T0413251

2020

Harris

New York

Manufacturers Directory

MERGENT
Exclusive Provider of
Dun & Bradstreet Library Solutions

dun & bradstreet

HOOVERS™   First Research    HARRIS INFOSOURCE™

Published January 2020 next update January 2021

Publisher

Mergent Inc.
444 Madison Ave
New York, NY 10022

©Mergent Inc All Rights Reserved
2020 Mergent Business Press
ISSN 1080-2614
ISBN 978-1-64141-638-2

TABLE OF CONTENTS

SUMMARY OF CONTENTS

Number of Companies.. 16,384
Number of Decision Makers 35,482
Minimum Number of Employees 5

EXPLANATORY NOTES

How to Cross-Reference in This Directory

Sequential Entry Numbers. Each establishment in the Geographic Section is numbered sequentially (G-0000). The number assigned to each establishment is referred to as its "entry number." To make cross-referencing easier, each listing in the Geographic, SIC, Alphabetic and Product Sections includes the establishment's entry number. To facilitate locating an entry in the Geographic Section, the entry numbers for the first listing on the left page and the last listing on the right page are printed at the top of the page next to the city name.

Source Suggestions Welcome

Although all known sources were used to compile this directory, it is possible that companies were inadvertently omitted. Your assistance in calling attention to such omissions would be greatly appreciated. A special form on the facing page will help you in the reporting process.

Analysis

Every effort has been made to contact all firms to verify their information. The one exception to this rule is the annual sales figure, which is considered by many companies to be confidential information. Therefore, estimated sales have been calculated by multiplying the nationwide average sales per employee for the firm's major SIC/NAICS code by the firm's number of employees. Nationwide averages for sales per employee by SIC/NAICS codes are provided by the U.S. Department of Commerce and are updated annually. All sales—sales (est)—have been estimated by this method. The exceptions are parent companies (PA), division headquarters (DH) and headquarter locations (HQ) which may include an actual corporate sales figure—sales (corporate-wide) if available.

Types of Companies

Descriptive and statistical data are included for companies in the entire state. These comprise manufacturers, machine shops, fabricators, assemblers and printers. Also identified are corporate offices in the state.

Employment Data

This directory contains companies with 5 or more employees in the manufacturing industry. The employment figure shown in the Geographic Section includes male and female employees and embraces all levels of the company: administrative, clerical, sales and maintenance. This figure is for the facility listed and does not include other plants or offices. It should be recognized that these figures represent an approximate year-round average. These employment figures are broken into codes A through G and used in the Product and SIC Sections to further help you in qualifying a company. Be sure to check the footnotes on the bottom of pages for the code breakdowns.

Standard Industrial Classification (SIC)

The Standard Industrial Classification (SIC) system used in this directory was developed by the federal government for use in classifying establishments by the type of activity they are engaged in. The SIC classifications used in this directory are from the 1987 edition published by the U.S. Government's Office of Management and Budget. The SIC system separates all activities into broad industrial divisions (e.g., manufacturing, mining, retail trade). It further subdivides each division. The range of manufacturing industry classes extends from two-digit codes (major industry group) to four-digit codes (product).

For example:

Industry Breakdown	Code	Industry, Product, etc.
*Major industry group	20	Food and kindred products
Industry group	203	Canned and frozen foods
*Industry	2033	Fruits and vegetables, etc.

*Classifications used in this directory

Only two-digit and four-digit codes are used in this directory.

Arrangement

1. The **Geographic Section** contains complete in-depth corporate data. This section is sorted by cities listed in alphabetical order and companies listed alphabetically within each city. A County/City Index for referencing cities within counties precedes this section.

IMPORTANT NOTICE: It is a violation of both federal and state law to transmit an unsolicited advertisement to a facsimile machine. Any user of this product that violates such laws may be subject to civil and criminal penalties, which may exceed $500 for each transmission of an unsolicited facsimile. Mergent Inc. provides fax numbers for lawful purposes only and expressly forbids the use of these numbers in any unlawful manner.

2. The **Standard Industrial Classification (SIC) Section** lists companies under approximately 500 four-digit SIC codes. An alphabetical and a numerical index precedes this section. A company can be listed under several codes. The codes are in numerical order with companies listed alphabetically under each code.

3. The **Alphabetic Section** lists all companies with their full physical or mailing addresses and telephone number.

4. The **Product Section** lists companies under unique Harris categories. An index preceding this section lists all product categories in alphabetical order. Companies can be listed under several categories.

USER'S GUIDE TO LISTINGS

GEOGRAPHIC SECTION

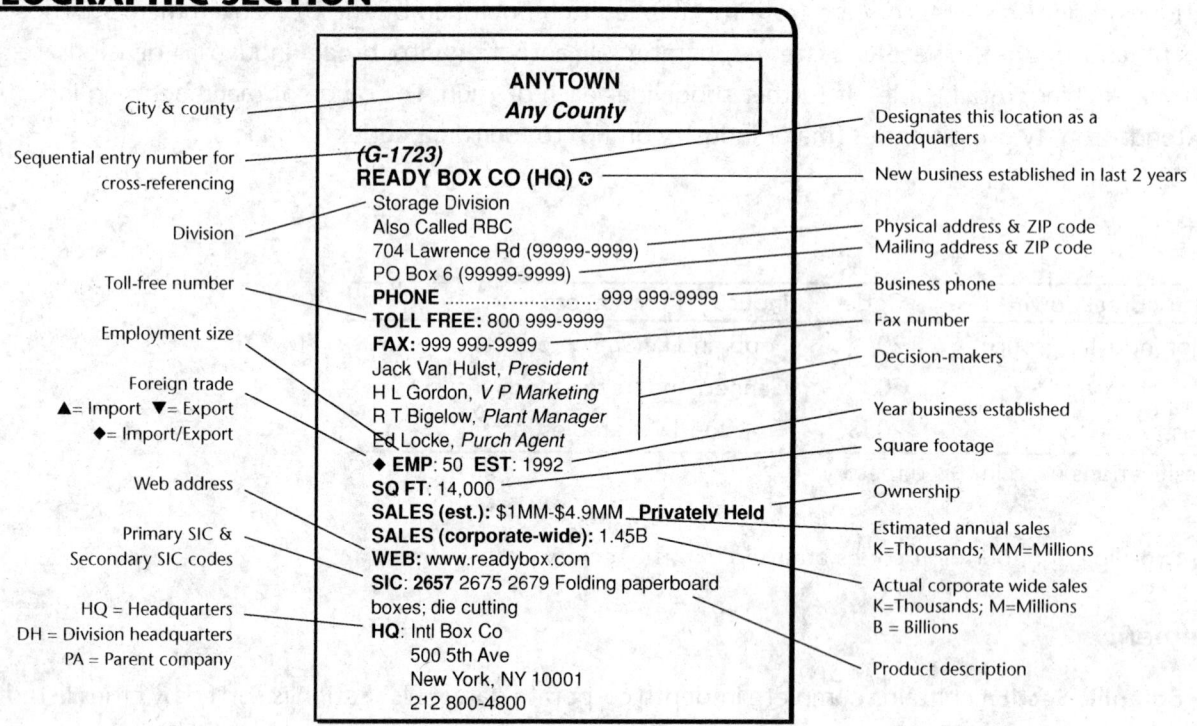

City & county

Sequential entry number for cross-referencing

Division

Toll-free number

Employment size

Foreign trade
▲= Import ▼= Export
◆= Import/Export

Web address

Primary SIC & Secondary SIC codes

HQ = Headquarters
DH = Division headquarters
PA = Parent company

ANYTOWN
Any County

(G-1723)
READY BOX CO (HQ) ✪
Storage Division
Also Called RBC
704 Lawrence Rd (99999-9999)
PO Box 6 (99999-9999)
PHONE 999 999-9999
TOLL FREE: 800 999-9999
FAX: 999 999-9999
Jack Van Hulst, *President*
H L Gordon, *V P Marketing*
R T Bigelow, *Plant Manager*
Ed Locke, *Purch Agent*
◆ **EMP:** 50 **EST:** 1992
SQ FT: 14,000
SALES (est.): $1MM-$4.9MM **Privately Held**
SALES (corporate-wide): 1.45B
WEB: www.readybox.com
SIC: 2657 2675 2679 Folding paperboard boxes; die cutting
HQ: Intl Box Co
500 5th Ave
New York, NY 10001
212 800-4800

Designates this location as a headquarters

New business established in last 2 years

Physical address & ZIP code
Mailing address & ZIP code

Business phone

Fax number

Decision-makers

Year business established

Square footage

Ownership

Estimated annual sales
K=Thousands; MM=Millions

Actual corporate wide sales
K=Thousands; M=Millions
B = Billions

Product description

SIC SECTION

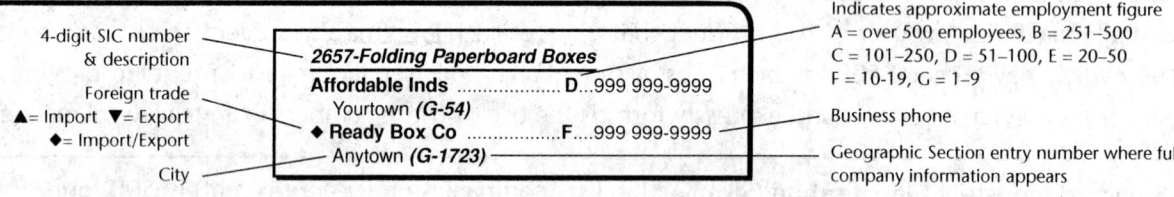

4-digit SIC number & description

Foreign trade
▲= Import ▼= Export
◆= Import/Export

City

2657-Folding Paperboard Boxes
Affordable Inds .... D...999 999-9999
Yourtown *(G-54)*
◆ **Ready Box Co** .... F....999 999-9999
Anytown *(G-1723)*

Indicates approximate employment figure
A = over 500 employees, B = 251–500
C = 101–250, D = 51–100, E = 20–50
F = 10-19, G = 1–9

Business phone

Geographic Section entry number where full company information appears

ALPHABETIC SECTION

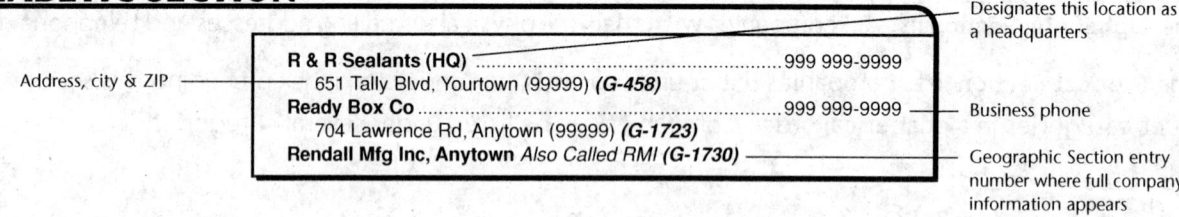

Address, city & ZIP

R & R Sealants (HQ) 999 999-9999
651 Tally Blvd, Yourtown (99999) *(G-458)*
Ready Box Co 999 999-9999
704 Lawrence Rd, Anytown (99999) *(G-1723)*
Rendall Mfg Inc, Anytown *Also Called RMI (G-1730)*

Designates this location as a headquarters

Business phone

Geographic Section entry number where full company information appears

PRODUCT SECTION

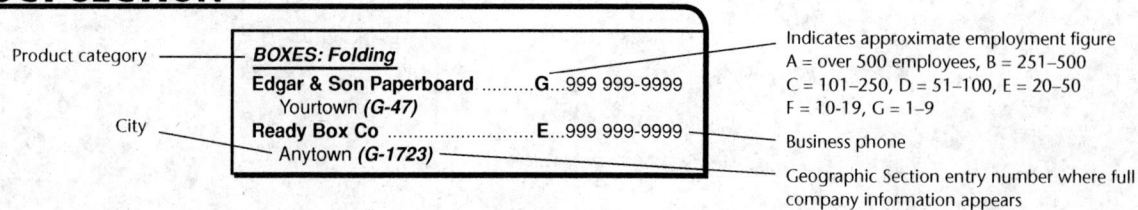

Product category

City

BOXES: Folding
Edgar & Son Paperboard ....G...999 999-9999
Yourtown *(G-47)*
Ready Box Co ....E...999 999-9999
Anytown *(G-1723)*

Indicates approximate employment figure
A = over 500 employees, B = 251–500
C = 101–250, D = 51–100, E = 20–50
F = 10-19, G = 1–9

Business phone

Geographic Section entry number where full company information appears

GEOGRAPHIC SECTION

Companies sorted by city in alphabetical order

In-depth company data listed

STANDARD INDUSTRIAL CLASSIFICATIONS

Alphabetical index of classifcation descriptions

Numerical index of classifcation descriptions

Companies sorted by SIC product groupings

ALPHABETIC SECTION

Company listings in alphabetical order

PRODUCT INDEX

Product categories listed in alphabetical order

PRODUCT SECTION

Companies sorted by product and manufacturing service classifications

GEOGRAPHIC

SIC

ALPHABETIC

PRDT INDEX

PRODUCT

New York
County Map

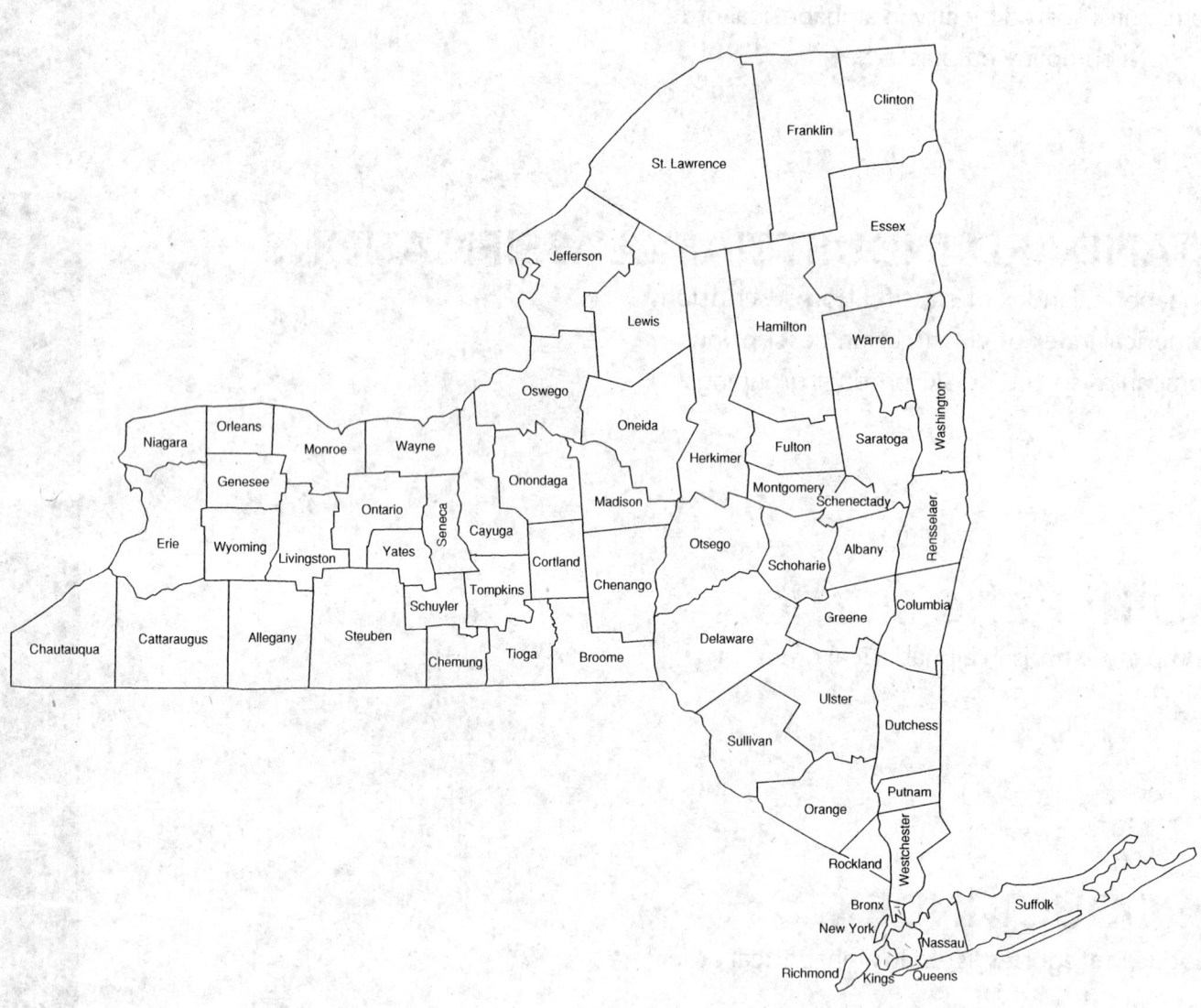

COUNTY/CITY CROSS-REFERENCE INDEX

	ENTRY #		ENTRY #		ENTRY #		ENTRY #		ENTRY #
Kings		**Nassau**		**Niagara**		Syracuse	(G-14807)	Lacona	(G-6747)
Brooklyn	(G-1410)	Albertson	(G-145)	Barker	(G-590)	Tully	(G-15207)	Mexico	(G-7866)
Lewis		Atlantic Beach	(G-452)	Burt	(G-3060)	**Ontario**		Oswego	(G-12408)
Beaver Falls	(G-760)	Baldwin	(G-530)	Gasport	(G-5136)	Bloomfield	(G-940)	Parish	(G-12495)
Castorland	(G-3206)	Bayville	(G-747)	Lewiston	(G-6919)	Canandaigua	(G-3124)	Phoenix	(G-12615)
Constableville	(G-3634)	Bellmore	(G-778)	Lockport	(G-7058)	Clifton Springs	(G-3479)	Pulaski	(G-12994)
Croghan	(G-3802)	Bethpage	(G-829)	Middleport	(G-7887)	Farmington	(G-4768)	Sandy Creek	(G-14154)
Harrisville	(G-5565)	Carle Place	(G-3169)	Newfane	(G-11894)	Fishers	(G-4796)	West Monroe	(G-15814)
Lowville	(G-7414)	Cedarhurst	(G-3238)	Niagara Falls	(G-11900)	Geneva	(G-5145)	Williamstown	(G-16115)
Lyons Falls	(G-7455)	East Meadow	(G-4131)	North Tonawanda	(G-12050)	Hall	(G-5500)	**Otsego**	
Livingston		East Norwich	(G-4152)	Ransomville	(G-13066)	Honeoye	(G-6068)	Cherry Valley	(G-3368)
Avon	(G-511)	East Rockaway	(G-4170)	Sanborn	(G-14136)	Manchester	(G-7527)	Cooperstown	(G-3638)
Caledonia	(G-3068)	East Williston	(G-4249)	Wilson	(G-16153)	Naples	(G-8206)	Edmeston	(G-4294)
Conesus	(G-3605)	Elmont	(G-4382)	Youngstown	(G-16384)	Oaks Corners	(G-12161)	Fly Creek	(G-4908)
Dansville	(G-3818)	Farmingdale	(G-4568)	**Oneida**		Phelps	(G-12601)	Morris	(G-8084)
Geneseo	(G-5143)	Floral Park	(G-4805)	Barneveld	(G-592)	Seneca Castle	(G-14361)	Oneonta	(G-12256)
Hemlock	(G-5830)	Franklin Square	(G-4958)	Blossvale	(G-955)	Stanley	(G-14611)	Richfield Springs	(G-13105)
Lakeville	(G-6773)	Freeport	(G-4976)	Boonville	(G-1102)	Victor	(G-15389)	Schenevus	(G-14319)
Leicester	(G-6908)	Garden City	(G-5089)	Camden	(G-3098)	**Orange**		Unadilla	(G-15220)
Lima	(G-6929)	Garden City Park	(G-5120)	Chadwicks	(G-3303)	Bullville	(G-3054)	West Burlington	(G-15758)
Livonia	(G-7054)	Glen Cove	(G-5186)	Clayville	(G-3454)	Campbell Hall	(G-3118)	**Putnam**	
Mount Morris	(G-8113)	Glen Head	(G-5205)	Clinton	(G-3482)	Central Valley	(G-3298)	Brewster	(G-1138)
Nunda	(G-12133)	Great Neck	(G-5359)	Forestport	(G-4928)	Chester	(G-3369)	Carmel	(G-3184)
Piffard	(G-12623)	Greenvale	(G-5460)	Holland Patent	(G-6033)	Cornwall	(G-3724)	Cold Spring	(G-3521)
Retsof	(G-13094)	Hempstead	(G-5831)	Marcy	(G-7564)	Cornwall On Hudson	(G-3733)	Mahopac	(G-7473)
York	(G-16362)	Hewlett	(G-5868)	Mc Connellsville	(G-7686)	Florida	(G-4821)	Patterson	(G-12515)
Madison		Hicksville	(G-5878)	New Hartford	(G-8236)	Godeffroy	(G-5302)	**Queens**	
Canastota	(G-3149)	Inwood	(G-6287)	New York Mills	(G-11831)	Goshen	(G-5304)	Arverne	(G-406)
Cazenovia	(G-3224)	Island Park	(G-6315)	Oriskany	(G-12384)	Greenwood Lake	(G-5478)	Astoria	(G-412)
Chittenango	(G-3402)	Jericho	(G-6571)	Oriskany Falls	(G-12400)	Harriman	(G-5544)	Bayside	(G-733)
De Ruyter	(G-3823)	Lawrence	(G-6886)	Remsen	(G-13083)	Highland Falls	(G-5966)	Bayside Hills	(G-746)
Erieville	(G-4484)	Levittown	(G-6912)	Rome	(G-13841)	Highland Mills	(G-5967)	Bellerose	(G-773)
Hamilton	(G-5526)	Lido Beach	(G-6927)	Sangerfield	(G-14155)	Huguenot	(G-6193)	College Point	(G-3531)
Morrisville	(G-8085)	Locust Valley	(G-7121)	Sauquoit	(G-14218)	Middletown	(G-7891)	Corona	(G-3734)
Munnsville	(G-8195)	Long Beach	(G-7134)	Sherrill	(G-14402)	Monroe	(G-8013)	Douglaston	(G-4028)
Oneida	(G-12244)	Lynbrook	(G-7423)	Stittville	(G-14734)	Montgomery	(G-8058)	East Elmhurst	(G-4103)
Wampsville	(G-15480)	Manhasset	(G-7530)	Utica	(G-15236)	Mountainville	(G-8193)	Elmhurst	(G-4331)
West Edmeston	(G-15760)	Massapequa	(G-7642)	Vernon	(G-15364)	New Hampton	(G-8232)	Far Rockaway	(G-4562)
Monroe		Massapequa Park	(G-7654)	Vernon Center	(G-15368)	New Windsor	(G-8357)	Floral Park	(G-4819)
Brockport	(G-1175)	Merrick	(G-7853)	Waterville	(G-15594)	Newburgh	(G-11857)	Flushing	(G-4831)
Churchville	(G-3407)	Mineola	(G-7954)	Westernville	(G-15942)	Pine Bush	(G-12625)	Forest Hills	(G-4914)
East Rochester	(G-4159)	New Hyde Park	(G-8249)	Westmoreland	(G-15960)	Pine Island	(G-12630)	Fresh Meadows	(G-5037)
Fairport	(G-4489)	North Baldwin	(G-12003)	Whitesboro	(G-16079)	Port Jervis	(G-12845)	Glen Oaks	(G-5214)
Gates	(G-5141)	North Bellmore	(G-12013)	Yorkville	(G-16375)	Rock Tavern	(G-13820)	Glendale	(G-5216)
Henrietta	(G-5853)	Oceanside	(G-12163)	**Onondaga**		Salisbury Mills	(G-14134)	Hollis	(G-6040)
Hilton	(G-5972)	Old Bethpage	(G-12213)	Baldwinsville	(G-539)	Slate Hill	(G-14463)	Howard Beach	(G-6139)
Honeoye Falls	(G-6070)	Old Westbury	(G-12222)	Brewerton	(G-1134)	Southfields	(G-14541)	Jackson Heights	(G-6419)
Mendon	(G-7851)	Oyster Bay	(G-12443)	Bridgeport	(G-1168)	Sparrow Bush	(G-14547)	Jamaica	(G-6423)
North Chili	(G-12021)	Plainview	(G-12659)	Camillus	(G-3107)	Sugar Loaf	(G-14769)	Kew Gardens	(G-6660)
Penfield	(G-12569)	Port Washington	(G-12859)	Cicero	(G-3415)	Tuxedo Park	(G-15216)	Laurelton	(G-6882)
Pittsford	(G-12635)	Rockville Centre	(G-13826)	Clay	(G-3451)	Unionville	(G-15234)	Little Neck	(G-6996)
Rochester	(G-13194)	Roosevelt	(G-14030)	De Witt	(G-3824)	Walden	(G-15456)	Long Island City	(G-7140)
Rush	(G-14069)	Roslyn	(G-14039)	East Syracuse	(G-4192)	Warwick	(G-15510)	Maspeth	(G-7585)
Scottsville	(G-14338)	Roslyn Heights	(G-14048)	Elbridge	(G-4295)	Washingtonville	(G-15523)	Middle Village	(G-7876)
Spencerport	(G-14551)	Sea Cliff	(G-14345)	Fabius	(G-4488)	West Point	(G-15834)	Oakland Gardens	(G-12159)
Webster	(G-15629)	Seaford	(G-14348)	Fayetteville	(G-4783)	Westtown	(G-15965)	Ozone Park	(G-12457)
West Henrietta	(G-15782)	South Hempstead	(G-14519)	Jamesville	(G-6555)	**Orleans**		Queens Village	(G-13016)
Montgomery		Syosset	(G-14777)	Jordan	(G-6630)	Albion	(G-152)	Rego Park	(G-13076)
Amsterdam	(G-316)	Uniondale	(G-15223)	Kirkville	(G-6724)	Holley	(G-6035)	Richmond Hill	(G-13107)
Canajoharie	(G-3120)	Valley Stream	(G-15332)	La Fayette	(G-6736)	Kendall	(G-6647)	Ridgewood	(G-13136)
Esperance	(G-4485)	Wantagh	(G-15482)	Liverpool	(G-7000)	Lyndonville	(G-7444)	Rockaway Beach	(G-13822)
Fonda	(G-4910)	West Hempstead	(G-15766)	Manlius	(G-7543)	Medina	(G-7727)	Rockaway Park	(G-13824)
Fort Plain	(G-4946)	Westbury	(G-15860)	Marcellus	(G-7560)	**Oswego**		Rosedale	(G-14036)
Fultonville	(G-5077)	Williston Park	(G-16147)	Memphis	(G-7835)	Bernhards Bay	(G-826)	Saint Albans	(G-14104)
Palatine Bridge	(G-12477)	Woodbury	(G-16166)	Nedrow	(G-8214)	Central Square	(G-3293)	South Ozone Park	(G-14521)
Saint Johnsville	(G-14116)	Woodmere	(G-16190)	North Syracuse	(G-12038)	Constantia	(G-3635)	South Richmond Hill	(G-14522)
Sprakers	(G-14564)	**New York**		Skaneateles	(G-14446)	Fulton	(G-5054)	Springfield Gardens	(G-14588)
		New York	(G-8387)	Skaneateles Falls	(G-14459)	Hannibal	(G-5542)	Sunnyside	(G-14770)
				Solvay	(G-14494)			Whitestone	(G-16086)

ENTRY#

- Woodhaven (G-16187)
- Woodside (G-16195)

Rensselaer

- Averill Park (G-505)
- Berlin (G-823)
- Castleton On Hudson (G-3200)
- Cropseyville (G-3803)
- Eagle Bridge (G-4071)
- East Greenbush (G-4113)
- Hoosick (G-6082)
- Hoosick Falls (G-6083)
- Nassau (G-8212)
- Petersburg (G-12600)
- Poestenkill (G-12801)
- Rensselaer (G-13084)
- Stephentown (G-14730)
- Troy (G-15162)
- Valley Falls (G-15331)
- West Sand Lake (G-15835)

Richmond

- Staten Island (G-14612)

Rockland

- Airmont (G-9)
- Blauvelt (G-925)
- Chestnut Ridge (G-3395)
- Congers (G-3606)
- Garnerville (G-5133)
- Haverstraw (G-5804)
- Hillburn (G-5970)
- Monsey (G-8033)
- Nanuet (G-8196)
- New City (G-8223)
- Nyack (G-12135)
- Orangeburg (G-12304)
- Palisades (G-12481)
- Pearl River (G-12529)
- Piermont (G-12622)
- Pomona (G-12806)
- Sloatsburg (G-14470)
- Spring Valley (G-14565)
- Stony Point (G-14743)
- Suffern (G-14756)
- Tallman (G-15031)
- Tappan (G-15033)
- Thiells (G-15065)
- Tomkins Cove (G-15079)
- Valley Cottage (G-15312)
- West Haverstraw (G-15764)
- West Nyack (G-15815)

Saratoga

- Ballston Lake (G-557)
- Ballston Spa (G-566)
- Clifton Park (G-3460)
- Corinth (G-3704)
- Galway (G-5082)
- Gansevoort (G-5083)
- Greenfield Center (G-5450)
- Halfmoon (G-5490)
- Malta (G-7494)
- Mechanicville (G-7690)
- Middle Grove (G-7872)
- Rexford (G-13095)
- Rock City Falls (G-13817)
- Round Lake (G-14062)
- Saratoga Springs (G-14161)
- Schuylerville (G-14323)
- South Glens Falls (G-14511)
- Stillwater (G-14733)
- Waterford (G-15533)
- Wilton (G-16156)

Schenectady

- Delanson (G-3958)
- Duanesburg (G-4043)
- Glenville (G-5270)
- Niskayuna (G-11994)
- Rotterdam Junction (G-14060)
- Schenectady (G-14244)
- Scotia (G-14328)

Schoharie

- Central Bridge (G-3259)
- Charlotteville (G-3328)
- Cobleskill (G-3497)
- Howes Cave (G-6144)
- Middleburgh (G-7886)
- Richmondville (G-13129)
- Schoharie (G-14321)
- Sharon Springs (G-14381)
- Sloansville (G-14469)
- Warnerville (G-15502)

Schuyler

- Beaver Dams (G-759)
- Burdett (G-3055)
- Cayuta (G-3223)
- Hector (G-5825)
- Montour Falls (G-8074)
- Odessa (G-12200)
- Rock Stream (G-13819)
- Watkins Glen (G-15613)
- Wayne (G-15628)

Seneca

- Interlaken (G-6283)
- Lodi (G-7131)
- Ovid (G-12423)
- Romulus (G-13878)
- Seneca Falls (G-14362)
- Waterloo (G-15550)

St. Lawrence

- Brasher Falls (G-1113)
- Canton (G-3163)
- Childwold (G-3401)
- Cranberry Lake (G-3801)
- Gouverneur (G-5316)
- Hammond (G-5528)
- Heuvelton (G-5867)
- Massena (G-7663)
- Norfolk (G-11997)
- North Lawrence (G-12033)
- Norwood (G-12131)
- Ogdensburg (G-12201)
- Potsdam (G-12936)
- South Colton (G-14503)
- Waddington (G-15447)

Steuben

- Addison (G-4)
- Arkport (G-393)
- Avoca (G-510)
- Bath (G-630)
- Campbell (G-3116)
- Corning (G-3705)
- Hammondsport (G-5529)
- Hornell (G-6102)
- Lindley (G-6986)
- Painted Post (G-12471)
- Wayland (G-15625)
- Woodhull (G-16189)

Suffolk

- Amityville (G-255)
- Aquebogue (G-364)
- Babylon (G-517)
- Bay Shore (G-641)
- Bayport (G-726)
- Bellport (G-791)
- Blue Point (G-956)
- Bohemia (G-958)
- Brentwood (G-1114)
- Bridgehampton (G-1164)
- Brightwaters (G-1170)
- Brookhaven (G-1405)
- Calverton (G-3076)
- Center Moriches (G-3245)
- Centereach (G-3249)
- Centerport (G-3254)
- Central Islip (G-3260)
- Cold Spring Harbor (G-3526)
- Commack (G-3576)
- Copiague (G-3643)
- Coram (G-3692)
- Cutchogue (G-3815)
- Deer Park (G-3825)
- Dix Hills (G-4008)
- East Hampton (G-4117)
- East Islip (G-4129)
- East Moriches (G-4140)
- East Northport (G-4141)
- East Patchogue (G-4153)
- East Quogue (G-4156)
- East Setauket (G-4176)
- Eastport (G-4251)
- Edgewood (G-4258)
- Farmingville (G-4781)
- Greenlawn (G-5451)
- Greenport (G-5456)
- Halesite (G-5488)
- Hampton Bays (G-5533)
- Hauppauge (G-5576)
- Holbrook (G-5982)
- Holtsville (G-6044)
- Huntington (G-6197)
- Huntington Station (G-6235)
- Islandia (G-6323)
- Islip (G-6349)
- Islip Terrace (G-6358)
- Jamesport (G-6490)
- Kings Park (G-6672)
- Lake Grove (G-6759)
- Lake Ronkonkoma (G-6770)
- Lindenhurst (G-6939)
- Lloyd Harbor (G-7055)
- Manorville (G-7551)
- Mastic (G-7674)
- Mastic Beach (G-7675)
- Mattituck (G-7676)
- Medford (G-7697)
- Melville (G-7751)
- Middle Island (G-7873)
- Miller Place (G-7945)
- Montauk (G-8054)
- Mount Sinai (G-8115)
- Nesconset (G-8218)
- North Babylon (G-12001)
- Northport (G-12099)
- Oakdale (G-12149)
- Patchogue (G-12496)
- Peconic (G-12545)
- Port Jeff STA (G-12832)
- Port Jefferson (G-12840)
- Quogue (G-13061)
- Ridge (G-13131)
- Riverhead (G-13171)
- Ronkonkoma (G-13882)
- Sag Harbor (G-14096)
- Sagaponack (G-14103)
- Saint James (G-14107)
- Sayville (G-14222)
- Selden (G-14350)
- Setauket (G-14376)
- Shelter Island (G-14385)
- Shirley (G-14410)
- Smithtown (G-14472)
- Southampton (G-14526)
- Southold (G-14542)
- Speonk (G-14561)
- Stony Brook (G-14737)
- Wading River (G-15448)
- Wainscott (G-15454)
- Water Mill (G-15528)
- West Babylon (G-15677)
- West Islip (G-15809)
- West Sayville (G-15838)
- Westhampton (G-15954)
- Westhampton Beach (G-15956)
- Wyandanch (G-16240)
- Yaphank (G-16254)

Sullivan

- Barryville (G-598)
- Bethel (G-827)
- Callicoon (G-3075)
- Cochecton (G-3501)
- Ferndale (G-4787)
- Hurleyville (G-6268)
- Jeffersonville (G-6569)
- Kauneonga Lake (G-6640)
- Liberty (G-6924)
- Livingston Manor (G-7053)
- Long Eddy (G-7139)
- Monticello (G-8069)
- Narrowsburg (G-8210)
- Rock Hill (G-13818)
- Roscoe (G-14035)
- South Fallsburg (G-14508)
- Thompsonville (G-15066)
- Westbrookville (G-15859)
- Wht Sphr Spgs (G-16108)
- Woodridge (G-16194)

Tioga

- Apalachin (G-362)
- Berkshire (G-821)
- Candor (G-3161)
- Lockwood (G-7120)
- Nichols (G-11993)
- Owego (G-12428)
- Spencer (G-14549)
- Waverly (G-15619)

Tompkins

- Dryden (G-4036)
- Etna (G-4486)
- Freeville (G-5033)
- Groton (G-5480)
- Ithaca (G-6360)
- Lansing (G-6840)
- Newfield (G-11897)
- Trumansburg (G-15199)

Ulster

- Accord (G-1)
- Bearsville (G-758)
- Bloomington (G-951)
- Boiceville (G-1100)
- Ellenville (G-4305)
- Gardiner (G-5127)
- High Falls (G-5954)
- Highland (G-5957)
- Kerhonkson (G-6658)
- Kingston (G-6677)
- Lake Katrine (G-6763)
- Marlboro (G-7579)
- Milton (G-7951)
- Mount Marion (G-8110)
- New Paltz (G-8305)
- Rifton (G-13167)
- Saugerties (G-14196)
- Shokan (G-14429)
- Stone Ridge (G-14735)
- Tillson (G-15078)
- Ulster Park (G-15218)
- Wallkill (G-15467)
- West Hurley (G-15808)
- Woodstock (G-16234)

Warren

- Bakers Mills (G-529)
- Brant Lake (G-1112)
- Chestertown (G-3393)
- Glens Falls (G-5239)
- Lake George (G-6756)
- Lake Luzerne (G-6765)
- North Creek (G-12031)
- Queensbury (G-13029)
- Warrensburg (G-15503)

Washington

- Argyle (G-391)
- Cambridge (G-3091)
- Cossayuna (G-3799)
- Fort Ann (G-4933)
- Fort Edward (G-4936)
- Granville (G-5348)
- Greenwich (G-5468)
- Hartford (G-5566)
- Hudson Falls (G-6183)
- Middle Granville (G-7867)
- Salem (G-14132)
- Whitehall (G-16076)

Wayne

- Clyde (G-3488)
- Lyons (G-7447)
- Macedon (G-7457)
- Marion (G-7568)
- Newark (G-11837)
- North Rose (G-12034)
- Ontario (G-12283)
- Palmyra (G-12485)
- Red Creek (G-13070)
- Savannah (G-14220)
- Sodus (G-14491)
- Walworth (G-15477)
- Williamson (G-16109)
- Wolcott (G-16161)

Westchester

- Amawalk (G-200)
- Ardsley (G-383)
- Armonk (G-395)
- Baldwin Place (G-538)

	ENTRY #		ENTRY #		ENTRY #		ENTRY #		ENTRY #
Bedford	(G-762)	Hartsdale	(G-5567)	Peekskill	(G-12548)	Valhalla	(G-15302)	Perry	(G-12595)
Bedford Hills	(G-765)	Hastings On Hudson	(G-5571)	Pelham	(G-12564)	Waccabuc	(G-15446)	Portageville	(G-12932)
Briarcliff Manor	(G-1161)	Hawthorne	(G-5809)	Pleasantville	(G-12795)	West Harrison	(G-15763)	Silver Springs	(G-14443)
Bronxville	(G-1399)	Irvington	(G-6305)	Port Chester	(G-12812)	White Plains	(G-15967)	Warsaw	(G-15507)
Buchanan	(G-2608)	Jefferson Valley	(G-6567)	Pound Ridge	(G-12991)	Yonkers	(G-16280)	Wyoming	(G-16249)
Chappaqua	(G-3322)	Katonah	(G-6633)	Purchase	(G-13001)	Yorktown Heights	(G-16363)		
Cortlandt Manor	(G-3792)	Larchmont	(G-6842)	Rye	(G-14076)			**Yates**	
Cross River	(G-3804)	Mamaroneck	(G-7499)	Rye Brook	(G-14087)	**Wyoming**		Branchport	(G-1111)
Croton Falls	(G-3805)	Mohegan Lake	(G-8008)	Scarsdale	(G-14233)	Arcade	(G-367)	Dresden	(G-4034)
Croton On Hudson	(G-3806)	Montrose	(G-8078)	Sleepy Hollow	(G-14464)	Attica	(G-455)	Dundee	(G-4045)
Dobbs Ferry	(G-4018)	Mount Kisco	(G-8086)	Somers	(G-14498)	Bliss	(G-939)	Himrod	(G-5976)
Eastchester	(G-4250)	Mount Vernon	(G-8119)	South Salem	(G-14525)	Castile	(G-3198)	Penn Yan	(G-12577)
Elmsford	(G-4391)	New Rochelle	(G-8315)	Tarrytown	(G-15039)	Gainesville	(G-5081)	Rushville	(G-14075)
Goldens Bridge	(G-5303)	North Salem	(G-12037)	Thornwood	(G-15067)	Java Village	(G-6564)		
Harrison	(G-5548)	Ossining	(G-12402)	Tuckahoe	(G-15203)	North Java	(G-12032)		

GEOGRAPHIC SECTION

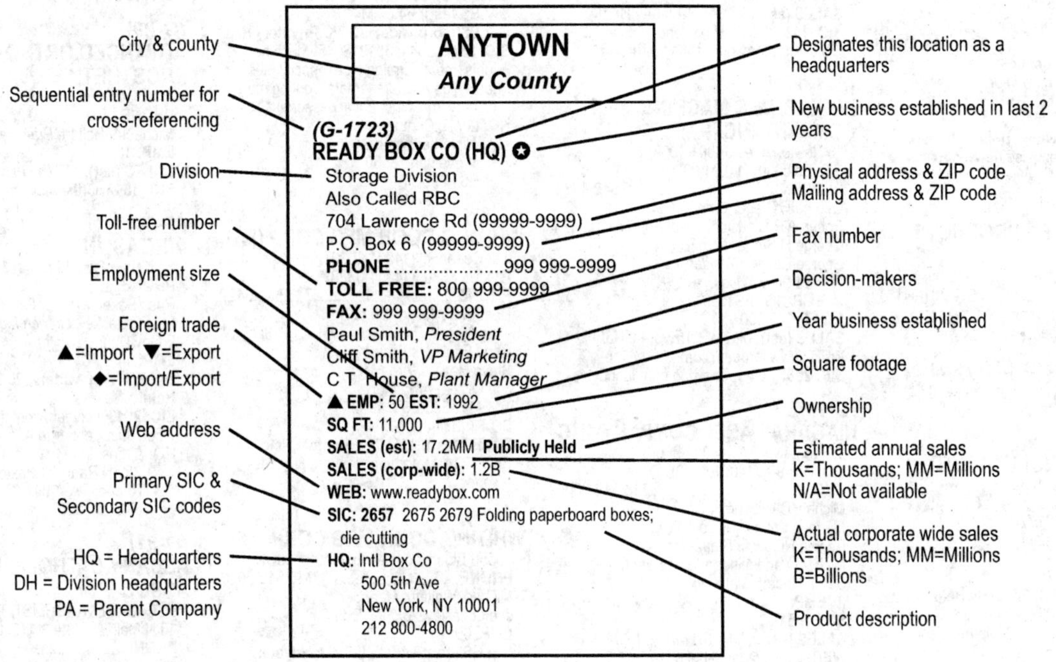
City & county
Sequential entry number for cross-referencing
Division
Toll-free number
Employment size
Foreign trade
▲=Import ▼=Export
◆=Import/Export
Web address
Primary SIC & Secondary SIC codes
HQ = Headquarters
DH = Division headquarters
PA = Parent Company
ANYTOWN
Any County
(G-1723)
READY BOX CO (HQ) ✪
Storage Division
Also Called RBC
704 Lawrence Rd (99999-9999)
P.O. Box 6 (99999-9999)
PHONE......................999 999-9999
TOLL FREE: 800 999-9999
FAX: 999 999-9999
Paul Smith, President
Cliff Smith, VP Marketing
C T House, Plant Manager
▲ EMP: 50 EST: 1992
SQ FT: 11,000
SALES (est): 17.2MM Publicly Held
SALES (corp-wide): 1.2B
WEB: www.readybox.com
SIC: 2657 2675 2679 Folding paperboard boxes; die cutting
HQ: Intl Box Co
500 5th Ave
New York, NY 10001
212 800-4800
Designates this location as a headquarters
New business established in last 2 years
Physical address & ZIP code
Mailing address & ZIP code
Fax number
Decision-makers
Year business established
Square footage
Ownership
Estimated annual sales
K=Thousands; MM=Millions
N/A=Not available
Actual corporate wide sales
K=Thousands; MM=Millions
B=Billions
Product description

See footnotes for symbols and codes identification.

- This section is in alphabetical order by city.
- Companies are sorted alphabetically under their respective cities.
- To locate cities within a county refer to the County/City Cross Reference Index.

IMPORTANT NOTICE: It is a violation of both federal and state law to transmit an unsolicited advertisement to a facsimile machine. Any user of this product that violates such laws may be subject to civil and criminal penalties which may exceed $500 for each transmission of an unsolicited facsimile. Harris InfoSource provides fax numbers for lawful purposes only and expressly forbids the use of these numbers in any unlawful manner.

Accord
Ulster County

(G-1)
VIC DEMAYOS INC
4967 Us Highway 209 (12404-5723)
P.O. Box 253 (12404-0253)
PHONE..................................845 626-4343
Vic De Mayo, *President*
Eugene De Mayo, *President*
EMP: 6 **EST:** 1964
SQ FT: 4,000
SALES (est): 225K **Privately Held**
SIC: 3111 5941 Accessory products, leather; sporting goods & bicycle shops

Adams
Jefferson County

(G-2)
GREAT LAKES CHEESE NY INC
23 Phelps St (13605-1096)
PHONE..................................315 232-4511
Gary Vanic, *Ch of Bd*
Hans Epprecht, *President*
John Epprecht, *Vice Pres*
Grant Crumb, *Plant Mgr*
Tracy Stuckey, *Purch Dir*
EMP: 79
SQ FT: 88,000
SALES (est): 19.2MM
SALES (corp-wide): 1.6B **Privately Held**
WEB: www.greatlakescheese.com
SIC: 2022 Cheese, natural & processed
PA: Great Lakes Cheese Co., Inc.
17825 Great Lakes Pkwy
Hiram OH 44234
440 834-2500

Adams Center
Jefferson County

(G-3)
R G KING GENERAL CONSTRUCTION
Also Called: Kings Quarry
13018 County Route 155 (13606-3104)
PHONE..................................315 583-3560
Ronald King, *President*
Bill King, *Vice Pres*
EMP: 5 **EST:** 1959
SALES (est): 508.2K **Privately Held**
SIC: 1442 Construction sand & gravel

Addison
Steuben County

(G-4)
CRAWFORD PRINT SHOP INC
6120 Herrington Rd (14801-9235)
PHONE..................................607 359-4970
Adam Crawford, *President*
EMP: 5
SALES: 220K **Privately Held**
WEB: www.crawfordsprintshop.com
SIC: 2752 Color lithography

(G-5)
HES INC
6303 Symonds Hill Rd (14801-9564)
PHONE..................................607 359-2974
John J Crane, *President*
EMP: 8
SQ FT: 10,000
SALES: 450K **Privately Held**
SIC: 3621 3599 Electric motor & generator parts; machine shop, jobbing & repair

Afton
Chenango County

(G-6)
BABYSAFE USA LLC
251 County Road 17 (13730-3111)
PHONE..................................877 367-4141
Sagi Ben-Dov, *Mng Member*
Jamie Baciuska,
Lynn Baciuska,
▲ **EMP:** 5
SQ FT: 8,000
SALES: 235K **Privately Held**
SIC: 3944 Baby carriages & restraint seats

(G-7)
COBRA OPERATING INDUSTRIES LLC
37 Main St (13730-3164)
PHONE..................................607 639-1700
Barbara A Wagner,
Richard W Wagner,
EMP: 6
SALES (est): 400K **Privately Held**
SIC: 3441 Fabricated structural metal

(G-8)
WAGNER NINEVEH INC
224 County Rd 26 (13730)
PHONE..................................607 693-2689
Jennifer Hartwell, *Assistant*
EMP: 11 **EST:** 2007
SALES (est): 1.4MM **Privately Held**
SIC: 2421 Sawmills & planing mills, general

Airmont
Rockland County

(G-9)
901 D LLC
360 Route 59 Ste 3 (10952-3416)
PHONE..................................845 369-1111
Pam Lucianna, *Purchasing*
Fred Sainclivier, *Project Engr*
Aldric Seguin, *Sales Executive*
Marvin Goldberg, *Director*
Francois Duverne,
EMP: 48
SALES (est): 14.9MM
SALES (corp-wide): 26.8MM **Privately Held**
WEB: www.901d.com
SIC: 3553 Cabinet makers' machinery
PA: Graycliff Partners, Lp
500 5th Ave Fl 47
New York NY 10110
212 300-2900

(G-10)
ART ESSENTIALS OF NEW YORK (PA)
25 Church Rd (10952-4108)
P.O. Box 38, Tallman (10982-0038)
PHONE....................................845 368-1100
Bella Jacobs, *President*
Arnold A Jacobs, *Shareholder*
EMP: 3
SQ FT: 1,400
SALES: 1MM **Privately Held**
WEB: www.artessentialsofnewyork.com
SIC: 2499 Decorative wood & woodwork

(G-11)
HANDY LAUNDRY PRODUCTS CORP (PA)
382 Route 59 Ste 318 (10952-3422)
PHONE.....................................845 701-1111
Shlome Masri, *President*
Aron Braun, *Principal*
▲ EMP: 6
SALES (est): 490.4K **Privately Held**
SIC: 2392 Laundry, garment & storage bags

(G-12)
I TRADE TECHNOLOGY LTD
3 Rustic Dr (10952-4722)
PHONE.....................................615 348-7233
Malkie Lebrecht, *Ch of Bd*
Shia Lebrecht, *Principal*
Andy Gordon,
EMP: 20
SALES (est): 5.8MM **Privately Held**
SIC: 3678 5999 5065 Electronic connectors; electronic parts & equipment; connectors, electronic

(G-13)
JOMAR INDUSTRIES INC
382 Route 59 Ste 352 (10952-3484)
P.O. Box 379, Monsey (10952-0379)
PHONE.....................................845 357-5773
Alan Marks, *President*
Nancy Lopez, *Sales Staff*
▲ EMP: 20
SQ FT: 4,000
SALES (est): 1.6MM **Privately Held**
WEB: www.jomarindustries.com
SIC: 3993 2395 5961 2759 Advertising novelties; art needlework: made from purchased materials; gift items, mail order; commercial printing

(G-14)
MINTED GREEN INC
85 Regina Rd (10952-4527)
PHONE.....................................845 458-1845
Chaim Rosenberg, *Ch of Bd*
EMP: 6 EST: 2015
SQ FT: 1,200
SALES: 2.8MM **Privately Held**
SIC: 3942 5092 5945 Dolls & stuffed toys; toys & games; toys & games

---
Akron
Erie County

(G-15)
AAKRON RULE CORP (PA)
8 Indianola Ave (14001-1199)
P.O. Box 418 (14001-0418)
PHONE.....................................716 542-5483
Danielle Robillard, *Ch of Bd*
Jon Merrick, *Vice Pres*
Devin Piscitelli, *Vice Pres*
George Vancleef, *Opers Mgr*
Jean Taylor, *Purch Mgr*
◆ EMP: 150 EST: 1967
SQ FT: 16,000
SALES (est): 44.9MM **Privately Held**
WEB: www.aakronline.com
SIC: 2499 3993 3952 3951 Rulers & rules, wood; paint sticks, wood; signs & advertising specialties; lead pencils & art goods; pens & mechanical pencils

(G-16)
COUNTY LINE STONE CO INC
4515 Crittenden Rd (14001-9517)
P.O. Box 150 (14001-0150)
PHONE.....................................716 542-5435

John Buyers Jr, *Vice Pres*
Bruce M Buyers, *Vice Pres*
EMP: 30
SQ FT: 20,000
SALES (est): 4.7MM **Privately Held**
SIC: 1429 5032 Sandstone, crushed & broken-quarrying; asphalt mixture

(G-17)
FORD GUM & MACHINE COMPANY INC (PA)
18 Newton Ave (14001-1099)
P.O. Box 330 (14001-0330)
PHONE.....................................716 542-4561
George H Stege, *Ch of Bd*
Robert A R Clouston, *Ch of Bd*
George H Stege, *Ch of Bd*
George Stege, *President*
Warren Clark, *Vice Pres*
▲ EMP: 100 EST: 1913
SQ FT: 125,000
SALES (est): 59.7MM **Privately Held**
WEB: www.fordgum.com
SIC: 2067 5441 Chewing gum; candy

(G-18)
NIAGARA LABEL COMPANY INC
12715 Lewis Rd (14001-9668)
P.O. Box 90 (14001-0090)
PHONE.....................................716 542-3000
Michael C Witmarsh, *CEO*
Marjorie Witmarsh, *Corp Secy*
Connie Ribbeck, *Prdtn Mgr*
Michele Vanderlinden, *Sales Staff*
Sarah Hobart, *Manager*
▲ EMP: 17
SQ FT: 5,000
SALES (est): 3MM **Privately Held**
WEB: www.niagaralabel.com
SIC: 2754 2759 Labels: gravure printing; labels & seals: printing

(G-19)
NIAGARA SPECIALTY METALS INC
12600 Clarence Center Rd (14001-9749)
P.O. Box 280 (14001-0280)
PHONE.....................................716 542-5552
Robert F Shabala Jr, *President*
Julie Majka, *General Mgr*
Tim Gelnett, *Vice Pres*
Timothy Gelnett, *Vice Pres*
Frank Cox, *Sales Staff*
◆ EMP: 37
SQ FT: 110,000
SALES (est): 14.5MM **Privately Held**
WEB: www.nsm-ny.com
SIC: 3312 Blast furnaces & steel mills

(G-20)
PERRYS ICE CREAM COMPANY INC
1 Ice Cream Plz (14001-1031)
PHONE.....................................716 542-5492
Robert Denning, *President*
Brian Perry, *Exec VP*
Wahidul Islam, *Engineer*
Rebecca Rackl, *Credit Staff*
Jodi Perry, *Human Res Dir*
▲ EMP: 300
SQ FT: 135,000
SALES (est): 75.9MM **Privately Held**
SIC: 2024 5145 Ice cream, bulk; snack foods

(G-21)
RE-AL INDUSTRIAL CORP
Also Called: D & E Industrial
5391 Crittenden Rd (14001-9598)
P.O. Box 37, Newfane (14108-0037)
PHONE.....................................716 542-4556
Richard Bottom, *President*
EMP: 8
SQ FT: 8,000
SALES: 700K **Privately Held**
WEB: www.d-eind.com
SIC: 3535 1796 Conveyors & conveying equipment; machinery installation

(G-22)
STRIPPIT INC (DH)
Also Called: L V D
12975 Clarence Center Rd (14001-1371)
PHONE.....................................716 542-4511
John P Lesebbre, *President*

Bruce Turner, *CFO*
Jerry Benning, *Sales Engr*
◆ EMP: 200
SQ FT: 255,000
SALES (est): 64.8MM
SALES (corp-wide): 73.7K **Privately Held**
SIC: 3542 3544 3549 3545 Machine tools, metal forming type; special dies, tools, jigs & fixtures; metalworking machinery; machine tool accessories
HQ: L.V.D. Company
Nijverheidslaan 2
Wevelgem 8560
564 305-11

(G-23)
WHITING DOOR MFG CORP (PA)
113 Cedar St (14001-1038)
P.O. Box 388 (14001-0388)
PHONE.....................................716 542-5427
Donald J Whiting, *Ch of Bd*
Greg Marek, *President*
Chris Ericksen, *Area Mgr*
Steve Hazard, *Area Mgr*
Joe Olszta, *Area Mgr*
▼ EMP: 330 EST: 1953
SQ FT: 371,000
SALES (est): 128MM **Privately Held**
SIC: 3714 Motor vehicle parts & accessories

(G-24)
WHITING DOOR MFG CORP
13550 Bloomingdale Rd (14001-9801)
PHONE.....................................716 542-3070
Michael Whiting, *Manager*
Joe Lukasiewizd, *Info Tech Dir*
EMP: 60
SALES (corp-wide): 128MM **Privately Held**
SIC: 3493 Coiled flat springs
PA: Whiting Door Mfg Corp
113 Cedar St
Akron NY 14001
716 542-5427

Akwesasne
Franklin County

(G-25)
OHSERASE MANUFACTURING LLC
26 Eagle Dr (13655-3235)
P.O. Box 1221 (13655-1221)
PHONE.....................................518 358-9309
Justin Tarbell, *Vice Pres*
▲ EMP: 23
SALES (est): 3MM **Privately Held**
SIC: 3999 Barber & beauty shop equipment

Albany
Albany County

(G-26)
ACCESSIBLE BATH TECH LLC
6 Albright Ave (12203-4802)
PHONE.....................................518 937-1518
Craig La Londe, *President*
EMP: 15
SALES: 950K **Privately Held**
SIC: 3999 Manufacturing industries

(G-27)
ACCUPRINT (PA)
2005 Western Ave Ste 1 (12203-5073)
PHONE.....................................518 456-2431
Donald Blais, *Owner*
EMP: 6
SALES (est): 537.1K **Privately Held**
SIC: 2752 Commercial printing, offset

(G-28)
ADIRONDACK SPCLTY ADHSIVES INC
4258 Albany St (12205-4614)
P.O. Box 13283 (12212-3283)
PHONE.....................................518 869-5736
Jerald Casey, *President*
EMP: 15

SQ FT: 7,500
SALES (est): 3.5MM **Privately Held**
WEB: www.adktapes.com
SIC: 2891 Adhesives

(G-29)
ADVANCED ORTHOTICS & PROSTHETH
350 Northern Blvd Ste 101 (12204-1091)
PHONE.....................................518 472-1023
Michael V Bolton, *Principal*
EMP: 13
SALES (est): 1.7MM **Privately Held**
SIC: 3842 Orthopedic appliances

(G-30)
AIRGAS INC
84 Karner Rd (12205-4730)
PHONE.....................................518 690-0068
Ross Baker, *Principal*
Lester Mackey, *Branch Mgr*
F Gay Dunn, *Co-Mgr*
EMP: 14
SALES (corp-wide): 125.9MM **Privately Held**
SIC: 2813 Oxygen, compressed or liquefied; nitrogen; argon
HQ: Airgas, Inc.
259 N Radnor Chester Rd # 100
Radnor PA 19087
610 687-5253

(G-31)
ALBANY CATHOLIC PRESS ASSOC
Also Called: EVANGELIST, THE
40 N Main Ave Ste 2 (12203-1481)
PHONE.....................................518 453-6688
James Breig, *Principal*
Bishop Hubbard, *Principal*
Stephanie Zebrowski, *Manager*
Barbra Oliver, *Manager*
Kathy Hughes, *Admin Asst*
EMP: 9
SQ FT: 10,000
SALES: 955.2K **Privately Held**
SIC: 2711 8661 Newspapers: publishing only, not printed on site; religious organizations

(G-32)
ALBANY LETTER SHOP INC
16 Van Zandt St Ste 20 (12207-1448)
P.O. Box 1003 (12201-1003)
PHONE.....................................518 434-1172
Fax: 518 434-6261
EMP: 6
SQ FT: 2,900
SALES (est): 41.6K **Privately Held**
SIC: 2752 Offset Printing

(G-33)
ALBANY MOLECULAR RESEARCH INC
21 Corporate Cir (12203-5154)
PHONE.....................................518 512-2234
Ronald Aungst, *Research*
Tracey Block, *Research*
Jaime Frattellone, *Research*
Emily Freeman, *Research*
Kathryn Golden, *Research*
EMP: 7
SALES (corp-wide): 137.4MM **Privately Held**
SIC: 2836 8731 Biological products, except diagnostic; commercial physical research
HQ: Albany Molecular Research, Inc.
26 Corporate Cir
Albany NY 12203

(G-34)
ALBANY MOLECULAR RESEARCH INC (HQ)
Also Called: Amri
26 Corporate Cir (12203-5121)
P.O. Box 15098 (12212-5098)
PHONE.....................................518 512-2000
Michael Mulhern, *CEO*
Christian Phillips, *General Mgr*
Julianne Zaremba, *General Mgr*
Ben Seisler, *Counsel*
Margalit Fine, *Exec VP*
◆ EMP: 277
SQ FT: 159,000

SALES: 570.4MM
SALES (corp-wide): 137.4MM **Privately
Held**
SIC: 2836 8731 Biological products, except diagnostic; biotechnical research,
commercial

**(G-35)
ALBANY MTAL FBRCATION
HOLDINGS**
67 Henry Johnson Blvd (12210-1413)
PHONE..................................518 463-5161
Dave Warzek, *Principal*
EMP: 7 EST: 2008
SALES (est): 1.1MM **Privately Held**
SIC: 3444 Sheet metalwork

**(G-36)
ALBANY STUDENT PRESS INC**
Also Called: A S P
1400 Washington Ave Cc329 (12222-0100)
PHONE..................................518 442-5665
Carey Qeen, *Manager*
EMP: 30
SALES: 12.4MM **Privately Held**
SIC: 2711 2741 Newspapers; miscellaneous publishing

**(G-37)
ALL-LIFTS INCORPORATED**
27-39 Thatcher St (12207-5016)
PHONE..................................518 465-3461
Steven R Dewey, *President*
Patrick Dewey, *Vice Pres*
Beth Wilson, *Accountant*
George Battistoni, *Sales Staff*
Brian Dewey, *Sales Staff*
EMP: 25 EST: 1966
SQ FT: 12,400
SALES (est): 6MM **Privately Held**
WEB: www.all-lifts.com
SIC: 2298 5063 3496 Slings, rope; electrical construction materials; chain, welded

**(G-38)
ALO ACQUISITION LLC (DH)**
26 Corporate Cir (12203-5121)
PHONE..................................518 464-0279
Thomas E D'Ambra, *Ch of Bd*
EMP: 4
SALES (est): 92.5MM
SALES (corp-wide): 137.4MM **Privately
Held**
SIC: 2833 5122 8733 Medicinals & botanicals; drugs & drug proprietaries; research
institute

**(G-39)
AMERICAN BOILER TANK WLDG
INC**
53 Pleasant St (12207-1317)
PHONE..................................518 463-5012
William A Novak, *President*
Bill Engel, *Buyer*
EMP: 20
SQ FT: 30,000
SALES: 5MM **Privately Held**
WEB: www.americanboiler.com
SIC: 3443 Fabricated plate work (boiler
shop)

**(G-40)
ANDREW J GEORGE**
Also Called: Cardinal Data/Lark Graphics
457 Madison Ave (12210-1002)
PHONE..................................518 462-4662
Andrew J George, *Owner*
EMP: 5
SQ FT: 1,750
SALES (est): 481.2K **Privately Held**
SIC: 2752 Commercial printing, lithographic

**(G-41)
ANSWERMGMT LLC**
90 State St (12207-1716)
PHONE..................................914 318-1301
John Lambros,
EMP: 5
SALES (est): 117.2K **Privately Held**
SIC: 7372 8742 Prepackaged software;
management consulting services

**(G-42)
ARCY PLASTIC LAMINATES INC
(PA)**
555 Patroon Creek Blvd (12206-5007)
P.O. Box 307, Waterford (12188-0307)
PHONE..................................518 235-0753
Robert Cecucci, *Asst Sec*
EMP: 40 EST: 1952
SQ FT: 31,000
SALES (est): 4.4MM **Privately Held**
SIC: 2541 Counter & sink tops

**(G-43)
ARDENT MILLS LLC**
Cargill
101 Normanskill St (12202-2155)
PHONE..................................518 447-1700
Paul Umstott, *Opers Staff*
Ian Hansberger, *Production*
Cody Meyers, *Manager*
EMP: 100
SALES (corp-wide): 473.4MM **Privately
Held**
WEB: www.cargill.com
SIC: 2041 0723 Flour & other grain mill
products; flour milling custom services
PA: Ardent Mills, Llc
1875 Lawrence St Ste 1400
Denver CO 80202
800 851-9618

**(G-44)
BARKER STEEL LLC**
126 S Port Rd (12202-1063)
P.O. Box 800, Coeymans (12045-0800)
PHONE..................................518 465-6221
David Legenbauer, *Branch Mgr*
EMP: 20
SALES (corp-wide): 25B **Publicly Held**
WEB: www.barker.com
SIC: 3449 8742 3441 Bars, concrete reinforcing: fabricated steel; management
consulting services; fabricated structural
metal
HQ: Barker Steel Llc
55 Sumner St Ste 1
Milford MA 01757
800 363-3953

**(G-45)
BELTRON PRODUCTS INC**
80 State St (12207-2541)
PHONE..................................888 423-5876
David Gold, *CFO*
EMP: 25
SALES (est): 899.6K **Privately Held**
SIC: 3629 Electronic generation equipment

**(G-46)
BEN WEITSMAN OF ALBANY
LLC**
300 Smith Blvd (12202-1090)
PHONE..................................518 462-4444
Adam Weitsman, *Mng Member*
Stephnen Green,
Daniel Innarella,
Joel Root,
EMP: 22 EST: 2013
SALES: 21MM
SALES (corp-wide): 179.2MM **Privately
Held**
SIC: 3559 3341 Recycling machinery;
copper smelting & refining (secondary)
PA: Weitsman Shredding, Llc
1 Recycle Dr
Owego NY 13827
607 687-7777

**(G-47)
BENWAY-HAWORTH-LWLR-
LACOSTA HE**
Also Called: Hearing Aid Office, The
21 Everett Rd (12205-1437)
PHONE..................................518 432-4070
Robert Lacosta, *President*
EMP: 12
SQ FT: 2,000
SALES (est): 1.4MM **Privately Held**
SIC: 3842 5999 Hearing aids; hearing aids

**(G-48)
BESPOKE SOFTWARE INC**
5 Sand Creek Rd (12205-1423)
P.O. Box 4406, Clifton Park (12065-0853)
PHONE..................................518 618-0746

Jennifer Clink, *General Mgr*
William Cornett, *Principal*
Amanda Bailey, *Marketing Staff*
EMP: 15
SALES (est): 1.7MM **Privately Held**
SIC: 7372 Prepackaged software

**(G-49)
BEST PALLET & CRATE LLC**
22 Railroad Ave (12205-5727)
PHONE..................................518 438-2945
Neil Manasse,
EMP: 6
SALES (est): 901K **Privately Held**
SIC: 2448 Pallets, wood & wood with metal

**(G-50)
BIMBO BAKERIES**
78 N Manning Blvd (12206-2294)
PHONE..................................518 463-2221
Joe Rebholtz, *Principal*
EMP: 16
SALES (est): 2.6MM **Privately Held**
SIC: 2051 Bread, cake & related products

**(G-51)
BIMBO BAKERIES USA INC**
40 Fuller Rd (12205-5122)
PHONE..................................518 489-4053
EMP: 18 **Privately Held**
WEB: www.gwbakeries.com
SIC: 2051 Bakery: wholesale or wholesale/retail combined
HQ: Bimbo Bakeries Usa, Inc
255 Business Center Dr # 200
Horsham PA 19044
215 347-5500

**(G-52)
BRIGAR X-PRESS SOLUTIONS
INC**
Also Called: Digital X-Press
5 Sand Creek Rd Ste 100 (12205-1400)
PHONE..................................518 438-7817
John J Mc Grath III, *CEO*
Jodi Hess, *President*
Thomas Newkirk, *Principal*
EMP: 70 EST: 1989
SQ FT: 60,000
SALES (est): 24.6MM **Privately Held**
WEB: www.brigarxpress.com
SIC: 2752 Commercial printing, offset

**(G-53)
BULLEX INC**
Also Called: Bullex Digital Safety
20 Corporate Cir Ste 3 (12203-5153)
PHONE..................................518 689-2023
Ryan O Donnell, *CEO*
Tom Rossi,
▲ EMP: 10
SALES (est): 12.6MM
SALES (corp-wide): 2.4MM **Privately
Held**
WEB: www.bullexsafety.com
SIC: 3569 8748 Firefighting apparatus;
safety training service
HQ: Lion Training Resources Group, Inc.
7200 Poe Ave Ste 400
Dayton OH 45414
937 898-1949

**(G-54)
BUSINESS FIRST OF NEW YORK**
Also Called: Business Review
2 Winners Cir 104 (12205-1181)
PHONE..................................518 640-6800
Caroline Jones, *General Mgr*
Todd Kehoe, *Research*
Kristina Feigel, *Graphic Designe*
EMP: 23
SALES (corp-wide): 1.3B **Privately Held**
SIC: 2711 Newspapers: publishing only,
not printed on site
HQ: Business First Of New York Inc
465 Main St Ste 100
Buffalo NY 14203
716 854-5822

**(G-55)
CALLANAN INDUSTRIES INC
(DH)**
8 Southwoods Blvd Ste 4 (12211-2554)
P.O. Box 15097 (12212-5097)
PHONE..................................518 374-2222
Jonas Havens, *President*

Dan Broomhall, *General Mgr*
Sheila Barkevich, *Vice Pres*
Todd Anson, *Plant Mgr*
Tim Hauck, *Plant Mgr*
▲ EMP: 205
SQ FT: 24,000
SALES (est): 102.2MM
SALES (corp-wide): 30.6B **Privately Held**
WEB: www.callanan.com
SIC: 3272 2951 Concrete products, precast; asphalt paving mixtures & blocks

**(G-56)
CAPITAL REGION WKLY
NEWSPAPERS**
Also Called: Advertiser
645 Albany Shaker Rd (12211-1158)
P.O. Box 15000 (12212-5000)
PHONE..................................518 877-7160
Patrick Smith, *President*
EMP: 29
SQ FT: 4,000
SALES (est): 1.6MM **Privately Held**
SIC: 2711 Newspapers, publishing & printing

**(G-57)
CAPITOL CITY SPECIALTIES CO**
10 Burdick Dr (12205-1467)
PHONE..................................518 486-8935
Michael Campagna, *Principal*
EMP: 8 EST: 2013
SALES (est): 759K **Privately Held**
SIC: 2099 Peanut butter

**(G-58)
CASCADES NEW YORK INC**
71 Fuller Rd (12205-5734)
PHONE..................................518 689-1020
Scott Reed, *Manager*
EMP: 25
SALES (corp-wide): 3.5B **Privately Held**
SIC: 2621 Paper mills
HQ: Cascades New York Inc.
1845 Emerson St
Rochester NY 14606
585 527-8110

**(G-59)
CHAMPLAIN HUDSON POWER
EX INC**
600 Broadway Fl 3 (12207-2235)
PHONE..................................518 465-0710
John Douglas, *CEO*
Donald Jensson, *President*
Scott Hargreaves, *CFO*
EMP: 7
SQ FT: 500
SALES (est): 540K **Privately Held**
SIC: 3568 Power transmission equipment

**(G-60)
CHARLES FREIHOFER BAKING
CO**
1 Prospect Rd (12206-2229)
PHONE..................................518 463-2221
Peter Rollins, *President*
EMP: 8
SALES (est): 1.1MM **Privately Held**
SIC: 2499 Bakers' equipment, wood

**(G-61)
CLEAR VIEW BAG COMPANY
INC**
5 Burdick Dr (12205-1405)
P.O. Box 11160 (12211-0160)
PHONE..................................518 458-7153
William J Romer, *Ch of Bd*
Deborah S Romer, *Vice Pres*
Len Smith, *QC Mgr*
Sherri Smith, *Administration*
EMP: 156 EST: 1957
SQ FT: 45,000
SALES (est): 27.9MM **Privately Held**
WEB: www.clearviewbag.com
SIC: 3081 2673 Polyethylene film; bags:
plastic, laminated & coated

**(G-62)
CMC-KUHNKE INC**
90 State St Ste 601 (12207-1706)
PHONE..................................518 694-3310
Heinz Grossjohann, *President*
Alex Grossjohann, *Vice Pres*
EMP: 12

SQ FT: 10,000
SALES (est): 2.4MM **Privately Held**
SIC: 3411 Food & beverage containers

(G-63)
CMP EXPORT CO INC
Also Called: Ticoniun
413 N Pearl St (12207-1311)
P.O. Box 350 (12201-0350)
PHONE..............................518 434-3147
Devon Howe, *President*
Dana Haugh, *Vice Pres*
Ed Civiok, *Treasurer*
Edward Civiok Jr, *Treasurer*
Maryjo Kaleda,
▲ **EMP:** 42
SALES (est): 3.9MM **Privately Held**
WEB: www.cmpindustries.com
SIC: 3843 Dental equipment & supplies

(G-64)
CMP INDUSTRIES LLC (PA)
Also Called: Ticonium Division
413 N Pearl St (12207-1311)
PHONE..............................518 434-3147
Devon Howe, *Mng Member*
Kirby Amick, *Technical Staff*
Elmer Rose, *Technical Staff*
◆ **EMP:** 40 **EST:** 1889
SQ FT: 90,000
SALES (est): 8.9MM **Privately Held**
WEB: www.cmpindustry.com
SIC: 3843 Dental equipment & supplies

(G-65)
CMP INDUSTRIES LLC
Also Called: Nobilium
413 N Pearl St (12207-1311)
PHONE..............................518 434-3147
William Regan, *Branch Mgr*
EMP: 5
SALES (corp-wide): 8.9MM **Privately Held**
WEB: www.cmpindustry.com
SIC: 3843 Dental laboratory equipment
PA: Cmp Industries Llc
      413 N Pearl St
      Albany NY 12207
      518 434-3147

(G-66)
COCA-COLA BTLG CO OF NY INC
38 Warehouse Row (12205-5757)
PHONE..............................518 459-2010
Dwayne St Claire, *COO*
Dwayne St Clair, *Opers Mgr*
Julie Francis, *Sales/Mktg Mgr*
EMP: 11
SALES (corp-wide): 31.8B **Publicly Held**
SIC: 2086 5149 Bottled & canned soft
drinks; groceries & related products
HQ: The Coca-Cola Bottling Company Of
New York Inc
2500 Windy Ridge Pkwy Se
Atlanta GA 30339
770 989-3000

(G-67)
COCCADOTTS INC
1179 Central Ave (12205-5436)
PHONE..............................518 438-4937
Rachel Dott, *Owner*
Luke Dott, *Treasurer*
EMP: 11
SALES (est): 982K **Privately Held**
SIC: 2051 Cakes, bakery: except frozen

(G-68)
COMMERCEHUB INC (HQ)
201 Fuller Rd Fl 6 (12203-3621)
PHONE..............................518 810-0700
Francis Poore, *President*
Mike Amend, *COO*
John Hinkle, *Exec VP*
Kathleen Conley, *Vice Pres*
Gavin Hogan, *Vice Pres*
EMP: 15 **EST:** 1997
SQ FT: 49,500
SALES: 111.1MM **Privately Held**
SIC: 7372 Prepackaged software
PA: Great Dane Parent, Llc
201 Fuller Rd Fl 6
Albany NY 12203
518 810-0700

(G-69)
DAVIES OFFICE REFURBISHING INC (PA)
40 Loudonville Rd (12204-1513)
PHONE..............................518 449-2040
William E Davies, *President*
Evelyn Davies, *Vice Pres*
David Wyman, *Accounts Exec*
Michael Nguyen, *CIO*
Melissa Kruzinski, *Administration*
▲ **EMP:** 135
SQ FT: 96,000
SALES (est): 38.1MM **Privately Held**
WEB: www.daviesoffice.com
SIC: 2522 7641 Office furniture, except
wood; office furniture repair & mainte-
nance

(G-70)
DIGITAL PAGE LLC
75 Benjamin St (12202-1137)
P.O. Box 216, Glenmont (12077-0216)
PHONE..............................518 446-9129
Eugene R Spada II,
EMP: 11
SQ FT: 2,000
SALES (est): 191.9K **Privately Held**
SIC: 2791 Typesetting

(G-71)
DURAVENT INC
10 Jupiter Ln (12205-4947)
PHONE..............................518 463-7284
Mike Winn, *President*
EMP: 24
SALES (corp-wide): 154.5MM **Privately Held**
SIC: 3444 Metal ventilating equipment
HQ: Duravent, Inc.
877 Cotting Ct
Vacaville CA 95688
800 835-4429

(G-72)
DYNAMIC SCREENPRINTING
12 Vatrano Rd (12205-3404)
PHONE..............................518 487-4256
Jeff Serge, *Mng Member*
EMP: 9
SALES (est): 829.3K **Privately Held**
SIC: 2261 Screen printing of cotton broad-
woven fabrics

(G-73)
EASY BOOK PUBLISHING INC
260 Osborne Rd Ste 3 (12211-1856)
P.O. Box 11455 (12211-0455)
PHONE..............................518 459-6281
Nydia Russum, *President*
John Russum, *Vice Pres*
EMP: 6
SQ FT: 1,500
SALES (est): 560.3K **Privately Held**
WEB: www.easy-book.net
SIC: 2741 Directories: publishing only, not
printed on site

(G-74)
EDP RENEWABLES NORTH AMER LLC
1971 Western Ave 230 (12203-5066)
PHONE..............................518 426-1650
Patrick Doyle, *Branch Mgr*
EMP: 8
SALES (corp-wide): 4.2B **Privately Held**
SIC: 3621 Windmills, electric generating
HQ: Edp Renewables North America Llc
808 Travis St Ste 700
Houston TX 77002
713 265-0350

(G-75)
EMPIRE AIR SPECIALTIES INC
40 Kraft Ave (12205-5428)
PHONE..............................518 689-4440
Robert J Miner, *President*
Rebecca Miner, *Treasurer*
EMP: 25
SQ FT: 5,500
SALES (est): 5.1MM **Privately Held**
SIC: 3444 Sheet metalwork

(G-76)
FASTSIGNS
1593 Central Ave (12205-2457)
PHONE..............................518 456-7446
James Pritchard, *Principal*
EMP: 10
SALES (est): 1.1MM **Privately Held**
SIC: 3993 Signs & advertising specialties

(G-77)
FINGERPRINT AMERICA INC
1843 Central Ave (12205-4796)
P.O. Box 12542 (12212-2542)
PHONE..............................518 435-1609
Chris Migliaro, *President*
EMP: 6
SQ FT: 3,000
SALES (est): 733.2K **Privately Held**
WEB: www.fingerprintamerica.com
SIC: 3999 Fingerprint equipment

(G-78)
FORT ORANGE PRESS INC
11 Sand Creek Rd (12205-1442)
PHONE..............................518 489-3233
Robert F Witko, *Ch of Bd*
Frank P Witko, *Ch of Bd*
Michael P Witko, *President*
William Dorsman, *Vice Pres*
Kenneth L Pleat, *Vice Pres*
EMP: 37 **EST:** 1905
SQ FT: 33,000
SALES (est): 11.4MM **Privately Held**
WEB: www.fortorangepress.com
SIC: 2752 2791 Commercial printing, off-
set; typesetting

(G-79)
GALAXY NUTRITIONAL FOODS INC
Also Called: Go Veggie
90 State St Ste 700 (12207-1707)
PHONE..............................401 667-5000
Rick Antonelli, *CEO*
◆ **EMP:** 21
SALES (est): 18.6MM
SALES (corp-wide): 50.9MM **Privately Held**
WEB: www.galaxyfoods.com
SIC: 2022 Cheese, natural & processed
PA: Greenspace Brands Inc
176 St George St
Toronto ON M5R 2
416 934-5034

(G-80)
GENERAL ELECTRIC COMPANY
11 Anderson Dr (12205-1401)
PHONE..............................518 459-4110
Gautam Naik, *Engineer*
Robert Hitchcock, *Manager*
EMP: 50
SQ FT: 1,680
SALES (corp-wide): 121.6B **Publicly Held**
SIC: 3629 7694 Electronic generation
equipment; electric motor repair
PA: General Electric Company
41 Farnsworth St
Boston MA 02210
617 443-3000

(G-81)
GREAT DANE PARENT LLC (PA)
201 Fuller Rd Fl 6 (12203-3621)
PHONE..............................518 810-0700
Francis Poore, *President*
EMP: 2
SALES (est): 111.1MM **Privately Held**
SIC: 7372 Prepackaged software

(G-82)
GREENBUSH TAPE & LABEL INC
40 Broadway Unit 31 (12202-1174)
P.O. Box 1488 (12201-1488)
PHONE..............................518 465-2389
Alfred Chenot, *Corp Secy*
James Chenot, *Vice Pres*
EMP: 35 **EST:** 1966
SQ FT: 75,000
SALES (est): 4.6MM **Privately Held**
WEB: www.greenbushlabel.com
SIC: 2759 2672 Labels & seals: printing;
coated & laminated paper

(G-83)
HANES SUPPLY INC
156 Railroad Ave Ste 3 (12205-5773)
PHONE..............................518 438-0139
Bill Kenny, *Manager*
EMP: 13
SALES (est): 2.3MM
SALES (corp-wide): 97.5MM **Privately Held**
SIC: 3496 Miscellaneous fabricated wire
products
PA: Hanes Supply, Inc.
55 James E Casey Dr
Buffalo NY 14206
716 826-2636

(G-84)
HANGER INC
1315 Central Ave (12205-5282)
PHONE..............................518 435-0840
EMP: 23
SALES (corp-wide): 1B **Publicly Held**
SIC: 3842 Surgical appliances & supplies
PA: Hanger, Inc.
10910 Domain Dr Ste 300
Austin TX 78758
512 777-3800

(G-85)
HEARST CORPORATION
Capital Newspaper Div
645 Albany Shaker Rd (12211-1158)
P.O. Box 15000 (12212-5000)
PHONE..............................518 454-5694
Gary Hahn, *Publisher*
Lisa Stevens, *Editor*
Will Waldron, *Editor*
David P White, *Vice Pres*
Charlie Hug, *Opers Staff*
EMP: 550
SALES (corp-wide): 8.3B **Privately Held**
WEB: www.hearstcorp.com
SIC: 2721 2752 2711 Periodicals: publish-
ing only; commercial printing, lithographic;
newspapers
PA: The Hearst Corporation
300 W 57th St Fl 42
New York NY 10019
212 649-2000

(G-86)
HOCKEY FACILITY
830 Albany Shaker Rd (12211-1054)
PHONE..............................518 452-7396
Paul Hebert, *Manager*
EMP: 5
SALES (est): 494.1K **Privately Held**
SIC: 2329 Hockey uniforms: men's, youths'
& boys'

(G-87)
HOEHN INC
Also Called: Hoehn.us
159 Chestnut St (12210-1905)
PHONE..............................518 463-8900
James G Hoehn Jr, *President*
Melissa Nigro, *Vice Pres*
EMP: 15
SALES: 1.6MM **Privately Held**
WEB: www.hoehn.com
SIC: 2339 2389 Women's & misses' ac-
cessories; men's miscellaneous acces-
sories

(G-88)
HP INC
5 Computer Dr S (12205-1608)
PHONE..............................650 857-1501
Charlene D Fitzgerald, *Branch Mgr*
EMP: 43
SALES (corp-wide): 58.4B **Publicly Held**
SIC: 3571 Personal computers (microcom-
puters)
PA: Hp, Inc.
1501 Page Mill Rd
Palo Alto CA 94304
650 857-1501

(G-89)
ION OPTICS INC
Also Called: Cosmo Optics
75 Benjamin St (12202-1137)
PHONE..............................518 339-6853
Brian Sebastian, *Principal*
EMP: 13

SALES (est): 1.2MM **Privately Held**
SIC: 3229 Lens blanks, optical

(G-90)
ISIMULATE LLC
43 New Scotland Ave (12208-3412)
PHONE..............................877 947-2831
Chris Kroboth, *Manager*
EMP: 5
SQ FT: 1,000
SALES (est): 500K **Privately Held**
SIC: 3845 Arc lamp units, electrotherapeutic (except IR & UV)

(G-91)
JASON LADANYE GUITAR PIANO & H
605 Park Ave (12208-3217)
PHONE..............................518 527-3973
Jason Ladanye, *Owner*
EMP: 50
SALES (est): 90.9K **Privately Held**
SIC: 3931 Harmonicas

(G-92)
JOHNSON CONTROLS INC
130 Railroad Ave (12205-5701)
PHONE..............................518 694-4822
Dave Ricci, *Accounts Exec*
John Desare, *Manager*
EMP: 9 **Privately Held**
SIC: 2531 Seats, automobile
HQ: Johnson Controls, Inc.
    5757 N Green Bay Ave
    Milwaukee WI 53209
    414 524-1200

(G-93)
KAL-HARBOUR INC
Also Called: Harbour Roads
11 Villa Rd (12204-2213)
P.O. Box 4087 (12204-0087)
PHONE..............................518 266-0690
Laura Harbour, *President*
EMP: 10 **Privately Held**
WEB: www.harbourroads.com
SIC: 2951 Asphalt paving mixtures & blocks
PA: Kal-Harbour Inc
    21 Arch St
    Watervliet NY 12189

(G-94)
KING ROAD MATERIALS INC (DH)
Also Called: King Paving
8 Southwoods Blvd (12211-2554)
P.O. Box 15097 (12212-5097)
PHONE..............................518 381-9995
Donald E Fane, *President*
EMP: 35 EST: 1959
SQ FT: 2,552
SALES (est): 21.8MM
SALES (corp-wide): 30.6B **Privately Held**
SIC: 2951 Asphalt & asphaltic paving mixtures (not from refineries)

(G-95)
KING ROAD MATERIALS INC
Cordell Rd (12212)
P.O. Box 12699 (12212-2699)
PHONE..............................518 382-5354
Mellisa Bennett, *Principal*
EMP: 15
SALES (corp-wide): 30.6B **Privately Held**
SIC: 3273 Ready-mixed concrete
HQ: King Road Materials, Inc.
    8 Southwoods Blvd
    Albany NY 12211
    518 381-9995

(G-96)
KRONOS INCORPORATED
16 Sage Est Ste 206 (12204-2241)
PHONE..............................518 459-5545
Frank Shipp, *Manager*
EMP: 36
SALES (corp-wide): 1B **Privately Held**
WEB: www.kronos.com
SIC: 7372 Prepackaged software
HQ: Kronos Incorporated
    900 Chelmsford St # 312
    Lowell MA 01851
    978 250-9800

(G-97)
LIDS CORPORATION
131 Colonie Ctr Spc 429 (12205-2751)
PHONE..............................518 459-7060
Dinelle Jackson, *Manager*
EMP: 5
SALES (corp-wide): 2.1B **Publicly Held**
WEB: www.hatworld.com
SIC: 2253 Hats & headwear, knit
HQ: Lids Corporation
    7555 Woodland Dr
    Indianapolis IN 46278

(G-98)
MCD METALS LLC
20 Corporate Cir Ste 2 (12203-5175)
PHONE..............................518 456-9694
Kevin Gleason, *President*
Jacek Wozniak, *Opers Mgr*
EMP: 11
SALES (est): 734.5K **Privately Held**
SIC: 3499 Shims, metal

(G-99)
MECHANICAL TECHNOLOGY INC (PA)
Also Called: MTI
325 Washington Avenue Ext (12205-5581)
PHONE..............................518 218-2550
David C Michaels, *Ch of Bd*
Frederick W Jones, *President*
James Prueitt, *Vice Pres*
Ann Hogle, *Purch Mgr*
Peter Opela, *Engineer*
EMP: 27 EST: 1961
SQ FT: 17,400
SALES: 7MM **Publicly Held**
SIC: 3829 Stress, strain & flaw detecting/measuring equipment; vibration meters, analyzers & calibrators

(G-100)
MOHAWK INNOVATIVE TECH INC (PA)
1037 Watervliet Shaker Rd (12205-2032)
PHONE..............................518 862-4290
Hooshang Heshmat, *President*
James F Walton II, *Chairman*
Melissa D Heshmat, *CFO*
Michael Genier, *Manager*
Michael Tomaszewski, *Admin Sec*
EMP: 12
SQ FT: 18,000
SALES (est): 3MM **Privately Held**
WEB: www.mohawkinnovative.com
SIC: 3714 8711 Axle housings & shafts, motor vehicle; engineering services

(G-101)
MOTOROLA SOLUTIONS INC
251 New Karner Rd (12205-4627)
PHONE..............................518 869-9517
EMP: 142
SALES (corp-wide): 5.7B **Publicly Held**
SIC: 3663 Mfg Communication Equipment
PA: Motorola Solutions, Inc.
    1303 E Algonquin Rd
    Schaumburg IL 60661
    847 576-5000

(G-102)
MPM AR LLC
22 Corporate Woods Blvd (12211-2374)
PHONE..............................518 233-3397
EMP: 3
SALES (est): 1.5MM
SALES (corp-wide): 2.7B **Publicly Held**
SIC: 2869 Silicones
HQ: Mpm Holdings Inc.
    260 Hudson River Rd
    Waterford NY 12188
    518 233-3330

(G-103)
MTI INSTRUMENTS INC
325 Washington Ave 3 (12206-3012)
PHONE..............................518 218-2550
Kevin G Lynch, *Principal*
Rick Jones, *Chairman*
EMP: 10

SALES (est): 4.7MM
SALES (corp-wide): 7MM **Publicly Held**
WEB: www.mtiinstruments.com
SIC: 3829 8731 Stress, strain & flaw detecting/measuring equipment; vibration meters, analyzers & calibrators; commercial research laboratory; engineering laboratory, except testing; energy research
PA: Mechanical Technology Incorporated
    325 Washington Avenue Ext
    Albany NY 12205
    518 218-2550

(G-104)
NEW YORK STATE ASSOC
Also Called: NYSASBO
453 New Karner Rd (12205-3821)
PHONE..............................518 434-2281
Korrin Wallim, *Manager*
Michael Borges, *Exec Dir*
EMP: 10
SALES: 2.2MM **Privately Held**
SIC: 7372 8699 Application computer software; membership organizations

(G-105)
NEWSPAPER TIMES UNION
Also Called: Capitol Newspaper
645 Albany Shaker Rd (12211-1158)
P.O. Box 15000 (12212-5000)
PHONE..............................518 454-5676
David White, *President*
Darrell Foster, *Prdtn Mgr*
Renee Bernard, *Sales Staff*
Kriston Delisio, *Sales Staff*
Herb Terns, *Advt Staff*
EMP: 12
SALES (est): 690K **Privately Held**
WEB: www.saratogasignature.com
SIC: 2711 Newspapers, publishing & printing

(G-106)
NINE PIN CIDERWORKS LLC
929 Broadway (12207-1305)
PHONE..............................518 449-9999
Alejandro Del Peral, *Mng Member*
Joshua Whelan, *Representative*
EMP: 10 EST: 2013
SALES (est): 911.4K **Privately Held**
SIC: 2099 Cider, nonalcoholic

(G-107)
NORTHEAST COMMERCIAL PRTG INC (PA)
Also Called: Eastern Offset
1237 Central Ave Ste 3 (12205-5328)
PHONE..............................518 459-5047
Anthony Mosca, *President*
EMP: 7
SQ FT: 4,000
SALES (est): 768.6K **Privately Held**
WEB: www.northeastcommercial.com
SIC: 2752 Commercial printing, offset

(G-108)
NORTHEASTERN AIR QUALITY INC
730 3rd St (12206-2007)
PHONE..............................518 857-3641
Robert Kelley, *President*
EMP: 12
SALES (est): 5MM **Privately Held**
SIC: 1389 Testing, measuring, surveying & analysis services

(G-109)
ORACLE AMERICA INC
Also Called: Sun Microsystems
7 Southwoods Blvd Ste 1 (12211-2526)
PHONE..............................518 427-9353
Leslie Woodin, *Sales/Mktg Mgr*
EMP: 52
SALES (corp-wide): 39.5B **Publicly Held**
SIC: 7372 Prepackaged software
HQ: Oracle America, Inc.
    500 Oracle Pkwy
    Redwood City CA 94065
    650 506-7000

(G-110)
OUR DAILY EATS LLC
10 Burdick Dr Ste 1 (12205-1457)
PHONE..............................518 810-8412
EMP: 12

SALES (est): 1.8MM **Privately Held**
SIC: 2068 Mfg Salted/Roasted Nuts/Seeds

(G-111)
PARK-OHIO INDS TRSRY CO INC (DH)
Also Called: Supply Technologies NY , Inc.
80 State St (12207-2541)
PHONE..............................212 966-3310
John A Chrzanowski, *Ch of Bd*
Samuel Laufer, *President*
▲ EMP: 18 EST: 1953
SQ FT: 10,000
SALES (est): 12.5MM
SALES (corp-wide): 1.6B **Publicly Held**
SIC: 3452 3599 5072 3451 Bolts, metal; rivets, metal; washers, metal; screws, metal; machine shop, jobbing & repair; bolts; rivets; washers (hardware); screws; screw machine products
HQ: Supply Technologies Llc
    6065 Parkland Blvd Ste 2
    Cleveland OH 44124
    440 947-2100

(G-112)
PATRICK RYANS MODERN PRESS
1 Colonie St (12207-2434)
PHONE..............................518 434-2921
Michael Ryan, *President*
Patrick Ryan, *Vice Pres*
EMP: 10 EST: 1946
SQ FT: 6,000
SALES (est): 1MM **Privately Held**
WEB: www.modernpress.com
SIC: 2752 2759 2791 Commercial printing, offset; letterpress printing; typesetting

(G-113)
PBR GRAPHICS INC
20 Railroad Ave Ste 1 (12205-5785)
PHONE..............................518 458-2909
Robert Cullum Jr, *President*
Robert G Cullum Sr, *Vice Pres*
Barbara Cullum, *Treasurer*
EMP: 9
SQ FT: 11,000
SALES: 920K **Privately Held**
SIC: 2752 Commercial printing, offset

(G-114)
PENGUIN RANDOM HOUSE LLC
80 State St (12207-2541)
PHONE..............................212 366-2377
David Shanks, *CEO*
EMP: 200
SALES (corp-wide): 75.3MM **Privately Held**
SIC: 2731 5942 Books: publishing only; book stores
HQ: Penguin Random House Llc
    1745 Broadway Frnt 1
    New York NY 10019
    212 782-9000

(G-115)
PHYLJOHN DISTRIBUTORS INC
Also Called: Gillette Creamery
6 Interstate Ave (12205-5309)
PHONE..............................518 459-2775
Frank Ogno, *Accounts Mgr*
Richard H Gillette, *Supervisor*
EMP: 10
SALES (est): 33.6MM **Privately Held**
WEB: www.gillettecreamery.com
SIC: 2024 Ice cream & frozen desserts
PA: Phyljohn Distributors, Inc.
    47 Steves Ln
    Gardiner NY 12525
    845 419-0900

(G-116)
PINE BUSH PRINTING CO INC
2005 Western Ave (12203-7016)
PHONE..............................518 456-2431
Don Blais, *President*
EMP: 7
SALES (est): 651.8K **Privately Held**
SIC: 2752 Commercial printing, offset

(G-117)
PRAXAIR INC
120 Railroad Ave (12205-5701)
PHONE..............................518 482-4360

GEOGRAPHIC

EMP: 20 **Privately Held**
SIC: 2813 Industrial gases
HQ: Praxair, Inc.
　　10 Riverview Dr
　　Danbury CT 06810
　　203 837-2000

(G-118)
PRECISION N AMER FD MCHY LLC
60 Commerce Ave Ste 42 (12206-2043)
PHONE.................................518 462-3387
Mark Altarac, *President*
▲ EMP: 12
SQ FT: 57,000
SALES (est): 2.4MM **Privately Held**
SIC: 3556 Food products machinery

(G-119)
PRINTING RESOURCES INC
Also Called: The Printing Company
100 Fuller Rd Ste 1 (12205-5760)
PHONE.................................518 482-2470
Darcy Harding, *President*
EMP: 20
SQ FT: 15,000
SALES (est): 2MM **Privately Held**
SIC: 2759 2791 2789 2752 Commercial
printing; typesetting; bookbinding & re-
lated work; commercial printing, litho-
graphic

(G-120)
R & J SHEET METAL DISTRIBUTORS
Also Called: R and J Sheet Metal
156 Orange St (12210)
PHONE.................................518 433-1525
Robert Gardner, *President*
EMP: 6
SALES (est): 969.1K **Privately Held**
SIC: 3444 Sheet metalwork

(G-121)
R R DONNELLEY & SONS COMPANY
Moore Graphics Services
4 Executive Park Dr Ste 2 (12203-3717)
PHONE.................................518 438-9722
Joe Benoit, *Manager*
EMP: 100
SALES (corp-wide): 6.8B **Publicly Held**
WEB: www.moore.com
SIC: 2759 Screen printing
PA: R. R. Donnelley & Sons Company
　　35 W Wacker Dr
　　Chicago IL 60601
　　312 326-8000

(G-122)
RAD SOAP CO LLC
8 Wolfert Ave (12204-2658)
PHONE.................................518 461-9667
Alexis Kerber,
EMP: 18 EST: 2011
SALES (est): 2.9MM **Privately Held**
SIC: 2841 Soap & other detergents

(G-123)
RAFF ENTERPRISES
12 Petra Ln Ste 6 (12205-4973)
PHONE.................................518 218-7883
Sean Raff, *Owner*
EMP: 8
SALES (est): 788.4K **Privately Held**
SIC: 2511 China closets

(G-124)
RATIONAL RETENTION LLC (PA)
Also Called: Rational Enterprises
2 Tower Pl Ste 13 (12203-3726)
PHONE.................................518 489-3000
Bob Conley, *Vice Pres*
Bernard Hillengas, *Vice Pres*
Melissa Faas, *Controller*
William W Duker, *Mng Member*
Leigh McEntire, *Manager*
EMP: 37
SALES (est): 3MM **Privately Held**
SIC: 7372 7374 Business oriented com-
puter software; data processing & prepa-
ration

(G-125)
RED HAWK FIRE & SECURITY LLC
14 Jetway Dr (12211-2806)
PHONE.................................518 877-7616
Richard Fuzy, *Pastor*
Steve Vallery, *Branch Mgr*
EMP: 6
SALES (corp-wide): 4.5B **Publicly Held**
SIC: 3699 Security control equipment &
systems
HQ: Red Hawk Fire & Security, Llc
　　5100 Town Center Cir # 350
　　Boca Raton FL 33486
　　877 387-0188

(G-126)
REM PRINTING INC
55 Railroad Ave (12205-5947)
PHONE.................................518 438-7338
Paul Remmert, *President*
Matthew Remmert, *VP Sales*
EMP: 6
SQ FT: 5,000
SALES: 600K **Privately Held**
WEB: www.remprinting.com
SIC: 2752 Commercial printing, offset

(G-127)
SCARANO BOAT BUILDING INC
194 S Port Rd (12202-1075)
PHONE.................................518 463-3401
John S Scarano, *President*
EMP: 45
SALES: 950K **Privately Held**
WEB: www.scaranoboat.com
SIC: 3732 Boat building & repairing

(G-128)
SCARANO BOATBUILDING INC
194 S Port Rd (12202-1075)
PHONE.................................518 463-3401
John Scarano, *President*
Rick Scarano, *Vice Pres*
EMP: 27
SQ FT: 90,000
SALES (est): 4.3MM **Privately Held**
SIC: 3732 Boat building & repairing

(G-129)
SCHNEIDER ELECTRIC USA INC
Also Called: Schneider Electric 124
501 New Karner Rd Ste 5 (12205-3882)
PHONE.................................518 452-2590
Michael Sokaris, *Manager*
EMP: 10
SALES (corp-wide): 177.9K **Privately Held**
WEB: www.squared.com
SIC: 3699 Electrical equipment & supplies
HQ: Schneider Electric Usa, Inc.
　　201 Wshington St Ste 2700
　　Boston MA 02108
　　978 975-9600

(G-130)
SOMML HEALTH INC
43 New Scotland Ave Mc25 (12208-3412)
PHONE.................................518 880-2170
EMP: 5 EST: 2015
SQ FT: 200
SALES (est): 171.6K **Privately Held**
SIC: 7372 Prepackaged software

(G-131)
STANLEY PAPER CO INC
1 Terminal St (12206-2283)
PHONE.................................518 489-1131
Matthew Jasinski II, *President*
Pearl Jasinski, *Corp Secy*
EMP: 11 EST: 1942
SQ FT: 6,000
SALES (est): 2.4MM **Privately Held**
SIC: 2679 5113 Conduits, fiber (pressed
pulp): from purchased material; industrial
& personal service paper

(G-132)
STEIN FIBERS LTD (PA)
4 Computer Dr W Ste 200 (12205-1630)
PHONE.................................518 489-5700
Sidney J Stein III, *Ch of Bd*
Peter J Spitalny, *President*
Napier Breen, *Engineer*
Allen Greenberg, *CFO*

Allen Greenburg, *CFO*
◆ EMP: 20
SQ FT: 4,600
SALES: 284.7MM **Privately Held**
WEB: www.steinfibers.com
SIC: 2824 Polyester fibers

(G-133)
STOP N SHOP LLC
911 Central Ave Ste 149 (12206-1350)
PHONE.................................518 512-9657
Efasto Bowl, *Mng Member*
EMP: 6
SALES (est): 148.8K **Privately Held**
SIC: 7372 Business oriented computer
software

(G-134)
TECHNICAL WLDG FABRICATORS LLC
27 Thatcher St (12207-3003)
PHONE.................................518 463-2229
Carol Boyer,
EMP: 10
SALES (est): 1.4MM **Privately Held**
SIC: 3315 Welded steel wire fabric

(G-135)
TEL TECHNOLOGY CENTER AMER LLC (DH)
255 Fuller Rd Ste 244 (12203-3663)
PHONE.................................512 424-4200
Hiroshi Takenaka,
▲ EMP: 22
SALES (est): 5.7MM **Privately Held**
SIC: 3674 Semiconductors & related de-
vices
HQ: Tokyo Electron U.S. Holdings, Inc.
　　2400 Grove Blvd
　　Austin TX 78741
　　512 424-1000

(G-136)
THERMOAURA INC
132b Railroad Ave Ste B (12205-5701)
PHONE.................................518 813-4997
Rutvik J Mehta, *President*
EMP: 11
SQ FT: 4,800
SALES: 500K **Privately Held**
SIC: 3674 Wafers (semiconductor devices)

(G-137)
TOKYO ELECTRON AMERICA INC
255 Fuller Rd Ste 214 (12203-3603)
PHONE.................................518 292-4200
Chris Krammer, *Branch Mgr*
EMP: 9 **Privately Held**
WEB: www.telusa.com
SIC: 3674 Semiconductors & related de-
vices
HQ: Tokyo Electron America, Inc.
　　2400 Grove Blvd
　　Austin TX 78741
　　512 424-1000

(G-138)
U ALL INC
9 Interstate Ave (12205-5320)
PHONE.................................518 438-2558
James Holodak, *President*
Susan Holodak, *Admin Sec*
EMP: 25
SQ FT: 10,000
SALES (est): 3.7MM **Privately Held**
WEB: www.allu.com
SIC: 2759 2395 5199 2396 Screen print-
ing; embroidery & art needlework; adver-
tising specialties; automotive & apparel
trimmings

(G-139)
UCC GUIDE INC (HQ)
Also Called: Ernst Publishing Co
99 Washington Ave (12210-2822)
PHONE.................................518 434-0909
Gregory E Teal, *CEO*
Jan Clark, *Vice Pres*
Kathryn Teal, *Vice Pres*
EMP: 10
SQ FT: 4,000

SALES (est): 2.1MM
SALES (corp-wide): 1.1B **Publicly Held**
WEB: www.ernstinfo.com
SIC: 2741 Miscellaneous publishing
PA: Black Knight, Inc.
　　601 Riverside Ave
　　Jacksonville FL 32204
　　904 854-5100

(G-140)
ULTREPET LLC
136c Fuller Rd (12205-5604)
PHONE.................................781 275-6400
M Scott Mellen, *President*
Carol C Forman, *Principal*
David B Spencer, *Chairman*
Leigh A Peritz, *Vice Pres*
Paul C Zordan, *Vice Pres*
▲ EMP: 65
SALES (est): 13.4MM
SALES (corp-wide): 51.9MM **Privately Held**
SIC: 3559 Plastics working machinery
PA: Wte Corporation
　　7 Alfred Cir
　　Bedford MA 01730
　　781 275-6400

(G-141)
WEST END IRON WORKS INC
4254 Albany St (12205-4684)
PHONE.................................518 456-1105
Eric R Frey, *President*
EMP: 5 EST: 1890
SQ FT: 9,000
SALES (est): 721.6K **Privately Held**
SIC: 3446 Architectural metalwork

(G-142)
WILD WORKS INCORPORATED
30 Railroad Ave (12205-5721)
PHONE.................................716 891-4197
William C Smith, *CEO*
EMP: 5
SALES (est): 536.4K **Privately Held**
SIC: 2891 Adhesives & sealants

(G-143)
YOGIBO LLC
120 Washington Avenue Ext # 23
(12203-5367)
PHONE.................................518 456-1762
David Ozmon, *Branch Mgr*
EMP: 14 **Privately Held**
SIC: 2519 Household furniture, except
wood or metal: upholstered
PA: Yogibo Llc
　　16 Celina Ave Unit 13
　　Nashua NH 03063

(G-144)
ZELA INTERNATIONAL CO
13 Manor St (12207-3008)
PHONE.................................518 436-1833
Ike Sukljian, *President*
John Sukljian, *Vice Pres*
Cristina Samuels, *VP Sales*
▲ EMP: 25
SQ FT: 60,000
SALES (est): 2.3MM **Privately Held**
WEB: www.zela.com
SIC: 2844 5122 Cosmetic preparations;
cosmetics

Albertson
Nassau County

(G-145)
BRAUN INDUSTRIES INC (PA)
Also Called: Braun Brush Company
43 Albertson Ave (11507-2102)
PHONE.................................516 741-6000
Lance W Cheney, *CEO*
Peter Lassen, *Director*
▲ EMP: 19 EST: 1875
SQ FT: 15,000
SALES: 3.2MM **Privately Held**
WEB: www.brush.com
SIC: 3991 Brooms & brushes

▲ = Import ▼=Export
◆ =Import/Export

(G-146)
BURT MILLWORK CORPORATION
85 Fairview Dr (11507-1007)
PHONE.....................718 257-4601
Eli Gordon, *President*
Seymour Gordon, *Vice Pres*
▲ **EMP:** 22
SQ FT: 42,500
SALES (est): 5.4MM **Privately Held**
SIC: 2431 Doors, wood; door shutters, wood; windows, wood

(G-147)
DAIGE PRODUCTS INC
1 Albertson Ave Ste 3 (11507-1444)
P.O. Box 223 (11507-0223)
PHONE.....................516 621-2100
I M Harris, *President*
Richard Fchinkel, *Vice Pres*
Ira Harris, *Personnel*
Harris Ike, *Administration*
EMP: 15
SQ FT: 3,500
SALES (est): 2.5MM **Privately Held**
WEB: www.daige.com
SIC: 3555 Printing trades machinery

(G-148)
PATSY STROCCHIA & SONS IRON WO
Also Called: Strocchia Iron Works
175 I U Willets Rd Ste 4 (11507-1342)
PHONE.....................516 625-8800
Ralph J Strocchia, *Ch of Bd*
Leonard D Strocchia, *Vice Pres*
Ralph Strocchia Jr, *Admin Sec*
EMP: 18 **EST:** 1922
SALES (est): 3.2MM **Privately Held**
SIC: 3441 Fabricated structural metal

(G-149)
PAYA PRINTING OF NY INC
87 Searingtown Rd (11507-1125)
PHONE.....................516 625-8346
Mohammad Samii, *President*
EMP: 5
SQ FT: 1,000
SALES (est): 472.3K **Privately Held**
SIC: 2754 2752 Commercial printing, gravure; commercial printing, lithographic

(G-150)
PELLA CORPORATION
Also Called: Pella Window Door
77 Albertson Ave Ste 2 (11507-2127)
PHONE.....................516 385-3622
Shanade Alton, *Branch Mgr*
EMP: 316
SALES (corp-wide): 1.7B **Privately Held**
SIC: 2431 Windows, wood
PA: Pella Corporation
102 Main St
Pella IA 50219
641 621-1000

(G-151)
PELLA CORPORATION
Also Called: Pella Window Door
77 Albertson Ave Ste 2 (11507-2127)
PHONE.....................516 385-3622
EMP: 316
SALES (corp-wide): 663.7MM **Privately Held**
SIC: 2431 Mfg Millwork
PA: Pella Corporation
102 Main St
Pella IA 50219
641 621-1000

Albion
Orleans County

(G-152)
3021743 HOLDINGS INC
Also Called: Freeze-Dry Foods Inc.
111 West Ave Ste 2 (14411-1500)
PHONE.....................585 589-6399
Alasdair Grant, *CEO*
Karen Richardson, *President*
Anna Marie Clift, *Controller*
▲ **EMP:** 40
SALES (est): 7.9MM
SALES (corp-wide): 2.7MM **Privately Held**
WEB: www.freeze-dry.com
SIC: 2038 Frozen specialties
PA: Freeze-Dry Foods Limited
115-710 Dorval Dr
Oakville ON L6K 3
905 844-1471

(G-153)
ALBION-HOLLEY PENNYSAVER INC
Also Called: Lake Country Media
170 N Main St (14411-1063)
P.O. Box 231 (14411-0231)
PHONE.....................585 589-5641
Karen Sawicz, *President*
Gary Hill, *Editor*
Tom Rivers, *Editor*
Marissa Olles, *Art Dir*
Jayme Privitera, *Graphic Designe*
EMP: 48
SQ FT: 22,000
SALES (est): 6.8MM **Privately Held**
SIC: 2791 2711 2741 Typesetting; job printing & newspaper publishing combined; miscellaneous publishing

(G-154)
AUSTIN INDUSTRIES INC
3871 Oak Orchard Rd (14411-9536)
PHONE.....................585 589-1353
Alan Austin, *President*
Vernon Carl Austin, *Vice Pres*
Denise Austin, *Treasurer*
Beverly Walthew, *Admin Sec*
EMP: 10
SQ FT: 7,200
SALES (est): 1.3MM **Privately Held**
SIC: 3542 5085 Machine tools, metal forming type; welding supplies; industrial tools

(G-155)
CDL MANUFACTURING INC
15661 Telegraph Rd (14411)
PHONE.....................585 589-2533
Kaz Laszewski, *President*
Steve Chiruck, *Vice Pres*
EMP: 5
SQ FT: 8,000
SALES (est): 662.1K **Privately Held**
WEB: www.cdlmfg.com
SIC: 3599 Machine shop, jobbing & repair

(G-156)
J PAHURA CONTRACTORS
415 East Ave (14411-1620)
PHONE.....................585 589-5793
James Pahura, *Owner*
EMP: 5
SALES (est): 210K **Privately Held**
SIC: 2951 Asphalt paving mixtures & blocks

(G-157)
L&M SPECIALTY FABRICATION
3816 Oak Orchard Rd (14411-9536)
P.O. Box 426, Elba (14058-0426)
PHONE.....................585 283-4847
Lee Shuknecht, *Managing Prtnr*
Matt Geissler, *Partner*
Sarah Geissler, *Principal*
EMP: 7
SALES (est): 666.4K **Privately Held**
SIC: 3523 Cabs, tractors & agricultural machinery

(G-158)
ORLEANS PALLET COMPANY INC
227 West Ave (14411-1520)
PHONE.....................585 589-0781
Shawn R Malark, *President*
EMP: 11
SQ FT: 65,000
SALES: 954K **Privately Held**
SIC: 2448 Pallets, wood

(G-159)
PENASACK MACHINE COMPANY INC
49 Sanford St (14411-1117)
P.O. Box 396 (14411-0396)
PHONE.....................585 589-7044
Gerard Damore, *Ch of Bd*
EMP: 40 **EST:** 1967
SQ FT: 35,000
SALES (est): 7.9MM **Privately Held**
SIC: 3441 Fabricated structural metal

(G-160)
RS AUTOMATION
Also Called: Richard Stacey Rs Automation
4015 Oak Orchard Rd (14411-9326)
PHONE.....................585 589-0199
Richard Stacey, *Owner*
Christina Farabella, *Purchasing*
EMP: 17
SQ FT: 12,000
SALES (est): 4.6MM **Privately Held**
SIC: 3441 5084 Fabricated structural metal; industrial machinery & equipment

(G-161)
SAINT-GOBAIN ADFORS AMER INC
14770 East Ave (14411-9709)
PHONE.....................585 589-4401
Joel Allen, *Branch Mgr*
EMP: 52
SALES (corp-wide): 215.9MM **Privately Held**
SIC: 2297 Nonwoven fabrics
HQ: Saint-Gobain Adfors America, Inc.
1795 Baseline Rd
Grand Island NY 14072
716 775-3900

(G-162)
WOODSIDE GRANITE INDUSTRIES
Also Called: Brigden Memorials
13890 Ridge Rd W (14411-9160)
PHONE.....................585 589-6500
Leo Lacroix, *President*
▲ **EMP:** 9
SQ FT: 1,500
SALES (est): 1.6MM **Privately Held**
SIC: 3272 5999 Grave markers, concrete; gravestones, finished

---

Alcove
Albany County

(G-163)
NEW YORK QUARRIES INC
305 Rte 111 (12007)
PHONE.....................518 756-3138
Nancy O'Brien, *President*
▲ **EMP:** 15
SQ FT: 1,200
SALES: 1.5MM **Privately Held**
WEB: www.newyorkquarries.com
SIC: 3281 1411 Granite, cut & shaped; limestone, dimension-quarrying

---

Alden
Erie County

(G-164)
AGRI SERVICES CO
13899 North Rd (14004-9779)
PHONE.....................716 937-6618
James Guarino, *Owner*
EMP: 5
SALES (est): 125K **Privately Held**
SIC: 3714 5531 Automotive wiring harness sets; truck equipment & parts

(G-165)
ALDEN AURORA GAS COMPANY INC
Also Called: Reserve Gas Company
13441 Railroad St (14004-1389)
P.O. Box 207 (14004-0207)
PHONE.....................716 937-9484
Edward Harris, *Ch of Bd*
James C Gorom, *President*
Paul Tryanowski, *Treasurer*
Jacqueline Harris, *Shareholder*
Bernice Rosenbloom, *Shareholder*
EMP: 8
SQ FT: 1,200
SALES (est): 575.6K **Privately Held**
SIC: 1381 Drilling oil & gas wells

(G-166)
BENNETT MANUFACTURING CO INC
13315 Railroad St (14004-1390)
PHONE.....................716 937-9161
Steven L Yellen, *Ch of Bd*
Richard D Yellen, *Vice Pres*
Toby F Yellen, *Treasurer*
Patricia Miller, *Human Res Mgr*
▲ **EMP:** 150
SQ FT: 100,000
SALES (est): 32.3MM **Privately Held**
WEB: www.bennettmfg.com
SIC: 3441 2842 Fabricated structural metal; specialty cleaning, polishes & sanitation goods

(G-167)
D J CROWELL CO INC
2815 Town Line Rd (14004-9676)
PHONE.....................716 684-3343
David C Bressette, *President*
Jeffrey Minotti, *Vice Pres*
EMP: 6 **EST:** 1900
SQ FT: 6,000
SALES: 500K **Privately Held**
SIC: 3599 Machine shop, jobbing & repair

(G-168)
DUNDAS-JAFINE INC
11099 Broadway St (14004-9517)
PHONE.....................716 681-9690
Debbie Patterson, *General Mgr*
David Jafine, *Vice Pres*
Bill Szajn, *CFO*
Colleen Ference, *Human Resources*
Dave Rockwell, *Sales Staff*
EMP: 50
SALES (corp-wide): 15.3MM **Privately Held**
WEB: www.dundasjafine.com
SIC: 3585 3564 3444 Heating equipment, complete; air conditioning equipment, complete; blowers & fans; sheet metalwork
PA: Dundas Jafine Inc
80 West Dr
Brampton ON L6T 3
905 450-7200

(G-169)
GAMMA NORTH CORPORATION
13595 Broadway St (14004-9736)
PHONE.....................716 902-5100
Matthew Baum, *President*
James Mitchell, *President*
Elliot Kracko, *Chairman*
Juan J Alpizar, *Senior VP*
Jose M Rodriguez, *Senior VP*
EMP: 50 **EST:** 2012
SALES (est): 9.3MM **Privately Held**
SIC: 3442 Store fronts, prefabricated, metal

(G-170)
HUBCO INC
2885 Commerce Dr (14004-8538)
PHONE.....................716 683-5940
Craig Huber, *President*
Paul Huber, *Vice Pres*
Mark Richardson, *Info Tech Mgr*
▲ **EMP:** 6
SQ FT: 6,000
SALES (est): 1MM **Privately Held**
WEB: www.hubcopads.com
SIC: 3569 3589 Assembly machines, non-metalworking; floor sanding machines, commercial

(G-171)
INTEGER HOLDINGS CORPORATION
Also Called: Greatbatch Medical
11900 Walden Ave (14004-9706)
PHONE.....................716 937-5100
Ed Voboril, *Chairman*
William Blarr, *Safety Mgr*

Nichole Davis, *Mfg Staff*
Patrick Guidry, *Senior Buyer*
Raul Diaz, *Buyer*
EMP: 23
SALES (corp-wide): 1.2B **Publicly Held**
SIC: 3841 Surgical & medical instruments
PA: Integer Holdings Corporation
    5830 Gran Pkwy Ste 1150
    Plano TX 75024
    214 618-5243

(G-172)
PHELINGER TOOL & DIE CORP
1254 Town Line Rd (14004-9672)
PHONE....................................716 685-1780
Gordon Phelinger, *President*
Scott Phelinger, *Vice Pres*
EMP: 7
SQ FT: 1,000
SALES (est): 1MM **Privately Held**
WEB: www.phelingertool.com
SIC: 3544 Special dies & tools; jigs & fix-
tures

(G-173)
RESERVE GAS COMPANY INC
13441 Railroad St (14004-1338)
P.O. Box 207 (14004-0207)
PHONE....................................716 937-9484
Sterlin Harris, *CEO*
James C Gorom, *President*
EMP: 8
SQ FT: 3,200
SALES (est): 1.2MM **Privately Held**
SIC: 1311 Natural gas production

(G-174)
SDR TECHNOLOGY INC
1613 Lindan Dr (14004-1113)
PHONE....................................716 583-1249
Charles Chauncey, *President*
EMP: 5
SALES (est): 381.2K **Privately Held**
SIC: 3663 Radio & TV communications
equipment

(G-175)
TURBOPRO INC
1284 Town Line Rd (14004-9672)
PHONE....................................716 681-8651
Joseph Bantle, *President*
Brenda Bantle, *Vice Pres*
EMP: 6
SALES (est): 1.2MM **Privately Held**
SIC: 3563 Air & gas compressors

(G-176)
**WEISBECK PUBLISHING
PRINTING**
Also Called: Alden Advertiser
13200 Broadway St (14004-1313)
PHONE....................................716 937-9226
Leonard A Weisbeck Jr, *President*
EMP: 5 **EST:** 1948
SQ FT: 1,748
SALES (est): 341.7K **Privately Held**
WEB: www.aldenadvertiser.com
SIC: 2711 Commercial printing & newspa-
per publishing combined; job printing &
newspaper publishing combined

Alexander
Genesee County

(G-177)
LENAPE ENERGY INC (PA)
Also Called: Leape Resources,
9489 Alexander Rd (14005-9795)
PHONE....................................585 344-1200
John Holko, *President*
Amy Holko, *Vice Pres*
EMP: 5
SQ FT: 3,200
SALES (est): 921.8K **Privately Held**
WEB: www.lenaperesources.com
SIC: 1381 1389 1382 4923 Drilling oil &
gas wells; haulage, oil field; gas com-
pressing (natural gas) at the fields; oil &
gas exploration services; gas transmis-
sion & distribution

(G-178)
LENAPE RESOURCES INC
9489 Alexander Rd (14005-9795)
PHONE....................................585 344-1200
John Holko, *President*
Amy Holko, *Vice Pres*
EMP: 10
SALES: 1MM
SALES (corp-wide): 921.8K **Privately
Held**
WEB: www.lenaperesources.com
SIC: 1382 4923 Oil & gas exploration
services; gas transmission & distribution
PA: Lenape Energy Inc
    9489 Alexander Rd
    Alexander NY 14005
    585 344-1200

(G-179)
RICHARD BAUER LOGGING
3936 Cookson Rd (14005-9718)
PHONE....................................585 343-4149
Richard Bauer, *Owner*
EMP: 5 **EST:** 1962
SALES (est): 292.4K **Privately Held**
SIC: 2411 Logging camps & contractors

Alexandria Bay
Jefferson County

(G-180)
**THOUSAND ISLANDS PRINTING
CO**
Also Called: Thousand Islands Sun
45501 St Rt 12 (13607)
P.O. Box 277 (13607-0277)
PHONE....................................315 482-2581
Jeanne Roy Snow, *President*
William F Roy, *Vice Pres*
Helethea Roy, *Treasurer*
EMP: 9 **EST:** 1901
SQ FT: 3,250
SALES (est): 696.9K **Privately Held**
SIC: 2711 Job printing & newspaper pub-
lishing combined

(G-181)
**THOUSAND ISLANDS WINERY
LLC**
43298 Seaway Ave Ste 1 (13607-2141)
PHONE....................................315 482-9306
Steven J Conaway,
Erika Conaway,
EMP: 22
SQ FT: 4,771
SALES (est): 3.3MM **Privately Held**
WEB: www.thousandislandswinery.com
SIC: 2084 Wines

Alfred
Allegany County

(G-182)
**SAXON GLASS TECHNOLOGIES
INC**
200 N Main St Ste 114 (14802-1000)
P.O. Box 575 (14802-0575)
PHONE....................................607 587-9630
Arun Varshneya, *President*
Darshana Varshneya, *Vice Pres*
EMP: 10
SQ FT: 4,500
SALES (est): 1.2MM **Privately Held**
WEB: www.saxonglass.com
SIC: 3211 Strengthened or reinforced
glass

Alfred Station
Allegany County

(G-183)
ASK CHEMICALS HI-TECH LLC
6329 Rte 21 (14803)
P.O. Box 788, Alfred (14802-0788)
PHONE....................................607 587-9146
Luiz Totti, *Exec VP*
Aris Chatziparaskeva, *Exec VP*

Edward Holzlein, *Plant Mgr*
Rick Glenn, *Controller*
Robert Gage, *Marketing Mgr*
▲ **EMP:** 112
SALES: 18MM **Privately Held**
SIC: 2899 Chemical preparations
HQ: Ask Chemicals Gmbh
    Reisholzstr. 16-18
    Hilden 40721
    211 711-030

(G-184)
**BUFFALO CRUSHED STONE
INC**
638 State Route 244 (14803-9766)
P.O. Box 38 (14803-0038)
PHONE....................................607 587-8102
Douglas Drake, *Manager*
EMP: 9
SALES (corp-wide): 651.9MM **Privately
Held**
SIC: 1442 Construction sand mining;
gravel mining
HQ: Buffalo Crushed Stone, Inc.
    500 Como Park Blvd
    Buffalo NY 14227
    716 826-7310

(G-185)
**NORTHERN TIMBER
HARVESTING LLC**
6042 State Route 21 (14803)
PHONE....................................585 233-7330
Adam Ricci,
EMP: 11
SQ FT: 10,000
SALES (est): 2.9MM **Privately Held**
SIC: 2411 Logging camps & contractors

Allegany
Cattaraugus County

(G-186)
**ALLEGANY LAMINATING AND
SUPPLY**
158 W Main St Ste A (14706-1223)
PHONE....................................716 372-2424
Charles Cousins, *President*
Wanda Cousins, *Corp Secy*
John Hare, *Supervisor*
EMP: 5
SQ FT: 8,300
SALES (est): 460K **Privately Held**
SIC: 2541 3088 Table or counter tops,
plastic laminated; partitions for floor at-
tachment, prefabricated: wood; cabinets,
except refrigerated: show, display, etc.:
wood; tubs (bath, shower & laundry),
plastic

(G-187)
E F LIPPERT CO INC
4451 S Nine Mile Rd (14706-9790)
PHONE....................................716 373-1100
Mary Stayer, *President*
Tom Stayer, *Vice Pres*
Carol Donahey, *Manager*
Sheila Taylor, *Manager*
Cinda Warner, *Admin Sec*
EMP: 13 **EST:** 1945
SQ FT: 500
SALES (est): 725.7K **Privately Held**
SIC: 1442 5261 Common sand mining;
gravel mining; sod; top soil

(G-188)
**HANSON AGGREGATES EAST
LLC**
4419 S Nine Mile Rd (14706-9790)
PHONE....................................716 372-1574
EMP: 6
SALES (est): 326.8K **Privately Held**
SIC: 3272 Mfg Concrete Products

(G-189)
I & S OF NY INC
4174 Route 417 (14706-9787)
P.O. Box 380 (14706-0380)
PHONE....................................716 373-7001
Frank Steven, *President*
EMP: 10
SQ FT: 6,000

SALES (est): 1.5MM **Privately Held**
SIC: 1389 Servicing oil & gas wells

(G-190)
POTTER LUMBER CO INC
3786 Potter Rd (14706-9410)
P.O. Box 10 (14706-0010)
PHONE....................................716 373-1260
Robert G Potter, *President*
Theodore Potter, *Vice Pres*
Mary Frances Potter, *Treasurer*
Lucy Benson, *Admin Sec*
EMP: 40 **EST:** 1910
SQ FT: 700
SALES (est): 5.8MM **Privately Held**
SIC: 2421 2426 Lumber: rough, sawed or
planed; hardwood dimension & flooring
mills

Almond
Allegany County

(G-191)
**HANSON AGGREGATES NEW
YORK LLC**
Also Called: Hanson Ready Mix Concrete
546 Clark Rd (14804)
PHONE....................................607 276-5881
Jeff Feenaughty, *Site Mgr*
Jeffrey Feenaughty, *Manager*
EMP: 5
SALES (corp-wide): 20.6B **Privately Held**
SIC: 3273 Ready-mixed concrete
HQ: Hanson Aggregates New York Llc
    8505 Freport Pkwy Ste 500
    Irving TX 75063

Altamont
Albany County

(G-192)
**ALTAMONT SPRAY WELDING
INC**
133 Lewis Rd (12009-3220)
PHONE....................................518 861-8870
Mark C Schrowang, *President*
Sandra E Schrowang, *Vice Pres*
EMP: 9
SQ FT: 9,000
SALES (est): 1.2MM **Privately Held**
WEB: www.altamontspraywelding.com
SIC: 3599 Machine shop, jobbing & repair

(G-193)
**CARVER SAND & GRAVEL LLC
(PA)**
494 Western Tpke Ste 1 (12009-2095)
PHONE....................................518 355-6034
Sybil Lindstead, *CFO*
Nancy Laraway, *Mng Member*
Michael Bath,
Carver Laraway,
EMP: 35 **EST:** 1995
SQ FT: 1,000
SALES (est): 17MM **Privately Held**
SIC: 1442 Construction sand & gravel

(G-194)
**INDIAN LADDER FARMSTEAD
BREWER**
287 Altamont Rd (12009-3542)
PHONE....................................518 577-1484
Dietrich Gehring,
EMP: 5
SQ FT: 875
SALES (est): 185.3K **Privately Held**
SIC: 2082 Beer (alcoholic beverage)

(G-195)
INOVA LLC
6032 Depot Rd (12009-4313)
P.O. Box 644 (12009-0644)
PHONE....................................518 861-3400
EMP: 15
SALES (est): 2.5MM **Privately Held**
SIC: 2599 Mfg Furniture/Fixtures

▲ = Import ▼=Export
◆ =Import/Export

(G-196)
MET WELD INTERNATIONAL LLC
5727 Ostrander Rd (12009-4209)
PHONE.................................518 765-2318
Dan Hill, *Opers Staff*
Jim Carter, *Purch Mgr*
Scott Kniffin, *Purch Mgr*
Maegan Lipinski, *Engineer*
Tad Ripley, *Engineer*
EMP: 70
SQ FT: 55,000
SALES (est): 18.4MM
SALES (corp-wide): 80.4MM **Privately Held**
WEB: www.metweldintl.com
SIC: 3444 Sheet metalwork
PA: Gavial Holdings, Inc.
1435 W Mccoy Ln
Santa Maria CA 93455
805 614-0060

(G-197)
REMARKABLE LIQUIDS LLC
6032 Depot Rd (12009-4313)
P.O. Box 122, Guilderland Center (12085-0122)
PHONE.................................518 861-5351
Jason Napoleon, *Opers Staff*
Maria Brand, *CFO*
Ben English, *Sales Staff*
Todd Harmon, *Sales Staff*
Matt Hartman, *Sales Staff*
EMP: 70
SALES (est): 13.1MM **Privately Held**
SIC: 2082 Beer (alcoholic beverage)

(G-198)
ROBERT PIKCILINGIS
Also Called: Candy Kraft
2575 Western Ave (12009-9488)
PHONE.................................518 355-1860
Robert Pikcilingis, *Owner*
EMP: 10
SQ FT: 4,000
SALES (est): 1MM **Privately Held**
SIC: 2064 2066 Chocolate candy, except solid chocolate; chocolate & cocoa products

(G-199)
RSB ASSOCIATES INC
Also Called: Bruno Associates
488 Picard Rd (12009-3519)
P.O. Box 14825, Albany (12212-4825)
PHONE.................................518 281-5067
Robert S Bruno Sr, *President*
Sean Bruno, *Vice Pres*
EMP: 11
SQ FT: 4,000
SALES: 650K **Privately Held**
SIC: 3554 Die cutting & stamping machinery, paper converting

Amawalk
Westchester County

(G-200)
PIC NIC LLC
51 Mahopac Ave (10501-1005)
PHONE.................................914 245-6500
Rick Rezzenico, *Partner*
EMP: 8
SALES (est): 947.6K **Privately Held**
SIC: 3556 Ice cream manufacturing machinery

Amenia
Dutchess County

(G-201)
CASCADE MOUNTAIN WINERY & REST
835 Cascade Rd (12501)
PHONE.................................845 373-9021
William Wetmore, *President*
EMP: 10 EST: 1972
SALES (est): 680K **Privately Held**
SIC: 2084 5812 Wines; eating places

(G-202)
GREY HOUSE PUBLISHING INC (PA)
4919 Route 22 (12501-5585)
P.O. Box B, Millerton (12546-0640)
PHONE.................................518 789-8700
Richard H Gottlieb, *Ch of Bd*
David Garoogian, *Editor*
Leslie McKenzie, *Vice Pres*
Yvonne Coburn, *Opers Mgr*
Rich Flaherty, *Accounts Mgr*
EMP: 26
SALES (est): 5.3MM **Privately Held**
WEB: www.greyhouse.com
SIC: 2741 2731 Miscellaneous publishing; book publishing

(G-203)
TIA LATTRELL
13 Powder House Rd (12501-5517)
PHONE.................................845 373-9494
Tia Lattrell, *Owner*
Frederic Latrell, *Owner*
EMP: 5
SALES (est): 261.5K **Privately Held**
SIC: 2024 Ice cream & frozen desserts

Amherst
Erie County

(G-204)
AIRSEP CORPORATION
Airsep Commercial Products Div
260 Creekside Dr Ste 100 (14228-2075)
PHONE.................................716 691-0202
EMP: 100
SALES (corp-wide): 1.1B **Publicly Held**
SIC: 3569 Mfg Oxygen Generators
HQ: Airsep Corporation
401 Creekside Dr
Amherst NY 14228
716 691-0202

(G-205)
ALLIED MOTION CONTROL CORP
495 Commerce Dr Ste 3 (14228-2311)
PHONE.................................716 242-7535
Richard Smith, *Principal*
EMP: 5
SALES (est): 504.7K **Privately Held**
SIC: 3621 Motors & generators

(G-206)
ALLIED MOTION SYSTEMS CORP (DH)
Also Called: Hathaway Prcess Instrmentation
495 Commerce Dr Ste 3 (14228-2311)
PHONE.................................716 691-5868
Ronald Meyer, *President*
EMP: 15
SQ FT: 13,000
SALES (est): 2.2MM
SALES (corp-wide): 6.4B **Publicly Held**
SIC: 3825 Electrical power measuring equipment
HQ: Qualitrol Company Llc
1385 Fairport Rd
Fairport NY 14450
586 643-3717

(G-207)
ALLIED MOTION TECHNOLOGIES INC (PA)
495 Commerce Dr Ste 3 (14228-2311)
PHONE.................................716 242-8634
Richard S Warzala, *Ch of Bd*
Robert P Maida, *Vice Pres*
Michael R Leach, *CFO*
Michael Leach, *CFO*
Brian Kelly, *Regl Sales Mgr*
▲ EMP: 221
SQ FT: 6,000
SALES: 310.6MM **Publicly Held**
WEB: www.alliedmotion.com
SIC: 3621 3825 Motors, electric; rotary converters (electrical equipment); function generators

(G-208)
ALLSAFE TECHNOLOGIES INC
290 Creekside Dr (14228-2031)
PHONE.................................716 691-0400
James Pokornowski, *President*
Frank Ortolano, *President*
Mike Chown, *Production*
Brian Hamp, *Production*
Robert P Pokornowski, *Treasurer*
▲ EMP: 65 EST: 1966
SQ FT: 35,000
SALES (est): 13.5MM **Privately Held**
WEB: www.allsafe.com
SIC: 3089 2759 Identification cards, plastic; commercial printing

(G-209)
AMERICAN BUSINESS FORMS INC
3840 E Robinson Rd # 249 (14228-2001)
PHONE.................................716 836-5111
Larry Zavadil, *Branch Mgr*
EMP: 30
SALES (corp-wide): 357.5MM **Privately Held**
SIC: 2752 Commercial printing, lithographic
PA: American Business Forms, Inc.
31 E Minnesota Ave
Glenwood MN 56334
320 634-5471

(G-210)
AMERICAN PRECISION INDS INCS (HQ)
45 Hazelwood Dr (14228-2224)
PHONE.................................716 691-9100
Scott Benigni, *President*
◆ EMP: 200
SQ FT: 106,800
SALES (est): 240.1MM
SALES (corp-wide): 6.4B **Publicly Held**
WEB: www.apischmidtbretten.com
SIC: 3677 3621 3625 3443 Coil windings, electronic; inductors, electronic; motors & generators; electromagnetic clutches or brakes; heat exchangers: coolers (after, inter), condensers, etc.; condensers, steam; separators, industrial process: metal plate
PA: Fortive Corporation
6920 Seaway Blvd
Everett WA 98203
425 446-5000

(G-211)
AMHERST STNLESS FBRICATION LLC
60 John Glenn Dr (14228-2118)
PHONE.................................716 691-7012
Gerald J Bogdan, *President*
Joseph B Huber, *Corp Secy*
Jim Mazur, *Engineer*
▼ EMP: 40 EST: 1945
SQ FT: 35,000
SALES (est): 13.5MM **Privately Held**
WEB: www.avinsfab.com
SIC: 3443 Tanks, lined: metal plate
PA: General Oil Equipment Co., Inc.
60 John Glenn Dr
Amherst NY 14228
716 691-7012

(G-212)
BEKAERT CORPORATION
Also Called: Advanced Coating Technologies
6000 N Bailey Ave Ste 9 (14226-5102)
PHONE.................................716 830-1321
Chandra Venkatraman, *Branch Mgr*
EMP: 20
SALES (corp-wide): 429.7MM **Privately Held**
WEB: www.bekaert.com
SIC: 3315 Wire & fabricated wire products
HQ: Bekaert Corporation
1395 S Marietta Pkwy Se 500-100
Marietta GA 30067
770 421-8520

(G-213)
BIRDAIR INC (HQ)
65 Lawrence Bell Dr # 100 (14221-7182)
PHONE.................................716 633-9500
Mitsuo Sugimoto, *President*
Carl Hoffner, *Manager*

◆ EMP: 60 EST: 1956
SQ FT: 20,000
SALES (est): 12.3MM **Privately Held**
SIC: 3448 Prefabricated metal buildings

(G-214)
BROOK & WHITTLE LIMITED
215 John Glenn Dr (14228-2227)
PHONE.................................716 691-4348
EMP: 14
SALES (corp-wide): 7.8MM **Privately Held**
SIC: 2671 Plastic film, coated or laminated for packaging
HQ: Brook & Whittle Limited
20 Carter Dr
Guilford CT 06437

(G-215)
CAIRE INC
260 Creekside Dr (14228-2047)
PHONE.................................716 691-0202
EMP: 27 **Privately Held**
SIC: 3842 3845 3841 Respirators; electromedical equipment; surgical & medical instruments
HQ: Caire Inc.
2200 Arprt Ind Dr Ste 500
Ball Ground GA 30107

(G-216)
CCA HOLDING INC
300 Corporate Pkwy (14226-1207)
PHONE.................................716 446-8800
Edward Bredniak, *President*
William F Sullivan, *Vice Pres*
◆ EMP: 245
SALES (est): 11.6MM **Privately Held**
SIC: 3313 Ferroalloys

(G-217)
CENTER FOR INQUIRY INC (PA)
Also Called: COUNCEL FOR SECULAR HUMANISM &
3965 Rensch Rd (14228-2743)
P.O. Box 664, Buffalo (14226-0664)
PHONE.................................716 636-4869
Paul Kurtz, *President*
Alice Pine, *Office Mgr*
Lauren Foster, *Manager*
Nora Hurley, *Producer*
James Underdown, *Exec Dir*
EMP: 15
SALES: 10.8MM **Privately Held**
WEB: www.centerforinquiry.net
SIC: 2721 Magazines: publishing only, not printed on site

(G-218)
CHART INDUSTRIES INC
Also Called: Airsep
260 Creekside Dr Ste 100 (14228-2047)
PHONE.................................716 691-0202
Ravi Bansal PHD, *CEO*
Angel Beiter, *VP Finance*
EMP: 25 **Publicly Held**
SIC: 3443 Fabricated plate work (boiler shop)
PA: Chart Industries, Inc.
3055 Torrington Dr
Ball Ground GA 30107

(G-219)
CRANE EQUIPMENT & SERVICE INC (HQ)
140 John Jmes Adubon Pkwy (14228-1183)
PHONE.................................716 689-5400
Jena Buer, *President*
Karen L Howard, *CFO*
Rakesh A Jobanputra, *Treasurer*
Timothy R Harvey, *Admin Sec*
EMP: 3 EST: 1997
SQ FT: 3,000
SALES (est): 29.9MM
SALES (corp-wide): 876.2MM **Publicly Held**
WEB: www.broussardla.com
SIC: 3531 Crane carriers
PA: Columbus Mckinnon Corporation
205 Crosspoint Pkwy
Getzville NY 14068
716 689-5400

G
E
O
G
R
A
P
H
I
C

(G-220)
DELPHI AUTOMOTIVE LLP
Also Called: Delphi Amherst Test Operations
4326 Ridge Lea Rd (14226-1016)
PHONE..................716 438-4886
EMP: 6
SALES (corp-wide): 571K **Privately Held**
SIC: 3714 Motor vehicle parts & accessories
PA: Aptiv International Holdings (Uk) Llp
Courteney Road
Gillingham ME8 0

(G-221)
ENHANCED TOOL INC
90 Pineview Dr (14228-2120)
PHONE..................716 691-5200
Michael Emmert, CEO
David M Healey, Vice Pres
EMP: 20
SQ FT: 6,000
SALES (est): 3.7MM **Privately Held**
WEB: www.enhancedtool.com
SIC: 3544 Special dies & tools

(G-222)
ESM GROUP INC (DH)
Also Called: E S M
300 Corporate Pkwy 118n (14226-1258)
PHONE..................716 446-8914
Gregory P Marzec, Ch of Bd
William F Sullivan, Exec VP
Charles A Zak, Exec VP
◆ EMP: 15 EST: 1988
SQ FT: 15,000
SALES (est): 25.8MM
SALES (corp-wide): 177.9K **Privately Held**
WEB: www.esmgroup.com
SIC: 2819 Industrial inorganic chemicals
HQ: Skw Stahl-Metallurgie Gmbh
Rathausplatz 11
Unterneukirchen 84579
863 462-7203

(G-223)
ESM II INC (DH)
300 Corporate Pkwy 118n (14226-1258)
PHONE..................716 446-8888
Charles F Wright, President
▲ EMP: 50
SALES (est): 13MM
SALES (corp-wide): 177.9K **Privately Held**
SIC: 3549 Metalworking machinery
HQ: Esm Group Inc.
300 Corporate Pkwy 118n
Amherst NY 14226
716 446-8914

(G-224)
ESM SPECIAL METALS & TECH INC
300 Corporate Pkwy 118n (14226-1207)
PHONE..................716 446-8914
Hartmut Meyer-Grnow, CEO
Sandyee Whipple, Principal
EMP: 20
SALES (est): 2.7MM **Privately Held**
SIC: 2819 Industrial inorganic chemicals

(G-225)
GENERAL OIL EQUIPMENT CO INC (PA)
60 John Glenn Dr (14228-2118)
PHONE..................716 691-7012
Gerald Bogdan, Ch of Bd
Joseph B Huber, President
Bob Gladwell, Purch Mgr
John Mendolia, Engineer
Christopher Bogdan, Project Engr
EMP: 49
SQ FT: 34,000
SALES (est): 13.5MM **Privately Held**
WEB: www.goe-avins.com
SIC: 3625 5084 7699 3443 Electric controls & control accessories, industrial; oil refining machinery, equipment & supplies; industrial machinery & equipment repair; tanks, lined: metal plate

(G-226)
GROVER CLEVELAND PRESS INC
2676 Sweet Home Rd (14228-2128)
PHONE..................716 564-2222
Michael Degen, President
Tom Degen, Vice Pres
EMP: 10 EST: 1947
SQ FT: 12,800
SALES: 2MM **Privately Held**
WEB: www.groverclevelandpress.com
SIC: 2752 2759 Commercial printing, offset; photo-offset printing; letterpress printing; embossing on paper

(G-227)
INTERNATIONAL IMAGING MTLS INC (PA)
Also Called: Iimak
310 Commerce Dr (14228-2396)
PHONE..................716 691-6333
Douglas Wagner, President
Susan R Stamp, Senior VP
Joseph Perna, CFO
◆ EMP: 370
SQ FT: 250,000
SALES (est): 162.3MM **Privately Held**
SIC: 3955 3555 Ribbons, inked: typewriter, adding machine, register, etc.; printing trades machinery

(G-228)
KISTLER INSTRUMENT CORPORATION
75 John Glenn Dr (14228-2171)
PHONE..................716 691-5100
Nick Wilks, Managing Dir
Mark Burzik, Opers Mgr
Nancy Woomer, Purch Mgr
Rande Caroll, Purch Agent
Andrew Cook, Engineer
EMP: 63
SALES (corp-wide): 478.9MM **Privately Held**
SIC: 3829 Measuring & controlling devices
HQ: Kistler Instrument Corporation
30280 Hudson Dr
Novi MI 48377
248 668-6900

(G-229)
LIBERTY DISPLAYS INC
4230b Ridge Lea Rd # 110 (14226-1063)
PHONE..................716 743-1757
Dean Rainer, President
EMP: 30
SQ FT: 57,000
SALES: 5MM **Privately Held**
SIC: 3999 Forms: display, dress & show

(G-230)
LOOMIS ROOT INC
135 Pineview Dr (14228-2231)
PHONE..................716 564-7668
Steven E Root, President
Judith Ryczek, Controller
▲ EMP: 11 EST: 1915
SQ FT: 13,000
SALES (est): 2.5MM **Privately Held**
SIC: 3053 5014 5084 Gaskets, packing & sealing devices; tire & tube repair materials; recapping machinery, for tires

(G-231)
MAHLE INDSTRBETEILIGUNGEN GMBH
Also Called: Delphi-T Compressor Engrg Ctr
4236 Ridge Lea Rd (14226-1016)
PHONE..................716 319-6700
Tim Skinner, Manager
EMP: 75
SALES (corp-wide): 504.6K **Privately Held**
SIC: 3714 Motor vehicle parts & accessories
HQ: Mahle Industriebeteiligungen Gmbh
Pragstr. 26-46
Stuttgart
711 501-0

(G-232)
MAHLE MANUFACTURING MGT INC (DH)
4236 Ridge Lea Rd (14226-1016)
PHONE..................248 735-3623
Bruce Moorehouse, CEO
▼ EMP: 5
SQ FT: 100
SALES (est): 6.6MM
SALES (corp-wide): 504.6K **Privately Held**
SIC: 3714 Motor vehicle parts & accessories
HQ: Mahle Industries, Incorporated
23030 Mahle Dr
Farmington Hills MI 48335
248 305-8200

(G-233)
MOTIVAIR CORPORATION
85 Woodridge Dr (14228-2221)
PHONE..................716 691-9222
Graham Whitmore, President
Kevin Werely, Sales Staff
Andrea Shorr, Mktg Dir
Anthony Frizalone, Director
Lindsay Kirsch, Admin Asst
▲ EMP: 20
SQ FT: 25,000
SALES (est): 6.1MM **Privately Held**
SIC: 3585 3443 Air conditioning condensers & condensing units; separators, industrial process: metal plate

(G-234)
NEXSTAR HOLDING CORP
Also Called: PHASE IL MARKETING DBA
275 Northpointe Pkwy (14228-1895)
PHONE..................716 929-9000
Gary Robinson, President
Richard S Elliott, Vice Pres
EMP: 5
SALES (est): 1MM **Privately Held**
SIC: 3564 Filters, air: furnaces, air conditioning equipment, etc.

(G-235)
NK MEDICAL PRODUCTS INC (PA)
80 Creekside Dr (14228-2027)
PHONE..................716 759-7200
Norman V Kurlander, President
▲ EMP: 5
SQ FT: 1,600
SALES (est): 1.2MM **Privately Held**
WEB: www.nkmedicalproducts.com
SIC: 2514 2599 Cribs: metal; hospital beds

(G-236)
NOVUM MEDICAL PRODUCTS NY LLC
80 Creekside Dr (14228-2027)
PHONE..................716 759-7200
Joe Mandella, President
Thomas Kosmowski, Natl Sales Mgr
Jennifer Cappello, Manager
▲ EMP: 10 EST: 2008
SALES (est): 1.1MM **Privately Held**
SIC: 2514 2599 Cribs: metal; hospital beds

(G-237)
OERLIKON BLZERS CATING USA INC
6000 N Bailey Ave Ste 9 (14226-5102)
PHONE..................716 270-2228
EMP: 40
SALES (corp-wide): 2.6B **Privately Held**
SIC: 3479 Coating of metals & formed products
HQ: Oerlikon Balzers Coating Usa Inc.
1700 E Golf Rd Ste 200
Schaumburg IL 60173
847 619-5541

(G-238)
OERLIKON METCO (US) INC
6000 N Bailey Ave (14226-5102)
PHONE..................716 270-2228
Dan Wisniewski, Branch Mgr
EMP: 8
SALES (corp-wide): 2.6B **Privately Held**
SIC: 3399 Powder, metal

HQ: Oerlikon Metco (Us) Inc.
1101 Prospect Ave
Westbury NY 11590
516 334-1300

(G-239)
ONY BIOTECH INC
1576 Sweet Home Rd (14228-2710)
PHONE..................716 636-9096
Edmund Egan, President
John Kaminski, Natl Sales Mgr
Dale Bloomberg, Marketing Mgr
Barbara Riso, Marketing Mgr
Marissa Watroba, Marketing Staff
EMP: 26
SQ FT: 8,000
SALES (est): 5.8MM **Privately Held**
WEB: www.ony.com
SIC: 2834 Pharmaceutical preparations

(G-240)
ORIGINAL CRUNCH ROLL FCTRY LLC
90 Sylvan Pkwy (14228-1109)
PHONE..................716 402-5030
Zachary Bohn, President
EMP: 5 EST: 2016
SALES (est): 199.1K **Privately Held**
SIC: 2013 Frozen meats from purchased meat

(G-241)
PANZARELLA PRTG & PACKG INC
Also Called: Ansel Printing & Packaging
310 Creekside Dr Ste 324 (14228-2039)
PHONE..................716 853-4480
Michael A Panzarella, President
Michael Panzarella, President
EMP: 5
SALES (est): 425.2K **Privately Held**
SIC: 2711 2732 2741 Commercial printing & newspaper publishing combined; book printing; posters: publishing & printing; guides: publishing & printing

(G-242)
SAINT-GBAIN ADVNCED CRMICS LLC
Boron Nitride Div
168 Creekside Dr (14228-2037)
PHONE..................716 691-2000
William Hill, Manager
EMP: 50
SALES (corp-wide): 215.9MM **Privately Held**
WEB: www.hexoloy.com
SIC: 3291 Abrasive products
HQ: Saint-Gobain Advanced Ceramics Llc
23 Acheson Dr
Niagara Falls NY 14303

(G-243)
SIEMENS INDUSTRY INC
85 Northpointe Pkwy (14228-1886)
PHONE..................716 568-0983
EMP: 87
SALES (corp-wide): 95B **Privately Held**
SIC: 3822 Air conditioning & refrigeration controls
HQ: Siemens Industry, Inc.
1000 Deerfield Pkwy
Buffalo Grove IL 60089
847 215-1000

(G-244)
STATURE ELECTRIC INC
495 Commerce Dr (14228-2311)
PHONE..................716 242-7535
Richard D Smith, President
Richard S Warzala, Vice Pres
Kenneth R Wyman, Treasurer
Susan M Chiarmonte, Admin Sec
EMP: 18
SALES (est): 1.7MM
SALES (corp-wide): 310.6MM **Publicly Held**
SIC: 3546 3621 Power-driven handtools; electric motor & generator parts; motors, electric
PA: Allied Motion Technologies Inc.
495 Commerce Dr Ste 3
Amherst NY 14228
716 242-8634

(G-245)
SUITE SOLUTIONS INC
100 Corporate Pkwy # 338 (14226-1200)
PHONE.............................716 929-3050
Alan Perlmutter, *President*
Edward F O'Gara, *Bd of Directors*
EMP: 25
SALES (est): 1.1MM **Privately Held**
SIC: 7372 7371 Prepackaged software;
custom computer programming services

(G-246)
SYNERGY TOOLING SYSTEMS INC (PA)
287 Commerce Dr (14228-2302)
PHONE.............................716 834-4457
Richard E Morrison Jr, *President*
Frank Zdinski, *VP Mfg*
Tim Chriswell, *Cust Mgr*
EMP: 35
SQ FT: 20,000
SALES (est): 5.8MM **Privately Held**
SIC: 3544 Special dies & tools

(G-247)
TARGETPROCESS INC (PA)
1325 Millersport Hwy (14221-2932)
P.O. Box 1845 (14226-7845)
PHONE.............................877 718-2617
Michael Dubakov, *President*
Lizz Enzinna, *Accounts Mgr*
John Manuele, *Accounts Exec*
Sergey Fishkin, *Sales Staff*
Peter Strasser, *Sales Staff*
EMP: 10
SALES (est): 827.5K **Privately Held**
SIC: 7372 Prepackaged software

(G-248)
THOMSON INDUSTRIES INC (PA)
45 Hazelwood Dr (14228-2224)
PHONE.............................716 691-9100
Dan Daniel, *CEO*
Brian Buzzard, *Engineer*
James Carlson, *Engineer*
John Maler, *Engineer*
EMP: 22
SALES (est): 16MM **Privately Held**
SIC: 3585 Heating equipment, complete

(G-249)
TRANSCONTINENTAL PRINTING GP
300 International Dr # 200 (14221-5781)
PHONE.............................716 626-3078
Louis J Continelli, *Branch Mgr*
EMP: 5
SALES (corp-wide): 1.5B **Privately Held**
SIC: 2752 Commercial printing, lithographic
PA: Imprimeries Transcontinental 2005
S.E.N.C.
1 Place Ville-Marie Bureau 3240
Montreal QC H3B 0
514 954-4000

(G-250)
TRI-METAL INDUSTRIES INC
100 Pineview Dr (14228-2120)
PHONE.............................716 691-3323
Donald Chatwin Jr, *President*
Douglas B Chatwin, *Treasurer*
EMP: 38
SQ FT: 33,000
SALES (est): 2MM **Privately Held**
SIC: 3444 Sheet metal specialties, not stamped

(G-251)
UFC BIOTECHNOLOGY INC
435 Creekside Dr Ste 1 (14228-2135)
PHONE.............................716 603-3652
Bayram Arman, *Ch of Bd*
EMP: 10
SALES (est): 1.6MM **Privately Held**
SIC: 2835 Microbiology & virology diagnostic products

(G-252)
ULTRA-SCAN CORPORATION
4240 Ridge Lea Rd Ste 10 (14226-1083)
PHONE.............................716 832-6269
EMP: 11
SQ FT: 12,600

SALES (est): 2MM **Privately Held**
SIC: 3575 Mfg Computer Terminals

(G-253)
WATSON BOWMAN ACME CORP
95 Pineview Dr (14228-2121)
PHONE.............................716 691-8162
Markus Burri, *President*
Mike Turchiarelli, *Finance*
Stephen Pabst, *Department Mgr*
◆ **EMP:** 150
SALES (est): 35MM
SALES (corp-wide): 71.7B **Privately Held**
WEB: www.wbacorp.com
SIC: 3441 2899 3568 Expansion joints
(structural shapes); iron or steel; concrete
curing & hardening compounds; power
transmission equipment
HQ: Basfin Corporation
100 Park Ave
Florham Park NJ 07932
973 245-6000

(G-254)
WELCOME MAGAZINE INC
4511 Harlem Rd (14226-3803)
PHONE.............................716 839-3121
Julie Kianof More, *President*
Margaret Ashley, *Manager*
EMP: 10
SQ FT: 500
SALES (est): 1MM **Privately Held**
WEB: www.welcome-magazine.com
SIC: 2721 Magazines: publishing only, not
printed on site

Amityville
Suffolk County

(G-255)
A & G PRECISION CORP
680 Albany Ave (11701-1123)
PHONE.............................631 957-5613
Gus Georgopoulos, *President*
Nick Georgopoulos, *Vice Pres*
EMP: 15
SALES: 1.5MM **Privately Held**
SIC: 3599 Machine shop, jobbing & repair

(G-256)
ANCON GEAR & INSTRUMENT CORP (PA)
29 Seabro Ave (11701-1201)
PHONE.............................631 694-5255
Joseph Markiewicz, *President*
Ed Markiewicz, *Vice Pres*
Micheal Chapman, *Opers Mgr*
Donna Scalice, *Admin Sec*
EMP: 18 **EST:** 1961
SQ FT: 6,000
SALES (est): 2.3MM **Privately Held**
WEB: www.ancongear.com
SIC: 3599 Machine shop, jobbing & repair

(G-257)
CALICO COTTAGE INC
210 New Hwy (11701-1116)
PHONE.............................631 841-2100
Mark Wurzel, *President*
Mark L Wurzel, *President*
David A Sank, *Exec VP*
Larry Wurzel, *Vice Pres*
Lawrence J Wurzel, *Vice Pres*
▼ **EMP:** 50
SQ FT: 45,000
SALES (est): 15.4MM **Privately Held**
WEB: www.calicocottage.com
SIC: 2064 Candy & other confectionery
products

(G-258)
CONTINENTAL INSTRUMENTS LLC
Also Called: Continental Access
355 Bayview Ave (11701-2801)
PHONE.............................631 842-9400
Ben Shour, *Controller*
Robert Weinstein, *Human Res Dir*
George Zamora, *Sales Staff*
Richard Soloway, *Mng Member*
John Banks,
EMP: 34
SQ FT: 90,000

SALES (est): 2.7MM
SALES (corp-wide): 102.9MM **Publicly Held**
SIC: 3625 Control equipment, electric
PA: Napco Security Technologies, Inc.
333 Bayview Ave
Amityville NY 11701
631 842-9400

(G-259)
CONTROL RESEARCH INC
Also Called: Cri Graphic
385 Bayview Ave Unit C (11701-2801)
PHONE.............................631 225-1111
Robert Slomkowski, *President*
Sheryl Young, *Office Mgr*
EMP: 5 **EST:** 1963
SQ FT: 10,000
SALES (est): 606.8K **Privately Held**
WEB: www.stageresearch.com
SIC: 2759 2395 Screen printing; embroidery & art needlework

(G-260)
CRAFTMASTER FLAVOR TECHNOLOGY
23 Albany Ave (11701-2829)
PHONE.............................631 789-8607
Thomas Massetti, *President*
Ellen McDonald, *Vice Pres*
Joseph Massetti, *Treasurer*
EMP: 10
SQ FT: 4,000
SALES (est): 1.4MM **Privately Held**
SIC: 2869 2087 Flavors or flavoring materials, synthetic; extracts, flavoring

(G-261)
CULTURE CLASH CORPORATION
393 Bayview Ave (11701-2801)
Rural Route 16 Juniper St (11701)
PHONE.............................631 933-8179
Asim Henry, *President*
Antone Reid, *Vice Pres*
EMP: 8
SQ FT: 12,000
SALES (est): 274K **Privately Held**
SIC: 2035 5812 Seasonings & sauces, except tomato & dry; dressings, salad: raw
& cooked (except dry mixes); mayonnaise; eating places

(G-262)
DANIEL DEMARCO AND ASSOC INC
25 Greene Ave (11701-2943)
PHONE.............................631 598-7000
Daniel Demarco, *Ch of Bd*
Dano Demarco, *General Mgr*
Gil D'Orazio, *Senior VP*
Rob Herzog, *Project Mgr*
Chris McCarthy, *Project Mgr*
EMP: 35
SALES (est): 8.9MM **Privately Held**
WEB: www.danieldemarco.com
SIC: 3429 1751 2499 Cabinet hardware;
cabinet building & installation; decorative
wood & woodwork

(G-263)
G MARKS HDWR LIQUIDATING CORP
Also Called: Marks USA
333 Bayview Ave (11701-2801)
PHONE.............................631 225-5400
George Marks, *President*
EMP: 90 **EST:** 1977
SQ FT: 35,000
SALES (est): 12.6MM
SALES (corp-wide): 102.9MM **Publicly Held**
WEB: www.marksusa.com
SIC: 3429 Locks or lock sets
PA: Napco Security Technologies, Inc.
333 Bayview Ave
Amityville NY 11701
631 842-9400

(G-264)
GKN AEROSPACE MONITOR INC
1000 New Horizons Blvd (11701-1138)
PHONE.............................562 619-8558
Daniele Cagnatel, *CEO*

Kevin L Cummings, *Ch of Bd*
Fran Novak, *President*
Eugenio Gallucci, *General Mgr*
David Maguire, *General Mgr*
▲ **EMP:** 275 **EST:** 1947
SQ FT: 238,000
SALES (est): 72.6MM
SALES (corp-wide): 11B **Privately Held**
WEB: www.monair.com
SIC: 3728 3769 Aircraft assemblies, sub-
assemblies & parts; guided missile &
space vehicle parts & auxiliary equipment
HQ: Gkn Limited
Po Box 4128
Redditch WORCS
152 751-7715

(G-265)
GRAND KNITTING MILLS INC (PA)
7050 New Horizons Blvd # 1 (11701-1179)
PHONE.............................631 226-5000
Fax: 631 226-8336
▲ **EMP:** 40 **EST:** 1910
SQ FT: 35,000
SALES (est): 2.9MM **Privately Held**
SIC: 2361 5137 Mfg Girl/Youth
Dresses/Blouses Whol Women's/Child's
Clothing

(G-266)
HABCO CORP
Also Called: Habco Sales
41 Ranick Dr E (11701-2844)
PHONE.............................631 789-1400
Herb Auleta, *CEO*
Steven Auleta, *President*
Philip Auleta, *Vice Pres*
Carol Auleta, *Treasurer*
▲ **EMP:** 50
SQ FT: 19,175
SALES: 9MM **Privately Held**
SIC: 2022 Processed cheese

(G-267)
HART SPECIALTIES INC
Also Called: New York Eye
5000 New Horizons Blvd (11701-1143)
P.O. Box 9003 (11701-9003)
PHONE.............................631 226-5600
Arthur Jankolovits, *Ch of Bd*
Lucy Korn, *Vice Pres*
Shannon Melendez, *Vice Pres*
Jan Phillips, *Vice Pres*
Jack Podesta, *Manager*
◆ **EMP:** 70
SQ FT: 25,000
SALES (est): 19.4MM **Privately Held**
WEB: www.newyorkeye.net
SIC: 3827 5995 Optical instruments & apparatus; optical goods stores

(G-268)
HEALTH CARE PRODUCTS
369 Bayview Ave (11701-2801)
PHONE.............................631 789-8228
Bruce Kutinsky, *President*
Joseph Bonaccorsi, *Exec VP*
Michael Stehn, *Vice Pres*
Tammy Froberg, *Exec Dir*
Lorelie Lee, *Technician*
EMP: 6 **EST:** 2017
SALES (est): 531.1K **Privately Held**
SIC: 2834 Pharmaceutical preparations

(G-269)
HELGEN INDUSTRIES INC
Also Called: De Santis Holster and Lea Gds
431 Bayview Ave (11701-2638)
PHONE.............................631 841-6300
Gene De Santis, *Ch of Bd*
Helen De Santis, *Vice Pres*
Beryl Garner, *Manager*
▲ **EMP:** 125
SQ FT: 14,000
SALES (est): 18.9MM **Privately Held**
WEB: www.desantisholster.com
SIC: 3199 3172 Holsters, leather; personal leather goods

(G-270)
HI-TECH PHARMACAL CO INC (HQ)
Also Called: Hi-Tech Pharmacal - An Akorn
369 Bayview Ave (11701-2801)
PHONE.............................631 789-8228

David S Seltzer, *President*
Gary M April, *President*
April Polikoff, *Counsel*
Kamel Egbaria, *Exec VP*
John Franolic, *Vice Pres*
▲ **EMP:** 192
SALES (est): 109.7MM
SALES (corp-wide): 694MM **Publicly Held**
WEB: www.hitechpharm.com
SIC: 2834 Pharmaceutical preparations
PA: Akorn, Inc.
    1925 W Field Ct Ste 300
    Lake Forest IL 60045
    847 279-6100

(G-271)
HI-TECH PHARMACAL CO INC
219 Dixon Ave (11701-2831)
PHONE......................................631 789-8228
EMP: 40
SALES (corp-wide): 694MM **Publicly Held**
SIC: 2834 Pharmaceutical preparations
HQ: Hi-Tech Pharmacal Co., Inc.
    369 Bayview Ave
    Amityville NY 11701
    631 789-8228

(G-272)
HI-TECH PHARMACAL CO INC
Also Called: Hi-Tech Pharmacal - An Akorn
26 Edison St (11701-2839)
PHONE......................................631 789-8228
Bernard Seltzer, *President*
Carmela Staugaitis, *Purch Mgr*
EMP: 12
SALES (corp-wide): 694MM **Publicly Held**
SIC: 2834 Pharmaceutical preparations
HQ: Hi-Tech Pharmacal Co., Inc.
    369 Bayview Ave
    Amityville NY 11701
    631 789-8228

(G-273)
HI-TECH PHARMACAL CO INC
Also Called: Hi-Tech Pharmacal - An Akorn
225 Dixon Ave (11701-2831)
PHONE......................................631 789-8228
David Seltzer, *Park Mgr*
EMP: 150
SALES (corp-wide): 694MM **Publicly Held**
SIC: 2834 Pharmaceutical preparations
HQ: Hi-Tech Pharmacal Co., Inc.
    369 Bayview Ave
    Amityville NY 11701
    631 789-8228

(G-274)
HITECH PHARM
369 Bayview Ave (11701-2801)
PHONE......................................631 789-8228
David S Seltzer, *President*
Sofia Ramos, *Engineer*
Luigi Schettino, *Engineer*
William Peters, *CFO*
Bruce Simpson, *Accounting Mgr*
EMP: 5
SALES (est): 523.5K **Privately Held**
SIC: 2834 Pharmaceutical preparations

(G-275)
IMC TEDDY FOOD SERVICE
Also Called: Sefi Fabricator
50 Ranick Dr E (11701-2822)
P.O. Box 338 (11701-0338)
PHONE......................................631 789-8881
Rasik Patel, *Partner*
Madelin Fernandez, *Purch Agent*
Suzane Girrsoli, *Human Res Dir*
EMP: 48
SALES (est): 7.2MM **Privately Held**
WEB: www.imcteddy.com
SIC: 3589 Commercial cooking & food-warming equipment

(G-276)
INNOGENIX INC
8200 New Horizons Blvd (11701-1152)
PHONE......................................631 450-4704
Manish Potti, *President*
Rajeshwarared Maareddy, *Manager*
EMP: 10

SALES (est): 542.7K **Privately Held**
SIC: 2834 Pharmaceutical preparations

(G-277)
INTERSTATE WOOD PRODUCTS INC
Also Called: Interstate Wood & Vinyl Pdts
1084 Sunrise Hwy (11701-2526)
PHONE......................................631 842-4488
Jennifer Cerullo, *CEO*
John Hokanson, *Manager*
EMP: 25
SQ FT: 8,500
SALES (est): 4.4MM
SALES (corp-wide): 28.4MM **Privately Held**
SIC: 2499 5031 3496 1799 Fencing, wood; fencing, wood; miscellaneous fabricated wire products; fence construction
PA: Amendola Industries, Inc.
    1084 Sunrise Hwy
    Amityville NY 11701

(G-278)
ISLAND LITE LOUVERS INC
35 Albany Ave (11701-2828)
PHONE......................................631 608-4250
EMP: 25
SALES (est): 3.6MM **Privately Held**
SIC: 3648 Mfg Lighting Equipment

(G-279)
JAXSON LLC
145 Dixon Ave Ste 1 (11701-2860)
PHONE......................................631 842-7775
EMP: 50
SALES (est): 7.2MM **Privately Held**
SIC: 3441 Fabricated structural metal

(G-280)
JAXSON ROLLFORMING INC
145 Dixon Ave Ste 1 (11701-2836)
PHONE......................................631 842-7775
Alexander Trink, *President*
▲ **EMP:** 37
SALES (est): 8MM **Privately Held**
WEB: www.jaxsonrollforming.com
SIC: 3446 5031 Fences, gates, posts & flagpoles; partitions & supports/studs, including accoustical systems; molding, all materials

(G-281)
JEFFREY JOHN
Also Called: Creative Compositions
25 Elm Pl (11701-2815)
PHONE......................................631 842-2850
John Jeffrey, *Owner*
EMP: 6
SALES (est): 349.6K **Privately Held**
SIC: 2499 Decorative wood & woodwork

(G-282)
JGM WHOLESALE BAKERY INC
26 Elm Pl (11701-2816)
PHONE......................................631 396-0131
Noris Moreira, *President*
Samuel Moreira, *Vice Pres*
EMP: 5
SALES (est): 153.8K **Privately Held**
SIC: 2051 Bakery: wholesale or wholesale/retail combined

(G-283)
KABCO PHARMACEUTICALS INC
2000 New Horizons Blvd (11701-1137)
PHONE......................................631 842-3600
Abu Kabir, *Ch of Bd*
Saiful Kibria, *President*
Liton Kabir, *Buyer*
Amir Hossain, *QC Mgr*
Belal Chowdhury, *Manager*
▲ **EMP:** 4
SQ FT: 30,000
SALES (est): 1.6MM **Privately Held**
WEB: www.kabco.org
SIC: 2834 Vitamin preparations

(G-284)
KDO INDUSTRIES INC
32 Ranick Dr W (11701-2825)
PHONE......................................631 608-4612
Lucelle Del Rosaio, *CEO*
George Koenig, *Vice Pres*

EMP: 7
SQ FT: 10,000
SALES (est): 1.6MM **Privately Held**
SIC: 3441 Fabricated structural metal

(G-285)
KEY CAST STONE COMPANY INC
113 Albany Ave (11701-2632)
PHONE......................................631 789-2145
Filippo Pedalino, *President*
John Gonzalez, *Treasurer*
Carmelo Cicero, *Admin Sec*
▲ **EMP:** 20 **EST:** 1958
SQ FT: 20,000
SALES (est): 3MM **Privately Held**
WEB: www.keycaststone.com
SIC: 3272 Precast terrazo or concrete products; steps, prefabricated concrete; sills, concrete

(G-286)
KLEER-FAX INC
750 New Horizons Blvd (11701-1130)
PHONE......................................631 225-1100
Elias Cruz, *CEO*
Louis Nigro, *President*
◆ **EMP:** 97
SQ FT: 50,000
SALES (est): 21.8MM **Privately Held**
WEB: www.kleer-fax.com
SIC: 2678 2677 3089 5943 Stationery products; envelopes; extruded finished plastic products; office forms & supplies; die-cut paper & board

(G-287)
L AND S PACKING CO
Also Called: Paesana
7000 New Horizons Blvd (11701-1148)
P.O. Box 709, Farmingdale (11735-0709)
PHONE......................................631 845-1717
Louis J Scaramelli III, *Ch of Bd*
Louis Scarmelli IV, *President*
Stan Staszewski, *General Mgr*
Jacqueline Massaro, *Exec VP*
Lorraine Scaramelli, *Exec VP*
▲ **EMP:** 72
SALES (est): 16.9MM **Privately Held**
WEB: www.paesana.com
SIC: 2033 2035 Olives: packaged in cans, jars, etc.; vegetables: packaged in cans, jars, etc.; maraschino cherries: packaged in cans, jars, etc.; spaghetti & other pasta sauce: packaged in cans, jars, etc.; pickles, sauces & salad dressings

(G-288)
L3HARRIS TECHNOLOGIES INC
1500 New Horizons Blvd (11701-1130)
PHONE......................................631 630-4200
James Smith, *President*
EMP: 1000
SALES (corp-wide): 6.8B **Publicly Held**
SIC: 3825 3812 3761 3699 Instruments to measure electricity; search & navigation equipment; guided missiles & space vehicles; electrical equipment & supplies; radio & TV communications equipment
PA: L3harris Technologies, Inc.
    1025 W Nasa Blvd
    Melbourne FL 32919
    321 727-9100

(G-289)
L3HARRIS TECHNOLOGIES INC
1500 New Horizons Blvd (11701-1130)
PHONE......................................631 630-4000
Frank Otto, *Branch Mgr*
EMP: 123
SALES (corp-wide): 6.8B **Publicly Held**
WEB: www.nycedo.com
SIC: 3625 Control equipment, electric
PA: L3harris Technologies, Inc.
    1025 W Nasa Blvd
    Melbourne FL 32919
    321 727-9100

(G-290)
LAMBRO INDUSTRIES INC (PA)
115 Albany Ave (11701-2632)
P.O. Box 367 (11701-0367)
PHONE......................................631 842-8088
Shiv Anand CPA, *Ch of Bd*
▲ **EMP:** 100
SQ FT: 56,000

SALES (est): 17.7MM **Privately Held**
WEB: www.lambro.net
SIC: 3444 Ventilators, sheet metal

(G-291)
LEMODE CONCEPTS INC
19 Elm Pl (11701-2815)
PHONE......................................631 841-0796
Robert Tolda, *President*
Bob Tolda, *President*
Susan Tolda, *Vice Pres*
EMP: 6
SALES (est): 430K **Privately Held**
WEB: www.lemodeconcepts.com
SIC: 2511 Kitchen & dining room furniture

(G-292)
LYNMAR PRINTING CORP
8600 New Horizons Blvd (11701-1154)
PHONE......................................631 957-8500
Lou Dilorenzo, *President*
Anthony Lisanti, *Vice Pres*
EMP: 8
SQ FT: 8,000
SALES (est): 1MM **Privately Held**
WEB: www.lynmarprinting.com
SIC: 2752 Commercial printing, offset

(G-293)
MADJEK INC
185 Dixon Ave (11701-2840)
PHONE......................................631 842-4475
R Freeman, *Vice Pres*
Robert Cummings, *Project Mgr*
Joe Corrente, *Engineer*
Elaine Moore, *Human Resources*
Mike Cuneo, *Network Mgr*
▲ **EMP:** 85
SALES (est): 14.4MM **Privately Held**
WEB: www.madjek.com
SIC: 2541 Store fixtures, wood

(G-294)
MAGNIFLOOD INC
7200 New Horizons Blvd (11701-1150)
PHONE......................................631 226-1000
Kenneth Greene, *President*
Omar Hernandez, *Engineer*
Anita Greene, *Admin Sec*
Frank Zarcone, *Analyst*
▲ **EMP:** 20 **EST:** 1977
SQ FT: 27,500
SALES (est): 4.7MM **Privately Held**
WEB: www.magniflood.com
SIC: 3646 Commercial indusl & institutional electric lighting fixtures

(G-295)
MASSAPQUA PRCSION MCHINING LTD
30 Seabro Ave (11701-1202)
PHONE......................................631 789-1485
Richard Beleski, *President*
EMP: 9
SQ FT: 7,000
SALES: 1.9MM **Privately Held**
SIC: 3599 Machine shop, jobbing & repair

(G-296)
METRO IRON CORP
4 Seabro Ave (11701-1202)
PHONE......................................631 842-5929
John Valente, *President*
Melissa Szatkowski, *Project Mgr*
Daniel Valente, *Project Mgr*
EMP: 7
SALES (est): 1.8MM **Privately Held**
WEB: www.metroiron.com
SIC: 3441 Fabricated structural metal

(G-297)
NAPCO SECURITY TECH INC (PA)
333 Bayview Ave (11701-2801)
PHONE......................................631 842-9400
Richard L Soloway, *Ch of Bd*
Michael Carrieri, *Senior VP*
Jorge Hevia, *Senior VP*
Thurmond Byron, *Vice Pres*
Al Depierro, *Vice Pres*
◆ **EMP:** 244 **EST:** 1969
SQ FT: 90,000

G
E
O
G
R
A
P
H
I
C

SALES: 102.9MM **Publicly Held**
WEB: www.napcosecurity.com
SIC: **3669** 3699 3429 1731 Emergency
alarms; fire alarm apparatus, electric; security control equipment & systems; door
locks, bolts & checks; safety & security
specialization; systems software development services

(G-298)
NEW BUSINESS SOLUTIONS INC
Also Called: Nbs
31 Sprague Ave (11701-2618)
PHONE.................................631 789-1500
Michele Ruggeri, *CEO*
George J Ruggeri, *President*
Gregory Pfaff, *Marketing Staff*
Justina Gartner, *Manager*
▲ EMP: 28
SALES (est): 5.7MM **Privately Held**
WEB: www.newbusinesssolutions.com
SIC: **2542** 2541 7389 Fixtures: display, of-
fice or store: except wood; store & office
display cases & fixtures; window trimming
service

(G-299)
OFFICIAL OFFSET CORPORATION
8600 New Horizons Blvd (11701-1183)
PHONE.................................631 957-8500
Benjamin Paulino, *Ch of Bd*
Frank Paulino, *Vice Pres*
Mary Paulino, *Admin Sec*
▼ EMP: 20 EST: 1957
SQ FT: 20,000
SALES: 4.5MM **Privately Held**
WEB: www.officialoffset.com
SIC: **2752** 2791 Commercial printing, off-
set; typesetting

(G-300)
OIL SOLUTIONS INTL INC
35 Mill St (11701-2819)
PHONE.................................631 608-8889
Dennis Traina, *Chairman*
EMP: 8
SALES (est): 160.7K **Privately Held**
SIC: **2911** Oils, lubricating

(G-301)
P & M LLC
Also Called: Sefi Fabricators
50 Ranick Dr E (11701-2822)
P.O. Box 338 (11701-0338)
PHONE.................................631 842-2200
Rasik Patel, *Mng Member*
EMP: 46 EST: 1997
SQ FT: 17,000
SALES (est): 10.2MM **Privately Held**
SIC: **3556** Food products machinery

(G-302)
PAULIN INVESTMENT COMPANY
8600 New Horizons Blvd (11701-1154)
PHONE.................................631 957-8500
Ben M Paulino, *Owner*
EMP: 27
SALES (est): 2.9MM **Privately Held**
SIC: **2759** Commercial printing

(G-303)
PEPSI BOTTLING VENTURES LLC
Also Called: Pepsico
550 New Horizons Blvd (11701-1139)
PHONE.................................631 226-9000
Carl Cariffunior, *General Mgr*
EMP: 40 **Privately Held**
SIC: **2086** Carbonated soft drinks, bottled
& canned
HQ: Pepsi Bottling Ventures Llc
4141 Parklake Ave Ste 600
Raleigh NC 27612
919 865-2300

(G-304)
PRECISION SIGNSCOM INC
Also Called: Precision Engraving Company
243 Dixon Ave (11701-2830)
PHONE.................................631 841-7500
Michael Anzalone, *Ch of Bd*
EMP: 51
SQ FT: 23,500

SALES (est): 8.2MM **Privately Held**
SIC: **3993** Signs, not made in custom sign
painting shops

(G-305)
RISING TIDE FUEL LLC
2 S Bay Ave (11701-4215)
PHONE.................................631 374-7361
Gene Monahan, *Principal*
EMP: 7
SALES (est): 1MM **Privately Held**
SIC: **2869** Fuels

(G-306)
SARAGA INDUSTRIES CORP
Also Called: Lenco
690 Albany Ave Unit D (11701-1199)
PHONE.................................631 842-4049
Robert Saraga, *President*
EMP: 6
SQ FT: 4,000
SALES (est): 988K **Privately Held**
WEB: www.lencocoolers.com
SIC: **3443** Heat exchangers, condensers &
components

(G-307)
STEIN INDUSTRIES INC
22 Sprague Ave (11701-2634)
PHONE.................................631 789-2222
Stuart Stein, *President*
Andrew Stein, *Vice Pres*
Andrew Jinks, *Manager*
EMP: 40 EST: 1937
SQ FT: 30,000
SALES (est): 5.8MM **Privately Held**
WEB: www.steinindustries.com
SIC: **2541** Wood partitions & fixtures

(G-308)
STRUCTURED 3D INC
188 Dixon Ave (11701-2812)
PHONE.................................346 704-2614
Mitchell Proux, *President*
EMP: 5
SALES (est): 190.4K **Privately Held**
SIC: **2759** Commercial printing

(G-309)
SUNDIAL BRANDS LLC
11 Ranick Dr S (11701-2823)
PHONE.................................631 842-8800
Richelieu Dennis, *CEO*
Nyema Tudman, *President*
Akhil Bhansali, *Vice Pres*
Rosario Lea De, *Vice Pres*
Cyrus Dennis, *Vice Pres*
▲ EMP: 215
SALES (est): 102.4MM
SALES (corp-wide): 58.3B **Privately Held**
SIC: **2844** Cosmetic preparations
PA: Unilever Plc
Unilever House
London EC4Y
207 822-5252

(G-310)
SUNDIAL FRAGRANCES & FLAVORS
11 Ranick Dr S (11701-2823)
PHONE.................................631 842-8800
Richelieu Dennis, *CEO*
Nyema S Tubman, *Ch of Bd*
Martha Dennis, *Treasurer*
EMP: 24
SQ FT: 50,000
SALES (est): 7.8MM **Privately Held**
WEB: www.nhexec.com
SIC: **2869** 5122 Perfumes, flavorings &
food additives; perfumes

(G-311)
SUNDIAL GROUP LLC
Also Called: Sundial Creations
11 Ranick Dr S (11701-2823)
PHONE.................................631 842-8800
Marry Dennis, *CEO*
Dennis Richelieu, *CEO*
Christine Williams, *Research*
Linda Hess, *Graphic Designe*
EMP: 40
SQ FT: 50,000
SALES (est): 13.7MM
SALES (corp-wide): 58.3B **Privately Held**
SIC: **2844** Cosmetic preparations

PA: Unilever N.V.
Weena 455
Rotterdam
102 174-000

(G-312)
TOPIDERM INC (PA)
5200 New Horizons Blvd (11701-1189)
PHONE.................................631 226-7979
Burt Shaffer, *Ch of Bd*
Bob Arnaiz, *Prdtn Mgr*
Carol Donaldson, *Purch Mgr*
Kathleen Sieger, *Purch Mgr*
Steven Pinsky, *CFO*
▲ EMP: 200
SALES (est): 58.4MM **Privately Held**
SIC: **2834** 2844 Pharmaceutical prepara-
tions; cosmetic preparations

(G-313)
TOPIX PHARMACEUTICALS INC (PA)
5200 New Horizons Blvd (11701-1189)
PHONE.................................631 226-7979
Brenda Wu, *President*
Burt Shaffer, *President*
Joe Ragosta, *VP Sales*
Laura Deutsch, *Sales Staff*
Eva Vermont, *Sales Staff*
▲ EMP: 150
SALES (est): 45MM **Privately Held**
WEB: www.topixpharm.com
SIC: **2834** Pharmaceutical preparations

(G-314)
TRITON BUILDERS INC
645 Broadway Ste T (11701-2118)
PHONE.................................631 841-2534
Stacy Guercia-Baldea, *President*
EMP: 20
SQ FT: 2,000
SALES: 6MM **Privately Held**
SIC: **3441** Fabricated structural metal

(G-315)
TRUE TYPE PRINTING CO INC
8600 New Horizons Blvd (11701-1154)
PHONE.................................718 706-6900
Lee Forlenza, *President*
EMP: 5
SALES (est): 431.8K **Privately Held**
SIC: **2752** Commercial printing, offset

Amsterdam
Montgomery County

(G-316)
AMSTERDAM PRINTING & LITHO INC
Go Promos
166 Wallins Corners Rd (12010-1817)
PHONE.................................518 842-6000
Melissa Santamaria, *Branch Mgr*
EMP: 15
SALES (corp-wide): 2.8B **Privately Held**
WEB: www.amsterdamprinting.com
SIC: **3993** 2752 2761 Advertising novel-
ties; commercial printing, lithographic;
manifold business forms
HQ: Amsterdam Printing & Litho, Inc.
166 Wallins Corners Rd
Amsterdam NY 12010
518 842-6000

(G-317)
AMSTERDAM PRINTING & LITHO INC
Baldwin Cooke
166 Wallins Corners Rd (12010-1817)
PHONE.................................518 842-6000
EMP: 49
SALES (corp-wide): 2.8B **Privately Held**
WEB: www.amsterdamprinting.com
SIC: **3993** 2752 2761 Advertising novel-
ties; commercial printing, lithographic;
manifold business forms
HQ: Amsterdam Printing & Litho, Inc.
166 Wallins Corners Rd
Amsterdam NY 12010
518 842-6000

(G-318)
BECKMANN CONVERTING INC (PA)
14 Park Dr (12010-5340)
P.O. Box 390 (12010-0390)
PHONE.................................518 842-0073
Klaus Beckmann, *CEO*
Peter Piusz, *Vice Pres*
Bill Wood, *Engineer*
Tony Tangerone, *Controller*
Gale Daley, *Supervisor*
▲ EMP: 44
SQ FT: 100,000
SALES (est): 6.3MM **Privately Held**
WEB: www.beckmannconverting.com
SIC: **2295** 2262 Leather, artificial or imita-
tion; fire resistance finishing: manmade &
silk broadwoven

(G-319)
BEECH-NUT NUTRITION COMPANY (DH)
1 Nutritious Pl (12010-8105)
PHONE.................................518 839-0300
Jeffrey Boutelle, *President*
Cheryl Benninger, *QC Mgr*
Marc Ruf, *Asst Controller*
Rachel Shapiro, *Human Res Mgr*
Debbie Wilder, *Human Resources*
◆ EMP: 295
SALES (est): 128MM
SALES (corp-wide): 1.3B **Privately Held**
SIC: **2032** Baby foods, including meats:
packaged in cans, jars, etc.
HQ: Hero Ag
Karl Roth-Strasse 8
Lenzburg AG 5600
628 855-111

(G-320)
BRETON INDUSTRIES INC (PA)
1 Sam Stratton Rd (12010-5243)
PHONE.................................518 842-3030
Alfred Damofal, *CEO*
Peter A Lewis, *Senior VP*
G Eric Lewis, *Vice Pres*
G Richard Lewis, *Treasurer*
EMP: 110
SQ FT: 55,000
SALES (est): 18.9MM **Privately Held**
WEB: www.bretonindustries.com
SIC: **2394** 2399 3443 2295 Tarpaulins,
fabric: made from purchased materials;
canvas awnings & canopies; canvas cov-
ers & drop cloths; shades, canvas: made
from purchased materials; aprons, breast
(harness); fabricated plate work (boiler
shop); coated fabrics, not rubberized; nar-
row fabric mills

(G-321)
CAPITOL CUPS INC
1030 Riverfront Ctr (12010-4616)
P.O. Box 710 (12010-0710)
PHONE.................................518 627-0051
Robert S Abrams, *President*
John Belfance Jr, *COO*
Robert N Sawyer, *CFO*
Robert L Thompson, *Controller*
EMP: 26
SQ FT: 10,000
SALES (est): 4.3MM **Privately Held**
WEB: www.capitolcups.com
SIC: **3089** Cups, plastic, except foam

(G-322)
CAPITOL PLASTIC PRODUCTS INC
1030 Riverfront Ctr (12010-4616)
P.O. Box 710 (12010-0710)
PHONE.................................518 627-0051
Robert Abrams, *Principal*
▼ EMP: 210
SALES (est): 9.2MM
SALES (corp-wide): 114.6MM **Privately Held**
SIC: **3085** Plastics bottles
PA: Cv Holdings, Llc
1030 Riverfront Ctr
Amsterdam NY 12010
518 627-0051

(G-323)
CRANESVILLE BLOCK CO INC (PA)
Also Called: Cranesville Ready-Mix
1250 Riverfront Ctr (12010-4602)
PHONE..............................518 684-6154
John A Tesiero III, *Ch of Bd*
Elizabeth Tesiero, *Corp Secy*
Brian Olpalka, *Store Mgr*
Steve Dillenbeck, *Purch Mgr*
Edward Arthurs, *Controller*
▲ EMP: 45 EST: 1947
SALES (est): 45MM **Privately Held**
SIC: 3271 3273 5211 Blocks, concrete or
cinder: standard; ready-mixed concrete;
concrete & cinder block; cement; masonry
materials & supplies

(G-324)
CSP TECHNOLOGIES INC (HQ)
1031 Riverfront Ctr (12010)
PHONE..............................518 627-0051
Robert Abrams, *CEO*
▲ EMP: 45
SALES (est): 14.5MM
SALES (corp-wide): 114.6MM **Privately
Held**
SIC: 3089 Plastic processing
PA: Cv Holdings, Llc
1030 Riverfront Ctr
Amsterdam NY 12010
518 627-0051

(G-325)
ELECTRIC CITY CONCRETE CO INC (HQ)
774 State Highway 5s (12010-7668)
P.O. Box 430 (12010-0430)
PHONE..............................518 887-5560
John A Tesiero Jr, *President*
Carol Whelly, *Vice Pres*
EMP: 25 EST: 1977
SALES (est): 1.5MM
SALES (corp-wide): 45MM **Privately
Held**
SIC: 3273 Ready-mixed concrete
PA: Cranesville Block Co., Inc.
1250 Riverfront Ctr
Amsterdam NY 12010
518 684-6154

(G-326)
EMBASSY MILLWORK INC
3 Sam Stratton Rd (12010-5243)
PHONE..............................518 839-0965
Michael Caruso, *President*
EMP: 12
SALES (est): 1.1MM **Privately Held**
SIC: 2421 Planing mill, independent: ex-
cept millwork

(G-327)
FIBER GLASS INDUSTRIES INC (PA)
Also Called: Fgi
69 Edson St (12010-5247)
PHONE..............................518 842-4000
John Menzel, *CEO*
Mike Lanham, *President*
◆ EMP: 75 EST: 1957
SQ FT: 60,000
SALES (est): 22.7MM **Privately Held**
SIC: 2221 Fiberglass fabrics; glass broad-
woven fabrics

(G-328)
FULMONT READY-MIX COMPANY INC (PA)
774 State Highway 5s (12010-7668)
PHONE..............................518 887-5560
Elizabeth Tesiero, *President*
John Tesiero III, *Vice Pres*
EMP: 16 EST: 1947
SALES: 1.1MM **Privately Held**
SIC: 3273 Ready-mixed concrete

(G-329)
GREAT ADIRONDACK YARN COMPANY
950 County Highway 126 (12010-6287)
PHONE..............................518 843-3381
Patti Subik, *Owner*
Paul Subik, *Vice Pres*
EMP: 10

SALES: 400K **Privately Held**
SIC: 2281 2253 5949 5199 Natural & animal fiber yarns, spun; sweaters &
sweater coats, knit; sewing & needlework;
yarns

(G-330)
HYPERBARIC TECHNOLOGIES INC
1 Sam Stratton Rd (12010-5243)
P.O. Box 69 (12010-0069)
PHONE..............................518 842-3030
Peter Lewis, *President*
Richard Lewis, *CFO*
EMP: 2
SQ FT: 5,000
SALES (est): 3.2MM **Privately Held**
SIC: 3443 Chambers & caissons

(G-331)
J H BUHRMASTER COMPANY INC
Also Called: Amsterdam Oil Heat
164 W Main St (12010-3130)
PHONE..............................518 843-1700
Donald L Hosier, *Sales/Mktg Mgr*
EMP: 8
SALES (corp-wide): 8.6MM **Privately
Held**
SIC: 3567 Industrial furnaces & ovens
PA: J. H. Buhrmaster Company, Inc.
421 Sacandaga Rd
Scotia NY 12302
518 382-0260

(G-332)
KC TAG CO
108 Edson St (12010-7213)
PHONE..............................518 842-6666
Kevin Collins, *Ch of Bd*
EMP: 8
SALES (est): 1.1MM **Privately Held**
SIC: 3089 Plastics products

(G-333)
LOSURDO FOODS INC
78 Sam Stratton Rd (12010-5244)
PHONE..............................518 842-1500
Maria Hammill, *Branch Mgr*
EMP: 25
SALES (corp-wide): 73.5MM **Privately
Held**
WEB: www.losurdofoods.com
SIC: 2099 Food preparations
PA: Losurdo Foods, Inc.
20 Owens Rd
Hackensack NJ 07601
201 343-6680

(G-334)
MCCLARY MEDIA INC
Also Called: Port Jackson Media
1 Venner Rd (12010-5617)
PHONE..............................800 453-6397
Kevin McClary, *Principal*
Geoff Dylong, *Principal*
Rich Kretser, *Principal*
Dave Warner, *Principal*
EMP: 5
SALES (est): 203.3K **Privately Held**
SIC: 2711 7313 Newspapers: publishing
only, not printed on site; magazine adver-
tising representative; newspaper advertis-
ing representative

(G-335)
MHXCO FOAM COMPANY LLC
120 Edson St (12010-7213)
P.O. Box 579 (12010-0579)
PHONE..............................518 843-8400
Stephen Trembley, *Mng Member*
EMP: 14
SALES: 3MM **Privately Held**
SIC: 3069 Foam rubber

(G-336)
MILLER PRINTING & LITHO INC
97 Guy Park Ave (12010-3225)
PHONE..............................518 842-0001
Scott Miller, *President*
EMP: 6
SQ FT: 9,000
SALES (est): 914.7K **Privately Held**
SIC: 2752 Commercial printing, offset

(G-337)
MILNOT HOLDING CORPORATION
1 Nutritious Pl (12010-8105)
PHONE..............................518 839-0300
Amy McGrath, *Human Res Dir*
EMP: 5
SALES (est): 502.2K
SALES (corp-wide): 1.3B **Privately Held**
SIC: 2099 Food preparations
HQ: Hero Ag
Karl Roth-Strasse 8
Lenzburg AG 5600
628 855-111

(G-338)
MOHAWK FABRIC COMPANY INC
96 Guy Park Ave (12010-3241)
P.O. Box 587 (12010-0587)
PHONE..............................518 842-3090
Gregory Needham, *President*
Dominic Wade, *Principal*
EMP: 15 EST: 1922
SQ FT: 35,000
SALES (est): 4.3MM **Privately Held**
WEB: www.mohawkfabric.com
SIC: 2258 Lace & warp knit fabric mills

(G-339)
MOHAWK RESOURCES LTD
65 Vrooman Ave (12010-5321)
P.O. Box 110 (12010-0110)
PHONE..............................518 842-1431
Steven Perlstein, *President*
Andrea Baldomar, *General Mgr*
Nancy Rogers, *Business Mgr*
Ron Veresko, *Engineer*
Ray Pedrick, *Sales Staff*
▲ EMP: 70
SQ FT: 55,000
SALES (est): 40.9MM **Privately Held**
WEB: www.mohawklifts.com
SIC: 3536 Hoists

(G-340)
MOHAWK SIGN SYSTEMS INC
5 Dandreano Dr (12010-5253)
P.O. Box 966, Schenectady (12301-0966)
PHONE..............................518 842-5303
Bettina Dill, *President*
Neal Dill, *Vice Pres*
Neale Dill, *Vice Pres*
EMP: 30 EST: 1946
SQ FT: 10,000
SALES (est): 2.5MM **Privately Held**
WEB: www.mohawksign.com
SIC: 3993 Signs, not made in custom sign
painting shops

(G-341)
NATIONWIDE TARPS INCORPORATED (PA)
Also Called: NTI Global
50 Willow St (12010-4219)
P.O. Box 189 (12010-0189)
PHONE..............................518 843-1545
Stephen Raeburn, *Ch of Bd*
Anita Raeburn, *Vice Pres*
April Smida, *Human Res Mgr*
Benal Raeburn, *Agent*
Steve Raeburn, *Executive*
▲ EMP: 75
SQ FT: 195,000
SALES (est): 15.9MM **Privately Held**
WEB: www.ntiglobal.com
SIC: 3081 2821 2394 2392 Polyethylene
film; plastics materials & resins; canvas &
related products; household furnishings;
solar cells

(G-342)
NORTH E RGGERS ERECTORS NY INC
178 Clizbe Ave (12010-2935)
PHONE..............................518 842-6377
Scott Egan, *President*
Michael Egan, *Vice Pres*
Charles Egan, *Treasurer*
Thomas Egan, *Admin Sec*
EMP: 40
SQ FT: 6,000
SALES (est): 7.7MM **Privately Held**
SIC: 3441 Fabricated structural metal

(G-343)
NORTHEASTERN WATER JET INC
4 Willow St (12010-4219)
PHONE..............................518 843-4988
Lenny Laporte, *President*
Andre Laporte, *Vice Pres*
EMP: 18
SQ FT: 176,000
SALES (est): 3.5MM **Privately Held**
WEB: www.newj.com
SIC: 3599 Machine shop, jobbing & repair

(G-344)
NOTEWORTHY INDUSTRIES INC
Also Called: Noteworthy Company, The
336 Forest Ave (12010-2723)
PHONE..............................518 842-2662
Elsa Buseck, *President*
John P Colangelo, *Vice Pres*
Adam Eagon, *Marketing Staff*
Anthony Constantino, *Officer*
Tina C Wells, *Author*
◆ EMP: 148 EST: 1971
SQ FT: 400,000
SALES: 18MM **Privately Held**
WEB: www.noteworthy.com
SIC: 2673 2679 Plastic bags: made from
purchased materials; paper products,
converted

(G-345)
POWER AND COMPOSITE TECH LLC
Also Called: P C T
200 Wallins Corners Rd (12010-1819)
PHONE..............................518 843-6825
Robert Mylott, *CEO*
Phil Day, *Managing Dir*
Joseph Day, *Vice Pres*
Bill Pabis, *Vice Pres*
Fabio Tucci, *Vice Pres*
▲ EMP: 90
SQ FT: 55,000
SALES (est): 24.2MM **Privately Held**
WEB: www.pactinc.com
SIC: 3621 Electric motor & generator parts
PA: Thayer Capital Partners, L.P.
1455 Penn Ave Nw Ste 350
Washington DC 20004

(G-346)
RAYCO OF SCHENECTADY INC
4 Sam Stratton Rd (12010)
PHONE..............................518 212-5113
Ed Legere, *President*
Michael Kilgalen, *Managing Prtnr*
Janis Legere, *Vice Pres*
EMP: 13
SQ FT: 6,000
SALES (est): 1.8MM **Privately Held**
SIC: 3471 Electroplating of metals or
formed products; polishing, metals or
formed products

(G-347)
SARATOGA HORSEWORKS LTD
57 Edson St (12010-5238)
P.O. Box 549 (12010-0549)
PHONE..............................518 843-6756
Michael Libertucci, *President*
Adrienne Libertucci, *Corp Secy*
EMP: 25
SQ FT: 15,000
SALES (est): 1.2MM **Privately Held**
WEB: www.horseworks.com
SIC: 2399 Horse & pet accessories, textile

(G-348)
TONCHE TIMBER LLC
3959 State Highway 30 (12010-6509)
PHONE..............................845 389-3489
Ronald Cohen, *Owner*
EMP: 6 EST: 2007
SALES (est): 398.1K **Privately Held**
SIC: 2411 Timber, cut at logging camp

(G-349)
TRI-VILLAGE PUBLISHERS INC
Also Called: Recorder, The
1 Venner Rd (12010-5617)
PHONE..............................518 843-1100
EMP: 60

SALES (est): 2.7MM **Privately Held**
WEB: www.recordernews.com
SIC: 2711 Newspapers: publishing only, not printed on site

(G-350)
TRIO CLEAN LLC
1451 State Highway 5s (12010-8341)
PHONE.................................518 627-4055
Dominic Wade,
Schuyler Wade,
EMP: 10
SALES (est): 438.6K **Privately Held**
SIC: 3582 Commercial laundry equipment

(G-351)
UNIVERSAL CUSTOM MILLWORK INC
3 Sam Stratton Rd (12010-5243)
PHONE.................................518 330-6622
EMP: 60
SQ FT: 50,000
SALES (est): 7.1MM **Privately Held**
WEB: www.ucmillwork.com
SIC: 2431 Millwork

(G-352)
VIDA-BLEND LLC
1430 State Highway 5s (12010-8184)
PHONE.................................518 627-4138
Freddy Luna, *Mng Member*
Edward Pragliabento, *Mng Member*
Michael Pragliabento, *Mng Member*
EMP: 20 **EST:** 2013
SALES (est): 3.5MM **Privately Held**
SIC: 2834 Vitamin, nutrient & hematinic preparations for human use

(G-353)
WESTROCK CONTAINER LLC
28 Park Dr (12010-5340)
PHONE.................................518 842-2450
Edward H Poulin, *Manager*
EMP: 60
SALES (corp-wide): 16.2B **Publicly Held**
SIC: 2411 2674 2621 2631 Wooden logs; shipping & shopping bags or sacks; kraft paper; container board; boxes, corrugated: made from purchased materials; boxes, solid fiber: made from purchased materials
HQ: Westrock Container, Llc
1601 Blairs Ferry Rd Ne
Cedar Rapids IA 52402
319 393-3610

(G-354)
WILLIAM J KLINE & SON INC (PA)
Also Called: Hamilton County News
1 Venner Rd (12010-5617)
PHONE.................................518 843-1100
Sidney Lefavour, *President*
Kevin McClary, *Publisher*
Brian Krohn, *General Mgr*
EMP: 90 **EST:** 1878
SQ FT: 30,000
SALES (est): 4.3MM **Privately Held**
SIC: 2711 2752 Newspapers: publishing only, not printed on site; commercial printing, lithographic

Ancram
Columbia County

(G-355)
SCHWEITZER-MAUDUIT INTL INC
2424 Route 82 (12502-5414)
P.O. Box 10 (12502-0010)
PHONE.................................518 329-4222
Gary Kennedy, *Manager*
EMP: 135 **Publicly Held**
SIC: 2141 2111 2621 Tobacco stemming & redrying; cigarettes; cigarette paper
PA: Schweitzer-Mauduit International, Inc.
100 N Point Ctr E Ste 600
Alpharetta GA 30022

Angelica
Allegany County

(G-356)
ANGELICA FOREST PRODUCTS INC
54 Closser Ave (14709-8746)
P.O. Box 685 (14709-0685)
PHONE.................................585 466-3205
David Chamberlain, *Principal*
EMP: 9 **EST:** 2011
SALES (est): 1MM **Privately Held**
SIC: 2421 Sawmills & planing mills, general

(G-357)
ANGELICA SPRING COMPANY INC
99 West Ave (14709-8713)
P.O. Box 681 (14709-0681)
PHONE.................................585 466-7892
William Geoppner, *President*
EMP: 17
SQ FT: 4,400
SALES (est): 3.2MM **Privately Held**
WEB: www.angelicaspringcompany.com
SIC: 3493 3496 Coiled flat springs; flat springs, sheet or strip stock; miscellaneous fabricated wire products

Angola
Erie County

(G-358)
ANGOLA PENNY SAVER INC
19 Center St (14006-1305)
PHONE.................................716 549-1164
James Austin, *Publisher*
EMP: 12
SQ FT: 5,950
SALES (est): 909.2K **Privately Held**
SIC: 2711 Newspapers, publishing & printing

(G-359)
GOYA FOODS INC
Also Called: Goya Foods Great Lakes
200 S Main St (14006-1534)
P.O. Box 152 (14006-0152)
PHONE.................................716 549-0076
Rafael Rodriguez, *General Mgr*
Robert J Drago Sr, *Principal*
Juan Rodriguez, *Engineer*
Luis Valencia, *Plant Engr*
EMP: 75
SALES (corp-wide): 1.1B **Privately Held**
SIC: 2033 2032 2035 2034 Canned fruits & specialties; canned specialties; pickles, sauces & salad dressings; dehydrated fruits, vegetables, soups; poultry slaughtering & processing
PA: Goya Foods, Inc.
350 County Rd
Jersey City NJ 07307
201 348-4900

(G-360)
POLYTEX INC
1305 Eden Evans Center Rd (14006-8839)
PHONE.................................716 549-5100
Jacob H Ilioha, *President*
▲ **EMP:** 100
SQ FT: 8,000
SALES (est): 5.9MM **Privately Held**
SIC: 2221 Fiberglass fabrics

(G-361)
TX RX SYSTEMS INC
8625 Industrial Pkwy (14006-9692)
PHONE.................................716 549-4700
David J Hessler, *Ch of Bd*
Anthony Delgobbo, *Plant Mgr*
Wayne Newman, *Plant Mgr*
Ken Pokigo, *Engineer*
Dennis Morgan, *CFO*
▲ **EMP:** 115 **EST:** 1976
SQ FT: 31,000

SALES (est): 23MM **Privately Held**
WEB: www.txrx.com
SIC: 3669 Intercommunication systems, electric
PA: Bird Technologies Group Inc.
30303 Aurora Rd
Solon OH 44139

Apalachin
Tioga County

(G-362)
TAYLOR BROTHERS INC
6 Jacobs Rd (13732)
PHONE.................................607 625-2828
Douglas Weist, *President*
EMP: 12
SQ FT: 10,000
SALES: 600K **Privately Held**
SIC: 2448 Pallets, wood; skids, wood

(G-363)
WATERMANS DISTILLERY LLC
6172 State Route 434 (13732-2459)
PHONE.................................607 258-0274
Michelle Alig, *Mng Member*
EMP: 5
SALES (est): 162.7K **Privately Held**
SIC: 2085 Grain alcohol for beverage purposes

Aquebogue
Suffolk County

(G-364)
ALTAIRE PHARMACEUTICALS INC
311 West Ln (11931)
P.O. Box 849 (11931-0849)
PHONE.................................631 722-5988
▲ **EMP:** 130
SALES (est): 32.5MM **Privately Held**
SIC: 2834 Pharmaceutical preparations

(G-365)
CRESCENT DUCK FARM INC
10 Edgar Ave (11931)
P.O. Box 500 (11931-0500)
PHONE.................................631 722-8700
Douglas H Corwin, *President*
Douglas Corwin, *Vice Pres*
Jeffrey Corwin, *Treasurer*
Janet Wedel, *Admin Sec*
▼ **EMP:** 50 **EST:** 1959
SQ FT: 6,000
SALES (est): 7.9MM **Privately Held**
SIC: 2015 4222 2011 Ducks, processed: fresh; refrigerated warehousing & storage; meat packing plants

(G-366)
PAUMANOK VINEYARDS LTD
1074 Main Rd Rte 25 (11931)
P.O. Box 741 (11931-0741)
PHONE.................................631 722-8800
Charles Massoud, *President*
Ursula Massoud, *Vice Pres*
Karen Kankel, *Sales Staff*
Salim Massoud, *Manager*
▲ **EMP:** 20
SQ FT: 9,000
SALES (est): 2.8MM **Privately Held**
WEB: www.paumanok.com
SIC: 2084 Wines; wine cellars, bonded: engaged in blending wines

Arcade
Wyoming County

(G-367)
AMERICAN PRECISION INDS INC
Surface Mounted Devices Div
95 North St (14009-9196)
P.O. Box 38 (14009-0038)
PHONE.................................585 496-5755
Kevin Heffler, *Branch Mgr*
EMP: 100

SALES (corp-wide): 6.4B **Publicly Held**
WEB: www.apischmidtbretten.com
SIC: 3677 Coil windings, electronic; inductors, electronic
HQ: American Precision Industries Inc.
45 Hazelwood Dr
Amherst NY 14228
716 691-9100

(G-368)
API HEAT TRANSFER INC
A P I Airtech Division
91 North St (14009-9196)
PHONE.................................585 496-5755
Jack Bellomo, *President*
Karl Anderson, *Branch Mgr*
EMP: 200
SQ FT: 85,000
SALES (corp-wide): 46.7MM **Privately Held**
WEB: www.apiheattransfer.com
SIC: 3443 Heat exchangers: coolers (after, inter), condensers, etc.
HQ: Api Heat Transfer Inc.
2777 Walden Ave Ste 1
Buffalo NY 14225
716 684-6700

(G-369)
BATAVIA ENCLOSURES INC
636 Main St (14009-1037)
PHONE.................................585 344-1797
Toll Free:.................................877 -
EMP: 6
SQ FT: 10,000
SALES (est): 1MM **Privately Held**
SIC: 3444 Mfg Sheet Metalwork

(G-370)
BLISS MACHINE INC
260 North St (14009-1206)
P.O. Box 145 (14009-0145)
PHONE.................................585 492-5128
William Kanner, *President*
Randy Kanner, *Vice Pres*
EMP: 18
SQ FT: 9,500
SALES (est): 3.6MM **Privately Held**
WEB: www.blissmachine.net
SIC: 3599 Machine shop, jobbing & repair

(G-371)
BRAUEN CONSTRUTION
1087 Chaffee Rd (14009-9779)
PHONE.................................585 492-0042
Floyd Brauen, *President*
EMP: 7 **EST:** 1983
SQ FT: 16,000
SALES (est): 1.1MM **Privately Held**
WEB: www.brauenmillwork.com
SIC: 2431 Woodwork, interior & ornamental

(G-372)
DEVIN MFG INC
40 Edward St (14009-1012)
P.O. Box 97 (14009-0097)
PHONE.................................585 496-5770
William A Devin, *President*
Anne Devin, *Vice Pres*
Erica Bigos, *Admin Sec*
▼ **EMP:** 17 **EST:** 1959
SQ FT: 17,400
SALES (est): 3.1MM **Privately Held**
WEB: www.devinmfg.com
SIC: 3599 3537 3494 3949 Machine shop, jobbing & repair; engine stands & racks, metal; valves & pipe fittings; target shooting equipment; targets, archery & rifle shooting

(G-373)
EMKAY TRADING CORP
Also Called: Emkay Bordeaux
58 Church St (14009-1117)
P.O. Box 174 (14009-0174)
PHONE.................................585 492-3800
Cathy Golman, *Branch Mgr*
EMP: 30
SQ FT: 51,500
SALES (corp-wide): 1.9MM **Privately Held**
WEB: www.emkaytrading.org
SIC: 2022 2026 Cheese, natural & processed; cream, sweet

GEOGRAPHIC

PA: Emkay Trading Corp
250 Clearbrook Rd Ste 127
Elmsford NY 10523
914 592-9000

(G-374)
GM PALMER INC
51 Edward St (14009-1012)
P.O. Box 343 (14009-0343)
PHONE......................585 492-2990
Greg Palmer, *President*
Mary Palmer, *Corp Secy*
◆ **EMP:** 15
SQ FT: 47,500
SALES (est): 10MM **Privately Held**
SIC: 2421 Fuelwood, from mill waste

(G-375)
GOWANDA - BTI LLC
Also Called: Chiptek
7426a Tanner Pkwy (14009-9758)
PHONE......................716 492-4081
Don McElheny,
EMP: 66
SALES: 7.6MM **Privately Held**
SIC: 3677 Electronic coils, transformers &
other inductors

(G-376)
J A YANSICK LUMBER CO INC
16 Rule Dr (14009-1019)
PHONE......................585 492-4312
James Yansick, *President*
EMP: 30 EST: 1966
SQ FT: 1,979
SALES (est): 3.1MM **Privately Held**
SIC: 2421 2426 Lumber: rough, sawed or
planed; hardwood dimension & flooring
mills

(G-377)
MAPLE GROVE CORP
Also Called: Maple Grove and Enterprises
7075 Route 98 (14009-9756)
P.O. Box 156 (14009-0156)
PHONE......................585 492-5286
Phillip M Hobin, *Ch of Bd*
Jen Hobin, *COO*
Ted Hobin Jr, *Vice Pres*
Xavier Reagan, *Accounting Mgr*
Michelle Hobin, *Admin Sec*
EMP: 25
SQ FT: 1,200
SALES (est): 5MM **Privately Held**
SIC: 7692 7213 Welding repair; coat sup-
ply

(G-378)
**NEIGHBOR TO NEIGHBOR
NEWS INC**
Also Called: Arcade Herald
223 Main St (14009-1209)
PHONE......................585 492-2525
Grant Hamilton, *President*
EMP: 9
SQ FT: 1,200
SALES (est): 360K **Privately Held**
SIC: 2711 Newspapers: publishing only,
not printed on site

(G-379)
NEW EAGLE SILO CORP
7648 Hurdville Rd (14009-1021)
PHONE......................585 492-1300
Leonard Johnson, *President*
EMP: 8 EST: 1967
SQ FT: 6,000
SALES: 400K **Privately Held**
SIC: 3531 Cement silos (batch plant)

(G-380)
PRESTOLITE ELECTRIC INC
400 Main St (14009-1189)
PHONE......................585 492-2278
Bill Brauen, *CEO*
Craig Bender, *Engrg Mgr*
David Little, *Engineer*
Jay Petri, *Electrical Engi*
Rebeccabecky Landphair, *Finance*
EMP: 150
SQ FT: 34,000
SALES (corp-wide): 1.2B **Privately Held**
SIC: 3694 Alternators, automotive

HQ: Prestolite Electric Incorporated
30120 Hudson Dr
Novi MI 48377
866 463-7078

(G-381)
STEEL & OBRIEN MFG INC
7869 Route 98 (14009-9601)
PHONE......................585 492-5800
Bryan Wells, *President*
Pete Beyette, *Vice Pres*
Scott Wells, *Vice Pres*
Tim Bainbridge, *Project Mgr*
Mike Lovelace, *Purch Agent*
▲ **EMP:** 72
SQ FT: 55,000
SALES (est): 15.6MM **Privately Held**
WEB: www.steelobrien.com
SIC: 3494 3492 Valves & pipe fittings; fluid
power valves & hose fittings

(G-382)
TPI ARCADE INC
7888 Route 98 (14009-9601)
PHONE......................585 492-0122
Jack Pohlman, *Ch of Bd*
Gerald Byrne, *Chairman*
Traci Hemmerlin, *Controller*
EMP: 75
SALES (est): 15.4MM
SALES (corp-wide): 501.5MM **Privately
Held**
WEB: www.tpicast.com
SIC: 3363 Aluminum die-castings
PA: Ligon Industries, Llc
1927 1st Ave N Ste 500
Birmingham AL 35203
205 322-3302

Ardsley
Westchester County

(G-383)
**ACORDA THERAPEUTICS INC
(PA)**
420 Saw Mill River Rd (10502-2605)
PHONE......................914 347-4300
Ron Cohen, *President*
David Lawrence, *Principal*
Lisa Bryant, *Business Mgr*
Shawn Carlson, *Business Mgr*
Christina D'Angelo, *Business Mgr*
▲ **EMP:** 241
SQ FT: 138,000
SALES: 471.4MM **Publicly Held**
WEB: www.acorda.com
SIC: 2834 8731 2836 Drugs acting on the
central nervous system & sense organs;
biotechnical research, commercial; bio-
logical products, except diagnostic

(G-384)
ADVANCED COMM SOLUTIONS
38 Ridge Rd (10502-2226)
PHONE......................914 693-5076
EMP: 5
SALES: 900K **Privately Held**
SIC: 3663 Mfg Radio/Tv Communication
Equipment

(G-385)
AMBULATORY MONITORING INC
731 Saw Mill River Rd # 3 (10502-1814)
P.O. Box 609 (10502-0609)
PHONE......................914 693-9240
Thomas Kazlauski, *President*
Linda Tavolacci, *Vice Pres*
Marie Calise, *Admin Asst*
EMP: 6
SQ FT: 1,000
SALES (est): 854.6K **Privately Held**
WEB: www.ambulatory-monitoring.com
SIC: 3841 Surgical & medical instruments

(G-386)
BIOTIE THERAPIES INC
420 Saw Mill River Rd (10502-2605)
PHONE......................650 244-4850
Timo Veromaa, *CEO*
Ian Massey, *President*
Mehdi Paborji, *COO*
EMP: 12
SQ FT: 5,500

SALES (est): 2.6MM **Publicly Held**
WEB: www.synosia.com
SIC: 2834 Druggists' preparations (phar-
maceuticals); tranquilizers or mental drug
preparations
PA: Acorda Therapeutics, Inc.
420 Saw Mill River Rd
Ardsley NY 10502

(G-387)
**BLINDTEK DESIGNER SYSTEMS
INC**
466 Saw Mill River Rd 2 (10502-2112)
PHONE......................914 347-7100
Lee Miller, *President*
Anthony Ash, *Vice Pres*
Steve Beamand, *Vice Pres*
Paul Berliner, *Technical Staff*
▲ **EMP:** 18 EST: 1998
SALES (est): 3MM **Privately Held**
SIC: 2591 Blinds vertical

(G-388)
DISTRIBUTORS VENDING CORP
Also Called: DVC Vending
2 Lawrence St (10502-2604)
PHONE......................914 472-8981
Mark Koerner, *President*
Raymond Cirino, *Vice Pres*
EMP: 14
SALES (est): 1.7MM **Privately Held**
SIC: 3581 Automatic vending machines

(G-389)
IRTRONICS INSTRUMENTS INC
132 Forest Blvd (10502-1031)
PHONE......................914 693-6291
John Jenkofsky, *President*
EMP: 10
SQ FT: 1,200
SALES: 870K **Privately Held**
SIC: 3822 3355 3672 Temperature sen-
sors for motor windings; aluminum wire &
cable; printed circuit boards

(G-390)
SUPRESTA US LLC (DH)
420 Saw Mill River Rd (10502-2605)
PHONE......................914 674-9434
Peggy Viehweger, *CEO*
Thomas Emignanelli, *CFO*
▼ **EMP:** 21
SALES: 19.9MM **Privately Held**
SIC: 2899 Fire retardant chemicals
HQ: Perimeter Solutions Lp
8000 Maryland Ave Ste 350
Saint Louis MO 63105
314 983-7500

Argyle
Washington County

(G-391)
**ADIRONDACK PLAS & RECYCL
INC**
453 County Route 45 (12809-3514)
PHONE......................518 746-9212
John Aspland, *CEO*
◆ **EMP:** 21
SQ FT: 125,000
SALES (est): 5.2MM **Privately Held**
SIC: 3089 3559 Plastic processing; recy-
cling machinery

(G-392)
ADIRONDACK SCENIC INC
Also Called: Adirondack Studios
439 County Route 45 Ste 1 (12809-3514)
PHONE......................518 638-8000
David Thomas Lloyd, *CEO*
Joel Krasnove, *COO*
Michael Blau, *Vice Pres*
Stephen Detmer, *Project Mgr*
Wayne Idecker, *Project Mgr*
▲ **EMP:** 100
SQ FT: 128,000
SALES: 180MM **Privately Held**
WEB: www.adirondackscenic.com
SIC: 2599 Factory furniture & fixtures

Arkport
Steuben County

(G-393)
HP HOOD LLC
25 Hurlbut St (14807-9706)
P.O. Box 474 (14807-0474)
PHONE......................607 295-8134
Keith Watson, *Production*
Freeman Covert, *Manager*
EMP: 100
SQ FT: 5,184
SALES (corp-wide): 2.2B **Privately Held**
WEB: www.hphood.com
SIC: 2026 2099 2022 Cottage cheese;
cream, sour; yogurt; food preparations;
cheese, natural & processed
PA: Hp Hood Llc
6 Kimball Ln Ste 400
Lynnfield MA 01940
617 887-8441

Arkville
Delaware County

(G-394)
**CATSKILL MOUNTAIN
PUBLISHING**
Also Called: Catskill Mountain News
43414 State Hwy 28 (12406)
P.O. Box 515 (12406-0515)
PHONE......................845 586-2601
Richard D Sanford, *President*
Laurie Sanford, *Vice Pres*
EMP: 11 EST: 1903
SALES (est): 761.1K **Privately Held**
WEB: www.catskillmountainnews.com
SIC: 2711 Newspapers: publishing only,
not printed on site

Armonk
Westchester County

(G-395)
**ARUMAI TECHNOLOGIES INC
(PA)**
175 King St (10504-1606)
PHONE......................914 217-0038
P Stephen Lamont, *CEO*
David J Colter, *CTO*
Gregory B Thagard, *CTO*
EMP: 12
SALES (est): 652.1K **Privately Held**
SIC: 7372 Prepackaged software

(G-396)
COLUMBIA CABINETS LLC (PA)
20 Maple Ave Ste F (10504-1859)
PHONE......................212 972-7550
Evan H Levey, *CEO*
EMP: 6
SALES (est): 1.1MM **Privately Held**
SIC: 2434 Wood kitchen cabinets

(G-397)
**IBM WORLD TRADE
CORPORATION (HQ)**
1 New Orchard Rd Ste 1 # 1 (10504-1722)
PHONE......................914 765-1900
Virginia M Rometty, *CEO*
Asif Samad, *Partner*
John P Gianukakis, *Principal*
James W Boyken, *Vice Pres*
Steve Jarrett, *Vice Pres*
EMP: 8
SQ FT: 417,000
SALES (est): 23.8B
SALES (corp-wide): 79.5B **Publicly Held**
WEB: www.lnn.com
SIC: 3577 3571 7377 7379 Computer
peripheral equipment; electronic comput-
ers; computer rental & leasing; computer
related maintenance services

PA: International Business Machines Corporation
1 New Orchard Rd Ste 1 # 1
Armonk NY 10504
914 499-1900

(G-398)
INTERNATIONAL BUS MCHS CORP
Also Called: IBM
20 Old Post Rd (10504-1314)
PHONE...................................914 499-2000
David Leftwich, *General Mgr*
Nancy Lewis, *Manager*
Zafer Karaca, *Director*
Andrew Liveris, *Bd of Directors*
EMP: 50
SALES (corp-wide): 79.5B **Publicly Held**
WEB: www.ibm.com
SIC: 7372 Prepackaged software
PA: International Business Machines Corporation
1 New Orchard Rd Ste 1 # 1
Armonk NY 10504
914 499-1900

(G-399)
JINGLEBELL INC
Also Called: JINGLENOG DBA
190 Byram Lake Rd (10504-1509)
PHONE...................................914 219-5395
Melissa Byrne, *President*
▲ **EMP:** 6 EST: 2008
SALES: 200K **Privately Held**
SIC: 3229 3231 7389 Christmas tree ornaments, from glass produced on-site; Christmas tree ornaments: made from purchased glass; design services

(G-400)
MAIN STREET CONNECT LLC
Also Called: Daily Voice
200 Business Park Dr # 209 (10504-1719)
PHONE...................................203 803-4110
John Haffey, *Editor*
Elizabeth Rivers, *Accounts Mgr*
Carll Tucker,
EMP: 10
SALES (est): 684.8K **Privately Held**
SIC: 2711 Newspapers, publishing & printing

(G-401)
PRODUCTION RESOURCE GROUP LLC (PA)
Also Called: Prg Integrated Solutions
200 Business Park Dr # 109 (10504-1751)
PHONE...................................877 774-7088
Jeremiah Harris, *CEO*
Matthew Carson, *CEO*
Stephan Paridaen, *President*
John Hovis, *COO*
Robert Manners, *Exec VP*
◆ **EMP:** 100
SQ FT: 140,000
SALES (est): 340.3MM **Privately Held**
WEB: www.prg.com
SIC: 3999 7922 Theatrical scenery; equipment rental, theatrical; lighting, theatrical

(G-402)
SUMMIT COMMUNICATIONS
28 Half Mile Rd (10504-1306)
PHONE...................................914 273-5504
Russell Dekker, *Owner*
EMP: 6
SALES (est): 283.9K **Privately Held**
SIC: 2741 Miscellaneous publishing

(G-403)
SURGICAL DESIGN CORP
Also Called: S D C
3 Macdonald Ave (10504-1935)
PHONE...................................914 273-2445
William Banko MD, *President*
Stanislava Banko, *Corp Secy*
Clara Santos, *Purchasing*
EMP: 15
SQ FT: 10,000
SALES (est): 2.1MM **Privately Held**
WEB: www.surgical.com
SIC: 3841 3851 3827 Surgical instruments & apparatus; instruments, microsurgical: except electromedical; ophthalmic goods; optical instruments & lenses

(G-404)
TRINITY PACKAGING CORPORATION (HQ)
357 Main St Unit 1 (10504-1717)
PHONE...................................914 273-4111
▲ **EMP:** 18
SQ FT: 9,000
SALES (est): 155.8MM
SALES (corp-wide): 311.6MM **Privately Held**
SIC: 2673 2679 Plastic bags: made from purchased materials; paper products, converted
PA: Proampac Pg Borrower Llc
12025 Tricon Rd
Cincinnati OH 45246
513 671-1777

(G-405)
VISANT SECONDARY HOLDINGS CORP (DH)
357 Main St (10504-1860)
PHONE...................................914 595-8200
Paul B Carousso, *Vice Pres*
David F Burgstahler, *Director*
Alexander Navab, *Director*
Charles P Pieper, *Director*
Susan C Schnabel, *Director*
EMP: 31
SALES (est): 831.7MM
SALES (corp-wide): 8.6B **Publicly Held**
SIC: 2741 Yearbooks: publishing & printing
HQ: Visant Holding Corp.
3601 Minnesota Dr Ste 400
Minneapolis MN 55435
914 595-8200

Arverne
Queens County

(G-406)
ARMOUR BEARER GROUP INC
Also Called: 2fish 5loaves Comminty Pantry
424 Beach 65th St (11692-1440)
PHONE...................................646 812-4487
Clinton Nixon, *President*
EMP: 5 EST: 2014
SALES (est): 234.8K **Privately Held**
SIC: 2099 Food preparations

(G-407)
DARRELL MITCHELL
Also Called: D.A.M. Construction, Company
704 Beach 67th St (11692-1314)
PHONE...................................646 659-7075
Darrell Mitchell, *Owner*
EMP: 5
SALES (est): 163.7K **Privately Held**
SIC: 1389 1799 8741 8742 Construction, repair & dismantling services; construction site cleanup; construction management; construction project management consultant

Ashville
Chautauqua County

(G-408)
CASTELLI AMERICA LLC
5151 Fairbanks Rd (14710-9796)
PHONE...................................716 782-2101
Jay Arcata, *Branch Mgr*
EMP: 80
SALES (corp-wide): 534MM **Privately Held**
SIC: 2022 Cheese, natural & processed
HQ: Castelli America, Llc
277 Fairfield Rd Ste 208
Fairfield NJ 07004
973 227-0002

(G-409)
CHAUTAUQUA MACHINE SPC LLC
1880 Open Meadows Rd (14710-9793)
PHONE...................................716 782-3276
Cindy Furlow, *Office Mgr*
Dennis Furlow,
EMP: 10
SQ FT: 8,000

SALES (est): 750K **Privately Held**
SIC: 3441 7692 Fabricated structural metal; automotive welding

(G-410)
CHAUTQUA PRCSION MACHINING INC
1287 Hunt Rd (14710-9612)
PHONE...................................716 763-3752
Jeff Christie, *President*
Eric Hewitt, *Facilities Mgr*
Craig Lassinger, *Engineer*
Mary Ann Attard, *Administration*
EMP: 12
SALES (est): 1.7MM **Privately Held**
SIC: 3599 Machine shop, jobbing & repair

(G-411)
THAYER TOOL & DIE INC
1718 Blckvlle Watts Flts (14710-9538)
PHONE...................................716 782-4841
Jennifer Nicklas, *President*
Donald Nichols, *Vice Pres*
EMP: 8
SQ FT: 5,000
SALES (est): 577.6K **Privately Held**
SIC: 3544 Special dies & tools

Astoria
Queens County

(G-412)
4 OVER 4COM INC
1941 46th St (11105-1101)
PHONE...................................718 932-2700
Taso Panagiotopoulos, *President*
Elizabeth Salazar, *Production*
Nancy Savescu, *Cust Mgr*
Hary Ayala, *CTO*
Chris Nava, *Executive Asst*
EMP: 6
SALES (est): 801.9K **Privately Held**
SIC: 2759 Post cards, picture: printing

(G-413)
AKI CABINETS INC
2636 2nd St (11102-4130)
PHONE...................................718 721-2541
Mujo Todic, *Ch of Bd*
Gloria Henderson, *Principal*
▲ **EMP:** 22
SALES (est): 2.6MM **Privately Held**
SIC: 2434 Wood kitchen cabinets

(G-414)
ALPS PROVISION CO INC
2270 45th St (11105-1336)
PHONE...................................718 721-4477
Giulio Sottovia, *President*
Leonardo Castorina, *Vice Pres*
Remo Tozzi, *Treasurer*
EMP: 27 EST: 1928
SQ FT: 12,500
SALES (est): 4.1MM **Privately Held**
WEB: www.alpsinstyle.com
SIC: 2013 5143 5147 Sausages & other prepared meats; cheese; meats, fresh

(G-415)
D & S SUPPLIES INC
2067 21st St (11105-3507)
PHONE...................................718 721-5256
Paul Melky, *President*
EMP: 17
SALES (est): 1.2MM **Privately Held**
SIC: 3679 Electronic loads & power supplies

(G-416)
D-LITE DONUTS
4519 Broadway (11103-1625)
PHONE...................................718 626-5953
George Kaparakos, *Owner*
EMP: 5 EST: 1995
SALES (est): 150K **Privately Held**
SIC: 2051 Doughnuts, except frozen

(G-417)
DF MAVENS INC
2420 49th St (11103-1017)
PHONE...................................347 813-4705
Malcolm Stogo, *Principal*
EMP: 20 EST: 2013

SALES (est): 970K **Privately Held**
SIC: 2024 Ice cream & frozen desserts

(G-418)
ECONOMY PUMP & MOTOR REPR INC
3652 36th St (11106-1304)
PHONE...................................718 433-2600
Elsie Domagala, *President*
EMP: 6
SALES (est): 835.5K **Privately Held**
SIC: 3433 3585 3586 5999 Heating equipment, except electric; heat pumps, electric; compressors for refrigeration & air conditioning equipment; measuring & dispensing pumps; motors, electric

(G-419)
ELECTROTECH SERVICE EQP CORP
2450 46th St (11103-1008)
PHONE...................................718 626-7700
Joseph Amendalara, *CEO*
EMP: 46
SQ FT: 15,000
SALES (est): 19.1MM **Privately Held**
SIC: 3613 5731 Switchgear & switchgear accessories; consumer electronic equipment

(G-420)
ELGRECO GT INC
2035 18th St Apt 2c (11105-4266)
PHONE...................................718 777-7922
Nikolaos Gkoufas, *Principal*
EMP: 8
SALES (est): 1.3MM **Privately Held**
SIC: 2673 2674 2656 2621 Plastic bags: made from purchased materials; paper bags: made from purchased materials; paper cups, plates, dishes & utensils; packaging paper

(G-421)
EMPIRE METAL FINISHING INC
2469 46th St (11103-1007)
PHONE...................................718 545-6700
Michael Vetrone, *President*
Lisa Vetrone, *Vice Pres*
EMP: 30 EST: 1922
SQ FT: 5,000
SALES (est): 2.9MM **Privately Held**
SIC: 3471 3499 3449 Gold plating; fire- or burglary-resistive products; miscellaneous metalwork

(G-422)
EXQUISITE GLASS & STONE INC
3117 12th St (11106-4801)
PHONE...................................718 937-9266
Buz Vaultz, *President*
EMP: 5
SQ FT: 900
SALES: 500K **Privately Held**
SIC: 3231 Decorated glassware: chipped, engraved, etched, etc.

(G-423)
FAME CONSTRUCTION INC
2388 Brklyn Queens Expy W (11103-1023)
PHONE...................................718 626-1000
Michael Andreou, *President*
EMP: 50
SQ FT: 1,700
SALES (est): 2MM **Privately Held**
SIC: 1389 Construction, repair & dismantling services

(G-424)
HELLAS STONE INC
3550 10th St (11106-5110)
PHONE...................................718 545-4716
Esdavros Cayioulis, *CEO*
▲ **EMP:** 5
SALES (est): 521K **Privately Held**
SIC: 2514 Kitchen cabinets: metal

(G-425)
INTER CRAFT CUSTOM FURNITURE
1431 Astoria Blvd (11102-3691)
PHONE...................................718 278-2573
Chipiv Savva, *President*
EMP: 9

G
E
O
G
R
A
P
H
I
C

SALES (est): 840K **Privately Held**
SIC: 2511 Wood household furniture

(G-426)
KJ ASTORIA GOURMET INC
3720 Broadway (11103-4057)
PHONE.................................718 545-6900
Kwang Hee Lee, *Principal*
EMP: 5
SALES (est): 179.4K **Privately Held**
SIC: 2037 Frozen fruits & vegetables

(G-427)
LEMODE PLUMBING & HEATING
3455 11th St (11106-5011)
PHONE.................................718 545-3336
Angelo Lemodetis, *Owner*
EMP: 30
SALES (est): 4.7MM **Privately Held**
SIC: 3494 Plumbing & heating valves

(G-428)
LENS LAB EXPRESS
SOUTHERN BLVD
3097 Steinway St Ste 301 (11103-3820)
PHONE.................................718 626-5184
Jeffery Nesses, *President*
EMP: 7
SALES (est): 925.8K **Privately Held**
SIC: 3851 5048 Ophthalmic goods; oph-
thalmic goods

(G-429)
MELITA CORP
3330 14th St (11106-4624)
PHONE.................................718 392-7280
EMP: 201
SQ FT: 44,000
SALES (est): 40.8MM **Privately Held**
SIC: 2051 5411 Bread, cake & related
products; grocery stores

(G-430)
MODERN ART FOUNDRY INC
Also Called: Jeffrey Spring Modern Art
1870 41st St (11105-1025)
PHONE.................................718 728-2030
Robert Spring, *President*
Jeffrey Spring, *Vice Pres*
Mary Jo Bursig, *Controller*
▲ EMP: 30
SQ FT: 14,000
SALES (est): 5MM **Privately Held**
WEB: www.modernartfoundry.com
SIC: 3366 3446 Castings (except die):
bronze; architectural metalwork

(G-431)
NIEBYLSKI BAKERY INC
2364 Steinway St (11105-1913)
PHONE.................................718 721-5152
Anthony Niebylski, *President*
Rose Niebylski, *Vice Pres*
EMP: 7
SALES: 500K **Privately Held**
SIC: 2051 5461 Bakery: wholesale or
wholesale/retail combined; bakeries

(G-432)
NY PHRMACY COMPOUNDING
CTR INC
3715 23rd Ave (11105-1993)
PHONE.................................201 403-5151
Wesam Abdrabouh, *President*
EMP: 5 EST: 2014
SALES (est): 549.5K **Privately Held**
SIC: 2834 Pharmaceutical preparations

(G-433)
OMNICARE ANESTHESIA PC
(PA)
3636 33rd St Ste 211 (11106-2329)
PHONE.................................718 433-0044
Evans Crevecoeur MD, *Ch of Bd*
Gina Duval, *Principal*
Donald Will, *Vice Pres*
EMP: 23
SALES (est): 4.9MM **Privately Held**
SIC: 3841 Anesthesia apparatus

(G-434)
PILATES DESIGNS LLC
3517 31st St (11106-2320)
PHONE.................................718 721-5929
Silvia Fuster, *Principal*

EMP: 9
SALES (est): 963.5K **Privately Held**
SIC: 3949 Sporting & athletic goods

(G-435)
QUATTRO FRAMEWORKS INC
4414 Astoria Blvd Fl 4 (11103-2005)
PHONE.................................718 361-2620
Sebastian Ramundo, *President*
EMP: 11
SALES (est): 623.7K **Privately Held**
SIC: 2499 Picture frame molding, finished

(G-436)
RAGO FOUNDATIONS LLC (PA)
1815 27th Ave (11102-3744)
P.O. Box 2027 (11102-0027)
PHONE.................................718 728-8436
Justin Chernoff,
▼ EMP: 35 EST: 1944
SALES (est): 6MM **Privately Held**
WEB: www.ragoshapewear.com
SIC: 2342 Foundation garments, women's

(G-437)
RAMEN & YAKITORI OKIDOKI
INC
3405 30th Ave (11103-4620)
PHONE.................................718 806-1677
Rennard A Madrazo, *Principal*
EMP: 8
SALES (est): 449.7K **Privately Held**
SIC: 2098 Noodles (e.g. egg, plain &
water), dry

(G-438)
REAL FACTORS INC
3049 Crescent St Apt H1b5 (11102-3236)
PHONE.................................206 963-6661
Colin George, *CEO*
Andrew Ermogenous, *Vice Pres*
Tom Hunter, *Vice Pres*
EMP: 7
SALES (est): 80.8K **Privately Held**
SIC: 7372 Prepackaged software
PA: 7park Data, Inc.
275 Madison Ave Ste Fl15
New York NY 10016

(G-439)
ROSENWACH TANK CO INC (PA)
Also Called: Rosenwach Group, The
4302 Ditmars Blvd (11105-1337)
PHONE.................................212 972-4411
Andrew Rosenwach, *Ch of Bd*
Wallace Rosenwach, *Principal*
George Vassiliades, *Principal*
Alice Rosenwach, *Treasurer*
Rose Castro, *Bookkeeper*
EMP: 35 EST: 1945
SQ FT: 23,000
SALES (est): 16.7MM **Privately Held**
SIC: 2449 3443 2531 Tanks, wood: coop-
ered; fabricated plate work (boiler shop);
public building & related furniture

(G-440)
SINGLECUT BEERSMITHS LLC
(PA)
1933 37th St (11105-1118)
PHONE.................................718 606-0788
Daniel Bronson, *General Mgr*
Rich Buceta, *Mng Member*
EMP: 14 EST: 2012
SALES (est): 3.1MM **Privately Held**
SIC: 3556 Brewers' & maltsters' machinery

(G-441)
SITECRAFT INC
Also Called: Rosenwach Tank Co
4302 Ditmars Blvd (11105-1337)
PHONE.................................718 729-4900
Andrew Rosenwach, *President*
EMP: 5
SQ FT: 10,000
SALES (est): 744.6K
SALES (corp-wide): 16.7MM **Privately**
Held
SIC: 2511 Wood lawn & garden furniture
PA: Rosenwach Tank Co. Inc.
4302 Ditmars Blvd
Astoria NY 11105
212 972-4411

(G-442)
STEINWAY AWNING II LLC (PA)
Also Called: Steinway Awnings
4230 24th St (11101-4608)
PHONE.................................718 729-2965
Cuzana Michalovicoug, *Executive*
EMP: 6
SQ FT: 4,000
SALES: 300K **Privately Held**
SIC: 2394 5999 Awnings, fabric: made
from purchased materials; canopies, fab-
ric: made from purchased materials;
awnings

(G-443)
VSHIP CO
3636 33rd St Ste 207 (11106-2329)
PHONE.................................718 706-8566
Vindu Koil, *President*
Ali Siddiqui, *Manager*
◆ EMP: 12
SALES (est): 1.1MM **Privately Held**
SIC: 3443 Containers, shipping (bombs,
etc.): metal plate

(G-444)
WAINLAND INC
2460 47th St (11103-1010)
PHONE.................................718 626-2233
Donald Wainland, *President*
Mark Wainland, *Vice Pres*
Neil Wainland, *Vice Pres*
Amel Mustajbasic, *Purch Mgr*
▲ EMP: 45
SALES (est): 8.9MM **Privately Held**
WEB: www.wainlands.com
SIC: 3645 3444 Residential lighting fix-
tures; sheet metalwork

(G-445)
WHITE COFFEE CORP
1835 38th St (11105-1076)
PHONE.................................718 204-7900
Carole White, *Ch of Bd*
Al Gaviria, *President*
Jonathan White, *Exec VP*
Gregory White, *Vice Pres*
Paul Harvey, *Plant Mgr*
▲ EMP: 85 EST: 1939
SALES (est): 29.6MM **Privately Held**
SIC: 2095 5149 Coffee roasting (except by
wholesale grocers); tea

(G-446)
WLF FOUNDERS CORPORATION
Also Called: Water Lilies
4510 19th Ave (11105-1034)
PHONE.................................718 777-8899
Chan Chin LI, *Chairman*
Tina Lee, *Purch Mgr*
Gary Cheung, *Natl Sales Mgr*
Al Greenwood, *VP Sales*
Luzia Chan, *Administration*
▲ EMP: 100
SQ FT: 48,000
SALES (est): 20.1MM **Privately Held**
WEB: www.waterliliesfood.com
SIC: 2038 Frozen specialties

Athens
Greene County

(G-447)
NORTHEAST TREATERS INC
796 Schoharie Tpke (12015-4306)
PHONE.................................518 945-2660
Frank Crowe, *Manager*
EMP: 25
SALES (corp-wide): 17MM **Privately**
Held
WEB: www.netreaters.com
SIC: 2491 Wood preserving
PA: Northeast Treaters, Inc.
201 Springfield Rd
Belchertown MA 01007
413 323-7811

(G-448)
NORTHEAST TREATERS NY LLC
796 Schoharie Tpke (12015-4306)
PHONE.................................518 945-2660
David A Reed, *Mng Member*
Douglas C Elder,

Charles Geiger,
Henry G Page Jr,
Richard White,
EMP: 20
SQ FT: 884
SALES (est): 2.4MM **Privately Held**
WEB: www.otda.state.ny.us
SIC: 2491 Structural lumber & timber,
treated wood

(G-449)
PECKHAM ASPHALT RESALE
CORP
Also Called: James Reed Sales
2 Union St (12015-1207)
PHONE.................................518 945-1120
EMP: 7
SALES (corp-wide): 171.1MM **Privately**
Held
SIC: 2951 Asphalt paving mixtures &
blocks
HQ: Peckham Asphalt Resale Corp.
20 Haarlem Ave Ste 200
White Plains NY 10603
914 949-2000

(G-450)
PECKHAM INDUSTRIES INC
Uninn St (12015)
PHONE.................................518 945-1120
John R Peckham, *Branch Mgr*
EMP: 5
SALES (corp-wide): 171.1MM **Privately**
Held
SIC: 2951 Asphalt paving mixtures &
blocks
PA: Peckham Industries, Inc.
20 Haarlem Ave Ste 200
White Plains NY 10603
914 949-2000

(G-451)
PECKHAM MATERIALS CORP
2 Union St Ext (12015-1298)
PHONE.................................518 945-1120
Mark Libruk, *Terminal Mgr*
Joe Widermuth, *Manager*
EMP: 20
SQ FT: 242
SALES (corp-wide): 171.1MM **Privately**
Held
SIC: 2951 Asphalt paving mixtures &
blocks
HQ: Peckham Materials Corp
20 Haarlem Ave Ste 200
White Plains NY 10603
914 686-2045

Atlantic Beach
Nassau County

(G-452)
ANCHOR COMMERCE TRADING
CORP
53 Dutchess Blvd (11509-1223)
P.O. Box 238 (11509-0238)
PHONE.................................516 881-3485
Meryl P Benin, *President*
EMP: 6 EST: 1976
SALES (est): 266.2K **Privately Held**
SIC: 3714 3533 2819 3823 Motor vehicle
parts & accessories; oil field machinery &
equipment; industrial inorganic chemicals;
computer interface equipment for indus-
trial process control

(G-453)
HORIZON APPAREL MFG INC
115 Bayside Dr (11509-1608)
PHONE.................................516 361-4878
Mark Hassin, *President*
Bonnie Hassin, *Vice Pres*
▲ EMP: 5
SQ FT: 800
SALES: 25MM **Privately Held**
SIC: 2211 Apparel & outerwear fabrics,
cotton

(G-454)
SMALL BUSINESS ADVISORS
INC
2005 Park St (11509-1235)
PHONE.................................516 374-1387

▲ = Import ▼=Export
◆ =Import/Export

Joseph Gelb, *President*
Barbara Goetz Gelb, *Shareholder*
EMP: 10
SALES (est): 465.8K **Privately Held**
SIC: 2721 8721 Periodicals; accounting, auditing & bookkeeping

---

Attica
Wyoming County

(G-455)
ATTICA MILLWORK INC
71 Market St (14011-1071)
P.O. Box 118 (14011-0118)
PHONE.....................................585 591-2333
Kevin Demars, *President*
Justin Papucci, *Vice Pres*
Thomas Wackenheim, *Shareholder*
▲ **EMP:** 19 **EST:** 1945
SQ FT: 65,000
SALES (est): 2.5MM **Privately Held**
WEB: www.atticamillwork.com
SIC: 2431 Millwork

(G-456)
ATTICA PACKAGE COMPANY INC
45 Windsor St (14011-1208)
P.O. Box 295 (14011-0295)
PHONE.....................................585 591-0510
Douglas W Domes, *President*
EMP: 10 **EST:** 1917
SQ FT: 16,000
SALES (est): 1.4MM **Privately Held**
SIC: 2411 5199 5211 Logging; sawdust; millwork & lumber

(G-457)
HLW ACRES LLC
Also Called: Hlw Acres Poultry Processing
1727 Exchange Street Rd (14011-9627)
PHONE.....................................585 591-0795
Hermann Weber, *Owner*
EMP: 9
SALES (est): 548.4K **Privately Held**
SIC: 2015 Poultry slaughtering & processing

(G-458)
PRECISION FABRICATION LLC
40 S Pearl St (14011-1207)
PHONE.....................................585 591-3449
Donald McCulloch, *Owner*
EMP: 5
SALES (est): 530K **Privately Held**
SIC: 3444 3448 Sheet metalwork; prefabricated metal components

---

Auburn
Cayuga County

(G-459)
4M PRECISION INDUSTRIES INC
4000 Technology Park Blvd (13021-9030)
PHONE.....................................315 252-8415
Margaret Morin, *President*
Daniel Morin, *Vice Pres*
Stephen C Morin, *Shareholder*
Edith Carroll Morin, *Admin Sec*
EMP: 44 **EST:** 1968
SQ FT: 55,000
SALES (est): 10.6MM **Privately Held**
WEB: www.4mprecision.com
SIC: 3469 Stamping metal for the trade

(G-460)
AUBURN CUSTOM MILLWORK INC
Also Called: SLC
315 Genesee St Ste 8 (13021-3150)
PHONE.....................................315 253-3843
Christopher Colella, *President*
EMP: 8
SALES (est): 1.4MM **Privately Held**
SIC: 2431 2541 Millwork; cabinets, lockers & shelving

(G-461)
AUBURN FOUNDRY INC
15 Wadsworth St (13021-2257)
P.O. Box 715 (13021-0715)
PHONE.....................................315 253-4441
David Boglione, *President*
Denise Boglione, *Admin Sec*
EMP: 17 **EST:** 1947
SQ FT: 60,000
SALES (est): 2.3MM **Privately Held**
WEB: www.auburnfoundry.com
SIC: 3321 Gray iron castings

(G-462)
AUBURN PUBLISHING CO
Also Called: Citizen , The
25 Dill St (13021-3605)
PHONE.....................................315 253-5311
Richard J Emanuel, *President*
David Wilcox, *Editor*
Lee Cunningham, *Creative Dir*
EMP: 85
SALES (est): 5.1MM
SALES (corp-wide): 593.9MM **Publicly Held**
SIC: 2711 Newspapers: publishing only, not printed on site; newspapers, publishing & printing
HQ: Lee Publications, Inc.
4600 E 53rd St
Davenport IA 52807
563 383-2100

(G-463)
AUBURN TANK & MANUFACTURING CO
Also Called: Atco EZ Dock
24 Mcmaster St (13021-2442)
P.O. Box 488 (13021-0488)
PHONE.....................................315 255-2788
Carl Weber, *President*
EMP: 14
SQ FT: 12,000
SALES (est): 2.2MM **Privately Held**
WEB: www.auburntank.com
SIC: 3444 Sheet metalwork

(G-464)
AUBURN VACUUM FORMING CO INC
40 York St (13021-1251)
P.O. Box 489 (13021-0489)
PHONE.....................................315 253-2440
Martin Pelchat, *President*
Paul Pucek, *CFO*
Jack Hutson, *Sales Staff*
Dan Debois, *Maintence Staff*
EMP: 19 **EST:** 1969
SQ FT: 71,000
SALES: 2.1MM
SALES (corp-wide): 3.2MM **Privately Held**
SIC: 3089 Injection molding of plastics
PA: Plastique M.P. Inc
250 Rue Gouin
Richmond QC
819 826-5921

(G-465)
AVSTAR FUEL SYSTEMS INC
15 Brookfield Pl (13021-2209)
PHONE.....................................315 255-1955
EMP: 8
SALES (est): 811.6K **Privately Held**
SIC: 2869 Fuels

(G-466)
BCS ACCESS SYSTEMS US LLC
2150 Crane Brook Dr (13021-9516)
PHONE.....................................315 258-3469
Jeffrey Webster, *Officer*
John Andrew Dale,
EMP: 278
SALES (est): 55MM **Privately Held**
SIC: 3469 Metal stampings
HQ: Bcs Automotive Interface Solutions Limited
3rd Floor 35 Soho Square
London W1D 3
121 526-4441

(G-467)
BIMBO BAKERIES USA INC
11 Corcoran Dr (13021-2213)
PHONE.....................................315 253-9782

Bill Bos, *Plant Mgr*
EMP: 100
SQ FT: 28,668 **Privately Held**
SIC: 2051 Bread, cake & related products
HQ: Bimbo Bakeries Usa, Inc
255 Business Center Dr # 200
Horsham PA 19044
215 347-5500

(G-468)
BO-MER PLASTICS LLC
13 Pulaski St (13021-1105)
PHONE.....................................315 252-7216
Thomas R Herbert, *President*
Scott Morin, *Engineer*
▼ **EMP:** 46 **EST:** 2001
SQ FT: 44,000
SALES (est): 10.5MM **Privately Held**
WEB: www.bo-mer.com
SIC: 3089 Thermoformed finished plastic products; plastic processing

(G-469)
BROOK NORTH FARMS INC
Also Called: Igk Equestrian
89 York St (13021-1135)
P.O. Box 1239, Weedsport (13166-1239)
PHONE.....................................315 834-9390
Carolyn Kyle, *CEO*
Peter Kyle, *President*
▲ **EMP:** 12
SALES (est): 2MM **Privately Held**
WEB: www.northbrookfarms.com
SIC: 2515 3496 5083 Mattresses & bedsprings; mats & matting; dairy machinery & equipment

(G-470)
COPPER JOHN CORPORATION
173 State St (13021-1841)
PHONE.....................................315 258-9269
Douglas A Springer, *President*
Eric Springer, *Vice Pres*
▲ **EMP:** 19
SQ FT: 11,000
SALES (est): 2.1MM **Privately Held**
WEB: www.copperjohn.com
SIC: 3949 Archery equipment, general

(G-471)
CURRIER PLASTICS INC
101 Columbus St (13021-3101)
PHONE.....................................315 255-1779
John Currier, *Ch of Bd*
Massimo A Leone, *President*
Ron Ringleben, *President*
James E Currier, *Vice Pres*
Gary Kieffer, *Vice Pres*
▲ **EMP:** 99
SQ FT: 60,000
SALES (est): 28.2MM **Privately Held**
WEB: www.currierplastics.com
SIC: 3089 Injection molding of plastics

(G-472)
DAIKIN APPLIED AMERICAS INC
Also Called: Applied Terminal Systems
4900 Technology Park Blvd (13021-8592)
PHONE.....................................315 253-2771
Rich Savage, *Plant Mgr*
Jeff Cusyck, *Engineer*
Andy Vezos, *Sales Mgr*
Jim Cullin, *Manager*
Patrick Schoof, *Manager*
EMP: 55 **Privately Held**
SIC: 3585 3822 3564 3561 Heating & air conditioning combination units; auto controls regulating residntl & coml environmt & applncs; blowers & fans; pumps & pumping equipment; fabricated pipe & fittings
HQ: Daikin Applied Americas Inc.
13600 Industrial Pk Blvd
Minneapolis MN 55441
763 553-5330

(G-473)
DEWITT PLASTICS INC
28 Aurelius Ave (13021-2231)
PHONE.....................................315 255-1209
David M Hess, *President*
Keith Kowal, *Prdtn Mgr*
George Clancy, *Maint Spvr*
Beatrice Hess, *Accounting Mgr*
▲ **EMP:** 11 **EST:** 1972

SALES (est): 2.7MM **Privately Held**
WEB: www.dewittplastics.com
SIC: 2821 Plasticizer/additive based plastic materials

(G-474)
EMCOM INC (PA)
Also Called: Electomechanical Componets
62 Columbus St Ste 4 (13021-3161)
PHONE.....................................315 255-5300
Endy China, *President*
Joseph Reding, *President*
Tony Pongipat, *Vice Pres*
Sue Galbally, *Buyer*
Ed Leaf, *Buyer*
▲ **EMP:** 100
SQ FT: 10,000
SALES (est): 21.8MM **Privately Held**
WEB: www.em-com.com
SIC: 3699 Electrical equipment & supplies

(G-475)
FINGER LAKES LEA CRAFTERS LLC
Also Called: Auburn Leathercrafters
42 Washington St Ste 1 (13021-2496)
PHONE.....................................315 252-4107
Anita Dungey, *Mng Member*
Alan Dungey, *Mng Member*
▼ **EMP:** 15
SQ FT: 13,000
SALES (est): 1.2MM **Privately Held**
WEB: www.auburndirect.com
SIC: 3199 5199 Dog furnishings: collars, leashes, muzzles, etc.: leather; sponges (animal)

(G-476)
FLP GROUP LLC
301 Clark St (13021-2236)
PHONE.....................................315 252-7583
Greg Kanane, *President*
EMP: 11 **EST:** 1928
SQ FT: 20,000
SALES (est): 2MM
SALES (corp-wide): 3.6MM **Privately Held**
WEB: www.fingerlakespress.com
SIC: 2752 2791 2789 2759 Commercial printing, offset; typesetting; bookbinding & related work; commercial printing; automotive & apparel trimmings
PA: Kinaneco., Inc.
2925 Milton Ave
Syracuse NY 13209
315 468-6201

(G-477)
GEN-WEST ASSOCIATES LLC
101 Columbus St (13021-3121)
PHONE.....................................315 255-1779
Louri Hapkins, *Principal*
Pat Craine, *Accountant*
EMP: 5
SALES (est): 569.3K **Privately Held**
SIC: 3089 Injection molding of plastics

(G-478)
HAMMOND & IRVING INC (PA)
254 North St (13021-1129)
PHONE.....................................315 253-6265
Edward Gallager, *President*
Edward C Gallagher, *Exec VP*
Barbara Zach, *Treasurer*
Denny Zach, *Agent*
Dave Bolak, *Supervisor*
▲ **EMP:** 85
SQ FT: 20,000
SALES (est): 24MM **Privately Held**
WEB: www.hammond-irving.com
SIC: 3462 Iron & steel forgings

(G-479)
INTERNATIONAL FIRE-SHIELD INC
194 Genesee St (13021-3360)
P.O. Box 7305 (13022-7305)
PHONE.....................................315 255-1006
Patrick D Bumpus, *CEO*
George Murray, *Ch of Bd*
EMP: 12
SALES (est): 2.2MM **Privately Held**
WEB: www.nyfs.com
SIC: 2899 Fire retardant chemicals

(G-480)
ITT LLC
Also Called: ITT Water Technology
1 Goulds Dr (13021-3134)
PHONE..................................315 258-4904
Louis Juliano, *Branch Mgr*
Michele Andrle, *Relations*
EMP: 58
SALES (corp-wide): 2.7B **Publicly Held**
SIC: 3625 Control equipment, electric
HQ: Itt Llc
　　1133 Westchester Ave N-100
　　White Plains NY 10604
　　914 641-2000

(G-481)
JACOBS PRESS INC
87 Columbus St (13021-3121)
P.O. Box 580 (13021-0580)
PHONE..................................315 252-4861
Michael K Trapani, *President*
Pat Nation, *Sales Staff*
Stacy Feocco, *Office Mgr*
Molly Trapani, *Admin Sec*
EMP: 10 **EST:** 1915
SQ FT: 7,228
SALES: 1.1MM **Privately Held**
WEB: www.jacobspress.com
SIC: 2752 Commercial printing, offset

(G-482)
JOHN G RUBINO INC
Also Called: GLEASON-AVERY
45 Aurelius Ave (13021-2249)
PHONE..................................315 253-7396
John G Rubino, *CEO*
John Rubino, *President*
Barbara Zelehowsky, *Manager*
▲ **EMP:** 30
SQ FT: 32,000
SALES: 3.7MM **Privately Held**
WEB: www.gleasonavery.com
SIC: 3621 3566 Motors, electric; speed
　　changers, drives & gears

(G-483)
JOHNSTON PRECISION INC
7 Frank Smith St (13021-1145)
PHONE..................................315 253-4181
Theodore Johnston, *President*
EMP: 5
SQ FT: 2,400
SALES (est): 602.3K **Privately Held**
SIC: 3599 Machine shop, jobbing & repair

(G-484)
MACK STUDIOS DISPLAYS INC
5500 Technology Park Blvd (13021-8555)
P.O. Box 917 (13021-0917)
PHONE..................................315 252-7542
Peter Maciulewicz, *CEO*
William Flynn, *Purchasing*
Chris Mason, *Human Res Dir*
Jill Doyon, *Manager*
Farrell Sutherland, *Manager*
EMP: 45
SQ FT: 125,000
SALES: 10.9MM **Privately Held**
WEB: www.mackstudios.com
SIC: 3999 Advertising display products

(G-485)
MATTEO & ANTONIO BARTOLOTTA
Also Called: Bartolotta Furniture
282 State St (13021-1144)
PHONE..................................315 252-2220
Matteo Bartolotta, *President*
EMP: 10
SQ FT: 4,000
SALES (est): 1MM **Privately Held**
SIC: 2512 2521 2434 Upholstered house-
　　hold furniture; wood office furniture; wood
　　kitchen cabinets

(G-486)
NEW HOPE MILLS INC
181 York St (13021-9009)
PHONE..................................315 252-2676
Dale E Weed, *President*
David J Weed, *Vice Pres*
EMP: 12 **EST:** 1823
SQ FT: 11,500

SALES (est): 1.1MM **Privately Held**
WEB: www.newhopemills.com
SIC: 2045 0723 Pancake mixes, prepared:
　　from purchased flour; flour milling custom
　　services

(G-487)
NEW HOPE MILLS MFG INC (PA)
181 York St (13021-9009)
PHONE..................................315 252-2676
Douglas Weed, *CEO*
Dale Weed, *President*
Dawn Korbel, *Sales Staff*
EMP: 50
SQ FT: 30,000
SALES (est): 9MM **Privately Held**
SIC: 2051 5461 Bakery products, partially
　　cooked (except frozen); bakeries

(G-488)
NUCOR STEEL AUBURN INC
25 Quarry Rd (13021-1146)
P.O. Box 2008 (13021-1077)
PHONE..................................315 253-4561
Dan Dimicco, *Chairman*
Luke Scott, *Safety Mgr*
John Bell, *Engineer*
Scott Scharett, *Engineer*
Ian Spitzer, *Engineer*
▲ **EMP:** 290
SQ FT: 300,000
SALES (est): 130.2MM
SALES (corp-wide): 25B **Publicly Held**
WEB: www.nucorauburn.com
SIC: 3312 Stainless steel
PA: Nucor Corporation
　　1915 Rexford Rd Ste 400
　　Charlotte NC 28211
　　704 366-7000

(G-489)
OWENS-BROCKWAY GLASS CONT INC
7134 County House Rd (13021-5901)
PHONE..................................315 258-3211
Steven Gabel, *Manager*
EMP: 210
SALES (corp-wide): 6.8B **Publicly Held**
SIC: 3221 Glass containers
HQ: Owens-Brockway Glass Container Inc.
　　1 Michael Owens Way
　　Perrysburg OH 43551
　　567 336-8449

(G-490)
PREDATOR MOUNTAINWEAR INC
324 Fire Lane 15 (13021-8680)
PHONE..................................315 727-3241
Lee Crossley, *President*
EMP: 5
SQ FT: 1,500
SALES: 1MM **Privately Held**
SIC: 2329 Ski & snow clothing: men's &
　　boys'

(G-491)
PRINTERY
55 Arterial W (13021-2730)
PHONE..................................315 253-7403
Pam Flaherty, *Owner*
EMP: 5
SALES (est): 190K **Privately Held**
SIC: 2261 Screen printing of cotton broad-
　　woven fabrics

(G-492)
R P M INDUSTRIES INC
Also Called: RPM Displays
26 Aurelius Ave (13021-2212)
PHONE..................................315 255-1105
Roger P Mueller, *President*
David Hess, *Vice Pres*
Martin Lynch, *Asst Treas*
Roy P Mueller, *VP Sales*
▲ **EMP:** 50 **EST:** 1925
SQ FT: 60,000
SALES (est): 49.2K **Privately Held**
WEB: www.rpmdisplays.com
SIC: 3089 5046 2499 Boxes, plastic;
　　plastic hardware & building products;
　　mannequins; shoe trees

(G-493)
ROBINSON CONCRETE INC (PA)
Also Called: Vitale Ready Mix Concrete
3486 Franklin Street Rd (13021-9348)
PHONE..................................315 253-6666
Michael Vitale Jr, *President*
Vincent Vitale, *Vice Pres*
William Rhodes, *Materials Mgr*
Paul F Vitale, *Admin Sec*
EMP: 50 **EST:** 1865
SQ FT: 2,500
SALES (est): 26.1MM **Privately Held**
SIC: 3273 3272 1442 Ready-mixed con-
　　crete; concrete products, precast; con-
　　struction sand & gravel

(G-494)
SCHOTT CORPORATION
Also Called: Fiber Optics Schott America
62 Columbus St (13021-3167)
PHONE..................................315 255-2791
Hinz Keiser, *Plant Mgr*
EMP: 64
SALES (corp-wide): 449.3K **Privately
Held**
SIC: 3229 3827 3674 Pressed & blown
　　glass; optical instruments & lenses; semi-
　　conductors & related devices
HQ: Schott Corporation
　　555 Taxter Rd Ste 470
　　Elmsford NY 10523
　　914 831-2200

(G-495)
SIMPLEX MANUFACTURING CO INC
105 Dunning Ave (13021-4403)
P.O. Box 279 (13021-0279)
PHONE..................................315 252-7524
Robert C Merritt, *President*
Bob Merritt, *Editor*
Richard C Merritt, *Vice Pres*
Carol Marsden, *Executive Asst*
EMP: 19 **EST:** 1918
SQ FT: 25,000
SALES (est): 3.2MM **Privately Held**
WEB: www.simplexco.com
SIC: 3469 Metal stampings

(G-496)
SUNNYCREST INC (PA)
58 Prospect St (13021-1699)
PHONE..................................315 252-7214
Robert Atkinson, *President*
William Atkinson, *Vice Pres*
Ron Shortsleeve, *Finance Mgr*
Eleanor Atkinson, *Admin Sec*
Tonya Vatter, *Admin Asst*
EMP: 30 **EST:** 1969
SQ FT: 53,000
SALES (est): 4.2MM **Privately Held**
WEB: www.sunnycrest.com
SIC: 3272 7261 Concrete products, pre-
　　cast; funeral service & crematories

(G-497)
T SHORE PRODUCTS LTD
Also Called: Shore Products Co
5 Eagle Dr (13021-8695)
PHONE..................................315 252-9174
Thomas H Tutt II, *President*
Marlene Tutt, *Vice Pres*
EMP: 6
SQ FT: 8,500
SALES: 800K **Privately Held**
SIC: 3536 3448 5461 Boat lifts; docks:
　　prefabricated metal; bakeries

(G-498)
TARO MANUFACTURING COMPANY INC
114 Clark St (13021-3325)
PHONE..................................315 252-9430
Mario Buttaro, *President*
Mark Buttaro, *Vice Pres*
Steve Buttaro, *Vice Pres*
Roxanne Foster, *Manager*
▲ **EMP:** 19
SQ FT: 17,000
SALES (est): 3.3MM **Privately Held**
WEB: www.taromfg.com
SIC: 3621 3694 3678 Rotors, for motors;
　　ignition apparatus & distributors; elec-
　　tronic connectors

(G-499)
TMS INTERNATIONAL LLC
25 Quarry Rd (13021-1146)
PHONE..................................315 253-8925
EMP: 5 **Privately Held**
SIC: 3312 Blast furnaces & steel mills
HQ: Tms International, Llc
　　2835 E Carson St Fl 3
　　Pittsburgh PA 15203
　　412 678-6141

(G-500)
TOWPATH MACHINE CORP
31 Allen St (13021-9004)
PHONE..................................315 252-0112
Patricia Hanford, *President*
George Hanford, *Treasurer*
EMP: 7
SQ FT: 3,000
SALES: 500K **Privately Held**
WEB: www.towpathmachine.com
SIC: 3599 Machine shop, jobbing & repair

(G-501)
UFP NEW YORK LLC (HQ)
Also Called: Universal Forest Products
11 Allen St (13021-9004)
PHONE..................................315 253-2758
Ralph Gschwind, *Principal*
Chris Luca, *Director*
EMP: 20
SALES (est): 11.8MM
SALES (corp-wide): 4.4B **Publicly Held**
WEB: www.ufpinc.com
SIC: 2439 Trusses, wooden roof
PA: Universal Forest Products, Inc.
　　2801 E Beltline Ave Ne
　　Grand Rapids MI 49525
　　616 364-6161

(G-502)
VOLPI MANUFACTURING USA CO INC
5 Commerce Way (13021-8557)
PHONE..................................315 255-1737
Max Kunz, *CEO*
Kurt Van, *Business Mgr*
Scott Kittelberger, *COO*
James Casasanta, *Engineer*
Thomas Baumann, *CFO*
◆ **EMP:** 38
SQ FT: 37,000
SALES (est): 6.4MM **Privately Held**
WEB: www.volpiusa.com
SIC: 3229 Glass fiber products
HQ: Volpi Ag
　　Wiesenstrasse 33
　　Schlieren ZH 8952
　　447 324-343

(G-503)
WEAVER MACHINE & TOOL CO INC
44 York St (13021-1136)
PHONE..................................315 253-4422
Victor Ianno, *President*
EMP: 15
SQ FT: 26,000
SALES (est): 3.1MM **Privately Held**
WEB: www.weavermachine.com
SIC: 3599 Machine shop, jobbing & repair

Aurora
Cayuga County

(G-504)
MACKENZIE-CHILDS LLC (PA)
3260 State Route 90 (13026-9769)
PHONE..................................315 364-6118
Lee Feldman, *CEO*
Colleen Miller, *Opers Staff*
Laura Heslop, *Buyer*
Julie Schneider, *Buyer*
Howard Cohen, *CFO*
◆ **EMP:** 150
SQ FT: 70,000
SALES (est): 37MM **Privately Held**
WEB: www.mackenzie-childs.com
SIC: 3263 2512 2511 Cookware, fine
　　earthenware; upholstered household fur-
　　niture; wood household furniture

Averill Park
Rensselaer County

(G-505)
518 PRINTS LLC
1548 Burden Lake Rd Ste 4 (12018-2818)
P.O. Box 632 (12018-0632)
PHONE................................518 674-5346
Jesse Brust, *Owner*
EMP: 6
SALES (est): 656.5K **Privately Held**
SIC: 2752 Commercial printing, lithographic

(G-506)
CAPITAL REG WKLY NEWSPPR GROUP
Also Called: Advertiser, The
29 Sheer Rd (12018-4722)
P.O. Box 70 (12018-0070)
PHONE................................518 674-2841
Charles Hug, *Principal*
Alyson Regan, *Principal*
Karen Demis, *Manager*
EMP: 10
SALES (est): 850K **Privately Held**
SIC: 2721 Periodicals: publishing only

(G-507)
GARMENT CARE SYSTEMS LLC
Also Called: Laura Star Service Center
55 Blue Heron Dr (12018-4600)
PHONE................................518 674-1826
James E Wells, *Mng Member*
▲ **EMP:** 6
SALES (est): 654.5K **Privately Held**
WEB: www.garmentcaresystems.com
SIC: 3499 Ironing boards, metal

(G-508)
L J VALENTE INC
8957 Ny Highway 66 (12018-5822)
PHONE................................518 674-3750
Anthony Valente, *President*
Steve A Valente, *Vice Pres*
EMP: 8
SALES (est): 1.5MM **Privately Held**
SIC: 2421 Building & structural materials, wood

(G-509)
NORTHERN CRUSHING LLC
167 Totem Lodge Rd (12018-3746)
PHONE................................518 365-8452
Patrick Kerwin,
EMP: 6
SALES (est): 218.3K **Privately Held**
SIC: 1442 Construction sand & gravel

Avoca
Steuben County

(G-510)
HAINES EQUIPMENT INC
20 Carrington St (14809-9766)
PHONE................................607 566-8531
Patricia Haines, *President*
EMP: 50
SQ FT: 50,000
SALES (est): 9.3MM **Privately Held**
WEB: www.hainesequipment.com
SIC: 3523 3565 3556 3535 Farm machinery & equipment; packaging machinery; food products machinery; conveyors & conveying equipment; tire cord & fabrics

Avon
Livingston County

(G-511)
B & B PRECISION MFG INC (PA)
310 W Main St (14414-1150)
P.O. Box 279 (14414-0279)
PHONE................................585 226-6226
Gerald Macintyre, *President*
Lawrence Bailey, *Treasurer*
Shelly Guerin, *Accounts Mgr*

EMP: 32 **EST:** 1976
SQ FT: 15,900
SALES (est): 5.5MM **Privately Held**
WEB: www.bbprecision.com
SIC: 3599 Machine shop, jobbing & repair

(G-512)
BARILLA AMERICA NY INC
100 Horseshoe Blvd (14414-1164)
PHONE................................585 226-5600
Kirk Trofholz, *Principal*
▲ **EMP:** 121
SALES (est): 19MM
SALES (corp-wide): 3MM **Privately Held**
SIC: 2099 Packaged combination products: pasta, rice & potato
HQ: Barilla America Inc.
885 Sunset Ridge Rd
Northbrook IL 60062

(G-513)
KRAFT HEINZ FOODS COMPANY
Also Called: Kraft Foods
140 Spring St (14414-1153)
PHONE................................585 226-4400
Greg Manning, *Manager*
Mary Boike, *Manager*
EMP: 450
SALES (corp-wide): 26.2B **Publicly Held**
WEB: www.kraftfoods.com
SIC: 2038 2099 Whipped topping, frozen; food preparations
HQ: Kraft Heinz Foods Company
1 Ppg Pl Fl 34
Pittsburgh PA 15222
412 456-5700

(G-514)
MONROE INDUSTRIES INC
5611 Tec Dr (14414-9562)
PHONE................................585 226-8230
John C Webster, *President*
EMP: 8
SALES (est): 720K **Privately Held**
SIC: 3281 Marble, building: cut & shaped

(G-515)
PENNY LANE PRINTING INC
Also Called: Penny Express
1471 Rte 15 (14414)
P.O. Box 340 (14414-0340)
PHONE................................585 226-8111
Steven Harrison, *President*
Kimberly Dougherty, *Vice Pres*
EMP: 54
SQ FT: 25,000
SALES: 4.5MM **Privately Held**
SIC: 2759 7319 Screen printing; distribution of advertising material or sample services

(G-516)
STAR HEADLIGHT LANTERN CO INC (PA)
455 Rochester St (14414-9503)
PHONE................................585 226-9500
Christopher D Jacobs, *Ch of Bd*
Christopher D Jacob, *President*
David W Jacobs, *President*
Elvis Pacavar, *Engineer*
Donna Stocking, *Human Res Dir*
◆ **EMP:** 146
SQ FT: 85,000
SALES (est): 31.6MM **Privately Held**
WEB: www.star1889.com
SIC: 3648 3669 Strobe lighting systems; railroad signaling devices, electric

Babylon
Suffolk County

(G-517)
A C J COMMUNICATIONS INC
Also Called: Beacon
65 Deer Park Ave Ste 2 (11702-2820)
PHONE................................631 587-5612
Carolyn James, *Principal*
◆ **EMP:** 15
SALES (est): 87.5K **Privately Held**
SIC: 2711 Newspapers: publishing only, not printed on site

(G-518)
BEDROCK LANDSCAPING MTLS CORP
Also Called: Bedrock Plus
454 Sunrise Hwy (11704-5906)
PHONE................................631 587-4950
David Cannetti, *President*
EMP: 9
SALES (est): 961.1K **Privately Held**
WEB: www.bedrockmaterial.com
SIC: 3291 Abrasive buffs, bricks, cloth, paper, stones, etc.

(G-519)
EAST PENN MANUFACTURING CO
790 Railroad Ave (11704-7820)
PHONE................................631 321-7161
Timothy Dunn, *Principal*
EMP: 6
SALES (corp-wide): 2.8B **Privately Held**
SIC: 3999 Barber & beauty shop equipment
PA: East Penn Manufacturing Co.
102 Deka Rd
Lyon Station PA 19536
610 682-6361

(G-520)
EDM MFG
141 John St Ste 600 (11702-2945)
PHONE................................631 669-1966
Dariusz Mejer, *Chairman*
EMP: 8
SALES (est): 833.9K **Privately Held**
SIC: 3599 Machine shop, jobbing & repair

(G-521)
JEWELERS MACHINIST CO INC
400 Columbus Ave (11704-5599)
PHONE................................631 661-5020
Raymond Pawloski, *President*
John Pawloski, *Vice Pres*
Kathleen Pawloski, *Admin Sec*
EMP: 7 **EST:** 1946
SQ FT: 3,000
SALES (est): 1MM **Privately Held**
WEB: www.threadgrind.com
SIC: 3599 Machine shop, jobbing & repair

(G-522)
M C PACKAGING CORPORATION
Also Called: M C Packaging Corp Plant
300 Governor Ave (11704-1900)
PHONE................................631 643-3763
EMP: 40
SALES (corp-wide): 22.9MM **Privately Held**
SIC: 2679 5113 2759 2657 Mfg Converted Paper Prdt Whol Indstl/Svc Paper Commercial Printing Mfg Folding Paperbrd Box Mfg Corrugated/Fiber Box
PA: M C Packaging Corporation
200 Adams Blvd
Farmingdale NY 11735
631 414-7840

(G-523)
PHARMAVANTAGE LLC
15 Lakeland Ave (11702-1409)
PHONE................................631 321-8171
Susan Capie,
▲ **EMP:** 6
SALES (est): 584.9K **Privately Held**
SIC: 2834 Druggists' preparations (pharmaceuticals)

(G-524)
PREMIER SYSTEMS LLC
41 John St Ste 6 (11702-2932)
PHONE................................631 587-9700
Joseph Pegno,
EMP: 6
SALES (est): 670K **Privately Held**
SIC: 3679 Electronic circuits

(G-525)
PREMIUM PROCESSING CORP
30 Kittiwake Ln (11702-4215)
PHONE................................631 232-1105
Keith Schmidt, *President*
Matthew Overholser, *Sales Staff*
EMP: 52
SQ FT: 30,000

SALES (est): 654.9K **Privately Held**
SIC: 2834 Vitamin preparations

Bainbridge
Chenango County

(G-526)
SHEHAWKEN ARCHERY CO INC
40 S Main St (13733-1216)
P.O. Box 187 (13733-0187)
PHONE................................607 967-8333
Fax: 607 967-2828
EMP: 12
SQ FT: 17,000
SALES (est): 720K **Privately Held**
SIC: 3949 Mfg Archery Equipment

(G-527)
TRIMAC MOLDING SERVICES
13 Pruyn St (13733-1155)
P.O. Box 176 (13733-0176)
PHONE................................607 967-2900
Linda Pickwick, *Partner*
Harold Pickwick, *Partner*
EMP: 9
SQ FT: 60,000
SALES (est): 1.3MM **Privately Held**
WEB: www.trimacmolding.com
SIC: 3089 Injection molding of plastics

(G-528)
UPTURN INDUSTRIES INC
2-4 Whitney Way (13733)
PHONE................................607 967-2923
Mike Horoszewski, *CEO*
Donna L Enck, *CEO*
Tomas Mahar, *Business Mgr*
Tom Mahar, *QC Dir*
▲ **EMP:** 31
SQ FT: 12,000
SALES (est): 5.1MM **Privately Held**
WEB: www.upturnindustries.com
SIC: 3599 Machine shop, jobbing & repair

Bakers Mills
Warren County

(G-529)
CHAD PIERSON
Also Called: Chad Pierson Logging & Trckg
Chad Pierson (12811)
P.O. Box 29 (12811-0029)
PHONE................................518 251-0186
Chad Pierson, *President*
EMP: 7
SQ FT: 5,600
SALES (est): 701K **Privately Held**
SIC: 2411 Logging

Baldwin
Nassau County

(G-530)
ELLIQUENCE LLC
2455 Grand Ave (11510-3556)
PHONE................................516 277-9000
Alan Ellman, *Mng Member*
▲ **EMP:** 19
SALES (est): 3.2MM **Privately Held**
SIC: 3841 Surgical & medical instruments

(G-531)
JAL SIGNS INC
Also Called: Sign-A-Rama
540 Merrick Rd (11510-3439)
PHONE................................516 536-7280
Agnes Lidner, *President*
Jim Lindner, *Manager*
James Lidner, *Admin Sec*
EMP: 10 **EST:** 1999
SALES (est): 1.3MM **Privately Held**
SIC: 3993 Signs & advertising specialties

(G-532)
MAKS PHARMA & DIAGNOSTICS INC
2365 Milburn Ave Bldg 2 (11510-3349)
PHONE................................631 270-1528

Sadathulla Shareef, *President*
Mohammad Ullah, *Vice Pres*
Sylwia Jabysz, *Admin Sec*
EMP: 3 **EST:** 2012
SQ FT: 2,200
SALES: 1MM **Privately Held**
SIC: 2834 Pharmaceutical preparations

(G-533)
ROSE FENCE INC
345 Sunrise Hwy (11510)
PHONE..................................516 223-0777
Scott Rose, *Branch Mgr*
EMP: 10
SALES (corp-wide): 13.6MM **Privately Held**
WEB: www.rosefence.com
SIC: 2499 5211 3496 3315 Fencing, wood; fencing; miscellaneous fabricated wire products; steel wire & related products
PA: Rose Fence, Inc.
345 W Sunrise Hwy
Freeport NY 11520
516 223-0777

(G-534)
RUSSCO METAL SPINNING CO INC
1020 Archer Pl (11510-3604)
PHONE..................................516 872-6055
EMP: 10
SQ FT: 5,300
SALES (est): 1.2MM **Privately Held**
SIC: 3469 Metal Spinning

(G-535)
SONIQUENCE LLC
Also Called: Ellusa
2473 Grand Ave (11510-3531)
PHONE..................................516 267-6400
Alan Ellman,
EMP: 10
SALES (est): 414.8K **Privately Held**
SIC: 3841 Surgical & medical instruments

(G-536)
SPORTS DEPOT INC
891 Hayes St (11510-4646)
PHONE..................................516 965-4668
Robert Smalley, *CEO*
EMP: 1
SALES: 1MM **Privately Held**
SIC: 2395 Embroidery products, except schiffli machine

(G-537)
TECHNICAL PACKAGING INC
2365 Milburn Ave (11510-3349)
P.O. Box 504 (11510-0504)
PHONE..................................516 223-2300
Don Romig, *President*
James Kane, *Vice Pres*
EMP: 15
SALES (est): 3.2MM **Privately Held**
WEB: www.technicalpackaging.com
SIC: 2653 2441 3053 3086 Boxes, corrugated: made from purchased materials; packing cases, wood: nailed or lock corner; packing materials; packaging & shipping materials, foamed plastic; packaging materials; corrugated & solid fiber boxes

Baldwin Place
Westchester County

(G-538)
GOODWILL INDS OF GREATER NY
80 Route 6 Unit 605 (10505-1033)
PHONE..................................914 621-0781
Herbert Wright, *Principal*
EMP: 161
SALES (corp-wide): 117.3MM **Privately Held**
SIC: 3999 Barber & beauty shop equipment
PA: Goodwill Industries Of Greater New York Inc
421 27th Ave
Astoria NY 11102
718 728-5400

Baldwinsville
Onondaga County

(G-539)
ACME SIGNS OF BALDWINSVILLE
3 Marble St (13027-2918)
PHONE..................................315 638-4865
Dennis Sick, *Owner*
EMP: 6
SALES (est): 271.7K **Privately Held**
SIC: 3993 4226 Signs & advertising specialties; special warehousing & storage

(G-540)
ADVANCED RECOVERY & RECYCL LLC
3475 Linda Ln (13027-9217)
PHONE..................................315 450-3301
Byron Tietjen, *President*
Peter Stockmann,
EMP: 10
SALES (est): 676.4K **Privately Held**
SIC: 2611 Pulp manufactured from waste or recycled paper

(G-541)
ANHEUSER-BUSCH LLC
2780 Brundage Rd (13027)
PHONE..................................315 638-0365
EMP: 5
SALES (est): 171.4K **Privately Held**
SIC: 2082 Malt beverages

(G-542)
ANHEUSER-BUSCH LLC
2885 Belgium Rd (13027-2797)
P.O. Box 200 (13027-0200)
PHONE..................................315 638-0365
Chris Lukaczyk, *Area Mgr*
Jesse Randolph, *Opers Mgr*
Penny Gallonio, *Safety Mgr*
Steven McCormick, *Opers-Prdtn-Mfg*
Charlie Hornsey, *Engineer*
EMP: 162
SALES (corp-wide): 1.5B **Privately Held**
WEB: www.hispanicbud.com
SIC: 2082 Beer (alcoholic beverage)
HQ: Anheuser-Busch, Llc
1 Busch Pl
Saint Louis MO 63118
800 342-5283

(G-543)
BACO CONTROLS INC (PA)
8431 Loop Rd (13027-1304)
P.O. Box 570, Cazenovia (13035-0570)
PHONE..................................315 635-2500
Thomas C Rogers, *President*
EMP: 10
SQ FT: 1,500
SALES (est): 1.8MM **Privately Held**
WEB: www.bacocontrols.com
SIC: 3625 Relays & industrial controls

(G-544)
CAPCO MARKETING
Also Called: Gourmet Connection
8417 Oswego Rd 177 (13027-8813)
P.O. Box 1727, Cicero (13039-1727)
PHONE..................................315 699-1687
Kirk Capece, *Owner*
EMP: 10
SALES (est): 452.4K **Privately Held**
WEB: www.capcomarketing.com
SIC: 2721 5812 Magazines: publishing & printing; eating places

(G-545)
COMPLEX BIOSYSTEMS INC
8417 Oswego Rd 201 (13027-8813)
PHONE..................................315 464-8007
Jacques Beaumont, *Owner*
EMP: 7
SQ FT: 600
SALES (est): 336K **Privately Held**
SIC: 3845 7371 7373 8711 Electrotherapeutic apparatus; computer software systems analysis & design, custom; computer-aided engineering (CAE) systems service; consulting engineer

(G-546)
COVERALL MANUFACTURING
Also Called: New Top Sales Company
3653 Hayes Rd (13027-8414)
PHONE..................................315 622-2852
Joseph Peta, *President*
EMP: 8
SALES (est): 789.9K **Privately Held**
WEB: www.golfcarcovers.com
SIC: 2394 Canvas & related products

(G-547)
FINGER LKES STIRS CABINETS LLC
7496 Kingdom Rd (13027-8782)
PHONE..................................315 638-3150
Jack Barton, *Principal*
Jason Barton, *Principal*
Brad Crosby, *Principal*
EMP: 5
SALES (est): 476.7K **Privately Held**
SIC: 2434 Wood kitchen cabinets

(G-548)
GIOVANNI FOOD CO INC (PA)
8800 Sixty Rd (13027-1235)
PHONE..................................315 457-2373
Louis J Dement, *Vice Pres*
Rod Young, *Production*
Katie Weber, *Purch Mgr*
Jeff Burch, *Project Engr*
David Monahan, *CFO*
◆ **EMP:** 70
SQ FT: 25,000
SALES (est): 13.9MM **Privately Held**
WEB: www.giovannifoods.com
SIC: 2033 Tomato products: packaged in cans, jars, etc.

(G-549)
INDIAN SPRINGS MFG CO INC
2095 W Genesee Rd (13027-8649)
P.O. Box 469 (13027-0469)
PHONE..................................315 635-6101
Maurice J Ferguson, *CEO*
Shawn Ferguson, *President*
Patricia Ferguson, *Admin Sec*
Robert Wolniak, *Admin Sec*
EMP: 18
SQ FT: 9,000
SALES (est): 4.9MM **Privately Held**
WEB: www.indiansprings.com
SIC: 2812 3599 Chlorine, compressed or liquefied; machine & other job shop work

(G-550)
KAYLON INDUSTRIES LLC
15 Downer St (13027-2819)
PHONE..................................315 303-2119
Christopher Leonard,
EMP: 5
SALES: 100K **Privately Held**
SIC: 3999 Manufacturing industries

(G-551)
METROPOLITAN SIGNS INC
3760 Patchett Rd (13027-9454)
P.O. Box 3062, Liverpool (13089-3062)
PHONE..................................315 638-1448
David R Razzante, *President*
EMP: 10 **EST:** 1970
SQ FT: 4,000
SALES: 600K **Privately Held**
WEB: www.metropolitansigns.com
SIC: 3993 Electric signs

(G-552)
PAPERWORKS INDUSTRIES INC
2900 Mclane Rd (13027-1319)
PHONE..................................315 638-4355
EMP: 234 **Privately Held**
SIC: 2653 Boxes, corrugated: made from purchased materials
PA: Paperworks Industries, Inc.
40 Monument Rd Ste 200
Bala Cynwyd PA 19004

(G-553)
SPECIALIZED PACKG GROUP INC (HQ)
Also Called: Paperworks
2900 Mclane Rd (13027-1319)
PHONE..................................315 638-4355
C Anderson Bolton, *CEO*
Clint Rutledge, *COO*

Scott Gomez, *CFO*
▲ **EMP:** 2
SALES (est): 43MM **Privately Held**
SIC: 2653 2657 Corrugated & solid fiber boxes; folding paperboard boxes

(G-554)
SPECIALIZED PACKG RADISSON LLC
8800 Sixty Rd (13027-1235)
PHONE..................................315 638-4355
Thomas Garland,
Carlton Highsmith,
EMP: 150 **EST:** 1998
SALES (est): 32.4MM **Privately Held**
SIC: 2653 2657 Boxes, solid fiber: made from purchased materials; folding paperboard boxes
HQ: The Specialized Packaging Group Inc
2900 Mclane Rd
Baldwinsville NY 13027
315 638-4355

(G-555)
SSAC INC
8242 Loop Rd (13027-1391)
PHONE..................................800 843-8848
Fax: 315 638-0333
EMP: 21
SALES (est): 3.3MM **Privately Held**
SIC: 3625 Mfg Relays/Industrial Controls

(G-556)
SYRASOFT LLC
6 Canton St (13027-2300)
PHONE..................................315 708-0341
Thomas Gardener, *Partner*
EMP: 10
SALES (est): 1.1MM **Privately Held**
WEB: www.syrasoft.com
SIC: 7372 7371 Prepackaged software; custom computer programming services

Ballston Lake
Saratoga County

(G-557)
ASTRO CHEMICAL COMPANY INC
3 Mill Rd (12019-2022)
P.O. Box 1250 (12019-0250)
PHONE..................................518 399-5338
Duane A Ball, *Ch of Bd*
Jay Arnold, *Vice Pres*
Scott Fuller, *VP Opers*
▲ **EMP:** 20
SQ FT: 24,000
SALES (est): 5.3MM **Privately Held**
WEB: www.astrochemical.com
SIC: 2891 Adhesives & sealants

(G-558)
BENNETT STAIR COMPANY INC
1021 State Route 50 (12019-1915)
PHONE..................................518 384-1554
Dave Bennett, *President*
Gayle Bennett, *Office Mgr*
EMP: 8
SQ FT: 2,800
SALES: 650K **Privately Held**
SIC: 2431 Staircases & stairs, wood; staircases, stairs & railings

(G-559)
CBM FABRICATIONS INC
15 Westside Dr (12019-2025)
PHONE..................................518 399-8023
Charles B McCormack II, *Ch of Bd*
Margaret Spoonogle, *Office Mgr*
EMP: 30
SQ FT: 8,100
SALES (est): 8.4MM **Privately Held**
WEB: www.cbmfab.com
SIC: 3441 7692 3599 3444 Fabricated structural metal; welding repair; machine shop, jobbing & repair; sheet metalwork

(G-560)
LAKESIDE CIDER MILL FARM INC
336 Schauber Rd (12019-2104)
PHONE..................................518 399-8359
Richard Pearce, *President*

Jeffrey Pearce, *Vice Pres*
EMP: 8 **EST:** 1944
SQ FT: 5,000
SALES (est): 1MM **Privately Held**
SIC: 2099 5812 5431 Cider, nonalcoholic; eating places; vegetable stands or markets

(G-561)
MERCURY PEN COMPANY INC
245 Eastline Rd (12019-1810)
PHONE..................................518 899-9653
Jody Gentilesco, *President*
▲ **EMP:** 7
SQ FT: 5,000
SALES: 216.6K **Privately Held**
WEB: www.mercurypen.com
SIC: 3951 Ball point pens & parts; penholders & parts; pencils & pencil parts, mechanical

(G-562)
NORTHEAST TONER INC
26 Walden Gln Fl 2 (12019-9234)
PHONE..................................518 899-5545
Gail Trietiak, *President*
Paul Trietiak, *Vice Pres*
EMP: 7
SALES (est): 1.1MM **Privately Held**
SIC: 3955 Print cartridges for laser & other computer printers

(G-563)
SIXNET LLC
331 Ushers Rd Ste 14 (12019-1546)
P.O. Box 767, Clifton Park (12065-0767)
PHONE..................................518 877-5173
Steve Schoenberg, *CEO*
Laura La Prairie, *Sales Dir*
Jill Teresi, *Cust Mgr*
Jacob Colegrove, *Manager*
Joe Slattery, *Technical Staff*
EMP: 80
SQ FT: 20,000
SALES (est): 12.3MM
SALES (corp-wide): 2B **Privately Held**
WEB: www.sixnetio.com
SIC: 3823 Computer interface equipment for industrial process control
HQ: Red Lion Controls, Inc.
20 Willow Springs Cir
York PA 17406
717 767-6961

(G-564)
SIXNET HOLDINGS LLC
331 Ushers Rd Ste 10 (12019-1546)
PHONE..................................518 877-5173
Hilton Nicholson,
▲ **EMP:** 5
SALES (est): 7.9MM
SALES (corp-wide): 2B **Privately Held**
SIC: 3823 Industrial instrmnts msrmnt display/control process variable
PA: Spectris Plc
Heritage House
Egham TW20
178 447-0470

(G-565)
TJB SUNSHINE ENTERPRISES
6 Redwood Dr (12019-2631)
PHONE..................................518 384-6483
Tom Brundige, *President*
EMP: 14
SALES (est): 1.1MM **Privately Held**
SIC: 2842 Window cleaning preparations

Ballston Spa
Saratoga County

(G-566)
ADVANCED COMFORT SYSTEMS INC
Also Called: ACS
12b Commerce Dr (12020-3631)
PHONE..................................518 884-8444
Roger M Kerr, *President*
▲ **EMP:** 10
SALES (est): 1.7MM **Privately Held**
WEB: www.advancedcomfortsys.com
SIC: 7372 1742 Application computer software; insulation, buildings

(G-567)
ALBATROS NORTH AMERICA INC
Also Called: Sepsa North America
6 Mccrea Hill Rd (12020-5515)
PHONE..................................518 381-7100
John Hanrahan, *CEO*
Nicholas Fuster, *President*
William D Kolberg, *Finance*
▲ **EMP:** 45
SQ FT: 36,000
SALES (est): 10.2MM **Privately Held**
WEB: www.sepsa.es
SIC: 3679 3699 Static power supply converters for electronic applications; security control equipment & systems

(G-568)
ALLYTEX LLC
540 Acland Blvd (12020-3074)
PHONE..................................518 376-7539
Alison Arakelian,
EMP: 5
SALES (est): 310.6K **Privately Held**
SIC: 2311 Men's & boys' suits & coats

(G-569)
APPLIED MATERIALS INC
10 Stonebreak Rd Ste 2 (12020-4505)
PHONE..................................518 245-1400
EMP: 6
SALES (corp-wide): 17.2B **Publicly Held**
SIC: 3674 Semiconductors & related devices
PA: Applied Materials, Inc.
3050 Bowers Ave
Santa Clara CA 95054
408 727-5555

(G-570)
BURNT HILLS FABRICATORS INC
318 Charlton Rd B (12020-3412)
P.O. Box 2, Burnt Hills (12027-0002)
PHONE..................................518 885-1115
James Fantauzzi, *President*
EMP: 15
SQ FT: 7,000
SALES (est): 3.1MM **Privately Held**
SIC: 3441 Fabricated structural metal

(G-571)
DEATH WISH COFFEE COMPANY LLC (PA)
100 Saratoga Village Blvd # 3
(12020-3737)
PHONE..................................518 400-1050
Michael Brown, *CEO*
Michael Pilkington, *COO*
Keith Abatto, *CFO*
EMP: 38 **EST:** 2013
SQ FT: 26,000
SALES (est): 14.3MM **Privately Held**
SIC: 2095 5499 Coffee extracts; coffee roasting (except by wholesale grocers); coffee

(G-572)
DIT PRINTS INCORPORATED
Also Called: Digital Imiging Technologies
27 Kent St Ste 53 (12020-1543)
PHONE..................................518 885-4400
Deborah Libratore Le Blanc, *President*
Paul Le Blanc, *General Mgr*
EMP: 5
SQ FT: 2,400
SALES (est): 452.7K **Privately Held**
SIC: 2759 Commercial printing

(G-573)
DURA-MILL INC
16 Stonebreak Rd (12020)
PHONE..................................518 899-2255
David Walrath, *President*
Scott Walrath, *Vice Pres*
Suzanne Walrath, *Controller*
EMP: 30
SALES: 8.2MM
SALES (corp-wide): 11.1B **Privately Held**
WEB: www.duramill.com
SIC: 3545 Cutting tools for machine tools
HQ: Ab Sandvik Coromant
Mossvagen 10
Sandviken 811 3
262 600-00

(G-574)
GLOBALFOUNDRIES US INC
107 Hermes Rd (12020-4534)
PHONE..................................408 462-3900
Debra Leach, *Vice Pres*
Buren Jason VA, *Mfg Mgr*
Der Heide Pau VA, *Mfg Mgr*
Jason Cargin, *Engineer*
Scott Michalski, *Engineer*
EMP: 19 **Privately Held**
SIC: 3369 3674 Nonferrous foundries; integrated circuits, semiconductor networks, etc.
HQ: Globalfoundries U.S. Inc.
2600 Great America Way
Santa Clara CA 95054

(G-575)
GREAT AMERICAN AWNING & PATIO
43 Round Lake Rd (12020)
PHONE..................................518 899-2300
Frank Rasalik, *President*
EMP: 15
SALES (est): 1.2MM **Privately Held**
SIC: 3271 Blocks, concrete: chimney or fireplace

(G-576)
HARVEST TECHNOLOGIES INC
36 Featherfoil Way (12020-4371)
PHONE..................................518 899-7124
Donna Morris, *Partner*
Turk Ellis, *Partner*
EMP: 2
SALES: 2MM **Privately Held**
SIC: 2611 Pulp manufactured from waste or recycled paper

(G-577)
IRWIN FUTURES LLC
608 Rock City Rd (12020-2502)
PHONE..................................518 884-9008
Linda Irwin, *Principal*
EMP: 5
SALES (est): 379.9K **Privately Held**
SIC: 2711 Newspapers, publishing & printing

(G-578)
JOHNSON CONTROLS INC
339 Brownell Rd (12020-3705)
PHONE..................................518 884-8313
David Bardsley, *Branch Mgr*
EMP: 95 **Privately Held**
SIC: 2531 Seats, automobile
HQ: Johnson Controls, Inc.
5757 N Green Bay Ave
Milwaukee WI 53209
414 524-1200

(G-579)
LANE ENTERPRISES INC
825 State Route 67 (12020-3604)
PHONE..................................518 885-4385
M J Cathers, *Branch Mgr*
EMP: 20
SALES (corp-wide): 71.1MM **Privately Held**
WEB: www.lanepipe.com
SIC: 3444 3449 Pipe, sheet metal; miscellaneous metalwork
PA: Lane Enterprises, Inc.
3905 Hartzdale Dr Ste 514
Camp Hill PA 17011
717 761-8175

(G-580)
LEMANS CORPORATION
Also Called: Drag Specialties
10 Mccrea Hill Rd (12020-5515)
PHONE..................................518 885-7500
Mike Cornell, *Manager*
EMP: 9
SALES (corp-wide): 651.6MM **Privately Held**
SIC: 3714 Acceleration equipment, motor vehicle
PA: Lemans Corporation
3501 Kennedy Rd
Janesville WI 53545
608 758-1111

(G-581)
MERIDIAN MANUFACTURING INC
27 Kent St Ste 103a (12020-1543)
PHONE..................................518 885-0450
Paul Michael, *President*
Robin Guarino, *Vice Pres*
Deane Vedder, *Manager*
EMP: 7
SQ FT: 8,100
SALES (est): 1.2MM **Privately Held**
SIC: 3599 Machine shop, jobbing & repair

(G-582)
MESSENGER PRESS
1826 Amsterdam Rd (12020-3323)
P.O. Box 376 (12020-0376)
PHONE..................................518 885-9231
Ed Bellamy, *Owner*
EMP: 8
SALES (est): 460K **Privately Held**
SIC: 2752 7336 Lithographing on metal; commercial art & graphic design

(G-583)
NORTH AMERICAN SVCS GROUP LLC (HQ)
Also Called: North American Service Group
1240 Saratoga Rd (12020-3500)
PHONE..................................518 885-1820
Frank Zilka, *President*
Rick Matteson, *General Mgr*
Jeff King, *Regional Mgr*
Tim Zilka, *COO*
Robert Pople, *Opers Mgr*
EMP: 15
SQ FT: 40,000
SALES (est): 5.6MM **Privately Held**
SIC: 3443 1799 Cryogenic tanks, for liquids & gases; service station equipment installation, maintenance & repair

(G-584)
NORTHWIND GRAPHICS
2453 State Route 9 (12020-4407)
PHONE..................................518 899-9651
Steve Richardson, *Owner*
EMP: 5
SQ FT: 3,500
SALES (est): 420.9K **Privately Held**
SIC: 2759 Screen printing

(G-585)
PREMIUM BLDG COMPONENTS INC
831 Rt 67 Bldg 46 (12020)
PHONE..................................518 885-0194
John Buyaskas, *Principal*
EMP: 20
SALES (corp-wide): 7.1MM **Privately Held**
SIC: 3713 Truck & bus bodies
PA: Premium Building Components, Inc.
527 Queensbury Ave
Queensbury NY 12804
518 792-0189

(G-586)
SAND HILL INDUSTRIES INC
Also Called: T-Shirt Graphics
12 Grove St (12020-1814)
PHONE..................................518 885-7991
Dennis Albright, *President*
Eileen Albright, *Vice Pres*
EMP: 6
SQ FT: 10,000
SALES (est): 560K **Privately Held**
WEB: www.t-shirtgraphics.com
SIC: 2759 2395 2752 3081 Screen printing; embroidery & art needlework; commercial printing, offset; unsupported plastics film & sheet

(G-587)
SPECIALTY SILICONE PDTS INC
3 Mccrea Hill Rd (12020-5511)
PHONE..................................518 885-8826
Susan Premo, *CEO*
Paul Dicaprio, *President*
Patricia S Babbie, *Senior VP*
Ned REO, *Senior VP*
Frederic E Sober, *Senior VP*
▲ **EMP:** 70
SQ FT: 52,000

SALES (est): 13.6MM **Publicly Held**
WEB: www.sspinc.com
SIC: 2869 2822 3714 2992 Silicones; silicone rubbers; motor vehicle parts & accessories; lubricating oils & greases
HQ: Heico Electronic Technologies Corp.
3000 Taft St
Hollywood FL 33021
954 987-6101

(G-588)
STEWARTS PROCESSING CORP
(PA)
2907 State Route 9 (12020-4201)
P.O. Box 435, Saratoga Springs (12866-0435)
PHONE..............................518 581-1200
Gary C Dake, *Ch of Bd*
Erik Kaehler, *District Mgr*
David Farr, *CFO*
Michael Cocca, *Treasurer*
Scott Corey, *Branch Mgr*
EMP: 85
SALES: 61.9MM **Privately Held**
SIC: 2026 2024 2086 Fluid milk; ice cream & ice milk; soft drinks: packaged in cans, bottles, etc.

(G-589)
WINDOW TECH SYSTEMS INC
15 Old Stonebreak Rd (12020-4900)
P.O. Box 2260 (12020-8260)
PHONE..............................518 899-9000
David L Bangert, *President*
Dave Bangert, *President*
Tracy Carpenter, *Sales Staff*
EMP: 22 **EST:** 1952
SQ FT: 30,000
SALES (est): 4.8MM **Privately Held**
WEB: www.windowtechsystems.net
SIC: 3442 3089 Screens, window, metal; windows, plastic

Barker
Niagara County

(G-590)
ATLANTIC TRANSFORMER INC
1674 Quaker Rd (14012-9616)
P.O. Box 276 (14012-0276)
PHONE..............................716 795-3258
John Khorrami, *President*
EMP: 10
SQ FT: 8,500
SALES: 400K **Privately Held**
WEB: www.mgs4u.com
SIC: 3677 Electronic transformers

(G-591)
JT PRECISION INC
8701 Haight Rd (14012-9630)
PHONE..............................716 795-3860
Jeff Thuman Sr, *President*
Richard Meyers, *Principal*
Sarah Munn, *Principal*
Cristine O'Keefe, *Officer*
EMP: 34
SALES: 3MM **Privately Held**
SIC: 3599 Machine shop, jobbing & repair

Barneveld
Oneida County

(G-592)
JET SEW CORPORATION
8119 State Route 12 (13304)
P.O. Box 326 (13304-0326)
PHONE..............................315 896-2683
Edward Wiehl, *President*
EMP: 15
SQ FT: 65,000
SALES: 550K **Privately Held**
WEB: www.jetsew.com
SIC: 3599 Custom machinery

(G-593)
METAL PARTS
MANUFACTURING INC
119 Remsen Rd (13304-2407)
PHONE..............................315 831-2530

William Noeth, *President*
Paul Lopus, *Admin Sec*
EMP: 5
SQ FT: 3,000
SALES (est): 375K **Privately Held**
WEB: www.mpminc.net
SIC: 3599 Machine shop, jobbing & repair

(G-594)
MOHAWK ELECTRO
TECHNIQUES INC
7677 Cameron Hill Rd (13304-1917)
PHONE..............................315 896-2661
Lee Broomfield, *President*
Fred Ingo, *Vice Pres*
EMP: 90
SQ FT: 5,000
SALES (est): 9.1MM **Privately Held**
SIC: 3677 Coil windings, electronic; electronic transformers

(G-595)
ROLLING STAR
MANUFACTURING INC
125 Liberty Ln (13304-2537)
P.O. Box 471 (13304-0471)
PHONE..............................315 896-4767
Jamie R Servello, *President*
Dean Beck, *Vice Pres*
EMP: 20
SQ FT: 2,728
SALES (est): 4MM **Privately Held**
WEB: www.customizedtrailers.com
SIC: 3715 Truck trailers

(G-596)
SQUARE STAMPING MFG CORP
108 Old Remsen Rd (13304)
P.O. Box 207 (13304-0207)
PHONE..............................315 896-2641
David Allen, *President*
Dan Hart, *General Mgr*
Jeffrey Gouger, *Treasurer*
Beth McGovern, *Office Mgr*
EMP: 35 **EST:** 1926
SQ FT: 25,000
SALES (est): 6.3MM **Privately Held**
WEB: www.squarestamping.com
SIC: 3469 Stamping metal for the trade

Barrytown
Dutchess County

(G-597)
STATION HILL OF BARRYTOWN
120 Station Hill Rd (12507-5018)
PHONE..............................845 758-5293
George Quasha, *President*
Susan Quasha, *Vice Pres*
Sam Truitt, *Exec Dir*
EMP: 6
SALES (est): 423.6K **Privately Held**
SIC: 2731 5961 Book publishing; book club, mail order; record &/or tape (music or video) club, mail order

Barryville
Sullivan County

(G-598)
N A R ASSOCIATES INC
128 Rte 55 (12719)
P.O. Box 233 (12719-0233)
PHONE..............................845 557-8713
Nick A Roes, *President*
Nancy Bennett, *Vice Pres*
EMP: 6
SALES (est): 537.5K **Privately Held**
WEB: www.nickroes.com
SIC: 2731 Book publishing

Batavia
Genesee County

(G-599)
ALICIA F HERDLEIN
Also Called: Extreme Streetwear
5450 E Main Street Rd (14020-9625)
PHONE..............................585 344-4411
Herdlein F Alicia, *Owner*
Alicia Herdlein, *Owner*
EMP: 5
SALES: 500K **Privately Held**
SIC: 2759 Screen printing

(G-600)
ALUDYNE NEW YORK LLC
Also Called: Automotive, LLC
4320 Federal Dr (14020-4104)
PHONE..............................248 728-8642
Andreas Weller, *CEO*
EMP: 15
SALES (est): 2.4MM
SALES (corp-wide): 1.3B **Privately Held**
WEB: www.automotivecorporation.com
SIC: 3714 Motor vehicle parts & accessories
HQ: Aludyne, Inc.
300 Galleria Ofcntr Ste 5
Southfield MI 48034
248 728-8642

(G-601)
AMADA TOOL AMERICA INC
4 Treadeasy Ave Ste A (14020-3010)
PHONE..............................585 344-3900
Hitoshi Iizuka, *President*
Michael Guerin, *Treasurer*
▲ **EMP:** 55
SQ FT: 50,000
SALES (est): 9.4MM **Privately Held**
SIC: 3544 Special dies & tools
HQ: Amada North America, Inc
7025 Firestone Blvd
Buena Park CA 90621

(G-602)
ARTISAN BOOT & SHOE CO LLC
3 Treadeasy Ave (14020-3009)
PHONE..............................585 813-2825
Nicole Porter,
EMP: 10
SQ FT: 60,000
SALES (est): 362.1K **Privately Held**
SIC: 3143 Work shoes, men's; orthopedic shoes, men's; dress shoes, men's

(G-603)
BATAVIA PRESS LLC
3817 W Main Street Rd (14020-9402)
PHONE..............................585 343-4429
Becky Almeter, *Partner*
Robert Hodgins,
EMP: 32
SALES (est): 1.5MM **Privately Held**
SIC: 2752 7389 2759 Business form & card printing, lithographic; document embossing; engrossing: diplomas, resolutions, etc.; invitation & stationery printing & engraving; security certificates: engraved

(G-604)
BILL SHEA ENTERPRISES INC
Also Called: Deluxe Machine & Tool Co
8825 Alexander Rd (14020-9581)
PHONE..............................585 343-2284
William Shea, *President*
Steven Shea, *Vice Pres*
EMP: 2
SQ FT: 20,000
SALES (est): 1.1MM **Privately Held**
WEB: www.trojanloaders.com
SIC: 3599 Machine shop, jobbing & repair

(G-605)
BONSAL AMERICAN INC
102 Cedar St (14020-3337)
PHONE..............................585 343-4741
David Trzybinski, *Branch Mgr*
EMP: 13
SQ FT: 28,069

SALES (corp-wide): 30.6B **Privately Held**
WEB: www.bonsalamerican.com
SIC: 3272 Concrete products
HQ: Bonsal American, Inc.
625 Griffith Rd Ste 100
Charlotte NC 28217
704 525-1621

(G-606)
BRACH MACHINE INC
4814 Ellicott Street Rd (14020-3420)
PHONE..............................585 343-9134
William H Brach, *President*
Nancy E Brach, *Vice Pres*
Nancy Brach, *Vice Pres*
▲ **EMP:** 12
SQ FT: 15,000
SALES (est): 1.5MM **Privately Held**
WEB: www.brachmachine.com
SIC: 3599 Machine shop, jobbing & repair

(G-607)
CARGILL INCORPORATED
8849 Wortendyke Rd (14020-9558)
PHONE..............................585 345-1160
Brent Brinegar, *Opers-Prdtn-Mfg*
EMP: 70
SALES (corp-wide): 114.7B **Privately Held**
WEB: www.cargill.com
SIC: 2048 Prepared feeds
PA: Cargill, Incorporated
15407 Mcginty Rd W
Wayzata MN 55391
952 742-7575

(G-608)
CHAPIN INTERNATIONAL INC
700 Ellicott St (14020-3744)
P.O. Box 549 (14021-0549)
PHONE..............................585 343-3140
Andris K Chapin, *Ch of Bd*
James W Campbell, *President*
James Grant, *Vice Pres*
Valerie De Lagenest, *Mktg Dir*
◆ **EMP:** 225
SQ FT: 710,000
SALES (est): 22.3MM
SALES (corp-wide): 50.1MM **Privately Held**
SIC: 3499 3524 3085 3563 Aerosol valves, metal; lawn & garden equipment; plastics bottles; air & gas compressors
PA: Chapin Manufacturing, Inc
700 Ellicott St Ste 3
Batavia NY 14020
585 343-3140

(G-609)
CHAPIN MANUFACTURING INC
(PA)
700 Ellicott St Ste 3 (14020-3794)
P.O. Box 549 (14021-0549)
PHONE..............................585 343-3140
James W Campbell, *Ch of Bd*
Andris K Chapin, *Ch of Bd*
James Grant, *Vice Pres*
William Campbell, *Plant Mgr*
Lena LI, *Opers Staff*
◆ **EMP:** 220
SQ FT: 710,000
SALES (est): 50.1MM **Privately Held**
WEB: www.chapinmfg.com
SIC: 3499 3524 3085 3563 Aerosol valves, metal; lawn & garden equipment; plastics bottles; air & gas compressors; spraying outfits: metals, paints & chemicals (compressor); spreaders, fertilizer

(G-610)
CHASSIX AUTOMOTIVE CORP
4320 Federal Dr (14020-4104)
PHONE..............................585 815-1700
EMP: 16
SALES (est): 2.2MM **Privately Held**
SIC: 3599 Machine shop, jobbing & repair

(G-611)
CONSOLIDATED CONTAINER CO
LLC
Also Called: Liquitane
14 Hall St (14020-3216)
PHONE..............................585 343-9351
Bob Henry, *Facilities Mgr*
EMP: 15

SALES (corp-wide): 14B **Publicly Held**
WEB: www.ccccllc.com
SIC: 3089 Plastic containers, except foam
HQ: Consolidated Container Company, Llc
2500 Windy Ridge Pkwy Se # 1400
Atlanta GA 30339
678 742-4600

(G-612)
COUNTRY FOLKS
123 N Spruce St (14020-2611)
PHONE..................................585 343-9721
Patrick Berg, *Principal*
EMP: 5
SALES (est): 196.4K **Privately Held**
SIC: 2711 Newspapers

(G-613)
EXIDE TECHNOLOGIES
Also Called: Exide Batteries
4330 Commerce Dr (14020-4117)
PHONE..................................585 344-0656
Deborah Cravatta, *Manager*
EMP: 9
SALES (corp-wide): 2.3B **Privately Held**
WEB: www.exideworld.com
SIC: 3691 3629 Lead acid batteries (storage batteries); battery chargers, rectifying or nonrotating
PA: Exide Technologies
13000 Deerfield Pkwy # 200
Milton GA 30004
678 566-9000

(G-614)
FONTRICK DOOR INC
9 Apollo Dr (14020-3001)
PHONE..................................585 345-6032
Michael J Fontaine, *CEO*
Jacob Mingle, *Engineer*
Judy Brown, *Bookkeeper*
EMP: 30
SQ FT: 26,000
SALES (est): 4.7MM **Privately Held**
WEB: www.fontrickdoor.com
SIC: 2431 1751 Doors & door parts & trim, wood; cabinet building & installation

(G-615)
GEORGIA-PACIFIC CORRUGARED LLC
4 Etreadeasy Ave (14020)
PHONE..................................585 343-3800
Andrew Perkins, *Manager*
Cherry Jim, *Maintence Staff*
EMP: 65
SALES (est): 10.9MM
SALES (corp-wide): 40.6B **Privately Held**
WEB: www.gp.com
SIC: 2611 Pulp manufactured from waste or recycled paper
HQ: Georgia-Pacific Llc
133 Peachtree St Nw
Atlanta GA 30303
404 652-4000

(G-616)
GRAHAM CORPORATION (PA)
20 Florence Ave (14020-3318)
PHONE..................................585 343-2216
James J Malvaso, *Ch of Bd*
James R Lines, *President*
Jeffrey Glajch, *Vice Pres*
Alan E Smith, *Vice Pres*
Richard Derosa, *Project Mgr*
◆ EMP: 269
SQ FT: 45,000
SALES (est): 91.8MM **Publicly Held**
WEB: www.graham-mfg.com
SIC: 3563 3585 3443 Vacuum pumps, except laboratory; compressors for refrigeration & air conditioning equipment; condensers, refrigeration; heat exchangers, condensers & components; heat exchangers, plate type; heat exchangers: coolers (after, inter), condensers, etc.

(G-617)
HEATH MANUFACTURING COMPANY
Also Called: Heath Outdoors Products
700 Elliott St (14020-3744)
PHONE..................................800 444-3140
EMP: 6

SALES (corp-wide): 50.1MM **Privately Held**
SIC: 2048 Bird food, prepared
HQ: Heath Manufacturing Company
140 Mill St Ste A
Coopersville MI 49404
616 997-8181

(G-618)
HODGINS ENGRAVING CO INC
3817 W Main Street Rd (14020-9402)
P.O. Box 728 (14021-0728)
PHONE..................................585 343-4444
Robert Hodgins, *President*
Kathleen Dixson, *President*
Becky Hodgins, *Cust Mgr*
◆ EMP: 70
SQ FT: 36,000
SALES (est): 12.7MM **Privately Held**
WEB: www.hodginsengraving.com
SIC: 3555 3953 Printing trades machinery; marking devices

(G-619)
LICKITY SPLITS
238 East Ave (14020-2704)
PHONE..................................585 345-6091
Fred Hamilton, *Partner*
Craig Hargrades, *Partner*
EMP: 8
SALES (est): 508K **Privately Held**
SIC: 2024 Ice cream & frozen desserts

(G-620)
MONDELEZ GLOBAL LLC
Also Called: Nabisco
4303 Federal Dr (14020-4105)
PHONE..................................585 345-3300
Phil Barter, *Branch Mgr*
Karen Holmstrom, *Manager*
Anthony Del Duca, *Maintence Staff*
EMP: 9 **Publicly Held**
SIC: 2099 5141 Food preparations; groceries, general line
HQ: Mondelez Global Llc
3 N Pkwy Ste 300
Deerfield IL 60015
847 943-4000

(G-621)
N Y WESTERN CONCRETE CORP
638 E Main St (14020-2812)
PHONE..................................585 343-6850
Joseph Penepent, *President*
Eugene Penepent, *Vice Pres*
Vincent Penepent, *Treasurer*
EMP: 5 EST: 1950
SQ FT: 2,000
SALES (est): 1.3MM **Privately Held**
SIC: 3273 Ready-mixed concrete

(G-622)
O-AT-KA MILK PRODUCTS COOP INC (PA)
700 Ellicott St (14020-3744)
P.O. Box 718 (14021-0718)
PHONE..................................585 343-0536
Robert Hall, *CEO*
Herbert Nobles, *Ch of Bd*
Bill Schreiber, *COO*
Dan Wolf, *COO*
Daniel Plinski, *Vice Pres*
◆ EMP: 277 EST: 1956
SQ FT: 205,000
SALES: 319.3MM **Privately Held**
WEB: www.oatkamilk.com
SIC: 2023 2021 2026 Concentrated skim milk; evaporated milk; dried nonfat milk; creamery butter; fluid milk

(G-623)
PINNACLE MANUFACTURING CO INC
56 Harvester Ave (14020-3357)
P.O. Box 1446 (14021-1446)
PHONE..................................585 343-5664
Kim Kisiel, *President*
Kevin Kisiel, *Vice Pres*
Luis Pulvino, *Plant Mgr*
▲ EMP: 25
SQ FT: 35,000

SALES (est): 5.9MM **Privately Held**
WEB: www.pinnaclemanufacturing.com
SIC: 3363 3364 Aluminum die-castings; zinc & zinc-base alloy die-castings

(G-624)
SEVEN SPRINGS GRAVEL PDTS LLC
8479 Seven Springs Rd (14020-9632)
PHONE..................................585 343-4336
Mike Doyle,
Carmen Pariso,
EMP: 6
SALES (est): 570K **Privately Held**
SIC: 1442 Gravel mining

(G-625)
STRONG FORGE & FABRICATION
20 Liberty St (14020-3208)
P.O. Box 803 (14021-0803)
PHONE..................................585 343-5251
Mitchell Strong, *President*
Brian Delillo, *Manager*
Deb Buchinger, *Executive*
EMP: 37
SALES (est): 7.2MM **Privately Held**
WEB: www.strongforge.com
SIC: 3599 Machine shop, jobbing & repair

(G-626)
SUMMIT LUBRICANTS INC
4d Treadeasy Ave (14020-3010)
P.O. Box 966 (14021-0966)
PHONE..................................585 815-0798
Ronald Krol, *President*
Danielle Brinkman, *Administration*
Cindy Turner,
▲ EMP: 47
SQ FT: 50,000
SALES (est): 14.7MM
SALES (corp-wide): 867.5MM **Publicly Held**
WEB: www.summitlubricants.com
SIC: 2992 Lubricating oils & greases
PA: Quaker Chemical Corporation
1 Quaker Park
Conshohocken PA 19428
610 832-4000

(G-627)
TOMPKINS METAL FINISHING INC
6 Apollo Dr (14020-3002)
PHONE..................................585 344-2600
Allen C Tompkins, *President*
John Tompkins, *Vice Pres*
John Abdoo, *Prdtn Mgr*
Bill Schuler, *Safety Mgr*
Jim McCarrick, *Engineer*
EMP: 80
SALES (est): 14.6MM **Privately Held**
SIC: 3471 Electroplating of metals or formed products

(G-628)
TRACO MANUFACTURING INC
4300 Commerce Dr (14020-4102)
PHONE..................................585 343-2434
Tracy Jachimowicz, *President*
Daniel Jachimowicz, *Vice Pres*
Alicia Jachimowicz, *Office Mgr*
EMP: 5
SQ FT: 16,500
SALES (est): 640.2K **Privately Held**
WEB: www.tracomfg.com
SIC: 2542 Partitions & fixtures, except wood

(G-629)
VISUAL IMPACT GRAPHICS INC
653 Ellicott St Ste 6 (14020-3746)
P.O. Box 236, Byron (14422-0236)
PHONE..................................585 548-7118
Tom Chapell, *President*
EMP: 6
SALES (est): 527.9K **Privately Held**
WEB: www.visualimpactonline.com
SIC: 3993 Signs & advertising specialties

Bath
Steuben County

(G-630)
BABCOCK CO INC
36 Delaware Ave (14810-1607)
PHONE..................................607 776-3341
Mark McConnell, *President*
J Ward McConnell, *Chairman*
Richard Hargraves, *Finance Mgr*
Valerie Boughey, *Officer*
EMP: 25
SQ FT: 107,000
SALES (est): 4.9MM **Privately Held**
SIC: 2499 Ladders, wood

(G-631)
BOMBARDIER TRNSP HOLDINGS USA
7940 State Route 415 (14810-7571)
PHONE..................................607 776-4791
Carl Drum, *Branch Mgr*
EMP: 60
SALES (corp-wide): 16.2B **Privately Held**
SIC: 3441 8711 3799 3585 Fabricated structural metal; engineering services; cars, off-highway: electric; refrigeration & heating equipment; electrical apparatus & equipment; electrical equipment & supplies
HQ: Bombardier Transportation (Holdings) Usa Inc.
1251 Waterfront Pl
Pittsburgh PA 15222
412 655-5700

(G-632)
CLARK SPECIALTY CO INC
36 Delaware Ave (14810-1607)
PHONE..................................607 776-3193
James L Presley, *Ch of Bd*
Robert Abbey, *Purch Mgr*
Susan Weaver, *Admin Sec*
EMP: 37 EST: 1946
SALES (est): 5.9MM **Privately Held**
WEB: www.clarkspecialty.com
SIC: 2542 3444 Telephone booths: except wood; sheet metalwork

(G-633)
GATEHOUSE MEDIA LLC
Also Called: Steuben Courier Advocate
10 W Steuben St (14810-1512)
PHONE..................................607 776-2121
Karen Causer, *Manager*
EMP: 7
SQ FT: 3,700
SALES (corp-wide): 1.5B **Privately Held**
WEB: www.gatehousemedia.com
SIC: 2711 Newspapers, publishing & printing
HQ: Gatehouse Media, Llc
175 Sullys Trl Fl 3
Pittsford NY 14534
585 598-0030

(G-634)
HANGER PRSTHETCS & ORTHO INC
47 W Steuben St (14810-1540)
PHONE..................................607 776-8013
Erico Webster, *General Mgr*
EMP: 7
SALES (corp-wide): 1B **Publicly Held**
SIC: 3842 Surgical appliances & supplies
HQ: Hanger Prosthetics & Orthotics, Inc.
10910 Domain Dr Ste 300
Austin TX 78758
512 777-3800

(G-635)
HANSON AGGREGATES NEW YORK LLC
7235 Sandpit Rd (14810-8172)
PHONE..................................607 776-7945
Dan Stone, *Manager*
EMP: 15
SALES (corp-wide): 20.6B **Privately Held**
SIC: 3273 Ready-mixed concrete
HQ: Hanson Aggregates New York Llc
8505 Freport Pkwy Ste 500
Irving TX 75063

G E O G R A P H I C

(G-636)
KEELER SERVICES
47 W Steuben St Ste 4 (14810-1540)
PHONE..........................607 776-5757
Mathew Keeler, *Owner*
EMP: 6
SQ FT: 6,270
SALES (est): 412.1K **Privately Held**
SIC: 3585 Heating & air conditioning combination units

(G-637)
KNIGHT STTLEMENT SAND GRAV LLC
7291 County Route 15 (14810-8245)
P.O. Box 191 (14810-0191)
PHONE..........................607 776-2048
Bryan Dickson,
Brett Dickson,
L Jay Dickson,
EMP: 38
SQ FT: 9,408
SALES: 6.3MM **Privately Held**
SIC: 3273 Ready-mixed concrete

(G-638)
LANE ENTERPRISES INC
Also Called: Lane Metal Products
16 May St (14810-9716)
PHONE..........................607 776-3366
Richard A Walter, *Manager*
EMP: 10
SQ FT: 18,416
SALES (corp-wide): 71.1MM **Privately Held**
WEB: www.lanepipe.com
SIC: 3443 Culverts, metal plate
PA: Lane Enterprises, Inc.
　3905 Hartzdale Dr Ste 514
　Camp Hill PA 17011
　717 761-8175

(G-639)
PHILIPS ELEC N AMER CORP
Philips Lighting
7265 State Route 54 (14810-9586)
PHONE..........................607 776-3692
Tony Stuart, *Manager*
EMP: 110
SALES (corp-wide): 20.8B **Privately Held**
WEB: www.usa.philips.com
SIC: 3645 3641 Residential lighting fixtures; electric lamps
HQ: Philips North America Llc
　3000 Minuteman Rd Ms1203
　Andover MA 01810
　978 659-3000

(G-640)
SMART SYSTEMS INC
320 E Washington St (14810-1323)
P.O. Box 158, Bohemia (11716-0158)
PHONE..........................607 776-5380
EMP: 20
SALES (est): 2.2MM **Privately Held**
SIC: 3711 5012 Mfg Motor Vehicle/Car Bodies Whol Autos/Motor Vehicles

---

Bay Shore
Suffolk County

(G-641)
3DFLAM INC
Also Called: LPI Envelope
1460 N Clinton Ave Ste I9 (11706-4057)
PHONE..........................631 647-2694
Frank Owad, *President*
Victoria Heikkila, *Treasurer*
EMP: 10 EST: 2008
SQ FT: 7,500
SALES (est): 1.9MM **Privately Held**
SIC: 2677 Envelopes

(G-642)
ABS TALKX INC
34 Cleveland Ave (11706-1223)
PHONE..........................631 254-9100
EMP: 8
SQ FT: 7,300
SALES (est): 1.2MM **Privately Held**
SIC: 3661 5999 4813 Mfg
Telephone/Telegraph Apparatus Ret Misc Merchandise Telephone Communications

(G-643)
ADEPTRONICS INCORPORATED
Also Called: Ziptswitch
281 Skip Ln Ste C (11706-1215)
PHONE..........................631 667-0659
EMP: 6
SALES: 850K **Privately Held**
SIC: 3625 Mfg Relays/Industrial Controls

(G-644)
AIR INDUSTRIES GROUP (PA)
1460 5th Ave (11706-4147)
PHONE..........................631 881-4920
Luciano Melluzzo, *CEO*
Michael N Taglich, *Chairman*
Michael E Recca, *CFO*
EMP: 53
SALES: 46.3MM **Publicly Held**
SIC: 3728 Aircraft body assemblies & parts; aircraft landing assemblies & brakes; aircraft assemblies, subassemblies & parts

(G-645)
AIR INDUSTRIES MACHINING CORP
1460 5th Ave (11706-4147)
PHONE..........................631 328-7000
Michael N Taglich, *Ch of Bd*
Luciano Melluzzo, *President*
▲ EMP: 115
SQ FT: 76,000
SALES (est): 19.3MM **Publicly Held**
SIC: 3728 Aircraft assemblies, subassemblies & parts
PA: Air Industries Group
　1460 5th Ave
　Bay Shore NY 11706

(G-646)
ALL STAR CARTS & VEHICLES INC
1565 5th Industrial Ct B (11706-3434)
PHONE..........................631 666-5581
Steven Kronrad, *President*
Gregory Kronrad, *Vice Pres*
Robert Kronrad, *Vice Pres*
EMP: 51
SQ FT: 25,000
SALES (est): 7.8MM **Privately Held**
WEB: www.allstarcarts.com
SIC: 2599 3792 3444 2451 Carts, restaurant equipment; travel trailers & campers; sheet metalwork; mobile homes

(G-647)
AMERICA NY RI WANG FD GROUP CO (PA)
30 Inez Dr (11706-2204)
PHONE..........................631 231-8999
Lian You Ye, *President*
Rita Sung, *Vice Pres*
Eddie Leung, *Senior Mgr*
▲ EMP: 38 EST: 2009
SALES: 10MM **Privately Held**
SIC: 2038 Ethnic foods, frozen

(G-648)
AMERICAN CHALLENGE ENTERPRISES
60 Corbin Ave Ste N (11706-1046)
PHONE..........................631 595-7171
Robert Laker Sr, *Ch of Bd*
Robert J Laker Jr, *President*
Bruce Laker, *Vice Pres*
▲ EMP: 5
SALES (est): 778.1K **Privately Held**
SIC: 2329 2339 Men's & boys' athletic uniforms; uniforms, athletic: women's, misses' & juniors'

(G-649)
AMERICAN PRIDE FASTENERS LLC
195 S Fehr Way (11706-1207)
PHONE..........................631 940-8292
Lynda Zacpal, *President*
George W Hughes III, *Vice Pres*
Nicholas Zacpal, *QC Mgr*
Anthony Manno, *Sales Mgr*
Kathy Sheridan, *Office Mgr*
▲ EMP: 20
SQ FT: 10,000

SALES: 4.2MM **Privately Held**
SIC: 3965 3452 5085 Fasteners; bolts, nuts, rivets & washers; fasteners & fastening equipment

(G-650)
ANBRIELLA SAND & GRAVEL CORP
145 S 4th St (11706-1230)
PHONE..........................631 586-2111
Ricky Starr, *President*
EMP: 42
SALES (est): 2MM **Privately Held**
SIC: 3273 Ready-mixed concrete

(G-651)
ANTENNA & RADOME RES ASSOC (PA)
15 Harold Ct (11706-2220)
P.O. Box 113, Old Bethpage (11804-0113)
PHONE..........................631 231-8400
Florence Isaacson, *President*
EMP: 50
SQ FT: 20,000
SALES (est): 19.6MM **Privately Held**
WEB: www.arra.com
SIC: 3679 Microwave components

(G-652)
ARTISTIC IRON WORKS INC
94 Saxon Ave Ste A (11706-7005)
PHONE..........................631 665-4285
Rick Portera, *President*
EMP: 8
SQ FT: 5,500
SALES: 1.5MM **Privately Held**
SIC: 3446 3312 2431 Stairs, fire escapes, balconies, railings & ladders; rails, steel or iron; staircases, stairs & railings

(G-653)
ASTRO ELECTROPLATING INC
171 4th Ave (11706-7303)
PHONE..........................631 968-0656
Neil Weinstein, *CEO*
John Jodoin, *Opers Mgr*
Jennifer Calderone, *Human Resources*
Rebecca Koretz, *Human Resources*
Nicole Wright, *Manager*
EMP: 38
SALES (est): 5MM **Privately Held**
SIC: 3471 Electroplating of metals or formed products

(G-654)
AWE TECHNOLOGIES LLC
261 W Main St (11706-8319)
PHONE..........................631 747-8448
Peter G Espina, *CEO*
Dipen N Sinha, *CTO*
William R Wheeler, *Exec Dir*
EMP: 5
SALES (est): 424.8K **Privately Held**
SIC: 3826 3829 5047 Analytical instruments; measuring & controlling devices; medical & hospital equipment

(G-655)
BAIRD MOLD MAKING INC
195 N Fehr Way Ste C (11706-1234)
PHONE..........................631 667-0322
John Baird, *President*
▲ EMP: 6
SQ FT: 3,000
SALES (est): 803.6K **Privately Held**
SIC: 3089 Molding primary plastic; injection molding of plastics

(G-656)
BFG MARINE INC
200 Candlewood Rd (11706-2217)
PHONE..........................631 586-5500
Glenn Burgos, *President*
Ellis W Konkel III, *Vice Pres*
Stanley Solow, *Manager*
EMP: 10 EST: 1959
SQ FT: 20,000
SALES (est): 2.3MM **Privately Held**
WEB: www.bfgmarine.com
SIC: 3429 5085 Marine hardware; industrial supplies

(G-657)
BIMBO BAKERIES USA INC
Also Called: Transportation Department
14 Spence St (11706-2207)
PHONE..........................631 951-5183
Phil Paturzo, *Vice Pres*
Anthony Maiorano, *Branch Mgr*
EMP: 32 **Privately Held**
WEB: www.gwbakeries.com
SIC: 2051 Bread, cake & related products
HQ: Bimbo Bakeries Usa, Inc
　255 Business Center Dr # 200
　Horsham PA 19044
　215 347-5500

(G-658)
BIMBO BAKERIES USA INC
30 Inez Dr (11706-2204)
PHONE..........................203 531-2311
James Montgomery, *Branch Mgr*
EMP: 50 **Privately Held**
WEB: www.englishmuffin.com
SIC: 2051 Doughnuts, except frozen; cakes, bakery: except frozen; pies, bakery: except frozen
HQ: Bimbo Bakeries Usa, Inc
　255 Business Center Dr # 200
　Horsham PA 19044
　215 347-5500

(G-659)
BONDY PRINTING CORP
Also Called: Sir Speedy
267 W Main St (11706-8319)
PHONE..........................631 242-1510
William Bondy Jr, *President*
Donna Bondy, *Vice Pres*
EMP: 5
SALES (est): 780.1K **Privately Held**
SIC: 2752 2791 2789 2759 Commercial printing, lithographic; typesetting; bookbinding & related work; commercial printing; automotive & apparel trimmings

(G-660)
CABLE MANAGEMENT SOLUTIONS INC
Also Called: Jette Group
291 Skip Ln (11706-1206)
PHONE..........................631 674-0004
Roger Jette, *President*
▲ EMP: 30
SQ FT: 3,500
SALES (est): 7.1MM **Privately Held**
WEB: www.snaketray.com
SIC: 3496 Miscellaneous fabricated wire products

(G-661)
CENTURY METAL PARTS CORP
230 S Fehr Way (11706-1208)
PHONE..........................631 667-0800
Frank Swierzbin, *President*
Thomas Larkin, *IT/INT Sup*
EMP: 25
SQ FT: 17,000
SALES (est): 4MM **Privately Held**
SIC: 3663 3451 Antennas, transmitting & communications; screw machine products

(G-662)
CHEM-TEK SYSTEMS INC
Also Called: Moldedtanks.com
208 S Fehr Way (11706-1208)
P.O. Box 222, Nesconset (11767-0222)
PHONE..........................631 253-3010
Shawn Sprague, *President*
EMP: 10
SQ FT: 4,000
SALES (est): 1MM **Privately Held**
SIC: 3089 Plastic & fiberglass tanks

(G-663)
CLAD METAL SPECIALTIES INC
1516 5th Industrial Ct (11706-3402)
PHONE..........................631 666-7750
Denise Marcoccia, *Exec VP*
Dominick Bodami, *Vice Pres*
EMP: 19
SQ FT: 13,500
SALES (est): 3.9MM **Privately Held**
WEB: www.cladmetal.com
SIC: 3479 Bonderizing of metal or metal products

▲ = Import ▼ =Export
◆ =Import/Export

(G-664)
COLONIAL LABEL SYSTEMS INC
Also Called: Colonial Rapid
50 Corbin Ave Ste L (11706-1047)
P.O. Box 812, Deer Park (11729-0976)
PHONE 631 254-0111
Ron Afzelius, *President*
EMP: 25
SALES (est): 4MM **Privately Held**
SIC: 2759 Commercial printing

(G-665)
COLONIE PLASTICS CORP
188 Candlewood Rd (11706-2219)
PHONE 631 434-6969
Paul Gurbatri, *President*
Laura Arzeno, *Opers Mgr*
Louie Passi, *Manager*
▲ EMP: 130
SQ FT: 11,500
SALES (est): 14.9MM **Privately Held**
WEB: www.colonieplastics.com
SIC: 3089 Injection molded finished plastic products

(G-666)
COLORFULLY YOURS INC
11 Grant Ave (11706-1007)
PHONE 631 242-8600
Joseph Lindner, *President*
Deborah Lindner, *Vice Pres*
EMP: 10
SQ FT: 5,000
SALES: 1.2MM **Privately Held**
WEB: www.colorfullyyours.com
SIC: 2752 Commercial printing, offset

(G-667)
COMMAND COMPONENTS CORPORATION
6 Cherry St (11706-7325)
PHONE 631 666-4411
Jerry Sukman, *President*
EMP: 8
SQ FT: 3,000
SALES (est): 1.2MM **Privately Held**
WEB: www.commandcomponents.com
SIC: 3643 Electric connectors

(G-668)
CYNCAL STEEL FABRICATORS INC
225 Pine Aire Dr (11706-1147)
PHONE 631 254-5600
Cynthia Callahan, *Owner*
EMP: 12 EST: 2014
SALES (est): 1.2MM **Privately Held**
SIC: 3441 Fabricated structural metal

(G-669)
D K P WOOD RAILINGS & STAIRS
1971 Union Blvd (11706-7956)
PHONE 631 665-8656
Dmitri Onishchuk, *President*
EMP: 11
SALES (est): 1MM **Privately Held**
SIC: 2431 Stair railings, wood

(G-670)
DAVID PEYSER SPORTSWEAR INC (PA)
Also Called: Weatherproof
90 Spence St (11706-2230)
P.O. Box 9171 (11706-9171)
PHONE 631 231-7788
Paul Peyser, *President*
Joshua Peyser, *Corp Secy*
Alan Peyser, *Vice Pres*
Pam Tyburski, *Manager*
▲ EMP: 245
SQ FT: 110,000
SALES (est): 88MM **Privately Held**
WEB: www.mvsport.com
SIC: 2329 Men's & boys' sportswear & athletic clothing

(G-671)
DECAL TECHNIQUES INC
40 Corbin Ave Ste I (11706-1048)
PHONE 631 491-1800
Eugene P Snyder, *President*
Terry Lomanto, *Vice Pres*

Helen Rider, *Admin Sec*
EMP: 8
SQ FT: 4,000
SALES (est): 600K **Privately Held**
WEB: www.decaltech.com
SIC: 2752 Decals, lithographed; posters, lithographed

(G-672)
DEER PARK SAND & GRAVEL CORP
145 S 4th St (11706-1200)
PHONE 631 586-2323
David Ciardullo, *President*
Joe Ciardullo, *Vice Pres*
Wendy Larose, *Bookkeeper*
EMP: 20
SQ FT: 4,000
SALES (est): 3.6MM **Privately Held**
SIC: 3273 5032 Ready-mixed concrete; gravel; sand, construction

(G-673)
DELTA POLYMERS INC
130 S 2nd St (11706-1036)
PHONE 631 254-6240
Razia Rana, *President*
Riasat Rana, *Vice Pres*
Shazia Rana, *Engineer*
EMP: 8
SQ FT: 10,000
SALES (est): 1.5MM **Privately Held**
WEB: www.deltapolymers.com
SIC: 2851 1752 Epoxy coatings; floor laying & floor work

(G-674)
DURO DYNE CORPORATION (HQ)
81 Spence St (11706-2206)
P.O. Box 9117 (11706-9117)
PHONE 631 249-9000
Randall Hinden, *President*
Eric Johannesen, *General Mgr*
Mike Peluso, *Manager*
Stephen Trant, *Info Tech Dir*
▲ EMP: 150 EST: 1952
SQ FT: 130,000
SALES (est): 34.2MM
SALES (corp-wide): 122.1MM **Privately Held**
SIC: 3585 Air conditioning equipment, complete; heating equipment, complete
PA: Dyne Duro National Corp
81 Spence St
Bay Shore NY 11706
631 249-9000

(G-675)
DURO DYNE MACHINERY CORP
81 Spence St (11706-2206)
P.O. Box 9117 (11706-9117)
PHONE 631 249-9000
Milton Hinden, *CEO*
Randall Hinden, *President*
Carole D'Agosta, *Vice Pres*
William Watman, *Vice Pres*
◆ EMP: 40
SQ FT: 25,000
SALES (est): 9.8MM
SALES (corp-wide): 122.1MM **Privately Held**
SIC: 3585 Air conditioning units, complete: domestic or industrial; heating equipment, complete
PA: Dyne Duro National Corp
81 Spence St
Bay Shore NY 11706
631 249-9000

(G-676)
DURO DYNE NATIONAL CORP (PA)
81 Spence St (11706-2206)
P.O. Box 9117 (11706-9117)
PHONE 631 249-9000
Randall Hinden, *President*
Bernard Hinden, *Director*
◆ EMP: 125
SQ FT: 35,000
SALES (est): 122.1MM **Privately Held**
SIC: 3585 Air conditioning equipment, complete; heating equipment, complete

(G-677)
E F IRON WORKS & CONSTRUCTION
241 N Fehr Way Ste 3 (11706-1233)
PHONE 631 242-4766
Ed Frage, *President*
EMP: 6
SALES: 390K **Privately Held**
WEB: www.efiron.com
SIC: 3446 1799 Architectural metalwork; ornamental metal work

(G-678)
EMPIRE INDUSTRIAL SYSTEMS CORP (PA)
40 Corbin Ave (11706-1048)
PHONE 631 242-4619
Shali Roufberg, *President*
EMP: 10
SQ FT: 7,500
SALES (est): 1.1MM **Privately Held**
SIC: 3443 1711 7699 3441 Boilers: industrial, power, or marine; boiler & furnace contractors; boiler repair shop; fabricated structural metal

(G-679)
EUR-PAC CORPORATION
1460 5th Ave (11706-4147)
PHONE 203 756-0102
Peter Rand, *Vice Pres*
Richard Rand, *Vice Pres*
EMP: 9 EST: 1947
SALES (est): 1.5MM **Publicly Held**
SIC: 3724 Aircraft engines & engine parts
PA: Air Industries Group
1460 5th Ave
Bay Shore NY 11706

(G-680)
FOOD BASKET USA COMPANY LTD
30 Inez Dr (11706-2204)
PHONE 631 231-8999
Charlie Gao, *Principal*
Eddie Leung, *CFO*
EMP: 20 EST: 2015
SALES (est): 891K **Privately Held**
SIC: 2038 Frozen specialties

(G-681)
FRED M LAWRENCE CO INC (PA)
Also Called: Lawrece Frames
45 Drexel Dr (11706-2201)
PHONE 631 617-6853
Vincent Lanci, *President*
Christopher Lanci, *President*
▲ EMP: 26
SQ FT: 25,000
SALES (est): 4MM **Privately Held**
WEB: www.photoframes.net
SIC: 2499 Picture & mirror frames, wood

(G-682)
INTER MOLDS INC
26 Cleveland Ave (11706-1223)
PHONE 631 667-8580
Victor Goncalves, *President*
Francisco Silva, *Vice Pres*
Douglas Cooper, *Treasurer*
Mario Santiago, *Admin Sec*
EMP: 6
SQ FT: 5,000
SALES (est): 700K **Privately Held**
WEB: www.intermolds.com
SIC: 3544 Forms (molds), for foundry & plastics working machinery

(G-683)
INTERFACE PRODUCTS CO INC
215 N Fehr Way Ste C (11706-1209)
PHONE 631 242-4605
George Miller, *President*
Mary Ann Harrell, *Office Mgr*
EMP: 8
SQ FT: 2,125
SALES (est): 770K **Privately Held**
SIC: 3534 Elevators & equipment

(G-684)
ISLIP MINITURE GOLF
500 E Main St (11706-8502)
PHONE 631 940-8900
Mike Flemming,

EMP: 8
SALES (est): 355.8K **Privately Held**
SIC: 3999 Miniatures

(G-685)
JERRY CARDULLO IRON WORKS INC
Also Called: Cardullo, J Iron Works
101 Spence St (11706-2208)
PHONE 631 242-8881
Jerry Cardullo, *President*
EMP: 12
SQ FT: 3,000
SALES (est): 880K **Privately Held**
SIC: 3446 Architectural metalwork

(G-686)
KENNEY MANUFACTURING DISPLAYS
Also Called: Kenny Mfg
1062 Bay Shore Ave (11706-2706)
PHONE 631 231-5563
Robert Kenney Sr, *President*
Michael Kenney, *Vice Pres*
Cathy Richard, *Production*
Brian Ohara, *Purch Mgr*
Lance Clifton, *Buyer*
EMP: 11
SALES (est): 1.8MM **Privately Held**
WEB: www.kenneydisplays.com
SIC: 3089 3578 Plastic containers, except foam; point-of-sale devices

(G-687)
LAMINATED WINDOW PRODUCTS INC
211 N Fehr Way (11706-1203)
PHONE 631 242-6883
Ismael Santiago, *President*
EMP: 10
SQ FT: 4,000
SALES: 800K **Privately Held**
SIC: 2391 2394 Draperies, plastic & textile: from purchased materials; shades, canvas: made from purchased materials

(G-688)
LANWOOD INDUSTRIES INC
Also Called: Fred Lawrence Co
45 Drexel Dr (11706-2201)
PHONE 718 786-3000
EMP: 30
SQ FT: 25,000
SALES (est): 193.4K **Privately Held**
SIC: 2499 2782 Mfg Wood Products Mfg Blankbooks/Binders

(G-689)
LASTICKS AEROSPACE INC
35 Washington Ave Ste E (11706-1027)
PHONE 631 242-8484
Guy T Russo, *President*
Keith Johns, *Vice Pres*
Luciano De Biassi, *QC Mgr*
EMP: 14
SQ FT: 5,000
SALES (est): 2.9MM **Privately Held**
WEB: www.lasticksaero.com
SIC: 3599 Machine shop, jobbing & repair

(G-690)
LEXAN INDUSTRIES INC
Also Called: Struthers Electronics
15 Harold Ct (11706-2220)
PHONE 631 434-7586
Florence Isaacson, *President*
EMP: 19
SQ FT: 11,000
SALES (est): 1.3MM **Privately Held**
SIC: 3679 3825 Microwave components; test equipment for electronic & electrical circuits

(G-691)
MBA ORTHOTICS INC
60 Corbin Ave Unit 60g (11706-1046)
PHONE 631 392-4755
Andrea Tamayo, *President*
Adriana Salcedo, *General Mgr*
EMP: 5
SALES: 300K **Privately Held**
SIC: 3131 Sole parts for shoes

(G-692)
MILEX PRECISION INC
66 S 2nd St Ste G (11706-1000)
PHONE.................................631 595-2393
Aeric Misko, *President*
Dagmar Misko, *Vice Pres*
EMP: 14
SQ FT: 4,000
SALES: 1.5MM **Privately Held**
SIC: 3728 3599 Aircraft parts & equipment; machine shop, jobbing & repair

(G-693)
MINICO INDUSTRIES INC
66a S 2nd St Ste A (11706)
PHONE.................................631 595-1455
Nicholas Chonis, *President*
Constantine Chonis, *Vice Pres*
Michael Chonis, *Treasurer*
EMP: 9
SQ FT: 4,500
SALES (est): 1.3MM **Privately Held**
WEB: www.minicoindustries.com
SIC: 3089 Injection molding of plastics

(G-694)
MOSTLY MICA INC
77 Cleveland Ave Ste A (11706-1239)
PHONE.................................631 586-4200
Alex Sanchez, *President*
Ron Sanchez, *Office Mgr*
EMP: 5
SQ FT: 1,500
SALES: 914K **Privately Held**
WEB: www.mostlymica.com
SIC: 2434 Wood kitchen cabinets

(G-695)
MV CORP INC
Also Called: M V Sport
88 Spence St Ste 90 (11706-2229)
P.O. Box 9171 (11706-9171)
PHONE.................................631 273-8020
Joshua Peyser, *Ch of Bd*
Alan Peyser, *Principal*
Paul Peyser, *Principal*
Todd Ferris, *Opers Mgr*
David Chin, *Assistant*
▲ EMP: 150
SQ FT: 40,000
SALES (est): 15.5MM
SALES (corp-wide): 88MM **Privately Held**
WEB: www.mvsport.com
SIC: 2311 2262 2759 2339 Men's & boys' suits & coats; screen printing: man-made fiber & silk broadwoven fabrics; screen printing; women's & misses' outerwear
PA: David Peyser Sportswear, Inc.
   90 Spence St
   Bay Shore NY 11706
   631 231-7788

(G-696)
NASSAU SUFFOLK BRD OF WOMENS
145 New York Ave (11706-3209)
PHONE.................................631 666-8835
Cris McNamara, *President*
EMP: 50
SALES (est): 1.7MM **Privately Held**
SIC: 2387 Apparel belts

(G-697)
NASSAU TOOL WORKS INC
1479 N Clinton Ave (11706-4051)
PHONE.................................631 328-7031
Michael N Taglich, *Ch of Bd*
Luciano Melluzzo, *President*
EMP: 50
SQ FT: 60,000
SALES (est): 8.4MM **Publicly Held**
SIC: 3599 3728 Machine shop, jobbing & repair; aircraft landing assemblies & brakes
PA: Air Industries Group
   1460 5th Ave
   Bay Shore NY 11706

(G-698)
POLY SCIENTIFIC R&D CORP
70 Cleveland Ave (11706-1282)
PHONE.................................631 586-0400
John J Caggiano, *Ch of Bd*
John H Arnold, *Exec VP*

Joseph Caggiano, *Vice Pres*
EMP: 40 EST: 1969
SQ FT: 22,000
SALES (est): 8.8MM **Privately Held**
WEB: www.polyrnd.com
SIC: 2869 5169 2819 Industrial organic chemicals; chemicals & allied products; industrial inorganic chemicals

(G-699)
POLYCAST INDUSTRIES INC
130 S 2nd St (11706-1036)
PHONE.................................631 595-2530
Razia Rana, *President*
Riasat Rana, *Vice Pres*
EMP: 5
SQ FT: 100,000
SALES: 1MM **Privately Held**
SIC: 3679 2992 2891 2821 Electronic circuits; lubricating oils & greases; adhesives & sealants; plastics materials & resins

(G-700)
PRECISION METALS CORP
221 Skip Ln (11706-1206)
PHONE.................................631 586-5032
Thomas J Figlozzi, *Ch of Bd*
Anna Maria Figlozzi, *Corp Secy*
Tony Figlozzi, *Vice Pres*
EMP: 45
SQ FT: 16,000
SALES (est): 14.5MM **Privately Held**
WEB: www.precisionmetalscorp.com
SIC: 3441 3599 3444 Fabricated structural metal; machine & other job shop work; sheet metalwork

(G-701)
PRESTIGELINE INC
5 Inez Dr (11706-2203)
P.O. Box 100 (11706-0703)
PHONE.................................631 273-3636
Scott Roth, *President*
Stuart Goldstein, *Senior VP*
Kenneth Golden, *Vice Pres*
▲ EMP: 82 EST: 1949
SQ FT: 150,000
SALES (est): 11.1MM **Privately Held**
WEB: www.prestigelineinc.com
SIC: 3645 5063 Residential lighting fixtures; lighting fixtures, residential

(G-702)
PROTO MACHINE INC
60 Corbin Ave Ste D (11706-1046)
PHONE.................................631 392-1159
EMP: 11
SQ FT: 3,600
SALES: 1.2MM **Privately Held**
SIC: 3599 Machining Full Service Job Shop

(G-703)
R G FLAIR CO INC
199 S Fehr Way (11706-1207)
PHONE.................................631 586-7311
Gerhard Raible, *President*
Dieter Thole, *Corp Secy*
Martin Sievers, *Vice Pres*
Chris Thole, *Manager*
▲ EMP: 22
SQ FT: 13,000
SALES (est): 3.7MM **Privately Held**
WEB: www.rgflair.com
SIC: 3469 3915 Stamping metal for the trade; jewelers' materials & lapidary work

(G-704)
RAN MAR ENTERPRISES LTD
143 Anchor Ln (11706-8121)
PHONE.................................631 666-4754
EMP: 12
SQ FT: 13,000
SALES (est): 1.4MM **Privately Held**
SIC: 2891 Manufacturer Converter And Packaging Of Self-Stick Adhesive Products

(G-705)
RFN INC
44 Drexel Dr (11706-2202)
PHONE.................................516 764-5100
Alex Treyger, *President*
EMP: 18

SALES: 1.5MM **Privately Held**
SIC: 2759 8742 Commercial printing; marketing consulting services

(G-706)
RICHMAR PRINTING INC
44 Drexel Dr (11706-2202)
PHONE.................................631 617-6915
EMP: 5
SALES (corp-wide): 559K **Privately Held**
SIC: 2752 Commercial printing, lithographic
PA: Richmar Printing, Inc.
   480 Canal St Ste 400
   New York NY

(G-707)
RIT PRINTING CORP
250 N Fairway (11706)
PHONE.................................631 586-6220
Anthony Buono, *President*
EMP: 10
SQ FT: 8,000
SALES (est): 1.7MM **Privately Held**
WEB: www.ritprinting.com
SIC: 2752 2759 Commercial printing, offset; commercial printing

(G-708)
ROCKET TECH FUEL CORP
20 Corbin Ave (11706-1004)
PHONE.................................516 810-8947
Richard Miller, *President*
Joseph Silhan, *Vice Pres*
EMP: 10 EST: 2004
SQ FT: 1,800
SALES: 90MM **Privately Held**
SIC: 1311 Crude petroleum & natural gas

(G-709)
ROMAN STONE CONSTRUCTION CO
85 S 4th St (11706-1210)
PHONE.................................631 667-0566
Thomas Montalbine, *President*
Eric Johnson, *Engineer*
Layne Urbas, *Treasurer*
Ryan Camberdella, *Sales Mgr*
EMP: 45 EST: 1903
SQ FT: 25,000
SALES (est): 9.3MM **Privately Held**
WEB: www.romanstoneco.com
SIC: 3272 Pipe, concrete or lined with concrete

(G-710)
ROYAL WINDOWS MFG CORP
Also Called: Royal Windows and Doors
1769 5th Ave Unit A (11706-1735)
PHONE.................................631 435-8888
Solomos Hajicharalambous, *Ch of Bd*
George Efthymiou, *Treasurer*
Efthymios Efthymiou, *Controller*
Solon Efthymiou, *Manager*
EMP: 27
SQ FT: 60,000
SALES (est): 4.4MM **Privately Held**
WEB: www.royalwindow.com
SIC: 2431 5031 1751 Windows, wood; doors, wood; doors & windows; window & door (prefabricated) installation

(G-711)
RUBIES COSTUME COMPANY INC
Also Called: Collegeville Imagineering
158 Candlewood Rd (11706-2219)
PHONE.................................631 777-3300
EMP: 100
SALES (corp-wide): 464.8MM **Privately Held**
SIC: 2389 7299 Mfg Costumes
PA: Rubie's Costume Company, Inc.
   12008 Jamaica Ave
   Richmond Hill NY 11418
   718 846-1008

(G-712)
RUBIES COSTUME COMPANY INC
Also Called: Rubie's Distribution Center
1 Holloween Hwy (11706)
PHONE.................................631 951-3688
Marc Beige, *Manager*
EMP: 120

SALES (corp-wide): 366.5MM **Privately Held**
SIC: 2389 7299 Costumes; costume rental
PA: Rubie's Costume Company, Inc.
   12008 Jamaica Ave
   Richmond Hill NY 11418
   718 846-1008

(G-713)
RUBIES COSTUME COMPANY INC
158 Candlewood Rd (11706-2219)
PHONE.................................631 435-7912
Philip Nastasi, *Manager*
EMP: 10
SALES (corp-wide): 366.5MM **Privately Held**
SIC: 2389 Costumes
PA: Rubie's Costume Company, Inc.
   12008 Jamaica Ave
   Richmond Hill NY 11418
   718 846-1008

(G-714)
SIW INC
271 Skip Ln (11706-1206)
PHONE.................................631 888-0130
Lisa Gurcan, *President*
Dominic Amorosa, *Vice Pres*
Dominick Amorosa, *Vice Pres*
▲ EMP: 12
SQ FT: 11,500
SALES (est): 2.1MM **Privately Held**
SIC: 3449 Bars, concrete reinforcing: fabricated steel

(G-715)
SMART USA INC (PA)
1440 5th Ave (11706-4147)
PHONE.................................631 969-1111
Jim Soleiman, *Ch of Bd*
Yosi Soleimany, *Vice Pres*
EMP: 15
SALES (est): 2.3MM **Privately Held**
SIC: 2671 3365 Thermoplastic coated paper for packaging; cooking/kitchen utensils, cast aluminum

(G-716)
SNAKE TRAY INTERNATIONAL LLC
Also Called: Snake Tray
291 Skip Ln (11706-1206)
PHONE.................................631 674-0004
Roger Jette, *Mng Member*
▲ EMP: 50
SALES (est): 633.3K **Privately Held**
SIC: 3661 Telephone & telegraph apparatus

(G-717)
STANDARD INDUSTRIAL WORKS INC
271 Skip Ln (11706-1206)
PHONE.................................631 888-0130
Paul Spotts, *President*
EMP: 10
SQ FT: 11,800
SALES: 700K **Privately Held**
SIC: 3444 Sheet metalwork

(G-718)
SUFFOLK COPY CENTER INC
Also Called: Suffolk Printing
26 W Main St (11706-8383)
PHONE.................................631 665-0570
William Beitch, *President*
Charles Beitch, *Vice Pres*
Florence Beitch, *Treasurer*
Jaclyn Giunta, *Admin Asst*
EMP: 6 EST: 1971
SQ FT: 4,000
SALES (est): 947.6K **Privately Held**
WEB: www.suffolkprinting.com
SIC: 2752 Commercial printing, offset

(G-719)
SUMMIT MANUFACTURING LLC (HQ)
Also Called: Summit Plastics
100 Spence St (11706-2231)
PHONE.................................631 952-1570
Louis Marinello, *President*
Ping Hsia, *Vice Pres*
Jim Judson, *Director*

◆ EMP: 7 EST: 2015
SALES (est): 6MM
SALES (corp-wide): 211.6MM **Privately Held**
SIC: 3089 Plastic containers, except foam
PA: Array Canada Inc
45 Progress Ave
Scarborough ON M1P 2
416 299-4865

(G-720)
SUMNER INDUSTRIES INC
Also Called: Ateco Products
309 Orinoco Dr (11706-7111)
PHONE................................631 666-7290
Jonathan Sumner, *President*
▼ EMP: 15
SQ FT: 10,000
SALES (est): 3.2MM **Privately Held**
SIC: 3728 Aircraft parts & equipment

(G-721)
TAPE-IT INC
233 N Fehr Way (11706-1203)
PHONE................................631 243-4100
Arnold Rabinowitz, *President*
Rabinowitz Arnold, *Data Proc Staff*
Arnold Robinwitz, *Director*
◆ EMP: 50
SQ FT: 55,000
SALES (est): 14.8MM **Privately Held**
WEB: www.tapeit.com
SIC: 2672 5113 5122 Tape, pressure sensitive: made from purchased materials; pressure sensitive tape; drugs, proprietaries & sundries

(G-722)
TENSATOR INC
Also Called: Tensator Group
260 Spur Dr S (11706-3917)
P.O. Box 400 (11706-0779)
PHONE................................631 666-0300
Alan McPherson, *CEO*
David Cohen, *Business Mgr*
Richard Scarpelli, *Opers Staff*
Miryam Korn, *Senior Buyer*
Cindy Ferrer, *Credit Staff*
◆ EMP: 94
SQ FT: 81,000
SALES (est): 22.6MM
SALES (corp-wide): 30.8MM **Privately Held**
WEB: www.lawrencemetal.com
SIC: 3446 Ornamental metalwork
HQ: Tensator Group Limited
Unit 7 Danbury Court
Milton Keynes BUCKS MK14
190 868-4600

(G-723)
TROJAN METAL FABRICATION INC (PA)
Also Called: Trojan Powder Coating
2215 Union Blvd (11706-8015)
PHONE................................631 968-5040
Carl Troiano, *CEO*
Keith Rein, *Vice Pres*
Chris Banach, *Plant Mgr*
Claudia Troiano, *Office Mgr*
Francisco Rodriguez, *Manager*
EMP: 46
SQ FT: 80,000
SALES (est): 6.4MM **Privately Held**
WEB: www.trojanpowder.com
SIC: 3479 Coating of metals & formed products

(G-724)
ULTIMATE STYLES OF AMERICA
27 Garfield Ave Unit A (11706-1052)
PHONE................................631 254-0219
David Goldstein, *President*
EMP: 12
SQ FT: 4,000
SALES (est): 1.3MM **Privately Held**
SIC: 2499 5712 Kitchen, bathroom & household ware: wood; cabinet work, custom

(G-725)
WOOD TALK
Also Called: Woodtalk Stairs & Rails
203 N Fehr Way Ste C (11706-1235)
PHONE................................631 940-3085
Scott Braun, *Principal*

EMP: 5
SALES (est): 487.2K **Privately Held**
SIC: 2431 Staircases, stairs & railings

Bayport
Suffolk County

(G-726)
CARE ENTERPRISES INC
435 Renee Dr (11705-1237)
PHONE................................631 472-8155
Lina Torre, *Vice Pres*
EMP: 6
SALES (est): 650K **Privately Held**
SIC: 3822 Air conditioning & refrigeration controls

(G-727)
CGW CORP (PA)
102 S Gillette Ave (11705-2239)
PHONE................................631 472-6600
George Werner, *President*
EMP: 7
SALES: 800K **Privately Held**
WEB: www.cgwcorp.com
SIC: 3825 Network analyzers

(G-728)
CHIMNEY DOCTORS AMERICAS CORP
738a Montauk Hwy (11705-1621)
PHONE................................631 868-3586
Nicole Newberg, *President*
EMP: 5
SQ FT: 500
SALES (est): 275.3K **Privately Held**
SIC: 3259 3271 3272 1799 Clay chimney products; blocks, concrete: chimney or fireplace; fireplace & chimney material: concrete; prefabricated fireplace installation

(G-729)
NATURES BOUNTY CO
Capsuleworks
10 Vitamin Dr (11705-1115)
PHONE................................631 472-2817
Michelle Classi, *Purchasing*
Sean Byers, *Supervisor*
Jose Ruiz, *Supervisor*
Peter Tinson, *Supervisor*
Clelia Trejo, *Supervisor*
EMP: 18 **Publicly Held**
SIC: 2833 Vitamins, natural or synthetic: bulk, uncompounded
HQ: The Nature's Bounty Co
2100 Smithtown Ave
Ronkonkoma NY 11779
631 200-2000

(G-730)
PLASTIC SOLUTIONS INC
158 Schenck Ave (11705)
PHONE................................631 234-9013
AVI Ben-Bassat, *Ch of Bd*
EMP: 32
SALES (est): 4.6MM **Privately Held**
SIC: 3089 3544 Plastic containers, except foam; special dies, tools, jigs & fixtures

(G-731)
STICKERSHOPCOM INC
Also Called: Labels, Stickers and More
582 Middle Rd (11705-1900)
PHONE................................631 563-4323
Stacy Ianson, *CEO*
EMP: 5
SALES (est): 741.2K **Privately Held**
SIC: 2679 5999 3993 2759 Tags & labels, paper; banners, flags, decals & posters; letters for signs, metal; poster & decal printing & engraving

(G-732)
WENNER BREAD PRODUCTS INC
Also Called: Wenner Bakery
33 Rajon Rd (11705-1101)
PHONE................................800 869-6262
Nancy Coppola, *Sales Staff*
EMP: 14

SALES (corp-wide): 105.7MM **Privately Held**
SIC: 2051 Bread, cake & related products
PA: Wenner Bread Products, Inc.
2001 Orville Dr N
Ronkonkoma NY 11779
800 869-6262

Bayside
Queens County

(G-733)
A T A BAGEL SHOPPE INC
Also Called: Bagel Club
20814 Cross Island Pkwy (11360-1187)
PHONE................................718 352-4948
Anthony Lombardo, *President*
EMP: 5
SALES (est): 270K **Privately Held**
SIC: 2051 5812 5461 Bagels, fresh or frozen; eating places; bagels

(G-734)
ABSOLUTE FITNESS US CORP
21337 39th Ave Ste 322 (11361-2071)
PHONE................................732 979-8582
Salvatore Naimo, *CEO*
Dina Destafano, *Director*
EMP: 100
SALES (est): 4.7MM **Privately Held**
SIC: 3949 Sporting & athletic goods

(G-735)
BAGEL CLUB INC
20521 35th Ave (11361-1245)
PHONE................................718 423-6106
Rosa Lombardo, *President*
EMP: 13
SALES (est): 1.5MM **Privately Held**
SIC: 2051 Bagels, fresh or frozen

(G-736)
CANAAN PRINTING INC
20007 46th Ave (11361-3018)
PHONE................................718 729-3100
Sang Miung Kim, *President*
EMP: 10 EST: 1980
SQ FT: 5,000
SALES (est): 840K **Privately Held**
WEB: www.canaanprinting.com
SIC: 2752 Commercial printing, offset

(G-737)
FREEMAN TECHNOLOGY INC
2355 Bell Blvd Apt 2h (11360-2051)
PHONE................................732 829-8345
Tim Freeman, *President*
EMP: 20 EST: 2012
SQ FT: 1,500
SALES: 2MM
SALES (corp-wide): 79.8MM **Privately Held**
SIC: 3829 Measuring & controlling devices
HQ: Freeman Technology Limited
1 Miller Court
Tewkesbury GLOS

(G-738)
G PESSO & SONS INC
20320 35th Ave (11361-1110)
PHONE................................718 224-9130
EMP: 8
SALES (est): 537.2K **Privately Held**
SIC: 2024 Ice cream, bulk

(G-739)
KASTOR CONSULTING INC
3919 218th St (11361-2331)
PHONE................................718 224-9109
Greg Manaris, *President*
EMP: 9
SALES (est): 780K **Privately Held**
WEB: www.kastor.com
SIC: 7372 Prepackaged software

(G-740)
NATIONAL PROSTHETIC ORTHOT
21441 42nd Ave Ste 3a (11361-2963)
PHONE................................718 767-8400
Fernando Perez, *President*
EMP: 9
SQ FT: 1,500

SALES (est): 900K **Privately Held**
SIC: 3842 Limbs, artificial; braces, orthopedic

(G-741)
NOTICIA HISPANOAMERICANA INC
3815 Bell Blvd (11361-2260)
PHONE................................516 223-5678
Cinthia Diaz, *Owner*
Silvana Diaz, *Publisher*
Jeovanny Mata, *Director*
▲ EMP: 30
SALES (est): 843.7K **Privately Held**
SIC: 2711 Newspapers

(G-742)
SCHNEPS PUBLICATIONS INC (PA)
Also Called: Forest Hills Courier
3815 Bell Blvd Ste 38 (11361-2260)
PHONE................................718 260-2500
Victoria A Schneps, *President*
Victoria Schneps, *Publisher*
Joshua Schneps, *Vice Pres*
Adele Udell, *Sales Mgr*
Eduardo Cerchiara, *Marketing Staff*
EMP: 36
SALES (est): 8.2MM **Privately Held**
SIC: 2711 Newspapers, publishing & printing

(G-743)
UL CORP
3812 Corporal Stone St # 2 (11361-2259)
PHONE................................201 203-4453
Hyung Ho Kim, *President*
Gary Johnson, *Engineer*
Isadore Netto, *Engineer*
Alex Hummel, *Project Engr*
Nikesha Phipps, *Project Engr*
EMP: 8
SALES (est): 1.2MM **Privately Held**
SIC: 3953 Marking devices

(G-744)
VF IMAGEWEAR INC
333 Pratt Ave (11359-1119)
PHONE................................718 352-2363
Martin Soto, *Manager*
EMP: 21
SALES (corp-wide): 13.8MM **Publicly Held**
WEB: www.vfsolutions.com
SIC: 2311 2326 2339 Men's & boys' uniforms; work uniforms; women's & misses' outerwear
HQ: Vf Imagewear, Inc.
545 Marriott Dr Ste 200
Nashville TN 37214
615 565-5000

(G-745)
YIAMAS DAIRY FARMS LLC
2 Bay Club Dr (11360-2957)
P.O. Box 605046 (11360-5046)
PHONE................................347 766-7177
Kostas Symeonidis, *President*
EMP: 6 EST: 2017
SALES (est): 446.3K **Privately Held**
SIC: 2026 Fermented & cultured milk products

Bayside Hills
Queens County

(G-746)
CATHAY GLOBAL CO INC
Also Called: Vactronics
5815 215th St (11364-1839)
PHONE................................718 229-0920
Fu Geng, *President*
Janet Jiang, *Vice Pres*
EMP: 6 EST: 1991
SQ FT: 2,000
SALES (est): 406.5K **Privately Held**
SIC: 3699 Electrical equipment & supplies

G E O G R A P H I C

Bayville
Nassau County

(G-747)
PLURIBUS PRODUCTS INC
1 Overlook Ave (11709-2113)
PHONE.................................718 852-1614
Peter V Martino, *President*
John V Martino, *Purchasing*
EMP: 32 **EST:** 1966
SQ FT: 50,000
SALES (est): 4.3MM **Privately Held**
SIC: 2531 2449 3341 Public building &
  related furniture; wood containers; sec-
  ondary nonferrous metals

Beacon
Dutchess County

(G-748)
ARCHITECTURAL GLASS INC
71 Maple St Apt 2 (12508-2034)
PHONE.................................845 831-3116
Michael Benzer, *President*
Jennifer Smith, *Vice Pres*
EMP: 10
SQ FT: 8,000
SALES (est): 605K **Privately Held**
WEB: www.glasstiles.com
SIC: 3229 Glassware, art or decorative

(G-749)
CHEMPRENE INC
483 Fishkill Ave (12508-1251)
P.O. Box 471 (12508-0471)
PHONE.................................845 831-2800
John Nicoletti, *President*
Motria Iverson, *Accounts Mgr*
▲ **EMP:** 110
SQ FT: 200,000
SALES (est): 41.1MM
SALES (corp-wide): 242.1K **Privately
Held**
WEB: www.chemprene.com
SIC: 3496 3069 3535 Conveyor
  belts; rubberized fabrics; rubber hard-
  ware; conveyors & conveying equipment;
  coated fabrics, not rubberized; investment
  holding companies, except banks
HQ: Ammeraal Beltech International Be-
  heer B.V.
  Comeniusstraat 8
  Alkmaar 1817
  725 751-212

(G-750)
CHEMPRENE HOLDING INC
483 Fishkill Ave (12508-1251)
PHONE.................................845 831-2800
Jami Goud, *Ch of Bd*
Paul Hamilton, *President*
▲ **EMP:** 180
SALES (est): 19.8MM **Privately Held**
SIC: 3496 3069 3535 2295 Conveyor
  belts; rubberized fabrics; conveyors &
  conveying equipment; coated fabrics, not
  rubberized

(G-751)
DOREL HAT CO (PA)
1 Main St (12508)
PHONE.................................845 831-5231
Salvatore Cumella, *CEO*
Ramon Moreno, *Vice Pres*
EMP: 35
SQ FT: 28,000
SALES (est): 1.6MM **Privately Held**
WEB: www.aldohats.com
SIC: 2353 Hats, trimmed: women's,
  misses' & children's

(G-752)
FCR LLC
Also Called: Recommunity
508 Fishkill Ave (12508-1255)
PHONE.................................845 926-1071
EMP: 7
SALES (corp-wide): 10B **Publicly Held**
SIC: 2611 Pulp manufactured from waste
  or recycled paper

HQ: Fcr, Llc
  809 W Hill St Ste B
  Charlotte NC 28208
  704 332-1603

(G-753)
**HUDSON VALLEY
CHOCOLATIER INC (PA)**
Also Called: Alps Sweet Shop
269 Main St (12508-2735)
PHONE.................................845 831-8240
Sally Craft, *President*
Terry Craft, *Vice Pres*
EMP: 14
SALES (est): 1.8MM **Privately Held**
WEB: www.alpssweetshop.com
SIC: 2064 5441 Candy & other confec-
  tionery products; candy

(G-754)
MORE GOOD
383 Main St (12508-3014)
PHONE.................................845 765-0115
EMP: 7
SALES (est): 654.8K **Privately Held**
SIC: 2099 Food preparations

(G-755)
NICHE DESIGN INC
Also Called: Niche Modern
310 Fishkill Ave Unit 11 (12508-2073)
P.O. Box 311 (12508-0311)
PHONE.................................212 777-2101
Jeremy Pyles, *CEO*
Brandy Burre, *Sales Associate*
Britney Malave, *Marketing Staff*
Shannon Doyle, *Manager*
EMP: 15
SALES (est): 20.1K **Privately Held**
WEB: www.nichenyc.com
SIC: 3229 Glass lighting equipment parts

(G-756)
SIEGFRIEDS CALL INC
20 Kent St 109 (12508-2042)
PHONE.................................845 765-2275
Scott H Bacon, *Partner*
Andrea Bacon, *Officer*
EMP: 6
SALES (est): 146.4K **Privately Held**
SIC: 3931 Brass instruments & parts

(G-757)
TIGA HOLDINGS INC
74 Dennings Ave (12508-3624)
PHONE.................................845 838-3000
Gary Santagata, *President*
Timothy Hochberj, *Vice Pres*
Michael J Siciliano, *Director*
EMP: 24
SQ FT: 2,300
SALES (est): 2.3MM **Privately Held**
WEB: www.tigallc.com
SIC: 3911 Jewelry, precious metal

Bearsville
Ulster County

(G-758)
**LIFELINK MONITORING CORP
(PA)**
3201 Route 212 (12409-5224)
P.O. Box 152 (12409-0152)
PHONE.................................845 336-2098
Arthur G Avedisian, *President*
John K Holland, *Chairman*
EMP: 20 **EST:** 1994
SQ FT: 25,000
SALES (est): 2.1MM **Privately Held**
WEB: www.llmi.com
SIC: 2835 In vitro & in vivo diagnostic sub-
  stances

Beaver Dams
Schuyler County

(G-759)
**M & H RESEARCH AND DEV
CORP**
Also Called: M&H Soaring
471 Post Creek Rd (14812-9124)
P.O. Box 368, Big Flats (14814-0368)
PHONE.................................607 734-2346
Claude M Sullivan, *President*
Hinz Weissembuehler, *Principal*
Karen Schlosser, *Vice Pres*
EMP: 6
SALES: 450K **Privately Held**
WEB: www.mandhsoaring.com
SIC: 3721 Gliders (aircraft)

Beaver Falls
Lewis County

(G-760)
**LYDALL PERFORMANCE MTLS
US INC**
Also Called: Interface Performance Mtls
9635 Main St (13305)
PHONE.................................315 346-3100
EMP: 12
SALES (corp-wide): 785.9MM **Publicly
Held**
SIC: 2679 Paper products, converted
HQ: Lydall Performance Materials (Us), Inc.
  216 Wohlsen Way
  Lancaster PA 17603

(G-761)
OMNIAFILTRA LLC
9567 Main St (13305)
P.O. Box 410 (13305-0410)
PHONE.................................315 346-7300
Gino Fronzoni, *President*
John Wheeler, *Controller*
◆ **EMP:** 37
SQ FT: 70,000
SALES (est): 12MM **Privately Held**
SIC: 2621 Paper mills

Bedford
Westchester County

(G-762)
**BEDFORD WDWRK
INSTLLATIONS INC**
200 Pound Ridge Rd (10506-1243)
PHONE.................................914 764-9434
EMP: 6
SALES (est): 440K **Privately Held**
SIC: 2493 Mfg Reconstituted Wood Prod-
  ucts

(G-763)
JSD COMMUNICATIONS INC
Also Called: Remodeling News
10 Colonel Thomas Ln (10506-1521)
P.O. Box 911 (10506-0911)
PHONE.................................914 588-1841
James F Duffy, *President*
EMP: 13
SALES (est): 500K **Privately Held**
WEB: www.remodelingconnection.com
SIC: 2721 Magazines: publishing only, not
  printed on site

(G-764)
LESANNE LIFE SCIENCES LLC
47 Brook Farm Rd (10506-1309)
PHONE.................................914 234-0860
Robert J Beckman,
Robert Beckman,
EMP: 5
SALES: 300K **Privately Held**
SIC: 2835 In vitro & in vivo diagnostic sub-
  stances

Bedford Hills
Westchester County

(G-765)
**BEDFORD PRECISION PARTS
CORP**
290 Adams St (10507-1910)
P.O. Box 357 (10507-0357)
PHONE.................................914 241-2211
Daniel L Kleinman, *President*
Paul Kleinman, *Chairman*
Evalyn S Kleinman, *Corp Secy*
David Kleinman, *Vice Pres*
Robert Kleinman, *Vice Pres*
EMP: 36 **EST:** 1965
SQ FT: 14,000
SALES (est): 5MM **Privately Held**
WEB: www.bedfordprecision.com
SIC: 3993 3563 Signs & advertising spe-
  cialties; spraying outfits: metals, paints &
  chemicals (compressor)

(G-766)
CUSTOM SPORTSWEAR CORP
Also Called: Sportswear Unlimited
375 Adams St (10507-2001)
PHONE.................................914 666-9200
Adam Giardina, *President*
Len Schlangel, *CFO*
Helen Bowers, *Manager*
EMP: 5 **EST:** 1988
SQ FT: 6,000
SALES (est): 500K **Privately Held**
WEB: www.sptunl.com
SIC: 2759 5136 Screen printing; uniforms,
  men's & boys'

(G-767)
**DAVID HOWELL PRODUCT
DESIGN**
Also Called: David Howell & Company
405 Adams St (10507-2066)
PHONE.................................914 666-4080
David Howell, *President*
Susan Howell, *Admin Sec*
EMP: 20 **EST:** 1978
SQ FT: 6,000
SALES (est): 2MM **Privately Held**
WEB: www.davidhowell.com
SIC: 3911 Jewelry, precious metal

(G-768)
DISPERSION TECHNOLOGY INC
364 Adams St (10507-2048)
PHONE.................................914 241-4777
Andrei Dukhin, *President*
EMP: 4
SQ FT: 3,000
SALES (est): 1.8MM **Privately Held**
SIC: 3829 Measuring & controlling devices

(G-769)
**EYEGLASS SERVICE
INDUSTRIES**
Also Called: Vision World
777 Bedford Rd (10507-1547)
PHONE.................................914 666-3150
Patricia Ausiello, *CEO*
EMP: 5
SALES (corp-wide): 7MM **Privately Held**
WEB: www.visionworld.com
SIC: 3841 5995 Surgical & medical instru-
  ments; opticians
PA: Eyeglass Service Industries Inc
  420 Sunrise Hwy
  Lynbrook NY 11563
  516 561-3937

(G-770)
MALCON INC
405 Adams St (10507-2066)
P.O. Box 463 (10507-0463)
PHONE.................................914 666-7146
Peter Malavenda, *President*
Frances Malavenda, *Corp Secy*
John Loguercio, *Manager*
EMP: 18
SQ FT: 15,000
SALES (est): 439.6K **Privately Held**
WEB: www.malcon.com
SIC: 3823 Panelboard indicators,
  recorders & controllers; receiver

(G-771)
PRODUCTION MILLING COMPANY
364 Adams St Ste 5 (10507-2047)
PHONE.....................914 666-0792
Frank G Servidio, *President*
EMP: 5
SQ FT: 1,900
SALES (est): 544.5K **Privately Held**
SIC: 3599 Machine shop, jobbing & repair

(G-772)
RAINBEAU RIDGE FARM
49 Davids Way (10507-2531)
PHONE.....................914 234-2197
Lisa Schwartz, *Owner*
Karen Sabath, *Partner*
Mark Schwartz, *Co-Owner*
EMP: 9
SQ FT: 6,000
SALES (est): 443.3K **Privately Held**
SIC: 2022 8299 Cheese, natural & processed; educational services

Bellerose
Queens County

(G-773)
ADVANTEX SOLUTIONS INC
24845 Jericho Tpke (11426-1912)
PHONE.....................718 278-2290
Giovanni Natale, *President*
Antonio Sferrazz, *Vice Pres*
EMP: 6
SALES (est): 1MM **Privately Held**
SIC: 3822 Temperature controls, automatic

(G-774)
DOWNRIGHT PRINTING CORP
8829 238th St (11426-1229)
PHONE.....................516 619-7200
Richard Reategui, *CEO*
EMP: 5
SALES (est): 92.3K **Privately Held**
SIC: 2752 Commercial printing, lithographic

(G-775)
LEIGH SCOTT ENTERPRISES INC
Also Called: Minuteman Press
24802 Union Tpke (11426-1837)
PHONE.....................718 343-5440
Scott Levine, *President*
Paris Vevgas, *Production*
EMP: 6
SALES (est): 1MM **Privately Held**
WEB: www.minutemanbellrose.com
SIC: 2752 2791 Commercial printing, lithographic; typesetting

(G-776)
RITNOA INC
24019 Jamaica Ave Ste 2 (11426-2040)
PHONE.....................212 660-2148
Shabbir Khan, *President*
EMP: 38 EST: 2006
SQ FT: 12,000
SALES (est): 3.1MM **Privately Held**
SIC: 7372 Business oriented computer software

(G-777)
ZINNIAS INC
24520 Grand Central Pkwy 4l
(11426-2712)
PHONE.....................718 746-8551
▲ EMP: 12
SQ FT: 3,800
SALES: 1.4MM **Privately Held**
SIC: 2369 2361 Girls And Childrens Outerwear, Nec, Nsk

Bellmore
Nassau County

(G-778)
ANDERSENS SPRING & WLDG CORP
2374 Merrick Rd (11710-3821)
PHONE.....................516 785-7337
Walter A Andersen Jr, *President*
EMP: 6 EST: 1951
SQ FT: 11,000
SALES (est): 421.4K **Privately Held**
SIC: 7692 7539 Welding repair; automotive welding; automotive springs, rebuilding & repair

(G-779)
ARNOLD TAYLOR PRINTING INC
2218 Brody Ln (11710-5102)
PHONE.....................516 781-0564
Carey Platt, *President*
EMP: 5 EST: 1963
SALES (est): 350K **Privately Held**
SIC: 2752 Commercial printing, offset

(G-780)
BELLMORE STEEL PRODUCTS CORP
2282 Bellmore Ave (11710-5627)
P.O. Box 825 (11710-0825)
PHONE.....................516 785-9667
Glenn S Suskind, *Ch of Bd*
EMP: 16
SQ FT: 3,000
SALES (est): 2.7MM **Privately Held**
SIC: 3441 Fabricated structural metal

(G-781)
DECAL MAKERS INC
2477 Merrick Rd (11710-5751)
PHONE.....................516 221-7200
EMP: 25 EST: 1923
SALES (est): 2.3MM **Privately Held**
SIC: 2752 3993 2396 Lithographic Commercial Printing Mfg Signs/Advertising Specialties Mfg Auto/Apparel Trimming

(G-782)
E J MANUFACTURING INC (PA)
2648 Grand Ave (11710-3553)
PHONE.....................516 313-9380
Elliot S Negrin, *Ch of Bd*
Jeff Negrin, *Vice Pres*
▲ EMP: 2
SQ FT: 8,000
SALES (est): 3MM **Privately Held**
SIC: 2326 Men's & boys' work clothing

(G-783)
HOT LINE INDUSTRIES INC (PA)
Also Called: Casttle Harbor
2648 Grand Ave (11710-3553)
PHONE.....................516 764-0400
Howard Negrin, *President*
Jeff Negrin, *Corp Secy*
Elliot Negrin, *Vice Pres*
◆ EMP: 16
SALES (est): 1.3MM **Privately Held**
WEB: www.hotlineindustries.com
SIC: 2339 Women's & misses' outerwear

(G-784)
METRO CITY GROUP INC
2283 Bellmore Ave (11710-5623)
PHONE.....................516 781-2500
Carlos Jaramillo, *President*
EMP: 4
SALES: 4.5MM **Privately Held**
SIC: 3423 1711 Plumbers' hand tools; carpenters' hand tools, except saws: levels, chisels, etc.; plumbing contractors

(G-785)
PAPERWORLD INC
3054 Lee Pl (11710-5034)
PHONE.....................516 221-2702
Carol Grubman, *President*
▲ EMP: 37
SALES (est): 7.7MM **Privately Held**
SIC: 2679 2675 Adding machine rolls, paper: made from purchased material; die-cut paper & board

(G-786)
PARABIT SYSTEMS INC
2677 Grand Ave (11710-3552)
P.O. Box 481, Roosevelt (11575-0481)
PHONE.....................516 378-4800
Robert Leiponis, *President*
Andrew Sherman, *Foreman/Supr*
Giselle Soriano, *Purch Agent*
Luckner Badio, *Accountant*
Olesya Maggio, *Accountant*
▲ EMP: 50
SQ FT: 25,000
SALES (est): 11.5MM **Privately Held**
SIC: 3699 3661 3578 2542 Security devices; telephone & telegraph apparatus; telephone station equipment & parts, wire; automatic teller machines (ATM); telephone booths: except wood

(G-787)
PURE KEMIKA LLC
2156 Legion St (11710-4915)
PHONE.....................718 745-2200
Luis F Becker, *Mng Member*
EMP: 6 EST: 2013
SQ FT: 1,000
SALES: 1.5MM **Privately Held**
SIC: 2899 Chemical preparations

(G-788)
RUSH GOLD MANUFACTURING LTD
Also Called: G R M
2400 Merrick Rd (11710-3821)
PHONE.....................516 781-3155
Harold Lazar, *President*
Shirley Lazar, *Admin Sec*
▲ EMP: 74
SQ FT: 10,000
SALES: 5MM **Privately Held**
SIC: 3499 3961 Novelties & giftware, including trophies; costume jewelry

(G-789)
SALISBURY SPORTSWEAR INC
2523 Marine Pl (11710-5107)
PHONE.....................516 221-9519
Herbert Margolis, *President*
EMP: 50
SALES (est): 3MM **Privately Held**
SIC: 2339 Sportswear, women's

(G-790)
SPEEDY SIGN A RAMA USA INC
Also Called: Sign-A-Rama
2956 Merrick Rd (11710-5760)
PHONE.....................516 783-1075
Michael Bolz, *President*
EMP: 5
SALES (est): 389.3K **Privately Held**
SIC: 3993 Signs & advertising specialties

Bellport
Suffolk County

(G-791)
50+ LIFESTYLE
146 S Country Rd Ste 4 (11713-2530)
PHONE.....................631 286-0058
Hon Frank C Trotta, *President*
Frank C Trotta, *Owner*
Mary Alice Graham, *Finance*
EMP: 8
SALES: 750K **Privately Held**
SIC: 2711 Newspapers, publishing & printing

(G-792)
ABLE ELECTRONICS INC
18 Sawgrass Dr (11713-1549)
PHONE.....................631 924-5386
Loraine Leverock, *CEO*
Elizabeth Padrazo, *Chairman*
Ann Konon, *Vice Pres*
Kenneth Levebrock, *Vice Pres*
Cody Valentin, *Sales Mgr*
EMP: 10
SQ FT: 995
SALES: 3.1MM **Privately Held**
SIC: 3674 Semiconductors & related devices

(G-793)
ALTERNATIVE SERVICE INC
Also Called: Alternative Parts
7 Sawgrass Dr (11713-1547)
PHONE.....................631 345-9500
Russell Drake, *President*
Ruseell Drake, *President*
John Cochrane, *Vice Pres*
▲ EMP: 15
SQ FT: 15,000
SALES (est): 1.9MM **Privately Held**
SIC: 3444 5084 7699 3541 Sheet metalwork; industrial machine parts; industrial machinery & equipment repair; machine tools, metal cutting type

(G-794)
AVS LAMINATES INC
Also Called: Steigercraft
99 Bellport Ave (11713-2106)
PHONE.....................631 286-2136
Alan Steiger, *President*
▲ EMP: 25
SQ FT: 20,800
SALES (est): 5.4MM **Privately Held**
WEB: www.steigercraft.com
SIC: 3732 Fishing boats: lobster, crab, oyster, etc.: small

(G-795)
C HOWARD COMPANY INC
1007 Station Rd (11713-1552)
PHONE.....................631 286-7940
Fax: 631 286-7947
EMP: 9 EST: 1934
SQ FT: 10,000
SALES (est): 520K **Privately Held**
SIC: 2064 Mfg Candy/Confectionery

(G-796)
CRAZ WOODWORKING ASSOC INC
24 Sawgrass Dr (11713-1549)
PHONE.....................631 205-1890
Peter Craz, *President*
Steve Lineberger, *Office Mgr*
EMP: 12
SQ FT: 12,000
SALES (est): 1.8MM **Privately Held**
SIC: 2499 Decorative wood & woodwork

(G-797)
EASTERN PRECISION MACHINING
11 Farber Dr Ste I (11713-1500)
PHONE.....................631 286-4758
Norbert G Schreiber, *President*
Annmarie Schreiber, *Vice Pres*
EMP: 5
SQ FT: 6,000
SALES (est): 653.8K **Privately Held**
WEB: www.easternprecisionmachining.com
SIC: 3728 3599 Aircraft parts & equipment; machine shop, jobbing & repair

(G-798)
EDGE DISPLAY GROUP ENTP INC
35 Sawgrass Dr Ste 2 (11713-1577)
PHONE.....................631 498-1373
Philip J Zellner, *President*
▼ EMP: 10 EST: 1999
SALES (est): 1MM **Privately Held**
SIC: 3993 Displays & cutouts, window & lobby

(G-799)
FIREWORKS BY GRUCCI INC
20 Pinehurst Dr (11713-1573)
PHONE.....................631 286-0088
Phil Grucci, *President*
Felix Grucci Jr, *President*
Donna Butler, *Vice Pres*
◆ EMP: 30
SQ FT: 6,000
SALES (est): 6.4MM **Privately Held**
SIC: 2899 Fireworks

(G-800)
HEINECK ASSOCIATES INC
28 Curtis Ave (11713-1120)
PHONE.....................631 207-2347
Andrew Heineck, *President*
Robin Rinehart, *Professor*
EMP: 6 EST: 2000

GEOGRAPHIC

SALES: 500K **Privately Held**
SIC: 7372 Prepackaged software

(G-801)
K INDUSTRIES INC (PA)
1107 Station Rd Ste 5a (11713-1562)
P.O. Box 542 (11713-0542)
PHONE...................................631 897-2125
Victor Schneider, *President*
EMP: 5
SQ FT: 10,000
SALES: 1MM **Privately Held**
SIC: 3443 Tanks, standard or custom fabricated: metal plate

(G-802)
MAEHR INDUSTRIES INC
14 Sawgrass Dr (11713-1549)
PHONE...................................631 924-1661
Michael Maehr, *President*
EMP: 12
SQ FT: 5,000
SALES: 1MM **Privately Held**
WEB: www.maehr.com
SIC: 3469 3599 Machine parts, stamped or pressed metal; machine shop, jobbing & repair

(G-803)
MCKEON ROLLING STL DOOR CO INC (PA)
44 Sawgrass Dr (11713-1549)
PHONE...................................631 803-3000
Joseph J McKeon, *President*
Dan Dodge, *Business Mgr*
David L Dodge, *Vice Pres*
Ashraf Gomaa, *Vice Pres*
Richard Fallon, *Controller*
▲ EMP: 48 EST: 1986
SALES (est): 7MM **Privately Held**
SIC: 3442 Metal doors; rolling doors for industrial buildings or warehouses, metal; fire doors, metal

(G-804)
MOTION MESSAGE INC
22 Sawgrass Dr Ste 4 (11713-1571)
PHONE...................................631 924-9500
William Sheridan, *President*
Irene Sheridan, *Admin Sec*
EMP: 10
SQ FT: 12,000
SALES (est): 1.1MM **Privately Held**
SIC: 3993 Electric signs

(G-805)
OPTISOURCE INTERNATIONAL INC
Also Called: Nu-Chem Laboratories
40 Sawgrass Dr Ste 1 (11713-1564)
PHONE...................................631 924-8360
Daryl Squicciarini, *President*
Anthony Zanghi, *Project Mgr*
John Delligatti, *Purch Agent*
Roseann Ullman, *Accounting Mgr*
John Perez, *Credit Staff*
▲ EMP: 30
SQ FT: 30,000
SALES: 13MM
SALES (corp-wide): 1.4MM **Privately Held**
WEB: www.1-800-optisource.com
SIC: 3851 Lens coating, ophthalmic
HQ: Essilor Laboratories Of America, Inc.
　　13515 N Stemmons Fwy
　　Dallas TX 75234
　　972 241-4141

(G-806)
PALLETS R US INC (PA)
555 Woodside Ave (11713-1220)
PHONE...................................631 758-2360
Nicholas Sorge, *Ch of Bd*
Thomas Sorge, *Vice Pres*
EMP: 50
SQ FT: 10,000
SALES (est): 7.9MM **Privately Held**
SIC: 2448 Pallets, wood

(G-807)
POLYMAG INC
685 Station Rd Ste 2 (11713-1697)
PHONE...................................631 286-4111
Deviveni Ratnam, *President*
▲ EMP: 20
SQ FT: 15,000

SALES (est): 2.9MM **Privately Held**
WEB: www.polymaginc.com
SIC: 3499 Magnets, permanent: metallic

(G-808)
THEGO CORPORATION
Also Called: Acme Marine Hoist
2 Mooring Dr (11713-2810)
PHONE...................................631 776-2472
EMP: 5 EST: 1948
SQ FT: 11,500
SALES: 1MM **Privately Held**
SIC: 3536 Mfg Marine Hoists

(G-809)
TORINO INDUS FABRICATION INC
4 Pinehurst Dr (11713-1573)
P.O. Box 2368, East Setauket (11733-0892)
PHONE...................................631 509-1640
Maria Passanante, *President*
Joseph Passanante, *Vice Pres*
EMP: 9
SALES (est): 505.7K **Privately Held**
SIC: 3441 Building components, structural steel

(G-810)
TORINO INDUSTRIAL INC
Also Called: Torino Industrial Fabrication
4 Pinehurst Dr (11713-1573)
P.O. Box 2368, East Setauket (11733-0892)
PHONE...................................631 509-1640
Vincent Sette, *Ch of Bd*
Keith Passanante, *Vice Pres*
Maria Passanante, *Treasurer*
Palmina Sette, *Shareholder*
EMP: 13
SQ FT: 10,000
SALES (est): 2.5MM **Privately Held**
WEB: www.torinoindustrial.com
SIC: 3449 Bars, concrete reinforcing: fabricated steel

Belmont
Allegany County

(G-811)
SUIT-KOTE CORPORATION
5628 Tuckers Corners Rd (14813-9604)
PHONE...................................585 268-7127
Paul Suit, *Branch Mgr*
EMP: 10
SALES (corp-wide): 272.8MM **Privately Held**
SIC: 2911 Asphalt or asphaltic materials, made in refineries
PA: Suit-Kote Corporation
　　1911 Lorings Crossing Rd
　　Cortland NY 13045
　　607 753-1100

Bemus Point
Chautauqua County

(G-812)
LAKESIDE INDUSTRIES INC
Also Called: Point Industrial
2 Lakeside Dr (14712-9310)
P.O. Box 9130 (14712-0913)
PHONE...................................716 386-3031
Roy Benson, *CEO*
Brad Benson, *President*
EMP: 10
SQ FT: 2,000
SALES: 950K **Privately Held**
SIC: 3599 Amusement park equipment

Bergen
Genesee County

(G-813)
DIEHL DEVELOPMENT INC
Also Called: Diehl Sand & Gravel
5922 N Lake Rd (14416-9507)
PHONE...................................585 494-2920

Keith Diehl, *President*
EMP: 5
SQ FT: 500
SALES (est): 1.8MM **Privately Held**
SIC: 1442 Gravel mining

(G-814)
GT INNOVATIONS LLC
7674 Swamp Rd (14416-9352)
PHONE...................................585 739-7659
Daniel Grastorf, *Owner*
EMP: 5
SALES (est): 693K **Privately Held**
SIC: 3444 Concrete forms, sheet metal

(G-815)
GUTHRIE HELI-ARC INC
Also Called: Guthrie Sales & Service
6276 Clinton Street Rd (14416-9738)
PHONE...................................585 548-5053
Margaret Ryan, *President*
Matthew Ryan, *Vice Pres*
EMP: 8
SQ FT: 4,500
SALES (est): 786.5K **Privately Held**
SIC: 7692 Welding repair

(G-816)
K2 PLASTICS INC
8210 Buffalo Rd (14416-9444)
PHONE...................................585 494-2727
Klaus Kremmin II, *President*
EMP: 5
SALES (est): 749.3K **Privately Held**
WEB: www.k2plasticsinc.com
SIC: 3089 Molding primary plastic; injection molding of plastics

(G-817)
LIBERTY PUMPS INC
7000 Appletree Ave (14416-9446)
PHONE...................................800 543-2550
Charles E Cook, *CEO*
Robyn Brookhart, *President*
Allan Davis, *Vice Pres*
Randall Waldron, *Vice Pres*
Jeffrey Cook, *Purch Mgr*
◆ EMP: 240 EST: 1965
SQ FT: 250,000
SALES: 125.1MM **Privately Held**
WEB: www.libertypumps.com
SIC: 3561 Pumps, domestic: water or sump

(G-818)
MILLERS MILLWORKS INC
Also Called: Millers Presentation Furniture
29 N Lake Ave (14416-9528)
P.O. Box 175 (14416-0175)
PHONE...................................585 494-1420
Greg Lumb, *President*
Nicole Robinson, *Office Admin*
Michelle Yoffee, *Office Admin*
EMP: 20 EST: 1996
SQ FT: 6,192
SALES: 2.1MM **Privately Held**
WEB: www.millersmillwork.com
SIC: 2521 Wood office furniture

(G-819)
ODYSSEY CONTROLS INC
6256 Clinton Street Rd (14416-9738)
P.O. Box 613 (14416-0613)
PHONE...................................585 548-9800
Danie T Harmon Jr, *Ch of Bd*
Andy Meyer, *Engineer*
EMP: 6
SALES (est): 974.7K **Privately Held**
SIC: 3613 Control panels, electric

(G-820)
SCOMAC INC
8629 Buffalo Rd (14416)
P.O. Box 455 (14416-0455)
PHONE...................................585 494-2200
Lawrence Scott, *President*
EMP: 12
SQ FT: 12,000
SALES (est): 1.9MM **Privately Held**
WEB: www.scomac.com
SIC: 3545 Diamond dressing & wheel crushing attachments

Berkshire
Tioga County

(G-821)
TIOGA HARDWOODS INC (PA)
12685 State Route 38 (13736-1930)
P.O. Box 195 (13736-0195)
PHONE...................................607 657-8686
Kevin Gillette, *President*
Randy Bowers, *Vice Pres*
Chad Cotterill, *Vice Pres*
Scott Snyder, *Vice Pres*
◆ EMP: 1
SQ FT: 20,000
SALES (est): 4.7MM **Privately Held**
WEB: www.tiogahardwoods.com
SIC: 2861 Hardwood distillates

(G-822)
TREIMAN PUBLICATIONS CORP
12724 State Route 38 (13736-1911)
PHONE...................................607 657-8473
Dov Trieman, *President*
EMP: 5
SALES (est): 287.1K **Privately Held**
SIC: 2741 Miscellaneous publishing

Berlin
Rensselaer County

(G-823)
COWEE FOREST PRODUCTS INC
28 Taylor Ave (12022)
P.O. Box 248 (12022-0248)
PHONE...................................518 658-2233
William Stallkamp, *President*
Arthur Bogen, *Vice Pres*
▲ EMP: 20 EST: 1898
SQ FT: 100,000
SALES: 2MM **Privately Held**
WEB: www.cowee.com
SIC: 2499 Novelties, wood fiber; carved & turned wood

(G-824)
GREEN RENEWABLE INC
28 Taylor Ave (12022)
P.O. Box 248 (12022-0248)
PHONE...................................518 658-2233
Sean M Gallivan, *President*
EMP: 40
SALES: 4.7MM **Privately Held**
SIC: 2499 Clothespins, wood

(G-825)
MILANESE COMMERCIAL DOOR LLC
28 Taylor Ave (12022-7740)
P.O. Box 560 (12022-0560)
PHONE...................................518 658-0398
Brian Milanese, *Principal*
EMP: 10 EST: 2007
SALES (est): 1.4MM **Privately Held**
SIC: 3442 5031 Metal doors; door frames, all materials

Bernhards Bay
Oswego County

(G-826)
MCINTOSH BOX & PALLET CO INC
741 State Route 49 (13028)
P.O. Box 76 (13028-0076)
PHONE...................................315 675-8511
Michael Milson, *Branch Mgr*
EMP: 60
SALES (corp-wide): 38.4MM **Privately Held**
WEB: www.mcintoshbox.com
SIC: 2448 2441 Pallets, wood; nailed wood boxes & shook
PA: Mcintosh Box & Pallet Co., Inc.
　　5864 Pyle Dr
　　East Syracuse NY 13057
　　315 446-9350

▲ = Import ▼ =Export
◆ =Import/Export

Bethel
Sullivan County

(G-827)
ALEXY ASSOCIATES INC
86 Jim Stephenson Rd (12720)
P.O. Box 70 (12720-0070)
PHONE..............................845 482-3000
Cornelius Alexy, *President*
Sharon Alexy, *Admin Sec*
EMP: 20
SALES: 200K **Privately Held**
WEB: www.aaultrasoniccleaners.com
SIC: 3699 7629 Cleaning equipment, ultrasonic, except medical & dental; electronic equipment repair

(G-828)
CAMPANELLIS POULTRY FARM INC
4 Perry Rd (12720)
PHONE..............................845 482-2222
Anthony Campanelli, *Owner*
EMP: 5
SALES: 1.7MM **Privately Held**
SIC: 2015 Poultry slaughtering & processing

Bethpage
Nassau County

(G-829)
A & M LITHO INC
4 Hunt Pl (11714-6411)
PHONE..............................516 342-9727
Anna Laperuta, *President*
EMP: 25
SALES: 2.5MM **Privately Held**
SIC: 2752 Commercial printing, offset

(G-830)
ABBLE AWNING CO INC
313 Broadway Ste 315 (11714-3003)
PHONE..............................516 822-1200
Thomas Catalano, *President*
John Catalano, *Vice Pres*
EMP: 9
SQ FT: 2,400
SALES: 500K **Privately Held**
WEB: www.abbleawning.com
SIC: 2394 Awnings, fabric: made from purchased materials; canopies, fabric: made from purchased materials

(G-831)
AC MOORE INCORPORATED
3988 Hempstead Tpke (11714-5603)
PHONE..............................516 796-5831
Fax: 516 796-5852
EMP: 5
SALES (corp-wide): 546.1MM **Privately Held**
SIC: 2499 5023 Mfg Wood Products Whol Homefurnishings
HQ: A.C. Moore Incorporated
130 A C Moore Dr
Berlin NJ 08009
856 768-4930

(G-832)
AGUA ENERVIVA LLC
Also Called: Agua Brands
15 Grumman Rd W Ste 1300 (11714-5029)
P.O. Box 1018 (11714-0019)
PHONE..............................516 597-5440
Michael Venuti, *President*
Carol Dollard, *COO*
Thomas Reynolds, *Finance*
EMP: 12
SALES (est): 1.5MM **Privately Held**
SIC: 2087 Beverage bases, concentrates, syrups, powders & mixes

(G-833)
BRUNSCHWIG & FILS LLC (HQ)
245 Central Ave (11714-3922)
PHONE..............................800 538-1880
Curtis Meier, *Manager*
Peter Smith,
▲ **EMP:** 14

SALES (est): 28.7MM
SALES (corp-wide): 197.2MM **Privately Held**
SIC: 2329 2211 Ski & snow clothing: men's & boys'; upholstery, tapestry & wall coverings: cotton
PA: Kravet Inc.
225 Cent Ave S
Bethpage NY 11714
516 293-2000

(G-834)
DRIMARK
999 S Oyster Bay Rd (11714-1038)
PHONE..............................516 484-6200
Charles Reichmann, *President*
EMP: 15
SALES (est): 3MM **Privately Held**
SIC: 2678 Stationery products

(G-835)
GRUMMAN FIELD SUPPORT SERVICES
S Oyster Bay Rd (11714)
PHONE..............................516 575-0574
Ed Sax, *Principal*
Brian Boyer, *Vice Pres*
Tony Miller, *Finance*
EMP: 70
SALES (est): 11.7MM **Publicly Held**
WEB: www.sperry.ngc.com
SIC: 3721 8731 Aircraft; commercial physical research
HQ: Northrop Grumman Systems Corporation
2980 Fairview Park Dr
Falls Church VA 22042
703 280-2900

(G-836)
HOWE MACHINE & TOOL CORP
236 Park Ave (11714-3709)
PHONE..............................516 931-5687
Paul Howe, *President*
Ryan Howe, *Vice Pres*
Janette Morrison, *Sales Staff*
EMP: 11
SQ FT: 11,500
SALES: 11.5MM **Privately Held**
WEB: www.howemachine.com
SIC: 3599 Machine shop, jobbing & repair

(G-837)
KREON INC
999 S Oyster Bay Rd # 105 (11714-1041)
PHONE..............................516 470-9522
Thomas Mindt, *CEO*
Darin Fowler, *President*
▲ **EMP:** 5
SALES (est): 1MM **Privately Held**
SIC: 3641 Electric lamps
HQ: Kreon
Industrieweg-Noord 1152
Oudsbergen 3660
898 197-80

(G-838)
MARK DRI PRODUCTS INC
999 S Oyster Bay Rd # 312 (11714-1038)
PHONE..............................516 484-6200
Charles Reichmann, *CEO*
Andre Reichmann, *President*
Kathy Bromer, *Marketing Staff*
Tatum Finnetan, *Executive*
▲ **EMP:** 200
SQ FT: 54,000
SALES (est): 23.5MM **Privately Held**
WEB: www.drimark.com
SIC: 3951 5112 Markers, soft tip (felt, fabric, plastic, etc.); pens &/or pencils

(G-839)
MELMONT FINE PRINGNG/GRAPHICS
6 Robert Ct Ste 24 (11714-1415)
P.O. Box 395, Old Bethpage (11804-0395)
PHONE..............................516 939-2253
Angela Melledy, *President*
EMP: 6
SALES: 150K **Privately Held**
SIC: 2711 7389 Newspapers, publishing & printing; printing broker

(G-840)
MLS SALES
226 10th St (11714-1703)
PHONE..............................516 681-2736
Mary Lafauci, *Owner*
EMP: 6
SALES: 120K **Privately Held**
SIC: 3679 Electronic components

(G-841)
NORTHROP GRUMMAN CORPORATION
660 Grumman Rd W (11714)
PHONE..............................703 280-2900
James Eng, *Engineer*
Scott Oishi, *Sales Mgr*
EMP: 702 **Publicly Held**
SIC: 3812 Search & navigation equipment
PA: Northrop Grumman Corporation
2980 Fairview Park Dr
Falls Church VA 22042

(G-842)
NORTHROP GRUMMAN SYSTEMS CORP
Also Called: Northrop Grumman Corporation
925 S Oyster Bay Rd (11714-3582)
PHONE..............................516 575-0574
Carl Johnson, *Vice Pres*
Scott Siegel, *Project Dir*
Dominic Anton, *Project Mgr*
Rich Turner, *Chief Engr*
Sam Ghannadi, *Engineer*
EMP: 1659 **Publicly Held**
WEB: www.sperry.ngc.com
SIC: 3721 8731 Aircraft; commercial physical research
HQ: Northrop Grumman Systems Corporation
2980 Fairview Park Dr
Falls Church VA 22042
703 280-2900

(G-843)
NORTHROP GRUMMAN SYSTEMS CORP
925 S Oyster Bay Rd (11714-3582)
PHONE..............................516 346-7100
Adam Spiers, *General Mgr*
Mindy Matusewicz, *Engineer*
David Wendrow, *Engineer*
Paul Mitrani, *Branch Mgr*
Mark Reeve, *Info Tech Dir*
EMP: 150 **Publicly Held**
WEB: www.sperry.ngc.com
SIC: 3812 Search & navigation equipment
HQ: Northrop Grumman Systems Corporation
2980 Fairview Park Dr
Falls Church VA 22042
703 280-2900

(G-844)
RAIN CATCHERS SEAMLESS GUTTERS
39 Park Ln (11714-5226)
PHONE..............................516 520-1956
Robert Dambrosio, *CEO*
EMP: 5
SALES (est): 413.1K **Privately Held**
SIC: 3272 Floor slabs & tiles, precast concrete

(G-845)
VENGO INC
999 S Oyster Bay Rd # 407 (11714-1044)
PHONE..............................866 526-7054
Brian Shimmerlik, *CEO*
Adam Gargenderg, *Vice Pres*
Adam Gartenberg, *Vice Pres*
Kevin Bende, *Sr Software Eng*
Shawn Sethi, *Sr Software Eng*
EMP: 6
SALES (est): 1.1MM **Privately Held**
SIC: 3581 Automatic vending machines

(G-846)
WILSONART INTL HOLDINGS LLC
999 S Oyster Bay Rd # 3305 (11714-1038)
PHONE..............................516 935-6980
Greg Martino, *Manager*
EMP: 20

SALES (corp-wide): 14.7B **Publicly Held**
WEB: www.wilsonart.com
SIC: 2821 2541 Plastics materials & resins; table or counter tops, plastic laminated
HQ: Wilsonart International Holdings Llc
2501 Wilsonart Dr
Temple TX 76504
254 207-7000

Big Flats
Chemung County

(G-847)
KG MOTORS INC
Also Called: Notubes.com
202 Daniel Zenker Dr (14814-8944)
PHONE..............................607 562-2877
Stan Koziatek, *CEO*
Erich Farnham, *Purch Agent*
Bob Nunnink, *Sales Staff*
Aaron Snyder, *Sales Staff*
Chris Currie, *Manager*
▲ **EMP:** 30
SALES: 15MM **Privately Held**
SIC: 3751 Bicycles & related parts

(G-848)
REYNOLDS MANUFACTURING INC
3298 State Rte 352 (14814)
PHONE..............................607 562-8936
Kasandra Reynolds, *Ch of Bd*
EMP: 17
SQ FT: 11,000
SALES (est): 3.9MM **Privately Held**
SIC: 3444 3469 Sheet metalwork; machine parts, stamped or pressed metal

(G-849)
X-GEN PHARMACEUTICALS INC (PA)
300 Daniel Zenker Dr (14814)
P.O. Box 445 (14814-0445)
PHONE..............................607 562-2700
Susan E Badia, *Ch of Bd*
Robin Liles, *Vice Pres*
Catherine Liles, *Treasurer*
David Potter, *Marketing Mgr*
▲ **EMP:** 3
SQ FT: 53,000
SALES (est): 3.9MM **Privately Held**
SIC: 2834 Pharmaceutical preparations

Binghamton
Broome County

(G-850)
A-LINE TECHNOLOGIES INC
197 Corporate Dr (13904-3214)
PHONE..............................607 772-2439
Alex Boyce, *President*
Frank J Boyce, *Vice Pres*
EMP: 10
SQ FT: 10,000
SALES: 1.1MM **Privately Held**
SIC: 3714 3599 Motor vehicle transmissions, drive assemblies & parts; machine shop, jobbing & repair

(G-851)
ALL AMERICAN BUILDING
109 Crestmont Rd (13905-3951)
PHONE..............................607 797-7123
Douglas E Hamm, *Owner*
EMP: 8
SALES (est): 783.7K **Privately Held**
SIC: 3448 Prefabricated metal buildings

(G-852)
ALL SPEC FINISHING INC
219 Clinton St (13905-2236)
P.O. Box 55 (13903-0055)
PHONE..............................607 770-9174
Anthony Milasi, *President*
Dennis Smith, *President*
Shirley Milasi, *Admin Sec*
EMP: 50
SQ FT: 80,000

SALES (est): 5.4MM **Privately Held**
WEB: www.allspecfinishing.com
SIC: 3479 7699 Painting, coating & hot dipping; painting of metal products; plastics products repair

(G-853)
AMERICAN QUALITY TECHNOLOGY
6 Emma St (13905-2508)
PHONE..................................607 777-9488
Gary Crounse, *President*
Jerome Luchuk, *CFO*
EMP: 12
SALES: 980K **Privately Held**
SIC: 3672 3679 3825 Printed circuit boards; electronic circuits; instruments to measure electricity

(G-854)
AMETEK INC
33 Lewis Rd Ste 6 (13905-1045)
PHONE..................................607 763-4700
Rodney Cogswell, *Mfg Mgr*
Susan Dodge, *Materials Mgr*
Robert Glydon, *Finance Mgr*
Kevin McLoughlin, *Comptroller*
Robert Hyland, *Branch Mgr*
EMP: 68
SALES (corp-wide): 4.8B **Publicly Held**
SIC: 3621 Motors & generators
PA: Ametek, Inc.
     1100 Cassatt Rd
     Berwyn PA 19312
     610 647-2121

(G-855)
ARNOLD-DAVIS LLC
Also Called: Harris Assembly Group
187 Indl Pk Dr (13904)
PHONE..................................607 772-1201
Thomas Davis, *CEO*
Linda Hansen, *Purch Agent*
Mike Novak, *Engineer*
Michael Querry, *Engineer*
Charlie Faciszewski, *Sales Mgr*
▲ **EMP:** 125
SQ FT: 30,000
SALES (est): 28.7MM **Privately Held**
WEB: www.harrisasm.com
SIC: 3679 Harness assemblies for electronic use: wire or cable

(G-856)
BARRETT PAVING MATERIALS INC
14 Brandywine St (13901-2203)
P.O. Box 2368 (13902-2368)
PHONE..................................607 723-5367
Gary Hoyt, *Manager*
EMP: 6
SQ FT: 1,144
SALES (corp-wide): 83.5MM **Privately Held**
WEB: www.barrettpaving.com
SIC: 2951 1442 Asphalt & asphaltic paving mixtures (not from refineries); construction sand & gravel
HQ: Barrett Paving Materials Inc.
     3 Becker Farm Rd Ste 307
     Roseland NJ 07068
     973 533-1001

(G-857)
BINGHAMTON BURIAL VAULT CO INC
1114 Porter Ave (13901-1628)
PHONE..................................607 722-4931
Brian Abbey, *President*
Janet Evenson, *Vice Pres*
EMP: 14
SQ FT: 10,000
SALES (est): 2MM **Privately Held**
SIC: 3272 Steps, prefabricated concrete; burial vaults, concrete or precast terrazzo

(G-858)
BINGHAMTON KNITTING CO INC
11 Alice St (13904-1587)
P.O. Box 1646 (13902-1646)
PHONE..................................607 722-6941
Douglas W Hardler, *President*
Craig Hardler, *Shareholder*
Julia Sherwood, *Admin Sec*
▲ **EMP:** 20 **EST:** 1922

SQ FT: 23,200
SALES: 1.1MM **Privately Held**
WEB: www.brimwick.com
SIC: 2253 Sweaters & sweater coats, knit

(G-859)
BINGHAMTON PRECAST & SUP CORP
18 Phelps St (13901-1858)
PHONE..................................607 722-0334
Jay Abbey, *Ch of Bd*
EMP: 50
SALES (est): 10.5MM **Privately Held**
WEB: www.binghamtonprecast.com
SIC: 3272 Pipe, concrete or lined with concrete

(G-860)
BINGHAMTON SIMULATOR CO INC
Also Called: B S C
151 Court St (13901-3502)
PHONE..................................607 321-2980
John Matthews, *CEO*
E Terry Lewis, *President*
Robin Laabs, *Principal*
Greg Stanton, *COO*
Barbara Blincoe, *Treasurer*
▲ **EMP:** 40
SQ FT: 14,000
SALES (est): 5.9MM **Privately Held**
WEB: www.bsc.com
SIC: 3571 3577 7699 7373 Electronic computers; graphic displays, except graphic terminals; aircraft & heavy equipment repair services; systems integration services; electrical equipment & supplies

(G-861)
BOCES BUSINESS OFFICE
Also Called: Broom Tioga Boces
435 Glenwood Rd (13905-1699)
PHONE..................................607 763-3300
Sandra Ruffo, *President*
EMP: 19
SALES (est): 2.2MM **Privately Held**
SIC: 2761 Continuous forms, office & business

(G-862)
BOKA PRINTING INC
12 Hall St (13903-2114)
PHONE..................................607 725-3235
Bob Carr, *Principal*
EMP: 7 **EST:** 2013
SALES (est): 931.9K **Privately Held**
SIC: 2752 Commercial printing, lithographic

(G-863)
BRAND BOX USA LLC
1 Chamberlain St (13904-1314)
PHONE..................................607 584-7682
EMP: 7
SALES (est): 626K **Privately Held**
SIC: 2653 Corrugated & solid fiber boxes

(G-864)
BSC ASSOCIATES LLC
151 Court St (13901-3502)
PHONE..................................607 321-2980
Greg Stanton,
Barbara Blincoe,
EMP: 19
SALES: 1.5MM **Privately Held**
SIC: 3699 Flight simulators (training aids), electronic

(G-865)
BW ELLIOTT MFG CO LLC
11 Beckwith Ave (13901-1726)
P.O. Box 773 (13902-0773)
PHONE..................................607 772-0404
Richard Allbritton, *CEO*
George Scherer, *President*
Ken Ozowski, *Vice Pres*
Tom Micha, *Purchasing*
Paul Smith, *Engineer*
▲ **EMP:** 295
SQ FT: 250,000

SALES (est): 78.7MM
SALES (corp-wide): 654.7MM **Publicly Held**
WEB: www.elliottmfg.com
SIC: 3492 3531 3568 Control valves, fluid power: hydraulic & pneumatic; construction machinery; shafts, flexible
PA: Actuant Corporation
     N86 W12500 Wstbrook Crssi St N 86
     Menomonee Falls WI 53051
     262 293-1500

(G-866)
C H THOMPSON COMPANY INC
69-93 Eldredge St (13902)
P.O. Box 333 (13902-0333)
PHONE..................................607 724-1094
Stacy Cacialli, *President*
Stacy Schraeder, *Vice Pres*
Joseph Talerico, *CFO*
Thomas Talerico, *Officer*
EMP: 65
SQ FT: 75,000
SALES (est): 8.1MM **Privately Held**
SIC: 3471 2396 3479 Anodizing (plating) of metals or formed products; automotive & apparel trimmings; painting, coating & hot dipping

(G-867)
CMP ADVNCED MECH SLTONS NY LLC
Also Called: Cmp New York
90 Bevier St (13904-1020)
PHONE..................................607 352-1712
Edward Zimmermann, *Business Mgr*
Steven Zimmermann, *Mng Member*
EMP: 130
SALES (est): 1.3MM
SALES (corp-wide): 1.6MM **Privately Held**
SIC: 3824 Mechanical & electromechanical counters & devices
PA: Cmp Ams (International) Limitee
     1241 Rue Des Cascades
     Chateauguay QC J6J 4
     450 691-5510

(G-868)
CREATIVE ORTHOTICS PROSTHETICS
65 Pennsylvania Ave 207 (13903-1651)
PHONE..................................607 771-4672
Thomas Kirk PHD, *CEO*
EMP: 9
SALES (corp-wide): 1B **Publicly Held**
SIC: 3842 5999 Limbs, artificial; orthopedic & prosthesis applications
HQ: Creative Orthotics & Prosthetics, Inc.
     1300 College Ave Ste 1
     Elmira NY 14901
     607 734-7215

(G-869)
CROWLEY FOODS INC (HQ)
93 Pennsylvania Ave (13903-1645)
PHONE..................................800 637-0019
John Kaned, *President*
▼ **EMP:** 31 **EST:** 1904
SALES (est): 185.8MM
SALES (corp-wide): 2.2B **Privately Held**
WEB: www.crowleyfoods.com
SIC: 2024 2026 Ice cream & frozen desserts; fermented & cultured milk products
PA: Hp Hood Llc
     6 Kimball Ln Ste 400
     Lynnfield MA 01940
     617 887-8441

(G-870)
D D & L INC
Also Called: E D I Window Systems
3 Alice St (13904-1502)
P.O. Box 2949 (13902-2949)
PHONE..................................607 729-9131
David P Smith, *President*
Richard Smith, *Vice Pres*
EMP: 17
SQ FT: 15,120
SALES (est): 1.7MM **Privately Held**
SIC: 3442 5211 Window & door frames; door & window products

(G-871)
DBASE LLC
100 Emerson Pkwy (13905-6625)
P.O. Box 917, Oxford (13830-0917)
PHONE..................................607 729-0234
Robert Thompson, *Principal*
Kathy Kolosky, *Engineer*
Paul McGee, *Sales Dir*
Martin Kay, *CTO*
Michael Rozlog,
EMP: 8 **EST:** 2011
SALES (est): 715.9K **Privately Held**
SIC: 7372 Application computer software

(G-872)
DLZ HOLDINGS SOUTH INC
27 Link Dr Ste D (13904-3208)
PHONE..................................607 723-1727
David Ziebarth, *Branch Mgr*
EMP: 14
SALES (corp-wide): 3.6MM **Privately Held**
WEB: www.insulatingcoatings.com
SIC: 2851 Lacquers, varnishes, enamels & other coatings
PA: Dlz Holdings South, Inc.
     956 S Us Highway 41
     Inverness FL 34450
     352 344-8741

(G-873)
ECK PLASTIC ARTS INC
87 Prospect Ave (13901-2616)
PHONE..................................607 722-3227
Robert L Eck Jr, *President*
Philip Willson, *Project Mgr*
▲ **EMP:** 25
SQ FT: 30,000
SALES (est): 5.5MM **Privately Held**
WEB: www.eckplastics.com
SIC: 3089 Injection molding of plastics; injection molded finished plastic products

(G-874)
ELECTRO FORM CORP
128 Bevier St (13904-1094)
PHONE..................................607 722-6404
Auguste Mathey Jr, *President*
Donna Kadaronak, *Office Mgr*
Donna Jadarondak, *Admin Sec*
EMP: 11
SQ FT: 6,000
SALES (est): 1.3MM **Privately Held**
SIC: 3599 Machine shop, jobbing & repair

(G-875)
EMS TECHNOLOGIES INC
71 Frederick St (13901-2563)
PHONE..................................607 723-3676
Clarence Hotchkiss, *Ch of Bd*
Mark Hotchkiss, *President*
Robert Phillips, *President*
Tom Costello, *Principal*
EMP: 40
SQ FT: 36,000
SALES (est): 9.7MM
SALES (corp-wide): 11.1MM **Privately Held**
WEB: www.emstech.com
SIC: 3672 Printed circuit boards
PA: Nelson Holdings Ltd
     71 Frederick St
     Binghamton NY 13901
     607 772-1794

(G-876)
ENJOY CITY NORTH INC
Also Called: Save Around
100 Emerson Pkwy (13905-6625)
P.O. Box 2399 (13902-2399)
PHONE..................................607 584-5061
Luke Stanton, *President*
Vik Mehta, *Partner*
Raymond H Stanton, *Principal*
Janine Drew, *Regional Mgr*
Jennifer Jones, *Regional Mgr*
EMP: 100
SALES (est): 5.9MM **Privately Held**
SIC: 2741 Miscellaneous publishing

▲ = Import ▼=Export
◆ =Import/Export

(G-877)
FELCHAR MANUFACTURING CORP (HQ)
Also Called: Norwich Manufacturing Division
196 Corporate Dr (13904-3295)
P.O. Box 3307, Williamsport PA (17701-0307)
PHONE..................607 723-4076
Jonathan Miller, *President*
Vince Bungo, *Vice Pres*
Steve Cole, *Vice Pres*
▲ EMP: 650
SQ FT: 40,000
SALES (est): 176.6MM
SALES (corp-wide): 307.3MM **Privately Held**
WEB: www.felchar.com
SIC: 3678 3089 3621 Electronic connectors; injection molding of plastics; motors & generators
PA: Shop Vac Corporation
2323 Reach Rd
Williamsport PA 17701
570 326-0502

(G-878)
FRATELLIS LLC
Also Called: New Horizons Bakery
20 Campbell Rd (13905-4304)
PHONE..................607 722-5663
Anthony Roma, *Principal*
Mary Roma, *Mng Member*
EMP: 21
SQ FT: 23,000
SALES (est): 850K **Privately Held**
SIC: 2051 2053 5142 5149 Bread, cake & related products; frozen bakery products, except bread; croissants, frozen; bakery products, frozen; bakery products

(G-879)
FRITO-LAY NORTH AMERICA INC
10 Spud Ln (13904-3299)
PHONE..................607 775-7000
Brian Stringer, *Opers-Prdtn-Mfg*
EMP: 85
SQ FT: 4,906
SALES (corp-wide): 64.6B **Publicly Held**
WEB: www.fritolay.com
SIC: 2096 2099 Potato chips & other potato-based snacks; food preparations
HQ: Frito-Lay North America, Inc.
7701 Legacy Dr
Plano TX 75024

(G-880)
GLOWA MANUFACTURING INC
6 Emma St (13905-2508)
PHONE..................607 770-0811
Jerry Glowa, *President*
Karen Glowa, *Vice Pres*
William Pomeroy, *Shareholder*
EMP: 47
SQ FT: 10,000
SALES (est): 5.3MM **Privately Held**
SIC: 3577 Computer peripheral equipment

(G-881)
HANGER PRSTHETCS & ORTHO INC
65 Pennsylvania Ave (13903-1651)
PHONE..................607 771-4672
EMP: 7
SALES (corp-wide): 1B **Publicly Held**
SIC: 3842 Limbs, artificial
HQ: Hanger Prosthetics & Orthotics, Inc.
10910 Domain Dr Ste 300
Austin TX 78758
512 777-3800

(G-882)
HP HOOD LLC
Also Called: Crowley Foods
93 Pennsylvania Ave (13903-1645)
PHONE..................607 772-6580
Joe Cervantes, *Senior VP*
EMP: 1660
SALES (corp-wide): 2.2B **Privately Held**
WEB: www.hphood.com
SIC: 2024 2026 Ice cream & frozen desserts; fermented & cultured milk products

PA: Hp Hood Llc
6 Kimball Ln Ste 400
Lynnfield MA 01940
617 887-8441

(G-883)
I 3 MANUFACTURING SERVICES INC
100 Eldredge St (13901-2631)
PHONE..................607 238-7077
James T Matthews, *President*
EMP: 5
SALES (est): 384.1K **Privately Held**
SIC: 3672 Printed circuit boards

(G-884)
I3 ASSEMBLY LLC
100 Eldredge St (13901-2631)
PHONE..................607 238-7077
James Matthews, *Mng Member*
EMP: 150 EST: 2015
SQ FT: 185,000
SALES (est): 15MM
SALES (corp-wide): 135MM **Privately Held**
SIC: 3672 Printed circuit boards
PA: I3 Electronics, Inc.
100 Eldredge St
Binghamton NY 13901
607 238-7077

(G-885)
I3 ELECTRONICS INC (PA)
100 Eldredge St (13901-2631)
PHONE..................607 238-7077
Jim Matthews Jr, *President*
James Thornton, *Opers Staff*
Raymond Brady, *Mfg Staff*
Thomas Eveges, *Mfg Staff*
Alan Fairchild, *Mfg Staff*
◆ EMP: 142 EST: 2013
SALES (est): 135MM **Privately Held**
SIC: 3672 Printed circuit boards

(G-886)
IHD MOTORSPORTS LLC
Also Called: Independence Harley-Davidson
1152 Upper Front St (13905-1119)
PHONE..................979 690-1669
James E Booth, *Mng Member*
EMP: 15 EST: 2014
SQ FT: 15,000
SALES (est): 2.6MM **Privately Held**
SIC: 3751 2396 Motorcycles & related parts; motorcycle accessories; automotive & apparel trimmings

(G-887)
ILLINOIS TOOL WORKS INC
33 Lewis Rd (13905-1048)
PHONE..................607 770-4945
Ron Skeeles, *General Mgr*
EMP: 20
SALES (corp-wide): 14.7B **Publicly Held**
SIC: 3444 Metal housings, enclosures, casings & other containers
PA: Illinois Tool Works Inc.
155 Harlem Ave
Glenview IL 60025
847 724-7500

(G-888)
INTEGRATED SOLAR TECH LLC
Also Called: Suntegra
120 Hawley St Ste 123 (13901-3904)
PHONE..................914 249-9364
Oliver Koehler, *CEO*
▲ EMP: 5
SQ FT: 500
SALES (est): 385.4K **Privately Held**
SIC: 3433 Solar heaters & collectors

(G-889)
IVI SERVICES INC
Also Called: Indian Valley
5 Pine Camp Dr (13904-3109)
PHONE..................607 729-5111
Wayne A Rozen, *CEO*
◆ EMP: 72 EST: 1940
SQ FT: 250,000

SALES (est): 13.8MM **Privately Held**
WEB: www.iviindustries.com
SIC: 2299 4225 4953 2673 Bagging, jute; general warehousing; recycling, waste materials; bags: plastic, laminated & coated; textile bags; broadwoven fabric mills, manmade

(G-890)
JANE LEWIS
Also Called: Sun Valley Printing
82 Castle Creek Rd (13901-1004)
PHONE..................607 722-0584
Jane Lewis, *Owner*
David A Lewis, *Co-Owner*
EMP: 6
SQ FT: 2,400
SALES: 250K **Privately Held**
SIC: 2752 2791 2789 Commercial printing, offset; typesetting; bookbinding & related work

(G-891)
JOHNSON OUTDOORS INC
Eureka Tents
625 Conklin Rd (13903-2700)
P.O. Box 966 (13902-0966)
PHONE..................607 779-2200
Mark Pecora, *Warehouse Mgr*
William Kelly, *Branch Mgr*
Nathan Hines, *Manager*
EMP: 175
SALES (corp-wide): 490.5MM **Publicly Held**
SIC: 2394 2393 5091 5941 Tents: made from purchased materials; knapsacks, canvas: made from purchased materials; camping equipment & supplies; camping equipment; canoe & kayak dealers; sporting & athletic goods
PA: Johnson Outdoors Inc.
555 Main St
Racine WI 53403
262 631-6600

(G-892)
JONES HUMDINGER
204 Hayes Rd (13905-5918)
PHONE..................607 771-6501
Steve Kallfelz, *Owner*
EMP: 15
SALES: 180K **Privately Held**
SIC: 2024 Ice cream & frozen desserts

(G-893)
LABRADOR STONE INC
11 Dutchess Rd (13901-1411)
PHONE..................570 465-2120
EMP: 7
SALES (est): 912.6K **Privately Held**
SIC: 1429 7389 Crushed & broken stone;

(G-894)
LEO P CALLAHAN INC
229 Lwer Stlla Ireland Rd (13905)
PHONE..................607 797-7314
James Callahan, *President*
EMP: 10 EST: 1960
SQ FT: 1,600
SALES (est): 1MM **Privately Held**
SIC: 2796 Color separations for printing

(G-895)
MASONITE INTERNATIONAL CORP
Also Called: Bwo of NY
28 Track Dr (13904-2717)
PHONE..................607 775-0615
Brian Shearer, *Sales Executive*
Brock Ryall, *Branch Mgr*
EMP: 12
SALES (corp-wide): 2.1B **Publicly Held**
WEB: www.bwimillwork.com
SIC: 2431 Millwork
PA: Masonite International Corporation
201 N Franklin St Ste 300
Tampa FL 33602
800 895-2723

(G-896)
MECHANICAL PWR CONVERSION LLC
Also Called: D&V Electronics USA
6 Emma St (13905-2508)
PHONE..................607 766-9620
David Eddy, *President*

EMP: 14
SQ FT: 10,000
SALES (est): 5MM
SALES (corp-wide): 472.8MM **Publicly Held**
WEB: www.eandmpower.com
SIC: 3679 Electronic loads & power supplies
PA: Motorcar Parts Of America Inc
2929 California St
Torrance CA 90503
310 212-7910

(G-897)
MELLEM CORPORATION
Also Called: Goldsmith
31 Lewis St Ste 1 (13901-3018)
PHONE..................607 723-0001
Gina McHugh, *President*
▲ EMP: 15
SQ FT: 750
SALES (est): 1.9MM **Privately Held**
SIC: 3911 5944 Jewelry, precious metal; jewelry, precious stones & precious metals

(G-898)
METAL FAB LLC
13 Spud Ln (13904-3210)
PHONE..................607 775-3200
Patrick Ryan, *Manager*
Janet Beal,
Rick Simon,
Eugene Taren,
EMP: 5
SQ FT: 9,500
SALES: 857K **Privately Held**
SIC: 3441 Fabricated structural metal

(G-899)
MORO CORPORATION
Also Called: Titchener Iron Works Division
23 Griswold St (13904-1511)
PHONE..................607 724-4241
Douglas Wilcox, *Branch Mgr*
EMP: 25
SQ FT: 7,368
SALES (corp-wide): 62MM **Publicly Held**
WEB: www.mcgregorindustries.com
SIC: 3446 Architectural metalwork
PA: Moro Corporation
994 Old Eagle School Rd # 1000
Wayne PA 19087
484 367-0300

(G-900)
MS MACHINING INC
Also Called: Mechanical Specialties Co
2 William St (13904-1418)
P.O. Box 2046 (13902-2046)
PHONE..................607 723-1105
Eugene Mazza, *President*
Jo Ann Risley, *Office Mgr*
EMP: 9 EST: 1956
SQ FT: 10,000
SALES (est): 1.5MM **Privately Held**
SIC: 3544 3599 Special dies & tools; custom machinery; machine shop, jobbing & repair

(G-901)
NELSON HOLDINGS LTD (PA)
71 Frederick St (13901-2529)
PHONE..................607 772-1794
Clarence Hotchkiss Jr, *Ch of Bd*
Mark Hotchkiss, *President*
Frederick Hotchkiss, *Vice Pres*
EMP: 1
SQ FT: 180,000
SALES (est): 11.1MM **Privately Held**
SIC: 3679 5261 7699 Electronic circuits; lawn & garden equipment; lawn mower repair shop

(G-902)
NIELSEN HARDWARE CORPORATION (PA)
Also Called: Nielsen/Sessions
71 Frederick St (13901-2529)
P.O. Box 773 (13902-0773)
PHONE..................607 821-1475
David Snavely, *Buyer*
Sonia Pelletier Moore, *CFO*
Gary Oliveira, *Manager*
◆ EMP: 25
SQ FT: 40,000

SALES (est): 5MM **Privately Held**
WEB: www.nielsensessions.com
SIC: 3429 Manufactured hardware (general)

(G-903)
PARLOR CITY PAPER BOX CO INC
2 Eldredge St (13901-2600)
P.O. Box 756 (13902-0756)
PHONE..............................607 772-0600
David L Culver, *Ch of Bd*
Bruce Culver, *Vice Pres*
Brian Culver, *Human Res Mgr*
EMP: 56
SQ FT: 140,000
SALES (est): 13MM **Privately Held**
WEB: www.pghcitypaper.com
SIC: 2653 2652 Corrugated & solid fiber boxes; setup paperboard boxes

(G-904)
PETER PAPASTRAT
Also Called: A A P C O Screen Prntng/Sprtwr
193 Main St (13905-2619)
P.O. Box 285 (13905-0285)
PHONE..............................607 723-8112
Peter Papastrat, *Owner*
EMP: 5
SQ FT: 6,000
SALES (est): 326.2K **Privately Held**
SIC: 2759 5699 Screen printing; customized clothing & apparel

(G-905)
RB CONVERTING INC
28 Track Dr (13904-2717)
PHONE..............................607 777-1325
Paul Haslett, *Branch Mgr*
EMP: 5 **Privately Held**
SIC: 2679 Paper products, converted
HQ: Rb Converting, Inc.
12855 Valley Branch Ln
Dallas TX 75234
800 543-7690

(G-906)
REYNOLDS BOOK BINDERY LLC
37 Milford St (13904-1615)
PHONE..............................607 772-8937
Fax: 607 772-0152
EMP: 11
SQ FT: 15,000
SALES (est): 720K **Privately Held**
SIC: 2789 Book Bindery Company

(G-907)
S L C INDUSTRIES INCORPORATED
63 Barlow Rd (13904-2722)
P.O. Box 116, Kirkwood (13795-0116)
PHONE..............................607 775-2299
Adam Milligan, *President*
Art Boyle, *President*
Michael Prozeralik, *Treasurer*
Thomas O Milligan, *Admin Sec*
EMP: 10
SQ FT: 20,000
SALES (est): 1.5MM **Privately Held**
WEB: www.slcindustries.com
SIC: 2759 2789 Screen printing; bookbinding & related work

(G-908)
SENSOR & DECONTAMINATION INC
Also Called: S D I
892 Powderhouse Rd (13903-7104)
P.O. Box 132 (13903-0132)
PHONE..............................301 526-8389
Barry R Jones, *President*
David Doetschman, *Corp Secy*
EMP: 10
SALES (est): 710K **Privately Held**
WEB: www.sensoranddecon.com
SIC: 2842 7389 Specialty cleaning preparations;

(G-909)
SOUTHERN TIER PLASTICS INC
Kirkwood Industrial Park (13902)
P.O. Box 2015 (13902-2015)
PHONE..............................607 723-2601
Joyce Gray, *President*
Douglas Gray, *Treasurer*

Barbara Gwyn, *Admin Sec*
▲ **EMP:** 72
SQ FT: 30,000
SALES (est): 14.8MM **Privately Held**
WEB: www.southerntierplastics.com
SIC: 3089 Injection molding of plastics

(G-910)
SUNY AT BINGHAMTON
Also Called: School of Management
Vestal Pkwy E (13901)
PHONE..............................607 777-2316
Gary Roodman, *Dean*
EMP: 73 **Privately Held**
SIC: 2731 8221 9411 Books: publishing only; university; administration of educational programs;
HQ: Suny At Binghamton
4400 Vestal Pkwy
Binghamton NY 13902
607 777-2000

(G-911)
SURESCAN CORPORATION
Also Called: X1000
100 Eldredge St (13901-2631)
PHONE..............................607 321-0042
Jim Matthews, *CEO*
John Percival, *President*
EMP: 23
SALES (est): 5.3MM
SALES (corp-wide): 135MM **Privately Held**
WEB: www.surescaneds.com
SIC: 3844 X-ray apparatus & tubes
PA: I3 Electronics, Inc.
100 Eldredge St
Binghamton NY 13901
607 238-7077

(G-912)
TCMF INC
Also Called: C.H. Thompson Finishing
69-93 Eldredge St (13901)
PHONE..............................607 724-1094
George Morgan, *President*
Brittany Morgan, *President*
Charles Morgan, *Vice Pres*
Trevor Morgan, *Admin Sec*
EMP: 75
SALES (est): 4.1MM **Privately Held**
SIC: 3471 2759 Plating & polishing; commercial printing

(G-913)
THOMAS F EGAN
Also Called: Craftsmen/Access Unlimited
570 Hance Rd (13903-5700)
PHONE..............................607 669-4822
Thomas Egan, *Owner*
Nancy Garrett, *Manager*
EMP: 26
SALES (est): 3.5MM **Privately Held**
WEB: www.accessunlimited.com
SIC: 3842 3999 Technical aids for the handicapped; wheelchair lifts

(G-914)
TRI CITY HIGHWAY PRODUCTS INC
111 Bevier St (13904-1013)
PHONE..............................607 722-2967
Martin A Galasso Jr, *CEO*
EMP: 30
SQ FT: 2,500
SALES (est): 5.2MM **Privately Held**
SIC: 2951 1442 Asphalt paving mixtures & blocks; construction sand & gravel

(G-915)
VIRTUSPHERE INC
7 Hillside Ave (13903-2025)
PHONE..............................607 760-2207
Nourakhmed Latypov, *CEO*
Nurulla Latypov, *President*
EMP: 11
SALES: 150K **Privately Held**
SIC: 7372 Educational computer software

(G-916)
WESTCODE INCORPORATED
2226 Airport Rd (13905-5912)
PHONE..............................607 766-9881
Edward J Widdowson, *CEO*
EMP: 25

SALES (corp-wide): 918.8MM **Privately Held**
WEB: www.westcodeus.com
SIC: 3743 Railroad equipment
HQ: Westcode Incorporated
223 Wilmington W
Chadds Ford PA 19317
610 738-1200

Blasdell
Erie County

(G-917)
B F G ELCPLTG AND MFG CO
3949 Jeffrey Blvd (14219-2334)
P.O. Box 825, Hamburg (14075-0825)
PHONE..............................716 362-0888
Minta Marie, *CEO*
EMP: 32
SALES (est): 255K **Privately Held**
SIC: 3999 Manufacturing industries

(G-918)
CARBON ACTIVATED CORPORATION
3774 Hoover Rd (14219-2302)
PHONE..............................716 677-6661
Chris Allen, *Branch Mgr*
EMP: 22 **Privately Held**
SIC: 2819 Industrial inorganic chemicals
PA: Carbon Activated Corporation
2250 S Central Ave
Compton CA 90220

(G-919)
KRIEGER DEFENSE GROUP LLC
4329 Oakwood Ave (14219-1222)
PHONE..............................716 485-1970
Troy Lapare, *Principal*
Joe Gutowski, *Principal*
EMP: 10
SALES (est): 362.1K **Privately Held**
SIC: 3812 Defense systems & equipment

(G-920)
REPUBLIC STEEL INC
Also Called: Lackawanna Hot Rolled Plant
3049 Lake Shore Rd (14219-1447)
PHONE..............................716 827-2800
Larry Braun, *General Mgr*
Tom Tyrrell, *Branch Mgr*
EMP: 360 **Privately Held**
SIC: 3312 Blast furnaces & steel mills
HQ: Republic Steel
2633 8th St Ne
Canton OH 44704
330 438-5435

(G-921)
SAMUEL SON & CO (USA) INC
250 Lake Ave (14219-1500)
PHONE..............................716 856-6500
Don Clark, *Branch Mgr*
EMP: 9
SALES (corp-wide): 1.8B **Privately Held**
SIC: 3312 Blast furnaces & steel mills
HQ: Samuel, Son & Co. (Usa) Inc.
1401 Davey Rd Ste 300
Woodridge IL 60517
630 783-8900

(G-922)
SOTEK INC
3590 Jeffrey Blvd (14219-2390)
PHONE..............................716 821-5961
John E Maurer, *President*
Michael Maurer, *Vice Pres*
Jim Carroll, *Opers Mgr*
John Rehac, *Manager*
Rick Pfalzer, *Maintence Staff*
▲ **EMP:** 52
SQ FT: 45,000
SALES (est): 9.3MM **Privately Held**
WEB: www.sotek.com
SIC: 3599 Machine shop, jobbing & repair

(G-923)
TRANSCO RAILWAY PRODUCTS INC
Milestrip Rd (14219)
P.O. Box 1968, Buffalo (14219-0168)
PHONE..............................716 824-1219
Tom Jakubowski, *Manager*

EMP: 23
SALES (corp-wide): 225.3B **Publicly Held**
SIC: 3743 Railroad equipment, except locomotives
HQ: Transco Railway Products Inc.
200 N La Salle St # 1550
Chicago IL 60601
312 427-2818

(G-924)
VALENTI DISTRIBUTING
84 Maple Ave (14219-1624)
PHONE..............................716 824-2304
John Valenti, *Principal*
EMP: 7
SALES (est): 23.6K **Privately Held**
SIC: 2064 Candy & other confectionery products

Blauvelt
Rockland County

(G-925)
AERCO INTERNATIONAL INC (HQ)
100 Oritani Dr (10913-1022)
PHONE..............................845 580-8000
James F Dagley, *President*
Fred Depuy, *Vice Pres*
Lou Vorsteveld, *Vice Pres*
Doug Hoover, *Facilities Mgr*
Ronald Lake, *Buyer*
▲ **EMP:** 153
SQ FT: 150,000
SALES (est): 36.5MM
SALES (corp-wide): 1.5B **Publicly Held**
WEB: www.aerco.com
SIC: 3443 3492 Heat exchangers, plate type; heat exchangers: coolers (after, inter), condensers, etc.; boilers: industrial, power, or marine; control valves, fluid power: hydraulic & pneumatic
PA: Watts Water Technologies, Inc.
815 Chestnut St
North Andover MA 01845
978 688-1811

(G-926)
ARTWILL GROUP LLC
344 Greenbush Rd (10913-1108)
PHONE..............................845 826-3692
Denise Weiner, *Mng Member*
EMP: 22
SALES (est): 646.2K **Privately Held**
SIC: 2759 Screen printing

(G-927)
CWS POWDER COATINGS COMPANY LP
2234 Bradley Hill Rd # 12 (10913-1014)
PHONE..............................845 398-2911
Cws Powder Coatings, *Partner*
Victoria Phillips, *Controller*
Jonathan Abrams, *Director*
▲ **EMP:** 9
SQ FT: 2,500
SALES (est): 2.4MM
SALES (corp-wide): 73.1MM **Privately Held**
SIC: 3399 Powder, metal
HQ: Cws Powder Coatings Gmbh
Katharinenstr. 61
Duren 52353
242 198-30

(G-928)
ERT SOFTWARE INC
4 Pine Glen Dr (10913-1150)
PHONE..............................845 358-5721
Roman Tenenbaum, *President*
EMP: 5
SALES: 1.5MM **Privately Held**
WEB: www.alivest.com
SIC: 7372 Prepackaged software

(G-929)
K-BINET INC
624 Route 303 (10913-1170)
PHONE..............................845 348-1149
Jay Kim, *President*
Ann Degli, *Admin Sec*
EMP: 8 **EST:** 2001

SALES (est): 680K **Privately Held**
SIC: 2434 Wood kitchen cabinets

(G-930)
LIGHTING N BEYOND LLC
628 Ste 303 (10913)
P.O. Box 539, Spring Valley (10977-0539)
PHONE.............................718 669-9142
Mike Oberlander,
EMP: 5
SQ FT: 6,000
SALES: 150K **Privately Held**
SIC: 3648 Lighting equipment

(G-931)
NEXBEV INDUSTRIES LLC (PA)
600 Bradley Hill Rd Ste 2 (10913-1171)
PHONE.............................646 648-1255
Charles Sessoms,
Antonio Johnson,
EMP: 10
SQ FT: 750
SALES: 50K **Privately Held**
SIC: 2086 Carbonated beverages, nonalcoholic: bottled & canned

(G-932)
RBHAMMERS CORP
Also Called: Heatherdell RB Hammers
500 Bradley Hill Rd (10913-1134)
PHONE.............................845 353-5042
Richard Tegtmeier, *President*
Brian Kobza, *Transportation*
◆ EMP: 10
SQ FT: 1,500
SALES (est): 5.8MM **Privately Held**
SIC: 3546 Hammers, portable: electric or
pneumatic, chipping, etc.

(G-933)
RYAN PRINTING INC
300 Corporate Dr Ste 6 (10913-1162)
PHONE.............................845 535-3235
Al Ryan, *President*
EMP: 26
SQ FT: 35,000
SALES (est): 5MM **Privately Held**
SIC: 2752 Commercial printing, offset

(G-934)
SWIVELIER COMPANY INC
Also Called: Point Electric Div
600 Bradley Hill Rd Ste 3 (10913-1171)
PHONE.............................845 353-1455
Michael I Schwartz, *President*
Louis M Cafarchio, *Admin Sec*
EMP: 70
SQ FT: 125,000
SALES (est): 10.8MM **Privately Held**
WEB: www.swivelier.com
SIC: 3646 3645 3643 Commercial indusl
& institutional electric lighting fixtures; residential lighting fixtures; current-carrying
wiring devices

(G-935)
TAPPAN WIRE & CABLE INC
(HQ)
100 Bradley Hill Rd (10913-1000)
P.O. Box 4000, Carrollton GA (30112-5050)
PHONE.............................845 353-9000
Stuart W Thorn, *Ch of Bd*
Darren Krych, *President*
Mike Luterzo, *Vice Pres*
Jerry Rosen, *CFO*
▲ EMP: 189 EST: 1978
SQ FT: 180,000
SALES (est): 46.5MM
SALES (corp-wide): 2.2B **Privately Held**
WEB: www.tappanwire.com
SIC: 3315 3643 3357 Wire & fabricated
wire products; current-carrying wiring devices; nonferrous wiredrawing & insulating
PA: Southwire Company, Llc
1 Southwire Dr
Carrollton GA 30119
770 832-4242

(G-936)
TRI-SEAL HOLDINGS INC
900 Bradley Hill Rd (10913-1163)
PHONE.............................845 353-3300
Paul Young, *Ch of Bd*
Diane Schweitzer, *Owner*
F Patrick Smith, *Chairman*

Jim Jackson, *Production*
Charles Greco, *QC Mgr*
EMP: 63 EST: 1946
SQ FT: 58,000
SALES (est): 9.1MM
SALES (corp-wide): 1.1B **Privately Held**
WEB: www.tri-seal.com
SIC: 3081 2821 Packing materials, plastic
sheet; plastics materials & resins
PA: Tekni-Plex, Inc.
460 E Swedesford Rd # 3000
Wayne PA 19087
484 690-1520

(G-937)
TRI-SEAL INTERNATIONAL INC
(HQ)
900 Bradley Hill Rd (10913-1163)
PHONE.............................845 353-3300
Anatoly Verdel, *President*
▲ EMP: 3
SALES (est): 1MM
SALES (corp-wide): 1.1B **Privately Held**
SIC: 2679 Egg cartons, molded pulp: made
from purchased material
PA: Tekni-Plex, Inc.
460 E Swedesford Rd # 3000
Wayne PA 19087
484 690-1520

(G-938)
VITS INTERNATIONAL INC
200 Corporate Dr (10913-1119)
PHONE.............................845 353-5000
Deirdre Ryder, *President*
◆ EMP: 40
SQ FT: 22,000
SALES: 20MM **Privately Held**
WEB: www.vitsamerica.com
SIC: 3555 Printing trades machinery

Bliss
Wyoming County

(G-939)
FIVE CORNERS REPAIR INC
6653 Hardys Rd (14024-9714)
PHONE.............................585 322-7369
Jason Sampson, *President*
Scott Lester, *Vice Pres*
EMP: 12
SALES: 950K **Privately Held**
SIC: 3441 Fabricated structural metal

Bloomfield
Ontario County

(G-940)
BENJAMIN SHERIDAN
CORPORATION (DH)
7629 State Route 5 And 20 (14469-9210)
PHONE.............................585 657-6161
Ken D'Arcy, *President*
EMP: 5
SQ FT: 224,000
SALES (est): 9.3MM **Publicly Held**
SIC: 3482 3484 Pellets & BB's, pistol & air
rifle ammunition; pellet & BB guns
HQ: Crosman Corporation
7629 State Route 5 And 20
Bloomfield NY 14469
585 657-6161

(G-941)
BRISTOL METALS INC
7817 State Route 5 And 20 (14469-9352)
PHONE.............................585 657-7665
Edward Gilligan, *President*
Kelly Gilligan, *Corp Secy*
EMP: 14
SQ FT: 15,000
SALES: 1.5MM **Privately Held**
SIC: 3441 Fabricated structural metal

(G-942)
CARVER CREEK ENTERPRISES
INC
2524 Cannan Rd (14469-9655)
PHONE.............................585 657-7511
Donald Dean, *President*

Thomas Dean, *Vice Pres*
EMP: 5
SQ FT: 1,764
SALES (est): 706.5K **Privately Held**
WEB: www.carvercreekent.com
SIC: 2511 Wood household furniture

(G-943)
COMMODORE MACHINE CO INC
26 Maple Ave (14469-9228)
PHONE.............................585 657-6916
George Brandoon, *Ch of Bd*
▲ EMP: 21 EST: 1970
SALES (est): 3.6MM **Privately Held**
SIC: 3089 Trays, plastic

(G-944)
CRESENT SERVICES INC
Also Called: Crescent Tank Mfg
2557 Cannan Rd (14469-9655)
P.O. Box 116 (14469-0116)
PHONE.............................585 657-4104
Robert Denome, *President*
EMP: 3
SQ FT: 11,000
SALES (est): 1.5MM **Privately Held**
SIC: 3589 Car washing machinery

(G-945)
CROSMAN CORPORATION (DH)
7629 State Route 5 And 20 (14469-9210)
PHONE.............................585 657-6161
Robert Beckwith, *CEO*
Sonia Nau, *Vice Pres*
David Swanson, *Vice Pres*
Jim Haremza, *Plant Mgr*
Marissa Wasickanin, *Production*
▲ EMP: 29
SQ FT: 224,000
SALES (est): 20.6MM **Publicly Held**
WEB: www.crosman.com
SIC: 3484 3482 3563 Pellet & BB guns;
pellets & BB's, pistol & air rifle ammunition; shot, steel (ammunition); air & gas
compressors
HQ: Cbcp Acquisition Corp.
60 One Wilton Rd Fl 2 Sixty
Westport CT 06880
203 221-1703

(G-946)
DOLCO LLC
Also Called: Commodore
26 Maple Ave (14469-9228)
PHONE.............................585 657-7777
George Braddon, *CEO*
Fritz Seager, *President*
Nicholas Calcagno, *Vice Pres*
Bill Bezek, *Project Mgr*
Brett Campbell, *Design Engr*
▲ EMP: 50
SQ FT: 35,000
SALES (est): 14.5MM
SALES (corp-wide): 1.1B **Privately Held**
SIC: 3089 2671 7336 Injection molding of
plastics; packaging paper & plastics film,
coated & laminated; package design
HQ: Dolco Packaging Corp.
101 Railroad Ave
Ridgefield NJ 07657

(G-947)
FURNITURE DOCTOR INC
7007 State Route 5 And 20 (14469-9322)
P.O. Box 519 (14469-0519)
PHONE.............................585 657-6941
Thomas Baker, *President*
Marfa Baker, *Corp Secy*
EMP: 9
SQ FT: 16,000
SALES (est): 847K **Privately Held**
WEB: www.thefurnituredoctoronline.com
SIC: 2511 2514 5712 5021 Wood household furniture; metal household furniture;
furniture stores; furniture; reupholstery &
furniture repair; interior decorating

(G-948)
TERPHANE HOLDINGS LLC (DH)
2754 W Park Dr (14469-9385)
PHONE.............................585 657-5800
Richard Composto, *Plant Mgr*
Linda Wilson, *Purch Mgr*
Renan Bergmann,
▼ EMP: 7

SALES (est): 14.6MM
SALES (corp-wide): 1.1B **Publicly Held**
SIC: 2821 5199 Plastics materials &
resins; packaging materials
HQ: Tredegar Film Products Corporation
1100 Boulders Pkwy # 200
North Chesterfield VA 23225
804 330-1000

(G-949)
TERPHANE LLC
2754 W Park Dr (14469-9385)
PHONE.............................585 657-5800
Renan Bergmann, *CEO*
Clyde McDonald, *Maint Spvr*
Glen Vonwald, *Production*
Linda Wilson, *Purch Mgr*
Gabriel Caridade, *Technical Mgr*
◆ EMP: 52
SQ FT: 100,000
SALES (est): 14.6MM
SALES (corp-wide): 1.1B **Publicly Held**
WEB: www.terphane.com
SIC: 2821 Polyesters
HQ: Terphane Holdings Llc
2754 W Park Dr
Bloomfield NY 14469

(G-950)
VELMEX INC
7550 State Route 5 And 20 (14469-9389)
PHONE.............................585 657-6151
Mitchel Evans, *President*
Tim Luzeckyj, *Production*
Manny Freshman, *Engineer*
Alan Lane, *Engineer*
Alayne Evans, *Treasurer*
EMP: 32
SQ FT: 15,500
SALES: 5.4MM **Privately Held**
WEB: www.velmex.com
SIC: 3545 Machine tool attachments & accessories

Bloomington
Ulster County

(G-951)
COBRA SYSTEMS INC
2669 New York 32 (12411)
PHONE.............................845 338-6675
Michael V Pavlov, *President*
▼ EMP: 10
SQ FT: 2,400
SALES (est): 1.6MM **Privately Held**
WEB: www.cobracoil.com
SIC: 3496 Barbed wire, made from purchased wire

Bloomville
Delaware County

(G-952)
ED BEACH FOREST
MANAGEMENT
2042 Scott Rd (13739-1203)
PHONE.............................607 538-1745
Edwin R Beach, *Principal*
EMP: 6 EST: 2010
SALES (est): 461K **Privately Held**
SIC: 2411 Logging

(G-953)
G HAYNES HOLDINGS INC
Also Called: Catskill Castings Co
51971 State Highway 10 (13739-2242)
P.O. Box 752 (13739-0752)
PHONE.............................607 538-1160
George Haynes, *President*
EMP: 9
SQ FT: 3,500
SALES (est): 423.5K **Privately Held**
WEB: www.catskillcastings.com
SIC: 3543 Foundry patternmaking

(G-954)
GREENE BRASS & ALUM FNDRY LLC
51971 State Highway 10 (13739-2242)
P.O. Box 752 (13739-0752)
PHONE..........................607 656-4204
Thomas Dodd, *Mng Member*
George Heynes,
EMP: 7
SALES: 1.1MM **Privately Held**
SIC: 3334 3363 7389 Primary aluminum; aluminum die-castings;

Blossvale
Oneida County

(G-955)
BLUEBAR OIL CO INC
8446 Mill Pond Way (13308)
PHONE..........................315 245-4328
David Link, *President*
EMP: 11
SQ FT: 2,000
SALES (est): 1MM **Privately Held**
SIC: 1389 5983 5172 Oil field services; fuel oil dealers; gasoline

---

Blue Point
Suffolk County

(G-956)
DEER PK STAIR BLDG MLLWK INC
51 Kennedy Ave (11715-1009)
P.O. Box 107 (11715-0107)
PHONE..........................631 363-5000
Michael Souto, *President*
Leita Souto, *Admin Sec*
EMP: 45
SQ FT: 30,000
SALES (est): 7.9MM **Privately Held**
WEB: www.deerparkstairs.com
SIC: 2431 5211 5031 Stair railings, wood; staircases & stairs, wood; lumber products; cabinets, kitchen; kitchen cabinets

(G-957)
SPECIALTY INK CO INC (PA)
Also Called: Aero Brand Inks
40 Harbour Dr (11715-1421)
P.O. Box 778, Deer Park (11729-0778)
PHONE..........................631 586-3666
Gary Werwa, *President*
▲ EMP: 16 EST: 1934
SQ FT: 15,000
SALES (est): 3.2MM **Privately Held**
WEB: www.specialtyink.com
SIC: 2899 3953 2893 Ink or writing fluids; pads, inking & stamping; printing ink

---

Bohemia
Suffolk County

(G-958)
A NATIONAL PRINTING CO INC
606 Johnson Ave Ste 31 (11716-2688)
PHONE..........................631 243-3395
Michael Orrach, *President*
EMP: 6
SALES (est): 371.6K **Privately Held**
SIC: 2752 Commercial printing, lithographic

(G-959)
A P MANUFACTURING
21 Floyds Run (11716-2155)
PHONE..........................909 228-3049
Jane P Sobota, *Owner*
EMP: 7
SALES (est): 336.5K **Privately Held**
SIC: 3599 Machine shop, jobbing & repair

(G-960)
ABACO STEEL PRODUCTS INC
40 Aero Rd Ste 4 (11716-2194)
PHONE..........................631 589-1800
Kenneth Podd, *President*

EMP: 4 EST: 1972
SQ FT: 10,000
SALES: 1.2MM **Privately Held**
WEB: www.abacosteel.com
SIC: 2542 2541 Shelving, office & store: except wood; partitions for floor attachment, prefabricated: except wood; cabinets, lockers & shelving

(G-961)
ABLE ENVIRONMENTAL SERVICES
1599 Ocean Ave (11716-1947)
PHONE..........................631 567-6585
Faith Barnard, *President*
EMP: 5
SALES (est): 550K **Privately Held**
SIC: 1382 Oil & gas exploration services

(G-962)
ABSOLUTE MANUFACTURING INC
Also Called: Absolute Engineering Company
210 Knickerbocker Ave (11716-3175)
PHONE..........................631 563-7466
Val Palzzynski, *President*
Carissa Pelczynski, *Accounts Exec*
EMP: 8
SQ FT: 5,000
SALES (est): 1MM **Privately Held**
SIC: 3599 Machine shop, jobbing & repair

(G-963)
ACCURATE MARINE SPECIALTIES
2200 Artic Ave (11716-2414)
PHONE..........................631 589-5502
Gary Lucas, *President*
Chip Watkins, *Corp Secy*
EMP: 6
SQ FT: 5,900
SALES (est): 959.8K **Privately Held**
SIC: 7694 5541 Motor repair services; marine service station

(G-964)
ACE CNTRACTING CONSULTING CORP
Also Called: Island Chimney Service
1650 Sycamore Ave Ste 18 (11716-1731)
PHONE..........................631 567-4752
Marc Jagerman, *President*
EMP: 9
SALES (est): 843.6K **Privately Held**
SIC: 3271 Blocks, concrete: chimney or fireplace

(G-965)
ACE MOLDING & TOOL INC
51 Floyds Run (11716-2155)
PHONE..........................631 567-2355
Americo Carnaxide, *President*
EMP: 5
SALES: 40K **Privately Held**
SIC: 3089 Molding primary plastic

(G-966)
ADVANCED CYBER SECURITY CORP
3880 Veterans Memorial Hw (11716-1038)
PHONE..........................866 417-9155
Daniel Delgiorno, *CEO*
EMP: 20
SALES (est): 1.1MM **Privately Held**
SIC: 7372 Operating systems computer software

(G-967)
AEROSPACE LIGHTING CORPORATION (DH)
355 Knickerbocker Ave (11716-3103)
PHONE..........................631 563-6400
Werner Lieberherr, *President*
Thomas P McCaffrey, *Senior VP*
Sean Cromie, *Vice Pres*
Wayne R Exton, *Vice Pres*
Steve Scover, *Vice Pres*
EMP: 100 EST: 1987
SQ FT: 60,000
SALES: 15.3MM
SALES (corp-wide): 66.5B **Publicly Held**
SIC: 3647 5063 Aircraft lighting fixtures; electrical apparatus & equipment

HQ: B/E Aerospace, Inc.
1400 Corporate Center Way
Wellington FL 33414
561 791-5000

(G-968)
ALL AMERICAN AWARDS INC
Also Called: All American Uniform
331 Knickerbocker Ave (11716-3134)
PHONE..........................631 567-2025
Frank Coppola, *President*
Jean Coppola, *Vice Pres*
Gina Fecile, *Office Mgr*
Dominic Coppola, *Manager*
EMP: 11
SQ FT: 10,000
SALES (est): 1.4MM **Privately Held**
SIC: 3914 5699 5199 2395 Trophies; uniforms & work clothing; advertising specialties; embroidery & art needlework

(G-969)
ALL ISLAND BLOWER & SHTMTL
1585 Smithtown Ave Unit C (11716-2406)
PHONE..........................631 567-7070
Brian Levine, *President*
Brian Higgins, *President*
EMP: 10
SQ FT: 4,000
SALES (est): 1.1MM **Privately Held**
SIC: 3444 Sheet metal specialties, not stamped

(G-970)
AM CAST INC (PA)
34 Aero Rd (11716-2902)
PHONE..........................631 750-1644
Tomaso Veneroso, *Ch of Bd*
Ray Redman, *COO*
Stephanie Veneroso, *Vice Pres*
Davide Berretti, *CFO*
Jenna Santaniello, *Admin Asst*
▲ EMP: 11
SQ FT: 3,500
SALES (est): 2MM **Privately Held**
WEB: www.amcastonline.com
SIC: 3364 Nonferrous die-castings except aluminum

(G-971)
AMPLITECH INC
620 Johnson Ave Ste 2 (11716-2658)
PHONE..........................631 521-7738
Fawad Maqbool, *CEO*
EMP: 8
SQ FT: 5,500
SALES: 1.2MM **Privately Held**
WEB: www.amplitechinc.com
SIC: 3663 Microwave communication equipment

(G-972)
AMPLITECH GROUP INC (PA)
620 Johnson Ave Ste 2 (11716-2658)
PHONE..........................631 521-7831
Fawad Maqbool, *Ch of Bd*
Louisa Sanfratello, *CFO*
EMP: 6 EST: 2002
SALES: 2.4MM **Publicly Held**
SIC: 3651 3663 Amplifiers: radio, public address or musical instrument; microwave communication equipment

(G-973)
ANDREA ELECTRONICS CORPORATION (PA)
620 Johnson Ave Ste 1b (11716-2636)
PHONE..........................631 719-1800
Douglas J Andrea, *Ch of Bd*
Corisa L Guiffre, *CFO*
Marybeth Loizos, *Accounts Exec*
◆ EMP: 9 EST: 1934
SQ FT: 3,000
SALES: 1.4MM **Publicly Held**
WEB: www.andreaelectronics.com
SIC: 3651 3663 3577 Microphones; mobile communication equipment; computer peripheral equipment

(G-974)
APEX SIGNAL CORPORATION
110 Wilbur Pl (11716-2402)
PHONE..........................631 567-1100
William Forman, *President*
Wayne Grandner, *COO*

Patty Angelos, *Manager*
EMP: 90
SALES (est): 9.5MM **Privately Held**
SIC: 3669 5065 Traffic signals, electric; electronic parts & equipment
PA: North Atlantic Industries, Inc.
110 Wilbur Pl
Bohemia NY 11716

(G-975)
ARCHIMEDES PRODUCTS INC
21 Floyds Run (11716-2155)
PHONE..........................631 589-1215
Jane Sobota, *President*
EMP: 8
SQ FT: 6,000
SALES (est): 760K **Privately Held**
WEB: www.cncarch.com
SIC: 3599 Machine shop, jobbing & repair

(G-976)
ARLAN DAMPER CORPORATION
1598 Lakeland Ave (11716-2198)
PHONE..........................631 589-7431
Albert A Sapio, *President*
EMP: 25 EST: 1961
SQ FT: 6,400
SALES (est): 4.8MM **Privately Held**
SIC: 3444 Sheet metal specialties, not stamped

(G-977)
B & H PRECISION FABRICATORS
95 Davinci Dr (11716-2601)
PHONE..........................631 563-9620
Dan Barthelomew, *President*
Deborah Barthelomew, *Vice Pres*
Debbie Bartholomew, *Officer*
EMP: 15
SQ FT: 5,000
SALES: 1MM **Privately Held**
SIC: 3444 Sheet metal specialties, not stamped

(G-978)
B/E AEROSPACE INC
355 Knickerbocker Ave (11716-3103)
PHONE..........................631 563-6400
Amin J Khoury, *Ch of Bd*
EMP: 30
SALES (corp-wide): 66.5B **Publicly Held**
SIC: 2531 3728 3647 Seats, aircraft; aircraft parts & equipment; aircraft lighting fixtures
HQ: B/E Aerospace, Inc.
1400 Corporate Center Way
Wellington FL 33414
561 791-5000

(G-979)
BAOMA INDUSTRIAL INC
840 Lincoln Ave Ste 6 (11716-4108)
PHONE..........................631 218-6515
EMP: 5 EST: 2017
SALES (est): 510.1K **Privately Held**
SIC: 2869 Perfumes, flavorings & food additives

(G-980)
BETA TRANSFORMER TECH CORP (DH)
40 Orville Dr Ste 2 (11716-2529)
PHONE..........................631 244-7393
Terrance M Paradie, *CEO*
Vincent Buffa, *President*
Sean P Maroney, *Treasurer*
Peter Grennan, *Sales Mgr*
Halle F Terrion, *Admin Sec*
EMP: 36
SQ FT: 30,000
SALES (est): 6.1MM
SALES (corp-wide): 3.8B **Publicly Held**
WEB: www.bttc-beta.com
SIC: 3612 Transformers, except electric
HQ: Data Device Corporation
105 Wilbur Pl
Bohemia NY 11716
631 567-5600

(G-981)
BGA TECHNOLOGY LLC
116 Wilbur Pl (11716-2402)
PHONE..........................631 750-4600
Michael Cody, *President*
EMP: 40

SALES (est): 3.6MM **Privately Held**
SIC: 3674 8734 Semiconductors & related
devices; testing laboratories

(G-982)
**BMG PRINTING AND
PROMOTION LLC**
170 Wilbur Pl Ste 700 (11716-2416)
PHONE..........................631 231-9200
Paulette Desimone, *Principal*
John L Melillo,
EMP: 8
SALES: 50K **Privately Held**
SIC: 2761 3993 2732 2752 Manifold
business forms; signs & advertising spe-
cialties; pamphlets: printing & binding, not
published on site; commercial printing,
offset; promotional printing, lithographic

(G-983)
**BULLITT MOBILE LLC
(PA)**
Also Called: Bullitt Group
80 Orville Dr Ste 100 (11716-2505)
PHONE..........................631 424-1749
Kit Newell, *Partner*
Bryan Bourff, *Vice Pres*
Janelle Stoner, *Vice Pres*
Gareth Drewery, *Technical Mgr*
Eliana Santos, *VP Bus Dvlpt*
EMP: 56
SQ FT: 1,200
SALES (est): 6.3MM
SALES (corp-wide): 85.6K **Privately Held**
SIC: 3663 Cellular radio telephone
HQ: Bullitt Mobile Limited
1 Valpy Street
Reading BERKS RG1 1
118 958-0449

(G-984)
C & H MACHINING INC
281 Knickerbocker Ave (11716-3103)
PHONE..........................631 582-6737
Cliff W Havel, *President*
Phillip A Russo, *Vice Pres*
EMP: 13
SQ FT: 6,000
SALES: 1.3MM **Privately Held**
SIC: 3599 Machine shop, jobbing & repair

(G-985)
C & M CIRCUITS INC
50 Orville Dr (11716-2548)
PHONE..........................631 589-0208
EMP: 24
SQ FT: 7,500
SALES (est): 1.7MM **Privately Held**
SIC: 3629 Mfg Electrical Industrial Appara-
tus

(G-986)
**CERTIFIED PRCSION MCHINING
INC**
70 Knickerbocker Ave # 4 (11716-3166)
PHONE..........................631 244-3671
Michael Staib, *President*
James Turano, *Vice Pres*
EMP: 6
SQ FT: 8,000
SALES (est): 784.2K **Privately Held**
SIC: 3599 Machine shop, jobbing & repair

(G-987)
CLIMATRONICS CORP (HQ)
606 Johnson Ave Ste 28 (11716-2419)
PHONE..........................541 471-7111
Thomas Pottberg, *President*
Joann Pottberg, *Corp Secy*
David W Gilmore, *Vice Pres*
James Riley Loftin, *CFO*
EMP: 14
SQ FT: 16,500
SALES (est): 1.4MM
SALES (corp-wide): 25.9MM **Privately
Held**
WEB: www.climatronics.com
SIC: 3829 Meteorological instruments
PA: Met One Instruments, Inc.
1600 Nw Washington Blvd
Grants Pass OR 97526
541 471-7111

(G-988)
**CLINTRAK CLINICAL LABELING
S (PA)**
Also Called: Eagle Business Systems
2800 Veterans Hwy (11716-1002)
PHONE..........................888 479-3900
Bob Scarth, *General Mgr*
Jamie Pieron, *Opers Mgr*
Joe Macdougall, *Production*
Pamela Jones-Nill, *QC Mgr*
Darlene Lombardo, *Human Res Dir*
▲ **EMP:** 55
SQ FT: 45,000
SALES (est): 10.1MM **Privately Held**
WEB: www.clintrak.com
SIC: 2754 Letter, circular & form: gravure
printing

(G-989)
**CMB WIRELESS GROUP LLC
(PA)**
116 Wilbur Pl (11716-2402)
PHONE..........................631 750-4700
Joseph Lucania, *CEO*
Rich Meigh, *Exec VP*
Vincent Vivolo Jr, *Exec VP*
Frank Pipolo, *Vice Pres*
Tom Doherty, *CFO*
▲ **EMP:** 280
SALES (est): 43.9MM **Privately Held**
SIC: 3663 Mobile communication equip-
ment

(G-990)
**CMS HEAT TRANSFER DIVISION
INC**
273 Knickerbocker Ave (11716-3103)
PHONE..........................631 968-0084
Chris Mauro, *President*
Steve White, *Vice Pres*
Kathy Beers, *Project Mgr*
Philip Varca, *Sr Project Mgr*
Marek Dolat, *Admin Sec*
EMP: 25
SQ FT: 16,000
SALES (est): 5.3MM **Privately Held**
WEB: www.cmsheattransfer.com
SIC: 3443 Finned tubes, for heat transfer;
heat exchangers, plate type

(G-991)
COTTONWOOD METALS INC
1625 Sycamore Ave Ste A (11716-1728)
PHONE..........................646 807-8674
Christopher Smith, *Chairman*
EMP: 20 **EST:** 2011
SQ FT: 15,000
SALES (est): 2.4MM **Privately Held**
SIC: 3441 Fabricated structural metal

(G-992)
CRAFT-TECH MFG CORP
1750 Artic Ave (11716-2423)
PHONE..........................631 563-4949
Joseph Desantis, *CEO*
Ralph Desantis Jr, *Vice Pres*
Ralph Desantis Sr, *Treasurer*
EMP: 7
SQ FT: 19,500
SALES (est): 840K **Privately Held**
SIC: 3444 Casings, sheet metal

(G-993)
**CREATIVE METAL
FABRICATORS**
360 Knickerbocker Ave # 13 (11716-3124)
PHONE..........................631 567-2266
Richard W Donovan, *President*
EMP: 7
SQ FT: 8,500
SALES (est): 600K **Privately Held**
SIC: 3446 Architectural metalwork

(G-994)
CUSTOM DESIGN METALS INC
1612 Locust Ave Ste C (11716-2100)
PHONE..........................631 563-2444
Robert Lyon, *President*
Richard Mellace, *Vice Pres*
EMP: 5
SQ FT: 7,500
SALES (est): 766.8K **Privately Held**
SIC: 3399 Metal powders, pastes & flakes

(G-995)
**CUSTOM HOUSE ENGRAVERS
INC**
Also Called: Village Plaquesmith, Ththe
104 Keyland Ct (11716-2656)
PHONE..........................631 567-3004
Terry McLean, *President*
Terry Mc Lean, *Principal*
Brian McLean, *Vice Pres*
▲ **EMP:** 6
SQ FT: 3,200
SALES: 1MM **Privately Held**
SIC: 2796 3089 3479 Engraving
platemaking services; engraving of plas-
tic; etching & engraving

(G-996)
**CUSTOM NUTRACEUTICALS
LLC (PA)**
80 Orville Dr Ste 112 (11716-2505)
PHONE..........................631 755-1388
Jason Mancuso,
EMP: 26
SALES: 8.9MM **Privately Held**
SIC: 2833 Drugs & herbs: grading, grinding
& milling

(G-997)
CYGNUS AUTOMATION INC
1605 9th Ave (11716-1202)
PHONE..........................631 981-0909
Sharon Dietrich, *President*
John Alessandro, *Vice Pres*
Mark Salerno, *Vice Pres*
Christian Dietrich, *Admin Sec*
EMP: 20
SQ FT: 6,000
SALES (est): 2.8MM **Privately Held**
SIC: 3629 3672 5063 Electronic genera-
tion equipment; printed circuit boards;
wire & cable

(G-998)
D & I FINISHING INC
1560 Ocean Ave Ste 7 (11716-1951)
PHONE..........................631 471-3034
Danny Guerrier, *President*
Barbara Guerrier, *General Mgr*
EMP: 6
SQ FT: 4,500
SALES: 400K **Privately Held**
SIC: 3479 1721 3471 Painting of metal
products; painting & paper hanging; fin-
ishing, metals or formed products

(G-999)
**DATA DEVICE CORPORATION
(DH)**
105 Wilbur Pl (11716-2426)
PHONE..........................631 567-5600
Terrance M Paradie, *CEO*
Vincent Buffa, *President*
Paul Stein, *President*
Frank Bloomfield, *Vice Pres*
John Santini, *Vice Pres*
▲ **EMP:** 320
SQ FT: 104,000
SALES (est): 135.4MM
SALES (corp-wide): 3.8B **Publicly Held**
WEB: www.ddc-web.com
SIC: 3577 3674 3677 Data conversion
equipment, media-to-media: computer;
modules, solid state; electronic transform-
ers
HQ: Ilc Industries, Llc
105 Wilbur Pl
Bohemia NY 11716
631 567-5600

(G-1000)
**DAVIS AIRCRAFT PRODUCTS
CO INC**
1150 Walnut Ave Ste 1 (11716-2168)
P.O. Box 525 (11716-0525)
PHONE..........................631 563-1500
Bruce T Davis, *CEO*
Douglas Davis, *Vice Pres*
Jill Davis, *Vice Pres*
Jason Kuhlken, *Purch Agent*
Judy Bender, *Purchasing*
▲ **EMP:** 143 **EST:** 1967
SQ FT: 30,000

SALES (est): 31.6MM **Privately Held**
WEB: www.davisaircraftproducts.com
SIC: 3724 3728 Aircraft engines & engine
parts; aircraft parts & equipment

(G-1001)
DAYTON T BROWN INC (PA)
Also Called: D T B
1175 Church St (11716-5014)
PHONE..........................631 589-6300
Dayton T Brown Jr, *Ch of Bd*
Richard Dunne, *President*
Tom Volpe, *Business Mgr*
Daniel Melore, *Senior VP*
Robert C Single, *Senior VP*
EMP: 273 **EST:** 1950
SQ FT: 250,000
SALES (est): 74.4MM **Privately Held**
WEB: www.daytontbrown.com
SIC: 3444 2741 8711 8734 Sheet metal
specialties, not stamped; technical manu-
als: publishing only, not printed on site;
technical papers: publishing only, not
printed on site; engineering services; test-
ing laboratories; measuring & controlling
devices

(G-1002)
DELTA LOCK COMPANY LLC
366 Central Ave (11716-3105)
PHONE..........................631 238-7035
Bob Bonstrom, *VP Sales*
▲ **EMP:** 14
SALES (est): 2.4MM **Privately Held**
SIC: 3429 Locks or lock sets

(G-1003)
**DENTON PRINTING
CORPORATION**
1650 Sycamore Ave Ste 28 (11716-1731)
PHONE..........................631 586-4333
Dennis Dornan, *President*
Patty Lyons, *Admin Sec*
EMP: 12
SQ FT: 8,000
SALES: 1.4MM **Privately Held**
WEB: www.dentonadvertising.com
SIC: 2752 Lithographing on metal; adver-
tising posters, lithographed

(G-1004)
DEROSA FABRICATIONS INC
250 Knickerbocker Ave (11716-3112)
PHONE..........................631 563-0640
Tony Derosa, *President*
Lorry Derosa, *Vice Pres*
EMP: 20
SQ FT: 12,500
SALES (est): 2.3MM **Privately Held**
SIC: 3599 Machine shop, jobbing & repair

(G-1005)
**DESIGN WORKS CRAFT INC
(PA)**
70 Orville Dr Ste 1 (11716-2547)
PHONE..........................631 244-5749
Daniel Knopp, *President*
▲ **EMP:** 10
SQ FT: 24,500
SALES (est): 4.6MM **Privately Held**
WEB: www.designworkscrafts.com
SIC: 3944 Craft & hobby kits & sets

(G-1006)
DESIGNS FOR VISION INC
4000 Veterans Mem Hwy (11716-1024)
PHONE..........................631 585-3300
Richard Feinbloom, *Chairman*
Tracy Mayer, *Design Engr Mgr*
Peter Murphy, *Treasurer*
Katie Kromberg, *Sales Mgr*
Alex Anderson, *Sales Staff*
▲ **EMP:** 130
SQ FT: 30,000
SALES (est): 27.6MM **Privately Held**
WEB: www.designsforvision.com
SIC: 3841 3851 Surgical & medical instru-
ments; ophthalmic goods

(G-1007)
EAGLE TELEPHONICS INC
3880 Veterans Mem Hwy (11716-1038)
PHONE..........................631 471-3600
Richard J Riccoboni, *Ch of Bd*
Don H Coleman, *COO*
Alexander Wenger, *Exec VP*

Frederic H Chapus, *Vice Pres*
EMP: 15
SQ FT: 10,000
SALES (est): 3.3MM **Privately Held**
WEB: www.eagletelephonics.com
SIC: 3661 6794 Telephones & telephone apparatus; patent owners & lessors

(G-1008)
EASTERN COLOR STRIPPING INC
Also Called: Eastern Color Imaging
666 Lanson St (11716-3427)
PHONE 631 563-3700
EMP: 10
SQ FT: 3,000
SALES (est): 1.1MM **Privately Held**
SIC: 2796 7335 Digital 4 Color Printing And Service Bureau

(G-1009)
EASTERN EXTERIOR WALL
869 Lincoln Ave (11716-4105)
PHONE 631 589-3880
Mike Collier, *Project Mgr*
Rob Young, *Sr Project Mgr*
Charlie Bona, *Manager*
EMP: 20
SALES (corp-wide): 172.4MM **Privately Held**
HQ: Wall Eastern Exterior Systems Inc
   645 Hamilton St Ste 300
   Allentown PA 18101
   610 868-5522

(G-1010)
EL-GEN LLC
7 Shirley St Unit 1 (11716-1735)
PHONE 631 218-3400
Gerard Verbiar, *Treasurer*
Roy J Mc Keen,
EMP: 5
SQ FT: 7,500
SALES (est): 400K **Privately Held**
WEB: www.elgenmfg.com
SIC: 2023 Dietary supplements, dairy & non-dairy based

(G-1011)
ELAN UPHOLSTERY INC
120b Wilbur Pl Ste B (11716-2404)
PHONE 631 563-0650
Alan Fogg, *President*
Ann Fogg, *President*
EMP: 10
SQ FT: 7,500
SALES (est): 1MM **Privately Held**
SIC: 2512 7641 Upholstered household furniture; upholstery work

(G-1012)
ELECTRO ALLOY RECOVERY INC
Also Called: Electro Waste Systems
130 Knickerbocker Ave M (11716-3171)
PHONE 631 879-7530
John Wellman, *President*
EMP: 8
SQ FT: 15,000
SALES: 2MM **Privately Held**
SIC: 3339 Gold refining (primary); platinum group metal refining (primary)

(G-1013)
FOSTER - GORDON MANUFACTURING
55 Knickerbocker Ave G (11716-3131)
PHONE 631 589-6776
Jonathan Gordon, *President*
Louren Gordon, *Vice Pres*
EMP: 8
SQ FT: 9,000
SALES (est): 978.2K **Privately Held**
SIC: 2789 2782 5112 5999 Beveling of cards; blankbooks & looseleaf binders; blank books; alcoholic beverage making equipment & supplies

(G-1014)
FURNITURE BY CRAFTMASTER LTD
1595 Ocean Ave Ste A9 (11716-1962)
PHONE 631 750-0658
Michael Ruggiero, *President*

Donna Agate, *Corp Secy*
EMP: 5
SQ FT: 3,600
SALES (est): 638.2K **Privately Held**
SIC: 2521 2512 Wood office furniture; upholstered household furniture

(G-1015)
GE AVIATION SYSTEMS LLC
1000 Macarthur Mem Hwy (11716)
P.O. Box 1000 (11716-0999)
PHONE 631 467-5500
Kathleen Moosmueller, *General Mgr*
Brett Rowles, *Manager*
EMP: 250
SALES (corp-wide): 121.6B **Publicly Held**
SIC: 3728 Aircraft parts & equipment
HQ: Ge Aviation Systems Llc
   1 Neumann Way
   Cincinnati OH 45215
   937 898-9600

(G-1016)
GE AVIATION SYSTEMS LLC
1000 Macarthur Mem Hwy (11716)
PHONE 513 243-9104
Rebecca Everett, *Branch Mgr*
EMP: 99
SALES (corp-wide): 121.6B **Publicly Held**
SIC: 3812 8731 Search & navigation equipment; electronic research
HQ: Ge Aviation Systems Llc
   1 Neumann Way
   Cincinnati OH 45215
   937 898-9600

(G-1017)
GFH ORTHOTIC & PROSTHETIC LABS
Also Called: Hutnick Rehab
161 Keyland Ct (11716-2621)
PHONE 631 467-3725
Glenn F Hutnick, *Ch of Bd*
EMP: 5 **EST:** 1979
SALES (est): 609.6K **Privately Held**
SIC: 3842 Limbs, artificial; braces, orthopedic

(G-1018)
GLENN WAYNE WHOLESALE BKY INC
Also Called: Glenn Wayne Bakery
1800 Artic Ave (11716-2443)
PHONE 631 289-9200
Glenn Alessi, *Ch of Bd*
Wayne Stelz, *President*
EMP: 85
SQ FT: 15,000
SALES (est): 18.5MM **Privately Held**
WEB: www.glennwayne.com
SIC: 2051 Bakery: wholesale or wholesale/retail combined

(G-1019)
GLOBAL PAYMENT TECH INC (PA)
Also Called: Gpt
170 Wilbur Pl Ste 600 (11716-2433)
PHONE 631 563-2500
Andre Soussa, *Ch of Bd*
William McMahon, *President*
Dennys Noriega, *Opers Staff*
▲ **EMP:** 25
SQ FT: 25,550
SALES (est): 12.2MM **Publicly Held**
WEB: www.gptx.com
SIC: 3581 Mechanisms & parts for automatic vending machines

(G-1020)
HW SPECIALTIES CO INC
210 Knickerbocker Ave B (11716-3175)
PHONE 631 589-0745
Kevin Anderson, *President*
Fred Wichelman, *Vice Pres*
EMP: 18 **EST:** 1969
SQ FT: 2,500
SALES: 1.4MM **Privately Held**
SIC: 3599 Machine shop, jobbing & repair

(G-1021)
ILC HOLDINGS INC (HQ)
105 Wilbur Pl (11716-2426)
PHONE 631 567-5600
Clifford P Lane, *CEO*
EMP: 9
SALES (est): 135.4MM
SALES (corp-wide): 3.8B **Publicly Held**
SIC: 3674 Semiconductors & related devices
PA: Transdigm Group Incorporated
   1301 E 9th St Ste 3000
   Cleveland OH 44114
   216 706-2960

(G-1022)
ILC INDUSTRIES INC
105 Wilbur Pl (11716-2426)
PHONE 631 567-5600
Dan Veenstra, *General Mgr*
Sadhan Mandal, *Engineer*
Julio Reyes, *Engineer*
John Stith, *Engineer*
Derek Pulis, *Senior Engr*
EMP: 20 **EST:** 2016
SALES (est): 861.9K **Privately Held**
SIC: 3999 Manufacturing industries

(G-1023)
ILC INDUSTRIES LLC (DH)
Also Called: I L C
105 Wilbur Pl (11716-2426)
PHONE 631 567-5600
Clifford P Lane, *CEO*
Mohamed Hamed, *Vice Pres*
Roy Heyder, *Senior Engr*
Ken Sheedy, *CFO*
Nancy Henzel, *Accountant*
▲ **EMP:** 17 **EST:** 2010
SQ FT: 150,000
SALES (est): 135.4MM
SALES (corp-wide): 3.8B **Publicly Held**
WEB: www.ilcindustries.com
SIC: 3674 Semiconductors & related devices
HQ: Ilc Holdings, Inc.
   105 Wilbur Pl
   Bohemia NY 11716
   631 567-5600

(G-1024)
INTELLIGENT TRAFFIC SYSTEMS
140 Keyland Ct Unit 1 (11716-2646)
PHONE 631 567-5994
Joseph Battista, *President*
Karen Battista, *Admin Sec*
EMP: 8
SQ FT: 3,200
SALES: 400K **Privately Held**
SIC: 3669 Signaling apparatus, electric

(G-1025)
J PERCOCO INDUSTRIES INC
Also Called: Mjs Woodworking
1546 Ocean Ave Ste 4 (11716-1938)
PHONE 631 312-4572
Jerolamo Percoco, *President*
EMP: 8
SQ FT: 15,000
SALES: 1MM **Privately Held**
SIC: 2511 2434 2431 Wood household furniture; wood kitchen cabinets; millwork

(G-1026)
JAMES D RUBINO INC
20 Jules Ct Ste 5 (11716-4106)
PHONE 631 244-8730
James D Rubino, *President*
EMP: 24
SALES (est): 3.3MM **Privately Held**
SIC: 3499 Fabricated metal products

(G-1027)
JANCO PRESS INC
20 Floyds Run (11716-2154)
PHONE 631 563-3003
Maurice Janco, *President*
Florence Janco, *Vice Pres*
Seth Janco, *Vice Pres*
EMP: 15 **EST:** 1967
SQ FT: 10,000
SALES (est): 3.6MM **Privately Held**
SIC: 2754 2759 Labels: gravure printing; labels & seals: printing; embossing on paper

(G-1028)
JEROME STVENS PHRMCUTICALS INC
Also Called: Jsp
60 Davinci Dr (11716-2633)
PHONE 631 567-1113
Ronald Steinlauf, *Chairman*
EMP: 15
SQ FT: 20,000
SALES (est): 4.6MM **Privately Held**
SIC: 2834 Druggists' preparations (pharmaceuticals)

(G-1029)
JOLIN MACHINING CORP
1561 Smithtown Ave (11716-2409)
PHONE 631 589-1305
John Lutjen, *President*
EMP: 12
SQ FT: 7,000
SALES (est): 2.1MM **Privately Held**
SIC: 3599 Machine shop, jobbing & repair

(G-1030)
JONATHAN LORD CORP
87 Carlough Rd Unit A (11716-2921)
PHONE 631 563-4445
Carole Kentrup, *Co-President*
Kathleen Dancik, *Co-President*
EMP: 12
SQ FT: 8,000
SALES (est): 2MM **Privately Held**
WEB: www.jonathanlord.com
SIC: 2052 2051 Cookies & crackers; cakes, bakery: except frozen

(G-1031)
L & J INTERIORS INC
35 Orville Dr Ste 3 (11716-2533)
PHONE 631 218-0838
Jerry Esquibel, *President*
Leon Esquibel, *Vice Pres*
Liz Vanderbilt, *Office Mgr*
EMP: 8
SALES (est): 870K **Privately Held**
WEB: www.ljinteriors.com
SIC: 2541 1742 Store fixtures, wood; drywall

(G-1032)
LED LUMINA USA LLC
116 Wilbur Pl (11716-2402)
PHONE 631 750-4433
Christina Bonlarron, *CFO*
John Bonlarron, *Mng Member*
▲ **EMP:** 1
SALES: 1MM **Privately Held**
SIC: 3229 Bulbs for electric lights

(G-1033)
LEETECH MANUFACTURING INC
105 Carlough Rd Unit C (11716-2914)
P.O. Box 281 (11716-0281)
PHONE 631 563-1442
Fred Vasta, *President*
EMP: 5
SALES (est): 583.7K **Privately Held**
SIC: 3599 Machine shop, jobbing & repair

(G-1034)
LEIDEL CORPORATION (PA)
Also Called: Pentaplastics
95 Orville Dr (11716-2501)
PHONE 631 244-0900
Paul Sachdev, *Ch of Bd*
Roger D Leidel, *President*
EMP: 28 **EST:** 1902
SQ FT: 14,000
SALES (est): 5.7MM **Privately Held**
WEB: www.leidelcorp.com
SIC: 3089 Injection molded finished plastic products; molding primary plastic

(G-1035)
LOGITEK INC
110 Wilbur Pl (11716-2402)
PHONE 631 567-1100
William Forman, *CEO*
EMP: 90 **EST:** 1969

SALES: 20MM **Privately Held**
WEB: www.naii.com
SIC: 3679 3825 3812 3674 Electronic circuits; instruments to measure electricity; search & navigation equipment; semiconductors & related devices; relays & industrial controls
PA: North Atlantic Industries, Inc.
110 Wilbur Pl
Bohemia NY 11716

(G-1036)
LONG ISLANDS BEST INC
1650 Sycamore Ave Ste 4b (11716-1731)
PHONE............................855 542-3785
John Bosco, *President*
EMP: 7
SALES: 119K **Privately Held**
SIC: 2741 Telephone & other directory publishing

(G-1037)
LOUGHLIN MANUFACTURING CORP
1601 9th Ave (11716-1202)
PHONE............................631 585-4422
Martin Loughlin, *President*
EMP: 14 **EST:** 1970
SQ FT: 5,000
SALES (est): 2.5MM **Privately Held**
SIC: 3599 Machine shop, jobbing & repair

(G-1038)
LSC PERIPHERALS INCORPORATED
415 Central Ave Ste F (11716-3118)
PHONE............................631 244-0707
Frank Villa, *President*
Roger Strolin, *Vice Pres*
EMP: 4
SQ FT: 4,000
SALES (est): 1.5MM **Privately Held**
SIC: 3577 Printers, computer

(G-1039)
LUCAS DENTAL EQUIPMENT CO INC
360 Knickerbocker Ave # 4 (11716-3124)
PHONE............................631 244-2807
Richard Lucas, *Ch of Bd*
Joyce Lucas, *President*
EMP: 14 **EST:** 1930
SQ FT: 20,000
SALES (est): 1.9MM **Privately Held**
SIC: 3843 Dental equipment

(G-1040)
LUX MUNDI CORP
1595 Ocean Ave Ste B12 (11716-1934)
PHONE............................631 244-4596
Henry Kleitsch, *President*
EMP: 8
SALES (est): 972.6K **Privately Held**
SIC: 3999 Candles

(G-1041)
MAGELLAN AEROSPACE NY INC
25 Aero Rd (11716-2901)
PHONE............................631 589-2440
Jerry Myszka, *Manager*
Daniel Constantinescu, *Supervisor*
EMP: 250
SALES (corp-wide): 732.9MM **Privately Held**
SIC: 3599 3728 5088 Machine shop, jobbing & repair; aircraft parts & equipment; aircraft equipment & supplies
HQ: Magellan Aerospace, New York, Inc.
9711 50th Ave
Corona NY 11368
718 699-4000

(G-1042)
MAGNAWORKS TECHNOLOGY INC
36 Carlough Rd Unit H (11716-2905)
PHONE............................631 218-3431
Stan Stromski, *Director*
EMP: 7
SALES (est): 638.4K **Privately Held**
WEB: www.magnaworkstechnology.com
SIC: 3499 Magnets, permanent: metallic

(G-1043)
MALHAME PUBLS & IMPORTERS INC
Also Called: Regina Press
180 Orville Dr Unit A (11716-2546)
PHONE............................631 694-8600
Robert Malhame, *President*
George E Malhame, *President*
Robert E Malhame, *Treasurer*
▲ **EMP:** 22 **EST:** 1889
SALES (est): 3.5MM **Privately Held**
WEB: www.malhame.com
SIC: 2731 5049 Books: publishing only; religious supplies

(G-1044)
MASS MDSG SELF SELECTION EQP
35 Orville Dr Ste 2 (11716-2533)
PHONE............................631 234-3300
Stephen D Jaha, *Ch of Bd*
Bob Panagos, *Vice Pres*
Peggy Djaha, *CPA*
Steph Friscia, *Office Mgr*
▲ **EMP:** 20 **EST:** 1961
SQ FT: 4,000
SALES (est): 3.4MM **Privately Held**
WEB: www.masmerch.com
SIC: 2542 1751 Partitions & fixtures, except wood; store fixture installation

(G-1045)
MCGUIGAN INC
Also Called: Concept Components
210 Knickerbocker Ave (11716-3175)
PHONE............................631 750-6222
James W McGuigan, *Ch of Bd*
Helene Strafford, *Controller*
EMP: 25
SQ FT: 9,000
SALES (est): 6.2MM **Privately Held**
WEB: www.mcguigan.com
SIC: 3566 3599 3724 Gears, power transmission, except automotive; custom machinery; aircraft engines & engine parts

(G-1046)
MED SERVICES INC
100 Knickerbocker Ave C (11716-3127)
PHONE............................631 218-6450
Steven Cortese, *President*
EMP: 78
SQ FT: 1,800
SALES (est): 155MM **Privately Held**
SIC: 3845 7699 Electromedical equipment; medical equipment repair, non-electric

(G-1047)
MONARCH METAL FABRICATION INC
1625 Sycamore Ave Ste A (11716-1728)
PHONE............................631 563-8967
James Carter, *President*
▼ **EMP:** 8
SQ FT: 17,000
SALES (est): 1.5MM **Privately Held**
WEB: www.monarchmetal.com
SIC: 3444 Sheet metalwork

(G-1048)
MPE GRAPHICS INC
Also Called: Milburn Printing
120 Wilbur Pl Ste A (11716-2440)
PHONE............................631 582-8900
Keith Quinn, *President*
Lisa Sullivan, *Director*
EMP: 11
SQ FT: 5,000
SALES (est): 1.5MM **Privately Held**
SIC: 2759 Commercial printing

(G-1049)
MTWLI PRECISION CORP
1605 Sycamore Ave Unit B (11716-1734)
PHONE............................631 244-3767
EMP: 5
SQ FT: 2,100
SALES: 200K **Privately Held**
SIC: 3549 Mfg Metalworking Machinery

(G-1050)
NATURES BOUNTY INC
90 Orville Dr (11716-2521)
PHONE............................631 567-9500

EMP: 8 **Publicly Held**
SIC: 2834 Vitamin preparations
HQ: Nature's Bounty, Inc.
2100 Smithtown Ave
Ronkonkoma NY 11779
631 200-2000

(G-1051)
NEW KIT ON THE BLOCK
100 Knickerbocker Ave K (11716-3127)
PHONE............................631 757-5655
Lee Holcomb, *President*
EMP: 5
SQ FT: 4,000
SALES (est): 369.2K **Privately Held**
WEB: www.thenewkitontheblock.com
SIC: 3993 5099 Signs & advertising specialties; signs, except electric

(G-1052)
NORTH ATLANTIC INDUSTRIES INC
50 Orville Dr Ste 3 (11716-2548)
PHONE............................631 567-1100
EMP: 38 **Privately Held**
SIC: 3825 Instruments to measure electricity
PA: North Atlantic Industries, Inc.
110 Wilbur Pl
Bohemia NY 11716

(G-1053)
NORTH ATLANTIC INDUSTRIES INC (PA)
110 Wilbur Pl (11716-2402)
PHONE............................631 567-1100
William Forman, *President*
Ernie Keith, *COO*
Lino Massafra, *Vice Pres*
Valerie Auciello, *Research*
Greg McCrea, *Senior Engr*
EMP: 137
SQ FT: 30,000
SALES: 62MM **Privately Held**
SIC: 3571 Electronic computers

(G-1054)
NORTH HILLS SIGNAL PROC CORP
40 Orville Dr (11716-2504)
PHONE............................631 244-7393
Estro Vitantonio, *CEO*
Warren Esanu, *Ch of Bd*
Leslie Brand, *CFO*
Marco M Elser, *Director*
▲ **EMP:** 23
SQ FT: 12,000
SALES (est): 708.8K
SALES (corp-wide): 6.3MM **Privately Held**
WEB: www.northhills-sp.com
SIC: 3679 Harness assemblies for electronic use: wire or cable
PA: North Hills Holding Company Llc
6851 Jericho Tpke Ste 170
Syosset NY 11791
516 682-7705

(G-1055)
NORTHROCK INDUSTRIES INC
31 Crossway E (11716-1204)
PHONE............................631 924-6130
Brian F Robertson, *President*
Alan Browning, *Treasurer*
Eric Rueb, *Admin Sec*
▲ **EMP:** 21
SQ FT: 12,000
SALES (est): 3.8MM **Privately Held**
WEB: www.northrockindustries.com
SIC: 3531 Construction machinery

(G-1056)
NYCON DIAMOND & TOOLS CORP
55 Knickerbocker Ave A (11716-3120)
PHONE............................855 937-6922
John Pierpaoli, *President*
EMP: 7
SQ FT: 2,000
SALES (est): 344.4K **Privately Held**
SIC: 3559 Concrete products machinery

(G-1057)
OLD WORLD MOULDINGS INC
821 Lincoln Ave (11716-4103)
PHONE............................631 563-8660
Alan D Havranek, *President*
EMP: 8 **EST:** 1966
SQ FT: 20,000
SALES: 2.4MM **Privately Held**
WEB: www.oldworldmouldings.com
SIC: 2431 Moldings, wood: unfinished & prefinished

(G-1058)
PACKAGING DYNAMICS LTD
35 Carlough Rd Ste 2 (11716-2913)
PHONE............................631 563-4499
Daniel Lehmann, *CEO*
Eric Lehmann, *President*
Pat Lehmann, *Admin Sec*
◆ **EMP:** 15
SALES (est): 3.5MM **Privately Held**
SIC: 3565 Packaging machinery

(G-1059)
PASSUR AEROSPACE INC
35 Orville Dr Ste 1 (11716-2533)
PHONE............................631 589-6800
G S Beckwith Gilbert, *Ch of Bd*
James Cole, *Vice Pres*
John Keller, *Vice Pres*
Leo Prusak, *Vice Pres*
Rick Haines, *Engineer*
EMP: 6
SQ FT: 3,000
SALES (est): 1.7MM
SALES (corp-wide): 14.8MM **Publicly Held**
WEB: www.passur.com
SIC: 3671 Cathode ray tubes, including rebuilt
PA: Passur Aerospace, Inc.
1 Landmark Sq Ste 1900
Stamford CT 06901
203 622-4086

(G-1060)
PDA PANACHE CORP
Also Called: P D A Panache
70 Knickerbocker Ave # 7 (11716-3151)
P.O. Box 577, Bellport (11713-0577)
PHONE............................631 776-0523
Paul Schiller, *President*
Lynn Schiller, *Vice Pres*
EMP: 5
SALES (est): 580K **Privately Held**
WEB: www.pdapanache.com
SIC: 3577 5941 5112 Input/output equipment, computer; sporting goods & bicycle shops; pens &/or pencils

(G-1061)
PERVI PRECISION COMPANY INC
220 Knickerbocker Ave # 1 (11716-3181)
PHONE............................631 589-5557
Carlos Perez, *Owner*
Silvia Perez, *Marketing Staff*
EMP: 6
SQ FT: 4,100
SALES (est): 888K **Privately Held**
SIC: 3469 3599 Machine parts, stamped or pressed metal; machine shop, jobbing & repair

(G-1062)
POWER CONNECTOR INC
140 Wilbur Pl Ste 4 (11716-2400)
PHONE............................631 563-7878
Andrew S Linder, *President*
Peter Spadaro, *General Mgr*
Arlene R Linder, *Vice Pres*
▲ **EMP:** 38
SQ FT: 32,000
SALES: 10MM **Privately Held**
SIC: 3678 Electronic connectors

(G-1063)
PRECISION ASSEMBLY TECH INC
Also Called: P.A.t
160 Wilbur Pl Ste 500 (11716-2437)
PHONE............................631 699-9400
Lorraine Caruso, *Principal*
Russell Gulotta, *Chairman*
Thomas Gulotta, *Vice Pres*

▲ **EMP:** 50
SQ FT: 25,000
SALES (est): 16.6MM **Privately Held**
WEB: www.pat-inc.com
SIC: 3679 Electronic circuits; harness assemblies for electronic use: wire or cable

(G-1064)
PRECISION CHARTS INC
Also Called: P C I
130 Wilbur Pl (11716-2404)
P.O. Box 456 (11716-0456)
PHONE..............................631 244-8295
Barry Spencer, *President*
Michael Lesh, *Vice Pres*
▲ **EMP:** 25
SQ FT: 30,000
SALES (est): 5.1MM **Privately Held**
WEB: www.pcicharts.com
SIC: 2621 Book, bond & printing papers

(G-1065)
PRECISION INDEX EQUIPMENT INC
1555 Ocean Ave Ste A (11716-1933)
PHONE..............................631 468-8776
Craig Block, *President*
EMP: 8
SQ FT: 5,000
SALES (est): 1MM **Privately Held**
WEB: www.precision-index-equip.com
SIC: 3599 Machine shop, jobbing & repair

(G-1066)
PRIMOPLAST INC
1555 Ocean Ave Ste E (11716-1933)
PHONE..............................631 750-0680
Eugene Ruoff, *President*
William Hayes, *Admin Sec*
EMP: 12
SQ FT: 1,000
SALES: 950K **Privately Held**
SIC: 3089 3531 Injection molded finished plastic products; construction machinery attachments

(G-1067)
PRO TORQUE
Also Called: J Rivera
1440 Church St (11716-5027)
PHONE..............................631 218-8700
Joseph Rivera, *President*
Lynn Dimino, *CFO*
EMP: 25
SQ FT: 165,000
SALES: 1.7MM **Privately Held**
WEB: www.jrivera.com
SIC: 3714 Motor vehicle transmissions, drive assemblies & parts

(G-1068)
PROTEX INTERNATIONAL CORP
Also Called: Securax
366 Central Ave (11716-3105)
PHONE..............................631 563-4250
David Wachsman, *CEO*
Rodney Surratt, *CFO*
▲ **EMP:** 75
SQ FT: 34,000
SALES (est): 13MM **Privately Held**
WEB: www.protex-intl.com
SIC: 3699 Security control equipment & systems

(G-1069)
QUEUE SOLUTIONS LLC
155 Knickerbocker Ave # 1 (11716-3150)
PHONE..............................631 750-6440
Richard Prigg, *Mng Member*
EMP: 10
SALES: 5MM **Privately Held**
SIC: 3842 Personal safety equipment

(G-1070)
REPELLEM CONSUMER PDTS CORP
Also Called: Ecosmartplastics
1626 Locust Ave Ste 6 (11716-2159)
PHONE..............................631 273-3992
Terry Feinberg, *President*
EMP: 10
SALES (est): 29.2K **Privately Held**
SIC: 2673 2392 Trash bags (plastic film): made from purchased materials; tablecloths: made from purchased materials

(G-1071)
ROAD CASES USA INC
1625 Sycamore Ave Ste A (11716-1728)
PHONE..............................631 563-0633
Lucille Maielna, *Office Mgr*
EMP: 20
SALES (est): 106.3K **Privately Held**
SIC: 3523 Farm machinery & equipment

(G-1072)
S G NEW YORK LLC (PA)
Also Called: Pennysaver News
2950 Vtrans Mem Hwy Ste 1 (11716-1030)
PHONE..............................631 665-4000
Jan Marasco, *Accounts Exec*
Richard Megenedy Jr,
Murray Rossby,
EMP: 33
SQ FT: 4,000
SALES (est): 5.3MM **Privately Held**
SIC: 2741 2711 Shopping news: publishing & printing; newspapers, publishing & printing

(G-1073)
SCHNEIDER ELECTRIC USA INC
1430 Church St Unit H (11716-5028)
PHONE..............................631 567-5710
Robyn Zavoli, *Branch Mgr*
Ken Jensen, *Manager*
EMP: 5
SALES (corp-wide): 177.9K **Privately Held**
SIC: 3643 3612 3823 3625 Bus bars (electrical conductors); connectors & terminals for electrical devices; power transformers, electric; controllers for process variables, all types; relays & industrial controls; motor controls, electric; relays, electric power; switches, electronic applications; electrical apparatus & equipment; power circuit breakers
HQ: Schneider Electric Usa, Inc.
   201 Wshington St Ste 2700
   Boston MA 02108
   978 975-9600

(G-1074)
SCIENTIFIC INDUSTRIES INC (PA)
80 Orville Dr Ste 102 (11716-2505)
PHONE..............................631 567-4700
Joseph G Cremonese, *Ch of Bd*
Helena R Santos, *President*
Robert P Nichols, *Admin Sec*
EMP: 33 **EST:** 1954
SQ FT: 19,000
SALES: 10.2MM **Publicly Held**
WEB: www.scind.com
SIC: 3821 Shakers & stirrers

(G-1075)
SECURITY DYNAMICS INC
Also Called: Sdi Cable
217 Knickerbocker Ave # 4 (11716-3132)
PHONE..............................631 392-1701
Huihua Wang, *Ch of Bd*
William Wang, *President*
▲ **EMP:** 12
SQ FT: 3,000
SALES (est): 3.3MM **Privately Held**
SIC: 3699 Security control equipment & systems

(G-1076)
SELECT CONTROLS INC
45 Knickerbocker Ave # 3 (11716-3119)
PHONE..............................631 567-9010
Robert Ufer, *President*
Diane Morris, *Corp Secy*
Carol Morris, *Office Mgr*
EMP: 32
SQ FT: 2,500
SALES (est): 5.7MM **Privately Held**
WEB: www.select-controls.com
SIC: 3823 3625 8711 3613 Industrial flow & liquid measuring instruments; industrial electrical relays & switches; consulting engineer; switchgear & switchboard apparatus

(G-1077)
SHAR-MAR MACHINE COMPANY
1648 Locust Ave Ste F (11716-2156)
PHONE..............................631 567-8040
Myron Rubin, *Owner*

EMP: 5
SQ FT: 3,200
SALES (est): 439.3K **Privately Held**
SIC: 3599 Machine shop, jobbing & repair

(G-1078)
SHORT RUN FORMS INC
171 Keyland Ct (11716-2621)
PHONE..............................631 567-7171
Steven Looney, *President*
Andrew Boccio, *Senior VP*
Robert Stumpo, *Vice Pres*
Eileen Holland, *Art Dir*
EMP: 60
SQ FT: 17,000
SALES (est): 8.3MM **Privately Held**
WEB: www.shortrunforms.com
SIC: 2759 5943 Business forms: printing; office forms & supplies

(G-1079)
SINN- TECH INDUSTRIES INC
125 Wilbur Pl Ste 210 (11716-2415)
PHONE..............................631 643-1171
Daniel Tierney, *Owner*
Robert Becker, *Director*
EMP: 10
SALES: 1MM **Privately Held**
WEB: www.sinn-tech.com
SIC: 3545 Machine tool accessories

(G-1080)
SMART HIGH VOLTAGE SOLUTIONS
390 Knickerbocker Ave # 6 (11716-3123)
P.O. Box 5135, Hauppauge (11788-0001)
PHONE..............................631 563-6724
Kevin R Smith, *President*
Hersh Ochakovski, *Exec VP*
▼ **EMP:** 16
SQ FT: 1,825
SALES: 2.5MM **Privately Held**
SIC: 3542 High energy rate metal forming machines

(G-1081)
SPECTRUM CRAFTS INC
Also Called: Janlynn Corporation, The
70 Orville Dr Ste 1 (11716-2547)
PHONE..............................631 244-5749
Daniel Knopp, *President*
EMP: 24 **EST:** 2013
SALES (est): 155.7K
SALES (corp-wide): 4.1MM **Privately Held**
SIC: 3944 Craft & hobby kits & sets
PA: Design Works Craft Inc.
   70 Orville Dr Ste 1
   Bohemia NY 11716
   631 244-5749

(G-1082)
STRUCTURAL INDUSTRIES INC
2950 Veterans Memorial Hw (11716-1037)
PHONE..............................631 471-5200
Stanley Hirsch, *CEO*
Jamie Hirsch, *President*
Cliff Burger, *Exec VP*
Judy Hirsch, *Vice Pres*
Judy Vietheer, *CFO*
▲ **EMP:** 180 **EST:** 1966
SQ FT: 70,000
SALES (est): 21.3MM **Privately Held**
WEB: www.structuralindustries.com
SIC: 2499 3089 3499 Picture frame molding, finished; plastic processing; picture frames, metal

(G-1083)
SYMBOL TECHNOLOGIES LLC
110 Orville Dr (11716-2506)
PHONE..............................631 738-2400
Ron Goldman, *Branch Mgr*
EMP: 15
SALES (corp-wide): 4.2B **Publicly Held**
WEB: www.symbol.com
SIC: 3577 Computer peripheral equipment
HQ: Symbol Technologies, Llc
   1 Zebra Plz
   Holtsville NY 11742
   631 737-6851

(G-1084)
T R P MACHINE INC
35 Davinci Dr Ste B (11716-2666)
PHONE..............................631 567-9620

Patrick Price, *President*
Roger Price, *Principal*
Thomas Price, *Vice Pres*
EMP: 25
SQ FT: 8,500
SALES (est): 3.9MM **Privately Held**
WEB: www.trpmachine.com
SIC: 3599 Machine shop, jobbing & repair

(G-1085)
TEMRICK INC
1605 Sycamore Ave Unit B (11716-1734)
PHONE..............................631 567-8860
Trevor Glausen Jr, *President*
Melissa Glausen, *Vice Pres*
EMP: 5 **EST:** 1978
SQ FT: 5,000
SALES: 550K **Privately Held**
SIC: 3599 7389 Machine shop, jobbing & repair; grinding, precision: commercial or industrial

(G-1086)
TOUCH ADJUST CLIP CO INC
1687 Roosevelt Ave (11716-1428)
PHONE..............................631 589-3077
Richard Haug Sr, *President*
Richard C Haug, *President*
▲ **EMP:** 9
SQ FT: 10,000
SALES: 1.3MM **Privately Held**
WEB: www.touchadjustclip.com
SIC: 3915 Jewel cutting, drilling, polishing, recutting or setting

(G-1087)
TREO INDUSTRIES INC
Also Called: Genie Fastener Mfg Co
35 Carlough Rd Ste 1 (11716-2913)
PHONE..............................631 737-4022
Thomas W Blank, *Ch of Bd*
Tim Blank, *President*
Eugenia Blank, *Treasurer*
EMP: 7
SQ FT: 8,000
SALES (est): 957.7K **Privately Held**
SIC: 3452 Bolts, nuts, rivets & washers

(G-1088)
TRIAD COUNTER CORP
1225 Church St (11716-5014)
PHONE..............................631 750-0615
Frank Simone, *President*
Peter Amari, *Vice Pres*
Kirk Ibsen, *Treasurer*
EMP: 20
SQ FT: 20,000
SALES (est): 2.8MM **Privately Held**
SIC: 2541 5031 1799 Counter & sink tops; kitchen cabinets; kitchen & bathroom remodeling

(G-1089)
TRIANGLE RUBBER CO INC
50 Aero Rd (11716-2909)
PHONE..............................631 589-9400
Thomas Barresi, *President*
Joseph Barresi Jr, *Vice Pres*
▲ **EMP:** 25
SQ FT: 13,000
SALES (est): 4.3MM **Privately Held**
WEB: www.trianglerubber.com
SIC: 3069 5085 3061 Molded rubber products; rubber goods, mechanical; mechanical rubber goods

(G-1090)
TRIPAR MANUFACTURING CO INC
2050 Artic Ave Ste A (11716-2432)
PHONE..............................631 563-0855
John M McNamara, *President*
EMP: 7
SALES: 1.3MM **Privately Held**
SIC: 3444 3599 Sheet metalwork; machine shop, jobbing & repair

(G-1091)
TRIPLE POINT MANUFACTURING
1371 Church St Ste 6 (11716-5026)
PHONE..............................631 218-4988
Bernard Lichtenberger, *President*
Erwin Stropagel, *Treasurer*
EMP: 7
SQ FT: 4,000

SALES: 671K **Privately Held**
WEB: www.tpmny.com
SIC: 3451 3599 Screw machine products; machine & other job shop work

(G-1092)
TUSK MANUFACTURING INC
1371 Church St Ste 1 (11716-5026)
PHONE.....................................631 567-3349
Kevin Zorn, *Vice Pres*
Karl Zorn, *Vice Pres*
EMP: 17 EST: 1979
SQ FT: 8,000
SALES: 2.2MM **Privately Held**
WEB: www.tuskmfg.com
SIC: 3812 Search & navigation equipment

(G-1093)
UNITED MACHINING INC
1595 Smithtown Ave Ste D (11716-2418)
P.O. Box 480 (11716-0480)
PHONE.....................................631 589-6751
Corey Vercellone, *President*
EMP: 6
SALES: 430K **Privately Held**
SIC: 3599 Machine shop, jobbing & repair

(G-1094)
UPTEK SOLUTIONS CORP
130 Knickerbocker Ave A (11716-3171)
PHONE.....................................631 256-5565
Lin Xu, *President*
Jeffrey Tian, *Vice Pres*
EMP: 13 EST: 2012
SALES (est): 1.9MM **Privately Held**
SIC: 3826 3699 Laser scientific & engineering instruments; laser systems & equipment

(G-1095)
VELP SCIENTIFIC INC
155 Keyland Ct (11716-2621)
PHONE.....................................631 573-6002
Stefano Casiraghi, *Sales Staff*
Stefano Casirachi, *Admin Sec*
▲ EMP: 5
SALES (est): 602.7K **Privately Held**
SIC: 3826 Analytical instruments

(G-1096)
VJ TECHNOLOGIES INC (PA)
Also Called: Vjt
89 Carlough Rd (11716-2903)
PHONE.....................................631 589-8800
Vijay Alreia, *Chairman*
Robert Kerwin, *Manager*
Satya Korlipara, *Admin Sec*
◆ EMP: 35
SQ FT: 30,000
SALES (est): 0 **Privately Held**
SIC: 3844 3812 3829 X-ray apparatus & tubes; search & detection systems & instruments; nuclear radiation & testing apparatus

(G-1097)
VYTEK INC
271 Knickerbocker Ave (11716-3103)
PHONE.....................................631 750-1770
Joan Crisafulli, *President*
EMP: 10
SALES (est): 1MM **Privately Held**
SIC: 3599 7539 Machine shop, jobbing & repair; machine shop, automotive

(G-1098)
WEMCO CASTING LLC
20 Jules Ct Ste 2 (11716-4106)
PHONE.....................................631 563-8050
Sharen Fenchel, *Owner*
EMP: 70
SQ FT: 2,000
SALES (est): 9.5MM **Privately Held**
WEB: www.wemcocastingllc.com
SIC: 3369 Nonferrous foundries

(G-1099)
Z WORKS INC
1395 Lakeland Ave Ste 10 (11716-3318)
PHONE.....................................631 750-0612
Zoltan Mata, *Owner*
Katalin Gergely, *Owner*
EMP: 5 EST: 2001

SALES (est): 552.4K **Privately Held**
WEB: www.z-works.com
SIC: 3544 Special dies, tools, jigs & fixtures

Boiceville
Ulster County

(G-1100)
STUCKI EMBROIDERY WORKS INC (PA)
Also Called: Am-Best Emblems
Rr 28 Box W (12412)
PHONE.....................................845 657-2308
Murray Fenwick, *President*
Ilse Fenwick, *Corp Secy*
Arthur Stucki, *Vice Pres*
EMP: 18 EST: 1924
SQ FT: 17,000
SALES (est): 2.3MM **Privately Held**
SIC: 2395 Swiss loom embroideries; emblems, embroidered

Bolivar
Allegany County

(G-1101)
KLEIN CUTLERY LLC
Also Called: Scissor Online
7971 Refinery Rd (14715-9605)
PHONE.....................................585 928-2500
Wayne J West,
▲ EMP: 60
SQ FT: 18,000
SALES (est): 8.4MM **Privately Held**
WEB: www.scissorsonline.com
SIC: 3421 Scissors, hand; shears, hand

Boonville
Oneida County

(G-1102)
3B TIMBER COMPANY INC
8745 Industrial Dr (13309)
P.O. Box 761 (13309-0761)
PHONE.....................................315 942-6580
Mark S Bourgeois, *President*
Gary S Bourgeois, *Vice Pres*
Gary Bourgeois, *Vice Pres*
Janet F Bourgeois, *Treasurer*
EMP: 19
SQ FT: 5,400
SALES (est): 2.2MM **Privately Held**
SIC: 2411 Poles, wood: untreated; posts, wood: hewn, round or split; piling, wood: untreated; wood chips, produced in the field

(G-1103)
BAILEY BOONVILLE MILLS INC
123 Mill St (13309-1115)
P.O. Box 257 (13309-0257)
PHONE.....................................315 942-2131
Delbert C Bailey, *President*
EMP: 7 EST: 1968
SALES (est): 721.6K **Privately Held**
SIC: 2048 5999 Prepared feeds; feed & farm supply

(G-1104)
BOONVILLE HERALD INC
Also Called: Boonvlle Hrald Adrndack Turist
105 E Schuyler St (13309-1103)
PHONE.....................................315 942-4449
Joe Kelly, *President*
EMP: 7 EST: 1800
SALES (est): 380.4K **Privately Held**
SIC: 2711 Newspapers: publishing only, not printed on site

(G-1105)
BOONVILLE MANUFACTURING CORP
13485 State Route 12 (13309-3530)
PHONE.....................................315 942-4368
Randy Anderson, *President*
EMP: 7
SQ FT: 8,000

SALES (est): 1MM **Privately Held**
SIC: 3053 Gaskets, all materials

(G-1106)
C J LOGGING EQUIPMENT INC
Also Called: CJ Motor Sports
8730 Industrial Dr (13309-4828)
P.O. Box 661 (13309-0661)
PHONE.....................................315 942-5431
Mark S Bourgeois, *Ch of Bd*
J Yates Hudson, *President*
Robert Martin Calfee III, *Chairman*
Gary S Bourgeois, *Vice Pres*
Linda Bourgeois, *Treasurer*
▲ EMP: 25
SALES (est): 7.7MM **Privately Held**
WEB: www.cjlogequip.com
SIC: 2411 Logging

(G-1107)
NORTHERN FOREST PDTS CO INC
9833 Crolius Dr (13309-5001)
PHONE.....................................315 942-6955
Jeffrey Crolius, *President*
Jay Crolius, *Vice Pres*
EMP: 7
SQ FT: 2,800
SALES (est): 530K **Privately Held**
SIC: 2431 2499 Millwork; decorative wood & woodwork

(G-1108)
PRESERVING CHRSTN PUBLICATIONS (PA)
12614 State Route 46 (13309)
P.O. Box 221 (13309-0221)
PHONE.....................................315 942-6617
Gerard Maicher, *President*
John Parrot, *Admin Sec*
EMP: 8
SQ FT: 6,300
SALES: 169.1K **Privately Held**
WEB: www.pcpbooks.com
SIC: 2731 Book publishing

(G-1109)
QUALITY DAIRY FARMS INC
Also Called: Mercer's Dairy
13584 State Route 12 (13309-3532)
PHONE.....................................315 942-2611
Dalton Givens, *President*
Ruth Mignerey, *Shareholder*
▼ EMP: 24
SQ FT: 9,600
SALES (est): 4.1MM **Privately Held**
SIC: 2024 Ice cream, bulk

(G-1110)
S M S C INC
Also Called: Central Adirondack Textiles
101 Water St (13309-1327)
PHONE.....................................315 942-4394
Fax: 315 942-4394
EMP: 6
SALES (est): 588.4K **Privately Held**
SIC: 3321 Gray/Ductile Iron Foundry

Branchport
Yates County

(G-1111)
HUNT COUNTRY VINEYARDS
4021 Italy Hill Rd (14418-9615)
PHONE.....................................315 595-2812
Art Hunt, *Owner*
Joyce Hunt, *Owner*
Matt Kelly, *Marketing Staff*
EMP: 25
SQ FT: 2,256
SALES (est): 880K **Privately Held**
WEB: www.huntcountryvineyards.com
SIC: 2084 Wines

Brant Lake
Warren County

(G-1112)
GAR WOOD CUSTOM BOATS
20 Duell Hill Rd (12815-2026)
PHONE.....................................518 494-2966
Thomas Turcotte, *Mng Member*
EMP: 8
SALES (est): 993.4K **Privately Held**
WEB: www.garwoodcustomboats.com
SIC: 3732 Boats, fiberglass: building & repairing

Brasher Falls
St. Lawrence County

(G-1113)
TRI-TOWN PACKING CORP
Helena Rd (13613)
P.O. Box 387, Winthrop (13697-0387)
PHONE.....................................315 389-5101
John Liberty, *President*
Thomas Liberty, *President*
Jeff Liberty, *Vice Pres*
EMP: 15 EST: 1977
SQ FT: 5,300
SALES: 1MM **Privately Held**
WEB: www.adirondacksmokedmeats.com
SIC: 2011 5147 Meat packing plants; meats & meat products

Brentwood
Suffolk County

(G-1114)
ALLIED AERO SERVICES INC
506 Grand Blvd (11717-7902)
PHONE.....................................631 277-9368
Larry Soech, *President*
Steven Leonard, *Vice Pres*
EMP: 6
SALES (est): 444.4K **Privately Held**
SIC: 3295 Minerals, ground or treated

(G-1115)
APPLAUSE COATING LLC
8b Grand Blvd (11717-5117)
PHONE.....................................631 231-5223
Barbara Pinto, *Mng Member*
EMP: 11
SALES: 750K **Privately Held**
SIC: 3479 Coating of metals & formed products

(G-1116)
BECKS CLASSIC MFG INC
50 Emjay Blvd Ste 14 (11717-3300)
PHONE.....................................631 435-3800
Warren Beck, *CEO*
Steven Beck, *President*
Kevin Beck, *Vice Pres*
Mary Closen, *Manager*
EMP: 100
SQ FT: 60,000
SALES (est): 12.2MM **Privately Held**
SIC: 2399 2341 2322 2676 Diapers, except disposable: made from purchased materials; panties: women's, misses', children's & infants'; underwear, men's & boys': made from purchased materials; sanitary paper products

(G-1117)
CUBITEK INC
95 Emjay Blvd Ste 2 (11717-3330)
PHONE.....................................631 665-6900
Daniel Hartman, *President*
Peter Hartman, *Vice Pres*
Judy Hartman, *Treasurer*
▼ EMP: 15
SQ FT: 500
SALES: 3.1MM **Privately Held**
SIC: 3599 Machine shop, jobbing & repair

(G-1118)
DATAGRAPHIC BUSINESS SYSTEMS
79 Emjay Blvd (11717-3323)
PHONE................................516 485-9069
Glenn M Schuster, *President*
Alex Chirivas, *Accounts Exec*
EMP: 6
SQ FT: 3,000
SALES (est): 1.4MM **Privately Held**
WEB: www.datagraphicdesign.com
SIC: 2621 5943 Business form paper; office forms & supplies

(G-1119)
DELSUR PARTS
112 Pheasant Cir (11717-5047)
PHONE................................631 630-1606
Carlos Fuentes, *Owner*
EMP: 5
SALES: 150K **Privately Held**
SIC: 3556 Food products machinery

(G-1120)
DORMITORY AUTHORITY - STATE NY
998 Crooked Hill Rd # 26 (11717-1019)
PHONE................................631 434-1487
Mallikarjuna Dokku, *Project Mgr*
R A Christopher Wue, *Project Mgr*
Terry McGowan, *Director*
EMP: 8
SALES (corp-wide): 2.1B **Privately Held**
SIC: 3599 Pump governors, for gas machines
PA: Dormitory Authority - State Of New York
   515 Broadway Ste 100
   Albany NY 12207
   518 257-3000

(G-1121)
EXPRESS CONCRETE INC
1250 Suffolk Ave (11717-4507)
PHONE................................631 273-4224
Bruno Palmieri, *President*
EMP: 6
SQ FT: 3,000
SALES (est): 706.5K **Privately Held**
SIC: 3272 Concrete products

(G-1122)
HY CERT SERVICES INC
122 Cain Dr (11717-1266)
P.O. Box 534, Miller Place (11764-0534)
PHONE................................631 231-7005
Richard Pecchio, *President*
EMP: 5
SALES (est): 517.4K **Privately Held**
SIC: 3491 Industrial valves

(G-1123)
INTERSTATE WINDOW CORPORATION
Also Called: Mannix
345 Crooked Hill Rd Ste 1 (11717-1020)
PHONE................................631 231-0800
Robert Salzer, *President*
Paul Greenstein, *Vice Pres*
Sue Hausner, *Vice Pres*
▲ **EMP:** 100
SQ FT: 51,000
SALES (est): 29MM **Privately Held**
WEB: www.mannixwindows.com
SIC: 3442 Window & door frames

(G-1124)
J & A USA INC
335 Crooked Hill Rd (11717-1041)
PHONE................................631 243-3336
Yunho Kim, *President*
Daniel Hwang, *Purchasing*
Sidney Park, *CFO*
◆ **EMP:** 9
SQ FT: 15,000
SALES (est): 1.6MM **Privately Held**
WEB: www.jausa.com
SIC: 3999 Barber & beauty shop equipment

(G-1125)
LLOYDS FASHIONS INC (PA)
335 Crooked Hill Rd (11717-1041)
PHONE................................631 435-3353
Lloyd Goldberg, *President*
Rita Goldberg, *Vice Pres*

▲ **EMP:** 58 **EST:** 1958
SQ FT: 22,000
SALES: 2.6MM **Privately Held**
SIC: 2353 2253 5137 Millinery; shawls, knit; women's & children's clothing

(G-1126)
PLASTIRUN CORPORATION
70 Emjay Blvd Bldg A (11717-3394)
PHONE................................631 273-2626
Jack Elyahouzadeh, *President*
Jacob Y Lavi, *Treasurer*
◆ **EMP:** 60 **EST:** 1982
SQ FT: 51,000
SALES (est): 14MM **Privately Held**
WEB: www.plastirun.com
SIC: 2656 2621 Straws, drinking: made from purchased material; paper mills; towels, tissues & napkins: paper & stock

(G-1127)
T S O GENERAL CORP
81 Emjay Blvd Unit 1 (11717-3329)
PHONE................................631 952-5320
Kirk Malandrakis, *President*
EMP: 20
SQ FT: 30,000
SALES: 2MM **Privately Held**
WEB: www.tsogen.com
SIC: 2759 Commercial printing

(G-1128)
THURO METAL PRODUCTS INC (PA)
21-25 Grand Blvd N (11717)
PHONE................................631 435-0444
Albert Thuro, *Ch of Bd*
David Thuro, *President*
Louis Krieger, *General Mgr*
Carolyn Thuro, *Corp Secy*
Sam Handle, *Vice Pres*
▲ **EMP:** 40 **EST:** 1971
SQ FT: 25,000
SALES (est): 12.2MM **Privately Held**
WEB: www.thurometal.com
SIC: 3451 3545 Screw machine products; machine tool attachments & accessories

(G-1129)
UNIWARE HOUSEWARE CORP (PA)
120 Wilshire Blvd Ste B (11717-8333)
PHONE................................631 242-7400
Lily Hsu, *President*
Roger Hsu, *Vice Pres*
▲ **EMP:** 23
SALES: 8.5MM **Privately Held**
SIC: 3634 Electric housewares & fans

(G-1130)
US NONWOVENS CORP
105 Emjay Blvd (11717-3323)
PHONE................................631 236-4491
▲ **EMP:** 142 **Privately Held**
SIC: 2842 Specialty cleaning, polishes & sanitation goods
PA: U.S. Nonwovens Corp.
   100 Emjay Blvd
   Brentwood NY 11717

(G-1131)
US NONWOVENS CORP
110 Emjay Blvd (11717-3322)
PHONE................................631 952-0100
Samuel Mehdizadeh, *Ch of Bd*
EMP: 230 **Privately Held**
SIC: 2842 Specialty cleaning, polishes & sanitation goods
PA: U.S. Nonwovens Corp.
   100 Emjay Blvd
   Brentwood NY 11717

(G-1132)
US NONWOVENS CORP (PA)
100 Emjay Blvd (11717-3322)
PHONE................................631 952-0100
Shervin Zade, *CEO*
Linda Naerheim, *Business Mgr*
Rody Mehdizadeh, *COO*
Michael Pischel, *CFO*
Thomas Ford, *Manager*
◆ **EMP:** 63
SQ FT: 35,000

SALES (est): 476.8MM **Privately Held**
WEB: www.usnonwovens.com
SIC: 2842 5169 2676 5999 Specialty cleaning, polishes & sanitation goods; detergents & soaps, except specialty cleaning; sanitary paper products; toiletries, cosmetics & perfumes

(G-1133)
V E POWER DOOR CO INC
140 Emjay Blvd (11717-3322)
P.O. Box 663, Commack (11725-0663)
PHONE................................631 231-4500
James Lanzarone, *CEO*
Philip Lanzarone, *President*
Evelyn Semar, *Corp Secy*
Susan Cruz, *Vice Pres*
Edward Lanzarone, *Vice Pres*
▲ **EMP:** 40
SQ FT: 23,000
SALES (est): 9.4MM **Privately Held**
SIC: 3699 Door opening & closing devices, electrical

Brewerton
Onondaga County

(G-1134)
AE FUND INC
Also Called: Frigo Design
5860 Mckinley Rd (13029-9691)
PHONE................................315 698-7650
Eric J Gantley, *President*
Anthony Verdi, *Exec VP*
Allan Issacs, *Vice Pres*
Melissa Govendo, *Executive Asst*
EMP: 30
SQ FT: 15,000
SALES: 6.6MM **Privately Held**
WEB: www.frigodesign.com
SIC: 3632 Refrigerator cabinets, household: metal & wood

(G-1135)
GEORDIE MAGEE UPHL & CANVAS
Also Called: Magee Canvas & Trailer Sales
Weber Rd (13029)
P.O. Box 656 (13029-0656)
PHONE................................315 676-7679
Geordie H Magee, *President*
EMP: 6
SQ FT: 4,400
SALES: 1.1MM **Privately Held**
WEB: www.mageetrailers.com
SIC: 2211 5999 Canvas; canvas products

(G-1136)
IRENE CERONE
Also Called: Brewerton Special Tee's
9600 Brewerton Rd (13029-8798)
P.O. Box 670 (13029-0670)
PHONE................................315 668-2899
Michael Cerone, *Owner*
Irene Cerone, *Co-Owner*
EMP: 7
SALES (est): 594.8K **Privately Held**
SIC: 2396 Screen printing on fabric articles

(G-1137)
ROBINSON CONCRETE INC
7020 Corporate Park Dr (13029)
PHONE................................315 676-4662
Michael J Vitale, *Principal*
EMP: 10
SALES (corp-wide): 26.1MM **Privately Held**
SIC: 3273 Ready-mixed concrete
PA: Robinson Concrete, Inc.
   3486 Franklin Street Rd
   Auburn NY 13021
   315 253-6666

Brewster
Putnam County

(G-1138)
ADVANCED PRECISION TECHNOLOGY
577 N Main St Ste 7 (10509-1240)
PHONE................................845 279-3540
Olaf Brauer, *President*
Christine Brauer, *Vice Pres*
EMP: 10
SQ FT: 6,800
SALES (est): 1.1MM **Privately Held**
SIC: 3444 3341 Sheet metalwork; secondary nonferrous metals

(G-1139)
AKZO NOBEL CHEMICALS LLC
Also Called: Croton River Center
281 Fields Ln (10509-2676)
PHONE................................845 276-8200
Cheryl Mahoney, *Office Mgr*
Elliot Band, *Manager*
EMP: 5
SALES (est): 1.4MM **Privately Held**
SIC: 2869 Industrial organic chemicals

(G-1140)
ALLIANCE CONTROL SYSTEMS INC
577 N Main St Ste 9 (10509-1240)
PHONE................................845 279-4430
Doug Homberg, *President*
▲ **EMP:** 8
SALES (est): 943.6K **Privately Held**
SIC: 3629 Electronic generation equipment

(G-1141)
AMPRO INTERNATIONAL INC
30 Coventry Ln (10509-4808)
PHONE................................845 278-4910
Floyd Pircio, *President*
Laura Arone, *Admin Sec*
EMP: 2
SQ FT: 1,000
SALES: 1MM **Privately Held**
SIC: 3679 Antennas, receiving

(G-1142)
BASE SYSTEMS INC
Also Called: Tower Computers
1606 Route 22 (10509-4014)
PHONE................................845 278-1991
EMP: 2
SQ FT: 3,000
SALES: 2MM **Privately Held**
SIC: 7372 5045 Ret & Whol Of Prepackaged Software

(G-1143)
BLACK & DECKER (US) INC
Also Called: Powers Fasteners
2 Powers Ln (10509-3633)
PHONE................................914 235-6300
Jeffrey R Powers, *Vice Pres*
Erica Duttera, *Opers Mgr*
Arthur Bernardon, *Purch Mgr*
Robert Antoinette, *Engineer*
Mark Ziegler, *Engineer*
EMP: 375
SALES (corp-wide): 13.9B **Publicly Held**
SIC: 3546 Power-driven handtools
HQ: Black & Decker (U.S.) Inc.
   1000 Stanley Dr
   New Britain CT 06053
   860 225-5111

(G-1144)
BREWSTER TRANSIT MIX CORP (PA)
31 Fields Ln (10509-3507)
P.O. Box 410 (10509-0410)
PHONE................................845 279-3738
Ted Petrillo, *President*
Henry Paparazzo, *Vice Pres*
Curtis Mc Gann, *Admin Sec*
▲ **EMP:** 80
SQ FT: 1,000
SALES (est): 10.6MM **Privately Held**
SIC: 3273 5032 Ready-mixed concrete; gravel; sand, construction

▲ = Import ▼ =Export
◆ =Import/Export

(G-1145)
BREWSTER TRANSIT MIX CORP
Fields Ln (10509)
P.O. Box 410 (10509-0410)
PHONE..............................845 279-3738
Jeff Chattin, *General Mgr*
EMP: 35
SALES (corp-wide): 10.6MM **Privately Held**
SIC: 3273 Ready-mixed concrete
PA: Brewster Transit Mix Corp
31 Fields Ln
Brewster NY 10509
845 279-3738

(G-1146)
DAIRY CONVEYOR CORP (PA)
38 Mount Ebo Rd S (10509-4005)
PHONE..............................845 278-7878
Gary Freudenberg, *Chairman*
Roland Debald, *Vice Pres*
Karl Horberg, *CFO*
Peter Debald, *Treasurer*
Jose Gomez, *VP Sales*
◆ **EMP:** 86 **EST:** 1954
SQ FT: 68,000
SALES (est): 26.8MM **Privately Held**
SIC: 3535 7699 Conveyors & conveying equipment; industrial machinery & equipment repair

(G-1147)
DUNMORE CORPORATION
3633 Danbury Rd (10509-4516)
PHONE..............................845 279-5061
Terry Jones, *Manager*
EMP: 75
SQ FT: 49,432 **Privately Held**
WEB: www.dunmore.com
SIC: 2621 3081 2672 Paper mills; plastic film & sheet; coated & laminated paper
HQ: Dunmore Corporation
145 Wharton Rd
Bristol PA 19007
215 781-8895

(G-1148)
ELSAG NORTH AMERICA LLC
7 Sutton Pl Ste A (10509-3537)
PHONE..............................877 773-5724
Greg Lewis, *Technical Mgr*
Ted Broach, *IT/INT Sup*
EMP: 5
SALES (corp-wide): 6.3MM **Privately Held**
SIC: 3829 Photogrammetrical instruments
PA: Elsag North America Llc
205 Creek Ridge Rd Ste H
Greensboro NC 27406
336 379-7135

(G-1149)
FEYEM USA INC
7 Sutton Pl (10509-3536)
PHONE..............................845 363-6253
Palma Settini, *President*
EMP: 5
SALES (est): 202.9K **Privately Held**
SIC: 2329 2331 Men's & boys' sportswear & athletic clothing; women's & misses' blouses & shirts

(G-1150)
HEALTHY N FIT INTL INC (PA)
7 Sutton Pl Ste A (10509-3537)
PHONE..............................800 338-5200
Robert Sepe Jr, *Ch of Bd*
Irene Sepe, *Vice Pres*
EMP: 13 **EST:** 1976
SALES (est): 2.5MM **Privately Held**
SIC: 2833 5122 Vitamins, natural or synthetic: bulk, uncompounded; vitamins & minerals

(G-1151)
HIPOTRONICS INC (HQ)
1650 Route 22 (10509-4013)
P.O. Box 414 (10509-0414)
PHONE..............................845 279-8091
Timothy H Powers, *CEO*
Richard Davies, *President*
Jeff Brown, *Vice Pres*
Reinold Grob, *Vice Pres*
Charles Consalvo, *Opers Mgr*
◆ **EMP:** 115 **EST:** 1962
SQ FT: 90,000

SALES (est): 33.5MM
SALES (corp-wide): 4.4B **Publicly Held**
WEB: www.hipotronics.com
SIC: 3825 3679 3829 3677 Test equipment for electronic & electrical circuits; test equipment for electronic & electric measurement; power supplies, all types: static; measuring & controlling devices; electronic coils, transformers & other inductors; electronic capacitors; semiconductors & related devices
PA: Hubbell Incorporated
40 Waterview Dr
Shelton CT 06484
475 882-4000

(G-1152)
HUDSON MACHINE WORKS INC
Also Called: H M W
30 Branch Rd (10509-4522)
PHONE..............................845 279-1413
Daniel R Ferguson, *Ch of Bd*
Michael Ferguson, *General Mgr*
Jennifer Ferguson, *Vice Pres*
Glenn Moss, *CFO*
Nancy Dally, *Mktg Dir*
EMP: 110 **EST:** 1892
SQ FT: 25,000
SALES (est): 18.4MM **Privately Held**
WEB: www.hudsonmachine.com
SIC: 3743 Railroad equipment

(G-1153)
LAMOTHERMIC CORP
391 Route 312 (10509-2328)
PHONE..............................845 278-6118
Amos Noach, *Ch of Bd*
Gideon Noach, *Vice Pres*
Tom Eng, *Manager*
Taylor Seymour, *Director*
EMP: 97
SQ FT: 42,000
SALES: 12MM **Privately Held**
WEB: www.lamothermic.com
SIC: 3369 Castings, except die-castings, precision

(G-1154)
MATERION ADVANCED MATERIALS
42 Mount Ebo Rd S (10509-4005)
PHONE..............................800 327-1355
Raymond Chan, *Branch Mgr*
EMP: 6
SALES (corp-wide): 1.2B **Publicly Held**
SIC: 3339 Primary nonferrous metals
HQ: Materion Advanced Materials Technologies And Services Inc.
2978 Main St
Buffalo NY 14214
800 327-1355

(G-1155)
MATERION BREWSTER LLC
42 Mount Ebo Rd S (10509-4005)
P.O. Box 1950 (10509-8950)
PHONE..............................845 279-0900
Richard Fager, *Mng Member*
Matthew Willson,
▲ **EMP:** 75
SQ FT: 36,000
SALES (est): 26.4MM
SALES (corp-wide): 1.2B **Publicly Held**
WEB: www.puretechinc.com
SIC: 3499 3674 Friction material, made from powdered metal; semiconductors & related devices
HQ: Materion Advanced Materials Technologies And Services Inc.
2978 Main St
Buffalo NY 14214
800 327-1355

(G-1156)
NOURYON FUNCTIONAL CHEM LLC
281 Fields Ln (10509-2676)
PHONE..............................845 276-8200
Ralph Sterling, *Vice Pres*
Ton B Chner, *Branch Mgr*
EMP: 88
SALES (corp-wide): 1.4B **Privately Held**
SIC: 2869 Industrial organic chemicals

HQ: Nouryon Functional Chemicals Llc
525 W Van Buren St Fl 16
Chicago IL 60607
312 544-7000

(G-1157)
PEDIFIX INC
301 Fields Ln (10509-2621)
PHONE..............................845 277-2850
Dennis Case, *President*
Jon Case, *Vice Pres*
Vivian Anschel-Weiss, *Manager*
▲ **EMP:** 25
SQ FT: 15,000
SALES (est): 4.9MM **Privately Held**
WEB: www.pedifix.com
SIC: 3143 3143 Orthopedic shoes, women's; orthopedic shoes, men's

(G-1158)
PRE CYCLED INC
1689 Route 22 (10509-4022)
P.O. Box 341 (10509-0341)
PHONE..............................845 278-7611
Daniel Horkan, *President*
Carol Horkan, *Vice Pres*
EMP: 5
SQ FT: 3,000
SALES (est): 830.5K **Privately Held**
WEB: www.pre-cycled.com
SIC: 2752 7389 Commercial printing, lithographic; advertising, promotional & trade show services

(G-1159)
UNILOCK NEW YORK INC (HQ)
51 International Blvd (10509-2343)
PHONE..............................845 278-6700
Edward Bryant, *President*
Sean O' Lary, *General Mgr*
Joseph Kerr, *Vice Pres*
Daniel Neviackas, *Sales Staff*
Jason Stafford, *Sales Staff*
▲ **EMP:** 8
SALES (est): 10.4MM
SALES (corp-wide): 127.8MM **Privately Held**
WEB: www.unilock.com
SIC: 3281 5211 3272 3271 Paving blocks, cut stone; paving stones; concrete products; concrete block & brick; asphalt paving mixtures & blocks
PA: Unilock Ltd
401 The West Mall Suite 610
Etobicoke ON M9C 5
416 646-5180

(G-1160)
VISTALAB TECHNOLOGIES INC
2 Geneva Rd (10509-2340)
PHONE..............................914 244-6226
Richard Scordato, *Ch of Bd*
Jeffrey E Calhoun, *Vice Pres*
Jeffrey Calhoun, *Vice Pres*
Jim Orcutt, *Vice Pres*
Edward Flynn, *CFO*
▲ **EMP:** 34
SQ FT: 25,000
SALES (est): 8.8MM **Privately Held**
SIC: 3821 Pipettes, hemocytometer

Briarcliff Manor
Westchester County

(G-1161)
HER MONEY MEDIA INC
4 Justine Ct (10510-2534)
PHONE..............................917 882-3284
Jean Chatzky, *CEO*
David Wieder, *President*
EMP: 8
SALES (est): 319.4K **Privately Held**
SIC: 2721 2741 Periodicals;

(G-1162)
THALLE INDUSTRIES INC (PA)
51 Route 100 (10510-1441)
PHONE..............................914 762-3415
Gregg J Pacchiana, *Ch of Bd*
Glenn Pacchiana, *Principal*
George Pacchiana, *Corp Secy*
Jeff Manganello, *Vice Pres*
EMP: 35
SQ FT: 720

SALES (est): 4.5MM **Privately Held**
SIC: 2951 3281 Asphalt paving mixtures & blocks; stone, quarrying & processing of own stone products

(G-1163)
YOGOLICIOUS INC
516 N State Rd (10510-1526)
PHONE..............................914 236-3455
EMP: 5
SALES (est): 273.3K
SALES (corp-wide): 559K **Privately Held**
SIC: 2026 Yogurt
PA: Yogolicious Inc.
59 Marble Ave Ste 1
Pleasantville NY

Bridgehampton
Suffolk County

(G-1164)
BRIDGEHAMPTON STEEL & WLDG INC
Also Called: Aand D Maintenance
27 Foster Ave (11932-4013)
P.O. Box 19 (11932-0019)
PHONE..............................631 537-2486
John Parry, *President*
Suzanne Parry, *Vice Pres*
EMP: 10
SQ FT: 3,000
SALES (est): 1.3MM **Privately Held**
SIC: 3443 1799 Fabricated plate work (boiler shop); welding on site

(G-1165)
COMERFORD HENNESSY AT HOME INC
Also Called: Comerford Collection
2442 Main St (11932)
P.O. Box 44 (11932-0044)
PHONE..............................631 537-6200
Karen Comerford, *President*
Michael Hennessy, *Vice Pres*
EMP: 5
SQ FT: 1,500
SALES (est): 584.1K **Privately Held**
SIC: 2511 Wood household furniture

(G-1166)
IRON HORSE GRAPHICS LTD
112 Maple Ln (11932-4056)
P.O. Box 3006 (11932-3006)
PHONE..............................631 537-3400
Grover Gatewood, *President*
EMP: 9
SQ FT: 2,200
SALES: 782.1K **Privately Held**
SIC: 2752 2759 Offset & photolithographic printing; commercial printing

(G-1167)
SAGAPONACK SAND & GRAVEL CORP
Also Called: Keith Grimes
Haines Path (11932)
P.O. Box 964, Montauk (11954-0801)
PHONE..............................631 537-2424
Keith Grimes, *President*
Susan Grimes, *Vice Pres*
EMP: 20
SALES: 403K **Privately Held**
SIC: 1442 Common sand mining; gravel mining

Bridgeport
Onondaga County

(G-1168)
POWER GNERATION INDUS ENGS INC
8927 Tyler Rd (13030-9727)
PHONE..............................315 633-9389
Mike Verdow, *President*
EMP: 22
SALES (est): 2.9MM **Privately Held**
SIC: 3621 Power generators

(G-1169)
SYRACUSE LETTER COMPANY INC
Also Called: Lettergraphics
1179 Oak Ln (13030-9779)
P.O. Box 1295, Syracuse (13201-1295)
PHONE..................................315 476-8328
Nancy Osborn, *President*
David L Osborn, *Chairman*
Bill Davidson, *Vice Pres*
▲ EMP: 15
SQ FT: 24,500
SALES (est): 1.6MM **Privately Held**
SIC: 2759 7331 7389 Promotional printing; direct mail advertising services; coupon redemption service

Brightwaters
Suffolk County

(G-1170)
ALLEN FIELD CO INC
256 Orinoco Dr Ste A (11718-1823)
PHONE..................................631 665-2782
Andrew Franzone, *CEO*
Andrew Franzone Jr, *Ch of Bd*
David Kassel, *Ch of Bd*
Harry Goodman, *Vice Pres*
▲ EMP: 12 EST: 1945
SQ FT: 20,000
SALES: 6MM **Privately Held**
WEB: www.allenfield.com
SIC: 3089 Handles, brush or tool: plastic; injection molded finished plastic products

(G-1171)
INDUSTRIAL MUNICIPAL EQUIPMENT (PA)
146 Concourse E (11718-1502)
PHONE..................................631 665-6712
Peter E Rising, *President*
Mary Rising, *Corp Secy*
EMP: 13
SQ FT: 3,000
SALES (est): 1.6MM **Privately Held**
WEB: www.imetest.com
SIC: 3826 Water testing apparatus

Broadalbin
Fulton County

(G-1172)
BROADALBIN MANUFACTURING CORP
Also Called: BMC
8 Pine St (12025-3128)
P.O. Box 398 (12025-0398)
PHONE..................................518 883-5313
James C Stark, *President*
Michael Deuel, *President*
Mike Deuel, *Vice Pres*
EMP: 23 EST: 1970
SQ FT: 8,000
SALES (est): 4.2MM **Privately Held**
SIC: 3599 7692 1761 Machine shop, jobbing & repair; welding repair; sheet metalwork

(G-1173)
EMVI INC
Also Called: Emvi Chocolate
111 Bellen Rd Ste 2 (12025-2101)
P.O. Box 598, Tuxedo Park (10987-0598)
PHONE..................................518 883-5111
Irina Gelman, *Principal*
EMP: 6
SALES (est): 431.6K **Privately Held**
SIC: 2066 Chocolate

(G-1174)
GL & RL LOGGING INC
713 Union Mills Rd (12025-1988)
PHONE..................................518 883-3936
George Lee, *President*
EMP: 15
SALES (est): 985.3K **Privately Held**
SIC: 2411 Timber, cut at logging camp

Brockport
Monroe County

(G-1175)
CUSTOM SERVICE SOLUTIONS INC
1900 Transit Way (14420-3006)
PHONE..................................585 637-3760
Paul Guglielmi, *CEO*
Diana Petranek, *CFO*
Tiffany Petranek, *Office Mgr*
EMP: 6
SQ FT: 4,200
SALES: 1.4MM **Privately Held**
WEB: www.customservicesolutions.com
SIC: 3545 Machine tool accessories

(G-1176)
HAMILTON MARKETING CORPORATION
5211 Lake Rd S (14420-9753)
PHONE..................................585 395-0678
Edward Hamilton, *President*
EMP: 5
SQ FT: 5,000
SALES (est): 564.9K **Privately Held**
SIC: 3825 Microwave test equipment

(G-1177)
HAMLIN BOTTLE & CAN RETURN INC
3423 Redman Rd (14420-9422)
PHONE..................................585 259-1301
Andriy Basisty, *President*
EMP: 7
SALES: 240K **Privately Held**
SIC: 2611 Pulp mills, mechanical & recycling processing

(G-1178)
JETS LEFROIS CORP
Also Called: Jets Lefrois Foods
56 High St (14420-2058)
PHONE..................................585 637-5003
Duncan Tsay, *President*
Rosalinc Tsay, *Vice Pres*
EMP: 6
SQ FT: 6,000
SALES (est): 630.1K **Privately Held**
SIC: 2033 2035 Barbecue sauce: packaged in cans, jars, etc.; relishes, vinegar

(G-1179)
ROCK IROQUOIS PRODUCTS INC
5251 Sweden Walker Rd (14420-9716)
PHONE..................................585 637-6834
Chris Pangrizio, *Manager*
EMP: 20
SALES (corp-wide): 30.6B **Privately Held**
SIC: 1429 Dolomitic marble, crushed & broken-quarrying
HQ: Iroquois Rock Products Inc.
1150 Penfield Rd
Rochester NY 14625
585 381-7010

Brocton
Chautauqua County

(G-1180)
CARBON GRAPHITE MATERIALS INC
Also Called: Cgm
115 Central Ave (14716-9771)
PHONE..................................716 792-7979
Ryan Walker, *President*
▲ EMP: 9
SALES (est): 2.2MM **Privately Held**
SIC: 3624 Carbon & graphite products

(G-1181)
JAMESTOWN PLASTICS INC (PA)
8806 Highland Ave (14716-9791)
P.O. Box U (14716-0680)
PHONE..................................716 792-4144
Jay J Baker, *Ch of Bd*
Marcy Pakulski, *Purch Mgr*
Brandy Smith, *QC Mgr*
James Barry, *Engineer*
Dale Akin, *Manager*
EMP: 90
SQ FT: 87,000
SALES (est): 18.1MM **Privately Held**
WEB: www.jamestownplastics.com
SIC: 3089 Plastic processing

Bronx
Bronx County

(G-1182)
527 FRANCO BAKERY CORPORATION
Also Called: Caribe Bakery
527 E 138th St (10454-4971)
PHONE..................................718 993-4200
Franco Guillermo, *President*
EMP: 5
SALES (est): 351.7K **Privately Held**
SIC: 2051 Bakery: wholesale or wholesale/retail combined

(G-1183)
872 HUNTS POINT PHARMACY INC
872 Hunts Point Ave (10474-5402)
PHONE..................................718 991-3519
EMP: 7
SALES (est): 631.6K **Privately Held**
SIC: 2834 Mfg Pharmaceutical Preparations

(G-1184)
A & L DOORS & HARDWARE LLC
375 E 163rd St Frnt 2 (10451-4391)
PHONE..................................718 585-8400
Nathan Lax, *Buyer*
Garry Schnitzler, *Purchasing*
Mark Kraus, *Office Mgr*
Leo Lichstein, *President*
EMP: 14
SQ FT: 16,000
SALES (est): 2.3MM **Privately Held**
WEB: www.urban-architectural-interiors.com
SIC: 3442 3429 7699 Metal doors; window & door frames; locks or lock sets; locksmith shop

(G-1185)
A & L SHTMTL FABRICATIONS CORP
1243 Oakpoint Ave (10474-6803)
PHONE..................................718 842-1600
Anatoly Lekhter, *President*
Marat Golnick, *Vice Pres*
EMP: 45
SQ FT: 37,500
SALES (est): 9.4MM **Privately Held**
WEB: www.aandlsheetmetal.com
SIC: 3444 Sheet metalwork

(G-1186)
A L EASTMOND & SONS INC (PA)
Also Called: Easco Boiler
1175 Leggett Ave (10474-6246)
PHONE..................................718 378-3000
Arlington Leon Eastmond, *Chairman*
Neil Thomasetti, *Manager*
EMP: 80 EST: 1914
SQ FT: 50,000
SALES (est): 15.4MM **Privately Held**
WEB: www.easco.com
SIC: 3443 7699 7629 Boilers: industrial, power, or marine; boiler repair shop; electrical repair shops

(G-1187)
A&S REFRIGERATION EQUIPMENT
557 Longfellow Ave (10474-6913)
PHONE..................................718 993-6030
Alexander Savinon, *President*
EMP: 5
SALES: 98K **Privately Held**
SIC: 3585 Refrigeration & heating equipment

(G-1188)
A1 INTERNATIONAL HEAT TREATING
905 Brush Ave (10465-1810)
P.O. Box 93, Valhalla (10595-0093)
PHONE..................................718 863-5552
Peter Palmero, *President*
John Palmero, *Vice Pres*
Theresa Palmero, *Manager*
EMP: 5
SQ FT: 2,000
SALES (est): 814.7K **Privately Held**
SIC: 3398 Metal heat treating

(G-1189)
ABOVE THE REST BAKING CORP
531-533 Bryant Ave (10474)
PHONE..................................718 313-9222
Natalie Darmanin, *President*
EMP: 60 EST: 2016
SALES: 7MM **Privately Held**
SIC: 2051 Bakery: wholesale or wholesale/retail combined

(G-1190)
AC AIR COOLING CO INC
Also Called: Air Conditioning
1637 Stillwell Ave (10461-2216)
PHONE..................................718 933-1011
Cac Dong Bui, *President*
Deonarine Sooknarain, *Vice Pres*
Maritza Matos, *Manager*
EMP: 15
SALES (est): 1.9MM **Privately Held**
SIC: 3585 Air conditioning units, complete: domestic or industrial

(G-1191)
ACA QUALITY BUILDING PDTS LLC
1322 Garrison Ave (10474-4710)
PHONE..................................718 991-2423
Rubin Goldklang, *Manager*
EMP: 25
SALES (corp-wide): 4.3MM **Privately Held**
SIC: 3446 Partitions & supports/studs, including accoustical systems
PA: Aca Quality Building Products Llc
920 Longfellow Ave
Bronx NY 10474
718 991-2423

(G-1192)
ACE BAG & BURLAP COMPANY INC
1601 Bronxdale Ave Frnt 4 (10462-3364)
PHONE..................................718 319-9300
Joseph Rochman Sr, *President*
Hyman Rochman, *Corp Secy*
Jerry Rochman, *Manager*
◆ EMP: 13
SQ FT: 60,000
SALES (est): 1.7MM **Privately Held**
SIC: 2393 2673 Textile bags; plastic bags: made from purchased materials

(G-1193)
ACE DROP CLOTH CANVAS PDTS INC
Also Called: Ace Drop Cloth Co
4216 Park Ave (10457-4201)
PHONE..................................718 731-1550
Jerry Mathios, *President*
Adam Mathios, *Vice Pres*
David Mathios, *Vice Pres*
Marc Mathios, *Vice Pres*
▲ EMP: 31
SQ FT: 35,000
SALES (est): 4.3MM **Privately Held**
WEB: www.acedropcloth.com
SIC: 2299 2326 2394 2393 Fibers, textile: recovery from textile mill waste & rags; work pants; work shirts: men's, youths' & boys'; cloth, drop (fabric): made from purchased materials; textile bags; socks

(G-1194)
ACE FIRE DOOR CORP
4000 Park Ave (10457-7318)
PHONE..................................718 901-0001
Aharon Blum, *President*

▲ = Import ▼=Export
◆ =Import/Export

Joseph Strulovich, *Vice Pres*
Irving Bauer, *Treasurer*
Nate Lax, *Controller*
Ziara Escalera, *Exec Dir*
EMP: 20
SQ FT: 20,000
SALES (est): 4MM **Privately Held**
SIC: 3442 2431 Fire doors, metal; doors, wood

(G-1195)
ACME AWNING CO INC
435 Van Nest Ave (10460-2876)
PHONE..............................718 409-1881
Lawrence Loiacono, *President*
Jay Loiacono, *Vice Pres*
EMP: 15 **EST:** 1924
SQ FT: 25,000
SALES: 1MM **Privately Held**
WEB: www.acmeawn.com
SIC: 2394 3089 5039 5999 Awnings, fabric: made from purchased materials; awnings, fiberglass & plastic combination; awnings; awnings

(G-1196)
ACTION PAPER CO INC
429 E 164th St (10456-6602)
P.O. Box 210 (10456-0210)
PHONE..............................718 665-1652
Larry Rossman, *President*
EMP: 8
SQ FT: 20,000
SALES (est): 1.3MM **Privately Held**
SIC: 2653 Boxes, corrugated: made from purchased materials

(G-1197)
ADDEO BAKERS INC
2372 Hughes Ave (10458-8148)
PHONE..............................718 367-8316
Lawrence Addeo, *President*
EMP: 12
SQ FT: 2,300
SALES (est): 730K **Privately Held**
SIC: 2051 5461 Bread, all types (white, wheat, rye, etc): fresh or frozen; bread

(G-1198)
ADVANCED CMPT SFTWR CONSULTING
2236 Pearsall Ave (10469-5436)
PHONE..............................718 300-3577
Mohammad Ziauddin, *President*
EMP: 5
SALES (est): 241.7K **Privately Held**
SIC: 7372 Prepackaged software

(G-1199)
ALBA FUEL CORP
2135 Wllmsbrdge Rd Fl 2 Flr 2 (10461)
PHONE..............................718 931-1700
Esad Kukaj, *President*
EMP: 5
SALES (est): 927.1K **Privately Held**
SIC: 1389 5172 Oil field services; fuel oil

(G-1200)
ALBERT MENIN INTERIORS LTD
2417 3rd Ave Fl 3 (10451-6339)
PHONE..............................212 876-3041
Emil Shikh, *President*
Clara Silva, *Manager*
EMP: 12
SQ FT: 1,500
SALES (est): 1.2MM **Privately Held**
WEB: www.albertmenin.com
SIC: 2519 5023 5713 5714 Household furniture, except wood or metal: upholstered; carpets; draperies; carpets; draperies

(G-1201)
ALLIED METAL SPINNING CORP
1290 Viele Ave (10474-7133)
PHONE..............................718 893-3300
Arlene Saunders, *Ch of Bd*
◆ **EMP:** 60
SQ FT: 80,000
SALES (est): 10.8MM **Privately Held**
WEB: www.alliedmetalusa.com
SIC: 3469 Cooking ware, except porcelain enamelled

(G-1202)
ALLWAY TOOLS INC
1255 Seabury Ave (10462-5534)
PHONE..............................718 792-3636
Brent Swenson, *President*
Tim Cheng, *VP Engrg*
EMP: 100
SALES (est): 6.8MM **Privately Held**
SIC: 3423 3425 Hand & edge tools; saw blades & handsaws
HQ: Linzer Products Corp.
248 Wyandanch Ave
West Babylon NY 11704
631 253-3333

(G-1203)
ALTYPE FIRE DOOR CORPORATION
886 E 149th St (10455-5012)
PHONE..............................718 292-3500
Harold Halman, *President*
Douglas Halamn, *Corp Secy*
Gary Halman, *Vice Pres*
EMP: 5
SQ FT: 12,000
SALES (est): 818.1K **Privately Held**
WEB: www.altypefiredoor.com
SIC: 3442 Fire doors, metal

(G-1204)
AMERICAN REFUSE SUPPLY INC
Also Called: American Hose & Hydralics
521 Longfellow Ave (10474-6913)
PHONE..............................718 893-8157
Tim Butler, *Manager*
EMP: 7
SALES (corp-wide): 2.2MM **Privately Held**
SIC: 3714 3562 Motor vehicle parts & accessories; ball & roller bearings
PA: American Refuse Supply Inc
700 21st Ave
Paterson NJ 07513
973 684-3225

(G-1205)
ANASIA INC
1175 Jerome Ave (10452-3331)
PHONE..............................718 588-1407
Victor Florencio, *President*
EMP: 5
SALES (est): 406.5K **Privately Held**
SIC: 2671 Packaging paper & plastics film, coated & laminated

(G-1206)
ANHEUSER-BUSCH COMPANIES LLC
510 Food Center Dr (10474-7047)
PHONE..............................718 589-2610
Nelson Jamel, *Vice Pres*
Ed Fitzmaurice, *Manager*
EMP: 7
SALES (corp-wide): 1.5B **Privately Held**
SIC: 2082 3411 Beer (alcoholic beverage); aluminum cans
HQ: Anheuser-Busch Companies, Llc
1 Busch Pl
Saint Louis MO 63118
314 632-6777

(G-1207)
ATLAS COATINGS CORP
820 E 140th St (10454-1904)
PHONE..............................718 402-2000
Michael Landau, *President*
Stephan Landau, *Vice Pres*
Jarred Thweatt, *Controller*
EMP: 64
SQ FT: 25,000
SALES (est): 5.9MM **Privately Held**
SIC: 2893 Printing ink

(G-1208)
AURA DETERGENT LLC (PA)
1746 Crosby Ave (10461-4902)
PHONE..............................718 824-2162
John Poppola, *Mng Member*
EMP: 8
SALES (est): 1.2MM **Privately Held**
SIC: 2841 Soap & other detergents

(G-1209)
BACO ENTERPRISES INC
1190 Longwood Ave (10474-5714)
P.O. Box 740487 (10474-0009)
PHONE..............................718 589-6225
Barry L Cohen, *President*
Brian Cohen, *Vice Pres*
David Cohen, *Vice Pres*
Marcial Mendez, *Sales Staff*
Phil Raffa, *Sales Staff*
▲ **EMP:** 80
SQ FT: 60,000
SALES (est): 31MM **Privately Held**
WEB: www.bacoent.com
SIC: 3449 3452 Bars, concrete reinforcing: fabricated steel; bolts, metal

(G-1210)
BANDIT INTERNATIONAL LTD
600 E 132nd St (10454-4639)
PHONE..............................718 402-2100
Albert Berkner, *President*
Sophie Berkner, *Vice Pres*
EMP: 15
SQ FT: 50,000
SALES (est): 1.1MM **Privately Held**
SIC: 2329 2339 5136 5137 Men's & boys' sportswear & athletic clothing; sportswear, women's; sportswear, men's & boys'; women's & children's sportswear & swimsuits

(G-1211)
BEEHIVE PRESS INC
3742 Boston Rd (10469-2633)
P.O. Box 409 (10469-0409)
PHONE..............................718 654-1200
Roger Denhoff, *President*
Peter Kirkel, *Vice Pres*
Alec Denhoff, *Sales Mgr*
EMP: 7 **EST:** 1927
SQ FT: 4,500
SALES: 1.2MM **Privately Held**
WEB: www.beehivepress.com
SIC: 2752 2791 Commercial printing, offset; typesetting

(G-1212)
BELMET PRODUCTS INC (PA)
1350 Garrison Ave (10474-4807)
PHONE..............................718 542-8220
Fred Collins, *President*
Angelo Demauro, *Vice Pres*
John Collins, *Opers Mgr*
Sal Monteleone, *Sales Mgr*
Catherine Goetz, *Cust Mgr*
EMP: 48 **EST:** 1919
SQ FT: 39,000
SALES (est): 3MM **Privately Held**
WEB: www.belmetproducts.com
SIC: 3469 3312 Stamping metal for the trade; blast furnaces & steel mills

(G-1213)
BEYOND BETTER FOODS LLC
Also Called: Eaten Lightened
101 Lincoln Ave Frnt 2 (10454-4415)
PHONE..............................212 888-1120
Michael Shoretz, *CEO*
Alexandra Wright, *Sales Staff*
EMP: 6 **EST:** 2012
SQ FT: 5,000
SALES (est): 1.8MM **Privately Held**
SIC: 2024 Ice cream, packaged: molded, on sticks, etc.

(G-1214)
BIMBO BAKERIES USA INC
5625 Broadway Frnt 2 (10463-5548)
PHONE..............................718 601-1561
EMP: 5
SALES (corp-wide): 13.7B **Privately Held**
SIC: 2051 Mfg Bread/Related Products
HQ: Bimbo Bakeries Usa, Inc
255 Business Center Dr # 200
Horsham PA 19044
215 347-5500

(G-1215)
BONK SAM UNFORMS CIVILIAN CAP
Also Called: Sam Bonk Uniform
131 Rose Feiss Blvd Fl 2 (10454-3662)
PHONE..............................718 585-0665
Sarah Bonk, *President*
Harry Bonk, *General Mgr*

(G-1209) (duplicate continued)

Rachel B Jones, *Vice Pres*
EMP: 50 **EST:** 1963
SQ FT: 18,000
SALES (est): 5.4MM **Privately Held**
SIC: 2353 Uniform hats & caps

(G-1216)
BORGATTIS RAVIOLI EGG NOODLES
632 E 187th St (10458)
PHONE..............................718 367-3799
Mario John Borgatti, *President*
Christopher Borgatti, *Vice Pres*
Mario Borgatti, *Associate*
EMP: 5
SQ FT: 500
SALES: 500K **Privately Held**
WEB: www.borgattis.com
SIC: 2098 2032 Noodles (e.g. egg, plain & water), dry; ravioli: packaged in cans, jars, etc.

(G-1217)
BRANDT EQUIPMENT LLC
Also Called: Brandt Industries
4461 Bronx Blvd (10470-1407)
PHONE..............................718 994-0800
Abe Reich,
EMP: 9
SQ FT: 10,000
SALES (est): 1.5MM **Privately Held**
WEB: www.brandtind.com
SIC: 2599 3843 Hospital furniture, except beds; dental equipment

(G-1218)
BRONX NEW WAY CORP
113 E Kingsbridge Rd (10468-7510)
PHONE..............................347 431-1385
Adel Maflahi, *Principal*
EMP: 6
SALES (est): 459.1K **Privately Held**
SIC: 3643 Outlets, electric: convenience

(G-1219)
BUILDING MANAGEMENT ASSOC INC
998 E 167th St Ofc (10459-2054)
PHONE..............................718 542-4779
Jaime Diaz, *Manager*
EMP: 36
SALES (corp-wide): 11.8MM **Privately Held**
SIC: 3822 Building services monitoring controls, automatic
PA: Building Management Associates, Inc.
885 Bruckner Blvd
Bronx NY 10459
718 617-2800

(G-1220)
CASA REDIMIX CONCRETE CORP
886 Edgewater Rd (10474-4906)
PHONE..............................718 589-1555
Lucy Figueroa, *President*
EMP: 14
SALES (est): 2.4MM **Privately Held**
SIC: 3273 Ready-mixed concrete

(G-1221)
CEC ELEVATOR CAB CORP
540 Manida St (10474-6818)
PHONE..............................718 328-3632
Carlos Vanga Sr, *President*
Nick Gretsuk, *Vice Pres*
Sharlette Leslie, *Production*
Rakesh Rampersaud, *Purch Agent*
Kam Chung, *Engineer*
EMP: 65
SQ FT: 30,000
SALES (est): 16.1MM **Privately Held**
WEB: www.cecelevator.com
SIC: 3534 7699 Elevators & equipment; elevators: inspection, service & repair

(G-1222)
CENTER SHEET METAL INC
1371 E Bay Ave (10474-7025)
PHONE..............................718 378-4476
Maureen O'Connor, *CEO*
Victor Gany, *President*
Glenn Gany, *VP Opers*
Keith Oliveri, *Technology*
EMP: 150

SQ FT: 45,000
SALES (est): 21.7MM **Privately Held**
SIC: 3444 Sheet metalwork

(G-1223)
CFS ENTERPRISES INC
Also Called: CFS Steel Company
650 E 132nd St (10454-4603)
PHONE..............................718 585-0500
James R Melvin Jr, *Ch of Bd*
EMP: 20
SQ FT: 40,000
SALES (est): 4.8MM
SALES (corp-wide): 94.6MM **Privately Held**
WEB: www.cfssteel.com
SIC: 3312 Blast furnaces & steel mills
PA: Re-Steel Supply Company, Inc.
　2000 Eddystone Indus Park
　Eddystone PA 19022
　610 876-8216

(G-1224)
CHARLES H BECKLEY INC (PA)
749 E 137th St (10454-3402)
PHONE..............................718 665-2218
Theodore W Marschke, *President*
Charles L Beckley, *Principal*
Ken Marschke, *Marketing Staff*
▲ **EMP:** 18 **EST:** 1932
SQ FT: 12,000
SALES (est): 2.1MM **Privately Held**
WEB: www.chbeckley.com
SIC: 2515 2511 Box springs, assembled; mattresses & foundations; wood household furniture

(G-1225)
CITY EVOLUTIONARY
336 Barretto St (10474-6718)
PHONE..............................718 861-7585
Matt Tan, *General Mgr*
EMP: 8
SALES (est): 546.6K **Privately Held**
SIC: 3449 Bars, concrete reinforcing: fabricated steel

(G-1226)
CITY JEANS INC
845 White Plins Rd Frnt 1 (10473)
PHONE..............................718 239-5353
Kyle Christianson, *Owner*
EMP: 5
SALES (corp-wide): 39.4MM **Privately Held**
SIC: 2329 Men's & boys' sportswear & athletic clothing
PA: City Jeans Inc
　1515 132nd St Fl 2nd
　College Point NY 11356
　718 359-2489

(G-1227)
COCA-COLA REFRESHMENTS USA INC
977 E 149th St (10455-5090)
PHONE..............................718 401-5200
Tom Druell, *Branch Mgr*
EMP: 20
SALES (corp-wide): 31.8B **Publicly Held**
WEB: www.cokecce.com
SIC: 2086 5149 Bottled & canned soft drinks; groceries & related products
HQ: Coca-Cola Refreshments Usa, Inc.
　2500 Windy Ridge Pkwy Se
　Atlanta GA 30339
　770 989-3000

(G-1228)
COLOR CARTON CORP
341 Canal Pl (10451-6091)
PHONE..............................718 665-0840
Nicholas F Loprinzi, *President*
Vincent Loprinzi, *Corp Secy*
Nicholas V Loprinzi, *Vice Pres*
Paul Locascio, *Sales Mgr*
Debbie Loprinzi, *Manager*
▲ **EMP:** 60 **EST:** 1960
SQ FT: 90,000
SALES (est): 7.3MM **Privately Held**
WEB: www.colorcarton.com
SIC: 2752 2653 2657 Commercial printing, offset; corrugated & solid fiber boxes; folding paperboard boxes

(G-1229)
COLUMBIA POOL ACCESSORIES INC
111 Bruckner Blvd (10454-4514)
PHONE..............................718 993-0389
Fax: 718 993-8323
▲ **EMP:** 5
SALES (est): 504K **Privately Held**
SIC: 3585 Mfg Refrigeration/Heating Equipment

(G-1230)
COMPLETE FIBER SOLUTIONS INC
1459 Bassett Ave (10461-2309)
PHONE..............................718 828-8900
Victor Desantis, *Principal*
Josh Brite, *Principal*
Chris Richard, *Principal*
EMP: 8
SALES (est): 161K **Privately Held**
SIC: 3357 3229 1731 Fiber optic cable (insulated); fiber optics strands; fiber optic cable installation

(G-1231)
CORAL MANAGEMENT CORP
Also Called: Total Machine and Welding
923 Bryant Ave (10474-4701)
PHONE..............................718 893-9286
EMP: 5
SALES: 320K **Privately Held**
SIC: 3449 Mfg Misc Structural Metalwork

(G-1232)
COVINGTON SOUND
2705 Kingsbridge Ter (10463-7456)
PHONE..............................646 256-7486
Velma Harris, *Owner*
EMP: 6
SALES: 570K **Privately Held**
SIC: 3651 Speaker systems

(G-1233)
CROSS BRONX OPTICAL
961 E 174th St (10460-5060)
PHONE..............................917 667-6611
Marina Pritsker, *Owner*
EMP: 5
SALES (est): 240.8K **Privately Held**
SIC: 3827 Optical instruments & lenses

(G-1234)
CUSTOM 101 PRINTS INC
3601 Bronxwood Ave (10469-1143)
PHONE..............................718 708-4425
Anthony Matthews, *CEO*
EMP: 10
SQ FT: 2,000
SALES: 300K **Privately Held**
SIC: 2759 Screen printing

(G-1235)
D B F ASSOCIATES
Also Called: August Graphics
1150 E 156th St (10474-6227)
PHONE..............................718 328-0005
Bruce Feldman, *President*
Debra Feldman, *General Mgr*
Debra Bashore, *Assistant VP*
EMP: 8 **EST:** 2001
SALES: 460K **Privately Held**
WEB: www.dbfassociates.com
SIC: 2759 Screen printing

(G-1236)
DALE PRESS INC
Also Called: Riverdale Press, The
5676 Riverdale Ave # 311 (10471-2138)
PHONE..............................718 543-6200
Bernard L Stein, *President*
Michael Hinman, *Editor*
Richard L Stein, *Vice Pres*
Therese Hall, *Manager*
Ira Gluckman, *Commissioner*
EMP: 25
SQ FT: 2,500
SALES (est): 1.5MM **Privately Held**
WEB: www.riverdalepress.com
SIC: 2711 Newspapers: publishing only, not printed on site

(G-1237)
DAYTON INDUSTRIES INC
1350 Garrison Ave (10474-4807)
PHONE..............................718 542-8144
J Fred Collins, *CEO*
Milovan Petrovic, *QC Dir*
Barbara Agovino, *Human Resources*
Catherine Goetz, *Office Mgr*
Dwayne Tucker, *Manager*
▲ **EMP:** 45 **EST:** 1980
SQ FT: 45,000
SALES (est): 11.9MM **Privately Held**
WEB: www.daytonind.com
SIC: 3469 3442 Stamping metal for the trade; metal doors, sash & trim

(G-1238)
DELBIA DO COMPANY INC (PA)
2550 Park Ave (10451-6014)
PHONE..............................718 585-2226
Daryl Do, *Vice Pres*
Jerry Chow, *Vice Pres*
▲ **EMP:** 9
SQ FT: 8,000
SALES (est): 1.8MM **Privately Held**
SIC: 2087 2844 Flavoring extracts & syrups; perfumes, natural or synthetic

(G-1239)
DELBIA DO COMPANY INC
11 Canal Pl (10451-6009)
PHONE..............................718 585-2226
Delbia Do, *Branch Mgr*
EMP: 13
SALES (corp-wide): 1.8MM **Privately Held**
SIC: 2844 2087 Perfumes & colognes; flavoring extracts & syrups
PA: Delbia Do Company Inc.
　2550 Park Ave
　Bronx NY 10451
　718 585-2226

(G-1240)
DELICIOSO COCO HELADO INC
849 Saint Anns Ave (10456-7633)
PHONE..............................718 292-1930
Alfred Thiebaud, *President*
Sophia Thiebaud, *Admin Sec*
EMP: 15
SQ FT: 20,000
SALES (est): 2.4MM **Privately Held**
SIC: 2024 5451 Ice cream, bulk; ice cream (packaged)

(G-1241)
DOMINIC DE NIGRIS INC
3255 E Tremont Ave Frnt (10461-5790)
PHONE..............................718 597-4460
Dominic De Nigris, *President*
Dan A De Nigris, *Vice Pres*
Dan C De Nigris, *Admin Sec*
EMP: 30
SQ FT: 2,910
SALES (est): 2.7MM **Privately Held**
SIC: 3281 1411 Monuments, cut stone (not finishing or lettering only); dimension stone

(G-1242)
DRYVE LLC
4515 Waldo Ave (10471-3933)
PHONE..............................646 279-3648
Erika Boyer,
EMP: 5 **EST:** 2016
SALES (est): 130.5K **Privately Held**
SIC: 2741 Miscellaneous publishing

(G-1243)
DUFOUR PASTRY KITCHENS INC
251 Locust Ave (10454-2004)
PHONE..............................718 402-8800
Fax: 718 402-7002
EMP: 24
SALES (est): 3.7MM **Privately Held**
SIC: 2038 2053 Mfg Frozen Specialties Mfg Frozen Bakery Products

(G-1244)
DUN-RITE SPCLIZED CARRIERS LLC
1561 Southern Blvd (10460-5602)
PHONE..............................718 991-1100
Brett Deutsch, *Vice Pres*

Phil Bracco, *Project Mgr*
Carl Panepinto, *Controller*
Anthony Conetta, *VP Finance*
Dawn RAO, *Mktg Dir*
EMP: 12
SALES: 1MM **Privately Held**
SIC: 3536 Hoists, cranes & monorails

(G-1245)
DURO BUSINESS SOLUTIONS INC
Also Called: Duro UAS
2417 3rd Ave Ste 806 (10451-6342)
PHONE..............................646 577-9537
Brian Wilson, *President*
EMP: 5 **EST:** 2015
SALES (est): 119.8K **Privately Held**
SIC: 3672 Printed circuit boards

(G-1246)
DWH&S INC
825 E 140th St (10454-1930)
PHONE..............................718 993-6405
Robert H Haber, *President*
David Haber, *Vice Pres*
Conrad Karbowniczak, *VP Sales*
Todd Stone, *Sales Staff*
▲ **EMP:** 50 **EST:** 1902
SQ FT: 40,000
SALES (est): 4.8MM **Privately Held**
WEB: www.habersilver.com
SIC: 3914 Silversmithing; hollowware, plated (all metals)

(G-1247)
E & J IRON WORKS INC
801 E 136th St (10454-3546)
PHONE..............................718 665-6040
Gerhard Teicht, *President*
Edmund Teicht, *General Mgr*
EMP: 20
SQ FT: 22,000
SALES (est): 3.8MM **Privately Held**
SIC: 3446 Gates, ornamental metal

(G-1248)
E H HURWITZ & ASSOCIATES
3000 Kingsbridge Ave (10463-5101)
PHONE..............................718 884-3766
EMP: 9 **EST:** 1978
SALES (est): 720K **Privately Held**
SIC: 7372 Prepackaged Software Services

(G-1249)
EASCO BOILER CORP
1175 Leggett Ave (10474-6294)
PHONE..............................718 378-3000
Arlington Leon Eastmond, *Ch of Bd*
Leon Eastmond, *President*
EMP: 30
SQ FT: 15,000
SALES (est): 5.3MM **Privately Held**
SIC: 3443 Fabricated plate work (boiler shop)

(G-1250)
EDWARD C LYONS COMPANY INC
Also Called: E C Lyons
3646 White Plains Rd Frnt (10467-5717)
PHONE..............................718 515-5361
Gary Owens, *President*
Cheryl Owens, *Vice Pres*
EMP: 7 **EST:** 1958
SQ FT: 5,000
SALES: 500K **Privately Held**
WEB: www.eclyons.com
SIC: 3423 Engravers' tools, hand

(G-1251)
EDWARD C MULLER CORP
Also Called: Edward C. Lyons
3646 White Plains Rd Frnt (10467-5717)
PHONE..............................718 881-7270
Gary Owens, *President*
Cheryl D Owens, *Vice Pres*
EMP: 15 **EST:** 1898
SQ FT: 3,600
SALES: 700K **Privately Held**
SIC: 3423 Engravers' tools, hand

(G-1252)
EDWARDS GRAPHIC CO INC
3801 Hudson Manor Ter 4s (10463-1105)
PHONE..............................718 548-6858

Jackie Ginsberg, *President*
Ed Edwards, *Vice Pres*
EMP: 5
SALES (est): 421.6K **Privately Held**
SIC: 2752 Commercial printing, offset

(G-1253)
EMERGENCY BEACON CORP
2564 Park Ave 1 (10451-6014)
PHONE..................................914 576-2700
Joan Goodman, *President*
George Ramos, *Vice Pres*
Patricia Wyllie, *Vice Pres*
EMP: 15
SALES: 1MM **Privately Held**
WEB: www.emergencybeaconcorp.com
SIC: 3812 Aircraft/aerospace flight instruments & guidance systems

(G-1254)
EMILIOR PHRM COMPOUNDING INC
Also Called: Haldey Phrm Compounding
3619 Provost Ave Fl 1 (10466-6145)
PHONE..................................646 350-0033
Emil J Haldey, *President*
EMP: 40
SALES (est): 4.9MM **Privately Held**
SIC: 2834 5912 Pharmaceutical preparations; drug stores & proprietary stores

(G-1255)
EVE SALES CORP
945 Close Ave (10473-4906)
PHONE..................................718 589-6800
Stuart Gale, *President*
◆ **EMP:** 13
SQ FT: 22,000
SALES (est): 3MM **Privately Held**
WEB: www.evesales.com
SIC: 2032 Mexican foods: packaged in cans, jars, etc.

(G-1256)
FIGUEROA CLARIBELL
Also Called: Family Printing
613 E Fordham Rd (10458-5026)
PHONE..................................718 772-8521
Claribell Figueroa, *Owner*
EMP: 5
SALES (est): 177.1K **Privately Held**
SIC: 2752 Commercial printing, lithographic

(G-1257)
FINEST CC CORP
3111 E Tremont Ave (10461-5705)
PHONE..................................917 574-4525
Larry Derasmo, *President*
EMP: 6
SQ FT: 1,000
SALES (est): 274.8K **Privately Held**
SIC: 3471 Electroplating of metals or formed products

(G-1258)
FIVE ISLANDS PUBLISHING INC
Also Called: Fire Island News
8 Fort Charles Pl (10463-6705)
P.O. Box 486, Ocean Beach (11770-0486)
PHONE..................................631 583-5345
Shawn Beqaj, *President*
Nicole Pressly, *Treasurer*
EMP: 10
SQ FT: 1,000
SALES (est): 369.8K **Privately Held**
SIC: 2711 Newspapers: publishing only, not printed on site

(G-1259)
FLAIR DISPLAY INC
3920 Merritt Ave (10466-2502)
PHONE..................................718 324-9330
Eugene Dilorenzo, *President*
Chris Dilorenzo, *Vice Pres*
Raymond Hand, *Vice Pres*
Betty Hood, *Assistant*
▲ **EMP:** 60 **EST:** 1953
SQ FT: 50,000
SALES (est): 8.7MM **Privately Held**
WEB: www.flairdisplay.com
SIC: 3993 Displays & cutouts, window & lobby; displays, paint process

(G-1260)
FOAM PRODUCTS INC
360 Southern Blvd (10454-1711)
PHONE..................................718 292-4830
Karen Ippolito, *President*
Frank Ippolito, *Vice Pres*
EMP: 20
SQ FT: 32,000
SALES (est): 4.3MM **Privately Held**
SIC: 3069 3086 Foam rubber; insulation or cushioning material, foamed plastic

(G-1261)
FOUR SASONS MULTI-SERVICES INC
3525 Decatur Ave Apt 2k (10467-1729)
PHONE..................................347 843-6262
Gabriel Gomez, *CEO*
EMP: 5
SQ FT: 100
SALES (est): 518.1K **Privately Held**
SIC: 2842 Specialty cleaning preparations

(G-1262)
FRA-RIK FORMICA FABG CO INC
1464 Blondell Ave Fl 2 (10461-2688)
PHONE..................................718 597-3335
Philip De Candido, *President*
Frank Maiore, *Vice Pres*
EMP: 9 **EST:** 1965
SQ FT: 5,000
SALES (est): 866.3K **Privately Held**
SIC: 2434 3299 Wood kitchen cabinets; mica products

(G-1263)
FUEL WATCHMAN SALES & SERVICE
Also Called: Full Timer
364 Jackson Ave (10454-1698)
P.O. Box 202, Garden City (11530-0202)
PHONE..................................718 665-6100
Benjamin Strysco, *President*
Tom Strysco, *Vice Pres*
Joan Strysco, *Admin Sec*
EMP: 10 **EST:** 1944
SALES (est): 1.8MM **Privately Held**
SIC: 3822 3669 Auto controls regulating residntl & coml environmt & applncs; smoke detectors

(G-1264)
GAL MANUFACTURING CO LLC (HQ)
Also Called: Vantage Elevator Solutions
50 E 153rd St (10451-2104)
PHONE..................................718 292-9000
Angelo Messina, *Mng Member*
Mark Boelhouwer, *Mng Member*
EMP: 62 **EST:** 2017
SALES (est): 123MM
SALES (corp-wide): 8B **Privately Held**
SIC: 3534 Elevators & moving stairways
PA: Golden Gate Private Equity Incorporated
  1 Embarcadero Ctr Fl 39
  San Francisco CA 94111
  415 983-2706

(G-1265)
GENERAL FIRE-PROOF DOOR CORP
913 Edgewater Rd (10474-4930)
PHONE..................................718 893-5500
Aaron Szabo, *President*
Rubin Kuszel, *Vice Pres*
EMP: 50 **EST:** 1921
SALES (est): 7.5MM **Privately Held**
SIC: 3442 Fire doors, metal

(G-1266)
GENERAL GALVANIZING SUP CO INC (PA)
652 Whittier St Fl Mezz (10474-6194)
PHONE..................................718 589-4300
Anthony Visentin, *President*
EMP: 53 **EST:** 1935
SQ FT: 10,000
SALES (est): 5.2MM **Privately Held**
SIC: 3471 5085 Electroplating & plating; fasteners & fastening equipment

(G-1267)
GOLDEN GLOW COOKIE CO INC
Also Called: Cookie Factory
1844 Givan Ave (10469-3155)
PHONE..................................718 379-6223
Rose Florio, *President*
Joan Florio, *Vice Pres*
Salvatore Florio Jr, *Vice Pres*
EMP: 20
SQ FT: 15,000
SALES (est): 3.1MM **Privately Held**
SIC: 2051 2052 Bakery: wholesale or wholesale/retail combined; cookies

(G-1268)
GOOD-O-BEVERAGE INC
Also Called: Coco Rico Southeast
1801 Boone Ave (10460-5101)
PHONE..................................718 328-6400
Steven Kucerak, *Principal*
Kersia Corporation, *Principal*
Jose Regalado, *Sales Mgr*
▲ **EMP:** 18 **EST:** 1942
SQ FT: 53,000
SALES (est): 5.1MM **Privately Held**
WEB: www.good-o.com
SIC: 2086 Soft drinks: packaged in cans, bottles, etc.

(G-1269)
GRAPHIC PRINTING
2376 Jerome Ave (10468-6401)
PHONE..................................718 701-4433
Joao Oliveira, *Owner*
EMP: 5
SALES (est): 213.3K **Privately Held**
SIC: 2759 Publication printing

(G-1270)
GRUBER DISPLAY CO INC
3920g Merritt Ave (10466-2502)
PHONE..................................718 882-8220
Jay Merkel, *President*
EMP: 15
SQ FT: 10,000
SALES: 750K **Privately Held**
SIC: 2759 Screen printing

(G-1271)
H W WILSON COMPANY INC
950 University Ave (10452-4297)
P.O. Box 602, Ipswich MA (01938-0602)
PHONE..................................718 588-8635
F Dixon Brooke Jr, *President*
J David Walker, *President*
Tim Collins, *Vice Pres*
EMP: 450 **EST:** 1898
SQ FT: 150,000
SALES (est): 24.2MM
SALES (corp-wide): 2.8B **Privately Held**
WEB: www.hwwilson.com
SIC: 2721 2731 Periodicals: publishing & printing; books: publishing & printing
HQ: Ebsco Publishing, Inc.
  10 Estes St
  Ipswich MA 01938
  978 356-6500

(G-1272)
HANGER PRSTHETCS & ORTHO INC
1250 Waters Pl (10461-2720)
PHONE..................................718 892-1103
Walt Meffert, *Branch Mgr*
EMP: 5
SALES (corp-wide): 1B **Publicly Held**
SIC: 3842 Surgical appliances & supplies
HQ: Hanger Prosthetics & Orthotics, Inc.
  10910 Domain Dr Ste 300
  Austin TX 78758
  512 777-3800

(G-1273)
HAT ATTACK INC (PA)
Also Called: Hat Attack I Bujibaja
4643 Bullard Ave Ste A (10470-1415)
PHONE..................................718 994-1000
William Gedney, *President*
Barbara J Gedney, *Vice Pres*
Bill Gedney, *Office Mgr*
Lillian Pimenteo, *Manager*
Lillian Dimentel, *Director*
◆ **EMP:** 20
SQ FT: 11,000

SALES: 5MM **Privately Held**
WEB: www.hatattack.com
SIC: 3111 2353 Bag leather; hats, caps & millinery

(G-1274)
HEALTHEE ENDEAVORS INC
3565c Boston Rd (10469-2500)
P.O. Box 690159 (10469-0761)
PHONE..................................718 653-5499
Junior Blake, *President*
Jennifer Blake, *Vice Pres*
Julian Reynolds, *Administration*
EMP: 7 **EST:** 1985
SALES: 400K **Privately Held**
SIC: 2833 Vitamins, natural or synthetic: bulk, uncompounded

(G-1275)
HEATING & BURNER SUPPLY INC
479 Walton Ave (10451-5337)
PHONE..................................718 665-0006
Bob Broker, *President*
Terrance Broker, *Vice Pres*
Eric Nelson, *Sales Staff*
EMP: 7
SQ FT: 10,000
SALES (est): 1.8MM **Privately Held**
WEB: www.heatingandburner.com
SIC: 3822 5063 Auto controls regulating residntl & coml environmt & applncs; motors, electric

(G-1276)
HIGH RIDGE NEWS LLC
5818 Broadway (10463-4105)
PHONE..................................718 548-7412
Atul Patel, *Owner*
EMP: 5
SALES (est): 268.4K **Privately Held**
SIC: 2711 Newspapers, publishing & printing

(G-1277)
I-TEM BRAND LLC
Also Called: Innovation By Temi
675 E 213th St Apt 1 (10467-5671)
PHONE..................................718 790-6927
Temitayo Adewuyi, *Mng Member*
EMP: 10 **EST:** 2017
SALES: 256.9K **Privately Held**
SIC: 3873 5094 5944 Watches, clocks, watchcases & parts; watches & parts, except crystals & jewels; watches & parts; watches

(G-1278)
IDEAL SIGNS INC
538 Wales Ave (10455-4510)
PHONE..................................718 292-9196
EMP: 5
SQ FT: 3,000
SALES (est): 396.1K **Privately Held**
SIC: 3993 Mfg Signs/Advertising Specialties

(G-1279)
IMPERIAL DAMPER & LOUVER CO
907 E 141st St (10454-2009)
PHONE..................................718 731-3800
Brad Mattes, *President*
Tom Tulley, *Vice Pres*
Myrna Garcia, *Prdtn Mgr*
Aida Rivera, *Office Mgr*
Jared Mattes, *Technician*
EMP: 35
SQ FT: 16,500
SALES (est): 6.6MM **Privately Held**
WEB: www.imperialdamper.com
SIC: 3444 3446 Metal ventilating equipment; louvers, ventilating

(G-1280)
INDEX INCORPORATED
415 Concord Ave (10455-4801)
PHONE..................................440 632-5400
Elias Wexler, *President*
Tom McCartney, *General Mgr*
EMP: 13
SQ FT: 3,500
SALES (est): 1.4MM **Privately Held**
WEB: www.zerointernational.com
SIC: 3052 Rubber & plastics hose & beltings

HQ: Schlage Lock Company Llc
11819 N Penn St
Carmel IN 46032
317 810-3700

(G-1281)
INDUSTRIAL PAPER TUBE INC
1335 E Bay Ave (10474-6992)
PHONE................................718 893-5000
Howard Kramer, *President*
John Costello, *Vice Pres*
EMP: 19
SQ FT: 50,000
SALES (est): 3.5MM **Privately Held**
WEB: www.mailingtubes-ipt.com
SIC: 3089 2655 Closures, plastic; tubes,
for chemical or electrical uses: paper or
fiber

(G-1282)
INFORM STUDIO INC
480 Austin Pl Frnt E (10455-5023)
PHONE................................718 401-6149
Patrick Eck, *President*
Emad Ebrahim, *Vice Pres*
Alicia Guthrie, *Office Mgr*
EMP: 10
SQ FT: 7,000
SALES (est): 1.7MM **Privately Held**
SIC: 2431 Interior & ornamental woodwork
& trim

(G-1283)
INNOVA INTERIORS INC
780 E 134th St Fl 2 (10454-3527)
PHONE................................718 401-2122
Leon Mace Natenzon, *President*
EMP: 20 EST: 2001
SALES (est): 1.2MM **Privately Held**
SIC: 2499 1751 Decorative wood & wood-
work; carpentry work

(G-1284)
IWEB DESIGN INC
1491 Metro Ave Ste 3i (10462)
PHONE................................805 243-8305
John Horne, *CEO*
Jon Jaskiel, *Vice Pres*
EMP: 10
SALES (est): 460K **Privately Held**
SIC: 3577 Encoders, computer peripheral
equipment

(G-1285)
**JEM THREADING SPECIALTIES
INC**
1059 Washington Ave (10456-6636)
P.O. Box 491, Lake Peekskill (10537-0491)
PHONE................................718 665-3341
Michael Rottenkolber, *President*
John Rottenkolber, *Vice Pres*
EMP: 5
SQ FT: 17,500
SALES (est): 652.8K **Privately Held**
SIC: 3965 3354 3452 Fasteners; rods,
extruded, aluminum; bolts, metal

(G-1286)
**JENNA CONCRETE
CORPORATION**
1465 Bronx River Ave (10472-1001)
PHONE................................718 842-5250
Carmine Valente, *President*
EMP: 30
SQ FT: 1,000
SALES (est): 6.3MM
SALES (corp-wide): 1.5B **Publicly Held**
SIC: 3272 3273 3271 Concrete products;
ready-mixed concrete; concrete block &
brick
PA: U.S. Concrete, Inc.
331 N Main St
Euless TX 76039
817 835-4105

(G-1287)
JENNA HARLEM RIVER INC
1465 Bronx River Ave (10472-1001)
PHONE................................718 842-5997
Carmine Valente, *President*
EMP: 5
SQ FT: 1,000
SALES (est): 454.9K **Privately Held**
SIC: 3272 3273 3271 Concrete products;
ready-mixed concrete; concrete block &
brick

(G-1288)
JOHN LANGENBACHER CO INC
888 Longfellow Ave (10474-4804)
PHONE................................718 328-0141
Harry Boyd, *President*
William Boyd, *President*
Larry Scherer, *Exec VP*
William Hudspeth, *CFO*
EMP: 50 EST: 1907
SQ FT: 100,000
SALES (est): 4.6MM **Privately Held**
SIC: 2431 5712 Millwork; custom made
furniture, except cabinets

(G-1289)
KD DIDS INC
Also Called: K D Dance
140 E 144th St (10451-5434)
PHONE................................718 402-2012
David E Lee, *President*
David Lee, *President*
EMP: 22
SQ FT: 6,000
SALES (est): 5.3MM **Privately Held**
WEB: www.kddance.com
SIC: 2253 5961 Shirts (outerwear), knit;
fitness & sporting goods, mail order

(G-1290)
KEMET PROPERTIES LLC
1179 E 224th St (10466-5834)
PHONE................................718 654-8079
EMP: 5
SALES (est): 529.7K **Privately Held**
SIC: 3675 Mfg Electronic Capacitors

(G-1291)
KENMAR SHIRTS INC (PA)
1415 Blondell Ave (10461-2622)
PHONE................................718 824-3880
Mark Greene, *President*
Karen Greene, *Corp Secy*
Irwin Haberman, *Vice Pres*
EMP: 20
SQ FT: 8,000
SALES (est): 1.7MM **Privately Held**
WEB: www.kenmarshirts.com
SIC: 2759 5136 5137 2396 Screen print-
ing; men's & boys' clothing; women's &
children's clothing; automotive & apparel
trimmings

(G-1292)
**KICKS CLOSET SPORTSWEAR
INC**
1031 Southern Blvd Frnt 2 (10459-3435)
PHONE................................347 577-0857
Ismail Abadi, *President*
EMP: 6 EST: 2014
SQ FT: 1,800
SALES (est): 2.7MM **Privately Held**
SIC: 2329 3149 2339 Men's & boys'
sportswear & athletic clothing; athletic
shoes, except rubber or plastic; women's
& misses' athletic clothing & sportswear

(G-1293)
KIRSCHNER BRUSH LLC
Also Called: Kbc
605 E 132nd St Frnt 3 (10454-4638)
PHONE................................718 292-1809
Israel Kirschner,
▲ EMP: 15 EST: 1939
SQ FT: 20,000
SALES (est): 900K **Privately Held**
SIC: 3991 Paint brushes

(G-1294)
KNJ FABRICATORS LLC
4341 Wickham Ave (10466-1809)
PHONE................................347 234-6985
Krishnadatt N Joe,
EMP: 10
SQ FT: 4,000
SALES (est): 900K **Privately Held**
SIC: 3441 Fabricated structural metal

(G-1295)
L & D MANUFACTURING CORP
Also Called: D & L Manufacturing
366 Canal Pl Frnt (10451-5911)
PHONE................................718 665-5226
Larry Weisel, *President*
Leon Weisel, *Vice Pres*
EMP: 6

SALES (est): 624.9K **Privately Held**
SIC: 2599 Restaurant furniture, wood or
metal

(G-1296)
**L A S REPLACEMENT PARTS
INC**
1645 Webster Ave (10457-8096)
PHONE................................718 583-4700
Alan Siegel, *President*
Lloyd Siegel, *Corp Secy*
EMP: 10 EST: 1946
SQ FT: 10,000
SALES (est): 1.5MM **Privately Held**
WEB: www.lasparts.com
SIC: 3432 1711 Plumbing fixture fittings &
trim; plumbing, heating, air-conditioning
contractors

(G-1297)
LA PRIMA BAKERY INC (PA)
765 E 182nd St (10460-1140)
PHONE................................718 584-4442
Sal Attina, *President*
Rocco Attina, *Vice Pres*
EMP: 19
SQ FT: 18,000
SALES (est): 1.2MM **Privately Held**
SIC: 2051 Bread, all types (white, wheat,
rye, etc): fresh or frozen

(G-1298)
LEADER SHEET METAL INC
759 E 133rd St Apt 2 (10454-3437)
PHONE................................347 271-4961
Jenny Dashevsky, *President*
EMP: 17
SALES (est): 3.2MM **Privately Held**
SIC: 3444 Sheet metalwork

(G-1299)
LEGACY USA LLC
Also Called: Legacy Manufacturing
415 Concord Ave (10455-4801)
PHONE................................718 292-5333
Michael Draper, *Opers Staff*
Jon Underwood, *Natl Sales Mgr*
Ashley Rojas, *Office Mgr*
Jacob Wexler, *Mng Member*
Becca Lisoski, *Manager*
EMP: 15 EST: 2016
SQ FT: 20,000
SALES (est): 700K **Privately Held**
SIC: 2891 Adhesives & sealants

(G-1300)
**LEMON BROTHERS
FOUNDATION INC**
Also Called: Not For Profit Chari
23b Debs Pl (10475-2575)
PHONE................................347 920-2749
Mohammed Rahman, *Principal*
EMP: 15
SALES (est): 24K **Privately Held**
SIC: 3999 Education aids, devices & sup-
plies

(G-1301)
LENON MODELS INC
300 W 245th St (10471-3902)
PHONE................................212 229-1581
Elise Hubsher, *President*
EMP: 5
SALES (est): 451.1K **Privately Held**
SIC: 3259 Architectural clay products

(G-1302)
LENS LAB
2124 Bartow Ave (10475-4615)
PHONE................................718 379-2020
Janet Bennis, *Manager*
EMP: 6
SALES (est): 266.2K **Privately Held**
SIC: 3851 Ophthalmic goods

(G-1303)
LINDA CAMPBELL
Also Called: Campbell's Print Shop
4420 Richardson Ave (10470-1545)
PHONE................................718 994-4026
Linda Campbell, *Owner*
EMP: 7 EST: 1998
SALES (est): 349.4K **Privately Held**
SIC: 2759 Circulars: printing

(G-1304)
LINO PRESS INC
652 Southern Blvd (10455-3637)
PHONE................................718 665-2625
Franklin Nunez, *Owner*
EMP: 20
SALES (est): 1.2MM **Privately Held**
SIC: 2741 Miscellaneous publishing

(G-1305)
M J M TOOLING CORP
Also Called: Sutter Machine Tool and Die
1059 Washington Ave (10456-6636)
PHONE................................718 292-3590
John Rottenkolber, *President*
Michael Rottenkolber, *Treasurer*
EMP: 9
SALES (est): 1.1MM **Privately Held**
SIC: 3544 Special dies & tools

(G-1306)
MARATHON ENTERPRISES INC
Also Called: House O'Weenies
787 E 138th St (10454-1989)
PHONE................................718 665-2560
Don Stacey, *Plant Mgr*
Allan Thoreson, *Manager*
EMP: 60
SALES (corp-wide): 19.4MM **Privately
Held**
WEB: www.sabrett.com
SIC: 2013 Frankfurters from purchased
meat
PA: Marathon Enterprises, Inc.
9 Smith St
Englewood NJ 07631
201 935-3330

(G-1307)
**MASON TRANSPARENT
PACKAGE INC**
1180 Commerce Ave (10462-5506)
PHONE................................718 792-6000
Richard Cole, *President*
Ellen Cole, *Vice Pres*
Kevin O'Connell, *Vice Pres*
Sylvia A Cole, *Admin Sec*
EMP: 30 EST: 1947
SQ FT: 25,000
SALES (est): 3.8MM **Privately Held**
WEB: www.masontransparent.com
SIC: 2671 2673 2759 Plastic film, coated
or laminated for packaging; plastic bags:
made from purchased materials; commer-
cial printing

(G-1308)
**MATERIALS DESIGN
WORKSHOP**
830 Barry St (10474-5707)
PHONE................................718 893-1954
Eugene Black, *President*
James Black, *Opers Mgr*
EMP: 14
SQ FT: 11,000
SALES (est): 2.1MM **Privately Held**
SIC: 2521 Cabinets, office: wood

(G-1309)
**MENSCH MILL & LUMBER CORP
(PA)**
Also Called: Mensch Supply
1261 Commerce Ave (10462-5527)
PHONE................................718 359-7500
Jeff Solomon, *CEO*
Howard Kahn, *Ch of Bd*
Dennis Martinez, *Buyer*
Yvette Menendez, *Controller*
Jack Maddalena, *Manager*
EMP: 20 EST: 1947
SQ FT: 20,000
SALES: 30.1MM **Privately Held**
WEB: www.menschmill.com
SIC: 2431 5211 5231 Millwork; lumber
products; paint, glass & wallpaper

(G-1310)
**MERCURY LOCK AND DOOR
SERVICE**
529 C Wortham St (10474)
PHONE................................718 542-7048
Howard Levine, *President*
EMP: 29 EST: 2010
SALES (est): 2.8MM **Privately Held**
SIC: 3442 Fire doors, metal

▲ = Import ▼=Export
◆ =Import/Export

(G-1311)
METALLINE FIRE DOOR CO INC (PA)
4110 Park Ave (10457-6017)
PHONE.................................718 583-2320
Lydia Rodriguez, *President*
William Rodriguez, *Vice Pres*
EMP: 20
SQ FT: 12,500
SALES (est): 4.9MM **Privately Held**
SIC: 3442 5072 Fire doors, metal; window & door frames; hardware

(G-1312)
METALWORKS INC
1303 Herschell St (10461-3622)
PHONE.................................718 319-0011
Michael Josephs, *Ch of Bd*
Jeff Dynhas, *Vice Pres*
Denise Josephs, *Admin Sec*
EMP: 30
SQ FT: 15,000
SALES (est): 3.6MM **Privately Held**
SIC: 3446 Architectural metalwork

(G-1313)
MIL & MIR STEEL PDTS CO INC
1210 Randall Ave (10474-6399)
PHONE.................................718 328-7596
William Miraglia, *President*
EMP: 6 **EST:** 1958
SQ FT: 5,000
SALES (est): 350K **Privately Held**
SIC: 3537 Lift trucks, industrial: fork, platform, straddle, etc.

(G-1314)
MILLENNIUM RMNFCTRED TONER INC
7 Bruckner Blvd (10454-4411)
PHONE.................................718 585-9887
Frank Garcia, *President*
Charles Baker, *Senior VP*
EMP: 11
SALES (est): 920K **Privately Held**
WEB: www.mrtoners.com
SIC: 2893 Printing ink

(G-1315)
MILLER BLAKER INC
620 E 132nd St (10454-4603)
PHONE.................................718 665-0500
Cliff Blaker, *Ch of Bd*
Lee Miller, *Senior VP*
Rabin Ramcharan, *Vice Pres*
Ernie Pitone, *Project Mgr*
Steve Samuels, *Project Mgr*
▲ **EMP:** 100
SQ FT: 50,000
SALES (est): 15MM **Privately Held**
WEB: www.millerblaker.com
SIC: 2431 2521 Interior & ornamental woodwork & trim; wood office furniture

(G-1316)
MISS GRIMBLE ASSOCIATES INC
Also Called: Grimble Bakery
909 E 135th St (10454-3611)
PHONE.................................718 665-2253
Errol Bier, *President*
EMP: 12
SQ FT: 15,000
SALES (est): 720K **Privately Held**
WEB: www.missgrimble.com
SIC: 2051 Bakery: wholesale or wholesale/retail combined

(G-1317)
MODULAR MEDICAL CORP
1513 Olmstead Ave (10462-4254)
PHONE.................................718 829-2626
Jeffery S Offner, *President*
Peter Wachs, *Vice Pres*
EMP: 30
SQ FT: 30,000
SALES (est): 1.3MM **Privately Held**
SIC: 3841 Surgical & medical instruments

(G-1318)
MONARCH ELECTRIC PRODUCTS INC
Also Called: Vicron Electronic Mfg
4077 Park Ave Fl 5 (10457-7310)
PHONE.................................718 583-7996

Fax: 718 299-9121
▲ **EMP:** 6 **EST:** 1946
SQ FT: 5,000
SALES (est): 500K **Privately Held**
SIC: 3643 Mfg Fluorescent Starting Switches

(G-1319)
MONTE PRESS INC
4808 White Plains Rd (10470-1102)
PHONE.................................718 325-4999
Barbara Deangelo, *President*
EMP: 5
SQ FT: 2,400
SALES (est): 320K **Privately Held**
SIC: 2752 Commercial printing, offset

(G-1320)
N & L FUEL CORP
2014 Blackrock Ave (10472-6104)
PHONE.................................718 863-3538
Nick Leandro, *Principal*
EMP: 9
SALES (est): 1MM **Privately Held**
SIC: 2869 Fuels

(G-1321)
NATIONAL EQUIPMENT CORPORATION
Also Called: Union Standard & Un Conf McHy
801 E 141st St (10454-1917)
PHONE.................................718 585-0200
Eddie Greenberg, *Manager*
EMP: 30
SALES (corp-wide): 10.6MM **Privately Held**
SIC: 3559 3565 5084 3556 Chemical machinery & equipment; pharmaceutical machinery; packaging machinery; processing & packaging equipment; confectionery machinery
PA: National Equipment Corporation
600 Mmaroneck Ave Ste 400
Harrison NY 10528
718 585-0200

(G-1322)
NATIONAL STEEL RULE DIE INC
441 Southern Blvd (10455-4906)
PHONE.................................718 402-1396
Frank G Curatolo, *President*
EMP: 14 **EST:** 1945
SQ FT: 5,000
SALES: 900K **Privately Held**
SIC: 3544 Dies, steel rule; special dies & tools

(G-1323)
NEW YORK BOTTLING CO INC
Also Called: Mayim Chaim Beverages
626 Whittier St (10474-6121)
PHONE.................................718 963-3232
Zvi Hold, *President*
Joseph Hold, *Vice Pres*
Racheal Hold, *Admin Sec*
Esta Kohn, *Admin Sec*
EMP: 12 **EST:** 1967
SQ FT: 10,000
SALES (est): 2.6MM **Privately Held**
SIC: 2086 Soft drinks: packaged in cans, bottles, etc.

(G-1324)
NEX-GEN READY MIX CORP
530 Faile St (10474-6908)
PHONE.................................347 231-0073
Salvatore Bullaro, *Chairman*
EMP: 7
SALES (est): 752K **Privately Held**
SIC: 3273 Ready-mixed concrete

(G-1325)
NOROC ENTERPRISES INC
415 Concord Ave (10455-4801)
PHONE.................................718 585-3230
Elias Wexler, *CEO*
Jerry Heid, *Vice Pres*
◆ **EMP:** 150 **EST:** 1928
SQ FT: 27,000
SALES (est): 20MM **Privately Held**
WEB: www.zerointernational.com
SIC: 3251 3053 Fireproofing tile, clay; gasket materials

(G-1326)
NORTH BRONX RETINAL & OPHTHLMI
3725 Henry Hudson Pkwy (10463-1527)
PHONE.................................347 535-4932
Daniel Chechik MD, *Ch of Bd*
EMP: 8
SALES (est): 849.8K **Privately Held**
SIC: 3851 Ophthalmic goods

(G-1327)
NYC BRONX INC
2490 Grand Concourse (10458-5201)
PHONE.................................917 417-0509
Prosper Ozies, *President*
EMP: 5
SQ FT: 2,000
SALES (est): 588K **Privately Held**
SIC: 2369 Girls' & children's outerwear

(G-1328)
OMC INC
4010 Park Ave (10457-7397)
PHONE.................................718 731-5001
James O'Halpin, *President*
Mike Checci, *Corp Secy*
Robert Moteti, *Vice Pres*
EMP: 110
SQ FT: 25,000
SALES (est): 19.1MM **Privately Held**
WEB: www.omcdrafting.com
SIC: 3444 Sheet metalwork

(G-1329)
OPERATIVE CAKE CORP
Also Called: Lady Linda Cakes
711 Brush Ave (10465-1839)
P.O. Box 1017 (10465-0623)
PHONE.................................718 278-5600
Matthew Jacobson, *President*
Mark Jacobson, *President*
Sam Jacobson, *Vice Pres*
EMP: 50
SQ FT: 60,000
SALES (est): 6.1MM
SALES (corp-wide): 41.6MM **Privately Held**
WEB: www.groceryhaulers.com
SIC: 2051 5149 Bread, cake & related products; bakery products
PA: Grocery Haulers, Inc.
485 Route 1 S
Iselin NJ 08830
732 499-3745

(G-1330)
P H CUSTOM WOODWORKING CORP
830 Barry St Fl 2nd (10474-5707)
PHONE.................................917 801-1444
Kazimierz Sperling, *President*
Daniel Sperling, *Principal*
Anna Sperling, *Vice Pres*
EMP: 23
SQ FT: 8,000
SALES: 3.2MM **Privately Held**
SIC: 2431 Interior & ornamental woodwork & trim; exterior & ornamental woodwork & trim

(G-1331)
PACIFIC DESIGNS INTL INC
2743 Webster Ave (10458-3705)
PHONE.................................718 364-2867
Edward Nerenberg, *President*
EMP: 7
SALES (est): 497.7K **Privately Held**
SIC: 3081 Floor or wall covering, unsupported plastic

(G-1332)
PARKCHESTER DPS LLC
2000 E Tremont Ave (10462-5703)
PHONE.................................718 823-4411
EMP: 107
SALES (est): 10MM **Privately Held**
SIC: 3841 Surgical & medical instruments

(G-1333)
PATIENT-WEAR LLC
3940 Merritt Ave (10466-2502)
PHONE.................................914 740-7770
Thomas A Keith, *President*
EMP: 8

SALES: 950K **Privately Held**
SIC: 2389 Apparel & accessories

(G-1334)
PELICAN PRODUCTS CO INC (PA)
1049 Lowell St (10459-2608)
PHONE.................................718 860-3220
Kenneth Silver, *President*
David Silver, *Vice Pres*
▲ **EMP:** 23 **EST:** 1946
SQ FT: 20,000
SALES (est): 2.8MM **Privately Held**
WEB: www.pelicanproducts.com
SIC: 3951 3089 Pens & mechanical pencils; novelties, plastic

(G-1335)
PEPSI-COLA BOTTLING CO NY INC
650 Brush Ave (10465-1804)
PHONE.................................718 892-1570
Michael Moral, *Manager*
EMP: 75
SALES (corp-wide): 64.6B **Publicly Held**
SIC: 2086 Soft drinks: packaged in cans, bottles, etc.
HQ: Pepsi-Cola Bottling Company Of New York, Inc.
11202 15th Ave
College Point NY 11356
718 392-1000

(G-1336)
PERRIGO COMPANY
1625 Bathgate Ave (10457-8101)
PHONE.................................718 960-9900
Todd W Kingma, *Exec VP*
Ange Francois, *Project Mgr*
Joseph C Papa, *Branch Mgr*
Vikrant Bandekar, *Manager*
Nesive Bell, *Manager*
EMP: 22 **Privately Held**
SIC: 2834 Analgesics
HQ: Perrigo Company
515 Eastern Ave
Allegan MI 49010
269 673-8451

(G-1337)
PERRIGO NEW YORK INC
455 Claremont Pkwy (10457-8301)
PHONE.................................718 901-2800
Oscar Camejo, *Manager*
EMP: 15 **Privately Held**
WEB: www.agis-group.com
SIC: 2834 Ointments
HQ: Perrigo New York, Inc.
1700 Bathgate Ave
Bronx NY 10457
718 960-9900

(G-1338)
PERRIGO NEW YORK INC (DH)
Also Called: Suppositoria Laboratory
1700 Bathgate Ave (10457-7512)
PHONE.................................718 960-9900
Joseph C Papa, *Ch of Bd*
Giora Carni, *President*
Mike Munoz, *Buyer*
Altin Leka, *QC Mgr*
Natalie Paz, *Engineer*
▲ **EMP:** 500
SQ FT: 300,000
SALES (est): 87.3MM **Privately Held**
WEB: www.agis-group.com
SIC: 2834 Ointments
HQ: Perrigo Company
515 Eastern Ave
Allegan MI 49010
269 673-8451

(G-1339)
PONCIO SIGNS
3007 Albany Cres (10463-5960)
PHONE.................................718 543-4851
Poncio Salcedo, *Owner*
EMP: 7 **EST:** 1962
SQ FT: 700
SALES (est): 290K **Privately Held**
SIC: 3993 Signs, not made in custom sign painting shops

(G-1340)
POORAN PALLET INC
319 Barretto St (10474-6722)
PHONE...................................718 938-7970
Zainool Pooran, *President*
EMP: 5
SQ FT: 5,000
SALES: 300K **Privately Held**
SIC: 2448 Pallets, wood & wood with metal

(G-1341)
PORK KING SAUSAGE INC
F22 Hunts Point Co Op Mkt (10474-7568)
PHONE...................................718 542-2810
Dominick Puntolillo, *President*
Frank Puntolillo, *Vice Pres*
EMP: 25
SQ FT: 10,000
SALES (est): 5.1MM **Privately Held**
SIC: 2013 Sausages & other prepared
meats

(G-1342)
**PRECISION ORNA IR WORKS
INC**
Also Called: Precision Furniture
1838 Adee Ave (10469-3245)
PHONE...................................718 379-5200
Joseph Napolitano, *President*
Anthony Napolitano, *Vice Pres*
Philip Napolitano, *Admin Sec*
EMP: 9
SQ FT: 40,000
SALES: 700K **Privately Held**
WEB: www.precisionfurniture.com
SIC: 2514 Household furniture: uphol-
stered on metal frames

(G-1343)
**PREMIER BRANDS AMERICA
INC**
555 E 242nd St (10470-1007)
PHONE...................................718 325-3000
Glenn Lee, *President*
EMP: 10
SALES (est): 1MM
SALES (corp-wide): 35.9MM **Privately
Held**
SIC: 3131 2842 3842 Footwear cut stock;
shoe polish or cleaner; orthopedic appli-
ances
PA: Premier Brands Of America Inc.
170 Hamilton Ave Ste 201
White Plains NY 10601
914 667-6200

(G-1344)
PREMIUM OCEAN LLC
1271 Ryawa Ave (10474-7114)
PHONE...................................917 231-1061
Esraim Basson,
Juliana Paparizou,
▲ EMP: 15
SALES (est): 4.1MM **Privately Held**
SIC: 2091 Seafood products: packaged in
cans, jars, etc.

(G-1345)
**PRONTO GAS HEATING SUPS
INC**
Also Called: Johnson Contrls Authorized Dlr
431 E 165th St Fl 2 (10456-6644)
PHONE...................................718 292-0707
Trifone A Demarinis, *Branch Mgr*
EMP: 9
SALES (est): 1.3MM
SALES (corp-wide): 4MM **Privately Held**
WEB: www.prontosupplies.com
SIC: 3829 5075 5074 Measuring & con-
trolling devices; warm air heating & air
conditioning; plumbing & hydronic heating
supplies
PA: Pronto Gas Heating Supplies Inc.
181 Chrystie St Frnt
New York NY 10002
212 777-3366

(G-1346)
**PULSE PLASTICS PRODUCTS
INC**
1156 E 165th St (10459-2613)
P.O. Box 427, New City (10956-0427)
PHONE...................................718 328-5224
Alan J Backelman, *President*
EMP: 25

SQ FT: 23,000
SALES: 1.5MM **Privately Held**
WEB: www.pulseplastics.com
SIC: 3089 Molding primary plastic; injec-
tion molding of plastics

(G-1347)
**QUALITY HM BRANDS
HOLDINGS LLC (PA)**
125 Rose Feiss Blvd (10454-3624)
PHONE...................................718 292-2024
Maurice Feiss, *Mng Member*
Thomas Bilbrough,
William J Haley,
▲ EMP: 3
SALES (est): 189.9MM **Privately Held**
SIC: 3645 5063 Residential lighting fix-
tures; lighting fixtures; lighting fixtures,
residential

(G-1348)
QUALITY MILLWORK CORP
425 Devoe Ave (10460-2309)
P.O. Box 479 (10460-0241)
PHONE...................................718 892-2250
Anthony Guarino, *President*
▲ EMP: 28
SQ FT: 45,000
SALES (est): 3.6MM **Privately Held**
SIC: 2431 Doors, wood

(G-1349)
R GOLDSMITH
1974 Mayflower Ave (10461-4007)
PHONE...................................718 239-1396
Claudine Bryan, *Branch Mgr*
EMP: 10
SALES (est): 486.8K **Privately Held**
SIC: 3914 Silversmithing

(G-1350)
REEFER TEK LLC
885a E 149th St Fl 2 (10455)
PHONE...................................347 590-1067
EMP: 12 EST: 2010
SQ FT: 12,000
SALES (est): 1.3MM **Privately Held**
SIC: 3559 Mfg Misc Industry Machinery

(G-1351)
RM BAKERY LLC
Also Called: Rollo Mio Artisan Bakery
220 Coster St (10474-7121)
PHONE...................................718 472-3036
Christian Mattheus, *Mng Member*
EMP: 31
SALES (est): 5.8MM **Privately Held**
SIC: 2051 Cakes, bakery: except frozen

(G-1352)
ROANWELL CORPORATION
2564 Park Ave (10451-6014)
PHONE...................................718 401-0288
Barbara Labarre, *CEO*
Jonathan Labarre, *President*
William Rathban, *Principal*
Yolibel Garcia, *Asst Controller*
Cheldwyn Simon, *Marketing Mgr*
▼ EMP: 45
SQ FT: 28,000
SALES: 6MM **Privately Held**
WEB: www.roanwellcorp.com
SIC: 3669 Intercommunication systems,
electric

(G-1353)
ROCKING THE BOAT INC
812 Edgewater Rd (10474-4902)
PHONE...................................718 466-5799
Amy Kantroitz, *President*
Victor Isayev, *Finance*
Adam Green, *Exec Dir*
Victoria Swedin, *Admin Asst*
EMP: 10
SALES: 3MM **Privately Held**
WEB: www.rockingtheboat.org
SIC: 3732 Non-motorized boat, building &
repairing

(G-1354)
S & S FASHIONS INC
941 Longfellow Ave (10474-4810)
PHONE...................................718 328-0001
Sageev Mangal, *President*
▲ EMP: 5
SQ FT: 18,000

SALES: 4MM **Privately Held**
SIC: 2329 Men's & boys' sportswear & athletic clothing

(G-1355)
S & S SOAP CO INC
815 E 135th St (10454-3584)
PHONE...................................718 585-2900
Zvi Sebrow, *President*
David Sebrow, *Vice Pres*
Joseph Sebrow, *Admin Sec*
EMP: 20 EST: 1930
SQ FT: 40,000
SALES (est): 4.6MM **Privately Held**
WEB: www.blutex.com
SIC: 2841 Detergents, synthetic organic or
inorganic alkaline

(G-1356)
**S & V RESTAURANT EQP MFRS
INC**
Also Called: Custom Cool
4320 Park Ave (10457-2442)
PHONE...................................718 220-1140
Sam Zeltser, *CEO*
Shlomo Zeltser, *President*
Vyacheslav Ulman, *Corp Secy*
Zelig Zeltser, *Vice Pres*
EMP: 46
SQ FT: 35,000
SALES (est): 9.7MM **Privately Held**
WEB: www.customcool.com
SIC: 3585 Refrigeration equipment, com-
plete

(G-1357)
S & V RESTAURANTS CORP
Also Called: Custom Cool
4320 Park Ave (10457-2442)
PHONE...................................718 220-1140
Sam Zeltser, *President*
EMP: 40
SALES (est): 3.3MM **Privately Held**
SIC: 2599 Carts, restaurant equipment

(G-1358)
SACCOMIZE INC
1554 Stillwell Ave (10461-2212)
PHONE...................................818 287-3000
Anthony Saccommanno, *President*
Thomas Saccommanno, *Vice Pres*
EMP: 9
SQ FT: 5,000
SALES (est): 789K **Privately Held**
WEB: www.saccomize.com
SIC: 3471 7542 Finishing, metals or
formed products; washing & polishing, au-
tomotive

(G-1359)
SANJAY PALLETS INC
424 Coster St (10474-6811)
PHONE...................................347 590-2485
Mohamed Salem Shaheed, *CEO*
EMP: 8
SALES (est): 1.1MM **Privately Held**
SIC: 2448 Pallets, wood & wood with metal

(G-1360)
SARABETHS KITCHEN LLC
1161 E 156th St (10474-6226)
PHONE...................................718 589-2900
Sarabeth Levine,
EMP: 7
SALES (est): 110.5K **Privately Held**
SIC: 2033 Jams, jellies & preserves: pack-
aged in cans, jars, etc.

(G-1361)
SBK PRESERVES INC
Also Called: Sarabeth's Bakery
1161 E 156th St (10474-6226)
PHONE...................................800 773-7378
William Levine, *Ch of Bd*
Suzanne B Levine, *Vice Pres*
Toni Walls,
▲ EMP: 40
SQ FT: 15,000
SALES (est): 6.4MM **Privately Held**
SIC: 2033 5149 5961 Jams, including imi-
tation: packaged in cans, jars, etc.; pick-
les, preserves, jellies & jams; food, mail
order

(G-1362)
SCACCIANOCE INC
Also Called: Daisy Brand Confectionery
1165 Burnett Pl (10474-5716)
PHONE...................................718 991-4462
Donald Beck, *President*
Anthony Scaccianoce, *Vice Pres*
▲ EMP: 10 EST: 1904
SQ FT: 10,000
SALES (est): 964.8K **Privately Held**
SIC: 2064 2068 Candy & other confec-
tionery products; salted & roasted nuts &
seeds

(G-1363)
**SIDCO FOOD DISTRIBUTION
CORP**
2324 Webster Ave (10458-7506)
P.O. Box 379, Fort Lee NJ (07024-0379)
PHONE...................................718 733-3939
Jose Negron, *Ch of Bd*
Lois Rodriguez, *Vice Pres*
EMP: 15
SQ FT: 10,000
SALES (est): 6MM **Privately Held**
SIC: 3556 1541 Food products machinery;
food products manufacturing or packing
plant construction

(G-1364)
**SIGMA MANUFACTURING INDS
INC**
1361 E Bay Ave (10474-7025)
PHONE...................................718 842-9180
Fax: 718 991-4094
EMP: 13
SQ FT: 12,000
SALES (est): 3MM **Privately Held**
SIC: 3599 Mfg Industrial Machinery

(G-1365)
**SIGNATURE METAL MBL MAINT
LLC**
791 E 132nd St (10454-3512)
PHONE...................................718 292-8280
Gary Swartz,
EMP: 100 EST: 2000
SALES (est): 16MM **Privately Held**
SIC: 3449 Miscellaneous metalwork

(G-1366)
**SML BROTHERS HOLDING
CORP**
820 E 140th St (10454-1904)
PHONE...................................718 402-2000
Michael Landau, *CEO*
Stephen Landau, *Admin Sec*
▲ EMP: 85 EST: 1976
SALES (est): 15.9MM **Privately Held**
WEB: www.polytexink.com
SIC: 3952 2851 2865 Ink, drawing: black
& colored; paints & paint additives; color
pigments, organic

(G-1367)
SPARROW MINING CO (PA)
3743 White Plains Rd (10467-5754)
PHONE...................................718 519-6600
Randolph Silverstein, *Partner*
David Silverstein, *Partner*
EMP: 7
SALES (est): 1.4MM **Privately Held**
SIC: 1442 Sand mining

(G-1368)
SPECIALTY STEEL FABG CORP
Also Called: Specialty Steel of America.
544 Casanova St (10474-6712)
PHONE...................................718 893-6326
Gregory Burns, *President*
Warren Wilhelm, *Vice Pres*
EMP: 14
SQ FT: 12,000
SALES (est): 2.4MM **Privately Held**
WEB: www.specialtysteelinternational.com
SIC: 3441 5051 5084 Fabricated struc-
tural metal; metals service centers & of-
fices; industrial machinery & equipment

(G-1369)
ST RAYMOND MONUMENT CO
2727 Lafayette Ave (10465-2228)
PHONE...................................718 824-3600
Raymond Carotenuto, *President*
Ethel Carotenuto, *Corp Secy*

EMP: 5 EST: 1971
SQ FT: 1,200
SALES (est): 403.6K **Privately Held**
SIC: **3272** 5999 Monuments, concrete; tombstones, precast terrazzo or concrete; monuments, finished to custom order

(G-1370)
STANDARD PAPER BOX MACHINE CO
347 Coster St Fl 2 (10474-6813)
PHONE..................718 328-3300
Aaron Adams, *Ch of Bd*
Bruce Adams, *President*
Larry Wilson, *Vice Pres*
Vicki Adams, *Treasurer*
▲ EMP: 25
SQ FT: 35,000
SALES (est): 3.6MM **Privately Held**
SIC: **3554** 3542 Box making machines, paper; die cutting & stamping machinery; paper converting; machine tools, metal forming type

(G-1371)
STARLITE PNT & VARNISH CO INC
Also Called: Starlight Paint Factory
724 E 140th St (10454-2405)
PHONE..................718 292-6420
Peter J Gorynski Jr, *President*
EMP: 5
SQ FT: 9,000
SALES (est): 2.5MM **Privately Held**
SIC: **2851** 5231 Paints & paint additives; paint

(G-1372)
STEVEN JOHN OPTICIANS
5901 Riverdale Ave (10471-1602)
PHONE..................718 543-3336
Steven John, *Owner*
EMP: 9
SALES (est): 670K **Privately Held**
SIC: **3827** Optical instruments & lenses

(G-1373)
SUPERMARKET EQUIPMENT DEPO INC
1135 Bronx River Ave (10472-3101)
P.O. Box 368, Mountain Dale (12763-0368)
PHONE..................718 665-6200
EMP: 7
SALES: 2.5MM **Privately Held**
SIC: **3585** Mfg Refrigeration/Heating Equipment

(G-1374)
SUPREME FIRE PROOF DOOR CO
391 Rider Ave (10451-5905)
PHONE..................718 665-4224
Wazier Mahmood, *President*
EMP: 10 EST: 1942
SQ FT: 2,500
SALES (est): 1.2MM **Privately Held**
SIC: **3442** Fire doors, metal

(G-1375)
SVYZ TRADING CORP
4320 Park Ave (10457-2442)
PHONE..................718 220-1140
Sam Zeltser, *Principal*
Zelk Zeltser, *Vice Pres*
Steve Ulman, *Admin Sec*
▲ EMP: 6
SQ FT: 5,000
SALES (est): 797.5K **Privately Held**
SIC: **3822** Refrigeration/air-conditioning defrost controls

(G-1376)
T J RONAN PAINT CORP
Also Called: Ronan Paints
749 E 135th St (10454-3408)
PHONE..................718 292-1100
Dennis Doran, *Ch of Bd*
John A Doran Jr, *Corp Secy*
▼ EMP: 25
SQ FT: 35,000
SALES (est): 5MM **Privately Held**
WEB: www.ronanpaints.com
SIC: **2851** Paints & paint additives

(G-1377)
T M INTERNATIONAL LLC
Also Called: Mazzella Blasting Mat Co
413 Faile St 15 (10474-6907)
P.O. Box 10930, Fairfield NJ (07004-6930)
PHONE..................718 842-0949
Frank Stagnito, *President*
EMP: 7
SQ FT: 45,000
SALES (est): 1MM **Privately Held**
WEB: www.tmi2001.com
SIC: **2298** Blasting mats, rope

(G-1378)
TANNENS
363 E 149th St (10455-3983)
PHONE..................718 292-4646
Mary Tannen, *Owner*
EMP: 7 EST: 1938
SQ FT: 1,875
SALES (est): 716.4K **Privately Held**
SIC: **2759** 5943 Letterpress printing; office forms & supplies

(G-1379)
TARA RIFIC SCREEN PRINTING INC
4197 Park Ave (10457-6033)
PHONE..................718 583-6864
Sandy Stein, *President*
Jason Holden, *Manager*
EMP: 7
SALES: 170K **Privately Held**
SIC: **2759** Screen printing

(G-1380)
TREMONT OFFSET INC
1500 Ericson Pl (10461-5414)
PHONE..................718 892-7333
Robert Del Greco, *President*
Janet Del Greco, *Vice Pres*
Janet Delgreco, *Vice Pres*
Janet Greco, *Vice Pres*
EMP: 9
SQ FT: 2,000
SALES (est): 1.3MM **Privately Held**
SIC: **2752** Commercial printing, offset

(G-1381)
TRENCH & MARINE PUMP CO INC
3466 Park Ave (10456-4307)
P.O. Box 543 (10456-0525)
PHONE..................212 423-9098
Herman Azia, *President*
Malcolm Azia, *Vice Pres*
Yvette Azia, *Treasurer*
EMP: 40 EST: 1918
SQ FT: 10,000
SALES (est): 1.8MM **Privately Held**
SIC: **3561** 3594 Pumps, domestic: water or sump; fluid power pumps & motors

(G-1382)
TROY SIGN & PRINTING
Also Called: Troy Sign Printing Center
4827 White Plains Rd (10470-1125)
PHONE..................718 994-4482
Leslie Peterson, *Owner*
EMP: 6
SALES (est): 497.8K **Privately Held**
SIC: **2752** Commercial printing, lithographic

(G-1383)
TRUXTON CORP
Also Called: Howard Formed Steel Pdts Div
1357 Lafayette Ave (10474-4846)
P.O. Box 225, Yonkers (10704-0225)
PHONE..................718 842-6000
Howard Schwartz, *President*
Steve Meier, *Sales Staff*
EMP: 5 EST: 1945
SQ FT: 5,000
SALES (est): 809.3K **Privately Held**
WEB: www.mailcart.com
SIC: **3799** Pushcarts & wheelbarrows

(G-1384)
TRYLON WIRE & METAL WORKS INC
526 Tiffany St (10474-6614)
PHONE..................718 542-4472
Mark Herrmann, *President*
EMP: 25

SQ FT: 20,000
SALES (est): 3.3MM **Privately Held**
SIC: **2542** 3496 3444 Stands, merchandise display: except wood; miscellaneous fabricated wire products; sheet metalwork

(G-1385)
TWI-LAQ INDUSTRIES INC
Also Called: Stone Glo Products
1345 Seneca Ave (10474-4611)
PHONE..................718 638-5860
Lorin Wels, *President*
Steven Wels, *Exec VP*
Robert Wels, *Vice Pres*
Maurice Silverman, *CPA*
EMP: 30
SQ FT: 30,000
SALES (est): 6.3MM **Privately Held**
WEB: www.stoneglo.com
SIC: **2842** Sanitation preparations

(G-1386)
UB WELDING CORP
2230 Dr Martin L King Jr (10453-1342)
PHONE..................347 688-5196
EMP: 8
SALES (est): 88.7K **Privately Held**
SIC: **7692** Welding repair

(G-1387)
UNITED FARM PROCESSING CORP (PA)
4366 Park Ave (10457-2442)
PHONE..................718 933-6060
Marvin Weinhaus, *President*
Stephen Leibowitz, *Vice Pres*
EMP: 150
SQ FT: 31,000
SALES (est): 5.2MM **Privately Held**
SIC: **2035** Pickled fruits & vegetables

(G-1388)
UNITED PICKLE PRODUCTS CORP
4366 Park Ave (10457-2442)
PHONE..................718 933-6060
Marvin Weishaus, *President*
Stephen Leibowitz, *Vice Pres*
Michael Liu, *CFO*
EMP: 49
SQ FT: 60,000
SALES: 25MM **Privately Held**
SIC: **2035** Vegetables, pickled

(G-1389)
VANITY FAIR BATHMART INC
2971 Webster Ave (10458-2424)
PHONE..................718 584-6700
John P O'Boyle, *President*
EMP: 10
SQ FT: 3,500
SALES (est): 1MM **Privately Held**
WEB: www.vanityfairbathmart.com
SIC: **3431** 3469 5023 5031 Bathroom fixtures, including sinks; kitchen fixtures & equipment: metal, except cast aluminum; kitchenware; lumber, plywood & millwork

(G-1390)
VELVET HEALING BY ALMA CORP
645 Melrose Ave Frnt 1 (10455-2552)
PHONE..................347 271-4220
Alfonsina Pena, *Owner*
EMP: 5
SALES (est): 265.8K **Privately Held**
SIC: **3221** Medicine bottles, glass

(G-1391)
VICTORIA PLATING CO INC
650 Tiffany St (10474-6289)
P.O. Box 740486 (10474-0009)
PHONE..................718 589-1550
Charles Antmann, *President*
Jeffrey S Higdon, *Vice Pres*
▲ EMP: 51 EST: 1947
SQ FT: 45,000
SALES (est): 5.3MM **Privately Held**
WEB: www.victoriaplating.com
SIC: **3471** Electroplating of metals or formed products

(G-1392)
VIELE MANUFACTURING CORP
1340 Viele Ave (10474-7134)
PHONE..................718 893-2200
Gary Hellinger, *CEO*
Emmauel Barrientos, *Manager*
◆ EMP: 500
SQ FT: 25,000
SALES (est): 65.1MM **Privately Held**
SIC: **3089** Injection molding of plastics

(G-1393)
VR BAGS INC
637 E 132nd St (10454-4602)
PHONE..................212 714-1494
Shida Najiri, *President*
EMP: 5
SALES (est): 69.2K **Privately Held**
SIC: **2392** Laundry, garment & storage bags

(G-1394)
WALDORF BAKERS INC
Also Called: Festival Bakers
909 E 135th St (10454-3611)
PHONE..................718 665-2253
Milton Bier, *Ch of Bd*
Errol M Bier, *President*
Nancy Bier, *Vice Pres*
EMP: 15
SQ FT: 13,328
SALES (est): 1MM **Privately Held**
SIC: **2051** Bread, cake & related products

(G-1395)
WALTERS & WALTERS INC
961 E 224th St (10466-4677)
PHONE..................347 202-8535
EMP: 7 EST: 2013
SALES (est): 92.3K **Privately Held**
SIC: **7692** Welding repair

(G-1396)
WENIG CORPORATION
230 Manida St Fl 2 (10474-7199)
PHONE..................718 542-3600
Fax: 718 542-3979
EMP: 30 EST: 1924
SQ FT: 50,000
SALES (est): 5.1MM **Privately Held**
SIC: **3444** Mfg Sheet Metalwork

(G-1397)
YANKEE CORP
Also Called: Yankee Wiping Cloth
1180 Randall Ave (10474-6217)
PHONE..................718 589-1377
Todd W Hooper, *Chairman*
Richard Kocher, *Vice Pres*
▲ EMP: 10
SQ FT: 16,250
SALES (est): 1.2MM **Privately Held**
SIC: **2299** 5093 7218 Fabrics: linen, jute, hemp, ramie; waste rags; wiping towel supply

(G-1398)
YULA CORPORATION
330 Bryant Ave (10474-7197)
PHONE..................718 991-0900
Larry Feldman, *CEO*
Fred Feldman, *President*
Raymond Levin, *Manager*
Matthew Feldman, *Director*
▲ EMP: 40 EST: 1926
SQ FT: 20,000
SALES (est): 10.1MM **Privately Held**
WEB: www.yulacorp.com
SIC: **3443** Heat exchangers, plate type

Bronxville
Westchester County

(G-1399)
ARTISANAL BRANDS INC (PA)
42 Forest Ln (10708-1936)
PHONE..................914 441-3591
Daniel W Dowe, *President*
EMP: 34
SQ FT: 10,000
SALES (est): 3.9MM **Publicly Held**
SIC: **2022** 5451 Natural cheese; cheese

(G-1400)
CLARK BOTANICALS INC
81 Pondfield Rd Ste 263 (10708-3818)
PHONE................................914 826-4319
Francesco Clark, *President*
EMP: 10
SALES (est): 1.3MM **Privately Held**
SIC: 2844 Cosmetic preparations

(G-1401)
LION E-MOBILITY NORTH AMER INC
6 Sherman Ave (10708-4219)
PHONE................................917 345-6365
Roland Bopp, *CEO*
EMP: 5
SALES: 500K **Privately Held**
SIC: 3679 Electronic components

(G-1402)
NOMAD EDITIONS LLC
123 Ellison Ave (10708-2728)
PHONE................................212 918-0992
Mark Edminston, *CEO*
Marjorie Martay, *Exec VP*
Samuel Spivy, *Vice Pres*
Cristine De Pedro, *CTO*
EMP: 18
SALES (est): 1MM **Privately Held**
SIC: 2759 Advertising literature: printing

(G-1403)
SOVEREIGN SERVICING SYSTEM LLC
1 Stone Pl Ste 200 (10708-3431)
PHONE................................914 779-1400
Stewart Alpert, *Principal*
EMP: 18
SALES (est): 1MM **Privately Held**
SIC: 1389 Roustabout service

(G-1404)
TOKENWORKS INC
26 Milburn St Fl 2 (10708-3402)
PHONE................................914 704-3100
Charles Cagliostro, *President*
EMP: 5
SALES: 500K **Privately Held**
WEB: www.tokenworks.com
SIC: 3577 Decoders, computer peripheral equipment

Brookhaven
Suffolk County

(G-1405)
AMNEAL PHARMACEUTICALS LLC
50 Horseblock Rd (11719-9509)
PHONE................................908 231-1911
EMP: 50
SALES (corp-wide): 430MM **Privately Held**
SIC: 2834 Mfg Pharmaceutical Preparations
PA: Amneal Pharmaceuticals, Llc
400 Crossing Blvd Fl 3
Bridgewater NJ 08807
631 952-0214

(G-1406)
AMNEAL PHARMACEUTICALS LLC
50 Horseblock Rd (11719-9509)
PHONE................................631 952-0214
EMP: 41
SALES (corp-wide): 1.6B **Publicly Held**
SIC: 2834 5122 Pharmaceutical preparations; pharmaceuticals
HQ: Amneal Pharmaceuticals Of New York, Llc
50 Horseblock Rd
Brookhaven NY 11719
908 947-3120

(G-1407)
AMNEAL PHARMACEUTICALS NY LLC (DH)
50 Horseblock Rd (11719-9509)
PHONE................................908 947-3120
Todd Branning, *CFO*
Cathy Cosham, *Human Res Mgr*

▲ EMP: 50
SQ FT: 75,000
SALES (est): 89.7MM
SALES (corp-wide): 1.6B **Publicly Held**
WEB: www.amneal.com
SIC: 2834 5122 Pharmaceutical preparations; pharmaceuticals

(G-1408)
GEOTECH ASSOCIATES LTD
20 Stiriz Rd (11719-9717)
PHONE................................631 286-0251
Michael Verruto Jr, *President*
Linda Billski, *Bookkeeper*
EMP: 6
SQ FT: 1,500
SALES: 600K **Privately Held**
SIC: 3272 Concrete stuctural support & building material

(G-1409)
LONG ISLAND PRECAST INC
20 Stiriz Rd (11719-9717)
PHONE................................631 286-0240
Michael Verruto, *Ch of Bd*
Chris Verruto, *Vice Pres*
Michael Cetta, *Plant Mgr*
EMP: 30
SQ FT: 1,500
SALES (est): 6.1MM **Privately Held**
WEB: www.li-precast.com
SIC: 3272 Concrete products, precast

Brooklyn
Kings County

(G-1410)
12PT PRINTING LLC
2053 E 1st St (11223-4026)
PHONE................................718 376-2120
Joseph Sutton, *Owner*
EMP: 5 EST: 2014
SALES (est): 205.1K **Privately Held**
SIC: 2752 Commercial printing, lithographic

(G-1411)
212KIDDISH INC
168 Spencer St (11205-3929)
PHONE................................718 705-7227
Joseph Kohn, *President*
Mendel Kohn, *Vice Pres*
EMP: 6 EST: 2010
SQ FT: 2,300
SALES: 4MM **Privately Held**
SIC: 2052 7389 Cookies & crackers; trade show arrangement

(G-1412)
21ST CENTURY SPIRITS CORP
137 12th St (11215)
PHONE................................718 499-0606
Byung J Park, *Ch of Bd*
EMP: 6
SALES (est): 479.7K **Privately Held**
SIC: 2085 Gin (alcoholic beverage)

(G-1413)
2P AGENCY USA INC
1674 E 22nd St Ste 1 (11229-1500)
PHONE................................212 203-5586
Robert Azaryev, *CEO*
EMP: 2
SQ FT: 1,000
SALES (est): 21.5MM
SALES (corp-wide): 221.1MM **Privately Held**
SIC: 3663 5999 Mobile communication equipment; mobile telephones & equipment
PA: 2p Commercial Agency S.R.O.
U Zvonarky 291/3
Praha 2 - Vinohrady

(G-1414)
388 ASSOCIATES INC
385 Harman St (11237-4701)
PHONE................................267 367-0990
Qi Wang, *Manager*
EMP: 5
SALES (est): 156.7K **Privately Held**
SIC: 2392 Household furnishings

(G-1415)
3PHASE INDUSTRIES LLC
Also Called: Token
481 Van Buren St Unit 9a (11221-3046)
PHONE................................347 763-2942
Will Kavesh,
Nicole Cornell,
EMP: 6
SQ FT: 4,000
SALES (est): 500K **Privately Held**
SIC: 2522 2519 Office furniture, except wood; household furniture, except wood or metal: upholstered

(G-1416)
3RD AVENUE DOUGHNUT INC
7111 3rd Ave (11209-1308)
PHONE................................718 748-3294
EMP: 10
SALES (est): 505.5K **Privately Held**
SIC: 2051 Mfg Bread/Related Products

(G-1417)
3V COMPANY INC
Also Called: Three V
110 Bridge St Ste 3 (11201-1575)
PHONE................................718 858-7333
Clara Crombo, *CEO*
Sam Gombo, *President*
Dan Gombo, *Vice Pres*
EMP: 47
SQ FT: 22,000
SALES (est): 8.1MM **Privately Held**
WEB: www.threev.com
SIC: 2087 2834 2099 2086 Syrups, flavoring (except drink); pharmaceutical preparations; food preparations; bottled & canned soft drinks

(G-1418)
40 STREET BAKING INC
8617 17th Ave (11214-3601)
PHONE................................212 683-4700
Mohammed Irfan,
EMP: 8
SALES (est): 467.5K **Privately Held**
SIC: 2051 Bread, cake & related products

(G-1419)
461 NEW LOTS AVENUE LLC
461 New Lots Ave (11207-6411)
P.O. Box 20540 (11202-0540)
PHONE................................347 303-9305
Desmond R John Sr,
EMP: 6
SALES (est): 331K **Privately Held**
SIC: 2759 7991 Commercial printing; spas

(G-1420)
5TH AVENUE PHARMACY INC
4818 5th Ave Ste 1 (11220-1936)
PHONE................................718 439-8585
Avraham Pudel, *President*
EMP: 9
SALES (est): 1.2MM **Privately Held**
SIC: 2834 Pharmaceutical preparations

(G-1421)
6727 11TH AVE CORP
Also Called: Prestige Printing Company
6727 11th Ave (11219-5904)
PHONE................................718 837-8787
Vincent Costanza, *President*
Luke Spano, *Vice Pres*
EMP: 10
SQ FT: 3,200
SALES (est): 1.5MM **Privately Held**
SIC: 2752 2759 Commercial printing, offset; offset & photolithographic printing; letterpress printing

(G-1422)
72 STEEL AND ALUMINIUM WORK
220 42nd St (11232-2814)
PHONE................................917 667-3033
Cheng X Lin, *Principal*
EMP: 6 EST: 2016
SALES (est): 386.1K **Privately Held**
SIC: 3479 Aluminum coating of metal products

(G-1423)
728 BERRIMAN LLC
728 Berriman St (11208-5402)
PHONE................................718 272-5000
David Minsky,
EMP: 5
SALES (est): 287.8K **Privately Held**
SIC: 3949 Golf equipment

(G-1424)
786 IRON WORKS CORP
50 Morgan Ave (11237-1605)
PHONE................................718 418-4808
Baudin Canka, *President*
EMP: 5
SQ FT: 5,000
SALES (est): 806.8K **Privately Held**
SIC: 3446 Fences or posts, ornamental iron or steel

(G-1425)
888 PHARMACY INC
4821 8th Ave (11220-2213)
PHONE................................718 871-8833
Larisa Golubets, *President*
EMP: 10 EST: 2012
SALES (est): 1.5MM **Privately Held**
SIC: 2834 Pharmaceutical preparations

(G-1426)
999 BAGELS INC
1410 86th St (11228-3408)
PHONE................................718 915-0742
Stefano Mannino, *CEO*
Salvatore Mannino, *Director*
EMP: 8
SALES (est): 678.7K **Privately Held**
SIC: 2051 5461 Bagels, fresh or frozen; bagels

(G-1427)
A & B FINISHING INC
401 Park Ave (11205-1406)
PHONE................................718 522-4702
Fax: 718 624-4916
EMP: 40
SQ FT: 20,000
SALES: 800K **Privately Held**
SIC: 2253 5199 2339 Knit Outerwear Mill Whol Nondurable Goods Mfg Women's/Misses' Outerwear

(G-1428)
A & L ASSET MANAGEMENT LTD
143 Alabama Ave (11207-2911)
PHONE................................718 566-1500
Meir Akerman, *CEO*
Eugene Loevinger, *Admin Sec*
EMP: 150
SQ FT: 120,000
SALES (est): 12.3MM **Privately Held**
SIC: 3999 Candles

(G-1429)
A & MT REALTY GROUP LLC
1979 Pacific St Fl 1 (11233-3803)
PHONE................................718 974-5871
Aboubacar Tounkara, *Mng Member*
EMP: 10
SALES: 1MM **Privately Held**
SIC: 1389 8741 Construction, repair & dismantling services; management services

(G-1430)
A & S ELECTRIC
952 Flushing Ave (11206-4720)
PHONE................................212 228-2030
EMP: 7 EST: 2011
SALES (est): 1.2MM **Privately Held**
SIC: 3699 1731 Mfg Electrical Equipment/Supplies Electrical Contractor

(G-1431)
A B S BRASS PRODUCTS INC
185 Moore St (11206-3707)
PHONE................................718 497-2115
Mark Azerrad, *President*
EMP: 11 EST: 1971
SQ FT: 6,000
SALES (est): 970K **Privately Held**
SIC: 3432 Plumbers' brass goods: drain cocks, faucets, spigots, etc.

(G-1432)
A BOGEN ENTERPRISES INC
1837 Coney Island Ave (11230-6546)
PHONE..................................718 951-9533
Mitchell A Bogen, *President*
▲ EMP: 7
SQ FT: 1,800
SALES (est): 28.2K Privately Held
SIC: 2329 5136 5611 Shirt & slack suits:
men's, youths' & boys'; men's & boys'
clothing; clothing accessories: men's &
boys'

(G-1433)
A G M DECO INC
305 Wallabout St 307 (11206-4325)
PHONE..................................718 624-6200
Leib Rosenberg, *Manager*
EMP: 15 Privately Held
SIC: 3442 Sash, door or window: metal
PA: A. G. M. Deco Inc.
741 Myrtle Ave
Brooklyn NY 11205

(G-1434)
A G M DECO INC (PA)
Also Called: Steiner Doors
741 Myrtle Ave (11205-4197)
PHONE..................................718 624-6200
Gabrielle Steiner, *President*
▲ EMP: 92
SQ FT: 2,000
SALES (est): 120MM Privately Held
SIC: 3442 Sash, door or window: metal

(G-1435)
A HEALTH OBSESSION LLC
2184 Mcdonald Ave (11223-3926)
PHONE..................................347 850-4587
Joseph Chehebar,
EMP: 30
SALES (est): 2.5MM
SALES (corp-wide): 9MM Privately Held
SIC: 2086 5149 Fruit drinks (less than
100% juice): packaged in cans, etc.; bev-
erages, except coffee & tea
PA: Jusbyjulie.Com Llc
2184 Mcdonald Ave
Brooklyn NY 11223
917 270-6040

(G-1436)
**A TO Z KOSHER MEAT
PRODUCTS CO**
Also Called: Empire National
123 Borinquen Pl (11211)
PHONE..................................718 384-7400
Edward Weinberg, *President*
Karen Weinberg, *Manager*
EMP: 20
SQ FT: 20,000
SALES (est): 2.6MM Privately Held
SIC: 2011 Meat packing plants

(G-1437)
**A VAN HOEK WOODWORKING
LIMITED**
71 Montrose Ave (11206-2005)
PHONE..................................718 599-4388
Andre Van Hoek, *President*
EMP: 5
SALES: 300K Privately Held
SIC: 2499 5712 Decorative wood & wood-
work; cabinet work, custom

(G-1438)
A&B IRON WORKS INC
137 Conover St (11231-1102)
PHONE..................................347 466-3193
Ashley Beygelman, *President*
Boris Beygelman, *Vice Pres*
EMP: 9
SALES: 150K Privately Held
SIC: 3315 Fence gates posts & fittings:
steel

(G-1439)
A-1 IRON WORKS INC
2413 Atlantic Ave (11233-3416)
PHONE..................................718 927-4766
Mario Palermo, *CEO*
Alberto Palermo, *President*
EMP: 6 EST: 1997
SQ FT: 4,000

SALES (est): 1.1MM Privately Held
SIC: 3312 Hot-rolled iron & steel products

(G-1440)
A-1 PRODUCTS INC
165 Classon Ave (11205-2636)
PHONE..................................718 789-1818
Imre Kaufman, *Principal*
EMP: 9
SQ FT: 7,000
SALES (est): 1.4MM Privately Held
WEB: www.a1prepaid.com
SIC: 3111 2789 3089 Cutting of leather;
paper cutting; plastic processing

(G-1441)
A-1 SKULL CAP CORP
Also Called: A1 Skullcaps
1212 36th St (11218-2010)
PHONE..................................718 633-9333
Henny Blau, *President*
▲ EMP: 25
SALES (est): 1.3MM Privately Held
WEB: www.skullcap.com
SIC: 2353 5999 Hats & caps; religious
goods

(G-1442)
A-ONE LAMINATING CORP
1636 Coney Island Ave 2b (11230-5808)
PHONE..................................718 266-6002
Sol Chaimovits, *CEO*
Ira Chaimovits, *Vice Pres*
Reizel Chaimovits, *Admin Sec*
▲ EMP: 6
SALES: 3MM Privately Held
SIC: 2295 2621 2672 Laminating of fab-
rics; asphalt paper, laminated; coated &
laminated paper

(G-1443)
**A-ONE MOVING & STORAGE
INC**
1725 Avenue M (11230-5303)
PHONE..................................718 266-6002
EMP: 25
SQ FT: 35,000
SALES (est): 3.5MM Privately Held
SIC: 2295 2257 Mfg Coated Fabrics Weft
Knit Fabric Mill

(G-1444)
**A-PLUS RESTAURANT
EQUIPMENT**
623 Sackett St (11217-3116)
PHONE..................................718 522-2656
Alex Picav, *Principal*
▼ EMP: 8
SALES (est): 879.2K Privately Held
SIC: 2599 Carts, restaurant equipment

(G-1445)
**A1 ORNAMENTAL IRON WORKS
INC**
61 Jefferson St (11206-6108)
PHONE..................................718 265-3055
Matt Barsily, *President*
EMP: 5
SALES (est): 386.2K Privately Held
SIC: 3446 Architectural metalwork

(G-1446)
AB FIRE INC
1554 61st St (11219-5431)
P.O. Box 230581 (11223-0581)
PHONE..................................917 416-6444
Ave Kay, *President*
EMP: 8
SALES (est): 618.8K Privately Held
SIC: 3711 Fire department vehicles (motor
vehicles), assembly of

(G-1447)
ABC ELASTIC CORP (PA)
Also Called: ABC Freight Solutions
889 Metropolitan Ave (11211-2513)
PHONE..................................718 388-2953
Morris Freund, *President*
Herman Freund, *Admin Sec*
EMP: 8 EST: 1966
SQ FT: 10,000
SALES (est): 2MM Privately Held
SIC: 2221 Elastic fabrics, manmade fiber &
silk

(G-1448)
ABETTER PROCESSING CORP
984 E 35th St (11210-3423)
PHONE..................................718 252-2223
EMP: 15
SALES (est): 919.1K Privately Held
SIC: 3471 Plating/Polishing Service

(G-1449)
ABLE ANODIZING CORP
1767 Bay Ridge Ave (11204-5016)
PHONE..................................718 252-0660
Brenda Clark, *Vice Pres*
Mary Di Nicola, *Treasurer*
EMP: 13 EST: 1962
SQ FT: 8,000
SALES: 2.3MM Privately Held
SIC: 3471 Anodizing (plating) of metals or
formed products

(G-1450)
ABLE NATIONAL CORP
49 Wyckoff Ave (11237-8001)
PHONE..................................718 386-8801
Abraham Katz, *President*
EMP: 20
SQ FT: 150,000
SALES (est): 4MM Privately Held
WEB: www.ablenational.com
SIC: 2675 3469 2891 Paper die-cutting;
metal stampings; adhesives & sealants

(G-1451)
ACCURATE KNITTING CORP
1478 E 26th St (11210-5233)
PHONE..................................646 552-2216
Chajim Philip Franzos, *President*
EMP: 7
SQ FT: 5,800
SALES (est): 1.2MM Privately Held
SIC: 2253 Sweaters & sweater coats, knit

(G-1452)
ACCURATE PRECAST
1957 Pitkin Ave (11207-3305)
PHONE..................................718 345-2910
Fred Lermer, *Principal*
EMP: 18
SALES (est): 2MM Privately Held
SIC: 3272 Precast terrazzo or concrete
products

(G-1453)
**ACCURATE SIGNS & AWNINGS
INC**
247 Prospect Ave Ste 2 (11215-8403)
PHONE..................................718 788-0302
EMP: 10
SQ FT: 4,000
SALES: 2MM Privately Held
SIC: 3993 Mfg Signs/Advertising Special-
ties

(G-1454)
ACE & JIG LLC (PA)
323 Dean St Ste 2 (11217-1906)
PHONE..................................347 227-0318
Nicole Mikeal, *Manager*
EMP: 8
SALES (est): 871.9K Privately Held
SIC: 2335 5137 Ensemble dresses:
women's, misses' & juniors'; scarves,
women's & children's; women's & chil-
dren's dresses, suits, skirts & blouses

(G-1455)
**ACME ARCHITECTURAL
PRODUCTS**
513 Porter Ave (11222)
PHONE..................................718 360-0700
Jack Teich, *President*
EMP: 500
SQ FT: 15,000
SALES (est): 25.4MM Privately Held
WEB: www.acmesteel.com
SIC: 3469 Spinning metal for the trade;
stamping metal for the trade

(G-1456)
**ACME ARCHITECTURAL PDTS
INC (PA)**
Also Called: Acme Architectural Walls
251 Lombardy St (11222-5516)
PHONE..................................718 384-7800
Jack Teich, *President*

Joel Licari, *Vice Pres*
Michael Teich, *Vice Pres*
Mark Teich, *Treasurer*
▲ EMP: 51
SQ FT: 250,000
SALES (est): 50.8MM Privately Held
WEB: www.acmearchitecturalwalls.com
SIC: 3442 3444 3446 Metal doors; sheet
metalwork; partitions & supports/studs, in-
cluding accoustical systems

(G-1457)
ACME PARTS INC
901 Elton St (11208-5315)
PHONE..................................718 649-1750
Allan Rodolitz, *President*
EMP: 26
SQ FT: 20,000
SALES (est): 3.3MM Privately Held
WEB: www.acmeparts.com
SIC: 3432 Plumbers' brass goods: drain
cocks, faucets, spigots, etc.

(G-1458)
ACME SMOKED FISH CORP (PA)
30 Gem St 56 (11222-2804)
PHONE..................................954 942-5598
Eric Caslow, *Ch of Bd*
Mark Brownstein, *Vice Pres*
David Caslow, *Vice Pres*
Robert Caslow, *Vice Pres*
Eduardo Carbajosa, *CFO*
◆ EMP: 100
SQ FT: 70,000
SALES (est): 18.6MM Privately Held
WEB: www.acmesmokedfish.com
SIC: 2091 Fish, smoked; fish, cured

(G-1459)
ACTIVE WORLD SOLUTIONS INC
Also Called: M/Wbe
609 Fountain Ave (11208-6006)
PHONE..................................718 922-9404
Alvaro Vazquez, *President*
Maria Vazquez, *Principal*
▲ EMP: 6
SALES (est): 696.9K Privately Held
SIC: 2759 2395 7389 Screen printing;
embroidery & art needlework; advertising,
promotional & trade show services

(G-1460)
ADEL ROOTSTEIN (USA) INC
145 18th St (11215-5313)
PHONE..................................718 499-5650
Patty Marino, *Manager*
EMP: 42
SQ FT: 16,572 Privately Held
SIC: 3999 Mannequins
HQ: Adel Rootstein (Usa) Inc
205 W 19th St
New York NY
212 645-2020

(G-1461)
ADIR PUBLISHING CO
1212 36th St (11218-2010)
PHONE..................................718 633-9437
Matt Fef, *Owner*
EMP: 10
SALES: 910K Privately Held
WEB: www.a1skullcap.com
SIC: 2731 Books: publishing & printing

(G-1462)
**ADRIATIC WOOD PRODUCTS
INC**
1994 Industrial Park Rd (11207-3335)
PHONE..................................718 922-4621
Anthony Grbic, *President*
John Grbic, *Vice Pres*
Chris Magas, *Sales Staff*
John Grisie, *CIO*
Miljenka Grbic, *Admin Sec*
▲ EMP: 38
SQ FT: 80,000
SALES (est): 4.5MM Privately Held
WEB: www.adriaticwood.com
SIC: 2431 Moldings, wood: unfinished &
prefinished

(G-1463)
ADS-N-COLOR INC
20 Jay St Ste 530 (11201-8324)
PHONE..................................718 797-0900
Anthony Masi, *President*

Nicholas Masi, *Vice Pres*
EMP: 50
SQ FT: 5,000
SALES (est): 3.5MM **Privately Held**
SIC: 2752 Commercial printing, offset

(G-1464)
ADVANCE CHEMICALS USA INC
1230 57th St (11219-4523)
PHONE....................................718 633-1030
Heldon Eross, *President*
EMP: 4
SQ FT: 2,000
SALES (est): 1MM **Privately Held**
SIC: 3087 Custom compound purchased resins

(G-1465)
ADVANCED READY MIX CORP
239 Ingraham St (11237-1512)
PHONE....................................718 497-5020
Rocco Mancione, *President*
EMP: 16
SALES (est): 2.8MM **Privately Held**
SIC: 3273 Ready-mixed concrete

(G-1466)
ADVANCED TRANSIT MIX CORP
610 Johnson Ave (11237-1312)
PHONE....................................718 497-5020
Milo Silberstein, *Principal*
EMP: 5
SALES (est): 259.6K **Privately Held**
SIC: 3273 Ready-mixed concrete

(G-1467)
ADVANTAGE WHOLESALE SUPPLY LLC
172 Empire Blvd Brooklyn (11225)
PHONE....................................718 284-5346
Michael Rubinstein, *Accounts Mgr*
Sholom Eckhaus, *Manager*
David Smetana,
EMP: 55 **EST:** 2011
SALES (est): 10.2MM **Privately Held**
SIC: 3429 Manufactured hardware (general)

(G-1468)
AEON AMERICA INC
68 Jay St Ste 201 (11201-8359)
PHONE....................................914 584-0275
Paul Hains, *President*
Kellen Quinn, *Director*
EMP: 8
SALES: 587.4K **Privately Held**
SIC: 2721 Magazines: publishing only, not printed on site

(G-1469)
AESTHONICS INC
Also Called: Remains Lighting
21 Belvidere St Fl 3 (11206-4501)
PHONE....................................646 723-2463
David Callegaros, *President*
David Calligeros, *Manager*
▲ **EMP:** 100
SQ FT: 50,000
SALES (est): 15.9MM **Privately Held**
SIC: 3645 3646 Residential lighting fixtures; commercial indusl & institutional electric lighting fixtures

(G-1470)
AFRO TIMES NEWSPAPER
Also Called: New American
1195 Atlantic Ave (11216-2709)
P.O. Box 160397 (11216-0397)
PHONE....................................718 636-9500
Tom Watkins, *Owner*
▲ **EMP:** 10
SQ FT: 7,500
SALES (est): 321.8K **Privately Held**
WEB: www.newamerican.com
SIC: 2711 Newspapers: publishing only, not printed on site

(G-1471)
AGE MANUFACTURERS INC
10624 Avenue D (11236-1910)
PHONE....................................718 927-0048
Yosel Avtzon, *President*
▲ **EMP:** 65 **EST:** 1958
SQ FT: 43,000

SALES (est): 5.6MM **Privately Held**
SIC: 3999 3131 2339 2337 Hair & hair-based products; footwear cut stock; trimmings (leather); shoe; scarves, hoods, headbands, etc.: women's; women's & misses' suits & coats

(G-1472)
AIR FLOW PUMP CORP
Also Called: Air Flow Pump Supply
8412 Foster Ave (11236-3205)
PHONE....................................718 241-2800
Joseph Weinstock, *President*
David Weinstock, *Vice Pres*
EMP: 8
SQ FT: 6,000
SALES: 1.5MM **Privately Held**
SIC: 3561 5084 Pumps & pumping equipment; water pumps (industrial)

(G-1473)
AIR SKATE & AIR JUMP CORP (PA)
Also Called: Solo
2208 E 5th St (11223-4827)
P.O. Box 7453, New York (10116-7453)
PHONE....................................212 967-1201
Morris Tawil, *CEO*
▲ **EMP:** 17
SALES (est): 6.2MM **Privately Held**
SIC: 3143 5139 Men's footwear, except athletic; footwear, athletic

(G-1474)
AJMADISON CORP
3605 13th Ave (11218-3707)
PHONE....................................718 532-1800
Michael Gross, *Ch of Bd*
Matthew Ortiz, *Editor*
▼ **EMP:** 55
SALES (est): 18.3MM **Privately Held**
SIC: 3639 7389 Major kitchen appliances, except refrigerators & stoves;

(G-1475)
ALADDIN BAKERS INC
Also Called: East Coast Pita Bakery
239 26th St (11232)
PHONE....................................718 499-1818
David Ross, *Sales Staff*
Donald Guzzi, *Manager*
EMP: 100
SALES (est): 9MM
SALES (corp-wide): 11.8MM **Privately Held**
WEB: www.aladdinbakers.com
SIC: 2051 Bread, cake & related products
PA: Aladdin Bakers, Inc.
240 25th St
Brooklyn NY 11232
718 499-1818

(G-1476)
ALBERT KEMPERLE INC
890 E 51st St (11203-6736)
PHONE....................................718 629-1084
Albert Kemperle, *Owner*
EMP: 20
SALES (corp-wide): 163.8MM **Privately Held**
SIC: 3465 Body parts, automobile: stamped metal
PA: Albert Kemperle, Inc.
8400 New Horizons Blvd
Amityville NY 11701
631 841-1241

(G-1477)
ALBEST METAL STAMPING CORP (PA)
1 Kent Ave (11249-1000)
PHONE....................................718 388-6000
Alexander Fischer, *President*
Nathan Hirsch, *Corp Secy*
Cheryl Francis, *Buyer*
◆ **EMP:** 44
SQ FT: 120,000
SALES (est): 7MM **Privately Held**
WEB: www.albest.com
SIC: 3469 3364 3089 3496 Stamping metal for the trade; nonferrous die-castings except aluminum; casting of plastic; miscellaneous fabricated wire products; aluminum die-castings

(G-1478)
ALBEST METAL STAMPING CORP
30 Wythe Ln (11249)
PHONE....................................718 388-6000
EMP: 21
SALES (corp-wide): 7MM **Privately Held**
SIC: 3469 Metal stampings
PA: Albest Metal Stamping Corp.
1 Kent Ave
Brooklyn NY 11249
718 388-6000

(G-1479)
ALBRIZIO INC
Also Called: Albrizio Couture
257 Varet St Ste Mgmt (11206-3859)
PHONE....................................212 719-5290
David Cicalese, *Chairman*
Ann Albrizio, *Executive*
EMP: 6 **EST:** 2010
SALES (est): 657.5K **Privately Held**
SIC: 2353 Millinery

(G-1480)
ALDO FRUSTACCI IRON WORKS INC
165 27th St (11232-1624)
PHONE....................................718 768-0707
Aldo Frustaci, *President*
EMP: 10 **EST:** 1979
SQ FT: 8,000
SALES (est): 1.3MM **Privately Held**
SIC: 3444 3441 3446 Sheet metalwork; fabricated structural metal; stairs, staircases, stair treads: prefabricated metal

(G-1481)
ALDOS IRON WORKS INC
75 Van Brunt St (11231-1428)
PHONE....................................718 834-0408
Enzo Frustaci, *President*
EMP: 7 **EST:** 1974
SQ FT: 2,700
SALES: 950K **Privately Held**
SIC: 3446 Architectural metalwork

(G-1482)
ALETA INDUSTRIES INC
40 Ash St (11222)
PHONE....................................718 349-0040
Zinovy Malinov, *President*
Michael Guitonowitz, *Vice Pres*
Alex Sandler, *Treasurer*
EMP: 18
SQ FT: 15,000
SALES (est): 2.9MM **Privately Held**
WEB: www.aletastjames.com
SIC: 3444 Sheet metalwork

(G-1483)
ALGEMEINER JOURNAL INC
508 Montgomery St (11225-3023)
P.O. Box 250746 (11225-0746)
PHONE....................................718 771-0400
Gershon Jacobson, *President*
EMP: 5
SALES (est): 374.5K **Privately Held**
WEB: www.algemeiner.com
SIC: 2711 Newspapers: publishing only, not printed on site

(G-1484)
ALL AMERICAN CONCRETE CORP
239 Ingraham St (11237-1512)
PHONE....................................718 497-3301
Walter Charles, *President*
Anne Kresse, *Vice Pres*
EMP: 4
SALES (est): 1.6MM **Privately Held**
SIC: 3271 Concrete block & brick

(G-1485)
ALL AMERICAN TRANSIT MIX CORP
46 Knickerbocker Ave (11237-1410)
PHONE....................................718 417-3654
Catherine Manzione, *President*
EMP: 9
SALES (est): 800K **Privately Held**
SIC: 3273 Ready-mixed concrete

(G-1486)
ALL OUT DIE CUTTING INC
49 Wyckoff Ave Ste 1 (11237-2650)
PHONE....................................718 346-6666
Abraham Katc, *President*
EMP: 25 **EST:** 1980
SQ FT: 20,000
SALES (est): 1.9MM **Privately Held**
SIC: 3544 3469 2891 2675 Special dies & tools; metal stampings; adhesives & sealants; die-cut paper & board

(G-1487)
ALL UNITED WINDOW CORP
97 Classon Ave (11205-1401)
PHONE....................................718 624-0490
Cooper Eng, *President*
EMP: 21
SQ FT: 10,000
SALES (est): 3.1MM **Privately Held**
WEB: www.allunitedwindow.com
SIC: 3442 5211 Storm doors or windows, metal; windows, storm: wood or metal

(G-1488)
ALLIED FOOD PRODUCTS INC (PA)
251 Saint Marks Ave (11238-3503)
P.O. Box 380305 (11238-0305)
PHONE....................................718 230-4227
Ernest Stern, *President*
David Weill, *Marketing Mgr*
Isaac Stern, *Director*
▲ **EMP:** 10
SQ FT: 10,000
SALES (est): 3.9MM **Privately Held**
WEB: www.alliedfoodproducts.com
SIC: 2034 2045 2099 5149 Soup mixes; cake mixes, prepared: from purchased flour; dessert mixes & fillings; gravy mixes, dry; salad dressing; mineral or spring water bottling

(G-1489)
ALLIED SAMPLE CARD CO INC
140 58th St Ste 7a (11220-2524)
PHONE....................................718 238-0523
Marc Trager, *President*
Thomas Firavanti, *Vice Pres*
EMP: 30 **EST:** 1938
SQ FT: 22,000
SALES (est): 1MM **Privately Held**
SIC: 2675 Cards, folders & mats: die-cut

(G-1490)
ALPHA INCORPORATED
265 80th St (11209-3611)
PHONE....................................718 765-1614
Michael Gerovich, *Owner*
EMP: 6 **EST:** 2010
SALES (est): 414.7K **Privately Held**
SIC: 3089 Identification cards, plastic

(G-1491)
ALPHA KNITTING MILLS INC
41 Varick Ave Ste Mgmt (11237-1521)
PHONE....................................718 628-6300
Rose Fuchs, *President*
Bernard Fried, *Corp Secy*
Alex Fried, *Vice Pres*
William Fried, *Vice Pres*
EMP: 15
SQ FT: 15,000
SALES (est): 1.2MM **Privately Held**
SIC: 2253 Knit outerwear mills

(G-1492)
ALPINE PAPER BOX CO INC
2246 Fulton St (11233-3306)
PHONE....................................718 345-4040
Anthony Caggiano, *President*
EMP: 30 **EST:** 1953
SQ FT: 15,000
SALES (est): 4.5MM **Privately Held**
SIC: 3499 2631 Boxes for packing & shipping, metal; paperboard mills

(G-1493)
ALTANA TECHNOLOGIES INC
81 Prospect St (11201-1473)
PHONE....................................516 263-0633
Evan Smith, *CEO*
Raphael Tehranian, *COO*
Peter Swatz, *CTO*
EMP: 8

▲ = Import ▼=Export
◆ =Import/Export

SALES (est): 186.1K **Privately Held**
SIC: 7372 5045 Prepackaged software; computers, peripherals & software

(G-1494)
ALTRONIX CORP
140 58th St Bldg A3w (11220-2521)
PHONE..............................718 567-8181
Jonathan Sohnis, *Ch of Bd*
Alan Forman, *President*
Gary Zatz, *Natl Sales Mgr*
Mark Salter, *Marketing Staff*
Alexandra Pancaldo, *Manager*
◆ **EMP:** 100
SQ FT: 52,000
SALES (est): 32.1MM **Privately Held**
SIC: 3699 3625 5063 Security control equipment & systems; control equipment, electric; burglar alarm systems

(G-1495)
AMBER BEVER INC
8604 Avenue M 1 (11236-4918)
PHONE..............................212 391-4911
Beverly Brown, *CEO*
Mark Brown, *President*
▲ **EMP:** 4
SQ FT: 1,500
SALES: 2MM **Privately Held**
SIC: 2339 Women's & misses' athletic clothing & sportswear

(G-1496)
AMBY INTERNATIONAL INC
1460 E 12th St (11230-6606)
PHONE..............................718 645-0964
Ben Wallerstein, *President*
▲ **EMP:** 5
SALES (est): 786.8K **Privately Held**
SIC: 2673 Plastic bags: made from purchased materials

(G-1497)
AMCO INTL MFG & DESIGN INC
10 Conselyea St (11211-2202)
PHONE..............................718 388-8668
Adam Milewski, *President*
EMP: 26
SALES: 950K **Privately Held**
SIC: 3691 Storage batteries

(G-1498)
AMERICAN CRAFT JEWELERS INC (PA)
3611 14th Ave Ste 522 (11218-3750)
PHONE..............................718 972-0945
Stanley Grimstein, *President*
EMP: 9
SQ FT: 2,000
SALES: 8MM **Privately Held**
SIC: 3911 Jewelry, precious metal

(G-1499)
AMERICAN MTAL STMPING SPINNING
72 N 15th St (11222-2802)
PHONE..............................718 384-1500
Stephanie Eisenberg, *President*
EMP: 15
SALES (est): 1.9MM **Privately Held**
SIC: 3469 Stamping metal for the trade; spinning metal for the trade

(G-1500)
AMERICAN PACKAGE COMPANY INC
Also Called: Ampaco
226 Franklin St (11222-1382)
PHONE..............................718 389-4444
Martin C Kofman, *President*
EMP: 40 **EST:** 1921
SQ FT: 120,000
SALES (est): 7.1MM **Privately Held**
SIC: 2652 3089 Setup paperboard boxes; boxes, plastic

(G-1501)
AMERICAN PRINT SOLUTIONS INC
561 President St (11215-1018)
PHONE..............................718 246-7800
Steven Klein, *Branch Mgr*
EMP: 5

SALES (est): 343K
SALES (corp-wide): 3.9MM **Privately Held**
SIC: 2752 Commercial printing, offset
PA: American Print Solutions Inc.
2233 Nostrand Ave Ste 7
Brooklyn NY 11210
718 208-2309

(G-1502)
AMERICAN PRINT SOLUTIONS INC (PA)
2233 Nostrand Ave Ste 7 (11210-3029)
PHONE..............................718 208-2309
Erica Braun, *President*
Isaac Braun, *Vice Pres*
Malki Lipshitz, *Treasurer*
Israel Izzy Braun, *Finance Dir*
Israel I Braun, *Finance*
EMP: 5
SQ FT: 20,000
SALES (est): 3.9MM **Privately Held**
SIC: 2754 5112 Business forms: gravure printing; business forms

(G-1503)
AMERICAN WOOD COLUMN CORP
913 Grand St (11211-2785)
PHONE..............................718 782-3163
Thomas Lupo, *President*
EMP: 8 **EST:** 1916
SQ FT: 12,000
SALES (est): 944.9K **Privately Held**
SIC: 2431 3299 Woodwork, interior & ornamental; ornamental & architectural plaster work

(G-1504)
AMIRAM DROR INC (PA)
Also Called: Black Hound
226 India St (11222-1804)
P.O. Box 170, Short Hills NJ (07078-0170)
PHONE..............................212 979-9505
Amiram Dror, *President*
EMP: 16
SQ FT: 7,500
SALES: 1.8MM **Privately Held**
WEB: www.blackhoundny.com
SIC: 2051 2064 2066 2033 Bakery: wholesale or wholesale/retail combined; chocolate candy, except solid chocolate; chocolate bars, solid; fruits & fruit products in cans, jars, etc.; chocolate; candy

(G-1505)
AMJ DOT LLC
Also Called: City Fashion, The
1726 E 7th St (11223-2216)
PHONE..............................718 775-3288
Assaf Joseth, *CEO*
Assaf Joseph, *CEO*
Ruth Elmann, *COO*
David Yakobov, *CFO*
▲ **EMP:** 7
SQ FT: 1,200
SALES (est): 2.4MM **Privately Held**
SIC: 2335 5621 Women's, juniors' & misses' dresses; women's clothing stores

(G-1506)
AMPLE HILLS CREAMERY INC (PA)
305 Nevins St (11215-1015)
PHONE..............................347 725-4061
Brian Smith, *CEO*
EMP: 25
SALES (est): 9.2MM **Privately Held**
SIC: 2024 Ice cream & frozen desserts

(G-1507)
AMPLE HILLS CREAMERY INC
623 Vanderbilt Ave (11238-3502)
PHONE..............................718 809-1678
EMP: 47
SALES (corp-wide): 9.2MM **Privately Held**
SIC: 2024 Ice cream & frozen desserts
PA: Ample Hills Creamery, Inc.
305 Nevins St
Brooklyn NY 11215
347 725-4061

(G-1508)
AMPLE HILLS HOLDINGS INC
305 Nevins St (11215-1015)
PHONE..............................347 725-4061
Brian Smith, *CEO*
EMP: 9
SALES (est): 957.6K **Privately Held**
SIC: 2024 6719 Ice cream & frozen desserts; investment holding companies, except banks

(G-1509)
AMPLIFY EDUCATION INC (PA)
Also Called: Projected
55 Washington St Ste 800 (11201-1066)
PHONE..............................212 213-8177
Larry Berger, *CEO*
Catherine Mackay, *President*
Laszlo Kopits, *Exec VP*
Jim Mylen, *Senior VP*
Alexandra Clarke, *Vice Pres*
◆ **EMP:** 500
SQ FT: 57,000
SALES (est): 243.4MM **Privately Held**
WEB: www.wirelessgeneration.com
SIC: 2731 8299 7372 Book publishing; educational services; educational computer software

(G-1510)
ANGEL-MADE IN HEAVEN INC
Also Called: 116 26 Street
116 26th St (11232-1405)
PHONE..............................718 832-4778
Morris Dahan, *President*
EMP: 9
SQ FT: 29,800
SALES (corp-wide): 1.3MM **Privately Held**
WEB: www.angelmih.com
SIC: 2339 Women's & misses' outerwear
PA: Angel-Made In Heaven, Inc.
525 Fashion Ave Rm 1710
New York NY 10018
212 869-5678

(G-1511)
ANIIWE INC
774 Rockaway Ave Apt 3k (11212-5830)
PHONE..............................347 683-1891
Tamaris King, *President*
Tiffany King, *Principal*
EMP: 5
SALES (est): 318.9K **Privately Held**
SIC: 3961 5139 2679 Bracelets, except precious metal; shoe accessories; wallboard, decorated: made from purchased material

(G-1512)
ANNE TAINTOR INC
Also Called: ATI
137 Montague St (11201-3548)
PHONE..............................718 483-9312
Anne Taintor, *President*
Nathan Janoff, *Vice Pres*
▲ **EMP:** 6
SALES (est): 643K **Privately Held**
WEB: www.annetaintor.com
SIC: 2771 2752 2678 7389 Greeting cards; post cards, picture: lithographed; poster & decal printing, lithographic; notebooks: made from purchased paper;

(G-1513)
ANNOINTED BUTY MINISTRIES LLC
1697 E 54th St (11234-3921)
P.O. Box 340437 (11234-0437)
PHONE..............................646 867-3796
Rachel Ineus, *CEO*
EMP: 5
SALES (est): 235.7K **Privately Held**
SIC: 2721 Periodicals

(G-1514)
ANU INDUSTRIES LLC
1414 Brooklyn Ave Apt 4f (11210-1868)
PHONE..............................201 735-7475
Yusef Assaan, *Principal*
EMP: 5
SALES (est): 213.6K **Privately Held**
SIC: 3999 Manufacturing industries

(G-1515)
ANYAS LICORICE INC
1027 Grand St (11211-1748)
PHONE..............................917 935-1916
Anya Skwarek, *Principal*
EMP: 7
SALES (est): 434.4K **Privately Held**
SIC: 2064 Candy & other confectionery products

(G-1516)
APEX AIRTRONICS INC (PA)
2465 Atlantic Ave (11207-2346)
P.O. Box 353, Woodmere (11598-0353)
PHONE..............................718 485-8560
William Rosenblum, *President*
▲ **EMP:** 28 **EST:** 1948
SQ FT: 14,000
SALES (est): 4.9MM **Privately Held**
SIC: 3663 Radio broadcasting & communications equipment

(G-1517)
APEX REAL HOLDINGS INC
Also Called: Pak 21
1640 40th St Ste A (11218-5541)
PHONE..............................877 725-2150
Mark Loewy, *President*
EMP: 8
SQ FT: 2,000
SALES (est): 115.7K **Privately Held**
WEB: www.pak21.com
SIC: 2392 Bags, garment storage: except paper or plastic film

(G-1518)
APOLLO WINDOWS & DOORS INC
1003 Metropolitan Ave (11211-2605)
PHONE..............................718 386-3326
Hang Hsin Cheng, *President*
Wen Tsui Ping, *Admin Sec*
EMP: 10
SQ FT: 20,000
SALES (est): 1MM **Privately Held**
WEB: www.apollowindows.com
SIC: 2431 Doors & door parts & trim, wood; windows & window parts & trim, wood

(G-1519)
APPLE CORE ELECTRONICS INC
991 Flushing Ave (11206-4721)
PHONE..............................718 628-4068
Michael Arnold, *President*
Gregory Arnold, *Vice Pres*
EMP: 11
SQ FT: 4,000
SALES (est): 1.8MM **Privately Held**
SIC: 3669 5065 Intercommunication systems, electric; intercommunication equipment, electronic

(G-1520)
APPLIED MINERALS INC (PA)
55 Washington St Ste 301 (11201-1077)
PHONE..............................212 226-4265
Mario Concha, *Ch of Bd*
John F Levy, *Vice Ch Bd*
Christopher T Carney, *CFO*
Yash Khanna, *CTO*
Sharad Mathur, *CTO*
EMP: 11
SALES: 4.8MM **Publicly Held**
WEB: www.atlasmining.com
SIC: 1459 2816 Clays, except kaolin & ball; iron oxide pigments (ochers, siennas, umbers)

(G-1521)
APPSBIDDER INC
55 Clark St 772 (11201-2415)
PHONE..............................917 880-4269
EMP: 5
SALES (est): 166.2K **Privately Held**
SIC: 7372 Prepackaged Software Services

(G-1522)
APSCO SPORTS ENTERPRISES INC
Also Called: Abercrombie & Fitch
50th St & 1st Av Bg 57 F5 (11232)
PHONE..............................718 965-9500
Philip Livoti, *President*

Phillip Livoti, *President*
Philip Di Pietro, *Vice Pres*
Vincent Dipietro, *Opers Mgr*
Christine De Chirico, *Controller*
▲ **EMP:** 60 **EST:** 1968
SQ FT: 30,000
SALES (est): 7.4MM **Privately Held**
SIC: 2396 Screen printing on fabric articles

(G-1523)
ARCHITCTRAL DSIGN ELEMENTS LLC
52 Box St (11222-1150)
PHONE..........................718 218-7800
Alan Paulenoff, *Mng Member*
Tess Cross, *Manager*
EMP: 7
SALES: 850K **Privately Held**
SIC: 3083 Laminated plastics plate & sheet

(G-1524)
ARCHITECTURAL COATINGS INC
538 Johnson Ave (11237-1226)
PHONE..........................718 418-9584
Nick Comaianni, *President*
Daniel France, *Vice Pres*
Margaret Karnick, *Admin Sec*
EMP: 18
SALES: 1.2MM **Privately Held**
SIC: 3599 Machine & other job shop work

(G-1525)
ARCTIC GLACIER NEWBURGH INC
335 Moffat St (11237-6408)
PHONE..........................718 456-2013
Vincent Losquadro, *Branch Mgr*
EMP: 7
SALES (corp-wide): 2.4B **Publicly Held**
SIC: 2097 Manufactured ice
HQ: Arctic Glacier Newburgh Inc.
225 Lake St
Newburgh NY 12550
845 561-0549

(G-1526)
ARES BOX LLC
63 Flushing Ave Unit 224 (11205-1073)
PHONE..........................718 858-8760
Mary Filippidis,
EMP: 85
SALES (est): 4.9MM **Privately Held**
SIC: 2671 Packaging paper & plastics film, coated & laminated

(G-1527)
ARES PRINTING AND PACKG CORP
Brooklyn Navy Yard Bldg (11205)
PHONE..........................718 858-8760
Mary Filippidis, *President*
Bob Filippidis, *Vice Pres*
George Filippidis, *Vice Pres*
Jerry Filippidis, *Vice Pres*
EMP: 125
SQ FT: 150,000
SALES (est): 16.6MM **Privately Held**
WEB: www.aresny.com
SIC: 2752 2653 Commercial printing, off-set; corrugated & solid fiber boxes; boxes, corrugated: made from purchased materials; display items, corrugated: made from purchased materials

(G-1528)
ARIMED ORTHOTICS PROSTHETICS (PA)
302 Livingston St (11217-1002)
P.O. Box 844628, Dallas TX (75284-4628)
PHONE..........................718 875-8754
Steven Mirones, *President*
Evelyn Neonakis, *Manager*
Frank Murtaugh, *Director*
EMP: 14
SQ FT: 10,000
SALES (est): 3.4MM **Privately Held**
WEB: www.arimed.com
SIC: 3842 5661 5999 7251 Orthopedic appliances; shoes, orthopedic; orthopedic & prosthesis applications; shoe repair shop

(G-1529)
ARISTA STEEL DESIGNS CORP
788 3rd Ave (11232-1418)
PHONE..........................718 965-7077
Steve Viglis, *President*
EMP: 5
SALES: 1,000K **Privately Held**
SIC: 3449 Bars, concrete reinforcing: fabricated steel

(G-1530)
ARISTOCRAT LIGHTING INC
104 Halleck St (11231-2100)
PHONE..........................718 522-0003
Leon Gross, *President*
Michael Gross, *Vice Pres*
EMP: 12 **EST:** 1983
SQ FT: 18,000
SALES (est): 1.5MM **Privately Held**
SIC: 3646 Commercial indusl & institutional electric lighting fixtures

(G-1531)
ARMADA NEW YORK LLC
141 Flushing Ave Unit 404 (11205-1338)
PHONE..........................718 852-8105
Anthony Wilson,
Jason Golob,
Cory Watson,
EMP: 11
SALES (est): 1.1MM **Privately Held**
SIC: 2431 2599 Millwork; factory furniture & fixtures

(G-1532)
ARNOLDS MEAT FOOD PRODUCTS
274 Heyward St (11206-2994)
PHONE..........................718 384-8071
Sheldon Dosik, *President*
Jason Judd, *Vice Pres*
EMP: 25
SALES (est): 3.8MM **Privately Held**
SIC: 2013 Sausages from purchased meat

(G-1533)
AROMASONG USA INC
35 Frost St (11211-1202)
PHONE..........................718 838-9669
Sam Neustein, *President*
EMP: 10
SALES (est): 599.5K **Privately Held**
SIC: 2844 2099 Bath salts; seasonings & spices

(G-1534)
ART BEDI-MAKKY FOUNDRY CORP
227 India St Ste 31 (11222-1803)
PHONE..........................718 383-4191
Istvan Makky, *President*
EMP: 8
SQ FT: 7,500
SALES: 400K **Privately Held**
SIC: 3366 Castings (except die): bronze

(G-1535)
ART DIGITAL TECHNOLOGIES LLC
85 Debevoise Ave (11222-5608)
PHONE..........................646 649-4820
Dan Bright,
EMP: 11
SALES (est): 1.8MM **Privately Held**
WEB: www.artdigitaltech.com
SIC: 2752 7336 Commercial printing, lithographic; commercial art & graphic design

(G-1536)
ARTEMIS STUDIOS INC
Also Called: Diane Artemis Studios
34 35th St Ste 2b (11232-2212)
PHONE..........................718 788-6022
Martin Kurant, *President*
EMP: 70 **EST:** 1964
SQ FT: 30,000
SALES (est): 5MM **Privately Held**
WEB: www.artemisstudios.com
SIC: 3999 3645 Shades, lamp or candle; residential lighting fixtures

(G-1537)
ARTHUR GLUCK SHIRTMAKERS INC
871 E 24th St (11210-2821)
PHONE..........................212 755-8165
Michael Spitzer, *President*
EMP: 10 **EST:** 1956
SALES: 1.5MM **Privately Held**
WEB: www.shirtcreations.com
SIC: 2321 Men's & boys' dress shirts

(G-1538)
ASA MANUFACTURING INC
3611 14th Ave (11218-3773)
PHONE..........................718 853-3033
Alex Klein, *President*
Sam Hershkovich, *Vice Pres*
EMP: 20
SQ FT: 4,000
SALES (est): 3.8MM **Privately Held**
WEB: www.par4shelters.com
SIC: 3915 Jewelry parts, unassembled

(G-1539)
ASAP RACK RENTAL INC
33 35th St St5 (11232-2022)
PHONE..........................718 499-4495
David Fox, *President*
EMP: 7
SQ FT: 6,000
SALES: 969.3K **Privately Held**
SIC: 2542 3537 5051 5021 Garment racks: except wood; industrial trucks & tractors; pipe & tubing, steel; racks

(G-1540)
ASHCO MANAGEMENT INC
1937 Mcdonald Ave (11223-1805)
PHONE..........................212 960-8428
Isaac Ashkenazie, *CEO*
EMP: 10 **EST:** 2011
SQ FT: 5,000
SALES (est): 396.5K **Privately Held**
SIC: 3732 5023 5731 Kayaks, building & repairing; kitchen tools & utensils; radio, television & electronic stores

(G-1541)
ASHLEY RESIN CORP
1171 59th St (11219-4909)
P.O. Box 190733 (11219-0733)
PHONE..........................718 851-8111
Nathan Freedman, *President*
Misem Moskobics, *Admin Sec*
◆ **EMP:** 5
SALES (est): 1.4MM **Privately Held**
WEB: www.ashleypoly.com
SIC: 2821 7389 Plastics materials & resins;

(G-1542)
ASPECT PRINTING INC
904 E 51st St (11203-6736)
PHONE..........................347 789-4284
Olga Belenkaya, *Ch of Bd*
Anatoly Fusman, *Manager*
EMP: 20
SALES (est): 2.7MM **Privately Held**
SIC: 2711 2759 Commercial printing & newspaper publishing combined; magazines: printing

(G-1543)
AT COPY INC
Also Called: Save Mor Copy Center
25 Flatbush Ave (11217-2499)
PHONE..........................718 624-6136
Bartholemew Tesoriero, *President*
Roberta Tesoriero, *Vice Pres*
EMP: 9
SQ FT: 3,300
SALES (est): 1.6MM **Privately Held**
SIC: 2752 Commercial printing, offset

(G-1544)
ATALLA HANDBAGS INC
559 79th St (11209-3709)
PHONE..........................718 965-5500
Sami Atalla, *President*
EMP: 4
SQ FT: 1,300
SALES: 1.1MM **Privately Held**
SIC: 3171 Handbags, women's

(G-1545)
ATELIER VIOLLET CORP
505 Driggs Ave (11211-2020)
PHONE..........................718 782-1727
Jean Paul Viollet, *President*
EMP: 6
SQ FT: 7,500
SALES (est): 945.2K **Privately Held**
WEB: www.atelierviollet.com
SIC: 2511 5712 2499 Wood household furniture; custom made furniture, except cabinets; decorative wood & woodwork

(G-1546)
ATERES PUBLISHING & BK BINDERY
Also Called: Ateres Book Binding
845 Bedford Ave (11205-2801)
PHONE..........................718 935-9355
Sam Greenfield, *President*
Simon Pollak, *Sales Executive*
Joseph Greenfield, *Admin Sec*
▲ **EMP:** 14 **EST:** 1975
SQ FT: 20,000
SALES (est): 1.6MM **Privately Held**
SIC: 2789 2731 Bookbinding & repairing: trade, edition, library, etc.; book publishing

(G-1547)
ATLANTIC ELECTRONIC TECH LLC
Also Called: Atlantic Electronic Technology
285 5th Ave Apt 2b (11215-2421)
PHONE..........................800 296-2177
Absalam Ottafa,
▲ **EMP:** 5
SQ FT: 1,500
SALES: 500K **Privately Held**
SIC: 3699 Security control equipment & systems

(G-1548)
ATLANTIC STAIRS CORP
Also Called: Design Interiors
284a Meserole St (11206-2242)
PHONE..........................718 417-8818
Stanley Majkut, *President*
Elizabeth Wozniak, *Admin Sec*
EMP: 6
SQ FT: 3,000
SALES (est): 797.4K **Privately Held**
WEB: www.atlanticstairs.com
SIC: 2431 Doors & door parts & trim, wood; staircases, stairs & railings

(G-1549)
ATLAS COATINGS GROUP CORP (PA)
4808 Farragut Rd (11203-6612)
PHONE..........................718 469-8787
Ben Berman, *CEO*
Jeff Berman, *President*
Lance Berman, *Vice Pres*
EMP: 75 **EST:** 2001
SALES (est): 4.7MM **Privately Held**
SIC: 2851 5231 Paints & paint additives; paint

(G-1550)
ATTIAS OVEN CORP
Also Called: Cannon Co
926 3rd Ave (11232-2002)
PHONE..........................718 499-0145
Simon Attias, *President*
Anna Dane, *Human Res Dir*
Carrie Gorelick, *Manager*
Kazumichi Narui, *Manager*
▲ **EMP:** 6
SQ FT: 5,000
SALES (est): 1MM **Privately Held**
WEB: www.attiasco.com
SIC: 3589 Commercial cooking & food-warming equipment

(G-1551)
AUDIBLE DIFFERENCE INC
Also Called: Audible Difference Lnc
110 8th St (11215-3116)
PHONE..........................212 662-4848
Erich R Bechtel, *President*
John Geraghty, *Project Engr*
EMP: 27

SALES (est): 5.4MM **Privately Held**
WEB: www.adigroup.net
SIC: 3699 Electric sound equipment

(G-1552)
AUDIO TECHNOLOGY NEW YORK INC
Also Called: Audiology
129 31st St (11232-1824)
PHONE...................................718 369-7528
▲ EMP: 10
SQ FT: 30,000
SALES (est): 1.7MM **Privately Held**
SIC: 3651 Mfg Home Audio/Video Equipment

(G-1553)
AVOOMO POWER LLC
1317 Avenue J (11230-3605)
PHONE...................................718 344-0404
Amir Friedlander, President
EMP: 10
SALES (est): 283.1K **Privately Held**
SIC: 3999 Manufacturing industries

(G-1554)
AZURRX BIOPHARMA INC
760 Parkside Ave Ste 304 (11226-1784)
PHONE...................................646 699-7855
Edward J Borkowski, Ch of Bd
James Sapirstein, President
Maged Shenouda, CFO
James E Pennington, Chief Mktg Ofcr
Daniel Dupret, Officer
EMP: 13
SQ FT: 687
SALES (est): 2.2MM **Privately Held**
SIC: 2834 Pharmaceutical preparations

(G-1555)
B & B SWEATER MILLS INC (PA)
1160 Flushing Ave (11237-1747)
PHONE...................................718 456-8693
Berl Biderman, President
Sol Biderman, Corp Secy
▲ EMP: 10 EST: 1954
SQ FT: 42,000
SALES (est): 975.4K **Privately Held**
SIC: 2253 5137 Sweaters & sweater coats, knit; sweaters, women's & children's

(G-1556)
B & K DYE CUTTING INC
245 Varet St (11206-3823)
PHONE...................................718 497-5216
EMP: 6
SQ FT: 5,000
SALES: 300K **Privately Held**
SIC: 2261 Dyeing & Cutting Materials

(G-1557)
B D B TYPEWRITER SUPPLY WORKS
6215 14th Ave (11219-5338)
PHONE...................................718 232-4800
Albert Brauner, Owner
EMP: 25 EST: 1948
SQ FT: 3,160
SALES (est): 1.3MM **Privately Held**
SIC: 2521 2752 Wood office furniture; commercial printing, lithographic

(G-1558)
BABY CENTRAL LLC
2436 Mcdonald Ave (11223-5231)
PHONE...................................718 372-2229
Mike Seda, Principal
EMP: 6 EST: 2007
SALES (est): 620K **Privately Held**
SIC: 2023 Baby formulas

(G-1559)
BACKSTAGE LLC (PA)
45 Main St Ste 416 (11201-1093)
PHONE...................................212 493-4243
Lisa Hamil, Editor
Michael Rieck, Senior VP
Luke Crowe, Vice Pres
James Reynolds, Vice Pres
Michael J Felman, CFO
EMP: 26
SALES: 11.5MM **Privately Held**
SIC: 2721 Magazines: publishing only, not printed on site

(G-1560)
BADER ENTERPRISE INC
Also Called: Better Candy Company
115 27th St (11232-1504)
PHONE...................................718 965-9434
Younis Bader, President
EMP: 8
SQ FT: 9,000
SALES (est): 999.4K **Privately Held**
SIC: 2064 Candy & other confectionery products

(G-1561)
BANNER SMOKED FISH INC
2715 W 15th St (11224-2705)
PHONE...................................718 449-1992
Abraham A Attias, Ch of Bd
Eddie Flores, Asst Controller
Alan Levitz, Admin Sec
▲ EMP: 54
SQ FT: 20,000
SALES (est): 6.3MM **Privately Held**
SIC: 2091 Fish, smoked

(G-1562)
BANNERBOY CORPORATION
424 3rd Ave A (11215-3112)
PHONE...................................646 691-6524
Adam McNichol, Managing Prtnr
Katie Holliday McVeay, Manager
EMP: 6
SALES (est): 230.6K **Privately Held**
SIC: 3993 Neon signs

(G-1563)
BARCLAY BROWN CORP
47 Lancaster Ave (11223-5533)
PHONE...................................718 376-7166
Gladys Hedaya, President
Maurice Hedaya, Vice Pres
EMP: 10
SALES (est): 792.5K **Privately Held**
WEB: www.barclaybrowncorp.com
SIC: 3161 3086 Satchels; packaging & shipping materials, foamed plastic

(G-1564)
BASS OIL & CHEMICAL LLC
136 Morgan Ave (11237-1220)
PHONE...................................718 628-4444
Leonard Roz, CEO
EMP: 17
SALES (est): 1.5MM **Privately Held**
SIC: 1389 Oil field services

(G-1565)
BASS OIL COMPANY INC
136 Morgan Ave (11237-1220)
PHONE...................................718 628-4444
Gregory Bass, Ch of Bd
EMP: 30
SQ FT: 28,000
SALES (est): 6.3MM **Privately Held**
SIC: 2899 5172 Antifreeze compounds; engine fuels & oils

(G-1566)
BATAMPTE PICKLE PRODUCTS INC (PA)
77 Brooklyn Terminal Mkt (11236-1511)
PHONE...................................718 251-2100
Barry Silberstein, President
Howard Silberstein, Corp Secy
Scott Silberstein, Vice Pres
EMP: 60 EST: 1955
SQ FT: 12,000
SALES (est): 8.7MM **Privately Held**
SIC: 2035 5149 Pickles, vinegar; pickles, preserves, jellies & jams

(G-1567)
BATOR BINTOR INC
42 Delevan St (11231-1808)
PHONE...................................347 546-6503
Max Connolly, President
EMP: 10
SALES (est): 528.9K **Privately Held**
WEB: www.batorbintor.com
SIC: 2431 2541 1521 Windows & window parts & trim, wood; cabinets, lockers & shelving; general remodeling, single-family houses

(G-1568)
BAYIT HOME AUTOMATION CORP
2906 Shell Rd Fl 2 (11224-3612)
PHONE...................................973 988-2638
Eliav Scaba, CEO
Marco Scaba, Principal
Charles Dayon, VP Sales
▲ EMP: 30
SALES (est): 3.9MM **Privately Held**
SIC: 3651 Video camera-audio recorders, household use

(G-1569)
BEDESSEE IMPORTS LTD
140 Varick Ave (11237-1219)
PHONE...................................718 272-1300
Verman Bedessee, Branch Mgr
EMP: 20
SALES (corp-wide): 25MM **Privately Held**
SIC: 2098 Noodles (e.g. egg, plain & water), dry
PA: Bedessee Imports Ltd
2 Golden Gate Crt
Scarborough ON M1P 3
416 292-2400

(G-1570)
BEDFORD DOWNING GLASS
220 Ingraham St Ste 2 (11237-1514)
PHONE...................................718 418-6409
Ingo Williams, Owner
▼ EMP: 9
SQ FT: 25,000
SALES: 605K **Privately Held**
SIC: 3229 5999 Glassware, art or decorative; art, picture frames & decorations

(G-1571)
BEIS MOSHIACH INC
744 Eastern Pkwy (11213-3409)
PHONE...................................718 778-8000
Menachem Hendel, President
Mm Hendel, Chief
Naftoli Greenfield, Admin Sec
EMP: 35
SALES (est): 3.3MM **Privately Held**
SIC: 2759 Publication printing

(G-1572)
BELTRAN ASSOCIATES INC
1133 E 35th St Ste 1 (11210-4243)
PHONE...................................718 252-2996
Michael Beltran, Ch of Bd
Ichael Beltran, Ch of Bd
Michael R Beltran, Ch of Bd
EMP: 40
SQ FT: 10,000
SALES (est): 9.1MM **Privately Held**
WEB: www.beltranassociates.com
SIC: 3564 Air purification equipment

(G-1573)
BELTRAN TECHNOLOGIES INC
1133 E 35th St (11210-4243)
PHONE...................................718 338-3311
Michael R Beltran, Ch of Bd
▲ EMP: 25
SALES (est): 5.4MM **Privately Held**
SIC: 3564 8711 Precipitators, electrostatic; engineering services

(G-1574)
BENCHMARK FURNITURE MFG
300 Dewitt Ave (11236-1912)
PHONE...................................718 257-4707
Sandy Marks, President
▲ EMP: 70
SQ FT: 50,000
SALES (est): 8.1MM **Privately Held**
WEB: www.benchmarkfurnituremfg.com
SIC: 2511 Wood household furniture

(G-1575)
BENNETT MULTIMEDIA INC
1087 Utica Ave (11203-5318)
PHONE...................................718 629-1454
David Newman, President
EMP: 10
SQ FT: 4,000
SALES (est): 870K **Privately Held**
SIC: 2752 Commercial printing, lithographic

(G-1576)
BENSON MILLS INC (PA)
140 58th St Ste 7j (11220-2538)
PHONE...................................718 236-6743
Keith Levy, Ch of Bd
Gabriel Levy, President
Ralph Levy, Vice Pres
◆ EMP: 22
SQ FT: 5,000
SALES (est): 2.4MM **Privately Held**
SIC: 2299 Fabrics: linen, jute, hemp, ramie

(G-1577)
BENTO BOX LLC
254 36th St Unit 6 (11232-2401)
PHONE...................................718 260-8200
Daniel Rapoport, Mng Member
EMP: 6
SALES (est): 552.2K **Privately Held**
SIC: 2511 Kitchen & dining room furniture

(G-1578)
BEST BOILERS INC
2402 Neptune Ave (11224-2316)
P.O. Box 240607 (11224-0607)
PHONE...................................718 372-4210
Aaron Ganguli, President
Raymond Miele, Treasurer
EMP: 10
SALES (est): 815K **Privately Held**
WEB: www.bestboilers.com
SIC: 3433 Boilers, low-pressure heating: steam or hot water

(G-1579)
BEST MEDICAL WEAR LTD
34 Franklin Ave Ste 301 (11205-1222)
PHONE...................................718 858-5544
Herman Schwartz, CEO
Gitty Schwartz, President
Gittel Schwartz, President
▲ EMP: 8 EST: 1997
SALES: 2.5MM **Privately Held**
WEB: www.bestmedicalwear.com
SIC: 2326 Work uniforms; medical & hospital uniforms, men's

(G-1580)
BESTMADE PRINTING LLC
Also Called: B M Printing
205 Keap St Apt 2 (11211-7970)
PHONE...................................718 384-0719
Shia Ostreicher, Owner
EMP: 10
SALES (est): 1MM **Privately Held**
SIC: 2759 Commercial printing

(G-1581)
BEVERAGE WORKS INCORPORATED
70 Hamilton Ave 8 (11231-1305)
PHONE...................................718 834-0500
Steve Dimario, Manager
EMP: 6
SALES (est): 426.9K **Privately Held**
SIC: 2086 Carbonated beverages, nonalcoholic: bottled & canned

(G-1582)
BEVERAGE WORKS NY INC
70 Hamilton Ave 8 (11231-1305)
PHONE...................................718 812-2034
Gerald Ponfigslione, Principal
EMP: 20 **Privately Held**
WEB: www.beverageworks.com
SIC: 2086 Bottled & canned soft drinks
PA: The Beverage Works Ny Inc
1800 State Route 34 # 203
Wall Township NJ 07719

(G-1583)
BIEN CUIT LLC
120 Smith St (11201-6217)
PHONE...................................718 852-0200
Alex Copeland, Office Mgr
David Golper, Mng Member
Elyse Hinojosa, Manager
EMP: 41
SALES: 3MM **Privately Held**
SIC: 2051 Bakery: wholesale or wholesale/retail combined

(G-1584)
BIGROW PAPER MFG CORP
Also Called: Bigrow Paper Product
930 Bedford Ave (11205-4502)
PHONE.................................718 624-4439
David Greenwald, *President*
▲ EMP: 10
SQ FT: 13,000
SALES (est): 1.4MM **Privately Held**
SIC: 2621 Business form paper; envelope
paper

(G-1585)
**BILLIE-ANN PLASTICS PKG
CORP**
360 Troutman St (11237-2614)
PHONE.................................718 497-3409
Toll Free:................................888 -
William Rubinstein, *President*
Joan Rubinstein, *Vice Pres*
▲ EMP: 30
SQ FT: 15,000
SALES (est): 5.4MM **Privately Held**
WEB: www.billieannplastics.com
SIC: 3089 Plastic processing

(G-1586)
BILLING CODING AND PRTG INC
455 Grant Ave (11208-3056)
PHONE.................................718 827-9409
Omirta Rickheeram, *President*
EMP: 7
SALES (est): 673.1K **Privately Held**
SIC: 2752 Commercial printing, litho-
graphic

(G-1587)
BINAH MAGAZINES CORP
207 Foster Ave (11230-2195)
PHONE.................................718 305-5200
Ruth Lichtenstein, *Principal*
Mendy Loevy, *Asst Controller*
Chanie Berger, *Director*
EMP: 50
SALES (est): 4.3MM **Privately Held**
SIC: 2721 Periodicals

(G-1588)
BINDLE AND KEEP
47 Hall St Ste 109 (11205-1315)
PHONE.................................917 740-5002
Daniel Friedman, *Owner*
EMP: 8 EST: 2013
SALES (est): 680K **Privately Held**
SIC: 2311 2337 Suits, men's & boys':
made from purchased materials; women's
& misses' suits & skirts

(G-1589)
BIOBAT INC (PA)
450 Clarkson Ave Msc129 (11203-2012)
PHONE.................................718 270-1011
Eva Cramer, *President*
EMP: 1 EST: 2011
SQ FT: 500
SALES (est): 2.2MM **Privately Held**
SIC: 2833 Medicinal chemicals

(G-1590)
BKLYNFAVORS PARTY PRINT
49 Sheridan Ave (11208-3022)
PHONE.................................718 277-0233
Dashawn Gables, *Sales Staff*
EMP: 5
SALES (est): 366.3K **Privately Held**
SIC: 2752 Commercial printing, litho-
graphic

(G-1591)
BKNY PRINTING CORP
105 Jamaica Ave (11207-2015)
PHONE.................................718 875-4219
Jose Andrade, *Ch of Bd*
EMP: 20
SALES (est): 2.1MM **Privately Held**
WEB: www.bknyprinting.com
SIC: 2759 Screen printing

(G-1592)
BLACKBIRDS BROOKLYN LLC
Also Called: Four &TWenty Blackbirds
597 Sackett St (11217-3116)
PHONE.................................917 362-4080
Kathryn Morrissette, *Administration*
Emily Elsen,

Melissa Elsen,
EMP: 25
SALES (est): 1MM **Privately Held**
SIC: 2051 Bakery: wholesale or whole-
sale/retail combined

(G-1593)
BLUE MARBLE ICE CREAM LLC
220 36th St Unit 33 (11232-2405)
PHONE.................................718 858-5551
Alexis Miesen, *Co-Owner*
Jennie Dundas, *Mng Member*
Vincent Biscaye, *Director*
EMP: 8
SALES (est): 1.2MM **Privately Held**
SIC: 2024 5451 Ice cream, bulk; ice
cream (packaged)

(G-1594)
**BLUE OCEAN FOOD TRADING
LLC**
154 42nd St (11232-3317)
PHONE.................................718 689-4291
Guo Wen Lin, *Mng Member*
EMP: 6
SALES (est): 445.5K **Privately Held**
SIC: 2091 Canned & cured fish & seafoods

(G-1595)
**BLUE RIDGE TEA & HERB CO
LTD**
22 Woodhull St Fl 2 (11231-2643)
PHONE.................................718 625-3100
Roger Rigolli, *President*
Troy Rigolli, *Vice Pres*
EMP: 9
SQ FT: 5,000
SALES (est): 1.1MM **Privately Held**
WEB: www.blueridgetea.com
SIC: 2099 Tea blending

(G-1596)
BLUE STAR BEVERAGES CORP
1099 Flushing Ave (11237-1830)
PHONE.................................718 381-3535
Albert Shtainer, *Principal*
▲ EMP: 9
SALES (est): 921.2K **Privately Held**
SIC: 2086 Carbonated beverages, nonal-
coholic: bottled & canned

(G-1597)
BLUEBERRY KNITTING INC (PA)
138 Ross St (11211-7808)
PHONE.................................718 599-6520
Phillip Werzberger, *President*
EMP: 35
SQ FT: 1,000
SALES (est): 2.4MM **Privately Held**
SIC: 2253 Sweaters & sweater coats, knit

(G-1598)
**BNC INNOVATIVE
WOODWORKING**
555 Liberty Ave (11207-3109)
PHONE.................................718 277-2800
Hyman Cassuto, *Owner*
EMP: 11
SQ FT: 11,202
SALES (est): 1.1MM **Privately Held**
SIC: 2431 Millwork

(G-1599)
BNEI ARAM SOBA INC
Also Called: Community Magazine
1616 Ocean Pkwy (11223-2144)
PHONE.................................718 645-4460
Jack Cohen, *President*
Aliza Parker, *Opers Mgr*
David Sitt, *Treasurer*
David N Sitt, *Treasurer*
Max Sharp, *Controller*
EMP: 11
SQ FT: 8,000
SALES (est): 1.1MM **Privately Held**
WEB: www.communitym.com
SIC: 2721 Magazines: publishing only, not
printed on site

(G-1600)
BNH LEAD EXAMINER CORP
199 Lee Ave Ste 481 (11211-8919)
PHONE.................................718 807-1365
Naftali Burger, *Ch of Bd*
EMP: 6

SALES (est): 280K **Privately Held**
SIC: 2711 Newspapers, publishing & printing

(G-1601)
BODY BUILDERS INC
Also Called: Red Line Networx Screen Prtg
5518 3rd Ave (11220-2609)
PHONE.................................718 492-7997
Richard Baez, *Ch of Bd*
EMP: 6
SALES (est): 565.7K **Privately Held**
SIC: 2759 Commercial printing

(G-1602)
**BOOKLINKS PUBLISHING SVCS
LLC**
55 Washington St Ste 253c (11201-1073)
PHONE.................................718 852-2116
Maria Villela, *President*
Marty Fluger, *Director*
Jose Schettino, *Bd of Directors*
EMP: 6
SQ FT: 5,000
SALES: 2MM **Privately Held**
SIC: 2731 Textbooks: publishing only, not
printed on site

(G-1603)
**BOOKLYN ARTISTS ALLIANCE
INC**
140 58th St Bldg B-7g (11220-2521)
PHONE.................................718 383-9621
Monica Johnson, *Principal*
M Ober, *Business Mgr*
Maya Taylor, *Business Mgr*
Richard Lee, *Manager*
Aimee Lusty, *Director*
EMP: 5
SALES: 330.3K **Privately Held**
WEB: www.booklyn.org
SIC: 2731 Books: publishing & printing

(G-1604)
BRACCI IRONWORKS INC
1440 Utica Ave (11203-6617)
PHONE.................................718 629-2374
Cory Bracci, *President*
Charlie Smith, *General Mgr*
Jonathan Bracci, *Vice Pres*
EMP: 10
SQ FT: 9,000
SALES: 1.6MM **Privately Held**
SIC: 3446 7692 Stairs, staircases, stair
treads: prefabricated metal; welding re-
pair

(G-1605)
BRAGLEY MFG CO INC
Also Called: Bragley Shipg Carrying Cases
924 Bergen St (11238-3301)
PHONE.................................718 622-7469
Neil Lurie, *President*
Vincent Lorello, *Vice Pres*
Leila Lurie, *Admin Sec*
EMP: 50 EST: 1946
SQ FT: 20,000
SALES (est): 4.8MM **Privately Held**
WEB: www.bragleycases.com
SIC: 2441 3089 3161 Cases, wood;
cases, plastic; luggage

(G-1606)
BRAZEN STREET LLC
734 Pennsylvania Ave (11207-6903)
PHONE.................................516 305-7951
Dr Ade Bushansky, *CEO*
Dr Tyrone Johnson, *CFO*
EMP: 50
SALES (est): 4.1MM **Privately Held**
SIC: 2082 Beer (alcoholic beverage)

(G-1607)
BRIDGE ENTERPRISES INC
544 Park Ave (11205-1600)
PHONE.................................718 625-6622
Sara Lev, *President*
EMP: 5
SALES (est): 415.9K **Privately Held**
SIC: 2732 Book music: printing & binding,
not published on site

(G-1608)
BRIDGE FULFILLMENT INC
445 Park Ave 204 (11205-2735)
PHONE.................................718 625-6622
Chaim Eigner, *Ch of Bd*
EMP: 3
SQ FT: 500
SALES: 2MM **Privately Held**
SIC: 2759 Commercial printing

(G-1609)
BRIGHT WAY SUPPLY INC
6302 Fort Hamilton Pkwy (11219-5122)
PHONE.................................718 833-2882
Phillip Lee, *Ch of Bd*
▲ EMP: 15
SQ FT: 10,000
SALES (est): 1.8MM **Privately Held**
SIC: 3677 Transformers power supply,
electronic type

(G-1610)
BRODER MFG INC
566 Johnson Ave (11237-1305)
P.O. Box 370182 (11237-0182)
PHONE.................................718 366-1667
Martin Broder, *President*
▲ EMP: 6
SQ FT: 6,000
SALES (est): 513.5K **Privately Held**
SIC: 2392 5162 Tablecloths & table set-
tings; plastics products

(G-1611)
BROOKLYN BANGERS LLC
111 Atlantic Ave Ste 1r (11201-6864)
PHONE.................................718 875-3535
Joseph Del Prete, *Mng Member*
Joseph D Prete, *Mng Member*
Saul Bolton,
Ben Daitz,
EMP: 17
SQ FT: 1,800
SALES (est): 186.3K **Privately Held**
SIC: 2013 5147 Sausages & other pre-
pared meats; meats & meat products

(G-1612)
BROOKLYN BREW SHOP LLC
81 Prospect St (11201-1473)
PHONE.................................718 874-0119
Stephen Valand,
▲ EMP: 12
SQ FT: 2,000
SALES: 3.5MM **Privately Held**
SIC: 3556 5084 Beverage machinery; in-
dustrial machinery & equipment

(G-1613)
BROOKLYN CASING CO INC
412 3rd St (11215-2882)
PHONE.................................718 522-0866
Morris Klasbole, *President*
EMP: 6
SALES (est): 410K **Privately Held**
SIC: 2013 Sausage casings, natural

(G-1614)
BROOKLYN CIRCUS (PA)
150 Nevins St (11217-2986)
PHONE.................................718 858-0919
Ouigi Theordore, *Owner*
Delon George, *Director*
Gabe Garcia, *Art Dir*
EMP: 10
SALES (est): 760.7K **Privately Held**
SIC: 2752 Letters, circular or form: litho-
graphed

(G-1615)
**BROOKLYN CSTM MET
FBRCTION INC**
48 Prospect Park Sw (11215-5915)
PHONE.................................718 499-1573
David Stanavich, *President*
EMP: 5
SALES (est): 498.4K **Privately Held**
SIC: 3499 Fabricated metal products

(G-1616)
BROOKLYN DENIM CO
85 N 3rd St (11249-3944)
PHONE.................................718 782-2600
Frank Pizzurro, *Principal*
EMP: 10

SALES (est): 980K **Privately Held**
SIC: 2211 2389 5651 Denims; apparel for handicapped; jeans stores

(G-1617)
BROOKLYN INDUSTRIES LLC
328 7th Ave (11215-4105)
PHONE..............................718 788-5250
Lindsey Stamps, *Manager*
EMP: 7
SALES (corp-wide): 20.6MM **Privately Held**
SIC: 3999 Barber & beauty shop equipment
PA: Brooklyn Industries Llc
45 Main St Ste 413
Brooklyn NY 11201
718 801-8900

(G-1618)
BROOKLYN JOURNAL PUBLICATIONS
Also Called: Brooklyn Heights Press
16 Court St 30 (11241-0102)
PHONE..............................718 422-7400
John Dozier Hasty, *President*
EMP: 20
SALES (est): 1MM **Privately Held**
WEB: www.brooklyneagle.net
SIC: 2711 Newspapers, publishing & printing

(G-1619)
BROOKLYN PRINTERS INC
1661 Nostrand Ave (11226-5515)
PHONE..............................718 511-7994
EMP: 9
SALES (est): 1.5MM **Privately Held**
SIC: 2752 Commercial printing, lithographic

(G-1620)
BROOKLYN RAIL INC
99 Commercial St Apt 15 (11222-1081)
PHONE..............................718 349-8427
Theodore Hann, *President*
Kara Rooney, *Associate*
EMP: 12
SALES: 743.9K **Privately Held**
WEB: www.brooklynrail.org
SIC: 2711 Newspapers

(G-1621)
BROOKLYN ROASTING WORKS LLC
45 Washington St (11201-1029)
PHONE..............................718 855-1000
EMP: 5 **Privately Held**
SIC: 2095 Coffee extracts
PA: Brooklyn Roasting Works Llc
50 John St
Brooklyn NY 11201

(G-1622)
BROOKLYN SWEET SPOT INC
366 Myrtle Ave Ste A (11205-2694)
PHONE..............................718 522-2577
Kiyomi Rodgers, *President*
EMP: 5 EST: 2013
SALES (est): 324.8K **Privately Held**
SIC: 2051 Cakes, bakery: except frozen

(G-1623)
BROOKLYN WINERY LLC (PA)
213 N 8th St (11211-2007)
PHONE..............................347 763-1506
Marisa Pellicci, *Sales Staff*
Rachel Schauman, *Sales Staff*
Jessica Wittwer, *Manager*
Bryan Leventhal,
EMP: 11
SALES (est): 2MM **Privately Held**
SIC: 2084 Wines

(G-1624)
BROOKLYNS BEST PASTA CO INC
7520 Avenue V (11234-6217)
PHONE..............................917 881-3007
Elena Trotta, *Principal*
EMP: 5 EST: 2018

SALES (est): 153.8K **Privately Held**
SIC: 2099 2033 5149 Pasta, uncooked: packaged with other ingredients; spaghetti & other pasta sauce: packaged in cans, jars, etc.; pasta & rice

(G-1625)
BROOKLYNWRAP INC
Also Called: Brooklynwrap Fresh Wraps
4714 Avenue N (11234-3710)
PHONE..............................718 258-8088
Yuewei Chen, *CEO*
Asone Waterman, *Manager*
EMP: 5
SALES (est): 451.2K **Privately Held**
SIC: 2099 5812 Dessert mixes & fillings; eating places

(G-1626)
BSD ALUMINUM FOIL LLC
260 Hewest St (11211)
PHONE..............................347 689-3875
Esther Klein, *President*
EMP: 25 EST: 2009
SQ FT: 100,000
SALES (est): 1.8MM **Privately Held**
SIC: 2621 3421 3353 Towels, tissues & napkins: paper & stock; table & food cutlery, including butchers'; aluminum sheet, plate & foil

(G-1627)
BUDD WOODWORK INC
54 Franklin St (11222-2089)
PHONE..............................718 389-1110
Serafin Caamano, *President*
Belen Caamano, *Shareholder*
EMP: 15 EST: 1952
SQ FT: 14,000
SALES (est): 2.3MM **Privately Held**
SIC: 2499 Decorative wood & woodwork

(G-1628)
BUNA BESTA TORTILLAS
219 Johnson Ave (11206-2713)
PHONE..............................347 987-3995
Francis Forgione, *Principal*
EMP: 6
SALES (est): 444.3K **Privately Held**
SIC: 2099 Tortillas, fresh or refrigerated

(G-1629)
BUPERIOD PBC
8 Brighton 15th St (11235-5840)
PHONE..............................917 406-9804
Vanessa Siverls, *CEO*
EMP: 5
SALES (est): 193.7K **Privately Held**
SIC: 2299 7389 Pads, fiber: henequen, sisal, istle;

(G-1630)
BUSHWICK BOTTLING LLC
465 Johnson Ave (11237-1201)
PHONE..............................929 666-3618
Randy Bresil,
EMP: 10 EST: 2017
SALES (est): 283.1K **Privately Held**
SIC: 3999 Manufacturing industries

(G-1631)
BUSHWICK KITCHEN LLC
630 Flushing Ave Fl 5 (11206-5026)
PHONE..............................917 297-1045
Jonathan Mines, *Sales Staff*
Casey Elsas, *Mng Member*
Ped Barbeau,
EMP: 5
SQ FT: 1,400
SALES: 500K **Privately Held**
SIC: 2035 Seasonings & sauces, except tomato & dry

(G-1632)
BUSINESS DIRECTORY INC
Also Called: Community Directory
137 Division Ave Ste A (11211-8270)
PHONE..............................718 486-8099
Shie Krausz, *President*
EMP: 10
SALES (est): 850K **Privately Held**
SIC: 2741 Telephone & other directory publishing

(G-1633)
BUSINESS MANAGEMENT SYSTEMS
Also Called: Fisau
1675 W 9th St Apt 4d (11223-1220)
PHONE..............................914 245-8558
Zak Kogan, *CEO*
Leonid Kogan, *President*
Mark Milyavsky, *Vice Pres*
Yakov Rudman, *Project Leader*
EMP: 11
SALES (est): 782.6K **Privately Held**
WEB: www.fisau.com
SIC: 7372 Business oriented computer software

(G-1634)
BUST INC
Also Called: Bust Magazine
253 36th St Unit 3 (11232-2415)
PHONE..............................212 675-1707
Laura Henzel, *President*
Debbie Stoller, *Vice Pres*
EMP: 5
SALES (est): 708.9K **Privately Held**
WEB: www.bust.com
SIC: 2721 Magazines: publishing & printing

(G-1635)
C B S FOOD PRODUCTS CORP
770 Chauncey St (11207-1120)
PHONE..............................718 452-2500
Bernard Steinberg, *Ch of Bd*
Chaim Stein, *President*
Phillip Shapiro, *Vice Pres*
EMP: 15 EST: 1939
SQ FT: 34,000
SALES (est): 5.6MM **Privately Held**
SIC: 2079 Cooking oils, except corn: vegetable refined; shortening & other solid edible fats

(G-1636)
C T A DIGITAL INC
36 Taaffe Pl (11205-1409)
PHONE..............................718 963-9845
Sol Markowitz, *Vice Pres*
Yuling Chang, *Buyer*
EMP: 12
SALES (corp-wide): 14K **Privately Held**
SIC: 3944 Video game machines, except coin-operated
PA: C T A Digital Inc.
326 State Route 208
Monroe NY 10950
845 513-0433

(G-1637)
CAB SIGNS INC
Also Called: Cab Plastics
38 Livonia Ave (11212-4011)
PHONE..............................718 479-2424
Christopher Bayer, *President*
Charles Bayer, *Vice Pres*
Chee Yong, *Manager*
EMP: 26
SQ FT: 14,000
SALES (est): 3.6MM **Privately Held**
WEB: www.cabplastics.com
SIC: 3993 Signs, not made in custom sign painting shops

(G-1638)
CABEZON DESIGN GROUP INC
197 Waverly Ave (11205-3605)
PHONE..............................718 488-9868
Kurt Lebeck, *President*
EMP: 7
SALES (est): 242K **Privately Held**
WEB: www.cabezondesign.com
SIC: 3446 Architectural metalwork

(G-1639)
CABINETS BY STANLEY INC
46 Hall St (11205)
PHONE..............................718 222-5861
Stanley Stryszowski, *CEO*
Lukasz Stryszowski, *Exec VP*
Tom Stryszowski, *Project Mgr*
EMP: 8
SALES (est): 568.9K **Privately Held**
SIC: 2434 Wood kitchen cabinets

(G-1640)
CALIPER STUDIO INC
75 Scott Ave (11237-1320)
PHONE..............................718 302-2427
Jonathan Taylor, *President*
Steve Lynch, *Vice Pres*
Michael Conlon, *Admin Sec*
EMP: 37
SALES (est): 1.4MM **Privately Held**
SIC: 3446 Architectural metalwork

(G-1641)
CAMEO METAL PRODUCTS INC
127 12th St (11215-3891)
PHONE..............................718 788-1106
Vito Di Maio, *Ch of Bd*
Antonio D Maio, *President*
Frank Spodnick, *General Mgr*
Anthony Di Maio, *Vice Pres*
▲ EMP: 40
SQ FT: 48,988
SALES (est): 8.2MM **Privately Held**
WEB: www.cameometal.com
SIC: 3559 3469 Metal finishing equipment for plating, etc.; metal stampings

(G-1642)
CANARSIE COURIER INC
1142 E 92nd St 44 (11236-3698)
PHONE..............................718 257-0600
Donna Marra, *Publisher*
Sandra Greco, *Principal*
Catherine Rosa, *Business Mgr*
EMP: 10
SALES (est): 706.1K **Privately Held**
WEB: www.canarsiecourier.com
SIC: 2711 Newspapers, publishing & printing

(G-1643)
CANDLE IN THE WINDOW INC
Also Called: Aura Essence
19 Vanderbilt Ave (11205-1113)
PHONE..............................718 852-5743
Marni Bouchardy, *Ch of Bd*
▲ EMP: 16
SALES (est): 1.1MM **Privately Held**
SIC: 3999 5199 Candles; candles

(G-1644)
CANNIZZARO SEAL & ENGRAVING CO
435 Avenue U (11223-4007)
P.O. Box 230304 (11223-0304)
PHONE..............................718 513-6125
Janet Cannizzaro, *President*
▲ EMP: 5
SQ FT: 1,200
SALES (est): 672K **Privately Held**
WEB: www.cannizzaroseal.com
SIC: 3953 5199 Embossing seals & hand stamps; gifts & novelties

(G-1645)
CAPUTO BAKERY INC
Also Called: Caputo's Bake Shop
329 Court St Ste 1 (11231-4390)
PHONE..............................718 875-6871
John Caputo, *President*
Francis Tunzi, *Vice Pres*
EMP: 5
SQ FT: 2,000
SALES (est): 300K **Privately Held**
SIC: 2051 5461 Bakery: wholesale or wholesale/retail combined; bakeries

(G-1646)
CARBON6 LLC
989 Pacific St (11238-3206)
PHONE..............................607 229-3611
John Paul Easley II,
EMP: 5
SALES (est): 77.3K **Privately Held**
SIC: 3911 Rings, finger: precious metal

(G-1647)
CARDINAL TANK CORP
Also Called: Cardinal Boiler and Tank
700 Hicks St (11231-1823)
PHONE..............................718 625-4350
William J Weidmann, *President*
EMP: 50
SQ FT: 31,000

SALES (est): 9.5MM **Privately Held**
WEB: www.cardinal-detecto.centralcaroli-
nascale.co
SIC: **3443** Fuel tanks (oil, gas, etc.): metal
plate

(G-1648)
CARECONNECTOR
177 Concord St Apt 2a (11201-2091)
PHONE.................................919 360-2987
Sima Pendharkar, *Principal*
EMP: 5
SALES (est): 199.7K **Privately Held**
SIC: **7372** Business oriented computer
software

(G-1649)
CARRY-ALL CANVAS BAG CO INC
1983 Coney Island Ave (11223-2328)
PHONE.................................718 375-4230
Michel Kraut, *President*
▲ EMP: 7
SQ FT: 3,800
SALES: 500K **Privately Held**
WEB: www.carryallbag.com
SIC: **3161** Traveling bags

(G-1650)
CARTER ENTERPRISES LLC (PA)
Also Called: Mil-Spec. Enterprises
4610 12th Ave (11219-2556)
PHONE.................................718 853-5052
Chaim Wolf, *Mng Member*
▲ EMP: 32
SALES (est): 61.2MM **Privately Held**
WEB: www.carterny.com
SIC: **2389** Men's miscellaneous acces-
sories

(G-1651)
CARTRIDGE EVOLUTION INC
140 58th St Bldg Bu4e (11220-2521)
PHONE.................................718 788-0678
Wyman Xu, *Ch of Bd*
EMP: 7
SALES (est): 844.4K **Privately Held**
SIC: **3955** Print cartridges for laser & other
computer printers

(G-1652)
CARTS MOBILE FOOD EQP CORP
Also Called: Cfe
113 8th St (11215-3115)
PHONE.................................718 788-5540
Jeno Rosenberg, *President*
Florence Rosenberg, *Corp Secy*
Joe Revitte, *Design Engr*
EMP: 22
SQ FT: 15,000
SALES (est): 4.1MM **Privately Held**
WEB: www.cartsfoodeqp.com
SIC: **2599** 3589 3556 Food wagons,
restaurant; carts, restaurant equipment;
commercial cooking & foodwarming
equipment; food products machinery

(G-1653)
CASA COLLECTION INC
106 Ferris St (11231-1066)
PHONE.................................718 694-0272
Roberto Gil, *President*
EMP: 5
SALES (est): 480K **Privately Held**
WEB: www.casacollection.com
SIC: **2434** 5712 Wood kitchen cabinets;
juvenile furniture

(G-1654)
CASA INNOVATIONS INC
Also Called: Shredder Essentials
155 Bay Ridge Ave (11220-5108)
PHONE.................................718 965-6600
Aron Abramson, *CEO*
Charles Sued, *President*
▲ EMP: 6
SQ FT: 5,300
SALES (est): 1.1MM **Privately Held**
SIC: **3678** Electronic connectors

(G-1655)
CATALINA PRODUCTS CORP (PA)
2455 Mcdonald Ave (11223-5232)
PHONE.................................718 336-8288
Victor Salama, *President*
Marie Mireille Salama, *Corp Secy*
Linda Reyzis, *Vice Pres*
Paul Yedin, *Vice Pres*
▲ EMP: 35 EST: 1968
SQ FT: 75,000
SALES (est): 2.1MM **Privately Held**
WEB: www.catalinabath.com
SIC: **2392** Shower curtains: made from
purchased materials

(G-1656)
CCC PUBLICATIONS INC
12020 Flatlands Ave (11207-8203)
PHONE.................................718 306-1008
AR Bernard, *CEO*
Robin Hogan, *General Mgr*
Karen Bernard, *Vice Pres*
EMP: 11
SQ FT: 2,500
SALES: 600K **Privately Held**
SIC: **2731** Book publishing
PA: Christian Cultural Center, Inc.
12020 Flatlands Ave
Brooklyn NY 11207

(G-1657)
CELONIS INC
1820 Avenue M Unit 544 (11230-5347)
PHONE.................................941 615-9670
Alexander Rinke, *CEO*
Panayiotis Vitakis, *Senior VP*
Anthony Deighton, *Chief Mktg Ofcr*
EMP: 5
SALES (est): 261.9K **Privately Held**
SIC: **7372** Prepackaged software

(G-1658)
CERTIFIED HEALTH PRODUCTS INC
67 35th St Unit C533 (11232-2248)
PHONE.................................718 339-7498
Gene Kisselman, *President*
Steve Zeltser, *Vice Pres*
EMP: 35
SQ FT: 12,000
SALES (est): 3.9MM **Privately Held**
SIC: **3069** Orthopedic sundries, molded
rubber

(G-1659)
CHAMBORD LLC
4302 Farragut Rd (11203-6520)
PHONE.................................718 859-1110
Daniel Faks, *President*
EMP: 20
SQ FT: 12,000
SALES (est): 1.3MM **Privately Held**
SIC: **2051** Bread, cake & related products

(G-1660)
CHAN KEE DRIED BEAN CURD INC
71 Steuben St (11205-2608)
PHONE.................................718 622-0820
Alex Luk, *President*
Tan Muneng Sing, *Principal*
Tran Van Track, *Principal*
EMP: 6
SQ FT: 1,000
SALES: 500K **Privately Held**
SIC: **2099** Tofu, except frozen desserts

(G-1661)
CHARLOTTE NEUVILLE DESIGN LLC
Also Called: Fashion Chef, The
882 3rd Ave (11232-1904)
PHONE.................................646 530-4570
Charlotte Neuville, *President*
EMP: 6
SQ FT: 2,000
SALES (est): 539.2K **Privately Held**
SIC: **2051** Cakes, bakery: except frozen

(G-1662)
CHEFS DELIGHT PACKING CO
94 N 8th St (11249-2802)
PHONE.................................718 388-8581
Bradford Karroll, *President*

Doug Karroll, *Vice Pres*
EMP: 13 EST: 1956
SQ FT: 3,000
SALES (est): 1.6MM **Privately Held**
SIC: **2011** Meat packing plants

(G-1663)
CIC INTERNATIONAL LTD
1118 42nd St (11219-1213)
P.O. Box 533, New York (10011)
PHONE.................................212 213-0089
S G Fassoulis, *President*
David Ceva, *Exec VP*
Joseph Ceva, *Exec VP*
James Chladek, *Vice Pres*
Robert Perry, *Vice Pres*
EMP: 98
SQ FT: 14,656
SALES (est): 6.5MM **Privately Held**
SIC: **3812** 3711 3482 3483 Aircraft/aero-
space flight instruments & guidance sys-
tems; military motor vehicle assembly;
small arms ammunition; ammunition com-
ponents; rocket launchers; helicopters

(G-1664)
CITY COOLING ENTERPRISES INC
1624 61st St (11204-2109)
PHONE.................................718 331-7400
Derick Pearlin, *President*
EMP: 8
SQ FT: 5,000
SALES (est): 1.1MM **Privately Held**
SIC: **3444** 1711 Sheet metalwork; heating
& air conditioning contractors

(G-1665)
CITY OF NEW YORK
Also Called: HRA Poster Project
4014 1st Ave Unit 3 (11232-2700)
PHONE.................................718 965-8787
David Hall, *Branch Mgr*
EMP: 30 **Privately Held**
WEB: www.nyc.gov
SIC: **2741** 9199 Shopping news: publish-
ing & printing; general government admin-
istration;
PA: City Of New York
City Hl
New York NY 10007
212 788-3000

(G-1666)
CITY OF NEW YORK
Also Called: Department of Sanitation
5602 19th Ave (11204-2049)
PHONE.................................718 236-2693
Jay Ryan, *Superintendent*
EMP: 117 **Privately Held**
WEB: www.nyc.gov
SIC: **2842** 9511 Sanitation preparations;
waste management program administra-
tion, government;
PA: City Of New York
City Hl
New York NY 10007
212 788-3000

(G-1667)
CITY SIGNS INC
1940 Mcdonald Ave (11223-1829)
PHONE.................................718 375-5933
Yehuda Mizrahi, *President*
Eyal Mizrahi, *Vice Pres*
Smadar Mizrahi, *Treasurer*
EMP: 5
SQ FT: 12,000
SALES (est): 636.1K **Privately Held**
WEB: www.citysignsinc.com
SIC: **3993** 2399 5999 Signs, not made in
custom sign painting shops; neon signs;
flags, fabric; awnings

(G-1668)
CITY SITES SPORTSWEAR INC (PA)
2421 Mcdonald Ave (11223-5230)
P.O. Box 230187 (11223-0187)
PHONE.................................718 375-2990
Sui Tong MA, *President*
David Schwitzer, *Corp Secy*
▲ EMP: 24
SQ FT: 8,000
SALES (est): 2.6MM **Privately Held**
SIC: **2339** Sportswear, women's

(G-1669)
CK PRINTING CORP
267 41st St (11232-2811)
PHONE.................................718 965-0388
Bo Wen Chen, *CEO*
EMP: 8
SALES (est): 855K **Privately Held**
SIC: **2752** Commercial printing, litho-
graphic

(G-1670)
CLASSIC ALBUM
343 Lorimer St (11206-1998)
PHONE.................................718 388-2818
Barry Himmel, *President*
EMP: 30
SQ FT: 12,500
SALES (est): 2.7MM **Privately Held**
SIC: **2782** 7221 2789 2759 Blankbooks
& looseleaf binders; photographic studios,
portrait; bookbinding & related work; com-
mercial printing

(G-1671)
CLASSIC ALBUM LLC
343 Lorimer St (11206-1998)
PHONE.................................718 388-2818
Barry Himmel,
▲ EMP: 75 EST: 1952
SQ FT: 10,000
SALES (est): 9.3MM **Privately Held**
SIC: **2782** 7221 Albums; photographic stu-
dios, portrait

(G-1672)
CNV ARCHITECTURAL COATINGS INC
538 Johnson Ave (11237-1226)
PHONE.................................718 418-9584
Nicola Comaianni, *President*
EMP: 6 EST: 2015
SQ FT: 10,000
SALES (est): 297.5K **Privately Held**
SIC: **3479** Metal coating & allied service

(G-1673)
CODE RED TRADING LLC
995 E 8th St Fl 3 (11230-3514)
PHONE.................................347 782-2608
Joseph Sasson, *Mng Member*
Alan Sasson,
David Sasson,
EMP: 50
SALES (est): 12MM **Privately Held**
SIC: **3944** Electronic games & toys

(G-1674)
COFFEE HOLDING COMPANY INC
4425 1st Ave (11232-4201)
PHONE.................................718 832-0800
R Gordon, *Principal*
David Gordon, *Vice Pres*
Fernando Lopez, *Warehouse Mgr*
Sam Elway, *Human Res Mgr*
Karen Gordon, *Bd of Directors*
▼ EMP: 8
SALES (est): 737.5K **Privately Held**
SIC: **2095** Roasted coffee

(G-1675)
COLONIAL REDI RECORD CORP
1225 36th St (11218-2023)
PHONE.................................718 972-7433
Joe Berkobits, *President*
EMP: 25
SQ FT: 12,000
SALES: 2.5MM **Privately Held**
SIC: **3993** Signs & advertising specialties

(G-1676)
COLUMBIA BUTTON NAILHEAD CORP
306 Stagg St 316 (11206-1702)
PHONE.................................718 386-3414
Robert Matz, *President*
Charles J Matz Jr, *Corp Secy*
EMP: 17 EST: 1946
SQ FT: 20,000
SALES (est): 2.2MM **Privately Held**
SIC: **3965** Studs, shirt, except
precious/semiprecious metal or stone;
buttons & parts; buckles & buckle parts

(G-1677)
COMBOLAND PACKING CORP
2 Cumberland St (11205-1040)
PHONE...............................718 858-4200
Marvin Eisenstadt, *President*
Ira Eisenstadt, *Vice Pres*
Stephen Mahabir, *Mfg Staff*
Tammi Cohn, *Manager*
Matthew Cauusco, *Planning*
EMP: 99
SALES (est): 8.8MM Privately Held
SIC: 2869 Perfumes, flavorings & food additives

(G-1678)
COMMODORE MANUFACUTRING CORP
Also Called: Commodore Tool
3913 2nd Ave (11232-2707)
PHONE...............................718 788-2600
Abraham Damast, *Branch Mgr*
EMP: 50
SALES (corp-wide): 26.8MM Privately Held
SIC: 3542 Machine tools, metal forming type
PA: Commodore Manufacutring Corporation
4312 2nd Ave
Brooklyn NY 11232
718 788-2600

(G-1679)
COMMON GOOD LLC
135 Kent Ave (11249-3154)
PHONE...............................646 246-1441
EMP: 5 EST: 2010
SALES (est): 668K Privately Held
SIC: 2844 Toilet preparations

(G-1680)
COMMUNITY NEWS GROUP LLC (PA)
Also Called: Bronx Times Reporter
1 Metrotech Ctr Fl 10 (11201-3949)
PHONE...............................718 260-2500
Les Goodstein, *CEO*
Jennifer Goodstein, *President*
Bill Egbert, *Editor*
Bill Roundy, *Editor*
Gayle Greenberg, *Accounts Exec*
EMP: 105
SQ FT: 14,000
SALES (est): 20.1MM Privately Held
SIC: 2711 Commercial printing & newspaper publishing combined; newspapers, publishing & printing

(G-1681)
CONFRTRNITY OF PRESCIOUS BLOOD
5300 Fort Hamilton Pkwy (11219)
PHONE...............................718 436-1120
Susan Pergolizzi, *Principal*
Austin Bennett, *Director*
EMP: 8
SALES (est): 690K Privately Held
WEB: www.confraternitypb.org
SIC: 2731 Books: publishing only

(G-1682)
CONSUMER FLAVORING EXTRACT CO
921 Mcdonald Ave (11218-5611)
PHONE...............................718 435-0201
Louis Fontana, *President*
EMP: 14 EST: 1962
SQ FT: 5,000
SALES (est): 1.8MM Privately Held
WEB: www.consumersflavoring.com
SIC: 2079 2087 Edible oil products, except corn oil; concentrates, flavoring (except drink)

(G-1683)
CONTINENTAL LATEX CORP
1489 Shore Pkwy Apt 1g (11214-6321)
PHONE...............................718 783-7883
George Miller, *President*
EMP: 10 EST: 1953
SALES (est): 800K Privately Held
SIC: 3069 3089 Air-supported rubber structures; plastic processing

(G-1684)
CONTROL ELECTROPOLISHING CORP
109 Walworth St (11205-2897)
P.O. Box 790385, Middle Village (11379-0385)
PHONE...............................718 858-6634
Nancy Zapata, *President*
EMP: 15 EST: 1959
SQ FT: 7,000
SALES: 1.2MM Privately Held
SIC: 3471 Polishing, metals or formed products

(G-1685)
CONVERGENT MED MGT SVCS LLC
7513 3rd Ave (11209-3103)
PHONE...............................718 921-6159
Anthony Pennacchio, *President*
EMP: 5
SALES (est): 553.2K Privately Held
SIC: 3674 Semiconductors & related devices

(G-1686)
COPY CAT
3177 Coney Island Ave A (11235-6443)
PHONE...............................718 934-2192
Horace Bryan, *President*
Araceli Bryan, *Vice Pres*
EMP: 5 EST: 1977
SQ FT: 3,000
SALES (est): 415.2K Privately Held
SIC: 3647 Vehicular lighting equipment

(G-1687)
COPY CORNER INC
200 Division Ave (11211)
PHONE...............................718 388-4545
Zalman Eizikovits, *President*
EMP: 5
SQ FT: 1,500
SALES (est): 410K Privately Held
SIC: 2754 2789 Commercial printing, gravure; bookbinding & related work

(G-1688)
CORNELL BEVERAGES INC
105 Harrison Pl (11237-1403)
PHONE...............................718 381-3000
Helene Hoffman, *President*
Allan Hoffman, *Vice Pres*
Donna Hoffman, *Treasurer*
EMP: 10
SALES (est): 1MM Privately Held
WEB: www.cornellbev.com
SIC: 2086 Soft drinks: packaged in cans, bottles, etc.

(G-1689)
CORONET PARTS MFG CO INC (PA)
883 Elton St (11208-5315)
PHONE...............................718 649-1750
Allan Rodolitz, *President*
Jeffrey Rodolitz, *President*
Mark Silfen, *General Mgr*
Joseph Thomas, *Purch Mgr*
Armand Salvati, *Sales Staff*
EMP: 20 EST: 1945
SQ FT: 15,000
SALES (est): 7.3MM Privately Held
WEB: www.coronetparts.com
SIC: 3432 5074 Plumbers' brass goods: drain cocks, faucets, spigots, etc.; plumbers' brass goods & fittings

(G-1690)
CORONET PARTS MFG CO INC
901 Elton St Fl 1 (11208-5315)
PHONE...............................718 649-1750
Joel Poretz, *Branch Mgr*
EMP: 20
SALES (corp-wide): 7.3MM Privately Held
WEB: www.coronetparts.com
SIC: 3432 Plumbers' brass goods: drain cocks, faucets, spigots, etc.
PA: Coronet Parts Mfg. Co. Inc.
883 Elton St
Brooklyn NY 11208
718 649-1750

(G-1691)
COSMIC ENTERPRISE
147 Rockaway Ave Ste A (11233-3289)
PHONE...............................718 342-6257
Marjorie Thorne, *Owner*
EMP: 6
SALES (est): 320K Privately Held
SIC: 2833 5499 Drugs & herbs: grading, grinding & milling; health & dietetic food stores

(G-1692)
COUNTY ENERGY CORP
65 S 11th St Apt 1e (11249-7003)
PHONE...............................718 626-7000
David Rosner, *President*
EMP: 4
SALES: 20MM Privately Held
SIC: 1311 4911 Natural gas production; electric services

(G-1693)
COURIER-LIFE INC
Also Called: Courier Life Publications
1 Metrotech Ctr (11201-3948)
PHONE...............................718 260-2500
Les Goodstein, *CEO*
Jennifer Goodstein, *President*
EMP: 218
SQ FT: 11,300
SALES (est): 10.9MM
SALES (corp-wide): 20.1MM Privately Held
WEB: www.courierlife.net
SIC: 2711 Newspapers: publishing only, not printed on site; newspapers, publishing & printing
PA: Community News Group Llc
1 Metrotech Ctr Fl 10
Brooklyn NY 11201
718 260-2500

(G-1694)
CRAFT PACKAGING INC
1274 49th St Ste 350 (11219-3011)
PHONE...............................718 633-4045
Fhia Rothstein, *President*
Rothstein Shia, *Owner*
EMP: 5
SALES (est): 445K Privately Held
SIC: 2671 Packaging paper & plastics film, coated & laminated

(G-1695)
CREAM BEBE
694 Myrtle Ave Ste 220 (11205)
PHONE...............................917 578-2088
Yossi Greenburg, *Owner*
EMP: 10
SALES (est): 380K Privately Held
SIC: 2361 Shirts: girls', children's & infants'

(G-1696)
CREATIONS IN LUCITE INC
165 Franklin Ave Apt 5 (11205-2760)
PHONE...............................718 871-2000
Davin Rand, *President*
David Rand, *President*
Shaye Gross, *Vice Pres*
EMP: 9
SALES (est): 150K Privately Held
WEB: www.creationsinlucite.com
SIC: 2821 Acrylic resins

(G-1697)
CREATIVE GOLD LLC
1425 37th St Ste 5 (11218-3771)
PHONE...............................718 686-2225
▲ EMP: 23 EST: 2003
SALES: 500K Privately Held
SIC: 3911 Manufacture Precious Metals

(G-1698)
CREATIVE SCENTS USA INC
183 Wilson St Ste 106 (11211-7578)
PHONE...............................718 522-5901
Adolf Kraus, *CEO*
EMP: 3
SALES: 2MM Privately Held
SIC: 2392 Household furnishings

(G-1699)
CREATIVE STONE MFG INC
349 Covert St (11237-6319)
PHONE...............................718 386-7425
Coronado BR, *Manager*

EMP: 5
SALES (corp-wide): 61.2MM Privately Held
SIC: 3272 Siding, precast stone
PA: Creative Stone Mfg., Inc.
11191 Calabash Ave
Fontana CA 92337
909 357-8295

(G-1700)
CREST LOCK CO INC
342 Herzl St (11212-4442)
PHONE...............................718 345-9898
Samuel Sheiman, *President*
▲ EMP: 15 EST: 1938
SQ FT: 20,000
SALES (est): 1.4MM Privately Held
WEB: www.crestlock.net
SIC: 3429 Luggage hardware

(G-1701)
CRITERION BELL & SPECIALTY
4312 2nd Ave (11232-3306)
PHONE...............................718 788-2600
Abraham Damast, *President*
Donald Damast, *Corp Secy*
Gary Damast, *Vice Pres*
EMP: 40
SQ FT: 30,000
SALES (est): 3.6MM Privately Held
SIC: 3499 3999 Novelties & specialties, metal; Christmas tree ornaments, except electrical & glass

(G-1702)
CROWN WOODWORKING CORP
583 Montgomery St (11225-3009)
PHONE...............................718 974-6415
Mendel Barber, *President*
EMP: 9
SALES: 350K Privately Held
SIC: 2431 Millwork

(G-1703)
CROWNBROOK ACC LLC (PA)
Also Called: American Conveyor
478 Albany Ave 113 (11203-1002)
PHONE...............................718 626-0760
Ron Schinik, *Mng Member*
Richard Dauphin,
▲ EMP: 40
SQ FT: 30,000
SALES (est): 9.7MM Privately Held
SIC: 3535 1799 Conveyors & conveying equipment; welding on site

(G-1704)
CRUSADER CANDLE CO INC
325 Nevins St Ste 327329 (11215-1084)
PHONE...............................718 625-0005
Paul J Morra, *President*
◆ EMP: 28 EST: 1946
SQ FT: 14,500
SALES: 5MM Privately Held
SIC: 3999 Candles

(G-1705)
CRYE PRECISION LLC
63 Flushing Ave (11205-1005)
PHONE...............................718 246-3838
Jean Gonzalez, *Buyer*
Eric Burt, *Engineer*
Steven Filipelli, *Controller*
Beth Rodriguez, *Cust Mgr*
Jeremy Morton, *Sales Staff*
▲ EMP: 185
SQ FT: 90,000
SALES (est): 53MM Privately Held
SIC: 3842 2311 5632 5699 Clothing, fire resistant & protective; military uniforms, men's & youths': purchased materials; policemen's uniforms: made from purchased materials; apparel accessories; customized clothing & apparel; textile & apparel services

(G-1706)
CT INDUSTRIAL SUPPLY CO INC
305 Ten Eyck St (11206-1724)
P.O. Box 60338 (11206-0338)
PHONE...............................718 417-3226
Charles Tolkin, *President*
EMP: 10
SALES (est): 1MM Privately Held
SIC: 3089 Garbage containers, plastic

(G-1707)
CTAC HOLDINGS LLC
68 35th Street Brooklyn (11232)
PHONE.....................212 924-2280
Anthony Cirone, *President*
EMP: 20
SALES (est): 2.4MM **Privately Held**
SIC: 2066 Chocolate

(G-1708)
CUMBERLAND PACKING CORP (PA)
2 Cumberland St (11205-1000)
PHONE.....................718 858-4200
Steven Eisenstadt, *CEO*
Jeffrey Eisenstadt, *Principal*
Rob Bowen, *Exec VP*
Ira Eisenstadt, *Senior VP*
Mike Briskey, *Vice Pres*
◆ EMP: 390
SQ FT: 13,000
SALES: 150MM **Privately Held**
WEB: www.cpack.com
SIC: 2869 Sweeteners, synthetic; flavors or flavoring materials, synthetic

(G-1709)
CURRICULUM ASSOCIATES LLC
55 Prospect St (11201-1497)
PHONE.....................978 313-1355
Stephanie Lawkins, *Manager*
EMP: 12
SALES (corp-wide): 14MM **Privately Held**
SIC: 2731 Book publishing
PA: Curriculum Associates, Llc
153 Rangeway Rd
North Billerica MA 01862
978 667-8000

(G-1710)
CUSTOM FIXTURES INC
129 13th St (11215-4603)
PHONE.....................718 965-1141
Michael Lerich, *President*
EMP: 9
SQ FT: 8,000
SALES (est): 960K **Privately Held**
WEB: www.customfixturesonline.com
SIC: 2542 Fixtures: display, office or store: except wood

(G-1711)
CUSTOM LAMPSHADES INC
Also Called: Creative Custom Shades
544 Park Ave Ste 503 (11205-1788)
P.O. Box 50186 (11205-0186)
PHONE.....................718 254-0500
Nachman Heller, *President*
EMP: 16 EST: 1979
SALES (est): 1.8MM **Privately Held**
SIC: 3645 5719 Lamp & light shades; lamps & lamp shades

(G-1712)
CUSTOM LUCITE CREATIONS INC
165 Franklin Ave Apt 5 (11205-2760)
PHONE.....................718 871-2000
David L Rand, *CEO*
EMP: 10
SALES (est): 943K **Privately Held**
SIC: 3089 Injection molding of plastics; plastic processing

(G-1713)
CUSTOM WOOD INC
770 E 94th St (11236-1817)
PHONE.....................718 927-4700
James Campo, *President*
EMP: 8 EST: 1980
SQ FT: 3,200
SALES: 750K **Privately Held**
SIC: 2541 2431 Store fixtures, wood; woodwork, interior & ornamental

(G-1714)
D & H AMAZING DEALS INC (PA)
Also Called: D&H
1233 39th St (11218-1932)
PHONE.....................347 318-3805
Daniel Fuchs, *President*
▲ EMP: 6

SALES: 5MM **Privately Held**
SIC: 2844 5731 Cosmetic preparations; radio, television & electronic stores

(G-1715)
D BEST SERVICE CO INC
Also Called: D Best Glass & Mirror
729 Church Ave (11218-3305)
PHONE.....................718 972-6133
William Omalley Jr, *President*
Grace Fradella O'Malley, *Admin Sec*
EMP: 7
SQ FT: 400
SALES (est): 947K **Privately Held**
SIC: 3429 1751 7699 Metal fasteners; window & door installation & erection; mirror repair shop

(G-1716)
D V S IRON & ALUMINUM WORKS
117 14th St (11215-4607)
PHONE.....................718 768-7961
Louis Di Janic, *President*
EMP: 9 EST: 1969
SQ FT: 1,000
SALES (est): 1.4MM **Privately Held**
SIC: 3446 Railings, prefabricated metal

(G-1717)
DADDARIO & COMPANY INC
Also Called: D'Addario & Company Inc
1000 Dean St Ste 410 (11238-3385)
PHONE.....................718 599-6660
EMP: 22
SALES (corp-wide): 180MM **Privately Held**
SIC: 3931 Musical instruments
PA: D'addario & Company, Inc.
595 Smith St
Farmingdale NY 11735
631 439-3300

(G-1718)
DAHILL DISTRIBUTORS INC
975 Dahill Rd (11204-1738)
PHONE.....................347 371-9453
Hirsch Stengel, *President*
EMP: 8
SQ FT: 500
SALES: 800K **Privately Held**
WEB: www.filmart.com
SIC: 3699 5199 Electrical equipment & supplies; general merchandise, non-durable

(G-1719)
DAILY WEAR SPORTSWEAR CORP (PA)
2308 Mcdonald Ave (11223-4739)
PHONE.....................718 972-0533
Isaac Abed, *President*
Joey Abed, *Vice Pres*
Michael Abed, *Vice Pres*
▲ EMP: 8
SQ FT: 20,000
SALES (est): 1MM **Privately Held**
SIC: 2339 Sportswear, women's

(G-1720)
DALY MEGHAN
78 5th Ave (11217-4647)
PHONE.....................347 699-3259
Meghan Daly, *Owner*
EMP: 10
SALES (est): 283.4K **Privately Held**
SIC: 2051 Bakery: wholesale or wholesale/retail combined

(G-1721)
DAMASCUS BAKERY INC (PA)
56 Gold St (11201-1297)
PHONE.....................718 855-1456
Edward Mafoud, *President*
David Mafoud, *Exec VP*
Tim Rizk, *Controller*
Wanda Hightower, *Human Res Mgr*
Edwin Turner, *Supervisor*
EMP: 91 EST: 1930
SQ FT: 20,000
SALES (est): 23.4MM **Privately Held**
WEB: www.damascusbakery.com
SIC: 2051 5149 Bakery: wholesale or wholesale/retail combined; bakery products

(G-1722)
DANET INC
Also Called: Russian Bazaar
8518 17th Ave Fl 2 (11214-2810)
PHONE.....................718 266-4444
Nathasha Shapiro, *President*
Anatoli Shapiro, *Vice Pres*
Margarita Shapiro, *Director*
EMP: 12
SALES (est): 490K **Privately Held**
WEB: www.danet.com
SIC: 2711 7319 Newspapers: publishing only, not printed on site; transit advertising services

(G-1723)
DANIEL O REICH INCORPORATED
Also Called: Reich Paper
7518 3rd Ave (11209-3104)
PHONE.....................718 748-6000
Dan Reich, *CEO*
Duke Reich, *President*
▲ EMP: 10
SQ FT: 4,800
SALES (est): 2.1MM **Privately Held**
WEB: www.oliveart.com
SIC: 2621 Paper mills

(G-1724)
DANIELS BATH & BEYOND
57 49th St (11232-4229)
PHONE.....................718 765-1915
EMP: 6
SALES (est): 403.6K **Privately Held**
SIC: 2391 2273 2392 Curtains & draperies; draperies, plastic & textile: from purchased materials; mats & matting; shower curtains: made from purchased materials

(G-1725)
DAPPER DADS INC
45 Rochester Ave (11233-3011)
PHONE.....................917 903-8045
Mario Daniels, *President*
Geayse Williams, *Vice Pres*
EMP: 5
SALES (est): 204.3K **Privately Held**
SIC: 2741 7389 Miscellaneous publishing;

(G-1726)
DAS YIDISHE LICHT INC
66 Middleton St Apt 1 (11206-5088)
PHONE.....................718 387-3166
Mike Kraus, *President*
EMP: 5
SQ FT: 1,500
SALES (est): 290K **Privately Held**
SIC: 2711 Newspapers: publishing only, not printed on site

(G-1727)
DAVEL SYSTEMS INC
1314 Avenue M (11230-5206)
PHONE.....................718 382-6024
David Liberman, *President*
EMP: 6
SALES (est): 477.1K **Privately Held**
SIC: 7372 Prepackaged software

(G-1728)
DAVES CBD LLC
28 Locust St Apt 202 (11206-4550)
PHONE.....................917 833-7306
Patrick Hannon,
EMP: 5 EST: 2017
SALES (est): 159.4K **Privately Held**
SIC: 3999

(G-1729)
DAWNEX INDUSTRIES INC
861 Park Ave (11206-7300)
PHONE.....................718 384-0199
Fax: 718 709-1331
EMP: 10
SALES (est): 600K **Privately Held**
SIC: 3089 Mfg Plastic Products

(G-1730)
DBG MEDIA
358 Classon Ave (11238-1306)
PHONE.....................718 599-6828
David Greaves, *Owner*
EMP: 8

SQ FT: 900
SALES (est): 230K **Privately Held**
WEB: www.ourtimepress.com
SIC: 2711 Newspapers: publishing only, not printed on site

(G-1731)
DE ANS PORK PRODUCTS INC (PA)
899 4th Ave (11232-2150)
PHONE.....................718 788-2464
Frank De Angelis, *President*
Anthony Gaglia, *Vice Pres*
Guy De Angelis, *Treasurer*
EMP: 25
SQ FT: 13,000
SALES (est): 2.8MM **Privately Held**
SIC: 2013 Sausages from purchased meat

(G-1732)
DEAN TRADING CORP
200 Junius St (11212-8103)
PHONE.....................718 485-0600
Robert Clemente, *Ch of Bd*
EMP: 18 EST: 1966
SQ FT: 20,000
SALES (est): 6.1MM **Privately Held**
SIC: 2299 Textile mill waste & remnant processing

(G-1733)
DELLET INDUSTRIES INC
1 43rd St Ste L8 (11232-2621)
PHONE.....................718 965-0101
Mike Brown, *Regional Mgr*
EMP: 16
SALES (est): 1.5MM **Privately Held**
SIC: 2599 Furniture & fixtures

(G-1734)
DELLS CHERRIES LLC
Also Called: Dell's Maraschino Cherries Co
175 Dikeman St Ste 177 (11231-1199)
PHONE.....................718 624-4380
Dana Bentz, *President*
Tom Bentz, *Vice Pres*
Ann Mondella, *Vice Pres*
Dominique Mondella, *Vice Pres*
EMP: 30 EST: 2016
SQ FT: 30,000
SALES (est): 942.1K **Privately Held**
SIC: 2033 Maraschino cherries: packaged in cans, jars, etc.

(G-1735)
DELLS CHERRIES LLC
81 Ferris St (11231-1105)
PHONE.....................718 624-4380
Dana Bentz, *President*
EMP: 30
SQ FT: 17,540
SALES (est): 2.2MM **Privately Held**
WEB: www.dellscherry.com
SIC: 2033 Maraschino cherries: packaged in cans, jars, etc.

(G-1736)
DELUXE TRAVEL STORE INC
Also Called: Deluxe Passport Express
5014 12th Ave (11219-3407)
PHONE.....................718 435-8111
Yitzchok Isaac Stern, *CEO*
EMP: 5
SALES (est): 282.8K **Privately Held**
SIC: 3161 3199 5099 Luggage; corners, luggage: leather; luggage

(G-1737)
DER YID INC
Also Called: Der Yid Publication
84 Bay St (11231)
P.O. Box 110556 (11211-0556)
PHONE.....................718 797-3900
Moses Freidman, *Owner*
Aron Friedman, *Editor*
EMP: 35
SQ FT: 2,900
SALES: 1.7MM **Privately Held**
SIC: 2731 Book publishing

(G-1738)
DESIGNS BY ROBERT SCOTT INC
Also Called: Closet Systems Group, The
810 Humboldt St Ste 3 (11222-1913)
PHONE..................718 609-2535
Robert S Feingold, *President*
Jason Kesselman, *Vice Pres*
EMP: 20
SQ FT: 16,000
SALES: 1.8MM **Privately Held**
WEB: www.robertscottinc.com
SIC: 2511 2521 2499 Wood household
furniture; wood office furniture; kitchen,
bathroom & household ware: wood

(G-1739)
DIANA KANE INCORPORATED
229 5th Ave Ste B (11215-7708)
PHONE..................718 638-6520
Diana Kane, *President*
EMP: 5
SQ FT: 600
SALES: 500K **Privately Held**
WEB: www.dianakane.com
SIC: 3911 5094 Jewelry, precious metal;
jewelry

(G-1740)
DIANE STUDIOS INC (PA)
34 35th St Ste 2b (11232-2212)
PHONE..................718 788-6007
Martin Kurant, *President*
▲ EMP: 55
SQ FT: 30,000
SALES (est): 4.4MM **Privately Held**
WEB: www.dianestudios.com
SIC: 3999 Shades, lamp or candle

(G-1741)
DIB MANAGMNT INC
Also Called: Airtech Lab
251 53rd St (11220-1716)
PHONE..................718 439-8190
Rollads Dib, *President*
EMP: 10
SALES (est): 1.1MM **Privately Held**
SIC: 2869 Fuels

(G-1742)
DICK BAILEY SERVICE INC
Also Called: Dick Bailey Printers
25 Chapel St Ste 602 (11201-1916)
P.O. Box 23030 (11202-3030)
PHONE..................718 522-4363
Richard Bailey, *President*
William Bailey, *Vice Pres*
Lynne Bailey, *Consultant*
EMP: 14
SALES (est): 2MM **Privately Held**
SIC: 2752 8111 Commercial printing, off-
set; legal services

(G-1743)
DIGIORANGE INC
Also Called: Shhhmouse
5620 1st Ave Ste 4 (11220-2519)
PHONE..................718 801-8244
▲ EMP: 8
SALES (est): 245.2K **Privately Held**
SIC: 3577 Computer peripheral equipment

(G-1744)
DIGITAC INC (PA)
2076 Ocean Pkwy (11223-4045)
PHONE..................732 215-4020
Jacob Elmann, *Ch of Bd*
▲ EMP: 15
SQ FT: 80,000
SALES (est): 2.5MM **Privately Held**
SIC: 3651 3089 3827 Video camera-
audio recorders, household use; plastic
kitchenware, tableware & houseware;
spyglasses

(G-1745)
DIGITAC LLC
Also Called: Ultratab
2076 Ocean Pkwy 2 (11223-4045)
PHONE..................732 669-7637
Jacob Elmann, *Principal*
EMP: 8 EST: 2012

SALES (est): 402.5K **Privately Held**
SIC: 3651 3571 5064 Video camera-
audio recorders, household use; personal
computers (microcomputers); video camera-audio recorders (camcorders)

(G-1746)
DIJIFI LLC
1166 Manhattan Ave # 100 (11222-1036)
PHONE..................646 519-2447
Jesse Crowder,
EMP: 11
SALES (est): 1.1MM **Privately Held**
SIC: 2754 Photogravure printing

(G-1747)
DIME TRADING INC
787 Kent Ave (11205-1517)
PHONE..................718 797-0303
Isamar Margareten, *President*
▲ EMP: 8
SALES (est): 1.5MM **Privately Held**
WEB: www.dimetrading.com
SIC: 2789 Trade binding services

(G-1748)
DINETTE DEPOT LTD
Also Called: Dining Furniture
350 Dewitt Ave (11207-6618)
P.O. Box 696, Bay Shore (11706-0845)
PHONE..................516 515-9623
Walter Lustig, *Partner*
Barry Lustig, *Partner*
▲ EMP: 75 EST: 1919
SQ FT: 60,000
SALES (est): 8.9MM **Privately Held**
SIC: 2511 Kitchen & dining room furniture

(G-1749)
DISPLAY PRESENTATIONS LTD
16 Court St Fl 14 (11241-1014)
PHONE..................631 951-4050
Stanley Zaneski, *Ch of Bd*
Fabian Zaneski, *President*
Stan Zaneski, *Vice Pres*
EMP: 52
SQ FT: 56,000
SALES (est): 6.1MM **Privately Held**
WEB: www.displaypresentations.net
SIC: 3993 Displays & cutouts, window &
lobby

(G-1750)
DIXIE FOAM LTD
Also Called: Dixiefoam Beds
1205 Manhattan Ave # 311 (11222-6155)
PHONE..................212 645-8999
MD Taracido-Bram, *President*
Roger Wade, *Sales Dir*
EMP: 5 EST: 1971
SQ FT: 2,000
SALES: 600K **Privately Held**
WEB: www.dixiefoam.com
SIC: 2515 Mattresses & bedsprings

(G-1751)
DKN READY MIX LLC
362 Maspeth Ave (11211-1704)
PHONE..................718 218-6418
Diane Macchio, *Owner*
EMP: 6
SALES (est): 884K **Privately Held**
SIC: 3271 Concrete block & brick

(G-1752)
DLC COMPREHENSIVE MEDICAL PC
979 Fulton St (11238-2346)
P.O. Box 216, Old Westbury (11568-0216)
PHONE..................718 857-1200
Katie Cheng, *Manager*
EMP: 10 EST: 1997
SALES (est): 692K **Privately Held**
SIC: 2741 5961 Miscellaneous publishing;
magazines, mail order

(G-1753)
DLX INDUSTRIES INC
Also Called: Columbia Seal N Sew
225 25th St (11232-1337)
PHONE..................718 272-9420
Martin Prince, *President*
Marc Stewart, *Vice Pres*
▲ EMP: 100 EST: 1950
SQ FT: 70,000

SALES (est): 12MM **Privately Held**
SIC: 3161 Attache cases; briefcases;
cases, carrying

(G-1754)
DOLCE VITE INTERNATIONAL LLC
386 12th St (11215-5002)
PHONE..................713 962-5767
Christina Summers, *Mng Member*
EMP: 5 EST: 2015
SALES (est): 227.9K **Privately Held**
SIC: 2066 Chocolate

(G-1755)
DOMANI FASHIONS CORP
86 S 1st St (11249-4171)
PHONE..................718 797-0505
Moses Rosenberg, *President*
Benjamin Schlesinger, *Vice Pres*
◆ EMP: 9
SQ FT: 3,000
SALES (est): 989K **Privately Held**
SIC: 2369 2253 Girls' & children's outer-
wear; sweaters & sweater coats, knit

(G-1756)
DOMESTIC CASING CO
410 3rd Ave (11215-3179)
PHONE..................718 522-1902
Morris Klagsbald, *Partner*
Harold Klagsbald, *Partner*
▲ EMP: 6 EST: 1956
SQ FT: 12,000
SALES (est): 1.9MM **Privately Held**
SIC: 2013 2011 Sausage casings, natural;
meat packing plants

(G-1757)
DONNE DIEU PAPER MILL INC
Also Called: Dieu Donne
63 Flushing Ave Unit 112 (11205-1069)
PHONE..................212 226-0573
Paul Wong, *Treasurer*
Bridget Donlon, *Program Mgr*
Kathleen Flynn, *Exec Dir*
John Shorb, *Exec Dir*
Dona Warner, *Director*
EMP: 7
SQ FT: 8,000
SALES: 688.8K **Privately Held**
WEB: www.dieudonne.org
SIC: 2621 8999 7999 Art paper; artist's
studio; arts & crafts instruction

(G-1758)
DOORTEC ARCHTCTURAL MET GL LLC
234 46th St (11220-1008)
PHONE..................718 567-2730
Boris Barskiy,
EMP: 27
SALES (corp-wide): 4.8MM **Privately Held**
SIC: 3444 Sheet metalwork
PA: Doortec Architectural Metal & Glass,
L.L.C.
303 Martin St
River Vale NJ 07675
201 497-5056

(G-1759)
DR JACOBS NATURALS LLC
2615 Coney Island Ave 2nd (11223-5501)
PHONE..................718 265-1522
Joe Aini, *Mng Member*
Joseph Abadi, *Associate*
EMP: 24
SALES (est): 263.5K **Privately Held**
SIC: 2841 Soap & other detergents

(G-1760)
DREAM STATUARY INC
Also Called: Original Dream Statuary
251 Cleveland St (11208-1004)
PHONE..................718 647-2024
Kumar Budhu, *President*
EMP: 6
SALES: 100K **Privately Held**
SIC: 3299 Statuary: gypsum, clay, papier
mache, metal, etc.; art goods: plaster of
paris, papier mache & scagliola

(G-1761)
DREAMS TO PRINT
Also Called: Hard Ten
10101 Foster Ave (11236-2107)
PHONE..................718 483-8020
Michael Azafrani, *Owner*
EMP: 1
SALES (est): 3MM **Privately Held**
SIC: 2731 Book clubs: publishing & print-
ing

(G-1762)
DRESSER-ARGUS INC
36 Bridge St (11201-1170)
PHONE..................718 643-1540
Warren Frank, *Ch of Bd*
Bonita Wetmore, *Admin Sec*
▲ EMP: 5
SQ FT: 6,000
SALES (est): 938.9K **Privately Held**
SIC: 3728 3423 Military aircraft equipment
& armament; hand & edge tools

(G-1763)
DRNS CORP
Also Called: Carousel ADS
140 58th St Ste 3f (11220-2561)
PHONE..................718 369-4530
Mark Nacson, *CEO*
Stephen S Franco, *President*
Stephen Franco, *Finance*
▲ EMP: 35
SQ FT: 19,500
SALES: 6MM **Privately Held**
WEB: www.directpromos.com
SIC: 2759 7389 Screen printing; embroi-
dering of advertising on shirts, etc.

(G-1764)
DURALL DOLLY LLC
48 Spencer St (11205-1737)
PHONE..................802 728-7121
EMP: 15 EST: 1981
SQ FT: 14,000
SALES (est): 990K **Privately Held**
SIC: 2599 Mfg Harwood Dollies

(G-1765)
DWECK INDUSTRIES INC (PA)
Also Called: Stephen Dweck Industries
2455 Mcdonald Ave Fl 2 (11223-5232)
P.O. Box 350520 (11235-0520)
PHONE..................718 615-1695
Edmond Dweck, *President*
Gregory Dweck, *Corp Secy*
Stephen Dweck, *Vice Pres*
EMP: 2
SQ FT: 8,000
SALES (est): 3MM **Privately Held**
WEB: www.stephendweck.com
SIC: 3911 Pearl jewelry, natural or cultured

(G-1766)
DWECK INDUSTRIES INC
2247 E 16th St Fl 2 (11229)
PHONE..................718 615-1695
Edmond Dweck, *Branch Mgr*
EMP: 36
SALES (corp-wide): 3MM **Privately Held**
WEB: www.stephendweck.com
SIC: 3915 Lapidary work, contract or other
PA: Dweck Industries, Inc.
2455 Mcdonald Ave Fl 2
Brooklyn NY 11223
718 615-1695

(G-1767)
DYNAMIC HEALTH LABS INC
Also Called: Pet Authority
110 Bridge St Ste 2 (11201-1575)
PHONE..................718 858-0100
Bruce Burwick, *President*
▲ EMP: 33
SQ FT: 24,000
SALES (est): 10.5MM **Privately Held**
SIC: 2037 Fruit juices

(G-1768)
DYNAMIC PACKAGING INC
1567 39th St (11218-4424)
PHONE..................718 388-0800
Stanley Freund, *Ch of Bd*
EMP: 10
SQ FT: 10,000

GEOGRAPHIC

SALES (est): 1.1MM **Privately Held**
WEB: www.dynamicpackaging.net
SIC: 2759 5113 Bags, plastic: printing;
bags, paper & disposable plastic

(G-1769)
DYNATABS LLC
Also Called: Www.dynatabs.com
1600 Ocean Pkwy Apt 1f (11230-7037)
PHONE.................................718 376-6084
Harold Baum, *Managing Dir*
Setty Baum, *CFO*
EMP: 11
SQ FT: 3,900
SALES (est): 1.3MM **Privately Held**
WEB: www.dynatabs.com
SIC: 2023 Dietary supplements, dairy &
non-dairy based

(G-1770)
E & F HOME FASHIONS INC (PA)
2154 E 71st St (11234-6225)
PHONE.................................718 968-9719
Elaine Roth, *President*
Fred Roth, *Corp Secy*
▲ **EMP:** 6
SALES (est): 456.5K **Privately Held**
SIC: 2392 5023 Tablecloths & table set-
tings; shower curtains: made from pur-
chased materials; linens & towels

(G-1771)
**E G M RESTAURANT
EQUIPMENT MFG**
688 Flushing Ave (11206-5025)
PHONE.................................718 782-9800
Scott Michaels, *President*
EMP: 7 **EST:** 1971
SQ FT: 2,500
SALES (est): 640K **Privately Held**
SIC: 3444 Restaurant sheet metalwork

(G-1772)
E GRAPHICS CORPORATION
160 Havemeyer St (11211-8772)
PHONE.................................718 486-9767
Esmeralda Lora, *President*
EMP: 5
SALES (est): 405.6K **Privately Held**
SIC: 2732 Book printing

(G-1773)
E S P METAL CRAFTS INC
379 Harman St (11237-4701)
PHONE.................................718 381-2443
Edward Grancagnolo, *President*
▲ **EMP:** 9
SALES: 1MM **Privately Held**
SIC: 3446 Railings, bannisters, guards,
etc.: made from metal pipe

(G-1774)
E-Z GLOBAL WHOLESALE INC
925 E 14th St (11230-3648)
PHONE.................................888 769-7888
Shakhim Mamedov, *President*
EMP: 5
SALES (est): 174.3K **Privately Held**
SIC: 3999 Manufacturing industries

(G-1775)
**EAST WEST GLOBAL
SOURCING INC**
425 Neptune Ave Apt 22a (11224-4587)
PHONE.................................917 887-2286
Michael Zeidner, *CEO*
EMP: 8
SQ FT: 2,000
SALES (est): 371K **Privately Held**
SIC: 3199 Leather garments

(G-1776)
**EASTERN FEATHER & DOWN
CORP**
Also Called: Yugo Landau
1027 Metropolitan Ave (11211-2710)
PHONE.................................718 387-4100
Joseph Landau, *President*
Yehoshua Weiner, *Vice Pres*
▲ **EMP:** 8
SQ FT: 45,000
SALES: 4MM **Privately Held**
SIC: 3999 Down (feathers)

(G-1777)
**EASTERN SILVER OF BORO
PARK**
4901 16th Ave (11204-1115)
PHONE.................................718 854-5600
Bernard Gelbstein, *President*
EMP: 5
SQ FT: 4,500
SALES: 1MM **Privately Held**
SIC: 3479 Engraving jewelry silverware, or
metal

(G-1778)
**EASTERN TRADING PARTNERS
CORP**
866 Eastern Pkwy Apt 2f (11213-3510)
PHONE.................................212 202-1451
Joe Vogel, *President*
EMP: 4 **EST:** 2009
SQ FT: 1,500
SALES: 3MM **Privately Held**
SIC: 3441 Building components, structural
steel

(G-1779)
EASY AERIAL INC
63 Flushing Ave (11205-1005)
PHONE.................................646 639-4410
Ido Gur, *CEO*
Ivan Stamatovski, *Chief Engr*
Daniel Sirkis,
EMP: 5 **EST:** 2017
SALES (est): 244.7K **Privately Held**
SIC: 3721 Aircraft

(G-1780)
ECOQUALITY INC
7608 Bay Pkwy (11214-1572)
PHONE.................................718 887-7876
EMP: 7
SALES (est): 94.4K **Privately Held**
SIC: 2656 Cups, paper: made from pur-
chased material

(G-1781)
**ED NEGRON FINE
WOODWORKING**
43 Hall St Fl 5 (11205-1315)
PHONE.................................718 246-1016
Ed Negron, *President*
EMP: 8
SALES (est): 722.4K **Privately Held**
SIC: 2431 2499 Millwork; decorative wood
& woodwork

(G-1782)
EDCO SUPPLY CORPORATION
323 36th St (11232-2599)
PHONE.................................718 788-8108
Carl Freyer, *CEO*
Arlene Amuso, *Human Res Mgr*
Louisa Susman, *Sales Staff*
Lydia Fraulo,
EMP: 53 **EST:** 1955
SQ FT: 25,000
SALES (est): 9.5MM **Privately Held**
WEB: www.edcosupply.com
SIC: 3081 5113 2673 Packing materials,
plastic sheet; pressure sensitive tape;
bags: plastic, laminated & coated

(G-1783)
**EDISON POWER & LIGHT CO
INC**
204 Van Dyke St 207 (11231)
PHONE.................................718 522-0002
Leon Gross, *President*
EMP: 14
SQ FT: 36,000
SALES (est): 1.8MM **Privately Held**
SIC: 3648 5719 Lighting equipment; light-
ing fixtures

(G-1784)
**EDSAL MACHINE PRODUCTS
INC (PA)**
126 56th St (11220-2575)
PHONE.................................718 439-9163
Evangelos S Tsevdos, *Ch of Bd*
Steven Tsevdos, *President*
Dessie Tsevdos, *Admin Sec*
▲ **EMP:** 12
SQ FT: 20,000

SALES (est): 1.8MM **Privately Held**
SIC: 3599 Machine shop, jobbing & repair

(G-1785)
EFS DESIGNS LLC
610 Smith St Ste 3 (11231-2113)
PHONE.................................718 852-9511
Michael Hutchinson, *Accountant*
Udoro Suarez, *Mng Member*
EMP: 6
SQ FT: 20,000
SALES: 591K **Privately Held**
SIC: 2262 2759 Screen printing: man-
made fiber & silk broadwoven fabrics;
screen printing

(G-1786)
EGM MFG INC
688 Flushing Ave (11206-5025)
PHONE.................................718 782-9800
Scott Michaels, *Principal*
EMP: 5
SALES (est): 230K **Privately Held**
SIC: 3999 Barber & beauty shop equip-
ment

(G-1787)
EKS MANUFACTURING INC
577 Wortman Ave (11208-5415)
P.O. Box 21325 (11202-1325)
PHONE.................................917 217-0784
William Socolov, *Owner*
EMP: 10
SALES (est): 1.1MM **Privately Held**
SIC: 3652 Phonograph records, prere-
corded

(G-1788)
EL DIARIO LLC
15 Metrotech Ctr Ste 7 (11201-3856)
PHONE.................................212 807-4600
Rossana Rosado, *CEO*
Luis Canarte, *Editor*
Ramon Frisneda, *Editor*
Ramon Vera, *Production*
Jeannette Belaustegui, *Sales Staff*
EMP: 122
SALES (est): 7.2MM **Privately Held**
WEB: www.eldiariony.com
SIC: 2711 Newspapers, publishing & print-
ing

(G-1789)
EL ERMAN INTERNATIONAL LTD
1205 E 29th St (11210-4630)
PHONE.................................212 444-9440
Shelley Cohen, *President*
Moshe Cohen, *Vice Pres*
David Elan, *Vice Pres*
◆ **EMP:** 3
SALES: 2MM
SALES (corp-wide): 61.4MM **Privately
Held**
SIC: 2844 5122 Face creams or lotions;
hair preparations
PA: E.L. Erman Cosmetic Production Ltd
3 Haplada
Ashdod 77524
885 325-37

(G-1790)
**ELECTRIC MOTORS AND
PUMPS INC**
466 Carroll St (11215-1012)
PHONE.................................718 935-9118
Jorge Fraticelli, *President*
Maria Fraticelli, *Vice Pres*
EMP: 7
SQ FT: 4,500
SALES (est): 790K **Privately Held**
SIC: 3469 5999 5084 Machine parts,
stamped or pressed metal; engine &
motor equipment & supplies; motors,
electric; plumbing & heating supplies;
pumps & pumping equipment

(G-1791)
ELECTRONIC DIE CORP
19th St Fl 2 Flr 2 (11232)
PHONE.................................718 455-3200
Joseph Assenza, *President*
Michael Reiss, *Principal*
Alfred Torez, *Treasurer*
EMP: 10
SQ FT: 10,000

SALES (est): 1.2MM **Privately Held**
WEB: www.electronicdiecorp.com
SIC: 3544 Special dies & tools

(G-1792)
**ELEGANT DESSERTS BY
METRO INC**
868 Kent Ave (11205-2702)
PHONE.................................718 388-1323
Martin Weisz, *President*
Benjamin Weisz, *Principal*
EMP: 12
SQ FT: 7,500
SALES: 830K **Privately Held**
SIC: 2024 Ices, flavored (frozen dessert)

(G-1793)
ELEGANT LINEN INC
200 60th St (11220-3712)
PHONE.................................718 492-0297
Benjamin Barber, *President*
Richard Citron, *Vice Pres*
▲ **EMP:** 30
SQ FT: 4,000
SALES (est): 3.3MM **Privately Held**
WEB: www.elegantlinen.com
SIC: 2392 Sheets, fabric: made from pur-
chased materials

(G-1794)
ELEMENT ST JOHNS CORP
764 Saint Johns Pl (11216-4694)
PHONE.................................917 349-2139
Michelle Abreu, *Principal*
EMP: 9 **EST:** 2015
SALES (est): 1.1MM **Privately Held**
SIC: 2819 Industrial inorganic chemicals

(G-1795)
ELEPATH INC
110 Kent Ave 9 (11249-2812)
PHONE.................................347 417-4975
Bryan Goldberg, *CFO*
EMP: 5
SALES (est): 333.2K **Privately Held**
SIC: 7372 Application computer software

(G-1796)
**ELEPHANTS CUSTOM
FURNITURE INC**
67 Van Dam St (11222-3806)
PHONE.................................917 509-3581
Gokhan Doguer, *President*
EMP: 51
SQ FT: 10,000
SALES (est): 8.3MM **Privately Held**
SIC: 2499 Decorative wood & woodwork

(G-1797)
ELRAMIDA HOLDINGS INC
2555 E 29th St (11235-2020)
PHONE.................................646 280-0503
Mark Harris, *CEO*
Eldar Rakhamineov, *Ch of Bd*
EMP: 22
SALES (est): 4.5MM **Privately Held**
SIC: 3537 Trucks, tractors, loaders, carri-
ers & similar equipment

(G-1798)
EMERALD HOLDINGS INC
Also Called: Emerald Knitting
63 Flushing Ave Unit 201 (11205-1072)
PHONE.................................718 797-4404
Michael Engle, *President*
Arnold Shulman, *Vice Pres*
▲ **EMP:** 5
SALES (est): 611.6K **Privately Held**
SIC: 2339 2253 Women's & misses' outer-
wear; knit outerwear mills

(G-1799)
EMES MOTOR INC
876 Metropolitan Ave (11211-2515)
PHONE.................................718 387-2445
Abraham Mertz, *President*
EMP: 5
SALES: 600K **Privately Held**
SIC: 3621 5999 Motors & generators; mo-
tors, electric

(G-1800)
EMILIA INTERIORS INC (PA)
867 E 52nd St (11203-6701)
PHONE.................................718 629-4202

Nicholas Vignapiano, *President*
Jennie Vignapiano, *Corp Secy*
EMP: 19
SQ FT: 20,000
SALES (est): 1.5MM **Privately Held**
WEB: www.girardemilia.com
SIC: 2511 Wood household furniture

(G-1801)
EMPIRE PRESS CO (PA)
550 Empire Blvd (11225-3131)
PHONE..................................718 756-9500
Mordechai Chein, *Owner*
Joe Katz, *Office Mgr*
EMP: 5
SQ FT: 6,000
SALES (est): 513.4K **Privately Held**
WEB: www.empirepress.com
SIC: 2791 2752 Typesetting; commercial
printing, offset

(G-1802)
EMPIRE TRANSIT MIX INC
430 Maspeth Ave (11211-1704)
PHONE..................................718 384-3000
Rocco Tomassetti, *Ch of Bd*
EMP: 40
SALES (est): 7.9MM **Privately Held**
SIC: 3273 Ready-mixed concrete

(G-1803)
EMUNAS SALES INC
947 E 27th St (11210-3727)
PHONE..................................718 621-3138
Usher Orzel, *President*
EMP: 16
SQ FT: 3,000
SALES (est): 422.2K **Privately Held**
SIC: 2323 Men's & boys' neckwear

(G-1804)
ENERGY AHEAD INC
693 E 2nd St (11218-5654)
PHONE..................................718 813-7338
Jehuda Klein, *Administration*
EMP: 9
SALES: 450K **Privately Held**
SIC: 3999 Manufacturing industries

(G-1805)
ENERGY CONSERVATION & SUP INC
Also Called: Ecs Global Solutions
55 Washington St Ste 324 (11201-1070)
PHONE..................................718 855-5888
Luther Garcia, *CEO*
Ricky Dweck, *Vice Pres*
Jim Crespo, *Project Mgr*
Elliot Levy, *Project Mgr*
Dina Depalma, *Accounts Mgr*
EMP: 35
SQ FT: 2,200
SALES (est): 18.3MM **Privately Held**
WEB: www.enerconsupply.com
SIC: 3646 Commercial indusl & institu-
tional electric lighting fixtures

(G-1806)
ENTERPRISE WOOD PRODUCTS INC
4710 18th Ave (11204-1260)
PHONE..................................718 853-9243
Jan Koegel, *President*
Leonard Rosenberg, *Treasurer*
EMP: 11
SQ FT: 7,500
SALES (est): 1.3MM **Privately Held**
SIC: 2434 Wood kitchen cabinets

(G-1807)
ENZO MANZONI LLC
2896 W 12th St (11224-2907)
PHONE..................................212 464-7000
Gene Isaac, *Director*
EMP: 5
SQ FT: 5,000
SALES (est): 400K **Privately Held**
SIC: 2326 5136 Work apparel, except uni-
forms; men's & boys' clothing; men's &
boys' sportswear & work clothing

(G-1808)
EPNER TECHNOLOGY INCORPORATED (PA)
25 Division Pl (11222-5204)
PHONE..................................718 782-5948
David Epner, *President*
Paul J Brancato, *General Mgr*
Stephen V Candiloro, *Corp Secy*
Steven A Candiloro Sr, *Vice Pres*
Heather Michella, *Manager*
▼ **EMP:** 40
SQ FT: 40,000
SALES (est): 6.2MM **Privately Held**
WEB: www.epner.com
SIC: 3471 Electroplating of metals or
formed products

(G-1809)
EPNER TECHNOLOGY INCORPORATED
78 Kingsland Ave (11222-5603)
PHONE..................................718 782-8722
David Epner, *Marketing Staff*
Stephen V Candiloro, *Systems Mgr*
EMP: 35
SALES (est): 2.2MM
SALES (corp-wide): 6.2MM **Privately
Held**
WEB: www.epner.com
SIC: 3471 Plating & polishing
PA: Epner Technology Incorporated
25 Division Pl
Brooklyn NY 11222
718 782-5948

(G-1810)
ERCOLE NYC INC (PA)
142 26th St (11232)
PHONE..................................212 675-2218
Ornella Pisano, *President*
▲ **EMP:** 18
SQ FT: 15,000
SALES (est): 1.6MM **Privately Held**
WEB: www.ercolehome.com
SIC: 3253 2511 Ceramic wall & floor tile;
tables, household: wood

(G-1811)
ESER REALTY CORP (PA)
62 Greenpoint Ave 64 (11222-2057)
PHONE..................................718 383-0565
Robert Frenkel, *Ch of Bd*
Morton Frenkel, *President*
◆ **EMP:** 50
SQ FT: 30,000
SALES (est): 5.4MM **Privately Held**
SIC: 3999 Feathers, renovating

(G-1812)
ESKAYEL INC
75 S 6th St (11249-6027)
PHONE..................................347 703-8084
Shannan Campanaro, *Principal*
EMP: 5
SALES (est): 411.9K **Privately Held**
SIC: 2299 2273 2679 8999 Broadwoven
fabrics: linen, jute, hemp & ramie; dyeing
& finishing of tufted rugs & carpets; wall-
paper; artist's studio

(G-1813)
ESQUIRE MECHANICAL CORP
79 Sandford St (11205)
PHONE..................................718 625-4006
EMP: 7
SQ FT: 5,000
SALES (est): 1.2MM **Privately Held**
SIC: 3556 Mfg Rotisseries

(G-1814)
ESS BEE INDUSTRIES INC
95 Evergreen Ave (11206-6124)
PHONE..................................718 894-5202
EMP: 30
SQ FT: 40,000
SALES (est): 2.3MM **Privately Held**
SIC: 2221 2392 5023 Manmade Broad-
woven Fabric Mill Mfg Household Fur-
nishings Whol Homefurnishings

(G-1815)
ESSENCE COMMUNICATIONS INC (PA)
Also Called: Essence Magazine
241 37th St Fl 1 (11232-2410)
PHONE..................................212 522-1212
Michelle Ebanks, *CEO*
Christian Juhl, *CEO*
Kyoko Matsushita, *CEO*
Barbara Britton, *President*
Clarence O Smith, *President*
▲ **EMP:** 119
SQ FT: 30,000
SALES (est): 30.6MM **Privately Held**
SIC: 2721 Magazines: publishing only, not
printed on site

(G-1816)
ESSEX WORKS LTD
446 Riverdale Ave (11207-6121)
PHONE..................................718 495-4575
Douglas Schickler, *President*
EMP: 19 **EST:** 1995
SQ FT: 3,000
SALES (est): 1.8MM **Privately Held**
WEB: www.essexworks.com
SIC: 3299 Architectural sculptures: gyp-
sum, clay, papier mache, etc.

(G-1817)
EURO WOODWORKING INC
303 Park Ave Fl 8 (11205-1307)
PHONE..................................718 246-9172
Wolfgang Michelitsch, *President*
EMP: 6
SALES (est): 611.9K **Privately Held**
SIC: 2434 Wood kitchen cabinets

(G-1818)
EVER-NU-METAL PRODUCTS INC
471 20th St (11215-6294)
P.O. Box 150572 (11215-0572)
PHONE..................................646 423-5833
Frank Gagliardi Jr, *President*
John Gagliardi, *General Mgr*
Rocco Gagliardi, *Corp Secy*
▲ **EMP:** 12
SQ FT: 14,000
SALES (est): 1.3MM **Privately Held**
WEB: www.evernumetal.com
SIC: 3471 Finishing, metals or formed
products

(G-1819)
EXCELLENT PHOTO COPIES (PA)
165 Hooper St (11211-7911)
PHONE..................................718 384-7272
Garbor Rubin, *President*
Joseph Weinberger, *Vice Pres*
EMP: 7
SQ FT: 600
SALES: 500K **Privately Held**
SIC: 2752 7334 Commercial printing, off-
set; photocopying & duplicating services

(G-1820)
EXCELLENT POLY INC
820 4th Ave (11232-1612)
PHONE..................................718 768-6555
Joshua Silber, *CEO*
Isaac Stern, *President*
Harry Weingarten, *Exec VP*
EMP: 15 **EST:** 1959
SQ FT: 55,000
SALES (est): 3.7MM **Privately Held**
WEB: www.excellentpoly.com
SIC: 2673 3081 Plastic bags: made from
purchased materials; unsupported plas-
tics film & sheet

(G-1821)
EXCELLENT PRINTING INC
Also Called: Excellent Photocopies
165 Hooper St (11211-7911)
PHONE..................................718 384-7272
Gubor Rubin, *President*
Joseph Weinburger, *Vice Pres*
EMP: 6
SALES (est): 486.3K **Privately Held**
WEB: www.yeshivanet.com
SIC: 2752 Commercial printing, litho-
graphic

(G-1822)
EXECUTIVE MACHINES INC
Also Called: Jeam Imports
882 3rd Ave Unit 8 (11232-1902)
P.O. Box 320150 (11232-0150)
PHONE..................................718 965-6600
Aron Abramson, *CEO*
Charles Sued, *President*
▲ **EMP:** 30
SQ FT: 20,000
SALES (est): 20K **Privately Held**
WEB: www.executivemachines.com
SIC: 3678 Electronic connectors

(G-1823)
EXPERT INDUSTRIES INC
848 E 43rd St (11210-3502)
PHONE..................................718 434-6060
Cynthia Rubinberg, *President*
Michael Rubinberg, *Vice Pres*
EMP: 25
SQ FT: 25,000
SALES (est): 4MM **Privately Held**
SIC: 3443 3556 3444 Tanks, standard or
custom fabricated: metal plate; vessels,
process or storage (from boiler shops):
metal plate; mixers, commercial, food;
sheet metalwork

(G-1824)
EY INDUSTRIES INC
Also Called: Ruckel Manufacturing Co
63 Flushing Ave Unit 331 (11205-1083)
PHONE..................................718 624-9122
Joseph Friedman, *President*
Beth Green, *Train & Dev Mgr*
EMP: 15 **EST:** 1937
SQ FT: 15,000
SALES (est): 980K **Privately Held**
WEB: www.yarmulka.com
SIC: 2392 Comforters & quilts: made from
purchased materials; pillowcases: made
from purchased materials; mattress pro-
tectors, except rubber; sheets, fabric:
made from purchased materials

(G-1825)
EZ NEWSLETTER LLC
1449 Bay Ridge Ave 2 (11219-6232)
PHONE..................................412 943-7777
Eric V Hileman, *Mng Member*
EMP: 10
SALES (est): 890K **Privately Held**
SIC: 7372 Prepackaged software

(G-1826)
EZ SYSTEMS US INC
215 Water St Gf (11201-1131)
PHONE..................................929 295-0699
Bertrand Maugain, *CEO*
Morten Ingebrigtsen, *Ch of Bd*
Eivind Hesjadalen, *CFO*
Monika Zimmermann, *Manager*
EMP: 105
SALES (est): 5MM
SALES (corp-wide): 9MM **Privately Held**
SIC: 7372 Business oriented computer
software
PA: Ez Systems As
Solligata 2
Porsgrunn 0254
355 870-20

(G-1827)
F R A M TECHNOLOGIES INC
3048 Bedford Ave (11210-3714)
PHONE..................................718 338-6230
Mordechai Plotsker, *President*
EMP: 6
SALES (est): 50.2K **Privately Held**
WEB: www.framtech.com
SIC: 7372 Prepackaged software

(G-1828)
FACTORY EAST
Also Called: Factory Nyc
723 Kent Ave (11249-7807)
PHONE..................................718 280-1558
Paul Outlaw, *Principal*
Shane Jezowski, *Project Mgr*
Jim Wines, *Project Mgr*
Nelson Cris, *Accounting Mgr*
Ryan Brennan, *Manager*
EMP: 20
SALES (est): 2.6MM **Privately Held**
SIC: 3542 Sheet metalworking machines

(G-1829)
FAIRVIEW BELL AND INTERCOM
502 Gravesend Neck Rd B (11223-4800)
PHONE..............................718 627-8621
Grzegorz Butny, *President*
Florence Kachman, *Manager*
EMP: 5
SQ FT: 600
SALES (est): 200K **Privately Held**
SIC: 3699 Security devices

(G-1830)
FALCONES COOKIE LAND LTD (PA)
Also Called: Falcone Food Distribution
1648 61st St (11204)
PHONE..............................718 236-4200
Carmine Falcone Jr, *Ch of Bd*
Angelo Falcone, *President*
Francis Falcone, *Vice Pres*
Mike Falcone, *Sales Staff*
EMP: 40
SQ FT: 24,000
SALES (est): 5.4MM **Privately Held**
SIC: 2052 Cookies

(G-1831)
FAMILY FUEL CO INC
1571 W 10th St (11204-6302)
PHONE..............................718 232-2009
Carol Maiden, *Chairman*
EMP: 5
SALES (est): 359.8K **Privately Held**
SIC: 2869 Fuels

(G-1832)
FANCY WINDOWS & DOORS MFG CORP
Also Called: Fancy Window & Door
312 Ten Eyck St (11206-1723)
PHONE..............................718 366-7800
Jin Hu Ye, *Ch of Bd*
Jackson Ye, *President*
Jian Xu Chong, *Shareholder*
▲ EMP: 7
SQ FT: 4,000
SALES (est): 935.5K **Privately Held**
SIC: 2431 Doors & door parts & trim, wood; windows & window parts & trim, wood

(G-1833)
FAUCETS AND MORE INCORPORATED
5318a 16th Ave Ste 106 (11204-1425)
PHONE..............................734 328-2387
Jack Branson, *President*
EMP: 6
SALES: 7MM **Privately Held**
SIC: 3432 Faucets & spigots, metal & plastic

(G-1834)
FAVORITE PLASTIC CORP
1465 Utica Ave (11234-1108)
PHONE..............................718 253-7000
Hershey Friedman, *President*
Mitch Kirschner, *Vice Pres*
▲ EMP: 110 EST: 1956
SQ FT: 75,000
SALES (est): 16.8MM **Privately Held**
WEB: www.favoriteplastics.com
SIC: 3081 3083 Plastic film & sheet; laminated plastics plate & sheet

(G-1835)
FAYDA MANUFACTURING CORP
Also Called: Fay Da Mott St
259 Meserole St (11206-2244)
PHONE..............................718 456-9331
Han Chieh Chou, *President*
Jame Chou, *Admin Mgr*
EMP: 10
SALES (est): 1.4MM **Privately Held**
SIC: 2051 Bread, cake & related products

(G-1836)
FAYE BERNARD LOUNGEWEAR
2604 Avenue M (11210-4611)
PHONE..............................718 951-7245
Faye Zola, *Partner*
Bernard Zola, *Partner*
EMP: 8
SQ FT: 2,000
SALES (est): 600K **Privately Held**
SIC: 2341 Nightgowns & negligees: women's & children's

(G-1837)
FELDMAN JEWELRY CREATIONS INC
4821 16th Ave (11204-1109)
PHONE..............................718 438-8895
Susan Feldman, *President*
Mordecai Feldman, *Vice Pres*
EMP: 5
SQ FT: 650
SALES (est): 490K **Privately Held**
SIC: 3911 Necklaces, precious metal; rings, finger: precious metal

(G-1838)
FENCE PLAZA CORP
1601 Nostrand Ave (11226-5101)
PHONE..............................718 469-2200
George Prince, *President*
EMP: 6
SQ FT: 300
SALES (est): 1.1MM **Privately Held**
WEB: www.fenceplaza.com
SIC: 3446 1799 5211 3441 Fences or posts, ornamental iron or steel; fence construction; fencing; fabricated structural metal

(G-1839)
FERRO FABRICATORS INC
1117 38th St (11218-1926)
PHONE..............................718 703-0007
Gregory Dec, *President*
EMP: 13 EST: 2003
SQ FT: 10,000
SALES (est): 2.4MM **Privately Held**
SIC: 3449 Bars, concrete reinforcing: fabricated steel

(G-1840)
FIBERWAVE CORPORATION
140 58th St Ste 37 (11220-2524)
PHONE..............................718 802-9011
John Romeo, *President*
Ed Kirchgessner, *CFO*
▲ EMP: 200
SALES (est): 31.8MM **Privately Held**
WEB: www.fiberwave.com
SIC: 3661 Fiber optics communications equipment

(G-1841)
FIELD WARES LLC
Also Called: Field Company
53 Bridge St Apt 410 (11201-7901)
PHONE..............................508 380-6545
Stephen Muscarella, *Mng Member*
Chris Muscarella,
EMP: 6
SQ FT: 1,000
SALES (est): 2MM **Privately Held**
SIC: 3321 Cooking utensils, cast iron

(G-1842)
FIL DOUX INC
227 5th Ave (11215-1202)
PHONE..............................212 202-1459
Leonardo Novik, *Ch of Bd*
Robert Pullen, *Human Res Mgr*
EMP: 10
SALES: 3MM **Privately Held**
SIC: 2299 Broadwoven fabrics: linen, jute, hemp & ramie

(G-1843)
FILTA CLEAN CO INC
Also Called: Belton Industries
107 Georgia Ave (11207-2401)
P.O. Box 70452 (11207-0452)
PHONE..............................718 495-3800
Tommy Weber, *President*
Ron Weber, *Vice Pres*
EMP: 35
SQ FT: 10,000
SALES (est): 9MM **Privately Held**
WEB: www.multidisplayandpanel.com
SIC: 3564 7349 Filters, air: furnaces, air conditioning equipment, etc.; air duct cleaning

(G-1844)
FINE AND RAW CHOCOLATE
288 Seigel St (11206-3813)
PHONE..............................718 366-3633
Daniel Sklaar, *Owner*
EMP: 5
SALES (est): 150K **Privately Held**
SIC: 2064 Candy bars, including chocolate covered bars

(G-1845)
FINELINE THERMOGRAPHERS INC
544 Park Ave Ste 308 (11205-1647)
PHONE..............................718 643-1100
Samuel Fried, *President*
Themmy Sixler, *Admin Sec*
EMP: 7
SQ FT: 7,000
SALES (est): 817.5K **Privately Held**
SIC: 2759 Thermography

(G-1846)
FINESSE CREATIONS INC
3004 Avenue J (11210-3838)
PHONE..............................718 692-2100
Esther Machlis, *President*
▲ EMP: 10
SQ FT: 2,500
SALES (est): 2.6MM **Privately Held**
WEB: www.finessecreations.com
SIC: 3599 5044 3569 Custom machinery; office equipment; baling machines, for scrap metal, paper or similar material

(G-1847)
FIRE FOX SECURITY CORP
2070 72nd St Apt B1 (11204-5823)
PHONE..............................917 981-9280
John Mansi, *President*
EMP: 5
SQ FT: 800
SALES: 250K **Privately Held**
SIC: 3699 5045 Security control equipment & systems; computers, peripherals & software

(G-1848)
FIVE BORO HOLDING LLC
1425 37th St Bsmt 3 (11218-3769)
PHONE..............................718 431-9500
Joey Cohen, *Mng Member*
EMP: 10
SQ FT: 18,000
SALES (est): 138.2K **Privately Held**
WEB: www.fiveboroughprinting.com
SIC: 2761 Computer forms, manifold or continuous

(G-1849)
FLARE MULTICOPY CORP
Also Called: Flare Multi Copy
1840 Flatbush Ave (11210-4831)
PHONE..............................718 258-8860
Steven Zeller, *President*
Sam Stempler, *Treasurer*
EMP: 22
SALES (est): 3.2MM **Privately Held**
SIC: 2752 2791 2789 2732 Commercial printing, offset; typesetting; bookbinding & related work; book printing

(G-1850)
FLATCUT LLC
68 Jay St Ste 901 (11201-8364)
PHONE..............................212 542-5732
Tomer Ben-Gal, *Principal*
Jay Schainholz, *Principal*
Deven Pravin Shah, *Marketing Staff*
EMP: 5
SALES (est): 523.8K **Privately Held**
SIC: 3498 3532 3496 Fabricated pipe & fittings; mining machinery; miscellaneous fabricated wire products

(G-1851)
FLAVOR PAPER LTD (PA)
Also Called: Flavor League
216 Pacific St (11201-5888)
PHONE..............................718 422-0230
Emily Cangie, *COO*
Walt Vayo, *VP Prdtn*
Todd Tilev, *VP Sales*
Julia Heydemann, *Director*
Jon Sherman, *Administration*
EMP: 13
SQ FT: 3,500
SALES (est): 1.2MM **Privately Held**
WEB: www.flavorleague.com
SIC: 2679 Wallpaper

(G-1852)
FLEAHEART INC
61 Greenpoint Ave Ste 403 (11222-1526)
PHONE..............................718 521-4958
Andrew Woodrum, *Ch of Bd*
EMP: 11
SALES (est): 1.3MM **Privately Held**
SIC: 2759 Commercial printing

(G-1853)
FLEETWOOD CABINET CO INC (PA)
673 Livonia Ave (11207-5407)
PHONE..............................516 379-2139
Eric Belgraier, *President*
EMP: 8 EST: 1948
SQ FT: 12,000
SALES: 1MM **Privately Held**
SIC: 2541 Cabinets, except refrigerated: show, display, etc.: wood; counters or counter display cases, wood; table or counter tops, plastic laminated; sink tops, plastic laminated

(G-1854)
FLICKINGER GLASSWORKS INC
175 Van Dyke St Ste 321ap (11231-1079)
PHONE..............................718 875-1531
Charles Flickinger, *President*
EMP: 8
SQ FT: 7,000
SALES (est): 1.1MM **Privately Held**
WEB: www.flickingerglassworks.com
SIC: 3231 5231 Glass sheet, bent: made from purchased glass; glass, leaded or stained

(G-1855)
FLUSHING BOILER & WELDING CO
8720 Ditmas Ave (11236-1606)
PHONE..............................718 463-1266
EMP: 7
SALES (est): 470K **Privately Held**
SIC: 7692 7699 5074 1799 Welding Repair Repair Services Whol Plumbing Equip/Supp Special Trade Contractor

(G-1856)
FLUSHING PHARMACY INC
414 Flushing Ave Ste 1 (11205-1548)
PHONE..............................718 260-8999
Michell Wifemen, *President*
EMP: 250
SALES (est): 326.2K **Privately Held**
SIC: 2834 5813 Druggists' preparations (pharmaceuticals); night clubs

(G-1857)
FOLENE PACKAGING LLC
2509 Avenue M (11210-4544)
P.O. Box 300965 (11230-0965)
PHONE..............................917 626-6740
Edward Weiss,
▲ EMP: 5
SALES (est): 586.6K **Privately Held**
SIC: 2671 Plastic film, coated or laminated for packaging

(G-1858)
FORD REGULATOR VALVE CORP
199 Varet St (11206-3704)
PHONE..............................718 497-3255
Joseph Tuzzolo, *President*
Paula Tuzollo, *Treasurer*
Michael Tuzzolo, *Marketing Staff*
EMP: 5 EST: 1889
SQ FT: 5,000
SALES (est): 520K **Privately Held**
WEB: www.fordregulatorvalve.com
SIC: 3494 5085 Valves & pipe fittings; industrial supplies

(G-1859)
FORO MARBLE CO INC
166 2nd Ave (11215-4619)
PHONE..............................718 852-2322

Joseph P Guido, *President*
Joseph A Guido Jr, *Exec VP*
Joan Foro, *Vice Pres*
Joan Guido, *Sales Executive*
EMP: 25 **EST:** 1965
SQ FT: 25,000
SALES (est): 4.4MM **Privately Held**
WEB: www.foromarble.net
SIC: 3272 5032 Tile, precast terrazzo or
concrete; tile, clay or other ceramic, ex-
cluding refractory

(G-1860)
FORTUNA VISUAL GROUP INC
Also Called: Fortune Sign
1334 39th St (11218-3616)
PHONE....................................646 383-8682
Anatoliy Kreychmar, *Principal*
EMP: 5 **EST:** 2011
SALES (est): 527.1K **Privately Held**
SIC: 3993 Signs & advertising specialties

(G-1861)
FOSTER REEVE & ASSOCIATES INC (PA)
1155 Manhattan Ave # 1011 (11222-6161)
PHONE....................................718 609-0090
Foster Reeve, *President*
Cathy Reilly, *CFO*
▲ **EMP:** 6
SALES (est): 5MM **Privately Held**
WEB: www.fraplaster.com
SIC: 3299 1742 Moldings, architectural:
plaster of paris; plastering, plain or orna-
mental

(G-1862)
FOUNTAIN TILE OUTLET INC
609 Fountain Ave Ste A (11208-6007)
PHONE....................................718 927-4555
Frank Lapetina, *Principal*
EMP: 6
SALES (est): 297.3K **Privately Held**
SIC: 2426 Flooring, hardwood

(G-1863)
FOUR S SHOWCASE MANUFACTURING
1044 Linwood St (11208-5422)
PHONE....................................718 649-4900
Tony Razi, *President*
Isabel Razi, *Vice Pres*
EMP: 8
SQ FT: 12,000
SALES (est): 931.7K **Privately Held**
WEB: www.4sshowcase.com
SIC: 2542 Office & store showcases & dis-
play fixtures

(G-1864)
FOX 416 CORP
Also Called: Fox's U-Bet Syrups
416 Thatford Ave (11212-5810)
PHONE....................................718 385-4600
David Fox, *Ch of Bd*
Karen Fox, *Corp Secy*
Susan Frank, *Controller*
Kelly Fox, *Executive*
EMP: 30 **EST:** 1900
SQ FT: 36,000
SALES (est): 6.7MM **Privately Held**
WEB: www.foxs-u-bet.com
SIC: 2087 2066 Syrups, flavoring (except
drink); chocolate coatings & syrup

(G-1865)
FRANKLIN POLY FILM INC
1149 56th St (11219-4504)
PHONE....................................718 492-3523
Isidore Handler, *President*
Rose Frankel, *Principal*
Israel Kahan, *Admin Sec*
▼ **EMP:** 39 **EST:** 1970
SQ FT: 26,000
SALES (est): 5.4MM **Privately Held**
SIC: 2673 3082 3081 Plastic bags: made
from purchased materials; unsupported
plastics profile shapes; unsupported plas-
tics film & sheet

(G-1866)
FRENCH & ITLN FURN CRAFTSMEN
Also Called: French Itln Furn Craftsmen Cor
999 Grand St (11211-2704)
PHONE....................................718 599-5000
Patrick F Molloy, *President*
EMP: 7
SQ FT: 6,000
SALES (est): 490K **Privately Held**
WEB: www.frenchanditalian.com
SIC: 2511 5712 Wood household furniture;
furniture stores

(G-1867)
FRESH FANATIC INC
88 Washington Ave (11205-1202)
PHONE....................................516 521-6574
Andrew Goldin, *CEO*
David Goldin, *President*
Dawa Tsering, *Technology*
EMP: 8
SALES (est): 1MM **Privately Held**
SIC: 2033 5146 5149 Fruit juices: fresh;
fish, fresh; sandwiches

(G-1868)
FRESH ICE CREAM COMPANY LLC
630 Flushing Ave 4 (11206-5026)
PHONE....................................347 603-6021
Gerard Tucci, *Manager*
EMP: 10 **Privately Held**
SIC: 2024 5143 Ice cream & frozen
desserts; ice cream & ices
PA: The Fresh Ice Cream Company Llc
278 6th St Apt 3b
Brooklyn NY 11215

(G-1869)
FRESH ICE CREAM COMPANY LLC (PA)
Also Called: Craft Collective
278 6th St Apt 3b (11215-3860)
PHONE....................................347 603-6021
Forbes Fisher, *President*
David Stein,
EMP: 20
SQ FT: 10,000
SALES (est): 4.2MM **Privately Held**
SIC: 2024 Ice cream & frozen desserts

(G-1870)
FRIENDLY STAR FUEL INC
889 3rd Ave (11232-1907)
PHONE....................................718 369-8801
Gurpal Cheema, *Principal*
EMP: 7
SALES (est): 674.4K **Privately Held**
SIC: 2869 Fuels

(G-1871)
FUTURE DIAGNOSTICS LLC
266 47th St (11220-1010)
PHONE....................................347 434-6700
Hindy Sobel, *Mng Member*
Charles Sobel, *Mng Member*
◆ **EMP:** 42
SQ FT: 20,000
SALES (est): 15MM **Privately Held**
SIC: 3841 Medical instruments & equip-
ment, blood & bone work

(G-1872)
FUTURE STAR DIGATECH
713 Monroe St (11221-2813)
PHONE....................................718 666-0350
Kertena Seabrook, *Owner*
EMP: 10
SALES (est): 760.6K **Privately Held**
SIC: 3577 Printers, computer

(G-1873)
FUZION CREATIONS INTL LLC
Also Called: Dj Expression
140 58th St Ste A (11220-2539)
PHONE....................................718 369-8800
Maney Douek, *President*
EMP: 50
SQ FT: 1,500
SALES (est): 5.2MM **Privately Held**
SIC: 3911 5094 Jewelry apparel; jewelry

(G-1874)
G S COMMUNICATIONS USA INC
Also Called: Gs Communications USA
179 Greenpoint Ave (11222-7088)
PHONE....................................718 389-7371
Helen Juszczak, *President*
David Pasirstein, *Vice Pres*
Louis Makowski, *Network Mgr*
EMP: 22
SQ FT: 11,250
SALES (est): 2MM **Privately Held**
WEB: www.gscomm.com
SIC: 3571 5734 Personal computers (mi-
crocomputers); computer & software
stores

(G-1875)
G Z G REST & KIT MET WORKS
120 13th St (11215-4604)
PHONE....................................718 788-8621
Gregory Uchatel, *President*
Alex Blyustein, *Vice Pres*
EMP: 15
SQ FT: 5,500
SALES (est): 920K **Privately Held**
SIC: 2599 Bar, restaurant & cafeteria furni-
ture; carts, restaurant equipment

(G-1876)
GAC EXPRESS INC
1310 52nd St (11219-3860)
PHONE....................................718 438-2227
EMP: 5
SALES (est): 343K **Privately Held**
SIC: 3661 Message concentrators

(G-1877)
GARCO MANUFACTURING CORP INC
4802 Farragut Rd (11203-6612)
PHONE....................................718 287-3330
EMP: 7 **EST:** 1960
SQ FT: 4,000
SALES (est): 64.5K **Privately Held**
SIC: 2851 Mfg Paints/Allied Products

(G-1878)
GARY GELBFISH MD
2502 Avenue I (11210-2830)
PHONE....................................718 258-3004
Gary Gelbfish, *Owner*
EMP: 8
SALES (est): 690K **Privately Held**
SIC: 3845 Surgical support systems: heart-
lung machine, exc. iron lung

(G-1879)
GCM METAL INDUSTRIES INC
454 Troutman St (11237-2604)
PHONE....................................718 386-4059
Baldo Ciaravino, *President*
EMP: 15
SALES (est): 1.4MM **Privately Held**
SIC: 3449 1791 5051 1799 Bars, con-
crete reinforcing: fabricated steel; struc-
tural steel erection; structural shapes, iron
or steel; ornamental metal work

(G-1880)
GCNS TECHNOLOGY GROUP INC (PA)
597 Rutland Rd (11203-1703)
PHONE....................................347 713-8160
Onyike Adjaero, *President*
EMP: 6
SALES (est): 1.3MM **Privately Held**
SIC: 3825 Network analyzers

(G-1881)
GDI CUSTOM MARBLE & GRAN INC
Also Called: Gdi
134 Avenue T (11223-3624)
PHONE....................................718 996-9100
Peter Desantis, *President*
▲ **EMP:** 10
SQ FT: 8,500
SALES (est): 1MM **Privately Held**
SIC: 3281 1743 Marble, building: cut &
shaped; granite, cut & shaped; tile instal-
lation, ceramic

(G-1882)
GENERAL VY-COAT LLC
1636 Coney Island Ave 2b (11230-5808)
PHONE....................................718 266-6002
Sol Chaimovits,
▲ **EMP:** 40
SQ FT: 80,000
SALES (est): 5.2MM **Privately Held**
SIC: 2851 3086 2821 Vinyl coatings,
strippable; plastics foam products; plas-
tics materials & resins

(G-1883)
GENIUS MEDIA GROUP INC
Also Called: Rap Genius
92 3rd St (11231-4808)
PHONE....................................509 670-7502
Thomas Lehman, *President*
EMP: 15
SALES (est): 1.4MM **Privately Held**
SIC: 2741 Miscellaneous publishing

(G-1884)
GHANI TEXTILES INC
2459 Coyle St Fl 2 (11235-1207)
PHONE....................................718 859-4561
Muhammad Aslam, *CEO*
▲ **EMP:** 1
SALES (est): 1MM **Privately Held**
SIC: 2299 Acoustic felts

(G-1885)
GHOSTEK LLC
140 58th St Ste 2g (11220-2486)
PHONE....................................855 310-3439
Vadim Mikhailov,
David Khanatayev,
EMP: 17 **EST:** 2015
SALES (est): 106.9K **Privately Held**
SIC: 3663 5731 Cellular radio telephone;
sound equipment, automotive

(G-1886)
GILLIES COFFEE COMPANY
150 19th St (11232-1005)
PHONE....................................718 499-7766
Donald N Schoenholt, *President*
Hy Chabbott, *Treasurer*
EMP: 17
SQ FT: 14,000
SALES (est): 3.3MM **Privately Held**
WEB: www.gilliescoffee.com
SIC: 2095 2099 Coffee roasting (except by
wholesale grocers); tea blending

(G-1887)
GIULIETTA LLC
649 Morgan Ave Ste 3h (11222-3765)
PHONE....................................212 334-1859
Sofia Sizzi, *Principal*
EMP: 5 **EST:** 2011
SALES (est): 489.4K **Privately Held**
SIC: 2339 Women's & misses' accessories

(G-1888)
GIUMENTA CORP (PA)
Also Called: Utility Brass & Bronze Div
42 2nd Ave (11215-3102)
PHONE....................................718 832-1200
Anthony J Giumenta, *President*
Anthony F Giumenta, *Vice Pres*
Stephen Giumenta, *Treasurer*
▼ **EMP:** 46
SQ FT: 55,000
SALES (est): 12.8MM **Privately Held**
SIC: 3446 Ornamental metalwork

(G-1889)
GIUMENTA CORP
Architectural Grille Division
42 2nd Ave (11215-3102)
PHONE....................................718 832-1200
Anthony Giumenta, *President*
EMP: 46
SALES (corp-wide): 12.8MM **Privately
Held**
SIC: 3446 Architectural metalwork
PA: Giumenta Corp.
42 2nd Ave
Brooklyn NY 11215
718 832-1200

(G-1890)
GLISSEN CHEMICAL CO INC (PA)
1321 58th St (11219-4594)
P.O. Box 190034 (11219-0034)
PHONE..................................718 436-4200
Joseph W Lehr, *President*
Barbara Lehr, *Exec VP*
EMP: 100 EST: 1930
SQ FT: 25,000
SALES (est): 15.6MM **Privately Held**
SIC: 2841 Detergents, synthetic organic or inorganic alkaline

(G-1891)
GLOBMARBLE LLC
2201 Neptune Ave Ste 5 (11224-2362)
PHONE..................................347 717-4088
Iryna Semenenko, *Mng Member*
◆ EMP: 6 EST: 2010
SALES: 316.8K **Privately Held**
SIC: 3544 5031 Industrial molds; molding, all materials

(G-1892)
GLOBUS CORK INC
141 Flushing Ave (11205-1338)
PHONE..................................347 963-4059
Jen Biscoe, *Vice Pres*
▲ EMP: 11
SALES (est): 1.5MM **Privately Held**
WEB: www.globuscork.com
SIC: 2499 Tiles, cork

(G-1893)
GMD SHIPYARD CORP (PA)
Brooklyn Navy Yard 276 (11205)
PHONE..................................718 260-9202
Alexander Gomez, *President*
EMP: 20
SALES: 15MM **Privately Held**
WEB: www.gmdshipyard.com
SIC: 3731 Shipbuilding & repairing

(G-1894)
GMS HICKS STREET CORPORATION
214 Hicks St (11201-4110)
PHONE..................................718 858-1010
Greg Markman, *Principal*
EMP: 40
SALES (est): 2.3MM **Privately Held**
SIC: 3088 Plastics plumbing fixtures

(G-1895)
GODDARD DESIGN CO
51 Nassau Ave Ste 1b (11222-3171)
PHONE..................................718 599-0170
Robert Goddard, *Owner*
Rosemary Heath, *Office Mgr*
EMP: 7
SQ FT: 2,000
SALES: 500K **Privately Held**
WEB: www.goddarddesign.com
SIC: 3648 3625 3669 Lighting equipment; control equipment, electric; intercommunication systems, electric

(G-1896)
GOLD & DIAMONDS WHOLESALE OUTL
4417 5th Ave (11220-6834)
PHONE..................................718 438-7888
Alex Gattif, *President*
EMP: 4
SALES: 2MM **Privately Held**
SIC: 3911 5094 Jewel settings & mountings, precious metal; diamonds (gems)

(G-1897)
GOLDEN CHOCOLATE INC
590 Smith St (11231-3819)
P.O. Box 88, Hewlett (11557-0088)
PHONE..................................718 330-1000
Robert Pincow, *Vice Pres*
EMP: 5
SQ FT: 7,000
SALES (est): 581.9K **Privately Held**
SIC: 2064 Candy & other confectionery products

(G-1898)
GOLDEN LEAVES KNITWEAR INC
43 Hall St Ste B3 (11205-1395)
PHONE..................................718 875-8235
Cheskel Gluck, *President*
▲ EMP: 40
SQ FT: 25,000
SALES: 2.3MM **Privately Held**
SIC: 2253 2339 Sweaters & sweater coats, knit; women's & misses' outerwear

(G-1899)
GOLDMARK INC
Also Called: Gold Mark Mfg Co
3611 14th Ave Ste B01 (11218-3750)
PHONE..................................718 438-0295
Shimson Jalas, *President*
EMP: 20
SQ FT: 20,000
SALES (est): 3.3MM **Privately Held**
WEB: www.goldmark.com
SIC: 3915 Jewelers' findings & materials

(G-1900)
GOODMAN MAIN STOPPER MFG CO
523 Atlantic Ave (11217-1913)
PHONE..................................718 875-5140
Joseph Petrone, *President*
EMP: 12 EST: 1897
SQ FT: 10,000
SALES (est): 159.6K **Privately Held**
SIC: 3494 5999 Valves & pipe fittings; medical apparatus & supplies

(G-1901)
GOTENNA INC
81 Willoughby St Fl 4 (11201-5232)
PHONE..................................718 360-4988
Daniela Perdomo, *President*
John Levy, *Principal*
Russ Dauer, *COO*
Jim Schueren, *Vice Pres*
Mike Nolfi, *Mfg Staff*
EMP: 13
SALES (est): 1.8MM **Privately Held**
SIC: 3679 Headphones, radio

(G-1902)
GOURMET CRAFTS INC
152 Highlawn Ave (11223-2636)
P.O. Box 200006 (11220-0006)
PHONE..................................718 372-0505
Borris Tulman, *President*
Eugene Tulman, *Vice Pres*
Eric Shkolnik, *CFO*
EMP: 16
SQ FT: 4,000
SALES: 925K **Privately Held**
WEB: www.thecrepeteam.com
SIC: 2099 Food preparations

(G-1903)
GOURMET TOAST CORP
345 Park Ave (11205-1389)
PHONE..................................718 852-4536
Jack Feld, *President*
EMP: 8 EST: 1958
SQ FT: 8,000
SALES: 600K **Privately Held**
SIC: 2099 2051 Bread crumbs, not made in bakeries; bread, cake & related products

(G-1904)
GOVERNMENT DATA PUBLICATION
1661 Mcdonald Ave (11230-6312)
PHONE..................................347 789-8719
Siegfried Lobel, *President*
EMP: 35
SQ FT: 10,000
SALES (est): 3MM **Privately Held**
WEB: www.govdata.com
SIC: 2731 2741 2721 2752 Books: publishing only; miscellaneous publishing; directories: publishing only, not printed on site; periodicals: publishing only; commercial printing, lithographic

(G-1905)
GRADO LABORATORIES INC
4614 7th Ave Ste 1 (11220-1499)
PHONE..................................718 435-5340

John A Grado, *President*
▲ EMP: 10 EST: 1953
SQ FT: 10,000
SALES (est): 1.8MM **Privately Held**
SIC: 3679 Phonograph needles; headphones, radio

(G-1906)
GRANADA ELECTRONICS INC
485 Kent Ave (11249-5927)
PHONE..................................718 387-1157
Nachman Brach, *President*
EMP: 6
SQ FT: 55,000
SALES (est): 540K **Privately Held**
SIC: 3651 Audio electronic systems; television receiving sets

(G-1907)
GRAND VISUAL LLC
188 Broadway (11211-6130)
PHONE..................................912 529-6215
Ben Putland, *COO*
Dan Dawson, *Director*
Jeremy Taylor, *Director*
David Wilkinson, *Director*
EMP: 7
SALES (est): 81.4K
SALES (corp-wide): 206MM **Privately Held**
SIC: 3999 Advertising display products
HQ: Talon Outdoor Limited
Holden House 57 Rathbone Place
London W1T 1
207 467-6799

(G-1908)
GRASS ROOTS JUICERY
336a Graham Ave (11211-3965)
PHONE..................................718 486-2838
Sabrina Diaz, *Principal*
EMP: 30 EST: 2015
SALES (est): 2.8MM **Privately Held**
SIC: 2037 5812 Frozen fruits & vegetables; eating places

(G-1909)
GREEN WAVE INTERNATIONAL INC
5423 1st Ave (11220-2503)
P.O. Box 90288 (11209-0288)
PHONE..................................718 499-3371
Kay Dan Wong, *President*
John Calarese Sr, *Exec Dir*
▲ EMP: 7
SQ FT: 12,000
SALES (est): 1MM **Privately Held**
SIC: 3263 Commercial tableware or kitchen articles, fine earthenware

(G-1910)
GREENEBUILD LLC
390a Lafayette Ave (11238)
PHONE..................................917 562-0556
Winston Greene,
EMP: 12
SALES (est): 755.8K **Privately Held**
SIC: 1442 Construction sand & gravel

(G-1911)
GREENTREE PHARMACY INC
291 7th Ave (11215-7263)
PHONE..................................718 768-2700
Julia Nudelman, *Owner*
EMP: 10 EST: 2013
SALES (est): 1.6MM **Privately Held**
SIC: 2834 5961 Pharmaceutical preparations; pharmaceuticals, mail order

(G-1912)
GROW COMPUTER INC
448 15th St Apt 1r (11215-5778)
PHONE..................................646 535-2037
Daniel Nelson, *CEO*
EMP: 7
SALES: 95K **Privately Held**
SIC: 3429 Manufactured hardware (general)

(G-1913)
GTM ALAP INC
2835 86th St (11223-4634)
PHONE..................................833 345-2748
Arshad Iqbal, *President*
EMP: 5

SALES (est): 156.9K **Privately Held**
SIC: 2759 Engraving

(G-1914)
H & H LABORATORIES INC (PA)
61 4th St (11231-4809)
PHONE..................................718 624-8041
George Hoffmann, *President*
▲ EMP: 14
SQ FT: 5,000
SALES (est): 1.6MM **Privately Held**
WEB: www.hhlabs.com
SIC: 2844 2841 Toilet preparations; soap & other detergents

(G-1915)
H & H LABORATORIES INC
409 Hoyt St (11231-4858)
PHONE..................................718 624-8041
George Hoffman, *Branch Mgr*
EMP: 5
SALES (corp-wide): 1.6MM **Privately Held**
SIC: 2844 2841 Toilet preparations; soap & other detergents
PA: H & H Laboratories Inc.
61 4th St
Brooklyn NY 11231
718 624-8041

(G-1916)
H T L & S LTD
Also Called: Peerless Envelopes & Prtg Co
5820 Fort Hamilton Pkwy (11219)
PHONE..................................718 435-4474
Sheldon Kustin, *Partner*
Lewis Kustin, *Partner*
EMP: 11 EST: 1933
SQ FT: 20,000
SALES: 700K **Privately Held**
SIC: 2752 2759 Commercial printing, offset; letterpress printing; flexographic printing

(G-1917)
H2GEAR FASHIONS LLC
1065 Shepherd Ave (11208-5713)
PHONE..................................347 787-7508
Henry Guindi,
Henry Naftali,
▲ EMP: 5
SQ FT: 350
SALES: 2.2MM **Privately Held**
SIC: 2339 Women's & misses' athletic clothing & sportswear

(G-1918)
HAGADAH PASSOVER BAKERY
814 Bergen St (11238-3702)
PHONE..................................718 638-1589
P Woodsberger, *Principal*
EMP: 8 EST: 2001
SALES (est): 453.6K **Privately Held**
SIC: 2051 Bread, cake & related products

(G-1919)
HALMARK ARCHITECTURAL FINSHG
353 Stanley Ave (11207-7601)
PHONE..................................718 272-1831
Hal Spergel, *President*
EMP: 24
SQ FT: 10,000
SALES (est): 2.9MM **Privately Held**
SIC: 3471 2843 3449 Finishing, metals or formed products; surface active agents; miscellaneous metalwork

(G-1920)
HALO INNOVATIONS INC
Also Called: Halo Sleep Systems
134 N 4th St (11249-3296)
PHONE..................................952 259-1500
Charles Dorsey, *CEO*
William Schmid, *Ch of Bd*
Bob Hiben, *CFO*
▲ EMP: 21
SALES (est): 24MM **Privately Held**
WEB: www.haloinnovations.com
SIC: 2341 Women's & children's nightwear

(G-1921)
HAMODIA CORP
324 Avenue I (11230-2618)
PHONE..................................718 338-5637
Ruth Lichtenstein, *Ch of Bd*

EMP: 5
SALES (est): 246.5K **Privately Held**
SIC: 2711 Newspapers, publishing & printing

(G-1922)
HAMODIA CORP
Also Called: Daily Newsppr For Torah Jewry
207 Foster Ave (11230-2195)
PHONE..............................718 853-9094
Ruth Lichtenstein, *CEO*
Aliza Agress, *Editor*
Tzippy Zager, *Editor*
EMP: 17 EST: 1998
SALES (est): 1MM **Privately Held**
SIC: 2711 Newspapers, publishing & printing

(G-1923)
HANA PASTRIES INC
34 35th St Unit 9 (11232-2212)
P.O. Box 320154 (11232-0154)
PHONE..............................718 369-7593
EMP: 6
SALES (est): 757.2K **Privately Held**
SIC: 2051 5411 Mfg Bread/Related Products Ret Groceries

(G-1924)
HANCO METAL PRODUCTS INC
25 Jay St (11201-1139)
PHONE..............................212 787-5992
Mark Meyer Hantman, *President*
Myles Hantman, *General Mgr*
Debra Hantman, *Corp Secy*
EMP: 10 EST: 1934
SQ FT: 2,000
SALES (est): 800K **Privately Held**
SIC: 3451 3432 Screw machine products; faucets & spigots, metal & plastic

(G-1925)
HANDMADE FRAMES INC
1013 Grand St Ste 2 (11211-1720)
PHONE..............................718 782-8364
Paul Baumann, *President*
Angel Lopez, *General Mgr*
Marilyn Gold, *Vice Pres*
EMP: 14
SQ FT: 9,000
SALES (est): 983.6K **Privately Held**
SIC: 3999 3952 Framed artwork; frames for artists' canvases

(G-1926)
HANDY TOOL & MFG CO INC
1205 Rockaway Ave (11236-2132)
P.O. Box 360524 (11236-0524)
PHONE..............................718 478-9203
Gennady Nekritin, *Project Engr*
Rochelle Sherman, *Treasurer*
EMP: 22 EST: 1948
SQ FT: 13,600
SALES (est): 5.8MM **Privately Held**
SIC: 3728 3544 Aircraft assemblies, subassemblies & parts; special dies, tools, jigs & fixtures

(G-1927)
HAVE YOUR CAKE KITCHEN LLC
Also Called: Rule Breaker Snacks
291 Union St Phb (11231)
PHONE..............................646 820-8074
Nancy Kalish, *Mng Member*
EMP: 7
SALES (est): 515K **Privately Held**
SIC: 2051 7389 Bakery: wholesale or wholesale/retail combined;

(G-1928)
HEALTHONE PHARMACY INC
119 Pennsylvania Ave (11207-2993)
PHONE..............................718 495-9015
Mel Springer, *President*
EMP: 15
SALES (est): 3.5MM **Privately Held**
SIC: 2834 Pharmaceutical preparations

(G-1929)
HEALTHY WAY OF LIFE MAGAZINE
1529 Voorhies Ave (11235-3912)
PHONE..............................718 616-1681
Boris Zat, *President*

EMP: 5
SALES (est): 300.9K **Privately Held**
SIC: 2721 Periodicals

(G-1930)
HECHT & SOHN GLASS CO INC
406 Willoughby Ave (11205-4509)
PHONE..............................718 782-8295
Abe Sabel, *President*
▲ **EMP:** 6
SQ FT: 11,000
SALES (est): 754K **Privately Held**
WEB: www.entrances.com
SIC: 3211 3231 Flat glass; doors, glass: made from purchased glass

(G-1931)
HENRYS DEALS INC
Also Called: Allstateelectronics
1002 Quentin Rd Ste 2009 (11223-2248)
PHONE..............................347 821-4685
David Matts, *CEO*
Simon Sarweh, *CEO*
EMP: 20
SALES (est): 1MM **Privately Held**
SIC: 3861 Photographic equipment & supplies

(G-1932)
HERCULES HEAT TREATING CORP
101 Classon Ave 113 (11205-1401)
PHONE..............................718 625-1266
Anthony Rizzo Jr, *President*
Joseph Rizzo, *COO*
Michelle Lupiani, *Receptionist*
EMP: 27
SQ FT: 25,000
SALES (est): 5.9MM **Privately Held**
WEB: www.herculesht.com
SIC: 3398 Metal heat treating

(G-1933)
HERMAN HALL COMMUNICATIONS
Also Called: Everybodys Carribbean Magazine
1630 Nostrand Ave (11226-5516)
PHONE..............................718 941-1879
Herman Hall, *President*
Helen Lucas, *Treasurer*
EMP: 12
SQ FT: 5,000
SALES: 500K **Privately Held**
SIC: 2721 Magazines: publishing only, not printed on site

(G-1934)
HERRIS GOURMET INC
536 Grand St (11211-3503)
PHONE..............................917 578-2308
Herman Franczoz, *Vice Pres*
EMP: 5
SQ FT: 2,500
SALES (est): 288.9K **Privately Held**
SIC: 2051 5812 5499 Cakes, bakery: except frozen; contract food services; gourmet food stores

(G-1935)
HERTLING TROUSERS INC
236 Greenpoint Ave (11222-2493)
PHONE..............................718 784-6100
Julius Hertling, *President*
▲ **EMP:** 40
SQ FT: 8,000
SALES (est): 4.4MM **Privately Held**
SIC: 2325 2253 Men's & boys' trousers & slacks; pants, slacks or trousers, knit

(G-1936)
HMO BEVERAGE CORPORATION
68 33rd St Unit 4 (11232-1912)
PHONE..............................917 371-6100
Georgios Papanastasatos, *Principal*
EMP: 8
SALES (est): 617.9K **Privately Held**
SIC: 2086 Carbonated beverages, nonalcoholic: bottled & canned

(G-1937)
HNC ENTERPRISES LLC
10624 Avenue D (11236-1910)
PHONE..............................904 448-9387

Isaac Autzon,
EMP: 5
SQ FT: 4,000
SALES (est): 1.5MM **Privately Held**
SIC: 2844 5122 Toilet preparations; cosmetics

(G-1938)
HOLLYWOOD SIGNS INC
388 3rd Ave (11215-2705)
PHONE..............................917 577-7333
Steve Kokonovich, *President*
EMP: 9
SALES (est): 690K **Privately Held**
SIC: 3993 Signs & advertising specialties

(G-1939)
HOLYOKE FITTINGS INC
850 Stanley Ave (11208-5226)
PHONE..............................718 649-0710
Allan Rodolitz, *President*
Jamie Hamm, *Natl Sales Mgr*
Nicole Pecchillo, *Sales Staff*
EMP: 15 EST: 1964
SQ FT: 18,000
SALES (est): 2MM **Privately Held**
WEB: www.holyokefittings.com
SIC: 3494 Valves & pipe fittings

(G-1940)
HOME REPORTER INC
Also Called: Home Reporter & Sunset News
8723 3rd Ave (11209-5103)
PHONE..............................718 238-6600
James F Griffin Jr, *President*
Alex Kalas, *Corp Secy*
Marvile Griffin, *Vice Pres*
EMP: 50 EST: 1956
SQ FT: 2,000
SALES (est): 2.3MM **Privately Held**
WEB: www.homereporter.net
SIC: 2711 Commercial printing & newspaper publishing combined

(G-1941)
HOME4U INC
152 Skillman St Apt 8 (11205-3906)
PHONE..............................347 262-7214
Abraham Goldstein, *CEO*
Joel Teitelbaum, *CFO*
▲ **EMP:** 7
SQ FT: 2,000
SALES (est): 413.3K **Privately Held**
SIC: 2541 Cabinets, lockers & shelving

(G-1942)
HONEYBEE ROBOTICS LTD (HQ)
Also Called: Honeybee Rbtics Crft Mechanisms
Suit Bldg 128 (11205)
PHONE..............................212 966-0661
Kiel Davis, *President*
Stephen Gorvan, *Chairman*
Jason Herman, *Vice Pres*
Erik Mumm, *Vice Pres*
Kris Zacny, *Vice Pres*
EMP: 44
SQ FT: 110,000
SALES (est): 11MM
SALES (corp-wide): 196.2MM **Privately Held**
WEB: www.honeybeerobotics.com
SIC: 3569 Robots, assembly line: industrial & commercial
PA: Ensign-Bickford Industries, Inc.
999 17th St Ste 900
Denver CO 80202
860 843-2000

(G-1943)
HOPSCOTCH TECHNOLOGIES INC
81 Prospect St (11201-1473)
PHONE..............................313 408-4285
Samantha John, *CEO*
Jocelyn Leavitt, *Principal*
Michael Hirshland, *Principal*
EMP: 5 EST: 2013
SALES (est): 60.9K **Privately Held**
SIC: 7372 Educational computer software

(G-1944)
HOSKIE CO INC
132 Harrison Pl (11237-1522)
PHONE..............................718 628-8672

Glenn Ho, *CEO*
◆ **EMP:** 80 EST: 2000
SQ FT: 38,000
SALES (est): 17.4MM **Privately Held**
WEB: www.hoskiecompanyinc.com
SIC: 2015 3999 Poultry slaughtering & processing; atomizers, toiletry

(G-1945)
HPI CO INC (PA)
1656 41st St (11218-5512)
P.O. Box 190418 (11219-0418)
PHONE..............................718 851-2753
Moshe Kenner, *President*
Peggy Oberland, *Vice Pres*
▲ **EMP:** 5
SQ FT: 3,000
SALES (est): 100K **Privately Held**
WEB: www.hpico.net
SIC: 3567 Industrial furnaces & ovens

(G-1946)
HUDSON POWER TRANSMISSION CO
241 Halsey St (11216-2403)
PHONE..............................718 622-3869
Lawrence Saft, *President*
EMP: 5
SQ FT: 880
SALES (est): 440K **Privately Held**
SIC: 3568 Power transmission equipment

(G-1947)
HUNTINGTON ICE & CUBE CORP (PA)
335 Moffat St (11237-6408)
PHONE..............................718 456-2013
Gaspar Piccolo, *Vice Pres*
EMP: 10
SALES (est): 1.1MM **Privately Held**
SIC: 2097 Block ice

(G-1948)
HYGRADE
30 Warsoff Pl (11205-1638)
PHONE..............................718 488-9000
Follman Lazar, *President*
EMP: 7
SALES (est): 139.5K **Privately Held**
SIC: 3842 7218 4959 Personal safety equipment; wiping towel supply; environmental cleanup services

(G-1949)
HYMAN PODRUSNICK CO INC
212 Foster Ave (11230-2197)
PHONE..............................718 853-4502
David Binder, *President*
Mae Binder, *Vice Pres*
▲ **EMP:** 5
SQ FT: 5,000
SALES (est): 649.2K **Privately Held**
SIC: 3469 3821 Household cooking & kitchen utensils, porcelain enameled; laboratory apparatus & furniture

(G-1950)
IAMMALIAMILLS LLC
Also Called: Malia Mills
32 33rd St Unit 13 (11232-1924)
PHONE..............................805 845-2137
Malian Mills,
Malia Mills,
EMP: 6
SALES (est): 646.2K **Privately Held**
SIC: 2253 Bathing suits & swimwear, knit

(G-1951)
ICESTONE LLC
63 Flushing Ave Unit 283b (11205-1079)
PHONE..............................718 624-4900
Dal Lamagna, *CEO*
Jana Milcikova, *President*
Arti Bhatt, *Vice Pres*
Alison Tester, *Purch Dir*
Erik Ramao, *Sales Staff*
▲ **EMP:** 37
SQ FT: 55,000
SALES (est): 6.7MM **Privately Held**
SIC: 3281 2541 1752 3499 Building stone products; counter & sink tops; ceramic floor tile installation; furniture parts, metal

(G-1952)
IEH CORPORATION
140 58th St Ste 8e (11220-2525)
PHONE.................................718 492-4440
David Offerman, *Ch of Bd*
Mark Iskin, *Purchasing*
Robert Romeo, *VP Engrg*
Robert Knoth, *CFO*
EMP: 168 **EST:** 1937
SQ FT: 20,400
SALES: 28.4MM **Privately Held**
WEB: www.iehcorp.com
SIC: 3678 Electronic connectors

(G-1953)
IMPERIAL FRAMES & ALBUMS LLC
8200 21st Ave (11214-2506)
PHONE.................................718 832-9793
Moshe Wigdder, *Mng Member*
▲ **EMP:** 5
SALES: 2.5MM **Privately Held**
WEB: www.imperialframes.com
SIC: 2499 Woodenware, kitchen & household

(G-1954)
IMPREMEDIA LLC (PA)
Also Called: La Raza
1 Metrotech Ctr Fl 18 (11201-3948)
PHONE.................................212 807-4600
Ivan Adaime, *Vice Pres*
Javier Casas, *CFO*
Marcelo Caro, *Sales Dir*
Sergio Fraire, *Creative Dir*
Fernando Lang, *Officer*
▲ **EMP:** 99
SALES (est): 65.3MM **Privately Held**
WEB: www.impremedia.com
SIC: 2711 Newspapers: publishing only, not printed on site

(G-1955)
INDIAN LARRY LEGACY
400 Union Ave (11211-3429)
PHONE.................................718 609-9184
EMP: 5
SALES: 500K **Privately Held**
SIC: 3751 Mfg Motorcycles/Bicycles

(G-1956)
INDUSTRIAL ELECTRONIC HARDWARE
140 58th St Ste 8e (11220-2525)
PHONE.................................718 492-4440
Bob Offman, *President*
EMP: 70
SALES (est): 6MM **Privately Held**
SIC: 3429 Manufactured hardware (general)

(G-1957)
INFANT FORMULA LABORATORY SVC
711 Livonia Ave (11207-5497)
PHONE.................................718 257-3000
Richard C Miller, *President*
EMP: 10 **EST:** 1947
SQ FT: 20,000
SALES (est): 1MM **Privately Held**
SIC: 2023 5149 Bottled baby formula; groceries & related products

(G-1958)
INK PUBLISHING CORPORATION
68 Jay St Ste 315 (11201-8360)
PHONE.................................347 294-1220
Kristian Knapp, *Sales Dir*
Phyll Castle, *Branch Mgr*
EMP: 5 **Privately Held**
SIC: 2721 Magazines: publishing only, not printed on site
HQ: Ink Publishing Corporation
800 Suth Dglas Rd Ste 250
Coral Gables FL 33134

(G-1959)
INK WELL
1440 Coney Island Ave (11230-4120)
PHONE.................................718 253-9736
Yosef Oratz, *Owner*
EMP: 5
SQ FT: 4,000

SALES (est): 340K **Privately Held**
SIC: 2752 Commercial printing, lithographic

(G-1960)
INLAND PAPER PRODUCTS CORP
Also Called: Wew Container
444 Liberty Ave (11207-3034)
P.O. Box 70137 (11207-0137)
PHONE.................................718 827-8150
Daniel Weicher, *President*
Joel Einbinoer, *Corp Secy*
▲ **EMP:** 20 **EST:** 1946
SQ FT: 30,000
SALES (est): 3.6MM **Privately Held**
SIC: 3083 Laminated plastics plate & sheet

(G-1961)
INTEGRA MICROSYSTEM 1988 INC
Also Called: All-Tech
61 Greenpoint Ave Ste 412 (11222-1526)
PHONE.................................718 609-6099
Israel Haber, *Ch of Bd*
EMP: 5
SQ FT: 1,000
SALES (est): 826.8K **Privately Held**
SIC: 3575 Computer terminals, monitors & components

(G-1962)
INTER METAL FABRICATORS INC
161 Dikeman St (11231-1105)
P.O. Box 290718 (11229-0718)
PHONE.................................718 852-4000
EMP: 13
SQ FT: 10,000
SALES (est): 1.9MM **Privately Held**
SIC: 3441 Structural Metal Fabrication

(G-1963)
INTERIOR METALS
Also Called: M&A Metals
255 48th St (11220-1011)
PHONE.................................718 439-7324
Michael Tommasi, *President*
Antonella Tommasi, *Corp Secy*
Paul Monte, *Project Mgr*
Flora Lopez, *Administration*
EMP: 27
SQ FT: 13,000
SALES (est): 4.7MM **Privately Held**
WEB: www.interiormetals.com
SIC: 3444 Radiator shields or enclosures, sheet metal

(G-1964)
INTERNATIONAL AIDS VACCINE INI
140 58th St (11220-2521)
PHONE.................................646 381-8066
EMP: 97
SALES (corp-wide): 72.3MM **Privately Held**
SIC: 2836 8731 Vaccines; commercial physical research
PA: International Aids Vaccine Initative Inc.
125 Broad St Fl 9th
New York NY 10004
212 847-1111

(G-1965)
INTERNATIONAL IDENTITY LLC
824 Park Ave Apt 1c (11206-5324)
PHONE.................................787 864-0379
Pedroalberto Sanchez, *President*
EMP: 5
SALES (est): 215.8K **Privately Held**
SIC: 7372 Prepackaged software

(G-1966)
INTERNATIONAL STONE ACCESSRS
703 Myrtle Ave (11205-3903)
PHONE.................................718 522-5399
Abraham Levy, *President*
Sanny Levy, *Vice Pres*
▲ **EMP:** 6
SQ FT: 7,500
SALES (est): 931.6K **Privately Held**
WEB: www.stonecityexpo.com
SIC: 3281 Marble, building: cut & shaped

(G-1967)
INTERNTIONAL FIREPROF DOOR INC
1005 Greene Ave (11221-2910)
PHONE.................................718 783-1310
Eric Arrow, *President*
EMP: 10
SQ FT: 7,500
SALES (est): 1.5MM **Privately Held**
WEB: www.firedoor.com
SIC: 3442 5251 Fire doors, metal; window & door frames; hardware

(G-1968)
INTERNTNAL AUTO VOLUNTARY UNTD
1956 Bay Ridge Ave Fl 2 (11204-4544)
PHONE.................................718 743-8732
Yuri Artemenko, *President*
EMP: 6
SALES (est): 292.2K **Privately Held**
SIC: 3714 Motor vehicle parts & accessories

(G-1969)
IQUIT CIG LLC
4014 13th Ave (11218-3502)
PHONE.................................718 475-1422
Zelman Pollak,
EMP: 6
SQ FT: 250
SALES (est): 335.6K **Privately Held**
SIC: 3999 Cigarette & cigar products & accessories

(G-1970)
IRX THERAPUETICS INC
140 58th St (11220-2521)
PHONE.................................347 442-0640
EMP: 6
SALES (est): 439.7K **Privately Held**
SIC: 2834 Pharmaceutical preparations

(G-1971)
ISSACS YISROEL
Also Called: Benchers Unlimited
4424 18th Ave (11204-1201)
PHONE.................................718 851-7430
Yisroel Issacs, *Owner*
EMP: 5
SALES: 600K **Privately Held**
WEB: www.benchers.com
SIC: 2759 5947 Imprinting; gifts & novelties

(G-1972)
IT COMMODITY SOURCING INC
Also Called: Federal Contract MGT Svcs
1640 E 22nd St (11210-5125)
PHONE.................................718 677-1577
EMP: 5
SALES (est): 370K **Privately Held**
SIC: 3663 Mfg Radio/Tv Communication Equipment

(G-1973)
ITAC LABEL & TAG CORP
179 Lexington Ave (11216-1114)
PHONE.................................718 625-2148
ARI Adler, *President*
EMP: 7
SQ FT: 17,500
SALES: 700K **Privately Held**
SIC: 2672 Labels (unprinted), gummed: made from purchased materials

(G-1974)
ITIN SCALE CO INC
4802 Glenwood Rd (11234-1106)
PHONE.................................718 336-5900
Samuel Racer, *President*
Lance Gregor, *Sales Mgr*
Patrick Fagan, *Manager*
◆ **EMP:** 20 **EST:** 1970
SQ FT: 4,500
SALES (est): 5.1MM **Privately Held**
WEB: www.itinscales.com
SIC: 3829 3699 3596 3821 Measuring & controlling devices; electrical equipment & supplies; scales & balances, except laboratory; laboratory apparatus & furniture; scales, except laboratory; commercial cooking & food service equipment

(G-1975)
IVALUA INC
195 Montague St (11201-3628)
PHONE.................................650 930-9710
Daniel Olivier Amzallag, *CEO*
EMP: 10
SALES (corp-wide): 34.6MM **Privately Held**
SIC: 7372 Business oriented computer software
HQ: Ivalua, Inc.
805 Veterans Blvd Ste 203
Redwood City CA 94063

(G-1976)
J & J BRONZE & ALUMINUM CAST
Also Called: All Cast Foundry
249 Huron St (11222-1801)
PHONE.................................718 383-2111
Vincent Grosso, *Vice Pres*
EMP: 34
SQ FT: 23,000
SALES (est): 4.2MM **Privately Held**
SIC: 3366 3365 3369 Castings (except die): bronze; aluminum & aluminum-based alloy castings; nonferrous foundries

(G-1977)
J H C FABRICATIONS INC (PA)
Also Called: Jhc Labresin
595 Berriman St (11208-5203)
P.O. Box 80377 (11208-0377)
PHONE.................................718 649-0065
Henry L Calamari, *President*
John Calamari, *Corp Secy*
▲ **EMP:** 28
SQ FT: 16,000
SALES (est): 3.9MM **Privately Held**
WEB: www.jhclabresin.com
SIC: 3821 3644 Laboratory furniture; insulators & insulation materials, electrical

(G-1978)
J H M ENGINEERING
4014 8th Ave (11232-3706)
PHONE.................................718 871-1810
J H Maliga, *Owner*
EMP: 25 **EST:** 1966
SQ FT: 15,000
SALES (est): 2MM **Privately Held**
SIC: 3841 3843 3845 3699 Surgical & medical instruments; dental equipment; electromedical equipment; electrical equipment & supplies

(G-1979)
J LOWY CO
Also Called: J Lowy Lea Skullcaps Mfg Co
940 E 19th St (11230-3805)
PHONE.................................718 338-7324
Jerry Lowy, *Owner*
▲ **EMP:** 8
SALES: 1MM **Privately Held**
WEB: www.kippott.com
SIC: 2386 5999 Hats & caps, leather; religious goods

(G-1980)
J M L PRODUCTIONS INC
162 Spencer St (11205-3929)
PHONE.................................718 643-1674
Jay Cohen, *President*
Michael Dymburt, *Admin Sec*
EMP: 60
SQ FT: 30,000
SALES (est): 2.3MM **Privately Held**
SIC: 2396 2759 Screen printing on fabric articles; screen printing

(G-1981)
J M P DISPLAY FIXTURE CO INC
760 E 96th St (11236-1821)
PHONE.................................718 649-0333
Joseph Cangelosi, *President*
Rosalie Angelosi, *Vice Pres*
EMP: 7
SQ FT: 7,200
SALES (est): 1.2MM **Privately Held**
SIC: 2541 Display fixtures, wood

(G-1982)
J R COOPERAGE CO INC
125 Division Pl (11222-5325)
PHONE...........................718 387-1664
Gustav Rosenberg, *President*
EMP: 8
SQ FT: 40,000
SALES: 170K **Privately Held**
SIC: 3412 Metal barrels, drums & pails

(G-1983)
JACKS GOURMET LLC
1000 Dean St Ste 214 (11238-3382)
PHONE...........................718 954-4681
Jack Silberstein, *CEO*
EMP: 12
SALES: 1.5MM **Privately Held**
SIC: 2013 Sausages & other prepared meats

(G-1984)
JACMAX INDUSTRIES LLC
Also Called: Expressive Scent
473 Wortman Ave (11208-5425)
PHONE...........................718 439-3743
Max Antar, *CEO*
Jack Eida, *President*
EMP: 5 EST: 2009
SQ FT: 150,000
SALES (est): 455.6K **Privately Held**
SIC: 2677 Envelopes

(G-1985)
JACOB INC
287 Keap St (11211-7477)
PHONE...........................646 450-3067
Solomon Breuer, *CEO*
EMP: 40
SQ FT: 8,000
SALES: 20MM **Privately Held**
SIC: 3554 Paper industries machinery

(G-1986)
JACOBS JUICE CORP
388 Avenue X Apt 2h (11223-6025)
PHONE...........................646 255-2860
Jacob Prig, *President*
EMP: 5
SALES (est): 183.4K **Privately Held**
SIC: 3999 Novelties, bric-a-brac & hobby kits

(G-1987)
JACOBY ENTERPRISES LLC
1615 54th St (11204-1438)
PHONE...........................718 435-0289
Abraham Jacobowitz, *Mng Member*
Shraga Jacobowitz, *Mng Member*
▲ EMP: 7
SQ FT: 1,500
SALES (est): 1.2MM **Privately Held**
WEB: www.jacobygems.com
SIC: 3911 5094 Bracelets, precious metal; cigarette lighters, precious metal; precious stones & metals; jewelry

(G-1988)
JAKES SNEAKERS INC
845 Classon Ave (11238-6103)
PHONE...........................718 233-1132
Jake Zebak, *President*
EMP: 1
SALES: 1.2MM **Privately Held**
SIC: 2393 5661 Cushions, except spring & carpet: purchased materials; children's shoes

(G-1989)
JAXIS INC (PA)
Also Called: Jaxi's Sportswear
1365 38th St (11218-3634)
PHONE...........................212 302-7611
Ezra Abed, *President*
Nathan Mann, *Vice Pres*
Eddy Mann, *Admin Sec*
EMP: 6
SQ FT: 1,100
SALES (est): 560K **Privately Held**
SIC: 2339 5137 Sportswear, women's; sportswear, women's & children's

(G-1990)
JAY TUROFF
Also Called: Jay-Art Nvelties/Tower Grafics
681 Coney Island Ave (11218-4306)
PHONE...........................718 856-7300

Jay Turoff, *Owner*
EMP: 11 EST: 1965
SQ FT: 3,500
SALES: 1.2MM **Privately Held**
SIC: 3993 7336 3961 Signs & advertising specialties; commercial art & graphic design; costume novelties

(G-1991)
JERRY TOMASELLI
Also Called: Express Tag & Label
141 32nd St (11232-1809)
PHONE...........................718 965-1400
Jerry Tomaselli, *Owner*
EMP: 10
SQ FT: 10,000
SALES: 500K **Privately Held**
SIC: 2679 Tags, paper (unprinted): made from purchased paper

(G-1992)
JEWELERS SOLDER SUPPLY INC
Also Called: Jewler's Solder Sheet & Wire
1362 54th St (11219-4291)
P.O. Box 190141 (11219-0141)
PHONE...........................718 637-1256
Michael Goldenberg, *Owner*
Connie Klinger, *Principal*
Rachel Goldenberg, *Vice Pres*
EMP: 11
SQ FT: 10,000
SALES: 145.2K **Privately Held**
SIC: 3356 Solder: wire, bar, acid core, & rosin core

(G-1993)
JEWISH HERITAGE FOR BLIND
1655 E 24th St (11229-2401)
PHONE...........................718 338-4999
Rabbi David Toiv, *President*
EMP: 8
SQ FT: 2,000
SALES (est): 607.1K **Privately Held**
WEB: www.jhftb.org
SIC: 2741 Miscellaneous publishing

(G-1994)
JEWISH JOURNAL
7014 13th Ave (11228-1604)
PHONE...........................718 630-9350
EMP: 5
SALES (est): 160K **Privately Held**
SIC: 2711 Newspapers-Publishing/Printing

(G-1995)
JEWISH PRESS INC
4915 16th Ave (11204-1115)
PHONE...........................718 330-1100
Sidney Klass, *President*
Jerry Greenwald, *Vice Pres*
Harry Rosenthal, *Vice Pres*
Irene Klass, *Admin Sec*
Jodie Maoz, *Associate*
EMP: 149 EST: 1949
SQ FT: 40,000
SALES (est): 9.6MM **Privately Held**
WEB: www.jewishpress.com
SIC: 2711 Newspapers: publishing only, not printed on site

(G-1996)
JO-MART CANDIES CORP
Also Called: Jo Mart Chocolates
2917 Avenue R (11229-2525)
PHONE...........................718 375-1277
Michael Rogak, *President*
EMP: 11 EST: 1946
SQ FT: 3,000
SALES (est): 1.5MM **Privately Held**
WEB: www.jomartchocolates.com
SIC: 2064 5441 2066 Candy & other confectionery products; candy; chocolate & cocoa products

(G-1997)
JOHN AUGULIARO PRINTING CO
Also Called: John V Auguliaro Printing
2533 Mcdonald Ave (11223-5232)
PHONE...........................718 382-5283
Justin Auguliaro, *President*
EMP: 8
SALES (est): 760K **Privately Held**
SIC: 2759 Commercial printing

(G-1998)
JOMAT NEW YORK INC
4100 1st Ave Ste 3 (11232-3303)
PHONE...........................718 369-7641
Marc Landman, *President*
EMP: 35
SQ FT: 12,000
SALES: 1MM **Privately Held**
SIC: 2339 2369 Women's & misses' outerwear; girls' & children's outerwear

(G-1999)
JORDACHE WOODWORKING CORP
276 Greenpoint Ave # 1303 (11222-2451)
PHONE...........................718 349-3373
Nicholas Jordache, *President*
EMP: 14
SALES (est): 500K **Privately Held**
SIC: 2434 2499 Wood kitchen cabinets; decorative wood & woodwork

(G-2000)
JOS H LOWENSTEIN AND SONS INC (PA)
420 Morgan Ave (11222-5705)
PHONE...........................718 388-5410
Stephen J Lowenstein, *Ch of Bd*
David Lowenstein, *President*
Sue Papish, *Exec VP*
Charles Garza, *Vice Pres*
Thomas Sowpel, *Vice Pres*
◆ EMP: 85 EST: 1897
SQ FT: 100,000
SALES (est): 15.6MM **Privately Held**
WEB: www.jhlowenstein.com
SIC: 2869 2865 Industrial organic chemicals; dyes, synthetic organic

(G-2001)
JOSEPH PAUL
Also Called: Perfect Publications
1064 Rogers Ave Apt 5 (11226-6234)
P.O. Box 1087, New York (10163-1087)
PHONE...........................718 693-4269
Joseph Paul, *Owner*
A Bourne, *Manager*
◆ EMP: 4
SALES (est): 340K **Privately Held**
SIC: 2752 Commercial printing, lithographic

(G-2002)
JOSEPH SHALHOUB & SON INC
1258 Prospect Ave (11218-1304)
PHONE...........................718 871-6300
Joseph Shalhoub Jr, *President*
Ray Shalhoub, *Vice Pres*
EMP: 14
SQ FT: 15,000
SALES (est): 710K **Privately Held**
SIC: 2064 Fruits: candied, crystallized, or glazed

(G-2003)
JOSEPH ZAKON WINERY LTD
Also Called: Kesser Wine
586 Montgomery St (11225-3130)
PHONE...........................718 604-1430
Joseph Zakon, *President*
EMP: 3
SQ FT: 5,000
SALES: 1.5MM **Privately Held**
SIC: 2084 Wines

(G-2004)
JOY OF LEARNING
992 Gates Ave (11221-3602)
PHONE...........................718 443-6463
C Clay Berry, *Owner*
EMP: 7
SALES: 200K **Privately Held**
SIC: 2211 Broadwoven fabric mills, cotton

(G-2005)
JOYA LLC
Also Called: Joya Studio
19 Vanderbilt Ave (11205-1113)
PHONE...........................718 852-6979
Bernard Bouchardy, *CEO*
Mayra Miranda, *Manager*
EMP: 15
SALES (est): 1.2MM **Privately Held**
SIC: 3999 Candles

(G-2006)
JOYVA CORP (PA)
53 Varick Ave (11237-1523)
PHONE...........................718 497-0170
Sanford Wiener, *CEO*
Sandra Quinones, *Office Mgr*
Richard Radutzky, *Manager*
◆ EMP: 75 EST: 1906
SQ FT: 26,370
SALES (est): 12.2MM **Privately Held**
WEB: www.joyva.com
SIC: 2099 2066 2064 Food preparations; chocolate & cocoa products; halvah (candy)

(G-2007)
JTA USA INC
63 Flushing Ave Unit 339 (11205-1084)
PHONE...........................718 722-0902
Alex Rub, *President*
EMP: 7
SQ FT: 2,000
SALES (est): 731.9K **Privately Held**
SIC: 3291 Wheels, abrasive

(G-2008)
JUDAICA PRESS INC
123 Ditmas Ave (11218-4930)
PHONE...........................718 972-6202
Gloria Goldman, *President*
Chaim Schneider, *Sales Mgr*
Aryeh Mezzi, *Manager*
▲ EMP: 8 EST: 1963
SQ FT: 2,325
SALES (est): 1.1MM **Privately Held**
WEB: www.judaicapress.com
SIC: 2731 Books: publishing only

(G-2009)
JUDIS LAMPSHADES INC
1495 E 22nd St (11210-5122)
PHONE...........................917 561-3921
Judith Sadan, *President*
Judi Sadan, *President*
EMP: 5 EST: 1998
SQ FT: 1,000
SALES: 310K **Privately Held**
WEB: www.judislampshades.com
SIC: 3645 Lamp shades, metal

(G-2010)
JUICES ENTERPRISES INC
1142 Nostrand Ave (11225-5414)
PHONE...........................718 953-1860
Patrick Brown, *President*
Juliet McNaughton, *President*
EMP: 6
SALES (est): 437.1K **Privately Held**
SIC: 2086 Carbonated beverages, nonalcoholic: bottled & canned

(G-2011)
JULIANS RECIPE LLC
42 West St Ste 2 (11222-6260)
PHONE...........................888 640-8880
Alexander Dzieduszycki, *Mng Member*
▲ EMP: 8
SQ FT: 1,100
SALES (est): 7.5MM **Privately Held**
SIC: 2038 Frozen specialties

(G-2012)
JULIUS COHEN JEWELERS INC
169 Richardson St (11222-5016)
PHONE...........................212 371-3050
Leslie Steinweiss, *President*
Anderson King, *Manager*
Parsley Steinweiss, *Director*
EMP: 7 EST: 1956
SALES (est): 909.8K **Privately Held**
WEB: www.juliuscohen.com
SIC: 3911 5944 Bracelets, precious metal; rings, finger: precious metal; pins (jewelry), precious metal; jewelry stores

(G-2013)
JUNIORS CHEESECAKE INC (PA)
386 Flatbush Avenue Ext (11201-5331)
PHONE...........................718 852-5257
Alan Rosen, *President*
Walter Rosen, *Chairman*
Kevin Rosen, *Vice Pres*
Anna Poselenova, *Opers Staff*
Nancy Weinberger, *Marketing Staff*

GEOGRAPHIC

EMP: 7
SQ FT: 30,000
SALES (est): 1.7MM **Privately Held**
WEB: www.juniorscheesecake.com
SIC: 2051 Cakes, pies & pastries

(G-2014)
JUS BY JULIE LLC (PA)
2184 Mcdonald Ave (11223-3926)
PHONE..........................718 266-3906
Jack Sardar, *Manager*
Sesar Maleh,
Elliot Maleh,
EMP: 2
SALES (est): 1.1MM **Privately Held**
SIC: 2033 Vegetable juices: fresh; fruit juices: fresh

(G-2015)
K & R ALLIED INC
Also Called: Allied K & R Broom & Brush Co
39 Pearl St Fl 2 (11201-8302)
PHONE..........................718 625-6610
Karl Chang, *President*
Kam Lau, *Vice Pres*
Cathy Chang, *Prgrmr*
EMP: 10 EST: 1974
SQ FT: 18,000
SALES (est): 1.1MM **Privately Held**
WEB: www.alliedkr.com
SIC: 3991 Brooms

(G-2016)
K & S CHILDRENS WEAR INC
Also Called: Elegant Sportswear
204 Wallabout St (11206-5418)
PHONE..........................718 624-0006
Thomas Klein, *President*
Jacob Klein, *Vice Pres*
EMP: 47
SQ FT: 20,000
SALES: 7.5MM **Privately Held**
SIC: 2253 2369 Sweaters & sweater coats, knit; jackets: girls', children's & infants'

(G-2017)
K DISPLAYS
1363 47th St (11219-2612)
PHONE..........................718 854-6045
Malvin Boehm, *President*
EMP: 10
SALES (est): 486.4K **Privately Held**
SIC: 3172 Cases, jewelry

(G-2018)
K M DRIVE LINE INC
966 Grand St (11211-2707)
PHONE..........................718 599-0628
Salvatore Bucchio, *President*
John Smith, *Accounts Mgr*
EMP: 8
SQ FT: 5,000
SALES (est): 1.2MM **Privately Held**
WEB: www.kmdriveline.com
SIC: 3714 5013 5531 Drive shafts, motor vehicle; motor vehicle supplies & new parts; automobile & truck equipment & parts

(G-2019)
K T A V PUBLISHING HOUSE INC
527 Empire Blvd (11225-3121)
PHONE..........................201 963-9524
Sol Scharfstein, *President*
Bernard Scharfstein, *Corp Secy*
▲ EMP: 13
SQ FT: 25,000
SALES (est): 1.3MM **Privately Held**
WEB: www.ktav.com
SIC: 2731 Books: publishing only

(G-2020)
KALE FACTORY INC
790 Washington Ave (11238-7706)
PHONE..........................917 363-6361
EMP: 6
SALES (est): 474.4K **Privately Held**
SIC: 2099 Food preparations

(G-2021)
KARO SHEET METAL INC
Also Called: Karosheet Metal
229 Russell St (11222-3004)
PHONE..........................718 542-8420
Kathleen Portman, *President*

EMP: 40
SQ FT: 10,000
SALES (est): 6.3MM **Privately Held**
SIC: 3444 Ducts, sheet metal; ventilators, sheet metal

(G-2022)
KEEMOTION LLC
81 Prospect St Fl 5 (11201-1473)
PHONE..........................914 458-3900
EMP: 9
SALES (est): 1.2MM
SALES (corp-wide): 1.1MM **Privately Held**
SIC: 3651 Video camera-audio recorders, household use
PA: Keemotion
Place Antoine-Louis Hennepin 6
Ottignies-Louvain-La-Neuve 1348

(G-2023)
KELLYS SHEET METAL INC
Also Called: Kelly Sheet Metal Shop
367 Kosciuszko St (11221-6667)
PHONE..........................718 774-4750
Collins Kelly, *President*
EMP: 10
SQ FT: 8,000
SALES: 1.5MM **Privately Held**
SIC: 3444 Sheet metalwork

(G-2024)
KENDI IRON WORKS INC
236 Johnson Ave (11206-2819)
PHONE..........................718 821-2722
Zadok Zvi, *President*
Anna Zvi, *Vice Pres*
EMP: 8
SQ FT: 16,500
SALES (est): 680.6K **Privately Held**
SIC: 3446 Ornamental metalwork

(G-2025)
KEURIG DR PEPPER INC
212 Wolcott St (11231-1130)
PHONE..........................718 246-6200
Joseph Poli, *CEO*
M McCrodden, *Financial Exec*
EMP: 8 **Publicly Held**
SIC: 2086 Soft drinks: packaged in cans, bottles, etc.
PA: Keurig Dr Pepper Inc.
53 South Ave
Burlington MA 01803

(G-2026)
KINFOLK STUDIOS INC
Also Called: Kinfolk Store, The
94 Wythe Ave (11249-1923)
PHONE..........................770 617-5592
Maceo McNeff, *President*
EMP: 14 **Privately Held**
SIC: 2599 Bar, restaurant & cafeteria furniture
PA: Kinfolk Studios Inc.
90 Wythe Ave
Brooklyn NY 11249

(G-2027)
KINFOLK STUDIOS INC (PA)
Also Called: Kinfolk Store
90 Wythe Ave (11249-1923)
PHONE..........................347 799-2946
Ryan Carney, *President*
EMP: 16
SQ FT: 900
SALES: 950K **Privately Held**
SIC: 2599 Bar, restaurant & cafeteria furniture

(G-2028)
KING RESEARCH INC
114 12th St Ste 1 (11215-3892)
PHONE..........................718 788-0122
◆ EMP: 23 EST: 1947
SQ FT: 23,500
SALES (est): 3.2MM **Privately Held**
SIC: 2842 2841 2844 3229 Mfg Polish/Sanitation Gd Mfg Soap/Other Detergent Mfg Toilet Preparations Mfg Pressed/Blown Glass

(G-2029)
KING SALES INC
284 Wallabout St (11206-4927)
PHONE..........................718 301-9862

David Schwimmer, *Owner*
▲ EMP: 10
SALES (est): 480.7K **Privately Held**
SIC: 2329 Athletic (warmup, sweat & jogging) suits: men's & boys'

(G-2030)
KING STEEL IRON WORK CORP
2 Seneca Ave (11237)
PHONE..........................718 384-7500
Eliran Galapo, *Vice Pres*
EMP: 15
SALES (est): 2.9MM **Privately Held**
SIC: 3441 Fabricated structural metal

(G-2031)
KINGS CNTY BRWERS CLLCTIVE LLC
381 Troutman St (11237-2613)
PHONE..........................917 207-2739
Anthony Bellis,
EMP: 10
SALES (est): 1.8MM **Privately Held**
SIC: 3556 2082 Brewers' & maltsters' machinery; brewers' grain

(G-2032)
KINGS FILM & SHEET INC
Also Called: Kings Specialty Co
482 Baltic St (11217-2508)
P.O. Box 170144 (11217-0144)
PHONE..........................718 624-7510
Forrest T Weisburst, *President*
Joel Leonard, *General Mgr*
EMP: 24
SQ FT: 15,000
SALES (est): 3.8MM **Privately Held**
WEB: www.kingsspecialty.com
SIC: 3081 Plastic film & sheet

(G-2033)
KMS CONTRACTING INC
Also Called: Sure Iron Works
86 Georgia Ave (11207-2402)
PHONE..........................718 495-6500
Steven Horn, *President*
EMP: 14
SQ FT: 11,500
SALES (est): 2.6MM **Privately Held**
WEB: www.sureiron.com
SIC: 3446 Architectural metalwork

(G-2034)
KODIAK STUDIOS INC
3030 Emmons Ave Apt 3t (11235-2226)
PHONE..........................718 769-5399
Alex Tish, *President*
EMP: 5
SALES (est): 384.4K **Privately Held**
WEB: www.kodiakstudios.com
SIC: 3299 Architectural sculptures: gypsum, clay, papier mache, etc.

(G-2035)
KON TAT GROUP CORPORATION
Also Called: Ametal International
1491 E 34th St (11234-2601)
PHONE..........................718 207-5022
Kong Tat Yee, *CEO*
David Kong, *Exec VP*
▼ EMP: 8
SQ FT: 4,000
SALES (est): 179.7K **Privately Held**
SIC: 7692 Welding repair

(G-2036)
KWADAIR LLC
137 Kent St (11222-2127)
PHONE..........................646 824-2511
▲ EMP: 5
SALES (est): 457.1K **Privately Held**
SIC: 3812 Aircraft/aerospace flight instruments & guidance systems

(G-2037)
KWESI LEGESSE LLC
Also Called: K.E.Y.S. Publishers
203 Remsen Ave (11212-1342)
PHONE..........................347 581-9872
Kayode Smith, *Co-Owner*
EMP: 5
SALES (est): 180.3K **Privately Held**
SIC: 2731 Book publishing

(G-2038)
KWIK TICKET INC (PA)
Also Called: Jon Barry Company Division
4101 Glenwood Rd (11210-2024)
PHONE..........................718 421-3800
Larry Spiewak, *Principal*
Vivian Martinez, *Opers Mgr*
Malky Jacobovits, *Office Mgr*
Ike Betesh, *Manager*
◆ EMP: 15
SQ FT: 30,000
SALES (est): 2MM **Privately Held**
WEB: www.kwikticket.com
SIC: 2752 Tags, lithographed; tickets, lithographed

(G-2039)
KWONG CHI METAL FABRICATION
166 41st St (11232-3320)
PHONE..........................718 369-6429
Larry Lang, *President*
EMP: 8
SALES (est): 400K **Privately Held**
SIC: 3479 3499 Coating of metals & formed products; fabricated metal products

(G-2040)
L & M UNISERV CORP
4416 18th Ave Pmb 133 (11204-1201)
PHONE..........................718 854-3700
Morris Wizel, *President*
EMP: 6
SALES (est): 527.3K **Privately Held**
SIC: 2759 Magazines: printing; catalogs: printing

(G-2041)
LA NEWYORKINA LLC
231 Court St (11201-6406)
PHONE..........................917 669-4591
EMP: 5
SALES (est): 212.8K **Privately Held**
SIC: 2024 Juice pops, frozen

(G-2042)
LADYBIRD BAKERY INC
1112 8th Ave (11215-4314)
PHONE..........................718 499-8108
Mary L Clemens, *Ch of Bd*
EMP: 6
SQ FT: 750
SALES (est): 634.9K **Privately Held**
WEB: www.twolittleredhens.com
SIC: 2051 2052 Bakery: wholesale or wholesale/retail combined; cookies & crackers

(G-2043)
LAGE INDUSTRIES CORPORATION
9814 Ditmas Ave (11236-1914)
PHONE..........................718 342-3400
Daniel Lage, *Owner*
EMP: 12 EST: 2014
SALES: 2MM **Privately Held**
SIC: 3273 Ready-mixed concrete

(G-2044)
LAGUNATIC MUSIC & FILMWORKS
Also Called: Blackheart Records
456 Johnson Ave 202 (11237-1202)
PHONE..........................212 353-9600
Kenny Laguna, *President*
Meryl Laguna, *Corp Secy*
Joan Jett, *Vice Pres*
Ed Sargent, *Manager*
EMP: 10
SALES (est): 878.9K **Privately Held**
WEB: www.blackheart.com
SIC: 2741 Music book & sheet music publishing

(G-2045)
LAMM INDUSTRIES INC
2513 E 21st St (11235-2903)
PHONE..........................718 368-0181
Vladimir Lamm, *President*
EMP: 6
SALES (est): 922.9K **Privately Held**
WEB: www.lammindustries.com
SIC: 3651 5731 Audio electronic systems; radio, television & electronic stores

(G-2046)
LANCASTER QUALITY PORK INC
5600 1st Ave Ste 6 (11220-2558)
PHONE.....................718 439-8822
David Kaplan, *President*
EMP: 16
SALES (est): 2.3MM **Privately Held**
SIC: **2013** 5147 5421 Prepared pork products from purchased pork; meat brokers; meat markets, including freezer provisioners

(G-2047)
LANOVES INC
72 Anthony St (11222-5329)
PHONE.....................718 384-1880
Sebastian Antoniuk, *President*
EMP: 8
SALES (est): 710K **Privately Held**
SIC: **2511** Wood household furniture

(G-2048)
LAYTON MANUFACTURING CORP (PA)
864 E 52nd St (11203-6702)
PHONE.....................718 498-6000
Steve Layton, *President*
Antonia Layton, *Vice Pres*
EMP: 24
SQ FT: 9,000
SALES (est): 5.3MM **Privately Held**
WEB: www.laytonmfg.com
SIC: **3585** 1711 5075 Air conditioning equipment, complete; heating & air conditioning contractors; air conditioning & ventilation equipment & supplies

(G-2049)
LAZER MARBLE & GRANITE CORP
1053 Dahill Rd (11204-1741)
PHONE.....................718 859-9644
Lazer Mechlovitz, *CEO*
Nachman Mechlovitz, *President*
Rene Shleifer, *Sales Staff*
▲ EMP: 7
SQ FT: 4,200
SALES (est): 1.2MM **Privately Held**
SIC: **3211** 3253 Building glass, flat; ceramic wall & floor tile

(G-2050)
LDI LIGHTING INC (PA)
240 Broadway Ste C (11211-8409)
PHONE.....................718 384-4490
Allen Mundle, *President*
EMP: 9
SQ FT: 5,000
SALES (est): 2.5MM **Privately Held**
SIC: **3646** Ornamental lighting fixtures, commercial

(G-2051)
LDI LIGHTING INC
193 Williamsburg St W A (11211-7984)
PHONE.....................718 384-4490
Alex Menzlowitz, *Branch Mgr*
EMP: 5
SALES (corp-wide): 2.5MM **Privately Held**
SIC: **3646** Commercial indusl & institutional electric lighting fixtures
PA: Ldi Lighting, Inc
240 Broadway Ste C
Brooklyn NY 11211
718 384-4490

(G-2052)
LE HOOK ROUGE LLC
275 Conover St Ste 3q-3p (11231-1035)
PHONE.....................212 947-6272
Esther Chen, *President*
▲ EMP: 1 EST: 2014
SQ FT: 10,000
SALES: 8MM **Privately Held**
SIC: **3911** Jewelry apparel

(G-2053)
LE LABO HOLDING LLC (HQ)
Also Called: Le Labo Fragrances
122 N 6th St Fl 2 (11249-3002)
PHONE.....................646 490-6200
Fabrice Penot,
▲ EMP: 30

SALES (est): 9.3MM **Publicly Held**
SIC: **2844** Perfumes & colognes

(G-2054)
LE LABO HOLDING LLC
80 39th St Fl Ground (11232-2614)
PHONE.....................646 719-1740
Jean B Mondesir Jr, *Principal*
EMP: 25 **Publicly Held**
SIC: **2844** Perfumes & colognes
HQ: Le Labo Holding Llc
122 N 6th St Fl 2
Brooklyn NY 11249
646 490-6200

(G-2055)
LEARNINGATEWAY LLC
106 Saint James Pl (11238-1831)
PHONE.....................212 920-7969
Catherine Gichenje, *President*
EMP: 5
SALES (est): 347.2K **Privately Held**
SIC: **7372** Educational computer software

(G-2056)
LED WAVES INC
4100 1st Ave Ste 3n (11232-3303)
PHONE.....................347 416-6182
Joel Slavis, *CEO*
▲ EMP: 12
SALES (est): 2.3MM **Privately Held**
SIC: **3641** 5063 Electric lamps; light bulbs & related supplies

(G-2057)
LEE PRINTING INC
188 Lee Ave (11211-8028)
PHONE.....................718 237-1651
Leo Wollner, *President*
EMP: 5
SQ FT: 1,800
SALES: 800K **Privately Held**
SIC: **2752** Commercial printing, offset

(G-2058)
LEE SPRING COMPANY LLC (HQ)
140 58th St Ste 3c (11220-2522)
PHONE.....................888 777-4647
Al Mangels Jr, *President*
Ralph Mascolo, *Vice Pres*
Laura Hoffman, *Production*
Elvis Jarvis, *QC Mgr*
Calvin Lin, *Engineer*
▲ EMP: 150
SQ FT: 33,000
SALES (est): 40.6MM **Privately Held**
WEB: www.leespring.com
SIC: **3495** 3493 3315 5085 Mechanical springs, precision; steel springs, except wire; steel wire & related products; industrial supplies
PA: Unimex Corporation
54 E 64th St
New York NY 10065
800 886-0390

(G-2059)
LEGION LIGHTING CO INC
221 Glenmore Ave (11207-3307)
PHONE.....................718 498-1770
Sheldon Bellovin, *President*
Evan Bellovin, *Vice Pres*
Michael Bellovin, *Vice Pres*
▲ EMP: 30 EST: 1946
SQ FT: 75,000
SALES: 7.3MM **Privately Held**
WEB: www.legionlighting.com
SIC: **3646** Fluorescent lighting fixtures, commercial

(G-2060)
LEHIGH CEMENT COMPANY LLC
63 Flushing Ave Unit 295 (11205-1080)
PHONE.....................718 522-0800
Joseph Basile, *Terminal Mgr*
Rocco Castania, *Manager*
EMP: 20
SALES (corp-wide): 20.6B **Privately Held**
WEB: www.lehighcement.com
SIC: **3273** Ready-mixed concrete
HQ: Lehigh Cement Company Llc
300 E John Carpenter Fwy
Irving TX 75062
877 534-4442

(G-2061)
LEITER SUKKAHS INC
1346 39th St (11218-3616)
PHONE.....................718 436-0303
Gitel Goldman, *President*
▲ EMP: 7
SQ FT: 8,000
SALES (est): 989.2K **Privately Held**
WEB: www.leiterssukkah.com
SIC: **2394** 5049 5999 Tents: made from purchased materials; religious supplies; tents; religious goods

(G-2062)
LENS LAB EXPRESS
Also Called: Vision Quest
482 86th St (11209-4708)
PHONE.....................718 921-5488
Sherri Smith, *Owner*
EMP: 6
SALES (est): 496.5K **Privately Held**
SIC: **3851** 5995 5049 Ophthalmic goods; opticians; optical goods

(G-2063)
LEO INTERNATIONAL INC
471 Sutter Ave (11207-3905)
PHONE.....................718 290-8005
Gary Stern, *President*
Richard Ward, *Officer*
▲ EMP: 25
SQ FT: 65,000
SALES (est): 6.9MM **Privately Held**
WEB: www.leointernational.com
SIC: **3498** Fabricated pipe & fittings

(G-2064)
LEWIS AVENUE LLC
172 5th Ave 111 (11217-3597)
PHONE.....................718 669-0579
Joseph Abdallah, *President*
EMP: 15
SALES (est): 586.5K **Privately Held**
SIC: **3429** Keys, locks & related hardware

(G-2065)
LEWIS MACHINE CO INC
Also Called: Lewis, S J Machine Co
209 Congress St (11201-6415)
PHONE.....................718 625-0799
Gene Wayda, *President*
EMP: 8 EST: 1933
SQ FT: 2,000
SALES: 750K **Privately Held**
SIC: **3599** Machine shop, jobbing & repair

(G-2066)
LIBERTY FABRICATION INC
226 Glenmore Ave (11207-3323)
PHONE.....................718 495-5735
Jimmy Hsu, *President*
EMP: 5
SALES (est): 757.8K **Privately Held**
SIC: **3315** Wire & fabricated wire products

(G-2067)
LIBERTY PANEL CENTER INC (PA)
Also Called: Liberty Panel & Home Center
1009 Liberty Ave (11208-2812)
PHONE.....................718 647-2763
Irwin Kandel, *President*
Cory Kandel, *Vice Pres*
Craig Kandel, *Vice Pres*
EMP: 19
SQ FT: 25,000
SALES (est): 2.5MM **Privately Held**
SIC: **2851** 5231 Paints & paint additives; paint, glass & wallpaper

(G-2068)
LIDDABIT SWEETS
330 Wythe Ave Apt 2g (11249-4153)
PHONE.....................917 912-1370
Liz Gutman, *Principal*
EMP: 6
SALES (est): 501.1K **Privately Held**
SIC: **2053** Buns, sweet: frozen

(G-2069)
LIFESTYLE-TRIMCO (PA)
Also Called: Lifestyle-Trimco Viaggo
323 Malta St (11207-8210)
PHONE.....................718 257-9101
Charles Rosenthal, *President*

Chuck Rosenthal, *Principal*
Lloyd Kielson, *Vice Pres*
▲ EMP: 39
SQ FT: 12,000
SALES: 18MM **Privately Held**
SIC: **3999** 2542 2541 5046 Mannequins; garment racks: except wood; garment racks, wood; mannequins; display equipment, except refrigerated; signs & advertising specialties

(G-2070)
LIGHT BLUE USA LLC
1421 Locust Ave (11230-5220)
PHONE.....................718 475-2515
Isaac Markowitz, *Director*
EMP: 8 EST: 2012
SALES (est): 390.5K **Privately Held**
SIC: **3674** 3648 1731 Light emitting diodes; lighting equipment; lighting contractor

(G-2071)
LIGHT PHONE INC (PA)
49 Bogart St Apt 44 (11206-3837)
PHONE.....................415 595-0044
Joe Hollier, *Founder*
Kaiwei Tang, *Founder*
EMP: 5
SALES: 500K **Privately Held**
SIC: **3669** Communications equipment

(G-2072)
LIGHT WAVES CONCEPT INC
Also Called: Led Waves
4100 1st Ave (11232-2609)
PHONE.....................212 677-6400
Joel Slavis, *President*
▲ EMP: 13
SALES: 2MM **Privately Held**
WEB: www.lightwavesconcept.com
SIC: **3646** 3544 Commercial indusl & institutional electric lighting fixtures; special dies, tools, jigs & fixtures

(G-2073)
LILIBRAND LLC
157 13th St 202 (11215-4702)
PHONE.....................212 239-8230
EMP: 6
SALES (est): 336.8K **Privately Held**
SIC: **3648** Lighting equipment

(G-2074)
LILLYS HOMESTYLE BAKESHOP INC
6210 9th Ave (11220-4726)
PHONE.....................718 491-2904
Ethan Lieberman, *Ch of Bd*
Mendel Brach, *President*
EMP: 60 EST: 2003
SALES (est): 9.8MM **Privately Held**
SIC: **2051** Bakery: wholesale or wholesale/retail combined

(G-2075)
LINDA TOOL & DIE CORPORATION
163 Dwight St (11231-1539)
PHONE.....................718 522-2066
Michael Di Marino, *President*
Linda Cataffo, *Vice Pres*
Arlene Di Marino, *Vice Pres*
Shlomo Mordechai, *Engineer*
Sandy Wise, *Office Mgr*
▲ EMP: 23
SQ FT: 17,500
SALES (est): 4.5MM **Privately Held**
WEB: www.lindatool.com
SIC: **3599** Machine shop, jobbing & repair

(G-2076)
LINDEN FORMS & SYSTEMS INC
40 S 6th St (11249-5938)
PHONE.....................212 219-1100
Leo Green, *President*
EMP: 25 EST: 1975
SQ FT: 8,000
SALES (est): 2MM **Privately Held**
SIC: **2761** 2759 Computer forms, manifold or continuous; commercial printing

(G-2077)
LION DIE-CUTTING CO INC
95 Dobbin St Ste 1 (11222-2851)
PHONE....................................718 383-8841
Leo Friedman, *President*
Moshe Lieberman, *Vice Pres*
EMP: 27 **EST:** 1958
SQ FT: 40,000
SALES: 3MM **Privately Held**
SIC: 2675 2621 Cutouts, cardboard, die-
cut: from purchased materials; card paper

(G-2078)
LION IN THE SUN PARK SLOPE
LTD
232 7th Ave (11215-3041)
PHONE....................................718 369-4006
Melinda Morris, *CEO*
David Morris, *Vice Pres*
EMP: 9
SQ FT: 2,000
SALES (est): 1.2MM **Privately Held**
WEB: www.lioninthesuninvitations.com
SIC: 2759 Invitation & stationery printing &
engraving; invitations: printing

(G-2079)
LITE BRITE MANUFACTURING
INC
575 President St (11215)
PHONE....................................718 855-9797
David Kabasso, *President*
Shaul Kabasso, *Vice Pres*
EMP: 15
SQ FT: 20,000
SALES (est): 1.2MM **Privately Held**
SIC: 3646 3643 Fluorescent lighting fix-
tures, commercial; current-carrying wiring
devices

(G-2080)
LIVID MAGAZINE
1055 Bedford Ave Apt 4c (11216-4730)
PHONE....................................929 340-7123
Daniel Watson, *Owner*
EMP: 11
SALES (est): 473.1K **Privately Held**
SIC: 2721 Magazines: publishing & printing

(G-2081)
LLCS PUBLISHING CORP
2071 Flatbush Ave Ste 189 (11234-4340)
PHONE....................................718 569-2703
Matt Cunningham, *Owner*
EMP: 10
SALES (est): 547.3K **Privately Held**
WEB: www.llcpublishing.com
SIC: 2741 Miscellaneous publishing

(G-2082)
LO & SONS INC
55 Prospect St (11201-1497)
PHONE....................................917 775-4025
Helen Lo, *CEO*
Jan Lo, *President*
▲ **EMP:** 10
SALES (est): 211.4K **Privately Held**
SIC: 3161 Traveling bags

(G-2083)
LONDON PARIS LTD
4211 13th Ave (11219-1334)
PHONE....................................718 564-4793
Elias Brach, *President*
▲ **EMP:** 7
SALES: 1.4MM **Privately Held**
SIC: 2329 Athletic (warmup, sweat & jog-
ging) suits: men's & boys'

(G-2084)
LOPEZ RESTORATIONS INC (PA)
394 Mcguinness Blvd Ste 4 (11222-1201)
PHONE....................................718 383-1555
Angel Lopez, *President*
EMP: 11
SQ FT: 3,500
SALES (est): 1.5MM **Privately Held**
SIC: 3952 Frames for artists' canvases

(G-2085)
LOPOPOLO IRON WORKS INC
2495 Mcdonald Ave (11223-5232)
PHONE....................................718 339-0572
Joseph Lopopolo, *President*
Mike Lopopolo, *Shareholder*

EMP: 7 **EST:** 1965
SQ FT: 4,000
SALES (est): 1.2MM **Privately Held**
SIC: 3446 Gates, ornamental metal

(G-2086)
LOTUS AWNINGS ENTERPRISES
INC
157 11th St (11215-3815)
PHONE....................................718 965-4824
Susana Merchan, *President*
EMP: 7
SQ FT: 5,000
SALES (est): 849.3K **Privately Held**
SIC: 3444 5999 Awnings & canopies;
awnings

(G-2087)
LOWEL-LIGHT
MANUFACTURING INC
140 58th St Ste 8c (11220-2524)
PHONE....................................718 921-0600
Marvin Seligman, *President*
▲ **EMP:** 40 **EST:** 1959
SQ FT: 34,000
SALES (est): 5.2MM **Privately Held**
WEB: www.lowel.com
SIC: 3861 3641 Photographic equipment
& supplies; electric lamps

(G-2088)
LTDM INCORPORATED
129 48th St (11232-4227)
PHONE....................................718 965-1339
Thomas Corrales, *Principal*
EMP: 5
SALES (est): 622.4K **Privately Held**
SIC: 2511 Wood household furniture

(G-2089)
LYN JO KITCHENS INC
1679 Mcdonald Ave (11230-6312)
PHONE....................................718 336-6060
Hal Grosshandler, *President*
EMP: 5
SQ FT: 2,400
SALES: 260K **Privately Held**
SIC: 2434 Wood kitchen cabinets

(G-2090)
LYNCH KNITTING MILLS INC
538 Johnson Ave (11237-1226)
PHONE....................................718 821-3436
EMP: 35 **EST:** 1965
SQ FT: 15,000
SALES (est): 3.3MM **Privately Held**
SIC: 2253 Knit Outerwear Mill

(G-2091)
M & C FURNITURE
Also Called: M C Kitchen & Bath
375 Park Ave (11205-2635)
PHONE....................................718 422-2136
Moshe Chayun, *President*
Erez Chayun, *Vice Pres*
▲ **EMP:** 6
SQ FT: 9,000
SALES (est): 846.2K **Privately Held**
WEB: www.fintec-usa.com
SIC: 2511 5031 1751 Wood household
furniture; kitchen cabinets; cabinet & fin-
ish carpentry

(G-2092)
M & D INSTALLERS INC (PA)
Also Called: M & D Fire Door
70 Flushing Ave Ste 1 (11205-1067)
PHONE....................................718 782-6978
Moshe Deutsch, *Ch of Bd*
David Posner, *President*
Jay Posner, *CFO*
Mendel Mandel, *Sales Staff*
▼ **EMP:** 52
SQ FT: 50,000
SALES: 30MM **Privately Held**
WEB: www.mdfiredoor.com
SIC: 3442 5211 5031 Fire doors, metal;
door & window products; metal doors,
sash & trim

(G-2093)
M & M FOOD PRODUCTS INC
Also Called: Flaum Appetizing
286 Scholes St (11206-1728)
PHONE....................................718 821-1970

Morris Grunhut, *Ch of Bd*
EMP: 14
SQ FT: 23,000
SALES (est): 940K **Privately Held**
WEB: www.flaumappetizing.com
SIC: 2099 Salads, fresh or refrigerated

(G-2094)
M & R WOODWORKING &
FINISHING
49 Withers St (11211-6891)
PHONE....................................718 486-5480
Robert Wieczorkowski, *President*
Milgorzata Wieczorkowski, *Vice Pres*
EMP: 7
SQ FT: 5,625
SALES: 500K **Privately Held**
SIC: 2499 Decorative wood & woodwork

(G-2095)
M B C METAL INC
Also Called: Milgo Industrial
68 Lombardy St (11222-5207)
PHONE....................................718 384-6713
Bruce Gitlin, *President*
EMP: 10
SQ FT: 5,000
SALES (est): 750K **Privately Held**
SIC: 3446 Architectural metalwork

(G-2096)
M B M MANUFACTURING INC
331 Rutledge St Ste 203 (11211-7546)
PHONE....................................718 769-4148
David Goldstein, *President*
Susan Goldstein, *Vice Pres*
▲ **EMP:** 15 **EST:** 1978
SQ FT: 25,000
SALES (est): 1.2MM **Privately Held**
SIC: 2253 Sweaters & sweater coats, knit

(G-2097)
M FACTORY USA INC
147 41st St Unit 8 (11232-2625)
PHONE....................................917 410-7878
Alessandro Lanaro, *President*
Tara Montoneri, *Director*
Rebecca Gieser, *Admin Sec*
EMP: 4 **EST:** 2016
SQ FT: 6,000
SALES (est): 3.6MM
SALES (corp-wide): 21.8MM **Privately**
Held
SIC: 3851 Eyeglasses, lenses & frames
PA: Tworoger Associates, Ltd.
594 Broadway Rm 801
New York NY 10012
212 965-4900

(G-2098)
MAC ARTSPRAY FINISHING
CORP
Also Called: Mac-Artspray Finshg
799 Sheffield Ave (11207-7797)
PHONE....................................718 649-3800
Howard Moskowitz, *President*
EMP: 12
SQ FT: 10,000
SALES: 800K **Privately Held**
SIC: 3479 Painting of metal products

(G-2099)
MACADAME INC
Also Called: Imakr Store New York
68 34th St Unit 6 (11232-2000)
PHONE....................................212 477-1930
Brian Quan, *Managing Dir*
Silvain Preumont, *Chairman*
EMP: 7
SALES (est): 195.4K **Privately Held**
SIC: 2754 Business forms: gravure printing

(G-2100)
MACEDONIA LTD
Also Called: Carlton Ice Cream Co
34 E 29th St (11226-5027)
PHONE....................................718 462-3596
Aristides Saketos, *President*
Zeno Gianopoulos, *Vice Pres*
▲ **EMP:** 12
SQ FT: 8,500
SALES (est): 2.1MM **Privately Held**
WEB: www.macedonia.com
SIC: 2024 5143 Ice cream, bulk; ice
cream & ices

(G-2101)
MAD SCNTSTS BRWING
PRTNERS LLC
Also Called: Sixpoint Brewery
40 Van Dyke St (11231-1529)
PHONE....................................347 766-2739
Shane Welch, *President*
Jeffrey Gorlechen, *Sales Staff*
David Ranly, *Supervisor*
▲ **EMP:** 25
SALES (est): 7.5MM **Privately Held**
SIC: 2082 Beer (alcoholic beverage)

(G-2102)
MADE CLOSE LLC
141 Meserole Ave (11222-2744)
PHONE....................................917 837-1357
David Mehlman, *CEO*
EMP: 6
SALES (est): 185.1K **Privately Held**
SIC: 2051 Bakery: wholesale or whole-
sale/retail combined

(G-2103)
MAJESTIC HOME IMPRVS DISTR
5902 Fort Hamilton Pkwy (11219-4834)
PHONE....................................718 853-5079
Man L Wong, *President*
▲ **EMP:** 5
SALES (est): 399.3K **Privately Held**
WEB: www.majesticimprovements.com
SIC: 2514 1521 Kitchen cabinets: metal;
single-family home remodeling, additions
& repairs

(G-2104)
MAKERBOT INDUSTRIES LLC
(DH)
1 Metrotech Ctr Fl 21 (11201-3949)
PHONE....................................347 334-6800
Jenny Lawton, *CEO*
▲ **EMP:** 150
SQ FT: 15,000
SALES (est): 101MM
SALES (corp-wide): 179MM **Privately**
Held
SIC: 3621 3625 5084 Motors & genera-
tors; actuators, industrial; industrial ma-
chinery & equipment
HQ: Stratasys, Inc.
7665 Commerce Way
Eden Prairie MN 55344
952 937-3000

(G-2105)
MALIA MILLS INC
32 33rd St Unit 13 (11232-1924)
PHONE....................................212 354-4200
EMP: 11
SALES (est): 654.2K **Privately Held**
SIC: 2339 5699 Mfg Women's/Misses'
Outerwear Ret Misc Apparel/Accessories

(G-2106)
MANGO USA INC
5620 1st Ave Ste 1 (11220-2519)
PHONE....................................718 998-6050
Kheder Fatiha, *CEO*
▲ **EMP:** 20 **EST:** 2006
SALES (est): 3.8MM **Privately Held**
SIC: 3144 3021 3149 2339 Dress shoes,
women's; canvas shoes, rubber soled;
athletic shoes, except rubber or plastic;
women's & misses' athletic clothing &
sportswear; women's & children's clothing

(G-2107)
MANHATTAN COMFORT INC (PA)
1482 Carroll St (11213-4514)
PHONE....................................908 888-0818
Schneur Lang, *President*
▲ **EMP:** 8
SALES: 10MM **Privately Held**
SIC: 2521 5712 Wood office furniture; fur-
niture stores

(G-2108)
MANHATTAN POLY BAG
CORPORATION
1228 47th St (11219-2501)
P.O. Box 370713 (11237-0713)
PHONE....................................917 689-7549
William Kaufman, *President*
Sylvia Kaufman, *Vice Pres*
Gary Kaufman, *Controller*

▲ = Import ▼ =Export
◆ =Import/Export

EMP: 32
SQ FT: 88,500
SALES (est): 3.9MM Privately Held
SIC: 2673 Plastic bags: made from purchased materials

(G-2109)
MANHATTAN SPECIAL BOTTLING
342 Manhattan Ave (11211-2404)
PHONE................................718 388-4144
Aurora Passaro, President
Louis Passaro, Exec VP
EMP: 10
SQ FT: 7,500
SALES (est): 1MM Privately Held
WEB: www.manhattanspecial.com
SIC: 2086 Soft drinks: packaged in cans, bottles, etc.

(G-2110)
MANNING LEWIS DIV RUBICON INDS
848 E 43rd St (11210-3502)
PHONE................................908 687-2400
Michael Rubinberg, President
EMP: 25
SALES (est): 1.2MM Privately Held
SIC: 3443 Fabricated plate work (boiler shop)

(G-2111)
MANZIONE READY MIX CORP
Also Called: Manzione Enterprises
46 Knickerbocker Ave (11237-1410)
PHONE................................718 628-3837
Rocco Manzione, President
Gary Snolpava, President
EMP: 4 EST: 1999
SQ FT: 45,000
SALES (est): 3MM Privately Held
SIC: 3273 Ready-mixed concrete

(G-2112)
MARAMONT CORPORATION (PA)
5600 1st Ave (11220-2550)
PHONE................................718 439-8900
George Chivari, President
Linda Jannzzkowski, CFO
▲ EMP: 420
SQ FT: 65,000
SALES (est): 101MM Privately Held
SIC: 2099 8322 Ready-to-eat meals, salads & sandwiches; salads, fresh or refrigerated; sandwiches, assembled & packaged: for wholesale market; individual & family services

(G-2113)
MARCY BUSINESS FORMS INC
1468 40th St (11218-3510)
PHONE................................718 935-9100
Samuel Roth, Ch of Bd
EMP: 5
SALES (est): 550K Privately Held
WEB: www.marcybusinessforms.com
SIC: 2761 Manifold business forms

(G-2114)
MARCY PRINTING INC
777 Kent Ave Ste A (11205-1543)
P.O. Box 110199 (11211-0199)
PHONE................................718 935-9100
Charles H Laufer, President
Jano Roth, Manager
EMP: 5
SQ FT: 12,000
SALES (est): 808.9K Privately Held
SIC: 2752 Commercial printing, offset; letters, circular or form: lithographed

(G-2115)
MARINA HOLDING CORP
Also Called: Venice Marina
3939 Emmons Ave (11235-1001)
PHONE................................718 646-9283
Chuck Rondot, Manager
EMP: 15
SQ FT: 6,000

SALES (est): 1.3MM
SALES (corp-wide): 1.3B Privately Held
WEB: www.venicemarina.com
SIC: 2339 5551 5541 Women's & misses' outerwear; boat dealers; gasoline service stations
PA: Jordache Enterprises Inc.
1400 Broadway Rm 1400 # 1400
New York NY 10018
212 643-8400

(G-2116)
MARLBOROUGH JEWELS INC
67 35th St Unit B516 (11232-2228)
P.O. Box 320673 (11232-0673)
PHONE................................718 768-2000
Donald Calaman, President
EMP: 8
SALES (est): 1MM Privately Held
SIC: 3961 5094 3911 Costume jewelry, ex. precious metal & semiprecious stones; jewelry; jewelry, precious metal

(G-2117)
MARLOW PRINTING CO INC
Also Called: Nap Industries
667 Kent Ave (11249-7530)
PHONE................................718 625-4948
Jack Freund, President
Morris Lowy, Vice Pres
EMP: 30 EST: 1977
SQ FT: 35,000
SALES (est): 3.9MM Privately Held
WEB: www.napind.com
SIC: 2759 2752 Flexographic printing; commercial printing, lithographic

(G-2118)
MARLY HOME INDUSTRIES USA INC
181 Lombardy St (11222-5417)
PHONE................................718 388-3030
EMP: 10
SALES (est): 190.2K Privately Held
SIC: 2824 2221 Polyester fibers; polyester broadwoven fabrics

(G-2119)
MAROVATO INDUSTRIES INC
108 Dobbin St (11222-2806)
PHONE................................718 389-0800
Margaret Rotondi, Ch of Bd
Marty Pietanza, Opers Mgr
Rosemarie Rotondi, Treasurer
▲ EMP: 15
SALES (est): 4MM Privately Held
WEB: www.marovato.com
SIC: 3441 8711 Building components, structural steel; structural engineering; mechanical engineering

(G-2120)
MARTIN GREENFIELD CLOTHIERS
Also Called: Greenfield Martin Clothiers
239 Varet St (11206-3823)
PHONE................................718 497-5480
Martin Greenfield, President
Jay Greenfield, Exec VP
Todd Greenfield, Vice Pres
▲ EMP: 140
SQ FT: 40,000
SALES (est): 15MM Privately Held
SIC: 2311 2325 Suits, men's & boys': made from purchased materials; jackets, tailored suit-type: men's & boys'; topcoats, men's & boys': made from purchased materials; slacks, dress: men's, youths' & boys'

(G-2121)
MASON WOODWORKS LLC
127 Chester Ave (11218-3021)
PHONE................................917 363-7052
Robert Mason, Principal
EMP: 5
SALES (est): 380.9K Privately Held
SIC: 2431 Millwork

(G-2122)
MASS APPEAL MAGAZINE
261 Vandervoort Ave (11211-1718)
PHONE................................718 858-0979
Adrian Moeller, Partner
Patrick Elasik, Partner
EMP: 7 EST: 1998

SQ FT: 1,100
SALES (est): 830.6K Privately Held
SIC: 2721 Magazines: publishing only, not printed on site

(G-2123)
MATCHABLES INC
Also Called: Bara Fashions
106 Green St Ste G1 (11222-1352)
PHONE................................718 389-9318
Raphael Blumenstock, President
Ruth Malach, Vice Pres
EMP: 10
SQ FT: 8,000
SALES (est): 750K Privately Held
SIC: 2253 Sweaters & sweater coats, knit

(G-2124)
MATERIAL PROCESS SYSTEMS INC
613 Berriman St (11208-5203)
PHONE................................718 302-3081
Steven Urbatsch, President
Matthew Josephs, Vice Pres
▲ EMP: 14
SALES (est): 1.8MM Privately Held
WEB: www.materialprocess.com
SIC: 2434 3446 Wood kitchen cabinets; architectural metalwork

(G-2125)
MATRIX STEEL COMPANY INC
50 Bogart St (11206-3818)
PHONE................................718 381-6800
EMP: 6
SALES (est): 1.5MM Privately Held
SIC: 3312 3321 Fabrication Structural Steel/Miscellaneous Ironworks

(G-2126)
MATTHEWS HATS
99 Kenilworth Pl Fl 1 (11210-2423)
PHONE................................718 859-4683
Larry S Matthews, Partner
Merrill Matthews, Partner
Benjamin Obler, Prdtn Mgr
EMP: 7
SALES (est): 410K Privately Held
SIC: 2353 Hats, trimmed: women's, misses' & children's

(G-2127)
MAXWELL BAKERY INC
2700 Atlantic Ave (11207-2819)
P.O. Box 76, New York (10028-0015)
PHONE................................718 498-2200
George Jograj, Owner
Earl Wheelin, General Mgr
EMP: 25
SQ FT: 10,000
SALES (est): 1.6MM Privately Held
WEB: www.maxwellbakery.com
SIC: 2051 Bakery: wholesale or wholesale/retail combined

(G-2128)
MDCARE911 LLC
Also Called: Gocare247
30 Main St Apt 5c (11201-8213)
PHONE................................917 640-4869
Anthony Schweinzer,
EMP: 5
SALES (est): 128.9K Privately Held
SIC: 7372 Home entertainment computer software

(G-2129)
MDS HOT BAGELS DELI INC
127 Church Ave (11218-3917)
PHONE................................718 438-5650
Alex Esalias, Manager
EMP: 7
SQ FT: 1,000
SALES (est): 435K Privately Held
SIC: 2051 5461 5411 Bagels, fresh or frozen; bagels; delicatessens

(G-2130)
MECHANICAL DISPLAYS INC
4420 Farragut Rd (11203-6522)
PHONE................................718 258-5588
Hugo Paulucci, President
Lou Nasti, Vice Pres
▲ EMP: 7
SQ FT: 7,500

SALES (est): 1MM Privately Held
WEB: www.mechanicaldisplays.com
SIC: 3944 7389 Trains & equipment, toy: electric & mechanical; convention & show services

(G-2131)
MECHON BEISS UVAS
1130 40th St (11218-2745)
PHONE................................718 436-1489
Shie Weisblum, President
EMP: 5
SALES (est): 291.6K Privately Held
SIC: 2791 Typesetting

(G-2132)
MEDI-TECH INTERNATIONAL CORP (PA)
Also Called: Spandage
26 Court St Ste 1301 (11242-1113)
PHONE................................800 333-0109
Jacqueline Fortunato, CEO
Victoria Lamantia, COO
Randy Walsh, Vice Pres
Amy Nikolich, Accounts Mgr
Clariel Francisco, Cust Mgr
▲ EMP: 4 EST: 1973
SQ FT: 1,000
SALES (est): 2.6MM Privately Held
WEB: www.medi-techintl.com
SIC: 3842 2339 Bandages: plastic, muslin, plaster of paris, etc.; dressings, surgical; maternity clothing

(G-2133)
MEEKER SALES CORP
551 Sutter Ave (11207-4001)
PHONE................................718 384-5400
Harvey Worth, President
EMP: 1
SQ FT: 150
SALES (est): 1.2MM Privately Held
SIC: 2514 Metal household furniture

(G-2134)
MEGA PLASTIC GROUP INC
2667 Coney Island Ave (11223-5520)
PHONE................................347 737-8444
Serkan Ozayar, CEO
▲ EMP: 30
SALES (est): 134.5K Privately Held
SIC: 2821 Plastics materials & resins

(G-2135)
MEISEL-PESKIN CO INC (PA)
349 Scholes St 353 (11206-1787)
PHONE................................718 497-1840
Garry Meisel, President
▲ EMP: 78 EST: 1934
SQ FT: 18,000
SALES (est): 4.9MM Privately Held
SIC: 3999 Furs, dressed: bleached, curried, scraped, tanned or dyed

(G-2136)
MENPIN SUPPLY CORP
1229 60th St (11219-4930)
PHONE................................718 415-4168
David Hiehs, President
EMP: 18 EST: 2016
SALES: 2.8MM Privately Held
SIC: 3589 Water filters & softeners, household type

(G-2137)
MENROSE USA LLC
Also Called: Milkboy
605 Montgomery St (11225-3129)
PHONE................................718 221-5540
EMP: 5 EST: 2014
SALES (est): 289.7K Privately Held
SIC: 2066 Chocolate

(G-2138)
MENUCHA PUBLISHERS INC
1221 38th St (11218-1928)
PHONE................................718 232-0856
Hirsch Traube, President
▲ EMP: 16
SALES (est): 1.6MM Privately Held
SIC: 2741 Miscellaneous publishing

(G-2139)
MERB LLC
Also Called: Belgian Boys USA
240 Kent Ave (11249-4121)
PHONE.................................631 393-3621
Michael Berro, *President*
Ricardo Dellajiovanna, *Vice Pres*
Greg Galel, *Marketing Mgr*
Anouck Gotlib, *Creative Dir*
EMP: 10 EST: 2013
SALES: 10MM **Privately Held**
SIC: 2099 Food preparations

(G-2140)
MERCADO GLOBAL INC
254 36th St Unit 41 (11232-2499)
PHONE.................................718 838-9908
Garrard Beeney, *Partner*
Meg Koglin, *Principal*
Leah Vinton, *Principal*
Ruth Degolia, *Exec Dir*
EMP: 4
SALES: 1.1MM **Privately Held**
WEB: www.mercadoglobal.org
SIC: 3961 Jewelry apparel, non-precious
metals

(G-2141)
MERCURY PAINT
CORPORATION (PA)
4808 Farragut Rd (11203-6612)
PHONE.................................718 469-8787
Jeff Berman, *President*
Wyatt Tichner, *Opers Mgr*
▲ **EMP:** 75 EST: 1961
SQ FT: 100,000
SALES: 17.7MM **Privately Held**
WEB: www.mercurypaintcorp.com
SIC: 2851 5231 Paints & paint additives;
paint

(G-2142)
MERCURY PLASTICS CORP
989 Utica Ave 995 (11203-4399)
PHONE.................................718 498-5400
William Wright, *President*
George Wright Jr, *Corp Secy*
▲ **EMP:** 20
SQ FT: 8,000
SALES (est): 3MM **Privately Held**
SIC: 3089 Molding primary plastic

(G-2143)
MERKOS LINYONEI CHINUCH
INC
Also Called: Merkos Bookstore
291 Kingston Ave (11213-3402)
PHONE.................................718 778-0226
Malka Ahern, *Manager*
EMP: 20
SALES (corp-wide): 950K **Privately Held**
WEB: www.chabad.org
SIC: 2731 Books: publishing only
PA: Merkos L'inyonei Chinuch, Inc.
770 Eastern Pkwy
Brooklyn NY 11213
718 774-4000

(G-2144)
MERZON LEATHER CO INC
810 Humboldt St Ste 2 (11222-1913)
PHONE.................................718 782-6260
Richard Merzon, *President*
▲ **EMP:** 150 EST: 1943
SQ FT: 50,000
SALES (est): 14.7MM **Privately Held**
SIC: 3161 3172 Cases, carrying; suit-
cases; camera carrying bags; personal
leather goods

(G-2145)
MESORAH PUBLICATIONS LTD
4401 2nd Ave (11232-4212)
PHONE.................................718 921-9000
Martin Zlotowitz, *President*
Jacob Brander, *Vice Pres*
Bernard Kempler, *MIS Dir*
Nosson Scherman, *Admin Sec*
▲ **EMP:** 43
SQ FT: 20,000
SALES (est): 8MM **Privately Held**
WEB: www.artscroll.com
SIC: 2731 Books: publishing only; pam-
phlets: publishing only, not printed on site

(G-2146)
METAL CRAFTS INC
Also Called: Metalcraft By N Barzel
650 Berriman St (11208-5304)
PHONE.................................718 443-3333
Norman Barzel, *President*
Norman Barsi, *President*
EMP: 6
SALES (est): 590K **Privately Held**
SIC: 3441 Fabricated structural metal

(G-2147)
METRO KITCHENS CORP
1040 E 45th St (11203-6542)
PHONE.................................718 434-1166
John Ciavattoni, *President*
Kevin Taflin, *Vice Pres*
▲ **EMP:** 11
SQ FT: 10,000
SALES (est): 880K **Privately Held**
WEB: www.metro-kitchens.com
SIC: 2434 5031 1751 Wood kitchen cabi-
nets; kitchen cabinets; cabinet & finish
carpentry

(G-2148)
METRO PRODUCTS & SERVICES
LLC (PA)
Also Called: Gumbusters of New York
1424 74th St (11228-2208)
PHONE.................................866 846-8486
Anthony Mule, *Owner*
Andrea Mule, *Co-Owner*
▲ **EMP:** 8
SQ FT: 5,000
SALES (est): 871.9K **Privately Held**
SIC: 2861 Gum & wood chemicals

(G-2149)
METROPOLITAN PACKG MFG
CORP
68 Java St (11222-1519)
PHONE.................................718 383-2700
Malka Katz, *President*
Herman Katz, *Vice Pres*
Abraham Katz, *VP Sales*
▲ **EMP:** 35 EST: 1964
SQ FT: 10,000
SALES (est): 6.8MM **Privately Held**
WEB: www.metropack.com
SIC: 2673 Plastic bags: made from pur-
chased materials

(G-2150)
MICHAEL BERNSTEIN DESIGN
ASSOC
361 Stagg St Fl 4 (11206-1734)
PHONE.................................718 456-9277
EMP: 20
SQ FT: 10,000
SALES (est): 1.6MM **Privately Held**
SIC: 2431 2434 Mfg Millwork Mfg Wood
Kitchen Cabinets

(G-2151)
MICHAEL STUART INC
199 Cook St (11206-3701)
PHONE.................................718 821-0704
Michael Stuart Fuchs, *President*
EMP: 20 EST: 1975
SQ FT: 20,000
SALES (est): 1.5MM **Privately Held**
SIC: 2369 2392 2211 2361 Girls' & chil-
dren's outerwear; tablecloths: made from
purchased materials; bathmats, cotton;
girls' & children's dresses, blouses &
shirts

(G-2152)
MICRO ESSENTIAL
LABORATORY
4224 Avenue H (11210-3518)
P.O. Box 100824 (11210-0824)
PHONE.................................718 338-3618
Joel Florin, *President*
Mark Florin, *Vice Pres*
Evelyn La Nier, *Office Mgr*
EMP: 30
SQ FT: 7,500
SALES (est): 7.3MM **Privately Held**
WEB: www.microessentiallab.com
SIC: 2672 Chemically treated papers:
made from purchased materials

(G-2153)
MILGO INDUSTRIAL INC (PA)
Also Called: Milgo/Bufkin
68 Lombardy St (11222-5234)
PHONE.................................718 388-6476
Bruce J Gitlin, *President*
Rose Gitlin, *Vice Pres*
Gina Jordan, *Vice Pres*
Barbara Kanter, *CFO*
EMP: 70 EST: 1918
SQ FT: 30,000
SALES (est): 11.6MM **Privately Held**
WEB: www.milgo-bufkin.com
SIC: 3446 3442 3398 Architectural metal-
work; metal doors, sash & trim; store
fronts, prefabricated, metal; brazing
(hardening) of metal

(G-2154)
MILGO INDUSTRIAL INC
514 Varick Ave (11222-5400)
PHONE.................................718 387-0406
Alex Kveton, *Branch Mgr*
EMP: 5
SALES (corp-wide): 11.6MM **Privately**
Held
WEB: www.milgo-bufkin.com
SIC: 3446 3442 3398 Architectural metal-
work; metal doors, sash & trim; brazing
(hardening) of metal
PA: Milgo Industrial Inc.
68 Lombardy St
Brooklyn NY 11222
718 388-6476

(G-2155)
MILLENNIUM STL RACK RNTALS
INC (PA)
253 Bond St (11217-2919)
PHONE.................................718 965-4736
Toll Free:.................................877 -
David Fox, *President*
Nicola Romero, *Manager*
▲ **EMP:** 9 EST: 1999
SALES (est): 1.1MM **Privately Held**
WEB: www.millenniumsteelservice.com
SIC: 2542 7359 Garment racks: except
wood; equipment rental & leasing

(G-2156)
MINDBODYGREEN LLC
45 Main St Ste 422 (11201-1093)
PHONE.................................347 529-6952
Jason Wacob,
Stephen Anderson,
EMP: 29
SQ FT: 2,500
SALES (est): 2.3MM **Privately Held**
SIC: 2741

(G-2157)
MINI-CIRCUITS FORT WAYNE
LLC
13 Neptune Ave (11235-4404)
P.O. Box 350166 (11235-0166)
PHONE.................................718 934-4500
Gerard Crepeau, *Purch Mgr*
Arthur Ackerman, *QC Mgr*
Wing Shum, *Engineer*
Marc Sweet, *Controller*
Lynn Fogel, *CTO*
EMP: 500
SALES (est): 66.2MM **Privately Held**
WEB: www.matchingpad.com
SIC: 3679 3678 3677 3674 Attenuators;
electronic connectors; electronic coils,
transformers & other inductors; semicon-
ductors & related devices; radio & TV
communications equipment; current-car-
rying wiring devices

(G-2158)
MISHPACHA MAGAZINE INC
5809 16th Ave (11204-2112)
PHONE.................................718 686-9339
Eli Peli, *President*
Rachel Bachrach, *Editor*
EMP: 5
SALES (est): 512.5K **Privately Held**
SIC: 2721 Magazines: publishing & printing

(G-2159)
MISS SPORTSWEAR INC
117 9th St (11215-3108)
PHONE.................................212 391-2535

Moses Fallas, *Ch of Bd*
EMP: 12 **Privately Held**
SIC: 2339 Women's & misses' athletic
clothing & sportswear
PA: M.I.S.S. Sportswear, Inc.
1410 Broadway Rm 703
New York NY 10018

(G-2160)
MISS SPORTSWEAR INC
Also Called: Miss Group, The
117 9th St (11215-3108)
PHONE.................................718 369-6012
Sammy Fallas, *Branch Mgr*
EMP: 12 **Privately Held**
SIC: 2339 Women's & misses' athletic
clothing & sportswear
PA: M.I.S.S. Sportswear, Inc.
1410 Broadway Rm 703
New York NY 10018

(G-2161)
MISSIONTEX INC
236 Greenpoint Ave Ste 12 (11222-2495)
PHONE.................................718 532-9053
Jay McLaughlin, *Principal*
▲ **EMP:** 5
SALES (est): 320K **Privately Held**
SIC: 2281 5949 5632 5651 Yarn spinning
mills; fabric stores piece goods; fur ap-
parel; family clothing stores

(G-2162)
MJK CUTTING INC
Also Called: M J K
117 9th St (11215-3108)
PHONE.................................718 384-7613
Wing Lau, *President*
EMP: 10
SALES (est): 750K **Privately Held**
SIC: 3552 Jacquard card cutting machines

(G-2163)
MJK ENTERPRISES LLC
Also Called: M & J Custom Lampshade Com-
pany
34 35th St (11232-2021)
PHONE.................................917 653-9042
Martin Kuranc, *Managing Prtnr*
EMP: 8 EST: 2011
SALES: 50MM **Privately Held**
SIC: 3648 Lanterns: electric, gas, carbide,
kerosene or gasoline

(G-2164)
MKJ COMMUNICATIONS INC
850 3rd Ave Ste 402 (11232-1523)
PHONE.................................212 206-0072
Jennifer Herman, *President*
EMP: 37
SQ FT: 3,500
SALES (est): 7.2MM **Privately Held**
SIC: 3669 Intercommunication systems,
electric

(G-2165)
MNN HOLDING COMPANY LLC
Also Called: Mother Nature & Partners
155 Water St Ste 616 (11201-1016)
PHONE.................................404 558-5251
Michael Jacobson, *CFO*
EMP: 18 **Privately Held**
SIC: 7372 8748 Publishers' computer soft-
ware; publishing consultant
PA: Mnn Holding Company, Llc
191 Peachtree St Ne Ste 4
Atlanta GA 30303

(G-2166)
MODERN PLASTIC BAGS MFG
INC
63 Flushing Ave Unit 303 (11205-1080)
PHONE.................................718 237-2985
Abrahm Stossel, *President*
EMP: 5
SQ FT: 3,000
SALES: 450K **Privately Held**
SIC: 2673 Plastic bags: made from pur-
chased materials

(G-2167)
MOES WEAR APPAREL INC
1020 E 48th St Ste 8 (11203-6605)
PHONE.................................718 940-1597
Selly Nessry, *President*
Jeff Saad, *Vice Pres*

Morris Saad, *Vice Pres*
▲ EMP: 13
SQ FT: 50,000
SALES (est): 2.1MM **Privately Held**
SIC: 2339 Women's & misses' outerwear

(G-2168)
MOLDOVA PICKLES & SALADS INC
1060 E 46th St (11203-6516)
PHONE.............................718 284-2220
Naum Zozulya, *President*
Vitality Pinchev, *Vice Pres*
▲ EMP: 5
SALES (est): 413K **Privately Held**
SIC: 2035 Pickles, vinegar

(G-2169)
MONFEFO LLC
630 Flushing Ave 5q (11206-5026)
PHONE.............................347 779-2600
Justin Monsul, *Mng Member*
EMP: 5 EST: 2016
SQ FT: 600
SALES: 300K **Privately Held**
SIC: 2086 Soft drinks: packaged in cans, bottles, etc.

(G-2170)
MONTROSE EQUIPMENT SALES INC
Also Called: Ace
202 N 10th St (11211-1109)
PHONE.............................718 388-7446
Emil Romotzki, *President*
Jack Pivovarov, *Corp Secy*
▲ EMP: 12
SQ FT: 8,000
SALES (est): 1.2MM **Privately Held**
SIC: 3541 Machine tools, metal cutting type

(G-2171)
MORCO PRODUCTS CORP
556 39th St (11232-3002)
PHONE.............................718 853-4005
Michael Morgan, *President*
Neil Falcone, *Vice Pres*
EMP: 15
SQ FT: 6,200
SALES (est): 1.1MM **Privately Held**
SIC: 3599 Machine shop, jobbing & repair

(G-2172)
MOTI INC
4118 13th Ave (11219-1333)
PHONE.............................718 436-4280
Mordechai Fleicher, *President*
▲ EMP: 16
SQ FT: 8,000
SALES (est): 1.2MM **Privately Held**
SIC: 3999 Wigs, including doll wigs, toupees or wiglets

(G-2173)
MOZNAIM PUBLISHING CO INC
Also Called: Moznaim Co
4304 12th Ave (11219-1301)
PHONE.............................718 853-0525
Menachem Wagshol, *President*
Moznaim Gross, *Superintendent*
Monshe Sternlicht, *Vice Pres*
▲ EMP: 6
SALES (est): 360K **Privately Held**
WEB: www.moznaim.com
SIC: 2731 5192 5999 Books: publishing only; books; religious goods

(G-2174)
MPL METAL INC
1560 Troy Ave (11203-6536)
PHONE.............................718 338-4952
Moises Robles, *Vice Pres*
EMP: 5
SALES (est): 512K **Privately Held**
SIC: 3499 Aerosol valves, metal

(G-2175)
MR DISPOSABLE INC
101 Richardson St Ste 2 (11211-1344)
PHONE.............................718 388-8574
Raymond Cora, *CEO*
Victor Morales, *Vice Pres*
Debbie Cora, *Admin Sec*
▲ EMP: 10

SALES: 400K **Privately Held**
WEB: www.mrdisposable.com
SIC: 2676 Diapers, paper (disposable): made from purchased paper

(G-2176)
MR GLASS TEMPERING LLC
38 15th St (11215-4610)
PHONE.............................718 576-3826
Raymond Gao,
Robert Liao,
EMP: 12
SQ FT: 10,000
SALES: 1.6MM **Privately Held**
SIC: 3211 Tempered glass

(G-2177)
MR PIEROGI LLC
126 12th St (11215-3817)
PHONE.............................718 499-7821
Leonard Sherman,
EMP: 11
SALES (est): 1.2MM **Privately Held**
SIC: 2013 Sausages & other prepared meats

(G-2178)
MR SIGN USA INC
1920 Atlantic Ave (11233-3004)
PHONE.............................718 218-3321
Michael Leivowitz, *President*
EMP: 15
SALES (est): 1.2MM **Privately Held**
SIC: 3993 Signs & advertising specialties

(G-2179)
MRCHOCOLATECOM LLC
Also Called: Jacques Torres Chocolate
66 Water St Ste 2 (11201-1048)
PHONE.............................718 875-9772
Jacques Torres, *Partner*
Keitaro Goto, *Partner*
Kris Kruid, *Partner*
Linda Lee, *Sales Dir*
Saida Chabla, *Marketing Staff*
▲ EMP: 18
SALES (est): 910K **Privately Held**
WEB: www.jacquestorres.com
SIC: 2064 5145 5441 Candy & other confectionery products; confectionery; candy, nut & confectionery stores

(G-2180)
MS PAPER PRODUCTS CO INC
930 Bedford Ave (11205-4502)
PHONE.............................718 624-0248
Solomon Schwimmer, *President*
EMP: 6 EST: 1970
SQ FT: 12,000
SALES: 500K **Privately Held**
SIC: 2631 Paperboard mills

(G-2181)
MTZ ENTERPRISES INC
870 39th St (11232)
PHONE.............................347 834-2716
Sam Brody, *President*
EMP: 10
SQ FT: 1,200
SALES: 2MM **Privately Held**
SIC: 3646 Commercial indusl & institutional electric lighting fixtures

(G-2182)
MY HANKY INC
680 81st St Apt 4d (11228-2833)
PHONE.............................646 321-0869
Frank Marino, *President*
EMP: 10
SQ FT: 500
SALES: 500K **Privately Held**
SIC: 2389 Handkerchiefs, except paper

(G-2183)
MYSTIC DISPLAY CO INC
909 Remsen Ave (11236-1624)
PHONE.............................718 485-2651
David Censi, *President*
Barry Censi, *Corp Secy*
Hank Lombardi, *Vice Pres*
▼ EMP: 2
SQ FT: 47,000
SALES: 8MM **Privately Held**
WEB: www.mysticdisplay.com
SIC: 3993 7319 Displays & cutouts, window & lobby; display advertising service

(G-2184)
N C IRON WORKS INC
1117 60th St (11219-4925)
PHONE.............................718 633-4660
Nicholas Sorrentino, *President*
EMP: 5
SQ FT: 3,900
SALES (est): 941.5K **Privately Held**
SIC: 3312 Hot-rolled iron & steel products

(G-2185)
NAGAD CABINETS INC
1039 Mcdonald Ave (11230-1020)
PHONE.............................718 382-7200
Naftali Grueberger, *President*
EMP: 5
SQ FT: 2,000
SALES (est): 745.6K **Privately Held**
SIC: 2434 Vanities, bathroom: wood

(G-2186)
NANOTRONICS IMAGING INC
63 Flushing Ave Unit 128 (11205-1059)
PHONE.............................212 401-6209
Matthew Putman, *CEO*
Jonathan Yancey, *Technology*
EMP: 20
SALES (corp-wide): 2.9MM **Privately Held**
SIC: 3826 Analytical instruments
PA: Nanotronics Imaging, Inc.
    2251 Front St Ste 109-111
    Cuyahoga Falls OH 44221
    330 926-9809

(G-2187)
NAP INDUSTRIES INC
Also Called: N A P
667 Kent Ave (11249-7500)
PHONE.............................718 625-4948
Leopold Lowy, *President*
Morris Lowy, *Chairman*
Jack Freund, *Vice Pres*
Leiby Freund, *Manager*
▲ EMP: 90
SQ FT: 55,000
SALES (est): 19.1MM **Privately Held**
SIC: 3081 Unsupported plastics film & sheet

(G-2188)
NARRATIVELY INC
30 John St (11201-1122)
PHONE.............................203 536-0332
Noah Rosenberg, *President*
EMP: 25 EST: 2012
SQ FT: 20,000
SALES (est): 1.3MM **Privately Held**
SIC: 2741

(G-2189)
NATIONAL DIE & BUTTON MOULD CO
Also Called: Eisen Bros
1 Kent Ave (11249-1014)
PHONE.............................201 939-7800
Louis Eisenpresser, *President*
George Eisenpresser, *Chairman*
EMP: 50 EST: 1911
SQ FT: 65,000
SALES (est): 5.1MM **Privately Held**
WEB: www.nailheads.com
SIC: 3965 3469 Buttons & parts; buckles & buckle parts; eyelets, metal: clothing, fabrics, boots or shoes; metal stampings

(G-2190)
NATIONAL PRFMCE SOLUTIONS INC
Also Called: Squeaky Clean
1043 78th St (11228-2611)
PHONE.............................718 833-4767
Lola Bizas, *Ch of Bd*
Jacob Kahle, *Principal*
Greg Bowman, *Co-Owner*
Michell Bowman, *Co-Owner*
Ryan Mullen, *Director*
EMP: 100
SQ FT: 400
SALES: 20.1MM **Privately Held**
SIC: 3993 Advertising artwork

(G-2191)
NATIONWIDE DAIRY INC
792 E 93rd St (11236-1831)
PHONE.............................347 689-8148
Eduard Magidov, *CEO*
◆ EMP: 5
SQ FT: 9,000
SALES (est): 423.4K **Privately Held**
SIC: 2023 Dry, condensed, evaporated dairy products

(G-2192)
NATURAL STONE & CABINET INC
1365 Halsey St (11237-6102)
PHONE.............................718 388-2988
Sally Lee, *Owner*
▲ EMP: 5
SALES (est): 423.1K **Privately Held**
SIC: 2522 Cabinets, office: except wood

(G-2193)
NAUTICAL MARINE PAINT CORP
Also Called: Nautical Paint
4802 Farragut Rd (11203-6690)
PHONE.............................718 462-7000
EMP: 25
SQ FT: 4,000
SALES (corp-wide): 15.8MM **Privately Held**
SIC: 2851 5231 Mfg Paints/Allied Products Ret Paint/Glass/Wallpaper
PA: Nautical Marine Paint Corp
    1999 Elizabeth St
    North Brunswick NJ 08902
    732 821-3200

(G-2194)
NB ELCTRCAL ENCLSURES MFRS INC
902 903 Shepherd Ave (11208)
PHONE.............................718 272-8792
Neville Bearam, *President*
Travis Maynard, *Business Mgr*
EMP: 7
SALES: 2MM **Privately Held**
SIC: 3441 Fabricated structural metal

(G-2195)
NCC NY LLC
1840 Mcdonald Ave (11223-1827)
PHONE.............................718 943-7000
Joey Haber,
Joe Nakash,
Ralph Nakash,
▲ EMP: 20 EST: 1999
SQ FT: 9,000
SALES (est): 4.8MM **Privately Held**
WEB: www.ehalacha.com
SIC: 3699 Extension cords
PA: Nakash Five Points Llc
    1400 Broadway Fl 15
    New York NY 10018

(G-2196)
NEO CABINETRY LLC
400 Liberty Ave (11207-3061)
PHONE.............................718 403-0456
Louis Doucet, *Owner*
EMP: 10
SALES (est): 1MM **Privately Held**
SIC: 2434 Wood kitchen cabinets

(G-2197)
NEO PLASTICS LLC
1007 Sheffield Ave (11207-8341)
PHONE.............................646 542-1499
Isak Bengiyat,
EMP: 12
SALES (est): 607.7K **Privately Held**
SIC: 3089 Plastic containers, except foam

(G-2198)
NEPTUNE MACHINE INC
521 Carroll St (11215-1011)
PHONE.............................718 852-4100
Nicholas G Karkas, *President*
John Karkas, *Vice Pres*
Camille Manzo, *Office Mgr*
Aris Fotopoulos, *Manager*
EMP: 20
SQ FT: 12,500
SALES (est): 3.8MM **Privately Held**
WEB: www.neptunemachine.com
SIC: 3599 Machine shop, jobbing & repair

(G-2199)
NEW AGE IRONWORKS INC
183 Van Siclen Ave (11207-2605)
PHONE................................718 277-1895
Yair Tapia, *President*
EMP: 10
SALES (est): 1.2MM **Privately Held**
SIC: 3441 Fabricated structural metal

(G-2200)
NEW ART PUBLICATIONS INC
Also Called: BOMB MAGAZINE
80 Hanson Pl Ste 703 (11217-2998)
PHONE................................718 636-9100
Betsy Sussler, *President*
Alexis Boehmler, *Principal*
Raluca Albu, *Editor*
Chantal McStay, *Assoc Editor*
Ryan Chapman, *Director*
EMP: 10
SALES: 1.8MM **Privately Held**
WEB: www.bombsite.com
SIC: 2721 Magazines: publishing only, not
printed on site

(G-2201)
NEW CONCEPTS OF NEW YORK
LLC
89 19th St 91 (11232-1055)
PHONE................................212 695-4999
Robert Schwartz,
▲ EMP: 20
SALES (est): 2.4MM **Privately Held**
WEB: www.newconceptsllc.com
SIC: 2339 Women's & misses' accessories

(G-2202)
NEW DIMENSION AWARDS INC
(PA)
6505 11th Ave (11219-5602)
PHONE................................718 236-8200
Joseph S Cardinale, *President*
EMP: 9
SQ FT: 16,000
SALES (est): 941.2K **Privately Held**
WEB: www.newdimensioninc.com
SIC: 3499 2796 Trophies, metal, except
silver; novelties & specialties, metal; en-
graving platemaking services

(G-2203)
NEW DIMENSIONS OFFICE
GROUP
Also Called: Acme Office Group
540 Morgan Ave (11222-5227)
PHONE................................718 387-0995
Ernest Eager, *President*
Bertran Teich, *Vice Pres*
Buddy Martin, *Treasurer*
Jack Teich, *Admin Sec*
EMP: 52
SQ FT: 20,000
SALES (est): 3.6MM **Privately Held**
SIC: 3446 2541 2522 2521 Architectural
metalwork; wood partitions & fixtures; of-
fice furniture, except wood; panel systems
& partitions (free-standing), office: wood

(G-2204)
NEW YORK CHRISTAN TIMES
INC
1061 Atlantic Ave (11238-2902)
P.O. Box 381066 (11238-8066)
PHONE................................718 638-6397
Dennis Dillon, *President*
Karen Granger, *Vice Pres*
EMP: 6
SALES (est): 492.3K **Privately Held**
SIC: 2759 Publication printing

(G-2205)
NEW YORK DAILY CHALLENGE
INC (PA)
1195 Atlantic Ave Fl 2 (11216-2709)
P.O. Box 160252 (11216-0252)
PHONE................................718 636-9500
Thomas H Watkins Jr, *President*
Duwad Philip, *Manager*
EMP: 20
SQ FT: 1,000
SALES (est): 1MM **Privately Held**
SIC: 2711 Newspapers: publishing only,
not printed on site

(G-2206)
NEW YORK DISTILLING CO LLC
405 Leonard St (11222-3910)
PHONE................................718 473-2955
▲ EMP: 497
SALES (corp-wide): 21.7MM **Privately
Held**
SIC: 2085 Distilled & blended liquors
PA: New York Distilling Company, Llc
511 8th St Apt 1l
Brooklyn NY 11215
917 893-7519

(G-2207)
NEW YORK DISTILLING CO LLC
(PA)
511 8th St Apt 1l (11215-4222)
PHONE................................917 893-7519
EMP: 3
SALES (est): 21.7MM **Privately Held**
SIC: 2085 Distilled & blended liquors

(G-2208)
NEW YORK HOSPITAL
DISPOSABLE
101 Richardson St Ste 1 (11211-1344)
PHONE................................718 384-1620
Rosa Ramos, *President*
Victor Cora, *President*
Zitzor Cora, *Admin Sec*
EMP: 20
SQ FT: 12,000
SALES (est): 1.7MM **Privately Held**
SIC: 2389 2326 Hospital gowns; men's &
boys' work clothing

(G-2209)
NEW YORK PASTA AUTHORITY
INC
640 Parkside Ave (11226-8414)
PHONE................................347 787-2130
Chavi Katzman, *Exec Dir*
EMP: 10
SALES (est): 629.3K **Privately Held**
SIC: 2033 Spaghetti & other pasta sauce:
packaged in cans, jars, etc.

(G-2210)
NEW YORK POPLIN LLC
4611 1st Ave (11232-4200)
PHONE................................718 768-3296
Wayne Yip, *Mng Member*
▲ EMP: 8
SQ FT: 8,000
SALES (est): 4.5MM **Privately Held**
SIC: 2221 Apparel & outerwear fabric,
manmade fiber or silk

(G-2211)
NEW YORK QRTRLY
FOUNDATION INC
322 76th St (11209-3106)
P.O. Box 470, Beacon (12508-0470)
PHONE................................917 843-8825
Raymond Hammond, *President*
Neil Smith, *Vice Pres*
Linda Tieber, *Treasurer*
Andrea Lockett, *Admin Sec*
EMP: 12
SALES: 52K **Privately Held**
SIC: 2731 7389 Book publishing;

(G-2212)
NEWCASTLE FABRICS CORP
Also Called: Newtown Finishing
86 Beadel St (11222-5232)
PHONE................................718 388-6600
Daniel Aldalezo, *Manager*
EMP: 5
SALES (corp-wide): 5.3MM **Privately
Held**
WEB: www.newcastlefabrics.com
SIC: 2269 7389 Finishing plants; textile &
apparel services
PA: Newcastle Fabrics Corp.
601 Ocean Ter
Staten Island NY 10301
718 782-5560

(G-2213)
NEWS REPORT INC
Also Called: Diyzeitung
1281 49th St Ste 3 (11219-3055)
PHONE................................718 851-6607
Albert Friedman, *Ch of Bd*

Rose Friedman, *Vice Pres*
EMP: 25
SALES (est): 1MM **Privately Held**
SIC: 2711 Newspapers: publishing only,
not printed on site; newspapers, publish-
ing & printing

(G-2214)
NEWYORK PEDORTHIC
ASSOCIATES
Also Called: Rosenbaum Foot
2102 63rd St (11204-3058)
PHONE................................718 236-7700
Mark Rosenbaum, *President*
EMP: 6
SALES (est): 854.9K **Privately Held**
SIC: 3069 Orthopedic sundries, molded
rubber

(G-2215)
NIFT GROUP INC
14 Woodbine St (11221-4302)
PHONE................................504 505-1144
Timothee Dumain, *Principal*
EMP: 1 EST: 2016
SALES: 3MM **Privately Held**
SIC: 7372 Business oriented computer
software

(G-2216)
NIGUN MUSIC
4116 13th Ave (11219-1333)
PHONE................................718 977-5700
EMP: 10 EST: 2017
SALES (est): 785.7K **Privately Held**
SIC: 2741 Miscellaneous publishing

(G-2217)
NLHE LLC
Also Called: Nanette Lepore
141 Flushing Ave 906 (11205-1338)
PHONE................................212 594-0012
Robert Savage, *CEO*
Erica Wolf, *President*
EMP: 50 EST: 2014
SALES (est): 265K **Privately Held**
SIC: 2339 5137 Sportswear, women's;
women's & children's clothing

(G-2218)
NOBLE CHECKS INC
1682 43rd St Apt 2 (11204-1059)
PHONE................................212 537-6241
Isaac Dresdner, *Ch of Bd*
EMP: 5
SALES (est): 678.1K **Privately Held**
WEB: www.noblechecks.com
SIC: 2759 Commercial printing

(G-2219)
NORDIC INTERIOR INC
26 Court St Ste 2211 (11242-1122)
PHONE................................718 456-7000
Helge Halvorsen, *President*
Lloyd Jacobsen, *Corp Secy*
Harald Haegeland, *Vice Pres*
Dieter Eckert, *Sr Project Mgr*
Gene Wong, *Manager*
▲ EMP: 150
SQ FT: 55,000
SALES (est): 20.7MM **Privately Held**
WEB: www.nordicinterior.com
SIC: 2431 1742 Woodwork, interior & or-
namental; drywall

(G-2220)
NORTHSIDE MEDIA GROUP LLC
55 Washington St Ste 652 (11201-1063)
PHONE................................917 318-6513
Brian Quinn, *Vice Pres*
Scott Stedman, *Mng Member*
EMP: 15
SALES: 2.4MM
SALES (corp-wide): 6MM **Privately Held**
SIC: 2721 Magazines: publishing & printing
PA: Zealot Networks, Inc.
2114 Narcissus Ct
Venice CA 90291
310 821-3737

(G-2221)
NOVEL BOX COMPANY LTD
5620 1st Ave Ste 4 (11220-2519)
PHONE................................718 965-2222
Moishe Sternhill, *President*
Abe Kwadrat, *Vice Pres*

◆ EMP: 25
SALES (est): 5.2MM **Privately Held**
WEB: www.novelbox.com
SIC: 2657 3469 3089 Folding paperboard
boxes; boxes, stamped metal; boxes,
plastic

(G-2222)
NOVOYE RSSKOYE SLOVO
PUBG CORP
Also Called: Russian Daily
2614 Voorhies Ave (11235-2414)
PHONE................................646 460-4566
Yuri Ivnitsky, *Ch of Bd*
Lawrence Weinberg, *President*
EMP: 52
SQ FT: 16,000
SALES (est): 2MM **Privately Held**
WEB: www.nrs.com
SIC: 2711 Newspapers: publishing only,
not printed on site

(G-2223)
NUVITE CHEMICAL
COMPOUNDS CORP
213 Freeman St 215 (11222-1404)
PHONE................................718 383-8351
Clifford Lester, *President*
Robert McHugh, *Vice Pres*
Gary Comodo, *Director*
EMP: 11
SQ FT: 7,000
SALES (est): 1MM **Privately Held**
WEB: www.nuvitechemical.com
SIC: 2842 Cleaning or polishing prepara-
tions

(G-2224)
NY CABINET FACTORY INC
6901 14th Ave (11228-1701)
PHONE................................718 256-6541
Vin Burratto, *President*
Frank Burratto, *Vice Pres*
EMP: 11 EST: 2015
SQ FT: 2,500
SALES: 2MM **Privately Held**
SIC: 2434 5211 Wood kitchen cabinets;
counter tops

(G-2225)
NY ORTHOPEDIC USA INC
63 Flushing Ave Unit 333 (11205-1083)
PHONE................................718 852-5330
Michael Rozenberg, *President*
Michael Blatt, *Vice Pres*
▲ EMP: 80
SQ FT: 24,000
SALES (est): 10MM **Privately Held**
WEB: www.nyorthousa.com
SIC: 3842 2389 5999 Personal safety
equipment; uniforms & vestments; med-
ical apparatus & supplies

(G-2226)
NYC COMMUNITY MEDIA LLC
Also Called: Villager, The
1 Metrotech Ctr N Fl 10 (11201-3875)
PHONE................................212 229-1890
Michael Shirey, *Art Dir*
Jennifer Goodstein,
EMP: 18
SQ FT: 1,200
SALES (est): 1.2MM **Privately Held**
SIC: 2711 Newspapers: publishing only,
not printed on site

(G-2227)
NYP HOLDINGS INC
Also Called: New York Post
1 Metrotech Ctr N Fl 10 (11201-3875)
PHONE................................718 260-2500
Cliff Luster, *Principal*
EMP: 60
SALES (corp-wide): 10B **Publicly Held**
SIC: 2711 Newspapers, publishing & print-
ing
HQ: Nyp Holdings, Inc.
1211 Ave Of The Americas
New York NY 10036

(G-2228)
OFFICE GRABS LLC
Also Called: Officegrabscom
1245 50th St Apt 4d (11219-3561)
PHONE................................347 678-3993

Moshe Rosenberg, *CFO*
EMP: 7
SALES (est): 94K **Privately Held**
SIC: 3577 Computer peripheral equipment

(G-2229)
OFFICE GRABS NY INC
1303 53rd St 105 (11219-3823)
PHONE.....................212 444-1331
Meir Barminka, *CEO*
Moshe Rosenberg, *President*
EMP: 6
SALES (est): 695K **Privately Held**
SIC: 2752 Commercial printing, lithographic

(G-2230)
OLOLLO INC
43 Hall St Ste B8 (11205-1395)
PHONE.....................877 701-0110
Regan Chen, *President*
▲ EMP: 7 EST: 2009
SQ FT: 10,000
SALES (est): 1MM **Privately Held**
SIC: 2519 Household furniture, except wood or metal: upholstered

(G-2231)
OMG CLEANERS INC
565 Coney Island Ave (11218-4303)
PHONE.....................718 282-2011
EMP: 5
SALES (est): 431.2K **Privately Held**
SIC: 2842 Drycleaning preparations

(G-2232)
ONE STORY INC
232 3rd St Ste A108 (11215-2708)
PHONE.....................917 816-3659
Maribeth Batcha, *President*
Hannah Tinti, *Vice Pres*
EMP: 8
SALES: 312.1K **Privately Held**
SIC: 2741 Miscellaneous publishing

(G-2233)
ORCHARD SAUSAGES INC
340 Johnson Ave (11206-2802)
PHONE.....................718 381-9388
Tom Sat, *President*
Zhao Ming SA, *Vice Pres*
EMP: 10
SQ FT: 10,000
SALES: 3MM **Privately Held**
SIC: 2013 Sausages & other prepared meats

(G-2234)
ORTEX HOME TEXTILE INC
Also Called: Ortex Home Textiles
523 E 82nd St (11236-3118)
PHONE.....................718 241-7298
Merry Lati, *President*
David Ausi, *Vice Pres*
▲ EMP: 6
SQ FT: 15,000
SALES (est): 6.4MM **Privately Held**
SIC: 2211 Sheets, bedding & table cloths: cotton

(G-2235)
ORTHOCRAFT INC
1477 E 27th St (11210-5308)
PHONE.....................718 951-1700
Herschel Sauber, *President*
EMP: 6
SQ FT: 800
SALES (est): 973.5K **Privately Held**
SIC: 3842 5999 Limbs, artificial; orthopedic appliances; orthopedic & prosthesis applications

(G-2236)
ORTHOPEDIC ARTS LABORATORY INC
141 Atlantic Ave Apt 1 (11201-5516)
PHONE.....................718 858-2400
Stephan Manucharian, *CEO*
EMP: 5
SQ FT: 850
SALES (est): 898.3K **Privately Held**
SIC: 3842 Limbs, artificial; prosthetic appliances

(G-2237)
OSO INDUSTRIES INC
1205 Manhattan Ave (11222-6154)
PHONE.....................917 709-2050
Eric Weil, *Principal*
EMP: 8
SALES (est): 318.5K **Privately Held**
SIC: 3999 Manufacturing industries

(G-2238)
OUTER IMAGE LLC
226 42nd St (11232-2814)
PHONE.....................914 420-3097
Laura Vardanian,
EMP: 8
SALES (est): 459.1K **Privately Held**
SIC: 3993 Signs & advertising specialties

(G-2239)
OUTREACH PUBLISHING CORP
546 Montgomery St (11225-3023)
PHONE.....................718 773-0525
Shlomo Lakein, *President*
Reuven Lakein, *General Mgr*
Reuben Lakein, *Vice Pres*
EMP: 7
SALES (est): 660K **Privately Held**
WEB: www.outreach770.com
SIC: 2741 Miscellaneous publishing

(G-2240)
P M BELTS USA INC
131 32nd St (11232-1809)
P.O. Box 320650 (11232-0650)
PHONE.....................800 762-3580
Gregory O'Neil, *President*
EMP: 45 EST: 1986
SQ FT: 12,500
SALES (est): 2.1MM **Privately Held**
WEB: www.pmbelt.com
SIC: 2387 Apparel belts

(G-2241)
P8H INC
Also Called: Paddle8
81 Prospect St 7 (11201-1473)
PHONE.....................212 343-1142
EMP: 40 EST: 2017
SALES: 20MM **Privately Held**
SIC: 7372 7389 Prepackaged Software Services Business Services

(G-2242)
PALAGONIA BAKERY CO INC
Also Called: Palagonia Italian Bread
508 Junius St (11212-7199)
PHONE.....................718 272-5400
Christopher Palagonia, *President*
▲ EMP: 100
SQ FT: 25,000
SALES (est): 13MM **Privately Held**
SIC: 2051 Bread, cake & related products

(G-2243)
PAP CHAT INC
3105 Quentin Rd (11234-4234)
PHONE.....................516 350-1888
Justin Schwartz, *CEO*
EMP: 5
SALES (est): 207.7K **Privately Held**
SIC: 7372 7389 Prepackaged software;

(G-2244)
PAPER SOLUTIONS INC
342 37th St (11232-2506)
PHONE.....................718 499-4666
Wing FAI Lam, *CEO*
▲ EMP: 3
SALES: 2MM **Privately Held**
SIC: 2621 Paper mills

(G-2245)
PAPERSTREET TECHNOLOGY INC
240 Kent Ave (11249-4121)
PHONE.....................704 773-5689
Matthew Decourcelle, *CEO*
Carter Lathrop, *Chief Engr*
EMP: 6
SQ FT: 200
SALES (est): 135.3K **Privately Held**
SIC: 7372 Application computer software

(G-2246)
PARADISE PLASTICS LLC
116 39th St (11232-2712)
PHONE.....................718 788-3733
Max Berg,
Judith Berg,
Ernest Grossberger,
Gabriella Grossberger,
EMP: 25 EST: 1952
SQ FT: 40,000
SALES (est): 5MM **Privately Held**
WEB: www.paradiseplastics.com
SIC: 2673 Plastic bags: made from purchased materials

(G-2247)
PARK AVE BLDG & ROOFG SUPS LLC
Also Called: Benjamin Moore Authorized Ret
2120 Atlantic Ave (11233-3162)
PHONE.....................718 403-0100
Bob Groeninger, *CEO*
Raymond Rivera, *President*
Eddy Philippe, *Vice Pres*
Bruce Pooler, *Opers Mgr*
ARI Rodriguez, *Warehouse Mgr*
EMP: 40
SQ FT: 15,000
SALES (est): 38.5MM **Privately Held**
SIC: 3531 5033 5231 Aerial work platforms: hydraulic/elec. truck/carrier mounted; roofing & siding materials; paint, glass & wallpaper

(G-2248)
PARK AVENUE SPORTSWEAR LTD (PA)
820 4th Ave (11232-1612)
PHONE.....................718 369-0520
Joseph Steg, *President*
Martin Perlstein, *Vice Pres*
EMP: 12 EST: 1962
SQ FT: 15,000
SALES (est): 1.9MM **Privately Held**
SIC: 2339 Sportswear, women's

(G-2249)
PARK SLOPE COPY CENTER
123 7th Ave (11215-1301)
PHONE.....................718 783-0268
Bob Kalb, *Owner*
Jon Kalb, *General Mgr*
EMP: 11
SALES: 123.6K **Privately Held**
SIC: 2752 Commercial printing, offset

(G-2250)
PATRICK MACKIN CUSTOM FURN
Also Called: Art Boards
612 Degraw St (11217-3112)
PHONE.....................718 237-2592
Patrick Mackin, *President*
▲ EMP: 7
SALES (est): 650K **Privately Held**
WEB: www.art-boards.com
SIC: 2511 5999 5199 Wood household furniture; art & architectural supplies; art goods & supplies

(G-2251)
PECORARO DAIRY PRODUCTS INC (PA)
287 Leonard St (11211-3618)
PHONE.....................718 388-2379
Cesare Pecoraro, *President*
Ralph Parlato, *Vice Pres*
EMP: 6
SQ FT: 4,000
SALES (est): 959.9K **Privately Held**
SIC: 2022 Natural cheese

(G-2252)
PEKING FOOD LLC
47 Stewart Ave (11237-1517)
PHONE.....................718 628-8080
Lawrence Wu, *Mng Member*
Teresa Wu,
▼ EMP: 30
SQ FT: 28,000
SALES (est): 4MM **Privately Held**
SIC: 2051 Bread, cake & related products

(G-2253)
PENN STATE MTAL FBRCTORS NO 2
810 Humboldt St Ste 1-B (11222-1914)
P.O. Box 185, East Rockaway (11518-0185)
PHONE.....................718 786-8814
Herbert Engler, *President*
EMP: 4
SQ FT: 7,500
SALES: 1MM **Privately Held**
SIC: 3531 3463 Construction machinery; pump & compressor forgings, nonferrous

(G-2254)
PERALTA METAL WORKS INC
602 Atkins Ave (11208-5202)
PHONE.....................718 649-8661
Omar Peralta, *President*
Yvette Peralta, *Vice Pres*
EMP: 8
SQ FT: 3,500
SALES (est): 1.5MM **Privately Held**
SIC: 3441 Fabricated structural metal

(G-2255)
PHILLIP TISSICHER
Also Called: Fao Printing
1688 Utica Ave (11234-1526)
PHONE.....................718 282-3310
Phillip Tissicher, *Owner*
EMP: 12
SALES (est): 113.7K **Privately Held**
SIC: 2752 Commercial printing, lithographic

(G-2256)
PHOENIX METAL DESIGNS INC
100 Hinsdale St (11207-2902)
PHONE.....................516 597-4100
Voula Nikitopoulos, *Chairman*
EMP: 5 EST: 2016
SALES: 747.7K **Privately Held**
SIC: 3446 Architectural metalwork

(G-2257)
PICTURE PERFECT FRAMING
1758 50th St (11204-1220)
PHONE.....................718 851-1884
Harry Gruber, *Owner*
Chaya Gruber, *Owner*
EMP: 5 EST: 1990
SALES: 30K **Privately Held**
SIC: 2499 3499 Picture & mirror frames, wood; picture frames, metal

(G-2258)
PILGRIM SURF & SUPPLY
68 N 3rd St (11249-3925)
PHONE.....................718 218-7456
Chris Gentile, *Owner*
EMP: 7
SALES (est): 580.2K **Privately Held**
SIC: 3949 Surfboards

(G-2259)
PILLOW PERFECTIONS LTD INC
252 Norman Ave Ste 101 (11222-6412)
PHONE.....................718 383-2259
Kenny Fried, *President*
▼ EMP: 8 EST: 1977
SQ FT: 7,000
SALES: 700K **Privately Held**
SIC: 2511 5712 Wood household furniture; furniture stores

(G-2260)
PINK BOX ACCESSORIES LLC
Also Called: Blue Box
940 40th St (11219-1025)
PHONE.....................718 435-2821
Mariano Uy,
Michael Uy,
▲ EMP: 5
SALES: 500K **Privately Held**
SIC: 3911 7389 Jewelry, precious metal;

(G-2261)
PINTRILL LLC
185 Wythe Ave (11249-3120)
PHONE.....................718 782-1000
Jordan Roswell, *Mng Member*
EMP: 11 EST: 2014
SALES (est): 1.1MM **Privately Held**
SIC: 3951 Pens & mechanical pencils

(G-2262)
PIPING SOLUTIONS INC
4601c 1st Ave (11232-4200)
PHONE...................................646 258-5381
Bella Safir, *President*
EMP: 5
SALES (est): 335.2K **Privately Held**
SIC: 3498 Piping systems for pulp paper & chemical industries

(G-2263)
PIROKE TRADE INC
1430 35th St Fl 2 (11218-3706)
PHONE...................................646 515-1537
Keitaro Maruyama, *President*
EMP: 5
SALES (est): 280K **Privately Held**
SIC: 2789 Trade binding services

(G-2264)
PIVOT RECORDS LLC
600 Johnson Ave (11237-1318)
P.O. Box 70276 (11207-0276)
PHONE...................................718 417-1213
EMP: 11
SALES (est): 490K **Privately Held**
SIC: 3652 Mfg Prerecorded Records/Tapes

(G-2265)
PLASTPAC INC
32 Walton St (11206-5056)
PHONE...................................908 272-7200
Mark Porges, *President*
EMP: 38
SALES (corp-wide): 9.3MM **Privately Held**
SIC: 3086 Plastics foam products
PA: Plastpac Inc
   30 Boright Ave
   Kenilworth NJ 07033
   908 272-7200

(G-2266)
PLATFORM EXPERTS INC
2938 Quentin Rd (11229-1825)
PHONE...................................646 843-7100
Joshua Newman, *President*
Zev Graber, *Manager*
EMP: 8
SQ FT: 4,000
SALES (est): 775.2K **Privately Held**
WEB: www.platformexperts.com
SIC: 7372 Prepackaged software

(G-2267)
PM SPIRITS LLC
505 Johnson Ave Apt 17 (11237-1209)
PHONE...................................347 689-4414
Nicolas Palazzi,
EMP: 12
SALES (est): 91.7K **Privately Held**
SIC: 2084 Brandy spirits

(G-2268)
POLYTECH POOL MFG INC
Also Called: Wet & Wild Pools & Spas
262 48th St 262 (11220-1012)
P.O. Box 544, Cedarhurst (11516-0544)
PHONE...................................718 492-8991
Fax: 718 439-1254
EMP: 10 EST: 1975
SQ FT: 60,000
SALES (est): 870K **Privately Held**
SIC: 3949 Mfg Sporting/Athletic Goods

(G-2269)
PONTI ROSSI INC
186 Franklin St Apt C16 (11222-1690)
PHONE...................................347 506-9616
Alessandro Capuano, *President*
EMP: 6
SALES (est): 227.7K **Privately Held**
SIC: 2099 Food preparations

(G-2270)
POP PRINTING INCORPORATED
299 24th St (11232-1309)
PHONE...................................212 808-7800
Stephen Stein, *Ch of Bd*
EMP: 13
SALES (est): 1.5MM **Privately Held**
SIC: 2752 Commercial printing, offset

(G-2271)
POST HERITAGE INC
266 90th St (11209-5714)
PHONE...................................646 286-7579
Ken Hew, *President*
EMP: 5 EST: 2016
SALES (est): 545.4K **Privately Held**
SIC: 2621 7389 7371 Book, bond & printing papers; printed circuitry graphic layout; custom computer programming services

(G-2272)
POTENTIAL POLY BAG INC
1253 Coney Island Ave (11230-3520)
PHONE...................................718 258-0800
Mark Katz, *President*
Jerry Millman, *Vice Pres*
▲ EMP: 9
SQ FT: 10,000
SALES (est): 1.6MM **Privately Held**
WEB: www.potentialpolybag.com
SIC: 3081 Polyethylene film

(G-2273)
POWERHOUSE CULTURAL ENTRMT INC
Also Called: Powerhouse Books
126a Front St (11201-1116)
PHONE...................................212 604-9074
Daniel Power, *CEO*
Craig Cohen, *President*
▲ EMP: 17
SQ FT: 10,200
SALES (est): 2.8MM **Privately Held**
WEB: www.powerhousebooks.com
SIC: 2731 Book publishing

(G-2274)
POWERMATE CELLULAR
140 58th St Ste 1d (11220-2525)
PHONE...................................718 833-9400
Fax: 718 567-7020
▲ EMP: 7
SALES (est): 730.8K **Privately Held**
SIC: 3661 Mfg Telephone/Telegraph Apparatus

(G-2275)
PPR DIRECT MARKETING LLC (PA)
74 20th St (11232-1101)
PHONE...................................718 965-8600
Robert Notine,
Richard Carvalho,
Margaret Hickey,
▲ EMP: 8 EST: 2010
SALES (est): 3.9MM **Privately Held**
SIC: 2389 Men's miscellaneous accessories

(G-2276)
PR & STONE & TILE INC
Also Called: Stone Crafters International
17 Beadel St (11222-5110)
PHONE...................................718 383-1115
Edward Rynkosky, *President*
Arakdiusz Rakowski, *Vice Pres*
EMP: 5
SALES: 900K **Privately Held**
SIC: 3281 Granite, cut & shaped

(G-2277)
PRECISION MTAL FABRICATORS INC
Also Called: PMF
236 39th St (11232-2820)
PHONE...................................718 832-9805
Dimitrios Theodoru, *President*
EMP: 12
SQ FT: 8,000
SALES (est): 2.2MM **Privately Held**
SIC: 3444 Sheet metalwork

(G-2278)
PRECISION PRODUCT INC
18 Steuben St (11205-1306)
PHONE...................................718 852-7127
Sonny K Chan, *President*
▲ EMP: 5
SQ FT: 6,000
SALES (est): 650.5K **Privately Held**
SIC: 3531 Construction machinery

(G-2279)
PREEBRO PRINTING
5319 Fort Hamilton Pkwy (11219-4036)
PHONE...................................718 633-7300
Zur Getter, *Owner*
EMP: 5
SALES (est): 556K **Privately Held**
WEB: www.preebroprinting.com
SIC: 2752 Commercial printing, offset

(G-2280)
PREMIUM ASSURE INC
1726 Mcdonald Ave Ste 201 (11230-6942)
PHONE...................................605 252-9999
Shulem Iskowitz, *Ch of Bd*
Nick Hager, *Principal*
EMP: 5 EST: 2017
SALES (est): 182.3K **Privately Held**
SIC: 3999 Hair & hair-based products

(G-2281)
PRESSED JUICE LLC (PA)
Also Called: East Coast Copacking
205 Clinton Ave Apt 12a (11205-3555)
PHONE...................................646 573-9157
Paul Baudier,
Donaldo Aragon,
EMP: 2
SALES: 1MM **Privately Held**
SIC: 2033 Fruit juices: packaged in cans, jars, etc.

(G-2282)
PRESSER KOSHER BAKING CORP
1720 Avenue M (11230-5358)
PHONE...................................718 375-5088
Sam Klein, *President*
EMP: 20
SQ FT: 2,500
SALES: 750K **Privately Held**
SIC: 2051 5461 Bakery: wholesale or wholesale/retail combined; bakeries

(G-2283)
PRESTIGE HANGERS STR FIXS CORP
1026 55th St (11219-4024)
PHONE...................................718 522-6777
Abe Minkosf, *President*
Mozes Parnes, *Manager*
EMP: 5
SQ FT: 5,000
SALES: 370K **Privately Held**
WEB: www.prestigestorefixtures.com
SIC: 3089 Clothes hangers, plastic

(G-2284)
PRIME FOOD PROCESSING CORP
300 Vandervoort Ave (11211-1715)
PHONE...................................718 963-2323
Albert Chan, *Ch of Bd*
Yee Hung Chan, *President*
◆ EMP: 80
SQ FT: 35,000
SALES (est): 12.5MM **Privately Held**
SIC: 2013 2037 Frozen meats from purchased meat; vegetables, quick frozen & cold pack, excl. potato products

(G-2285)
PRIMO FROZEN DESSERTS INC
Also Called: Ices Queen
1633 Utica Ave (11234-1524)
PHONE...................................718 252-2312
Dan Lazzaro, *CEO*
Dominick Lazzaro, *Vice Pres*
EMP: 8
SQ FT: 4,500
SALES: 400K **Privately Held**
SIC: 2024 Ices, flavored (frozen dessert)

(G-2286)
PRIMO PLASTICS INC
162 Russell St (11222-3619)
P.O. Box 220187 (11222-0187)
PHONE...................................718 349-1000
John Primo, *President*
Pete Krutros, *Vice Pres*
▲ EMP: 20
SQ FT: 7,800

SALES: 2.6MM **Privately Held**
SIC: 2673 5113 Plastic bags: made from purchased materials; bags, paper & disposable plastic

(G-2287)
PRINCE SEATING CORP
1355 Atlantic Ave (11216-2810)
PHONE...................................718 363-2300
Abe Belsky, *President*
Henry Bodner, *Vice Pres*
▲ EMP: 45
SQ FT: 80,000
SALES: 15MM **Privately Held**
WEB: www.chairfactory.net
SIC: 2521 Wood office chairs, benches & stools; chairs, office: padded, upholstered or plain: wood; stools, office: wood

(G-2288)
PRINT HOUSE INC
Also Called: Printhouse, The
538 Johnson Ave (11237-1226)
PHONE...................................718 443-7500
Sholom Laine, *Ch of Bd*
Yaakov Laine, *Executive*
▲ EMP: 60
SQ FT: 71,000
SALES (est): 14.3MM **Privately Held**
SIC: 2752 Commercial printing, lithographic

(G-2289)
PRINT MALL
4122 16th Ave (11204-1052)
PHONE...................................718 437-7700
Sara Olewski, *Owner*
EMP: 5
SALES (est): 450.4K **Privately Held**
WEB: www.invitations123.com
SIC: 2759 Invitation & stationery printing & engraving

(G-2290)
PRINT SEFORIM BZUL INC
8 Lynch St Apt 6r (11206-5528)
PHONE...................................718 679-1011
EMP: 6
SALES (est): 135.1K **Privately Held**
SIC: 2752 Commercial printing, lithographic

(G-2291)
PRINTING FACTORY LLC
1940 Utica Ave (11234-3214)
PHONE...................................718 451-0500
Lisa Blitman,
EMP: 12
SALES (est): 891K **Privately Held**
SIC: 2732 Book printing

(G-2292)
PRINTING MAX NEW YORK INC
2282 Flatbush Ave (11234-4518)
P.O. Box 340369 (11234-0369)
PHONE...................................718 692-1400
George Blair, *Principal*
EMP: 6
SALES (est): 588K **Privately Held**
SIC: 2759 Screen printing

(G-2293)
PRINTING SALES GROUP LIMITED
Also Called: Flair Printers
1856 Flatbush Ave (11210-4831)
PHONE...................................718 258-8860
Steven Zuller, *President*
EMP: 20
SALES (est): 1.7MM **Privately Held**
SIC: 2752 Commercial printing, offset

(G-2294)
PRINTOUT COPY CORP
829 Bedford Ave (11205-2801)
PHONE...................................718 855-4040
Sinai Roth, *President*
Jacob Sabel, *Vice Pres*
Surie Lebovits, *Manager*
EMP: 21
SQ FT: 3,500
SALES (est): 5MM **Privately Held**
SIC: 2752 Commercial printing, offset

(G-2295)
PRINTUTOPIA
393 Prospect Ave (11215-5608)
P.O. Box 150528 (11215-0528)
PHONE...................................718 788-1545
Hamlet Villa, *General Mgr*
EMP: 10
SALES (est): 810.9K **Privately Held**
SIC: 2752 Commercial printing, offset

(G-2296)
PROCESSING FOUNDATION INC
400 Jay St 175 (11201-5116)
PHONE...................................415 748-2679
Ben Fry, *President*
Daniel Shiffman, *Treasurer*
Casey Reas, *Admin Sec*
EMP: 6
SALES: 40.4K **Privately Held**
SIC: 7372 Educational computer software

(G-2297)
PRODUCTAND DESIGN INC
63 Flushing Ave Unit 322 (11205-1082)
PHONE...................................718 858-2440
John Milich, *President*
▲ **EMP:** 10
SALES: 2MM **Privately Held**
SIC: 3441 8712 Fabricated structural
    metal; architectural services

(G-2298)
PROFOOT INC (PA)
74 20th St Fl 2 (11232-1101)
PHONE...................................718 965-8600
Leonard Feldman, *President*
Robert Notine, *Corp Secy*
Larry Brown, *Vice Pres*
Richard Carvalho, *Vice Pres*
Pamela Cress, *Vice Pres*
◆ **EMP:** 72
SQ FT: 35,000
SALES (est): 32.3MM **Privately Held**
WEB: www.profootcare.com
SIC: 3842 Orthopedic appliances; foot ap-
    pliances, orthopedic

(G-2299)
PROFORMANCE FOODS INC
42 West St Apt 316 (11222-6261)
PHONE...................................703 869-3413
Ryan Wiltse, *President*
EMP: 7
SALES: 2MM **Privately Held**
SIC: 2096 Potato chips & similar snacks

(G-2300)
PROJECT ENERGY SAVERS LLC
Also Called: PES Group
68 Jay St Ste 517 (11201-8362)
PHONE...................................718 596-6448
Marcy Rubenstein, *Bookkeeper*
Joshua Wolfe, *Mng Member*
Joshua F Wolfe, *Manager*
Mark Wolfe,
EMP: 14
SALES: 1.2MM **Privately Held**
SIC: 2731 8748 Textbooks: publishing
    only, not printed on site; energy conserva-
    tion consultant

(G-2301)
**PROMOTIONAL DEVELOPMENT
INC**
Also Called: P D I
909 Remsen Ave (11236-1624)
PHONE...................................718 485-8550
Henry Lombardi, *President*
Anthony Valentine, *Vice Pres*
Richard Lauro, *Engineer*
Hyogin Bang, *Design Engr*
David Censi, *CFO*
▲ **EMP:** 80
SQ FT: 60,000
SALES (est): 12.9MM **Privately Held**
WEB: www.promotionaldevelopment.com
SIC: 3999 3993 Advertising display prod-
    ucts; signs & advertising specialties

(G-2302)
PROTECTIVE LINING CORP
601 39th St (11232-3101)
PHONE...................................718 854-3838
Steven Howard, *President*
Morton Howard, *Vice Pres*

▲ **EMP:** 65 **EST:** 1950
SQ FT: 28,000
SALES: 14.8MM **Privately Held**
WEB: www.prolining.com
SIC: 2673 Plastic bags: made from pur-
    chased materials

(G-2303)
PROVISION SUPPLY LLC (PA)
Also Called: Ezcontacts.com
1153 55th St (11219-4117)
PHONE...................................347 623-0237
Joel Lefkowitz, *President*
EMP: 13
SALES (est): 13.1MM **Privately Held**
SIC: 3851 Protective eyeware

(G-2304)
PROVISIONAIRE & CO LLC
Also Called: Field Trip Jerky
630 Flushing Ave Fl 4 (11206-5026)
P.O. Box 710, Westport CT (06881-0710)
PHONE...................................646 681-8600
Todd Tolis, *Sales Dir*
Thomas Donigan, *Manager*
Maxwell Fiedel, *Manager*
M Scott Fiesinger,
Matthew Levey,
EMP: 20
SALES (est): 2.5MM **Privately Held**
SIC: 2013 Snack sticks, including jerky:
    from purchased meat

(G-2305)
PURE ACOUSTICS INC
18 Fuller Pl (11215-6007)
PHONE...................................718 788-4411
Rami Ezratty, *CEO*
EMP: 7 **EST:** 2003
SALES: 2MM **Privately Held**
SIC: 3651 Speaker systems

(G-2306)
PURE PLANET WATERS LLC
4809 Avenue N Ste 185 (11234-3711)
PHONE...................................718 676-7900
Denise Piccolo,
Gary Cucuza,
EMP: 10
SQ FT: 2,000
SALES: 1MM **Privately Held**
SIC: 3589 5999 5078 5074 Water filters
    & softeners, household type; water purifi-
    cation equipment, household type; water
    treatment equipment, industrial; water pu-
    rification equipment; drinking water cool-
    ers, mechanical; water purification
    equipment

(G-2307)
PUREGRAB LLC
294 Hoyt St (11231-4908)
PHONE...................................718 935-1959
Ryan Paul, *Mng Member*
Ryan Cleofe, *Mng Member*
EMP: 5
SALES (est): 156.7K **Privately Held**
SIC: 2391 Curtains & draperies

(G-2308)
**PUTNAM ROLLING LADDER CO
INC**
444 Jefferson St (11237-2326)
PHONE...................................718 381-8219
Henry Skiba, *Manager*
EMP: 17
SALES (corp-wide): 3.4MM **Privately
Held**
WEB: www.putnamrollingladder.com
SIC: 2499 Ladders, wood
PA: Putnam Rolling Ladder Co Inc
    32 Howard St
    New York NY 10013
    212 226-5147

(G-2309)
QUALITY FOAM INC
137 Gardner Ave (11237-1107)
PHONE...................................718 381-3644
Paul Minarsky, *President*
Kyle Minarsky, *Vice Pres*
◆ **EMP:** 12
SALES (est): 1.6MM **Privately Held**
WEB: www.qualityfoamproducts.com
SIC: 2515 Mattresses, containing felt, foam
    rubber, urethane, etc.

(G-2310)
QUALITY NATURE INC
8225 5th Ave Ste 215 (11209-4508)
PHONE...................................718 484-4666
Sagie Gernshteyn, *President*
EMP: 5
SQ FT: 300
SALES: 733.6K **Privately Held**
SIC: 2834 Vitamin, nutrient & hematinic
    preparations for human use

(G-2311)
**QUALITY STAINLESS STEEL NY
INC (PA)**
865 63rd St (11220-4727)
PHONE...................................718 748-1785
Hong Guang Huang, *Ch of Bd*
EMP: 10
SALES (est): 1.1MM **Privately Held**
SIC: 3312 Stainless steel

(G-2312)
QUALITY STRAPPING INC
55 Meadow St (11206-1700)
PHONE...................................718 418-1111
Imre Oberlander, *President*
Aharon L Grossman, *Vice Pres*
Abraham Stern, *CFO*
Ben Friedman, *Sales Staff*
▲ **EMP:** 58
SQ FT: 60,000
SALES: 5.4MM **Privately Held**
WEB: www.qualitystrapping.com
SIC: 3559 Plastics working machinery

(G-2313)
**QUALITY WOODWORKING
CORP**
260 Butler St (11217-3006)
PHONE...................................718 875-3437
Joseph Borruso Sr, *President*
Denise Jacob, *Office Mgr*
Anthony Borruso, *Admin Sec*
EMP: 19 **EST:** 1943
SQ FT: 16,000
SALES (est): 2.7MM **Privately Held**
SIC: 2431 Millwork

(G-2314)
**QUEEN ANN MACARONI MFG
CO INC**
Also Called: Queen Ann Ravioli
7205 18th Ave (11204-5634)
PHONE...................................718 256-1061
Alfred Ferrara, *President*
Anna Ferrara, *Vice Pres*
EMP: 7
SQ FT: 4,000
SALES (est): 628.1K **Privately Held**
WEB:
www.queenannravioliandmacaroni.com
SIC: 2098 5499 Macaroni products (e.g.
    alphabets, rings & shells), dry; gourmet
    food stores

(G-2315)
QUIP NYC INC
45 Main St Ste 616 (11201-1099)
PHONE...................................917 331-3993
Simon Enever, *President*
Shane Pittson, *Marketing Mgr*
EMP: 9
SALES (est): 463.5K **Privately Held**
SIC: 2844 3634 Toothpastes or powders,
    dentifrices; toothbrushes, electric

(G-2316)
QUIST INDUSTRIES LTD
204 Van Dyke St Ste 320a (11231-1005)
P.O. Box 150083 (11215-0083)
PHONE...................................718 243-2800
Rebecca Steinman, *President*
EMP: 10
SQ FT: 3,500
SALES (est): 837.3K **Privately Held**
WEB: www.quistindustries.com
SIC: 2759 2395 Letterpress & screen
    printing; emblems, embroidered

(G-2317)
R & F BOARDS & DIVIDERS INC
1678 57th St (11204-1800)
PHONE...................................718 331-1529
EMP: 5

SALES (est): 350.7K **Privately Held**
SIC: 3081 Mfg Unsupported Plastic
    Film/Sheet

(G-2318)
R & H BAKING CO INC
19 5th St (11231-4514)
PHONE...................................718 852-1768
Humayun Kabir, *Owner*
EMP: 25 **EST:** 2003
SQ FT: 15,000
SALES: 1.5MM **Privately Held**
WEB: www.kabirbakery.com
SIC: 2051 Bakery: wholesale or whole-
    sale/retail combined

(G-2319)
R H GUEST INC
1300 Church Ave (11226-2602)
PHONE...................................718 675-7600
Robert Guest, *President*
Gloria Caprio, *Corp Secy*
EMP: 8
SQ FT: 1,000
SALES: 1.7MM **Privately Held**
WEB: www.rhgexhibits.com
SIC: 2542 2541 8412 Showcases (not re-
    frigerated): except wood; showcases, ex-
    cept refrigerated: wood; museum

(G-2320)
**R HOCHMAN PAPERS
INCORPORATED**
68 35th St (11232-2019)
PHONE...................................516 466-6414
Ronald Hochman, *President*
Erik Rimalovski, *COO*
▲ **EMP:** 11
SALES (est): 9.8MM **Privately Held**
WEB: www.hochmanpapers.com
SIC: 2752 Commercial printing, offset

(G-2321)
RAGNATELLI INC
Also Called: Elite Woodworking
300 Dewitt Ave (11236-1912)
PHONE...................................718 765-4050
Lucio Ragnatelli, *President*
John P Ragnatelli, *Vice Pres*
EMP: 40
SQ FT: 12,000
SALES: 3MM **Privately Held**
SIC: 2431 Millwork

(G-2322)
RAGS KNITWEAR LTD
850 Metropolitan Ave (11211-2515)
P.O. Box 420, Lynbrook (11563-0420)
PHONE...................................718 782-8417
Paul Gross, *President*
EMP: 10
SQ FT: 40,000
SALES: 980K **Privately Held**
SIC: 2253 Sweaters & sweater coats, knit

(G-2323)
RAHARNEY CAPITAL LLC
325 Gold St Fl 502 (11201-3040)
PHONE...................................212 220-9084
Sean Murray, *Mng Member*
EMP: 5
SALES (est): 171.1K **Privately Held**
SIC: 2721 Magazines: publishing only, not
    printed on site

(G-2324)
RAILINGS BY NEW STAR BRASS
Also Called: J Ironwork
26 Cobeck Ct (11223-6147)
PHONE...................................516 358-1153
Carlo Lopopolo, *President*
Al Grancagnolo, *President*
Mary Ann Harmon, *Purchasing*
EMP: 20
SQ FT: 25,000
SALES (est): 3.8MM **Privately Held**
SIC: 3446 Architectural metalwork

(G-2325)
RAINBOW PLASTICS INC
371 Vandervoort Ave (11211-1712)
PHONE...................................718 218-7288
Maggie Zheng, *Vice Pres*
▲ **EMP:** 13
SALES (est): 2MM **Privately Held**
SIC: 3089 Garbage containers, plastic

(G-2326)
RAINBOW POLY BAG CO INC
179 Morgan Ave (11237-1015)
PHONE..............................718 386-3500
Gladys Harmanoglu, *President*
Hikmet Harmanoglu, *Vice Pres*
EMP: 40
SQ FT: 50,000
SALES (est): 7.5MM **Privately Held**
WEB: www.rainbowpolybag.com
SIC: 2673 3081 Plastic bags: made from purchased materials; unsupported plastics film & sheet

(G-2327)
RAPID-LITE FIXTURE CORPORATION
249 Huron St (11222-7175)
PHONE..............................347 599-2600
Joel Eskin, *Ch of Bd*
EMP: 10 **EST:** 1946
SQ FT: 4,500
SALES (est): 1.5MM **Privately Held**
WEB: www.rapidlite.com
SIC: 3645 3646 5063 5719 Residential lighting fixtures; commercial indusl & institutional electric lighting fixtures; lighting fixtures, residential; lighting fixtures, commercial & industrial; lighting fixtures

(G-2328)
RAWPOTHECARY INC
630 Flushing Ave (11206-5026)
PHONE..............................917 783-7770
Stephanie Walzack, *President*
EMP: 8 **EST:** 2013
SALES (est): 722.5K **Privately Held**
SIC: 2099 5812 Ready-to-eat meals, salads & sandwiches; eating places

(G-2329)
RAY GOLD SHADE INC
16 Wellington Ct (11230-2424)
PHONE..............................718 377-8892
Martin Rosenbaum, *President*
Sonia Rosenbaum, *Vice Pres*
EMP: 10
SQ FT: 18,000
SALES (est): 813.2K **Privately Held**
WEB: www.goldrayshades.com
SIC: 3999 Shades, lamp or candle

(G-2330)
RB WYATT MFG CO INC
2518 Ralph Ave (11234-5519)
P.O. Box 340296 (11234-0296)
PHONE..............................718 209-9682
Joseph Dalcamo Jr, *President*
Joseph Accettulli, *Vice Pres*
Brian Grant, *Vice Pres*
EMP: 10
SQ FT: 4,000
SALES (est): 2MM **Privately Held**
SIC: 3231 Doors, glass: made from purchased glass

(G-2331)
RBW STUDIO LLC
Also Called: Rich Brilliant Willing
67 34th St Unit 5 (11232-2010)
PHONE..............................212 388-1621
Theodore Richardson, *President*
Alex Williams, *Vice Pres*
Alexander Williams, *Vice Pres*
Charles Brill, *CFO*
Wesley Damgo, *Bookkeeper*
EMP: 25
SQ FT: 2,000
SALES (est): 4.2MM **Privately Held**
SIC: 3699 Christmas tree lighting sets, electric

(G-2332)
REAR VIEW SAFETY INC
1797 Atlantic Ave (11233-3040)
PHONE..............................855 815-3842
Gila Newman, *CEO*
Joseph Schechter, *Exec VP*
Priscilla Vela, *Cust Mgr*
▲ **EMP:** 25
SQ FT: 6,000
SALES (est): 5.1MM
SALES (corp-wide): 90.1MM **Privately Held**
SIC: 3861 Cameras & related equipment

PA: Safe Fleet Investments Llc
6800 E 163rd St
Belton MO 64012
844 258-8178

(G-2333)
RECORDED ANTHLOGY OF AMRCN MUS
Also Called: New World Records
20 Jay St Ste 1001 (11201-8346)
PHONE..............................212 290-1695
Herman E Krawitz, *President*
Auther Moorhaed, *Treasurer*
Russell Platt, *Controller*
Paul Tai, *Director*
▲ **EMP:** 12
SALES (est): 1.2MM **Privately Held**
WEB: www.newworldrecords.org
SIC: 3652 Pre-recorded records & tapes

(G-2334)
RECYCLED BROOKLYN GROUP LLC
236 Van Brunt St (11231-1211)
P.O. Box 310492 (11231-0492)
PHONE..............................917 902-0662
Matthew Lostice,
Alberto Baudo,
Nilesh Dawda,
Andrea De Sanctis,
Marco Gentilucci,
EMP: 14
SQ FT: 8,000
SALES (est): 1.2MM **Privately Held**
SIC: 2511 5712 Wood household furniture; furniture stores

(G-2335)
REDI RECORDS PAYROLL
1225 36th St (11218-2023)
PHONE..............................718 854-6990
Joe Burke, *President*
EMP: 10 **EST:** 1947
SALES (est): 594.9K **Privately Held**
SIC: 2752 Calendars, lithographed

(G-2336)
REGIONAL MGT & CONSULTING INC
79 Bridgewater St (11222-3818)
PHONE..............................718 599-3718
Henryk Jarosz, *President*
Bogdan Szczurek, *Exec VP*
EMP: 10
SQ FT: 4,200
SALES (est): 1.3MM **Privately Held**
SIC: 3292 5033 Asbestos products; insulation materials

(G-2337)
REISMAN BROS BAKERY INC
Also Called: Reismans Bros. Bakery
110 Avenue O (11204-6591)
P.O. Box 40112 (11204-0112)
PHONE..............................718 331-1975
Bernat Reisman, *Ch of Bd*
Larry Fisler, *Vice Pres*
Esther Friedman, *Admin Sec*
EMP: 15
SQ FT: 4,000
SALES (est): 4MM **Privately Held**
WEB: www.reismansbakery.com
SIC: 2051 5411 Bakery: wholesale or wholesale/retail combined; cakes, bakery: except frozen; supermarkets

(G-2338)
REMARKETY INC (PA)
81 Prospect St (11201-1473)
PHONE..............................800 570-7564
Yoel Presman, *President*
EMP: 3
SQ FT: 600
SALES: 1.2MM **Privately Held**
SIC: 7372 Home entertainment computer software

(G-2339)
REMEDIES SURGICAL SUPPLIES
331 Rutledge St Ste 204 (11211-7546)
PHONE..............................718 599-5301
Mordchai Hirsch, *President*
EMP: 7
SQ FT: 2,000

SALES (est): 4.5MM **Privately Held**
SIC: 3634 3069 Humidifiers, electric: household; medical & laboratory rubber sundries & related products

(G-2340)
REMSEN GRAPHICS CORP
52 Court St 2 (11201-4901)
PHONE..............................718 643-7500
Greg Vellanti, *President*
Frank Vellanti, *Vice Pres*
Piero Galluzzo, *Admin Sec*
EMP: 5
SQ FT: 1,200
SALES: 1MM **Privately Held**
SIC: 2752 7389 Offset & photolithographic printing

(G-2341)
RENE PORTIER INC
3611 14th Ave Ste 6 (11218-3750)
PHONE..............................718 853-7896
EMP: 9
SQ FT: 6,000
SALES (est): 1MM **Privately Held**
SIC: 2339 Mfg Women's/Misses' Outerwear

(G-2342)
REVIVN PUBLIC BENEFIT CORP
63 Flushing Ave Unit 231 (11205-1074)
PHONE..............................347 762-8193
John Fazzolari, *President*
Vatsal Patel, *Manager*
EMP: 15 **EST:** 2014
SALES (est): 1.9MM **Privately Held**
SIC: 7372 3571 Application computer software; electronic computers

(G-2343)
RHOSEY LLC
Also Called: Rose Gourmet
1677 Mcdonald Ave (11230-6312)
PHONE..............................718 382-1226
Kevin Ronan,
EMP: 5
SALES (est): 469.1K **Privately Held**
SIC: 2045 2038 5142 Doughs, frozen or refrigerated: from purchased flour; ethnic foods, frozen; packaged frozen goods

(G-2344)
RICHARD MANUFACTURING CO INC
63 Flushing Ave Unit 327 (11205-1083)
PHONE..............................718 254-0958
Solomon Mayer, *President*
Janet Mayer, *Admin Sec*
EMP: 8 **EST:** 1943
SALES: 200K **Privately Held**
SIC: 2326 2339 Aprons, work, except rubberized & plastic: men's; aprons, except rubber or plastic: women's, misses', juniors'

(G-2345)
RINI TANK & TRUCK SERVICE
327 Nassau Ave (11222-3811)
PHONE..............................718 384-6606
Richard V Rini, *President*
EMP: 16
SQ FT: 10,000
SALES (est): 978.7K **Privately Held**
SIC: 7692 Welding repair

(G-2346)
RIOT NEW MEDIA GROUP INC
147 Prince St Ste 1 (11201-3022)
PHONE..............................604 700-4896
Jeffrey O'Neal, *CEO*
Josh Corman, *Editor*
Amanda Nelson, *Editor*
Kelly Jensen, *Assoc Editor*
Alex Baker, *Director*
EMP: 6
SALES (est): 516.3K **Privately Held**
SIC: 2741

(G-2347)
RIVA JEWELRY MANUFACTURING INC
140 58th St Ste 8b (11220-2524)
PHONE..............................718 361-3100
Ted Doudak, *President*
John Badee, *Engineer*

Jim Sartori, *CFO*
Remon Soliman, *Security Mgr*
Edgar Andrade, *Manager*
▲ **EMP:** 125
SQ FT: 20,000
SALES (est): 22.3MM **Privately Held**
WEB: www.rivajewelry.com
SIC: 3911 Jewelry apparel

(G-2348)
RIVERSIDE MACHINERY COMPANY (PA)
Also Called: Sns Machinery
140 53rd St (11232-4319)
PHONE..............................718 492-7400
Simon Srybnik, *President*
Louis Srybnik, *Vice Pres*
Saul Waller, *Treasurer*
Jay B Srybnik, *Admin Sec*
EMP: 5
SQ FT: 30,000
SALES (est): 4.3MM **Privately Held**
SIC: 3599 Machine shop, jobbing & repair

(G-2349)
RIVERSIDE MACHINERY COMPANY
132 54th St (11220-2506)
PHONE..............................718 492-7400
Simon Srybnik, *Manager*
EMP: 20
SQ FT: 35,060
SALES (corp-wide): 4.3MM **Privately Held**
SIC: 3549 5084 Metalworking machinery; industrial machinery & equipment
PA: Riverside Machinery Company Inc
140 53rd St
Brooklyn NY 11232
718 492-7400

(G-2350)
ROB HERSCHENFELD DESIGN INC
304 Boerum St (11206-3590)
PHONE..............................718 456-6801
Rob Herschenfeld, *President*
EMP: 10
SQ FT: 10,000
SALES (est): 1.2MM **Privately Held**
SIC: 2512 1522 Upholstered household furniture; remodeling, multi-family dwellings

(G-2351)
ROBIN INDUSTRIES LTD
56 N 3rd St (11249-3925)
PHONE..............................718 218-9616
Monica Vega, *President*
EMP: 11
SQ FT: 10,000
SALES (est): 1.2MM **Privately Held**
WEB: www.robinindustries.com
SIC: 3632 1711 Household refrigerators & freezers; heating & air conditioning contractors

(G-2352)
ROGER MICHAEL PRESS INC (PA)
499 Van Brunt St Ste 6b (11231-1053)
P.O. Box 27176 (11202-7176)
PHONE..............................732 752-0800
Michael Held, *President*
Deborah Held, *Vice Pres*
▲ **EMP:** 61
SQ FT: 20,000
SALES (est): 200K **Privately Held**
WEB: www.mrogerpress.com
SIC: 2782 2789 Bookbinding & related work; looseleaf binders & devices

(G-2353)
ROMANTIC TIMES INC
Also Called: Romantic Times Magazine
9 Ridgewood Pl (11237-5912)
PHONE..............................718 237-1097
Kathryn Falk, *President*
EMP: 17
SQ FT: 6,000
SALES (est): 2.1MM **Privately Held**
WEB: www.romantictimes.com
SIC: 2721 5942 Magazines: publishing & printing; book stores

(G-2354)
ROODE HOEK & CO INC
55 Ferris St (11231-1194)
PHONE..............................718 522-5921
EMP: 13 EST: 2000
SALES: 750K Privately Held
SIC: 2431 Mfg Wooden Architectural Components
PA: E.R. Butler & Co., Inc.
   55 Prince St Frnt A
   New York NY 10012

(G-2355)
ROSE SOLOMON CO
63 Flushing Ave Unit 330 (11205-1083)
PHONE..............................718 855-1788
Mendel Reichman, President
▲ EMP: 21 EST: 1908
SQ FT: 7,000
SALES (est): 1.1MM Privately Held
SIC: 2389 5049 2869 Burial garments; religious supplies; industrial organic chemicals

(G-2356)
ROTH CLOTHING CO INC (PA)
300 Penn St (11211-7405)
PHONE..............................718 384-4927
Mates Roth, President
▲ EMP: 3
SQ FT: 30,000
SALES: 1.2MM Privately Held
SIC: 2389 2311 Clergymen's vestments; suits, men's & boys': made from purchased materials

(G-2357)
ROTH DESIGN & CONSULTING INC
Also Called: Roth's Metal Works
132 Bogart St (11206)
PHONE..............................718 209-0193
Arnold Roth, President
Jake Roth, Vice Pres
EMP: 40
SQ FT: 40,000
SALES (est): 7MM Privately Held
SIC: 3441 8711 1791 Fabricated structural metal; building construction consultant; structural engineering; structural steel erection

(G-2358)
ROYAL CLOTHING CORP
1316 48th St Apt 1 (11219-3167)
PHONE..............................718 436-5841
Abraham Sports, President
Joseph Schwartz, Buyer
EMP: 6
SQ FT: 2,000
SALES: 2MM Privately Held
SIC: 2311 5611 Suits, men's & boys': made from purchased materials; suits, men's

(G-2359)
ROYAL CROWN FINANCIAL
1028 Dahill Rd (11204-1742)
PHONE..............................718 234-7237
Milton Schwartz, Vice Pres
EMP: 6
SALES (est): 201.4K Privately Held
SIC: 2086 Soft drinks: packaged in cans, bottles, etc.

(G-2360)
ROYAL KOSHER FOODS LLC
1464 45th St Ste 1a (11219-2243)
PHONE..............................347 221-1867
Yitzchok Podrigal,
EMP: 6
SALES (est): 110.5K Privately Held
SIC: 2099 Food preparations

(G-2361)
ROYAL MOLDS INC
1634 Marine Pkwy (11234-4217)
PHONE..............................718 382-7686
EMP: 15 EST: 1946
SQ FT: 10,000
SALES (est): 1.1MM Privately Held
SIC: 3544 3423 Mfg Dies/Tools/Jigs/Fixtures Mfg Hand/Edge Tools

(G-2362)
ROYAL SWEET BAKERY INC
119 49th St (11232-4229)
PHONE..............................718 567-7770
Mikhail Yusim, President
◆ EMP: 10
SALES (est): 1.1MM Privately Held
SIC: 2051 Bakery: wholesale or wholesale/retail combined

(G-2363)
RPI OF INDIANA INC
123 Varick Ave (11237-1216)
PHONE..............................330 279-2421
Adrienne Cooper, CEO
Mike McVicker, President
EMP: 31
SALES (est): 5.9MM Privately Held
WEB: www.rpicontainers.com
SIC: 3443 Dumpsters, garbage

(G-2364)
RUBICON INDUSTRIES CORP (PA)
848 E 43rd St (11210-3500)
PHONE..............................718 434-4700
Michael Rubinberg, President
Matthew Rubinberg, General Mgr
▲ EMP: 24
SQ FT: 20,000
SALES (est): 4.7MM Privately Held
WEB: www.rubiconhx.com
SIC: 3585 Evaporative condensers, heat transfer equipment

(G-2365)
RUS AUTO PARTS INC
Also Called: Bdtrims
508 Coney Island Ave (11218-3409)
PHONE..............................800 410-2669
Alex Kobzar, President
EMP: 5
SALES (est): 388.7K Privately Held
SIC: 3089 Automotive parts, plastic

(G-2366)
RUSSIAN MIX INC
2225 Benson Ave Apt 74 (11214-5245)
PHONE..............................347 385-7198
EMP: 5
SALES (est): 345.8K Privately Held
SIC: 3273 Ready-mixed concrete

(G-2367)
RUSSKAYA REKLAMA INC
2699 Coney Island Ave (11235-5004)
PHONE..............................718 769-3000
Paul Reklama, President
EMP: 20
SALES (est): 1.1MM Privately Held
SIC: 2711 Newspapers, publishing & printing

(G-2368)
RYBA GENERAL MERCHANDISE INC
63 Flushing Ave Unit 332 (11205-1083)
PHONE..............................718 522-2028
Sam Ryba, President
Marvin Ryba, Vice Pres
Chaya Knopfler, Admin Sec
◆ EMP: 7
SQ FT: 25,000
SALES (est): 710K Privately Held
WEB: www.rybagen.com
SIC: 2325 5136 Slacks, dress: men's, youths' & boys'; men's & boys' clothing; shirts, men's & boys'

(G-2369)
S & J SHEET METAL SUPPLY
70 Grand Ave (11205-2505)
PHONE..............................718 384-0800
David Gottlieb, Branch Mgr
EMP: 5
SALES (corp-wide): 107.4MM Privately Held
SIC: 3444 5033 Sheet metalwork; roofing & siding materials
PA: S. & J. Sheet Metal Supply Inc.
   526 E 134th St
   Bronx NY 10454
   718 993-0460

(G-2370)
S & S MACHINERY CORP (PA)
Also Called: CAM Machinery Co
140 53rd St (11232-4319)
PHONE..............................718 492-7400
Simon Srybnik, President
Louis Srybnik, Vice Pres
▲ EMP: 100
SQ FT: 100,000
SALES (est): 11.4MM Privately Held
WEB: www.sandsmachinery.com
SIC: 3541 3549 5084 3545 Machine tools, metal cutting type; metalworking machinery; metalworking machinery; machine tools & accessories; machine tool accessories

(G-2371)
S & S MACHINERY CORP
132 54th St (11220-2506)
PHONE..............................718 492-7400
Al Testa, Branch Mgr
EMP: 40
SALES (corp-wide): 11.4MM Privately Held
WEB: www.sandsmachinery.com
SIC: 3541 3549 5084 Machine tools, metal cutting type; metalworking machinery; machine tools & accessories; metalworking machinery
PA: S. & S. Machinery Corp.
   140 53rd St
   Brooklyn NY 11232
   718 492-7400

(G-2372)
S & S PRTG DIE-CUTTING CO INC
488 Morgan Ave Ste A (11222-5703)
PHONE..............................718 388-8990
Felix Sikar, President
▲ EMP: 14
SQ FT: 21,000
SALES (est): 1.4MM Privately Held
WEB: www.printdiecut.com
SIC: 3469 7389 2759 2675 Stamping metal for the trade; metal cutting services; letterpress printing; die-cut paper & board; coated & laminated paper

(G-2373)
S & T MACHINE INC
970 E 92nd St Fl 1 (11236-1720)
PHONE..............................718 272-2484
Saverio Accardi, President
Tinal Accardi, Vice Pres
EMP: 15
SQ FT: 5,000
SALES (est): 1.5MM Privately Held
SIC: 3444 Sheet metal specialties, not stamped

(G-2374)
S & W LADIES WEAR
3611 14th Ave Ste 601 (11218-3750)
PHONE..............................718 431-2800
Elias Bochner, Owner
EMP: 7 EST: 2015
SALES (est): 124.7K Privately Held
SIC: 3144 Boots, canvas or leather: women's

(G-2375)
S & W METAL TRADING CORP
1601 E 7th St (11230-7002)
PHONE..............................212 719-5070
Abraham Slomovics, President
Abraham Weisz, Vice Pres
EMP: 8
SQ FT: 1,000
SALES (est): 960.6K Privately Held
SIC: 3339 3341 Primary nonferrous metals; secondary nonferrous metals

(G-2376)
S D Z METAL SPINNING STAMPING
1807 Pacific St (11233-3505)
PHONE..............................718 778-3600
Kenny Mersand, President
EMP: 15
SQ FT: 10,000
SALES: 971.2K Privately Held
SIC: 3469 Spinning metal for the trade; stamping metal for the trade

(G-2377)
S HELLERMAN INC (PA)
242 Green St (11222-1208)
PHONE..............................718 622-2995
Robert Hellerman, President
Joseph Hellerman, Vice Pres
EMP: 11
SQ FT: 20,000
SALES: 750K Privately Held
SIC: 2299 Textile mill waste & remnant processing

(G-2378)
S2 SPORTSWEAR INC
4100 1st Ave Ste 5n (11232-3303)
PHONE..............................347 335-0713
Saul Chakkall, CEO
Albert Zayat, Vice Pres
Ronnie Chakkall, CFO
▲ EMP: 10 EST: 2014
SQ FT: 6,000
SALES: 1.3MM Privately Held
SIC: 2339 5137 Sportswear, women's; sportswear, women's & children's

(G-2379)
SABBSONS INTERNATIONAL INC
Also Called: Simple Elegance New York
474 50th St (11220-1913)
PHONE..............................718 360-1947
Isaac Sabbagh, CEO
Abraham I Sabbagh, Vice Pres
Victor Sabbagh, CFO
◆ EMP: 10
SALES (est): 492.2K Privately Held
SIC: 2299 Linen fabrics

(G-2380)
SAFCORE LLC
23 Van Dam St (11222-4509)
PHONE..............................917 627-5263
Safwat Riad,
EMP: 10
SALES (est): 322.9K Privately Held
SIC: 2519 Household furniture

(G-2381)
SAHADI FINE FOODS INC
4215 1st Ave (11232-3300)
PHONE..............................718 369-0100
Pat Whelan, Managing Dir
Vin Campbell, Info Tech Dir
Audrey Sahadi, Director
Charles Sahadi, Director
Robert Sahadi, Director
◆ EMP: 22
SQ FT: 116,000
SALES (est): 4.8MM Privately Held
WEB: www.sahadifinefoods.com
SIC: 2068 2032 5149 5145 Nuts: dried, dehydrated, salted or roasted; seeds: dried, dehydrated, salted or roasted; beans & bean sprouts, canned, jarred, etc.; fruits, dried; nuts, salted or roasted

(G-2382)
SALTY ROAD INC
190 Bedford Ave 404 (11249-2904)
PHONE..............................347 673-3925
Marisa Wu, CEO
EMP: 8
SALES (est): 696.3K Privately Held
SIC: 2064 Candy & other confectionery products

(G-2383)
SANGSTER FOODS INC
225 Parkside Ave Apt 3p (11226-1352)
PHONE..............................212 993-9129
Lily Golberg, Director
Peter Sangster, Director
Tania Sangster, Director
EMP: 10
SALES (est): 324.6K Privately Held
SIC: 2032 2043 2091 5149 Ethnic foods: canned, jarred, etc.; infants' foods, cereal type; canned & cured fish & seafoods; health foods; instant coffee

(G-2384)
SARUG INC
2055 Mcdonald Ave (11223-2821)
PHONE..............................718 339-2791
Henrik Zylberstein, President

EMP: 55
SQ FT: 3,000
SALES (est): 3.3MM **Privately Held**
SIC: 2253 Sweaters & sweater coats, knit

(G-2385)
SAS MAINTENANCE SERVICES INC
8435 Bay 16th St Ste A (11214-2844)
PHONE..............................718 837-2124
Maria Locascio, *President*
EMP: 17
SALES: 2.8MM **Privately Held**
WEB: www.sasmaint.com
SIC: 3471 Cleaning, polishing & finishing

(G-2386)
SCHLESS BOTTLES INC (PA)
4616 16th Ave (11204-1104)
PHONE..............................718 236-2790
Mark Schlesinger, *Ch of Bd*
Judy Schlesinger, *President*
▲ **EMP:** 16
SQ FT: 40,000
SALES (est): 3.8MM **Privately Held**
SIC: 3085 Plastics bottles

(G-2387)
SCHNEPS MEDIA LLC (PA)
1 Metrotech Ctr (11201-3948)
PHONE..............................718 224-5863
Victoria Schneps, *President*
EMP: 2
SALES (est): 2.7MM **Privately Held**
SIC: 2711 Newspapers

(G-2388)
SCHOOL NEWS NATIONWIDE INC
490 E 28th St (11226-7826)
PHONE..............................718 753-9920
Bill Tinglin, *President*
Ron Glick, *Principal*
Harlan Levine, *Principal*
Bill McNamara, *Principal*
Morris Tinglin, *Principal*
EMP: 6
SALES (est): 368.1K **Privately Held**
SIC: 2711 Newspapers: publishing only, not printed on site

(G-2389)
SCHWARTZ TEXTILE LLC
Also Called: Tag Manufacturing
160 7th St (11215-3107)
PHONE..............................718 499-8243
Mitchell Schwartz, *President*
Marc Schwartz, *Vice Pres*
Irving Schwartz,
▲ **EMP:** 25 **EST:** 1948
SQ FT: 60,000
SALES (est): 2.1MM **Privately Held**
SIC: 2329 2321 Sweaters & sweater jackets: men's & boys'; men's & boys' furnishings

(G-2390)
SCIENTIFIC COMPONENTS CORP (PA)
Also Called: Mini-Circuits
13 Neptune Ave (11235-4404)
P.O. Box 350199 (11235-0199)
PHONE..............................718 934-4500
Alicia Kaylie, *CEO*
Gloria Kaylie, *Corp Secy*
Ted C Heil, *COO*
CHI Shum, *Vice Pres*
Steven Feigenbaum, *Materials Mgr*
▲ **EMP:** 475
SQ FT: 50,000
SALES (est): 147MM **Privately Held**
WEB: www.minicircuits.com
SIC: 3679 Electronic switches; electronic circuits

(G-2391)
SCIENTIFIC COMPONENTS CORP
Also Called: Mini Circuits
2450 Knapp St (11235-1006)
PHONE..............................718 368-2060
EMP: 264
SALES (corp-wide): 147MM **Privately Held**
SIC: 3679 Electronic circuits

PA: Scientific Components Corp
13 Neptune Ave
Brooklyn NY 11235
718 934-4500

(G-2392)
SCR GROUP NY INC
2799 Coney Island Ave 2f (11235-5015)
PHONE..............................516 601-3174
Rital Saban, *CEO*
EMP: 6
SALES (est): 236.5K **Privately Held**
SIC: 3851 Eyeglasses, lenses & frames

(G-2393)
SEASONS SOYFOOD INC
605 Degraw St (11217-3120)
PHONE..............................718 797-9896
Johnny Hong, *President*
▲ **EMP:** 8
SALES (est): 500K **Privately Held**
SIC: 2099 Tofu, except frozen desserts

(G-2394)
SEOUL SHOPPING BAG INC
10001 Avenue D (11236-1900)
PHONE..............................718 439-9226
Han Woo, *President*
EMP: 9 **EST:** 2010
SALES (est): 1.3MM **Privately Held**
SIC: 2674 Shipping & shopping bags or sacks

(G-2395)
SEPHARDIC YELLOW PAGES
2150 E 4th St (11223-4037)
PHONE..............................718 998-0299
David Benhorren, *Owner*
EMP: 20 **EST:** 1998
SALES (est): 1.6MM **Privately Held**
SIC: 2759 2741 Publication printing; miscellaneous publishing

(G-2396)
SERGE DUCT DESIGNS INC
535 Dean St Apt 124 (11217-5207)
PHONE..............................718 783-7799
Serge Rozenbaum, *President*
Micha Rozenbaug, *Vice Pres*
EMP: 20
SALES (est): 3.3MM **Privately Held**
SIC: 3549 Metalworking machinery

(G-2397)
SETTEPANI INC (PA)
Also Called: Settepani Bakery
602 Lorimer St (11211-2220)
PHONE..............................718 349-6524
Nino Settepani, *President*
Biagio Settepani, *Vice Pres*
Antonio Settepani, *Admin Sec*
EMP: 28
SQ FT: 5,000
SALES (est): 700K **Privately Held**
WEB: www.settepani.com
SIC: 2051 5461 Bakery: wholesale or wholesale/retail combined; bakeries

(G-2398)
SETTON BROTHERS INC
326 Troy Ave (11213-4634)
PHONE..............................646 902-6011
Yoel Setton, *President*
▲ **EMP:** 6
SQ FT: 2,000
SALES: 3MM **Privately Held**
SIC: 2389 Men's miscellaneous accessories

(G-2399)
SG BLOCKS INC (PA)
195 Montague St Fl 14 (11201-3631)
PHONE..............................646 240-4235
Paul M Galvin, *Ch of Bd*
Mahesh S Shetty, *President*
Rockey L Butler, *Vice Pres*
Gerald Sheeran, *CFO*
Stevan Armstrong, *CTO*
▼ **EMP:** 12
SALES (est): 8.1MM **Publicly Held**
WEB: www.newvalley.com
SIC: 2448 5032 8711 8741 Cargo containers, wood & metal combination; building blocks; engineering services; construction management

(G-2400)
SH LEATHER NOVELTY COMPANY
123 Clymer St Bsmt (11249-6708)
PHONE..............................718 387-7742
Shiee Handler, *President*
Solmen Delowitz, *Vice Pres*
Feiga Handler, *Treasurer*
EMP: 3 **EST:** 1954
SQ FT: 4,000
SALES: 1MM **Privately Held**
SIC: 2387 Apparel belts

(G-2401)
SHAKUFF LLC
34 35th St Unit 29 (11232-2209)
PHONE..............................212 675-0383
Joseph Sidof, *President*
EMP: 6
SALES (est): 142.3K **Privately Held**
SIC: 3648 Lighting equipment

(G-2402)
SHALAM IMPORTS INC (PA)
Also Called: Shalamex
1552 Dahill Rd Ste B (11204-3572)
PHONE..............................718 686-6271
Sasson Shalam, *President*
Abraham Shalam, *Vice Pres*
◆ **EMP:** 12 **EST:** 1955
SQ FT: 1,800
SALES (est): 1.3MM **Privately Held**
SIC: 2674 Shipping bags or sacks, including multiwall & heavy duty

(G-2403)
SHANGHAI STOVE INC
78 Gerry St 82 (11206-4326)
PHONE..............................718 599-4583
James Wong, *President*
EMP: 15
SALES (est): 1.6MM **Privately Held**
SIC: 3444 Restaurant sheet metalwork

(G-2404)
SHAREMETHODS LLC
1 N 4th Pl Apt 19i (11249-3340)
PHONE..............................877 742-7366
Eric Hoffert, *CEO*
EMP: 11
SALES (est): 616.2K **Privately Held**
WEB: www.sharemethods.com
SIC: 7372 Prepackaged software

(G-2405)
SHIELD SECURITY DOORS LTD
300 Cadman Plz W Fl 12 (11201-3226)
PHONE..............................202 468-3308
Samuel Fish, *President*
EMP: 5
SALES: 1MM **Privately Held**
SIC: 3699 5072 Security control equipment & systems; security devices; security devices, locks

(G-2406)
SHOWERAY CO
1857 E 8th St (11223-3234)
PHONE..............................718 965-3633
Abraham Grazi, *President*
Jack Grazi, *Vice Pres*
Maurice Grazi, *Admin Sec*
EMP: 100 **EST:** 1938
SQ FT: 60,000
SALES (est): 3.7MM **Privately Held**
SIC: 2392 2391 Shower curtains: made from purchased materials; tablecloths: made from purchased materials; mattress protectors, except rubber; curtains & draperies

(G-2407)
SIGN & SIGNS
783 Coney Island Ave (11218-5380)
PHONE..............................718 941-6200
Ali Chashir, *Principal*
EMP: 6
SALES (est): 427.4K **Privately Held**
SIC: 3993 Electric signs

(G-2408)
SIGN GROUP INC
Also Called: Boro Park Signs
5215 New Utrecht Ave (11219-3829)
PHONE..............................718 438-7103

Ushe Steinmetz, *President*
Solomon Gutter, *Admin Sec*
EMP: 25
SQ FT: 9,000
SALES (est): 3MM **Privately Held**
WEB: www.signgroup.com
SIC: 3993 Electric signs

(G-2409)
SIGN HEAVEN CORP
160 25th St (11232-1409)
PHONE..............................718 499-4423
Simon Purke, *President*
EMP: 5
SALES (est): 27.1K **Privately Held**
WEB: www.signheavenny.com
SIC: 3993 Signs & advertising specialties

(G-2410)
SIGN WORLD INC
1194 Utica Ave (11203-5997)
PHONE..............................212 619-9000
Herman Weiss, *President*
Carl Weiss, *Corp Secy*
EMP: 25 **EST:** 1964
SQ FT: 10,000
SALES (est): 1.9MM **Privately Held**
SIC: 3993 2752 Signs & advertising specialties; commercial printing, lithographic

(G-2411)
SIGNS & DECAL CORP
410 Morgan Ave (11211-1640)
PHONE..............................718 486-6400
Abdulrasul M Khalfan, *President*
Abdulrasul Khalfan, *President*
Tazzim Khalfan, *Vice Pres*
Andres Carrera, *Project Mgr*
Manoj Garimella, *Engineer*
▲ **EMP:** 30
SQ FT: 25,000
SALES (est): 5.6MM **Privately Held**
WEB: www.signsanddecal.com
SIC: 3993 Displays & cutouts, window & lobby; signs, not made in custom sign painting shops

(G-2412)
SILKY TONES INC
777 Kent Ave Ste 213 (11205-1585)
PHONE..............................718 218-5598
EMP: 5
SALES (est): 225.4K **Privately Held**
SIC: 2251 Women's hosiery, except socks

(G-2413)
SILLY PHILLIE CREATIONS INC
Also Called: Swisse Cheeks
140 58th St Ste 6f (11220-2526)
PHONE..............................718 492-6300
Richard S'Dao, *President*
Phyllis G S'Dao, *Vice Pres*
Phyllis Sdao, *Vice Pres*
▲ **EMP:** 30
SQ FT: 30,000
SALES (est): 2.9MM **Privately Held**
WEB: www.sillyphillie.com
SIC: 2392 2361 2369 Household furnishings; girls' & children's dresses, blouses & shirts; sun suits: girls', children's & infants'

(G-2414)
SILVER OAK PHARMACY INC
5105 Church Ave (11203-3511)
PHONE..............................718 922-3400
Axay B Joshi, *Principal*
EMP: 6
SALES (est): 536.7K **Privately Held**
SIC: 2834 Pharmaceutical preparations

(G-2415)
SILVERMAN & GORF INC
60 Franklin Ave (11205-1594)
PHONE..............................718 625-1309
Edward Gorf, *President*
Harry Moorer, *Vice Pres*
EMP: 6
SQ FT: 30,000
SALES (est): 490K **Privately Held**
SIC: 3471 Plating of metals or formed products

(G-2416)
SILVERSTONE SHTMTL FBRICATIONS
66 Huntington St (11231)
PHONE................718 422-0380
Rustem Duka, *President*
EMP: 5
SQ FT: 10,000
SALES (est): 1MM **Privately Held**
SIC: 3441 Fabricated structural metal

(G-2417)
SIMON LIU INC
280 24th St (11232-1310)
PHONE................718 567-2011
Simon Liu, *President*
▲ EMP: 12
SQ FT: 7,500
SALES (est): 907.5K **Privately Held**
WEB: www.simonliuinc.com
SIC: 3952 5999 Artists' equipment; artists' supplies & materials

(G-2418)
SIMON S DECORATING INC
911 Avenue N (11230-5719)
PHONE................718 339-2931
Simon Poldanl, *President*
EMP: 5
SALES (est): 442.9K **Privately Held**
SIC: 2512 Upholstered household furniture

(G-2419)
SIMPLE ELEGANCE NEW YORK INC
474 50th St (11220-1913)
PHONE................718 360-1947
Isaac Sabbagh, *President*
Victor Sabbagh, *Vice Pres*
Abraham Sabbagh, *CFO*
▲ EMP: 15
SQ FT: 6,000
SALES (est): 1.1MM **Privately Held**
SIC: 2299 5131 Linen fabrics; linen piece goods, woven

(G-2420)
SINCERUS LLC
2478 Mcdonald Ave (11223-5233)
PHONE................800 419-2804
Marc Poirier,
EMP: 5
SQ FT: 5,000
SALES (est): 229.7K **Privately Held**
SIC: 2834 Pharmaceutical preparations

(G-2421)
SING AH POULTRY
114 Sackett St (11231-1414)
PHONE................718 625-7253
Perry Chen, *Owner*
EMP: 5
SQ FT: 2,400
SALES (est): 311.4K **Privately Held**
SIC: 2015 Poultry, slaughtered & dressed

(G-2422)
SING TAO NEWSPAPERS NY LTD
5317 8th Ave (11220-3259)
PHONE................212 431-9030
Rick Ho, *Manager*
EMP: 10 **Privately Held**
WEB: www.nysingtao.com
SIC: 2711 Newspapers
PA: Sing Tao Newspapers New York Ltd.
188 Lafayette St
New York NY 10013

(G-2423)
SING TAO NEWSPAPERS NY LTD
905 Flushing Ave Fl 2 (11206-4602)
PHONE................718 821-0123
Patrick Seto, *Facilities Mgr*
EMP: 30
SQ FT: 20,900 **Privately Held**
WEB: www.nysingtao.com
SIC: 2711 Newspapers, publishing & printing
PA: Sing Tao Newspapers New York Ltd.
188 Lafayette St
New York NY 10013

(G-2424)
SITA FINISHING INC
Also Called: Sita Knitting
207 Starr St Ste 1 (11237-2639)
PHONE................718 417-5295
Loan Sita, *President*
Ioan Sita, *President*
George Sita, *Vice Pres*
▲ EMP: 10
SQ FT: 8,000
SALES (est): 1MM **Privately Held**
WEB: www.sitafashion.com
SIC: 2211 Canvas

(G-2425)
SLAVA INDUSTRIES INCORPORATED (PA)
Also Called: Nfk International
555 16th St (11215-5914)
PHONE................718 499-4850
Nevio Kovacevic, *Principal*
Ilaria Sialino, *CFO*
▲ EMP: 2
SQ FT: 1,200
SALES (est): 38MM **Privately Held**
SIC: 2512 2514 Upholstered household furniture; metal household furniture

(G-2426)
SLEEPING PARTNERS INTL INC
Also Called: Sleeping Partners Home Fashion
140 58th St Ste 3e (11220-2522)
PHONE................212 254-1515
Salvatore Stoch, *Ch of Bd*
Terry Pierson, *Bookkeeper*
▲ EMP: 15
SQ FT: 25,000
SALES (est): 5MM **Privately Held**
SIC: 2392 Household furnishings

(G-2427)
SLEEPY HEAD INC
230 3rd St (11215-2714)
PHONE................718 237-9655
EMP: 10
SQ FT: 17,000
SALES (est): 720K **Privately Held**
SIC: 2369 Mfg Girl/Youth Outerwear

(G-2428)
SLN GROUP INC
2172 E 26th St (11229-4955)
PHONE................718 677-5969
Luiza Shamilova, *Principal*
EMP: 5
SALES (est): 421.2K **Privately Held**
SIC: 3679 Electronic components

(G-2429)
SLOANE DESIGN INC
226 52nd St (11220-1715)
PHONE................212 539-0184
Sloane Madureira, *President*
Tim Chapman, *Vice Pres*
EMP: 5 EST: 2005
SALES (est): 275.4K **Privately Held**
SIC: 2752 Commercial printing, lithographic

(G-2430)
SMARTONERS INC (PA)
289 Keap St Ste A (11211-7459)
PHONE................718 975-0197
Aidel Appel, *President*
EMP: 4
SQ FT: 3,000
SALES (est): 8MM **Privately Held**
SIC: 3955 Print cartridges for laser & other computer printers

(G-2431)
SMITH STREET BREAD CO LLC
17 5th St (11231-4514)
PHONE................718 797-9712
Mark Rubin, *Mng Member*
EMP: 12
SQ FT: 500
SALES (est): 1MM **Privately Held**
SIC: 2051 Bread, cake & related products

(G-2432)
SOCIAL BICYCLES LLC
Also Called: Sobi
55 Prospect St Ste 304 (11201-1497)
PHONE................917 746-7624
Dara Khosrowshahi, *CEO*
Daniel Toy, *General Mgr*
Avra Van Der Zee, *COO*
Jeffrey Yu, *Engineer*
Edward Rayner, *CFO*
▲ EMP: 25
SQ FT: 700
SALES (est): 10.3MM
SALES (corp-wide): 11.2B **Publicly Held**
SIC: 3751 7372 Bicycles & related parts; prepackaged software
PA: Uber Technologies, Inc.
1455 Market St Fl 4
San Francisco CA 94103
415 612-8582

(G-2433)
SOCKBIN
718 Avenue U (11223-4134)
PHONE................917 519-1119
Andrew Muller, *Owner*
EMP: 6
SALES (est): 247.4K **Privately Held**
SIC: 2252 Socks

(G-2434)
SOCKS AND MORE OF NY INC
1605 Avenue Z Fl 1 (11235-3809)
PHONE................718 769-1785
Irene Dubrovsky, *Chairman*
EMP: 9
SALES (est): 997.4K **Privately Held**
SIC: 2252 Socks

(G-2435)
SOHO LETTERPRESS INC
68 35th St Unit 6 (11232-2211)
PHONE................718 788-2518
Anne Noonan, *President*
EMP: 12
SALES (est): 1.1MM **Privately Held**
WEB: www.soholetterpress.com
SIC: 2759 Letterpress printing

(G-2436)
SOLA HOME EXPO INC
172 Neptune Ave (11235-5317)
PHONE................718 646-3383
Sergiy Orlov, *President*
▲ EMP: 6
SALES (est): 80K **Privately Held**
SIC: 3431 Bathroom fixtures, including sinks

(G-2437)
SOLAR ENERGY SYSTEMS LLC (PA)
1205 Manhattan Ave # 1210 (11222-6156)
PHONE................718 389-1545
David Buckner, *President*
Christopher Moustakis, *Vice Pres*
EMP: 12
SQ FT: 1,300
SALES (est): 4MM **Privately Held**
WEB: www.solaresystems.com
SIC: 3433 1711 Solar heaters & collectors; solar energy contractor

(G-2438)
SOLARWATERWAY INC
Also Called: Solarelectricway
254 36th St Ste C453 (11232-2544)
PHONE................888 998-5337
Jacqueline Sarway, *President*
Murray Sarway, *Vice Pres*
▲ EMP: 33
SQ FT: 9,000
SALES (est): 4.8MM **Privately Held**
SIC: 3645 3646 5063 Residential lighting fixtures; commercial indusl & institutional electric lighting fixtures; lighting fixtures

(G-2439)
SOLARZ BROS PRINTING CORP
231 Norman Ave Ste 105 (11222-1559)
PHONE................718 383-1330
Sbigniew Solarz, *Principal*
EMP: 6
SALES (est): 399.8K **Privately Held**
SIC: 2752 Commercial printing, offset

(G-2440)
SOLENIS LLC
Also Called: Ashland Water Technologies
761 Humboldt St (11222-3001)
PHONE................718 383-1717
Peter Coster, *Branch Mgr*
EMP: 9
SALES (corp-wide): 767.2MM **Privately Held**
SIC: 2899 Water treating compounds
HQ: Solenis Llc
3 Beaver Valley Rd # 500
Wilmington DE 19803
866 337-1533

(G-2441)
SONAAL INDUSTRIES INC
210 Kingsland Ave (11222-4303)
PHONE................718 383-3860
Rana P Mukhopadhyay, *Principal*
EMP: 7
SALES (est): 205.5K **Privately Held**
SIC: 3999 Manufacturing industries

(G-2442)
SOTO SAKE CORPORATION
18 Bridge St Ste 4i (11201-1107)
PHONE................305 781-3906
William Melnyk, *Director*
Daniel Rubinoff, *Director*
EMP: 8 EST: 2015
SALES (est): 403K **Privately Held**
SIC: 2086 Water, pasteurized: packaged in cans, bottles, etc.

(G-2443)
SOURCE TECHNOLOGIES
9728 3rd Ave (11209-7742)
PHONE................718 708-0305
Nick Anthony, *Owner*
EMP: 12
SQ FT: 2,000
SALES: 1MM **Privately Held**
SIC: 3599 Machine & other job shop work

(G-2444)
SOUTH CENTRAL BOYZ
2568 Bedford Ave Apt 1a (11226-7071)
PHONE................718 496-7270
Keith Bessor, *President*
EMP: 5
SALES (est): 280K **Privately Held**
SIC: 2389 7389 Costumes;

(G-2445)
SPACE 150
20 Jay St Ste 928 (11201-8354)
PHONE................612 332-6458
EMP: 120 EST: 2003
SALES (est): 11.6MM **Privately Held**
SIC: 2741 Misc Publishing

(G-2446)
SPFM CORP (PA)
Also Called: Spray Market, The
162 2nd Ave (11215-4619)
PHONE................718 788-6800
Jacob Kloc, *President*
Ann Marie Wolf, *Administration*
EMP: 5 EST: 2011
SALES: 500K **Privately Held**
SIC: 3563 Spraying & dusting equipment

(G-2447)
SPREAD-MMMS LLC
545 Prospect Pl Apt 10d (11238-4271)
P.O. Box 4, New York (10029-0004)
PHONE................917 727-8116
EMP: 6
SALES (est): 414.9K **Privately Held**
SIC: 2099 Mfg Food Preparations

(G-2448)
ST JOHN
1700 Saint Johns Pl (11233-4906)
PHONE................718 771-4541
EMP: 5 EST: 2010
SALES (est): 363.4K **Privately Held**
SIC: 2339 Mfg Women's/Misses' Outerwear

(G-2449)
STAG BROTHERS CAST STONE CO
909 E 51st St (11203-6735)
PHONE................718 629-0975
Sal Stagliano, *President*
EMP: 8
SALES: 310K **Privately Held**
SIC: 3272 Concrete products

(G-2450)
STAMPS & SIGNS ONLINE CORP
622 Broadway (11206-4381)
PHONE...............................718 218-0050
Ben Follman, *CEO*
EMP: 8
SALES (est): 987.1K **Privately Held**
SIC: 3993 5999 Signs & advertising specialties; trophies & plaques

(G-2451)
STAPLEX COMPANY INC
777 5th Ave (11232-1695)
PHONE...............................718 768-3333
James J Cussani Jr, *President*
Gregory Cussani, *Vice Pres*
David Hill, *Vice Pres*
R Powers, *Vice Pres*
▲ EMP: 20 EST: 1949
SQ FT: 20,000
SALES (est): 4.3MM **Privately Held**
SIC: 3579 3821 Stapling machines (hand or power); laboratory apparatus & furniture

(G-2452)
STAR COMPOSITION SERVICES INC
170 Hewes St (11211-8001)
PHONE...............................212 684-4001
Jacob Weiss, *President*
▲ EMP: 5 EST: 1970
SQ FT: 800
SALES (est): 500K **Privately Held**
SIC: 2791 7374 Typesetting, computer controlled; computer graphics service

(G-2453)
STARLINER SHIPPING & TRAVEL
5305 Church Ave Ste 1 (11203-3638)
PHONE...............................718 385-1515
Rhea Murray, *President*
Leighton Murray, *Vice Pres*
Blueth Murray-Ogunnoiki, *Vice Pres*
Anthia Murray, *Treasurer*
▼ EMP: 7
SALES (est): 540K **Privately Held**
SIC: 2599 Ship furniture

(G-2454)
STEALTH ARCHTCTRAL WINDOWS INC
Also Called: Stealth Window
232 Varet St (11206-3862)
PHONE...............................718 821-6666
Barry Borgen, *President*
EMP: 19
SQ FT: 52,000
SALES (est): 2.1MM **Privately Held**
WEB: www.avantguards.com
SIC: 2431 Windows, wood

(G-2455)
STEALTH INC
1129 E 27th St (11210-4620)
PHONE...............................718 252-7900
Jack Edelstein, *President*
EMP: 16
SQ FT: 3,000
SALES (est): 1.7MM **Privately Held**
SIC: 2326 Industrial garments, men's & boys'

(G-2456)
STEELCRAFT MANUFACTURING CO
Also Called: Steel Craft
352 Pine St (11208-2807)
PHONE...............................718 277-2404
Louis Massa, *President*
Christopher Hansen, *Principal*
Keith Flynn, *Persnl Mgr*
Janice Burke, *Info Tech Mgr*
EMP: 11 EST: 1945
SQ FT: 9,000
SALES (est): 962.3K **Privately Held**
SIC: 3444 2541 2514 Radiator shields or enclosures, sheet metal; wood partitions & fixtures; kitchen cabinets: metal

(G-2457)
STEELDECK NY INC
141 Banker St (11222-3147)
PHONE...............................718 599-3700

Philip Parsons, *President*
Gail Moorcroft, *Vice Pres*
▲ EMP: 15 EST: 2001
SQ FT: 20,000
SALES (est): 3.2MM **Privately Held**
SIC: 3999 5049 2541 2531 Stage hardware & equipment, except lighting; theatrical equipment & supplies; partitions for floor attachment, prefabricated: wood; theater furniture

(G-2458)
STEELMASTERS INC
135 Liberty Ave (11212-8008)
PHONE...............................718 498-2854
Matthew Rosio, *President*
Anthony Masi, *Vice Pres*
EMP: 23
SQ FT: 14,000
SALES (est): 3MM **Privately Held**
SIC: 3442 Rolling doors for industrial buildings or warehouses, metal

(G-2459)
STEELSTONE GROUP LLC
Also Called: Gourmia
3611 14th Ave Ste 540 (11218-3773)
PHONE...............................888 552-0033
Naphtali Biegeleisen, *CEO*
EMP: 6
SALES (est): 59MM **Privately Held**
SIC: 3631 Household cooking equipment

(G-2460)
STEINBOCK-BRAFF INC
Also Called: Kat Nap Products
3611 14th Ave (11218-3773)
PHONE...............................718 972-6500
Corey Steinbock, *President*
▲ EMP: 30 EST: 1933
SQ FT: 80,000
SALES (est): 3.8MM **Privately Held**
WEB: www.sleepmattress.com
SIC: 2515 5021 Mattresses & foundations; household furniture

(G-2461)
STIEGELBAUER ASSOCIATES INC (PA)
63 Flushing Ave Unit 280 (11205-1078)
PHONE...............................718 624-0835
Michael Stiegelbauer, *President*
Dawn Stiegelbauer, *Corp Secy*
Steven Paone, *Vice Pres*
Kimberly Amato, *Marketing Staff*
EMP: 30
SQ FT: 180,000
SALES (est): 4.1MM **Privately Held**
SIC: 3999 Theatrical scenery

(G-2462)
STONE AND BATH GALLERY
868 39th St (11232-3230)
PHONE...............................718 438-4500
Samuel Stru, *Owner*
▲ EMP: 8
SALES (est): 298.7K **Privately Held**
SIC: 3261 3251 Bathroom accessories/fittings, vitreous china or earthenware; brick & structural clay tile

(G-2463)
STREET BEAT SPORTSWEAR INC (PA)
Also Called: Visual F-X
462 Kent Ave Fl 2 (11249-5922)
PHONE...............................718 302-1500
Albert Papouchado, *President*
Allen Smith, *CFO*
▲ EMP: 10
SQ FT: 66,000
SALES (est): 3.6MM **Privately Held**
SIC: 2339 Sportswear, women's

(G-2464)
STUDIO 21 LA INC
13 42nd St Fl 5 (11232-2616)
PHONE...............................718 965-6579
▲ EMP: 20
SQ FT: 5,000
SALES (est): 1.4MM **Privately Held**
SIC: 2531 5399 5712 Mfg Public Building Furniture Ret Misc General Merchandise Ret Furniture

(G-2465)
STUDIO 40 INC
810 Humboldt St Ste 4 (11222-1913)
PHONE...............................212 420-8631
Richard Temerian, *President*
EMP: 6 **Privately Held**
SIC: 3446 Architectural metalwork
PA: Studio 40 Inc
40 Great Jones St Apt 1
New York NY 10012

(G-2466)
STUHRLING ORIGINAL LLC
449 20th St (11215-6247)
PHONE...............................718 840-5760
Israel Jacobson, *Controller*
Evan Szanzer, *Chief Mktg Ofcr*
Sam Friedman, *Creative Dir*
Chaim Fischer, *Executive*
Pearl Neuwirth, *Executive Asst*
◆ EMP: 25
SQ FT: 20,000
SALES (est): 10MM **Privately Held**
SIC: 3873 5094 Watches, clocks, watchcases & parts; clocks, watches & parts; watches & parts

(G-2467)
STURDY STORE DISPLAYS INC
110 Beard St (11231-1502)
PHONE...............................718 389-9919
Michael Fried, *President*
Jacob Brauner, *Vice Pres*
Moshe Nathan Neuman, *Controller*
▲ EMP: 23
SQ FT: 35,000
SALES (est): 3.2MM **Privately Held**
WEB: www.sturdystoredisplays.com
SIC: 2542 Partitions & fixtures, except wood

(G-2468)
STYLIST PLEATING CORP
107 Vanderveer St Apt 3b (11207-2155)
PHONE...............................718 384-8181
Kenneth Stier, *President*
EMP: 18
SQ FT: 11,000
SALES (est): 879.8K **Privately Held**
SIC: 2395 Permanent pleating & pressing, for the trade

(G-2469)
SUN MING JAN INC
145 Noll St (11206-4714)
PHONE...............................718 418-8221
Ben Chen, *CEO*
▲ EMP: 10 EST: 1999
SALES (est): 949.6K **Privately Held**
SIC: 2013 Sausages & other prepared meats

(G-2470)
SUNBURST STUDIOS INC
584 3rd Ave (11215-4612)
PHONE...............................718 768-6360
Ihor Nykolak, *President*
Peter Friedman, *Treasurer*
EMP: 5 EST: 1976
SQ FT: 3,600
SALES: 400K **Privately Held**
WEB: www.sunburststudio.com
SIC: 3231 8999 Stained glass: made from purchased glass; cut & engraved glassware: made from purchased glass; art restoration

(G-2471)
SUPER NEON LIGHT CO INC
7813 16th Ave (11214-1085)
PHONE...............................718 236-5667
James Coccaro Jr, *President*
Hovannes Moussati, *Business Mgr*
Christian Buncher, *Opers Dir*
Marina Josifoski, *Finance*
David Shrm-CP, *Human Res Mgr*
EMP: 8 EST: 1939
SQ FT: 1,600
SALES (est): 936.2K **Privately Held**
SIC: 3993 Neon signs

(G-2472)
SUPER SAUCES INC
553 Prospect Ave (11215-6020)
PHONE...............................347 497-2537
Andrew Suzuka, *CEO*

EMP: 5
SALES (est): 139.9K **Privately Held**
SIC: 2033 Tomato sauce: packaged in cans, jars, etc.

(G-2473)
SUPERIOR BLOCK CORP
Also Called: Glenwood Masonry Products
761 E 42nd St (11210-2012)
PHONE...............................718 421-0900
Constance Cincotta, *President*
EMP: 10
SQ FT: 75,000
SALES (est): 1.8MM **Privately Held**
SIC: 3271 Concrete block & brick

(G-2474)
SUPERIOR ELEC ENCLOSURE INC
16 Spencer St (11205-1605)
PHONE...............................718 797-9090
Harris Grant, *President*
EMP: 7
SALES (est): 1MM **Privately Held**
SIC: 3444 Metal housings, enclosures, casings & other containers

(G-2475)
SUPERIOR FIBER MILLS INC
181 Lombardy St (11222-5417)
P.O. Box 306, East Norwich (11732-0306)
PHONE...............................718 782-7500
Helen Burney, *President*
Henry Burney, *Vice Pres*
EMP: 40
SQ FT: 125,000
SALES (est): 5.1MM **Privately Held**
WEB: www.superiorfibers.com
SIC: 2299 2221 Batts & batting: cotton mill waste & related material; broadwoven fabric mills, manmade

(G-2476)
SUPREME BOILERS INC
9221 Ditmas Ave (11236-1711)
PHONE...............................718 342-2220
Aaron Ganguli, *President*
David Rakst, *Vice Pres*
EMP: 5 EST: 2007
SALES (est): 540K **Privately Held**
SIC: 3443 Boiler & boiler shop work

(G-2477)
SUPREME LIGHTING DESIGN LLC
5308 13th Ave (11219-5198)
PHONE...............................718 812-3347
David Goldstein,
EMP: 15
SALES (est): 587.6K **Privately Held**
SIC: 3612 Distribution transformers, electric

(G-2478)
SUPREME POLY PLASTICS INC
299 Meserole St (11206-1732)
PHONE...............................718 456-9300
Abe Eilander, *President*
EMP: 25
SQ FT: 45,000
SALES (est): 3.9MM **Privately Held**
WEB: www.supremepoly.com
SIC: 2673 Plastic bags: made from purchased materials

(G-2479)
SURE-KOL REFRIGERATOR CO INC
490 Flushing Ave (11205-1615)
PHONE...............................718 625-0601
Steven Waslin, *President*
David J Waslin, *Corp Secy*
Jack Waslin, *Vice Pres*
EMP: 10 EST: 1947
SQ FT: 13,000
SALES (est): 1.5MM **Privately Held**
SIC: 3632 Household refrigerators & freezers

(G-2480)
SURPRISE PLASTICS INC
124 57th St (11220-2576)
PHONE...............................718 492-6355
Fax: 718 492-0258
▲ EMP: 115

SQ FT: 48,000
SALES (est): 16.8MM **Privately Held**
SIC: 3089 Mfg Plastic Products

(G-2481)
SURTIC MINING COMPANY LLC
1825 Foster Ave (11230-1834)
PHONE..................................718 434-0477
Herman Graham, *CEO*
Bruce Benn, *COO*
Venicia Fletchman, *Exec VP*
EMP: 14
SALES: 31.2MM **Privately Held**
SIC: 1041 7389 Open pit gold mining;

(G-2482)
SWEATER BRAND INC
Also Called: Domain
86 S 1st St (11249-4171)
PHONE..................................718 797-0505
Moshe Rosenberg, *Manager*
EMP: 6
SALES (corp-wide): 3.2MM **Privately Held**
SIC: 2253 Sweaters & sweater coats, knit
PA: Sweater Brand Inc.
22 Wallenberg Cir
Monsey NY
718 797-0505

(G-2483)
SYNERGY DIGITAL
43 Hall St (11205-1315)
PHONE..................................718 643-2742
Fax: 718 643-9212
EMP: 15
SALES (est): 720K **Privately Held**
SIC: 3691 Mfg Storage Batteries

(G-2484)
T & L TRADING CO
17 Meserole St (11206-1901)
PHONE..................................718 782-5550
David Tang, *Owner*
▲ EMP: 5
SQ FT: 5,000
SALES (est): 675.8K **Privately Held**
SIC: 2621 Stationery, envelope & tablet papers; bond paper

(G-2485)
T M I PLASTICS INDUSTRIES INC
28 Wythe Ave (11249-1036)
PHONE..................................718 383-0363
Sam Yuen, *President*
▲ EMP: 15
SALES (est): 2.2MM **Privately Held**
SIC: 2673 Plastic bags: made from purchased materials

(G-2486)
T MIX INC
6217 5th Ave (11220-4611)
PHONE..................................646 379-6814
Lin Jian, *CEO*
EMP: 6
SALES (est): 688.6K **Privately Held**
SIC: 3273 Ready-mixed concrete

(G-2487)
T&K PRINTING INC
Also Called: T & K Printing
262 44th St (11232-2816)
PHONE..................................718 439-9454
Hien Khuu, *President*
EMP: 10
SALES (est): 1.8MM **Privately Held**
SIC: 3577 2759 Optical scanning devices; commercial printing

(G-2488)
TAAM TOV FOODS INC
Also Called: Ko-Sure Food Distributors
188 28th St (11232-1604)
PHONE..................................718 788-8880
Meyer Thurm, *President*
Max Thurm, *Vice Pres*
Sam Sherer, *Treasurer*
▲ EMP: 7
SALES (est): 723.9K **Privately Held**
SIC: 2022 Cheese spreads, dips, pastes & other cheese products

(G-2489)
TABLE TOPS PAPER CORP
47 Hall St Ste C-2 (11205-1315)
P.O. Box 220443 (11222-0443)
PHONE..................................718 831-6440
Ben Ruiz, *President*
EMP: 8
SALES: 660K **Privately Held**
SIC: 2759 5111 5999 Financial note & certificate printing & engraving; printing & writing paper; alarm signal systems

(G-2490)
TABLET PUBLISHING COMPANY INC
Also Called: Tablet Newspaper, The
1712 10th Ave (11215-6215)
PHONE..................................718 965-7333
Monsignor Anthony Danna, *Publisher*
Ed Wilkinson, *Principal*
Leonard W Kaiser, *Business Mgr*
Carrie White, *Manager*
EMP: 25 EST: 1908
SQ FT: 18,000
SALES (est): 1.4MM **Privately Held**
SIC: 2711 2741 Newspapers: publishing only, not printed on site; miscellaneous publishing

(G-2491)
TAI SENG
106 Lexington Ave (11238-1412)
PHONE..................................718 399-6311
▲ EMP: 6
SALES (est): 330K **Privately Held**
SIC: 2673 Mfg Bags-Plastic/Coated Paper

(G-2492)
TALMU NY LLC
266 47th St (11220-1010)
PHONE..................................347 434-6700
Reuven Sobel,
Warren Vogel,
EMP: 6
SALES (est): 330.7K **Privately Held**
SIC: 3639 5149 Major kitchen appliances, except refrigerators & stoves; coffee & tea

(G-2493)
TARGUM PRESS USA INC
Also Called: Horizons Magazine
1946 59th St (11204-2389)
PHONE..................................248 355-2266
Sydney Choncow, *President*
David Dombey, *Admin Sec*
EMP: 8
SALES (est): 584.8K **Privately Held**
SIC: 2731 Book publishing

(G-2494)
TAYLOR TANK COMPANY INC
848 E 43rd St (11210-3502)
PHONE..................................718 434-1300
Michael Rubinberg, *President*
Cynthia Rubinberg, *Admin Sec*
EMP: 30 EST: 1947
SQ FT: 20,000
SALES (est): 4.7MM
SALES (corp-wide): 4.7MM **Privately Held**
WEB: www.rubiconhx.com
SIC: 3443 Tanks, standard or custom fabricated: metal plate
PA: Rubicon Industries Corp.
848 E 43rd St
Brooklyn NY 11210
718 434-4700

(G-2495)
TECHNICAL LIBRARY SERVICE INC
Also Called: Talas
330 Morgan Ave (11211-2716)
PHONE..................................212 219-0770
Jacob Salik, *Ch of Bd*
Marjorie Salik, *President*
▲ EMP: 11 EST: 1962
SQ FT: 25,000
SALES (est): 1.7MM **Privately Held**
WEB: www.talas-nyc.com
SIC: 2653 8231 5199 Corrugated boxes, partitions, display items, sheets & pad; boxes, corrugated: made from purchased materials; libraries; law library; packaging materials

(G-2496)
TECHNIPOLY MANUFACTURING INC
Also Called: T M I of New York
20 Wythe Ave (11249-1036)
PHONE..................................718 383-0363
Kam San Yuen, *Owner*
Lip Foo Yee, *Vice Pres*
Allen Yuen, *Admin Sec*
EMP: 28
SQ FT: 16,000
SALES (est): 4.4MM **Privately Held**
SIC: 2673 2752 Plastic bags: made from purchased materials; commercial printing, lithographic

(G-2497)
TECNOLUX INCORPORATED
103 14th St (11215-4607)
PHONE..................................718 369-3900
David Ablon, *President*
▲ EMP: 7
SQ FT: 10,000
SALES (est): 710K **Privately Held**
WEB: www.tecnolux.com
SIC: 3648 Lighting equipment

(G-2498)
TEKA FINE LINE BRUSHES INC
3691 Bedford Ave (11229-1703)
PHONE..................................718 692-2928
Terry Ettkins, *President*
EMP: 7 EST: 1970
SALES (est): 860.6K **Privately Held**
WEB: www.tekabrush.com
SIC: 3991 Hair pencils (artists' brushes)

(G-2499)
TELLER PRINTING CORP
317 Division Ave (11211-7307)
PHONE..................................718 486-3662
James Teller, *President*
EMP: 6
SALES (est): 595.1K **Privately Held**
SIC: 2752 Commercial printing, lithographic

(G-2500)
THATS MY GIRL INC (PA)
80 39th St Ste 501 (11232-2604)
P.O. Box 230317 (11223-0317)
PHONE..................................212 695-0020
Salomon Salem, *President*
Raymond Kassin, *Vice Pres*
EMP: 10
SQ FT: 800
SALES (est): 2.4MM **Privately Held**
SIC: 2361 Girls' & children's dresses, blouses & shirts

(G-2501)
THE EARTH TIMES FOUNDATION
195 Adams St Apt 6j (11201-1808)
PHONE..................................718 297-0488
Pranay Gupte, *President*
Ranjit Sahni, *Treasurer*
Jon Quint, *Director*
EMP: 5
SALES: 984.9K **Privately Held**
SIC: 2711 Newspapers, publishing & printing

(G-2502)
THEMIS CHIMNEY INC
190 Morgan Ave (11237-1014)
PHONE..................................718 937-4716
Mark Papadimitriou, *President*
EMP: 12
SQ FT: 12,000
SALES (est): 2.4MM **Privately Held**
SIC: 3443 3444 Liners/lining; sheet metalwork

(G-2503)
THOMPSON OVERHEAD DOOR CO INC
47 16th St (11215-4613)
PHONE..................................718 788-2470
Olav M Thompson, *President*
Edward Thompson, *Corp Secy*
EMP: 15 EST: 1952
SQ FT: 16,000

SALES (est): 2.3MM **Privately Held**
SIC: 3442 5211 Rolling doors for industrial buildings or warehouses, metal; door & window products

(G-2504)
TIE KING INC (PA)
Also Called: Jimmy Sales
243 44th St (11232-2815)
PHONE..................................718 768-8484
Jimmy Azizo, *President*
David Azizo, *General Mgr*
Solomon Azizo, *Treasurer*
Steven Azizo, *Manager*
Jack Azizo, *Admin Sec*
▲ EMP: 50
SQ FT: 20,000
SALES (est): 5.5MM **Privately Held**
WEB: www.thetieking.com
SIC: 2323 Men's & boys' neckties & bow ties

(G-2505)
TIMES ONE INC
5415 8th Ave (11220-3229)
PHONE..................................718 686-8988
EMP: 5
SALES (est): 561.9K **Privately Held**
SIC: 3915 Jewel preparing: instruments, tools, watches & jewelry

(G-2506)
TIN RAGE PRODUCTIONS INC
123 7th Ave (11215-1301)
PHONE..................................718 398-0787
Wessel Van Huyssteen, *Chairman*
EMP: 5
SALES (est): 442.7K **Privately Held**
SIC: 3356 Tin

(G-2507)
TLC INDUSTRIES INC
600 Smith St (11231-2116)
PHONE..................................718 596-2842
Theodore Ferrara, *President*
EMP: 10
SALES (est): 411.2K **Privately Held**
SIC: 3531 Excavators: cable, clamshell, crane, derrick, dragline, etc.

(G-2508)
TLI IMPORT INC
151 2nd Ave (11215-4615)
PHONE..................................917 578-4568
Nouri Arabi, *President*
EMP: 6 EST: 2010
SALES (est): 331.6K **Privately Held**
SIC: 2221 Textile warping, on a contract basis

(G-2509)
TONER-N-MORE INC
2220 65th St Ste 103 (11204-4035)
PHONE..................................718 232-6200
Yoni Glatzer, *President*
EMP: 5
SQ FT: 10,000
SALES (est): 650.3K **Privately Held**
WEB: www.tonernmore.com
SIC: 3861 Toners, prepared photographic (not made in chemical plants)

(G-2510)
TOOLS & STAMPING CORP
Also Called: Balint Tool
48 Eagle St (11222-1013)
P.O. Box 220375 (11222-0375)
PHONE..................................718 392-4040
Ernest Feldman, *President*
Judah Feldman, *Vice Pres*
EMP: 5 EST: 1960
SALES (est): 390K **Privately Held**
WEB: www.jnet.com
SIC: 3469 3544 3429 Stamping metal for the trade; special dies & tools; luggage hardware

(G-2511)
TOPOO INDUSTRIES INCORPORATED
2847 W 21st St (11224-2301)
PHONE..................................718 331-3755
▲ EMP: 8
SALES (est): 743.8K **Privately Held**
SIC: 3999 Manufacturing industries

(G-2512)
TOPRINT LTD
6110 7th Ave　(11220-4286)
PHONE..................718 439-0469
Thomas Corey, *Principal*
EMP: 5
SALES (est): 340K　**Privately Held**
SIC: 2759　Commercial printing

(G-2513)
TOTAL METAL RESOURCE
Also Called: Pmrnyc
175 Bogart St　(11206-1720)
PHONE..................718 384-7818
Scott Behr, *President*
EMP: 10
SALES (est): 1.5MM　**Privately Held**
SIC: 3499　Fabricated metal products

(G-2514)
TOURA LLC
392 2nd St Apt 2　(11215-7185)
PHONE..................646 652-8668
Kathleen Schnoor, *Principal*
Aaron Radin,
EMP: 10
SALES (est): 730.4K　**Privately Held**
SIC: 3663　Mobile communication equipment

(G-2515)
TOWER ISLES FROZEN FOODS LTD
Also Called: Tower Isles Patties
2025 Atlantic Ave　(11233-3131)
P.O. Box 330625　(11233-0625)
PHONE..................718 495-2626
Patrick Jolly, *President*
James Jobson, *Vice Pres*
Inna Lysloff, *Manager*
EMP: 73　**EST:** 1969
SQ FT: 32,600
SALES: 20MM　**Privately Held**
WEB: www.towerislespatties.com
SIC: 2013　Boneless meat, from purchased meat

(G-2516)
TRANSCNTINENTAL ULTRA FLEX INC
975 Essex St　(11208-5419)
PHONE..................718 272-9100
Eli Blatt, *CEO*
Dan B Kochba, *General Mgr*
Keith Hoffer, *QC Mgr*
Steve Lippsett, *Engineer*
Todd Addison, *Treasurer*
◆ **EMP:** 270
SQ FT: 115,000
SALES (est): 53.2MM
SALES (corp-wide): 1.6B　**Privately Held**
WEB: www.ultraflex.com
SIC: 2759　2671　2752　Flexographic printing; packaging paper & plastics film, coated & laminated; commercial printing, lithographic
PA: Transcontinental Inc
　1 Place Ville-Marie Bureau 3240
　Montreal QC H3B 0
　514 954-4000

(G-2517)
TRANSLAND SOURCING LLC
5 Lynch St　(11249-9223)
PHONE..................718 596-5704
EMP: 4
SALES: 5MM　**Privately Held**
SIC: 3571　Mfg Electronic Computers

(G-2518)
TRI STATE SHEARING BENDING INC
366 Herzl St　(11212-4442)
P.O. Box 120002　(11212-0002)
PHONE..................718 485-2200
Alan Blaier, *President*
Michele Blaier, *Vice Pres*
EMP: 15
SQ FT: 12,000
SALES (est): 3.7MM　**Privately Held**
SIC: 3446　Stairs, staircases, stair treads: prefabricated metal

(G-2519)
TRI-STATE FOOD JOBBERS INC
5600 1st Ave Unit A5　(11220-2550)
PHONE..................718 921-1211
Maor Ohana, *President*
EMP: 6　**EST:** 2009
SALES: 2.6MM　**Privately Held**
SIC: 3497　Foil containers for bakery goods & frozen foods

(G-2520)
TRICO MANUFACTURING CORP
196 Dupont St　(11222-1241)
PHONE..................718 349-6565
Elizabeth Fling, *President*
EMP: 6　**EST:** 2000
SQ FT: 7,000
SALES (est): 484.1K　**Privately Held**
SIC: 3429　Door locks, bolts & checks; door opening & closing devices, except electrical

(G-2521)
TRIMET COAL LLC
1615 Avenue I Apt 420　(11230-3041)
PHONE..................718 951-3654
EMP: 21
SALES (est): 1.3MM　**Privately Held**
SIC: 1241　Coal Mining Services

(G-2522)
TRIPI ENGRAVING CO INC
Also Called: Royal Engraving
60 Meserole Ave　(11222-2638)
PHONE..................718 383-6500
Phil Tripi, *President*
Salvatore Trivelli, *Manager*
EMP: 25
SQ FT: 10,000
SALES (est): 2.2MM　**Privately Held**
SIC: 2759　5112　5943　2796　Engraving; stationery; stationery stores; platemaking services; typesetting; commercial printing, lithographic

(G-2523)
TRIPLE J BEDDING LLC
63 Flushing Ave Unit 331　(11205-1083)
PHONE..................718 643-8005
Joseph Friedman, *CEO*
▲ **EMP:** 7
SALES (est): 26K　**Privately Held**
SIC: 2511　Wood household furniture

(G-2524)
TRM LINEN INC
1546 59th St　(11219-5028)
PHONE..................718 686-6075
Chaim Cohen, *Ch of Bd*
▼ **EMP:** 5
SALES (est): 547.5K　**Privately Held**
SIC: 2299　5961　Linen fabrics; mail order house

(G-2525)
TROVE INC
20 Jay St Ste 846　(11201-8306)
PHONE..................212 268-2046
EMP: 14
SALES (est): 1.4MM　**Privately Held**
SIC: 3999　5199　Fire extinguishers, portable; gifts & novelties

(G-2526)
TRU-TONE METAL PRODUCTS INC
1261 Willoughby Ave　(11237-2904)
PHONE..................718 386-5960
James P Murtha, *President*
Catherine Murtha, *Vice Pres*
EMP: 20　**EST:** 1947
SQ FT: 5,000
SALES (est): 2.3MM　**Privately Held**
SIC: 3471　Anodizing (plating) of metals or formed products; coloring & finishing of aluminum or formed products

(G-2527)
TUNECORE INC (PA)
45 Main St Ste 705　(11201-1075)
P.O. Box 20256　(11202-0256)
PHONE..................646 651-1060
Scott Ackerman, *CEO*
Shelby Kennedy, *Vice Pres*
Gillian Morris, *Vice Pres*

Matt Barrington, *CFO*
Jake Smith, *Marketing Staff*
EMP: 33
SALES (est): 1.7MM　**Privately Held**
SIC: 3651　Music distribution apparatus

(G-2528)
TUNECORE INC
63 Pearl St　(11201-1147)
PHONE..................646 651-1060
Scott Ackermann, *CEO*
EMP: 15
SALES (corp-wide): 1.7MM　**Privately Held**
SIC: 2741　Miscellaneous publishing
PA: Tunecore, Inc.
　45 Main St Ste 705
　Brooklyn NY 11201
　646 651-1060

(G-2529)
TUROFF TOWER GRAPHICS INC
Also Called: Tower Sales Co
681 Coney Island Ave　(11218-4306)
PHONE..................718 856-7300
Jay Turoff, *President*
Rose Turoff, *Corp Secy*
Georgina Snyder, *Vice Pres*
EMP: 14　**EST:** 1969
SQ FT: 1,000
SALES (est): 1.3MM　**Privately Held**
SIC: 3993　Neon signs

(G-2530)
TUV TAAM CORP
502 Flushing Ave　(11205-1616)
PHONE..................718 855-2207
Aaron Nutovich, *President*
Rivka Nutovich, *Treasurer*
Lea Gold, *Admin Sec*
▲ **EMP:** 50
SQ FT: 10,000
SALES (est): 7.1MM　**Privately Held**
SIC: 2099　2038　Tortillas, fresh or refrigerated; salads, fresh or refrigerated; frozen specialties

(G-2531)
TWI WATCHES LLC
Also Called: Akribos Watches
4014 1st Ave Unit 10　(11232-2700)
PHONE..................718 663-3969
Ben Rosenbaum, *Sales Dir*
Chaim Sischer, *Mng Member*
▲ **EMP:** 35
SALES (est): 2MM　**Privately Held**
SIC: 3873　Watches, clocks, watchcases & parts

(G-2532)
TWIN MARQUIS INC (HQ)
7 Bushwick Pl　(11206-2815)
PHONE..................718 386-6868
Hyung Kyun Kim, *Ch of Bd*
Jing Lin, *Engineer*
Lillian Chan, *Director*
Chung Pun Tang, *Admin Sec*
▲ **EMP:** 65
SQ FT: 33,000
SALES: 40.3MM
SALES (corp-wide): 5.3B　**Privately Held**
WEB: www.twinmarquis.com
SIC: 2098　2099　2035　Noodles (e.g. egg, plain & water), dry; noodles, fried (Chinese); pickles, sauces & salad dressings
PA: Cj Cheiljedang Corp.
　330 Dongho-Ro, Jung-Gu
　Seoul　04560
　822 674-0111

(G-2533)
TWO WORLDS ARTS LTD
307 Kingsland Ave　(11222-3708)
PHONE..................212 929-2210
Jean Chau, *Manager*
EMP: 6
SALES (corp-wide): 931.1K　**Privately Held**
SIC: 2512　Upholstered household furniture
PA: Two Worlds Arts Ltd
　122 W 18th St
　New York NY 10011
　212 929-2210

(G-2534)
ULTRAPEDICS LTD (PA)
355 Ovington Ave Ste 104　(11209-1457)
P.O. Box 90384　(11209-0384)
PHONE..................718 748-4806
Eric Schwelke, *President*
EMP: 7
SQ FT: 3,400
SALES (est): 1.1MM　**Privately Held**
SIC: 3842　5999　Prosthetic appliances; artificial limbs

(G-2535)
UNIFIED SOLUTIONS FOR CLG INC
1829 Pacific St　(11233-3505)
P.O. Box 110162　(11211-0162)
PHONE..................718 782-8800
Mendel Jacobowitz, *President*
Lipa Jacobowitz, *Vice Pres*
EMP: 15　**EST:** 2009
SALES (est): 3.1MM　**Privately Held**
SIC: 2869　Butadiene (industrial organic chemical)

(G-2536)
UNIFORMS BY PARK COATS INC
790 3rd Ave　(11232-1510)
PHONE..................718 499-1182
Nick Haymandos, *President*
Despina Haymandos, *Vice Pres*
EMP: 28　**EST:** 1973
SQ FT: 8,000
SALES (est): 2.7MM　**Privately Held**
WEB: www.uniformsbypark.com
SIC: 2311　2337　Men's & boys' uniforms; uniforms, except athletic: women's, misses' & juniors'

(G-2537)
UNIMEX CORPORATION
Lee Spring Company Division
1462 62nd St　(11219-5413)
PHONE..................718 236-2222
Albert Mangels, *President*
EMP: 160
SALES (corp-wide): 40.6MM　**Privately Held**
SIC: 3495　Mechanical springs, precision
PA: Unimex Corporation
　54 E 64th St
　New York NY 10065
　800 886-0390

(G-2538)
UNITED GEMDIAM INC
Also Called: UGI
1537 52nd St　(11219-3910)
PHONE..................718 851-5083
Morris Friedman, *President*
Isaac Friedman, *Office Mgr*
EMP: 43
SQ FT: 5,000
SALES (est): 2.8MM　**Privately Held**
WEB: www.ugi.com
SIC: 3915　5094　Diamond cutting & polishing; diamonds (gems)

(G-2539)
UNITED PLASTICS INC
640 Humboldt St Ste 1　(11222-4121)
P.O. Box 220363　(11222-0363)
PHONE..................718 389-2255
Gary Mayo, *Manager*
EMP: 7
SALES (corp-wide): 1.5MM　**Privately Held**
SIC: 2673　3089　Plastic bags: made from purchased materials; plastic processing
PA: United Plastics, Inc
　219 Nassau Ave
　Brooklyn NY
　718 389-2255

(G-2540)
UNITED TRANSIT MIX INC
318 Boerum St　(11206-3505)
P.O. Box 370647　(11237-0647)
PHONE..................718 416-3400
Tony Mastronardi, *President*
EMP: 14
SALES (est): 4MM　**Privately Held**
SIC: 3273　Ready-mixed concrete

(G-2541)
UNITED WIND INC
155 Water St (11201-1016)
PHONE...................888 313-3353
Russell Tencer, *CEO*
Aaron Lubowitz, *COO*
Philip Futernik, *CTO*
Tyler Petit, *Director*
EMP: 20 EST: 2013
SALES (est): 3.7MM Privately Held
SIC: 3443 Wind tunnels

(G-2542)
UNIVERSAL COOLERS INC
120 13th St (11215-4604)
PHONE...................718 788-8621
Gregory Uchitel, *Ch of Bd*
▲ EMP: 6 EST: 1995
SALES (est): 1.2MM Privately Held
SIC: 3585 Parts for heating, cooling & refrigerating equipment

(G-2543)
UNIVERSAL FIRE PROOF DOOR
1171 Myrtle Ave (11206-6007)
PHONE...................718 455-8442
Abelardo Galicia, *President*
EMP: 25
SQ FT: 24,000
SALES (est): 5.4MM Privately Held
SIC: 3442 Fire doors, metal

(G-2544)
UNIVERSAL PARENT AND YOUTH
Also Called: Upayori
1530 Pa Ave Apt 17e (11239-2620)
PHONE...................917 754-2426
Vincent Riggins, *Exec Dir*
EMP: 10
SALES (est): 537.8K Privately Held
SIC: 3585 Refrigeration & heating equipment

(G-2545)
UNIVERSAL SCREENING ASSOCIATES
Also Called: USA Tees.com
6509 11th Ave (11219-5602)
PHONE...................718 232-2744
David Cardinale, *President*
Adam Kokoni, *Graphic Designe*
Eugene Polishchuk, *Graphic Designe*
▲ EMP: 12
SQ FT: 500
SALES: 500K Privately Held
SIC: 2759 Screen printing

(G-2546)
UNIVERSAL STEEL FABRICATORS
90 Junius St (11212-8029)
PHONE...................718 342-0782
Harvinder Paul, *President*
Emilio Franza, *Treasurer*
EMP: 15
SQ FT: 3,500
SALES: 1MM Privately Held
SIC: 3446 5051 1799 Architectural metalwork; structural shapes, iron or steel; fence construction

(G-2547)
UPBEAT UPHOLSTERY & DESIGN LLC
344 Stagg St (11206-1725)
PHONE...................347 480-3980
Simcha Fern, *Mng Member*
EMP: 7
SQ FT: 7,000
SALES (est): 1.5MM Privately Held
SIC: 2431 7641 2434 Millwork; reupholstery; wood kitchen cabinets

(G-2548)
US CONCRETE INC
Also Called: Kings Material
692 Mcdonald Ave (11218-4914)
PHONE...................718 438-6800
Robert Bruzzese, *Branch Mgr*
EMP: 20
SALES (corp-wide): 1.5B Publicly Held
SIC: 3273 Ready-mixed concrete

PA: U.S. Concrete, Inc.
331 N Main St
Euless TX 76039
817 835-4105

(G-2549)
US SWEETENERS CORP
133-48 St (11232)
PHONE...................718 854-8714
Raizy Geller, *President*
Moses Geller, *CFO*
Joel Geller, *Officer*
EMP: 35
SALES: 35MM Privately Held
SIC: 2061 Granulated cane sugar

(G-2550)
VAAD LHAFOTZAS SICHOES
788 Eastern Pkwy (11213-3409)
PHONE...................718 778-5436
Zalmen Chanin, *President*
Nachman Shapiro, *Treasurer*
Sholom Jacobson, *Admin Sec*
▲ EMP: 13 EST: 1967
SQ FT: 10,000
SALES: 1MM Privately Held
SIC: 2731 Books: publishing only

(G-2551)
VAN BLARCOM CLOSURES INC (PA)
156 Sanford St (11205)
PHONE...................718 855-3810
Vincent Scuderi Jr, *Ch of Bd*
Ron Camuto, *Vice Pres*
Joe Scuderi, *Production*
Michael Scuderi, *Purch Mgr*
Anthony Scuderi, *QC Mgr*
▲ EMP: 195 EST: 1947
SQ FT: 160,000
SALES: 49.3MM Privately Held
WEB: www.vbcpkg.com
SIC: 3089 3466 3549 Closures, plastic; caps, plastic; closures, stamped metal; bottle caps & tops, stamped metal; jar tops & crowns, stamped metal; assembly machines, including robotic

(G-2552)
VAN LEEUWEN ARTISAN ICE CREAM
56 Dobbin St (11222-3110)
PHONE...................718 701-1630
Ben Van Leeuwen, *Principal*
▲ EMP: 7
SALES (est): 446K Privately Held
SIC: 2024 Ice cream & frozen desserts

(G-2553)
VAN RIP INC
67 West St Ste 705 (11222-5393)
PHONE...................415 529-5403
Abhishek Pruisken, *CEO*
Marco De Leon, *CFO*
EMP: 22
SQ FT: 1,600
SALES: 1.7MM Privately Held
SIC: 2066 2038 Chocolate; waffles, frozen

(G-2554)
VERSO INC
20 Jay St Ste 1010 (11201-8346)
PHONE...................718 246-8160
Jacob Stevens, *Director*
EMP: 8
SQ FT: 2,500
SALES: 959.9K
SALES (corp-wide): 2.2MM Privately Held
SIC: 2731 Book publishing
PA: New Left Books Limited
6 Meard Street
London W1F 0
207 437-3546

(G-2555)
VIAMEDIA CORPORATION
2610 Atlantic Ave (11207-2415)
PHONE...................718 485-7792
James Underwood, *President*
Michael Underwood, *Vice Pres*
EMP: 5
SQ FT: 3,200
SALES (est): 254.1K Privately Held
WEB: www.via-indy.com
SIC: 2741 Miscellaneous publishing

(G-2556)
VICTORIA FINE FOODS LLC (DH)
443 E 100th St (11236-2103)
PHONE...................718 649-1635
Tim Shanley, *CEO*
Brian Dean, *President*
Gerald Aquilina,
◆ EMP: 100 EST: 2011
SQ FT: 90,000
SALES (est): 39.3MM
SALES (corp-wide): 1.7B Publicly Held
SIC: 2035 2099 2033 5149 Pickles, sauces & salad dressings; spices, including grinding; canned fruits & specialties; pasta & rice
HQ: Victoria Fine Foods Holding Company
443 E 100th St
Brooklyn NY 11236
718 649-1635

(G-2557)
VICTORIA FINE FOODS HOLDING CO (HQ)
443 E 100th St (11236-2103)
PHONE...................718 649-1635
Tim Shanley, *CEO*
Brian Dean, *President*
EMP: 4
SQ FT: 90,000
SALES (est): 39.3MM
SALES (corp-wide): 1.7B Publicly Held
SIC: 2035 2099 2033 5149 Pickles, sauces & salad dressings; spices, including grinding; canned fruits & specialties; pasta & rice
PA: B&G Foods, Inc.
4 Gatehall Dr Ste 110
Parsippany NJ 07054
973 401-6500

(G-2558)
VIKING MAR WLDG SHIP REPR LLC
14 Raleigh Pl (11226-4218)
PHONE...................718 758-4116
Floyd Ricketts,
EMP: 10
SALES (est): 520.5K Privately Held
SIC: 3731 Shipbuilding & repairing

(G-2559)
VINEGAR HILL ASSET LLC
436 E 34th St (11203-5034)
PHONE...................718 469-0342
EMP: 5 EST: 2015
SALES (est): 91.3K Privately Held
SIC: 2099 Vinegar

(G-2560)
VINELAND KOSHER POULTRY INC
Also Called: Poultry Dist
5600 1st Ave A7 (11220-2550)
PHONE...................718 921-1347
EMP: 10
SALES (corp-wide): 8.4MM Privately Held
SIC: 2015 5144 Poultry Processing Whol Poultry/Products
PA: Vineland Kosher Poultry Inc
1050 S Mill Rd
Vineland NJ 08360
856 692-1871

(G-2561)
VIRGINIA DARE EXTRACT CO INC (PA)
Also Called: V & E Kohnstamm & Co Div
882 3rd Ave Unit 2 (11232-1902)
PHONE...................718 788-6320
Howard Smith Jr, *President*
Stephen Balter, *Vice Pres*
Scott Taylor, *Accounts Exec*
Chrisandra Harvey,
◆ EMP: 152
SQ FT: 165,000
SALES (est): 42.9MM Privately Held
SIC: 2087 Extracts, flavoring

(G-2562)
VIRTUALAPT CORP
45 Main St Ste 613 (11201-1099)
PHONE...................917 293-3173

Bryan Colin, *CEO*
EMP: 14
SALES (est): 440.2K Privately Held
SIC: 3812 Search & detection systems & instruments; distance measuring equipment

(G-2563)
VIRTUVENT INC
81 Prospect St Fl 7 (11201-1473)
PHONE...................855 672-8677
Devin Drake, *Chairman*
Saul Sutcher, *COO*
EMP: 7 EST: 2012
SQ FT: 2,000
SALES (est): 450.6K Privately Held
SIC: 7372 7389 Business oriented computer software;

(G-2564)
VISITAINER CORP
Also Called: Plastifold Industries Division
148 Classon Ave (11205-2637)
PHONE...................718 636-0300
William Lefkovitz, *President*
EMP: 25 EST: 1962
SQ FT: 30,000
SALES (est): 2.5MM Privately Held
SIC: 2657 3089 Folding paperboard boxes; plastic containers, except foam

(G-2565)
VITAROSE CORP OF AMERICA
2615 Nostrand Ave Ste 1 (11210-4643)
PHONE...................718 951-9700
Joe Derose, *President*
EMP: 6 EST: 1959
SQ FT: 2,625
SALES: 1MM Privately Held
SIC: 2541 3231 3089 3444 Window backs, store or lunchroom, prefabricated: wood; products of purchased glass; awnings, fiberglass & plastic combination; awnings & canopies

(G-2566)
VITO & SONS BAKERY
Also Called: Mima S Bakery
1423 72nd St (11228-1711)
PHONE...................201 617-8501
Fax: 201 864-3088
EMP: 10
SALES (est): 612.1K Privately Held
SIC: 2051 Mfg Bread/Related Products

(G-2567)
VLINE INC
81 Prospect St (11201-1473)
PHONE...................512 222-5464
Jack Strong, *CEO*
EMP: 5
SALES (est): 325.4K Privately Held
SIC: 7372 Utility computer software

(G-2568)
VOLCKENING INC (PA)
6700 3rd Ave (11220-5296)
PHONE...................718 748-0294
William J Schneider, *Ch of Bd*
Frederick C Schneider, *President*
Henry Schneider, *Vice Pres*
EMP: 45
SQ FT: 30,000
SALES (est): 6.6MM Privately Held
WEB: www.volckening.com
SIC: 3565 3991 Packaging machinery; brushes, household or industrial

(G-2569)
VOODOO MANUFACTURING INC
361 Stagg St Ste 408 (11206-1743)
PHONE...................646 893-8366
Max Friefeld, *CEO*
Oliver Ortlieb, *Marketing Staff*
Nicole Hartmann, *Executive*
EMP: 30
SALES (est): 100K Privately Held
SIC: 3555 Printing trades machinery

(G-2570)
VPULSE INC
191 Nassau Ave (11222-3509)
PHONE...................646 729-5675
William Ruhnke, *CEO*
EMP: 5

SALES (est): 369.7K **Privately Held**
SIC: 3089 Ducting, plastic

(G-2571)
VSG INTERNATIONAL LLC
Also Called: Kustom Collabo
196 Clinton Ave Apt A2 (11205-3411)
PHONE.............................718 300-8171
Yusef Sirius-El, *Mng Member*
Nicholas Vasilopoulos,
▲ **EMP:** 5 **EST:** 2012,
SQ FT: 5,000
SALES (est): 298.1K **Privately Held**
SIC: 3149 Athletic shoes, except rubber or
plastic

(G-2572)
W E W CONTAINER CORPORATION
189 Wyona St (11207-3009)
PHONE.............................718 827-8150
Daniel Weicher, *Branch Mgr*
EMP: 20
SALES (corp-wide): 3.5MM **Privately Held**
SIC: 2673 2671 Bags: plastic, laminated &
coated; plastic film, coated or laminated
for packaging
PA: W E W Container Corporation
200 Bradford St
Brooklyn NY
718 827-8150

(G-2573)
W W TRADING CO INC
50 Franklin Ave (11205-1504)
PHONE.............................718 935-1085
Han Thuong Luong, *Ch of Bd*
EMP: 5
SALES (est): 356K **Privately Held**
SIC: 3537 Trucks: freight, baggage, etc.:
industrial, except mining

(G-2574)
WALTER P SAUER LLC
Also Called: Morris Fine Furniture Workshop
276 Grndpint Ave Ste 8400 (11222)
PHONE.............................718 937-0600
Anthony Morris,
EMP: 43
SQ FT: 2,100
SALES (est): 2.6MM **Privately Held**
WEB: www.walterpsauer.com
SIC: 2511 Wood household furniture

(G-2575)
WARNACO INC
70 Washington St Fl 10 (11201-1442)
PHONE.............................718 722-3000
Smitty Seelall, *Branch Mgr*
EMP: 10
SALES (corp-wide): 9.6B **Publicly Held**
WEB: www.warnaco.com
SIC: 2341 2321 2253 2329 Panties:
women's, misses', children's & infants';
women's & children's nightwear; men's &
boys' dress shirts; shirts (outerwear), knit;
sweaters & sweater coats, knit; athletic
(warmup, sweat & jogging) suits: men's &
boys'; underwear, men's & boys': made
from purchased materials; brassieres
HQ: Warnaco Inc.
501 Fashion Ave Fl 14
New York NY 10018
212 287-8000

(G-2576)
WATERMARK DESIGNS HOLDINGS LTD
350 Dewitt Ave (11207-6618)
PHONE.............................718 257-2800
AVI Abel, *President*
Jack Abel, *Vice Pres*
▲ **EMP:** 55
SQ FT: 20,000
SALES (est): 9.4MM **Privately Held**
SIC: 3431 3432 Bathroom fixtures, includ-
ing sinks; plumbing fixture fittings & trim

(G-2577)
WAZER INC
141 Flushing Ave (11205-1338)
PHONE.............................201 580-6486
Nisan Lerea, *CEO*
Matthew Nowicki, *Admin Sec*
EMP: 25 **EST:** 2016

SALES (est): 171.3K **Privately Held**
SIC: 3541 7389 Numerically controlled
metal cutting machine tools;

(G-2578)
WEICRO GRAPHICS INC
Also Called: Able Printing
2190 Brigham St Apt 2h (11229-5644)
PHONE.............................631 253-3360
Sanford Weiss, *President*
Lucyna Mleczko, *Vice Pres*
EMP: 22
SALES (est): 3.2MM **Privately Held**
WEB: www.lemontreestationery.com
SIC: 2752 2759 Commercial printing, off-
set; commercial printing

(G-2579)
WEINFELD SKULL CAP MFG CO INC
Also Called: A Weinfeld Skull Cap Mfg
6022 14th Ave (11219-5006)
PHONE.............................718 854-3864
Mendel Weinfeld, *President*
▲ **EMP:** 8
SQ FT: 180
SALES (est): 804.2K **Privately Held**
SIC: 2353 Hats & caps

(G-2580)
WETLOOK DETAILING INC
1125 Banner Ave Apt 11a (11235-5267)
PHONE.............................212 390-8877
Dylan Valentine, *COO*
EMP: 8 **EST:** 2016
SALES (est): 400.6K **Privately Held**
SIC: 3589 Car washing machinery

(G-2581)
WG SHEET METAL CORP
341 Amber St (11208-5104)
PHONE.............................718 235-3093
Andy Tolta, *Admin Sec*
EMP: 5
SALES: 700K **Privately Held**
SIC: 3444 Sheet metalwork

(G-2582)
WHITLEY EAST LLC
Brooklyn Navy Yd Bg 2 Fl (11205)
PHONE.............................718 403-0050
William McShane, *General Mgr*
EMP: 79 **Privately Held**
WEB: www.capsyscorp.com
SIC: 2452 Modular homes, prefabricated,
wood
HQ: Whitley East, Llc
64 Hess Rd
Leola PA 17540
717 656-2081

(G-2583)
WIDE FLANGE INC
176 27th St (11232-1625)
PHONE.............................718 492-8705
Joyce Cavagnaro, *President*
Blaze Bono, *Vice Pres*
EMP: 11
SQ FT: 5,500
SALES (est): 1.8MM **Privately Held**
SIC: 3449 Bars, concrete reinforcing: fabri-
cated steel

(G-2584)
WIGGBY PRECISION MACHINE CORP
140 58th St Ste 56 (11220-2526)
PHONE.............................718 439-6900
Ronald Wiggberg, *CEO*
Robert G Wiggberg, *Corp Secy*
EMP: 30 **EST:** 1949
SALES (est): 4.4MM **Privately Held**
SIC: 3599 Machine shop, jobbing & repair

(G-2585)
WILLIAM BROOKS WOODWORKING
856 Saratoga Ave (11212-4350)
PHONE.............................718 495-9767
William Brooks, *Owner*
EMP: 10
SALES: 275K **Privately Held**
SIC: 2434 Wood kitchen cabinets

(G-2586)
WILLIAM HARVEY STUDIO INC
214 N 8th St (11211-2008)
PHONE.............................718 599-4343
William Harvey, *President*
Reed Harvey, *Admin Sec*
EMP: 5
SQ FT: 2,500
SALES (est): 290K **Privately Held**
WEB: www.williamharveydesign.com
SIC: 2392 Household furnishings

(G-2587)
WILLIAM KANES MFG CORP
23 Alabama Ave (11207-2303)
PHONE.............................718 346-1515
William Kanes, *President*
EMP: 7
SQ FT: 5,000
SALES: 500K **Privately Held**
SIC: 3444 3599 Sheet metalwork; ma-
chine shop, jobbing & repair

(G-2588)
WILLIAMSBURG BULLETIN
136 Ross St (11211-7705)
PHONE.............................718 387-0123
EMP: 6
SALES (est): 370K **Privately Held**
SIC: 2711 Commercial printing & newspa-
per publishing combined

(G-2589)
WINDOW-FIX INC
331 37th St Fl 1 (11232-2505)
PHONE.............................718 854-3475
Ernesto Cappello, *President*
John Cappello, *Vice Pres*
EMP: 20
SALES (est): 3.3MM **Privately Held**
SIC: 3211 1751 7699 Window glass, clear
& colored; window & door installation &
erection; window blind repair services

(G-2590)
WINDOWMAN INC (USA)
460 Kingsland Ave (11222-1906)
PHONE.............................718 246-2626
Bruce Schmutter, *President*
EMP: 6
SALES: 2MM **Privately Held**
WEB: www.windowmanusa.com
SIC: 3442 3699 1796 1751 Metal doors,
sash & trim; door opening & closing de-
vices, electrical; installing building equip-
ment; window & door installation &
erection; safety & security specialization

(G-2591)
WINDOWS MEDIA PUBLISHING LLC
369 Remsen Ave (11212-1245)
PHONE.............................917 732-7892
Mark McLean,
EMP: 25
SALES (est): 834.9K **Privately Held**
SIC: 2731 Books: publishing & printing

(G-2592)
WINTER WATER FACTORY
191 33rd St (11232-2109)
PHONE.............................646 387-3247
Stefanie Lynen, *Owner*
Todd Warnock, *Opers Staff*
EMP: 6
SALES (est): 250K **Privately Held**
SIC: 2253 Dresses, knit

(G-2593)
WONTON FOOD INC (PA)
220 Moore St 222 (11206-3708)
PHONE.............................718 628-6868
Norman Wong, *CEO*
Ching Sun Wong, *Ch of Bd*
Randy Drake, *Vice Pres*
Yuzhou Ll, *Vice Pres*
Foo Kam Wong, *Vice Pres*
▲ **EMP:** 160
SQ FT: 55,000
SALES (est): 80.3MM **Privately Held**
WEB: www.wontonfood.com
SIC: 2099 2052 5149 Noodles, fried (Chi-
nese); cookies; canned goods: fruit, veg-
etables, seafood, meats, etc.

(G-2594)
WOODWARD/WHITE INC
45 Main St Ste 820 (11201-1076)
PHONE.............................718 509-6082
Bradley Silberberg, *Branch Mgr*
EMP: 10
SALES (corp-wide): 11.3MM **Privately Held**
SIC: 2731 Book publishing
PA: Woodward/White, Inc.
801 Broad St Ste 950
Augusta GA 30901
803 648-0300

(G-2595)
WORLD CHEESE CO INC
178 28th St (11232-1604)
PHONE.............................718 965-1700
Leo S Thurm, *President*
Meyer Thurm, *President*
Yudi Sherer, *Sales Staff*
Florence Greenberg, *Exec Sec*
◆ **EMP:** 16
SQ FT: 25,000
SALES (est): 4.9MM **Privately Held**
SIC: 2022 Natural cheese; cheese
spreads, dips, pastes & other cheese
products

(G-2596)
WORLD JOURNAL LLC
6007 8th Ave (11220-4337)
PHONE.............................718 871-5000
Boby Chou, *CEO*
EMP: 12
SALES (corp-wide): 53.3MM **Privately Held**
WEB: www.wjnews.net
SIC: 2711 Newspapers, publishing & print-
ing
HQ: World Journal Llc
14107 20th Ave Fl 2
Whitestone NY 11357
718 746-8889

(G-2597)
WORLDWIDE RESOURCES INC
1908 Avenue O (11230-6721)
PHONE.............................718 760-5000
David Pick, *President*
EMP: 16
SQ FT: 1,200
SALES (est): 1MM **Privately Held**
SIC: 3324 Aerospace investment castings,
ferrous

(G-2598)
Y & A TRADING INC
Also Called: Sukkah Center
1365 38th St (11218-3634)
PHONE.............................718 436-6333
Joe Biston, *President*
▲ **EMP:** 10
SALES (est): 771.9K **Privately Held**
WEB: www.sukkah.com
SIC: 2394 5999 Canvas & related prod-
ucts; religious goods

(G-2599)
YALOZ MOULD & DIE CO INC
Also Called: Yaloz Mold & Die
239 Java St Fl 2 (11222-1893)
PHONE.............................718 389-1131
Yehuda Leon Yaloz, *President*
EMP: 30 **EST:** 1964
SQ FT: 45,000
SALES (est): 2.6MM **Privately Held**
SIC: 2542 3429 Fixtures, store: except
wood; manufactured hardware (general)

(G-2600)
YEPES FINE FURNITURE
72 Van Dam St (11222-3807)
PHONE.............................718 383-0221
Tiberio Yepes, *Owner*
EMP: 20
SALES (est): 1.4MM **Privately Held**
SIC: 2512 5712 Upholstered household
furniture; furniture stores

(G-2601)
YOFAH RELIGIOUS ARTICLES INC
2001 57th St Ste 1 (11204-2035)
PHONE.............................718 435-3288

▲ = Import ▼=Export
◆ =Import/Export

Jacob Leser, *President*
▲ EMP: 13
SQ FT: 2,000
SALES: 1.4MM **Privately Held**
SIC: 3911 Rosaries or other small religious articles, precious metal

(G-2602)
YORK FUEL INCORPORATED
1760 Flatbush Ave (11210-4203)
PHONE..................................718 951-0202
Gurmeet Singh Buttar, *President*
EMP: 6
SALES (est): 601.3K **Privately Held**
SIC: 2869 Fuels

(G-2603)
YS MARKETING INC (PA)
Also Called: Numed
2004 Mcdonald Ave (11223-2819)
PHONE..................................718 778-6080
Joel Silberstein, *President*
EMP: 20
SALES: 20MM **Privately Held**
SIC: 2834 Pharmaceutical preparations

(G-2604)
Z-STUDIOS DSIGN FBRICATION LLC
30 Haven Pl (11233-3408)
PHONE..................................347 512-4210
Zachary Zaus,
EMP: 5
SQ FT: 2,500
SALES: 200K **Privately Held**
SIC: 3446 Architectural metalwork

(G-2605)
ZIPARI INC
45 Main St Ste 406 (11201-1084)
PHONE..................................855 558-7884
Mark Nathan, *CEO*
Jyoti Mokal, *Engineer*
Janelle Taylor, *Marketing Staff*
Alex Rud, *Software Engr*
Yuri Weinstock, *Software Engr*
EMP: 50
SALES (est): 895.4K **Privately Held**
SIC: 7372 Application computer software

(G-2606)
ZOOMERS INC (PA)
Also Called: Planet Motherhood
32 33rd St (11232-1901)
PHONE..................................718 369-2656
Gary Jay Schulman, *CEO*
Deborah Schulman, *President*
Wayne Sternberg, *Vice Pres*
▲ EMP: 35
SQ FT: 20,000
SALES (est): 3.3MM **Privately Held**
SIC: 2339 Maternity clothing

Brownville
Jefferson County

(G-2607)
FLORELLE TISSUE CORPORATION
1 Bridge St (13615-7765)
PHONE..................................647 997-7405
Harry Minas, *President*
▲ EMP: 50
SALES (est): 1.2MM **Privately Held**
SIC: 2676 Towels, napkins & tissue paper products

Buchanan
Westchester County

(G-2608)
CONTINENTAL BUCHANAN LLC
350 Broadway (10511-1000)
PHONE..................................703 480-3800
Ike Preston, *President*
Dennis Romps, *CFO*
▲ EMP: 100

SALES (est): 9.5MM **Privately Held**
SIC: 2493 3275 2891 Building board & wallboard, except gypsum; building board, gypsum; sealing compounds for pipe threads or joints

(G-2609)
LAFARGE NORTH AMERICA INC
350 Broadway (10511-1000)
PHONE..................................914 930-3027
Criss Fraley, *Opers-Prdtn-Mfg*
EMP: 100
SALES (corp-wide): 27.6B **Privately Held**
SIC: 3241 3275 Cement, hydraulic; gypsum products
HQ: Lafarge North America Inc.
8700 W Bryn Mawr Ave
Chicago IL 60631
773 372-1000

(G-2610)
SILVA CABINETRY INC
12 White St Ste C (10511-1665)
PHONE..................................914 737-7697
Antonio Dasilva, *President*
EMP: 25
SALES (est): 2.9MM **Privately Held**
SIC: 2434 Wood kitchen cabinets

Buffalo
Erie County

(G-2611)
240 MICHIGAN STREET INC
Also Called: Garb-El Products Co
96 Darwin Dr (14226-4509)
PHONE..................................716 434-6010
James Carbone, *President*
EMP: 10
SQ FT: 19,000
SALES (est): 2MM **Privately Held**
WEB: www.garb-el.com
SIC: 3589 Garbage disposers & compactors, commercial

(G-2612)
260 OAK STREET INC
260 Oak St (14203-1626)
PHONE..................................877 852-4676
Glenn Snyder, *Ch of Bd*
EMP: 5
SQ FT: 6,233
SALES (est): 376.8K **Privately Held**
SIC: 2542 Cabinets: show, display or storage: except wood

(G-2613)
5TH & OCEAN CLOTHING INC
160 Delaware Ave (14202-2404)
PHONE..................................716 604-9000
Luis Leiter Jr, *Mng Member*
Alex A Leiter, *Director*
◆ EMP: 115
SQ FT: 40,000
SALES (est): 10.2MM
SALES (corp-wide): 606.1MM **Privately Held**
WEB: www.5thocean.com
SIC: 2339 Women's & misses' accessories
PA: New Era Cap Co., Inc.
160 Delaware Ave
Buffalo NY 14202
716 604-9000

(G-2614)
760 NL HOLDINGS
760 Northland Ave (14211-1041)
PHONE..................................716 821-1391
Tim George, *Principal*
EMP: 30 EST: 1996
SQ FT: 20,000
SALES (est): 8.4MM **Privately Held**
WEB: www.nfcf.net
SIC: 3441 Fabricated structural metal

(G-2615)
A J M ENTERPRISES
348 Cayuga Rd (14225-1927)
PHONE..................................716 626-7294
Jarek Chelpinski, *Partner*
EMP: 10
SALES (est): 546.9K **Privately Held**
SIC: 3915 Jewelers' castings

(G-2616)
A-FAB INITIATIVES INC
99 Bud Mil Dr (14206-1801)
PHONE..................................716 877-5257
Edward Raimonde, *President*
◆ EMP: 12
SALES (est): 975.1K **Privately Held**
SIC: 3441 3354 Fabricated structural metal; aluminum extruded products

(G-2617)
ACCESS PRODUCTS INC
241 Main St Ste 100 (14203-2703)
PHONE..................................800 679-4022
Kenneth E J Szekely, *President*
Sean Morrison, *Principal*
David Murray, *Vice Pres*
Lance Mitchell, *Sales Staff*
EMP: 6
SALES: 5.3MM **Privately Held**
SIC: 3272 Building materials, except block or brick: concrete

(G-2618)
ACME NIPPLE MFG CO INC
1930 Elmwood Ave (14207-1902)
PHONE..................................716 873-7491
John Hurley, *President*
EMP: 8
SQ FT: 10,000
SALES (est): 1MM **Privately Held**
SIC: 3321 Pressure pipe & fittings, cast iron

(G-2619)
ACME SCREENPRINTING LLC
247 Cayuga Rd Ste 25e (14225-1949)
PHONE..................................716 565-1052
Joe Stepason,
EMP: 7
SALES (est): 303.2K **Privately Held**
SIC: 2759 Screen printing

(G-2620)
ADCO CIRCUITS INC
Also Called: E J E Research Div
160 Lawrence Bell Dr # 122 (14221-7897)
PHONE..................................716 668-6600
John Nemcek, *Vice Pres*
Edward Vrana, *Vice Pres*
EMP: 6
SALES (corp-wide): 26.9MM **Privately Held**
WEB: www.adcocircuits.com
SIC: 3674 3679 3672 Microprocessors; electronic circuits; printed circuit boards
PA: Adco Circuits, Inc.
2868 Bond St
Rochester Hills MI 48309
248 853-6620

(G-2621)
ADM MILLING CO
250 Ganson St (14203-3048)
P.O. Box 487 (14240-0487)
PHONE..................................716 849-7333
Charles Bayless, *Vice Pres*
Andreas Martin, *Vice Pres*
Brad Heald, *Plant Mgr*
Yvette Ceser, *Manager*
George Siradis, *Manager*
EMP: 75
SALES (corp-wide): 64.3B **Publicly Held**
WEB: www.admmilling.com
SIC: 2041 Grain mills (except rice)
HQ: Adm Milling Co.
8000 W 110th St Ste 300
Overland Park KS 66210
913 491-9400

(G-2622)
ADPRO SPORTS LLC
55 Amherst Villa Rd (14225-1432)
PHONE..................................716 854-5116
Ron Raccuia, *President*
Thomas Naples, *Exec VP*
Jeffrey Diebel, *Senior VP*
Paul Schintzius, *Senior VP*
Abby Camacho, *Sales Staff*
EMP: 76 EST: 1990
SALES (est): 1.1MM **Privately Held**
SIC: 2329 2339 3949 Men's & boys' sportswear & athletic clothing; women's & misses' athletic clothing & sportswear; team sports equipment

(G-2623)
ADSCO MANUFACTURING CORP
4979 Lake Ave (14219-1398)
PHONE..................................716 827-5450
Gustav Linda, *President*
James Treantis, *Controller*
EMP: 60
SQ FT: 32,000
SALES (est): 12.1MM **Privately Held**
WEB: www.adscomfg.com
SIC: 3441 Expansion joints (structural shapes), iron or steel

(G-2624)
ADVANCED MACHINE DESIGN CO INC
45 Roberts Ave (14206-3130)
PHONE..................................716 826-2000
Heinrich Moelbert, *Ch of Bd*
Reiner Moelbert, *President*
Ursula Moelbert, *Corp Secy*
EMP: 30
SQ FT: 102,000
SALES (est): 5.9MM **Privately Held**
WEB: www.amd-co.com
SIC: 3541 3542 8711 3549 Machine tool replacement & repair parts, metal cutting types; machine tools, metal forming type; presses: hydraulic & pneumatic, mechanical & manual; shearing machines, power; industrial engineers; metalworking machinery; cutlery

(G-2625)
AEP ENVIRONMENTAL LLC
2495 Main St Ste 230 (14214-2156)
PHONE..................................716 446-0739
Lynn Zier, *Mng Member*
Anthony Zier, *Admin Sec*
Scott Meacham,
Kenneth Pronti,
EMP: 10
SALES: 500K **Privately Held**
SIC: 3646 2844 5122 5047 Commercial indusl & institutional electric lighting fixtures; toilet preparations; drugs, proprietaries & sundries; medical & hospital equipment; household furnishings

(G-2626)
ALLEN BOAT CO INC
370 Babcock St Rear (14206-2802)
PHONE..................................716 842-0800
Thomas Allen Jr, *President*
Michael Huffman, *Vice Pres*
Sharon Hicok, *Controller*
EMP: 6 EST: 1961
SQ FT: 10,000
SALES (est): 997.3K **Privately Held**
WEB: www.allenboatco.com
SIC: 3732 2394 Sailboats, building & repairing; sails: made from purchased materials

(G-2627)
ALLIED CIRCUITS LLC
22 James E Casey Dr (14206-2367)
PHONE..................................716 551-0285
Chris Aquiline,
Chris Scinta,
Tom Wagner,
EMP: 50
SQ FT: 10,400
SALES: 9.6MM **Privately Held**
WEB: www.alliedcircuits.com
SIC: 3613 Panelboards & distribution boards, electric

(G-2628)
AMBIND CORP
Cheektowaga (14225)
P.O. Box 886 (14231-0886)
PHONE..................................716 836-4365
David Spiezer, *President*
EMP: 5
SALES (est): 660.1K **Privately Held**
SIC: 2241 Bindings, textile

(G-2629)
AMERICAN CITY BUS JOURNALS INC
465 Main St Ste 100 (14203-1717)
PHONE..................................716 541-1654
Jack Connors, *Principal*

Dawn Taibbi, *Accounts Exec*
Donna Collins, *Senior Editor*
EMP: 32
SALES (corp-wide): 1.3B **Privately Held**
SIC: 2711 Newspapers: publishing only, not printed on site
HQ: American City Business Journals, Inc.
120 W Morehead St Ste 400
Charlotte NC 28202
704 973-1000

(G-2630)
AMERICAN DOUGLAS METALS INC
Also Called: Afab Initiative
99 Bud Mil Dr (14206-1801)
PHONE..............................716 856-3170
Edward Raimonde, *CEO*
Kevin Blake, *Branch Mgr*
EMP: 12
SQ FT: 29,700
SALES (corp-wide): 27.4MM **Privately Held**
WEB: www.americandouglasmetals.com
SIC: 1099 3353 3291 Aluminum ore mining; aluminum sheet, plate & foil; abrasive products
PA: American Douglas Metals, Inc.
783 Thorpe Rd
Orlando FL 32824
407 855-6590

(G-2631)
AMERICAN IMAGES INC
25 Imson St (14210-1615)
PHONE..............................716 825-8888
Steve Wojtkowiak, *President*
EMP: 10
SALES (est): 1.4MM **Privately Held**
SIC: 2397 Schiffli machine embroideries

(G-2632)
AMETA INTERNATIONAL CO LTD
2221 Kenmore Ave Ste 108 (14207-1360)
PHONE..............................416 992-8036
EMP: 6 EST: 2013
SALES (est): 571.4K
SALES (corp-wide): 8MM **Privately Held**
SIC: 3699 Security control equipment & systems
PA: Ameta International Co. Ltd
80 Shields Crt
Markham ON L3R 9
905 415-1234

(G-2633)
AMHERST MEDIA INC
175 Rano St Ste 200 (14207-2176)
P.O. Box 538 (14213-0538)
PHONE..............................716 874-4450
Craig Alesse, *President*
EMP: 5
SALES (est): 705K **Privately Held**
WEB: www.amherstmedia.com
SIC: 2731 7812 Books: publishing only; video production

(G-2634)
ANDUJAR ASBESTOS AND LEAD
473 4th St (14201-1603)
PHONE..............................716 228-6757
Alfredo Andjujar, *President*
EMP: 9 EST: 2015
SQ FT: 24,000
SALES: 200K **Privately Held**
SIC: 3292 Asbestos products

(G-2635)
ANNESE & ASSOCIATES INC
500 Corporate Pkwy # 106 (14226-1263)
PHONE..............................716 972-0076
Raymond Apy, *Branch Mgr*
EMP: 8
SALES (corp-wide): 96.1MM **Privately Held**
SIC: 3577 Data conversion equipment, media-to-media: computer
HQ: Annese & Associates, Inc.
747 Pierce Rd Ste 2
Clifton Park NY 12065
518 877-7058

(G-2636)
ANTIQUES & COLLECTIBLE AUTOS
35 Dole St (14210-1603)
PHONE..............................716 825-3990
Joseph Trombley, *President*
EMP: 3
SALES: 1.6MM **Privately Held**
WEB: www.acrods.com
SIC: 3711 Automobile bodies, passenger car, not including engine, etc.

(G-2637)
ANTONICELLI VITO RACE CAR
3883 Broadway St (14227-1105)
PHONE..............................716 684-2205
Vito Antonicelli, *Owner*
EMP: 5
SQ FT: 6,000
SALES (est): 75K **Privately Held**
SIC: 3711 Motor vehicles & car bodies

(G-2638)
API HEAT TRANSF THERMASYS CORP (DH)
2777 Walden Ave (14225-4788)
PHONE..............................716 684-6700
Joseph Cordosi, *President*
◆ **EMP:** 169
SALES (est): 185.8MM
SALES (corp-wide): 46.7MM **Privately Held**
SIC: 3443 3714 Heat exchangers: coolers (after, inter), condensers, etc.; radiators & radiator shells & cores, motor vehicle
HQ: Api Heat Transfer Company
2777 Walden Ave Ste 1
Buffalo NY 14225
716 684-6700

(G-2639)
API HEAT TRANSFER COMPANY (DH)
2777 Walden Ave Ste 1 (14225-4788)
PHONE..............................716 684-6700
Mike Laisure, *President*
Sean Burley, *Project Engr*
Rick Andrzejewski, *Design Engr*
Victor Guardiola, *Controller*
Theresa Carbajal, *Administration*
EMP: 10 EST: 2005
SALES (est): 505.8MM
SALES (corp-wide): 46.7MM **Privately Held**
SIC: 3443 Heat exchangers: coolers (after, inter), condensers, etc.
HQ: Api Heat Transfer Intermediate Holdings, Llc
2777 Walden Ave Ste 1
Buffalo NY 14225
716 684-6700

(G-2640)
API HEAT TRANSFER INC (DH)
2777 Walden Ave Ste 1 (14225-4788)
PHONE..............................716 684-6700
Michael Laisure, *President*
Tom Gorman, *Vice Pres*
John Malone, *Vice Pres*
Sean Parker, *Vice Pres*
Joel Xue, *Opers Dir*
◆ **EMP:** 300
SQ FT: 112,000
SALES: 320MM
SALES (corp-wide): 46.7MM **Privately Held**
WEB: www.apiheattransfer.com
SIC: 3443 Fabricated plate work (boiler shop)
HQ: Api Heat Transfer Company
2777 Walden Ave Ste 1
Buffalo NY 14225
716 684-6700

(G-2641)
APPLE IMPRINTS APPAREL INC
2336 Bailey Ave (14211-1738)
PHONE..............................716 893-1130
Jack Lipomi, *President*
Kevin Lipomi, *Vice Pres*
▲ **EMP:** 22 EST: 1981
SQ FT: 15,000

SALES (est): 2.8MM **Privately Held**
WEB: www.appleimprints.com
SIC: 2396 7319 Screen printing on fabric articles; display advertising service

(G-2642)
APPLINCE INSTALLATION SVC CORP (PA)
3190 Genesee St (14225-2607)
PHONE..............................716 884-7425
Paul Glowlacki, *CEO*
Wayne Stoutner, *President*
EMP: 24
SALES (est): 14MM **Privately Held**
SIC: 3631 5085 7699 Household cooking equipment; industrial supplies; restaurant equipment repair

(G-2643)
ARCHER-DANIELS-MIDLAND COMPANY
Also Called: ADM
250 Ganson St (14203-3048)
P.O. Box 487 (14240-0487)
PHONE..............................716 849-7333
Brad Heald, *Branch Mgr*
Andrew Van Thyne, *Manager*
EMP: 100
SALES (corp-wide): 64.3B **Publicly Held**
WEB: www.admworld.com
SIC: 2041 Flour & other grain mill products
PA: Archer-Daniels-Midland Company
77 W Wacker Dr Ste 4600
Chicago IL 60601
312 634-8100

(G-2644)
ASSOCIATED PUBLISHING COMPANY (HQ)
61 John Muir Dr (14228-1147)
PHONE..............................325 676-4032
Robert N Allen III, *President*
EMP: 40
SALES (est): 6.8MM
SALES (corp-wide): 8.3B **Privately Held**
WEB:
www.associatedpublishingcompany.com
SIC: 2741 Directories, telephone: publishing only, not printed on site
PA: The Hearst Corporation
300 W 57th St Fl 42
New York NY 10019
212 649-2000

(G-2645)
ATECH-SEH METAL FABRICATOR
330 Greene St (14206-1025)
PHONE..............................716 895-8888
EMP: 20
SALES (est): 2MM **Privately Held**
SIC: 3444 Sheet metalwork

(G-2646)
ATHENEX INC (PA)
1001 Main St Ste 600 (14203-1009)
PHONE..............................716 427-2950
Johnson Y N Lau, *Ch of Bd*
Timothy Cook, *Senior VP*
David Cutler, *Vice Pres*
Mary Hughes, *Vice Pres*
Joe Mase, *Vice Pres*
EMP: 77
SQ FT: 51,000
SALES: 89.1MM **Publicly Held**
WEB: www.kinexpharma.com
SIC: 2834 8731 Pharmaceutical preparations; medical research, commercial

(G-2647)
ATHENEX PHARMACEUTICAL DIV LLC (PA)
1001 Main St Ste 600 (14203-1009)
PHONE..............................877 463-7823
Tom Moutvic, *Vice Pres*
Randoll Sze, *CFO*
James Bennett, *Consultant*
EMP: 14
SALES (est): 2.9MM **Privately Held**
SIC: 2834 Powders, pharmaceutical; solutions, pharmaceutical

(G-2648)
AURUBIS BUFFALO INC
600 Military Rd (14207)
PHONE..............................716 879-6700
Raymond Mercer, *President*
EMP: 11
SALES (corp-wide): 11.9B **Privately Held**
SIC: 3351 Copper rolling & drawing
HQ: Aurubis Buffalo, Inc.
70 Sayre St
Buffalo NY 14207
716 879-6700

(G-2649)
AURUBIS BUFFALO INC (HQ)
70 Sayre St (14207-2225)
P.O. Box 981 (14240-0981)
PHONE..............................716 879-6700
Raymond Mercer, *President*
Naveed Moghadam, *Business Mgr*
Jurgen Schachler, *COO*
Bonnie Rizzo, *Vice Pres*
Angela Seidler, *Vice Pres*
▲ **EMP:** 277
SQ FT: 1,214,500
SALES (est): 172.8MM
SALES (corp-wide): 11.9B **Privately Held**
WEB: www.luvata.com
SIC: 3351 Copper rolling & drawing
PA: Aurubis Ag
Hovestr. 50
Hamburg 20539
407 883-0

(G-2650)
AUSTIN AIR SYSTEMS LIMITED
500 Elk St (14210-2208)
PHONE..............................716 856-3700
Richard Taylor, *President*
Joyce Taylor, *Vice Pres*
Joe Pache, *Info Tech Mgr*
◆ **EMP:** 60
SQ FT: 173,000
SALES (est): 19.5MM **Privately Held**
SIC: 3564 Air purification equipment

(G-2651)
AVALON COPY CENTERS AMER INC
Also Called: Avalon Document Services
741 Main St (14203-1321)
PHONE..............................716 995-7777
Lewis Airth, *Managing Prtnr*
Andrew Guffey, *Managing Prtnr*
Aimee Tarin, *Accounts Exec*
Hilary Kleppe, *Branch Mgr*
David Landrum, *Director*
EMP: 25
SALES (corp-wide): 19MM **Privately Held**
SIC: 2741 7375 7336 7334 Art copy: publishing & printing; information retrieval services; commercial art & graphic design; photocopying & duplicating services
PA: Avalon Copy Centers Of America, Inc.
901 N State St
Syracuse NY 13208
315 471-3333

(G-2652)
AVANTI ADVANCED MFG CORP
673 Ontario St (14207-1614)
PHONE..............................716 791-9001
Jim WEI, *Ch of Bd*
▲ **EMP:** 10 EST: 2013
SALES (est): 810.6K **Privately Held**
SIC: 3089 Injection molding of plastics

(G-2653)
B & K COMPONENTS LTD
2100 Old Union Rd (14227-2725)
PHONE..............................323 776-4277
John L Beyer III, *President*
Dr Charles A Marchetta, *Admin Sec*
▲ **EMP:** 70 EST: 1981
SQ FT: 18,500
SALES (est): 9.5MM **Privately Held**
WEB: www.bkcomp.com
SIC: 3651 Audio electronic systems

(G-2654)
B & P JAYS INC
Also Called: Mecca Printing
19 N Hill Dr (14224-2582)
PHONE..............................716 668-8408
EMP: 5

▲ = Import ▼=Export
◆ =Import/Export

SQ FT: 1,400
SALES: 200K **Privately Held**
SIC: 2752 Offset Printing

(G-2655)
BARRON GAMES INTL CO LLC
84 Aero Dr Ste 5 (14225-1435)
PHONE.................................716 630-0054
Gregory Bacorn, *President*
Anna Bacorn, *Vice Pres*
Anna Zykina, *Vice Pres*
Alyssa Chawgo, *Office Mgr*
◆ EMP: 11
SQ FT: 4,500
SALES: 2MM **Privately Held**
WEB: www.barrongames.com/
SIC: 3944 5092 Electronic games & toys;
video games

(G-2656)
BATAVIA PRECISION GLASS LLC
231 Currier Ave (14212-2262)
PHONE.................................585 343-6050
Steve Barber,
EMP: 6
SQ FT: 9,000
SALES (est): 63K **Privately Held**
SIC: 3231 8748 Leaded glass; business
consulting

(G-2657)
BATES JACKSON ENGRAVING CO INC
17 Elm St 21 (14203-2605)
PHONE.................................716 854-3000
Rozanne Flammer, *CEO*
Edward Flammer, *President*
Carolyn Owen, *VP Finance*
EMP: 35 EST: 1903
SQ FT: 19,000
SALES (est): 3.7MM **Privately Held**
SIC: 2759 2752 2791 Engraving; com-
mercial printing, offset; typesetting

(G-2658)
BATTENFELD-AMERICAN INC
1575 Clinton St (14206-3064)
P.O. Box 728, North Tonawanda (14120-
0728)
PHONE.................................716 822-8410
John A Bellanti Sr, *CEO*
Barbara A Bellanti, *Ch of Bd*
Barbara Bellanti, *President*
Debbi Carpenter, *Vice Pres*
Florence Bellanti, *Admin Sec*
▼ EMP: 38
SQ FT: 110,000
SALES (est): 9.2MM
SALES (corp-wide): 44.4MM **Privately Held**
WEB: www.battenfeld-grease.com
SIC: 2992 Oils & greases, blending & com-
pounding
PA: Battenfeld Management, Inc.
1174 Erie Ave
North Tonawanda NY 14120
716 695-2100

(G-2659)
BEAR METAL WORKS INC
39 Scoville Ave (14206-2932)
P.O. Box 2528 (14240-2528)
PHONE.................................716 824-4350
Barrett E Price, *Ch of Bd*
Gloria Gau, *Project Mgr*
Catherine Jasinski, *Admin Sec*
EMP: 10 EST: 1999
SALES (est): 2.4MM **Privately Held**
SIC: 3441 Fabricated structural metal

(G-2660)
BEKA WORLD LP
258 Sonwil Dr (14225-5516)
PHONE.................................716 685-3717
EMP: 7
SALES (corp-wide): 3.5B **Publicly Held**
SIC: 2992 Lubricating oils & greases
HQ: Beka World Lp
2775 N Hills Dr Ne
Atlanta GA 30305
404 841-1133

(G-2661)
BELRIX INDUSTRIES INC
3590 Jeffrey Blvd (14219-2390)
PHONE.................................716 821-5964
Gail Maurer, *President*
EMP: 6
SQ FT: 15,000
SALES (est): 1.1MM **Privately Held**
WEB: www.belrix.com
SIC: 3469 Machine parts, stamped or
pressed metal

(G-2662)
BETTER WIRE PRODUCTS INC
680 New Babcock St (14206-2201)
PHONE.................................716 883-3377
William Breeser, *President*
Steve Bennett, *Opers Staff*
Lynn Youngman, *Sales Staff*
▲ EMP: 35 EST: 1952
SQ FT: 30,000
SALES (est): 8.2MM **Privately Held**
SIC: 3496 Miscellaneous fabricated wire
products

(G-2663)
BFG MANUFACTURING SERVICES INC
3949 Jeffrey Blvd (14219-2334)
P.O. Box 825, Hamburg (14075-0825)
PHONE.................................716 362-0888
Minta Marie, *Branch Mgr*
EMP: 27
SALES (est): 3.5MM
SALES (corp-wide): 12.6MM **Privately Held**
WEB: www.bfgelectroplating.com
SIC: 3471 Electroplating of metals or
formed products
PA: Bfg Manufacturing Services, Inc.
701 Martha St
Punxsutawney PA 15767
814 938-9164

(G-2664)
BIG HEART PET BRANDS
Del Monte Foods
243 Urban St (14211-1532)
PHONE.................................716 891-6566
Greg Pastore, *General Mgr*
Todd Verost, *Opers Mgr*
Bill Pasquale, *Safety Mgr*
Sean McGloin, *Purch Mgr*
Barbara Schumacher, *Purch Agent*
EMP: 31
SALES (corp-wide): 7.8B **Publicly Held**
WEB: www.kraftfoods.com
SIC: 2066 Chocolate & cocoa products
HQ: Big Heart Pet Brands, Inc.
1 Maritime Plz Fl 2
San Francisco CA 94111
415 247-3000

(G-2665)
BMC LLC
3155 Broadway St (14227-1034)
PHONE.................................716 681-7755
Richard Neal, *President*
▲ EMP: 24 EST: 1972
SQ FT: 4,500
SALES (est): 2.5MM **Privately Held**
SIC: 3084 Plastics pipe

(G-2666)
BROOK & WHITTLE LIMITED
215 John Glenn Dr (14228-2227)
PHONE.................................716 853-1688
Andrew Sharp, *Sales Mgr*
EMP: 120
SALES (corp-wide): 7.8MM **Privately Held**
SIC: 2671 4789 Plastic film, coated or
laminated for packaging; cargo loading &
unloading services
HQ: Brook & Whittle Limited
20 Carter Dr
Guilford CT 06437

(G-2667)
BRYANT MACHINE & DEVELOPMENT
63 Stanley St (14206-1017)
PHONE.................................716 894-8282
Michael Denz, *President*
Matthew Bryant Jr, *Corp Secy*

EMP: 10
SQ FT: 8,000
SALES: 200K **Privately Held**
SIC: 3599 Machine shop, jobbing & repair

(G-2668)
BRYANT MACHINE CO INC
63 Stanley St (14206-1017)
PHONE.................................716 894-8282
Kip Laviolette, *President*
Erica Laviolette, *Office Mgr*
EMP: 10 EST: 1946
SQ FT: 5,000
SALES (est): 1MM **Privately Held**
WEB: www.bryantmachine.com
SIC: 3599 Machine shop, jobbing & repair

(G-2669)
BRYANT MANUFACTURING WNY INC
63 Stanley St (14206-1017)
PHONE.................................716 894-8282
Kip A Laviolette, *CEO*
EMP: 6
SALES (est): 950K **Privately Held**
SIC: 3599 Machine shop, jobbing & repair

(G-2670)
BUFFALO ARMORY LLC
1050 Military Rd (14217-2528)
PHONE.................................716 935-6346
John Bastiste, *President*
EMP: 5
SALES (est): 832.4K **Privately Held**
SIC: 3398 Metal heat treating

(G-2671)
BUFFALO BLENDS INC (PA)
1400 William St (14206-1813)
PHONE.................................716 825-4422
Timothy Sheehy, *President*
Kevin Prise, *Treasurer*
▲ EMP: 22 EST: 1999
SQ FT: 35,000
SALES (est): 3.2MM **Privately Held**
WEB: www.buffaloblends.com
SIC: 2087 Beverage bases, concentrates,
syrups, powders & mixes

(G-2672)
BUFFALO CRUSHED STONE INC (HQ)
500 Como Park Blvd (14227-1606)
PHONE.................................716 826-7310
Steven B Detwiler, *Ch of Bd*
David Firmstone, *Vice Pres*
Jamie Hypnarowski, *Vice Pres*
Melissa Garman, *Shareholder*
EMP: 40
SQ FT: 25,000
SALES (est): 32.6MM
SALES (corp-wide): 651.9MM **Privately Held**
SIC: 1422 Crushed & broken limestone
PA: New Enterprise Stone & Lime Co., Inc.
3912 Brumbaugh Rd
New Enterprise PA 16664
814 224-6883

(G-2673)
BUFFALO FINISHING WORKS INC
1255 Niagara St (14213-1501)
PHONE.................................716 893-5266
John Warchocki, *President*
Ulrike Warchocki, *Vice Pres*
EMP: 5
SQ FT: 7,000
SALES: 250K **Privately Held**
SIC: 3479 Painting of metal products;
enameling, including porcelain, of metal
products

(G-2674)
BUFFALO GAMES LLC
220 James E Casey Dr (14206-2362)
PHONE.................................716 827-8393
Nagendra Raina, *Mng Member*
EMP: 75
SQ FT: 88,000
SALES (est): 1.9MM **Privately Held**
SIC: 3944 Games, toys & children's vehi-
cles

HQ: Buffalo Holding Corp.
220 James E Casey Dr
Buffalo NY 14206
716 464-5263

(G-2675)
BUFFALO LAW JOURNAL
465 Main St Ste 100 (14203-1717)
PHONE.................................716 541-1600
Kim Schaus, *General Mgr*
EMP: 6
SALES (est): 310K **Privately Held**
WEB: www.buffalolawjournal.com
SIC: 2711 Newspapers: publishing only,
not printed on site

(G-2676)
BUFFALO LINING & FABRICATING
73 Gillette Ave (14214-2702)
PHONE.................................716 883-6500
Bruce F Meyers, *President*
James Meyers, *Vice Pres*
EMP: 6 EST: 1956
SQ FT: 12,000
SALES (est): 695.3K **Privately Held**
SIC: 3069 Molded rubber products

(G-2677)
BUFFALO METAL CASTING CO INC
1875 Elmwood Ave (14207-1997)
PHONE.................................716 874-6211
John Klodzinski, *President*
Justin Klodzinski, *General Mgr*
Jennifer Patterson, *Manager*
EMP: 40
SQ FT: 80,000
SALES (est): 7.6MM **Privately Held**
WEB: www.buffalometalcasting.com
SIC: 3369 Castings, except die-castings,
precision

(G-2678)
BUFFALO METAL FABRICATING CORP
50 Wecker St (14215-3897)
PHONE.................................716 892-7800
Nicholas Moroczko, *President*
Alfreda Moroczko, *Corp Secy*
Morgan Moroczko, *Vice Pres*
EMP: 15
SQ FT: 50,000
SALES (est): 2.4MM **Privately Held**
WEB: www.buffalometalfab.com
SIC: 3441 Fabricated structural metal

(G-2679)
BUFFALO METAL FINISHING CO
135 Dart St (14213-1087)
P.O. Box 1012 (14213-7012)
PHONE.................................716 883-2751
Frank Bonare, *President*
EMP: 14 EST: 1941
SQ FT: 11,000
SALES: 500K **Privately Held**
SIC: 3471 3479 Plating of metals or
formed products; polishing, metals or
formed products; anodizing (plating) of
metals or formed products; painting of
metal products

(G-2680)
BUFFALO NEWS INC
1 News Plz (14203-2994)
P.O. Box 100 (14240-0100)
PHONE.................................716 849-4401
Stanford Lipsey, *CEO*
Karen Colville, *President*
Warren Colville, *President*
Bruce Andriatch, *Editor*
Paul Ehret, *Editor*
▲ EMP: 900 EST: 2009
SQ FT: 1,000
SALES: 186.5K
SALES (corp-wide): 225.3B **Publicly Held**
WEB: www.berkshirehathaway.com
SIC: 2711 Newspapers, publishing & print-
ing
PA: Berkshire Hathaway Inc.
3555 Farnam St Ste 1140
Omaha NE 68131
402 346-1400

(G-2681)
BUFFALO NEWSPRESS INC
200 Broadway St (14204-1439)
P.O. Box 648 (14240-0648)
PHONE...................716 852-1600
Warren T Colville, *President*
Mark Korzelius, *President*
Michael A Kibler, *Chairman*
Joan Holzman, *Vice Pres*
Marcus Regoord, *Vice Pres*
EMP: 120
SQ FT: 80,000
SALES (est): 22.8MM **Privately Held**
WEB: www.buffalonewspress.com
SIC: 2759 Newspapers: printing; advertis-
ing literature: printing

(G-2682)
**BUFFALO SCALE AND SUP CO
INC**
280 Seneca St (14204-2012)
P.O. Box 140 (14205-0140)
PHONE...................716 847-2880
Frederick Wilhelm, *President*
Manaswini Somashekhar, *President*
EMP: 6
SQ FT: 5,500
SALES (est): 1.1MM **Privately Held**
WEB: www.buffaloscale.com
SIC: 3596 Scales & balances, except labo-
ratory

(G-2683)
**BUFFALO SPREE PUBLISHING
INC (PA)**
1738 Elmwood Ave Ste 103 (14207-2465)
PHONE...................716 783-9119
Laurence Levite, *CEO*
Theresa Clair, *CFO*
Betty Tata, *Accounts Exec*
Marianne Potratz, *Manager*
Chastity O'Shei, *Creative Dir*
EMP: 25
SQ FT: 10,000
SALES (est): 2.3MM **Privately Held**
WEB: www.buffalospree.com
SIC: 2721 Magazines: publishing only, not
printed on site

(G-2684)
**BUFFALO STANDARD PRINTING
CORP**
Also Called: Am-Pol Eagle
3620 Harlem Rd Ste 5 (14215-2042)
PHONE...................716 835-9454
Irene Harzewski, *President*
EMP: 10 **EST:** 1958
SALES (est): 709.7K **Privately Held**
SIC: 2711 Commercial printing & newspa-
per publishing combined; job printing &
newspaper publishing combined

(G-2685)
BUFLOVAK LLC (PA)
750 E Ferry St (14211-1106)
PHONE...................716 895-2100
Mike Durusky, *Plant Mgr*
Tami McNamara, *Purch Mgr*
Dave Bielecki, *Controller*
Debbie Hacken, *Natl Sales Mgr*
Michael Bieger, *Mng Member*
◆ **EMP:** 28
SQ FT: 225,000
SALES (est): 11.7MM **Privately Held**
WEB: www.buffalotechnologies.com
SIC: 3556 5084 3567 3443 Food prod-
ucts machinery; industrial machinery &
equipment; industrial furnaces & ovens;
fabricated plate work (boiler shop)

(G-2686)
**BUSINESS FIRST OF NEW YORK
(DH)**
465 Main St Ste 100 (14203-1793)
PHONE...................716 854-5822
Jack Connors, *President*
EMP: 44
SQ FT: 10,000
SALES: 4.5MM
SALES (corp-wide): 1.3B **Privately Held**
SIC: 2711 Newspapers: publishing only,
not printed on site

HQ: American City Business Journals, Inc.
120 W Morehead St Ste 400
Charlotte NC 28202
704 973-1000

(G-2687)
**BUXTON MACHINE AND TOOL
CO INC**
2181 Elmwood Ave (14216-1002)
PHONE...................716 876-2312
James P Hettrick, *President*
Mildred Di Luca, *Admin Sec*
EMP: 12 **EST:** 1984
SQ FT: 12,000
SALES (est): 1.8MM **Privately Held**
SIC: 3599 Machine shop, jobbing & repair

(G-2688)
**C S BUSINESS SYSTEMS INC
(PA)**
1236 Main St (14209-2197)
PHONE...................716 886-6521
Michael I Choo, *President*
Kim Cooper, *Human Res Mgr*
Tom Massimi, *Info Tech Dir*
Nicole Jablonski, *Admin Asst*
▲ **EMP:** 25
SQ FT: 35,000
SALES (est): 8.8MM **Privately Held**
WEB: www.csbusiness.com
SIC: 3678 3357 5045 Electronic connec-
tors; nonferrous wiredrawing & insulating;
computer peripheral equipment

(G-2689)
CALSPAN CORPORATION (HQ)
4455 Genesee St (14225-1955)
P.O. Box 400 (14225)
PHONE...................716 631-6955
Robert Jacobson, *President*
Louis H Knotts, *President*
John Yurtchuk, *Chairman*
Peter Sauer, *COO*
Ruthanne Armstrong, *Senior VP*
◆ **EMP:** 129
SQ FT: 170,200
SALES (est): 43.3MM
SALES (corp-wide): 78.4MM **Privately
Held**
WEB: www.windtunnel.com
SIC: 3721 Research & development on air-
craft by the manufacturer
PA: Calspan Holdings, Llc
4455 Genesee St
Buffalo NY 14225
716 631-6955

(G-2690)
CALSPAN HOLDINGS LLC (PA)
4455 Genesee St (14225-1955)
P.O. Box 400 (14225)
PHONE...................716 631-6955
Louis Knotts, *CEO*
Peter Sauer, *CFO*
EMP: 12
SQ FT: 170,200
SALES (est): 78.4MM **Privately Held**
SIC: 3721 Research & development on air-
craft by the manufacturer

(G-2691)
**CAMELLIA GENERAL
PROVISION CO**
Also Called: Camellia Foods
1333 Genesee St (14211-2227)
PHONE...................716 893-5352
Peter J Cichocki, *Ch of Bd*
Edmund J Cichocki Jr, *President*
Eric Cichocki, *Vice Pres*
Patrick Cichocki, *Vice Pres*
Kathleen Cichocki, *Admin Sec*
EMP: 46 **EST:** 1937
SQ FT: 40,000
SALES: 10MM **Privately Held**
WEB: www.camelliafoods.com
SIC: 2013 5147 Sausage casings, natural;
bologna from purchased meat; smoked
meats from purchased meat; meats,
fresh; meats, cured or smoked

(G-2692)
CARAUSTAR INDUSTRIES INC
25 Dewberry Ln (14227-2709)
PHONE...................716 874-0393
Lynn Ramsey, *Branch Mgr*

EMP: 8
SALES (corp-wide): 3.8B **Publicly Held**
SIC: 2655 Tubes, fiber or paper: made
from purchased material
HQ: Caraustar Industries, Inc.
5000 Austell Powder Sprin
Austell GA 30106
770 948-3101

(G-2693)
CCL LABEL INC
685 Howard St (14206-2210)
P.O. Box 550 (14240-0550)
PHONE...................716 852-2155
Roy Graham, *Plant Mgr*
Matt Piejda, *Buyer*
Gale Podsiadlo, *Buyer*
James August, *QC Mgr*
Peter Lowry, *Engineer*
EMP: 150
SQ FT: 25,883
SALES (corp-wide): 3.9B **Privately Held**
WEB: www.avery.com
SIC: 2672 2671 Adhesive papers, labels
or tapes: from purchased material; pack-
aging paper & plastics film, coated & lami-
nated
HQ: Ccl Label, Inc.
161 Worcester Rd Ste 603
Framingham MA 01701
508 872-4511

(G-2694)
CENO TECHNOLOGIES INC
1234 Delaware Ave (14209-1463)
PHONE...................716 885-5050
Scott Patrick, *President*
Alan Rowdon, *Vice Pres*
EMP: 5
SALES (est): 661.9K **Privately Held**
SIC: 3531 Construction machinery

(G-2695)
CERTAINTEED CORPORATION
Pipe and Plastic Div
231 Ship Canal Pkwy (14218-1026)
PHONE...................716 827-7560
Bob Kearful, *Branch Mgr*
EMP: 400
SALES (corp-wide): 215.9MM **Privately
Held**
WEB: www.certainteed.net
SIC: 3089 Extruded finished plastic prod-
ucts
HQ: Certainteed Llc
20 Moores Rd
Malvern PA 19355
610 893-5000

(G-2696)
**CHOCOLATE DELIVERY
SYSTEMS INC (PA)**
1800 Elmwood Ave (14207-2449)
PHONE...................716 877-3146
Timothy Thill, *President*
Anne Rosa, *Vice Pres*
▲ **EMP:** 32
SALES (est): 16.6MM **Privately Held**
SIC: 2064 Candy bars, including chocolate
covered bars

(G-2697)
CILYOX INC
Also Called: New Rosen Printing
345 Broadway St (14204-1541)
PHONE...................716 853-3809
Michael Cimato, *President*
Bryan Knox, *Vice Pres*
EMP: 10 **EST:** 1963
SQ FT: 43,000
SALES (est): 1.3MM **Privately Held**
SIC: 2752 Commercial printing, offset

(G-2698)
CLEARVIEW SOCIAL INC
77 Goodell St Ste 430 (14203-1257)
PHONE...................801 414-7675
Adrian Dayton, *CEO*
Chris Lafleur, *COO*
Austin Clark, *Sales Mgr*
Alex Fenner, *Regl Sales Mgr*
Seth Weinert, *Sales Staff*
EMP: 5 **EST:** 2013
SALES (est): 188.8K **Privately Held**
SIC: 7372 Business oriented computer
software

(G-2699)
CLEVELAND BIOLABS INC
73 High St (14203-1149)
PHONE...................716 849-6810
Yakov Kogan, *CEO*
Lea Verny, *Ch of Bd*
Jian Zhang, *Partner*
Glenn Hart, *General Mgr*
John Szydlo, *Finance Dir*
EMP: 19
SQ FT: 32,000
SALES: 1.1MM **Privately Held**
WEB: www.cbiolabs.com
SIC: 2834 8731 Pharmaceutical prepara-
tions; biological research

(G-2700)
COBEY INC (PA)
1 Ship Canal Pkwy (14218-1024)
PHONE...................716 362-9550
John J Obey, *Ch of Bd*
Robert J Castle, *Vice Pres*
Neil Ackerman, *Project Mgr*
Eric Butler, *Project Mgr*
John Kranock, *Engineer*
▲ **EMP:** 110
SQ FT: 117,000
SALES (est): 48.1MM **Privately Held**
WEB: www.cobey.com
SIC: 3498 Fabricated pipe & fittings

(G-2701)
COGNIGEN CORPORATION
Also Called: Cognigen Acquisition
1780 Wehrle Dr Ste 110 (14221-7000)
PHONE...................716 633-3463
Jill Fiedler-Kelly, *President*
Drew Rokitka, *COO*
Ted Grasela, *Exec VP*
Cindy Welawander, *Exec VP*
Joel Owen, *Vice Pres*
EMP: 65
SALES (est): 8MM **Publicly Held**
SIC: 2834 8999 Druggists' preparations
(pharmaceuticals); scientific consulting
PA: Simulations Plus, Inc.
42505 10th St W Ste 103
Lancaster CA 93534

(G-2702)
COHENS BAKERY INC
Also Called: Al Cohens Famous Rye Bread
Bky
1132 Broadway St (14212-1502)
PHONE...................716 892-8149
Mark Didomenico, *President*
John J Blando, *Vice Pres*
Gary East Abrook, *Accountant*
EMP: 45
SQ FT: 25,000
SALES (est): 5.7MM **Privately Held**
SIC: 2045 5149 2051 Doughs & batters:
from purchased flour; groceries & related
products; bread, cake & related products

(G-2703)
COLAD GROUP LLC
693 Seneca St Fl 5 (14210-1324)
PHONE...................716 961-1776
Rick Prochaska, *Production*
F Martin Anson, *Mng Member*
J Todd Anson,
EMP: 81
SALES: 7.6MM
SALES (corp-wide): 18.3MM **Privately
Held**
WEB: www.colad.com
SIC: 2782 2671 2752 2759 Blankbooks
& looseleaf binders; packaging paper &
plastics film, coated & laminated; com-
mercial printing, lithographic; commercial
printing; signs & advertising specialties
PA: Bindagraphics, Inc.
2701 Wilmarco Ave
Baltimore MD 21223
410 362-7200

(G-2704)
COMET FLASHER INC (PA)
1 Babcock St (14210-2253)
PHONE...................716 821-9595
James Casey, *President*
Devon Saltsman, *Project Mgr*
Nancy Banks, *Manager*
Jamie Rybij, *Admin Sec*
EMP: 9

SALES (est): 1.5MM **Privately Held**
SIC: 3669 Traffic signals, electric

(G-2705)
COMMERCIAL PRINT & IMAGING
4778 Main St (14226-4020)
PHONE.................................716 597-0100
Kevin Preston, *President*
John A Polvino, *Vice Pres*
EMP: 25
SQ FT: 6,500
SALES (est): 3.4MM **Privately Held**
SIC: 2752 Commercial printing, offset

(G-2706)
COMMITMENT 2000 INC
Also Called: Father Sam's Bakery
105 Msgr Valente Dr (14206-1815)
PHONE.................................716 439-1206
William A Sam, *Ch of Bd*
Samuel Sam, *Vice Pres*
Nick Sam, *Plant Mgr*
Matt Sam, *Safety Mgr*
Anthony Sinicki, *Warehouse Mgr*
EMP: 40 EST: 1977
SQ FT: 40,000
SALES (est): 8.9MM **Privately Held**
WEB: www.fathersams.com
SIC: 2051 Bread, all types (white, wheat, rye, etc): fresh or frozen

(G-2707)
COMPLEMAR PRINT LLC
Also Called: Merrill Press
3034 Genesee St (14225-2641)
PHONE.................................716 875-7238
Michael Gotthelf, *President*
Christine Gotthelf, *Vice Pres*
Joan Gotthelf, *Admin Sec*
EMP: 12
SQ FT: 7,000
SALES (est): 1.8MM
SALES (corp-wide): 27.7MM **Privately Held**
WEB: www.quickbizcards.com
SIC: 2752 Commercial printing, offset
PA: Complemar Partners, Inc.
   500 Lee Rd Ste 200
   Rochester NY 14606
   585 647-5800

(G-2708)
CONAX TECHNOLOGIES LLC (PA)
2300 Walden Ave (14225-4765)
PHONE.................................716 684-4500
Trey Wilson, *Regl Sales Mgr*
Heather Craig, *Sales Staff*
Robert Fox, *Mng Member*
Michael Ferraro, *Manager*
Timothy Webster,
EMP: 126
SQ FT: 83,000
SALES (est): 18.9MM **Privately Held**
WEB: www.conaxbuffalo.com
SIC: 3823 Industrial process control instruments

(G-2709)
CONNIES LAUNDRY
1494 S Park Ave (14220-1075)
PHONE.................................716 822-2800
Froncell Clifton, *Owner*
EMP: 5
SQ FT: 1,000
SALES (est): 500K **Privately Held**
SIC: 2842 Laundry cleaning preparations

(G-2710)
COOKIEBAKER LLC
1 Robert Rich Way (14213-1701)
PHONE.................................716 878-8000
Sam Stolbun, *President*
EMP: 6
SALES (est): 498.8K **Privately Held**
SIC: 2099 Food preparations

(G-2711)
COOPER TURBOCOMPRESSOR INC (DH)
3101 Broadway St (14227-1034)
P.O. Box 209 (14225-0209)
PHONE.................................716 896-6600
Jeff Altamari, *Vice Pres*
Frank Athearn, *Vice Pres*
Ron Flecknoe, *Vice Pres*

Ray Plachta, *Vice Pres*
Ed Roper, *Vice Pres*
▲ EMP: 485
SQ FT: 273,000
SALES (est): 61MM **Publicly Held**
SIC: 3511 3563 Turbines & turbine generator sets; air & gas compressors

(G-2712)
CRANDALL FILLING MACHINERY INC
80 Gruner Rd (14227-1007)
PHONE.................................716 897-3486
David Reed, *President*
Heather Wood, *Treasurer*
Dian Reed, *Shareholder*
EMP: 6 EST: 1906
SQ FT: 7,000
SALES (est): 804.5K **Privately Held**
SIC: 3565 Packaging machinery

(G-2713)
CROSBY COMPANY
183 Pratt St (14204-1519)
PHONE.................................716 852-3522
Peter W Crosby, *CEO*
Jack Spencer, *Buyer*
Sean McCarthy, *Treasurer*
Jason Crosby, *Admin Sec*
Richard Daeing, *Admin Sec*
EMP: 50
SQ FT: 300,000
SALES (est): 10.8MM **Privately Held**
WEB: www.crosbycompany.com
SIC: 3469 Stamping metal for the trade

(G-2714)
CRYSTAL ROCK LLC
100 Stradtman St Ste 1 (14206-2665)
PHONE.................................716 626-7460
Tom Gawel, *Division Mgr*
EMP: 25
SALES (corp-wide): 2.2B **Privately Held**
SIC: 2086 Water, pasteurized: packaged in cans, bottles, etc.
HQ: Crystal Rock Llc
   1050 Buckingham St
   Watertown CT 06795

(G-2715)
CURTIS L MACLEAN L C (HQ)
Also Called: Maclean Curtis
50 Thielman Dr (14206-2364)
PHONE.................................716 898-7800
Duncan Mac Lean, *CEO*
Paul Hojnacki, *President*
Bob Filipski, *Facilities Mgr*
Mark Bettinger, *Mfg Staff*
Zachary Dailey, *Engineer*
EMP: 300
SALES (est): 53.8MM
SALES (corp-wide): 1.2B **Privately Held**
SIC: 3714 Motor vehicle engines & parts
PA: Mac Lean-Fogg Company
   1000 Allanson Rd
   Mundelein IL 60060
   847 566-0010

(G-2716)
CURTIS SCREW CO INC
50 Thielman Dr (14206-2364)
PHONE.................................716 898-7800
John Hoskins, *Chairman*
EMP: 36
SALES (est): 7.9MM **Privately Held**
SIC: 3451 Screw machine products

(G-2717)
CUSTOM CANVAS MANUFACTURING CO
775 Seneca St (14210-1487)
PHONE.................................716 852-6372
Anthony L Guido Jr, *President*
Phyllis Guido, *Vice Pres*
William Sal Guido, *Prdtn Mgr*
▲ EMP: 28 EST: 1961
SQ FT: 32,000
SALES (est): 3.2MM **Privately Held**
SIC: 2394 7699 Canvas covers & drop cloths; liners & covers, fabric: made from purchased materials; tarpaulins, fabric: made from purchased materials; tents: made from purchased materials; tent repair shop

(G-2718)
D & G WELDING INC
249 Hertel Ave (14207-2153)
PHONE.................................716 873-3088
Toll Free:.................................888
David M Black, *President*
EMP: 5
SQ FT: 2,300
SALES (est): 566.6K **Privately Held**
SIC: 7692 3498 Welding repair; pipe fittings, fabricated from purchased pipe

(G-2719)
D-C THEATRICKS
747 Main St (14203-1321)
PHONE.................................716 847-0180
David Dejac, *Partner*
Douglas Caskey, *Partner*
EMP: 5
SQ FT: 4,600
SALES (est): 430K **Privately Held**
WEB: www.costume.com
SIC: 2389 5699 5136 5137 Theatrical costumes; costumes, masquerade or theatrical; men's & boys' clothing; women's & children's clothing

(G-2720)
DAN TRENT COMPANY INC
Also Called: D & D Printing
1728 Clinton St (14206-3151)
PHONE.................................716 822-1422
Daniel Trent, *President*
EMP: 5 EST: 1970
SQ FT: 5,610
SALES (est): 1MM **Privately Held**
SIC: 2752 Commercial printing, offset

(G-2721)
DARLING INGREDIENTS INC
2000 William St (14206-2415)
PHONE.................................716 895-0655
Robert Fader, *Manager*
Hem Mehta, *Network Enginr*
EMP: 19
SALES (corp-wide): 3.3B **Publicly Held**
WEB: www.darlingii.com
SIC: 2077 Animal & marine fats & oils
PA: Darling Ingredients Inc.
   5601 N Macarthur Blvd
   Irving TX 75038
   972 717-0300

(G-2722)
DAVIS
283 Minnesota Ave (14215-1013)
PHONE.................................716 833-4678
Arthur L Davis, *Principal*
EMP: 9
SALES (est): 668.9K **Privately Held**
SIC: 2389 Clergymen's vestments

(G-2723)
DECK BROS INC
88 Beacon St (14220-1162)
PHONE.................................716 852-0262
Ronald P Kellner, *President*
Karl J Kellner, *Vice Pres*
EMP: 25
SALES: 3MM **Privately Held**
SIC: 3599 7692 Machine shop, jobbing & repair; welding repair

(G-2724)
DELAWARE VALLEY FORGE CO INC
247 Rano St (14207-2149)
PHONE.................................716 447-9140
Margaret Duggan, *President*
Michael Duggan, *Vice Pres*
William Simon Jr, *Vice Pres*
EMP: 5
SALES (est): 497.6K **Privately Held**
SIC: 3462 Iron & steel forgings

(G-2725)
DELAWARE VALLEY FORGE INC
241 Rano St (14207-2149)
P.O. Box 220, Kenmore (14217-0220)
PHONE.................................716 447-9140
Margaret Duggan, *President*
EMP: 20
SALES (est): 1.7MM **Privately Held**
SIC: 3462 Iron & steel forgings

(G-2726)
DENNY MACHINE CO INC
20 Norris St (14207-2207)
PHONE.................................716 873-6865
Leonard Deni, *President*
Frank Deni, *President*
Joseph Deni, *Vice Pres*
Laura Kelahan, *Controller*
Jennie Deni, *Admin Sec*
EMP: 45 EST: 1957
SQ FT: 10,000
SALES (est): 7.6MM **Privately Held**
WEB: www.deni.com
SIC: 3599 Machine shop, jobbing & repair

(G-2727)
DERRICK CORPORATION (PA)
Also Called: Derrick Equipment
590 Duke Rd (14225-5102)
PHONE.................................716 683-9010
James W Derrick, *Ch of Bd*
William W Derrick, *President*
Alan Bishop, *Division Mgr*
Jake Jacobs, *Division Mgr*
Jarrod Rice, *Area Mgr*
◆ EMP: 200 EST: 1951
SQ FT: 210,000
SALES (est): 185.2MM **Privately Held**
WEB: www.derrickcorp.com
SIC: 3533 Oil & gas field machinery

(G-2728)
DESIGNERS FOLDING BOX CORP
84 Tennessee St (14204-2797)
PHONE.................................716 853-5141
Jeffrey P Winney, *President*
Sandra Wright, *Purchasing*
Jeff Winney, *Pub Rel Mgr*
James Winney, *Treasurer*
Teri McAndrews, *Admin Sec*
EMP: 25 EST: 1950
SQ FT: 38,000
SALES (est): 2.5MM **Privately Held**
WEB: www.designersfoldingbox.com
SIC: 2657 Folding paperboard boxes

(G-2729)
DILESE INTERNATIONAL INC
Also Called: Choco-Logo
141 Broadway St (14203-1629)
PHONE.................................716 855-3500
Daniel Johnson, *President*
EMP: 10
SQ FT: 10,000
SALES (est): 1MM **Privately Held**
WEB: www.chocologo.com
SIC: 2066 2064 Chocolate; candy & other confectionery products

(G-2730)
DKM SALES LLC
Also Called: Dkm Ad Art
1352 Genesee St (14211-2296)
PHONE.................................716 893-7777
Ken Krzeminski, *Partner*
Scott Tanyi, *Plant Mgr*
Jan Gannon, *Sales Staff*
Ryan Carpenter, *Manager*
Andrew Wood, *Graphic Designe*
EMP: 40
SQ FT: 65,000
SALES (est): 5.2MM **Privately Held**
WEB: www.dkm-sales.com
SIC: 2759 3993 2399 Screen printing; advertising novelties; banners, made from fabric

(G-2731)
DUALL FINISHING INC
53 Hopkins St (14220-2130)
PHONE.................................716 827-1707
Richard Duman, *President*
EMP: 8
SALES: 325K **Privately Held**
SIC: 3549 Metalworking machinery

(G-2732)
DURO-SHED INC (PA)
721 Center Rd (14224-2181)
PHONE.................................585 344-0800
Dave Delagrange, *President*
EMP: 33
SQ FT: 6,000

SALES (est): 2.6MM **Privately Held**
WEB: www.duro-shed.com
SIC: 2452 Prefabricated wood buildings

(G-2733)
E B ATLAS STEEL CORP
120 Tonawanda St (14207-3117)
PHONE................................716 876-0900
Brian Hogle, *President*
EMP: 16
SQ FT: 7,000
SALES (est): 3.5MM **Privately Held**
SIC: 3441 Fabricated structural metal

(G-2734)
E I DU PONT DE NEMOURS & CO
Also Called: Dupont
3115 River Rd (14207-1059)
P.O. Box 88 (14207-0088)
PHONE................................716 876-4420
John A Wacek, *Engineer*
P V Crane, *Senior Engr*
Sharon Laskowski, *Corp Comm Staff*
Bobby Lawson, *Manager*
Greg Palermo, *Supervisor*
EMP: 50
SALES (corp-wide): 30.6B **Publicly Held**
WEB: www.dupont.com
SIC: 2823 2253 2821 Cellulosic man-
made fibers; knit outerwear mills; plastics
materials & resins
HQ: E. I. Du Pont De Nemours And Com-
pany
974 Centre Rd Bldg 735
Wilmington DE 19805
302 485-3000

(G-2735)
EAC HOLDINGS OF NY CORP
701 Willet Rd (14218-3756)
PHONE................................716 822-2500
Kristine Ramming, *President*
Stuart Weintraub, *General Mgr*
Betty Ramming, *Chairman*
James Kintzel, *Corp Secy*
▼ **EMP:** 23
SQ FT: 70,000
SALES (est): 3MM **Privately Held**
WEB: www.electroabrasives.com
SIC: 3291 Abrasive grains

(G-2736)
EAST CAST ORTHTICS PROSTHETICS
505 Delaware Ave (14202-1309)
PHONE................................716 856-5192
Vincent Benenati, *President*
Larry Benenati, *Vice Pres*
EMP: 12
SALES (est): 1.1MM **Privately Held**
SIC: 3842 Orthopedic appliances

(G-2737)
EASTERN NIAGRA RADIOLOGY
899 Main St (14203-1109)
PHONE................................716 882-6544
Joseph Serghany MD, *Partner*
Cynithia Selmensburger, *Admin Sec*
EMP: 22
SALES (est): 300K **Privately Held**
SIC: 3829 Medical diagnostic systems, nu-
clear

(G-2738)
EASTMAN MACHINE COMPANY
779 Washington St (14203-1396)
PHONE................................716 856-2200
Robert L Stevenson, *CEO*
Trevor Stevenson, *Vice Pres*
Wade Stevenson, *Vice Pres*
Michael Herman, *Opers Mgr*
Kristina Ettinger, *Export Mgr*
◆ **EMP:** 110 **EST:** 1888
SQ FT: 130,000
SALES (est): 36.3MM **Privately Held**
WEB: www.eastmancuts.com
SIC: 3552 Textile machinery

(G-2739)
EDWIN J MCKENICA & SONS INC
Also Called: E.J. McKenica & Sons
1200 Clinton St (14206-2824)
PHONE................................716 823-4646
Trent McKenica, *CEO*
Richard E McKenica, *Ch of Bd*

Glenn Milbrand, *President*
Bob Brigham, *General Mgr*
Robert Brigham, *General Mgr*
▲ **EMP:** 15 **EST:** 1974
SQ FT: 28,000
SALES (est): 3.6MM **Privately Held**
SIC: 3599 Machine shop, jobbing & repair

(G-2740)
ELECTRO ABRASIVES LLC
701 Willet Rd (14218-3798)
PHONE................................716 822-2500
Kristine L Ramming, *President*
Leonardo Curimbaba, *General Mgr*
Brian Hauer, *Opers Mgr*
Jim Pierowicz, *Manager*
◆ **EMP:** 20
SALES (est): 3.4MM **Privately Held**
SIC: 3291 Abrasive products

(G-2741)
ELWOOD SPECIALTY PRODUCTS INC
2180 Elmwood Ave (14216-1003)
PHONE................................716 877-6622
Peter McGennis Jr, *President*
Bill Easton, *Mfg Staff*
EMP: 13
SQ FT: 20,000
SALES (est): 1.5MM **Privately Held**
WEB: www.coolsac.com
SIC: 3842 Clothing, fire resistant & protec-
tive

(G-2742)
EM-KAY MOLDS INC
398 Ludington St (14206-1446)
PHONE................................716 895-6180
Richard Boehler, *President*
C F Boehler, *Vice Pres*
EMP: 6
SQ FT: 24,000
SALES: 400K **Privately Held**
SIC: 3089 Injection molding of plastics;
molding primary plastic

(G-2743)
EMCOM INDUSTRIES INC
235 Genesee St (14204-1456)
PHONE................................716 852-3711
Daniel A Higgins, *President*
EMP: 5
SQ FT: 40,000
SALES: 290K **Privately Held**
SIC: 3322 3599 Malleable iron foundries;
machine shop, jobbing & repair

(G-2744)
EMPIRE INNOVATION GROUP LLC
410 Main St Ste 5 (14202-3735)
PHONE................................716 852-5000
Nicolas Knab,
EMP: 10
SALES (est): 1MM **Privately Held**
SIC: 7372 Application computer software

(G-2745)
ENGINEERED COMPOSITES INC
Also Called: Armor Tile
55 Roberts Ave (14206-3119)
PHONE................................716 362-0295
Daniel Bolubash, *President*
Roman Bolubash, *Vice Pres*
Jeff Hansen, *Prdtn Mgr*
Aaron Boljkovac, *Manager*
David Holmes, *Manager*
▲ **EMP:** 30
SQ FT: 43,000
SALES (est): 11.8MM **Privately Held**
WEB: www.armortile.com
SIC: 3089 Floor coverings, plastic

(G-2746)
ENRG INC
155 Chandler St 5 (14207-2405)
PHONE................................716 873-2939
John Olenick, *President*
Tim Curry, *Manager*
EMP: 15
SQ FT: 13,000
SALES: 1.5MM **Privately Held**
WEB: www.enrg-inc.com
SIC: 3299 3674 Ceramic fiber; solid state
electronic devices

(G-2747)
ENTERPRISE FOLDING BOX CO INC
75 Isabelle St (14207-1739)
PHONE................................716 876-6421
Andrew Baranyi, *CEO*
Lynette Ovitt, *President*
Aj Baranyi, *Office Mgr*
Lynette Lodestro, *Branch Mgr*
Victoria Csicser, *Manager*
EMP: 24
SQ FT: 100,000
SALES (est): 8.9MM **Privately Held**
WEB: www.enterprisebox.com
SIC: 2631 Folding boxboard

(G-2748)
ESENSORS INC
4240 Ridge Lea Rd Ste 37 (14226-1083)
PHONE................................716 837-8719
Darold Wobschall, *President*
Bryan Schutjer, *VP Bus Dvlpt*
Peter Williams, *Controller*
Kevin Klos, *Info Tech Mgr*
EMP: 10
SQ FT: 2,000
SALES (est): 1.6MM **Privately Held**
WEB: www.eesensors.com
SIC: 3823 Industrial instrmnts msrmnt dis-
play/control process variable

(G-2749)
ESM GROUP INC
300 Corporate Pkwy 118n (14226-1258)
P.O. Box 128, Valencia PA (16059-0128)
PHONE................................724 265-1766
Charles Wright, *President*
EMP: 6
SALES (corp-wide): 177.9K **Privately
Held**
WEB: www.esmgroup.com
SIC: 2819 Industrial inorganic chemicals
HQ: Esm Group Inc.
300 Corporate Pkwy 118n
Amherst NY 14226
716 446-8914

(G-2750)
F X GRAPHIX INC
3043 Delaware Ave (14217-2059)
PHONE................................716 871-1511
Thomas Giambra, *President*
Pamela Gittins, *Partner*
EMP: 6
SQ FT: 1,600
SALES (est): 686.4K **Privately Held**
WEB: www.fxgraphix.com
SIC: 2395 7336 Embroidery products, ex-
cept schiffli machine; commercial art &
graphic design

(G-2751)
FAMOUS DOUGHNUTS INC
3043 Main St (14214-1333)
PHONE................................716 834-6356
Richard Roehm Sr, *President*
EMP: 8
SQ FT: 6,000
SALES (est): 791.7K **Privately Held**
SIC: 2051 Doughnuts, except frozen

(G-2752)
FIBRON PRODUCTS INC
Also Called: Real Wood Tiles
170 Florida St (14208-1250)
PHONE................................716 886-2378
Robert C Oshei Jr, *President*
EMP: 50 **EST:** 1949
SQ FT: 65,000
SALES (est): 3.5MM **Privately Held**
SIC: 2499 2426 Handles, wood; hardwood
dimension & flooring mills

(G-2753)
FLASHFLO MANUFACTURING INC
88 Hopkins St (14220-2131)
PHONE................................716 826-9500
Lawrence Speiser, *President*
EMP: 10
SALES (est): 1.7MM **Privately Held**
SIC: 3599 Machine shop, jobbing & repair

(G-2754)
FLEXIBLE LIFELINE SYSTEMS INC
100 Stradman St (14206-2666)
PHONE................................716 896-4949
Murry Mike Mumau, *President*
Austin Townsend, *General Mgr*
Megan Quinn, *Vice Pres*
EMP: 44 **EST:** 2017
SALES (est): 1.7MM **Privately Held**
SIC: 3842 Surgical appliances & supplies

(G-2755)
FLEXLUME SIGN CORPORATION
1464 Main St (14209-1780)
P.O. Box 804 (14209-0804)
PHONE................................716 884-2020
Alfred P Rowell Sr, *CEO*
Alfred P Rowell Jr, *President*
Shirley J Rowell, *Corp Secy*
Michelle Holland, *Administration*
EMP: 9
SQ FT: 22,000
SALES (est): 1.2MM **Privately Held**
WEB: www.flexlume.com
SIC: 3993 1799 Electric signs; sign instal-
lation & maintenance

(G-2756)
FOLAM TOOL CO INC
35 Burgundy Ter (14228-1334)
PHONE................................716 688-1347
Adrien Malof, *CEO*
Adrien P Malof, *President*
EMP: 5
SQ FT: 10,000
SALES: 90K **Privately Held**
WEB: www.folamtoolco.com
SIC: 3541 Machine tools, metal cutting
type

(G-2757)
FORSYTH INDUSTRIES INC
1195 Colvin Blvd (14223-1909)
PHONE................................716 652-1070
EMP: 29 **EST:** 1890
SQ FT: 50,000
SALES (est): 4.2MM **Privately Held**
SIC: 3469 3315 Mfg Metal Stampings Mfg
Steel Wire/Related Products

(G-2758)
FPPF CHEMICAL CO INC (PA)
117 W Tupper St Ste 1 (14201-2171)
PHONE................................716 856-9607
Christopher Lory, *President*
Mark Jacobs, *Sales Staff*
EMP: 8
SQ FT: 4,000
SALES (est): 1.7MM **Privately Held**
WEB: www.fppf.com
SIC: 2911 2899 Fuel additives; antifreeze
compounds

(G-2759)
FRANK WARDYNSKI & SONS INC
336 Peckham St (14206-1717)
PHONE................................716 854-6083
Raymond F Wardynski, *Ch of Bd*
Michael Wardynski, *Manager*
EMP: 40
SQ FT: 24,000
SALES (est): 6.8MM **Privately Held**
WEB: www.wardynski.com
SIC: 2013 5149 2011 Sausage casings,
natural; canned goods: fruit, vegetables,
seafood, meats, etc.; meat packing plants

(G-2760)
FREDERICK MACHINE REPAIR INC
405 Ludington St (14206-1445)
PHONE................................716 332-0104
Alan Frederick, *President*
Jennifer Kelly, *Vice Pres*
EMP: 8
SQ FT: 11,000
SALES (est): 1.3MM **Privately Held**
SIC: 3599 Machine shop, jobbing & repair

(G-2761)
FRONTIER HT-DIP GLVANIZING INC
1740 Elmwood Ave (14207-2410)
P.O. Box 199 (14207-0199)
PHONE..................................716 875-2091
Lewis G Pierce, *President*
▲ EMP: 18
SQ FT: 65,000
SALES (est): 3.2MM **Privately Held**
WEB: www.frontierhdgalvanizing.com
SIC: 3479 Galvanizing of iron, steel or end-formed products

(G-2762)
FRONTIER HYDRAULICS CORP
1738 Elmwood Ave Ste 2 (14207-2465)
PHONE..................................716 694-2070
Steve M Jackson, *President*
EMP: 12 EST: 1963
SQ FT: 10,000
SALES: 750K **Privately Held**
WEB: www.frontierhydraulics.com
SIC: 3511 Hydraulic turbines

(G-2763)
FULL CIRCLE STUDIOS LLC
710 Main St (14202-1915)
PHONE..................................716 875-7740
Kevin Crosby, *General Mgr*
Jim Phillips, *Founder*
Terry Fisher,
EMP: 7
SALES (est): 864.1K **Privately Held**
WEB: www.fullcirclestudios.com
SIC: 3699 Electronic training devices

(G-2764)
GALLAGHER PRINTING INC
Also Called: Rocket Communications
2518 Delaware Ave (14216-1702)
PHONE..................................716 873-2434
David Gallagher, *President*
Dean Gallagher, *Corp Secy*
Daryl Gallagher, *Vice Pres*
Dennis Gallagher, *Treasurer*
EMP: 30 EST: 1969
SQ FT: 30,000
SALES (est): 3.6MM **Privately Held**
WEB: www.gallagherprinting.com
SIC: 2752 2711 6513 Commercial printing, offset; newspapers; apartment building operators

(G-2765)
GALLE & ZINTER INC
Also Called: Galle Mamorial
3405 Harlem Rd (14225-2019)
PHONE..................................716 833-4212
Paul Zinter, *President*
Rick Zinter, *Principal*
Tina Zinter, *Admin Sec*
EMP: 7
SQ FT: 2,198
SALES (est): 534.7K **Privately Held**
SIC: 3272 Monuments & grave markers, except terrazo

(G-2766)
GAN KAVOD INC
300 International Dr (14221-5781)
P.O. Box 1000, New Hartford (13413-0709)
PHONE..................................716 633-2820
Patricia A Hays, *Principal*
EMP: 33
SALES: 5.4MM **Privately Held**
SIC: 3843 Enamels, dentists'

(G-2767)
GARLAND TECHNOLOGY LLC (PA)
199 Delaware Ave (14202-2113)
P.O. Box 711 (14205-0711)
PHONE..................................716 242-8500
Christopher Bihary, *CEO*
Erica Tank, *President*
Marcus Austin, *Partner*
Katelyn Hemingway, *Partner*
Samantha Schlein, *Partner*
EMP: 20
SALES (est): 3.3MM **Privately Held**
SIC: 3572 Computer storage devices

(G-2768)
GAY SHEET METAL DIES INC
301 Hinman Ave (14216-1093)
PHONE..................................716 877-0208
Dolores Dewey, *President*
EMP: 8 EST: 1936
SQ FT: 6,500
SALES (est): 1.3MM **Privately Held**
SIC: 3469 3544 Stamping metal for the trade; die sets for metal stamping (presses)

(G-2769)
GEAR MOTIONS INCORPORATED
Also Called: Oliver Gear
1120 Niagara St (14213-1714)
PHONE..................................716 885-1080
Mike Barron, *Branch Mgr*
EMP: 22
SALES (corp-wide): 18MM **Privately Held**
WEB: www.gearmotions.com
SIC: 3462 Gears, forged steel
PA: Gear Motions Incorporated
1750 Milton Ave
Syracuse NY 13209
315 488-0100

(G-2770)
GEMTROL INC
1800 Broadway St Bldg 1c (14212-2001)
PHONE..................................716 894-0716
Jeffrey Dombek, *President*
EMP: 8
SQ FT: 4,400
SALES (est): 1.4MM **Privately Held**
WEB: www.gemtrol.com
SIC: 3625 Electric controls & control accessories, industrial

(G-2771)
GENERAL MILLS INC
54 S Michigan Ave (14203-3086)
PHONE..................................716 856-6060
Heather Kelly, *Project Engr*
Joanne Thompson, *Corp Comm Staff*
Allen Brown, *Director*
EMP: 50
SALES (corp-wide): 16.8B **Publicly Held**
WEB: www.generalmills.com
SIC: 2041 Flour: blended, prepared or self-rising; flour mixes
PA: General Mills, Inc.
1 General Mills Blvd
Minneapolis MN 55426
763 764-7600

(G-2772)
GENERAL MILLS INC
315 Ship Canal Pkwy (14218-1018)
PHONE..................................716 856-6060
Bernice Greene, *Project Mgr*
EMP: 58
SALES (corp-wide): 16.8B **Publicly Held**
SIC: 2043 Wheat flakes: prepared as cereal breakfast food
PA: General Mills, Inc.
1 General Mills Blvd
Minneapolis MN 55426
763 764-7600

(G-2773)
GENERAL MOTORS LLC
2995 River Rd 2 (14207-1059)
PHONE..................................716 879-5000
Nicole Peltier, *Materials Mgr*
Loren Bonville, *Engineer*
Keith Carver, *Engineer*
Kim Chilcott, *Engineer*
John Ciavatta, *Engineer*
EMP: 900 **Publicly Held**
SIC: 3714 Motor vehicle parts & accessories
HQ: General Motors Llc
300 Renaissance Ctr L1
Detroit MI 48243

(G-2774)
GENESEE RESERVE BUFFALO LLC
300 Bailey Ave (14210-2211)
P.O. Box 20619, Rochester (14602-0619)
PHONE..................................716 824-3116
Bob Victor,

EMP: 30
SALES (est): 2.5MM **Privately Held**
SIC: 2491 Structural lumber & timber, treated wood

(G-2775)
GIBRALTAR INDUSTRIES INC (PA)
3556 Lake Shore Rd # 100 (14219-1400)
P.O. Box 2028 (14219-0228)
PHONE..................................716 826-6500
William P Montague, *Ch of Bd*
Frank G Heard, *Vice Ch Bd*
William T Bosway, *President*
Dean Stewart, *General Mgr*
Pat Burns, *COO*
◆ EMP: 82
SALES: 1B **Publicly Held**
WEB: www.gibraltar1.com
SIC: 3499 3316 3441 3398 Strapping, metal; cold finishing of steel shapes; strip steel, cold-rolled: from purchased hot-rolled; sheet, steel, cold-rolled: from purchased hot-rolled; bars, steel, cold finished, from purchased hot-rolled; fabricated structural metal; metal heat treating

(G-2776)
GLAXOSMITHKLINE LLC
17 Mahogany Dr (14221-2420)
PHONE..................................716 913-5679
EMP: 26
SALES (corp-wide): 39.5B **Privately Held**
SIC: 2834 Pharmaceutical preparations
HQ: Glaxosmithkline Llc
5 Crescent Dr
Philadelphia PA 19112
215 751-4000

(G-2777)
GLOBALQUEST SOLUTIONS INC
2813 Wehrle Dr Ste 3 (14221-7384)
PHONE..................................716 601-3524
Aaron Fox, *President*
Michael Morlock, *CTO*
EMP: 12
SQ FT: 2,000
SALES (est): 3.4MM **Privately Held**
WEB: www.globalquestinc.com
SIC: 7372 Business oriented computer software

(G-2778)
GOERGEN-MACKWIRTH CO INC
765 Hertel Ave (14207-1992)
P.O. Box 750 (14207-0750)
PHONE..................................716 874-4800
Jeffrey Mertz, *President*
Patricia Mertz, *Admin Sec*
EMP: 45
SQ FT: 24,000
SALES (est): 11.1MM **Privately Held**
WEB: www.goergenmackwirth.com
SIC: 3444 1761 Sheet metalwork; sheet metalwork

(G-2779)
GOODNATURE PRODUCTS INC
149 Bud Mil Dr (14206-1801)
PHONE..................................800 875-3381
Dale Wettlaufer, *President*
Diane Massett, *Accounting Mgr*
Lori Sonnenfeld, *Human Res Mgr*
Pete Whitehead, *VP Sales*
Eric Tyler, *Accounts Exec*
EMP: 30
SQ FT: 18,000
SALES (est): 6MM **Privately Held**
WEB: www.goodnature.com
SIC: 3634 3556 Juice extractors, electric; pasteurizing equipment, dairy machinery

(G-2780)
GRAPHIC CNTRLS ACQISITION CORP (DH)
400 Exchange St (14204-2064)
P.O. Box 1271 (14240-1271)
PHONE..................................716 853-7500
Sam Heleba, *CEO*
Michael Gaglio, *Exec VP*
Mark Ginter, *Mfg Spvr*
Paul Poeller, *Mfg Spvr*
Gary Toomy, *Opers Staff*
◆ EMP: 275
SQ FT: 235,000

SALES (est): 128.7MM **Privately Held**
WEB: www.graphiccontrols.com
SIC: 2752 2679 Tag, ticket & schedule printing: lithographic; paper products, converted
HQ: Graphic Controls Holdings, Inc.
400 Exchange St
Buffalo NY 14204
716 853-7500

(G-2781)
GRAPHIC CONTROLS HOLDINGS INC (HQ)
400 Exchange St (14204-2064)
P.O. Box 1271 (14240-1271)
PHONE..................................716 853-7500
Samuel Heleba, *CEO*
Ryokei Tsuryta, *Ch of Bd*
Thomas Reardon, *Corp Secy*
Paul Pohlman, *Prdtn Mgr*
Gail Toy, *Credit Staff*
EMP: 12
SQ FT: 235,000
SALES: 138MM **Privately Held**
SIC: 2752 6719 2679 Tag, ticket & schedule printing: lithographic; investment holding companies, except banks; paper products, converted

(G-2782)
GREAT LAKES ORTHPD LABS INC
1031 Main St (14203-1014)
PHONE..................................716 893-4116
Thomas F Daley, *President*
Marc A Edelstein, *Vice Pres*
Marc Edelstein, *Vice Pres*
EMP: 7
SQ FT: 1,400
SALES (est): 946.2K **Privately Held**
SIC: 3842 Limbs, artificial; orthopedic appliances; braces, orthopedic

(G-2783)
GREAT LAKES PLASTICS CO INC
2371 Broadway St (14212-2313)
P.O. Box 2820 (14240-2820)
PHONE..................................716 896-3100
EMP: 28 EST: 1946
SQ FT: 28,000
SALES (est): 4.4MM **Privately Held**
WEB: www.greatlakesplastic.com
SIC: 3082 3081 Rods, unsupported plastic; unsupported plastics film & sheet

(G-2784)
GREAT LAKES PRESSED STEEL CORP
1400 Niagara St (14213-1302)
PHONE..................................716 885-4037
Timothy O Nichols, *President*
Maryjane Nichols, *Vice Pres*
Andrew Nichols, *Manager*
Mary Jane Nichols, *Admin Sec*
EMP: 20
SQ FT: 25,000
SALES (est): 3.6MM **Privately Held**
WEB: www.glpscorp.com
SIC: 3469 3544 Stamping metal for the trade; dies, steel rule

(G-2785)
GREEN APPLE COURAGE INC
Also Called: BP Magazine
374 Delaware Ave Ste 240 (14202-1623)
P.O. Box 59 (14205-0059)
PHONE..................................716 614-4673
Joanne Doan, *Ch of Bd*
EMP: 3 EST: 2004
SALES: 1.3MM **Privately Held**
SIC: 2721 Magazines: publishing & printing

(G-2786)
GROWTECH INDUSTRIES LLC (PA)
3100 Lake Shore Rd (14219-1408)
PHONE..................................315 335-9692
Rich Stapleton, *Mng Member*
William Jacobi,
▼ EMP: 9
SQ FT: 20,000
SALES: 1.8MM **Privately Held**
SIC: 3523 Farm machinery & equipment

(G-2787)
HABASIT AMERICA INC
1400 Clinton St (14206-2919)
PHONE..................................716 824-8484
Carol Paget, *Production*
Ray Adams, *Credit Staff*
Tim Eldridge, *Branch Mgr*
Fred Dahl, *Manager*
Bob Gladczak, *Manager*
EMP: 75
SQ FT: 50,000
SALES (corp-wide): 708MM **Privately Held**
WEB: www.habasit.com
SIC: 3496 3052 Conveyor belts; rubber & plastics hose & beltings
HQ: Habasit America, Inc.
 805 Satellite Blvd Nw
 Suwanee GA 30024
 678 288-3600

(G-2788)
HADLEY EXHIBITS INC (PA)
1700 Elmwood Ave (14207-2408)
PHONE..................................716 874-3666
Theodore K Johnson, *President*
Ralph Allen, *Vice Pres*
Greg Kerl, *Prdtn Mgr*
Scott Calhoun, *Sales Mgr*
Grzegorz Pilip, *Graphiç Designe*
EMP: 87
SQ FT: 180,000
SALES (est): 13.1MM **Privately Held**
WEB: www.hadleyexhibits.com
SIC: 3993 Displays & cutouts, window & lobby

(G-2789)
HAGNER INDUSTRIES INC
95 Botsford Pl (14216-2601)
PHONE..................................716 873-5720
Peter Hagner, *President*
EMP: 8
SQ FT: 3,800
SALES (est): 400K **Privately Held**
SIC: 3599 1799 Machine shop, jobbing & repair; welding on site

(G-2790)
HAKSON SAFETY WEARS INC
111 Colgate Ave (14220)
PHONE..................................613 667-3015
Muhamad Aslam, *President*
EMP: 10
SQ FT: 3,000
SALES: 500K **Privately Held**
SIC: 3842 Clothing, fire resistant & protective

(G-2791)
HAMBURG FINISHING WORKS INC
3949 Jeffrey Blvd (14219-2334)
PHONE..................................716 362-0888
Frank Marie, *President*
Jeffrey Grube, *Corp Secy*
EMP: 5
SALES (est): 348.3K **Privately Held**
SIC: 3471 Electroplating of metals or formed products

(G-2792)
HANKIN BROTHERS CAP CO
Also Called: Han-Kraft Uniform Headwear
1910 Genesee St (14211-1818)
PHONE..................................716 892-8840
Benjamin Hankin, *Partner*
Richard Hankin, *Partner*
EMP: 10
SQ FT: 2,800
SALES (est): 1MM **Privately Held**
SIC: 2353 Uniform hats & caps

(G-2793)
HARMAC MEDICAL PRODUCTS INC (PA)
2201 Bailey Ave (14211-1797)
PHONE..................................716 897-4500
John F Somers, *President*
David Rozanski, *Buyer*
Lou Ann Digiacomo, *Manager*
▲ EMP: 400
SQ FT: 80,000

SALES (est): 104.9MM **Privately Held**
WEB: www.harmac.com
SIC: 3841 Surgical & medical instruments

(G-2794)
HAROLD WOOD CO INC
329 Hinman Ave (14216-1096)
PHONE..................................716 873-1535
Richard L Wood, *President*
Jane Wood, *Admin Sec*
EMP: 5 EST: 1927
SQ FT: 3,200
SALES (est): 607.9K **Privately Held**
WEB: www.haroldwood.com
SIC: 3479 Name plates: engraved, etched, etc.

(G-2795)
HARPER INTERNATIONAL CORP
4455 Genesee St Ste 123 (14225-1965)
PHONE..................................716 276-9900
Tom Kittell, *CEO*
Charles Miller, *President*
Diana Robbins, *Vice Pres*
John Pace, *Purch Mgr*
Elizabeth Wruck, *Purchasing*
◆ EMP: 100 EST: 1988
SALES: 50MM **Privately Held**
WEB: www.harperintl.com
SIC: 3567 Industrial furnaces & ovens

(G-2796)
HEALTH MATTERS AMERICA INC
2501 Broadway St Ste 2 (14227-1054)
P.O. Box 1482 (14225-8482)
PHONE..................................716 235-8772
Jerry Zeifman, *President*
▲ EMP: 14
SALES (est): 1.6MM **Privately Held**
SIC: 2393 Tea bags, fabric: made from purchased materials

(G-2797)
HEINTZ & WEBER CO INC
150 Reading St (14220-2156)
PHONE..................................716 852-7171
Steven D Desmond, *CEO*
Suzanne M Desmond, *Exec VP*
EMP: 7
SQ FT: 12,500
SALES (est): 860.7K **Privately Held**
WEB: www.webersmustard.com
SIC: 2035 Pickles, vinegar; mustard, prepared (wet); relishes, fruit & vegetable

(G-2798)
HI-TEMP FABRICATION INC
15 Lawrence Bell Dr (14221-7075)
PHONE..................................716 852-5655
Shelly Kent, *President*
Dave Schedlbauer, *Vice Pres*
John Lent, *Sales Mgr*
EMP: 13
SQ FT: 40,000
SALES (est): 2.1MM **Privately Held**
WEB: www.hi-tempfab.com
SIC: 2493 Hardboard & fiberboard products

(G-2799)
HOHL MACHINE & CONVEYOR CO INC
Also Called: Hohlveyor
1580 Niagara St (14213-1102)
PHONE..................................716 882-7210
Richard Milazzo, *President*
Carl Milazzo, *Principal*
EMP: 50
SQ FT: 30,000
SALES (est): 11.9MM **Privately Held**
SIC: 3599 3535 Machine & other job shop work; belt conveyor systems, general industrial use

(G-2800)
HOOD INDUSTRIES INC
580 Tifft St (14220-1813)
PHONE..................................716 836-0301
Steven R Doraski, *President*
EMP: 10
SQ FT: 60,000
SALES (est): 1.4MM **Privately Held**
SIC: 2449 Shipping cases & drums, wood: wirebound & plywood

(G-2801)
HOSPIRA INC
2501 Walden Ave (14225)
PHONE..................................716 684-9400
James Prosser, *Branch Mgr*
EMP: 193
SALES (corp-wide): 53.6B **Publicly Held**
SIC: 2834 Druggists' preparations (pharmaceuticals)
HQ: Hospira, Inc.
 275 N Field Dr
 Lake Forest IL 60045
 224 212-2000

(G-2802)
HUTCHINSON INDUSTRIES INC
Rodgard
92 Msgr Valente Dr (14206-1822)
PHONE..................................716 852-1435
Bill Barrett, *Branch Mgr*
EMP: 30
SALES (corp-wide): 8.4B **Publicly Held**
SIC: 3069 Medical & laboratory rubber sundries & related products
HQ: Hutchinson Industries, Inc.
 460 Southard St
 Trenton NJ 08638
 609 394-1010

(G-2803)
HYDRO-AIR COMPONENTS INC
Also Called: Zehnder Rittling
100 Rittling Blvd (14220-1885)
PHONE..................................716 827-6510
Scott Pallotta, *CEO*
Bill Boquard, *Vice Pres*
Robert Daigler, *Vice Pres*
Andrew Kiesling, *Production*
Dave Polisoto, *Senior Engr*
▲ EMP: 130
SQ FT: 80,000
SALES (est): 36.4MM
SALES (corp-wide): 688.9MM **Privately Held**
SIC: 3585 1711 Refrigeration & heating equipment; plumbing, heating, air-conditioning contractors
PA: Zehnder Group Ag
 Moortalstrasse 1
 GrAnichen AG
 628 551-500

(G-2804)
I ON YOUTH
115 Godfrey St (14215-2361)
PHONE..................................716 832-6509
Marilyn Nixon, *President*
EMP: 5
SALES (est): 304.6K **Privately Held**
SIC: 2721 Periodicals

(G-2805)
ICYNENE US ACQUISITION CORP
438 Main St Ste 100 (14202-3207)
PHONE..................................800 758-7325
Bill Sommers, *CFO*
EMP: 4
SALES (est): 2.3MM
SALES (corp-wide): 11.9MM **Publicly Held**
SIC: 2899 Foam charge mixtures
PA: Ffl Partners, Llc
 1 Maritime Plz Fl 22
 San Francisco CA 94111
 415 402-2100

(G-2806)
IMAGE TECH
96 Donna Lea Blvd (14221-3104)
PHONE..................................716 635-0167
Joan Hudack, *Owner*
EMP: 15
SALES (est): 520K **Privately Held**
SIC: 3999 Pet supplies

(G-2807)
IMMCO DIAGNOSTICS INC
640 Ellicott St Fl 3 (14203-1245)
PHONE..................................716 691-0091
EMP: 9 **Privately Held**
SIC: 3231 2835 8071 Mfg Products-Purchased Glass Mfg Diagnostic Substances Medical Laboratory

HQ: Immco Diagnostics, Inc.
 60 Pineview Dr
 Buffalo NY 14228
 716 691-0091

(G-2808)
IN ROOM PLUS INC
2495 Main St Ste 217 (14214-2154)
PHONE..................................716 838-9433
Mike Amrose, *CEO*
Wanda Jones, *President*
Kim Hamilton, *Director*
Elizabeth Jones, *Director*
Lori Kempski, *Director*
▼ EMP: 32
SQ FT: 21,000
SALES (est): 5.3MM **Privately Held**
WEB: www.inroomplus.com
SIC: 2064 Candy & other confectionery products

(G-2809)
INDUSTRIAL SUPPORT INC
36 Depot St (14206-2204)
PHONE..................................716 662-2954
David P Sullivan, *President*
▲ EMP: 75
SQ FT: 55,000
SALES (est): 16.9MM **Privately Held**
WEB: www.industrialsupportinc.com
SIC: 3441 5999 2541 Fabricated structural metal; electronic parts & equipment; wood partitions & fixtures

(G-2810)
INGERSOLL-RAND COMPANY
3101 Broadway St (14227-1034)
P.O. Box 209 (14217-0209)
PHONE..................................716 896-6600
Linda McDonnell, *Business Mgr*
Pasquale Cariello, *Project Mgr*
Brian Fleming, *Project Mgr*
Duane Schmitz, *Project Mgr*
Peter Quartararo, *Opers Mgr*
EMP: 40 **Privately Held**
SIC: 3563 Air & gas compressors
HQ: Ingersoll-Rand Company
 800 Beaty St Ste B
 Davidson NC 28036
 704 655-4000

(G-2811)
INSTANTWHIP OF BUFFALO INC
2117 Genesee St (14211-1907)
PHONE..................................716 892-7031
John Beck, *General Mgr*
EMP: 20
SALES (corp-wide): 47.5MM **Privately Held**
SIC: 2099 2035 2026 2022 Food preparations; pickles, sauces & salad dressings; fluid milk; cheese, natural & processed; sample distribution
HQ: Instantwhip Of Buffalo, Inc
 2200 Cardigan Ave
 Columbus OH 43215
 614 488-2536

(G-2812)
INSTY-PRINTS OF BUFFALO INC (PA)
265 Franklin St (14202-1901)
PHONE..................................716 853-6483
David Metz, *President*
Jim Metz, *Vice Pres*
Tom Metz, *Treasurer*
EMP: 7
SQ FT: 3,500
SALES (est): 1.2MM **Privately Held**
SIC: 2752 Commercial printing, lithographic

(G-2813)
INTERIOR SOLUTIONS OF WNY LLC
472 Franklin St (14202-1302)
PHONE..................................716 332-0372
Jan Malof,
EMP: 9
SALES (est): 1MM **Privately Held**
SIC: 2521 Chairs, office: padded, upholstered or plain: wood

(G-2814)
INTERNATIONAL PAPER COMPANY
100 Bud Mil Dr (14206-1802)
PHONE..............................716 852-2144
Pam Regans, *Branch Mgr*
EMP: 15
SALES (corp-wide): 23.3B **Publicly Held**
WEB: www.tin.com
SIC: 2653 Corrugated & solid fiber boxes
PA: International Paper Company
6400 Poplar Ave
Memphis TN 38197
901 419-9000

(G-2815)
J D COUSINS INC
667 Tifft St (14220-1890)
PHONE..............................716 824-1098
Gregory N Pauly, *CEO*
George Morris, *Exec VP*
Mike Heim, *Foreman/Supr*
Jim Howard, *Info Tech Mgr*
EMP: 24 EST: 1904
SQ FT: 30,000
SALES (est): 5.4MM **Privately Held**
WEB: www.jdcousins.com
SIC: 3443 Fabricated plate work (boiler shop)

(G-2816)
JAYS FURNITURE PRODUCTS INC
321 Ramsdell Ave (14216-1030)
PHONE..............................716 876-8854
James Gianni, *President*
Dean Gianni, *Plant Mgr*
Janie Gianni, *Admin Sec*
EMP: 30
SQ FT: 25,000
SALES (est): 5.2MM **Privately Held**
WEB: www.jaysfurnitureproducts.com
SIC: 2531 2512 2431 Benches for public buildings; upholstered household furniture; millwork

(G-2817)
JBREN CORP
Also Called: Lancaster Tanks and Steel Pdts
107 Dorothy St (14206-2939)
PHONE..............................716 332-5928
John Brennan, *CEO*
EMP: 16
SALES (est): 2.6MM **Privately Held**
SIC: 3443 Water tanks, metal plate

(G-2818)
JCCO ENTERPRISES
348 Cayuga Rd (14225-1927)
PHONE..............................716 626-0892
Adam Chelpinski, *Owner*
EMP: 10
SALES (est): 899.6K **Privately Held**
SIC: 3911 Jewelry, precious metal

(G-2819)
JENTSCH & CO INC
107 Dorothy St (14206-2939)
PHONE..............................716 852-4111
Christopher Jentsch, *President*
Walter Peters, *Corp Secy*
EMP: 6 EST: 1931
SQ FT: 28,500
SALES (est): 944.3K **Privately Held**
WEB: www.jentschandcompany.com
SIC: 3441 Fabricated structural metal

(G-2820)
JERRY MILLER MOLDED SHOES INC (PA)
Also Called: Jerry Miller I.D. Shoes
36 Mason St (14213-1505)
PHONE..............................716 881-3920
Hussain Syed, *President*
Sarah Syed, *Vice Pres*
◆ EMP: 11
SQ FT: 26,000
SALES (est): 1.2MM **Privately Held**
WEB: www.jerrymillershoes.com
SIC: 3143 3144 Orthopedic shoes, men's; orthopedic shoes, women's

(G-2821)
JERSEY EXPRESS INC
3080 Main St (14214-1304)
PHONE..............................716 834-6151
EMP: 15
SALES (est): 1.4MM **Privately Held**
SIC: 2389 Mfg Apparel/Accessories

(G-2822)
JET-BLACK SEALERS INC
Also Called: Sealmaster
555 Ludwig Ave (14227-1026)
P.O. Box 7257 (14240-7257)
PHONE..............................716 891-4197
William C Smith, *Ch of Bd*
Eric Moggaffin, *Sales Mgr*
Rosemary Smith, *Admin Sec*
EMP: 6
SQ FT: 6,400
SALES (est): 1.4MM **Privately Held**
WEB: www.sealmasterbuffalo.com
SIC: 2951 Asphalt paving mixtures & blocks

(G-2823)
JOHNSON CONTROLS INC
130 John Muir Dr Ste 100 (14228-1139)
PHONE..............................716 688-7340
Harold Witschi, *Branch Mgr*
EMP: 50 **Privately Held**
SIC: 3822 Auto controls regulating residntl & coml environmt & applncs
HQ: Johnson Controls, Inc.
5757 N Green Bay Ave
Milwaukee WI 53209
414 524-1200

(G-2824)
JOHNSON MANUFACTURING COMPANY
Also Called: SA Day Buffalo Flux Facility
1489 Niagara St (14213-1103)
P.O. Box 1084, Tonawanda (14151-1084)
PHONE..............................716 881-3030
Jackson Bowling, *General Mgr*
EMP: 10 **Privately Held**
WEB: www.johnsonmfg.com
SIC: 2899 Fluxes: brazing, soldering, galvanizing & welding
PA: Johnson Manufacturing Company, Inc
114 Lost Grove Rd
Princeton IA 52768

(G-2825)
JRB MACHINE-TOOL INC
5647 Seneca St (14224-3747)
P.O. Box 285, Lancaster (14086-0285)
PHONE..............................716 206-0355
Richard Betschen, *President*
Jane Betschen, *Vice Pres*
▲ EMP: 7
SALES (est): 814.9K **Privately Held**
SIC: 3599 Machine shop, jobbing & repair

(G-2826)
JUST LAMPS OF NEW YORK INC
334 Harris Hill Rd Apt 1 (14221-7473)
PHONE..............................716 626-2240
Dave Bethell, *CEO*
Eric Lanham, *President*
Eric Laham, *General Mgr*
Mark Murray, *CFO*
Dave Fromm, *Controller*
EMP: 12
SALES (est): 2.2MM **Privately Held**
WEB: www.justlamps.us.com
SIC: 3861 Projectors, still or motion picture, silent or sound

(G-2827)
K & E FABRICATING COMPANY INC
40 Stanley St (14206-1018)
PHONE..............................716 829-1829
Peter Fasolino, *President*
Dennis Abrahamson, *Office Mgr*
EMP: 12
SQ FT: 10,000
SALES (est): 2.7MM **Privately Held**
SIC: 3441 Fabricated structural metal

(G-2828)
K D M DIE COMPANY INC
620 Elk St (14210-2237)
PHONE..............................716 828-9000

Gary Posluszny, *CEO*
Carl Posluszny, *Treasurer*
EMP: 17
SQ FT: 32,000
SALES (est): 2.5MM **Privately Held**
SIC: 3544 3599 Special dies & tools; machine shop, jobbing & repair

(G-2829)
K-TECHNOLOGIES INC
4090 Jeffrey Blvd (14219-2338)
PHONE..............................716 828-4444
Jeffrey Kryszak, *President*
Julie Bodkin, *Engineer*
EMP: 40
SQ FT: 5,400
SALES (est): 4MM **Privately Held**
WEB: www.k-technologies.net
SIC: 3824 Electromechanical counters

(G-2830)
KEHR-BUFFALO WIRE FRAME CO INC
Also Called: Rogers Industrial Spring
127 Kehr St (14211-1522)
P.O. Box 806, Grand Island (14072-0806)
PHONE..............................716 897-2288
George Rogers, *President*
James Rogers III, *Vice Pres*
EMP: 30
SQ FT: 27,000
SALES (est): 4.7MM **Privately Held**
WEB: www.kbwf.net
SIC: 3496 Miscellaneous fabricated wire products

(G-2831)
KELLER BROS & MILLER INC
401 Franklin St (14202-1586)
PHONE..............................716 854-2374
Ralph Salerno, *President*
EMP: 9
SQ FT: 8,600
SALES (est): 1.6MM **Privately Held**
WEB: www.kbmprinting.com
SIC: 2752 Commercial printing, offset

(G-2832)
KEY TECH FINISHING
2929 Main St Ste 2 (14214-1760)
PHONE..............................716 832-1232
Jack Karet, *President*
Jennifer Masse, *General Mgr*
Joan Karet, *Corp Secy*
EMP: 30
SQ FT: 80,000
SALES (est): 2.2MM
SALES (corp-wide): 8.7MM **Privately Held**
WEB: www.keyfinishing.com
SIC: 3471 Electroplating of metals or formed products; electroplating & plating
PA: Keystone Corporation
144 Milton St
Buffalo NY 14210
800 880-9747

(G-2833)
KEYNOTE SYSTEMS CORPORATION
2810 Sweet Home Rd (14228-1347)
PHONE..............................716 564-1332
Leonard Gostowski, *President*
EMP: 5
SALES (est): 560.8K **Privately Held**
SIC: 7372 Prepackaged software

(G-2834)
KEYSTONE CORPORATION (PA)
144 Milton St (14210-1644)
PHONE..............................800 880-9747
Jack A Karet, *President*
Joan Karet, *Corp Secy*
Michael Karet, *Vice Pres*
Sam Goorevich, *Sales Mgr*
EMP: 40 EST: 1923
SQ FT: 45,000
SALES (est): 8.7MM **Privately Held**
WEB: www.keyfinishing.com
SIC: 3471 Electroplating of metals or formed products; electroplating & plating; anodizing (plating) of metals or formed products

(G-2835)
KITTINGER COMPANY INC
4675 Transit Rd (14221-6022)
PHONE..............................716 876-1000
Raymond C Bialkowski, *CEO*
EMP: 50
SQ FT: 60,000
SALES (est): 7.8MM **Privately Held**
WEB: www.kittingerfurniture.com
SIC: 2521 2512 2511 Wood office furniture; upholstered household furniture; wood household furniture

(G-2836)
KNOLL INC
Also Called: Datesweiser
1700 Broadway St (14212-2031)
PHONE..............................716 891-1700
EMP: 60 **Publicly Held**
SIC: 2521 Wood office furniture
PA: Knoll, Inc.
1235 Water St
East Greenville PA 18041

(G-2837)
KOCH METAL SPINNING CO INC
74 Jewett Ave (14214-2421)
PHONE..............................716 835-3631
Eric Koch, *President*
Mark Kuercvoerser, *QC Mgr*
▼ EMP: 52 EST: 1939
SQ FT: 50,000
SALES (est): 4.3MM **Privately Held**
WEB: www.kochmetalspinning.com
SIC: 3469 Spinning metal for the trade

(G-2838)
KOEHLR-GIBSON MKG GRAPHICS INC
Also Called: Koehler-Gibson Mkg & Graphics
875 Englewood Ave (14223-2334)
PHONE..............................716 838-5960
David Koehler, *President*
EMP: 20
SQ FT: 13,000
SALES (est): 2.7MM **Privately Held**
SIC: 3953 2796 Date stamps, hand: rubber or metal; postmark stamps, hand: rubber or metal; printing dies, rubber or plastic, for marking machines; photoengraving plates, linecuts or halftones

(G-2839)
KOHLER AWNING INC
2600 Walden Ave (14225-4736)
PHONE..............................716 685-3333
John M Kohler, *President*
Craig Kohler, *Corp Secy*
Jesse W Kohler, *Vice Pres*
EMP: 30 EST: 1924
SQ FT: 2,182
SALES (est): 4.4MM **Privately Held**
WEB: www.kohlerawning.com
SIC: 2394 7699 Awnings, fabric: made from purchased materials; awning repair shop

(G-2840)
KYNTEC CORPORATION
2100 Old Union Rd (14227-2725)
PHONE..............................716 810-6956
Patrick Lee, *Ch of Bd*
Scott Taylor, *President*
Gerald Spyche, *Vice Pres*
Rich Ryan, *Treasurer*
John Sperrazza, *Sales Staff*
EMP: 6 EST: 2012
SALES (est): 1.3MM **Privately Held**
SIC: 3569 3484 3531 Industrial shock absorbers; rifles or rifle parts, 30 mm. & below; aircraft hardware; marine related equipment

(G-2841)
L LLC
106 Soldiers Pl (14222-1261)
PHONE..............................716 885-3918
Liz Valenti, *Comptroller*
Mohsen Lachaal, *Mng Member*
EMP: 20 EST: 2001
SALES (est): 2.1MM **Privately Held**
SIC: 2079 Olive oil

(G-2842)
LABATT USA LLC
79 Perry St Ste 1 (14203-3079)
PHONE................................716 604-1050
Glen Walter, *President*
Thomas Cardella, *Vice Pres*
James Pendegrat,
▲ EMP: 60
SALES (est): 7.9MM **Privately Held**
SIC: 2082 Beer (alcoholic beverage)
HQ: North American Breweries, Inc.
　　445 Saint Paul St
　　Rochester NY 14605

(G-2843)
LACTALIS AMERICAN GROUP INC
2375 S Park Ave (14220-2653)
PHONE................................716 827-2622
Sean Paul Quiblier, *Principal*
EMP: 100
SALES (corp-wide): 355.8K **Privately Held**
SIC: 2022 Natural cheese
HQ: Lactalis American Group, Inc.
　　2376 S Park Ave
　　Buffalo NY 14220
　　716 823-6262

(G-2844)
LACTALIS AMERICAN GROUP INC (DH)
Also Called: Sorrento Lactalis
2376 S Park Ave (14220-2670)
PHONE................................716 823-6262
Frederick Bouisset, *CEO*
Charmaine Derosa, *District Mgr*
Pierre Lorieau, *Vice Pres*
Paul Peterson, *Vice Pres*
Suzanne Risman, *Vice Pres*
◆ EMP: 500
SALES (est): 622.7MM
SALES (corp-wide): 355.8K **Privately Held**
WEB: www.lactalisamericangroup.com
SIC: 2022 Natural cheese
HQ: Parmalat Spa
　　Via Delle Nazioni Unite 4
　　Collecchio PR 43044
　　052 180-81

(G-2845)
LAFARGE NORTH AMERICA INC
575 Ohio St (14203-3119)
PHONE................................716 854-5791
Edward Hickey, *Manager*
EMP: 5
SALES (corp-wide): 27.6B **Privately Held**
WEB: www.lafargenorthamerica.com
SIC: 3273 Ready-mixed concrete
HQ: Lafarge North America Inc.
　　8700 W Bryn Mawr Ave
　　Chicago IL 60631
　　773 372-1000

(G-2846)
LAKESHORE CARBIDE INC
1959 Maple Rd (14221-2754)
PHONE................................716 462-4349
Carl Ciesla, *Chairman*
EMP: 6
SALES (est): 694.6K **Privately Held**
SIC: 2819 Carbides

(G-2847)
LANDIES CANDIES CO INC
2495 Main St Ste 350 (14214-2154)
PHONE................................716 834-8212
Larry Szrama, *President*
Andrew Gaiek, *Vice Pres*
Dennis Hussak, *Marketing Staff*
▲ EMP: 10
SALES (est): 1.8MM **Privately Held**
WEB: www.landiescandies.com
SIC: 2064 Candy & other confectionery products

(G-2848)
LASEOPTICS CORP
300 International Dr # 100 (14221-5781)
PHONE................................716 462-5078
Samuel John, *President*
EMP: 14
SALES (est): 1.1MM **Privately Held**
SIC: 2298 Cable, fiber

(G-2849)
LIME ENERGY CO
1a Elk Terminal (14204-4200)
PHONE................................704 892-4442
Adam Procell, *Branch Mgr*
EMP: 8
SALES (corp-wide): 272.2MM **Publicly Held**
SIC: 3274 Lime
HQ: Lime Energy Co.
　　4 Gateway Ctr Fl 4 # 4
　　Newark NJ 07102
　　201 416-2575

(G-2850)
LINE WARD CORPORATION
157 Seneca Creek Rd (14224-2347)
PHONE................................716 675-7373
Cheryl Gustavel, *President*
Roger Gustavel, *Vice Pres*
EMP: 5
SQ FT: 3,000
SALES: 1.4MM **Privately Held**
WEB: www.lineward.com
SIC: 3531 Construction machinery

(G-2851)
LITELAB CORP (PA)
251 Elm St (14203-1603)
PHONE................................716 856-4300
Frederick A Spaulding, *CEO*
Dawn M Casati, *Corp Secy*
Lawrence Christ, *COO*
Michael Heaverlo, *Mfg Dir*
Dawn Csati, *Controller*
▲ EMP: 140
SQ FT: 80,000
SALES (est): 37.6MM **Privately Held**
WEB: www.litelab.com
SIC: 3646 3645 Commercial indusl & institutional electric lighting fixtures; residential lighting fixtures

(G-2852)
LOCKHOUSE DISTILLERY
41 Columbia St Ste 3 (14204-2100)
PHONE................................716 768-4898
Chad Vosseller, *President*
Thomas Jablonski, *Partner*
Jon Mirro, *Vice Pres*
EMP: 6
SALES (est): 292.6K **Privately Held**
SIC: 2085 Distilled & blended liquors

(G-2853)
LOY L PRESS INC
Also Called: Allegra Printing
3959 Union Rd (14225-4253)
PHONE................................716 634-5966
Richard Delong, *President*
Joyce S Delong, *Vice Pres*
EMP: 5
SQ FT: 1,894
SALES (est): 887.2K **Privately Held**
SIC: 2752 2791 2789 2759 Commercial printing, offset; typesetting; bookbinding & related work; commercial printing

(G-2854)
M A MOSLOW & BROS INC
375 Norfolk Ave (14215-3108)
PHONE................................716 896-2950
David Moslow, *President*
Joe Moslow, *Vice Pres*
▲ EMP: 40
SQ FT: 21,000
SALES (est): 4.3MM **Privately Held**
WEB: www.moslowbros.com
SIC: 2499 Trophy bases, wood

(G-2855)
M K ULRICH CONSTRUCTION INC
Also Called: Bison Iron & Step
1601 Harlem Rd (14206-1923)
PHONE................................716 893-5777
Don Ulrich, *President*
Marie Ulrich, *Vice Pres*
EMP: 12
SQ FT: 4,800
SALES: 900K **Privately Held**
SIC: 3272 1799 Ornamental metal work; steps, prefabricated concrete

(G-2856)
MACNEIL POLYMERS INC (PA)
3155 Broadway St (14227-1034)
PHONE................................716 681-7755
Richard Neil, *President*
EMP: 15 EST: 2000
SQ FT: 35,097
SALES (est): 1MM **Privately Held**
WEB: www.macneilpolymers.com
SIC: 2821 Plastics materials & resins

(G-2857)
MAGAZINES & BROCHURES INC
Also Called: Labels X Press
2205 Kenmore Ave Ste 107 (14207-1329)
PHONE................................716 875-9699
Craig Boggs, *President*
Scott Boggs, *Treasurer*
EMP: 5
SALES (est): 538.7K **Privately Held**
WEB: www.labelsxpress.com
SIC: 2759 2752 Labels & seals: printing; commercial printing, lithographic

(G-2858)
MAGNESIUM TECHNOLOGIES CORP
266 Elmwood Ave (14222-2202)
P.O. Box 818 (14222)
PHONE................................905 689-7361
Bernie Rumbold, *CEO*
EMP: 13
SALES (corp-wide): 1.2B **Privately Held**
SIC: 3295 Magnesite, crude: ground, calcined or dead-burned
HQ: Opta Minerals (Usa) Inc.
　　4807 Rockside Rd Ste 400
　　Independence OH 44131
　　330 659-3003

(G-2859)
MAGTROL INC
70 Gardenville Pkwy W (14224-1394)
PHONE................................716 668-5555
William A Mulroy III, *President*
Thomas Rymarczyk, *General Mgr*
◆ EMP: 50 EST: 1953
SQ FT: 35,000
SALES (est): 12.1MM **Privately Held**
WEB: www.magtrol.com
SIC: 3625 3568 3825 3823 Brakes, electromagnetic; clutches, except vehicular; instruments to measure electricity; industrial instrmnts msrmnt display/control process variable; motor vehicle parts & accessories; aircraft & motor vehicle measurement equipment

(G-2860)
MAKE-WAVES INSTRUMENT CORP (PA)
4172 Vinewood Dr (14221-7518)
PHONE................................716 681-7524
John R Patterson, *President*
Brian Cory, *Vice Pres*
▲ EMP: 25
SQ FT: 36,000
SALES (est): 2.4MM **Privately Held**
WEB: www.makewavesinstrumentcorp.com
SIC: 3825 3829 3641 3545 Tachometer generators; gauges, motor vehicle: oil pressure, water temperature; electric lamps; machine tool accessories; valves & pipe fittings; gaskets, packing & sealing devices

(G-2861)
MARKIN TUBING LP
Also Called: Markin Tubing Division
400 Ingham Ave (14218-2536)
PHONE................................585 495-6211
Tom Stamper, *Manager*
EMP: 17 **Privately Held**
SIC: 3312 3317 Tubes, steel & iron; steel pipe & tubes
PA: Markin Tubing, Lp
　　1 Markin Ln
　　Wyoming NY 14591

(G-2862)
MASSIMO FRIEDMAN INC
Also Called: Great Arrow Graphics
2495 Main St Ste 457 (14214-2154)
PHONE................................716 836-0408
Alan Friedman, *President*

Donna M Massimo, *Corp Secy*
Lisa Samar, *Vice Pres*
EMP: 20
SALES (est): 2.2MM **Privately Held**
WEB: www.greatarrow.com
SIC: 2771 Greeting cards

(G-2863)
MAXSECURE SYSTEMS INC
300 International Dr # 100 (14221-5781)
PHONE................................800 657-4336
Ken Szekely, *President*
Ken Lawrence, *Admin Sec*
EMP: 3 EST: 1997
SALES: 1.3MM **Privately Held**
WEB: www.max-secure.com
SIC: 2531 Public building & related furniture

(G-2864)
MC IVOR MANUFACTURING INC
400 Ingham Ave (14218-2536)
P.O. Box 13 (14220-0013)
PHONE................................716 825-1808
Bruce Mc Ivor, *President*
EMP: 6
SQ FT: 13,000
SALES (est): 632.2K **Privately Held**
SIC: 3599 Machine shop, jobbing & repair

(G-2865)
MESSER LLC
101 Katherine St (14210-2005)
PHONE................................716 847-0748
Jack Pederson, *Opers-Prdtn-Mfg*
EMP: 40
SALES (corp-wide): 1.4B **Privately Held**
SIC: 2813 Nitrogen; oxygen, compressed or liquefied
HQ: Messer Llc
　　200 Somerset Corp Blvd # 7000
　　Bridgewater NJ 08807
　　908 464-8100

(G-2866)
MINEO & SAPIO MEATS INC
Also Called: Minero & Sapio Sausage
410 Connecticut St (14213-2641)
PHONE................................716 884-2398
Michael Pierro, *President*
Nadine Pierro, *Treasurer*
EMP: 6
SALES (est): 1.4MM **Privately Held**
WEB: www.mineosapio.com
SIC: 2013 5421 Sausages & other prepared meats; meat markets, including freezer provisioners

(G-2867)
MIRION TECH CONAX NUCLEAR INC
Also Called: Ist Conax Nuclear
402 Sonwil Dr (14225-5530)
PHONE................................716 681-1973
Iain Wilson, *CEO*
Mike Freed, *COO*
Jack Pacheco, *CFO*
Mike Brumbaugh, *CIO*
Emmanuelle Lee, *General Counsel*
EMP: 23
SQ FT: 26,200
SALES (est): 4.8MM **Privately Held**
WEB: www.mirion.com
SIC: 3829 Nuclear radiation & testing apparatus
HQ: Mirion Technologies (Ist) Corporation
　　315 Daniel Zenker Dr # 204
　　Horseheads NY 14845
　　607 562-4300

(G-2868)
MOBILEAPP SYSTEMS LLC
4 Grand View Trl (14217)
PHONE................................716 667-2780
EMP: 5 EST: 2012
SALES (est): 310.6K **Privately Held**
SIC: 7372 Prepackaged software

(G-2869)
MOD-PAC CORP (PA)
1801 Elmwood Ave Ste 1 (14207-2496)
PHONE................................716 898-8480
Kevin T Keane, *Ch of Bd*
Daniel G Keane, *President*
Robert J McKenna, *Principal*
Howard Zemsky, *Principal*

▲ = Import ▼=Export
◆ =Import/Export

David B Lupp, *COO*
◆ **EMP:** 160
SQ FT: 333,000
SALES: 59.2MM **Privately Held**
WEB: www.modpac.com
SIC: 2657 5999 Food containers, folding:
 made from purchased material; alarm &
 safety equipment stores

(G-2870)
MOD-PAC CORP
 1801 Elmwood Ave Ste 1 (14207-2496)
 P.O. Box 1907, Blasdell (14219-0107)
PHONE.............................716 447-9013
Leo Eckman, *Manager*
EMP: 100
SALES (corp-wide): 59.2MM **Privately
Held**
WEB: www.modpac.com
SIC: 2754 2752 Commercial printing,
 gravure; commercial printing, lithographic
PA: Mod-Pac Corp.
 1801 Elmwood Ave Ste 1
 Buffalo NY 14207
 716 898-8480

(G-2871)
MONO-SYSTEMS INC
 180 Hopkins St (14220-1854)
PHONE.............................716 821-1344
Jim Sutton, *Manager*
EMP: 30
SALES (corp-wide): 16.9MM **Privately
Held**
WEB: www.monosystems.com
SIC: 3443 3643 3549 Cable trays, metal
 plate; current-carrying wiring devices;
 metalworking machinery
PA: Mono-Systems, Inc.
 4 International Dr # 280
 Rye Brook NY 10573
 914 934-2075

(G-2872)
**MOOGS MEDICAL DEVICES
GROUP**
 251 Seneca St (14204-2013)
PHONE.............................716 652-2000
Martin Berardi, *President*
George Cameron, *Vice Pres*
John Manzella, *Engineer*
John Schaf, *Engineer*
Jennifer Walter, *Controller*
▲ **EMP:** 6
SALES (est): 166.8K **Privately Held**
SIC: 3841 5047 Inhalation therapy equip-
 ment; medical & hospital equipment

(G-2873)
MRI NORTHTOWNS GROUP PC
Also Called: Northtown Imaging
 199 Park Club Ln Ste 300 (14221-5269)
PHONE.............................716 836-4646
James Rinaldi, *Manager*
EMP: 11
SALES (corp-wide): 2.2MM **Privately
Held**
WEB: www.lockportmri.com
SIC: 3231 Medical & laboratory glassware:
 made from purchased glass
PA: Mri Northtown's Group Pc
 1020 Youngs Rd Ste 120w
 Williamsville NY 14221
 716 689-4406

(G-2874)
MULLER TOOL INC
 74 Anderson Rd (14225-4979)
PHONE.............................716 895-3658
Gary D Reisweber, *President*
Bruce Reisweber, *Vice Pres*
Paul Banko, *QC Mgr*
EMP: 20 **EST:** 1941
SQ FT: 12,000
SALES (est): 3.3MM **Privately Held**
WEB: www.mullertool.com
SIC: 3599 3451 Machine shop, jobbing &
 repair; screw machine products

(G-2875)
MULTISORB TECH INTL LLC (PA)
 325 Harlem Rd (14224-1825)
PHONE.............................716 824-8900
James Renda, *President*
Mark Wilger, *Warehouse Mgr*
Sarah Cook, *Opers Staff*

Peter Taliaferro, *Production*
Nicholas Wawrowski, *Production*
EMP: 1
SALES (est): 30.6MM **Privately Held**
SIC: 2819 Industrial inorganic chemicals

(G-2876)
**MULTISORB TECHNOLOGIES
INC**
Also Called: Ecto Tech Automation
 10 French Rd (14227)
PHONE.............................716 656-1402
John S Cullen, *CEO*
EMP: 30
SALES (corp-wide): 320.9MM **Privately
Held**
SIC: 2819 Industrial inorganic chemicals
HQ: Multisorb Technologies, Inc.
 325 Harlem Rd
 Buffalo NY 14224
 716 824-8900

(G-2877)
MUNSCHAUER INC
 330 Greene St (14206-1025)
 P.O. Box 686 (14240-0686)
PHONE.............................716 895-8888
Grace W Munschauer, *Ch of Bd*
Grace Munschauer, *President*
EMP: 16 **EST:** 2008
SALES (est): 3MM **Privately Held**
SIC: 3442 Window & door frames

(G-2878)
N MAKE MOLD INC
Also Called: Chocolate Delivery Systems
 85 River Rock Dr Ste 202 (14207-2170)
PHONE.............................716 877-3146
Timothy Thill, *President*
▲ **EMP:** 50
SALES (est): 16MM
SALES (corp-wide): 16.6MM **Privately
Held**
SIC: 2064 Candy bars, including chocolate
 covered bars
PA: Chocolate Delivery Systems, Inc.
 1800 Elmwood Ave
 Buffalo NY 14207
 716 877-3146

(G-2879)
NAS QUICK SIGN INC
Also Called: North American Signs Buffalo
 1628 Elmwood Ave (14207-3014)
PHONE.............................716 876-7599
Frank Strada, *President*
Agnes Strada, *Shareholder*
EMP: 9
SQ FT: 7,000
SALES (est): 1.3MM **Privately Held**
SIC: 3993 Signs, not made in custom sign
 painting shops; electric signs

(G-2880)
NEW AVON LLC
 433 Thorncliff Rd (14223-1128)
PHONE.............................716 572-4842
Kathy Gleason, *Principal*
EMP: 12 **Privately Held**
SIC: 2844 Toilet preparations
HQ: New Avon Llc
 1 Liberty Plz Fl 25
 New York NY 10006
 212 282-6000

(G-2881)
**NEW BUFFALO SHIRT FACTORY
INC**
 1979 Harlem Rd (14212-2410)
PHONE.............................716 436-5839
John Weiss, *President*
David Swart, *Director*
Pamela Thayer, *Director*
EMP: 8
SQ FT: 14,000
SALES: 1MM **Privately Held**
SIC: 2759 Screen printing

(G-2882)
NEW ERA CAP CO INC
 160 Delaware Ave (14202-2404)
PHONE.............................716 604-9000
Michael Thorton, *Manager*
EMP: 300

SALES (corp-wide): 606.1MM **Privately
Held**
WEB: www.neweracap.com
SIC: 2353 Uniform hats & caps; baseball
 caps
PA: New Era Cap Co., Inc.
 160 Delaware Ave
 Buffalo NY 14202
 716 604-9000

(G-2883)
NEW ERA CAP CO INC (PA)
 160 Delaware Ave (14202-2404)
PHONE.............................716 604-9000
Christopher Koch, *Ch of Bd*
Peter M Augustine, *President*
Valerie Koch, *Corp Secy*
Jessica Mahoney, *Production*
Denise Tatford, *Production*
◆ **EMP:** 326 **EST:** 1920
SQ FT: 120,000
SALES (est): 606.1MM **Privately Held**
WEB: www.neweracap.com
SIC: 2353 Uniform hats & caps; baseball
 caps

(G-2884)
NIAGARA FIBERGLASS INC
 88 Okell St (14220-2133)
 P.O. Box 1088 (14220-8088)
PHONE.............................716 822-3921
Stephen Gale, *President*
Philip O'Donnell, *Vice Pres*
EMP: 45
SQ FT: 23,000
SALES: 2.3MM **Privately Held**
SIC: 3089 3544 Molding primary plastic;
 special dies, tools, jigs & fixtures

(G-2885)
NIAGARA GEAR CORPORATION
 941 Military Rd (14217-2590)
PHONE.............................716 874-3131
Matthew Babisz, *President*
Robert C Barden, *Vice Pres*
Marcia Iore, *Finance Mgr*
EMP: 25 **EST:** 1952
SQ FT: 30,000
SALES (est): 4.2MM **Privately Held**
WEB: www.niagaragear.com
SIC: 3566 Gears, power transmission, ex-
 cept automotive

(G-2886)
NIAGARA PUNCH & DIE CORP
 176 Gruner Rd (14227-1090)
PHONE.............................716 896-7619
Jay Czerniak, *President*
Jean Czerniak, *Admin Sec*
EMP: 8 **EST:** 1956
SQ FT: 5,000
SALES (est): 1.7MM **Privately Held**
WEB: www.npd123.com
SIC: 3544 Special dies & tools

(G-2887)
NIAGARA TRANSFORMER CORP
 1747 Dale Rd (14225-4964)
 P.O. Box 233 (14225-0233)
PHONE.............................716 896-6500
John F Darby, *President*
Sheldon Kennedy, *Vice Pres*
Stan Hatch, *Opers Mgr*
Rose Joralemon, *Opers Staff*
David Baca, *Engineer*
▲ **EMP:** 85 **EST:** 1928
SQ FT: 100,000
SALES (est): 28MM **Privately Held**
WEB: www.niagaratransformer.com
SIC: 3612 Power transformers, electric

(G-2888)
NIAGARA TYING SERVICE INC
 176 Dingens St (14206-2308)
PHONE.............................716 825-0066
Albert J Barrato, *President*
Antoinette Barrato, *Admin Sec*
▲ **EMP:** 38
SALES (est): 5.8MM **Privately Held**
WEB: www.niagaratyingservice.com
SIC: 2013 Sausage casings, natural

(G-2889)
**NICKEL CITY STUDIOS PHOTO
JOUR**
 45 Linwood Ave (14209-2203)
PHONE.............................716 200-0956
Rich Mattingly, *Principal*
EMP: 5
SALES (est): 430.3K **Privately Held**
SIC: 3356 Nickel

(G-2890)
NORAZZA INC
 3938 Broadway St (14227-1104)
PHONE.............................716 706-1160
Thomas J Sperazza, *CEO*
Gregory Tramont, *Controller*
Kevin Bowman, *VP Sales*
▲ **EMP:** 10
SALES (est): 2.5MM **Privately Held**
WEB: www.norazza.com
SIC: 3577 3861 Computer peripheral
 equipment; photographic equipment &
 supplies

(G-2891)
NORSE ENERGY CORP USA
 3556 Lake Shore Rd # 700 (14219-1445)
PHONE.............................716 568-2048
EMP: 5 **EST:** 1993
SALES (est): 690K **Privately Held**
SIC: 1382 Oil/Gas Exploration Services

(G-2892)
**NORTHROP GRUMMAN INTL
TRDG INC**
Also Called: Land Self Prtction Systems Div
 1740 Wehrle Dr (14221-7032)
PHONE.............................716 626-7233
Brian Schmidt, *Sales Staff*
Joe Downie, *Manager*
Joseph Downie, *Director*
EMP: 6
SALES (est): 569.5K **Publicly Held**
SIC: 3699 Flight simulators (training aids),
 electronic
HQ: Northrop Grumman Overseas Holding,
 Inc.
 2980 Fairview Park Dr
 Falls Church VA 22042
 703 280-4069

(G-2893)
**NORTHROP GRUMMAN
SYSTEMS CORP**
 1740 Wehrle Dr (14221-7032)
PHONE.............................716 626-4600
Angelo Genco, *General Mgr*
Tim Green, *Principal*
Lisa Lane, *Opers Mgr*
Walter Bird, *Engineer*
Kevin Ditondo, *Engineer*
EMP: 99 **Publicly Held**
SIC: 3812 Search & navigation equipment
HQ: Northrop Grumman Systems Corpora-
 tion
 2980 Fairview Park Dr
 Falls Church VA 22042
 703 280-2900

(G-2894)
**OEHLERS WLDG &
FABRICATION INC**
 242 Elk St (14210-2102)
PHONE.............................716 821-1800
Mark Appelbaum, *President*
EMP: 15
SQ FT: 45,000
SALES: 1.4MM **Privately Held**
SIC: 3441 Fabricated structural metal

(G-2895)
**OERLIKON BLZERS CATING
USA INC**
 6000 N Bailey Ave Ste 3 (14226-5102)
PHONE.............................716 564-8557
John Jesnowski, *Branch Mgr*
EMP: 30
SALES (corp-wide): 2.6B **Privately Held**
WEB: www.balzers.com
SIC: 3479 3471 Coating of metals &
 formed products; finishing, metals or
 formed products

GEOGRAPHIC

HQ: Oerlikon Balzers Coating Usa Inc.
1700 E Golf Rd Ste 200
Schaumburg IL 60173
847 619-5541

(G-2896)
OLIVER GEAR INC
1120 Niagara St (14213-1790)
PHONE.............................716 885-1080
Sam Haines, *President*
Mike Barron, *Vice Pres*
Barbara Stone, *CFO*
EMP: 25
SQ FT: 21,000
SALES (est): 6MM
SALES (corp-wide): 18MM **Privately Held**
WEB: www.gearmotions.com
SIC: 3566 7699 Gears, power transmission, except automotive; industrial equipment services
PA: Gear Motions Incorporated
1750 Milton Ave
Syracuse NY 13209
315 488-0100

(G-2897)
ONEIDA SALES & SERVICE INC
Also Called: Oneida Concrete Products
155 Commerce Dr (14218-1041)
PHONE.............................716 822-8205
Frederick Saia, *President*
EMP: 40
SALES (est): 9.5MM **Privately Held**
WEB: www.oneidagroup.com
SIC: 3531 1799 3496 Concrete plants; fence construction; miscellaneous fabricated wire products

(G-2898)
ONY INC BAIRD RESEARCHPARK
1576 Sweet Home Rd (14228-2710)
PHONE.............................716 636-9096
Edmond Egan, *President*
Cathleen Conley, *Business Mgr*
EMP: 30 EST: 2010
SALES (est): 1.7MM **Privately Held**
SIC: 2834 Druggists' preparations (pharmaceuticals)

(G-2899)
ORBITAL HOLDINGS INC
2775 Broadway St Ste 200 (14227-1043)
PHONE.............................951 360-7100
Jerry Jacobs, *Vice Pres*
▲ EMP: 20
SQ FT: 35,160
SALES (est): 3MM **Privately Held**
WEB: www.avf.com
SIC: 3449 3429 Miscellaneous metalwork; manufactured hardware (general)
HQ: Avf Group Inc.
2775 Broadway St Ste 200
Cheektowaga NY 14227

(G-2900)
OTIS BEDDING MFG CO INC (PA)
80 James E Casey Dr (14206-2367)
PHONE.............................716 825-2599
John Roma Sr, *President*
John Roma Jr, *Vice Pres*
Carol Roma, *Treasurer*
▲ EMP: 20 EST: 1882
SQ FT: 40,000
SALES (est): 2.5MM **Privately Held**
WEB: www.otisbed.com
SIC: 2515 5712 Mattresses, innerspring or box spring; mattresses

(G-2901)
P & G STEEL PRODUCTS CO INC
54 Gruner Rd (14227-1092)
PHONE.............................716 896-7900
David E Ponkow, *Chairman*
Andrew Ponkow, *Exec VP*
Thomas Brush, *CFO*
▲ EMP: 100 EST: 1955
SQ FT: 75,000
SALES: 25MM **Privately Held**
WEB: www.pgsteel.com
SIC: 3469 3544 4961 Stamping metal for the trade; special dies, tools, jigs & fixtures; steam & air-conditioning supply

(G-2902)
P J R INDUSTRIES INC
Also Called: Southside Precast Products
1951 Hamburg Tpke Ste 17 (14218-1047)
PHONE.............................716 825-9300
Richard Workman, *President*
Paul Rossi, *CFO*
EMP: 32
SQ FT: 18,500
SALES: 3.5MM **Privately Held**
WEB: www.southsideprecast.com
SIC: 3272 Concrete products, precast

(G-2903)
P P I BUSINESS FORMS INC
94 Spaulding St (14220-1238)
PHONE.............................716 825-1241
Fax: 716 685-4740
EMP: 9
SQ FT: 9,500
SALES (est): 900K **Privately Held**
SIC: 2761 Manifold Busines Forms

(G-2904)
PACKAGE PRINT TECHNOLOGIES
1831 Niagara St (14207-3112)
PHONE.............................716 871-9905
Kim Koehler, *President* .
Tony Collini, *General Mgr*
▲ EMP: 10
SQ FT: 5,000
SALES (est): 3.7MM **Privately Held**
WEB: www.packageprinttech.com
SIC: 3555 3069 Printing trades machinery; printers' rolls & blankets: rubber or rubberized fabric

(G-2905)
PAR-FOAM PRODUCTS INC
239 Van Rensselaer St (14210-1345)
PHONE.............................716 855-2066
Kaushik A Shah, *President*
Rolandd J Neuffer, *Vice Pres*
Kathleen Lopez, *Department Mgr*
Kevin Eick, *Manager*
Timothy Halas, *Loan*
EMP: 130
SQ FT: 64,000
SALES (est): 14.7MM **Privately Held**
SIC: 3069 3714 3086 Foam rubber; motor vehicle parts & accessories; plastics foam products

(G-2906)
PARK AVENUE IMPRINTS LLC (PA)
2955 S Park Ave (14218-2613)
PHONE.............................716 822-5737
James Roorda, *Mng Member*
EMP: 6
SQ FT: 1,200
SALES (est): 592.2K **Privately Held**
SIC: 2759 Screen printing

(G-2907)
PARKSIDE CANDY CO INC (PA)
3208 Main St Ste 1 (14214-1379)
PHONE.............................716 833-7540
Phillip J Buffamonte, *President*
EMP: 17
SALES (est): 1.9MM **Privately Held**
WEB: www.parksidecandy.com
SIC: 2066 5441 Chocolate bars, solid; chocolate candy, solid; candy

(G-2908)
PARRINELLO PRINTING INC
84 Aero Dr (14225-1435)
PHONE.............................716 633-7780
Colleen Parrinello, *President*
EMP: 14
SALES (est): 2.1MM **Privately Held**
SIC: 2752 Commercial printing, offset

(G-2909)
PDI CONE CO INC
Also Called: Dutchtreat
69 Leddy St (14210-2134)
PHONE.............................716 825-8750
Geoge Page, *Principal*
EMP: 67
SALES (est): 8.2MM **Privately Held**
SIC: 2052 Cones, ice cream

(G-2910)
PELLICANO SPECIALTY FOODS INC
195 Reading St (14220-2157)
P.O. Box 34, Lake View (14085-0034)
PHONE.............................716 822-2366
Mario Pellicano, *President*
Jim Kalec, *Vice Pres*
EMP: 18 EST: 1996
SALES: 4MM **Privately Held**
SIC: 2099 Food preparations

(G-2911)
PENINSULA PLASTICS LTD
161 Marine Dr Apt 6e (14202-4214)
P.O. Box 1179 (14202)
PHONE.............................716 854-3050
Craig Bolton, *Owner*
EMP: 54
SALES (est): 2.1MM **Privately Held**
WEB: www.penplast.com
SIC: 3089 Injection molding of plastics

(G-2912)
PEOPLES CHOICE M R I
125 Galileo Dr (14221-2776)
PHONE.............................716 681-7377
Vafeem Iqbal, *President*
Vaseem Iqbal, *Med Doctor*
EMP: 10
SALES (est): 827.1K **Privately Held**
WEB: www.peoplesmri.com
SIC: 3577 Magnetic ink & optical scanning devices

(G-2913)
PERAFLEX HOSE INC
155 Great Arrow Ave Ste 4 (14207-3010)
PHONE.............................716 876-8806
Newell Kraik, *President*
Mark Montgomery, *Director*
▲ EMP: 15
SQ FT: 13,000
SALES (est): 2.9MM **Privately Held**
WEB: www.peraflex.com
SIC: 3052 5085 Rubber & plastics hose & beltings; industrial supplies

(G-2914)
PERKINS INTERNATIONAL INC (HQ)
672 Delaware Ave (14209-2202)
PHONE.............................309 675-1000
Michael J Baunton, *CEO*
Dan Hagan, *Analyst*
EMP: 5
SALES (est): 3.1MM
SALES (corp-wide): 54.7B **Publicly Held**
WEB: www.tuckaway.com
SIC: 3519 Internal combustion engines
PA: Caterpillar Inc.
510 Lake Cook Rd Ste 100
Deerfield IL 60015
224 551-4000

(G-2915)
PERMA TECH INC
363 Hamburg St (14204-2086)
PHONE.............................716 854-0707
Richard E Lund Jr, *President*
EMP: 22
SQ FT: 45,000
SALES (est): 3MM **Privately Held**
WEB: www.permatechinc.com
SIC: 2394 3441 3089 Awnings, fabric: made from purchased materials; fabricated structural metal; doors, folding: plastic or plastic coated fabric

(G-2916)
PHILCOM LTD
1144 Military Rd (14217-2232)
PHONE.............................716 875-8005
Bruce G Phillips, *Ch of Bd*
Karen Phillips, *Vice Pres*
EMP: 1
SALES (est): 3.8MM **Privately Held**
SIC: 3089 Boxes, plastic

(G-2917)
PHILPAC CORPORATION (PA)
1144 Military Rd (14217-2232)
PHONE.............................716 875-8005
Bruce G Phillips, *President*
Karen Phillips, *Corp Secy*

Jason Sleggs, *Sales Staff*
Shannon Dunn, *Manager*
Stephen Dysert, *Manager*
EMP: 50
SALES (est): 14.1MM **Privately Held**
SIC: 2653 5085 3086 2655 Boxes, corrugated: made from purchased materials; packing, industrial; padding, foamed plastic; fiber cans, drums & similar products; nailed wood boxes & shook

(G-2918)
PIERCE ARROW DRAPERY MFG
Also Called: Pierce Arrow Draperies
1685 Elmwood Ave Ste 312 (14207-2435)
PHONE.............................716 876-3023
Robert Merkel, *President*
EMP: 5
SQ FT: 2,000
SALES (est): 526.5K **Privately Held**
SIC: 2221 Draperies & drapery fabrics, manmade fiber & silk

(G-2919)
PII HOLDINGS INC (DH)
2150 Elmwood Ave (14207-1910)
PHONE.............................716 876-9951
Mike McLelland, *CEO*
Ray Baran, *Treasurer*
EMP: 2
SALES (est): 208MM
SALES (corp-wide): 2.9B **Privately Held**
SIC: 3089 3822 6719 Molding primary plastic; temperature controls, automatic; investment holding companies, except banks
HQ: Berwind Consolidated Holdings, Inc.
3000 Ctr Sq W 1500 Mkt St
Philadelphia PA 19102
215 563-2800

(G-2920)
PLANT SCIENCE LABORATORIES LLC
649 Wyoming Ave (14215-2631)
PHONE.............................716 228-4553
Mike Tarnharb, *Mng Member*
EMP: 6
SALES (est): 1MM **Privately Held**
SIC: 2833 Vitamins, natural or synthetic: bulk, uncompounded

(G-2921)
PLASLOK CORP
3155 Broadway St (14227-1034)
PHONE.............................716 681-7755
Richard A Neil, *President*
EMP: 43
SQ FT: 75,000
SALES: 7MM **Privately Held**
SIC: 2821 Molding compounds, plastics

(G-2922)
PLASTIC SYS/GR BFLO INC
465 Cornwall Ave (14215-3125)
PHONE.............................716 835-7555
Daniel McNamara, *President*
Sean Lobue, *General Mgr*
EMP: 5 EST: 1980
SQ FT: 9,200
SALES (est): 697.1K **Privately Held**
WEB: www.plasticsystems.com
SIC: 3089 Plastic containers, except foam; trays, plastic; thermoformed finished plastic products; cases, plastic

(G-2923)
POINTMAN LLC (PA)
Also Called: Swremote
403 Main St Ste 200 (14203-2107)
PHONE.............................716 842-1439
Stephen Kiernan, *President*
Steven B Raines, *COO*
Steven Raines, *Vice Pres*
Sean Briceland, *Software Engr*
Steve Kiernan, *Director*
EMP: 5
SQ FT: 18,000
SALES: 1.6MM **Privately Held**
SIC: 7372 5734 5045 Business oriented computer software; software, business & non-game; computer software

▲ = Import ▼=Export
◆ =Import/Export

(G-2924)
POL-TEK INDUSTRIES LTD
2300 Clinton St (14227-1735)
PHONE................................716 823-1502
Martin Ostrowski, *CEO*
Wanda Ostrowski, *Corp Secy*
Natalie Handzlik, *Office Mgr*
EMP: 15
SQ FT: 11,000
SALES (est): 2MM **Privately Held**
WEB: www.pol-tek.com
SIC: 3599 Machine shop, jobbing & repair

(G-2925)
POWER UP MANUFACTURING INC
275 N Pointe Pkwy Ste 100 (14228-1895)
PHONE................................716 876-4890
Dean T Wright, *President*
◆ **EMP:** 25
SQ FT: 15,000
SALES (est): 3.5MM **Privately Held**
WEB: www.powerupmfg.com
SIC: 3069 Battery boxes, jars or parts,
hard rubber

(G-2926)
POWERFLOW INC
1714 Broadway St (14212-2090)
P.O. Box 905 (14240-0905)
PHONE................................716 892-1014
Douglas K Ward, *Ch of Bd*
▲ **EMP:** 66 **EST:** 1978
SQ FT: 55,000
SALES: 33MM **Privately Held**
WEB: www.powerflowinc.com
SIC: 3714 Motor vehicle parts & acces-
sories

(G-2927)
PRAXAIR DISTRIBUTION INC
345 Evans St Apt A (14221-5654)
PHONE................................716 879-2185
Ken Genova, *Engineer*
Matthew Mooney, *Engineer*
Oscar Ashu Eta Jr, *Branch Mgr*
Kehinde Akinyemi, *Administration*
Jennifer Linker, *Analyst*
EMP: 5 **Privately Held**
SIC: 2813 Industrial gases
HQ: Praxair Distribution, Inc.
10 Riverview Dr
Danbury CT 06810
203 837-2000

(G-2928)
PRECISION PHOTO-FAB INC
Also Called: Switzer
4020 Jeffrey Blvd (14219-2393)
PHONE................................716 821-9393
Bernie Switzer, *President*
Joseph Dunlop, *Vice Pres*
Adam Switzer, *Vice Pres*
EMP: 55
SQ FT: 20,000
SALES (est): 12.4MM **Privately Held**
WEB: www.precisionphotofab.com
SIC: 3469 Metal stampings

(G-2929)
PRECISION SPCLTY FBRCTIONS LLC
51 N Gates Ave (14218-1029)
PHONE................................716 824-2108
Dennis Switzer,
John Maher,
EMP: 20
SALES (est): 2.9MM **Privately Held**
SIC: 3441 Fabricated structural metal

(G-2930)
PREMIER MACHINING TECH INC
2100 Old Union Rd (14227-2725)
PHONE................................716 608-1311
William G Belcher, *President*
Kimberly Belcher, *Admin Sec*
EMP: 8
SQ FT: 18,500
SALES: 1.2MM **Privately Held**
SIC: 3599 Machine shop, jobbing & repair

(G-2931)
PRINCE RUBBER & PLAS CO INC (PA)
137 Arthur St (14207-2098)
PHONE................................225 272-1653
S Warren Prince Jr, *Ch of Bd*
John G Putnam, *Admin Sec*
▲ **EMP:** 45
SQ FT: 35,000
SALES (est): 10.7MM **Privately Held**
WEB: www.princerp.com
SIC: 3069 3089 3084 3053 Hard rubber
& molded rubber products; plastic pro-
cessing; plastics pipe; gaskets, packing &
sealing devices

(G-2932)
PRINTED IMAGE
1906 Clinton St (14206-3206)
PHONE................................716 821-1880
Richard Zavarella, *Owner*
EMP: 5
SQ FT: 3,000
SALES (est): 496.2K **Privately Held**
SIC: 2752 Commercial printing, litho-
graphic

(G-2933)
PRINTING PREP INC
707 Washington St (14203-1308)
PHONE................................716 852-5011
Harold S Leader, *President*
John Wulf, *Executive*
EMP: 32
SQ FT: 11,365
SALES (corp-wide): 2.6MM **Privately
Held**
WEB: www.printleader.us
SIC: 2752 Commercial printing, litho-
graphic
PA: Printing Prep, Inc
12 E Tupper St
Buffalo NY
716 852-5011

(G-2934)
PRO-GEAR CO INC
1120 Niagara St (14213-1714)
PHONE................................716 684-3811
Gary Rackley, *President*
EMP: 5
SQ FT: 6,500
SALES (est): 377.2K
SALES (corp-wide): 18MM **Privately
Held**
SIC: 3462 Gears, forged steel
PA: Gear Motions Incorporated
1750 Milton Ave
Syracuse NY 13209
315 488-0100

(G-2935)
PROMETHEUS BOOKS INC
25 Chapel Woods (14221-1812)
PHONE................................716 691-0133
Jonathan Kurtz, *President*
▲ **EMP:** 30
SALES (est): 3.2MM **Privately Held**
WEB: www.prometheusbooks.com
SIC: 2731 Books: publishing only

(G-2936)
PROTECTIVE INDUSTRIES INC (DH)
Also Called: Caplugs
2150 Elmwood Ave (14207-1910)
PHONE................................716 876-9951
David Williams, *President*
Rob Kennery, *Vice Pres*
Brad Longstreth, *Vice Pres*
Kennery Rob, *Vice Pres*
James Ray, *VP Opers*
◆ **EMP:** 343
SQ FT: 80,000
SALES (est): 208MM
SALES (corp-wide): 2.9B **Privately Held**
WEB: www.mokon.com
SIC: 3089 3822 Molding primary plastic;
temperature controls, automatic
HQ: Pii Holdings, Inc.
2150 Elmwood Ave
Buffalo NY 14207
716 876-9951

(G-2937)
PROTECTIVE INDUSTRIES INC
Mokon
2510 Elmwood Ave (14217-2223)
PHONE................................716 876-9951
Robert Kennery, *General Mgr*
EMP: 55
SALES (corp-wide): 2.9B **Privately Held**
WEB: www.mokon.com
SIC: 3822 Temperature controls, automatic
HQ: Protective Industries, Inc.
2150 Elmwood Ave
Buffalo NY 14207
716 876-9951

(G-2938)
PVS CHEMICAL SOLUTIONS INC
55 Lee St (14210-2109)
PHONE................................716 825-5762
Patrick Murphy, *Opers Mgr*
Chris Cancilla, *Facilities Mgr*
Jane Lamanna, *Engineer*
Brice Eidson, *Personnel Assit*
EMP: 51
SALES (corp-wide): 558.5MM **Privately
Held**
SIC: 2819 2899 Sulfur chloride; chemical
preparations
HQ: Pvs Chemical Solutions, Inc.
10900 Harper Ave
Detroit MI 48213

(G-2939)
QLS SOLUTIONS GROUP INC
701 Seneca St Ste 600 (14210-1361)
PHONE................................716 852-2203
Gary Skalyo, *President*
EMP: 24
SQ FT: 30,000
SALES (est): 4.3MM **Privately Held**
WEB: www.qualitylaser.com
SIC: 3955 3861 Print cartridges for laser &
other computer printers; reproduction ma-
chines & equipment

(G-2940)
QTA MACHINING INC
Also Called: Quick Turn Around Machining
876 Bailey Ave (14206-2300)
PHONE................................716 862-8108
Suzanne M Pelczynski, *President*
Roxanne Pelczynski, *Vice Pres*
EMP: 12
SQ FT: 10,000
SALES (est): 2.1MM **Privately Held**
WEB: www.qtanow.com
SIC: 3599 Machine shop, jobbing & repair

(G-2941)
QUAKER BONNET INC
54 Irving Pl (14201-1521)
PHONE................................716 885-7208
Elizabeth Kolken, *President*
Ben Kolken, *Vice Pres*
EMP: 5 **EST:** 1930
SQ FT: 4,400
SALES (est): 494.2K **Privately Held**
WEB: www.quakerbonnet.com
SIC: 2051 2052 2024 Bakery: wholesale
or wholesale/retail combined; cookies; ice
cream & frozen desserts

(G-2942)
QUALITY BINDERY SERVICE INC
501 Amherst St (14207-2913)
PHONE................................716 883-5185
Kathleen Hartmans, *President*
EMP: 34
SQ FT: 4,000
SALES (est): 4.1MM **Privately Held**
SIC: 2789 Trade binding services

(G-2943)
QUEEN CITY MALTING LLC
644 N Forest Rd (14221-4965)
PHONE................................716 481-1313
Joseph S Kirby Jr, *CEO*
EMP: 7
SALES (est): 262.8K **Privately Held**
SIC: 2083 Malt

(G-2944)
QUEEN CITY MANUFACTURING INC
333 Henderson Ave (14217-1538)
PHONE................................716 877-1102
Robert Maranto, *President*
Joseph Mallare, *Vice Pres*
Steve Nappo, *Vice Pres*
▲ **EMP:** 5
SALES (est): 1.4MM **Privately Held**
WEB: www.queencitymanufacturing.com
SIC: 2821 Melamine resins, melamine-
formaldehyde

(G-2945)
R & A INDUSTRIAL PRODUCTS
Also Called: R&A Prods
30 Cornelia St (14210-1202)
PHONE................................716 823-4300
Tony Onello, *President*
EMP: 5
SQ FT: 2,600
SALES: 376.6K **Privately Held**
SIC: 3061 Mechanical rubber goods

(G-2946)
R & B MACHINERY CORP
400 Kennedy Rd Ste 3 (14227-1073)
PHONE................................716 894-3332
Fax: 716 894-3335
EMP: 4
SQ FT: 28,000
SALES (est): 2.2MM **Privately Held**
SIC: 3559 Mfg Misc Industry Machinery

(G-2947)
RAPID RAYS PRINTING & COPYING
300 Broadway St (14204-1433)
P.O. Box 442 (14205-0442)
PHONE................................716 852-0550
Raymond Wellence, *President*
Kathleen Wellence, *Vice Pres*
EMP: 9 **EST:** 1973
SQ FT: 4,100
SALES (est): 1.1MM **Privately Held**
WEB: www.rapidrays.com
SIC: 2752 Commercial printing, offset

(G-2948)
RAPID SERVICE ENGRAVING CO
1593 Genesee St (14211-1634)
PHONE................................716 896-4555
James F Egloff, *President*
John F Egloff, *Admin Sec*
EMP: 6
SQ FT: 6,000
SALES (est): 578.8K **Privately Held**
SIC: 2796 2752 Photoengraving plates,
linecuts or halftones; commercial printing,
lithographic

(G-2949)
RAPISTAK CORPORATION
1 Alliance Dr (14218-2529)
PHONE................................716 822-2804
Nathan Pautorek, *CEO*
EMP: 7
SALES (est): 1.7MM **Privately Held**
WEB: www.rapistak.com
SIC: 3531 Dozers, tractor mounted: mate-
rial moving

(G-2950)
REALTIMETRADERSCOM
1325 N Forest Rd Ste 240 (14221-2143)
P.O. Box 387, Getzville (14068-0387)
PHONE................................716 632-6600
Andrew Marthiasan, *President*
EMP: 33 **EST:** 1995
SQ FT: 2,000
SALES (est): 1.4MM **Privately Held**
SIC: 2711 7375 Newspapers; information
retrieval services

(G-2951)
REIMANN & GEORGER CORPORATION
1849 Harlem Rd (14212-2401)
PHONE................................716 895-1156
E Eric Von Dungen, *Principal*
Donna Cooke, *Supervisor*
▲ **EMP:** 42
SQ FT: 38,000

G
E
O
G
R
A
P
H
I
C

SALES (est): 17.7MM **Privately Held**
WEB: www.rgcproducts.com
SIC: 3536 3546 Hoists; boat lifts; power-driven handtools

(G-2952)
REUSE ACTION INCORPORATED
279 Northampton St (14208-2304)
PHONE..................................716 949-0900
Michael Gainer, *Principal*
EMP: 5
SALES (est): 579.6K **Privately Held**
SIC: 3822 Building services monitoring controls, automatic

(G-2953)
RICH HOLDINGS INC
1 Robert Rich Way (14213-1701)
PHONE..................................716 878-8000
Christopher T Dunstan, *Principal*
◆ **EMP:** 75
SALES (est): 7.5MM **Privately Held**
SIC: 2053 Frozen bakery products, except bread

(G-2954)
RICH PRODUCTS CORPORATION (PA)
1 Robert Rich Way (14213-1701)
P.O. Box 245 (14240-0245)
PHONE..................................716 878-8000
Bill Gisel, *CEO*
Kim Burke, *President*
Ray Burke, *President*
Richard Ferranti, *President*
Jeff Kim, *President*
◆ **EMP:** 1375 **EST:** 1993
SQ FT: 60,000
SALES (est): 3.8B **Privately Held**
WEB: www.richs.com
SIC: 2092 2053 2023 2099 Fresh or frozen packaged fish; shrimp, frozen: prepared; shellfish, frozen: prepared; frozen bakery products, except bread; dry, condensed, evaporated dairy products; whipped topping, dry mix; cream substitutes; dessert mixes & fillings

(G-2955)
RIGIDIZED METALS CORPORATION
Also Called: Rigidized-Metal
658 Ohio St (14203-3185)
PHONE..................................716 849-4703
Richard S Smith Jr, *Ch of Bd*
Richard S Smith III, *President*
James Halliday, *Business Mgr*
Douglas F Lum, *Treasurer*
▲ **EMP:** 48 **EST:** 1940
SQ FT: 58,060
SALES (est): 22.7MM **Privately Held**
WEB: www.rigidized.com
SIC: 3469 3444 2796 Rigidizing metal; sheet metalwork; platemaking services

(G-2956)
RLP HOLDINGS INC
Also Called: Belt Maintenance Systems
1049 Military Rd (14217-2228)
PHONE..................................716 852-0832
Joe Hooley, *President*
Joseph Hooley, *Branch Mgr*
▲ **EMP:** 8
SQ FT: 18,000
SALES (est): 2.4MM **Privately Held**
SIC: 3535 Conveyors & conveying equipment

(G-2957)
ROBERTS-GORDON LLC (DH)
Also Called: RG
1250 William St (14206-1819)
P.O. Box 44 (14240-0044)
PHONE..................................716 852-4400
Mark J Dines, *President*
Richard G Jasiura, *CFO*
Richard Jasiura, *CFO*
Angela Dipasquale, *Controller*
▲ **EMP:** 100 **EST:** 1998
SQ FT: 107,000
SALES (est): 90MM
SALES (corp-wide): 303.1MM **Privately Held**
WEB: www.rg-inc.com
SIC: 3675 3433 Condensers, electronic; unit heaters, domestic

HQ: Specified Air Solutions Llc
1250 William St
Buffalo NY 14206
716 852-4400

(G-2958)
ROBINSON KNIFE
2615 Walden Ave (14225-4735)
PHONE..................................716 685-6300
Robert Skerker, *CEO*
EMP: 11
SALES (est): 1.5MM **Privately Held**
SIC: 3089 Plastic kitchenware, tableware & houseware

(G-2959)
ROCKET COMMUNICATIONS INC
Also Called: Buffalo Rocket
2507 Delaware Ave (14216)
PHONE..................................716 873-2594
David Gallagher, *CEO*
Dennis Gallagher, *Vice Pres*
Dean Gallagher, *Treasurer*
Daryl Gallagher, *Admin Sec*
EMP: 12 **EST:** 1996
SQ FT: 30,000
SALES (est): 727.5K **Privately Held**
WEB: www.buffalorocket.com
SIC: 2711 Newspapers, publishing & printing

(G-2960)
RODGARD CORPORATION
92 Msgr Valente Dr (14206-1822)
PHONE..................................716 852-1435
Richard E Hauck, *Ch of Bd*
EMP: 30
SALES (est): 32.4K
SALES (corp-wide): 803.2MM **Publicly Held**
WEB: www.rodgard.com
SIC: 2821 Elastomers, nonvulcanizable (plastics)
PA: Astronics Corporation
130 Commerce Way
East Aurora NY 14052
716 805-1599

(G-2961)
ROLLERS INC
2495 Main St Ste 359 (14214-2154)
PHONE..................................716 837-0700
Frank Reppenhagen, *Owner*
EMP: 9
SALES (est): 640K **Privately Held**
WEB: www.rollers.com
SIC: 2515 3555 5085 Mattresses, containing felt, foam rubber, urethane, etc.; printing trade parts & attachments; industrial supplies

(G-2962)
ROSINA FOOD PRODUCTS INC (HQ)
Also Called: Ceoentano
170 French Rd (14227-2777)
PHONE..................................716 668-0123
Russell A Corigliano, *Ch of Bd*
James Corigliano, *Ch of Bd*
Rosina Markey, *Principal*
Greg Setter, *Senior VP*
Frank Corigliano, *Vice Pres*
EMP: 178
SQ FT: 60,000
SALES (est): 35.6MM **Privately Held**
SIC: 2013 5812 Sausages & other prepared meats; eating places

(G-2963)
ROSINA HOLDING INC (PA)
170 French Rd (14227-2717)
PHONE..................................716 668-0123
Russell A Corigliano, *Ch of Bd*
Todd Palczewski, *Research*
Frank Corigliano, *Treasurer*
Randy Bernick, *VP Finance*
Dorothy Buchanan, *Credit Staff*
EMP: 3
SQ FT: 40,000
SALES (est): 49.1MM **Privately Held**
SIC: 2013 Sausages & other prepared meats

(G-2964)
ROSS L SPORTS SCREENING INC
2756 Seneca St (14224-1866)
PHONE..................................716 824-5350
Dave Cellino, *Owner*
Jason Cellino, *Sales Staff*
EMP: 15 **EST:** 1973
SALES (est): 477.9K **Privately Held**
SIC: 2759 Screen printing

(G-2965)
ROUGH BROTHERS HOLDING CO (HQ)
Also Called: Sunlight US Co., Inc.
3556 Lake Shore Rd # 100 (14219-1445)
PHONE..................................716 826-6500
Frank Heard, *President*
Paul M Murray, *Senior VP*
Kenneth W Smith, *CFO*
Timothy F Murphy, *Treasurer*
EMP: 8
SALES (est): 113.4MM
SALES (corp-wide): 1B **Publicly Held**
SIC: 3499 3316 3441 3398 Strapping, metal; cold finishing of steel shapes; fabricated structural metal; metal heat treating
PA: Gibraltar Industries, Inc.
3556 Lake Shore Rd # 100
Buffalo NY 14219
716 826-6500

(G-2966)
ROYAL BEDDING CO BUFFALO INC
Also Called: Restonic
201 James E Casey Dr (14206-2363)
PHONE..................................716 895-1414
Thomas Comer Jr, *President*
Shannon Brogan, *Manager*
▲ **EMP:** 25
SQ FT: 110,000
SALES (est): 5MM **Privately Held**
SIC: 2515 Mattresses, innerspring or box spring; box springs, assembled

(G-2967)
RWB CONTROLS INC
471 Connecticut St (14213-2645)
PHONE..................................716 897-4341
Fax: 716 882-1575
EMP: 6
SQ FT: 4,000
SALES (est): 600K **Privately Held**
SIC: 3823 5063 Mfg Industrial Process Control Instruments & Displays

(G-2968)
S & H MACHINE COMPANY INC
83 Clyde Ave (14215-2237)
PHONE..................................716 834-1194
EMP: 5
SQ FT: 5,500
SALES: 400K **Privately Held**
SIC: 3599 Machine Shop

(G-2969)
S J B FABRICATION
430 Kennedy Rd (14227-1032)
PHONE..................................716 895-0281
Sean Brubckman, *Owner*
EMP: 10
SALES (est): 310.1K **Privately Held**
SIC: 7692 Welding repair

(G-2970)
S J MCCULLAGH INC (PA)
Also Called: McCullagh Coffee
245 Swan St (14204-2051)
PHONE..................................716 856-3473
Warren E Emblidge Jr, *President*
Carol Emblidge, *Admin Sec*
▲ **EMP:** 50
SQ FT: 16,000
SALES (est): 11.7MM **Privately Held**
SIC: 2095 5113 5149 Coffee roasting (except by wholesale grocers); cups, disposable plastic & paper; groceries & related products; dried or canned foods; sugar, refined; chocolate

(G-2971)
SAFETEC OF AMERICA INC
887 Kensington Ave (14215-2720)
PHONE..................................716 895-1822

Scott A Weinstein, *CEO*
Peter Weinstein, *Vice Pres*
Anthony Gioia, *Production*
Allyson Devonshire, *Human Res Mgr*
Ken Bianchi, *Sales Executive*
▲ **EMP:** 60
SQ FT: 80,000
SALES: 10.3MM **Privately Held**
WEB: www.safetec.com
SIC: 2842 2834 Specialty cleaning, polishes & sanitation goods; drugs affecting parasitic & infective diseases

(G-2972)
SAFETY-KLEEN SYSTEMS INC
60 Katherine St (14210-2006)
PHONE..................................716 855-2212
James Drozdowski, *Branch Mgr*
EMP: 16
SQ FT: 24,259
SALES (corp-wide): 3.3B **Publicly Held**
SIC: 2992 Re-refining lubricating oils & greases
HQ: Safety-Kleen Systems, Inc.
2600 N Central Expy # 400
Richardson TX 75080
972 265-2000

(G-2973)
SAHLEN PACKING COMPANY INC
318 Howard St (14206-2760)
P.O. Box 280 (14240-0280)
PHONE..................................716 852-8677
Joseph E Sahlen, *Ch of Bd*
Christopher Cauley, *Vice Pres*
David Miller, *Controller*
James Bowen, *CPA*
Mark Battistoni, *Regl Sales Mgr*
▲ **EMP:** 85 **EST:** 1869
SQ FT: 53,789
SALES (est): 15.5MM **Privately Held**
WEB: www.sahlen.com
SIC: 2011 Sausages from meat slaughtered on site; hams & picnics from meat slaughtered on site; bacon, slab & sliced from meat slaughtered on site

(G-2974)
SALIT SPECIALTY REBAR INC
1050 Military Rd (14217-2528)
PHONE..................................716 299-1990
Steven Cohen, *CEO*
Kevin Cornell, *VP Sales*
Sheri Otis, *Manager*
Richard Huza, *Business Dir*
Jeanette Fedkiw, *Admin Asst*
▼ **EMP:** 25
SALES (est): 15MM
SALES (corp-wide): 89.6MM **Privately Held**
SIC: 3441 Fabricated structural metal
PA: Myer Salit Limited
7771 Stanley Ave
Niagara Falls ON L2G 0
905 354-5691

(G-2975)
SCHULER-SUBRA INC
Also Called: Eskay Metal Fabricating
83 Doat St (14211-2048)
PHONE..................................716 893-3100
Jeff Subra, *President*
EMP: 6 **EST:** 1944
SQ FT: 16,500
SALES (est): 648.9K **Privately Held**
WEB: www.specialtystainless.com
SIC: 3441 Fabricated structural metal

(G-2976)
SCHUTTE-BUFFALO HAMMERMILL LLC
Also Called: Schutte-Buffalo Hammer Mill
61 Depot St (14206-2203)
PHONE..................................716 855-1202
Chris Berardi, *President*
Jim Klopfer, *Vice Pres*
Matthew Moliterno, *Engineer*
▲ **EMP:** 25 **EST:** 1933
SQ FT: 22,500
SALES (est): 8.9MM
SALES (corp-wide): 9.5MM **Privately Held**
WEB: www.hammermills.com
SIC: 3531 Hammer mills (rock & ore crushing machines), portable

PA: Mber Ventures, Inc.
61 Depot St
Buffalo NY 14206
716 855-1555

(G-2977)
SCREW COMPRESSOR TECH INC
158 Ridge Rd (14218-1035)
PHONE..................716 827-6600
John Zahner, *President*
EMP: 13
SALES (est): 2.3MM **Privately Held**
SIC: 3563 Air & gas compressors

(G-2978)
SECOND AMENDMENT FOUNDATION
Also Called: Gun Week
267 Linwood Ave Ste A (14209-1816)
PHONE..................716 885-6408
Joseph Tartaro, *President*
Peggy Tartaro, *Editor*
EMP: 5
SALES (corp-wide): 3.9MM **Privately Held**
WEB: www.saf.org
SIC: 2711 Newspapers, publishing & printing
PA: Second Amendment Foundation Inc
12500 Ne 10th Pl
Bellevue WA 98005
425 454-7012

(G-2979)
SERVICE CANVAS CO INC
149 Swan St Unit 155 (14203-2624)
PHONE..................716 853-0558
Jerald H Eron, *President*
EMP: 12 **EST:** 1946
SQ FT: 80,000
SALES (est): 1.2MM **Privately Held**
WEB: www.servicecanvas.com
SIC: 2394 Canopies, fabric: made from purchased materials
PA: Synthetic Textiles Inc
398 Broadway St
Buffalo NY 14204

(G-2980)
SERVICE MFG GROUP INC (PA)
400 Scajaquada St (14211-1722)
PHONE..................716 893-1482
Linda Casoni, *CEO*
Vito Casoni, *President*
Bridget Kashmer, *Info Tech Mgr*
EMP: 12
SQ FT: 150,000
SALES (est): 8.4MM **Privately Held**
WEB: www.t-smg.com
SIC: 3625 3444 Relays & industrial controls; sheet metal specialties, not stamped

(G-2981)
SERVICE MFG GROUP INC
Also Called: Smg Control Systems
400 Scajaquada St (14211-1722)
PHONE..................716 893-1482
George Smith, *Opers-Prdtn-Mfg*
EMP: 35
SALES (est): 4.4MM
SALES (corp-wide): 8.4MM **Privately Held**
WEB: www.t-smg.com
SIC: 3444 Sheet metalwork
PA: The Service Manufacturing Group Inc
400 Scajaquada St
Buffalo NY 14211
716 893-1482

(G-2982)
SIEMENS INDUSTRY INC
85 Northpointe Pkwy Ste 8 (14228-1886)
PHONE..................716 568-0983
Patrick Parlane, *Branch Mgr*
EMP: 50
SALES (corp-wide): 95B **Privately Held**
WEB: www.sibt.com
SIC: 3585 7373 1541 Heating equipment, complete; computer integrated systems design; industrial buildings & warehouses
HQ: Siemens Industry, Inc.
1000 Deerfield Pkwy
Buffalo Grove IL 60089
847 215-1000

(G-2983)
SIMREX CORPORATION
1223 William St (14206-1805)
PHONE..................716 206-0174
Donna Neuperger, *President*
Michael Aquilino, *Exec VP*
Frank Neuperger, *Vice Pres*
Dan Smyntek, *Engineer*
▼ **EMP:** 8
SQ FT: 3,200
SALES (est): 1.3MM **Privately Held**
SIC: 3669 3661 Intercommunication systems, electric; modems

(G-2984)
SMARTPILL CORPORATION
847 Main St (14203-1109)
PHONE..................716 882-0701
David Barthel, *President*
EMP: 31
SQ FT: 7,500
SALES (est): 3.7MM **Privately Held**
WEB: www.smartpill.com
SIC: 3826 Analytical instruments

(G-2985)
SOMERSET PRODUCTION CO LLC
338 Harris Hill Rd # 102 (14221-7470)
PHONE..................716 932-6480
Thomas H O'Neil Jr,
William A Ziegler,
EMP: 7
SQ FT: 6,000
SALES (est): 627.6K **Privately Held**
SIC: 1382 Oil & gas exploration services

(G-2986)
SOMMER AND SONS PRINTING INC
2222 S Park Ave (14220-2296)
P.O. Box 3, Bowmansville (14026-0003)
PHONE..................716 822-4311
EMP: 11
SQ FT: 10,000
SALES (est): 1.6MM **Privately Held**
SIC: 2754 Commercial Printing

(G-2987)
SOPARK CORP (PA)
3300 S Park Ave (14218-3530)
PHONE..................716 822-0434
Gerald Murak, *Ch of Bd*
Kiruba Hanmugam, *President*
Andrea Heinold, *Controller*
▲ **EMP:** 85
SQ FT: 28,000
SALES (est): 11MM **Privately Held**
WEB: www.sopark.com
SIC: 3672 3679 3621 3694 Printed circuit boards; electronic circuits; motors, electric; engine electrical equipment

(G-2988)
SOROC TECHNOLOGY CORP
1051 Clinton St (14206-2823)
PHONE..................716 849-5913
Rudy Cheddie, *President*
EMP: 2
SALES (est): 1MM
SALES (corp-wide): 240.9MM **Privately Held**
WEB: www.soroc.com
SIC: 7372 Prepackaged software
PA: Soroc Technology Inc
607 Chrislea Rd
Woodbridge ON L4L 8
905 265-8000

(G-2989)
SORRENTO LACTALIS INC
2376 S Park Ave (14220-2670)
PHONE..................716 823-6262
John J Zielinski, *CFO*
James Binner, *Manager*
EMP: 11
SALES (est): 767.7K
SALES (corp-wide): 355.8K **Privately Held**
SIC: 2022 Natural cheese
HQ: Lactalis American Group, Inc.
2376 S Park Ave
Buffalo NY 14220
716 823-6262

(G-2990)
SOUND VIDEO SYSTEMS WNY LLC
1720 Military Rd (14217-1148)
PHONE..................716 684-8200
Joseph Caprino,
▲ **EMP:** 10
SALES (est): 1.4MM **Privately Held**
SIC: 3651 Household audio & video equipment

(G-2991)
SPECIFIED AIR SOLUTIONS LLC (HQ)
1250 William St (14206-1819)
P.O. Box 44 (14240-0044)
PHONE..................716 852-4400
Charley Brown, *CEO*
EMP: 26
SALES (est): 90.1MM
SALES (corp-wide): 303.1MM **Privately Held**
SIC: 3585 3567 Heating equipment, complete; paint baking & drying ovens
PA: Madison Industries Holdings Llc
500 W Madison St Ste 3890
Chicago IL 60661
312 277-0156

(G-2992)
STEPHEN M KIERNAN
Also Called: Big Bear
701 Seneca St Ste 300 (14210-1351)
PHONE..................716 836-6300
Stephen M Kiernan, *CEO*
David M Thiemecke, *COO*
EMP: 40
SALES (est): 1.6MM **Privately Held**
SIC: 2395 Embroidery & art needlework

(G-2993)
STETRON INTERNATIONAL INC (PA)
90 Broadway St Ste 1 (14203-1687)
PHONE..................716 854-3443
Edward R Steger, *Ch of Bd*
Monique Steger, *President*
Caroline A Steger, *Exec VP*
Roy T Chao, *Senior VP*
▲ **EMP:** 14
SQ FT: 13,000
SALES (est): 3MM **Privately Held**
WEB: www.stetron.com
SIC: 3679 8734 3676 3674 Electronic circuits; electronic loads & power supplies; electronic switches; testing laboratories; electronic resistors; semiconductors & related devices; printed circuit boards; relays & industrial controls

(G-2994)
STORYBOOKS FOREVER
4 Magnolia Ave (14220-2005)
P.O. Box 1234 (14220-8234)
PHONE..................716 822-7845
Dan Devlin, *Owner*
EMP: 14 **EST:** 2001
SALES (est): 530.2K **Privately Held**
SIC: 2731 Book publishing

(G-2995)
SUIT-KOTE CORPORATION
505 Como Park Blvd (14227-1605)
PHONE..................716 683-8850
Gary Thompson, *Branch Mgr*
Brandon Padbury, *Manager*
EMP: 15
SALES (corp-wide): 272.8MM **Privately Held**
WEB: www.suit-kote.com
SIC: 2843 Surface active agents
PA: Suit-Kote Corporation
1911 Lorings Crossing Rd
Cortland NY 13045
607 753-1100

(G-2996)
SUPER PRICE CHOPPER INC
1580 Genesee St (14211-1635)
PHONE..................716 893-3323
AK Kaid, *President*
EMP: 11
SALES (est): 485.7K **Privately Held**
SIC: 3751 Motorcycles & related parts

(G-2997)
SURMET CERAMICS CORPORATION
699 Hertel Ave Ste 290 (14207-2341)
PHONE..................716 875-4091
Timothy Davis, *CEO*
EMP: 17
SALES (est): 2MM
SALES (corp-wide): 11.5MM **Privately Held**
SIC: 3297 Graphite refractories: carbon bond or ceramic bond
PA: Surmet, Corp.
31 B St
Burlington MA 01803
781 345-5721

(G-2998)
SWEETWORKS INC (PA)
Also Called: Niagara Chocolates
3500 Genesee St (14225-5015)
PHONE..................716 634-4545
Philip Terranova, *CEO*
Leanne Khoury, *Business Mgr*
Andrew Ingham, *Opers Mgr*
Jeffrey Geiger, *Prdtn Mgr*
Bob Dunn, *Purch Mgr*
◆ **EMP:** 138
SQ FT: 115,000
SALES (est): 138.1MM **Privately Held**
WEB: www.sweetworks.net
SIC: 2066 2067 2064 Chocolate; chewing gum; candy & other confectionery products; chocolate candy, except solid chocolate; lollipops & other hard candy

(G-2999)
SYNTHETIC TEXTILES INC (PA)
398 Broadway St (14204-1546)
P.O. Box 1465 (14240-1465)
PHONE..................716 842-2598
Jerald H Eron, *President*
EMP: 14
SQ FT: 88,000
SALES (est): 1.4MM **Privately Held**
WEB: www.synthetictextile.com
SIC: 3083 Plastic finished products, laminated

(G-3000)
SYSTEMS DRS C3 INC (DH)
485 Cayuga Rd (14225-1368)
PHONE..................716 631-6200
Alan Dietrich, *President*
Jason Rinsky, *Vice Pres*
Richard A Schneider, *Treasurer*
Vance Conway, *Technical Staff*
Mark S Newman, *Director*
EMP: 300
SQ FT: 300,000
SALES (est): 137.6MM
SALES (corp-wide): 9.2B **Privately Held**
WEB: www.drs-ewns.com
SIC: 3812 8713 Radar systems & equipment;
HQ: Leonardo Drs, Inc.
2345 Crystal Dr Ste 1000
Arlington VA 22202
703 416-8000

(G-3001)
T M MACHINE INC
176 Reading St (14220-2198)
PHONE..................716 822-0817
Theodore S Michalski, *President*
Dennis Michalski, *Vice Pres*
EMP: 9
SQ FT: 7,000
SALES: 1.5MM **Privately Held**
SIC: 3599 Machine shop, jobbing & repair

(G-3002)
TAILORED COATINGS INC
1800 Brdwy St Bldg 2a (14212)
PHONE..................716 893-4869
David R Mohamed, *Ch of Bd*
Fred Tafelski, *Principal*
EMP: 22
SALES (est): 3.6MM **Privately Held**
SIC: 3479 Painting of metal products

(G-3003)
TCHNOLOGIES N MRC AMEERICA LLC
Also Called: M R C
25 Roberts Ave (14206-3130)
PHONE..................................716 822-4300
Lynn Leimkuehler, *Vice Pres*
James Leimkuehler,
EMP: 9 **EST:** 1980
SQ FT: 150,000
SALES (est): 1.3MM **Privately Held**
SIC: 3599 7699 Machine shop, jobbing & repair; industrial machinery & equipment repair

(G-3004)
TECTRAN MFG INC (HQ)
2345 Walden Ave Ste 1 (14225-4770)
PHONE..................................800 776-5549
Bruce McKie, *Ch of Bd*
▲ **EMP:** 86
SALES: 19.4MM **Privately Held**
WEB: www.tectran.com
SIC: 3713 Truck bodies & parts

(G-3005)
TEGNA INC
Also Called: W G R Z - T V Channel 2
259 Delaware Ave (14202-2008)
PHONE..................................716 849-2222
Jim Toellner, *General Mgr*
Jeffrey Beacham, *Accounts Exec*
Dan Meyers, *Director*
Heather Waldman, *Author*
EMP: 130
SALES (corp-wide): 2.2B **Publicly Held**
WEB: www.gannett.com
SIC: 2711 4833 Newspapers; television broadcasting stations
PA: Tegna Inc.
8350 Broad St Ste 2000
Tysons VA 22102
703 873-6600

(G-3006)
TENT AND TABLE COM LLC
2845 Bailey Ave (14215-3242)
PHONE..................................716 570-0258
▲ **EMP:** 15
SALES: 7MM **Privately Held**
SIC: 3999 Mfg Misc Products

(G-3007)
TERRAPIN STATION LTD
1172 Hertel Ave (14216-2704)
PHONE..................................716 874-6677
Barry Cohen, *President*
Robert Colsanti, *Vice Pres*
EMP: 13
SALES (est): 1.2MM **Privately Held**
WEB: www.terrapinstationbuffalo.com
SIC: 2337 Women's & misses' suits & coats

(G-3008)
THE CHOCOLATE SHOP
871 Niagara St (14213-2114)
PHONE..................................716 882-5055
Vincent Caruana, *Owner*
James Vincent, *Manager*
EMP: 6
SQ FT: 3,500
SALES (est): 381.6K **Privately Held**
WEB: www.chocolateshopandmore.com
SIC: 2066 5441 Chocolate & cocoa products; candy

(G-3009)
THERMAL FOAMS/SYRACUSE INC (PA)
2101 Kenmore Ave (14207-1695)
PHONE..................................716 874-6474
William F Wopperer, *Ch of Bd*
John P Jeffery, *President*
Dennis Brady, *Vice Pres*
David Wopperer, *Vice Pres*
Larry Brady, *Treasurer*
▲ **EMP:** 2
SQ FT: 150,000
SALES (est): 5.8MM **Privately Held**
SIC: 3086 Insulation or cushioning material, foamed plastic

(G-3010)
TIEDEMANN WALDEMAR INC
Also Called: Roofing Consultant
1720 Military Rd Ste 2 (14217-1148)
PHONE..................................716 875-5665
Waldemar Tiedemann, *President*
EMP: 11 **EST:** 1964
SALES (est): 1.1MM **Privately Held**
SIC: 2431 1761 Millwork; roofing contractor

(G-3011)
TIME RELEASE SCIENCES INC
Also Called: Trs Packaging
205 Dingens St (14206-2309)
PHONE..................................716 823-4580
Jeffrey Dorn, *Ch of Bd*
▲ **EMP:** 22
SALES (est): 4.6MM **Privately Held**
SIC: 2671 Packaging paper & plastics film, coated & laminated

(G-3012)
TMP TECHNOLOGIES INC (PA)
Also Called: Advanced Foam Products Div
1200 Northland Ave (14215-3835)
PHONE..................................716 895-6100
Jeffrey T Doran, *Ch of Bd*
Gary R Ashe, *Vice Pres*
Kirk Dorn, *Vice Pres*
Don Phister, *Vice Pres*
Robert Schultz, *Plant Mgr*
▼ **EMP:** 65
SQ FT: 47,000
SALES (est): 21.3MM **Privately Held**
WEB: www.tmptech.com
SIC: 3069 3086 2834 2821 Sponge rubber & sponge rubber products; molded rubber products; foam rubber; plastics foam products; pharmaceutical preparations; plastics materials & resins

(G-3013)
TOMRIC SYSTEMS INC
85 River Rock Dr (14207-2178)
PHONE..................................716 854-6050
Timothy Thill, *Ch of Bd*
◆ **EMP:** 14
SALES (est): 443.1K
SALES (corp-wide): 16.6MM **Privately Held**
SIC: 2064 Candy & other confectionery products
PA: Chocolate Delivery Systems, Inc.
1800 Elmwood Ave
Buffalo NY 14207
716 877-3146

(G-3014)
TOOLING ENTERPRISES INC
680 New Babcock St Ste 1 (14206-2285)
PHONE..................................716 842-0445
Eugene Joseph, *President*
EMP: 10
SQ FT: 21,000
SALES (est): 1.3MM **Privately Held**
SIC: 3469 3544 Stamping metal for the trade; special dies, tools, jigs & fixtures

(G-3015)
TOP SEEDZ LLC
247 Cayuga Rd (14225-1900)
PHONE..................................716 380-2612
Rebecca Brady, *Mng Member*
EMP: 5 **EST:** 2017
SALES: 300K **Privately Held**
SIC: 2052 Cookies & crackers

(G-3016)
TOVIE ASARESE ROYAL PRTG CO
351 Grant St (14213-1423)
PHONE..................................716 885-7692
Ottoviano Asarese, *President*
EMP: 7 **EST:** 1952
SQ FT: 1,500
SALES (est): 964.4K **Privately Held**
SIC: 2752 2759 Commercial printing, offset; letterpress printing

(G-3017)
TRANE US INC
45 Earhart Dr Ste 103 (14221-7809)
PHONE..................................716 626-1260
Joseph Goungo, *Sales Engr*
Ronald Gerster, *Branch Mgr*
EMP: 50 **Privately Held**
SIC: 3585 Refrigeration & heating equipment
HQ: Trane U.S. Inc.
3600 Pammel Creek Rd
La Crosse WI 54601
608 787-2000

(G-3018)
TRANSCO RAILWAY PRODUCTS INC
Milestrip Rd Rr 179 (14219)
P.O. Box 1968, Blasdell (14219-0168)
PHONE..................................716 825-1663
Rfick Heldt, *Manager*
EMP: 20
SALES (corp-wide): 225.3B **Publicly Held**
SIC: 3743 Railroad equipment
HQ: Transco Railway Products Inc.
200 N La Salle St # 1550
Chicago IL 60601
312 427-2818

(G-3019)
TRICO HOLDING CORPORATION (DH)
Also Called: Trico Products
50 Thielman Dr (14206-2364)
PHONE..................................716 852-5700
Thomas F Plocinik, *President*
Robert Young, *CFO*
Thomas E Schmitt, *Treasurer*
Linda Boylan, *Controller*
John Cummings, *Manager*
EMP: 2000
SALES (est): 243MM
SALES (corp-wide): 332.6MM **Privately Held**
SIC: 3399 3469 3714 3089 Powder, metal; stamping metal for the trade; motor vehicle parts & accessories; injection molding of plastics
HQ: Trico Products Corporation
3255 W Hamlin Rd
Rochester Hills MI 48309
248 371-1700

(G-3020)
TRINITY PACKAGING CORPORATION
Cello-Pack Spclty Flms Lmntion
55 Innsbruck Dr (14227-2703)
PHONE..................................716 668-3111
Craig Miller, *Vice Pres*
EMP: 26
SALES (corp-wide): 311.6MM **Privately Held**
SIC: 3081 2673 Unsupported plastics film & sheet; bags: plastic, laminated & coated
HQ: Trinity Packaging Corporation
357 Main St Unit 1
Armonk NY 10504
914 273-4111

(G-3021)
TRIPP PLATING WORKS INC
1491 William St (14206-1807)
PHONE..................................716 894-2424
Steven E Jagielo, *President*
Cherie Jagielo, *Vice Pres*
EMP: 7 **EST:** 1922
SQ FT: 6,000
SALES (est): 776.4K **Privately Held**
SIC: 3471 Electroplating of metals or formed products; polishing, metals or formed products; buffing for the trade

(G-3022)
TRU MOLD SHOES INC
42 Breckenridge St (14213-1555)
PHONE..................................716 881-4484
Ahmed Syed, *President*
Wayne Weisedel, *General Mgr*
Andrea Syed, *Vice Pres*
Sarah Syed, *Vice Pres*
EMP: 15
SQ FT: 11,000
SALES (est): 4.3MM **Privately Held**
WEB: www.trumold.com
SIC: 3143 3144 Orthopedic shoes, men's; orthopedic shoes, women's

(G-3023)
TWENTY-FIRST CENTURY PRESS INC
501 Cornwall Ave (14215-3125)
PHONE..................................716 837-0800
Tracy B Lach, *President*
Mary Crimmen, *Vice Pres*
▲ **EMP:** 18 **EST:** 1979
SQ FT: 40,000
SALES (est): 3.4MM **Privately Held**
SIC: 2752 2789 Commercial printing, offset; photo-offset printing; binding only: books, pamphlets, magazines, etc.

(G-3024)
TYSON DELI INC (HQ)
Also Called: MGM
665 Perry St (14210-1355)
PHONE..................................716 566-3189
Howard Zemsky, *Chairman*
Eric Naber, *Plant Mgr*
EMP: 450
SQ FT: 85,000
SALES (est): 34.1MM
SALES (corp-wide): 42.4B **Publicly Held**
SIC: 2011 Meat packing plants
PA: Tyson Foods, Inc.
2200 W Don Tyson Pkwy
Springdale AR 72762
479 290-4000

(G-3025)
U S SUGAR CO INC
692 Bailey Ave (14206-3003)
PHONE..................................716 828-1170
Tom Ferlito, *CEO*
Ed Jackson, *Senior VP*
Vernessa Roberts, *Vice Pres*
Steve Ward, *Vice Pres*
◆ **EMP:** 50
SQ FT: 300,000
SALES (est): 18.6MM **Privately Held**
SIC: 2099 Sugar

(G-3026)
UC COATINGS LLC (PA)
2250 Fillmore Ave (14214-2119)
P.O. Box 1066 (14215-6066)
PHONE..................................716 833-9366
Eric Degenfelder, *CEO*
Thuy N Murray, *Corp Secy*
Tim Cutler, *Exec VP*
Shawn Naffky, *Accounting Mgr*
Paulette Welker, *Cust Mgr*
▼ **EMP:** 27 **EST:** 1951
SQ FT: 30,000
SALES (est): 3.9MM **Privately Held**
WEB: www.uccoatings.com
SIC: 2851 Wood fillers or sealers; lacquers, varnishes, enamels & other coatings

(G-3027)
UNICELL BODY COMPANY INC (PA)
571 Howard St (14206-2195)
PHONE..................................716 853-8628
Roger J Martin, *Ch of Bd*
Scott Vader, *President*
Ernie Deufemi, *General Mgr*
Anthony Lista, *General Mgr*
Tony Lista, *General Mgr*
EMP: 45 **EST:** 1963
SQ FT: 67,000
SALES: 20MM **Privately Held**
WEB: www.unicell.com
SIC: 3713 5013 Truck bodies (motor vehicles); truck parts & accessories

(G-3028)
UNIFORM NAMEMAKERS INC
55 Amherst Villa Rd (14225-1432)
PHONE..................................716 626-5474
Warren Clark, *President*
EMP: 10
SQ FT: 7,000
SALES (est): 550K **Privately Held**
WEB: www.uniformnamemakers.com
SIC: 2395 Embroidery & art needlework

(G-3029)
UNILOCK LTD
510 Smith St (14210-1288)
PHONE..................................716 822-6074
David Mc Intyre, *Branch Mgr*

EMP: 20
SALES (corp-wide): 127.8MM **Privately Held**
SIC: 3271 Paving blocks, concrete
PA: Unilock Ltd
401 The West Mall Suite 610
Etobicoke ON M9C 5
416 646-5180

(G-3030)
UNITED RICHTER ELECTRICAL MTRS
106 Michigan Ave (14204-2111)
PHONE..................................716 855-1945
Thomas Weiner, *President*
John Cook, *Vice Pres*
Judith Weiner, *Admin Sec*
EMP: 10
SQ FT: 10,000
SALES (est): 1.7MM **Privately Held**
SIC: 7694 5063 Electric motor repair; power transmission equipment, electric

(G-3031)
UPSTATE FARMS DAIRY LLC
25 Anderson Rd (14225-4905)
PHONE..................................716 892-3156
Larry Webster, *CEO*
EMP: 250
SALES (est): 5.5MM
SALES (corp-wide): 903.7MM **Privately Held**
SIC: 2026 Fermented & cultured milk products
PA: Upstate Niagara Cooperative, Inc.
25 Anderson Rd
Buffalo NY 14225
716 892-3156

(G-3032)
UPSTATE NIAGARA COOP INC (PA)
Also Called: Bison Products
25 Anderson Rd (14225-4905)
P.O. Box 650 (14225-0650)
PHONE..................................716 892-3156
Larry Webster, *CEO*
Daniel Wolf, *President*
Kim Pickard, *General Mgr*
Sherrie Green, *Regional Mgr*
Jim Murphy, *Vice Pres*
EMP: 55 **EST:** 1930
SALES: 903.7MM **Privately Held**
SIC: 2026 Fermented & cultured milk products

(G-3033)
UPSTATE NIAGARA COOP INC
Also Called: Upstate Milk Co-Operatives
1730 Dale Rd (14225-4921)
P.O. Box 650 (14225-0650)
PHONE..................................716 892-2121
Larry Darch, *Principal*
Brenda Melligan, *Manager*
Colleen Keller, *Executive*
EMP: 200
SQ FT: 53,690
SALES (corp-wide): 903.7MM **Privately Held**
SIC: 2023 2026 Ice cream mix, unfrozen: liquid or dry; fluid milk
PA: Upstate Niagara Cooperative, Inc.
25 Anderson Rd
Buffalo NY 14225
716 892-3156

(G-3034)
V LAKE INDUSTRIES INC
1555 Niagara St (14213-1101)
PHONE..................................716 885-9141
Keith McCoy, *President*
David Russell, *Project Mgr*
EMP: 8
SQ FT: 24,000
SALES (est): 1.3MM **Privately Held**
SIC: 3599 Machine shop, jobbing & repair

(G-3035)
VENT-A-KILN CORPORATION
Also Called: Vent-A-Fume
51 Botsford Pl Ste 1 (14216-2641)
PHONE..................................716 876-2023
Susan Lee, *President*
EMP: 5
SQ FT: 1,200

SALES (est): 882.5K **Privately Held**
WEB: www.ventakiln.com
SIC: 3564 Blowers & fans

(G-3036)
VERMONT MEDICAL INC
Also Called: Vermed
400 Exchange St (14204-2064)
PHONE..................................802 463-9976
Hurley Blakeney, *CEO*
Rich Kalich, *President*
Thomas Salmon, *Vice Pres*
Patrick Boylan, *Treasurer*
George Nostrand, *Admin Sec*
▲ **EMP:** 160
SQ FT: 44,800
SALES (est): 30.4MM **Privately Held**
SIC: 3823 3845 Electrodes used in industrial process measurement; electromedical equipment

(G-3037)
VINCENT MARTINO DENTAL LAB
74 Ransier Dr (14224-2244)
PHONE..................................716 674-7800
Vincent Martino, *President*
Deborah Martino, *Admin Sec*
EMP: 10 **EST:** 1976
SQ FT: 800
SALES: 300K **Privately Held**
SIC: 3843 8072 Orthodontic appliances; orthodontic appliance production

(G-3038)
VISIMETRICS CORPORATION
2290 Kenmore Ave (14207-1312)
PHONE..................................716 871-7070
Kenneth Luczkiewicz, *President*
William Umiker, *Vice Pres*
EMP: 8
SQ FT: 22,000
SALES (est): 1MM **Privately Held**
WEB: www.visicnc.com
SIC: 3599 Machine shop, jobbing & repair

(G-3039)
VOYAGER EMBLEMS INC
Also Called: Voyager Custom Products
701 Seneca St Ste D (14210-1351)
PHONE..................................416 255-3421
Donald B Grant, *Ch of Bd*
Sally Grant, *President*
Mark King, *VP Sales*
Thomas Maloney, *Admin Sec*
EMP: 108 **EST:** 1965
SQ FT: 38,000
SALES (est): 5.3MM
SALES (corp-wide): 1.6MM **Privately Held**
WEB: www.voyager-emblems.com
SIC: 2395 Emblems, embroidered
HQ: Grant Emblems Limited
55 Fieldway Rd Suite A
Etobicoke ON M8Z 3
416 255-3421

(G-3040)
VULCAN STEAM FORGING CO
247 Rano St (14207-2189)
P.O. Box 87 (14207-0087)
PHONE..................................716 875-3680
Michael Duggan, *President*
Jered Fitch, *Opers Mgr*
Frank Attea, *Opers Staff*
▲ **EMP:** 27
SQ FT: 30,000
SALES (est): 5.6MM **Privately Held**
WEB: www.vulcansf.com
SIC: 3462 Flange, valve & pipe fitting forgings, ferrous

(G-3041)
WARD INDUSTRIAL EQUIPMENT INC (PA)
Also Called: Ward Iron Works Limited
1051 Clinton St (14206-2823)
PHONE..................................716 856-6966
Guy Nelson, *President*
▲ **EMP:** 1
SQ FT: 500
SALES (est): 4.3MM **Privately Held**
WEB: www.devansco.com
SIC: 3535 5084 Bulk handling conveyor systems; industrial machinery & equipment

(G-3042)
WEB ASSOCIATES INC
1255 Niagara St (14213-1501)
PHONE..................................716 883-3377
William E Breeser, *President*
EMP: 6
SALES (est): 480.3K **Privately Held**
WEB: www.betterwire.com
SIC: 3315 3469 Wire & fabricated wire products; metal stampings

(G-3043)
WEBB-MASON INC
300 Airborne Pkwy Ste 210 (14225-1491)
PHONE..................................716 276-8792
Jon Webber, *Manager*
EMP: 23
SALES (corp-wide): 113.5MM **Privately Held**
SIC: 2752 Business form & card printing, lithographic
PA: Webb-Mason, Inc.
10830 Gilroy Rd
Hunt Valley MD 21031
410 785-1111

(G-3044)
WENDT CORPORATION
2555 Walden Ave (14225-4737)
PHONE..................................716 391-1200
Thomas A Wendt Sr, *CEO*
Mike Fialkowski, *President*
Joseph Nuchereno, *Project Mgr*
Ethan Willard, *Sales Engr*
William Closee, *Manager*
◆ **EMP:** 100
SQ FT: 66,000
SALES (est): 37.4MM **Privately Held**
SIC: 3599 Custom machinery

(G-3045)
WEST METAL WORKS INC
Also Called: W M W
68 Hayes Pl (14210-1614)
PHONE..................................716 895-4900
James Stermer, *President*
Jennifer Stermer, *Vice Pres*
EMP: 20 **EST:** 1946
SALES (est): 3.7MM **Privately Held**
WEB: www.westmetalworks.com
SIC: 7692 3559 3443 3449 Welding repair; chemical machinery & equipment; plate work for the metalworking trade; miscellaneous metalwork

(G-3046)
WESTERN NEW YORK FAMILY MAG
3147 Delaware Ave Ste B (14217-2077)
P.O. Box 3147 (14240-3147)
PHONE..................................716 836-3486
Michelle J Miller, *Owner*
EMP: 5
SALES (est): 532.7K **Privately Held**
WEB: www.wnyfamilymagazine.com
SIC: 2721 Magazines: publishing only, not printed on site

(G-3047)
WILCRO INC
90 Earhart Dr Ste 19 (14221-7802)
PHONE..................................716 632-4204
Richard Crooks Sr, *President*
Richard Crooks Jr, *Vice Pres*
Robert Crooks, *Admin Sec*
EMP: 9
SALES (est): 514.8K **Privately Held**
WEB: www.wilcro.com
SIC: 3571 2796 Personal computers (microcomputers); engraving on copper, steel, wood or rubber: printing plates

(G-3048)
WILLARD MACHINE
73 Forest Ave (14213-1093)
PHONE..................................716 885-1630
Jeffrey Rathmann, *President*
EMP: 13
SQ FT: 10,000
SALES (est): 1.2MM **Privately Held**
WEB: www.willardmachine.com
SIC: 3599 Machine shop, jobbing & repair

(G-3049)
WILLIAM S HEIN & CO INC
Also Called: Metro Center Western New York
1575 Main St (14209-1513)
PHONE..................................716 882-2600
Kevin Marmion, *President*
EMP: 100
SALES (corp-wide): 40.4K **Privately Held**
WEB: www.foreign-law.com
SIC: 2731 Books: publishing only
PA: William S. Hein & Co., Inc.
2350 N Forest Rd Ste 14a
Getzville NY 14068
716 882-2600

(G-3050)
WINTERS INSTRUMENTS INC (HQ)
Also Called: Winters Instruments
455 Cayuga Rd Ste 650 (14225-1317)
PHONE..................................281 880-8607
Jeffrey Smith, *President*
Dharmesh Bhardwaj, *Regional Mgr*
Brian McClure, *Exec VP*
Thom Milligan, *Vice Pres*
Brian Best, *Opers Mgr*
▲ **EMP:** 45
SQ FT: 10,000
SALES (est): 5.1MM
SALES (corp-wide): 10.2MM **Privately Held**
SIC: 3823 5084 Industrial instrmnts msrmnt display/control process variable; instruments & control equipment
PA: Winters Instruments Ltd
121 Railside Rd
North York ON M3A 1
416 444-2345

(G-3051)
X-L ENVELOPE AND PRINTING INC
701 Seneca St Ste 100 (14210-1376)
P.O. Box 344 (14224-0344)
PHONE..................................716 852-2135
EMP: 11
SQ FT: 20,000
SALES (est): 2.3MM **Privately Held**
SIC: 2677 2752 Mfg Envelopes Lithographic Commercial Printing

(G-3052)
YOUNG & SWARTZ INC
39 Cherry St (14204-1298)
PHONE..................................716 852-2171
Raphael Winzig, *President*
Paul Winzig, *Master*
EMP: 10 **EST:** 1886
SQ FT: 15,000
SALES (est): 1.2MM **Privately Held**
SIC: 3991 5198 Brushes, household or industrial; paint brushes, rollers, sprayers

(G-3053)
YR BLANC & CO LLC
Also Called: Renovatio Med & Surgical Sups
25 Eltham Dr (14226-4108)
PHONE..................................716 800-3999
Yves-Richard Blanc, *CEO*
EMP: 5
SALES (est): 764.4K **Privately Held**
SIC: 2899 3589 1781 5078 ; sewage & water treatment equipment; water well servicing; drinking water coolers, mechanical

---

Bullville
Orange County

(G-3054)
WOODARDS CONCRETE PRODUCTS INC
629 Lybolt Rd (10915)
P.O. Box 8 (10915-0008)
PHONE..................................845 361-3471
Robert Zwart, *President*
Gayle Cortright, *Corp Secy*
Allen Zwart, *Vice Pres*
Steve Zwart, *Vice Pres*
EMP: 25 **EST:** 1955
SQ FT: 14,000

SALES (est): 4.3MM **Privately Held**
WEB: www.woodardsconcrete.com
SIC: **3272** Concrete products, precast; septic tanks, concrete; steps, prefabricated concrete

Burdett
Schuyler County

(G-3055)
ATWATER ESTATE VINEYARDS LLC
5055 State Route 414 (14818-9816)
PHONE..................................607 546-8463
Ted Marks, *Partner*
Stacy Yeater, *Accountant*
Denise Clappier, *Manager*
Amanda Gumtow, *Manager*
EMP: 20 EST: 2000
SQ FT: 672
SALES (est): 2.3MM **Privately Held**
WEB: www.atwatervineyards.com
SIC: **2084** Wines

(G-3056)
DAMIANI WINE CELLARS LLC
4704 State Route 414 (14818-9779)
PHONE..................................607 546-5557
Antoinette Di Ciaccio, *Manager*
Brandy Ahouse, *Manager*
EMP: 6
SALES (est): 769.9K **Privately Held**
SIC: **2084** Wines

(G-3057)
FINGER LAKES DISTILLING
4676 State Route 414 (14818-9730)
PHONE..................................607 546-5510
Brian McKenzie, *President*
EMP: 17
SALES (est): 1.9MM **Privately Held**
SIC: **2085** Distilled & blended liquors

(G-3058)
J R DILL WINERY LLC
4922 State Route 414 (14818-9729)
PHONE..................................607 546-5757
Jeff Dill, *Mng Member*
EMP: 5 EST: 2010
SALES (est): 403.4K **Privately Held**
SIC: **2084** Wines

Burke
Franklin County

(G-3059)
CREST HAVEN PRECAST INC
4925 State Route 11 (12917-2410)
PHONE..................................518 483-4750
Gary Boileau, *President*
Eva Boileau, *Vice Pres*
EMP: 7
SALES: 800K **Privately Held**
SIC: **3271** Blocks, concrete or cinder: standard

Burt
Niagara County

(G-3060)
NOURYON SURFACE CHEMISTRY
2153 Lockport Olcott Rd (14028-9788)
PHONE..................................716 778-8554
Gordon Martens, *Manager*
EMP: 8
SALES (corp-wide): 1.4B **Privately Held**
WEB: www.akzo-nobel.com
SIC: **2869** 2899 Industrial organic chemicals; chemical preparations
HQ: Nouryon Surface Chemistry
　525 W Van Buren St # 1600
　Chicago IL 60607
　312 544-7000

(G-3061)
SCHULZE VINEYARDS & WINERY LLC
2090 Coomer Rd (14028-9733)
PHONE..................................716 778-8090
Anne Schulze,
EMP: 13
SALES: 578K **Privately Held**
SIC: **2084** Wines

Byron
Genesee County

(G-3062)
OXBO INTERNATIONAL CORPORATION (DH)
7275 Batavia Byron Rd (14422-9599)
PHONE..................................585 548-2665
Gary C Stich, *CEO*
Richard Glazier, *Ch of Bd*
Paul Dow, *Vice Pres*
Andrew Talbott, *Vice Pres*
Jenny Southwick, *Buyer*
▲ EMP: 100
SQ FT: 43,500
SALES (est): 51MM
SALES (corp-wide): 51.4MM **Privately Held**
WEB: www.oxbocorp.com
SIC: **3523** 5083 Farm machinery & equipment; farm & garden machinery
HQ: Ploeger Oxbo Group B.V.
　Electronweg 5
　Roosendaal
　165 319-333

Cairo
Greene County

(G-3063)
B & B FOREST PRODUCTS LTD
251 Route 145 (12413-2659)
P.O. Box 907 (12413-0907)
PHONE..................................518 622-0811
William Fabian, *President*
▼ EMP: 13 EST: 1993
SALES (est): 1.3MM **Privately Held**
SIC: **2411** Logging

(G-3064)
BILBEE CONTROLS INC
628 Main St (12413)
PHONE..................................518 622-3033
EMP: 12
SQ FT: 12,000
SALES: 1.5MM **Privately Held**
SIC: **3822** Mfg Environmental Controls

(G-3065)
JRS FUELS INC
8037 Route 32 (12413-2526)
PHONE..................................518 622-9939
John Vandenburgh, *Principal*
EMP: 5
SALES (est): 652.4K **Privately Held**
SIC: **2869** Fuels

(G-3066)
K & B WOODWORKING INC
133 Rolling Meadow Rd (12413-2201)
PHONE..................................518 634-7253
Peter Vogel, *President*
Richard Vogel, *Corp Secy*
Rick Vogel, *Treasurer*
EMP: 9
SQ FT: 10,000
SALES (est): 726K **Privately Held**
WEB: www.kbwoodworking.com
SIC: **2511** 2499 Wood household furniture; decorative wood & woodwork

(G-3067)
OAK VALLEY LOGGING INC
558 Frank Hitchcock Rd (12413-2626)
P.O. Box 1260 (12413-1260)
PHONE..................................518 622-8249
Glenn Defrancesco, *Chairman*
EMP: 6
SALES (est): 381.6K **Privately Held**
SIC: **2411** Logging camps & contractors

Caledonia
Livingston County

(G-3068)
ADVIS INC
2218 River Rd (14423-9518)
PHONE..................................585 568-0100
Mark F Bocko, *CEO*
Donna REA, *Business Mgr*
EMP: 9
SALES: 950K **Privately Held**
SIC: **3674** Semiconductors & related devices

(G-3069)
COMMODITY RESOURCE CORPORATION
2773 Caledonia Leroy Rd (14423-9538)
P.O. Box 576, Lakeville (14480-0576)
PHONE..................................585 538-9500
Leslie Cole, *President*
EMP: 12
SALES (est): 1.9MM **Privately Held**
WEB: www.crcconnect.com
SIC: **2875** 2048 Fertilizers, mixing only; feed premixes

(G-3070)
GULDENSCHUH LOGGING & LBR LLC
143 Wheatland Center Rd (14423-9750)
P.O. Box 191 (14423-0191)
PHONE..................................585 538-4750
Don Guldenschuh, *Mng Member*
Donald Guldenschuh,
EMP: 9
SQ FT: 50,000
SALES (est): 1.4MM **Privately Held**
SIC: **2426** 2411 5099 5211 Furniture stock & parts, hardwood; logging; timber products, rough; lumber products

(G-3071)
HORNS & HALOS CFT BREWING LLC
3154 State St (14423-1222)
PHONE..................................585 507-7248
Justin Caccamise,
John Kabrovski,
EMP: 20
SQ FT: 8,200
SALES (est): 671.8K **Privately Held**
SIC: **2082** Near beer

(G-3072)
RHETT M CLARK INC
Also Called: Gregson-Clark
3213 Lehigh St (14423-1073)
PHONE..................................585 538-9570
Rhett M Clark, *President*
EMP: 6
SQ FT: 5,000
SALES (est): 1MM **Privately Held**
SIC: **3524** 5083 Lawn & garden equipment; lawn & garden machinery & equipment

(G-3073)
SPECIALIZED PRINTED FORMS INC
Also Called: Spforms
352 Center St (14423-1202)
P.O. Box 118 (14423-0118)
PHONE..................................585 538-2381
Kevin Johnston, *General Mgr*
Russell Shepard, *Plant Mgr*
Amy McAleavey, *Purchasing*
Mike Randall, *Sales Staff*
▲ EMP: 20 EST: 1951
SQ FT: 135,000
SALES (est): 3.6MM
SALES (corp-wide): 400.7MM **Publicly Held**
WEB: www.spforms.com
SIC: **2761** Continuous forms, office & business
PA: Ennis, Inc.
　2441 Presidential Pkwy
　Midlothian TX 76065
　972 775-9801

(G-3074)
TSS FOAM INDUSTRIES CORP
2770 W Main St (14423-9560)
P.O. Box 119 (14423-0119)
PHONE..................................585 538-2321
Samuel L Dilberto Jr, *Ch of Bd*
Ann Pringle, *Purch Mgr*
EMP: 15
SQ FT: 60,000
SALES (est): 2.7MM **Privately Held**
SIC: **3086** 5047 7389 Packaging & shipping materials, foamed plastic; medical & hospital equipment; sewing contractor

Callicoon
Sullivan County

(G-3075)
CATSKILL DELAWARE PUBLICATIONS (PA)
Also Called: Sullivan County Democrat
5 Lower Main St (12723-5000)
P.O. Box 308 (12723-0308)
PHONE..................................845 887-5200
Frederick W Stabbert III, *President*
EMP: 19 EST: 1900
SQ FT: 5,704
SALES: 1MM **Privately Held**
WEB: www.sc-democrat.com
SIC: **2711** 2752 Commercial printing & newspaper publishing combined; commercial printing, lithographic

Calverton
Suffolk County

(G-3076)
ACME MARINE HOIST INC
Also Called: Thego
800 Burman Blvd (11933-3024)
PHONE..................................631 472-3030
Norman Marcioch, *President*
▼ EMP: 8 EST: 1958
SQ FT: 11,500
SALES (est): 719.2K **Privately Held**
WEB: www.acmemarinehoist.com
SIC: **3536** Hoists, cranes & monorails

(G-3077)
BONSAL AMERICAN INC
931 Burman Blvd (11933-3027)
PHONE..................................631 208-8073
John Cardona, *Principal*
EMP: 20
SALES (corp-wide): 30.6B **Privately Held**
WEB: www.bonsalamerican.com
SIC: **3272** Concrete products
HQ: Bonsal American, Inc.
　625 Griffith Rd Ste 100
　Charlotte NC 28217
　704 525-1621

(G-3078)
COASTAL PIPELINE PRODUCTS CORP
55 Twomey Ave (11933-1374)
P.O. Box 575 (11933-0575)
PHONE..................................631 369-4000
Alexander Koke, *President*
▲ EMP: 50
SQ FT: 32,000
SALES (est): 10.6MM **Privately Held**
WEB: www.coastalpipeline.com
SIC: **3272** Concrete products, precast

(G-3079)
COOKING WITH CHEF MICHELLE LLC
Also Called: Ms. Michelles
4603 Middle Country Rd (11933-4104)
PHONE..................................516 662-2324
Michelle Gilette-Kelly, *President*
Michelle Marie Gilette-Kelly, *President*
Christopher Kelly, *CFO*
EMP: 6
SQ FT: 8,400
SALES: 229.6K **Privately Held**
SIC: **2052** 5149 Cookies; crackers, cookies & bakery products

(G-3080)
EAST END COUNTRY KITCHENS INC
Also Called: Pezera Associates
121 Edwards Ave (11933-1602)
PHONE....................631 727-2258
Henry Pazera, *President*
EMP: 10
SALES (est): 1.2MM **Privately Held**
SIC: 2434 Wood kitchen cabinets

(G-3081)
GLOBAL MARINE POWER INC
Also Called: Hustler Powerboats
221 Scott Ave (11933-3039)
PHONE....................631 208-2933
Joe Logiudice, *Owner*
John Cunningham, *Vice Pres*
Paul Logiudice, *Vice Pres*
Richard Logiudice, *Vice Pres*
EMP: 40
SQ FT: 32,000
SALES (est): 8.3MM **Privately Held**
WEB: www.hustlerpowerboats.com
SIC: 3089 3732 5551 Plastic boats &
other marine equipment; boat building &
repairing; boat dealers

(G-3082)
LUMINATI AEROSPACE LLC
400 David Ct (11933-3007)
PHONE....................631 574-2616
Daniel Preston, *CEO*
April Chapple, *Vice Pres*
EMP: 16
SALES (est): 998.5K **Privately Held**
SIC: 3721 Research & development on air-
craft by the manufacturer

(G-3083)
PELLA CORPORATION
Also Called: Reilly Windows & Doors
901 Burman Blvd (11933-3027)
PHONE....................631 208-0710
Michael P Reilly, *Chairman*
EMP: 126
SALES (corp-wide): 1.7B **Privately Held**
SIC: 2431 5211 5031 2499 Millwork; mill-
work & lumber; doors & windows; decora-
tive wood & woodwork; window & door
(prefabricated) installation
PA: Pella Corporation
102 Main St
Pella IA 50219
641 621-1000

(G-3084)
RACING INDUSTRIES INC
901 Scott Ave (11933-3033)
PHONE....................631 905-0100
Ameet Bambani, *President*
▲ EMP: 20
SQ FT: 20,000
SALES (est): 4.5MM **Privately Held**
WEB: www.racingindustries.com
SIC: 3465 Body parts, automobile:
stamped metal

(G-3085)
ROAR BIOMEDICAL INC
4603 Middle Country Rd (11933-4104)
PHONE....................631 591-2749
Robert Brocia, *Branch Mgr*
EMP: 5
SALES (corp-wide): 2.6MM **Privately
Held**
SIC: 2836 5122 Biological products, ex-
cept diagnostic; biologicals & allied prod-
ucts
PA: Roar Biomedical Inc
3960 Broadway
New York NY 10032
212 280-2983

(G-3086)
STONY BROOK MFG CO INC (PA)
652 Scott Ave (11933-3046)
PHONE....................631 369-9530
Ella Scaife, *President*
Marek Hyrycz, *Vice Pres*
Graham Scaife, *Vice Pres*
EMP: 30
SQ FT: 11,000

SALES (est): 5.1MM **Privately Held**
WEB: www.stonybrookmfg.com
SIC: 3317 Steel pipe & tubes

(G-3087)
SUFFOLK CEMENT PRECAST INC (PA)
1813 Middle Rd (11933)
P.O. Box 261 (11933-0261)
PHONE....................631 727-4432
Kenneth Lohr, *President*
EMP: 9
SQ FT: 500
SALES (est): 1MM **Privately Held**
SIC: 3273 Ready-mixed concrete

(G-3088)
SUFFOLK CEMENT PRODUCTS INC
1843 Middle Rd (11933-1450)
PHONE....................631 727-2317
Mark A Lohr, *Ch of Bd*
Linda Hagen, *Vice Pres*
EMP: 29
SQ FT: 4,500
SALES (est): 17.2MM **Privately Held**
WEB: www.suffolkcement.com
SIC: 3273 3271 Ready-mixed concrete;
blocks, concrete or cinder: standard

(G-3089)
TEBBENS STEEL LLC
800 Burman Blvd (11933-3024)
PHONE....................631 208-8330
Thomas A Tebbens II, *Mng Member*
Elsie Tebbens,
EMP: 18 EST: 1959
SQ FT: 9,000
SALES (est): 4.8MM **Privately Held**
SIC: 3449 8711 Miscellaneous metalwork;
structural engineering

(G-3090)
US HOISTS CORP
Also Called: Acme Marine
800 Burman Blvd (11933-3024)
PHONE....................631 472-3030
Thomas A Tebbens II, *President*
Kelly Tebbens, *Vice Pres*
◆ EMP: 7
SALES (est): 1.1MM **Privately Held**
SIC: 3536 Hoists, cranes & monorails

Cambridge
Washington County

(G-3091)
B & J LUMBER CO INC
1075 State Route 22 (12816-2501)
PHONE....................518 677-3845
John Merriman, *President*
Barbara Merriman, *Vice Pres*
EMP: 5 EST: 1955
SALES: 100K **Privately Held**
SIC: 2421 5989 0115 Sawmills & planing
mills, general; wood (fuel); corn

(G-3092)
CAMBRIDGE-PACIFIC INC
Also Called: CTX Printing
891 State Rd 22 (12816)
P.O. Box 159 (12816-0159)
PHONE....................518 677-5988
Chris Belnap, *President*
▲ EMP: 33 EST: 1986
SQ FT: 12,000
SALES (est): 6.7MM **Privately Held**
WEB: www.cpacific.com
SIC: 2677 Envelopes

(G-3093)
COMMON SENSE NATURAL SOAP
7 Pearl St (12816-1127)
PHONE....................518 677-0224
Robert Racine, *Owner*
EMP: 30 EST: 2014
SALES (est): 5.5MM **Privately Held**
SIC: 2844 Toilet preparations

(G-3094)
EASTERN CASTINGS CO
2 Pearl St (12816-1107)
P.O. Box 129 (12816-0129)
PHONE....................518 677-5610
Anthony McDonald, *President*
Andrew Nolan, *Treasurer*
EMP: 15
SQ FT: 25,000
SALES (est): 2.3MM **Privately Held**
SIC: 3365 Aluminum foundries

(G-3095)
ED LEVIN INC
Also Called: Ed Levin Jewelry
52 W Main St (12816-1158)
PHONE....................518 677-8595
Peter Tonjes, *President*
Lisa A Saunders, *Principal*
EMP: 25
SQ FT: 10,000
SALES: 2MM **Privately Held**
WEB: www.edlevinjewelry.com
SIC: 3911 Jewelry, precious metal

(G-3096)
ROBERT RACINE (PA)
Also Called: Common Sense Natural Soap
41 N Union St (12816-1025)
PHONE....................518 677-0224
Robert Racine, *Owner*
▲ EMP: 37
SALES (est): 7MM **Privately Held**
WEB: www.commonsensefarm.com
SIC: 2841 2844 Soap & other detergents;
toilet preparations

(G-3097)
WAYMOR1 INC
Hc 22 (12816)
PHONE....................518 677-8511
Susan H Morris, *Owner*
Wayne R Morris, *Owner*
EMP: 50
SALES (corp-wide): 46.7MM **Privately
Held**
SIC: 2679 2676 Paper products, con-
verted; sanitary paper products
PA: Waymor1, Inc.
879 State Rte 22
Cambridge NY 12816

Camden
Oneida County

(G-3098)
CAMDEN NEWS INC
Also Called: Queens Central News
39 Main St (13316-1301)
P.O. Box 117 (13316-0117)
PHONE....................315 245-1849
James Van Winkle, *President*
EMP: 5 EST: 1974
SQ FT: 7,000
SALES (est): 400.5K **Privately Held**
SIC: 2711 Newspapers: publishing only,
not printed on site

(G-3099)
CAMDEN WIRE CO INC
Also Called: International Wire Group
12 Masonic Ave (13316-1294)
PHONE....................315 245-3800
Rodney Kent, *President*
Donald De Kay, *VP Finance*
EMP: 700 EST: 1929
SQ FT: 400,000
SALES (est): 115MM
SALES (corp-wide): 2.9B **Privately Held**
SIC: 3351 3357 Wire, copper & copper
alloy; nonferrous wiredrawing & insulating
HQ: International Wire Group, Inc.
12 Masonic Ave
Camden NY 13316

(G-3100)
DAVIS LOGGING & LUMBER
1450 Curtiss Rd (13316-5006)
PHONE....................315 245-1040
Leonard Davis, *Principal*
EMP: 5 EST: 1985
SALES (est): 354.8K **Privately Held**
SIC: 2411 Logging

(G-3101)
INTERNATIONAL WIRE GROUP (HQ)
12 Masonic Ave (13316-1202)
PHONE....................315 245-3800
Gregory Smith, *President*
EMP: 15 EST: 2011
SALES (est): 493.5MM
SALES (corp-wide): 2.9B **Privately Held**
SIC: 3351 Wire, copper & copper alloy
PA: Atlas Holdings, Llc
100 Northfield St
Greenwich CT 06830
203 622-9138

(G-3102)
INTERNATIONAL WIRE GROUP INC (DH)
Also Called: Bare Wire Division
12 Masonic Ave (13316-1202)
PHONE....................315 245-2000
Rodney D Kent, *Ch of Bd*
Geoff Kent, *Vice Pres*
Glenn J Holler, *CFO*
Donald F Dekay, *VP Finance*
▲ EMP: 300
SALES (est): 493.5MM
SALES (corp-wide): 2.9B **Privately Held**
SIC: 3357 Nonferrous wiredrawing & insu-
lating
HQ: International Wire Group
12 Masonic Ave
Camden NY 13316
315 245-3800

(G-3103)
KEVIN REGAN LOGGING LTD
1011 Hillsboro Rd (13316-4518)
P.O. Box 439 (13316-0439)
PHONE....................315 245-3890
Kevin Regan, *President*
EMP: 5
SALES (est): 585.6K **Privately Held**
SIC: 2411 1629 Logging; land clearing
contractor

(G-3104)
OMEGA WIRE INC (DH)
Also Called: Bare Wire Div
12 Masonic Ave (13316-1202)
P.O. Box 131 (13316-0131)
PHONE....................315 245-3800
Rodney D Kent, *President*
Peter Ernenwein, *Vice Pres*
Donald De Kay, *VP Finance*
▲ EMP: 325
SQ FT: 200,000
SALES (est): 99.6MM
SALES (corp-wide): 2.9B **Privately Held**
WEB: www.omegawire.com
SIC: 3351 Wire, copper & copper alloy

(G-3105)
OWI CORPORATION
Also Called: Bare Wire Division
12 Masonic Ave (13316-1202)
P.O. Box 131 (13316-0131)
PHONE....................315 245-4305
Rodney Kent, *President*
Donald De Kay, *VP Finance*
▲ EMP: 6
SALES (est): 816.7K
SALES (corp-wide): 2.9B **Privately Held**
SIC: 3351 Wire, copper & copper alloy
HQ: International Wire Group, Inc.
12 Masonic Ave
Camden NY 13316

(G-3106)
PERFORMANCE WIRE & CABLE INC
9482 State Route 13 (13316-4947)
P.O. Box 126 (13316-0126)
PHONE....................315 245-2594
Steven Benjamin, *President*
Teresa Benjamin, *Principal*
EMP: 13
SQ FT: 37,500
SALES (est): 2.5MM **Privately Held**
WEB: www.performancewire.com
SIC: 3357 Nonferrous wiredrawing & insu-
lating

Camillus
Onondaga County

(G-3107)
AQUARII INC
17 Genesee St (13031-1126)
PHONE..................................315 672-8807
Ray Carrock, *President*
Hannah Carrock, *Marketing Mgr*
EMP: 8
SALES (est): 1.6MM **Privately Held**
SIC: 3646 Commercial indusl & institutional electric lighting fixtures

(G-3108)
CLEARSTEP TECHNOLOGIES LLC
213 Emann Dr (13031-2009)
PHONE..................................315 952-3628
Scott Buehler,
EMP: 7 EST: 2007
SQ FT: 2,000
SALES: 1.8MM **Privately Held**
WEB: www.clearsteptech.com
SIC: 2741 Technical manual & paper publishing

(G-3109)
KSA MANUFACTURING LLC
5050 Smoral Rd (13031-9726)
PHONE..................................315 488-0809
Adam Kudlick,
Jane Kudlick,
▲ **EMP:** 12
SQ FT: 8,500
SALES (est): 1.4MM **Privately Held**
WEB: www.ksamanufacturing.com
SIC: 3492 Hose & tube fittings & assemblies, hydraulic/pneumatic

(G-3110)
STEVE POLI SALES
Also Called: Imprinted Sportswear
102 Farmington Dr (13031-2113)
PHONE..................................315 487-0394
Steve Poli, *Owner*
EMP: 5
SALES (est): 283.6K **Privately Held**
SIC: 2261 Screen printing of cotton broadwoven fabrics

(G-3111)
TOSCH PRODUCTS LTD
25 Main St (13031-1126)
PHONE..................................315 672-3040
Todd Oudemool, *President*
Dirk J Oudemool,
EMP: 6
SQ FT: 12,000
SALES: 500K **Privately Held**
WEB: www.toschltd.com
SIC: 3949 Lacrosse equipment & supplies, general

(G-3112)
UPSTATE TUBE INC
5050 Smoral Rd (13031-9726)
PHONE..................................315 488-5636
Michael Kudlick, *President*
Kristy Kudlick, *Principal*
Tyler Kudlick, *Vice Pres*
EMP: 5
SALES (est): 424.5K **Privately Held**
SIC: 3492 Fluid power valves & hose fittings

(G-3113)
WESTROCK - SOUTHERN CONT LLC
100 Southern Dr (13031-1578)
PHONE..................................315 487-6111
Dave Atkwell, *Manager*
EMP: 120
SALES (corp-wide): 16.2B **Publicly Held**
WEB: www.southerncontainer.com
SIC: 2653 3412 Boxes, corrugated: made from purchased materials; metal barrels, drums & pails
HQ: Westrock - Southern Container, Llc
1000 Abernathy Rd Ste 125
Atlanta GA 30328
770 448-2193

(G-3114)
WESTROCK RKT LLC
100 Southern Dr (13031-1578)
PHONE..................................315 487-6111
David Ray, *Manager*
EMP: 13
SALES (corp-wide): 16.2B **Publicly Held**
SIC: 2631 Paperboard mills
HQ: Westrock Rkt, Llc
1000 Abernathy Rd Ste 125
Atlanta GA 30328
770 448-2193

(G-3115)
WESTROCK RKT LLC
4914 W Genesee St (13031-2374)
PHONE..................................770 448-2193
David Atwell, *Plant Mgr*
EMP: 161
SALES (corp-wide): 16.2B **Publicly Held**
WEB: www.rocktenn.com
SIC: 2653 Boxes, corrugated: made from purchased materials
HQ: Westrock Rkt, Llc
1000 Abernathy Rd Ste 125
Atlanta GA 30328
770 448-2193

Campbell
Steuben County

(G-3116)
KRAFT HEINZ FOODS COMPANY
Kraft Foods
8596 Main St (14821-9636)
PHONE..................................607 527-4584
Kenneth Blake, *Principal*
Henry Mapes, *Branch Mgr*
EMP: 350
SALES (corp-wide): 26.2B **Publicly Held**
WEB: www.kraftfoods.com
SIC: 2022 2026 Cheese, natural & processed; fluid milk
HQ: Kraft Heinz Foods Company
1 Ppg Pl Fl 34
Pittsburgh PA 15222
412 456-5700

(G-3117)
UPSTATE FARMS CHEESE LLC
8600 Main St (14821)
PHONE..................................607 527-4584
Tim Reagan, *Plant Mgr*
EMP: 180
SALES (est): 4.2MM
SALES (corp-wide): 903.7MM **Privately Held**
SIC: 2022 Processed cheese
PA: Upstate Niagara Cooperative, Inc.
25 Anderson Rd
Buffalo NY 14225
716 892-3156

Campbell Hall
Orange County

(G-3118)
MCNEILLY WOOD PRODUCTS INC
120 Neelytown Rd (10916-2807)
PHONE..................................845 457-9651
Timothy R Mc Neilly, *President*
Daniel J Mc Neilly, *Vice Pres*
Daniel J McNeilly, *Vice Pres*
Jeryl Mc Neilly, *Manager*
Ann Mc Neilly, *Admin Sec*
EMP: 45 EST: 1947
SQ FT: 12,000
SALES (est): 7MM **Privately Held**
WEB: www.mcneillywoodproducts.com
SIC: 2441 2448 5031 Nailed wood boxes & shook; pallets, wood; skids, wood; lumber: rough, dressed & finished

Canaan
Columbia County

(G-3119)
HILLTOWN PORK INC (PA)
12948 State Route 22 (12029-2118)
PHONE..................................518 781-4050
Richard A Beckwith, *President*
Edwin S Beckwith, *Vice Pres*
Robert A Beckwith, *Admin Sec*
EMP: 16
SALES (est): 1.7MM **Privately Held**
SIC: 2011 2013 Pork products from pork slaughtered on site; sausages & other prepared meats

Canajoharie
Montgomery County

(G-3120)
GRAVYMASTER INC
Also Called: Dryden & Palmer Co
101 Erie Blvd (13317-1148)
PHONE..................................203 453-1893
Stephen A Besse, *President*
Debbie Haig, *Purchasing*
EMP: 44
SQ FT: 31,000
SALES (est): 4.6MM **Privately Held**
WEB: www.gravy.com
SIC: 2064 2035 2099 Candy & other confectionery products; seasonings & sauces, except tomato & dry; food preparations

(G-3121)
RICHARDSON BRANDS COMPANY (HQ)
Also Called: Richardson Foods
101 Erie Blvd (13317-1148)
PHONE..................................800 839-8938
Arnold J D'Angelo, *CEO*
Tracey Burton, *Vice Pres*
Kathy Hiserodt, *Vice Pres*
John Almaviva, *Opers Mgr*
Harold Rabe, *Warehouse Mgr*
▲ **EMP:** 150
SQ FT: 180,000
SALES (est): 30.1MM
SALES (corp-wide): 481.6MM **Privately Held**
WEB: www.richardsonbrands.com
SIC: 2064 Candy & other confectionery products
PA: Founders Equity, Inc.
545 5th Ave Rm 401
New York NY 10017
212 829-0900

(G-3122)
W W CUSTOM CLAD INC (PA)
337 E Main St (13317-1221)
PHONE..................................518 673-3322
Charles E Wright, *President*
Christopher Watson, *Vice Pres*
▲ **EMP:** 3
SQ FT: 12,000
SALES (est): 5.7MM **Privately Held**
WEB: www.wwcustomclad.com
SIC: 3479 Coating of metals & formed products

(G-3123)
W W CUSTOM CLAD INC
75 Creek St (13317-1446)
PHONE..................................518 673-3322
EMP: 62
SQ FT: 23,804
SALES (corp-wide): 5.7MM **Privately Held**
WEB: www.wwcustomclad.com
SIC: 3479 Coating of metals & formed products
PA: W. W. Custom Clad, Inc.
337 E Main St
Canajoharie NY 13317
518 673-3322

Canandaigua
Ontario County

(G-3124)
AKOUSTIS INC
5450 Campus Dr Ste 100 (14424-8260)
PHONE..................................585 919-3073
Mary Winters, *Opers Staff*
EMP: 30
SALES (corp-wide): 1.4MM **Publicly Held**
SIC: 3674 4813 Integrated circuits, semiconductor networks, etc.; data telephone communications
HQ: Akoustis, Inc.
9805 Northcross Center Ct A
Huntsville NC 28078
704 997-5735

(G-3125)
BADGE MACHINE PRODUCTS INC
2491 Brickyard Rd (14424-7969)
PHONE..................................585 394-0330
Gail Flugel, *President*
Christian Flugel, *Vice Pres*
Kathy Flugel, *Vice Pres*
Francis Flugel, *Treasurer*
Allison Leet, *Controller*
EMP: 30
SQ FT: 24,000
SALES (est): 5.2MM **Privately Held**
WEB: www.badgemachine.com
SIC: 3599 Machine shop, jobbing & repair

(G-3126)
BRISTOL CORE INC
5310 North St (14424-6900)
P.O. Box 507 (14424-0507)
PHONE..................................585 919-0302
Morgan Curtice, *President*
EMP: 18
SALES (est): 3.5MM **Privately Held**
SIC: 2621 Bristols

(G-3127)
CANANDAIGUA MSGNR INCORPORTED (PA)
Also Called: Daily Messenger
73 Buffalo St (14424-1001)
PHONE..................................585 394-0770
George Ewing Jr, *President*
George Ewing Sr, *Chairman*
Lynn Brown, *Sls & Mktg Exec*
John Bowman, *Manager*
EMP: 200
SALES (est): 12.2MM **Privately Held**
SIC: 2711 2752 Newspapers: publishing only, not printed on site; commercial printing, lithographic

(G-3128)
CARGES ENTPS OF CANANDAIGUA
Also Called: Canandaigua Quick Print
330 S Main St (14424-2117)
PHONE..................................585 394-2600
Elizabeth Carges, *President*
Kevin Carges, *Vice Pres*
Robert Carges, *Vice Pres*
EMP: 6
SQ FT: 2,000
SALES (est): 1.1MM **Privately Held**
WEB: www.quickprntny.com
SIC: 2752 7334 Commercial printing, offset; photocopying & duplicating services

(G-3129)
CONSTELLATION BRANDS INC
3325 Marvin Sands Dr (14424-8405)
PHONE..................................585 393-4880
EMP: 31
SALES (corp-wide): 8.1B **Publicly Held**
WEB: www.cbrands.com
SIC: 2084 Wines, brandy & brandy spirits
PA: Constellation Brands, Inc.
207 High Point Dr # 100
Victor NY 14564
585 678-7100

▲ = Import ▼=Export
◆ =Import/Export

(G-3130)
DENNIES MANUFACTURING INC
2543 State Route 21 (14424-8718)
PHONE.................................585 393-4646
Richard Warkentin, *President*
Cindy Baxter, *Human Resources*
EMP: 27
SQ FT: 10,000
SALES (est): 5.2MM **Privately Held**
SIC: 3599 3441 7692 Machine shop, jobbing & repair; fabricated structural metal; welding repair

(G-3131)
DOUGS MACHINE SHOP INC
2304 Brickyard Rd (14424-7975)
P.O. Box 699 (14424-0699)
PHONE.................................585 905-0004
Douglas Leonard, *Ch of Bd*
EMP: 8 EST: 2008
SALES (est): 1MM **Privately Held**
SIC: 3599 Machine shop, jobbing & repair

(G-3132)
FINGER LAKES EXTRUSION CORP
Also Called: Flex Tubing
2437 State Route 21 (14424-8716)
PHONE.................................585 905-0632
William Scott, *President*
▲ EMP: 21 EST: 1998
SQ FT: 56,000
SALES: 5.6MM **Privately Held**
WEB: www.flextubing.com
SIC: 3089 3082 Extruded finished plastic products; tubes, unsupported plastic

(G-3133)
GATEHOUSE MEDIA LLC
Mpnnow
73 Buffalo St (14424-1001)
PHONE.................................585 394-0770
Beth Kesel, *General Mgr*
Patty Emmi, *Sales Staff*
Carl Helbig, *Branch Mgr*
EMP: 100
SALES (corp-wide): 1.5B **Privately Held**
WEB: www.gatehousemedia.com
SIC: 2711 2752 Newspapers, publishing & printing; commercial printing, lithographic
HQ: Gatehouse Media, Llc
175 Sullys Trl Fl 3
Pittsford NY 14534
585 598-0030

(G-3134)
GROSSGLOCKNER INC
Also Called: Artisan Meats
2640 Brickyard Rd (14424-7966)
PHONE.................................585 266-4960
Josef Brunner, *CEO*
Craig Funk, *General Mgr*
EMP: 6
SALES (est): 476.3K **Privately Held**
SIC: 2013 Sausages from purchased meat

(G-3135)
JUST RIGHT CARBINES LLC
231 Saltonstall St (14424-8301)
PHONE.................................585 261-5331
Richard J Cutri,
EMP: 6
SALES: 900K **Privately Held**
SIC: 3999 Manufacturing industries

(G-3136)
MOORE PRINTING COMPANY INC
9 Coy St (14424-1595)
PHONE.................................585 394-1533
Donna Miller, *President*
Burton Moore, *President*
EMP: 8
SQ FT: 3,500
SALES (est): 1MM **Privately Held**
SIC: 2752 2759 Commercial printing, offset; letterpress printing

(G-3137)
MURCADOM CORPORATION
Also Called: Fire Curtain Technologies
5711 Thomas Rd (14424-7988)
PHONE.................................585 412-2176
Jason Murphy, *CEO*
Timothy Wigton, *Opers Staff*

Paul Yarnall, *Director*
EMP: 10
SALES (est): 1MM **Privately Held**
SIC: 3272 7389 Building materials, except block or brick: concrete; business services

(G-3138)
PACTIV LLC
2651 Brickyard Rd (14424-7990)
PHONE.................................585 394-5125
Sam Aversa, *Engineer*
Margaret Finucane, *Branch Mgr*
EMP: 238
SALES (corp-wide): 14.1MM **Privately Held**
SIC: 2673 3089 5113 Food storage & frozen food bags, plastic; food storage & trash bags (plastic); food casings, plastic; containers, paper & disposable plastic; cups, disposable plastic & paper; dishes, disposable plastic & paper
HQ: Pactiv Llc
1900 W Field Ct
Lake Forest IL 60045
847 482-2000

(G-3139)
PACTIV LLC
Also Called: Canandaigua Technology Center
5250 North St (14424-1026)
PHONE.................................585 393-3149
David Class, *Branch Mgr*
EMP: 800
SALES (corp-wide): 14.1MM **Privately Held**
WEB: www.pactiv.com
SIC: 3089 Tableware, plastic; composition stone, plastic; doors, folding: plastic or plastic coated fabric
HQ: Pactiv Llc
1900 W Field Ct
Lake Forest IL 60045
847 482-2000

(G-3140)
PLURES TECHNOLOGIES INC (PA)
4070 County Road 16 (14424-8314)
PHONE.................................585 905-0554
Aaron Dobrinsky, *President*
EMP: 1
SALES: 5.5MM **Privately Held**
SIC: 3674 Integrated circuits, semiconductor networks, etc.

(G-3141)
QUICKPRINT
330 S Main St (14424-2117)
PHONE.................................585 394-2600
Kevin Carges, *CEO*
Robert Carges, *Vice Pres*
EMP: 5
SALES (est): 362.8K **Privately Held**
SIC: 2752 Commercial printing, offset

(G-3142)
SELECT FABRICATORS INC
5310 North St Ste 5 (14424-6900)
P.O. Box 119 (14424-0119)
PHONE.................................585 393-0650
David A Yearsley, *President*
Eleanor Yearsley, *Vice Pres*
Gary W Winch, *CFO*
Sandra Winch, *Admin Sec*
▼ EMP: 15 EST: 2000
SQ FT: 19,728
SALES (est): 2.3MM **Privately Held**
WEB: www.selectfabricatorsinc.com
SIC: 2393 3812 2673 2394 Duffle bags, canvas: made from purchased materials; aircraft/aerospace flight instruments & guidance systems; bags: plastic, laminated & coated; tents: made from purchased materials

(G-3143)
SKYOP LLC
5297 Parkside Dr Ste 440c (14424-7501)
PHONE.................................585 598-4737
Brian Pitre,
Daniel Albert,
EMP: 10 EST: 2013
SALES (est): 172.8K **Privately Held**
SIC: 7372 Educational computer software

(G-3144)
TIMBER FRAMES INC
5557 State Route 64 (14424-9382)
PHONE.................................585 374-6405
Alan R Milanette, *President*
EMP: 7 EST: 1976
SQ FT: 800
SALES (est): 1.4MM **Privately Held**
WEB: www.timberframesinc.com
SIC: 2439 1751 Structural wood members; framing contractor

(G-3145)
WOLFE PUBLICATIONS INC (PA)
Also Called: Messenger Post Media
73 Buffalo St (14424-1001)
PHONE.................................585 394-0770
Kathy Hammond, *President*
Marie Ewing, *Vice Pres*
John Bowman, *Prdtn Mgr*
Tom Wheeler, *Sales Mgr*
Dawn Zona, *Executive*
EMP: 104 EST: 1956
SQ FT: 17,500
SALES (est): 7.7MM **Privately Held**
WEB: www.mpnewspapers.com
SIC: 2711 Commercial printing & newspaper publishing combined

(G-3146)
YOUNG EXPLOSIVES CORP
Also Called: Display Fireworks
2165 New Michigan Rd (14424-7918)
P.O. Box 18653, Rochester (14618-0653)
PHONE.................................585 394-1783
James R Young, *President*
▲ EMP: 70 EST: 1949
SQ FT: 400
SALES (est): 12.2MM **Privately Held**
WEB: www.youngexplosives.com
SIC: 2899 7999 Fireworks; fireworks display service

Canaseraga
Allegany County

(G-3147)
BEAVER CREEK INDUSTRIES INC
11530 White Rd (14822-9607)
PHONE.................................607 545-6382
Gary Bajus, *President*
Ethan Flint, *Publisher*
Gary Bajus II, *Vice Pres*
Mary Bajus, *Treasurer*
Mitch Wing, *Prgrmr*
EMP: 9
SQ FT: 8,000
SALES: 1MM **Privately Held**
SIC: 2431 Interior & ornamental woodwork & trim

(G-3148)
WILSON BEEF FARMS LLC
10751 Hess Rd (14822-9701)
PHONE.................................607 545-8308
Christopher Wilson, *Owner*
Chris Wilson, *Mng Member*
EMP: 10
SQ FT: 6,000
SALES (est): 886.2K **Privately Held**
WEB: www.wilsonbeeffarms.com
SIC: 2013 5421 Sausages & other prepared meats; meat markets, including freezer provisioners

---

Canastota
Madison County

(G-3149)
BLADING SERVICES UNLIMITED LLC
40 Madison Blvd (13032-3500)
PHONE.................................315 875-5313
Stephen Stevens,
EMP: 12
SALES (est): 2.2MM **Privately Held**
SIC: 3599 Machine shop, jobbing & repair

(G-3150)
CALLANAN INDUSTRIES INC
6375 Tuttle Rd (13032-4168)
PHONE.................................315 697-9569
Tim Hauck, *Principal*
EMP: 25
SALES (est): 30.6B **Privately Held**
SIC: 3272 Concrete products, precast
HQ: Callanan Industries, Inc.
8 Southwoods Blvd Ste 4
Albany NY 12211
518 374-2222

(G-3151)
CANASTOTA PUBLISHING CO INC
130 E Center St (13032-1307)
P.O. Box 388 (13032-0388)
PHONE.................................315 697-9010
Patrick Milmoe, *President*
EMP: 5
SQ FT: 3,200
SALES (est): 765K **Privately Held**
SIC: 2752 Commercial printing, offset

(G-3152)
DEBRUCQUE CLEVELAND TRAMRAIL S
3 Technology Blvd (13032-3517)
PHONE.................................315 697-5160
Ron Debrucque, *Mng Member*
EMP: 6
SQ FT: 4,500
SALES (est): 1MM **Privately Held**
SIC: 3536 Cranes & monorail systems

(G-3153)
OWL WIRE & CABLE LLC
3127 Seneca Tpke (13032-3514)
PHONE.................................315 697-2011
Philip J Kemper, *President*
Robert J Ratti, *Chairman*
Frank Russo, *CFO*
▲ EMP: 180 EST: 1951
SQ FT: 400,000
SALES (est): 66.7MM
SALES (corp-wide): 225.3B **Publicly Held**
WEB: www.owlwire.com
SIC: 3496 Miscellaneous fabricated wire products
HQ: The Marmon Group Llc
181 W Madison St Ste 2600
Chicago IL 60602

(G-3154)
PRIME MATERIALS RECOVERY INC
51 Madison Blvd (13032-3501)
PHONE.................................315 697-5251
Francis Pratt, *Branch Mgr*
EMP: 8
SALES (corp-wide): 157.5MM **Privately Held**
SIC: 3441 Fabricated structural metal
PA: Prime Materials Recovery Inc.
99 E River Dr
East Hartford CT 06108
860 622-7626

(G-3155)
S K CIRCUITS INC (PA)
340 Rosewood Cir (13032-1556)
PHONE.................................703 376-8718
Vijay K Kodali, *President*
EMP: 12
SALES (est): 1.6MM **Privately Held**
SIC: 3672 Printed circuit boards

(G-3156)
SALARINOS ITALIAN FOODS INC
Also Called: Basilio's
110 James St (13032-1410)
P.O. Box 565 (13032-0565)
PHONE.................................315 697-9766
Vincent Salamone Jr, *President*
Debra Salamone, *Vice Pres*
EMP: 10
SQ FT: 4,050
SALES (est): 1.2MM **Privately Held**
SIC: 2013 2038 Sausages from purchased meat; pizza, frozen

(G-3157)
SIDE HILL FARMERS COOP INC
8275 State Route 13 (13032-4470)
PHONE................................315 697-9862
Paul O'Mara, *President*
Kirsten Tolman, *Treasurer*
EMP: 20
SALES: 1MM **Privately Held**
SIC: 2011 Meat packing plants

(G-3158)
THERMOLD CORPORATION
7059 Harp Rd (13032-4583)
PHONE................................315 697-3924
Jeremy Schwimmer, *Ch of Bd*
Dan Emmons, *President*
Michael Dunn, *Vice Pres*
Daniel Emmons, *VP Engrg*
▲ EMP: 106 EST: 1945
SQ FT: 35,000
SALES (est): 29.5MM **Privately Held**
WEB: www.thermold.com
SIC: 3089 Molding primary plastic; injection molding of plastics

(G-3159)
TRICON PIPING SYSTEMS INC
2 Technology Blvd (13032-3520)
P.O. Box 361 (13032-0361)
PHONE................................315 697-8787
Hugh Roszel, *President*
▼ EMP: 12 EST: 1999
SALES (est): 3.2MM **Privately Held**
WEB: www.triconpiping.com
SIC: 3317 Steel pipe & tubes

(G-3160)
VICTORY SIGNS INC
8915 Old State Route 13 (13032-5417)
PHONE................................315 762-0220
Anthony Deperno, *President*
Jennifer Deperno, *Vice Pres*
EMP: 8
SQ FT: 2,000
SALES (est): 1.1MM **Privately Held**
SIC: 3993 Signs, not made in custom sign painting shops

Candor
Tioga County

(G-3161)
H L ROBINSON SAND & GRAVEL (PA)
535 Ithaca Rd (13743)
P.O. Box 121 (13743-0121)
PHONE................................607 659-5153
Hannah L Robinson, *President*
EMP: 18
SQ FT: 5,000
SALES: 2.6MM **Privately Held**
SIC: 1442 Sand mining; gravel mining

(G-3162)
MARCELLUS ENERGY SERVICES LLC
3 Mill St Ste 6 (13743)
PHONE................................607 236-0038
Gloria Tubbs, *Mng Member*
EMP: 20 EST: 2012
SALES (est): 1.3MM **Privately Held**
SIC: 1389 Oil field services

Canton
St. Lawrence County

(G-3163)
BIMBO BAKERIES USA INC
19 Miner St Ste D (13617-1231)
PHONE................................315 379-9069
EMP: 18 **Privately Held**
SIC: 2051 Bakery: wholesale or wholesale/retail combined
HQ: Bimbo Bakeries Usa, Inc
　255 Business Center Dr # 200
　Horsham PA 19044
　215 347-5500

(G-3164)
COMMERCIAL PRESS INC
6589 Us Highway 11 (13617-3980)
P.O. Box 367 (13617-0367)
PHONE................................315 274-0028
David Charleson, *President*
Tracy Charleson, *Vice Pres*
EMP: 6
SQ FT: 1,200
SALES (est): 809.4K **Privately Held**
SIC: 2752 2759 Commercial printing, offset; commercial printing

(G-3165)
CORNING INCORPORATED
334 County Route 16 (13617-3135)
PHONE................................315 379-3200
Joseph Neubert, *Plant Mgr*
Matthew Mitchell, *Opers Staff*
Daniel Cassavaw, *Engineer*
David Jenne, *Sales Staff*
Carlos Duran, *Manager*
EMP: 86
SALES (corp-wide): 11.2B **Publicly Held**
WEB: www.corning.com
SIC: 3229 3211 Pressed & blown glass; flat glass
PA: Corning Incorporated
　1 Riverfront Plz
　Corning NY 14831
　607 974-9000

(G-3166)
FRAZER COMPUTING INC
6196 Us Highway 11 (13617-3967)
P.O. Box 569 (13617-0569)
PHONE................................315 379-3500
Michael Frazer, *Owner*
Corey Griffin, *Software Dev*
Jake Morley, *Director*
Nicole Gilson, *Executive Asst*
EMP: 26
SALES (est): 4MM **Privately Held**
WEB: www.frazercomputing.com
SIC: 7372 Business oriented computer software

(G-3167)
ST LAWRENCE COUNTY NEWSPAPERS (HQ)
Also Called: Courier Observer
1 Main St Ste 103 (13617-1279)
P.O. Box 409, Ogdensburg (13669-0409)
PHONE................................315 393-1003
Chuck Kelley, *General Mgr*
Brenda Labrake, *Business Mgr*
Debra Peters, *Accounts Exec*
▲ EMP: 60
SQ FT: 15,000
SALES (est): 5.6MM
SALES (corp-wide): 32MM **Privately Held**
WEB: www.courierobserver.com
SIC: 2711 2752 Commercial printing & newspaper publishing combined; commercial printing, lithographic
PA: Johnson Newspaper Corporation
　260 Washington St
　Watertown NY
　315 782-1000

Cape Vincent
Jefferson County

(G-3168)
METALCRAFT MARINE US INC
583 E Broadway St (13618-4152)
P.O. Box 961 (13618-0961)
PHONE................................315 501-4015
Tom Wroe, *President*
Michael Allen, *General Mgr*
Paul Cooledge, *Project Mgr*
Rob Phippen, *Controller*
Bob Clark, *Admin Sec*
▼ EMP: 17
SQ FT: 4,000
SALES: 547K
SALES (corp-wide): 13.4MM **Privately Held**
SIC: 3732 3731 Boat building & repairing; shipbuilding & repairing; barges, building & repairing; combat vessels, building & repairing; fireboats, building & repairing

PA: Metal Craft Marine Incorporated
　347 Wellington St
　Kingston ON K7K 6
　613 549-7747

Carle Place
Nassau County

(G-3169)
ALPHA WOLF LLC
241 Rushmore Ave (11514-1428)
PHONE................................516 778-5812
Michael Chalavoutis, *President*
Lorraine Chalavoutis, *Vice Pres*
EMP: 5 EST: 2015
SALES: 100K **Privately Held**
SIC: 2086 Mineral water, carbonated: packaged in cans, bottles, etc.

(G-3170)
APOLLO ORTHOTICS CORP
320 Westbury Ave (11514-1607)
PHONE................................516 333-3223
Caleb Lee, *CEO*
EMP: 5
SALES: 500K **Privately Held**
SIC: 3842 Orthopedic appliances

(G-3171)
BEE GREEN INDUSTRIES INC
322 Westbury Ave (11514-1607)
PHONE................................516 334-3525
Harold Livine, *President*
EMP: 6
SALES (est): 312.1K **Privately Held**
SIC: 3999 Manufacturing industries

(G-3172)
BIOTEMPER
Also Called: Biotemper Plus
516 Mineola Ave (11514-1716)
PHONE................................516 302-7985
Nadeem Khan, *Administration*
EMP: 5 EST: 2015
SALES (est): 229.7K **Privately Held**
SIC: 2833 Medicinal chemicals

(G-3173)
FORMED PLASTICS INC
207 Stonehinge Ln (11514-1743)
P.O. Box 347 (11514-0347)
PHONE................................516 334-2300
Patrick K Long, *President*
Stephen Zamprelli, *President*
Beth Long, *Exec VP*
David Long, *Exec VP*
Matthew Desmond, *Vice Pres*
EMP: 80 EST: 1946
SQ FT: 74,000
SALES (est): 20.3MM **Privately Held**
WEB: www.formedplastics.com
SIC: 3089 Plastic processing

(G-3174)
GENNARIS ITLN FRENCH BKY INC
Also Called: Cardinali Bakery
465 Westbury Ave (11514-1401)
PHONE................................516 997-8968
Giuseppe A Mauro, *President*
Mary Lou Makelski, *Admin Sec*
EMP: 6
SALES (est): 759.1K **Privately Held**
SIC: 2051 5461 Bread, cake & related products; bakeries

(G-3175)
JOHNSON & HOFFMAN LLC
40 Voice Rd (11514-1511)
P.O. Box 343 (11514-0343)
PHONE................................516 742-3333
Brad Ansary, *President*
Jerry Bentivegna, *Vice Pres*
Jo Dimino, *Purch Agent*
Larry Zettwoch, *VP Sales*
Jeff Cohen, *Mktg Dir*
EMP: 70
SQ FT: 65,000
SALES (est): 14.7MM **Privately Held**
WEB: www.aecjh.com
SIC: 3469 Metal stampings

(G-3176)
LOW-COST MFG CO INC
318 Westbury Ave (11514-1607)
P.O. Box 147 (11514-0147)
PHONE................................516 627-3282
Harold Rothlin, *President*
Freddy Malamud, *General Mgr*
Muriel Debeaumont, *Controller*
▲ EMP: 6
SQ FT: 4,000
SALES (est): 1MM **Privately Held**
WEB: www.lowcostmfg.com
SIC: 3564 5087 Purification & dust collection equipment; laundry equipment & supplies

(G-3177)
M&M PRINTING INC
Also Called: MARsid-M&m Group, The
245 Westbury Ave (11514-1604)
PHONE................................516 796-3020
Barry Caputo, *President*
Sidney Halpern, *Vice Pres*
Dan Magorrian, *Marketing Mgr*
Chris Brunner, *Executive*
EMP: 15
SALES (est): 1.6MM **Privately Held**
SIC: 2752 Commercial printing, offset

(G-3178)
MARKET PLACE PUBLICATIONS
Also Called: J & F Advertising
234 Silverlake Blvd Ste 2 (11514-1644)
PHONE................................516 997-7909
Gonzalez Jose, *Principal*
EMP: 40 EST: 1987
SALES (est): 1.5MM **Privately Held**
SIC: 2711 7313 Newspapers; newspaper advertising representative

(G-3179)
MARSID GROUP LTD
Also Called: Marsid Press
245 Westbury Ave (11514-1604)
PHONE................................516 334-1603
Sidney Halpern, *President*
▼ EMP: 9
SALES (est): 1.3MM **Privately Held**
WEB: www.mmprint.com
SIC: 2752 Commercial printing, offset

(G-3180)
RAYANA DESIGNS INC
288 Westbury Ave (11514-1605)
PHONE................................718 786-2040
Andreas Vassiliou, *President*
Andreas Fiorentino, *Corp Secy*
Mihran Panossian, *Vice Pres*
Dennis Fiorentino, *Admin Sec*
EMP: 20
SALES (est): 2.7MM **Privately Held**
WEB: www.rayanadesigns.com
SIC: 3479 Engraving jewelry silverware, or metal

(G-3181)
SCIENTIFIC SOLUTIONS GLOBL LLC
326 Westbury Ave (11514-1607)
PHONE................................516 543-3376
Felicia Accius, *Manager*
Aurangzeb Pirzada,
EMP: 10 EST: 2017
SQ FT: 3,600
SALES: 500K **Privately Held**
SIC: 2844 Cosmetic preparations

(G-3182)
TEXTURED FD INNVATIONS TFI LLC
552 Westbury Ave (11514-1747)
PHONE................................515 731-3663
Carol Letzter, *Principal*
John Amato, *Principal*
EMP: 6
SALES (est): 185.1K **Privately Held**
SIC: 2038 2024 2037 0751 Frozen specialties; ice cream & frozen desserts; frozen fruits & vegetables; slaughtering: custom livestock services; marine fats, oils & meals

(G-3183)
VINCENTS FOOD CORP
179 Old Country Rd (11514-1907)
PHONE..................................516 481-3544
Anthony Marisi, *President*
Robert Marisi, *Treasurer*
EMP: 12
SALES (est): 720K **Privately Held**
SIC: 2033 Tomato sauce: packaged in cans, jars, etc.

Carmel
Putnam County

(G-3184)
BIODESIGN INC OF NEW YORK (PA)
1 Sunset Rdg (10512-1118)
P.O. Box 1050 (10512-8050)
PHONE..................................845 454-6610
Susanne Ruddnick PHD, *President*
Michael Payne PHD, *Vice Pres*
EMP: 15
SQ FT: 26,000
SALES (est): 1.2MM **Privately Held**
WEB: www.biodesignofny.com
SIC: 3821 3829 Laboratory apparatus & furniture; measuring & controlling devices

(G-3185)
EASTERN JUNGLE GYM INC (PA)
30 Commerce Dr (10512-3026)
PHONE..................................845 878-9800
Scott Honigsberg, *President*
Rolf Zimmerman, *President*
Mark Honigsberg, *Vice Pres*
Barbara Hobbs,
◆ **EMP:** 30
SQ FT: 30,000
SALES (est): 6.3MM **Privately Held**
WEB: www.playsystem.com
SIC: 3949 5941 Playground equipment; playground equipment

(G-3186)
J & J TL DIE MFG & STAMPG CORP
594 Horsepound Rd (10512-4703)
PHONE..................................845 228-0242
Ronald C Johnson, *President*
EMP: 5 **EST:** 1981
SQ FT: 4,800
SALES (est): 554.9K **Privately Held**
SIC: 3599 Machine shop, jobbing & repair

(G-3187)
JAMES A STALEY CO INC
5 Bowen Ct (10512-4535)
PHONE..................................845 878-3344
James A Staley, *President*
J David Mori, *Vice Pres*
Kevin Loffredo, *Engineer*
Wayne Ackert, *Sales Staff*
Chris Staley, *Manager*
EMP: 18
SQ FT: 15,800
SALES (est): 5.2MM **Privately Held**
WEB: www.staleyco.com
SIC: 3829 7699 Aircraft & motor vehicle measurement equipment; testers for checking hydraulic controls on aircraft; fuel system instruments, aircraft; aircraft & heavy equipment repair services; hydraulic equipment repair

(G-3188)
NORTHEAST MESA LLC (PA)
10 Commerce Dr (10512-3026)
PHONE..................................845 878-9344
Giulio Burra,
Phil Waylonis,
EMP: 12 **EST:** 1995
SQ FT: 8,400
SALES (est): 2.1MM **Privately Held**
WEB: www.northeastmesa.com
SIC: 3271 Blocks, concrete: landscape or retaining wall

(G-3189)
PATTERSON BLACKTOP CORP
Also Called: Peckham Materials
1181 Route 6 (10512-1645)
P.O. Box 849 (10512-0849)
PHONE..................................845 628-3425
Kurt Gabrielson, *Branch Mgr*
EMP: 6
SALES (corp-wide): 171.1MM **Privately Held**
SIC: 2951 Asphalt paving mixtures & blocks
HQ: Patterson Blacktop Corp
20 Haarlem Ave
White Plains NY 10603

(G-3190)
PRECISION ARMS INC
Also Called: Time Precision
421 Route 52 (10512-6063)
PHONE..................................845 225-1130
Art Cocchia, *President*
Steven Cocchia, *Vice Pres*
EMP: 6
SQ FT: 3,500
SALES (est): 524.2K **Privately Held**
WEB: www.precisionarms.com
SIC: 3599 7699 Machine shop, jobbing & repair; gunsmith shop

(G-3191)
TPA COMPUTER CORP
531 Route 52 Apt 4 (10512-6073)
PHONE..................................877 866-6044
Steven Barnes, *President*
EMP: 10
SQ FT: 1,000
SALES (est): 1.2MM **Privately Held**
WEB: www.tpacomputer.com
SIC: 7372 5734 Application computer software; computer & software stores

(G-3192)
TRAFFIC LANE CLOSURES LLC
1214 Route 52 Ste 1 (10512-4569)
P.O. Box 726, Brewster (10509-0726)
PHONE..................................845 228-6100
Ralph M Rosenfeld, *General Mgr*
Teresa Rosenfeld, *Mng Member*
EMP: 13
SQ FT: 3,800
SALES: 1.7MM **Privately Held**
WEB: www.trafficlaneclosures.com
SIC: 3669 1611 7359 3679 Highway signals, electric; highway signs & guardrails; work zone traffic equipment (flags, cones, barrels, etc.); attenuators; soil erosion control fabrics

Carthage
Jefferson County

(G-3193)
A B C MC CLEARY SIGN CO INC
40230 State Route 3 (13619-9727)
PHONE..................................315 493-3550
Ronald Moore, *President*
Jo Anne Moore, *Corp Secy*
EMP: 11
SQ FT: 15,000
SALES (est): 792.9K **Privately Held**
SIC: 3993 Electric signs

(G-3194)
CARTHAGE FIBRE DRUM INC (PA)
14 Hewitt Dr (13619-1101)
P.O. Box 109 (13619-0109)
PHONE..................................315 493-2730
Timothy Wright, *President*
Cathy Wright, *Corp Secy*
Ford Wright Sr, *Vice Pres*
EMP: 15 **EST:** 1915
SQ FT: 1,509
SALES (est): 2.5MM **Privately Held**
SIC: 2655 Fiber cans, drums & similar products

(G-3195)
CEM MACHINE INC (PA)
571 W End Ave (13619-1038)
PHONE..................................315 493-4258
Mark Robinson, *President*

Jason Flint, *Engineer*
Timothy Nettles, *Treasurer*
Roxanne Robinson, *Treasurer*
▲ **EMP:** 48
SQ FT: 80,000
SALES (est): 6.9MM **Privately Held**
WEB: www.cem-machine.com
SIC: 3599 Machine shop, jobbing & repair

(G-3196)
CHAMPION MATERIALS INC (PA)
502 S Washington St (13619-1533)
P.O. Box 127 (13619-0127)
PHONE..................................315 493-2654
James D Uhlinger Jr, *Ch of Bd*
EMP: 6
SALES (est): 6.2MM **Privately Held**
WEB: www.championmaterials.com
SIC: 3273 5211 Ready-mixed concrete; sand & gravel

(G-3197)
DAVID JOHNSON
Also Called: Poly Can
Deer River Rd (13619)
PHONE..................................315 493-4735
David Johnson, *Owner*
EMP: 12
SQ FT: 12,000
SALES: 2MM **Privately Held**
SIC: 3085 Plastics bottles

Castile
Wyoming County

(G-3198)
DON BECK INC
5249 State Route 39 (14427-9518)
PHONE..................................585 493-3040
Richard T Beck, *President*
EMP: 6
SALES (est): 994.1K **Privately Held**
SIC: 3523 Farm machinery & equipment

Castle Creek
Broome County

(G-3199)
A D BOWMAN & SON LUMBER CO
1737 Us Highway 11 (13744-1107)
PHONE..................................607 692-2595
Melvin Bowman, *Ch of Bd*
Joanne Bowman, *President*
Joel Bowman, *Vice Pres*
EMP: 28
SALES (est): 4.3MM **Privately Held**
SIC: 2426 2448 2421 Lumber, hardwood dimension; pallets, wood & wood with metal; sawmills & planing mills, general

Castleton On Hudson
Rensselaer County

(G-3200)
CELL-NIQUE CORPORATION
22 Hamilton Way (12033-1015)
PHONE..................................203 856-8550
Dan Ratner, *CEO*
◆ **EMP:** 1
SQ FT: 1,000,000
SALES (est): 3.1MM **Privately Held**
WEB: www.cell-nique.com
SIC: 2086 Iced tea & fruit drinks, bottled & canned

(G-3201)
CURTIS PRTG CO THE DEL PRESS
1528 Columbia Tpke (12033-9584)
PHONE..................................518 477-4820
Richard Lieberman, *President*
Bruce Curtis, *Principal*
EMP: 5

SALES (est): 609.8K **Privately Held**
WEB: www.curtisprinting.com
SIC: 2759 Letterpress printing

(G-3202)
DANCING DEER BAKING CO LLC
22 Hamilton Way (12033-1015)
PHONE..................................617 442-7300
Kevin McGahren, *CEO*
EMP: 50
SALES (est): 15.2MM **Privately Held**
WEB: www.dancingdeer.com
SIC: 2051 2052 Bakery: wholesale or wholesale/retail combined; cookies & crackers

(G-3203)
MOORADIAN HYDRAULICS & EQP CO (PA)
1190 Route 9 (12033-9686)
PHONE..................................518 766-3866
Richard Mooradian, *President*
Thomas Mooradian, *Vice Pres*
EMP: 12
SQ FT: 17,200
SALES (est): 2.5MM **Privately Held**
SIC: 7692 7699 5085 Welding repair; hydraulic equipment repair; hose, belting & packing

(G-3204)
SAXTON CORPORATION
1320 Route 9 (12033-9686)
PHONE..................................518 732-7705
Mike Kellog, *President*
EMP: 30
SALES (est): 2.7MM **Privately Held**
SIC: 3993 Signs & advertising specialties

(G-3205)
VIWIT PHARMACEUTICALS INC
1600 Brookview Station Rd (12033-3123)
PHONE..................................201 701-9787
Keene WEI, *President*
Augie Aswan, *Manager*
EMP: 5
SQ FT: 2,000
SALES (est): 300.7K **Privately Held**
SIC: 2834 Pharmaceutical preparations

Castorland
Lewis County

(G-3206)
BLACK RIVER WOODWORKING LLC
4773 State Route 410 (13620-2301)
PHONE..................................315 376-8405
Melvin Hess,
Brian Ball,
Ronald Hess,
EMP: 5 **EST:** 1993
SQ FT: 6,000
SALES (est): 550K **Privately Held**
SIC: 2511 Wood household furniture

(G-3207)
DANIEL & LOIS LYNDAKER LOGGING
10460 Monnat School Rd (13620-1270)
PHONE..................................315 346-6527
Lois Lyndaker, *Principal*
EMP: 8 **EST:** 2010
SALES (est): 806K **Privately Held**
SIC: 2411 Logging

(G-3208)
LYNDAKER TIMBER HARVESTING LLC
10204 State Route 812 (13620-1268)
PHONE..................................315 346-1328
David R Lyndaker,
Anita Lyndaker,
EMP: 11
SALES (est): 1.2MM **Privately Held**
SIC: 2411 Timber, cut at logging camp

Cato
Cayuga County

(G-3209)
ZAPPALA FARMS AG SYSTEMS INC
11404 Schuler Rd (13033-4276)
PHONE..........................315 626-6293
James R Zappala, *President*
Samuel Zappala, *Vice Pres*
John R Zappala, *Admin Sec*
Cathy Zappala,
EMP: 30
SALES (est): 2.4MM **Privately Held**
SIC: 3523 5531 Farm machinery & equipment; automotive accessories

Catskill
Greene County

(G-3210)
CIMENT ST-LAURENT INC
Also Called: St Lawrence Cement Co
6446 Route 9w (12414-5322)
P.O. Box 31 (12414-0031)
PHONE..........................518 943-4040
Georges Hubin, *Branch Mgr*
EMP: 140
SALES (corp-wide): 30.6B **Privately Held**
SIC: 3241 Masonry cement
HQ: Groupe Crh Canada Inc
2300 Steeles Ave W Bureau 400
Concord ON L4K 5
877 332-3006

(G-3211)
GOLUB CORPORATION
Also Called: Price Chopper Pharmacy
320 W Bridge St (12414-1730)
PHONE..........................518 943-3903
Kathleen Bryant, *Branch Mgr*
EMP: 21
SALES (corp-wide): 3.6B **Privately Held**
SIC: 3751 Motorcycles & related parts
PA: The Golub Corporation
461 Nott St
Schenectady NY 12308
518 355-5000

(G-3212)
LEHIGH CEMENT COMPANY
120 Alpha Rd (12414-6902)
PHONE..........................518 943-5940
Cheryl McElroy, *Manager*
EMP: 20
SALES (corp-wide): 367.6MM **Privately Held**
WEB: www.gfcement.com
SIC: 3273 5032 Ready-mixed concrete; cement
HQ: Lehigh Cement Company
313 Warren St
Glens Falls NY 12801
518 792-1137

(G-3213)
LEHIGH NORTHEAST CEMENT CO
120 Alpha Rd (12414-6902)
PHONE..........................518 792-1137
Cheryl McElroy, *Principal*
Kerry Dietrich, *Manager*
EMP: 6
SQ FT: 3,648
SALES (est): 786.3K **Privately Held**
SIC: 3273 Ready-mixed concrete

(G-3214)
MARK T WESTINGHOUSE
Also Called: Pro Printers of Greene County
138 Grandview Ave (12414-1934)
PHONE..........................518 678-3262
Mark T Westinghouse, *Owner*
EMP: 6 **EST:** 1970
SQ FT: 2,000
SALES: 600K **Privately Held**
SIC: 2752 2759 Commercial printing, offset; letterpress printing

(G-3215)
MOUNTAIN T-SHIRTS INC
Also Called: Mountain T-Shirts & Sign Works
8 W Bridge St (12414-1620)
PHONE..........................518 943-4533
Craig Remaley, *President*
Daniel Webster, *Corp Secy*
Michael Marciante, *Treasurer*
EMP: 6
SALES (est): 380K **Privately Held**
WEB: www.mountaintshirts.com
SIC: 2396 2261 5136 5199 Printing & embossing on plastics fabric articles; printing of cotton broadwoven fabrics; men's & boys' clothing; gifts & novelties

(G-3216)
PECKHAM INDUSTRIES INC
7065 Us Highway 9w (12414-5311)
P.O. Box 146, Ashland (12407-0146)
PHONE..........................518 943-0155
Gary Metcalf, *Principal*
EMP: 18
SALES (corp-wide): 171.1MM **Privately Held**
SIC: 2951 Concrete, asphaltic (not from refineries)
PA: Peckham Industries, Inc.
20 Haarlem Ave Ste 200
White Plains NY 10603
914 949-2000

(G-3217)
WILLIAM MOON IRON WORKS INC
Also Called: Moon, Wm
80 Main St (12414-1805)
PHONE..........................518 943-3861
Paul Moon, *President*
EMP: 10
SQ FT: 6,000
SALES: 450K **Privately Held**
SIC: 3599 Machine shop, jobbing & repair

(G-3218)
WOLFGANG B GOURMET FOODS INC
117 Cauterskill Ave (12414-1748)
PHONE..........................518 719-1727
Wolfgang Brandl, *President*
Penelope Queen, *Vice Pres*
Dr Fereidoon Behin, *Shareholder*
EMP: 14
SQ FT: 10,000
SALES (est): 2.4MM **Privately Held**
SIC: 2033 Spaghetti & other pasta sauce: packaged in cans, jars, etc.

Cattaraugus
Cattaraugus County

(G-3219)
ADAMS LUMBER CO INC
6052 Adams Rd (14719-9567)
PHONE..........................716 358-2815
John Adams, *President*
Dennis Adams, *Treasurer*
EMP: 16 **EST:** 1961
SQ FT: 10,000
SALES (est): 2.1MM **Privately Held**
SIC: 2421 Lumber: rough, sawed or planed

(G-3220)
CHESTER-JENSEN COMPANY
124 S Main St (14719-1240)
PHONE..........................610 876-6276
Albert Gimbrone, *Opers-Prdtn-Mfg*
EMP: 40
SQ FT: 52,232
SALES (corp-wide): 5.1MM **Privately Held**
WEB: www.chester-jensen.com
SIC: 3556 Food products machinery
PA: Chester-Jensen Company
345 Tilghman St
Chester PA 19013
610 876-6276

(G-3221)
P & C GAS MEASUREMENTS SERVICE
Also Called: P & C Service
9505 Tannery Rd (14719-9761)
PHONE..........................716 257-3412
James Perkins, *CEO*
Marie Robbons, *Manager*
EMP: 11
SQ FT: 5,000
SALES (est): 826.6K **Privately Held**
SIC: 1389 Oil sampling service for oil companies

(G-3222)
SETTERSTIX INC
261 S Main St (14719-1312)
PHONE..........................716 257-3451
Eric Pritchard, *President*
Scott Turner, *Prdtn Mgr*
Ron Wasmund, *Controller*
▼ **EMP:** 43
SALES (est): 12.2MM **Privately Held**
SIC: 2679 Paperboard products, converted

Cayuta
Schuyler County

(G-3223)
WAGNER HARDWOODS LLC
6307 St Route 224 (14824)
P.O. Box 68 (14824-0068)
PHONE..........................607 594-3321
Les Wagner, *Branch Mgr*
EMP: 200 **Privately Held**
WEB: www.wagner-hardwoods.com
SIC: 2421 Sawmills & planing mills, general
PA: Wagner Hardwoods Llc
6052 County Road 20
Friendship NY 14739

Cazenovia
Madison County

(G-3224)
BYS PUBLISHING LLC
118 Albany St (13035-1257)
PHONE..........................315 655-9431
Brent Selleck,
◆ **EMP:** 5
SALES (est): 316.5K **Privately Held**
SIC: 2741 Miscellaneous publishing

(G-3225)
CONTINENTAL CORDAGE CORP (DH)
75 Burton St (13035-1156)
P.O. Box 623 (13035-0623)
PHONE..........................315 655-9800
Rodney D Kent, *President*
▲ **EMP:** 100
SQ FT: 60,000
SALES (est): 5.8MM
SALES (corp-wide): 2.9B **Privately Held**
WEB: www.iwgbwd.com
SIC: 2298 3357 3496 3356 Cordage: abaca, sisal, henequen, hemp, jute or other fiber; nonferrous wiredrawing & insulating; miscellaneous fabricated wire products; nonferrous rolling & drawing; copper rolling & drawing; steel wire & related products

(G-3226)
D R CORNUE WOODWORKS
3206 Us Route 20 (13035-8408)
PHONE..........................315 655-9463
Dale R Cornue, *Owner*
EMP: 6
SQ FT: 6,000
SALES: 600K **Privately Held**
SIC: 2431 Doors, wood; woodwork, interior & ornamental; windows, wood

(G-3227)
FITZSIMMONS SYSTEMS INC
53 Nelson St (13035-1306)
PHONE..........................315 214-7010
Lowell Todd Fitzsimmons, *President*

▼ **EMP:** 13
SQ FT: 1,500
SALES (est): 2.2MM **Privately Held**
WEB: www.fuelstoragetank.com
SIC: 2899 Chemical preparations

(G-3228)
KNOWLES CAZENOVIA INC (HQ)
Also Called: Dli
2777 Us Route 20 (13035-8444)
PHONE..........................315 655-8710
Michael P Busse, *Ch of Bd*
David Wightman, *President*
Jon Keenan, *Production*
Tim Brauner, *Engineer*
Brian Nagle, *Engineer*
▲ **EMP:** 179
SQ FT: 120,000
SALES (est): 34MM
SALES (corp-wide): 826.9MM **Publicly Held**
WEB: www.dilabs.com
SIC: 3675 Electronic capacitors
PA: Knowles Corporation
1151 Maplewood Dr
Itasca IL 60143
630 250-5100

(G-3229)
MADISON COUNTY DISTILLERY LLC
2420 Rte 20 (13035-8438)
PHONE..........................315 391-6070
Patrick Ruddy,
EMP: 5
SALES (est): 205K **Privately Held**
SIC: 2085 Gin (alcoholic beverage); vodka (alcoholic beverage)

(G-3230)
MALL INC
4876 Bethel Rd (13035-9621)
PHONE..........................315 751-9490
Peter Burr, *CEO*
Steven Petrocelli, *President*
EMP: 2
SALES: 5.5MM **Privately Held**
SIC: 7372 Application computer software

(G-3231)
MARQUARDT SWITCHES INC (DH)
2711 Us Route 20 (13035-9405)
PHONE..........................315 655-8050
Harold Marquardt, *Ch of Bd*
Kirk Wardell, *President*
John Jelfo, *CFO*
Peter Mitchell, *Admin Sec*
▲ **EMP:** 200 **EST:** 1981
SQ FT: 98,000
SALES: 250MM
SALES (corp-wide): 711.6K **Privately Held**
WEB: www.switches.com
SIC: 3613 3625 Switchgear & switchboard apparatus; switches, electric power
HQ: Marquardt Gmbh
SchloBstr. 16
Rietheim-Weilheim 78604
742 499-0

(G-3232)
PDJ INC
Also Called: Johnson Bros Lumber
2550 E Ballina Rd (13035-8475)
PHONE..........................315 655-8824
Paul Johnson, *President*
Judith Johnson, *Vice Pres*
Kara Connellan, *Office Spvr*
Heather Johnson, *Admin Sec*
EMP: 30
SQ FT: 39,400
SALES (est): 5.3MM **Privately Held**
SIC: 2421 Lumber: rough, sawed or planed

(G-3233)
PEAKS COFFEE COMPANY
3264 Rte 20 (13035-8408)
P.O. Box 539 (13035-0539)
PHONE..........................315 565-1900
Kelsey Ball, *Co-Owner*
Samuel Bender, *Co-Owner*
EMP: 5
SQ FT: 1,100

SALES (est): 169.2K **Privately Held**
SIC: 2095 Coffee roasting (except by wholesale grocers)

(G-3234)
PRICET PRINTING
3852 Charles Rd (13035-4505)
PHONE................315 655-0369
Nathan Hoak, *President*
EMP: 6
SALES (est): 726.3K **Privately Held**
SIC: 2752 Commercial printing, lithographic

(G-3235)
STK ELECTRONICS INC
Also Called: Air-O-Tronics
2747 Rte 20 (13035-8444)
PHONE................315 655-8476
Bill Merlini, *Ch of Bd*
Peter M Kip, *Principal*
Peter Mitchell, *Principal*
William Merlini, *CFO*
▲ EMP: 40
SQ FT: 20,000
SALES (est): 9.4MM **Privately Held**
WEB: www.stkelectronics.com
SIC: 3675 5063 Electronic capacitors; electrical apparatus & equipment; circuit breakers

(G-3236)
TRONSER INC
3066 John Trush Jr Blvd (13035-9541)
PHONE................315 655-9528
Michael Tronser, *President*
James Dowd, *Vice Pres*
James Biando, *Mfg Staff*
Peter Mitchell, *Admin Sec*
▲ EMP: 6
SQ FT: 7,000
SALES (est): 1.4MM
SALES (corp-wide): 9.7MM **Privately Held**
WEB: www.tronser.com
SIC: 3675 Electronic capacitors
PA: Alfred Tronser Gmbh
Quellenweg 14
Engelsbrand 75331
708 279-80

(G-3237)
VOLTRONICS LLC
Also Called: Trimmer Capacitor Company, The
2777 Us Route 20 (13035-8444)
PHONE................410 749-2424
Aaron Goldberg, *General Mgr*
EMP: 48 EST: 1963
SQ FT: 200,000
SALES (est): 8.2MM
SALES (corp-wide): 6.9B **Publicly Held**
WEB: www.variablecap.com
SIC: 3675 Electronic capacitors
PA: Dover Corporation
3005 Highland Pkwy # 200
Downers Grove IL 60515
630 541-1540

Cedarhurst
Nassau County

(G-3238)
ABLE KITCHEN
Also Called: Able Kitchen Supplies
540 Willow Ave Unit B (11516-2211)
PHONE................877 268-1264
Schulman Joseph, *Owner*
Raquel Walt, *Marketing Mgr*
EMP: 15
SALES (est): 994.2K **Privately Held**
SIC: 2434 Wood kitchen cabinets

(G-3239)
GLOBAL SECURITY TECH LLC
123 Grove Ave Ste 222 (11516-2302)
PHONE................917 838-4507
Yoram Curiel, *CEO*
Victor Franco, *President*
Samuel Franco, *VP Sales*
Ivan Ivanov, *Marketing Staff*
Victor Dabah,
EMP: 10

SALES (est): 73.2K **Privately Held**
SIC: 3089 Identification cards, plastic

(G-3240)
M & M BAGEL CORP
Also Called: Bagelry
507 Central Ave (11516-2010)
PHONE................516 295-1222
Vincent Matuozzi, *President*
Robert Madorsky, *Vice Pres*
EMP: 12
SALES (est): 1MM **Privately Held**
SIC: 2051 5461 Bagels, fresh or frozen; bagels

(G-3241)
MARK F ROSENHAFT N A O
538 Central Ave (11516-2127)
PHONE................516 374-1010
Mark F Rosenhaft, *Owner*
EMP: 8
SALES (est): 429.8K **Privately Held**
SIC: 3851 5999 Eyes, glass & plastic; miscellaneous retail stores

(G-3242)
NANO VIBRONIX INC (PA)
601 Chestnut St (11516-2228)
PHONE................516 374-8330
Harold Jacobs, *President*
EMP: 6
SALES (est): 1.7MM **Privately Held**
SIC: 3841 Surgical & medical instruments

(G-3243)
NJR MEDICAL DEVICES
390 Oak Ave (11516-1824)
P.O. Box 582, New York (10021-0034)
PHONE................440 258-8204
Nicholas Pastron, *CEO*
EMP: 20
SALES (est): 2.2MM **Privately Held**
SIC: 3841 Suction therapy apparatus

(G-3244)
SOLAR THIN FILMS INC (PA)
Also Called: Stf
445 Central Ave Unit 366 (11516-2077)
PHONE................212 629-8260
Robert M Bubin, *CEO*
▲ EMP: 28
SALES (est): 3.9MM **Publicly Held**
SIC: 3674 Photovoltaic devices, solid state

Center Moriches
Suffolk County

(G-3245)
DIAMOND PRECAST PRODUCTS INC
170 Railroad Ave (11934-1906)
PHONE................631 874-3777
Rick Cerrone, *President*
Dominic Iannuci, *Treasurer*
Ronald Notaranonio, *Admin Sec*
EMP: 15 EST: 1999
SALES (est): 1.8MM **Privately Held**
SIC: 3272 Precast terrazo or concrete products

(G-3246)
ISLAND READY MIX INC
170 Railroad Ave (11934-1906)
PHONE................631 874-3777
Rice Cerrone, *President*
Dominic Iannuci, *Treasurer*
Ronald Notarantonio, *Admin Sec*
EMP: 25 EST: 1961
SALES (est): 4.5MM **Privately Held**
WEB: www.islandreadymix.com
SIC: 3273 3272 Ready-mixed concrete; concrete products, precast

(G-3247)
RED TAIL MOULDING & MLLWK LLC
23 Frowein Rd Ste 1 (11934-1606)
PHONE................516 852-4613
Tom Smith,
EMP: 3
SALES: 1.2MM **Privately Held**
SIC: 2431 Doors & door parts & trim, wood

(G-3248)
SPECIALTY PRODUCTS INC
15 Frowein Rd Bldg E2 (11934-1609)
P.O. Box 1164, Westhampton Beach (11978-7164)
PHONE................866 869-4335
Vincent Immordino, *CEO*
Linda Bonhof, *President*
EMP: 20
SQ FT: 10,000
SALES: 10MM **Privately Held**
SIC: 3089 5199 Injection molded finished plastic products; general merchandise, non-durable

Centereach
Suffolk County

(G-3249)
A M S SIGN DESIGNS
2360 Middle Country Rd (11720-3523)
PHONE................631 467-7722
Mark Saccone, *Owner*
Suzanna Saccone, *Co-Owner*
EMP: 5
SALES (est): 415.3K **Privately Held**
SIC: 3993 Signs & advertising specialties

(G-3250)
CALIBRATION TECHNOLOGIES INC
30 Woodland Blvd (11720-3636)
PHONE................631 676-6133
Thomas J Accardi, *President*
EMP: 5
SALES (est): 526K **Privately Held**
SIC: 3629 Electrical industrial apparatus

(G-3251)
I FIX SCREEN
203 Centereach Mall (11720-2751)
PHONE................631 421-1938
Alberto Cruz, *Principal*
EMP: 6 EST: 2013
SALES (est): 421.2K **Privately Held**
SIC: 3442 Screen & storm doors & windows

(G-3252)
QUANTA ELECTRONICS INC
48 Fran Ln (11720-4441)
PHONE................631 961-9953
Martin Czerniewski, *President*
EMP: 12
SALES (est): 1.4MM **Privately Held**
SIC: 3663 Radio & TV communications equipment

(G-3253)
WIN SET TECHNOLOGIES LLC
2364 Middle Country Rd (11720-3502)
P.O. Box 2007, Miller Place (11764-8786)
PHONE................631 234-7077
Philip Settepani,
Frederick Winter III,
▼ EMP: 10 EST: 2001
SQ FT: 3,000
SALES: 750K **Privately Held**
WEB: www.winset.net
SIC: 3542 Presses: forming, stamping, punching, sizing (machine tools)

Centerport
Suffolk County

(G-3254)
BLONDIE S BAKESHOP INC
90 Washington Dr (11721-1831)
PHONE................631 424-4545
Jeff Kennaugh, *President*
EMP: 8
SALES (est): 592.2K **Privately Held**
SIC: 2051 Bakery: wholesale or wholesale/retail combined

(G-3255)
FORUM PUBLISHING CO
Also Called: Marketer's Forum Magazine
383 E Main St (11721-1538)
PHONE................631 754-5000

Martin B Stevens, *Owner*
EMP: 9
SQ FT: 3,000
SALES: 1.4MM **Privately Held**
WEB: www.forum123.com
SIC: 2721 Trade journals: publishing & printing

(G-3256)
LEESA DESIGNS LTD
31 Glenn Cres (11721-1715)
P.O. Box 488 (11721-0488)
PHONE................631 261-3991
Helen L Dello-Iacona, *President*
Helen L Dello-Iacora, *President*
Sara Mazzola, *Treasurer*
EMP: 5 EST: 1997
SALES: 200K **Privately Held**
SIC: 2339 Neckwear & ties: women's, misses' & juniors'

(G-3257)
MSP TECHNOLOGYCOM LLC
77 Bankside Dr (11721-1738)
PHONE................631 424-7542
Walter Stark, *CEO*
Jeanne Connor-Stark,
EMP: 3
SQ FT: 1,200
SALES (est): 1.2MM **Privately Held**
WEB: www.msptechnology.com
SIC: 3585 5075 Humidifiers & dehumidifiers; dehumidifiers, except portable

(G-3258)
SURVIVAL INC
90 Washington Dr Ste C (11721-1831)
PHONE................631 385-5060
Sanjay Lakhani, *President*
Rebecca Lakhani, *Vice Pres*
▲ EMP: 8
SALES (est): 1MM **Privately Held**
WEB: www.survivalrules.com
SIC: 2339 Women's & misses' outerwear

Central Bridge
Schoharie County

(G-3259)
AMERICAN STANDARD MFG INC
Also Called: Asm
106 Industrial Park Ln (12035)
P.O. Box 164 (12035-0164)
PHONE................518 868-2512
Coleman Vickary, *Chairman*
Aaron Haig, *Prdtn Mgr*
Bob Zieschang, *Sales Staff*
Sharon Miller, *Software Dev*
Connie Vickary, *Admin Sec*
EMP: 25
SQ FT: 28,000
SALES (est): 6MM **Privately Held**
WEB: www.amrstd.com
SIC: 3499 2542 Machine bases, metal; partitions & fixtures, except wood

Central Islip
Suffolk County

(G-3260)
AH ELCTRONIC TEST EQP REPR CTR
7 Olive St (11722-4017)
PHONE................631 234-8979
Audley Haynes, *Principal*
Nicole Johnson, *COO*
EMP: 12 **Privately Held**
WEB: www.ahelectronics.com
SIC: 1389 3825 7629 Testing, measuring, surveying & analysis services; standards & calibration equipment for electrical measuring; electronic equipment repair
PA: Ah Electronic Test Equipment Repair Center Inc
374 Islip Ave Ste 201
Islip NY 11751

(G-3261)
ALPHAMED BOTTLES INC
300 S Technology Dr (11722-4400)
PHONE................631 524-5577

Subhakar Viyala, *President*
Pavan Vemula, *Opers Mgr*
▲ **EMP:** 21
SQ FT: 26,000
SALES: 8MM **Privately Held**
SIC: 3085 Plastics bottles

(G-3262)
ASCENT PHARMACEUTICALS INC (HQ)
400 S Technology Dr (11722-4402)
PHONE..................................631 851-0550
Sudhakar Viviyala, *CEO*
▲ **EMP:** 96
SALES (est): 21.5MM **Privately Held**
SIC: 2834 Pharmaceutical preparations

(G-3263)
AUTRONIC PLASTICS INC
Also Called: API
1150 Motor Pkwy (11722-1217)
PHONE..................................516 333-7577
Michael Lax, *President*
Tim Keuning, *President*
Agjah I Libohova, *Research*
Jerzy Prochnicki, *Manager*
Karen Ledoux, *Executive*
▲ **EMP:** 120
SQ FT: 55,000
SALES (est): 37.9MM **Privately Held**
WEB: www.apisolution.com
SIC: 3089 5162 Injection molding of plastics; plastics products

(G-3264)
AVCO INDUSTRIES INC
120 Windsor Pl (11722-3331)
P.O. Box 416, Huntington Station (11746-0338)
PHONE..................................631 851-1555
Gil Korine, *Ch of Bd*
▲ **EMP:** 15
SQ FT: 40,000
SALES (est): 9.8MM **Privately Held**
SIC: 2679 Pressed fiber & molded pulp products except food products

(G-3265)
BERKSHIRE TRANSFORMER (PA)
Also Called: Custom Power Systems
77 Windsor Pl Ste 18 (11722-3334)
PHONE..................................631 467-5328
Paul Alessandrini, *Owner*
EMP: 5
SALES (est): 916.7K **Privately Held**
SIC: 3679 3612 Electronic loads & power supplies; transformers, except electric

(G-3266)
BI NUTRACEUTICALS INC
120 Hoffman Ln (11749-5008)
PHONE..................................631 232-1105
Bob Harvey, *Manager*
EMP: 52
SALES (corp-wide): 23MM **Privately Held**
WEB: www.botanicals.com
SIC: 2834 Vitamin preparations
HQ: Bi Nutraceuticals, Inc.
2384 E Pacifica Pl
Rancho Dominguez CA 90220
310 669-2100

(G-3267)
CELLU TISSUE - LONG ISLAND LLC
555 N Research Pl (11722-4417)
PHONE..................................631 232-2626
Russell C Taylor,
▲ **EMP:** 210
SALES (est): 22.5MM **Publicly Held**
SIC: 2676 Sanitary paper products
HQ: Cellu Tissue Holdings, Inc.
12725 Morris Road Ext
Alpharetta GA 30004

(G-3268)
CENTRAL ISLIP PHARMACY INC
1629 Islip Ave (11722-2701)
PHONE..................................631 234-6039
Ronald Goodstadt, *Principal*
EMP: 7

SALES (est): 847.4K **Privately Held**
SIC: 2834 Adrenal pharmaceutical preparations

(G-3269)
COLOR CARD LLC
Also Called: Limo-Print.com
1065 Islip Ave (11722-4203)
PHONE..................................631 232-1300
Robert Haller Sr, *President*
Marilyn Haller, *Vice Pres*
EMP: 18
SQ FT: 110,000
SALES (est): 1.5MM **Privately Held**
SIC: 2752 5961 2759 Business form & card printing, lithographic; cards, mail order; invitations: printing

(G-3270)
CREATIVE HOME FURNISHINGS (PA)
Also Called: Dakotah
250 Creative Dr (11722-4404)
PHONE..................................631 582-8000
Gunther Bartsch, *President*
◆ **EMP:** 3
SALES (est): 8.1MM **Privately Held**
WEB: www.dakotah.com
SIC: 2392 Cushions & pillows

(G-3271)
CVD EQUIPMENT CORPORATION (PA)
Also Called: C V D
355 S Technology Dr (11722-4416)
PHONE..................................631 981-7081
Leonard A Rosenbaum, *Ch of Bd*
Steven Aragon, *COO*
William Linss, *Vice Pres*
Max Shatalov, *Vice Pres*
Karlheinz Strobl, *Vice Pres*
▲ **EMP:** 199
SQ FT: 130,000
SALES: 24.3MM **Publicly Held**
WEB: www.cvdequipment.com
SIC: 3674 Semiconductors & related devices

(G-3272)
CVD EQUIPMENT CORPORATION
Also Called: Conceptronic
355 S Technology Dr (11722-4416)
PHONE..................................631 582-4365
Leonard Rosenbaum, *President*
EMP: 15
SALES (corp-wide): 24.3MM **Publicly Held**
WEB: www.cvdequipment.com
SIC: 3559 3567 Semiconductor manufacturing machinery; heating units & devices, industrial: electric
PA: Cvd Equipment Corporation
355 S Technology Dr
Central Islip NY 11722
631 981-7081

(G-3273)
EUGENE G DANNER MFG INC
Also Called: Danner, Eg Mfg
160 Oval Dr (11749-1403)
PHONE..................................631 234-5261
Eugene G Danner, *President*
Josephine Danner, *Corp Secy*
Michael Danner, *Vice Pres*
▲ **EMP:** 38 **EST:** 1948
SQ FT: 31,000
SALES (est): 7.9MM **Privately Held**
WEB: www.dannermfg.com
SIC: 3089 Aquarium accessories, plastic

(G-3274)
FAR EASTERN COCONUT COMPANY
200 Corporate Plz 201a (11749-1552)
PHONE..................................631 851-8800
Richard Martino, *President*
Mitchell Bauman, *Treasurer*
▲ **EMP:** 10
SQ FT: 2,000
SALES (est): 640K **Privately Held**
SIC: 2099 Coconut, desiccated & shredded

(G-3275)
FHA FIREDOOR CORP
32 Windsor Pl (11722-3302)
PHONE..................................718 366-1700
Paul Sklar, *CEO*
EMP: 5
SALES (est): 581.8K **Privately Held**
SIC: 3442 Metal doors, sash & trim

(G-3276)
FREEPORT PAPER INDUSTRIES INC
120 Windsor Pl (11722-3331)
PHONE..................................631 851-1555
Gil Korine, *Ch of Bd*
◆ **EMP:** 60
SQ FT: 40,000
SALES (est): 14.1MM **Privately Held**
SIC: 2621 Paper mills

(G-3277)
GMR MANUFACTURING INC
Also Called: George Raum Manufacturing
101 Windsor Pl Unit D (11722-3329)
PHONE..................................631 582-2600
George Raum, *President*
EMP: 6 **EST:** 1976
SQ FT: 2,300
SALES (est): 520.4K **Privately Held**
SIC: 3599 Machine shop, jobbing & repair

(G-3278)
INVAGEN PHARMACEUTICALS INC
550 S Research Pl (11722-4415)
PHONE..................................631 949-6367
Fakiha Rana, *Branch Mgr*
EMP: 150
SALES (corp-wide): 1.6B **Privately Held**
SIC: 2834 Tablets, pharmaceutical
HQ: Invagen Pharmaceuticals Inc.
7 Oser Ave Ste 4
Hauppauge NY 11788
631 231-3233

(G-3279)
ISLAND RECYCLING CORP
228 Blydenburg Rd (11749-5006)
PHONE..................................631 234-6688
Mary Dimatteo, *President*
EMP: 5
SQ FT: 10,000
SALES (est): 572.3K **Privately Held**
SIC: 3341 Recovery & refining of nonferrous metals

(G-3280)
ISLANDIA MRI ASSOCIATES PC
200 Corporate Plz Ste 203 (11749-1507)
PHONE..................................631 234-2828
Joel Reiter, *President*
EMP: 15
SALES (est): 1.5MM **Privately Held**
SIC: 3826 Magnetic resonance imaging apparatus

(G-3281)
J&R FUEL OF LI INC
97 W Suffolk Ave (11722-2143)
PHONE..................................631 234-1959
James R Reed, *Owner*
EMP: 5
SALES (est): 385.2K **Privately Held**
SIC: 2869 Fuels

(G-3282)
LENARO PAPER CO INC
31 Windsor Pl (11722-3301)
PHONE..................................631 439-8800
Leonard Aronica, *Ch of Bd*
Anthony J Aronica, *Vice Pres*
◆ **EMP:** 18 **EST:** 1970
SQ FT: 143,000
SALES (est): 9.2MM **Privately Held**
WEB: www.lenaropaper.com
SIC: 2621 5111 Paper mills; fine paper

(G-3283)
M & M MOLDING CORP
250 Creative Dr (11722-4404)
PHONE..................................631 582-1900
Mathias Meinzinger, *President*
John McLaughlin, *CFO*
Gunther Bartsch, *Treasurer*
Richie Janiencz, *Manager*

▲ **EMP:** 200 **EST:** 1977
SQ FT: 50,000
SALES (est): 27.2MM **Privately Held**
SIC: 3089 Injection molded finished plastic products

(G-3284)
MONARCH GRAPHICS INC
1065 Islip Ave (11722-4203)
PHONE..................................631 232-1300
Marilyn Haller, *President*
Robert Haller, *Vice Pres*
Melissa Cruz, *Prdtn Mgr*
EMP: 18
SQ FT: 11,000
SALES (est): 2.4MM **Privately Held**
WEB: www.monarchgraphics.com
SIC: 2752 Commercial printing, lithographic

(G-3285)
NATIONWIDE EXHIBITOR SVCS INC
Also Called: Nationwide Displays
110 Windsor Pl (11722-3331)
PHONE..................................631 467-2034
Steven Griffith, *President*
Frank Vesce, *General Mgr*
William Griffith, *Vice Pres*
Steve Graffeo, *Project Mgr*
John Griffith, *Manager*
EMP: 10
SQ FT: 20,000
SALES (est): 2MM **Privately Held**
SIC: 3993 3999 2542 Displays & cutouts, window & lobby; advertising display products; fixtures: display, office or store: except wood

(G-3286)
QUALITY ENCLOSURES INC (PA)
101 Windsor Pl Unit H (11722-3339)
PHONE..................................631 234-0115
Manny Schwartz, *Ch of Bd*
Michael Schwartz, *President*
Steve Schwartz, *General Mgr*
▲ **EMP:** 23
SQ FT: 27,000
SALES (est): 6.4MM **Privately Held**
WEB: www.qualityenclosures.com
SIC: 3088 3231 Plastics plumbing fixtures; products of purchased glass

(G-3287)
RICHARD RUFFNER
Also Called: Dynamic Printing
69 Carleton Ave (11722-3018)
PHONE..................................631 234-4600
Richard Ruffner, *Owner*
Rosie Dejesus, *Exec Dir*
EMP: 15
SQ FT: 6,000
SALES (est): 1.1MM **Privately Held**
SIC: 2759 7349 5943 2789 Commercial printing; building maintenance services; office forms & supplies; bookbinding & related work; manifold business forms; commercial printing, lithographic

(G-3288)
SPECTRUM CATALYSTS INC
69 Windsor Pl (11722-3300)
P.O. Box 472, Smithtown (11787-0472)
PHONE..................................631 560-3683
John Plunkett, *President*
Michael Plunkett, *Senior VP*
EMP: 5 **EST:** 2001
SQ FT: 100,000
SALES: 1MM **Privately Held**
SIC: 3559 Chemical machinery & equipment

(G-3289)
SYNERGY RESOURCES INC
320 Carleton Ave Ste 6200 (11722-4538)
PHONE..................................631 665-2050
Gene Caiola, *Ch of Bd*
Mark Lilly, *Principal*
Lou Miranda, *Vice Pres*
Tania S George, *Technology*
EMP: 65
SQ FT: 3,500

▲ = Import ▼=Export
◆ =Import/Export

SALES: 12MM **Privately Held**
WEB: www.synergyresources.net
SIC: 7372 Business oriented computer software

(G-3290)
SYSTEM OF AME BINDING
95 Hoffman Ln (11749-5020)
PHONE..................631 390-8560
William Stross, *Vice Pres*
EMP: 9
SALES (est): 1.5MM **Privately Held**
SIC: 3111 Bookbinders' leather

(G-3291)
UNITED BAKING CO INC
16 Bronx Ave (11722-2406)
PHONE..................631 413-5116
EMP: 17 **Privately Held**
SIC: 2052 Cookies & crackers
PA: United Baking Co., Inc.
41 Natcon Dr
Shirley NY 11967

(G-3292)
VANGUARD METALS INC
135 Brightside Ave (11722-2709)
P.O. Box 666 (11722-0666)
PHONE..................631 234-6500
Joel Frank, *President*
Helene Frank, *Vice Pres*
EMP: 15
SQ FT: 6,000
SALES: 1.6MM **Privately Held**
WEB: www.vanguardmetals.com
SIC: 3451 3599 Screw machine products; machine shop, jobbing & repair

Central Square
Oswego County

(G-3293)
ALLOY METAL PRODUCTS LLC
193 Us Route 11 (13036-9760)
P.O. Box 2 (13036-0002)
PHONE..................315 676-2405
James Thayer, *Mng Member*
▲ **EMP:** 10
SQ FT: 14,000
SALES: 1MM **Privately Held**
WEB: www.alloymetalproducts.com
SIC: 3714 Motor vehicle parts & accessories

(G-3294)
AMERITOOL MFG INC
64 Corporate Park Dr (13036-9595)
P.O. Box 213 (13036-0213)
PHONE..................315 668-2172
Jerome E Beck, *President*
Cheryl Joyce, *Vice Pres*
▲ **EMP:** 20
SALES (est): 3.9MM **Privately Held**
SIC: 3593 Fluid power cylinders & actuators

(G-3295)
NASIFF ASSOCIATES INC
841 County Route 37 (13036-2133)
P.O. Box 88, Brewerton (13029-0088)
PHONE..................315 676-2346
Roger Nasiff, *President*
William Heaney, *VP Engrg*
EMP: 6
SALES (est): 1.1MM **Privately Held**
WEB: www.nasiff.com
SIC: 3841 8711 Diagnostic apparatus, medical; professional engineer

(G-3296)
TORRINGTON INDUSTRIES INC
Also Called: Mid-State Ready Mix
90 Corporate Park Dr (13036-9595)
PHONE..................315 676-4662
Theodore Zoli, *President*
EMP: 6
SALES (corp-wide): 1.9MM **Privately Held**
SIC: 3273 Ready-mixed concrete
PA: Torrington Industries Inc
112 Wall St
Torrington CT 06790
860 489-9261

(G-3297)
UPSTATE INSULATED GLASS INC
47 Weber Rd (13036-2109)
PHONE..................315 475-4960
James R Markert, *President*
EMP: 6
SQ FT: 3,100
SALES: 800K **Privately Held**
SIC: 3231 1793 5231 Insulating units, multiple-glazed; made from purchased glass; glass & glazing work; glass

Central Valley
Orange County

(G-3298)
DAVID YURMAN ENTERPRISES LLC
484 Evergreen Ct (10917-6716)
PHONE..................845 928-8660
EMP: 9
SALES (corp-wide): 46.9MM **Privately Held**
SIC: 3911 Mfg Precious Metal Jewelry
PA: David Yurman Enterprises Llc
24 Vestry St
New York NY 10013
212 896-1550

(G-3299)
ELIZABETH ARDEN INC
214 Red Apple Ct (10917-6605)
PHONE..................845 810-2175
April Lee, *Principal*
EMP: 199 **Publicly Held**
SIC: 2844 Toilet preparations
HQ: Elizabeth Arden, Inc.
880 Sw 145th Ave Ste 200
Pembroke Pines FL 33027

(G-3300)
SCHILLER STORES INC
Also Called: Lecreuset of America
869 Adirondack Way (10917-6205)
PHONE..................845 928-4316
Marcia York, *Branch Mgr*
EMP: 5 **Privately Held**
WEB: www.lecreusetofamerica.com
SIC: 3269 Cookware: stoneware, coarse earthenware & pottery
PA: Schiller Stores Inc
509 Tanger Mall Dr
Riverhead NY 11901

(G-3301)
VF OUTDOOR LLC
Also Called: North Face
461 Dune Rd (10917-6201)
PHONE..................845 928-4900
Justin Dobson, *Manager*
Justin Dodson, *Manager*
EMP: 25
SALES (corp-wide): 13.8MM **Publicly Held**
WEB: www.thenorthface.com
SIC: 2329 2339 Men's & boys' leather, wool & down-filled outerwear; women's & misses' outerwear
HQ: Vf Outdoor, Llc
2701 Harbor Bay Pkwy
Alameda CA 94502
510 618-3500

(G-3302)
WOODBURY PRINTING PLUS + INC
96 Turner Rd (10917-4001)
PHONE..................845 928-6610
Frank Collins, *President*
EMP: 5
SQ FT: 3,800
SALES: 450K **Privately Held**
WEB: www.wprintingplus.com
SIC: 2752 7334 2791 3993 Commercial printing, offset; photocopying & duplicating services; typesetting; signs & advertising specialties

Chadwicks
Oneida County

(G-3303)
NEW YORK STATE TOOL CO INC
3343 Oneida St (13319)
PHONE..................315 737-8985
David Wilsey, *President*
Matthew Wilsey, *President*
EMP: 11
SQ FT: 6,000
SALES (est): 1.7MM **Privately Held**
WEB: www.nystool.com
SIC: 3599 Machine shop, jobbing & repair

(G-3304)
WILLIAMS TOOL INC
9372 Elm St (13319-3515)
P.O. Box 430 (13319-0430)
PHONE..................315 737-7226
Ray Williams, *President*
Bob Prichard, *Prdtn Mgr*
Dan Petrie, *Manager*
EMP: 38 **EST:** 1957
SQ FT: 17,000
SALES: 3.3MM **Privately Held**
WEB: www.wmstool.com
SIC: 3599 Machine shop, jobbing & repair

Chaffee
Erie County

(G-3305)
DIAMOND SAW WORKS INC (PA)
12290 Olean Rd (14030-9767)
PHONE..................716 496-7417
James Ziemer, *President*
James M Ziemer, *President*
Ed Duschen, *Engineer*
Jim Montgomery, *Engineer*
Al Epperson, *Regl Sales Mgr*
▲ **EMP:** 50
SQ FT: 55,000
SALES (est): 4.8MM **Privately Held**
WEB: www.diamondsaw.com
SIC: 3425 Saw blades & handsaws

(G-3306)
DONALD STEFAN
Also Called: Stefan & Sons Welding
3428 W Yorkshire Rd (14030-9619)
PHONE..................716 492-1110
Donald Stefan, *Owner*
EMP: 5
SALES (est): 140.3K **Privately Held**
SIC: 7692 3441 Welding repair; fabricated structural metal

(G-3307)
HART TO HART INDUSTRIES INC
Also Called: Arcade Glass Works
13520 Chaffee Curriers Rd (14030-9701)
PHONE..................716 492-2709
Bill Harter, *President*
EMP: 5
SQ FT: 3,500
SALES: 516.1K **Privately Held**
SIC: 3444 3089 Awnings & canopies; window frames & sash, plastic

(G-3308)
UFP NEW YORK LLC
Also Called: Universal Forest Products
13989 E Schutt Rd (14030-9763)
PHONE..................716 496-5484
Steve Slowik, *Branch Mgr*
EMP: 40
SQ FT: 18,720
SALES (corp-wide): 4.4B **Publicly Held**
WEB: www.ufpinc.com
SIC: 2439 Trusses, wooden roof
HQ: Ufp New York, Llc
11 Allen St
Auburn NY 13021
315 253-2758

Champlain
Clinton County

(G-3309)
BOW INDUSTRIAL CORPORATION
178 W Service Rd (12919-4440)
PHONE..................518 561-0190
Samuel Bern, *President*
▼ **EMP:** 96
SQ FT: 60,000
SALES (est): 1.4MM **Privately Held**
SIC: 3088 Plastics plumbing fixtures

(G-3310)
BURTON CORPORATION
Also Called: Burton Snowboards
21 Lawrence Paquette Dr (12919-4857)
PHONE..................802 862-4500
EMP: 100
SALES (corp-wide): 188.4MM **Privately Held**
WEB: www.burton.com
SIC: 3949 Sporting & athletic goods
PA: The Burton Corporation
180 Queen City Park Rd
Burlington VT 05401
802 862-4500

(G-3311)
ELEGANCE COATING LTD
33 W Service Rd Ste 100 (12919-4438)
PHONE..................518 298-2888
Norman Morin, *President*
Yoland Cloutier, *Vice Pres*
EMP: 65 **EST:** 2007
SALES: 6MM **Privately Held**
SIC: 3479 Coating of metals & formed products

(G-3312)
GREAT WESTERN MALTING CO
16 Beeman Way (12919-4965)
PHONE..................800 496-7732
Will Jackson, *President*
▲ **EMP:** 9
SALES (est): 412.1K **Privately Held**
SIC: 2083 Malt

(G-3313)
HUMANWARE USA INC (PA)
1 Ups Way (12919-4569)
P.O. Box 800 (12919-0800)
PHONE..................800 722-3393
Phillip Rance, *President*
Greg Brown, *CFO*
EMP: 75
SQ FT: 3,800
SALES (est): 10.1MM **Privately Held**
SIC: 3851 Eyeglasses, lenses & frames

(G-3314)
KOREGON ENTERPRISES INC
Also Called: Nite Train R
102 W Service Rd (12919-4440)
PHONE..................450 218-6836
H J Park, *President*
▲ **EMP:** 5
SQ FT: 3,300
SALES (est): 655.4K **Privately Held**
WEB: www.nitetrain-r.com
SIC: 3699 5047 Electrical equipment & supplies; incontinent care products & supplies

(G-3315)
MODERN MECHANICAL FAB INC
100 Walnut St Ste 7 (12919-5337)
PHONE..................518 298-5177
Heather Trombly, *President*
▲ **EMP:** 9
SALES (est): 1.5MM **Privately Held**
WEB: www.modmechfab.com
SIC: 3441 Fabricated structural metal

(G-3316)
STARCYL USA CORP
348 State Route 11 (12919-4816)
PHONE..................877 782-7295
Terry Allardin, *President*
EMP: 15
SQ FT: 10,000

SALES (est): 3.6MM **Privately Held**
SIC: 3593 Fluid power cylinders, hydraulic or pneumatic

(G-3317)
TESTORI INTERIORS INC
107 Lwrnce Paqtte Indstrl (12919)
PHONE.....................518 298-4400
Lindo Lapegna, *CEO*
Peter George, *Principal*
Ajay Thakker, *CFO*
◆ **EMP:** 43 EST: 2000
SQ FT: 100,000
SALES (est): 8.9MM **Privately Held**
SIC: 2531 Public building & related furniture

(G-3318)
UNI SOURCE TECHNOLOGY
1320 Rt 9 (12919)
PHONE.....................514 748-8888
Lawrence Rutenberg, *Branch Mgr*
EMP: 10
SALES (corp-wide): 4.7MM **Privately Held**
SIC: 3812 Defense systems & equipment
PA: Unisource Technology Inc
         9010 Av Ryan
         Dorval QC H9P 2
         514 748-8888

(G-3319)
UNIQUE PACKAGING CORPORATION
11320 State Route 9 # 3807 (12919-5062)
P.O. Box 219, Plattsburgh (12901-0219)
PHONE.....................514 341-5872
Fred Povitz, *President*
Earl Povitz, *Opers Staff*
EMP: 5
SALES (est): 496.8K **Privately Held**
SIC: 3053 3172 Packing materials; cases, jewelry

(G-3320)
UNIVERSAL INTERIORS LLC
107 Lawrence Paquette Dr (12919-4862)
PHONE.....................518 298-4400
Ajay Thakker, *President*
EMP: 11
SALES (est): 349.6K **Privately Held**
SIC: 2519 2531 Fiberglass & plastic furniture; public building & related furniture

(G-3321)
WATER SPLASH INC
25 Locust St Ste 421 (12919-5001)
PHONE.....................800 936-3430
Gokhan Celik, *CEO*
Tara Menon, *Manager*
▲ **EMP:** 5
SALES (est): 364.4K **Privately Held**
SIC: 3999 Manufacturing industries

Chappaqua
Westchester County

(G-3322)
AIR ENGINEERING FILTERS INC
17 Memorial Dr (10514-3528)
P.O. Box 174 (10514-0174)
PHONE.....................914 238-5945
Pam Rubin, *President*
EMP: 9
SQ FT: 2,000
SALES (est): 1.2MM **Privately Held**
SIC: 3564 Filters, air: furnaces, air conditioning equipment, etc.

(G-3323)
CONSTRUCTION TECHNOLOGY INC (PA)
17 Green Ln (10514-2739)
PHONE.....................914 747-8900
Richard Levine, *President*
EMP: 22
SQ FT: 1,000
SALES (est): 1.9MM **Privately Held**
SIC: 7372 Prepackaged software

(G-3324)
DECORATIVE HARDEWARE
180 Hunts Ln (10514-2602)
P.O. Box 627 (10514-0627)
PHONE.....................914 238-5251
Ronald Lawrence Prezener, *President*
Marie Anne Prezener, *Vice Pres*
▲ **EMP:** 10
SQ FT: 2,000
SALES (est): 1.3MM **Privately Held**
WEB: www.decorative-hardware.com
SIC: 3429 Furniture builders' & other household hardware; furniture hardware

(G-3325)
INSIGHT UNLIMITED INC
660 Quaker Rd (10514-1505)
PHONE.....................914 861-2090
Shmuel Kliger, *President*
EMP: 6
SALES (est): 282K **Privately Held**
SIC: 7372 Prepackaged software

(G-3326)
NANORX INC
6 Devoe Pl (10514-3601)
PHONE.....................914 671-0224
Palayakopai Raghavan, *President*
EMP: 2
SALES: 1MM **Privately Held**
SIC: 2834 Medicines, capsuled or ampuled

(G-3327)
WIDGETWORKS UNLIMITED LLC
395 Millwood Rd (10514-1100)
PHONE.....................914 666-6395
Russell Todd,
EMP: 5
SALES: 100K **Privately Held**
SIC: 3651 Speaker systems

Charlotteville
Schoharie County

(G-3328)
FLY-TYERS CARRY-ALL LLC
Also Called: Folstaf Company, The
112 Meade Rd (12036-1612)
PHONE.....................607 821-1460
Lee Stoliar,
EMP: 5
SQ FT: 850
SALES (est): 611.9K **Privately Held**
WEB: www.folstaf.com
SIC: 3949 5091 Fishing equipment; fishing tackle, general; fishing equipment & supplies; fishing tackle

Chateaugay
Franklin County

(G-3329)
AGRI-MARK INC
39 Mccadam Ln (12920-4306)
P.O. Box 900 (12920-0900)
PHONE.....................518 497-6644
Ron Davis, *Manager*
Tom Sorrell, *Director*
EMP: 100
SALES (corp-wide): 382MM **Privately Held**
WEB: www.agrimark.net
SIC: 2022 Natural cheese
PA: Agri-Mark, Inc.
         40 Shattuck Rd Ste 301
         Andover MA 01810
         978 552-5500

Chatham
Columbia County

(G-3330)
CRAFTECH
5 Dock St (12037)
PHONE.....................518 828-5011
Linda Geblanski, *CEO*
Erwin Gerard, *Owner*
EMP: 55

SALES (est): 2.6MM **Privately Held**
SIC: 2821 3089 Molding compounds, plastics; molding primary plastic

(G-3331)
KLING MAGNETICS INC
343 State Route 295 (12037-3713)
P.O. Box 348 (12037-0348)
PHONE.....................518 392-4000
Jody Rael, *President*
▲ **EMP:** 20
SQ FT: 20,000
SALES (est): 2.2MM **Privately Held**
SIC: 3993 3089 2752 3944 Advertising novelties; novelties, plastic; commercial printing, lithographic; games, toys & children's vehicles

(G-3332)
RAPID INTELLECT GROUP INC
77 Church St Apt B (12037-1341)
P.O. Box 131, Stuyvesant Falls (12174-0131)
PHONE.....................518 929-3210
Steve Grzeskow, *President*
Peter Grzeskow, *Vice Pres*
EMP: 12 EST: 1997
SALES (est): 766.1K **Privately Held**
SIC: 2731 Books: publishing only

(G-3333)
SONOCO-CRELLIN INTL INC (HQ)
87 Center St (12037-1032)
PHONE.....................518 392-2000
Bob Puechl, *Vice Pres*
Michael Tucker, *Vice Pres*
Lee Rabenburg, *Finance*
▲ **EMP:** 500
SQ FT: 70,000
SALES: 190.6MM
SALES (corp-wide): 5.3B **Publicly Held**
SIC: 3089 Molding primary plastic
PA: Sonoco Products Company
         1 N 2nd St
         Hartsville SC 29550
         843 383-7000

Chazy
Clinton County

(G-3334)
JP SIGNS
9592 State Route 9 Ste 1 (12921-3113)
PHONE.....................518 569-3907
Jessica Macnerland, *Owner*
EMP: 5
SALES: 150K **Privately Held**
SIC: 3993 7389 5699 Signs & advertising specialties; printers' services: folding, collating; T-shirts, custom printed

(G-3335)
PLASTITEL USA INC
641 Ridge Rd Bldg 7 (12921-2420)
PHONE.....................800 667-2313
Denis Deshaies, *CEO*
EMP: 9 EST: 2014
SALES (est): 1.4MM
SALES (corp-wide): 10MM **Privately Held**
SIC: 3089 Thermoformed finished plastic products
PA: Produits Plastitel Inc, Les
         2604 Rue Debray
         Montreal QC H7S 2
         450 687-0060

Cheektowaga
Erie County

(G-3336)
ACCOLADE USA INC (PA)
Also Called: Level Wear
60 Industrial Pkwy # 397 (14227-2774)
PHONE.....................302 257-5688
Hilton Ngo, *President*
Lily Guo, *Superintendent*
Stephen Tsao, *CFO*
EMP: 12
SQ FT: 100,000

SALES (est): 1MM **Privately Held**
SIC: 2211 Apparel & outerwear fabrics, cotton

(G-3337)
ADEMCO INC
Also Called: ADI Global Distribution
307 Cayuga Rd Ste 160 (14225-1985)
PHONE.....................716 631-2197
Susan Jackson, *Manager*
EMP: 5
SALES (corp-wide): 4.8B **Publicly Held**
WEB: www.honeywell.com
SIC: 3724 3669 3822 Aircraft engines & engine parts; emergency alarms; auto controls regulating residntl & coml environmt & applncs
HQ: Ademco Inc.
         1985 Douglas Dr N
         Golden Valley MN 55422
         800 468-1502

(G-3338)
AMERICAN CTR FOR EDMOCRACY LLC
435 Cleveland Dr (14225-1009)
PHONE.....................716 803-1118
Larry Pegiza, *President*
EMP: 5
SALES (est): 117.2K
SALES (corp-wide): 5.1MM **Privately Held**
SIC: 7372 Prepackaged software
PA: Gap Technologies, Inc
         431 Cleveland Dr
         Buffalo NY 14225
         716 803-1111

(G-3339)
AVF GROUP INC (DH)
2775 Broadway St Ste 200 (14227-1043)
PHONE.....................951 360-7111
Jerry Jacobs, *President*
▲ **EMP:** 14
SALES (est): 3MM **Privately Held**
WEB: www.avf.com
SIC: 2542 Partitions & fixtures, except wood

(G-3340)
BUFFALO COMPRESSED AIR INC
2727 Broadway St Ste 3a (14227-1070)
P.O. Box 1215, Lockport (14095-1215)
PHONE.....................716 783-8673
Greg Fuer, *Principal*
EMP: 7
SALES (est): 1.1MM **Privately Held**
SIC: 3563 Air & gas compressors

(G-3341)
COMAIRCO EQUIPMENT INC (DH)
3250 Union Rd (14227-1044)
PHONE.....................716 656-0211
Roland Nadeau, *President*
Edward Murphy, *Vice Pres*
EMP: 7
SQ FT: 6,000
SALES (est): 6.5MM
SALES (corp-wide): 11.8MM **Privately Held**
WEB: www.comairco.com
SIC: 3563 Air & gas compressors
HQ: Equipement Comairco Ltee
         5535 Rue Ernest-Cormier
         Montreal QC H7C 2
         450 665-8780

(G-3342)
CRS NUCLEAR SERVICES LLC
840 Aero Dr Ste 150 (14225-1451)
PHONE.....................716 810-0688
Kevin Connor, *Mng Member*
▲ **EMP:** 12
SALES: 5.4MM **Privately Held**
SIC: 2834 Pharmaceutical preparations

(G-3343)
CULINARY ARTS SPECIALTIES INC
Also Called: Cas
2268 Union Rd (14227-2726)
PHONE.....................716 656-8943
Arthur L Keller, *President*

Andrew P Keller, *Vice Pres*
Jonathan Polly, *Purch Mgr*
Gus Walters, *Manager*
EMP: 85
SQ FT: 50,000
SALES (est): 20.5MM **Privately Held**
SIC: 2053 Cakes, bakery: frozen

(G-3344)
DERRICK CORPORATION
2540 Walden Ave (14225-4744)
PHONE................,716 685-4892
EMP: 297
SALES (corp-wide): 185.2MM **Privately Held**
SIC: 3533 Derricks, oil or gas field
PA: Derrick Corporation
590 Duke Rd
Buffalo NY 14225
716 683-9010

(G-3345)
DORM COMPANY CORPORATION
Also Called: Dorm Co.
575 Kennedy Rd Ste 2 (14227-1040)
P.O. Box 485, Clarence Center (14032-0485)
PHONE................502 551-6195
Jeff Gawronski, *President*
▲ **EMP:** 5
SQ FT: 6,000
SALES (est): 1MM **Privately Held**
SIC: 2431 Dormers, wood

(G-3346)
DPM OF WESTERN NEW YORK LLC
340 Nagel Dr (14225-4731)
PHONE................716 684-3825
Thomas Salisbury, *Ch of Bd*
Michael Orth, *Purch Mgr*
Tom Salisbury, *CFO*
Deron Bauer, *Accounts Exec*
Denise Poole, *Accounts Exec*
EMP: 73
SALES (est): 11.6MM
SALES (corp-wide): 29MM **Privately Held**
SIC: 2752 Commercial printing, lithographic
HQ: Dpm Of Western New York Llc
3235 Grand Island Blvd
Grand Island NY 14072
716 775-8001

(G-3347)
ECOLAB INC
3719 Union Rd Ste 121 (14225-4250)
PHONE................716 683-6298
Dave Beckwith, *Branch Mgr*
EMP: 17
SALES (corp-wide): 14.6B **Publicly Held**
WEB: www.ecolab.com
SIC: 2841 Soap & other detergents
PA: Ecolab Inc.
1 Ecolab Pl
Saint Paul MN 55102
800 232-6522

(G-3348)
FLUID HANDLING LLC
Standard Xchange
175 Standard Pkwy (14227-1233)
PHONE................716 897-2800
Joseph McMara, *Branch Mgr*
EMP: 240 **Publicly Held**
WEB: www.ittind.com
SIC: 3443 Industrial vessels, tanks & containers
HQ: Fluid Handling, Llc
175 Standard Pkwy
Cheektowaga NY 14227
716 897-2800

(G-3349)
FLUID HANDLING LLC (HQ)
Also Called: Xylem
175 Standard Pkwy (14227-1233)
PHONE................716 897-2800
Ken Napolitano, *President*
Rita Nair, *General Mgr*
Gary Ross, *Counsel*
Christine Duane, *Vice Pres*
Paul Stellato, *Vice Pres*
◆ **EMP:** 1

SALES (est): 256.7MM **Publicly Held**
SIC: 3561 Pumps & pumping equipment

(G-3350)
GEMINI MANUFACTURES
160 Holtz Dr (14225)
PHONE................716 633-0306
Todd Lehmann, *Partner*
Irene Turski, *Partner*
EMP: 14
SQ FT: 4,200
SALES (est): 860K **Privately Held**
SIC: 3915 Jewelers' materials & lapidary work

(G-3351)
GF PACKAGING LLC (PA)
2727 Broadway St Ste 3 (14227-1070)
PHONE................716 692-2705
Val Sracine, *Mng Member*
▲ **EMP:** 30 **EST:** 1946
SQ FT: 50,000
SALES (est): 3MM **Privately Held**
SIC: 2542 Counters or counter display cases: except wood

(G-3352)
HAMMOND MANUFACTURING CO INC
475 Cayuga Rd (14225-1309)
PHONE................716 630-7030
Robert F Hammond, *CEO*
Marc A Dube, *Principal*
Damon Accurso, *Sales Mgr*
Scott Woofter, *Sales Staff*
Kathy Jakubowski, *Supervisor*
▲ **EMP:** 14
SQ FT: 17,000
SALES (est): 3.5MM
SALES (corp-wide): 110.3MM **Privately Held**
WEB: www.hammfg.com
SIC: 3677 5063 Transformers power supply, electronic type; electrical apparatus & equipment; transformers, electric
PA: Hammond Manufacturing Company Limited
394 Edinburgh Rd N
Guelph ON N1H 1
519 822-2960

(G-3353)
HANZLIAN SAUSAGE INCORPORATED
Also Called: Hanzlian Sausage Deli
2351 Genesee St (14225-2839)
PHONE................716 891-5247
David Hanzlian, *President*
George J Hanzlian Jr, *Vice Pres*
EMP: 8
SQ FT: 7,800
SALES (est): 876K **Privately Held**
SIC: 2013 Sausages & other prepared meats

(G-3354)
HUGH F MCPHERSON INC
Also Called: Franklin's Printing
70 Innsbruck Dr (14227-2735)
PHONE................716 668-6107
Hugh F McPherson, *President*
Barbara L McPherson, *Vice Pres*
EMP: 7
SALES (est): 870.9K **Privately Held**
SIC: 2752 2791 7331 Commercial printing, lithographic; typesetting; mailing service

(G-3355)
MP CAROLL INC
4822 Genesee St (14225-2494)
PHONE................716 683-8520
Michael Carrol, *President*
◆ **EMP:** 12
SALES (est): 2.1MM **Privately Held**
SIC: 2426 Flooring, hardwood

(G-3356)
MULTI-HEALTH SYSTEMS INC
Indus Pkwy Ste 70660 60 (14227)
P.O. Box 950, North Tonawanda (14120-0950)
PHONE................800 456-3003
Steven J Stein, *Branch Mgr*
Amy Patenaude, *Consultant*
Janice Sneath, *Consultant*

EMP: 90
SALES (corp-wide): 21MM **Privately Held**
WEB: www.mhs.com
SIC: 3695 2741 Computer software tape & disks: blank, rigid & floppy; miscellaneous publishing
PA: Multi-Health Systems Inc
3770 Victoria Park Ave
North York ON M2H 3
416 492-2627

(G-3357)
NEVILLE MFG SVC & DIST INC (PA)
2320 Clinton St (14227-1735)
PHONE................716 834-3038
Patrick Crowe, *President*
Joe Venturo, *VP Engrg*
EMP: 24 **EST:** 1951
SQ FT: 4,000
SALES (est): 4MM **Privately Held**
SIC: 2448 Pallets, wood; skids, wood

(G-3358)
NOVATECH INC
190 Gruner Rd (14227-1022)
PHONE................716 892-6682
John Popovich, *President*
John Popovich Jr, *Vice Pres*
EMP: 20
SQ FT: 8,000
SALES (est): 3.4MM **Privately Held**
WEB: www.novatechmachining.com
SIC: 3545 Precision tools, machinists'

(G-3359)
PROSTHETICS BY NELSON INC (PA)
Also Called: Nelson Prsthtics Orthotics Lab
2959 Genesee St (14225-2653)
PHONE................716 894-6666
Christopher Vandusen, *President*
EMP: 16
SQ FT: 8,500
SALES (est): 2.2MM **Privately Held**
SIC: 3842 5999 Limbs, artificial; orthopedic appliances; orthopedic & prosthesis applications

(G-3360)
REDLAND FOODS CORP
40 Sonwil Dr (14225-2425)
PHONE................716 288-9061
Eva Mounsteven, *Director*
▲ **EMP:** 12
SALES (est): 982K **Privately Held**
SIC: 2099 Emulsifiers, food

(G-3361)
SMG METAL PRODUCTS LLC
390 Cayuga Rd (14225-1940)
PHONE................716 633-6439
Jay Bozer, *Manager*
EMP: 8
SALES (est): 1.6MM **Privately Held**
SIC: 3444 Sheet metalwork

(G-3362)
STEREO ADVANTAGE INC
Also Called: Advantage Wood Shop
45 Boxwood Ln (14227-2707)
PHONE................716 656-7161
Anthony Ragusa Jr, *Partner*
EMP: 10
SALES (corp-wide): 42.3MM **Privately Held**
SIC: 2541 Store & office display cases & fixtures
PA: Stereo Advantage, Inc.
1955 Wehrle Dr Ste B
Williamsville NY 14221
716 204-2346

(G-3363)
SUPERIOR GLOVE WORKS USA LTD
2345 Walden Ave Ste 600 (14225-4752)
PHONE................716 626-9500
Lynne Jordan, *Principal*
Dan Duffey, *Sales Staff*
EMP: 30
SALES (est): 2.8MM **Privately Held**
SIC: 3842 Gloves, safety

(G-3364)
TECTRAN INC
2345 Walden Ave Ste 100 (14225-4770)
PHONE................800 776-5549
Bruce McKie, *President*
Chris Dacey, *Engineer*
EMP: 9
SALES (est): 1.1MM **Privately Held**
SIC: 3699 3799 Cleaning equipment, ultrasonic, except medical & dental; carriages, horse drawn

(G-3365)
WITT PREPARATIONS LLC
65 Inns Brook Rd (14227)
P.O. Box 514, Elma (14059-0514)
PHONE................716 948-4002
Michael Wittman, *Mng Member*
EMP: 6
SALES: 900K **Privately Held**
SIC: 3559 3471 Metal finishing equipment for plating, etc.; sand blasting of metal parts

---

Chemung
Chemung County

(G-3366)
VULCRAFT OF NEW YORK INC (HQ)
621 M St (14825)
P.O. Box 280 (14825-0280)
PHONE................607 529-9000
Peggy Peters, *Principal*
Ray Napolitan, *Exec VP*
Chris La Cava, *Marketing Staff*
EMP: 121
SQ FT: 300,000
SALES (est): 63.3MM
SALES (corp-wide): 25B **Publicly Held**
WEB: www.nucor.com
SIC: 3441 Expansion joints (structural shapes), iron or steel
PA: Nucor Corporation
1915 Rexford Rd Ste 400
Charlotte NC 28211
704 366-7000

Chenango Bridge
Broome County

(G-3367)
ATWOOD TOOL & MACHINE INC
39 Kattelville Rd (13745)
PHONE................607 648-6543
H Blair Atwood, *President*
Brent Atwood, *Vice Pres*
David Atwood, *Treasurer*
Laurie Atwood, *Treasurer*
Donna Ackerman, *Office Mgr*
EMP: 22 **EST:** 1963
SQ FT: 23,000
SALES (est): 3.3MM **Privately Held**
WEB: www.atwoodknives.com
SIC: 3599 Machine shop, jobbing & repair

Cherry Valley
Otsego County

(G-3368)
THISTLE HILL WEAVERS
143 Baxter Rd (13320-2431)
PHONE................518 284-2729
Rabbit Goody, *Owner*
Jill Maney, *Manager*
EMP: 5
SALES (est): 465.2K **Privately Held**
WEB: www.thistlehillweavers.com
SIC: 2299 Hand woven fabrics

G
E
O
G
R
A
P
H
I
C

Chester
Orange County

(G-3369)
ADVERTISER PUBLICATIONS INC
Also Called: Marketplace, The
148 State Route 17m (10918)
PHONE....................................845 783-1111
Howard Kaplan, *President*
Seth Kaplan, *Vice Pres*
Steve Herman, *Manager*
EMP: 13
SQ FT: 2,200
SALES: 1.9MM **Privately Held**
SIC: 2711 7331 7313 Newspapers: publishing only, not printed on site; direct mail advertising services; newspaper advertising representative

(G-3370)
AMSCAN INC
Also Called: Amscan Everyday Warehouse
47 Elizabeth Dr (10918-1367)
PHONE....................................845 469-9116
EMP: 11
SALES (corp-wide): 2.4B **Publicly Held**
SIC: 2656 Plates, paper: made from purchased material
HQ: Amscan Inc.
80 Grasslands Rd Ste 3
Elmsford NY 10523
914 345-2020

(G-3371)
BRAKEWELL STL FABRICATORS INC
55 Leone Ln (10918-1363)
PHONE....................................845 469-9131
Dan Doyle, *President*
Dave Bendlin, *Project Mgr*
Robert McGrath, *Project Mgr*
William Valentin, *Project Mgr*
Frank Versace, *Project Mgr*
EMP: 45
SQ FT: 26,000
SALES: 7MM **Privately Held**
WEB: www.brakewell.com
SIC: 3411 3499 Metal cans; metal ladders

(G-3372)
BYK USA INC
48 Leone Ln (10918-1362)
PHONE....................................845 469-5800
Stephan Glander, *Branch Mgr*
EMP: 29
SALES (corp-wide): 385.1K **Privately Held**
SIC: 2819 Industrial inorganic chemicals
HQ: Byk Usa Inc.
524 S Cherry St
Wallingford CT 06492
203 265-2086

(G-3373)
COMMUNITY PRODUCTS LLC
Also Called: Community Playthings
359 Gibson Hill Rd (10918-2321)
PHONE....................................845 658-7720
William Wiser, *Purchasing*
John Rhodes, *Branch Mgr*
EMP: 23
SALES (corp-wide): 100.5MM **Privately Held**
SIC: 3842 Surgical appliances & supplies
PA: Community Products, Llc
101 Woodcrest Dr
Rifton NY 12471
845 658-8799

(G-3374)
COMMUNITY PRODUCTS LLC
24 Elizabeth Dr (10918-1366)
PHONE....................................845 572-3433
Ben Maendel, *Branch Mgr*
EMP: 18
SALES (corp-wide): 100.5MM **Privately Held**
SIC: 3842 Orthopedic appliances
PA: Community Products, Llc
101 Woodcrest Dr
Rifton NY 12471
845 658-8799

(G-3375)
DURASOL SYSTEMS INC (HQ)
445 Bellvale Rd (10918-3115)
PHONE....................................845 610-1100
Vince Best, *President*
Paolo Galliani, *President*
Frank Dorr, *Vice Pres*
Trace Feinstein, *Vice Pres*
Tim Robinson, *Vice Pres*
◆ **EMP:** 51
SQ FT: 65,000
SALES (est): 17.9MM
SALES (corp-wide): 32.1MM **Privately Held**
WEB: www.durasol.com
SIC: 2394 Awnings, fabric: made from purchased materials
PA: Bat Spa
Via H. Ford 2
Noventa Di Piave VE 30020
042 165-672

(G-3376)
EMPIRE EMULSIONS LLC
1297 Craigville Rd (10918-4524)
P.O. Box 9 (10918-0009)
PHONE....................................845 610-5350
Skip Swiantek, *Mng Member*
EMP: 9
SALES (est): 741.2K **Privately Held**
SIC: 2952 Asphalt felts & coatings

(G-3377)
F A ALPINE WINDOWS MFG
1683 State Route 17m (10918-1020)
PHONE....................................845 469-5700
Larry Maddaloni, *President*
▲ **EMP:** 10
SALES (est): 1.6MM **Privately Held**
WEB: www.faalpinewindowmfg.com
SIC: 3442 Metal doors

(G-3378)
G SCHIRMER INC
Also Called: Music Sales
2 Old Rt 17 (10918)
P.O. Box 572 (10918-0572)
PHONE....................................845 469-4699
John Castaldo, *Exec VP*
Jeffrey Duncan, *Exec VP*
Ella Winfield, *Manager*
Chris Coviello, *Manager*
Anders Nelsson, *Director*
EMP: 50
SALES (corp-wide): 13.9MM **Privately Held**
WEB: www.schirmer.com
SIC: 2741 Music books: publishing only, not printed on site
HQ: G Schirmer Inc
180 Madison Ave Ste 2400
New York NY 10016
212 254-2100

(G-3379)
GREEN ENERGY CONCEPTS INC
37 Elkay Dr Ste 51 (10918-3025)
P.O. Box 1023, Harriman (10926-1023)
PHONE....................................845 238-2574
Richard Mueller, *President*
Joanne Camacho, *QC Mgr*
▲ **EMP:** 6
SALES: 950K **Privately Held**
SIC: 3646 Commercial indusl & institutional electric lighting fixtures

(G-3380)
KE DURASOL AWNINGS INC
445 Bellvale Rd (10918-3115)
PHONE....................................845 610-1100
Paolo Galliani, *President*
Vince Best, *Principal*
EMP: 12
SALES (est): 1.1MM **Privately Held**
SIC: 2394 Canvas & related products

(G-3381)
NEXANS ENERGY USA INC
Also Called: Industrial Cables
25 Oakland Ave (10918-1011)
PHONE....................................845 469-2141
Gordon Thursfield, *President*
Steve Hall, *Principal*
Sande Aivaliotis, *Vice Pres*
Alain Blezy, *Plant Mgr*
Julie Land, *CFO*
◆ **EMP:** 160
SQ FT: 350,000
SALES (est): 56.3MM **Privately Held**
SIC: 3496 Cable, uninsulated wire: made from purchased wire
HQ: Nexans Canada Inc
140 Allstate Pky Suite 300
Markham ON L3R 0
905 944-4300

(G-3382)
PDJ COMPONENTS INC
35 Brookside Ave (10918-1409)
PHONE....................................845 469-9191
George W Ketchum, *CEO*
Pamela Ketchum, *Vice Pres*
Christin Keating, *Personnel*
EMP: 40
SQ FT: 30,000
SALES (est): 7.2MM **Privately Held**
WEB: www.pdjtruss.com
SIC: 2439 2499 Trusses, wooden roof; trusses, except roof: laminated lumber; decorative wood & woodwork

(G-3383)
REPRO MED SYSTEMS INC
Also Called: RMS Medical Products
24 Carpenter Rd Ste 1 (10918-1065)
PHONE....................................845 469-2042
R John Fletcher, *Ch of Bd*
Donald B Pettigrew, *President*
Manuel Marques, *COO*
John Toomey, *Vice Pres*
Craig S Ross, *VP Sls/Mktg*
▲ **EMP:** 73
SALES (est): 17.3MM **Privately Held**
SIC: 3841 Suction therapy apparatus

(G-3384)
RIC-LO PRODUCTIONS LTD
Also Called: Lycian Stage Lighting
1144 Kings Hwy (10918-3100)
P.O. Box 214, Sugar Loaf (10981-0214)
PHONE....................................845 469-2285
Richard F Logothetis, *Chairman*
▲ **EMP:** 43
SQ FT: 17,400
SALES (est): 8.3MM **Privately Held**
SIC: 3648 3641 Stage lighting equipment; electric lamps

(G-3385)
S A BAXTER LLC (PA)
37 Elkay Dr Ste 33 (10918-3025)
PHONE....................................845 469-7995
Scott Baxter,
▲ **EMP:** 3
SALES: 2MM **Privately Held**
SIC: 3446 5072 Architectural metalwork; builders' hardware

(G-3386)
SATIN FINE FOODS INC
32 Leone Ln (10918-1362)
PHONE....................................845 469-1034
Kevin O' Reilly, *Ch of Bd*
◆ **EMP:** 75
SQ FT: 96,000
SALES (est): 5.5MM **Privately Held**
SIC: 2064 Candy & other confectionery products

(G-3387)
STERIS CORPORATION
23 Elizabeth Dr (10918-1367)
PHONE....................................845 469-4087
Tracy Wild, *QC Mgr*
EMP: 8 **Privately Held**
SIC: 3842 Surgical appliances & supplies
HQ: Steris Corporation
5960 Heisley Rd
Mentor OH 44060
440 354-2600

(G-3388)
STRAUS COMMUNICATIONS
Also Called: Straus Newspaper
20 West Ave Ste 201 (10918-1053)
PHONE....................................845 782-4000
Stan Martin, *Manager*
EMP: 15

SALES (est): 806.9K
SALES (corp-wide): 2.5MM **Privately Held**
WEB: www.strausnews.com
SIC: 2711 Newspapers, publishing & printing
PA: Straus Communications
57 W 57th St Ste 1204
New York NY
212 751-0400

(G-3389)
STRAUS NEWSPAPERS INC
20 West Ave (10918-1032)
PHONE....................................845 782-4000
Jeanne Straus, *President*
Juan Ayala, *Principal*
Tia Bertolotti, *Finance*
Lori Marrie, *Sales Staff*
Rick Sophia, *Director*
EMP: 24 EST: 1991
SALES (est): 1.7MM **Privately Held**
SIC: 2711 Newspapers

(G-3390)
TELE-VUE OPTICS INC
32 Elkay Dr (10918-3001)
PHONE....................................845 469-4551
Albert Nagler, *CEO*
David Nagler, *President*
Sandy Nagler, *Vice Pres*
▲ **EMP:** 20
SQ FT: 14,000
SALES (est): 4.1MM **Privately Held**
WEB: www.televue.com
SIC: 3827 Optical instruments & apparatus

(G-3391)
THEODORE A RAPP ASSOCIATES
728 Craigville Rd (10918-4014)
PHONE....................................845 469-2100
Theodore A Rapp, *President*
EMP: 7
SALES (est): 718.8K **Privately Held**
SIC: 3651 Microphones

(G-3392)
TRISTATE CONTRACT SALES LLC
164 Dug Rd (10918-2652)
PHONE....................................845 782-2614
Ross Elliot, *Principal*
EMP: 5
SALES (est): 442.6K **Privately Held**
SIC: 2434 Vanities, bathroom: wood

Chestertown
Warren County

(G-3393)
CETTEL STUDIO OF NEW YORK INC
636 Atateka Dr (12817-2010)
PHONE....................................518 494-3622
Peter Heonis, *President*
EMP: 6
SALES: 350K **Privately Held**
SIC: 3843 Orthodontic appliances

(G-3394)
PECKHAM MATERIALS CORP
5983 State Route 9 (12817-2513)
PHONE....................................518 494-2313
John McClure, *Opers-Prdtn-Mfg*
EMP: 10
SQ FT: 208
SALES (corp-wide): 171.1MM **Privately Held**
SIC: 2951 5032 Asphalt paving mixtures & blocks; brick, stone & related material
HQ: Peckham Materials Corp
20 Haarlem Ave Ste 200
White Plains NY 10603
914 686-2045

Chestnut Ridge
Rockland County

(G-3395)
MEHRON INC
Also Called: Lechler Labs
100 Red Schoolhouse Rd C2
(10977-7056)
PHONE......................845 426-1700
Martin Melik, *President*
Gene Flaharty, *Sales Mgr*
Stephanie Ferreira, *Mktg Dir*
▲ **EMP:** 35 **EST:** 1932
SQ FT: 15,000
SALES (est): 12MM **Privately Held**
WEB: www.mehron.com
SIC: 2844 Cosmetic preparations

(G-3396)
**PAR PHARMACEUTICAL INC
(DH)**
1 Ram Ridge Rd (10977-6714)
PHONE......................845 573-5500
Paul V Campanelli, *CEO*
Thomas J Haughey, *President*
Kenneth I Sawyer, *Principal*
Michael A Tropiano, *Exec VP*
Joseph Barbarite, *Senior VP*
▲ **EMP:** 277 **EST:** 1978
SQ FT: 92,000
SALES (est): 170.3MM **Privately Held**
SIC: 2834 Druggists' preparations (pharmaceuticals)
HQ: Par Pharmaceutical Companies, Inc.
1 Ram Ridge Rd
Chestnut Ridge NY 10977
845 573-5500

(G-3397)
**PAR PHRMCEUTICAL
COMPANIES INC (DH)**
1 Ram Ridge Rd (10977-6714)
PHONE......................845 573-5500
Paul V Campanelli, *CEO*
Tony Pera, *President*
Tony Cere, *General Mgr*
Jamie Dannhauser, *General Mgr*
Soraya Garcia, *General Mgr*
EMP: 38 **EST:** 2012
SALES (est): 227.4MM **Privately Held**
SIC: 2834 Pharmaceutical preparations
HQ: Endo Health Solutions Inc.
1400 Atwater Dr
Malvern PA 19355
484 216-0000

(G-3398)
**PAR STERILE PRODUCTS LLC
(DH)**
6 Ram Ridge Rd (10977-6713)
PHONE......................845 573-5500
Paul V Campanelli, *CEO*
Michael Tropiano, *CFO*
Thomas J Haughey,
Morgan Stanley Investments,
Peter Jenkins,
EMP: 32
SALES (est): 71.2MM **Privately Held**
WEB: www.jhppharma.com
SIC: 2834 Pharmaceutical preparations
HQ: Par Pharmaceutical, Inc.
1 Ram Ridge Rd
Chestnut Ridge NY 10977
845 573-5500

(G-3399)
TELEDYNE LECROY INC (HQ)
700 Chestnut Ridge Rd (10977-6435)
PHONE......................845 425-2000
Sean B O'Connor, *CEO*
Tyler Cox, *Vice Pres*
Kevin Fitzgerald, *Vice Pres*
Roberto Petrillo, *Vice Pres*
Kevin Prusso, *Vice Pres*
▲ **EMP:** 204
SQ FT: 95,000
SALES (est): 184.1MM
SALES (corp-wide): 2.9B **Publicly Held**
WEB: www.lecroy.com
SIC: 3825 3829 Oscillographs & oscilloscopes; measuring & controlling devices

PA: Teledyne Technologies Inc
1049 Camino Dos Rios
Thousand Oaks CA 91360
805 373-4545

(G-3400)
**U S PLYCHMICAL OVERSEAS
CORP**
584 Chestnut Ridge Rd # 586
(10977-5646)
PHONE......................845 356-5530
David Cherry, *President*
Bruce W Gebhardt, *General Mgr*
Richard E Knipe Jr, *VP Sales*
EMP: 20
SQ FT: 20,000
SALES (est): 3.2MM **Privately Held**
WEB: www.uspoly.com
SIC: 2842 Cleaning or polishing preparations; sanitation preparations

Childwold
St. Lawrence County

(G-3401)
LEATHER ARTISAN
Also Called: Artisan Bags
9740 State Highway 3 (12922-2028)
PHONE......................518 359-3102
Thomas Amoroso, *Partner*
EMP: 5
SQ FT: 7,000
SALES (est): 630.1K **Privately Held**
WEB: www.leatherartisan.com
SIC: 3172 5699 5199 Personal leather goods; leather garments; leather, leather goods & furs

Chittenango
Madison County

(G-3402)
A L SEALING
2280 Osborne Rd (13037-8791)
PHONE......................315 699-6900
John C Thomas, *Ch of Bd*
EMP: 5
SALES (est): 312.3K **Privately Held**
SIC: 3053 Gaskets & sealing devices

(G-3403)
**ARISE AT MARSHALL FARMS
INC**
1972 New Boston Rd (13037-9600)
PHONE......................315 687-6727
Jennifer Schulz, *Branch Mgr*
Ron Champion, *Info Tech Mgr*
EMP: 5
SALES (est): 378K
SALES (corp-wide): 298.6K **Privately Held**
SIC: 3699 Grids, electric
PA: Arise At Marshall Farms, Inc.
635 James St Ste 1
Syracuse NY 13203
315 472-3171

(G-3404)
**CONSOLDTED PRECISION PDTS
CORP**
901 E Genesee St (13037-1325)
PHONE......................315 687-0014
Renae Wallace, *Mfg Mgr*
Mark Gaspari, *Manager*
EMP: 350
SALES (corp-wide): 6.9B **Privately Held**
SIC: 3365 3324 Aluminum foundries; steel investment foundries
HQ: Consolidated Precision Products Corp.
1621 Euclid Ave Ste 1850
Cleveland OH 44115
216 453-4800

(G-3405)
CPP - GUAYMAS
901 E Genesee St (13037-1325)
PHONE......................315 687-0014
Carl Bratt, *General Mgr*
Ramses Valdes, *Manager*
EMP: 200

SQ FT: 1,000
SALES (est): 24.3MM
SALES (corp-wide): 6.9B **Privately Held**
WEB: www.escocorp.com
SIC: 3559 Foundry, smelting, refining & similar machinery
HQ: Cpp-Syracuse, Inc.
901 E Genesee St
Chittenango NY 13037
315 687-0014

(G-3406)
CPP-SYRACUSE INC (DH)
901 E Genesee St (13037-1325)
PHONE......................315 687-0014
James Stewart, *CEO*
Bart Sgroi, *Info Tech Mgr*
▲ **EMP:** 30 **EST:** 1947
SQ FT: 95,000
SALES (est): 70.6MM
SALES (corp-wide): 6.9B **Privately Held**
SIC: 3324 3369 3356 Aerospace investment castings, ferrous; nonferrous foundries; nonferrous rolling & drawing
HQ: Consolidated Precision Products Corp.
1621 Euclid Ave Ste 1850
Cleveland OH 44115
216 453-4800

Churchville
Monroe County

(G-3407)
**AMA PRECISION SCREENING
INC**
456 Sanford Rd N (14428-9503)
PHONE......................585 293-0820
George Pietropaolo, *President*
EMP: 18
SALES (est): 2.3MM **Privately Held**
WEB: www.amatech.com
SIC: 2759 Screen printing

(G-3408)
**AMERICAN PACKAGING
CORPORATION**
100 Apc Dr (14428-9655)
PHONE......................585 537-4650
Brendan O'Hara, *Manager*
EMP: 112
SALES (corp-wide): 280.5MM **Privately Held**
SIC: 2671 Paper coated or laminated for packaging
PA: American Packaging Corporation
100 Apc Way
Columbus WI 53925
920 623-2291

(G-3409)
BURNT MILL SMITHING
127 Burnt Mill Rd (14428-9405)
PHONE......................585 293-2380
Dennis Schrieber, *Owner*
Dennis Schriber, *Owner*
EMP: 5
SALES (est): 295K **Privately Held**
WEB: www.burnt-mill.com
SIC: 3949 5941 Sporting & athletic goods; sporting goods & bicycle shops

(G-3410)
**CUSTOM MOLDING SOLUTIONS
INC**
456 Sanford Rd N (14428-9503)
PHONE......................585 293-1702
Dwight Campbell, *President*
EMP: 22
SALES (est): 4.7MM **Privately Held**
SIC: 3089 Injection molding of plastics

(G-3411)
DYNAK INC
530 Savage Rd (14428-9614)
PHONE......................585 271-2255
EMP: 13
SQ FT: 25,000
SALES: 2MM **Privately Held**
SIC: 3599 Mfg Industrial Machinery

(G-3412)
**INLAND VACUUM INDUSTRIES
INC (PA)**
35 Howard Ave (14428-8008)
P.O. Box 373 (14428-0373)
PHONE......................585 293-3330
Peter C Yu, *Ch of Bd*
Lusanne Lam, *Vice Pres*
Cindy Oliver, *Officer*
▲ **EMP:** 12
SQ FT: 1,000
SALES (est): 1.7MM **Privately Held**
WEB: www.inlandvacuum.com
SIC: 2992 Lubricating oils & greases

(G-3413)
INTEK PRECISION
539 Attridge Rd (14428-9712)
PHONE......................585 293-0853
Susan Kurucz, *Partner*
Paul Kurucz, *Partner*
EMP: 8
SQ FT: 3,000
SALES: 200K **Privately Held**
WEB: www.intekprecision.com
SIC: 3544 Special dies & tools

(G-3414)
QUALICOAT INC
14 Sanford Rd N (14428-9503)
PHONE......................585 293-2650
Michael Pontarelli, *Ch of Bd*
Sharon Cubitt, *Office Mgr*
▲ **EMP:** 80
SQ FT: 48,000
SALES (est): 10.2MM **Privately Held**
WEB: www.qualicoat.com
SIC: 3479 Coating of metals & formed products; painting of metal products

Cicero
Onondaga County

(G-3415)
ADD ASSOCIATES INC (PA)
Also Called: Image Press, The
6333 Daedalus Rd (13039-8889)
PHONE......................315 449-3474
Toll Free:......................888 -
Chris Arnone, *President*
Lonnie Dahl, *Vice Pres*
EMP: 8
SQ FT: 10,000
SALES (est): 1.1MM **Privately Held**
SIC: 2752 Commercial printing, lithographic

(G-3416)
AWNING MART INC
Also Called: Monroe Sign & Awning
5665 State Route 31 (13039-8513)
PHONE......................315 699-5928
Doug Loguidice, *President*
EMP: 8
SQ FT: 4,400
SALES (est): 823.9K **Privately Held**
SIC: 2394 1799 5199 5999 Awnings, fabric: made from purchased materials; awning installation; canvas products; awnings; canvas products

(G-3417)
CLINTONS DITCH COOP CO INC
8478 Pardee Rd (13039-8531)
PHONE......................315 699-2695
Ronald Anania, *President*
Bill Fitzgerald, *Vice Pres*
Tim Tenney, *Vice Pres*
Thomas Houseknecht, *Treasurer*
Cynthia Van Auken, *Human Resources*
EMP: 155
SQ FT: 250,000
SALES: 62.6MM **Privately Held**
WEB: www.clintonsditch.com
SIC: 2086 Soft drinks: packaged in cans, bottles, etc.

(G-3418)
DAF OFFICE NETWORKS INC
6121 Jemola Runne (13039-8238)
PHONE......................315 699-7070
David A Farabee, *President*
EMP: 9

GEOGRAPHIC

SALES (est): 1MM **Privately Held**
SIC: 2521 5112 5044 Wood office furniture; office supplies; office equipment

(G-3419)
EJ GROUP INC
6177 S Bay Rd (13039-9303)
PHONE..................................315 699-2601
EMP: 9 **Privately Held**
SIC: 3446 Architectural metalwork
PA: Ej Group, Inc.
　301 Spring St
　East Jordan MI 49727

(G-3420)
GIBAR INC
7838 Brewerton Rd (13039-9536)
PHONE..................................315 452-5656
EMP: 220
SALES (corp-wide): 9MM **Privately Held**
SIC: 3421 Table & food cutlery, including butchers'
PA: Gibar, Inc
　1 Technology Pl
　East Syracuse NY 13057
　315 432-4546

(G-3421)
LIBERTY MACHINE & TOOL
7908 Ontario Ave (13039-9759)
PHONE..................................315 699-3242
Thomas Burgmeier, *Owner*
EMP: 1
SQ FT: 2,500
SALES: 1MM **Privately Held**
SIC: 3599 Machine shop, jobbing & repair

(G-3422)
PAUL DE LIMA COMPANY INC
8550 Pardee Rd (13039-8519)
PHONE..................................315 457-3725
Adam Drescher, *Vice Pres*
Jim Sarner, *Vice Pres*
Steve Zaremba, *CFO*
Peter Sansone, *Human Res Dir*
Karen Huntley, *Mktg Dir*
EMP: 23
SALES (corp-wide): 14.5MM **Privately Held**
SIC: 2095 Roasted coffee
PA: Paul De Lima Company, Inc.
　7546 Morgan Rd Ste 1
　Liverpool NY 13090
　315 457-3725

(G-3423)
R & B FABRICATION INC
7282 State Route 31 (13039-9708)
PHONE..................................315 640-9901
Robert Bellinger, *President*
Beth Bellinger, *Principal*
Robert Schneider, *Vice Pres*
Carly Barrett, *Manager*
EMP: 10 EST: 2017
SALES: 50K **Privately Held**
SIC: 7692 7699 7353 1541 Welding repair; automotive welding; industrial equipment services; cranes & aerial lift equipment, rental or leasing; prefabricated building erection, industrial

(G-3424)
THERMAL FOAMS/SYRACUSE INC
6173 S Bay Rd (13039-9303)
P.O. Box 1981 (13039-1981)
PHONE..................................315 699-8734
John Jeffery, *Branch Mgr*
EMP: 25 **Privately Held**
SIC: 3086 Plastics foam products
PA: Thermal Foams/Syracuse, Inc.
　2101 Kenmore Ave
　Buffalo NY 14207

╔══════════════════════════════╗
Clarence
Erie County
╚══════════════════════════════╝

(G-3425)
ANABEC INC
9393 Main St (14031-1912)
P.O. Box 433 (14031-0433)
PHONE..................................716 759-1674
Stephen Meyers, *President*

Nancy Ewing, *Vice Pres*
EMP: 5 EST: 1995
SQ FT: 3,200
SALES (est): 792.5K **Privately Held**
WEB: www.anabec.com
SIC: 2899 Chemical preparations

(G-3426)
ATHENEX PHARMA SOLUTIONS LLC
11342 Main St (14031-1718)
PHONE..................................877 463-7823
Stephen A Panaro, *CEO*
Nicholas Bidwell, *Project Mgr*
Mark Czopp, *Project Mgr*
Tim Umland, *Project Mgr*
Sharon Stoyell, *Pharmacist*
EMP: 8 EST: 2012
SQ FT: 18,000
SALES (est): 2.8MM
SALES (corp-wide): 89.1MM **Publicly Held**
SIC: 2834 Pharmaceutical preparations
PA: Athenex, Inc.
　1001 Main St Ste 600
　Buffalo NY 14203
　716 427-2950

(G-3427)
BUFFALO CRUSHED STONE INC
91 Barton Rd (14031-1837)
P.O. Box 827, Buffalo (14231-0827)
PHONE..................................716 632-6963
Greg Kramer, *President*
EMP: 32
SQ FT: 3,895
SALES (corp-wide): 651.9MM **Privately Held**
SIC: 1422 Crushed & broken limestone
HQ: Buffalo Crushed Stone, Inc.
　500 Como Park Blvd
　Buffalo NY 14227
　716 826-7310

(G-3428)
DIMAR MANUFACTURING CORP
10123 Main St (14031-2164)
P.O. Box 597 (14031-0597)
PHONE..................................716 759-0351
Gregory A Fry, *President*
Thomas J Kowalski, *CFO*
EMP: 140
SQ FT: 93,000
SALES: 17MM **Privately Held**
WEB: www.dimarmfg.com
SIC: 3499 3444 Furniture parts, metal; sheet metalwork

(G-3429)
DRESCHER PAPER BOX INC
10425 Keller Rd (14031-1057)
PHONE..................................716 854-0288
J Baird Langworthy, *President*
John Langworthy, *Exec VP*
EMP: 14 EST: 1867
SALES (est): 2.5MM **Privately Held**
WEB: www.drescherpuzzle.com
SIC: 2652 3944 Setup paperboard boxes; games, toys & children's vehicles; puzzles

(G-3430)
DYNABRADE INC (PA)
8989 Sheridan Dr (14031-1490)
PHONE..................................716 631-0100
Walter N Welsch, *Ch of Bd*
Ned T Librock, *President*
Steven D Briggs, *Vice Pres*
Hardy Hamann, *Vice Pres*
Scott Nolt, *Terminal Mgr*
▲ EMP: 175
SQ FT: 95,000
SALES (est): 30.4MM **Privately Held**
WEB: www.dynabrade.com
SIC: 3546 Power-driven handtools

(G-3431)
EASTERN HILLS PRINTING (PA)
9195 Main St (14031-1931)
PHONE..................................716 741-3300
Geoffrey Mohring, *CEO*
EMP: 9
SQ FT: 400
SALES (est): 954.2K **Privately Held**
SIC: 2752 Commercial printing, offset

(G-3432)
EASTERN MANUFACTURING INC
9530 Cobblestone Dr (14031-2413)
PHONE..................................716 741-4572
Barbara Gomlar, *President*
EMP: 10
SQ FT: 8,000
SALES (est): 1.3MM **Privately Held**
SIC: 3441 Fabricated structural metal

(G-3433)
ELECTROCHEM SOLUTIONS INC (DH)
10000 Wehrle Dr (14031-2086)
PHONE..................................716 759-5800
Joseph Flanagan, *Exec VP*
Thomas J Mazza, *Treasurer*
Timothy G McEvoy, *Admin Sec*
◆ EMP: 53
SALES (est): 45.9MM
SALES (corp-wide): 1.2B **Publicly Held**
SIC: 3692 Primary batteries, dry & wet
HQ: Greatbatch Ltd.
　10000 Wehrle Dr
　Clarence NY 14031
　612 331-6750

(G-3434)
EXCEL INDUSTRIES INC
11737 Main St (14031)
P.O. Box 409 (14031-0409)
PHONE..................................716 542-5468
Francis Nicholas, *President*
Donald Nicholas, *Vice Pres*
Diana Fiske, *Treasurer*
Craig Nicholas, *Office Mgr*
Ivy L Nicholas, *Shareholder*
EMP: 40 EST: 1947
SQ FT: 35,000
SALES (est): 6.2MM **Privately Held**
WEB: www.excelindustriesinc.com
SIC: 3599 3441 Machine shop, jobbing & repair; fabricated structural metal

(G-3435)
INTEGER HOLDINGS CORPORATION
Engineered Components Division
4098 Barton Rd (14031-1814)
PHONE..................................716 759-5200
Jennifer Nebelecky, *Engineer*
Mark Zawodzinski, *Accounting Mgr*
Charles Wemhoff, *Manager*
Laura Roskopf, *Director*
EMP: 100
SALES (corp-wide): 1.2B **Publicly Held**
WEB: www.greatbatch.com
SIC: 3841 3842 Surgical instruments & apparatus; surgical appliances & supplies
PA: Integer Holdings Corporation
　5830 Gran Pkwy Ste 1150
　Plano TX 75024
　214 618-5243

(G-3436)
MEDIMA LLC
Also Called: Medima Metals
5727 Strickler Rd (14031-1372)
PHONE..................................716 741-0400
Barry Lazar, *Mng Member*
Diane Locche, *Manager*
▲ EMP: 250
SALES: 425MM **Privately Held**
SIC: 3339 3313 Silicon & chromium; ferroalloys

(G-3437)
OEM SOLUTIONS INC
4995 Rockhaven Dr (14031-2438)
PHONE..................................716 864-9324
▲ EMP: 4
SQ FT: 3,000
SALES: 1MM **Privately Held**
SIC: 3469 3699 Metal Stamping And Electrical Equipment And Supplies

(G-3438)
PALLET SERVICES INC (PA)
4055 Casillio Pkwy (14031-2047)
P.O. Box 911, Tonawanda (14151-0911)
PHONE..................................716 873-7700
Donald Matre, *CEO*
Ronald A Matre, *Vice Pres*
Mike Hanel, *Plant Mgr*

EMP: 120 EST: 1997
SALES (est): 23MM **Privately Held**
WEB: www.palletservices.com
SIC: 2448 Wood pallets & skids

(G-3439)
PEAK MOTION INC
11190 Main St (14031-1702)
PHONE..................................716 534-4925
Douglas Webster, *President*
EMP: 7
SALES (est): 1.5MM **Privately Held**
WEB: www.peakmotion.com
SIC: 3499 3544 Aerosol valves, metal; special dies, tools, jigs & fixtures

(G-3440)
PRECIMED INC
Also Called: Greatbatch Medical
10000 Wehrle Dr (14031-2086)
PHONE..................................716 759-5600
Patrick White, *CEO*
Patrick Berdoz, *President*
EMP: 46
SQ FT: 2,000
SALES (est): 4.5MM
SALES (corp-wide): 1.2B **Publicly Held**
WEB: www.precimed.com
SIC: 3841 5047 Surgical & medical instruments; medical & hospital equipment
HQ: Greatbatch Ltd.
　10000 Wehrle Dr
　Clarence NY 14031
　612 331-6750

(G-3441)
RLS HOLDINGS INC
11342 Main St (14031-1718)
PHONE..................................716 418-7274
Stephen A Panaro PHD, *President*
EMP: 5
SALES (est): 799K **Privately Held**
SIC: 2834 Pharmaceutical preparations

(G-3442)
RODAC USA CORP
5605 Kraus Rd (14031-1342)
PHONE..................................716 741-3931
EMP: 25
SALES (est): 2.2MM **Privately Held**
SIC: 3648 Mfg Lighting Equipment

(G-3443)
WAVE FLOAT ROOMS LLC
4817 Kraus Rd (14031-1507)
PHONE..................................844 356-2876
Craig Silver,
EMP: 8
SALES: 1.4MM **Privately Held**
SIC: 3999 Hot tub & spa covers

╔══════════════════════════════╗
Clarence Center
Erie County
╚══════════════════════════════╝

(G-3444)
CLARENCE RESINS AND CHEMICALS
9585 Keller Rd (14032-9230)
PHONE..................................716 406-9804
James G Lawrence, *President*
EMP: 8
SQ FT: 800
SALES (est): 1.2MM **Privately Held**
SIC: 2821 5169 Plastics materials & resins; synthetic resins, rubber & plastic materials

(G-3445)
EXACTA LLC
8955 Williams Ct (14032-9414)
PHONE..................................716 406-2303
Peter Buchbinder, *Owner*
James B Schleer, *Mng Member*
EMP: 9
SQ FT: 1,200
SALES (est): 1MM **Privately Held**
WEB: www.exacta.com
SIC: 3555 Copy holders, printers'

(G-3446)
J R PRODUCTS INC
9680 County Rd (14032-9240)
PHONE..................................716 633-7565

▲ = Import ▼=Export
◆ =Import/Export

Doug Rouba, *President*
Brian Roba, *VP Sales*
▲ **EMP:** 9
SALES (est): 730K **Privately Held**
WEB: www.jrprvinc.com
SIC: 3949 Camping equipment & supplies

(G-3447)
JW BURG MACHINE & TOOL INC
7430 Rapids Rd (14032-9501)
P.O. Box 372 (14032-0372)
PHONE................................716 434-0015
Joe Burg, *President*
EMP: 8
SALES (est): 265.7K **Privately Held**
SIC: 3599 Machine shop, jobbing & repair

(G-3448)
MALYN INDUSTRIAL CERAMICS INC
8640 Roll Rd (14032-9139)
P.O. Box 469 (14032-0469)
PHONE................................716 741-1510
Michael Malyn, *President*
Pat Malyn, *Vice Pres*
Laura Case, *Accountant*
EMP: 7
SQ FT: 7,000
SALES (est): 930K **Privately Held**
WEB: www.malyn.com
SIC: 3291 3432 Grinding balls, ceramic; plumbing fixture fittings & trim

(G-3449)
TECHNIFLO CORPORATION
9730 County Rd (14032-9651)
P.O. Box 307, Clarence (14031-0307)
PHONE................................716 741-3500
Richard F Whitesell, *CEO*
EMP: 9 **EST:** 1975
SQ FT: 8,000
SALES (est): 1.8MM **Privately Held**
SIC: 3625 Noise control equipment

(G-3450)
UNICENTER MILLWORK INC
9605 Clarence Center Rd (14032-9748)
PHONE................................716 741-8201
Terrance Reilly, *President*
EMP: 9
SALES (est): 680K **Privately Held**
SIC: 2431 Millwork

Clay
Onondaga County

(G-3451)
MS SPARES LLC
8055 Evesborough Dr (13041-9140)
PHONE................................607 223-3024
Michael Slater, *President*
EMP: 5
SALES (est): 559.5K **Privately Held**
SIC: 3061 3599 3444 7692 Mechanical rubber goods; machine & other job shop work; sheet metalwork; welding repair

Clayton
Jefferson County

(G-3452)
AMERICAN METALCRAFT MARINE
690 Riverside Dr (13624-1043)
P.O. Box 961, Cape Vincent (13618-0961)
PHONE................................315 686-9891
Kenneth I Johnson, *President*
Leon Rusho Jr, *Vice Pres*
▼ **EMP:** 7 **EST:** 1997
SALES (est): 567.9K **Privately Held**
WEB: www.americanmetalcraftmarine.com
SIC: 3732 Boat building & repairing

(G-3453)
COYOTE MOON LLC (PA)
Also Called: Coyote Moon Vineyards
17371 County Route 3 (13624-2193)
P.O. Box 497 (13624-0497)
PHONE................................315 686-5600
Kristina Ives, *Pub Rel Staff*

Phillip Randazzo,
Elena Comiskey, *Assistant*
EMP: 12
SALES (est): 2.2MM **Privately Held**
SIC: 2084 5182 5921 Wines; wine; wine

Clayville
Oneida County

(G-3454)
BARRETT PAVING MATERIALS INC
363 Rasbach Rd (13322-2538)
PHONE................................315 737-9471
Michael Labuz, *Sales Staff*
Robert Bard, *Branch Mgr*
EMP: 13
SALES (corp-wide): 83.5MM **Privately Held**
WEB: www.barrettpaving.com
SIC: 2951 1429 3272 1422 Asphalt & asphaltic paving mixtures (not from refineries); igneous rock, crushed & broken-quarrying; concrete products; crushed & broken limestone
HQ: Barrett Paving Materials Inc.
    3 Becker Farm Rd Ste 307
    Roseland NJ 07068
    973 533-1001

(G-3455)
CLAYVILLE ICE CO INC
2514 Foundry Pl (13322-1600)
P.O. Box 12 (13322-0012)
PHONE................................315 839-5405
Gareth A Evans, *President*
EMP: 8
SQ FT: 17,000
SALES (est): 340.1K **Privately Held**
SIC: 2097 Block ice; ice cubes

(G-3456)
HMI METAL POWDERS
Also Called: Pratt With ME Hmi Met Powders
2395 Main St (13322-1102)
P.O. Box 294 (13322-0294)
PHONE................................315 839-5421
John Letisky, *Treasurer*
EMP: 120
SQ FT: 140,000
SALES (est): 14.7MM **Privately Held**
SIC: 3312 Blast furnaces & steel mills

(G-3457)
HOMOGENEOUS METALS INC
Also Called: Hmi Metal Powders
2395 Main St (13322-1102)
P.O. Box 294 (13322-0294)
PHONE................................315 839-5421
Mark Hewko, *Ch of Bd*
Greg Treacy, *Ch of Bd*
Mark Huwko, *General Mgr*
Mark Bernat, *Analyst*
▲ **EMP:** 56 **EST:** 1965
SQ FT: 129,000
SALES (est): 14.3MM
SALES (corp-wide): 66.5B **Publicly Held**
WEB: www.hmipowder.com
SIC: 3312 Billets, steel
PA: United Technologies Corporation
    10 Farm Springs Rd
    Farmington CT 06032
    860 728-7000

(G-3458)
VALLEY CREEK SIDE INC
Also Called: Valley Signs
1960 State Route 8 (13322-1312)
P.O. Box 287 (13322-0287)
PHONE................................315 839-5526
EMP: 7
SALES (est): 240K **Privately Held**
SIC: 3993 Mfg Signs/Advertising Specialties

(G-3459)
WOLAK INC
2360 King Rd (13322-1214)
PHONE................................315 839-5366
J Wolak, *President*
EMP: 7 **EST:** 1941
SQ FT: 20,000

SALES (est): 560K **Privately Held**
SIC: 2541 Counter & sink tops

Clifton Park
Saratoga County

(G-3460)
ADVANCED MFG TECHNIQUES
453 Kinns Rd (12065-2408)
P.O. Box 617 (12065-0617)
PHONE................................518 877-8560
Steve Petronis, *President*
Richard Carusone, *Vice Pres*
EMP: 7
SQ FT: 10,000
SALES (est): 1.1MM **Privately Held**
WEB: www.advmfgtech.com
SIC: 3599 3699 Machine shop, jobbing & repair; electrical equipment & supplies

(G-3461)
ANTHROPOSOPHIC PRESS INC (PA)
15 Greenridge Dr (12065-6628)
PHONE................................518 851-2054
Gordon Edwards, *Ch of Bd*
Michael Dobson, *President*
Christopher Bamford, *Admin Sec*
▲ **EMP:** 2
SQ FT: 6,500
SALES (est): 1.1MM **Privately Held**
SIC: 2731 5192 5961 Books: publishing only; books; books, mail order (except book clubs)

(G-3462)
ATLANTIC PROJECTS COMPANY INC
5 Southside Dr Ste 11s (12065-3870)
P.O. Box 782 (12065-0782)
PHONE................................518 878-2065
Judith Brodeur, *CFO*
EMP: 10 **EST:** 1999
SALES (est): 1.6MM
SALES (corp-wide): 482.1MM **Publicly Held**
SIC: 3511 Hydraulic turbines
HQ: Atlantic Projects Company Limited
    3 Marine Road
    Dun Laoghaire

(G-3463)
BOBRICK WASHROOM EQUIPMENT INC
200 Commerce Dr (12065-1399)
PHONE................................518 877-7444
Rich Ross, *Manager*
Ashley Hillard, *Director*
EMP: 100
SALES (corp-wide): 97.9MM **Privately Held**
SIC: 2542 5074 3446 Partitions & fixtures, except wood; plumbing & hydronic heating supplies; architectural metalwork
HQ: Bobrick Washroom Equipment, Inc.
    6901 Tujunga Ave
    North Hollywood CA 91605
    818 764-1000

(G-3464)
G&G LED LLC
10 Corprate Dr Clifton Pa Clifton Park (12065)
PHONE................................800 285-6780
Cory Baright, *VP Opers*
Patrick Tully, *Prdtn Mgr*
Brandon Smith, *Mfg Staff*
Caleb Peterson, *Engineer*
Carrie Jackson, *Accounting Mgr*
EMP: 23 **EST:** 2010
SQ FT: 12,000
SALES (est): 5.4MM **Privately Held**
SIC: 3646 Commercial indusl & institutional electric lighting fixtures

(G-3465)
JOHNSON CONTROLS
1399 Vischer Ferry Rd (12065)
PHONE................................518 952-6040
Dan Bullis, *Manager*
EMP: 30 **Privately Held**
WEB: www.simplexgrinnell.com
SIC: 3669 Emergency alarms

HQ: Johnson Controls Fire Protection Lp
    6600 Congress Ave
    Boca Raton FL 33487
    561 988-7200

(G-3466)
LASERTECH CRTRIDGE RE-BUILDERS
7 Longwood Dr (12065-7614)
PHONE................................518 373-1246
Enn Epner, *Owner*
William Hougeich, *Vice Pres*
EMP: 9
SALES (est): 400K **Privately Held**
SIC: 3861 5734 Toners, prepared photographic (not made in chemical plants); computer & software stores

(G-3467)
M MANASTRIP-M CORPORATION
821 Main St (12065-1002)
PHONE................................518 664-2089
David Scagnelli, *President*
George Scagnelli, *Buyer*
EMP: 5
SQ FT: 3,000
SALES (est): 453.3K **Privately Held**
WEB: www.manastrip.com
SIC: 3498 3451 3494 Manifolds, pipe: fabricated from purchased pipe; screw machine products; valves & pipe fittings

(G-3468)
MICROB PHASE SERVICES
Also Called: Brittish American Envmtl
14 Nottingham Way S (12065-1727)
PHONE................................518 877-8948
Ron Shongar, *Owner*
EMP: 15
SALES (est): 830K **Privately Held**
SIC: 3822 Auto controls regulating residntl & coml environmt & applncs

(G-3469)
NYI BUILDING PRODUCTS INC (PA)
5 Southside Dr Ste 204 (12065-3870)
PHONE................................518 458-7500
Jay Torani, *Principal*
Susanne Brook, *Vice Pres*
▲ **EMP:** 16
SQ FT: 1,500
SALES (est): 4.1MM **Privately Held**
WEB: www.nyionline.com
SIC: 3315 5169 Nails, spikes, brads & similar items; adhesives & sealants

(G-3470)
PRINT & GRAPHICS GROUP
12 Fire Rd Ste 3 (12065-3130)
PHONE................................518 371-4649
Frank Papasso, *Owner*
EMP: 6
SALES (est): 468.9K **Privately Held**
SIC: 2752 Commercial printing, offset

(G-3471)
PVC INDUSTRIES INC
107 Pierce Rd (12065-1310)
PHONE................................518 877-8670
Louis F Simonini, *President*
EMP: 30
SQ FT: 65,000
SALES (est): 951.3K **Privately Held**
WEB: www.pvcindustries.com
SIC: 3089 Windows, plastic; window frames & sash, plastic
PA: Sturbridge Associates Iii Llc
    185 Union Ave
    Providence RI 02909

(G-3472)
SENSIO AMERICA
800 Route 146 Ste 175 (12065-3945)
PHONE................................877 501-5337
Paul Bardwell, *General Mgr*
Terry V Delong, *Principal*
EMP: 15
SALES (est): 2.3MM **Privately Held**
SIC: 3648 Lighting equipment

(G-3473)
SENSIO AMERICA LLC (PA)
800 Route 146 Ste 175 (12065-3945)
PHONE...............................877 501-5337
Terry Delong, *Vice Pres*
▲ EMP: 14
SQ FT: 7,000
SALES: 5.2MM **Privately Held**
SIC: 3648 Lighting equipment

(G-3474)
SHMALTZ BREWING COMPANY
6 Fairchild Sq 1 (12065-1254)
PHONE...............................518 406-5430
Greg Chanese, *Mktg Dir*
Matt Polacheck, *Director*
▲ EMP: 34
SALES (est): 5.5MM **Privately Held**
SIC: 2082 Beer (alcoholic beverage)

(G-3475)
ST SILICONES CORPORATION
821 Main St (12065-1002)
PHONE...............................518 406-3208
David A Scagnelli, *President*
EMP: 15
SALES (est): 1MM **Privately Held**
SIC: 3841 Surgical & medical instruments

(G-3476)
THE GRAMECY GROUP
4 Gramecy Ct (12065-2329)
PHONE...............................518 348-1325
Bill Sommers, *Owner*
EMP: 8
SALES (est): 721.8K **Privately Held**
WEB: www.gramecy.com
SIC: 2759 3479 Commercial printing;
name plates: engraved, etched, etc.

(G-3477)
WESTCHESTER VALVE & FITTING CO
741 Pierce Rd (12065-1302)
PHONE...............................914 762-6600
Tom Selfridge, *Owner*
EMP: 5
SALES (est): 280.2K **Privately Held**
SIC: 3494 Valves & pipe fittings

(G-3478)
WORLDWIDE GAS TURBINE PDTS INC
Also Called: Gt Parts & Services
300 Commerce Dr (12065-1317)
PHONE...............................518 877-7200
Anthony Campana, *CEO*
Stephen P Campana, *Ch of Bd*
Sean Moran, *Sales Engr*
Antoinette Campana, *Admin Sec*
EMP: 8
SQ FT: 1,200
SALES (est): 1.9MM **Privately Held**
SIC: 3511 Turbines & turbine generator
sets

Clifton Springs
Ontario County

(G-3479)
MERCHANDISER INC
70 Stephens St (14432-1051)
P.O. Box 642 (14432-0642)
PHONE...............................315 462-6411
Cheryl Tears, *President*
James Tears, *Vice Pres*
EMP: 5
SQ FT: 1,792
SALES: 450K **Privately Held**
WEB: www.themerchandiser.net
SIC: 2759 2711 Publication printing; news-
papers

(G-3480)
RJ WELDING & FABRICATING INC
2300 Wheat Rd (14432-9312)
PHONE...............................315 523-1288
Robert Crosby, *Principal*
EMP: 5
SALES (est): 556.2K **Privately Held**
SIC: 7692 Welding repair

(G-3481)
TOWNLINE MACHINE CO INC
3151 Manchester (14432)
PHONE...............................315 462-3413
Scott Converse, *President*
Patrick Converse, *Treasurer*
EMP: 22
SQ FT: 25,000
SALES: 3MM **Privately Held**
SIC: 3545 Precision tools, machinists'

Clinton
Oneida County

(G-3482)
GERMANIUM CORP AMERICA INC
34 Robinson Rd (13323-1419)
PHONE...............................315 853-4900
Gregory P Evans, *Ch of Bd*
▲ EMP: 11
SALES (est): 1.5MM
SALES (corp-wide): 229.6MM **Privately Held**
WEB: www.indium.com
SIC: 3341 2819 Secondary nonferrous
metals; chemicals, high purity: refined
from technical grade
PA: Indium Corporation Of America
34 Robinson Rd
Clinton NY 13323
800 446-3486

(G-3483)
INDIUM CORPORATION OF AMERICA (PA)
34 Robinson Rd (13323-1419)
P.O. Box 269, Utica (13503-0269)
PHONE...............................800 446-3486
Gregory P Evans, *CEO*
William N Macartney III, *Ch of Bd*
Ross Bemtson, *President*
Don Olejarczyk, *Opers Mgr*
Michael Schmitt, *Production*
▲ EMP: 45 EST: 1934
SQ FT: 12,000
SALES (est): 229.6MM **Privately Held**
WEB: www.indium.com
SIC: 3356 Solder: wire, bar, acid core, &
rosin core

(G-3484)
POWER LINE CONSTRUCTORS INC
24 Robinson Rd (13323-1419)
P.O. Box 385 (13323-0385)
PHONE...............................315 853-6183
David L Critelli, *President*
En M Critelli, *Exec VP*
Steven M Critelli, *Exec VP*
Allen Kobbe, *Vice Pres*
Michael E Lopata, *Vice Pres*
EMP: 30
SQ FT: 7,500
SALES (est): 7.4MM **Privately Held**
WEB: www.powerlineconstructors.com
SIC: 3669 Traffic signals, electric

(G-3485)
SANTUCCI CUSTOM LIGHTING
2943 Lumbard Rd (13323-4527)
PHONE...............................866 853-1929
Marilyn Santucci, *CEO*
EMP: 10 EST: 2018
SALES: 1MM **Privately Held**
SIC: 3646 Chandeliers, commercial

(G-3486)
TENNEY MEDIA GROUP (PA)
Also Called: Omp Printing & Graphics
28 Robinson Rd (13323-1419)
P.O. Box 325 (13323-0325)
PHONE...............................315 853-5569
Claudia Cleary, *Ch of Bd*
Patrick Dowdall, *COO*
Robert Tenney, *Admin Sec*
EMP: 70
SQ FT: 25,000
SALES (est): 3.9MM **Privately Held**
WEB: www.psaver.com
SIC: 2711 Newspapers

Clinton Corners
Dutchess County

(G-3487)
CLINTON VINEYARDS INC
450 Schultzville Rd (12514-2402)
PHONE...............................845 266-5372
Phyllis Feder, *President*
EMP: 5
SALES (est): 425.6K **Privately Held**
WEB: www.clintonvineyards.com
SIC: 2084 Wines

Clyde
Wayne County

(G-3488)
ADVANCED ATOMIZATION TECH LLC
Also Called: Aatech
124 Columbia St (14433-1049)
PHONE...............................315 923-2341
Leanne Collazzo, *General Mgr*
Bill Kohberger, *Engineer*
Jeffery Caster, *Project Engr*
Christopher Harrison, *CFO*
James Mazzarell, *CTO*
EMP: 300
SQ FT: 60,000
SALES (est): 136MM
SALES (corp-wide): 14.3B **Publicly Held**
SIC: 3724 Aircraft engines & engine parts
PA: Parker-Hannifin Corporation
6035 Parkland Blvd
Cleveland OH 44124
216 896-3000

(G-3489)
ENERGY PANEL STRUCTURES INC
Also Called: Fingerlakes Construction
10269 Old Route 31 (14433-9777)
PHONE...............................315 923-7777
Kirt Burghdorf, *Vice Pres*
Duane Hix, *Engineer*
EMP: 7
SALES (corp-wide): 190.3MM **Privately Held**
SIC: 3448 2452 Prefabricated metal build-
ings; prefabricated wood buildings
HQ: Energy Panel Structures, Inc.
603 N Van Gordon Ave
Graettinger IA 51342
712 859-3219

(G-3490)
ENERGY PANEL STRUCTURES INC
Also Called: Fingerlakes Construction
10269 Old Route 31 (14433-9777)
PHONE...............................585 343-1777
Kirt Burghdorf, *Vice Pres*
EMP: 6
SALES (corp-wide): 190.3MM **Privately Held**
SIC: 3448 2452 Prefabricated metal build-
ings; prefabricated wood buildings
HQ: Energy Panel Structures, Inc.
603 N Van Gordon Ave
Graettinger IA 51342
712 859-3219

(G-3491)
FUEL EFFICIENCY LLC
101 Davis Pkwy (14433)
PHONE...............................315 923-2511
Joseph Connelly,
Karen Connelly,
EMP: 8
SQ FT: 12,700
SALES (est): 1.4MM **Privately Held**
WEB: www.fuelefficiency.com
SIC: 3443 Boilers: industrial, power, or ma-
rine; boiler shop products: boilers, smoke-
stacks, steel tanks

(G-3492)
MEADE MACHINE CO INC
31 Ford St (14433-1306)
PHONE...............................315 923-1703

Mark Clinton Meade, *President*
Elizabeth Meade, *Vice Pres*
EMP: 6 EST: 1943
SQ FT: 8,000
SALES: 800K **Privately Held**
SIC: 3599 7539 Machine shop, jobbing &
repair; machine shop, automotive

(G-3493)
MODERN BLOCK LLC
2440 Wyne Zandra Rose Vly (14433)
PHONE...............................315 923-7443
Andy Martin,
Glen S Martin,
EMP: 8
SALES: 600K **Privately Held**
SIC: 3271 Concrete block & brick

(G-3494)
PARKER-HANNIFIN CORPORATION
Also Called: Parker-Hannifin Aerospace
124 Columbia St (14433-1049)
PHONE...............................631 231-3737
James Steurrys, *Engineer*
David Wright, *Manager*
EMP: 248
SALES (corp-wide): 14.3B **Publicly Held**
SIC: 3728 Aircraft parts & equipment
PA: Parker-Hannifin Corporation
6035 Parkland Blvd
Cleveland OH 44124
216 896-3000

(G-3495)
THOMAS ELECTRONICS INC (PA)
208 Davis Pkwy (14433-9550)
PHONE...............................315 923-2051
David A Ketchum, *President*
Dennis Young, *President*
Douglas Ketchum, *Exec VP*
Doug Ketchum, *Vice Pres*
Scott Hughes, *Facilities Mgr*
▲ EMP: 160
SQ FT: 71,180
SALES (est): 22.5MM **Privately Held**
SIC: 3671 Cathode ray tubes, including re-
built

Clymer
Chautauqua County

(G-3496)
CUSTOM SHIPPING PRODUCTS INC
8661 Knowlton Rd (14724-9706)
P.O. Box 245 (14724-0245)
PHONE...............................716 355-4437
John Holthouse, *President*
Shelly Schenck, *Corp Secy*
Mike Schenck, *Vice Pres*
EMP: 10
SQ FT: 3,000
SALES: 890K **Privately Held**
SIC: 2448 Pallets, wood

Cobleskill
Schoharie County

(G-3497)
CLAPPER HOLLOW DESIGNS INC
369 N Grand St (12043-4140)
PHONE...............................518 234-9561
Michael Lambert, *President*
Brigette Belka, *Vice Pres*
EMP: 20
SQ FT: 10,000
SALES (est): 1.6MM **Privately Held**
SIC: 3952 Frames for artists' canvases

(G-3498)
COBLESKILL STONE PRODUCTS INC (PA)
112 Rock Rd (12043-5738)
P.O. Box 220 (12043-0220)
PHONE...............................518 234-0221
Emil Galasso, *Chairman*
Michael Galasso, *Vice Pres*

▲ = Import ▼=Export
◆ =Import/Export

Daniel Kleeschulte, *Vice Pres*
Michael Moore, *Vice Pres*
Craig Watson, *Admin Sec*
EMP: 15 **EST:** 1954
SQ FT: 5,000
SALES (est): 115.2MM
SALES (corp-wide): 126.7MM **Privately Held**
WEB: www.cobleskillstone.com
SIC: 1422 Crushed & broken limestone

(G-3499)
EFJ INC
Also Called: Mill Services
128 Macarthur Ave (12043-3603)
PHONE..............................518 234-4799
Daniel W Holt, *President*
James Place, *Vice Pres*
EMP: 60 **EST:** 1993
SQ FT: 80,000
SALES: 10.6MM **Privately Held**
WEB: www.millservices.com
SIC: 2431 Millwork

(G-3500)
T A S SALES SERVICE LLC
105 Kenyon Rd (12043-5713)
PHONE..............................518 234-4919
Thomas Sachs, *Principal*
EMP: 9
SALES (est): 1.1MM **Privately Held**
SIC: 1389 Gas field services

Cochecton
Sullivan County

(G-3501)
COCHECTON MILLS INC (PA)
30 Depot Rd (12726-5221)
PHONE..............................845 932-8282
Dennis E Nearing, *President*
Mike Dickinson, *Warehouse Mgr*
EMP: 20
SQ FT: 8,500
SALES (est): 3.3MM **Privately Held**
SIC: 2048 2041 Poultry feeds; livestock
feeds; flour & other grain mill products

(G-3502)
JML QUARRIES INC
420 Bernas Rd (12726-5423)
PHONE..............................845 932-8206
Rodney Cornelius, *President*
EMP: 25
SQ FT: 2,000
SALES (est): 3.2MM **Privately Held**
SIC: 1422 Crushed & broken limestone

(G-3503)
MASTEN ENTERPRISES LLC (PA)
420 Bernas Rd (12726-5423)
PHONE..............................845 932-8206
John Bernas, *Principal*
Mauren Cowger, *Manager*
EMP: 150 **EST:** 2000
SQ FT: 2,000
SALES (est): 12.2MM **Privately Held**
SIC: 1429 Grits mining (crushed stone)

(G-3504)
SULLIVAN CONCRETE INC
Also Called: Sullivan Structures
420 Bernas Rd (12726-5423)
PHONE..............................845 888-2235
John Bernas, *President*
EMP: 12
SQ FT: 2,000
SALES (est): 2.7MM **Privately Held**
WEB: www.sullivanstructures.com
SIC: 3273 Ready-mixed concrete

Coeymans
Albany County

(G-3505)
TRACEY WELDING CO INC
29 Riverview Dr (12045-7719)
P.O. Box 799 (12045-0799)
PHONE..............................518 756-6309

Richard Tracey, *President*
Richard J Tracey, *Vice Pres*
EMP: 8
SQ FT: 15,200
SALES (est): 1.3MM **Privately Held**
WEB: www.traceywelding.com
SIC: 7692 Welding repair

Cohoes
Albany County

(G-3506)
ELECTRONIC COATING TECH INC (PA)
1 Mustang Dr Ste 4 (12047-4867)
PHONE..............................518 688-2048
Tom Charlton, *President*
Art Perkowski, *Manager*
▲ **EMP:** 12
SALES (est): 1.6MM **Privately Held**
SIC: 3479 3672 Coating of metals &
formed products; coating of metals with
silicon; printed circuit boards

(G-3507)
JAY MOULDING CORPORATION
7 Bridge Ave Ste 1 (12047-4799)
PHONE..............................518 237-4200
Christy Smagala, *President*
Richard Smagala, *Shareholder*
EMP: 10
SQ FT: 9,000
SALES: 1MM **Privately Held**
WEB: www.jaymoulding.com
SIC: 3083 Thermosetting laminates: rods,
tubes, plates & sheet; thermoplastic lami-
nates: rods, tubes, plates & sheet

(G-3508)
LINDE GAS NORTH AMERICA LLC
Also Called: Lifegas
10 Arrowhead Ln (12047-4812)
PHONE..............................518 713-2015
Casey Hilligas, *Branch Mgr*
EMP: 40 **Privately Held**
SIC: 2813 Nitrogen; oxygen, compressed
or liquefied
HQ: Linde Gas North America Llc
200 Somerset Corp Blvd # 7000
Bridgewater NJ 08807

(G-3509)
MATHESON TRI-GAS INC
15 Green Mountain Dr (12047-4807)
PHONE..............................518 203-5003
Scott Kallman, *Branch Mgr*
EMP: 5 **Privately Held**
SIC: 2813 Nitrogen
HQ: Matheson Tri-Gas, Inc.
150 Allen Rd Ste 302
Basking Ridge NJ 07920
908 991-9200

(G-3510)
MOHAWK FINE PAPERS INC (PA)
465 Saratoga St (12047-4626)
P.O. Box 497 (12047-0497)
PHONE..............................518 237-1740
Thomas D O'Connor, *Ch of Bd*
John F Haren, *President*
Walter Duignan, *Vice Chairman*
Kevin P Richard, *COO*
Dolph Beyer, *Vice Pres*
▲ **EMP:** 300 **EST:** 1876
SQ FT: 207,000
SALES (est): 240.1MM **Privately Held**
WEB: www.mohawkpaper.com
SIC: 2672 2621 Coated & laminated
paper; paper mills; uncoated paper

(G-3511)
NORLITE LLC
Also Called: Norlite Corporation
628 Saratoga St (12047-4644)
P.O. Box 694 (12047-0694)
PHONE..............................518 235-0030
Michael Ferraro, *Corp Secy*
Robert O'Brien, *Mng Member*
EMP: 325 **EST:** 1973
SQ FT: 5,000

SALES (est): 40.4MM
SALES (corp-wide): 179.1K **Privately Held**
WEB: www.norliteagg.com
SIC: 3295 Shale, expanded
HQ: Tradebe Environmental Services, Llc
1433 E 83rd Ave Ste 200
Merrillville IN 46410

(G-3512)
PEAK PERFORMANCE DESIGN LLC
Also Called: Create Prosthetics
1 Mustang Dr Ste 2 (12047-4856)
PHONE..............................518 302-9198
Daniel Kelleher, *CFO*
EMP: 7 **EST:** 2016
SALES (est): 273.3K **Privately Held**
SIC: 3842 3577 Prosthetic appliances;
printers & plotters

(G-3513)
PRECISION VALVE & AUTOMTN INC (PA)
Also Called: PVA
1 Mustang Dr Ste 3 (12047-4867)
PHONE..............................518 371-2684
Anthony J Hynes, *Ch of Bd*
Ryan Livingston, *Regional Mgr*
Craig Tuttle, *Mfg Dir*
Sean Farrell, *Opers Staff*
Thomas Benware, *Engineer*
▲ **EMP:** 190
SQ FT: 115,000
SALES (est): 34.1MM **Privately Held**
WEB: www.pva.net
SIC: 3491 Industrial valves

(G-3514)
REO WELDING INC
5 New Cortland St (12047-2628)
PHONE..............................518 238-1022
Robert J REO Jr, *President*
Michael REO, *Vice Pres*
EMP: 17
SQ FT: 6,000
SALES (est): 4.7MM **Privately Held**
WEB: www.reowelding.com
SIC: 3441 7692 Fabricated structural
metal; welding repair

(G-3515)
SCHONWETTER ENTERPRISES INC
Also Called: Bilinski Sausage Mfg Co
41 Lark St (12047-4618)
PHONE..............................518 237-0171
Steven M Schonwetter, *Ch of Bd*
Peter McNulty, *Plant Mgr*
Sagar Agarwal, *QC Mgr*
Steven Schonwetter, *Mktg Dir*
Kevin Oconnor, *Marketing Staff*
EMP: 25
SQ FT: 20,000
SALES (est): 5MM **Privately Held**
WEB: www.bilinski.com
SIC: 2013 Sausages from purchased meat

(G-3516)
SHELTER ENTERPRISES INC
8 Saratoga St (12047-3109)
P.O. Box 618 (12047-0618)
PHONE..............................518 237-4100
Jeffory J Myers, *Principal*
▲ **EMP:** 60
SQ FT: 110,000
SALES (est): 14.7MM **Privately Held**
WEB: www.shelter-ent.com
SIC: 3086 2452 Insulation or cushioning
material, foamed plastic; prefabricated
buildings, wood

(G-3517)
SIGN STUDIO INC
98 Niver St Ste 3 (12047-4734)
PHONE..............................518 266-0877
Ronald Levesque, *CEO*
EMP: 12
SALES (est): 1.4MM **Privately Held**
SIC: 3993 Signs, not made in custom sign
painting shops

(G-3518)
TROYS LANDSCAPE SUPPLY CO INC
1266 Loudon Rd (12047)
PHONE..............................518 785-1526
Troy Miller, *President*
Monica Mickman, *Vice Pres*
EMP: 11
SQ FT: 2,520
SALES (est): 1MM **Privately Held**
SIC: 3271 Blocks, concrete: landscape or
retaining wall

(G-3519)
VITAL SIGNS & GRAPHICS CO INC
251 Saratoga St (12047-3120)
PHONE..............................518 237-8372
Alexander Coloruotolo, *President*
EMP: 5
SQ FT: 1,200
SALES (est): 546K **Privately Held**
SIC: 3993 7336 Signs, not made in cus-
tom sign painting shops; graphic arts &
related design

(G-3520)
W N VANALSTINE & SONS INC (PA)
Also Called: Macaran Printed Products
18 New Cortland St (12047-2628)
PHONE..............................518 237-1436
Nicholas V Alstine, *President*
William N Van Astine III, *Chairman*
Edward Wixted, *CFO*
Patrick Degnan, *Sales Executive*
Lois Johnson, *Marketing Mgr*
EMP: 75 **EST:** 1952
SQ FT: 52,000
SALES (est): 16.3MM **Privately Held**
WEB: www.printandapply.com
SIC: 2759 5199 Flexographic printing;
packaging materials

Cold Spring
Putnam County

(G-3521)
MID-HUDSON CONCRETE PDTS INC
3504 Route 9 (10516-3862)
PHONE..............................845 265-3141
Joe Giachinta, *President*
Katie Demarco, *Marketing Staff*
EMP: 10
SQ FT: 3,000
SALES (est): 1.5MM **Privately Held**
WEB:
www.midhudsonconcreteproducts.com
SIC: 3272 Concrete products, precast;
septic tanks, concrete

(G-3522)
OLD SOULS INC
Also Called: Lam-Tek Millwork Fabricators
63 Main St (10516-3014)
PHONE..............................845 809-5886
Ralph Karabec, *President*
Annabelle Karabec, *Vice Pres*
Judy Grosso, *Admin Sec*
EMP: 5
SALES (est): 556.8K **Privately Held**
WEB: www.oldsouls.com
SIC: 2431 2541 2434 Millwork; wood par-
titions & fixtures; wood kitchen cabinets

(G-3523)
PUTNAM CNTY NEWS RECORDER LLC
3 Stone St (10516-3020)
P.O. Box 185 (10516-0185)
PHONE..............................845 265-2468
Kimberly Hyatt, *Assoc Editor*
Elizabeth Ailes, *Editor*
EMP: 12 **EST:** 1939
SALES (est): 639.1K **Privately Held**
WEB: www.pcnr.com
SIC: 2711 Newspapers: publishing only,
not printed on site

G E O G R A P H I C

(G-3524)
RIVERVIEW INDUSTRIES INC
3012 Route 9 Ste 1 (10516-3675)
PHONE......................845 265-5284
Kevin Reichard, *President*
Paul Reichard, *Vice Pres*
EMP: 7
SALES (est): 949.4K **Privately Held**
SIC: 3548 7538 7549 Welding apparatus;
general truck repair; high performance
auto repair & service

(G-3525)
**SCANGA WOODWORKING
CORP**
22 Corporate Park W (10516)
PHONE......................845 265-9115
Laura Hammond, *Ch of Bd*
Hugo Scanga, *President*
John Scagna, *Vice Pres*
Mark Scagna, *Vice Pres*
Josh Hammond, *Project Mgr*
▲ EMP: 38
SQ FT: 9,000
SALES (est): 6.2MM **Privately Held**
SIC: 2431 Moldings, wood: unfinished &
prefinished

Cold Spring Harbor
Suffolk County

(G-3526)
**CIRRUS HEALTHCARE
PRODUCTS LLC (PA)**
60 Main St Ste A (11724-1433)
P.O. Box 220 (11724-0220)
PHONE......................631 692-7600
Drew O'Connell,
▲ EMP: 28
SALES (est): 6MM **Privately Held**
WEB: www.cirrushealthcare.com
SIC: 3842 Ear plugs

(G-3527)
DANI ACCESSORIES INC
204 Lawrence Hill Rd (11724-1910)
PHONE......................631 692-4505
Daniel Montefusco, *President*
EMP: 30
SQ FT: 4,000
SALES (est): 2MM **Privately Held**
SIC: 3171 Handbags, women's

(G-3528)
**NYC VINYL SCREEN PRINTING
INC (PA)**
204 Lawrence Hill Rd (11724-1910)
PHONE......................718 784-1360
Daniel Montefusco, *President*
▼ EMP: 1
SALES (est): 1.4MM **Privately Held**
SIC: 2759 Commercial printing

(G-3529)
PRINT CENTER INC
3 Harbor Rd Ste 21 (11724-1514)
PHONE......................718 643-9559
Robert Hershon, *President*
EMP: 6
SALES (est): 479K **Privately Held**
WEB: www.rhinography.com
SIC: 2752 Commercial printing, litho-
graphic

Colden
Erie County

(G-3530)
O & S MACHINE & TOOL CO INC
8143 State Rd (14033-9713)
P.O. Box 303 (14033-0303)
PHONE......................716 941-5542
Philip J Schueler, *President*
EMP: 9 EST: 1977
SQ FT: 5,000
SALES (est): 1MM **Privately Held**
SIC: 3599 Machine shop, jobbing & repair

College Point
Queens County

(G-3531)
A ANGONOA INC (PA)
11505 15th Ave (11356-1597)
P.O. Box 560089 (11356-0089)
PHONE......................718 762-4466
Peter Zampieri, *President*
John Armao, *Plant Mgr*
Christopher Desantis, *Sales Staff*
Mike Kroczynski, *Manager*
Eileen Rapp, *Manager*
EMP: 110
SQ FT: 60,000
SALES (est): 14.5MM **Privately Held**
WEB: www.angonoa.com
SIC: 2051 Bread, cake & related products

(G-3532)
AABACS GROUP INC
1509 132nd St (11356-2441)
PHONE......................718 961-3577
Michael Shin, *Principal*
EMP: 10
SALES (est): 990.8K **Privately Held**
SIC: 3699 Security control equipment &
systems

(G-3533)
**ABC WINDOWS AND SIGNS
CORP**
12606 18th Ave (11356-2326)
PHONE......................718 353-6210
Lin Yang, *Ch of Bd*
EMP: 12 EST: 2010
SALES (est): 1.3MM **Privately Held**
SIC: 3993 Signs, not made in custom sign
painting shops

(G-3534)
**AEROSPACE WIRE & CABLE
INC**
12909 18th Ave (11356-2407)
PHONE......................718 358-2345
Richard Chen, *President*
CHI Chung Chen, *Shareholder*
CHI Chen, *Shareholder*
▲ EMP: 30
SQ FT: 3,500
SALES (est): 7.2MM **Privately Held**
WEB: www.aerospacewire.com
SIC: 3315 Wire, steel: insulated or ar-
mored; cable, steel: insulated or armored

(G-3535)
AFC INDUSTRIES INC
1316 133rd Pl Ste 1 (11356-2024)
PHONE......................718 747-0237
Anat Barnes, *Chairman*
Gary Jacobs, *Controller*
Jay Katz, *Marketing Staff*
Dawn Nelson, *Office Mgr*
Rotlevi Amir, *Executive*
▲ EMP: 100
SQ FT: 20,000
SALES (est): 11MM **Privately Held**
WEB: www.afcindustries.com
SIC: 2599 Hospital furniture, except beds

(G-3536)
**AMERICAN ORTHOTIC LAB CO
INC**
924 118th St (11356-1557)
PHONE......................718 961-6487
Kevin John Renart, *President*
EMP: 7
SQ FT: 1,080
SALES (est): 917.5K **Privately Held**
SIC: 3544 Industrial molds

(G-3537)
BEL AIRE OFFSET CORP
Also Called: Bel Aire Printing
1853 College Point Blvd (11356-2220)
PHONE......................718 539-8333
Carmine Nicoletti, *President*
EMP: 5
SQ FT: 5,000
SALES (est): 693.5K **Privately Held**
WEB: www.belaireprintingcorp.com
SIC: 2752 Commercial printing, offset

(G-3538)
**CANADA DRY BOTTLING CO NY
LP (PA)**
11202 15th Ave (11356-1428)
PHONE......................718 358-2000
Harold A Honickman, *Partner*
▲ EMP: 58
SQ FT: 85,000
SALES (est): 51.4MM **Privately Held**
SIC: 2086 Bottled & canned soft drinks

(G-3539)
**CAPITAL KIT CAB & DOOR
MFRS**
Also Called: Capital Ktchens Cab Doors Mfrs
1425 128th St (11356-2335)
PHONE......................718 886-0303
Tom Catalanotto Sr, *President*
Steven Catalanotto, *Corp Secy*
Tom Catalanotto Jr, *Vice Pres*
EMP: 7
SQ FT: 10,000
SALES (est): 700K **Privately Held**
WEB: www.capitalkitchens.com
SIC: 2434 2431 5031 1751 Wood kitchen
cabinets; doors, wood; kitchen cabinets;
cabinet & finish carpentry

(G-3540)
CITY STORE GATES MFG CORP
Also Called: None
1520 129th St (11356-2400)
PHONE......................718 939-9700
Vincent Greco Jr, *Ch of Bd*
Daniel Ocallaghan, *Sales Dir*
▲ EMP: 25
SQ FT: 35,000
SALES (est): 6.6MM **Privately Held**
SIC: 3446 5211 1799 3429 Gates, orna-
mental metal; door & window products;
fence construction; manufactured hard-
ware (general); millwork

(G-3541)
**EAST COAST
THERMOGRAPHERS INC**
1558 127th St Ste 1 (11356-2347)
PHONE......................718 321-3211
Barry Schwartz, *President*
EMP: 30
SQ FT: 6,000
SALES (est): 2MM **Privately Held**
SIC: 2759 3953 2752 Thermography;
marking devices; commercial printing, lith-
ographic

(G-3542)
FILLING EQUIPMENT CO INC
1539 130th St (11356-2481)
PHONE......................718 445-2111
Robert A Hampton, *President*
EMP: 11 EST: 1959
SQ FT: 6,800
SALES (est): 2.7MM **Privately Held**
WEB: www.fillingequipment.com
SIC: 3565 5084 Bottling machinery: filling,
capping, labeling; industrial machinery &
equipment

(G-3543)
GMD INDUSTRIES INC
Also Called: Designer Glass
12920 18th Ave (11356-2408)
PHONE......................718 445-8779
Jorge Rodriguez, *President*
Maria Rodriguez, *Vice Pres*
Raquel Rodriguez, *Sales Staff*
▲ EMP: 8
SQ FT: 1,500
SALES (est): 1.1MM **Privately Held**
WEB: www.gmdindustries.com
SIC: 3231 Decorated glassware: chipped,
engraved, etched, etc.; mirrored glass

(G-3544)
IN-HOUSE INC
1535 126th St Ste 3 (11356-2346)
PHONE......................718 445-9007
Joseph Passarella, *President*
Andrew Schwalb, *Director*
EMP: 10
SQ FT: 5,000

SALES: 1.5MM **Privately Held**
SIC: 2752 2791 2789 2732 Commercial
printing, offset; typesetting; bookbinding &
related work; book printing

(G-3545)
INK-IT PRINTING INC
Also Called: Ink-It Prtg Inc/Angle Offset
1535 126th St Ste 1 (11356-2346)
PHONE......................718 229-5590
Michael Igoe, *President*
EMP: 8
SQ FT: 750
SALES (est): 701.8K **Privately Held**
SIC: 2752 Commercial printing, offset

(G-3546)
INTER-FENCE CO INC
1520 129th St (11356-2400)
PHONE......................718 939-9700
Vincent Greco Sr, *President*
Vincent Greco Jr, *Vice Pres*
Susan Hutter, *Vice Pres*
Thomas A Greco, *Treasurer*
Angela Greco, *Admin Sec*
EMP: 40
SQ FT: 35,000
SALES (est): 5.4MM **Privately Held**
SIC: 3442 3446 Metal doors; gates, orna-
mental metal

(G-3547)
**ISLAND CIRCUITS
INTERNATIONAL**
1318 130th St Fl 2 (11356-1917)
PHONE......................516 625-5555
Maurizio Lanza, *Branch Mgr*
EMP: 7
SALES (corp-wide): 1.8MM **Privately
Held**
SIC: 3679 Electronic circuits
PA: Island Circuits International
100 E 2nd St Ste 201
Mineola NY 11501
516 625-5555

(G-3548)
JAD CORP OF AMERICA
2048 119th St (11356-2123)
PHONE......................718 762-8900
Joseph A Dussich Jr, *President*
Henry Schaeffer, *CFO*
Trina Laxa, *Controller*
Trina Yapching, *Controller*
Chris Panzarella, *Sales Mgr*
EMP: 50
SQ FT: 45,000
SALES (est): 24.4MM **Privately Held**
WEB: www.jad.com
SIC: 2673 5087 5169 Trash bags (plastic
film): made from purchased materials;
cleaning & maintenance equipment &
supplies; chemicals & allied products

(G-3549)
**JPMORGAN CHASE BANK NAT
ASSN**
13207 14th Ave (11356-2001)
PHONE......................718 767-3592
Yessenia Salce, *Agent*
EMP: 6
SALES (corp-wide): 131.4B **Publicly
Held**
SIC: 3578 Automatic teller machines (ATM)
HQ: Jpmorgan Chase Bank, National Asso-
ciation
1111 Polaris Pkwy
Columbus OH 43240
614 436-3055

(G-3550)
LAHOYA ENTERPRISE INC
Also Called: Kourosh
1842 College Point Blvd (11356-2221)
PHONE......................718 886-8799
Kourosh Tehrani, *Ch of Bd*
▲ EMP: 30
SALES (est): 2MM **Privately Held**
SIC: 2339 Women's & misses' outerwear

(G-3551)
LIBERTY CONTROLS INC
1505 132nd St Fl 2 (11356-2441)
PHONE......................718 461-0600
Charles Papalcure, *President*
David Derose, *Project Mgr*

▲ = Import ▼=Export
◆ =Import/Export

EMP: 7 EST: 1998
SALES (est): 1.3MM **Privately Held**
WEB: www.liberty-controls.com
SIC: 3829 Measuring & controlling devices

(G-3552)
M T M PRINTING CO INC
2321 College Point Blvd (11356-2596)
PHONE..............................718 353-3297
Steven Kolman, *President*
Tracy Kolman, *Vice Pres*
EMP: 14 EST: 1940
SQ FT: 5,500
SALES (est): 2.7MM **Privately Held**
WEB: www.mtmprinting.com
SIC: 2752 2759 Commercial printing, off-
set; letterpress printing

(G-3553)
MATIC INDUSTRIES INC
1540 127th St (11356-2332)
PHONE..............................718 886-5470
Roland Tatzel, *President*
EMP: 7
SALES (est): 580K **Privately Held**
SIC: 3599 Machine shop, jobbing & repair

(G-3554)
MINT-X PRODUCTS
CORPORATION
2048 119th St (11356-2123)
PHONE..............................877 646-8224
Joseph Dussich, *President*
Gary Price, *General Mgr*
James Dussich, *Vice Pres*
Bill Wertz, *Vice Pres*
Rich Wilson, *Director*
EMP: 10
SALES: 10MM **Privately Held**
SIC: 2673 Food storage & trash bags
(plastic)

(G-3555)
MRS BAKING DISTRIBUTION
CORP
1825 127th St (11356-2333)
PHONE..............................718 460-6700
Steven Borg, *Principal*
Ira Lampert, *Principal*
Brandon Schops, *Sales Staff*
Frank Massimo, *Info Tech Dir*
EMP: 8
SALES (est): 1.2MM **Privately Held**
SIC: 2051 Bread, cake & related products

(G-3556)
NAS CP CORP (DH)
Also Called: Interplex Nas Electronics
1434 110th St Apt 4a (11356-1445)
PHONE..............................718 961-6757
Jack Seidler, *President*
John Pease, *Exec VP*
Irving Klein, *Treasurer*
▲ **EMP:** 45
SQ FT: 41,000
SALES (est): 27.1MM **Privately Held**
SIC: 3544 3471 3825 Dies & die holders
for metal cutting, forming, die casting;
plating of metals or formed products; test
equipment for electronic & electric meas-
urement
HQ: Interplex Industries, Inc.
231 Ferris Ave
Rumford RI 02916
718 961-6212

(G-3557)
OLIVE LED LIGHTING INC
1310 111th St (11356-1453)
PHONE..............................718 746-0830
Junho Lee, *President*
◆ **EMP:** 7
SQ FT: 8,800
SALES (est): 977.1K **Privately Held**
SIC: 3648 5063 Lighting equipment; light
bulbs & related supplies

(G-3558)
PARKMATIC CAR PRKG
SYSTEMS LLC
2025 130th St (11356-2700)
PHONE..............................800 422-5438
EMP: 5

SALES (corp-wide): 3.5MM **Privately
Held**
SIC: 3559 Parking facility equipment &
supplies
PA: Parkmatic Car Parking Systems, Llc
47-10 A 32nd Pl
Long Island City NY 11101
516 224-7700

(G-3559)
PEPSI-COLA BOTTLING CO NY
INC (HQ)
11202 15th Ave (11356-1496)
PHONE..............................718 392-1000
William Wilson, *Ch of Bd*
Patricia Cioppa, *General Mgr*
Robert Sherman, *Vice Pres*
Bill Donovan, *Warehouse Mgr*
Thomas Obrien, *Opers Staff*
EMP: 550
SQ FT: 400,000
SALES (est): 7B
SALES (corp-wide): 64.6B **Publicly Held**
SIC: 2086 Carbonated soft drinks, bottled
& canned
PA: Pepsico, Inc.
700 Anderson Hill Rd
Purchase NY 10577
914 253-2000

(G-3560)
PRECISION GEAR
INCORPORATED
11207 14th Ave (11356-1407)
PHONE..............................718 321-7200
M Briggs Forelli, *President*
William Girimonte, *Vice Pres*
Phillip Carlu, *Engineer*
David Kaczmarkiewicz, *Engineer*
Cowell Michael, *Engineer*
▲ **EMP:** 147
SQ FT: 56,000
SALES (est): 46.6MM **Privately Held**
WEB: www.precisiongearinc.com
SIC: 3728 Aircraft power transmission
equipment; beaching gear, aircraft

(G-3561)
QUALITY LIFE INC
2047 129th St (11356-2725)
PHONE..............................718 939-5787
Ping Ping Huang, *Ch of Bd*
▲ **EMP:** 15
SALES (est): 1.1MM **Privately Held**
SIC: 3634 Massage machines, electric, ex-
cept for beauty/barber shops

(G-3562)
RAINBOW LEATHER INC
1415 112th St (11356-1435)
PHONE..............................718 939-8762
Richard Lipson, *President*
Danny Pilpe, *Vice Pres*
Maria LI, *Prdtn Mgr*
▲ **EMP:** 10 **EST:** 1981
SQ FT: 8,000
SALES (est): 1.8MM **Privately Held**
WEB: www.rainbowleather.com
SIC: 3111 Embossing of leather

(G-3563)
SCHUSTER & RICHARD
LABORTORIES
Also Called: Schuster & Richard Lab
1420 130th St (11356-2416)
PHONE..............................718 358-8607
Charles Boudiette, *President*
EMP: 6 EST: 1946
SQ FT: 1,500
SALES (est): 540K **Privately Held**
SIC: 3842 Foot appliances, orthopedic

(G-3564)
SIGN CITY OF NEW YORK INC
13212 11th Ave (11356-1958)
P.O. Box 527015, Flushing (11352-7015)
PHONE 718 661-1118
EMP: 5
SALES (est): 74.2K **Privately Held**
SIC: 3993 Signs & advertising specialties

(G-3565)
SPACE SIGN
1525 132nd St (11356-2441)
PHONE..............................718 961-1112

Chang Kon Hahn, *President*
Joyce Hahn, *Vice Pres*
EMP: 11
SQ FT: 5,000
SALES (est): 1.3MM **Privately Held**
WEB: www.spacesign.com
SIC: 3993 3089 3444 1799 Electric
signs; awnings, fiberglass & plastic com-
bination; awnings, sheet metal; awning in-
stallation; awnings

(G-3566)
SRTECH INDUSTRY CORP
12019 Ketch Ct (11356-1151)
PHONE..............................718 496-7001
S Chung, *President*
EMP: 25
SQ FT: 5,000
SALES: 3MM **Privately Held**
SIC: 3663 Amplifiers, RF power & IF

(G-3567)
TAG ENVELOPE CO INC
1419 128th St (11356-2335)
PHONE..............................718 389-6844
Geraldine Wald, *President*
Eric Wald, *Vice Pres*
Ian Wald, *Vice Pres*
EMP: 22 EST: 1919
SQ FT: 10,000
SALES: 3MM **Privately Held**
SIC: 2621 2679 Envelope paper; tags,
paper (unprinted): made from purchased
paper

(G-3568)
ZERED INC (PA)
12717 20th Ave (11356-2317)
PHONE..............................718 353-7464
Hakjin Han, *President*
James Han, *Director*
▲ **EMP:** 10
SALES (est): 1.3MM **Privately Held**
SIC: 3211 Plate glass, polished & rough

Collins
Erie County

(G-3569)
COUNTRY SIDE SAND &
GRAVEL (HQ)
Taylor Hollow Rd (14034)
PHONE..............................716 988-3271
Daniel Gernatt Jr, *President*
EMP: 1 EST: 1964
SQ FT: 10,000
SALES (est): 1.2MM
SALES (corp-wide): 29.8MM **Privately
Held**
SIC: 1442 Sand mining; gravel mining
PA: Gernatt Asphalt Products, Inc.
13870 Taylor Hollow Rd
Collins NY 14034
716 532-3371

(G-3570)
EAST END
1995 Lenox Rd (14034-9785)
PHONE..............................716 532-2622
Cheryl Whiteparker, *Owner*
EMP: 10
SALES (est): 1.1MM **Privately Held**
WEB: www.eastend.com
SIC: 2111 Cigarettes

(G-3571)
GERNATT ASPHALT PRODUCTS
INC (PA)
Also Called: Gernatt Companies
13870 Taylor Hollow Rd (14034-9713)
PHONE..............................716 532-3371
Daniel R Gernatt Jr, *Ch of Bd*
Randall Best, *Vice Pres*
Rick Marzullo, *Sales Staff*
Susan Degolier, *Office Mgr*
EMP: 20
SQ FT: 10,000
SALES (est): 29.8MM **Privately Held**
WEB: www.gernatt.com
SIC: 1442 Construction sand & gravel

(G-3572)
STEEL CITY SALT LLC
13870 Taylor Hollow Rd (14034-9713)
PHONE..............................716 532-0000
Bill Schmitz, *Principal*
EMP: 6 EST: 2014
SALES: 500K **Privately Held**
SIC: 1479 Rock salt mining

Colonie
Albany County

(G-3573)
COLONIE BLOCK AND SUPPLY
CO
124 Lincoln Ave (12205-4917)
PHONE..............................518 869-8411
Thomas Gentile, *President*
Donald Countermine, *Vice Pres*
Marlene Countermine, *Treasurer*
EMP: 5 EST: 1935
SQ FT: 5,000
SALES (est): 693.3K **Privately Held**
SIC: 3271 5032 Blocks, concrete or cin-
der: standard; masons' materials

(G-3574)
GERALD MCGLONE
17 Zoar Ave (12205-3531)
PHONE..............................518 482-2613
Gerald McGlone, *Owner*
EMP: 5
SALES (est): 423.6K **Privately Held**
SIC: 2679 Wallpaper

(G-3575)
SNYDERS NEON DISPLAYS INC
Also Called: Snyder Neon & Plastic Signs
5 Highland Ave (12205-5458)
PHONE..............................518 857-4100
Mary Elizabeth Orminski, *President*
Mark Orminski, *Vice Pres*
EMP: 6 EST: 1931
SQ FT: 5,800
SALES: 230K **Privately Held**
SIC: 3993 7389 Signs, not made in cus-
tom sign painting shops; crane & aerial lift
service

Commack
Suffolk County

(G-3576)
AMNEAL PHARMACEUTICALS
NY LLC
360 Moreland Rd Ste C (11725-5707)
PHONE..............................631 952-0214
Mircea Curticapean, *Manager*
EMP: 6
SALES (corp-wide): 1.6B **Publicly Held**
SIC: 2834 Pharmaceutical preparations
HQ: Amneal Pharmaceuticals Of New York,
Llc
50 Horseblock Rd
Brookhaven NY 11719
908 947-3120

(G-3577)
AVENTURA TECHNOLOGIES
INC (PA)
48 Mall Dr (11725-5704)
PHONE..............................631 300-4000
Frances Cabasso, *CEO*
Kevin A Lichtman, *Vice Pres*
Jonathan Lasker, *Opers Mgr*
Ed Matulik, *Sales Engr*
Jeffrey Burmeister, *Sales Staff*
◆ **EMP:** 40
SQ FT: 40,000
SALES (est): 17.4MM **Privately Held**
WEB: www.ati247.com
SIC: 3577 3812 1731 Computer periph-
eral equipment; search & navigation
equipment; voice, data & video wiring
contractor; closed circuit television instal-
lation

G
E
O
G
R
A
P
H
I
C

(G-3578)
AVERY BIOMEDICAL DEVICES INC
61 Mall Dr Ste 1 (11725-5725)
PHONE..................................631 864-1600
Martin Dobelle, *CEO*
Antonio Martins, *CEO*
Claire Dobelle, *President*
Rommel Caguicla, *Technical Mgr*
Linda Towler, *CFO*
EMP: 16
SQ FT: 4,000
SALES (est): 1.7MM **Privately Held**
WEB: www.dobelle.com
SIC: 3841 Surgical instruments & apparatus

(G-3579)
BEYER GRAPHICS INC
30 Austin Blvd Ste A (11725-5747)
PHONE..................................631 543-3900
Jose Beyer, *CEO*
William Beyer Sr, *Ch of Bd*
Daniel Byer, *CFO*
Doreen Ullger, *Sales Staff*
Dan Beyer, *IT/INT Sup*
▲ EMP: 99
SQ FT: 40,000
SALES (est): 35.9MM **Privately Held**
SIC: 2752 2791 2789 7374 Commercial printing, offset; typesetting; bookbinding & related work; computer graphics service

(G-3580)
BREN-TRNICS BATTERIES INTL INC
10 Brayton Ct (11725-3104)
PHONE..................................631 499-5155
Leo A Brenna, *President*
EMP: 6
SALES (est): 805K **Privately Held**
SIC: 3691 Batteries, rechargeable

(G-3581)
BREN-TRNICS BATTERIES INTL LLC
10 Brayton Ct (11725-3104)
PHONE..................................631 499-5155
Leo Brenna, *President*
EMP: 20
SQ FT: 94,000
SALES (est): 2.4MM **Privately Held**
SIC: 3691 Alkaline cell storage batteries

(G-3582)
BREN-TRONICS INC
10 Brayton Ct (11725-3104)
PHONE..................................631 499-5155
SAI W Fung, *President*
Sylvain Lhuissier, *Vice Pres*
Leigh Straub, *Opers Staff*
John Bungart, *QC Dir*
Peter Burke, *Engineer*
◆ EMP: 200 **EST:** 1973
SQ FT: 80,000
SALES (est): 56.2MM **Privately Held**
WEB: www.bren-tronics.com
SIC: 3691 3692 3699 Storage batteries; primary batteries, dry & wet; electrical equipment & supplies

(G-3583)
CLEAN GAS SYSTEMS INC
368 Veterans Memorial Hwy 3a
(11725-4338)
PHONE..................................631 467-1600
Anil M Shah, *President*
EMP: 20
SQ FT: 4,000
SALES (est): 4.3MM **Privately Held**
WEB: www.cgscgs.com
SIC: 3564 8711 7389 Air purification equipment; pollution control engineering; air pollution measuring service

(G-3584)
COMFORT CARE TEXTILES INC (HQ)
368 Veterans Memorial Hwy # 5
(11725-4322)
PHONE..................................631 543-0531
Scott Janicola, *Chairman*
▲ EMP: 40
SQ FT: 26,000

SALES (est): 6.5MM
SALES (corp-wide): 11.9MM **Privately Held**
SIC: 2295 Coated fabrics, not rubberized
PA: Jan Lew Textile Corp
368 Veterans Memorial Hwy # 5
Commack NY 11725
631 543-0531

(G-3585)
CORAL COLOR PROCESS LTD
50 Mall Dr (11725-5704)
PHONE..................................631 543-5200
Edward Aiello, *President*
Edie Dinapoli, *Managing Dir*
Ediedie D Npolis, *Vice Pres*
Bill Sayrafe, *Prdtn Mgr*
EMP: 37
SQ FT: 20,000
SALES (est): 13MM **Privately Held**
SIC: 2752 Commercial printing, offset

(G-3586)
DOCTOR PAVERS
34 Redleaf Ln (11725-5516)
PHONE..................................516 342-6016
Roberto A Mendonca, *Owner*
EMP: 5
SALES (est): 346.2K **Privately Held**
SIC: 2951 Asphalt paving mixtures & blocks

(G-3587)
FACTORY WHEEL WAREHOUSE INC
57 Mall Dr (11725-5703)
PHONE..................................516 605-2131
EMP: 9 **EST:** 2012
SALES (est): 887.7K **Privately Held**
SIC: 3714 5013 5015 5085 Motor vehicle wheels & parts; wheel rims, motor vehicle; wheels, motor vehicle; wheels, motor vehicle; wheels, used: motor vehicle; bearings, bushings, wheels & gears

(G-3588)
FOREST RESEARCH INSTITUTE INC
49 Mall Dr (11725-5722)
PHONE..................................631 858-5200
Forest Labs, *Principal*
Richard Del Bosco, *Manager*
EMP: 11 **EST:** 2008
SALES (est): 1.4MM **Privately Held**
SIC: 2834 Pharmaceutical preparations

(G-3589)
GASSER & SONS INC (PA)
440 Moreland Rd (11725-5778)
PHONE..................................631 543-6600
Richard F Gasser, *Chairman*
Jack Gasser, *Vice Pres*
Robert Perez, *Mfg Staff*
▲ EMP: 145 **EST:** 1916
SQ FT: 30,000
SALES (est): 35.3MM **Privately Held**
WEB: www.gasser.com
SIC: 3469 Stamping metal for the trade

(G-3590)
GEMINI PHARMACEUTICALS INC
87 Modular Ave Ste 1 (11725-5718)
PHONE..................................631 543-3334
Andrew Finamore, *President*
Mark Gaeta, *COO*
Michael Finamore, *Vice Pres*
Brian Finamore, *Treasurer*
Clyde Granger, *Director*
▲ EMP: 260
SALES: 36.4MM **Privately Held**
WEB: www.geminipharm.com
SIC: 2834 2833 Pharmaceutical preparations; vitamins, natural or synthetic: bulk, uncompounded

(G-3591)
HAROME DESIGNS LLC
75 Modular Ave (11725-5705)
PHONE..................................631 864-1900
Alan J Cohen, *Mng Member*
EMP: 22
SALES (est): 1.2MM **Privately Held**
SIC: 2519 Household furniture, except wood or metal: upholstered

(G-3592)
HOBART CORPORATION
71 Mall Dr Ste 1 (11725-5728)
PHONE..................................631 864-3440
Paul Todoro, *Manager*
EMP: 24
SALES (corp-wide): 14.7B **Publicly Held**
WEB: www.hobartcorp.com
SIC: 3639 5084 7629 7699 Major kitchen appliances, except refrigerators & stoves; food product manufacturing machinery; electrical repair shops; restaurant equipment repair
HQ: Hobart Llc
701 S Ridge Ave
Troy OH 45373
937 332-3000

(G-3593)
ISLAND AUDIO ENGINEERING
7 Glenmere Ct (11725-5607)
PHONE..................................631 543-2372
George Alexandrovich, *Owner*
EMP: 5 **EST:** 1972
SALES (est): 397.3K **Privately Held**
SIC: 3677 Inductors, electronic

(G-3594)
MAKERS NUTRITION LLC
71s Mall Dr (11725-5703)
PHONE..................................844 625-3771
EMP: 6
SALES (est): 533.3K
SALES (corp-wide): 25MM **Privately Held**
SIC: 2023 Dietary supplements, dairy & non-dairy based
PA: Makers Nutrition Llc
315 Oser Ave Ste 1
Hauppauge NY 11788
631 456-5397

(G-3595)
MALOYA LASER INC
65a Mall Dr Ste 1 (11725-5726)
PHONE..................................631 543-2327
Reto Hug, *President*
Marc Anderes, *Vice Pres*
Roger Hug, *VP Sales*
EMP: 27
SQ FT: 22,500
SALES (est): 6.1MM **Privately Held**
WEB: www.maloyalaser.com
SIC: 3444 Mail (post office) collection or storage boxes, sheet metal

(G-3596)
ROPACK USA INC
49 Mall Dr (11725-5722)
PHONE..................................631 482-7777
Yves Massicotta, *CEO*
EMP: 10 **EST:** 2015
SALES (est): 1.8MM **Privately Held**
SIC: 2834 Pharmaceutical preparations

(G-3597)
RPF ASSOCIATES INC
Also Called: Signs By Tomorrow
2155 Jericho Tpke Ste A (11725-2919)
PHONE..................................631 462-7446
Ron Facchiano, *President*
EMP: 5
SQ FT: 1,250
SALES (est): 665.5K **Privately Held**
SIC: 3993 Signs & advertising specialties

(G-3598)
SETTONS INTL FOODS INC (PA)
Also Called: Setton Farms
85 Austin Blvd (11725-5701)
PHONE..................................631 543-8090
Joshua Setton, *CEO*
Morris Setton, *Exec VP*
Jeff Gibbons, *Plant Mgr*
Keven Macdonald, *Maint Spvr*
Alfredo Nunez, *Maint Spvr*
◆ EMP: 70 **EST:** 1971
SQ FT: 55,000
SALES (est): 22.9MM **Privately Held**
WEB: www.settonfarms.com
SIC: 2034 2068 2099 2066 Dried & dehydrated fruits; nuts: dried, dehydrated, salted or roasted; food preparations; chocolate & cocoa products; candy & other confectionery products

(G-3599)
SIMPLY NATURAL FOODS LLC
Also Called: Simply Lite Foods
74 Mall Dr (11725-5711)
PHONE..................................631 543-9600
Abe Rach,
Russ Asaro,
▲ EMP: 200
SQ FT: 55,000
SALES (est): 20.9MM **Privately Held**
WEB: www.simplylite.com
SIC: 3556 2064 2066 Food products machinery; candy & other confectionery products; chocolate & cocoa products

(G-3600)
US NONWOVENS CORP
360 Moreland Rd (11725-5707)
PHONE..................................631 952-0100
EMP: 386 **Privately Held**
SIC: 2842 Specialty cleaning, polishes & sanitation goods
PA: U.S. Nonwovens Corp.
100 Emjay Blvd
Brentwood NY 11717

(G-3601)
VEHICLE TRACKING SOLUTIONS LLC
152 Veterans Memorial Hwy (11725-3634)
PHONE..................................631 586-7400
John Cunningham, *President*
Glenn Reed, *COO*
Marty Cruz, *Opers Mgr*
Karen Cunningham, *CFO*
Ryan Wilkinson, *CTO*
EMP: 50
SQ FT: 17,000
SALES (est): 12.5MM **Privately Held**
WEB: www.vehicletrackingsolutions.com
SIC: 7372 Prepackaged software

(G-3602)
VITA-GEN LABORATORIES LLC
71s Mall Dr (11725-5703)
PHONE..................................631 450-4357
Eric Haller, *Mng Member*
EMP: 5
SALES (est): 506.1K **Privately Held**
SIC: 2834 Vitamin, nutrient & hematinic preparations for human use; medicines, capsuled or ampuled

(G-3603)
WELLMILL LLC
Also Called: Vitamix Laboratories
69 Mall Dr Ste 1 (11725-5727)
P.O. Box 12413, Hauppauge (11788-0509)
PHONE..................................631 465-9245
Michael Kochitz, *Mng Member*
John Greenough, *Director*
David Grudzinski, *Administration*
Steven Browne,
EMP: 25
SQ FT: 25,000
SALES: 3MM **Privately Held**
SIC: 2834 Vitamin preparations

(G-3604)
WICKERS SPORTSWEAR INC (PA)
Also Called: Wickers Performance Wear
88 Wyandanch Blvd (11725-4310)
PHONE..................................631 543-1640
Anthony Mazzenga, *CEO*
Diane Basso, *President*
Carol Mazzenga, *Principal*
Maryann D'Erario, *Treasurer*
▲ EMP: 9
SQ FT: 2,000
SALES (est): 1.5MM **Privately Held**
WEB: www.wickers.com
SIC: 2322 2341 Underwear, men's & boys': made from purchased materials; women's & children's underwear

Conesus
Livingston County

(G-3605)
EAGLE CREST VINEYARD LLC
Also Called: O-Neh-Da Vineyard
7107 Vineyard Rd (14435-9521)
PHONE..................................585 346-5760
Elizabeth Goldstone,
▲ EMP: 5
SQ FT: 20,000
SALES (est): 605.7K Privately Held
SIC: 2084 0172 Wines; grapes

Congers
Rockland County

(G-3606)
AKTINA CORP
360 N Route 9w (10920-1420)
PHONE..................................845 268-0101
George Zacharopoulos, President
Nicholas Zacharopoulos, Vice Pres
Joan Zacharopoulos, Admin Sec
▼ EMP: 28
SQ FT: 15,000
SALES (est): 6.1MM Privately Held
WEB: www.aktina.com
SIC: 3841 Surgical & medical instruments

(G-3607)
ANKA TOOL & DIE INC
150 Wells Ave (10920-2096)
PHONE..................................845 268-4116
Agnes Karl, Corp Secy
Anton Karl Jr, Vice Pres
Ingrid Capasso, Office Mgr
▲ EMP: 35 EST: 1970
SQ FT: 6,400
SALES (est): 5.8MM Privately Held
WEB: www.ankatool.com
SIC: 3544 3089 Special dies & tools; injection molding of plastics

(G-3608)
APTARGROUP INC
Also Called: Aptar Congers
250 N Route 303 (10920-1450)
PHONE..................................845 639-3700
Alla Itenberg, QC Mgr
Kevin Hoover, Engineer
Alex Theodorakis, Branch Mgr
Rafek Dawod, Manager
Jaimee Given, Manager
EMP: 150 Publicly Held
SIC: 3586 Measuring & dispensing pumps
PA: Aptargroup, Inc.
    265 Exchange Dr Ste 100
    Crystal Lake IL 60014

(G-3609)
BEAN KING INTERNATIONAL LLC
36 N Route 9w (10920-2459)
PHONE..................................845 268-3135
Faustino Larios, Mng Member
Jose Moreno, Mng Member
▲ EMP: 10
SALES: 4MM Privately Held
SIC: 3523 Driers (farm): grain, hay & seed

(G-3610)
BOURGHOL BROTHERS INC
73 Lake Rd (10920-2323)
P.O. Box 80 (10920-0080)
PHONE..................................845 268-9752
Charles Bourghol, President
Alexander Bourghol, Treasurer
EMP: 7
SQ FT: 1,200
SALES (est): 1.1MM Privately Held
WEB: www.bourgholbrosjewelers.com
SIC: 3911 5944 Jewelry, precious metal; jewelry, precious stones & precious metals

(G-3611)
CELTIC SHEET METAL INC
Also Called: Celtic Industries
100 Brenner Dr Unit C (10920-1322)
PHONE..................................845 267-3400
Elizabeth Cunney, President
William Raber, Project Mgr
Owen Tierney, Foreman/Supr
EMP: 40
SQ FT: 20,000
SALES (est): 8.1MM Privately Held
WEB: www.celticsheetmetal.com
SIC: 3444 Sheet metalwork

(G-3612)
CHARTWELL PHARMA NDA B2 HOLDIN
77 Brenner Dr (10920-1307)
PHONE..................................845 268-5000
Kimberly Ezdebski, Vice Pres
EMP: 5
SALES (est): 229.7K Privately Held
SIC: 2834 Tablets, pharmaceutical

(G-3613)
CHARTWELL PHARMACEUTICALS LLC
77 Brenner Dr (10920-1307)
PHONE..................................845 268-5000
David I Chipkin, COO
Yali Elkin, Exec VP
Francis Ezdebski, Vice Pres
Kimberly Ezdebski, Vice Pres
EMP: 75
SALES (est): 18.2MM Privately Held
SIC: 2834 Pharmaceutical preparations

(G-3614)
F M GROUP INC
100 Wells Ave (10920-2042)
P.O. Box 48 (10920-0048)
PHONE..................................845 589-0102
Josef Feldman, President
Solomon Feldman, Marketing Staff
EMP: 10
SALES (est): 1.6MM Privately Held
WEB: www.functionalmaterials.com
SIC: 2899 2865 Ink or writing fluids; dyes & pigments

(G-3615)
HUDSON VALLEY COATINGS LLC
175 N Route 9w Ste 12 (10920-1780)
PHONE..................................845 398-1778
Joseph Montana,
EMP: 5 EST: 2008
SALES (est): 396.2K Privately Held
SIC: 3479 Coating of metals with plastic or resins

(G-3616)
INDUS PRECISION MANUFACTURING
50 N Harrison Ave Ste 9 (10920-1952)
PHONE..................................845 268-0782
Shylamma Mathew, Chairman
Abraham Mathew, Vice Pres
EMP: 14
SALES: 450K Privately Held
SIC: 3599 Machine shop, jobbing & repair

(G-3617)
LINDEN COOKIES INC
25 Brenner Dr (10920-1307)
PHONE..................................845 268-5050
Paul L Sturz, President
C Ronald Sturz, Vice Pres
EMP: 50 EST: 1960
SQ FT: 33,000
SALES (est): 10.1MM Privately Held
WEB: www.lindencookies.com
SIC: 2052 Cookies

(G-3618)
STAR KAY WHITE INC (PA)
151 Wells Ave (10920-1398)
PHONE..................................845 268-2600
Walter Katzenstein, Principal
Benjamin Katzenstein, Vice Pres
George Granada, Mfg Staff
Carissa Coslit, Buyer
John Benzinger, Research
◆ EMP: 65 EST: 1890
SQ FT: 45,000

SALES (est): 14.3MM Privately Held
WEB: www.starkaywhite.com
SIC: 2087 Flavoring extracts & syrups

(G-3619)
VALOIS OF AMERICA INC
250 N Route 303 (10920-1450)
PHONE..................................845 639-3700
Alex Thoedorakis, President
Pamela Moran, Sales Staff
▲ EMP: 150
SQ FT: 3,500
SALES (est): 19.4MM Publicly Held
WEB: www.aptargroup.com
SIC: 3586 Measuring & dispensing pumps
PA: Aptargroup, Inc.
    265 Exchange Dr Ste 100
    Crystal Lake IL 60014

(G-3620)
VITANE PHARMACEUTICALS INC
125 Wells Ave (10920-2036)
PHONE..................................845 267-6700
Mohammed Hassan, CEO
Ezz Hamza, President
Mohammed Mathloob, Technical Staff
Sandra Childs, Admin Asst
◆ EMP: 24
SQ FT: 15,000
SALES: 7.4MM Privately Held
SIC: 2834 Pharmaceutical preparations

Conklin
Broome County

(G-3621)
ARDAGH METAL PACKAGING USA INC
379 Broome Corporate Pkwy (13748-1513)
PHONE..................................607 584-3300
EMP: 126
SALES (corp-wide): 242.1K Privately Held
SIC: 3411 Metal cans
HQ: Ardagh Metal Packaging Usa Inc.
    600 N Bell Ave Ste 200
    Carnegie PA 15106

(G-3622)
CBA GROUP LLC
33 Broome Corporate Pkwy (13748-1510)
P.O. Box 825, Binghamton (13902-0825)
PHONE..................................607 779-7522
Jeroen Schmits, President
Patrick J Gillard, President
Koen A Gieskes, Vice Pres
EMP: 1000
SALES: 4.7MM
SALES (corp-wide): 1.5B Privately Held
SIC: 3559 Electronic component making machinery
HQ: Francisco Partners, L.P.
    1 Letterman Dr Bldg C
    San Francisco CA 94129
    415 418-2900

(G-3623)
DOLMEN
216 Broome Corporate Pkwy (13748-1506)
PHONE..................................912 596-1537
Steve Hanratty, Principal
EMP: 10
SALES (est): 400K Privately Held
SIC: 3999 Manufacturing industries

(G-3624)
E-SYSTEMS GROUP LLC
Also Called: SMC
100 Progress Pkwy (13748-1320)
PHONE..................................607 775-1100
Harry Bradley, Opers Staff
Christopher Larocca, Sales Staff
Harry Bradley, Mng Member
Frans De Coster, Manager
Bill Wentz, Manager
▲ EMP: 26 EST: 1952
SQ FT: 30,000

SALES (est): 5.5MM
SALES (corp-wide): 48.4MM Privately Held
WEB: www.smcplus.com
SIC: 2521 2522 5045 3571 Wood office furniture; office furniture, except wood; computers, peripherals & software; computer peripheral equipment; electronic computers; partitions & fixtures, except wood
PA: Engineered Data Products Holdings, Llc
    6800 W 117th Ave
    Broomfield CO 80020
    303 465-2800

(G-3625)
INTERNATIONAL PAPER COMPANY
1240 Conklin Rd (13748-1407)
PHONE..................................607 775-1550
David Davenport, Sls & Mktg Exec
Edward Badyna, Manager
EMP: 150
SALES (corp-wide): 23.3B Publicly Held
SIC: 2653 2656 2631 2611 Boxes, corrugated: made from purchased materials; food containers (liquid tight), including milk cartons; cartons, milk: made from purchased material; container, packaging & boxboard; container board; packaging board; pulp mills; printing paper
PA: International Paper Company
    6400 Poplar Ave
    Memphis TN 38197
    901 419-9000

(G-3626)
NEWSPAPER PUBLISHER LLC
Also Called: Independent Baptist Voice
1035 Conklin Rd (13748-1102)
P.O. Box 208 (13748-0208)
PHONE..................................607 775-0472
Don Einstein, President
EMP: 10
SQ FT: 15,000
SALES (est): 540.1K Privately Held
WEB: www.automarketpaper.com
SIC: 2711 2791 7011 Newspapers: publishing only, not printed on site; typesetting; bed & breakfast inn

(G-3627)
PERFORATED SCREEN SURFACES
216 Broome Corporate Pkwy (13748-1506)
PHONE..................................866 866-8690
Davis Fleming, President
EMP: 20
SALES (est): 3.2MM Privately Held
SIC: 3443 Perforating on heavy metal

(G-3628)
S & T KNITTING CO INC (PA)
Also Called: Derby Fashion Center
1010 Conklin Rd (13748-1004)
P.O. Box 1512, Binghamton (13902-1512)
PHONE..................................607 722-7558
Richard Horner, President
Bridgette Harvey, Admin Sec
EMP: 27 EST: 1958
SQ FT: 65,000
SALES (est): 1.9MM Privately Held
SIC: 2253 5651 Sweaters & sweater coats, knit; family clothing stores

(G-3629)
TIN INC
1240 Conklin Rd (13748-1407)
PHONE..................................607 775-1550
Edward Badyna, Manager
EMP: 88
SALES (corp-wide): 23.3B Publicly Held
WEB: www.tin.com
SIC: 2653 Boxes, corrugated: made from purchased materials
HQ: Tin Inc.
    6400 Poplar Ave
    Memphis TN 38197

(G-3630)
TOOLROOM EXPRESS INC
Also Called: Four Square Tool
1010 Conklin Rd (13748-1004)
PHONE..................................607 723-5373
Richard Haddock, President

Jake Haddock, *Mktg Dir*
Shelly Haddock, *Manager*
▲ **EMP:** 55
SQ FT: 20,000
SALES (est): 11.2MM **Privately Held**
WEB: www.toolroomexpress.com
SIC: 3089 3599 Injection molding of plastics; machine shop, jobbing & repair

(G-3631)
UI ACQUISITION HOLDING CO (PA)
33 Broome Corporate Pkwy (13748-1510)
PHONE........................607 779-7522
Jean-Luc Pelissier, *President*
Keith O'Leary, *Vice Pres*
EMP: 2
SALES (est): 143.3MM **Privately Held**
SIC: 3559 Electronic component making machinery

(G-3632)
UI HOLDING COMPANY (HQ)
33 Broome Corporate Pkwy (13748-1510)
P.O. Box 825, Binghamton (13902-0825)
PHONE........................607 779-7522
Jeroen Schmits, *President*
Koen A Gieskes, *Vice Pres*
Maxim Factourovich, *Engineer*
Patrick J Gillard, *CFO*
EMP: 3
SALES (est): 155.9MM **Privately Held**
SIC: 3559 Electronic component making machinery

(G-3633)
UNIVERSAL INSTRUMENTS CORP (DH)
33 Broome Corporate Pkwy (13748-1510)
PHONE........................800 842-9732
Jean-Luc Pelissier, *CEO*
Jeff Knight, *General Mgr*
Keith O'Leary, *CFO*
Jay Smith, *Controller*
Andrew Wittbrodt, *Cust Mgr*
◆ **EMP:** 200
SALES (est): 139.8MM **Privately Held**
WEB: www3.uic.com
SIC: 3559 Electronic component making machinery

Constableville
Lewis County

(G-3634)
GOT WOOD
5748 W Main St (13325-1801)
PHONE........................315 405-3384
EMP: 6
SALES (est): 426K **Privately Held**
SIC: 2411 Logging

Constantia
Oswego County

(G-3635)
BRIDGEPORT METALCRAFT INC
567 County Route 23 (13044-2737)
P.O. Box 470 (13044-0470)
PHONE........................315 623-9597
Donald Deitz Jr, *President*
Cristy Deitz, *Vice Pres*
EMP: 5 EST: 1965
SQ FT: 5,000
SALES (est): 550K **Privately Held**
WEB: www.bridgeportmetalcraft.com
SIC: 3469 Spinning metal for the trade

(G-3636)
MICHAEL P MMARR
Also Called: Mike's Custom Cabinets
1358 State Route 49 (13044-2769)
P.O. Box 91 (13044-0091)
PHONE........................315 623-9380
Michael Marr, *Owner*
Michael P Marr, *Owner*
EMP: 9

SALES: 325K **Privately Held**
SIC: 2434 5211 2541 Wood kitchen cabinets; cabinets, kitchen; wood partitions & fixtures

(G-3637)
UNITED WIRE TECHNOLOGIES INC
1804 State Route 49 (13044-2604)
P.O. Box 502, Cleveland (13042-0502)
PHONE........................315 623-7203
James E Ransom, *Ch of Bd*
Paul Coates, *President*
Donald Ransom, *Vice Pres*
Michael Ransom, *CFO*
▲ **EMP:** 15
SQ FT: 17,000
SALES (est): 2.6MM **Privately Held**
SIC: 3357 Nonferrous wiredrawing & insulating

Cooperstown
Otsego County

(G-3638)
BREWERY OMMEGANG LTD
656 County Highway 33 (13326-4737)
PHONE........................607 286-4144
Simon Thorpe, *President*
Tara Aitchison, *COO*
Rick Debar, *Technical Mgr*
Chance Nichols, *CFO*
Mike Albin, *Finance*
▲ **EMP:** 30
SQ FT: 35,000
SALES (est): 6.6MM **Privately Held**
WEB: www.ommegang.com
SIC: 2082 Beer (alcoholic beverage)

(G-3639)
COOPERSTOWN BAT COMPANY INC
118 Main St (13326-1225)
P.O. Box 415 (13326-0415)
PHONE........................607 547-2415
Timothy Haney, *President*
Sharon Oberriter, *President*
Don Oberriter, *Vice Pres*
EMP: 15
SQ FT: 4,000
SALES: 1.6MM **Privately Held**
WEB: www.cooperstownbat.com
SIC: 3949 Baseball equipment & supplies, general

(G-3640)
DUVEL MORTGAGE USA INC
656 County Highway 33 (13326-4737)
PHONE........................607 267-6121
Tom Gardner, *Executive*
EMP: 5
SALES (est): 238.4K **Privately Held**
SIC: 2082 Malt beverages

(G-3641)
VANBERG & DEWULF CO INC
52 Pioneer St Ste 4 (13326-1231)
PHONE........................607 547-8184
Don Feinberg, *Principal*
▲ **EMP:** 6
SALES (est): 399.9K **Privately Held**
SIC: 2082 Beer (alcoholic beverage)

Copake
Columbia County

(G-3642)
HIGH VOLTAGE INC
31 County Route 7a (12516-1214)
PHONE........................518 329-3275
Stephen Peschel, *Ch of Bd*
Michael Peschel, *Chairman*
James Grayson, *Vice Pres*
EMP: 32
SQ FT: 23,760
SALES (est): 8.1MM **Privately Held**
WEB: www.hvinc.com
SIC: 3826 Analytical instruments

Copiague
Suffolk County

(G-3643)
ACTION MACHINED PRODUCTS INC
1355 Bangor St (11726-2911)
PHONE........................631 842-2333
Edward G Korndoerfer, *President*
EMP: 13
SQ FT: 8,750
SALES (est): 2.3MM **Privately Held**
SIC: 3451 Screw machine products

(G-3644)
AJES PHARMACEUTICALS LLC
11a Lincoln St (11726-1530)
PHONE........................631 608-1728
Asha Patel,
Jatendra Patel,
▼ **EMP:** 20
SQ FT: 25,000
SALES (est): 4.1MM **Privately Held**
SIC: 2833 5499 Vitamins, natural or synthetic: bulk, uncompounded; health & dietetic food stores

(G-3645)
ARCHITECTURAL FIBERGLASS CORP
1395 Marconi Blvd (11726-2814)
P.O. Box 116 (11726-0116)
PHONE........................631 842-4772
Charles Wittman, *President*
EMP: 22
SALES (est): 2.1MM **Privately Held**
WEB: www.afcornice.com
SIC: 2295 5999 Varnished glass & coated fiberglass fabrics; fiberglass materials, except insulation

(G-3646)
ARGENCORD MACHINE CORP INC
10 Reith St (11726-1414)
PHONE........................631 842-8990
Emilio Benenati, *Ch of Bd*
Gustavo Sanchez, *COO*
Steven Peltier, *CFO*
EMP: 7 EST: 1967
SQ FT: 10,000
SALES: 300K **Privately Held**
SIC: 3599 Machine shop, jobbing & repair

(G-3647)
ART PRECISION METAL PRODUCTS
1465 S Strong Ave (11726-3253)
PHONE........................631 842-8889
Steven Triola, *President*
EMP: 10
SQ FT: 13,500
SALES (est): 1.8MM **Privately Held**
SIC: 3599 3469 3444 3544 Machine shop, jobbing & repair; spinning metal for the trade; sheet metalwork; special dies & tools

(G-3648)
ASTRA PRODUCTS INC
6 Bethpage Rd (11726-1413)
P.O. Box 479, Baldwin (11510-0479)
PHONE........................631 464-4747
Mark Bogin, *President*
Jeffrey Bogin, *Vice Pres*
▲ **EMP:** 6
SQ FT: 4,000
SALES: 3MM **Privately Held**
SIC: 3081 5162 Plastic film & sheet; plastics sheets & rods

(G-3649)
BALDWIN MACHINE WORKS INC
20 Grant Ave 2040 (11726-3817)
PHONE........................631 842-9110
Kenneth Roblin, *President*
▲ **EMP:** 6
SQ FT: 6,000

SALES (est): 758.2K **Privately Held**
SIC: 3541 3545 Drill presses; machine tool accessories; drills (machine tool accessories); drilling machine attachments & accessories

(G-3650)
D & C CLEANING INC
1095 Campagnoli Ave (11726-2309)
PHONE........................631 789-5659
EMP: 12
SALES (est): 763.6K **Privately Held**
SIC: 3635 Mfg Home Vacuum Cleaners

(G-3651)
ELWOOD INTERNATIONAL INC
89 Hudson St (11726-1505)
P.O. Box 180 (11726-0180)
PHONE........................631 842-6600
Stuart Roll, *Ch of Bd*
Richard Roll, *President*
EMP: 18
SQ FT: 37,000
SALES (est): 4.4MM **Privately Held**
WEB: www.elwoodintl.com
SIC: 2035 Seasonings & sauces, except tomato & dry

(G-3652)
ENGINEERED METAL PRODUCTS INC
10 Reith St (11726-1414)
PHONE........................631 842-3780
Gustavo Sanchez, *President*
EMP: 9
SALES (est): 549.3K **Privately Held**
SIC: 3728 Aircraft assemblies, subassemblies & parts

(G-3653)
GABILA & SONS MFG INC
Also Called: Gabila's Knishes
100 Wartburg Ave (11726-2919)
PHONE........................631 789-2220
Elliott Gabay, *President*
Sophie Levy, *Chairman*
EMP: 50 EST: 1921
SQ FT: 20,000
SALES (est): 7.4MM **Privately Held**
SIC: 2051 Bakery: wholesale or wholesale/retail combined; knishes, except frozen

(G-3654)
GABILA FOOD PRODUCTS INC
100 Wartburg Ave (11726-2919)
PHONE........................631 789-2220
Elliot Gabay, *President*
EMP: 50
SALES: 7MM **Privately Held**
SIC: 2043 Cereal breakfast foods

(G-3655)
GLOBE GRINDING CORP
1365 Akron St (11726-2909)
PHONE........................631 694-1970
Jeffrey Rapisarda, *President*
Robert Rapisarda, *Vice Pres*
EMP: 10
SQ FT: 10,000
SALES (est): 2MM **Privately Held**
SIC: 3599 Machine & other job shop work

(G-3656)
H & M LEASING CORP
1245 Marconi Blvd (11726-2815)
PHONE........................631 225-5246
Mark Field, *President*
Marc B Field, *President*
EMP: 6
SALES (est): 670K **Privately Held**
SIC: 3444 Bins, prefabricated sheet metal

(G-3657)
HARBOR WLDG & FABRICATION CORP
30 Railroad Ave (11726-2708)
PHONE........................631 667-1880
Joseph Awing, *President*
EMP: 11
SALES: 1.8MM **Privately Held**
SIC: 3449 Bars, concrete reinforcing: fabricated steel

(G-3658)
HERMANN GERDENS INC
1725 N Strongs Rd (11726-2926)
PHONE.....................631 841-3132
Joseph Gerdens, *President*
EMP: 6 **EST:** 1987
SALES (est): 735.1K **Privately Held**
SIC: 3444 Sheet metalwork

(G-3659)
HOLLYWOOD ADVG BANNERS INC
Also Called: Hollywood Banners
539 Oak St (11726-3215)
PHONE.....................631 842-3000
Timothy Cox, *President*
EMP: 24
SALES (est): 2.8MM **Privately Held**
SIC: 3993 Signs & advertising specialties

(G-3660)
HOLLYWOOD BANNERS INC
539 Oak St (11726-3261)
PHONE.....................631 842-3000
Daniel F Mahoney, *Ch of Bd*
Mike Hartman, *Sales Staff*
Christopher O'Shea, *Sales Staff*
Tony Connelli, *Graphic Designe*
EMP: 30
SQ FT: 22,000
SALES (est): 3.8MM **Privately Held**
WEB: www.hollywoodbanners.com
SIC: 3993 Signs & advertising specialties

(G-3661)
JAF CONVERTERS INC
60 Marconi Blvd (11726-2098)
PHONE.....................631 842-3131
John Flandina, *CEO*
Emily Flandina, *Admin Sec*
▲ **EMP:** 45
SQ FT: 10,000
SALES (est): 5.9MM **Privately Held**
WEB: www.jafstamp.com
SIC: 3993 Signs & advertising specialties

(G-3662)
LONG ISLAND TOOL & DIE INC
1445 S Strong Ave (11726-3227)
PHONE.....................631 225-0600
Richard Cohen, *Principal*
EMP: 5
SALES (est): 396.8K **Privately Held**
SIC: 3544 Special dies & tools

(G-3663)
MALISA BRANKO INC
95 Garfield Ave (11726-3222)
PHONE.....................631 225-9741
Branko Malisa, *President*
Regina Malisa, *Corp Secy*
EMP: 12
SQ FT: 5,600
SALES (est): 1.3MM **Privately Held**
SIC: 3599 Machine shop, jobbing & repair

(G-3664)
MARK - 10 CORPORATION
11 Dixon Ave (11726-1902)
PHONE.....................631 842-9200
William Fridman, *President*
EMP: 20
SQ FT: 12,000
SALES (est): 5.2MM **Privately Held**
WEB: www.mark-10.com
SIC: 3823 5084 8731 Electrolytic conductivity instruments, industrial process; industrial process control instruments; industrial machinery & equipment; electronic research

(G-3665)
NELL-JOY INDUSTRIES INC (PA)
8 Reith St Ste 10 (11726-1414)
PHONE.....................631 842-8989
Emilio L Benenati, *CEO*
Steven Peltier, *President*
Stephen Manz, *QC Mgr*
Melissa Gavin, *Controller*
Sandra Origoni, *Sales Mgr*
EMP: 32
SQ FT: 35,000
SALES (est): 3.4MM **Privately Held**
SIC: 3724 5088 Aircraft engines & engine parts; aircraft & space vehicle supplies & parts; aeronautical equipment & supplies

(G-3666)
NORTH EAST FINISHING CO INC
Also Called: Nefco
245 Ralph Ave (11726-1514)
PHONE.....................631 789-8000
Bill Dechirico, *President*
Donna Ward, *Corp Secy*
Joseph Ricchetti, *Vice Pres*
EMP: 11
SQ FT: 7,500
SALES (est): 1.2MM **Privately Held**
SIC: 3471 Finishing, metals or formed products

(G-3667)
P & L DEVELOPMENT LLC
Also Called: Pl Developments
33 Ralph Ave (11726-1532)
PHONE.....................631 693-8000
Julie Anne Solis, *General Mgr*
EMP: 80 **Privately Held**
SIC: 2834 Druggists' preparations (pharmaceuticals)
PA: P & L Development, Llc
609 Cantiague Rock Rd 2a
Westbury NY 11590

(G-3668)
PIPER PLASTICS CORP (PA)
102 Ralph Ave (11726-1510)
PHONE.....................631 842-6889
Andrew Weiss, *President*
Charles Weiss, *Vice Pres*
EMP: 23 **EST:** 1963
SQ FT: 16,000
SALES (est): 2.4MM **Privately Held**
WEB: www.piper-plastics.com
SIC: 3089 3479 Molding primary plastic; coating of metals with plastic or resins

(G-3669)
PIPER PLASTICS CORP
105 Ralph Ave (11726-1511)
PHONE.....................631 842-6889
Andrew Weiss, *Branch Mgr*
EMP: 6
SALES (corp-wide): 2.4MM **Privately Held**
SIC: 3089 Molding primary plastic
PA: Piper Plastics Corp
102 Ralph Ave
Copiague NY 11726
631 842-6889

(G-3670)
PRECISION ELECTRONICS INC
1 Di Tomas Ct (11726-1943)
PHONE.....................631 842-4900
Dominick Scaringella, *President*
Joseph Corrigan, *Vice Pres*
Joseph A Whalen Jr, *Treasurer*
Rita Scaringella, *Admin Sec*
EMP: 15 **EST:** 1955
SQ FT: 13,000
SALES: 3.5MM **Privately Held**
WEB: www.precisionelect.com
SIC: 3677 3625 3612 Coil windings, electronic; electronic transformers; relays, for electronic use; voltage regulators, transmission & distribution

(G-3671)
PROTOFAST HOLDING CORP
182 N Oak St (11726-1223)
PHONE.....................631 753-2549
Marco Gil, *President*
EMP: 6
SQ FT: 5,600
SALES (est): 700K **Privately Held**
SIC: 3444 Sheet metalwork

(G-3672)
QUALITY CANDLE MFG CO INC
121 Cedar St (11726-1201)
PHONE.....................631 842-8475
Joseph Arnone, *President*
EMP: 10 **EST:** 1955
SQ FT: 6,000
SALES (est): 870K **Privately Held**
WEB: www.qualitycandlecompany.com
SIC: 3999 Candles

(G-3673)
REESE MANUFACTURING INC
16 Reith St (11726-1414)
PHONE.....................631 842-3780
Emilio Benenati, *President*
Terri Martin, *Vice Pres*
EMP: 8
SALES (est): 367.8K **Privately Held**
SIC: 3728 Aircraft body assemblies & parts

(G-3674)
RMW FILTRATION PRODUCTS CO LLC
230 Lambert Ave (11726-3207)
P.O. Box 573, Lindenhurst (11757-0573)
PHONE.....................631 226-9412
EMP: 3
SQ FT: 4,000
SALES: 2MM **Privately Held**
SIC: 3599 Custom Machine Shop

(G-3675)
SCAN-A-CHROME COLOR INC
555 Oak St (11726-3215)
PHONE.....................631 532-6146
Brian Geiger, *President*
EMP: 5
SALES (est): 697.5K **Privately Held**
SIC: 2759 7336 7389 Commercial printing; commercial art & graphic design;

(G-3676)
SEAL REINFORCED FIBERGLASS INC (PA)
19 Bethpage Rd (11726-1421)
PHONE.....................631 842-2230
Patrick Kaler, *President*
Kevin Kaler, *Vice Pres*
Timothy Kaler, *Shareholder*
Helen Kaler, *Admin Sec*
Laura Kaler, *Admin Asst*
EMP: 28 **EST:** 1961
SQ FT: 20,000
SALES: 3MM **Privately Held**
WEB: www.sealfiberglass.com
SIC: 3089 Molding primary plastic; plastic processing

(G-3677)
SEAL REINFORCED FIBERGLASS INC
23 Bethpage Rd (11726-1421)
PHONE.....................631 842-2230
Thomas Kaler, *Branch Mgr*
EMP: 9
SQ FT: 11,000
SALES (corp-wide): 3MM **Privately Held**
WEB: www.sealfiberglass.com
SIC: 3089 Molding primary plastic
PA: Seal Reinforced Fiberglass, Inc.
19 Bethpage Rd
Copiague NY 11726
631 842-2230

(G-3678)
SIGN SHOP INC
1272 Montauk Hwy Ste A (11726-4908)
PHONE.....................631 226-4145
John Prete, *President*
Bill Prete, *Vice Pres*
EMP: 6
SQ FT: 6,500
SALES: 500K **Privately Held**
WEB: www.thesignshopinc.com
SIC: 2759 7389 2752 Screen printing; lettering & sign painting services; commercial printing, lithographic

(G-3679)
STEEL CRAFT ROLLING DOOR
5 Di Tomas Ct (11726-1943)
PHONE.....................631 608-8662
Joan Palmieri, *Manager*
EMP: 10
SALES (est): 1.3MM **Privately Held**
SIC: 3325 Steel foundries

(G-3680)
SUNRISE DOOR SOLUTIONS
Also Called: Sunrise Installation
1215 Sunrise Hwy (11726-1405)
PHONE.....................631 464-4139
EMP: 5
SALES (est): 466.7K **Privately Held**
SIC: 3442 Mfg Metal Doors/Sash/Trim

(G-3681)
SWISS TOOL CORPORATION
100 Court St (11726-1287)
PHONE.....................631 842-7766
Anton Croenlein, *President*
Anna Croenlein, *Corp Secy*
Walli Amato, *Executive*
EMP: 40
SQ FT: 20,000
SALES (est): 7.5MM **Privately Held**
WEB: www.swisstoolcorp.com
SIC: 3354 Aluminum extruded products

(G-3682)
TATRA MFG CORPORATION
30 Railroad Ave (11726-2717)
PHONE.....................631 691-1184
Joseph Tyminski, *President*
Lana Tyminski, *Corp Secy*
EMP: 15
SQ FT: 10,000
SALES (est): 2.5MM **Privately Held**
SIC: 3444 Sheet metalwork

(G-3683)
TII INDUSTRIES INC
1385 Akron St (11726-2932)
PHONE.....................631 789-5000
T Roach, *Principal*
Walter R Fay, *Vice Pres*
Alex Feezer, *Vice Pres*
Thomas Smith, *Vice Pres*
Jaclyn Porter, *Accounting Mgr*
EMP: 11 **EST:** 2013
SALES (est): 803.9K **Privately Held**
SIC: 3999 Manufacturing industries

(G-3684)
TOBAY PRINTING CO INC
1361 Marconi Blvd (11726-2898)
PHONE.....................631 842-3300
Robert Rogers, *President*
Jean Rogers, *Vice Pres*
Chuck Williams, *Sales Executive*
Nancy Cummings, *Representative*
EMP: 40
SALES (est): 6.1MM **Privately Held**
WEB: www.tobayprinting.com
SIC: 2732 2752 2796 2791 Book printing; commercial printing, lithographic; platemaking services; typesetting; bookbinding & related work

(G-3685)
TRIL INC
320 Pioxi St (11726-2132)
PHONE.....................631 645-7989
Sushe Zhang, *Principal*
Xiaoling Wang, *Vice Pres*
EMP: 9
SALES (est): 651.2K **Privately Held**
SIC: 3841 Surgical & medical instruments

(G-3686)
VALLE SIGNS AND AWNINGS
55 Decker St (11726-1401)
PHONE.....................516 408-3440
Oscar Valle, *Owner*
EMP: 10
SALES (est): 1.1MM **Privately Held**
SIC: 3993 Electric signs

(G-3687)
VIBRATION ELIMINATOR CO INC (PA)
15 Dixon Ave (11726-1902)
PHONE.....................631 841-4000
Stuart Levy, *President*
Don Warick Jr, *Vice Pres*
Donald Warick, *Vice Pres*
Lenny Roytman, *Engineer*
Kevin Tur, *Manager*
▲ **EMP:** 41 **EST:** 1933
SQ FT: 13,000
SALES (est): 6.3MM **Privately Held**
WEB: www.veco-ny.com
SIC: 3625 Noise control equipment

(G-3688)
VIN MAR PRECISION METALS INC
1465 S Strong Ave (11726-3210)
PHONE.....................631 563-6608
Catherine Leo, *President*
Anthony Leo, *Vice Pres*

EMP: 15
SQ FT: 6,000
SALES (est): 2.5MM **Privately Held**
WEB: www.vin-mar.com
SIC: 3444 Sheet metal specialties, not stamped

(G-3689)
W A BAUM CO INC
620 Oak St (11726-3217)
P.O. Box 209 (11726-0209)
PHONE..................................631 226-3940
William A Baum Jr, *Ch of Bd*
John C Baum Sr, *President*
James M Baum, *Vice Pres*
Michael Hayes, *Vice Pres*
Margaret Faber, *Export Mgr*
▲ EMP: 80 EST: 1916
SQ FT: 31,000
SALES (est): 11.7MM **Privately Held**
WEB: www.wabaum.com
SIC: 3841 Blood pressure apparatus

(G-3690)
WORLDWIDE ARNTCAL CMPNENTS INC (PA)
10 Reith St (11726-1414)
PHONE..................................631 842-3780
Steven Peltier, *President*
Carol Peltier, *Treasurer*
▼ EMP: 25
SQ FT: 10,000
SALES (est): 4MM **Privately Held**
WEB: www.aeronauticalcomponents.com
SIC: 3812 5088 Search & navigation equipment; aircraft equipment & supplies

(G-3691)
WORLDWIDE ARNTCAL CMPNENTS INC
Also Called: Beryllium Manufacturing
10 Reith St (11726-1414)
P.O. Box 407, Lindenhurst (11757-0407)
PHONE..................................631 842-3780
Steve Paltier, *CFO*
EMP: 6
SALES (est): 275.5K
SALES (corp-wide): 4MM **Privately Held**
WEB: www.aeronauticalcomponents.com
SIC: 3812 5088 Search & navigation equipment; transportation equipment & supplies
PA: Worldwide Aeronautical Components Inc.
10 Reith St
Copiague NY 11726
631 842-3780

Coram
Suffolk County

(G-3692)
BAYSHORE WIRE PRODUCTS CORP
480 Mill Rd (11727-4108)
PHONE..................................631 451-8825
Socratis Stavropoulos, *President*
EMP: 11
SQ FT: 11,000
SALES (est): 1.3MM **Privately Held**
SIC: 3496 Miscellaneous fabricated wire products

(G-3693)
HAMPTON TRANSPORT INC
3655 Route 112 (11727-4123)
PHONE..................................631 716-4445
Keith Lewin, *President*
EMP: 12 EST: 1993
SALES (est): 100K **Privately Held**
SIC: 2399 4119 Horse harnesses & riding crops, etc.: non-leather; local passenger transportation

(G-3694)
ISLAND INDUSTRIES CORP
480 Mill Rd (11727-4108)
PHONE..................................631 451-8825
Socratis Stavropoulos, *President*
▲ EMP: 7
SQ FT: 20,000
SALES (est): 1.3MM **Privately Held**
SIC: 3315 Wire & fabricated wire products

(G-3695)
NATURES VALUE INC (PA)
468 Mill Rd (11727-4108)
PHONE..................................631 846-2500
Oscar Ramjeet, *CEO*
Joe Kramer, *CFO*
▲ EMP: 300
SQ FT: 224,000
SALES (est): 82.3MM **Privately Held**
WEB: www.naturesvalue.com
SIC: 2834 Vitamin preparations

(G-3696)
NEW YORK FAN COIL LLC
7 Chesapeake Bay Rd (11727-2004)
PHONE..................................646 580-1344
Seth Rubin,
EMP: 8
SALES (est): 862.9K **Privately Held**
SIC: 3677 Electronic coils, transformers & other inductors

(G-3697)
NOTO INDUSTRIAL CORP
11 Thomas St (11727-3153)
PHONE..................................631 736-7600
John Noto, *President*
EMP: 8 EST: 2010
SALES (est): 1MM **Privately Held**
SIC: 3535 Conveyors & conveying equipment

(G-3698)
PREMIUM MULCH & MATERIALS INC
482 Mill Rd (11727-4108)
PHONE..................................631 320-3666
Nicholas Sorge, *President*
EMP: 10
SALES (est): 91K **Privately Held**
SIC: 2499 Mulch or sawdust products, wood

(G-3699)
SHARONANA ENTERPRISES INC
52 Sharon Dr (11727-1923)
PHONE..................................631 875-5619
Orlando Vizcaino, *Principal*
EMP: 20
SALES (est): 1MM **Privately Held**
SIC: 2541 Store & office display cases & fixtures

(G-3700)
SUFFOLK INDUS RECOVERY CORP
Also Called: Pk Metals
3542 Route 112 (11727-4101)
PHONE..................................631 732-6403
Philip L Fava, *CEO*
Richard Smith, *Vice Pres*
Cathy Finn, *Payroll Mgr*
Mike Eberl, *Manager*
EMP: 65 EST: 1934
SALES (est): 14.7MM **Privately Held**
WEB: www.pkmetals.com
SIC: 2611 4212 Pulp mills, mechanical & recycling processing; garbage collection & transport, no disposal

Corfu
Genesee County

(G-3701)
BAILEY ELC MTR & PUMP SUP LLC
2186 Main Rd (14036-9650)
PHONE..................................585 418-5051
Glen Bailey, *Mng Member*
EMP: 8
SQ FT: 3,000
SALES (est): 1.9MM **Privately Held**
SIC: 7694 Electric motor repair

(G-3702)
DELAVAL INC
Also Called: Beck, Don
850 Main Rd (14036-9753)
PHONE..................................585 599-4696
Donald M Beck, *Branch Mgr*
John Donnelly, *Branch Mgr*

EMP: 18
SQ FT: 8,100 **Privately Held**
WEB: www.donbeckinc.com
SIC: 3556 Milk processing machinery
HQ: Delaval Inc.
11100 N Congress Ave
Kansas City MO 64153
816 891-7700

(G-3703)
IDEAL BURIAL VAULT COMPANY
1166 Vision Pkwy (14036-9794)
PHONE..................................585 599-2242
George Tilley, *President*
EMP: 8 EST: 1953
SQ FT: 4,500
SALES (est): 1.3MM **Privately Held**
SIC: 3272 Burial vaults, concrete or pre-cast terrazzo

Corinth
Saratoga County

(G-3704)
CURTIS/PALMER HYDROELECTRIC LP
15 Pine St (12822-1319)
PHONE..................................518 654-6297
David Liebetreu, *Plant Mgr*
EMP: 11
SALES (est): 1.6MM **Publicly Held**
SIC: 3629 Power conversion units, a.c. to d.c.: static-electric
PA: Atlantic Power Corporation
3 Allied Dr Ste 220
Dedham MA 02026

Corning
Steuben County

(G-3705)
CORNING INCORPORATED (PA)
1 Riverfront Plz (14831-0002)
PHONE..................................607 974-9000
Wendell P Weeks, *Ch of Bd*
Kevin G Corliss, *Counsel*
James P Clappin, *Exec VP*
Clark S Kinlin, *Exec VP*
David L Morse, *Exec VP*
◆ EMP: 946 EST: 1851
SALES: 11.2B **Publicly Held**
WEB: www.corning.com
SIC: 3229 3357 3661 3674 Glass fiber products; glass tubes & tubing; TV tube blanks, glass; fiber optic cable (insulated); telephone & telegraph apparatus; semi-conductors & related devices

(G-3706)
CORNING INCORPORATED
Decker Bldg (14831-0001)
PHONE..................................607 974-9000
Jamie Houghton, *Branch Mgr*
EMP: 51
SALES (corp-wide): 11.2B **Publicly Held**
WEB: www.corning.com
SIC: 3229 Pressed & blown glass
PA: Corning Incorporated
1 Riverfront Plz
Corning NY 14831
607 974-9000

(G-3707)
CORNING INCORPORATED
1 Riverfront Plz (14831-0002)
PHONE..................................607 974-9000
Dick Jack, *General Mgr*
Han Jung Han Yim, *Analyst*
EMP: 45
SALES (corp-wide): 11.2B **Publicly Held**
WEB: www.corning.com
SIC: 3229 Pressed & blown glass
PA: Corning Incorporated
1 Riverfront Plz
Corning NY 14831
607 974-9000

(G-3708)
CORNING INCORPORATED
Hp-Ab-01-A9b (14831-0001)
PHONE..................................607 248-1200

Fred Judge, *Dept Chairman*
Kirk Gregg, *Officer*
EMP: 48
SALES (corp-wide): 11.2B **Publicly Held**
SIC: 3229 3661 3674 3357 Glass fiber products; glass tubes & tubing; TV tube blanks, glass; telephone & telegraph apparatus; semiconductors & related devices; fiber optic cable (insulated)
PA: Corning Incorporated
1 Riverfront Plz
Corning NY 14831
607 974-9000

(G-3709)
CORNING INCORPORATED
1 W Market St Ste 601 (14830-2673)
PHONE..................................607 974-4488
John Holliday, *Branch Mgr*
EMP: 6
SALES (corp-wide): 11.2B **Publicly Held**
WEB: www.corning.com
SIC: 3229 Pressed & blown glass
PA: Corning Incorporated
1 Riverfront Plz
Corning NY 14831
607 974-9000

(G-3710)
CORNING INCORPORATED
1 Museum Way (14830-2253)
PHONE..................................607 974-8496
Sean Keenan, *Engineer*
John O'Hare, *Comms Mgr*
Pete Knott, *Manager*
EMP: 20
SQ FT: 7,500
SALES (corp-wide): 11.2B **Publicly Held**
WEB: www.corning.com
SIC: 3229 Pressed & blown glass
PA: Corning Incorporated
1 Riverfront Plz
Corning NY 14831
607 974-9000

(G-3711)
CORNING INTERNATIONAL CORP (HQ)
1 Riverfront Plz (14831-0002)
PHONE..................................607 974-9000
Wendell P Weeks, *CEO*
John W Loose, *Ch of Bd*
James W Wheat, *President*
Kirk P Gregg, *Vice Pres*
Kenneth C KAO, *Vice Pres*
▼ EMP: 7
SQ FT: 15,000
SALES (est): 619.9MM
SALES (corp-wide): 11.2B **Publicly Held**
WEB: www.corningware.com
SIC: 3229 5945 Pressed & blown glass; ceramics supplies
PA: Corning Incorporated
1 Riverfront Plz
Corning NY 14831
607 974-9000

(G-3712)
CORNING OPTCAL CMMNCATIONS LLC
22 W 3rd St (14830-3114)
P.O. Box 2306, Hickory NC (28603-2306)
PHONE..................................607 974-7543
Justin Green, *Sales Staff*
Tony Tripeny, *Manager*
Kim Hamilton, *Manager*
EMP: 12
SALES (corp-wide): 11.2B **Publicly Held**
WEB: www.corningcablesystems.com
SIC: 3357 Communication wire
HQ: Corning Optical Communications Llc
4200 Corning Pl
Charlotte NC 28216
828 901-5000

(G-3713)
CORNING SPECIALTY MTLS INC
1 Riverfront Plz (14831-0002)
PHONE..................................607 974-9000
Wendell P Weeks, *Ch of Bd*
EMP: 2

▲ = Import ▼=Export
◆ =Import/Export

SALES (est): 1.5MM
SALES (corp-wide): 11.2B **Publicly Held**
SIC: 3357 3229 3674 Fiber optic cable (insulated); glass fiber products; glass tubes & tubing; TV tube blanks, glass; semiconductors & related devices
PA: Corning Incorporated
1 Riverfront Plz
Corning NY 14831
607 974-9000

(G-3714)
CORNING VITRO CORPORATION
Also Called: Corning Consumer Products Co
1 Riverfront Plz (14830-2556)
PHONE..............................607 974-8605
Peter Campanella, *President*
John W Loose, *President*
Hayward R Gipson, *Senior VP*
Thomas E Blumer, *Vice Pres*
Dawn M Cross, *Vice Pres*
◆ **EMP:** 4593
SALES (est): 228.8MM
SALES (corp-wide): 11.2B **Publicly Held**
WEB: www.corning.com
SIC: 3229 3469 Pressed & blown glass; household cooking & kitchen utensils, metal
PA: Corning Incorporated
1 Riverfront Plz
Corning NY 14831
607 974-9000

(G-3715)
GATEHOUSE MEDIA LLC
Also Called: Leader, The
34 W Pulteney St (14830-2211)
P.O. Box 1017 (14830-0817)
PHONE..............................607 936-4651
Denny Bruen, *Principal*
Becky Jenkins, *Bookkeeper*
Heather Falkey, *Manager*
Breenna Hilton, *Manager*
EMP: 85
SALES (corp-wide): 1.5B **Privately Held**
WEB: www.the-leader.com
SIC: 2711 Newspapers, publishing & printing
HQ: Gatehouse Media, Llc
175 Sullys Trl Fl 3
Pittsford NY 14534
585 598-0030

(G-3716)
HERFF JONES LLC
262 W 2nd St (14830-2438)
PHONE..............................607 936-2366
Virginia Caumlake, *Manager*
EMP: 25
SALES (corp-wide): 1.1B **Privately Held**
WEB: www.herffjones.com
SIC: 2741 Yearbooks: publishing & printing
HQ: Herff Jones, Llc
4501 W 62nd St
Indianapolis IN 46268
800 419-5462

(G-3717)
KABRICS
2737 Forest Hill Dr (14830-3690)
PHONE..............................607 962-6344
Kathy Wilson, *Owner*
EMP: 8
SALES (est): 300K **Privately Held**
SIC: 2395 Embroidery & art needlework

(G-3718)
MULTIMEDIA SERVICES INC
11136 River Rd 40 (14830-9324)
PHONE..............................607 936-3186
Richard Bartholomew, *President*
Daniel Flatt, *Vice Pres*
Rick Bartholomew, *Human Res Mgr*
Ralph Begeal, *Sales Staff*
Robin Savard, *Administration*
EMP: 21
SQ FT: 13,000
SALES (est): 4.8MM **Privately Held**
SIC: 2752 Commercial printing, offset

(G-3719)
PANELOGIC INC
366 Baker Street Ext (14830-1639)
PHONE..............................607 962-6319
George Welch, *CEO*
Douglas Brown, *President*

EMP: 32
SQ FT: 14,500
SALES (est): 8.1MM **Privately Held**
WEB: www.panelogic.com
SIC: 3625 Electric controls & control accessories, industrial

(G-3720)
RYERS CREEK CORP
Also Called: Mill, The
1330 Mill Dr (14830-9020)
PHONE..............................607 523-6617
Graham Howard, *Manager*
EMP: 20
SQ FT: 7,500
SALES (est): 2.2MM **Privately Held**
WEB: www.gotothemill.com
SIC: 2499 3999 Novelties, wood fiber; tobacco pipes, pipestems & bits

(G-3721)
STORFLEX HOLDINGS INC
Also Called: Storflex Fixture
392 Pulteney St (14830-2134)
PHONE..............................607 962-2137
Timothy Purdie, *Ch of Bd*
Connie Santell, *Treasurer*
▼ **EMP:** 152
SQ FT: 160,000
SALES (est): 41.7MM **Privately Held**
WEB: www.storflex.com
SIC: 3585 Refrigeration & heating equipment

(G-3722)
TOBEYCO MANUFACTURING CO INC
165 Cedar St (14830-2603)
PHONE..............................607 962-2446
Stephen Tobey, *President*
EMP: 12
SQ FT: 16,000
SALES (est): 880K **Privately Held**
SIC: 3599 3479 Machine & other job shop work; machine shop, jobbing & repair; painting, coating & hot dipping

(G-3723)
VITRIX INC
Also Called: Vitrix Hot Glass and Crafts
77 W Market St (14830-2526)
PHONE..............................607 936-8707
Thomas Kelly, *President*
EMP: 6
SALES (est): 683.4K **Privately Held**
WEB: www.vitrixhotglass.com
SIC: 3231 5719 Products of purchased glass; glassware

Cornwall
Orange County

(G-3724)
ADVANCE D TECH INC
2 Mill St Stop 19 (12518-1265)
P.O. Box 38 (12518-0038)
PHONE..............................845 534-8248
Samuel Brach, *President*
EMP: 10
SQ FT: 6,000
SALES (est): 1.5MM **Privately Held**
SIC: 3545 Diamond cutting tools for turning, boring, burnishing, etc.

(G-3725)
ASPIRE ONE COMMUNICATIONS LLC
245 Main St Ste 8 (12518-1598)
PHONE..............................201 281-2998
Steven Mandel,
EMP: 12
SQ FT: 20,000
SALES (est): 4MM **Privately Held**
SIC: 2721 8999 Magazines: publishing & printing; communication services

(G-3726)
ASPIRE ONE COMMUNICATIONS INC
246 Main St (12518-1568)
P.O. Box 496 (12518-0496)
PHONE..............................845 534-6110
Steven Mandel, *President*

Sophia Koutsiaftis, *Publisher*
Valerie Mangan, *Manager*
Michael Mazzola, *Director*
EMP: 9
SALES: 2MM **Privately Held**
SIC: 2721 7389 Magazines: publishing & printing;

(G-3727)
BOEING DISTRIBUTION SVCS INC
Also Called: Klx Aerospace Solutions
45 Quaker Ave Ste 203 (12518-2146)
PHONE..............................845 534-0401
Joan Nissen, *Branch Mgr*
EMP: 15
SALES (corp-wide): 101.1B **Publicly Held**
SIC: 3812 Search & navigation equipment
HQ: Boeing Distribution Services, Inc.
3760 W 108th St Unit 1
Hialeah FL 33018
561 383-5100

(G-3728)
COSTUME ARMOUR INC
Also Called: Christo Vac
2 Mill St Stop 1 (12518-1265)
P.O. Box 85 (12518-0085)
PHONE..............................845 534-9120
Nino Novellino, *President*
Susan Truncale, *Admin Asst*
EMP: 16 EST: 1962
SQ FT: 20,000
SALES (est): 1.7MM **Privately Held**
WEB: www.costumearmour.com
SIC: 2389 3999 Theatrical costumes; theatrical scenery

(G-3729)
MOMN POPS INC
13 Orr Hatch (12518-1727)
PHONE..............................845 567-0640
EMP: 25
SALES (est): 3.6MM **Privately Held**
SIC: 2064 2066 Mfg Candy/Confectionery & Chocolate/Cocoa Products

(G-3730)
NEW YORK STATE FOAM ENRGY LLC
2 Commercial Dr (12518-1484)
P.O. Box 175 (12518-0175)
PHONE..............................845 534-4656
Bryan Bender, *Financial Exec*
Jeanine Nicholson, *Office Mgr*
Dennis Bender,
EMP: 8
SALES (est): 1.2MM **Privately Held**
SIC: 3086 1742 Insulation or cushioning material, foamed plastic; acoustical & insulation work

(G-3731)
NEWS OF THE HIGHLANDS INC (PA)
Also Called: Cornwall Local
35 Hasbrouck Ave (12518-1603)
P.O. Box 518 (12518-0518)
PHONE..............................845 534-7771
Constantine Eristoff, *President*
Anne Phipps Sidamon-Eristoff, *Vice Pres*
Henry J Sylvestri, *Treasurer*
EMP: 14
SALES (est): 767.4K **Privately Held**
WEB: www.newsofthehighlands.com
SIC: 2711 Commercial printing & newspaper publishing combined

(G-3732)
RANDOB LABS LTD
45 Quaker Ave Ste 207 (12518-2146)
P.O. Box 440 (12518-0440)
PHONE..............................845 534-2197
Jim Creagan, *President*
EMP: 3
SALES (est): 1.6MM **Privately Held**
SIC: 2834 Vitamin, nutrient & hematinic preparations for human use

Cornwall On Hudson
Orange County

(G-3733)
EXECUTIVE SIGN CORP
43 Boulevard (12520-1809)
PHONE..............................212 397-4050
Isaac Goldman, *Owner*
EMP: 6
SALES (est): 385.1K **Privately Held**
WEB: www.executivesigncorp.com
SIC: 3993 Signs, not made in custom sign painting shops

Corona
Queens County

(G-3734)
BONO SAWDUST SUPPLY CO INC
Also Called: Bono Sawdust Co
3330 127th Pl (11368-1508)
PHONE..............................718 446-1374
Fax: 718 446-6715
EMP: 6 EST: 1931
SQ FT: 12,000
SALES (est): 750K **Privately Held**
SIC: 2421 2842 Mfg Sawdust & Shavings

(G-3735)
CAZAR PRINTING & ADVERTISING
4215 102nd St (11368-2460)
PHONE..............................718 446-4606
Herman Cazar, *Owner*
▲ **EMP:** 5
SALES (est): 320K **Privately Held**
SIC: 2752 Commercial printing, lithographic

(G-3736)
CORONA PLUMBING & HTG SUP INC
10466 Roosevelt Ave (11368-2328)
PHONE..............................718 424-4133
Apolinar A Ferreira, *Ch of Bd*
EMP: 5
SALES (est): 118.3K **Privately Held**
SIC: 3432 1711 Plumbing fixture fittings & trim; hydronics heating contractor

(G-3737)
CORONA READY MIX INC
5025 97th Pl (11368-3028)
PHONE..............................718 271-5940
Paul Melis, *President*
John Vasilantonakis, *Vice Pres*
EMP: 10
SQ FT: 6,500
SALES (est): 1.5MM **Privately Held**
SIC: 3273 Ready-mixed concrete

(G-3738)
DELICIOUS FOODS INC
11202 Roosevelt Ave (11368-2624)
PHONE..............................718 446-9352
Berminder Chahal, *President*
EMP: 11
SALES (est): 910.2K **Privately Held**
WEB: www.deliciousasianfood.com
SIC: 2038 2032 5812 Ethnic foods, frozen; ethnic foods: canned, jarred, etc.; caterers

(G-3739)
GREEN ZONE FOOD SERVICE INC
9906 Christie Ave 3a (11368-3149)
PHONE..............................917 709-1728
Jian Lin, *CEO*
Ryan Su, *Vice Pres*
EMP: 6 EST: 2015
SQ FT: 2,000
SALES (est): 243.4K **Privately Held**
SIC: 2086 Carbonated beverages, nonalcoholic: bottled & canned; soft drinks: packaged in cans, bottles, etc.

(G-3740)
IMAGE IRON WORKS INC
5050 98th St (11368-3023)
PHONE......................................718 592-8276
Sigi Fredo Gomez, *President*
EMP: 8
SALES (est): 720K **Privately Held**
SIC: 3312 Hot-rolled iron & steel products

(G-3741)
JASON & JEAN PRODUCTS INC
104 Corona Ave (11368)
PHONE......................................718 271-8300
Chin Ho Kim, *President*
EMP: 10
SQ FT: 6,000
SALES (est): 809K **Privately Held**
SIC: 3999 Hair & hair-based products

(G-3742)
KENAN INTERNATIONAL TRADING
Also Called: Moo Goong Hwa
10713 Northern Blvd (11368-1235)
PHONE......................................718 672-4922
Young Kim, *President*
▲ EMP: 5
SQ FT: 6,720
SALES (est): 648.1K **Privately Held**
WEB: www.kenandigital.com
SIC: 3444 3993 2759 5999 Awnings,
sheet metal; signs & advertising special-
ties; commercial printing; awnings

(G-3743)
MAGELLAN AEROSPACE BETHEL INC
9711 50th Ave (11368-2740)
PHONE......................................203 798-9373
James Butyniec, *CEO*
Paul Heide, *General Mgr*
Carey Leuis, *Opers Mgr*
Tom Heis, *Engineer*
Paul Murphy, *Engineer*
▲ EMP: 125
SQ FT: 37,250
SALES (est): 19.4MM
SALES (corp-wide): 732.9MM **Privately Held**
WEB: www.ambel.net
SIC: 3728 3599 3724 Aircraft assemblies,
subassemblies & parts; machine & other
job shop work; aircraft engines & engine
parts
PA: Magellan Aerospace Corporation
3160 Derry Rd E
Mississauga ON L4T 1
905 677-1889

(G-3744)
MAGELLAN AEROSPACE NY INC (HQ)
9711 50th Ave (11368-2740)
P.O. Box 847256, Boston MA (02284-7256)
PHONE......................................718 699-4000
N Murray Edwards, *Ch of Bd*
John Marcello, *Ch of Bd*
James S Butyniec, *President*
Hon William G Davis, *Counsel*
Jo-Ann Ball, *Vice Pres*
▲ EMP: 200 EST: 1939
SQ FT: 205,000
SALES: 45.1MM
SALES (corp-wide): 732.9MM **Privately Held**
WEB: www.magellan.aero
SIC: 3812 3769 3489 3728 Search &
navigation equipment; guided missile &
space vehicle parts & auxiliary equip-
ment; ordnance & accessories; aircraft
assemblies, subassemblies & parts
PA: Magellan Aerospace Corporation
3160 Derry Rd E
Mississauga ON L4T 1
905 677-1889

(G-3745)
MILAN PROVISION CO INC
10815 Roosevelt Ave (11368-2538)
PHONE......................................718 899-7678
Sal Laurita, *President*
EMP: 20
SQ FT: 3,000
SALES (est): 2.1MM **Privately Held**
SIC: 2013 Sausages & other prepared
meats

(G-3746)
MOGA TRADING COMPANY INC
57 Granger St (11368)
PHONE......................................718 760-2966
Paul Cheng, *President*
EMP: 7
SALES (est): 571.2K **Privately Held**
SIC: 2392 Household furnishings

(G-3747)
NATURAL DREAMS LLC
5312 104th St (11368-3222)
PHONE......................................718 760-4202
Kaston Etal, *President*
EMP: 5
SALES (est): 334.8K **Privately Held**
SIC: 2515 Mattresses & bedsprings

(G-3748)
RUTCARELE INC
3449 110th St (11368-1333)
PHONE......................................347 830-5353
Alex Rovira, *CEO*
EMP: 8
SALES: 950K **Privately Held**
SIC: 3999 Manufacturing industries

(G-3749)
S S PRECISION GEAR & INSTR
4512 104th St (11368-2890)
PHONE......................................718 457-7474
Salvatore Silvestri, *President*
Michael Silvestri, *General Mgr*
EMP: 7
SQ FT: 2,500
SALES: 500K **Privately Held**
SIC: 3545 Machine tool accessories

(G-3750)
SOLAR SCREEN CO INC
5311 105th St (11368-3297)
PHONE......................................718 592-8222
Miles Joseph, *President*
EMP: 9 EST: 1955
SQ FT: 10,000
SALES: 2MM **Privately Held**
WEB: www.solar-screen.com
SIC: 2591 Window shades

(G-3751)
UNITED STEEL PRODUCTS INC
3340 127th Pl (11368-1508)
PHONE......................................718 478-5330
Fred Budetti, *President*
Alfred Franza, *Vice Pres*
Alfredo Franza, *Vice Pres*
Todd Rigolli, *CFO*
Nicholas Henry, *Sales Associate*
▲ EMP: 80
SQ FT: 22,000
SALES: 9.1MM **Privately Held**
WEB: www.unitedsteelproducts.com
SIC: 3442 1542 7699 Metal doors; com-
mercial & office building contractors; door
& window repair

(G-3752)
YONG JI PRODUCTIONS INC
10219 44th Ave (11368-2430)
PHONE......................................917 559-4616
Wanchang Yin, *President*
EMP: 20
SALES (est): 1.2MM **Privately Held**
SIC: 2311 Men's & boys' suits & coats

Cortland
Cortland County

(G-3753)
ACTUANT CORPORATION
Also Called: Cortland
44 River St (13045-2311)
PHONE......................................607 753-8276
John Stidd, *CEO*
EMP: 47
SALES (corp-wide): 654.7MM **Publicly Held**
SIC: 3593 Fluid power cylinders, hydraulic
or pneumatic

PA: Actuant Corporation
N86 W12500 Wstbrook Crssi St N 86
Menomonee Falls WI 53051
262 293-1500

(G-3754)
ALPLA INC
106 Central Ave (13045-2754)
PHONE......................................607 250-8101
John Mulvaney, *Supervisor*
EMP: 5
SALES (est): 416.3K **Privately Held**
SIC: 3085 Plastics bottles

(G-3755)
BFMA HOLDING CORPORATION
37 Huntington St (13045-3096)
PHONE......................................607 753-6746
Barry W Florescue, *Ch of Bd*
EMP: 9
SQ FT: 3,000
SALES (est): 1.1MM **Privately Held**
SIC: 2841 5122 5131 5139 Soap: granu-
lated, liquid, cake, flaked or chip; toi-
letries; sewing accessories; shoe
accessories; display equipment, except
refrigerated; packaging & labeling serv-
ices

(G-3756)
BORGWARNER MORSE TEC LLC
3690 Luker Rd (13045-9397)
PHONE......................................607 257-6700
Roger Wood, *Branch Mgr*
EMP: 90 **Privately Held**
WEB: www.borgwarnermorsetec.com
SIC: 3714 Motor vehicle parts & acces-
sories
HQ: Borgwarner Morse Tec Llc
800 Warren Rd
Ithaca NY 14850
607 257-6700

(G-3757)
BP DIGITAL IMAGING LLC
Also Called: Carbon Copies
87 Main St (13045-2610)
P.O. Box 5396 (13045-5396)
PHONE......................................607 753-0022
Betsy Allen, *Mng Member*
Jeff Czimmer, *IT/INT Sup*
▼ EMP: 8
SQ FT: 1,800
SALES: 500K **Privately Held**
SIC: 2752 Photolithographic printing

(G-3758)
CORTLAND CABLE COMPANY INC
44 River St (13045-2335)
P.O. Box 330 (13045-0330)
PHONE......................................607 753-8276
John Stidd, *CEO*
Richard Nye, *Vice Pres*
Bob Keohane, *Plant Engr*
Luis Padilla, *VP Sales*
◆ EMP: 50
SALES (est): 49.7K
SALES (corp-wide): 654.7MM **Publicly Held**
WEB: www.cortlandcable.com
SIC: 3496 3357 2823 Cable, uninsulated
wire: made from purchased wire; nonfer-
rous wiredrawing & insulating; cellulosic
manmade fibers
HQ: Cortland Company, Inc.
44 River St
Cortland NY 13045

(G-3759)
CORTLAND COMPANY INC (HQ)
44 River St (13045-2311)
P.O. Box 330 (13045-0330)
PHONE......................................607 753-8276
John A Stidd, *CEO*
John Thomas, *President*
Sam Bull, *Vice Pres*
John G Greco, *Vice Pres*
Stephen A Breen, *CFO*
EMP: 64

SALES (est): 44.8MM
SALES (corp-wide): 654.7MM **Publicly Held**
WEB: www.actuant.com
SIC: 2298 5063 Ropes & fiber cables; wire
& cable; electronic wire & cable
PA: Actuant Corporation
N86 W12500 Wstbrook Crssi St N 86
Menomonee Falls WI 53051
262 293-1500

(G-3760)
CORTLAND LINE MFG LLC
3736 Kellogg Rd (13045-8818)
PHONE......................................607 756-2851
John Wilson, *President*
Ralph Canfield, *CFO*
EMP: 40
SALES (est): 2.7MM **Privately Held**
SIC: 2298 5941 5091 Fishing lines, nets,
seines: made in cordage or twine mills;
fishing equipment; fishing equipment &
supplies

(G-3761)
CORTLAND MACHINE AND TOOL CO
60 Grant St (13045-2173)
P.O. Box 27 (13045-0027)
PHONE......................................607 756-5852
Stan Pierce, *President*
Debbie Hoyt, *Human Res Mgr*
Scott Rogers, *Technology*
EMP: 11 EST: 1913
SQ FT: 10,000
SALES: 900K **Privately Held**
SIC: 3599 Machine shop, jobbing & repair

(G-3762)
CORTLAND PLASTICS INTL LLC
211 S Main St (13045)
PHONE......................................607 662-0120
Kay Breed, *Controller*
Patrick Dessein, *Mng Member*
David Erwin,
Rick Esposito,
EMP: 26
SALES (est): 5.6MM **Privately Held**
SIC: 3085 Plastics bottles

(G-3763)
CORTLAND READY MIX INC
6 Locust Ave Ofc Rte 13 (13045-1412)
PHONE......................................607 753-3063
Michael Saunders, *President*
EMP: 12 EST: 1944
SQ FT: 4,000
SALES: 200K
SALES (corp-wide): 7.8MM **Privately Held**
WEB: www.saundersconcrete.com
SIC: 3273 Ready-mixed concrete
PA: Saunders Concrete Co. Inc.
5126 S Onondaga Rd
Nedrow NY 13120
315 469-3217

(G-3764)
CORTLAND STANDARD PRINTING CO
110 Main St (13045-6607)
P.O. Box 5548 (13045-5548)
PHONE......................................607 756-5665
Kevin R Howe, *President*
Evan Geibel, *Publisher*
F M Catalano, *Chief*
Ann G Howe, *Vice Pres*
Mike Riley, *Accounts Mgr*
EMP: 65 EST: 1867
SQ FT: 15,000
SALES (est): 4.4MM **Privately Held**
WEB: www.cortlandstandard.com
SIC: 2711 2791 Newspapers: publishing
only, not printed on site; typesetting

(G-3765)
CVILLE YOGHURT INC
3156 Byrne Hollow Xing (13045-6621)
PHONE......................................315 430-4966
EMP: 5
SALES (est): 408.3K **Privately Held**
SIC: 2026 Fluid milk

(G-3766)
FORKEY CONSTRUCTION & FABG INC
3690 Luker Rd (13045-9397)
PHONE..................................607 849-4879
Charles Forkey, *President*
EMP: 30
SQ FT: 27,000
SALES (est): 7.9MM **Privately Held**
SIC: 3469 Machine parts, stamped or pressed metal

(G-3767)
GRAPH-TEX INC
46 Elm St (13045-2225)
P.O. Box 109 (13045-0109)
PHONE..................................607 756-7791
Brent Riley, *President*
EMP: 10
SALES (corp-wide): 3.1MM **Privately Held**
WEB: www.graph-tex.com
SIC: 2759 Screen printing
PA: Graph-Tex, Inc.
  24 Court St
  Cortland NY 13045
  607 756-1875

(G-3768)
GRAPH-TEX INC (PA)
24 Court St (13045-2685)
P.O. Box 109 (13045-0109)
PHONE..................................607 756-1875
Brent Riley, *President*
EMP: 8
SQ FT: 3,600
SALES (est): 3.1MM **Privately Held**
WEB: www.graph-tex.com
SIC: 2759 5941 5091 Screen printing; sporting goods & bicycle shops; sporting & recreation goods

(G-3769)
GRAPHICS PLUS PRINTING INC
215 S Main St (13045-3266)
PHONE..................................607 299-0500
Robert Eckard, *President*
EMP: 24
SQ FT: 47,000
SALES (est): 5.6MM **Privately Held**
SIC: 2752 2759 7336 Commercial printing, offset; screen printing; art design services

(G-3770)
GUTCHESS HARDWOODS INC
890 Mclean Rd (13045-9393)
PHONE..................................607 753-3393
EMP: 9 **EST:** 2015
SALES (est): 1MM **Privately Held**
SIC: 2421 Sawmills & planing mills, general

(G-3771)
GUTCHESS LUMBER CO INC (PA)
890 Mclean Rd (13045-9393)
PHONE..................................607 753-3393
Gary H Gutchess, *Ch of Bd*
Matthew F Gutchess, *President*
Andrew Middleton, *Plant Mgr*
Jeffrey D Breed, *Treasurer*
◆ **EMP:** 250 **EST:** 1904
SQ FT: 3,500
SALES: 150MM **Privately Held**
WEB: www.gutchess.com
SIC: 2421 2426 Building & structural materials, wood; lumber, hardwood dimension

(G-3772)
ITHACA PREGANCY CENTER
4 Church St (13045-2710)
PHONE..................................607 753-3909
EMP: 5
SALES (est): 477K
SALES (corp-wide): 183.1K **Privately Held**
SIC: 2835 Pregnancy test kits
PA: Ithaca Pregancy Center
  210 W Green St
  Ithaca NY 14850
  607 273-4673

(G-3773)
JACKSONS WELDING LLC
Also Called: Jacksons Welding Service & Sls
215 N Homer Ave (13045)
PHONE..................................607 756-2725
EMP: 7
SQ FT: 8,000
SALES (est): 252.2K **Privately Held**
SIC: 7692 5084 1799 Welding Repair Whol Industrial Equipment Trade Contractor

(G-3774)
JM MURRAY CENTER INC (PA)
823 State Route 13 Ste 1 (13045-8731)
PHONE..................................607 756-9913
Floyd Moon, *President*
Jerry Gebhard, *General Mgr*
Judy O Brien, *Vice Pres*
Dale Davis, *Vice Pres*
Gerald Gebhard, *Vice Pres*
▲ **EMP:** 110
SQ FT: 110,000
SALES: 17.8MM **Privately Held**
WEB: www.jmmurray.com
SIC: 2673 3843 7349 Bags: plastic, laminated & coated; dental equipment & supplies; building maintenance services

(G-3775)
MARIETTA CORPORATION (HQ)
Also Called: Marietta Hospitality
37 Huntington St (13045-3098)
P.O. Box 5250 (13045-5250)
PHONE..................................607 753-6746
Donald W Sturdivant, *CEO*
Chris Calhoun, *Senior VP*
Beth Corl, *Senior VP*
Ray Ferretti, *Senior VP*
David Hempson, *Senior VP*
◆ **EMP:** 500
SQ FT: 550,000
SALES (est): 364.4MM
SALES (corp-wide): 256.4MM **Privately Held**
SIC: 2844 2834 2541 Cosmetic preparations; toilet preparations; druggists' preparations (pharmaceuticals); store & office display cases & fixtures
PA: Marietta Holding Corporation, Inc.
  37 Huntington St
  Cortland NY 13045
  607 753-6746

(G-3776)
MARIETTA CORPORATION
106 Central Ave (13045-2754)
PHONE..................................607 753-0982
Greg Rudy, *Branch Mgr*
EMP: 350
SALES (corp-wide): 256.4MM **Privately Held**
SIC: 2841 7389 Soap: granulated, liquid, cake, flaked or chip; packaging & labeling services
HQ: Marietta Corporation
  37 Huntington St
  Cortland NY 13045
  607 753-6746

(G-3777)
MARIETTA CORPORATION
Also Called: Packaging Avantage/Marietta La
37 Huntington St (13045-3098)
P.O. Box 5006 (13045-5006)
PHONE..................................323 589-8181
Greg Mullen, *Branch Mgr*
EMP: 600
SALES (corp-wide): 256.4MM **Privately Held**
SIC: 2841 5122 5131 5139 Soap: granulated, liquid, cake, flaked or chip; toiletries; toilet articles; toilet preparations; perfumes; sewing accessories; hair accessories; shoe accessories; display equipment, except refrigerated; packaging & labeling services
HQ: Marietta Corporation
  37 Huntington St
  Cortland NY 13045
  607 753-6746

(G-3778)
MCCONNAUGHAY TECHNOLOGIES
Also Called: Cortland Asphalt Products
1911 Lorings Crossing Rd (13045-9747)
PHONE..................................607 753-1100
Frank Suits Jr, *President*
Larry Ostermeyer, *Vice Pres*
▲ **EMP:** 8
SQ FT: 15,000
SALES (est): 1.4MM
SALES (corp-wide): 272.8MM **Privately Held**
WEB: www.mcconnaughay.com
SIC: 2951 Asphalt paving mixtures & blocks
PA: Suit-Kote Corporation
  1911 Lorings Crossing Rd
  Cortland NY 13045
  607 753-1100

(G-3779)
PALL CORPORATION
Also Called: Pall Trinity Micro
3643 State Route 281 (13045-3591)
P.O. Box 2030 (13045-0930)
PHONE..................................607 753-6041
David Berger, *President*
Terrance Edwards, *Buyer*
Jay Jackson, *Buyer*
Todd Nielson, *Engineer*
Pete Pinkowski, *Engineer*
EMP: 750
SALES (corp-wide): 19.8B **Publicly Held**
WEB: www.pall.com
SIC: 3842 3841 3569 3599 Surgical appliances & supplies; surgical & medical instruments; IV transfusion apparatus; filters; filters, general line: industrial; filter elements, fluid, hydraulic line; air intake filters, internal combustion engine, except auto; gasoline filters, internal combustion engine, except auto; oil filters, internal combustion engine, except automotive; filters: oil, fuel & air, motor vehicle; perforated metal, stamped
HQ: Pall Corporation
  25 Harbor Park Dr
  Port Washington NY 11050
  516 484-5400

(G-3780)
PALL CORPORATION
3669 State Route 281 (13045-8957)
PHONE..................................607 753-6041
Angela Griffin, *Engineer*
Brian Palermo, *Engineer*
Jacques Joseph, *Branch Mgr*
EMP: 750
SALES (corp-wide): 19.8B **Publicly Held**
WEB: www.pall.com
SIC: 3842 Surgical appliances & supplies
HQ: Pall Corporation
  25 Harbor Park Dr
  Port Washington NY 11050
  516 484-5400

(G-3781)
PALL CORPORATION
Also Called: Pall's Advnced Sprtons Systems
839 State Route 13 Ste 12 (13045-8998)
P.O. Box 2030 (13045-0930)
PHONE..................................607 753-6041
Carl Boise, *Principal*
Michael Fox, *Engineer*
EMP: 750
SALES (corp-wide): 19.8B **Publicly Held**
SIC: 3842 Surgical appliances & supplies
HQ: Pall Corporation
  25 Harbor Park Dr
  Port Washington NY 11050
  516 484-5400

(G-3782)
PAUL BUNYAN PRODUCTS INC
890 Mclean Rd (13045-9393)
PHONE..................................315 696-6164
Judith Greene, *President*
William Oustad, *Vice Pres*
Margaret Hudson, *Treasurer*
EMP: 20
SQ FT: 36,000
SALES (est): 3.8MM **Privately Held**
SIC: 2448 Pallets, wood

(G-3783)
PRECISION EFORMING LLC
839 State Route 13 Ste 1 (13045-8999)
PHONE..................................607 753-7730
Scott Selbach,
Doug Ondrack,
EMP: 13
SQ FT: 7,000
SALES (est): 2MM **Privately Held**
WEB: www.precisioneforming.com
SIC: 3542 Electroforming machines

(G-3784)
PYROTEK INCORPORATED
641 State Route 13 (13045-8836)
PHONE..................................607 756-3050
Thomas Howard, *Manager*
EMP: 97
SALES (corp-wide): 565.8MM **Privately Held**
SIC: 3365 Aluminum foundries
PA: Pyrotek Incorporated
  705 W 1st Ave
  Spokane WA 99201
  509 926-6212

(G-3785)
QUADRA FLEX CORP
Also Called: Quadra Flex Quality Labels
1955 State Route 13 (13045-9619)
P.O. Box 286 (13045-0286)
PHONE..................................607 758-7066
David Masri, *President*
Christopher Meddaugh, *Vice Pres*
Thresa Meddaugh, *Treasurer*
Ben Masri, *Director*
Elizabeth Masri, *Admin Sec*
EMP: 5
SQ FT: 2,500
SALES: 700K **Privately Held**
WEB: www.quadraflex.com
SIC: 2759 2679 Labels & seals: printing; labels, paper: made from purchased material

(G-3786)
REDDING-HUNTER INC
Also Called: Redding Reloading Equipment
1089 Starr Rd (13045-8806)
PHONE..................................607 753-3331
Richard W Beebe, *President*
Robin Sharpless, *Exec VP*
Gerald Gebhard, *Vice Pres*
Fred Muller, *Opers Staff*
▼ **EMP:** 25
SQ FT: 15,000
SALES (est): 4.7MM **Privately Held**
WEB: www.redding-reloading.com
SIC: 3484 3599 Small arms; machine shop, jobbing & repair

(G-3787)
SAUNDERS CONCRETE CO INC
Also Called: Cortland Ready Mix
6 Locust Ave (13045-1412)
PHONE..................................607 756-7905
Wilbur Hayes, *Manager*
EMP: 15
SALES (corp-wide): 7.8MM **Privately Held**
SIC: 3273 Ready-mixed concrete
PA: Saunders Concrete Co. Inc.
  5126 S Onondaga Rd
  Nedrow NY 13120
  315 469-3217

(G-3788)
SELLCO INDUSTRIES INC
58 Grant St (13045-2174)
P.O. Box 70 (13045-0070)
PHONE..................................607 756-7594
George Delorenzo Jr, *President*
Marilyn De Lorenzo, *Vice Pres*
EMP: 20
SQ FT: 19,000
SALES (est): 2.5MM **Privately Held**
WEB: www.sellcoinc.com
SIC: 3993 2782 2399 2396 Signs & advertising specialties; looseleaf binders & devices; banners, made from fabric; automotive & apparel trimmings

(G-3789)
SUIT-KOTE CORPORATION (PA)
1911 Lorings Crossing Rd (13045-9775)
PHONE..................................607 753-1100

GEOGRAPHIC

Frank H Suits Jr, *President*
Harvey Andersen, *General Mgr*
Earl Koon, *General Mgr*
Scott Harris, *Vice Pres*
Dan Quinlan, *Vice Pres*
◆ **EMP:** 200
SQ FT: 10,000
SALES (est): 272.8MM **Privately Held**
WEB: www.suit-kote.com
SIC: 2951 1611 Asphalt & asphaltic paving
  mixtures (not from refineries); highway &
  street paving contractor

(G-3790)
TECHNOLOGIES APPLICATION
LLC
Also Called: Glyph Production Technologies
3736 Kellogg Rd (13045-8818)
PHONE......................607 275-0345
Rebecca Ebhardt, *Marketing Mgr*
Liran Shathi,
▲ **EMP:** 14
SQ FT: 15,000
SALES: 7MM **Privately Held**
WEB: www.glyphtech.com
SIC: 3572 Computer storage devices

(G-3791)
WILBEDONE INC
1133 State Route 222 (13045-9352)
PHONE......................607 756-8813
Thomas L Beames, *President*
David Motyl, *Manager*
EMP: 33
SQ FT: 18,000
SALES (est): 5.2MM **Privately Held**
WEB: www.wilbedone.com
SIC: 2541 Counter & sink tops

Cortlandt Manor
Westchester County

(G-3792)
ABLE INDUSTRIES INC
Also Called: Able Wire Co
18 Brook Ln (10567-6502)
PHONE......................914 739-5685
Warren Button, *President*
Patricia Button, *Admin Sec*
▲ **EMP:** 12 **EST:** 1980
SQ FT: 18,000
SALES (est): 1.1MM **Privately Held**
WEB: www.ablewire.com
SIC: 3315 Wire, steel: insulated or ar-
  mored

(G-3793)
DURANM INC
101 Dale Ave (10567-1617)
PHONE......................914 774-3367
Martin F Duran, *CEO*
EMP: 5
SALES (est): 626.1K **Privately Held**
SIC: 3272 Floor slabs & tiles, precast con-
  crete

(G-3794)
ELMSFORD SHEET METAL
WORKS INC
23 Arlo Ln (10567-2631)
PHONE......................914 739-6300
Donald J Trier, *President*
EMP: 75
SQ FT: 24,000
SALES (est): 12.5MM
SALES (corp-wide): 31.8B **Privately Held**
WEB: www.elmsfordsheetmetal.com
SIC: 3444 7389 7699 Sheet metal spe-
  cialties, not stamped; metal cutting serv-
  ices; metal reshaping & replating services
HQ: Engie North America Inc.
  1990 Post Oak Blvd # 1900
  Houston TX 77056
  713 636-0000

(G-3795)
GC MOBILE SERVICES INC
Also Called: G C Mobile Svces
32 William Puckey Dr (10567-6216)
PHONE......................914 736-9730
Garth Cooperman, *President*
EMP: 6

SALES: 250K **Privately Held**
SIC: 7692 Welding repair

(G-3796)
HIGHRANGE FUELS INC
96 Oregon Rd (10567-1246)
PHONE......................914 930-8300
Sajan Augustine, *Principal*
EMP: 7
SALES (est): 457.8K **Privately Held**
SIC: 2869 Fuels

(G-3797)
MINES PRESS INC
Also Called: Iscream
231 Croton Ave (10567-5284)
PHONE......................888 559-2634
Steven Mines, *Ch of Bd*
Daniel Mines, *Ch of Bd*
Cynthia Mines, *Corp Secy*
Suzanne Shwab, *Purch Agent*
Carl Hutt, *CFO*
▲ **EMP:** 115 **EST:** 1933
SQ FT: 100,000
SALES (est): 31.9MM **Privately Held**
WEB: www.minespress.com
SIC: 2752 2759 2789 2791 Commercial
  printing, offset; letterpress printing; gold
  stamping on books; typesetting

(G-3798)
PRONTO PRINTER
2085 E Main St Ste 3 (10567-2616)
PHONE......................914 737-0800
John P Marvin, *Owner*
EMP: 6 **EST:** 1974
SQ FT: 7,000
SALES: 650K **Privately Held**
SIC: 2752 Photo-offset printing

Cossayuna
Washington County

(G-3799)
FRONHOFER TOOL COMPANY
INC
4197 County Rd 48 (12823)
P.O. Box 84 (12823-0084)
PHONE......................518 692-2496
Paul Fronhofer II, *Ch of Bd*
Kyle Fronhofer, *Vice Pres*
EMP: 30
SQ FT: 10,000
SALES: 5MM **Privately Held**
WEB: www.fronhofertool.com
SIC: 3599 Machine shop, jobbing & repair

Coxsackie
Greene County

(G-3800)
DUCOMMUN
AEROSTRUCTURES NY INC
171 Stacey Rd (12051-2613)
PHONE......................518 731-2791
Michael D Grosso, *CEO*
Anthony J Reardon, *Ch of Bd*
Hugh J Quigley, *President*
Paul Burton, *Vice Pres*
EMP: 270
SQ FT: 65,000
SALES (est): 50.7MM
SALES (corp-wide): 629.3MM **Publicly**
Held
WEB: www.dynabil.com
SIC: 3728 Aircraft parts & equipment
HQ: Ducommun Aerostructures, Inc.
  268 E Gardena Blvd
  Gardena CA 90248
  310 380-5390

Cranberry Lake
St. Lawrence County

(G-3801)
FORM A ROCKLAND PLASTICS
INC
7152 Main St (12927)
P.O. Box 670 (12927-0670)
PHONE......................315 848-3300
Donald Lashomb II, *President*
Cynthia Whitmore Lashomb, *Treasurer*
EMP: 5 **EST:** 1963
SQ FT: 6,000
SALES (est): 623.7K **Privately Held**
SIC: 3089 3172 Plastic containers, except
  foam; key cases

Croghan
Lewis County

(G-3802)
GRAND SLAM SAFETY LLC
9793 Bridge St (13327)
P.O. Box 35 (13327-0035)
PHONE......................315 301-4039
Robert K Lyndaker, *President*
Brian Graves, *Plant Engr*
Bob Chamberlain, *Marketing Staff*
Robert Chamberlain,
Mick Lehman,
EMP: 15
SALES: 300K **Privately Held**
SIC: 3949 Sporting & athletic goods

Cropseyville
Rensselaer County

(G-3803)
R J VALENTE GRAVEL INC
3349 Rte 2 (12052)
PHONE......................518 279-1001
Tim Banks, *Branch Mgr*
EMP: 29
SALES (corp-wide): 19.4MM **Privately**
Held
SIC: 1442 Construction sand & gravel
PA: R. J. Valente Gravel, Inc.
  1 Madison St
  Troy NY 12180
  518 432-4470

Cross River
Westchester County

(G-3804)
VEPO SOLUTIONS LLC
3 Fairview Ct (10518-1127)
PHONE......................914 384-2121
Alan Seiler, *President*
EMP: 5 **EST:** 2017
SALES: 2MM **Privately Held**
SIC: 3824 7371 Water meters; computer
  software development & applications

Croton Falls
Westchester County

(G-3805)
GARY STOCK CORPORATION
597 Rte 22 (10519)
P.O. Box 609 (10519-0609)
PHONE......................914 276-2700
Gary Stock, *President*
EMP: 7
SALES (est): 1MM **Privately Held**
WEB: www.gstockco.com
SIC: 2759 Promotional printing

Croton On Hudson
Westchester County

(G-3806)
BLUE PIG ICE CREAM FACTORY
121 Maple St (10520-2538)
PHONE......................914 271-3850
Julia Horowitz, *Owner*
EMP: 5
SALES: 250K **Privately Held**
SIC: 2024 5812 Ice cream & frozen
  desserts; ice cream stands or dairy bars

(G-3807)
DALEE BOOKBINDING CO INC
Also Called: Creations In Canvas
10 Croton Lake Rd (10520-3615)
PHONE......................914 965-1660
David Hutter, *President*
EMP: 16 **EST:** 1965
SQ FT: 12,000
SALES (est): 2MM **Privately Held**
WEB: www.daleebook.com
SIC: 2789 2782 Binding only: books, pam-
  phlets, magazines, etc.; blankbooks

(G-3808)
GENERAL SPLICE
CORPORATION
Hwy 129 (10520)
P.O. Box 868 (10520-0868)
PHONE......................914 271-5131
Ralph Milano, *President*
Nicole Milano, *Treasurer*
EMP: 6
SQ FT: 7,000
SALES (est): 1MM **Privately Held**
SIC: 3535 Conveyors & conveying equip-
  ment

(G-3809)
HEPA-HAT INCORPORATED
31 Park Trl (10520-2211)
PHONE......................914 271-9747
James Breen, *President*
Carol Breen, *Vice Pres*
EMP: 10
SALES: 50K **Privately Held**
SIC: 2353 7389 Hats & caps;

Crown Point
Essex County

(G-3810)
MOUNTAIN FOREST PRODUCTS
INC
3281 Nys Route 9n (12928-2405)
PHONE......................518 597-3674
Kevin Mero, *President*
Vicki Mero, *Corp Secy*
EMP: 6
SQ FT: 1,152
SALES (est): 733.8K **Privately Held**
SIC: 2411 Logging

Cuba
Allegany County

(G-3811)
D F STAUFFER BISCUIT CO INC
8670 Farnsworth Rd (14727-9720)
P.O. Box 12002, York PA (17402-0672)
PHONE......................585 968-2700
EMP: 50
SALES (corp-wide): 11.6B **Privately Held**
SIC: 2052 Mfg Cookies/Crackers
HQ: D F Stauffer Biscuit Co Inc
  360 S Belmont St
  York PA 17403
  717 815-4600

(G-3812)
DEMING ELECTRO-PLATING
CORP
5 Woodruff St (14727-1020)
PHONE......................585 968-2355
Barbara Deming, *President*

▲ = Import ▼=Export
◆ =Import/Export

Bruce L Deming, *Vice Pres*
Michael L Demming, *Vice Pres*
Michael Deming, *Director*
EMP: 6 **EST:** 1947
SQ FT: 22,000
SALES: 500K **Privately Held**
SIC: 3471 Electroplating of metals or
formed products

(G-3813)
EMPIRE CHEESE INC
4520 County Road 6 (14727-9598)
PHONE..................................585 968-1552
Gary Vanic, *CEO*
John Epprecht, *Corp Secy*
Russell Mullins, *Vice Pres*
Shelley Williamson, *Purch Agent*
Bozena Lukomski, *QC Mgr*
▲ **EMP:** 175
SQ FT: 100,000
SALES (est): 92.1MM
SALES (corp-wide): 1.6B **Privately Held**
WEB: www.empirecheese.com
SIC: 2022 Natural cheese
PA: Great Lakes Cheese Co., Inc.
17825 Great Lakes Pkwy
Hiram OH 44234
440 834-2500

(G-3814)
SPS MEDICAL SUPPLY CORP
Also Called: Sterilator Company
31 Water St Ste 1 (14727-1030)
PHONE..................................585 968-2377
Shawn Doyle, *Branch Mgr*
EMP: 10
SALES (corp-wide): 918.1MM **Publicly Held**
SIC: 3842 3821 Sterilizers, hospital & surgical; autoclaves, laboratory
HQ: Sps Medical Supply Corp.
6789 W Henrietta Rd
Rush NY 14543
585 359-0130

Cutchogue
Suffolk County

(G-3815)
DI BORGHESE CASTELLO LLC
17150 County Road 48 (11935-1041)
P.O. Box 957 (11935-0957)
PHONE..................................631 734-5111
Marco Borghese, *Mng Member*
EMP: 10
SALES (est): 811.1K **Privately Held**
WEB: www.castellodiborghese.com
SIC: 2084 Wines

(G-3816)
PELLEGRINI VINEYARDS LLC
23005 Main Rd (11935-1331)
PHONE..................................631 734-4111
Rita Pellegrini, *Partner*
John Larsen, *Manager*
EMP: 5
SALES (est): 533.4K **Privately Held**
WEB: www.pellegrinivineyards.com
SIC: 2084 Wines

(G-3817)
PUGLIESE VINEYARDS INC
34515 Main Rd Rte 25 (11935)
P.O. Box 467 (11935-0467)
PHONE..................................631 734-4057
Patricia Pugliese, *President*
EMP: 5
SALES (est): 473.3K **Privately Held**
WEB: www.pugliesevineyards.com
SIC: 2084 Wines

Dansville
Livingston County

(G-3818)
DANSVILLE LOGGING & LUMBER
10903 State Route 36 (14437-9444)
PHONE..................................585 335-5879
Timothy Rauber, *President*
EMP: 23

SQ FT: 900
SALES: 1.4MM **Privately Held**
SIC: 2421 Lumber: rough, sawed or planed

(G-3819)
GPM ASSOCIATES LLC
Also Called: Forbes Products
10 Forbes St (14437-9268)
PHONE..................................585 335-3940
Kevin Webster, *Marketing Staff*
Michelle Pragle, *Executive*
Mark McDermott,
EMP: 20
SALES (corp-wide): 15.5MM **Privately Held**
SIC: 2782 3089 2752 2393 Blankbooks & looseleaf binders; novelties, plastic; commercial printing, lithographic; textile bags
PA: Gpm Associates Llc
45 High Tech Dr
Rush NY 14543
585 334-4800

(G-3820)
JUST IN TIME CNC MACHINING
88 Ossian St (14437-9101)
PHONE..................................585 335-2010
Kelly Alexander, *President*
EMP: 14
SQ FT: 10,000
SALES (est): 1.6MM **Privately Held**
SIC: 3599 Machine shop, jobbing & repair

Davenport
Delaware County

(G-3821)
GREENE LUMBER CO LP
16991 State Highway 23 (13750-8304)
PHONE..................................607 278-6101
Jeffrey Meyer,
EMP: 35
SQ FT: 13,888
SALES (est): 5.8MM
SALES (corp-wide): 340.3MM **Privately Held**
SIC: 2421 Lumber: rough, sawed or planed
PA: Baillie Lumber Co., L.P.
4002 Legion Dr
Hamburg NY 14075
800 950-2850

Dayton
Cattaraugus County

(G-3822)
ALPINE WATER USA LLC
70 Park Dr N (14041)
PHONE..................................203 912-9723
Alexander Muhr, *Mng Member*
EMP: 5
SALES (est): 362.6K **Privately Held**
SIC: 2086 Water, pasteurized: packaged in cans, bottles, etc.

De Ruyter
Madison County

(G-3823)
USA BODY INC
994 Middle Lake Rd (13052-1244)
PHONE..................................315 852-6123
Bruce Macrae, *President*
Kristine Macrae, *Admin Sec*
EMP: 8
SALES (est): 1.5MM **Privately Held**
SIC: 3713 Truck bodies (motor vehicles)

De Witt
Onondaga County

(G-3824)
MAXI COMPANIES INC
4317 E Genesee St (13214-2114)
PHONE..................................315 446-1002

Charles C Giancola, *President*
▼ **EMP:** 6
SALES (est): 536.3K **Privately Held**
SIC: 3582 Dryers, laundry: commercial, including coin-operated

Deer Park
Suffolk County

(G-3825)
514 ADAMS CORPORATION
Also Called: Adams Press
305 Suburban Ave (11729-6806)
PHONE..................................516 352-6948
Daniel Rummo, *President*
Chris Rummo, *Vice Pres*
Theresa Rummo, *Admin Sec*
EMP: 7
SALES (est): 1MM **Privately Held**
SIC: 2752 2791 2789 Commercial printing, offset; typesetting; bookbinding & related work

(G-3826)
ABLE WELDBUILT INDUSTRIES INC
1050 Grand Blvd (11729-5710)
PHONE..................................631 643-9700
Steve Laganas, *President*
EMP: 15
SALES (est): 3.4MM **Privately Held**
SIC: 3713 Truck & bus bodies

(G-3827)
ABRA-KA-DATA SYSTEMS LTD
39 W Jefryn Blvd Ste 1 (11729-5792)
PHONE..................................631 667-5550
Robert A Berding, *Ch of Bd*
Kenneth Berding, *President*
Dorothy Berding, *Admin Sec*
▲ **EMP:** 22
SQ FT: 15,000
SALES (est): 2.2MM **Privately Held**
SIC: 2761 Manifold business forms

(G-3828)
ACEM CORP
45 W Jefryn Blvd Ste 107 (11729-5722)
PHONE..................................631 242-2440
John Makowski, *CEO*
EMP: 4
SALES (est): 2.5MM **Privately Held**
WEB: www.acemcasino.com
SIC: 2511 2514 Wood game room furniture; metal game room furniture

(G-3829)
AD MAKERS LONG ISLAND INC
60 E Jefryn Blvd Ste 3 (11729-5798)
PHONE..................................631 595-9100
Arthur Lituchy, *President*
Henry Houston, *Vice Pres*
EMP: 10
SQ FT: 1,500
SALES (est): 930K **Privately Held**
WEB: www.admadvertising.com
SIC: 3993 7311 Signs & advertising specialties; advertising agencies

(G-3830)
ADVANCED STRUCTURES CORP (PA)
235 W Industry Ct (11729-4688)
PHONE..................................631 667-5000
Linda Frank, *President*
Tina Lang, *Controller*
EMP: 15
SQ FT: 22,000
SALES (est): 3.8MM **Privately Held**
WEB: www.advancedstructurescorp.com
SIC: 3469 3083 Metal stampings; laminated plastic sheets

(G-3831)
AERO SPECIALTIES MANUFACTURING
20 Burt Dr (11729-5770)
PHONE..................................631 242-7200
Donald Carter, *President*
Elizabeth A Smith, *Vice Pres*
EMP: 12 **EST:** 1999
SQ FT: 1,400

SALES: 3.4MM **Privately Held**
SIC: 3599 Machine shop, jobbing & repair

(G-3832)
AKZO NOBEL COATINGS INC
1014 Grand Blvd Ste 6 (11729-5782)
PHONE..................................631 242-6020
Patrick McDonald, *Manager*
EMP: 6
SALES (corp-wide): 11.3B **Privately Held**
WEB: www.nam.sikkens.com
SIC: 2851 Paints & allied products
HQ: Akzo Nobel Coatings Inc.
8220 Mohawk Dr
Strongsville OH 44136
440 297-5100

(G-3833)
ALL COLOR BUSINESS SPC LTD
305 Suburban Ave (11729-6806)
PHONE..................................516 420-0649
William Bogue, *Ch of Bd*
EMP: 6
SALES (est): 760K **Privately Held**
SIC: 2752 Commercial printing, lithographic

(G-3834)
ALL-COLOR OFFSET PRINTERS INC
Also Called: All Color Business Specialties
305 Suburban Ave (11729-6806)
PHONE..................................516 420-0649
William Bogue, *President*
Tim Dorman, *Vice Pres*
EMP: 5
SQ FT: 2,500
SALES (est): 967.1K **Privately Held**
SIC: 2752 Commercial printing, offset

(G-3835)
ALLSTATE GASKET & PACKING INC
31 Prospect Pl (11729-3713)
PHONE..................................631 254-4050
Angelo Romano, *President*
▲ **EMP:** 17
SQ FT: 2,000
SALES (est): 2.4MM **Privately Held**
WEB: www.allstategasket.com
SIC: 3053 5085 3443 Gaskets, all materials; industrial supplies; fabricated plate work (boiler shop)

(G-3836)
ALLSTATE SIGN & PLAQUE CORP
70 Burt Dr (11729-5702)
P.O. Box 725 (11729-0725)
PHONE..................................631 242-2828
David Fick, *President*
Mark Fick, *Vice Pres*
Peter Fick, *Treasurer*
EMP: 15 **EST:** 1956
SQ FT: 15,000
SALES: 2.6MM **Privately Held**
WEB: www.allstatesign.com
SIC: 3993 2796 Signs, not made in custom sign painting shops; engraving platemaking services

(G-3837)
AMERICAN RACING HEADERS INC
Also Called: Arh
880 Grand Blvd (11729-5708)
PHONE..................................631 608-1427
Nick Filippides, *CEO*
Jose Cruz, *Principal*
EMP: 30 **EST:** 2011
SALES (est): 6.8MM **Privately Held**
SIC: 3542 Headers

(G-3838)
AMERICAN SEALING TECHNOLOGY
31 Prospect Pl (11729-3713)
P.O. Box 545, Levittown (11756-0545)
PHONE..................................631 254-0019
EMP: 12
SQ FT: 10,000
SALES (est): 960K **Privately Held**
SIC: 3053 Mfg Gaskets/Packing/Sealing Devices

GEOGRAPHIC

(G-3839)
ANAND PRINTING MACHINERY INC
188 W 16th St (11729-4909)
PHONE..................................631 667-3079
Amand Kumar, *President*
EMP: 1
SALES: 8MM **Privately Held**
SIC: 3555 Printing trades machinery

(G-3840)
ANTHONY MANNO & CO INC
307 Skidmore Rd Ste 2 (11729-7117)
P.O. Box 32, Freeport (11520-0032)
PHONE..................................631 445-1834
Anthony Manno, *President*
Russell Fragala, *Senior VP*
EMP: 7
SQ FT: 5,000
SALES (est): 644.2K **Privately Held**
SIC: 3452 Screws, metal

(G-3841)
ARMA CONTAINER CORP
65 N Industry Ct (11729-4601)
PHONE..................................631 254-1200
Bruce Margolis, *CEO*
Howard Gottfried, *Vice Pres*
Kim Geraci, *VP Bus Dvlpt*
Jack Hausman, *Treasurer*
Wayne Margolis, *General Counsel*
▼ EMP: 50 EST: 1946
SQ FT: 70,000
SALES (est): 12.7MM **Privately Held**
WEB: www.armacontainer.com
SIC: 2653 Boxes, corrugated: made from
   purchased materials

(G-3842)
ARTHUR BROWN W MFG CO
49 E Industry Ct Ste I (11729-4711)
P.O. Box 755, Saint James (11780-0755)
PHONE..................................631 243-5594
Philip Sabatino, *President*
Anthony Sabatino, *Vice Pres*
EMP: 15
SQ FT: 8,000
SALES (est): 2.2MM **Privately Held**
WEB: www.arthurwbrown.com
SIC: 2511 Wood household furniture

(G-3843)
AUTO DATA SYSTEMS INC (PA)
Also Called: Auto Data Labels
44 W Jefryn Blvd Ste K (11729-4721)
PHONE..................................631 667-2382
Scott Saal, *President*
▼ EMP: 21
SQ FT: 3,000
SALES: 2.2MM **Privately Held**
SIC: 2679 5131 Tags & labels, paper; la-
   bels

(G-3844)
AUTO MARKET PUBLICATIONS INC
1641 Deer Park Ave Ste 5 (11729-5209)
PHONE..................................631 667-0500
Corey Franklin, *President*
EMP: 8
SALES (est): 640.2K **Privately Held**
SIC: 2741 Telephone & other directory
   publishing

(G-3845)
BEST WAY TOOLS BY ANDERSON INC
171 Brook Ave (11729-7204)
PHONE..................................631 586-4702
Arleen Anderson CPA, *CEO*
Wayne Anderson, *President*
Warren Anderson, *Vice Pres*
Paul Cassutti, *Vice Pres*
Austen Anderson, *VP Sales*
EMP: 4
SQ FT: 15,000
SALES: 8MM **Privately Held**
WEB: www.bestwaytools.com
SIC: 3423 5072 Hand & edge tools; hard-
   ware

(G-3846)
BIMBO BAKERIES
955 Grand Blvd (11729-5707)
PHONE..................................631 274-4906

EMP: 8
SALES (est): 545.2K **Privately Held**
SIC: 2051 Bread, cake & related products

(G-3847)
BLI INTERNATIONAL INC
Also Called: Allegiant Health
75 N Industry Ct (11729-4601)
PHONE..................................631 940-9000
Brian LI, *President*
Robert Naughton, *General Mgr*
Lee Rudibaugh, *Senior VP*
Jerry Maleh, *Vice Pres*
John Zhong, *Vice Pres*
EMP: 130
SALES (est): 38.2MM **Privately Held**
SIC: 2834 Tablets, pharmaceutical

(G-3848)
BLUE SKIES
859 Long Island Ave (11729-3426)
PHONE..................................631 392-1140
Lisa Delvecchio, *Owner*
EMP: 5
SALES (est): 419.7K **Privately Held**
SIC: 3577 Printers & plotters

(G-3849)
BRENSEKE GEORGE WLDG IR WORKS
Also Called: Brenseke's
915 Long Island Ave Ste A (11729-3731)
PHONE..................................631 271-4870
Carol Brenseke, *President*
George Brenseke, *Vice Pres*
EMP: 6
SALES: 800K **Privately Held**
SIC: 7692 Welding repair

(G-3850)
BROOKS LITHO DIGITAL GROUP INC
35 W Jefryn Blvd Ste A (11729-5784)
PHONE..................................631 789-4500
David Brooks, *President*
Linda Brooks, *Vice Pres*
EMP: 5
SQ FT: 500
SALES (est): 929.2K **Privately Held**
WEB: www.brookslitho.com
SIC: 2752 2791 2789 2759 Commercial
   printing, offset; typesetting; bookbinding &
   related work; commercial printing

(G-3851)
CHALLENGE GRAPHICS SVCS INC (PA)
22 Connor Ln (11729-7234)
PHONE..................................631 586-0171
Anthony Brancato, *Ch of Bd*
Jim McLoone, *General Mgr*
Joseph Brancato, *Vice Pres*
Kurt Hochreiter, *Prdtn Mgr*
Roseann Brancato, *Treasurer*
EMP: 42
SQ FT: 32,000
SALES (est): 6.6MM **Privately Held**
SIC: 2752 2791 2789 Lithographing on
   metal; typesetting; bookbinding & related
   work

(G-3852)
CHAPMAN SKATEBOARD CO INC
Also Called: New York Skateboards
87 N Industry Ct Ste A (11729-4607)
PHONE..................................631 321-4773
Greg Chapman, *President*
Christine Chapman, *Vice Pres*
Chappy Chapman, *Sales Mgr*
Glenn Chapman, *Administration*
▲ EMP: 5
SQ FT: 2,000
SALES (est): 582.4K **Privately Held**
WEB: www.chapmanskateboards.com
SIC: 3949 5941 Skates & parts, roller;
   skateboarding equipment

(G-3853)
CONTINENTAL KNITTING MILLS
Also Called: La-Mar Fashions
156 Brook Ave (11729-7251)
PHONE..................................631 242-5330
Pat Marini, *President*
Jennifer Marini, *Vice Pres*

EMP: 5
SQ FT: 4,000
SALES: 300K **Privately Held**
SIC: 2329 2339 5131 Men's & boys'
   sportswear & athletic clothing; women's &
   misses' athletic clothing & sportswear;
   sportswear, women's; knit fabrics

(G-3854)
COUSINS FURNITURE & HM IMPRVS
Also Called: Cousin's Furniture
515 Acorn St (11729-3601)
PHONE..................................631 254-3752
Joaquim L Rodrigues, *President*
Ilidio Rodrigues, *Vice Pres*
Barton Bienenstock, *Executive*
EMP: 42
SQ FT: 10,200
SALES (est): 5.6MM **Privately Held**
SIC: 2511 2431 Wood household furniture;
   millwork

(G-3855)
CREATIVE JUICES PRTG GRAPHICS
Also Called: Bigposters.com
35 W Jefryn Blvd Ste A (11729-5784)
PHONE..................................631 249-2211
Michael Karmatz, *President*
EMP: 12 EST: 1997
SQ FT: 2,300
SALES (est): 1.7MM **Privately Held**
SIC: 2752 Commercial printing, litho-
   graphic

(G-3856)
CTI SOFTWARE INC
44 W Jefryn Blvd Ste P (11729-4721)
PHONE..................................631 253-3550
Eric Meyn, *Ch of Bd*
EMP: 13
SALES (est): 716.7K **Privately Held**
WEB: www.ctisoftware.com
SIC: 7372 Prepackaged software

(G-3857)
CURIOUSLY CREATIVE CANDLES
1067 Long Island Ave (11729-3801)
PHONE..................................631 586-1700
Christine M Lehat, *President*
EMP: 14 EST: 1999
SALES (est): 1.1MM **Privately Held**
SIC: 3999 Candles

(G-3858)
D W S ASSOCIATES INC
Also Called: D W S Printing
89 N Industry Ct (11729-4601)
PHONE..................................631 667-6666
Thomas Staib, *President*
Andrew Staib, *Vice Pres*
Craig Pace, *Sales Dir*
Sal Addotta, *Manager*
EMP: 36
SQ FT: 20,000
SALES (est): 10.7MM **Privately Held**
WEB: www.dwsprinting.com
SIC: 2752 Commercial printing, offset

(G-3859)
DAVINCI DESIGNS INC
Also Called: Davinci Dsgns Distinctive Furn
20 Lucon Dr Unit A (11729-5789)
PHONE..................................631 595-1095
Ralph Vinci, *CEO*
Chris Vinci, *Vice Pres*
Patricia Kennedy, *Manager*
EMP: 15
SQ FT: 3,000
SALES (est): 1.5MM **Privately Held**
WEB: www.davincidesigns.com
SIC: 2522 2521 Office furniture, except
   wood; wood office furniture

(G-3860)
DEER PARK DRIVESHAFT & HOSE
Also Called: Deer Park Drv Shaft & Hose Co
85 Brook Ave Ste C (11729-7202)
PHONE..................................631 667-4091
Nick Monastero, *President*
Richard Desena, *Vice Pres*
EMP: 4

SALES: 1MM **Privately Held**
SIC: 3714 3052 5013 Drive shafts, motor
   vehicle; axles, motor vehicle; automobile
   hose, plastic; automotive supplies & parts

(G-3861)
DEER PARK MACARONI CO INC (PA)
Also Called: Dpr Food Service
1882 Deer Park Ave (11729-4318)
PHONE..................................631 667-4600
Ernest Oliviero, *President*
Tom McDonald, *Vice Pres*
Tom Messina, *Client Mgr*
Christopher Litrel, *Admin Sec*
EMP: 12 EST: 1949
SQ FT: 5,000
SALES (est): 2MM **Privately Held**
WEB: www.deerparkravioli.com
SIC: 2098 Macaroni & spaghetti

(G-3862)
DEER PARK MACARONI CO INC
Also Called: Deer Park Ravioli & Macaroni
1882 Deer Park Ave (11729-4318)
PHONE..................................631 667-4600
Earnest Olivero, *Manager*
EMP: 10
SALES (est): 833.4K
SALES (corp-wide): 2MM **Privately Held**
WEB: www.deerparkravioli.com
SIC: 2098 5149 Noodles (e.g. egg, plain &
   water), dry; pasta & rice
PA: Deer Park Macaroni Co Inc
   1882 Deer Park Ave
   Deer Park NY 11729
   631 667-4600

(G-3863)
DESIGN DISTRIBUTORS INC
300 Marcus Blvd (11729-4500)
PHONE..................................631 242-2000
Stuart J Avrick, *Ch of Bd*
Adam G Avrick, *President*
Mark F Rice, *Vice Pres*
▲ EMP: 85 EST: 1962
SQ FT: 80,000
SALES (est): 19.1MM **Privately Held**
SIC: 2759 2752 7331 Envelopes: printing;
   commercial printing, lithographic; direct
   mail advertising services

(G-3864)
DOVER MARINE MFG & SUP CO INC
98 N Industry Ct (11729-4602)
PHONE..................................631 667-4300
Theodore Cerrito, *President*
Lisa Cerrito, *Treasurer*
EMP: 5
SQ FT: 5,000
SALES (est): 480K **Privately Held**
WEB: www.dovermfg.com
SIC: 3429 Marine hardware

(G-3865)
DP MURPHY CO INC
945 Grand Blvd (11729-5707)
PHONE..................................631 673-9400
Timothy M Schratwieser, *President*
Rudy Markowitz, *Plant Mgr*
John Van Wyk, *Opers Mgr*
Hiram Quezada, *Prgrmr*
Adriane Gray, *Director*
EMP: 66 EST: 1873
SQ FT: 20,000
SALES (est): 8.8MM **Privately Held**
WEB: www.dpmurphy.com
SIC: 2752 7374 7331 2791 Commercial
   printing, offset; data processing service;
   mailing service; typesetting; bookbinding
   & related work

(G-3866)
EAST COAST EMBROIDERY LTD
74 Brook Ave Ste 1 (11729-7227)
PHONE..................................631 254-3878
Susan Simione, *President*
EMP: 7
SALES: 750K **Privately Held**
SIC: 2395 Embroidery products, except
   schiffli machine

▲ = Import ▼ =Export
◆ =Import/Export

(G-3867)
EAST COAST ORTHOIC & PROS COR (PA)
75 Burt Dr (11729-5701)
PHONE..............................516 248-5566
Vincent A Benenati, *CEO*
Lawrence J Benenati, *President*
John Fernandez, *Opers Mgr*
Thomas Giordano, *Opers Mgr*
Robert Lea, *Facilities Mgr*
▲ EMP: 70 EST: 1997
SALES (est): 12.7MM **Privately Held**
WEB: www.ec-op.com
SIC: 3842 Orthopedic appliances

(G-3868)
EC WOOD & COMPANY INC
110 E Industry Ct (11729-4706)
PHONE..............................718 388-2287
Joseph Fontana, *President*
EMP: 15
SQ FT: 13,000
SALES (est): 1.4MM **Privately Held**
SIC: 2434 Wood kitchen cabinets

(G-3869)
ELITE CELLULAR ACCESSORIES INC
61 E Industry Ct (11729-4725)
PHONE..............................877 390-2502
John Nordstrom, *President*
Stephen Conlon, *Exec VP*
EMP: 30
SQ FT: 10,000
SALES (est): 2.7MM **Privately Held**
SIC: 3663 5065 5731 Mobile communication equipment; intercommunication equipment; electronic; video cameras, recorders & accessories

(G-3870)
ELSENER ORGAN WORKS INC
120 E Jefryn Blvd Ste A (11729-5723)
PHONE..............................631 254-2744
Josephine Elsener, *President*
EMP: 7 EST: 2004
SQ FT: 5,000
SALES: 500K **Privately Held**
WEB: www.elsenerorganworks.com
SIC: 3931 Musical instruments

(G-3871)
EMBASSY DINETTES INC
78 E Industry Ct (11729-4704)
PHONE..............................631 253-2292
Michael Walman, *Vice Pres*
◆ EMP: 5
SQ FT: 15,000
SALES (est): 456.8K **Privately Held**
SIC: 2514 Dinette sets: metal

(G-3872)
EMPIRE INDUSTRIAL BURNER SVC
550 Brook Ave (11729-6802)
PHONE..............................631 242-4619
Edward Roufberg, *President*
Rose Marie Price, *Administration*
EMP: 10
SQ FT: 37,000
SALES: 1MM
SALES (corp-wide): 1.1MM **Privately Held**
SIC: 3433 1711 Burners, furnaces, boilers & stokers; boiler maintenance contractor; heating systems repair & maintenance
PA: Empire Industrial Systems Corp.
40 Corbin Ave
Bay Shore NY 11706
631 242-4619

(G-3873)
FLOW X RAY CORPORATION
Also Called: Flow Dental
100 W Industry Ct (11729-4604)
PHONE..............................631 242-9729
Howard Wolf, *President*
Martin B Wolf, *Chairman*
Arlene Wolf, *Vice Pres*
Geri Cheselka, *Export Mgr*
Carolyn Price, *CFO*
▲ EMP: 96 EST: 1974
SQ FT: 70,000
SALES (est): 13.4MM **Privately Held**
SIC: 3844 X-ray apparatus & tubes

(G-3874)
FORCE DIGITAL MEDIA INC
39 W Jefryn Blvd Ste 2 (11729-5792)
PHONE..............................631 243-0243
John Mazzio, *President*
EMP: 5
SALES (est): 189.8K **Privately Held**
SIC: 2759 7336 Commercial printing; package design

(G-3875)
FORMATS UNLIMITED INC
Also Called: Mf Digital
19 W Jefryn Blvd Ste 2 (11729-5749)
PHONE..............................631 249-9200
Anthony Cosentino, *Ch of Bd*
Joyce Cosentino, *Vice Pres*
John McGrath, *Sales Staff*
Shawn Florman, *Technical Staff*
Jayne Hessel, *Officer*
EMP: 10
SQ FT: 2,500
SALES (est): 1.9MM **Privately Held**
WEB: www.formats-unlimited.com
SIC: 7372 5045 3572 5065 Prepackaged software; disk drives; disk drives, computer; diskettes, computer

(G-3876)
FOSSIL INDUSTRIES INC
44 W Jefryn Blvd Ste A (11729-4721)
PHONE..............................631 254-9200
Howard Decesare, *President*
Mark Decesare, *Vice Pres*
Linda Peters, *Accounts Exec*
▼ EMP: 25
SQ FT: 25,000
SALES (est): 2.9MM **Privately Held**
WEB: www.fossilinc.com
SIC: 3993 Signs, not made in custom sign painting shops

(G-3877)
FUTURE SPRAY FINISHING CO
78 Brook Ave Ste A (11729-7226)
PHONE..............................631 242-6252
Josephine Galea, *Owner*
EMP: 5
SQ FT: 4,500
SALES (est): 364K **Privately Held**
SIC: 3479 Coating of metals & formed products

(G-3878)
GLOBAL STEEL PRODUCTS CORP (HQ)
95 Marcus Blvd (11729-4501)
PHONE..............................631 586-3455
Peter Rolla, *President*
Adrienne Rolla, *Treasurer*
◆ EMP: 150
SQ FT: 85,000
SALES: 19.1MM
SALES (corp-wide): 201.7MM **Privately Held**
SIC: 2542 3446 3443 3442 Partitions for floor attachment, prefabricated: except wood; architectural metalwork; fabricated plate work (boiler shop); metal doors, sash & trim
PA: ltr Industries, Inc
441 Saw Mill River Rd
Yonkers NY 10701
914 964-7063

(G-3879)
HI-TEMP BRAZING INC
539 Acorn St (11729-3601)
PHONE..............................631 491-4917
Raymond M Gentner, *President*
Raymond M Gentner III, *Opers Mgr*
EMP: 30
SQ FT: 7,500
SALES (est): 6.3MM **Privately Held**
WEB: www.hitempbrazing.com
SIC: 3398 Brazing (hardening) of metal

(G-3880)
HIGHLAND ORGANIZATION CORP
435 Unit 23 Brook Ave (11729)
PHONE..............................631 991-3240
Marc Piacenti, *President*
Jennifer McGee, *Comptroller*

EMP: 35 EST: 1999
SQ FT: 3,200
SALES: 5MM **Privately Held**
SIC: 2431 Millwork

(G-3881)
HRD METAL PRODUCTS INC
120 E Jefryn Blvd Ste A (11729-5723)
PHONE..............................631 243-6700
Hector Lasalle, *President*
Martin Michie, *Vice Pres*
EMP: 8
SQ FT: 4,000
SALES: 800K **Privately Held**
SIC: 3444 Sheet metalwork

(G-3882)
ICE CUBE INC (PA)
171 E Industry Ct Ste B (11729-4732)
PHONE..............................613 254-0071
Cono Simino, *President*
EMP: 7
SALES (est): 848.3K **Privately Held**
SIC: 2097 Ice cubes

(G-3883)
ISLAND INSTRUMENT CORPORATION
65 Burt Dr (11729-5701)
PHONE..............................631 243-0550
Patrick McKeever, *President*
Dawn Bannwarth, *Office Mgr*
EMP: 5
SQ FT: 12,500
SALES (est): 1.2MM **Privately Held**
WEB: www.sonnart.com
SIC: 3599 Machine shop, jobbing & repair

(G-3884)
J & J SWISS PRECISION INC
160 W Industry Ct Ste F (11729-4677)
P.O. Box 408 (11729-0408)
PHONE..............................631 243-5584
John Dojlidko, *President*
Tom Mak, *QC Mgr*
John Mroz, *Treasurer*
EMP: 30
SQ FT: 10,000
SALES (est): 4.7MM **Privately Held**
SIC: 3599 3451 Machine shop, jobbing & repair; screw machine products

(G-3885)
JAMAR PRECISION PRODUCTS CO
5 Lucon Dr (11729-5711)
PHONE..............................631 254-0234
James Lewandoski, *President*
Joy Lewandoski, *Vice Pres*
EMP: 12
SQ FT: 10,500
SALES (est): 726K **Privately Held**
SIC: 3599 Machine shop, jobbing & repair

(G-3886)
JAMCO AEROSPACE INC
121a E Industry Ct (11729-4705)
PHONE..............................631 586-7900
Jack Lee, *CEO*
Linette Lee, *President*
Ronald Lee, *QC Mgr*
Erin Hung, *Manager*
Hanna LI, *Admin Sec*
EMP: 50
SQ FT: 30,000
SALES (est): 11MM **Privately Held**
WEB: www.jamco-aerospace.com
SIC: 3728 Aircraft parts & equipment

(G-3887)
JAVCON MACHINE INC
255 Skidmore Rd (11729-7102)
PHONE..............................631 586-1890
Eric Clauss, *President*
EMP: 9 EST: 1977
SALES: 1.5MM **Privately Held**
SIC: 3599 Machine shop, jobbing & repair

(G-3888)
JED LIGHTS INC (HQ)
10 Connor Ln (11729-7210)
PHONE..............................516 812-5001
Doug Flank, *Manager*
EMP: 10
SQ FT: 10,000

SALES (est): 4.9MM
SALES (corp-wide): 10.1MM **Privately Held**
SIC: 3648 5063 3053 3052 Lighting equipment; lighting fittings & accessories; gasket materials; rubber & plastics hose & beltings
PA: Green Logic Led Electrical Supply Inc.
75 Marine St
Farmingdale NY 11735
516 280-2854

(G-3889)
JOHN J MAZUR INC
94 E Jefryn Blvd Ste K (11729-5728)
PHONE..............................631 242-4554
John J Mazur Jr, *President*
EMP: 15 EST: 1957
SQ FT: 15,000
SALES (est): 2.3MM **Privately Held**
SIC: 3599 Machine shop, jobbing & repair

(G-3890)
JUSTIN GREGORY INC
94 E Jefryn Blvd Ste E (11729-5728)
PHONE..............................631 249-5187
Justin Gregory, *CEO*
Renee Levin, *President*
EMP: 6
SALES (est): 639.9K **Privately Held**
SIC: 3111 Accessory products, leather

(G-3891)
KENWIN SALES CORP
Also Called: Levitt Industrial Textile
86 W Industry Ct (11729-4610)
P.O. Box 7150, Hicksville (11802-7150)
PHONE..............................516 933-7553
Beth Foley, *CEO*
Andrew Kanter, *President*
EMP: 8
SQ FT: 6,000
SALES (est): 1MM **Privately Held**
WEB: www.levittextiles.com
SIC: 3965 Fasteners

(G-3892)
KONAR PRECISION MFG INC
62 S 2nd St Ste F (11729-4716)
PHONE..............................631 242-4466
Daruisz Konarski, *President*
Slawomir Konarski, *Vice Pres*
Monika Konarska, *Accounting Mgr*
Karol Konarski, *Office Mgr*
EMP: 5
SQ FT: 2,000
SALES: 500K **Privately Held**
SIC: 3599 Machine shop, jobbing & repair

(G-3893)
L & K GRAPHICS INC
Also Called: Minuteman Press
1917 Deer Park Ave (11729-3302)
PHONE..............................631 667-2269
Richard Crockett, *Ch of Bd*
Robert Mason, *President*
EMP: 6
SQ FT: 2,000
SALES (est): 1MM **Privately Held**
SIC: 2752 Commercial printing, lithographic

(G-3894)
L MILLER DESIGN INC
Also Called: Bank Displays.com
100 E Jefryn Blvd Ste F (11729-5729)
PHONE..............................631 242-1163
Robert L Miller, *President*
Leena Miller, *Corp Secy*
Mike Malone, *Vice Pres*
John Giachetti, *Director*
EMP: 7
SALES: 650K **Privately Held**
WEB: www.lmillerdesign.com
SIC: 3993 7319 Signs & advertising specialties; display advertising service

(G-3895)
LA STRADA DANCE FOOTWEAR INC
770 Grand Blvd Ste 1 (11729-5725)
PHONE..............................631 242-1401
Daniel Cerasuolo, *President*
Linda O'Shea, *Corp Secy*
EMP: 6
SQ FT: 3,300

SALES: 350K **Privately Held**
SIC: 3149 2252 Ballet slippers; socks

(G-3896)
LESLY ENTERPRISE & ASSOCIATES
29 Columbo Dr (11729-1808)
P.O. Box 190 (11729-0190)
PHONE..............................631 988-1301
Lesly Senat, *Principal*
EMP: 5
SALES: 50K **Privately Held**
SIC: 3721 Aircraft

(G-3897)
LEVON GRAPHICS CORP
301 Suburban Ave (11729-6806)
P.O. Box 148, Farmingdale (11735-0148)
PHONE..............................631 753-2022
Donna A Dickran, *Ch of Bd*
Harry L Dickran, *President*
Elizabeth Meisser, *Admin Asst*
EMP: 80
SALES (est): 12.2MM **Privately Held**
WEB: www.levongraphics.com
SIC: 2752 2759 Commercial printing, offset; commercial printing

(G-3898)
LIGHTING SCULPTURES INC
Also Called: Versaponents
66 N Industry Ct (11729-4602)
PHONE..............................631 242-3387
Chet Yaswen, *President*
Laura Yaswen, *Vice Pres*
EMP: 10
SALES: 2.3MM **Privately Held**
SIC: 3648 Lighting equipment

(G-3899)
LONG ISLAND METALFORM INC
12 Lucon Dr (11729-5712)
PHONE..............................631 242-9088
George Seitz Jr, *President*
EMP: 14
SQ FT: 14,000
SALES (est): 2.8MM **Privately Held**
WEB: www.longislandmetalform.com
SIC: 3469 Spinning metal for the trade

(G-3900)
LUCIA GROUP INC
45 W Jefryn Blvd Ste 108 (11729-5722)
PHONE..............................631 392-4900
Craig Lucia, *President*
Guly Rothwell, *Project Mgr*
▲ **EMP:** 5 **EST:** 1994
SQ FT: 1,000
SALES (est): 610K **Privately Held**
WEB: www.theluciagroup.com
SIC: 2522 2542 Office furniture, except wood; shelving, office & store: except wood

(G-3901)
LYNNE B ENTERPRISES INC
Also Called: Apogee
593 Acorn St Ste B (11729-3613)
PHONE..............................631 254-6975
Lynn Nicoali, *President*
Dominick Persichilli, *Production*
Keith Stegemann, *Engineer*
Ted Rykowski, *Design Engr*
Nicole Enlow, *CFO*
EMP: 25
SQ FT: 30,000
SALES (est): 8.8MM **Privately Held**
WEB: www.apogeetranslite.com
SIC: 3548 3646 Welding apparatus; commercial indusl & institutional electric lighting fixtures

(G-3902)
M H STRYKE CO INC
181 E Industry Ct Ste A (11729-4718)
PHONE..............................631 242-2660
Kenneth Winter, *President*
EMP: 10 **EST:** 1931
SQ FT: 3,000
SALES (est): 760.5K **Privately Held**
SIC: 3965 Fasteners, snap

(G-3903)
MARKSMEN MANUFACTURING CORP
355 Marcus Blvd (11729-4509)
PHONE..............................800 305-6942
Peter Guttieri, *President*
◆ **EMP:** 48 **EST:** 1966
SQ FT: 14,800
SALES (est): 11.1MM **Privately Held**
WEB: www.marksmenmfg.com
SIC: 3452 3599 Bolts, metal; machine shop, jobbing & repair

(G-3904)
MASTER CRAFT FINISHERS INC
30 W Jefryn Blvd Ste 1 (11729-4730)
PHONE..............................631 586-0540
Roger J Fox, *President*
Jay Adriaenssens, *Vice Pres*
EMP: 40 **EST:** 1969
SQ FT: 15,000
SALES (est): 4.5MM **Privately Held**
SIC: 3479 3471 2396 Coating of metals & formed products; finishing, metals or formed products; automotive & apparel trimmings

(G-3905)
MCG ELECTRONICS INC
Also Called: McG Surge Protection
12 Burt Dr (11729-5778)
PHONE..............................631 586-5125
Michael Coyle, *President*
Cecilia Coyle, *Vice Pres*
Dion Neri, *Engineer*
Sue Baron, *Sales Mgr*
Anthony Biondo, *Sales Mgr*
▼ **EMP:** 50
SQ FT: 10,000
SALES (est): 7.9MM **Privately Held**
WEB: www.mcgsurge.com
SIC: 3674 Semiconductors & related devices

(G-3906)
MD INTERNATIONAL INDUSTRIES
Also Called: M D I Industries
120 E Jefryn Blvd Ste Aa (11729-5739)
PHONE..............................631 254-3100
Martin Michie, *Owner*
Laurie Frank, *Office Mgr*
Blanche Michie, *Shareholder*
EMP: 24
SQ FT: 10,000
SALES (est): 4.5MM **Privately Held**
WEB: www.mdiindustries.com
SIC: 3728 3444 Aircraft parts & equipment; sheet metalwork

(G-3907)
MODERN PACKAGING INC
505 Acorn St (11729-3601)
PHONE..............................631 595-2437
Syed Zaki Hossai, *Ch of Bd*
Towhidul Islam, *General Mgr*
Jaroslaw Dabek, *Vice Pres*
Jerry Dabek, *Vice Pres*
Mike Esterbrook, *Purchasing*
▲ **EMP:** 62
SQ FT: 20,000
SALES (est): 14.1MM **Privately Held**
WEB: www.modernpackaginginc.com
SIC: 3599 3565 5084 Custom machinery; packaging machinery; packaging machinery & equipment

(G-3908)
NANZ CUSTOM HARDWARE INC
105 E Jefryn Blvd (11729-5713)
PHONE..............................212 367-7000
Kristen Ricci, *Manager*
EMP: 125
SALES (corp-wide): 24.1MM **Privately Held**
WEB: www.nanz.com
SIC: 3429 5031 Door opening & closing devices, except electrical; building materials, interior
PA: Nanz Custom Hardware, Inc.
20 Vandam St Fl 5l
New York NY 10013
212 367-7000

(G-3909)
NATIONAL COMPUTER & ELECTRONIC
Also Called: Nceec
367 Bay Shore Rd Ste D (11729-7244)
PHONE..............................631 242-7222
Neal Morofsky, *Chairman*
Lynn Nicolai, *Vice Pres*
EMP: 8
SQ FT: 5,000
SALES (est): 859K **Privately Held**
WEB: www.ncee.com
SIC: 3469 Electronic enclosures, stamped or pressed metal

(G-3910)
NELCO LABORATORIES INC
154 Brook Ave (11729-7251)
P.O. Box 58 (11729-0058)
PHONE..............................631 242-0082
April Catanzaro, *President*
Noelle Park, *Vice Pres*
EMP: 22 **EST:** 1971
SQ FT: 6,800
SALES (est): 3.2MM **Privately Held**
WEB: www.nelcolabs.com
SIC: 2836 Allergens, allergenic extracts

(G-3911)
NEW WOP RECORDS
Also Called: Artists, Doo Wop
317 W 14th St (11729-6301)
PHONE..............................631 617-9732
Giro Manuele, *Owner*
EMP: 5
SALES (est): 210K **Privately Held**
SIC: 3651 Household audio & video equipment

(G-3912)
NIJON TOOL CO INC
12 Evergreen Pl 12 # 12 (11729-3708)
PHONE..............................631 242-3434
Franklin Trama, *President*
John Burns, *Vice Pres*
EMP: 10
SQ FT: 12,500
SALES (est): 870K **Privately Held**
SIC: 3544 Special dies & tools

(G-3913)
NUTEC COMPONENTS INC
81 E Jefryn Blvd Ste A (11729-5733)
PHONE..............................631 242-1224
Rene H Schnetzler, *President*
Glenn Stanley, *Vice Pres*
EMP: 15
SQ FT: 10,500
SALES (est): 3.6MM **Privately Held**
WEB: www.nutec1.com
SIC: 3823 Industrial instrmnts msrmnt display/control process variable

(G-3914)
NUTRA SOLUTIONS USA INC
Also Called: Nsusa
1019 Grand Blvd (11729-5709)
PHONE..............................631 392-1900
Latiful Hakue, *CEO*
Kalsar Sultana, *Principal*
EMP: 25
SALES (est): 9.5MM **Privately Held**
SIC: 2833 7389 Vitamins, natural or synthetic: bulk, uncompounded; packaging & labeling services

(G-3915)
NY FROYO LLC
324 W 19th St (11729-6342)
PHONE..............................516 312-4588
EMP: 5
SALES (est): 254.2K **Privately Held**
SIC: 2024 Yogurt desserts, frozen

(G-3916)
OCEAN CARDIAC MONITORING
38 W 17th St (11729-3902)
PHONE..............................631 777-3700
Roberto Garcia, *Owner*
EMP: 5
SALES (est): 561.6K **Privately Held**
SIC: 3845 Patient monitoring apparatus

(G-3917)
PAULS RODS & RESTOS INC
131 Brook Ave Ste 13 (11729-7221)
PHONE..............................631 665-7637
Paul R Dimauro, *Principal*
EMP: 6
SALES (est): 830.5K **Privately Held**
SIC: 3531 Automobile wrecker hoists

(G-3918)
PHOTO MEDIC EQUIPMENT INC
Also Called: Precise Optics
3 Saxwood St Ste E (11729-4700)
PHONE..............................631 242-6600
Len Corso, *Ch of Bd*
R Hannington, *Purchasing*
Ann Alonzo, *Controller*
R Corso, *Marketing Staff*
Gordon Kellogg, *Systems Mgr*
EMP: 90
SQ FT: 50,000
SALES (est): 7.7MM **Privately Held**
WEB: www.preciseoptics.com
SIC: 3844 X-ray apparatus & tubes

(G-3919)
PLX INC
Also Called: P L X
40 W Jefryn Blvd (11729-4720)
PHONE..............................631 586-4190
Jack Lipkins, *President*
Zvi Bleier, *Vice Pres*
Kasia Karolczuk, *Prdtn Mgr*
Zechariah Gajadhar, *Engineer*
Kevin Cavanagh, *Technology*
EMP: 40 **EST:** 1953
SALES: 7.1MM **Privately Held**
WEB: www.plxinc.com
SIC: 3827 Optical instruments & apparatus

(G-3920)
PNC SPORTS
1880 Deer Park Ave (11729-4318)
PHONE..............................516 665-2244
Richard Knowles, *Principal*
EMP: 7
SALES (est): 688.1K **Privately Held**
SIC: 3949 Sporting & athletic goods

(G-3921)
PRECISION CNC
71 E Jefryn Blvd (11729-5713)
PHONE..............................631 847-3999
Sal Napolitano, *Owner*
EMP: 6
SALES (est): 782.4K **Privately Held**
SIC: 3728 Aircraft parts & equipment

(G-3922)
PRINT MARKET INC
66 E Jefryn Blvd Ste 1 (11729-5760)
PHONE..............................631 940-8181
EMP: 8
SALES (est): 62.8K **Privately Held**
SIC: 2752 Lithographic Commercial Printing

(G-3923)
PROFESSIONAL MANUFACTURERS
475 Brook Ave (11729-7208)
P.O. Box 282 (11729-0282)
PHONE..............................631 586-2440
Richard Lizio, *President*
EMP: 10 **EST:** 1959
SALES (est): 960K **Privately Held**
SIC: 3843 Dental equipment & supplies

(G-3924)
PVH CORP
Also Called: Van Heusen
1358 The Arches Cir (11729-7069)
PHONE..............................631 254-8200
Shannon Wright, *Branch Mgr*
EMP: 9
SALES (corp-wide): 9.6B **Publicly Held**
SIC: 2321 Men's & boys' dress shirts
PA: Pvh Corp.
200 Madison Ave Bsmt 1
New York NY 10016
212 381-3500

(G-3925)
R E F PRECISION PRODUCTS
517 Acorn St Ste A (11729-3610)
PHONE..................................631 242-4471
Robert Fleece, *Partner*
Raymond Crisafulli, *Partner*
EMP: 17
SQ FT: 3,600
SALES (est): 2.2MM **Privately Held**
WEB: www.refprecisionproducts.com
SIC: 3599 Custom machinery; machine shop, jobbing & repair

(G-3926)
RAINBOW POWDER COATING CORP
86 E Industry Ct (11729-4704)
PHONE..................................631 586-4019
Ron Vincent, *President*
EMP: 5
SQ FT: 5,800
SALES (est): 496.4K **Privately Held**
SIC: 3471 Finishing, metals or formed products

(G-3927)
REFLEX OFFSET INC
305 Suburban Ave (11729-6806)
PHONE..................................516 746-4142
John Banks, *President*
Richard Banks, *Vice Pres*
EMP: 8
SQ FT: 5,400
SALES (est): 1MM **Privately Held**
WEB: www.reflexoffset.com
SIC: 2752 Commercial printing, offset

(G-3928)
RINALDI PRECISION MACHINE
Also Called: R P M
43 Crossway Dr (11729-6225)
PHONE..................................631 242-4141
Angelo Rinaldi, *President*
EMP: 10
SQ FT: 1,700
SALES (est): 1.6MM **Privately Held**
SIC: 3599 Machine shop, jobbing & repair

(G-3929)
ROSEMONT PRESS INCORPORATED
35 W Jefryn Blvd Ste A (11729-5784)
PHONE..................................212 239-4770
Czarina Anif, *Branch Mgr*
EMP: 9
SALES (corp-wide): 8.2MM **Privately Held**
WEB: www.rosemontpress.com
SIC: 2741 Miscellaneous publishing
PA: Rosemont Press Incorporated
253 Church St Apt 2
New York NY 10013
212 239-4770

(G-3930)
ROSS METAL FABRICATORS INC
225 Marcus Blvd (11729-4503)
P.O. Box 12308, Hauppauge (11788-0615)
PHONE..................................631 586-7000
Richard Ross, *President*
Ron Reid, *Vice Pres*
Lawrence Perez, *Treasurer*
EMP: 40 EST: 1969
SQ FT: 30,000
SALES (est): 6.6MM
SALES (corp-wide): 43.4MM **Privately Held**
SIC: 3443 Metal parts
PA: Charles Ross & Son Company
710 Old Willets Path
Hauppauge NY 11788
631 234-0500

(G-3931)
RSM ELECTRON POWER INC (PA)
Also Called: Sensitron Semiconductor
221 W Industry Ct (11729-4605)
PHONE..................................631 586-7600
Steve Saunders, *President*
Isaac Tubbs, *Sales Associate*
▲ EMP: 225 EST: 1969
SQ FT: 18,000
SALES: 49MM **Privately Held**
WEB: www.sensitron.com
SIC: 3674 Integrated circuits, semiconductor networks, etc.

(G-3932)
SCHENCK CORPORATION (DH)
535 Acorn St (11729-3698)
PHONE..................................631 242-4010
Lars Kuenne, *President*
Uwe Grimm, *CFO*
Patrise Heins, *Manager*
Emil Je Wisekal, *Supervisor*
Tarek El-Sawaf, *Business Dir*
◆ EMP: 70
SQ FT: 40,000
SALES (est): 25.9MM
SALES (corp-wide): 4.4B **Privately Held**
SIC: 3545 3829 Balancing machines (machine tool accessories); measuring & controlling devices
HQ: Schenck Industrie-Beteiligungen Ag
C/O Dr. Thomas Hefti
Glarus GL
556 402-544

(G-3933)
SCHENCK USA CORP (DH)
535 Acorn St (11729-3601)
PHONE..................................631 242-4010
Lars Kuenne, *President*
Ronald Kapps, *Facilities Mgr*
Uwe Grimm, *CFO*
Patrise Heins, *Manager*
Joe Murray, *Director*
▲ EMP: 60
SQ FT: 44,000
SALES (est): 20MM
SALES (corp-wide): 4.4B **Privately Held**
WEB: www.schenck-usa.com
SIC: 3545 3829 Balancing machines (machine tool accessories); measuring & controlling devices
HQ: Schenck Corporation
535 Acorn St
Deer Park NY 11729
631 242-4010

(G-3934)
SCIENTIFIC COMPONENTS CORP
Also Called: Mini Circuits Lab
161 E Industry Ct (11729-4705)
PHONE..................................631 243-4901
Al Chasinov, *Branch Mgr*
EMP: 40
SALES (corp-wide): 147MM **Privately Held**
SIC: 3825 Instruments to measure electricity
PA: Scientific Components Corp
13 Neptune Ave
Brooklyn NY 11235
718 934-4500

(G-3935)
SECTOR MICROWAVE INDS INC
999 Grand Blvd (11729-5799)
PHONE..................................631 242-2245
Victor H Nelson, *President*
Thomas J Nelson, *Vice Pres*
Jim Tracy, *Manager*
Patricia Nelson, *Admin Sec*
▼ EMP: 55
SQ FT: 28,000
SALES (est): 8.7MM **Privately Held**
SIC: 3643 Electric switches

(G-3936)
SHARON MANUFACTURING CO INC
540 Brook Ave (11729-6802)
PHONE..................................631 242-8870
Robert Stamm, *President*
EMP: 8
SQ FT: 7,500
SALES (est): 1.7MM **Privately Held**
SIC: 3469 3565 Machine parts, stamped or pressed metal; bag opening, filling & closing machines

(G-3937)
SOMERS STAIN GLASS INC
108 Brook Ave Ste A (11729-7238)
PHONE..................................631 586-7772
Ronald Somers, *President*
Tricia Somers, *Office Mgr*
EMP: 10
SQ FT: 10,000
SALES: 700K **Privately Held**
SIC: 3231 3229 Stained glass: made from purchased glass; lamp parts & shades, glass

(G-3938)
SOUNDCOAT COMPANY INC (DH)
1 Burt Dr (11729-5756)
PHONE..................................631 242-2200
Louis Nenninger, *CEO*
Elizabeth Orlando, *Treasurer*
◆ EMP: 65 EST: 1963
SQ FT: 70,000
SALES (est): 14.9MM
SALES (corp-wide): 305.9MM **Privately Held**
WEB: www.soundcoat.com
SIC: 3086 2299 3625 3296 Insulation or cushioning material, foamed plastic; acoustic felts; noise control equipment; mineral wool

(G-3939)
SPEAQUA CORP
46 W Jefryn Blvd (11729-4736)
PHONE..................................858 334-9042
Steven Patsis, *President*
Steve Patsis, *Vice Pres*
EMP: 40
SQ FT: 20,000
SALES (est): 1.9MM **Privately Held**
SIC: 3651 Loudspeakers, electrodynamic or magnetic

(G-3940)
SUFFOLK COMMUNITY COUNCIL INC (PA)
819 Grand Blvd Ste 1 (11729-5780)
PHONE..................................631 434-9277
Judith Pannullo, *Director*
EMP: 9
SQ FT: 2,000
SALES (est): 194.3K **Privately Held**
WEB: www.suffolkcommunitycouncil.org
SIC: 2721 8322 Periodicals: publishing only; individual & family services

(G-3941)
TEK PRECISION CO LTD
205 W Industry Ct (11729-4613)
PHONE..................................631 242-0330
John Krause, *CEO*
Steve Longobardi, *President*
Randall Strauss, *Vice Pres*
Pat Sweeney, *Production*
Sharon Valles, *Purch Mgr*
EMP: 24
SQ FT: 21,000
SALES: 10.4MM **Privately Held**
WEB: www.tekprecision.com
SIC: 3728 Aircraft assemblies, subassemblies & parts

(G-3942)
TRI-STATE WINDOW FACTORY CORP
360 Marcus Blvd (11729-4504)
PHONE..................................631 667-8600
John Kypreos, *President*
EMP: 75
SQ FT: 31,000
SALES (est): 13.8MM **Privately Held**
SIC: 3089 1761 1751 Windows, plastic; siding contractor; window & door (prefabricated) installation

(G-3943)
ULTRA THIN READY TO BAKE PIZZA
Also Called: Ultra Thin Pzza Shlls Fltbrads
151 E Industry Ct (11729-4705)
PHONE..................................516 679-6655
Cherise Kramer, *Partner*
Douglas Bronsky, *Mng Member*
EMP: 30
SQ FT: 15,000
SALES (est): 5.6MM **Privately Held**
SIC: 2099 Pizza, refrigerated: except frozen

(G-3944)
UNICEL CORPORATION
235 W Industry Ct (11729-4605)
PHONE..................................760 741-3912
Michael Henderson, *President*
▲ EMP: 30 EST: 1978
SQ FT: 13,000
SALES (est): 4.8MM **Privately Held**
WEB: www.unicelcorp.com
SIC: 3469 Honeycombed metal

(G-3945)
UNIVERSAL SHIELDING CORP
20 W Jefryn Blvd (11729-5769)
PHONE..................................631 667-7900
Irwin Newman, *Ch of Bd*
Michael Newman, *Vice Pres*
Michael Rance, *Manager*
EMP: 50
SQ FT: 20,000
SALES (est): 12.7MM **Privately Held**
WEB: www.universalshielding.com
SIC: 3448 3469 3444 Buildings, portable: prefabricated metal; metal stampings; sheet metalwork

(G-3946)
UNIVERSAL SIGNS AND SVC INC
435 Brook Ave Unit 2 (11729-6826)
PHONE..................................631 446-1121
Marcos Marmol, *President*
EMP: 27
SQ FT: 20,000
SALES (est): 3MM **Privately Held**
SIC: 3993 Signs, not made in custom sign painting shops

(G-3947)
UNLIMITED INDUSTRIES INC
44 W Jefryn Blvd Ste Q2 (11729-4721)
PHONE..................................631 665-5800
Joseph Leone, *President*
EMP: 8
SALES (est): 935.4K **Privately Held**
SIC: 3999 Manufacturing industries

(G-3948)
USA SIGNS OF AMERICA INC
172 E Industry Ct (11729-4706)
PHONE..................................631 254-6900
John Prahalis, *President*
Lynn Loder, *Vice Pres*
EMP: 75
SALES (est): 7.3MM **Privately Held**
WEB: www.usasignsofamerica.com
SIC: 3993 Signs & advertising specialties

(G-3949)
VEJA ELECTRONICS INC (PA)
Also Called: Stack Electronics
46 W Jefryn Blvd Ste A (11729-4736)
PHONE..................................631 321-6086
Steven Patsis, *CEO*
Steve Patsis, *President*
▲ EMP: 100
SQ FT: 40,000
SALES (est): 32.6MM **Privately Held**
WEB: www.stackny.com
SIC: 3644 5063 5065 Terminal boards; electrical fittings & construction materials; electronic parts

(G-3950)
VERSAPONENTS INC
Also Called: Writing Sculptures
66 N Industry Ct (11729-4602)
PHONE..................................631 242-3387
Chet Yaswen, *President*
Laura Yaswen, *Vice Pres*
EMP: 16
SQ FT: 4,500
SALES (est): 2.5MM **Privately Held**
SIC: 3646 Commercial indusl & institutional electric lighting fixtures

(G-3951)
VINYL MATERIALS INC
365 Bay Shore Rd (11729-7201)
PHONE..................................631 586-9444
Alex Folkman, *President*
Joseph Folkman, *Vice Pres*
Roop Narine Dhanrag, *Controller*
EMP: 50
SQ FT: 65,000

SALES (est): 8.2MM **Privately Held**
SIC: 3081 5162 3089 Vinyl film & sheet; plastics products; plastic processing

(G-3952)
VISUAL MILLWORK & FIX MFG INC
95 Marcus Blvd (11729-4501)
PHONE..................................718 267-7800
Mario Fichera Sr, *CEO*
Mario Fichera Jr, *Vice Pres*
Lydia Fichara, *CFO*
Roy White, *CFO*
EMP: 60
SQ FT: 50,000
SALES (est): 6.6MM **Privately Held**
WEB: www.visualdisplayinc.com
SIC: 2542 Office & store showcases & display fixtures

(G-3953)
WESTROCK RKT LLC
140 W Industry Ct (11729-4604)
PHONE..................................631 586-6000
Ron Byers, *General Mgr*
EMP: 130
SQ FT: 120,000
SALES (corp-wide): 16.2B **Publicly Held**
WEB: www.rocktenn.com
SIC: 2653 5113 Boxes, corrugated: made from purchased materials; bags, paper & disposable plastic
HQ: Westrock Rkt, Llc
    1000 Abernathy Rd Ste 125
    Atlanta GA 30328
    770 448-2193

(G-3954)
WOLF X-RAY CORPORATION
100 W Industry Ct (11729-4604)
PHONE..................................631 242-9729
Martin Wolf, *President*
Hugo Burbano, *Purchasing*
◆ **EMP:** 60 **EST:** 1931
SQ FT: 80,000
SALES (est): 10.2MM **Privately Held**
WEB: www.wolfxray.com
SIC: 3844 X-ray apparatus & tubes

(G-3955)
WOLO MFG CORP
1 Saxwood St Ste 1 # 1 (11729-4779)
PHONE..................................631 242-0333
Stanley Solow, *President*
◆ **EMP:** 21
SQ FT: 10,000
SALES (est): 4.1MM **Privately Held**
SIC: 3429 3714 3647 Motor vehicle hardware; motor vehicle parts & accessories; vehicular lighting equipment

(G-3956)
WORLD LLC
Also Called: Wmw Machinery Company
513 Acorn St Ste B (11729-3611)
PHONE..................................631 940-9121
Cornel Circiumaru, *Mng Member*
▼ **EMP:** 15
SQ FT: 8,000
SALES: 1.5MM **Privately Held**
SIC: 3541 Machine tools, metal cutting type

(G-3957)
ZACMEL GRAPHICS LLC
500 Brook Ave Ste B (11729-6835)
PHONE..................................631 944-6031
David Warheit,
EMP: 7 **EST:** 2003
SALES (est): 1MM **Privately Held**
SIC: 2752 7336 Commercial printing, offset; commercial art & graphic design

Delanson
Schenectady County

(G-3958)
BENZSAY & HARRISON INC
Railroad Ave (12053)
P.O. Box 272 (12053-0272)
PHONE..................................518 895-2311
Rudolph Benzsay, *President*
Sema Benzsay, *Admin Sec*

EMP: 6
SQ FT: 25,000
SALES: 900.1K **Privately Held**
WEB: www.bh-inc.com
SIC: 2819 Aluminum compounds

(G-3959)
ELECTRCAL INSTRUMENTATION CTRL
1253 Youngs Rd (12053-1711)
P.O. Box 24, Duanesburg (12056-0024)
PHONE..................................518 861-5789
Michael Weiss, *President*
EMP: 11
SALES: 2MM **Privately Held**
SIC: 3823 Industrial process control instruments

(G-3960)
HARVEST HOMES INC
1331 Cole Rd (12053-3109)
PHONE..................................518 895-2341
Timothy O Brien, *Ch of Bd*
Henry Walthery, *General Mgr*
Robert A Guay, *Vice Pres*
Don Smith, *Regl Sales Mgr*
Gary Shufelt, *Info Tech Mgr*
EMP: 35
SQ FT: 27,000
SALES: 4.5MM **Privately Held**
SIC: 2452 2439 Panels & sections, prefabricated, wood; structural wood members

Delevan
Cattaraugus County

(G-3961)
HALEY CONCRETE INC (PA)
10413 Delevan Elton Rd (14042-9613)
PHONE..................................716 492-0849
Lawrence Haley II, *President*
Lawrence Haley III, *Admin Sec*
EMP: 15
SQ FT: 1,250
SALES (est): 2MM **Privately Held**
SIC: 3273 4212 Ready-mixed concrete; local trucking, without storage

(G-3962)
KENDOR MUSIC INC
21 Grove St (14042-9682)
P.O. Box 278 (14042-0278)
PHONE..................................716 492-1254
Craig Cornwall, *President*
Jackie Cornwall, *Finance Mgr*
EMP: 12
SQ FT: 10,000
SALES (est): 1MM **Privately Held**
WEB: www.kendormusic.com
SIC: 2741 Music, sheet: publishing & printing

Delhi
Delaware County

(G-3963)
DELAWARE COUNTY TIMES INC
56 Main St (13753-1121)
PHONE..................................607 746-2176
Donald F Bishop II, *President*
Thomas Shaffer, *Manager*
EMP: 6
SALES (est): 468.8K **Privately Held**
SIC: 2711 2721 Newspapers: publishing only, not printed on site; periodicals

(G-3964)
EXCELSIOR PUBLICATIONS
133 Main St (13753-1219)
PHONE..................................607 746-7600
Francis P Ruggiero, *President*
EMP: 5 **EST:** 1999
SALES (est): 479.5K **Privately Held**
SIC: 2721 Magazines: publishing & printing

(G-3965)
FRIESLNDCMPINA INGRDNTS N AMER
40196 State Hwy 10 Delhi (13753)
PHONE..................................607 746-0196
Don Combs, *Principal*
EMP: 35
SALES (corp-wide): 13.2B **Privately Held**
SIC: 2023 Baby formulas
HQ: Frieslandcampina Ingredients North America, Inc
    61 S Paramus Rd Ste 535
    Paramus NJ 07652
    201 655-7780

(G-3966)
SAPUTO DAIRY FOODS USA LLC
Also Called: Morningstar Foods
40236 State Highway 10 (13753-3207)
P.O. Box 1 (13753-0001)
PHONE..................................607 746-2141
Elizabeth Banburen, *Manager*
EMP: 100
SALES (corp-wide): 3.7B **Privately Held**
WEB: www.morningstarfoods.com
SIC: 2026 Milk processing (pasteurizing, homogenizing, bottling)
HQ: Saputo Dairy Foods Usa, Llc
    2711 N Haske Ave Ste 3700
    Dallas TX 75204
    214 863-2300

(G-3967)
SPORTSFIELD SPECIALTIES INC (PA)
Also Called: Promats Athletics
41155 State Highway 10 (13753-3213)
P.O. Box 231 (13753-0231)
PHONE..................................607 746-8911
Wayne Oliver, *President*
Alex Fletcher, *Regional Mgr*
Michael Mercadante, *Regional Mgr*
Ed Rosa, *Vice Pres*
Edward Rosa, *Vice Pres*
EMP: 45
SQ FT: 46,000
SALES (est): 10.8MM **Privately Held**
WEB: www.sportsfieldspecialties.com
SIC: 3949 Sporting & athletic goods

Delmar
Albany County

(G-3968)
COMMUNITY MEDIA GROUP LLC (PA)
Also Called: Spotlight Newspaper
125 Adams St (12054-3211)
PHONE..................................518 439-4949
Bill Decker, *Consultant*
John A McIntyre Jr,
David B Tyler Jr,
EMP: 7
SALES (est): 1.9MM **Privately Held**
SIC: 2711 Newspapers, publishing & printing

(G-3969)
SANZDRANZ LLC (PA)
Also Called: Gatherer's Gourmet Granola
83 Dumbarton Dr (12054-4418)
PHONE..................................518 894-8625
Sandro Gerbini, *President*
EMP: 5 **EST:** 2010
SQ FT: 3,700
SALES (est): 231K **Privately Held**
SIC: 2043 Cereal breakfast foods

Depew
Erie County

(G-3970)
AUBURN-WATSON CORP (PA)
3295 Walden Ave (14043-2313)
PHONE..................................716 876-8000
Wayne Watson, *President*
Natalie Watson, *Vice Pres*
EMP: 10 **EST:** 1946
SQ FT: 8,000

SALES (est): 1.2MM **Privately Held**
SIC: 2434 1751 Wood kitchen cabinets; cabinet building & installation

(G-3971)
BISON STEEL INCORPORATED
2 Main St Ste 103 (14043-3323)
P.O. Box 454 (14043-0454)
PHONE..................................716 683-0900
Edwin C Bailey, *President*
Gus Schiralli, *Admin Sec*
▲ **EMP:** 5
SQ FT: 27,000
SALES (est): 786.2K **Privately Held**
SIC: 3496 Miscellaneous fabricated wire products

(G-3972)
BMG SYSTEMS
4779 Transit Rd 169 (14043-4915)
P.O. Box 1307, Orchard Park (14127-8307)
PHONE..................................716 432-5160
EMP: 14
SALES (est): 2.5MM **Privately Held**
SIC: 3444 Sheet metalwork

(G-3973)
BUFFALO ENVELOPE INC
Also Called: Buffalo Envelope Company
2914 Walden Ave Ste 300 (14043-2694)
PHONE..................................716 686-0100
Dany Paradis, *Principal*
Sandy Morley, *COO*
EMP: 12
SQ FT: 12,800
SALES (est): 2.8MM
SALES (corp-wide): 147.9MM **Privately Held**
SIC: 2677 5112 Envelopes; envelopes
PA: Supremex Inc
    7213 Rue Cordner
    Lasalle QC H8N 2
    514 595-0555

(G-3974)
BUFFALO POWER ELECTRONICS CTR
166 Taylor Dr Ste 1 (14043-2021)
PHONE..................................716 651-1600
William Gates, *Ch of Bd*
Dennis M Cascio, *President*
Frank Stasio, *Vice Pres*
EMP: 15
SQ FT: 38,000
SALES (est): 4.9MM **Privately Held**
WEB: www.buffalopower.com
SIC: 3612 5065 Transformers, except electric; transformers, electronic

(G-3975)
BUFFALO TUNGSTEN INC
Also Called: Bti
2 Main St (14043-3323)
P.O. Box 397 (14043-0397)
PHONE..................................716 683-9170
Ralph V Showalter, *Ch of Bd*
Jeffrey Showalter, *Engineer*
Travis Showalter, *Accounting Mgr*
Diane Shopwalter, *Admin Sec*
◆ **EMP:** 60
SQ FT: 500,000
SALES (est): 17.6MM **Privately Held**
WEB: www.buffalotungsten.com
SIC: 3399 2819 Powder, metal; tungsten carbide powder, except abrasive or metallurgical

(G-3976)
CASCADES NEW YORK INC
3241 Walden Ave (14043-2848)
PHONE..................................716 681-1560
Tom Derkovitz, *Manager*
EMP: 25
SALES (corp-wide): 3.5B **Privately Held**
WEB: www.metrowaste.com
SIC: 2621 Paper mills
HQ: Cascades New York Inc.
    1845 Emerson St
    Rochester NY 14606
    585 527-8110

(G-3977)
CUSTOM COUNTERTOPS INC (PA)
3192 Walden Ave (14043-2846)
PHONE..................................716 685-2871

Gloria Marino, *President*
EMP: 8
SALES: 750K **Privately Held**
WEB: www.custmcounter tops.com
SIC: 3131 2541 Counters; wood partitions & fixtures

(G-3978)
D R M MANAGEMENT INC (PA)
Also Called: Fresh Bake Pizza Co
3430 Transit Rd (14043-4853)
PHONE................................716 668-0333
Ronald Digiore, *President*
Daniel J Digiore, *Vice Pres*
Mark Digiore, *Admin Sec*
EMP: 48
SQ FT: 1,200
SALES (est): 5.4MM **Privately Held**
WEB: www.drminc.us
SIC: 2038 8741 2099 Pizza, frozen; restaurant management; pizza, refrigerated: except frozen

(G-3979)
DESU MACHINERY CORPORATION
200 Gould Ave (14043-3134)
P.O. Box 245 (14043-0245)
PHONE................................716 681-5798
Martin W Golden II, *CEO*
Mark L Dalquist, *President*
Thomas Depczynski, *Sls & Mktg Exec*
EMP: 85
SALES (est): 8MM **Privately Held**
SIC: 3556 3565 Packing house machinery; bottling machinery: filling, capping, labeling

(G-3980)
ELMAR INDUSTRIES INC
200 Gould Ave (14043-3138)
P.O. Box 245 (14043-0245)
PHONE................................716 681-5650
Martin W Golden II, *Ch of Bd*
Mark L Dahlquist, *Ch of Bd*
David Zolnowski, *Purch Mgr*
Mark Vaughn, *Engineer*
Tom Depczynski, *Marketing Mgr*
▲ **EMP:** 62
SQ FT: 21,000
SALES (est): 19.2MM **Privately Held**
WEB: www.elmarworldwide.com
SIC: 3565 Packaging machinery

(G-3981)
FIBRIX LLC
Buffalo Batt A Div of Polyeste
3307 Walden Ave (14043-2347)
PHONE................................716 683-4100
Bob Heilman, *Manager*
EMP: 50
SQ FT: 43,000
SALES (corp-wide): 74MM **Privately Held**
WEB: www.leggett.com
SIC: 2299 2824 2221 Batting, wadding, padding & fillings; pillow fillings: curled hair, cotton waste, moss, hemp tow; organic fibers, noncellulosic; broadwoven fabric mills, manmade
HQ: Fibrix, Llc
1820 Evans St Ne
Conover NC 28613

(G-3982)
FLADO ENTERPRISES INC
Also Called: Quality Quick Signs
1380 French Rd Ste 6 (14043-4800)
PHONE................................716 668-6400
Christopher R Flejtuch, *President*
EMP: 7
SQ FT: 7,000
SALES (est): 794.3K **Privately Held**
WEB: www.qualityquicksigns.com
SIC: 3993 Signs, not made in custom sign painting shops

(G-3983)
FRUIT FRESH UP INC
2928 Walden Ave Ste 2 (14043-2615)
PHONE................................716 683-3200
Ronald J Santora, *President*
Michael Grabowski, *Prdtn Mgr*
EMP: 35
SQ FT: 10,000

SALES (est): 6MM **Privately Held**
WEB: www.fruitfreshup.com
SIC: 2015 2499 2064 Egg processing; picture & mirror frames, wood; candy & other confectionery products

(G-3984)
HARPER INTERNATIONAL CORP
99 Sheldon Ave (14043-3532)
PHONE................................716 276-9900
Charles Miller, *President*
EMP: 6
SALES (est): 779.4K **Privately Held**
SIC: 3567 Industrial furnaces & ovens

(G-3985)
HOWDEN NORTH AMERICA INC (PA)
Also Called: Howdens
2475 George Urban Blvd # 120 (14043-2022)
PHONE................................330 867-8540
Matthew Ingle, *CEO*
Karl Kimmerling, *President*
Will Samuel, *Chairman*
Tara V Norman, *IT/INT Sup*
◆ **EMP:** 85 **EST:** 1980
SALES (est): 224.5MM **Privately Held**
WEB: www.howdenbuffalo.com
SIC: 3564 3568 Exhaust fans: industrial or commercial; couplings, shaft: rigid, flexible, universal joint, etc.

(G-3986)
LEGNO VENETO USA
3283 Walden Ave (14043-2311)
PHONE................................716 651-9169
James Carol II, *Owner*
James Caroll, *Owner*
▲ **EMP:** 9
SQ FT: 26,000
SALES (est): 1MM **Privately Held**
WEB: www.lvwoodfloors.com
SIC: 2426 Flooring, hardwood

(G-3987)
LEICA MICROSYSTEMS INC
Also Called: Opd
3362 Walden Ave (14043-2475)
P.O. Box 123, Cragsmoor (12420-0123)
PHONE................................716 686-3000
John Burgess, *Branch Mgr*
Tom Tonner, *Manager*
EMP: 8
SALES (corp-wide): 19.8B **Publicly Held**
SIC: 3827 Optical instruments & apparatus; microscopes, except electron, proton & corneal
HQ: Leica Microsystems Inc.
1700 Leider Ln
Buffalo Grove IL 60089
847 405-0123

(G-3988)
MOLDCRAFT INC
240 Gould Ave (14043-3130)
PHONE................................716 684-1126
John Chase, *President*
Henry Lewandowski, *Treasurer*
Sharon Winkler, *Office Mgr*
Jimmy Gray, *Admin Sec*
EMP: 20
SQ FT: 8,000
SALES: 3.8MM **Privately Held**
WEB: www.moldcraftinc.com
SIC: 3544 Forms (molds), for foundry & plastics working machinery

(G-3989)
NIAGARA REFINING LLC
5661 Transit Rd (14043-3227)
P.O. Box 398 (14043-0398)
PHONE................................716 706-1400
▲ **EMP:** 27
SALES (est): 7.9MM **Privately Held**
SIC: 2819 Tungsten carbide powder, except abrasive or metallurgical

(G-3990)
NORTHEAST METROLOGY CORP
4490 Broadway (14043-2904)
PHONE................................716 827-3770
Basil Korbut, *President*
EMP: 10
SQ FT: 6,120

SALES (est): 2MM **Privately Held**
WEB: www.vantek-nem.com
SIC: 3825 8734 Test equipment for electronic & electric measurement; testing laboratories

(G-3991)
OSMOSE HOLDINGS INC
2475 George Urban Blvd (14043-2022)
PHONE................................716 882-5905
James R Spengler Jr, *President*
Laura A Podkulski, *Admin Sec*
◆ **EMP:** 1335
SALES (est): 187.4MM
SALES (corp-wide): 43B **Publicly Held**
WEB: www.fireretardanttreatedwood.com
SIC: 2491 Preserving (creosoting) of wood
HQ: Oaktree Capital Management, L.P.
333 S Grand Ave Ste 2800
Los Angeles CA 90071

(G-3992)
PCB GROUP INC
Also Called: ICP
3425 Walden Ave (14043-2417)
PHONE................................716 684-0001
Mike Lally, *CEO*
James F Lally, *Ch of Bd*
John Betzig, *Opers Mgr*
Larry Dick, *Opers Mgr*
Brandon Jones, *Purch Mgr*
EMP: 50
SQ FT: 64,000
SALES (est): 124.4MM
SALES (corp-wide): 778MM **Publicly Held**
SIC: 3679 3823 Transducers, electrical; industrial instrmnts msrmnt display/control process variable
PA: Mts Systems Corporation
14000 Technology Dr
Eden Prairie MN 55344
952 937-4000

(G-3993)
PCB PIEZOTRONICS INC
Larson Davis
3425 Walden Ave (14043-2495)
PHONE................................716 684-0001
Chris Rasmussen, *Buyer*
Jeff Williams, *Sales Staff*
EMP: 10
SALES (corp-wide): 778MM **Publicly Held**
SIC: 3829 Measuring & controlling devices
HQ: Pcb Piezotronics, Inc.
3425 Walden Ave
Depew NY 14043
716 684-0001

(G-3994)
PCB PIEZOTRONICS INC
Industrl Mntrng Instrmntatn Dv
3425 Walden Ave (14043-2495)
PHONE................................716 684-0003
Erick Yax, *Manager*
EMP: 400
SALES (corp-wide): 778MM **Publicly Held**
WEB: www.pcb.com
SIC: 3679 5063 Electronic circuits; electrical apparatus & equipment
HQ: Pcb Piezotronics, Inc.
3425 Walden Ave
Depew NY 14043
716 684-0001

(G-3995)
QMC TECHNOLOGIES INC
4388 Broadway (14043-2998)
PHONE................................716 681-0810
James A Serafin, *President*
Rachael S Serafin, *General Mgr*
Bob Serafin, *Vice Pres*
Cathy Wawrzyniak, *Bookkeeper*
▲ **EMP:** 16
SQ FT: 5,500
SALES (est): 4.8MM **Privately Held**
WEB: www.qmctechnologies.com
SIC: 3599 Machine shop, jobbing & repair

(G-3996)
REICHERT INC
Also Called: Reichert Technologies
3362 Walden Ave Ste 100 (14043-2437)
PHONE................................716 686-4500

Bruce Wilson, *Ch of Bd*
Timothy Levindofske, *President*
Ralph Nicosia, *President*
Karen Garbacz, *General Mgr*
Jerry C Cirino, *Vice Pres*
▲ **EMP:** 147
SQ FT: 48,000
SALES (est): 46.4MM
SALES (corp-wide): 4.8B **Publicly Held**
WEB: www.leicams.com
SIC: 3841 Surgical & medical instruments
PA: Ametek, Inc.
1100 Cassatt Rd
Berwyn PA 19312
610 647-2121

(G-3997)
RMF PRINT MANAGEMENT GROUP
786 Terrace Blvd Ste 3 (14043-3729)
P.O. Box 329, Lancaster (14086-0329)
PHONE................................716 683-4351
Tony Cirelli, *VP Sales*
Sharon Doherty, *Manager*
EMP: 13
SALES (est): 1.7MM **Privately Held**
SIC: 2752 Commercial printing, offset

Deposit
Broome County

(G-3998)
CANNONSVILLE LUMBER INC
199 Old Route 10 (13754-2100)
PHONE................................607 467-3380
Adolf Schaffer Jr, *President*
EMP: 5 **EST:** 1998
SALES (est): 695.9K **Privately Held**
SIC: 2421 Sawmills & planing mills, general
PA: Schaefer Enterprises Of Deposit, Inc.
315 Old Route 10
Deposit NY 13754

(G-3999)
COURIER PRINTING CORP
24 Laurel Bank Ave Ste 2 (13754-1244)
PHONE................................607 467-2191
Hilton Evans, *President*
Sarah Evans, *Admin Sec*
EMP: 30 **EST:** 1848
SQ FT: 55,000
SALES: 1.8MM **Privately Held**
WEB: www.courierprintingcorp.com
SIC: 2752 Commercial printing, offset

(G-4000)
INTEGRATED WOOD COMPONENTS INC
Also Called: Iwci
791 Airport Rd (13754-1277)
P.O. Box 145 (13754-0145)
PHONE................................607 467-1739
John Kamp, *President*
Tom Stobert, *Corp Secy*
Gerard Kamp, *Vice Pres*
Cork Faulkner, *Accounts Exec*
Charlie Hopkins, *Accounts Exec*
EMP: 49
SQ FT: 2,800
SALES (est): 5.8MM **Privately Held**
SIC: 2541 Wood partitions & fixtures

(G-4001)
SANFORD STONE LLC
185 Latham Rd (13754-1271)
P.O. Box 313 (13754-0313)
PHONE................................607 467 1313
George W Sanford,
EMP: 21
SALES (est): 2.5MM **Privately Held**
SIC: 3281 Cut stone & stone products

(G-4002)
SCHAEFER ENTPS DEPOSIT INC (PA)
315 Old Route 10 (13754-2106)
PHONE................................607 467-4990
Larry Schaefer, *President*
EMP: 30
SALES (est): 7.6MM **Privately Held**
SIC: 1422 Cement rock, crushed & broken-quarrying

(G-4003)
SCHAEFER LOGGING INC
315 Old Route 10 (13754-2106)
PHONE....................................607 467-4990
Larry Schaefer, *President*
EMP: 10
SALES (est): 1MM **Privately Held**
SIC: 2411 5411 Logging; convenience
stores
PA: Schaefer Enterprises Of Deposit, Inc.
315 Old Route 10
Deposit NY 13754

(G-4004)
WALTER R TUCKER ENTPS LTD
Also Called: E-Z Red Co
8 Leonard Way (13754-1240)
P.O. Box 80 (13754-0080)
PHONE....................................607 467-2866
Mark Tucker, *President*
Bob Cacciabeve, *Exec VP*
▲ EMP: 25 EST: 1966
SQ FT: 13,000
SALES (est): 6.1MM **Privately Held**
WEB: www.ezred.com
SIC: 3825 3824 3991 3629 Battery
testers, electrical; test equipment for elec-
tronic & electric measurement; liquid me-
ters; brushes, except paint & varnish;
battery chargers, rectifying or nonrotating;
motor vehicle supplies & new parts; test-
ing equipment, electrical: automotive

Derby
Erie County

(G-4005)
GREYLINE SIGNS INC
6681 Schuyler Dr (14047-9644)
PHONE....................................716 947-4526
Linda Scritchfield, *President*
Everett Scritchfield, *Vice Pres*
EMP: 5
SALES (est): 430K **Privately Held**
SIC: 3993 Signs & advertising specialties

(G-4006)
NEW ERA CAP CO INC
8061 Erie Rd (14047-9503)
PHONE....................................716 549-0445
Eileen Beiter, *COO*
EMP: 10
SALES (corp-wide): 606.1MM **Privately
Held**
SIC: 2353 Uniform hats & caps; baseball
caps
PA: New Era Cap Co., Inc.
160 Delaware Ave
Buffalo NY 14202
716 604-9000

Dexter
Jefferson County

(G-4007)
**VENUS MANUFACTURING CO
INC (PA)**
349 Lakeview Dr (13634)
P.O. Box 551 (13634-0551)
PHONE....................................315 639-3100
Roger Reifensnyder, *CEO*
Michael J Hennegan, *President*
▲ EMP: 90
SQ FT: 14,000
SALES (est): 6.2MM **Privately Held**
WEB: www.venusswimwear.com
SIC: 2339 Bathing suits: women's, misses'
& juniors'

Dix Hills
Suffolk County

(G-4008)
A & D TOOL INC
30 Pashen Pl (11746-6600)
PHONE....................................631 243-4339
Dimitrios Margiellos, *President*
Tatiana Labate, *Corp Secy*

EMP: 7
SALES: 360K **Privately Held**
WEB: www.adtool.com
SIC: 3544 Forms (molds), for foundry &
plastics working machinery

(G-4009)
ALTERNATIVES FOR CHILDREN
600 S Service Rd (11746-6015)
PHONE....................................631 271-0777
Vivienne Viera, *Director*
EMP: 31
SALES (corp-wide): 17.4MM **Privately
Held**
SIC: 3949 Windsurfing boards (sailboards)
& equipment
PA: Alternatives For Children
14 Research Way
East Setauket NY 11733
631 331-6400

(G-4010)
**AUTHORITY TRANSPORTATION
INC**
Also Called: Authority On Transportation
167 Oakfield Ave (11746-6327)
PHONE....................................888 933-1268
Jinya Kato, *Principal*
David Lipsky, *Principal*
EMP: 12
SQ FT: 40,000
SALES (est): 1MM **Privately Held**
SIC: 3716 Motor homes

(G-4011)
MAYFLOWER SPLINT CO
16 Arbor Ln (11746-5127)
P.O. Box 381, Huntington Station (11746-
0309)
PHONE....................................631 549-5131
Inge Krueger, *Owner*
EMP: 25
SALES (est): 1.6MM **Privately Held**
SIC: 3842 Surgical appliances & supplies

(G-4012)
MCG GRAPHICS INC
101 Village Hill Dr (11746-8335)
PHONE....................................631 499-0730
Michael Goldsmith, *President*
EMP: 6
SQ FT: 800
SALES (est): 747.1K **Privately Held**
SIC: 2752 2754 Commercial printing, litho-
graphic; commercial printing, gravure

(G-4013)
**PREMIERE LIVING PRODUCTS
LLC**
22 Branwood Dr (11746-5710)
PHONE....................................631 873-4337
Sandy Cohen, *Mng Member*
◆ EMP: 10
SALES (est): 524.9K **Privately Held**
SIC: 2511 Storage chests, household:
wood

(G-4014)
PRINTING X PRESS IONS
5 Dix Cir (11746-6033)
PHONE....................................631 242-1992
EMP: 7
SALES: 1.5MM **Privately Held**
SIC: 2752 Lithographic Commercial Print-
ing

(G-4015)
SENTRY DEVICES CORP
33 Rustic Gate Ln (11746-6136)
PHONE....................................631 491-3191
Alex Feibush, *President*
EMP: 5
SALES (est): 400K **Privately Held**
SIC: 3669 1731 Burglar alarm apparatus,
electric; marine horns, electric; fire detec-
tion & burglar alarm systems specializa-
tion

(G-4016)
TREBOR INSTRUMENT CORP
39 Balsam Dr (11746-7724)
PHONE....................................631 423-7026
Zygmunt Grzesiak, *President*
EMP: 8
SQ FT: 2,200

SALES (est): 855.5K **Privately Held**
WEB: www.treborinst.com
SIC: 3599 Machine shop, jobbing & repair

(G-4017)
**YING KE YOUTH AGE GROUP
INC**
1 Campbell Dr (11746-7901)
PHONE....................................929 402-8458
Mark Bestercy, *Vice Pres*
EMP: 12
SALES (est): 241.2K **Privately Held**
SIC: 3751 5137 5065 Motor scooters &
parts; women's & children's clothing; elec-
tronic parts & equipment

Dobbs Ferry
Westchester County

(G-4018)
**NOURYON SURFACE
CHEMISTRY**
Also Called: Akzo Nobel Central Research
7 Livingstone Ave (10522-3401)
PHONE....................................914 674-5008
G Thompson, *Branch Mgr*
EMP: 250
SALES (corp-wide): 1.4B **Privately Held**
WEB: www.akzo-nobel.com
SIC: 2819 8731 2899 Industrial inorganic
chemicals; commercial physical research;
chemical preparations
HQ: Nouryon Surface Chemistry
525 W Van Buren St # 1600
Chicago IL 60607
312 544-7000

(G-4019)
REMBAR COMPANY LLC
67 Main St (10522-2152)
P.O. Box 67 (10522-0067)
PHONE....................................914 693-2620
Frank H Firor, *CEO*
Walter Pastor, *President*
Gertrude Donnelly, *Vice Pres*
Audra Haase, *Vice Pres*
▼ EMP: 23
SQ FT: 8,000
SALES (est): 3.1MM **Privately Held**
WEB: www.rembar.com
SIC: 3297 3399 Nonclay refractories;
metal powders, pastes & flakes

(G-4020)
SUN SCIENTIFIC INC
145 Palisade St (10522-1617)
PHONE....................................914 479-5108
Sundram Ravikumar, *President*
Shridhar Shanmugam, *COO*
David Hildenbrand, *Vice Pres*
Arti Ravikumar, *Vice Pres*
Vikram Ravikumar, *Planning*
EMP: 7
SQ FT: 1,500
SALES (est): 660.8K **Privately Held**
SIC: 3845 Electromedical equipment

(G-4021)
W H WHITE PUBLICATIONS INC
Also Called: Rivertowns Enterprise
95 Main St (10522-1673)
PHONE....................................914 725-2500
Deborah White, *President*
EMP: 8 EST: 1981
SALES (est): 368.9K **Privately Held**
SIC: 2711 Newspapers, publishing & print-
ing

Dolgeville
Herkimer County

(G-4022)
**GEHRING TRICOT
CORPORATION (PA)**
Also Called: Gehring Textiles
68 Ransom St (13329-1461)
P.O. Box 272 (13329-0272)
PHONE....................................315 429-8551
George G Gehring Jr, *President*
Brenda Gehring, *Principal*

Marie Bevilaqua, *Vice Pres*
William Christmann, *Vice Pres*
Paul Gutowski, *Vice Pres*
▲ EMP: 71 EST: 1952
SQ FT: 50,000
SALES (est): 64MM **Privately Held**
SIC: 2258 2262 Dyeing & finishing lace
goods & warp knit fabric; tricot fabrics; fin-
ishing plants, manmade fiber & silk fab-
rics

(G-4023)
**GEHRING TRICOT
CORPORATION**
68 Ransom St Ste 272 (13329-1461)
PHONE....................................315 429-8551
Robert Lumley, *Vice Pres*
Ray Moissonnier, *QC Dir*
Paul Gutowski, *Controller*
Richard Patrick, *Data Proc Dir*
EMP: 125
SALES (corp-wide): 64MM **Privately
Held**
SIC: 2257 2258 Dyeing & finishing circular
knit fabrics; warp & flat knit products
PA: Gehring Tricot Corporation
68 Ransom St
Dolgeville NY 13329
315 429-8551

(G-4024)
**NORTH HUDSON WOODCRAFT
CORP**
152 N Helmer Ave (13329-2826)
P.O. Box 192 (13329-0192)
PHONE....................................315 429-3105
Jeffrey C Slifka, *Ch of Bd*
William Slifka, *Treasurer*
Michael Jorrey, *Controller*
EMP: 50 EST: 1871
SQ FT: 100,000
SALES (est): 7.4MM **Privately Held**
WEB: www.northhudsonwoodcraft.com
SIC: 2426 3995 Furniture dimension
stock, hardwood; burial caskets

(G-4025)
**RAWLINGS SPORTING GOODS
CO INC**
Also Called: Adirondack Rawlings
52 Mckinley Ave (13329-1139)
PHONE....................................315 429-8511
Ronald Van Dergroef, *Principal*
Kevin Griffin, *Purch Agent*
Robert Johnson, *Engineer*
EMP: 52
SQ FT: 62,884
SALES (corp-wide): 74.3MM **Privately
Held**
SIC: 3949 Sporting & athletic goods
HQ: Rawlings Sporting Goods Company,
Inc.
510 Maryville University
Saint Louis MO 63141

(G-4026)
REAL DESIGN INC
187 S Main St (13329-1455)
PHONE....................................315 429-3071
Sam Camardello, *President*
EMP: 10
SALES: 400K **Privately Held**
WEB: www.realdesigninc.com
SIC: 3429 Furniture hardware

(G-4027)
TUMBLE FORMS INC (PA)
1013 Barker Rd (13329-2401)
P.O. Box 266 (13329-0266)
PHONE....................................315 429-3101
Dave Faulchner, *General Mgr*
EMP: 132
SQ FT: 25,200
SALES (est): 13.2MM **Privately Held**
SIC: 3842 Surgical appliances & supplies

Douglaston
Queens County

(G-4028)
SALVADOR COLLETTI BLANK
25141 Van Zandt Ave (11362-1735)
PHONE....................................718 217-6725

Salvador Colletti, *Principal*
EMP: 5
SALES (est) 240.9K **Privately Held**
SIC: 2099 Food preparations

(G-4029)
SPRINGFIELD CONTROL SYSTEMS
4056 Douglaston Pkwy (11363-1507)
PHONE..............................718 631-0870
William Boettjer, *President*
EMP: 8
SALES (est): 680K **Privately Held**
SIC: 3823 Temperature measurement instruments, industrial

(G-4030)
TAMKA SPORT LLC
225 Beverly Rd (11363-1122)
PHONE..............................718 224-7820
Kathleen Derienzo, *Mng Member*
EMP: 8
SALES: 90K **Privately Held**
SIC: 2329 2339 Men's & boys' athletic uniforms; uniforms, athletic: women's, misses' & juniors'

Dover Plains
Dutchess County

(G-4031)
CENTRAL DOVER DEVELOPMENT
247 Dover Furnace Rd (12522-5773)
PHONE..............................917 709-3266
Wayne Tanner, *President*
Elaine Tanner, *Vice Pres*
EMP: 4
SALES: 1MM **Privately Held**
SIC: 1442 0191 Gravel mining; general farms, primarily crop

(G-4032)
J & J LOG & LUMBER CORP
528 Old State Route 22 (12522-5821)
P.O. Box 1139 (12522-1139)
PHONE..............................845 832-6535
Randolph L Williams, *CEO*
◆ **EMP:** 80
SQ FT: 10,200
SALES (est): 15.6MM **Privately Held**
SIC: 2421 2426 Sawmills & planing mills, general; hardwood dimension & flooring mills

(G-4033)
PALUMBO BLOCK CO INC
365 Dover Furnace Rd (12522-5775)
P.O. Box 810 (12522-0810)
PHONE..............................845 832-6100
Fortunato Palumbo, *President*
Anthony Palumbo, *Vice Pres*
Mary Palumbo, *Vice Pres*
Tony Palumbo, *Vice Pres*
Mary Palumbo Sprong, *Vice Pres*
EMP: 25
SQ FT: 28,000
SALES (est): 4.6MM **Privately Held**
SIC: 3271 5082 5211 Blocks, concrete or cinder: standard; masonry equipment & supplies; masonry materials & supplies

Dresden
Yates County

(G-4034)
ABTEX CORPORATION
89 Main St (14441-9708)
P.O. Box 188 (14441-0188)
PHONE..............................315 536-7403
D Mark Fultz, *President*
Christian Donovan, *Opers Mgr*
Lyle Adler, *Controller*
Steve Gleason, *Sales Associate*
John Roman, *Manager*
EMP: 21
SQ FT: 20,000

SALES (est): 4.4MM **Privately Held**
WEB: www.abtex.com
SIC: 3991 3541 Brushes, household or industrial; machine tools, metal cutting type

(G-4035)
FAULKNER TRUSS COMPANY INC
1830 King Hill Rd (14441)
P.O. Box 407, Hammondsport (14840-0407)
PHONE..............................315 536-8894
Richard C Faulkner, *Ch of Bd*
EMP: 5
SALES (est): 573.2K **Privately Held**
SIC: 2439 Trusses, wooden roof

Dryden
Tompkins County

(G-4036)
AMISH STRUCTURE
32 North St (13053-8514)
P.O. Box 2 (13053-0002)
PHONE..............................607 257-1070
Virginia Jordan, *Partner*
Christoper Jordan, *Partner*
EMP: 10
SALES (est): 1.1MM **Privately Held**
SIC: 2421 Outdoor wood structural products

(G-4037)
BAGELOVERS INC
42 Elm St (13053-9623)
P.O. Box 62 (13053-0062)
PHONE..............................607 844-3683
Charles Tallman, *President*
Gary Westphal, *Vice Pres*
EMP: 18
SQ FT: 12,500
SALES (est): 2.4MM **Privately Held**
SIC: 2051 5142 Bagels, fresh or frozen; packaged frozen goods

(G-4038)
HENRY NEWMAN LLC
Also Called: Ithaca Ice Company, The
39 Elm St Rear Bldg (13053)
P.O. Box 333, Ithaca (14851-0333)
PHONE..............................607 273-8512
Henry Newman, *Owner*
Charles Everhart, *Principal*
EMP: 10
SQ FT: 4,800
SALES (est): 284.7K **Privately Held**
SIC: 2097 5999 Ice cubes; ice

(G-4039)
INTEGRATED WATER MANAGEMENT
Also Called: I W M
289 Cortland Rd (13053-9517)
P.O. Box 523 (13053-0523)
PHONE..............................607 844-4276
David Duffett, *President*
▲ **EMP:** 5
SQ FT: 3,700
SALES (est): 1MM **Privately Held**
SIC: 3589 Water treatment equipment, industrial

(G-4040)
ROSCOE BROTHERS INC
15 Freeville Rd (13053-9537)
PHONE..............................607 844-3750
Chris Roscoe, *President*
Nick Roscoe, *Vice Pres*
EMP: 13 **EST:** 2014
SALES: 1MM **Privately Held**
SIC: 2452 7389 Prefabricated buildings, wood;

(G-4041)
STURGES ELEC PDTS CO INC
Also Called: Sepco-Sturges Electronics
23 North St (13053)
P.O. Box 532 (13053-0532)
PHONE..............................607 844-8604
James Koch, *President*
EMP: 45
SQ FT: 15,000

SALES (est): 6.2MM **Privately Held**
WEB: www.sturgeselectronics.com
SIC: 3679 Harness assemblies for electronic use: wire or cable

(G-4042)
STURGES ELECTRONICS LLC
23 North St (13053)
P.O. Box 532 (13053-0532)
PHONE..............................607 844-8604
Gary Nelson, *President*
EMP: 16
SALES (est): 232.3K **Privately Held**
SIC: 3679 Harness assemblies for electronic use: wire or cable

Duanesburg
Schenectady County

(G-4043)
AMERICAN CAR SIGNS INC
1483 W Duane Lake Rd (12056-2713)
PHONE..............................518 227-1173
Eulaila Kulikoff, *CEO*
EMP: 6
SALES: 50K **Privately Held**
SIC: 3993 Electric signs

(G-4044)
CUSTOM DESIGN KITCHENS INC
1700 Duanesburg Rd (12056-4310)
PHONE..............................518 355-4446
Terry Zarrillo, *President*
Dawn Zarrillo, *Corp Secy*
EMP: 10
SQ FT: 10,000
SALES (est): 920K **Privately Held**
SIC: 2541 5031 5211 3131 Cabinets, except refrigerated: show, display, etc.: wood; kitchen cabinets; cabinets, kitchen; counter tops; counters

Dundee
Yates County

(G-4045)
EAST BRANCH WINERY INC (PA)
Also Called: Mc Gregor Vineyard Winery
5503 Dutch St (14837-9746)
PHONE..............................607 292-3999
Robert Mc Gregor, *President*
David Payne, *Shareholder*
Marge Mc Gregor, *Admin Sec*
EMP: 8
SQ FT: 2,000
SALES (est): 402K **Privately Held**
SIC: 2084 0172 Wines; grapes

(G-4046)
FINGER LAKES MEDIA INC
Also Called: The Observer
45 Water St (14837)
P.O. Box 127 (14837-0127)
PHONE..............................607 243-7600
George Lawson, *President*
EMP: 12
SALES (est): 510.3K **Privately Held**
WEB: www.fingerlakesmedia.com
SIC: 2711 Newspapers, publishing & printing

(G-4047)
HERMANN J WIEMER VINEYARD
3962 Rte 14 (14837)
P.O. Box 38 (14837-0038)
PHONE..............................607 243-7971
Hermann J Wiemer, *President*
Osker Bynke, *Mktg Dir*
▲ **EMP:** 5
SALES (est): 514.4K **Privately Held**
WEB: www.wiemer.com
SIC: 2084 0172 Wines; grapes

(G-4048)
HICKORY ROAD LAND CO LLC
Also Called: Hickory Hollow Wind Cellars
5289 Route 14 (14837)
P.O. Box 37 (14837-0037)
PHONE..............................607 243-9114
Edward Woodland, *Mng Member*
Suzanne Kendall, *Manager*

EMP: 5
SALES (est): 437.3K **Privately Held**
SIC: 2084 Wines

Dunkirk
Chautauqua County

(G-4049)
AMCOR RIGID PACKAGING USA LLC
1 Cliffstar Ave (14048-2800)
PHONE..............................716 366-2440
Bryan Cotton, *Branch Mgr*
EMP: 50 **Privately Held**
WEB: www.slpcamericas.com
SIC: 3089 Plastic containers, except foam
HQ: Amcor Rigid Packaging Usa, Llc
40600 Ann Arbor Rd E # 201
Plymouth MI 48170

(G-4050)
CHAUTAUQUA CIRCUITS INC
855 Main St (14048-3505)
PHONE..............................716 366-5771
William E Wragge, *President*
EMP: 6
SALES (est): 250K **Privately Held**
SIC: 3672 Printed circuit boards

(G-4051)
CHAUTAUQUA WOODS CORPORATION
134 Franklin Ave (14048-2806)
P.O. Box 130 (14048-0130)
PHONE..............................716 366-3808
Bia Khan, *President*
Donna Bolling, *Office Mgr*
EMP: 40
SQ FT: 50,000
SALES: 1.2MM **Privately Held**
WEB: www.chautauquawoods.com
SIC: 2431 Doors, wood

(G-4052)
CLIFFSTAR LLC (DH)
Also Called: Cott Beverages
1 Cliffstar Dr (14048-2800)
PHONE..............................716 366-6100
Monica Consonery, *Exec VP*
Kevin Sanvidge, *Exec VP*
Richard Star, *Exec VP*
Kevin M Sanvidge, *VP Admin*
Glenn Mann, *QA Dir*
◆ **EMP:** 700
SALES (est): 612.3MM **Privately Held**
SALES (corp-wide): 3.3B **Privately Held**
SIC: 2033 2086 Fruit juices: fresh; bottled & canned soft drinks; pasteurized & mineral waters, bottled & canned
HQ: Refresco Beverages Us Inc.
8112 Woodland Center Blvd
Tampa FL 33614
813 313-1800

(G-4053)
DUNKIRK CONSTRUCTION PRODUCTS
852 Main St (14048-3506)
P.O. Box 149 (14048-0149)
PHONE..............................716 366-5220
EMP: 5
SQ FT: 3,800
SALES (est): 643.3K **Privately Held**
SIC: 3273 Mfg Ready-Mixed Concrete

(G-4054)
DUNKIRK METAL PRODUCTS WNY LLC (PA)
3575 Chadwick Dr (14048-9652)
PHONE..............................716 366-2555
Joe Shull, *President*
Jeaai Gaulhv, *Partner*
Nathaniel Organ, *Engineer*
▼ **EMP:** 22 **EST:** 1946
SQ FT: 50,000
SALES (est): 5.8MM **Privately Held**
SIC: 3469 Metal stampings

GEOGRAPHIC

(G-4055)
DUNKIRK SPECIALTY STEEL LLC
830 Brigham Rd (14048-3473)
P.O. Box 319 (14048-0319)
PHONE......................................716 366-1000
Dennis Oates, *President*
Wendel Crosby, *General Mgr*
Connie Carlson, *COO*
William W Beible Jr, *Senior VP*
Paul A McGrath, *VP Admin*
◆ EMP: 166
SALES (est): 36.5MM **Publicly Held**
WEB: www.dunkirkspecialtysteel.com
SIC: 3312 Stainless steel
PA: Universal Stainless & Alloy Products,
    Inc.
    600 Mayer St
    Bridgeville PA 15017

(G-4056)
ECR INTERNATIONAL INC
Dunkirk Division
85 Middle Rd (14048-1311)
P.O. Box 32 (14048-0032)
PHONE......................................716 366-5500
Thomas Poweski, *Manager*
Dennis Keppel, *Technician*
EMP: 130
SQ FT: 17,087
SALES (corp-wide): 107.2MM **Privately Held**
WEB: www.ecrinternational.com
SIC: 3433 3443 Boilers, low-pressure
    heating: steam or hot water; fabricated
    plate work (boiler shop)
PA: Ecr International, Inc.
    2201 Dwyer Ave
    Utica NY 13501
    315 797-1310

(G-4057)
FFC HOLDING CORP SUBSIDIARIES
1 Ice Cream Dr (14048-3300)
PHONE......................................716 366-5400
Kenneth A Johnson, *President*
Bob Bogdanowicz, *Purch Mgr*
EMP: 352
SQ FT: 280,000
SALES (est): 29.3MM **Privately Held**
SIC: 2024 Ice cream & frozen desserts

(G-4058)
FIELDBROOK FOODS CORPORATION (HQ)
1 Ice Cream Dr (14048-3300)
P.O. Box 1318 (14048-6318)
PHONE......................................716 366-5400
Kenneth A Johnson, *CEO*
Mark McLenithan, *COO*
Staci Kring, *Senior VP*
Kevin Grismore, *Vice Pres*
David Hall, *Vice Pres*
◆ EMP: 229
SQ FT: 234,000
SALES (est): 95.4MM
SALES (corp-wide): 744.5MM **Privately Held**
SIC: 2024 Ice cream, bulk
PA: Wells Enterprises, Inc.
    1 Blue Bunny Dr Sw
    Le Mars IA 51031
    712 546-4000

(G-4059)
INX INTERNATIONAL INK CO
3257 Middle Rd (14048-9745)
PHONE......................................716 366-6010
Sue Colston, *Branch Mgr*
EMP: 21 **Privately Held**
SIC: 2893 Printing ink
HQ: Inx International Ink Co.
    150 N Martingale Rd # 700
    Schaumburg IL 60173
    630 382-1800

(G-4060)
LAKESIDE PRECISION INC
208 Dove St (14048-1598)
PHONE......................................716 366-5030
Christopher Anson, *CEO*
Hugh Graves, *Opers Dir*
EMP: 22 **EST:** 1963
SQ FT: 11,300

SALES: 1.7MM **Privately Held**
WEB: www.lakesideprecision.com
SIC: 3599 Machine shop, jobbing & repair;
    custom machinery

(G-4061)
NESTLE PURINA PETCARE COMPANY
Also Called: Nestle Purina Factory
3800 Middle Rd (14048-9750)
PHONE......................................716 366-8080
Ron Bowers, *Branch Mgr*
EMP: 300
SALES (corp-wide): 92B **Privately Held**
WEB: www.purina.com
SIC: 2047 Dog food
HQ: Nestle Purina Petcare Company
    1 Checkerboard Sq
    Saint Louis MO 63164
    314 982-1000

(G-4062)
OBSERVER DAILY SUNDAY NEWSPPR
Also Called: The Observer
10 E 2nd St (14048-1602)
P.O. Box 391 (14048-0391)
PHONE......................................716 366-3000
Karl T Davis, *General Mgr*
James Austin, *Plant Mgr*
Janice Gee, *Director*
EMP: 100
SALES (est): 13.8MM **Privately Held**
WEB: www.observertoday.com
SIC: 2752 2711 Commercial printing, litho-
    graphic; newspapers

(G-4063)
PERSCH SERVICE PRINT INC (PA)
11 W 3rd St (14048)
P.O. Box 232 (14048-0232)
PHONE......................................716 366-2677
Robert H Persch, *President*
Margaret T Persch, *Treasurer*
Margaret P Triaga, *Admin Sec*
EMP: 9 **EST:** 1911
SALES (est): 1.4MM **Privately Held**
SIC: 2752 7334 Commercial printing, off-
    set; photocopying & duplicating services

(G-4064)
REM-TRONICS INC
659 Brigham Rd (14048-2361)
PHONE......................................716 934-2697
Abe M Kadis, *President*
Clayton Spaeth, *General Mgr*
EMP: 58
SQ FT: 20,000
SALES (est): 9.7MM **Privately Held**
WEB: www.rem-tronics.com
SIC: 3679 Electronic circuits

(G-4065)
REXFORD SERVICES INC
4849 W Lake Rd (14048-9613)
PHONE......................................716 366-6671
William Rexford, *President*
Trisha Rexford, *Vice Pres*
EMP: 5
SALES (est): 680.7K **Privately Held**
SIC: 3713 Specialty motor vehicle bodies

(G-4066)
SHAANT INDUSTRIES INC
134 Franklin Ave (14048-2806)
P.O. Box 130 (14048-0130)
PHONE......................................716 366-3654
Khalid Khan, *President*
◆ EMP: 40
SQ FT: 50,000
SALES (est): 7.1MM **Privately Held**
WEB: www.ultrapak.net
SIC: 3081 2671 Polyvinyl film & sheet;
    packaging paper & plastics film, coated &
    laminated

(G-4067)
SPECIAL METALS CORPORATION
100 Willowbrook Ave (14048-3479)
P.O. Box 304 (14048-0304)
PHONE......................................716 366-5663
Fred A Schweizer, *Opers Staff*
Don Borowski, *Manager*

EMP: 60
SALES (corp-wide): 225.3B **Publicly Held**
SIC: 3542 3463 3462 3341 Forging ma-
    chinery & hammers; extruding machines
    (machine tools), metal; die casting ma-
    chines; nonferrous forgings; iron & steel
    forgings; secondary nonferrous metals
HQ: Special Metals Corporation
    4832 Richmond Rd Ste 100
    Warrensville Heights OH 44128
    216 755-3030

(G-4068)
X PRESS SCREEN PRINTING
4867 W Lake Rd (14048-9613)
PHONE......................................716 679-7788
Chad Rizzo, *President*
EMP: 7
SALES (est): 584.7K **Privately Held**
SIC: 2759 Commercial printing

Durham
Greene County

(G-4069)
ADVANCED YARN TECHNOLOGIES INC
Also Called: Cidega American Trim
4750 State Hwy 145 (12422-5306)
PHONE......................................518 239-6600
Richard Gangi, *President*
Daniel Gangi, *Vice Pres*
Sebastian Gangi, *Vice Pres*
EMP: 50
SALES (est): 5.8MM **Privately Held**
SIC: 2281 5199 Yarn spinning mills; fab-
    rics, yarns & knit goods

(G-4070)
AMERICAN TRIM MFG INC
4750 State Hwy 145 (12422-5306)
PHONE......................................518 239-8151
Richard Gangi, *President*
Daniel Gangi, *Vice Pres*
Sabastian Gangi, *Vice Pres*
▲ EMP: 50
SQ FT: 30,000
SALES (est): 12.5MM **Privately Held**
SIC: 2241 Trimmings, textile

Eagle Bridge
Rensselaer County

(G-4071)
EAGLE BRIDGE MACHINE & TL INC
135 State Route 67 (12057)
P.O. Box 95 (12057-0095)
PHONE......................................518 686-4541
Robert Farrara, *President*
Raymond Farrara, *Corp Secy*
▲ EMP: 35 **EST:** 1965
SQ FT: 12,000
SALES (est): 4.4MM **Privately Held**
WEB: www.eaglebridgemachine.com
SIC: 3599 3743 Machine shop, jobbing &
    repair; railroad equipment

(G-4072)
MORCON INC (PA)
Also Called: Morcon Tissue
62 Owlkill Rd (12057-2609)
PHONE......................................518 677-8511
Joseph Raccuia, *President*
Tim Goodbred, *Vice Pres*
Brian Stidd, *Controller*
EMP: 90
SALES: 40MM **Privately Held**
SIC: 2621 Tissue paper

(G-4073)
PROFESSIONAL PACKG SVCS INC
Also Called: Pro Pack
62 Owlkill Rd (12057-2609)
PHONE......................................518 677-5100
Ronald Dooley, *President*
Lorraine Dooley, *Corp Secy*
EMP: 30

SQ FT: 25,000
SALES (est): 5.6MM **Privately Held**
SIC: 2653 2631 3086 Boxes, corrugated:
    made from purchased materials; paper-
    board mills; plastics foam products

(G-4074)
PROPAK INC
70 Owlkill Rd (12057)
PHONE......................................518 677-5100
Jack Baratta, *Principal*
EMP: 6
SALES (est): 588.4K **Privately Held**
SIC: 2652 Setup paperboard boxes

(G-4075)
STRATO TRANSIT COMPONENTS LLC
155 State Route 67 (12057)
PHONE......................................518 686-4541
Michael Foxx,
Michael Corridon,
Steven Foxx,
▲ EMP: 9
SALES (est): 1.1MM **Privately Held**
SIC: 3743 Railroad equipment

Earlville
Chenango County

(G-4076)
EARLVILLE PAPER BOX CO INC
19 Clyde St (13332)
P.O. Box 130 (13332-0130)
PHONE......................................315 691-2131
EMP: 20
SQ FT: 7,200
SALES (est): 4.1MM **Privately Held**
WEB: www.earlvillepaperbox.com
SIC: 2652 Setup paperboard boxes

East Amherst
Erie County

(G-4077)
ELITE ROASTERS INC (PA)
Also Called: Elite Coffee Roasters
8600 Transit Rd Ste 1b (14051-2615)
PHONE......................................716 626-0307
Gerald Dewes, *CFO*
William Klein, *Director*
EMP: 20 **EST:** 2015
SALES (est): 8MM **Privately Held**
SIC: 2095 5149 7389 Roasted coffee;
    coffee, green or roasted; packaging & la-
    beling services

(G-4078)
INTEGRTED WORK ENVRONMENTS LLC
Also Called: Iwe
6346 Everwood Ct N (14051-2032)
P.O. Box 1514, Williamsville (14231-1514)
PHONE......................................716 725-5088
Evan M Casey, *Mng Member*
EMP: 7
SALES (est): 974.7K **Privately Held**
SIC: 3821 5047 5049 Laboratory appara-
    tus & furniture; medical laboratory equip-
    ment; laboratory equipment, except
    medical or dental

(G-4079)
SUPERIOR EXTERIORS OF BUFFALO
57 Insbrook Ct (14051-1496)
PHONE......................................716 873-1000
Salvatore Dinatale, *President*
EMP: 10
SQ FT: 15,000
SALES (est): 1MM **Privately Held**
SIC: 3444 Awnings & canopies

(G-4080)
SWEET MELODYS LLC
8485 Transit Rd (14051-1059)
PHONE......................................716 580-3227
Chuck Incorvia,
▲ EMP: 20

2020 Harris
New York Manufacturers Directory

▲ = Import ▼ =Export
◆ =Import/Export

SALES (est): 2MM **Privately Held**
SIC: 2024 Dairy based frozen desserts

East Aurora
Erie County

(G-4081)
AMERICAN PRECISION INDS INC
Also Called: API Delevan
270 Quaker Rd (14052-2192)
P.O. Box 449 (14052-0449)
PHONE...............................716 652-3600
Daniel A Raskas, *President*
Jim Bingel, *Branch Mgr*
EMP: 95
SALES (corp-wide): 6.4B **Publicly Held**
WEB: www.apischmidtbretten.com
SIC: 3677 Coil windings, electronic; inductors, electronic
HQ: American Precision Industries Inc.
45 Hazelwood Dr
Amherst NY 14228
716 691-9100

(G-4082)
ASTRONICS CORPORATION (PA)
130 Commerce Way (14052-2164)
PHONE...............................716 805-1599
Peter J Gundermann, *President*
James F Mulato, *President*
David R Burney, *Exec VP*
James S Kramer, *Exec VP*
Mark A Peabody, *Exec VP*
▲ EMP: 171
SQ FT: 125,000
SALES: 803.2MM **Publicly Held**
SIC: 3728 3647 Aircraft parts & equipment; aircraft lighting fixtures

(G-4083)
AURORA TECHNICAL SERVICES LTD
11970 Parker Rd (14052-9533)
P.O. Box 103 (14052-0103)
PHONE...............................716 652-1463
Karen Wright, *President*
Steven Wright, *Vice Pres*
EMP: 5
SQ FT: 1,100
SALES (est): 651.1K **Privately Held**
WEB: www.auroratechserv.com
SIC: 3829 3825 Ultrasonic testing equipment; meters: electric, pocket, portable, panelboard, etc.

(G-4084)
COLDEN CLOSET LLC
1375 Boies Rd (14052-9726)
PHONE...............................716 713-6125
Kevin Lindberg, *Owner*
EMP: 9
SALES (est): 1MM **Privately Held**
SIC: 2673 Wardrobe bags (closet accessories): from purchased materials

(G-4085)
DIREKT FORCE LLC
455 Olean Rd Ste 3 (14052-9791)
PHONE...............................716 652-3022
Kurt Knolle, *Mng Member*
EMP: 25 EST: 2001
SQ FT: 7,000
SALES (est): 4.9MM **Privately Held**
WEB: www.direktforce.com
SIC: 3492 3593 3443 Control valves, fluid power: hydraulic & pneumatic; fluid power cylinders, hydraulic or pneumatic; fabricated plate work (boiler shop)

(G-4086)
EVERFAB INC
12928 Big Tree Rd (14052-9524)
PHONE...............................716 655-1550
Alan L Everett, *Ch of Bd*
Lee Everett, *Vice Pres*
Scott Everett, *Vice Pres*
Scott Johnson, *Mfg Mgr*
Eric Valentine, *QC Mgr*
EMP: 55
SQ FT: 45,000

SALES (est): 12.1MM **Privately Held**
WEB: www.everfab.com
SIC: 2821 3441 3545 3544 Elastomers, nonvulcanizable (plastics); molding compounds, plastics; fabricated structural metal; machine tool accessories; special dies, tools, jigs & fixtures; machine & other job shop work

(G-4087)
EXTEN II LLC
127 Elm St (14052-2535)
P.O. Box 875, Orchard Park (14127-0875)
PHONE...............................716 895-2214
Richard Swanson, *President*
EMP: 18
SALES (est): 2.3MM **Privately Held**
SIC: 3714 Motor vehicle parts & accessories

(G-4088)
F M EDM INC
210 Pennsylvania Ave (14052-2919)
P.O. Box 773 (14052-0773)
PHONE...............................716 655-1784
Mark Marin, *President*
▲ EMP: 3
SQ FT: 4,000
SALES: 1MM **Privately Held**
WEB: www.fmedm.com
SIC: 3544 Special dies & tools

(G-4089)
GRANT HAMILTON (PA)
Also Called: East Aurora Advertiser
710 Main St (14052-2406)
P.O. Box 5 (14052-0005)
PHONE...............................716 652-0320
Grant Hamilton, *Owner*
EMP: 15
SQ FT: 2,850
SALES (est): 1MM **Privately Held**
WEB: www.eastaurorany.com
SIC: 2741 5943 Newsletter publishing; office forms & supplies

(G-4090)
GUARDIAN SYSTEMS TECH INC
659 Oakwood Ave (14052-2511)
PHONE...............................716 481-5597
Edward Seebald, *CEO*
Meighan Lloyd, *Principal*
EMP: 10
SALES (est): 649.6K **Privately Held**
SIC: 3699 Electrical equipment & supplies

(G-4091)
LUMINESCENT SYSTEMS INC (HQ)
Also Called: L S I
130 Commerce Way (14052-2191)
PHONE...............................716 655-0800
Peter Gundermann, *President*
Frank Johns, *Vice Pres*
James Kramer, *Vice Pres*
Richard Miller, *Vice Pres*
John Drenning, *Bd of Directors*
EMP: 300
SALES (est): 63.3MM
SALES (corp-wide): 803.2MM **Publicly Held**
SIC: 3647 3646 3648 3577 Aircraft lighting fixtures; commercial indusl & institutional electric lighting fixtures; lighting equipment; computer peripheral equipment
PA: Astronics Corporation
130 Commerce Way
East Aurora NY 14052
716 805-1599

(G-4092)
MATTEL INC
Also Called: Fisher-Price
636 Girard Ave (14052-1824)
P.O. Box 1169 (14052-7169)
PHONE...............................310 252-2000
Jerry Drinkard, *Principal*
Ron Baker, *Vice Pres*
Shari Wollman, *Vice Pres*
Jamie Hert, *Engineer*
Mike Ruppenthal, *Engineer*
EMP: 34
SALES (corp-wide): 4.5B **Publicly Held**
SIC: 3944 Games, toys & children's vehicles

PA: Mattel, Inc.
333 Continental Blvd
El Segundo CA 90245
310 252-2000

(G-4093)
MOOG INC
Also Called: Moog Industrial Group
300 Jamison Rd (14052)
PHONE...............................716 687-4954
Keith Mazierski, *Purch Mgr*
Mark Smith, *Buyer*
Lawrence Chow, *Engineer*
Robert Muir, *Engineer*
Darvin Remington, *Engineer*
EMP: 300
SALES (corp-wide): 2.9B **Publicly Held**
WEB: www.moog.com
SIC: 3492 3721 Fluid power valves & hose fittings; aircraft
PA: Moog Inc.
400 Jamison Rd
Elma NY 14059
716 805-2604

(G-4094)
MOOG INC
Moog Systems Group
7021 Seneca St (14052)
PHONE...............................716 805-8100
Michael Baczkowski, *Vice Pres*
Monte T Lyons, *Opers Staff*
Mike Ratajczak, *Opers Staff*
Blaine Sheffer, *Opers Staff*
Nicole Wodka-Cook, *Opers Staff*
EMP: 225
SALES (corp-wide): 2.9B **Publicly Held**
WEB: www.moog.com
SIC: 3812 Search & navigation equipment
PA: Moog Inc.
400 Jamison Rd
Elma NY 14059
716 805-2604

(G-4095)
NORTHERN DESIGN INC
12990 Old Big Tree Rd (14052-9525)
PHONE...............................716 652-7071
Robert Lippert, *President*
Gabor Bertalan, *Vice Pres*
EMP: 6
SQ FT: 550
SALES (est): 500K **Privately Held**
WEB: www.northerndesign.com
SIC: 3544 Forms (molds), for foundry & plastics working machinery; dies & die holders for metal cutting, forming, die casting

(G-4096)
SLOSSON EDUCTL PUBLICATIONS
538 Buffalo Rd (14052-9456)
P.O. Box 280 (14052-0280)
PHONE...............................716 652-0930
Steven Slosson, *President*
Janet Slosson, *Chairman*
EMP: 12
SQ FT: 2,400
SALES (est): 1.2MM **Privately Held**
WEB: www.slosson.com
SIC: 2741 8748 8299 Miscellaneous publishing; publishing consultant; arts & crafts schools

(G-4097)
WEST FALLS MACHINE CO INC
Also Called: West Falls Machine Co 1
11692 E Main Rd (14052-9597)
PHONE...............................716 655-0440
Matthew Creps, *CEO*
Mary Ann George, *Vice Pres*
EMP: 15
SQ FT: 15,000
SALES (est): 2.7MM **Privately Held**
SIC: 3599 3471 Machine shop, jobbing & repair; chromium plating of metals or formed products

East Berne
Albany County

(G-4098)
RUDY STEMPEL & FAMILY SAWMILL
73 Stempel Ln (12059-2843)
PHONE...............................518 872-0431
Rudolph Stempel, *President*
EMP: 6
SALES (est): 528.5K **Privately Held**
SIC: 2421 Sawmills & planing mills, general

East Bethany
Genesee County

(G-4099)
SANDVOSS FARMS LLC
Also Called: First Light Farm & Creamery
10198 East Rd (14054-9754)
PHONE...............................585 297-7044
Peter R Sandvoss, *Owner*
Peter Sandvoss,
Stephen Sandvoss,
EMP: 8
SALES (est): 378.9K **Privately Held**
SIC: 2022 Natural cheese

East Concord
Erie County

(G-4100)
MCEWAN TRUCKING & GRAV PRODUC
11696 Route 240 (14055-9717)
PHONE...............................716 609-1828
Mary McEwan, *Principal*
EMP: 6
SALES (est): 545.1K **Privately Held**
SIC: 1442 Construction sand & gravel

(G-4101)
WENDELS POULTRY FARM
12466 Vaughn St (14055-9747)
PHONE...............................716 592-2299
Martin Wendel, *Partner*
Denise Wendel, *Partner*
David Wendel, *Partner*
EMP: 8
SQ FT: 12,000
SALES (est): 928.6K **Privately Held**
SIC: 2015 0254 Poultry, processed; poultry hatcheries

East Durham
Greene County

(G-4102)
GLAXOSMITHKLINE LLC
Also Called: Glaxosmthkline Cnsmr Heathcare
3169 Route 145 (12423-1416)
PHONE...............................518 239-6901
Max Van Veem, *Vice Pres*
Max Van Vessem, *Branch Mgr*
EMP: 75
SALES (corp-wide): 39.5B **Privately Held**
SIC: 3843 2834 Dental equipment & supplies; procaine pharmaceutical preparations
HQ: Glaxosmithkline Llc
5 Crescent Dr
Philadelphia PA 19112
215 751-4000

G
E
O
G
R
A
P
H
I
C

East Elmhurst
Queens County

(G-4103)
ARM CONSTRUCTION COMPANY INC
10001 27th Ave (11369-1647)
PHONE...........................646 235-6520
Abdul Motaleb, *President*
EMP: 5
SALES: 383K **Privately Held**
SIC: 1389 7389 Construction, repair & dis-
mantling services;

(G-4104)
BROTHERS ROOFING SUPPLIES CO
10514 Astoria Blvd (11369-2097)
PHONE...........................718 779-0280
Robert Kersch, *Ch of Bd*
Michael Kersch, *Vice Pres*
EMP: 20 EST: 1969
SQ FT: 16,000
SALES (est): 4.3MM **Privately Held**
WEB: www.brothersroofingsupply.com
SIC: 3444 Metal roofing & roof drainage
equipment

(G-4105)
CITROS BUILDING MATERIALS CO
10514 Astoria Blvd (11369-2027)
PHONE...........................718 779-0727
Bobby Kersh, *President*
EMP: 40
SQ FT: 1,600
SALES (est): 5.2MM **Privately Held**
SIC: 3444 Skylights, sheet metal

(G-4106)
DOROSE NOVELTY CO INC
Also Called: Dorose Albums
3107 103rd St (11369-2013)
PHONE...........................718 451-3088
Sam Krauthamer, *President*
Alex Brodsky, *Vice Pres*
Regina Krauthamer, *Treasurer*
EMP: 14 EST: 1958
SALES (est): 1.1MM **Privately Held**
SIC: 2782 Albums

(G-4107)
I RAUCHS SONS INC
3220 112th St (11369-2590)
PHONE...........................718 507-8844
Milton Levine, *President*
Joel Levine, *Corp Secy*
EMP: 21 EST: 1903
SQ FT: 12,000
SALES (est): 3.5MM **Privately Held**
SIC: 3444 Sheet metalwork

(G-4108)
KESSO FOODS INC
Also Called: Mediterranean Thick Yogurt
7720 21st Ave (11370-1219)
PHONE...........................718 777-5303
Fotini Kessissoglou, *President*
EMP: 5
SALES: 100K **Privately Held**
SIC: 2026 5143 Fluid milk; yogurt

(G-4109)
LIBERTY AWNINGS & SIGNS INC
Also Called: Empire Signs
7705 21st Ave (11370-1250)
PHONE...........................347 203-1470
Panayiotis Panayi, *CEO*
EMP: 2
SQ FT: 5,000
SALES: 2.3MM **Privately Held**
SIC: 3993 Advertising artwork

(G-4110)
MOON GATES COMPANY
3243 104th St (11369-2515)
PHONE...........................718 426-0023
EMP: 6
SQ FT: 2,000

SALES (est): 400K **Privately Held**
SIC: 3446 1791 Mfg Architectural Metalwork Structural Steel Erection

(G-4111)
T RJ SHIRTS INC
3050 90th St (11369-1706)
PHONE...........................347 642-3071
Femd Rocky, *Principal*
EMP: 6
SALES (est): 487.3K **Privately Held**
SIC: 2331 T-shirts & tops, women's: made
from purchased materials

(G-4112)
WESTCHSTR CRNKSHFT GRNDNG
Also Called: Westchster Crankshaft Grinding
3263 110th St (11369-2525)
PHONE...........................718 651-3900
Marco Albanese, *Vice Pres*
▲ EMP: 9
SALES (est): 1.1MM **Privately Held**
SIC: 3599 Crankshafts & camshafts, ma-
chining

East Greenbush
Rensselaer County

(G-4113)
AUTOMATED & MGT SOLUTIONS LLC
743 Columbia Tpke (12061-2266)
PHONE...........................518 833-0315
Francis Clifford, *Mng Member*
Sharon Hemmes, *Information Mgr*
EMP: 7 EST: 2011
SALES: 900K **Privately Held**
SIC: 7372 Application computer software;
operating systems computer software

(G-4114)
GARELICK FARMS LLC
504 Third Avenue Ext (12061)
PHONE...........................518 283-0820
Bill Hogan, *Branch Mgr*
EMP: 210 **Publicly Held**
SIC: 2026 Cottage cheese
HQ: Garelick Farms, Llc
1199 W Central St Ste 1
Franklin MA 02038
508 528-9000

(G-4115)
LEONARD CARLSON
Also Called: Carlson, L A Co
90 Waters Rd (12061-3422)
PHONE...........................518 477-4710
Leonard Carlson, *Owner*
▲ EMP: 6 EST: 1956
SQ FT: 6,000
SALES: 425K **Privately Held**
SIC: 3931 Organs, all types: pipe, reed,
hand, electronic, etc.

(G-4116)
SABIC INNOVATIVE PLASTICS
1 Gail Ct (12061-1750)
PHONE...........................713 448-7474
Charles Lin, *General Mgr*
Narendra Mansharamani, *Principal*
Jason Fuller, *Project Mgr*
David Clay, *Materials Mgr*
Dominic Bruno, *Safety Mgr*
EMP: 36 EST: 2012
SALES (est): 5.9MM **Privately Held**
SIC: 2821 Plastics materials & resins

East Hampton
Suffolk County

(G-4117)
BISTRIAN CEMENT CORPORATION
225 Springs Fireplace Rd (11937-4823)
P.O. Box 5048 (11937-6079)
PHONE...........................631 324-1123
Barry Bistrian, *President*
Betsy Avallone, *Shareholder*
Bruce Bistrian, *Shareholder*

Pat Bistrian, *Shareholder*
Barbara Borg, *Shareholder*
EMP: 12
SQ FT: 20,000
SALES: 1.7MM **Privately Held**
SIC: 3272 3259 Septic tanks, concrete;
drain tile, clay

(G-4118)
C E KING & SONS INC
10 Saint Francis Pl (11937-4330)
PHONE...........................631 324-4944
Clarence E King III, *President*
David King, *Treasurer*
Deanna King, *Admin Sec*
Deanna Tikkanen, *Admin Sec*
EMP: 7
SQ FT: 1,650
SALES: 600K **Privately Held**
WEB: www.kingsawnings.com
SIC: 2394 5999 Awnings, fabric: made
from purchased materials; fire extinguish-
ers

(G-4119)
CHESU INC
81 Newtown Ln (11937-2323)
PHONE...........................239 564-2803
Chet Borgida, *President*
Susan Borgida, *Vice Pres*
EMP: 10 EST: 2012
SALES (est): 1MM **Privately Held**
SIC: 3086 5111 7389 Packaging & ship-
ping materials, foamed plastic; printing
paper; notary publics

(G-4120)
EAST HAMPTON IND NEWS INC
Also Called: East Hampton Independent The
74 Montauk Hwy Unit 19 (11937-3268)
PHONE...........................631 324-2500
James Mackim, *President*
James Mackim, *Publisher*
Jodi Della Femina, *Vice Pres*
Lee Minitree, *Treasurer*
R Mott, *Executive*
EMP: 28
SQ FT: 1,400
SALES (est): 1.6MM **Privately Held**
WEB: www.indyeastend.com
SIC: 2711 Newspapers, publishing & print-
ing

(G-4121)
EAST HAMPTON STAR INC
153 Main St (11937-2716)
P.O. Box 5002 (11937-6005)
PHONE...........................631 324-0002
Helen Rattray, *President*
EMP: 40 EST: 1886
SQ FT: 6,400
SALES (est): 2.9MM **Privately Held**
WEB: www.easthamptonstar.com
SIC: 2711 Commercial printing & newspa-
per publishing combined; newspapers,
publishing & printing

(G-4122)
ELIE TAHARI LTD
1 Main St (11937-2701)
PHONE...........................631 329-8883
Brenda Bolin, *Branch Mgr*
EMP: 75
SALES (corp-wide): 171.9MM **Privately Held**
SIC: 2337 Suits: women's, misses' & jun-
iors'
PA: Elie Tahari Ltd.
16 Bleeker St
Millburn NJ 07041
973 671-6300

(G-4123)
IRONY LIMITED INC (PA)
Also Called: Hedges and Gardens
53 Sag Harbor Tpke (11937-4905)
PHONE...........................631 329-4065
Robert Linker, *President*
Elizabeth Linker, *Vice Pres*
EMP: 2
SQ FT: 2,200

SALES (est): 1.2MM **Privately Held**
SIC: 3441 7641 3446 1799 Fabricated
structural metal; antique furniture repair &
restoration; stairs, staircases, stair treads:
prefabricated metal; ornamental metal
work

(G-4124)
KEENERS EAST END LITHO INC
10 Prospect Blvd (11937-5800)
P.O. Box 1798, Sag Harbor (11963-0063)
PHONE...........................631 324-8565
Charles Keener, *President*
Lynn Keener, *Corp Secy*
Greg Keener, *Vice Pres*
EMP: 8
SALES (est): 679.6K **Privately Held**
SIC: 2752 Commercial printing, offset

(G-4125)
LURIA COMMUNICATIONS INC
Also Called: Card Pak Start Up
31 Shorewood Dr Fl 1 (11937-3402)
PHONE...........................631 329-4922
Jay Blatt, *President*
Vicki Luria, *Vice Pres*
EMP: 8
SALES: 500K **Privately Held**
SIC: 2721 7311 7331 Trade journals: pub-
lishing only, not printed on site; advertis-
ing agencies; mailing list brokers

(G-4126)
NATURPATHICA HOLISTIC HLTH INC
74 Montauk Hwy Unit 23 (11937-3268)
PHONE...........................631 329-8792
Barbara Close, *CEO*
EMP: 100
SQ FT: 750
SALES (est): 4.4MM **Privately Held**
SIC: 2844 Cosmetic preparations

(G-4127)
SABIN METAL CORPORATION (PA)
300 Pantigo Pl Ste 102 (11937-2630)
PHONE...........................631 329-1695
Andrew Sabin, *President*
Jonathan Sabin, *Exec VP*
Kevin Beirne, *Vice Pres*
John Jonat, *Vice Pres*
Scott Yarnes, *Opers Mgr*
▲ EMP: 14 EST: 1945
SQ FT: 4,000
SALES (est): 39.9MM **Privately Held**
WEB: www.sabinmetal.com
SIC: 3341 Secondary precious metals

(G-4128)
STAR READY MIX EAST INC
225 Springs Fireplace Rd (11937-4823)
P.O. Box 371, Medford (11763-0371)
PHONE...........................631 289-8787
Thomas Hess, *President*
EMP: 15
SALES (est): 1.1MM **Privately Held**
SIC: 3273 Ready-mixed concrete

East Islip
Suffolk County

(G-4129)
KEY CONTAINER CORP
135 Hollins Ln (11730-3006)
PHONE...........................631 582-3847
Frank Giaquinko, *President*
EMP: 6
SALES: 800K **Privately Held**
SIC: 2653 Corrugated & solid fiber boxes

(G-4130)
QUALIFIED MANUFACTURING CORP
15 Amber Ct (11730-3801)
PHONE...........................631 249-4440
EMP: 11 EST: 1970
SQ FT: 7,000
SALES (est): 1.4MM **Privately Held**
SIC: 3599 Mfg Industrial Machinery

East Meadow
Nassau County

(G-4131)
ARTYS SPRNKLR SVC INSTLLATION
234 E Meadow Ave Unit B (11554-2455)
PHONE...................................516 538-4371
Arthur R Wolf, *President*
Helen Wolf, *Treasurer*
EMP: 13
SALES (est): 700K **Privately Held**
SIC: 3432 Lawn hose nozzles & sprinklers

(G-4132)
CHV PRINTED COMPANY
1905 Hempstead Tpke B (11554-1047)
PHONE...................................516 997-1101
Andrew Mazzone, *Principal*
EMP: 19
SALES (est): 1.8MM **Privately Held**
SIC: 2752 Commercial printing, offset

(G-4133)
COMPLETE ORTHOPEDIC SVCS INC
325 Merrick Ave Ste 1 (11554-1556)
PHONE...................................516 357-9113
Noreen Diaz, *Ch of Bd*
Alexandra Divito, *Sales Staff*
Anne Feret, *Practice Mgr*
EMP: 20
SALES (est): 2.7MM **Privately Held**
SIC: 3842 Braces, orthopedic

(G-4134)
DATASONIC INC
1413 Cleveland Ave (11554-4405)
PHONE...................................516 248-7330
Richard Mintz, *President*
EMP: 5
SALES (est): 320K **Privately Held**
SIC: 3669 Burglar alarm apparatus, electric

(G-4135)
EATON CORPORATION
280 Bellmore Rd (11554-3538)
PHONE...................................516 353-3017
John Pierro, *Principal*
EMP: 222 **Privately Held**
SIC: 3625 Motor controls & accessories
HQ: Eaton Corporation
    1000 Eaton Blvd
    Cleveland OH 44122
    440 523-5000

(G-4136)
HI TECH SIGNS OF NY INC
415 E Meadow Ave (11554-3952)
PHONE...................................516 794-7880
Scott Abrecht, *President*
EMP: 5
SQ FT: 2,000
SALES (est): 615.5K **Privately Held**
SIC: 3993 5999 Signs, not made in custom sign painting shops; banners, flags, decals & posters

(G-4137)
HIBU INC (DH)
90 Merrick Ave Ste 530 (11554-1575)
PHONE...................................516 730-1900
Mike Pocock, *CEO*
John Condron, *Ch of Bd*
Joseph Walsh, *President*
Bob Wigley, *Chairman*
Mark Payne, *COO*
◆ **EMP:** 200
SQ FT: 30,000
SALES (est): 1.8B **Privately Held**
SIC: 2741 Directories: publishing & printing
HQ: Yell Limited
    3 Forbury Place
    Reading BERKS RG1 3
    800 555-444

(G-4138)
JOHN PRIOR
2545 Hempstead Tpke # 402 (11554-2144)
PHONE...................................516 520-9801
John Prior, *Principal*

Barbara Gordon, *Human Resources*
Maria Lawrence, *Sales Mgr*
Ronald Prior, *Sales Executive*
EMP: 8 **EST:** 2007
SALES (est): 716.9K **Privately Held**
SIC: 3999 Manufacturing industries

(G-4139)
PJ DECORATORS INC
257 Pontiac Pl (11554-1231)
PHONE...................................516 735-9693
David Brill, *President*
EMP: 25
SALES (est): 2MM **Privately Held**
SIC: 2591 5023 5719 Drapery hardware & blinds & shades; vertical blinds; vertical blinds

East Moriches
Suffolk County

(G-4140)
TATES WHOLESALE LLC
Also Called: Tate's Bake Shop
62 Pine St (11940-1117)
PHONE...................................631 780-6511
Kathleen King, *President*
Thomas Pawluk, *CFO*
EMP: 130
SALES (est): 21.3MM **Publicly Held**
SIC: 2051 Bakery: wholesale or wholesale/retail combined
PA: Mondelez International, Inc.
    3 Parkway North Blvd # 300
    Deerfield IL 60015

East Northport
Suffolk County

(G-4141)
ADVANTAGE ORTHOTICS INC
337 Larkfield Rd (11731-2904)
PHONE...................................631 368-1754
Claire Ann Ketcham, *Principal*
EMP: 9
SALES (est): 1.1MM **Privately Held**
SIC: 3842 Orthopedic appliances

(G-4142)
ARCHITCTRAL MLLWK INSTALLATION
590 Elwood Rd (11731-5629)
PHONE...................................631 499-0755
EMP: 23
SALES: 2MM **Privately Held**
SIC: 2431 2439 Mfg Millwork Mfg Structural Wood Members

(G-4143)
COMPUTER CONVERSIONS CORP
6 Dunton Ct (11731-1704)
PHONE...................................631 261-3300
Stephen Renard, *President*
Dave Varrone, *General Mgr*
Paul Waldman, *Vice Pres*
Les Levy, *Project Engr*
Karin Hazin, *Accounts Mgr*
EMP: 32
SQ FT: 5,000
SALES (est): 7.6MM **Privately Held**
WEB: www.computer-conversions.com
SIC: 3571 Electronic computers

(G-4144)
EAST TO WEST ARCHITECTRAL PDTS
103 Tinton Pl Ste 1a (11731-5330)
PHONE...................................631 433-9690
Dean Nichol, *President*
EMP: 1
SALES: 3MM **Privately Held**
WEB: www.easttowestsales.com
SIC: 3996 Hard surface floor coverings

(G-4145)
FASTNET SOFTWARE INTL INC
459 Elwood Rd (11731-4006)
PHONE...................................888 740-7790
Uzma Abbas, *President*

EMP: 10
SALES (est): 813.4K **Privately Held**
SIC: 7372 Business oriented computer software

(G-4146)
FORTE NETWORK
Also Called: Forte Security Group
75 Lockfield Rd (11731)
PHONE...................................631 390-9050
Richard Allen, *President*
EMP: 40
SALES (est): 4.2MM **Privately Held**
SIC: 3699 Security control equipment & systems

(G-4147)
ISLAND SILKSCREEN INC
Also Called: Connie's T Shirt Shop
328 Larkfield Rd (11731-2945)
PHONE...................................631 757-4567
Mike Sambur, *President*
EMP: 5
SALES (est): 458.4K **Privately Held**
SIC: 2759 Screen printing

(G-4148)
JORDAN PANEL SYSTEMS CORP (PA)
196 Laurel Rd Unit 2 (11731-1441)
PHONE...................................631 754-4900
John A Finamore Sr, *President*
▼ **EMP:** 25
SQ FT: 5,000
SALES (est): 10MM **Privately Held**
WEB: www.jordanpanel.com
SIC: 3499 1761 1793 5033 Aerosol valves, metal; roofing, siding & sheet metal work; glass & glazing work; roofing, asphalt & sheet metal

(G-4149)
LOUDON LTD
Also Called: Minuteman Press
281 Larkfield Rd (11731-2417)
PHONE...................................631 757-4447
Kathy Loudon, *President*
EMP: 5
SQ FT: 1,800
SALES (est): 708.5K **Privately Held**
SIC: 2752 2791 Commercial printing, lithographic; typesetting

(G-4150)
MONASANI SIGNS INC
Also Called: Mr Sign
22 Compton St (11731-5510)
PHONE...................................631 266-2635
William Monahan, *President*
EMP: 5
SQ FT: 1,500
SALES: 400K **Privately Held**
SIC: 3993 7532 Signs & advertising specialties; truck painting & lettering

(G-4151)
READY CHECK GLO INC
23 Bruce Ln Ste E (11731-2701)
PHONE...................................516 547-1849
Celestina Pugliese, *CEO*
EMP: 5 **EST:** 2010
SALES: 175K **Privately Held**
SIC: 2752 7389 Menus, lithographed;

East Norwich
Nassau County

(G-4152)
GOLDEN EGRET LLC
38 Cord Pl (11732-1155)
P.O. Box 314 (11732-0314)
PHONE...................................516 922-2839
Walter Belous, *Mng Member*
▲ **EMP:** 6
SALES (est): 766.7K **Privately Held**
SIC: 3313 Tungsten carbide powder

East Patchogue
Suffolk County

(G-4153)
GLOBAL HANGER & DISPLAY INC
14 Hewlett Ave (11772-5407)
PHONE...................................631 475-5900
Sandy Stoll, *Principal*
▲ **EMP:** 6
SALES (est): 575.9K **Privately Held**
SIC: 3089 Plastics products

(G-4154)
HUNTER METAL INDUSTRIES INC
Also Called: Hunter Displays
14 Hewlett Ave (11772-5499)
PHONE...................................631 475-5900
Sandy Stoll, *CEO*
Kevin Kasper, *General Mgr*
Ken Kasper, *Vice Pres*
Susan Anastasia, *Accounting Mgr*
James Reed, *Sales Mgr*
EMP: 100 **EST:** 1951
SQ FT: 75,000
SALES (est): 15.7MM **Privately Held**
WEB: www.hunterdisplays.com
SIC: 2542 2541 Fixtures: display, office or store: except wood; display fixtures, wood

(G-4155)
PROGRESSIVE ORTHOTICS LTD
285 Sills Rd Bldg 8c (11772-8800)
PHONE...................................631 447-3860
Bruce Goodman, *Branch Mgr*
EMP: 12
SALES (corp-wide): 905.9K **Privately Held**
WEB: www.progressiveorthotics.com
SIC: 3842 5999 Orthopedic appliances; orthopedic & prosthesis applications
PA: Progressive Orthotics Ltd
    280 Middle Country Rd G
    Selden NY 11784
    631 732-5556

East Quogue
Suffolk County

(G-4156)
EAST COAST MINES LTD
Also Called: East Coast Mines & Material
2 Lewis Rd (11942)
PHONE...................................631 653-5445
William Tintle, *President*
EMP: 20
SQ FT: 5,000
SALES (est): 2.9MM **Privately Held**
SIC: 1442 5261 5032 Construction sand & gravel; top soil; brick, stone & related material

(G-4157)
HAMPTON SHIPYARDS INC
7 Carter Ln (11942-4334)
P.O. Box 3007 (11942-2008)
PHONE...................................631 653-6777
Fred Scopinich, *President*
Doris Scopinich, *Vice Pres*
EMP: 10 **EST:** 1956
SQ FT: 21,000
SALES (est): 1.1MM **Privately Held**
SIC: 3732 Boat building & repairing

(G-4158)
SITEWATCH TECHNOLOGY LLC
22 Sunset Ave (11942-4200)
PHONE...................................207 778-3246
Fred York, *Principal*
David B Horn,
EMP: 6
SALES (est): 590.8K **Privately Held**
SIC: 3678 Electronic connectors

East Rochester
Monroe County

(G-4159)
ART PARTS SIGNS INC
100 Lincoln Pkwy (14445-1450)
PHONE..........................585 381-2134
Patricia Ransco, *President*
EMP: 7
SQ FT: 8,000
SALES: 500K **Privately Held**
SIC: 3993 Signs, not made in custom sign
painting shops

(G-4160)
CARPENTIER INDUSTRIES LLC
Also Called: Rochester Magnet
119 Despatch Dr (14445-1447)
PHONE..........................585 385-5550
Andrew Carpentier, *President*
Jill Marefka, *Accounts Mgr*
Melissa Winslow, *Office Mgr*
▲ EMP: 15
SQ FT: 10,000
SALES (est): 2.2MM **Privately Held**
WEB: www.rochestermagnet.com
SIC: 3499 Magnets, permanent: metallic

(G-4161)
EKOSTINGER INC
140 Despatch Dr (14445-1448)
PHONE..........................585 739-0450
Parr Wiegel, *CEO*
Steve Smith, *Exec VP*
Scott Leffert, *Vice Pres*
Ania Makuch, *Vice Pres*
Steven Chatwin, *Officer*
EMP: 11 EST: 2012
SQ FT: 13,500
SALES (est): 1.1MM **Privately Held**
SIC: 3713 Truck bodies & parts

(G-4162)
FERRO CORPORATION
603 W Commercial St (14445-2253)
P.O. Box 389 (14445-0389)
PHONE..........................585 586-8770
Daniel Dickmann, *Research*
Richard Veeder, *Branch Mgr*
EMP: 35
SQ FT: 30,000
SALES (corp-wide): 1.6B **Publicly Held**
WEB: www.ferro.com
SIC: 2819 Industrial inorganic chemicals
PA: Ferro Corporation
6060 Parkland Blvd # 250
Mayfield Heights OH 44124
216 875-5600

(G-4163)
FILTROS LTD
Also Called: Filtros Plant
603 W Commercial St (14445-2253)
P.O. Box 389 (14445-0389)
PHONE..........................585 586-8770
Byron Anderson, *CEO*
Allan Schilling, *Vice Pres*
Scott Stranford, *QC Mgr*
Ken Speed, *Manager*
EMP: 35 EST: 1999
SQ FT: 45,000
SALES (est): 5.6MM **Privately Held**
WEB: www.filtrosltd.com
SIC: 3255 3564 3297 3264 Clay refracto-
ries; blowers & fans; nonclay refractories;
porcelain electrical supplies

(G-4164)
HOERCHER INDUSTRIES INC
A1 Country Club Rd Ste 1 (14445-2230)
PHONE..........................585 398-2982
Lawrence Hoercher, *President*
EMP: 5
SQ FT: 3,500
SALES (est): 360K **Privately Held**
SIC: 3599 Electrical discharge machining
(EDM)

(G-4165)
IDEAL MANUFACTURING INC
80 Bluff Dr (14445-1300)
PHONE..........................585 872-7190
Ben Stroyer, *President*

Arthur Stroyer, *Vice Pres*
Nancy Balentine, *Office Admin*
▼ EMP: 32
SQ FT: 7,000
SALES (est): 9.1MM **Privately Held**
SIC: 2515 Foundations & platforms

(G-4166)
KRONENBERGER MFG CORP
115 Despatch Dr (14445-1447)
P.O. Box 650 (14445-0650)
PHONE..........................585 385-2340
Gunter Kronenberger, *President*
Eric Kronenberger, *Vice Pres*
Kevin Kronenberger, *Vice Pres*
EMP: 45
SQ FT: 40,000
SALES (est): 7.5MM **Privately Held**
SIC: 3599 Machine shop, jobbing & repair

(G-4167)
LINCDOC LLC
Also Called: Lincware
401 Main St (14445-1718)
PHONE..........................585 563-1669
Darren Mathis, *CEO*
Rob Tiernan, *VP Sales*
Cristin Donaher, *Business Anlyst*
Cara Chatellier, *Marketing Staff*
Adam Lenio, *Creative Dir*
EMP: 7
SALES (est): 468.7K **Privately Held**
SIC: 7372 Prepackaged software

(G-4168)
OMNI-ID USA INC
333 W Cmmrcl St 333-150 (14445)
PHONE..........................585 299-5990
Tony Kington, *President*
Ed Nabrotzky, *Exec VP*
Andre Cote, *Senior VP*
Tracy Gay, *Vice Pres*
EMP: 37
SALES (est): 6.8MM **Privately Held**
WEB: www.omni-id.com
SIC: 3825 Radio frequency measuring
equipment

(G-4169)
RICHARDS & WEST INC
Also Called: Rw Manufacturing Company
501 W Commercial St Ste 1 (14445-2258)
PHONE..........................585 461-4088
John R Keim, *Ch of Bd*
Gary Keim, *Vice Pres*
John E Miner, *Vice Pres*
EMP: 54 EST: 1982
SQ FT: 10,000
SALES (est): 8.5MM **Privately Held**
WEB: www.rwmfg.com
SIC: 3911 7631 5944 Jewelry, precious
metal; jewelry repair services; jewelry,
precious stones & precious metals

East Rockaway
Nassau County

(G-4170)
ADULTS AND CHILDREN WITH LEARN
22 Alice Ct (11518-1902)
PHONE..........................516 593-8230
EMP: 34
SALES (corp-wide): 85.3MM **Privately Held**
SIC: 3999 Barber & beauty shop equip-
ment
PA: Adults And Children With Learning And
Developmental Disabilities, Inc.
807 S Oyster Bay Rd
Bethpage NY 11714
516 822-0028

(G-4171)
CIRCUITS & SYSTEMS INC
Also Called: Arlyn Scales
59 2nd St (11518-1236)
PHONE..........................516 593-4301
Arnold Gordon, *President*
Lynne Gordon, *Corp Secy*
▲ EMP: 22 EST: 1977
SQ FT: 6,000

SALES (est): 5.4MM **Privately Held**
WEB: www.chaverware.com
SIC: 3596 7373 Scales & balances, ex-
cept laboratory; computer-aided design
(CAD) systems service

(G-4172)
DAWN PAPER CO INC (PA)
Also Called: Dawn Printing Company
4 Leonard Dr (11518-1609)
PHONE..........................516 596-9110
Stephen Kucker, *President*
Jonathan Greenberg, *Vice Pres*
Marla Perrino, *Vice Pres*
EMP: 12
SQ FT: 5,000
SALES (est): 2.4MM **Privately Held**
SIC: 2752 5113 5085 Commercial print-
ing, lithographic; bags, paper & dispos-
able plastic; boxes, crates, etc., other
than paper

(G-4173)
FK SAFETY GEAR INC
736 Stranton Ave (11518)
PHONE..........................516 233-9628
Muhammad Rafique, *President*
Saadia Khan, *Senior VP*
Khalid Mehmood, *Vice Pres*
EMP: 6
SQ FT: 60,000
SALES: 100K **Privately Held**
SIC: 3842 Personal safety equipment

(G-4174)
STERLING PIERCE COMPANY INC
395 Atlantic Ave (11518-1423)
PHONE..........................516 593-1170
William Burke, *President*
Isabel Burke, *Vice Pres*
Michael Arguelles, *Manager*
▼ EMP: 29
SQ FT: 5,000
SALES (est): 3.3MM **Privately Held**
WEB: www.sterlingpierce.com
SIC: 2789 2732 2752 Binding only:
books, pamphlets, magazines, etc.; book
printing; commercial printing, lithographic

(G-4175)
STYLEBUILT ACCESSORIES INC (PA)
Also Called: Stylebuilt Acesries
45 Rose Ln (11518-2126)
PHONE..........................917 439-0578
Jonathan Greenfield, *President*
Jerome Greenfield, *Vice Pres*
Jackie Greenfield, *Treasurer*
▲ EMP: 12 EST: 1946
SQ FT: 65,000
SALES: 950K **Privately Held**
WEB: www.stylebuilt.com
SIC: 3499 Novelties & specialties, metal

East Setauket
Suffolk County

(G-4176)
B & Z TECHNOLOGIES LLC
Also Called: Bnz Tech
7 Technology Dr (11733-4000)
PHONE..........................631 675-9666
Javed Siddiqui, *President*
Asma Siddiqui, *CFO*
EMP: 7
SQ FT: 2,000
SALES: 2MM **Privately Held**
WEB: www.bnztech.com
SIC: 3812 Antennas, radar or communica-
tions; radar systems & equipment

(G-4177)
BASF CORPORATION
Also Called: BASF The Chemical Company
361 Sheep Pasture Rd (11733-3614)
PHONE..........................631 689-0200
Meredith Culver, *Branch Mgr*
Anthony Asselta, *Manager*
EMP: 157
SALES (corp-wide): 71.7B **Privately Held**
SIC: 2869 Industrial organic chemicals

HQ: Basf Corporation
100 Park Ave
Florham Park NJ 07932
973 245-6000

(G-4178)
FLAGPOLES INCORPORATED
95 Gnarled Hollow Rd (11733-1934)
P.O. Box 833 (11733-0643)
PHONE..........................631 751-5500
Jack Seferian, *CEO*
Haig Seferian, *Principal*
Gregory Seferian, *Vice Pres*
▼ EMP: 90
SQ FT: 96,000
SALES (est): 19.1MM **Privately Held**
WEB: www.flagpole.net
SIC: 3446 3441 3354 Flagpoles, metal;
fabricated structural metal; aluminum ex-
truded products

(G-4179)
GEOMETRIC CIRCUITS INC
10 Technology Dr Unit 7 (11733-4063)
PHONE..........................631 249-0230
John Pollina, *President*
Kurt J Meyer, *Corp Secy*
EMP: 60
SALES (est): 7.8MM **Privately Held**
WEB: www.geometriccircuits.com
SIC: 3672 Printed circuit boards

(G-4180)
MARK GOLDBERG PROSTHETIC
9 Technology Dr (11733-4000)
PHONE..........................631 689-6606
Mark E Goldberg, *President*
EMP: 14
SALES (est): 1.7MM **Privately Held**
SIC: 3842 8021 5999 Limbs, artificial;
prosthodontist; artificial limbs

(G-4181)
MILLER MOHR DISPLAY INC
12 Technology Dr Unit 6 (11733-4049)
PHONE..........................631 941-2769
Marilyn Mohr, *President*
Miller Mohr, *Principal*
EMP: 5
SALES: 950K **Privately Held**
SIC: 3993 Displays & cutouts, window &
lobby

(G-4182)
MML SOFTWARE LTD
Also Called: Finance Manager
45 Research Way Ste 207 (11733-6401)
PHONE..........................631 941-1313
Ron Bovich, *President*
Andrew Miller, *President*
Mercedes Burgos, *Vice Pres*
Sophia Koehler, *Finance Mgr*
Wendy Gottlieb, *Mktg Coord*
EMP: 20
SQ FT: 5,000
SALES (est): 2.2MM **Privately Held**
WEB: www.financemgr.com
SIC: 7372 6163 Application computer soft-
ware; loan brokers

(G-4183)
PENETRON INTERNATIONAL LTD
45 Research Way Ste 203 (11733-6401)
PHONE..........................631 941-9700
Robert G Reuera, *CEO*
Vicki Denninger, *COO*
Grant Urban, *Sales Mgr*
Vanessa Georgiades, *Sales Staff*
Michelle Staria, *Sales Staff*
▲ EMP: 14
SQ FT: 60,000
SALES (est): 5.5MM **Privately Held**
WEB: www.penetron.com
SIC: 2899 Waterproofing compounds

(G-4184)
POLE-TECH CO INC
Also Called: Poletech Flagpole Manufaturer
97 Gnarled Hollow Rd (11733-1980)
P.O. Box 715 (11733-0770)
PHONE..........................631 689-5525
Karnik M Seferian, *Ch of Bd*
Ralph Barbarite, *Vice Pres*
Melanie Veen, *Manager*
◆ EMP: 17

SQ FT: 20,000
SALES (est): 4.7MM **Privately Held**
WEB: www.poletech.com
SIC: 3446 Flagpoles, metal

(G-4185)
PRINTING SPECTRUM INC
12 Research Way Ste 1 (11733-3531)
PHONE..................................631 689-1010
James Altebrando, *Ch of Bd*
EMP: 12
SQ FT: 10,000
SALES (est): 2MM **Privately Held**
WEB: www.printingspectrum.com
SIC: 2752 Commercial printing, offset

(G-4186)
SARTEK INDUSTRIES INC
Also Called: Snr Cctv Systems Division
17 N Belle Mead Ave Ste 1 (11733-3466)
PHONE..................................631 473-3555
Carl Saieva, *President*
EMP: 6
SQ FT: 5,200
SALES: 950.3K **Privately Held**
WEB: www.sarind.com
SIC: 3663 1731 Television closed circuit
   equipment; closed circuit television instal-
   lation

(G-4187)
SKYLINE LLC
16 Hulse Rd Ste 1 (11733-3645)
PHONE..................................631 403-4131
Louis Bove, *Mng Member*
Lawrence Schreiber,
EMP: 20
SALES: 3.5MM **Privately Held**
SIC: 3295 Perlite, aggregate or expanded

(G-4188)
TIMES BEACON RECORD
NEWSPAPERS (PA)
Also Called: Village Times, The
185 Route 25a Ste 4 (11733-2870)
P.O. Box 707 (11733-0769)
PHONE..................................631 331-1154
Leah E Dunaief, *President*
Leah Dunaief, *Owner*
EMP: 16 EST: 1973
SALES (est): 2MM **Privately Held**
SIC: 2711 Newspapers: publishing only,
   not printed on site

(G-4189)
TUCKER JONES HOUSE INC
1 Enterprise Dr (11733-4086)
P.O. Box 231 (11733-0231)
PHONE..................................631 642-9092
Donna Sucilsky, *President*
EMP: 20
SQ FT: 8,000
SALES (est): 2.3MM **Privately Held**
WEB: www.tavernpuzzle.com
SIC: 3944 Puzzles

(G-4190)
VISION QUEST LIGHTING INC
Also Called: E-Quest Lighting
12 Satterly Rd (11733-3722)
PHONE..................................631 737-4800
Larry Lieberman, *Ch of Bd*
Torrey Bievenour, *Vice Pres*
Janelle Norton, *Vice Pres*
▲ EMP: 33
SQ FT: 2,500
SALES (est): 8.7MM **Privately Held**
WEB: www.vql.com
SIC: 3645 3646 Residential lighting fix-
   tures; fluorescent lighting fixtures, resi-
   dential; garden, patio, walkway & yard
   lighting fixtures: electric; fluorescent light-
   ing fixtures, commercial

(G-4191)
ZEPPELIN ELECTRIC COMPANY
INC
26 Deer Ln (11733-3407)
PHONE..................................631 928-9467
William Zeppelin, *President*
EMP: 7
SQ FT: 1,250
SALES: 525.4K **Privately Held**
SIC: 3625 1731 Relays & industrial con-
   trols; electronic controls installation

East Syracuse
Onondaga County

(G-4192)
A NUCLIMATE QULTY SYSTEMS
INC
6295 E Molloy Rd Ste 3 (13057-1072)
PHONE..................................315 431-0226
Edward Campagna Jr, *President*
John Dimillo, *Vice Pres*
James Miller, *VP Engrg*
EMP: 19
SALES (est): 2.3MM **Privately Held**
SIC: 3585 3433 Heating equipment, com-
   plete; heating & air conditioning combina-
   tion units; heating equipment, except
   electric

(G-4193)
ALBERT F STAGER INC
6805 Crossbow Dr (13057-1006)
PHONE..................................315 434-7240
EMP: 5
SALES (corp-wide): 473.7MM **Privately
Held**
SIC: 3081 Plastic film & sheet
HQ: Albert F Stager Inc
   3815 California Rd
   Orchard Park NY 14127
   716 667-6000

(G-4194)
ALLEN TOOL PHOENIX INC
6821 Ellicott Dr (13057-1148)
P.O. Box 3024, Liverpool (13089-3024)
PHONE..................................315 463-7533
Cheryl Maines, *President*
Heath Severn, *Engineer*
Nick Grevelding, *Administration*
EMP: 20
SQ FT: 18,000
SALES (est): 3.5MM **Privately Held**
WEB: www.allentoolphoenix.com
SIC: 3599 7692 Machine shop, jobbing &
   repair; welding repair

(G-4195)
ANAREN INC (HQ)
6635 Kirkville Rd (13057-9672)
PHONE..................................315 432-8909
Lawrence A Sala, *President*
Mark P Burdick, *President*
David E Kopf, *President*
Jeff Liebl, *President*
Bo Jensen, *General Mgr*
▲ EMP: 300
SQ FT: 159,000
SALES (est): 316.7MM
SALES (corp-wide): 2.8B **Publicly Held**
WEB: www.anaren.com
SIC: 3679 Electronic circuits; microwave
   components
PA: Ttm Technologies, Inc.
   200 Sandpointe Ave # 400
   Santa Ana CA 92707
   714 327-3000

(G-4196)
ARMSTRONG MOLD
CORPORATION (PA)
6910 Manlius Center Rd (13057-8507)
PHONE..................................315 437-1517
John Alfred Armstrong, *CEO*
Peter Armstrong, *President*
Mark Garofano, *President*
Jeffrey Forrest, *COO*
John Armstrong, *Vice Pres*
▼ EMP: 50
SQ FT: 90,000
SALES (est): 19.8MM **Privately Held**
WEB: www.armstrongmold.com
SIC: 3365 3089 3543 Aluminum & alu-
   minum-based alloy castings; injection
   molding of plastics; industrial patterns

(G-4197)
ARMSTRONG MOLD
CORPORATION
5860 Fisher Rd (13057-2962)
PHONE..................................315 437-1517
John Alfred Armstrong, *Principal*
Greg Mork, *Engineer*
EMP: 75

SQ FT: 31,060
SALES (corp-wide): 19.8MM **Privately
Held**
WEB: www.armstrongmold.com
SIC: 3599 3365 3089 3543 Custom machinery; machine shop, jobbing & repair;
   aluminum & aluminum-based alloy castings; injection molding of plastics; industrial patterns
PA: Armstrong Mold Corporation
   6910 Manlius Center Rd
   East Syracuse NY 13057
   315 437-1517

(G-4198)
ASSA ABLOY ENTRANCE
SYSTEMS US
Also Called: Besam Entrance Solutions
28 Corporate Cir Ste 1 (13057-1283)
PHONE..................................315 492-6600
Shane Stone, *Branch Mgr*
EMP: 22
SALES (corp-wide): 9.3B **Privately Held**
SIC: 3699 1796 3442 Door opening &
   closing devices, electrical; installing build-
   ing equipment; metal doors
HQ: Assa Abloy Entrance Systems Us Inc.
   1900 Airport Rd
   Monroe NC 28110
   704 290-5520

(G-4199)
AURORA STONE GROUP LLC
114 Marcy St (13057-2143)
PHONE..................................315 471-6869
Sondra Murphy,
EMP: 10 EST: 2011
SALES (est): 922.9K **Privately Held**
SIC: 3281 1743 Granite, cut & shaped;
   marble installation, interior

(G-4200)
BK PRINTING INC
Also Called: Speedpro Imaging
6507 Basile Rowe (13057-2928)
PHONE..................................315 565-5396
Robert Kellher, *President*
Lori Parker, *CFO*
EMP: 7 EST: 2010
SQ FT: 5,000
SALES: 700K **Privately Held**
SIC: 2752 Commercial printing, litho-
   graphic

(G-4201)
BRISTOL-MYERS SQUIBB
COMPANY
6000 Thompson Rd (13057-5050)
P.O. Box 4755, Syracuse (13221-4755)
PHONE..................................315 432-2000
Helen Shareshian, *Project Mgr*
Robert E Ward, *Opers Staff*
Fran Sidnam, *Mfg Staff*
Steven Lee, *Branch Mgr*
Matthew Cadin, *Manager*
EMP: 40
SALES (corp-wide): 22.5B **Publicly Held**
WEB: www.bms.com
SIC: 2834 Druggists' preparations (phar-
   maceuticals)
PA: Bristol-Myers Squibb Company
   430 E 29th St Fl 14
   New York NY 10016
   212 546-4000

(G-4202)
CARRIER CORPORATION
Carrier Transicold
1201 Kinne St (13057)
P.O. Box 4805, Syracuse (13221-4805)
PHONE..................................315 432-6000
Nick Pinchuk, *Manager*
Alan Knight, *Manager*
EMP: 293
SALES (corp-wide): 66.5B **Publicly Held**
WEB: www.carrier.com
SIC: 3585 Air conditioning equipment,
   complete
HQ: Carrier Corporation
   13995 Pasteur Blvd
   Palm Beach Gardens FL 33418
   800 379-6484

(G-4203)
CARRIER CORPORATION
Transicold
Carrier Pkwy Bldg Tr 20 (13057)
P.O. Box 4805, Syracuse (13221-4805)
PHONE..................................315 432-3844
Nick Pinchuk, *President*
Scott Lindsay, *Engineer*
EMP: 293
SALES (corp-wide): 66.5B **Publicly Held**
WEB: www.carrier.com
SIC: 3585 Lockers, refrigerated
HQ: Carrier Corporation
   13995 Pasteur Blvd
   Palm Beach Gardens FL 33418
   800 379-6484

(G-4204)
CLEARWOOD CUSTOM
CARPENTRY AND
617 W Manlius St Ste 1 (13057-2276)
PHONE..................................315 432-8422
Kyle Latray, *Mng Member*
Andrew McDonald,
EMP: 30
SQ FT: 33,856
SALES: 5.1MM **Privately Held**
WEB: www.clearwoodccm.com
SIC: 2431 2434 Millwork; wood kitchen
   cabinets

(G-4205)
DAIRY FARMERS AMERICA INC
5001 Brittonfield Pkwy (13057-9201)
P.O. Box 4844, Syracuse (13221-4844)
PHONE..................................816 801-6440
Ona Coker, *Export Mgr*
Jennifer Lastowicka, *Accountant*
Nichole Owens, *Corp Comm Staff*
David Geisler, *Manager*
EMP: 41
SALES (corp-wide): 13.6B **Privately Held**
WEB: www.dfamilk.com
SIC: 2026 Milk processing (pasteurizing,
   homogenizing, bottling)
PA: Dairy Farmers Of America, Inc.
   1405 N 98th St
   Kansas City KS 66111
   816 801-6455

(G-4206)
DATACOM SYSTEMS INC
9 Adler Dr (13057-1201)
PHONE..................................315 463-9541
Kevin Formby, *President*
Timothy Crofton, *President*
Sam Lanzafane, *Chairman*
Joe Sullivan, *Vice Pres*
Morris De Lorenzo, *Buyer*
EMP: 33
SQ FT: 16,000
SALES (est): 7.1MM **Privately Held**
WEB: www.datacomsystems.com
SIC: 3571 Electronic computers

(G-4207)
DEAN FOODS COMPANY
6867 Schuyler Rd (13057-9752)
PHONE..................................315 452-5001
Leah Curcio, *Principal*
Tom Trudeau, *Director*
EMP: 87 **Publicly Held**
SIC: 2026 Milk processing (pasteurizing,
   homogenizing, bottling)
PA: Dean Foods Company
   2711 N Haskell Ave # 340
   Dallas TX 75204

(G-4208)
E F THRESH INC
6000 Galster Rd (13057-2917)
PHONE..................................315 437-7301
Eric F Thresh, *President*
Janet Thresh, *Corp Secy*
William Thresh, *Vice Pres*
EMP: 6
SQ FT: 35,000
SALES: 728K **Privately Held**
SIC: 2541 6512 Cabinets, except refriger-
   ated: show, display, etc.: wood; commer-
   cial & industrial building operation

(G-4209)
FALK PRECISION INC
5917 Fisher Rd (13057-2912)
PHONE..................................315 437-4545

Tracy Foltz, *Ch of Bd*
EMP: 30
SQ FT: 15,000
SALES (est): 3.8MM **Privately Held**
WEB: www.falkprecision.com
SIC: 3599 Machine shop, jobbing & repair

(G-4210)
FBM GALAXY INC
6741 Old Collamer Rd (13057-1119)
PHONE.....................315 463-5144
Glen Markam, *Manager*
EMP: 18
SALES (corp-wide): 2B **Publicly Held**
WEB: www.spi-co.com
SIC: 3089 3296 3554 Plastic processing;
fiberglass insulation; die cutting & stamp-
ing machinery, paper converting
HQ: Fbm Galaxy, Inc.
1650 Manheim Pike Ste 202
Lancaster PA 17601
717 569-3900

(G-4211)
FIBERONE LLC
5 Technology Pl Ste 4 (13057-9738)
PHONE.....................315 434-8877
Liz Castaneda, *General Mgr*
Craig Mead,
EMP: 15 **EST:** 2000
SALES (est): 2MM **Privately Held**
SIC: 2298 Cable, fiber

(G-4212)
GEI INTERNATIONAL INC
Also Called: Gaebel Enterprises
100 Ball St (13057-2359)
P.O. Box 6849, Syracuse (13217-6849)
PHONE.....................315 463-9261
Peter Anderson, *President*
Maureen Anderson, *Vice Pres*
EMP: 20 **EST:** 1960
SALES (est): 2.3MM **Privately Held**
WEB: www.geionline.com
SIC: 3423 3531 5199 3829 Rules or
rulers, metal; scrapers (construction ma-
chinery); art goods & supplies; measuring
& controlling devices

(G-4213)
GREENWOOD WINERY LLC
6475 Collamer Rd (13057-1031)
P.O. Box 2949, Syracuse (13220-2949)
PHONE.....................315 432-8132
Tom Greenwood, *Owner*
Robyn Bombard, *Sales Mgr*
EMP: 30
SALES: 800K **Privately Held**
SIC: 2084 2066 Wines; chocolate

(G-4214)
**H F W COMMUNICATIONS INC
(HQ)**
Also Called: Holstein World
6437 Collamer Rd Ste 1 (13057-1559)
PHONE.....................315 703-7979
Scott Smith, *CEO*
Joel Hastings, *President*
John Montandon, *President*
Art Sweum, *Vice Pres*
EMP: 15
SALES (est): 5.8MM **Privately Held**
SIC: 2721 Trade journals: publishing &
printing
PA: Multi-Ag Media L.L.C.
6437 Collamer Rd
East Syracuse NY
315 703-7979

(G-4215)
HANGER INC
6620 Fly Rd Ste 203 (13057-4282)
PHONE.....................518 438-4546
EMP: 23
SALES (corp-wide): 1B **Publicly Held**
SIC: 3842 Surgical appliances & supplies
PA: Hanger, Inc.
10910 Domain Dr Ste 300
Austin TX 78758
512 777-3800

(G-4216)
HERCULES CANDY CO
Also Called: Hercules Gift & Gourmet
720 W Manlius St (13057-2158)
PHONE.....................315 463-4339

Terry L Andrianos, *Partner*
EMP: 8
SALES: 232K **Privately Held**
WEB: www.herculescandy.com
SIC: 2064 5441 5149 Candy & other con-
fectionery products; candy; chocolate

(G-4217)
**HONEYWELL INTERNATIONAL
INC**
7000 Airways Park Dr # 4 (13057-9413)
PHONE.....................315 463-7208
Michael Lyons, *Manager*
EMP: 10
SALES (corp-wide): 41.8B **Publicly Held**
WEB: www.ondemandcorp.com
SIC: 3724 Aircraft engines & engine parts
PA: Honeywell International Inc.
300 S Tryon St
Charlotte NC 28202
973 455-2000

(G-4218)
**INDUSTRIAL FABRICATING
CORP (PA)**
6201 E Molloy Rd (13057-1021)
PHONE.....................315 437-3353
Myron R Kocan, *President*
Richard Stukey, *Buyer*
EMP: 33
SQ FT: 60,000
SALES (est): 14MM **Privately Held**
WEB: www.industrialfabricating.com
SIC: 3441 3444 Fabricated structural
metal; sheet metalwork

(G-4219)
**INDUSTRIAL FABRICATING
CORP**
4 Collamer Cir (13057-1102)
PHONE.....................315 437-8234
Gary Cristal, *Manager*
EMP: 29
SQ FT: 32,886
SALES (corp-wide): 14MM **Privately
Held**
WEB: www.industrialfabricating.com
SIC: 3443 Weldments
PA: Industrial Fabricating Corp
6201 E Molloy Rd
East Syracuse NY 13057
315 437-3353

(G-4220)
INFICON INC (HQ)
2 Technology Pl (13057-9714)
PHONE.....................315 434-1100
Darren Lee, *General Mgr*
Jeffrey Newbery, *General Mgr*
Hoang Cao, *Vice Pres*
Ulrich Doebler, *Vice Pres*
URS Waelchli, *Vice Pres*
▲ **EMP:** 250
SQ FT: 135,000
SALES (est): 6.7MM
SALES (corp-wide): 410.4MM **Privately
Held**
WEB: www.inficon.com
SIC: 3823 3812 Industrial process control
instruments; search & navigation equip-
ment
PA: Inficon Holding Ag
Hintergasse 15b
Bad Ragaz SG 7310
813 004-980

(G-4221)
INFICON HOLDING AG
2 Technology Pl (13057-9714)
PHONE.....................315 434-1100
Timothy Karandy, *Engineer*
Peter G Maier, *CFO*
EMP: 7
SALES (est): 448K **Privately Held**
SIC: 3823 Industrial process control instru-
ments

(G-4222)
INFITEC INC
6500 Badgley Rd (13057-9667)
P.O. Box 2956, Syracuse (13220-2956)
PHONE.....................315 433-1150
George W Ehegartner, *Ch of Bd*
David Lawrie, *Vice Pres*
Bob Eichenlaub, *Purch Mgr*

Garry White, *Project Engr*
◆ **EMP:** 60
SQ FT: 22,000
SALES: 4.8MM **Privately Held**
WEB: www.infitec.com
SIC: 3625 3822 Timing devices, elec-
tronic; auto controls regulating residntl &
coml environmt & applncs

(G-4223)
J W STEVENS CO INC
6059 Corporate Dr (13057-1040)
PHONE.....................315 472-6311
Jeff Salanger, *Vice Pres*
Ed Gilson, *Sales Mgr*
EMP: 6
SALES (est): 711.8K **Privately Held**
SIC: 3443 Boiler shop products: boilers,
smokestacks, steel tanks

(G-4224)
JE MILLER INC
747 W Manlius St (13057-2177)
PHONE.....................315 437-6811
Dennis J Hile, *President*
Robert Leroy, *General Mgr*
Barbara Hile, *Vice Pres*
EMP: 16 **EST:** 1951
SQ FT: 15,000
SALES (est): 3.5MM **Privately Held**
WEB: www.jemiller.com
SIC: 3625 3585 Relays & industrial con-
trols; air conditioning units, complete: do-
mestic or industrial

(G-4225)
KERNER AND MERCHANT
104 Johnson St (13057-2840)
PHONE.....................315 463-8023
Benjamin R Merchant, *President*
Albert H Arnold, *Admin Sec*
EMP: 7
SQ FT: 3,600
SALES: 300K **Privately Held**
SIC: 3931 7699 Pipes, organ; organ tun-
ing & repair

(G-4226)
**MICROWAVE FILTER COMPANY
INC (PA)**
6743 Kinne St (13057-1269)
PHONE.....................315 438-4700
Paul W Mears, *CEO*
Robert R Andrews, *Ch of Bd*
Sherry Bell, *General Mgr*
Carl F Fahrenkrug Jr, *Exec VP*
Richard L Jones, *CFO*
EMP: 35 **EST:** 1967
SQ FT: 40,000
SALES: 3.3MM **Publicly Held**
WEB: www.microwavefilter.com
SIC: 3677 3679 Filtration devices, elec-
tronic; microwave components

(G-4227)
MUTUAL LIBRARY BINDERY INC
6295 E Molloy Rd Ste 3 (13057-1104)
P.O. Box 6026, Syracuse (13217-6026)
PHONE.....................315 455-6638
Otto E Rausch, *President*
Robert Rausch, *Vice Pres*
Stephen Rausch, *Vice Pres*
EMP: 25 **EST:** 1915
SALES (est): 2.5MM **Privately Held**
SIC: 2789 Bookbinding & repairing: trade,
edition, library, etc.

(G-4228)
NIAGARA SCIENTIFIC INC
Also Called: Schroeder Machine Div
6743 Kinne St (13057-1215)
P.O. Box 146 (13057-0146)
PHONE.....................315 437-0821
Carl Fahrenkrug, *President*
Milo Peterson, *Exec VP*
Richard Jones, *CFO*
EMP: 44
SQ FT: 16,000
SALES (est): 7MM
SALES (corp-wide): 3.3MM **Publicly Held**
WEB: www.microwavefilter.com
SIC: 3565 3826 Carton packing machines;
environmental testing equipment

PA: Microwave Filter Company, Inc.
6743 Kinne St
East Syracuse NY 13057
315 438-4700

(G-4229)
NIDEC MOTOR CORPORATION
Advanced Motors & Drives
6268 E Molloy Rd (13057-1047)
PHONE.....................315 434-9303
EMP: 17 **Privately Held**
SIC: 3621 Motors, electric
HQ: Nidec Motor Corporation
8050 West Florissant Ave
Saint Louis MO 63136

(G-4230)
**POWER-FLO TECHNOLOGIES
INC**
Also Called: Auburn Armature
6500 New Venture Gear Dr (13057-1076)
PHONE.....................315 399-5801
Mike Capfllo, *Manager*
EMP: 93
SALES (corp-wide): 57MM **Privately
Held**
WEB: www.auburnarmature.com
SIC: 7694 Armature rewinding shops
PA: Power-Flo Technologies, Inc.
270 Park Ave
New Hyde Park NY 11040
516 812-6800

(G-4231)
PPC BROADBAND INC (HQ)
6176 E Molloy Rd (13057-4010)
P.O. Box 278 (13057-0278)
PHONE.....................315 431-7200
Dave Jackson, *CEO*
Jose Rosa, *General Mgr*
Brian Kelly, *Vice Pres*
Al Moran, *Vice Pres*
Michael Reed, *Vice Pres*
◆ **EMP:** 500 **EST:** 1992
SALES: 350MM
SALES (corp-wide): 2.5B **Publicly Held**
WEB: www.ppc-online.com
SIC: 3678 Electronic connectors
PA: Belden Inc.
1 N Brentwood Blvd Fl 15
Saint Louis MO 63105
314 854-8000

(G-4232)
RAYMOND CORPORATION
6533 Chrysler Ln (13057-1375)
PHONE.....................315 643-5000
Jim Schaefer, *Branch Mgr*
EMP: 30 **Privately Held**
SIC: 3535 3537 7359 Conveyors & con-
veying equipment; industrial trucks & trac-
tors; equipment rental & leasing
HQ: The Raymond Corporation
22 S Canal St
Greene NY 13778
607 656-2311

(G-4233)
**REYNOLDS TECH
FABRICATORS INC**
6895 Kinne St (13057-1217)
PHONE.....................315 437-0532
Joan J Reynolds, *CEO*
EMP: 37
SQ FT: 35,000
SALES (est): 6.8MM **Privately Held**
SIC: 3559 3471 Refinery, chemical pro-
cessing & similar machinery; plating of
metals or formed products

(G-4234)
RICHLAR INDUSTRIES INC
Also Called: Richlar Custom Foam Div
6741 Old Collamer Rd (13057-1119)
PHONE.....................315 463-5144
Richard Bruntarger, *President*
EMP: 18
SQ FT: 32,000
SALES (est): 3.1MM **Privately Held**
SIC: 3089 3296 3554 Plastic processing;
fiberglass insulation; die cutting & stamp-
ing machinery, paper converting

▲ = Import ▼=Export
◆ =Import/Export

(G-4235)
SAAB DEFENSE AND SEC USA LLC
5717 Enterprise Pkwy (13057-2953)
PHONE..............................315 445-5009
Laurence Harris, *Principal*
Magnus Rnberg, *Exec VP*
Jay Abendroth, *Vice Pres*
Anders Carp, *Vice Pres*
Lena Eliasson, *Vice Pres*
EMP: 14
SALES (corp-wide): 3.6B **Privately Held**
SIC: 3812 Search & detection systems & instruments
HQ: Saab Defense And Security Usa Llc
20700 Loudoun County Pkwy # 100
Ashburn VA 20147
703 406-7200

(G-4236)
SBB INC
1 Gm Dr Ste 5 (13057)
PHONE..............................315 422-2376
Robert McKenty, *Principal*
Brian Kearney, *Engineer*
EMP: 5
SALES (est): 1.2MM **Privately Held**
SIC: 3564 Air purification equipment

(G-4237)
SEABOARD GRAPHIC SERVICES LLC
Also Called: Minuteman Press
6881 Schuyler Rd (13057-9752)
PHONE..............................315 652-4200
Melinda Kuhn, *CFO*
Lawrence Kuhn, *Mng Member*
EMP: 25
SALES (est): 4.6MM **Privately Held**
WEB: www.seaboardgraphics.com
SIC: 2752 Commercial printing, lithographic

(G-4238)
SHAKO INC
6191 E Molloy Rd (13057-1038)
PHONE..............................315 437-1294
Brian Mayfield, *Principal*
EMP: 8
SALES (est): 892.9K **Privately Held**
SIC: 3535 Pneumatic tube conveyor systems

(G-4239)
STF SERVICES INC
26 Corporate Cir Ste 2 (13057-1105)
PHONE..............................315 463-8506
Michael Smith, *President*
John Siedlicki, *COO*
EMP: 50
SQ FT: 20,000
SALES (est): 4.5MM
SALES (corp-wide): 1.8B **Privately Held**
WEB: www.superforms.com
SIC: 2731 2741 Books: publishing only; miscellaneous publishing
HQ: The Bureau Of National Affairs Inc
1801 S Bell St Ste Cn110
Arlington VA 22202
703 341-3000

(G-4240)
SULLIVAN BAZINET BONGIO INC
Also Called: S B B
6295 E Molloy Rd Ste 3 (13057-1072)
PHONE..............................315 437-6500
John Bazinet, *Partner*
Vincent Bongio, *Partner*
Mike Sullivan, *Partner*
Brandon Bogart, *General Mgr*
Sheila Cooperider, *Office Mgr*
EMP: 30
SALES (est): 7.9MM **Privately Held**
WEB: www.sbbinc.com
SIC: 3564 Air purification equipment

(G-4241)
SYRACUSE CORRUGATED BOX CORP
302 Stoutenger St (13057-2841)
P.O. Box 126 (13057-0126)
PHONE..............................315 437-9901
David R Wilde, *President*
Charles Wilde, *Vice Pres*

John Wilde, *Admin Sec*
EMP: 14 EST: 1969
SQ FT: 24,000
SALES (est): 2.5MM **Privately Held**
SIC: 2653 Boxes, corrugated: made from purchased materials

(G-4242)
THE PRS GROUP INC (PA)
Also Called: Political Risk Services, The
5010 Campuswood Dr # 204 (13057-1233)
PHONE..............................315 431-0511
Christopher McKee, *CEO*
Sharon Ryan, *Editor*
Christa Mosher, *Production*
Dianna Spinner, *Treasurer*
Louis Carroll, *Director*
EMP: 10 EST: 2000
SALES (est): 848.3K **Privately Held**
WEB: www.prsgroup.com
SIC: 2721 Periodicals: publishing & printing; statistical reports (periodicals): publishing & printing

(G-4243)
TPC INC
6780 Nthrn Blvd Ste 401 (13057)
P.O. Box 2581, Syracuse (13220-2581)
PHONE..............................315 438-8605
Max Bablok, *President*
EMP: 6
SALES (est): 24.3MM **Privately Held**
SIC: 3728 Aircraft parts & equipment

(G-4244)
TRANE US INC
15 Technology Pl (13057-9816)
PHONE..............................315 234-1500
Tyler Malm, *Sales Engr*
Mike Carey, *Branch Mgr*
EMP: 36
SQ FT: 4,500 **Privately Held**
SIC: 3585 Refrigeration & heating equipment
HQ: Trane U.S. Inc.
3600 Pammel Creek Rd
La Crosse WI 54601
608 787-2000

(G-4245)
TYCO SIMPLEXGRINNELL
6731 Collamer Rd Ste 4 (13057-9715)
PHONE..............................315 437-9664
Kevin Hache, *Branch Mgr*
EMP: 40
SALES (corp-wide): 1.3B **Privately Held**
SIC: 3569 3491 Sprinkler systems, fire: automatic; automatic regulating & control valves
PA: Tyco Simplexgrinnell
1501 Nw 51st St
Boca Raton FL 33431
561 988-3658

(G-4246)
UNITED TECHNOLOGIES CORP
6304 Carrier Pkwy (13057-6300)
PHONE..............................315 432-7849
Leo Rubio, *Manager*
EMP: 9
SALES (corp-wide): 66.5B **Publicly Held**
SIC: 3724 Aircraft engines & engine parts
PA: United Technologies Corporation
10 Farm Springs Rd
Farmington CT 06032
860 728-7000

(G-4247)
UNIVERSAL STEP INC
5970 Butternut Dr (13057-8526)
PHONE..............................315 437-7611
David Smith, *President*
William Smith, *Principal*
EMP: 5 EST: 2009
SALES (est): 595.1K **Privately Held**
SIC: 3272 Steps, prefabricated concrete

(G-4248)
VILLAGE DECORATION LTD
20 Corporate Cir (13057-1015)
PHONE..............................315 437-2522
Michael Robinson, *President*
Shawn Robinson, *Plant Mgr*
EMP: 30
SQ FT: 13,500

SALES: 1.5MM **Privately Held**
SIC: 3599 Machine & other job shop work

East Williston
Nassau County

(G-4249)
NORTH AMERICAN PIPE CORP
Also Called: Jekerda Sales
156 High St (11596-1418)
PHONE..............................516 338-2863
Jamie Hebert, *Manager*
EMP: 10 **Publicly Held**
SIC: 3354 3084 Pipe, extruded, aluminum; plastics pipe
HQ: North American Pipe Corporation
2801 Post Oak Blvd # 600
Houston TX 77056

Eastchester
Westchester County

(G-4250)
W D TECHNOLOGY INC
42 Water St Ste B (10709-5502)
PHONE..............................914 779-8738
Vincent Rende, *President*
EMP: 6
SQ FT: 1,000
SALES: 1.5MM **Privately Held**
SIC: 3679 3825 Liquid crystal displays (LCD); radio frequency measuring equipment

Eastport
Suffolk County

(G-4251)
EASTPORT FEEDS INC
140 E Moriches Blvd (11941-1122)
P.O. Box 127 (11941-0127)
PHONE..............................631 325-0077
Donald Dixon, *Sales/Mktg Mgr*
Jed Brambley, *Manager*
EMP: 9
SQ FT: 84,942
SALES (est): 983K
SALES (corp-wide): 711.5K **Privately Held**
SIC: 2048 Prepared feeds
PA: Eastport Feeds, Inc.
10 Edgar Ave
Aquebogue NY 11931
631 722-8700

(G-4252)
MEDIA TECHNOLOGIES LTD
220 Sonata Ct (11941-1617)
PHONE..............................631 467-7900
Rainer Zopfy, *President*
EMP: 12
SQ FT: 6,800
SALES (est): 2.4MM **Privately Held**
WEB: www.mediatechmail.com
SIC: 3652 5044 Compact laser discs, prerecorded; duplicating machines

Eden
Erie County

(G-4253)
AARFID LLC (PA)
3780 Yochum Rd (14057-9519)
PHONE..............................716 992-3999
Chad Carpenter, *President*
EMP: 5
SALES (est): 1MM **Privately Held**
SIC: 7372 3695 Business oriented computer software; magnetic & optical recording media

(G-4254)
E B TROTTNOW MACHINE SPC
8955 Woodside Dr (14057-1460)
PHONE..............................716 694-0600
EMP: 18 EST: 1948

SQ FT: 55,000
SALES (est): 3MM **Privately Held**
SIC: 3599 Mfg Industrial Machinery

(G-4255)
EDEN TOOL & DIE INC
2721 Hemlock Rd (14057-1390)
P.O. Box 296 (14057-0296)
PHONE..............................716 992-4240
James Rettig, *President*
Gary Rettig, *Vice Pres*
Raymond Rettig, *Admin Sec*
▼ EMP: 8
SALES (est): 1MM **Privately Held**
SIC: 3544 Special dies & tools

(G-4256)
JOHN F RAFTER INC
Also Called: Jf Rafter The Lexington Co
2746 W Church St (14057-1011)
P.O. Box 300 (14057-0300)
PHONE..............................716 992-3425
John Rafter Jr, *President*
EMP: 5
SQ FT: 2,500
SALES (est): 567.8K **Privately Held**
SIC: 3452 Screws, metal

(G-4257)
MUSTANG-MAJOR TOOL & DIE CO
3243 N Boston Rd (14057-9500)
PHONE..............................716 992-9200
David Kolodczak, *President*
EMP: 6 EST: 1965
SQ FT: 8,200
SALES (est): 800K **Privately Held**
WEB: www.mmtooldie.com
SIC: 3544 Special dies & tools

Edgewood
Suffolk County

(G-4258)
ABH NATURES PRODUCTS INC
131 Heartland Blvd (11717-8315)
PHONE..............................631 249-5783
Jahirul Islam, *President*
Harsh Vyas, *CFO*
Sahina Islam, *Director*
EMP: 28
SQ FT: 40,000
SALES (est): 8.3MM **Privately Held**
WEB: www.abhnature.com
SIC: 2833 Vitamins, natural or synthetic: bulk, uncompounded

(G-4259)
ABH PHARMA INC
131 Heartland Blvd (11717-8315)
PHONE..............................866 922-4669
Frank Cantone, *CEO*
EMP: 70 EST: 2016
SALES (est): 9MM **Privately Held**
SIC: 2834 Pharmaceutical preparations

(G-4260)
ADVANCE FOOD SERVICE CO INC
200 Heartland Blvd (11717-8380)
PHONE..............................631 242-4800
Milton Schwartz, *Corp Secy*
Daniel Schwartz, *Vice Pres*
EMP: 200
SQ FT: 60,000
SALES (est): 30MM **Privately Held**
SIC: 3589 Cooking equipment, commercial

(G-4261)
ALL ISLAND MEDIA INC (PA)
Also Called: Pennysaver/Town Crier
1 Rodeo Dr (11717-8318)
P.O. Box 506, Bohemia (11716-0506)
PHONE..............................631 698-8400
Paul E Gregory, *Principal*
Robert Sussi, *Vice Pres*
Arleen Butler, *Sales Mgr*
Scott Willman, *Cust Mgr*
Jerry Beagelman, *Accounts Exec*
EMP: 136
SQ FT: 20,000

SALES (est): 10.3MM **Privately Held**
WEB: www.allislandmedia.com
SIC: 2711 Newspapers, publishing & printing

(G-4262)
AZTEC TOOL CO INC
180 Rodeo Dr (11717-8340)
PHONE....................................631 243-1144
Stewart Swiss, *President*
James Evarts, *Vice Pres*
EMP: 20
SQ FT: 24,000
SALES (est): 3.9MM **Privately Held**
WEB: www.aztectool.com
SIC: 3089 Injection molding of plastics

(G-4263)
BIOCHEMICAL DIAGNOSTICS INC
180 Heartland Blvd (11717-8314)
PHONE....................................631 595-9200
Allen Panetz, *President*
Amir Forooqi, *Corp Secy*
EMP: 25
SQ FT: 30,000
SALES (est): 4.1MM **Privately Held**
WEB: www.biochemicaldiagnostics.com
SIC: 3841 2835 Diagnostic apparatus, medical; in vitro & in vivo diagnostic substances

(G-4264)
CASTELLA IMPORTS INC (PA)
120 Wilshire Blvd Ste A (11717-8333)
PHONE....................................631 231-5500
Vasilios Valsamos, *Ch of Bd*
Chris Valsamos, *Vice Pres*
Carole Williams, *Sales Staff*
John Casares, *Mktg Coord*
Melissa Grebe, *Mktg Coord*
◆ **EMP:** 159
SQ FT: 110,000
SALES (est): 71.2MM **Privately Held**
WEB: www.castellaimports.com
SIC: 2099 5149 Food preparations; specialty food items

(G-4265)
COMPAC DEVELOPMENT CORPORATION
Also Called: Miller Stuart
91 Heartland Blvd (11717-8330)
PHONE....................................631 881-4903
Scott Cullen, *General Mgr*
EMP: 85
SALES (est): 5.4MM
SALES (corp-wide): 83.9MM **Publicly Held**
WEB: www.compac-rf.com
SIC: 3469 Electronic enclosures, stamped or pressed metal
PA: Cpi Aerostructures, Inc.
91 Heartland Blvd
Edgewood NY 11717
631 586-5200

(G-4266)
CPI AEROSTRUCTURES INC (PA)
91 Heartland Blvd (11717-8330)
PHONE....................................631 586-5200
Eric Rosenfeld, *Ch of Bd*
Douglas McCrosson, *President*
Charles Munna, *VP Opers*
Christine Madigan, *Buyer*
Vincent Tieniber, *QC Mgr*
EMP: 140 **EST:** 1980
SQ FT: 171,000
SALES: 83.9MM **Publicly Held**
WEB: www.cpiaero.com
SIC: 3728 Aircraft assemblies, subassemblies & parts

(G-4267)
FLEXIM AMERICAS CORPORATION (HQ)
250 Executive Dr Ste V (11717-8354)
PHONE....................................631 492-2300
Jens Hilpert, *President*
John Obrien, *Vice Pres*
EMP: 12
SQ FT: 7,250

SALES (est): 2.5MM
SALES (corp-wide): 53.1MM **Privately Held**
SIC: 3823 Industrial instrmnts msrmnt display/control process variable
PA: Flexim Flexible IndustriemeBtechnik Gmbh
Boxberger Str. 4
Berlin 12681
309 366-7660

(G-4268)
FORERUNNER TECHNOLOGIES INC (PA)
150 Executive Dr Ste M (11717-8323)
PHONE....................................631 337-2100
Jim Wallace, *President*
Stephen Spencer, *Vice Pres*
Michael Viola, *Vice Pres*
Dan Esposito, *Project Mgr*
Matthew Ali, *Sales Staff*
▲ **EMP:** 45
SQ FT: 8,000
SALES (est): 19.6MM **Privately Held**
SIC: 3661 7371 4813 4899 Telephone & telegraph apparatus; computer software development & applications; telephone communication, except radio; data communication services; electronic parts & equipment; communication services

(G-4269)
GLOBAL MARKET DEVELOPMENT INC
Also Called: Accusonic Voice Systems
200 Executive Dr Ste G (11717-8322)
PHONE....................................631 667-1000
Anthony Mazzeo, *President*
Philip Glickman, *Exec VP*
Phillip Glickman, *Vice Pres*
Johanna Morales, *Controller*
▲ **EMP:** 30
SQ FT: 4,200
SALES (est): 6.1MM **Privately Held**
WEB: www.accusonicproducts.com
SIC: 3651 Loudspeakers, electrodynamic or magnetic

(G-4270)
IBA INDUSTRIAL INC
Also Called: Rdi
151 Heartland Blvd (11717-8315)
PHONE....................................631 254-6800
Richard A Galloway, *Ch of Bd*
Frederic Genin, *President*
Rick Galloway, *Vice Pres*
Plato Apergis, *Engineer*
Dylan Brown, *Design Engr*
▲ **EMP:** 41 **EST:** 1958
SQ FT: 42,000
SALES (est): 13.2MM
SALES (corp-wide): 192.1MM **Privately Held**
WEB: www.e-beam-rdi.com
SIC: 3699 5065 Electron linear accelerators; electronic parts & equipment
PA: Ion Beam Application
Chemin Du Cyclotron 3
Ottignies-Louvain-La-Neuve 1348
104 758-11

(G-4271)
IMPRESSART
100 Executive Dr Ste D (11717-8328)
PHONE....................................631 940-9530
EMP: 15
SALES (est): 699.9K **Privately Held**
SIC: 3999 Mfg Misc Products

(G-4272)
INTERNATIONAL LEISURE PDTS INC
191 Rodeo Dr (11717-8319)
PHONE....................................631 254-2155
Larry Schwimmer, *President*
▲ **EMP:** 20
SALES (est): 1.8MM
SALES (corp-wide): 19.2MM **Privately Held**
SIC: 3949 Billiard & pool equipment & supplies, general
PA: Swimline Corp.
191 Rodeo Dr
Edgewood NY 11717
631 254-2155

(G-4273)
KELTA INC (PA)
141 Rodeo Dr (11717-8378)
PHONE....................................631 789-5000
Parag Mehta, *President*
Dwight Tabor, *Sales Mgr*
Jyotindra Mehta, *Admin Sec*
▲ **EMP:** 22
SQ FT: 25,000
SALES (est): 103.5MM **Privately Held**
SIC: 3089 3643 3661 Plastic hardware & building products; current-carrying wiring devices; telephone & telegraph apparatus

(G-4274)
KINPLEX CORP
Also Called: Tables Manufacturing
200 Heartland Blvd (11717-8380)
PHONE....................................631 242-4800
EMP: 50
SALES (corp-wide): 86.3MM **Privately Held**
SIC: 3589 2599 3556 Mfg Service Industry Machinery Mfg Furniture/Fixtures Mfg Food Products Machinery
PA: Kinplex Corp.
200 Heartland Blvd
Edgewood NY 11788
631 242-4800

(G-4275)
MERIT ELECTRONIC DESIGN CO INC
Also Called: Medco
190 Rodeo Dr (11717-8317)
PHONE....................................631 667-9699
Guy Intoci, *President*
Cheryl Sickles, *CFO*
▲ **EMP:** 115
SQ FT: 20,000
SALES (est): 43.7MM **Privately Held**
WEB: www.medcomfg.com
SIC: 3679 Electronic circuits

(G-4276)
NIKON INSTRUMENTS INC
200 Executive Dr Ste A (11717-8322)
PHONE....................................631 845-7620
EMP: 5 **Privately Held**
SIC: 3826 Analytical instruments
HQ: Nikon Instruments Inc.
1300 Walt Whitman Rd Fl 2
Melville NY 11747
631 547-4200

(G-4277)
POLY-FLEX CORP (PA)
250 Executive Dr Ste S (11717-8354)
PHONE....................................631 586-9500
Barry Neustein, *President*
Talbert Paola, *Principal*
▲ **EMP:** 10
SQ FT: 8,000
SALES (est): 1.9MM **Privately Held**
WEB: www.poly-flexcorp.com
SIC: 2759 Envelopes: printing

(G-4278)
POLYGEN PHARMACEUTICALS INC
41 Mercedes Way Unit 17 (11717-8334)
PHONE....................................631 392-4044
Zhoumin Li, *President*
Bipin Sharma, *Director*
EMP: 22
SQ FT: 32,000
SALES (est): 4.9MM **Privately Held**
SIC: 2834 Pharmaceutical preparations

(G-4279)
PRO-TECH CATINGS SOLUTIONS INC
250 Executive Dr Ste H (11717-8354)
PHONE....................................631 707-9400
Alvelio Farington, *President*
EMP: 5
SALES (est): 123.9K **Privately Held**
SIC: 3479 Etching & engraving

(G-4280)
RSQUARED NY INC
100 Heartland Blvd (11717-8313)
P.O. Box 807, Deer Park (11729-0971)
PHONE....................................631 521-8700
Altaf Hirji, *President*

▲ **EMP:** 98
SQ FT: 30,000
SALES (est): 13.7MM **Privately Held**
WEB: www.redvisuals.com
SIC: 3993 Advertising artwork

(G-4281)
S G NEW YORK LLC
Also Called: Penny Saver News
1 Rodeo Dr (11717-8318)
PHONE....................................631 698-8400
Bob Sussy, *Manager*
EMP: 17
SALES (corp-wide): 5.3MM **Privately Held**
SIC: 2711 Newspapers, publishing & printing
PA: S G New York Llc
2950 Vtrans Mem Hwy Ste 1
Bohemia NY 11716
631 665-4000

(G-4282)
SATCO PRODUCTS INC (PA)
Also Called: Satco Lighting
110 Heartland Blvd (11717-8303)
PHONE....................................631 243-2022
Herbert Gildin, *CEO*
William Gildin, *Ch of Bd*
Phil Alexander, *General Mgr*
Alan Ginsberg, *General Mgr*
Luis Melendez, *General Mgr*
◆ **EMP:** 63
SQ FT: 80,000
SALES (est): 32.1MM **Privately Held**
WEB: www.satco.com
SIC: 3641 5063 Electric lamps; electrical apparatus & equipment; lighting fixtures

(G-4283)
SUPPLEMENT MFG PARTNER INC
250 Executive Dr Ste L (11717-8354)
PHONE....................................516 368-2656
William Kartwright, *CEO*
Steve Milano, *Managing Prtnr*
EMP: 11
SALES (est): 514.4K **Privately Held**
SIC: 2833 Vitamins, natural or synthetic: bulk, uncompounded

(G-4284)
SWIMLINE CORP (PA)
191 Rodeo Dr (11717-8319)
PHONE....................................631 254-2155
Herman Schwimmer, *Ch of Bd*
Larry Schwimmer, *President*
Dennis Smith, *General Mgr*
Maria N Glenis, *Opers Mgr*
Shelby Schwimmer, *Marketing Staff*
◆ **EMP:** 125
SALES (est): 19.2MM **Privately Held**
SIC: 3949 3081 Swimming pools, plastic; unsupported plastics film & sheet

(G-4285)
SWIMLINE INTERNATIONAL CORP
191 Rodeo Dr (11717-8319)
PHONE....................................631 254-2155
Larry Schwimmer, *President*
Cynthia Schwimmer, *Vice Pres*
◆ **EMP:** 125
SALES (est): 9.7MM
SALES (corp-wide): 19.2MM **Privately Held**
SIC: 3423 Leaf skimmers or swimming pool rakes
PA: Swimline Corp.
191 Rodeo Dr
Edgewood NY 11717
631 254-2155

(G-4286)
SYLHAN LLC (PA)
210 Rodeo Dr (11717-8317)
PHONE....................................631 243-6600
Bob Luisi, *Vice Pres*
Ronald Manganiello,
Edward N Epstein,
▲ **EMP:** 20
SQ FT: 20,000
SALES (est): 2MM **Privately Held**
WEB: www.sylhan.com
SIC: 3599 Machine shop, jobbing & repair

▲ = Import ▼=Export
◆ =Import/Export

(G-4287)
TII TECHNOLOGIES INC (HQ)
141 Rodeo Dr (11717-8378)
PHONE..................................516 364-9300
Parag Mehta, *President*
Clint Blundon, *Vice Pres*
Nisar Chaudhry, *Vice Pres*
Luca Evans, *Vice Pres*
Kurt Weber, *Opers Staff*
▲ **EMP:** 29
SQ FT: 25,000
SALES (est): 10.4MM
SALES (corp-wide): 103.5MM **Privately
Held**
WEB: www.tiinettech.com
SIC: 3089 3643 3661 Plastic hardware &
building products; lightning protection
equipment; telephone & telegraph appa-
ratus
PA: Kelta, Inc.
141 Rodeo Dr
Edgewood NY 11717
631 789-5000

(G-4288)
TIME BASE CORPORATION (PA)
Also Called: Time Base Consoles
170 Rodeo Dr (11717-8317)
PHONE..................................631 293-4068
Jansen Hahn, *President*
Frank Lapallo, *Vice Pres*
Daniel Giebel, *Senior Engr*
Michelle Vales, *Admin Asst*
EMP: 47
SQ FT: 20,000
SALES (est): 45.2MM **Privately Held**
SIC: 2517 5712 Wood television & radio
cabinets; cabinet work, custom

(G-4289)
**TOGA MANUFACTURING INC
(HQ)**
200 Heartland Blvd (11717-8379)
PHONE..................................631 242-4800
Alice Schwartz, *President*
Penny Schwartz Hutner, *Vice Pres*
Daniel Schwartz, *Vice Pres*
▲ **EMP:** 4
SQ FT: 40,000
SALES (est): 9.1MM
SALES (corp-wide): 77.7MM **Privately
Held**
SIC: 3589 Commercial cooking & food-
warming equipment
PA: Kinplex Corp.
325 Wireless Blvd Ste 1
Hauppauge NY 11788
631 242-4800

(G-4290)
US ALLIANCE PAPER INC
101 Heartland Blvd (11717-8315)
PHONE..................................631 254-3030
John Sarraf, *President*
Jeanette Provan, *General Mgr*
Donna Dagrosa, *COO*
Steve Saraf, *Vice Pres*
Steve Sarrafzadeh, *Vice Pres*
▲ **EMP:** 220
SQ FT: 250,000
SALES (est): 67.4MM **Privately Held**
WEB: www.usalliancepaper.com
SIC: 2621 Paper mills

(G-4291)
**WAYNE INTEGRATED TECH
CORP**
160 Rodeo Dr (11717-8317)
PHONE..................................631 242-0213
Helen Moks, *CEO*
Joseph V Moks Jr, *Vice Pres*
Joseph Moks, *VP Opers*
Karen Moks, *Office Mgr*
EMP: 38
SQ FT: 15,000
SALES (est): 8.1MM **Privately Held**
WEB: www.gowayne.com
SIC: 3443 3444 3599 Containers, ship-
ping (bombs, etc.): metal plate; metal
housings, enclosures, casings & other
containers; machine shop, jobbing & re-
pair

(G-4292)
WEICO WIRE & CABLE INC
Also Called: Magnet Wire Division
161 Rodeo Dr (11717-8359)
PHONE..................................631 254-2970
Theodore Weill, *President*
Ellen Moore, *Controller*
▲ **EMP:** 28
SQ FT: 35,000
SALES: 12.5K **Privately Held**
SIC: 3496 Cable, uninsulated wire: made
from purchased wire

(G-4293)
**WELDING METALLURGY INC
(HQ)**
91 Heartland Blvd (11717-8330)
PHONE..................................631 586-5200
Douglas McCrosson, *President*
Vincent Palazzolo, *CFO*
EMP: 55
SQ FT: 173,000
SALES (est): 21.4MM
SALES (corp-wide): 83.9MM **Publicly
Held**
WEB: www.weldingmet.com
SIC: 3441 Fabricated structural metal
PA: Cpi Aerostructures, Inc.
91 Heartland Blvd
Edgewood NY 11717
631 586-5200

Edmeston
Otsego County

(G-4294)
BISHOP PRINT SHOP INC
Also Called: Ecclesiastical Press
9 East St (13335-2436)
PHONE..................................607 965-8155
Michael Lampron, *President*
EMP: 9 **EST:** 1949
SALES (est): 1.4MM **Privately Held**
WEB: www.bishopprintshop.com
SIC: 2752 2893 Commercial printing, off-
set; letterpress or offset ink

Elbridge
Onondaga County

(G-4295)
**ACCURATE MCHNING
INCORPORATION**
Also Called: Acrolite
251 State Route 5 (13060)
P.O. Box 1010 (13060-1010)
PHONE..................................315 689-1428
Ronald E Drake Sr, *President*
Heather Moore, *Engineer*
Natalie Duffy, *Office Mgr*
Matthew R Drake, *Admin Sec*
EMP: 19
SQ FT: 13,600
SALES (est): 4.4MM **Privately Held**
WEB: www.acrolite.com
SIC: 3599 Machine shop, jobbing & repair

(G-4296)
ALLRED & ASSOCIATES INC
321 Rte 5 W (13060)
PHONE..................................315 252-2559
Jimmie B Allred III, *President*
Andy Morabito, *Info Tech Dir*
EMP: 40
SALES (est): 8.1MM **Privately Held**
WEB: www.evi-inc.com
SIC: 3083 Laminated plastic sheets

(G-4297)
DUCK FLATS PHARMA
245 E Main St (13060-8706)
P.O. Box 101 (13060-0101)
PHONE..................................315 689-3407
Luana Pescokoplowitz, *Owner*
EMP: 9
SALES (est): 570K **Privately Held**
SIC: 2678 Tablets & pads, book & writing:
from purchased materials

(G-4298)
TESSY PLASTICS CORP
488 State Route 5 (13060-9501)
PHONE..................................315 689-3924
Roland Beck, *President*
EMP: 750
SALES (corp-wide): 334.6MM **Privately
Held**
SIC: 3089 Injection molding of plastics
PA: Tessy Plastics Corp.
700 Visions Dr
Skaneateles NY 13152
315 689-3924

Elizabethtown
Essex County

(G-4299)
**DENTON PUBLICATIONS INC
(PA)**
Also Called: Free Trader
14 Hand Ave (12932)
P.O. Box 338 (12932-0338)
PHONE..................................518 873-6368
Daniel Alexander, *President*
Gayle Alexander, *Vice Pres*
Maureen Lindsay, *Accounting Mgr*
Lin Jones, *Admin Sec*
Kelly Bresett, *Graphic Designe*
EMP: 80 **EST:** 1948
SQ FT: 11,000
SALES (est): 6MM **Privately Held**
WEB: www.denpubs.com
SIC: 2711 2752 Commercial printing &
newspaper publishing combined; com-
mercial printing, lithographic

(G-4300)
E C C CORP
7 Church St (12932)
P.O. Box 567 (12932-0567)
PHONE..................................518 873-6494
Peter Belzer, *President*
▲ **EMP:** 6
SQ FT: 5,304
SALES: 1MM **Privately Held**
SIC: 3944 Banks, toy

(G-4301)
HALFWAY HOUSE LLC
7158 Us Route 9 (12932)
PHONE..................................518 873-2198
Tina Croff, *Partner*
Gifford Croff, *Partner*
EMP: 7
SALES (est): 680.1K **Privately Held**
SIC: 2599 Bar, restaurant & cafeteria furni-
ture

Elka Park
Greene County

(G-4302)
CHURCH COMMUNITIES NY INC
Also Called: Community Playthings
2255 Platte Clove Rd (12427-1014)
PHONE..................................518 589-5103
Martin Mathis, *Branch Mgr*
EMP: 40
SALES (corp-wide): 11MM **Privately Held**
WEB:
www.churchcommunitiesfoundation.org
SIC: 3944 3842 Games, toys & children's
vehicles; orthopedic appliances
PA: Church Communities Ny Inc.
101 Woodcrest Dr
Rifton NY 12471
845 658-7700

(G-4303)
CHURCH COMMUNITIES NY INC
Also Called: Community Playthings
Platte Clove Rd (12427)
PHONE..................................518 589-5103
Martin Mathis, *Branch Mgr*
EMP: 40

SALES (corp-wide): 11MM **Privately
Held**
WEB:
www.churchcommunitiesfoundation.org
SIC: 3944 3842 Games, toys & children's
vehicles; orthopedic appliances
PA: Church Communities Ny Inc.
101 Woodcrest Dr
Rifton NY 12471
845 658-7700

(G-4304)
COMMUNITY PRODUCTS LLC
2255 Platte Clove Rd (12427-1014)
PHONE..................................518 589-5103
EMP: 21
SALES (corp-wide): 100.5MM **Privately
Held**
WEB: www.communityplaythings.com
SIC: 3842 3942 Surgical appliances &
supplies; dolls & stuffed toys
PA: Community Products, Llc
101 Woodcrest Dr
Rifton NY 12471
845 658-8799

Ellenville
Ulster County

(G-4305)
BROSS QUALITY PAVING
4 Kossar Pl (12428-2414)
PHONE..................................845 532-7116
Julio Moya, *Partner*
EMP: 6
SALES (est): 479.2K **Privately Held**
SIC: 2951 Asphalt paving mixtures &
blocks

(G-4306)
**DEVIL DOG MANUFACTURING
CO INC (PA)**
23 Market St (12428-2107)
P.O. Box 588 (12428-0588)
PHONE..................................845 647-4411
Carl J Rosenstock, *President*
Richard Rosenstock, *Vice Pres*
Herbert Rosenstock, *Treasurer*
Nelson Rosenstock, *Shareholder*
Stanley Rosenstock, *Admin Sec*
▲ **EMP:** 6 **EST:** 1952
SQ FT: 30,000
SALES (est): 18.5MM **Privately Held**
WEB: www.sportwear.com
SIC: 2369 Jeans: girls', children's & infants'

(G-4307)
JM ORIGINALS INC
Also Called: Sbi Enterprises
70 Berme Rd (12428-5605)
P.O. Box 563 (12428-0563)
PHONE..................................845 647-3003
Martha Arginsky, *President*
Myrna Jargowsky, *Vice Pres*
◆ **EMP:** 140 **EST:** 1976
SQ FT: 35,000
SALES (est): 13.4MM **Privately Held**
WEB: www.jmoriginals.com
SIC: 2361 5137 5641 2369 Girls' & chil-
dren's dresses, blouses & shirts; women's
& children's clothing; children's wear;
girls' & children's outerwear

(G-4308)
**MASTER JUVENILE PRODUCTS
INC**
Also Called: Sbi Enterprises
70 Berme Rd (12428-5605)
PHONE..................................845 647-8400
Irwin Arginsky, *President*
EMP: 10
SQ FT: 40,000
SALES (est): 869.9K **Privately Held**
WEB: www.pogosticks.com
SIC: 3944 Games, toys & children's vehi-
cles

(G-4309)
OPTIMUM WINDOW MFG CORP
28 Canal St (12428-1226)
PHONE..................................845 647-1900
Candido Perez, *Ch of Bd*
Maria E Perez, *Corp Secy*
Elias Perez, *Sales Staff*

GEOGRAPHIC

Paula F Fabbro, *Executive*
Esther Robles, *Executive*
◆ **EMP:** 37
SALES (est): 10MM **Privately Held**
WEB: www.optimumwindow.com
SIC: 3442 Screen & storm doors & windows

(G-4310)
REED SYSTEMS LTD
17 Edwards Pl (12428-1601)
P.O. Box 209 (12428-0209)
PHONE....................................845 647-3660
James Reed, *President*
Joan E Reed, *Vice Pres*
EMP: 15 **EST:** 1977
SQ FT: 1,600
SALES: 4.9MM **Privately Held**
WEB: www.reedsystemsltd.com
SIC: 3399 Powder, metal

(G-4311)
ROCK MOUNTAIN FARMS INC
11 Spring St (12428-1329)
PHONE....................................845 647-9084
Karen Osterhoudt, *President*
Howard Osterhoudt, *Vice Pres*
EMP: 5
SALES (est): 540K **Privately Held**
SIC: 1442 6519 Gravel mining; landholding office

Ellicottville
Cattaraugus County

(G-4312)
AMERICAN LCKR SEC SYSTEMS INC
12 Martha St (14731-9714)
PHONE....................................716 699-2773
Fax: 716 699-2775
EMP: 25
SQ FT: 4,800
SALES (corp-wide): 30.1MM **Privately Held**
SIC: 3581 Mfg Vending Machines
PA: American Locker Security Systems, Inc.
700 Freeport Pkwy Ste 300
Coppell TX 75019
817 329-1600

(G-4313)
ELLICOTTVILLE DISTILLERY LLC
5462 Robbins Rd (14731-9764)
P.O. Box 1471 (14731-1471)
PHONE....................................716 597-6121
Bryan Scharf, *President*
EMP: 6
SALES (est): 370.2K **Privately Held**
SIC: 2085 Distilled & blended liquors

(G-4314)
FITZPATRICK AND WELLER INC
12 Mill St (14731-9614)
P.O. Box 490 (14731-0490)
PHONE....................................716 699-2393
Gregory J Fitzpatrick, *Ch of Bd*
Dana G Fitzpatrick, *Chairman*
Daniel Fitzpatrick, *Vice Pres*
Greg Fitzpatrick, *Vice Pres*
Dave Hellwig, *Prdtn Mgr*
▼ **EMP:** 85 **EST:** 1892
SQ FT: 220,000
SALES (est): 14.9MM **Privately Held**
WEB: www.fitzweller.com
SIC: 2426 Furniture dimension stock, hardwood

(G-4315)
NORTH PK INNOVATIONS GROUP INC
6442 Route 242 E (14731-9742)
P.O. Box 900 (14731-0900)
PHONE....................................716 699-2031
William Northrup, *CEO*
Lori Northrup, *Chairman*
▲ **EMP:** 20
SQ FT: 13,000

SALES (est): 4.9MM **Privately Held**
SIC: 3829 5075 Measuring & controlling devices; warm air heating & air conditioning

Ellington
Chautauqua County

(G-4316)
ELLIOT INDUSTRIES INC
Leach Rd (14732)
P.O. Box 420 (14732-0420)
PHONE....................................716 287-3100
Thomas A Elliot, *President*
Ann Elliot, *Treasurer*
EMP: 8
SQ FT: 5,000
SALES (est): 550K **Privately Held**
SIC: 3296 Fiberglass insulation

Elma
Erie County

(G-4317)
COMGRAPH SALES SERVICE
7491 Clinton St (14059-8807)
PHONE....................................716 601-7243
Brian Schiemant, *Owner*
EMP: 5
SALES (est): 542.7K **Privately Held**
SIC: 2759 Commercial printing

(G-4318)
FREDERICK COON INC
Also Called: Elma Press
5751 Clinton St (14059-9424)
PHONE....................................716 683-6812
Frederick H Coon Jr, *President*
Douglas Coon, *Vice Pres*
Joel Coon, *Vice Pres*
Betty Coon, *Treasurer*
EMP: 23
SQ FT: 2,708
SALES: 900K **Privately Held**
SIC: 2752 2759 Commercial printing, offset; letterpress printing

(G-4319)
GENERAL WELDING & FABG INC (PA)
991 Maple Rd (14059-9530)
PHONE....................................716 652-0033
Mark S Andol, *President*
Ed Pierrot, *Sales Staff*
Sue Shotwell, *Marketing Staff*
EMP: 3
SQ FT: 14,000
SALES (est): 6MM **Privately Held**
SIC: 7692 3715 5531 Welding repair; truck trailers; truck equipment & parts

(G-4320)
KENS SERVICE & SALES INC
11500 Clinton St (14059-8830)
PHONE....................................716 683-1155
Kenneth Kelchlin Jr, *President*
Matt Kelchlin, *Vice Pres*
EMP: 14 **EST:** 1955
SQ FT: 25,000
SALES (est): 2.8MM **Privately Held**
SIC: 3799 All terrain vehicles (ATV)

(G-4321)
MOOG INC (PA)
Also Called: MOOG-FTS
400 Jamison Rd (14059-9596)
P.O. Box 18, East Aurora (14052-0018)
PHONE....................................716 805-2604
John R Scannell, *Ch of Bd*
Mark J Trabert, *President*
Martin Bobak, *General Mgr*
Richard A Aubrecht, *Vice Pres*
Linda Kasperek, *Project Mgr*
◆ **EMP:** 2100 **EST:** 1951
SQ FT: 22,000

SALES: 2.9B **Publicly Held**
WEB: www.moog.com
SIC: 3812 3492 3625 3769 Aircraft control systems, electronic; fluid power valves for aircraft; relays & industrial controls; actuators, industrial; guided missile & space vehicle parts & auxiliary equipment; aircraft parts & equipment; surgical & medical instruments

(G-4322)
MOOG INC
160 Jamison Rd (14059)
PHONE....................................716 687-4778
Dave Golda, *Manager*
EMP: 25
SALES (corp-wide): 2.9B **Publicly Held**
SIC: 3625 Relays & industrial controls
PA: Moog Inc.
400 Jamison Rd
Elma NY 14059
716 805-2604

(G-4323)
MOOG INC
6860 Seneca St (14059-9520)
PHONE....................................716 687-7825
Lisa Landahl, *Sales Staff*
Rick Huftalen, *Manager*
Rick Roncone, *Administration*
EMP: 11
SALES (est): 2MM **Privately Held**
SIC: 3812 Search & navigation equipment

(G-4324)
MOOG INC
Also Called: Moog Space and Defense Group
500 Jamison Rd Plt20 (14059-9497)
PHONE....................................716 687-5486
Rhonda McCroskey, *Production*
James Saczuk, *Project Engr*
Brandon Denton, *Design Engr*
Todd Salzler, *Design Engr*
Bill Watt, *Electrical Engi*
EMP: 453
SALES (corp-wide): 2.9B **Publicly Held**
SIC: 3812 Aircraft control systems, electronic
PA: Moog Inc.
400 Jamison Rd
Elma NY 14059
716 805-2604

(G-4325)
R W PUBLICATIONS DIV OF WTRHS (PA)
Also Called: Akron-Corfu Pennysaver
6091 Seneca St Bldg C (14059-9807)
PHONE....................................716 714-5620
Robert Rozeski Sr, *President*
Thomas Rybczynski, *Vice Pres*
Cheryl Kowalski, *Treasurer*
EMP: 30 **EST:** 1961
SQ FT: 5,800
SALES (est): 12.9MM **Privately Held**
WEB: www.rwpennysaver.com
SIC: 2711 2741 Newspapers, publishing & printing; miscellaneous publishing

(G-4326)
R W PUBLICATIONS DIV OF WTRHS
Also Called: Pennysavers Rw Publications
6091 Seneca St Bldg C (14059-9807)
PHONE....................................716 714-5620
Meg Bourdette, *General Mgr*
EMP: 20
SALES (corp-wide): 12.9MM **Privately Held**
WEB: www.rwpennysaver.com
SIC: 2711 Newspapers, publishing & printing
PA: R W Publications Div Of Waterhouse Publication Inc
6091 Seneca St Bldg C
Elma NY 14059
716 714-5620

(G-4327)
SERVOTRONICS INC (PA)
1110 Maple Rd (14059-9573)
PHONE....................................716 655-5990
Kenneth D Trbovich, *Ch of Bd*
James Takacs, *COO*
Salvatore Sanfilippo, *Senior VP*
James C Takacs, *Senior VP*

Michael F McKee, *VP Opers*
EMP: 125 **EST:** 1959
SQ FT: 83,000
SALES: 47.8MM **Publicly Held**
WEB: www.servotronics.com
SIC: 3728 3769 3421 3492 Aircraft parts & equipment; guided missile & space vehicle parts & auxiliary equipment; cutlery; electrohydraulic servo valves, metal

(G-4328)
STEUBEN FOODS INCORPORATED (PA)
1150 Maple Rd (14059-9597)
PHONE....................................718 291-3333
Kenneth Schlossberg, *President*
Cook Alciati, *Counsel*
Tyson Prince, *Counsel*
Jeffrey Sokal, *Vice Pres*
Bruce Budinoff, *Vice Pres*
EMP: 17
SQ FT: 10,000
SALES (est): 115.3MM **Privately Held**
SIC: 2032 2026 Puddings, except meat: packaged in cans, jars, etc.; yogurt; milk drinks, flavored

(G-4329)
STEUBEN FOODS INCORPORATED
1150 Maple Rd (14059-9597)
PHONE....................................716 655-4000
Norman Bower, *Branch Mgr*
EMP: 200
SALES (corp-wide): 115.3MM **Privately Held**
SIC: 2026 Milk processing (pasteurizing, homogenizing, bottling)
PA: Steuben Foods, Incorporated
1150 Maple Rd
Elma NY 14059
718 291-3333

(G-4330)
STONY MANUFACTURING INC
591 Pound Rd (14059-9602)
PHONE....................................716 652-6730
James A Wyzykiewicz, *President*
Michael C Wyzykiewicz, *Vice Pres*
Ronald P Wyzykiewicz, *Vice Pres*
EMP: 9
SQ FT: 12,500
SALES (est): 1.5MM **Privately Held**
SIC: 3599 Machine shop, jobbing & repair

Elmhurst
Queens County

(G-4331)
4 STAR BRANDS INC
7416 Grand Ave (11373-4460)
P.O. Box 1193, Port Washington (11050-7193)
PHONE....................................516 944-0472
Frank Iemmiti, *President*
Anthony Iemmiti, *Vice Pres*
Sal Iemmiti, *Vice Pres*
Victor Iemmiti, *Vice Pres*
EMP: 7
SALES (est): 449K **Privately Held**
SIC: 2086 Iced tea & fruit drinks, bottled & canned

(G-4332)
BUFFALO PROVISIONS CO INC
4009 76th St (11373-1033)
PHONE....................................718 292-4300
Rene Armendariz, *President*
Staci Armendariz, *Vice Pres*
Andres Mendez, *Manager*
EMP: 15
SQ FT: 10,000
SALES (est): 1.6MM **Privately Held**
SIC: 2013 Sausages from purchased meat

(G-4333)
COACH INC
90 Queens Blvd (11373)
PHONE....................................718 760-0624
EMP: 14
SALES (corp-wide): 4.1B **Publicly Held**
SIC: 3171 Mfg Women's Handbags/Purses

PA: Coach, Inc.
516 W 34th St Bsmt 5
New York NY 10001
212 594-1850

(G-4334)
FEDERAL SAMPLE CARD CORP
4520 83rd St (11373-3599)
PHONE..................................718 458-1344
Michael Cronin, *President*
Mike Maguire, *Engineer*
Steve Gallardo, *Manager*
Tatiana Smith, *Technology*
Keith Bates, *Asst Director*
EMP: 100
SQ FT: 40,000
SALES (est): 7.4MM **Privately Held**
SIC: 2782 3999 Sample books; advertising display products

(G-4335)
GO GO APPLE INC
4126 Benham St (11373-1750)
PHONE..................................646 264-8909
EMP: 5
SALES (est): 176.7K **Privately Held**
SIC: 3571 Mfg Electronic Computers

(G-4336)
MAJESTIC CURTAINS LLC
4410 Ketcham St Apt 2g (11373-3686)
PHONE..................................718 898-0774
Robert Connor,
Barbara Tisdale,
EMP: 7
SALES: 660K **Privately Held**
SIC: 2391 1799 Curtains & draperies; window treatment installation

(G-4337)
PENNER ELBOW COMPANY INC
4700 76th St (11373-2946)
PHONE..................................718 526-9000
Sheldon Flatow, *President*
EMP: 12
SQ FT: 10,000
SALES (est): 1.4MM **Privately Held**
SIC: 3444 3321 Elbows, for air ducts, stovepipes, etc.: sheet metal; pressure pipe & fittings, cast iron

(G-4338)
ROKON TECH LLC
5223 74th St (11373-4108)
PHONE..................................718 429-0729
Manfred Konrad, *Mng Member*
EMP: 5
SALES (est): 611.6K **Privately Held**
SIC: 3534 Elevators & moving stairways

Elmira
Chemung County

(G-4339)
AFI CYBERNETICS CORPORATION
713 Batavia St (14904-2011)
PHONE..................................607 732-3244
Kenneth Doyle, *President*
Tracy Haines, *Purch Agent*
Tim Blampied, *Sales Dir*
EMP: 28
SQ FT: 25,000
SALES (est): 6MM **Privately Held**
WEB: www.aficybernetics.com
SIC: 3625 Electric controls & control accessories, industrial

(G-4340)
AIR-FLO MFG CO INC
365 Upper Oakwood Ave (14903-1127)
PHONE..................................607 733-8284
Charles Musso Jr, *President*
Tom Musso, *Vice Pres*
Kevin Foster, *Opers Mgr*
Lisa Brady, *Purch Mgr*
Velma Andrews, *Accountant*
EMP: 75
SQ FT: 60,000
SALES (est): 33MM **Privately Held**
WEB: www.air-flo.com
SIC: 3531 Construction machinery

(G-4341)
CARBAUGH TOOL COMPANY INC
126 Philo Rd W (14903-9755)
PHONE..................................607 739-3293
Harold Dota, *President*
EMP: 30 EST: 1966
SQ FT: 10,600
SALES (est): 4.6MM **Privately Held**
SIC: 3599 3544 Machine shop, jobbing & repair; special dies & tools

(G-4342)
CARBIDE-USA LLC
100 Home St (14904-1859)
P.O. Box 4005 (14904-0005)
PHONE..................................607 331-9353
EMP: 8
SALES (est): 1.2MM **Privately Held**
SIC: 2819 Carbides

(G-4343)
CENTER FOR ORTHOTIC & PROSTHET
1141 Broadway St (14904-2542)
PHONE..................................607 215-0847
Don Dixon, *Branch Mgr*
EMP: 6
SALES (est): 528.5K
SALES (corp-wide): 11.7MM **Privately Held**
SIC: 3842 Limbs, artificial
PA: Center For Orthotic & Prosthetic Care Of North Carolina, Inc.
4702 Creekstone Dr
Durham NC 27703
919 797-1230

(G-4344)
COMMUNITY GLASS INC
139 W 17th St (14903-1215)
PHONE..................................607 737-8860
Patrick M Crouse, *President*
EMP: 7
SALES (est): 624.9K **Privately Held**
SIC: 3231 Products of purchased glass

(G-4345)
CONCRETE DESIGNS INC
2770 County Route 60 (14901-9464)
PHONE..................................607 738-0309
Kenneth Elston, *President*
EMP: 8
SALES: 500K **Privately Held**
SIC: 2899 1771 Foam charge mixtures; patio construction, concrete

(G-4346)
COURSER INC
802 County Road 64 # 100 (14903-7984)
PHONE..................................607 739-3861
Daniel Herman, *Ch of Bd*
Christophe Seeley, *Engineer*
Christopher Seeley, *Engineer*
Steve Seeley, *Finance Mgr*
Dan Herman, *Human Res Mgr*
EMP: 25
SQ FT: 50,000
SALES (est): 4.6MM **Privately Held**
WEB: www.courser.com
SIC: 3599 Machine shop, jobbing & repair

(G-4347)
CREATIVE ORTHOTICS & PROSTHET (DH)
1300 College Ave Ste 1 (14901-1154)
PHONE..................................607 734-7215
Vinit Asar, *Ch of Bd*
John Renz, *President*
EMP: 14
SALES (est): 37.9MM
SALES (corp-wide): 1B **Publicly Held**
WEB: www.creativeoandp.com
SIC: 3842 5999 5047 Limbs, artificial; artificial limbs; hospital equipment & furniture
HQ: Hanger Prosthetics & Orthotics, Inc.
10910 Domain Dr Ste 300
Austin TX 78758
512 777-3800

(G-4348)
EASTERN METAL OF ELMIRA INC (PA)
1430 Sullivan St (14901-1698)
PHONE..................................607 734-2295
Kevin Harrison, *Ch of Bd*
Rodney Kerrick, *Data Proc Dir*
▼ EMP: 80 EST: 1947
SALES (est): 19.2MM **Privately Held**
WEB: www.usa-sign.com
SIC: 3993 7336 Signs & advertising specialties; graphic arts & related design

(G-4349)
EASTSIDE OXIDE CO
211 Judson St (14901-3308)
PHONE..................................607 734-1253
Greg Wheeler, *Principal*
John Short, *Principal*
EMP: 40
SALES (est): 1.6MM **Privately Held**
WEB: www.eastsiderailnow.org
SIC: 3471 Finishing, metals or formed products

(G-4350)
ELMIRA HEAT TREATING INC
407 S Kinyon St (14904-2398)
PHONE..................................607 734-1577
Terry Youngs, *CEO*
Richard Youngs, *President*
Ann Borden, *Manager*
EMP: 40 EST: 1962
SQ FT: 20,000
SALES (est): 9.9MM **Privately Held**
WEB: www.elmiraht.com
SIC: 3398 Tempering of metal

(G-4351)
F M HOWELL & COMPANY (PA)
Also Called: Howell Packaging
79 Pennsylvania Ave (14904-1455)
P.O. Box 286 (14902-0286)
PHONE..................................607 734-6291
Katherine H Roehlke, *CEO*
Trevor Ball, *Vice Pres*
Pamela Brayton, *Vice Pres*
Douglas M McGinnis, *Vice Pres*
T Brett Powell, *Vice Pres*
▲ EMP: 74 EST: 1883
SQ FT: 168,000
SALES: 36.3MM **Privately Held**
WEB: www.howellpkg.com
SIC: 2657 2671 7389 2652 Folding paperboard boxes; thermoplastic coated paper for packaging; packaging & labeling services; setup paperboard boxes

(G-4352)
FENNELL INDUSTRIES LLC (PA)
Also Called: United Dividers
108 Stephens Pl (14901-1539)
PHONE..................................607 733-6693
Tom Fennell, *Owner*
Kevin Fennell, *Purchasing*
Patrick Sullivan, *Purchasing*
Martin Fennell, *Mng Member*
Thomas Fennell,
EMP: 30 EST: 1967
SQ FT: 13,500
SALES (est): 9.1MM **Privately Held**
SIC: 2653 Boxes, corrugated: made from purchased materials; partitions, corrugated: made from purchased materials

(G-4353)
GEORGE CHILSON LOGGING
54 Franklin St (14904-1738)
PHONE..................................607 732-1558
George Chilson, *Owner*
EMP: 1
SALES: 1.6MM **Privately Held**
SIC: 2411 Logging camps & contractors

(G-4354)
HANGER PRSTHETCS & ORTHO INC
Also Called: Hanger Clinic
1300 College Ave Ste 1 (14901-1154)
PHONE..................................607 795-1220
Sheryl Price, *Manager*
EMP: 99
SALES (corp-wide): 1B **Publicly Held**
SIC: 3842 Limbs, artificial

HQ: Hanger Prosthetics & Orthotics, Inc.
10910 Domain Dr Ste 300
Austin TX 78758
512 777-3800

(G-4355)
HARDINGE INC (HQ)
1 Hardinge Dr (14903-1946)
PHONE..................................607 734-2281
Christopher Disantis, *Ch of Bd*
Charles P Dougherty, *President*
Richard R Burkhart, *Principal*
B Christopher Disantis, *Principal*
Ryan J Levenson, *Principal*
◆ EMP: 277
SALES: 317.9MM **Privately Held**
WEB: www.hardinge.com
SIC: 3541 3545 3553 3549 Machine tools, metal cutting type; lathes; grinding, polishing, buffing, lapping & honing machines; collets (machine tool accessories); lathes, wood turning: including accessories; metalworking machinery
PA: Hardinge Holdings, Llc
79 W Paces Ferry Rd Nw
Atlanta GA 30305
404 419-2670

(G-4356)
HAUN WELDING SUPPLY INC
1100 Sullivan St (14901-1640)
PHONE..................................607 846-2289
Mike Cesaro, *Manager*
EMP: 8
SALES (corp-wide): 65.7MM **Privately Held**
SIC: 7692 5999 5169 Welding repair; welding supplies; industrial gases
PA: Haun Welding Supply, Inc.
5921 Court Street Rd
Syracuse NY 13206
315 463-5241

(G-4357)
HILLIARD CORPORATION (PA)
100 W 4th St (14901-2190)
P.O. Box 866 (14902-0866)
PHONE..................................607 733-7121
Arie J Van Den Blink, *Ch of Bd*
Gene A Ebbrecht, *President*
Steven J Chesebro, *Exec VP*
Michael V Cantando, *Vice Pres*
David Ochab, *Vice Pres*
◆ EMP: 277 EST: 1905
SQ FT: 326,000
SALES (est): 106.5MM **Privately Held**
SIC: 3564 3569 3823 Purification & dust collection equipment; filters; industrial instrmnts msrmnt display/control process variable

(G-4358)
HILLIARD CORPORATION
1420 College Ave (14901-1153)
PHONE..................................607 733-7121
Arie J Van Den Blink, *Branch Mgr*
EMP: 9
SALES (corp-wide): 106.5MM **Privately Held**
SIC: 3564 3569 3823 Purification & dust collection equipment; filters; industrial instrmnts msrmnt display/control process variable
PA: The Hilliard Corporation
100 W 4th St
Elmira NY 14901
607 733-7121

(G-4359)
I D MACHINE INC
Also Called: I Do Machining
1580 Lake St (14901-1248)
PHONE..................................607 796-2549
John Meier, *Ch of Bd*
EMP: 7
SALES (est): 1.1MM **Privately Held**
WEB: www.idomachining.com
SIC: 3599 Machine shop, jobbing & repair

(G-4360)
JRSMM LLC
Also Called: Jetwrx Rotable Services
1316 College Ave (14901-1169)
P.O. Box 282 (14902-0282)
PHONE..................................607 331-1549
Robert Salluzzo, *CFO*

GEOGRAPHIC

EMP: 6
SQ FT: 12,000
SALES (est): 313.4K **Privately Held**
SIC: 3728 Aircraft parts & equipment

(G-4361)
KITCHEN SPECIALTY CRAFTSMEN
2366 Corning Rd (14903-1045)
PHONE............................607 739-0833
Douglas Wells, *President*
Kenneth Wells, *Vice Pres*
Phillis Wells, *Treasurer*
EMP: 9 **EST:** 1968
SALES (est): 1.1MM **Privately Held**
SIC: 2541 Table or counter tops, plastic laminated

(G-4362)
MCWANE INC
Also Called: Kennedy Valve Division
1021 E Water St (14901-3332)
P.O. Box 931 (14902-0931)
PHONE............................607 734-2211
Arne Feyling, *General Mgr*
David Adams, *Safety Mgr*
Gene Patterson, *Purch Mgr*
Brad Bidlack, *Engineer*
Dan Burczynski, *Engineer*
EMP: 376
SALES (corp-wide): 1.2B **Privately Held**
WEB: www.mcwane.com
SIC: 3491 3561 3321 5085 Industrial valves; pumps & pumping equipment; gray & ductile iron foundries; valves & fittings
PA: Mcwane, Inc.
   2900 Highway 280 S # 300
   Birmingham AL 35223
   205 414-3100

(G-4363)
MEGA TOOL & MFG CORP
1023 Caton Ave (14904-2620)
PHONE............................607 734-8398
Craig Spencer, *President*
Mary Lou Spencer, *Admin Sec*
Mary Spencer, *Admin Sec*
EMP: 25 **EST:** 1965
SQ FT: 18,000
SALES (est): 3.4MM **Privately Held**
WEB: www.megatool-mfg.com
SIC: 3599 3469 7692 3544 Machine shop, jobbing & repair; machine parts, stamped or pressed metal; welding repair; special dies, tools, jigs & fixtures

(G-4364)
PC SOLUTIONS & CONSULTING
407 S Walnut St (14904-1637)
PHONE............................607 735-0466
Roy Brotherhood, *President*
Katherine Brotherhood, *Vice Pres*
EMP: 5
SQ FT: 1,800
SALES (est): 787.8K **Privately Held**
WEB: www.powerpcs.com
SIC: 3575 7371 Computer terminals, monitors & components; custom computer programming services

(G-4365)
QUICKER PRINTER INC
210 W Gray St (14901-2907)
P.O. Box 1257 (14902-1257)
PHONE............................607 734-8622
Robert Lavarnway Jr, *President*
EMP: 7
SQ FT: 5,000
SALES (est): 1.2MM **Privately Held**
WEB: www.quickerprinter.com
SIC: 2752 2791 Commercial printing, offset; typesetting

(G-4366)
RAINBOW LETTERING
1329 College Ave (14901-1133)
PHONE............................607 732-5751
George Malone, *Owner*
Tom Wolfe, *Owner*
EMP: 5
SALES: 150K **Privately Held**
SIC: 2396 2759 Screen printing on fabric articles; screen printing

(G-4367)
SEPAC INC
Also Called: Placid Industries
1580 Lake St Ste 1 (14901-1255)
PHONE............................607 732-2030
John H Meier, *President*
Martha Zoerb, *Accounting Mgr*
▲ **EMP:** 35
SQ FT: 17,352
SALES (est): 9.3MM **Privately Held**
SIC: 3568 Power transmission equipment

(G-4368)
STAR-GAZETTE FUND INC
Also Called: Elmira Star-Gazette
310 E Church St (14901-2704)
PHONE............................607 734-5151
Monte I Trammer, *President*
EMP: 150
SALES: 20MM
SALES (corp-wide): 2.9B **Publicly Held**
SIC: 2711 Newspapers, publishing & printing
HQ: Gannett Satellite Information Network, Llc
   7950 Jones Branch Dr
   Mc Lean VA 22102
   703 854-6000

(G-4369)
SURFACE FINISH TECHNOLOGY
215 Judson St (14901-3308)
PHONE............................607 732-2909
John Short, *President*
Linda Short, *Corp Secy*
Jack Slocum, *Engineer*
Carrie Roadarmel, *CFO*
Laura Walters, *Human Res Mgr*
EMP: 35
SQ FT: 18,000
SALES (est): 4.3MM **Privately Held**
WEB: www.surfacefinishtech.com
SIC: 3471 Finishing, metals or formed products

(G-4370)
TDS FITNESS EQUIPMENT CORP
Also Called: New York Barbell
160 Home St (14904-1811)
P.O. Box 4189 (14904-0189)
PHONE............................607 733-6789
T D Seethapathy, *President*
Thuggini D Seethapathy, *President*
▲ **EMP:** 10
SQ FT: 100,000
SALES (est): 3.8MM **Privately Held**
WEB: www.tdsfitnessequipment.com
SIC: 3949 5091 5941 Dumbbells & other weightlifting equipment; exercise equipment; exercise equipment; exercise equipment

(G-4371)
TDS FOUNDRY CORPORATION
160 Home St (14904-1811)
PHONE............................607 733-6789
EMP: 9
SALES (est): 267.3K **Privately Held**
SIC: 3949 Exercise equipment

(G-4372)
WINCHESTER OPTICAL COMPANY (DH)
1935 Lake St (14901-1239)
P.O. Box 1515 (14902-1515)
PHONE............................607 734-4251
Ben E Lynch, *President*
Michael P Lynch, *Vice Pres*
Mike Lynch, *Vice Pres*
Deborah Lynch, *Treasurer*
Matt Medwid, *Sales Mgr*
EMP: 41
SQ FT: 32,500
SALES (est): 12.8MM
SALES (corp-wide): 1.4MM **Privately Held**
WEB: www.winoptical.com
SIC: 3851 5048 Frames, lenses & parts, eyeglass & spectacle; ophthalmic goods
HQ: Essilor Laboratories Of America Holding Co., Inc.
   13555 N Stemmons Fwy
   Dallas TX 75234
   214 496-4141

(G-4373)
WRIGHTCUT EDM & MACHINE INC
951 Carl St (14904-2662)
PHONE............................607 733-5018
Byron Wright, *President*
Michelle Wright, *Vice Pres*
EMP: 9
SQ FT: 3,500
SALES (est): 1.3MM **Privately Held**
WEB: www.wrightcutedm.com
SIC: 3599 Machine shop, jobbing & repair

Elmira Heights
Chemung County

(G-4374)
ANCHOR GLASS CONTAINER CORP
151 E Mccanns Blvd (14903-1955)
P.O. Box 849, Elmira (14902-0849)
PHONE............................607 737-1933
EMP: 370
SALES (corp-wide): 264.1K **Privately Held**
WEB: www.anchorglass.com
SIC: 3221 Glass containers
HQ: Anchor Glass Container Corporation
   401 E Jackson St Ste 1100
   Tampa FL 33602

(G-4375)
CAF USA INC
300 E 18th St (14903-1333)
PHONE............................607 737-3004
Jesus Isturiz, *General Mgr*
Hoyos V Manuel, *General Mgr*
Adriana Ramirez, *General Mgr*
Lou Tartaglia, *Vice Pres*
Fernando Branger, *Terminal Mgr*
EMP: 100
SALES (corp-wide): 1.6B **Privately Held**
SIC: 3743 Railroad equipment
HQ: Caf Usa, Inc.
   1401 K St Nw Ste 1003
   Washington DC 20005
   202 898-4848

(G-4376)
FINGER LAKES TRAFFIC CTRL LLC
160 E 14th St (14903-1318)
PHONE............................607 795-7458
Carina Southard,
EMP: 35
SALES (est): 1.1MM **Privately Held**
SIC: 3669 Pedestrian traffic control equipment

(G-4377)
GOLOS PRINTING INC
110 E 9th St (14903-1733)
PHONE............................607 732-1896
Thomas L Golos Sr, *President*
Thomas L Corp Sr, *President*
Hank Corp, *Vice Pres*
EMP: 6 **EST:** 1921
SQ FT: 10,000
SALES: 300K **Privately Held**
SIC: 2752 2759 Commercial printing, offset; letterpress printing

(G-4378)
MOTOR COMPONENTS LLC
2243 Corning Rd (14903-1031)
PHONE............................607 737-8011
Reeve Howland, *Facilities Mgr*
Dave Demarco, *Controller*
Jane Allen, *HR Admin*
Anita Mawhir, *HR Admin*
Kris Miller, *Manager*
▲ **EMP:** 68
SQ FT: 300,000
SALES (est): 18.8MM
SALES (corp-wide): 38.3MM **Privately Held**
WEB: www.motorcomponents.com
SIC: 3714 Motor vehicle wheels & parts
PA: Bam Enterprises, Inc.
   2937 Alt Blvd
   Grand Island NY 14072
   716 773-7634

(G-4379)
SERVICE MACHINE & TOOL COMPANY
206 E Mccanns Blvd (14903-1958)
P.O. Box 2118 (14903-0118)
PHONE............................607 732-0413
Keith Knowlden, *President*
Axieann Knowlden, *Corp Secy*
Hal Fitzsimmons, *Tech/Comp Coord*
▲ **EMP:** 25
SALES (est): 4.8MM **Privately Held**
WEB: www.servicemachinetool.com
SIC: 3599 Machine shop, jobbing & repair

(G-4380)
STAMPED FITTINGS INC
217 Lenox Ave (14903-1118)
PHONE............................607 733-9988
Shana Graham, *President*
Mike Graham, *Vice Pres*
Chad Briggs, *VP Opers*
▲ **EMP:** 25 **EST:** 1997
SQ FT: 25,000
SALES (est): 4.8MM **Privately Held**
WEB: www.stampedfittings.com
SIC: 3469 Stamping metal for the trade

(G-4381)
SWIFT GLASS CO INC
131 22nd St (14903-1329)
P.O. Box 879, Elmira (14902-0879)
PHONE............................607 733-7166
Daniel J Burke, *President*
Kevin Wheeler, *Opers Mgr*
Jim Darling, *Sales Mgr*
Helen Faulkner, *Sales Associate*
▲ **EMP:** 85 **EST:** 1882
SQ FT: 80,000
SALES (est): 18MM **Privately Held**
WEB: www.swiftglass.com
SIC: 3231 Scientific & technical glassware: from purchased glass

---

Elmont
Nassau County

(G-4382)
ARCHITECTURAL SIGN GROUP INC
145 Meacham Ave (11003-2633)
PHONE............................516 326-1800
Abbas Jaffer, *President*
Rehana Jaffer, *Vice Pres*
EMP: 5
SQ FT: 8,000
SALES (est): 759.5K **Privately Held**
WEB: www.archsigngroup.com
SIC: 3993 1611 Electric signs; letters for signs, metal; highway & street sign installation

(G-4383)
AWT SUPPLY CORP
Also Called: American Printing Eqp & Sup
153 Meacham Ave (11003-2633)
P.O. Box 356, Franklin Square (11010-0356)
PHONE............................516 437-9105
Greg Mandel, *President*
Josh Solomon, *Vice Pres*
Max Mandel, *Exec Dir*
▲ **EMP:** 8
SQ FT: 45,000
SALES (est): 1.5MM **Privately Held**
WEB: www.americanprintingequipment.com
SIC: 3555 5051 3546 Printing trades machinery; wire; power-driven handtools

(G-4384)
ELMONT NORTH LITTLE LEAGUE
1532 Clay St (11003-1046)
PHONE............................516 775-8210
Ronald Levin, *Owner*
Tom Laietta, *Vice Pres*
EMP: 7
SALES (est): 462.1K **Privately Held**
SIC: 2721 Trade journals: publishing only, not printed on site

▲ = Import ▼ = Export
◆ = Import/Export

(G-4385)
GM INSULATION CORP
1345 Rosser Ave (11003-3244)
P.O. Box 2188, New Hyde Park (11040-8188)
PHONE..............................516 354-6000
Izabel Skugor, *President*
EMP: 13
SALES (est): 2.4MM **Privately Held**
SIC: 2295 Sealing or insulating tape for pipe: coated fiberglass

(G-4386)
MARTIN ORNA IR WORKS II INC
266 Elmont Rd (11003-1600)
PHONE..............................516 354-3923
Martin Boventre, *President*
Charles Cascio, *Principal*
EMP: 5 **EST:** 1962
SQ FT: 5,000
SALES (est): 630.2K **Privately Held**
SIC: 3446 Architectural metalwork

(G-4387)
PROFESSNAL SPT PBLICATIONS INC
570 Elmont Rd (11003-3535)
PHONE..............................516 327-9500
Michael Shabsels, *Ch of Bd*
EMP: 20
SALES (est): 1.7MM **Privately Held**
SIC: 2741 Miscellaneous publishing

(G-4388)
PROFESSNAL SPT PBLICATIONS INC
Also Called: Pspi
570 Elmont Rd Ste 202 (11003-3535)
PHONE..............................516 327-9500
EMP: 100
SALES (corp-wide): 22.6MM **Privately Held**
WEB: www.pspsports.com
SIC: 2721 Periodicals
PA: Professional Sports Publications Inc.
519 8th Ave
New York NY 10018
212 697-1460

(G-4389)
SAPIENZA PASTRY INC
Also Called: Sapienza Bake Shop
1376 Hempstead Tpke (11003-2539)
PHONE..............................516 352-5232
Paul Sapienza, *President*
EMP: 25
SQ FT: 3,600
SALES (est): 3.3MM **Privately Held**
SIC: 2051 5461 2099 2052 Bakery: wholesale or wholesale/retail combined; bakeries; food preparations; cookies & crackers

(G-4390)
TIMELY SIGNS INC
2135 Linden Blvd Ste C (11003-3900)
PHONE..............................516 285-5339
Eugene Goldsmith, *President*
EMP: 6
SQ FT: 2,000
SALES (est): 600K **Privately Held**
SIC: 3993 Displays & cutouts, window & lobby

Elmsford
Westchester County

(G-4391)
A GATTY PRODUCTS INC
Also Called: A Gatty Svce
1 Warehouse Ln (10523-1538)
P.O. Box 725 (10523-0725)
PHONE..............................914 592-3903
Andy Gattyan, *President*
Eva Gattyan, *Vice Pres*
EMP: 6
SQ FT: 5,000
SALES (est): 396K **Privately Held**
SIC: 3639 1799 Trash compactors, household; hydraulic equipment, installation & service

(G-4392)
ADL DATA SYSTEMS INC
565 Taxter Rd Ste 100 (10523-2300)
PHONE..............................914 591-1800
David Pollack, *President*
Aaron Weg, *Vice Pres*
Shelley Pollack, *Human Res Mgr*
Olinda Montoro, *Admin Asst*
EMP: 40
SQ FT: 13,000
SALES (est): 5.1MM **Privately Held**
WEB: www.adldata.com
SIC: 7372 Business oriented computer software

(G-4393)
ANCHOR TECH PRODUCTS CORP
4 Vernon Ln Ste 2 (10523-1947)
PHONE..............................914 592-0240
Dan Esposito, *President*
Steve Ebanks, *Manager*
▲ **EMP:** 20
SQ FT: 3,000
SALES (est): 2MM **Privately Held**
SIC: 3052 Vacuum cleaner hose, rubber; vacuum cleaner hose, plastic; v-belts, rubber

(G-4394)
ARTINA GROUP INC
250 Clearbrook Rd Ste 245 (10523-1332)
P.O. Box 681, Tarrytown (10591-0681)
PHONE..............................914 592-1850
INA Shapiro, *President*
Nicholas Colucci, *Exec VP*
Richard Horn, *Vice Pres*
Mark Spinozza, *Controller*
Stephanie Boyle, *Executive Asst*
EMP: 34 **EST:** 1971
SQ FT: 25,000
SALES (est): 6.4MM **Privately Held**
SIC: 2752 Business forms, lithographed

(G-4395)
BEST PRICED PRODUCTS INC
250 Clearbrook Rd Ste 240 (10523-1332)
P.O. Box 1174, White Plains (10602-1174)
PHONE..............................914 345-3800
Linda Goldberg, *President*
EMP: 5
SQ FT: 30,000
SALES (est): 445.3K **Privately Held**
WEB: www.bpp2.com
SIC: 3999 Novelties, bric-a-brac & hobby kits

(G-4396)
BH COFFEE COMPANY LLC (PA)
Also Called: Barrie House Coffee & Tea
4 Warehouse Ln (10523-1541)
PHONE..............................914 377-2500
David Goldstein, *CEO*
Paul Goldstein, *President*
Ronald Goldstein, *Vice Pres*
George Ercolino, *CFO*
Shay Zohar, *Sales Staff*
▲ **EMP:** 100 **EST:** 1934
SQ FT: 35,000
SALES (est): 24.4MM **Privately Held**
WEB: www.barriehouse.com
SIC: 2095 Coffee roasting (except by wholesale grocers)

(G-4397)
C & F IRON WORKS INC
14 N Payne St Ste 1 (10523-1839)
PHONE..............................914 592-2450
Fernando Pastilha, *President*
EMP: 15
SQ FT: 1,600
SALES (est): 800K **Privately Held**
SIC: 3446 Railings, bannisters, guards, etc.: made from metal pipe

(G-4398)
C & F STEEL DESIGN
14 N Payne St Ste 2 (10523-1841)
PHONE..............................914 592-3928
Arthur Boino, *CEO*
EMP: 18
SALES (est): 2.7MM **Privately Held**
SIC: 3446 Fences, gates, posts & flagpoles

(G-4399)
CENTRAL COCA-COLA BTLG CO INC (DH)
555 Taxter Rd Ste 550 (10523-2331)
PHONE..............................914 789-1100
Brock John F, *CEO*
Betty Sams Christian, *Ch of Bd*
Malcolm Bruni, *Vice Pres*
Culhane John J, *Vice Pres*
Palmer Vicki, *Vice Pres*
▲ **EMP:** 300
SQ FT: 2,000
SALES (est): 256.7MM
SALES (corp-wide): 31.8B **Publicly Held**
SIC: 2086 8741 Bottled & canned soft drinks; management services
HQ: Coca-Cola Refreshments Usa, Inc.
2500 Windy Ridge Pkwy Se
Atlanta GA 30339
770 989-3000

(G-4400)
COCA-COLA BTLG CO OF NY INC
111 Fairview Pk Dr Ste 1 (10523-1536)
PHONE..............................914 789-1572
Edward Bryan, *Branch Mgr*
EMP: 18
SALES (corp-wide): 31.8B **Publicly Held**
SIC: 2086 Bottled & canned soft drinks
HQ: The Coca-Cola Bottling Company Of New York Inc
2500 Windy Ridge Pkwy Se
Atlanta GA 30339
770 989-3000

(G-4401)
COCA-COLA BTLG CO OF NY INC
115 Fairview Pk Dr Ste 1 (10523-1535)
PHONE..............................914 789-1580
Margerite Lopiccollo, *Principal*
EMP: 10
SALES (corp-wide): 31.8B **Publicly Held**
SIC: 2086 Bottled & canned soft drinks
HQ: The Coca-Cola Bottling Company Of New York Inc
2500 Windy Ridge Pkwy Se
Atlanta GA 30339
770 989-3000

(G-4402)
CONWAY IMPORT CO INC
Also Called: Conway Dressing For Success
4 Warehouse Ln Ste 142 (10523-1568)
PHONE..............................914 592-1312
Leo Maccaro, *Branch Mgr*
EMP: 5
SALES (corp-wide): 13MM **Privately Held**
WEB: www.conwaydressings.com
SIC: 2035 Mayonnaise
PA: Conway Import Co., Inc.
11051 W Addison St
Franklin Park IL 60131
800 323-8801

(G-4403)
CORAL BLOOD SERVICE
525 Executive Blvd # 285 (10523-1240)
PHONE..............................800 483-4888
Rose Shaw, *Vice Pres*
EMP: 15
SALES (est): 1.7MM **Privately Held**
SIC: 2836 Plasmas

(G-4404)
CRAFTERS WORKSHOP INC
116 S Central Ave Ste 1 (10523-3503)
PHONE..............................914 345-2838
Jaime Echt, *President*
▼ **EMP:** 9
SQ FT: 3,000
SALES (est): 512.4K **Privately Held**
WEB: www.thecraftersworkshop.com
SIC: 3953 Stencils, painting & marking

(G-4405)
CRONIN ENTERPRISES INC
Also Called: Minuteman Press
70 E Main St Ste 2 (10523-3146)
PHONE..............................914 345-9600
Gary Cronin, *President*
Jacquiline Cronin, *Vice Pres*
EMP: 9

SQ FT: 4,000
SALES (est): 1.2MM **Privately Held**
SIC: 2752 Commercial printing, lithographic

(G-4406)
CUSTOM PINS INC
150 Clearbrook Rd Ste 139 (10523-1148)
PHONE..............................888 922-9378
James Zendman, *President*
EMP: 6
SALES (est): 493.3K **Privately Held**
WEB: www.custompins.com
SIC: 3961 Pins (jewelry), except precious metal

(G-4407)
EMKAY TRADING CORP (PA)
250 Clearbrook Rd Ste 127 (10523-1332)
P.O. Box 504 (10523-0504)
PHONE..............................914 592-9000
Howard Kravitz, *President*
Ruth Kravitz, *Vice Pres*
EMP: 2
SQ FT: 2,500
SALES (est): 1.9MM **Privately Held**
WEB: www.emkaytrading.org
SIC: 2022 Cheese, natural & processed

(G-4408)
ENGAGEMENT TECHNOLOGY LLC
33 W Main St Ste 303 (10523-2413)
PHONE..............................914 591-7600
Gloria Golle, *Controller*
Nick Gazivoda, *VP Sales*
Bruce Bolger,
EMP: 10
SALES (est): 1.4MM **Privately Held**
SIC: 3679 Electronic loads & power supplies

(G-4409)
FABRICATION ENTERPRISES INC
250 Clearbrook Rd Ste 240 (10523-1332)
P.O. Box 1500, White Plains (10602-1500)
PHONE..............................914 591-9300
Elliott Goldberg, *President*
Dean Marano, *Vice Pres*
Linda Green, *VP Prdtn*
Kathleen Renna, *Opers Staff*
Brendan Fahey, *Accounts Mgr*
◆ **EMP:** 45
SQ FT: 30,000
SALES (est): 50MM **Privately Held**
WEB: www.fabricationenterprises.com
SIC: 3841 2297 Physiotherapy equipment, electrical; nonwoven fabrics

(G-4410)
HUDSON SOFTWARE CORPORATION
3 W Main St Ste 106 (10523-2414)
PHONE..............................914 773-0400
Glenn Polin, *President*
Mike Gulley, *COO*
Ralph Santoni, *Manager*
EMP: 35
SQ FT: 6,000
SALES (est): 2.8MM **Privately Held**
WEB: www.hudsonsoft.com
SIC: 7372 7371 7374 Prepackaged software; custom computer programming services; service bureau, computer

(G-4411)
HYPRES INC (PA)
175 Clearbrook Rd (10523-1109)
PHONE..............................914 592-1190
Richard E Hitt Jr, *Ch of Bd*
Richard Hitt, *President*
Deepnarayan Gupta, *President*
Oleg Mukhanov, *President*
Timur Filippov, *Research*
EMP: 37
SQ FT: 17,250
SALES (est): 11MM **Privately Held**
WEB: www.hypres.com
SIC: 3679 Electronic circuits

(G-4412)
IRON ART INC
14 N Payne St (10523-1835)
PHONE..............................914 592-7977

Fernando Pastilha, *President*
EMP: 5
SALES: 200K **Privately Held**
SIC: 3446 Ornamental metalwork

(G-4413)
JAM PRINTING PUBLISHING INC
11 Clearbrook Rd Ste 133 (10523-1126)
PHONE.................................914 345-8400
Judith Millman, *President*
EMP: 7
SALES (est): 949.8K **Privately Held**
WEB: www.jamprinting.com
SIC: 2752 Commercial printing, litho-
graphic

(G-4414)
KEURIG DR PEPPER INC
55 Hunter Ln (10523-1334)
PHONE.................................914 846-2300
Sam Suleiman, *Warehouse Mgr*
EMP: 100 **Publicly Held**
SIC: 2086 Soft drinks: packaged in cans,
bottles, etc.
PA: Keurig Dr Pepper Inc.
5301 Legacy Dr
Plano TX 01803

(G-4415)
MAGNETIC ANALYSIS
CORPORATION (PA)
Also Called: M A C
103 Fairview Pk Dr Ste 2 (10523-1544)
PHONE.................................914 530-2000
Jl Vitulli, *Ch of Bd*
William S Gould III, *Chairman*
Keith Brandt, *District Mgr*
Fred Fundy, *District Mgr*
John Hobbs, *District Mgr*
▲ EMP: 90 EST: 1928
SQ FT: 26,000
SALES: 25MM **Privately Held**
WEB: www.mac-ndt.com
SIC: 3829 Testing equipment: abra-
sion, shearing strength, etc.; instruments
to measure electricity

(G-4416)
MASTER IMAGE PRINTING INC
75 N Central Ave Ste 202 (10523-2548)
PHONE.................................914 347-4400
John Sabatino, *President*
Mary Jane Yollen, *Vice Pres*
EMP: 5
SQ FT: 5,000
SALES: 1MM **Privately Held**
WEB: www.masterimage.com
SIC: 2759 2752 2396 2679 Labels &
seals: printing; commercial printing, litho-
graphic; automotive & apparel trimmings;
labels, paper: made from purchased ma-
terial

(G-4417)
MASTERDISK CORPORATION
134 S Central Ave Ste C (10523-3539)
PHONE.................................212 541-5022
Douglas Levine, *CEO*
Laksham Fernando, *Treasurer*
EMP: 15
SQ FT: 10,000
SALES: 981K **Privately Held**
WEB: www.masterdisk.com
SIC: 3652 3651 2851 Master records or
tapes, preparation of; household audio &
video equipment; vinyl coatings, strip-
pable

(G-4418)
MOTTS LLP (HQ)
Also Called: Motts
55 Hunter Ln (10523-1334)
P.O. Box 869077, Plano TX (75086-9077)
PHONE.................................972 673-8088
Jim Baldwin, *General Counsel*
Larry D Young,
◆ EMP: 250
SQ FT: 160,000
SALES (est): 208.7MM **Publicly Held**
WEB: www.maunalai.com
SIC: 2033 5149 2087 Fruit juices: pack-
aged in cans, jars, etc.; apple sauce:
packaged in cans, jars, etc.; beverage
concentrates; cocktail mixes, nonalcoholic

(G-4419)
NANOVIBRONIX INC
525 Executive Blvd (10523-1240)
PHONE.................................914 233-3004
William Stern, *CEO*
EMP: 12
SALES: 318K **Privately Held**
SIC: 3845 Ultrasonic medical equipment,
except cleaning

(G-4420)
NOVAMED-USA INC
4 Westchester Plz 137 (10523-1612)
PHONE.................................914 789-2100
Carol Schuler, *Exec VP*
▲ EMP: 40
SQ FT: 30,000
SALES (est): 5.9MM **Privately Held**
SIC: 3841 3845 Catheters; patient moni-
toring apparatus

(G-4421)
OLYMPIA SPORTS COMPANY
INC
Also Called: Olympia Company
500 Executive Blvd # 170 (10523-1239)
PHONE.................................914 347-4737
Roger Heumann, *President*
Ed Brodsky, *Vice Pres*
Peter Kiernan, *Vice Pres*
▲ EMP: 10
SQ FT: 7,200
SALES (est): 1.3MM **Privately Held**
WEB: www.olympiagloves.com
SIC: 3949 Gloves, sport & athletic: boxing,
handball, etc.

(G-4422)
PRESS EXPRESS
400 Executive Blvd # 146 (10523-1243)
PHONE.................................914 592-3790
Al Tiso, *President*
EMP: 5
SALES (est): 408.6K **Privately Held**
SIC: 2741 7313 Miscellaneous publishing;
printed media advertising representatives

(G-4423)
RADON TESTING CORP OF
AMERICA (PA)
Also Called: R T C A
2 Hayes St (10523-2502)
PHONE.................................914 345-3380
Michael Osterer, *CEO*
Nancy Bredhoff, *President*
Alan S Bandes, *Vice Pres*
Mark A Goodman, *Vice Pres*
Dante Galan, *Lab Dir*
EMP: 18
SQ FT: 4,500
SALES (est): 2.6MM **Privately Held**
WEB: www.rtca.com
SIC: 3821 Laboratory apparatus & furniture

(G-4424)
RALPH MARTINELLI
Also Called: Suburban Marketing Assoc
100 Clearbrook Rd Ste 170 (10523-1135)
PHONE.................................914 345-3055
Ralph Martinelli, *Owner*
EMP: 30
SALES (est): 1.3MM **Privately Held**
WEB: www.sub-pub.com
SIC: 2721 Magazines: publishing only, not
printed on site

(G-4425)
RAW INDULGENCE LTD
Also Called: Raw Revolution
44 Executive Blvd Ste 205 (10523-1336)
P.O. Box 359, Hawthorne (10532-0359)
PHONE.................................866 498-4671
David Friedman, *CEO*
Alice Benedetto, *President*
Wai Wu, *Principal*
▲ EMP: 14
SQ FT: 3,000
SALES (est): 2.9MM **Privately Held**
SIC: 2099 Food preparations

(G-4426)
RELIABLE AUTMTC SPRNKLR
CO INC (PA)
103 Fairview Pk Dr Ste 1 (10523-1523)
PHONE.................................800 431-1588

Frank J Fee III, *President*
Jim Daly, *Vice Pres*
Candida M Fee, *Vice Pres*
Kevin T Fee, *Vice Pres*
Michael R Fee, *Vice Pres*
◆ EMP: 350 EST: 1920
SQ FT: 64,000
SALES (est): 389.2MM **Privately Held**
SIC: 3569 Sprinkler systems, fire: auto-
matic

(G-4427)
SAVE O SEAL CORPORATION
INC
90 E Main St (10523-3218)
P.O. Box 553 (10523-0553)
PHONE.................................914 592-3031
Tullio Muscariello, *President*
Rose Muscariello, *Vice Pres*
EMP: 7
SQ FT: 3,000
SALES (est): 1.2MM **Privately Held**
SIC: 3565 5085 Packaging machinery;
knives, industrial

(G-4428)
SCHOTT CORPORATION (DH)
555 Taxter Rd Ste 470 (10523-2363)
PHONE.................................914 831-2200
Linda S Mayer, *Ch of Bd*
Dr Andreas F Liebenberg, *President*
Nikhil Krishna, *Business Mgr*
George Giatras, *Vice Pres*
Manfred Jaeckel, *Vice Pres*
◆ EMP: 70
SQ FT: 70,000
SALES (est): 752.6MM **Privately Held**
SALES (corp-wide): 449.3K **Privately**
Held
SIC: 3211 3829 3221 3229 Flat glass;
measuring & controlling devices; glass
containers; glass fiber products
HQ: Schott Ag
Hattenbergstr. 10
Mainz 55122
613 166-0

(G-4429)
SCHOTT GEMTRON
CORPORATION
555 Taxter Rd Ste 470 (10523-2352)
PHONE.................................423 337-3522
Linda S Mayer, *President*
EMP: 194
SALES (corp-wide): 449.3K **Privately**
Held
SIC: 3211 Flat glass
HQ: Schott Gemtron Corporation
615 Highway 68
Sweetwater TN 37874
423 337-3522

(G-4430)
SCHOTT LITHOTEC USA CORP
555 Taxter Rd Ste 470 (10523-2352)
PHONE.................................845 463-5300
Patrick Markschlaeger, *President*
EMP: 80
SQ FT: 36,115
SALES (est): 5.7MM **Privately Held**
SIC: 3674 Semiconductors & related de-
vices

(G-4431)
SCHOTT NORTH AMERICA INC
(DH)
555 Taxter Rd Ste 470 (10523-2352)
PHONE.................................914 831-2200
Greg Wolters, *CEO*
Tony Cappabianca, *Business Mgr*
Patrick Gallagher, *Business Mgr*
David Gibson, *Director*
Manfred Jaeckel, *Admin Sec*
▲ EMP: 60 EST: 1998
SQ FT: 23,000
SALES (est): 529.9MM
SALES (corp-wide): 449.3K **Privately**
Held
WEB: www.us.schott.com
SIC: 3229 Pressed & blown glass
HQ: Schott Corporation
555 Taxter Rd Ste 470
Elmsford NY 10523
914 831-2200

(G-4432)
SCHOTT SOLAR PV LLC
Also Called: Schott Solar Pv, Inc.
555 Taxter Rd Ste 470 (10523-2352)
PHONE.................................888 457-6527
Mark Finocchario, *President*
Hans-Juergen Gebel, *Vice Pres*
Manfred Jaeckel, *Admin Sec*
▲ EMP: 8
SALES (est): 804.4K
SALES (corp-wide): 449.3K **Privately**
Held
SIC: 3674 3211 Solar cells; flat glass
HQ: Schott Solar Ag
Hattenbergstr. 10
Mainz
613 166-0

(G-4433)
SIGN WORKS INCORPORATED
150 Clearbrook Rd Ste 118 (10523-1142)
PHONE.................................914 592-0700
Lynn Feiner, *President*
Rosanne Bocknik, *CFO*
Anthony Martinelli, *Marketing Staff*
EMP: 25
SQ FT: 11,000
SALES (est): 2.7MM **Privately Held**
SIC: 3993 1799 Signs, not made in cus-
tom sign painting shops; sign installation
& maintenance

(G-4434)
SML ACQUISITION LLC
33 W Main St Ste 505 (10523-2453)
PHONE.................................914 592-3130
Robert B Wetzel, *President*
EMP: 179 EST: 2011
SQ FT: 35,000
SALES (est): 12.5MM **Privately Held**
SIC: 2844 Toilet preparations

(G-4435)
SPOTLIGHT PUBLICATIONS LLC
100 Clearbrook Rd Ste 170 (10523-1135)
PHONE.................................914 345-9473
Catherine Colon, *Publisher*
John Jordan, *Principal*
Barbara Begley, *Marketing Staff*
EMP: 5
SALES (est): 470K **Privately Held**
SIC: 2721 Magazines: publishing only, not
printed on site

(G-4436)
TRANE US INC
3 Westchester Plz Ste 198 (10523-1623)
PHONE.................................914 593-0303
Terry Connor, *Manager*
EMP: 5 **Privately Held**
SIC: 3585 Refrigeration & heating equip-
ment
HQ: Trane U.S. Inc.
3600 Pammel Creek Rd
La Crosse WI 54601
608 787-2000

(G-4437)
TRI-STATE METALS LLC
Also Called: Tsm
41 N Lawn Ave (10523-2632)
PHONE.................................914 347-8157
Ray Ayerbe, *Webmaster*
EMP: 10
SQ FT: 10,000
SALES (est): 2.2MM **Privately Held**
SIC: 3444 Culverts, flumes & pipes

(G-4438)
U E SYSTEMS INCORPORATED
(PA)
14 Hayes St (10523-2536)
PHONE.................................914 592-1220
Michael Osterer, *Ch of Bd*
Blake Canham, *Regional Mgr*
Joe Edelen, *Regional Mgr*
Jacob Law, *Regional Mgr*
Mike Naro, *Regional Mgr*
EMP: 30
SALES (est): 10.7MM **Privately Held**
WEB: www.uesystems.com
SIC: 3829 3812 3699 Ultrasonic testing
equipment; search & navigation equip-
ment; electrical equipment & supplies

▲ = Import ▼=Export
◆ =Import/Export

(G-4439)
VITERION CORPORATION
565 Taxter Rd Ste 175 (10523-2371)
PHONE.............................914 333-6033
Toru Ide, *President*
EMP: 16 **EST:** 2012
SALES (est): 2.5MM **Privately Held**
SIC: 3841 Surgical & medical instruments

(G-4440)
WESTINGHOUSE A BRAKE TECH CORP
Also Called: Metro Service Center
4 Warehouse Ln Ste 144 (10523-1556)
PHONE.............................914 347-8650
Doug Cavallo, *Manager*
EMP: 13
SALES (corp-wide): 4.3B **Publicly Held**
WEB: www.wabco-rail.com
SIC: 3743 Rapid transit cars & equipment
PA: Westinghouse Air Brake Technologies
Corporation
30 Isabella St
Pittsburgh PA 15212
412 825-1000

(G-4441)
WHITE PLAINS MARBLE INC
186 E Main St (10523-3302)
PHONE.............................914 347-6000
John Bargellini, *President*
EMP: 7
SQ FT: 5,000
SALES (est): 700K **Privately Held**
SIC: 3281 1743 Marble, building: cut & shaped; statuary, marble; terrazzo, tile, marble, mosaic work

---

Endicott
Broome County

(G-4442)
311 INDUSTRIES CORP
434 Airport Rd (13760-4406)
PHONE.............................607 846-4520
John Galli, *President*
▲ **EMP:** 6
SALES (est): 193.9K **Privately Held**
SIC: 3089 Boot or shoe products, plastic

(G-4443)
AMPHENOL CABLES ON DEMAND CORP
20 Valley St (13760-3600)
PHONE.............................607 321-2115
R Adam Norwitt, *CEO*
▲ **EMP:** 10
SQ FT: 10,000
SALES: 4MM
SALES (corp-wide): 8.2B **Publicly Held**
SIC: 3678 Electronic connectors
PA: Amphenol Corporation
358 Hall Ave
Wallingford CT 06492
203 265-8900

(G-4444)
AMPHENOL INTRCONNECT PDTS CORP (HQ)
20 Valley St (13760-3600)
PHONE.............................607 754-4444
Richard Adam Norwitt, *CEO*
Martin H Loeffler, *President*
Edward G Jepsen, *CFO*
Diana Reardon, *Treasurer*
Kathy Malloy, *Credit Staff*
▲ **EMP:** 5
SQ FT: 140,000
SALES: 79.6MM
SALES (corp-wide): 8.2B **Publicly Held**
WEB: www.amphenol-aipc.com
SIC: 3679 Harness assemblies for electronic use: wire or cable
PA: Amphenol Corporation
358 Hall Ave
Wallingford CT 06492
203 265-8900

(G-4445)
BAE SYSTEMS CONTROLS INC (DH)
1098 Clark St (13760-2815)
PHONE.............................607 770-2000
Ehtisham Siddiqui, *CEO*
Robert Murphy, *Principal*
Joyce Sherwood, *Principal*
Thomas Grady, *Opers Mgr*
Bruce Gervais, *Opers Staff*
▲ **EMP:** 1400 **EST:** 2000
SALES (est): 453.2MM
SALES (corp-wide): 21.6B **Privately Held**
WEB: www.baesystemscontrols.com
SIC: 3812 Aircraft/aerospace flight instruments & guidance systems

(G-4446)
CHAKRA COMMUNICATIONS INC
32 Washington Ave (13760-5305)
PHONE.............................607 748-7491
Jim Arnold, *Branch Mgr*
EMP: 20 **Privately Held**
WEB: www.chakracentral.com
SIC: 2752 7334 2791 2789 Commercial printing, offset; photocopying & duplicating services; typesetting; bookbinding & related work; commercial printing
HQ: Chakra Communications, Inc.
80 W Drullard Ave
Lancaster NY 14086

(G-4447)
CROWLEY FABG MACHINING CO INC (PA)
403 N Nanticoke Ave (13760-4138)
PHONE.............................607 484-0299
Thomas Crowley, *President*
Mike Crowley, *General Mgr*
Jim Macuch, *Purch Agent*
Karen Crowley, *Accountant*
Mike Dalessi, *Marketing Staff*
EMP: 33
SQ FT: 30,000
SALES (est): 5.6MM **Privately Held**
WEB: www.crowleyfab.com
SIC: 3599 Machine shop, jobbing & repair

(G-4448)
DATUM ALLOYS INC
407 Airport Rd (13760-4405)
PHONE.............................607 239-6274
Ben Scott, *President*
Duncan Watey, *Vice Pres*
◆ **EMP:** 6
SQ FT: 800
SALES (est): 746.9K **Privately Held**
SIC: 3291 Abrasive metal & steel products

(G-4449)
ELTEE TOOL & DIE CO
404 E Franklin St (13760-4124)
PHONE.............................607 748-4301
William Andrew Keeler, *Owner*
EMP: 10
SQ FT: 10,000
SALES (est): 1.4MM **Privately Held**
SIC: 3559 Automotive related machinery

(G-4450)
ENDICOTT INTERCONNECT TECH INC
Also Called: Ei
1701 North St (13760-5587)
P.O. Box 5250, Binghamton (13902-5250)
PHONE.............................866 820-4820
James J Mc Namara Jr, *Ch of Bd*
Michael Cummings, *President*
William Lynn, *CFO*
Brad Van Brunt, *Sales Staff*
James W Orband, *Admin Sec*
▲ **EMP:** 600
SQ FT: 1,400,000
SALES (est): 90.2K **Privately Held**
WEB: www.endicottinterconnect.com
SIC: 3674 Semiconductors & related devices

(G-4451)
ENDICOTT PRECISION INC
1328-30 Campville Rd (13760-4414)
PHONE.............................607 754-7076
Tammie Romich, *General Mgr*
Douglas Walters, *General Mgr*
Manuel Oliveira, *Chairman*
Debbie Anderson, *Vice Pres*
Dolores Oliveira, *Vice Pres*
EMP: 125
SQ FT: 85,000
SALES: 16.6MM **Privately Held**
WEB: www.endicottprecision.com
SIC: 3444 3443 3599 3469 Sheet metalwork; fabricated plate work (boiler shop); weldments; custom machinery; metal stampings

(G-4452)
ENDICOTT RESEARCH GROUP INC
2601 Wayne St (13760-3207)
PHONE.............................607 754-9187
Nathan Burd, *President*
Scott Barney, *Vice Pres*
Greg Cleveland, *Engineer*
Michael Kretzmer, *Engineer*
Tim Delucca, *CFO*
EMP: 64
SQ FT: 30,000
SALES (est): 15MM **Privately Held**
WEB: www.ergpower.com
SIC: 3629 Power conversion units, a.c. to d.c.: static-electric; inverters, nonrotating: electrical

(G-4453)
ENGINEERING MFG TECH LLC
101 Delaware Ave (13760-6106)
PHONE.............................607 754-7111
Wyoma Chambala, *Vice Pres*
Michael Nowalk, *Vice Pres*
Luis Townsend, *Comptroller*
EMP: 90 **EST:** 1946
SQ FT: 80,000
SALES (est): 19MM **Privately Held**
WEB: www.endicottmachine.com
SIC: 3444 3599 3496 3469 Sheet metalwork; machine & other job shop work; miscellaneous fabricated wire products; metal stampings

(G-4454)
FADEC ALLIANCE LLC
1098 Clark St (13760-2815)
PHONE.............................607 770-3342
Steven McCullough, *President*
EMP: 122
SALES: 122MM **Privately Held**
SIC: 3724 Aircraft engines & engine parts

(G-4455)
FAMBUS INC
Also Called: Village Printing
2800 Watson Blvd (13760-3512)
PHONE.............................607 785-3700
David Labelle, *President*
Maureen Labelle, *Office Mgr*
EMP: 6
SQ FT: 2,100
SALES (est): 590K **Privately Held**
WEB: www.fambus.com
SIC: 2752 7334 Commercial printing, offset; photocopying & duplicating services

(G-4456)
FELIX ROMA & SONS INC
2 S Page Ave (13760-4693)
P.O. Box 5547 (13763-5547)
PHONE.............................607 748-3336
Eugene F Roma, *President*
Eugene Romask, *Vice Pres*
EMP: 60
SQ FT: 43,000
SALES (est): 8.1MM **Privately Held**
WEB: www.felixroma.com
SIC: 2051 Bakery: wholesale or wholesale/retail combined; bread, all types (white, wheat, rye, etc): fresh or frozen; rolls, bread type: fresh or frozen

(G-4457)
G B INTERNATIONAL TRDG CO LTD
408 Airport Rd (13760-4494)
PHONE.............................607 785-0938
August Garufy, *President*
◆ **EMP:** 250
SQ FT: 30,000
SALES (est): 40.9MM **Privately Held**
WEB: www.gbint.com
SIC: 3629 5065 5999 Power conversion units, a.c. to d.c.: static-electric; electronic parts & equipment; electronic parts & equipment

(G-4458)
GEORGE INDUSTRIES LLC (PA)
1 S Page Ave (13760-4695)
PHONE.............................607 748-3371
Jon Cohen, *President*
Kellen Kafka, *Engineer*
John Ferro, *Finance*
Don Leonard, *Manager*
Kathy Snyder, *Information Mgr*
EMP: 67
SQ FT: 100,000
SALES (est): 16.8MM **Privately Held**
WEB: www.georgeindustries.com
SIC: 3441 Fabricated structural metal

(G-4459)
I3 ELECTRONICS INC
Huron Campus 1500 1700 (13760)
PHONE.............................607 238-7077
Jim Matthews Jr, *Branch Mgr*
EMP: 53
SALES (corp-wide): 135MM **Privately Held**
SIC: 3672 Printed circuit boards
PA: I3 Electronics, Inc.
100 Eldredge St
Binghamton NY 13901
607 238-7077

(G-4460)
JARETS STUFFED CUPCAKES
116 Oak Hill Ave (13760-2810)
PHONE.............................607 658-9096
EMP: 8 **EST:** 2015
SALES (est): 406.6K **Privately Held**
SIC: 2051 Bread, cake & related products

(G-4461)
JAX SIGNS AND NEON INC
108 Odell Ave (13760)
PHONE.............................607 727-3420
James E Taber, *Ch of Bd*
EMP: 7
SALES (est): 831.4K **Privately Held**
SIC: 3993 Electric signs

(G-4462)
JD TOOL INC
205 Harrison Ave (13760-5119)
PHONE.............................607 786-3129
Jeffrey Dibble, *President*
Mandy Esposito, *Office Mgr*
EMP: 3
SALES: 1.8MM **Privately Held**
WEB: www.jdtool.net
SIC: 3545 Tools & accessories for machine tools

(G-4463)
JIM ROMAS BAKERY INC
202 N Nanticoke Ave (13760-4135)
PHONE.............................607 748-7425
James Roma, *President*
Carl Roma, *Vice Pres*
EMP: 30
SQ FT: 5,200
SALES: 800K **Privately Held**
SIC: 2051 5411 Bakery: wholesale or wholesale/retail combined; delicatessens

(G-4464)
MEDSIM-EAGLE SIMULATION INC
811 North St (13760-5127)
PHONE.............................607 658-9354
Nimrod Goor, *President*
Christopher Paulsen, *Vice Pres*
EMP: 12
SALES (est): 692.5K **Privately Held**
WEB: www.medsim.com
SIC: 3571 3577 7373 Electronic computers; graphic displays, except graphic terminals; systems integration services
HQ: Medsim Inc
741 Curlew Rd
Delray Beach FL 33444

(G-4465)
MICROCHIP TECHNOLOGY INC
3301 Country Club Rd (13760-3401)
PHONE....................607 785-5992
EMP: 166
SALES (corp-wide): 5.3B Publicly Held
SIC: 3674 Semiconductors & related devices
PA: Microchip Technology Inc
2355 W Chandler Blvd
Chandler AZ 85224
480 792-7200

(G-4466)
NEW VISION INDUSTRIES INC
1239 Campville Rd (13760-4424)
P.O. Box 570, Apalachin (13732-0570)
PHONE....................607 687-7700
Michael R Copt, President
Betsy Copt, Vice Pres
EMP: 18
SQ FT: 4,100
SALES (est): 5.5MM Privately Held
WEB: www.newvisionindustries.com
SIC: 3569 3441 Assembly machines, non-metalworking; fabricated structural metal

(G-4467)
NORTH POINT TECHNOLOGY LLC
816 Buffalo St (13760-1780)
PHONE....................866 885-3377
Tyler Johnson, IT/INT Sup
Brian Middaugh, IT/INT Sup
Robert P Lee,
EMP: 10
SALES (est): 726K Privately Held
WEB: www.northpointusa.com
SIC: 3625 Relays & industrial controls

(G-4468)
PALMER INDUSTRIES INC
2320 Lewis St (13760-6157)
PHONE....................607 754-8741
Jeck Palmer Jr, Manager
EMP: 7
SALES (corp-wide): 2.2MM Privately Held
WEB: www.palmerind.com
SIC: 3842 3534 Wheelchairs; elevators & moving stairways
PA: Palmer Industries Inc
509 Paden St
Endicott NY 13760
607 754-2957

(G-4469)
PALMER INDUSTRIES INC (PA)
509 Paden St (13760-4631)
P.O. Box 5707 (13763-5707)
PHONE....................607 754-2957
Jack Palmer Sr, President
Jack Palmer Jr, General Mgr
▲ EMP: 20
SALES (est): 2.2MM Privately Held
WEB: www.palmerind.com
SIC: 3842 Wheelchairs

(G-4470)
PALMER INDUSTRIES INC
1 Heath St (13760-6110)
P.O. Box 5707 (13763-5707)
PHONE....................607 754-8741
Jack Palmer Jr, Manager
EMP: 6
SALES (corp-wide): 2.2MM Privately Held
WEB: www.palmerind.com
SIC: 3842 Wheelchairs
PA: Palmer Industries Inc
509 Paden St
Endicott NY 13760
607 754-2957

(G-4471)
PHOTONIX TECHNOLOGIES INC
48 Washington Ave (13760-5305)
PHONE....................607 786-4600
John Urban, President
Sam Cucci, Vice Pres
EMP: 12
SQ FT: 2,500
SALES: 1,000K Privately Held
WEB: www.photonixtechnologies.com
SIC: 3825 Test equipment for electronic & electric measurement

(G-4472)
SAM A LUPO & SONS INC (PA)
1219 Campville Rd (13760-4411)
P.O. Box 5721 (13763-5721)
PHONE....................800 388-5352
Sam A Lupo Jr, President
Stephen J Lupo, Vice Pres
EMP: 3
SALES (est): 8.7MM Privately Held
WEB: www.spiedies.com
SIC: 2011 5411 Meat by-products from meat slaughtered on site; delicatessens

(G-4473)
SMARTYS CORNER
501 W Main St (13760-4621)
PHONE....................607 239-5276
Laura Cla, Principal
EMP: 6 EST: 2008
SALES (est): 435.9K Privately Held
SIC: 2024 Ice cream, bulk

(G-4474)
TIOGA TOOL INC (PA)
160 Glendale Dr (13760-3704)
PHONE....................607 785-6005
Jeff Rudler, President
Tracy Smith, Office Mgr
EMP: 16 EST: 1965
SQ FT: 5,500
SALES (est): 2.7MM Privately Held
WEB: www.tiogatool.com
SIC: 3599 1799 Machine shop, jobbing & repair; welding on site

(G-4475)
TNTPAVING
1077 Taft Ave (13760-7201)
PHONE....................607 372-4911
Dale Thomas, Owner
EMP: 5
SALES (est): 204.9K Privately Held
SIC: 2952 Asphalt felts & coatings

(G-4476)
TRUEBITE INC
129 Squires Ave (13760-2936)
PHONE....................607 786-3184
Ed Calafut, President
▲ EMP: 12
SALES (est): 825K Privately Held
WEB: www.fotofiles.com
SIC: 3545 Drills (machine tool accessories)

(G-4477)
VESTAL ELECTRONIC DEVICES LLC
635 Dickson St (13760-4527)
PHONE....................607 773-8461
Walter H Kintner Jr, Mng Member
▲ EMP: 17
SQ FT: 110,000
SALES: 3.4MM Privately Held
WEB: www.vestalelectronics.com
SIC: 3679 3356 Electronic circuits; tin & tin alloy bars, pipe, sheets, etc.

(G-4478)
WEDDING GOWN PRESERVATION CO
707 North St (13760-5011)
PHONE....................607 748-7999
Michael Schapiro, Owner
Susan Schapiro, Vice Pres
Sue Schapiro, Human Res Mgr
EMP: 60
SALES (est): 7.3MM Privately Held
WEB: www.gownpreservation.com
SIC: 2842 Drycleaning preparations

Endwell
Broome County

(G-4479)
EMPIRE PLASTICS INC
2011 E Main St (13760-5622)
PHONE....................607 754-9132
John Witinski Sr, President
John Witinski Jr, Vice Pres
EMP: 33 EST: 1958
SQ FT: 11,000

SALES (est): 5.4MM Privately Held
SIC: 3599 3699 2821 Machine shop, jobbing & repair; laser welding, drilling & cutting equipment; thermosetting materials; acrylic resins; nylon resins; polytetrafluoroethylene resins (teflon)

(G-4480)
J T SYSTEMATIC
Also Called: Just In Time Company
39 Valley St (13760-3659)
PHONE....................607 754-0929
Roger Carr, Owner
EMP: 5
SQ FT: 6,000
SALES: 350K Privately Held
SIC: 3089 3999 3544 3599 Injection molded finished plastic products; models, general, except toy; industrial molds; machine shop, jobbing & repair

(G-4481)
LIGHTSPIN TECHNOLOGIES INC
616 Lowell Dr (13760-2525)
PHONE....................301 656-7600
Jared Bowling, President
Richard Clayton, Chairman
EMP: 6
SALES: 1MM Privately Held
WEB: www.polychip.com
SIC: 3674 Semiconductors & related devices

(G-4482)
PROGRESSIVE TOOL COMPANY INC
3221 Lawndale St (13760-3593)
PHONE....................607 748-8294
Gordon E Markoff, CEO
Ronald G Markoff, President
Sandra J Roloson, Corp Secy
Lorraine Markoff, Vice Pres
Pat Crowley, Plant Mgr
EMP: 35 EST: 1956
SQ FT: 15,900
SALES (est): 5MM Privately Held
SIC: 3599 Machine shop, jobbing & repair

(G-4483)
PTC PRECISION LLC
3221 Lawndale St (13760-3523)
PHONE....................607 748-8294
Donald Cornwell, President
EMP: 21 EST: 2017
SQ FT: 30,000
SALES: 5MM
SALES (corp-wide): 13.7MM Privately Held
SIC: 3545 Precision tools, machinists'
PA: Dj Acquisition Management Corp.
6364 Dean Pkwy
Ontario NY 14519
585 265-3000

Erieville
Madison County

(G-4484)
MADISON MFG & MCH INC
3882 Sanderson Rd (13061-4166)
PHONE....................315 922-4476
Mark Russitano, Principal
EMP: 8 EST: 2017
SALES (est): 235K Privately Held
SIC: 3999 Manufacturing industries

Esperance
Montgomery County

(G-4485)
US SANDER LLC
4131 Rte 20 (12066)
P.O. Box 335 (12066-0335)
PHONE....................518 875-9157
Gary Rudolph, Mng Member
David Rudolph,
Peggy Rudolph,
EMP: 9
SQ FT: 10,000

SALES (est): 1.8MM Privately Held
WEB: www.ussander.com
SIC: 3553 Sanding machines, except portable floor sanders: woodworking

---

Etna
Tompkins County

(G-4486)
W F SAUNDERS & SONS INC
Also Called: Saunders Concrete
30 Pinckney Rd (13062)
PHONE....................607 257-6930
Bob Saunders, Owner
EMP: 9
SALES (est): 879.6K Privately Held
SALES (corp-wide): 7.7MM Privately Held
SIC: 3273 Ready-mixed concrete
PA: W F Saunders & Sons Inc
5126 S Onondaga Rd
Nedrow NY 13120
315 469-3217

Evans Mills
Jefferson County

(G-4487)
PETER S CURTIS
Also Called: Curtis Furniture Company
25465 Ny State Rt 342 (13637)
PHONE....................315 782-7363
Peter Curtis, Owner
EMP: 6
SALES (est): 659.4K Privately Held
WEB: www.curtisfurniture.com
SIC: 2511 Wood household furniture

Fabius
Onondaga County

(G-4488)
VILLAGE WROUGHT IRON INC
7756 Main St (13063-9749)
PHONE....................315 683-5589
Gary Host, President
Adam Host, Vice Pres
EMP: 12
SQ FT: 15,000
SALES (est): 1.9MM Privately Held
SIC: 3446 Architectural metalwork

Fairport
Monroe County

(G-4489)
BERNARD HALL
Also Called: Minuteman Press
10 Perinton Hills Mall (14450-3621)
PHONE....................585 425-3340
Bernard Hall, Owner
EMP: 5
SALES (est): 527.1K Privately Held
SIC: 2752 2791 2789 Commercial printing, lithographic; typesetting; bookbinding & related work

(G-4490)
BREED ENTERPRISES INC
34 Water St (14450-1549)
PHONE....................585 388-0126
Ronald Reding, President
Bruce Caruana, Vice Pres
EMP: 5
SALES: 1.1MM Privately Held
WEB: www.bullittmansparts.com
SIC: 3599 Machine shop, jobbing & repair

(G-4491)
CAM-TECH INDUSTRIES INC
95 Estates Dr W (14450-8425)
PHONE....................585 425-2090
Thomas Collier, President
Richard Vice, Vice Pres
EMP: 21 EST: 1982
SQ FT: 30,000

▲ = Import ▼=Export
◆ =Import/Export

SALES (est): 3.8MM **Privately Held**
WEB: www.camtechindustries.com
SIC: 3451 Screw machine products

(G-4492)
CASA LARGA VINEYARDS (PA)
27 Emerald Hill Cir (14450-9504)
P.O. Box 400 (14450-0400)
PHONE..........................585 223-4210
Ann Colaruotolo, *President*
Andrew Colaruotolo, *President*
John Colaruotolo, *Vice Pres*
EMP: 30
SALES (est): 3.2MM **Privately Held**
WEB: www.casalarga.com
SIC: 2084 5921 7299 Wines; wine; banquet hall facilities

(G-4493)
CASA LARGA VINEYARDS
2287 Turk Hill Rd (14450-9579)
P.O. Box 400 (14450-0400)
PHONE..........................585 223-4210
Ann Colaruottolo, *Manager*
EMP: 7
SALES (corp-wide): 3.2MM **Privately Held**
WEB: www.casalarga.com
SIC: 2084 Wines
PA: Casa Larga Vineyards
27 Emerald Hill Cir
Fairport NY 14450
585 223-4210

(G-4494)
CORNING TROPEL CORPORATION
60 Oconnor Rd (14450-1328)
PHONE..........................585 377-3200
Curt Weinstein, *Ch of Bd*
John Burning, *President*
Dan Gales, *Mfg Mgr*
Robert Grejda, *Engineer*
John Limner, *Engineer*
EMP: 195
SQ FT: 100,000
SALES (est): 28.6MM
SALES (corp-wide): 11.2B **Publicly Held**
WEB: www.tropel.com
SIC: 3841 3827 3229 Ophthalmic instruments & apparatus; optical instruments & lenses; pressed & blown glass
PA: Corning Incorporated
1 Riverfront Plz
Corning NY 14831
607 974-9000

(G-4495)
D BAG LADY INC
183 Perinton Pkwy (14450-9104)
PHONE..........................585 425-8095
Debra Perry, *President*
EMP: 8
SQ FT: 8,500
SALES (est): 1.2MM **Privately Held**
WEB: www.dbaglady.com
SIC: 2673 Plastic bags: made from purchased materials

(G-4496)
DAVIS INTERNATIONAL INC
388 Mason Rd (14450-9561)
PHONE..........................585 421-8175
Timothy M McGraw, *President*
James R Davis, *Principal*
EMP: 12
SQ FT: 5,000
SALES (est): 1.6MM **Privately Held**
WEB: www.davisinternational.net
SIC: 3555 5084 Printing trades machinery; printing trades machinery, equipment & supplies

(G-4497)
FITSMO LLC
108 Packetts Gln (14450-2150)
PHONE..........................585 519-1956
Anthony Messana, *Mng Member*
EMP: 6
SALES (est): 327.6K **Privately Held**
SIC: 3949 7389 Sporting & athletic goods;

(G-4498)
HANDONE STUDIOS INC
388 Mason Rd (14450-9561)
PHONE..........................585 421-8175

Jim Davis, *President*
Anatol Topolewski, *Purch Mgr*
EMP: 9
SQ FT: 6,000
SALES: 300K **Privately Held**
SIC: 2759 Screen printing

(G-4499)
IRON SMOKE WHISKEY LLC
111 Parce Ave Ste 5 (14450-1467)
PHONE..........................585 388-7584
Thomas J Brunett, *President*
EMP: 6 EST: 2015
SALES (est): 566.5K **Privately Held**
SIC: 2085 Bourbon whiskey

(G-4500)
J & N COMPUTER SERVICES INC
1387 Fairport Rd Ste 900j (14450-2087)
PHONE..........................585 388-8780
Nancy E Jacobsen, *Ch of Bd*
Jerry Jacobsen, *General Mgr*
Adam Pierce, *Technology*
EMP: 11
SQ FT: 3,000
SALES (est): 4.1MM **Privately Held**
SIC: 3571 5734 Electronic computers; computer & software stores

(G-4501)
JASCO HEAT TREATING INC
75 Macedon Center Rd (14450-9763)
P.O. Box 60620, Rochester (14606-0620)
PHONE..........................585 388-0071
Eugine W Baldino, *CEO*
Kenneth Marvald, *Admin Sec*
EMP: 23
SQ FT: 50,000
SALES (est): 5.8MM **Privately Held**
WEB: www.jascotools.com
SIC: 3398 Metal heat treating

(G-4502)
LAHR RECYCLING & RESINS INC
Also Called: Lahr Plastics
164 Daley Rd (14450-9524)
PHONE..........................585 425-8608
Craig A Lahr, *President*
EMP: 15
SQ FT: 20,000
SALES (est): 1.8MM **Privately Held**
SIC: 3087 Custom compound purchased resins

(G-4503)
LIDESTRI BEVERAGES LLC (PA)
Also Called: Dundeespirits
815 Whitney Rd W (14450-1030)
PHONE..........................585 377-7700
Giovanni Lidestri, *CEO*
Barbara Jackson, *Manager*
▲ EMP: 19
SALES (est): 3MM **Privately Held**
SIC: 2099 Food preparations

(G-4504)
LIDESTRI FOODS INC (PA)
Also Called: Lidestri Food and Drink
815 Whitney Rd W (14450-1030)
PHONE..........................585 377-7700
John Lidestri, *CEO*
Joe Ferrigno, *Principal*
Robert Schiefer, *Principal*
Edward Salzano, *Vice Pres*
Mark Scoville, *Vice Pres*
◆ EMP: 400 EST: 1974
SQ FT: 260,000
SALES (est): 247.9MM **Privately Held**
WEB: www.francescorinaldi.com
SIC: 3221 2033 Bottles for packing, bottling & canning: glass; canned fruits & specialties; spaghetti & other pasta sauce: packaged in cans, jars, etc.

(G-4505)
LMG NATIONAL PUBLISHING INC (HQ)
350 Willowbrook Office Pa (14450-4222)
P.O. Box 580, Middletown (10940-0580)
PHONE..........................585 598-6874
Leslie Hinton, *Ch of Bd*
EMP: 27

SALES (est): 15.9MM
SALES (corp-wide): 1.5B **Privately Held**
SIC: 2711 2752 Newspapers, publishing & printing; commercial printing, lithographic
PA: New Media Investment Group Inc.
1345 Avenue Of The Americ
New York NY 10105
212 479-3160

(G-4506)
MASTERCRAFT DECORATORS INC
320 Macedon Center Rd (14450-9759)
PHONE..........................585 223-5150
James Yonosko, *President*
▲ EMP: 40
SQ FT: 6,000
SALES: 5MM **Privately Held**
WEB: www.guildlines.com
SIC: 2759 Screen printing

(G-4507)
MICROGEN SYSTEMS INC
3 Railroad St Ste D (14450-1563)
PHONE..........................585 214-2426
Robert Andosca, *CEO*
Michael Perrotta, *CFO*
EMP: 8
SQ FT: 3,000
SALES (est): 758.7K **Privately Held**
SIC: 3676 Electronic resistors

(G-4508)
MOSER BAER TECHNOLOGIES INC
6 Camborne Cir (14450-8963)
PHONE..........................585 749-0480
Gopalan Rajeswaran, *CEO*
EMP: 12
SQ FT: 12,000
SALES (est): 177.4K **Privately Held**
SIC: 3674 Semiconductors & related devices
PA: Moser Baer India Limited
No-43/A B, Phase-3
New Delhi DL 11002

(G-4509)
MURPHY MANUFACTURING CO INC
38 West Ave (14450-2159)
P.O. Box 119 (14450-0119)
PHONE..........................585 223-0100
Gordon D Murphy Sr, *President*
Donna Faust, *Database Admin*
▲ EMP: 5 EST: 1946
SQ FT: 6,500
SALES (est): 360K **Privately Held**
WEB: www.murphymanufacturing.com
SIC: 3451 3491 Screw machine products; industrial valves

(G-4510)
OMEGA TOOL MEASURING MCHS INC (PA)
101 Perinton Pkwy (14450-9104)
PHONE..........................585 598-7800
Michael R Nuccitelli, *CEO*
Chris Nuccitelli, *President*
Mark Higgins, *Exec VP*
Ronald S Ricotta, *Vice Pres*
Jay Nuccitelli, *VP Opers*
▲ EMP: 35
SQ FT: 100,000
SALES: 30MM **Privately Held**
WEB: www.parlec.com
SIC: 3541 3545 Numerically controlled metal cutting machine tools; machine tool accessories

(G-4511)
ORACLE AMERICA INC
Sun Microsystems
345 Woodcliff Dr Ste 1 (14450-4210)
PHONE..........................585 317-4648
Kevin Regan, *Manager*
EMP: 55
SALES (corp-wide): 39.5B **Publicly Held**
SIC: 7372 Prepackaged software
HQ: Oracle America, Inc.
500 Oracle Pkwy
Redwood City CA 94065
650 506-7000

(G-4512)
PARKER-HANNIFIN CORPORATION
Also Called: Chomerics Div
83 Estates Dr W (14450-8425)
PHONE..........................585 425-7000
Patrick Malone, *CEO*
EMP: 126
SALES (corp-wide): 14.3B **Publicly Held**
SIC: 3594 Fluid power pumps & motors
PA: Parker-Hannifin Corporation
6035 Parkland Blvd
Cleveland OH 44124
216 896-3000

(G-4513)
PARLEC LLC
101 Perinton Pkwy Fl 1 (14450-9182)
PHONE..........................585 425-4400
Joe Odea, *Mng Member*
EMP: 80 EST: 2017
SQ FT: 100,000
SALES (est): 2.5MM **Privately Held**
SIC: 3545 Machine tool accessories
PA: Techniks, Llc
9930 E 56th St
Indianapolis IN 46236

(G-4514)
PENNSAUKEN PACKING COMPANY LLC
815 Whitney Rd W (14450-1030)
PHONE..........................585 377-7700
Giovanni Lidestri, *CEO*
EMP: 7
SALES (est): 332.7K
SALES (corp-wide): 247.9MM **Privately Held**
SIC: 3221 Food containers, glass
PA: Lidestri Foods, Inc.
815 Whitney Rd W
Fairport NY 14450
585 377-7700

(G-4515)
PERFORMANCE DESIGNED BY PETERS
Also Called: Poerformance Design
7 Duxbury Hts (14450-3331)
PHONE..........................585 223-9062
Peter R Geib, *President*
Todd Geib, *Vice Pres*
EMP: 19
SALES: 5MM **Privately Held**
SIC: 3714 Motor vehicle parts & accessories

(G-4516)
QUALITROL COMPANY LLC (HQ)
Also Called: Otiwti
1385 Fairport Rd (14450-1399)
PHONE..........................586 643-3717
Ronald Meyer, *President*
John Piper, *President*
Jay Cunningham, *Vice Pres*
Joseph Mbuyi, *Vice Pres*
Jim Niederst, *Opers Mgr*
▲ EMP: 111
SQ FT: 50,000
SALES (est): 110.8MM
SALES (corp-wide): 6.4B **Publicly Held**
WEB: www.qualitrolcorp.com
SIC: 3829 Measuring & controlling devices
PA: Fortive Corporation
6920 Seaway Blvd
Everett WA 98203
425 446-5000

(G-4517)
QUALTECH TOOL & MACHINE INC
1000 Turk Hill Rd Ste 292 (14450-8755)
P.O. Box 356 (14450-0356)
PHONE..........................585 223-9227
Anita Palmer, *President*
Richard T Palmer III, *Vice Pres*
EMP: 10 EST: 1979
SQ FT: 10,500
SALES (est): 1.4MM **Privately Held**
SIC: 3599 Machine shop, jobbing & repair

(G-4518)
R STEINER TECHNOLOGIES INC
180 Perinton Pkwy (14450-9107)
PHONE..........................585 425-5912

Rudolph Steiner, *CEO*
Andy Nolan, *President*
EMP: 20
SQ FT: 12,000
SALES: 1.5MM **Privately Held**
WEB: www.steinertechnologies.com
SIC: 3541 Machine tools, metal cutting
　type

(G-4519)
SCAIFE ENTERPRISES INC
Also Called: Petrillo's Bakery
4 Chillon Ct (14450-4642)
PHONE..................................585 454-5231
EMP: 18
SALES (est): 2MM **Privately Held**
SIC: 2051 Mfg Bread/Related Products

(G-4520)
SENDEC CORP
Sendec Corp Product Division
151 Perinton Pkwy (14450-9104)
PHONE..................................585 425-5965
David Sestito, *General Mgr*
Thomas Tette, *Executive*
EMP: 22 **Privately Held**
WEB: www.sendec.com
SIC: 3679 Microwave components
HQ: Sendec Corp.
　345 Pomroys Dr
　Windber PA 15963
　585 425-3390

(G-4521)
SENECA TEC INC
73 Country Corner Ln (14450-3034)
PHONE..................................585 381-2645
John Kidd, *President*
James Kidd, *Vice Pres*
Art Trimble, *Vice Pres*
EMP: 9
SQ FT: 1,500
SALES (est): 765.7K **Privately Held**
WEB: www.senecatec.com
SIC: 3861 3841 Photographic processing
　equipment & chemicals; surgical & med-
　ical instruments

(G-4522)
SIEMENS PRODUCT LIFE MGMT SFTW
345 Woodcliff Dr (14450-4210)
PHONE..................................585 389-8699
Len Carlson, *Sales Mgr*
EMP: 34
SALES (corp-wide): 95B **Privately Held**
SIC: 7372 Business oriented computer
　software
HQ: Siemens Industry Software Inc.
　5800 Granite Pkwy Ste 600
　Plano TX 75024
　972 987-3000

(G-4523)
STEINER TECHNOLOGIES INC
180 Perinton Pkwy (14450-9107)
PHONE..................................585 425-5910
Andrew Nolan, *President*
EMP: 19 **EST:** 2008
SALES (est): 3.9MM **Privately Held**
SIC: 3545 Cutting tools for machine tools

(G-4524)
STREAMLINE PRECISION INC
205 Turk Hill Park (14450-8728)
PHONE..................................585 421-9050
Kelly Palladino, *President*
Robert Levitsky, *Vice Pres*
Tom Gore, *Engineer*
EMP: 8
SQ FT: 1,000
SALES (est): 926.4K **Privately Held**
SIC: 3545 Precision tools, machinists'

(G-4525)
STREAMLINE PRECISION INC
Also Called: Streamline Machine
1000 Turk Hill Rd Ste 205 (14450-8755)
PHONE..................................585 421-9050
Robert Levitsky, *President*
EMP: 6
SALES (est): 650K **Privately Held**
SIC: 3545 Precision tools, machinists'

(G-4526)
SUHOR INDUSTRIES INC (PA)
Also Called: Si Funeral Services
72 Oconnor Rd (14450-1328)
PHONE..................................585 377-5100
Joe Suhor, *President*
Jay Muller, *Plant Mgr*
Ted Hart, *Treasurer*
Trinh Huynh, *Sales Staff*
Steve Williams, *Technology*
▲ **EMP:** 14
SQ FT: 4,250
SALES (est): 2.2MM **Privately Held**
WEB: www.wilbertservices.com
SIC: 3272 Burial vaults, concrete or pre-
　cast terrazzo

(G-4527)
THALES LASER SA
78 Schuyler Baldwin Dr (14450-9100)
PHONE..................................585 223-2370
Ariane Andreani, *General Mgr*
EMP: 65
SALES (est): 3.4MM **Privately Held**
SIC: 3674 Semiconductors & related de-
　vices

(G-4528)
VIDEK INC
1387 Fairport Rd 1000c (14450-2004)
PHONE..................................585 377-0377
Thomas Slechta, *President*
Jim Reda, *Vice Pres*
Doug Farrell, *Purchasing*
Moreen Jorjensen, *Controller*
EMP: 25
SQ FT: 14,861
SALES (est): 5.5MM **Privately Held**
WEB: www.videk.com/
SIC: 3827 3829 Optical test & inspection
　equipment; measuring & controlling de-
　vices

(G-4529)
VOLT TEK INC
111 Parce Ave (14450-1467)
PHONE..................................585 377-2050
Fax: 585 377-2654
▲ **EMP:** 15
SALES (est): 1.4MM **Privately Held**
SIC: 3644 Mfg Nonconductive Wiring De-
　vices

(G-4530)
WORKPLACE INTERIORS LLC
400 Packetts Lndg (14450-1576)
PHONE..................................585 425-7420
Chad Mucha, *Project Mgr*
Scott Maccaull, *Mng Member*
EMP: 20 **EST:** 2015
SQ FT: 16,000
SALES: 16.7MM **Privately Held**
SIC: 2522 5021 Office furniture, except
　wood; office furniture

(G-4531)
XACTIV INC
Also Called: Torrey Pines Research
71 Perinton Pkwy (14450-9104)
PHONE..................................585 288-7220
Peter Mason, *President*
Chuck Synborski, *Exec VP*
EMP: 19
SQ FT: 21,000
SALES (est): 4.4MM **Privately Held**
SIC: 3624 3721 8731 8711 Carbon &
　graphite products; research & develop-
　ment on aircraft by the manufacturer;
　commercial physical research; engineer-
　ing services; scientific consulting

Falconer
Chautauqua County

(G-4532)
AJ GENCO MCH SP MCHY RDOUT SVC
Also Called: A J Gnco Mch Shp/Mchnery
Rdout
235 Carter St (14733-1409)
PHONE..................................716 664-4925
Anthony J Genco, *President*
EMP: 10

SQ FT: 23,940
SALES: 610K **Privately Held**
SIC: 3599 7692 3444 Machine shop, job-
　bing & repair; welding repair; sheet metal-
　work

(G-4533)
ALLIED INSPECTION SERVICES LLC
4 Carter St (14733-1406)
PHONE..................................716 489-3199
Scott M Lynn, *Director*
EMP: 13
SALES (est): 2MM **Privately Held**
SIC: 3569 Sprinkler systems, fire: auto-
　matic

(G-4534)
ARCONIC INC
Also Called: Alcoa
2632 S Work St Ste 24 (14733-1705)
PHONE..................................716 358-6451
EMP: 8
SALES (corp-wide): 12.9B **Publicly Held**
SIC: 3542 Mfg Machine Tools-Forming
PA: Arconic Inc.
　390 Park Ave Fl 12
　New York NY 15212
　212 836-2758

(G-4535)
BARTON TOOL INC
1864 Lyndon Blvd (14733-1735)
P.O. Box 17 (14733-0017)
PHONE..................................716 665-2801
Jo Anne Barton, *President*
John Barton, *Vice Pres*
EMP: 7
SQ FT: 20,000
SALES (est): 1.1MM **Privately Held**
WEB: www.bartontool.com
SIC: 3089 3599 Injection molding of plas-
　tics; machine shop, jobbing & repair

(G-4536)
CHAUTAUQUA SIGN CO INC
2164 Allen Street Ext (14733-1703)
PHONE..................................716 665-2222
Gregory J Winter, *President*
EMP: 8
SALES (est): 805.1K **Privately Held**
WEB:
www.chautauquasportshalloffame.org
SIC: 3993 Signs & advertising specialties

(G-4537)
CPI OF FALCONER INC
1890 Lyndon Blvd (14733-1731)
PHONE..................................716 664-4444
EMP: 22
SQ FT: 20,000
SALES (est): 266.7K **Privately Held**
SIC: 3089 3965 Mfg Plastic Products Mfg
　Fasteners/Buttons/Pins

(G-4538)
ELLISON BRONZE INC
125 W Main St (14733-1698)
PHONE..................................716 665-6522
Peter Stark, *Ch of Bd*
Mark Graves, *President*
Billy Emerson, *Vice Pres*
Roger Overend, *Vice Pres*
James Chau, *Purch Mgr*
◆ **EMP:** 59 **EST:** 1913
SQ FT: 65,000
SALES (est): 12.1MM **Privately Held**
WEB: www.ellisonbronze.com
SIC: 3442 Metal doors

(G-4539)
EMC TECH INC
1984 Allen Street Ext (14733-1717)
PHONE..................................716 488-9071
Eric Corey, *Vice Pres*
Scott Schuler, *Marketing Staff*
EMP: 13
SALES (est): 1.4MM **Privately Held**
SIC: 3552 3585 Dyeing, drying & finishing
　machinery & equipment; air conditioning
　equipment, complete

(G-4540)
FALCON CHAIR AND TABLE INC
121 S Work St (14733-1433)
P.O. Box 8 (14733-0008)
PHONE..................................716 664-7136
EMP: 49
SQ FT: 23,000
SALES (est): 4.7MM **Privately Held**
SIC: 2511 Mfg Wood Household Furniture

(G-4541)
FALCONER ELECTRONICS INC
421 W Everett St (14733-1647)
PHONE..................................716 665-4176
Roger E Hall, *President*
Janine Hall, *Vice Pres*
Scott Johnson, *Manager*
EMP: 61
SQ FT: 20,000
SALES (est): 10.8MM **Privately Held**
WEB: www.falconer-electronics.com
SIC: 3672 5065 Printed circuit boards;
　electronic parts

(G-4542)
HANSON AGGREGATES EAST LLC
4419 S 9 Mile Rd (14733)
P.O. Box 473 (14733-0473)
PHONE..................................716 372-1574
Mike Shumack, *Manager*
EMP: 17
SALES (corp-wide): 20.6B **Privately Held**
SIC: 3273 Ready-mixed concrete
HQ: Hanson Aggregates East Llc
　3131 Rdu Center Dr
　Morrisville NC 27560
　919 380-2500

(G-4543)
HANSON SIGN SCREEN PRCESS CORP
Also Called: Hanson Sign Companies
82 Carter St (14733-1406)
PHONE..................................716 661-3900
Edward Sullivan, *CEO*
EMP: 34 **EST:** 1949
SQ FT: 25,000
SALES: 4.6MM **Privately Held**
WEB: www.hansonsign.com
SIC: 3993 Signs, not made in custom sign
　painting shops

(G-4544)
INSCAPE (NEW YORK) INC (HQ)
Also Called: Inscape Archtectural Interiors
221 Lister Ave 1 (14733-1459)
PHONE..................................716 665-6210
Rod Turgeon, *CEO*
Craig Dunlop, *Ch of Bd*
Nic Balderi, *Vice Pres*
Bryan Berndt, *Vice Pres*
Kent Smallwood, *CFO*
◆ **EMP:** 82
SALES (est): 20.7MM
SALES (corp-wide): 67.4MM **Privately
Held**
SIC: 2542 3442 3441 3449 Partitions for
　floor attachment, prefabricated: except
　wood; metal doors; fabricated structural
　metal; custom roll formed products;
PA: Inscape Corporation
　67 Toll Rd
　Holland Landing ON L9N 1
　905 836-7676

(G-4545)
INSCAPE INC
221 Lister Ave (14733-1459)
PHONE..................................716 665-6210
Kristen Johnson, *Business Mgr*
Hethre Strickland, *Business Mgr*
Aziz Hirji, *CFO*
Dennis Dyke, *Marketing Staff*
William Kuppinger, *Manager*
EMP: 40
SQ FT: 130,000
SALES: 2MM **Privately Held**
SIC: 2522 2542 Office furniture, except
　wood; partitions & fixtures, except wood

(G-4546)
JAMES TOWN MACADAM INC
1946 New York Ave (14733-1739)
PHONE..................................716 665-4504

Jim Ells, *Principal*
EMP: 56
SQ FT: 2,000
SALES (est): 5.2MM **Privately Held**
SIC: 3273 Ready-mixed concrete

(G-4547)
JAMESTOWN CONTAINER CORP (PA)
14 Deming Dr (14733-1697)
P.O. Box 8, Jamestown (14702-0008)
PHONE.................................716 665-4623
Bruce Janowsky, *Ch of Bd*
Joseph R Palmeri, *Vice Pres*
Michelle Minko, *Purchasing*
Lou Petitti, *Engineer*
Dick Weimer, *Treasurer*
▼ **EMP:** 110
SQ FT: 100,000
SALES (est): 148.3MM **Privately Held**
WEB: www.jamestowncontainer.com
SIC: 2653 3086 Boxes, corrugated: made from purchased materials; packaging & shipping materials, foamed plastic

(G-4548)
JAMESTOWN IRON WORKS INC
2022 Allen Street Ext (14733-1793)
PHONE.................................716 665-2818
David W Maher, *President*
Michelle Maher, *Manager*
EMP: 16 EST: 1881
SQ FT: 3,600
SALES (est): 4.3MM **Privately Held**
SIC: 3321 3599 Ductile iron castings; machine shop, jobbing & repair

(G-4549)
LANDPRO EQUIPMENT LLC (PA)
1756 Lindquist Dr (14733-9710)
PHONE.................................716 665-3110
Tracy Buck, *President*
Ryan Payment, *Vice Pres*
EMP: 41
SALES (est): 13.6MM **Privately Held**
SIC: 3523 Farm machinery & equipment

(G-4550)
MONOFRAX LLC
1870 New York Ave (14733-1797)
PHONE.................................716 483-7200
Bill Andrews, *President*
Robert Walrod, *Purchasing*
Alan Lindquist, *Manager*
◆ **EMP:** 250
SQ FT: 300,000
SALES (est): 50.4MM
SALES (corp-wide): 940.5K **Privately Held**
WEB: www.monofrax.com
SIC: 3297 Nonclay refractories
PA: Callista Holdings Gmbh & Co. Kg
Steinstr. 48
Munchen 81667
892 314-1600

(G-4551)
PREMIER PRCISION MACHINING LLC
Also Called: Rand Machine Products
2072 Allen Street Ext (14733-1709)
PHONE.................................716 665-5217
Gregory Wales, *Principal*
EMP: 40 EST: 2017
SALES (est): 12MM **Privately Held**
SIC: 3812 3599 Defense systems & equipment; machine & other job shop work

(G-4552)
RAND MACHINE PRODUCTS, INC.
2072 Allen Street Ext (14733-1709)
P.O. Box 72 (14733-0072)
PHONE.................................716 665-5217
EMP: 133 EST: 1964
SALES (est): 27MM **Privately Held**
WEB: www.randmachine.com
SIC: 3544 3494 3743 3599 Special dies, tools, jigs & fixtures; special dies & tools; valves & pipe fittings; industrial locomotives & parts; custom machinery

(G-4553)
RAPID REMOVAL LLC
1599 Route 394 (14733-9716)
P.O. Box 498 (14733-0498)
PHONE.................................716 665-4663
Brian Hasson,
EMP: 10 EST: 2010
SALES (est): 563.7K **Privately Held**
SIC: 2851 Removers & cleaners

(G-4554)
REYNOLDS PACKAGING MCHY INC
Also Called: Csi
2632 S Work St Ste 24 (14733-1705)
PHONE.................................716 358-6451
Fax: 716 358-6459
EMP: 55 **Privately Held**
SIC: 3565 3643 3466 Mfg Packaging Machinery Mfg Conductive Wiring Devices Mfg Crowns/Closures
HQ: Reynolds Packaging Machinery Inc.
2632 S Work St Ste 24
Falconer NY 14733

(G-4555)
SKF USA INC
Also Called: SKF Aeroengine North America
1 Maroco St (14733-9705)
P.O. Box 263 (14733-0263)
PHONE.................................716 661-2869
Steve Koehler, *Branch Mgr*
Bruce Sweeney, *Manager*
EMP: 61
SALES (corp-wide): 9.5B **Privately Held**
WEB: www.skfusa.com
SIC: 3562 3769 Ball bearings & parts; guided missile & space vehicle parts & auxiliary equipment
HQ: Skf Usa Inc.
890 Forty Foot Rd
Lansdale PA 19446
267 436-6000

(G-4556)
SKF USA INC
Also Called: MRC Bearings
1 Maroco St (14733-9705)
PHONE.................................716 661-2600
Rolf Jacobson, *Branch Mgr*
EMP: 61
SALES (corp-wide): 9.5B **Privately Held**
WEB: www.skfusa.com
SIC: 3053 3829 3562 Gaskets & sealing devices; oil seals, rubber; vibration meters, analyzers & calibrators; ball bearings & parts
HQ: Skf Usa Inc.
890 Forty Foot Rd
Lansdale PA 19446
267 436-6000

(G-4557)
SKF USA INC
Also Called: SKF Aeroengine North America
1 Maroco St (14733-9705)
PHONE.................................716 661-2600
Steve Koehler, *Branch Mgr*
EMP: 61
SALES (corp-wide): 9.5B **Privately Held**
WEB: www.skfusa.com
SIC: 3562 3769 Ball bearings & parts; guided missile & space vehicle parts & auxiliary equipment
HQ: Skf Usa Inc.
890 Forty Foot Rd
Lansdale PA 19446
267 436-6000

(G-4558)
STUART MOLD & MANUFACTURING
560 N Work St (14733-1115)
PHONE.................................716 488-9765
Randall Stuart, *President*
Charles Stuart, *Vice Pres*
EMP: 12
SQ FT: 10,000
SALES (est): 1.3MM **Privately Held**
WEB: www.stumold.com
SIC: 3089 Injection molding of plastics

(G-4559)
STUART TOOL & DIE INC
600 N Work St (14733-1117)
PHONE.................................716 488-1975
Ronald Rothleder, *President*
Patrick J Degnan, *Vice Pres*
Pj Degnan, *Vice Pres*
Dawn Delahoy, *Office Mgr*
Jim Manno, *Administration*
EMP: 40
SQ FT: 10,000
SALES: 9MM **Privately Held**
WEB: www.stu-t-d.com
SIC: 3544 Industrial molds; special dies & tools; jigs & fixtures

(G-4560)
TRUCK-LITE CO LLC (HQ)
310 E Elmwood Ave (14733-1421)
P.O. Box 387, Jamestown (14702-0387)
PHONE.................................716 665-6214
Douglas Wolma, *President*
Brian Kupchella, *COO*
David McKean, *Exec VP*
Jeff Church, *Maint Spvr*
Ken Patterson, *Purchasing*
◆ **EMP:** 373
SALES (est): 363MM
SALES (corp-wide): 11.1B **Privately Held**
SIC: 3648 Lighting equipment
PA: Penske Corporation
2555 S Telegraph Rd
Bloomfield Hills MI 48302
248 648-2000

(G-4561)
TRUCK-LITE SUB INC
310 E Elmwood Ave (14733-1421)
PHONE.................................800 888-7095
George Baldwin, *Principal*
Jeff Caulfield, *Regional Mgr*
Frank Mangifesto, *Regional Mgr*
John Cecco, *Vice Pres*
Michael Mulroy, *Vice Pres*
EMP: 7 EST: 2015
SALES (est): 152.4K **Privately Held**
SIC: 3799 Transportation equipment

Far Rockaway
Queens County

(G-4562)
BUSINESS ADVISORY SERVICES
Also Called: Universal Water Technology
1104 Bay 25th St (11691-1749)
PHONE.................................718 337-3740
Michael Walfish, *President*
David Weis, *Vice Pres*
EMP: 5
SALES: 750K **Privately Held**
SIC: 3589 Water treatment equipment, industrial

(G-4563)
EAZY LOCKS LLC
1914 Mott Ave (11691-4102)
PHONE.................................718 327-7770
Carl Roberts, *CEO*
EMP: 6
SQ FT: 1,700
SALES: 1.1MM **Privately Held**
SIC: 3429 Locks or lock sets

(G-4564)
EMPIRE PUBLISHING INC
Also Called: West End Journal
1525 Central Ave Ste 1 (11691-4020)
PHONE.................................516 829-4000
Jerome Lippman, *President*
EMP: 15
SQ FT: 2,000
SALES (est): 870.4K **Privately Held**
SIC: 2711 Newspapers: publishing only, not printed on site

(G-4565)
FAR ROCKAWAY DRUGS INC
Also Called: Ocean Park Drugs & Surgical
1727 Seagirt Blvd (11691-4513)
PHONE.................................718 471-2500
Russell Shvartsshteyn, *President*
Steven Blick, *Vice Pres*
EMP: 16

SQ FT: 4,000
SALES (est): 2.8MM **Privately Held**
WEB: www.mynucare.com
SIC: 3842 5912 Surgical appliances & supplies; drug stores & proprietary stores

(G-4566)
J P R PHARMACY INC
Also Called: Vista Pharmacy & Surgical
529 Beach 20th St (11691-3645)
PHONE.................................718 327-0600
Jeffrey Rosenberg, *President*
Russell Shvartsshteyn, *Vice Pres*
EMP: 11
SQ FT: 800
SALES: 4.6MM **Privately Held**
SIC: 3842 5912 Surgical appliances & supplies; drug stores & proprietary stores

(G-4567)
ROCKAWAY STAIRS LTD
1011 Bay 24th St (11691-1801)
PHONE.................................718 945-0047
Nollah Pastor, *President*
EMP: 5
SALES (est): 334.7K **Privately Held**
SIC: 2431 Stair railings, wood

Farmingdale
Nassau County

(G-4568)
A & J MACHINE & WELDING INC
6040 New Hwy (11735)
PHONE.................................631 845-7586
Ahalya Narine, *Manager*
EMP: 15 **Privately Held**
SIC: 7692 Welding repair
PA: A & J Machine & Welding Inc.
8776 130th St
Jamaica NY

(G-4569)
A R V PRECISION MFG INC
60 Baiting Place Rd Ste B (11735-6228)
PHONE.................................631 293-9643
Fred Freyre, *President*
EMP: 5
SQ FT: 2,000
SALES (est): 885.1K **Privately Held**
SIC: 3679 3599 3089 Electronic circuits; machine shop, jobbing & repair; injection molded finished plastic products

(G-4570)
AAA CATALYTIC RECYCLING INC
345 Eastern Pkwy (11735-2713)
PHONE.................................631 920-7944
Drew Vecchionem, *CEO*
▲ **EMP:** 10
SALES: 10MM **Privately Held**
SIC: 3339 Platinum group metal refining (primary)

(G-4571)
ABBE LABORATORIES INC
1095 Broadhollow Rd Ste E (11735-4815)
PHONE.................................631 756-2223
Eleanor Posner, *President*
Robert Posner, *Corp Secy*
EMP: 10
SALES (est): 1.9MM **Privately Held**
WEB: www.abbelabs.com
SIC: 2844 5122 Face creams or lotions; cosmetics

(G-4572)
AC ENVELOPE INC
51 Heisser Ln Ste B (11735-3321)
PHONE.................................516 420-0646
Bob Kuhlmann, *President*
Gene Greenlaw, *Managing Prtnr*
William Bogue, *Corp Secy*
EMP: 5
SALES (est): 500K **Privately Held**
SIC: 3555 5112 2759 2752 Presses, envelope, printing; envelopes; commercial printing; commercial printing, lithographic

(G-4573)
ADORE FLOORS INC
5 Dubon Ct (11735-1007)
PHONE....................................631 843-0900
Jerry Brennan, *Sales Dir*
▲ EMP: 5 EST: 2009
SALES (est): 141.5K **Privately Held**
SIC: 3292 5032 3089 Tile, vinyl asbestos; tile & clay products; floor coverings, plastic

(G-4574)
AIRFLEX CORP
965 Conklin St (11735-2412)
PHONE....................................631 752-1219
Jonathan Fogelman, *President*
EMP: 89
SQ FT: 10,000
SALES (est): 17.7MM **Privately Held**
SIC: 3446 Architectural metalwork

(G-4575)
AIRFLEX INDUSTRIAL INC (PA)
965 Conklin St (11735-2412)
PHONE....................................631 752-1234
Jonathan Fogelman, *Ch of Bd*
EMP: 41 EST: 1997
SQ FT: 10,000
SALES (est): 16.4MM **Privately Held**
WEB: www.airflexind.com
SIC: 3446 3822 3365 Louvers, ventilating; damper operators: pneumatic, thermostatic, electric; aluminum & aluminum-based alloy castings

(G-4576)
AIRFLEX INDUSTRIAL INC
937 Conklin St (11735-2412)
PHONE....................................631 752-1234
Jonathan Fogelman, *Branch Mgr*
EMP: 6
SALES (corp-wide): 16.4MM **Privately Held**
SIC: 3446 Louvers, ventilating
PA: Airflex Industrial, Inc.
965 Conklin St
Farmingdale NY 11735
631 752-1234

(G-4577)
ALA SCIENTIFIC INSTRUMENTS INC
60 Marine St Ste 1 (11735-5660)
PHONE....................................631 393-6401
Alan Kriegstein, *President*
Andrew Pomerantz, *Vice Pres*
Kim Forrest, *Administration*
EMP: 13
SQ FT: 6,000
SALES (est): 2.5MM **Privately Held**
WEB: www.alascience.com
SIC: 3841 5047 Surgical & medical instruments; medical equipment & supplies

(G-4578)
ALL AMERICAN FUNDING & REF LLC
345 Eastern Pkwy (11735-2713)
PHONE....................................516 978-7531
Andrew Vecchione, *Mng Member*
Frank Ponte,
Joe Ponte,
Frank Tuzzo,
EMP: 6
SALES: 18MM **Privately Held**
SIC: 3339 5093 Precious metals; metal scrap & waste materials

(G-4579)
ALL STAR SHEET METAL INC
25 Rome St (11735-6601)
PHONE....................................718 456-1567
Christine Benazic, *CEO*
Enrik Benazic, *President*
EMP: 15
SQ FT: 5,200
SALES (est): 2.5MM **Privately Held**
SIC: 3444 Sheet metalwork

(G-4580)
ALLOY METAL WORKS INC
146 Verdi St (11735-6324)
PHONE....................................631 694-8163
Phillip Rajotte Jr, *President*
EMP: 5
SQ FT: 2,500
SALES: 250K **Privately Held**
SIC: 3441 Fabricated structural metal

(G-4581)
ALPHA MANUFACTURING CORP
152 Verdi St (11735-6324)
PHONE....................................631 249-3700
George Sparacio, *President*
EMP: 10
SQ FT: 6,000
SALES: 1MM **Privately Held**
SIC: 3599 Machine shop, jobbing & repair

(G-4582)
AMANA TOOL CORP
Also Called: Age Timberline Mamba
120 Carolyn Blvd (11735-1525)
PHONE....................................631 752-1300
Eitan Spiegel, *President*
Aaron Einstein, *Chairman*
John P McInerney, *Vice Pres*
Zygmunt L Milewski, *Vice Pres*
Eric Einstein, *Mfg Dir*
◆ EMP: 52
SQ FT: 80,000
SALES (est): 9.9MM **Privately Held**
WEB: www.amanatool.com
SIC: 3425 Saw blades & handsaws

(G-4583)
AMERICAN AEROSPACE CONTRLS INC
Also Called: A A C
570 Smith St (11735-1115)
PHONE....................................631 694-5100
Ruth Gitlin, *CEO*
Susan Brosnan, *General Mgr*
Philip Koch, *Opers Staff*
Celeste Morrissey, *QC Mgr*
Camille Cavallo, *Manager*
EMP: 47 EST: 1965
SQ FT: 16,000
SALES: 10MM **Privately Held**
WEB: www.a-a-c.com
SIC: 3812 Search & navigation equipment

(G-4584)
AMERICAN VISUALS INC
Also Called: American Visual Display
90 Gazza Blvd (11735-1402)
PHONE....................................631 694-6104
Morris Charnow, *President*
EMP: 7
SQ FT: 8,200
SALES (est): 825.6K **Privately Held**
WEB: www.americanvisuals.com
SIC: 3993 3089 Displays & cutouts, window & lobby; plastic processing

(G-4585)
ANDREA SYSTEMS LLC
140 Finn Ct (11735-1107)
PHONE....................................631 390-3140
Tony Macri, *QC Mgr*
Luis Rivera, *Electrical Engi*
Robert J Carton, *Sales Mgr*
Frank Randazzo, *Mng Member*
Heather Hinkley, *Manager*
EMP: 23
SQ FT: 15,000
SALES: 5MM **Privately Held**
WEB: www.andreasystems.com
SIC: 3669 Intercommunication systems, electric

(G-4586)
ARBE MACHINERY INC
54 Allen Blvd (11735-5623)
PHONE....................................631 756-2477
Artin Karakaya, *President*
Burc Karakaya, *Vice Pres*
◆ EMP: 10
SQ FT: 30,000
SALES (est): 2.3MM **Privately Held**
SIC: 3559 5084 3599 Jewelers' machines; industrial machinery & equipment; machine shop, jobbing & repair

(G-4587)
AURI NUTRASCIENCE INC
155 Rome St (11735-6610)
PHONE....................................631 454-0020
Abu S Hossain, *Ch of Bd*
EMP: 8
SALES (est): 1.1MM **Privately Held**
SIC: 2834 Pharmaceutical preparations

(G-4588)
AUSCO INC
425 Smith St Ste 1 (11735-1124)
PHONE....................................516 944-9882
Kenneth Bram, *Ch of Bd*
Jackie Gregus, *General Mgr*
Thai Tong, *Vice Pres*
Glenn Davis, *Mfg Mgr*
Cliff Lestrange, *QA Dir*
EMP: 100
SQ FT: 11,000
SALES (est): 25.1MM **Privately Held**
WEB: www.auscoinc.com
SIC: 3728 Aircraft assemblies, subassemblies & parts

(G-4589)
AUTEL US INC (HQ)
Also Called: Autel North America
175 Central Ave Ste 200 (11735-6917)
PHONE....................................631 923-2620
Arthur Jacobsen, *CEO*
▲ EMP: 5 EST: 2011
SQ FT: 20,000
SALES: 1.8MM
SALES (corp-wide): 60.8MM **Privately Held**
SIC: 3694 Automotive electrical equipment
PA: Autel Intelligent Technology Corp., Ltd.
8th Floor, Building B1, Zhiyuan Xueyuan Road, Xili, Nanshan Shenzhen 51805
755 861-4777

(G-4590)
AVANTI FURNITURE CORP
497 Main St (11735-3579)
PHONE....................................516 293-8220
Joan Bagnasco, *President*
Kevin Bagnasco, *Treasurer*
▲ EMP: 12
SQ FT: 10,000
SALES (est): 1.6MM **Privately Held**
SIC: 2512 Chairs: upholstered on wood frames

(G-4591)
BDR CREATIVE CONCEPTS INC
141 Central Ave Ste B (11735-6903)
PHONE....................................516 942-7768
Ronald Cohen, *President*
Pearl Cohen, *Vice Pres*
Tiffany Unruh, *Manager*
Bruce Beckerman, *Shareholder*
Debra Beckerman, *Shareholder*
EMP: 14
SQ FT: 7,000
SALES (est): 1.7MM **Privately Held**
WEB: www.bdrcc.com
SIC: 2759 Poster & decal printing & engraving

(G-4592)
BESCOR VIDEO ACCESSORIES LTD
244 Route 109 (11735-1503)
PHONE....................................631 420-1717
Douglas Brandwin, *President*
▲ EMP: 16
SQ FT: 8,000
SALES (est): 3.1MM **Privately Held**
SIC: 3861 5065 5043 Cameras & related equipment; video equipment, electronic; photographic cameras, projectors, equipment & supplies

(G-4593)
BEVERAGE WORKS NJ INC
16 Dubon Ct (11735-1008)
PHONE....................................631 293-3501
Jeffrey Brown, *VP Opers*
Iies Hantman, *Manager*
Joe Deland, *Manager*
EMP: 20 **Privately Held**
WEB: www.beverageworks.com
SIC: 2086 Bottled & canned soft drinks
PA: The Beverage Works Ny Inc
1800 State Route 34 # 203
Wall Township NJ 07719

(G-4594)
BST UNITED CORP
185 Marine St (11735-5609)
PHONE....................................631 777-2110
Khaled Shahriar, *President*
Sabina Khaleq, *Vice Pres*
Tony Pahm, *Vice Pres*
EMP: 12
SALES: 250K **Privately Held**
SIC: 3089 Blow molded finished plastic products

(G-4595)
C & C BINDERY CO INC
Also Called: C&C Diecuts
25 Central Ave Unit B (11735-6920)
PHONE....................................631 752-7078
Joe Spalone, *President*
EMP: 30
SQ FT: 11,000
SALES (est): 4.7MM **Privately Held**
SIC: 2789 Binding only: books, pamphlets, magazines, etc.

(G-4596)
CANDID LITHO PRINTING LTD (PA)
210 Route 109 (11735-1503)
PHONE....................................212 431-3800
Howard Weinstein, *President*
Omar Martinez, *President*
Scott Weinstein, *Corp Secy*
Lewis Rosenberg, *Vice Pres*
Shauna Weinstein, *CFO*
EMP: 60 EST: 1964
SQ FT: 109,285
SALES (est): 18.1MM **Privately Held**
WEB: www.candidlitho.com
SIC: 2752 Commercial printing, offset

(G-4597)
CANDID WORLDWIDE LLC (HQ)
210 Route 109 (11735-1503)
PHONE....................................212 799-5300
David Stadler, *CEO*
Howard Weinstein, *President*
EMP: 7
SALES (est): 7.1MM
SALES (corp-wide): 18.1MM **Privately Held**
SIC: 2759 Posters, including billboards: printing
PA: Candid Litho Printing Ltd.
210 Route 109
Farmingdale NY 11735
212 431-3800

(G-4598)
CHIM-CAP CORP
120 Schmitt Blvd (11735-1424)
PHONE....................................800 262-9622
Fred Giumenta Jr, *President*
▲ EMP: 20
SQ FT: 40,000
SALES (est): 3.8MM **Privately Held**
WEB: www.chimcapcorp.com
SIC: 3272 Fireplace & chimney material: concrete; chimney caps, concrete

(G-4599)
CIGAR OASIS LLC
79 Heisser Ct (11735-3310)
PHONE....................................516 520-5258
Albert P Foundos, *President*
Christine Beno, *Vice Pres*
Donna Oswald, *Vice Pres*
Philip Foundos, *Treasurer*
▲ EMP: 5
SQ FT: 2,000
SALES (est): 569.2K **Privately Held**
SIC: 3911 Cigar & cigarette accessories

(G-4600)
COCO ARCHITECTUREAL GRILLES
173 Allen Blvd (11735-5616)
PHONE....................................631 482-9449
Jim Coco, *President*
EMP: 5
SALES (est): 675K **Privately Held**
SIC: 3441 Fabricated structural metal

(G-4601)
COLONIAL PRECISION MACHINERY
Also Called: Colonial Electric
134 Rome St (11735-6607)
PHONE..................................631 249-0738
James Tormey, *President*
Scott Tormey, *Vice Pres*
EMP: 7
SQ FT: 15,000
SALES (est): 650K **Privately Held**
SIC: 3469 Machine parts, stamped or pressed metal

(G-4602)
COMMERCE SPRING CORP
143 Allen Blvd (11735-5616)
PHONE..................................631 293-4844
Bruno Rotellini, *President*
EMP: 12
SQ FT: 10,000
SALES (est): 1.2MM **Privately Held**
WEB: www.commercespring.com
SIC: 3495 Wire springs

(G-4603)
COSMO ELECTRONIC MACHINE CORP
Also Called: D & L Electronic Die
113 Gazza Blvd (11735-1421)
PHONE..................................631 249-2535
Kenneth Arutt, *President*
Bruce Mc Kee, *Vice Pres*
EMP: 50
SQ FT: 3,000
SALES (est): 5.2MM **Privately Held**
SIC: 3544 Special dies & tools

(G-4604)
COSMOS ELECTRONIC MACHINE CORP (PA)
140 Schmitt Blvd (11735-1461)
PHONE..................................631 249-2535
Kenneth Arutt, *President*
Bruce McKee, *Vice Pres*
Elvin Cerritos, *Production*
EMP: 43
SQ FT: 20,000
SALES (est): 8.6MM **Privately Held**
SIC: 3567 Industrial furnaces & ovens

(G-4605)
CRISRAY PRINTING CORP
50 Executive Blvd Ste A (11735-4710)
PHONE..................................631 293-3770
Raymond J Marro, *President*
Anthony Conti, *Vice Pres*
Chris Marro, *Vice Pres*
Patricia Marro, *Vice Pres*
EMP: 30 EST: 1971
SQ FT: 10,000
SALES (est): 5MM **Privately Held**
WEB: www.crisray.com
SIC: 2759 Labels & seals: printing

(G-4606)
CURTISS-WRIGHT CONTROLS
Also Called: Curtiss-Wrght Intgrted Sensing
175 Central Ave Ste 100 (11735-6917)
P.O. Box 7751, Philadelphia PA (19101-7751)
PHONE..................................631 756-4740
Thomas P Quinly, *COO*
Jasbir Arneja, *Opers Staff*
EMP: 14
SALES (corp-wide): 2.4B **Publicly Held**
SIC: 3674 Semiconductors & related devices
HQ: Curtiss-Wright Controls Integrated Sensing, Inc.
28965 Avenue Penn
Valencia CA 91355

(G-4607)
CURTISS-WRIGHT FLOW CONTROL (HQ)
Also Called: Target Rock
1966 Broadhollow Rd Ste E (11735-1726)
PHONE..................................631 293-3800
Martin Benante, *Ch of Bd*
David Linton, *President*
Robert Queenan, *Division Mgr*
David C Adams, *COO*
Joseph Callaghan, *Vice Pres*
◆ EMP: 236 EST: 1950

SQ FT: 100,000
SALES (est): 404MM
SALES (corp-wide): 2.4B **Publicly Held**
SIC: 3491 3494 Industrial valves; valves & pipe fittings
PA: Curtiss-Wright Corporation
130 Harbour Place Dr # 300
Davidson NC 28036
704 869-4600

(G-4608)
CURTISS-WRIGHT FLOW CTRL CORP
1966 Broadhollow Rd Ste E (11735-1726)
P.O. Box 379 (11735-0379)
PHONE..................................631 293-3800
Mike Grant, *Mfg Staff*
William Hughes, *Purchasing*
Steve Jung, *Branch Mgr*
Anthony Lewis, *Manager*
Lisa Demers, *Technician*
EMP: 160
SALES (corp-wide): 2.4B **Publicly Held**
SIC: 3491 Industrial valves
HQ: Curtiss-Wright Flow Control Service, Llc
1966 Broadhollow Rd Ste E
Farmingdale NY 11735
631 293-3800

(G-4609)
CUSTOM DOOR & MIRROR INC
Also Called: Flex Supply
148 Milbar Blvd (11735-1425)
PHONE..................................631 414-7725
Angelo Sciubba, *Ch of Bd*
Philip Sciubba, *Vice Pres*
▲ EMP: 20 EST: 1996
SQ FT: 17,000
SALES: 3MM **Privately Held**
WEB: www.paniflex.com
SIC: 3089 2431 Doors, folding: plastic or plastic coated fabric; millwork

(G-4610)
CUSTOM METAL INCORPORATED
Also Called: Custom Metal Fabrication
59 Central Ave Ste 8 (11735-6902)
PHONE..................................631 643-4075
Stephen Pratt, *President*
Nancy Pratt, *Corp Secy*
EMP: 11
SALES: 1.4MM **Privately Held**
WEB: www.custommetalfabrication.com
SIC: 3469 Machine parts, stamped or pressed metal

(G-4611)
CUSTOM SITECOM LLC
Also Called: Buckle Down
470 Smith St (11735-1105)
PHONE..................................631 420-4238
Eric Swope, *COO*
Jason Dorf,
▲ EMP: 11
SALES (est): 2MM **Privately Held**
SIC: 3714 Motor vehicle parts & accessories

(G-4612)
DADDARIO & COMPANY INC (PA)
595 Smith St (11735-1120)
P.O. Box 290 (11735-0290)
PHONE..................................631 439-3300
James D'Addario, *Ch of Bd*
Rick Drumm, *President*
John D'Addario III, *Exec VP*
John D'Addario Jr, *Vice Pres*
David Via, *Vice Pres*
◆ EMP: 700
SQ FT: 110,000
SALES (est): 180MM **Privately Held**
WEB: www.daddario.com
SIC: 3931 Guitars & parts, electric & non-electric; strings, musical instrument

(G-4613)
DAKOTA SYSTEMS MFG CORP
Also Called: Dakota Wall
1885 New Hwy Ste 2 (11735-1518)
PHONE..................................631 249-5811
Edward Owsinski, *President*
Jimmy Eowinski, *Bookkeeper*

EMP: 6
SQ FT: 3,000
SALES (est): 1.1MM **Privately Held**
SIC: 2542 3312 Partitions & fixtures, except wood; stainless steel

(G-4614)
DESKTOP PUBLISHING CONCEPTS
Also Called: Toledo Graphics Group
855 Conklin St Ste T (11735-2409)
P.O. Box 34 (11735-0034)
PHONE..................................631 752-1934
Nicholas Sachs, *President*
EMP: 12
SQ FT: 2,500
SALES (est): 1.3MM **Privately Held**
WEB: www.toledogroup.com
SIC: 2791 7336 Typesetting; graphic arts & related design

(G-4615)
DIGICOM INTERNATIONAL INC
145 Rome St (11735-6610)
PHONE..................................631 249-8999
Chia I Chen, *CEO*
Michelle Chiu, *Accounts Mgr*
Jammy Chen, *Executive*
▲ EMP: 15
SQ FT: 20,000
SALES (est): 3MM **Privately Held**
SIC: 3571 5045 Electronic computers; computer peripheral equipment

(G-4616)
DIGITAL MATRIX CORP
34 Sarah Dr Ste B (11735-1218)
PHONE..................................516 481-7990
Alex Greenspan, *President*
Jan Berman, *Vice Pres*
Alexsandr Davelman, *Engineer*
Joel Berman, *Treasurer*
Lorraine Berman, *Shareholder*
EMP: 21
SQ FT: 20,000
SALES (est): 3.7MM **Privately Held**
WEB: www.galvanics.com
SIC: 3559 Electroplating machinery & equipment

(G-4617)
DINEWISE INC
500 B Cuntry Blvd Ste 400 (11735)
PHONE..................................631 694-1111
Paul A Roman, *Ch of Bd*
Thomas McNeill, *CFO*
EMP: 2
SQ FT: 5,330
SALES: 6.7MM **Privately Held**
SIC: 2032 2011 5499 Chicken broth: packaged in cans, jars, etc.; chicken soup: packaged in cans, jars, etc.; beef products from beef slaughtered on site; gourmet food stores

(G-4618)
DUCON TECHNOLOGIES INC
110 Bi County Blvd # 124 (11735-3923)
PHONE..................................631 420-4900
Aron Govil, *Branch Mgr*
EMP: 45
SALES (est): 2.9MM
SALES (corp-wide): 431.5MM **Privately Held**
SIC: 3564 3537 Blowers & fans; industrial trucks & tractors
PA: Ducon Technologies Inc.
5 Penn Plz
New York NY 10001
631 694-1700

(G-4619)
DYNAMIC PRODUCTS INC
500 Eastern Pkwy Ste 2 (11735-2445)
PHONE..................................631 270-4833
Mark Rubin, *President*
EMP: 5
SALES (est): 374.3K **Privately Held**
SIC: 3494 Valves & pipe fittings

(G-4620)
E B INDUSTRIES LLC (PA)
90 Carolyn Blvd (11735-1525)
PHONE..................................631 293-8565
Cory Yaeger, *Project Mgr*
John Delalio, *Business Dir*

Steven M Delalio,
Devorah Lisnoff, *Executive Asst*
Jerry Bianco,
EMP: 25 EST: 1965
SQ FT: 16,000
SALES (est): 3.1MM **Privately Held**
WEB: www.ebindustries.com
SIC: 7692 Welding repair

(G-4621)
E B INDUSTRIES LLC
90 Carolyn Blvd (11735-1525)
PHONE..................................631 293-8565
Steven Delalio, *Mng Member*
EMP: 25
SALES (est): 411.8K
SALES (corp-wide): 3.1MM **Privately Held**
WEB: www.ebindustries.com
SIC: 7692 Welding repair
PA: E B Industries, Llc
90 Carolyn Blvd
Farmingdale NY 11735
631 293-8565

(G-4622)
EAST CAST ENVMTL RSTRATION INC
136 Allen Blvd (11735-5659)
PHONE..................................631 600-2000
Edwin Rincon, *President*
EMP: 5
SQ FT: 15,000
SALES: 1MM **Privately Held**
SIC: 3826 Differential thermal analysis instruments

(G-4623)
EDLAW PHARMACEUTICALS INC
195 Central Ave Ste B (11735-6904)
PHONE..................................631 454-6888
Scott Giroux, *General Mgr*
Bonnie Hilton Green, *Principal*
▼ EMP: 20
SQ FT: 6,500
SALES (est): 3.4MM **Privately Held**
SIC: 2834 Pharmaceutical preparations

(G-4624)
EEG ENTERPRISES INC
586 Main St (11735-3546)
PHONE..................................516 293-7472
Philip McLaughlin, *President*
Bill McLaughlin, *President*
William Jorden, *Vice Pres*
Frank Zovko, *Engineer*
Eric McErlain, *Sales Dir*
EMP: 12
SQ FT: 5,000
SALES (est): 2.1MM **Privately Held**
WEB: www.eegent.com
SIC: 3663 Cable television equipment; television antennas (transmitting) & ground equipment

(G-4625)
ENZO LIFE SCIENCES INC (HQ)
Also Called: Enzo Diagnostics
10 Executive Blvd (11735-4710)
PHONE..................................631 694-7070
Elazar Rabbani, *Ch of Bd*
Michael Garofalo, *General Mgr*
Barry W Weiner, *Exec VP*
Herbert Bass, *Vice Pres*
Jeannette Beneteau, *Opers Staff*
EMP: 30
SQ FT: 40,000
SALES (est): 12.8MM
SALES (corp-wide): 81.1MM **Publicly Held**
SIC: 2835 2834 5049 In vitro & in vivo diagnostic substances; pharmaceutical preparations; laboratory equipment, except medical or dental
PA: Enzo Biochem, Inc.
527 Madison Ave Rm 901
New York NY 10022
212 583-0100

(G-4626)
ENZO LIFE SCIENCES INTL INC
10 Executive Blvd (11735-4710)
PHONE..................................610 941-0430
Robert Zipkin, *President*
Ira Taffer, *Vice Pres*

◆ **EMP:** 28
SQ FT: 20,000
SALES (est): 3.6MM
SALES (corp-wide): 81.1MM **Publicly Held**
WEB: www.biomol.com
SIC: 2834 Pharmaceutical preparations
HQ: Enzo Life Sciences, Inc.
　　10 Executive Blvd
　　Farmingdale NY 11735

(G-4627)
EVANS MANUFACTURING LLC
595 Smith St (11735-1116)
P.O. Box 290 (11735-0290)
PHONE.....................631 439-3300
James D'Addario,
John D'Addario Jr,
Robert Dodaro,
Michael Russo,
Domenick Scarfogliero,
▲ **EMP:** 75 **EST:** 1995
SQ FT: 110,000
SALES (est): 6MM **Privately Held**
WEB: www.dadario.com
SIC: 3931 Heads, drum

(G-4628)
FABCO INDUSTRIES INC
24 Central Dr (11735-1202)
PHONE.....................631 393-6024
Dominic Chang, *President*
John Markee, *Treasurer*
John Peters Jr, *Admin Sec*
EMP: 9
SQ FT: 10,000
SALES (est): 145K **Privately Held**
SIC: 3589 4953 Water treatment equipment, industrial; refuse systems

(G-4629)
FARMINGDALE IRON WORKS INC
105 Florida St (11735-6305)
PHONE.....................631 249-5995
John Cardullo, *President*
Vita Cardullo, *Corp Secy*
EMP: 6 **EST:** 1959
SQ FT: 4,500
SALES (est): 642.4K **Privately Held**
SIC: 3441 Fabricated structural metal

(G-4630)
FERRARO MANUFACTURING COMPANY
150 Central Ave (11735-6900)
PHONE.....................631 752-1509
Joseph Ferraro, *President*
EMP: 6
SALES (est): 800.9K **Privately Held**
WEB: www.ferrarofirm.com
SIC: 3599 Machine shop, jobbing & repair

(G-4631)
FIBER FOOT APPLIANCES INC
34 Sarah Dr Ste A (11735-1218)
PHONE.....................631 465-9199
Jeffrey Fiber, *President*
Allan Fiber, *Treasurer*
Helene Fiber, *Admin Sec*
EMP: 13
SQ FT: 6,500
SALES (est): 1.4MM **Privately Held**
SIC: 3842 Foot appliances, orthopedic

(G-4632)
FOREST LABS
210 Sea Ln (11735-3900)
PHONE.....................631 755-1185
Shankar Hariharan, *Exec VP*
EMP: 8
SALES (est): 711.9K **Privately Held**
SIC: 2834 Pharmaceutical preparations

(G-4633)
FRUITCROWN PRODUCTS CORP (PA)
250 Adams Blvd (11735-6615)
PHONE.....................631 694-5800
Robert E Jagenburg, *President*
Bruce Jagenburg, *Vice Pres*
Gregory Newman, *Safety Mgr*
Catherine Samluk, *Research*
Larry Merola, *Controller*
▼ **EMP:** 45

SQ FT: 40,000
SALES (est): 18.6MM **Privately Held**
WEB: www.fruitcrown.com
SIC: 2099 Food preparations

(G-4634)
FUN INDUSTRIES OF NY
111 Milbar Blvd (11735-1426)
PHONE.....................631 845-3805
Bryan Spodek, *Principal*
EMP: 5
SALES (est): 1.3MM **Privately Held**
SIC: 3999 Manufacturing industries

(G-4635)
GAMMA INSTRUMENT CO INC
34 Sarah Dr Ste B (11735-1218)
PHONE.....................516 486-5526
John Schurr, *President*
William Hansen, *Vice Pres*
EMP: 7
SALES: 500K **Privately Held**
SIC: 3599 Machine shop, jobbing & repair

(G-4636)
GAVIN MFG CORP
25 Central Ave Unit A (11735-6920)
PHONE.....................631 467-0040
Christopher Gavin, *President*
Brian Gavin, *Vice Pres*
Michael Gavin, *Vice Pres*
Ryan Gavin, *Vice Pres*
EMP: 45 **EST:** 1953
SQ FT: 15,000
SALES (est): 7.7MM **Privately Held**
WEB: www.gavinmfgcorp.com
SIC: 2679 2653 2657 Paper products, converted; paperboard products, converted; corrugated & solid fiber boxes; folding paperboard boxes

(G-4637)
GILD-RITE INC
51 Carolyn Blvd (11735-1527)
PHONE.....................631 752-9000
Howard Schneider, *President*
Morris D Schneider, *Chairman*
Roert Schneider, *Vice Pres*
Sylvia K Zang, *Treasurer*
EMP: 5
SQ FT: 7,000
SALES: 250K
SALES (corp-wide): 12.4MM **Privately Held**
SIC: 2789 Gilding books, cards or paper
PA: Leather Craftsmen, Inc.
　　6 Dubon Ct
　　Farmingdale NY 11735
　　631 752-9000

(G-4638)
GLISSADE NEW YORK LLC
399 Smith St (11735-1106)
PHONE.....................631 756-4800
Jed Leadman,
▲ **EMP:** 25
SQ FT: 30,000
SALES (est): 3.3MM **Privately Held**
WEB: www.glissade.com
SIC: 2514 2434 Medicine cabinets & vanities: metal; vanities, bathroom: wood

(G-4639)
GOLDMARK PRODUCTS INC
855 Conklin St Ste D (11735-2409)
PHONE.....................631 777-3343
EMP: 30
SQ FT: 5,000
SALES (est): 3.2MM **Privately Held**
SIC: 3911 3339 Mfg Precious Metal Jewelry Primary Nonferrous Metal Producer

(G-4640)
GREAT ROCK AUTOMATION INC
99 Rome St (11735-6606)
PHONE.....................631 270-1508
Dona Kiessel, *Opers Mgr*
Dario Morales, *Engineer*
EMP: 13
SALES (est): 2.1MM **Privately Held**
SIC: 3433 5074 Boilers, low-pressure heating: steam or hot water; boilers, steam

(G-4641)
GREEN LOGIC LED ELEC SUP INC (PA)
Also Called: Gllusa
75 Marine St (11735-5604)
PHONE.....................516 280-2854
George Geffen, *CEO*
Daniel Yu, *Vice Pres*
Donald Geffen, *Marketing Staff*
Marvin Yu,
EMP: 38
SALES (est): 10.1MM **Privately Held**
SIC: 3674 Light emitting diodes

(G-4642)
GUSTBUSTER LTD
Also Called: Sunbuster
855 Conklin St Ste O (11735-2409)
PHONE.....................631 391-9000
Steven Asman, *President*
▲ **EMP:** 8
SQ FT: 17,000
SALES (est): 2MM **Privately Held**
WEB: www.gustbuster.com
SIC: 3999 Umbrellas, canes & parts

(G-4643)
HAHNS OLD FASHIONED CAKE CO
75 Allen Blvd (11735-5614)
PHONE.....................631 249-3456
Regina C Hahn, *President*
Andrew M Hahn, *Corp Secy*
EMP: 12
SQ FT: 4,550
SALES: 1MM **Privately Held**
WEB: www.crumbcake.net
SIC: 2051 5149 Cakes, bakery: except frozen; bakery products

(G-4644)
HIRSCH OPTICAL CORP
91 Carolyn Blvd (11735-1409)
PHONE.....................516 752-2211
Harold M Rothstein, *President*
Ken Mittel, *Exec VP*
Kenneth Mitel, *Vice Pres*
Michael Weinstein, *Vice Pres*
EMP: 60 **EST:** 1978
SQ FT: 12,000
SALES (est): 6.8MM **Privately Held**
WEB: www.hirschoptical.com
SIC: 3851 Eyeglasses, lenses & frames

(G-4645)
HORNE PRODUCTS INC
144 Verdi St (11735-6324)
PHONE.....................631 293-0773
John Hind, *President*
Joanne Incalcatera, *Corp Secy*
Patricia A O'Neill, *Vice Pres*
EMP: 6
SQ FT: 2,200
SALES (est): 991.9K **Privately Held**
WEB: www.horneproducts.com
SIC: 3743 5088 Railroad equipment; railroad equipment & supplies

(G-4646)
HURON TL CUTTER GRINDING INC
2045 Wellwood Ave (11735-1212)
PHONE.....................631 420-7000
James Cosenza, *President*
Richard Cosenza, *Vice Pres*
Blanche Silbert, *Admin Sec*
Danielle Avena, *Administration*
EMP: 30 **EST:** 1955
SQ FT: 25,000
SALES: 4MM **Privately Held**
WEB: www.hurontool.com
SIC: 3545 3841 3568 3423 Tools & accessories for machine tools; knives, surgical; power transmission equipment; hand & edge tools

(G-4647)
I J WHITE CORPORATION
20 Executive Blvd (11735-4710)
PHONE.....................631 293-3788
Peter J White, *Ch of Bd*
Niv Eldor, *COO*
Andy Cohn, *Vice Pres*
Roy Berntsen, *Plant Mgr*
Frank Vecchio, *Purch Mgr*

▼ **EMP:** 70 **EST:** 1919
SQ FT: 42,500
SALES (est): 23.7MM **Privately Held**
WEB: www.ijwhite.com
SIC: 3535 Conveyors & conveying equipment

(G-4648)
IMPRESSIVE IMPRINTS INC
195 Central Ave N (11735-6904)
PHONE.....................631 293-6161
Howard Lang, *President*
EMP: 5 **EST:** 1961
SQ FT: 3,000
SALES (est): 551K **Privately Held**
SIC: 3993 Signs & advertising specialties

(G-4649)
INNOVATIVE AUTOMATION INC
595 Smith St (11735-1116)
P.O. Box 290 (11735-0290)
PHONE.....................631 439-3300
James D'Addario, *President*
John D'Addario Jr, *Vice Pres*
EMP: 12
SQ FT: 25,000
SALES (est): 1.4MM **Privately Held**
WEB: www.innovativeautomation.net
SIC: 3545 Machine tool attachments & accessories

(G-4650)
INSTANT VERTICALS INC
330 Broadhollow Rd (11735-4807)
PHONE.....................631 501-0001
Michael Moran, *President*
John Joy, *Vice Pres*
Eileen Schulze, *Office Mgr*
EMP: 10
SALES (est): 1.2MM **Privately Held**
WEB: www.instantverticals.com
SIC: 2591 1799 Window blinds; window treatment installation

(G-4651)
INTELLIGENT CTRL SYSTEMS LLC
208 Route 109 Ste 211 (11735-1536)
PHONE.....................516 340-1011
Jack Hammer, *Chief Engr*
Michael Ruff,
Celso Monge,
EMP: 5
SALES (est): 382.7K **Privately Held**
SIC: 3699 Electrical equipment & supplies

(G-4652)
INTERNATIONAL KEY SUPPLY LLC
Also Called: Ik Supply
224 Sherwood Ave (11735-1718)
PHONE.....................631 983-6096
Sean McAuliffe, *Partner*
Neil Healey, *Opers Mgr*
Anna Blinova, *Manager*
EMP: 10
SALES: 1.2MM **Privately Held**
SIC: 3429 3694 3643 Keys & key blanks; automotive electrical equipment; connectors & terminals for electrical devices

(G-4653)
ISOLATION DYNAMICS CORP
Also Called: Idc
50 Boening Plz (11735-1519)
P.O. Box 361, Merrick (11566-0361)
PHONE.....................631 491-5670
Max Borrasso, *President*
EMP: 20
SALES (est): 3.9MM **Privately Held**
WEB: www.isolator.us
SIC: 3493 Steel springs, except wire

(G-4654)
J M HALEY CORP
151 Toledo St Ste 1 (11735-6640)
PHONE.....................631 845-5200
John Ackerson, *President*
Steven Cardona, *Project Mgr*
Pavel Kaliadka, *Project Mgr*
Cynthia Bissoon, *Administration*
EMP: 140 **EST:** 1972
SQ FT: 10,000

▲ = Import ▼=Export
◆ =Import/Export

SALES: 16MM **Privately Held**
WEB: www.jmhaleycorp.com
SIC: 3441 Fabricated structural metal

(G-4655)
J P PRINTING INC (PA)
Also Called: Minuteman Press
331 Main St (11735-3508)
PHONE..................................516 293-6110
Jeff Miller, *President*
Douglas Harlan, *Vice Pres*
Susan Miller, *Vice Pres*
Thomas Cronin, *Manager*
EMP: 5
SQ FT: 1,200
SALES: 385K **Privately Held**
SIC: 2752 5943 Commercial printing, lithographic; office forms & supplies

(G-4656)
JAMES WOERNER INC
130 Allen Blvd (11735-5617)
PHONE..................................631 454-9330
James Woerner, *President*
Barbara Woerner, *Vice Pres*
EMP: 6
SQ FT: 7,000
SALES (est): 1MM **Privately Held**
SIC: 3498 3441 7538 Fabricated pipe & fittings; fabricated structural metal; general automotive repair shops

(G-4657)
JANED ENTERPRISES
48 Allen Blvd Unit B (11735-5642)
PHONE..................................631 694-4494
Joseph Pileri, *CEO*
Claudia Montuori, *President*
EMP: 15
SQ FT: 14,000
SALES (est): 2.5MM **Privately Held**
WEB: www.janed.net
SIC: 3449 Miscellaneous metalwork

(G-4658)
JUNK IN MY TRUNK INC
266 Route 109 (11735-1503)
PHONE..................................631 420-5865
Tomasz Myszke, *Principal*
EMP: 5
SALES (est): 583.7K **Privately Held**
SIC: 3161 Trunks

(G-4659)
K SIDRANE INC
24 Baiting Place Rd (11735-6227)
PHONE..................................631 393-6974
Neil Sidrane, *Chairman*
Andrew Hersh, *Accounts Mgr*
▲ EMP: 45 EST: 1948
SQ FT: 10,000
SALES (est): 12MM **Privately Held**
SIC: 2679 2671 2672 Tags & labels, paper; packaging paper & plastics film, coated & laminated; coated & laminated paper; adhesive papers, labels or tapes: from purchased material

(G-4660)
KABAR MANUFACTURING CORP (HQ)
140 Schmitt Blvd (11735-1461)
PHONE..................................631 694-6857
Bruce Mc Kee, *President*
Ken Arutt, *Treasurer*
Antoinette Mander, *Administration*
Paolo Bruschi, *Maintence Staff*
▲ EMP: 45 EST: 1945
SQ FT: 12,000
SALES (est): 11.2MM
SALES (corp-wide): 8.6MM **Privately Held**
WEB: www.cosmos-kabar.com
SIC: 3565 3559 Packaging machinery; plastics working machinery
PA: Cosmos Electronic Machine Corp.
140 Schmitt Blvd
Farmingdale NY 11735
631 249-2535

(G-4661)
KABAR MANUFACTURING CORP
113 Gazza Blvd (11735-1421)
PHONE..................................631 694-1036
Bruce Mc Kee, *President*

EMP: 30
SALES (corp-wide): 8.6MM **Privately Held**
WEB: www.cosmos-kabar.com
SIC: 3559 Plastics working machinery
HQ: Kabar Manufacturing Corp.
140 Schmitt Blvd
Farmingdale NY 11735
631 694-6857

(G-4662)
KAZAC INC
Also Called: Corzane Cabinets
55 Allen Blvd Ste C (11735-5643)
PHONE..................................631 249-7299
Fax: 631 249-1454
EMP: 5
SQ FT: 4,200
SALES: 450K **Privately Held**
SIC: 2511 2521 Mfg Wood Household Furniture Mfg Wood Office Furniture

(G-4663)
KEDCO INC
Also Called: Kedco Wine Storage Systems
564 Smith St (11735-1115)
PHONE..................................516 454-7800
Helene Windt, *President*
David Windt, *Corp Secy*
Ken Windt, *Vice Pres*
EMP: 12 EST: 1970
SQ FT: 20,000
SALES (est): 2MM **Privately Held**
SIC: 3585 2599 3556 Refrigeration & heating equipment; bar, restaurant & cafeteria furniture; beverage machinery

(G-4664)
KELLY WINDOW SYSTEMS INC
460 Smith St (11735-1105)
PHONE..................................631 420-8500
Carl J Giugliano, *President*
Frank Giugliano, *Vice Pres*
Pat Giugliano, *Vice Pres*
EMP: 32
SQ FT: 20,000
SALES (est): 4.6MM **Privately Held**
WEB: www.kellywindows.com
SIC: 2431 3442 Windows, wood; metal doors, sash & trim

(G-4665)
KEM MEDICAL PRODUCTS CORP (PA)
400 Broadhollow Rd Ste 2 (11735-4824)
PHONE..................................631 454-6565
Douglas A Kruger, *President*
Joseph Ebenstein, *Vice Pres*
EMP: 3
SQ FT: 2,500
SALES (est): 1.4MM **Privately Held**
WEB: www.kemmed.com
SIC: 3842 3829 Personal safety equipment; measuring & controlling devices

(G-4666)
KINEMOTIVE CORPORATION
222 Central Ave Ste 1 (11735-6958)
PHONE..................................631 249-6440
Arthur Szeglin, *Ch of Bd*
William Niedzwiecki, *President*
Charles Szeglin, *Principal*
Engin Oge, *Vice Pres*
Amber Garcia, *Purchasing*
EMP: 48 EST: 1959
SQ FT: 20,000
SALES (est): 9.8MM **Privately Held**
WEB: www.kinemotive.com
SIC: 3492 3452 3599 3568 Fluid power valves & hose fittings; screws, metal; bellows, industrial: metal; couplings, shaft: rigid, flexible, universal joint, etc.; pivots, power transmission; precision springs; pressure transducers

(G-4667)
L P R PRECISION PARTS & TLS CO
108 Rome St Ste 1 (11735-6637)
PHONE..................................631 293-7334
Tarquin Rattotti Jr, *President*
Tarquin Rattotti Sr, *Principal*
Lucy Rattotti, *Corp Secy*
EMP: 10
SQ FT: 5,000

SALES (est): 1.7MM **Privately Held**
WEB: www.lprprecision.com
SIC: 3599 Machine shop, jobbing & repair

(G-4668)
LA MAR LIGHTING CO INC
485 Smith St (11735-1106)
P.O. Box 9013 (11735-9013)
PHONE..................................631 777-7700
Jeffrey Goldstein, *CEO*
Barry Kugel, *Ch of Bd*
Bill Phillips, *Vice Pres*
Carolyn Goldstein, *Controller*
William Phillips, *VP Sales*
▲ EMP: 46 EST: 1957
SQ FT: 40,000
SALES: 13.9MM **Privately Held**
WEB: www.lamarlighting.com
SIC: 3646 3641 3648 Fluorescent lighting fixtures, commercial; electric lamps; lighting equipment

(G-4669)
LADY BURD EXCLUSIVE COSMT INC (PA)
Also Called: Lady Burd Private Label Cosmt
44 Executive Blvd Ste 1 (11735-4706)
PHONE..................................631 454-0444
Roberta Burd, *Chairman*
Allan Burd, *Vice Pres*
Christina Burd, *Vice Pres*
Lawrence Burd, *Vice Pres*
Tina Burd, *Vice Pres*
▲ EMP: 109
SQ FT: 40,000
SALES (est): 20.8MM **Privately Held**
WEB: www.ladyburd.com
SIC: 2844 Cosmetic preparations

(G-4670)
LEATHER CRAFTSMEN INC (PA)
6 Dubon Ct (11735-1008)
PHONE..................................631 752-9000
Howard Schneider, *President*
Joseph Fiore, *Vice Pres*
Robert Schneider, *Admin Sec*
EMP: 70
SQ FT: 18,000
SALES (est): 12.4MM **Privately Held**
WEB: www.leathercraftsmen.com
SIC: 2782 Albums

(G-4671)
LOGOMAX INC
242 Route 109 Ste B (11735-1500)
PHONE..................................631 420-0484
Victor Rouse, *President*
Annette Regan, *Sales Staff*
EMP: 4
SALES: 1.1MM **Privately Held**
WEB: www.logomaxusa.com
SIC: 2759 Screen printing

(G-4672)
LONG BLOCKCHAIN CORP (PA)
12 Dubon Ct Ste 1 (11735-1025)
PHONE..................................855 542-2832
Shamyl Malik, *Ch of Bd*
Peter Dydensborg, *Vice Pres*
EMP: 20
SQ FT: 5,000
SALES: 4.4MM **Privately Held**
SIC: 2086 Iced tea & fruit drinks, bottled & canned

(G-4673)
LOS OLIVOS LTD
105 Bi County Blvd (11735-3919)
PHONE..................................631 773-6439
Ester Alvarado, *Ch of Bd*
EMP: 135
SALES (est): 3.2MM **Privately Held**
SIC: 3556 Smokers, food processing equipment

(G-4674)
M C PACKAGING CORPORATION (PA)
120-200 Adams Blvd (11735)
PHONE..................................631 694-3012
Robert M Silverberg, *Ch of Bd*
Marc Silverberg, *President*
Jonathan Clair, *Vice Pres*
▲ EMP: 135 EST: 1966
SQ FT: 9,000

SALES (est): 48.9MM **Privately Held**
WEB: www.mcpkg.com
SIC: 2679 Cardboard products, except die-cut

(G-4675)
MACHINIT INC
400 Smith St (11735-1105)
PHONE..................................631 454-9297
Tony Kusturic, *President*
Edward Grcic, *General Mgr*
EMP: 4
SALES (est): 2MM **Privately Held**
SIC: 2253 Knit outerwear mills

(G-4676)
MAN PRODUCTS INC
99 Milbar Blvd Unit 1 (11735-1407)
PHONE..................................631 789-6500
Attilio Mancusi, *President*
EMP: 30
SALES (est): 4.4MM **Privately Held**
WEB: www.manproducts.com
SIC: 3448 Prefabricated metal buildings

(G-4677)
MAROTTA DENTAL STUDIO INC
130 Finn Ct (11735-1107)
PHONE..................................631 249-7520
Leonard Marotta, *President*
Steven Pigliacelli, *Vice Pres*
Chris Marotta, *Treasurer*
EMP: 40
SQ FT: 15,000
SALES (est): 7MM **Privately Held**
WEB: www.marottadental.com
SIC: 3843 8021 8072 Dental materials; offices & clinics of dentists; dental laboratories

(G-4678)
MART-TEX ATHLETICS INC
180 Allen Blvd (11735-5617)
PHONE..................................631 454-9583
Richard Marte, *President*
Raymond Marte Jr, *Corp Secy*
Peter Rasp Sr, *Sales Mgr*
EMP: 35
SQ FT: 15,000
SALES (est): 3.5MM **Privately Held**
WEB: www.mart-tex.com
SIC: 2759 Screen printing

(G-4679)
MAZZA CLASSICS INCORPORATED
117 Gazza Blvd (11735-1415)
PHONE..................................631 390-9060
Jim Rivera, *President*
EMP: 7
SQ FT: 5,000
SALES: 500K **Privately Held**
SIC: 2512 Upholstered household furniture

(G-4680)
MEMORY PROTECTION DEVICES INC
200 Broadhollow Rd Ste 4 (11735-4814)
PHONE..................................631 249-0001
Thomas Blaha, *President*
Charles Engelstein, *Chairman*
Daniel Lynch, *Vice Pres*
Dan Lynch, *Info Tech Mgr*
EMP: 10
SQ FT: 3,000
SALES: 7MM **Privately Held**
WEB: www.memoryprotectiondevices.com
SIC: 3089 Battery cases, plastic or plastic combination

(G-4681)
METADURE PARTS & SALES INC
Also Called: Sbcontract.com
165 Gazza Blvd (11735-1415)
PHONE..................................631 249-2141
Gary Templeton, *President*
Nicholas Picon, *Manager*
EMP: 12
SQ FT: 10,000
SALES (est): 2.2MM **Privately Held**
SIC: 3728 Military aircraft equipment & armament

GEOGRAPHIC

(G-4682)

METROPLTAN DATA SLTONS MGT INC

279 Conklin St (11735-2608)
P.O. Box 11394, Newark NJ (07101-4394)
PHONE.................................516 586-5520
John Dankowitz, *President*
Patricia Dankowitz, *Administration*
EMP: 11
SQ FT: 1,500
SALES (est): 2MM **Privately Held**
SIC: 3089 Identification cards, plastic

(G-4683)

MICHBI DOORS INC

Also Called: Open & Shut Doors
175 Marine St (11735-5609)
PHONE.................................631 231-9050
Michelle Bianculli, *President*
Doug Hommel, *Vice Pres*
Suzanne Mutone, *Vice Pres*
Jeannette Cambridge, *Project Mgr*
Christopher Bianculli, *CFO*
EMP: 56 **EST:** 1981
SALES (est): 8.3MM **Privately Held**
WEB: www.michbidoors.com
SIC: 2431 3231 3442 Millwork; products of purchased glass; metal doors, sash & trim

(G-4684)

MILLER TECHNOLOGY INC

61 Gazza Blvd (11735-1401)
PHONE.................................631 694-2224
Walter Miller Jr, *President*
Joane Miller, *Treasurer*
EMP: 5 **EST:** 1954
SQ FT: 3,000
SALES: 250K **Privately Held**
SIC: 3089 3369 3599 Casting of plastic; castings, except die-castings, precision; machine shop, jobbing & repair

(G-4685)

MINUTEMAN PRESS INTL INC (PA)

61 Executive Blvd (11735-4710)
PHONE.................................631 249-1370
Robert Titus, *CEO*
Roy W Titus, *Ch of Bd*
Vance Ferratusco, *General Mgr*
Cyndi Hurst, *General Mgr*
Jose Reyna, *General Mgr*
◆ **EMP:** 50 **EST:** 1975
SQ FT: 30,000
SALES: 23.4MM **Privately Held**
SIC: 2752 Commercial printing, lithographic

(G-4686)

MIRAGE MOULDING MFG INC

Also Called: Mirage Moulding & Supply
160 Milbar Blvd (11735-1425)
PHONE.................................631 843-6168
Hashim Ismailzadah, *President*
▲ **EMP:** 11
SALES (est): 1.2MM **Privately Held**
SIC: 3089 Molding primary plastic

(G-4687)

MISONIX OPCO INC (PA)

1938 New Hwy (11735-1214)
PHONE.................................631 694-9555
Stavros G Vizirgianakis, *CEO*
Sharon Klugewicz, *COO*
Robert S Ludecker, *Senior VP*
Joseph J Brennan, *Vice Pres*
Joseph Brennan, *Vice Pres*
▲ **EMP:** 85
SQ FT: 34,400
SALES: 38.8MM **Publicly Held**
WEB: www.misonix.com
SIC: 3841 3845 3677 Surgical & medical instruments; electromedical equipment; electronic coils, transformers & other inductors

(G-4688)

MKT329 INC

Also Called: Superior Packaging
565 Broadhollow Rd Ste 5 (11735-4826)
P.O. Box 667, North Bellmore (11710-0667)
PHONE.................................631 249-5500
Marlene Tallon, *President*

▲ **EMP:** 21 **EST:** 2014
SQ FT: 121
SALES (est): 3.6MM **Privately Held**
SIC: 2653 Boxes, corrugated: made from purchased materials

(G-4689)

MOREY PUBLISHING

Also Called: Long Island Press
20 Hempstead Tpke Unit B (11735-2043)
PHONE.................................516 284-3300
Jed Morey, *Ch of Bd*
Joanna Austin, *Publisher*
Jon Sasala, *Editor*
Alexandra Magno, *Marketing Staff*
EMP: 30
SALES (est): 4.4MM **Privately Held**
SIC: 2741 Miscellaneous publishing

(G-4690)

NAMEPLATE MFRS OF AMER

65 Toledo St (11735-6620)
PHONE.................................631 752-0055
Bill Williams, *CEO*
Darren Cash, *COO*
EMP: 40
SQ FT: 8,000
SALES (est): 4.6MM **Privately Held**
WEB: www.nameplateamerica.com
SIC: 3479 3993 2752 2671 Name plates: engraved, etched, etc.; signs & advertising specialties; commercial printing, lithographic; packaging paper & plastics film, coated & laminated

(G-4691)

NATIONWIDE SALES AND SERVICE

303 Smith St Ste 4 (11735-1110)
PHONE.................................631 491-6625
Mark Genoa, *Ch of Bd*
Scott Genoa, *Vice Pres*
▲ **EMP:** 10
SQ FT: 10,000
SALES (est): 1.8MM **Privately Held**
WEB: www.shopnss.com
SIC: 3635 5087 5722 Household vacuum cleaners; janitors' supplies; vacuum cleaning systems; vacuum cleaners

(G-4692)

NEIGHBOR NEWSPAPERS

565 Broadhollow Rd Ste 3 (11735-4826)
PHONE.................................631 226-2636
Richard A Freedman, *Principal*
EMP: 7 **EST:** 2008
SALES (est): 402.3K **Privately Held**
SIC: 2711 Commercial printing & newspaper publishing combined

(G-4693)

NEILSON INTERNATIONAL INC

144 Allen Blvd Ste B (11735-5644)
P.O. Box 784, Hicksville (11802-0784)
PHONE.................................631 454-0400
Kamlesh Mehta, *President*
▲ **EMP:** 3
SQ FT: 8,000
SALES: 1MM **Privately Held**
WEB: www.neilsoninc.com
SIC: 2211 Print cloths, cotton

(G-4694)

NETECH CORPORATION

Also Called: Biomedical & Industrial
110 Toledo St (11735-6623)
PHONE.................................631 531-0100
Mohan Das, *President*
EMP: 11
SQ FT: 4,500
SALES (est): 2.1MM **Privately Held**
WEB: www.gonetech.com
SIC: 3845 Electromedical equipment

(G-4695)

NOGA DAIRIES INC

Also Called: Dairy Delite
175 Price Pkwy (11735-1318)
PHONE.................................516 293-5448
Eli Paz, *CEO*
Zami Leinson, *President*
▲ **EMP:** 10
SQ FT: 22,000
SALES (est): 1.3MM **Privately Held**
SIC: 2026 2022 Yogurt; spreads, cheese

(G-4696)

NUTRASCIENCE LABS INC

70 Carolyn Blvd (11735-1525)
PHONE.................................631 247-0660
Steve Rolfes, *CEO*
Ryan Gillen, *Accounts Exec*
Samantha Lucchi, *Sales Staff*
Brian Lambert, *Manager*
Christopher Bennett, *Art Dir*
EMP: 27 **EST:** 2014
SALES (est): 1.3MM
SALES (corp-wide): 73.2MM **Publicly Held**
SIC: 2833 2834 Botanical products, medicinal: ground, graded or milled; druggists' preparations (pharmaceuticals)
PA: Twinlab Consolidated Holdings Inc.
4800 T Rex Ave Ste 305
Boca Raton FL 33431
561 443-4301

(G-4697)

ORICS INDUSTRIES INC

240 Smith St (11735-1113)
PHONE.................................718 461-8613
Ori Cohen, *Ch of Bd*
▲ **EMP:** 50
SQ FT: 15,000
SALES (est): 24.2MM **Privately Held**
WEB: www.orics.com
SIC: 3565 3841 Packaging machinery; surgical & medical instruments

(G-4698)

ORLANDI INC (PA)

Also Called: Orlandi Scented Products
131 Executive Blvd (11735-4719)
PHONE.................................631 756-0110
Sven Dobler, *Ch of Bd*
Per Dobler, *Vice Pres*
Camilla Gilfillan, *Vice Pres*
Val Marinelli, *Vice Pres*
Douglas M Whitaker, *Vice Pres*
▲ **EMP:** 100
SQ FT: 80,000
SALES (est): 34.5MM **Privately Held**
WEB: www.orlandi-usa.com
SIC: 3993 3999 7389 2752 Signs & advertising specialties; novelties, bric-a-brac & hobby kits; packaging & labeling services; commercial printing, lithographic

(G-4699)

ORLANDI INC

121 Executive Blvd (11735-4719)
PHONE.................................631 756-0110
Sven Dobler, *President*
EMP: 50
SQ FT: 45,500
SALES (corp-wide): 34.5MM **Privately Held**
SIC: 3993 3999 7389 2752 Signs & advertising specialties; novelties, bric-a-brac & hobby kits; packaging & labeling services; commercial printing, lithographic
PA: Orlandi, Inc.
131 Executive Blvd
Farmingdale NY 11735
631 756-0110

(G-4700)

OSI PHARMACEUTICALS LLC

500 Bi County Blvd # 118 (11735-3959)
PHONE.................................631 847-0175
EMP: 84
SALES (corp-wide): 10.4B **Privately Held**
SIC: 2834 Mfg Pharmaceutical Preparations
HQ: Osi Pharmaceuticals, Llc
1 Bioscience Way Dr
Farmingdale NY 11735
631 962-2000

(G-4701)

OSI PHARMACEUTICALS LLC (DH)

1 Bioscience Way Dr (11735)
PHONE.................................631 962-2000
Colin Goddard PHD, *CEO*
Gabriel Leung, *President*
Anker Lundemose MD PHD, *President*
Robert L Simon, *Exec VP*
Linda E Amper PHD, *Senior VP*
◆ **EMP:** 7

SALES (est): 74.1MM **Privately Held**
WEB: www.osip.com
SIC: 2834 8731 Drugs affecting neoplasms & endocrine systems; drugs acting on the central nervous system & sense organs; commercial physical research
HQ: Astellas Us Holding, Inc.
1 Astellas Way
Northbrook IL 60062
224 205-8800

(G-4702)

PCX AEROSTRUCTURES LLC

60 Milbar Blvd (11735-1406)
PHONE.................................631 467-2632
EMP: 25
SALES (corp-wide): 100MM **Privately Held**
SIC: 3441 Structural Metal Fabrication
PA: Pcx Aerostructures, Llc
300 Fenn Rd
Newington CT 06111
860 666-2471

(G-4703)

PEDINOL PHARMACAL INC

30 Banfi Plz N (11735-1528)
PHONE.................................800 733-4665
Richard Strauss, *Ch of Bd*
EMP: 8
SALES (est): 732.3K **Privately Held**
SIC: 2834 Pharmaceutical preparations

(G-4704)

PEERLESS INSTRUMENT CO INC

1966 Broadhollow Rd Ste D (11735-1726)
PHONE.................................631 396-6500
Martin R Benante, *CEO*
David Linton, *President*
Frederic Borah, *General Mgr*
Vincent Materese, *Finance Dir*
EMP: 109 **EST:** 1938
SQ FT: 55,000
SALES (est): 22.5MM
SALES (corp-wide): 2.4B **Publicly Held**
WEB: www.peerlessny.com
SIC: 3829 7389 3825 3625 Measuring & controlling devices; design services; instruments to measure electricity; relays & industrial controls
PA: Curtiss-Wright Corporation
130 Harbour Place Dr # 300
Davidson NC 28036
704 869-4600

(G-4705)

PHARBEST PHARMACEUTICALS INC

14 Engineers Ln Ste 1 (11735-1219)
PHONE.................................631 249-5130
Munir Islam, *President*
Tausif Islam, *Marketing Staff*
Intekhab Ahmed, *Manager*
Nishant Parikh, *Manager*
▲ **EMP:** 41
SQ FT: 22,000
SALES (est): 8MM **Privately Held**
WEB: www.pharbestusa.com
SIC: 2834 Druggists' preparations (pharmaceuticals)

(G-4706)

PHARMALIFE INC

130 Gazza Blvd (11735-1420)
PHONE.................................631 249-4040
Larry Sayage, *President*
EMP: 5 **EST:** 1999
SQ FT: 4,300
SALES (est): 692.9K **Privately Held**
SIC: 2834 Vitamin, nutrient & hematinic preparations for human use

(G-4707)

PHOENIX LABORATORIES INC

200 Adams Blvd (11735-6615)
PHONE.................................516 822-1230
Melvin Rich, *President*
Stephen R Stern, *Exec VP*
Charlotte Rich, *Admin Sec*
EMP: 180 **EST:** 1966
SQ FT: 40,000

SALES (est): 25MM **Privately Held**
WEB: www.phoenixlaboratories.com
SIC: 2834 Vitamin, nutrient & hematinic preparations for human use; vitamin preparations

(G-4708)
PINTAIL COFFEE INC
1776 New Hwy (11735-1513)
PHONE.................................631 396-0808
Stuart Kessler, *Principal*
Stephen Jackson, *Manager*
EMP: 8 **EST:** 2013
SALES (est): 186.7K **Privately Held**
SIC: 2095 5149 5499 Coffee roasting (except by wholesale grocers); coffee, green or roasted; coffee

(G-4709)
PIRNAT PRECISE METALS INC
Also Called: F & M Precise Metals Co
127 Marine St (11735-5609)
PHONE.................................631 293-9169
Frank Pirnat, *President*
Mark Pirnat, *Vice Pres*
EMP: 7 **EST:** 1967
SQ FT: 10,000
SALES (est): 1.2MM **Privately Held**
SIC: 3444 Sheet metalwork

(G-4710)
PLASCAL CORP
361 Eastern Pkwy (11735-2713)
P.O. Box 590 (11735-0590)
PHONE.................................516 249-2200
Mark Hurd, *CEO*
Fred Hurd, *President*
Sheldon Eskowitz, *Corp Secy*
Thomas Blackler, *Vice Pres*
Raymond Brown, *Vice Pres*
▲ **EMP:** 4 **EST:** 1975
SQ FT: 75,000
SALES: 6MM **Privately Held**
WEB: www.plascal.com
SIC: 3081 Vinyl film & sheet

(G-4711)
PLATINUM PRINTING & GRAPHICS
70 Carolyn Blvd Ste C (11735-1525)
PHONE.................................631 249-3325
Paul Currao, *President*
EMP: 5 **EST:** 1996
SALES (est): 477.7K **Privately Held**
SIC: 2752 Commercial printing, offset

(G-4712)
POLYPLASTIC FORMS INC
49 Gazza Blvd (11735-1401)
PHONE.................................631 249-5011
Thomas Garrett, *President*
Diane Garrett, *Corp Secy*
Richard Garrett, *Vice Pres*
Nancy Behrens, *Administration*
EMP: 35
SQ FT: 10,000
SALES (est): 5.2MM **Privately Held**
WEB: www.polyplasticforms.com
SIC: 3993 Displays & cutouts, window & lobby; signs, not made in custom sign painting shops

(G-4713)
POSILLICO MATERIALS LLC
1750 New Hwy (11735-1562)
PHONE.................................631 249-1872
Joseph K Posillico, *CEO*
Michael J Posillico, *President*
Mario A Posillico, *Chairman*
Joseph D Posillico, *Senior VP*
Paul F Posillico, *Senior VP*
EMP: 11 **EST:** 1971
SQ FT: 2,500
SALES (est): 13.6MM
SALES (corp-wide): 161.9MM **Privately Held**
SIC: 2951 Asphalt & asphaltic paving mixtures (not from refineries)
PA: Posillico Civil, Inc.
1750 New Hwy
Farmingdale NY 11735
631 249-1872

(G-4714)
PRECIPART CORPORATION (HQ)
120 Finn Ct Ste 2 (11735-1121)
PHONE.................................631 694-3100
John P Walter, *President*
Thomas Kiriyanthan, *Production*
Navin Boradia, *Project Engr*
John Kustan, *Manager*
Slawomir Liebert, *Supervisor*
EMP: 216
SQ FT: 16,200
SALES (est): 43.5MM **Privately Held**
WEB: www.precipart.com
SIC: 3566 Gears, power transmission, except automotive

(G-4715)
PRECISION ENVELOPE CO INC
Also Called: H & R Precision
110 Schmitt Blvd 7a (11735-6961)
PHONE.................................631 694-3990
Gilbert M Colombo Jr, *President*
Jane Colombo, *Corp Secy*
Diana Hall, *Bookkeeper*
EMP: 9
SQ FT: 7,000
SALES (est): 1.2MM **Privately Held**
SIC: 2759 2752 Envelopes: printing; stationery: printing; business forms, lithographed

(G-4716)
PROMPT PRINTING INC
160 Rome St (11735-6609)
PHONE.................................631 454-6524
Fax: 631 454-6370
EMP: 6 **EST:** 1980
SQ FT: 2,000
SALES: 370K **Privately Held**
SIC: 2752 Lithographic Commercial Printing

(G-4717)
PROOF INDUSTRIES INC
125 Rome St (11735-6606)
PHONE.................................631 694-7663
Vincent Cacioppo, *President*
EMP: 9
SQ FT: 3,000
SALES (est): 1.3MM **Privately Held**
WEB: www.proofroof.com
SIC: 2439 5999 1751 Trusses, wooden roof; awnings; window & door (prefabricated) installation

(G-4718)
PROPER CHEMICAL LTD
280 Smith St (11735-1113)
PHONE.................................631 420-8000
Emil Backstrom, *President*
EMP: 5
SQ FT: 20,000
SALES (est): 400K **Privately Held**
SIC: 2833 Medicinal chemicals

(G-4719)
QUALITY STAIR BUILDERS INC
95 Schmitt Blvd (11735-1403)
PHONE.................................631 694-0711
Esta Topal, *President*
Sherri Sugar, *Corp Secy*
EMP: 16
SQ FT: 10,000
SALES (est): 2.2MM **Privately Held**
SIC: 2431 Staircases & stairs, wood

(G-4720)
QUICK SIGN F X
6 Powell St (11735-4019)
PHONE.................................516 249-6531
Steve Levine, *President*
EMP: 13
SALES (est): 853.7K **Privately Held**
SIC: 3993 Signs & advertising specialties

(G-4721)
R & J GRAPHICS INC
45 Central Ave (11735-6901)
PHONE.................................631 293-6611
John Merendino, *President*
Ann Merendino, *Admin Sec*
EMP: 16
SQ FT: 15,000
SALES (est): 2.6MM **Privately Held**
SIC: 2752 Commercial printing, offset

(G-4722)
R D PRINTING ASSOCIATES INC
1865 New Hwy Ste 1 (11735-1501)
PHONE.................................631 390-5964
Ralph Demartino Jr, *President*
EMP: 14
SQ FT: 10,000
SALES (est): 1.4MM **Privately Held**
SIC: 2752 Commercial printing, offset

(G-4723)
RAILWORKS CORPORATION
Signals & Communications
83 Central Ave (11735-6901)
PHONE.................................904 296-5055
Tim Orlandi, *Branch Mgr*
Marcia Calvitto, *Admin Asst*
EMP: 6
SALES (corp-wide): 1.4B **Privately Held**
SIC: 3612 Signaling transformers, electric
HQ: Railworks Corporation
5 Penn Plz
New York NY 10001
212 502-7900

(G-4724)
RIPI PRECISION CO INC (PA)
92 Toledo St (11735-6623)
PHONE.................................631 694-2453
Michael Percibali, *President*
EMP: 15
SQ FT: 12,000
SALES (est): 2.8MM **Privately Held**
SIC: 3599 Machine shop, jobbing & repair

(G-4725)
ROBOCOM US LLC (HQ)
Also Called: Robocom Systems International
1111 Broadhollow Rd # 100 (11735-4819)
PHONE.................................631 861-2045
Fred Radcliffe, *President*
Richard Adamo, *Vice Pres*
Raymond Oconnor, *Vice Pres*
Kathleen Poulos, *Controller*
Michael Ciani, *Prgrmr*
EMP: 13
SQ FT: 4,000
SALES: 7MM
SALES (corp-wide): 7.7MM **Privately Held**
WEB: www.avantce.com
SIC: 7372 Prepackaged software
PA: Avantc, Llc
3838 Tamiami Trl N # 416
Naples FL 34103
407 312-8445

(G-4726)
ROLI RETREADS INC
Also Called: Roli Tire and Auto Repair
212 E Carmans Rd Unit A (11735-4722)
PHONE.................................631 694-7670
Richard Bucci, *Owner*
Laura Lavender, *Controller*
EMP: 20
SQ FT: 6,500
SALES (est): 4.2MM **Privately Held**
WEB: www.rolitire.com
SIC: 3011 7549 Tire & inner tube materials & related products; automotive maintenance services

(G-4727)
ROTA PACK INC
34 Sarah Dr Ste B (11735-1218)
PHONE.................................631 274-1037
Adrian Spirea, *Ch of Bd*
EMP: 11
SALES: 525K **Privately Held**
WEB: www.rotaindustries.com
SIC: 3565 3535 Packaging machinery; conveyors & conveying equipment

(G-4728)
ROZAL INDUSTRIES INC
151 Marine St (11735-5609)
PHONE.................................631 420-4277
Brian Casio, *President*
Gary Grieber, *Vice Pres*
EMP: 47
SALES (est): 4MM **Privately Held**
SIC: 3599 Machine shop, jobbing & repair

(G-4729)
RS PRECISION INDUSTRIES INC
295 Adams Blvd (11735-6632)
PHONE.................................631 420-0424
Robert Savitzky, *President*
Michael Edgmon, *General Mgr*
Lily Savitzky, *Admin Sec*
EMP: 24
SQ FT: 6,700
SALES (est): 5.4MM **Privately Held**
WEB: www.rsprecision.com
SIC: 3599 Machine shop, jobbing & repair

(G-4730)
S & V KNITS INC
117 Marine St (11735-5607)
PHONE.................................631 752-1595
EMP: 30
SQ FT: 14,000
SALES (est): 2.8MM **Privately Held**
SIC: 2253 2339 Knit Outerwear Mill Mfg Women's/Misses' Outerwear

(G-4731)
SEANAIR MACHINE CO INC
95 Verdi St (11735-6320)
PHONE.................................631 694-2820
Laura Abel Nawrocki, *Ch of Bd*
Dorothy Abel, *President*
Thomas J Nawrochi, *Vice Pres*
EMP: 18 **EST:** 1955
SQ FT: 16,000
SALES (est): 3.3MM **Privately Held**
SIC: 3599 Machine shop, jobbing & repair

(G-4732)
SIMTEC INDUSTRIES CORPORATION
65 Marine St Ste A (11735-5638)
PHONE.................................631 293-0080
Jean J Simon, *President*
EMP: 6
SALES: 1MM **Privately Held**
SIC: 3552 Textile machinery

(G-4733)
SKYLINE CUSTOM CABINETRY INC
200 Verdi St Unit A (11735-6337)
PHONE.................................631 393-2983
Lisa Mumalo, *Principal*
EMP: 5
SALES (est): 506.1K **Privately Held**
SIC: 2434 Wood kitchen cabinets

(G-4734)
SMITH GRAPHICS INC
40 Florida St (11735-6301)
PHONE.................................631 420-4180
Rick Smith, *President*
Sarah Silva, *Office Mgr*
▲ **EMP:** 8
SQ FT: 2,500
SALES: 1.2MM **Privately Held**
WEB: www.smithgraphicsinc.com
SIC: 3993 Signs & advertising specialties

(G-4735)
SOURCE ENVELOPE INC
104 Allen Blvd Ste I (11735-5627)
PHONE.................................866 284-0707
EMP: 9
SQ FT: 2,000
SALES (est): 963.4K **Privately Held**
SIC: 2752 2759 Lithographic And Letterpress Printing

(G-4736)
SPACE COAST SEMICONDUCTOR INC
1111 Broadhollow Rd Fl 3 (11735-4881)
PHONE.................................631 414-7131
Anthony Tamborrino, *Director*
EMP: 10
SALES (est): 672.2K **Privately Held**
WEB: www.spacecoastsemi.com
SIC: 3679 Electronic circuits

(G-4737)
SPECIALTY CONVEYOR CORP
132 Gazza Blvd (11735-1420)
PHONE.................................347 707-0490
Constantin Lutas, *Principal*
EMP: 5

SALES (est): 690K **Privately Held**
SIC: 3535 Belt conveyor systems, general industrial use

(G-4738)
SPECTRA POLYMERS & COLOR SPC
77 Marine St (11735-5604)
PHONE..................................631 694-6943
Bethany Reilly, *Controller*
EMP: 10
SALES (est): 409.5K **Privately Held**
SIC: 2821 Molding compounds, plastics

(G-4739)
STANDWILL PACKAGING INC
220 Sherwood Ave (11735-1718)
PHONE..................................631 752-1236
William Standwill Jr, *President*
Janet Kelso, *Receptionist*
▲ **EMP:** 25 **EST:** 1976
SQ FT: 15,000
SALES (est): 4MM **Privately Held**
WEB: www.standwill.com
SIC: 2752 2759 Commercial printing, offset; commercial printing

(G-4740)
STAR MOLD CO INC
125 Florida St (11735-6307)
PHONE..................................631 694-2283
Guenther Merz, *President*
EMP: 6
SQ FT: 2,400
SALES (est): 320K **Privately Held**
SIC: 3544 Industrial molds

(G-4741)
STEPHEN J LIPKINS INC
855 Conklin St Ste A (11735-2409)
PHONE..................................631 249-8866
Jonathan Lipkins, *President*
EMP: 5 **EST:** 1968
SQ FT: 2,800
SALES (est): 420K **Privately Held**
SIC: 3915 Jewel cutting, drilling, polishing, recutting or setting; jewelry polishing for the trade

(G-4742)
STERLING INDUSTRIES INC
410 Eastern Pkwy (11735-2431)
PHONE..................................631 753-3070
Brian Lewis, *President*
EMP: 25
SALES (est): 4.4MM **Privately Held**
SIC: 3444 Sheet metalwork

(G-4743)
SUNDIAL BRANDS
1 Adams Blvd (11735-6611)
PHONE..................................631 842-8800
EMP: 7 **EST:** 2015
SALES (est): 1.4MM **Privately Held**
SIC: 2844 Toilet preparations

(G-4744)
SUPERIOR METAL & WOODWORK INC
70 Central Ave (11735-6906)
PHONE..................................631 465-9004
John Cipri, *President*
Joseph Cipri, *Vice Pres*
James Santora, *Project Mgr*
EMP: 25
SQ FT: 12,500
SALES: 6.5MM **Privately Held**
SIC: 3446 Architectural metalwork

(G-4745)
SUPERIOR MOTION CONTROLS INC
40 Smith St (11735-1005)
PHONE..................................516 420-2921
Frank Grieco, *CEO*
Tony Reda, *Engineer*
Rich Neuman, *Sales Staff*
Rich Neunman, *Marketing Staff*
EMP: 40
SQ FT: 20,000
SALES: 9.6MM **Privately Held**
WEB: www.superior-ny.com
SIC: 3728 3679 3462 Aircraft assemblies, subassemblies & parts; electronic loads & power supplies; iron & steel forgings

(G-4746)
SWIMWEAR ANYWHERE INC (PA)
Also Called: Carmen Mark Valvo Swimwear
85 Sherwood Ave (11735-1717)
PHONE..................................631 420-1400
Rosemarie Dilorenzo, *Chairman*
Joseph Dilorenzo, *COO*
Bob Colasante, *Prdtn Mgr*
Arthur Conway, *Opers Staff*
Brenda Blackman, *VP Sales*
◆ **EMP:** 75 **EST:** 1998
SALES: 52MM **Privately Held**
SIC: 2339 Bathing suits: women's, misses' & juniors'

(G-4747)
SYNTHO PHARMACEUTICALS INC
230 Sherwood Ave (11735-1718)
PHONE..................................631 755-9898
Hosneara Malik, *President*
Tithi Malik, *Director*
EMP: 6
SQ FT: 10,000
SALES: 3MM **Privately Held**
WEB: www.synthopharmaceutical.com
SIC: 2834 Pharmaceutical preparations

(G-4748)
T A TOOL & MOLDING INC
Also Called: Konrad Design
185 Marine St (11735-5609)
PHONE..................................631 293-0172
Ludwig Konrad, *President*
Maryann Konrad, *Vice Pres*
EMP: 18
SALES (est): 2.7MM **Privately Held**
SIC: 3089 3544 Injection molding of plastics; industrial molds

(G-4749)
TANGENT MACHINE & TOOL CORP
108 Gazza Blvd (11735-1489)
PHONE..................................631 249-3088
Joseph Scafidi, *President*
Joseph A Scafidi, *President*
Charles C Piola, *CFO*
EMP: 17 **EST:** 1953
SQ FT: 30,000
SALES (est): 3.5MM **Privately Held**
SIC: 3599 3728 Machine shop, jobbing & repair; aircraft parts & equipment

(G-4750)
TAPE PRINTERS INC
155 Allen Blvd Ste A (11735-5640)
PHONE..................................631 249-5585
Alexander J Kruk, *President*
▲ **EMP:** 15
SQ FT: 10,000
SALES (est): 2.8MM **Privately Held**
WEB: www.tapeprinters.com
SIC: 2759 Bag, wrapper & seal printing & engraving; labels & seals: printing

(G-4751)
TELEPHONICS CORPORATION
Also Called: Communications Systems Div
815 Broadhollow Rd (11735-3937)
PHONE..................................631 755-7659
Robert Hirner, *Mfg Staff*
EMP: 99
SALES (corp-wide): 1.5B **Publicly Held**
SIC: 3661 Telephone & telegraph apparatus
HQ: Telephonics Corporation
　　815 Broadhollow Rd
　　Farmingdale NY 11735
　　631 755-7000

(G-4752)
TELEPHONICS CORPORATION (HQ)
815 Broadhollow Rd (11735-3937)
PHONE..................................631 755-7000
Kevin McSweeney, *President*
Jack Sullivan, *General Mgr*
Alan Bryan, *Principal*
Bill Glusing, *Senior VP*
Michael Anderson, *Vice Pres*
▲ **EMP:** 667
SQ FT: 160,000

SALES: 335MM
SALES (corp-wide): 1.9B **Publicly Held**
SIC: 3669 3661 3679 3812 Intercommunication systems, electric; telephone & telegraph apparatus; electronic circuits; radar systems & equipment; air traffic control systems & equipment, electronic; radio & TV communications equipment
PA: Griffon Corporation
　　712 5th Ave Fl 18
　　New York NY 10019
　　212 957-5000

(G-4753)
TELEPHONICS CORPORATION
Also Called: Command Systems Division
815 Broadhollow Rd (11735-3937)
PHONE..................................631 755-7000
Joseph Battaglia, *CEO*
EMP: 99
SALES (corp-wide): 1.5B **Publicly Held**
SIC: 3699 Electronic training devices
HQ: Telephonics Corporation
　　815 Broadhollow Rd
　　Farmingdale NY 11735
　　631 755-7000

(G-4754)
THERMAL PROCESS CNSTR CO
19 Engineers Ln (11735-1207)
PHONE..................................631 293-6400
Al Gupta, *President*
EMP: 22
SQ FT: 10,000
SALES (est): 1.5MM **Privately Held**
SIC: 3567 3497 Incinerators, metal: domestic or commercial; metal foil & leaf

(G-4755)
TIGER SUPPLY INC
99 Sherwood Ave (11735-1717)
PHONE..................................631 293-2700
Anthony Davanzo, *President*
EMP: 6
SALES (est): 955.2K **Privately Held**
WEB: www.tigersupplyinc.com
SIC: 3843 Dental equipment & supplies

(G-4756)
TIME-CAP LABORATORIES INC
Also Called: Custom Coatings
7 Michael Ave (11735-3921)
PHONE..................................631 753-9090
Mark Saldanha, *Ch of Bd*
Irene McGregor, *President*
Robert Azzara, *COO*
Sam Chacko, *Manager*
Joseph Perez, *Technology*
▲ **EMP:** 160
SQ FT: 45,000
SALES: 60.9MM **Privately Held**
SIC: 2834 Proprietary drug products
PA: Marksans Pharma Limited
　　11th Floor Grandeur, Off Veera Desai
　　Extension Road,
　　Mumbai MH 40005

(G-4757)
TIN BOX COMPANY OF AMERICA INC (PA)
216 Sherwood Ave (11735-1718)
PHONE..................................631 845-1600
Lloyd Roth, *President*
Andy Siegel, *Vice Pres*
Michael Siegel, *Vice Pres*
Stephen Siegel, *CFO*
Mary Rogers, *Sales Staff*
▲ **EMP:** 25
SQ FT: 20,000
SALES (est): 5.6MM **Privately Held**
SIC: 2631 5051 Container, packaging & boxboard; tin & tin base metals, shapes, forms, etc.

(G-4758)
TRI-FLEX LABEL CORP
48 Allen Blvd Unit A (11735-5642)
PHONE..................................631 293-0411
Kevin Duckman, *President*
Kevin Duckham, *President*
Gene Saraniero, *Manager*
Ed Webster, *Director*
▲ **EMP:** 20
SQ FT: 6,000

SALES (est): 4.4MM **Privately Held**
WEB: www.triflexlabel.com
SIC: 2672 2679 Labels (unprinted), gummed: made from purchased materials; labels, paper: made from purchased material

(G-4759)
TRI-SUPREME OPTICAL LLC
Also Called: Tri Supreme Optical
91 Carolyn Blvd (11735-1527)
PHONE..................................631 249-2020
Jay Graber,
Phil Feldman,
▲ **EMP:** 95
SQ FT: 18,000
SALES (est): 12.5MM
SALES (corp-wide): 1.4MM **Privately Held**
WEB: www.essilor.com
SIC: 3851 5049 Lenses, ophthalmic; optical goods
HQ: Essilor Of America, Inc.
　　13555 N Stemmons Fwy
　　Dallas TX 75234
　　214 496-4000

(G-4760)
TRONIC PLATING CO INC
37 Potter St (11735-4200)
PHONE..................................516 293-7883
Herbert Buckstone, *President*
Stanley J Buckstone, *Vice Pres*
EMP: 11 **EST:** 1955
SQ FT: 6,000
SALES: 629.2K **Privately Held**
SIC: 3471 Electroplating of metals or formed products: finishing, metals or formed products

(G-4761)
VELOCITY PHARMA LLC
210-220 Sea Ln (11735)
PHONE..................................631 393-2905
Ankur Shah, *President*
Arthur Valeeva, *Opers Mgr*
Nicholas Monte, *Director*
▲ **EMP:** 8
SQ FT: 20,000
SALES: 5MM **Privately Held**
SIC: 2834 Vitamin, nutrient & hematinic preparations for human use

(G-4762)
VITA-NAT INC
298 Adams Blvd (11735-6615)
PHONE..................................631 293-6000
Mohd M Alam, *President*
Khurshid Anwar, *Vice Pres*
▲ **EMP:** 6
SQ FT: 7,000
SALES: 861.1K **Privately Held**
SIC: 2834 Vitamin, nutrient & hematinic preparations for human use

(G-4763)
W R P WELDING LTD
Also Called: Ramick Welding
126 Toledo St (11735-6625)
PHONE..................................631 249-8859
William R Pontecorvo, *President*
EMP: 6 **EST:** 1963
SQ FT: 3,500
SALES (est): 542.1K **Privately Held**
SIC: 7692 Brazing

(G-4764)
WALNUT PACKAGING INC
450 Smith St (11735-1105)
PHONE..................................631 293-3836
Jose Alvarado, *President*
EMP: 21
SQ FT: 14,000
SALES (est): 3.3MM **Privately Held**
WEB: www.wpiplasticbags.com
SIC: 3086 Packaging & shipping materials, foamed plastic

(G-4765)
WEL MADE ENTERPRISES INC
1630 New Hwy (11735-1510)
PHONE..................................631 752-1238
EMP: 14 **EST:** 1950
SQ FT: 1,800
SALES: 1.1MM **Privately Held**
SIC: 3272 Mfg Concrete Products

2020 Harris
New York Manufacturers Directory

▲ = Import ▼=Export
◆ =Import/Export

(G-4766)
XYLON INDUSTRIES INC
79 Florida St (11735-6305)
PHONE..................................631 293-4717
Joseph Jones, *President*
EMP: 5
SQ FT: 4,200
SALES: 850K **Privately Held**
SIC: 3842 2431 Radiation shielding
aprons, gloves, sheeting, etc.; millwork

(G-4767)
ZINGS COMPANY LLC
250 Adams Blvd (11735-6615)
PHONE..................................631 454-0339
Robert Jagenburg,
EMP: 5
SALES (est): 385.1K **Privately Held**
WEB: www.zingsco.com
SIC: 2024 Juice pops, frozen

Farmington
Ontario County

(G-4768)
BADGER TECHNOLOGIES INC
5829 County Road 41 (14425-9103)
PHONE..................................585 869-7101
Manoj Shekar, *President*
Jim Harris, *General Mgr*
▲ EMP: 63
SQ FT: 15,000
SALES (est): 9.4MM **Privately Held**
WEB: www.badgertech.com
SIC: 3672 Printed circuit boards

(G-4769)
CROSMAN CORPORATION
1360 Rural Rte 8 (14425)
PHONE..................................585 398-3920
Steve Burley, *Branch Mgr*
EMP: 30 **Publicly Held**
SIC: 3484 3482 3563 Pellet & BB guns;
pellets & BB's, pistol & air rifle ammuni-
tion; shot, steel (ammunition); air & gas
compressors
HQ: Crosman Corporation
7629 State Route 5 And 20
Bloomfield NY 14469
585 657-6161

(G-4770)
EBSCO INDUSTRIES INC
Global Point Products
5815 County Road 41 (14425-9103)
PHONE..................................585 398-2000
David Testa, *Vice Pres*
EMP: 5
SALES (corp-wide): 2.8B **Privately Held**
WEB: www.ebscoind.com
SIC: 3861 Photographic equipment & sup-
plies
PA: Ebsco Industries, Inc.
5724 Highway 280 E
Birmingham AL 35242
205 991-6600

(G-4771)
EMORY MACHINE & TOOL CO INC
6176 Hunters Dr (14425-1122)
PHONE..................................585 436-9610
EMP: 45
SQ FT: 30,000
SALES (est): 4.4MM **Privately Held**
SIC: 3599 3451 Mfg Industrial Machinery
Mfg Screw Machine Products

(G-4772)
HANSEN STEEL
Also Called: Hansen Metal Fabrications
6021 County Road 41 (14425-8938)
P.O. Box 25100 (14425-0100)
PHONE..................................585 398-2020
Thomas Hansen, *Owner*
EMP: 25
SQ FT: 13,500
SALES (est): 3.7MM **Privately Held**
SIC: 3441 7692 3444 Fabricated struc-
tural metal; welding repair; sheet metal-
work

(G-4773)
HOFF ASSOCIATES MFG REPS INC
Also Called: Global Point Technology
5815 County Road 41 (14425-9103)
PHONE..................................585 398-2000
John J Hoff, *President*
Dawn Wicks, *Purch Mgr*
Dan Webb, *Sales Staff*
▲ EMP: 22
SQ FT: 22,000
SALES (est): 5.2MM **Privately Held**
WEB: www.globalpointusa.com
SIC: 3679 Harness assemblies for elec-
tronic use: wire or cable

(G-4774)
INGLESIDE MACHINE CO INC
1120 Hook Rd (14425-8956)
PHONE..................................585 924-3046
Jan Marie Veomett, *Ch of Bd*
EMP: 80
SQ FT: 40,000
SALES (est): 11.6MM **Privately Held**
WEB: www.inglesidemachine.com
SIC: 7692 3599 Welding repair; machine
shop, jobbing & repair

(G-4775)
MINITEC FRAMING SYSTEMS LLC
5602 County Road 41 (14425-9101)
PHONE..................................585 924-4690
Susan Paeth, *General Mgr*
Jason Cooley, *Foreman/Supr*
Matt Hoad, *Engineer*
Mike Taylor, *Sales Engr*
Andrew Moles,
▲ EMP: 26 EST: 1998
SQ FT: 53,000
SALES: 3.5MM **Privately Held**
SIC: 3354 Aluminum extruded products

(G-4776)
NEXTGEN BUILDING COMPONENTS
6080 Collett Rd (14425-9531)
PHONE..................................585 924-7171
Catherine Morse, *President*
EMP: 35 EST: 2016
SALES (est): 104.8K **Privately Held**
SIC: 3441 Building components, structural
steel

(G-4777)
ROCHESTER ASPHALT MATERIALS
5929 Loomis Rd (14425-9526)
PHONE..................................585 924-7360
Daniel Coe, *Branch Mgr*
EMP: 60
SALES (corp-wide): 30.6B **Privately Held**
SIC: 3273 Ready-mixed concrete
HQ: Rochester Asphalt Materials Inc
1150 Penfield Rd
Rochester NY 14625
585 381-7010

(G-4778)
ROCHESTER LUMBER COMPANY
Also Called: Trusses & Trim Division
6080 Collett Rd (14425-9531)
PHONE..................................585 924-7171
Paul Rickner, *Branch Mgr*
EMP: 30
SALES (corp-wide): 9.6MM **Privately Held**
SIC: 2439 2431 3442 Trusses, wooden
roof; doors, wood; staircases & stairs,
wood; metal doors, sash & trim
PA: Rochester Lumber Company
2040 East Ave
Rochester NY 14610
585 473-8080

(G-4779)
TCS ELECTRONICS INC
1124 Corporate Dr (14425-9570)
PHONE..................................585 337-4301
Jim Harris, *General Mgr*
Renee Strong, *Manager*
EMP: 27

SALES (est): 6MM **Privately Held**
SIC: 3672 3679 Circuit boards, television
& radio printed; harness assemblies for
electronic use: wire or cable

(G-4780)
VR FOOD EQUIPMENT INC
5801 County Road 41 (14425-9103)
P.O. Box 25428 (14425-0428)
PHONE..................................315 531-8133
Steven A Von Rhedey, *Ch of Bd*
Isaac Von Rhedey, *Vice Pres*
Steven P Von Rhedey, *Vice Pres*
Peter Von Rhedey, *CFO*
▲ EMP: 10
SQ FT: 15,000
SALES (est): 2.5MM **Privately Held**
WEB: www.vrfoodequipment.com
SIC: 3556 5084 Food products machinery;
food industry machinery

Farmingville
Suffolk County

(G-4781)
BUD BARGER ASSOC INC
Also Called: Carduner Sales Company
3 Mount Mckinley Ave (11738-2107)
PHONE..................................631 696-6703
Bud Barger, *President*
EMP: 5
SALES (est): 602K **Privately Held**
SIC: 3679 Electronic components

(G-4782)
MIND DESIGNS INC (PA)
5 Gregory Ct (11738-4202)
PHONE..................................631 563-3644
Anibal Rodriguez, *President*
Dorothea Rodriguez, *CFO*
Joshua Rodriguez, *Officer*
EMP: 8
SQ FT: 8,800
SALES (est): 1.5MM **Privately Held**
WEB: www.mindglow.com
SIC: 2431 5211 Planing mill, millwork;
cabinets, kitchen

Fayetteville
Onondaga County

(G-4783)
DATA KEY COMMUNICATION LLC
7573 Hunt Ln (13066-2560)
PHONE..................................315 445-2347
Judy Flannagan, *Mng Member*
Carole Jesiolowski, *Manager*
EMP: 15
SALES (est): 1.4MM **Privately Held**
WEB: www.datakeyllc.com
SIC: 2721 7375 7371 Magazines: pub-
lishing only, not printed on site; informa-
tion retrieval services; custom computer
programming services

(G-4784)
JENLOR LTD
523 E Genesee St (13066-1536)
P.O. Box 495 (13066-0495)
PHONE..................................315 637-9080
Joseph Ophir, *President*
▲ EMP: 10
SQ FT: 5,000
SALES (est): 1.4MM **Privately Held**
WEB: www.jenlor-samatic.com
SIC: 3679 Electronic circuits

(G-4785)
P B & H MOULDING CORPORATION
7121 Woodchuck Hill Rd (13066-9714)
PHONE..................................315 455-1756
Timothy Orcutt, *President*
Douglas Hatch, *Vice Pres*
Jo Dean Hall Orcutt, *Vice Pres*
EMP: 22
SQ FT: 33,000

SALES (est): 2.6MM **Privately Held**
WEB: www.pbhmoulding.com
SIC: 2499 Picture frame molding, finished

Felts Mills
Jefferson County

(G-4786)
CRANESVILLE BLOCK CO INC
Also Called: Drum Ready-Mix
23903 Cemetery Rd (13638-3113)
P.O. Box 210 (13638-0210)
PHONE..................................315 773-2296
Robert Vancoughnett, *Manager*
EMP: 35
SALES (corp-wide): 45MM **Privately Held**
SIC: 3271 3273 Blocks, concrete or cin-
der: standard; ready-mixed concrete
PA: Cranesville Block Co., Inc.
1250 Riverfront Ctr
Amsterdam NY 12010
518 684-6154

Ferndale
Sullivan County

(G-4787)
CHIPITA AMERICA INC
Also Called: Mamma Says
1243 Old Route 17 (12734-5422)
PHONE..................................845 292-2540
Ed McDermott, *Manager*
EMP: 50
SALES (corp-wide): 355.8K **Privately Held**
SIC: 2052 Cookies
HQ: Chipita America, Inc.
1 Westbrook Corporate Ctr
Westchester IL 60154
708 731-2434

(G-4788)
DC FABRICATION & WELDING INC
17 Radcliff Rd (12734-5300)
PHONE..................................845 295-0215
Dan Coutermash, *President*
Bill Fredrick, *Treasurer*
EMP: 6
SQ FT: 8,000
SALES: 600K **Privately Held**
SIC: 7692 Welding repair

(G-4789)
GETEC INC
624 Harris Rd (12734-5135)
P.O. Box 583 (12734-0583)
PHONE..................................845 292-0800
Jean Bader, *President*
Hans Bader Jr, *Vice Pres*
Christa Bader, *Project Engr*
▲ EMP: 15
SQ FT: 10,000
SALES: 3.1MM **Privately Held**
WEB: www.getec.com
SIC: 3621 Generators & sets, electric

(G-4790)
HUDSON VALLEY FOIE GRAS LLC
80 Brooks Rd (12734-5101)
PHONE..................................845 292-2500
Michael Ginor,
EMP: 12 EST: 2008
SALES (est): 2.2MM **Privately Held**
SIC: 2015 Ducks, processed; ducks,
processed: canned; ducks, processed:
fresh; ducks, processed: frozen

Feura Bush
Albany County

(G-4791)
MESSER LLC
76 W Yard Rd (12067-9739)
PHONE..................................518 439-8187
Paul L Giudice, *Project Mgr*

John Cox, *Branch Mgr*
Miguel Lamar, *Technical Staff*
EMP: 55
SALES (corp-wide): 1.4B **Privately Held**
SIC: 2813 Nitrogen; oxygen, compressed or liquefied
HQ: Messer Llc
　　200 Somerset Corp Blvd # 7000
　　Bridgewater NJ 08807
　　908 464-8100

(G-4792)
OWENS CORNING SALES LLC
1277 Feura Bush Rd (12067-1719)
P.O. Box 98, Delmar (12054-0098)
PHONE......................518 475-3600
Craig Burroughs, *Branch Mgr*
EMP: 465
SQ FT: 1,860 **Publicly Held**
WEB: www.owenscorning.com
SIC: 3229 3296 Pressed & blown glass; mineral wool
HQ: Owens Corning Sales, Llc
　　1 Owens Corning Pkwy
　　Toledo OH 43659
　　419 248-8000

Fillmore
Allegany County

(G-4793)
CUBA SPECIALTY MFG CO INC
Also Called: Tackle Factory
81 S Genesee St (14735-8700)
P.O. Box 195 (14735-0195)
PHONE......................585 567-4176
Dana R Pickup, *President*
Stephen Fentz, *President*
Edward Fox, *President*
Michelle Popovice, *Controller*
▲ **EMP:** 10 **EST:** 1931
SQ FT: 23,000
SALES (est): 1.6MM **Privately Held**
SIC: 3496 Traps, animal & fish

(G-4794)
PRIMESOUTH INC
11537 Route 19 (14735)
PHONE......................585 567-4191
John Kingston, *Manager*
EMP: 10 **EST:** 1991
SALES (est): 740K **Privately Held**
SIC: 3825 Electrical power measuring equipment

Findley Lake
Chautauqua County

(G-4795)
OUR OWN CANDLE COMPANY INC (PA)
10349 Main St (14736-9722)
P.O. Box 99 (14736-0099)
PHONE......................716 769-5000
Lawrence S Gross, *President*
Kurt M Duska, *Vice Pres*
◆ **EMP:** 12
SALES (est): 2MM **Privately Held**
SIC: 3999 Shades, lamp or candle; candles

Fishers
Ontario County

(G-4796)
GORBEL INC (PA)
600 Fishers Run (14453)
P.O. Box 593 (14453-0593)
PHONE......................585 924-6262
David Reh, *CEO*
Brian D Reh, *Ch of Bd*
Betty Dolce, *General Mgr*
David Butwid, *Vice Pres*
Todd Ferguson, *Foreman/Supr*
▲ **EMP:** 130 **EST:** 1977
SQ FT: 64,000

SALES (est): 75.2MM **Privately Held**
WEB: www.gorbel.com
SIC: 3536 Cranes, industrial plant

Fishkill
Dutchess County

(G-4797)
ACADIA STAIRS
73 Route 9 Ste 3 (12524-2944)
PHONE......................845 765-8600
Michelle Cioffredi, *President*
▲ **EMP:** 8
SALES (est): 1.3MM **Privately Held**
SIC: 3441 Fabricated structural metal

(G-4798)
CRANESVILLE BLOCK CO INC
70 Route 9 (12524-2962)
PHONE......................845 896-5687
John Tesrro, *CEO*
EMP: 20
SQ FT: 3,960
SALES (corp-wide): 45MM **Privately Held**
PA: Cranesville Block Co., Inc.
　　1250 Riverfront Ctr
　　Amsterdam NY 12010
　　518 684-6154

(G-4799)
ENTERPRISE BAGELS INC
Also Called: Bagel Shoppe, The
986 Main St Ste 3 (12524-3508)
PHONE......................845 896-3823
Joe Raffele, *CEO*
EMP: 12
SALES (est): 1.4MM **Privately Held**
SIC: 2051 Bagels, fresh or frozen

(G-4800)
FAMILY HEARING CENTER
18 Westage Dr Ste 16 (12524-2289)
PHONE......................845 897-3059
Lori Biasotti, *Owner*
EMP: 5
SALES (est): 440.6K **Privately Held**
SIC: 3842 8049 Hearing aids; audiologist

(G-4801)
MONTFORT BROTHERS INC
44 Elm St (12524-1804)
PHONE......................845 896-6694
Jacqueline Montfort, *President*
Bob Armstrong, *General Mgr*
Karen Piga, *Executive Asst*
EMP: 30
SQ FT: 15,000
SALES (est): 6.4MM **Privately Held**
WEB: www.montfortgroup.com
SIC: 3271 Blocks, concrete or cinder: standard

(G-4802)
N SKETCH BUILD INC
982 Main St Ste 4-130 (12524-3506)
PHONE......................800 975-0597
Jacqueline Ellison, *Ch of Bd*
Jacqueline Jolly, *Director*
◆ **EMP:** 9
SALES (est): 934.3K **Privately Held**
SIC: 2499 Decorative wood & woodwork

(G-4803)
NERAK SYSTEMS INC
4 Stage Door Rd (12524-2423)
PHONE......................914 763-8259
Volker Brandt, *President*
Peter Pralle, *Vice Pres*
Simone Wakefield, *CFO*
▲ **EMP:** 15
SQ FT: 100,000
SALES (est): 4.4MM
SALES (corp-wide): 96.1K **Privately Held**
WEB: www.nerak-systems.com
SIC: 3535 5084 Conveyors & conveying equipment; materials handling machinery
HQ: Nerak Gmbh Fordertechnik
　　Brigitta 5
　　Hambühren 29313
　　508 494-40

(G-4804)
SUBURBAN PUBLISHING INC (PA)
Also Called: Hudson Valley Magazine
1 Summit Ct Ste 200a (12524-1370)
PHONE......................845 463-0542
Dan Burnside, *Publisher*
Angelo Martinello, *Chairman*
Robert Martinella, *Vice Pres*
Robert Martinelli, *Vice Pres*
EMP: 12
SQ FT: 3,000
SALES (est): 1.1MM **Privately Held**
WEB: www.hudsonvalleymagazine.com
SIC: 2721 Magazines: publishing only, not printed on site

Floral Park
Nassau County

(G-4805)
ALLIANCE SERVICES CORP
23 Van Siclen Ave (11001-2012)
PHONE......................516 775-7600
Frank De Oliveira, *President*
Peter Smith, *General Mgr*
Victor De Oliveira, *Vice Pres*
EMP: 14
SQ FT: 18,000
SALES: 1.6MM **Privately Held**
WEB: www.alliancewelding.com
SIC: 7692 Welding repair

(G-4806)
ALLIANCE WELDING & STEEL FABG
15 Van Siclen Ave (11001-2012)
PHONE......................516 775-7600
Victor De Oliveira, *President*
Frank De Oliveira, *Corp Secy*
EMP: 18
SQ FT: 18,000
SALES (est): 2.4MM **Privately Held**
SIC: 3444 7692 Sheet metalwork; welding repair

(G-4807)
ALLOMATIC PRODUCTS COMPANY
Also Called: Sales Department
102 Jericho Tpke Ste 104 (11001-2035)
PHONE......................516 775-0330
Bob Clark, *Vice Pres*
Bob Tichy, *Marketing Mgr*
Israel Tabaksblat, *Marketing Staff*
John Butz, *Manager*
EMP: 5 **Privately Held**
WEB: www.allomatic.com
SIC: 3714 Motor vehicle parts & accessories
HQ: Allomatic Products Company Inc
　　609 E Chaney St
　　Sullivan IN 47882
　　800 686-4729

(G-4808)
AUTOMATED BLDG MGT SYSTEMS INC (PA)
Also Called: Honeywell Authorized Dealer
54 Cherry Ln (11001-1611)
PHONE......................516 216-5603
Alkesh Amin, *President*
EMP: 40
SQ FT: 2,000
SALES: 27.5MM **Privately Held**
WEB: www.abmsys.com
SIC: 3822 Temperature controls, automatic

(G-4809)
BARCLAY TAGG RACING
86 Geranium Ave (11001-3035)
PHONE......................631 404-8269
Barclay Tagg, *Owner*
EMP: 30
SALES (est): 1.1MM **Privately Held**
SIC: 3721 Aircraft

(G-4810)
C & A SERVICE INC (PA)
Also Called: Citrus and Allied Essences
65 S Tyson Ave (11001-1821)
PHONE......................516 354-1200

Richard Pisano Jr, *President*
◆ **EMP:** 5
SALES (est): 1.1MM **Privately Held**
SIC: 2899 2911 Chemical preparations; aromatic chemical products

(G-4811)
CB PUBLISHING LLC
Also Called: CB Products
50 Carnation Ave Bldg 2-1 (11001-1741)
P.O. Box 280, New Hyde Park (11040-0280)
PHONE......................516 354-4888
Clifford Brechner, *President*
EMP: 7
SQ FT: 1,400
SALES (est): 577.4K **Privately Held**
WEB: www.cbproducts.com
SIC: 2731 Books: publishing only

(G-4812)
CITRUS AND ALLIED ESSENCES LTD (PA)
Also Called: C&A Aromatics
65 S Tyson Ave (11001-1898)
PHONE......................516 354-1200
Stephen Pisano, *CEO*
Richard C Pisano Jr, *CEO*
Grace Alloca, *Principal*
Arthur Curran, *Principal*
Ann E Heller, *Principal*
◆ **EMP:** 29
SQ FT: 11,000
SALES (est): 24MM **Privately Held**
WEB: www.citrusandallied.com
SIC: 2087 2899 2911 Flavoring extracts & syrups; chemical preparations; aromatic chemical products

(G-4813)
CREATRON SERVICES INC
Also Called: Lanel
504 Cherry Ln (11001-1646)
PHONE......................516 437-5119
Isidore Epstein, *President*
Alan Rosen, *Vice Pres*
EMP: 20 **EST:** 1965
SQ FT: 10,000
SALES (est): 1.4MM **Privately Held**
SIC: 3861 Photographic equipment & supplies

(G-4814)
DECREE SIGNS & GRAPHICS INC
Also Called: Manhattan Signs
91 Tulip Ave Apt Kd1 (11001-1983)
PHONE......................973 278-3603
Anthony Decrescenzo, *President*
EMP: 15
SALES (est): 1.7MM **Privately Held**
SIC: 3993 Signs, not made in custom sign painting shops

(G-4815)
EASTERN UNIT EXCH RMNFACTURING
186 Beech St (11001-3318)
P.O. Box 180346, Richmond Hill (11418-0346)
PHONE......................718 739-7113
Chester Brown, *President*
Mehendra Sarwan, *Manager*
EMP: 15 **EST:** 1976
SQ FT: 5,000
SALES (est): 1.8MM **Privately Held**
SIC: 3694 Alternators, automotive; generators, automotive & aircraft; motors, starting: automotive & aircraft

(G-4816)
P T E INC
36 Ontario Rd (11001-4113)
PHONE......................516 775-3839
Gustave Loos, *President*
EMP: 19 **EST:** 1957
SQ FT: 10,125
SALES (est): 1.8MM **Privately Held**
SIC: 3599 Machine shop, jobbing & repair

(G-4817)
TWO BILLS MACHINE & TOOL CO
17 Concord St (11001-2819)
PHONE......................516 437-2585

▲ = Import ▼=Export
◆ =Import/Export

Wilhelm Sangen, *President*
Frederick Sangen, *Vice Pres*
EMP: 11
SQ FT: 7,000
SALES (est): 1.3MM **Privately Held**
SIC: 3599 Machine shop, jobbing & repair

(G-4818)
WETPAINTCOM INC
Also Called: Wet Paint
9523 242nd St (11001-3906)
PHONE..................................206 859-6300
Ben Elowitz, *CEO*
Bert Hogue, *CFO*
EMP: 38
SALES (est): 2.7MM
SALES (corp-wide): 4.5MM **Publicly Held**
WEB: www.wetpaint.com
SIC: 7372 7371 Prepackaged software;
custom computer programming services
PA: X Function Inc
45 W 89th St Apt 4a
New York NY 10024
212 231-0092

Floral Park
Queens County

(G-4819)
INDIRA FOODS INC
25503 Hillside Ave # 255 (11004)
PHONE..................................718 343-1500
Indira Mathur, *President*
EMP: 10
SALES (est): 820K **Privately Held**
SIC: 2032 Italian foods: packaged in cans,
jars, etc.

(G-4820)
S & J TRADING INC
8030 263rd St (11004-1517)
P.O. Box 40337, Glen Oaks (11004-0337)
PHONE..................................718 347-1323
Surinder Chawla, *President*
▲ **EMP:** 8
SALES: 800K **Privately Held**
SIC: 3299 5063 5033 Mica products;
electrical apparatus & equipment; roofing,
siding & insulation

Florida
Orange County

(G-4821)
BRACH KNITTING MILLS INC
12 Roosevelt Ave (10921-1808)
P.O. Box 13 (10921-0013)
PHONE..................................845 651-4450
Shea Brach, *President*
EMP: 15 **EST:** 1965
SQ FT: 32,000
SALES: 500K **Privately Held**
SIC: 2251 2331 Panty hose; tights,
women's; shirts, women's & juniors':
made from purchased materials

(G-4822)
**CONVERGENT CNNCTIVITY
TECH INC**
1751 State Route 17a (10921-1061)
P.O. Box 454 (10921-0454)
PHONE..................................845 651-5250
Joseph T Moore, *Ch of Bd*
▲ **EMP:** 5
SALES (est): 789.9K **Privately Held**
SIC: 3357 Nonferrous wiredrawing & insu-
lating

(G-4823)
**EMPIRE VENTILATION EQP CO
INC (PA)**
9 Industrial Dr (10921-1000)
PHONE..................................718 728-2143
George R Taylor, *President*
Linda L Taylor, *Vice Pres*
Robert Warnken, *CFO*
Robert E Warnken, *Treasurer*
Brian G Taylor, *Admin Sec*
EMP: 12 **EST:** 1936
SQ FT: 15,000

SALES: 1.5MM **Privately Held**
WEB: www.empirevent.com
SIC: 3444 Ventilators, sheet metal

(G-4824)
H&F PRODUCTS INC
12 Roosevelt Ave (10921-1808)
P.O. Box 71 (10921-0071)
PHONE..................................845 651-6100
Rivkah Brach, *Ch of Bd*
Herman Brach, *President*
Joe Brach, *CFO*
EMP: 30
SQ FT: 15,000
SALES: 1.5MM **Privately Held**
SIC: 2099 Food preparations

(G-4825)
ISLAND NAMEPLATE INC
124 S Main St (10921-1818)
P.O. Box 548 (10921-0548)
PHONE..................................845 651-4005
Joseph C Sicina III, *President*
EMP: 5
SQ FT: 1,860
SALES: 260K **Privately Held**
SIC: 3993 Name plates: except engraved,
etched, etc.: metal

(G-4826)
REMEE PRODUCTS CORP (PA)
Also Called: Remfo
1751 State Route 17a (10921-1061)
PHONE..................................845 651-4431
Elias Muhlrad, *President*
Steve N Luciana, *President*
Eric Muhlrad, *COO*
Bill Cullen, *Vice Pres*
Glenn La Perle, *VP Opers*
◆ **EMP:** 95
SQ FT: 125,000
SALES (est): 30.9MM **Privately Held**
SIC: 3357 Nonferrous wiredrawing & insu-
lating

(G-4827)
ZIRCAR CERAMICS INC (PA)
100 N Main St Ste 2 (10921-1329)
P.O. Box 519 (10921-0519)
PHONE..................................845 651-6600
Phil Hamling, *President*
David Hamling, *Vice Pres*
Jay Magnelli, *Prdtn Mgr*
▲ **EMP:** 34
SQ FT: 30,000
SALES (est): 7.2MM **Privately Held**
WEB: www.zircarceramics.com
SIC: 3297 Nonclay refractories

(G-4828)
ZIRCAR REFR COMPOSITES INC
14 Golden Hill Ter (10921-1116)
PHONE..................................845 651-2200
Julie Sterns, *Branch Mgr*
EMP: 12 **Privately Held**
WEB: www.zrci.com
SIC: 2493 Reconstituted wood products
PA: Zircar Refractory Composites, Inc.
46 Jayne St
Florida NY 10921

(G-4829)
**ZIRCAR REFR COMPOSITES INC
(PA)**
46 Jayne St (10921-1109)
P.O. Box 489 (10921-0489)
PHONE..................................845 651-4481
Tom Hamling, *Ch of Bd*
Peter Hamling, *President*
▲ **EMP:** 8
SQ FT: 4,000
SALES (est): 3.3MM **Privately Held**
WEB: www.zrci.com
SIC: 3297 Nonclay refractories

(G-4830)
ZIRCAR ZIRCONIA INC
87 Meadow Rd (10921-1112)
P.O. Box 287 (10921-0287)
PHONE..................................845 651-3040
Craig Hamling, *President*
Clare Hamling, *Vice Pres*
Kyra Hamling, *Buyer*
David Hoskins, *Sales Staff*
▲ **EMP:** 24
SQ FT: 20,800

SALES (est): 3.8MM **Privately Held**
WEB: www.zircarzirconia.com
SIC: 3297 Nonclay refractories

Flushing
Queens County

(G-4831)
5 STARS PRINTING CORP
13330 32nd Ave (11354-1921)
PHONE..................................718 461-4612
S K Han, *President*
EMP: 10
SALES (est): 894.5K **Privately Held**
WEB: www.bocasoccer.com
SIC: 2759 Commercial printing

(G-4832)
AB SEAFOOD TRADING INC
3129 Higgins St (11354-2503)
PHONE..................................718 353-8848
Dian Yan Lin, *CEO*
EMP: 5
SALES (est): 274.7K **Privately Held**
SIC: 2092 Fresh or frozen packaged fish

(G-4833)
**ACCREDO HEALTH
INCORPORATED**
14330 38th Ave Apt 1f (11354-5720)
PHONE..................................718 353-3012
Nakia Jefferson, *Branch Mgr*
EMP: 5
SALES (corp-wide): 141.6B **Publicly
Held**
SIC: 2833 Medicinals & botanicals
HQ: Accredo Health, Incorporated
1640 Century Center Pkwy # 110
Memphis TN 38134

(G-4834)
**ACE PRINTING & PUBLISHING
INC**
Also Called: Ace Printing Co
14951 Roosevelt Ave (11354-4939)
PHONE..................................718 939-0040
Sung N Kang, *CEO*
EMP: 10
SQ FT: 3,000
SALES (est): 800K **Privately Held**
SIC: 2752 Offset & photolithographic print-
ing

(G-4835)
AIR EXPORT MECHANICAL
4108 Parsons Blvd Apt 4r (11355-1940)
PHONE..................................917 709-5310
Gricelio Nosquera, *President*
EMP: 5
SALES (est): 480K **Privately Held**
SIC: 3564 Filters, air: furnaces, air condi-
tioning equipment, etc.

(G-4836)
ALBERT SIY
Also Called: Avant Garde Screen Printing Co
13508 Booth Memorial Ave (11355-5009)
PHONE..................................718 359-0389
Albert Siy, *Owner*
EMP: 8
SALES (est): 1MM **Privately Held**
SIC: 2752 2759 2396 Commercial print-
ing, lithographic; screen printing; automo-
tive & apparel trimmings

(G-4837)
ALL ABOUT ART INC
4128 Murray St (11355-1055)
PHONE..................................718 321-0755
Gee Book Jeung, *President*
EMP: 11
SALES (est): 900K **Privately Held**
WEB: www.myallaboutart.com
SIC: 2395 2261 Embroidery products, ex-
cept schiffli machine; finishing plants, cot-
ton

(G-4838)
**AMERICAN AUTO ACC
INCRPORATION (PA)**
3506 Leavitt St Apt Clc (11354-2967)
PHONE..................................718 886-6600

Henry Hsu, *President*
Betty L Hsu, *Vice Pres*
EMP: 20
SQ FT: 50,000
SALES (est): 1.5MM **Privately Held**
WEB: www.3aracing.com
SIC: 3714 5013 Motor vehicle parts & ac-
cessories; motor vehicle supplies & new
parts

(G-4839)
**AMERICAN STD SHTMTL SUP
CORP**
13324 36th Rd (11354-4413)
PHONE..................................718 888-9350
Dezhao Zhao, *Principal*
EMP: 10
SALES (est): 955K **Privately Held**
SIC: 3444 3334 1711 Sheet metalwork;
primary aluminum; ventilation & duct work
contractor

(G-4840)
**ARRINGEMENT INTERNATIONAL
INC**
16015 45th Ave (11358-3135)
PHONE..................................347 323-7974
WEI Huang, *President*
EMP: 6 **EST:** 2013
SQ FT: 1,500
SALES (est): 200K **Privately Held**
SIC: 3911 Jewelry, precious metal

(G-4841)
BEST CONCRETE MIX CORP
3510 College Point Blvd (11354-2719)
PHONE..................................718 463-5500
Michael Emanuele, *President*
EMP: 35
SQ FT: 20,000
SALES (est): 6.2MM **Privately Held**
SIC: 3273 Ready-mixed concrete

(G-4842)
CHINESE MEDICAL REPORT INC
3907 Prince St Ste 5b (11354-5308)
PHONE..................................718 359-5676
Ava Lee, *President*
▲ **EMP:** 5
SALES (est): 250.9K **Privately Held**
WEB: www.chinesemedical.com
SIC: 2711 Newspapers

(G-4843)
CHRISTIAN PRESS INC
14317 Franklin Ave (11355-2116)
PHONE..................................718 886-4400
Young-Choon Chang, *President*
EMP: 5
SQ FT: 1,200
SALES: 250K **Privately Held**
SIC: 2711 8661 Newspapers, publishing &
printing; miscellaneous denomination
church

(G-4844)
CITIC INTL (USA) TRAVEL INC
13633 37th Ave Ste 2a (11354-4562)
PHONE..................................718 888-9577
Fuxing Chong, *President*
EMP: 6
SALES: 400K **Privately Held**
SIC: 7372 4724 Application computer soft-
ware; travel agencies

(G-4845)
COFIRE PAVING CORPORATION
12030 28th Ave (11354-1049)
PHONE..................................718 463-1403
Ross J Holland, *President*
John D Ficarelli, *Treasurer*
Robert Ficarelli, *Admin Sec*
EMP: 30 **EST:** 1946
SQ FT: 29,000
SALES (est): 4.6MM **Privately Held**
SIC: 2951 1611 Asphalt paving mixtures &
blocks; surfacing & paving

(G-4846)
**COURTLANDT BOOT JACK CO
INC**
3334 Prince St (11354-2731)
PHONE..................................718 445-6200
John K Parlante Jr, *President*
▲ **EMP:** 35 **EST:** 1940

SQ FT: 30,000
SALES (est): 4.3MM **Privately Held**
SIC: 3199 2387 Holsters, leather; apparel belts

(G-4847)
DELICIAS ANDINAS FOOD CORP
5750 Maspeth Ave (11378-2212)
PHONE................................718 416-2922
Manuel Midonda, *President*
Juanita Midonda, *Vice Pres*
EMP: 32
SALES (est): 5.5MM **Privately Held**
SIC: 2051 Bakery: wholesale or whole-sale/retail combined

(G-4848)
DIGITAL ONE USA INC
Also Called: Akhon Samoy Weekly
7230 Roosevelt Ave (11372-6335)
PHONE................................718 396-4890
Kazi S Hoque, *President*
EMP: 15
SALES (est): 809.1K **Privately Held**
SIC: 2711 Newspapers

(G-4849)
EASY ANALYTIC SOFTWARE INC (PA)
Also Called: Easi
7359 196th St (11366-1810)
PHONE................................718 740-7930
Robert Katz, *President*
Greg Gergen, *Vice Pres*
Edward Sussman, *Vice Pres*
Ed Sussman, *Officer*
EMP: 9
SALES (est): 849.7K **Privately Held**
WEB: www.easidemographics.com
SIC: 7372 Prepackaged software

(G-4850)
EXCELSIOR MLT-CLTURAL INST INC
13340 Roosevelt Ave 7g (11354-5221)
P.O. Box 14332, Augusta GA (30919-0332)
PHONE................................706 627-4285
Rhonda Jackson, *CEO*
Ronald Nurse, *Director*
EMP: 14
SALES (est): 822.5K **Privately Held**
SIC: 3812 Cabin environment indicators

(G-4851)
FERRARA BROS LLC (HQ)
12005 31st Ave (11354-2516)
PHONE................................718 939-3030
William J Sandbrook, *President*
EMP: 20 EST: 1969
SQ FT: 16,000
SALES (est): 12.1MM
SALES (corp-wide): 1.5B **Publicly Held**
WEB: www.ferraraconcrete.com
SIC: 3273 5211 5033 Ready-mixed con-crete; masonry materials & supplies; roof-ing, siding & insulation
PA: U.S. Concrete, Inc.
331 N Main St
Euless TX 76039
817 835-4105

(G-4852)
FIBER USA CORP
13620 38th Ave Ste 11f (11354-4232)
PHONE................................718 888-1512
Pengyu Zhu, *President*
EMP: 8
SQ FT: 3,000
SALES (est): 1.8MM
SALES (corp-wide): 22.6MM **Privately Held**
SIC: 2653 5093 Corrugated & solid fiber boxes; plastics scrap
PA: Jiangyin Mighty Chemical Fiber Co., Ltd.
No.131, Dudian Village, Hongxing Vil-lage, Xuxiake Town
Jiangyin 21440
510 869-2183

(G-4853)
FLUSHING IRON WELD INC
13125 Maple Ave (11355-4224)
PHONE................................718 359-2208
Dario Toro, *President*
Hector Munoz, *Vice Pres*

Paula Munoz, *Manager*
EMP: 20
SQ FT: 5,000
SALES: 2.5MM **Privately Held**
SIC: 3446 Architectural metalwork

(G-4854)
GLOBAL GRAPHICS INC
Also Called: Wen Hwa Printing
3711 Prince St Ste D (11354-4428)
PHONE................................718 939-4967
Rong Fang, *President*
Chen Wang, *Manager*
EMP: 10
SALES: 500K **Privately Held**
SIC: 2752 Commercial printing, litho-graphic

(G-4855)
GROUP INTERNATIONAL LLC
14711 34th Ave (11354-3755)
PHONE................................718 475-8805
John Liriano, *CEO*
EMP: 5
SALES (est): 169.2K **Privately Held**
SIC: 2043 Infants' foods, cereal type

(G-4856)
H H B BAKERY OF LITTLE NECK
Also Called: Richer's Bakery
24914 Horace Harding Expy (11362-2050)
PHONE................................718 631-7004
Eugene Stanko, *President*
EMP: 5
SALES (est): 230K **Privately Held**
SIC: 2051 Bakery: wholesale or whole-sale/retail combined

(G-4857)
H&L COMPUTERS INC
13523 Northern Blvd (11354-4006)
PHONE................................516 873-8088
Bothen Lin, *President*
EMP: 20
SQ FT: 5,000
SALES (est): 1.6MM **Privately Held**
SIC: 3571 Electronic computers

(G-4858)
HAIR COLOR RESEARCH GROUP INC
13320 Whitestone Expy (11354-2509)
PHONE................................718 445-6026
Armando Petruccelli, *President*
EMP: 26
SALES (est): 2.5MM **Privately Held**
SIC: 3999 Hair & hair-based products

(G-4859)
HISUN OPTOELECTRONICS CO LTD
Also Called: Hisun Led
4109 College Point Blvd (11355-4226)
PHONE................................718 886-6966
Eugene L Yu, *President*
▲ **EMP:** 15
SALES (est): 1.8MM **Privately Held**
SIC: 3674 Light emitting diodes

(G-4860)
HOME IDEAL INC
4528 159th St (11358-3148)
PHONE................................718 762-8998
Henry Chin, *President*
Cheryl Lyn, *Corp Secy*
Winston Lyn, *Vice Pres*
EMP: 7 EST: 1980
SALES: 300K **Privately Held**
SIC: 2434 5712 1751 2541 Wood kitchen cabinets; cabinets, except custom made: kitchen; cabinet building & installation; wood partitions & fixtures

(G-4861)
INTER PACIFIC CONSULTING CORP
Also Called: Ipcc
14055 34th Ave Apt 3n (11354-3038)
PHONE................................718 460-2787
John Tsao, *President*
▲ **EMP:** 5
SALES: 1MM **Privately Held**
SIC: 3499 5023 Picture frames, metal; frames & framing, picture & mirror

(G-4862)
INTERCULTURAL ALLIANCE ARTISTS
Also Called: Iaas , The
4510 165th St (11358-3229)
P.O. Box 4378, New York (10163-4378)
PHONE................................917 406-1202
Gabrielle David, *President*
Stephanie Agosto, *Vice Pres*
Michelle Aragon, *Vice Pres*
Joan Edmonds Ashman, *Vice Pres*
Naydene Brickus, *Vice Pres*
EMP: 5
SALES: 11.8K **Privately Held**
SIC: 2721 Magazines: publishing & printing

(G-4863)
INTREPID CONTROL SERVICE INC
2904 Francis Lewis Blvd (11358-1536)
PHONE................................718 886-8771
William Varrone, *President*
James Colleran, *Corp Secy*
Andrew Manesis, *Vice Pres*
Dean Pecoraro, *Vice Pres*
EMP: 5
SQ FT: 750
SALES (est): 961.1K **Privately Held**
SIC: 3822 Temperature controls, automatic

(G-4864)
J D STEWARD INC
4537 162nd St (11358-3157)
PHONE................................718 358-0169
Dominick Savino, *President*
Jean Stephens, *Vice Pres*
Joseph Savino, *Treasurer*
EMP: 5
SALES (est): 900K **Privately Held**
WEB: www.jdsteward.com
SIC: 3498 Fabricated pipe & fittings

(G-4865)
JOHN A VASSILAROS & SON INC
Also Called: Vassilaros Coffee
2905 120th St (11354-2505)
PHONE................................718 886-4140
John Vassilaros, *President*
Irene Vassilaros, *Vice Pres*
George Kasselakis, *Sales Executive*
EMP: 42
SQ FT: 25,000
SALES (est): 11MM **Privately Held**
WEB: www.vassilaroscoffee.com
SIC: 2095 Coffee roasting (except by wholesale grocers)

(G-4866)
KALEL PARTNERS LLC
7012 170th St Ste 101 (11365-3332)
PHONE................................347 561-7804
Todd Friedman, *CEO*
EMP: 15
SALES (est): 474K **Privately Held**
SIC: 2741 Miscellaneous publishing

(G-4867)
KEPCO INC
13140 Maple Ave (11355-4225)
PHONE................................718 461-7000
Martin Kupferberg, *President*
EMP: 90
SALES (corp-wide): 77.5MM **Privately Held**
SIC: 3612 Power & distribution transform-ers
PA: Kepco, Inc.
13138 Sanford Ave
Flushing NY 11355
718 461-7000

(G-4868)
KOREA TIMES NEW YORK INC
15408 Nthrn Blvd Ste 2b (11354)
PHONE................................718 961-7979
Jae Chang, *President*
EMP: 7
SALES (corp-wide): 85.3MM **Privately Held**
SIC: 2711 Newspapers: publishing only, not printed on site

HQ: The Korea Times New York Inc
3710 Skillman Ave
Long Island City NY 11101
718 784-4526

(G-4869)
KOREAN YELLOW PAGES
14809 Northern Blvd (11354-4346)
PHONE................................718 461-0073
Gwanseo Pak, *Owner*
▲ **EMP:** 10
SALES: 300K **Privately Held**
SIC: 2741 Telephone & other directory publishing

(G-4870)
LEVI STRAUSS & CO
13432 Blossom Ave (11355-4639)
PHONE................................917 213-6263
Chip Bergh, *Branch Mgr*
EMP: 19
SALES (corp-wide): 5.5B **Publicly Held**
SIC: 2325 Jeans: men's, youths' & boys'
PA: Levi Strauss & Co.
1155 Battery St
San Francisco CA 94111
415 501-6000

(G-4871)
LIFE WATCH TECHNOLOGY INC
Also Called: My Life My Health
42-10 Polen St Ste 412 (11355)
PHONE................................917 669-2428
Jiping Zhu, *CEO*
EMP: 56
SQ FT: 1,200
SALES (est): 2MM **Privately Held**
SIC: 3873 Watches & parts, except crys-tals & jewels

(G-4872)
LONG ISLAND PIPE SUPPLY INC
Also Called: LONG ISLAND PIPE SUPPLY OF ALBANY
5858 56th St (11378-3106)
PHONE................................718 456-7877
David Pargon, *Manager*
EMP: 6
SALES (corp-wide): 2.6B **Privately Held**
WEB: www.lipipe.com
SIC: 3498 Fabricated pipe & fittings
HQ: Miles Moss Of Albany, Inc.
586 Commercial Ave
Garden City NY 11530
516 222-8008

(G-4873)
LOOSELEAF LAW PUBLICATIONS INC
4308 162nd St (11358-3131)
P.O. Box 650042, Fresh Meadows (11365-0042)
PHONE................................718 359-5559
Warren Taylor, *President*
Hilary McKeon, *General Mgr*
Michael Loughrey, *Vice Pres*
Tina Macgowan, *Production*
Hilliary McKeon, *Manager*
EMP: 10
SQ FT: 5,000
SALES: 1MM **Privately Held**
WEB: www.looseleaflaw.com
SIC: 2731 5961 Books: publishing only; books, mail order (except book clubs)

(G-4874)
MIKKELLER NYC
12001 Roosevelt Ave (11368-1653)
PHONE................................917 572-0357
James Raras, *Exec VP*
EMP: 5
SALES (est): 224.5K **Privately Held**
SIC: 2082 Malt beverages

(G-4875)
MILESTONE CONSTRUCTION CORP
13620 38th Ave Ste 11j (11354-4232)
PHONE................................718 459-8500
Mike S Lee, *Ch of Bd*
EMP: 6
SALES (est): 487.2K **Privately Held**
SIC: 1442 Construction sand & gravel

(G-4876)
NATURAL LAB INC
13538 39th Ave Ste 4 (11354-4423)
PHONE..................718 321-8848
Michael Chang, *Manager*
▲ EMP: 6
SALES (est): 543.2K **Privately Held**
SIC: 2099 5149 Food preparations; organic & diet foods

(G-4877)
NEW STAR BAKERY
4121a Kissena Blvd (11355-3138)
PHONE..................718 961-8868
Huantang Liang, *Owner*
EMP: 20
SALES (est): 1.2MM **Privately Held**
SIC: 2051 Bread, cake & related products

(G-4878)
NEW YORK IL BO INC
Also Called: Korean New York Daily, The
4522 162nd St Fl 2 (11358-3280)
PHONE..................718 961-1538
Grace Chung, *CEO*
▲ EMP: 15
SALES (est): 120K **Privately Held**
SIC: 2711 Newspapers: publishing only, not printed on site

(G-4879)
NEW YORK TIMES COMPANY
1 New York Times Plz (11354-1200)
PHONE..................718 281-7000
Thomas P Lombardo, *Plant Mgr*
Mike Joyce, *Foreman/Supr*
David Perpich, *Nurse*
EMP: 12
SALES (corp-wide): 1.7B **Publicly Held**
WEB: www.nytco.com
SIC: 2711 Commercial printing & newspaper publishing combined
PA: The New York Times Company
620 8th Ave Bsmt 1
New York NY 10018
212 556-1234

(G-4880)
NORTH AMERICA PASTEL ARTISTS
13303 41st Ave Apt 1a (11355-5840)
PHONE..................718 463-4701
Jason Chang, *President*
EMP: 8
SALES: 3K **Privately Held**
SIC: 3952 Pastels, artists'

(G-4881)
NORTH SHORE NEON SIGN CO INC
4649 54th Ave (11378-1011)
PHONE..................718 937-4848
Nancy Byrnes, *Accountant*
Tom Brown, *Manager*
EMP: 30
SALES (corp-wide): 13.5MM **Privately Held**
WEB: www.northshoreneon.com
SIC: 3993 1799 Electric signs; sign installation & maintenance
PA: North Shore Neon Sign Co. Inc.
295 Skidmore Rd
Deer Park NY 11729
631 667-2500

(G-4882)
P S PIBBS INC
Also Called: Pibbs Industries
13315 32nd Ave (11354-1909)
PHONE..................718 445-8046
Damiano Petruccelli, *CEO*
Biagio Petruccelli, *President*
Sunny Thomas, *President*
Antonio Petruccelli, *Vice Pres*
Nancy Petruccelli, *Purch Agent*
◆ EMP: 100
SQ FT: 30,000
SALES (est): 12MM **Privately Held**
WEB: www.pibbs.com
SIC: 3999 2844 Barber & beauty shop equipment; shampoos, rinses, conditioners: hair; hair preparations, including shampoos; face creams or lotions

(G-4883)
PALADINO PRTG & GRAPHICS INC
20009 32nd Ave (11361-1037)
PHONE..................718 279-6000
Vincent Paladino, *President*
EMP: 9
SQ FT: 1,000
SALES (est): 1.2MM **Privately Held**
SIC: 2752 Commercial printing, lithographic

(G-4884)
PALMBAY LTD
4459 Kissena Blvd Apt 6h (11355-3065)
PHONE..................718 424-3388
Wenchao Tao, *President*
◆ EMP: 6
SQ FT: 20,000
SALES (est): 817.3K **Privately Held**
WEB: www.disposablewear.com
SIC: 2384 2252 Robes & dressing gowns; slipper socks

(G-4885)
PARIS WEDDING CENTER CORP (PA)
42-53 42 55 Main St (11355)
PHONE..................347 368-4085
Yuki Lin, *President*
▲ EMP: 12
SALES (est): 888.6K **Privately Held**
SIC: 2335 Wedding gowns & dresses

(G-4886)
PEACE TIMES WEEKLY INC
14527 33rd Ave (11354-3145)
PHONE..................718 762-6500
Yongil Park, *President*
Joseph Aahn, *President*
▲ EMP: 5
SALES: 346.3K **Privately Held**
SIC: 2711 Newspapers: publishing only, not printed on site

(G-4887)
PERRY PLASTICS INC
3050 Whitestone Expy # 300 (11354-1964)
PHONE..................718 747-5600
Irwing Laub, *President*
Aaron Laub, *Vice Pres*
▼ EMP: 10
SALES (est): 902.3K **Privately Held**
SIC: 2295 Chemically coated & treated fabrics

(G-4888)
PRIME COOK (WTTC) INC (PA)
15038 Jewel Ave (11367-1434)
PHONE..................646 881-0068
Jun Chen, *President*
EMP: 3
SALES (est): 17.8MM **Privately Held**
SIC: 3262 China cookware

(G-4889)
PRIME RESEARCH SOLUTIONS LLC
Also Called: Turkprime
7328 136th St (11367-2827)
PHONE..................917 836-7941
Leonid Litman, *Principal*
Jonathan Robinson, *Principal*
EMP: 11
SALES (est): 155K **Privately Held**
SIC: 7372 8999 Educational computer software; scientific consulting

(G-4890)
S&L AEROSPACE METALS LLC
12012 28th Ave (11354-1049)
PHONE..................718 326-1821
Jerry Wang, *President*
Ted Varvatsas, *Exec VP*
Carlos Quintana, *Vice Pres*
Alan Wang, *Vice Pres*
Angelo Borgia, *Program Mgr*
EMP: 100 EST: 1946
SQ FT: 50,000
SALES (est): 26.3MM **Privately Held**
WEB: www.slaerospace.com
SIC: 3728 Aircraft assemblies, subassemblies & parts

(G-4891)
SANFORD PRINTING INC
13335 41st Rd (11355-3667)
PHONE..................718 461-1202
Paul Peng, *President*
▲ EMP: 5
SALES (est): 696K **Privately Held**
SIC: 2752 Commercial printing, offset

(G-4892)
SHENZHEN XNHDINGSHENG TECH LTD
4112a Main St 2fd09 (11355)
PHONE..................510 506-5753
Suye Guo,
EMP: 20
SALES (est): 504.6K **Privately Held**
SIC: 3999 Manufacturing industries

(G-4893)
SNAPP TOO ENTERPRISE
3312 211th St (11361-1523)
PHONE..................718 224-5252
Edward Porzelt, *Owner*
EMP: 6
SALES (est): 330K **Privately Held**
SIC: 2086 Bottled & canned soft drinks

(G-4894)
SPEEDY ENTERPRISE USA CORP (PA)
4111 162nd St (11358-4124)
PHONE..................718 463-3000
Harolyn Paik, *Principal*
EMP: 6
SALES (est): 502.2K **Privately Held**
SIC: 2752 Commercial printing, offset

(G-4895)
STARK AQUARIUM PRODUCTS CO INC
Also Called: Stark Fish
2914 122nd St (11354-2530)
PHONE..................718 445-5357
Edith Starkman, *President*
Omiros Gioroukos, *Vice Pres*
▲ EMP: 21 EST: 1977
SQ FT: 20,000
SALES (est): 2.7MM **Privately Held**
WEB: www.starkproducts.com
SIC: 3231 Aquariums & reflectors, glass

(G-4896)
SUNRISE TILE INC
13309 35th Ave (11354-2712)
PHONE..................718 939-0538
Kathy Chen, *Manager*
▲ EMP: 8
SALES (est): 797.4K **Privately Held**
SIC: 2273 1752 Carpets & rugs; wood floor installation & refinishing

(G-4897)
TABI INC
488 Onderdonk Ave Apt 1l (11385-1547)
PHONE..................347 701-1051
Diego Tenesaca, *President*
EMP: 6
SALES (est): 199.3K **Privately Held**
SIC: 7372 Application computer software

(G-4898)
TEMPCO GLASS FABRICATION LLC
13110 Maple Ave (11355-4223)
PHONE..................718 461-6888
Steven Powell, *General Mgr*
Johnson Chen, *General Mgr*
Shirley Shaw, *Sales Staff*
▲ EMP: 56 EST: 2012
SALES: 7MM **Privately Held**
SIC: 3211 Building glass, flat

(G-4899)
TILCON NEW YORK INC
Also Called: Flushing Terminal
3466 College Point Blvd (11354-2717)
PHONE..................845 480-3249
EMP: 63
SALES (corp-wide): 30.6B **Privately Held**
SIC: 1429 Dolomitic marble, crushed & broken quarrying

HQ: Tilcon New York Inc.
9 Entin Rd
Parsippany NJ 07054
973 366-7741

(G-4900)
TONGLI PHARMACEUTICALS USA INC (PA)
4260 Main St Apt 6f (11355-4737)
PHONE..................212 842-8837
Mingli Yao, *Ch of Bd*
Ailing Zhao, *Admin Sec*
EMP: 11
SALES (est): 11.1MM **Publicly Held**
SIC: 2834 Pharmaceutical preparations

(G-4901)
TRIBORO BAGEL CO INC
Also Called: Bagel Oasis
18312 Horace Harding Expy (11365-2123)
PHONE..................718 359-9245
Abe Moskowitz, *President*
Mike Edelstein, *Corp Secy*
EMP: 20 EST: 1961
SQ FT: 1,200
SALES (est): 1MM **Privately Held**
WEB: www.bageloasis.com
SIC: 2051 Bakery: wholesale or wholesale/retail combined; bagels, fresh or frozen

(G-4902)
TWINKLE LIGHTING INC
13114 40th Rd (11354-5137)
PHONE..................718 225-0939
Fuchun Lin, *President*
Cheng Zhi Lai, *Sales Mgr*
EMP: 5
SALES (est): 471.6K **Privately Held**
SIC: 3646 Commercial indusl & institutional electric lighting fixtures

(G-4903)
UNITED SATCOM INC
4555 Robinson St (11355-3444)
PHONE..................718 359-4100
Ted Park, *President*
EMP: 7
SQ FT: 3,500
SALES: 1.5MM **Privately Held**
SIC: 3663 Microwave communication equipment

(G-4904)
UNITED STEEL PRODUCTS INC
Also Called: Ronmar
3340 127th Pl (11368-1508)
PHONE..................914 968-7782
EMP: 60
SALES (est): 24.8K **Privately Held**
SIC: 3442 3446 Mfg Metal Doors/Sash/Trim Mfg Architectural Metalwork

(G-4905)
WARODEAN CORPORATION
Also Called: Loosesleeve Law Publications
4308 162nd St (11358-3131)
P.O. Box 650042, Fresh Meadows (11365-0042)
PHONE..................718 359-5559
Michael Loughrey, *President*
EMP: 8
SQ FT: 1,750
SALES (est): 690K **Privately Held**
SIC: 2731 Textbooks: publishing & printing

(G-4906)
WOLSKI WOOD WORKS INC
14134 78th Rd Apt 3c (11367-3331)
PHONE..................718 577-9816
Tadeusz Wolski, *President*
EMP: 7
SALES (est): 177.1K **Privately Held**
SIC: 2421 Outdoor wood structural products

(G-4907)
YELLOW E HOUSE INC
Also Called: Gatecomusa
18812 Northern Blvd (11358-2811)
PHONE..................718 888-2000
Stephan Cho, *CEO*
EMP: 7
SQ FT: 3,000

SALES (est): 499.7K **Privately Held**
SIC: 3571 5045 7629 5945 Electronic computers; computers, peripherals & software; business machine repair, electric; hobby, toy & game shops

Fly Creek
Otsego County

(G-4908)
ADIRONDACK LEATHER PDTS INC
196 Cemetery Rd (13337)
P.O. Box 180 (13337-0180)
PHONE..................................607 547-5798
Gregory M O Neil, *CEO*
Darlene O Neil, *Vice Pres*
EMP: 10
SALES (est): 1.4MM **Privately Held**
WEB: www.adirondackleatherproducts.com
SIC: 3199 7389 Holsters, leather; leggings or chaps, canvas or leather; leather belting & strapping;

(G-4909)
FLY CREEK CDER MILL ORCHRD INC
288 Goose St (13337-2314)
PHONE..................................607 547-9692
Brenda Michaels, *President*
Howard Michaels, *Vice Pres*
EMP: 5
SALES (est): 485.8K **Privately Held**
SIC: 2022 2033 2037 2084 Cheese, natural & processed; canned fruits & specialties; frozen fruits & vegetables; wines; gift shop

Fonda
Montgomery County

(G-4910)
KASSON & KELLER INC
Also Called: Kas-Kel
60 School St (12068-4809)
P.O. Box 777 (12068-0777)
PHONE..................................518 853-3421
William Keller III, *Ch of Bd*
Dan Novak, *COO*
James P Keller, *Exec VP*
Ashley Gray, *Sales Staff*
John McGuire, *Sales Staff*
▲ **EMP:** 900 **EST:** 1946
SQ FT: 60,000
SALES (est): 169.2MM **Privately Held**
WEB: www.kas-kel.com
SIC: 3442 3089 1521 3231 Window & door frames; windows, plastic; single-family housing construction; products of purchased glass

(G-4911)
KEYMARK CORPORATION
1188 Cayadutta St (12068)
P.O. Box 626 (12068-0626)
PHONE..................................518 853-3421
William L Keller III, *Ch of Bd*
Tony Maiolo, *COO*
James P Keller, *Exec VP*
Bob Channell, *Vice Pres*
Sterling Gartung, *Maint Spvr*
▲ **EMP:** 600 **EST:** 1964
SQ FT: 250,000
SALES (est): 228.8MM **Privately Held**
WEB: www.keymarkcorp.com
SIC: 3354 3479 3471 Aluminum extruded products; painting of metal products; anodizing (plating) of metals or formed products

(G-4912)
TEMPER CORPORATION (PA)
544 Persse Rd (12068-7700)
P.O. Box 1127 (12068-1127)
PHONE..................................518 853-3467
John Rode, *President*
Alice Stanawich, *Manager*
Matt Townes, *Manager*
EMP: 25
SQ FT: 30,000

SALES (est): 4.2MM **Privately Held**
WEB: www.tempercorp.com
SIC: 3493 3053 Steel springs, except wire; gaskets & sealing devices

(G-4913)
TEMPER CORPORATION
Temper Axle Products
544 Persse Rd (12068-7700)
PHONE..................................518 853-3467
John Rhode, *President*
EMP: 5
SALES (corp-wide): 4.2MM **Privately Held**
WEB: www.tempercorp.com
SIC: 3714 Axles, motor vehicle
PA: Temper Corporation
544 Persse Rd
Fonda NY 12068
518 853-3467

Forest Hills
Queens County

(G-4914)
2H INTERNATIONAL CORP
6766 108th St Apt D1 (11375-2904)
PHONE..................................347 623-9380
June LI, *Manager*
EMP: 5
SALES: 300K **Privately Held**
SIC: 2337 Women's & misses' suits & coats

(G-4915)
AIGNER CHOCOLATES (PA)
10302 Metropolitan Ave (11375-6734)
PHONE..................................718 544-1850
Peter Aigner, *Ch of Bd*
EMP: 6
SQ FT: 2,000
SALES (est): 952.9K **Privately Held**
WEB: www.aignerchocolates.com
SIC: 2064 2066 Chocolate candy, except solid chocolate; chocolate candy, solid

(G-4916)
ALLROUND LOGISTICS INC (PA)
Also Called: Allround Maritime Services
7240 Ingram St (11375-5927)
PHONE..................................718 544-8945
Roland Meier, *President*
Ellen Meier, *Vice Pres*
Charlie Boon, *Treasurer*
Jody Barton, *Asst Sec*
◆ **EMP:** 5
SQ FT: 3,600
SALES: 1.7MM **Privately Held**
WEB: www.allroundlogistics.com
SIC: 3534 Escalators, passenger & freight

(G-4917)
ARIEL TIAN LLC
253 W 35th St Fl 8 Flr 8 (11375)
P.O. Box 296, New York (10018-0005)
PHONE..................................212 457-1266
LI Tian, *Mng Member*
EMP: 5 **EST:** 2015
SALES: 100K **Privately Held**
SIC: 3111 7389 Accessory products, leather; styling of fashions, apparel, furniture, textiles, etc.

(G-4918)
COMBINE GRAPHICS CORP
10714 Queens Blvd (11375-4249)
PHONE..................................212 695-4044
Charles Caminiti, *President*
Louis Zafonte, *Vice Pres*
EMP: 5
SQ FT: 2,300
SALES (est): 574.3K **Privately Held**
SIC: 2752 Commercial printing, offset

(G-4919)
DENTAL TRIBUNE AMERICA LLC
11835 Queens Blvd Ste 400 (11375-7211)
PHONE..................................212 244-7181
Travis Gittens, *Business Mgr*
Nadine Dehmel, *Vice Pres*
Humberto Estrada, *Sales Staff*
Grzegorz Rosiak, *Sales Staff*

Eric Seid,
EMP: 14
SALES (est): 2.7MM **Privately Held**
SIC: 2759 Publication printing

(G-4920)
HANGER INC
Also Called: Hanger Prosthectics Orthotics
11835 Queens Blvd Ste LI3 (11375-7205)
PHONE..................................718 575-5504
Joe Nieto, *Manager*
Joe N Nieto, *Manager*
EMP: 8
SALES (corp-wide): 1B **Publicly Held**
SIC: 3842 5999 Surgical appliances & supplies; artificial limbs
PA: Hanger, Inc.
10910 Domain Dr Ste 300
Austin TX 78758
512 777-3800

(G-4921)
HI-TECH ADVANCED SOLUTIONS INC
10525 65th Ave Apt 4h (11375-1802)
PHONE..................................718 926-3488
Nison B Isaak, *President*
EMP: 10
SALES: 100K **Privately Held**
SIC: 3571 Electronic computers

(G-4922)
LOYALTYPLANT INC (PA)
70 23 Juno St (11375)
PHONE..................................551 221-2701
Vasilii Diachenko, *President*
EMP: 10
SALES (est): 399.2K **Privately Held**
SIC: 7372 Business oriented computer software

(G-4923)
NATIVE AMERCN ENRGY GROUP INC
7211 Austin St Ste 288 (11375-5354)
PHONE..................................718 408-2323
Raj Nanvaan, *Principal*
Linda Chontos, *Officer*
EMP: 6
SALES (est): 495.9K **Privately Held**
SIC: 1382 Oil & gas exploration services

(G-4924)
NATURE ONLY INC
10420 Queens Blvd Apt 3b (11375-3602)
PHONE..................................917 922-6539
EMP: 9
SALES (est): 780K **Privately Held**
SIC: 2844 Mfg Natural Rash Creams For Kids & Facial Creams

(G-4925)
NEW YORK TYPING & PRINTING CO
10816 72nd Ave (11375-5653)
PHONE..................................718 268-7900
Jay Goldstin, *President*
EMP: 5 **EST:** 1981
SALES (est): 380K **Privately Held**
SIC: 2752 7338 Commercial printing, offset; secretarial & typing service

(G-4926)
PRESTON GLASS INDUSTRIES INC
Also Called: P G I
10420 Queens Blvd Apt 17a (11375-3610)
PHONE..................................718 997-8888
Ashish Karnavat, *President*
EMP: 20 **EST:** 1995
SALES (est): 1.3MM **Privately Held**
SIC: 3641 Electrodes, cold cathode fluorescent lamp

(G-4927)
WILSON & WILSON GROUP
Also Called: Wilson N Wilson Group & RES
6514 110th St (11375-1424)
PHONE..................................212 729-4736
Pius Wilson, *Principal*
EMP: 5
SALES: 25K **Privately Held**
SIC: 3577 Computer peripheral equipment

Forestport
Oneida County

(G-4928)
NIRVANA INC
1 Nirvana Plz (13338)
PHONE..................................315 942-4900
Mozafar Rafizadeh, *President*
Mansur Rafizadeh, *Vice Pres*
MO Rafizadeh, *Vice Pres*
Edward Wiehl, *Vice Pres*
▲ **EMP:** 160
SQ FT: 250,000
SALES (est): 68MM **Privately Held**
WEB: www.nirvanaspring.com
SIC: 2086 Mineral water, carbonated: packaged in cans, bottles, etc.; water, pasteurized: packaged in cans, bottles, etc.

(G-4929)
TOWN OF OHIO
Also Called: Town of Ohio Highway Garage
N Lake Rd (13338)
PHONE..................................315 392-2055
Fred Reuter, *Manager*
EMP: 24
SQ FT: 2,066 **Privately Held**
SIC: 3531 Snow plow attachments
PA: Town Of Ohio
234 Nellis Rd
Cold Brook NY 13324
315 826-7912

Forestville
Chautauqua County

(G-4930)
BAILEY MANUFACTURING CO LLC
10987 Bennett State Rd (14062-9714)
PHONE..................................716 965-2731
John Hines, *President*
Dona Hines,
EMP: 50 **EST:** 2002
SQ FT: 40,000
SALES (est): 10.8MM **Privately Held**
SIC: 3469 Metal stampings

(G-4931)
MERRITT ESTATE WINERY INC
2264 King Rd (14062-9703)
PHONE..................................716 965-4800
William T Merritt, *President*
Jason Merritt, *Corp Secy*
EMP: 15
SQ FT: 20,000
SALES (est): 2.4MM **Privately Held**
WEB: www.merrittestatewinery.com
SIC: 2084 Wines

(G-4932)
P S M GROUP INC
Also Called: Pit Stop Motorsports
17 Main St (14062-9998)
P.O. Box 500 (14062-0500)
PHONE..................................716 532-6686
Jeffrey A Furash, *President*
EMP: 20 **EST:** 1978
SALES (est): 1.7MM **Privately Held**
WEB: www.burningasphalt.com
SIC: 2842 7948 Specialty cleaning, polishes & sanitation goods; race track operation

Fort Ann
Washington County

(G-4933)
JEWELRY BY SARAH BELLE
10394 State Route 149 (12827-1900)
PHONE..................................518 793-1626
Sarah Maynard, *Principal*
EMP: 5 **EST:** 2010
SALES (est): 362.7K **Privately Held**
SIC: 3911 Jewelry apparel

▲ = Import ▼=Export
◆ =Import/Export

(G-4934)
PETTEYS LUMBER
Also Called: A Petteys Lumber
10247 State Route 149 (12827-1804)
PHONE..................................518 792-5943
Alvin Petteys, *Owner*
EMP: 7
SALES: 370K **Privately Held**
SIC: 2421 2426 Lumber: rough, sawed or planed; hardwood dimension & flooring mills

---

Fort Drum
Jefferson County

(G-4935)
BLACK RIVER GENERATIONS LLC
Also Called: Reenergy Black River
4515 2nd St (13602)
P.O. Box 849 (13602-0849)
PHONE..................................315 773-2314
EMP: 23 **EST:** 2010
SALES (est): 9.8MM **Privately Held**
SIC: 3822 Mfg Environmental Controls

Fort Edward
Washington County

(G-4936)
A HYATT BALL CO LTD
School St (12828)
P.O. Box 342 (12828-0342)
PHONE..................................518 747-0272
Robert Simpson, *President*
EMP: 7
SQ FT: 12,000
SALES (est): 1.3MM **Privately Held**
SIC: 3562 3949 Ball bearings & parts; billiard & pool equipment & supplies, general

(G-4937)
BURNHAM POLYMERIC INC
Also Called: Burnhams, The
1408 Route 9 (12828-2459)
P.O. Box 317, Glens Falls (12801-0317)
PHONE..................................518 792-3040
Warren Burnham Jr, *President*
William Wulfken, *Vice Pres*
Matt Perkins, *Opers Mgr*
EMP: 7
SQ FT: 8,400
SALES (est): 1.1MM **Privately Held**
WEB: www.burnhams.com
SIC: 3089 Extruded finished plastic products

(G-4938)
D K MACHINE INC
48 Sullivan Pkwy (12828-1027)
PHONE..................................518 747-0626
Daniel Komarony, *President*
Scott Lufkin, *Engineer*
Theresa Komarony, *Admin Sec*
EMP: 10
SQ FT: 8,500
SALES (est): 1.7MM **Privately Held**
WEB: www.dkmachine.com
SIC: 3599 5085 Machine shop, jobbing & repair; industrial supplies

(G-4939)
EASM MACHINE WORKS LLC
35 Sullivan Pkwy (12828-1028)
PHONE..................................518 747-5326
Elizabeth Miller, *Mng Member*
EMP: 40
SALES (est): 1.5MM **Privately Held**
SIC: 2621 2611 Paper mills; pulp mills

(G-4940)
IRVING CONSUMER PRODUCTS INC (DH)
Also Called: Irving Tissue Div
1 Eddy St (12828-1711)
PHONE..................................518 747-4151
J K Irving, *Principal*
Arthur L Irving, *Vice Pres*
John Irving, *Director*

▲ **EMP:** 300
SQ FT: 700,000
SALES (est): 115.9MM
SALES (corp-wide): 2.8B **Privately Held**
SIC: 2621 Towels, tissues & napkins: paper & stock
HQ: Irving Consumer Products Limited
100 Prom Midland
Dieppe NB E1A 6
506 858-7777

(G-4941)
PALLETS INC
99 1/2 East St (12828-1813)
P.O. Box 326 (12828-0326)
PHONE..................................518 747-4177
Clinton Binley, *President*
Arthur Binley III, *Chairman*
Marvin Horowitz, *Admin Sec*
EMP: 45 **EST:** 1942
SQ FT: 100,000
SALES (est): 6.6MM **Privately Held**
WEB: www.palletsincorporated.com
SIC: 2448 2421 Pallets, wood; sawmills & planing mills, general; lumber: rough, sawed or planed

(G-4942)
PARKER MACHINE COMPANY INC
28 Sullivan Pkwy (12828-1027)
PHONE..................................518 747-0675
Tammy Aust, *President*
Patrick A Whaley, *Vice Pres*
EMP: 17
SQ FT: 17,400
SALES: 3.9MM **Privately Held**
WEB: www.parkermachine.com
SIC: 3599 5251 Machine shop, jobbing & repair; tools

(G-4943)
RFB ASSOCIATES INC
Also Called: Bruno Associates
35 Sullivan Pkwy (12828-1028)
P.O. Box 14825, Albany (12212-4825)
PHONE..................................518 271-0551
Robert Bruno Sr, *President*
Sean P Bruno Sr, *Vice Pres*
EMP: 12
SQ FT: 60,000
SALES: 3MM **Privately Held**
SIC: 3559 3569 3565 3552 Automotive related machinery; assembly machines, non-metalworking; packaging machinery; textile machinery

(G-4944)
STONEGATE STABLESS
106 Reynolds Rd (12828-9244)
PHONE..................................518 746-7133
William Johnson, *Owner*
EMP: 8
SALES (est): 540.6K **Privately Held**
SIC: 2399 Horse harnesses & riding crops, etc.: non-leather

(G-4945)
TYMETAL CORP
1109 State Route 4 (12828-2825)
PHONE..................................518 692-9930
John T Hedbring, *President*
Alex Thomson, *Manager*
EMP: 23 **Privately Held**
WEB: www.tymetal.com
SIC: 3446 3441 Fences, gates, posts & flagpoles; fabricated structural metal
HQ: Tymetal Corp.
678 Wilbur Ave
Greenwich NY 12834
518 692-9930

Fort Plain
Montgomery County

(G-4946)
ELITE PRECISE MANUFACTURER LLC
55 Willett St (13339-1178)
PHONE..................................518 993-3040
Ross Stevenson, *Principal*
EMP: 8
SQ FT: 10,000

SALES (est): 430.9K **Privately Held**
SIC: 3599 Machine & other job shop work

(G-4947)
PERFORMANCE PRECISION MFG LLC
55 Willett St (13339-1178)
PHONE..................................518 993-3033
Joeseph Stevenson, *Owner*
EMP: 8
SALES (est): 952.2K **Privately Held**
SIC: 3999 Manufacturing industries

Frankfort
Herkimer County

(G-4948)
C-FLEX BEARING CO INC
104 Industrial Dr (13340-1139)
PHONE..................................315 895-7454
D Joanne Willcox, *President*
Wayne Smith, *Vice Pres*
EMP: 10 **EST:** 1994
SQ FT: 6,200
SALES: 1.4MM **Privately Held**
WEB: www.c-flex.com
SIC: 3568 3812 3556 3825 Bearings, bushings & blocks; search & navigation equipment; food products machinery; instruments to measure electricity

(G-4949)
DI SANOS CREATIVE CANVAS INC
113 W Main St (13340-1007)
PHONE..................................315 894-3137
John Di Sano, *President*
EMP: 5
SQ FT: 2,400
SALES (est): 425.3K **Privately Held**
WEB: www.disanoscreativecanvas.com
SIC: 2394 5999 5091 Awnings, fabric: made from purchased materials; canvas covers & drop cloths; awnings; canvas products; boat accessories & parts

(G-4950)
F E HALE MFG CO
120 Benson Pl (13340-3752)
P.O. Box 186 (13340-0186)
PHONE..................................315 894-5490
Jim Benson, *President*
Michelle Keib, *Natl Sales Mgr*
Brooke Benson, *Admin Sec*
EMP: 65 **EST:** 1907
SQ FT: 80,000
SALES (est): 11.6MM **Privately Held**
WEB: www.halebookcases.com
SIC: 2521 Bookcases, office: wood

(G-4951)
FIBERDYNE LABS INC
127 Business Park Dr (13340-3700)
PHONE..................................315 895-8470
A Peter Polus III, *CEO*
Carl Fredlund, *President*
Chad A Polus, *President*
Jeffrey Sperl, *General Mgr*
James Bunnell, *VP Mfg*
▲ **EMP:** 80
SQ FT: 20,000
SALES: 10.5MM **Privately Held**
WEB: www.fiberdyne.com
SIC: 3357 4899 4822 Fiber optic cable (insulated); communication signal enhancement network system; telegraph & other communications

(G-4952)
JBF STAINLESS LLC
1963 Country Mile (13340-4567)
P.O. Box 632, Cazenovia (13035-0632)
PHONE..................................315 569-2800
John Feldmeier, *President*
Margaret Feldmeier, *Principal*
Ron Zawtocki, *Vice Pres*
Dana Farrell, *Plant Mgr*
Scott Blais, *Engineer*
EMP: 26
SALES (est): 7.2MM **Privately Held**
SIC: 3324 Steel investment foundries

(G-4953)
MAPLEHURST BAKERIES LLC
Also Called: Granny's Kitchens
178 Industrial Park Dr (13340-4745)
PHONE..................................315 735-5000
EMP: 280
SALES (corp-wide): 36.8B **Privately Held**
SIC: 2051 2053 Bread, cake & related products; doughnuts, frozen
HQ: Maplehurst Bakeries, Llc
50 Maplehurst Dr
Brownsburg IN 46112
317 858-9000

(G-4954)
MOHAWK VALLEY MANUFACTURING
2237 Broad St (13340-5101)
PHONE..................................315 797-0851
EMP: 7
SALES (est): 630K **Privately Held**
SIC: 3556 Mfg Food Products Machinery

(G-4955)
PRECISION POLISH LLC
144 Adams St (13340-3751)
PHONE..................................315 894-3792
Jack Dunderdale, *Vice Pres*
Michelle Williams, *Manager*
Nial Williams, *Executive*
EMP: 25
SALES: 1.4MM **Privately Held**
SIC: 3441 Fabricated structural metal

(G-4956)
SOFT-NOZE USA INC
2216 Broad St (13340-5100)
PHONE..................................315 732-2726
Brett Truett, *President*
Krista Petrowski, *Finance Mgr*
Haris Dervisevic, *Technology*
▲ **EMP:** 5
SQ FT: 4,500
SALES (est): 819.4K **Privately Held**
WEB: www.softnoze.com
SIC: 3625 Electric controls & control accessories, industrial

(G-4957)
TURBO MACHINED PRODUCTS LLC
102 Industrial Dr (13340-1139)
PHONE..................................315 895-3010
John A Kabot Jr, *President*
Robert Partmell, *Vice Pres*
Brett Brewer, *Engineer*
Jeffrey Evatt, *Engineer*
Charles Gross, *Engineer*
EMP: 35
SQ FT: 20,000
SALES (est): 8.1MM **Privately Held**
WEB: www.turbomp.com
SIC: 3824 3511 Impeller & counter driven flow meters; turbines & turbine generator sets & parts

---

Franklin Square
Nassau County

(G-4958)
A & G FOOD DISTRIBUTORS LLC
372 Doris Ave (11010-1325)
PHONE..................................917 939-3457
Rocco Macri, *President*
▲ **EMP:** 3 **EST:** 2009
SALES: 1.5MM **Privately Held**
SIC: 2032 Italian foods: packaged in cans, jars, etc.

(G-4959)
BONURA AND SONS IRON WORKS
957 Lorraine Dr (11010-1812)
PHONE..................................718 381-4100
EMP: 15
SALES (est): 1.2MM **Privately Held**
SIC: 3312 1799 Blast Furnace-Steel Works Trade Contractor

(G-4960)
D C I TECHNICAL INC
475 Franklin Ave Fl 2 (11010-1228)
PHONE..................................516 355-0464
Andrea Mannheim, *President*
Harold Adler, *Vice Pres*
Merideth Hilton, *Vice Pres*
Sidney Platt, *Vice Pres*
EMP: 12
SQ FT: 2,700
SALES (est): 882.8K **Privately Held**
SIC: 2731 2741 Books: publishing & printing; miscellaneous publishing

(G-4961)
LESSOILCOM
672 Dogwood Ave (11010-3247)
P.O. Box 20988, Floral Park (11002-0988)
PHONE..................................516 319-5052
Mike Gregoretti, *Principal*
EMP: 6
SALES (est): 340.2K **Privately Held**
SIC: 1241 Bituminous coal mining services, contract basis

(G-4962)
MOVIN ON SOUNDS AND SEC INC
Also Called: M O S S Communications
636 Hempstead Tpke (11010-4326)
PHONE..................................516 489-2350
Bruce Cirillo, *President*
Mark Rock, *Manager*
Jean Ulsheimer, *Manager*
Paul Cirillo, *Officer*
EMP: 35 **EST:** 1976
SALES (est): 6.6MM **Privately Held**
WEB: www.movinon.com
SIC: 3663 Radio & TV communications equipment

(G-4963)
NYCOM BUSINESS SOLUTIONS INC
804 Hempstead Tpke (11010-4321)
PHONE..................................516 345-6000
Jerry Sperduto, *President*
EMP: 3
SQ FT: 800
SALES: 1.2MM **Privately Held**
SIC: 3663 Cellular radio telephone

(G-4964)
STUDENT LIFELINE INC
Also Called: Student Safety Books
922 Hempstead Tpke (11010-3628)
P.O. Box 570200, Whitestone (11357-0200)
PHONE..................................516 327-0800
Richard Signarino, *President*
EMP: 42
SQ FT: 2,200
SALES (est): 4.1MM **Privately Held**
WEB: www.studentlifeline.com
SIC: 2741 Miscellaneous publishing

Franklinville
Cattaraugus County

(G-4965)
BUFFALO CRUSHED STONE INC
Rr 16 (14737)
P.O. Box 106 (14737-0106)
PHONE..................................716 566-9636
John Lentz, *Manager*
EMP: 11
SALES (corp-wide): 651.9MM **Privately Held**
SIC: 1442 5032 Gravel mining; stone, crushed or broken
HQ: Buffalo Crushed Stone, Inc.
500 Como Park Blvd
Buffalo NY 14227
716 826-7310

(G-4966)
CATTARAUGUS CONTAINERS INC
21 Elm St 23 (14737-1052)
P.O. Box 174 (14737-0174)
PHONE..................................716 676-2000

Jane Lemke, *President*
Paul Wagner, *Vice Pres*
Tammy Mooney, *Controller*
EMP: 33
SQ FT: 33,000
SALES: 3.8MM **Privately Held**
SIC: 2653 2657 5113 Boxes, corrugated: made from purchased materials; folding paperboard boxes; corrugated & solid fiber boxes

(G-4967)
ONTARIO KNIFE COMPANY
26 Empire St (14737-1099)
PHONE..................................716 676-5527
Nicholas D Trbovich Jr, *CEO*
Kenneth Trbovich, *Ch of Bd*
Nicholas D Trbovich, *Chairman*
Cari Jaroslawsky, *Treasurer*
◆ **EMP:** 63
SQ FT: 10,000
SALES: 6.5MM
SALES (corp-wide): 47.8MM **Publicly Held**
WEB: www.ontarioknife.com
SIC: 3421 Knife blades & blanks
PA: Servotronics, Inc.
1110 Maple Rd
Elma NY 14059
716 655-5990

Fredonia
Chautauqua County

(G-4968)
CDF INDSTRIAL PCKG SLTIONS INC
134 Clinton Ave (14063-1406)
PHONE..................................716 672-2984
Jeremy Poehler, *Ch of Bd*
Thomas J Ivory, *President*
Richard Ivory, *Vice Pres*
Vickie Ivory, *Treasurer*
Mary Ivory, *Admin Sec*
EMP: 18
SQ FT: 26,000
SALES (est): 3MM **Privately Held**
SIC: 2448 Pallets, wood

(G-4969)
FREDONIA PENNYSAVER INC (PA)
Also Called: Lakeshore Pennysaver
276 W Main St Ste 1 (14063-2099)
P.O. Box 493 (14063-0493)
PHONE..................................716 679-1509
Thomas K Webb Jr, *President*
Maureen Webb, *Vice Pres*
EMP: 5
SQ FT: 1,000
SALES (est): 805.8K **Privately Held**
WEB: www.fredoniapennysaver.com
SIC: 2741 2711 Guides: publishing only, not printed on site; newspapers, publishing & printing

(G-4970)
GREAT LAKES SPECIALITES
9491 Route 60 (14063-9729)
P.O. Box 351 (14063-0351)
PHONE..................................716 672-4622
Michael J Gloss, *Owner*
EMP: 20
SQ FT: 10,000
SALES (est): 1.8MM **Privately Held**
SIC: 2448 2449 2441 Pallets, wood; wood containers; nailed wood boxes & shook

(G-4971)
TUBE FABRICATION COMPANY INC
183 E Main St Ste 10 (14063-1435)
PHONE..................................716 673-1871
Daniel Sturniolo, *President*
EMP: 12
SALES (est): 2.2MM **Privately Held**
SIC: 3498 5051 Tube fabricating (contract bending & shaping); tubing, metal

(G-4972)
URBAN TECHNOLOGIES INC
3451 Stone Quarry Rd (14063-9722)
PHONE..................................716 672-2709
John Urbanik, *President*
EMP: 5
SALES (est): 676.5K **Privately Held**
SIC: 3677 Electronic transformers; inductors, electronic

(G-4973)
WOODBURY VINEYARDS INC
Also Called: Noble Vintages
3215 S Roberts Rd (14063-9417)
PHONE..................................716 679-9463
Joseph Carney, *Branch Mgr*
Maria Pizzino,
EMP: 5
SALES (corp-wide): 1.7MM **Privately Held**
WEB: www.woodburyvineyards.com
SIC: 2084 Wines
PA: Woodbury Vineyards, Inc.
2001 Crocker Rd Ste 440
Westlake OH 44145
440 835-2828

Freedom
Cattaraugus County

(G-4974)
GUTCHESS FREEDOM INC
10699 Maple Grove Rd (14065-9774)
PHONE..................................716 492-2824
Larry Lines, *Manager*
EMP: 70 **EST:** 2007
SALES (est): 8.3MM
SALES (corp-wide): 150MM **Privately Held**
SIC: 2421 Custom sawmill
PA: Gutchess Lumber Co., Inc.
890 Mclean Rd
Cortland NY 13045
607 753-3393

(G-4975)
GUTCHESS LUMBER CO INC
10699 Maple Grove Rd (14065-9774)
PHONE..................................716 492-2824
EMP: 43
SQ FT: 2,940
SALES (corp-wide): 150MM **Privately Held**
SIC: 2421 Sawmills & planing mills, general
PA: Gutchess Lumber Co., Inc.
890 Mclean Rd
Cortland NY 13045
607 753-3393

Freeport
Nassau County

(G-4976)
5TH AVENUE CHOCOLATIERE LLC
114 Church St (11520-3833)
PHONE..................................516 868-8070
Joseph Whaley,
▲ **EMP:** 20 **EST:** 2015
SALES: 3MM **Privately Held**
SIC: 2066 Chocolate

(G-4977)
5TH AVENUE CHOCOLATIERE LTD (PA)
114 Church St (11520-3833)
PHONE..................................212 935-5454
Joseph E Whaley, *President*
John Whaley, *Vice Pres*
▲ **EMP:** 4
SQ FT: 4,500
SALES: 1.6MM **Privately Held**
SIC: 2064 2066 5441 Candy & other confectionery products; chocolate & cocoa products; candy

(G-4978)
A PROMOS USA INC
Also Called: Aarrow Promotions
143 E Merrick Rd (11520-4017)
PHONE..................................516 377-0186
Mindy Younger, *Ch of Bd*
Debbie Mandel, *Vice Pres*
EMP: 12
SQ FT: 1,000
SALES: 1.5MM **Privately Held**
SIC: 2759 Screen printing

(G-4979)
ACCESS DISPLAY GROUP INC
Also Called: Swing Frame
151 S Main St (11520-3845)
PHONE..................................516 678-7772
Charles Abrams, *President*
Barbara Abrams, *Vice Pres*
Jessica Malarkey, *Sales Staff*
Brain McAuley, *Info Tech Dir*
Brian McAley, *Info Tech Mgr*
▲ **EMP:** 14
SQ FT: 6,000
SALES (est): 3MM **Privately Held**
WEB: www.swingframe.com
SIC: 3499 Picture frames, metal

(G-4980)
AIRMARINE ELECTROPLATING CORP
388 Woodcleft Ave (11520-6379)
PHONE..................................516 623-4406
Ernest Rieger III, *President*
EMP: 6
SALES (est): 724.4K **Privately Held**
WEB: www.airmarine.com
SIC: 3471 Electroplating of metals or formed products

(G-4981)
ALABASTER GROUP INC
188 N Main St (11520-2232)
PHONE..................................516 867-8223
Orna Alabaster, *President*
Zeev Alabaster, *Vice Pres*
EMP: 5
SQ FT: 7,300
SALES (est): 356.4K **Privately Held**
SIC: 2791 7336 7389 Typesetting; graphic arts & related design; printing broker

(G-4982)
ALL AMERICAN METAL CORPORATION
200 Buffalo Ave (11520-4732)
P.O. Box 108 (11520-0108)
PHONE..................................516 223-1760
Bernard Pechter, *President*
▲ **EMP:** 8
SQ FT: 50,000
SALES (est): 4.8MM **Privately Held**
WEB: www.allamericanmetal.com
SIC: 2542 Partitions for floor attachment, prefabricated: except wood

(G-4983)
ALL AMERICAN METAL CORPORATION
200 Buffalo Ave (11520-4732)
P.O. Box 108 (11520-0108)
PHONE..................................516 623-0222
EMP: 32
SALES (corp-wide): 5MM **Privately Held**
SIC: 2542 3446 Mfg Partitions/Fixtures-Nonwood Mfg Architectural Metalwork
PA: All American Metal Corporation
200 Buffalo Ave
Freeport NY 11520
516 223-1760

(G-4984)
ALPHA FASTENERS CORP
154 E Merrick Rd (11520-4020)
PHONE..................................516 867-6188
Koula Perdios, *President*
Archie Perdios, *Vice Pres*
Michael Perdios, *Vice Pres*
▲ **EMP:** 5
SQ FT: 3,000
SALES (est): 795.3K **Privately Held**
SIC: 3451 Screw machine products

▲ = Import ▼=Export
◆ =Import/Export

(G-4985)
ANNA YOUNG ASSOC LTD
Also Called: Lombardi Design & Mfg
100 Doxsee Dr (11520-4716)
PHONE..................................516 546-4400
Carl M Lombardi, *President*
▲ EMP: 150
SQ FT: 50,000
SALES (est): 56.6MM **Privately Held**
WEB: www.lombardi.cc
SIC: 3089 Injection molded finished plastic products

(G-4986)
ATLAZ INTERNATIONAL LTD
244 E Merrick Rd (11520-4029)
PHONE..................................516 239-1854
Loretta Zalta, *President*
Adam Zalta, *Vice Pres*
Andre Zalta, *Vice Pres*
EMP: 11
SALES (est): 2.3MM **Privately Held**
WEB: www.atlaz.com
SIC: 3577 5045 5112 Computer peripheral equipment; computer peripheral equipment; stationery & office supplies

(G-4987)
BELLO LLC
178 Hanse Ave (11520-4609)
PHONE..................................516 623-8800
John Alair Garcia, *Mng Member*
EMP: 144 EST: 2016
SQ FT: 65,000
SALES (est): 17.8MM **Privately Held**
SIC: 2053 Frozen bakery products, except bread

(G-4988)
BRAMSON HOUSE INC
151 Albany Ave (11520-4710)
PHONE..................................516 764-5006
Jules Abramson, *CEO*
Ellis Abramson, *President*
Betty Abramson, *Vice Pres*
Patty Abramson, *Accounting Mgr*
Neal Wilkinson, *Sales Mgr*
◆ EMP: 120
SQ FT: 80,000
SALES (est): 17MM **Privately Held**
WEB: www.bramsonhouse.com
SIC: 2392 2391 Bedspreads & bed sets: made from purchased materials; curtains & draperies

(G-4989)
CASTLEREAGH PRINTCRAFT INC
Also Called: Castle Reagh Print Craft
320 Buffalo Ave (11520-4711)
P.O. Box 9062 (11520-9062)
PHONE..................................516 623-1728
James Vollaro, *President*
Robert Quadrino, *Vice Pres*
Steven Quadrino, *Vice Pres*
Donna Vollaro, *CFO*
EMP: 70
SQ FT: 35,000
SALES (est): 9.5MM **Privately Held**
WEB: www.printcraftonline.com
SIC: 3555 2791 2789 2752 Printing trades machinery; typesetting; bookbinding & related work; commercial printing, lithographic

(G-4990)
CELLGEN INC
55 Commercial St (11520-2831)
PHONE..................................516 889-9300
Nicholas Capriotti, *CEO*
EMP: 9
SALES (est): 332K **Privately Held**
SIC: 3621 Generators & sets, electric

(G-4991)
DART AWNING INC
365 S Main St (11520-5114)
PHONE..................................516 544-2082
Thomas Hart, *President*
Richard Hart, *Admin Sec*
EMP: 7
SQ FT: 5,000
SALES (est): 1.5MM **Privately Held**
WEB: www.dartawnings.com
SIC: 3444 5999 Awnings, sheet metal; awnings

(G-4992)
DORAL REFINING CORP
533 Atlantic Ave (11520-5211)
PHONE..................................516 223-3684
Stephen Faliks, *President*
Alan Zaret, *Vice Pres*
EMP: 20
SQ FT: 10,000
SALES (est): 6MM **Privately Held**
WEB: www.doralcorp.com
SIC: 3339 Precious metals

(G-4993)
EDR INDUSTRIES INC
Also Called: Wil-Nic
100 Commercial St (11520-2832)
PHONE..................................516 868-1928
Don Capriglione, *President*
Christopher Cullinan, *Vice Pres*
EMP: 19
SQ FT: 10,000
SALES (est): 3.4MM **Privately Held**
SIC: 3599 Machine shop, jobbing & repair

(G-4994)
FARBER PLASTICS INC
162 Hanse Ave (11520-4644)
PHONE..................................516 378-4860
Lewis Farber, *President*
Yoni Oratz, *Purchasing*
Nicole Western, *Sales Staff*
Kc Calderone, *Office Mgr*
EMP: 23
SALES (est): 4.6MM **Privately Held**
SIC: 3089 Plastic processing

(G-4995)
FARBER TRUCKING CORP
162 Hanse Ave (11520-4644)
PHONE..................................516 378-4860
Lewis Farber, *President*
EMP: 23
SQ FT: 35,000
SALES (est): 3MM **Privately Held**
SIC: 3081 Plastic film & sheet

(G-4996)
FORM-TEC INC
216 N Main St Ste E (11520-2200)
PHONE..................................516 867-0200
Howard Lebow, *President*
EMP: 20
SQ FT: 10,000
SALES (est): 3.6MM **Privately Held**
WEB: www.form-tec.com
SIC: 3089 Molding primary plastic

(G-4997)
FORSYTHE COSMETIC GROUP LTD
Also Called: Forsythe Licensing
10 Niagara Ave (11520-4704)
P.O. Box 431, Lawrence (11559-0431)
PHONE..................................516 239-4200
Harriet Rose, *Ch of Bd*
Michael Rose, *President*
Marlyn Roquemore, *Exec VP*
Whitney Matza, *Vice Pres*
Cathy Cheong, *Sales Staff*
◆ EMP: 50
SQ FT: 20,000
SALES (est): 15.8MM **Privately Held**
WEB: www.cosmeticgroup.com
SIC: 2844 Cosmetic preparations

(G-4998)
FREEPORT SCREEN & STAMPING
31 Hanse Ave (11520-4601)
PHONE..................................516 379-0330
Stan Papot, *President*
▲ EMP: 20
SQ FT: 13,500
SALES (est): 2.4MM **Privately Held**
SIC: 3469 2759 2396 Metal stampings; screen printing; automotive & apparel trimmings

(G-4999)
GLENN FOODS INC (PA)
Also Called: Glenny's
371 S Main St Ste 119-405 (11520-5114)
PHONE..................................516 377-1400
Glenn Schacher, *President*
Philip Fruchter, *Vice Pres*

Steven Fruchter, *Treasurer*
▼ EMP: 10
SALES (est): 880K **Privately Held**
WEB: www.glennys.com
SIC: 2099 Food preparations

(G-5000)
GREENFIELD DIE CASTING CORP
99 Doxsee Dr (11520-4717)
PHONE..................................516 623-9230
Peter Greenfield, *President*
Michael Greenfield, *Vice Pres*
Douglas Greenfield, *Admin Sec*
EMP: 50
SQ FT: 56,000
SALES (est): 7.3MM **Privately Held**
SIC: 3364 3369 Zinc & zinc-base alloy die-castings; nonferrous foundries

(G-5001)
GREENFIELD INDUSTRIES INC
99 Doxsee Dr (11520-4717)
PHONE..................................516 623-9230
Peter Greenfield, *President*
Douglas Greenfield, *Vice Pres*
Michael Greenfield, *Vice Pres*
▲ EMP: 75
SQ FT: 70,000
SALES (est): 12.2MM **Privately Held**
WEB: www.greenfieldny.com
SIC: 3363 Aluminum die-castings

(G-5002)
HARWITT INDUSTRIES INC
61 S Main St Unit A (11520-3864)
PHONE..................................516 623-9787
Louis Harwitt, *President*
EMP: 13 EST: 2002
SALES (est): 920K **Privately Held**
SIC: 3599 Machine & other job shop work

(G-5003)
INTEX COMPANY INC (PA)
Also Called: Semtex Industrial
80 Commercial St (11520-2832)
PHONE..................................516 223-0200
Henrietta Rivman, *President*
EMP: 61
SQ FT: 20,000
SALES (est): 6.6MM **Privately Held**
SIC: 3674 5065 Semiconductors & related devices; electronic parts

(G-5004)
LAMAR PLASTICS PACKAGING LTD
216 N Main St Ste F (11520-2200)
PHONE..................................516 378-2500
Lawrence Aronson, *Ch of Bd*
Marc Aronson, *President*
Josh Aronson, *Vice Pres*
Linda Tino, *Traffic Mgr*
Barry Reimel, *VP Sales*
▲ EMP: 60 EST: 1966
SQ FT: 60,000
SALES (est): 10.3MM **Privately Held**
SIC: 3086 3993 Packaging & shipping materials, foamed plastic; displays & cutouts, window & lobby

(G-5005)
MARCON ELECTRONIC SYSTEMS LLC
152 Westend Ave (11520-5245)
PHONE..................................516 633-6396
Grace Connelly,
EMP: 6
SALES: 750K **Privately Held**
SIC: 3679 Electronic circuits

(G-5006)
MARCON SERVICES
152 Westend Ave (11520-5245)
PHONE..................................516 223-8019
Grace Connelly, *Owner*
EMP: 6
SALES (est): 66.5K **Privately Held**
WEB: www.graceconnelly.com
SIC: 3674 Semiconductors & related devices

(G-5007)
MELTO METAL PRODUCTS CO INC
37 Hanse Ave (11520-4696)
PHONE..................................516 546-8866
Bernard Liebman, *Ch of Bd*
Peter Sheridan, *Vice Pres*
▲ EMP: 35
SQ FT: 15,000
SALES (est): 8.6MM **Privately Held**
WEB: www.meltometalproducts.com
SIC: 3444 Sheet metalwork

(G-5008)
MICA INTERNATIONAL LTD
126 Albany Ave (11520-4702)
PHONE..................................516 378-3400
Fax: 516 379-0560
EMP: 12
SQ FT: 5,500
SALES (est): 820K **Privately Held**
SIC: 2511 Mfg Wood Household Furniture

(G-5009)
MIDBURY INDUSTRIES INC
86 E Merrick Rd (11520-4034)
PHONE..................................516 868-0600
Diane Jones, *President*
Michael Natilli Jr, *Vice Pres*
EMP: 15
SQ FT: 10,000
SALES (est): 900K **Privately Held**
WEB: www.midbury.com
SIC: 3089 Injection molding of plastics

(G-5010)
NEW YORK VANITY AND MFG CO
10 Henry St (11520-3910)
PHONE..................................718 417-1010
Teddy Foukalas, *President*
Tony Fotou, *Shareholder*
▲ EMP: 25
SQ FT: 30,000
SALES (est): 3.6MM **Privately Held**
WEB: www.nyvanity.com
SIC: 2434 Vanities, bathroom: wood

(G-5011)
ON TIME PLASTICS INC
121 Henry St (11520-3821)
PHONE..................................516 442-4280
Franklin Toribio, *President*
EMP: 7
SALES: 600K **Privately Held**
SIC: 3083 Thermoplastic laminates: rods, tubes, plates & sheet

(G-5012)
ONDRIVESUS CORP
216 N Main St Bldg B2 (11520-2200)
PHONE..................................516 771-6777
Dennis G Berg, *CEO*
D Lee Berg, *President*
Jayne Berg, *Vice Pres*
Don Grandone, *Engineer*
◆ EMP: 35
SQ FT: 11,000
SALES (est): 10.1MM **Privately Held**
WEB: www.ondrives.us
SIC: 3566 Speed changers, drives & gears

(G-5013)
ORAMAAX DENTAL PRODUCTS INC
216 N Main St Ste A (11520-2200)
PHONE..................................516 771-8514
Robert Endelson, *President*
EMP: 15
SQ FT: 12,500
SALES (est): 1.4MM **Privately Held**
WEB: www.flosscard.com
SIC: 3843 5047 Dental equipment & supplies; dental equipment & supplies

(G-5014)
PENTHOUSE MANUFACTURING CO INC
Also Called: Penthouse Group, The
225 Buffalo Ave (11520-4709)
PHONE..................................516 379-1300
William Ostrower, *President*
▲ EMP: 350 EST: 1952

GEOGRAPHIC

SALES (est): 32.7MM **Privately Held**
SIC: 3172 2399 Cosmetic bags; powder puffs & mitts

(G-5015)
PHOENIX METAL PRODUCTS INC
100 Bennington Ave (11520-3927)
PHONE..............................516 546-4200
Robert Wolf, *President*
◆ **EMP:** 10
SQ FT: 10,000
SALES (est): 1.8MM **Privately Held**
WEB: www.phoenixmetalproducts.com
SIC: 3469 Metal stampings

(G-5016)
PRESTI READY MIX CONCRETE INC
Also Called: Presti Stone and Mason
210 E Merrick Rd (11520-4029)
PHONE..............................516 378-6006
Joseph Prestigiacomo, *President*
EMP: 7
SQ FT: 2,500
SALES (est): 1.2MM **Privately Held**
SIC: 3273 3531 Ready-mixed concrete; bituminous, cement & concrete related products & equipment

(G-5017)
PRIMELITE MANUFACTURING CORP
407 S Main St (11520-5194)
PHONE..............................516 868-4411
Benjamin Heit, *President*
EMP: 9 **EST:** 1962
SQ FT: 12,000
SALES: 1.1MM **Privately Held**
WEB: www.primelite-mfg.com
SIC: 3646 Commercial indusl & institutional electric lighting fixtures

(G-5018)
QUALITY LINEALS USA INC
105 Bennington Ave Ste 1 (11520-3946)
PHONE..............................516 378-6577
Jill Kaiserman, *President*
EMP: 43
SQ FT: 40,000 **Privately Held**
SIC: 3544 Dies, plastics forming
PA: Quality Lineals Usa, Inc.
1 Kees Pl
Merrick NY 11566

(G-5019)
RAND & PASEKA MFG CO INC
10 Hanse Ave (11520-4602)
PHONE..............................516 867-1500
Marc Schwab, *President*
Andrea Schwab, *Senior VP*
EMP: 22
SQ FT: 19,000
SALES (est): 3.3MM **Privately Held**
SIC: 3911 Rosaries or other small religious articles, precious metal

(G-5020)
RSC MOLDING INC
75 Hanse Ave (11520-4608)
PHONE..............................516 351-9871
Deborah Leo, *President*
Stephen Leo, *Vice Pres*
EMP: 35
SALES (est): 2.3MM
SALES (corp-wide): 6.8MM **Privately Held**
WEB: www.rsc-ny.com
SIC: 3089 Injection molding of plastics
PA: Retail Solution Center, Inc.
273 Sea Cliff Ave
Sea Cliff NY 11579
516 771-7000

(G-5021)
SAJ OF FREEPORT CORP
Also Called: Love & Quiches Desserts
178 Hanse Ave (11520-4609)
PHONE..............................516 623-8800
Irwin Axelrod, *CEO*
Susan Axelrod, *Chairman*
Joan Axelrod, *Vice Pres*
Michael Goldstein, *Vice Pres*
Albert Mayden, *Vice Pres*
▼ **EMP:** 250 **EST:** 1974

SALES (est): 69.7MM **Privately Held**
WEB: www.loveandquiches.com
SIC: 2051 Bread, cake & related products

(G-5022)
SEA ISLE CUSTOM ROD BUILDERS
495 Guy Lombardo Ave (11520-6293)
PHONE..............................516 868-8855
Robert Feuring, *President*
EMP: 7
SQ FT: 1,710
SALES: 900K **Privately Held**
SIC: 3949 5941 Fishing tackle, general; fishing equipment

(G-5023)
SEMITRONICS CORP (HQ)
80 Commercial St (11520-2832)
PHONE..............................516 223-0200
Henrietta Rivman, *President*
Phil Balducci, *Opers Staff*
Paul Kurland, *QC Mgr*
EMP: 45
SQ FT: 10,000
SALES: 6.1MM
SALES (corp-wide): 6.6MM **Privately Held**
WEB: www.semitronics.com
SIC: 3674 5065 Semiconductors & related devices; electronic parts & equipment
PA: Intex Company Inc
80 Commercial St
Freeport NY 11520
516 223-0200

(G-5024)
SEVILLE CENTRAL MIX CORP (PA)
157 Albany Ave (11520-4710)
PHONE..............................516 868-3000
Peter Scalamandre, *Ch of Bd*
Joseph L Scalamandre, *Vice Pres*
EMP: 5 **EST:** 1979
SQ FT: 8,000
SALES (est): 7.8MM **Privately Held**
WEB: www.sevillecentralmix.com
SIC: 3273 Ready-mixed concrete

(G-5025)
SIGNATURE INDUSTRIES INC
32 Saint Johns Pl (11520-4618)
PHONE..............................516 771-8182
Emil Petschauer, *President*
Ante Vulin, *Vice Pres*
James Calderon, *Treasurer*
EMP: 15
SALES (est): 1.8MM **Privately Held**
WEB: www.signatureindustries.com
SIC: 3993 Signs, not made in custom sign painting shops

(G-5026)
SNOW CRAFT 216 INC
216 N Main St Ste F (11520-2200)
PHONE..............................718 757-6121
Jonathan Apes, *Owner*
EMP: 10
SALES (est): 1.5MM **Privately Held**
SIC: 2822 Polyethylene, chlorosulfonated (hypalon)

(G-5027)
TEENA CREATIONS INC
10 Hanse Ave (11520-4628)
PHONE..............................516 867-1500
Jules Rand, *President*
Michael Rand, *Treasurer*
Mark Schwab, *Admin Sec*
EMP: 5
SQ FT: 19,000
SALES (est): 520K **Privately Held**
SIC: 3911 Jewelry, precious metal

(G-5028)
TEMREX CORPORATION (PA)
300 Buffalo Ave (11520-4720)
P.O. Box 182 (11520-0182)
PHONE..............................516 868-6221
Alda Levander, *CEO*
Ethan Levander, *President*
Ruth Fusci, *Admin Sec*
EMP: 37
SQ FT: 5,000

SALES (est): 4.5MM **Privately Held**
WEB: www.temrex.com
SIC: 3843 Dental equipment & supplies

(G-5029)
THREE STAR OFFSET PRINTING
188 N Main St (11520-2232)
PHONE..............................516 867-8223
Zeev Alabaster, *President*
Orna Alabaster, *Corp Secy*
EMP: 10 **EST:** 1958
SQ FT: 7,300
SALES (est): 1.9MM **Privately Held**
SIC: 2752 Photo-offset printing; commercial printing, offset

(G-5030)
TRIUMPH ACTUATION SYSTEMS LLC
417 S Main St (11520-5144)
PHONE..............................516 378-0162
EMP: 55
SALES (corp-wide): 3.8B **Publicly Held**
SIC: 3593 3728 3724 3594 Mfg Fluid Power Cylinder Mfg Aircraft Parts/Equip Mfg Aircraft Engine/Part Mfg Fluid Power Pump/Mtr Whol Industrial Equip
HQ: Triumph Actuation Systems, Llc
4520 Hampton Rd
Clemmons NC 27012
336 766-9036

(G-5031)
UNIQUE DISPLAY MFG CORP (PA)
216 N Main St Ste D (11520-2200)
PHONE..............................516 546-3800
Philip Boxer, *President*
Eleanor Boxer, *Corp Secy*
EMP: 8 **EST:** 1976
SQ FT: 50,000
SALES (est): 925.1K **Privately Held**
SIC: 3993 Displays & cutouts, window & lobby

(G-5032)
WL CONCEPTS & PRODUCTION INC
1 Bennington Ave (11520-3953)
PHONE..............................516 565-5151
William Levine, *President*
James Levine, *Vice Pres*
Walter Nikles, *VP Opers*
Sabrina Issagholian, *Production*
Marian Keilson, *Director*
▲ **EMP:** 24
SQ FT: 4,500
SALES (est): 1.1MM **Privately Held**
WEB: www.wlconcepts.com
SIC: 3993 Signs & advertising specialties

Freeville
Tompkins County

(G-5033)
FREEVILLE PUBLISHING CO INC
Also Called: Cortland-Ithaca Subn Shopper
9 Main St (13068-9599)
P.O. Box 210 (13068-0210)
PHONE..............................607 844-9119
Michael Down, *President*
EMP: 10 **EST:** 1949
SQ FT: 1,998
SALES (est): 809.7K **Privately Held**
SIC: 2741 2752 2759 Shopping news: publishing only, not printed on site; commercial printing, offset; commercial printing

(G-5034)
GENOA SAND & GRAVEL LNSG
390 Peruville Rd (13068-9732)
PHONE..............................607 533-4551
EMP: 5
SALES (est): 210K **Privately Held**
SIC: 1442 Construction Sand/Gravel

(G-5035)
INCODEMA3D LLC
330 Main St (13068-9701)
P.O. Box 429 (13068-0429)
PHONE..............................607 269-4390
Terry Posecznick, *Controller*

Matt Pugh, *Manager*
Roxanne Andrian, *Director*
Scott Volk, *Director*
Illa Burbank, *Officer*
EMP: 38
SALES: 5MM **Privately Held**
SIC: 2759 Commercial printing

(G-5036)
WEAVER WIND ENERGY LLC
7 Union St (13068-3201)
PHONE..............................607 379-9463
Art Weaver, *President*
EMP: 5
SQ FT: 5,000
SALES (est): 526.4K **Privately Held**
SIC: 3511 Turbines & turbine generator sets

Fresh Meadows
Queens County

(G-5037)
AMERICAN CIGAR
6940 Fresh Meadow Ln (11365-3422)
PHONE..............................718 969-0008
Allen Schuster, *President*
EMP: 6
SALES (est): 450K **Privately Held**
WEB: www.smokeyscigars.com
SIC: 2121 Cigars

(G-5038)
CDML COMPUTER SERVICES LTD
5343 198th St (11365-1719)
PHONE..............................718 428-9063
Leonard Kaplan, *President*
EMP: 6
SALES: 281.3K **Privately Held**
WEB: www.cdml.com
SIC: 7372 7371 Prepackaged software; custom computer programming services

(G-5039)
DYNAMIC DECISIONS INC (PA)
18519 64th Ave (11365-2707)
PHONE..............................908 755-5000
Alan Fan, *President*
▲ **EMP:** 35
SQ FT: 6,500
SALES (est): 3.8MM **Privately Held**
WEB: www.ddidynex.com
SIC: 3571 3577 Electronic computers; computer peripheral equipment

(G-5040)
EXCEL TECHNOLOGY INC
5317 Hollis Court Blvd (11365-1727)
PHONE..............................718 423-7262
Allan Chan, *Branch Mgr*
EMP: 9 **Publicly Held**
SIC: 3674 Semiconductors & related devices
HQ: Excel Technology, Inc.
125 Middlesex Tpke
Bedford MA 01730
781 266-5700

(G-5041)
FRENCH ASSOCIATES INC
Also Called: French Pdts Frnch Pickle Works
7339 172nd St (11366-1420)
PHONE..............................718 387-9880
Seymour Rosen, *President*
Jerry Rosen, *Vice Pres*
EMP: 10 **EST:** 1919
SQ FT: 20,000
SALES (est): 650K **Privately Held**
WEB: www.frenchassociates.com
SIC: 2035 5199 5149 Pickles, vinegar; general merchandise, non-durable; groceries & related products

(G-5042)
HACULLA NYC INC
6805 Fresh Meadow Ln (11365-3438)
PHONE..............................718 886-3163
Jonathan Koon, *Principal*
EMP: 10 **EST:** 2014
SALES (est): 530K **Privately Held**
SIC: 2329 Men's & boys' sportswear & athletic clothing

▲ = Import ▼ =Export
◆ =Import/Export

(G-5043)
KOON ENTERPRISES LLC
6805 Fresh Madow Ln Ste B (11365)
PHONE..............................718 886-3163
Jonathan M Koon, *Mng Member*
Katherine Koon,
EMP: 5
SALES: 1.2MM Privately Held
SIC: 2389 Costumes

(G-5044)
KOONICHI INC
6805 Fresh Madow Ln Ste B (11365)
PHONE..............................718 886-8338
Jonathan Koon, *President*
Katherine Koon, *Vice Pres*
Raymond Koon, *CFO*
▲ **EMP: 7**
SQ FT: 2,500
SALES (est): 590K Privately Held
WEB: www.koonichi.com
SIC: 3089 Automotive parts, plastic

(G-5045)
RYBA SOFTWARE INC
7359 186th St (11366-1719)
PHONE..............................718 264-9352
Alexander J Ryba, *Principal*
EMP: 5
SALES (est): 198.4K Privately Held
SIC: 7372 Prepackaged software

(G-5046)
STAIRWORLD INC
5635 175th Pl B (11365-1627)
PHONE..............................718 441-9722
Kenneth Franklin, *President*
John Franklin, *Vice Pres*
EMP: 5
SALES (est): 665.1K Privately Held
WEB: www.stairworld.com
SIC: 2431 Stair railings, wood; staircases
& stairs, wood

(G-5047)
TOROTRON CORPORATION
18508 Union Tpke Ste 101 (11366-1700)
PHONE..............................718 428-6992
Oscar Zanger, *President*
Steve Bortnicker, *Controller*
Miriam Zanger, *Admin Sec*
EMP: 8 EST: 1950
SQ FT: 3,000
SALES: 350K Privately Held
SIC: 3679 Electronic circuits

(G-5048)
VR CONTAINMENT LLC
17625 Union Tpke Ste 175 (11366-1515)
PHONE..............................917 972-3441
EMP: 6 EST: 2012
SALES (est): 644K Privately Held
SIC: 3442 3446 Metal doors; gates, orna-
mental metal

Frewsburg
Chautauqua County

(G-5049)
**ARTISAN MANAGEMENT
GROUP INC**
39 Venman St (14738-9565)
PHONE..............................716 569-4094
Kevin Delong, *President*
EMP: 7
SALES: 950K Privately Held
SIC: 3544 3599 Special dies, tools, jigs &
fixtures; machine shop, jobbing & repair

(G-5050)
COLBURNS AC RFRGN
17 White Dr (14738-9553)
P.O. Box 9430 (14738-1443)
PHONE..............................716 569-3695
George M Colburn, *President*
EMP: 10
SQ FT: 3,600
SALES: 1.9MM Privately Held
SIC: 3585 7623 Heating & air conditioning
combination units; refrigeration repair
service

(G-5051)
MONARCH PLASTICS INC
225 Falconer St (14738-9506)
P.O. Box 648 (14738-0648)
PHONE..............................716 569-2175
Donald Olander, *President*
Bambi L Muro, *Executive*
▲ **EMP: 30 EST:** 1960
SQ FT: 16,000
SALES (est): 5.7MM Privately Held
WEB: www.monarchplastic.com
SIC: 3089 Molding primary plastic

Friendship
Allegany County

(G-5052)
FRIENDSHIP DAIRIES LLC
6701 County Road 20 (14739-8660)
PHONE..............................585 973-3031
Ron Klein, *President*
Tim Bentley, *CTO*
EMP: 250
SQ FT: 15,000
SALES (est): 39.8MM
SALES (corp-wide): 3.7B Privately Held
WEB: www.deanfoods.com
SIC: 2023 2022 Dry, condensed, evapo-
rated dairy products; cheese, natural &
processed
HQ: Saputo Dairy Foods Usa, Llc
2711 N Haske Ave Ste 3700
Dallas TX 75204
214 863-2300

(G-5053)
**WAGNER HARDWOODS LLC
(PA)**
6052 County Road 20 (14739-8664)
PHONE..............................607 229-8198
Les Wagner, *Principal*
EMP: 8
SALES (est): 22.5MM Privately Held
SIC: 2421 Sawmills & planing mills, gen-
eral

Fulton
Oswego County

(G-5054)
ATTIS ETHANOL FULTON LLC
376 Owens Rd (13069)
PHONE..............................315 593-0500
Stephanie Burke,
EMP: 85
SALES (est): 204.5K
**SALES (corp-wide): 890.2K Publicly
Held**
SIC: 2869 2046 Ethyl alcohol, ethanol;
corn oil products
PA: Attis Industries Inc.
12540 Broadwell Rd # 2104
Milton GA 30004
678 580-5661

(G-5055)
**C & C METAL FABRICATIONS
INC**
159 Hubbard St (13069-1247)
PHONE..............................315 598-7607
Judy Davis, *Manager*
John F Sharkey IV,
EMP: 19
SQ FT: 32,000
SALES (est): 3.2MM Privately Held
WEB: www.candcfabrication.com
SIC: 3441 Fabricated structural metal

(G-5056)
**CANFIELD MACHINE & TOOL
LLC**
121 Howard Rd (13069-4278)
PHONE..............................315 593-8062
Debra Canfield, *Director*
Chris Canfield,
EMP: 41
SQ FT: 24,000
SALES (est): 5.7MM Privately Held
SIC: 3599 Machine shop, jobbing & repair

(G-5057)
D-K MANUFACTURING CORP
Also Called: DK
551 W 3rd St S (13069-2824)
P.O. Box 600 (13069-0600)
PHONE..............................315 592-4327
Norman W Kesterke, *President*
Donald L Kesterke, *General Mgr*
EMP: 20
SQ FT: 30,000
SALES (est): 2MM Privately Held
WEB: www.d-kmfg.com
SIC: 3469 3599 Stamping metal for the
trade; machine shop, jobbing & repair

(G-5058)
DOT PUBLISHING
Also Called: Fulton Daily News
117 Cayuga St (13069-1709)
PHONE..............................315 593-2510
Monica Mackenzie, *President*
EMP: 10
SQ FT: 2,048
SALES (est): 581.9K Privately Held
SIC: 2711 Newspapers, publishing & print-
ing

(G-5059)
FULTON NEWSPAPERS INC
Also Called: Fulton Patriot
67 S 2nd St (13069-1725)
PHONE..............................315 598-6397
Vincent R Caravan, *President*
Ronald Caravan, *Vice Pres*
EMP: 20
SQ FT: 8,000
SALES (est): 928.2K Privately Held
SIC: 2711 2752 2791 2789 Newspapers:
publishing only, not printed on site; com-
mercial printing, offset; typesetting; book-
binding & related work

(G-5060)
FULTON SCREEN PRINTING
2 Harris St (13069-4937)
PHONE..............................315 593-2220
Tom Brady, *Partner*
Bonnie Macintyre, *Partner*
EMP: 5
SQ FT: 3,000
SALES (est): 494K Privately Held
WEB: www.fultonscreen.com
SIC: 2759 Screen printing

(G-5061)
FULTON TOOL CO INC
802 W Broadway Ste 1 (13069-1522)
PHONE..............................315 598-2900
Bruce Phelps, *President*
Barbara Phelps, *Corp Secy*
Peter Russell, *Vice Pres*
EMP: 21 EST: 1959
SQ FT: 32,000
SALES (est): 4.3MM Privately Held
WEB: www.fultontool.com
SIC: 3599 Machine shop, jobbing & repair

(G-5062)
**GONE SOUTH CONCRETE
BLOCK INC**
Also Called: John Deere Authorized Dealer
2809 State Route 3 (13069-5805)
P.O. Box 787 (13069-0787)
PHONE..............................315 598-2141
Thomas S Venezia, *President*
Dale Smith, *Vice Pres*
EMP: 30
SQ FT: 2,000
SALES (est): 6.7MM Privately Held
SIC: 3271 5211 5082 Blocks, concrete or
cinder: standard; lumber & other building
materials; construction & mining machin-
ery

(G-5063)
HAUN WELDING SUPPLY INC
214 N 4th St (13069-1216)
PHONE..............................315 592-5012
Patty Sasso, *Manager*
EMP: 7
SQ FT: 1,938
**SALES (corp-wide): 65.7MM Privately
Held**
SIC: 7692 5084 Welding repair; welding
machinery & equipment

PA: Haun Welding Supply, Inc.
5921 Court Street Rd
Syracuse NY 13206
315 463-5241

(G-5064)
HUHTAMAKI INC
Huhtamaki Consumer Packaging
100 State St (13069-2518)
PHONE..............................315 593-5311
Dietmar Johann, *Opers Mgr*
Stephanie Holly, *Accounts Mgr*
Dale Abbascia, *Sales Staff*
Derrill Hutchison, *Sales Staff*
Frederique Laborde, *Info Tech Mgr*
EMP: 585
SALES (corp-wide): 3.5B Privately Held
SIC: 2621 Pressed pulp products
HQ: Huhtamaki, Inc.
9201 Packaging Dr
De Soto KS 66018
913 583-3025

(G-5065)
IVES FARM MARKET
Also Called: Ives Slaughterhouse
2652 Rr 176 (13069)
PHONE..............................315 592-4880
Ronald Ives, *Owner*
Jean Ives, *Partner*
EMP: 5
SALES (est): 360K Privately Held
SIC: 2011 5411 5421 Meat packing
plants; grocery stores; meat markets, in-
cluding freezer provisioniers

(G-5066)
JOHN CRANE INC
2314 County Route 4 (13069-3659)
PHONE..............................315 593-6237
John Crane, *Branch Mgr*
EMP: 64
SALES (corp-wide): 4.2B Privately Held
SIC: 3053 Gaskets & sealing devices
HQ: John Crane Inc.
227 W Monroe St Ste 1800
Chicago IL 60606
312 605-7800

(G-5067)
K&NS FOODS USA LLC
607 Phillips St (13069-1520)
PHONE..............................315 598-8080
Jimmy Koid, *Mng Member*
▲ **EMP: 30 EST:** 2012
SALES (est): 7.6MM
**SALES (corp-wide): 1.9MM Privately
Held**
SIC: 2015 Chicken, processed: frozen
PA: K&N's Foods (Private) Limited
Second Floor
Lahore

(G-5068)
KENWELL CORPORATION
871 Hannibal St (13069-4186)
P.O. Box 207 (13069-0207)
PHONE..............................315 592-4263
Roger Horning Jr, *President*
Bruce Horning, *Vice Pres*
Bob Flack, *Manager*
EMP: 52 EST: 1970
SQ FT: 13,000
SALES (est): 10.8MM Privately Held
WEB: www.kenwellcorp.com
SIC: 3599 Machine shop, jobbing & repair

(G-5069)
**KRENGEL MANUFACTURING CO
INC**
Also Called: American Marking Systems
121 Fulton Ave Fl 2 (13069)
PHONE..............................212 227-1901
EMP: 18
SALES (est): 980K Privately Held
SIC: 3953 Mfg Marking Devices

(G-5070)
**LYDALL PERFORMANCE MTLS
US INC**
2885 State Route 481 (13069-4221)
PHONE..............................315 592-8100
Richard Isbell, *QC Dir*
Debra Morris, *Technology*
EMP: 219

SALES (corp-wide): 785.9MM **Publicly Held**
WEB: www.sealinfo.com
SIC: 3053 Gaskets, packing & sealing devices
HQ: Lydall Performance Materials (Us), Inc.
216 Wohlsen Way
Lancaster PA 17603

(G-5071)
MESSER MERCHANT PRODUCTION LLC
370 Owens Rd (13069-4619)
PHONE...........................315 593-1360
Richard Olinger, *Principal*
EMP: 9 **Privately Held**
SIC: 2813 Carbon dioxide
HQ: Messer Merchant Production, Llc
575 Mountain Ave
New Providence NJ 07974

(G-5072)
NET & DIE INC
24 Foster St (13069)
P.O. Box 240 (13069-0240)
PHONE...........................315 592-4311
Richard N Shatrau, *President*
Helena Rockwood, *Corp Secy*
EMP: 38 **EST:** 1963
SQ FT: 30,000
SALES (est): 6.7MM **Privately Held**
SIC: 3599 Machine shop, jobbing & repair

(G-5073)
NORTH END PAPER CO INC
702 Hannibal St (13069-1020)
PHONE...........................315 593-8100
William F Shafer III, *President*
EMP: 7
SQ FT: 40,000
SALES (est): 1.1MM
SALES (corp-wide): 8.7MM **Privately Held**
WEB: www.flowercitytissue.com
SIC: 2621 Tissue paper
PA: Flower City Tissue Mills Company, Inc.
700 Driving Park Ave
Rochester NY 14613
585 458-9200

(G-5074)
NORTHERN BITUMINOUS MIX INC
32 Silk Rd (13069-4862)
P.O. Box 787 (13069-0787)
PHONE...........................315 598-2141
Thomas Venezia Sr, *President*
EMP: 6
SQ FT: 2,000
SALES (est): 784K **Privately Held**
SIC: 2951 Asphalt & asphaltic paving mixtures (not from refineries)

(G-5075)
PATHFINDER INDUSTRIES INC
117 N 3rd St (13069-1256)
PHONE...........................315 593-2483
Marsha Ives, *President*
Maribeth Myers, *Vice Pres*
EMP: 21
SQ FT: 22,000
SALES (est): 4.6MM **Privately Held**
WEB: www.pathfinderind.com
SIC: 3444 Sheet metalwork

(G-5076)
UNIVERSAL METAL WORKS LLC
159 Hubbard St (13069-1247)
PHONE...........................315 598-7607
John F Sharkey IV,
EMP: 19
SALES: 4.5MM **Privately Held**
SIC: 3441 Fabricated structural metal

Fultonville
Montgomery County

(G-5077)
ANDERSON INSTRUMENT CO INC (HQ)
156 Auriesville Rd (12072-2031)
PHONE...........................518 922-5315
Andrew Hider, *CEO*
Larry Byrnes, *Vice Pres*
Brigitt Fauve, *Vice Pres*
Deanne Brassard, *Purch Agent*
Ashish Maharjan, *Engineer*
▲ **EMP:** 70
SQ FT: 40,000
SALES (est): 23.2MM
SALES (corp-wide): 6.4B **Publicly Held**
WEB: www.andinst.com
SIC: 3823 5084 3822 3625 Controllers for process variables, all types; industrial machinery & equipment; auto controls regulating residntl & coml environmt & applncs; relays & industrial controls
PA: Fortive Corporation
6920 Seaway Blvd
Everett WA 98203
425 446-5000

(G-5078)
CONSOLIDATED BARRICADES INC
179 Dillenbeck Rd (12072-3311)
PHONE...........................518 922-7944
Joseph Melideo, *President*
EMP: 8
SQ FT: 7,000
SALES (est): 1.2MM **Privately Held**
WEB: www.consolidatedbarricades.com
SIC: 3499 Barricades, metal

(G-5079)
FULTONVILLE MACHINE & TOOL CO
73 Union St (12072-1836)
P.O. Box 426 (12072-0426)
PHONE...........................518 853-4441
Randolf C Snyder, *President*
Patricia Snyder, *Corp Secy*
EMP: 11 **EST:** 1945
SQ FT: 18,000
SALES (est): 1.2MM **Privately Held**
SIC: 3599 Machine shop, jobbing & repair

(G-5080)
MOHAWK RIVER LEATHER WORKS
32 Broad St (12072)
PHONE...........................518 853-3900
Joseph H Sicilia, *President*
Robert Hojohn, *Vice Pres*
EMP: 17
SQ FT: 3,534
SALES (est): 2.6MM **Privately Held**
SIC: 3111 Coloring of leather

Gainesville
Wyoming County

(G-5081)
DRASGOW INC
4150 Poplar Tree Rd (14066-9723)
PHONE...........................585 786-3603
Karl Drasgow, *President*
Bryan Schabloski, *Production*
Crystal Hilton, *Info Tech Mgr*
EMP: 25
SQ FT: 17,946
SALES (est): 1.7MM **Privately Held**
SIC: 3599 Machine shop, jobbing & repair

Galway
Saratoga County

(G-5082)
WHALENS HORSERADISH PRODUCTS
1710 Route 29 (12074-2213)
PHONE...........................518 587-6404
Kim Bibens, *President*
EMP: 5 **EST:** 2013
SALES (est): 450.7K **Privately Held**
SIC: 2035 Horseradish, prepared

Gansevoort
Saratoga County

(G-5083)
AUREONIC
13 Whispering Pines Rd (12831-1443)
PHONE...........................518 791-9331
Shawn Lescault, *CEO*
Nicholas Karker, *Co-Owner*
Patrick Roden, *Co-Owner*
Robert Schramm, *Co-Owner*
Ian Tucker, *CFO*
EMP: 5
SALES (est): 350K **Privately Held**
SIC: 3823 7389 Combustion control instruments;

(G-5084)
PALLETTE STONE CORPORATION
269 Ballard Rd (12831-1597)
PHONE...........................518 584-2421
Thomas Longe, *President*
D Alan Collins, *Corp Secy*
EMP: 40
SQ FT: 3,000
SALES (est): 9.1MM
SALES (corp-wide): 33.1MM **Privately Held**
SIC: 3281 2951 3241 5032 Cut stone & stone products; concrete, bituminous; portland cement; stone, crushed or broken; asphalt mixture; concrete & cinder block; paving stones; concrete & cinder block
PA: D A Collins Environmental Services Llc
269 Ballard Rd
Wilton NY 12831
518 664-9855

(G-5085)
RASP INCORPORATED
8 Dukes Way (12831-1668)
PHONE...........................518 747-8020
Ronald Richards, *Ch of Bd*
Michael Close, *Treasurer*
Jeff Bruno, *Sr Project Mgr*
EMP: 27 **EST:** 1995
SQ FT: 8,000
SALES (est): 6.4MM **Privately Held**
WEB: www.rasp-controls.com
SIC: 3625 Industrial controls: push button, selector switches, pilot

(G-5086)
ROCK HILL BAKEHOUSE LTD
21 Saratoga Rd (12831)
PHONE...........................518 743-1627
Matthew Funiciello, *President*
Michael London, *Vice Pres*
Adam Witt, *Treasurer*
Wendy London, *Admin Sec*
EMP: 30
SALES (est): 2.7MM **Privately Held**
WEB: www.rockhillbakehouse.com
SIC: 2051 5461 Bread, all types (white, wheat, rye, etc): fresh or frozen; bread

(G-5087)
STONE BRIDGE IRON AND STL INC
426 Purinton Rd (12831-2193)
PHONE...........................518 695-3752
Brian Carmer, *Principal*
Britt Carmer, *Exec VP*
Mark Hutchinson, *Vice Pres*
Kevin Parucki, *Manager*

Nancy Carmer, *Admin Sec*
▲ **EMP:** 60
SQ FT: 45,000
SALES (est): 17.3MM **Privately Held**
WEB: www.stonebridgeiron.com
SIC: 3441 Building components, structural steel

(G-5088)
TRUARC FABRICATION
1 Commerce Park Dr (12831-2239)
PHONE...........................518 691-0430
Cris Edgrely, *President*
Bill Lorrain, *Manager*
EMP: 9
SALES (est): 956.8K **Privately Held**
SIC: 3599 Flexible metal hose, tubing & bellows

Garden City
Nassau County

(G-5089)
AAR ALLEN SERVICES INC
AAR Aircraft Component
747 Zeckendorf Blvd (11530-2188)
PHONE...........................516 222-9000
Rob Bruinsna, *General Mgr*
EMP: 39
SALES (corp-wide): 2B **Publicly Held**
SIC: 3728 Aircraft parts & equipment
HQ: Aar Allen Services, Inc.
1100 N Wood Dale Rd
Wood Dale IL 60191

(G-5090)
ATLAS SWITCH CO INC
969 Stewart Ave (11530-4816)
PHONE...........................516 222-6280
Gina Paradise, *President*
Chad Zepeda, *Engineer*
Art Metz, *Bookkeeper*
Barry Mednick, *Technology*
EMP: 33
SQ FT: 30,000
SALES (est): 11.2MM **Privately Held**
WEB: www.atlasswitch.com
SIC: 3613 3699 Switches, electric power except snap, push button, etc.; electrical equipment & supplies

(G-5091)
BEYOND AIR INC
825 E Gate Blvd Ste 320 (11530-2135)
PHONE...........................516 665-8200
Steven A Lisi, *Ch of Bd*
Amir Avniel, *President*
Douglas Beck, *CFO*
EMP: 18
SALES: 7.7MM **Privately Held**
SIC: 3841 Surgical & medical instruments

(G-5092)
BHARAT ELECTRONICS LIMITED
53 Hilton Ave (11530-2806)
PHONE...........................516 248-4021
Siva Muthuswamy, *Manager*
EMP: 7
SALES (corp-wide): 1.6B **Privately Held**
WEB: www.bel-india.com
SIC: 3674 Solid state electronic devices
PA: Bharat Electronics Limited
Outer Ring Road, Nagavara
Bengaluru KA 56004
802 503-9266

(G-5093)
BRISTOL-MYERS SQUIBB COMPANY
1000 Stewart Ave (11530-4814)
PHONE...........................516 832-2191
Richard Serafin, *Branch Mgr*
EMP: 225
SALES (corp-wide): 22.5B **Publicly Held**
WEB: www.bms.com
SIC: 2834 Pharmaceutical preparations
PA: Bristol-Myers Squibb Company
430 E 29th St Fl 14
New York NY 10016
212 546-4000

(G-5094)
CAMPUS COURSE PAKS INC
1 South Ave Fl 1 # 1 (11530-4213)
PHONE..................................516 877-3967
Wayne Piskin, *President*
EMP: 5
SQ FT: 1,500
SALES (est): 237.4MM **Privately Held**
WEB: www.ccpaks.com
SIC: 2731 Books: publishing only

(G-5095)
DILLMEIER ENTERPRISES INC
106 7th St Ste 201 (11530-5718)
PHONE..................................800 325-0596
EMP: 18
SALES (corp-wide): 23MM **Privately Held**
SIC: 3231 Products of purchased glass
PA: Dillmeier Enterprises, Inc.
2903 Industrial Park Rd
Van Buren AR 72956
800 325-0596

(G-5096)
DYNA-EMPIRE INC
1075 Stewart Ave (11530-4871)
PHONE..................................516 222-2700
G Patrick Mc Carthy, *President*
Richard Shaper, *Vice Pres*
Saf Samad, *Mfg Mgr*
Syd Crossley, *Opers Staff*
Janine Harty, *Accounting Mgr*
▲ EMP: 145 EST: 1941
SQ FT: 52,000
SALES (est): 29.4MM **Privately Held**
WEB: www.dyna-empire.com
SIC: 3724 3728 3829 3823 Aircraft engines & engine parts; aircraft landing assemblies & brakes; measuring & controlling devices; industrial instrmnts msrmnt display/control process variable; search & navigation equipment

(G-5097)
EDGEWOOD INDUSTRIES INC
635 Commercial Ave (11530-6409)
PHONE..................................516 227-2447
Frank Suppa, *President*
EMP: 6
SALES (est): 551.9K **Privately Held**
SIC: 3271 Concrete block & brick

(G-5098)
EURO FINE PAPER INC
220 Nassau Blvd (11530-5500)
PHONE..................................516 238-5253
Tom McShea Sr, *President*
EMP: 8
SALES (est): 640K **Privately Held**
SIC: 2621 Paper mills

(G-5099)
EUROPEAN MARBLE WORKS CO INC
Also Called: Puccio Marble and Onyx
54 Nassau Blvd (11530-4139)
PHONE..................................718 387-9778
Paul Puccio, *President*
John Puccio, *Vice Pres*
▲ EMP: 12 EST: 1956
SQ FT: 70,000
SALES (est): 1.3MM **Privately Held**
SIC: 3281 Cut stone & stone products

(G-5100)
EXERGY LLC
320 Endo Blvd Unit 1 (11530-6747)
PHONE..................................516 832-9300
Jordan Finkelstein, *President*
Bob Scott, *President*
Edward Loring, *General Mgr*
Robert Scott, *Vice Pres*
Dennis Cheung, *Prdtn Mgr*
EMP: 37
SQ FT: 20,000
SALES (est): 7.2MM **Privately Held**
WEB: www.exergyllc.com
SIC: 3443 8711 Heat exchangers, condensers & components; consulting engineer

(G-5101)
H&E SERVICE CORP
Also Called: Gimbel & Associates
400 Garden Cy Plz Ste 405 (11530)
PHONE..................................646 472-1936
Roger Gimbel, *President*
Gail Steiger, *Executive Asst*
William Martin, *Sr Consultant*
EMP: 98 EST: 1960
SQ FT: 30,000
SALES (est): 5.4MM **Privately Held**
SIC: 2752 Commercial printing, offset

(G-5102)
ISSCO CORPORATION (PA)
Also Called: Industrial SEC Systems Contrls
111 Cherry Valley Ave # 410 (11530-1570)
PHONE..................................212 732-8748
Arthur R Katon, *President*
Marsha Katon, *Corp Secy*
EMP: 16
SQ FT: 14,000
SALES (est): 1.5MM **Privately Held**
SIC: 3699 Security control equipment & systems

(G-5103)
L & M PUBLICATIONS INC
Also Called: Freeport Baldwin Leader
2 Endo Blvd (11530-6707)
PHONE..................................516 378-3133
Linda Laursen Toscano, *President*
Paul Laursen, *Vice Pres*
John Laursen, *Shareholder*
EMP: 33
SALES (est): 1.7MM **Privately Held**
WEB: www.merricklife.com
SIC: 2711 7313 Newspapers: publishing only, not printed on site; newspaper advertising representative

(G-5104)
LIFETIME BRANDS INC (PA)
1000 Stewart Ave (11530-4814)
PHONE..................................516 683-6000
Robert B Kay, *CEO*
Marian Finnigan, *CEO*
Jeffrey Siegel, *Ch of Bd*
Daniel Siegel, *President*
Joe Arria, *Vice Pres*
◆ EMP: 277
SQ FT: 159,000
SALES: 704.5MM **Publicly Held**
WEB: www.lifetimebrands.com
SIC: 3421 5023 5719 Cutlery; home furnishings; kitchen tools & utensils; stainless steel flatware; kitchenware; cutlery; glassware

(G-5105)
LITMOR PUBLISHING CORP (PA)
Also Called: Litmor Publications
821 Franklin Ave Ste 208 (11530-4519)
PHONE..................................516 931-0012
Margaret Norris, *Publisher*
Edward Norris, *General Mgr*
EMP: 15
SQ FT: 3,000
SALES (est): 1.3MM **Privately Held**
SIC: 2711 2791 2752 Newspapers, publishing & printing; typesetting; commercial printing, lithographic

(G-5106)
M AND J HAIR CENTER INC
Also Called: Natural Image Hair Concepts
1103 Stewart Ave Ste 100 (11530-4886)
PHONE..................................516 872-1010
Jean Dreyfuss, *President*
EMP: 15
SQ FT: 1,600
SALES (est): 1.4MM **Privately Held**
WEB: www.mjhair.com
SIC: 3999 Wigs, including doll wigs, toupees or wiglets

(G-5107)
MCQUILLING PARTNERS INC (PA)
1035 Stewart Ave Ste 100 (11530-4825)
PHONE..................................516 227-5718
John F Desantes, *Ch of Bd*
Peter Neave, *Managing Dir*
Tom Schmidt, *CTO*
EMP: 26 EST: 1964

SALES (est): 3.5MM **Privately Held**
WEB: www.mcquilling.com
SIC: 3731 Tankers, building & repairing

(G-5108)
MILES MOSS OF ALBANY INC (HQ)
586 Commercial Ave (11530-6418)
PHONE..................................516 222-8008
Robert Moss, *President*
Phil Lonetto, *Sales Staff*
EMP: 28
SQ FT: 35,000
SALES: 53.6MM
SALES (corp-wide): 2.6B **Privately Held**
WEB: www.lipipe.com
SIC: 3498 5074 Fabricated pipe & fittings; plumbing fittings & supplies
PA: Core & Main Lp
1830 Craig Park Ct
Saint Louis MO 63146
314 432-4700

(G-5109)
MILES MOSS OF NEW YORK INC (PA)
Also Called: LI Pipe Supply
586 Commercial Ave (11530-6418)
PHONE..................................516 222-8008
Robert Moss, *CEO*
Larry Greenberg, *General Mgr*
Brian Coyle, *Sales Mgr*
Frank Anselmo, *Sales Staff*
Tommy LI, *Sales Staff*
EMP: 40
SQ FT: 35,000
SALES (est): 30.5MM **Privately Held**
SIC: 3498 Fabricated pipe & fittings

(G-5110)
MITCO MANUFACTURING
605 Locust St (11530-6552)
PHONE..................................516 745-9236
▲ EMP: 7 EST: 2011
SALES (est): 441K **Privately Held**
SIC: 3999 Manufacturing industries

(G-5111)
OPTIONLINE LLC
100 Hilton Ave Apt 23 (11530-1564)
PHONE..................................516 218-3225
Luiz Grossmann, *President*
EMP: 25
SALES (est): 694.2K **Privately Held**
SIC: 2721 7375 Periodicals: publishing only; statistical reports (periodicals): publishing only; on-line data base information retrieval

(G-5112)
PUCCIO DESIGN INTERNATIONAL
Also Called: Puccio European Marble & Onyx
54 Nassau Blvd (11530-4139)
PHONE..................................516 248-6426
Paul Puccio, *President*
EMP: 15 EST: 1968
SQ FT: 4,000
SALES (est): 170.8K **Privately Held**
WEB: www.puccio.info
SIC: 3281 Furniture, cut stone

(G-5113)
RICHNER COMMUNICATIONS INC (PA)
Also Called: Prime Time
2 Endo Blvd (11530-6707)
PHONE..................................516 569-4000
Stuart Richner, *CEO*
Robert Kern, *General Mgr*
Tony Bellissimo, *Editor*
Jeff Bessen, *Editor*
Scott Brinton, *Editor*
EMP: 130
SQ FT: 90,000
SALES (est): 14.2MM **Privately Held**
SIC: 2711 Commercial printing & newspaper publishing combined; newspapers, publishing & printing

(G-5114)
ROBECO/ASCOT PRODUCTS INC
100 Ring Rd W (11530-3219)
PHONE..................................516 248-1521

EMP: 0
SALES (est): 1.2MM **Privately Held**
SIC: 3081 Unsupported Plastics Film And Sheet, Nsk

(G-5115)
SEVIROLI FOODS INC (PA)
385 Oak St (11530-6543)
PHONE..................................516 222-6220
Joseph Seviroli Jr, *Ch of Bd*
Paul Vertullo, *COO*
Alan Bronstein, *Vice Pres*
Dave Sammons, *Vice Pres*
Bert Singh, *Purch Mgr*
▲ EMP: 200
SALES (est): 78.1MM **Privately Held**
WEB: www.seviroli.com
SIC: 2038 Frozen specialties

(G-5116)
SOFTWARE ENGINEERING AMER INC (PA)
Also Called: Sea
1325 Franklin Ave Ste 545 (11530-1631)
PHONE..................................516 328-7000
Salvatore Simeone, *President*
Josephine Day, *Treasurer*
Colleen Simeone, *Treasurer*
John Brennan, *Accounts Mgr*
Gloria Sicignano, *Sales Staff*
EMP: 65
SQ FT: 40,000
SALES (est): 9.6MM **Privately Held**
WEB: www.seasoft.com
SIC: 7372 Prepackaged software

(G-5117)
STANDARD WEDDING BAND CO
951 Franklin Ave (11530-2909)
PHONE..................................516 294-0954
Walter E Soderlund, *President*
Mabel T Soderlund, *Treasurer*
EMP: 6
SALES: 500K **Privately Held**
SIC: 3911 Rings, finger: precious metal

(G-5118)
THERMAL TECH DOORS INC (PA)
576 Brook St (11530-6416)
PHONE..................................516 745-0100
Emanuel Karavas, *President*
Stephanos Kourtis, *Vice Pres*
Stavros Giannopoulos, *CFO*
EMP: 40
SQ FT: 25,000
SALES (est): 5MM **Privately Held**
SIC: 3442 Sash, door or window: metal

(G-5119)
WON & LEE INC
Also Called: Unicorn Graphics
971 Stewart Ave (11530-4816)
PHONE..................................516 222-0712
Jong Suk Lee, *President*
Jong Hoon Lee, *Vice Pres*
▲ EMP: 35
SQ FT: 30,000
SALES (est): 6.8MM **Privately Held**
WEB: www.unicorngraphics.com
SIC: 2759 2789 2752 2741 Calendars: printing; bookbinding & related work; commercial printing, lithographic; miscellaneous publishing; ink, printers'

Garden City Park
Nassau County

(G-5120)
DENTON STONEWORKS INC
94 Denton Ave (11040-4036)
P.O. Box 3807, New Hyde Park (11040-8807)
PHONE..................................516 746-1500
Boguslaw Kaczor, *CEO*
EMP: 14
SQ FT: 15,000
SALES (est): 1.8MM **Privately Held**
SIC: 3281 Cut stone & stone products

(G-5121)
GRACE LOVE INC
202 Atlantic Ave Ste C (11040-5032)
PHONE....................................646 402-4325
Andrew Giangrandi, *COO*
EMP: 15
SALES (est): 2.1MM **Privately Held**
SIC: 2037 Frozen fruits & vegetables

(G-5122)
NEW YORK PACKAGING II LLC
Also Called: Redi Bag USA
135 Fulton Ave (11040-5305)
P.O. Box 1039, New Hyde Park (11040-7039)
PHONE....................................516 746-0600
Jeffrey Rabiea, *President*
Michael Zapf, *CFO*
▲ **EMP:** 25
SALES (est): 36.8MM **Privately Held**
SIC: 2673 Plastic bags: made from purchased materials

(G-5123)
PERFECT GEAR & INSTRUMENT
125 Railroad Ave (11040-5016)
PHONE....................................516 873-6122
Karen Hearne, *Principal*
EMP: 24
SALES (corp-wide): 90.2MM **Privately Held**
SIC: 3462 Gears, forged steel
HQ: Perfect Gear & Instrument Corp
250 Duffy Ave
Hicksville NY 11801
516 328-3330

(G-5124)
SQUARE ONE PUBLISHERS INC
115 Herricks Rd (11040-5341)
PHONE....................................516 535-2010
Rudy Shur, *President*
▲ **EMP:** 12
SQ FT: 8,000
SALES (est): 2.3MM **Privately Held**
SIC: 2731 Books: publishing only

(G-5125)
WINDOWCRAFT INC
77 2nd Ave (11040-5030)
PHONE....................................516 294-3580
Joseph Daniels, *President*
Jerry Zachariah, *Engineer*
▲ **EMP:** 18
SQ FT: 6,000
SALES (est): 3.1MM **Privately Held**
SIC: 2591 Window shades

(G-5126)
YORK INDUSTRIES INC
303 Nassau Blvd (11040-5213)
PHONE....................................516 746-3736
Lee E Smith, *Ch of Bd*
Paul Byers, *Vice Pres*
Roseanne Squillace, *Buyer*
Frank Filadelfo, *VP Engrg*
Maria Maqueda, *VP Sales*
EMP: 50 **EST:** 1942
SQ FT: 9,000
SALES (est): 10.8MM **Privately Held**
WEB: www.york-ind.com
SIC: 3829 3568 3462 3429 Measuring & controlling devices; ball joints, except aircraft & automotive; iron & steel forgings; manufactured hardware (general); hand & edge tools; tire cord & fabrics

---

Gardiner
Ulster County

(G-5127)
BYCMAC CORP
Also Called: Kiss My Face
144 Main St (12525-5245)
P.O. Box 224 (12525-0224)
PHONE....................................845 255-0884
Robert Macleod, *President*
Steve Byckiewicz, *Exec VP*
Mary Abrahamsen, *Department Mgr*
Kelly Szeli, *Admin Sec*
◆ **EMP:** 45 **EST:** 1979
SQ FT: 20,000

SALES (est): 9.5MM **Privately Held**
WEB: www.kissmyface.com
SIC: 2844 Cosmetic preparations

(G-5128)
DAVID KUCERA INC
42 Steves Ln (12525-5319)
PHONE....................................845 255-1044
David Kucera, *President*
Ann Marie Cramer, *Manager*
EMP: 35
SQ FT: 15,000
SALES (est): 6.6MM **Privately Held**
WEB: www.davidkucerainc.com
SIC: 3272 Concrete products, precast

(G-5129)
GLASSON SCULPTURE WORKS
23 Shaft Rd (12525-5115)
PHONE....................................845 255-2969
EMP: 5
SALES (est): 311.9K **Privately Held**
SIC: 3299 Mfg Nonmetallic Mineral Products
PA: Glasson Sculpture Works
612 S 11th St
Laramie WY 82070

(G-5130)
S P INDUSTRIES INC
Also Called: Sp Scientific
815 Rte 208 (12525)
P.O. Box 48330, Newark NJ (07101-8530)
PHONE....................................845 255-5000
Dan De Beau, *Branch Mgr*
Paul W Coiteux, *Technical Staff*
EMP: 82
SQ FT: 7,200
SALES (corp-wide): 1.4B **Privately Held**
WEB: www.virtis.com
SIC: 3821 Laboratory apparatus & furniture
HQ: S P Industries, Inc.
935 Mearns Rd
Warminster PA 18974
215 672-7800

(G-5131)
TUTHILLTOWN SPIRITS LLC
14 Gristmill Ln (12525-5528)
P.O. Box 320 (12525-0320)
PHONE....................................845 255-1527
Brian Lee,
Ralph Erenzo,
▲ **EMP:** 15
SALES (est): 2.9MM
SALES (corp-wide): 1.7B **Privately Held**
SIC: 2085 Distilled & blended liquors
HQ: William Grant & Sons Limited
Phoenix Crescent
Bellshill

(G-5132)
UTILITY CANVAS INC (PA)
2686 Route 44 55 (12525)
PHONE....................................845 255-9290
Hal Grano, *President*
Jillian Kaufman, *Vice Pres*
EMP: 6
SQ FT: 4,000
SALES (est): 1MM **Privately Held**
SIC: 2394 Canvas & related products

Garnerville
Rockland County

(G-5133)
A & W METAL WORKS INC
55 W Railroad Ave 5 (10923-1261)
P.O. Box 276 (10923-0276)
PHONE....................................845 352-2346
Martin Weinstock, *Admin Sec*
EMP: 10 **EST:** 2016
SALES (est): 400K **Privately Held**
SIC: 3999 Manufacturing industries

(G-5134)
FIRST DUE FIRE EQUIPMENT INC
130 W Ramapo Rd (10923-2134)
PHONE....................................845 222-1329
David Leiser, *CEO*
Mike Humphrey, *General Mgr*
EMP: 10

SALES (est): 1.9MM **Privately Held**
WEB: www.jeffola.com
SIC: 3569 Firefighting apparatus & related equipment; firefighting apparatus

(G-5135)
SPECTACLE BREWING LLC
55 W Rr Ave Ste 25 (10923)
P.O. Box 395 (10923-0395)
PHONE....................................845 942-8776
Jeff O'Neil, *Owner*
EMP: 16
SALES: 4.8MM **Privately Held**
SIC: 2082 Beer (alcoholic beverage)

Gasport
Niagara County

(G-5136)
AG-PAK INC
8416 Telegraph Rd (14067-9246)
P.O. Box 304 (14067-0304)
PHONE....................................716 772-2651
James W Currie, *CEO*
Andy Currie, *President*
◆ **EMP:** 15
SQ FT: 14,000
SALES (est): 3.2MM **Privately Held**
WEB: www.agpak.com
SIC: 3556 Food products machinery

(G-5137)
GASPORT WELDING & FABG INC
8430 Telegraph Rd (14067-9246)
P.O. Box 410 (14067-0410)
PHONE....................................716 772-7205
Edward J Wojtkowski Jr, *President*
Beverly Wojtkowski, *Corp Secy*
EMP: 10
SQ FT: 14,000
SALES (est): 1.6MM **Privately Held**
SIC: 3443 7692 3441 Tanks, standard or custom fabricated: metal plate; hoppers, metal plate; containers, shipping (bombs, etc.): metal plate; welding repair; fabricated structural metal

(G-5138)
MAKIPLASTIC
4904 Gasport Rd (14067-9506)
P.O. Box 2 (14067-0002)
PHONE....................................716 772-2222
Scott Brauer, *Owner*
EMP: 5
SALES (est): 420.7K **Privately Held**
SIC: 3949 Bait, artificial: fishing

(G-5139)
MILNE MFG INC
8411 State St (14067-9246)
P.O. Box 159 (14067-0159)
PHONE....................................716 772-2536
Ann Cain, *Branch Mgr*
EMP: 11
SALES (corp-wide): 3MM **Privately Held**
WEB: www.mmplastics.com
SIC: 3089 7389 Injection molding of plastics; telephone answering service
PA: M M Plastic (Mfg) Company, Inc
1301 Blundell Rd
Mississauga ON L4Y 1
905 277-5514

(G-5140)
WOLFE LUMBER MILL INC
8416 Ridge Rd (14067-9415)
PHONE....................................716 772-7750
David C Caldwell, *President*
Sandy Lawrence, *Admin Sec*
EMP: 7
SQ FT: 11,000
SALES: 800K **Privately Held**
SIC: 2449 2448 2431 Fruit crates, wood: wirebound; pallets, wood; millwork

---

Gates
Monroe County

(G-5141)
KEYES MACHINE WORKS INC
147 Park Ave (14606-3818)
PHONE....................................585 426-5059
John Ritchie, *President*
Fraser Ritchie, *Vice Pres*
EMP: 5
SQ FT: 2,500
SALES: 490K **Privately Held**
SIC: 3544 3599 7699 Special dies & tools; custom machinery; industrial equipment services

(G-5142)
R D A CONTAINER CORPORATION
70 Cherry Rd (14624-2592)
PHONE....................................585 247-2323
Alan P Brant, *Ch of Bd*
Steve Douglass, *Dept Chairman*
Kevin Deyager, *Prdtn Mgr*
Theodre Brant, *Treasurer*
Jay Stewart, *VP Sales*
EMP: 42 **EST:** 1967
SQ FT: 103,000
SALES (est): 9.3MM **Privately Held**
WEB: www.rdacontainer.com
SIC: 2653 3086 2449 Boxes, corrugated: made from purchased materials; packaging & shipping materials, foamed plastic; rectangular boxes & crates, wood

---

Geneseo
Livingston County

(G-5143)
DEER RUN ENTERPRISES INC
Also Called: Deer Run Winery
3772 W Lake Rd (14454-9743)
PHONE....................................585 346-0850
George Kuyon, *President*
EMP: 6
SQ FT: 4,000
SALES (est): 684K **Privately Held**
WEB: www.deerrunwinery.com
SIC: 2084 Wines

(G-5144)
LIVINGSTON COUNTY NEWS
122 Main St (14454-1230)
PHONE....................................585 243-1234
Tom Turanvull, *President*
EMP: 7
SALES (est): 317.3K
SALES (corp-wide): 32MM **Privately Held**
WEB: www.ogd.com
SIC: 2711 Newspapers, publishing & printing
PA: Johnson Newspaper Corporation
260 Washington St
Watertown NY
315 782-1000

Geneva
Ontario County

(G-5145)
ALLESON OF ROCHESTER INC
Also Called: Don Alleson Athletic
833 Canandaigua Rd Ste 40 (14456-2015)
PHONE....................................315 548-3635
Lyla Bousfiou, *Opers-Prdtn-Mfg*
EMP: 40
SQ FT: 53,685
SALES (corp-wide): 429MM **Privately Held**
SIC: 2329 2339 Athletic (warmup, sweat & jogging) suits: men's & boys'; athletic clothing: women's, misses' & juniors'
HQ: Alleson Of Rochester, Inc.
111 Badger Ln
Statesville NC 28625
585 272-0606

(G-5146)
BERRYFIELD BOTTLING LLC
3655 Berry Fields Rd (14456-9500)
PHONE.....................315 781-2749
Doreen Kennedy, *Accounts Mgr*
EMP: 35
SALES (est): 1MM **Privately Held**
SIC: 2037 Fruit juices

(G-5147)
BILLSBORO WINERY
4760 State Route 14 (14456-9746)
PHONE.....................315 789-9538
Kim Aliberti, *President*
Deanna Fello, *Manager*
EMP: 6 EST: 1999
SALES (est): 529.4K **Privately Held**
SIC: 2084 Wines

(G-5148)
CCMI INC
88 Middle St (14456-1836)
P.O. Box 148 (14456-0148)
PHONE.....................315 781-3270
Wells C Lewis, *President*
Anthony Lewis, *President*
James Hartman, *Treasurer*
Rose Hammond Hoose, *Manager*
EMP: 8
SQ FT: 7,500
SALES (est): 1MM **Privately Held**
WEB: www.ccmi-reedco.com
SIC: 2821 7389 Plastics materials &
resins; packaging & labeling services

(G-5149)
CCN INTERNATIONAL INC
200 Lehigh St (14456-1096)
PHONE.....................315 789-4400
Charles Richard Conoyer, *President*
Anne Nenneau, *Exec VP*
Michael Hryzak, *Vice Pres*
Tim Bowman, *VP Mfg*
Mike Kelsey, *VP Mfg*
▼ EMP: 74 EST: 1970
SQ FT: 85,000
SALES (est): 10.6MM **Privately Held**
WEB: www.ccnintl.com
SIC: 2521 Desks, office: wood

(G-5150)
CHERIBUNDI INC (PA)
1 Montorency Way (14456)
PHONE.....................800 699-0460
Mike Hagan, *CEO*
Ed Maguire, *Vice Pres*
Roger Morse, *Plant Mgr*
Michelle Grech, *Chief Mktg Ofcr*
Joelle Morris, *Analyst*
EMP: 21
SQ FT: 8,300
SALES (est): 4.9MM **Privately Held**
SIC: 2037 2033 2086 Fruit juices; fruit
juice concentrates, frozen; fruit juices:
fresh; fruit drinks (less than 100% juice):
packaged in cans, etc.

(G-5151)
COMMUNITY MEDIA GROUP INC
Also Called: Finger Lakes Times
218 Genesee St (14456-2323)
P.O. Box 393 (14456-0393)
PHONE.....................315 789-3333
EMP: 90 **Privately Held**
SIC: 2711 Newspapers, publishing & print-
ing
PA: Community Media Group Inc.
805 S Logan St
West Frankfort IL 62896

(G-5152)
ENVIROFORM RECYCLED PDTS INC
287 Gambee Rd (14456-1025)
P.O. Box 553 (14456-0553)
PHONE.....................315 789-1810
Robert L Bates, *President*
Joe Bates, *Project Mgr*
EMP: 9
SQ FT: 5,000
SALES (est): 2.5MM **Privately Held**
WEB: www.enviroform.com
SIC: 3069 Molded rubber products; rubber
automotive products

(G-5153)
FAHY-WILLIAMS PUBLISHING INC
171 Reed St (14456-2137)
P.O. Box 1080 (14456-8080)
PHONE.....................315 781-6820
Kevin Fahy, *President*
Tim Braden, *Vice Pres*
Trisha McKenna, *Office Mgr*
EMP: 13
SQ FT: 3,200
SALES (est): 2MM **Privately Held**
WEB: www.fwpi.com
SIC: 2721 Magazines: publishing only, not
printed on site

(G-5154)
FINGER LAKES RADIOLOGY LLC
196 North St (14456-1651)
PHONE.....................315 787-5399
Andre Forcier,
EMP: 6
SALES (est): 1.3MM **Privately Held**
SIC: 3826 Magnetic resonance imaging
apparatus

(G-5155)
GENEVA GRANITE CO INC (PA)
272 Border City Rd (14456-1988)
P.O. Box 834 (14456-0834)
PHONE.....................315 789-8142
Ralph Fratto Jr, *President*
Joseph Fratto, *Corp Secy*
Jean Fratto, *Vice Pres*
EMP: 15
SQ FT: 1,200
SALES (est): 2.7MM **Privately Held**
SIC: 3281 1771 Curbing, paving & walk-
way stone; concrete work; curb construc-
tion

(G-5156)
GENEVA PRINTING COMPANY INC
40 Castle St (14456-2679)
P.O. Box 751 (14456-0751)
PHONE.....................315 789-8191
Ronald Alcock, *President*
Jo Ellen Alcock, *Vice Pres*
EMP: 8
SQ FT: 7,500
SALES (est): 1.4MM **Privately Held**
WEB: www.genevaprinting.com
SIC: 2752 Commercial printing, offset

(G-5157)
GUARDIAN INDUSTRIES LLC
50 Forge Ave (14456-1281)
PHONE.....................315 787-7000
Dean Cambell, *Principal*
Steve Legg, *Sales Staff*
Tom Olstead, *Director*
EMP: 332
SALES (corp-wide): 40.6B **Privately Held**
WEB: www.guardian.com
SIC: 3211 Flat glass
HQ: Guardian Industries, Llc
2300 Harmon Rd
Auburn Hills MI 48326
248 340-1800

(G-5158)
HANGER PRSTHETCS & ORTHO INC
787 State Route 5 And 20 (14456-2001)
PHONE.....................315 789-4810
Thomas Kirk PHD, *CEO*
EMP: 5
SALES (corp-wide): 1B **Publicly Held**
SIC: 3842 Limbs, artificial; braces, ortho-
pedic
HQ: Hanger Prosthetics & Orthotics, Inc.
10910 Domain Dr Ste 300
Austin TX 78758
512 777-3800

(G-5159)
MCINTOSH BOX & PALLET CO INC
40 Doran Ave (14456-1224)
PHONE.....................315 789-8750
Vayeli Rivera, *Manager*
EMP: 18

SQ FT: 14,400
SALES (corp-wide): 38.4MM **Privately Held**
WEB: www.mcintoshbox.com
SIC: 2441 2448 Shipping cases, wood:
nailed or lock corner; wood pallets & skids
PA: Mcintosh Box & Pallet Co., Inc.
5864 Pyle Dr
East Syracuse NY 13057
315 446-9350

(G-5160)
NEGYS NEW LAND VINYRD WINERY
Also Called: Three Brothers Winery
623 Lerch Rd Ste 1 (14456-9295)
PHONE.....................315 585-4432
Nancy Burdick, *President*
Dave Mansfield, *Owner*
Erica Ridley, *General Mgr*
Dale Nagy, *Vice Pres*
Jon Mansfield, *Assistant*
EMP: 7
SALES (est): 100K **Privately Held**
SIC: 2084 5921 Wines; wine

(G-5161)
R M REYNOLDS
Also Called: Point of Sale Outfitters
504 Exchange St (14456-3407)
PHONE.....................315 789-7365
R M Reynolds, *Owner*
EMP: 5
SQ FT: 5,500
SALES (est): 342.1K **Privately Held**
SIC: 3911 5094 Jewelry, precious metal;
jewelry

(G-5162)
SENECA FOODS CORPORATION
Also Called: Vegetable Operations
100 Gambee Rd (14456-1099)
PHONE.....................315 781-8733
Warren Fredericksen, *Plant Mgr*
Gary Hadyk, *Plant Mgr*
Mark Forsting, *Engineer*
Katie Gushlaw, *Human Res Mgr*
Jocelyn Cinamella, *Sales Staff*
EMP: 150
SALES (corp-wide): 1.2B **Publicly Held**
SIC: 2033 Sauerkraut: packaged in cans,
jars, etc.; vegetables: packaged in cans,
jars, etc.
PA: Seneca Foods Corporation
3736 S Main St
Marion NY 14505
315 926-8100

(G-5163)
SENECA TRUCK & TRAILER INC
2200 State Route 14 (14456-9511)
PHONE.....................315 781-1100
Patrick O'Connor, *President*
Patrick O Connor, *President*
EMP: 6
SALES (est): 350K **Privately Held**
WEB: www.senecatruck.com
SIC: 3715 Truck trailers

(G-5164)
TRAMWELL INC
Also Called: Graphic Connections
70 State St (14456-1760)
PHONE.....................315 789-2762
William D Whitwell, *President*
Nancy F Whitwell, *Vice Pres*
EMP: 5
SQ FT: 4,000
SALES (est): 300K **Privately Held**
SIC: 2261 Screen printing of cotton broad-
woven fabrics

(G-5165)
VANCE METAL FABRICATORS INC
251 Gambee Rd (14456-1025)
PHONE.....................315 789-5626
Joseph A Hennessy, *Ch of Bd*
William Dobbin Jr, *Chairman*
Len Visco, *Opers Mgr*
Brian Mott, *Safety Mgr*
Roy Stonesifer, *Foreman/Supr*
▲ EMP: 85 EST: 1880
SQ FT: 36,000

SALES (est): 39MM **Privately Held**
WEB: www.vancemetal.com
SIC: 3441 3444 Fabricated structural
metal; sheet metalwork

(G-5166)
VENTOSA VINEYARDS LLC
3440 State Route 96a (14456-9209)
PHONE.....................315 719-0000
Lenny Cecere, *Owner*
Jennifer Fish, *CFO*
EMP: 6
SALES (est): 1MM **Privately Held**
SIC: 2084 Wines

(G-5167)
ZOTOS INTERNATIONAL INC
Joico Laboritoriies
300 Forge Ave (14456-1294)
PHONE.....................315 781-3207
Herb Nieporent, *Principal*
EMP: 289
SALES (corp-wide): 22.7B **Privately Held**
WEB: www.zotos.com
SIC: 2844 Hair preparations, including
shampoos; cosmetic preparations
HQ: Zotos International, Inc.
100 Tokeneke Rd
Darien CT 06820
203 655-8911

Genoa
Cayuga County

(G-5168)
STONE WELL BODIES & MCH INC
625 Sill Rd (13071-4182)
PHONE.....................315 497-3512
Luigi Sposito, *CEO*
Todd Mix, *COO*
▼ EMP: 37
SQ FT: 30,000
SALES (est): 4.7MM **Privately Held**
WEB: www.stonewellbodies.com
SIC: 3715 3441 8711 Truck trailers; fabri-
cated structural metal; engineering serv-
ices

Germantown
Columbia County

(G-5169)
ON THE DOUBLE INC
Also Called: John Patrick
178 Viewmont Rd (12526-5808)
PHONE.....................518 431-3571
Walter Fleming, *Ch of Bd*
EMP: 5
SALES (est): 446.8K **Privately Held**
SIC: 2339 2329 Women's & misses' ath-
letic clothing & sportswear; men's & boys'
sportswear & athletic clothing

Gerry
Chautauqua County

(G-5170)
COBBE INDUSTRIES INC
Also Called: Valley Industries
1397 Harris Hollow Rd (14740-9515)
PHONE.....................716 287-2661
Daniel W Cobbe, *President*
EMP: 30 EST: 1976
SQ FT: 22,000
SALES (est): 4.3MM **Privately Held**
WEB: www.valleyindustries.com
SIC: 3469 3441 Metal stampings; fabri-
cated structural metal

(G-5171)
SWANSON LUMBER
5273 N Hill Rd (14740-9521)
PHONE.....................716 499-1726
Charles Swanson, *Owner*
EMP: 5
SQ FT: 2,688

SALES (est): 352K **Privately Held**
SIC: 2421 Sawmills & planing mills, general

(G-5172)
UNIVERSAL TOOLING CORPORATION
4533 Route 60 (14740-9540)
P.O. Box 364 (14740-0364)
PHONE..................................716 985-4691
Nichole Segrue, *CEO*
Warren Piazza, *President*
Mike Swanson, *Vice Pres*
EMP: 13 **EST:** 1981
SQ FT: 10,630
SALES (est): 1.5MM **Privately Held**
WEB: www.u-t-c.com
SIC: 3544 3545 Forms (molds), for foundry & plastics working machinery; dies, plastics forming; machine tool accessories

Getzville
Erie County

(G-5173)
C M INSURANCE COMPANY INC
Also Called: Columbus McKinnon
205 Crosspoint Pkwy (14068-1605)
PHONE..................................716 689-5409
Timothy T Tevens, *President*
Robert Friedl, *CFO*
Timothy Harvey, *Admin Sec*
EMP: 4
SQ FT: 2,900
SALES (est): 1MM
SALES (corp-wide): 876.2MM **Publicly Held**
WEB: www.columbusmckinnon.com
SIC: 3536 Hoists, cranes & monorails
PA: Columbus Mckinnon Corporation
    205 Crosspoint Pkwy
    Getzville NY 14068
    716 689-5400

(G-5174)
COLUMBUS MCKINNON CORPORATION (PA)
205 Crosspoint Pkwy (14068-1605)
PHONE..................................716 689-5400
Ernest R Verebelyi, *Ch of Bd*
Mark D Morelli, *President*
Linda Wrobel, *President*
Benjamin Auyeung, *Vice Pres*
Bert A Brant, *Vice Pres*
◆ **EMP:** 145 **EST:** 1875
SALES: 876.2MM **Publicly Held**
WEB: www.cmworks.com
SIC: 3536 3496 3535 3537 Hoists; cranes, industrial plant; cranes, overhead traveling; chain, welded; conveyor belts; conveyors & conveying equipment; tables, lift: hydraulic

(G-5175)
COLUMBUS MCKINNON CORPORATION
Also Called: Coffing
205 Crosspoint Pkwy (14068-1605)
PHONE..................................716 689-5400
EMP: 134
SALES (corp-wide): 876.2MM **Publicly Held**
WEB: www.cmworks.com
SIC: 3536 3496 3535 3537 Hoists; cranes, industrial plant; cranes, overhead traveling; chain, welded; conveyor belts; conveyors & conveying equipment; tables, lift: hydraulic
PA: Columbus Mckinnon Corporation
    205 Crosspoint Pkwy
    Getzville NY 14068
    716 689-5400

(G-5176)
COLUMBUS MCKINNON CORPORATION
Also Called: Yale
205 Crosspoint Pkwy (14068-1605)
PHONE..................................716 689-5400
EMP: 134

SALES (corp-wide): 876.2MM **Publicly Held**
WEB: www.cmworks.com
SIC: 3536 3496 3535 3537 Hoists; cranes, industrial plant; cranes, overhead traveling; chain, welded; conveyor belts; conveyors & conveying equipment; tables, lift: hydraulic
PA: Columbus Mckinnon Corporation
    205 Crosspoint Pkwy
    Getzville NY 14068
    716 689-5400

(G-5177)
INTEL CORPORATION
55 Dodge Rd (14068-1205)
PHONE..................................408 765-8080
Raman Parthasarathy, *Engineer*
Mike Brunner, *Branch Mgr*
EMP: 60
SALES (corp-wide): 70.8B **Publicly Held**
WEB: www.intel.com
SIC: 3674 7372 Microprocessors; application computer software
PA: Intel Corporation
    2200 Mission College Blvd
    Santa Clara CA 95054
    408 765-8080

(G-5178)
MISSION CRITICAL ENERGY INC
1801 N French Rd (14068-1032)
PHONE..................................716 276-8465
Mark Dettmer, *President*
EMP: 5
SALES (est): 478.8K **Privately Held**
SIC: 3511 Turbines & turbine generator sets

(G-5179)
NINAS CUSTARD
2577 Millersport Hwy (14068-1445)
PHONE..................................716 636-0345
Merry Scioli, *Partner*
EMP: 30
SALES (est): 3.6MM **Privately Held**
SIC: 2024 Ice cream & frozen desserts

(G-5180)
OLD DUTCHMANS WROUGH IRON INC
2800 Millersport Hwy (14068-1449)
P.O. Box 632 (14068-0632)
PHONE..................................716 688-2034
Keith Deck, *Principal*
▲ **EMP:** 6
SQ FT: 2,416
SALES (est): 100K **Privately Held**
WEB: www.oldutchman.com
SIC: 3446 Architectural metalwork

(G-5181)
PETIT PRINTING CORP
42 Hunters Gln (14068-1264)
PHONE..................................716 871-9490
Richard Petit, *President*
EMP: 8
SQ FT: 14,000
SALES: 540K **Privately Held**
WEB: www.petitprinting.com
SIC: 2752 Commercial printing, offset

(G-5182)
SPX FLOW US LLC
105 Crosspoint Pkwy (14068-1603)
PHONE..................................716 692-3000
EMP: 900
SALES (corp-wide): 2B **Publicly Held**
SIC: 3556 8742 Food products machinery; food & beverage consultant
HQ: Spx Flow Us, Llc
    135 Mount Read Blvd
    Rochester NY 14611
    585 436-5550

(G-5183)
U S ENERGY DEVELOPMENT CORP (PA)
2350 N Forest Rd (14068-1296)
PHONE..................................716 636-0401
Joseph M Jayson, *Ch of Bd*
Douglas Walch, *President*
Jerry Jones, *Opers Mgr*
EMP: 53

SALES (corp-wide): 876.2MM **Publicly Held**
WEB: www.cmworks.com
SIC: 3536 3496 3535 3537 Hoists; cranes, industrial plant; cranes, overhead traveling; chain, welded; conveyor belts; conveyors & conveying equipment; tables, lift: hydraulic
PA: Columbus Mckinnon Corporation
    205 Crosspoint Pkwy
    Getzville NY 14068
    716 689-5400

(G-5184)
WILLIAM S HEIN & CO INC (PA)
Also Called: METRO STORAGE CENTER
2350 N Forest Rd Ste 14a (14068-1296)
PHONE..................................716 882-2600
William S Hein Jr, *Ch of Bd*
Kevin Marmion, *President*
William Hein, *Vice Pres*
Shane Marmion, *Vice Pres*
Susan H Mc Clinton, *Vice Pres*
EMP: 115
SQ FT: 140,000
SALES: 40.4K **Privately Held**
WEB: www.foreign-law.com
SIC: 2731 5942 3572 Books: publishing only; book stores; computer storage devices

Ghent
Columbia County

(G-5185)
J D HANDLING SYSTEMS INC
1346 State Route 9h (12075-3415)
PHONE..................................518 828-9676
Joseph Cardinale Jr, *President*
Joseph Cardinale Sr, *Shareholder*
Diane Cardinale, *Admin Sec*
▲ **EMP:** 12
SQ FT: 53,000
SALES: 1.5MM **Privately Held**
WEB: www.jdhand.com
SIC: 3535 5599 Conveyors & conveying equipment; utility trailers

Glen Cove
Nassau County

(G-5186)
A LOSEE & SONS
68 Landing Rd (11542-1844)
PHONE..................................516 676-3060
Allan Losee, *President*
Mark Losee, *Treasurer*
EMP: 7
SQ FT: 3,000
SALES: 500K **Privately Held**
SIC: 2431 Woodwork, interior & ornamental

(G-5187)
ALLEN PICKLE WORKS INC
36 Garvies Point Rd (11542-2821)
PHONE..................................516 676-0640
Ronald Horman, *President*
Nick Horman, *Vice Pres*
EMP: 19
SQ FT: 20,000
SALES (est): 9MM **Privately Held**
SIC: 2035 Pickles, vinegar

(G-5188)
ALLIED MAKER
108 Glen Cove Ave (11542-2832)
PHONE..................................516 200-9145
Ryden Rizzo, *Principal*
Catie Buhler, *Manager*
EMP: 14
SALES (est): 1.8MM **Privately Held**
SIC: 3993 Signs & advertising specialties

(G-5189)
AUGUST THOMSEN CORP
36 Sea Cliff Ave (11542-3635)
PHONE..................................516 676-7100
Jeffrey G Schneider, *President*
Douglas J Schneider, *Vice Pres*
Douglass Schneider, *Sales Dir*
Ingrid Schneider, *Shareholder*
◆ **EMP:** 40 **EST:** 1905
SQ FT: 25,000

SALES (est): 8.3MM **Privately Held**
WEB: www.atecousa.com
SIC: 3365 Cooking/kitchen utensils, cast aluminum

(G-5190)
COMMUNITY CPONS FRNCHISING INC
100 Carney St Ste 2 (11542-3687)
PHONE..................................516 277-1968
Matthew Rosencrans, *President*
Dennis Bernstein, *Sales Mgr*
Stu Golden, *Regl Sales Mgr*
EMP: 25
SQ FT: 3,200
SALES: 3.5MM **Privately Held**
SIC: 2741 7313 Miscellaneous publishing; newspaper advertising representative

(G-5191)
COMPS INC
3 School St Ste 101b (11542-2548)
P.O. Box 255, Sea Cliff (11579-0255)
PHONE..................................516 676-0400
Keith Larson, *President*
EMP: 12
SALES (est): 887.8K **Privately Held**
WEB: www.compsny.com
SIC: 2741 Miscellaneous publishing

(G-5192)
EXPO FURNITURE DESIGNS INC
Also Called: Expo Lighting Design
1 Garvies Point Rd (11542-2821)
PHONE..................................516 674-1420
Brian Landau, *President*
Maria Landau, *Admin Sec*
▲ **EMP:** 10
SQ FT: 5,000
SALES: 900K **Privately Held**
WEB: www.expodesigninc.com
SIC: 3648 5063 5072 Lighting fixtures, except electric: residential; lighting fixtures; hardware

(G-5193)
G SICURANZA LTD
4 East Ave (11542-3917)
PHONE..................................516 759-0259
Gaetano Sicuranza, *Ch of Bd*
EMP: 5
SALES (est): 555.1K **Privately Held**
SIC: 3432 Plumbing fixture fittings & trim

(G-5194)
GADDIS INDUSTRIAL EQUIPMENT
Also Called: Gaddis Engineering
140 Pratt Oval (11542-1482)
P.O. Box 915, Locust Valley (11560-0915)
PHONE..................................516 759-3100
M Francis Gaddis, *President*
Marie B Gaddis, *Treasurer*
Paul Gaddis, *Asst Treas*
L C Hills, *Admin Sec*
EMP: 12
SALES (est): 1.2MM **Privately Held**
SIC: 3053 Packing materials

(G-5195)
GLEN PLAZA MARBLE & GRAN INC
75 Glen Cove Ave Ste A (11542-3261)
PHONE..................................516 671-1100
Frank Caruso, *President*
Joe Caruso, *Corp Secy*
Angelo Caruso, *Vice Pres*
▲ **EMP:** 7
SQ FT: 7,500
SALES (est): 702.1K **Privately Held**
SIC: 3281 5032 5999 5211 Granite, cut & shaped; marble, building: cut & shaped; granite building stone; marble building stone; monuments & tombstones; tile, ceramic

(G-5196)
KORE INFRASTRUCTURE LLC (PA)
4 High Pine (11542-1422)
PHONE..................................646 532-9060
Cornelius Shields, *Mng Member*
David Harding, *Officer*
EMP: 3
SQ FT: 3,000

SALES (est): 2.5MM **Privately Held**
SIC: 2869 4953 Fuels; recycling, waste materials

(G-5197)
NORESCO INDUSTRIAL GROUP INC
3 School St Ste 103 (11542-2548)
PHONE....................516 759-3355
Daan Hu, *President*
Julie Lee, *Exec VP*
▲ EMP: 40
SALES (est): 9.1MM **Privately Held**
WEB: www.norescoindustrial.com
SIC: 3321 5013 5084 3322 Ductile iron castings; automotive supplies & parts; industrial machinery & equipment; malleable iron foundries

(G-5198)
PLEATCO LLC
28 Garvies Point Rd (11542-2821)
PHONE....................516 609-0200
Howard Smith, *President*
John Antretter, *Vice Pres*
Mary Villegas, *VP Opers*
▲ EMP: 80
SQ FT: 21,000
SALES (est): 31.2MM **Privately Held**
SIC: 3589 Swimming pool filter & water conditioning systems

(G-5199)
PROFESSIONAL TAPE CORPORATION
100 Pratt Oval (11542-1482)
P.O. Box 234271, Great Neck (11023-4271)
PHONE....................516 656-5519
Morris Kamkar, *President*
▲ EMP: 4
SQ FT: 10,000
SALES: 7MM **Privately Held**
WEB: www.proftapeco.com
SIC: 3695 7819 5099 Magnetic tape; video tape or disk reproduction; video & audio equipment

(G-5200)
SHERCO SERVICES LLC
2 Park Pl Ste A (11542-2566)
PHONE....................516 676-3028
Shawn Sheridan,
EMP: 10
SALES (est): 1.2MM **Privately Held**
SIC: 3537 Trucks, tractors, loaders, carriers & similar equipment

(G-5201)
SLANTO MANUFACTURING INC
40 Garvies Point Rd (11542-2887)
PHONE....................516 759-5721
Mel Dubin, *President*
EMP: 25
SALES (est): 1.6MM **Privately Held**
SIC: 3442 Baseboards, metal

(G-5202)
STEVENSON PRINTING CO INC
1 Brewster St Ste 2 (11542-2556)
PHONE....................516 676-1233
Anthony Messineo, *President*
Cindy Messineo Hawxhurst, *Vice Pres*
Glenn Messineo, *Vice Pres*
EMP: 6 EST: 1909
SQ FT: 12,800
SALES (est): 800.8K **Privately Held**
WEB: www.printingedgemarketing.com
SIC: 2752 Commercial printing, offset

(G-5203)
SUNNYSIDE DECORATIVE PRINTS CO
Also Called: Etcetera Wallpapers
67 Robinson Ave (11542-2944)
PHONE....................516 671-1935
Douglas Fletcher Jr, *President*
Melissa Wolf, *Manager*
EMP: 9
SQ FT: 12,000
SALES (est): 1.2MM **Privately Held**
SIC: 2679 Wallpaper

(G-5204)
WELLS RUGS INC
Also Called: Wells, George Ruggery
44 Sea Cliff Ave (11542-3627)
PHONE....................516 676-2056
Joseph Misiak, *President*
EMP: 6
SALES (est): 404.7K **Privately Held**
SIC: 2273 Carpets & rugs

Glen Head
Nassau County

(G-5205)
DEANGELIS LTD
262 Glen Head Rd (11545-1974)
PHONE....................212 348-8225
Kenneth Deangelis, *President*
Kayel Deangelis, *Vice Pres*
EMP: 50 EST: 1957
SQ FT: 1,500
SALES (est): 4.8MM **Privately Held**
SIC: 2512 2391 Upholstered household furniture; draperies, plastic & textile: from purchased materials

(G-5206)
GLOBAL PACKAGING SERVICES LLC
67 Kissam Ln (11545-1013)
PHONE....................646 648-0355
Richard Loos,
EMP: 5 EST: 2011
SALES (est): 240.3K **Privately Held**
SIC: 3565 Packaging machinery

(G-5207)
HALM INSTRUMENT CO INC
180 Glen Head Rd (11545-1924)
PHONE....................516 676-6700
Floyd A Lyon, *President*
Stephen P Lyon, *Vice Pres*
Steven Lyon, *Vice Pres*
Donald Schanck, *Vice Pres*
EMP: 76 EST: 1945
SQ FT: 32,000
SALES (est): 5MM **Privately Held**
SIC: 3555 Printing presses

(G-5208)
INTERNATIONAL NEWSPPR PRTG CO
Also Called: International Newspaper Prntng
18 Carlisle Dr (11545-2120)
PHONE....................516 626-6095
EMP: 25 EST: 1932
SQ FT: 12,500
SALES (est): 3.1MM **Privately Held**
SIC: 2752 Offset Printing

(G-5209)
LOMIN CONSTRUCTION COMPANY
Also Called: O'Neil Construction
328 Glen Cove Rd (11545-2273)
PHONE....................516 759-5734
Steven O'Neil, *Partner*
EMP: 6
SALES (est): 490K **Privately Held**
SIC: 3531 1629 1611 Pavers; tennis court construction; surfacing & paving

(G-5210)
NEW ART SIGNS CO INC
78 Plymouth Dr N (11545-1127)
PHONE....................718 443-0900
Steven Weiss, *President*
EMP: 5
SALES (est): 350K **Privately Held**
SIC: 3993 2759 Signs & advertising specialties; screen printing

(G-5211)
NIRX MEDICAL TECHNOLOGIES LLC
15 Cherry Ln (11545-2215)
PHONE....................516 676-6479
Doug Maxwell, *Branch Mgr*
EMP: 15

SALES (corp-wide): 1.6MM **Privately Held**
WEB: www.nirx.net
SIC: 3845 Position emission tomography (PET scanner)
PA: Nirx Medical Technologies, Llc
7083 Hollywood Blvd Fl 4
Los Angeles CA 90028
424 264-0556

(G-5212)
NORTH SHORE MONUMENTS INC
667 Cedar Swamp Rd Ste 5 (11545-2267)
PHONE....................516 759-2156
Hugh A Tanchuck, *President*
Maggie L Tanchuck, *President*
EMP: 6
SQ FT: 3,100
SALES (est): 734.4K **Privately Held**
WEB: www.northshoremonuments.com
SIC: 3281 5999 1799 Granite, cut & shaped; monuments & tombstones; sandblasting of building exteriors

(G-5213)
PURE GHEE INC (PA)
33 Cherry St (11545-1803)
PHONE....................917 214-5431
Mahesh K Maheshwari, *President*
Sucheta Maheshwari, *Senior VP*
Raj Maheshwari, *Marketing Staff*
EMP: 8 EST: 1988
SALES: 2MM **Privately Held**
SIC: 2021 5143 Butter oil; butter

Glen Oaks
Queens County

(G-5214)
BAYSIDE BEEPERS & CELLULAR
25607 Hillside Ave (11004-1617)
PHONE....................718 343-3888
Albert Castro, *Owner*
EMP: 5 EST: 2013
SALES (est): 335.2K **Privately Held**
SIC: 3663 4812 Pagers (one-way); cellular telephone services

(G-5215)
WYNCO PRESS ONE INC
Also Called: Minuteman Press
7839 268th St (11004-1330)
PHONE....................516 354-6145
Jeff Wheeler, *President*
EMP: 6
SQ FT: 1,000
SALES: 750K **Privately Held**
SIC: 2752 2791 2789 Commercial printing, lithographic; typesetting; bookbinding & related work

Glendale
Queens County

(G-5216)
A & S WINDOW ASSOCIATES INC
8819 76th Ave (11385-7992)
PHONE....................718 275-7900
Alan Herman, *President*
▲ EMP: 20 EST: 1952
SQ FT: 14,000
SALES (est): 3.2MM **Privately Held**
WEB: www.aswindowassociates.com
SIC: 3442 Storm doors or windows, metal

(G-5217)
ALFA CARD INC
7915 Cooper Ave (11385-7528)
PHONE....................718 326-7107
George Chase, *President*
Judy Chase, *Vice Pres*
EMP: 8
SQ FT: 1,400
SALES (est): 385K **Privately Held**
WEB: www.alfacard.com
SIC: 2754 Business form & card printing, gravure

(G-5218)
ALLEN WILLIAM & COMPANY INC
Also Called: Alvin J Bart
7119 80th St Ste 8315 (11385-7733)
PHONE....................212 675-6461
Fax: 718 821-2486
EMP: 200 EST: 1884
SALES (est): 24MM **Privately Held**
SIC: 2678 2752 Mfg Stationery Products Lithographic Commercial Printing

(G-5219)
BOWE INDUSTRIES INC (PA)
Also Called: Changes
8836 77th Ave (11385-7826)
PHONE....................718 441-6464
Daniel Barasch, *CEO*
Marek Kiyashka, *President*
Daniel Baresch, *Purchasing*
Carol Delmastro, *Controller*
Michael Olsten, *Human Res Dir*
◆ EMP: 100 EST: 1976
SQ FT: 62,000
SALES (est): 53.9MM **Privately Held**
SIC: 2321 2331 2361 Men's & boys' furnishings; T-shirts & tops, women's: made from purchased materials; shirts, women's & juniors': made from purchased materials; t-shirts & tops: girls', children's & infants'; shirts: girls', children's & infants'

(G-5220)
BOWE INDUSTRIES INC
8836 77th Ave (11385-7826)
PHONE....................718 441-6464
Michael Ohlsten, *Branch Mgr*
EMP: 75
SALES (corp-wide): 53.9MM **Privately Held**
SIC: 2321 Men's & boys' furnishings
PA: Bowe Industries Inc.
8836 77th Ave
Glendale NY 11385
718 441-6464

(G-5221)
C F PETERS CORP
7030 80th St Ste 2 (11385-7735)
PHONE....................718 416-7800
Dr Don Gillespie, *Vice Pres*
Richie Anichiarico, *Warehouse Mgr*
Shili Uddin, *Finance*
Evelyn Hinrichsen, *Director*
▲ EMP: 27 EST: 1948
SQ FT: 7,200
SALES (est): 3.3MM **Privately Held**
WEB: www.petersedition.com
SIC: 2741 Music book & sheet music publishing

(G-5222)
CIDC CORP
Also Called: Ocs Industries
5605 Cooper Ave (11385-5737)
PHONE....................718 342-5820
Henry Gutman, *President*
▲ EMP: 15
SALES (est): 2MM **Privately Held**
SIC: 2514 3433 Cabinets, radio & television: metal; heating equipment, except electric

(G-5223)
COTTON EMPORIUM INC (PA)
8000 Cooper Ave Ste 8 (11385-7734)
PHONE....................718 894-3365
Josef Moshevili, *President*
Nana Moshevili, *Vice Pres*
▲ EMP: 8
SQ FT: 8,500
SALES (est): 2MM **Privately Held**
SIC: 2329 Sweaters & sweater jackets: men's & boys'

(G-5224)
FM BRUSH CO INC
7002 72nd Pl (11385-7307)
PHONE....................718 821-5939
Fred J Mink Jr, *Ch of Bd*
Beatrice Mink, *Corp Secy*
Jeffrey A Mink, *Vice Pres*
Carolyn Koster, *Traffic Mgr*
Patricia Hanna, *Credit Mgr*
▲ EMP: 120 EST: 1929

SQ FT: 20,000
SALES (est): 16.2MM **Privately Held**
WEB: www.fmbrush.com
SIC: 3991 Brushes, household or industrial

(G-5225)
FRED M VELEPEC CO INC
7172 70th St (11385-7246)
PHONE..................................718 821-6636
Fredric A Velepec, *President*
Gerda Velepec, *Vice Pres*
EMP: 21 **EST:** 1942
SQ FT: 6,000
SALES (est): 1.8MM **Privately Held**
SIC: 3545 Tools & accessories for machine tools

(G-5226)
GLENDALE ARCHITECTURAL WD PDTS
Also Called: Glendale Products
7102 80th St (11385-7715)
PHONE..................................718 326-2700
Vincenzo Alcamo, *President*
EMP: 30
SALES (est): 4.2MM **Privately Held**
WEB: www.glendalecustomfurniture.com
SIC: 2521 2511 Wood office furniture; wood household furniture

(G-5227)
GLENRIDGE FABRICATORS INC
7945 77th Ave (11385-7522)
PHONE..................................718 456-2297
Albert Putre, *Ch of Bd*
Kampta Persaud, *Vice Pres*
EMP: 10 **EST:** 1977
SQ FT: 36,000
SALES (est): 2.1MM **Privately Held**
SIC: 3441 3443 1799 Fabricated structural metal; weldments; welding on site

(G-5228)
MARK I PUBLICATIONS INC
Also Called: Queens Chronicle
7119 80th St Ste 8201 (11385-7733)
P.O. Box 747769, Rego Park (11374-7769)
PHONE..................................718 205-8000
Mark Wilder, *President*
Stanley Merzon, *Vice Pres*
EMP: 50
SQ FT: 1,800
SALES (est): 3.5MM **Privately Held**
WEB: www.qchron.com
SIC: 2711 Newspapers, publishing & printing

(G-5229)
NEW DAY WOODWORK INC
Also Called: John Bossone
8861 76th Ave (11385-7910)
PHONE..................................718 275-1721
Jay Levtow, *President*
EMP: 30
SQ FT: 14,000
SALES (est): 2.5MM **Privately Held**
WEB: www.newdaywoodwork.com
SIC: 2511 Wood household furniture

(G-5230)
NORTH STAR KNITTING MILLS INC
7030 80th St (11385-7737)
PHONE..................................718 894-4848
EMP: 7
SQ FT: 12,500
SALES: 900K **Privately Held**
SIC: 2253 5199 Knit Outerwear Mill Whol Nondurable Goods

(G-5231)
PHOENIX ENVMTL SVCS CORP
7314 88th St (11385-7950)
PHONE..................................718 381-8100
Frank Garibaldi, *President*
Michael Alexander, *Vice Pres*
Michael McLaughlin, *Vice Pres*
EMP: 18
SALES (est): 144.7K **Privately Held**
SIC: 3444 Sheet metalwork

(G-5232)
ROLLING GATE SUPPLY CORP
7919 Cypress Ave (11385-6038)
PHONE..................................718 366-5258

Miguel Molinare, *President*
▲ **EMP:** 9
SALES (est): 970K **Privately Held**
SIC: 3315 Steel wire & related products

(G-5233)
T & R KNITTING MILLS INC (PA)
8000 Cooper Ave Ste 6 (11385-7734)
PHONE..................................718 497-4017
Rocco Marini, *President*
▲ **EMP:** 40
SQ FT: 100,000
SALES (est): 20MM **Privately Held**
SIC: 2253 Sweaters & sweater coats, knit

(G-5234)
TIBANA FINISHING INC
7107 65th Pl Apt 1l (11385-6320)
PHONE..................................718 417-5375
Tiberija Miksa, *President*
◆ **EMP:** 20
SALES (est): 2.2MM **Privately Held**
WEB: www.tibana.com
SIC: 2329 2331 Men's & boys' sportswear & athletic clothing; women's & misses' blouses & shirts

Glenmont
Albany County

(G-5235)
AIR PRODUCTS AND CHEMICALS INC
461 River Rd (12077-4307)
PHONE..................................518 463-4273
Micheal Joczak, *Branch Mgr*
James Dwyer, *Administration*
EMP: 53
SQ FT: 8,624
SALES (corp-wide): 8.9B **Publicly Held**
WEB: www.airproducts.com
SIC: 2813 Oxygen, compressed or liquefied
PA: Air Products And Chemicals, Inc.
7201 Hamilton Blvd
Allentown PA 18195
610 481-4911

(G-5236)
DEMARTINI OIL EQUIPMENT SVC
214 River Rd (12077-4604)
P.O. Box 9 (12077-0009)
PHONE..................................518 463-5752
James Demartini, *President*
James De Martini, *President*
Marianne Carner, *Vice Pres*
Mathew Carner, *Treasurer*
EMP: 6 **EST:** 1945
SQ FT: 4,000
SALES (est): 1.1MM **Privately Held**
SIC: 3713 7699 Truck bodies (motor vehicles); industrial machinery & equipment repair

(G-5237)
INNOVATIVE MUNICIPAL PDTS US
Also Called: Innovative Surface Solutions
454 River Rd (12077-4306)
PHONE..................................800 387-5777
Greg Baun, *President*
Scott Fearis, *Manager*
▲ **EMP:** 30
SALES: 20MM **Privately Held**
SIC: 2819 Industrial inorganic chemicals
HQ: Innovative Building Products Inc
78 Orchard Rd
Ajax ON L1S 6
905 427-0318

(G-5238)
J & D WALTER DISTRIBUTORS INC
Also Called: J & D Walter Wholesale Distrg
6 Old River Rd (12077-4312)
P.O. Box 340 (12077-0340)
PHONE..................................518 449-1606
James F Walter, *President*
Chris Walter, *Vice Pres*
Patricia Walter, *Treasurer*
▲ **EMP:** 10 **EST:** 1973

SQ FT: 20,000
SALES (est): 1.4MM **Privately Held**
SIC: 2253 3151 5013 Jackets, knit; leather gloves & mittens; motorcycle parts

Glens Falls
Warren County

(G-5239)
AMES GOLDSMITH CORP
21 Rogers St (12801-3803)
PHONE..................................518 792-7435
Bill Hamelin, *President*
Steve Macy, *Vice Pres*
Mike Delsignore, *Project Engr*
Lisa Davis, *Controller*
Michael Herman, *Controller*
EMP: 16
SALES (corp-wide): 32MM **Privately Held**
SIC: 3399 2819 3339 2869 Silver powder; flakes, metal; catalysts, chemical; primary nonferrous metals; industrial organic chemicals
PA: Ames Goldsmith Corp.
50 Harrison Ave
South Glens Falls NY 12803
518 792-5808

(G-5240)
ANDRITZ INC
Also Called: Ahlstrom Kamyr
13 Pruyns Island Dr (12801-4706)
PHONE..................................518 745-2988
Michael Kingsley, *Manager*
EMP: 20
SALES (corp-wide): 6.9B **Privately Held**
SIC: 2611 Pulp manufactured from waste or recycled paper
HQ: Andritz Inc.
500 Technology Dr
Canonsburg PA 15317
724 597-7801

(G-5241)
ANGIODYNAMICS INC
10 Glens Fls Technical Pa (12801)
PHONE..................................518 792-4112
Mark Frost, *President*
Kevin Williams, *Supervisor*
EMP: 275
SALES (corp-wide): 270.6MM **Publicly Held**
SIC: 3841 Surgical & medical instruments
PA: Angiodynamics, Inc.
14 Plaza Dr
Latham NY 12110
518 795-1400

(G-5242)
BARTON MINES COMPANY LLC (PA)
Also Called: Barton International
6 Warren St (12801-4531)
PHONE..................................518 798-5462
Charles Bracken, *Ch of Bd*
William Flint, *President*
Christopher McGuirk, *Vice Pres*
Scott Beavers, *Purchasing*
Bill Flint, *VP Business*
◆ **EMP:** 150 **EST:** 1996
SQ FT: 5,000
SALES (est): 145.9MM **Privately Held**
WEB: www.barton.com
SIC: 1499 3291 5085 Garnet mining; coated abrasive products; abrasives

(G-5243)
BRENNANS QUICK PRINT INC
Also Called: Bqp
6 Collins Dr (12804-1493)
P.O. Box 4221, Queensbury (12804-0221)
PHONE..................................518 793-4999
Sue Brennan, *President*
EMP: 6
SALES (est): 691K **Privately Held**
WEB: www.bqprinting.com
SIC: 2752 Commercial printing, offset

(G-5244)
C R BARD INC
Glens Falls Manufacturing
289 Bay Rd (12804-2015)
PHONE..................................518 793-2531
Jason Gaeve, *Branch Mgr*
EMP: 960
SALES (corp-wide): 15.9B **Publicly Held**
WEB: www.crbard.com
SIC: 3841 3845 Surgical & medical instruments; electromedical equipment
HQ: C. R. Bard, Inc.
1 Becton Dr
Franklin Lakes NJ 07417
908 277-8000

(G-5245)
CONVERTER DESIGN INC (PA)
25 Murdock Ave (12801-2456)
PHONE..................................518 745-7138
Jim Wood, *President*
EMP: 1
SALES (est): 1.2MM **Privately Held**
SIC: 3599 Custom machinery

(G-5246)
COOPERS CAVE ALE CO S-CORP
2 Sagamore St (12801-3179)
PHONE..................................518 792-0007
Edward Bethel, *Partner*
Patricia Bethel, *Partner*
EMP: 15 **EST:** 1999
SALES (est): 2.1MM **Privately Held**
WEB: www.cooperscaveale.com
SIC: 2082 Beer (alcoholic beverage)

(G-5247)
DOHENY NICE AND EASY
Also Called: Doheny's Mobil
150 Broad St (12801-4253)
PHONE..................................518 793-1733
EMP: 8
SALES (est): 380K **Privately Held**
SIC: 2086 Mfg Bottled/Canned Soft Drinks

(G-5248)
ERBESSD RELIABILITY LLC
Also Called: Erbessd Reliability Instrs
2c Glens Falls Tech Park (12801-3864)
PHONE..................................518 874-2700
Michael Howard, *President*
EMP: 27
SALES (est): 1.5MM **Privately Held**
SIC: 3829 Measuring & controlling devices

(G-5249)
FLOMATIC CORPORATION
Also Called: Flomatic Valves
15 Pruyns Island Dr (12801-4706)
PHONE..................................518 761-9797
Bo Andersson, *President*
Nick Farrara, *Exec VP*
Brian Allen, *Engineer*
Don Gabris, *Manager*
◆ **EMP:** 50
SQ FT: 50,000
SALES (est): 10.6MM
SALES (corp-wide): 21.8MM **Privately Held**
WEB: www.flomatic.com
SIC: 3494 3491 Valves & pipe fittings; water works valves
HQ: Boshart Industries Inc
25 Whaley Ave
Milverton ON N0K 1
519 595-4444

(G-5250)
GLENS FALLS NEWSPAPERS INC
76 Lawrence St (12801-3741)
P.O. Box 2157 (12801-2157)
PHONE..................................518 792-3131
James Marshall, *Principal*
Caitlin Currier, *Sales Staff*
Kathleen Moore, *Analyst*
EMP: 6
SALES (est): 358K **Privately Held**
SIC: 2711 Newspapers, publishing & printing

(G-5251)
GLENS FALLS PRINTING LLC
51 Hudson Ave (12801-4347)
PHONE..................................518 793-0555
George Beyerbach,
Barbara Beyerbach,
Robert Beyerbach,
EMP: 12 **EST:** 1966
SQ FT: 4,800
SALES (est): 2.6MM **Privately Held**
SIC: 2752 Commercial printing, offset

(G-5252)
JUST BEVERAGES LLC
31 Broad St (12801-4301)
P.O. Box 4392, Queensbury (12804-0392)
PHONE..................................480 388-1133
Stephen Mager, *Engineer*
Jim Jacobs, *CFO*
EMP: 11
SALES (est): 1.3MM **Privately Held**
SIC: 2086 Mineral water, carbonated:
packaged in cans, bottles, etc.

(G-5253)
KADANT INC
436 Quaker Rd (12804-1535)
PHONE..................................518 793-8801
Eric Gerrebos, *Chief Engr*
Jeff Bachand, *Branch Mgr*
Thomas Kozloski, *Associate*
EMP: 12
SALES (corp-wide): 633.7MM **Publicly Held**
SIC: 3554 Paper industries machinery
PA: Kadant Inc.
1 Technology Park Dr # 210
Westford MA 01886
978 776-2000

(G-5254)
KMA CORPORATION
153 Maple St Ste 5 (12801-3796)
PHONE..................................518 743-1330
Eric Ukauf, *President*
▲ **EMP:** 9
SALES (est): 1.2MM **Privately Held**
SIC: 3599 Machine shop, jobbing & repair

(G-5255)
LEE ENTERPRISES INCORPORATED
Also Called: Post Star
76 Lawrence St (12801-3741)
P.O. Box 2157 (12801-2157)
PHONE..................................518 792-3131
Terry Doomes, *President*
Greg Brownell, *Editor*
Adam Colver, *Editor*
Lisa Malan, *Editor*
Patti Crotty, *Sales Mgr*
EMP: 160
SQ FT: 5,000
SALES (est): 10.3MM
SALES (corp-wide): 593.9MM **Publicly Held**
SIC: 2711 Newspapers: publishing only,
not printed on site
HQ: Lee Publications, Inc.
4600 E 53rd St
Davenport IA 52807
563 383-2100

(G-5256)
LEHIGH CEMENT COMPANY (DH)
Also Called: Lehigh Northeast Cement
313 Warren St (12801-3820)
P.O. Box 440 (12801-0440)
PHONE..................................518 792-1137
Helmut S Erhard, *Ch of Bd*
Dan Harrington, *President*
Keith Jones, *Business Mgr*
Kenneth Slater, *Plant Mgr*
Richard Walraven, *Production*
▲ **EMP:** 122
SQ FT: 20,000
SALES (est): 21.6MM
SALES (corp-wide): 367.6MM **Privately Held**
WEB: www.gfcement.com
SIC: 3241 Portland cement; masonry cement

HQ: Dyckerhoff Gmbh
Biebricher Str. 68
Wiesbaden 65203
611 676-0

(G-5257)
LEHIGH CEMENT COMPANY LLC
313 Lower Warren St (12804)
PHONE..................................518 792-1137
EMP: 35
SALES (corp-wide): 20.6B **Privately Held**
WEB: www.lehighcement.com
SIC: 3241 Portland cement
HQ: Lehigh Cement Company Llc
300 E John Carpenter Fwy
Irving TX 75062
877 534-4442

(G-5258)
MEDTEK SKIN CARE INC (PA)
Also Called: Phototherapeutix
206 Glen St Ste 5 (12801-3585)
PHONE..................................518 745-7264
Fax: 518 745-1402
EMP: 40
SQ FT: 9,000
SALES (est): 4.4MM **Privately Held**
SIC: 3648 Mfg U V A Tanning Systems And
Ultraviolet Medical Systems

(G-5259)
MILLER MECHANICAL SERVICES INC
55-57 Walnut St (12801)
P.O. Box 504 (12801-0504)
PHONE..................................518 792-0430
Elizabeth Miller, *President*
Ken Lofton, *Superintendent*
Frank Burkhardt, *Engineer*
Myles Miller, *Controller*
Elaine Lambert, *Administration*
EMP: 20
SQ FT: 2,240
SALES (est): 5.6MM **Privately Held**
WEB: www.millermech.com
SIC: 3542 Machine tools, metal forming type

(G-5260)
NATIONAL VAC ENVMTL SVCS CORP
80 Park Rd (12804-7614)
PHONE..................................518 743-0563
Roger Letendre, *Branch Mgr*
EMP: 20
SALES (corp-wide): 9.6MM **Privately Held**
SIC: 3589 Vacuum cleaners & sweepers,
electric: industrial
PA: National Vacuum Environmental Services Corp.
408 47th St
Niagara Falls NY 14304
716 773-1167

(G-5261)
NAVILYST MEDICAL INC
10 Glens Fls Technical Pa (12801)
PHONE..................................800 833-9973
Amy Wolfe, *Manager*
▲ **EMP:** 670
SALES (est): 150.8MM
SALES (corp-wide): 270.6MM **Publicly Held**
SIC: 3841 Surgical & medical instruments
PA: Angiodynamics, Inc.
14 Plaza Dr
Latham NY 12110
518 795-1400

(G-5262)
OAK LONE PUBLISHING CO INC
Also Called: Chronicle, The
15 Ridge St (12801-3608)
P.O. Box 153 (12801-0153)
PHONE..................................518 792-1126
Mark Frost, *President*
Patricia Maddock, *Vice Pres*
EMP: 27
SQ FT: 5,280
SALES (est): 1.9MM **Privately Held**
WEB: www.loneoak.com
SIC: 2711 Newspapers, publishing & printing

(G-5263)
PACTIV CORPORATION
6 Haskell Ave (12801-3854)
P.O. Box 148 (12801-0148)
PHONE..................................518 743-3100
Christopher G Angus, *Vice Pres*
EMP: 207
SALES (corp-wide): 14.1MM **Privately Held**
WEB: www.pactiv.com
SIC: 3089 Thermoformed finished plastic products
HQ: Pactiv Llc
1900 W Field Ct
Lake Forest IL 60045
847 482-2000

(G-5264)
PACTIV LLC
18 Peck Ave (12801-3833)
PHONE..................................518 793-2524
Gene Tomzzac, *Plant Mgr*
Paul Ostwald, *Manager*
Brian Williams, *MIS Dir*
EMP: 110
SALES (corp-wide): 14.1MM **Privately Held**
WEB: www.pactiv.com
SIC: 2673 3497 3089 Food storage &
trash bags (plastic); trash bags (plastic
film): made from purchased materials;
food storage & frozen food bags, plastic;
metal foil & leaf; plastic containers, except
foam; plastic kitchenware, tableware &
houseware
HQ: Pactiv Llc
1900 W Field Ct
Lake Forest IL 60045
847 482-2000

(G-5265)
PRECISION EXTRUSION INC
12 Glens Fls Technical Pa (12801)
PHONE..................................518 792-1199
Michael J Badera, *Ch of Bd*
Barbara Samiley, *Human Resources*
Rob Phillips, *Director*
EMP: 35
SQ FT: 15,000
SALES (est): 5.7MM
SALES (corp-wide): 7.9B **Privately Held**
WEB: www.precisionextrusion.com
SIC: 3089 Extruded finished plastic products
HQ: Pexco Llc
6470 E Johns Rssng 430
Johns Creek GA 30097
770 777-8540

(G-5266)
REVOLUTION LIGHTING LLC
211 Warren St Ste 1 (12801-3713)
P.O. Box 306 (12801-0306)
PHONE..................................518 779-3655
George B Studnicky IV, *President*
EMP: 5 **EST:** 2013
SALES (est): 348.5K **Privately Held**
SIC: 3648 Lighting equipment

(G-5267)
UMICORE ELEC MTLS USA INC
9 Pruyns Island Dr (12801-4706)
PHONE..................................518 792-7700
Marc Grynberg, *CEO*
Martin Boarder, *Chairman*
Stephan Csoma, *Exec VP*
Filip Platteeuw, *CFO*
▲ **EMP:** 110
SALES (est): 27.7MM
SALES (corp-wide): 3.7B **Privately Held**
SIC: 3339 Silver refining (primary)
HQ: Umicore Usa Inc.
3600 Glenwood Ave Ste 250
Raleigh NC 27612

(G-5268)
UMICORE USA INC
9 Pruyns Island Dr (12801-4706)
PHONE..................................919 874-7171
Allen Molvar, *Branch Mgr*
EMP: 25
SALES (corp-wide): 3.7B **Privately Held**
SIC: 3339 5051 5052 5169 Cobalt refining (primary); nonferrous metal sheets,
bars, rods, etc.; metallic ores; industrial
chemicals; metal scrap & waste materials

HQ: Umicore Usa Inc.
3600 Glenwood Ave Ste 250
Raleigh NC 27612

(G-5269)
VIBRO-LASER INSTRS CORP LLC
2c Glens Falls Tech Park (12801-3864)
PHONE..................................518 874-2700
Megh McCane Howard,
EMP: 5
SALES (est): 284.4K **Privately Held**
SIC: 3823 Analyzers, industrial process type

Glenville
Schenectady County

(G-5270)
BIOSOIL FARM INC
204 Glenville Industrial (12302-1072)
PHONE..................................518 344-4920
Chad Currin, *President*
Andrew McCarty, *CFO*
EMP: 6 **EST:** 2017
SQ FT: 12,000
SALES: 100K **Privately Held**
SIC: 2875 Fertilizers, mixing only

(G-5271)
DSM NUTRITIONAL PRODUCTS LLC
Fortitech
300 Tech Park (12302-7107)
PHONE..................................518 372-5155
Chris Nulmerrick, *Manager*
EMP: 152
SALES (corp-wide): 10.6B **Privately Held**
SIC: 2834 3295 2087 Vitamin, nutrient &
hematinic preparations for human use;
minerals, ground or treated; flavoring extracts & syrups
HQ: Dsm Nutritional Products, Llc
45 Waterview Blvd
Parsippany NJ 07054
800 526-0189

(G-5272)
INTERNATIONAL PAPER COMPANY
803 Corporation Park (12302-1057)
PHONE..................................518 372-6461
EMP: 92
SALES (corp-wide): 23.3B **Publicly Held**
WEB: www.tin.com
SIC: 2653 Boxes, corrugated: made from
purchased materials
PA: International Paper Company
6400 Poplar Ave
Memphis TN 38197
901 419-9000

(G-5273)
STARFIRE SYSTEMS INC
8 Sarnowski Dr (12302-3504)
PHONE..................................518 899-9336
Andrew Skinner, *CEO*
Richard M Saburro, *Ch of Bd*
Mark Hofmann, *Vice Pres*
Milt Kussler, *Engineer*
▲ **EMP:** 12
SALES (est): 2.3MM **Privately Held**
WEB: www.starfiresystems.com
SIC: 3299 8731 Ceramic fiber; commercial
physical research

Glenwood
Erie County

(G-5274)
LK INDUSTRIES INC
9731 Center St (14069-9611)
PHONE..................................716 941-9202
Larry Krzeminski, *President*
Lawrence Krzeminski, *General Mgr*
EMP: 5
SQ FT: 3,000
SALES: 600K **Privately Held**
SIC: 3541 Machine tools, metal cutting type

GEOGRAPHIC

Gloversville
Fulton County

(G-5275)
ADIRONDACK STAINED GLASS WORKS
29 W Fulton St Ste 6　(12078-2937)
PHONE......................................518 725-0387
Donald Dwyer, *President*
Brenda Dwyer, *Treasurer*
Patrick Duell, *Admin Sec*
EMP: 6
SQ FT: 9,600
SALES: 275K　**Privately Held**
SIC: 3231　Stained glass: made from purchased glass

(G-5276)
AMERICAN TARGET MARKETING INC
11 Cayadutta St　(12078-3816)
PHONE......................................518 725-4369
Richard Denero, *President*
Al Parillo, *Treasurer*
EMP: 31
SQ FT: 18,000
SALES: 700K　**Privately Held**
SIC: 3151　Leather gloves & mittens

(G-5277)
ANDROME LEATHER INC
21 Foster St　(12078-1600)
P.O. Box 826　(12078-0826)
PHONE......................................518 773-7945
Frank A Garguilo, *President*
Christopher Garguilo, *Vice Pres*
▲ EMP: 15
SQ FT: 10,000
SALES (est): 1.9MM　**Privately Held**
SIC: 3111　2843　Finishing of leather; leather finishing agents

(G-5278)
AVANTI CONTROL SYSTEMS INC
1 Hamilton St Fl 2　(12078-2321)
P.O. Box 113　(12078-0113)
PHONE......................................518 921-4368
Timothy M Tesiero, *President*
EMP: 6
SALES (est): 1.3MM　**Privately Held**
SIC: 3613　8711　Control panels, electric; engineering services

(G-5279)
BEEBIE PRINTING & ART AGCY INC
40 E Pine St　(12078-4339)
P.O. Box 1277　(12078-0011)
PHONE......................................518 725-4528
Craig J Beebie, *President*
EMP: 7
SQ FT: 10,000
SALES (est): 761.8K　**Privately Held**
SIC: 2759　7336　Screen printing; graphic arts & related design

(G-5280)
CALLAWAY GOLF BALL OPRTONS INC
Also Called: Spalding Sports Worldwide
Crossroads Industrial Par　(12078)
PHONE......................................518 773-2255
Mark Marvel, *Branch Mgr*
EMP: 130
SALES (corp-wide): 1.2B　**Publicly Held**
WEB: www.topflite.com
SIC: 3949　Golf equipment
HQ: Callaway Golf Ball Operations, Inc.
425 Meadow St
Chicopee MA 01013
413 536-1200

(G-5281)
COLONIAL TANNING CORPORATION (PA)
8 Wilson St 810　(12078-1500)
P.O. Box 1068　(12078-0009)
PHONE......................................518 725-7171
William Studenic, *President*
▲ EMP: 10　EST: 1971
SQ FT: 50,000

SALES (est): 1.6MM　**Privately Held**
SIC: 3111　Tanneries, leather

(G-5282)
CURTIN-HEBERT CO INC
Also Called: Curtin-Hebert Machines
11 Forest St　(12078-3999)
P.O. Box 511　(12078-0005)
PHONE......................................518 725-7157
James Curtin, *Ch of Bd*
EMP: 11　EST: 1908
SQ FT: 11,000
SALES (est): 1.9MM　**Privately Held**
WEB: www.curtinhebert.com
SIC: 3559　Rubber working machinery, including tires; leather working machinery; metal pickling equipment

(G-5283)
FOWNES BROTHERS & CO INC
204 County Highway 157　(12078-6043)
PHONE......................................518 752-4411
Rennie Sanges, *Branch Mgr*
EMP: 30
SALES (corp-wide): 66.2MM　**Privately Held**
SIC: 3151　2381　5136　5137　Gloves, leather: dress or semidress; gloves, woven or knit: made from purchased materials; gloves, men's & boys'; gloves, women's & children's; gloves, sport & athletic: boxing, handball, etc.
PA: Fownes Brothers & Co Inc
16 E 34th St Fl 5
New York NY 10016
800 345-6837

(G-5284)
HALO OPTICAL PRODUCTS INC
9 Phair St Ste 1　(12078-4328)
P.O. Box 1369　(12078-0011)
PHONE......................................518 773-4256
Peter Leonardi, *President*
EMP: 65　EST: 1964
SQ FT: 32,000
SALES (est): 8.5MM　**Privately Held**
SIC: 3827　Optical instruments & apparatus

(G-5285)
HOHENFORST SPLITTING CO INC
152 W Fulton St　(12078-2799)
PHONE......................................518 725-0012
Robert Hohenforst, *President*
Loretta Hohenforst, *Vice Pres*
EMP: 6
SQ FT: 6,000
SALES (est): 780.2K　**Privately Held**
SIC: 3111　Cutting of leather

(G-5286)
HUDSON DYING & FINISHING LLC
68 Harrison St　(12078-4732)
PHONE......................................518 752-4389
Mark Shore,
EMP: 30
SALES (est): 2MM　**Privately Held**
SIC: 2389　Men's miscellaneous accessories

(G-5287)
KENNYETTO GRAPHICS INC
137 E State St Ext　(12078-6038)
PHONE......................................518 883-6360
Lawrence Monks, *President*
Shirley Kraft, *Manager*
EMP: 30
SALES (est): 3.5MM　**Privately Held**
WEB: www.kennyettographics.com
SIC: 3993　Signs & advertising specialties

(G-5288)
LITCHFIELD FABRICS OF NC (PA)
111 Woodside Ave　(12078-2741)
PHONE......................................518 773-9500
William Conroy, *President*
Dale Steenburgh, *CFO*
Morris Evans, *Treasurer*
EMP: 3
SQ FT: 2,000
SALES (est): 3.2MM　**Privately Held**
SIC: 2258　Tricot fabrics

(G-5289)
PROTECH (LLC)
Also Called: Pro-TEC V I P
11 Cayadutta St　(12078-3816)
PHONE......................................518 725-7785
Al Parillo, *Mng Member*
Richard Denero,
EMP: 26
SALES (est): 2.3MM　**Privately Held**
SIC: 3151　5699　Gloves, leather: work; work clothing

(G-5290)
SAMCO LLC
122 S Main St　(12078)
PHONE......................................518 725-4705
Richard Warner,
EMP: 50
SQ FT: 30,000
SALES (est): 4.8MM　**Privately Held**
SIC: 3151　Gloves, leather: dress or semidress

(G-5291)
SOMERSET DYEING & FINISHING
68 Harrison St　(12078-4732)
P.O. Box 1189　(12078-0010)
PHONE......................................518 773-7383
Edward Falk, *Corp Secy*
EMP: 42
SQ FT: 24,000
SALES: 5.5MM　**Privately Held**
SIC: 2258　Dyeing & finishing lace goods & warp knit fabric

(G-5292)
SOMERSET INDUSTRIES INC (PA)
Also Called: CJ Indstries A Div Smrset Inds
68 Harrison St　(12078-4732)
P.O. Box 1189　(12078-0010)
PHONE......................................518 773-7383
Ed Falk, *CEO*
Edward Falk, *Treasurer*
▲ EMP: 32
SQ FT: 35,000
SALES (est): 12.8MM　**Privately Held**
WEB: www.somersetindustries.com
SIC: 2258　Lace & warp knit fabric mills

(G-5293)
STEPHEN MILLER GEN CONTRS INC
Also Called: Miller's Ready Mix
301 Riceville Rd　(12078-6958)
P.O. Box 291, Mayfield　(12117-0291)
PHONE......................................518 661-5601
Stephen Miller, *CEO*
EMP: 25　EST: 1971
SQ FT: 640
SALES (est): 5.8MM　**Privately Held**
SIC: 3273　1541　1761　1542　Ready-mixed concrete; industrial buildings, new construction; roofing, siding & sheet metal work; nonresidential construction

(G-5294)
TAYLOR MADE GROUP LLC
93 South Blvd　(12078-4730)
PHONE......................................518 725-0681
Dennis Flint, *CEO*
Jason Pajonk-Taylor, *President*
Robert Khalife, *CFO*
John Taylor, *Admin Sec*
▲ EMP: 47
SQ FT: 5,000
SALES: 15MM
SALES (corp-wide): 2.4B　**Publicly Held**
SIC: 3231　3429　Windshields, glass: made from purchased glass; manufactured hardware (general); marine hardware
HQ: Lippert Components, Inc.
3501 County Road 6 E
Elkhart IN 46514
574 312-7480

(G-5295)
TAYLOR PRODUCTS INC (PA)
66 Kingsboro Ave　(12078-3415)
P.O. Box 1190　(12078-0190)
PHONE......................................518 773-9312
James W Taylor, *Ch of Bd*
Dennis F Flint, *President*
Robert Khalife, *CFO*

Mike Oathout, *Marketing Mgr*
▲ EMP: 2
SQ FT: 20,000
SALES (est): 5.4MM　**Privately Held**
SIC: 3231　Tempered glass: made from purchased glass; safety glass: made from purchased glass

(G-5296)
TIC TAC TOES MFG CORP
1 Hamilton St　(12078-2321)
P.O. Box 953　(12078-0953)
PHONE......................................518 773-8187
Robert Winig, *President*
▲ EMP: 75
SQ FT: 75,000
SALES (est): 9.5MM　**Privately Held**
WEB: www.tictactoes.com
SIC: 3143　3144　Men's footwear, except athletic; women's footwear, except athletic

(G-5297)
TRADITION LEATHER INC
Also Called: Tradition Leather Co
41 W 11th Ave　(12078-1320)
PHONE......................................518 725-2555
Michael De Magistris, *President*
EMP: 20
SALES (est): 161.1K　**Privately Held**
SIC: 3111　Tanneries, leather

(G-5298)
WADSWORTH LOGGING INC
3095 State Highway 30　(12078-7601)
P.O. Box 177, Northville　(12134-0177)
PHONE......................................518 863-6870
Stephen S Wadsworth, *President*
EMP: 10　EST: 1996
SALES (est): 901K　**Privately Held**
SIC: 2411　Logging camps & contractors

(G-5299)
WASHBURNS DAIRY INC
145 N Main St　(12078-3078)
P.O. Box 1318, Dunkirk　(14048-6318)
PHONE......................................518 725-0629
Richard J Washburn, *President*
Alfred J Washburn, *Corp Secy*
Bill Washburn, *Vice Pres*
William Washburn, *Vice Pres*
EMP: 45
SQ FT: 6,000
SALES (est): 4.9MM　**Privately Held**
SIC: 2024　5143　Ice cream & ice milk; ice cream & ices

(G-5300)
WILLIAM B COLLINS COMPANY
Also Called: Leader Herald, The
8 E Fulton St　(12078-3227)
PHONE......................................518 773-8272
George Ogden Nutting, *President*
Patty Older, *Editor*
Paul Wagner, *Editor*
Robert M Nutting, *Vice Pres*
William C Nutting, *Vice Pres*
EMP: 70　EST: 1961
SQ FT: 15,000
SALES (est): 7.7MM　**Privately Held**
WEB: www.lhprint.com
SIC: 2711　Commercial printing & newspaper publishing combined
HQ: The Ogden Newspapers Inc
1500 Main St
Wheeling WV 26003
304 233-0100

(G-5301)
WOOD & HYDE LEATHER CO INC
68 Wood St　(12078-1695)
P.O. Box 786　(12078-0007)
PHONE......................................518 725-7105
Randall Doerter, *CEO*
James Keiffer, *President*
Thomas Porter, *CFO*
◆ EMP: 30
SQ FT: 266,000
SALES (est): 3.5MM　**Privately Held**
WEB: www.woodandhyde.com
SIC: 3111　Tanneries, leather

▲ = Import　▼=Export
◆ =Import/Export

Godeffroy
Orange County

(G-5302)
PHOTONSTRING INC
35 Shore Dr (12729-2215)
PHONE....................................917 966-5717
EMP: 6
SALES (est): 694.9K Privately Held
SIC: 3661 Fiber optics communications equipment

Goldens Bridge
Westchester County

(G-5303)
GUITAR SPECIALIST INC
307 Rte 22 (10526-1009)
P.O. Box 405 (10526-0405)
PHONE....................................914 401-9052
Doug J Proper, *President*
Sharon E Proper, *Admin Sec*
EMP: 5
SQ FT: 1,500
SALES (est): 327.2K Privately Held
WEB: www.guitarspecialist.com
SIC: 3931 7699 Guitars & parts, electric & nonelectric; musical instrument repair services

Goshen
Orange County

(G-5304)
ALTAN ROBOTECH (USA) INC
224a Main St (10924-2157)
PHONE....................................866 291-1101
Alfred D'Souza, *CEO*
EMP: 8 EST: 2017
SALES (est): 638K Privately Held
SIC: 3699 Household electrical equipment

(G-5305)
BIMBO BAKERIES USA INC
Also Called: Stroehmann Bakeries 72
9 Police Dr (10924-6730)
PHONE....................................845 294-5282
Phil Tobin, *Manager*
EMP: 19 Privately Held
SIC: 2051 5149 Breads, rolls & buns; groceries & related products
HQ: Bimbo Bakeries Usa, Inc
255 Business Center Dr # 200
Horsham PA 19044
215 347-5500

(G-5306)
BLASER PRODUCTION INC
31 Hatfield Ln (10924-6712)
PHONE....................................845 294-3200
Peter Blaser, *Ch of Bd*
Nick Blaser, *Vice Pres*
▲ EMP: 11
SALES (est): 15.1MM
SALES (corp-wide): 106.7MM Privately Held
WEB: www.blaser.com
SIC: 2992 Lubricating oils
HQ: Blaser Swisslube Holding Corp
31 Hatfield Ln
Goshen NY 10924

(G-5307)
BLASER SWISSLUBE HOLDING CORP (HQ)
31 Hatfield Ln (10924-6712)
PHONE....................................845 294-3200
Peter Blaser, *CEO*
Ulrich Krahenbuhl, *President*
Punit Gupta, *Managing Dir*
Richard Surico, *Vice Pres*
Linda Aldorasi, *Controller*
◆ EMP: 16
SQ FT: 40,000
SALES (est): 73.6MM
SALES (corp-wide): 106.7MM Privately Held
SIC: 2992 Lubricating oils

PA: Koras Ag
Winterseistrasse 22
RUegsauschachen BE 3415
344 600-101

(G-5308)
FG GALASSI MOULDING CO INC
699 Pulaski Hwy (10924-6009)
P.O. Box 700, Pine Island (10969-0700)
PHONE....................................845 258-2100
John Petromilli, *President*
Linda Petromilli, *Sales Staff*
▲ EMP: 9
SQ FT: 11,000
SALES (est): 1MM Privately Held
WEB: www.fggalassi.com
SIC: 2499 Picture & mirror frames, wood

(G-5309)
GLITTER SLIMES LLC
51 Greenwich Ave (10924-2032)
PHONE....................................845 772-1113
Nicolette Waltzer, *Mng Member*
EMP: 6
SALES (est): 578.9K Privately Held
SIC: 3944 Games, toys & children's vehicles

(G-5310)
JUNO CHEFS
Also Called: Milmar Food Group
1 6 1/2 Station Rd (10924-6723)
PHONE....................................845 294-5400
Julius Spessot, *President*
Luisa Spessot, *President*
Barry Werk, *Purchasing*
Mary Ellermakinen, *Human Res Mgr*
EMP: 65
SQ FT: 25,000
SALES (est): 12.7MM Privately Held
WEB: www.junofoundation.org
SIC: 2038 Breakfasts, frozen & packaged

(G-5311)
MILMAR FOOD GROUP II LLC
1 6 1/2 Station Rd (10924-6777)
PHONE....................................845 294-5400
Roy Makinen, *Exec VP*
Martin Hoffman,
▲ EMP: 250
SQ FT: 66,000
SALES (est): 58.3MM Privately Held
WEB: www.milmarfoodgroup.com
SIC: 2038 8748 Frozen specialties; business consulting

(G-5312)
ORIGINAL TUBE TSHIRT
185 Ridge Rd (10924-5306)
PHONE....................................845 291-7031
Ellen Cohen, *Owner*
EMP: 7
SALES (est): 53.6K Privately Held
SIC: 2396 Screen printing on fabric articles

(G-5313)
SKIN ATELIER INC
Also Called: Skinprint
1997 Route 17m (10924-5229)
PHONE....................................845 294-1202
Robert P Manzo, *President*
James Hannan, *Vice Pres*
Kate Ricciardi, *Marketing Staff*
▼ EMP: 10
SQ FT: 4,000
SALES (est): 1.9MM Privately Held
WEB: www.skinprint.com
SIC: 2844 Toilet preparations

(G-5314)
TILCON NEW YORK INC
Also Called: Goshen Quarry
2 Quarry Rd (10924-6045)
PHONE....................................845 615-0216
Bob Portice, *Manager*
EMP: 63
SALES (corp-wide): 30.6B Privately Held
SIC: 1429 Dolomitic marble, crushed & broken-quarrying
HQ: Tilcon New York Inc.
9 Entin Rd
Parsippany NJ 07054
973 366-7741

(G-5315)
VALUE FRAGRANCES & FLAVORS INC
7 Musket Ct (10924)
PHONE....................................845 294-5726
Alexander Vernon, *President*
Gerald Vernon, *CFO*
EMP: 18
SQ FT: 30,000
SALES (est): 15MM Privately Held
SIC: 2869 Perfumes, flavorings & food additives

Gouverneur
St. Lawrence County

(G-5316)
BAKERY & COFFEE SHOP
274 W Main St (13642-1333)
PHONE....................................315 287-1829
John Yerdon, *Owner*
EMP: 5
SALES: 230K Privately Held
SIC: 2051 Bakery: wholesale or wholesale/retail combined

(G-5317)
CARGILL INCORPORATED
19 Starbuck St (13642-1626)
P.O. Box 209 (13642-0209)
PHONE....................................315 287-0241
Edward Hoffman, *Sales/Mktg Mgr*
EMP: 20
SQ FT: 3,978
SALES (corp-wide): 114.7B Privately Held
WEB: www.cargill.com
SIC: 2048 Prepared feeds
PA: Cargill, Incorporated
15407 Mcginty Rd W
Wayzata MN 55391
952 742-7575

(G-5318)
CIVES CORPORATION
Also Called: Cives Steel Company Nthrn Div
8 Church St (13642-1416)
PHONE....................................315 287-2200
Jamie Sherrod, *Project Mgr*
Kim Pistolesi, *Accounting Dir*
Ted Totten, *Manager*
EMP: 150
SALES (corp-wide): 651.3MM Privately Held
WEB: www.cives.com
SIC: 3441 1791 Fabricated structural metal; structural steel erection
PA: Cives Corporation
3700 Mansell Rd Ste 500
Alpharetta GA 30022
770 993-4424

(G-5319)
CLEARWATER PAPER CORPORATION
4921 State Highway 58 (13642-3207)
PHONE....................................315 287-1200
John E Keel, *Human Resources*
Jeremery Bartholomew, *Branch Mgr*
EMP: 85 Publicly Held
SIC: 2621 Paper mills
PA: Clearwater Paper Corporation
601 W Riverside Ave # 1100
Spokane WA 99201

(G-5320)
DUNN PAPER - NATURAL DAM INC
4921 St Rt 58 (13642-3207)
PHONE....................................315 287-1200
Brent Earnshaw, *President*
Donald Venette, *Production*
Al Magnan, *CFO*
EMP: 88
SALES: 48MM
SALES (corp-wide): 139.6MM Privately Held
SIC: 2621 Specialty papers
HQ: Dunn Paper, Inc.
218 Riverview St
Port Huron MI 48060
810 984-5521

(G-5321)
IMERYS USA INC
16a Main St Hailesboro Rd (13642-3360)
P.O. Box 479 (13642-0479)
PHONE....................................315 287-0780
Bob Snyder, *Branch Mgr*
EMP: 17
SQ FT: 30,000
SALES (corp-wide): 3MM Privately Held
SIC: 1411 Granite, dimension-quarrying
HQ: Imerys Usa, Inc.
100 Mansell Ct E Ste 300
Roswell GA 30076
770 645-3300

(G-5322)
RIVERSIDE IRON LLC
26 Water St (13642)
PHONE....................................315 535-4864
Eric Tessmer, *President*
EMP: 12
SALES (est): 777.7K Privately Held
SIC: 3441 3446 3449 Dam gates, metal plate; architectural metalwork; miscellaneous metalwork

Gowanda
Cattaraugus County

(G-5323)
TTE FILTERS LLC (HQ)
1 Magnetic Pkwy (14070-1526)
P.O. Box 111 (14070-0111)
PHONE....................................716 532-2234
Claude Badawy, *President*
Thomas Norsen, *CFO*
Susan Szucs, *Director*
EMP: 8
SALES: 1.5MM
SALES (corp-wide): 18.7MM Privately Held
SIC: 3677 Filtration devices, electronic
PA: Gowanda Holdings, Llc
1 Magnetic Pkwy
Gowanda NY 14070
716 532-2234

Grand Island
Erie County

(G-5324)
ABRAXIS BIOSCIENCE LLC
3159 Staley Rd (14072-2028)
PHONE....................................716 773-0800
Mark Forell, *Manager*
EMP: 7
SALES (corp-wide): 15.2B Privately Held
SIC: 2834 Pharmaceutical preparations
HQ: Abraxis Bioscience, Llc
11755 Wilshire Blvd Fl 20
Los Angeles CA 90025

(G-5325)
ASI SIGN SYSTEMS INC
2957 Alt Blvd (14072-1220)
PHONE....................................716 775-0104
Keith Joslyn, *Plant Mgr*
Robin Wright, *Controller*
Bethany Bernatovicz, *Human Res Mgr*
Andy Bernatovicz, *Branch Mgr*
EMP: 7
SALES (corp-wide): 20.7MM Privately Held
SIC: 3993 Signs & advertising specialties
PA: Asi Sign Systems, Inc.
8181 Jetstar Dr Ste 110
Irving TX 75063
214 352-9140

(G-5326)
BAM ENTERPRISES INC (PA)
2937 Alt Blvd (14072-1285)
P.O. Box 310 (14072-0310)
PHONE....................................716 773-7634
Gary Moose, *CEO*
Victor Alfiero, *CFO*
Diane Zachwieja, *Technical Staff*
EMP: 2
SQ FT: 310,000
SALES (est): 38.3MM Privately Held
SIC: 3714 Motor vehicle wheels & parts

(G-5327)
DPM OF WESTERN NEW YORK LLC (HQ)
Also Called: Dual Print & Mail, LLC
3235 Grand Island Blvd (14072-1284)
PHONE..................................716 775-8001
Michael Vitch, *CEO*
Thomas Salisbury, *Ch of Bd*
Joanne Sabio, *Vice Pres*
Steven Gaertner, *Production*
EMP: 76
SALES (est): 12.6MM
SALES (corp-wide): 29MM **Privately Held**
SIC: 2752 Commercial printing, lithographic
PA: Compu-Mail, Llc
3235 Grand Island Blvd
Grand Island NY 14072
716 775-8001

(G-5328)
DYLIX CORPORATION
347 Lang Blvd (14072-3123)
PHONE..................................716 773-2985
Nathaniel G Bargar, *President*
Bryan Barrett, *Mfg Mgr*
Victor Sears, *Engineer*
Roger Brath, *Sales Engr*
EMP: 25
SALES (est): 4.8MM **Privately Held**
WEB: www.dylixcorp.com
SIC: 3829 Pressure transducers

(G-5329)
FAST BY GAST INC
120 Industrial Dr (14072-1270)
PHONE..................................716 773-1536
Paul Gast, *President*
Dana Gast, *Vice Pres*
▲ EMP: 9
SQ FT: 4,240
SALES (est): 1.2MM **Privately Held**
WEB: www.fastbygast.com
SIC: 3714 Motor vehicle parts & accessories

(G-5330)
FRESENIUS KABI USA LLC
3159 Staley Rd (14072-2028)
PHONE..................................716 773-0053
Peter Martinez, *Vice Pres*
Rob Lawson, *Facilities Mgr*
Lyn Davey, *Accountant*
Frank Harmon, *Director*
Mark Schimley, *Maintence Staff*
EMP: 450
SALES (corp-wide): 38.3B **Privately Held**
WEB: www.appdrugs.com
SIC: 2834 Pharmaceutical preparations
HQ: Fresenius Kabi Usa, Inc.
3 Corporate Dr
Lake Zurich IL 60047
847 969-2700

(G-5331)
FRESENIUS KABI USA LLC
3159 Staley Rd (14072-2028)
PHONE..................................716 773-0800
Corey Carpenter, *Production*
Michael Dudek, *Production*
Scott Gorenflo, *Engineer*
Michael Grisanti, *Accountant*
Frank Harmon, *Branch Mgr*
EMP: 35
SALES (corp-wide): 38.3B **Privately Held**
SIC: 2834 Pharmaceutical preparations
HQ: Fresenius Kabi Usa, Llc
3 Corporate Dr Fl 3 # 3
Lake Zurich IL 60047
847 550-2300

(G-5332)
GRAND ISLAND ANIMAL HOSPITAL
Also Called: Grand Island Research & Dev
2323 Whitehaven Rd (14072-1505)
PHONE..................................716 773-7645
Robert Harper, *President*
Lysa P Posner Dvm, *Principal*
EMP: 20
SALES (est): 1.5MM **Privately Held**
SIC: 3999 0742 Pet supplies; veterinary services, specialties

(G-5333)
INVITROGEN CORP
3175 Staley Rd (14072-2090)
P.O. Box 68 (14072-0068)
PHONE..................................716 774-6700
Mary McCormick, *Principal*
Lisa De Vaul, *Marketing Mgr*
EMP: 6 EST: 2016
SALES (est): 119.8K **Privately Held**
SIC: 2836 Biological products, except diagnostic

(G-5334)
ISLECHEM LLC
2801 Long Rd (14072-1244)
PHONE..................................716 773-8401
Daniel Canavan, *Vice Pres*
Dale Kunze, *Vice Pres*
Kevin Rader, *Project Mgr*
John Dahl, *Manager*
Ron Stacy, *Manager*
▲ EMP: 37
SALES: 8.2MM **Privately Held**
WEB: www.islechem.com
SIC: 2869 8731 Industrial organic chemicals; commercial physical research

(G-5335)
JR ENGINEERING ENTERPRISE LLC
2141 Bedell Rd (14072-1614)
PHONE..................................716 909-2693
Tila Roger M, *Vice Pres*
Jessey Rajah Roger, *Mng Member*
EMP: 2
SALES: 1MM **Privately Held**
SIC: 3564 7349 7389 Exhaust fans: industrial or commercial; exhaust hood or fan cleaning;

(G-5336)
LIFE TECHNOLOGIES CORPORATION
3175 Staley Rd (14072-2028)
PHONE..................................716 774-6700
Lyle Turner, *Vice Pres*
Chris Crannell, *Facilities Mgr*
Sonia Llarenas, *Mfg Staff*
Tracy Bronson, *Production*
Dulce Santos, *Production*
EMP: 100
SALES (corp-wide): 24.3B **Privately Held**
SIC: 3826 Analytical instruments
HQ: Life Technologies Corporation
5781 Van Allen Way
Carlsbad CA 92008
760 603-7200

(G-5337)
MESSER LLC
3279 Grand Island Blvd (14072-1216)
PHONE..................................716 773-7552
Jeff Schutrum, *Manager*
EMP: 60
SALES (corp-wide): 1.4B **Privately Held**
SIC: 3825 3625 3567 3561 Instruments to measure electricity; relays & industrial controls; industrial furnaces & ovens; pumps & pumping equipment; machine tool accessories
HQ: Messer Llc
200 Somerset Corp Blvd # 7000
Bridgewater NJ 08807
908 464-8100

(G-5338)
NIDEC INDUS AUTOMTN USA LLC
Also Called: Emerson Control Techniques
359 Lang Blvd Bldg B (14072-3123)
PHONE..................................716 774-1193
EMP: 30
SALES (corp-wide): 13.9B **Privately Held**
SIC: 3566 3823 Mfg Indstrl Machinery & Equip Process Control Instrmnts
HQ: Nidec Industrial Automation Usa, Llc
7078 Shady Oak Rd
Eden Prairie MN 55344
952 995-8000

(G-5339)
NRD LLC
2937 Alt Blvd (14072-1292)
P.O. Box 310 (14072-0310)
PHONE..................................716 773-7634
Douglas J Fiegel, *President*
Mike Nuhn, *Engineer*
Jeanne Treat, *Engineer*
John Glynn, *Sales Staff*
Pam May, *Office Mgr*
▲ EMP: 50
SQ FT: 32,000
SALES (est): 10.4MM
SALES (corp-wide): 38.3MM **Privately Held**
WEB: www.nrdstaticcontrol.com
SIC: 3629 3669 3499 Static elimination equipment, industrial; smoke detectors; fire- or burglary-resistive products
PA: Bam Enterprises, Inc.
2937 Alt Blvd
Grand Island NY 14072
716 773-7634

(G-5340)
OCCIDENTAL CHEMICAL CORP
2801 Long Rd (14072-1244)
PHONE..................................716 773-8100
Charles G Radar, *Branch Mgr*
EMP: 30
SALES (corp-wide): 18.9B **Publicly Held**
WEB: www.oxychem.com
SIC: 2812 Alkalies & chlorine
HQ: Occidental Chemical Corporation
14555 Dallas Pkwy Ste 400
Dallas TX 75254
972 404-3800

(G-5341)
R R DONNELLEY & SONS COMPANY
Also Called: Moore Business Forms
300 Lang Blvd (14072-3122)
PHONE..................................716 773-0647
Jeffrey Gebhart, *Branch Mgr*
EMP: 56
SALES (corp-wide): 6.8B **Publicly Held**
WEB: www.moore.com
SIC: 2759 Commercial printing
PA: R. R. Donnelley & Sons Company
35 W Wacker Dr
Chicago IL 60601
312 326-8000

(G-5342)
R R DONNELLEY & SONS COMPANY
Also Called: Moore Research Center
3235 Grand Island Blvd (14072-1284)
PHONE..................................716 773-0300
Anthony D Joseph, *Vice Pres*
EMP: 65
SALES (corp-wide): 6.8B **Publicly Held**
WEB: www.moore.com
SIC: 2761 Manifold business forms
PA: R. R. Donnelley & Sons Company
35 W Wacker Dr
Chicago IL 60601
312 326-8000

(G-5343)
SAINT-GOBAIN ADFORS AMER INC (DH)
Also Called: Saint-Gobain-Paris France
1795 Baseline Rd (14072-2010)
PHONE..................................716 775-3900
John Bedell, *CEO*
◆ EMP: 55
SALES (est): 151.4MM
SALES (corp-wide): 215.9MM **Privately Held**
WEB: www.sgtf.com
SIC: 2297 Nonwoven fabrics

(G-5344)
STARLINE USA INC
3036 Alt Blvd (14072-1274)
PHONE..................................716 773-0100
Joshua Lapsker, *CEO*
Ron Lapsker, *Chairman*
Jeffrey Hassler, *Director*
EMP: 120
SQ FT: 80,000
SALES (est): 15.9MM **Privately Held**
SIC: 2396 Printing & embossing on plastics fabric articles

(G-5345)
THERMO FISHER SCIENTIFIC INC
3175 Staley Rd (14072-2028)
PHONE..................................716 774-6700
Andrew Larsen, *Business Mgr*
Jennifer Pendola, *Project Mgr*
Darren Tower, *Mfg Mgr*
Justin Jones, *Mfg Staff*
Santo Libero, *Accounts Mgr*
EMP: 7
SALES (corp-wide): 24.3B **Publicly Held**
SIC: 3826 Analytical instruments
PA: Thermo Fisher Scientific Inc.
168 3rd Ave
Waltham MA 02451
781 622-1000

(G-5346)
TULLY PRODUCTS INC
2065 Baseline Rd (14072-2060)
PHONE..................................716 773-3166
Richard Ray, *President*
EMP: 5
SQ FT: 8,000
SALES: 500K **Privately Held**
SIC: 3089 Trays, plastic

(G-5347)
US PEROXIDE
1815 Love Rd Ste 1 (14072-2248)
PHONE..................................716 775-5585
Eric Poomi, *Project Mgr*
Paul Faulise, *Manager*
EMP: 7
SALES (est): 1.2MM **Privately Held**
SIC: 2819 Peroxides, hydrogen peroxide

Granville
Washington County

(G-5348)
CENTRAL TIMBER CO INC
Also Called: Central Timber Research/Devt
9088 State Route 22 (12832-4805)
PHONE..................................518 638-6338
Ralph Jameson II, *President*
EMP: 5
SQ FT: 52,704
SALES (est): 326.6K **Privately Held**
SIC: 2411 Logging

(G-5349)
LOCKER MASTERS INC
10329 State Route 22 (12832-5024)
PHONE..................................518 288-3203
Martha Lyng, *President*
William Lyng, *Treasurer*
Allan Lyng, *Admin Sec*
EMP: 12
SQ FT: 12,000
SALES: 600K **Privately Held**
SIC: 2542 7699 Lockers (not refrigerated): except wood; industrial machinery & equipment repair

(G-5350)
MANCHESTER NEWSPAPER INC (PA)
Also Called: Whitehall Times
14 E Main St (12832-1334)
P.O. Box 330 (12832-0330)
PHONE..................................518 642-1234
John Manchester, *President*
Lisa Manchester, *Vice Pres*
Renae McKittrick, *Advt Staff*
Dee Carroll, *Manager*
EMP: 33 EST: 1875
SQ FT: 10,000
SALES: 3.8MM **Privately Held**
WEB: www.manchesternewspapers.com
SIC: 2711 Newspapers: publishing only, not printed on site

(G-5351)
MANCHESTER WOOD INC
1159 County Route 24 (12832)
P.O. Box 180 (12832-0180)
PHONE..................................518 642-9518
Edward Eriksen, *President*
Luke Eriksen, *Vice Pres*
Priscilla Eriksen, *Treasurer*
Laurie Grottoli, *Accountant*

EMP: 148
SQ FT: 54,000
SALES (est): 21.6MM Privately Held
WEB: www.manchesterwood.com
SIC: 2511 Chairs, household, except up-
holstered: wood

(G-5352)
**METTOWEE LUMBER &
PLASTICS CO**
82 Church St (12832-1662)
PHONE..................................518 642-1100
Henry V Derminden IV, President
Robert Vanderminden Jr, Vice Pres
Kait McNulty, Marketing Mgr
Rick Doyle, Manager
EMP: 250 EST: 1936
SQ FT: 20,000
SALES (est): 19.5MM
SALES (corp-wide): 55.6MM Privately
Held
SIC: 2421 0811 3089 Sawmills & planing
mills, general; timber tracts; plastic pro-
cessing
PA: Telescope Casual Furniture, Inc.
82 Church St
Granville NY 12832
518 642-1100

(G-5353)
MUDDY TRAIL JERKY CO
85 Quaker St (12832-1532)
PHONE..................................518 642-2194
Mary Louise Lussier, Principal
EMP: 6
SALES (est): 427.9K Privately Held
SIC: 2013 Sausages & other prepared
meats

(G-5354)
NORTH AMERICAN SLATE INC
50 Columbus St (12832-1024)
PHONE..................................518 642-1702
Robert Tatko, President
EMP: 7 EST: 1998
SQ FT: 3,500
SALES (est): 495.1K Privately Held
SIC: 3281 Slate products

(G-5355)
**SAINT-GOBAIN PRFMCE PLAS
CORP**
1 Sealants Park (12832-1652)
PHONE..................................518 642-2200
Bob Shear, Branch Mgr
EMP: 150
SALES (corp-wide): 215.9MM Privately
Held
SIC: 2891 3086 2821 2671 Sealants;
plastics foam products; plastics materials
& resins; packaging paper & plastics film,
coated & laminated
HQ: Saint-Gobain Performance Plastics
Corporation
31500 Solon Rd
Solon OH 44139
440 836-6900

(G-5356)
WESTERN SLATE INC (PA)
33 Dekalb Rd (12832-5500)
PHONE..................................802 287-2210
Jeffrey Harrison, President
Colleen Harrison, Vice Pres
EMP: 25
SALES: 1.5MM Privately Held
WEB: www.westernslate.com
SIC: 1429 Slate, crushed & broken-quarry-
ing

(G-5357)
WINN MANUFACTURING INC
12 Burtis Ave (12832-1341)
P.O. Box 308 (12832-0308)
PHONE..................................518 642-3515
Steve Winn, President
Sandra Winn, Vice Pres
EMP: 6 EST: 1995
SQ FT: 4,500
SALES: 500K Privately Held
SIC: 3599 Machine shop, jobbing & repair

Great Bend
Jefferson County

(G-5358)
**HANSON AGGREGATES EAST
LLC**
County Rt 47 (13643)
P.O. Box 130, Watertown (13601-0130)
PHONE..................................315 493-3721
Dan Oconnor, Superintendent
EMP: 15
SQ FT: 910
SALES (corp-wide): 20.6B Privately Held
SIC: 3281 Limestone, cut & shaped
HQ: Hanson Aggregates East Llc
3131 Rdu Center Dr
Morrisville NC 27560
919 380-2500

Great Neck
Nassau County

(G-5359)
**ADVANCED BARCODE TECH
INC**
Also Called: ABT
175 E Shore Rd Ste 228 (11023-2434)
PHONE..................................516 570-8100
Charles Bibas, President
Stephen A Bauman, President
Dafna Bibas, Vice Pres
EMP: 16
SQ FT: 7,500
SALES (est): 3.8MM Privately Held
WEB: www.abtworld.com
SIC: 3577 7371 Bar code (magnetic ink)
printers; computer software development

(G-5360)
AFP MANUFACTURING CORP
9 Park Pl (11021-5034)
PHONE..................................516 466-6464
Attilio F Petrocelli, Principal
EMP: 22 EST: 2009
SALES (est): 4.4MM Privately Held
SIC: 3999 Manufacturing industries

(G-5361)
ALFRED BUTLER INC
107 Grace Ave (11021-1608)
PHONE..................................516 829-7460
Jerome Butler, President
▲ EMP: 16
SQ FT: 8,000
SALES (est): 1.8MM Privately Held
WEB: www.alfredbutler.com
SIC: 3911 Rings, finger: precious metal

(G-5362)
ALFRED KHALILY INC
Also Called: Alfa Chem
2 Harbor Way (11024-2117)
PHONE..................................516 504-0059
Alfred Khalily, President
Farry Khallily, Vice Pres
Freshteh Khalily, Treasurer
▲ EMP: 14
SQ FT: 5,000
SALES (est): 2.7MM Privately Held
WEB: www.alfachem1.com
SIC: 2834 Pharmaceutical preparations

(G-5363)
ALLURE FASHIONS INC
8 Barstow Rd Apt 2e (11021-3543)
PHONE..................................516 829-2470
Jay Confino, President
Abdool S Ali, Vice Pres
EMP: 2
SQ FT: 800
SALES: 1.5MM Privately Held
SIC: 2341 Women's & children's nightwear

(G-5364)
AMERICAN APPAREL LTD
15 Cuttermill Rd Ste 145 (11021-3252)
PHONE..................................516 504-4559
Kishore Hemrajani, President
EMP: 8
SQ FT: 1,000

SALES (est): 550.5K Privately Held
SIC: 2326 Men's & boys' work clothing

(G-5365)
APPLICATION RESOURCES INC
Also Called: Stratusoft
15 Cuttermill Rd Ste 529 (11021)
PHONE..................................516 636-6200
Eran Mertans, CEO
Eran D Mertens, Manager
EMP: 5
SALES (est): 438.6K Privately Held
WEB: www.stratusoft.com
SIC: 7372 Prepackaged software

(G-5366)
**ARCADIA CHEM PRESERVATIVE
LLC**
100 Great Neck Rd Apt 5b (11021-3349)
PHONE..................................516 466-5258
Richard Rofe, Mng Member
EMP: 5
SQ FT: 3,000
SALES (est): 5.8MM Privately Held
SIC: 2869 5169 Industrial organic chemi-
cals; alkalines & chlorine; drilling mud; in-
dustrial chemicals; silicon lubricants

(G-5367)
ARGON CORP (PA)
160 Great Neck Rd (11021-3304)
PHONE..................................516 487-5314
Moshe Albaum, CEO
Mike Forde, COO
Michele Kilcommons, Purch Mgr
Leonid Fabisevich, Design Engr
Craig Kernaghan, Technical Staff
▲ EMP: 18
SQ FT: 10,000
SALES (est): 7MM Privately Held
WEB: www.argoncorp.com
SIC: 3571 8731 Electronic computers;
computer (hardware) development

(G-5368)
**AUTOMOTIVE LEATHER GROUP
LLC**
17 Barstow Rd Ste 206 (11021-2213)
PHONE..................................516 627-4000
Bob Kamali, Mng Member
EMP: 10
SQ FT: 5,000
SALES (est): 398.3K Privately Held
SIC: 3111 Accessory products, leather

(G-5369)
AVANTE
35 Hicks Ln (11024-2026)
PHONE..................................516 782-4888
Arash Ouriel, Partner
Albert Alishahi, Partner
▲ EMP: 6
SALES (est): 567.4K Privately Held
WEB: www.avante.net
SIC: 2371 Fur goods

(G-5370)
BEAUTY AMERICA LLC
10 Bond St Ste 296 (11021-2454)
PHONE..................................917 744-1430
AVI Sivan,
EMP: 30
SALES: 1.9MM Privately Held
SIC: 3823 4813 Viscosimeters, industrial
process type;

(G-5371)
**BRILLIANT STARS COLLECTION
INC**
150 Great Neck Rd Ste 400 (11021-3309)
PHONE..................................516 365-9000
Rodney Rahmani, President
EMP: 5
SQ FT: 13,000
SALES (est): 444.9K Privately Held
WEB: www.brilliantstars.com
SIC: 3911 Jewelry, precious metal

(G-5372)
CADDY CONCEPTS INC
15 Cuttermill Rd (11021-3252)
PHONE..................................516 570-6279
▲ EMP: 10
SALES (est): 1MM Privately Held
SIC: 2392 Mfg Household Furnishings

(G-5373)
**CARDONA INDUSTRIES USA
LTD (PA)**
505 Northern Blvd Ste 213 (11021-5112)
P.O. Box 7778, Delray Beach FL (33482-
7778)
PHONE..................................516 466-5200
Ben Feinsod, President
Edward Streim, Chairman
Douglas Knapp, Vice Pres
▲ EMP: 8
SQ FT: 2,500
SALES (est): 1.3MM Privately Held
SIC: 3369 5094 White metal castings
(lead, tin, antimony), except die; jewelers'
findings

(G-5374)
CARNELS PRINTING INC
Also Called: Carnel Printing and Copying
21 Schenck Ave Apt 3ba (11021-3644)
PHONE..................................516 883-3355
Kay W Ray, President
EMP: 6
SQ FT: 2,500
SALES (est): 903.4K Privately Held
SIC: 2752 2791 2789 Commercial print-
ing, offset; typesetting; bookbinding & re-
lated work

(G-5375)
CHAMELEON GEMS INC
98 Cuttermill Rd Ste 398n (11021-3009)
PHONE..................................516 829-3333
Aaron Hakimian, CEO
Abraham Hakimian, President
EMP: 12
SALES (est): 1.6MM Privately Held
SIC: 3911 Jewelry, precious metal

(G-5376)
CLASSIC CREATIONS INC
Also Called: Viducci
1 Linden Pl Ste 409 (11021-2640)
PHONE..................................516 498-1991
Tony Nemati, Owner
EMP: 5
SALES (est): 412.2K Privately Held
SIC: 3915 Jewel cutting, drilling, polishing,
recutting or setting

(G-5377)
**COLONIAL TAG & LABEL CO
INC**
425 Northern Blvd Ste 36 (11021-4803)
PHONE..................................516 482-0508
Eric Kono, President
John Kono, Director
▲ EMP: 13 EST: 1966
SQ FT: 10,000
SALES (est): 7.8MM Privately Held
WEB: www.cdscds.com
SIC: 2241 2759 Labels, woven; tags:
printing

(G-5378)
CONFORMER PRODUCTS INC
60 Cuttermill Rd Ste 411 (11021-3104)
PHONE..................................516 504-6300
Marvin Makofsky, CEO
EMP: 13
SALES (est): 2.2MM Privately Held
SIC: 2677 Envelopes

(G-5379)
**CONNIE FRENCH CLEANERS
INC**
Also Called: Connie Cleaners
801 Middle Neck Rd (11024-1932)
PHONE..................................516 487-1343
Michael Estivo, President
EMP: 9 EST: 1938
SQ FT: 2,000
SALES (est): 1.1MM Privately Held
SIC: 2842 7219 Drycleaning preparations;
garment alteration & repair shop

(G-5380)
DALCOM USA LTD
Also Called: Dalfon
11 Middle Neck Rd Ste 301 (11021-2301)
PHONE..................................516 466-7733
Fred Hakim, President
EMP: 11
SQ FT: 4,000

GEOGRAPHIC

SALES: 2.5MM **Privately Held**
WEB: www.dalfon.com
SIC: 2326 Men's & boys' work clothing

(G-5381)
DENNIS METALS INC
33 Edgewood Pl (11024-1805)
PHONE..................................516 487-5747
Dennis Grossman, *Manager*
EMP: 5
SALES (corp-wide): 2.1MM **Privately Held**
SIC: 3339 Precious metals
PA: Dennis Metals Inc
    42 W 39th St Fl 14
    New York NY
    516 487-5747

(G-5382)
DSR INTERNATIONAL CORP
107 Northern Blvd Ste 401 (11021-4312)
PHONE..................................631 427-2600
Thil NA, *Principal*
Harvey Drill, *Sales Staff*
▲ **EMP:** 6
SALES (est): 565.6K **Privately Held**
SIC: 3315 5063 Cable, steel: insulated or armored; electronic wire & cable
HQ: Dsr Corp
    7 Noksansaneopjung-Ro 192beon-Gil,
    Gangseo-Gu
    Busan 46753

(G-5383)
EXPEDI-PRINTING INC
41 Red Brook Rd (11024-1437)
PHONE..................................516 513-0919
Shiann Jong Chen, *Chairman*
▲ **EMP:** 145
SQ FT: 130,000
SALES (est): 14.7MM **Privately Held**
WEB: www.expedi.com
SIC: 2759 Newspapers: printing; periodicals: printing

(G-5384)
F L DEMETER INC
12 N Gate Rd (11023-1313)
PHONE..................................516 487-5187
Debra Janke, *President*
Mark Crames, *Vice Pres*
▲ **EMP:** 25
SQ FT: 3,000
SALES (est): 5.3MM **Privately Held**
SIC: 2844 5122 Perfumes & colognes; cosmetics, perfumes & hair products

(G-5385)
FAB INDUSTRIES CORP (HQ)
98 Cuttermill Rd Ste 412 (11021-3006)
PHONE..................................516 498-3200
Steven Myers, *President*
Sam Hiatt, *Vice Pres*
Jerry Deese, *CFO*
David A Miller, *CFO*
Beth Myers, *Treasurer*
EMP: 307 **EST:** 1961
SQ FT: 2,409
SALES (est): 27.9MM **Privately Held**
WEB: www.fab-industries.com
SIC: 2258 2211 Warp & flat knit products; sheets, bedding & table cloths: cotton

(G-5386)
FABRIC RESOURCES INTL LTD (PA)
9 Park Pl (11021-5034)
PHONE..................................516 829-4550
Steven Richman, *President*
◆ **EMP:** 16 **EST:** 1939
SQ FT: 5,500
SALES (est): 2.8MM **Privately Held**
SIC: 2221 2262 2231 2295 Broadwoven fabric mills, manmade; finishing plants, manmade fiber & silk fabrics; broadwoven fabric mills, wool; coated fabrics, not rubberized

(G-5387)
FIRST QLTY PACKG SOLUTIONS LLC (PA)
80 Cuttermill Rd Ste 500 (11021-3108)
PHONE..................................516 829-3030
EMP: 15

SALES (est): 6.2MM **Privately Held**
SIC: 3086 Packaging & shipping materials, foamed plastic

(G-5388)
FIRST QUALITY PRODUCTS INC (HQ)
80 Cuttermill Rd Ste 500 (11021-3108)
P.O. Box 270, Mc Elhattan PA (17748-0270)
PHONE..................................516 829-4949
Nasser Damaghi, *Ch of Bd*
Jeff Loedding, *Prdtn Mgr*
Dennis Dobrowolski, *Opers Staff*
Larry Schul, *Opers Staff*
Shawn Brown, *Engineer*
◆ **EMP:** 11
SQ FT: 6,000
SALES (est): 335.1MM **Privately Held**
SIC: 2676 Sanitary paper products

(G-5389)
FLEXTRADE SYSTEMS INC (PA)
111 Great Neck Rd Ste 314 (11021-5403)
PHONE..................................516 627-8993
Vijay Kedia, *President*
Vikas Kedia, *Managing Dir*
Vishal Pandya, *COO*
Shailendra Balani, *Senior VP*
Jamie Benincasa, *Senior VP*
EMP: 140
SALES (est): 115.9MM **Privately Held**
WEB: www.flextrade.com
SIC: 7372 Business oriented computer software

(G-5390)
FORMULA 4 MEDIA LLC
17 Barstow Rd Ste 305 (11021-2213)
P.O. Box 231318 (11023-0318)
PHONE..................................516 305-4709
Jeff Nott, *CEO*
Cara Griffin, *Chief*
EMP: 10 **EST:** 2007
SALES (est): 269.9K **Privately Held**
SIC: 2721 Magazines: publishing only, not printed on site

(G-5391)
FULLER SPORTSWEAR CO INC
10 Grenfell Dr (11020-1429)
PHONE..................................516 773-3353
Robert Feinerman, *President*
Aaron Feinerman, *Corp Secy*
Robin Feinerman, *Vice Pres*
EMP: 6 **EST:** 1960
SQ FT: 50,000
SALES (est): 550K **Privately Held**
SIC: 2331 Blouses, women's & juniors': made from purchased material

(G-5392)
GEMORO INC
98 Cuttermill Rd Ste 446s (11021-3023)
PHONE..................................212 768-8844
Dennis Hakim, *President*
EMP: 5
SALES (est): 478.5K **Privately Held**
WEB: www.gemoro.com
SIC: 3911 5094 Jewelry, precious metal; jewelry & precious stones

(G-5393)
ILICO JEWELRY INC
98 Cuttermill Rd Ste 396 (11021-3008)
PHONE..................................516 482-0201
Michael Ilian, *President*
Rodney Ilian, *Vice Pres*
Rebecca Ilian, *Admin Sec*
EMP: 5
SQ FT: 1,200
SALES (est): 505.2K **Privately Held**
SIC: 3911 Jewelry, precious metal

(G-5394)
INTERNATIONAL CASEIN CORP CAL
111 Great Neck Rd Ste 218 (11021-5408)
PHONE..................................516 466-4363
Marvin Match, *President*
Vance Perry, *Vice Pres*
EMP: 5
SQ FT: 1,500
SALES (est): 480.5K **Privately Held**
SIC: 2821 Plastics materials & resins

(G-5395)
IRIDIUM INDUSTRIES INC
Also Called: Artube
17 Barstow Rd Ste 302 (11021-2213)
PHONE..................................516 504-9700
Jacques Sassouni, *Principal*
EMP: 50
SALES (corp-wide): 37.5MM **Privately Held**
SIC: 3089 3083 Plastic containers, except foam; laminated plastics plate & sheet
PA: Iridium Industries, Inc.
    147 Forge Rd
    East Stroudsburg PA 18301
    570 476-8800

(G-5396)
JAY-AIMEE DESIGNS INC
1 Great Neck Rd Ste 1 # 1 (11021-3323)
PHONE..................................718 609-0333
Isaac Matalon, *CEO*
Shlomi Matalon, *President*
EMP: 175
SQ FT: 4,000
SALES (est): 25.5MM **Privately Held**
WEB: www.jayaimee.com
SIC: 3911 Earrings, precious metal

(G-5397)
KALATI COMPANY INC
10 Bond St Ste 1 (11021-2455)
PHONE..................................516 423-9132
Rami Kalati, *Principal*
EMP: 6
SALES (est): 17.5K **Privately Held**
SIC: 2273 Carpets & rugs

(G-5398)
KAMALI AUTOMOTIVE GROUP INC
17 Barstow Rd Ste 206 (11021-2213)
PHONE..................................516 627-4000
Joseph Kamali, *Vice Pres*
EMP: 10
SALES (est): 398.3K **Privately Held**
SIC: 3111 Upholstery leather

(G-5399)
KAMALI GROUP INC
17 Barstow Rd Ste 206 (11021-2213)
PHONE..................................516 627-4000
Bahman Kamali, *Ch of Bd*
Bob Kamali, *Principal*
Joseph Kamali, *Vice Pres*
Ruth Kamali, *Vice Pres*
Selena Lau, *Vice Pres*
▲ **EMP:** 5
SQ FT: 3,000
SALES (est): 32.2K **Privately Held**
WEB: www.kamaligroup.com
SIC: 2399 3111 Automotive covers, except seat & tire covers; accessory products, leather

(G-5400)
LE VIAN CORP (PA)
Also Called: Arusha Tanzanite
235 Great Neck Rd (11021-3301)
PHONE..................................516 466-7200
Moosa Levian, *President*
Allen Levian, *Opers Staff*
Jonathan Levian, *Sales Mgr*
Cheryl Layton, *Sales Executive*
Mathew Banilivi, *Manager*
▲ **EMP:** 106 **EST:** 1998
SQ FT: 7,000
SALES (est): 31.2MM **Privately Held**
WEB: www.levian.com
SIC: 3911 Jewelry, precious metal

(G-5401)
LINO INTERNATIONAL INC
Also Called: Lino Metal
111 Great Neck Rd 300a (11021-5403)
PHONE..................................516 482-7100
Ling Hong LI, *President*
EMP: 7
SALES: 5MM **Privately Held**
SIC: 3312 Pipes, iron & steel

(G-5402)
MANHATTAN SHADE & GLASS CO INC (PA)
37 Pond Park Rd (11023-2011)
PHONE..................................212 288-5616

Steven Schulman, *President*
Morine Shulman, *Principal*
Douglas Schulman, *Vice Pres*
Mitchell Schulman, *Vice Pres*
▼ **EMP:** 33 **EST:** 1964
SQ FT: 3,500
SALES (est): 6.8MM **Privately Held**
WEB: www.manhattanshade.com
SIC: 2591 3211 Shade, curtain & drapery hardware; window glass, clear & colored

(G-5403)
MEDISONIC INC
57 Watermill Ln Ste 296 (11021-4234)
PHONE..................................516 653-2345
AVI Sivan, *CEO*
Faiza Masroor, *Admin Sec*
EMP: 10
SQ FT: 850
SALES: 175K **Privately Held**
SIC: 2844 Toilet preparations

(G-5404)
NAVA GLOBAL PARTNERS INC
347 Great Neck Rd (11021-4220)
PHONE..................................516 737-7127
Jiemin Fan, *Ch of Bd*
EMP: 5
SALES (est): 313.5K **Privately Held**
SIC: 2844 Toilet preparations

(G-5405)
NIBMOR PROJECT LLC
11 Middle Neck Rd (11021-2312)
PHONE..................................718 374-5091
Jennifer Love, *CEO*
Marcia Bell, *Opers Mgr*
EMP: 14
SALES (est): 2.3MM **Privately Held**
SIC: 2066 Chocolate

(G-5406)
NUTEK DISPOSABLES INC
80 Cuttermill Rd Ste 500 (11021-3108)
PHONE..................................516 829-3030
EMP: 6 **Privately Held**
SIC: 2676 Sanitary paper products
HQ: Nutek Disposables, Inc.
    121 North Rd
    Mc Elhattan PA 17748
    570 769-6900

(G-5407)
OAKWOOD PUBLISHING CO
10 Bond St Ste 1 (11021-2455)
PHONE..................................516 482-7720
EMP: 7
SQ FT: 3,000
SALES: 100K **Privately Held**
SIC: 2741 Misc Publishing

(G-5408)
OLD DUTCH MUSTARD CO INC (PA)
Also Called: Pilgrim Foods Co
98 Cuttermill Rd Ste 260s (11021-3033)
PHONE..................................516 466-0522
Charles R Santich, *Ch of Bd*
Paul Santich, *President*
Renate Santich, *Vice Pres*
◆ **EMP:** 6 **EST:** 1915
SQ FT: 3,000
SALES (est): 15.2MM **Privately Held**
SIC: 2099 2033 2035 Vinegar; fruit juices: concentrated, hot pack; fruit juices: fresh; fruit juices: packaged in cans, jars, etc.; mustard, prepared (wet)

(G-5409)
ORO AVANTI INC (PA)
250 Kings Point Rd (11024-1022)
PHONE..................................516 487-5185
Hersel Sarraf, *President*
Gidion Sarraf, *Vice Pres*
EMP: 7
SALES (est): 1.7MM **Privately Held**
SIC: 3295 Minerals, ground or treated

(G-5410)
OZ BAKING COMPANY LTD
114 Middle Neck Rd (11021-1245)
PHONE..................................516 466-5114
Ofer Zur, *Ch of Bd*
EMP: 8
SALES (est): 568.7K **Privately Held**
SIC: 2051 Bread, cake & related products

▲ = Import ▼=Export
◆ =Import/Export

(G-5411)
PAMA ENTERPRISES INC
60 Cuttermill Rd Ste 411 (11021-3104)
PHONE..................................516 504-6300
Marvin A Makofsky, *President*
EMP: 5
SALES (est) 619.1K **Privately Held**
SIC: 3993 2752 Advertising novelties;
commercial printing, lithographic

(G-5412)
PEARL LEATHER GROUP LLC
17 Barstow Rd Ste 206 (11021-2213)
PHONE..................................516 627-4047
Bob Kamali,
John Ruggeiro,
▲ EMP: 50
SQ FT: 4,000
SALES (est): 10MM **Privately Held**
SIC: 3111 Leather processing

(G-5413)
PENFLI INDUSTRIES INC
11 Woodland Pl (11021-1035)
PHONE..................................212 947-6080
Anton Fischman, *President*
Joe Fischman, *Vice Pres*
▲ EMP: 15 EST: 1978
SALES (est): 1.6MM **Privately Held**
WEB: www.penfliusa.com
SIC: 2326 5136 2339 5137 Men's &
boys' work clothing; men's & boys' cloth-
ing; women's & misses' athletic clothing &
sportswear; women's & children's clothing

(G-5414)
PREMIER INGRIDIENTS INC
3 Johnstone Rd (11021-1507)
PHONE..................................516 641-6763
Dennis Provda, *CEO*
▲ EMP: 4 EST: 2010
SALES: 1.3MM **Privately Held**
SIC: 2999 Waxes, petroleum: not produced
in petroleum refineries

(G-5415)
**PRESTIGE BOX CORPORATION
(PA)**
115 Cuttermill Rd (11021-3101)
P.O. Box 220428 (11022-0428)
PHONE..................................516 773-3115
Sherry Warren, *Principal*
Ray Turin, *Vice Pres*
EMP: 38 EST: 1963
SQ FT: 12,000
SALES (est): 49.7MM **Privately Held**
SIC: 2657 2653 2631 2652 Folding pa-
perboard boxes; boxes, corrugated: made
from purchased materials; boxboard;
setup paperboard boxes

(G-5416)
**PROGRESSIVE COLOR
GRAPHICS**
122 Station Rd (11023-1723)
PHONE..................................212 292-8787
Hugo Saltini, *President*
Stuart Linzer, *Vice Pres*
EMP: 41
SQ FT: 28,000
SALES (est): 4.2MM **Privately Held**
SIC: 2752 Offset & photolithographic print-
ing

(G-5417)
**ROCKMILLS STEEL PRODUCTS
CORP**
3 Hayden Ave (11024-2011)
P.O. Box 234838 (11023-4838)
PHONE..................................718 366-8300
Ann O'Brien, *President*
Daniel Obrien, *Shareholder*
Mary Obrien, *Shareholder*
EMP: 15
SALES (est): 3.7MM **Privately Held**
WEB: www.rockmillsboilers.com
SIC: 3433 Boilers, low-pressure heating:
steam or hot water

(G-5418)
ROSECORE DIVISION
Also Called: Corey Rugs
11 Grace Ave Ste 100 (11021-2417)
P.O. Box 855, Plainview (11803-0855)
PHONE..................................516 504-4530

Fax: 516 504-4542
EMP: 10
SALES (est): 820K **Privately Held**
SIC: 2273 Mfg Carpets/Rugs

(G-5419)
ROYAL JEWELRY MFG INC (PA)
825 Northern Blvd Fl 2 (11021-5321)
PHONE..................................212 302-2500
Parviz Hakimian, *President*
Ben Hakimian, *Vice Pres*
Ronnie Kalatizadeh, *Vice Pres*
David Zar, *Vice Pres*
Ken Hakimian, *Sales Staff*
▲ EMP: 46
SQ FT: 9,000
SALES (est): 7.2MM **Privately Held**
WEB: www.royaljewelrymfg.com
SIC: 3911 5094 5944 Jewelry, precious
metal; jewelry; jewelry stores

(G-5420)
S KASHI & SONS INC
175 Great Neck Rd Ste 204 (11021-3313)
PHONE..................................212 869-9393
Sarah Kashi, *President*
Elie Kashi, *Vice Pres*
Henry Hakimian, *Sales Executive*
Ronen Kashi, *Admin Sec*
▲ EMP: 15
SQ FT: 1,300
SALES (est): 2.4MM **Privately Held**
WEB: www.skashi.com
SIC: 3911 5094 Jewelry, precious metal;
precious stones & metals

(G-5421)
SAMUEL B COLLECTION INC
98 Cuttermill Rd Ste 234s (11021-3033)
PHONE..................................516 466-1826
Neda Behnam, *President*
Samuel Behnam, *Vice Pres*
▲ EMP: 10
SALES: 6MM **Privately Held**
SIC: 3911 5094 Jewelry, precious metal;
jewelry

(G-5422)
SCARGUARD LABS LLC
15 Barstow Rd (11021-2211)
PHONE..................................516 482-8050
Joel Studin, *CEO*
Steve Levinson, *VP Opers*
Richard E Pino, *CFO*
Jaclyn Politi, *Administration*
EMP: 12
SQ FT: 5,000
SALES (est): 3.1MM **Privately Held**
SIC: 2834 Pharmaceutical preparations

(G-5423)
**SSJJJ MANUFACTURING LLC
(PA)**
98 Cuttermill Rd Ste 412 (11021-3006)
PHONE..................................516 498-3200
Steven Myers,
Beth Myers,
EMP: 352
SALES (est): 15MM **Privately Held**
SIC: 2258 2211 Warp & flat knit products;
lace & lace products; bedspreads; lace:
made on lace machines; bed sets, lace;
sheets, bedding & table cloths: cotton

(G-5424)
STANDARD GROUP (PA)
Also Called: Southern Standard Cartons
1010 Nthrn Blvd Ste 236 (11021)
PHONE..................................718 335-5500
Brian McCoy, *Superintendent*
Andrew Palmer, *Superintendent*
Mark Sweeney, *Superintendent*
Steven D Levkoff, *Chairman*
Michael Arnette, *Counsel*
▲ EMP: 44
SQ FT: 115,000
SALES (est): 62.3MM **Privately Held**
SIC: 2657 Folding paperboard boxes

(G-5425)
STANDARD GROUP LLC (HQ)
Also Called: Southern Standard Cartoons
1010 Nthrn Blvd Ste 236 (11021)
PHONE..................................718 507-6430
Louis Cortes, *Vice Pres*
Joseph Rebecca,

Steven Levkoff,
▲ EMP: 235 EST: 2009
SQ FT: 115,000
SALES (est): 47.5MM **Privately Held**
WEB: www.thestandardgroup.com
SIC: 2657 Folding paperboard boxes

(G-5426)
STAR SPORTS CORP
Also Called: American Turf Monthly
747 Middle Neck Rd # 103 (11024-1950)
PHONE..................................516 773-4075
Allen Hakim, *President*
Joe Girardi, *Editor*
EMP: 20
SQ FT: 2,500
SALES (est): 900K **Privately Held**
WEB: www.carteriley.com
SIC: 2711 Newspapers

(G-5427)
STYLECRAFT INTERIORS INC
22 Watermill Ln (11021-4235)
PHONE..................................516 487-2133
Fred Reindl, *President*
Matthew Reindl, *Treasurer*
EMP: 10
SQ FT: 5,000
SALES: 600K **Privately Held**
WEB: www.stylecraftinteriors.com
SIC: 3843 2521 Cabinets, dental; cabi-
nets, office: wood

(G-5428)
TONI INDUSTRIES INC
Also Called: Hbs
111 Great Neck Rd Ste 305 (11021-5403)
PHONE..................................212 921-0700
Ophelia Chung, *President*
Neil Blumstein, *Vice Pres*
EMP: 14 EST: 2002
SALES: 18MM **Privately Held**
SIC: 2339 Athletic clothing: women's,
misses' & juniors'

(G-5429)
UNIQUE OVERSEAS INC
425 Northern Blvd Ste 22 (11021-4803)
PHONE..................................516 466-9792
Raju Shewakramani, *President*
Ragu Ramani, *Principal*
◆ EMP: 8
SALES (est): 894K **Privately Held**
WEB: www.uniqueoverseas.com
SIC: 3199 Equestrian related leather arti-
cles

(G-5430)
UNIVERSAL METALS INC
98 Cuttermill Rd Ste 428 (11021-3006)
PHONE..................................516 829-0896
Pushpa Kochar, *CEO*
Hira Kochar, *Vice Pres*
◆ EMP: 5
SALES (est): 1.9MM **Privately Held**
SIC: 3399 Metal fasteners

(G-5431)
**WEGO INTERNATIONAL
FLOORS LLC**
239 Great Neck Rd (11021-3301)
PHONE..................................516 487-3510
Bert Eshaghpour, *CEO*
Barry Okun, *CFO*
EMP: 11 EST: 2015
SALES (est): 604.7K
SALES (corp-wide): 704.7MM **Privately
Held**
SIC: 2491 5023 Flooring, treated wood
block; wood flooring
PA: Wego Chemical Group Inc.
239 Great Neck Rd
Great Neck NY 11021
516 487-3510

Green Island
Albany County

(G-5432)
ARCADIA MFG GROUP INC (PA)
80 Cohoes Ave (12183-1505)
PHONE..................................518 434-6213
William T Sumner, *Ch of Bd*

Michael Werner, *President*
Kimberly Maher, *Opers Staff*
Lou Ann Norelli, *Controller*
Michael Warner, *Sales Executive*
▲ EMP: 44
SQ FT: 20,000
SALES (est): 10.8MM **Privately Held**
WEB: www.arcadiasupply.com
SIC: 3498 3446 3444 3999 Fabricated
pipe & fittings; ornamental metalwork;
sheet metalwork; cigar lighters, except
precious metal

(G-5433)
CASE GROUP LLC
Also Called: Case Window and Door
195 Cohoes Ave (12183-1501)
PHONE..................................518 720-3100
Russell Brooks, *Mng Member*
Gerhard Loeffel,
◆ EMP: 36
SQ FT: 50,000
SALES (est): 5MM **Privately Held**
WEB: www.casewindow.com
SIC: 2431 Doors & door parts & trim, wood

(G-5434)
CRYSTAL IS INC (HQ)
70 Cohoes Ave Ste 1b (12183-1531)
PHONE..................................518 271-7375
Larry Felton, *CEO*
Steven Berger, *President*
Eoin Connolly, *Vice Pres*
Keith Evans, *Vice Pres*
Ben Jamison, *Vice Pres*
EMP: 45
SQ FT: 10,500
SALES (est): 10.4MM **Privately Held**
WEB: www.crystal-is.com
SIC: 3679 Electronic crystals

(G-5435)
**GENERAL CONTROL SYSTEMS
INC**
60 Cohoes Ave Ste 101 (12183-1553)
PHONE..................................518 270-8045
Clay Robinson, *President*
Peter Pritchard, *Business Mgr*
Jason Baniak, *Engineer*
Christen Egan, *Engineer*
Randy Powell, *Engineer*
EMP: 50
SQ FT: 24,000
SALES (est): 12.2MM **Privately Held**
WEB: www.gcontrol.net
SIC: 3625 Industrial controls: push button,
selector switches, pilot

(G-5436)
**GREEN ISLAND POWER
AUTHORITY**
20 Clinton St (12183-1117)
PHONE..................................518 273-0661
John J Brown, *Chairman*
Robert Bourgeois, *Fire Chief*
Micheal Cocca, *Vice Chairman*
Dave Filieau, *Supervisor*
Maggie Alix,
EMP: 11
SQ FT: 8,400
SALES: 5.8MM **Privately Held**
WEB: www.villageofgreenisland.com
SIC: 3699 Electrical equipment & supplies

(G-5437)
**HUERSCH MARKETING GROUP
LLC**
70 Cohoes Ave Ste 4 (12183-1533)
PHONE..................................518 874-1045
Thomas R Huerter, *CEO*
EMP: 12
SALES (est): 775.2K **Privately Held**
SIC: 2711 Commercial printing & newspa-
per publishing combined

(G-5438)
LAI INTERNATIONAL INC
1 Tibbits Ave (12183-1430)
PHONE..................................763 780-0060
Michael Bagel, *Manager*
EMP: 27 **Privately Held**
SIC: 3728 Aircraft assemblies, subassem-
blies & parts

GEOGRAPHIC

PA: Lai International, Inc.
4255 Pheasant Ridge Dr Ne # 405
Minneapolis MN 55449

(G-5439)
LYDALL PERFORMANCE MTLS INC
68 George St (12183-1113)
PHONE..................518 273-6320
EMP: 11
SALES (corp-wide): 785.9MM **Publicly Held**
SIC: 3569 Filters
HQ: Lydall Performance Materials, Inc.
134 Chestnut Hill Rd
Rochester NH 03867
603 332-4600

(G-5440)
LYDALL THERMAL/ACOUSTICAL INC
68 George St (12183-1113)
PHONE..................518 273-6320
Donald Ackerman, *QC Mgr*
Tim Lintz, *Design Engr*
Tim Reilly, *Controller*
Susan Pratt, *Human Resources*
Terrence Dingman, *Director*
◆ **EMP:** 115
SQ FT: 300,000
SALES (est): 30.6MM
SALES (corp-wide): 785.9MM **Publicly Held**
WEB: www.lydall.com
SIC: 2211 Cotton broad woven goods
PA: Lydall, Inc.
1 Colonial Rd
Manchester CT 06042
860 646-1233

(G-5441)
RELIABLE BROTHERS INC
185 Cohoes Ave (12183-1501)
PHONE..................518 273-6732
Kyle Buchakjiar, *Ch of Bd*
Vahan Buchakjian, *President*
EMP: 30
SALES (est): 5.3MM **Privately Held**
SIC: 2013 5147 Meat extracts from purchased meat; meats, fresh

(G-5442)
ROSS PRECISION MFG INC
1 Tibbits Ave (12183-1430)
PHONE..................518 273-3912
William F Ross, *President*
R Andrew Ross, *Vice Pres*
EMP: 10
SALES (est): 833.5K **Privately Held**
SIC: 3366 Machinery castings: copper or copper-base alloy

Greene
Chenango County

(G-5443)
AMERICAN BLADE MFG LLC
Also Called: Greene Brass & Aluminum Fndry
47 Birdsall St (13778-1053)
P.O. Box 220 (13778-0220)
PHONE..................607 656-4204
Tom Todd, *Manager*
EMP: 8
SALES (est): 886K
SALES (corp-wide): 1.3MM **Privately Held**
WEB: www.charleslay.com
SIC: 3366 3365 Bronze foundry; aluminum foundries
PA: American Blade Manufacturing Llc
138 Roundhouse Rd
Oneonta NY 13820
607 432-4518

(G-5444)
CROSS COUNTRY MFG INC
2355 Rte 206 (13778)
P.O. Box 565 (13778-0565)
PHONE..................607 656-4103
Frank M Hanrahan, *Branch Mgr*
EMP: 15

SALES (corp-wide): 6.9MM **Privately Held**
WEB: www.crosscountrymfg.com
SIC: 3715 Truck trailers
PA: Cross Country Manufacturing, Inc.
2355 State Highway 206
Greene NY 13778
607 656-4103

(G-5445)
G C CONTROLS INC
1408 County Road 2 (13778-2257)
PHONE..................607 656-4117
Mert Gilbert, *Ch of Bd*
Steven Gilbert, *Principal*
Dan Snowberger, *Vice Pres*
EMP: 40
SQ FT: 12,000
SALES (est): 8MM **Privately Held**
WEB: www.gccontrols.com
SIC: 3625 Electric controls & control accessories, industrial; control equipment, electric; timing devices, electronic

(G-5446)
GREENE TECHNOLOGIES INC
Grand & Clinton St (13778)
PHONE..................607 656-4166
Carol M Rosenkrantz, *Chairman*
EMP: 100
SQ FT: 49,000
SALES (est): 17.8MM **Privately Held**
WEB: www.greenetech.biz
SIC: 3444 3479 3471 3469 Sheet metalwork; coating of metals & formed products; electroplating of metals or formed products; polishing, metals or formed products; metal stampings

(G-5447)
RAPP SIGNS INC
3979 State Route 206 (13778-2134)
PHONE..................607 656-8167
Ronald J Rapp, *President*
David Rapp, *Principal*
Lorraine Detweiler, *Manager*
EMP: 13
SALES (est): 1.3MM **Privately Held**
SIC: 3993 1799 Signs, not made in custom sign painting shops; sign installation & maintenance

(G-5448)
RAYMOND CORPORATION (DH)
22 S Canal St (13778)
P.O. Box 130 (13778-0130)
PHONE..................607 656-2311
Michael G Field, *President*
Joerg Klose, *General Mgr*
Tom Wasser, *Superintendent*
Louis J Callea, *Counsel*
John Leshinski, *Counsel*
◆ **EMP:** 800
SQ FT: 325,000
SALES (est): 766.1MM **Privately Held**
WEB: www.raymondcorp.com
SIC: 3535 7359 3537 Conveyors & conveying equipment; belt conveyor systems, general industrial use; pneumatic tube conveyor systems; equipment rental & leasing; aircraft & industrial truck rental services; lift trucks, industrial: fork, platform, straddle, etc.
HQ: Raymond Consolidated Corporation
22 S Canal St
Greene NY 13778
800 235-7200

(G-5449)
RAYMOND SALES CORPORATION (DH)
22 S Canal St (13778-1244)
P.O. Box 130 (13778-0130)
PHONE..................607 656-2311
James Malvaso, *Principal*
EMP: 9
SQ FT: 325,000
SALES (est): 50MM **Privately Held**
SIC: 3537 5084 Forklift trucks; materials handling machinery
HQ: The Raymond Corporation
22 S Canal St
Greene NY 13778
607 656-2311

Greenfield Center
Saratoga County

(G-5450)
PECKHAM INDUSTRIES INC
430 Coy Rd (12833-1042)
PHONE..................518 893-2176
William H Peckham, *Branch Mgr*
EMP: 18
SALES (corp-wide): 171.1MM **Privately Held**
SIC: 2951 Concrete, asphaltic (not from refineries)
PA: Peckham Industries, Inc.
20 Haarlem Ave Ste 200
White Plains NY 10603
914 949-2000

Greenlawn
Suffolk County

(G-5451)
ALL CULTURES INC
Also Called: American Culture
12 Gates St (11740-1427)
PHONE..................631 293-3143
Louis Guaneri, *CEO*
◆ **EMP:** 35
SQ FT: 30,000
SALES (est): 6MM **Privately Held**
WEB: www.americanculturehair.com
SIC: 2844 Hair preparations, including shampoos; shampoos, rinses, conditioners: hair

(G-5452)
BAE SYSTEMS INFO & ELEC SYS
450 Pulaski Rd (11740-1606)
PHONE..................631 912-1525
John Amedo, *Engineer*
Kenneth Baron, *Engineer*
Joe Damm, *Engineer*
Scott Esbin, *Engineer*
Vincent Marino, *Engineer*
EMP: 10
SALES (corp-wide): 21.6B **Privately Held**
WEB: www.iesi.na.baesystems.com
SIC: 3812 Search & navigation equipment
HQ: Bae Systems Information And Electronic Systems Integration Inc.
65 Spit Brook Rd
Nashua NH 03060
603 885-4321

(G-5453)
BAE SYSTEMS PLC
1 Hazeltine Way (11740)
PHONE..................631 261-7000
Jay Santana, *Opers Mgr*
Stephen Harran, *Purchasing*
Tom Altamura, *Engineer*
Raymond Bayh, *Engineer*
Anthony Costa, *Engineer*
EMP: 25
SALES (corp-wide): 21.6B **Privately Held**
SIC: 3812 Search & navigation equipment
PA: Bae Systems Plc
6 Carlton Gardens
London
125 237-3232

(G-5454)
MB PLASTICS INC (PA)
130 Stony Hollow Rd (11740-1511)
PHONE..................718 523-1180
Milton Bassin, *President*
▲ **EMP:** 22 **EST:** 1964
SQ FT: 15,000
SALES (est): 2.4MM **Privately Held**
SIC: 2821 3911 Plastics materials & resins; jewelry apparel

(G-5455)
MEDICAL TECHNOLOGY PRODUCTS
33a Smith St (11740-1219)
PHONE..................631 285-6640
Thomas J Hartnett Jr, *Ch of Bd*
David Hawkins, *Admin Sec*

EMP: 8
SQ FT: 5,000
SALES (est): 1MM **Privately Held**
SIC: 3841 Surgical & medical instruments

Greenport
Suffolk County

(G-5456)
125-127 MAIN STREET CORP
Also Called: Mills, William J & Company
125 Main St 127 (11944-1421)
P.O. Box 2126 (11944-0978)
PHONE..................631 477-1500
William J Mills III, *President*
Robert Hills, *Vice Pres*
Tom Beatty, *Sales Staff*
Jamie Mills, *Sales Executive*
EMP: 18 **EST:** 1880
SQ FT: 25,000
SALES (est): 2MM **Privately Held**
WEB: www.millscanvas.com
SIC: 2394 Awnings, fabric: made from purchased materials; sails: made from purchased materials

(G-5457)
REFLECTIVE IMAGE
74605 Main Rd (11944-2623)
PHONE..................631 477-3368
Kristin Voneiff, *Owner*
William Voneiff, *Co-Owner*
EMP: 5
SALES (est): 391.3K **Privately Held**
WEB: www.reflectiveimages.org
SIC: 3993 Signs & advertising specialties

(G-5458)
STIDD SYSTEMS INC
220 Carpenter St (11944-1406)
P.O. Box 87 (11944-0087)
PHONE..................631 477-2400
Walter A Gezari, *President*
Robert J Digregorio, *Vice Pres*
David J Wilberding, *Vice Pres*
Deborah Pontino, *Purch Mgr*
Ian Strachan, *Engineer*
▼ **EMP:** 36
SQ FT: 62,000
SALES: 10MM **Privately Held**
WEB: www.stidd.com
SIC: 2531 Vehicle furniture

(G-5459)
WOODEN BOATWORKS
190 Sterling St Unit 2 (11944-1454)
PHONE..................631 477-6507
Robert Wahl, *Principal*
EMP: 6
SALES (est): 737.8K **Privately Held**
SIC: 3732 Boat building & repairing

Greenvale
Nassau County

(G-5460)
CALL FORWARDING TECHNOLOGIES
55 Northern Blvd Ste 3b (11548-1301)
PHONE..................516 621-3600
Charles Hart, *President*
EMP: 7
SQ FT: 600
SALES (est): 810K **Privately Held**
SIC: 3661 Telephones & telephone apparatus

(G-5461)
DALMA DRESS MFG CO INC
3 Carman Rd (11548-1123)
PHONE..................212 391-8296
EMP: 25
SQ FT: 5,500
SALES (est): 1.7MM **Privately Held**
SIC: 2335 2339 Mfg Women's/Misses' Dresses Mfg Women's/Misses' Outerwear

(G-5462)
INCREDIBLE SCENTS INC
1 Plaza Rd Ste 202 (11548-1059)
PHONE..............................516 656-3300
Howard Rabinowitz, *President*
Richard Davi, *Exec VP*
EMP: 5 **EST:** 1999
SQ FT: 1,500
SALES (est): 10MM **Privately Held**
WEB: www.incrediblescents.com
SIC: 3841 Surgical & medical instruments

(G-5463)
ROMAN IRON WORKS INC
15 Plaza Rd (11548-1085)
PHONE..............................516 621-1103
Maria McKinley, *President*
James Mancuso, *President*
EMP: 12 **EST:** 1953
SQ FT: 10,000
SALES (est): 2MM **Privately Held**
SIC: 3441 3446 1791 Fabricated structural metal; joists, open web steel: long-span series; architectural metalwork; stairs, fire escapes, balconies, railings & ladders; iron work, structural

(G-5464)
SLANT/FIN CORPORATION (PA)
100 Forest Dr (11548-1295)
PHONE..............................516 484-2600
Melvin Dubin, *Ch of Bd*
Adam Dubin, *Chairman*
Henry Noga, *Purch Agent*
Robert Viets, *Buyer*
Perry Labarbera, *Engineer*
▲ **EMP:** 374 **EST:** 1949
SQ FT: 200,000
SALES (est): 79.4MM **Privately Held**
WEB: www.slantfin.com
SIC: 3433 3443 Heating equipment, except electric; fabricated plate work (boiler shop)

(G-5465)
SLANTCO MANUFACTURING INC (HQ)
100 Forest Dr (11548-1205)
PHONE..............................516 484-2600
Melvin Dubin, *President*
Selwyn Steinberg, *Senior VP*
Donald Brown, *Treasurer*
Maria Matuszewski, *Supervisor*
Delcy Brooks, *Admin Sec*
EMP: 7 **EST:** 1976
SQ FT: 150,000
SALES (est): 1.3MM
SALES (corp-wide): 79.4MM **Privately Held**
SIC: 3443 Heat exchangers: coolers (after, inter), condensers, etc.
PA: Slant/Fin Corporation
100 Forest Dr
Greenvale NY 11548
516 484-2600

(G-5466)
WIN WOOD CABINETRY INC
200 Forest Dr Ste 7 (11548-1216)
PHONE..............................516 304-2216
Frank Lin, *President*
▲ **EMP:** 8
SALES (est): 454.3K **Privately Held**
SIC: 2434 Wood kitchen cabinets

Greenville
Greene County

(G-5467)
CLASSIC AUTO CRAFTS INC
Also Called: Town Line Auto
6501 State Route 32 (12083-2212)
P.O. Box 10 (12083-0010)
PHONE..............................518 966-8003
John Dolce, *President*
EMP: 8
SALES (est): 1.3MM **Privately Held**
WEB: www.townlineauto.com
SIC: 3599 Machine shop, jobbing & repair

Greenwich
Washington County

(G-5468)
BDP INDUSTRIES INC (PA)
Also Called: BELT DEWATERING PRESS
354 State Route 29 (12834-4518)
P.O. Box 118 (12834-0118)
PHONE..............................518 695-6851
Albert J Schmidt, *President*
Socrates Fronhofer, *Vice Pres*
Kelly Falk, *Purchasing*
Steve Dobert, *Engineer*
Carl Fronhofer, *Treasurer*
EMP: 49 **EST:** 1978
SALES (est): 18.2MM **Privately Held**
WEB: www.bdpindustries.com
SIC: 3523 3545 3542 Turf & grounds equipment; turf equipment, commercial; machine tool accessories; machine tools, metal forming type

(G-5469)
BETTERBEE INC
Also Called: Southern Adirondack Honey Co.
8 Meader Rd (12834-2734)
PHONE..............................518 314-0575
Erica Stevens, *CEO*
Margaret A Stevens, *President*
Justin Stevens, *Exec VP*
John Rath, *Engineer*
Leah Sargood, *Sales Mgr*
◆ **EMP:** 15
SQ FT: 3,500
SALES (est): 2.4MM **Privately Held**
WEB: www.betterbee.com
SIC: 2499 3999 Beekeeping supplies, wood; candles

(G-5470)
ESSITY PROF HYGIENE N AMER LLC
72 County Route 53 (12834-2214)
PHONE..............................518 692-8434
Glenn Jones, *Branch Mgr*
EMP: 50
SALES (corp-wide): 13.1B **Privately Held**
WEB: www.scatissue.com
SIC: 2621 Napkin stock, paper
HQ: Essity Professional Hygiene North America Llc
984 Winchester Rd
Neenah WI 54956
920 727-3770

(G-5471)
FORT MILLER GROUP INC
688 Wilbur Ave (12834-4413)
P.O. Box 98, Schuylerville (12871-0098)
PHONE..............................518 695-5000
John T Hedbring, *Ch of Bd*
John Marcelle, *Exec VP*
Mary A Spiezio, *Vice Pres*
Mark Bold, *Plant Mgr*
Brian Myers, *Safety Mgr*
▲ **EMP:** 420
SQ FT: 160,000
SALES (est): 134MM **Privately Held**
WEB: www.fortmiller.com
SIC: 3272 3441 Concrete products, precast; fabricated structural metal
PA: The Fort Miller Service Corp
688 Wilbur Ave
Greenwich NY 12834

(G-5472)
FORT MILLER SERVICE CORP (PA)
688 Wilbur Ave (12834-4413)
P.O. Box 98, Schuylerville (12871-0098)
PHONE..............................518 695-5000
John T Hedbring, *Ch of Bd*
Mary Ann Spiezio, *Vice Pres*
Scott Harrigan, *VP Engrg*
Richard Schumaker, *CFO*
▼ **EMP:** 12
SQ FT: 10,000
SALES (est): 156.7MM **Privately Held**
SIC: 3272 3271 5211 1799 Concrete products, precast; burial vaults, concrete or precast terrazzo; concrete block & brick; concrete & cinder block; fence construction

(G-5473)
HOLLINGSWORTH & VOSE COMPANY
3235 County Rte 113 (12834)
PHONE..............................518 695-8000
Donald Wagner, *Opers-Prdtn-Mfg*
EMP: 160
SQ FT: 3,594
SALES (corp-wide): 726MM **Privately Held**
WEB: www.hovo.com
SIC: 2621 3053 Filter paper; gasket materials
PA: Hollingsworth & Vose Company
112 Washington St
East Walpole MA 02032
508 850-2000

(G-5474)
NORTHAST CTR FOR BEKEEPING LLC
Also Called: Betterbee
8 Meader Rd (12834-2734)
PHONE..............................800 632-3379
Christopher Cripps,
Joseph Cali,
John Rath,
◆ **EMP:** 19
SALES (est): 1.6MM **Privately Held**
SIC: 2499 5191 3999 Beekeeping supplies, wood; beekeeping supplies (non-durable); beekeepers' supplies

(G-5475)
PHANTOM LABORATORY INC
Also Called: Phantom Laboratory, The
2727 State Route 29 (12834-3212)
P.O. Box 511, Salem (12865-0511)
PHONE..............................518 692-1190
Joshua Levy, *President*
Bonnie Hanlon, *Vice Pres*
Julie Simms, *Vice Pres*
Megan Stalter, *Cust Mgr*
EMP: 15
SQ FT: 65,000
SALES: 750K **Privately Held**
WEB: www.phantomlab.com
SIC: 3844 X-ray apparatus & tubes

(G-5476)
SOUTHERN ADRNDCK FBR PRDCRS CP
2532 State Route 40 (12834-2300)
PHONE..............................518 692-2700
Mary Jeanne Packer, *President*
EMP: 5
SALES (est): 50K **Privately Held**
SIC: 2299 Textile goods

(G-5477)
TYMETAL CORP (HQ)
678 Wilbur Ave (12834-4413)
P.O. Box 139, Schuylerville (12871-0139)
PHONE..............................518 692-9930
John T Hedbring, *President*
Rob Douglas, *President*
Fran Kyer, *Exec VP*
Bruce Gill, *Engineer*
Gary Lamphere, *Engineer*
EMP: 30
SQ FT: 25,000
SALES: 15MM **Privately Held**
WEB: www.tymetal.com
SIC: 3446 3441 Fences, gates, posts & flagpoles; fabricated structural metal

Greenwood Lake
Orange County

(G-5478)
AUTOMATED ELEVATOR SYSTEMS
659 Jersey Ave (10925-2014)
PHONE..............................845 595-1063
Jacqueline Doyle, *Principal*
EMP: 20
SALES (est): 527.2K **Privately Held**
SIC: 3534 Elevators & moving stairways

(G-5479)
BARNABY PRINTS INC (PA)
673 Jersey Ave (10925-2014)
P.O. Box 98 (10925-0098)
PHONE..............................845 477-2501
Robert Brodhurst, *President*
William Neuhaus, *Treasurer*
EMP: 15
SQ FT: 12,000
SALES (est): 1.1MM **Privately Held**
SIC: 2759 2396 Screen printing; automotive & apparel trimmings

Groton
Tompkins County

(G-5480)
BAY HORSE INNOVATIONS NYINC
130 Cayuga St (13073-1002)
PHONE..............................607 898-3337
Gene Velten, *President*
EMP: 7
SALES (est): 513.2K **Privately Held**
SIC: 3713 Truck & bus bodies

(G-5481)
C & D ASSEMBLY INC
107 Corona Ave (13073-1206)
PHONE..............................607 898-4275
Jeffrey Cronk, *President*
Candice Dann, *Treasurer*
▲ **EMP:** 42
SQ FT: 10,600
SALES (est): 9.5MM **Privately Held**
WEB: www.cdassembly.com
SIC: 3672 8731 Printed circuit boards; electronic research

(G-5482)
CAYUGA TOOL AND DIE INC
182 Newman Rd (13073-8712)
PHONE..............................607 533-7400
Judson Bailey, *President*
Becky Bailey, *Treasurer*
EMP: 9
SQ FT: 3,680
SALES (est): 664.9K **Privately Held**
SIC: 3599 Machine shop, jobbing & repair

(G-5483)
MARTINEZ SPECIALTIES INC
205 Bossard Rd (13073-9779)
PHONE..............................607 898-3053
Philip Martinez, *President*
Dorothy Martinez, *Vice Pres*
Jamie Young, *Vice Pres*
EMP: 8
SALES (est): 1.1MM **Privately Held**
SIC: 3694 Ignition apparatus & distributors

(G-5484)
PYLANTIS NEW YORK LLC
102 E Cortland St (13073-1108)
PHONE..............................310 429-5911
Jeff Toolan, *CEO*
Eli Gill, *COO*
Matt Ruttenberg,
EMP: 5 **EST:** 2012
SALES (est): 348.9K **Privately Held**
SIC: 3089 Injection molding of plastics

Guilderland
Albany County

(G-5485)
CUSTOM PRTRS GUILDERLAND INC
Also Called: Guilderland Printing
2210 Western Ave (12084-9701)
PHONE..............................518 456-2811
Joyce Ragone, *President*
Thomas Ragone, *Vice Pres*
EMP: 15
SQ FT: 4,000
SALES (est): 3.2MM **Privately Held**
SIC: 2752 Commercial printing, lithographic

Guilderland Center
Albany County

(G-5486)
INOVA LLC
2 Van Buren Blvd Bldg 19 (12085-7703)
P.O. Box 20 (12085-0020)
PHONE..................................866 528-2804
Loren Sherman,
▲ **EMP:** 35
SQ FT: 39,000
SALES (est): 5.9MM **Privately Held**
SIC: 2511 2599 2531 Bed frames, except
water bed frames: wood; hotel furniture;
school furniture

Halcottsville
Delaware County

(G-5487)
ALTA INDUSTRIES LTD
Also Called: Alta Log Homes
46966 State Hwy 30 (12438)
P.O. Box 88 (12438-0088)
PHONE..................................845 586-3336
Frank Mann, *President*
David S Mann, *Vice Pres*
David Mann, *Vice Pres*
Heather Davie, *Production*
EMP: 16
SQ FT: 7,000
SALES (est): 2.4MM **Privately Held**
WEB: www.altaloghomes.com
SIC: 2452 Log cabins, prefabricated, wood

Halesite
Suffolk County

(G-5488)
**MANUFACTURERS INDEXING
PDTS**
Also Called: Mip
53 Gristmill Ln (11743-2134)
PHONE..................................631 271-0956
Charles Busk Jr, *President*
EMP: 9 **EST:** 1964
SQ FT: 12,000
SALES (est): 787.7K **Privately Held**
SIC: 2821 2675 Vinyl resins; die-cut paper
& board

(G-5489)
ROSE FENCE INC
356 Bay Ave (11743-1141)
PHONE..................................516 790-2308
EMP: 88
SALES (corp-wide): 13.6MM **Privately
Held**
SIC: 3496 Fencing, made from purchased
wire
PA: Rose Fence, Inc.
345 W Sunrise Hwy
Freeport NY 11520
516 223-0777

Halfmoon
Saratoga County

(G-5490)
ADVANCE ENERGY TECH INC
1 Solar Dr (12065-3402)
PHONE..................................518 371-2140
Timothy K Carlo, *Ch of Bd*
EMP: 27 **EST:** 1965
SQ FT: 30,000
SALES (est): 6.3MM **Privately Held**
WEB: www.advanceet.com
SIC: 3585 Parts for heating, cooling & re-
frigerating equipment

(G-5491)
CAPITAL DISTRICT STAIRS INC
45 Dunsbach Rd (12065-7906)
PHONE..................................518 383-2449
Alex Nikiforov, *President*

EMP: 7
SALES (est): 1MM **Privately Held**
WEB: www.capitaldistrictstairs.com
SIC: 2431 Staircases & stairs, wood; stair
railings, wood

(G-5492)
EBELING ASSOCIATES INC (PA)
Also Called: Control Global Solutions
9 Corporate Dr Ste 1 (12065-8636)
PHONE..................................518 688-8700
Allan Robison, *President*
James Colunio, *CIO*
Scott Ebeling, *Systems Analyst*
EMP: 17
SQ FT: 5,500
SALES (est): 2.2MM **Privately Held**
WEB: www.execontrol.com
SIC: 7372 Prepackaged software

(G-5493)
INFO LABEL INC
12 Enterprise Ave (12065-3424)
P.O. Box 1168, Clifton Park (12065-0804)
PHONE..................................518 664-0791
Mark Dufort, *President*
Brad Bosco, *Manager*
EMP: 15
SQ FT: 7,000
SALES (est): 2.2MM **Privately Held**
WEB: www.infolabel.net
SIC: 2759 5084 Labels & seals: printing;
printing trades machinery, equipment &
supplies

(G-5494)
**INTERSOURCE MANAGEMENT
GROUP (PA)**
7 Corporate Dr Ste 3 (12065-8612)
PHONE..................................518 372-6798
Dan Cong, *Vice Pres*
Nancy Sheridan, *Project Mgr*
Robert Dybas, *Manager*
EMP: 6
SALES (est): 1.9MM **Privately Held**
SIC: 3511 Turbines & turbine generator
sets & parts

(G-5495)
MOTOROLA SOLUTIONS INC
7 Deer Run Holw (12065-5664)
PHONE..................................518 348-0833
Carolely Urgenson, *Principal*
EMP: 148
SALES (corp-wide): 7.3B **Publicly Held**
WEB: www.motorola.com
SIC: 3663 Radio broadcasting & communi-
cations equipment
PA: Motorola Solutions, Inc.
500 W Monroe St Ste 4400
Chicago IL 60661
847 576-5000

(G-5496)
MOVINADS & SIGNS LLC
1771 Route 9 (12065-2413)
PHONE..................................518 378-3000
Rob Potter, *President*
EMP: 5 **EST:** 2007
SQ FT: 4,000
SALES (est): 300K **Privately Held**
SIC: 3993 Signs & advertising specialties

(G-5497)
REQUEST INC
Also Called: Request Multimedia
14 Corporate Dr Ste 6 (12065-8607)
PHONE..................................518 899-1254
Peter M Cholnoky, *President*
Lavoy Gary, *Technology*
EMP: 30
SQ FT: 8,100
SALES (est): 5MM **Privately Held**
WEB: www.request.com
SIC: 3651 Home entertainment equipment,
electronic

(G-5498)
REQUEST SERIOUS PLAY LLC
14 Corporate Dr (12065-8607)
PHONE..................................518 899-1254
Barry Evans, *Principal*
EMP: 7
SALES (est): 680K **Privately Held**
SIC: 3651 Home entertainment equipment,
electronic

(G-5499)
SAVE MORE BEVERAGE CORP
Also Called: Uptown
1512 Route 9 Ste 1 (12065-8664)
PHONE..................................518 371-2520
Harold Rockowitz, *President*
Robert Popp, *Treasurer*
EMP: 8
SALES: 2.5MM **Privately Held**
SIC: 2086 5921 5149 5181 Carbonated
beverages, nonalcoholic: bottled &
canned; beer (packaged); soft drinks;
beer & other fermented malt liquors

Hall
Ontario County

(G-5500)
MILLCO WOODWORKING LLC
1710 Railroad Pl (14463-9005)
P.O. Box 38 (14463-0038)
PHONE..................................585 526-6844
Charles L Millerd,
Mark M Millerd,
EMP: 11
SQ FT: 6,290
SALES (est): 1.6MM **Privately Held**
WEB: www.millcowoodworking.com
SIC: 2434 2431 Wood kitchen cabinets;
millwork

Hamburg
Erie County

(G-5501)
ABASCO INC
5225 Southwestern Blvd (14075-3524)
P.O. Box 247 (14075-0247)
PHONE..................................716 649-4790
Frank A Saeli Jr, *President*
Michael Saeli, *Vice Pres*
Bill Seipel, *Vice Pres*
Bev Nappo, *Purch Mgr*
William G Seipel, *Marketing Mgr*
▲ **EMP:** 30 **EST:** 1962
SALES (est): 8.4MM **Privately Held**
WEB: www.abasco.net
SIC: 3613 3449 Control panels, electric;
miscellaneous metalwork

(G-5502)
CAPITAL CONCRETE INC
5690 Camp Rd (14075-3706)
PHONE..................................716 648-8001
Rosanne Lettieri, *President*
EMP: 6
SALES (est): 864.4K **Privately Held**
SIC: 3273 Ready-mixed concrete

(G-5503)
CLASSIC AWNINGS INC
Also Called: Classic Awnings and Tent Co
1 Elmview Ave (14075-3761)
P.O. Box 583 (14075-0583)
PHONE..................................716 649-0390
David Vesneske, *President*
EMP: 15
SQ FT: 5,000
SALES: 750K **Privately Held**
WEB: www.classicawnings.com
SIC: 2394 7359 Awnings, fabric: made
from purchased materials; tent & tarpaulin
rental

(G-5504)
E-ONE INC
4760 Camp Rd (14075-2604)
PHONE..................................716 646-6790
Jeffrey Hermann, *Branch Mgr*
Alan Hollister, *Director*
EMP: 70 **Publicly Held**
SIC: 3537 Industrial trucks & tractors
HQ: E-One, Inc.
1601 Sw 37th Ave
Ocala FL 34474
352 237-1122

(G-5505)
EATON BROTHERS CORP
3530 Lakeview Rd (14075-6160)
P.O. Box 60 (14075-0060)
PHONE..................................716 649-8250
Ralph D Allen, *President*
Gary Allen, *Exec VP*
Christopher Allen, *Shareholder*
▲ **EMP:** 9
SQ FT: 21,000
SALES (est): 2.1MM **Privately Held**
WEB: www.eatonbrothers.com
SIC: 3524 3272 Lawn & garden tractors &
equipment; tombstones, precast terrazzo
or concrete

(G-5506)
EL-DON BATTERY POST INC
4109 Saint Francis Dr (14075-1722)
PHONE..................................716 627-3697
Gary K Logsdon, *President*
EMP: 5
SALES (est): 827.4K **Privately Held**
SIC: 3691 5063 Storage batteries; batter-
ies

(G-5507)
EMCS LLC
4414 Manor Ln (14075-1117)
PHONE..................................716 523-2002
Ed Monacelli, *President*
Rob Haefner, *Vice Pres*
EMP: 7
SALES (est): 839.5K **Privately Held**
SIC: 3572 Computer storage devices

(G-5508)
EVENHOUSE PRINTING
4783 Southwestern Blvd (14075-1926)
PHONE..................................716 649-2666
Robin L Evenhouse, *Partner*
EMP: 7
SALES (est): 783K **Privately Held**
WEB: www.evenhouseprinting.com
SIC: 2752 Commercial printing, litho-
graphic

(G-5509)
**GATEWAY PRTG & GRAPHICS
INC**
3970 Big Tree Rd (14075-1320)
PHONE..................................716 823-3873
Jeffery Donner, *President*
Eugene Donner, *Corp Secy*
Brian Lattimore, *Production*
Dennis Oddi, *Accounts Exec*
Brenda Blazek, *Admin Sec*
EMP: 28 **EST:** 1966
SQ FT: 20,000
SALES (est): 4.8MM **Privately Held**
WEB: www.gatewayprints.com
SIC: 2752 2791 2789 2761 Commercial
printing, offset; typesetting; bookbinding &
related work; manifold business forms

(G-5510)
JOBS WEEKLY INC
Also Called: Wny Jobs.com
31 Buffalo St Ste 2 (14075-5000)
PHONE..................................716 648-5627
Thomas Kluckhohn, *President*
Sherry Becker, *Vice Pres*
Carl Kluckhohn, *Vice Pres*
Steve Kluckhohn, *Treasurer*
Susan O'Connor, *Manager*
EMP: 11
SALES: 1MM **Privately Held**
WEB: www.wnyjobs.com
SIC: 2711 Newspapers, publishing & print-
ing

(G-5511)
K & H INDUSTRIES INC
160 Elmview Ave (14075-3763)
PHONE..................................716 312-0088
Joseph Pinker Jr, *Ch of Bd*
Karl A Baake, *President*
John Herc, *Vice Pres*
Joe Powers, *Technical Mgr*
Wendy Caparco, *Engineer*
▲ **EMP:** 35 **EST:** 1960
SQ FT: 100,000

▲ = Import ▼=Export
◆ =Import/Export

SALES (est): 7.9MM **Privately Held**
WEB: www.khindustries.com
SIC: 3641 3643 3599 3089 Lamps, fluorescent, electric; plugs, electric; connectors & terminals for electrical devices; electrical discharge machining (EDM); injection molding of plastics

(G-5512)
KRAGEL CO INC
Also Called: Custom Bags Unlimited
23 Lake St (14075-4940)
P.O. Box 71 (14075-0071)
PHONE.....................................716 648-1344
Jim Bednasz, *President*
EMP: 7
SQ FT: 4,980
SALES (est): 181.5K **Privately Held**
SIC: 2221 2393 2394 Nylon broadwoven fabrics; textile bags; liners & covers, fabric: made from purchased materials

(G-5513)
KUSTOM KORNER
Also Called: West Herr Automotive Group
5140 Camp Rd (14075-2704)
PHONE.....................................716 646-0173
Scott Beiler, *President*
Eric Zimmerman, *General Mgr*
EMP: 13
SALES (est): 1.3MM **Privately Held**
SIC: 3465 Body parts, automobile: stamped metal

(G-5514)
NITRO MANUFACTURING LLC
106 Evans St Ste E (14075-6169)
PHONE.....................................716 646-9900
Bill Frascella, *Manager*
EMP: 10
SALES (est): 246.8K **Privately Held**
SIC: 3999 Barber & beauty shop equipment

(G-5515)
ON THE MARK DIGITAL PRINTING &
5758 S Park Ave (14075-3739)
PHONE.....................................716 823-3373
Mark Poydock, *President*
EMP: 5
SALES (est): 626.7K **Privately Held**
SIC: 3993 Signs & advertising specialties

(G-5516)
PRAXAIR INC
5322 Scranton Rd (14075-2935)
PHONE.....................................716 649-1600
Troy Raybold, *Research*
Jim Hodgson, *Manager*
EMP: 20 **Privately Held**
SIC: 2813 Industrial gases
HQ: Praxair, Inc.
10 Riverview Dr
Danbury CT 06810
203 837-2000

(G-5517)
QUALITY GRINDING INC
7223 Boston State Rd (14075-6932)
PHONE.....................................716 480-3766
Herbert Pineau, *Principal*
EMP: 7 EST: 2009
SALES (est): 1.3MM **Privately Held**
SIC: 3599 Crankshafts & camshafts, machining

(G-5518)
QUEST MANUFACTURING INC
5600 Camp Rd (14075-3706)
PHONE.....................................716 312-8000
Michael J O'Brien, *President*
Kimberly M Leach, *Principal*
Eric Pachol, *Engineer*
Matt Sharpless, *Sales Staff*
Gloria Obrien, *Manager*
EMP: 30 EST: 1998
SQ FT: 17,700
SALES (est): 702.2K **Privately Held**
WEB: www.questmanufacturing.com
SIC: 3312 Stainless steel

(G-5519)
QUEST MANUFACTURING INC
5600 Camp Rd (14075-3706)
PHONE.....................................716 312-8000

Kimberly M Leach, *Principal*
EMP: 20
SALES (est): 2.8MM **Privately Held**
SIC: 3999 Manufacturing industries

(G-5520)
ROLY DOOR SALES INC
5659 Herman Hill Rd (14075-6909)
PHONE.....................................716 877-1515
EMP: 5 EST: 1952
SALES (est): 328.6K **Privately Held**
SIC: 3442 Mfg Metal Doors/Sash/Trim

(G-5521)
SINCLAIR TECHNOLOGIES INC (DH)
5811 S Park Ave 3 (14075-3738)
PHONE.....................................716 874-3682
Valerie Sinclair, *Ch of Bd*
David Ralston, *President*
David Savel, *CFO*
Andrea Sinclair, *Treasurer*
Dorothy F Sinclair, *Admin Sec*
EMP: 21 EST: 1960
SQ FT: 36,000
SALES (est): 1.7MM **Privately Held**
WEB: www.sinctech.com
SIC: 3663 5065 3674 3643 Antennas, transmitting & communications; communication equipment; amateur radio communications equipment; semiconductors & related devices; current-carrying wiring devices; switchgear & switchboard apparatus; nonferrous wiredrawing & insulating
HQ: Sinclair Technologies Inc
85 Mary St
Aurora ON L4G 6
905 727-0165

(G-5522)
STAUB MACHINE COMPANY INC
Also Called: Staub Square
206 Lake St (14075-4471)
PHONE.....................................716 649-4211
Anthony J Staub, *Ch of Bd*
Tony Staub, *President*
Jim Staub, *Prdtn Mgr*
Erik Bauerlein, *Marketing Mgr*
EMP: 20
SQ FT: 1,500
SALES (est): 4.1MM **Privately Held**
WEB: www.staubmachine.com
SIC: 3599 Machine shop, jobbing & repair

(G-5523)
TERRANCE BROWN
4625 Ironwood Dr (14075-2112)
PHONE.....................................716 648-6171
Terrance Brown, *Principal*
EMP: 5
SALES (est): 212.7K **Privately Held**
SIC: 2711 Newspapers, publishing & printing

(G-5524)
WILLIAM R SHOEMAKER INC
399 Pleasant Ave (14075-4719)
PHONE.....................................716 649-0511
William R Shoemaker, *President*
Vera Shoemaker, *Treasurer*
EMP: 5
SQ FT: 1,800
SALES (est): 708.8K **Privately Held**
SIC: 3569 Firefighting apparatus

(G-5525)
WORLDWIDE PROTECTIVE PDTS LLC
4255 Mckinley Pkwy (14075-1052)
PHONE.....................................877 678-4568
Joseph A Milot Jr, *President*
▲ EMP: 110
SALES (est): 41.5MM
SALES (corp-wide): 1.6B **Privately Held**
WEB: www.wwprotective.com
SIC: 2381 Gloves: work: woven or knit, made from purchased materials
HQ: Protective Industrial Products, Inc.
968 Albany Shaker Rd
Latham NY 12110
518 861-0133

Hamilton
Madison County

(G-5526)
COSSITT CONCRETE PRODUCTS INC
6543 Middleport Rd (13346-2275)
P.O. Box 379 (13346-0379)
PHONE.....................................315 824-2700
Lance Kenyon, *President*
EMP: 10 EST: 1947
SQ FT: 1,500
SALES (est): 2MM **Privately Held**
SIC: 3272 3273 5211 3271 Concrete stuctural support & building material; ready-mixed concrete; lumber & other building materials; architectural concrete: block, split, fluted, screen, etc.

(G-5527)
JAMES MORRIS
Also Called: Madison Manufacturing
6697 Airport Rd (13346-2118)
PHONE.....................................315 824-8519
James Morris, *Owner*
Bob Britton, *General Mgr*
EMP: 30
SQ FT: 6,000
SALES (est): 2.8MM **Privately Held**
WEB: www.jamesmorris.net
SIC: 3559 Electronic component making machinery

Hammond
St. Lawrence County

(G-5528)
YESTERYEARS VINTAGE DOORS LLC
66 S Main St (13646-3201)
PHONE.....................................315 324-5250
Erica Demick, *Natl Sales Mgr*
Howard Demick,
EMP: 9
SQ FT: 5,760
SALES (est): 1.2MM **Privately Held**
WEB: www.vintagedoors.com
SIC: 2431 Doors, wood

Hammondsport
Steuben County

(G-5529)
HEARTWOOD SPECIALTIES INC
10249 Gibson Rd (14840-9431)
PHONE.....................................607 654-0102
Bruce G Bozman, *President*
EMP: 7 EST: 1983
SQ FT: 5,000
SALES (est): 680K **Privately Held**
SIC: 2521 2541 Wood office furniture; wood partitions & fixtures

(G-5530)
HERON HILL VINEYARDS INC (PA)
Also Called: Heron Hill Winery
9301 County Route 76 (14840-9685)
PHONE.....................................607 868-4241
John Engle Jr, *CEO*
Christy Dann, *CFO*
EMP: 33
SQ FT: 8,640
SALES (est): 2.5MM **Privately Held**
WEB: www.heronhill.com
SIC: 2084 5812 0172 Wines; eating places; grapes

(G-5531)
KEUKA BREWING CO LLC
8572 Briglin Rd (14840-9633)
PHONE.....................................607 868-4648
Richard Musso, *President*
Mark Goodwin, *Manager*
EMP: 8
SALES (est): 678K **Privately Held**
SIC: 2082 Beer (alcoholic beverage)

(G-5532)
KONSTANTIN D FRANK& SONS VINI
Also Called: Vinifera Wine Cellard
9749 Middle Rd (14840-9462)
PHONE.....................................607 868-4884
Fred Frank, *President*
Karen Smolos, *Engineer*
Hilda Volz, *Admin Sec*
▲ EMP: 30 EST: 1953
SALES (est): 3.9MM **Privately Held**
WEB: www.drfrankwines.com
SIC: 2084 0172 Wines; grapes

Hampton Bays
Suffolk County

(G-5533)
BROCK AWNINGS LTD
211 E Montauk Hwy Ste 1 (11946-2035)
PHONE.....................................631 765-5200
Earl Brock, *President*
EMP: 10 EST: 1975
SQ FT: 8,000
SALES: 693.1K **Privately Held**
WEB: www.brockawnings.com
SIC: 2394 5999 5199 5091 Awnings, fabric: made from purchased materials; canvas products; canvas products; boat accessories & parts

---

Hancock
Delaware County

(G-5534)
BEAVER MOUNTAIN LOG HOMES INC
200 Beaver Mountain Dr (13783-1748)
PHONE.....................................607 467-2700
Drew Prochazka, *Business Mgr*
Kenneth Clark, *Branch Mgr*
EMP: 5
SALES (corp-wide): 5.2MM **Privately Held**
SIC: 2452 Log cabins, prefabricated, wood
PA: Beaver Mountain Log Homes Inc
1740 County Highway 48
Deposit NY
607 467-2758

(G-5535)
COBLESKILL STONE PRODUCTS INC
Also Called: Hancock Quarry/Asphalt
1565 Green Flats Rd (13783)
PHONE.....................................607 637-4271
Ray Althiser, *Branch Mgr*
EMP: 10
SALES (corp-wide): 126.7MM **Privately Held**
WEB: www.cobleskillstone.com
SIC: 1422 2951 Crushed & broken limestone; asphalt & asphaltic paving mixtures (not from refineries)
PA: Cobleskill Stone Products, Inc.
112 Rock Rd
Cobleskill NY 12043
518 234-0221

(G-5536)
COMPREHENSIVE DENTAL TECH
Rr 1 Box 69 (13783)
PHONE.....................................607 467-4456
Marie Benjamin, *President*
Mike Archer, *Vice Pres*
EMP: 4
SQ FT: 2,700
SALES: 1.3MM **Privately Held**
SIC: 7372 8021 Prepackaged software; offices & clinics of dentists

(G-5537)
MALLERY LUMBER LLC
158 Labarre St (13783)
PHONE.....................................607 637-2236
Les Wagner, *President*
EMP: 7
SQ FT: 2,000

**G
E
O
G
R
A
P
H
I
C**

SALES (est): 69.2K **Privately Held**
SIC: 2421 Kiln drying of lumber

(G-5538)
PETERS LLC
5259 Peas Eddy Rd (13783-4237)
PHONE.....................607 637-5470
Dore Brooks, *Buyer*
Claire Conarro, *Buyer*
Van Peters,
Beverly Peters,
EMP: 5
SALES (est): 360K **Privately Held**
SIC: 2411 Logging

(G-5539)
RUSSELL BASS
Also Called: Russell Bass & Son Lumber
59 Saw Mill Rd (13783)
P.O. Box 718 (13783-0718)
PHONE.....................607 637-5253
Russell Bass, *Partner*
EMP: 15
SALES (est): 1.3MM **Privately Held**
SIC: 2421 2411 Sawmills & planing mills,
general; logging

(G-5540)
VAN CPETERS LOGGING INC
4480 Peas Eddy Rd (13783-4232)
PHONE.....................607 637-3574
Van Peters, *Principal*
EMP: 6
SALES (est): 515.7K **Privately Held**
SIC: 2411 Logging

Hannacroix
Greene County

(G-5541)
MODERN METAL FABRICATORS INC
799 Cr 111 (12087)
PHONE.....................518 966-4142
Brian Kinn, *President*
EMP: 7
SALES (est): 228.5K **Privately Held**
SIC: 2522 Office furniture, except wood

Hannibal
Oswego County

(G-5542)
ACRO-FAB LTD
55 Rochester St (13074-3139)
P.O. Box 184 (13074-0184)
PHONE.....................315 564-6688
Mike Combes, *Ch of Bd*
Martin Victory, *Corp Secy*
Darrell Baker, *Vice Pres*
EMP: 23
SQ FT: 12,000
SALES (est): 3.1MM **Privately Held**
WEB: www.acro-fab.com
SIC: 7692 3444 3599 Welding repair;
sheet metalwork; machine shop, jobbing
& repair

(G-5543)
WOOD-MIZER HOLDINGS INC
8604 State Route 104 (13074-2125)
PHONE.....................315 564-5722
David Scott, *Branch Mgr*
EMP: 7
SQ FT: 7,200
SALES (corp-wide): 133.2MM **Privately Held**
WEB: www.lastec.com
SIC: 3553 Woodworking machinery
PA: Wood-Mizer Holdings, Inc.
8180 W 10th St
Indianapolis IN 46214
317 271-1542

Harriman
Orange County

(G-5544)
HOME MAIDE INCORPORATED
1 Short St (10926-3311)
PHONE.....................845 837-1700
Edward Fennessy, *CEO*
EMP: 10
SALES (est): 477K **Privately Held**
SIC: 3556 Ovens, bakery

(G-5545)
JOHNSON CONTROLS
4 Commerce Dr S Ste 3 (10926-3108)
PHONE.....................845 774-4120
Steve Walsh, *Manager*
Teresa Brown, *Admin Asst*
EMP: 5 **Privately Held**
WEB: www.simplexgrinnell.com
SIC: 3669 5087 1731 1711 Emergency
alarms; firefighting equipment; fire detec-
tion & burglar alarm systems specializa-
tion; fire sprinkler system installation
HQ: Johnson Controls Fire Protection Lp
6600 Congress Ave
Boca Raton FL 33487
561 988-7200

(G-5546)
PREMIER INK SYSTEMS INC
2 Commerce Dr S (10926-3101)
PHONE.....................845 782-5802
Tyring Marcus, *Owner*
EMP: 48
SALES (corp-wide): 16.5MM **Privately Held**
SIC: 2759 Screen printing
PA: Premier Ink Systems, Inc.
10420 N State St
Harrison OH 45030
513 367-2300

(G-5547)
TAKASAGO INTL CORP USA
114 Commerce Dr S (10926-3101)
PHONE.....................845 751-0622
Zachary Bergoine, *Buyer*
Dana Drevitson, *Branch Mgr*
EMP: 100 **Privately Held**
SIC: 2844 Concentrates, perfume
HQ: Takasago International Corporation
(U.S.A)
4 Volvo Dr
Rockleigh NJ 07647
201 767-9001

Harrison
Westchester County

(G-5548)
CASTLE FUELS CORPORATION
440 Mamaroneck Ave (10528-2418)
PHONE.....................914 381-6600
Michael Romita, *CEO*
EMP: 39
SALES (est): 4.6MM **Privately Held**
SIC: 2869 Fuels

(G-5549)
CEMAC FOODS CORP
8 Cayuga Trl (10528-1820)
PHONE.....................914 835-0526
Thomas May, *President*
Helen Nash May, *Corp Secy*
Mel Persily, *Vice Pres*
Mildred Nash, *CFO*
EMP: 16
SQ FT: 3,000
SALES (est): 1.6MM **Privately Held**
WEB: www.cemacfoods.com
SIC: 2022 Natural cheese; imitation
cheese

(G-5550)
CHEMLUBE INTERNATIONAL LLC
500 Mmaroneck Ave Ste 306 (10528)
PHONE.....................914 381-5800
Robert Nobel, *CEO*

Robert Cowen, *Vice Pres*
Rob Kress, *Vice Pres*
Scott Ruliffson, *Manager*
◆ **EMP:** 13 **EST:** 2012
SQ FT: 5,300
SALES (est): 4.7MM **Privately Held**
SIC: 2992 5172 5169 Lubricating oils &
greases; lubricating oils & greases; chem-
icals & allied products

(G-5551)
CHEMLUBE MARKETING INC
500 Mamaroneck Ave (10528-1633)
PHONE.....................914 381-5800
Robert Nobel, *Ch of Bd*
◆ **EMP:** 13
SQ FT: 5,300
SALES (est): 5.4MM **Privately Held**
WEB: www.sopetra.com
SIC: 2992 5172 5169 Lubricating oils &
greases; lubricating oils & greases; chem-
icals & allied products

(G-5552)
DAL-TILE CORPORATION
31 Oakland Ave (10528-3709)
PHONE.....................914 835-1801
Brian Scocio, *Manager*
EMP: 7
SALES (corp-wide): 9.9B **Publicly Held**
WEB: www.mohawk.com
SIC: 3253 5032 Ceramic wall & floor tile;
ceramic wall & floor tile
HQ: Dal-Tile Corporation
7834 C F Hawn Fwy
Dallas TX 75217
214 398-1411

(G-5553)
GGP PUBLISHING INC
105 Calvert St Ste 201 (10528-3138)
P.O. Box 635, Larchmont (10538-0635)
PHONE.....................914 834-8896
Generosa Gina Protano, *Partner*
EMP: 10
SALES: 1MM **Privately Held**
WEB: www.ggppublishing.com
SIC: 2731 Books: publishing only

(G-5554)
GRACE ASSOCIATES INC
470 West St (10528-2510)
PHONE.....................718 767-9000
Anthony Grace, *President*
Richard Grace, *Vice Pres*
EMP: 5
SQ FT: 1,500
SALES (est): 639.3K **Privately Held**
SIC: 3271 3272 2951 Concrete block &
brick; concrete products; asphalt paving
mixtures & blocks

(G-5555)
MARTINELLI HOLDINGS LLC
Also Called: Today Media
4 Ellsworth Ave Apt 2 (10528-3142)
PHONE.....................302 504-1361
Dianne Green, *Branch Mgr*
EMP: 50
SALES (corp-wide): 15K **Privately Held**
SIC: 2721 Magazines: publishing only, not
printed on site
PA: Martinelli Holdings Llc
3301 Lancaster Pike 5c
Wilmington DE 19805
302 656-1809

(G-5556)
NATIONAL EQUIPMENT CORPORATION (PA)
Also Called: Union Standard Eqp Co Div
600 Mmaroneck Ave Ste 400 (10528)
PHONE.....................718 585-0200
Arthur A Greenberg, *Ch of Bd*
Andrew Greenberg, *President*
John Greenberg, *President*
Charles Greenberg, *Exec VP*
◆ **EMP:** 18
SQ FT: 260,000
SALES (est): 10.6MM **Privately Held**
SIC: 3559 5084 3556 Chemical machin-
ery & equipment; processing & packaging
equipment; confectionery machinery

(G-5557)
PACE POLYETHYLENE MFG CO INC (PA)
46 Calvert St (10528-3238)
P.O. Box 385 (10528-0385)
PHONE.....................914 381-3000
Stan Nathanson, *President*
Marc Lawrence, *Vice Pres*
EMP: 20
SQ FT: 1,500
SALES (est): 5.2MM **Privately Held**
SIC: 3081 Polyethylene film

(G-5558)
PROFESSIONAL MEDICAL DEVICES
10 Century Trl (10528-1702)
PHONE.....................914 835-0614
EMP: 10
SALES: 500K **Privately Held**
SIC: 3841 Mfg Surgical/Medical Instru-
ments

(G-5559)
SPRINGFIELD OIL SERVICES INC (PA)
550 Mmaroneck Ave Ste 503 (10528)
PHONE.....................914 315-6812
Bentley Blum, *President*
Mary Irwin, *Vice Pres*
▲ **EMP:** 18
SQ FT: 1,000
SALES (est): 1.2MM **Privately Held**
SIC: 1382 Oil & gas exploration services

(G-5560)
SS&C FINANCIAL SERVICES LLC (DH)
1 South Rd (10528-3309)
PHONE.....................914 670-3600
William Stone, *CEO*
Hans Hufschmid, *Principal*
Vernon Barback, *COO*
Martin Veilleux, *CFO*
Janice Hou, *Accountant*
EMP: 105
SQ FT: 24,000
SALES (est): 66MM
SALES (corp-wide): 3.4B **Publicly Held**
WEB: www.globeop.com
SIC: 7372 Prepackaged software
HQ: Ss&C Technologies, Inc.
80 Lamberton Rd
Windsor CT 06095
860 298-4500

(G-5561)
STILLTHEONE DISTILLERY LLC
500 Mmaroneck Ave Ste 205 (10528)
PHONE.....................914 217-0347
EMP: 6
SALES (est): 448.9K **Privately Held**
SIC: 2085 Distilled & blended liquors

(G-5562)
TREO BRANDS LLC
106 Calvert St (10528-3131)
PHONE.....................914 341-1850
Robert Golden, *CEO*
Brian O'Byrne, *President*
EMP: 12
SQ FT: 3,800
SALES: 1MM **Privately Held**
SIC: 2086 Carbonated beverages, nonal-
coholic: bottled & canned

(G-5563)
UNIVERSAL REMOTE CONTROL INC (PA)
Also Called: Urc
500 Mmaroneck Ave Ste 502 (10528)
PHONE.....................914 835-4484
Chang Park, *Chairman*
Brett Kozlowski, *Sales Engr*
Brian High, *Manager*
Jonathan Bell, *Technical Staff*
Elvin Lopez, *Technical Staff*
◆ **EMP:** 60
SQ FT: 11,000
SALES (est): 16.6MM **Privately Held**
WEB: www.universalremote.com
SIC: 3678 Electronic connectors

(G-5564)
VALUE SPRING TECHNOLOGY INC
521 Harrison Ave (10528-1431)
PHONE..............................917 705-4658
EMP: 15
SALES (est): 305.2K **Privately Held**
SIC: 7372 Prepackaged Software Services

Harrisville
Lewis County

(G-5565)
CIVES CORPORATION
Also Called: Viking-Cives
14331 Mill St (13648-3331)
PHONE..............................315 543-2321
Larry Jeroscko, *General Mgr*
Steve Rider, *General Mgr*
Andrew Mitchell, *Project Engr*
EMP: 75
SQ FT: 46,000
SALES (corp-wide): 651.3MM **Privately Held**
WEB: www.cives.com
SIC: 3531 Snow plow attachments
PA: Cives Corporation
3700 Mansell Rd Ste 500
Alpharetta GA 30022
770 993-4424

Hartford
Washington County

(G-5566)
RICHARD STEWART
4495 State Rte 149 (12838)
P.O. Box 18 (12838-0018)
PHONE..............................518 632-5363
Richard Stewart, *Owner*
Mary Stewart, *Owner*
EMP: 5
SALES (est): 445.1K **Privately Held**
SIC: 3523 Dairy equipment (farm)

Hartsdale
Westchester County

(G-5567)
APOGEE POWER USA INC
7 Verne Pl (10530-1026)
PHONE..............................202 746-2890
Michael Harper, *CEO*
John Hollins, *President*
Dr Kc Tsai, *Mfg Mgr*
EMP: 10
SALES (est): 14.6K **Privately Held**
SIC: 3825 3621 Electrical energy measuring equipment; storage battery chargers, motor & engine generator type

(G-5568)
SIGN HERE ENTERPRISES LLC
Also Called: Sign-A-Rama
28 N Central Ave Rear (10530-2407)
PHONE..............................914 328-3111
David Reichenberg,
EMP: 5
SALES (est): 350K **Privately Held**
SIC: 3993 Signs & advertising specialties

(G-5569)
TAPEMAKER SUPPLY COMPANY LLC
22 Sherbrooke Rd (10530-2938)
PHONE..............................914 693-3407
Ronald Huppert, *Mng Member*
EMP: 7
SALES (est): 407.8K **Privately Held**
WEB: www.tapemakersupply.com
SIC: 2759 Commercial printing

(G-5570)
TLC VISION (USA) CORPORATION
Also Called: Blinds To Go
150 Central Park Ave (10530)
PHONE..............................914 395-3949
Steven Shiller, *Owner*
EMP: 5
SALES (corp-wide): 1.2B **Privately Held**
SIC: 2591 Window blinds
HQ: Tlc Vision (Usa) Corporation
16305 Swingley Ridge Rd # 300
Chesterfield MO 63017
636 534-2300

Hastings On Hudson
Westchester County

(G-5571)
ALTERNATIVE TECHNOLOGY CORP
Also Called: Marketfax Information Services
1 North St Ste 1 # 1 (10706-1542)
P.O. Box 357 (10706-0357)
PHONE..............................914 478-5900
Tom Kadala, *CEO*
EMP: 5
SQ FT: 3,000
SALES: 1.2MM **Privately Held**
WEB: www.marketfax.com
SIC: 3661 5065 4822 7375 Facsimile equipment; facsimile equipment; facsimile transmission services; information retrieval services

(G-5572)
FLOGIC INC
Also Called: F Logic
25 Chestnut Dr (10706-1901)
PHONE..............................914 478-1352
Julius Funaro, *President*
Michael Piscatelli, *Vice Pres*
EMP: 13
SALES (est): 1.2MM **Privately Held**
WEB: www.flinc.com
SIC: 7372 Prepackaged software

(G-5573)
IN2GREEN LLC
14 Bellair Dr (10706-1102)
PHONE..............................914 693-5054
Lori Slater, *Mng Member*
EMP: 5 EST: 2009
SALES (est): 533.4K **Privately Held**
SIC: 2211 Blankets & blanketings, cotton

(G-5574)
JAMES RICHARD SPECIALTY CHEM
24 Ridge St (10706-2702)
PHONE..............................914 478-7500
Katrine Barth, *President*
Rebecca Yoftahie, *Manager*
EMP: 6
SQ FT: 1,300
SALES: 3MM **Privately Held**
WEB: www.rjsconline.com
SIC: 2842 Specialty cleaning, polishes & sanitation goods

(G-5575)
LORENA CANALS USA INC
104 Burnside Dr (10706-3013)
PHONE..............................844 567-3622
Delia Elbaum, *General Mgr*
▲ **EMP:** 3
SQ FT: 3,000
SALES: 1MM
SALES (corp-wide): 5.7MM **Privately Held**
SIC: 2273 5023 Carpets & rugs; rugs
PA: Lorena Canals Sl.
Calle Pere Ponce De Leon 4
Sant Just Desvern 08960

Hauppauge
Suffolk County

(G-5576)
A & Z PHARMACEUTICAL INC
180 Oser Ave (11788-3736)
PHONE..............................631 952-3802
Frank Berstler, *Vice Pres*
EMP: 90
SALES (est): 5.6MM **Privately Held**
SIC: 2834 8734 Pills, pharmaceutical; testing laboratories
PA: A & Z Pharmaceutical Inc.
350 Wireless Blvd Ste 200
Hauppauge NY 11788

(G-5577)
A & Z PHARMACEUTICAL INC (PA)
350 Wireless Blvd Ste 200 (11788-3947)
PHONE..............................631 952-3802
Emma LI, *CEO*
Xu Xiaoxian, *Ch of Bd*
Frank Berstler, *Senior VP*
Xian Chen, *Vice Pres*
Kevin McCourt, *Vice Pres*
◆ **EMP:** 450
SQ FT: 73,000
SALES (est): 154.9MM **Privately Held**
SIC: 2834 Vitamin, nutrient & hematinic preparations for human use

(G-5578)
ADVANCE TABCO INC (HQ)
325 Wireless Blvd Ste 1 (11788-3973)
PHONE..............................631 242-8270
Alice Schwartz, *Ch of Bd*
Penny Schwartz-Hutner, *President*
Daniel Schwartz, *Vice Pres*
Ryan Fee, *Purch Mgr*
Ron Dambrosio, *Marketing Staff*
◆ **EMP:** 85
SQ FT: 70,000
SALES (est): 20.1MM
SALES (corp-wide): 77.7MM **Privately Held**
SIC: 3589 3431 Commercial cooking & foodwarming equipment; metal sanitary ware
PA: Kinplex Corp.
325 Wireless Blvd Ste 1
Hauppauge NY 11788
631 242-4800

(G-5579)
ADVANCED BACK TECHNOLOGIES
89 Ste F Cabot Ct (11788)
PHONE..............................631 231-0076
David F Cuccia, *President*
EMP: 5 EST: 1997
SALES (est): 944.3K **Privately Held**
SIC: 3841 Surgical & medical instruments

(G-5580)
ADVANCED TESTING TECH INC (PA)
Also Called: A T T I
110 Ricefield Ln (11788-2008)
PHONE..............................631 231-8777
Hector M Gavilla, *Chairman*
Eli Levi, *Exec VP*
Tom Lingenfelter, *Vice Pres*
Angelo Stano, *Prdtn Mgr*
EMP: 180
SQ FT: 6,000
SALES (est): 32.7MM **Privately Held**
WEB: www.attinet.com
SIC: 3825 8711 Test equipment for electronic & electric measurement; electrical or electronic engineering

(G-5581)
AIPING PHARMACEUTICAL INC
350w Wireless Blvd (11788-3959)
PHONE..............................631 952-3802
Jing Zou, *Principal*
Frank Berstler, *Vice Pres*
EMP: 5
SALES (est): 449.4K **Privately Held**
SIC: 2834 2899 Tablets, pharmaceutical; gelatin: edible, technical, photographic or pharmaceutical

(G-5582)
ALADDIN PACKAGING LLC
115 Engineers Rd Ste 100 (11788-4005)
PHONE..............................631 273-4747
Jeff Russell, *VP Sales*
Moshe Wercberger, *Sales Associate*
Jerry Levovitz, *Marketing Staff*
Abraham Mandell, *Mng Member*
Joel Endzweig,
▲ **EMP:** 60
SQ FT: 75,000
SALES: 31.1MM **Privately Held**
SIC: 2673 Cellophane bags, unprinted; made from purchased materials

(G-5583)
ALLCRAFT FABRICATORS INC
150 Wireless Blvd (11788-3955)
PHONE..............................631 951-4100
Douglas Donaldson, *President*
Darren J Winter, *Exec VP*
Atul Shah, *Sales Staff*
Adriana Nolasco, *Executive Asst*
EMP: 75 EST: 1964
SALES (est): 12.1MM **Privately Held**
SIC: 2522 Office furniture, except wood

(G-5584)
ALLEN MACHINE PRODUCTS INC
120 Ricefield Ln Ste 100 (11788-2033)
PHONE..............................631 630-8800
Peter Allen, *Ch of Bd*
Eric Lazarus, *Managing Dir*
Richard Pettenato, *Vice Pres*
Michael Kellwick, *Purch Mgr*
Bernie Salter, *CFO*
▲ **EMP:** 50
SQ FT: 30,000
SALES: 5.9MM **Privately Held**
WEB: www.allenmachine.com
SIC: 3469 3444 Machine parts, stamped or pressed metal; sheet metalwork

(G-5585)
ALUFOIL PRODUCTS CO INC
135 Oser Ave Ste 3 (11788-3722)
PHONE..............................631 231-4141
Howard Lent, *Ch of Bd*
Elliot Lent, *Vice Pres*
Estelle Lent, *Shareholder*
Barbara Sherman, *Shareholder*
◆ **EMP:** 18 EST: 1945
SQ FT: 45,000
SALES: 3.7MM **Privately Held**
WEB: www.alufoil.com
SIC: 3497 3353 Foil, laminated to paper or other materials; foil, aluminum

(G-5586)
ALVIO-US CORP
89 Cabot Ct Ste M (11788-3719)
PHONE..............................631 664-0618
Joseph Tilton, *President*
EMP: 5
SALES (est): 479.3K **Privately Held**
SIC: 3442 1522 5031 5211 Metal doors, sash & trim; residential construction; doors & windows; lumber & other building materials; nonresidential construction

(G-5587)
AMERICAN ACCESS CARE LLC
32 Central Ave (11788-4734)
PHONE..............................631 582-9729
Thea Hemback, *Manager*
EMP: 11
SALES (corp-wide): 18.9B **Privately Held**
WEB: www.americanaccesscare.com
SIC: 3844 X-ray apparatus & tubes
HQ: American Access Care, L.L.C.
40 Valley Stream Pkwy
Malvern PA 19355
717 235-0181

(G-5588)
AMERICAN CHIMNEY SUPPLIES INC
129 Oser Ave Ste B (11788-3813)
PHONE..............................631 434-2020
Chris Arbucci, *President*
▲ **EMP:** 6 EST: 1993
SQ FT: 21,000

SALES (est): 1.1MM **Privately Held**
SIC: 3312 3272 3259 Stainless steel;
chimney caps, concrete; clay chimney
products

(G-5589)
AMERICAN DIAGNOSTIC CORP
Also Called: A D C
55 Commerce Dr (11788-3931)
PHONE..............................631 273-6155
Marc Blitstein, *President*
Neal Weingart, *Vice Pres*
Tony Morena, *Human Res Dir*
Charles McRae, *Sales Staff*
Steve Kelly, *Marketing Mgr*
◆ **EMP:** 77
SALES (est): 15.8MM **Privately Held**
WEB: www.adctoday.com
SIC: 3841 Blood pressure apparatus;
stethoscopes & stethographs

(G-5590)
AMERICAN HLTH
FORMULATIONS INC (HQ)
Also Called: Summit Vitamins
45 Adams Ave (11788-3605)
PHONE..............................631 392-1756
Jimmy Wang, *President*
Lisa Wang, *CFO*
John Mullins, *Sales Dir*
Giancarlo Denegri, *Sales Mgr*
Hank Cheatham, *Sales Staff*
EMP: 6
SQ FT: 20,000
SALES (est): 1.2MM **Privately Held**
SIC: 2834 2869 Vitamin preparations;
sweeteners, synthetic

(G-5591)
AMERICAN INTRMDAL CONT
MFG LLC
Also Called: Aicm
150 Motor Pkwy Ste 401 (11788-5108)
PHONE..............................631 774-6790
Pat Marron, *President*
EMP: 8
SQ FT: 200
SALES (est): 888.5K **Privately Held**
SIC: 2655 Fiber shipping & mailing con-
tainers

(G-5592)
ARC SYSTEMS INC
2090 Joshuas Path (11788-4764)
PHONE..............................631 582-8020
Robert Miller, *President*
Clifford Miller, *Treasurer*
John Grant, *Manager*
Kathie Mooney, *Manager*
▲ **EMP:** 33 **EST:** 1967
SQ FT: 12,000
SALES (est): 6.3MM **Privately Held**
WEB: www.arcsystemsinc.com
SIC: 3621 3694 3724 Motors, electric;
electric motor & generator parts; battery
charging alternators & generators; aircraft
engines & engine parts

(G-5593)
ARKAY PACKAGING
CORPORATION (PA)
700 Veterans Memorial Hwy # 300
(11788-2929)
PHONE..............................631 273-2000
Mitchell Kaneff, *Chairman*
Walter Shiels, *COO*
Brian Hopkins, *Plant Mgr*
Mel Bohince, *Project Mgr*
Charles Zilavy, *Production*
▲ **EMP:** 40
SQ FT: 5,000
SALES (est): 42.4MM **Privately Held**
WEB: www.arkay.com
SIC: 2657 Folding paperboard boxes

(G-5594)
ARTEMIS INC
36 Central Ave (11788-4734)
PHONE..............................631 232-2424
Yuly Margulis, *CEO*
Alex Margulis, *Vice Pres*
Alexander Margulis, *Vice Pres*
Michael Schorr, *Engineer*
Mike Schorr, *Engineer*
▲ **EMP:** 7 **EST:** 1999

SQ FT: 9,000
SALES (est): 1.4MM **Privately Held**
WEB: www.artemis.com
SIC: 3674 3812 Integrated circuits, semi-
conductor networks, etc.; radar systems &
equipment

(G-5595)
ARTISTIC PRODUCTS LLC
345 Oser Ave (11788-3607)
PHONE..............................631 435-0200
Richard Leifer,
Bradley Brighton,
Robert S Leifer,
▲ **EMP:** 45
SQ FT: 50,000
SALES (est): 7.7MM **Privately Held**
WEB: www.artistic-products.com
SIC: 2522 Desks, office: except wood

(G-5596)
ATLANTIC ESSENTIAL PDTS INC
7 Oser Ave Ste 1 (11788-3811)
PHONE..............................631 434-8333
Maxim G Uvarov, *Ch of Bd*
Pailla Rebby, *Vice Pres*
Selven Sam, *Vice Pres*
EMP: 57 **EST:** 1999
SQ FT: 22,000
SALES (est): 11.2MM **Privately Held**
WEB: www.atlanticep.com
SIC: 2834 7389 Vitamin preparations;
packaging & labeling services

(G-5597)
ATLANTIC ULTRAVIOLET CORP
375 Marcus Blvd (11788-2026)
PHONE..............................631 234-3275
Hilary Boehme, *President*
Thomas Dituro, *Vice Pres*
Celeste Kopp, *Treasurer*
Ronald Henderson, *Director*
Anne Wysocki, *Admin Sec*
◆ **EMP:** 30 **EST:** 1963
SALES (est): 7.1MM **Privately Held**
WEB: www.ultraviolet.com
SIC: 3589 3641 Water purification equip-
ment, household type; ultraviolet lamps

(G-5598)
AUTOMATIC CONNECTOR INC
375 Oser Ave (11788-3607)
PHONE..............................631 543-5000
David Lax, *President*
EMP: 19
SALES (est): 3.1MM **Privately Held**
WEB: www.automaticconnector.com
SIC: 3678 3643 Electronic connectors;
electric connectors

(G-5599)
AVM PRINTING INC
Also Called: Printers 3
43 Corporate Dr (11788-2048)
PHONE..............................631 351-1331
Anthony Viscuso, *President*
EMP: 13
SQ FT: 6,000
SALES: 2MM **Privately Held**
SIC: 2752 Commercial printing, litho-
graphic

(G-5600)
BACTOLAC PHARMACEUTICAL
INC (PA)
7 Oser Ave Ste 1 (11788-3811)
PHONE..............................631 951-4908
Pailla M Reddy, *President*
Renee Reynolds, *Vice Pres*
Chiru Reddy, *Purchasing*
Vanessa Jackson, *Manager*
Mariola Frigillana, *Supervisor*
▲ **EMP:** 200
SQ FT: 5,000
SALES (est): 100MM **Privately Held**
WEB: www.bactolac.com
SIC: 2834 Vitamin preparations

(G-5601)
BACTOLAC PHARMACEUTICAL
INC
620 Old Willets Path (11788-4103)
PHONE..............................631 951-4908
Pailla M Reddy, *President*
Alex Villedrouin, *Controller*
EMP: 50

SALES (corp-wide): 100MM **Privately
Held**
SIC: 2834 Vitamin preparations
PA: Bactolac Pharmaceutical Inc.
7 Oser Ave Ste 1
Hauppauge NY 11788
631 951-4908

(G-5602)
BARRONS EDUCATIONAL
SERIES INC (PA)
Also Called: B.E.S. Publishing
250 Wireless Blvd (11788-3924)
PHONE..............................631 434-3311
Jennifer Giammusso, *Editor*
Manuel H Barron, *Chairman*
Christopher Ciaschini, *Prdtn Dir*
Bob Labarbara, *Credit Mgr*
Jackie Raab, *Sales Mgr*
◆ **EMP:** 125
SQ FT: 75,000
SALES (est): 26.2MM **Privately Held**
WEB: www.barronseduc.com
SIC: 2731 5942 Books: publishing only;
book stores

(G-5603)
BETAPAST HOLDINGS LLC
110 Nicon Ct (11788-4212)
PHONE..............................631 582-6740
Wayne R Demmons, *CEO*
Joseph Yanosik, *President*
Linda Okvist, *Production*
Brian Rosengrant, *QC Dir*
John Calma, *Engineer*
EMP: 70 **EST:** 1966
SQ FT: 10,000
SALES (est): 11.7MM **Privately Held**
WEB: www.betatronix.com
SIC: 3823 3676 Potentiometric self-bal-
ancing inst., except X-Y plotters; elec-
tronic resistors

(G-5604)
BIO-BOTANICA INC (PA)
75 Commerce Dr (11788-3943)
PHONE..............................631 231-0987
Frank D'Amelio Sr, *CEO*
Josephine Perricone, *President*
Mark Sysler, *Senior VP*
Frank D'Amelio Jr, *Vice Pres*
Jonathan Selzer, *Vice Pres*
◆ **EMP:** 100
SQ FT: 100,000
SALES (est): 33.3MM **Privately Held**
SIC: 2833 2834 2844 Alkaloids & other
botanical based products; drugs & herbs:
grading, grinding & milling; botanical
products, medicinal: ground, graded or
milled; extracts of botanicals: powdered,
pilular, solid or fluid; toilet preparations

(G-5605)
BLACK & DECKER (US) INC
180 Oser Ave Ste 100 (11788-3709)
PHONE..............................631 952-2008
Joe Rufino, *Branch Mgr*
EMP: 7
SALES (corp-wide): 13.9B **Publicly Held**
WEB: www.dewalt.com
SIC: 3546 Power-driven handtools
HQ: Black & Decker (U.S.) Inc.
1000 Stanley Dr
New Britain CT 06053
860 225-5111

(G-5606)
BLUE STAR PRODUCTS INC
355 Marcus Blvd Ste 2 (11788-2027)
PHONE..............................631 952-3204
Gerald Jacino Sr, *President*
EMP: 12
SQ FT: 15,000
SALES (est): 1.3MM **Privately Held**
WEB: www.bluestar-products.com
SIC: 3559 Automotive maintenance equip-
ment

(G-5607)
BRICK-IT INC
17 Central Ave (11788-4733)
PHONE..............................631 244-3993
Ronald F Trezza, *President*
James Kulp, *Sales Staff*
▼ **EMP:** 5
SQ FT: 10,000

SALES (est): 1MM **Privately Held**
WEB: www.brickit.com
SIC: 3291 5211 Coated abrasive products;
brick

(G-5608)
BRICKIT
17 Central Ave (11788-4733)
PHONE..............................631 727-8977
Robert Dolinsk,
Robert Dolinsky,
EMP: 20
SALES (est): 3.3MM **Privately Held**
SIC: 3271 Brick, concrete

(G-5609)
BYSTRONIC INC
185 Commerce Dr (11788-3916)
PHONE..............................631 231-1212
Ulrich Troesch, *Principal*
Paul Kraus, *Regl Sales Mgr*
EMP: 8
SALES (corp-wide): 1.8B **Privately Held**
SIC: 3541 Machine tools, metal cutting
type
HQ: Bystronic Inc.
200 Airport Rd
Elgin IL 60123
847 214-0300

(G-5610)
C & C CUSTOM METAL
FABRICATORS
2 N Hoffman Ln (11788-2735)
PHONE..............................631 235-9646
Chris Drago, *President*
EMP: 6
SQ FT: 1,500
SALES (est): 483.7K **Privately Held**
SIC: 3441 Fabricated structural metal

(G-5611)
CASTELLA IMPORTS INC
60 Davids Dr (11788-2041)
PHONE..............................631 231-5500
EMP: 32 **Privately Held**
SIC: 2099 5149 Food preparations; spe-
cialty food items
PA: Castella Imports, Inc.
120 Wilshire Blvd Ste A
Edgewood NY 11717

(G-5612)
CENTRAL SEMICONDUCTOR
CORP
145 Adams Ave (11788-3603)
PHONE..............................631 435-1110
W S Radgowski, *CEO*
Susan M Ryan, *President*
Maryanne Liberto, *COO*
Tom Hambel, *Vice Pres*
Steven Radgowski, *Vice Pres*
▲ **EMP:** 80
SQ FT: 30,000
SALES (est): 23.9MM **Privately Held**
WEB: www.centralsemi.com
SIC: 3674 Integrated circuits, semiconduc-
tor networks, etc.

(G-5613)
CHARL INDUSTRIES INC
225 Engineers Rd (11788-4020)
PHONE..............................631 234-0100
Richard Coronato Sr, *President*
Mark Moldowsky, *QC Mgr*
Kitt Tyson, *Manager*
Charlotte Coronato, *Admin Sec*
EMP: 40
SQ FT: 44,000
SALES (est): 8.1MM **Privately Held**
WEB: www.charlco.com
SIC: 3599 Machine shop, jobbing & repair

(G-5614)
CHARLES ROSS & SON
COMPANY (PA)
Also Called: Ross Metal Fabricators Div
710 Old Willets Path (11788-4193)
P.O. Box 12308 (11788-0615)
PHONE..............................631 234-0500
Richard Ross, *President*
Joseph Martorana, *President*
Bogard Lagman, *Exec VP*
Teston Kerry, *Vice Pres*
Dave Almeida, *Purch Mgr*

▲ **EMP:** 60 **EST:** 1840
SQ FT: 50,000
SALES (est): 43.4MM **Privately Held**
WEB: www.cosmeticmixers.com
SIC: 3443 3586 3559 5084 Fabricated plate work (boiler shop); measuring & dispensing pumps; chemical machinery & equipment; pharmaceutical machinery; industrial machinery & equipment

(G-5615)
CIRCOR AEROSPACE INC
Aerodyne Controls
425 Rabro Dr Ste 1 (11788-4245)
PHONE..............................631 737-1900
Daniel R Godin, *Division Mgr*
Frank Filangeri, *Mfg Staff*
Cory Jordan, *Project Engr*
Jeff Horning, *Design Engr*
Melody Pagotto, *Marketing Staff*
EMP: 70
SALES (corp-wide): 1.1B **Publicly Held**
SIC: 3483 3829 3728 Ammunition, except for small arms; measuring & controlling devices; aircraft parts & equipment
HQ: Circor Aerospace, Inc.
2301 Wardlow Cir
Corona CA 92880

(G-5616)
CITATION HEALTHCARE LABELS LLC (HQ)
55 Engineers Rd (11788-4007)
PHONE..............................631 293-4646
Richard Bolnick, *President*
Frederick Youngs, *COO*
Kelly Logiudice, *QC Mgr*
Ann Sisalli, *Senior Mgr*
EMP: 3
SALES (est): 4.7MM
SALES (corp-wide): 27.8MM **Privately Held**
SIC: 2759 Labels & seals: printing
PA: Advanced Web Technologies, Llc
600 Hoover St Ne Ste 500
Minneapolis MN 55413
612 706-3700

(G-5617)
CLEANSE TEC
360 Oser Ave (11788-3608)
PHONE..............................718 346-9111
Steven Feig, *President*
Bob Clark, *Senior VP*
Bruce Hittner, *Vice Pres*
Kenneth Mack, *Manager*
Michelle Webb, *Manager*
EMP: 29
SALES (est): 7.4MM **Privately Held**
WEB: www.soapman.com
SIC: 2841 2842 Detergents, synthetic organic or inorganic alkaline; specialty cleaning, polishes & sanitation goods

(G-5618)
CLICK IT INC
85 Corporate Dr (11788-2021)
PHONE..............................631 686-2900
James J Carey, *CEO*
Vincent Pastore, *Technical Staff*
EMP: 60
SALES (est): 11.2MM **Privately Held**
WEB: www.clickitinc.com
SIC: 3663 Television closed circuit equipment

(G-5619)
COBHAM LONG ISLAND INC
Integrted Electronic Solutions
350 Kennedy Dr (11788-4014)
PHONE..............................631 231-9100
Ed Godan, *Engineer*
William Billbrown, *Branch Mgr*
EMP: 120
SALES (corp-wide): 2.3B **Privately Held**
SIC: 3679 3621 3674 3577 Electronic circuits; motors & generators; semiconductors & related devices; computer peripheral equipment
HQ: Cobham Long Island Inc.
35 S Service Rd
Plainview NY 11803
516 694-6700

(G-5620)
COCA-COLA BTLG CO OF NY INC
375 Wireless Blvd (11788-3940)
PHONE..............................631 434-3535
Mike Chidester, *Manager*
EMP: 50
SALES (corp-wide): 31.8B **Publicly Held**
SIC: 2086 Bottled & canned soft drinks
HQ: The Coca-Cola Bottling Company Of New York Inc
2500 Windy Ridge Pkwy Se
Atlanta GA 30339
770 989-3000

(G-5621)
COLONIAL WIRE & CABLE CO INC (PA)
40 Engineers Rd (11788-4079)
PHONE..............................631 234-8500
Thomas J Walsh III, *President*
Thomas J Walsh Jr, *Chairman*
George Stubbs, *Corp Secy*
EMP: 55 **EST:** 1944
SQ FT: 100,000
SALES (est): 11.3MM **Privately Held**
WEB: www.colonialwire.com
SIC: 3357 Nonferrous wiredrawing & insulating

(G-5622)
COLONIAL WIRE CABLE CO NJ (PA)
40 Engineers Rd (11788-4079)
PHONE..............................631 234-8500
Thomas Walsh II, *Ch of Bd*
EMP: 5
SALES (est): 820.6K **Privately Held**
SIC: 3357 Nonferrous wiredrawing & insulating

(G-5623)
COMME-CI COMME-CA AP GROUP
Also Called: Male Power Apparel
380 Rabo Dr (11788)
PHONE..............................631 300-1035
Sam Baker, *President*
Marybeth Healy, *Vice Pres*
▲ **EMP:** 21
SQ FT: 12,000
SALES (est): 3.1MM **Privately Held**
WEB: www.malepower.com
SIC: 2322 2329 2339 2341 Underwear, men's & boys': made from purchased materials; bathing suits & swimwear: men's & boys'; bathing suits: women's, misses' & juniors'; panties: women's, misses', children's & infants'

(G-5624)
COMMUNICATION POWER CORP
80 Davids Dr Ste 3 (11788-2002)
PHONE..............................631 434-7306
Daniel P Myer, *President*
Richard Myer, *General Mgr*
Fred Winter, *Engineer*
Tuna Djemil, *Manager*
Maryann Russell, *Manager*
▲ **EMP:** 36
SQ FT: 11,000
SALES (est): 8.6MM **Privately Held**
WEB: www.cpcamps.com
SIC: 3663 3651 5065 Amplifiers, RF power & IF; household audio & video equipment; communication equipment

(G-5625)
CONTRACT PHARMACAL CORP
110 Plant Ave Ste 3 (11788-3830)
PHONE..............................631 231-4610
Mark Wolf, *Manager*
Tania Dejesus, *Manager*
EMP: 20
SQ FT: 48,000
SALES (corp-wide): 290.5MM **Privately Held**
SIC: 2834 Pharmaceutical preparations
PA: Contract Pharmacal Corp.
135 Adams Ave
Hauppauge NY 11788
631 231-4610

(G-5626)
CONTRACT PHARMACAL CORP
1324 Motor Pkwy (11749-5262)
PHONE..............................631 231-4610
Jeff Reingold, *Mktg Dir*
Mark Wolf, *Manager*
EMP: 125
SALES (corp-wide): 290.5MM **Privately Held**
SIC: 2834 Pharmaceutical preparations
PA: Contract Pharmacal Corp.
135 Adams Ave
Hauppauge NY 11788
631 231-4610

(G-5627)
CONTRACT PHARMACAL CORP
250 Kennedy Dr (11788-4002)
PHONE..............................631 231-4610
Matt Wolf, *CEO*
EMP: 50
SALES (corp-wide): 290.5MM **Privately Held**
SIC: 2834 Pharmaceutical preparations
PA: Contract Pharmacal Corp.
135 Adams Ave
Hauppauge NY 11788
631 231-4610

(G-5628)
CONTRACT PHARMACAL CORP
145 Oser Ave (11788-3725)
PHONE..............................631 231-4610
Mark Wolf, *President*
EMP: 79
SALES (corp-wide): 290.5MM **Privately Held**
SIC: 2834 Pharmaceutical preparations
PA: Contract Pharmacal Corp.
135 Adams Ave
Hauppauge NY 11788
631 231-4610

(G-5629)
CONTRACT PHARMACAL CORP
160 Commerce Dr (11788-3944)
PHONE..............................631 231-4610
Mark Wolf, *Manager*
EMP: 181
SALES (corp-wide): 290.5MM **Privately Held**
SIC: 2834 Vitamin preparations
PA: Contract Pharmacal Corp.
135 Adams Ave
Hauppauge NY 11788
631 231-4610

(G-5630)
CONTRACT PHARMACAL CORP
150 Commerce Dr (11788-3930)
PHONE..............................631 231-4610
Mark Wolf, *Manager*
EMP: 19
SALES (corp-wide): 290.5MM **Privately Held**
SIC: 2834 Pharmaceutical preparations
PA: Contract Pharmacal Corp.
135 Adams Ave
Hauppauge NY 11788
631 231-4610

(G-5631)
CROSSTEX INTERNATIONAL INC (HQ)
10 Ranick Rd (11788-4209)
PHONE..............................631 582-6777
Gary Steinberg, *CEO*
Bill French, *General Mgr*
Mitchell Steinberg, *Exec VP*
Jackie Beltrani, *Vice Pres*
Sheldon Fisher, *Vice Pres*
◆ **EMP:** 75
SQ FT: 63,000
SALES (est): 49.3MM
SALES (corp-wide): 918.1MM **Publicly Held**
WEB: www.crosstex.com
SIC: 3843 2621 5047 2842 Dental equipment & supplies; toweling tissue, paper; dentists' professional supplies; specialty cleaning, polishes & sanitation goods; soap & other detergents; sanitary paper products

PA: Cantel Medical Corp.
150 Clove Rd Ste 36
Little Falls NJ 07424
973 890-7220

(G-5632)
CROSSTEX INTERNATIONAL INC
2095 Express Dr N (11788-5308)
PHONE..............................631 582-6777
Jessica Lauper, *Manager*
EMP: 10
SALES (corp-wide): 918.1MM **Publicly Held**
SIC: 3843 Dental equipment & supplies
HQ: Crosstex International, Inc.
10 Ranick Rd
Hauppauge NY 11788
631 582-6777

(G-5633)
CURRAN MANUFACTURING CORP (PA)
Also Called: Royal Products
200 Oser Ave (11788-3724)
PHONE..............................631 273-1010
F Allan Curran, *Ch of Bd*
Robert Curran, *Vice Pres*
Christopher Jakubowsky, *VP Opers*
Linda Michaels, *Purch Mgr*
Lynn Telis, *Director*
▲ **EMP:** 49 **EST:** 1946
SALES (est): 10.2MM **Privately Held**
WEB: www.airchucks.com
SIC: 3545 5084 Machine tool attachments & accessories; machine tools & accessories

(G-5634)
CURRAN MANUFACTURING CORP
Also Called: Royal Products
210 Oser Ave (11788-3724)
PHONE..............................631 273-1010
Allan Curran, *President*
EMP: 50
SALES (est): 5.8MM
SALES (corp-wide): 10.2MM **Privately Held**
WEB: www.airchucks.com
SIC: 3545 Machine tool attachments & accessories
PA: Curran Manufacturing Corp
200 Oser Ave
Hauppauge NY 11788
631 273-1010

(G-5635)
DEPCO INC
20 Newton Pl (11788-4752)
PHONE..............................631 582-1995
Greg Minuto, *CEO*
David W Bean, *President*
▲ **EMP:** 10
SQ FT: 20,000
SALES (est): 1.9MM **Privately Held**
SIC: 2822 Silicone rubbers

(G-5636)
DEUTSCH RELAYS
55 Engineers Rd (11788-4007)
PHONE..............................631 342-1700
Thomas M Sadusky, *President*
Serge Belot, *Vice Pres*
Keith Gaedje, *Engineer*
EMP: 14
SALES (est): 1.8MM **Privately Held**
SIC: 3625 Relays & industrial controls

(G-5637)
DISC GRAPHICS INC
30 Gilpin Ave (11788-4724)
PHONE..............................631 300-1129
Margaret Krumholz, *President*
EMP: 150
SALES (corp-wide): 81.3MM **Privately Held**
SIC: 2657 Folding paperboard boxes
HQ: Disc Graphics, Inc.
10 Gilpin Ave
Hauppauge NY 11788
631 234-1400

(G-5638)
DISC GRAPHICS INC (HQ)
Also Called: Oliver Disc
10 Gilpin Ave (11788-4770)
PHONE.................................631 234-1400
Donald Sinkin, *CEO*
Margaret Krumholz, *President*
Stephen Frey, *Senior VP*
John A Rebecchi, *Senior VP*
Bruno Foglia, *Vice Pres*
▲ EMP: 100
SALES (est): 58.3MM
SALES (corp-wide): 81.3MM **Privately Held**
WEB: www.discgraphics.com
SIC: 2657 Folding paperboard boxes
PA: Oliver Printing & Packaging Co., Llc
　　1760 Enterprise Pkwy
　　Twinsburg OH 44087
　　330 425-7890

(G-5639)
DISPLAY LOGIC USA INC
40 Oser Ave Ste 4 (11788-3807)
PHONE.................................631 406-1922
Keith Morton, *CEO*
Andrew Blum, *Partner*
Nir Levy, *COO*
EMP: 9 EST: 2012
SALES (est): 1.4MM **Privately Held**
SIC: 3823 Digital displays of process variables

(G-5640)
DOCTOR PRINT INC (PA)
Also Called: Dr Print
18 Commerce Dr Ste 1 (11788-3975)
PHONE.................................631 873-4560
Mitch Cohen, *CEO*
Anthony Bulla, *Vice Pres*
Dan Leverich, *Vice Pres*
Will Chimienti, *Executive*
Brendan Sweeney, *Executive*
EMP: 20
SQ FT: 4,000
SALES (est): 2.7MM **Privately Held**
SIC: 2759 Laser printing

(G-5641)
DRI RELAYS INC (HQ)
Also Called: First Switchtech
60 Commerce Dr (11788-3929)
PHONE.................................631 342-1700
Michel Nespoulous, *President*
Donna Schildt, *Buyer*
Donna Vazquez, *Buyer*
Charles Peterson, *Engineer*
Joanne Dice, *Accountant*
▲ EMP: 100
SALES (est): 23MM **Privately Held**
SIC: 3625 Relays, for electronic use
PA: Financiere De Societes Techniques
　　17 Rue Vicq D Azir
　　Paris 10e Arrondissement
　　142 039-420

(G-5642)
DRIVE SHAFT SHOP INC
210 Blydenburg Rd Unit A (11749-5022)
PHONE.................................631 348-1818
Frank J Rehak III, *President*
EMP: 10
SQ FT: 1,600
SALES (est): 840K **Privately Held**
WEB: www.driveshaftshop.com
SIC: 3714 Drive shafts, motor vehicle; axle
　　housings & shafts, motor vehicle; axles,
　　motor vehicle; hydraulic fluid power
　　pumps for auto steering mechanism

(G-5643)
EATING EVOLVED INC
135 Ricefield Ln (11788-2046)
PHONE.................................516 510-2601
EMP: 7 EST: 2015
SALES (est): 732.5K **Privately Held**
SIC: 2066 Chocolate & cocoa products

(G-5644)
EBC TECHNOLOGIES LLC
Also Called: Theautopartsshop.com
200 Motor Pkwy Ste D26 (11788-5116)
PHONE.................................631 729-8182
Jay Talluri, *CEO*
EMP: 55

SALES: 5MM **Privately Held**
SIC: 3571 Electronic computers

(G-5645)
ELECTRONIC MACHINE PARTS LLC
Also Called: Emp
400 Oser Ave Ste 2050 (11788-3671)
PHONE.................................631 434-3700
Tim McAdam, *Vice Pres*
Maureen McAdam, *Mng Member*
Maureen Ramert,
EMP: 13
SALES (est): 3.1MM **Privately Held**
WEB: www.empregister.com
SIC: 3625 3823 3714 Control equipment,
　　electric; industrial instrmnts msrmnt display/control process variable; motor vehicle parts & accessories

(G-5646)
ELECTRONIC PRINTING INC
1200 Prime Pl (11788-4761)
P.O. Box 1439, New York (10276-1439)
PHONE.................................631 218-2200
John Kwiecinski, *President*
Eileen Abrams, *Office Mgr*
Paul Kwiecinski, *Shareholder*
EMP: 7
SQ FT: 9,000
SALES (est): 1.2MM **Privately Held**
WEB: www.epi-printing.com
SIC: 2752 Commercial printing, lithographic

(G-5647)
EMBASSY INDUSTRIES INC
Also Called: Franklin Manufacturing Div
315 Oser Ave Ste 1 (11788-3680)
PHONE.................................631 435-0209
Robert Ramistella, *President*
Richard Horowitz, *Chairman*
Richard Cisek, *Cust Svc Dir*
◆ EMP: 170 EST: 1950
SQ FT: 75,000
SALES (est): 19.1MM
SALES (corp-wide): 629.1MM **Privately Held**
WEB: www.embassyind.com
SIC: 3433 1711 3567 Heating equipment,
　　except electric; plumbing, heating, airconditioning contractors; industrial furnaces & ovens
PA: Mestek, Inc.
　　260 N Elm St
　　Westfield MA 01085
　　470 898-4533

(G-5648)
ET OAKES CORPORATION
686 Old Willets Path (11788-4102)
PHONE.................................631 232-0002
W Peter Oakes, *Ch of Bd*
Robert Peck, *Vice Pres*
EMP: 20
SQ FT: 25,000
SALES (est): 5.2MM **Privately Held**
WEB: www.oakes.com
SIC: 3556 3531 5084 3599 Cutting,
　　chopping, grinding, mixing & similar machinery; construction machinery; food product manufacturing machinery; machine shop, jobbing & repair

(G-5649)
FB LABORATORIES INC
Also Called: Futurebiotics
70 Commerce Dr (11788-3962)
PHONE.................................631 963-6450
Saiful Kibria, *President*
Kerilee Crennan, *Purch Mgr*
Margaret Artes, *Purchasing*
▲ EMP: 50 EST: 2010
SALES (est): 11.4MM **Privately Held**
SIC: 2834 Vitamin preparations

(G-5650)
FINISH LINE TECHNOLOGIES INC (PA)
50 Wireless Blvd (11788-3954)
PHONE.................................631 666-7300
Henry J Krause, *President*
◆ EMP: 28
SQ FT: 60,000
SALES: 11.2MM **Privately Held**
SIC: 2992 Lubricating oils & greases

(G-5651)
FIXTURES 2000 INC
Also Called: Premier Store Fixtures
400 Oser Ave Ste 350 (11788-3632)
P.O. Box 14177 (11788-0401)
PHONE.................................631 236-4100
Jose Tellez, *President*
Oswaldo Zurita, *Senior VP*
Nelson Goodman, *Vice Pres*
◆ EMP: 280
SQ FT: 230,978
SALES (est): 67.2MM **Privately Held**
WEB: www.premierfixtures.com
SIC: 2542 Fixtures, store: except wood

(G-5652)
FLUID MECHANISMS HAUPPAUGE INC
225 Engineers Rd (11788-4020)
PHONE.................................631 234-0100
Richard Coronato, *President*
Charlotte Coronato, *Corp Secy*
EMP: 35 EST: 1962
SQ FT: 44,000
SALES (est): 9.8MM **Privately Held**
SIC: 3728 Aircraft parts & equipment

(G-5653)
FORECAST CONSOLES INC
681 Old Willets Path (11788-4109)
PHONE.................................631 253-9000
William Haberman, *President*
Ryan Haberman, *General Mgr*
Janet Haberman, *CFO*
▲ EMP: 24
SQ FT: 21,000
SALES (est): 4MM **Privately Held**
WEB: www.forecast-consoles.com
SIC: 2511 2531 2521 2541 Console tables: wood; public building & related furniture; wood office furniture; shelving, office & store, wood; office furniture, except wood

(G-5654)
FOREST LABORATORIES LLC
45 Adams Ave (11788-3605)
PHONE.................................212 421-7850
EMP: 54 **Privately Held**
SIC: 2834 Mfg Pharmaceutical Preparations
HQ: Forest Laboratories, Llc
　　909 3rd Ave Fl 23
　　New York NY 10022
　　212 421-7850

(G-5655)
FUNGILAB INC
89 Cabot Ct Ste K (11788-3719)
PHONE.................................631 750-6361
Ernest Buira, *CEO*
Joan Buira, *President*
◆ EMP: 5
SQ FT: 10,000
SALES: 1MM
SALES (corp-wide): 2.9MM **Privately Held**
SIC: 3821 Laboratory apparatus & furniture
PA: Fungi Lab Sa
　　Calle Constitucio (Pg Ind Les Grases),
　　64 - Nave 15
　　Sant Feliu De Llobregat 08980
　　936 853-500

(G-5656)
FUTUREBIOTICS LLC
70 Commerce Dr (11788-3936)
PHONE.................................631 273-6300
Steve Welling, *COO*
Steve Tuohey, *Research*
Cindy Warsaw, *Controller*
Saiful Kaibria, *Mng Member*
Martin Gora, *Software Dev*
◆ EMP: 25
SALES (est): 5.4MM **Privately Held**
WEB: www.futurebiotics.com
SIC: 2834 Medicines, capsuled or ampuled

(G-5657)
GENERAL SEMICONDUCTOR INC
150 Motor Pkwy Ste 101 (11788-5167)
PHONE.................................631 300-3818
Linda Perry, *Executive*
EMP: 6 EST: 2015

SALES (est): 313.3K **Privately Held**
SIC: 3674 Semiconductors & related devices

(G-5658)
GENERIC PHARMACEUTICAL SVCS
Also Called: Gpsi
1324 Motor Pkwy Ste 114 (11749-5226)
PHONE.................................631 348-6900
Harold Grossman, *President*
James Hassenfeld, *Corp Secy*
Paul Buchbauer, *Vice Pres*
Ann Costanza, *Officer*
Robyn Wolf, *Officer*
▲ EMP: 38
SQ FT: 20,000
SALES (est): 6.7MM **Privately Held**
WEB: www.poucher.com
SIC: 2834 Pharmaceutical preparations

(G-5659)
GEOSYNC MICROWAVE INC
320 Oser Ave (11788-3608)
PHONE.................................631 760-5567
Arthur Faverio, *President*
Stephen Philips, *Vice Pres*
Israel Moskovitch, *Engineer*
Faisal Zahidi, *Engineer*
Richard Bova, *Consultant*
EMP: 5
SQ FT: 4,000
SALES (est): 1.2MM **Privately Held**
WEB: www.geosyncmicrowave.com
SIC: 3663 Satellites, communications

(G-5660)
GES GES
89 Cabot Ct Ste A (11788-3719)
PHONE.................................631 291-9624
Sarken Dressler, *Project Mgr*
EMP: 5
SALES (est): 604.7K **Privately Held**
SIC: 2834 Liniments

(G-5661)
GLARO INC
735 Calebs Path Ste 1 (11788-4201)
PHONE.................................631 234-1717
Neal Glass, *President*
Robert Betensky, *Exec VP*
Kerry Betensky, *Vice Pres*
Jonathan Leonhardt, *Accounts Exec*
Lin Hou, *Admin Asst*
▲ EMP: 60 EST: 1945
SQ FT: 50,000
SALES (est): 9.6MM **Privately Held**
WEB: www.glaro.com
SIC: 2542 Office & store showcases & display fixtures

(G-5662)
GOURMET FACTORY INC
55 Corporate Dr (11788-2021)
PHONE.................................631 231-4548
Andromahi Kangadis, *Owner*
Ana Martinez, *Accountant*
Andrew Marsano, *Sales Staff*
Brian Yarmeisch, *Manager*
EMP: 5
SALES: 110.5K **Privately Held**
SIC: 2079 Cooking oils, except corn: vegetable refined

(G-5663)
GRAND PRIX LITHO INC
400 Oser Ave Ste 2300 (11788-3674)
PHONE.................................631 242-4182
Craig Lennon, *President*
EMP: 25 EST: 1968
SALES: 4MM **Privately Held**
WEB: www.grandprixlitho.com
SIC: 2752 Commercial printing, offset

(G-5664)
GSE COMPOSITES INC
110 Oser Ave (11788-3820)
P.O. Box 13248 (11788-0593)
PHONE.................................631 389-1300
EMP: 14
SALES (est): 1.9MM **Privately Held**
SIC: 3089 Mfg Plastic Products

▲ = Import ▼=Export
◆ =Import/Export

(G-5665)
HAIG PRESS INC
Also Called: Haig Graphic Communications
690 Old Willets Path (11788-4102)
PHONE..............................631 582-5800
James Kalousdian, *Ch of Bd*
Steve Kalousdian, *Vice Pres*
EMP: 44
SQ FT: 30,000
SALES: 7.9MM **Privately Held**
WEB: www.haiggraphic.com
SIC: 2752 2789 2759 Commercial print-
ing, offset; bookbinding & related work;
commercial printing

(G-5666)
HALLMARK HLTH CARE
SLTIONS LLC
200 Motor Pkwy Ste D26 (11788-5116)
PHONE..............................516 513-0959
Isaac Ullatil, *CEO*
Shiv Prakash Bidlur,
Jayasekhar Talluri,
EMP: 10
SQ FT: 2,400
SALES: 3MM **Privately Held**
SIC: 7372 Prepackaged software

(G-5667)
HARMONIC DRIVE LLC
89 Cabot Ct Ste A (11788-3719)
PHONE..............................631 231-6630
Douglas Olson, *President*
EMP: 6 **Privately Held**
WEB: www.harmonic-drive.com
SIC: 3566 Speed changers, drives & gears
HQ: Harmonic Drive L.L.C.
247 Lynnfield St
Peabody MA 01960

(G-5668)
HAUPPAUGE COMPUTER
WORKS INC (HQ)
Also Called: Hauppauge Cmpt Dgtal Erope
Sarl
909 Motor Pkwy (11788-5250)
PHONE..............................631 434-1600
Kenneth Plotkin, *Ch of Bd*
Sheila Easop, *Prdtn Mgr*
Gerald Tucciarone, *CFO*
Brice Washington, *Technical Staff*
▲ EMP: 25
SQ FT: 85,000
SALES: 9MM **Publicly Held**
WEB: www.happage.com
SIC: 3577 7371 Computer peripheral
equipment; custom computer program-
ming services

(G-5669)
HAUPPAUGE DIGITAL INC (PA)
909 Motor Pkwy (11788-5250)
PHONE..............................631 434-1600
Kenneth Plotkin, *Ch of Bd*
John Casey, *President*
Ron Petralia, *Vice Pres*
Gerald Tucciarone, *CFO*
Cheryl Willins, *Controller*
▲ EMP: 28
SALES: 34MM **Publicly Held**
WEB: www.hauppage.com
SIC: 3577 Computer peripheral equipment

(G-5670)
HI-TRON SEMICONDUCTOR
CORP
85 Engineers Rd (11788-4003)
PHONE..............................631 231-1500
Mel Lax, *President*
Mindy Lax, *Admin Sec*
EMP: 20 EST: 1964
SQ FT: 42,000
SALES (est): 1.4MM **Privately Held**
SIC: 3674 Semiconductors & related de-
vices

(G-5671)
HILORD CHEMICAL
CORPORATION
70 Engineers Rd (11788-4076)
PHONE..............................631 234-7373
Donald Balbinder, *President*
Cody Sickle, *Vice Pres*
Shawnee Sicke, *Treasurer*
Michael Lani, *Information Mgr*

Terry Sickle, *Admin Sec*
▲ EMP: 26 EST: 1970
SQ FT: 37,000
SALES (est): 6.3MM **Privately Held**
WEB: www.hilord.com
SIC: 3861 2822 3479 Toners, prepared
photographic (not made in chemical
plants); ethylene-propylene rubbers,
EPDM polymers; coating electrodes

(G-5672)
HOHMANN & BARNARD INC
(DH)
30 Rasons Ct (11788-4206)
P.O. Box 5270 (11788-0270)
PHONE..............................631 234-0600
Ronald P Hohmann Sr, *Principal*
Christopher Hohmann, *Corp Secy*
Joseph C Carr, *Director*
Gene Toombs, *Director*
▲ EMP: 25
SQ FT: 55,000
SALES (est): 43.4MM
SALES (corp-wide): 225.3B **Publicly**
Held
WEB: www.foamfiller.com
SIC: 3496 3462 3315 Clips & fasteners,
made from purchased wire; iron & steel
forgings; steel wire & related products
HQ: Mitek Industries, Inc.
16023 Swinly Rdg
Chesterfield MO 63017
314 434-1200

(G-5673)
HUCKLEBERRY INC
Also Called: Minuteman Press
655 Old Willets Path (11788-4105)
PHONE..............................631 630-5450
Robin Eschenberg, *President*
EMP: 6
SALES (est): 1.1MM **Privately Held**
SIC: 2752 Commercial printing, litho-
graphic

(G-5674)
I MEGLIO CORP
1140 Motor Pkwy Ste C (11788-5255)
PHONE..............................631 617-6900
Barbara Khanat, *President*
David Suarez, *Vice Pres*
EMP: 30
SALES: 67MM **Privately Held**
SIC: 2431 5031 Millwork; millwork

(G-5675)
ICONIX INC
40 Oser Ave Ste 4 (11788-3807)
PHONE..............................516 513-1420
Jacob Kohn, *Ch of Bd*
Debbie Koebel, *Bookkeeper*
Brian Baker, *Sales Mgr*
Lori Morra, *Sales Staff*
EMP: 18
SQ FT: 6,200
SALES: 9.1MM **Privately Held**
SIC: 3699 5065 Electrical equipment &
supplies; electronic parts & equipment

(G-5676)
INNOVATIVE LABS LLC
85 Commerce Dr (11788-3902)
PHONE..............................631 231-5522
Frank Amelio Sr, *CEO*
Frank D Amelio Jr, *President*
Dean Lafemina, *Vice Pres*
EMP: 60
SQ FT: 25,000
SALES: 10MM **Privately Held**
WEB: www.innovativelabsny.com
SIC: 2834 Tablets, pharmaceutical; medi-
cines, capsuled or ampuled

(G-5677)
INNOVATIVE VIDEO TECH INC
Also Called: Invid Tech
355 Oser Ave (11788-3607)
PHONE..............................631 388-5700
Joe Troiano, *President*
Lou Giannizzero, *Accounts Mgr*
◆ EMP: 13
SQ FT: 10,000
SALES (est): 1.5MM **Privately Held**
SIC: 3699 Security control equipment &
systems

(G-5678)
INVAGEN PHARMACEUTICALS
INC (DH)
7 Oser Ave Ste 4 (11788-3811)
PHONE..............................631 231-3233
Sudhakar Vidiyala, *President*
Kiran Kanneganti, *Research*
Bala Vattikuti, *Research*
Amina Ali, *Human Res Mgr*
Ram Kathuroju, *Research Analys*
▲ EMP: 330
SQ FT: 150,000
SALES (est): 117.2MM
SALES (corp-wide): 1.6B **Privately Held**
SIC: 2834 5122 Pharmaceutical prepara-
tions; pharmaceuticals

(G-5679)
J & M PACKAGING INC
Also Called: Baron Packaging
21 Newton Rd (11788-1646)
P.O. Box 5783 (11788-0164)
PHONE..............................631 608-3069
Melissa Vincente, *CEO*
John Vincente, *Vice Pres*
EMP: 10
SQ FT: 7,500
SALES (est): 162.8K **Privately Held**
SIC: 2653 2449 3086 Boxes, corrugated:
made from purchased materials; rectan-
gular boxes & crates, wood; plastics foam
products

(G-5680)
JACK MERKEL INC
1720 Express Dr S (11788-5302)
PHONE..............................631 234-2600
Jack Merkel, *President*
Scott Merkel, *General Mgr*
EMP: 5
SQ FT: 6,000
SALES: 800K **Privately Held**
SIC: 3599 7538 Machine shop, jobbing &
repair; engine repair; engine rebuilding:
automotive

(G-5681)
JOSH PACKAGING INC
245 Marcus Blvd Ste 1 (11788-2000)
PHONE..............................631 822-1660
Abraham Golshirazian, *Ch of Bd*
Abe Gulsh, *President*
Nejat Rahmani, *Vice Pres*
▲ EMP: 20
SQ FT: 30,000
SALES (est): 5MM **Privately Held**
SIC: 2673 5113 5162 Plastic bags: made
from purchased materials; industrial &
personal service paper; plastics materials

(G-5682)
KILTRONX ENVIRO SYSTEMS
CORP
330 Motor Pkwy 15thfl (11788-5104)
PHONE..............................917 971-7177
Garu Beutler, *President*
Arlen Cabale, *Controller*
EMP: 30
SQ FT: 1,500
SALES: 400K **Privately Held**
SIC: 2295 Chemically coated & treated
fabrics

(G-5683)
KINGS PARK ASPHALT
CORPORATION
201 Moreland Rd Ste 2 (11788-3922)
PHONE..............................631 269-9774
Michael Farino, *President*
James Farino, *Corp Secy*
Paul Farino, *Vice Pres*
EMP: 5
SQ FT: 1,000
SALES (est): 649.2K **Privately Held**
SIC: 2951 Asphalt paving blocks (not from
refineries)

(G-5684)
KINPLEX CORP (PA)
325 Wireless Blvd Ste 1 (11788-3973)
PHONE..............................631 242-4800
Penny Hunter, *President*
Penny S Hunter, *President*
Daniel Schwartz, *Vice Pres*
Byron Galloway, *Elder*

◆ EMP: 50
SALES (est): 77.7MM **Privately Held**
SIC: 3589 Commercial cooking & food-
warming equipment

(G-5685)
KLD LABS INC
55 Cabot Ct (11788-3717)
PHONE..............................631 549-4222
Steven Magnus, *President*
Carlo Sgroi, *Engineer*
Joseph Schipper, *Sr Software Eng*
Tom O'Brien, *Director*
EMP: 40
SQ FT: 20,000
SALES (est): 9.4MM **Privately Held**
WEB: www.kldlabs.com
SIC: 3829 7373 Measuring & controlling
devices; computer integrated systems de-
sign

(G-5686)
L3 TECHNOLOGIES INC
Narda-Miteq Division
435 Moreland Rd (11788-3926)
PHONE..............................631 231-1700
Joe Merenda, *President*
John Mega, *Division Pres*
EMP: 300
SALES (corp-wide): 6.8B **Publicly Held**
SIC: 3663 Telemetering equipment, elec-
tronic
HQ: L3 Technologies, Inc.
600 3rd Ave Fl 34
New York NY 10016
212 697-1111

(G-5687)
L3 TECHNOLOGIES INC
Also Called: L-3 Narda-Miteq
100 Davids Dr (11788-2043)
PHONE..............................631 436-7400
Steven Skpock, *President*
EMP: 700
SALES (corp-wide): 6.8B **Publicly Held**
SIC: 3663 3769 3661 3651 Radio & TV
communications equipment; guided mis-
sile & space vehicle parts & auxiliary
equipment; telephone & telegraph appa-
ratus; household audio & video equip-
ment; current-carrying wiring devices
HQ: L3 Technologies, Inc.
600 3rd Ave Fl 34
New York NY 10016
212 697-1111

(G-5688)
L3 TECHNOLOGIES INC
Also Called: Narda Satellite Networks
435 Moreland Rd (11788-3926)
PHONE..............................631 231-1700
Margaret Pawelko, *Administration*
EMP: 100
SQ FT: 60,000
SALES (corp-wide): 6.8B **Publicly Held**
SIC: 3663 8748 5731 Telemetering equip-
ment, electronic; communications consult-
ing; antennas, satellite dish
HQ: L3 Technologies, Inc.
600 3rd Ave Fl 34
New York NY 10016
212 697-1111

(G-5689)
L3 TECHNOLOGIES INC
Also Called: L-3 Narda-Miteq
330 Oser Ave (11788-3630)
PHONE..............................631 436-7400
Aksel Kiiss, *Manager*
EMP: 100
SALES (corp-wide): 6.8B **Publicly Held**
SIC: 3663 Radio broadcasting & communi-
cations equipment
HQ: L3 Technologies, Inc.
600 3rd Ave Fl 34
New York NY 10016
212 697-1111

(G-5690)
LA FLOR PRODUCTS COMPANY
INC (PA)
Also Called: La Flor Spices
25 Hoffman Ave (11788-4717)
PHONE..............................631 851-9601
Ruben La Torre Sr, *President*
Dan La Torre, *Exec VP*

Justin Latorre, *Exec VP*
Ruben La Torre Jr, *Vice Pres*
Chris Pappas, *Vice Pres*
▲ **EMP:** 44
SQ FT: 90,000
SALES: 9MM **Privately Held**
WEB: www.laflor.com
SIC: 2099 Seasonings & spices; seasonings: dry mixes

(G-5691)
**LEHNEIS ORTHOTICS
PROSTHETIC**
517 Route 111 Ste 300 (11788-4338)
PHONE..................................516 790-1897
Alfred Lehneis, *President*
EMP: 9
SALES (corp-wide): 5MM **Privately Held**
WEB: www.lehneis.com
SIC: 3842 5047 5999 Limbs, artificial;
medical equipment & supplies; artificial
limbs
PA: Lehneis Orthotics & Prosthetic Associates Ltd
13 Bedells Landing Rd
Roslyn NY
516 621-7277

(G-5692)
LISTEC VIDEO CORP (PA)
90 Oser Ave (11788-3800)
PHONE..................................631 273-3029
William J Littler, *Ch of Bd*
Joanne Camarda, *President*
Raymond Blumenthal, *Vice Pres*
EMP: 5
SQ FT: 3,000
SALES (est): 450.1K **Privately Held**
WEB: www.listecny.com
SIC: 3663 5099 Radio & TV communications equipment; video & audio equipment

(G-5693)
LIVING WELL INNOVATIONS INC
115 Engineers Rd (11788-4005)
PHONE..................................646 517-3200
Arthur Danziger, *President*
EMP: 6
SQ FT: 4,000
SALES (est): 4MM **Privately Held**
SIC: 2731 5192 Book publishing; books

(G-5694)
LNK INTERNATIONAL INC
22 Arkay Dr (11788-3708)
PHONE..................................631 435-3500
EMP: 100
SALES (corp-wide): 103.7MM **Privately Held**
SIC: 2834 Pharmaceutical preparations
PA: L.N.K. International Inc.
60 Arkay Dr
Hauppauge NY 11788
631 435-3500

(G-5695)
LNK INTERNATIONAL INC
100 Ricefield Ln (11788-2008)
PHONE..................................631 435-3500
Chudgar Pk, *Manager*
EMP: 100
SALES (corp-wide): 103.7MM **Privately Held**
SIC: 2834 Pharmaceutical preparations
PA: L.N.K. International Inc.
60 Arkay Dr
Hauppauge NY 11788
631 435-3500

(G-5696)
LNK INTERNATIONAL INC
325 Kennedy Dr (11788-4006)
PHONE..................................631 435-3500
Joseph J Mollica, *President*
EMP: 100
SALES (corp-wide): 103.7MM **Privately Held**
SIC: 2834 Pharmaceutical preparations
PA: L.N.K. International Inc.
60 Arkay Dr
Hauppauge NY 11788
631 435-3500

(G-5697)
LNK INTERNATIONAL INC
145 Ricefield Ln (11788-2007)
PHONE..................................631 543-3787
Pk Chudgar, *Manager*
EMP: 100
SALES (corp-wide): 103.7MM **Privately Held**
SIC: 2834 Pharmaceutical preparations
PA: L.N.K. International Inc.
60 Arkay Dr
Hauppauge NY 11788
631 435-3500

(G-5698)
LNK INTERNATIONAL INC
40 Arkay Dr (11788-3708)
PHONE..................................631 435-3500
Shaji Kumar Varghese, *Branch Mgr*
EMP: 100
SALES (corp-wide): 103.7MM **Privately Held**
SIC: 2834 Pharmaceutical preparations
PA: L.N.K. International Inc.
60 Arkay Dr
Hauppauge NY 11788
631 435-3500

(G-5699)
LNK INTERNATIONAL INC
55 Arkay Dr (11788-3707)
PHONE..................................631 231-4020
Joseph J Mollica Sr, *Branch Mgr*
EMP: 100
SALES (corp-wide): 103.7MM **Privately Held**
SIC: 2834 Pharmaceutical preparations
PA: L.N.K. International Inc.
60 Arkay Dr
Hauppauge NY 11788
631 435-3500

(G-5700)
LOURDES INDUSTRIES INC (PA)
65 Hoffman Ave (11788-4798)
PHONE..................................631 234-6600
William J Jakobsen, *Ch of Bd*
Bruce Jacobson, *Vice Pres*
Peter McKenna, *Vice Pres*
Paul Vaughan, *Opers Mgr*
Kevin Cullinan, *Mfg Staff*
EMP: 90 **EST:** 1954
SQ FT: 26,000
SALES (est): 21.4MM **Privately Held**
SIC: 3795 3492 3643 3724 Tanks & tank components; fluid power valves & hose fittings; current-carrying wiring devices; aircraft engines & engine parts; engineering services

(G-5701)
LOURDES SYSTEMS INC
21 Newton Pl (11788-4815)
PHONE..................................631 234-7077
George Powell, *Ch of Bd*
Peter Maguire, *President*
George Meyerle, *Vice Pres*
Peter McKenna, *Treasurer*
EMP: 12
SQ FT: 5,000
SALES (est): 1.3MM **Privately Held**
SIC: 3542 Machine tools, metal forming type

(G-5702)
M&C ASSOCIATES LLC
700 Vets Memrl Hwy 335 (11788)
PHONE..................................631 467-8760
Lou Marianacci, *President*
Leanora Gordon, *Principal*
Karen Ferraro, *Vice Pres*
Kelly Palacios, *Vice Pres*
Susan Garafola, *Opers Staff*
EMP: 40
SALES (est): 6.9MM **Privately Held**
SIC: 3571 Electronic computers

(G-5703)
MACHINERY MOUNTINGS INC
41 Sarah Dr (11788)
PHONE..................................631 851-0480
Bernard H Kass, *President*
Steven Kass, *Vice Pres*
Wayne Kass, *Vice Pres*
EMP: 14

SALES (est): 1.6MM **Privately Held**
SIC: 3499 Machine bases, metal

(G-5704)
MAGGIO DATA FORMS
1735 Express Dr S (11788)
PHONE..................................631 348-0343
Robert Maggio, *President*
James Maggio, *Vice Pres*
EMP: 110
SQ FT: 30,000
SALES (est): 16MM **Privately Held**
WEB: www.maggio.com
SIC: 2761 Manifold business forms

(G-5705)
MAKAMAH ENTERPRISES INC
Also Called: S.W.H. Precision Industries
89 Cabot Ct Ste C (11788-3719)
PHONE..................................631 231-0200
Christopher J Thomas, *President*
▲ **EMP:** 10
SALES (est): 1.2MM **Privately Held**
SIC: 3599 Machine shop, jobbing & repair

(G-5706)
MAKERS NUTRITION LLC (PA)
315 Oser Ave Ste 1 (11788-3680)
PHONE..................................631 456-5397
Jason Provenzano, *President*
Stephen Finnegan, *Senior VP*
John Skijus, *Accounts Exec*
EMP: 25 **EST:** 2014
SALES: 25MM **Privately Held**
SIC: 2023 Dietary supplements, dairy & non-dairy based

(G-5707)
MANHATTAN SHADE & GLASS CO INC
135 Ricefield Ln (11788-2046)
PHONE..................................212 288-5616
EMP: 32
SALES (corp-wide): 6.8MM **Privately Held**
WEB: www.manhattanshade.com
SIC: 3231 3211 2591 Products of purchased glass; window glass, clear & colored; shade, curtain & drapery hardware
PA: Manhattan Shade & Glass Co. Inc.
37 Pond Park Rd
Great Neck NY 11023
212 288-5616

(G-5708)
MASON INDUSTRIES INC (PA)
Also Called: M I
350 Rabro Dr (11788-4237)
P.O. Box 410, Smithtown (11787-0410)
PHONE..................................631 348-0282
Norm Mason, *Ch of Bd*
Patrick Lama, *Vice Pres*
Patricia Gerwycki, *Export Mgr*
Jenny King, *Purchasing*
Ian Azrak, *Engineer*
◆ **EMP:** 165 **EST:** 1958
SQ FT: 60,000
SALES (est): 51.6MM **Privately Held**
WEB: www.mercer-rubber.com
SIC: 3625 3829 3052 3069 Noise control equipment; measuring & controlling devices; rubber hose; hard rubber & molded rubber products; fabricated structural metal; electronic connectors

(G-5709)
MASON INDUSTRIES INC
33 Ranick Rd Ste 1 (11788-4250)
PHONE..................................631 348-0282
Patricia Gowicki, *Manager*
EMP: 7
SALES (corp-wide): 51.6MM **Privately Held**
SIC: 3625 Noise control equipment
PA: Mason Industries, Inc.
350 Rabro Dr
Hauppauge NY 11788
631 348-0282

(G-5710)
MCKEE FOODS CORPORATION
111 Serene Pl (11788-3534)
PHONE..................................631 979-9364
EMP: 609

SALES (corp-wide): 1.6B **Privately Held**
WEB: www.mckeefoods.com
SIC: 2051 Cakes, bakery: except frozen
PA: Mckee Foods Corporation
10260 Mckee Rd
Collegedale TN 37315
423 238-7111

(G-5711)
MEDICAL ACTION INDUSTRIES INC
150 Motor Pkwy Ste 205 (11788-5180)
PHONE..................................631 231-4600
Carmine Morello, *Vice Pres*
Paul Meringola, *Manager*
EMP: 215 **Publicly Held**
WEB: www.medical-action.com
SIC: 3842 4226 5999 5047 Sponges, surgical; sterilizers, hospital & surgical; surgical appliances & supplies; special warehousing & storage; medical apparatus & supplies; hospital equipment & furniture
HQ: Medical Action Industries Inc.
25 Heywood Rd
Arden NC 28704
631 231-4600

(G-5712)
MELLAND GEAR INSTR OF HUPPAUGE
225 Engineers Rd (11788-4020)
PHONE..................................631 234-0100
Richard Coronato Sr, *CEO*
Richard C Coronato, *CEO*
Charlotte Coronato, *Admin Sec*
EMP: 35 **EST:** 1959
SQ FT: 44,000
SALES (est): 5.7MM **Privately Held**
SIC: 3824 3545 Mechanical counters; precision tools, machinists'

(G-5713)
MERCER RUBBER CO
350 Rabro Dr (11788-4257)
PHONE..................................631 348-0282
Norman J Mason, *President*
Mary P Ryan, *Corp Secy*
Pat Lama, *Vice Pres*
Mae Ryan, *Controller*
▲ **EMP:** 150 **EST:** 1866
SQ FT: 60,000
SALES (est): 25MM
SALES (corp-wide): 51.6MM **Privately Held**
WEB: www.mercer-rubber.com
SIC: 3069 3052 Expansion joints, rubber; rubber hose
PA: Mason Industries, Inc.
350 Rabro Dr
Hauppauge NY 11788
631 348-0282

(G-5714)
MERGENCE STUDIOS LTD
135 Ricefield Ln (11788-2046)
PHONE..................................212 288-5616
▲ **EMP:** 12
SALES (est): 1.5MM **Privately Held**
SIC: 2241 Narrow Fabric Mill Misc Personal Services

(G-5715)
METAL DYNAMICS INTL CORP
Also Called: Mdi
25 Corporate Dr (11788-2021)
P.O. Box 13248 (11788-0593)
PHONE..................................631 231-1153
Daniel Shybunko, *President*
Tomas Scully, *Principal*
Anne D Shybunko-Moore, *Principal*
Tom Scully, *Sales Mgr*
◆ **EMP:** 5
SQ FT: 28,600
SALES (est): 723.1K **Privately Held**
WEB: www.metaldynamicsintl.com
SIC: 3728 Aircraft parts & equipment

(G-5716)
MICROCAD TRNING CONSULTING INC
77 Arkay Dr Ste C2 (11788-3742)
PHONE..................................631 291-9484
Michael F Frey, *Branch Mgr*
EMP: 7 **Privately Held**

SIC: 7372 Prepackaged software
PA: Microcad Training & Consulting, Inc.
440 Arsenal St Ste 3
Watertown MA

(G-5717)
MICROCHIP TECHNOLOGY INC
80 Arkay Dr Ste 100 (11788-3705)
PHONE..........................631 233-3280
Daniel Thornton, *Engineer*
Dan Levesser, *Manager*
Marco Forcone, *Senior Mgr*
EMP: 6
SALES (corp-wide): 5.3B Publicly Held
WEB: www.microchip.com
SIC: 3674 Microcircuits, integrated (semi-conductor)
PA: Microchip Technology Inc
2355 W Chandler Blvd
Chandler AZ 85224
480 792-7200

(G-5718)
MICROSOFT CORPORATION
2929 Expressway Dr N # 300 (11749-5302)
PHONE..........................516 380-1531
Brett Tanzer, *Manager*
EMP: 100
SALES (corp-wide): 125.8B Publicly
Held
WEB: www.microsoft.com
SIC: 7372 Application computer software
PA: Microsoft Corporation
1 Microsoft Way
Redmond WA 98052
425 882-8080

(G-5719)
MILSO INDUSTRIES INC
25 Engineers Rd (11788-4019)
PHONE..........................631 234-1133
Al Orsi, *Branch Mgr*
EMP: 12
SQ FT: 10,000
SALES (corp-wide): 1.6B Publicly Held
SIC: 3995 5087 Burial caskets; caskets
HQ: Milso Industries Inc.
534 Union St
Brooklyn NY 11215
718 624-4593

(G-5720)
MINI GRAPHICS INC
Also Called: Mgi
140 Commerce Dr (11788-3948)
PHONE..........................516 223-6464
James Delise, *CEO*
Charles J Delise, *Principal*
Steven Delise, *Principal*
Mark Dlhopolsky, *Project Mgr*
George Heinsohn, *Purch Mgr*
EMP: 100
SALES (est): 23.3MM Privately Held
WEB: www.minigraphics.net
SIC: 2759 Commercial printing

(G-5721)
MMC ENTERPRISES CORP
175 Commerce Dr Ste E (11788-3920)
PHONE..........................800 435-1088
Jin Sun, *President*
▲ EMP: 8
SALES (est): 972.6K Privately Held
SIC: 3826 Instruments measuring magnetic & electrical properties

(G-5722)
MOBILE FLEET INC (PA)
10 Commerce Dr (11788-3968)
P.O. Box 1240, Farmingdale (11735-0855)
PHONE..........................631 206-2920
Robert E Squicciarini Sr, *CEO*
Jennifer Clark, *Principal*
Kevin Walker, *Vice Pres*
Matt Tannenbaum, *CFO*
Daniel Bittner, *Cust Mgr*
▼ EMP: 43
SQ FT: 16,500
SALES: 15MM Privately Held
SIC: 3647 Automotive lighting fixtures

(G-5723)
MONITOR ELEVATOR PRODUCTS LLC
Also Called: Monitor Controls
125 Ricefield Ln (11788-2007)
PHONE..........................631 543-4334
Paul Horney, *President*
Steve Goldberg, *General Mgr*
Kathryn Byszewski, *Vice Pres*
Bill Higbee, *Production*
Mike Sable, *Controller*
▲ EMP: 65 EST: 2011
SQ FT: 30,000
SALES (est): 16.6MM
SALES (corp-wide): 52MM Privately
Held
WEB: www.mcontrols.com
SIC: 3534 Elevators & equipment
PA: Innovation Industries, Inc.
3500 E Main St
Russellville AR 72802
800 843-1004

(G-5724)
MTC INDUSTRIES INC (PA)
255 Oser Ave Ste 1 (11788-3765)
PHONE..........................631 274-4818
Jimmy Wang, *CEO*
Rodger Jonas, *Vice Pres*
Lisa Wang, *CFO*
Matthew Lee, *Sales Mgr*
Emma Karp, *Marketing Staff*
◆ EMP: 10
SQ FT: 15,000
SALES (est): 4.3MM Privately Held
WEB: www.mtcindustries.com
SIC: 2834 Pharmaceutical preparations

(G-5725)
NATUS MEDICAL INCORPORATED
Also Called: Neometrics
150 Motor Pkwy Ste 106 (11788-5167)
PHONE..........................631 457-4430
Joe Amato, *Principal*
Drew Davies, *Exec VP*
Ivan Pandiyan, *Vice Pres*
Doni Antonelli, *Project Mgr*
Christina Rossi, *Consultant*
EMP: 8
SALES (corp-wide): 530.8MM Publicly
Held
SIC: 3845 Electromedical equipment
PA: Natus Medical Incorporated
6701 Koll Center Pkwy # 12
Pleasanton CA 94566
925 223-6700

(G-5726)
NEOPOST USA INC
415 Oser Ave Ste K (11788-3637)
PHONE..........................631 435-9100
Joanne Lafrance, *Principal*
EMP: 50
SALES (corp-wide): 38.4MM Privately
Held
SIC: 3579 7359 7629 Postage meters; business machine & electronic equipment rental services; business machine repair, electric
HQ: Neopost Usa Inc.
478 Wheelers Farms Rd
Milford CT 06461
203 301-3400

(G-5727)
NEW HORIZON GRAPHICS INC
1200 Prime Pl (11788-4761)
PHONE..........................631 231-8055
Anthony Guida, *Chairman*
Annette Guida, *Corp Secy*
Anthony Trapani, *Plant Mgr*
Frank Montwill, *Production*
EMP: 45
SQ FT: 25,000
SALES (est): 10.4MM Privately Held
WEB: www.newhorizongraphic.com
SIC: 2752 2675 Commercial printing, offset; cards, folders & mats: die-cut

(G-5728)
NOVA SCIENCE PUBLISHERS INC
415 Oser Ave Ste N (11788-3678)
PHONE..........................631 231-7269

Frank Columbus, *President*
Nadezhda Columbus, *Vice Pres*
Harold G Carmona, *Manager*
EMP: 12
SALES (est): 1.9MM Privately Held
SIC: 2721 2731 Magazines: publishing only, not printed on site; book publishing

(G-5729)
NUBIAN HERITAGE
367 Old Willets Path (11788-1217)
PHONE..........................631 265-3551
Edwin McCray, *Owner*
EMP: 5
SALES (est): 274.2K Privately Held
SIC: 3999 5199 Fire extinguishers, portable; gifts & novelties

(G-5730)
OLAN LABORATORIES INC
Also Called: Prolocksusa
20 Newton Pl (11788-4752)
PHONE..........................631 582-2082
Maurice Gregory Minuto, *President*
Lisa Minuto, *Vice Pres*
EMP: 9
SQ FT: 20,000
SALES: 1.7MM Privately Held
SIC: 2844 Cosmetic preparations; hair preparations, including shampoos

(G-5731)
OLD WILLIAMSBURGH CORP
100 Wireless Blvd (11788-3955)
PHONE..........................631 952-0100
Shervin Zade, *CEO*
Michael Pischel, *CFO*
EMP: 60
SALES (est): 3.5MM Privately Held
SIC: 2844 Toilet preparations

(G-5732)
OLDCASTLE BUILDINGENVELOPE INC
895 Motor Pkwy (11788-5232)
PHONE..........................631 234-2200
Dan Dahill, *General Mgr*
Gina Rizzo, *Human Res Mgr*
Daniel Dahill, *Branch Mgr*
EMP: 125
SALES (corp-wide): 30.6B Privately Held
WEB: www.crh.ie
SIC: 3231 5231 Tempered glass: made from purchased glass; insulating glass: made from purchased glass; glass
HQ: Oldcastle Buildingenvelope, Inc.
5005 Lndn B Jnsn Fwy 10
Dallas TX 75244
214 273-3400

(G-5733)
OLYMPIC MANUFACTURING INC
195 Marcus Blvd (11788-3702)
PHONE..........................631 231-8900
Donald Molloy Jr, *President*
EMP: 20
SQ FT: 6,000
SALES (est): 2.1MM Privately Held
SIC: 3444 Sheet metalwork

(G-5734)
ORBIT INTERNATIONAL CORP (PA)
80 Cabot Ct (11788-3771)
PHONE..........................631 435-8300
Mitchell Binder, *President*
Theresa Riebe, *Purch Agent*
David Goldman, *CFO*
John Goodfellow, *Manager*
Mark Tublisky, *Admin Sec*
EMP: 90
SQ FT: 60,000
SALES (est): 26.5MM Publicly Held
WEB: www.orbitintl.com
SIC: 3679 3674 3643 3577 Power supplies, all types: static; solid state electronic devices; current-carrying wiring devices; computer peripheral equipment; computer terminals

(G-5735)
ORBIT INTERNATIONAL CORP
Tulip Development Laboratory
80 Cabot Ct (11788-3771)
PHONE..........................631 435-8300
Mitchell Binder, *Branch Mgr*

EMP: 53
SALES (corp-wide): 26.5MM Publicly
Held
SIC: 3679 Static power supply converters for electronic applications
PA: Orbit International Corp.
80 Cabot Ct
Hauppauge NY 11788
631 435-8300

(G-5736)
PARKER-HANNIFIN CORPORATION
Also Called: Electronics Systems Division
300 Marcus Blvd (11788-2044)
PHONE..........................631 231-3737
Donald Washkewicz, *President*
Dana Klein, *Buyer*
Steve Rooney, *Purchasing*
Pete Ho, *Engineer*
Rusty Newhouse, *Engineer*
EMP: 335
SQ FT: 150,000
SALES (corp-wide): 14.3B Publicly Held
WEB: www.parker.com
SIC: 3594 Fluid power pumps & motors
PA: Parker-Hannifin Corporation
6035 Parkland Blvd
Cleveland OH 44124
216 896-3000

(G-5737)
PDF SEAL INCORPORATED
280 Oser Ave (11788-3610)
PHONE..........................631 595-7035
Jaroslaw Dabek, *Ch of Bd*
Syed Zaki Hossain, *Vice Pres*
EMP: 25
SALES: 10MM Privately Held
SIC: 2631 Container, packaging & boxboard

(G-5738)
PEELLE COMPANY (PA)
373 Smithtown Byp 311 (11788-2516)
PHONE..........................631 231-6000
Henry E Peelle III, *President*
Michael J Ryan, *Vice Pres*
R B Peelle Jr, *Admin Sec*
▲ EMP: 7 EST: 1905
SQ FT: 6,000
SALES (est): 9.8MM Privately Held
SIC: 3499 Aerosol valves, metal

(G-5739)
PEER SOFTWARE INCORPORATED (PA)
1363 Veterans Hwy Ste 44 (11788-3046)
PHONE..........................631 979-1770
Paul J Marsala, *Principal*
EMP: 8
SALES (est): 2.7MM Privately Held
SIC: 7372 Prepackaged software

(G-5740)
PETER KWASNY INC
400 Oser Ave Ste 1650 (11788-3669)
PHONE..........................727 641-1462
Hans Peter Kwasny, *President*
▲ EMP: 6
SALES (est): 657K Privately Held
SALES (corp-wide): 71.1MM Privately
Held
SIC: 2851 Paints & allied products
PA: Peter Kwasny Gmbh
Heilbronner Str. 96
Gundelsheim 74831
626 995-0

(G-5741)
PINDER INTERNATIONAL INC (PA)
1140 Motor Pkwy Ste A (11788-5255)
PHONE..........................631 273-0324
Jatinder Dhall, *Ch of Bd*
▲ EMP: 5
SQ FT: 15,000
SALES (est): 769.4K Privately Held
SIC: 2231 Apparel & outerwear broadwoven fabrics

(PA)=Parent Co (HQ)=Headquarters (DH)=Div Headquarters
✪ = New Business established in last 2 years

2020 Harris
New York Manufacturers Directory

223

GEOGRAPHIC

(G-5742)
PIROD INC
Also Called: Valmont Site Pro 1
15 Oser Ave (11788-3808)
PHONE..................................631 231-7660
Joe Catapano, *General Mgr*
Joseph Cadapano, *Branch Mgr*
EMP: 33
SALES (corp-wide): 2.7B **Publicly Held**
SIC: 3441 Fabricated structural metal
HQ: Pirod Inc.
　　1545 Pidco Dr
　　Plymouth IN 46563
　　574 936-7221

(G-5743)
PNEUMERCATOR COMPANY INC
1785 Express Dr N (11788-5303)
PHONE..................................631 293-8450
Jonathan Levy, *President*
Dave McGarvey, *Natl Sales Mgr*
▲ **EMP:** 35 **EST:** 1914
SQ FT: 11,500
SALES (est): 7.1MM **Privately Held**
WEB: www.pneumercator.com
SIC: 3823 Gas flow computers, industrial
　　process type; pressure gauges, dial &
　　digital

(G-5744)
POLY CRAFT INDUSTRIES CORP
40 Ranick Rd (11788-4209)
PHONE..................................631 630-6731
Samuel Brach, *President*
Sylvia Brach, *Admin Sec*
▲ **EMP:** 25
SQ FT: 13,000
SALES (est): 5.9MM **Privately Held**
SIC: 2673 5113 Plastic bags: made from
　　purchased materials; bags, paper & dis-
　　posable plastic

(G-5745)
POSITIVE PROMOTIONS INC (PA)
15 Gilpin Ave (11788-4723)
PHONE..................................631 648-1200
Nelson Taxel, *CEO*
Rafael Valerio, *Editor*
Tom Zimmerman, *Vice Pres*
Michelle Hamilton, *Purchasing*
Natasha Jinks, *Purchasing*
◆ **EMP:** 200 **EST:** 1962
SQ FT: 60,000
SALES (est): 63.9MM **Privately Held**
SIC: 2752 Commercial printing, litho-
　　graphic

(G-5746)
PRECARE CORP (PA)
Also Called: Premier Care Industries
150 Marcus Blvd (11788-3723)
PHONE..................................631 667-1055
Ouri Neman, *CEO*
Matthew Neman, *Vice Pres*
Gregg Walker, *Vice Pres*
Candace Hassel, *Admin Asst*
▲ **EMP:** 5
SQ FT: 35,000
SALES (est): 20.5MM **Privately Held**
SIC: 2621 2676 Tissue paper; napkins,
　　sanitary: made from purchased paper; di-
　　apers, paper (disposable): made from
　　purchased paper; tampons, sanitary:
　　made from purchased paper

(G-5747)
PRECISION LABEL CORPORATION
50 Marcus Blvd (11788-3730)
PHONE..................................631 270-4490
Bradley A Cohn, *CEO*
EMP: 12
SALES (est): 2.1MM **Privately Held**
SIC: 2759 2679 Labels & seals: printing;
　　labels, paper: made from purchased ma-
　　terial

(G-5748)
PRELOAD CONCRETE STRUCTURES
60 Commerce Dr (11788-3929)
PHONE..................................631 231-8100
Andrew E Tripp Jr, *President*

Nancy Coll, *Corp Secy*
Jack Hornstein, *Vice Pres*
EMP: 42
SQ FT: 29,000
SALES (est): 6.9MM **Privately Held**
WEB: www.preload.com
SIC: 3272 Tanks, concrete

(G-5749)
PREMIER WOODWORKING INC
400 Oser Ave (11788-3619)
P.O. Box 14177 (11788-0401)
PHONE..................................631 236-4100
Jose Tellez, *President*
Carlos Zurita, *Vice Pres*
▲ **EMP:** 35
SQ FT: 230,000
SALES: 2.5MM **Privately Held**
SIC: 2541 Wood partitions & fixtures

(G-5750)
PRINTERS 3 INC
43 Corporate Dr Ste 2 (11788-2048)
PHONE..................................631 351-1331
Sal Viscuso, *Ch of Bd*
Anthony Viscuso, *President*
Christal Viscuso, *Corp Secy*
Sal Milazzo, *Sales Staff*
EMP: 10
SQ FT: 4,200
SALES (est): 1.7MM **Privately Held**
SIC: 2752 Commercial printing, offset

(G-5751)
PROFILE PRINTING & GRAPHICS (PA)
275 Marcus Blvd (11788-2022)
PHONE..................................631 273-2727
Michael Munda, *President*
EMP: 7
SQ FT: 3,000
SALES (est): 558.9K **Privately Held**
WEB: www.profileprinting.com
SIC: 2752 Commercial printing, offset

(G-5752)
QUOIZEL INC
590 Old Willets Path # 1 (11788-4119)
PHONE..................................631 436-4402
EMP: 27
SALES (corp-wide): 165.2MM **Privately Held**
SIC: 3645 5063 8741 Mfg Residential
　　Lighting Fixtures Whol Electrical Equip-
　　ment Management Services
PA: Quoizel, Inc.
　　6 Corporate Pkwy
　　Goose Creek SC 29445
　　843 553-6700

(G-5753)
RCE MANUFACTURING LLC
110 Nicon Ct (11788-4212)
PHONE..................................631 856-9005
SAI Fung, *Mng Member*
EMP: 35
SQ FT: 10,000
SALES (est): 464.8K **Privately Held**
SIC: 3672 Printed circuit boards

(G-5754)
RENTSCHLER BIOTECHNOLOGIE GMBH
400 Oser Ave Ste 1650 (11788-3669)
PHONE..................................631 656-7137
Nikolaus F Rentschler, *CEO*
EMP: 5
SALES (est): 426.6K **Privately Held**
SIC: 2836 Biological products, except diag-
　　nostic

(G-5755)
ROTRONIC INSTRUMENT CORP (DH)
135 Engineers Rd Ste 150 (11788-4018)
P.O. Box 11241 (11788-0703)
PHONE..................................631 348-6844
Patrick J Lafarie, *Senior VP*
David P Love, *Vice Pres*
Jay Crum, *Regl Sales Mgr*
Mike McGinn, *Regl Sales Mgr*
Tommy Lebla, *Marketing Staff*
▲ **EMP:** 18

SALES (est): 2.2MM
SALES (corp-wide): 177.9K **Privately Held**
WEB: www.rotronic-usa.com
SIC: 3823 Temperature measurement in-
　　struments, industrial; temperature instru-
　　ments: industrial process type; humidity
　　instruments, industrial process type
HQ: Rotronic Ag
　　Grindelstrasse 6
　　Bassersdorf ZH 8303
　　448 381-111

(G-5756)
RSM ELECTRON POWER INC
Also Called: Sensitron Semiconductor
100 Engineers Rd Ste 100 # 100
(11788-4023)
PHONE..................................631 586-7600
Steve Saunders, *Branch Mgr*
EMP: 145
SQ FT: 40,000
SALES (est): 17.2MM
SALES (corp-wide): 49MM **Privately Held**
SIC: 3674 Semiconductors & related de-
　　vices
PA: Rsm Electron Power, Inc.
　　221 W Industry Ct
　　Deer Park NY 11729
　　631 586-7600

(G-5757)
SANTA FE MANUFACTURING CORP
225 Engineers Rd (11788-4020)
PHONE..................................631 234-0100
Richard Coronato Sr, *President*
Charlotte Coronato, *Vice Pres*
EMP: 5
SQ FT: 44,000
SALES (est): 605.2K **Privately Held**
SIC: 3728 3827 Aircraft parts & equip-
　　ment; optical instruments & lenses

(G-5758)
SAPTALIL PHARMACUETICALS INC
45 Davids Dr (11788-2038)
PHONE..................................631 231-2751
Polireddy Dondeti, *CEO*
Tanya Akimova, *Vice Pres*
EMP: 6
SALES (est): 409.1K **Privately Held**
SIC: 2834 5122 Pharmaceutical prepara-
　　tions; pharmaceuticals

(G-5759)
SAPTALIS PHARMACEUTICALS LLC (PA)
45 Davids Dr (11788-2038)
PHONE..................................631 231-2751
Polireddy Dondeti, *President*
Tatiana Akimova, *Exec VP*
Serap Ozelkan, *Surgery Dir*
EMP: 22
SQ FT: 10,000
SALES (est): 3.6MM **Privately Held**
SIC: 2834 Pharmaceutical preparations

(G-5760)
SCALAMANDRE WALLPAPER INC
Also Called: Scalamandre Silks
350 Wireless Blvd (11788-3947)
PHONE..................................631 467-8800
▲ **EMP:** 401
SQ FT: 30,000
SALES (est): 40.2MM **Privately Held**
SIC: 2621 5198 2231 2221 Paper Mill
　　Whol Paints/Varnishes Wool Brdwv Fab-
　　ric Mill Manmad Brdwv Fabric Mill Cotton
　　Brdwv Fabric Mill

(G-5761)
SCHNEIDER OPTICS INC (HQ)
285 Oser Ave (11788-3616)
PHONE..................................631 761-5000
Dwight Lindsey, *CEO*
Ira Tiffen, *Vice Pres*
Ron Engvaldsen, *Mfg Dir*
Anthony Paccione, *Production*
Joe Lee, *Purchasing*
▲ **EMP:** 26
SQ FT: 11,000

SALES: 16MM
SALES (corp-wide): 76.7MM **Privately Held**
WEB: www.schneideroptics.com
SIC: 3827 Optical instruments & lenses
PA: Jos. Schneider Optische Werke Gmbh
　　Ringstr. 132
　　Bad Kreuznach 55543
　　671 601-0

(G-5762)
SCIEGEN PHARMACEUTICALS INC (HQ)
7 Oser Ave (11788-3811)
PHONE..................................631 951-4908
Pailla Malla Reddy, *CEO*
Venkata Reddy, *Vice Pres*
Amit Rathi, *Warehouse Mgr*
Krishna Mohan Chilakamarthy, *QC Dir*
Raghuram Pannala, *Director*
▲ **EMP:** 70
SQ FT: 89,000
SALES (est): 15MM
SALES (corp-wide): 100MM **Privately Held**
SIC: 2834 Vitamin preparations
PA: Bactolac Pharmaceutical Inc.
　　7 Oser Ave Ste 1
　　Hauppauge NY 11788
　　631 951-4908

(G-5763)
SCOTTS COMPANY LLC
65 Engineers Rd (11788-4003)
PHONE..................................631 478-6843
Peter Pirro, *Principal*
EMP: 8
SALES (corp-wide): 2.6B **Publicly Held**
SIC: 2873 Fertilizers: natural (organic), ex-
　　cept compost
HQ: The Scotts Company Llc
　　14111 Scottslawn Rd
　　Marysville OH 43040
　　937 644-0011

(G-5764)
SIGN A RAMA INC
Also Called: Sign-A-Rama
663 Old Willets Path C (11788-4117)
PHONE..................................631 952-3324
Jim Reardon, *Manager*
EMP: 6
SALES (corp-wide): 39.4MM **Privately Held**
WEB: www.franchisemart.com
SIC: 3993 Signs & advertising specialties
HQ: Sign A Rama Inc.
　　2121 Vista Pkwy
　　West Palm Beach FL 33411
　　561 640-5570

(G-5765)
SIGN DESIGN GROUP NEW YORK INC
47 Wireless Blvd (11788-3939)
PHONE..................................718 392-0779
Mazher Khalfan, *Ch of Bd*
▲ **EMP:** 18
SALES (est): 3.2MM **Privately Held**
WEB: www.sdgny.com
SIC: 3993 Electric signs

(G-5766)
SIMA TECHNOLOGIES LLC
345 Oser Ave (11788-3607)
PHONE..................................412 828-9130
Richard Leifer,
Robert S Leifer,
▲ **EMP:** 7
SQ FT: 27,000
SALES (est): 976K **Privately Held**
WEB: www.simacorp.com
SIC: 3651 3861 5999 3577 Household
　　audio & video equipment; photographic
　　processing equipment & chemicals; mo-
　　bile telephones & equipment; computer
　　peripheral equipment; electrical equip-
　　ment & supplies; motors & generators

(G-5767)
SIR INDUSTRIES INC
208 Blydenburg Rd Unit C (11749-5023)
PHONE..................................631 234-2444
Stanley Rabinowitz, *President*
▲ **EMP:** 6
SQ FT: 7,000

▲ = Import ▼ =Export
◆ =Import/Export

SALES: 30.4K **Privately Held**
SIC: 3648 5063 5719 Stage lighting equipment; light bulbs & related supplies; lighting fixtures

(G-5768)
SPACE-CRAFT WORLDWIDE INC
47 Wireless Blvd (11788-3939)
PHONE...............................631 603-3000
Mazher Khalfan, *President*
Jaime Reinado, *Purchasing*
Shawn Gomes, *Engineer*
Eddy Vasquez, *Design Engr*
Megan Howard, *Director*
▲ EMP: 40
SALES (est): 10.5MM **Privately Held**
SIC: 2541 Store & office display cases & fixtures

(G-5769)
SPECTRON GLASS & ELECTRONICS
595 Old Willets Path A (11788-4112)
PHONE...............................631 582-5600
Robert S Marshall, *Ch of Bd*
Pascal Lemarie, *Vice Pres*
Randy Bublitz, *QC Mgr*
Denise Nostro, *Comptroller*
Jennifer Marshall, *Human Res Mgr*
▲ EMP: 17
SQ FT: 16,000
SALES (est): 3.1MM **Privately Held**
WEB: www.spectronsensors.com
SIC: 3679 3674 Electronic switches; semiconductors & related devices
PA: Spectron Systems Technology Inc
595 Old Willets Path A
Hauppauge NY 11788
631 582-5600

(G-5770)
SPECTRON SYSTEMS TECHNOLOGY (PA)
595 Old Willets Path A (11788-4113)
PHONE...............................631 582-5600
Robert Marshall, *President*
Nancy Chereb, *Treasurer*
EMP: 13
SQ FT: 14,000
SALES (est): 3.1MM **Privately Held**
WEB: www.tiltsensors.com
SIC: 3674 Semiconductors & related devices

(G-5771)
SPECTRUM BRANDS INC
Also Called: United Pet Group
2100 Pacific St (11788-4737)
PHONE...............................631 232-1200
Mark Stern, *Branch Mgr*
EMP: 275
SALES (corp-wide): 3.1B **Publicly Held**
SIC: 3999 Pet supplies
HQ: Spectrum Brands, Inc.
3001 Deming Way
Middleton WI 53562
608 275-3340

(G-5772)
SPECTRUM THIN FILMS INC
135 Marcus Blvd (11788-3702)
PHONE...............................631 901-1010
Anthony Pirera, *President*
Kenneth Riccardi, *Technical Staff*
EMP: 35
SQ FT: 3,400
SALES (est): 12.6MM **Privately Held**
WEB: www.spectrumthinfilms.com
SIC: 3827 5049 Lenses, optical: all types except ophthalmic; optical goods

(G-5773)
SPELLMAN HGH-VOLTAGE ELEC CORP (PA)
475 Wireless Blvd (11788-3951)
PHONE...............................631 630-3000
Eric Marko, *Vice Pres*
David Gillispie, *VP Opers*
Andres Rocha, *Plant Mgr*
John Martino, *Facilities Mgr*
Mike Butler, *Opers Staff*
EMP: 500
SQ FT: 100,000

SALES (est): 297.2MM **Privately Held**
SIC: 3679 Electronic loads & power supplies

(G-5774)
STANDARD MICROSYSTEMS CORP (HQ)
Also Called: Smsc
80 Arkay Dr Ste 100 (11788-3774)
PHONE...............................631 435-6000
Christine King, *President*
Jennifer Innella, *Principal*
David Coller, *Senior VP*
Aaron L Fisher, *Senior VP*
Walter Siegel, *Senior VP*
▲ EMP: 61 EST: 1971
SQ FT: 200,000
SALES (est): 116.6MM
SALES (corp-wide): 5.3B **Publicly Held**
SIC: 3674 Microcircuits, integrated (semiconductor)
PA: Microchip Technology Inc
2355 W Chandler Blvd
Chandler AZ 85224
480 792-7200

(G-5775)
STAR QUALITY PRINTING INC
Also Called: Star Communications
270 Oser Ave (11788-3610)
PHONE...............................631 273-1900
Alka Parikh, *Ch of Bd*
Kalpesh Parikh, *President*
Adhish Parikh, *Vice Pres*
▲ EMP: 12
SQ FT: 7,500
SALES (est): 2.8MM **Privately Held**
WEB: www.sqprinting.com
SIC: 2752 Commercial printing, offset

(G-5776)
STERLING NORTH AMERICA INC
Also Called: Sterling Digital Print
270 Oser Ave (11788-3610)
PHONE...............................631 243-6933
Ed McAllister, *Ch of Bd*
Martin Sanchez, *Manager*
EMP: 28
SQ FT: 40,000
SALES (est): 6.7MM **Privately Held**
SIC: 2752 Commercial printing, offset

(G-5777)
SUMMIT APPAREL INC (PA)
Also Called: Royal Apparel
91 Cabot Ct (11788-3717)
PHONE...............................631 213-8299
Morad Mayeri, *Ch of Bd*
Abraham Mayeri, *Vice Pres*
▲ EMP: 48
SQ FT: 25,000
SALES (est): 10MM **Privately Held**
WEB: www.summitapparel.com
SIC: 2253 Dresses, knit

(G-5778)
SUPERIOR WASHER & GASKET CORP (PA)
170 Adams Ave (11788-3612)
P.O. Box 5407 (11788-0407)
PHONE...............................631 273-8282
Allan Lippolis, *Principal*
Robert Lippolis, *Purchasing*
Peter Anderson, *Sales Staff*
Michelle Card, *Sales Staff*
Ryan Jackson, *Sales Staff*
EMP: 65 EST: 1972
SQ FT: 42,000
SALES (est): 16.5MM **Privately Held**
WEB: www.superiorwasher.com
SIC: 3452 Washers, metal; washers

(G-5779)
SUPERITE GEAR INSTR OF HPPAUGE (PA)
225 Engineers Rd (11788-4020)
PHONE...............................631 234-0100
Richard Coronato Sr, *President*
Barbara Knox, *Human Res Mgr*
Charlotte Coronato, *Admin Sec*
EMP: 8
SQ FT: 44,000
SALES (est): 2.4MM **Privately Held**
SIC: 3462 Gears, forged steel

(G-5780)
SYMWAVE INC (DH)
80 Arkay Dr (11788-3705)
PHONE...............................949 542-4400
Yossi Cohen, *President*
Jun Ye, *Vice Pres*
Adam Spice, *CFO*
Christopher Thomas, *CTO*
EMP: 5
SALES (est): 733K
SALES (corp-wide): 5.3B **Publicly Held**
WEB: www.symwave.com
SIC: 3674 Semiconductors & related devices
HQ: Standard Microsystems Corporation
80 Arkay Dr Ste 100
Hauppauge NY 11788
631 435-6000

(G-5781)
TARSIA TECHNICAL INDUSTRIES
Also Called: TTI
93 Marcus Blvd (11788-3712)
PHONE...............................631 231-8322
Joe Tarsia, *President*
EMP: 7
SALES (est): 664.2K **Privately Held**
WEB: www.ttind.com
SIC: 3599 Machine shop, jobbing & repair

(G-5782)
TECHNIMETAL PRECISION INDS
195 Marcus Blvd (11788-3796)
PHONE...............................631 231-8900
Donald T Molloy, *President*
Stephen J Miller, *Exec VP*
EMP: 50 EST: 1967
SQ FT: 27,000
SALES (est): 8.9MM **Privately Held**
WEB: www.tpimetals.com
SIC: 3444 Sheet metal specialties, not stamped

(G-5783)
TELEBYTE INC (PA)
355 Marcus Blvd Ste 2 (11788-2027)
PHONE...............................631 423-3232
Dr Kenneth S Schneider, *Ch of Bd*
Michael Breneisen, *President*
Reinhold Neufeld, *Controller*
EMP: 25
SQ FT: 3,500
SALES (est): 5.4MM **Privately Held**
WEB: www.telebyteusa.com
SIC: 3669 Intercommunication systems, electric

(G-5784)
THREAD CHECK INC
390 Oser Ave Ste 2 (11788-3682)
PHONE...............................631 231-1515
Hyman Jack Kipnes, *President*
Glenn Belmonte, *General Mgr*
Jack Kipnes, *General Mgr*
Irving Kipnes, *Vice Pres*
Christine Bretanus, *Director*
EMP: 99
SQ FT: 74,000
SALES (est): 11.5MM **Privately Held**
WEB: www.threadcheck.com
SIC: 3552 5084 3823 Thread making machines, spinning machinery; industrial machinery & equipment; industrial instrmnts msrmnt display/control process variable

(G-5785)
TIFFEN COMPANY LLC
Also Called: Tiffen Co, The
80 Oser Ave (11788-3809)
PHONE...............................631 273-2500
EMP: 9
SALES (corp-wide): 23.4MM **Privately Held**
SIC: 3861 Photographic equipment & supplies
PA: The Tiffen Company Llc
90 Oser Ave
Hauppauge NY 11788
631 273-2500

(G-5786)
TIFFEN COMPANY LLC (PA)
90 Oser Ave (11788-3809)
PHONE...............................631 273-2500
Andrew Tiffen, *Prdtn Mgr*

Jose Rosado, *Sales Staff*
Steve Tiffen, *Mng Member*
Peter Roberto, *Info Tech Dir*
Karen Romanelli,
▲ EMP: 105
SALES (est): 23.4MM **Privately Held**
WEB: www.tiffen.com
SIC: 3861 Photographic equipment & supplies

(G-5787)
TOTAL DEFENSE INC
1393 Veterans Memorial Hw (11788-3068)
PHONE...............................631 257-3258
Robert Walters, *CEO*
Lawrence Guerin, *Vice Pres*
EMP: 65
SQ FT: 3,947
SALES (est): 2.4MM
SALES (corp-wide): 60MM **Privately Held**
SIC: 7372 Prepackaged software
PA: Appriver, Llc
1101 Glf Brz Pkwy Ste 200
Gulf Breeze FL 32561
850 932-5338

(G-5788)
TUNAVERSE MEDIA INC
750 Veterans Hwy Ste 200 (11788-2943)
PHONE...............................631 778-8350
Ross Pirtle, *President*
Hal Denton, *Vice Pres*
Tom Diemidil, *Vice Pres*
EMP: 8
SALES: 500K **Privately Held**
SIC: 7372 Prepackaged software

(G-5789)
TWINCO MFG CO INC (PA)
30 Commerce Dr (11788-3904)
PHONE...............................631 231-0022
John A Schatz, *President*
Ellen Wilcken, *Vice Pres*
Jennifer Tuorto, *Human Resources*
▲ EMP: 44 EST: 1965
SQ FT: 50,000
SALES: 9.3MM **Privately Held**
WEB: www.twincomfg.com
SIC: 3669 3469 3599 3743 Railroad signaling devices, electric; machine parts, stamped or pressed metal; machine & other job shop work; railroad equipment

(G-5790)
UNIFLEX HOLDINGS LLC (PA)
1600 Caleds Ext Ste 135 (11788)
PHONE...............................516 932-2000
Rob Cunningham,
▲ EMP: 10
SALES (est): 13.5MM **Privately Held**
WEB: www.uflineart.com
SIC: 2673 2674 2672 Plastic & pliofilm bags; bags: uncoated paper & multiwall; coated & laminated paper

(G-5791)
UNITED-GUARDIAN INC (PA)
230 Marcus Blvd (11788-3731)
P.O. Box 18050 (11788-8850)
PHONE...............................631 273-0900
Kenneth H Globus, *Ch of Bd*
Peter A Hiltunen, *Vice Pres*
Robert S Rubinger, *CFO*
Andrea Young, *Controller*
Donna Vigilante, *Manager*
EMP: 31
SQ FT: 50,000
SALES: 14.4MM **Publicly Held**
WEB: www.u-g.com
SIC: 2834 2844 Pharmaceutical preparations; cosmetic preparations

(G-5792)
UNIVERSAL PACKG SYSTEMS INC (PA)
Also Called: Paklab
380 Townline Rd Ste 130 (11788-2800)
PHONE...............................631 543-2277
Andrew Young III, *Ch of Bd*
Alan Kristel, *COO*
Jeffery Morlando, *CFO*
William Wachtel, *Admin Sec*
◆ EMP: 750
SQ FT: 115,000

SALES (est): 359.7MM **Privately Held**
SIC: 2844 7389 3565 2671 Cosmetic preparations; packaging & labeling services; bottling machinery: filling, capping, labeling; plastic film, coated or laminated for packaging

(G-5793)
UNLIMITED INK INC
595 Old Willets Path B (11788-4114)
PHONE..........................631 582-0696
Josh Disamone, *President*
EMP: 20
SALES (est): 934.8K **Privately Held**
SIC: 2759 5699 Screen printing; sports apparel

(G-5794)
US NONWOVENS CORP
85 Nicon Ct (11788-4213)
PHONE..........................631 232-0001
EMP: 128 **Privately Held**
SIC: 2842 Specialty cleaning, polishes & sanitation goods
PA: U.S. Nonwovens Corp.
　100 Emjay Blvd
　Brentwood NY 11717

(G-5795)
VEHICLE MANUFACTURERS INC
Also Called: Skyguard
1300 Veterans Hwy Ste 110 (11788-3077)
PHONE..........................631 851-1700
George J Wafer, *CEO*
Scott Wafer, *President*
Angelo Addesso, *COO*
EMP: 22
SALES: 10MM **Privately Held**
SIC: 3069 Rubber automotive products

(G-5796)
VETRA SYSTEMS CORPORATION
275 Marcus Blvd Unit J (11788-2022)
PHONE..........................631 434-3185
Jonas Ulenas, *President*
Paul Sabatino, *Vice Pres*
Valdas Douba, *Shareholder*
Nigole Ulenas, *Shareholder*
EMP: 8
SALES (est): 1.3MM **Privately Held**
WEB: www.vetra.com
SIC: 3823 5084 Computer interface equipment for industrial process control; controllers for process variables, all types; conveyor systems

(G-5797)
VISIONTRON CORP
720 Old Willets Path (11788-4102)
PHONE..........................631 582-8600
Lisa Torsiello, *President*
Kevin McDonald, *Business Mgr*
Joseph Torsiello, *Vice Pres*
Laurence Torsiello, *Vice Pres*
Charles Hansen, *Mfg Dir*
◆ **EMP:** 25
SQ FT: 20,000
SALES (est): 6.1MM **Privately Held**
WEB: www.visiontron.com
SIC: 3669 Intercommunication systems, electric

(G-5798)
W & H STAMPINGS INC
45 Engineers Rd (11788-4019)
PHONE..........................631 234-6161
Ernest E Hoffmann, *President*
Ron Marcisak, *General Mgr*
EMP: 28 **EST:** 1956
SQ FT: 33,000
SALES: 1MM **Privately Held**
WEB: www.whstamp.com
SIC: 3469 Stamping metal for the trade

(G-5799)
WATSON PRODUCTIONS LLC
Also Called: Skyline New York
740 Old Willets Path # 400 (11788-4121)
PHONE..........................516 334-9766
Robert Watson,
▼ **EMP:** 12

SALES (est): 2.4MM **Privately Held**
WEB: www.watsonproductions.com
SIC: 3577 Graphic displays, except graphic terminals

(G-5800)
WIDEX USA INC (DH)
Also Called: Widex International
185 Commerce Dr (11788-3916)
P.O. Box 6077, Long Island City (11106-0077)
PHONE..........................718 360-1000
Jake Haycock, *President*
▲ **EMP:** 87
SALES (est): 22.9MM
SALES (corp-wide): 177.9K **Privately Held**
SIC: 3842 Hearing aids
HQ: Widex A/S
　Nymollevej 6
　Lynge　3540
　443 556-00

(G-5801)
WILBAR INTERNATIONAL INC
50 Cabot Ct (11788-3716)
PHONE..........................631 951-9800
Steven Cohen, *President*
Coral Paige, *Marketing Mgr*
▲ **EMP:** 100
SQ FT: 20,000
SALES (est): 27.1MM **Privately Held**
SIC: 3949 Swimming pools, plastic; swimming pools, except plastic

(G-5802)
WOODBINE PRODUCTS INC
110 Plant Ave (11788-3830)
PHONE..........................631 586-3770
EMP: 20
SQ FT: 20,000
SALES (est): 2.4MM **Publicly Held**
SIC: 3812 Operates As A Manufacturer Of Navigation Equipment Specializing In Aerospace Acceleration Indicators Or Systems Components
HQ: Welding Metallurgy, Inc.
　360 Motor Pkwy Ste 100
　Hauppauge NY 11717
　631 253-0500

(G-5803)
WORLD TRADING CENTER INC
115 Engineers Rd Ste 200 (11788-4005)
PHONE..........................631 273-3330
Arthur W Danziger Jr, *President*
◆ **EMP:** 8
SQ FT: 4,000
SALES (est): 1.5MM **Privately Held**
WEB: www.wtcco.com
SIC: 2511 3699 3634 Wood household furniture; household electrical equipment; housewares, excluding cooking appliances & utensils

Haverstraw
Rockland County

(G-5804)
BRADS ORGANIC LLC
7 Hoover Ave (10927-1068)
PHONE..........................845 429-9080
Brad Smith, *Vice Pres*
Jeffrey Smith, *Mng Member*
▲ **EMP:** 2
SALES: 3MM
SALES (corp-wide): 27MM **Privately Held**
SIC: 2033 2099 2095 2096 Jams, including imitation: packaged in cans, jars, etc.; spaghetti & other pasta sauce: packaged in cans, jars, etc.; maple syrup; coffee roasting (except by wholesale grocers); corn chips & other corn-based snacks
PA: First International Health Foods, Ltd.
　7 Hoover Ave
　Haverstraw NY 10927
　845 429-9080

(G-5805)
JAGUAR INDUSTRIES INC
89 Broadway (10927-1144)
P.O. Box 385 (10927-0385)
PHONE..........................845 947-1800

Marvin Kigler, *President*
EMP: 15
SQ FT: 15,000
SALES: 8MM **Privately Held**
SIC: 3351 5065 3643 3357 Wire, copper & copper alloy; electronic parts & equipment; current-carrying wiring devices; nonferrous wiredrawing & insulating; laminated plastics plate & sheet

(G-5806)
ROCKLAND INSULATED WIRE CABLE
87 Broadway (10927-1144)
P.O. Box 111 (10927-0111)
PHONE..........................845 429-3103
Lawrence Kigler, *President*
EMP: 7 **EST:** 1956
SQ FT: 10,000
SALES (est): 1.2MM **Privately Held**
SIC: 3357 Nonferrous wiredrawing & insulating

(G-5807)
ROSS ELECTRONICS LTD
12 Maple Ave (10927-1824)
PHONE..........................718 569-6643
Reuven Lakein, *President*
▲ **EMP:** 20 **EST:** 2010
SALES: 12MM **Privately Held**
SIC: 3699 5999 Electrical equipment & supplies; electronic parts & equipment

(G-5808)
TILCON NEW YORK INC
Also Called: Haverstraw Quarry
66 Scratchup Rd (10927)
PHONE..........................845 638-3594
EMP: 63
SALES (corp-wide): 30.6B **Privately Held**
SIC: 2951 Asphalt paving mixtures & blocks
HQ: Tilcon New York Inc.
　9 Entin Rd
　Parsippany NJ 07054
　973 366-7741

Hawthorne
Westchester County

(G-5809)
ASTRA TOOL & INSTRUMENT MFG
369 Bradhurst Ave (10532-1141)
PHONE..........................914 747-3863
Greg Unmann, *President*
Greg Unman, *President*
EMP: 22 **EST:** 1950
SQ FT: 10,000
SALES: 2.9MM **Privately Held**
WEB: www.astratool.net
SIC: 3841 3599 Surgical & medical instruments; machine shop, jobbing & repair

(G-5810)
BIOMED PHARMACEUTICALS INC
Also Called: Soleo Health
4 Skyline Dr Ste 5 (10532-2192)
PHONE..........................914 592-0525
Drew Walk, *CEO*
John Ginzler, *CFO*
EMP: 8
SALES (est): 1.1MM
SALES (corp-wide): 56.4MM **Privately Held**
SIC: 2834 5912 Druggists' preparations (pharmaceuticals); drug stores & proprietary stores
PA: Soleo Health Holdings, Inc.
　950 Calcon Hook Rd Ste 19
　Sharon Hill PA 19079
　888 244-2340

(G-5811)
COCA-COLA REFRESHMENTS USA INC
3 Skyline Dr (10532-2174)
PHONE..........................914 592-0806
John Krause, *Project Mgr*
Brian Winn, *Branch Mgr*
EMP: 8

SALES (corp-wide): 31.8B **Publicly Held**
SIC: 2086 Bottled & canned soft drinks
HQ: Coca-Cola Refreshments Usa, Inc.
　2500 Windy Ridge Pkwy Se
　Atlanta GA 30339
　770 989-3000

(G-5812)
FOUR BROTHERS ITALIAN BAKERY
Also Called: Sinapi's Italian Ice
332 Elwood Ave (10532-1217)
PHONE..........................914 741-5434
Pat Sinapi, *President*
Angelo Sinapi, *Vice Pres*
Anthony Sinapi, *Treasurer*
Luigi Sinapi, *Admin Sec*
EMP: 5
SALES (est): 469.6K **Privately Held**
SIC: 2024 5143 Ices, flavored (frozen dessert); ice cream & ices

(G-5813)
GAS TURBINE CONTROLS CORP
6 Skyline Dr Ste 150 (10532-8102)
P.O. Box 104, Ardsley (10502-0104)
PHONE..........................914 693-0830
Peter Zinman, *Ch of Bd*
John Santacroce, *COO*
Robyn Howard, *Opers Mgr*
Richard Posem, *CFO*
▲ **EMP:** 25
SALES (est): 3MM **Privately Held**
SIC: 3625 Relays & industrial controls

(G-5814)
J JAMNER SURGICAL INSTRS INC
Also Called: Jarit Surgical Instruments
40 Saw Mill River Rd # 12 (10532-1535)
PHONE..........................914 592-9051
EMP: 23
SQ FT: 15,000
SALES (est): 3.1MM **Publicly Held**
SIC: 3841 Mfg Surgical/Medical Instruments
PA: Integra Lifesciences Holdings Corporation
　311 Enterprise Dr
　Plainsboro NJ 08536

(G-5815)
JOHNSON CONTROLS INC
8 Skyline Dr Ste 115 (10532-2151)
PHONE..........................914 593-5200
Rick Salon, *Manager*
EMP: 20 **Privately Held**
SIC: 3822 Energy cutoff controls, residential or commercial types
HQ: Johnson Controls, Inc.
　5757 N Green Bay Ave
　Milwaukee WI 53209
　414 524-1200

(G-5816)
KRYTEN IRON WORKS INC
3 Browns Ln Ste 201 (10532-1546)
PHONE..........................914 345-0990
EMP: 8
SALES (est): 1.4MM **Privately Held**
SIC: 3441 3446 Structural Metal Fabrication Mfg Architectural Metalwork

(G-5817)
LITHO DYNAMICS INC
17 Saw Mill River Rd (10532-1503)
PHONE..........................914 769-1759
Kenneth Giustino, *President*
Ed Martin, *Vice Pres*
Joseph Giustino, *Shareholder*
EMP: 6
SQ FT: 10,000
SALES: 400K **Privately Held**
SIC: 2752 Commercial printing, offset

(G-5818)
LUDL ELECTRONIC PRODUCTS LTD
Also Called: Lep
171 Brady Ave Ste 2 (10532-2217)
PHONE..........................914 769-6111
Helmut Ludl, *Ch of Bd*
Dirk Ludl, *President*
Mark Ludl, *President*

Petra H Ludl, *Corp Secy*
Jim Mullian, *Manager*
▼ **EMP:** 25
SQ FT: 23,000
SALES: 2K **Privately Held**
WEB: www.ludl.com
SIC: 3825 Instruments to measure electricity

(G-5819)
MWSI INC (PA)
12 Skyline Dr Ste 230 (10532-2138)
PHONE..........................914 347-4200
Mark Wasserman, *President*
EMP: 70
SQ FT: 12,160
SALES (est): 3.9MM **Privately Held**
SIC: 3961 5094 3911 Costume jewelry, ex. precious metal & semiprecious stones; jewelry; jewelry, precious metal

(G-5820)
NYSCO PRODUCTS LLC
211 Saw Mill River Rd (10532-1509)
P.O. Box 725, Bronx (10473-0725)
PHONE..........................718 792-9000
Barry Kramer, *Principal*
Charles Levin, *Vice Pres*
Glenn Smith, *Vice Pres*
Patricia Albright, *Human Res Dir*
Fazeena Baksh, *Marketing Staff*
▲ **EMP:** 60
SQ FT: 80,000
SALES (est): 11.8MM **Privately Held**
WEB: www.nysco.com
SIC: 3993 Signs & advertising specialties

(G-5821)
PEPSICO
3 Skyline Dr (10532-2174)
PHONE..........................419 252-0247
Daniel Lemire, *Engineer*
Shannon Thomas, *Senior Engr*
Kathy Dean, *Human Res Mgr*
Timothy Eremin, *Senior Mgr*
Terry Houston, *Executive*
EMP: 17
SALES (est): 2.8MM **Privately Held**
SIC: 2086 Carbonated soft drinks, bottled & canned

(G-5822)
PRINCETEL INC
Also Called: Wendon Engineering
200 Saw Mill River Rd (10532-1523)
PHONE..........................914 579-2410
Boying Zhang, *Branch Mgr*
EMP: 14
SALES (corp-wide): 11.6MM **Privately Held**
SIC: 3678 3621 Electronic connectors; sliprings, for motors or generators
PA: Princetel, Inc.
    2560 E State Street Ext
    Hamilton NJ 08619
    609 588-8801

(G-5823)
SCHMERSAL INC
15 Skyline Dr Ste 230 (10532-2152)
PHONE..........................914 347-4775
Gary Ferguson, *Managing Dir*
Sagar Bhosale, *Managing Dir*
David Upton, *Business Mgr*
Bruce Eylmann, *Purch Mgr*
Paresh Gadre, *Engineer*
◆ **EMP:** 26
SQ FT: 10,000
SALES (est): 5.2MM
SALES (corp-wide): 276.4MM **Privately Held**
WEB: www.schmersal.com
SIC: 3625 Motor control accessories, including overload relays
HQ: K. A. Schmersal Gmbh & Co. Kg
    Moddinghofe 30
    Wuppertal 42279
    202 647-40

(G-5824)
U X WORLD INC
245 Saw Mill River Rd # 106 (10532-1547)
PHONE..........................914 375-6167
Vinod Pulkayath, *President*
EMP: 5
SQ FT: 300

SALES: 140K **Privately Held**
SIC: 7372 Prepackaged software

Hector
Schuyler County

(G-5825)
HAZLITTS 1852 VINEYARDS INC
Also Called: Hazlitt 1852 Vineyards
5712 State Route 414 (14841-9714)
P.O. Box 53 (14841-0053)
PHONE..........................607 546-9463
Doug Hazlitt, *CEO*
Elaine Hazlitt, *President*
Jerome Hazlitt, *President*
Fred Wickham, *Vice Pres*
Leigh Triner, *Treasurer*
EMP: 48
SQ FT: 4,500
SALES (est): 7.1MM **Privately Held**
WEB: www.hazlitt1852.com
SIC: 2084 0172 Wines; grapes

(G-5826)
LAFAYETTE CHATEAU
Also Called: Chateau La Fayette Reneau
Rr 414 (14841)
PHONE..........................607 546-2062
Richard Reno, *Owner*
EMP: 25
SQ FT: 5,000
SALES (est): 2MM **Privately Held**
WEB: www.clrwine.com
SIC: 2084 Wines

(G-5827)
RED NEWT CELLARS INC
3675 Tichenor Rd (14841-9675)
PHONE..........................607 546-4100
David Whiting, *President*
Terri Myers, *Business Mgr*
Katie Thompson, *Manager*
EMP: 10
SQ FT: 13,000
SALES (est): 2.8MM **Privately Held**
WEB: www.rednewt.com
SIC: 2084 Wines

(G-5828)
STANDING STONE VINEYARDS
9934 State Route 414 (14841-9727)
PHONE..........................607 582-6051
Martha Macinski, *Owner*
Tom Macinski, *Co-Owner*
EMP: 6
SALES (est): 438.6K **Privately Held**
WEB: www.standingstonewines.com
SIC: 2084 5921 Wines; wine

(G-5829)
TICKLE HILL WINERY
3831 Ball Diamond Rd (14841-9629)
PHONE..........................607 546-7740
Valerie Rosbaugh, *Owner*
EMP: 5
SALES (est): 268.2K **Privately Held**
SIC: 2084 Wines

Hemlock
Livingston County

(G-5830)
ITT CORPORATION
4847 Main St (14466-9714)
PHONE..........................585 269-7109
Rosario Pitta, *Branch Mgr*
EMP: 46
SALES (corp-wide): 2.7B **Publicly Held**
WEB: www.ittind.com
SIC: 3625 Control equipment, electric
HQ: Itt Llc
    1133 Westchester Ave N-100
    White Plains NY 10604
    914 641-2000

Hempstead
Nassau County

(G-5831)
ANHUI SKYWORTH LLC
44 Kensington Ct (11550-2126)
PHONE..........................917 940-6903
Fuzhen Ang, *Mng Member*
Fuzhen Wang, *Mng Member*
▲ **EMP:** 65
SALES (est): 1.8MM **Privately Held**
SIC: 2392 5023 Cushions & pillows; pillowcases

(G-5832)
ARIC SIGNS & AWNINGS INC
153 Baldwin Rd (11550-6818)
PHONE..........................516 350-0409
Ivan Arizaga-Rodrig, *Owner*
EMP: 5
SALES (est): 347.6K **Privately Held**
SIC: 3993 Signs & advertising specialties

(G-5833)
ARNELL INC
73 High St (11550-3817)
PHONE..........................516 486-7098
Doug Riebl, *President*
Ron Riebl, *Vice Pres*
EMP: 6 **EST:** 1956
SQ FT: 4,300
SALES (est): 910.3K **Privately Held**
SIC: 3469 3544 Metal stampings; special dies, tools, jigs & fixtures

(G-5834)
BP BEYOND PRINTING INC
117 Fulton Ave (11550-3706)
PHONE..........................516 328-2700
Christine Persaud, *Ch of Bd*
EMP: 6
SALES (est): 859K **Privately Held**
SIC: 2752 2759 Commercial printing, offset; commercial printing

(G-5835)
CENTURY-TECH INC
32 Intersection St (11550-1306)
PHONE..........................718 326-9400
EMP: 13 **Privately Held**
SIC: 3561 Mfg Pumps/Pumping Equipment
PA: Century-Tech Inc.
    5825 63rd St
    Hempstead NY 11550

(G-5836)
GENERAL REFINING & SEMLT CORP
Also Called: Grc
59 Madison Ave (11550-4813)
PHONE..........................516 538-4747
Richard Spera, *President*
Elen Han, *Human Res Mgr*
EMP: 7
SQ FT: 10,000
SALES (est): 1MM **Privately Held**
SIC: 3339 3341 Gold refining (primary); silver refining (primary); platinum group metal refining (primary); secondary non-ferrous metals

(G-5837)
GENERAL REFINING CORPORATION
59 Madison Ave (11550-4813)
PHONE..........................516 538-4747
Peter Spera, *Principal*
EMP: 8
SALES (est): 850K **Privately Held**
SIC: 3339 Gold refining (primary)

(G-5838)
HEMPSTEAD SENTINEL INC
Also Called: Sentinel Printing
55 Chasner St (11550-4807)
P.O. Box 305 (11551-0305)
PHONE..........................516 486-5000
Glenn Boehmer, *President*
Joan Boehmer, *Admin Sec*
EMP: 13 **EST:** 1859
SQ FT: 7,000

SALES (est): 2.6MM **Privately Held**
SIC: 2752 Commercial printing, offset

(G-5839)
ICELL INCORPORATED
133 Fulton Ave (11550-3710)
PHONE..........................516 590-0007
Arpreet Sanhi, *President*
EMP: 127
SQ FT: 4,000
SALES (est): 10MM **Privately Held**
SIC: 3663 Mobile communication equipment

(G-5840)
JEM SIGN CORP (PA)
Also Called: Tee Pee Signs
470 S Franklin St (11550-7419)
PHONE..........................516 867-4466
Jeraldine Eid, *President*
Teddy Eid, *Vice Pres*
EMP: 5
SQ FT: 3,700
SALES (est): 725.6K **Privately Held**
WEB: www.teepeesigns.com
SIC: 3993 7532 5999 1799 Electric signs; truck painting & lettering; trophies & plaques; sign installation & maintenance

(G-5841)
JONICE INDUSTIRES
95 Angevine Ave (11550-5618)
PHONE..........................516 640-4283
EMP: 5
SALES (est): 232.3K **Privately Held**
SIC: 2299 Broadwoven fabrics: linen, jute, hemp & ramie

(G-5842)
KING CRACKER CORP
Also Called: Cristina
307 Peninsula Blvd (11550-4912)
PHONE..........................516 539-9251
Leonard Morales, *President*
EMP: 15
SALES (est): 450K **Privately Held**
SIC: 2051 5149 Bread, cake & related products; bakery products

(G-5843)
LONG ISLAND READY MIX
75 Chasner St (11550-4807)
PHONE..........................516 485-5260
Steve Welti, *Owner*
EMP: 5
SALES (est): 223.5K **Privately Held**
SIC: 3273 Ready-mixed concrete

(G-5844)
MAGER & GOUGELMAN INC
230 Hilton Ave Ste 112 (11550-8116)
PHONE..........................212 661-3939
Henry P Gougleman, *President*
EMP: 8
SALES (corp-wide): 855.4K **Privately Held**
WEB: www.artificial-eyes.com
SIC: 3851 Eyes, glass & plastic
PA: Mager & Gougelman Inc
    345 E 37th St Rm 316
    New York NY 10016
    212 661-3939

(G-5845)
MILLENNIUM SIGNS & DISPLAY INC
90 W Graham Ave (11550-6102)
PHONE..........................516 292-8000
Sajjad Khalfan, *President*
▲ **EMP:** 25
SQ FT: 35,000
SALES (est): 4MM **Privately Held**
WEB: www.msdny.com
SIC: 3993 Signs & advertising specialties

(G-5846)
NASSAU COUNTY PUBLICATIONS
Also Called: Beacon Newspapers
5 Centre St (11550-2422)
PHONE..........................516 481-5400
Peter Hoegl, *President*
EMP: 5

G
E
O
G
R
A
P
H
I
C

SALES (est): 352.4K **Privately Held**
SIC: 2711 Newspapers: publishing only, not printed on site

(G-5847)
PLANT-TECH2O INC
30 Chasner St (11550-4808)
P.O. Box 520 (11551-0520)
PHONE..............................516 483-7845
William Lyon, *President*
EMP: 5
SQ FT: 5,000
SALES: 500K **Privately Held**
SIC: 3523 7359 7389 1791 Farm machinery & equipment; live plant rental; plant care service; exterior wall system installation

(G-5848)
PURE GOLDS FAMILY CORP
1 Brooklyn Rd (11550-6619)
PHONE..............................516 483-5600
Steven Gold, *Ch of Bd*
Howard Gold, *Vice Pres*
Neil Gold, *CFO*
Paul Altamore, *Natl Sales Mgr*
Nikhil Bhowmik, *Technician*
◆ **EMP:** 75 **EST:** 1932
SQ FT: 75,000
SALES (est): 18.3MM **Privately Held**
WEB: www.goldshorseradish.com
SIC: 2035 2099 Seasonings & sauces, except tomato & dry; horseradish, prepared; Worcestershire sauce; mustard, prepared (wet); food preparations

(G-5849)
RELIABLE PRESS II INC
Also Called: Printing
73 Sealey Ave (11550-1240)
PHONE..............................718 840-5812
Ira Cohen, *President*
Sam Kowlessar, *Manager*
▲ **EMP:** 16
SALES (est): 1.1MM **Privately Held**
SIC: 2741 Miscellaneous publishing

(G-5850)
T-REX SUPPLY CORPORATION
1 Fulton Ave Ste 120 (11550-3646)
PHONE..............................516 308-0505
EMP: 6
SALES (est): 967.7K **Privately Held**
SIC: 3559 Special Industry Machinery, Nec, Nsk

(G-5851)
ULTIMATE SIGNS & DESIGNS INC
86 Sewell St (11550-5432)
PHONE..............................516 481-0800
Michael Peras, *President*
Shanna Peras, *Vice Pres*
Arlene Meli, *Project Mgr*
Marguerite Martinek, *Accounting Mgr*
Alice Adkins, *Office Mgr*
EMP: 26
SQ FT: 10,000
SALES (est): 3.8MM **Privately Held**
WEB: www.ultimatesigns.com
SIC: 3993 Electric signs

(G-5852)
WOODMOTIF INC
Also Called: Woodmotif Cabinetry
42 Chasner St (11550-4820)
PHONE..............................516 564-8325
George Dimitriadis, *President*
EMP: 10
SALES (est): 1.3MM **Privately Held**
SIC: 2521 2511 2499 Wood office furniture; wood household furniture; decorative wood & woodwork

Henrietta
Monroe County

(G-5853)
AGRINETIX CMPT SYSTEMS LLC
Also Called: Agrinetix, LLC
370 Summit Point Dr 1a (14467-9629)
PHONE..............................877 978-5477
Richard Wildman, *CEO*

Maureen Hough, *Business Mgr*
Christine Wildman, *Mng Member*
EMP: 12
SALES (est): 1.5MM **Privately Held**
SIC: 7372 Business oriented computer software

(G-5854)
ANGIOTECH BIOCOATINGS CORP
336 Summit Point Dr (14467-9607)
PHONE..............................585 321-1130
Richard Whitbourne, *Ch of Bd*
Richard Richmond, *President*
John F Lanzafame, *President*
Carolyn Eastman, *Vice Pres*
Gerard Whitbourne, *Vice Pres*
▲ **EMP:** 45
SQ FT: 13,000
SALES (est): 4MM
SALES (corp-wide): 278.3MM **Privately Held**
WEB: www.angiotech.com
SIC: 3479 2891 2851 Painting, coating & hot dipping; adhesives & sealants; paints & allied products
PA: Angiotech Pharmaceuticals, Inc
355 Burrard St Suite 1100
Vancouver BC V6C 2
604 221-7676

(G-5855)
ARGON MEDICAL DEVICES INC
336 Summit Point Dr (14467-9607)
PHONE..............................585 321-1130
EMP: 8
SALES (corp-wide): 243.4MM **Privately Held**
SIC: 3845 3842 3841 Electromedical equipment; surgical appliances & supplies; surgical & medical instruments
HQ: Argon Medical Devices, Inc.
2600 Dallas Pkwy Ste 440
Frisco TX 75034
903 675-9321

(G-5856)
HYDROACOUSTICS INC
999 Lehigh Station Rd # 100 (14467-9389)
PHONE..............................585 359-1000
EMP: 16
SQ FT: 45,000
SALES (est): 4.3MM
SALES (corp-wide): 3.7MM **Privately Held**
WEB: www.hydroacoustics.com
SIC: 3594 Fluid power pumps & motors
PA: Hai Technologies Inc.
999 Lehigh Station Rd # 100
Henrietta NY 14467

(G-5857)
KONECRANES INC
1020 Lehigh Station Rd # 4 (14467-9369)
PHONE..............................585 359-4450
Christina Moss, *Manager*
EMP: 12
SALES (corp-wide): 3.6B **Privately Held**
WEB: www.kciusa.com
SIC: 3536 7699 Cranes, industrial plant; industrial machinery & equipment repair
HQ: Konecranes, Inc.
4401 Gateway Blvd
Springfield OH 45502

(G-5858)
LAKE IMAGE SYSTEMS INC
205 Summit Point Dr Ste 2 (14467-9631)
PHONE..............................585 321-3630
Scott Stevens, *President*
Martin Keats, *President*
Paul Stinson, *Exec VP*
Paul Smith, *Senior VP*
Paul Dehond, *Engineer*
EMP: 17
SQ FT: 7,500
SALES: 5.5MM **Privately Held**
WEB: www.lakeimage.com
SIC: 3861 3554 7371 Cameras & related equipment; paper industries machinery; computer software development
PA: Lake Image Systems Limited
1 The Forum Icknield Way Industrial Estate
Tring HERTS HP23

(G-5859)
ORAFOL AMERICAS INC
Also Called: Reflexite Precision Tech Ctr
200 Park Centre Dr (14467)
PHONE..............................585 272-0309
Stephen Meissner, *Engineer*
Steven Scott, *Branch Mgr*
EMP: 25
SALES (corp-wide): 661.1MM **Privately Held**
WEB: www.reflexite.com
SIC: 3081 Vinyl film & sheet
HQ: Orafol Americas Inc.
1100 Oracal Pkwy
Black Creek GA 31308
912 851-5000

(G-5860)
TDG ACQUISTION CO LLC (PA)
Also Called: Six15 Technologies
336 Summit Point Dr Ste 1 (14467-9607)
PHONE..............................585 500-4625
Geoffrey Furman, *Design Engr*
Steve Hornos, *Manager*
Richard Ryan,
EMP: 23
SALES (est): 2.9MM **Privately Held**
SIC: 3357 Aircraft wire & cable, nonferrous

(G-5861)
TUCKER PRINTERS INC
270 Middle Rd (14467-9312)
PHONE..............................585 359-3030
Joe R Davis, *CEO*
Daniel A Tucker, *President*
Peter Ashe, *Vice Pres*
Jennifer Collier, *Project Mgr*
Kathy Howell, *Purch Agent*
EMP: 82 **EST:** 1997
SQ FT: 60,000
SALES (est): 20.6MM
SALES (corp-wide): 6.8B **Publicly Held**
WEB: www.tuckerprinters.com
SIC: 2752 Commercial printing, offset
HQ: Consolidated Graphics, Inc.
5858 Westheimer Rd # 200
Houston TX 77057
713 787-0977

(G-5862)
TURNER UNDGRD INSTLLATIONS INC
1233 Lehigh Station Rd (14467-9254)
PHONE..............................585 359-2531
Robert Turner, *President*
Rhett Turner, *Vice Pres*
Abraham Brouk, *Project Mgr*
Jane Peers, *Admin Sec*
EMP: 30
SQ FT: 11,000
SALES: 10.5MM **Privately Held**
SIC: 1381 Directional drilling oil & gas wells

Herkimer
Herkimer County

(G-5863)
HEIDELBERG GROUP INC
3056 State Hwy Rte 28 N (13350)
P.O. Box 787 (13350-0787)
PHONE..............................315 866-0999
Boyd Bissell, *President*
Philip Kernan, *COO*
John Catalic, *Vice Pres*
▲ **EMP:** 40
SQ FT: 8,000
SALES (est): 7.3MM **Privately Held**
WEB: www.heidelbergbakingco.com
SIC: 2051 Bakery: wholesale or wholesale/retail combined

(G-5864)
HERKIMER DIAMOND MINES INC
800 Mohawk St (13350-2261)
PHONE..............................315 891-7355
Renee Scialdo Schevat, *Ch of Bd*
EMP: 25
SALES (est): 3.2MM **Privately Held**
WEB: www.herkimerdiamond.com
SIC: 1499 5094 Gemstone & industrial diamond mining; diamonds (gems)

(G-5865)
HERKIMER TOOL & MACHINING CORP
Also Called: Herkimer Tool & Equipment Co
125 Marginal Rd (13350-2305)
PHONE..............................315 866-2110
F Ellis Green Jr, *President*
Francis E Green III, *Vice Pres*
Nancy J Green, *Admin Sec*
EMP: 10
SQ FT: 14,000
SALES (est): 1.3MM **Privately Held**
SIC: 3599 Machine shop, jobbing & repair

(G-5866)
LENNONS LITHO INC
Also Called: Mohawk Valley Printing Co
234 Kast Hill Rd (13350-4402)
PHONE..............................315 866-3156
Robert J Lennon, *Ch of Bd*
Elfrieda Lennon, *Treasurer*
EMP: 10
SQ FT: 6,400
SALES (est): 730K **Privately Held**
WEB: www.mohawkvalleyprinting.com
SIC: 2752 2759 Commercial printing, offset; commercial printing; letterpress printing

Heuvelton
St. Lawrence County

(G-5867)
LOSURDO FOODS INC
Also Called: Losurdo Creamery
34 Union St (13654-2200)
PHONE..............................315 344-2444
Michael Losurdo Sr, *President*
Antonio Fazzino, *Vice Pres*
Marc Losurdo, *Vice Pres*
Michael Losurdo Jr, *Vice Pres*
Maria Losurdo, *Treasurer*
EMP: 150
SQ FT: 75,000
SALES (est): 19.1MM
SALES (corp-wide): 73.5MM **Privately Held**
WEB: www.losurdofoods.com
SIC: 2022 Natural cheese
PA: Losurdo Foods, Inc.
20 Owens Rd
Hackensack NJ 07601
201 343-6680

Hewlett
Nassau County

(G-5868)
ABS METAL CORP
58 Holly Rd (11557-1411)
PHONE..............................646 302-9018
Alan Minchenberg, *Principal*
EMP: 5 **EST:** 2012
SALES (est): 491.2K **Privately Held**
SIC: 3471 Finishing, metals or formed products

(G-5869)
ALGAFUEL AMERICA
289 Meadowview Ave (11557-2106)
PHONE..............................516 295-2257
Allan Roffe, *Principal*
EMP: 7
SALES (est): 464.7K **Privately Held**
SIC: 2911 Diesel fuels

(G-5870)
LADY BRASS CO INC
1717 Broadway Unit 2 (11557-1682)
PHONE..............................516 887-8040
Lauren Brasco, *President*
EMP: 6
SALES (est): 1.1MM **Privately Held**
SIC: 2337 2326 Uniforms, except athletic: women's, misses' & juniors'; work uniforms

▲ = Import ▼=Export
◆ =Import/Export

(G-5871)
LIFEWATCH INC
Also Called: Lifewatch Personal Mergency
1344 Broadway Ste 106 (11557-1356)
PHONE..................................800 716-1433
Evan Sirlin, *President*
Art Sirlin, *Vice Pres*
Art Mitchell, *Treasurer*
EMP: 10
SALES: 700K **Privately Held**
WEB: www.lifewatch.net
SIC: 3669 5063 5999 Emergency alarms;
alarm systems; alarm signal systems

(G-5872)
NEW PRIMECARE
1184 Broadway (11557-2322)
PHONE..................................516 822-4031
Fred Tylutki, *CFO*
EMP: 6
SALES (est): 403.2K **Privately Held**
SIC: 3845 Laser systems & equipment,
medical

(G-5873)
TORSAF PRINTERS INC
Also Called: Minuteman Press
1313 Broadway (11557-2115)
PHONE..................................516 569-5577
David Toron, *President*
Michael Toron, *Corp Secy*
EMP: 6
SQ FT: 4,800
SALES (est): 1MM **Privately Held**
SIC: 2752 2791 Commercial printing, litho-
graphic; typesetting

(G-5874)
UNITED PIPE NIPPLE CO INC
1602 Lakeview Dr (11557-1818)
PHONE..................................516 295-2468
Roger Desimone, *CEO*
Selma Dolgov, *President*
▲ EMP: 15
SQ FT: 25,000
SALES: 5MM **Privately Held**
WEB: www.unitedpipenipple.com
SIC: 3494 Pipe fittings

(G-5875)
VENUS PRINTING COMPANY
1420 Kew Ave (11557-1413)
PHONE..................................212 967-8900
Erwin Goodman, *President*
Carol Goodman, *Treasurer*
Tom Shields, *Manager*
EMP: 15
SALES (est): 1MM **Privately Held**
SIC: 2759 Commercial printing

(G-5876)
WASHINGTON FOUNDRIES INC
1434 Vian Ave (11557-1423)
PHONE..................................516 374-8447
Jyotsna Kejriwal, *CEO*
Ramesh Kejriwal, *President*
EMP: 4
SQ FT: 2,100
SALES (est): 1.1MM **Privately Held**
SIC: 3674 Semiconductors & related de-
vices

(G-5877)
YES WERE NUTS LTD
Also Called: I'M Nuts
1215 Broadway (11557-2001)
PHONE..................................516 374-1940
Catherine Davi, *President*
EMP: 6
SQ FT: 2,500
SALES (est): 423.3K **Privately Held**
SIC: 2066 Chocolate

Hicksville
Nassau County

(G-5878)
AIR TECHNIQUES INC
70 Cantiague Rock Rd (11801-1163)
P.O. Box 870 (11802-0870)
PHONE..................................516 433-7676
Tiffany Crain, *Sales Staff*
Matthew Scott, *Sales Staff*

Harry Nagle, *Branch Mgr*
Robert Rilling, *Technical Staff*
EMP: 9
SALES (corp-wide): 294.1MM **Privately
Held**
SIC: 3843 Dental equipment
HQ: Air Techniques, Inc.
1295 Walt Whitman Rd
Melville NY 11747
516 433-7676

(G-5879)
AJAX WIRE SPECIALTY CO INC
119 Bloomingdale Rd (11801-6508)
PHONE..................................516 935-2333
Patricia Ellner, *CEO*
David Ellner, *President*
EMP: 15
SQ FT: 5,000
SALES: 1MM **Privately Held**
SIC: 3495 Wire springs

(G-5880)
ALL ISLAND MEDIA INC
Also Called: Carrier News
325 Duffy Ave Unit 2 (11801-3644)
PHONE..................................516 942-8400
Robert Sussi, *Branch Mgr*
EMP: 26
SALES (corp-wide): 10.3MM **Privately
Held**
WEB: www.allislandmedia.com
SIC: 2711 Newspapers, publishing & print-
ing
PA: All Island Media, Inc.
1 Rodeo Dr
Edgewood NY 11717
631 698-8400

(G-5881)
ALL THE RAGE INC
147 W Cherry St Unit 1 (11801-3885)
P.O. Box 20249, Huntington Station
(11746-0854)
PHONE..................................516 605-2001
Michael J Demarco, *President*
EMP: 7
SQ FT: 3,000
SALES (est): 4MM **Privately Held**
SIC: 3911 Jewelry apparel

(G-5882)
**ALLIED PHARMACY PRODUCTS
INC**
100 Tec St Unit F (11801-3650)
PHONE..................................516 374-8862
Stuart Meadow, *Principal*
EMP: 5
SALES (est): 671.2K **Privately Held**
SIC: 2834 5047 Pharmaceutical prepara-
tions; medical & hospital equipment

(G-5883)
APPLIED POWER SYSTEMS INC
Also Called: A P S
124 Charlotte Ave (11801-2620)
PHONE..................................516 935-2230
James Murphy, *CEO*
Les Doti, *Vice Pres*
Andres Romay, *Vice Pres*
Randall Kramer, *Med Doctor*
Richard Radocha, *Med Doctor*
▲ EMP: 25
SALES (est): 4.8MM **Privately Held**
WEB: www.appliedps.com
SIC: 3679 3677 3629 3823 Power sup-
plies, all types: static; transformers power
supply, electronic type; inverters, nonro-
tating: electrical; controllers for process
variables, all types; frequency converters
(electric generators)

(G-5884)
APX TECHNOLOGIES INC
264 Duffy Ave (11801-3605)
PHONE..................................516 433-1313
Yuval Ofek, *President*
Jennie Bueche, *Consultant*
Talia Ofek, *Director*
▲ EMP: 20
SQ FT: 3,500
SALES (est): 3MM **Privately Held**
SIC: 3679 Harness assemblies for elec-
tronic use: wire or cable; electronic loads
& power supplies

(G-5885)
**ARSTAN PRODUCTS
INTERNATIONAL**
Also Called: Apx Arstan Products
264 Duffy Ave (11801-3605)
PHONE..................................516 433-1313
Yuval Ofek, *President*
David Baum, *Executive*
EMP: 15
SQ FT: 3,500
SALES (est): 969.3K **Privately Held**
WEB: www.apxonline.com
SIC: 3679 3612 Power supplies, all types:
static; transformers, except electric

(G-5886)
AUTO-MAT COMPANY INC
69 Hazel St (11801-5340)
PHONE..................................516 938-7373
Timothy S Browner, *President*
Marilyn Browner, *Corp Secy*
Roger Browner, *Vice Pres*
EMP: 21 EST: 1956
SQ FT: 12,000
SALES (est): 1.5MM **Privately Held**
SIC: 2273 5013 7532 Automobile floor
coverings, except rubber or plastic; auto-
motive supplies & parts; interior repair
services

(G-5887)
BALANCE ENTERPRISES INC
12 W Cherry St (11801-3802)
PHONE..................................516 822-3183
Robert Philips, *President*
Robert Phillips, *Store Dir*
EMP: 8
SALES (est): 455.5K **Privately Held**
SIC: 3999 Education aids, devices & sup-
plies

(G-5888)
BATTSCO LLC
190 Lauman Ln Unit A (11801-6570)
PHONE..................................516 586-6544
Fred Hentschel, *Managing Prtnr*
John R Garnett, *Mng Member*
▲ EMP: 5
SQ FT: 2,500
SALES: 2MM **Privately Held**
SIC: 3691 Storage batteries

(G-5889)
BEBITZ USA INC
2 Reiter Ave (11801-5234)
PHONE..................................516 280-8378
Dhruv Kochhar, *President*
Daulat R Tannan, *Vice Pres*
Ashish Tannan, *Manager*
◆ EMP: 7
SALES (corp-wide): 25.4MM **Privately
Held**
SIC: 3312 Hot-rolled iron & steel products
HQ: Flanschenwerk Bebitz Gmbh
Lebendorfer StraBe 1
Konnern 06420
346 914-00

(G-5890)
C Q COMMUNICATIONS INC
Also Called: Cq Magazine
17 W John St Unit 1 (11801-1004)
PHONE..................................516 681-2922
Richard Ross, *President*
S Del Grosso, *Accounting Dir*
Catherine M Ross, *Admin Sec*
EMP: 22
SQ FT: 10,000
SALES (est): 3.1MM **Privately Held**
WEB: www.cq-vhf.com
SIC: 2721 Magazines: publishing only, not
printed on site

(G-5891)
**CAMBRIDGE KITCHENS MFG
INC**
280 Duffy Ave Unit 1 (11801-3656)
PHONE..................................516 935-5100
Neoklis Vasiliades, *President*
Barbara Narene, *Admin Sec*
EMP: 15
SQ FT: 32,000
SALES: 2.6MM **Privately Held**
WEB: www.cambridgekitchens.com
SIC: 2434 Wood kitchen cabinets

(G-5892)
CANBIOLA INC (PA)
960 S Broadway Ste 120 (11801-5028)
PHONE..................................954 253-4443
Rolv E Heggenhougen, *President*
Greg Partin, *CTO*
EMP: 7
SALES (est): 930.5K **Privately Held**
SIC: 2834 Pharmaceutical preparations

(G-5893)
**CLASSIC COLOR GRAPHICS INC
(PA)**
268 N Broadway Unit 8 (11801-2923)
P.O. Box 599, Jericho (11753-0599)
PHONE..................................516 822-9090
Daniel Fischer, *President*
Meryl Fischer, *Treasurer*
EMP: 7
SALES (est): 508.8K **Privately Held**
SIC: 2752 Commercial printing, offset

(G-5894)
CLASSIC COLOR GRAPHICS INC
87 Broadway (11801-4272)
PHONE..................................516 822-9090
Dan Fisher, *President*
Barry Moscowitz, *Accountant*
EMP: 5
SALES (corp-wide): 508.8K **Privately
Held**
SIC: 2752 Commercial printing, litho-
graphic
PA: Classic Color Graphics, Inc
268 N Broadway Unit 8
Hicksville NY 11801
516 822-9090

(G-5895)
**CLEARY CUSTOM CABINETS
INC**
794 S Broadway (11801-5017)
PHONE..................................516 939-2475
Tom Cleary, *President*
Lora Cleary, *Vice Pres*
EMP: 15
SALES (est): 2.1MM **Privately Held**
WEB: www.clearycustomcabinets.com
SIC: 2434 Wood kitchen cabinets

(G-5896)
COOPER LIGHTING LLC
Also Called: Neo Ray Lighting Products
100 Andrews Rd Ste 1 (11801-1725)
PHONE..................................516 470-1000
Harry Mangru, *Buyer*
Aida Rivera, *Design Engr*
Dennis Detore, *Controller*
Lisa Goodman,
▲ EMP: 110 EST: 2007
SALES (est): 15MM **Privately Held**
WEB: www.neoray-lighting.com
SIC: 3646 3645 Commercial indusl & insti-
tutional electric lighting fixtures; residen-
tial lighting fixtures
HQ: Cooper Industries Unlimited Company
41 A B Drury Street
Dublin

(G-5897)
**CORAL GRAPHIC SERVICES
INC (DH)**
Also Called: Coral Graphic Svce
840 S Broadway (11801-5066)
PHONE..................................516 576-2100
David Liess, *Ch of Bd*
Frank Cappo, *President*
Anthony Justice, *Info Tech Mgr*
▲ EMP: 171
SQ FT: 56,000
SALES (est): 77.3MM
SALES (corp-wide): 75.3MM **Privately
Held**
SIC: 2752 Commercial printing, offset
HQ: Dynamic Graphic Finishing, Inc.
945 Horsham Rd
Horsham PA 19044
215 441-8880

(G-5898)
CRAIG ENVELOPE CORP
220 Miller Pl (11801-1826)
PHONE...................................718 786-4277
Lawrence Aaronson, *President*
Susan Aaronson, *Corp Secy*
Robert Aaronson, *COO*
EMP: 39
SQ FT: 20,000
SALES (est): 6MM **Privately Held**
SIC: 2752 2759 Commercial printing, off-set; letterpress printing

(G-5899)
CREATIVE MODELS & PROTOTYPES
160 Lauman Ln Unit A (11801-6557)
PHONE...................................516 433-6828
Deborah Dinoia, *President*
William Dinoia, *Manager*
EMP: 8
SALES: 40K **Privately Held**
SIC: 3999 Models, general, except toy

(G-5900)
CROWN EQUIPMENT CORPORATION
Also Called: Crown Lift Trucks
5 Charlotte Ave Ste 1 (11801-3607)
PHONE...................................516 822-5100
Jim Casey, *Manager*
EMP: 68
SALES (corp-wide): 3.4B **Privately Held**
SIC: 3537 Lift trucks, industrial: fork, plat-form, straddle, etc.
PA: Crown Equipment Corporation
44 S Washington St
New Bremen OH 45869
419 629-2311

(G-5901)
DELTA SHEET METAL CORP
940 S Oyster Bay Rd (11801-3518)
PHONE...................................718 429-5805
Peter J Pappas, *President*
Eva Georgopoulos, *Vice Pres*
EMP: 202
SALES (est): 29.8MM **Privately Held**
SIC: 3444 Ducts, sheet metal

(G-5902)
DESIGNATRONICS INCORPORATED (PA)
Also Called: Sdp/Si
250 Duffy Ave Unit A (11801-3654)
PHONE...................................516 328-3300
Michael Walsh, *Ch of Bd*
Richard Kufner, *President*
Sue Anderson, *Exec VP*
Robert Lindemann, *Vice Pres*
Hitoshi Tanaka, *Vice Pres*
◆ EMP: 2
SQ FT: 40,000
SALES (est): 90.2MM **Privately Held**
WEB: www.designatronics.com
SIC: 3824 3559 3545 3625 Mechanical & electromechanical counters & devices; electronic component making machinery; cams (machine tool accessories); relays & industrial controls; iron & steel forgings

(G-5903)
E-BEAM SERVICES INC (PA)
270 Duffy Ave Ste H (11801-3600)
PHONE...................................516 622-1422
Paul R Minbiole, *President*
Mary C Daly, *Vice Pres*
Kim Hill, *Engineer*
Mary Daly, *Admin Sec*
▲ EMP: 4
SQ FT: 2,000
SALES: 5MM **Privately Held**
WEB: www.e-beamservices.com
SIC: 3671 Electron beam (beta ray) gener-ator tubes

(G-5904)
EISEMAN-LUDMAR CO INC
56 Bethpage Dr (11801-1502)
PHONE...................................516 932-6990
Andrew Ludmar, *President*
Carol Ludmar, *Vice Pres*
David Ludmar, *Vice Pres*
EMP: 10
SQ FT: 4,200

SALES (est): 891.8K **Privately Held**
WEB: www.elcaccessories.com
SIC: 2395 2241 Embroidery & art needle-work; lace & decorative trim, narrow fabric

(G-5905)
EMPIRE STEEL WORKS INC
110a New South Rd (11801-5223)
P.O. Box 111, Lynbrook (11563-0111)
PHONE...................................516 561-3500
Shaneeza Lila, *President*
EMP: 10
SALES (est): 1.7MM **Privately Held**
SIC: 3312 3446 Structural shapes & pil-ings, steel; fences or posts, ornamental iron or steel

(G-5906)
ESCHEN PRSTHETIC ORTHOTIC LABS
299 Duffy Ave (11801-3653)
PHONE...................................516 871-0029
Andrew Meyers, *President*
EMP: 10
SALES (est): 1.6MM **Privately Held**
SIC: 3842 Surgical appliances & supplies

(G-5907)
FLEXFIT LLC
350 Karin Ln Unit A (11801-5360)
PHONE...................................516 932-8800
John Michael, *Credit Mgr*
Allison Jeon, *Sales Staff*
Austin OH, *Sales Staff*
Peter Choi, *Marketing Staff*
Wayanna Kim, *Marketing Staff*
▲ EMP: 60
SALES (est): 70.7MM **Privately Held**
SIC: 2353 Hats & caps

(G-5908)
FOOT LOCKER RETAIL INC
Also Called: Champs Sports
358 Broadway Mall (11801-2709)
PHONE...................................516 827-5306
Jamie Blas, *Manager*
EMP: 10
SALES (corp-wide): 7.9B **Publicly Held**
WEB: www.venatorgroup.com
SIC: 2389 5611 Men's miscellaneous ac-cessories; clothing, sportswear, men's & boys'
HQ: Foot Locker Retail, Inc.
330 W 34th St
New York NY 10001
800 991-6815

(G-5909)
FOUGERA PHARMACEUTICALS INC
55 Cantiague Rock Rd (11801-1126)
P.O. Box 2006, Melville (11747-0103)
PHONE...................................631 454-7677
Robert Faivre, *Managing Dir*
EMP: 158
SALES (corp-wide): 51.9B **Privately Held**
SIC: 2834 Druggists' preparations (phar-maceuticals)
HQ: Fougera Pharmaceuticals Inc.
60 Baylis Rd
Melville NY 11747
631 454-7677

(G-5910)
GE POLYMERSHAPES
120 Andrews Rd (11801-1704)
PHONE...................................516 433-4092
Mike Grimm, *Manager*
◆ EMP: 10
SALES (est): 878.8K **Privately Held**
SIC: 2295 Resin or plastic coated fabrics

(G-5911)
GIM ELECTRONICS CORP
270 Duffy Ave Ste H (11801-3600)
PHONE...................................516 942-3382
Mark Douenias, *President*
William Cardenas, *Vice Pres*
EMP: 15
SQ FT: 7,800
SALES (est): 10MM **Privately Held**
WEB: www.gimelectronics.com
SIC: 3572 5961 Computer storage de-vices; computer equipment & electronics, mail order

(G-5912)
GLOBAL GLASS CORP
134 Woodbury Rd (11801-3025)
PHONE...................................516 681-2309
Jack Flax, *President*
▲ EMP: 6
SQ FT: 2,000
SALES (est): 662.4K **Privately Held**
SIC: 3211 3231 5231 5719 Flat glass; products of purchased glass; glass; mir-rors; glass & glazing work

(G-5913)
GLOPAK USA CORP (PA)
35 Engel St Ste B (11801-2648)
PHONE...................................844 445-6725
Kenneth Wang, *CEO*
Nicole Scott, *Opers Staff*
Angela Hua, *Purch Mgr*
Colleen McLoughlin, *Accounts Mgr*
Elyse Scott, *Manager*
▲ EMP: 34
SALES (est): 35MM **Privately Held**
SIC: 3221 Bottles for packing, bottling & canning: glass

(G-5914)
GOLFING MAGAZINE
Also Called: Long Island Golfer Magazine
22 W Nicholai St Ste 200 (11801-3881)
PHONE...................................516 822-5446
John Glozek Jr, *President*
▲ EMP: 8
SALES (est): 411K **Privately Held**
WEB: www.ligolfer.com
SIC: 2721 5736 Magazines: publishing only, not printed on site; sheet music

(G-5915)
HANAN PRODUCTS COMPANY INC
196 Miller Pl (11801-1826)
PHONE...................................516 938-1000
Stuart M Hanan, *President*
Francis Hanan, *Vice Pres*
Brian Krucenski, *Mfg Staff*
Ryan Hanan, *Accounts Mgr*
Doris Hanan, *Admin Sec*
▼ EMP: 20 EST: 1950
SQ FT: 23,000
SALES (est): 3.9MM **Privately Held**
WEB: www.hananproducts.com
SIC: 2026 Whipped topping, except frozen or dry mix

(G-5916)
HICKSVILLE MACHINE WORKS CORP
761 S Broadway (11801-5098)
PHONE...................................516 931-1524
Gioachino Jack Spiezio, *Ch of Bd*
Betty Spiezio, *Admin Sec*
EMP: 18
SQ FT: 35,000
SALES (est): 3.8MM **Privately Held**
WEB: www.hicksvillemachine.com
SIC: 3728 Aircraft assemblies, subassem-blies & parts

(G-5917)
JOHN E POTENTE & SONS INC
114 Woodbury Rd Unit 1 (11801-3047)
PHONE...................................516 935-8585
Eugene Potente, *CEO*
Ralph J Potente, *President*
Saverio Potente, *Vice Pres*
EMP: 6 EST: 1925
SQ FT: 5,000
SALES (est): 1MM **Privately Held**
SIC: 3272 Concrete products, precast

(G-5918)
KINGFORM CAP COMPANY INC
121 New South Rd (11801-5230)
PHONE...................................516 822-2501
Leonard Ochs, *President*
Kirk Epps, *Vice Pres*
▲ EMP: 60 EST: 1955
SQ FT: 33,000
SALES (est): 6.7MM **Privately Held**
WEB: www.kingformcap.com
SIC: 2353 Uniform hats & caps

(G-5919)
KOZY SHACK ENTERPRISES LLC (HQ)
83 Ludy St (11801-5114)
PHONE...................................516 870-3000
Robert Striano, *Principal*
Marcial Vargas, *Opers Staff*
Joanne Caridi, *Admin Sec*
◆ EMP: 250 EST: 1967
SQ FT: 70,000
SALES (est): 87.8MM
SALES (corp-wide): 6.8B **Privately Held**
WEB: www.kozyshack.com
SIC: 2099 5149 Desserts, ready-to-mix; gelatin dessert preparations; groceries & related products
PA: Land O'lakes, Inc.
4001 Lexington Ave N
Arden Hills MN 55126
651 375-2222

(G-5920)
KOZY SHACK ENTERPRISES LLC
Also Called: Freshway Distributors
50 Ludy St (11801-5115)
PHONE...................................516 870-3000
John Ievolo, *Manager*
EMP: 200
SALES (corp-wide): 6.8B **Privately Held**
WEB: www.kozyshack.com
SIC: 2099 5149 2024 Desserts, ready-to-mix; gelatin dessert preparations; gro-ceries & related products; ice cream & frozen desserts
HQ: Kozy Shack Enterprises, Llc
83 Ludy St
Hicksville NY 11801
516 870-3000

(G-5921)
KUNO STEEL PRODUCTS CORP
132 Duffy Ave (11801-3640)
PHONE...................................516 938-8500
Kuno Weckenmann, *President*
Irmgard Weckenmann, *Corp Secy*
EMP: 10
SQ FT: 1,500
SALES: 1.2MM **Privately Held**
WEB: www.kunosteel.com
SIC: 3441 Building components, structural steel

(G-5922)
LAND OLAKES INC
50 Ludy St (11801-5115)
PHONE...................................516 681-2980
EMP: 9
SALES (corp-wide): 6.8B **Privately Held**
SIC: 2099 Food preparations
PA: Land O'lakes, Inc.
4001 Lexington Ave N
Arden Hills MN 55126
651 375-2222

(G-5923)
LEATHER INDEXES CORP
174a Miller Pl (11801-1826)
P.O. Box 1350, Port Washington (11050-7350)
PHONE...................................516 827-1900
Paul Ellenberg, *President*
Kay Ellenberg, *Vice Pres*
EMP: 60
SQ FT: 15,000
SALES: 1.5MM **Privately Held**
SIC: 2678 2782 2675 Stationery prod-ucts; blankbooks & looseleaf binders; die-cut paper & board

(G-5924)
M F MANUFACTURING ENTERPRISES
2 Ballad Ln (11801-4529)
PHONE...................................516 822-5135
Michael Funk, *CEO*
Fern Funk, *Vice Pres*
EMP: 5
SALES (est): 325K **Privately Held**
SIC: 3469 Machine parts, stamped or pressed metal

▲ = Import ▼=Export
◆ =Import/Export

(G-5925)
MARCAL PRINTING INC
Also Called: PIP Printing
85 N Broadway (11801-2948)
PHONE................................516 942-9500
EMP: 6
SQ FT: 3,000
SALES (est): 940.3K **Privately Held**
SIC: 2752 Offset Printing

(G-5926)
MARIAH METAL PRODUCTS INC
89 Tec St (11801-3618)
PHONE................................516 938-9783
Raymond O Leary, *President*
EMP: 5
SQ FT: 2,000
SALES (est): 676.2K **Privately Held**
SIC: 3444 Sheet metalwork

(G-5927)
MARIGOLD SIGNS INC
Also Called: Sign-A-Rama
485 S Broadway Ste 34 (11801-5071)
PHONE................................516 433-7446
Vincent Marino, *President*
Robert Goldaber, *Vice Pres*
EMP: 10
SALES (est): 1.3MM **Privately Held**
SIC: 3993 Signs & advertising specialties

(G-5928)
MARKWIK CORP
309 W John St (11801-1024)
PHONE................................516 470-1990
Jane A Groene, *President*
Taylor Groene, *General Mgr*
EMP: 18 EST: 1949
SQ FT: 9,000
SALES (est): 2.3MM **Privately Held**
WEB: www.markwik.com
SIC: 3089 Plastic hardware & building
products

(G-5929)
MICRO CONTACTS INC (PA)
1 Enterprise Pl Unit E (11801-2694)
PHONE................................516 433-4830
Gerald F Tucci, *Ch of Bd*
Michael F Tucci, *President*
Robert Stinson, *General Mgr*
Steven Klekman, *Vice Pres*
Philip Uruburu, *Vice Pres*
▲ EMP: 50 EST: 1963
SQ FT: 40,000
SALES (est): 10MM **Privately Held**
WEB: www.microcontacts.com
SIC: 3643 Contacts, electrical

(G-5930)
MISON CONCEPTS INC
485 S Broadway Ste 33 (11801-5071)
PHONE................................516 933-8000
Joseph Jaroff, *President*
Bhavani Morganstern, *Vice Pres*
▲ EMP: 8
SQ FT: 2,000
SALES (est): 690K **Privately Held**
WEB: www.mison.com
SIC: 3446 Architectural metalwork

(G-5931)
MOD-A-CAN INC (PA)
178 Miller Pl (11801-1890)
PHONE................................516 931-8545
Stan Buoninfante, *President*
Stan L Buoninfante, *President*
Roberta Wolfe, *General Mgr*
Michael Iannotta, *Vice Pres*
John Niedfeld, *Foreman/Supr*
EMP: 55 EST: 1966
SQ FT: 19,400
SALES (est): 11.5MM **Privately Held**
WEB: www.modacan.com
SIC: 3812 Aircraft flight instruments

(G-5932)
MULTI PACKAGING SOLUTIONS INC
325 Duffy Ave Unit 1 (11801-3644)
PHONE................................516 488-2000
Michael Greenberg, *Branch Mgr*
EMP: 113

SALES (corp-wide): 14.8B **Publicly Held**
SIC: 2671 Packaging paper & plastics film,
coated & laminated
HQ: Multi Packaging Solutions, Inc.
150 E 52nd St Fl 28
New York NY 10022

(G-5933)
NASSAU CANDY DISTRIBUTORS INC (HQ)
Also Called: Nassau Candy Specialty
530 W John St (11801-1039)
PHONE................................516 433-7100
Lesley Stier, *President*
Barry Rosenbaum, *President*
Les Stier, *COO*
Pashka Bellia, *Vice Pres*
Guastella Maryann, *Vice Pres*
◆ EMP: 180
SQ FT: 300,000
SALES (est): 196.4MM
SALES (corp-wide): 212MM **Privately Held**
WEB: www.nassaucandy.com
SIC: 2064 Candy & other confectionery
products
PA: Nassau-Sosnick Distribution Company
Llc
258 Littlefield Ave
South San Francisco CA 94080
650 952-2226

(G-5934)
NY EMBROIDERY INC
Also Called: New York Embroidery & Monogram
25 Midland Ave (11801-1509)
PHONE................................516 822-6456
John La Rocca, *President*
▲ EMP: 20
SALES (est): 1.5MM **Privately Held**
WEB: www.nyembroidery.com
SIC: 2395 Embroidery & art needlework

(G-5935)
OLMSTEAD PRODUCTS CORP
1 Jefry Ln (11801-5394)
PHONE................................516 681-3700
Jack Tepper, *President*
Nicholas Lucarello, *Vice Pres*
▲ EMP: 12 EST: 1954
SQ FT: 7,000
SALES (est): 2.1MM **Privately Held**
SIC: 3556 Food products machinery

(G-5936)
OXYGEN INC (PA)
Also Called: Rodan
6 Midland Ave (11801-1510)
PHONE................................516 433-1144
Daniel Joory, *President*
Ronnie Zubli, *Corp Secy*
Kenny Miller, *Production*
◆ EMP: 9
SQ FT: 2,000
SALES (est): 1.1MM **Privately Held**
SIC: 2369 Bathing suits & swimwear: girls',
children's & infants'

(G-5937)
OYSTER BAY PUMP WORKS INC
78 Midland Ave Unit 1 (11801-1537)
P.O. Box 725 (11802-0725)
PHONE................................516 933-4500
Patrick Gaillard, *CEO*
▲ EMP: 18
SALES (est): 5.2MM **Privately Held**
WEB: www.obpw.com
SIC: 3561 3829 3589 Pumps & pumping
equipment; medical diagnostic systems,
nuclear; liquor dispensing equipment &
systems

(G-5938)
P & F BAKERS INC
640 S Broadway (11801-5016)
PHONE................................516 931-6821
P Zamparelli, *CEO*
EMP: 10
SALES (est): 543.8K **Privately Held**
SIC: 2026 Bakers' cheese

(G-5939)
PAL ALUMINUM INC (PA)
Also Called: Pal Industries
230 Duffy Ave Unit B (11801-3641)
PHONE................................516 937-1990
Pana Giotis Mar Neris, *President*
Laurel Marneris, *Vice Pres*
EMP: 3
SQ FT: 70,000
SALES (est): 4.7MM
SALES (corp-wide): 5MM **Privately Held**
SIC: 3444 5033 5031 Metal roofing & roof
drainage equipment; gutters, sheet metal;
roof deck, sheet metal; siding, except
wood; doors

(G-5940)
PAL MANUFACTURING CORP
230 Duffy Ave Unit B (11801-3641)
PHONE................................516 937-1990
Laurel Marneris, *President*
Panagiotis Marneris, *Vice Pres*
EMP: 28
SQ FT: 70,000
SALES (est): 4.5MM **Privately Held**
WEB: www.palwindows.com
SIC: 3442 3231 Storm doors or windows,
metal; products of purchased glass

(G-5941)
PB08 INC
40 Bloomingdale Rd (11801-6507)
PHONE................................347 866-7353
Jajtar Kular, *Owner*
Neeraj Sherma, *Principal*
EMP: 2
SALES (est): 3MM **Privately Held**
SIC: 3537 Trucks: freight, baggage, etc.:
industrial, except mining

(G-5942)
PEDRE CORP (PA)
Also Called: Pedre Watch
270 Duffy Ave Ste G (11801-3600)
PHONE................................212 868-2935
R Peter Gunshor, *President*
Anthony Scott, *Prdtn Mgr*
◆ EMP: 31
SQ FT: 10,000
SALES (est): 5.5MM **Privately Held**
WEB: www.pedrewatch.com
SIC: 3873 Watches, clocks, watchcases &
parts

(G-5943)
PERFECT GEAR & INSTRUMENT (HQ)
250 Duffy Ave (11801-3654)
PHONE................................516 328-3330
Morton Hoffman, *President*
Joseph Rubenfeld, *Vice Pres*
EMP: 10
SALES (est): 1.9MM
SALES (corp-wide): 90.2MM **Privately Held**
SIC: 3462 Gears, forged steel
PA: Designatronics Incorporated
250 Duffy Ave Unit A
Hicksville NY 11801
516 328-3300

(G-5944)
PETRO INC
477 W John St (11801-1029)
PHONE................................516 686-1900
Rodney Roberts, *Branch Mgr*
EMP: 9 **Publicly Held**
SIC: 1389 Oil field services
HQ: Petro, Inc.
9 W Broad St Ste 310
Stamford CT 06902
203 325-5400

(G-5945)
REPAPERS CORPORATION (PA)
268 N Broadway Unit 9 (11801-2923)
PHONE................................305 691-1635
Paula Maddux, *Director*
Andres Patino, *Officer*
◆ EMP: 19
SALES (est): 10.7MM **Privately Held**
SIC: 2611 Pulp manufactured from waste
or recycled paper

(G-5946)
SAMSON TECHNOLOGIES CORP (HQ)
278 Duffy Ave Unit B (11801-3642)
PHONE................................631 784-2200
Richard Ash, *Ch of Bd*
Scott Goodman, *President*
David Hakim, *General Mgr*
Derek Ash, *Business Mgr*
David Ash, *COO*
◆ EMP: 52
SALES (est): 14.2MM
SALES (corp-wide): 266.4MM **Privately Held**
WEB: www.samsontech.com
SIC: 3651 3931 5099 5065 Sound reproducing equipment; musical instruments;
musical instruments; sound equipment,
electronic
PA: Sam Ash Music Corporation
278 Duffy Ave Unit A
Hicksville NY 11801
516 932-6400

(G-5947)
SCIARRA LABORATORIES INC
48509 S Broadway (11801)
PHONE................................516 933-7853
John J Sciarra, *President*
Christopher J Sciarra, *Vice Pres*
Sara Beaulieu, *Office Mgr*
EMP: 6
SALES (est): 1.3MM **Privately Held**
WEB: www.sciarralabs.com
SIC: 2834 Pharmaceutical preparations

(G-5948)
SI PARTNERS INC
15 E Carl St Unit 1 (11801-4290)
PHONE................................516 433-1415
Amit Singhvi, *President*
▲ EMP: 7
SALES (est): 837.8K **Privately Held**
SIC: 3355 Aluminum wire & cable

(G-5949)
STS REFILL AMERICA LLC
399 W John St Unit A (11801-1043)
PHONE................................516 934-8008
Shahar Turgeman,
Mark Freedman,
Uri Hason,
Scott Robert,
▲ EMP: 6
SQ FT: 2,500
SALES (est): 451K **Privately Held**
WEB: www.stsrefill.com
SIC: 3951 Cartridges, refill: ball point pens

(G-5950)
SUNQUEST PHARMACEUTICALS INC
385 W John St Ste 1 (11801-1033)
PHONE................................855 478-6779
Atul Sharma, *President*
EMP: 17
SALES (est): 4.2MM **Privately Held**
SIC: 2834 Pharmaceutical preparations

(G-5951)
TAMPERPROOF SCREW COMPANY INC
30 Laurel St (11801-2641)
PHONE................................516 931-1616
Lewis Friedman, *President*
George Friedman, *Corp Secy*
Alaina Picitelli, *Vice Pres*
▲ EMP: 12
SQ FT: 5,000
SALES: 2.3MM **Privately Held**
WEB: www.tamperproof.com
SIC: 3452 Screws, metal

(G-5952)
TJ SIGNS UNLIMITED LLC
Also Called: American Signcrafters
327 New South Rd (11801-5226)
PHONE................................631 273-4800
Jeffrey Petersen, *CEO*
Jonathan Bell, *President*
Lisa Johnson, *President*
EMP: 130
SALES (est): 276.5K **Privately Held**
SIC: 3993 Signs & advertising specialties

(G-5953)
VIRAJ - USA INC (HQ)
2 Reiter Ave (11801-5234)
PHONE.................................516 280-8380
Dhruv Kochhar, *President*
Daulat Tannan, *Vice Pres*
◆ EMP: 6
SALES (est): 712.6K **Privately Held**
SIC: 3312 Stainless steel

High Falls
Ulster County

(G-5954)
ALE-TECHNIQUES INC
2452 Lucas Tpke Ste B (12440-5926)
PHONE.................................845 687-7200
Daniel Ale, *CEO*
EMP: 15
SQ FT: 35,000
SALES (est): 1.3MM **Privately Held**
SIC: 3545 Machine tool accessories

(G-5955)
DELTA PRESS INC
2426 Lucas Tpke (12440-5920)
PHONE.................................212 989-3445
Joel Sachs, *President*
EMP: 30
SALES (est): 2.5MM **Privately Held**
WEB: www.deltapress.com
SIC: 2752 Commercial printing, offset

(G-5956)
ULSTER COUNTY PRESS OFFICE
Also Called: Blue Stone Press
1209 State Route 213 (12440-5714)
P.O. Box 149, Stone Ridge (12484-0149)
PHONE.................................845 687-4480
Lori Childerss, *President*
Gregory Childress, *Principal*
EMP: 5
SALES (est): 463.5K **Privately Held**
WEB: www.ulstercountypress.com
SIC: 2711 Commercial printing & newspaper publishing combined; newspapers, publishing & printing

Highland
Ulster County

(G-5957)
BAD SEED CIDER CO LLC
465 Pancake Hollow Rd (12528-2338)
PHONE.................................914 474-4422
EMP: 7 EST: 2012
SALES (est): 626.9K **Privately Held**
SIC: 2084 Wines

(G-5958)
BORABORA FRUIT JUICES INC
255 Milton Xrds (12528-2256)
P.O. Box 383, Pound Ridge (10576-0383)
PHONE.................................914 438-8744
Michael Heath, *President*
EMP: 8
SQ FT: 10,000
SALES (est): 1MM **Privately Held**
SIC: 2086 Bottled & canned soft drinks

(G-5959)
GORDON FIRE EQUIPMENT LLC
3199 Us Highway 9w (12528-2633)
PHONE.................................845 691-5700
Mary Anne Hein, *Mng Member*
EMP: 6
SALES (est): 807K **Privately Held**
SIC: 2899 Fire retardant chemicals

(G-5960)
HUDSON VALLEY TECH DEV CTR INC
Also Called: Manufacturing & Tech Entp Ctr
180 South St (12528-2439)
PHONE.................................845 391-8214
Tom Phillips, *Exec Dir*
EMP: 15
SQ FT: 5,000

SALES: 1.2MM **Privately Held**
WEB: www.hvtdc.org
SIC: 3679 8711 Electronic circuits; consulting engineer

(G-5961)
M M TOOL AND MANUFACTURING
175 Chapel Hill Rd (12528-2105)
PHONE.................................845 691-4140
Matt Mc Cluskey, *President*
Kenneth P Castelo, *Director*
EMP: 8
SQ FT: 10,000
SALES: 1.2MM **Privately Held**
SIC: 3585 Air conditioning equipment, complete; air conditioning units, complete; domestic or industrial

(G-5962)
PRISM SOLAR TECHNOLOGIES INC (HQ)
180 South St (12528-2439)
PHONE.................................845 883-4200
Randy Stewart, *CEO*
David Waserstein, *Ch of Bd*
Carolyn Lewandowski, *Corp Secy*
Jose Castillo, *Research*
Paul Hauser, *Engineer*
▲ EMP: 38
SQ FT: 93,000
SALES (est): 4.9MM **Publicly Held**
SIC: 3433 Solar heaters & collectors

(G-5963)
SELUX CORPORATION
5 Lumen Ln (12528-1903)
P.O. Box 1060 (12528-8060)
PHONE.................................845 691-7723
Juergen Hess, *Ch of Bd*
Peter Stanway, *President*
Michael Seckler, *Vice Pres*
Claus Kinder, *VP Opers*
Randy Adams, *Plant Mgr*
◆ EMP: 164
SQ FT: 85,000
SALES: 37.8MM
SALES (corp-wide): 144.1K **Privately Held**
WEB: www.selux.com
SIC: 3646 Commercial indusl & institutional electric lighting fixtures
HQ: Selux Benelux
    Grotesteenweg 50
    Kontich 2550

(G-5964)
ULTRA-TAB LABORATORIES INC
50 Toc Dr (12528-1506)
PHONE.................................845 691-8361
Rick Polonski, *Plant Mgr*
Dennis Borerrello, *Manager*
EMP: 29
SALES (est): 5.2MM
SALES (corp-wide): 3.3MM **Privately Held**
WEB: www.ultratablabs.com
SIC: 2834 Pharmaceutical preparations
PA: Ultra-Tab Laboratories, Inc.
    521 Main St
    New Paltz NY 12561
    845 255-2496

(G-5965)
ZUMTOBEL LIGHTING INC (DH)
3300 Route 9w (12528-2630)
PHONE.................................845 691-6262
Kevin Maddy, *CEO*
Matthew Boucher, *Managing Dir*
Bill Simoni, *Vice Pres*
Stacey Dellasala, *Project Mgr*
Nirmal Kurup, *Materials Mgr*
▲ EMP: 130
SQ FT: 80,000
SALES: 44MM
SALES (corp-wide): 1.3B **Privately Held**
WEB: www.zumtobel.com
SIC: 3646 Commercial indusl & institutional electric lighting fixtures
HQ: Zumtobel Lighting Gmbh
    SchweizerstraBe 30
    Dornbirn 6850
    557 239-00

Highland Falls
Orange County

(G-5966)
SKD TACTICAL INC
291 Main St (10928-1803)
PHONE.................................845 897-2889
Dani Seuk, *CEO*
Joe Seuk, *Vice Pres*
Jo Seuk, *Administration*
▲ EMP: 6 EST: 1999
SALES: 1.5MM **Privately Held**
SIC: 2399 Military insignia, textile

Highland Mills
Orange County

(G-5967)
ALL MERCHANDISE DISPLAY CORP
Also Called: AM Display
4 Pheasant Run (10930-2140)
PHONE.................................718 257-2221
Eddie Minkoff, *President*
Abraham J Minkoff, *Vice Pres*
EMP: 7
SALES (est): 627.8K **Privately Held**
SIC: 2541 Display fixtures, wood

(G-5968)
M &L INDUSTRY OF NY INC
583 State Route 32 Ste 1u (10930-5229)
PHONE.................................845 827-6255
EMP: 9
SALES (est): 770K **Privately Held**
SIC: 2441 Mfg Wood Boxes/Shook

(G-5969)
SPEYSIDE HOLDINGS LLC
911 State Route 32 (10930-2309)
P.O. Box 1007 (10930-1007)
PHONE.................................845 928-2221
Anthony Williams, *Chairman*
EMP: 25
SALES (est): 855.3K **Privately Held**
SIC: 1442 Construction sand & gravel

Hillburn
Rockland County

(G-5970)
MERCO HACKENSACK INC
Also Called: Merco Tape
201 Route 59 Ste D2 (10931-1189)
PHONE.................................845 357-3699
David Rose, *President*
Adam Riskin, *Vice Pres*
Eleanor Rose, *Sales Staff*
Marcy Michelman, *Director*
Dana Saunders, *Products*
◆ EMP: 6 EST: 1972
SQ FT: 18,000
SALES: 4.7MM **Privately Held**
WEB: www.maskingtape.com
SIC: 2672 Tape, pressure sensitive: made from purchased materials

(G-5971)
SYMMETRY MEDICAL INC
201 Route 59 Bldg E (10931-1190)
P.O. Box 1187 (10931-1187)
PHONE.................................845 368-4573
EMP: 8
SALES (corp-wide): 697.6MM **Privately Held**
SIC: 3841 Surgical & medical instruments
HQ: Symmetry Medical Inc.
    3724 N State Road 15
    Warsaw IN 46582

Hilton
Monroe County

(G-5972)
CUDDEBACK MACHINING INC
18 Draffin Rd (14468-9708)
PHONE.................................585 392-5889
Lawrence Cuddeback, *President*
Sandra Cuddeback, *Admin Sec*
EMP: 7
SQ FT: 4,200
SALES (est): 1.1MM **Privately Held**
WEB: www.cuddebackmachining.com
SIC: 3496 3544 Miscellaneous fabricated wire products; special dies & tools

(G-5973)
MONROE FLUID TECHNOLOGY INC
36 Draffin Rd (14468-9717)
PHONE.................................585 392-3434
Alan Christodaro, *President*
Paul Silloway, *Prdtn Mgr*
Alan Eckard, *Technology*
▲ EMP: 25
SALES: 10MM **Privately Held**
SIC: 2992 2899 2841 Lubricating oils; cutting oils, blending: made from purchased materials; chemical preparations; soap & other detergents

(G-5974)
OMEGA CONSOLIDATED CORPORATION
101 Heinz St (14468-1226)
PHONE.................................585 392-9262
Martin Hunte, *President*
Robert Hunte, *Vice Pres*
Thomas Hunte, *Vice Pres*
▼ EMP: 20 EST: 1981
SQ FT: 30,000
SALES (est): 3.1MM **Privately Held**
WEB: www.omegacon.com
SIC: 3541 Machine tools, metal cutting type

(G-5975)
WILLIAM J RYAN
Also Called: Ryan Printing
1365 Hamlin Parma Townline (14468-9749)
PHONE.................................585 392-6200
William Ryan, *Owner*
EMP: 5
SQ FT: 3,000
SALES: 200K **Privately Held**
WEB: www.ryanprinting.com
SIC: 2752 7334 2759 Commercial printing, offset; photocopying & duplicating services; commercial printing

Himrod
Yates County

(G-5976)
LAPP MANAGEMENT CORP
Also Called: Wood-Tex Products
3700 Route 14 (14842-9802)
PHONE.................................607 243-5141
Barbara Lapp, *President*
EMP: 7
SQ FT: 12,000
SALES (est): 1.2MM **Privately Held**
WEB: www.woodtexproducts.com
SIC: 2452 Prefabricated buildings, wood

(G-5977)
WOOD TEX PRODUCTS LLC
3700 Route 14 (14842-9802)
PHONE.................................607 243-5141
Greg Chapman, *Opers Staff*
Rob Neu, *Sales Staff*
Kurt Hess, *Manager*
Paul Farmer, *Creative Dir*
Kent Lapp,
EMP: 54
SALES: 7.2MM **Privately Held**
SIC: 2452 Prefabricated buildings, wood

▲ = Import ▼=Export
◆ =Import/Export

Hobart
Delaware County

(G-5978)
HATHERLEIGH COMPANY LTD
62545 State Highway 10 (13788-3019)
PHONE.................................607 538-1092
Frederic Flach, *Ch of Bd*
Anna Krusinski, *Manager*
EMP: 9
SALES: 8.7K **Privately Held**
WEB: www.bodysculptingbible.com
SIC: 2721 7812 Trade journals: publishing only, not printed on site; audio-visual program production

(G-5979)
SPECGX LLC
Also Called: Mallinckrodt Pharmaceuticals
172 Railroad Ave (13788)
PHONE.................................607 538-9124
Joseph Welch, *Engineer*
Laura Ashline, *Senior Engr*
Jim Walter, *Manager*
Mike Vanzandt, *Manager*
Andrew Dougherty, *Maintence Staff*
EMP: 630 **Privately Held**
WEB: www.mallinckrodt.com
SIC: 2834 Pharmaceutical preparations
HQ: Specgx Llc
385 Marshall Ave
Saint Louis MO 63119
314 654-2000

Hogansburg
Franklin County

(G-5980)
JACOBS TOBACCO COMPANY
Also Called: Jacobs Manufacturing
344 Frogtown Rd (13655-3137)
PHONE.................................518 358-4948
Roseley Jacobs, *Owner*
Tisha Thompson, *Marketing Mgr*
EMP: 24
SALES (est): 4.3MM **Privately Held**
SIC: 2111 Cigarettes

(G-5981)
OHSERASE MANUFACTURING LLC
393 Frogtown Rd (13655-3138)
P.O. Box 550 (13655-0550)
PHONE.................................518 358-9309
Justin Tarbell, *Vice Pres*
▲ EMP: 8
SALES (est): 93.5K **Privately Held**
SIC: 3999 Barber & beauty shop equipment

Holbrook
Suffolk County

(G-5982)
ACCENT SPEAKER TECHNOLOGY LTD
Also Called: Nola Speaker
1511 Lincoln Ave (11741-2216)
PHONE.................................631 738-2540
Carl Marchisotto, *CEO*
▲ EMP: 7
SALES (est): 1MM **Privately Held**
SIC: 3651 Speaker systems

(G-5983)
ACCURATE INDUSTRIAL MACHINING
1711 Church St (11741-5921)
PHONE.................................631 242-0566
Jerome Bricker, *President*
Marguerite Bricker, *Corp Secy*
▲ EMP: 20
SQ FT: 30,000
SALES (est): 2.7MM **Privately Held**
SIC: 3599 5084 Machine shop, jobbing & repair; industrial machinery & equipment

(G-5984)
ADVANCED DOOR SOLUTIONS INC
Also Called: Advanced Doors
1363 Lincoln Ave Ste 7 (11741-2274)
PHONE.................................631 773-6100
James McGonigle, *President*
Lauren McGonigle, *Admin Mgr*
EMP: 7
SQ FT: 2,300
SALES: 1MM **Privately Held**
SIC: 3442 7699 1796 1793 Metal doors, sash & trim; lock & key services; lock parts made to individual order; installing building equipment; glass & glazing work; window & door installation & erection

(G-5985)
ALWAYS BAKED FRESH INC
331 Dante Ct Ste F (11741-3800)
PHONE.................................631 648-0811
Victoria Kim, *Principal*
EMP: 8 EST: 2008
SALES (est): 430.8K **Privately Held**
SIC: 2051 Cakes, bakery: except frozen

(G-5986)
BNM PRODUCT SERVICE
1561 Lincoln Ave (11741-2217)
PHONE.................................631 750-1586
Sergio Lorenzo, *President*
EMP: 5
SALES (est): 673.5K **Privately Held**
SIC: 3545 Machine tool accessories

(G-5987)
BRZOZKA INDUSTRIES INC
Also Called: Felber Metal Fabricators
790 Broadway Ave (11741-4906)
PHONE.................................631 588-8164
Waldmar Brazozka, *CEO*
Hans Felber, *President*
EMP: 10
SQ FT: 3,600
SALES (est): 1.8MM **Privately Held**
SIC: 3444 Sheet metalwork

(G-5988)
CAREFREE KITCHENS INC
925 Lincoln Ave Ste 1 (11741-2200)
PHONE.................................631 567-2120
Leonard Daino, *President*
Carolina Daino, *Vice Pres*
EMP: 5
SALES (est): 440K **Privately Held**
SIC: 2434 5031 5211 Wood kitchen cabinets; kitchen cabinets; cabinets, kitchen

(G-5989)
CJN MACHINERY CORP
917 Lincoln Ave Ste 13 (11741-2250)
PHONE.................................631 244-8030
Josephine Chillemi, *President*
Josephine Chllemi, *President*
EMP: 7
SQ FT: 4,000
SALES (est): 1.6MM **Privately Held**
SIC: 3599 Machine shop, jobbing & repair

(G-5990)
CLEAN ROOM DEPOT INC
1730 Church St (11741-5918)
PHONE.................................631 589-3033
Ken Lorello, *President*
Alexis Lorello, *Vice Pres*
EMP: 10
SQ FT: 3,600
SALES (est): 1.9MM **Privately Held**
WEB: www.cleanroomdepot.com
SIC: 3822 Auto controls regulating residntl & coml environmt & applncs

(G-5991)
COIL STAMPING INC
1340 Lincoln Ave Ste 1 (11741-2255)
PHONE.................................631 588-3040
Edward Kiss, *President*
EMP: 15
SALES (est): 1.6MM **Privately Held**
WEB: www.coilstamping.com
SIC: 3469 Metal stampings

(G-5992)
COLORSPEC COATINGS INTL INC
1716 Church St (11741-5918)
P.O. Box 493, Bohemia (11716-0493)
PHONE.................................631 472-8251
Lisa Bancalari, *President*
Robert Pein, *Vice Pres*
▲ EMP: 10
SQ FT: 5,200
SALES (est): 1.2MM **Privately Held**
WEB: www.colorspeccoatings.com
SIC: 2491 Preserving (creosoting) of wood

(G-5993)
CRYSTALIZATIONS SYSTEMS INC
1401 Lincoln Ave (11741-2215)
PHONE.................................631 467-0090
Patricia Ellenwood, *President*
Nelson Young, *Admin Sec*
EMP: 15
SQ FT: 12,000
SALES (est): 2.4MM **Privately Held**
SIC: 3499 Fire- or burglary-resistive products

(G-5994)
CTB ENTERPRISE LLC
1170 Lincoln Ave Unit 7 (11741-2286)
PHONE.................................631 563-0088
Tom Passaro, *Mng Member*
EMP: 10
SALES (est): 814.3K **Privately Held**
WEB: www.ctbenterprise.com
SIC: 3826 Instruments measuring magnetic & electrical properties

(G-5995)
DATA DISPLAY USA INC
1330 Lincoln Ave Ste 2 (11741-2268)
P.O. Box 5135, Brookings SD (57006-5135)
PHONE.................................631 218-2130
Marie Neville, *CEO*
Kevin Neville, *President*
▲ EMP: 120
SQ FT: 5,000
SALES: 13.3MM
SALES (corp-wide): 569.7MM **Publicly Held**
WEB: www.data-display.com
SIC: 3993 Signs & advertising specialties
HQ: Daktronics Ireland Co. Limited
Deerpark Industrial Estate
Ennis V95 X

(G-5996)
DEVOS LTD (PA)
Also Called: Guaranteed Returns
100 Colin Dr (11741-4306)
PHONE.................................800 473-2138
Paul Nick, *President*
Darren Volkes, *Exec VP*
Robert Schaltenbrand, *Vice Pres*
Chris Sellitto, *Vice Pres*
Charles Gurriera, *Controller*
▲ EMP: 113
SQ FT: 120,000
SALES (est): 21.7MM **Privately Held**
SIC: 2834 Pharmaceutical preparations

(G-5997)
DYNOCOAT INC
1738 Church St (11741-5918)
PHONE.................................631 244-9344
Patrick Dimaio, *President*
Donald Cowdell, *Vice Pres*
EMP: 10
SQ FT: 6,500
SALES: 850K **Privately Held**
WEB: www.dynocoat.com
SIC: 3479 Coating of metals & formed products

(G-5998)
ELECTRONIC SYSTEMS INC
Also Called: Esi
1742 Church St (11741-5918)
PHONE.................................631 589-4389
Gregory Quirk, *President*
EMP: 4
SALES: 1.2MM **Privately Held**
SIC: 3571 Electronic computers

(G-5999)
ENCORE REFINING AND RECYCLEING
1120 Lincoln Ave (11741-2260)
PHONE.................................631 319-1910
Joseph Crisera, *Partner*
Robert Gaslindo, *Partner*
EMP: 9
SALES (est): 432.3K **Privately Held**
SIC: 3341 Secondary precious metals

(G-6000)
IMAGE TYPOGRAPHY INC
Also Called: Starfire Printing
751 Coates Ave Ste 31 (11741-6039)
P.O. Box 5250, Miller Place (11764-7901)
PHONE.................................631 218-6932
James Bryant, *President*
EMP: 5
SALES (est): 484K **Privately Held**
WEB: www.starfireprinting.com
SIC: 2759 Commercial printing

(G-6001)
INGHAM INDUSTRIES INC
Also Called: Authentic Parts
1363 Lincoln Ave Ste 1 (11741-2274)
PHONE.................................631 242-2493
Donna Miller, *President*
EMP: 3
SQ FT: 2,500
SALES: 1MM **Privately Held**
WEB: www.authelectric.com
SIC: 3699 5065 5251 3429 Chimes, electric; intercommunication equipment, electronic; builders' hardware; manufactured hardware (general)

(G-6002)
INNOVATIVE POWER PRODUCTS INC
1170 Lincoln Ave Unit 7 (11741-2286)
PHONE.................................631 563-0088
Thomas Passaro Jr, *President*
Thomas Dowling, *Vice Pres*
EMP: 30
SQ FT: 5,200
SALES (est): 3.4MM **Privately Held**
SIC: 3679 Passive repeaters; electronic circuits

(G-6003)
ISLAND COMPONENTS GROUP INC
101 Colin Dr Unit 4 (11741-4332)
PHONE.................................631 563-4224
Demetris Agrotis, *CEO*
Roy Koch, *General Mgr*
EMP: 17
SQ FT: 5,000
SALES: 2MM **Privately Held**
WEB: www.islandcomponents.com
SIC: 3621 Motors, electric; electric motor & generator parts; electric motor & generator auxillary parts

(G-6004)
LATIUM USA TRADING LLC (PA)
Also Called: Four Seasons Sunrooms Windows
5005 Veterans Mem Hwy (11741-4506)
PHONE.................................631 563-4000
Shaun Kennedy, *President*
EMP: 70
SALES (est): 46.7MM **Privately Held**
SIC: 3448 Sunrooms, prefabricated metal

(G-6005)
LAWN ELEMENTS INC
1150 Lincoln Ave Ste 4 (11741-2251)
PHONE.................................631 656-9711
Veronica Concilio, *Principal*
EMP: 11 EST: 2010
SALES (est): 1.5MM **Privately Held**
SIC: 2819 Industrial inorganic chemicals

(G-6006)
LIBERTY LABEL MFG INC
21 Peachtree Ct (11741-4615)
PHONE.................................631 737-2365
Mike Fernandez, *President*
Lawrence Fernandez, *Vice Pres*
EMP: 15

SALES (est): 1.9MM **Privately Held**
WEB: www.libertylabel.com
SIC: 2754 2752 2672 Labels: gravure printing; commercial printing, lithographic; coated & laminated paper

(G-6007)
LONG ISLAND ANALYTICAL LABS
110 Colin Dr (11741-4306)
PHONE...............................631 472-3400
Mike Veraldi, *President*
Domenik Veraldi Jr, *Vice Pres*
Jim Aufiero, *Manager*
EMP: 18 **EST:** 1998
SQ FT: 6,000
SALES (est): 3.7MM **Privately Held**
WEB: www.lialinc.com
SIC: 3822 Auto controls regulating residntl & coml environmt & applncs

(G-6008)
M C PRODUCTS
Also Called: Division of Emergency Services
1330 Lincoln Ave Ste 2 (11741-2268)
P.O. Box 821 (11741-0821)
PHONE...............................631 471-4070
William Barnes, *President*
Jennifer Riccobono, *Mktg Dir*
EMP: 25
SALES (est): 4.2MM **Privately Held**
WEB: www.mcproducts.com
SIC: 3674 Semiconductors & related devices

(G-6009)
MARKETPLACE SLUTIONS GROUP LLC
48 Nimbus Rd Ste 303 (11741-4417)
PHONE...............................631 868-0111
Paul Pensabene, *Mng Member*
EMP: 25
SQ FT: 30,000
SALES: 4MM **Privately Held**
SIC: 2032 8742 8748 Italian foods: packaged in cans, jars, etc.; management consulting services; business consulting

(G-6010)
METALS BUILDING PRODUCTS
5005 Veterans Mem Hwy (11741-4506)
PHONE...............................844 638-2527
Shaun Kennedy, *President*
EMP: 19
SALES (est): 8MM
SALES (corp-wide): 46.7MM **Privately Held**
SIC: 3448 Prefabricated metal buildings
PA: Latium Usa Trading Llc
5005 Veterans Mem Hwy
Holbrook NY 11741
631 563-4000

(G-6011)
METALSMITH INC
1340 Lincoln Ave Ste 13 (11741-2255)
PHONE...............................631 467-1500
Jeff Smith, *President*
EMP: 5
SQ FT: 3,500
SALES (est): 420K **Privately Held**
SIC: 3444 Sheet metalwork

(G-6012)
MICROMATTER TECH INC USA
Also Called: Calmetrics
1340 Lincoln Ave Ste 6 (11741-2255)
PHONE...............................631 580-2522
Frank Ferrandino, *Branch Mgr*
EMP: 9
SALES (corp-wide): 783.8K **Privately Held**
SIC: 3479 Aluminum coating of metal products
PA: Micromatter Technologies Inc. Usa
603 Davis St Apt 2008
Austin TX 78701
631 580-2522

(G-6013)
NATIONAL ENERGY AUDITS LLC
1069 Main St 321 (11741-1618)
PHONE...............................631 883-3407
Steven Bendjy, *Principal*
EMP: 5

SALES (est): 445.4K **Privately Held**
SIC: 3677 Transformers power supply, electronic type

(G-6014)
NBTY INC
4320 Veterans Mem Hwy (11741-4504)
PHONE...............................631 200-2062
Denise Roman, *Marketing Staff*
Masae Tokiwa-Durben, *Marketing Staff*
George Brandenberger, *Department Mgr*
Kristi Latuso, *Manager*
Dragos Lynn, *Manager*
EMP: 9
SALES (est): 563.4K **Privately Held**
SIC: 2833 Medicinals & botanicals

(G-6015)
OMICRON TECHNOLOGIES INC
1736 Church St (11741-5918)
PHONE...............................631 434-7697
Bob Levine, *President*
John Kennedy, *Vice Pres*
EMP: 20
SALES (est): 901.2K **Privately Held**
SIC: 3999 Manufacturing industries

(G-6016)
READ MANUFACTURING COMPANY INC
330 Dante Ct (11741-3845)
PHONE...............................631 567-4487
Ronald H Read Sr, *CEO*
Heather Read-Connor, *President*
EMP: 21
SQ FT: 10,000
SALES: 2.6MM **Privately Held**
WEB: www.readmfg.com
SIC: 3444 3479 Sheet metal specialties, not stamped; painting, coating & hot dipping

(G-6017)
RIP-IT RIP-IT SHRED-IT CORP
920 Lincoln Ave Unit 8 (11741-2257)
P.O. Box 222, Yaphank (11980-0222)
PHONE...............................516 818-5825
Joseph Taormino, *Principal*
EMP: 6 **EST:** 2008
SALES (est): 164.4K **Privately Held**
SIC: 2789 Paper cutting

(G-6018)
ROADIE PRODUCTS INC
Also Called: Hybrid Cases
1121 Lincoln Ave Unit 20 (11741-2264)
P.O. Box 98, Oakdale (11769-0098)
PHONE...............................631 567-8588
Frank Maiella, *President*
▲ **EMP:** 25
SQ FT: 15,000
SALES (est): 4.7MM **Privately Held**
WEB: www.islandcases.com
SIC: 3161 3171 Musical instrument cases; handbags, women's

(G-6019)
RV PRINTING
39 Portside Dr (11741-5814)
PHONE...............................631 567-8658
Robert Viola, *Owner*
EMP: 7
SALES (est): 1.4MM **Privately Held**
SIC: 2752 Commercial printing, lithographic

(G-6020)
SELECT-A-FORM INC
4717 Veterans Mem Hwy (11741-4515)
PHONE...............................631 981-3076
Dave Walters, *President*
John Candia, *Vice Pres*
EMP: 52
SQ FT: 17,000
SALES (est): 4.6MM **Privately Held**
SIC: 2759 2761 2752 Business forms: printing; manifold business forms; color lithography

(G-6021)
SOLAR METROLOGY LLC
1340 Lincoln Ave Ste 6 (11741-2255)
PHONE...............................845 247-4701
Francis Reilly,
EMP: 9

SALES (est): 640.8K **Privately Held**
SIC: 3823 Industrial instrmnts msrmnt display/control process variable

(G-6022)
STERLING SHELF LINERS INC
836 Grundy Ave (11741-2606)
PHONE...............................631 676-5175
Jason Sterling, *President*
EMP: 5
SALES (est): 187.6K **Privately Held**
SIC: 2542 2392 Shelving, office & store: except wood; placemats, plastic or textile

(G-6023)
SUMMIT TECHNOLOGIES LLC
Also Called: Summit Laser Products
723 Broadway Ave (11741-4955)
PHONE...............................631 590-1040
Steven Hecht, *Mng Member*
Mike Kosiah,
▲ **EMP:** 38
SQ FT: 25,300
SALES (est): 3.7MM **Privately Held**
WEB: www.uninetimaging.com
SIC: 3955 Print cartridges for laser & other computer printers
PA: Uninet Imaging, Inc.
3232 W El Segundo Blvd
Hawthorne CA 90250

(G-6024)
SUPERIOR WELDING
331 Dante Ct Ste G (11741-3800)
PHONE...............................631 676-2751
Steve Takats, *Executive*
EMP: 7
SALES (est): 802.6K **Privately Held**
SIC: 3599 Machine shop, jobbing & repair

(G-6025)
SYMBOL TECHNOLOGIES LLC
25 Andrea Rd (11741-4310)
PHONE...............................631 218-3907
James Rawson, *Manager*
EMP: 16
SALES (corp-wide): 4.2B **Publicly Held**
WEB: www.symbol.com
SIC: 3577 Magnetic ink & optical scanning devices
HQ: Symbol Technologies, Llc
1 Zebra Plz
Holtsville NY 11742
631 737-6851

(G-6026)
TENS MACHINE COMPANY INC
800 Grundy Ave (11741-2606)
PHONE...............................631 981-3321
Toni Coffaro, *President*
Fabio Berlingieri, *Vice Pres*
Mike Berlingieri, *Vice Pres*
Salvatore Berlingieri, *Vice Pres*
Tom Crescenzo, *Manager*
EMP: 28
SQ FT: 9,620
SALES: 5.5MM **Privately Held**
WEB: www.tensmachine.com
SIC: 3728 Aircraft parts & equipment

(G-6027)
TRUSTFORT LLC
4250 Veterans Memorial Hw (11741-4020)
PHONE...............................781 787-0906
Atindra Barua, *Mng Member*
Marguerite Larkin, *Manager*
EMP: 3
SALES: 1MM **Privately Held**
SIC: 7372 Business oriented computer software

Holland
Erie County

(G-6028)
BUFFALO POLYMER PROCESSORS INC
42 Edgewood Dr (14080-9784)
PHONE...............................716 537-3153
Miro O Staroba, *Ch of Bd*
EMP: 40
SQ FT: 180,000

SALES (est): 7MM **Privately Held**
SIC: 3089 Injection molding of plastics; plastic processing

(G-6029)
INEX INC
9229 Olean Rd (14080-9773)
PHONE...............................716 537-2270
Michael Kasprzyk, *President*
Corry McCluer, *Info Tech Mgr*
EMP: 9
SALES (est): 1.6MM **Privately Held**
WEB: www.schunk-inex.com
SIC: 3443 Fabricated plate work (boiler shop)

(G-6030)
PRO-TECK COATING INC
7785 Olean Rd (14080-9709)
P.O. Box 372 (14080-0372)
PHONE...............................716 537-2619
Wayne Rutkowski Sr, *President*
Jeff Weber, *Vice Pres*
EMP: 13
SQ FT: 22,000
SALES (est): 1.1MM **Privately Held**
WEB: www.proteckcoating.com
SIC: 3479 Coating of metals with plastic or resins; coating of metals & formed products

(G-6031)
STAROBA PLASTICS INC
42 Edgewood Dr (14080-9784)
PHONE...............................716 537-3153
Miro Staroba, *CEO*
Barbara Staroba, *Vice Pres*
EMP: 125
SALES (est): 17.9MM **Privately Held**
SIC: 3089 Injection molding of plastics

(G-6032)
UHMAC INC
136 N Main St (14080-9704)
PHONE...............................716 537-2343
James McBride, *President*
Rhonda B Juhasz, *Corp Secy*
EMP: 10
SQ FT: 9,973
SALES (est): 1.6MM **Privately Held**
WEB: www.uhmac.com
SIC: 3542 Rebuilt machine tools, metal forming types

Holland Patent
Oneida County

(G-6033)
CUSTOM KLEAN CORP
Also Called: Pressure Washer Sales
8890 Boak Rd E (13354-3608)
PHONE...............................315 865-8101
Paul Sears, *President*
EMP: 15
SQ FT: 30,000
SALES (est): 1.8MM **Privately Held**
WEB: www.pressurewashersales.com
SIC: 3589 7363 High pressure cleaning equipment; domestic help service

(G-6034)
STEFFEN PUBLISHING INC
Also Called: Adirondack Home News
9584 Main St (13354-3819)
P.O. Box 403 (13354-0403)
PHONE...............................315 865-4100
Fax: 315 865-4000
EMP: 100
SQ FT: 20,000
SALES (est): 4.4MM **Privately Held**
SIC: 2711 2752 2732 2731 Newspapers-Publish/Print Lithographic Coml Print Book Printing Book-Publishing/Printing Periodical-Publish/Print

Holley
Orleans County

(G-6035)
AMY PAK PUBLISHING INC
3997 Roosevelt Hwy (14470-9201)
PHONE.................................585 964-8188
Amy Pak, *Principal*
EMP: 8
SALES (est): 742.3K **Privately Held**
SIC: 2741 Miscellaneous publishing

(G-6036)
ORLEANS CUSTOM PACKING INC
101 Cadbury Way (14470-1079)
PHONE.................................585 314-8227
Donald Ward, *Ch of Bd*
EMP: 6
SALES (est): 622.4K **Privately Held**
SIC: 2011 Meat packing plants

(G-6037)
PRECISION PACKAGING PDTS INC
88 Nesbitt Dr (14470-1078)
PHONE.................................585 638-8200
Michael Evans, *CEO*
Kerry Kyle, *Plant Mgr*
▲ **EMP:** 110
SQ FT: 68,000
SALES (est): 19.2MM
SALES (corp-wide): 8.6B **Publicly Held**
WEB: www.prepackpro.com
SIC: 3089 Plastic containers, except foam
PA: Newell Brands Inc.
221 River St Ste 13
Hoboken NJ 07030
201 610-6600

(G-6038)
SEAWARD CANDIES
3588 N Main Street Rd (14470-9305)
PHONE.................................585 638-6761
Donna Seaward,
EMP: 6
SALES: 75K **Privately Held**
SIC: 2064 5441 Candy & other confectionery products; candy

(G-6039)
WADDINGTON NORTH AMERICA INC
Also Called: Wna-Holley
88 Nesbitt Dr (14470-1078)
PHONE.................................585 638-8200
Kevin Haines, *Principal*
EMP: 150
SALES (corp-wide): 2.9B **Privately Held**
SIC: 3089 Air mattresses, plastic
HQ: Waddington North America, Inc.
50 E Rivercenter Blvd # 650
Covington KY 41011

Hollis
Queens County

(G-6040)
BORDEN & RILEY PAPER CO INC
18410 Jamaica Ave Ste W3 (11423-2434)
PHONE.................................718 454-9494
Zoila P Woodward, *President*
Juan Guerra, *Vice Pres*
▲ **EMP:** 25
SQ FT: 31,500
SALES (est): 5.2MM **Privately Held**
WEB: www.bordenandriley.com
SIC: 2675 Die-cut paper & board

(G-6041)
CHINA RUITAI INTL HOLDINGS LTD
8710 Clover Pl (11423-1252)
PHONE.................................718 740-2278
James Herbst, *Principal*
EMP: 3
SALES: 43.1MM **Privately Held**
SIC: 2869 Industrial organic chemicals

(G-6042)
CRUMBRUBBER TECHNOLOGY INC
18740 Hollis Ave (11423-2808)
PHONE.................................718 468-3988
Angelo Reali, *President*
Michael Reali, *Vice Pres*
EMP: 10
SQ FT: 60,000
SALES: 5MM **Privately Held**
SIC: 3559 4953 Recycling machinery; recycling, waste materials

(G-6043)
G & J RDYMX & MASNRY SUP INC
18330 Jamaica Ave (11423-2302)
PHONE.................................718 454-0800
John Cervoni, *President*
John Cerzoni, *President*
EMP: 12
SQ FT: 80,000
SALES (est): 1.2MM **Privately Held**
SIC: 3273 Ready-mixed concrete

Holtsville
Suffolk County

(G-6044)
ADVANCE PHARMACEUTICAL INC (PA)
895 Waverly Ave (11742-1109)
PHONE.................................631 981-4600
Tasrin Hossain, *President*
Liaquat Hossain, *Vice Pres*
EMP: 85
SQ FT: 80,000
SALES: 9MM **Privately Held**
SIC: 2834 Druggists' preparations (pharmaceuticals)

(G-6045)
BLACKSTONE INTERNATIONAL INC
Also Called: Ocean Stone and Fireplace
180 Long Island Ave (11742-1815)
PHONE.................................631 289-5490
Joseph Karatas, *President*
Victoria Nook, *Opers Mgr*
EMP: 5 **EST:** 2016
SALES (est): 121.6K **Privately Held**
SIC: 3272 5023 5074 5719 Fireplaces, concrete; fireplace equipment & accessories; fireplaces, prefabricated; fireplace equipment & accessories

(G-6046)
BROOKHAVEN INSTRUMENTS CORP
750 Blue Point Rd (11742-1896)
PHONE.................................631 758-3200
Walther Tscharnuter, *CEO*
Joe Pozzolano, *Ch of Bd*
Bruce Weiner, *President*
Michael Anderson, *Chief Engr*
Scott Lee, *Engineer*
EMP: 24
SQ FT: 15,000
SALES (est): 5MM **Privately Held**
WEB: www.bic.com
SIC: 3826 Analytical instruments

(G-6047)
C & H PRECISION TOOLS INC
194 Morris Ave Ste 20 (11742-1451)
PHONE.................................631 758-3806
Donald Schwabe, *President*
EMP: 20
SALES (est): 1.9MM **Privately Held**
SIC: 3469 Metal stampings

(G-6048)
CUTTING EDGE METAL WORKS
12 Long Island Ave (11742-1803)
PHONE.................................631 981-8333
Tom Richards, *Owner*
Lou Tancredi, *Vice Pres*
EMP: 24
SALES: 3.1MM **Privately Held**
SIC: 3444 Sheet metalwork

(G-6049)
DANTEC DYNAMICS INC
750 Blue Point Rd (11742-1832)
PHONE.................................631 654-1290
Kim D Jensen, *President*
EMP: 8
SQ FT: 6,000
SALES (est): 1.4MM
SALES (corp-wide): 177.9K **Privately Held**
WEB: www.dantecmt.com
SIC: 3826 Analytical instruments
HQ: Dantec Dynamics A/S
Tonsbakken 16-18
Skovlunde 2740
445 780-00

(G-6050)
KOEHLER INSTRUMENT COMPANY INC (PA)
85 Corporate Dr (11742-2007)
PHONE.................................631 589-3800
Roy Westerhaus, *Ch of Bd*
Stephen Foster, *Mfg Mgr*
Vivek Shahu, *Technical Mgr*
Jesse Kelly, *Engineer*
Yong Luo, *Engineer*
▲ **EMP:** 55
SQ FT: 28,500
SALES (est): 9.7MM **Privately Held**
WEB: www.koehlerinstrument.com
SIC: 3823 Industrial instrmnts msrmnt display/control process variable

(G-6051)
OASIS COSMETIC LABS INC
182 Long Island Ave (11742-1815)
PHONE.................................631 758-0038
Thomas Murray, *President*
EMP: 10
SALES: 2MM **Privately Held**
SIC: 2844 Cosmetic preparations

(G-6052)
SCREEN THE WORLD INC
Also Called: Crazy Hatter
658 Blue Point Rd (11742-1848)
PHONE.................................631 475-0023
Jeff Liebowitz, *President*
EMP: 12
SQ FT: 5,000
SALES (est): 1.5MM **Privately Held**
WEB: www.crazyhatter.com
SIC: 2759 2395 Screen printing; art needlework: made from purchased materials

(G-6053)
STARFIRE PRINTING INC
28 Washington Ave (11742-1027)
PHONE.................................631 736-1495
EMP: 5
SALES (est): 230K **Privately Held**
SIC: 2759 Commercial Printing

(G-6054)
SYMBOL TECHNOLOGIES LLC (HQ)
Also Called: Symbol Technologies Delaware
1 Zebra Plz (11742-1300)
PHONE.................................631 737-6851
Edward Fitzpatrick, *CEO*
Paul Kiernen, *Principal*
Timothy T Yates, *CFO*
Cary Schmiedel, *Treasurer*
Tony Russo, *Software Engr*
▲ **EMP:** 1800 **EST:** 1987
SQ FT: 299,000
SALES (est): 1.1B
SALES (corp-wide): 4.2B **Publicly Held**
WEB: www.symbol.com
SIC: 3577 Optical scanning devices
PA: Zebra Technologies Corporation
3 Overlook Pt
Lincolnshire IL 60069
847 634-6700

(G-6055)
TANGRAM COMPANY LLC
125 Corporate Dr (11742-2007)
PHONE.................................631 758-0460
Philip Gillette,
John Takakjian,
▼ **EMP:** 25
SQ FT: 32,000

SALES: 6.4MM **Privately Held**
WEB: www.tangramco.com
SIC: 2819 2899 Industrial inorganic chemicals; chemical preparations

(G-6056)
TELXON CORPORATION (DH)
1 Zebra Plz (11742-1300)
PHONE.................................631 738-2400
John W Paxton, *Ch of Bd*
Kenneth A Cassady, *President*
David H Briggs, *Vice Pres*
Woody M McGee, *CFO*
▲ **EMP:** 35 **EST:** 1969
SALES (est): 83.8MM
SALES (corp-wide): 4.2B **Publicly Held**
WEB: www.telxon.com
SIC: 3571 7373 3663 Personal computers (microcomputers); systems integration services; radio & TV communications equipment
HQ: Symbol Technologies, Llc
1 Zebra Plz
Holtsville NY 11742
631 737-6851

(G-6057)
TOPAZ INDUSTRIES INC
130 Corporate Dr (11742-2005)
PHONE.................................631 207-0700
Craig Stowell, *President*
▲ **EMP:** 10
SQ FT: 3,000
SALES (est): 2.2MM **Privately Held**
SIC: 2899 Salt

(G-6058)
WEISS INSTRUMENTS INC
905 Waverly Ave (11742-1109)
PHONE.................................631 207-1200
William Weiss, *CEO*
John Weiss, *President*
Kenneth Goodwin, *General Mgr*
Phillip J Weiss, *Chairman*
Josh Kalish, *Engineer*
▲ **EMP:** 100 **EST:** 1882
SQ FT: 50,000
SALES (est): 25.6MM **Privately Held**
WEB: www.weissinstruments.com
SIC: 3823 3829 Temperature instruments: industrial process type; pressure gauges, dial & digital; measuring & controlling devices

(G-6059)
ZEBRA TECHNOLOGIES ENTP CORP
1 Zebra Plz (11742-1325)
PHONE.................................800 722-6234
Anders Gustafsson, *CEO*
Celia Bershadsky, *Project Mgr*
Anthony Lasala, *Mfg Staff*
Michael Smiley, *CFO*
Kristen Ludwig, *Human Resources*
EMP: 39
SALES (est): 23MM
SALES (corp-wide): 4.2B **Publicly Held**
SIC: 3577 1541 5088 Computer peripheral equipment; prefabricated building erection, industrial; transportation equipment & supplies
PA: Zebra Technologies Corporation
3 Overlook Pt
Lincolnshire IL 60069
847 634-6700

Homer
Cortland County

(G-6060)
ALBANY INTERNATIONAL CORP
156 S Main St (13077-1600)
PHONE.................................607 749-7226
Glen Gutierrez, *Buyer*
Deborah Burkwit, *Engineer*
Jay Jandris, *Engineer*
Gary R Seales, *Manager*
EMP: 115

SALES (corp-wide): 982.4MM **Publicly Held**
WEB: www.albint.com
SIC: 2298 3089 2284 Cordage & twine; extruded finished plastic products; thread mills
PA: Albany International Corp.
　　216 Airport Dr
　　Rochester NH 03867
　　603 330-5850

(G-6061)
DEWEY MACHINE & TOOL INC
49 James St (13077-1221)
PHONE.................................607 749-3930
Chris Dewey, *President*
EMP: 6
SQ FT: 2,000
SALES (est): 864.4K **Privately Held**
SIC: 3599 Machine shop, jobbing & repair

(G-6062)
F M L INDUSTRIES INC
10 Hudson St (13077-1043)
P.O. Box 398 (13077-0398)
PHONE.................................607 749-7273
Paul Dries, *President*
EMP: 9
SQ FT: 12,000
SALES (est): 1.4MM **Privately Held**
SIC: 7692 3444 3599 Welding repair; sheet metalwork; machine shop, jobbing & repair

(G-6063)
HASKELL MACHINE & TOOL INC
5 S Fulton St (13077-1232)
P.O. Box 8 (13077-0008)
PHONE.................................607 749-2421
James E Harris, *President*
Roberta J Harris, *Vice Pres*
EMP: 10 EST: 1947
SQ FT: 7,000
SALES (est): 1.4MM **Privately Held**
WEB: www.haskellmachine.com
SIC: 3599 7692 Machine shop, jobbing & repair; welding repair

(G-6064)
HOMER IRON WORKS LLC
5130 Us Route 11 (13077-9528)
PHONE.................................607 749-3963
Mike Park,
EMP: 7
SQ FT: 2,100
SALES: 700K **Privately Held**
SIC: 3441 7692 7538 Fabricated structural metal; welding repair; general automotive repair shops

(G-6065)
HOMER LOGGING CONTRACTOR
6176 Sunnyside Dr (13077-9321)
PHONE.................................607 753-8553
Steve Hubbard, *Principal*
EMP: 5
SALES (est): 339.5K **Privately Held**
SIC: 2411 Logging camps & contractors

(G-6066)
PHOTON VISION SYSTEMS INC (PA)
1 Technology Pl (13077-1549)
PHONE.................................607 749-2689
Thomas L Vogelsong, *President*
Jeffrey J Zarnowski, *COO*
EMP: 15 EST: 1997
SALES (est): 1.6MM **Privately Held**
SIC: 3571 Electronic computers

(G-6067)
SOLIDUS INDUSTRIES INC
Also Called: Pb Industries
6849 N Glen Haven Rd (13077-9522)
PHONE.................................607 749-4540
Frank Girardi, *President*
EMP: 96
SQ FT: 28,000
SALES (est): 13MM **Privately Held**
WEB: www.pb-industries.com
SIC: 3444 3469 3479 2396 Sheet metalwork; machine parts, stamped or pressed metal; coating of metals & formed products; automotive & apparel trimmings

---

Honeoye
Ontario County

(G-6068)
CY PLASTICS WORKS INC
8601 Main St (14471-9603)
P.O. Box 560 (14471-0560)
PHONE.................................585 229-2555
Andy Molodetz, *President*
Jeff Egburtson, *Mfg Staff*
John Cavagnaro, *Engineer*
Peter Malinowski, *Controller*
David Rubin, *Director*
▲ **EMP:** 70
SQ FT: 35,000
SALES (est): 11.7MM **Privately Held**
SIC: 3089 3544 3842 3949 Injection molding of plastics; special dies, tools, jigs & fixtures; industrial molds; surgical appliances & supplies; sporting & athletic goods

(G-6069)
ROOME TECHNOLOGIES INC
4796 Honeoye Business Par (14471-8808)
P.O. Box 742 (14471-0742)
PHONE.................................585 229-4437
David Roome, *President*
EMP: 7
SQ FT: 8,500
SALES: 2MM **Privately Held**
WEB: www.roometechnologies.com
SIC: 3564 Filters, air: furnaces, air conditioning equipment, etc.

Honeoye Falls
Monroe County

(G-6070)
BRANSON ULTRASONICS CORP
475 Quaker Meeting Hse Rd (14472-9754)
PHONE.................................585 624-8000
John Bielaski, *Project Engr*
Craig Birrittella, *Manager*
EMP: 20
SQ FT: 78,580
SALES (corp-wide): 17.4B **Publicly Held**
WEB: www.bransonic.com
SIC: 3699 Cleaning equipment, ultrasonic, except medical & dental
HQ: Branson Ultrasonics Corporation
　　41 Eagle Rd Ste 1
　　Danbury CT 06810
　　203 796-0400

(G-6071)
EQUICENTER INC
3247 Rush Mendon Rd (14472-9333)
PHONE.................................585 742-2522
Jonathan Friedlander, *President*
EMP: 30
SALES: 1.3MM **Privately Held**
SIC: 3199 Equestrian related leather articles

(G-6072)
GRAVER TECHNOLOGIES LLC
300 W Main St (14472-1197)
PHONE.................................585 624-1330
Herbert J Ego, *General Mgr*
EMP: 40
SQ FT: 34,000
SALES (est): 9.4MM
SALES (corp-wide): 225.3B **Publicly Held**
SIC: 3569 Filters, general line: industrial
HQ: Graver Technologies Llc
　　200 Lake Dr
　　Newark DE 19702

(G-6073)
HANSON AGGREGATES PA LLC
2049 County Rd 6 (14472)
PHONE.................................585 624-3800
Douglas Fuess, *Manager*
EMP: 35
SALES (corp-wide): 20.6B **Privately Held**
SIC: 2951 1442 5032 Asphalt & asphaltic paving mixtures (not from refineries); gravel mining; brick, stone & related material

---

HQ: Hanson Aggregates Pennsylvania, Llc
　　7660 Imperial Way
　　Allentown PA 18195
　　610 366-4626

(G-6074)
HANSON AGGREGATES PA LLC
2049 Honeoye Falls 6 Rd (14472-8913)
P.O. Box 151 (14472-0151)
PHONE.................................585 624-1220
Mike Clark, *Branch Mgr*
EMP: 30
SALES (corp-wide): 20.6B **Privately Held**
SIC: 1442 5999 1422 5032 Gravel mining; stones, crystalline: rough; crushed & broken limestone; asphalt mixture
HQ: Hanson Aggregates Pennsylvania, Llc
　　7660 Imperial Way
　　Allentown PA 18195
　　610 366-4626

(G-6075)
HONEOYE FALLS DISTILLERY LLC (PA)
168 W Main St (14472-1135)
PHONE.................................201 780-4618
Scott M Stanton, *Mng Member*
John D Marshall,
Robert Teal Schlegel,
EMP: 12 EST: 2014
SQ FT: 7,000
SALES (est): 200K **Privately Held**
SIC: 2085 Applejack (alcoholic beverage)

(G-6076)
K & H PRECISION PRODUCTS INC
45 Norton St (14472-1032)
PHONE.................................585 624-4894
Steven Hogarth, *President*
Alex Ferguson, *Vice Pres*
George Reeners, *CFO*
EMP: 40
SQ FT: 20,000
SALES (est): 8.1MM **Privately Held**
WEB: www.kandhprecision.com
SIC: 3543 3089 3599 3544 Industrial patterns; injection molded finished plastic products; machine shop, jobbing & repair; special dies, tools, jigs & fixtures; nonferrous foundries

(G-6077)
KADDIS MANUFACTURING CORP
Enerco Plant
1175 Bragg St (14472-8602)
P.O. Box 92985, Rochester (14692-9085)
PHONE.................................585 624-3070
Bruce Whitmore, *Manager*
EMP: 8
SALES (corp-wide): 6.5MM **Privately Held**
WEB: www.kaddis.com
SIC: 3451 3621 3568 Screw machine products; motors & generators; power transmission equipment
PA: Kaddis Manufacturing Corp.
　　293 Patriot Way
　　Rochester NY 14624
　　585 464-9000

(G-6078)
MICROPEN TECHNOLOGIES CORP
Also Called: MICROPEN DIVISION
93 Papermill St (14472-1252)
PHONE.................................585 624-2610
Edwin P Petrazzolo, *Ch of Bd*
William Grande, *Vice Pres*
Eric Van Wormer, *Vice Pres*
Vanwormer Eric, *Opers Staff*
Leigh Barry, *Purchasing*
▼ **EMP:** 75
SQ FT: 38,000
SALES: 13.6MM **Privately Held**
WEB: www.ohmcraft.com
SIC: 3676 3625 Electronic resistors; resistors & resistor units

(G-6079)
RUSH GRAVEL CORP
130 Kavanaugh Rd (14472-9599)
PHONE.................................585 533-1740
Marie Schillinger, *Treasurer*

David Schillinger Jr, *Shareholder*
Timothy Schillinger, *Shareholder*
EMP: 8
SALES (est): 770K **Privately Held**
WEB: www.rushgravel.com
SIC: 1442 Sand mining; gravel mining

(G-6080)
SOUTHCO INC
Honeoye Falls Div
250 East St (14472-1298)
PHONE.................................585 624-2545
Don Fisher, *Opers Spvr*
Paul Soldo, *Mfg Staff*
Joseph Werner, *Engineer*
Jeffrey Williamson, *Engineer*
Ryan Zargiel, *Engineer*
EMP: 400
SQ FT: 40,000
SALES (corp-wide): 653.8MM **Privately Held**
WEB: www.southco.com
SIC: 3429 3452 Metal fasteners; bolts, nuts, rivets & washers
HQ: Southco, Inc.
　　210 N Brinton Lake Rd
　　Concordville PA 19331
　　610 459-4000

(G-6081)
STEVER-LOCKE INDUSTRIES INC
Also Called: Metal Stampings
179 N Main St (14472-1056)
PHONE.................................585 624-3450
Elaine R Davin, *President*
Mick Davin, *General Mgr*
▲ **EMP:** 9
SQ FT: 22,000
SALES (est): 5.6MM **Privately Held**
WEB: www.steverlocke.com
SIC: 3469 3672 3643 Metal stampings; wiring boards; current-carrying wiring devices

---

Hoosick
Rensselaer County

(G-6082)
VPS CONTROL SYSTEMS INC
19 Hill Rd (12089)
P.O. Box 249 (12089-0249)
PHONE.................................518 686-0019
Peter Schaaphok, *President*
Duane Goodermote, *Engineer*
Ingrid Schaaphok, *Admin Sec*
EMP: 14
SQ FT: 6,625
SALES: 1MM **Privately Held**
WEB: www.flexballcables.com
SIC: 3625 Electric controls & control accessories, industrial

---

Hoosick Falls
Rensselaer County

(G-6083)
GRAPHITEK INC
4883 State Route 67 (12090-4829)
P.O. Box 131, Glenmont (12077-0131)
PHONE.................................518 686-5966
Al Randle, *President*
Thierry Guerlain, *Vice Pres*
EMP: 18
SQ FT: 8,500
SALES: 3.5MM **Privately Held**
WEB: www.graphitek.com
SIC: 3993 Signs & advertising specialties

(G-6084)
LOVEJOY CHAPLET CORPORATION
12 River St (12090-1815)
P.O. Box 66 (12090-0066)
PHONE.................................518 686-5232
Peter McGuire, *President*
Lisa McGuire, *Vice Pres*
Margaret Sargood, *Admin Asst*
EMP: 28 EST: 1911
SQ FT: 20,000

2020 Harris
New York Manufacturers Directory
▲ = Import ▼=Export
◆ =Import/Export

SALES (est): 4.2MM **Privately Held**
WEB: www.lovejoychaplet.com
SIC: 3599 Machine shop, jobbing & repair

(G-6085)
LYDALL PERFORMANCE MTLS US INC
12 Davis St (12090-1006)
PHONE..................................518 686-3400
James Lynch, *Branch Mgr*
EMP: 60
SALES (corp-wide): 785.9MM **Publicly Held**
WEB: www.sealinfo.com
SIC: 2631 3053 Paperboard mills; gaskets, packing & sealing devices
HQ: Lydall Performance Materials (Us), Inc.
216 Wohlsen Way
Lancaster PA 17603

(G-6086)
OAK-MITSUI INC
1 Mechanic St Bldg 2 (12090-1011)
PHONE..................................518 686-8060
EMP: 54 **Privately Held**
SIC: 3497 Copper foil
HQ: Oak Mitsui, Inc.
29 Battleship Road Ext
Camden SC 29020
518 686-4961

(G-6087)
OAK-MITSUI TECHNOLOGIES LLC
80 1st St (12090-1631)
P.O. Box 501 (12090-0501)
PHONE..................................518 686-4961
John Yavis, *IT/INT Sup*
Fujio Kuwako,
▲ EMP: 30
SALES (est): 4.6MM **Privately Held**
WEB: www.oakmitsui.com
SIC: 3497 Copper foil
HQ: Oak Mitsui, Inc.
29 Battleship Road Ext
Camden SC 29020
518 686-4961

(G-6088)
SAINT-GOBAIN PRFMCE PLAS CORP
14 Mccaffrey St (12090-1819)
PHONE..................................518 686-7301
Chris Lower, *Manager*
EMP: 177
SALES (corp-wide): 215.9MM **Privately Held**
SIC: 2821 Plastics materials & resins
HQ: Saint-Gobain Performance Plastics Corporation
31500 Solon Rd
Solon OH 44139
440 836-6900

(G-6089)
SAINT-GOBAIN PRFMCE PLAS CORP
1 Liberty St (12090-1019)
P.O. Box 320 (12090)
PHONE..................................518 686-7301
Pat Traynor, *Branch Mgr*
EMP: 190
SALES (corp-wide): 215.9MM **Privately Held**
SIC: 2821 Polytetrafluoroethylene resins (teflon)
HQ: Saint-Gobain Performance Plastics Corporation
31500 Solon Rd
Solon OH 44139
440 836-6900

Hopewell Junction
Dutchess County

(G-6090)
APPLIED MATERIALS INC
2531 Route 52 (12533-3227)
PHONE..................................845 227-5000
Ofer Nakash, *Opers Staff*
Mark Gilliam, *Manager*
EMP: 50

SALES (corp-wide): 17.2B **Publicly Held**
WEB: www.appliedmaterials.com
SIC: 3674 Semiconductors & related devices
PA: Applied Materials, Inc.
3050 Bowers Ave
Santa Clara CA 95054
408 727-5555

(G-6091)
BEECH GROVE TECHNOLOGY INC
11 Sandy Pines Blvd (12533-8211)
P.O. Box 406, Stormville (12582-0406)
PHONE..................................845 223-6844
Carol Petvai, *President*
Steve Petvai, *Vice Pres*
EMP: 5
SQ FT: 1,500
SALES (est): 480K **Privately Held**
SIC: 3674 Semiconductors & related devices

(G-6092)
EMAGIN CORPORATION (PA)
700 South Dr Ste 201 (12533-4026)
PHONE..................................845 838-7900
Andrew G Sculley, *CEO*
Jill J Wittels, *Ch of Bd*
Jeffrey P Lucas, *President*
Amalkumar Ghosh, *Senior VP*
Oliver Prache, *Senior VP*
EMP: 105
SQ FT: 42,000
SALES: 26.2MM **Publicly Held**
WEB: www.emagin.com
SIC: 3674 Light emitting diodes

(G-6093)
FRITTERS & BUNS INC
236 Blue Hill Rd (12533-6659)
PHONE..................................845 227-6609
EMP: 8 EST: 1985
SALES (est): 400K **Privately Held**
SIC: 2051 Mfg Bread/Related Products

(G-6094)
GLOBALFOUNDRIES US 2 LLC (DH)
2070 Route 52 (12533-3507)
PHONE..................................512 457-3900
Sanjay Jha, *CEO*
John Toy, *Human Res Dir*
EMP: 143
SALES (est): 1.1MM **Privately Held**
SIC: 3674 Semiconductors & related devices

(G-6095)
GLOBALFOUNDRIES US INC
2070 Route 52 (12533-3507)
PHONE..................................512 457-3900
Rashi Garg, *Program Mgr*
David Brown, *Manager*
Brendan Chudy, *Manager*
Timothy Powers, *Manager*
Michael Mendicino, *Director*
EMP: 23 **Privately Held**
SIC: 3559 3674 Semiconductor manufacturing machinery; semiconductors & related devices
HQ: Globalfoundries U.S. Inc.
2600 Great America Way
Santa Clara CA 95054

(G-6096)
HOPEWELL PRECISION INC
19 Ryan Rd (12533-8322)
P.O. Box 551 (12533-0551)
PHONE..................................845 221-2737
Richard Skeen, *President*
Donna Cznarty, *Admin Sec*
EMP: 22
SQ FT: 25,000
SALES (est): 4.6MM **Privately Held**
WEB: www.hopewell-precision.com
SIC: 3663 Studio equipment, radio & television broadcasting

(G-6097)
INTERNATIONAL BUS MCHS CORP
Also Called: IBM
10 North Dr (12533)
PHONE..................................800 426-4968

Bill Lafontaine, *General Mgr*
Doug Warinner, *Vice Pres*
Rich Burda, *Engineer*
William Corbin, *Engineer*
Ethan Gallagher, *Engineer*
EMP: 170
SALES (corp-wide): 79.5B **Publicly Held**
WEB: www.ibm.com
SIC: 3674 Semiconductors & related devices
PA: International Business Machines Corporation
1 New Orchard Rd Ste 1 # 1
Armonk NY 10504
914 499-1900

(G-6098)
KLA CORPORATION
20 Corporate Park Rd C (12533-6557)
PHONE..................................845 897-1723
Matt Brown, *Manager*
EMP: 12
SALES (corp-wide): 4.5B **Publicly Held**
WEB: www.tencor.com
SIC: 3674 Semiconductors & related devices
PA: Kla Corporation
1 Technology Dr
Milpitas CA 95035
408 875-3000

(G-6099)
LIFE MEDICAL TECHNOLOGIES LLC
2070 Rte 52 21a Bldg 320a (12533)
PHONE..................................845 894-2121
EMP: 10
SALES (est): 660K **Privately Held**
SIC: 3069 Mfg Fabricated Rubber Products

(G-6100)
PHILLIP J ORTIZ MANUFACTURING
44 Railroad Ave (12533-7318)
P.O. Box 116 (12533-0116)
PHONE..................................845 226-7030
Barry Ortiz, *President*
EMP: 6
SQ FT: 10,000
SALES (est): 506.7K **Privately Held**
SIC: 7692 3714 Welding repair; motor vehicle parts & accessories

(G-6101)
SPECTRAL SYSTEMS LLC (PA)
35 Corporate Park Rd (12533-6558)
PHONE..................................845 896-2200
Scott Little, *President*
Laurie Robinson, *Accounting Mgr*
Carlos Guajardo, *Sales Mgr*
Robert Accomando, *Technology*
Bruce Capuano,
EMP: 47
SALES: 11MM **Privately Held**
SIC: 3827 Optical instruments & apparatus

Hornell
Steuben County

(G-6102)
BOMBARDIER TRANSPORTATION
1 William K Jackson Ln (14843-1457)
PHONE..................................607 324-0216
Dave Sharma, *Branch Mgr*
EMP: 60
SALES (corp-wide): 16.2B **Privately Held**
SIC: 3441 3743 Fabricated structural metal; railroad equipment, except locomotives
HQ: Bombardier Transportation (Holdings) Usa Inc.
1251 Waterfront Pl
Pittsburgh PA 15222
412 655-5700

(G-6103)
DOLOMITE PRODUCTS COMPANY INC
Also Called: A.L. Blades
7610 County Road 65 (14843-9626)
PHONE..................................607 324-3636
Jonathan Cook, *Sales Staff*
Andrew Crane, *Sales Staff*
EMP: 16
SALES (corp-wide): 30.6B **Privately Held**
SIC: 2951 Paving mixtures
HQ: Dolomite Products Company Inc.
1150 Penfield Rd
Rochester NY 14625
315 524-1998

(G-6104)
DYCO ELECTRONICS INC
7775 Industrial Park Rd (14843-9673)
PHONE..................................607 324-2030
Gregory D Georgek, *President*
Randy Drake, *General Mgr*
Allan Klus, *Engineer*
Anthony Gala, *Design Engr*
Karla Dungan, *Manager*
EMP: 80
SQ FT: 30,000
SALES (est): 14.7MM **Privately Held**
WEB: www.dycoelectronics.com
SIC: 3612 Specialty transformers

(G-6105)
DYCO MANUFACTURING LLC
Also Called: Dyco Electronics
7775 Industrial Park Rd (14843-9673)
PHONE..................................607 324-2030
Thomas Norsen,
Gregory Georgek,
Donald McElheny,
EMP: 63
SALES (est): 1.7MM **Privately Held**
SIC: 3999 Manufacturing industries

(G-6106)
FORTITUDE INDUSTRIES INC
Also Called: A T M
7200 County Route 70a (14843-9303)
PHONE..................................607 324-1500
Margaret E Walsh, *President*
Tom Connors, *Vice Pres*
Barry Walsh, *Vice Pres*
Rob Crowley, *Prdtn Mgr*
Gina Bixby, *Buyer*
▲ EMP: 65
SQ FT: 13,500
SALES (est): 11MM **Privately Held**
SIC: 3625 Electromagnetic clutches or brakes

(G-6107)
GATEHOUSE MEDIA LLC
Also Called: Evening Tribune
32 Broadway Mall (14843-1920)
PHONE..................................607 324-1425
Kelly Luvinson, *Manager*
EMP: 101
SALES (corp-wide): 1.5B **Privately Held**
WEB: www.gatehousemedia.com
SIC: 2711 Newspapers, publishing & printing
HQ: Gatehouse Media, Llc
175 Sullys Trl Fl 3
Pittsford NY 14534
585 598-0030

(G-6108)
GRAY MANUFACTURING INDS LLC
Also Called: G M I
6258 Ice House Rd (14843-9739)
P.O. Box 126 (14843-0126)
PHONE..................................607 281-1325
David Gray, *CEO*
Tim Wilcox, *Project Engr*
Marie Stewart, *Administration*
▲ EMP: 17
SQ FT: 15,000
SALES (est): 6.3MM **Privately Held**
SIC: 3743 Railroad equipment

(G-6109)
LOGO PRINT COMPANY
135 Seneca St (14843-1341)
PHONE..................................607 324-5403
Chris O'Dell, *President*

G E O G R A P H I C

EMP: 7
SALES (est): 23.6K **Privately Held**
SIC: 2752 Commercial printing, lithographic

(G-6110)
SENECA MEDIA INC (PA)
Also Called: Genesee County Express
32 Broadway Mall (14843-1920)
PHONE..................................607 324-1425
George Sample, *President*
Micheal Wnek, *President*
Sandy Eveland, *Accounting Mgr*
EMP: 75
SALES (est): 6.2MM **Privately Held**
WEB: www.eveningtribune.com
SIC: 2711 8661 Newspapers, publishing & printing; religious organizations

(G-6111)
STERN & STERN INDUSTRIES INC
188 Thacher St (14843-1293)
P.O. Box 556 (14843-0556)
PHONE..................................607 324-4485
Peter B Thornton, *Ch of Bd*
Stanley Cone, *Vice Pres*
Lee Kessler, *Vice Pres*
Joanne Prouty, *Vice Pres*
EMP: 100
SALES (est): 28.3MM **Privately Held**
WEB: www.sternandstern.com
SIC: 2221 Manmade & synthetic broadwoven fabrics

(G-6112)
TRANSIT AIR INC
Also Called: Transitair Systems
1 William K Jackson Ln (14843-1693)
PHONE..................................607 324-0216
Dave Sharma, *President*
Thomas J Martin, *Vice Pres*
Allen Wright, *Vice Pres*
Raghav Sharma, *Director*
Bryce Gaynes, *Admin Sec*
▲ EMP: 25 EST: 1991
SQ FT: 50,000
SALES (est): 8.2MM **Privately Held**
SIC: 3585 3822 3613 Air conditioning equipment, complete; auto controls regulating residntl & coml environmt & applncs; control panels, electric

---

Horseheads
Chemung County

(G-6113)
BEECHER EMSSN SLTN TCHNLGS LLC (PA)
Also Called: Ward Diesel Filter Systems
1250 Schweizer Rd (14845-9017)
PHONE..................................607 796-0149
Scott Beecher, *President*
John Meier, *Principal*
EMP: 17
SQ FT: 12,000
SALES (est): 2.3MM **Privately Held**
WEB: www.warddiesel.com
SIC: 3564 Air purification equipment

(G-6114)
BELDEN INC
Also Called: Lrc Electronics
224 N Main St Ste 4 (14845-1766)
PHONE..................................607 796-5600
Larry Zuber, *Branch Mgr*
EMP: 400
SALES (corp-wide): 2.5B **Publicly Held**
WEB: www.tnb.com
SIC: 3663 3678 3643 Cable television equipment; electronic connectors; current-carrying wiring devices
PA: Belden Inc.
  1 N Brentwood Blvd Fl 15
  Saint Louis MO 63105
  314 854-8000

(G-6115)
BENNETT DIE & TOOL INC
130 Wygant Rd (14845-1564)
PHONE..................................607 739-5629
Jim Mc Millen, *President*
Brian Bennett, *Vice Pres*

Jim Pittman, *Plant Mgr*
Jim McMillen, *Mktg Dir*
Jane Mc Millen, *Manager*
EMP: 40
SQ FT: 25,000
SALES (est): 6MM **Privately Held**
WEB: www.bdandt.com
SIC: 3544 Special dies & tools; jigs & fixtures

(G-6116)
CAMERON BRIDGE WORKS LLC
727 Blostein Blvd (14845-2739)
PHONE..................................607 734-9456
Christopher Goll, *President*
EMP: 20
SALES (est): 4.2MM
SALES (corp-wide): 27.9MM **Privately Held**
SIC: 3441 Fabricated structural metal for bridges
PA: Cameron Manufacturing & Design, Inc.
  727 Blostein Blvd
  Horseheads NY 14845
  607 739-3606

(G-6117)
CAMERON MFG & DESIGN INC (PA)
727 Blostein Blvd (14845-2739)
P.O. Box 478 (14845-0478)
PHONE..................................607 739-3606
Christopher Goll, *President*
Ronald Johnson, *President*
Guy Loomis, *Plant Mgr*
Joshua Roloson, *Plant Mgr*
Melissa Patrick, *Purch Agent*
▲ EMP: 205
SQ FT: 106,000
SALES (est): 27.9MM **Privately Held**
WEB: www.camfab.com
SIC: 3441 Fabricated structural metal

(G-6118)
CEMECON INC
315 Daniel Zenker Dr (14845-1008)
PHONE..................................607 562-2363
Gary Lake, *President*
Jeffrey Barlow, *Engineer*
▲ EMP: 40
SALES (est): 4.7MM **Privately Held**
SIC: 3999 Manufacturing industries

(G-6119)
CROWN TANK COMPANY LLC
60 Electric Pkwy (14845-1424)
PHONE..................................855 276-9682
EMP: 11
SALES (est): 1.2MM **Privately Held**
SIC: 3443 Fuel tanks (oil, gas, etc.): metal plate

(G-6120)
DAVID HELSING
Also Called: Horseheads Printing
2077 Grand Central Ave (14845-2893)
PHONE..................................607 796-2681
David Helsing, *Owner*
EMP: 5
SQ FT: 3,200
SALES (est): 320K **Privately Held**
SIC: 2752 7336 2789 Lithographing on metal; commercial art & graphic design; bookbinding & related work

(G-6121)
EM PFAFF & SON INC
204 E Franklin St (14845-2425)
PHONE..................................607 739-3691
Susan Alexander, *President*
John Alexander, *Vice Pres*
EMP: 19 EST: 1944
SQ FT: 21,000
SALES (est): 2.7MM **Privately Held**
SIC: 2431 2434 Millwork; wood kitchen cabinets

(G-6122)
EMHART GLASS MANUFACTURING INC
74 Kahler Rd (14845-1022)
PHONE..................................607 734-3671
Jonathan Chan, *Project Mgr*
Celeste Quint, *Purch Mgr*

Scott Briggs, *Engineer*
Ramon Rodriguez, *Engineer*
Jeffrey Wheeler, *Engineer*
EMP: 150
SALES (corp-wide): 3B **Privately Held**
WEB: www.emhartglass.com
SIC: 3559 Glass making machinery: blowing, molding, forming, etc.
HQ: Emhart Glass Manufacturing Inc.
  123 Great Pond Dr
  Windsor CT 06095
  860 298-7340

(G-6123)
FENNELL SPRING COMPANY LLC
295 Hemlock St (14845-2721)
PHONE..................................607 739-3541
Thomas Fennell, *Mng Member*
Martin Fennell,
EMP: 60
SQ FT: 75,000
SALES: 10MM **Privately Held**
SIC: 3495 Precision springs

(G-6124)
FUEL ENERGY SERVICES USA LTD
250 Ltta Brook Indus Pkwy (14845)
PHONE..................................607 846-2650
Mitchell Liivam, *CEO*
EMP: 22
SALES (est): 5.3MM **Privately Held**
SIC: 2869 1389 2911 7699 Fuels; oil field services; oils, fuel; pumps & pumping equipment repair; industrial equipment cleaning

(G-6125)
GAS FIELD SPECIALISTS INC
224 N Main St (14845-1766)
PHONE..................................716 378-6422
Brad West, *Branch Mgr*
Lisa Springstead, *Manager*
EMP: 51
SALES (corp-wide): 44.6MM **Privately Held**
SIC: 1389 Oil field services; gas field services
PA: Gas Field Specialists, Inc.
  2107 State Route 44 S
  Shinglehouse PA 16748
  814 698-2122

(G-6126)
MICATU INC
315 Daniel Zenker Dr # 202 (14845-1008)
PHONE..................................888 705-8836
Michael Oshetski, *CEO*
EMP: 5
SALES (est): 1.3MM **Privately Held**
SIC: 3827 Optical instruments & lenses

(G-6127)
MIRION TECH IMAGING LLC
Also Called: Mirion Tech Imging Systems Div
315 Daniel Zenker Dr (14845-1008)
PHONE..................................607 562-4300
David Stewart, *President*
Seth Rosen, *Admin Sec*
Emmanuelle Lee, *Asst Sec*
EMP: 23 EST: 2015
SQ FT: 15,000
SALES (est): 3.6MM **Privately Held**
SIC: 3663 Radio & TV communications equipment
PA: Mirion Technologies, Inc.
  3000 Executive Pkwy # 518
  San Ramon CA 94583

(G-6128)
MIRION TECHNOLOGIES IST CORP (HQ)
Also Called: Imaging and Sensing Technology
315 Daniel Zenker Dr # 204 (14845-1008)
PHONE..................................607 562-4300
Thomas Logan, *CEO*
David Stewart, *President*
Alan Ravizza, *Managing Dir*
Tim Pelot, *Vice Pres*
Jack Pacheco, *CFO*
EMP: 70
SQ FT: 105,000

SALES (est): 26.8MM **Privately Held**
WEB: www.mirion.com
SIC: 3679 3861 3829 3812 Electronic circuits; photographic equipment & supplies; nuclear radiation & testing apparatus; search & navigation equipment; computer peripheral equipment

(G-6129)
MRC GLOBAL (US) INC
224 N Main St Bldg 13-1 (14845-1766)
PHONE..................................607 739-8575
James Griffith, *Branch Mgr*
EMP: 11 **Publicly Held**
SIC: 1311 Crude petroleum & natural gas
HQ: Mrc Global (Us) Inc.
  1301 Mckinney St Ste 2300
  Houston TX 77010
  877 294-7574

(G-6130)
ORTHSTAR ENTERPRISES INC
119 Sing Sing Rd (14845-1073)
P.O. Box 459, Big Flats (14814-0459)
PHONE..................................607 562-2100
EMP: 65
SALES (est): 3.5MM **Privately Held**
SIC: 7372 7379 3812 3823 Prepackaged Software Svc Computer Related Svcs Mfg Search/Navgatn Equip Mfg Process Cntrl Instr

(G-6131)
PEPSI-COLA METRO BTLG CO INC
Also Called: Pepsico
140 Wygant Rd (14845-9126)
PHONE..................................607 795-2122
Drew White, *Facilities Mgr*
Brian Morgan, *Manager*
EMP: 85
SALES (corp-wide): 64.6B **Publicly Held**
WEB: www.pbg.com
SIC: 2086 Carbonated soft drinks, bottled & canned
HQ: Pepsi-Cola Metropolitan Bottling Company, Inc.
  1111 Westchester Ave
  White Plains NY 10604
  914 767-6000

(G-6132)
PHOTONIC CONTROLS LLC
500 1st Ctr Ste 2 (14845)
PHONE..................................607 562-4585
EMP: 14
SQ FT: 6,250
SALES: 1.8MM **Privately Held**
SIC: 3229 Electronic & Optical Product Design Services

(G-6133)
REPSOL OIL & GAS USA LLC
337 Daniel Zenker Dr (14845-1008)
PHONE..................................607 562-4000
Hitesh Shah, *Project Mgr*
Kelly Byzitter, *Foreman/Supr*
Chad Work, *Foreman/Supr*
Adam Walker, *Engineer*
Dominik Wells, *Engineer*
EMP: 5
SALES (corp-wide): 1.5B **Privately Held**
SIC: 1311 Natural gas production
HQ: Repsol Oil & Gas Usa, Llc
  2455 Tech Forest Blvd
  Spring TX 77381
  832 442-1000

(G-6134)
RIMCO PLASTICS CORP
316 Colonial Dr (14845-9034)
PHONE..................................607 739-3864
Robert Reimsnyder, *President*
Nancy Kosalek, *Corp Secy*
Lester Reimsnyder III, *Vice Pres*
EMP: 25 EST: 1966
SQ FT: 48,000
SALES (est): 4.6MM **Privately Held**
WEB: www.rimcoplastics.com
SIC: 3089 3086 Plastic processing; plastics foam products

(G-6135)
ROCHESTER COCA COLA BOTTLING
Also Called: Coca-Cola
210 Industrial Park Rd (14845-9024)
PHONE.....................................607 739-5678
John Kelley, *Branch Mgr*
EMP: 35
SQ FT: 23,000
SALES (corp-wide): 31.8B **Publicly Held**
SIC: 2086 Bottled & canned soft drinks
HQ: Rochester Coca Cola Bottling Corp
300 Oak St
Pittston PA 18640
570 655-2874

(G-6136)
SCHLUMBERGER TECHNOLOGY CORP
224 N Main St Bldg S (14845-1766)
PHONE.....................................607 378-0105
EMP: 200 **Publicly Held**
SIC: 1382 1389 3825 3824 Geophysical exploration, oil & gas field; geological exploration, oil & gas field; well logging; cementing oil & gas well casings; pumping of oil & gas wells; oil field services; measuring instruments & meters, electric; meters: electric, pocket, portable, panelboard, etc.; controls, revolution & timing instruments; counters, revolution; oil & gas field machinery; measuring & dispensing pumps
HQ: Schlumberger Technology Corp
300 Schlumberger Dr
Sugar Land TX 77478
281 285-8500

(G-6137)
SILICON CARBIDE PRODUCTS INC
361 Daniel Zenker Dr (14845-1008)
PHONE.....................................607 562-8599
Martin Metzger, *President*
Mark Whitmer, *Vice Pres*
▲ **EMP:** 30
SALES (est): 4.8MM **Privately Held**
WEB: www.siliconcarbideproducts.com
SIC: 3297 Cement: high temperature, refractory (nonclay)

(G-6138)
SYNTHES USA LLC
35 Airport Rd (14845-1067)
PHONE.....................................607 271-2500
Becky Lucas, *QC Mgr*
Rob Parmenter, *Engineer*
Doug Robertson, *Engineer*
Ron Lerner, *Manager*
Brooks Bellows, *Technician*
EMP: 150
SALES (corp-wide): 81.5B **Publicly Held**
SIC: 3842 Surgical appliances & supplies
HQ: Synthes Usa, Llc
1302 Wrights Ln E
West Chester PA 19380
610 719-5000

Howard Beach
Queens County

(G-6139)
FPL FBRCTORS ERCTORS GROUP LLC
15633 88th St (11414-2702)
PHONE.....................................917 334-6968
Frank Losaho, *Mng Member*
EMP: 1
SALES: 3MM **Privately Held**
SIC: 3441 Fabricated structural metal

(G-6140)
GRILLMASTER INC
15314 83rd St Apt 1 (11414-1863)
PHONE.....................................718 272-9191
Anne Cohen, *CEO*
Sherman Moss, *President*
Evelyn Kelly, *Manager*
EMP: 50
SQ FT: 20,000

SALES (est): 7.8MM **Privately Held**
SIC: 3585 3822 3446 Parts for heating, cooling & refrigerating equipment; auto controls regulating residntl & coml environmt & applncs; architectural metalwork

(G-6141)
RAK FINISHING CORP
15934 83rd St (11414-2933)
PHONE.....................................718 416-4242
John Muncan, *CEO*
Jon Muncan, *CEO*
Julianna Muncan, *President*
EMP: 48
SQ FT: 7,000
SALES (est): 3MM **Privately Held**
SIC: 2339 7389 Service apparel, washable: women's; textile & apparel services

(G-6142)
VIP PRINTING
16040 95th St (11414-3801)
PHONE.....................................718 641-9361
Victor Ingrassia, *Owner*
EMP: 5
SALES: 150K **Privately Held**
SIC: 2752 Commercial printing, lithographic

(G-6143)
VPJ PUBLICATION INC
Also Called: Forum South, The
15519 Lahn St (11414-2858)
PHONE.....................................718 845-3221
Patricia Adams, *President*
EMP: 25
SQ FT: 1,000
SALES (est): 948.3K **Privately Held**
SIC: 2711 Newspapers, publishing & printing

Howes Cave
Schoharie County

(G-6144)
W KINTZ PLASTICS INC (HQ)
Also Called: K P I Plastics
165 Caverns Rd (12092-1907)
PHONE.....................................518 296-8513
Edwin Kintz, *Ch of Bd*
Roger Cusano, *Engineer*
Lawrence Kath, *CFO*
Brian Hulbert, *Manager*
Paul Petersen, *Prgrmr*
◆ **EMP:** 10 **EST:** 1976
SQ FT: 60,000
SALES (est): 2.4MM
SALES (corp-wide): 21.3MM **Privately Held**
WEB: www.kintz.com
SIC: 3089 Injection molding of plastics; plastic processing
PA: Universal Plastics Corporation
75 Whiting Farms Rd
Holyoke MA 01040
413 592-4791

Hudson
Columbia County

(G-6145)
A & S WOODWORKING INC
9 Partition St (12534-3111)
PHONE.....................................518 821-0832
Arthur Cincotti, *CEO*
EMP: 7
SQ FT: 900
SALES: 5MM **Privately Held**
SIC: 2511 Wood household furniture

(G-6146)
A COLARUSSO AND SON INC (PA)
Also Called: Colarusso Blacktop Co
91 Newman Rd (12534-4040)
P.O. Box 302 (12534-0302)
PHONE.....................................518 828-3218
Peter G Colarusso Jr, *President*
Robert Colarusso, *Corp Secy*
Gary Graziano, *Vice Pres*
Robert Butler, *Project Mgr*

David Laspada, *VP Engrg*
EMP: 20 **EST:** 1912
SQ FT: 10,000
SALES (est): 11.7MM **Privately Held**
WEB: www.acolarusso.com
SIC: 2951 5032 1611 1771 Asphalt & asphaltic paving mixtures (not from refineries); asphalt mixture; stone, crushed or broken; highway & street construction; concrete work; construction sand & gravel

(G-6147)
ARCHER-DANIELS-MIDLAND COMPANY
Also Called: ADM
201 State Route 23b (12534-4009)
P.O. Box 398 (12534-0398)
PHONE.....................................518 828-4691
Andy Spirek, *Branch Mgr*
Mark Eisler, *Branch Mgr*
EMP: 50
SALES (corp-wide): 64.3B **Publicly Held**
SIC: 2041 Flour & other grain mill products
PA: Archer-Daniels-Midland Company
77 W Wacker Dr Ste 4600
Chicago IL 60601
312 634-8100

(G-6148)
ARCHER-DANIELS-MIDLAND COMPANY
Also Called: ADM
Ste B Rr 23 (12534)
P.O. Box 398 (12534-0398)
PHONE.....................................518 828-4691
Mark Eisler, *Manager*
EMP: 52
SALES (corp-wide): 64.3B **Publicly Held**
WEB: www.admworld.com
SIC: 2041 5149 Flour & other grain mill products; flour
PA: Archer-Daniels-Midland Company
77 W Wacker Dr Ste 4600
Chicago IL 60601
312 634-8100

(G-6149)
ATMOST REFRIGERATION CO INC (PA)
Also Called: R T F Manufacturing
793 Route 66 (12534-3410)
PHONE.....................................518 828-2180
Thomas Finck, *Principal*
Ashley Finck, *Marketing Staff*
▲ **EMP:** 5
SQ FT: 25,000
SALES (est): 3.3MM **Privately Held**
WEB: www.rtfmanufacturing.com
SIC: 3585 Refrigeration equipment, complete

(G-6150)
BERKSHIRE BUSINESS FORMS INC
829 Route 66 (12534-3406)
P.O. Box 118, Troy (12181-0118)
PHONE.....................................518 828-2600
Nancy Linton, *President*
Jeffrey C Linton, *Vice Pres*
John S Linton, *VP Mfg*
EMP: 12 **EST:** 1960
SQ FT: 15,000
SALES: 1.2MM **Privately Held**
SIC: 2759 Commercial printing

(G-6151)
CRAFTECH INDUSTRIES INC
8 Dock St (12534-2003)
P.O. Box 636 (12534-0636)
PHONE.....................................518 828-5001
Barbara Gerard, *President*
Irving Gerard, *Vice Pres*
Dean West, *Sales Mgr*
Tara Sterritt, *Cust Mgr*
EMP: 55 **EST:** 1966
SQ FT: 18,500
SALES (est): 13.1MM **Privately Held**
WEB: www.craftechind.com
SIC: 3451 3089 3452 Screw machine products; injection molding of plastics; bolts, nuts, rivets & washers

(G-6152)
DAILY MAIL & GREENE CNTY NEWS (HQ)
1 Hudson City Ctr Ste 202 (12534-2355)
P.O. Box 484, Catskill (12414-0484)
PHONE.....................................518 943-2100
Roger Coleman, *President*
Michael J Spitz, *Superintendent*
Robert Van, *Superintendent*
Raymond Pignone, *Principal*
Amy J Block, *Business Mgr*
EMP: 15 **EST:** 1951
SQ FT: 5,000
SALES (est): 4.4MM
SALES (corp-wide): 32MM **Privately Held**
WEB: www.thedailymail.org
SIC: 2711 Newspapers, publishing & printing
PA: Johnson Newspaper Corporation
260 Washington St
Watertown NY
315 782-1000

(G-6153)
DIGITAL FABRICATION WKSHP INC
99 S 3rd St Ste 2 (12534-2171)
PHONE.....................................518 249-6500
EMP: 7
SALES (est): 466.5K **Privately Held**
SIC: 2499 Decorative wood & woodwork

(G-6154)
DINOSAW INC (PA)
340 Power Ave (12534-2442)
PHONE.....................................518 828-9942
Henry J Warchol Jr, *CEO*
Gregg S Warchol, *President*
Scott Myers, *Sales Mgr*
Allison Coon, *Admin Sec*
EMP: 25
SQ FT: 14,000
SALES (est): 3.9MM **Privately Held**
WEB: www.dinosaw.com
SIC: 3425 3545 5085 3541 Saw blades & handsaws; machine tool accessories; industrial tools; machine tools, metal cutting type

(G-6155)
EMSIG MANUFACTURING CORP
160 Fairview Ave Ste 915 (12534-8404)
PHONE.....................................518 828-7301
James Feane, *Manager*
EMP: 11
SALES (corp-wide): 24.7MM **Privately Held**
SIC: 3965 5131 Buttons & parts; buttons
PA: Emsig Manufacturing Corp.
263 W 38th St Fl 5
New York NY 10018
718 784-7717

(G-6156)
FLANDERS PRECISIONAIRE NY
1 Vapor Trl (12534-4077)
PHONE.....................................518 751-5640
Philip L Whitaker, *Chairman*
EMP: 5
SALES (est): 905K **Privately Held**
SIC: 3564 Air cleaning systems

(G-6157)
FOSTER REFRIGERATORS ENTP
300 Fairview Ave (12534-1214)
PHONE.....................................518 671-6036
James Dinardi, *President*
EMP: 10
SALES: 1.8MM **Privately Held**
SIC: 3585 7623 Refrigeration equipment, complete; refrigeration service & repair

(G-6158)
GOLUB CORPORATION
Also Called: Price Chopper Pharmacy
351 Fairview Ave Ste 3 (12534-1259)
PHONE.....................................518 822-0076
Stacey McGovern, *Branch Mgr*
EMP: 26
SALES (corp-wide): 3.6B **Privately Held**
SIC: 3751 Motorcycles & related parts

G E O G R A P H I C

PA: The Golub Corporation
461 Nott St
Schenectady NY 12308
518 355-5000

(G-6159)
H & H HULLS INC
35 Industrial Tract Anx (12534-1505)
PHONE..................................518 828-1339
Thomas Halpin, *President*
EMP: 5
SQ FT: 2,604
SALES (est): 452.3K **Privately Held**
SIC: 3089 Injection molded finished plastic
products

(G-6160)
HOLCIM (US) INC
4303 Us Route 9 (12534-4032)
PHONE..................................518 828-8478
Melanie Pulcher, *Principal*
EMP: 6
SALES (corp-wide): 27.6B **Privately Held**
SIC: 3241 Portland cement
HQ: Holcim (Us) Inc.
8700 W Bryn Mawr Ave
Chicago IL 60631
773 372-1000

(G-6161)
HRI METALS LLC
1233 Us Route 9 (12534-3226)
PHONE..................................518 822-1013
Paul Harpis, *President*
EMP: 5
SALES (est): 223.9K **Privately Held**
SIC: 3444 5211 Metal roofing & roof
drainage equipment; roofing material

(G-6162)
HUDSON FABRICS LLC
128 2nd Street Ext (12534-1626)
PHONE..................................518 671-6100
Mark Schur,
EMP: 15
SALES (est): 1.6MM **Privately Held**
SIC: 2258 Tricot fabrics

(G-6163)
HUDSON VALLEY CREAMERY
LLC
2986 Us Route 9 (12534-4407)
PHONE..................................518 851-2570
Vincent Laurencon, *Facilities Mgr*
Bonnie Kelleher, *Purch Agent*
Veronica Madey,
▲ EMP: 10 EST: 2010
SALES (est): 1.2MM **Privately Held**
SIC: 2022 Cheese, natural & processed

(G-6164)
J V PRECISION INC
3031 Us Route 9 (12534-4320)
PHONE..................................518 851-3200
Dorothy Jahns, *President*
Scott Valentine, *Vice Pres*
Lisa Valentine, *Treasurer*
EMP: 6
SQ FT: 5,400
SALES (est): 999.2K **Privately Held**
WEB: www.jvprecision.com
SIC: 3624 Electrodes, thermal & elec-
trolytic uses: carbon, graphite

(G-6165)
JEM WDWKG & CABINETS INC
250 Falls Rd (12534-3323)
PHONE..................................518 828-5361
Neil Schnelwar, *Chairman*
EMP: 19 EST: 2007
SALES (est): 2.4MM **Privately Held**
SIC: 2431 Millwork

(G-6166)
JOHNNYS IDEAL PRINTING CO
Also Called: Johnny's Ideal Prntng Co
17 Kline St (12534-1408)
PHONE..................................518 828-6666
John Brodowski, *President*
Virginia Brodowski, *Treasurer*
EMP: 6
SALES (est): 792.5K **Privately Held**
SIC: 2752 2759 2791 2789 Commercial
printing, offset; letterpress printing; type-
setting; bookbinding & related work

(G-6167)
JOHNSON ACQUISITION CORP
(HQ)
Also Called: Chatham Courier, The
364 Warren St (12534-2419)
P.O. Box 635 (12534-0635)
PHONE..................................518 828-1616
Roger Coleman, *President*
Pamela Geskie, *Sales Staff*
Kate Lisa, *Manager*
EMP: 12
SQ FT: 35,000
SALES: 401.9K
SALES (corp-wide): 32MM **Privately
Held**
WEB: www.registerstar.com
SIC: 2711 Commercial printing & newspa-
per publishing combined
PA: Johnson Newspaper Corporation
260 Washington St
Watertown NY
315 782-1000

(G-6168)
JONAS LOUIS PAUL STUDIOS
INC
304 Miller Rd (12534-4522)
PHONE..................................518 851-2211
David Merritt, *President*
Pam Merritt, *Admin Sec*
EMP: 6 EST: 1942
SQ FT: 10,000
SALES (est): 429.3K **Privately Held**
WEB: www.jonasstudios.com
SIC: 3299 Statuary: gypsum, clay, papier
mache, metal, etc.

(G-6169)
LB FURNITURE INDUSTRIES
LLC
99 S 3rd St (12534-2172)
PHONE..................................518 828-1501
Wayne Vanmburger, *Purchasing*
Dan Coffman, *CFO*
Simon F Segal,
▲ EMP: 150
SQ FT: 300,000
SALES (est): 13.2MM **Privately Held**
WEB: www.lbempire.com
SIC: 2599 3469 Restaurant furniture,
wood or metal; household cooking &
kitchen utensils, metal

(G-6170)
MELTZ LUMBER CO OF
MELLENVILLE
483 Route 217 (12534-3640)
PHONE..................................518 672-7021
Emil Meltz Jr, *President*
Jeffory Meltz, *Vice Pres*
Betty Lou Meltz, *Admin Sec*
EMP: 20
SALES (est): 2.7MM **Privately Held**
SIC: 2421 5211 Sawmills & planing mills,
general; millwork & lumber

(G-6171)
MICOSTA ENTERPRISES INC
Also Called: Easy H2b
3007 County Route 20 (12534-3384)
PHONE..................................518 822-9708
Steven A McKay, *President*
EMP: 8
SQ FT: 350
SALES (est): 811.4K **Privately Held**
WEB: www.micostaent.com
SIC: 2053 2066 Pies, bakery: frozen;
chocolate bars, solid

(G-6172)
MODERN FARMER MEDIA INC
403 Warren St (12534-2414)
PHONE..................................518 828-7447
EMP: 10 EST: 2012
SALES (est): 1.3MM **Privately Held**
SIC: 2721 7371 Periodicals-
Publishing/Printing Custom Computer
Programing

(G-6173)
OVERHEAD DOOR
CORPORATION
W McGuire Co
1 Hudson Ave (12534-2807)
PHONE..................................518 828-7652
Rich Moore, *Manager*
EMP: 100 **Privately Held**
WEB: www.overheaddoor.com
SIC: 3442 2431 5084 3842 Garage
doors, overhead: metal; doors, wood; ma-
terials handling machinery; surgical appli-
ances & supplies; packaging machinery;
prefabricated metal buildings
HQ: Overhead Door Corporation
2501 S State Hwy 121 Ste
Lewisville TX 75067
469 549-7100

(G-6174)
PERIODICAL SERVICES CO INC
351 Fairview Ave Ste 300 (12534-1259)
PHONE..................................518 822-9300
Marcia Scneider, *President*
Rob Koskey, *Vice Pres*
EMP: 15 EST: 2013
SALES: 3MM **Privately Held**
SIC: 2721 Magazines: publishing only, not
printed on site

(G-6175)
PGS MILLWORK INC (PA)
32 Hickory Ln (12534-1297)
PHONE..................................518 828-2608
Thomas Spurge, *CEO*
Mara Lopez, *Counsel*
Scott Manchester, *Vice Pres*
Mike Frasca, *Project Mgr*
Larry Hess, *Project Mgr*
▲ EMP: 65
SQ FT: 44,000
SALES (est): 6.6MM **Privately Held**
WEB: www.pgsmillwork.com
SIC: 2431 2434 2499 5211 Woodwork,
interior & ornamental; wood kitchen cabi-
nets; decorative wood & woodwork; mill-
work & lumber

(G-6176)
PRINCTON ARCHTCTURAL
PRESS LLC (HQ)
202 Warren St (12534-2185)
PHONE..................................518 671-6100
Kevin Lippert,
▲ EMP: 16
SALES: 5.2MM
SALES (corp-wide): 29.9MM **Privately
Held**
SIC: 2731 2678 Books: publishing only;
stationery products
PA: The Mcevoy Group Llc
680 2nd St
San Francisco CA 94107
415 537-4200

(G-6177)
SATURN INDUSTRIES INC (PA)
157 Union Tpke (12534-1524)
P.O. Box 367 (12534-0367)
PHONE..................................518 828-9956
Maryanne Lee, *President*
John Lee, *Vice Pres*
EMP: 40 EST: 1959
SQ FT: 25,000
SALES: 3.5MM **Privately Held**
SIC: 3624 3599 3544 3769 Electrodes,
thermal & electrolytic uses: carbon,
graphite; machine & other job shop work;
special dies, tools, jigs & fixtures; guided
missile & space vehicle parts & auxiliary
equipment; current-carrying wiring de-
vices

(G-6178)
SAUSBIERS AWNING SHOP INC
43 8th St (12534-2901)
PHONE..................................518 828-3748
William M Harp, *President*
EMP: 8 EST: 1902
SQ FT: 4,000

SALES: 700K **Privately Held**
SIC: 2394 5999 7532 Awnings, fabric:
made from purchased materials; fire extinguishers; upholstery & trim shop, automotive; tops (canvas or plastic);
installation or repair: automotive

(G-6179)
SERVOTEC USA LLC
1 Industrial Tract Anx # 3 (12534-1514)
PHONE..................................518 671-6120
Thomas Tanguay,
EMP: 6
SALES (est): 900.9K **Privately Held**
WEB: www.servotecusa.com
SIC: 3542 Presses: hydraulic & pneumatic,
mechanical & manual

(G-6180)
SMITH CONTROL SYSTEMS INC
1839 Route 9h (12534-3374)
PHONE..................................518 828-7646
Thomas H Smith Sr, *President*
Kirt Coonradt, *Vice Pres*
Michael Keating, *Vice Pres*
Thomas H Smith Jr, *Treasurer*
Bill Farley, *Prgrmr*
EMP: 17
SQ FT: 10,000
SALES (est): 4.5MM **Privately Held**
WEB: www.smithcontrol.com
SIC: 3613 Control panels, electric

(G-6181)
TWIN COUNTIES PRO PRINTERS
INC
59 Fairview Ave (12534-2334)
PHONE..................................518 828-3278
David Scott, *President*
Linda D Scott, *CFO*
Ryan Scott, *Sales Mgr*
EMP: 10
SQ FT: 3,500
SALES (est): 1.1MM **Privately Held**
WEB: www.pro-printers.com
SIC: 2752 7334 Commercial printing, off-
set; photocopying & duplicating services

(G-6182)
UFP NEW YORK LLC
Also Called: Universal Forest Products
11 Falls Industrial Pk Rd (12534-3377)
PHONE..................................518 828-2888
Rich Flinn, *General Mgr*
EMP: 35
SALES (corp-wide): 4.4B **Publicly Held**
WEB: www.ufpinc.com
SIC: 2439 Trusses, wooden roof
HQ: Ufp New York, Llc
11 Allen St
Auburn NY 13021
315 253-2758

Hudson Falls
Washington County

(G-6183)
CASTLE POWER SOLUTIONS
LLC
5 Depot St (12839-1907)
PHONE..................................518 743-1000
Maureen Losito, *President*
◆ EMP: 14
SQ FT: 3,200
SALES: 3MM **Privately Held**
SIC: 3699 Electrical equipment & supplies

(G-6184)
COLOR-AID CORPORATION
38 La Fayette St Ste 2 (12839-1247)
PHONE..................................212 673-5500
Richard O'Brien, *President*
Raymond O'Brien, *Vice Pres*
EMP: 8
SQ FT: 8,500
SALES (est): 1.2MM **Privately Held**
WEB: www.coloraid.com
SIC: 2752 Commercial printing, litho-
graphic

(G-6185)
DIMENSIONAL MILLS INC
337 Main St (12839-1513)
PHONE...................................518 746-1047
David Lafountain, *President*
EMP: 5 **EST:** 1992
SALES (est): 600K **Privately Held**
SIC: 2448 Wood pallets & skids

(G-6186)
DWA PALLET INC
Also Called: Dimensional Mills
337 Main St (12839-1513)
PHONE...................................518 746-1047
Daniel Ellsworth, *President*
EMP: 9
SALES (est): 951K **Privately Held**
SIC: 2448 Pallets, wood

(G-6187)
GENERAL ELECTRIC COMPANY
446 Lock 8 Way 8th (12839)
PHONE...................................518 746-5750
Stephen Smith, *Branch Mgr*
EMP: 425
SALES (corp-wide): 121.6B **Publicly Held**
SIC: 3629 Capacitors, fixed or variable
PA: General Electric Company
41 Farnsworth St
Boston MA 02210
617 443-3000

(G-6188)
GL&V USA INC
27 Allen St (12839-1901)
PHONE...................................518 747-2444
Eve Lacroix, *General Mgr*
Brian Marauszwski, *Engineer*
Robert Schiavi, *Engineer*
Ben Barr, *Accounts Mgr*
Laurie Baker, *Info Tech Dir*
EMP: 103
SALES (corp-wide): 110MM **Privately Held**
WEB: www.glv.com
SIC: 3554 Paper industries machinery
HQ: Gl&V Usa Inc.
1 Cellu Dr Ste 200
Nashua NH 03063
603 882-2711

(G-6189)
GRANVILLE GLASS & GRANITE
131 Revere Rd (12839)
PHONE...................................518 812-0492
Kyle Suchan, *President*
Scott Suchan, *Vice Pres*
EMP: 5
SALES (est): 514.4K **Privately Held**
SIC: 3231 Products of purchased glass

(G-6190)
HAANEN PACKARD MACHINERY INC (PA)
16 Allen St (12839-1941)
PHONE...................................518 747-2330
Michael Haanen, *President*
EMP: 8 **EST:** 1972
SQ FT: 3,500
SALES (est): 1.8MM **Privately Held**
SIC: 3554 3559 Paper industries machinery; plastics working machinery

(G-6191)
NORTH-EAST MACHINE INC
4160 State Route 4 (12839-3716)
PHONE...................................518 746-1837
Tracy Stevenson, *President*
EMP: 7
SQ FT: 4,000
SALES: 450K **Privately Held**
SIC: 3599 Machine shop, jobbing & repair

(G-6192)
PECKHAM MATERIALS CORP
438 Vaughn Rd (12839-9644)
PHONE...................................518 747-3353
John R Peckham, *President*
Marc Chenier, *Technician*
EMP: 30

SALES (corp-wide): 171.1MM **Privately Held**
SIC: 1429 3531 2952 2951 Igneous rock, crushed & broken-quarrying; asphalt plant, including gravel-mix type; asphalt felts & coatings; asphalt paving mixtures & blocks; highway & street construction
HQ: Peckham Materials Corp
20 Haarlem Ave Ste 200
White Plains NY 10603
914 686-2045

Huguenot
Orange County

(G-6193)
ELEMENTIS SRL INC (DH)
Also Called: Summitreheis
15 Big Pond Rd (12746-5003)
P.O. Box 626 (12746-0626)
PHONE...................................845 692-3914
Piyush J Patel, *Ch of Bd*
Suresh Patel, *President*
◆ **EMP:** 110
SQ FT: 106,000
SALES (est): 19.6MM
SALES (corp-wide): 822.2MM **Privately Held**
SIC: 2819 Industrial inorganic chemicals
HQ: Srlh Holdings, Inc.
15 Big Pond Rd
Huguenot NY 12746
929 529-7951

(G-6194)
SOMERVILLE ACQUISITIONS CO INC
Also Called: Summit Research Laboratories
15 Big Pond Rd (12746-5003)
P.O. Box F (12746-0626)
PHONE...................................845 856-5261
EMP: 10
SALES (corp-wide): 27.3MM **Privately Held**
SIC: 2819 Manufactures Aluminum Compounds
PA: Somerville Acquisitions Co., Inc.
45 River Rd Ste 300
Flemington NJ 08822
908 782-9500

(G-6195)
SOMERVILLE TECH GROUP INC
15 Big Pond Rd (12746-5003)
P.O. Box F (12746-0626)
PHONE...................................908 782-9500
Piyush J Patel, *CEO*
EMP: 100
SALES (est): 5.9MM **Privately Held**
SIC: 2819 Aluminum compounds

(G-6196)
SRLH HOLDINGS INC (HQ)
15 Big Pond Rd (12746-5003)
PHONE...................................929 529-7951
Piyush J Patel, *CEO*
Suresh Patel, *President*
Michael Dodds, *CFO*
EMP: 111
SALES (est): 22MM
SALES (corp-wide): 822.2MM **Privately Held**
SIC: 2819 Industrial inorganic chemicals
PA: Elementis Plc
Caroline House
London WC1V
207 067-2999

Huntington
Suffolk County

(G-6197)
ACWORTH FOUNDATION
775 Park Ave Ste 255 (11743-7538)
PHONE...................................631 784-7802
Brian Acworth, *Owner*
EMP: 3
SALES: 1.2MM **Privately Held**
SIC: 2515 Foundations & platforms

(G-6198)
ADL DESIGN INC
4 W Mall Dr (11743-6440)
PHONE...................................516 949-6658
David Gabbay, *CEO*
Yvette Feist, *President*
▲ **EMP:** 2
SALES: 2MM **Privately Held**
SIC: 3144 Dress shoes, women's

(G-6199)
ANIMAL PANTRY
741 W Jericho Tpke (11743-6150)
PHONE...................................631 673-3666
Andrew Mistler, *Owner*
EMP: 5 **EST:** 2013
SALES (est): 250.8K **Privately Held**
SIC: 3999 Pet supplies

(G-6200)
APS ENTERPRISE SOFTWARE INC
775 Park Ave (11743-3976)
PHONE...................................631 784-7720
Peter Thiermann, *President*
Michael Sullivan, *Principal*
Steffen Heinke, *Treasurer*
EMP: 22
SALES (est): 1.2MM **Privately Held**
SIC: 7372 Prepackaged software

(G-6201)
BERJEN METAL INDUSTRIES LTD
645 New York Ave Unit 1 (11743-4266)
PHONE...................................631 673-7979
Robert Sentura, *President*
Barbara Santoro, *Vice Pres*
Robert J Santoro, *Admin Sec*
EMP: 6
SALES (est): 935.8K **Privately Held**
WEB: www.berjen.com
SIC: 3444 1761 Sheet metalwork; sheet metalwork

(G-6202)
BOA SECURITY TECHNOLOGIES CORP
Also Called: Boa Handcuff Company
586 New York Ave Unit 3 (11743-4269)
PHONE...................................516 480-6822
Alan Lurie, *President*
Alvin MA, *Vice Pres*
EMP: 5
SQ FT: 4,000
SALES: 406.5K **Privately Held**
WEB: www.cuffmaxx.com
SIC: 3429 Handcuffs & leg irons

(G-6203)
COOCOO SMS INC
356 New York Ave Ste 1 (11743-3304)
PHONE...................................646 459-4260
John J Tunney III, *Mng Member*
Larry Prager,
Ryan Thompson,
EMP: 11
SALES (est): 500K **Privately Held**
SIC: 7372 Prepackaged software

(G-6204)
DEJANA TRCK UTILITY EQP CO LLC
Also Called: Dejana Truck & Utility Eqp Co
743 Park Ave (11743-3912)
PHONE...................................631 549-0944
Fax: 631 549-0945
EMP: 25 **Publicly Held**
SIC: 3711 Mfg Motor Vehicle/Car Bodies
HQ: Dejana Truck & Utility Equipment Company, Llc
490 Pulaski Rd
Kings Park NY 11754
631 544-9000

(G-6205)
FAD INC
Also Called: Fad Treasures
630 New York Ave Ste B (11743-4289)
PHONE...................................631 385-2460
Allan Axelowitz, *President*
Donna Axelowitz, *Admin Sec*
▲ **EMP:** 27
SQ FT: 6,000

SALES (est): 3.3MM **Privately Held**
WEB: www.fad-treasures.com
SIC: 2339 5137 5632 Women's & misses' accessories; women's & children's accessories; women's accessory & specialty stores

(G-6206)
HARBORSIDE PRESS
94 N Woodhull Rd (11743-2829)
PHONE...................................631 470-4967
Anthony Cutrone, *President*
Leslie Dubin, *Vice Pres*
Frank Buchner, *CTO*
Susan Reckling, *Senior Editor*
EMP: 7
SALES (est): 92.3K **Privately Held**
SIC: 2741 Miscellaneous publishing

(G-6207)
INTEGRATED CONTROL CORP
Also Called: Kitchen Technology
748 Park Ave (11743-3900)
PHONE...................................631 673-5100
Roberta Vaccaro Salerno, *President*
Roberta Salerno, *President*
Mark Salerno, *CTO*
▲ **EMP:** 34
SQ FT: 5,000
SALES (est): 9MM **Privately Held**
WEB: www.integratedcontrol.com
SIC: 3823 Industrial instrmnts msrmnt display/control process variable

(G-6208)
J A T PRINTING INC
Also Called: Minuteman Press
46 Gerard St Unit 2 (11743-6944)
PHONE...................................631 427-1155
John Titus, *President*
Gina Titus, *Vice Pres*
EMP: 6
SALES (est): 777.9K **Privately Held**
SIC: 2752 Commercial printing, lithographic

(G-6209)
JURIS PUBLISHING INC
52 Elm St Ste 7 (11743-3488)
PHONE...................................631 351-5430
Charles Kitzen, *President*
Michael Kitzen, *Vice Pres*
▲ **EMP:** 12 **EST:** 1994
SALES (est): 1.4MM **Privately Held**
WEB: www.jurispub.com
SIC: 2731 Books: publishing only

(G-6210)
LADY-N-TH-WNDOW CHOCOLATES INC
Also Called: Bon Bons Chocolatier
319 Main St (11743-6914)
PHONE...................................631 549-1059
Mary Alice Meinersman, *President*
Susanna Fasolino, *Vice Pres*
Susannah Meinersman, *Vice Pres*
EMP: 10
SQ FT: 4,200
SALES (est): 1.3MM **Privately Held**
WEB: www.bonbonschocolatier.com
SIC: 2066 2064 5441 5947 Chocolate; candy & other confectionery products; candy; gift, novelty & souvenir shop

(G-6211)
LIBERTY INSTALL INC
27 W Neck Rd (11743-2618)
PHONE...................................631 651-5655
Sheri Stevens, *President*
EMP: 11
SALES (est): 465.6K **Privately Held**
SIC: 3841 Surgical & medical instruments

(G-6212)
LONG ISLAND CMNTY NWSPPERS INC
Also Called: Long Islndr Nrth/Sth Pblctns
322 Main St (11743-6923)
PHONE...................................631 427-7000
Peter Sloggatt, *Manager*
EMP: 12
SALES (corp-wide): 7.4MM **Privately Held**
WEB: www.antonnews.com
SIC: 2711 Newspapers, publishing & printing

(PA)=Parent Co (HQ)=Headquarters (DH)=Div Headquarters
✪ = New Business established in last 2 years

2020 Harris
New York Manufacturers Directory

241

GEOGRAPHIC

PA: Long Island Community Newspapers Inc.
132 E 2nd St
Mineola NY 11501
516 482-4490

(G-6213)
LONG ISLANDER NEWSPAPERS LLC
46 Green St Ste A (11743-3325)
PHONE...................................631 427-7000
Michael Schenkler,
EMP: 7
SALES (est): 366K **Privately Held**
SIC: 2711 Newspapers

(G-6214)
MORETTA CILENTO LTD LBLTY CO
Also Called: Gianni's Chicken Burgers
80 W Neck Rd (11743-2622)
PHONE...................................631 386-8654
Ginacarlo Moretta, *President*
EMP: 5
SALES (est): 170.4K **Privately Held**
SIC: 2038 Frozen specialties

(G-6215)
NORTHROP GRUMMAN SYSTEMS CORP
70 Dewey St (11743-7126)
PHONE...................................631 423-1014
Ray Schubnel, *Manager*
Mary Westerling, *Administration*
EMP: 7 **Publicly Held**
WEB: www.sperry.ngc.com
SIC: 3812 Search & navigation equipment
HQ: Northrop Grumman Systems Corporation
2980 Fairview Park Dr
Falls Church VA 22042
703 280-2900

(G-6216)
PASSIVE-PLUS INC
48 Elm St (11743-3402)
PHONE...................................631 425-0938
Lisa Beyel, *President*
Steve Beyel, *Vice Pres*
▲ **EMP:** 18
SALES (est): 1.7MM **Privately Held**
SIC: 3679 3675 3676 3674 Microwave components; electronic capacitors; electronic resistors; magnetohydrodynamic (MHD) devices

(G-6217)
PHOTO AGENTS LTD
Also Called: Country Printer, The
716 New York Ave (11743-4413)
PHONE...................................631 421-0258
Gary Lerman, *President*
EMP: 5
SALES (est): 439.2K **Privately Held**
WEB: www.thecountryprinter.com
SIC: 2759 2752 Commercial printing; commercial printing, lithographic

(G-6218)
QUANTUM MECHANICS NY LLC
40 Hennessey Dr (11743-3828)
PHONE...................................917 519-7077
EMP: 8
SALES (est): 382.1K **Privately Held**
SIC: 3572 Computer storage devices

(G-6219)
RED ONYX INDUSTRIAL PDTS LLC
23 Green St Ste 310 (11743-3363)
PHONE...................................516 459-6035
▲ **EMP:** 5 EST: 2009
SALES (est): 326.8K **Privately Held**
SIC: 3493 Leaf springs: automobile, locomotive, etc.

(G-6220)
ROBOT FRUIT INC
40 Radcliff Dr (11743-2649)
PHONE...................................631 423-7250
Thomas Vieweg, *CEO*
EMP: 12 EST: 2012
SALES (est): 603.1K **Privately Held**
SIC: 7372 Application computer software

(G-6221)
ROLLSON INC
10 Smugglers Cv (11743-1616)
PHONE...................................631 423-9578
Rudolph Creteur, *President*
Tom Perry, *Vice Pres*
EMP: 25 EST: 1938
SQ FT: 15,000
SALES (est): 2.7MM **Privately Held**
WEB: www.rollson.com
SIC: 3429 3444 3446 Marine hardware; sheet metalwork; architectural metalwork

(G-6222)
ROTRONIC INSTRUMENT CORP
160 E Main St Ste 1 (11743-7401)
PHONE...................................631 427-3898
Michael Foran, *Vice Pres*
Steve Chenal, *Regl Sales Mgr*
Ryan Smith, *Regl Sales Mgr*
Mihcael Foran, *Sales Engr*
J Lafarie, *Branch Mgr*
EMP: 8
SALES (corp-wide): 177.9K **Privately Held**
SIC: 3823 Industrial instrmnts msrmnt display/control process variable
HQ: Rotronic Instrument Corp.
135 Engineers Rd Ste 150
Hauppauge NY 11788
631 348-6844

(G-6223)
SC TEXTILES INC
Also Called: Affiliated Services Group
434 New York Ave (11743-3438)
PHONE...................................631 944-6262
Stephen S Cohen, *President*
EMP: 2
SQ FT: 3,500
SALES: 4MM **Privately Held**
SIC: 3679 Electronic loads & power supplies

(G-6224)
SELECT PRODUCTS HOLDINGS LLC (PA)
1 Arnold Dr Unit 3 (11743-3981)
P.O. Box 707 (11743-0707)
PHONE...................................631 421-6000
Simon Roozrokh, *CEO*
David Darouvar, *CFO*
▲ **EMP:** 49
SQ FT: 80,000
SALES (est): 12.6MM **Privately Held**
SIC: 2676 Towels, napkins & tissue paper products

(G-6225)
STEVEN KRAUS ASSOCIATES INC
9 Private Rd (11743-2243)
PHONE...................................631 923-2033
Steven Kraus, *President*
EMP: 5
SQ FT: 2,500
SALES: 475K **Privately Held**
SIC: 2542 Office & store showcases & display fixtures

(G-6226)
TELEPHONICS CORPORATION
Tlsi Division
770 Park Ave (11743-3974)
PHONE...................................631 549-6000
Mark Supko, *President*
Peter A Wolfe, *Senior VP*
Joseph Obiedzenski, *Opers Staff*
Jerry Golden, *Purch Agent*
Andrew Bosworth, *Engineer*
EMP: 30
SALES (corp-wide): 1.9B **Publicly Held**
SIC: 3679 3674 Electronic circuits; semiconductors & related devices
HQ: Telephonics Corporation
815 Broadhollow Rd
Farmingdale NY 11735
631 755-7000

(G-6227)
TELEPHONICS CORPORATION
780 Park Ave (11743-4516)
PHONE...................................631 470-8800
Stephen Maroney, *Director*
EMP: 99

SALES (corp-wide): 1.5B **Publicly Held**
SIC: 3699 Electronic training devices
HQ: Telephonics Corporation
815 Broadhollow Rd
Farmingdale NY 11735
631 755-7000

(G-6228)
TELEPHONICS TLSI CORP
780 Park Ave (11743-4516)
P.O. Box 35 (11743-0035)
PHONE...................................631 470-8854
Marshall Lacoff, *Senior VP*
Michelle Azadi, *Buyer*
Douglas Romeo, *Engineer*
Rudy Rupe, *Engineer*
Char Plattner, *Human Res Dir*
EMP: 200
SQ FT: 20,000
SALES (est): 6.8MM
SALES (corp-wide): 1.9B **Publicly Held**
SIC: 3674 Microcircuits, integrated (semiconductor)
HQ: Telephonics Corporation
815 Broadhollow Rd
Farmingdale NY 11735
631 755-7000

(G-6229)
TLSI INCORPORATED
780 Park Ave (11743-4516)
PHONE...................................631 470-8880
Zhigang MA, *President*
Kevin McSweeney, *COO*
Keith Keating, *Senior Mgr*
Dianne Delvecchio, *Administration*
EMP: 65
SALES (est): 8.2MM
SALES (corp-wide): 1.5B **Publicly Held**
SIC: 3674 3679 Semiconductors & related devices; electronic circuits
HQ: Telephonics Corporation
815 Broadhollow Rd
Farmingdale NY 11735
631 755-7000

(G-6230)
UNITED DATA SYSTEMS INC
Also Called: American Lpg Systems
202 E Main St Ste 302 (11743-2966)
PHONE...................................631 549-6900
Erling Kristiansen, *Ch of Bd*
▲ **EMP:** 8
SQ FT: 11,500
SALES (est): 565.8K **Privately Held**
WEB: www.udsystems.com
SIC: 7372 5045 Prepackaged software; computer software

(G-6231)
VALLEY INDUSTRIAL PRODUCTS INC
152 New York Ave (11743-2185)
PHONE...................................631 385-9300
Laurel B Phelan, *CEO*
Laurel Phelan, *Ch of Bd*
Alberta Barth Dwyer, *Treasurer*
EMP: 35 EST: 1965
SQ FT: 14,000
SALES (est): 12.5MM **Privately Held**
WEB: www.valleyindustrialtape.com
SIC: 2672 2671 2241 Tape, pressure sensitive: made from purchased materials; packaging paper & plastics film, coated & laminated; narrow fabric mills

(G-6232)
VDC ELECTRONICS INC
Also Called: Batteryminder
155 W Carver St Ste 2 (11743-3376)
PHONE...................................631 423-8220
Sheryl Ross, *Ch of Bd*
▲ **EMP:** 12
SALES (est): 1.7MM **Privately Held**
SIC: 3621 Storage battery chargers, motor & engine generator type

(G-6233)
VENCO SALES INC
755 Park Ave Ste 300 (11743-3979)
PHONE...................................631 754-0782
John Venini, *President*
Frank Brecher, *Sales Staff*
John Ruggiero, *Sales Staff*
Sue Zarcone, *Sales Staff*
Deirdre Watson, *Administration*

EMP: 20
SALES (est): 2.5MM **Privately Held**
SIC: 3494 Plumbing & heating valves

(G-6234)
WEBINFINITY AMERICAS INC (PA)
315 Main St Unit 4 (11743-6941)
PHONE...................................516 331-5180
James F Hodgkinson, *Ch of Bd*
Chris Becwar, *Partner*
Will Hodgkinson, *Vice Pres*
EMP: 13 EST: 2012
SALES (est): 7.8MM **Privately Held**
SIC: 3823 Digital displays of process variables

Huntington Station
Suffolk County

(G-6235)
AEROBIC WEAR INC
16 Depot Rd (11746-1737)
PHONE...................................631 673-1830
Bradley Rosen, *President*
EMP: 5
SQ FT: 6,200
SALES: 527.8K **Privately Held**
WEB: www.aerobicwear.com
SIC: 2339 2369 Athletic clothing: women's, misses' & juniors'; girls' & children's outerwear

(G-6236)
AMERICAN CULTURE HAIR INC
159 E 2nd St (11746-1430)
PHONE...................................631 242-3142
Louis Guarneri, *President*
▲ **EMP:** 22
SALES (est): 2.1MM **Privately Held**
SIC: 3999 Hair & hair-based products

(G-6237)
AMERICAN TCHNCAL CERAMICS CORP (DH)
Also Called: Atc
1 Norden Ln (11746-2140)
PHONE...................................631 622-4700
John Lawing, *CEO*
John S Gilbertson, *Principal*
Richard Monsorno, *Senior VP*
David B Ott, *Senior VP*
Kathleen M Kelly, *Vice Pres*
◆ **EMP:** 440
SQ FT: 18,000
SALES (est): 182.7MM **Publicly Held**
WEB: www.atceramics.com
SIC: 3672 3675 Printed circuit boards; electronic capacitors
HQ: Avx Corporation
1 Avx Blvd
Fountain Inn SC 29644
864 967-2150

(G-6238)
AMERICAN TCHNCAL CERAMICS CORP
17 Stepar Pl (11746-2141)
PHONE...................................631 622-4700
Ned Patel, *Production*
Yardley Cornet, *Purch Agent*
Robert Clark, *QC Mgr*
Allen Hagan, *Engineer*
Ed Scully, *Engineer*
EMP: 400 **Publicly Held**
WEB: www.atceramics.com
SIC: 3675 Electronic capacitors
HQ: American Technical Ceramics Corp.
1 Norden Ln
Huntington Station NY 11746
631 622-4700

(G-6239)
AUTO SPORT DESIGNS INC
203 W Hills Rd (11746-3147)
PHONE...................................631 425-1555
Tom Papadopoulos, *President*
Tomas Papadopoulos, *President*
▲ **EMP:** 11
SQ FT: 30,000

SALES (est): 2.1MM **Privately Held**
WEB: www.autosportdesigns.com
SIC: 3711 5511 5531 Automobile assembly, including specialty automobiles; new & used car dealers; speed shops, including race car supplies

(G-6240)
BC COMMUNICATIONS INC
Also Called: Sign Depot Distribution
211 Depot Rd (11746-2488)
PHONE......................631 549-8833
Suzanne Cranz, *President*
William F Cranz, *President*
Suzanne Vautier, *Vice Pres*
EMP: 1
SQ FT: 10,500
SALES (est): 1MM **Privately Held**
WEB: www.signdepotsales.com
SIC: 3993 Signs & advertising specialties

(G-6241)
CALIFORNIA FRAGRANCE COMPANY
Also Called: Aromafloria
171 E 2nd St (11746-1430)
PHONE......................631 424-4023
Sharon Christie, *President*
Liz Flaherty, *Controller*
◆ **EMP:** 30
SQ FT: 30,000
SALES (est): 7.5MM **Privately Held**
SIC: 2844 Cosmetic preparations

(G-6242)
COMCO PLASTICS INC
11 Stepar Pl (11746-2103)
PHONE......................718 849-9000
Michael French, *President*
John C French, *President*
Rovena Prifti, *Controller*
▲ **EMP:** 36 **EST:** 1956
SQ FT: 20,000
SALES (est): 4.3MM **Privately Held**
WEB: www.comcoplastics.com
SIC: 3081 3082 Unsupported plastics film & sheet; rods, unsupported plastic

(G-6243)
COMPLETE SEC & CONTRLS INC
100 Hillwood Dr (11746-1345)
PHONE......................631 421-7200
Steve Krishnayah, *President*
EMP: 18
SQ FT: 7,000
SALES (est): 175.3K **Privately Held**
WEB: www.completesecuritycorp.com
SIC: 3644 Noncurrent-carrying wiring services

(G-6244)
DC CONTRACTING & BUILDING CORP
136 Railroad St (11746-1540)
PHONE......................631 385-1117
Dean Confessore, *President*
EMP: 13
SQ FT: 5,000
SALES (est): 1.7MM **Privately Held**
SIC: 2431 Woodwork, interior & ornamental

(G-6245)
DILLNER PRECAST INC
200 W 9th St (11746-1667)
PHONE......................631 421-9130
John Dillner, *President*
EMP: 5
SQ FT: 4,000
SALES (corp-wide): 1MM **Privately Held**
SIC: 3272 Concrete products, precast
PA: Dillner Precast Inc
14 Meadow Ln
Lloyd Harbor NY 11743
631 421-9130

(G-6246)
FORMAC WELDING INC
42 W Hills Rd (11746-2304)
PHONE......................631 421-5525
Joel Mc Elearney, *President*
Maureen Mc Elearney, *Admin Sec*
EMP: 7
SQ FT: 3,800

SALES (est): 866.2K **Privately Held**
SIC: 7692 Welding repair

(G-6247)
FOUR-WAY PALLET CORP
191 E 2nd St (11746-1430)
PHONE......................631 351-3401
Leonard Koppelman, *President*
EMP: 28
SALES (est): 3.5MM **Privately Held**
SIC: 2448 7699 5084 Pallets, wood & wood with metal; pallet repair; materials handling machinery

(G-6248)
HART SPORTS INC
4 Roxanne Ct (11746-1122)
PHONE......................631 385-1805
James Hart, *President*
EMP: 6
SALES (est): 411.7K **Privately Held**
SIC: 3949 Hockey equipment & supplies, general

(G-6249)
I A S NATIONAL INC
Also Called: Hercules
95 W Hills Rd (11746-3197)
PHONE......................631 423-6900
Michael Flaxman, *President*
▼ **EMP:** 20
SALES (est): 2.8MM **Privately Held**
WEB: www.hercules.com
SIC: 3589 2899 Car washing machinery; chemical preparations

(G-6250)
ISLAND AUTOMATED GATE CO LLC
125 W Hills Rd (11746-3144)
PHONE......................631 425-0196
Stan Osowski,
EMP: 3
SALES: 1MM **Privately Held**
SIC: 3569 Bridge or gate machinery, hydraulic

(G-6251)
JOHN LAROCCA & SON INC
Also Called: E C Sumereau & Sons
290 Broadway (11746-1403)
PHONE......................631 423-5256
John Larocca, *President*
EMP: 6 **EST:** 1856
SQ FT: 10,000
SALES (est): 741.9K **Privately Held**
WEB: www.ecsumereau.com
SIC: 3471 Electroplating of metals or formed products

(G-6252)
KELMAR SYSTEMS INC
284 Broadway (11746-1497)
PHONE......................631 421-1230
Andrew Marglin, *President*
Laurie Franz, *Vice Pres*
Joan Marglin, *Admin Sec*
EMP: 16
SQ FT: 4,500
SALES (est): 1.4MM **Privately Held**
WEB: www.kelmarsystems.com
SIC: 3861 Sound recording & reproducing equipment, motion picture

(G-6253)
MELBOURNE C FISHER YACHT SAILS
Also Called: Doyle Sails
1345 New York Ave Ste 2 (11746-1751)
PHONE......................631 673-5055
Mark Washeim, *President*
Diana Malkin'washeim, *Vice Pres*
▼ **EMP:** 6
SALES (est): 722.7K **Privately Held**
SIC: 2394 Sails: made from purchased materials

(G-6254)
MICROSOFT CORPORATION
160 Walt Whitman Rd 1006b (11746-4160)
PHONE......................631 760-2340
EMP: 5
SALES (corp-wide): 125.8B **Publicly Held**
SIC: 7372 Prepackaged software

PA: Microsoft Corporation
1 Microsoft Way
Redmond WA 98052
425 882-8080

(G-6255)
NEW YORK DIGITAL CORPORATION
33 Walt Whitman Rd # 117 (11746-3678)
PHONE......................631 630-9798
Salil Bandy, *President*
EMP: 11
SQ FT: 30,000
SALES (est): 830K **Privately Held**
SIC: 3679 Electronic loads & power supplies

(G-6256)
NORTH SHORE PALLET INC
191 E 2nd St (11746-1430)
PHONE......................631 673-4700
EMP: 8
SALES (est): 1.2MM **Privately Held**
SIC: 2448 Pallets, wood & wood with metal

(G-6257)
ROTTKAMP TENNIS INC
100 Broadway (11746-1448)
PHONE......................631 421-0040
Richard Rottkamp, *President*
EMP: 25
SALES (est): 1.7MM **Privately Held**
SIC: 3949 Tennis equipment & supplies

(G-6258)
RUBBER STAMP X PRESS
7 Bradford Pl (11747-1043)
PHONE......................631 423-1322
Ilene Schleichkorn, *Chairman*
EMP: 5
SALES (est): 380.4K **Privately Held**
SIC: 3953 Embossing seals & hand stamps

(G-6259)
SCENT-A-VISION INC
171 E 2nd St (11746-1430)
PHONE......................631 424-4905
Sharon Christie, *President*
EMP: 23
SQ FT: 5,000
SALES (est): 3.3MM **Privately Held**
WEB: www.aromafloria.com
SIC: 2844 5122 Toilet preparations; perfumes

(G-6260)
SELECTRODE INDUSTRIES INC (PA)
230 Broadway (11746-1403)
PHONE......................631 547-5470
Joe Paternoster, *Ch of Bd*
Paul Paternoster, *President*
John Koziar, *Mfg Staff*
Randy Bruckner, *Technology*
Matthew Garuccio, *Director*
◆ **EMP:** 95
SQ FT: 26,000
SALES (est): 21.6MM **Privately Held**
WEB: www.selectrode.com
SIC: 3356 3496 Nonferrous rolling & drawing; miscellaneous fabricated wire products

(G-6261)
SUPER SWEEP INC (PA)
Also Called: SMS
20 Railroad St Unit 1 (11746-1296)
PHONE......................631 223-8205
Michael Marglin, *Ch of Bd*
EMP: 12
SALES (est): 2.6MM **Privately Held**
SIC: 3354 Aluminum extruded products

(G-6262)
SWISSWAY INC
123 W Hills Rd (11746-3155)
PHONE......................631 351-5350
Gerard Cavalier Jr, *President*
Rosemary Schwinn, *Asst Office Mgr*
EMP: 25 **EST:** 1963
SQ FT: 10,000
SALES (est): 3.7MM **Privately Held**
WEB: www.swisswayinc.com
SIC: 3599 Machine shop, jobbing & repair

(G-6263)
TECHNOPAVING NEW YORK INC
270 Broadway (11746-1561)
PHONE......................631 351-6472
Christine Brown, *President*
EMP: 7
SALES (est): 716.1K **Privately Held**
SIC: 3531 Pavers

(G-6264)
TEQUIPMENT INC
Also Called: T E Q
7 Norden Ln (11746-2102)
PHONE......................516 922-3508
Robert Sugarman, *President*
Christine Sugarman, *Corp Secy*
George Tsenes, *Vice Pres*
Frank Falconeri, *Warehouse Mgr*
Paul Cangelosi, *Opers Staff*
EMP: 100
SQ FT: 40,000
SALES (est): 21.2MM **Privately Held**
WEB: www.tequipment.com
SIC: 7372 Educational computer software

(G-6265)
VAIRE LLC
200 E 2nd St Ste 34 (11746-1464)
PHONE......................631 271-4933
Robert Pearl,
EMP: 6
SQ FT: 23,000
SALES (est): 1.1MM **Privately Held**
SIC: 3652 5211 Compact laser discs, prerecorded; bathroom fixtures, equipment & supplies

(G-6266)
WALSH & HUGHES INC (PA)
Also Called: Velvetop Products
1455 New York Ave (11746-1706)
PHONE......................631 427-5904
John B Walsh, *President*
Linda J Walsh, *Treasurer*
EMP: 8 **EST:** 1968
SQ FT: 3,800
SALES (est): 1.7MM **Privately Held**
WEB: www.velvetop.com
SIC: 2891 5941 5032 5091 Sealants; tennis goods & equipment; clay construction materials, except refractory; sporting & recreation goods

(G-6267)
Z-CAR-D CORP
Also Called: Sign-A-Rama
403 Oakwood Rd (11746-7207)
PHONE......................631 424-2077
Dawn M Tiritter-Bent, *Ch of Bd*
Michael Ziccardi, *Vice Pres*
EMP: 28
SQ FT: 15,000
SALES (est): 3.1MM **Privately Held**
WEB: www.ssar.com
SIC: 3993 Signs & advertising specialties

Hurleyville
Sullivan County

(G-6268)
MONGIELLO SALES INC
250 Hilldale Rd (12747-5301)
P.O. Box 320 (12747-0320)
PHONE......................845 436-4200
Anthony Mongiello, *President*
Felicia Ramos-Peters, *Pub Rel Mgr*
Gary Kudrowitz, *Manager*
▼ **EMP:** 40
SALES (est): 4.1MM **Privately Held**
SIC: 2022 Natural cheese

(G-6269)
MONGIELLOS ITLN CHEESE SPC LLC
Also Called: Formaggio Italian Cheese
250 Hilldale Rd (12747-5301)
P.O. Box 320 (12747-0320)
PHONE......................845 436-4200
Anthony Mongiello, *CEO*
John Jmongiello, *COO*
Daniela Nixon, *Controller*
Anna Rose Mongiello, *Manager*

Annarose Mongiello, *Manager*
EMP: 150
SQ FT: 65,000
SALES: 25.6MM **Privately Held**
SIC: 2022 Cheese, natural & processed

Hyde Park
Dutchess County

(G-6270)
CASTINO CORPORATION
1300 Route 9g (12538-2076)
PHONE............................845 229-0341
Eric Castaldo, *Principal*
EMP: 6 **EST:** 2011
SALES (est): 590.9K **Privately Held**
SIC: 3089 Plastics products

(G-6271)
HARMON AND CASTELLA PRINTING
29 Travis Rd (12538-2751)
PHONE............................845 471-9163
Frank Castella, *President*
Karen Castella, *Vice Pres*
EMP: 13
SALES (est): 2.2MM **Privately Held**
WEB: www.hcprinting.com
SIC: 2752 2759 Commercial printing, offset; letterpress printing

(G-6272)
HYDE PARK BREWING CO INC
4076 Albany Post Rd (12538-1934)
PHONE............................845 229-8277
Carmelo Decicco, *President*
EMP: 20
SQ FT: 4,000
SALES (est): 2MM **Privately Held**
WEB: www.hydeparkbrewing.com
SIC: 2082 5812 Beer (alcoholic beverage); eating places

(G-6273)
NEW CITY PRESS INC
202 Comforter Blvd (12538-2977)
PHONE............................845 229-0335
Patrick Markey, *General Mgr*
Gary Brandal, *Manager*
Tom Masters, *Director*
EMP: 5
SALES (est): 441.2K **Privately Held**
WEB: www.newcitypress.com
SIC: 2731 Books: publishing only

(G-6274)
RIVERWOOD SIGNS BY DANDEV DESI
7 Maple Ln (12538-1223)
PHONE............................845 229-0282
Kathleen Hinz-Shaffer, *President*
EMP: 5
SALES: 100K **Privately Held**
SIC: 3993 7336 7389 Signs & advertising specialties; commercial art & graphic design; design, commercial & industrial

(G-6275)
VICTORIA PRECISION INC
78 Travis Rd (12538-2753)
PHONE............................845 473-9309
Vincent Slaninka, *President*
EMP: 5
SQ FT: 3,000
SALES (est): 270K **Privately Held**
WEB: www.victoriaprecisioninc.com
SIC: 3599 Machine shop, jobbing & repair

Ilion
Herkimer County

(G-6276)
ACORN PRODUCTS CORP
27 Pleasant Ave (13357-1115)
PHONE............................315 894-4868
John Thayer, *President*
EMP: 15 **EST:** 2008
SALES (est): 1.5MM **Privately Held**
SIC: 2396 Printing & embossing on plastics fabric articles

(G-6277)
FERMER PRECISION INC
114 Johnson Rd (13357-3899)
PHONE............................315 822-6371
Stewart Bunce, *President*
Rick Bunce, *General Mgr*
John Tofani, *Vice Pres*
EMP: 72
SQ FT: 60,000
SALES: 8MM **Privately Held**
WEB: www.fermerprecision.com
SIC: 3599 Electrical discharge machining (EDM); machine shop, jobbing & repair

(G-6278)
ILION PLASTICS INC
27 Pleasant Ave (13357-1115)
PHONE............................315 894-4868
Steve Quinn, *President*
Kathy Quinn, *President*
EMP: 16
SQ FT: 10,000
SALES: 800K **Privately Held**
SIC: 3089 Injection molding of plastics

(G-6279)
JAMES WIRE DIE CO
138 West St (13357-2250)
PHONE............................315 894-3233
R B Roux, *President*
Alex Roux, *Vice Pres*
EMP: 5
SALES: 100K **Privately Held**
SIC: 3544 Special dies & tools

(G-6280)
ORIGINAL HRKMER CNTY CHESE INC
Also Called: Herkimer Cheese
2745 State Route 51 (13357-4299)
P.O. Box 310, Herkimer (13350-0310)
PHONE............................315 895-7428
Sheldon Basloe, *President*
Norma Basloe, *Corp Secy*
Robert Basloe, *Vice Pres*
Ray Kenniston, *Purchasing*
Michael Basloe, *VP Sales*
EMP: 60 **EST:** 1949
SQ FT: 22,913
SALES (est): 7.7MM **Privately Held**
WEB: www.herkimerfoods.com
SIC: 2022 2099 Natural cheese; gelatin dessert preparations; dessert mixes & fillings

(G-6281)
REMINGTON ARMS COMPANY LLC
14 Hoefler Ave (13357-1888)
PHONE............................315 895-3482
Laird G Williams, *Principal*
Steven Taylor, *Safety Dir*
Kyle Luke, *Opers Mgr*
Rosann Barone, *Buyer*
John Burress, *Buyer*
EMP: 850
SALES (corp-wide): 28B **Privately Held**
WEB: www.remington.com
SIC: 3484 8711 Guns (firearms) or gun parts, 30 mm. & below; engineering services
HQ: Remington Arms Company, Llc
     870 Remington Dr
     Madison NC 27025
     336 548-8700

(G-6282)
REVIVAL INDUSTRIES INC
126 Old Forge Rd (13357-4200)
PHONE............................315 868-1085
Richard Jackson, *President*
Edward R Jackson, *Vice Pres*
EMP: 17
SQ FT: 16,000
SALES (est): 1MM **Privately Held**
WEB: www.revivalindustries.com
SIC: 2426 2499 Gun stocks, wood; handles, poles, dowels & stakes: wood; novelties, wood fiber

Interlaken
Seneca County

(G-6283)
AMERICANA VINEYARDS & WINERY
4367 E Covert Rd (14847-9720)
PHONE............................607 387-6801
Joseph Gober, *President*
Earl Newhart, *Vice Pres*
EMP: 15
SALES: 750K **Privately Held**
SIC: 2084 Wines

(G-6284)
HIPSHOT PRODUCTS INC
Also Called: Melissa
8248 State Route 96 (14847-9655)
PHONE............................607 532-9404
David Borisoff, *President*
Zack Singer, *Engineer*
Kathy Ware, *Director*
▲ **EMP:** 15 **EST:** 1981
SALES (est): 2MM **Privately Held**
WEB: www.hipshotproducts.com
SIC: 3931 5736 Guitars & parts, electric & nonelectric; musical instrument stores

(G-6285)
LUCAS VINEYARDS INC
3862 County Road 150 (14847-9805)
PHONE............................607 532-4825
Ruth Lucas, *President*
Jeffrey Houck, *Vice Pres*
EMP: 12
SALES (est): 1.8MM **Privately Held**
WEB: www.lucasvineyards.com
SIC: 2084 0172 5921 Wines; grapes; liquor stores

(G-6286)
PINE TREE FARMS INC
3714 Cayuga St (14847-9607)
P.O. Box 254 (14847-0254)
PHONE............................607 532-4312
Mark Stillions, *President*
Joelle Stillions, *Corp Secy*
Neal Stillions, *Vice Pres*
Michelle Griego-Stillions, *Sales Mgr*
EMP: 30
SQ FT: 14,000
SALES (est): 4.7MM **Privately Held**
WEB: www.pinetreefarmsinc.com
SIC: 2048 Bird food, prepared

Inwood
Nassau County

(G-6287)
APEX ARIDYNE CORP
168 Doughty Blvd (11096-2010)
P.O. Box 960670 (11096-0670)
PHONE............................516 239-4400
Edward Schlussel, *President*
EMP: 5
SALES (corp-wide): 8.6MM **Privately Held**
SIC: 2258 2257 Lace & warp knit fabric mills; weft knit fabric mills
PA: Apex Aridyne Corp.
     2350 Long Dairy Rd
     Graham NC
     516 239-4400

(G-6288)
ARLEE LIGHTING CORP
125 Doughty Blvd (11096-2003)
PHONE............................516 595-8558
Pinchaf Gralla, *President*
▲ **EMP:** 4
SALES (est): 2.7MM **Privately Held**
SIC: 3646 Commercial indusl & institutional electric lighting fixtures

(G-6289)
AUDIOSAVINGS INC
Also Called: Rockville Pro
600 Bayview Ave Ste 200 (11096-1625)
PHONE............................888 445-1555
Shmuel Freund, *Ch of Bd*

▼ **EMP:** 12
SALES (est): 2.1MM **Privately Held**
SIC: 3651 Household audio & video equipment

(G-6290)
AUTARKIC HOLDINGS INC
Also Called: Laundrylux
461 Doughty Blvd (11096-1344)
PHONE............................516 371-4400
John Sabino, *CEO*
Neal Milch, *Ch of Bd*
Cody Milch, *President*
Archie Abrams, *CFO*
Zach Yaeger, *Sales Associate*
EMP: 80
SALES (est): 10.3MM **Privately Held**
SIC: 3633 3582 Household laundry machines, including coin-operated; commercial laundry equipment; commercial laundry equipment; dryers, laundry: commercial, including coin-operated

(G-6291)
EXCEL PAINT APPLICATORS INC
555 Doughty Blvd (11096-1031)
PHONE............................347 221-1968
P C Sekar, *President*
▲ **EMP:** 45
SQ FT: 48,000
SALES (est): 4.9MM **Privately Held**
SIC: 3991 Brooms & brushes

(G-6292)
EXCELLENT ART MFG CORP
Also Called: Neva Slip
531 Bayview Ave (11096-1703)
PHONE............................718 388-7075
Marshall Korn, *President*
David Korn, *Vice Pres*
▲ **EMP:** 16 **EST:** 1929
SQ FT: 25,000
SALES (est): 1.8MM **Privately Held**
SIC: 3949 2273 2392 Sporting & athletic goods; carpets & rugs; mattress pads

(G-6293)
FIBERALL CORP
449 Sheridan Blvd (11096-1203)
PHONE............................516 371-5200
Isaac Zilber, *President*
Sophie Zilber, *Vice Pres*
Tony Recchia, *VP Sales*
▲ **EMP:** 25
SQ FT: 8,000
SALES (est): 5MM **Privately Held**
WEB: www.fiberall.com
SIC: 3357 Nonferrous wiredrawing & insulating

(G-6294)
GENERAL DIARIES CORPORATION
56 John St (11096-1353)
PHONE............................516 371-2244
Mark Lebo, *President*
▲ **EMP:** 15 **EST:** 1953
SALES (est): 2MM **Privately Held**
WEB: www.dallasnews.com
SIC: 2782 2678 Memorandum books, printed; diaries; desk pads, paper: made from purchased materials

(G-6295)
HASTINGS HIDE INC
Also Called: A J Hollander Enterprises
372 Doughty Blvd (11096-1337)
PHONE............................516 295-2400
Howard Ganz, *President*
EMP: 6
SALES (est): 891.1K
SALES (corp-wide): 1.7MM **Privately Held**
SIC: 3111 5159 4731 Leather tanning & finishing; hides; agents, shipping
PA: Hastings Hide, Inc.
     231 Road 3168
     Hastings NE 68901
     402 463-5308

(G-6296)
INWOOD MATERIAL
1 Sheridan Blvd (11096-1807)
PHONE............................516 371-1842
Frank Sciarrino, *President*
EMP: 11

SALES (est): 1.7MM **Privately Held**
SIC: 3273 5082 Ready-mixed concrete; masonry equipment & supplies

(G-6297)
LES CHATEAUX DE FRANCE INC
1 Craft Ave (11096-1609)
PHONE..................................516 239-6795
Gerald Shapiro, *President*
Marie Cuscianna, *Vice Pres*
EMP: 28
SQ FT: 7,000
SALES (est): 3.4MM **Privately Held**
SIC: 2038 Snacks, including onion rings, cheese sticks, etc.

(G-6298)
MGR EQUIPMENT CORP
22 Gates Ave (11096-1612)
PHONE..................................516 239-3030
Gerald Ross, *President*
Robert Ross, *Corp Secy*
George Mauder, *Vice Pres*
▼ **EMP:** 25
SQ FT: 40,000
SALES (est): 4.3MM **Privately Held**
WEB: www.mgrequip.com
SIC: 3585 Ice making machinery

(G-6299)
N3A CORPORATION
345 Doughty Blvd (11096-1348)
PHONE..................................516 284-6799
Niall Alli, *CEO*
Adrienne Alli, *CFO*
▲ **EMP:** 100 **EST:** 2007
SQ FT: 100,000
SALES (est): 9.3MM **Privately Held**
SIC: 2676 2599 Towels, napkins & tissue paper products; hotel furniture

(G-6300)
NEA MANUFACTURING CORP
345 Doughty Blvd (11096-1348)
PHONE..................................516 371-4200
Sheik Alli, *President*
▲ **EMP:** 37
SQ FT: 4,000
SALES (est): 4.6MM **Privately Held**
SIC: 3672 3679 3677 3678 Printed circuit boards; electronic switches; electronic transformers; electronic connectors; household audio & video equipment; current-carrying wiring devices

(G-6301)
NOEL ASSOC
114 Henry St Ste A (11096-2350)
PHONE..................................516 371-5420
EMP: 5
SALES (est): 300K **Privately Held**
SIC: 3993 Mfg Signs/Advertising Specialties

(G-6302)
PLUSLUX LLC
Also Called: Wascomat of America
461 Doughty Blvd (11096-1344)
PHONE..................................516 371-4400
Neal Milch,
EMP: 7
SALES (est): 337.5K **Privately Held**
SIC: 3633 Household laundry machines, including coin-operated

(G-6303)
SCY MANUFACTURING INC
600 Bayview Ave Ste 200 (11096-1625)
PHONE..................................516 986-3083
◆ **EMP:** 3 **EST:** 2013
SQ FT: 900
SALES: 8MM **Privately Held**
SIC: 3651 Mfg Home Audio/Video Equipment

Irving
Chautauqua County

(G-6304)
SENECA NATION ENTERPRISE
11482 Route 20 (14081-9539)
PHONE..................................716 934-7430
Todd Gates, *Treasurer*

Mike Gates, *Manager*
EMP: 12
SALES (est): 1.4MM **Privately Held**
SIC: 2111 5172 Cigarettes; gasoline

Irvington
Westchester County

(G-6305)
ABYRX INC
1 Bridge St Ste 121 (10533-1553)
PHONE..................................914 357-2600
John Pacifico, *President*
Aniq Darr, *Vice Pres*
Jenny Enrico, *Opers Mgr*
Richard Kronenthal, *Officer*
EMP: 11 **EST:** 2013
SALES (est): 1.5MM **Privately Held**
SIC: 3841 Surgical instruments & apparatus

(G-6306)
CITY GEAR INC
213 Taxter Rd (10533-1111)
P.O. Box 210, South Orleans MA (02662-0210)
PHONE..................................914 450-4746
John Clark, *President*
Ingred Roberg, *Vice Pres*
▼ **EMP:** 6
SQ FT: 3,000
SALES (est): 825.8K **Privately Held**
SIC: 3599 Machine shop, jobbing & repair

(G-6307)
ELI CONSUMER HEALTHCARE LLC
Also Called: Tummyzen
90 N Broadway (10533-3200)
PHONE..................................914 943-3107
Hasan Ansari,
EMP: 10 **EST:** 2017
SALES (est): 940.7K **Privately Held**
SIC: 2023 Dietary supplements, dairy & non-dairy based

(G-6308)
FEINKIND INC
Also Called: REFINEDKIND PET PRODUCTS
17 Algonquin Dr (10533-1007)
PHONE..................................800 289-6136
Josh Feinkind, *CEO*
▲ **EMP:** 1
SQ FT: 65,000
SALES: 1MM **Privately Held**
SIC: 2511 Novelty furniture: wood

(G-6309)
GUTTZ CORPORATION OF AMERICA
Also Called: Gutts Corporation of America
50 S Buckhout St Ste 104 (10533-2217)
PHONE..................................914 591-9600
Robert H Cohen, *President*
Ronald Roemer, *Vice Pres*
Jane Berger, *Manager*
EMP: 13
SQ FT: 7,000
SALES (est): 1.5MM **Privately Held**
WEB: www.marketvis.com
SIC: 3955 Print cartridges for laser & other computer printers

(G-6310)
HAIR VENTURES LLC (PA)
Also Called: Hairstory
94 Fargo Ln (10533-1202)
PHONE..................................718 664-7689
Eli Halliwell, *CEO*
Erica Halliwell, *CFO*
EMP: 11
SALES (est): 1.1MM **Privately Held**
SIC: 2844 Hair preparations, including shampoos

(G-6311)
NATIONAL RES MKTG COUNCIL INC
Also Called: Research Report For Food Svc
1 Bridge St Ste 44 (10533-1560)
P.O. Box 285 (10533-0285)
PHONE..................................914 591-4297

Keith Gellman, *President*
Silvia Drenger, *Real Est Agnt*
Evan Kalt, *Real Est Agnt*
Renee Pisarz, *Real Est Agnt*
Natalie Werner, *Real Est Agnt*
EMP: 9
SQ FT: 1,600
SALES (est): 60.1K **Privately Held**
WEB: www.foodservicereport.com
SIC: 2741 Miscellaneous publishing

(G-6312)
ORTHOCON INC
1 Bridge St Ste 121 (10533-1553)
PHONE..................................914 357-2600
John J Pacifico, *President*
David J Hart, *Vice Pres*
Stephen Hall, *CFO*
EMP: 23 **EST:** 2006
SALES (est): 2.9MM **Privately Held**
SIC: 3841 Surgical & medical instruments

(G-6313)
PECO PALLET INC (HQ)
50 S Buckhout St Ste 301 (10533-2219)
PHONE..................................914 376-5444
Joseph Dagnese, *CEO*
David Lee, *President*
Jeff Euritt, *Vice Pres*
Denneen Ford, *Vice Pres*
Adrian Potgieter, *Vice Pres*
EMP: 24 **EST:** 1997
SQ FT: 5,000
SALES (est): 32.8MM **Privately Held**
WEB: www.pecopallet.com
SIC: 2448 7359 Pallets, wood; pallet rental services

(G-6314)
SPX COOLING TECHNOLOGIES INC
50 S Buckhout St Ste 204 (10533-2201)
PHONE..................................914 697-5030
Bart Petterson, *Manager*
EMP: 8
SALES (corp-wide): 1.5B **Publicly Held**
WEB: www.cts.spx.com
SIC: 3443 Fabricated plate work (boiler shop)
HQ: Spx Cooling Technologies, Inc.
7401 W 129th St
Overland Park KS 66213
913 664-7400

Island Park
Nassau County

(G-6315)
BHI ELEVATOR CABS INC
74 Alabama Ave (11558-1116)
PHONE..................................516 431-5665
Rick Hart, *President*
Brian Holodar, *Principal*
EMP: 10
SALES (est): 2.8MM **Privately Held**
SIC: 3534 Elevators & equipment

(G-6316)
ECOLOGICAL LABORATORIES INC (PA)
4 Waterford Rd (11558-1022)
P.O. Box 369 (11558-0369)
PHONE..................................516 823-3441
Michael Richter, *CEO*
Delvia Lukito, *President*
Barry Richter, *President*
Doug Dent, *Vice Pres*
Brett Richter, *Vice Pres*
▲ **EMP:** 55
SQ FT: 5,500
SALES (est): 13.4MM **Privately Held**
WEB: www.propump.com
SIC: 2899 2836 5169 Water treating compounds; biological products, except diagnostic; chemicals & allied products

(G-6317)
F & B PHOTO OFFSET CO INC (PA)
4 California Pl N (11558-2215)
P.O. Box 366 (11558-0366)
PHONE..................................516 431-5433
Frank Naudus, *President*

EMP: 5
SQ FT: 6,000
SALES: 1MM **Privately Held**
SIC: 2752 2759 Commercial printing, offset; letterpress printing

(G-6318)
H D M LABS INC
153 Kingston Blvd (11558-1926)
PHONE..................................516 431-8357
Hardat Singh, *President*
Anuj Doshi, *General Mgr*
EMP: 5 **EST:** 1993
SQ FT: 1,600
SALES (est): 879.9K **Privately Held**
WEB: www.hdmlabsinc.com
SIC: 3829 Medical diagnostic systems, nuclear

(G-6319)
MASTER PRINTING USA INC
192 New York Ave (11558-2248)
PHONE..................................718 456-0962
Zbigniew Kaminski, *Ch of Bd*
EMP: 10
SALES (est): 1.1MM **Privately Held**
SIC: 2752 Commercial printing, offset

(G-6320)
NATHAN BERRIE & SONS INC
Also Called: Naomi Manufacturing
3956 Long Beach Rd (11558-1146)
P.O. Box 240 (11558-0240)
PHONE..................................516 432-8500
Stanley Berrie, *President*
Suzanne Berrie, *Admin Sec*
EMP: 9 **EST:** 1944
SQ FT: 4,000
SALES (est): 1.1MM **Privately Held**
SIC: 3915 Jewelers' findings & materials

(G-6321)
NORTHFELD PRECISION INSTR CORP
Also Called: NORTH FIELD
4400 Austin Blvd (11558-1621)
P.O. Box 550 (11558-0550)
PHONE..................................516 431-1112
Donald Freedman, *Ch of Bd*
Paul Defeo, *COO*
Andrew Mollitor, *Engineer*
Charles Florio, *Sales Staff*
Patty Maura, *Sales Staff*
EMP: 32
SQ FT: 15,000
SALES (est): 8.3MM **Privately Held**
WEB: www.northfield.com
SIC: 3545 Chucks: drill, lathe or magnetic (machine tool accessories)

(G-6322)
SOUTH SHORE TRIBUNE INC
4 California Pl N (11558-2215)
P.O. Box 366 (11558-0366)
PHONE..................................516 431-5628
Frank Naudus, *President*
EMP: 6
SQ FT: 6,000
SALES (est): 253.5K
SALES (corp-wide): 1MM **Privately Held**
SIC: 2711 Commercial printing & newspaper publishing combined; newspapers, publishing & printing
PA: F & B Photo Offset Co Inc
4 California Pl N
Island Park NY 11558
516 431-5433

Islandia
Suffolk County

(G-6323)
A & L MACHINE COMPANY INC
200 Blydenburg Rd Ste 9 (11749-5011)
PHONE..................................631 463-3111
Horst Ehinger, *President*
George Ramos, *Principal*
EMP: 7 **EST:** 1963
SQ FT: 4,000
SALES (est): 1MM **Privately Held**
WEB: www.anlmachine.com
SIC: 3599 Machine shop, jobbing & repair

(G-6324)
ARK SCIENCES INC
1601 Veterans Hwy Ste 315 (11749-1543)
PHONE..............................646 943-1520
Joseph Tosini, *President*
EMP: 5
SALES (est): 621.3K **Privately Held**
SIC: 2834 Veterinary pharmaceutical preparations

(G-6325)
BI NUTRACEUTICALS INC
85 Hoffman Ln (11749-5019)
PHONE..............................631 533-4934
Robin Corcella, *Purchasing*
EMP: 6
SALES (est): 451.4K
SALES (corp-wide): 23MM **Privately Held**
SIC: 2087 2833 5122 5149 Flavoring extracts & syrups; medicinals & botanicals; vitamins & minerals; pharmaceuticals; medicinals & botanicals; seasonings; sauces & extracts; spices & seasonings; flavourings & fragrances
HQ: Bi Nutraceuticals, Inc.
　　2384 E Pacifica Pl
　　Rancho Dominguez CA 90220
　　310 669-2100

(G-6326)
BIG APPLE SIGN CORP
Also Called: Big Apple Visual Group
3 Oval Dr (11749-1402)
PHONE..............................631 342-0303
Mimoh Kwatra, *Design Engr*
Amir Khalfan, *Branch Mgr*
EMP: 35
SALES (corp-wide): 18.2MM **Privately Held**
WEB: www.bigapplegroup.com
SIC: 3993 2399 3552 Signs, not made in custom sign painting shops; displays & cutouts, window & lobby; banners, made from fabric; silk screens for textile industry
PA: Big Apple Sign Corp.
　　247 W 35th St Rm 400
　　New York NY 10001
　　212 629-3650

(G-6327)
CA INC
1 Ca Plz Ste 100 (11749-5303)
PHONE..............................800 225-5224
Michael P Gregoire, *CEO*
Sean Bucknall, *Vice Chairman*
Carolyn Kaminsky, *Business Mgr*
George Cox, *Vice Pres*
Edith Latour, *Vice Pres*
EMP: 6
SALES (corp-wide): 20.8B **Publicly Held**
SIC: 7372 Business oriented computer software; application computer software
HQ: Ca, Inc.
　　520 Madison Ave
　　New York NY 10022
　　800 225-5224

(G-6328)
CENTURY DIRECT LLC
15 Enter Ln (11749-4811)
PHONE..............................212 763-0600
Michael Kellogg, *Principal*
Michael Vignola, *Vice Pres*
Thomas McNeill, *CFO*
Jim Kiernan, *Persnl Mgr*
Bill Abrams, *VP Sales*
▲ **EMP:** 200
SQ FT: 80,000
SALES (est): 41.6MM **Privately Held**
WEB: www.centltr.com
SIC: 2759 7331 7379 Commercial printing; direct mail advertising services; computer related maintenance services

(G-6329)
CES INDUSTRIES INC
95 Hoffman Ln Ste S (11749-5020)
PHONE..............................631 782-7088
Mitchell B Nesenoff, *CEO*
Edward J Ermler, *Vice Pres*
EMP: 40 EST: 1968
SQ FT: 20,000
SALES (est): 6.7MM **Privately Held**
WEB: www.cesindustries.com
SIC: 3699 Electronic training devices

(G-6330)
DISPLAY MARKETING GROUP INC
170 Oval Dr Ste B (11749-1419)
PHONE..............................631 348-4450
Steven Larit, *President*
EMP: 35
SQ FT: 24,000
SALES (est): 5.2MM **Privately Held**
SIC: 3993 Displays & cutouts, window & lobby

(G-6331)
DUETTO INTEGRATED SYSTEMS INC
Also Called: Dis
85 Hoffman Ln Ste Q (11749-5019)
PHONE..............................631 851-0102
Carmela Faraci, *Office Mgr*
Gary Sortino, *Manager*
EMP: 10
SQ FT: 2,000
SALES (est): 1.5MM **Privately Held**
SIC: 3599 Custom machinery

(G-6332)
FLEXBAR MACHINE CORPORATION
Also Called: Mediflex
250 Gibbs Rd (11749-2697)
PHONE..............................631 582-8440
Jon Adler, *President*
Juanita Adler, *Corp Secy*
Robert Adler, *Vice Pres*
Keith Donaldson, *Purchasing*
Maria V Blando, *Info Tech Mgr*
▲ **EMP:** 27
SQ FT: 10,500
SALES (est): 6.3MM **Privately Held**
WEB: www.flexbar.com
SIC: 3545 3841 Machine tool attachments & accessories; surgical & medical instruments

(G-6333)
GREAT SHOES INC
72 Bridge Rd (11749-1411)
PHONE..............................718 813-1945
EMP: 10
SALES (corp-wide): 881.6K **Privately Held**
SIC: 3021 Rubber & plastics footwear
PA: Great Shoes Inc
　　19615c 65th Cres Apt 1a
　　Fresh Meadows NY 11365
　　718 813-1945

(G-6334)
I E D CORP
88 Bridge Rd (11749)
PHONE..............................631 348-0424
Martin Ramage, *President*
Robert Jaffe, *Engineer*
EMP: 10
SQ FT: 5,000
SALES (est): 1.5MM **Privately Held**
SIC: 3674 3625 Microprocessors; relays & industrial controls

(G-6335)
ICD PUBLICATIONS INC (PA)
Also Called: Hotel Business
1377 Motor Pkwy Ste 410 (11749-5258)
PHONE..............................631 246-9300
Ian Gittlitz, *President*
James Schultz, *Publisher*
Stefani O'Connor, *Editor*
Christina Trauthwein, *Editor*
Cynthia Evans, *Vice Pres*
EMP: 25
SQ FT: 10,000
SALES (est): 3.5MM **Privately Held**
WEB: www.icdnet.com
SIC: 2721 7313 Magazines: publishing only, not printed on site; magazine advertising representative

(G-6336)
INNOVANT INC (PA)
Also Called: Innovant Group
37 W 20th St Ste 1101 (11749)
PHONE..............................212 929-4883
Charles Braham, *President*
Garrett Pluck, *Vice Pres*
Mary Hudson, *Controller*

Carl Clark, *Branch Mgr*
Joan Gullans, *Admin Sec*
▲ **EMP:** 6
SALES (est): 47.5MM **Privately Held**
WEB: www.innovant.com
SIC: 2521 Wood office furniture

(G-6337)
JEG ONLINE VENTURES LLC
Also Called: Electricsolenoidvalves.com
85 Hoffman Ln Ste B (11749-5019)
PHONE..............................800 983-8230
Jose Germade, *Principal*
▲ **EMP:** 14 EST: 2011
SALES (est): 2.2MM **Privately Held**
SIC: 3491 Solenoid valves

(G-6338)
JIT INTERNATIONAL INC
Also Called: Just In Time Electronics
62 Bridge Rd (11749-1411)
PHONE..............................631 761-5551
Kenneth Pedroli, *Ch of Bd*
EMP: 5
SALES (est): 389.1K **Privately Held**
SIC: 3625 Industrial electrical relays & switches

(G-6339)
JOMART ASSOCIATES INC
170 Oval Dr Ste A (11749-1419)
PHONE..............................212 627-2153
Walter Waltman, *President*
Peter Batterson, *Vice Pres*
Evelyn Giman, *Admin Sec*
EMP: 30
SQ FT: 1,200
SALES (est): 2.8MM **Privately Held**
WEB: www.jomartassociates.com
SIC: 2759 Commercial printing

(G-6340)
METRO DOOR INC (DH)
Also Called: Metro Service Solutions
2929 Express Dr N 300b (11749-5306)
PHONE..............................800 669-3667
Scott McCermott, *President*
Scott McDermott, *President*
Jim Karcher, *Co-Founder*
Christine M Vetrano, *CFO*
Gayle Capozzi, *Director*
▼ **EMP:** 80 EST: 1999
SQ FT: 17,200
SALES (est): 22.4MM
SALES (corp-wide): 6.8B **Publicly Held**
WEB: www.metrodoor.com
SIC: 3446 1799 Fences, gates, posts & flagpoles; fence construction

(G-6341)
MULTIFOLD DIE CTNG FINSHG CORP
555 Raymond Dr (11749-4844)
PHONE..............................631 232-1235
William Collins, *Ch of Bd*
Christine Collins, *President*
EMP: 5
SALES (est): 618K **Privately Held**
SIC: 3544 Special dies & tools

(G-6342)
OLIVE BRANCH FOODS LLC
3124 Express Dr S (11749-5013)
PHONE..............................631 343-7070
Jeffrey Siegel, *CEO*
Ron Loeb, *President*
Harry Shufrin, *CFO*
Patty Amato, *Director*
Ron Logiudice, *Director*
EMP: 8
SALES (est): 83K **Privately Held**
SIC: 2033 Olives: packaged in cans, jars, etc.

(G-6343)
PRINTEX PACKAGING CORPORATION
555 Raymond Dr (11749-4844)
PHONE..............................631 234-4300
David Heller, *President*
Joel Heller, *President*
Carol Heller, *Vice Pres*
Tom Vollmuth, *Vice Pres*
Alex Diaz, *Manager*
▲ **EMP:** 70
SQ FT: 40,000

SALES (est): 19.8MM **Privately Held**
WEB: www.printexpackaging.com
SIC: 3089 3086 2671 Boxes, plastic; packaging & shipping materials, foamed plastic; packaging paper & plastics film, coated & laminated

(G-6344)
SOCKET PRODUCTS MFG CORP
175 Bridge Rd (11749-5202)
PHONE..............................631 232-9870
Sol Kellner, *President*
EMP: 5
SQ FT: 5,000
SALES (est): 835K **Privately Held**
SIC: 3452 3545 Screws, metal; nuts, metal; bolts, metal; sockets (machine tool accessories)

(G-6345)
SONOTEC US INC
190 Blydenburg Rd (11749-5015)
PHONE..............................631 415-4758
Christopher Portelli, *President*
Cristy Baldwin, *Office Mgr*
EMP: 120 EST: 2013
SALES: 1MM
SALES (corp-wide): 355.8K **Privately Held**
SIC: 3674 Solid state electronic devices
HQ: Sonotec Gmbh
　　Nauendorfer Str. 2
　　Halle (Saale) 06112
　　345 133-170

(G-6346)
WHITSONS FOOD SVC BRONX CORP
1800 Motor Pkwy (11749-5216)
PHONE..............................631 424-2700
Robert Whitcomb, *President*
Scott Berry, *District Mgr*
Beth Bunster, *Corp Secy*
Douglas Whitcomb, *Vice Pres*
John Whitcomb, *Vice Pres*
EMP: 350
SQ FT: 65,000
SALES (est): 47.7MM **Privately Held**
SIC: 2068 2099 Salted & roasted nuts & seeds; food preparations; peanut butter

(G-6347)
ZAHK SALES INC
Also Called: Project Visual
75 Hoffman Ln Ste A (11749-5027)
PHONE..............................631 851-0851
Husein Kermalli, *President*
▲ **EMP:** 7
SALES (est): 623K **Privately Held**
WEB: www.zahk.com
SIC: 3444 1752 Sheet metalwork; wood floor installation & refinishing

(G-6348)
ZYDOC MED TRANSCRIPTION LLC
1455 Veterans Memorial Hw (11749-4836)
PHONE..............................631 273-1963
Lisa Robbins, *Opers Mgr*
Sue Schmitt, *Opers Staff*
James Maisel, *Mng Member*
Stan Esikoff, *Bd of Directors*
Richard Barna, *Manager*
EMP: 11
SQ FT: 2,500
SALES (est): 636.1K **Privately Held**
WEB: www.transcriber.org
SIC: 7372 Prepackaged software

Islip
Suffolk County

(G-6349)
ADVANCED PAVEMENT GROUP CORP (PA)
2 W Beech St (11751-1513)
PHONE..............................631 277-8400
Ken Roy Jr, *President*
Michael Kmiec, *CFO*
EMP: 9
SALES: 7.2MM **Privately Held**
SIC: 2951 Asphalt paving mixtures & blocks

(G-6350)
AINES MANUFACTURING CORP
96 E Bayberry Rd (11751-4903)
PHONE...................................631 471-3900
▼ EMP: 30
SQ FT: 10,000
SALES (est): 4.3MM **Privately Held**
SIC: 3661 Mfg Telephone/Telegraph Apparatus

(G-6351)
COOKIES UNITED LLC
141 Freeman Ave (11751-1428)
PHONE...................................631 581-4000
Michael Strauss, *Marketing Staff*
Louis Avignone, *Mng Member*
▲ EMP: 120
SQ FT: 80,000
SALES (est): 6.4MM **Privately Held**
SIC: 2052 Cookies & crackers
PA: United Baking Co., Inc.
41 Natcon Dr
Shirley NY 11967

(G-6352)
EUGENIA SELECTIVE LIVING INC
122 Freeman Ave (11751-1417)
PHONE...................................631 277-1461
Edward Smith, *President*
Eugenia Smith, *Admin Sec*
EMP: 10
SQ FT: 5,000
SALES (est): 1.2MM **Privately Held**
WEB: www.selectiveliving.com
SIC: 2511 2519 2521 2522 Wood household furniture; furniture, household: glass, fiberglass & plastic; wood office furniture; office furniture, except wood; laboratory equipment, except medical or dental; cabinet & finish carpentry

(G-6353)
JIMCO LAMP & MANUFACTURING CO
Also Called: Jimco Lamp Company
181 Freeman Ave (11751-1400)
PHONE...................................631 218-2152
Marlo Lorenz, *Branch Mgr*
EMP: 8 **Privately Held**
SIC: 3999 3645 Shades, lamp or candle; table lamps
HQ: Jimco Lamp & Manufacturing Co
11759 Highway 63 N Ste B
Bono AR 72416
870 935-6820

(G-6354)
MEADES WELDING AND FABRICATING
331 Islip Ave (11751)
PHONE...................................631 581-1555
Michelle Mede, *President*
EMP: 5
SALES (est): 195.3K **Privately Held**
SIC: 7692 5046 Welding repair; commercial cooking & food service equipment

(G-6355)
MJB PRINTING CORP
Also Called: Mod Printing
280 Islip Ave (11751-2818)
PHONE...................................631 581-0177
Jeanine Bazata, *President*
Michael Bazata, *Treasurer*
EMP: 5 EST: 1960
SQ FT: 2,800
SALES (est): 717.9K **Privately Held**
SIC: 2752 Commercial printing, offset

(G-6356)
RIKE ENTERPRISES INC
Also Called: Corpkit Legal Supplies
46 Taft Ave (11751-2112)
PHONE...................................631 277-8338
Richard Jansen, *President*
Arlene Leonbruno, *Accountant*
Sue Schelling, *Accountant*
Dan Odwyer, *Sales Mgr*
▲ EMP: 15
SALES (est): 1.7MM **Privately Held**
WEB: www.corpkit.com
SIC: 2759 5112 Commercial printing; office supplies

(G-6357)
T J SIGNS UNLIMITED LLC (PA)
Also Called: American Signcrafters
327 New S Rd (11751)
PHONE...................................631 273-4800
Jeff Petersen, *President*
Jonathan Bell, *Vice Pres*
Anthony Lipari, *Vice Pres*
Valerie Mayer, *Vice Pres*
EMP: 50
SQ FT: 20,000
SALES: 25MM **Privately Held**
WEB: www.americansigncrafters.com
SIC: 3993 1799 7389 Electric signs; neon signs; sign installation & maintenance; personal service agents, brokers & bureaus

Islip Terrace
Suffolk County

(G-6358)
BARRASSO & SONS TRUCKING INC
160 Floral Park St (11752-1399)
PHONE...................................631 581-0360
Michael Barrasso, *President*
Joseph Longo, *Corp Secy*
Andres Ocampo, *Technology*
Anthony Barrasso, *Director*
Ernie Tsakiris, *Executive*
EMP: 30 EST: 1996
SQ FT: 2,500
SALES (est): 7.2MM **Privately Held**
SIC: 3271 5211 5032 Blocks, concrete or cinder: standard; brick; brick, stone & related material

(G-6359)
NIKE INC
2675 Sunrise Hwy (11752-2119)
PHONE...................................631 960-0184
John Grasselino, *Branch Mgr*
EMP: 38
SALES (corp-wide): 39.1B **Publicly Held**
SIC: 3021 Rubber & plastics footwear
PA: Nike, Inc.
1 Sw Bowerman Dr
Beaverton OR 97005
503 671-6453

Ithaca
Tompkins County

(G-6360)
ADVANCED DIGITAL INFO CORP
10 Brown Rd (14850-1287)
PHONE...................................607 266-4000
James H Watson Jr, *Principal*
EMP: 50
SALES (corp-wide): 402.6MM **Privately Held**
SIC: 3672 Printed circuit boards
HQ: Advanced Digital Information Corporation
11431 Willows Rd Ne
Redmond WA 98052
425 881-8004

(G-6361)
ADVION INC (PA)
61 Brown Rd Ste 100 (14850-1247)
PHONE...................................607 266-9162
David Patterson, *President*
Thomas R Kurz, *President*
Rosemary French, *General Mgr*
Mark Allen PH, *Vice Pres*
Gary Williams, *Vice Pres*
EMP: 20
SQ FT: 16,500
SALES (est): 13.1MM **Privately Held**
SIC: 3826 Mass spectrometers

(G-6362)
ALPINE MACHINE INC
1616 Trumansburg Rd (14850)
PHONE...................................607 272-1344
Richard Hoffman, *President*
David Osburn, *Corp Secy*
William Osburn, *Vice Pres*

Russell Timblin, *Vice Pres*
EMP: 15 EST: 1981
SQ FT: 6,000
SALES (est): 2MM **Privately Held**
WEB: www.alpinemachine.com
SIC: 3599 7692 3541 3444 Machine shop, jobbing & repair; welding repair; machine tools, metal cutting type; sheet metalwork

(G-6363)
ARNOLD PRINTING CORP
604 W Green St (14850-5250)
P.O. Box 217 (14851-0217)
PHONE...................................607 272-7800
Robert Becker Jr, *President*
Chris Becker, *Vice Pres*
Christian J Becker, *Vice Pres*
Richard Korf, *Treasurer*
EMP: 18 EST: 1963
SQ FT: 8,000
SALES (est): 2.8MM **Privately Held**
SIC: 2752 Commercial printing, offset

(G-6364)
BEETNPATH LLC
Also Called: Grainful
950 Danby Rd Ste 150 (14850-5793)
PHONE...................................607 319-5585
Andrew Scirri, *President*
Anthony Eisenhut, *Mng Member*
EMP: 6
SALES (est): 165K **Privately Held**
SIC: 2038 Breakfasts, frozen & packaged; lunches, frozen & packaged; dinners, frozen & packaged

(G-6365)
BENNETT DIE & TOOL INC
113 Brewery Ln (14850-8814)
PHONE...................................607 273-2836
James McMillen, *President*
Brian Bennett, *Vice Pres*
EMP: 16
SALES (est): 1.2MM **Privately Held**
SIC: 3544 Dies & die holders for metal cutting, forming, die casting; special dies & tools

(G-6366)
BIGWOOD SYSTEMS INC
35 Thornwood Dr Ste 400 (14850-1284)
PHONE...................................607 257-0915
Hsiao-Dong Chiang, *President*
Pat Causgrove, *General Mgr*
Bin Wang, *Engineer*
Gilburt Chiang, *Director*
EMP: 7
SALES (est): 651.6K **Privately Held**
WEB: www.bigwood-systems.com
SIC: 7372 Application computer software

(G-6367)
BIN OPTICS
20 Thornwood Dr Ste 100 (14850-1265)
PHONE...................................604 257-3200
Chet Warzynski, *Director*
EMP: 5
SALES (est): 332.6K **Privately Held**
SIC: 3089 Lenses, except optical: plastic

(G-6368)
BINOPTICS LLC (DH)
9 Brown Rd (14850-1247)
PHONE...................................607 257-3200
Alex Behfar, *CEO*
William Fritz, *COO*
Norman Kwong, *Exec VP*
Christopher Smith, *CFO*
▼ EMP: 35
SQ FT: 28,600
SALES (est): 16.9MM **Publicly Held**
WEB: www.binoptics.com
SIC: 3827 Optical instruments & lenses

(G-6369)
BIONIC EYE TECHNOLOGIES INC
239 Cherry St Ste 1b (14850-5024)
PHONE...................................845 505-5254
Richard Birney, *CEO*
EMP: 9
SALES (est): 492.3K **Privately Held**
SIC: 3842 Implants, surgical

(G-6370)
BOLTON POINT WTR TRTMNT PLANT
1402 E Shore Dr (14850-8506)
PHONE...................................607 277-0660
Paul Tunison, *Manager*
Steve Ridole, *Manager*
EMP: 5 EST: 2008
SALES (est): 509.3K **Privately Held**
SIC: 3589 Water treatment equipment, industrial

(G-6371)
BORGWARNER INC
780 Warren Rd (14850-1242)
PHONE...................................607 257-1800
Roger Wood, *President*
Frank Dimarco, *Senior Buyer*
John Bulzacchelli, *Engineer*
Chris Haesloop, *Engineer*
Magaly Wooten, *Engineer*
EMP: 30
SALES (corp-wide): 10.5B **Publicly Held**
SIC: 3714 Motor vehicle parts & accessories
PA: Borgwarner Inc.
3850 Hamlin Rd
Auburn Hills MI 48326
248 754-9200

(G-6372)
BORGWARNER MORSE TEC INC
780 Warren Rd (14850-1242)
PHONE...................................607 266-5111
Timothy M Manganello, *CEO*
EMP: 90 **Privately Held**
WEB: www.borgwarnermorsetec.com
SIC: 3714 Motor vehicle parts & accessories
HQ: Borgwarner Morse Tec Llc
800 Warren Rd
Ithaca NY 14850
607 257-6700

(G-6373)
BSU INC
445 E State St (14850-4409)
PHONE...................................607 272-8100
Catalina Chamseddine, *CEO*
Ahmad Chamseddine, *COO*
Dorothy Slocum, *Controller*
Dottie Highfield, *Accounts Mgr*
Michael Nutting, *Manager*
EMP: 29
SQ FT: 17,000
SALES: 3.5MM **Privately Held**
WEB: www.bsuinc.com
SIC: 3672 5065 8711 Printed circuit boards; electronic parts & equipment; engineering services

(G-6374)
CAYUGA WOODEN BOATWORKS INC
381 Enfield Main Rd (14850-9346)
P.O. Box 301, Cayuga (13034-0301)
PHONE...................................315 253-7447
Phil Walker, *General Mgr*
Ken Anderson, *Principal*
Kenneth Anderson, *Manager*
EMP: 21
SQ FT: 10,000
SALES (est): 3.4MM **Privately Held**
WEB: www.cwbw.com
SIC: 3732 7699 Boat building & repairing; boat repair

(G-6375)
CBORD GROUP INC (HQ)
950 Danby Rd Ste 100c (14850-5795)
PHONE...................................607 257-2410
Max Steinhardt, *President*
Tim Tighe, *President*
Bruce Lane, *Exec VP*
Karen Sammon, *Senior VP*
Larry Delaney, *Vice Pres*
EMP: 250
SQ FT: 40,000
SALES (est): 134.5MM
SALES (corp-wide): 5.1B **Publicly Held**
WEB: www.cbord.com
SIC: 7372 5045 Application computer software; computer peripheral equipment; computers

PA: Roper Technologies, Inc.
6901 Prof Pkwy E Ste 200
Sarasota FL 34240
941 556-2601

(G-6376)
CORNELL UNIVERSITY
Also Called: Cornell University Press
512 E State St (14850-4412)
P.O. Box 6525 (14851-6525)
PHONE..................................607 277-2338
Camille Andrews, *Librarian*
John G Ackerman, *Director*
David Mermi, *Professor*
EMP: 51
SALES (corp-wide): 4B Privately Held
SIC: 2731 8221 Textbooks: publishing
only, not printed on site; university
PA: Cornell University
308 Duffield Hall
Ithaca NY 14853
607 254-4636

(G-6377)
CORNELL UNIVERSITY
Also Called: Cornell Laboratory Ornithology
159 Sapsucker Woods Rd (14850-1923)
PHONE..................................607 254-2473
John Fitzpatrick, *Director*
EMP: 20
SALES (corp-wide): 4B Privately Held
SIC: 2721 8221 Periodicals; university
PA: Cornell University
308 Duffield Hall
Ithaca NY 14853
607 254-4636

(G-6378)
DAILY CORNELL SUN
Also Called: Dail Cornell Sun, The
139 W State St (14850-5427)
PHONE..................................607 273-0746
John Marcham, *President*
Josh Girsky, *Editor*
Nicole Hamilton, *Editor*
Jack Kantor, *Editor*
Cameron Pollack, *Editor*
EMP: 25
SQ FT: 7,020
SALES (est): 1.4MM Privately Held
WEB: www.cornellsun.com
SIC: 2711 Newspapers: publishing only,
not printed on site; newspapers, publish-
ing & printing

(G-6379)
DUKE COMPANY
7 Hall Rd (14850-8732)
PHONE..................................607 347-4455
Steven Dudley, *Principal*
EMP: 8
SALES (est): 178K Privately Held
SIC: 3272 7353 Building materials, except
block or brick: concrete; earth moving
equipment, rental or leasing

(G-6380)
F M ABDULKY INC (PA)
527 W Seneca St (14850-4033)
PHONE..................................607 272-7373
Fareed M Abdulky, *President*
Fareed Abdulky, *President*
Lamia Abdulky, *Vice Pres*
EMP: 13
SQ FT: 4,000
SALES (est): 1.2MM Privately Held
WEB: www.abdulky.com
SIC: 3911 Jewelry, precious metal

(G-6381)
F M ABDULKY INC
Also Called: Buffalo Finishing Company
527 W Seneca St (14850-4033)
PHONE..................................607 272-7373
Don Covert, *Manager*
EMP: 6
SQ FT: 2,616
SALES (corp-wide): 1.2MM Privately
Held
WEB: www.abdulky.com
SIC: 3911 Jewelry, precious metal
PA: F M Abdulky Inc
527 W Seneca St
Ithaca NY 14850
607 272-7373

(G-6382)
GLYCOBIA INC
33 Thornwood Dr Ste 104 (14850-1275)
PHONE..................................607 339-0051
Matthew Delisa, *President*
EMP: 5
SALES (est): 299K Privately Held
SIC: 2834 Pharmaceutical preparations

(G-6383)
GRATITUDE & COMPANY INC
215 N Cayuga St Ste 71 (14850-4323)
PHONE..................................607 277-3188
Julie Umbach, *President*
EMP: 6
SALES (est): 895K Privately Held
WEB: www.giftsofgratitude.com
SIC: 2621 Specialty papers

(G-6384)
HANGER PRSTHETCS & ORTHO INC
Also Called: Creative Orthotics Prosthetics
310 Taughannock Blvd 1a (14850-3251)
PHONE..................................607 277-6620
Thomas Kirk PHD, *CEO*
EMP: 10
SALES (corp-wide): 1B Publicly Held
SIC: 3842 Surgical appliances & supplies
HQ: Hanger Prosthetics & Orthotics, Inc.
10910 Domain Dr Ste 300
Austin TX 78758
512 777-3800

(G-6385)
INCODEMA INC
407 Cliff St (14850-2009)
PHONE..................................607 277-7070
Sean Whittaker, *CEO*
Mike Wargo, *COO*
Will Elmer, *Buyer*
Jeremy Woodman, *QC Mgr*
Benny Benjamin, *Engineer*
▼ EMP: 47
SQ FT: 30,000
SALES (est): 11.3MM Privately Held
SIC: 3444 Sheet metal specialties, not
stamped

(G-6386)
INDUSTRIAL MACHINE REPAIR
1144 Taughannock Blvd (14850-9573)
PHONE..................................607 272-0717
Martin J Sullivan, *Owner*
EMP: 6
SALES (est): 219.6K Privately Held
SIC: 3823 Computer interface equipment
for industrial process control

(G-6387)
INTERNATIONAL CENTER FOR POSTG
Also Called: Icpme-Ithaca Center
179 Graham Rd Ste E (14850-1141)
PHONE..................................607 257-5860
Kenneth Zeserson,
EMP: 9
SALES (est): 697.8K
SALES (corp-wide): 705MM Privately
Held
WEB: www.radinfonet.com
SIC: 2721 8741 Periodicals: publishing
only; management services
HQ: Jobson Medical Information Llc
395 Hudson St Fl 3
New York NY 10014
212 274-7000

(G-6388)
INTERNATIONAL CLIMBING MCHS
630 Elmira Rd (14850-8745)
PHONE..................................607 288-4001
Samuel J Maggio, *President*
Carolina Osorio Gil, *Manager*
EMP: 5
SALES (est): 644.5K Privately Held
SIC: 3599 Custom machinery

(G-6389)
ITHACA JOURNAL NEWS CO INC
123 W State St Ste 1 (14850-5479)
PHONE..................................607 272-2321
Sherman Bodner, *President*

EMP: 50 EST: 1815
SQ FT: 6,000
SALES (est): 7.4MM
SALES (corp-wide): 2.9B Publicly Held
WEB: www.ithaca.gannett.com
SIC: 2711 Commercial printing & newspa-
per publishing combined; newspapers,
publishing & printing
PA: Gannett Co., Inc.
7950 Jones Branch Dr
Mc Lean VA 22102
703 854-6000

(G-6390)
JOE MORO
Also Called: Moro Design
214 Fayette St (14850-5263)
PHONE..................................607 272-0591
Joe Moro, *Owner*
EMP: 5
SALES (est): 170K Privately Held
SIC: 3949 Bowling equipment & supplies

(G-6391)
KIONIX INC
36 Thornwood Dr (14850-1263)
PHONE..................................607 257-1080
Nader Sadrzadeh, *President*
Paul Bryan, *Exec VP*
Timothy J Davis, *Exec VP*
Kenneth N Salky, *Exec VP*
Kenneth Hager, *Vice Pres*
▲ EMP: 185
SQ FT: 60,000
SALES (est): 52.4MM Privately Held
WEB: www.kionix.com
SIC: 3674 Semiconductors & related de-
vices
PA: Rohm Company Limited
21, Mizosakicho, Saiin, Ukyo-Ku
Kyoto KYO 615-0

(G-6392)
LIQUID STATE BREWING CO INC
620 W Green St (14850-5250)
PHONE..................................607 319-6209
Jamey Tielens, *President*
Benjamin Brotman, *Vice Pres*
EMP: 5
SQ FT: 5,325
SALES (est): 83K Privately Held
SIC: 2082 Near beer

(G-6393)
M2 RACE SYSTEMS INC
53 Enfield Main Rd (14850-9367)
PHONE..................................607 882-9078
Ron Mielbrecht, *President*
Beth Mielbrecht, *Vice Pres*
EMP: 6
SQ FT: 7,500
SALES (est): 706.3K Privately Held
WEB: www.m2race.com
SIC: 3714 Cylinder heads, motor vehicle

(G-6394)
MADISON PRINTING CORP
Also Called: Instant Printing Service
704 W Buffalo St (14850-3300)
PHONE..................................607 273-3535
Angelo Digiacomo, *President*
Molly Digiacomo, *Vice Pres*
EMP: 5 EST: 1972
SQ FT: 1,600
SALES (est): 592.3K Privately Held
SIC: 2752 Commercial printing, offset

(G-6395)
MAG INC
Also Called: Momentummedia Sports Pubg
20 Eastlake Rd (14850-9786)
PHONE..................................607 257-6970
Mark Goldberg, *President*
Penny Small, *Financial Exec*
Mike Townsend, *Advt Staff*
EMP: 25
SQ FT: 3,600
SALES (est): 3.3MM Privately Held
WEB: www.momentummedia.com
SIC: 2721 Magazines: publishing only, not
printed on site

(G-6396)
MEZMERIZ INC
33 Thornwood Dr Ste 100 (14850-1275)
PHONE..................................607 216-8140

Bradley N Treat, *President*
Scott Adams, *Vice Pres*
EMP: 5
SALES (est): 935K Privately Held
SIC: 3679 Electronic components

(G-6397)
MITEGEN LLC
95 Brown Rd Ste 1034 (14850-1277)
P.O. Box 3867 (14852-3867)
PHONE..................................607 266-8877
Robert E Thorne,
EMP: 5
SALES: 200K Privately Held
WEB: www.mitegen.com
SIC: 3844 X-ray apparatus & tubes

(G-6398)
MPL INC
41 Dutch Mill Rd (14850-9785)
PHONE..................................607 266-0480
Shane French, *CEO*
Michelle French, *Ch of Bd*
EMP: 39
SQ FT: 15,000
SALES (est): 11.1MM Privately Held
WEB: www.mplinc.com
SIC: 3672 Printed circuit boards

(G-6399)
MULTIWIRE LABORATORIES LTD
95 Brown Rd 1018266a (14850-1294)
PHONE..................................607 257-3378
Donald Bilderback, *President*
Becky Bilderback, *Vice Pres*
▼ EMP: 6
SQ FT: 2,668
SALES (est): 855.4K Privately Held
WEB: www.multiwire.com
SIC: 3844 3826 X-ray apparatus & tubes;
analytical instruments

(G-6400)
NCR CORPORATION
950 Danby Rd (14850-5778)
PHONE..................................607 273-5310
Malcom Unsworth, *Branch Mgr*
EMP: 247
SALES (corp-wide): 6.4B Publicly Held
WEB: www.ncr.com
SIC: 2752 3577 Commercial printing, litho-
graphic; computer peripheral equipment
PA: Ncr Corporation
864 Spring St Nw
Atlanta GA 30308
937 445-5000

(G-6401)
NEW SKI INC
Also Called: Ithaca Times
109 N Cayuga St Ste A (14850-4340)
P.O. Box 27 (14851-0027)
PHONE..................................607 277-7000
James Belinski, *President*
EMP: 30
SQ FT: 2,000
SALES (est): 1.3MM Privately Held
WEB: www.ithacatimes.com
SIC: 2711 Newspapers: publishing only,
not printed on site

(G-6402)
NEWCHEM INC
Also Called: Newcut
407 Cliff St (14850-2009)
PHONE..................................315 331-7680
Sean Whittaker, *President*
Illa Burbank, *CFO*
Kirk Cranston, *Manager*
EMP: 22
SALES (est): 4MM Privately Held
SIC: 3479 Etching, photochemical

(G-6403)
ONGWEOWEH CORP (PA)
5 Barr Rd (14850-9117)
P.O. Box 3300 (14852-3300)
PHONE..................................607 266-7070
Frank C Bonamie, *Ch of Bd*
Justin M Bennett, *President*
Troy Williams, *General Mgr*
Crystal Collins, *Accounts Mgr*
Jon Kearney, *Manager*
EMP: 56
SQ FT: 1,000

▲ = Import ▼=Export
◆ =Import/Export

SALES (est): 182.2MM **Privately Held**
WEB: www.ongweoweh.com
SIC: 2448 Wood pallets & skids

(G-6404)
PERFORMANCE SYSTEMS CONTG INC
124 Brindley St (14850-5064)
PHONE..................................607 277-6240
Greg Thomas, *President*
Gregory Thomas,
EMP: 50
SQ FT: 20,000
SALES (est): 4.5MM **Privately Held**
WEB: www.pscontracting.com
SIC: 3825 Energy measuring equipment, electrical

(G-6405)
PETRUNIA LLC
Also Called: Petrune
126 E State St (14850-5542)
PHONE..................................607 277-1930
Dominica Brookman, *Mng Member*
EMP: 5
SALES (est): 628.5K **Privately Held**
SIC: 2339 Women's & misses' accessories

(G-6406)
POROUS MATERIALS INC
Also Called: Advance Pressure Products
20 Dutch Mill Rd (14850-9199)
PHONE..................................607 257-5544
Krishna M Gupta, *President*
Vaishnav Davey, *Project Mgr*
Sam Wright, *Technology*
Sudha Gupta, *Admin Sec*
Terri Murray, *Technician*
EMP: 17
SQ FT: 10,000
SALES (est): 2MM **Privately Held**
WEB: www.pmiapp.com
SIC: 3826 Laser scientific & engineering instruments

(G-6407)
PRECISION FILTERS INC (PA)
240 Cherry St (14850-5099)
PHONE..................................607 277-3550
Douglas Firth, *Ch of Bd*
Donald Chandler, *President*
Paul Costantini, *Vice Pres*
Alan Szary, *Vice Pres*
Stephen Finney, *Senior Engr*
EMP: 35
SQ FT: 15,500
SALES (est): 6.6MM **Privately Held**
WEB: www.pfinc.com
SIC: 3825 Test equipment for electronic & electric measurement

(G-6408)
PURITY ICE CREAM CO INC
700 Cascadilla St Ste A (14850-3255)
PHONE..................................607 272-1545
Bruce Lane, *President*
Heather Lane, *Vice Pres*
EMP: 18 **EST:** 1936
SQ FT: 10,000
SALES (est): 2MM **Privately Held**
WEB: www.purityicecream.com
SIC: 2024 5143 5812 2026 Ice cream, bulk; ice cream & ices; ice cream stands or dairy bars; fluid milk

(G-6409)
RHEONIX INC (PA)
10 Brown Rd Ste 103 (14850-1287)
PHONE..................................607 257-1242
Gregory J Galvin PHD, *Ch of Bd*
Richard A Montagna PHD, *Senior VP*
Peng Zhou PHD, *Senior VP*
John Brenner Ms, *Vice Pres*
Kenny Salky, *Vice Pres*
EMP: 60
SALES (est): 13.3MM **Privately Held**
WEB: www.rheonix.com
SIC: 3826 Analytical instruments

(G-6410)
RPS HOLDINGS INC
99 Eastlake Rd (14850-9786)
PHONE..................................607 257-7778
David Johnson, *President*
EMP: 22

SALES (est): 1.6MM **Privately Held**
WEB: www.rpsolutions.com
SIC: 7372 Business oriented computer software

(G-6411)
STORK H & E TURBO BLADING INC
334 Comfort Rd (14850-8626)
P.O. Box 177 (14851-0177)
PHONE..................................607 277-4968
John Slocum, *Ch of Bd*
Ben Tepeek, *CFO*
▲ **EMP:** 170 **EST:** 1976
SQ FT: 49,046
SALES (est): 42.4MM
SALES (corp-wide): 19.1B **Publicly Held**
WEB: www.he-machinery.com
SIC: 3511 Turbines & turbine generator sets
HQ: Stork Turbo Blading B.V.
Kamerlingh Onnesstraat 21
Sneek 8606
880 891-290

(G-6412)
THERM INCORPORATED
1000 Hudson Street Ext (14850-5999)
PHONE..................................607 272-8500
Robert R Sprole III, *Ch of Bd*
Valerie Daugherty, *General Mgr*
Rodney Ross, *Purch Agent*
Joe Harding, *Project Engr*
Valerie Talcott, *Manager*
▲ **EMP:** 200
SQ FT: 130,000
SALES (est): 52.3MM **Privately Held**
WEB: www.therm.com
SIC: 3724 Aircraft engines & engine parts

(G-6413)
TOMPKINS WEEKLY INC
36 Besemer Rd (14850-9638)
PHONE..................................607 539-7100
James Graney, *Principal*
EMP: 6
SALES (est): 317.3K **Privately Held**
SIC: 2711 Newspapers

(G-6414)
TRANSACT TECHNOLOGIES INC
Also Called: Ithaca Peripherals
20 Bomax Dr (14850-1200)
PHONE..................................607 257-8901
Donald Brooks, *Vice Pres*
Dick Cole, *Vice Pres*
Andy Hoffman, *Vice Pres*
Michael Kachala, *Vice Pres*
Steve Hilsdorf, *Project Engr*
EMP: 94
SQ FT: 70,000 **Publicly Held**
WEB: www.transact-tech.com
SIC: 3577 Printers, computer
PA: Transact Technologies Incorporated
2319 Whitney Ave Ste 3b
Hamden CT 06518

(G-6415)
TRANSACTION PRINTER GROUP
108 Woodcrest Ter (14850-6224)
PHONE..................................607 274-2500
Dana Wardlaw, *Principal*
EMP: 5 **EST:** 2009
SALES (est): 522.2K **Privately Held**
SIC: 2752 Commercial printing, lithographic

(G-6416)
VANGUARD GRAPHICS LLC
Also Called: Vanguard Printing
17 Hallwoods Rd (14850-8787)
P.O. Box 736, Fort Washington PA (19034-0736)
PHONE..................................607 272-1212
Steve Rossi, *President*
Laura Black, *Vice Pres*
William Post, *Vice Pres*
Bill Post, *Plant Mgr*
Lynn Hickey, *Purch Agent*
EMP: 140
SALES (est): 5.4MM
SALES (corp-wide): 7.1MM **Privately Held**
SIC: 2752 Commercial printing, offset

PA: Kappa Media, Llc
40 Skippack Pike
Fort Washington PA 19034
215 643-5800

(G-6417)
VECTOR MAGNETICS LLC
236 Cherry St (14850-5023)
PHONE..................................607 273-8351
Arthur Kuckes, *CEO*
Rahn Pitzer, *President*
David Mohler, *VP Opers*
David Mohler, *VP Opers*
EMP: 25
SQ FT: 12,000
SALES (est): 4.4MM **Privately Held**
SIC: 3829 Magnetometers

(G-6418)
ZYMTRNIX CATALYTIC SYSTEMS INC
526 N Campus (14853-6007)
PHONE..................................607 351-2639
Stephane Corgie, *CEO*
EMP: 6 **EST:** 2013
SALES (est): 729.3K **Privately Held**
SIC: 2869 Enzymes
PA: Zymtronix, Llc
526 N Campus 414a 1 Weill
Ithaca NY 14853
607 351-2639

Jackson Heights
Queens County

(G-6419)
CITYPHARMA INC
7316 Roosevelt Ave (11372-6336)
PHONE..................................917 832-6035
Lynn Youn, *President*
EMP: 5
SALES (est): 392.1K **Privately Held**
SIC: 2834 Pharmaceutical preparations

(G-6420)
KARISHMA FASHIONS INC
Also Called: Lavanya
3708 74th St (11372-6338)
PHONE..................................718 565-5404
Shiv Dass, *President*
EMP: 5
SQ FT: 1,500
SALES: 300K **Privately Held**
SIC: 2395 Embroidery & art needlework

(G-6421)
PROMETHEUS INTERNATIONAL INC
3717 74th St Ste 2f (11372-6320)
PHONE..................................718 472-0700
Sayedd Rabb, *President*
Monjur Hossain, *Manager*
EMP: 16 **EST:** 1989
SALES (est): 567.3K **Privately Held**
SIC: 2711 Commercial printing & newspaper publishing combined

(G-6422)
WEEKLY AJKAL
3707 74th St Ste 8 (11372-6308)
PHONE..................................718 565-2100
Jakaria Masud, *Owner*
EMP: 10
SALES (est): 375.8K **Privately Held**
SIC: 2711 Newspapers

Jamaica
Queens County

(G-6423)
ABBOTT INDUSTRIES INC (PA)
Also Called: Woodmaster Industries
9525 149th St (11435-4511)
PHONE..................................718 291-0800
Leonard Grossman, *Ch of Bd*
Jeffrey Grossman, *Vice Pres*
Cindy Ackerman, *Controller*
▲ **EMP:** 350 **EST:** 1958
SQ FT: 225,000

SALES (est): 36.8MM **Privately Held**
SIC: 2499 2541 3089 2542 Wooden-ware, kitchen & household; store fixtures, wood; plastic hardware & building products; office & store showcases & display fixtures; fryers, electric: household; heating units, for electric appliances; can openers, electric; food mixers, electric: household; miscellaneous fabricated wire products

(G-6424)
ACCORD PIPE FABRICATORS INC
9226 180th St (11433-1427)
PHONE..................................718 657-3900
Harry Schwarz, *President*
Thomas S Bloom, *Vice Pres*
EMP: 35
SQ FT: 40,000
SALES (est): 5.5MM **Privately Held**
SIC: 3498 5051 Fabricated pipe & fittings; pipe & tubing, steel

(G-6425)
AMERICAN TORQUE INC
10522 150th St (11435-5018)
PHONE..................................718 526-2433
Marsha McCarthy, *President*
Marcia McCarthy, *Vice Pres*
EMP: 10
SQ FT: 4,000
SALES (est): 1MM **Privately Held**
SIC: 3566 Torque converters, except automotive

(G-6426)
ATLAS CONCRETE BATCHING CORP
9511 147th Pl (11435-4507)
PHONE..................................718 523-3000
Thomas Polsinelli, *Principal*
EMP: 100
SQ FT: 12,000
SALES (est): 9MM **Privately Held**
SIC: 3273 Ready-mixed concrete

(G-6427)
ATLAS TRANSIT MIX CORP
9511 147th Pl (11435-4507)
PHONE..................................718 523-3000
Mary Polsinelli, *President*
Vincent Polsinelli, *Corp Secy*
Tom Polsinelli, *Vice Pres*
EMP: 150
SQ FT: 12,000
SALES (est): 900K **Privately Held**
SIC: 3273 Ready-mixed concrete

(G-6428)
B & R SHEET
10652 157th St (11433-2050)
PHONE..................................718 558-5544
Rohan Rampersaud, *Principal*
EMP: 5 **EST:** 2014
SALES (est): 502.1K **Privately Held**
SIC: 3444 1761 Sheet metalwork; sheet metalwork

(G-6429)
BAUERSCHMIDT & SONS INC
11920 Merrick Blvd (11434-2296)
PHONE..................................718 528-3500
Fred Bauerschmidt, *Ch of Bd*
Robert Bauerschmidt, *Treasurer*
Christina Vicario, *Bookkeeper*
Patty Bauerschmidt, *Manager*
▲ **EMP:** 70 **EST:** 1948
SQ FT: 28,000
SALES (est): 11.4MM **Privately Held**
WEB: www.bauerschmidtandsons.com
SIC: 2541 2431 2521 2434 Office fixtures, wood; cabinets, except refrigerated: show, display, etc.: wood; woodwork, interior & ornamental; wood office furniture; wood kitchen cabinets

(G-6430)
CAPITOL AWNING CO INC
Also Called: Capitol Awning & Shade Co
10515 180th St (11433-1818)
PHONE..................................212 505-1717
Michael Catalano, *President*
Fred Catalano Jr, *President*
Phil Catalano, *Vice Pres*
Ryan Catalano, *Treasurer*

EMP: 18
SQ FT: 8,000
SALES (est): 2MM **Privately Held**
WEB: www.capitolawning.com
SIC: 2394 Awnings, fabric: made from purchased materials

(G-6431)
CENTURY TOM INC
10416 150th St (11435-4924)
PHONE.....................347 654-3179
Yanru Lin, *CEO*
EMP: 4 **EST:** 2012
SALES: 1.7MM **Privately Held**
SIC: 2023 Dietary supplements, dairy & non-dairy based

(G-6432)
CHEMCLEAN CORPORATION
13045 180th St (11434-4107)
PHONE.....................718 525-4500
Bernard Esquenet, *President*
Paul N Crispin, *Principal*
Alcides Martinez, *Bookkeeper*
Brian Alexander, *Sales Executive*
Crispin Paul, *Supervisor*
▲ **EMP:** 28 **EST:** 1943
SQ FT: 30,000
SALES (est): 5.8MM **Privately Held**
WEB: www.chemclean.com
SIC: 2842 Cleaning or polishing preparations

(G-6433)
CIRCLE 5 DELI CORP
13440 Guy R Brewer Blvd (11434-3728)
PHONE.....................718 525-5687
Yahya Alsaidi, *Principal*
EMP: 8
SALES (est): 455.7K **Privately Held**
SIC: 2051 Bakery, for home service delivery

(G-6434)
CITY MASON CORP
Also Called: Three Star Supply
10417 148th St (11435-4921)
PHONE.....................718 658-3796
Anthony Scaccia, *Ch of Bd*
Frank Landen Jr, *President*
EMP: 15
SQ FT: 20,000
SALES (est): 1.1MM **Privately Held**
SIC: 3272 Concrete products

(G-6435)
CITY POST EXPRESS INC
17518 147th Ave (11434-5402)
P.O. Box 405, Fairfield CT (06824-0405)
PHONE.....................718 995-8690
Robert Swords, *Principal*
▲ **EMP:** 9
SALES (est): 866.5K **Privately Held**
SIC: 2741 Miscellaneous publishing

(G-6436)
CLASSIQUE PERFUMES INC
139 01 Archer Ave (11435)
PHONE.....................718 657-8200
EMP: 3
SQ FT: 9,500
SALES: 1.2MM **Privately Held**
SIC: 2844 Mfrs Colognes Perfumes & Cosmetics

(G-6437)
CONCORD EXPRESS CARGO INC
17214 119th Ave (11434-2260)
PHONE.....................718 276-7200
Chris Okafor, *CEO*
Margaret Jones, *Admin Sec*
▼ **EMP:** 5
SALES (est): 642.5K **Privately Held**
SIC: 2448 Cargo containers, wood & wood with metal

(G-6438)
CORKHILL MANUFACTURING CO INC
Also Called: Corkhill Grp
13121 Merrick Blvd (11434-4133)
PHONE.....................718 528-7413
Dennis Wugalter, *President*
Dennis Kourkoumelis, *General Mgr*

EMP: 8 **EST:** 1947
SQ FT: 7,000
SALES (est): 1.5MM **Privately Held**
SIC: 3442 Storm doors or windows, metal

(G-6439)
CRS REMANUFACTURING CO INC
9440 158th St (11433-1017)
PHONE.....................718 739-1720
Pratab Angira, *President*
Balkrishna Angira, *Vice Pres*
▲ **EMP:** 10
SALES (est): 920K **Privately Held**
SIC: 3714 Power steering equipment, motor vehicle

(G-6440)
D AND D SHEET METAL CORP
9510 218th St Ste 4 (11429-1216)
PHONE.....................718 465-7585
EMP: 12
SALES (est): 960K **Privately Held**
SIC: 3444 Mfg Sheet Metalwork

(G-6441)
EXPRESSIONS PUNCHING & DIGITIZ
Also Called: Expression Embroidery
9315 179th Pl (11433-1425)
PHONE.....................718 291-1177
George Hanakis, *President*
Evelyn Hanakis, *Vice Pres*
EMP: 9
SQ FT: 7,000
SALES: 980K **Privately Held**
SIC: 2395 Embroidery products, except schiffli machine; embroidery & art needlework

(G-6442)
FORTUNE POLY PRODUCTS INC
17910 93rd Ave (11433-1406)
PHONE.....................718 361-0767
Roger Truong, *President*
▲ **EMP:** 14
SQ FT: 25,000
SALES (est): 2.5MM **Privately Held**
SIC: 2673 Plastic bags: made from purchased materials

(G-6443)
FRANCHET METAL CRAFT INC
17832 93rd Ave (11433-1489)
PHONE.....................718 658-6400
Frank Grodio, *President*
EMP: 6
SQ FT: 4,000
SALES: 700K **Privately Held**
SIC: 3444 Sheet metal specialties, not stamped

(G-6444)
GLEANER COMPANY LTD
Also Called: Jamaican Weekly Gleaner
9205 172nd St Fl 2 (11433-1218)
PHONE.....................718 657-0788
Sheila Alexander, *Director*
EMP: 5
SALES (est): 510.2K **Privately Held**
WEB: www.gleaner-classifieds.com
SIC: 2711 Newspapers, publishing & printing
HQ: Gleaner Company (Canada) Inc, The
1390 Eglinton Ave W Suite 2
Toronto ON M6C 2
416 784-3002

(G-6445)
GOURMET BOUTIQUE LLC (PA)
14402 158th St (11434-4214)
PHONE.....................718 977-1200
Robert Liberto, *CEO*
Jan Sussman, *President*
Leo Maglasang, *QA Dir*
Jere Dudley, *VP Sales*
Jody Crystall, *Cust Svc Dir*
▲ **EMP:** 217
SQ FT: 60,000
SALES: 64MM **Privately Held**
WEB: www.gourmetboutique.com
SIC: 2099 Food preparations

(G-6446)
H & H FURNITURE CO
11420 101st Ave (11419-1139)
PHONE.....................718 850-5252
John Hassan, *Principal*
EMP: 5
SALES (est): 330K **Privately Held**
SIC: 2512 Upholstered household furniture

(G-6447)
H G MAYBECK CO INC
17930 93rd Ave Ste 2 (11433-1405)
PHONE.....................718 297-4410
John Arapis, *President*
Chris Arapis, *Vice Pres*
Len Golombek, *Sales Mgr*
▲ **EMP:** 30
SQ FT: 26,000
SALES (est): 4.2MM **Privately Held**
SIC: 2393 2673 Canvas bags; bags: plastic, laminated & coated

(G-6448)
HILLSIDE PRINTING INC
Also Called: Printing Express
16013 Hillside Ave (11432-3982)
PHONE.....................718 658-6719
Joseph Randazzo, *President*
EMP: 10
SQ FT: 2,000
SALES: 1MM **Privately Held**
WEB: www.hillsideprinting.com
SIC: 2752 Commercial printing, offset

(G-6449)
IMPLADENT LTD (PA)
19845 Foothill Ave (11423-1611)
PHONE.....................718 465-1810
Maurice Valen, *President*
Virginia Valen, *Vice Pres*
Johnny Yuen, *Sales Staff*
Gisele Sasson, *Admin Sec*
EMP: 8
SALES (est): 1.9MM **Privately Held**
WEB: www.impladentltd.com
SIC: 3843 3069 5047 Dental equipment & supplies; medical & laboratory rubber sundries & related products; dental equipment & supplies

(G-6450)
J SUSSMAN INC
10910 180th St (11433-2622)
PHONE.....................718 297-0228
David Sussman, *President*
Steve Sussman, *Vice Pres*
Bibi Ortiz, *Executive*
▼ **EMP:** 45 **EST:** 1906
SQ FT: 55,000
SALES (est): 11.4MM **Privately Held**
WEB: www.jsussmaninc.com
SIC: 3442 3354 Window & door frames; aluminum extruded products

(G-6451)
JAMAICA IRON WORKS INC
10847 Merrick Blvd (11433-2992)
PHONE.....................718 657-4849
Robert Pape, *President*
EMP: 10 **EST:** 1927
SQ FT: 2,000
SALES (est): 830K **Privately Held**
SIC: 3446 Fences or posts, ornamental iron or steel

(G-6452)
JONATHAN METAL & GLASS LTD
17816 104th Ave (11433-1825)
PHONE.....................718 846-8000
Wilfred Smith, *President*
Nerone Qela, *Project Mgr*
Antonio Gonzalez, *Purchasing*
Shakero Porter, *Office Mgr*
▲ **EMP:** 151
SALES: 44.3MM **Privately Held**
SIC: 3446 Bank fixtures, ornamental metal; brasswork, ornamental: structural; grillwork, ornamental metal

(G-6453)
LIBERTY READY MIX INC
9533 150th St (11435-4501)
PHONE.....................718 526-1700
Giabomo Gisonda, *President*

EMP: 12
SALES (est): 1.6MM **Privately Held**
SIC: 3273 Ready-mixed concrete

(G-6454)
LITE-MAKERS INC
10715 180th St (11433-2617)
PHONE.....................718 739-9300
John Iorio, *President*
Gary Iorio, *Treasurer*
▲ **EMP:** 30
SQ FT: 12,000
SALES (est): 4.7MM **Privately Held**
WEB: www.litemakers.com
SIC: 3646 Chandeliers, commercial

(G-6455)
MACHINA DEUS LEX INC
15921 Grand Central Pkwy (11432-1128)
PHONE.....................917 577-0972
Glen Kieser, *President*
EMP: 6
SALES (est): 150K **Privately Held**
SIC: 2421 Silo stock, wood: sawed

(G-6456)
MAIA SYSTEMS LLC
8344 Parsons Blvd Ste 101 (11432-1642)
PHONE.....................718 206-0100
Jack Najyb, *President*
EMP: 6
SALES (est): 846.4K **Privately Held**
SIC: 3661 3577 5734 Telephone sets, all types except cellular radio; computer peripheral equipment; computer & software stores

(G-6457)
MANIFESTATION-GLOW PRESS INC
8471 Parsons Blvd (11432-2543)
PHONE.....................718 380-5259
IA Konopiaty, *Ch of Bd*
Abakash Konopiaty, *President*
EMP: 5
SALES (est): 666.8K **Privately Held**
WEB: www.heart-light.com
SIC: 2752 Commercial printing, offset

(G-6458)
MAUCERI SIGN INC
Also Called: Mauceri Sign & Awning Co
16725 Rockaway Blvd (11434-5266)
PHONE.....................718 656-7700
James V Mauceri, *President*
Carol Caruso, *General Mgr*
EMP: 18
SQ FT: 14,000
SALES (est): 2.6MM **Privately Held**
SIC: 3993 2394 5999 Signs, not made in custom sign painting shops; awnings, fabric: made from purchased materials; awnings

(G-6459)
METAL WORKS OF NY INC
11603 Merrick Blvd (11434-1825)
PHONE.....................718 525-9440
Vincent Sabatino, *President*
Danny Sabatino, *Treasurer*
EMP: 5
SALES (est): 520K **Privately Held**
SIC: 3441 Fabricated structural metal

(G-6460)
METEOR EXPRESS INC
16801 Rockaway Blvd # 202 (11434-5287)
PHONE.....................718 551-9177
Ning Fang, *CEO*
EMP: 15
SALES (est): 1.2MM **Privately Held**
SIC: 3537 Trucks: freight, baggage, etc.: industrial, except mining

(G-6461)
MINUTEMAN PRESS INTL INC
24814 Union Tpke (11426)
PHONE.....................718 343-5440
Rob Schiffman, *Manager*
EMP: 5
SALES (corp-wide): 23.4MM **Privately Held**
SIC: 2752 Commercial printing, lithographic

▲ = Import ▼=Export
◆ =Import/Export

PA: Minuteman Press International, Inc.
61 Executive Blvd
Farmingdale NY 11735
631 249-1370

(G-6462)
MOUNTAIN SIDE FARMS INC
15504 Liberty Ave (11433-1038)
PHONE.....................718 526-3442
Henry Schwartz, *President*
EMP: 30 **EST:** 1981
SQ FT: 500
SALES (est): 29.8K **Privately Held**
SIC: 2026 Milk processing (pasteurizing, homogenizing, bottling)

(G-6463)
NEW YORK STEEL SERVICES CO
18009 Liberty Ave (11433-1434)
PHONE.....................718 291-7770
George Cromwell, *Owner*
EMP: 5
SALES (est): 390K **Privately Held**
SIC: 3449 Bars, concrete reinforcing: fabricated steel

(G-6464)
PATI INC
Also Called: Airport Press, The
Jfk Intl Airprt Hngar 16 (11430)
PHONE.....................718 244-6788
Fax: 718 995-3432
EMP: 10
SQ FT: 1,000
SALES (est): 790K **Privately Held**
SIC: 2721 Periodicals-Publishing/Printing

(G-6465)
PRECISION READY MIX INC
14707 Liberty Ave (11435-4727)
PHONE.....................718 658-5600
Frank Scaccia, *President*
EMP: 6
SQ FT: 700
SALES (est): 500K **Privately Held**
SIC: 3273 Ready-mixed concrete

(G-6466)
PREMIUM SWEETS USA INC
16803 Hillside Ave (11432-4340)
PHONE.....................718 739-6000
Babu Khan, *CEO*
EMP: 8
SALES (est): 610.7K **Privately Held**
SIC: 2064 5145 Candy & other confectionery products; candy

(G-6467)
QUEENS READY MIX INC
14901 95th Ave (11435-4521)
PHONE.....................718 526-4919
Tony Mastronardi, *President*
Jerry Mastronardi, *Vice Pres*
EMP: 7
SALES (est): 1MM **Privately Held**
SIC: 3273 Ready-mixed concrete

(G-6468)
R & M THERMOFOIL DOORS INC
14830 94th Ave (11435-4516)
PHONE.....................718 206-4991
Robby Moyal, *Ch of Bd*
EMP: 5
SALES (est): 643.2K **Privately Held**
SIC: 2434 Wood kitchen cabinets

(G-6469)
RAYS RESTAURANT & BAKERY INC
12325 Jamaica Ave (11418-2640)
PHONE.....................718 441-7707
Ray Manharalall, *CEO*
▲ **EMP:** 6
SQ FT: 3,100
SALES (est): 320K **Privately Held**
SIC: 2051 Bakery: wholesale or wholesale/retail combined

(G-6470)
REHABILITATION INTERNATIONAL
15350 89th Ave Apt 1101 (11432-3977)
PHONE.....................212 420-1500
Tomas Lagerwall, *President*

EMP: 5
SQ FT: 4,000
SALES: 182.2K **Privately Held**
SIC: 3663

(G-6471)
ROSCO INC (PA)
Also Called: Rosco Vision Systems
9021 144th Pl (11435-4227)
PHONE.....................718 526-2601
Sol Englander, *Chairman*
Gertrude Englander, *Corp Secy*
Ben Englander, *Vice Pres*
Danny Englander, *Vice Pres*
Joe Ippolito, *Plant Mgr*
◆ **EMP:** 153
SQ FT: 85,000
SALES (est): 33.8MM **Privately Held**
WEB: www.roscomirrors.com
SIC: 3231 3714 3429 Mirrors, truck & automobile: made from purchased glass; motor vehicle parts & accessories; manufactured hardware (general)

(G-6472)
ROSCO COLLISION AVOIDANCE INC
9021 144th Pl (11435-4227)
PHONE.....................718 526-2601
Daniel Englander, *VP Finance*
EMP: 8
SALES (est): 2MM **Privately Held**
SIC: 3861 Cameras & related equipment

(G-6473)
SKY LAUNDROMAT INC
8615 Ava Pl Apt 4e (11432-2954)
PHONE.....................718 639-7070
David Mendoza, *President*
EMP: 33
SQ FT: 5,000
SALES: 660K **Privately Held**
SIC: 2211 7215 Laundry nets; laundry, coin-operated

(G-6474)
SSRJA LLC
Also Called: Five Star Printing
10729 180th St (11433-2617)
PHONE.....................718 725-7020
Savithri Somwaru,
Anand Jagessar,
Seelochini S Liriano,
Javier Rojas,
EMP: 11
SQ FT: 10,000
SALES: 3MM **Privately Held**
SIC: 2711 Newspapers, publishing & printing

(G-6475)
STAR MOUNTAIN JFK INC
Also Called: Star Mountain Coffee
Federal Cir Bldg 141 (11430)
PHONE.....................718 553-6787
Carmen Ham, *President*
EMP: 5
SALES: 350K **Privately Held**
SIC: 2095 Roasted coffee

(G-6476)
SUGARBEAR CUPCAKES
14552 159th St (11434-4220)
PHONE.....................917 698-9005
Louise Torbert, *Principal*
EMP: 8
SALES (est): 315K **Privately Held**
SIC: 2051 Bread, cake & related products

(G-6477)
SUNBILT SOLAR PDTS BY SUSSMAN
10910 180th St (11433-2622)
PHONE.....................718 297-0228
Steven Sussman, *President*
David Sussman, *Vice Pres*
EMP: 55
SQ FT: 80,000
SALES (est): 5.7MM **Privately Held**
SIC: 3448 Sunrooms, prefabricated metal

(G-6478)
TECHNICAL SERVICE INDUSTRIES
Also Called: ABC Casting
17506 Devonshire Rd 5n (11432-2949)
PHONE.....................212 719-9800
Mitch Altman, *President*
Michael Hooks, *Vice Pres*
EMP: 27
SQ FT: 3,500
SALES (est): 3MM **Privately Held**
SIC: 3911 Jewelry, precious metal

(G-6479)
TEE PEE FENCE AND RAILING
Also Called: Tee Pee Fence & Rail
9312 179th Pl (11433-1426)
PHONE.....................718 658-8323
Tom Pendergast, *President*
Jim Pendergast, *Manager*
EMP: 15
SQ FT: 15,000
SALES: 1.3MM **Privately Held**
SIC: 3446 Fences or posts, ornamental iron or steel; railings, prefabricated metal

(G-6480)
THE SANDHAR CORP
16427 Highland Ave (11432-3555)
PHONE.....................718 523-0819
Hardev Sandhu, *President*
Shawinder Sandhu, *Vice Pres*
EMP: 7 **EST:** 1990
SALES (est): 413.8K **Privately Held**
SIC: 2711 Newspapers

(G-6481)
TRIPLE H CONSTRUCTION INC
10737 180th St (11433-2617)
PHONE.....................516 280-8252
Hesham Hassane, *President*
Venaal Hassane, *Vice Pres*
Nazim Koch, *Sr Project Mgr*
EMP: 22 **EST:** 2011
SALES: 700K **Privately Held**
SIC: 3446 1751 Fences or posts, ornamental iron or steel; window & door installation & erection

(G-6482)
TRU-ART SIGN CO INC
Also Called: Signs By Sunrise
10515 180th St (11433-1818)
PHONE.....................718 658-5068
Lawrence Amatulli, *President*
EMP: 12
SALES (corp-wide): 1.3MM **Privately Held**
SIC: 3993 Signs & advertising specialties
PA: Tru-Art Sign Co. Inc.
187 N Main St
Freeport NY
516 378-0066

(G-6483)
TURBO EXPRESS INC
16019 Rockaway Blvd Ste D (11434-5100)
PHONE.....................718 723-3686
Gilberto Rosario, *Principal*
EMP: 5
SALES (est): 239.2K **Privately Held**
SIC: 2741 Miscellaneous publishing

(G-6484)
UNIKE PRODUCTS INC
18230 Wexford Ter Apt 2m (11432-3119)
PHONE.....................347 686-4616
Nancy Roger, *CEO*
▼ **EMP:** 5
SALES: 100K **Privately Held**
SIC: 2844 Hair preparations, including shampoos; shampoos, rinses, conditioners: hair; oral preparations; toothpastes or powders, dentifrices

(G-6485)
URDU TIMES
16920 Hillside Ave (11432-4435)
PHONE.....................718 297-8700
Khalil Ur Rehman, *President*
EMP: 6
SALES (est): 198.5K **Privately Held**
SIC: 2711 Newspapers

(G-6486)
VICK CONSTRUCTION INC
1489014 90th Ave Apt 1f (11435)
PHONE.....................718 313-7625
Vick Mansukh, *President*
EMP: 5
SQ FT: 400
SALES: 80K **Privately Held**
SIC: 1389 Construction, repair & dismantling services

(G-6487)
WAYNE DECORATORS INC
14409 Rockaway Blvd Apt 1 (11436-1602)
PHONE.....................718 529-4200
Louis Sapodin, *President*
Alex Greenberg, *Vice Pres*
EMP: 8
SQ FT: 2,000
SALES (est): 617.1K **Privately Held**
SIC: 2391 2392 2393 Draperies, plastic & textile: from purchased materials; bedspreads & bed sets: made from purchased materials; pillows, bed: made from purchased materials; cushions, except spring & carpet: purchased materials

(G-6488)
WHITNEY FOODS INC
Also Called: Kissle
15504 Liberty Ave (11433-1038)
PHONE.....................718 291-3333
Henry Schwartz, *Ch of Bd*
Kenneth Schlossberg, *Vice Ch Bd*
D Bruce Budinoff, *Vice Pres*
Robert E Braks, *Treasurer*
EMP: 16
SALES (est): 1.5MM
SALES (corp-wide): 115.3MM **Privately Held**
SIC: 2026 Yogurt
PA: Steuben Foods, Incorporated
1150 Maple Rd
Elma NY 14059
718 291-3333

(G-6489)
X-TREME READY MIX INC
17801 Liberty Ave (11433-1432)
PHONE.....................718 739-3384
Michael Falco, *Ch of Bd*
EMP: 9
SALES (est): 1.2MM **Privately Held**
SIC: 3531 Mixers, concrete

Jamesport
Suffolk County

(G-6490)
NORTH HOUSE VINEYARDS INC
Also Called: Jamesport Vineyards
1216 Main Rd Rte 25a (11947)
P.O. Box 842 (11947-0842)
PHONE.....................631 779-2817
Ronald B Goerler, *President*
Ann Marie Goerler, *Treasurer*
▲ **EMP:** 5
SALES (est): 427.4K **Privately Held**
WEB: www.jamesportvineyards.com
SIC: 2084 Wines

Jamestown
Chautauqua County

(G-6491)
ACCESS ELEVATOR & LIFT INC (PA)
1209 E 2nd St (14701-1952)
PHONE.....................716 483-3696
Sean Fenton, *President*
EMP: 1
SALES: 1.8MM **Privately Held**
SIC: 3534 Elevators & equipment

(G-6492)
ALL METAL SPECIALTIES INC
300 Livingston Ave (14701-2665)
PHONE.....................716 664-6009
Raymond Anderson, *President*
EMP: 21 **EST:** 1953

(PA)=Parent Co (HQ)=Headquarters (DH)=Div Headquarters
✪ = New Business established in last 2 years

2020 Harris
New York Manufacturers Directory

251

GEOGRAPHIC

SQ FT: 18,500
SALES (est): 3.2MM **Privately Held**
WEB: www.allmetalspecialties.com
SIC: 3444 Sheet metalwork

(G-6493)
ALLIED INDUSTRIAL PRODUCTS CO
Also Called: Allied Industries
880 E 2nd St (14701-3824)
PHONE...................................716 664-3893
Greg Bender, *Manager*
EMP: 6
SALES (est): 297.3K
SALES (corp-wide): 90K **Privately Held**
SIC: 3599 Machine shop, jobbing & repair
PA: Allied Industrial Products Co
180 W Olive St
Long Beach NY

(G-6494)
ANDERSON PRECISION INC
20 Livingston Ave (14701-2844)
PHONE...................................716 484-1148
Steven Godfrey, *President*
Jason Carlson, *Prdtn Mgr*
John McCool, *Engineer*
Matt Satterfield, *Engineer*
Elise Bland, *Accountant*
▲ EMP: 83
SQ FT: 80,000
SALES (est): 21.3MM **Privately Held**
WEB: www.andersonprecision.com
SIC: 3451 3494 Screw machine products;
valves & pipe fittings

(G-6495)
ARTONE LLC (PA)
Also Called: Artone Furniture By Design
1089 Allen St (14701-2327)
PHONE...................................716 664-2232
Michael Calimeri, *President*
Sebastian Calimeri, *Exec VP*
Sebastian Calimeri, *Vice Pres*
James Tharp, *Plant Engr*
Sally Donisi, *Controller*
▲ EMP: 77
SQ FT: 240,000
SALES: 12.3MM **Privately Held**
WEB: www.artonemfg.com
SIC: 2521 2522 2531 2541 Wood office
furniture; office furniture, except wood;
public building & related furniture; wood
partitions & fixtures; wood kitchen cabi-
nets; upholstered household furniture

(G-6496)
BELLA INTERNATIONAL INC
111 W 2nd St Ste 4000 (14701-5207)
PHONE...................................716 484-0102
Stephen Pownell, *Principal*
EMP: 5
SALES (est): 508.3K **Privately Held**
WEB: www.bellayre.com
SIC: 2835 In vitro & in vivo diagnostic sub-
stances

(G-6497)
BIOPOOL US INC
Also Called: Trinity Biotech Distribution
2823 Girts Rd (14701-9666)
P.O. Box 1059 (14702-1059)
PHONE...................................716 483-3851
Ian Woodwards, *CEO*
William Reese, *Admin Sec*
▲ EMP: 48
SALES (est): 7MM **Privately Held**
SIC: 2835 In vitro & in vivo diagnostic sub-
stances
HQ: Trinity Biotech, Inc.
2823 Girts Rd
Jamestown NY 14701
800 325-3424

(G-6498)
BLACKSTONE ADVANCED TECH LLC
86 Blackstone Ave (14701-2202)
PHONE...................................716 665-5410
Richard Turner, *Manager*
Charles Viers, *General Mgr*
Sarah Drake, *Finance*
Jennifer Masse, *Director*
EMP: 101

SALES: 26.8MM **Privately Held**
SIC: 3444 3441 3443 Sheet metalwork;
fabricated structural metal; fabricated
plate work (boiler shop)

(G-6499)
BNO INTL TRDG CO INC
505 Chautauqua Ave (14701-7615)
P.O. Box 97 (14702-0097)
PHONE...................................716 487-1900
Benjamin N Okwumabua, *President*
Benjamin Okwumabua, *President*
Constance Okwumabua, *Vice Pres*
EMP: 4
SQ FT: 100,000
SALES: 2.5MM **Privately Held**
WEB: www.bnointl.com
SIC: 3669 5063 Highway signals, electric;
signaling equipment, electrical

(G-6500)
BUSH INDUSTRIES INC (PA)
1 Mason Dr (14701-9200)
P.O. Box 460 (14702-0460)
PHONE...................................716 665-2000
Jim Garde, *CEO*
Stephen Pettia, *President*
Mark Weppner, *Exec VP*
Jill Curley-Holshous, *Vice Pres*
Wende Parrish, *Vice Pres*
◆ EMP: 234 EST: 1959
SQ FT: 440,000
SALES (est): 80.9MM **Privately Held**
WEB: www.bushindustries.com
SIC: 2511 2521 Wood household furniture;
desks, office: wood; cabinets, office:
wood; bookcases, office: wood; panel
systems & partitions (free-standing), of-
fice: wood

(G-6501)
CITY OF JAMESTOWN
Also Called: Jamestown Public Works
200 E 3rd St Ste 4 (14701-5433)
PHONE...................................716 483-7545
Jeffrey Lehman, *Director*
Mark Schlemmer, *Director*
EMP: 55 **Privately Held**
SIC: 3531 Road construction & mainte-
nance machinery
PA: City Of Jamestown
200 E 3rd St
Jamestown NY 14701
716 483-7538

(G-6502)
CLEANING TECH GROUP LLC
Blackstone-Ney Ultrasonics
9 N Main St (14701-5213)
P.O. Box 220 (14702-0220)
PHONE...................................716 665-2340
Timothy Piazza, *President*
EMP: 50 **Privately Held**
SIC: 3569 3559 Blast cleaning equipment,
dustless; degreasing machines, automo-
tive & industrial
HQ: Cleaning Technologies Group, Llc
4933 Provident Dr
West Chester OH 45246

(G-6503)
CNTRY CROSS COMMUNICATIONS LLC
Also Called: W K Z A 106.9 K I S S-F M
106 W 3rd St Ste 106 # 106 (14701-5105)
PHONE...................................386 758-9696
John Newman, *Mng Member*
EMP: 10
SALES (est): 1.1MM **Privately Held**
WEB: www.1069kissfm.com
SIC: 3663 Radio receiver networks

(G-6504)
CONTAINER TSTG SOLUTIONS LLC
17 Tiffany Ave (14701-1953)
PHONE...................................716 487-3300
Brian Johnson, *Branch Mgr*
EMP: 15 **Privately Held**
SIC: 2834 Solutions, pharmaceutical
PA: Container Testing Solutions Llc
17 Lester St
Sinclairville NY 14782

(G-6505)
COPPER RIDGE OIL INC
111 W 2nd St Ste 404 (14701-5229)
P.O. Box 626, Olean (14760-0626)
PHONE...................................716 372-4021
Greg Thropp, *President*
EMP: 8
SALES (est): 950K **Privately Held**
SIC: 1381 Drilling oil & gas wells

(G-6506)
DAWSON METAL COMPANY INC
Also Called: Dawson Doors
825 Allen St (14701-3998)
PHONE...................................716 664-3811
David G Dawson, *Principal*
Rick Carlson, *Vice Pres*
Mike Restivo, *Vice Pres*
Laura Snow, *Production*
Tad Henderson, *Project Engr*
EMP: 110 EST: 1945
SQ FT: 100,000
SALES: 13.1MM **Privately Held**
WEB: www.dawsondoors.com
SIC: 3444 3442 Sheet metalwork; metal
doors, sash & trim; sash, door or window:
metal; moldings & trim, except automo-
bile: metal

(G-6507)
ECKO FIN & TOOLING INC
221 Hopkins Ave Ste 2 (14701-2252)
PHONE...................................716 487-0200
Steve Rauschenberger, *CEO*
Lance Rauschenberger, *Vice Pres*
▼ EMP: 11
SALES: 1.3MM **Privately Held**
SIC: 3542 Machine tools, metal forming
type

(G-6508)
EL GRECO WOODWORKING INC (PA)
106 E 1st St Ste 1 (14701-5499)
PHONE...................................716 483-0315
George Theofilactidis, *President*
Constantina Kathleen Theofilac, *Corp Secy*
Dimitri Theofilactidis, *Vice Pres*
EMP: 20 EST: 1975
SQ FT: 100,000
SALES (est): 2.7MM **Privately Held**
WEB: www.elgrecofurniture.com
SIC: 2511 Chairs, household, except up-
holstered: wood

(G-6509)
ELECTRIC MOTOR SPECIALTY INC
Also Called: Electric Motor Specialties
490 Crescent St (14701-3828)
P.O. Box 111, Dewittville (14728-0111)
PHONE...................................716 487-1458
William L Allen, *President*
EMP: 6
SALES (est): 551.3K **Privately Held**
SIC: 7694 5063 Electric motor repair; mo-
tors, electric

(G-6510)
EMCO FINISHING PRODUCTS INC
470 Crescent St (14701-3897)
PHONE...................................716 483-1176
Daniel S Alexander, *President*
Barbara L Sheldon, *Admin Sec*
▲ EMP: 9 EST: 1999
SQ FT: 14,000
SALES (est): 2.3MM **Privately Held**
SIC: 2851 Lacquer: bases, dopes, thinner

(G-6511)
FRED SANTUCCI INC
Also Called: Industrial Welding & Fabg Co
121 Jackson Ave E (14701-2441)
PHONE...................................716 483-1411
Frederick A Santucci, *President*
Marybeth Santucci, *Corp Secy*
Susan Wilston, *Manager*
EMP: 14
SQ FT: 12,000
SALES (est): 2.6MM **Privately Held**
SIC: 3441 7692 Fabricated structural
metal; welding repair

(G-6512)
GENCO JOHN
Also Called: S & S Enterprises
71 River St (14701-3806)
PHONE...................................716 483-5446
John Genco, *Owner*
EMP: 6
SQ FT: 21,000
SALES (est): 588.9K **Privately Held**
SIC: 3599 1541 7692 3541 Machine
shop, jobbing & repair; dry cleaning plant
construction; welding repair; machine
tools, metal cutting type

(G-6513)
GRACE WHEELER
Also Called: Superior Bat Company
118 E 1st St (14701-5430)
P.O. Box 3331 (14702-3331)
PHONE...................................716 483-1254
Grace Wheeler, *Owner*
EMP: 6
SQ FT: 26,000
SALES (est): 522.3K **Privately Held**
SIC: 3949 Baseball equipment & supplies,
general; softball equipment & supplies

(G-6514)
GREEN PROSTHETICS & ORTHOTICS
1290 E 2nd St (14701-1915)
PHONE...................................716 484-1088
Michelle Lohrke, *Opers-Prdtn-Mfg*
EMP: 7
SALES (corp-wide): 1.9MM **Privately Held**
SIC: 3842 5999 Limbs, artificial; artificial
limbs
PA: Green Prosthetics & Orthotics, Inc
2241 Peninsula Dr
Erie PA 16506
814 833-2311

(G-6515)
HANSON AGGREGATES NEW YORK LLC
2237 Allen Street Ext (14701-9632)
PHONE...................................716 665-4620
Scott Wheaton, *Manager*
EMP: 15
SALES (corp-wide): 20.6B **Privately Held**
SIC: 3273 Ready-mixed concrete
HQ: Hanson Aggregates New York Llc
8505 Freport Pkwy Ste 500
Irving TX 75063

(G-6516)
HOPES WINDOWS INC
84 Hopkins Ave (14701-2223)
P.O. Box 580 (14702-0580)
PHONE...................................716 665-5124
Randy Manita, *President*
Jim Cave, *Regional Mgr*
John Brown, *Vice Pres*
Brian Whalen, *Vice Pres*
John D Fafinski, *VP Mfg*
▲ EMP: 250
SQ FT: 228,000
SALES (est): 60.7MM **Privately Held**
SIC: 3442 Sash, door or window: metal

(G-6517)
HYTECH TOOL & DIE INC
2202 Washington St (14701-2028)
PHONE...................................716 488-2796
William Swanson, *President*
▲ EMP: 8
SQ FT: 6,625
SALES (est): 1.4MM
SALES (corp-wide): 3.1MM **Privately Held**
WEB: www.hytechmold.com
SIC: 3544 Dies & die holders for metal cut-
ting, forming, die casting; industrial molds
PA: Hytech Tool & Design Co
12076 Edinboro Rd
Edinboro PA 16412
814 734-6000

(G-6518)
INTERNATIONAL ORD TECH INC
101 Harrison St (14701-6614)
PHONE...................................716 664-1100
Tammy H Snyder, *President*
Fred Callahan, *Vice Pres*

John Hedman, *Vice Pres*
Sandy Alexander, *Cust Mgr*
◆ **EMP:** 90
SALES (est): 13.3MM **Privately Held**
WEB: www.iotusa.net
SIC: 3469 3398 2874 Metal stampings;
metal heat treating; phosphates

(G-6519)
JAMESTOWN ADVANCED PDTS CORP
2855 Girts Rd (14701-9666)
PHONE..............................716 483-3406
Wendi Lodestro, *Ch of Bd*
Wendi A Lodestro, *Ch of Bd*
Lee Lodestro, *Vice Pres*
Todd Corkery, *Representative*
EMP: 46
SALES (est): 16.2MM **Privately Held**
WEB: www.jamestownadvanced.com
SIC: 3444 Sheet metalwork

(G-6520)
JAMESTOWN AWNING INC
313 Steele St (14701-6287)
PHONE..............................716 483-1435
Mark Saxton, *President*
EMP: 9 **EST:** 1964
SQ FT: 5,000
SALES (est): 896.4K **Privately Held**
SIC: 2394 Awnings, fabric: made from purchased materials

(G-6521)
JAMESTOWN BRONZE WORKS INC
174 Hopkins Ave (14701-2290)
PHONE..............................716 665-2302
Robert R Knobloch, *President*
Wolfgang Michael Dunker, *Vice Pres*
▼ **EMP:** 5
SQ FT: 10,000
SALES: 500K **Privately Held**
WEB: www.jamestownbronze.com
SIC: 3369 3479 Nonferrous foundries;
etching on metals

(G-6522)
JAMESTOWN FAB STL & SUP INC
1034 Allen St (14701-2302)
PHONE..............................716 665-2227
Mel Duggan, *President*
Malachai Ives, *Vice Pres*
Lee Luce, *Vice Pres*
Sue Livermore, *HR Admin*
EMP: 6
SQ FT: 20,000
SALES: 1.2MM **Privately Held**
SIC: 3446 Fire escapes, metal; railings,
bannisters, guards, etc.: made from metal
pipe; stairs, staircases, stair treads: prefabricated metal; fences or posts, ornamental iron or steel

(G-6523)
JAMESTOWN KITCHEN & BATH INC
1085 E 2nd St (14701-2243)
PHONE..............................716 665-2299
Donald Proctor, *President*
Lora Proctor, *Admin Sec*
EMP: 7
SQ FT: 15,000
SALES (est): 1.2MM **Privately Held**
SIC: 3281 5712 Bathroom fixtures, cut
stone; cabinet work, custom

(G-6524)
JAMESTOWN METAL PRODUCTS LLC
178 Blackstone Ave (14701-2297)
PHONE..............................716 665-5313
Richard McLeod, *President*
Christian Davis, *Project Mgr*
Kristen Swan, *Project Mgr*
David Gniwecki, *Engineer*
Paul Jagoda, *Engineer*
▲ **EMP:** 105
SQ FT: 165,000
SALES (est): 27.2MM
SALES (corp-wide): 50MM **Privately Held**
SIC: 3821 Laboratory equipment: fume
hoods, distillation racks, etc.

PA: Institutional Casework, Incorporated
1865 Hwy 641 North Paris
Paris TN 38242
731 642-4251

(G-6525)
JAMESTOWN SCIENTIFIC INDS LLC
1300 E 2nd St (14701-1915)
PHONE..............................716 665-3224
Kelly Haight, *Facilities Mgr*
Bob Trusler, *Plant Engr*
John Pflaumer,
EMP: 13
SALES (est): 2.1MM **Privately Held**
WEB: www.jamestownscientific.com
SIC: 3069 Medical & laboratory rubber
sundries & related products

(G-6526)
JEFFREY D MENOFF DDS PC
785 Fairmount Ave (14701-2608)
PHONE..............................716 665-1468
Jeffrey D Menoff, *President*
EMP: 8
SALES (est): 681.3K **Privately Held**
SIC: 3843 Enamels, dentists'

(G-6527)
JOHNSON MCH & FIBR PDTS CO INC
142 Hopkins Ave (14701-2208)
PHONE..............................716 665-2003
Michael Marshall, *President*
Dale L Marshall, *Principal*
Brian Maloy, *Manager*
EMP: 15
SQ FT: 11,000
SALES (est): 2.8MM **Privately Held**
SIC: 3599 3541 Machine shop, jobbing &
repair; screw machines, automatic

(G-6528)
LAKESIDE CAPITAL CORPORATION
Also Called: Dahlstrom Roll Form
402 Chandler St Ste 2 (14701-3890)
P.O. Box 446 (14702-0446)
PHONE..............................716 664-2555
Robert G White, *Ch of Bd*
▲ **EMP:** 21
SQ FT: 73,800
SALES (est): 6.5MM **Privately Held**
WEB: www.dahlstromrollform.com
SIC: 3449 Custom roll formed products

(G-6529)
LARSON METAL MANUFACTURING CO
Also Called: Design Craft Division
1831 Mason Dr (14701-9290)
P.O. Box 1182 (14702-1182)
PHONE..............................716 665-6807
Melda W Larson, *President*
William E Larson, *Vice Pres*
EMP: 6
SQ FT: 31,000
SALES: 1MM **Privately Held**
SIC: 2522 Office furniture, except wood

(G-6530)
LYN JO ENTERPRISES LTD
Also Called: Standard Portable
136 Fredrick Blvd (14701-4270)
PHONE..............................716 753-2776
Julie Baraniewicz, *President*
EMP: 7
SALES: 750K **Privately Held**
WEB: www.standardportable.com
SIC: 3496 3699 Lamp frames, wire; trouble lights

(G-6531)
MASON CARVINGS INC
2871 Ivystone Dr (14701-9783)
PHONE..............................716 484-7884
Sam Mason, *President*
Thomas Mason, *Vice Pres*
Robert Parasiliti, *Manager*
Mary Jo Mason, *Admin Sec*
EMP: 8 **EST:** 1927
SQ FT: 18,000
SALES: 350K **Privately Held**
SIC: 2426 Carvings, furniture: wood

(G-6532)
MASTER MACHINE INCORPORATED
155 Blackstone Ave (14701-2203)
PHONE..............................716 487-2555
Steven Carolus, *President*
▲ **EMP:** 14
SQ FT: 15,000
SALES (est): 1.4MM **Privately Held**
SIC: 3599 Machine shop, jobbing & repair

(G-6533)
MILES MACHINE INC
85 Jones And Gifford Ave (14701-2826)
PHONE..............................716 484-6026
Richard Page, *President*
Michael Page, *Vice Pres*
EMP: 11
SQ FT: 5,000
SALES: 1MM **Privately Held**
SIC: 3599 Machine shop, jobbing & repair

(G-6534)
NATIONAL WIRE & METAL TECH INC
22 Carolina St (14701-2311)
PHONE..............................716 661-9180
Bump Hedman, *President*
John Hedman, *Vice Pres*
Tammy Snyder, *Vice Pres*
Lucy Hedman, *Treasurer*
Sara Hays, *Info Tech Mgr*
▲ **EMP:** 25
SQ FT: 80,000
SALES (est): 4.8MM **Privately Held**
SIC: 3469 2392 Perforated metal,
stamped; mops, floor & dust

(G-6535)
OGDEN NEWSPAPERS INC
Also Called: Post-Journal, The
15 W 2nd St (14701-5215)
P.O. Box 190 (14702-0190)
PHONE..............................716 487-1111
Michael Bird, *President*
James Austin, *Manager*
EMP: 200 **Privately Held**
SIC: 2711 Commercial printing & newspaper publishing combined
HQ: The Ogden Newspapers Inc
1500 Main St
Wheeling WV 26003
304 233-0100

(G-6536)
POST JOURNAL
412 Murray Ave (14701-4742)
PHONE..............................716 487-1111
Debra Brunner, *Principal*
EMP: 14
SALES (est): 1.1MM **Privately Held**
SIC: 2711 Commercial printing & newspaper publishing combined; newspapers,
publishing & printing

(G-6537)
PREMIER FINISHING INC
85 Jones And Gifford Ave (14701-2826)
PHONE..............................716 484-6271
Jack Sase, *President*
Gary Samson, *General Mgr*
EMP: 11 **EST:** 2013
SALES (est): 548.3K **Privately Held**
SIC: 3471 Plating of metals or formed
products

(G-6538)
PRODUCTO CORPORATION
Also Called: Ring Division Producto Machine
2980 Turner Rd (14701-9024)
P.O. Box 490 (14702)
PHONE..............................716 484-7131
Newman Marsilius, *President*
Alan Smith, *Engineer*
Maynard L Cotter, *Branch Mgr*
EMP: 113
SQ FT: 40,800
SALES (corp-wide): 65.8MM **Privately Held**
WEB: www.ringprecision.com
SIC: 3541 3542 3544 Machine tools,
metal cutting type; machine tools, metal
forming type; special dies, tools, jigs & fixtures

HQ: The Producto Corporation
800 Union Ave
Bridgeport CT 06607
203 366-3224

(G-6539)
ROLLFORM OF JAMESTOWN INC
Also Called: Precision Locker
181 Blackstone Ave (14701-2203)
PHONE..............................716 665-5310
Edward F Ruttenberg, *President*
Al Perone, *Prdtn Mgr*
▲ **EMP:** 17
SQ FT: 43,000
SALES (est): 4.6MM **Privately Held**
WEB: www.rollform.com
SIC: 3449 Custom roll formed products

(G-6540)
SHRED CENTER
20 Carroll St (14701-4755)
PHONE..............................716 664-3052
Ronald Mazonie, *Owner*
EMP: 6 **EST:** 2008
SALES (est): 557K **Privately Held**
SIC: 3559 Tire shredding machinery

(G-6541)
SPARTAN PUBLISHING INC
Also Called: Southern Tier Pennysaver
2 Harding Ave (14701-4778)
PHONE..............................716 664-7373
Robert V Stanley, *President*
Sandra Stanley, *Treasurer*
EMP: 12
SQ FT: 4,000
SALES (est): 530K **Privately Held**
SIC: 2711 Newspapers, publishing & printing

(G-6542)
SPRAY-TECH FINISHING INC
443 Buffalo St (14701-2262)
PHONE..............................716 664-6317
David Dawson, *President*
Guy Lombardo, *Treasurer*
Harold Andersen, *Admin Sec*
EMP: 11
SQ FT: 80,000
SALES: 1.1MM **Privately Held**
WEB: www.spraytechfinishing.com
SIC: 2952 Coating compounds, tar

(G-6543)
STAR TUBING CORP
53 River St (14701-3806)
P.O. Box 904 (14702-0904)
PHONE..............................716 483-1703
Gary F Johnson, *President*
Gary Johnson, *President*
Sandra Johnson, *Vice Pres*
Charles A Lawson, *Shareholder*
EMP: 6
SQ FT: 46,000
SALES (est): 1.3MM **Privately Held**
WEB: www.startubing.com
SIC: 3498 Tube fabricating (contract bending & shaping)

(G-6544)
SUHOR INDUSTRIES INC
Also Called: GM Pre Cast Products
584 Buffalo St (14701-2307)
PHONE..............................716 483-6818
Joel Suhor, *President*
EMP: 5
SALES (corp-wide): 2.2MM **Privately Held**
WEB: www.wilbertservices.com
SIC: 3272 Burial vaults, concrete or precast terrazzo
PA: Suhor Industries, Inc.
72 Oconnor Rd
Fairport NY 14450
585 377-5100

(G-6545)
SUIT-KOTE CORPORATION
57 Lister St (14701-2701)
PHONE..............................716 664-3750
George Ginter, *Branch Mgr*
EMP: 35

SALES (corp-wide): 272.8MM **Privately Held**
WEB: www.suit-kote.com
SIC: 2951 1611 Asphalt & asphaltic paving mixtures (not from refineries); highway & street paving contractor
PA: Suit-Kote Corporation
　　1911 Lorings Crossing Rd
　　Cortland NY 13045
　　607 753-1100

(G-6546)
SUNSET RIDGE HOLDINGS INC
Also Called: Electric Motor Specialty
490-496 Crescent St (14701)
PHONE.................................716 487-1458
Rebecca Ames, *President*
EMP: 5
SALES: 230K **Privately Held**
SIC: 7694 7699 Armature rewinding shops; pumps & pumping equipment repair

(G-6547)
SUPERIOR ENERGY SERVICES INC
1720 Foote Avenue Ext (14701-9385)
PHONE.................................716 483-0100
EMP: 7 **Publicly Held**
SIC: 1389 Servicing oil & gas wells
PA: Superior Energy Services, Inc.
　　1001 La St Ste 2900
　　Houston TX 77002

(G-6548)
SUPERIOR STL DOOR TRIM CO INC
154 Fairmount Ave (14701-2866)
PHONE.................................716 665-3256
Ellen Connell, *President*
Bevan Connell, *Vice Pres*
Matthew Ekstrom, *Sales Staff*
EMP: 15
SALES: 5MM **Privately Held**
SIC: 3442 Metal doors, sash & trim

(G-6549)
SUPERIOR WOOD TURNINGS
118 E 1st St (14701-5430)
P.O. Box 3341 (14702-3341)
PHONE.................................716 483-1254
Shane Goodwill, *Partner*
Doug Wheeler, *Partner*
EMP: 16
SQ FT: 30,000
SALES (est): 1.9MM **Privately Held**
WEB: www.superiorwoodturnings.com
SIC: 2499 Carved & turned wood

(G-6550)
TITANX ENGINE COOLING INC
2258 Allen Street Ext (14701-2330)
PHONE.................................716 665-7129
Stefan Nordstrm, *CEO*
Matthew Moore, *President*
Ulf Hellgesson, *Vice Pres*
Mats Hman, *Vice Pres*
Jonas Nilsson, *Vice Pres*
▲ **EMP:** 320
SALES (est): 141.4MM
SALES (corp-wide): 237.5MM **Privately Held**
SIC: 3714 Air conditioner parts, motor vehicle
HQ: Titanx Engine Cooling Ab
　　Klockskogsvagen 9
　　Solvesborg 294 7
　　456 550-00

(G-6551)
UPSTATE NIAGARA COOP INC
223 Fluvanna Ave (14701-2050)
PHONE.................................716 484-7178
Michael Conklin, *Manager*
EMP: 20
SALES (corp-wide): 903.7MM **Privately Held**
SIC: 2026 0241 5143 Milk processing (pasteurizing, homogenizing, bottling); milk production; dairy products, except dried or canned
PA: Upstate Niagara Cooperative, Inc.
　　25 Anderson Rd
　　Buffalo NY 14225
　　716 892-3156

(G-6552)
VAC AIR SERVICE INC
Also Called: Ameri Serv South
1295 E 2nd St (14701-1914)
P.O. Box 940 (14702-0940)
PHONE.................................716 665-2206
EMP: 11
SQ FT: 4,000
SALES (est): 1.4MM **Privately Held**
SIC: 3563 Mfg Air/Gas Compressors

(G-6553)
WEBER-KNAPP COMPANY (PA)
441 Chandler St (14701-3895)
PHONE.................................716 484-9135
Rex Mc Cray, *Ch of Bd*
Leila Bell, *Business Mgr*
Donald Pangborn, *Senior VP*
Larry Troxell, *Foreman/Supr*
Rhonda Johnson, *Opers Staff*
▲ **EMP:** 102 **EST:** 1920
SQ FT: 146,000
SALES (est): 16.6MM **Privately Held**
WEB: www.weberknapp.com
SIC: 3429 Furniture hardware

(G-6554)
WILSTON ENTERPRISES INC
Also Called: Industrial Welding & Fabg Co
121 Jackson Ave (14701-2441)
PHONE.................................716 483-1411
Susan L Wilston, *President*
Eugene Wilston, *Vice Pres*
EMP: 18 **EST:** 2007
SALES (est): 1.6MM **Privately Held**
SIC: 3441 Building components, structural steel

Jamesville
Onondaga County

(G-6555)
B & B LUMBER COMPANY INC (PA)
4800 Solvay Rd (13078-9530)
P.O. Box 420 (13078-0420)
PHONE.................................866 282-0582
Jeffrey H Booher, *Ch of Bd*
Brent Booher, *Principal*
Brigham Booher, *Principal*
Pat Buff, *Principal*
Gary R Booher, *Vice Pres*
EMP: 130
SQ FT: 300,000
SALES (est): 21.4MM **Privately Held**
SIC: 2448 2421 2426 Pallets, wood; lumber: rough, sawed or planed; hardwood dimension & flooring mills

(G-6556)
B&B ALBANY PALLET COMPANY LLC
4800 Solvay Rd (13078-9530)
P.O. Box 420 (13078-0420)
PHONE.................................315 492-1786
Ruth Manasse, *Vice Pres*
Michael Parvis, *Mfg Staff*
Jane Diehl, *Accountant*
Eric Smith,
EMP: 30 **EST:** 1966
SQ FT: 9,500
SALES (est): 3.7MM
SALES (corp-wide): 21.4MM **Privately Held**
SIC: 2448 Pallets, wood
PA: B & B Lumber Company Inc.
　　4800 Solvay Rd
　　Jamesville NY 13078
　　866 282-0582

(G-6557)
CHRISTIANA MILLWORK INC (PA)
4755 Jamesville Rd (13078)
PHONE.................................315 492-9099
Lawrence J Christiana, *President*
Ross Tuzzo Lino, *President*
EMP: 26
SQ FT: 26,000
SALES (est): 4.1MM **Privately Held**
SIC: 2431 Millwork

(G-6558)
HANSON AGGREGATES NEW YORK LLC
2237 Allen St (13078)
PHONE.................................716 665-4620
Roger Hutchinson, *Sales Mgr*
Scott Wheaton, *Manager*
EMP: 10
SALES (corp-wide): 20.6B **Privately Held**
SIC: 3273 Ready-mixed concrete
HQ: Hanson Aggregates New York Llc
　　8505 Freport Pkwy Ste 500
　　Irving TX 75063

(G-6559)
HANSON AGGREGATES NEW YORK LLC
4800 Jamesville Rd (13078)
P.O. Box 513 (13078-0513)
PHONE.................................315 469-5501
Dan Meehan, *Vice Pres*
EMP: 120
SALES (corp-wide): 20.6B **Privately Held**
SIC: 3273 Ready-mixed concrete
HQ: Hanson Aggregates New York Llc
　　8505 Freport Pkwy Ste 500
　　Irving TX 75063

(G-6560)
HANSON AGGREGATES PA LLC
4800 Jamesville Rd (13078)
P.O. Box 513 (13078-0513)
PHONE.................................315 469-5501
Liz Simmons, *Office Mgr*
Gary Eno, *Branch Mgr*
EMP: 20
SALES (corp-wide): 20.6B **Privately Held**
SIC: 1442 1422 Common sand mining; crushed & broken limestone
HQ: Hanson Aggregates Pennsylvania, Llc
　　7660 Imperial Way
　　Allentown PA 18195
　　610 366-4626

(G-6561)
PREMIER HARDWOOD PRODUCTS INC
4800 Solvay Rd (13078-9530)
P.O. Box 420 (13078-0420)
PHONE.................................315 492-1786
Brigham Booher, *Ch of Bd*
Lawrence G English, *President*
Jeffrey Booher, *Vice Pres*
Russ Shamblen, *Purch Agent*
Gary Booher, *Treasurer*
EMP: 50
SQ FT: 80,000
SALES (est): 9.5MM **Privately Held**
WEB: www.premierhardwood.com
SIC: 2426 Hardwood dimension & flooring mills

(G-6562)
ROBINSON CONCRETE INC
3537 Apulia Rd (13078-9663)
PHONE.................................315 492-6200
Micheal Vitale, *President*
EMP: 12
SALES (corp-wide): 26.1MM **Privately Held**
SIC: 3273 Ready-mixed concrete
PA: Robinson Concrete, Inc.
　　3486 Franklin Street Rd
　　Auburn NY 13021
　　315 253-6666

(G-6563)
U-CUT ENTERPRISES INC
4800 Solvay Rd (13078-9530)
P.O. Box 420 (13078-0420)
PHONE.................................315 492-9316
Brigham Booher, *Co-Owner*
Brent Booher, *Co-Owner*
Pat Buff, *Co-Owner*
EMP: 22
SQ FT: 8,000
SALES: 2.5MM **Privately Held**
WEB: www.u-cut.com
SIC: 3599 Machine shop, jobbing & repair

Java Village
Wyoming County

(G-6564)
FARRANT SCREW MACHINE PRODUCTS
Gulf Rd (14083)
P.O. Box 135 (14083-0135)
PHONE.................................585 457-3213
Thomas Farrant, *President*
EMP: 7
SQ FT: 13,000
SALES: 1MM **Privately Held**
SIC: 3599 Machine shop, jobbing & repair

Jay
Essex County

(G-6565)
ADIRONDACK LIFE INC (PA)
Also Called: Adirondack Life Magazine
Rr 9 Box North (12941)
P.O. Box 410 (12941-0410)
PHONE.................................518 946-2191
Barry Silverstein, *President*
Janine Sorrell, *Business Mgr*
Marty Kilburn, *Director*
Betsy Folwell, *Creative Dir*
EMP: 18
SALES (est): 1.8MM **Privately Held**
WEB: www.adirondacklife.com
SIC: 2721 Magazines: publishing only, not printed on site

(G-6566)
ADIRONDACK LIFE INC
Also Called: Adirondack Life Magazine
12961 Nys Route 9n (12941-5715)
PHONE.................................518 946-2191
Linda Bedard, *Advt Staff*
Barry Silverstein, *Branch Mgr*
EMP: 8
SALES (est): 790.9K
SALES (corp-wide): 1.8MM **Privately Held**
SIC: 2721 Magazines: publishing only, not printed on site
PA: Adirondack Life Inc
　　Rr 9 Box North
　　Jay NY 12941
　　518 946-2191

Jefferson Valley
Westchester County

(G-6567)
GEORGE PONTE INC (PA)
Also Called: Gpi Equipment Company
500 E Main St (10535-1100)
PHONE.................................914 243-4202
George Ponte, *President*
EMP: 5
SQ FT: 4,000
SALES (est): 728.5K **Privately Held**
WEB: www.gpiusa.com
SIC: 3559 5084 Pharmaceutical machinery; materials handling machinery

(G-6568)
LONGSTEM ORGANIZERS INC
380 E Main St (10535-1200)
P.O. Box 22 (10535-0022)
PHONE.................................914 777-2174
Alison Albanese, *President*
Gregery Alabnese, *Vice Pres*
▲ **EMP:** 6
SQ FT: 4,500
SALES (est): 600K **Privately Held**
SIC: 3449 Miscellaneous metalwork

Jeffersonville
Sullivan County

(G-6569)
A S A PRECISION CO INC
295 Jffersonville N Br Rd (12748-5825)
PHONE...............................845 482-4870
Steve Schmidt, *President*
Rich Schmidt, *Vice Pres*
EMP: 6 **EST:** 1961
SQ FT: 6,400
SALES (est): 780K **Privately Held**
SIC: 3826 Analytical instruments

(G-6570)
JEFFERSONVILLE VOLUNTEER
49 Callicoon Center Rd (12748)
P.O. Box 396 (12748-0396)
PHONE...............................845 482-3110
Dawnree Hauschild, *Chairman*
EMP: 50
SALES: 515.1K **Privately Held**
SIC: 3713 Ambulance bodies

Jericho
Nassau County

(G-6571)
BAMBERGER POLYMERS INC (HQ)
2 Jericho Plz Ste 109 (11753-1681)
PHONE...............................516 622-3600
Dennis Don, *Principal*
Steve Goldberg, *Exec VP*
Michael Pignataro, *Vice Pres*
Paul Coco, *CFO*
◆ **EMP:** 40
SQ FT: 10,000
SALES (est): 31.9MM **Privately Held**
SIC: 2821 Plastics materials & resins

(G-6572)
BANDEC LLC
Also Called: Kd Panels
366 N Broadway Ste 410 (11753-2000)
PHONE...............................516 627-1971
EMP: 5
SALES (est): 420.9K **Privately Held**
SIC: 2452 Panels & sections, prefabri-
cated, wood
PA: Keding Enterprises Co., Ltd.
16f, 69, Kaung Fu Rd., Sec. 2,
New Taipei City TAP 24158

(G-6573)
CFFCO USA INC
55 Jericho Tpke Ste 302 (11753-1013)
PHONE...............................718 747-1118
James Yan, *CEO*
Juan Lopez, *Vice Pres*
▲ **EMP:** 7
SQ FT: 1,800
SALES: 11MM **Privately Held**
WEB: www.cffco.com
SIC: 2499 Fencing, docks & other outdoor
wood structural products

(G-6574)
CLOUDSCALE365 INC (PA)
30 Jericho Executive Plz (11753-1057)
PHONE...............................888 608-6245
Pat Hannon, *COO*
Eric Church, *CTO*
EMP: 4 **EST:** 2015
SALES (est): 1.8MM **Privately Held**
SIC: 7372 Business oriented computer
software

(G-6575)
CONTINENTAL KRAFT CORP
100 Jericho Quadrangle # 219
(11753-2708)
PHONE...............................516 681-9090
Peter J Bogan, *Ch of Bd*
David Landau, *President*
Steve Roth, *Treasurer*
▼ **EMP:** 6
SQ FT: 2,264

SALES (est): 998.3K **Privately Held**
WEB: www.continentalkraft.com
SIC: 2631 Kraft linerboard

(G-6576)
DARBY DENTAL SUPPLY
105 Executive Ct (11753)
PHONE...............................516 688-6421
Gary Rosenberg, *Principal*
Anthony Ricigilano, *Vice Pres*
Rich Parent, *Analyst*
EMP: 9
SALES (est): 1.7MM **Privately Held**
SIC: 3843 Dental equipment & supplies

(G-6577)
ELARA FDSRVICE DISPOSABLES LLC
Also Called: Elara Brands
420 Jericho Tpke Ste 320 (11753-1319)
PHONE...............................877 893-3244
Daniel Grinberg, *President*
Ernesto Grinberg, *Chairman*
Donna Cherulnik, *Vice Pres*
Darci Rodriguez, *Vice Pres*
Maria Buono, *Controller*
▲ **EMP:** 7
SALES (est): 12MM **Privately Held**
SIC: 3089 5113 Work gloves, plastic;
bags, paper & disposable plastic

(G-6578)
EVENT JOURNAL INC
366 N Broadway Ste 209 (11753-2000)
PHONE...............................516 470-1811
Dawn Strain, *President*
Laura Miller, *Manager*
William Frank, *Director*
Catherine Kaczmarczyk, *Creative Dir*
EMP: 10
SALES (est): 570.5K **Privately Held**
SIC: 2711 Newspapers, publishing & print-
ing

(G-6579)
EXCHANGE MY MAIL INC
30 Jericho Executive Plz 100c
(11753-1025)
PHONE...............................516 605-1835
Sal Dipiazza, *CEO*
Steven Daneshgar, *Exec VP*
EMP: 15
SQ FT: 2,500
SALES (est): 1.7MM **Privately Held**
WEB: www.exchangemymail.com
SIC: 7372 Application computer software

(G-6580)
FIRETRONICS INC (PA)
50 Jericho Tpke (11753-1014)
PHONE...............................516 997-5151
Gail Miller, *President*
John Moreno, *Accountant*
EMP: 7
SALES (est): 575.6K **Privately Held**
SIC: 3669 Fire detection systems, electric

(G-6581)
HAZEN HOLDINGS LLC
425 N Broadway Unit 700 (11753-5034)
P.O. Box 700 (11753-0700)
PHONE...............................607 542-9365
Andrew Hazen, *Mng Member*
EMP: 5
SALES: 250K **Privately Held**
SIC: 2821 Plastics materials & resins

(G-6582)
HEALTH CARE COMPLIANCE (HQ)
30 Jericho Executive Plz 400c
(11753-1098)
PHONE...............................516 478-4100
Mitchell Diamond, *CEO*
Benjamin Diamond, *President*
Lise Rauzi Chc, *Vice Pres*
Ben Diamond, *Vice Pres*
Deborah Shapiro, *Vice Pres*
EMP: 17
SQ FT: 5,350
SALES (est): 3.3MM
SALES (corp-wide): 231.6MM **Publicly Held**
WEB: www.hccsonline.com
SIC: 7372 Educational computer software

PA: Healthstream, Inc.
500 11th Ave N Ste 1000
Nashville TN 37203
615 301-3100

(G-6583)
IMACOR INC
50 Jericho Tpke Ste 105 (11753-1014)
PHONE...............................516 393-0970
Scott Roth, *President*
Jenn Kujawski, *Exec VP*
EMP: 20
SALES (est): 2.8MM **Privately Held**
SIC: 3845 Ultrasonic scanning devices,
medical

(G-6584)
INTERNATIONAL TIME PRODUCTS
410 Jericho Tpke Ste 110 (11753-1318)
PHONE...............................516 931-0005
Raymond T D'Alessio, *Owner*
EMP: 6
SALES (est): 240K **Privately Held**
SIC: 3172 Watch straps, except metal

(G-6585)
KPP LTD
Also Called: Admor Blinds & Window Fashion
200 Robbins Ln Unit C2 (11753-2341)
PHONE...............................516 338-5201
Michael Parker, *President*
Dan Kossman, *Vice Pres*
Rita Parker, *Treasurer*
EMP: 7
SQ FT: 1,700
SALES (est): 1MM **Privately Held**
WEB: www.admorblinds.com
SIC: 2591 7641 Blinds vertical; reuphol-
stery & furniture repair

(G-6586)
NCR CORPORATION
30 Jericho Executive Plz (11753-1057)
PHONE...............................516 876-7200
Paul Buscemi, *Manager*
EMP: 200
SALES (corp-wide): 6.4B **Publicly Held**
WEB: www.ncr.com
SIC: 3571 7622 Electronic computers;
radio & television repair
PA: Ncr Corporation
864 Spring St Nw
Atlanta GA 30308
937 445-5000

(G-6587)
NYB DISTRIBUTORS INC (PA)
37 17th St (11753-2403)
PHONE...............................516 937-0666
Sam Suresh, *President*
EMP: 7 **EST:** 2012
SALES (est): 4.1MM **Privately Held**
SIC: 2023 8049 Dietary supplements,
dairy & non-dairy based; nutrition special-
ist

(G-6588)
PARKSIDE PRINTING CO INC
4 Tompkins Ave (11753-1920)
PHONE...............................516 933-5423
William Goldstein, *President*
Ellen Goldstein, *Corp Secy*
EMP: 10
SQ FT: 10,000
SALES (est): 1MM **Privately Held**
SIC: 2752 Commercial printing, litho-
graphic

(G-6589)
PITNEY BOWES INC
200 Robbins Ln Unit B2 (11753-2341)
PHONE...............................516 822-0900
Dan Hindman, *Branch Mgr*
EMP: 35
SALES (corp-wide): 3.5B **Publicly Held**
SIC: 3579 7359 Postage meters; business
machine & electronic equipment rental
services
PA: Pitney Bowes Inc.
3001 Summer St Ste 3
Stamford CT 06905
203 356-5000

(G-6590)
PRODUCT STATION INC
366 N Broadway Ste 410 (11753-2000)
PHONE...............................516 942-4220
Scott Roberts, *President*
Peter Oliveto, *Vice Pres*
EMP: 11
SALES (est): 1.1MM **Privately Held**
SIC: 3613 Distribution cutouts

(G-6591)
RAMLER INTERNATIONAL LTD
471 N Broadway 132 (11753-2106)
PHONE...............................516 353-3106
Garry Ramler, *President*
Gail Gordon, *Director*
▲ **EMP:** 24
SALES: 12MM **Privately Held**
SIC: 2599 Hotel furniture

(G-6592)
RESOURCE CAPITAL FUNDS LP
2 Jericho Plz Ste 103 (11753-1661)
PHONE...............................631 692-9111
Sherri Croasdale, *Branch Mgr*
EMP: 5
SALES (corp-wide): 110.1K **Privately Held**
SIC: 1481 Mine development, nonmetallic
minerals
PA: Resource Capital Funds Lp
1400 16th St Ste 200
Denver CO 80202
720 946-1444

(G-6593)
ROYCE ASSOCIATES A LTD PARTNR
Also Called: ROYCE ASSOCIATES A LIM-
ITED PARTNERSHIP
366 N Broadway Ste 400 (11753-2000)
PHONE...............................516 367-6298
Joanna Moskowitz, *Manager*
EMP: 5
SALES (corp-wide): 21.7MM **Privately Held**
SIC: 2869 3089 2842 2851 Industrial or-
ganic chemicals; plastic processing; pol-
ishing preparations & related products;
varnishes; chemical preparations
PA: Royce Associates, A Limited Partner-
ship
35 Carlton Ave
East Rutherford NJ 07073
201 438-5200

(G-6594)
SD EAGLE GLOBAL INC
2 Kay St (11753-2648)
PHONE...............................516 822-1778
Shaojun Liu, *President*
EMP: 7
SALES (est): 409.9K **Privately Held**
SIC: 2211 Denims

(G-6595)
SJ ASSOCIATES INC (PA)
500 N Broadway Ste 159 (11753-2111)
PHONE...............................516 942-3232
Bruce Joseph, *President*
EMP: 25
SQ FT: 3,000
SALES (est): 5.1MM **Privately Held**
SIC: 3559 5065 Electronic component
making machinery; electronic parts

(G-6596)
SKD DISTRIBUTION CORP
28 Westchester Ave (11753-1442)
PHONE...............................718 525-6000
Richard Marks, *President*
Anderson Huang, *Vice Pres*
Harold Marks, *Vice Pres*
▲ **EMP:** 30 **EST:** 1931
SQ FT: 45,000
SALES (est): 4.9MM **Privately Held**
SIC: 3089 3086 Novelties, plastic; plastics
foam products

(G-6597)
VERTARIB INC
Also Called: Thermacon Tank Insulation
471 N Broadway Ste 196 (11753-2106)
PHONE...............................561 683-0888
Alan Dinow, *CEO*

EMP: 5 **Privately Held**
SIC: 3443 Tank towers, metal plate
PA: Vertarib Inc.
  9005 Southern Blvd
  West Palm Beach FL 33411

(G-6598)
WAGNERS LLC (PA)
366 N Broadway Ste 402 (11753-2027)
P.O. Box 54 (11753-0054)
PHONE...............................516 933-6580
Harry Tyre, *President*
Donald P Corr, *Senior VP*
Danielle Traietta, *Engineer*
Maggie Keller, *Controller*
Brenda Lontine, *Manager*
EMP: 6
SQ FT: 1,500
SALES: 50MM **Privately Held**
WEB: www.wagnerproducts.com
SIC: 2048 Bird food, prepared

Johnson City
Broome County

(G-6599)
GAGNE ASSOCIATES INC
41 Commercial Dr (13790-4111)
P.O. Box 487 (13790-0487)
PHONE...............................800 800-5954
Mary Ann Holland, *Ch of Bd*
Jeff Sampson, *President*
William Coak, *Vice Pres*
Michelle Clark, *VP Mfg*
Cary Dunlay, *VP Sales*
▲ **EMP:** 25 **EST:** 1961
SQ FT: 37,250
SALES (est): 5.3MM **Privately Held**
WEB: www.gagneinc.com
SIC: 3089 5063 Plastic hardware & build-
  ing products; lighting fittings & acces-
  sories

(G-6600)
GANNETT CO INC
Also Called: Gannett NY Production Facility
10 Gannett Dr (13790-2260)
PHONE...............................607 352-2702
Ellen Zitis, *Accounts Exec*
Jay Laurino, *Marketing Staff*
Kevin Crane, *Manager*
EMP: 100
SALES (corp-wide): 2.9B **Publicly Held**
WEB: www.gannett.com
SIC: 2741 Miscellaneous publishing
PA: Gannett Co., Inc.
  7950 Jones Branch Dr
  Mc Lean VA 22102
  703 854-6000

(G-6601)
HI-TECH INDUSTRIES NY INC
23 Ozalid Rd (13790-2306)
PHONE...............................607 217-7361
Douglas Gardner, *Ch of Bd*
Douglas P Sterns, *President*
EMP: 28 **EST:** 1999
SQ FT: 8,900
SALES (est): 3.7MM **Privately Held**
SIC: 3444 3599 Sheet metalwork; ma-
  chine shop, jobbing & repair

(G-6602)
INNOVATION ASSOCIATES INC
711 Innovation Way (13790-1724)
PHONE...............................607 798-9376
Mary Reno, *CEO*
Joseph Harry Boyer, *Chairman*
Thomas Boyer, *COO*
Doyle Jensen, *Exec VP*
Phil L Samples, *Vice Pres*
▲ **EMP:** 150
SALES (est): 57.8MM **Privately Held**
WEB: www.innovat.com
SIC: 3559 8711 Pharmaceutical machin-
  ery; consulting engineer

(G-6603)
J H ROBOTICS INC
109 Main St (13790-2482)
PHONE...............................607 729-3758
John F Hartman, *Ch of Bd*
Thomas Burgin, *Vice Pres*
EMP: 35

SQ FT: 41,000
SALES (est): 9.7MM **Privately Held**
WEB: www.jhrobotics.com
SIC: 3494 3569 3545 Valves & pipe fit-
  tings; robots, assembly line: industrial &
  commercial; machine tool accessories

(G-6604)
KLEMMT ORTHOTICS & PROSTHETICS
Also Called: Klemmt Orthopaedic Services
130 Oakdale Rd (13790-1758)
PHONE...............................607 770-4400
Marcus Klemmt, *President*
Julie Klemmt, *Principal*
EMP: 8 **EST:** 1965
SQ FT: 3,000
SALES (est): 999.3K **Privately Held**
SIC: 3842 5999 Orthopedic appliances;
  prosthetic appliances; orthopedic & pros-
  thesis applications

(G-6605)
KNUCKLEHEAD EMBROIDERY INC
800 Valley Plz Ste 4 (13790-1046)
PHONE...............................607 797-2725
Dave Cobb, *President*
Diane Cobb, *Vice Pres*
Matt Heier, *Treasurer*
Bridget Heier, *Admin Sec*
EMP: 5
SQ FT: 1,500
SALES: 500K **Privately Held**
WEB: www.knuckleheadinc.com
SIC: 2262 5699 2759 2395 Embossing:
  manmade fiber & silk broadwoven fabrics;
  customized clothing & apparel; screen
  printing; art needlework: made from pur-
  chased materials

(G-6606)
NORTH POINT TECHNOLOGIES
520 Columbia Dr Ste 105 (13790-3305)
PHONE...............................607 238-1114
Robert Lee, *Owner*
Lisa Lee, *Co-Owner*
Richard J Wrobleski, *Administration*
EMP: 26
SALES (est): 3.9MM **Privately Held**
SIC: 3625 Industrial controls: push button,
  selector switches, pilot

(G-6607)
PELLA CORPORATION
Also Called: Pella Window Door
800 Valley Plz Ste 5 (13790-1046)
PHONE...............................607 223-2023
Chris Ward, *Branch Mgr*
EMP: 316
SALES (corp-wide): 1.7B **Privately Held**
SIC: 2431 Windows, wood
PA: Pella Corporation
  102 Main St
  Pella IA 50219
  641 621-1000

(G-6608)
ROB SALAMIDA COMPANY INC
71 Pratt Ave Ste 1 (13790-2255)
PHONE...............................607 729-4868
Robert A Salamida, *President*
▲ **EMP:** 19
SQ FT: 9,136
SALES (est): 3.7MM **Privately Held**
WEB: www.spiedie.com
SIC: 2035 2099 Seasonings & sauces, ex-
  cept tomato & dry; food preparations

(G-6609)
UPSTATE OFFICE LIQUIDATORS INC
Also Called: Upstate Office Furniture
718 Azon Way (13790-1725)
PHONE...............................607 722-9234
Sylvia J Kerber, *President*
Wayne Kerber Jr, *Vice Pres*
▲ **EMP:** 11
SQ FT: 45,000
SALES (est): 1.9MM **Privately Held**
WEB: www.upstateofficefurniture.com
SIC: 2521 Wood office furniture

Johnstown
Fulton County

(G-6610)
ARROW LEATHER FINISHING INC
228 Pleasant Ave (12095-1107)
PHONE...............................518 762-3121
Joseph De Cristofaro, *President*
▲ **EMP:** 50
SQ FT: 18,000
SALES (est): 6.7MM **Privately Held**
SIC: 3111 Finishing of leather

(G-6611)
BENJAMIN MOORE & CO
Union Ave Ext (12095)
P.O. Box 220 (12095-0220)
PHONE...............................518 736-1723
Riki Johnson, *Sales Staff*
Robert Nowicki, *Manager*
EMP: 40
SQ FT: 2,403
SALES (corp-wide): 225.3B **Publicly Held**
WEB: www.benjaminmoore.com
SIC: 2851 5198 Paints & allied products;
  paints
HQ: Benjamin Moore & Co.
  101 Paragon Dr
  Montvale NJ 07645
  201 573-9600

(G-6612)
CALLAWAY GOLF BALL OPRTONS INC
Also Called: Spalding Sports Worldwide
115 Corporate Dr (12095-4062)
PHONE...............................518 725-5744
Joan Sowle, *Branch Mgr*
EMP: 15
SALES (corp-wide): 1.2B **Publicly Held**
WEB: www.topflite.com
SIC: 3949 Golf equipment; basketball
  equipment & supplies, general
HQ: Callaway Golf Ball Operations, Inc.
  425 Meadow St
  Chicopee MA 01013
  413 536-1200

(G-6613)
CARVILLE NATIONAL LEATHER CORP
10 Knox Ave (12095-2715)
P.O. Box 142 (12095-0142)
PHONE...............................518 762-1634
Hugh Carville, *CEO*
Robert Carville, *President*
Jennifer Carville, *Finance Dir*
▲ **EMP:** 15
SQ FT: 64,000
SALES (est): 2.1MM **Privately Held**
SIC: 3111 5199 Finishing of leather; color-
  ing of leather; leather, leather goods &
  furs

(G-6614)
ELECTRO-METRICS CORPORATION
231 Enterprise Rd (12095-3340)
PHONE...............................518 762-2600
Leslie Apple, *CEO*
▼ **EMP:** 34
SQ FT: 42,500
SALES (est): 7.8MM **Privately Held**
WEB: www.emihq.com
SIC: 3663 Radio & TV communications
  equipment

(G-6615)
EMPIRE ARCHTCTURAL SYSTEMS INC
125 Belzano Rd (12095-9755)
PHONE...............................518 773-5109
Paul Lusenhop, *President*
EMP: 35
SQ FT: 40,000
SALES (est): 4.1MM **Privately Held**
SIC: 2541 3442 Store fronts, prefabri-
  cated: wood; store fronts, prefabricated,
  metal

(G-6616)
EUPHRATES INC
230 Enterprise Rd (12095-3338)
P.O. Box 977 (12095-0977)
PHONE...............................518 762-3488
Hamdi Ulukaya, *President*
▲ **EMP:** 87
SALES: 34MM **Privately Held**
WEB: www.euphrates.com
SIC: 2022 Natural cheese

(G-6617)
FAGE USA HOLDINGS (HQ)
1 Opportunity Dr (12095-3349)
PHONE...............................518 762-5912
Anthanasios Filippou, *CEO*
David Marino, *Opers Staff*
Robert Shea, *CFO*
Christos Koloventzos, *Treasurer*
◆ **EMP:** 5 **EST:** 2000
SALES (est): 221.8MM
SALES (corp-wide): 146.3MM **Privately Held**
SIC: 2026 5143 Yogurt; yogurt
PA: Fage Greece Dairy Industry Single
  Member S.A.
  35 Ermou
  Metamorfosi 14452
  210 289-2555

(G-6618)
HAWKINS FABRICS INC (PA)
328 N Perry St (12095-1210)
P.O. Box 351, Gloversville (12078-0351)
PHONE...............................518 773-9550
Alex Willart, *President*
James Batty, *President*
▲ **EMP:** 38 **EST:** 1981
SQ FT: 50,000
SALES (est): 12.1MM **Privately Held**
WEB: www.safeind.com
SIC: 2259 2231 Gloves, knit, except dress
  & semidress gloves; mittens, knit; work
  gloves, knit; broadwoven fabric mills, wool

(G-6619)
HUDSON INDUSTRIES CORPORATION
Also Called: Milligan & Higgins Div
100 Maple Ave (12095-1041)
P.O. Box 506 (12095-0506)
PHONE...............................518 762-4638
Ron Kormanek, *Branch Mgr*
EMP: 40
SQ FT: 36,025 **Privately Held**
WEB: www.milligan1868.com
SIC: 2891 Glue
HQ: Hudson Industries Corporation
  271 Us Highway 46 F207
  Fairfield NJ 07004
  973 402-0100

(G-6620)
JAG MANUFACTURING INC
26 Grecco Dr (12095-1067)
P.O. Box 957 (12095-0957)
PHONE...............................518 762-9558
Joseph A Galea, *President*
Kelly L Galea, *Vice Pres*
▲ **EMP:** 45
SQ FT: 10,000
SALES (est): 5.2MM **Privately Held**
SIC: 3949 3732 2394 2393 Golf equip-
  ment; boat building & repairing; canvas &
  related products; textile bags; broadwo-
  ven fabric mills, manmade

(G-6621)
KAMALI LEATHER LLC
204 Harrison St (12095-4072)
PHONE...............................518 762-2522
Mark Towne, *Manager*
EMP: 9
SALES: 1.1MM
SALES (corp-wide): 4.6MM **Privately Held**
SIC: 3199 Boxes, leather
PA: Kamali Leather Llc
  44 Hillside Ave
  Manhasset NY 11030
  516 627-6505

▲ = Import ▼=Export
◆ =Import/Export

(G-6622)
LEE DYEING COMPANY NC INC
Also Called: Merrimac Leasing
328 N Perry St (12095-1210)
P.O. Box 100 (12095-0100)
PHONE..................................518 736-5232
Morris Evans, *President*
EMP: 10
SQ FT: 76,063
SALES (est): 1.3MM **Privately Held**
WEB: www.leedyeing.com
SIC: 2261 Embossing cotton broadwoven
fabrics

(G-6623)
**PEACEFUL VALLEY MAPLE
FARM (PA)**
116 Lagrange Rd (12095-4031)
PHONE..................................518 762-0491
Stephen M Savage, *Owner*
EMP: 5
SALES: 100K **Privately Held**
SIC: 2099 Maple syrup

(G-6624)
**PEARL LEATHER FINISHERS
INC (PA)**
11 Industrial Pkwy 21 (12095-1046)
P.O. Box 709 (12095-0709)
PHONE..................................518 762-4543
Carmen F Ruggiero, *CEO*
Theresa Cook, *Admin Asst*
▲ EMP: 18
SQ FT: 20,000
SALES (est): 7.1MM **Privately Held**
WEB: www.pearlleather.com
SIC: 3111 Leather tanning & finishing

(G-6625)
**PIONEER WINDOW HOLDINGS
INC**
200 Union Ave (12095-3336)
P.O. Box 70 (12095-0070)
PHONE..................................518 762-5526
Vincent Amato, *President*
EMP: 50 **Privately Held**
WEB: www.pwindows.com
SIC: 3442 3354 Storm doors or windows,
metal; aluminum extruded products
PA: Pioneer Window Holdings, Inc.
3 Expressway Plz Ste 221
Roslyn Heights NY 11577

(G-6626)
R H CROWN CO INC
100 N Market St (12095-2126)
PHONE..................................518 762-4589
Michael Gray, *President*
Richard Reynolds, *Exec VP*
EMP: 30 EST: 1965
SQ FT: 58,000
SALES (est): 9.6MM **Privately Held**
SIC: 2911 7349 Oils, lubricating; janitorial
service, contract basis

(G-6627)
SILK SCREEN ART INC
1 School St (12095-2198)
PHONE..................................518 762-8423
David P Sponenberg, *President*
Guy B Sponenberg, *Vice Pres*
EMP: 12
SQ FT: 20,000
SALES (est): 870K **Privately Held**
SIC: 2759 Screen printing

(G-6628)
**SIMCO LEATHER
CORPORATION**
99 Pleasant Ave (12095-1720)
P.O. Box 509 (12095-0509)
PHONE..................................518 762-7100
Gerald Simek, *President*
▲ EMP: 20
SQ FT: 45,000
SALES (est): 3MM **Privately Held**
SIC: 3111 Tanneries, leather

(G-6629)
SPRAY NINE CORPORATION
309 W Montgomery St (12095-2435)
P.O. Box 290 (12095-0290)
PHONE..................................800 477-7299
EMP: 80
SQ FT: 82,000

SALES (est): 12MM **Privately Held**
WEB: www.spraynine.com
SIC: 2842 Cleaning or polishing prepara-
tions

Jordan
Onondaga County

(G-6630)
OMEGA WIRE INC
Also Called: Bare Wire Div
24 N Beaver St (13080-9531)
PHONE..................................315 689-7115
C Knapp, *Manager*
EMP: 90
SALES (corp-wide): 2.9B **Privately Held**
WEB: www.omegawire.com
SIC: 3351 3366 3315 Wire, copper & cop-
per alloy; copper foundries; steel wire &
related products
HQ: Omega Wire, Inc.
12 Masonic Ave
Camden NY 13316
315 245-3800

(G-6631)
WECARE ORGANICS LLC (PA)
9293 Bonta Bridge Rd (13080-9430)
PHONE..................................315 689-1937
Jeffrey Leblanc, *President*
Mike Leblanc, *President*
Owen Sheehan, *Vice Pres*
EMP: 24
SALES (est): 9.5MM **Privately Held**
SIC: 2869 Plasticizers, organic: cyclic &
acyclic

Jordanville
Herkimer County

(G-6632)
HANSON AGGREGATES PA INC
237 Kingdom Rd (13361-2603)
PHONE..................................315 858-1100
Kevin Smith, *Superintendent*
EMP: 30
SQ FT: 2,944
SALES (corp-wide): 20.6B **Privately Held**
SIC: 1442 1422 Common sand mining;
crushed & broken limestone
HQ: Hanson Aggregates Pennsylvania, Llc
7660 Imperial Way
Allentown PA 18195
610 366-4626

Katonah
Westchester County

(G-6633)
HOME TECH LLC
13 Catherine Pl (10536-3001)
PHONE..................................914 301-5408
Barry Miller,
EMP: 6
SALES: 1MM **Privately Held**
SIC: 3663 3699 Television monitors; secu-
rity devices

(G-6634)
LIGHF INC
42 Quicks Ln (10536-1006)
PHONE..................................917 803-3323
Todd Okolovitch, *President*
EMP: 7
SALES (est): 152.8K **Privately Held**
SIC: 7372 Application computer software

(G-6635)
MICHEL DESIGN WORKS LTD
Also Called: Michel Design Works USA
41 Katonah Ave Ste 209 (10536-2194)
P.O. Box 1227, Ocala FL (34478-1227)
PHONE..................................914 763-2244
Larry Hanson, *Credit Mgr*
Debbie McKeough, *Sales Dir*
Deborah Michel, *Creative Dir*
EMP: 15

SALES (est): 1.6MM
SALES (corp-wide): 402.3K **Privately
Held**
SIC: 2731 2844 Books: publishing only;
toilet preparations
PA: Michel Design Works Ltd.
2875 Route 35 Ste 6s-3
Katonah NY 10536
914 763-3245

(G-6636)
NEU GROUP INC (PA)
135 Katonah Ave Ste 2 (10536-2157)
PHONE..................................914 232-4068
Joseph Neu, *CEO*
EMP: 10
SALES: 3MM **Privately Held**
WEB: www.itreasurer.com
SIC: 2741 Newsletter publishing

(G-6637)
NOVA PACKAGING LTD INC
7 Sunrise Ave (10536-2301)
PHONE..................................914 232-8406
Greg Scott, *President*
EMP: 37
SALES (est): 4.8MM **Privately Held**
SIC: 2671 3081 2673 Packaging paper &
plastics film, coated & laminated; unsup-
ported plastics film & sheet; bags: plastic,
laminated & coated

(G-6638)
RECORD REVIEW LLC
Also Called: Bedford Pund Rdge Rcord Re-
view
16 The Pkwy Fl 3 (10536-1550)
PHONE..................................914 244-0533
Deborah White, *Mng Member*
Rob Astorino, *Executive*
EMP: 10
SALES (est): 429.3K **Privately Held**
SIC: 2711 Newspapers, publishing & print-
ing

(G-6639)
US AUTHENTIC LLC
11 Mt Holly Rd E (10536-2400)
PHONE..................................914 767-0295
Shaul Dover, *Mng Member*
▲ EMP: 6 EST: 2000
SQ FT: 4,000
SALES (est): 600.5K **Privately Held**
WEB: www.flightjacket.com
SIC: 2386 Garments, sheep-lined

Kauneonga Lake
Sullivan County

(G-6640)
B H M METAL PRODUCTS CO
Horseshoe Lake Rd (12749)
PHONE..................................845 292-5297
Robert Gordon, *Owner*
EMP: 6 EST: 1947
SQ FT: 15,000
SALES: 100K **Privately Held**
SIC: 3469 3441 3312 3679 Metal stamp-
ings; fabricated structural metal; tool & die
steel & alloys; electronic circuits

Keeseville
Clinton County

(G-6641)
ESSEX BOX & PALLET CO INC
49 Industrial Park Rd (12944-2936)
PHONE..................................518 834-7279
Michael Lemza, *President*
EMP: 22
SQ FT: 19,000
SALES (est): 2.8MM **Privately Held**
WEB: www.essexboxandpallet.com
SIC: 2449 2448 2499 Wood containers;
pallets, wood; handles, poles, dowels &
stakes: wood

(G-6642)
**INTERNATIONAL MTLS & SUPS
INC**
56 Industrial Park Rd (12944-2937)
PHONE..................................518 834-9899
David Kruse, *President*
John Burns, *Vice Pres*
Martin Caouette, *Vice Pres*
Jeffrey Kinblom, *Vice Pres*
David Rumble, *Vice Pres*
▼ EMP: 5 EST: 2001
SALES (est): 454.7K
SALES (corp-wide): 1.2B **Privately Held**
SIC: 2869 Industrial organic chemicals
HQ: Virginia Materials Inc.
3306 Peterson St
Norfolk VA 23509
800 321-2282

(G-6643)
**LOREMANSS EMBROIDERY
ENGRAV**
Also Called: Loreman's
1599 Front St (12944-3510)
P.O. Box 546 (12944-0546)
PHONE..................................518 834-9205
Thomas H Loreman, *Mng Member*
Donald Loreman Sr,
EMP: 12
SQ FT: 7,000
SALES: 1.7MM **Privately Held**
WEB: www.loremans.com
SIC: 2261 2759 7389 2395 Screen print-
ing of cotton broadwoven fabrics; screen
printing; engraving service; embroidery &
art needlework; automotive & apparel
trimmings

(G-6644)
MURRAY LOGGING LLC
1535 Route 9 (12944-2848)
PHONE..................................518 834-7372
Robert Murray,
James Murray,
EMP: 5
SALES (est): 379.4K **Privately Held**
SIC: 2411 Logging camps & contractors

(G-6645)
**PEPSI-COLA METRO BTLG CO
INC**
Also Called: Pepsico
1524 Route 9 (12944-2890)
PHONE..................................518 834-7811
Michael Bear, *Manager*
Jim Banker, *Manager*
EMP: 400
SALES (corp-wide): 64.6B **Publicly Held**
WEB: www.pbg.com
SIC: 2086 Carbonated soft drinks, bottled
& canned
HQ: Pepsi-Cola Metropolitan Bottling Com-
pany, Inc.
1111 Westchester Ave
White Plains NY 10604
914 767-6000

(G-6646)
**UPSTATE RECORDS
MANAGEMENT LLC**
1729 Front St (12944-3620)
PHONE..................................518 834-1144
Barbara Davidson,
EMP: 5
SALES: 125K **Privately Held**
SIC: 7372 Prepackaged software

Kendall
Orleans County

(G-6647)
**DMD MACHINING TECHNOLOGY
INC**
17231 Roosevelt Hwy (14476-9762)
PHONE..................................585 659-8180
David Hofer, *President*
EMP: 5
SALES: 250K **Privately Held**
SIC: 3599 Machine shop, jobbing & repair

Kenmore
Erie County

(G-6648)
ARMENTO INCORPORATED
Also Called: Armento Architectural Arts
1011 Military Rd (14217-2225)
P.O. Box 39, Buffalo (14217-0039)
PHONE....................716 875-2423
Robert W Pierce, *President*
EMP: 6 EST: 1946
SQ FT: 5,000
SALES (est): 1MM **Privately Held**
SIC: 3446 Ornamental metalwork

(G-6649)
DENNYS DRIVE SHAFT SERVICE
1189 Military Rd (14217-1845)
PHONE....................716 875-6640
Dennis Bringhurst, *President*
Mary Bringhurst, *Vice Pres*
EMP: 8
SALES (est): 1MM **Privately Held**
WEB: www.dennysdriveshaft.com
SIC: 3714 7538 Drive shafts, motor vehicle; general automotive repair shops

(G-6650)
HARGRAVE DEVELOPMENT
Also Called: Hargraves Bus MGT Consulting
84 Shepard Ave (14217-1914)
PHONE....................716 877-7880
Lawrence Tanner, *Owner*
Lloyd Tanner, *Principal*
EMP: 15
SALES (est): 597.2K **Privately Held**
SIC: 1499 8742 Miscellaneous nonmetallic minerals; business consultant

(G-6651)
HERRMANN GROUP LLC
Also Called: Identity Ink & Custom Tee
2320 Elmwood Ave (14217-2645)
PHONE....................716 876-9798
William Herrmann,
EMP: 5
SALES (est): 473.6K **Privately Held**
SIC: 2759 3552 3949 5136 Screen printing; embroidery machines; sporting & athletic goods; men's & boys' clothing; clothing, sportswear, men's & boys'

(G-6652)
HORACE J METZ
Also Called: Insty Trints
2385 Elmwood Ave (14217-2648)
PHONE....................716 873-9103
Horace J Metz, *Owner*
Jim Metz, *Manager*
EMP: 7 EST: 1976
SALES (est): 280.2K **Privately Held**
SIC: 2759 Commercial printing

(G-6653)
HULLEY HOLDING COMPANY INC (PA)
Also Called: Hulley Woodworking Company
2500 Elmwood Ave (14217-2223)
PHONE....................716 332-3982
John Hulley, *President*
EMP: 13
SQ FT: 6,400
SALES: 1MM **Privately Held**
WEB: www.hulleywoodworking.com
SIC: 2431 Millwork

(G-6654)
KEN-TON OPEN MRI PC
2882 Elmwood Ave (14217-1325)
PHONE....................716 876-7000
Joseph Serghany, *Ch of Bd*
Dr H Chen Park, *Principal*
EMP: 7
SALES (est): 670K **Privately Held**
SIC: 3841 8071 2835 Diagnostic apparatus, medical; testing laboratories; in vivo diagnostics

(G-6655)
W H JONES & SON INC
1208 Military Rd (14217-1833)
PHONE....................716 875-8233
Elizabeth Jones, *Ch of Bd*

W Todd Jones, *President*
Kevin B Jones, *Vice Pres*
Peter W Jones, *Vice Pres*
EMP: 10
SQ FT: 6,800
SALES: 737.7K **Privately Held**
SIC: 3599 Custom machinery

(G-6656)
ZENGER PARTNERS LLC
1881 Kenmore Ave (14217-2523)
PHONE....................716 876-2284
Joseph Zenger,
EMP: 37
SQ FT: 12,000
SALES: 3.1MM **Privately Held**
SIC: 2752 2791 2789 Commercial printing, offset; typesetting; bookbinding & related work

Kennedy
Chautauqua County

(G-6657)
CARGILL INCORPORATED
1029 Poland Center Rd (14747-9708)
PHONE....................716 665-6570
Tim Decker, *Branch Mgr*
EMP: 7
SALES (corp-wide): 114.7B **Privately Held**
WEB: www.growmarkfs.com
SIC: 2048 Prepared feeds
PA: Cargill, Incorporated
15407 Mcginty Rd W
Wayzata MN 55391
952 742-7575

Kerhonkson
Ulster County

(G-6658)
BARRA & TRUMBORE INC
40 Old Mine Rd (12446-2641)
PHONE....................845 626-5442
David Barra, *President*
Martin Trumbore, *Vice Pres*
▲ **EMP:** 8
SALES (est): 725.2K **Privately Held**
WEB: www.barratrumbore.com
SIC: 3281 Cut stone & stone products

(G-6659)
DAVES PRECISION MACHINE SHOP
56 Webster Ave (12446-2672)
PHONE....................845 626-7263
David Seymour, *Owner*
EMP: 12
SQ FT: 1,500
SALES (est): 540K **Privately Held**
SIC: 3599 Machine shop, jobbing & repair

Kew Gardens
Queens County

(G-6660)
A & B COLOR CORP (PA)
Also Called: Soho Guilds
8204 Lefferts Blvd # 356 (11415-1731)
PHONE....................718 441-5482
William Rabinowitz, *President*
EMP: 6
SQ FT: 2,500
SALES (est): 239.5K **Privately Held**
SIC: 2851 5198 Paints & allied products; paints

(G-6661)
AD-VANTAGE PRINTING INC
12034 Queens Blvd Vd (11415-1230)
PHONE....................718 820-0688
Francene Biderman, *President*
EMP: 11

SALES (est): 2.1MM **Privately Held**
WEB: www.advantages.net
SIC: 2752 5199 7336 Commercial printing, offset; advertising specialties; graphic arts & related design

(G-6662)
CUMMINS - ALLISON CORP
8002 Kew Gardens Rd # 402 (11415-3613)
PHONE....................718 263-2482
EMP: 64
SALES (corp-wide): 390.1MM **Privately Held**
SIC: 3579 3519 Perforators (office machines); internal combustion engines
PA: Cummins-Allison Corp
852 Feehanville Dr
Mount Prospect IL 60056
800 786-5528

(G-6663)
CUZINS DUZIN CORP
8420 Austin St Apt 3a (11415-2213)
P.O. Box 313073, Jamaica (11431-3073)
PHONE....................347 724-6200
Todd Jones, *Manager*
EMP: 8
SALES: 76K **Privately Held**
SIC: 2051 Doughnuts, except frozen

(G-6664)
I D E PROCESSES CORPORATION (PA)
106 81st Ave (11415-1108)
PHONE....................718 544-1177
Fax: 718 575-8050
▲ **EMP:** 17
SQ FT: 500
SALES: 2.1MM **Privately Held**
SIC: 3625 Mfg Silencers & Industrial Noise Control Equipment

(G-6665)
ISRAELI YELLOW PAGES
12510 Queens Blvd Ste 14 (11415-1522)
PHONE....................718 520-1000
Assaf Ran, *CEO*
EMP: 20
SALES (est): 756.9K **Privately Held**
SIC: 2741 Telephone & other directory publishing

(G-6666)
JACK L POPKIN & CO INC
12510 84th Rd (11415-2202)
PHONE....................718 361-6700
Leonard F Popkin, *President*
Debra Z Popkin, *Admin Sec*
EMP: 8 EST: 1947
SQ FT: 6,000
SALES: 1.6MM **Privately Held**
SIC: 3861 7699 Printing equipment, photographic; printing trades machinery & equipment repair

(G-6667)
JG INNOVATIVE INDUSTRIES INC
8002 Kew Gardens Rd # 5002 (11415-3600)
PHONE....................718 784-7300
Joseph Gottlieb, *Ch of Bd*
EMP: 8
SALES (est): 964.5K **Privately Held**
SIC: 3999 Advertising display products

(G-6668)
MANHOLE BRRIER SEC SYSTEMS INC
Also Called: Mbss
8002 Kew Gardens Rd # 901 (11415-3600)
PHONE....................516 741-1032
Michael Manoussos, *CEO*
John Messer, *President*
EMP: 22 EST: 2001
SQ FT: 5,000
SALES (est): 3.6MM **Privately Held**
SIC: 3699 Security devices

Kill Buck
Cattaraugus County

(G-6669)
DONVER INCORPORATED
4185 Killbuck Rd (14748)
P.O. Box 181 (14748-0181)
PHONE....................716 945-1910
Donald A Vershay, *President*
Patricia B Vershay, *Vice Pres*
EMP: 18
SQ FT: 900
SALES: 4.3MM **Privately Held**
SIC: 2421 3713 2491 2426 Sawmills & planing mills, general; truck & bus bodies; wood preserving; hardwood dimension & flooring mills

Kinderhook
Columbia County

(G-6670)
AMERICAN BIO MEDICA CORP (PA)
122 Smith Rd (12106-2819)
PHONE....................518 758-8158
Melissa A Waterhouse, *CEO*
Richard P Koskey, *Ch of Bd*
Edmund M Jaskiewicz, *President*
Douglas Casterlin, *Vice Pres*
Melissa Waterhouse, *Vice Pres*
EMP: 65
SQ FT: 30,000
SALES: 3.8MM **Publicly Held**
WEB: www.americanbiomedica.com
SIC: 2834 3841 Pharmaceutical preparations; diagnostic apparatus, medical

King Ferry
Cayuga County

(G-6671)
LAKE VIEW MANUFACTURING LLC
Also Called: Aurora Shoe Company
1690 State Route 90 N (13081-9713)
P.O. Box 430, Aurora (13026-0430)
PHONE....................315 364-7892
David Binns, *President*
EMP: 10
SQ FT: 5,000
SALES (est): 1.3MM **Privately Held**
SIC: 3143 3144 Men's footwear, except athletic; women's footwear, except athletic

Kings Park
Suffolk County

(G-6672)
DEJANA TRCK UTILITY EQP CO LLC (HQ)
490 Pulaski Rd (11754-1317)
PHONE....................631 544-9000
Peter Dejana, *President*
Elizabeth Peck, *Business Mgr*
Michael Sitkin, *Prdtn Mgr*
Nicholas Allen, *Parts Mgr*
Brian Costa, *Parts Mgr*
EMP: 150
SQ FT: 25,000
SALES (est): 36.1MM **Publicly Held**
SIC: 3711 5531 Truck & tractor truck assembly; truck equipment & parts

(G-6673)
HANSA PLASTICS INC
8 Meadow Glen Rd (11754-1312)
PHONE....................631 269-9050
Harold Schmidt, *President*
Nellie Schmidt, *Corp Secy*
Peter Schmidt Jr, *Vice Pres*
Harald Schmidt, *Design Engr*
▲ **EMP:** 10 EST: 1961
SQ FT: 5,000

▲ = Import ▼=Export
◆ =Import/Export

SALES (est): 1.8MM Privately Held
WEB: www.hansasystemsusa.com
SIC: 3089 Injection molding of plastics

(G-6674)
KINGS PARK READY MIX CORP
140 Old Northport Rd E (11754-4211)
PHONE..................................631 269-4330
Claudio Valente, President
EMP: 15
SALES: 2MM Privately Held
SIC: 3273 Ready-mixed concrete

(G-6675)
PELKOWSKI PRECAST CORP
294a Old Northport Rd (11754-4200)
PHONE..................................631 269-5727
Tom Pelkowski, President
Bob Pelkowski, Vice Pres
Bryan Pelkowski, Treasurer
Bill Pelkowski, Admin Sec
EMP: 17
SQ FT: 400
SALES (est): 2.7MM Privately Held
SIC: 3272 Concrete products, precast;
septic tanks, concrete; manhole covers or
frames, concrete; covers, catch basin:
concrete

(G-6676)
R SCHLEIDER CONTRACTING
CORP
135 Old Northport Rd (11754-4200)
PHONE..................................631 269-4249
Ray Schleider, President
Loretta Schleider, Vice Pres
EMP: 5 EST: 1969
SQ FT: 2,500
SALES (est): 853.6K Privately Held
SIC: 2951 5169 Road materials, bitumi-
nous (not from refineries); industrial salts
& polishes

Kingston
Ulster County

(G-6677)
ALCOA FASTENING SYSTEMS
1 Corporate Dr (12401-5536)
PHONE..................................845 334-7203
Klaus Kleinfeld, Principal
▲ EMP: 130
SQ FT: 40,000
SALES (est): 21.5MM Privately Held
SIC: 3452 Bolts, nuts, rivets & washers

(G-6678)
ARCONIC FSTENING SYSTEMS
RINGS
Also Called: Kingston Operations
1 Corporate Dr (12401-5536)
PHONE..................................800 278-4825
Charles Redlich, Engineer
Eileen Larocca, Human Res Mgr
David Hanson, Manager
Paul Ohama, Manager
EMP: 5 EST: 2016
SALES (est): 135.1K Privately Held
SIC: 3353 Aluminum sheet, plate & foil

(G-6679)
ARMOR DYNAMICS INC
138 Maple Hill Rd (12401-8616)
PHONE..................................845 658-9200
Bernard C Schaeffer, President
David Gagnon, CFO
EMP: 15
SALES: 1.5MM Privately Held
SIC: 3711 Cars, armored, assembly of

(G-6680)
BESICORP LTD (PA)
1151 Flatbush Rd (12401-7011)
PHONE..................................845 336-7700
William Seils, President
Frederic M Zinn Sr, President
Michael F Zinn, Chairman
EMP: 13 EST: 1998
SQ FT: 8,000
SALES (est): 6.2MM Privately Held
SIC: 3674 4911 3585 Photovoltaic de-
vices, solid state; electric services; refrig-
eration & heating equipment

(G-6681)
C & G OF KINGSTON INC
25 Cornell St (12401-3625)
P.O. Box 1458 (12402-1458)
PHONE..................................845 331-0148
Clyde E Wonderly, CEO
Gloria M Wonderly, Admin Sec
EMP: 60
SQ FT: 20,000
SALES (est): 5.2MM Privately Held
WEB: www.wonderlys.com
SIC: 2391 2392 Draperies, plastic & tex-
tile: from purchased materials; bed-
spreads & bed sets: made from
purchased materials

(G-6682)
C S I G INC
721 Broadway Ste 270 (12401-3449)
PHONE..................................845 383-3800
Andrew Peck, CEO
Jonathan Peck, CEO
Tim Peck, Vice Pres
Timothy Peck, Vice Pres
EMP: 9
SQ FT: 1,450
SALES (est): 650K Privately Held
WEB: www.csiginc.com
SIC: 7372 Application computer software

(G-6683)
CALLANAN INDUSTRIES INC
737 Flatbush Rd (12401-7313)
PHONE..................................845 331-6868
Randy Anson, Manager
EMP: 25
SALES (corp-wide): 30.6B Privately Held
WEB: www.callanan.com
SIC: 3272 3281 2951 1442 Concrete
products, precast; stone, quarrying & pro-
cessing of own stone products; asphalt
paving mixtures & blocks; construction
sand & gravel
HQ: Callanan Industries, Inc.
8 Southwoods Blvd Ste 4
Albany NY 12211
518 374-2222

(G-6684)
CENTER FOR PROSTHETIC
144 Pine St Ste 110 (12401-4946)
PHONE..................................845 336-7762
Jones Zinter, Branch Mgr
EMP: 5
SALES (est): 396.4K Privately Held
SIC: 3842 Prosthetic appliances
PA: Center For Prosthetic & Orthotic De-
sign, Inc.
149 S Lake Ave
Albany NY 12208

(G-6685)
CHARLTON PRECISION
PRODUCTS
461 Sawkill Rd (12401-1229)
P.O. Box 500, Mount Marion (12456-0500)
PHONE..................................845 338-2351
Robert Charlton, President
Bonnie Charlton, Vice Pres
Nancy Charlton, Shareholder
Katherine Charlton, Admin Sec
EMP: 8 EST: 1962
SQ FT: 4,000
SALES: 1.2MM Privately Held
WEB: www.charltonprecision.com
SIC: 3643 Current-carrying wiring devices

(G-6686)
CITY OF KINGSTON
Also Called: Kingston Wste Wtr Trment Plant
91 E Strand St (12401-6001)
PHONE..................................845 331-2490
Allen Winchell, Director
EMP: 11 Privately Held
WEB: www.kingstonez.com
SIC: 3589 9511 Sewage & water treat-
ment equipment;
PA: City Of Kingston
420 Broadway
Kingston NY 12401
845 334-3935

(G-6687)
CRANESVILLE BLOCK CO INC
637 E Chester St (12401-1738)
PHONE..................................845 331-1775

Will Longto, Principal
EMP: 25
SQ FT: 4,262
SALES (corp-wide): 45MM Privately
Held
SIC: 3273 Ready-mixed concrete
PA: Cranesville Block Co., Inc.
1250 Riverfront Ctr
Amsterdam NY 12010
518 684-6154

(G-6688)
DAILY FREEMAN
79 Hurley Ave (12401-2898)
PHONE..................................845 331-5000
Jan Dewey, Publisher
Sam Daleo, Principal
EMP: 11
SALES (est): 486K Privately Held
SIC: 2711 Newspapers, publishing & print-
ing

(G-6689)
DIRT T SHIRTS INC
444 Old Neighborhood Rd (12401-1508)
PHONE..................................845 336-4230
John Stote, President
Scott Winter, Vice Pres
William Stote, Treasurer
John Stote III, Admin Sec
EMP: 40
SQ FT: 25,000
SALES (est): 3.5MM Privately Held
SIC: 2396 2395 Screen printing on fabric
articles; art goods for embroidering,
stamped: purchased materials

(G-6690)
EAST COAST CULTURES LLC
906 State Route 28 (12401-7264)
P.O. Box 220147, Brooklyn (11222-0147)
PHONE..................................917 261-3010
EMP: 10
SALES (est): 932K Privately Held
SIC: 2086 Mfg Bottled/Canned Soft Drinks

(G-6691)
FABTECHNY LLC
401 Sawkill Rd Blgda (12401-1229)
PHONE..................................845 338-2000
Frank Buffa, Mng Member
EMP: 15 EST: 2013
SALES (est): 432.3K Privately Held
SIC: 3599 Industrial machinery

(G-6692)
FARM TO TABLE COMMUNITY
INC (PA)
Also Called: Farm Bridge, The
750 Enterprise Dr (12401-7027)
PHONE..................................845 383-1761
James Hyland, CEO
Stephani Vanwagenen, Manager
EMP: 28
SQ FT: 30,000
SALES: 5MM Privately Held
SIC: 2099 5199 Almond pastes; packag-
ing materials

(G-6693)
HEALTHALLIANCE HOSPITAL
Also Called: Benedictine Hospital
105 Marys Ave (12401-5848)
PHONE..................................845 338-2500
Jeffrey Murphy, Manager
EMP: 7
SALES (corp-wide): 1.6B Privately Held
SIC: 3821 Laboratory apparatus & furniture
HQ: Healthalliance Hospital Mary's Avenue
Campus
105 Marys Ave
Kingston NY 12401
845 338-2500

(G-6694)
HUCK INTERNATIONAL INC
Also Called: Arconic Fastening Systems
1 Corporate Dr (12401-5536)
PHONE..................................845 331-7300
Garvin Wells, Opers Mgr
Steven Boderck, Branch Mgr
EMP: 203

SALES (corp-wide): 14B Publicly Held
WEB: www.huck.com
SIC: 3452 3594 3546 Bolts, nuts, rivets &
washers; fluid power pumps & motors;
power-driven handtools
HQ: Huck International, Inc.
3724 E Columbia St
Tucson AZ 85714
520 519-7400

(G-6695)
KEEGAN ALES LLC
20 Saint James St (12401-4534)
PHONE..................................845 331-2739
Patrick Sylvester, Advt Staff
Tommy Keegan, Mng Member
EMP: 13
SALES (est): 1.1MM Privately Held
WEB: www.keeganales.com
SIC: 2082 Beer (alcoholic beverage)

(G-6696)
KINGSTON HOOPS SUMMER
68 Glen St (12401-6406)
P.O. Box 2606 (12402-2606)
PHONE..................................845 401-6830
Charlene Laday Hill, Owner
EMP: 8
SALES: 24K Privately Held
SIC: 3494 Valves & pipe fittings

(G-6697)
KNIGHTLY ENDEAVORS
319 Wall St Ste 2 (12401-3884)
PHONE..................................845 340-0949
John Reeder, Owner
Kelly Laverty,
EMP: 11 EST: 1996
SALES (est): 789.1K Privately Held
WEB: www.knightly.com
SIC: 2211 Apparel & outerwear fabrics,
cotton

(G-6698)
LABELLA PASTA INC
906 State Route 28 (12401-7264)
PHONE..................................845 331-9130
Nancy Covello, President
Dennis Covello, President
EMP: 7
SQ FT: 4,800
SALES (est): 709.5K Privately Held
WEB: www.labellapasta.com
SIC: 2099 Pasta, uncooked: packaged with
other ingredients

(G-6699)
LHV PRECAST INC
540 Ulster Landing Rd (12401-6963)
PHONE..................................845 336-8880
Henry Killian, CEO
Robert Willis, President
James Willis, Vice Pres
Mike Venett, Plant Engr
Karen Bennett, Admin Asst
EMP: 50 EST: 1979
SQ FT: 30,000
SALES (est): 8.9MM Privately Held
WEB: www.lhvprecast.com
SIC: 3272 Concrete products, precast

(G-6700)
LOCAL MEDIA GROUP INC
Also Called: Times Herald-Record
34 John St (12401-3822)
PHONE..................................845 340-4910
EMP: 12
SALES (corp-wide): 1.2B Publicly Held
SIC: 2711 Newspapers-Publishing/Printing
HQ: Local Media Group, Inc.
40 Mulberry St
Middletown NY 10940
845 341-1100

(G-6701)
LUMINARY PUBLISHING INC
314 Wall St (12401-3820)
PHONE..................................845 334-8600
Jason Stern, President
Nina Shengold, Editor
Amara Projansky, Vice Pres
Robert Pina, Accounts Exec
Anne Wygal, Accounts Exec
EMP: 15
SQ FT: 1,000

SALES (est): 1.8MM **Privately Held**
WEB: www.chronogram.com
SIC: 2721 2741 Magazines: publishing &
printing; art copy & poster publishing

(G-6702)
M & E MFG CO INC
19 Progress St (12401-3611)
P.O. Box 1548 (12402-1548)
PHONE...........................845 331-7890
Jeffrey Weinberger, *CEO*
Don Hall, *President*
EMP: 55
SQ FT: 54,000
SALES: 6.1MM **Privately Held**
WEB: www.zframerack.com
SIC: 3441 Fabricated structural metal

(G-6703)
MILLROCK TECHNOLOGY INC
39 Kieffer Ln Ste 2 (12401-2210)
PHONE...........................845 339-5700
Taylor Thompson, *Chairman*
Mary Anne Whitnas, *Accounts Mgr*
◆ EMP: 20
SQ FT: 12,000
SALES (est): 4.4MM **Privately Held**
WEB: www.millrocktech.com
SIC: 3585 Refrigeration equipment, complete

(G-6704)
NORTHAST COML WIN TRTMENTS INC
Also Called: Wonderly Company, The
25 Cornell St (12401-3625)
PHONE...........................845 331-0148
Al Parsons, *CEO*
Pat Schweikart, *CFO*
EMP: 65
SALES (est): 6.6MM **Privately Held**
SIC: 2391 Cottage sets (curtains): made
from purchased materials

(G-6705)
NORTHEAST DATA
619 State Route 28 (12401-7466)
P.O. Box 316, West Hurley (12491-0316)
PHONE...........................845 331-5554
Mark Wachtel, *Principal*
EMP: 5
SALES (est): 1MM **Privately Held**
SIC: 3559 Tire shredding machinery
PA: National Waste Management Holdings,
　Inc.
　5920 N Florida Ave
　Hernando FL 34442
　352 489-6912

(G-6706)
PEARSON EDUCATION INC
317 Wall St (12401-3819)
PHONE...........................845 340-8700
Dan Cooper, *Manager*
EMP: 27
SALES (corp-wide): 5.3B **Privately Held**
WEB: www.phgenit.com
SIC: 2731 Book publishing
HQ: Pearson Education, Inc.
　221 River St
　Hoboken NJ 07030
　201 236-7000

(G-6707)
R & F HANDMADE PAINTS INC
84 Ten Broeck Ave (12401-3921)
PHONE...........................845 331-3112
Richard Frumess, *President*
Kevin Lavin, *Vice Pres*
Darin Seim, *Opers Staff*
Jim Haskin, *Treasurer*
Kelly McGrath, *Education*
▲ EMP: 12
SQ FT: 5,000
SALES (est): 1MM **Privately Held**
SIC: 3952 5199 Lead pencils & art goods;
artists' materials

(G-6708)
ROBERT TABATZNIK ASSOC INC (PA)
Also Called: American Printing and Off Sups
867 Flatbush Rd (12401-7315)
PHONE...........................845 336-4555
Patricia Tabatznik, *Ch of Bd*
Buzz McKernan, *General Mgr*

Robert Tabatznik, *Sales Mgr*
Sarah Sprague, *Manager*
Carlos Canadilla, *Products*
EMP: 10
SQ FT: 7,300
SALES (est): 3.7MM **Privately Held**
WEB: www.rtachicago.com
SIC: 2752 5112 Commercial printing, offset; office supplies

(G-6709)
SOLVENTS COMPANY INC
9 Cornell St (12401-3623)
P.O. Box 2376 (12402-2376)
PHONE...........................631 595-9300
Batia Shellef, *President*
Cindy Kouhout, *Exec Dir*
EMP: 10 EST: 2013
SALES (est): 1.8MM **Privately Held**
SIC: 2911 2869 2899 2842 Solvents;
non-aromatic chemical products; industrial organic chemicals; chlorinated solvents; orange oil; degreasing solvent

(G-6710)
SPIEGEL WOODWORKS INC
Also Called: S A W
418 Old Neighborhood Rd (12401-1508)
PHONE...........................845 336-8090
Gary Spiegel, *President*
EMP: 10
SQ FT: 12,000
SALES: 1.6MM **Privately Held**
WEB: www.sawmoulding.com
SIC: 2431 2421 Moldings, wood: unfinished & prefinished; doors, wood;
sawmills & planing mills, general

(G-6711)
STATEBOOK LLC
185 Fair St Ste 2 (12401-0503)
P.O. Box 3659 (12402-3659)
PHONE...........................845 383-1991
Calandra Cruickshank, *Principal*
Dana Valdez, *Opers Staff*
EMP: 5
SALES (est): 315.8K **Privately Held**
SIC: 2741

(G-6712)
STAVO INDUSTRIES INC (PA)
Also Called: Ertel Alsop
132 Flatbush Ave (12401-2202)
PHONE...........................845 331-4552
George T Quigley, *Vice Pres*
Jason Neese, *Purch Mgr*
Ryan Bell, *Engineer*
Ivan I Schwartz, *Engineer*
Bill Kearney, *VP Sales*
▲ EMP: 17 EST: 1966
SQ FT: 15,000
SALES (est): 9.8MM **Privately Held**
WEB: www.ertelalsop.com
SIC: 3569 3561 3443 Filters, general line:
industrial; industrial pumps & parts; tanks,
standard or custom fabricated: metal
plate

(G-6713)
STAVO INDUSTRIES INC
Also Called: Ertel Engineering Co
132 Flatbush Ave (12401-2202)
PHONE...........................845 331-5389
George Quigley, *Vice Pres*
EMP: 45
SALES (est): 6.3MM
SALES (corp-wide): 9.8MM **Privately
Held**
WEB: www.ertelalsop.com
SIC: 3569 Filters
PA: Stavo Industries, Inc.
　132 Flatbush Ave
　Kingston NY 12401
　845 331-4552

(G-6714)
TIMELY SIGNS OF KINGSTON INC (PA)
154 Clinton Ave Fl 1 (12401-4922)
PHONE...........................845 331-8710
Gerard Beichert, *President*
Jeff Zduniak, *Principal*
Joe Beichert, *Vice Pres*
EMP: 12
SQ FT: 15,000

SALES (est): 833.3K **Privately Held**
WEB: www.timelysigns.com
SIC: 3993 Signs, not made in custom sign
painting shops

(G-6715)
TORTILLA HEAVEN INC
Also Called: Armadillo Bar & Grill
97 Abeel St (12401-6009)
PHONE...........................845 339-1550
Merle Borenstein, *President*
EMP: 20
SQ FT: 3,200
SALES (est): 2.2MM **Privately Held**
SIC: 2099 5812 Tortillas, fresh or refrigerated; Mexican restaurant

(G-6716)
TRI STATE HARDWOODS LTD
54 Breezy Hill Rd (12401-8426)
P.O. Box 779, Stone Ridge (12484-0779)
PHONE...........................845 687-7814
Ted G Peck, *President*
Michael Shipman, *Vice Pres*
EMP: 8
SALES (est): 1.6MM **Privately Held**
SIC: 2421 Sawmills & planing mills, general

(G-6717)
ULSTER PRECISION INC
100 Lipton St (12401-2600)
PHONE...........................845 338-0995
Selma Boris, *President*
Harold Hill, *Exec VP*
Lenore Eckhardt, *Vice Pres*
Jill Boris, *Admin Sec*
Lou Distasi,
EMP: 20
SQ FT: 16,000
SALES (est): 3.8MM **Privately Held**
SIC: 3444 3441 3645 Sheet metal specialties, not stamped; fabricated structural
metal; residential lighting fixtures

(G-6718)
ULSTER PUBLISHING CO INC (PA)
Also Called: Woodstock Times
322 Wall St Fl 1 (12401-3820)
P.O. Box 3329 (12402-3329)
PHONE...........................845 334-8205
Geddy Sveikauskas, *President*
EMP: 20 EST: 1972
SQ FT: 2,500
SALES (est): 3.4MM **Privately Held**
WEB: www.ulsterpublishing.com
SIC: 2711 2721 Newspapers: publishing
only, not printed on site; magazines: publishing only, not printed on site

(G-6719)
UNIVERSAL METAL FABRICATORS
Also Called: Reliance Gayco
27 Emerick St (12401-3009)
PHONE...........................845 331-8248
James Hassett, *President*
EMP: 10
SQ FT: 50,000
SALES (est): 2MM **Privately Held**
WEB: www.urminc.com
SIC: 3555 3599 3569 3532 Printing
trades machinery; machine shop, jobbing
& repair; separators for steam, gas, vapor
or air (machinery); mining machinery

(G-6720)
URBAN PRECAST LLC
6 Kieffer Ln (12401-2206)
PHONE...........................845 331-6299
Tom Auringer,
EMP: 50 EST: 2012
SALES (est): 177.7K **Privately Held**
SIC: 3272 Concrete products, precast

(G-6721)
USHECO INC
138 Maple Hill Rd (12401-8616)
PHONE...........................845 658-9200
Bernarr C Schaeffer, *CEO*
Wayne M Schaeffer, *President*
Lorene Schaeffer, *Vice Pres*
EMP: 16
SQ FT: 40,000

SALES (est): 1.3MM **Privately Held**
WEB: www.usheco.com
SIC: 3089 Injection molding of plastics;
plastic processing

(G-6722)
VINCENT CONIGLIARO
Also Called: Salvin Company
308 State Route 28 (12401-7445)
PHONE...........................845 340-0489
Vincent Conigliaro, *Owner*
EMP: 15
SQ FT: 12,000
SALES (est): 860K **Privately Held**
SIC: 3648 5719 1731 5731 Lighting
equipment; lighting, lamps & accessories;
lighting contractor; radio, television &
electronic stores; audio electronic systems

(G-6723)
WORKSHOP ART FABRICATION
117 Tremper Ave (12401-3619)
P.O. Box 1009 (12402-1009)
PHONE...........................845 331-0385
Vincent Didonato, *President*
Andrew Tharmer, *President*
EMP: 12
SALES: 1MM **Privately Held**
SIC: 3562 Casters

┌─────────────────────────────┐
│　　　　　**Kirkville**　　　　　│
│　　　*Onondaga County*　　　　│
└─────────────────────────────┘

(G-6724)
MANTH-BROWNELL INC
1120 Fyler Rd (13082-9445)
PHONE...........................315 687-7263
Wesley R Skinner Jr, *Ch of Bd*
Rob Pike, *Vice Pres*
Glenn Spaarling, *CFO*
Glenn Sparling, *CFO*
John Skinner, *Admin Sec*
EMP: 180 EST: 1951
SQ FT: 140,000
SALES (est): 45.2MM **Privately Held**
WEB: www.manth.com
SIC: 3451 Screw machine products

(G-6725)
NECESSITY SYSTEMS LLC
203 Creek View Path (13082-9488)
PHONE...........................907 322-4084
Gregory Walker, *Mng Member*
EMP: 2
SALES: 1.5MM **Privately Held**
SIC: 3721 Autogiros

(G-6726)
STANLEY INDUSTRIAL EQP LLC
8094 Saintsville Rd (13082-9325)
PHONE...........................315 656-8733
Thomas Stanley, *Mng Member*
EMP: 6
SQ FT: 5,200
SALES (est): 1.2MM **Privately Held**
SIC: 3537 Forklift trucks

(G-6727)
TITAN STEEL CORP
6333 N Kirkville Rd (13082-3300)
P.O. Box 10 (13082-0010)
PHONE...........................315 656-7046
Gretchen K Conway, *President*
Jeff Kealin, *Vice Pres*
EMP: 12
SALES (est): 2.7MM **Privately Held**
SIC: 3441 Building components, structural
steel

┌─────────────────────────────┐
│　　　　　**Kirkwood**　　　　　│
│　　　*Broome County*　　　　　│
└─────────────────────────────┘

(G-6728)
ACTIVE MANUFACTURING INC
32 Laughlin Rd (13795)
P.O. Box 332 (13795-0332)
PHONE...........................607 775-3162
Frank Sweetay, *President*
EMP: 12
SQ FT: 2,000

▲ = Import ▼=Export
◆ =Import/Export

SALES (est): 1.4MM **Privately Held**
SIC: 3599 3999 Machine shop, jobbing &
repair; models, general, except toy

(G-6729)
AKRATURN MFG INC
1743 Us Route 11 (13795-1637)
PHONE...................................607 775-2802
Douglas Gardner, *President*
Douglas Sterns, *Corp Secy*
David Gardner, *Vice Pres*
EMP: 51
SQ FT: 60,000
SALES (est): 5.2MM **Privately Held**
WEB: www.akraturn.com
SIC: 3599 Machine shop, jobbing & repair

(G-6730)
BELDEN MANUFACTURING INC
Also Called: Dan Ann Associates
1813 Us Route 11 (13795-1608)
PHONE...................................607 238-0998
Jerry Wilson, *President*
Kate Molesky, *Office Mgr*
EMP: 20
SQ FT: 6,000
SALES: 3MM **Privately Held**
SIC: 3599 Machine shop, jobbing & repair

(G-6731)
FUSE ELECTRONICS INC
1223 Us Route 11 (13795-1641)
PHONE...................................607 352-3222
Susane Lewis, *CEO*
Patricia Mancinelli, *Ch of Bd*
Susanne Lewis, *Manager*
EMP: 7
SALES (est): 1MM **Privately Held**
SIC: 3677 Electronic coils, transformers &
other inductors

(G-6732)
TRINIC LLC
40 Grossett Dr (13795-1006)
PHONE...................................607 775-1948
EMP: 14
SALES (est): 2.6MM **Privately Held**
SIC: 3272 Concrete products

La Fargeville
Jefferson County

(G-6733)
HP HOOD LLC
20700 State Route 411 (13656-3228)
P.O. Box 141 (13656-0141)
PHONE...................................315 658-2132
Chantelle Davis, *Production*
Bob Shrader, *IT/INT Sup*
EMP: 300
SALES (corp-wide): 2.2B **Privately Held**
SIC: 2026 Fluid milk
PA: Hp Hood Llc
6 Kimball Ln Ste 400
Lynnfield MA 01940
617 887-8441

(G-6734)
JOHNSON S SAND GRAVEL INC
23284 County Route 3 (13656-3111)
PHONE...................................315 771-1450
Rusty Johnson, *Principal*
EMP: 6
SALES (est): 542.4K **Privately Held**
SIC: 1442 Construction sand & gravel

(G-6735)
**THOUSAND ISLAND READY MIX
CON**
38760 State Route 180 (13656-3108)
PHONE...................................315 686-3203
Thomas Dillenbeck, *President*
Steven Dillenbeck, *Vice Pres*
EMP: 8 EST: 1964
SQ FT: 2,988
SALES (est): 1.3MM **Privately Held**
WEB: www.thousandislandsconcrete.com
SIC: 3273 Ready-mixed concrete

La Fayette
Onondaga County

(G-6736)
BOULAY FABRICATION INC
Rr 20 Box West (13084)
P.O. Box 508 (13084-0508)
PHONE...................................315 677-5247
Timothy Foody, *President*
Daniel Foody, *Vice Pres*
Connie Foody, *Admin Sec*
EMP: 12
SQ FT: 14,000
SALES (est): 2.1MM **Privately Held**
WEB: www.boulayfab.com
SIC: 3613 Control panels, electric

(G-6737)
BYRNE DAIRY INC (PA)
2394 Us Route 11 (13084-9583)
P.O. Box 176 (13084-0176)
PHONE...................................315 475-2121
Carl Byrne, *Ch of Bd*
Scott Smith, *General Mgr*
William M Byrne Jr, *Principal*
Rick Decarr, *Vice Pres*
Eric Greiner, *Vice Pres*
EMP: 300 EST: 1932
SQ FT: 32,000
SALES (est): 313.7MM **Privately Held**
WEB: www.byrnedairy.com
SIC: 2026 2024 Milk processing (pasteur-
izing, homogenizing, bottling); ice cream,
packaged: molded, on sticks, etc.; ice
cream, bulk

(G-6738)
ICHOR THERAPEUTICS INC
2521 Us Route 11 (13084-3352)
PHONE...................................315 677-8400
Kelsey Moody, *CEO*
EMP: 5
SALES (est): 464.4K **Privately Held**
SIC: 2834 Pharmaceutical preparations

Lackawanna
Erie County

(G-6739)
**ALLIANCE INNOVATIVE MFG
INC**
1 Alliance Dr (14218-2529)
PHONE...................................716 822-1626
Richard St John, *President*
Jeanine Zaleski, *Controller*
EMP: 34
SQ FT: 35,000
SALES: 7MM **Privately Held**
SIC: 3599 Machine shop, jobbing & repair

(G-6740)
CERTAINTEED CORPORATION
231 Ship Canal Pkwy (14218-1026)
PHONE...................................716 823-3684
EMP: 226
SALES (corp-wide): 215.9MM **Privately
Held**
SIC: 3221 Glass containers
HQ: Certainteed Llc
20 Moores Rd
Malvern PA 19355
610 893-5000

(G-6741)
LINITA DESIGN & MFG CORP
1951 Hamburg Tpke Ste 24 (14218-1047)
P.O. Box 1101, Buffalo (14201-6101)
PHONE...................................716 566-7753
Carlos Vera, *President*
Eva Vera, *Shareholder*
EMP: 50
SQ FT: 80,000
SALES: 10.6MM **Privately Held**
SIC: 3441 7389 7692 8711 Dam gates,
metal plate; design services; welding re-
pair; engineering services

(G-6742)
PAGE FRONT GROUP INC
2703 S Park Ave (14218-1511)
P.O. Box 756, Buffalo (14205-0756)
PHONE...................................716 823-8222
William Delmont, *President*
Beverly Mazur, *Corp Secy*
EMP: 6
SQ FT: 1,500
SALES (est): 400.8K **Privately Held**
SIC: 2711 Newspapers: publishing only,
not printed on site

(G-6743)
QUIKRETE COMPANIES LLC
Also Called: Quikrete-Buffalo
11 N Steelawanna Ave (14218-1114)
PHONE...................................716 213-2027
Tom Kostelny, *Sales Mgr*
Chuck Olgin, *Manager*
EMP: 30
SQ FT: 26,293 **Privately Held**
WEB: www.quikrete.com
SIC: 3272 Concrete products
HQ: The Quikrete Companies Llc
5 Concourse Pkwy Ste 1900
Atlanta GA 30328
404 634-9100

(G-6744)
RJS MACHINE WORKS INC
1611 Electric Ave (14218-3021)
PHONE...................................716 826-1778
Ronald J Szewczyk, *President*
EMP: 6
SQ FT: 9,000
SALES: 470K **Privately Held**
SIC: 3599 Machine shop, jobbing & repair

(G-6745)
**SAMPLA BELTING NORTH AMER
LLC**
61 N Gates Ave (14218-1029)
PHONE...................................716 667-7450
Stefan Cristian Balint,
◆ EMP: 40
SQ FT: 39,000
SALES: 10MM **Privately Held**
SIC: 3496 Conveyor belts
PA: Megadyne America, Llc
11016 Granite St
Charlotte NC 28273

(G-6746)
WELDED TUBE USA INC
2537 Hamburg Tpke (14218-2557)
PHONE...................................716 828-1111
Robert Mandel, *CEO*
▲ EMP: 60 EST: 2013
SALES (est): 19MM
SALES (corp-wide): 244.3MM **Privately
Held**
SIC: 3317 Steel pipe & tubes
PA: Welded Tube Of Canada Corp
111 Rayette Rd
Concord ON L4K 2.
905 669-1111

Lacona
Oswego County

(G-6747)
VANHOUTEN MOTORSPORTS
27 Center Rd (13083-4127)
PHONE...................................315 387-6312
Henry E Van Houten, *Principal*
EMP: 6
SALES (est): 656.9K **Privately Held**
SIC: 3531 Automobile wrecker hoists

Lagrangeville
Dutchess County

(G-6748)
**GRAPHICS SLUTION
PROVIDERS INC (PA)**
Also Called: Brewster Coachworks
115 Barmore Rd (12540-6601)
P.O. Box 55 (12540-0055)
PHONE...................................845 677-5088

Theresa Brewster, *President*
Alexander S Brewster, *Vice Pres*
Jack Brewster, *Vice Pres*
EMP: 10
SQ FT: 2,500
SALES: 2.5MM **Privately Held**
WEB: www.graphics-solutions.com
SIC: 2499 7373 Novelties, wood fiber;
value-added resellers, computer systems

(G-6749)
INTENTIONS JEWELRY LLC
83 Miller Hill Dr (12540-5641)
PHONE...................................845 226-4650
Janice Janssen, *Consultant*
Bob Baff,
Shareane Baff,
EMP: 5
SALES (est): 406.6K **Privately Held**
SIC: 3911 Jewelry, precious metal

(G-6750)
**MACRO TOOL & MACHINE
COMPANY**
1397 Route 55 (12540-5118)
PHONE...................................845 223-3824
Daniel Siegel, *President*
Gisela Siegel, *Corp Secy*
Roland Siegel, *Vice Pres*
EMP: 8
SQ FT: 30,000
SALES: 500K **Privately Held**
WEB: www.macrotool.com
SIC: 3599 Amusement park equipment;
machine shop, jobbing & repair

(G-6751)
**MICROCAD TRNING
CONSULTING INC**
1110 Route 55 Ste 209 (12540-5048)
PHONE...................................617 923-0500
Agustin Fernandez, *Principal*
EMP: 7 **Privately Held**
SIC: 7372 8243 Prepackaged software;
software training, computer
PA: Microcad Training & Consulting, Inc.
440 Arsenal St Ste 3
Watertown MA

(G-6752)
PARAGON AQUATICS
Also Called: KDI Paragon
1351 Route 55 Unit 1 (12540-5128)
PHONE...................................845 452-5500
Thomas A Saldarelli, *Principal*
Devin Hare, *Safety Mgr*
▲ EMP: 50
SQ FT: 38,000
SALES (est): 9MM
SALES (corp-wide): 17.4B **Publicly Held**
WEB: www.paragonaquatics.com
SIC: 3449 3446 Miscellaneous metalwork;
railings, prefabricated metal
HQ: Pentair Water Pool And Spa, Inc.
1620 Hawkins Ave
Sanford NC 27330
919 566-8000

(G-6753)
**PENTAIR WATER POOL AND
SPA INC**
Paragon Aquatics
341 Route 55 (12540)
PHONE...................................845 452-5500
Thomas Saldarelli, *President*
EMP: 45
SALES (corp-wide): 17.4B **Publicly Held**
WEB: www.pentairpool.com
SIC: 3589 3561 Swimming pool filter &
water conditioning systems; pumps, do-
mestic: water or sump
HQ: Pentair Water Pool And Spa, Inc.
1620 Hawkins Ave
Sanford NC 27330
919 566-8000

(G-6754)
STYLES AVIATION INC (PA)
Also Called: Sky Geek
30 Airway Dr Ste 2 (12540-5254)
PHONE...................................845 677-8185
Steven T Styles, *CEO*
Virginia R Styles, *Vice Pres*
Sherri Palm, *Treasurer*
▲ EMP: 5

(PA)=Parent Co (HQ)=Headquarters (DH)=Div Headquarters
✪ = New Business established in last 2 years

2020 Harris
New York Manufacturers Directory

261

GEOGRAPHIC

SQ FT: 5,000
SALES (est): 5.9MM **Privately Held**
SIC: 3728 5088 Aircraft parts & equipment; aircraft equipment & supplies

(G-6755)
TYMOR PARK
249 Duncan Rd (12540-5845)
PHONE......................................845 724-5691
Robert Mattes, *Director*
EMP: 5
SALES: 7.9K **Privately Held**
WEB: www.unionvaleny.us
SIC: 2531 Picnic tables or benches, park

Lake George
Warren County

(G-6756)
ADIRONDACK WINERY LLC
285 Canada St (12845-1400)
PHONE......................................518 668-9463
Mike Pardy, *Principal*
EMP: 5
SALES (est): 25.2K **Privately Held**
SIC: 2084 Wines

(G-6757)
LEATHER OUTLET
1656 State Route 9 (12845-3440)
PHONE......................................518 668-0328
Kevin Clint, *Owner*
EMP: 8
SALES (est): 653.7K **Privately Held**
SIC: 3199 Leather goods

(G-6758)
PERFORMANCE CUSTOM TRAILER
230 Lockhart Mountain Rd (12845-4904)
P.O. Box 106, Hadley (12835-0106)
PHONE......................................518 504-4021
William Bunting, *President*
Diane Bunting, *Treasurer*
EMP: 7
SQ FT: 3,000
SALES (est): 1.2MM **Privately Held**
SIC: 3799 Boat trailers

Lake Grove
Suffolk County

(G-6759)
LUCKY LOUS INC
24 State St (11755-1714)
PHONE......................................631 672-1932
Lou T Camassa, *President*
Maria Camassa, *Treasurer*
EMP: 7 EST: 2014
SALES: 80K **Privately Held**
SIC: 2099 Dessert mixes & fillings

(G-6760)
SPEEDWAY LLC
2825 Middle Country Rd (11755-2105)
PHONE......................................631 738-2536
Jaswante Kor, *Branch Mgr*
EMP: 15 **Publicly Held**
SIC: 1311 Crude petroleum production
HQ: Speedway Llc
500 Speedway Dr
Enon OH 45323
937 864-3000

(G-6761)
SUNDOWN SKI & SPORT SHOP INC (PA)
3060 Middle Country Rd (11755-2106)
PHONE......................................631 737-8600
Winfred Breuer, *President*
Michael Rahatigan, *Vice Pres*
Michael Rhatigan, *Vice Pres*
▲ **EMP:** 55
SQ FT: 13,000
SALES (est): 8MM **Privately Held**
SIC: 2511 5091 Wood lawn & garden furniture; skiing equipment

(G-6762)
VANS INC
313 Smith Haven Mall (11755-1201)
PHONE......................................631 724-1011
Sean Dunne, *Branch Mgr*
EMP: 10
SALES (corp-wide): 13.8MM **Publicly Held**
SIC: 3021 5699 Canvas shoes, rubber soled; uniforms & work clothing
HQ: Vans, Inc.
1588 S Coast Dr
Costa Mesa CA 92626
855 909-8267

Lake Katrine
Ulster County

(G-6763)
COBRA MANUFACTURING CORP
68 Leggs Mills Rd (12449-5145)
P.O. Box 209, Bloomington (12411-0209)
PHONE......................................845 514-2505
Michael V Pavlov, *President*
Hillarie Pavlov, *Treasurer*
▲ **EMP:** 9 EST: 2000
SALES (est): 1.2MM **Privately Held**
SIC: 3315 Barbed & twisted wire

(G-6764)
WCD WINDOW COVERINGS INC
1711 Ulster Ave (12449-5426)
P.O. Box 723 (12449-0723)
PHONE......................................845 336-4511
Drew Wonderly, *President*
EMP: 50
SQ FT: 14,000
SALES: 1.3MM **Privately Held**
WEB: www.wcd-drapery.com
SIC: 2391 5021 2591 Draperies, plastic & textile; from purchased materials; beds & bedding; drapery hardware & blinds & shades

Lake Luzerne
Warren County

(G-6765)
KETCHUM MANUFACTURING CO INC
11 Town Shed Rd (12846)
P.O. Box 10 (12846-0010)
PHONE......................................518 696-3331
Gary Powers, *President*
Lisa Podwirny, *Vice Pres*
Helen A Powers, *Admin Sec*
EMP: 13 EST: 1964
SQ FT: 8,000
SALES: 1.2MM **Privately Held**
WEB: www.ketchummfg.com
SIC: 3999 Identification tags, except paper

Lake Placid
Essex County

(G-6766)
COMSEC VENTURES INTERNATIONAL
17 Tamarack Ave (12946-1607)
PHONE......................................518 523-1600
William H Borland, *President*
Tina Preston, *Manager*
EMP: 6
SQ FT: 1,700
SALES (est): 458.2K **Privately Held**
SIC: 3699 4822 4215 7929 Security control equipment & systems; telegraph & other communications; courier services, except by air; entertainers & entertainment groups

(G-6767)
LAKE PLACID ADVERTISERS WKSHP
Also Called: Sir Speedy
Cold Brook Plz (12946)
P.O. Box 631 (12946-0631)
PHONE......................................518 523-3359
Tom Connors, *President*
Adele Pierce, *Vice Pres*
EMP: 20
SQ FT: 2,000
SALES: 4.5MM **Privately Held**
SIC: 2752 2759 2791 Commercial printing, lithographic; commercial printing; typesetting

(G-6768)
SUGAR SHACK DESERT COMPANY INC
2567 Main St (12946-3305)
PHONE......................................518 523-7540
Gina D Cimaglia, *CEO*
EMP: 6
SALES (est): 290K **Privately Held**
SIC: 2099 Sugar

Lake Pleasant
Hamilton County

(G-6769)
WILT INDUSTRIES INC
2452 State Route 8 (12108)
P.O. Box 679 (12108-0679)
PHONE......................................518 548-4961
Daniel Wilt, *President*
Richard Wilt, *Vice Pres*
EMP: 6 EST: 1949
SQ FT: 10,000
SALES (est): 1.1MM **Privately Held**
WEB: www.wiltindustries.com
SIC: 3559 Glass making machinery: blowing, molding, forming, etc.

Lake Ronkonkoma
Suffolk County

(G-6770)
HONEYWELL INTERNATIONAL INC
1859 Lakeland Ave (11779-7420)
PHONE......................................631 471-2202
Gail Cino, *Manager*
EMP: 5
SALES (corp-wide): 41.8B **Publicly Held**
WEB: www.adilink.com
SIC: 3724 Aircraft engines & engine parts
PA: Honeywell International Inc.
300 S Tryon St
Charlotte NC 28202
973 455-2000

(G-6771)
J F B & SONS LITHOGRAPHERS
1700 Ocean Ave (11779-6570)
PHONE......................................631 467-1444
Joseph Brown, *President*
Randall Brown, *Corp Secy*
Gary Brown, *Vice Pres*
Dennis Ganzak, *CFO*
EMP: 75
SQ FT: 43,000
SALES (est): 3.9MM
SALES (corp-wide): 301.1MM **Privately Held**
SIC: 2752 Commercial printing, lithographic
HQ: Earth Color New York, Inc.
249 Pomeroy Rd
Parsippany NJ 07054
973 884-1300

Lake View
Erie County

(G-6772)
EFFECTIVE SLLING SOLUTIONS LLC
1898 Hanley Dr (14085-9704)
PHONE......................................716 771-8503
Ben Kaukus, *Mng Member*
EMP: 5
SALES: 94K **Privately Held**
SIC: 2759 Screen printing

Lakeville
Livingston County

(G-6773)
ARCHER-DANIELS-MIDLAND COMPANY
Also Called: ADM
3401 Rochester Rd (14480-9762)
PHONE......................................585 346-2311
Lee Robinson, *Branch Mgr*
EMP: 7
SALES (corp-wide): 64.3B **Publicly Held**
WEB: www.admworld.com
SIC: 2041 Flour & other grain mill products
PA: Archer-Daniels-Midland Company
77 W Wacker Dr Ste 4600
Chicago IL 60601
312 634-8100

(G-6774)
CONESUS LAKE ASSOCIATION INC
5828 Big Tree Rd (14480)
P.O. Box 637 (14480-0637)
PHONE......................................585 346-6864
Greg Foust, *Ch of Bd*
George Coolbaugh, *President*
Burt Lyon, *Treasurer*
EMP: 30
SALES: 122.3K **Privately Held**
SIC: 3599 2511 Machine & other job shop work; wood household furniture

(G-6775)
S & R TOOL INC
6066 Stone Hill Rd (14480-9712)
PHONE......................................585 346-2029
Samuel Dandrea, *President*
Richard Panipinto, *Vice Pres*
EMP: 6
SQ FT: 10,428
SALES (est): 1MM **Privately Held**
SIC: 3599 Machine shop, jobbing & repair

(G-6776)
SWEETENERS PLUS LLC
5768 Sweeteners Blvd (14480-9741)
P.O. Box 520 (14480-0520)
PHONE......................................585 728-3770
Christian Modesti, *CEO*
Mark Rudolph, *QC Mgr*
Pamela Smith, *Controller*
Mark Farrell, *Manager*
▲ **EMP:** 70
SQ FT: 30,000
SALES (est): 38.3MM **Privately Held**
WEB: www.sweetenersplus.com
SIC: 2062 Cane sugar refining

Lakewood
Chautauqua County

(G-6777)
ARCHROCK INC
305 E Fairmount Ave Ste 4 (14750-2000)
PHONE......................................716 763-1553
Mike Czerniak, *Business Mgr*
Mike Czernika, *Manager*
EMP: 15 **Publicly Held**
WEB: www.exterran.com
SIC: 1389 5084 Gas compressing (natural gas) at the fields; compressors, except air conditioning

▲ = Import　▼=Export
◆ =Import/Export

PA: Archrock Inc.
9807 Katy Fwy Ste 100
Houston TX 77024

(G-6778)
ARRO MANUFACTURING LLC
4687 Gleason Rd (14750)
P.O. Box 19 (14750-0019)
PHONE..................................716 763-6203
Scott Bauer, *Mng Member*
Deborah Bauer,
EMP: 18
SALES (est): 765.1K **Privately Held**
SIC: 3544 3469 Punches, forming & stamping; metal stampings

(G-6779)
ARRO TOOL & DIE INC
4687 Gleason Rd (14750)
PHONE..................................716 763-6203
James R Lindell, *President*
Eric Corey, *Vice Pres*
Jeff A Lindell, *Vice Pres*
Richard Morris, *Vice Pres*
▼ **EMP:** 19 **EST:** 1952
SQ FT: 23,000
SALES (est): 2.9MM **Privately Held**
WEB: www.arrotool.com
SIC: 3544 3469 Special dies & tools; metal stampings

(G-6780)
CLASSIC BRASS INC
2051 Stoneman Cir (14750-9779)
P.O. Box 3563, Jamestown (14702-3563)
PHONE..................................716 763-1400
J Christopher Creighton, *President*
▲ **EMP:** 56
SQ FT: 30,050
SALES (est): 9.2MM **Privately Held**
SIC: 3429 Furniture builders' & other household hardware

(G-6781)
CUMMINS INC
4720 Baker St (14750-9772)
PHONE..................................716 456-2111
Maria Jones, *Opers Mgr*
Jonathan Martin, *Engineer*
Kevin Millward, *Engineer*
Dana Bogt, *Branch Mgr*
Rita Jackson, *Technology*
EMP: 800
SQ FT: 1,733
SALES (corp-wide): 23.7B **Publicly Held**
WEB: www.cummins.com
SIC: 3519 Internal combustion engines
PA: Cummins Inc.
500 Jackson St
Columbus IN 47201
812 377-5000

(G-6782)
DLH ENERGY SERVICE LLC
4422 W Fairmount Ave (14750-9705)
P.O. Box 40, Ashville (14710-0040)
PHONE..................................716 410-0028
Charles Dubose,
EMP: 3
SQ FT: 1,000
SALES: 5MM **Privately Held**
SIC: 1389 Oil field services

(G-6783)
QUALITY MANUFACTURING SYS LLC
1995 Stoneman Cir (14750-9776)
PHONE..................................716 763-0988
Patsy Jo Kosinski, *Partner*
EMP: 6
SQ FT: 12,000
SALES (est): 1.1MM **Privately Held**
SIC: 3569 Assembly machines, non-metalworking

(G-6784)
R R DONNELLEY & SONS COMPANY
Also Called: Moore Business Forms
112 Winchester Rd (14750-1739)
P.O. Box 137 (14750-0137)
PHONE..................................716 763-2613
EMP: 12
SALES (corp-wide): 6.9B **Publicly Held**
SIC: 2759 Commercial Printing

PA: R. R. Donnelley & Sons Company
35 W Wacker Dr Ste 3650
Chicago IL 60601
312 326-8000

(G-6785)
R-CO PRODUCTS CORPORATION
1855 Big Tree Rd (14750-9759)
PHONE..................................800 854-7657
Edward Roemer Jr, *President*
Erika Roemer, *Treasurer*
Katy Lord, *Admin Sec*
EMP: 13
SQ FT: 30,000
SALES (est): 2.5MM **Privately Held**
SIC: 2891 Sealants

(G-6786)
ULRICH PLANFILING EQP CORP
2120 4th Ave (14750-9727)
P.O. Box 135 (14750-0135)
PHONE..................................716 763-1815
Daniel Berry, *President*
Jamie Carlson, *Vice Pres*
Reid Van Every, *Plant Mgr*
Barbara Sauer, *Purch Mgr*
Eric Livengood, *Marketing Staff*
▼ **EMP:** 40
SQ FT: 42,400
SALES (est): 7.7MM **Privately Held**
WEB: www.ulrichcorp.com
SIC: 2522 Office cabinets & filing drawers: except wood

(G-6787)
WATER STREET BRASS CORPORATION
4515 Gleason Rd (14750-9748)
P.O. Box 463 (14750-0463)
PHONE..................................716 763-0059
Mathew Churchill, *President*
▲ **EMP:** 22
SALES (est): 2.7MM **Privately Held**
SIC: 3429 Furniture hardware

Lancaster
Erie County

(G-6788)
A & T TOOLING LLC
91 Beach Ave (14086-1658)
PHONE..................................716 601-7299
Maureen Hassenbohler,
EMP: 5
SALES: 250K **Privately Held**
SIC: 3543 Industrial patterns

(G-6789)
ADVANCED ASSEMBLY SERVICES INC
44 Knollwood Dr (14086-4459)
PHONE..................................716 217-8144
Tim Kosmowski, *President*
Ra Kosmowski, *Vice Pres*
EMP: 6 **EST:** 2000
SQ FT: 5,000
SALES (est): 823K **Privately Held**
WEB:
www.advancedassemblyservices.com
SIC: 3999 Barber & beauty shop equipment

(G-6790)
ADVANCED THERMAL SYSTEMS INC
15 Enterprise Dr (14086-9773)
PHONE..................................716 681-1800
Edward W Patnode, *Ch of Bd*
Eugene Miliczky, *President*
EMP: 40
SQ FT: 31,000
SALES (est): 8.5MM **Privately Held**
WEB: www.advancedthermal.net
SIC: 3494 3568 3498 3441 Expansion joints pipe; ball joints, except aircraft & automotive; fabricated pipe & fittings; fabricated structural metal

(G-6791)
AFTER 50 INC
5 W Main St Ste 2 (14086-2174)
PHONE..................................716 832-9300
Bonnie Degweck, *President*
Phyllis Goasiti, *Vice Pres*
EMP: 5
SALES: 500K **Privately Held**
SIC: 2711 Newspapers, publishing & printing

(G-6792)
AIR SYSTEM PRODUCTS INC
Also Called: AFP Industries
51 Beach Ave (14086-1658)
PHONE..................................716 683-0435
Patrick Scanlon, *President*
Henry Bourg, *President*
Mike Zacharko, *Manager*
▲ **EMP:** 12
SQ FT: 17,000
SALES (est): 1.7MM **Privately Held**
WEB: www.airsyspro.com
SIC: 3491 Industrial valves

(G-6793)
ALCO PLASTICS INC
35 Ward Rd (14086-9779)
PHONE..................................716 683-3020
Raymond Mazurczyk, *President*
EMP: 20 **EST:** 1971
SQ FT: 25,000
SALES (est): 3.1MM **Privately Held**
SIC: 2673 Plastic bags: made from purchased materials

(G-6794)
ALDEN OPTICAL LABORATORY INC
6 Lancaster Pkwy (14086-9713)
PHONE..................................716 937-9181
Charles H Creighton, *President*
Helen Creighton, *Treasurer*
EMP: 16
SQ FT: 8,000
SALES: 2.4MM **Privately Held**
WEB: www.aldenoptical.com
SIC: 3851 Ophthalmic goods

(G-6795)
APPLE RUBBER PRODUCTS INC (PA)
Also Called: Express Seal Div
310 Erie St (14086-9504)
PHONE..................................716 684-6560
Steven L Apple, *President*
Carol Malaney, *Vice Pres*
Terry Jacus, *Director*
▲ **EMP:** 130
SQ FT: 11,000
SALES (est): 32.8MM **Privately Held**
WEB: www.applerubber.com
SIC: 3069 Molded rubber products

(G-6796)
APPLE RUBBER PRODUCTS INC
Also Called: Expresseal
204 Cemetery Rd (14086-9798)
PHONE..................................716 684-7649
Steven Apple, *President*
EMP: 110
SQ FT: 49,668
SALES (est): 12.2MM
SALES (corp-wide): 32.8MM **Privately Held**
WEB: www.applerubber.com
SIC: 3069 3061 3053 Hard rubber & molded rubber products; molded rubber products; mechanical rubber goods; gaskets, packing & sealing devices
PA: Apple Rubber Products, Inc.
310 Erie St
Lancaster NY 14086
716 684-6560

(G-6797)
BABULA CONSTRUCTION INC
5136 William St (14086-9447)
PHONE..................................716 681-0886
Stanley Babula, *President*
Janet Babula, *Vice Pres*
EMP: 7

SALES: 300K **Privately Held**
SIC: 1389 Construction, repair & dismantling services

(G-6798)
BIMBO BAKERIES USA INC
2900 Commerce Pkwy (14086-1741)
PHONE..................................716 706-0450
George Weston, *Owner*
EMP: 18 **Privately Held**
WEB: www.gwbakeries.com
SIC: 2051 Bread, cake & related products
HQ: Bimbo Bakeries Usa, Inc
255 Business Center Dr # 200
Horsham PA 19044
215 347-5500

(G-6799)
BUFFALO FILTER LLC
5900 Genesee St (14086-9024)
PHONE..................................716 835-7000
Samantha Bonano, *CEO*
Samantha Palmerton, *Vice Pres*
Greg Pepe, *Vice Pres*
David McKay, *Opers Staff*
Paul Daniels, *Production*
▲ **EMP:** 85
SQ FT: 15,000
SALES (est): 20.8MM
SALES (corp-wide): 859.6MM **Publicly Held**
WEB: www.buffalofilter.com
SIC: 3841 3845 3699 3564 Surgical & medical instruments; laser systems & equipment, medical; electrical equipment & supplies; blowers & fans
PA: Conmed Corporation
525 French Rd
Utica NY 13502
315 797-8375

(G-6800)
CASEY MACHINE CO INC
74 Ward Rd (14086-9779)
PHONE..................................716 651-0150
Thomas Radziwon, *Ch of Bd*
Ronald C Radziwon, *President*
Peter Szulc, *Vice Pres*
Russell Reczek, *QC Mgr*
John Shamrock, *Treasurer*
EMP: 95 **EST:** 1976
SQ FT: 15,000
SALES (est): 18.4MM **Privately Held**
WEB: www.caseymachine.com
SIC: 3599 Machine shop, jobbing & repair

(G-6801)
CLASSIC & PERFORMANCE SPC
Also Called: Classic Tube
80 Rotech Dr (14086-9755)
PHONE..................................716 759-1800
Paul Fix, *President*
Lauren J Fix, *Vice Pres*
EMP: 24
SQ FT: 20,000
SALES (est): 4MM **Privately Held**
WEB: www.classictube.com
SIC: 3714 Exhaust systems & parts, motor vehicle

(G-6802)
DELFT PRINTING INC
1000 Commerce Pkwy (14086-1707)
PHONE..................................716 683-1100
Kamal C Jowdy, *President*
Kamal Jowdy, *CFO*
EMP: 7
SQ FT: 2,200
SALES: 800K **Privately Held**
WEB: www.delftprinting.com
SIC: 2759 Commercial printing

(G-6803)
DIVERSIFIED MANUFACTURING INC
4401 Walden Ave (14086-9013)
PHONE..................................716 681-7670
Walt Kempa, *Branch Mgr*
EMP: 15
SALES (corp-wide): 23.5MM **Privately Held**
WEB: www.dmimfg.com
SIC: 3441 Fabricated structural metal

G E O G R A P H I C

PA: Diversified Manufacturing Inc.
410 Ohio St
Lockport NY 14094
716 434-5585

(G-6804)
EASTERN AIR PRODUCTS LLC
Also Called: Engineered Air Products
41 Ward Rd (14086-9779)
PHONE..................................716 391-1866
Jeffrey Browne, *President*
Peter Baran, *Vice Pres*
Michael Arno, *CFO*
▲ **EMP:** 18 **EST:** 2009
SQ FT: 12,500
SALES: 3.2MM **Privately Held**
SIC: 3563 Air & gas compressors including
vacuum pumps

(G-6805)
**ERIE ENGINEERED PRODUCTS
INC**
3949 Walden Ave (14086-1472)
PHONE..................................716 206-0204
Barry Newman, *Ch of Bd*
Mark Folmsbee, *Vice Pres*
Lorne Weil, *Shareholder*
Sandra Whiteford,
EMP: 47
SQ FT: 88,000
SALES: 3.9MM **Privately Held**
WEB: www.containers-cases.com
SIC: 3443 3441 3412 3411 Containers,
shipping (bombs, etc.): metal plate; fabri-
cated structural metal; metal barrels,
drums & pails; metal cans; plastic con-
tainers, except foam; battery cases, plas-
tic or plastic combination; boxes, plastic;
buckets, plastic

(G-6806)
FBC CHEMICAL CORPORATION
4111 Walden Ave (14086-1599)
PHONE..................................716 681-1581
Laura Augustine, *Sales Staff*
Joe Villafranca, *Manager*
EMP: 5
SQ FT: 4,000
SALES (corp-wide): 54MM **Privately
Held**
WEB: www.fbcchem.com
SIC: 2842 5169 Cleaning or polishing
preparations; chemicals & allied products
PA: Fbc Chemical Corporation
634 Route 228
Mars PA 16046
724 625-3116

(G-6807)
FLOWNET LLC
580 Lake Ave (14086-9627)
PHONE..................................716 685-4036
EMP: 6
SALES (est): 288K **Privately Held**
SIC: 1311 Natural gas production

(G-6808)
GOOD EARTH INC
5960 Broadway St (14086-9531)
PHONE..................................716 684-8111
Gunter Burkhardt, *President*
Cornelia Orffeo, *Vice Pres*
EMP: 6
SALES (est): 824.5K **Privately Held**
WEB: www.goodearth.net
SIC: 2833 Organic medicinal chemicals:
bulk, uncompounded

(G-6809)
**GOOD EARTH ORGANICS CORP
(PA)**
5960 Broadway St (14086-9531)
P.O. Box 290 (14086-0290)
PHONE..................................716 684-8111
Guenter H Burkhardt, *Ch of Bd*
Andreas G Burkhardt, *Vice Pres*
Bernhard G Burkhardt, *Vice Pres*
Eva Burkhardt, *Vice Pres*
Cornelia Orffeo, *Purchasing*
▲ **EMP:** 20
SQ FT: 180,000
SALES: 17MM **Privately Held**
WEB: www.goodearth.org
SIC: 3523 Planting machines, agricultural

(G-6810)
HC BRILL CO INC
3765 Walden Ave (14086-1405)
PHONE..................................716 685-4000
Bob Craiglow, *Vice Pres*
EMP: 8
SALES (est): 1.2MM **Privately Held**
SIC: 2033 Canned fruits & specialties

(G-6811)
ILLINOIS TOOL WORKS INC
United Silicone Div
4471 Walden Ave (14086-9754)
PHONE..................................716 681-8222
Joseph Wukovits, *Branch Mgr*
EMP: 155
SALES (corp-wide): 14.7B **Publicly Held**
SIC: 3559 Plastics working machinery
PA: Illinois Tool Works Inc.
155 Harlem Ave
Glenview IL 60025
847 724-7500

(G-6812)
KZ PRECISION INC
Also Called: K Z Precision
1 Mason Pl (14086-1615)
PHONE..................................716 683-3202
Kenneth Zwara, *President*
EMP: 15
SQ FT: 7,500
SALES (est): 931.7K **Privately Held**
WEB: www.kzprecision.com
SIC: 3599 Machine shop, jobbing & repair

(G-6813)
LAFARGE NORTH AMERICA INC
6125 Genesee St (14086-9722)
PHONE..................................716 651-9235
Ron Morgan, *Manager*
EMP: 25
SALES (corp-wide): 27.6B **Privately Held**
WEB: www.lafargenorthamerica.com
SIC: 3241 1442 Cement, hydraulic; con-
struction sand & gravel
HQ: Lafarge North America Inc.
8700 W Bryn Mawr Ave
Chicago IL 60631
773 372-1000

(G-6814)
LANCASTER KNIVES INC (PA)
165 Court St (14086-2399)
PHONE..................................716 683-5050
Scott C Cant, *President*
Allen A Turton, *Engineer*
Rick Sinnott, *Supervisor*
▲ **EMP:** 48 **EST:** 1896
SQ FT: 46,000
SALES (est): 8.6MM **Privately Held**
WEB: www.lancasterknives.com
SIC: 3423 3545 3469 3541 Knives, agri-
cultural or industrial; shear knives; ma-
chine parts, stamped or pressed metal;
machine tools, metal cutting type

(G-6815)
LANCE VALVES
15 Enterprise Dr (14086-9749)
PHONE..................................716 681-5825
Eugene Miliczky, *Vice Pres*
Geoffrey Schrott, *Manager*
EMP: 8 **EST:** 1974
SQ FT: 6,000
SALES (est): 966.3K **Privately Held**
WEB: www.lancevalves.com
SIC: 3494 Valves & pipe fittings

(G-6816)
**MANHASSET TOOL & DIE CO
INC**
4270 Walden Ave (14086-9770)
PHONE..................................716 684-6066
Mark Fenimore, *President*
EMP: 10 **EST:** 1955
SALES (est): 1MM **Privately Held**
WEB: www.manhassettool.com
SIC: 3544 3542 Jigs & fixtures; jigs: in-
spection, gauging & checking; die sets for
metal stamping (presses); dies & die
holders for metal cutting, forming, die
casting; punching & shearing machines;
bending machines

(G-6817)
**MARKAR ARCHITECTURAL
PRODUCTS**
Also Called: Adams Ridge
68 Ward Rd (14086-9779)
PHONE..................................716 685-4104
Fax: 716 685-3919
EMP: 8 **Privately Held**
SIC: 3442 Mfg Metal Doors/Sash/Trim

(G-6818)
MOLDTECH INC
1900 Commerce Pkwy (14086-1735)
PHONE..................................716 685-3344
H Wayne Gerhart, *Ch of Bd*
Rob Paladichuk, *Vice Pres*
James H Wittman, *CFO*
James Wittman, *CFO*
▲ **EMP:** 45
SQ FT: 35,000
SALES (est): 15.7MM **Privately Held**
SIC: 3069 3061 Molded rubber products;
mechanical rubber goods

(G-6819)
**ORFFEO PRINTING & IMAGING
INC**
99 Cambria St (14086-1952)
P.O. Box 426 (14086-0426)
PHONE..................................716 681-5757
Gregory Orffeo, *Ch of Bd*
EMP: 5
SQ FT: 27,000
SALES (est): 2.7MM **Privately Held**
SIC: 2752 7331 Commercial printing, off-
set; direct mail advertising services

(G-6820)
**PALMA TOOL & DIE COMPANY
INC**
40 Ward Rd (14086-9779)
PHONE..................................716 681-4464
William D Tate Sr, *President*
Jeff Parks, *General Mgr*
Thomas Owczarak, *Vice Pres*
Stanley Blaszak, *Admin Sec*
EMP: 42
SQ FT: 23,000
SALES (est): 7.5MM **Privately Held**
WEB: www.palmatool.com
SIC: 3544 Special dies & tools

(G-6821)
**PARKER-HANNIFIN
CORPORATION**
4087 Walden Ave (14086-1512)
PHONE..................................716 686-6400
Alicia Carrasco, *Engineer*
Mark Harvey, *Electrical Engi*
Craig Dillworth, *Manager*
William Allhusen, *Sr Software Eng*
EMP: 126
SALES (corp-wide): 14.3B **Publicly Held**
SIC: 3594 Fluid power pumps
PA: Parker-Hannifin Corporation
6035 Parkland Blvd
Cleveland OH 44124
216 896-3000

(G-6822)
**PARKER-HANNIFIN
CORPORATION**
Finite Airtek Filtration
4087 Walden Ave (14086-1512)
PHONE..................................716 685-4040
Dale Zimmerman, *Regional Mgr*
Randy Peccia, *Engineer*
Rick Woodring, *Branch Mgr*
EMP: 82
SALES (corp-wide): 14.3B **Publicly Held**
WEB: www.parker.com
SIC: 3569 3714 3564 Filters; motor vehi-
cle parts & accessories; blowers & fans
PA: Parker-Hannifin Corporation
6035 Parkland Blvd
Cleveland OH 44124
216 896-3000

(G-6823)
**PARKER-HANNIFIN
CORPORATION**
Purification, Dehydration
4087 Walden Ave (14086-1512)
PHONE..................................716 685-4040

Jon Hilberg, *Branch Mgr*
EMP: 85
SALES (corp-wide): 14.3B **Publicly Held**
WEB: www.parker.com
SIC: 3585 3567 Refrigeration & heating
equipment; industrial furnaces & ovens
PA: Parker-Hannifin Corporation
6035 Parkland Blvd
Cleveland OH 44124
216 896-3000

(G-6824)
**PERFORMANCE ADVANTAGE
CO INC**
6 W Main St Lowr Rear (14086-2110)
P.O. Box 306 (14086-0306)
PHONE..................................716 683-7413
Richard Young, *President*
James Everett, *General Mgr*
Barb Kozurkiewicz, *Accounting Mgr*
Michael McGuire, *Sales Staff*
EMP: 15
SQ FT: 13,000
SALES (est): 2.2MM **Privately Held**
WEB: www.pactoolmounts.com
SIC: 3089 Plastic hardware & building
products

(G-6825)
PFANNENBERG INC
68 Ward Rd (14086-9779)
PHONE..................................716 685-6866
Andreas Pfannenberg, *President*
Laura Chasalow, *Vice Pres*
Ken Surdej, *Prdtn Mgr*
Brian Glynn, *Buyer*
Paul Smith, *Research*
◆ **EMP:** 52
SQ FT: 65,000
SALES (est): 15.5MM
SALES (corp-wide): 1.7MM **Privately
Held**
WEB: www.pfannenbergusa.com
SIC: 3585 Air conditioning units, complete:
domestic or industrial
PA: Pfannenberg Group Holding Gmbh
Werner-Witt-Str. 1
Hamburg 21035
407 341-20

(G-6826)
**PFANNENBERG
MANUFACTURING LLC**
68 Ward Rd (14086-9779)
PHONE..................................716 685-6866
William Baron, *President*
Laura Chasalow, *Vice Pres*
Jennifer Bialasik, *Vice Pres*
Earl Rogalski, *Vice Pres*
EMP: 60
SQ FT: 57,000
SALES (est): 2.1MM **Privately Held**
SIC: 3585 Refrigeration & heating equip-
ment

(G-6827)
PRZ TECHNOLOGIES INC
5490 Broadway St (14086-2220)
P.O. Box 369 (14086-0369)
PHONE..................................716 683-1300
Walt Przybyl, *President*
Mike Gergich, *Purch Mgr*
Aaron Lajoie, *Engineer*
Karan Andrea, *Accountant*
EMP: 15
SALES (est): 2.8MM **Privately Held**
SIC: 3545 Machine tool attachments & ac-
cessories

(G-6828)
RAM PRECISION TOOL INC
139 Gunnville Rd (14086-9017)
PHONE..................................716 759-8722
Joseph Walter, *President*
Barbara M Walter, *Vice Pres*
EMP: 6
SQ FT: 6,000
SALES (est): 836K **Privately Held**
WEB: www.ramprecisiontool.com
SIC: 3599 Machine shop, jobbing & repair

▲ = Import ▼=Export
◆ =Import/Export

(G-6829)
RICHARDS MACHINE TOOL CO INC
36 Nichter Rd (14086-9708)
PHONE..................................716 683-3380
EMP: 23
SQ FT: 18,000
SALES (est): 2.5MM **Privately Held**
SIC: 3599 Machine shop, jobbing & repair

(G-6830)
RMF PRINTING TECHNOLOGIES INC
Also Called: Ogilvie Press
50 Pearl St (14086-1922)
PHONE..................................716 683-7500
Monica Castano, Ch of Bd
Juan Carlos Yanez, CFO
▲ EMP: 50
SQ FT: 140,000
SALES (est): 19.3MM **Privately Held**
WEB: www.rmfprinttechnology.com
SIC: 2752 Commercial printing, lithographic

(G-6831)
ROLITE MFG INC
10 Wendling Ct (14086-9766)
PHONE..................................716 683-0259
Ron Roberts, President
Ronald Roberts, President
Thomas Debbins, Vice Pres
Nick Debbins, Project Mgr
Mike Bailey, Sales Staff
▲ EMP: 25
SQ FT: 65,000
SALES (est): 7MM **Privately Held**
WEB: www.rolitemfg.com
SIC: 3469 3449 Stamping metal for the trade; custom roll formed products

(G-6832)
S3J ELECTRONICS LLC
2000 Commerce Pkwy (14086-1733)
PHONE..................................716 206-1309
EMP: 20
SALES (est): 4.2MM **Privately Held**
SIC: 3674 Mfg Semiconductors/Related Devices

(G-6833)
SECURE INTERNATIONAL
100 W Drullard Ave Ste 3 (14086-1670)
PHONE..................................716 206-2500
Robert Eising, President
◆ EMP: 8
SALES (est): 688.7K **Privately Held**
SIC: 2051 Bakery: wholesale or wholesale/retail combined

(G-6834)
SEIBEL MODERN MFG & WLDG CORP
38 Palmer Pl (14086-2144)
PHONE..................................716 683-1536
Leon A Seibel, Ch of Bd
Mark Seibel, Vice Pres
Lynne M Sobkowiak, Manager
▲ EMP: 85 EST: 1945
SQ FT: 70,000
SALES (est): 20.9MM **Privately Held**
WEB: www.seibelmodern.com
SIC: 3441 3443 Fabricated structural metal; fabricated plate work (boiler shop)

(G-6835)
SILICONE PRODUCTS & TECHNOLOGY
4471 Walden Ave (14086-9754)
PHONE..................................716 684-1155
Kim Jackson, President
EMP: 150
SALES (est): 11.1MM **Privately Held**
SIC: 2822 3544 Silicone rubbers; special dies, tools, jigs & fixtures

(G-6836)
STUTZMAN MANAGEMENT CORP
11 Saint Joseph St (14086-1800)
PHONE..................................800 735-2013
Gerard Sheldon, President
EMP: 15
SQ FT: 32,000

SALES (est): 2.3MM **Privately Held**
SIC: 3443 Fuel tanks (oil, gas, etc.): metal plate

(G-6837)
UNITED SILICONE INC
4471 Walden Ave (14086-9778)
PHONE..................................716 681-8222
Donato Curcio, President
Robert Le Posa, Vice Pres
Don Fink, Opers Mgr
Joe Fisher, Opers Mgr
David Loos, Purch Agent
◆ EMP: 81
SQ FT: 80,000
SALES (est): 14MM **Privately Held**
SIC: 3953 Pads, inking & stamping

(G-6838)
W N R PATTERN & TOOL INC
21 Pavement Rd (14086-9595)
PHONE..................................716 681-9334
Gary Machniak, President
Jeffrey Tucker, Vice Pres
EMP: 6
SQ FT: 6,000
SALES (est): 360K **Privately Held**
SIC: 3544 3543 Industrial molds; forms (molds), for foundry & plastics working machinery; industrial patterns

(G-6839)
WEB-TECH PACKAGING INC
500 Commerce Pkwy (14086-1793)
PHONE..................................716 684-4520
David C Rost, President
William Rost, Shareholder
Kathleen Visciano, Shareholder
EMP: 16
SQ FT: 10,000
SALES (est): 3.3MM **Privately Held**
SIC: 2679 Labels, paper: made from purchased material

Lansing
Tompkins County

(G-6840)
CAYUGA CRUSHED STONE INC
87 Portland Point Rd (14882)
P.O. Box 41 (14882-0041)
PHONE..................................607 533-4273
Thomas Besemer, President
Matthew Besemer, Vice Pres
EMP: 20
SQ FT: 1,200
SALES (est): 3.3MM **Privately Held**
SIC: 1422 Crushed & broken limestone

(G-6841)
METAL IMPROVEMENT COMPANY LLC
Also Called: IMR Test Labs
131 Woodsedge Dr (14882-8940)
PHONE..................................607 533-7000
Peter Damian, Branch Mgr
EMP: 69
SALES (corp-wide): 2.4B **Publicly Held**
SIC: 3398 Shot peening (treating steel to reduce fatigue)
HQ: Metal Improvement Company, Llc
80 E Rte 4 Ste 310
Paramus NJ 07652
201 843-7800

Larchmont
Westchester County

(G-6842)
MAGIC REED
723 Larchmont Acres Apt D (10538-7363)
PHONE..................................914 630-4006
Kathy Sheinhouse, Principal
EMP: 11
SALES (est): 1.4MM **Privately Held**
SIC: 3931 Musical instruments

(G-6843)
SOGGY DOGGY PRODUCTIONS LLC
50 Chestnut Ave (10538-3534)
PHONE..................................877 504-4811
Joanna Rein, Mng Member
▲ EMP: 4
SALES (est): 2MM **Privately Held**
SIC: 3999 Pet supplies

(G-6844)
WAX JAMS LLC
66 E Brookside Dr (10538-1735)
PHONE..................................914 834-7886
Daniel Demasi, Principal
EMP: 14
SALES (est): 1.7MM **Privately Held**
SIC: 2033 Jams, jellies & preserves: packaged in cans, jars, etc.

(G-6845)
ZWUITS INC
2005 Palmer Ave (10538-2437)
PHONE..................................929 387-2323
Habib Ferdous, Principal
EMP: 10
SALES (est): 396.1K **Privately Held**
SIC: 2386 Leather & sheep-lined garments

Latham
Albany County

(G-6846)
AB ENGINE
4a Northway Ln (12110-4809)
PHONE..................................518 557-3510
Alexander Bakharev, Principal
EMP: 8
SALES (est): 370K **Privately Held**
SIC: 3519 Internal combustion engines

(G-6847)
ACCUMETRICS ASSOCIATES INC
6 British American Blvd # 100
(12110-1467)
PHONE..................................518 393-2200
John M Reschovsky, President
Todd Haver, Engineer
Sandra Reschovsky, Director
EMP: 17
SQ FT: 5,000
SALES (est): 2.9MM **Privately Held**
WEB: www.accumetrix.com
SIC: 3674 Semiconductors & related devices

(G-6848)
ANGIODYNAMICS INC (PA)
14 Plaza Dr (12110-2166)
PHONE..................................518 795-1400
James C Clemmer, President
Brent J Boucher, Senior VP
Chad T Campbell, Senior VP
Heather J Daniels-Cariveau, Senior VP
Benjamin H Davis, Senior VP
EMP: 277
SQ FT: 55,000
SALES: 270.6MM **Publicly Held**
WEB: www.angiodynamics.com
SIC: 3841 Surgical & medical instruments

(G-6849)
BRITISH AMERICAN PUBLISHING
19 British American Blvd (12110-6405)
PHONE..................................518 786-6000
Bernard F Conners, Chairman
Francis Coughlin, Treasurer
John T De Graff, Admin Sec
EMP: 60
SALES: 17MM **Privately Held**
WEB: www.bapublish.com
SIC: 2731 Books: publishing only

(G-6850)
BULLOCK BOYS LLC
400 Old Loudon Rd (12110-2908)
PHONE..................................518 783-6161
James Morrell, CEO
EMP: 15
SQ FT: 25,500

SALES (est): 858.3K **Privately Held**
SIC: 2599 Bar, restaurant & cafeteria furniture

(G-6851)
CALLANAN INDUSTRIES INC
Also Called: Clemente Latham Concrete
9 Fonda Rd (12110)
PHONE..................................518 785-5666
Mark Clemente, Manager
EMP: 8
SALES (corp-wide): 30.6B **Privately Held**
WEB: www.callanan.com
SIC: 3272 Concrete products, precast
HQ: Callanan Industries, Inc.
8 Southwoods Blvd Ste 4
Albany NY 12211
518 374-2222

(G-6852)
CARR MANUFACTURING JEWELERS
Also Called: Carr Jewelers
22 West Ln (12110-5320)
PHONE..................................518 783-6093
W James Dix, President
James E Dix, Vice Pres
Gloria Dix, Treasurer
EMP: 5
SALES (est): 347.1K **Privately Held**
SIC: 3911 7631 5944 Jewelry, precious metal; jewelry repair services; jewelry stores

(G-6853)
D & W DIESEL INC
51 Sicker Rd Ste 3 (12110-1505)
PHONE..................................518 437-1300
Jeffrey Hartgraves, Manager
EMP: 12
SALES (corp-wide): 98.5MM **Privately Held**
WEB: www.dwdiesel.com
SIC: 3519 Diesel engine rebuilding
PA: D & W Diesel, Inc.
1503 Clark Street Rd
Auburn NY 13021
315 253-5300

(G-6854)
DAVIS VISION INC (HQ)
Also Called: Versant Health
711 Troy Schenectady Rd # 301
(12110-2488)
PHONE..................................800 328-4728
Kirk Rothrock, CEO
Danny Bentley, President
Lora Shumate, President
Tonya Boldezar, Export Mgr
Brian Silverberg, CFO
▲ EMP: 3
SQ FT: 20,000
SALES: 186.3MM
SALES (corp-wide): 1.6B **Privately Held**
WEB: www.davisvision.com
SIC: 3851 Eyeglasses, lenses & frames; frames & parts, eyeglass & spectacle
PA: Centerbridge Partners, L.P.
375 Park Ave Fl 13
New York NY 10152
212 672-5000

(G-6855)
EAZYLIFT ALBANY LLC
836 Troy Schenectady Rd (12110-2424)
P.O. Box 340 (12110-0340)
PHONE..................................518 452-6929
Theresa Farrigan,
▲ EMP: 5
SALES: 950K **Privately Held**
SIC: 3534 Elevators & moving stairways

(G-6856)
EMERGENT POWER INC (HQ)
968 Albany Shaker Rd (12110-1401)
PHONE..................................201 441-3590
Andrew Marsh, President
EMP: 5
SALES (est): 17.8MM
SALES (corp-wide): 174.6MM **Publicly Held**
SIC: 2679 Fuel cell forms, cardboard: made from purchased material

GEOGRAPHIC

PA: Plug Power Inc.
968 Albany Shaker Rd
Latham NY 12110
518 782-7700

(G-6857)
G AND G SERVICE
21 Nelson Ave (12110-1805)
PHONE..................................518 785-9247
Greg Gilbert,
EMP: 5
SALES (est): 305.8K **Privately Held**
SIC: 3089 Plastics products

(G-6858)
HEAROS LLC
968 Albany Shaker Rd (12110-1401)
PHONE..................................844 432-7327
Joe Milot,
EMP: 5
SALES: 2MM **Privately Held**
SIC: 3842 Ear plugs

(G-6859)
HOWMEDICA OSTEONICS CORP
2 Northway Ln (12110-4820)
PHONE..................................518 783-1880
Steve Bulger, *Branch Mgr*
EMP: 9
SALES (corp-wide): 13.6B **Publicly Held**
SIC: 3842 Surgical appliances & supplies
HQ: Howmedica Osteonics Corp.
325 Corporate Dr
Mahwah NJ 07430
201 831-5000

(G-6860)
IMPERIAL POOLS INC (PA)
33 Wade Rd (12110-2613)
PHONE..................................518 786-1200
William Churchman, *CEO*
John V Maiuccoro, *President*
Katie Maiuccoro, *Principal*
Robert Burke, *Vice Pres*
Gary Maiuccoro, *Vice Pres*
◆ **EMP:** 123 **EST:** 1966
SQ FT: 100,000
SALES (est): 70.3MM **Privately Held**
WEB: www.imperialpools.com
SIC: 3949 5091 Swimming pools, except
plastic; swimming pools, equipment &
supplies

(G-6861)
KAFKO (US) CORP
787 Watervliet Shaker Rd (12110-2211)
PHONE..................................877 721-7665
Mark Laven, *President*
EMP: 5
SALES (est): 403K
SALES (corp-wide): 177.3MM **Privately
Held**
SIC: 3999 Manufacturing industries
PA: Latham International, Inc.
787 Watervliet Shaker Rd
Latham NY 12110
518 783-7776

(G-6862)
KJCKD INC (PA)
Also Called: Camelot Print & Copy Centers
630 Columbia St Ext Ste 2 (12110-3063)
PHONE..................................518 435-9696
John Derboghossian, *CEO*
Cristene Derboghossian, *COO*
EMP: 3 **EST:** 2015
SQ FT: 20,000
SALES (est): 1.2MM **Privately Held**
SIC: 2752 7334 7374 7336 Photo-offset
printing; photocopying & duplicating serv-
ices; optical scanning data service; com-
mercial art & graphic design; posters:
publishing & printing

(G-6863)
**KOVATCH MOBILE EQUIPMENT
CORP**
Walter Truck Division
68 Sicker Rd (12110-1560)
PHONE..................................518 785-0900
John Kovatch, *President*
EMP: 12
SQ FT: 31,000 **Publicly Held**
SIC: 3711 Fire department vehicles (motor
vehicles), assembly of; snow plows
(motor vehicles), assembly of

HQ: Kovatch Mobile Equipment Corp.
1 Industrial Complex
Nesquehoning PA 18240
570 669-9461

(G-6864)
**LA TORRE ORTHOPEDIC
LABORATORY (PA)**
960 Troy Schenectady Rd (12110-1609)
PHONE..................................518 786-8655
Timothy Lacy, *Owner*
EMP: 18
SALES (est): 2.3MM **Privately Held**
SIC: 3842 Orthopedic appliances

(G-6865)
**LATHAM INTERNATIONAL INC
(PA)**
787 Watervliet Shaker Rd (12110-2211)
PHONE..................................518 783-7776
Mark Laven, *President*
Ron Crowley, *VP Opers*
Allan Boaz, *Opers Staff*
Cary Oden, *Purchasing*
Frederick Wunning, *Controller*
◆ **EMP:** 1 **EST:** 2004
SQ FT: 90,000
SALES (est): 177.3MM **Privately Held**
WEB: www.pacificpools.com
SIC: 3086 3081 Plastics foam products;
vinyl film & sheet

(G-6866)
**LATHAM INTERNATIONAL MFG
CORP**
Also Called: Latham Pool Products
787 Watervliet Shaker Rd (12110-2211)
PHONE..................................800 833-3800
Scott Rajeski, *CEO*
EMP: 500
SALES (est): 127.2K **Privately Held**
SIC: 3949 Swimming pools, except plastic
HQ: Pamplona Capital Management Llc
375 Park Ave Fl 17
New York NY 10152
212 207-6820

(G-6867)
**LATHAM POOL PRODUCTS INC
(DH)**
787 Watervliet Shaker Rd (12110-2211)
P.O. Box 550, Jane Lew WV (26378-0550)
PHONE..................................518 951-1000
Scott Rajeski, *CEO*
John McGough, *Vice Pres*
Piontkowski Richard, *Vice Pres*
David Holihan, *Prdtn Mgr*
Kristi Carder, *Purch Mgr*
▼ **EMP:** 252
SQ FT: 25,000
SALES (est): 139.8MM **Privately Held**
SIC: 3949 Swimming pools, except plastic
HQ: Pamplona Capital Management Llc
375 Park Ave Fl 17
New York NY 10152
212 207-6820

(G-6868)
LATHAM POOL PRODUCTS INC
Also Called: Latham Manufacturing
787 Watervliet Shaker Rd (12110-2211)
PHONE..................................260 432-8731
Bill Reynolds, *Vice Pres*
Krysti Rivenburg, *Purch Agent*
Kristen Hladik, *Buyer*
Matt Geyman, *Branch Mgr*
Narvela Cook, *Manager*
EMP: 44 **Privately Held**
SIC: 3086 Plastics foam products
HQ: Latham Pool Products, Inc.
787 Watervliet Shaker Rd
Latham NY 12110

(G-6869)
**LATORRE ORTHOPEDIC
LABORATORY**
960 Troy Schenectady Rd (12110-1609)
PHONE..................................518 786-8655
Timothy Lacy, *President*
EMP: 15
SALES (est): 930K **Privately Held**
SIC: 3842 Orthopedic appliances; pros-
thetic appliances

(G-6870)
**MARKTECH INTERNATIONAL
CORP (PA)**
Also Called: Marktech Optoelectronics
3 Northway Ln N Ste 1 (12110-2232)
PHONE..................................518 956-2980
Mark G Campito, *Ch of Bd*
Clive A Sofe, *President*
Joseph Andrascik, *Vice Pres*
▲ **EMP:** 25
SALES (est): 3.1MM **Privately Held**
WEB: www.marktechopto.com
SIC: 3674 Semiconductors & related de-
vices

(G-6871)
PEPSI BEVERAGES CO
Also Called: Pepsico
421 Old Niskayuna Rd (12110-1566)
PHONE..................................518 782-2150
Denise Kanganis, *Human Resources*
EMP: 6 **EST:** 2010
SALES (est): 670.2K **Privately Held**
SIC: 2086 Carbonated soft drinks, bottled
& canned

(G-6872)
**PHILIPS MEDICAL SYSTEMS MR
(DH)**
Also Called: Philips Healthcare
450 Old Niskayuna Rd (12110-1569)
PHONE..................................518 782-1122
Stephen H Rusckowski, *CEO*
Leo Blecher, *President*
Richard Stevens, *President*
Thomas J O'Brien, *Exec VP*
John Hartsock, *Engineer*
◆ **EMP:** 400
SQ FT: 146,000
SALES (est): 206MM
SALES (corp-wide): 20.8B **Privately Held**
SIC: 3674 3679 3845 Integrated circuits,
semiconductor networks, etc.; cryogenic
cooling devices for infrared detectors,
masers; cores, magnetic; magnetic reso-
nance imaging device, nuclear

(G-6873)
PIP INC
Also Called: PIP Printing
968 Albany Shaker Rd (12110-1401)
PHONE..................................518 861-0133
Allan Piper, *Ch of Bd*
EMP: 6 **EST:** 1994
SALES (est): 756.4K **Privately Held**
SIC: 2752 Commercial printing, offset

(G-6874)
PLUG POWER INC (PA)
968 Albany Shaker Rd (12110-1428)
PHONE..................................518 782-7700
George C McNamee, *Ch of Bd*
Andrew J Marsh, *President*
Keith C Schmid, *COO*
Gerard L Conway Jr, *Senior VP*
Jose Luis Crespo, *Vice Pres*
▲ **EMP:** 277 **EST:** 1997
SQ FT: 140,000
SALES: 174.6MM **Publicly Held**
WEB: www.plugpower.com
SIC: 3629 3674 Electrochemical genera-
tors (fuel cells); fuel cells, solid state

(G-6875)
RESPONSELINK INC
Also Called: Responselink of Albany
31 Dussault Dr (12110-2303)
PHONE..................................518 424-7776
Jason Kutey, *President*
EMP: 6
SALES (est): 381.5K **Privately Held**
SIC: 3841 Surgical & medical instruments

(G-6876)
TIRE CONVERSION TECH INC
874 Albany Shaker Rd (12110-1416)
PHONE..................................518 372-1600
Garen Szablewski, *CEO*
Jeff Henry, *Vice Pres*
▲ **EMP:** 25
SQ FT: 10,000
SALES (est): 4.3MM **Privately Held**
WEB: www.tire-conversion.com
SIC: 3069 Custom compounding of rubber
materials

(G-6877)
TRANE US INC
301 Old Niskayuna Rd # 1 (12110-2276)
PHONE..................................518 785-1315
William Seward, *Branch Mgr*
EMP: 35 **Privately Held**
SIC: 3585 Refrigeration & heating equip-
ment
HQ: Trane U.S. Inc.
3600 Pammel Creek Rd
La Crosse WI 54601
608 787-2000

(G-6878)
TRANSTECH SYSTEMS INC (PA)
900 Albany Shaker Rd (12110-1416)
PHONE..................................518 370-5558
David Apkarian, *CEO*
Donald Colosimo, *Treasurer*
Adam Cartner, *Manager*
David Dussault, *Director*
Kevin Lynch, *Director*
▼ **EMP:** 28
SQ FT: 14,000
SALES: 3.9MM **Privately Held**
WEB: www.transtechsys.com
SIC: 3823 8731 Industrial instrmnts
msrmnt display/control process variable;
commercial physical research

(G-6879)
**UL INFORMATION & INSIGHTS
INC (DH)**
23 British American Blvd # 2 (12110-1429)
PHONE..................................518 640-9200
Lou Desorbo, *President*
Gabriel Guzman, *Project Mgr*
Crystal Nussbaumer, *Project Mgr*
Dave Spore, *Project Mgr*
Emily Swartz, *Project Mgr*
EMP: 39
SALES (est): 10.1MM
SALES (corp-wide): 29.7MM **Privately
Held**
WEB: www.thewercs.com
SIC: 7372 8748 Business oriented com-
puter software; business consulting
HQ: UL Llc
333 Pfingsten Rd
Northbrook IL 60062
847 272-8800

(G-6880)
VINYL WORKS INC
33 Wade Rd (12110-2613)
PHONE..................................518 786-1200
EMP: 50 **EST:** 1971
SALES (est): 4.1MM **Privately Held**
WEB: www.thevinylworks.com
SIC: 2394 Liners & covers, fabric: made
from purchased materials

(G-6881)
**WILLIAM BOYD PRINTING CO
INC**
Also Called: Boyd Printing Company
4 Weed Rd Ste 1 (12110-2939)
PHONE..................................518 339-5832
EMP: 120 **EST:** 1889
SQ FT: 81,000
SALES (est): 4.9MM **Privately Held**
SIC: 2711 2752 Commercial printing &
newspaper publishing combined; com-
mercial printing, lithographic

Laurelton
Queens County

(G-6882)
EPIC PHARMA LLC
22715 N Conduit Ave (11413-3134)
PHONE..................................718 276-8600
Towanda Williams, *Buyer*
Kevin Shook, *Controller*
Steven Kurtis, *Manager*
Marina Krylov, *Info Tech Mgr*
Paul Cook, *Director*
▲ **EMP:** 160
SQ FT: 110,000
SALES (est): 68.8MM **Privately Held**
SIC: 2834 Pharmaceutical preparations

(G-6883)
NOVARTIS CORPORATION
22715 N Conduit Ave (11413-3134)
PHONE.................718 276-8600
Kumar Rathnam, *Vice Pres*
EMP: 56
SALES (corp-wide): 51.9B **Privately Held**
WEB: www.novartis.com
SIC: 2834 Pharmaceutical preparations
HQ: Novartis Corporation
1 S Ridgedale Ave Ste 1 # 1
East Hanover NJ 07936
212 307-1122

(G-6884)
NOVARTIS PHARMACEUTICALS CORP
22715 N Conduit Ave (11413-3134)
PHONE.................718 276-8600
EMP: 8
SALES (est): 2.2MM
SALES (corp-wide): 49.4B **Privately Held**
SIC: 2834 Pharmaceutical Preparations
PA: Novartis Ag
Lichtstrasse 35
Basel BS 4056
613 241-111

(G-6885)
PURACAP LABORATORIES LLC
Also Called: Blu Pharmaceuticals
22715 N Conduit Ave (11413-3134)
PHONE.................270 586-6386
Sharon Luster,
EMP: 9
SALES (est): 2.1MM **Privately Held**
SIC: 2834 Druggists' preparations (pharmaceuticals)
HQ: Puracap International Llc
1001 Durham Ave Ste 200
South Plainfield NJ 07080
908 941-5456

Lawrence
Nassau County

(G-6886)
JOHN J RICHARDSON
Also Called: Gad Systems
12 Bernard St (11559-1245)
PHONE.................516 538-6339
John J Richardson, *Owner*
EMP: 15
SQ FT: 4,000
SALES: 900K **Privately Held**
SIC: 3695 Computer software tape & disks: blank, rigid & floppy

(G-6887)
M W MICROWAVE CORP
45 Auerbach Ln (11559-2529)
PHONE.................516 295-1814
Mariam Wiesenfeld, *President*
EMP: 12 **EST:** 1970
SQ FT: 10,000
SALES (est): 1MM **Privately Held**
SIC: 3679 Waveguides & fittings; microwave components

(G-6888)
MEDITUB INCORPORATED
11 Wedgewood Ln (11559-1427)
P.O. Box 668 (11559-0668)
PHONE.................866 633-4882
Joseph Swartz, *President*
EMP: 10
SALES (est): 683.7K **Privately Held**
SIC: 3272 Bathtubs, concrete
PA: Spa World Corporation
5701 Nw 35th Ave
Miami FL 33142

(G-6889)
MOTIVA ENTERPRISES LLC
Also Called: Motiva Sales Terminal
74 East Ave (11559-1025)
PHONE.................516 371-4780
Mario Dantinio, *Manager*
EMP: 7 **Privately Held**
WEB: www.motivaenterprises.com
SIC: 2911 Petroleum refining

HQ: Motiva Enterprises Llc
500 Dallas St Fl 9
Houston TX 77002
713 277-8000

(G-6890)
PREMIER SKIRTING PRODUCTS INC
Also Called: Premier Skrting Tblecloths Too
241 Mill St (11559-1209)
PHONE.................516 239-6581
Ross Yudin, *CEO*
Beth Yudin, *President*
Linda Ehrlich, *Corp Secy*
EMP: 16 **EST:** 1962
SQ FT: 8,500
SALES (est): 1.5MM **Privately Held**
WEB: www.premierskirting.com
SIC: 2392 Tablecloths: made from purchased materials; napkins, fabric & nonwoven: made from purchased materials

(G-6891)
RICHNER COMMUNICATIONS INC
Also Called: Oceanside-Island Park Herald
379 Central Ave (11559-1607)
P.O. Box 220 (11559-0220)
PHONE.................516 569-4000
Alex Costello, *Editor*
Rhonda Glickman, *Vice Pres*
Cliff Richner, *Branch Mgr*
EMP: 5
SALES (corp-wide): 14.2MM **Privately Held**
SIC: 2711 Newspapers, publishing & printing
PA: Richner Communications, Inc.
2 Endo Blvd
Garden City NY 11530
516 569-4000

(G-6892)
SEVILLE CENTRAL MIX CORP
101 Johnson Rd (11559)
PHONE.................516 239-8333
Peter Buck, *Manager*
EMP: 30
SALES (corp-wide): 7.8MM **Privately Held**
WEB: www.sevillecentralmix.com
SIC: 3273 Ready-mixed concrete
PA: Seville Central Mix Corp.
157 Albany Ave
Freeport NY 11520
516 868-3000

(G-6893)
TG PEPPE INC
Also Called: Doery Awning Co
299 Rockaway Tpke Unit B (11559-1269)
PHONE.................516 239-7852
Thomas Peppe, *President*
Gregory Peppe, *Vice Pres*
Sabrina Peppe, *Office Mgr*
EMP: 8
SQ FT: 6,000
SALES (est): 985K **Privately Held**
SIC: 2394 7699 Awnings, fabric: made from purchased materials; awning repair shop

(G-6894)
VILLAGE HERALD
379 Central Ave (11559-1607)
PHONE.................516 569-4403
Nathan Rodriguez, *Executive*
EMP: 5
SALES (est): 165.6K **Privately Held**
SIC: 2711 Newspapers, publishing & printing

Le Roy
Genesee County

(G-6895)
ALUMINUM INJECTION MOLD CO LLC
8741 Lake Street Rd Ste 4 (14482-9381)
PHONE.................585 502-6087
Gerald Ayers,
Tom Bergman,
EMP: 8

SQ FT: 12,000
SALES (est): 1.5MM **Privately Held**
WEB: www.aluminuminjectionmold.com
SIC: 3089 Injection molded finished plastic products; injection molding of plastics

(G-6896)
BATAVIA LEGAL PRINTING INC
7 Bank St (14482-1413)
P.O. Box 57, Stafford (14143-0057)
PHONE.................585 768-2100
Susan Duyssen, *President*
EMP: 5
SQ FT: 4,000
SALES: 350K **Privately Held**
WEB: www.batavialegal.com
SIC: 2759 Laser printing

(G-6897)
CK COATINGS
57 North St Ste 150 (14482-1143)
P.O. Box 203 (14482-0203)
PHONE.................585 502-0425
Linda Wright, *Owner*
EMP: 5
SALES (est): 487.6K **Privately Held**
SIC: 3827 Optical instruments & lenses

(G-6898)
DOLOMITE PRODUCTS COMPANY INC
8250 Golf Rd (14482)
PHONE.................585 768-7295
Matt McCormick, *Manager*
EMP: 12
SQ FT: 9,122
SALES (corp-wide): 30.6B **Privately Held**
WEB: www.dolomitegroup.com
SIC: 2951 Paving mixtures
HQ: Dolomite Products Company Inc.
1150 Penfield Rd
Rochester NY 14625
315 524-1998

(G-6899)
DRAY ENTERPRISES INC
Also Called: Le Roy Pennysaver
1 Church St (14482-1017)
P.O. Box 190 (14482-0190)
PHONE.................585 768-2201
David J Grayson Jr, *President*
Danette L Grayson, *Admin Sec*
EMP: 14
SQ FT: 16,000
SALES (est): 1MM **Privately Held**
WEB: www.leroyny.com
SIC: 2711 7389 Newspapers: publishing only, not printed on site; embroidering of advertising on shirts, etc.

(G-6900)
DUZMOR PAINTING INC
Also Called: Finishing Line, The
7959 E Main Rd (14482-9726)
P.O. Box 135 (14482-0135)
PHONE.................585 768-4760
Peter Mc Quillen, *President*
Judy Mc Quillen, *Vice Pres*
EMP: 6
SQ FT: 10,000
SALES (est): 878.6K **Privately Held**
WEB: www.thefinishinglineco.com
SIC: 3479 Painting of metal products

(G-6901)
ICON DESIGN LLC
9 Lent Ave (14482-1009)
PHONE.................585 768-6040
Wendell Castle, *President*
EMP: 25
SALES (est): 2.9MM **Privately Held**
WEB: www.icondesign.com
SIC: 2511 Wood household furniture

(G-6902)
LAPP INSULATOR COMPANY LLC ✪
130 Gilbert St (14482-1392)
PHONE.................585 768-6221
Ing Bernhard Kahl, *CEO*
EMP: 1 **EST:** 2019
SALES (est): 1.2MM **Privately Held**
SIC: 3264 3644 Insulators, electrical: porcelain; noncurrent-carrying wiring services; insulators & insulation materials, electrical

(G-6903)
LEROY PLASTICS INC
20 Lent Ave (14482-1010)
PHONE.................585 768-8158
Ernest Truax, *President*
◆ **EMP:** 61 **EST:** 1971
SQ FT: 62,305
SALES: 7.3MM **Privately Held**
WEB: www.leroyplastics.com
SIC: 3498 Fabricated pipe & fittings

(G-6904)
MARMACH MACHINE INC
11 Lent Ave (14482)
PHONE.................585 768-8800
John M Lynch, *President*
EMP: 6
SALES (est): 940.3K **Privately Held**
SIC: 3451 Screw machine products

(G-6905)
ORCON INDUSTRIES CORP (PA)
8715 Lake Rd (14482-9396)
PHONE.................585 768-7000
Bruce E Olson, *Ch of Bd*
Gale Hastings, *Exec VP*
Cheryl Le Blanc, *Vice Pres*
▲ **EMP:** 75
SQ FT: 98,000
SALES (est): 17.6MM **Privately Held**
WEB: www.orconind.com
SIC: 2653 3086 7336 Corrugated & solid fiber boxes; packaging & shipping materials, foamed plastic; chart & graph design

(G-6906)
PFISTERER LAPP LLC
130 Gilbert St (14482-1352)
PHONE.................585 768-6221
Bernhard Kahl, *CEO*
Rob Johnson, *COO*
Tom Zembsch, *Project Mgr*
Eric Kress, *QA Dir*
Veronika Capek, *CFO*
◆ **EMP:** 125
SQ FT: 651,000
SALES (est): 25MM **Privately Held**
WEB: www.lappinsulator.com
SIC: 3264 3644 Insulators, electrical: porcelain; noncurrent-carrying wiring services; insulators & insulation materials, electrical

(G-6907)
T S P CORP
Also Called: Thom McGinnes Excavating Plbg
78 One Half Lake St (14482)
PHONE.................585 768-6769
Thomas W McGinnis, *President*
EMP: 10
SQ FT: 1,000
SALES: 550K **Privately Held**
SIC: 3531 Plows: construction, excavating & grading

Leicester
Livingston County

(G-6908)
CPAC INC (DH)
Also Called: Stanley Home Products
2364 State Route 20a (14481-9734)
P.O. Box 175 (14481-0175)
PHONE.................585 382-3223
Thomas N Hendrickson, *Principal*
Jos J Coronas, *Director*
◆ **EMP:** 50
SQ FT: 31,262
SALES (est): 49.1MM
SALES (corp-wide): 79MM **Privately Held**
SIC: 3991 2392 2841 2844 Brooms & brushes; mops, floor & dust; soap & other detergents; shampoos, rinses, conditioners: hair; photographic equipment & supplies; specialty cleaning preparations

(G-6909)
CPAC EQUIPMENT INC
2364 State Route 20a (14481-9734)
P.O. Box 175 (14481-0175)
PHONE.................585 382-3223

Thomas Weldgen, *CEO*
Natalie Gayton, *Controller*
EMP: 16
SQ FT: 15,000
SALES (est): 2.3MM **Privately Held**
WEB: www.cpacequipment.com
SIC: 3843 Sterilizers, dental; dental equipment; glue, dental
PA: Integrated Medical Technologies, Inc.
   2422 E Washington St # 103
   Bloomington IL 61704
   309 662-3614

(G-6910)
FISHERS STORAGE SHEDS
7854 Alverson Rd (14481-9617)
PHONE...............................585 382-9580
Wayne Fisher, *Partner*
Jesse Fisher, *Partner*
Leon Fisher, *Partner*
EMP: 6
SALES: 566.4K **Privately Held**
WEB: www.fishers-storage-sheds.com
SIC: 2452 Prefabricated wood buildings

(G-6911)
SENECA FOODS CORPORATION
Also Called: Comstock Food
5705 Rte 36 (14481)
P.O. Box 278 (14481-0278)
PHONE...............................585 658-2211
Gary Ellis, *Plant Mgr*
Cameron Ellis, *Warehouse Mgr*
Michael Mallaber, *Purch Mgr*
Flo Mullen, *QC Mgr*
Mike Hanchette, *Manager*
EMP: 40
SALES (corp-wide): 1.2B **Publicly Held**
SIC: 2033 Canned fruits & specialties
PA: Seneca Foods Corporation
   3736 S Main St
   Marion NY 14505
   315 926-8100

Levittown
Nassau County

(G-6912)
APOGEE RETAIL NY
3041 Hempstead Tpke (11756-1332)
PHONE...............................516 731-1727
EMP: 5 **EST:** 2010
SALES (est): 417.4K **Privately Held**
SIC: 2329 Men's & boys' clothing

(G-6913)
BEYOND BEAUTY BASICS LLC
3359 Hempstead Tpke (11756-1342)
PHONE...............................516 731-7100
Claudie Oslian, *Mng Member*
EMP: 15
SALES (est): 1.7MM **Privately Held**
SIC: 2899 Core wash or wax

(G-6914)
CCZ READY MIX CONCRETE CORP
2 Loring Rd (11756-1516)
PHONE...............................516 579-7352
Michael Zampini, *President*
EMP: 5
SALES (est): 531.3K **Privately Held**
SIC: 3273 Ready-mixed concrete

(G-6915)
GLITNIR TICKETING INC
Also Called: Glitner Ticketing
3 Snapdragon Ln (11756-3315)
PHONE...............................516 390-5168
Gordon Krstacic, *CEO*
EMP: 5
SALES (est): 488.9K **Privately Held**
WEB: www.glitnir.com
SIC: 7372 Prepackaged software

(G-6916)
KB MILLWORK INC
36 Grey Ln (11756-4411)
P.O. Box 395 (11756-0395)
PHONE...............................516 280-2183
Kenneth Wright, *President*
EMP: 5
SQ FT: 1,200

SALES: 1.5MM **Privately Held**
SIC: 2431 Millwork

(G-6917)
UNIVERSAL ARMOR SYSTEMS CORP
Also Called: 2nd Skin Armor
9 Tanners Ln (11756-4703)
PHONE...............................631 838-1836
Stephen Moran, *CEO*
EMP: 26
SALES (est): 1.9MM **Privately Held**
SIC: 3728 9711 Aircraft parts & equipment; national security

Lewis
Essex County

(G-6918)
UPSTONE MATERIALS INC
Also Called: Lewis Sand & Gravel
Rr 9 (12950)
PHONE...............................518 873-2275
Ron Haugh, *Manager*
EMP: 9
SALES (corp-wide): 83.5MM **Privately Held**
WEB: www.graymont-ab.com
SIC: 2951 3273 3272 3241 Asphalt paving mixtures & blocks; ready-mixed concrete; concrete products; cement, hydraulic
HQ: Upstone Materials Inc.
   111 Quarry Rd
   Plattsburgh NY 12901
   518 561-5321

Lewiston
Niagara County

(G-6919)
450 RIDGE ST INC
Also Called: Mellen Pressroom & Bindery
450 Ridge St (14092-1206)
PHONE...............................716 754-2789
Ruth Koheil, *President*
EMP: 7
SQ FT: 1,488
SALES (est): 656.1K **Privately Held**
SIC: 2731 2752 2732 Books: publishing & printing; commercial printing, lithographic; book printing

(G-6920)
EASTON PHARMACEUTICALS INC
736 Center St Ste 5 (14092-1706)
PHONE...............................347 284-0192
Joseph Slechta, *President*
Peter Rothbart, *Treasurer*
EMP: 6 **EST:** 1998
SALES (est): 173.3K **Privately Held**
SIC: 2834 8731 Ointments; commercial physical research; commercial research laboratory; medical research, commercial

(G-6921)
EDWIN MELLEN PRESS INC
442 Center St (14092-1604)
PHONE...............................716 754-2796
EMP: 38
SALES (est): 1.6MM **Privately Held**
SIC: 2731 Books-Publishing/Printing

(G-6922)
PROTOCASE INCORPORATED
210 S 8th St (14092-1702)
PHONE...............................866 849-3911
Steve Lilley, *President*
Doug Milburn, *Vice Pres*
Colin Poushay, *Research*
Patricia McCann, *Controller*
Christa Carey, *Technical Staff*
EMP: 138
SALES: 8.6MM **Privately Held**
WEB: www.protocase.com
SIC: 3499 3466 Furniture parts, metal; crowns & closures

(G-6923)
PSR PRESS LTD
Also Called: Mellen Press, The
415 Ridge St (14092-1205)
P.O. Box 450 (14092-0450)
PHONE...............................716 754-2266
Herbert Richardson, *CEO*
EMP: 12
SQ FT: 2,000
SALES (est): 1.2MM **Privately Held**
WEB: www.mellenpress.com
SIC: 2731 Books: publishing only

Liberty
Sullivan County

(G-6924)
IDEAL SNACKS CORPORATION
89 Mill St (12754-2038)
PHONE...............................845 292-7000
Zeke Alenick, *President*
Steven Van Poucke, *Vice Pres*
◆ **EMP:** 200
SQ FT: 250,000
SALES (est): 55.5MM **Privately Held**
WEB: www.idealsnacks.com
SIC: 2096 Potato chips & similar snacks

(G-6925)
MAJOR-IPC INC
53 Webster Ave (12754-2005)
P.O. Box 350 (12754-0350)
PHONE...............................845 292-2200
David Feldman, *President*
▲ **EMP:** 5 **EST:** 1976
SQ FT: 9,800
SALES (est): 785.5K **Privately Held**
SIC: 3089 3441 Plastic processing; fabricated structural metal

(G-6926)
NEVERSINK STEEL CORP
Also Called: Liberty Iron Works
12 Asthalter Rd (12754-2617)
PHONE...............................845 292-4611
Barbara Siegel, *President*
Joseph G Siegel, *Vice Pres*
Joseph Siegel, *Vice Pres*
EMP: 8
SALES (est): 1.7MM **Privately Held**
SIC: 3441 7389 1791 Fabricated structural metal; crane & aerial lift service; iron work, structural

Lido Beach
Nassau County

(G-6927)
AIRLINE CONTAINER SERVICES
Also Called: Airline Container Svces
354 Harbor Dr (11561-4907)
PHONE...............................516 371-4125
R Dino Persaud, *President*
Gomattie Persaud, *Vice Pres*
▲ **EMP:** 7
SALES (est): 1.1MM **Privately Held**
SIC: 2448 Cargo containers, wood & wood with metal

(G-6928)
MARVEL DAIRY WHIP INC
258 Lido Blvd (11561-5024)
PHONE...............................516 889-4232
Pauline Seremetis, *President*
EMP: 5
SALES (est): 312.6K **Privately Held**
SIC: 2024 5451 Ice cream, bulk; ice cream (packaged)

Lima
Livingston County

(G-6929)
BEARS MANAGEMENT GROUP INC
Also Called: Bears Playgrounds
7577 E Main St (14485-9735)
PHONE...............................585 624-5694

C Daniel Bears, *President*
Trey Socash, *General Mgr*
Marcie Bears, *Vice Pres*
EMP: 18
SQ FT: 2,000
SALES (est): 1.3MM **Privately Held**
WEB: www.bearsplaygrounds.com
SIC: 3949 Playground equipment

(G-6930)
CORNEAL DESIGN CORPORATION
3288 Plank Rd (14485-9408)
PHONE...............................301 670-7076
Daniel L Bell, *President*
Linda Adkins, *Manager*
EMP: 10
SQ FT: 4,000
SALES (est): 1.3MM **Privately Held**
SIC: 3851 Contact lenses

(G-6931)
EAST MAIN ASSOCIATES
Also Called: Lakelands Concrete
7520 E Main St (14485-9731)
PHONE...............................585 624-1990
Todd Clarke, *President*
EMP: 60
SQ FT: 28,720
SALES: 270K **Privately Held**
SIC: 3272 Concrete products, precast

(G-6932)
LAKELANDS CONCRETE PDTS INC
7520 E Main St (14485-9731)
PHONE...............................585 624-1990
Todd Clarke, *President*
Geoff Lawrence, *Engineer*
Jennifer French, *Office Mgr*
EMP: 49
SQ FT: 40,000
SALES (est): 8MM **Privately Held**
WEB: www.lakelandsconcrete.com
SIC: 3272 Concrete products, precast

(G-6933)
NORTHEAST CONVEYORS INC
7620 Evergreen St (14485-9727)
P.O. Box 55, Le Roy (14482-0055)
PHONE...............................585 768-8912
Paul Hastings, *Ch of Bd*
Guy Bianchi, *Vice Pres*
Michael Schaffer, *Vice Pres*
Beth Bartz, *Treasurer*
Derek Bowman, *Sales Associate*
EMP: 17
SQ FT: 8,024
SALES (est): 5.4MM **Privately Held**
WEB: www.neind.com
SIC: 3535 Conveyors & conveying equipment
PA: Northeast Industrial Technologies, Inc.
   7115 W Main Rd Ste 2
   Le Roy NY 14482

(G-6934)
P & H THERMOTECH INC
1883 Heath Markham Rd (14485-9529)
P.O. Box 585 (14485-0585)
PHONE...............................585 624-1310
Dave Howes, *CEO*
Ray Platt, *President*
EMP: 5
SALES (est): 461.8K **Privately Held**
SIC: 2796 Platemaking services

(G-6935)
SMIDGENS INC
7336 Community Dr (14485-9772)
PHONE...............................585 624-1486
Rita Villa, *President*
Gary Villa, *Vice Pres*
EMP: 8
SQ FT: 3,000
SALES (est): 1.1MM **Privately Held**
WEB: www.smidgens.com
SIC: 3599 Machine shop, jobbing & repair

(G-6936)
SUPERIOR WALLS UPSTATE NY INC (PA)
7574 E Main St (14485-9731)
PHONE...............................585 624-9390
Gary T Hess, *President*

▲ = Import ▼=Export
◆ =Import/Export

Dan Nizzi, *Sales Mgr*
EMP: 44
SQ FT: 200,000
SALES (est): 13.9MM **Privately Held**
SIC: 3272 Precast terrazo or concrete
products

Limestone
Cattaraugus County

(G-6937)
CASE BROTHERS INC
370 Quinn Rd (14753-9713)
P.O. Box 181 (14753-0181)
PHONE..................................716 925-7172
Thomas A Case, *President*
EMP: 9
SALES (est): 949.7K **Privately Held**
SIC: 1389 Oil & gas field services

(G-6938)
JAY LITTLE OIL WELL SERVI
5460 Nichols Run (14753-9774)
PHONE..................................716 925-8905
Jay Little, *Principal*
EMP: 5
SALES (est): 333.2K **Privately Held**
SIC: 1389 Well logging

Lindenhurst
Suffolk County

(G-6939)
**ALRO MACHINE TOOL & DIE CO
INC**
Also Called: Alro Machine Company
585 W Hoffman Ave (11757-4032)
PHONE..................................631 226-5020
Steven Young, *President*
Ronald Young, *Founder*
Elizabeth Young, *Corp Secy*
EMP: 15 **EST:** 1960
SQ FT: 22,000
SALES (est): 3.1MM **Privately Held**
SIC: 3599 Machine shop, jobbing & repair

(G-6940)
**ANTHONY MANUFACTURING
INC**
34 Gear Ave (11757-1005)
PHONE..................................631 957-9424
Jon Hatz, *President*
Benjamin Hatz, *Shareholder*
Melanie Hatz, *Shareholder*
Sandy Hatz, *Shareholder*
Kevin Jampolis, *Shareholder*
EMP: 9
SQ FT: 12,000
SALES (est): 1.2MM **Privately Held**
WEB: www.keithmachinery.com
SIC: 3547 5084 Rolling mill machinery; in-
dustrial machinery & equipment

(G-6941)
AUTO BODY SERVICES LLC
400 W Hoffman Ave (11757-4038)
PHONE..................................631 431-4640
Michael Moretti, *Officer*
EMP: 12
SALES: 5MM **Privately Held**
SIC: 3563 3444 5013 Spraying outfits:
metals, paints & chemicals (compressor);
booths, spray: prefabricated sheet metal;
body repair or paint shop supplies, auto-
motive

(G-6942)
**AUTODYNE MANUFACTURING
CO INC**
200 N Strong Ave (11757-3629)
PHONE..................................631 957-5858
Lindsay Howe, *Ch of Bd*
Shari Kramberg, *Treasurer*
EMP: 10
SALES: 2MM **Privately Held**
WEB: www.autodyne.com
SIC: 3674 Solid state electronic devices

(G-6943)
**BUXTON MEDICAL EQUIPMENT
CORP**
1178 Route 109 (11757-1004)
PHONE..................................631 957-4500
Carl Newman, *President*
▲ **EMP:** 30
SALES (est): 5.3MM **Privately Held**
WEB: www.buxtonmed.com
SIC: 3841 Surgical & medical instruments

(G-6944)
**CANFIELD ELECTRONICS INC
(PA)**
6 Burton Pl (11757-1812)
PHONE..................................631 585-4100
Lynn Zaun, *President*
▼ **EMP:** 20
SQ FT: 15,000
SALES (est): 3.3MM **Privately Held**
WEB: www.canfieldelectronics.com
SIC: 3679 5065 Electronic circuits; elec-
tronic parts & equipment

(G-6945)
CAROB INDUSTRIES INC
215 W Hoffman Ave (11757-4096)
PHONE..................................631 225-0900
Robert A Levey, *President*
EMP: 10
SQ FT: 8,000
SALES: 1.2MM **Privately Held**
SIC: 2431 Millwork

(G-6946)
CRYSTAL FUSION TECH INC
185 W Montauk Hwy (11757-5654)
P.O. Box 1298, West Babylon (11704-
0298)
PHONE..................................631 253-9800
Ray Doran, *President*
EMP: 21
SALES (est): 3.5MM **Privately Held**
SIC: 2899 Water treating compounds

(G-6947)
D & D ELC MTRS & CMPSR INC
127 E Hoffman Ave (11757-5012)
PHONE..................................631 991-3001
Dennis Opaka Jr, *President*
Douglas Woelk, *Sales Mgr*
EMP: 15
SQ FT: 10,000
SALES (est): 3.6MM **Privately Held**
SIC: 7694 Electric motor repair

(G-6948)
**DELANEY MACHINE PRODUCTS
LTD**
150 S Alleghany Ave Ste A (11757-5062)
PHONE..................................631 225-1032
Bob Delaney, *President*
Sharon Delaney, *Vice Pres*
EMP: 6
SQ FT: 10,000
SALES: 850K **Privately Held**
SIC: 3599 Machine shop, jobbing & repair

(G-6949)
DERMATECH LABS INC
165 S 10th St (11757-4505)
PHONE..................................631 225-1700
Dan Bryle, *President*
▲ **EMP:** 10
SQ FT: 11,000
SALES (est): 940K **Privately Held**
SIC: 2844 5122 Cosmetic preparations;
cosmetics

(G-6950)
**DINE RITE SEATING PRODUCTS
INC**
165 E Hoffman Ave Unit 3 (11757-5036)
PHONE..................................631 226-8899
Phil Driesen, *President*
EMP: 20
SALES (est): 3.6MM **Privately Held**
SIC: 2599 7641 Restaurant furniture,
wood or metal; upholstery work

(G-6951)
**DULCETTE TECHNOLOGIES
LLC**
2 Hicks St (11757-1007)
PHONE..................................631 752-8700
Luke Verdet, *Director*
Mel Blum,
Eric Saltsberg,
Ashish Tandakar,
EMP: 7
SQ FT: 1,500
SALES (est): 641.2K
SALES (corp-wide): 77.3MM **Privately
Held**
WEB: www.dulcettetech.com
SIC: 2869 Sweeteners, synthetic
PA: Camlin Fine Sciences Limited
Plot No.F/11 & F/12, Opposite Seepz
Main Gate,
Mumbai MH 40009
226 700-1000

(G-6952)
**ELITE SEMI CONDUCTOR
PRODUCTS**
860 N Richmond Ave (11757-3007)
PHONE..................................631 884-8400
Robert Kravitz, *President*
Edward Kravitz, *Vice Pres*
Joan Kravitz, *Vice Pres*
EMP: 8
SQ FT: 5,000
SALES (est): 1.2MM **Privately Held**
WEB: www.elitesemi.com
SIC: 3674 Integrated circuits, semiconduc-
tor networks, etc.

(G-6953)
JOHNNY MICA INC
116 E Hoffman Ave (11757-5029)
PHONE..................................631 225-5213
John Desimini, *President*
Karla Desimini, *Corp Secy*
EMP: 5
SALES (est): 692.6K **Privately Held**
WEB: www.johnnymica.com
SIC: 2541 5031 1799 1751 Cabinets, ex-
cept refrigerated: show, display, etc.:
wood; kitchen cabinets; counter top instal-
lation; cabinet & finish carpentry

(G-6954)
**LINDENHURST FABRICATORS
INC**
117 S 13th St (11757-4546)
PHONE..................................631 226-3737
Charles Rogers, *President*
EMP: 8
SQ FT: 17,500
SALES (est): 1.6MM **Privately Held**
SIC: 3441 Fabricated structural metal

(G-6955)
LINEAR SIGNS INC
Also Called: Vista Visual Group
275 W Hoffman Ave Ste 1 (11757-4081)
PHONE..................................631 532-5330
Mike Shroff, *President*
Sohel Vakil, *Vice Pres*
Mobin Shroff, *Marketing Staff*
EMP: 15 **EST:** 1994
SQ FT: 7,000
SALES (est): 2.3MM **Privately Held**
SIC: 3993 Signs, not made in custom sign
painting shops

(G-6956)
**LONGO COMMERCIAL
CABINETS INC**
Also Called: Longo Cabinets
829 N Richmond Ave (11757-3008)
PHONE..................................631 225-4290
Robert Longo, *President*
Sandy Giuffrida, *Purch Mgr*
EMP: 50 **EST:** 1966
SQ FT: 22,000
SALES (est): 5.5MM **Privately Held**
SIC: 2541 2521 2434 Store fixtures,
wood; wood office furniture; wood kitchen
cabinets

(G-6957)
MAR-A-THON FILTERS INC
369 41st St (11757-2713)
PHONE..................................631 957-4774

John Reinbold, *President*
Sean Boyle, *General Mgr*
Thomas Cornell, *Corp Secy*
EMP: 6
SQ FT: 7,000
SALES (est): 846.7K **Privately Held**
SIC: 3364 3599 5046 Nonferrous die-
castings except aluminum; machine &
other job shop work; commercial cooking
& food service equipment

(G-6958)
MARIA DIONISIO WELDING INC
71 W Montauk Hwy (11757-5751)
PHONE..................................631 956-0815
Maria Dionisio, *President*
EMP: 5
SALES (est): 118.1K **Privately Held**
SIC: 7692 Welding repair

(G-6959)
MATTHEW-LEE CORPORATION
149 Pennsylvania Ave (11757-5052)
PHONE..................................631 226-0100
John Ferrigno, *President*
Matthew Ferrigno, *Corp Secy*
EMP: 10 **EST:** 1972
SQ FT: 13,000
SALES (est): 638K **Privately Held**
WEB: www.mattlee.com
SIC: 2759 Screen printing

(G-6960)
MIDDLEBY CORPORATION
Also Called: Marsal & Sons
175 E Hoffman Ave (11757-5013)
PHONE..................................631 226-6688
Carl Ferrara, *Treasurer*
Joseph Ferrera, *Branch Mgr*
EMP: 33
SALES (corp-wide): 2.7B **Publicly Held**
SIC: 3444 Restaurant sheet metalwork
PA: The Middleby Corporation
1400 Toastmaster Dr
Elgin IL 60120
847 741-3300

(G-6961)
**MODERN CRAFT BAR REST
EQUIP**
Also Called: Modern Craft Bar Rest Equip
165 E Hoffman Ave Unit 3 (11757-5036)
PHONE..................................631 226-5647
John Venticinque, *President*
Heidee Venticinque, *Admin Sec*
EMP: 7
SALES (est): 959.7K **Privately Held**
WEB: www.moderncraft.com
SIC: 2599 5046 2542 Bar, restaurant &
cafeteria furniture; commercial cooking &
food service equipment; bar fixtures, ex-
cept wood

(G-6962)
**NAS-TRA AUTOMOTIVE INDS
INC**
Also Called: Nastra Automotive
3 Sidney Ct (11757-1011)
PHONE..................................631 225-1225
James Lambert, *Ch of Bd*
Americo De Rocchis, *President*
Antonio Abbatiello, *Corp Secy*
Tim Nolan, *Plant Mgr*
Theresa Bartolotta, *Office Mgr*
▲ **EMP:** 150 **EST:** 1978
SQ FT: 60,000
SALES (est): 24.1MM **Privately Held**
WEB: www.nastra.com
SIC: 3714 3694 3625 Motor vehicle parts
& accessories; engine electrical equip-
ment; relays & industrial controls

(G-6963)
NEW FINE CHEMICALS INC
35 W Hoffman Ave (11757-4012)
PHONE..................................631 321-8151
Jim Haseez, *Director*
EMP: 7 **EST:** 2017
SALES (est): 304.1K **Privately Held**
SIC: 2899 Chemical preparations

(G-6964)
NEXGEN ENVIRO SYSTEMS INC
190 E Hoffman Ave Ste D (11757-5017)
PHONE..................................631 226-2930
Michael Robbins, *President*

Jason Robbins, *Vice Pres*
▲ **EMP:** 3
SALES: 1.1MM **Privately Held**
WEB: www.nexgenenviro.com
SIC: 3826 Environmental testing equipment

(G-6965)
NICOLIA CONCRETE PRODUCTS INC
Also Called: Nicolia of Long Island
640 Muncy St (11757-4318)
P.O. Box 1120, West Babylon (11704-0120)
PHONE..................................631 669-0700
R Glenn Schroeder, *Principal*
Robert Nicolia, *Chairman*
Antonio Nicolia, *Vice Pres*
Gian Nicolia, *Vice Pres*
Ed Cirella, *CFO*
▲ **EMP:** 53
SQ FT: 22,000
SALES (est): 6.9MM **Privately Held**
SIC: 3271 3272 2951 5211 Paving blocks, concrete; concrete products; asphalt paving mixtures & blocks; masonry materials & supplies

(G-6966)
NICOLIA READY MIX INC (PA)
615 Cord Ave (11757-4314)
P.O. Box 1065, West Babylon (11704-0065)
PHONE..................................631 669-7000
Roberto Nicolia, *Ch of Bd*
Antonio Nicolia, *President*
Frank Nicolia, *Vice Pres*
Gian Pierro Nicolia, *Vice Pres*
Sandy Nicolia, *Vice Pres*
EMP: 80 EST: 1980
SQ FT: 5,500
SALES (est): 18.5MM **Privately Held**
WEB: www.nicoliareadymix.com
SIC: 3273 Ready-mixed concrete

(G-6967)
NICOLIA READY MIX INC
615 Cord Ave (11757-4314)
PHONE..................................631 669-7000
EMP: 30
SALES (corp-wide): 18.5MM **Privately Held**
WEB: www.nicoliareadymix.com
SIC: 3273 Ready-mixed concrete
PA: Nicolia Ready Mix, Inc.
615 Cord Ave
Lindenhurst NY 11757
631 669-7000

(G-6968)
NICOLOCK PAVING STONES LLC (HQ)
612 Muncy St (11757-4318)
PHONE..................................631 669-0700
Robert Nicolia, *President*
Craig Luna, *Project Mgr*
Michael Telischak, *Mfg Staff*
Nino Nicolia, *VP Bus Dvlpt*
Jim Beck, *Sales Staff*
▲ **EMP:** 59
SALES: 35.4MM
SALES (corp-wide): 35.6MM **Privately Held**
SIC: 3272 Concrete products
PA: Nicolia Industries, Inc.
615 Cord Ave
Lindenhurst NY 11757
631 888-2200

(G-6969)
PACE UP PHARMACEUTICALS LLC
200 Bangor St (11757-3644)
PHONE..................................631 450-4495
Ming Yang,
EMP: 9
SALES (est): 1.3MM **Privately Held**
SIC: 2834 Druggists' preparations (pharmaceuticals)

(G-6970)
PRIDE LINES LTD
651 W Hoffman Ave (11757-4034)
PHONE..................................631 225-0033
Fax: 631 225-0099
EMP: 8

SQ FT: 8,000
SALES (est): 720K **Privately Held**
SIC: 3944 Manufactures Toy Trains

(G-6971)
RUSSELL PLASTICS TECH CO INC
521 W Hoffman Ave (11757-4052)
PHONE..................................631 963-8602
Alexander Bozza, *Ch of Bd*
EMP: 110
SQ FT: 58,000
SALES (est): 18.8MM **Privately Held**
WEB: www.russellplastics.com
SIC: 3089 Injection molding of plastics
HQ: Vaupell Holdings, Inc.
1144 Nw 53rd St
Seattle WA 98107

(G-6972)
SIMS STEEL CORPORATION
650 Muncy St (11757-4396)
PHONE..................................631 587-8670
William Sims, *President*
EMP: 25
SQ FT: 4,000
SALES (est): 6.3MM **Privately Held**
WEB: www.simssteel.com
SIC: 3449 Miscellaneous metalwork

(G-6973)
STEELFLEX ELECTRO CORP
145 S 13th St (11757-4546)
PHONE..................................516 226-4466
Philip Rine, *President*
Anthony Rine, *Vice Pres*
EMP: 60 EST: 1968
SQ FT: 25,000
SALES (est): 7.4MM **Privately Held**
SIC: 3357 Nonferrous wiredrawing & insulating

(G-6974)
STEINWAY PASTA & GELATI INC
146 Albany Ave (11757-3628)
PHONE..................................718 246-5414
Vincenzo Arpaia, *President*
▲ **EMP:** 15
SALES (est): 2.1MM **Privately Held**
SIC: 2099 5149 Packaged combination products: pasta, rice & potato; pasta & rice

(G-6975)
STJ ORTHOTIC SERVICES INC (PA)
Also Called: S T J Orthotic Svces
920 Wellwood Ave Ste B (11757-1246)
PHONE..................................631 956-0181
James De Francisco, *President*
Steven Levitz, *Vice Pres*
EMP: 12
SQ FT: 14,000
SALES: 3.5MM **Privately Held**
WEB: www.stjorthotic.com
SIC: 3842 Orthopedic appliances

(G-6976)
STRUX CORP
Also Called: Art Foam
100 Montauk Hwy (11757-5835)
PHONE..................................516 768-3969
Robert Kjeldsen, *President*
EMP: 25 EST: 1970
SQ FT: 30,000
SALES (est): 2.1MM **Privately Held**
WEB: www.strux.com
SIC: 3083 3675 3086 Laminated plastics plate & sheet; electronic capacitors; plastics foam products

(G-6977)
SUFFOLK GRANITE MANUFACTURING
Also Called: Suffolk Monument Mfg
25 Gear Ave (11757-1006)
PHONE..................................631 226-4774
Martin Solomon, *President*
EMP: 20
SQ FT: 17,500

SALES (est): 2.1MM **Privately Held**
WEB: www.uk-engineering.net
SIC: 3281 1423 1411 Monuments, cut stone (not finishing or lettering only); crushed & broken granite; dimension stone

(G-6978)
SUPERBOATS INC
694 Roosevelt Ave (11757-5820)
PHONE..................................631 226-1761
John H Coen, *President*
EMP: 6
SQ FT: 10,000
SALES: 600K **Privately Held**
SIC: 3732 5551 7699 Boats, fiberglass: building & repairing; boat dealers; boat repair

(G-6979)
SUPERIOR AGGRAGATES SUPPLY LLC
612 Muncy St (11757-4318)
PHONE..................................516 333-2923
Robert Nicolia,
Antonio L Nicolia,
Franco A Nicolia,
Gian P Nicolia,
Sandy N Nicolia,
EMP: 30
SALES: 2.9MM **Privately Held**
SIC: 3272 Precast terrazo or concrete products

(G-6980)
TENTINA WINDOW FASHIONS INC
1186 Route 109 (11757-1088)
P.O. Box 617 (11757-0617)
PHONE..................................631 957-9585
Frank J Miritello, *CEO*
Andrea Miritello, *President*
Jeffery Miritello, *Vice Pres*
Neil Miritello, *Treasurer*
Stephanie Miritello, *Admin Sec*
EMP: 105
SQ FT: 40,000
SALES (est): 11.4MM **Privately Held**
WEB: www.tentina.com
SIC: 2591 Window blinds; window shades

(G-6981)
VELIS ASSOCIATES INC (PA)
151 S 14th St (11757-4432)
PHONE..................................631 225-4220
Suriya Khan, *Chairman*
Brian Mastoberti, *Vice Pres*
EMP: 3
SALES (est): 5.3MM **Privately Held**
SIC: 3534 Elevators & equipment

(G-6982)
VIKING ATHLETICS LTD
80 Montauk Hwy Ste 1 (11757-5800)
PHONE..................................631 957-8000
David C Kjeldsen, *CEO*
Ben Porter, *General Mgr*
▲ **EMP:** 40 EST: 1995
SQ FT: 28,000
SALES (est): 4.1MM **Privately Held**
WEB: www.vikingathletics.com
SIC: 3949 5949 2759 Sporting & athletic goods; needlework goods & supplies; screen printing

(G-6983)
VIKING TECHNOLOGIES LTD
80 E Montauk Hwy (11757)
PHONE..................................631 957-8000
David Kjeldsen, *President*
EMP: 45 EST: 1959
SQ FT: 35,000
SALES: 10MM **Privately Held**
WEB: www.cardwellcondenser.com
SIC: 3629 3674 3675 Condensers, fixed or variable; semiconductors & related devices; electronic capacitors

(G-6984)
VILLAGE LANTERN BAKING CORP
155 N Wellwood Ave (11757-4085)
PHONE..................................631 225-1690
Linda Gramer, *Principal*
Thomas Lorch, *Principal*

EMP: 8
SALES (est): 655.7K **Privately Held**
SIC: 2051 Bread, cake & related products

(G-6985)
VISUAL CITI INC (PA)
305 Henry St (11757-4315)
PHONE..................................631 482-3030
Abbas Devji, *President*
Fazle Abbas Deyjiyani, *Chairman*
Samina Devji, *Vice Pres*
Mufaddal Boxwala, *Project Mgr*
Sandra Ventura, *Human Resources*
▲ **EMP:** 125
SQ FT: 28,000
SALES (est): 36.8MM **Privately Held**
WEB: www.visualciti.com
SIC: 3993 Displays & cutouts, window & lobby

Lindley
Steuben County

(G-6986)
LINDLEY WOOD WORKS INC
9625 Morgan Creek Rd (14858-9780)
P.O. Box 5 (14858-0005)
PHONE..................................607 523-7786
Peter McIntosh, *President*
Peter Mc Intosh, *President*
Keith Mc Intosh, *Vice Pres*
Mary Mc Intosh, *Admin Sec*
EMP: 15
SQ FT: 10,000
SALES (est): 2.3MM **Privately Held**
SIC: 2448 Pallets, wood

Little Falls
Herkimer County

(G-6987)
BURROWS PAPER CORPORATION
Also Called: Burrows Paper Mill
730 E Mill St (13365)
PHONE..................................315 823-2300
Fred Scarano, *Manager*
EMP: 70
SALES (corp-wide): 164.8MM **Privately Held**
WEB: www.burrowspaper.com
SIC: 2621 Paper mills
PA: Burrows Paper Corporation
501 W Main St Ste 1
Little Falls NY 13365
800 272-7122

(G-6988)
BURROWS PAPER CORPORATION
Also Called: Mohawk Valley Mill
489 W Main St (13365)
PHONE..................................315 823-2300
Duane Judd, *Manager*
EMP: 66
SALES (corp-wide): 164.8MM **Privately Held**
WEB: www.burrowspaper.com
SIC: 2621 Tissue paper; specialty papers
PA: Burrows Paper Corporation
501 W Main St Ste 1
Little Falls NY 13365
800 272-7122

(G-6989)
IDEAL WOOD PRODUCTS INC
Also Called: Ideal Stair Parts
225 W Main St (13365-1800)
PHONE..................................315 823-1124
Bruce Mang, *President*
▲ **EMP:** 40
SQ FT: 14,000
SALES (est): 6.1MM **Privately Held**
WEB: www.idealstairparts.com
SIC: 2431 Staircases & stairs, wood

(G-6990)
PEMS TOOL & MACHINE INC
125 Southern Ave (13365-1906)
PHONE..................................315 823-3595

Isabella Stone, *Ch of Bd*
Roger Schulze, *Engineer*
EMP: 31
SQ FT: 17,500
SALES (est): 7.5MM **Privately Held**
WEB: www.pemstoolandmachine.com
SIC: 3599 3549 Machine shop, jobbing &
repair; metalworking machinery

(G-6991)
PRETTY FUEL INC
29 W Lansing St (13365-1317)
PHONE..............................315 823-4063
Gamdur Narain, *Principal*
EMP: 5
SALES (est): 360.6K **Privately Held**
SIC: 2869 Fuels

(G-6992)
**R D S MOUNTAIN VIEW
TRUCKING**
Also Called: R D Drive and Shop
1600 State Route 5s (13365-5405)
P.O. Box 924 (13365-0924)
PHONE..............................315 823-4265
Randall Dawley, *Owner*
EMP: 7 **EST:** 2000
SALES (est): 745.9K **Privately Held**
SIC: 2611 Soda pulp

(G-6993)
SUNBELT INDUSTRIES INC (PA)
540 E Mill St (13365-2027)
P.O. Box 584 (13365-0584)
PHONE..............................315 823-2947
Earl Mannion, *President*
EMP: 10
SQ FT: 36,000
SALES (est): 1.2MM **Privately Held**
SIC: 3291 5085 Abrasive grains; abra-
sives

(G-6994)
**TWIN RIVERS PAPER COMPANY
LLC**
501 W Main St Ste 1 (13365-1829)
PHONE..............................315 823-2300
EMP: 282 **Privately Held**
SIC: 2621 Paper mills
PA: Twin Rivers Paper Company Llc
82 Bridge Ave
Madawaska ME 04756

(G-6995)
**VINCENT MANUFACTURING CO
INC**
560 E Mill St (13365-2027)
P.O. Box 306 (13365-0306)
PHONE..............................315 823-0280
Todd R Vincent, *President*
Alan N Vincent, *President*
Todd Vincent, *President*
Linda B Vincent, *Vice Pres*
EMP: 11 **EST:** 1892
SQ FT: 50,000
SALES: 800K **Privately Held**
SIC: 2299 5169 Batts & batting: cotton mill
waste & related material; polyurethane
products

Little Neck
Queens County

(G-6996)
ANGEL TIPS NAIL SALON
25473 Horace Harding Expy (11362-1816)
PHONE..............................718 225-8300
Sun Kim, *Owner*
EMP: 6
SALES (est): 542.8K **Privately Held**
SIC: 2844 7231 Manicure preparations;
manicurist, pedicurist

(G-6997)
E GLUCK CORPORATION (PA)
Also Called: Armitron Watch Div
6015 Little Neck Pkwy (11362-2500)
PHONE..............................718 784-0700
Eugen Gluck, *President*
Rachel Fredman, *Partner*
Stanislav Kravets, *Editor*
Sidney Gluck, *Exec VP*
Jerry Dikowitz, *Vice Pres*

▲ **EMP:** 122 **EST:** 1957
SQ FT: 200,000
SALES (est): 68.9MM **Privately Held**
WEB: www.egluck.com
SIC: 3873 5094 Watches & parts, except
crystals & jewels; clocks, assembly of;
watches & parts; clocks

(G-6998)
RENEWABLE ENERGY INC
6 Cornell Ln (11363-1939)
PHONE..............................718 690-2691
EMP: 6
SALES (est): 518.5K **Privately Held**
SIC: 3674 Mfg Semiconductors/Related
Devices

Little Valley
Cattaraugus County

(G-6999)
**LITTLE VALLEY SAND &
GRAVEL**
8984 New Albion Rd (14755)
P.O. Box 164 (14755-0164)
PHONE..............................716 938-6676
John R Charlesworth, *President*
Jay Charlesworth, *Treasurer*
Mary Charlesworth, *Admin Sec*
EMP: 7
SQ FT: 5,000
SALES (est): 687.1K **Privately Held**
SIC: 1442 4212 Construction sand mining;
gravel mining; local trucking, without stor-
age

Liverpool
Onondaga County

(G-7000)
**BARRETT PAVING MATERIALS
INC**
4530 Wetzel Rd (13090-2517)
PHONE..............................315 652-4585
Frank Simmons, *Finance*
Dan McAdams, *Sales Staff*
EMP: 30
SQ FT: 12,368
SALES (corp-wide): 83.5MM **Privately
Held**
WEB: www.barrettpaving.com
SIC: 2951 Asphalt paving mixtures &
blocks
HQ: Barrett Paving Materials Inc.
3 Becker Farm Rd Ste 307
Roseland NJ 07068
973 533-1001

(G-7001)
**BODYCOTE SYRACUSE HEAT
TREATIN**
4629 Crossroads Park Dr (13088-3515)
PHONE..............................315 451-0000
John H Mac Allister, *Ch of Bd*
George Stupp, *Vice Pres*
EMP: 23 **EST:** 1932
SQ FT: 30,000
SALES (est): 5.6MM
SALES (corp-wide): 935.8MM **Privately
Held**
WEB: www.syracuseheattreating.com
SIC: 3398 Brazing (hardening) of metal
HQ: Bodycote Usa, Inc.
12700 Park Central Dr # 700
Dallas TX 75251
214 904-2420

(G-7002)
BRANNOCK DEVICE CO INC
116 Luther Ave (13088-6726)
PHONE..............................315 475-9862
Salvatore A Leonardi Jr, *President*
Tim Follett, *Vice Pres*
EMP: 20 **EST:** 1929
SQ FT: 10,000
SALES (est): 2.5MM **Privately Held**
WEB: www.brannock.com
SIC: 3842 Foot appliances, orthopedic

(G-7003)
C & G VIDEO SYSTEMS INC (PA)
7778 Tirrell Hill Cir (13220-2508)
P.O. Box 2476, Syracuse (13220-2476)
PHONE..............................315 452-1490
Charles F Bisesi, *President*
Gail Bisesi, *Vice Pres*
EMP: 5
SQ FT: 3,600
SALES: 1MM **Privately Held**
SIC: 3699 1731 Security control equip-
ment & systems; electrical welding equip-
ment; electrical work

(G-7004)
C SPEED LLC (PA)
316 Commerce Blvd (13088-4511)
PHONE..............................315 453-1043
David Lysack, *President*
Michael Lesmerises, *Project Mgr*
Brian D Sherry -, *Engineer*
Kevin Francis -, *Engineer*
Pat McHenry, *Engineer*
EMP: 32
SQ FT: 5,000
SALES (est): 6.9MM **Privately Held**
WEB: www.cspeed.com
SIC: 3812 8711 3825 Search & navigation
equipment; electrical or electronic engi-
neering; instruments to measure electric-
ity

(G-7005)
CARGILL INCORPORATED
7700 Maltage Dr (13090-2513)
PHONE..............................315 622-3533
Hugh Fordyce, *Branch Mgr*
EMP: 25
SQ FT: 27,466
SALES (corp-wide): 114.7B **Privately
Held**
WEB: www.cargill.com
SIC: 2048 Prepared feeds
PA: Cargill, Incorporated
15407 Mcginty Rd W
Wayzata MN 55391
952 742-7575

(G-7006)
**CASCADE HELMETS HOLDINGS
INC**
4697 Crssrads Pk Dr Ste 1 (13088)
PHONE..............................315 453-3073
Bill Brine, *CEO*
Steve Moore, *COO*
EMP: 8
SALES (est): 2.7MM **Privately Held**
SIC: 3949 Helmets, athletic

(G-7007)
**CAYUGA PRESS CORTLAND
INC**
4707 Dey Rd (13088-3510)
PHONE..............................888 229-8421
Thomas Quartier, *President*
EMP: 32 **EST:** 2011
SALES (est): 342K **Privately Held**
SIC: 2752 2741 Commercial printing, off-
set; miscellaneous publishing

(G-7008)
CREATIVE COSTUME CO
3804 Rivers Pointe Way (13090-4917)
PHONE..............................212 564-5552
Susan Handler, *Partner*
Linda Carcaci, *Partner*
EMP: 7
SALES (est): 877.3K **Privately Held**
WEB: www.creativecostume.com
SIC: 2389 Costumes

(G-7009)
EAGLE COMTRONICS INC
7665 Henry Clay Blvd (13088-3507)
P.O. Box 2457, Syracuse (13220-2457)
PHONE..............................315 451-3313
William Devendorf, *CEO*
Timothy Devendorf, *President*
Gary Clark, *Engineer*
Glenn Sparling, *CFO*
Shawn-Marie Visconti, *Accounting Mgr*
▲ **EMP:** 200 **EST:** 1975
SQ FT: 100,000

SALES (est): 38.8MM **Privately Held**
WEB: www.eaglecomtronics.com
SIC: 3663 Cable television equipment

(G-7010)
**FAYETTE STREET COATINGS
INC**
1 Burr Dr (13088)
PHONE..............................315 488-5401
Bill Udovich, *Branch Mgr*
EMP: 11
SALES (corp-wide): 51.8MM **Publicly
Held**
SIC: 2851 Paints & allied products
HQ: Fayette Street Coatings, Inc.
1250 Justin Rd
Rockwall TX 75087
315 488-5401

(G-7011)
**HEARTH CABINETS AND MORE
LTD**
4483 Buckley Rd (13088-2506)
P.O. Box 2700 (13089-2700)
PHONE..............................315 641-1197
Richard D Hovey, *President*
EMP: 2
SALES (est): 2.3MM **Privately Held**
SIC: 2434 Wood kitchen cabinets

(G-7012)
**HSM PACKAGING
CORPORATION**
4529 Crown Rd (13090-3541)
PHONE..............................315 476-7996
Sheila M Martin, *CEO*
Homer S Martin III, *COO*
Jessica T Pletka, *CFO*
Casey Driscoll, *Auditor*
Brian Nelepovitz, *Supervisor*
▲ **EMP:** 58
SQ FT: 30,000
SALES (est): 13.9MM **Privately Held**
WEB: www.hsmpackaging.com
SIC: 2657 Folding paperboard boxes

(G-7013)
**ILLUMINATION TECHNOLOGIES
INC**
4172 Choke Cherry Way (13090-1122)
PHONE..............................315 463-4673
Michael Muehlemann, *President*
Daniel Muehlemann, *VP Business*
Jean Vurraro, *Manager*
EMP: 10
SQ FT: 6,000
SALES (est): 2.1MM **Privately Held**
WEB: www.illuminationtech.com
SIC: 3648 Lighting equipment

(G-7014)
INFIMED INC (PA)
Also Called: Varian Medical Systems
121 Metropolitan Park Dr (13088-5335)
PHONE..............................315 453-4545
Robert Kluge, *CEO*
Norman Shoenfeld, *Ch of Bd*
Amy L Ryan, *President*
Danielle Berube, *Sales Staff*
Carrie Christian, *Sales Staff*
▲ **EMP:** 64
SQ FT: 26,000
SALES (est): 8.8MM **Privately Held**
WEB: www.digitalxrayimages.com
SIC: 3845 Electromedical equipment

(G-7015)
INFO QUICK SOLUTIONS
7460 Morgan Rd (13090-3979)
PHONE..............................315 463-1400
Bernie Owens, *President*
Corinne Kopec, *Prgrmr*
Thomas Decker, *Director*
EMP: 50
SALES (est): 4.9MM **Privately Held**
SIC: 7372 Prepackaged software

(G-7016)
**INTEGRATED MEDICAL
DEVICES**
549 Electronics Pkwy # 200 (13088-4391)
PHONE..............................315 457-4200
Stephen L Esposito, *President*
EMP: 7
SQ FT: 4,400

G
E
O
G
R
A
P
H
I
C

SALES (est): 976.4K **Privately Held**
WEB: www.qrstech.com
SIC: 3845 Electrocardiographs

(G-7017)
IRONSHORE HOLDINGS INC
Also Called: Lipe Automation
290 Elwood Davis Rd (13088-2100)
PHONE.............................315 457-1052
Robert Offley, *CEO*
Jay Lacey, *President*
Andrew Pilcicki, *Production*
Campbell McIntire, *Shareholder*
EMP: 16 EST: 2001
SQ FT: 27,000
SALES (est): 1.3MM **Privately Held**
SIC: 3599 Machine shop, jobbing & repair

(G-7018)
JOHN MEZZALINGUA ASSOC LLC (PA)
Also Called: Jma Wireless
7645 Henry Clay Blvd (13088-3512)
P.O. Box 678 (13088-0678)
PHONE.............................315 431-7100
Michael Tierney, *Counsel*
Shawn Chawgo, *Vice Pres*
Eli Fischer, *Vice Pres*
Brian Foley, *Vice Pres*
Todd Landry, *Vice Pres*
▲ **EMP:** 150
SALES (est): 154.3MM **Privately Held**
SIC: 3663 Antennas, transmitting & communications; airborne radio communications equipment

(G-7019)
JT SYSTEMS INC
8132 Oswego Rd (13090-1500)
P.O. Box 2575 (13089-2575)
PHONE.............................315 622-1980
Jit Turakhia, *Ch of Bd*
Manda Turakhia, *Admin Sec*
EMP: 10
SQ FT: 1,700
SALES (est): 2.7MM **Privately Held**
WEB: www.jtsystemsinc.com
SIC: 3564 Air purification equipment; ventilating fans: industrial or commercial

(G-7020)
LOCKHEED MARTIN CORPORATION
497 Electronics Pkwy (13088-5394)
PHONE.............................315 456-3386
Steven Montagne, *General Mgr*
Peter Morin, *Principal*
Carl Bannar, *Vice Pres*
Kyle Cavorley, *Engineer*
Andrew Cleary, *Engineer*
EMP: 25 **Publicly Held**
SIC: 3812 Search & navigation equipment
PA: Lockheed Martin Corporation
6801 Rockledge Dr
Bethesda MD 20817

(G-7021)
LOCKHEED MARTIN CORPORATION
497 Electronics Pkwy # 5 (13088-5394)
P.O. Box 4840, Syracuse (13221-4840)
PHONE.............................315 456-0123
T S Kires, *Principal*
Jeanette Hoskins, *Engineer*
Chad Lindke, *Engineer*
Francis Pieniazek, *Engineer*
Philip Scalzetti, *Engineer*
EMP: 2200 **Publicly Held**
WEB: www.lockheedmartin.com
SIC: 3761 3812 Rockets, space & military, complete; navigational systems & instruments
PA: Lockheed Martin Corporation
6801 Rockledge Dr
Bethesda MD 20817

(G-7022)
LOCKHEED MARTIN GLOBAL INC (HQ)
Also Called: Lmgi
497 Electronics Pkwy # 5 (13088-5394)
PHONE.............................315 456-2982
Dale M Johnson, *President*
Zachary Parmely, *General Mgr*
Karen Barrett, *Admin Sec*

EMP: 31
SALES (est): 486.2MM **Publicly Held**
SIC: 3812 Search & navigation equipment

(G-7023)
LOCKHEED MARTIN OVERSEAS
497 Electronics Pkwy # 7 (13088-5394)
P.O. Box 4840, Syracuse (13221-4840)
PHONE.............................315 456-0123
Kwame Otieku, *Principal*
Linda Raymond, *Branch Mgr*
EMP: 14 **Publicly Held**
SIC: 3812 Sonar systems & equipment; radar systems & equipment
HQ: Lockheed Martin Overseas Services Corporation
6801 Rockledge Dr
Bethesda MD 20817

(G-7024)
MCAULIFFE PAPER INC
100 Commerce Blvd (13088-4500)
PHONE.............................315 453-2222
Charles Thiaville, *President*
Mary Y Maltbie, *Vice Pres*
EMP: 35 EST: 1920
SQ FT: 40,000
SALES (est): 3.5MM **Privately Held**
WEB: www.mcauliffepad.com
SIC: 2759 Business forms: printing

(G-7025)
MERCER MILLING CO
4698 Crossroads Park Dr (13088-3598)
PHONE.............................315 701-1334
Bill Colten, *President*
Scott Lyndaker, *Opers Staff*
Jeff Matuszczak, *Purchasing*
▲ **EMP:** 36 EST: 1829
SQ FT: 60,000
SALES (est): 16.7MM **Privately Held**
SIC: 2834 2833 Intravenous solutions; botanical products, medicinal: ground, graded or milled

(G-7026)
MIDSTATE PRINTING CORP
4707 Dey Rd (13088-3510)
PHONE.............................315 475-4101
John Williams III, *President*
Robert Williams, *Vice Pres*
Lee Boyce, *Project Mgr*
Thomas Keehfus, *CFO*
Michael Curbelo, *Sales Executive*
EMP: 49 EST: 1935
SQ FT: 28,000
SALES (est): 1.3MM
SALES (corp-wide): 52.9K **Privately Held**
WEB: www.midstateprinting.com
SIC: 2752 Commercial printing, offset
PA: Qpc-Mpc Consolidation, Inc.
4707 Dey Rd
Liverpool NY 13088
315 475-4101

(G-7027)
MODERN DECAL CO
8146 Soule Rd (13090-1536)
PHONE.............................315 622-2778
William J Hitchcock, *Owner*
Kathleen Hitchcock, *Co-Owner*
EMP: 6
SALES: 220K **Privately Held**
SIC: 2759 3993 Decals: printing; name plates: except engraved, etched, etc.: metal

(G-7028)
NANOPV CORPORATION
7526 Morgan Rd (13090-3502)
PHONE.............................609 851-3666
Anna Selvan John, *President*
EMP: 188 **Privately Held**
SIC: 3433 Solar heaters & collectors
PA: Nanopv Corporation
122 Mountainview Rd
Ewing NJ 08560

(G-7029)
PACKAGING CORPORATION AMERICA
Also Called: Pca/Syracuse, 384
4471 Steelway Blvd S (13090-3508)
P.O. Box 584 (13088-0584)
PHONE.............................315 457-6780
Joseph Armentrout, *General Mgr*

Julie Clark, *Controller*
Teresa Bashore, *Branch Mgr*
EMP: 130
SQ FT: 144,672
SALES (corp-wide): 7B **Publicly Held**
WEB: www.packagingcorp.com
SIC: 2653 Boxes, corrugated: made from purchased materials
PA: Packaging Corporation Of America
1 N Field Ct
Lake Forest IL 60045
847 482-3000

(G-7030)
PACTIV LLC
4471 Steelway Blvd S (13090-3517)
P.O. Box 584 (13088-0584)
PHONE.............................315 457-6780
Teresa J Bashore, *Manager*
EMP: 130
SALES (corp-wide): 14.1MM **Privately Held**
WEB: www.pactiv.com
SIC: 2653 Boxes, corrugated: made from purchased materials; boxes, solid fiber: made from purchased materials
HQ: Pactiv Llc
1900 W Field Ct
Lake Forest IL 60045
847 482-2000

(G-7031)
PAUL DE LIMA COMPANY INC (PA)
Also Called: Paul De Lima Coffee Company
7546 Morgan Rd Ste 1 (13090-3532)
PHONE.............................315 457-3725
Paul W Delima Jr, *CEO*
William J Drescher Jr, *Ch of Bd*
Ron Chrysler, *Vice Pres*
Peter Miller, *Vice Pres*
Heidi Phillips, *Prdtn Mgr*
▲ **EMP:** 55
SQ FT: 15,000
SALES (est): 14.5MM **Privately Held**
WEB: www.delimacoffee.com
SIC: 2095 5149 Coffee roasting (except by wholesale grocers); coffee, green or roasted

(G-7032)
PERFORMANCE LACROSSE GROUP INC (HQ)
4697 Crossroads Park Dr (13088-3515)
PHONE.............................315 453-3073
Stephen Moore, *President*
Steve Moore, *COO*
▲ **EMP:** 8
SALES: 1.2MM
SALES (corp-wide): 149.6MM **Privately Held**
WEB: www.sporthelmets.com
SIC: 3949 Helmets, athletic
PA: Old Bh Inc.
100 Domain Dr
Exeter NH 03833
603 430-2111

(G-7033)
POINTWISE INFORMATION SERVICE
223 1st St (13088-5140)
P.O. Box 11457, Syracuse (13218-1457)
PHONE.............................315 457-4111
Richard C Jaquin, *Owner*
EMP: 10
SQ FT: 1,000
SALES (est): 837.2K **Privately Held**
SIC: 2721 Periodicals: publishing only

(G-7034)
PRAXAIR DISTRIBUTION INC
4560 Morgan Pl (13090-3522)
PHONE.............................315 457-5821
Todd Saumier, *Principal*
EMP: 7 **Privately Held**
SIC: 2813 5984 5169 Oxygen, compressed or liquefied; nitrogen; liquefied petroleum gas dealers; oxygen; industrial gases; acetylene
HQ: Praxair Distribution, Inc.
10 Riverview Dr
Danbury CT 06810
203 837-2000

(G-7035)
PRECISION SYSTEMS MFG INC
4855 Executive Dr (13088-5378)
PHONE.............................315 451-3480
Theodore Jeske, *President*
Jamie Williams, *QC Mgr*
EMP: 48
SQ FT: 40,000
SALES (est): 11MM **Privately Held**
WEB: www.psmi.org
SIC: 3599 3444 7389 3549 Machine shop, jobbing & repair; sheet metalwork; design, commercial & industrial; metalworking machinery; special dies, tools, jigs & fixtures

(G-7036)
PRINT SOLUTIONS PLUS INC
7325 Oswego Rd (13090-3717)
PHONE.............................315 234-3801
Darren Petragnani, *President*
EMP: 6
SALES (est): 772.3K **Privately Held**
SIC: 2752 Commercial printing, offset

(G-7037)
QRS TECHNOLOGIES INC
549 Electronics Pkwy (13088-6059)
PHONE.............................315 457-5300
Steve Esposito, *Owner*
EMP: 5
SALES (est): 329.1K **Privately Held**
SIC: 3845 Electromedical apparatus

(G-7038)
ROBERTS OFFICE FURN CNCPTS INC
7327 Henry Clay Blvd (13088-3529)
PHONE.............................315 451-9185
Robert L Barcza, *CEO*
R Scott Barcza, *President*
EMP: 25
SQ FT: 76,000
SALES (est): 4.8MM **Privately Held**
WEB: www.robertsofc.com
SIC: 2522 7641 Office furniture, except wood; office furniture repair & maintenance

(G-7039)
SCAPA NORTH AMERICA
Also Called: Great Lakes Technologies
1111 Vine St (13088-5301)
PHONE.............................315 413-1111
Stuart Ganslaw,
Angelo Labbadia,
Steve Lennon,
▲ **EMP:** 20
SQ FT: 70,000
SALES: 10.5MM
SALES (corp-wide): 401.1MM **Privately Held**
WEB: www.greatlakestechnologies.com
SIC: 3081 Unsupported plastics film & sheet
HQ: Scapa Tapes North America Llc
111 Great Pond Dr
Windsor CT 06095
860 688-8000

(G-7040)
SOLENIS LLC
Also Called: Ashland Water Technologies
911 Old Liverpool Rd (13088-1504)
PHONE.............................315 461-4730
EMP: 9
SALES (corp-wide): 767.2MM **Privately Held**
SIC: 2899 Chemical preparations
HQ: Solenis Llc
3 Beaver Valley Rd # 500
Wilmington DE 19803
866 337-1533

(G-7041)
STALLION TECHNOLOGIES INC
4324 Loveland Dr (13090-6862)
PHONE.............................315 622-1176
Marshall MA, *President*
EMP: 8
SALES (est): 520K **Privately Held**
WEB: www.stalliontech.com
SIC: 3861 Photographic equipment & supplies

(G-7042)
STAMPCRETE INTERNATIONAL LTD
Also Called: Stampcrete Decorative Concrete
325 Commerce Blvd (13088-4595)
PHONE..................................315 451-2837
Karen Reith, *President*
Bob Williams, *Vice Pres*
▼ EMP: 20
SQ FT: 10,000
SALES (est): 7MM **Privately Held**
SIC: 3469 Metal stampings

(G-7043)
SYRACUSE PLASTICS LLC
7400 Morgan Rd (13090-3902)
PHONE..................................315 637-9881
Thomas Falcone,
Joseph R Falcone Sr,
Joseph R Falcone Jr,
Thomas R Falcone,
▲ EMP: 150 EST: 1953
SQ FT: 55,000
SALES (est): 34.7MM **Privately Held**
SIC: 3089 Injection molding of plastics

(G-7044)
TACTAIR FLUID CONTROLS INC
4806 W Taft Rd (13088-4810)
PHONE..................................315 451-3928
Dudley D Johnson, *Ch of Bd*
Christopher L Sax, *Mfg Mgr*
Stacy Field, *Production*
Tony Ilacqua, *Senior Buyer*
Theresa Beard, *Buyer*
EMP: 240
SQ FT: 70,000
SALES (est): 50.9MM
SALES (corp-wide): 3.8B **Publicly Held**
WEB: www.tactair.com
SIC: 3492 3593 Fluid power valves for aircraft; fluid power actuators, hydraulic or pneumatic
HQ: Young & Franklin, Inc.
    942 Old Liverpool Rd
    Liverpool NY 13088
    315 457-3110

(G-7045)
THERMO CIDTEC INC
Also Called: Cid Technologies
101 Commerce Blvd (13088-4507)
PHONE..................................315 451-9410
Seth H Hoogasian, *Ch of Bd*
Mike Pilon, *General Mgr*
Mark Ptaszek, *Purch Agent*
Suraj Bhaskaran, *Engineer*
EMP: 30
SQ FT: 14,000
SALES (est): 10MM
SALES (corp-wide): 24.3B **Publicly Held**
SIC: 3861 3674 Photographic equipment & supplies; solid state electronic devices
HQ: Thermo Vision Corp
    8 Forge Pkwy Ste 4
    Franklin MA 02038

(G-7046)
VANSANTIS DEVELOPMENT INC
4595 Morgan Pl (13090-3521)
PHONE..................................315 461-0113
Bill Vanauken, *President*
EMP: 40
SQ FT: 16,356
SALES (est): 5.6MM **Privately Held**
SIC: 2448 Pallets, wood

(G-7047)
WARD STEEL COMPANY INC
4591 Morgan Pl (13090-3511)
P.O. Box 628 (13088-0628)
PHONE..................................315 451-4566
John E Ward, *President*
Terrance Ward, *Vice Pres*
Derek Ward, *Project Mgr*
EMP: 25
SQ FT: 28,000
SALES (est): 7MM **Privately Held**
SIC: 3441 Building components, structural steel

(G-7048)
WARNER ENERGY LLC (PA)
7526 Morgan Rd (13090-3502)
PHONE..................................315 457-3828
Zach Drescher, *Vice Pres*
Steven Toomey, *Administration*
EMP: 8
SALES (est): 3.8MM **Privately Held**
SIC: 3674 Solar cells

(G-7049)
WHITACRE ENGINEERING COMPANY
4522 Wetzel Rd (13090-2548)
PHONE..................................315 622-1075
Samuel Conley, *Branch Mgr*
EMP: 7
SQ FT: 48,359
SALES (corp-wide): 10MM **Privately Held**
SIC: 3441 Fabricated structural metal
PA: Whitacre Engineering Company
    4645 Rebar Ave Ne
    Canton OH 44705
    330 455-8505

(G-7050)
XTO INCORPORATED (PA)
110 Wrentham Dr (13088-4503)
PHONE..................................315 451-7807
Donald G Kreiger, *CEO*
Ric Sill, *President*
Bryon Hoffman, *Business Mgr*
D Keith Krieger, *Vice Pres*
Don Knoop, *Purch Mgr*
▲ EMP: 65
SQ FT: 38,000
SALES (est): 14.6MM **Privately Held**
WEB: www.xtoinc.com
SIC: 3053 5085 3549 Gaskets & sealing devices; adhesives, tape & plasters; seals, industrial; metalworking machinery

(G-7051)
YOUNG & FRANKLIN INC (HQ)
942 Old Liverpool Rd (13088-5596)
PHONE..................................315 457-3110
Chuck Roberts, *Purch Mgr*
Peter Kaido, *Engineer*
Mike Mossotti, *Engineer*
Doug Nolan, *Design Engr*
Vince Ouellette, *Design Engr*
EMP: 100 EST: 1918
SQ FT: 70,000
SALES: 73MM
SALES (corp-wide): 3.8B **Publicly Held**
SIC: 3492 3625 3728 3593 Control valves, aircraft: hydraulic & pneumatic; control valves, fluid power: hydraulic & pneumatic; actuators, industrial; aircraft parts & equipment; fluid power cylinders & actuators
PA: Transdigm Group Incorporated
    1301 E 9th St Ste 3000
    Cleveland OH 44114
    216 706-2960

Livingston
Columbia County

(G-7052)
F H STICKLES & SON INC
2590 Rr 9 (12541)
P.O. Box 600 (12541-0600)
PHONE..................................518 851-9048
Bernard F Stickles Jr, *President*
EMP: 15 EST: 1928
SQ FT: 1,000
SALES (est): 2.4MM **Privately Held**
SIC: 3273 5032 Ready-mixed concrete; sand, construction; gravel

Livingston Manor
Sullivan County

(G-7053)
FLOUR POWER BAKERY CAFE
87 Debruce Rd (12758-2001)
PHONE..................................917 747-6895
Rowley, *President*

Denise Rowley, *Admin Sec*
EMP: 5
SALES (est): 275K **Privately Held**
SIC: 2051 Bakery: wholesale or wholesale/retail combined

Livonia
Livingston County

(G-7054)
FINGER LAKES TIMBER CO INC
6274 Decker Rd (14487)
PHONE..................................585 346-2990
Ronald Munson, *President*
Aaron Munson, *Vice Pres*
EMP: 6
SQ FT: 1,000
SALES (est): 907.2K **Privately Held**
SIC: 2411 Logging

Lloyd Harbor
Suffolk County

(G-7055)
DILLNER PRECAST INC (PA)
14 Meadow Ln (11743-9721)
PHONE..................................631 421-9130
John Dillner, *President*
Maureen Dillner, *Corp Secy*
EMP: 5
SALES: 1MM **Privately Held**
SIC: 3272 Concrete products, precast

(G-7056)
KANNALIFE SCIENCES INC
4 Knoll Ct (11743-9731)
PHONE..................................516 669-3219
EMP: 5
SALES (est): 514.4K **Privately Held**
SIC: 2834 2833 2835 Mfg Pharmaceutical Preparations Mfg Medicinal/Botanical Products Mfg Diagnostic Substances

Locke
Cayuga County

(G-7057)
COTE HARDWOOD PRODUCTS INC (PA)
Also Called: Cote Wood Products
4725 Cat Path Rd (13092-4135)
PHONE..................................607 898-5737
Pierre Cote, *President*
Carl Cote, *Vice Pres*
Paulette Cote, *Treasurer*
EMP: 13
SALES: 950K **Privately Held**
SIC: 2421 Lumber: rough, sawed or planed

Lockport
Niagara County

(G-7058)
6478 RIDGE ROAD LLC
6251 S Transit Rd (14094-6332)
PHONE..................................716 625-8400
Somers G Sherman, *President*
EMP: 24
SALES (est): 2.4MM **Privately Held**
SIC: 3281 Granite, cut & shaped

(G-7059)
ALLVAC
695 Ohio St (14094-4221)
PHONE..................................716 433-4411
Reginald C Buri, *Principal*
Don Bailey, *Executive*
▲ EMP: 11 EST: 2012
SALES (est): 2.3MM **Privately Held**
SIC: 3312 Stainless steel

(G-7060)
ARROWHEAD SPRING VINEYARDS LLC
4746 Townline Rd (14094-9604)
PHONE..................................716 434-8030
Duncan Ross,
EMP: 5
SALES (est): 441K **Privately Held**
WEB: www.duncanrossphoto.com
SIC: 2084 Wines

(G-7061)
BARRY STEEL FABRICATION INC (PA)
30 Simonds St (14094-4111)
P.O. Box 579 (14095-0579)
PHONE..................................716 433-2144
Steven R Barry, *President*
Jody Barry, *Vice Pres*
EMP: 34
SQ FT: 8,400
SALES (est): 11.6MM **Privately Held**
WEB: www.barrysteel.com
SIC: 3441 1791 Fabricated structural metal; structural steel erection

(G-7062)
BUFFALO MACHINE TLS OF NIAGARA
4935 Lockport Rd (14094-9630)
PHONE..................................716 201-1310
Theresa Silva, *President*
Joseph Silva, *Vice Pres*
EMP: 11
SQ FT: 25,000
SALES: 500K **Privately Held**
WEB: www.bmt-usa.com
SIC: 3542 Machine tools, metal forming type

(G-7063)
CANDLELIGHT CABINETRY INC
Also Called: Renaissance Import
24 Michigan St (14094-2628)
PHONE..................................716 434-2114
Robert Sanderson, *Ch of Bd*
John Yakich, *President*
EMP: 210
SQ FT: 40,000
SALES (est): 26.6MM **Privately Held**
WEB: www.candlelightcab.com
SIC: 2434 Wood kitchen cabinets

(G-7064)
CHAMELEON COLOR CARDS LTD
6530 S Transit Rd (14094-6334)
PHONE..................................716 625-9452
Phyllis Duha, *President*
Emeric J Duha, *Corp Secy*
▲ EMP: 55
SQ FT: 16,000
SALES (est): 10.4MM
SALES (corp-wide): 67.8MM **Privately Held**
WEB: www.duhagroup.com
SIC: 3993 Displays, paint process
PA: Duha Color Services Limited
    750 Bradford St
    Winnipeg MB R3H 0
    204 786-8961

(G-7065)
CNHI LLC
Also Called: Union Sun & Journal
135 Main St Ste 1 (14094-3728)
PHONE..................................716 439-9222
Denise Young, *Branch Mgr*
EMP: 33 **Privately Held**
SIC: 2711 Newspapers: publishing only, not printed on site
HQ: Cnhi, Llc
    445 Dexter Ave
    Montgomery AL 36104

(G-7066)
CUSTOM LASER INC (PA)
6747 Akron Rd (14094-5316)
P.O. Box 962 (14095-0962)
PHONE..................................716 434-8600
Gary Brockman, *President*
Jason Walling, *Sales Staff*
Ken Hammond, *Manager*
Greg Brockman, *Executive*
EMP: 30

SQ FT: 9,000
SALES (est): 4.5MM Privately Held
WEB: www.customlaserinc.com
SIC: 7692 3479 Welding repair; etching & engraving

(G-7067)
DELPHI THERMAL SYSTEMS
350 Upper Mountain Rd (14094-1861)
PHONE................................716 439-2454
EMP: 11 EST: 2014
SALES (est): 1.6MM Privately Held
SIC: 3714 Mfg Motor Vehicle Parts/Accessories

(G-7068)
DERN MOORE MACHINE COMPANY INC
151 S Niagara St (14094-1907)
PHONE................................716 433-6243
Ken Moore, President
Sally J Moore, Vice Pres
EMP: 9
SQ FT: 10,000
SALES (est): 840K Privately Held
WEB: www.moorewashsystems.com
SIC: 3599 Machine shop, jobbing & repair

(G-7069)
DOBRIN INDUSTRIES INC (PA)
210 Walnut St Ste 22 (14094-3713)
PHONE................................800 353-2229
Paul Dobrin, President
EMP: 5
SQ FT: 5,000
SALES (est): 853.1K Privately Held
WEB: www.time-frames.com
SIC: 3499 Picture frames, metal

(G-7070)
DOUGLAS PATTERSON & SONS INC
Also Called: Paterson, Douglas G & Sons
1 Oakhurst St (14094-1910)
P.O. Box 826 (14095-0826)
PHONE................................716 433-8100
Mark Patterson, Partner
Brian Patterson, Partner
EMP: 5
SQ FT: 5,000
SALES (est): 784.4K Privately Held
SIC: 3281 Cut stone & stone products

(G-7071)
E & R MACHINE INC
211 Grand St (14094-2198)
P.O. Box 499 (14095-0499)
PHONE................................716 434-6639
Garry E Sauls, Ch of Bd
EMP: 30 EST: 1961
SALES (est): 5.5MM Privately Held
WEB: www.er-machine.com
SIC: 3599 Machine shop, jobbing & repair

(G-7072)
E Z ENTRY DOORS INC
5299 Enterprise Dr (14094-1853)
PHONE................................716 434-3440
Roger W Grear, President
Patricia R Grear, Vice Pres
EMP: 12
SQ FT: 5,000
SALES (est): 2.2MM Privately Held
WEB: www.ezentrydoors.com
SIC: 3534 Elevators & equipment

(G-7073)
EMPRO NIAGARA INC
5027 Ridge Rd (14094-8948)
PHONE................................716 433-2769
Willa L Hand, President
Willa Hand, President
Will Hand, Principal
Melissa Hand, Vice Pres
EMP: 6 EST: 1966
SALES: 500K Privately Held
WEB: www.emproniagara.com
SIC: 3441 Fabricated structural metal

(G-7074)
ENTERTRON INDUSTRIES INC
99 Robinson Pl (14094-4617)
PHONE................................716 772-7216
Stephen Luft, President
EMP: 24 EST: 1979

SQ FT: 6,000
SALES (est): 220.5K Privately Held
WEB: www.entertron.com
SIC: 3625 3672 Electric controls & control accessories, industrial; printed circuit boards

(G-7075)
FISHING VALLEY LLC
7217 N Canal Rd (14094-9411)
PHONE................................716 523-6158
Anna Zhalyalotdinova,
EMP: 5
SALES (est): 175.6K Privately Held
SIC: 3949 Bait, artificial; fishing

(G-7076)
FREEDOM RUN WINERY INC
5138 Lower Mountain Rd (14094-9767)
PHONE................................716 433-4136
Larry Manning, Manager
EMP: 7
SALES (est): 715.8K Privately Held
SIC: 2084 Wines

(G-7077)
GLOBAL ABRASIVE PRODUCTS INC (PA)
62 Mill St (14094-2460)
PHONE................................716 438-0047
John Sidebottom, President
John T Sidebottom, President
Laurie J Sidebottom, Vice Pres
Carolyn Payne, Executive Asst
EMP: 40
SALES (est): 5MM Privately Held
WEB: www.preson.com
SIC: 3291 Coated abrasive products; sandpaper

(G-7078)
GM COMPONENTS HOLDINGS LLC
Also Called: Gmch Lockport Ptc
200 Upper Mountain Rd (14094-1819)
PHONE................................716 439-2237
Pat Murtha, Branch Mgr
EMP: 209 Publicly Held
SIC: 3714 Air conditioner parts, motor vehicle; defrosters, motor vehicle; heaters, motor vehicle; radiators & radiator shells & cores, motor vehicle
HQ: Gm Components Holdings, Llc
300 Renaissance Ctr
Detroit MI 48243

(G-7079)
GM COMPONENTS HOLDINGS LLC
Also Called: Gmch Lockport
200 Upper Mountain Rd (14094-1819)
PHONE................................716 439-2463
Ronald Pirtle, Branch Mgr
EMP: 300 Publicly Held
SIC: 3629 3714 3585 3563 Condensers, for motors or generators; motor vehicle parts & accessories; refrigeration & heating equipment; air & gas compressors
HQ: Gm Components Holdings, Llc
300 Renaissance Ctr
Detroit MI 48243

(G-7080)
GM COMPONENTS HOLDINGS LLC
Also Called: General Mtr Cmponents Holdings
200 Upper Mountain Rd # 7 (14094-1819)
PHONE................................716 439-2011
Anita Mullen, Branch Mgr
EMP: 300 Publicly Held
SIC: 3629 3714 3585 3563 Condensers, for motors or generators; motor vehicle parts & accessories; refrigeration & heating equipment; air & gas compressors
HQ: Gm Components Holdings, Llc
300 Renaissance Ctr
Detroit MI 48243

(G-7081)
GM COMPONENTS HOLDINGS LLC
Also Called: Integrated Indus Resources
200 Upper Mountain Rd # 10 (14094-1819)
PHONE................................716 439-2402

Mark Inchiosa, Branch Mgr
EMP: 75 Publicly Held
WEB: www.delphiauto.com
SIC: 3053 Gaskets & sealing devices
HQ: Gm Components Holdings, Llc
300 Renaissance Ctr
Detroit MI 48243

(G-7082)
GOODING CO INC
Also Called: Insert Outsert Experts, The
5568 Davison Rd (14094-9090)
PHONE................................716 266-6252
Greg Hamilton, Corp Secy
Joseph Haas, Exec VP
Craig Curran, Vice Pres
▼ EMP: 42 EST: 1957
SQ FT: 26,500
SALES: 6.4MM
SALES (corp-wide): 323.1MM Privately Held
WEB: www.goodingcoinc.com
SIC: 2679 2752 2621 Tags & labels, paper; commercial printing, offset; wrapping & packaging papers; packaging paper
HQ: Nosco, Inc
2199 N Delany Rd
Gurnee IL 60031
847 336-4200

(G-7083)
HTI RECYCLING LLC (PA)
Also Called: Manufacturing
490 Ohio St (14094-4220)
PHONE................................716 433-9294
Derek Martin,
EMP: 22
SALES (est): 8MM Privately Held
SIC: 3069 Reclaimed rubber (reworked by manufacturing processes)

(G-7084)
J M CANTY INC
6100 Donner Rd (14094-9227)
PHONE................................716 625-4227
Thomas Canty, Ch of Bd
Jean Canty, Vice Pres
Brittney Canty, Engineer
Rich Marinelli, Engineer
Kathy Hurley, CIO
EMP: 30
SQ FT: 38,000
SALES (est): 8MM Privately Held
WEB: www.jmcanty.com
SIC: 3443 3648 2891 Vessels, process or storage (from boiler shops): metal plate; lighting equipment; sealants

(G-7085)
JACK J FLORIO JR
Also Called: Micro Graphics
36b Main St (14094-3607)
PHONE................................716 434-9123
Jack J Florio Jr, Owner
EMP: 5
SALES (est): 462.6K Privately Held
SIC: 2752 2754 2759 2791 Commercial printing, offset; commercial printing, gravure; commercial printing; typesetting; bookbinding & related work; automotive & apparel trimmings

(G-7086)
JONATHAN BROSE
Also Called: Steamworks
51 Canal St (14094-2817)
PHONE................................716 417-8978
Jonathan Brose, Mng Member
EMP: 8
SALES: 160K Privately Held
SIC: 2095 5812 Roasted coffee; coffee shop

(G-7087)
LAFARGE NORTH AMERICA INC
400 Hinman Rd (14094-9276)
P.O. Box 510 (14095-0510)
PHONE................................716 772-2621
Harry McCormick, Manager
Matthew Stoll, Director
EMP: 30
SQ FT: 47,480
SALES (corp-wide): 27.6B Privately Held
WEB: www.lafargenorthamerica.com
SIC: 3241 Cement, hydraulic

HQ: Lafarge North America Inc.
8700 W Bryn Mawr Ave
Chicago IL 60631
773 372-1000

(G-7088)
MAHLE BEHR TROY INC
350 Upper Mountain Rd (14094-1861)
PHONE................................716 439-3039
EMP: 126
SALES (corp-wide): 504.6K Privately Held
SIC: 3714 Motor vehicle parts & accessories
HQ: Mahle Behr Troy Inc.
2700 Daley Dr
Troy MI 48083
248 743-3700

(G-7089)
MAHLE BEHR USA INC
Also Called: Delphi Thrmal Lckport Model Sp
350 Upper Mountain Rd (14094-1861)
PHONE................................716 439-2011
Rick Dunbar, Engineer
Dave Patterson, Branch Mgr
EMP: 450
SALES (corp-wide): 504.6K Privately Held
SIC: 3714 Motor vehicle parts & accessories
HQ: Mahle Behr Usa Inc.
2700 Daley Dr
Troy MI 48083
248 743-3700

(G-7090)
MERRITT MACHINERY LLC
10 Simonds St (14094-4111)
PHONE................................716 434-5558
Anna McCann,
◆ EMP: 20 EST: 1977
SQ FT: 30,000
SALES (est): 4.6MM Privately Held
WEB: www.merrittpmi.com
SIC: 3553 Woodworking machinery

(G-7091)
METAL CLADDING INC
230 S Niagara St (14094-1927)
PHONE................................716 434-5513
Alexander F Robb, CEO
Raymond S Adornetto, CFO
Deborah Reimer, Admin Sec
▲ EMP: 87 EST: 1945
SQ FT: 70,000
SALES (est): 14.5MM Privately Held
WEB: www.metalcladding.com
SIC: 3479 3089 Coating of metals with plastic or resins; coating, rust preventive; plastic hardware & building products; plastic & fiberglass tanks

(G-7092)
METRO GROUP INC
Also Called: Retailer
8 South St (14094-4412)
PHONE................................716 434-4055
Bernard Bradpiece, President
Mark Botsford, District Mgr
Andrew Firmin, Accounts Mgr
Steve Ludwig, Accounts Mgr
EMP: 5 EST: 1948
SQ FT: 1,500
SALES (est): 246K Privately Held
SIC: 2741 Guides: publishing only, not printed on site; shopping news: publishing only, not printed on site

(G-7093)
MILWARD ALLOYS INC
500 Mill St (14094-1712)
PHONE................................716 434-5536
Johanna Van De Mark, President
Allen Van De Mark, Vice Pres
Johanna V Mark, Plant Mgr
David Summerlee, Plant Mgr
Kevin Kristy, Maint Spvr
◆ EMP: 37
SQ FT: 60,000
SALES: 5MM Privately Held
WEB: www.milward.com
SIC: 3351 3365 Bands, copper & copper alloy; aluminum & aluminum-based alloy castings

(G-7094)
MODERN-TEC MANUFACTURING INC
4935 Lockport Rd (14094-9630)
PHONE..................................716 625-8700
Christopher Matyas, *President*
EMP: 5
SQ FT: 11,000
SALES (est): 654K **Privately Held**
SIC: 3599 Air intake filters, internal combustion engine, except auto; machine shop, jobbing & repair

(G-7095)
MOLEY MAGNETICS INC
5202 Commerce Dr (14094-1862)
PHONE..................................716 434-4023
John S Moley, *CEO*
Ronald Slaby, *Vice Pres*
Nick Moley, *Opers Staff*
Susan Davis, *Purch Agent*
Brandon Darnell, *Engineer*
▲ EMP: 12
SALES (est): 1.2MM **Privately Held**
SIC: 3621 Electric motor & generator parts

(G-7096)
NIAGARA COOLER INC
6605 Slyton Settlement Rd (14094-1144)
PHONE..................................716 434-1235
Joseph Loiacano, *President*
EMP: 7
SQ FT: 5,000
SALES (est): 1MM **Privately Held**
WEB: www.niagaracooler.com
SIC: 3443 Fabricated plate work (boiler shop)

(G-7097)
NIAGARA FIBERBOARD INC
140 Van Buren St (14094-2437)
P.O. Box 520 (14095-0520)
PHONE..................................716 434-8881
Stephen W Halas, *Ch of Bd*
Kevin Cain, *Vice Pres*
EMP: 23
SQ FT: 60,000
SALES (est): 4.1MM **Privately Held**
WEB: www.niagarafiberboard.com
SIC: 2493 2631 Fiberboard, other vegetable pulp; paperboard mills

(G-7098)
NIAGARA PRECISION INC
233 Market St (14094-2917)
PHONE..................................716 439-0956
Roger Hood, *President*
Dennis Hood, *Vice Pres*
Barbara Hood, *Admin Sec*
EMP: 24
SQ FT: 12,000
SALES (est): 4MM **Privately Held**
WEB: www.niagaraprecision.net
SIC: 3599 Machine shop, jobbing & repair

(G-7099)
NORTON PULPSTONES INCORPORATED
120 Church St (14094-2825)
P.O. Box 408, Mountville PA (17554-0408)
PHONE..................................716 433-9400
Glen Smith, *Branch Mgr*
EMP: 8
SALES (corp-wide): 1.1MM **Privately Held**
SIC: 2611 Mechanical pulp, including groundwood & thermomechanical
PA: Norton Pulpstones Incorporated
604 Lindsay Cir
Villanova PA 19085
610 964-0544

(G-7100)
ONTARIO LABEL GRAPHICS INC
6444 Ridge Rd (14094-1015)
PHONE..................................716 434-8505
Richard E Verheyn, *President*
Rose M Verheyn, *Vice Pres*
EMP: 12
SQ FT: 9,000
SALES (est): 1.5MM **Privately Held**
SIC: 2759 Labels & seals: printing

(G-7101)
PIVOT PUNCH CORPORATION
6550 Campbell Blvd (14094-9228)
PHONE..................................716 625-8000
Robert H King Jr, *CEO*
Christopher C King, *President*
Robert H King, *Chairman*
Christopher King, *Vice Pres*
Cameron May, *Vice Pres*
EMP: 87 EST: 1945
SQ FT: 32,500
SALES: 7.2MM **Privately Held**
WEB: www.pivotpunch.com
SIC: 3544 Punches, forming & stamping

(G-7102)
PRECISE PUNCH CORPORATION
6550 Campbell Blvd (14094-9210)
PHONE..................................716 625-8000
Robert H King Jr, *President*
Christopher King, *Vice Pres*
Joseph La Monto, *Accounting Mgr*
EMP: 11
SQ FT: 3,000
SALES (est): 1.1MM **Privately Held**
SIC: 3544 Punches, forming & stamping

(G-7103)
ROSS JC INC
6722 Lincoln Ave (14094-6220)
PHONE..................................716 439-1161
John Ross, *President*
Natalie Ross, *Vice Pres*
EMP: 5
SQ FT: 5,452
SALES: 400K **Privately Held**
SIC: 3545 Machine tool accessories

(G-7104)
ROYALTON MILLWORK & DESIGN
7526 Tonawanda Creek Rd (14094-9350)
PHONE..................................716 439-4092
Thomas Herberger, *President*
EMP: 5
SQ FT: 10,000
SALES (est): 743.3K **Privately Held**
SIC: 2431 Doors & door parts & trim, wood; windows & window parts & trim, wood; moldings & baseboards, ornamental & trim; staircases, stairs & railings

(G-7105)
RUBBERFORM RECYCLED PDTS LLC
75 Michigan St (14094-2629)
PHONE..................................716 478-0404
Bill Robbins, *CEO*
Susie Robbins, *Accounts Mgr*
Tianna Cialone, *Manager*
Kristin Gugino, *Manager*
Deborah A Robbins,
▼ EMP: 14
SQ FT: 30,000
SALES (est): 3.4MM **Privately Held**
WEB: www.rubberform.com
SIC: 3069 Reclaimed rubber (reworked by manufacturing processes)

(G-7106)
SENTRY METAL BLAST INC
Also Called: Sentry Metal Services
553 West Ave (14094-4116)
P.O. Box 160 (14095-0160)
PHONE..................................716 285-5241
Gary D Verost, *President*
James Verost, *Vice Pres*
Mark Verost, *Vice Pres*
EMP: 30
SQ FT: 47,000
SALES (est): 7.1MM **Privately Held**
WEB: www.sentrymetal.com
SIC: 3441 3479 Fabricated structural metal; coating of metals & formed products

(G-7107)
SPRING LAKE WINERY LLC
7373 Rochester Rd (14094-1627)
PHONE..................................716 439-5253
Tamre Varallo,
EMP: 7
SALES: 41K **Privately Held**
SIC: 2084 Wines, brandy & brandy spirits

(G-7108)
SUMMIT MSP LLC
6042 Old Beattie Rd (14094-7943)
PHONE..................................716 433-1014
J Butcher, *Mng Member*
John Butcher, *Mng Member*
Cookie Butcher,
EMP: 7
SALES (est): 776.9K **Privately Held**
WEB: www.summitprintmail.com
SIC: 2752 Commercial printing, offset

(G-7109)
SUMMIT MSP LLC
6042 Old Beattie Rd (14094-7943)
PHONE..................................716 433-1014
John Butcher, *General Mgr*
Rose Butcher, *Mng Member*
EMP: 8
SQ FT: 1,500
SALES: 767K **Privately Held**
SIC: 2752 Commercial printing, offset

(G-7110)
TDY INDUSTRIES LLC
Also Called: ATI Specialty Materials
695 Ohio St (14094-4221)
PHONE..................................716 433-4411
H Dalton, *Branch Mgr*
EMP: 35
SQ FT: 438 **Publicly Held**
WEB: www.alleghenyludlum.com
SIC: 3312 3339 Stainless steel; primary nonferrous metals
HQ: Tdy Industries, Llc
1000 Six Ppg Pl
Pittsburgh PA 15222
412 394-2800

(G-7111)
TED WESTBROOK
Also Called: Westbrook Machinery
4736 Mapleton Rd (14094-9621)
PHONE..................................716 625-4443
Ted Westbrook, *Owner*
EMP: 1 EST: 1995
SALES: 1MM **Privately Held**
SIC: 3599 Machine shop, jobbing & repair

(G-7112)
TITANIUM DEM REMEDIATION GROUP
4907 I D A Park Dr (14094-1833)
P.O. Box 471 (14095-0471)
PHONE..................................716 433-4100
EMP: 12
SALES (est): 4.6MM **Privately Held**
SIC: 3356 Nonferrous Rolling/Drawing

(G-7113)
TORRENT EMS LLC
190 Walnut St (14094-3710)
PHONE..................................716 312-4099
Michael Dehn, *CEO*
Louise Cadwalader, *Treasurer*
EMP: 16
SALES (est): 4.3MM
SALES (corp-wide): 13.8MM **Privately Held**
SIC: 3577 Computer peripheral equipment
PA: Trek, Inc.
190 Walnut St
Lockport NY 14094
716 438-7555

(G-7114)
TREK INC (PA)
190 Walnut St (14094-3710)
PHONE..................................716 438-7555
Toshio Uehara, *CEO*
Mike Dehn, *President*
Louise Cadwalader, *VP Finance*
Bruce T Williams, *Director*
John Carney, *Admin Sec*
EMP: 16
SQ FT: 30,330
SALES: 13.8MM **Privately Held**
SIC: 3825 Instruments to measure electricity

(G-7115)
TWIN LAKE CHEMICAL INC
520 Mill St (14094-1794)
P.O. Box 411 (14095-0411)
PHONE..................................716 433-3824

James J Hodan, *President*
▲ EMP: 18
SQ FT: 10,000
SALES (est): 3.9MM **Privately Held**
WEB: www.twinlakechemical.com
SIC: 2869 Industrial organic chemicals

(G-7116)
ULRICH SIGN CO INC
177 Oakhurst St (14094-1920)
PHONE..................................716 434-0167
C McCaffrey, *President*
Christopher McCaffrey, *President*
Joe Reinhart, *General Mgr*
EMP: 21 EST: 1939
SQ FT: 6,000
SALES (est): 2MM **Privately Held**
WEB: www.ulrichsigns.com
SIC: 3993 Neon signs; signs, not made in custom sign painting shops

(G-7117)
VANCHLOR COMPANY INC (PA)
45 Main St (14094-2838)
PHONE..................................716 434-2624
Richard G Shotell, *Ch of Bd*
Dirk A Van De Mark, *Vice Pres*
Jody Musolino, *Office Mgr*
◆ EMP: 12 EST: 1960
SALES (est): 2.7MM **Privately Held**
WEB: www.vanchlor.com
SIC: 2819 Aluminum chloride

(G-7118)
VANCHLOR COMPANY INC
555 W Jackson St (14094-1744)
PHONE..................................716 434-2624
Richard Shotell, *Branch Mgr*
EMP: 16
SQ FT: 30,839
SALES (corp-wide): 2.7MM **Privately Held**
WEB: www.vanchlor.com
SIC: 2819 Aluminum chloride
PA: Vanchlor Company, Inc.
45 Main St
Lockport NY 14094
716 434-2624

(G-7119)
VANDEMARK CHEMICAL INC (PA)
1 N Transit Rd (14094-2323)
PHONE..................................716 433-6764
Michael Kucharski, *CEO*
Paul Ameis, *COO*
Chris Banach, *Safety Mgr*
David Rodems, *CFO*
Clyde Ferguson, *Manager*
◆ EMP: 85 EST: 1951
SQ FT: 13,770
SALES (est): 24.1MM **Privately Held**
WEB: www.vdmchemical.com
SIC: 2869 Industrial organic chemicals

Lockwood
Tioga County

(G-7120)
H F CARY & SONS
70 Reniff Rd (14859-9753)
PHONE..................................607 598-2563
Lewis A Cary, *Owner*
EMP: 5
SALES: 250K **Privately Held**
SIC: 3272 Septic tanks, concrete

Locust Valley
Nassau County

(G-7121)
ALPHA 6 DISTRIBUTIONS LLC
Also Called: Arctix
11 Oyster Bay Rd (11560-2322)
PHONE..................................516 801-8290
Judy Ward, *CFO*
Matthew Bruderman, *Mng Member*
▲ EMP: 12
SQ FT: 3,000

SALES (est): 24.3MM **Privately Held**
SIC: 2329 5137 2339 Athletic (warmup, sweat & jogging) suits: men's & boys'; women's & children's clothing; women's & misses' athletic clothing & sportswear

(G-7122)
FARMTOBOTTLE LLC
4 Valley Rd (11560-2603)
PHONE................................631 944-8422
EMP: 5
SALES (est): 177.7K **Privately Held**
SIC: 2086 2037 Fruit drinks (less than 100% juice): packaged in cans, etc.; fruit juices

(G-7123)
FERA PHARMACEUTICALS LLC
134 Birch Hill Rd (11560-1833)
PHONE................................516 277-1449
Andrew Pras, *Sales Staff*
Frank J Dellafer,
Janet Dellafera,
EMP: 12
SQ FT: 800
SALES: 2.8MM **Privately Held**
SIC: 2834 Pharmaceutical preparations

(G-7124)
FILESTREAM INC
257 Buckram Rd (11560-1906)
P.O. Box 93, Glen Head (11545-0093)
PHONE................................516 759-4100
Yao Chu, *President*
EMP: 10
SQ FT: 1,200
SALES: 2MM **Privately Held**
WEB: www.filestream.com
SIC: 7372 Application computer software; business oriented computer software; educational computer software

(G-7125)
FOREST IRON WORKS INC
3 Elm St Ste A (11560-2149)
PHONE................................516 671-4229
Mario Gallo, *President*
EMP: 8
SQ FT: 13,000
SALES (est): 1.4MM **Privately Held**
SIC: 3446 Architectural metalwork

(G-7126)
HENRY DESIGN STUDIOS INC
129 Birch Hill Rd Ste 2 (11560-1841)
PHONE................................516 801-2760
Henry Perlstein, *President*
Henri Rayski, *Vice Pres*
Elka Perlstein, *Treasurer*
EMP: 7
SQ FT: 1,400
SALES: 1MM **Privately Held**
SIC: 3911 Jewelry, precious metal

(G-7127)
JK MANUFACTURING INC
115 Forest Ave Unit 22 (11560-4001)
PHONE................................212 683-3535
Joe Rubens, *Owner*
EMP: 9
SALES (est): 809K **Privately Held**
SIC: 3911 Jewelry, precious metal

(G-7128)
NAK INTERNATIONAL CORP (PA)
108 Forest Ave Ste 1 (11560-1743)
PHONE................................516 334-6245
Allan Seligson, *President*
Mark Zurick, *VP Admin*
Dick Kline, *Vice Pres*
Dean Musi, *Vice Pres*
▲ **EMP:** 58 **EST:** 1986
SALES (est): 14MM **Privately Held**
SIC: 3463 Nonferrous forgings

(G-7129)
STANDARD BOTS COMPANY
18 Pomeroy Ln (11560-1039)
PHONE................................646 876-2687
Evan Beard, *CEO*
▲ **EMP:** 6
SALES (est): 290.3K **Privately Held**
SIC: 3549 Assembly machines, including robotic

(G-7130)
T G S INC
6 Wildwood Ct (11560-1108)
PHONE................................516 629-6905
Rajesh Raichoudhury, *CEO*
EMP: 5
SALES (est): 285.9K **Privately Held**
WEB: www.tgs.com
SIC: 2731 Books: publishing & printing

Lodi
Seneca County

(G-7131)
LAMOREAUX LANDING WI
Also Called: Wagner Farms
9224 State Route 414 (14860-9641)
PHONE................................607 582-6162
Brenda Clawson, *Chief Engr*
Kevin Butler, *Sales Staff*
Mark Wagner,
EMP: 70
SQ FT: 4,070
SALES (est): 5.2MM **Privately Held**
WEB: www.lamoreauxwine.com
SIC: 2084 Wines

(G-7132)
WAGNER VINEYARDS LLC
9322 State Route 414 (14860-9641)
PHONE................................607 582-6976
Laura Lee, *Pub Rel Staff*
John Wagner, *Manager*
EMP: 5
SALES: 900K **Privately Held**
SIC: 2084 Wines

(G-7133)
WAGNER VINEYARDS & BREWING CO
Also Called: Ginny Lee Cafe
9322 State Route 414 (14860-9641)
PHONE................................607 582-6574
Stanley Wagner, *Owner*
Brent Wojnowski, *Manager*
EMP: 30
SQ FT: 1,200
SALES (est): 3MM **Privately Held**
WEB: www.wagnervineyards.com
SIC: 2084 0172 2082 Wines; grapes; malt beverages

Long Beach
Nassau County

(G-7134)
AIR TITE MANUFACTURING INC
Also Called: Focus Point Windows & Doors
724 Park Pl Ste B (11561-2158)
P.O. Box 149 (11561-0149)
PHONE................................516 897-0295
Fax: 516 897-0299
EMP: 120
SQ FT: 40,000
SALES (est): 1.6MM **Privately Held**
SIC: 3442 Mfg Storm Doors & Windows Metal

(G-7135)
BARRIER BREWING COMPANY LLC
612 W Walnut St (11561-2919)
PHONE................................516 316-4429
Evan Klein, *Administration*
EMP: 5 **EST:** 2012
SALES (est): 335K **Privately Held**
SIC: 2082 Malt beverages

(G-7136)
ECHO APPELLATE PRESS INC (PA)
30 W Park Ave Ste 200 (11561-2018)
PHONE................................516 432-3601
Stuart Davis, *President*
Joyce Davis, *Corp Secy*
EMP: 6
SQ FT: 4,500
SALES: 763K **Privately Held**
WEB: www.echoappellate.com
SIC: 2752 Commercial printing, offset

(G-7137)
INNOVATION IN MOTION INC
Also Called: Iim Global
780 Long Beach Blvd (11561-2238)
PHONE................................407 878-7561
David Jones, *CEO*
Thomas Szoke, *COO*
Daniel Fovzati, *Director*
Andrash Vago, *Director*
▼ **EMP:** 6
SQ FT: 10,000
SALES (est): 421.1K
SALES (corp-wide): 3.8MM **Publicly Held**
SIC: 3663 7371 3559 Mobile communication equipment; computer software development & applications; screening equipment, electric
PA: Ipsidy Inc.
670 Long Beach Blvd
Long Beach NY 11561
516 274-8700

(G-7138)
IPSIDY INC (PA)
670 Long Beach Blvd (11561-2237)
PHONE................................516 274-8700
Philip D Beck, *Ch of Bd*
Stuart Stoller, *CFO*
Paul Whittle, *CIO*
Thomas Szoke, *CTO*
Graham Arad, *General Counsel*
EMP: 19
SALES: 3.8MM **Publicly Held**
SIC: 7372 7371 Prepackaged software; computer software development & applications

---

Long Eddy
Sullivan County

(G-7139)
DEDECO INTERNATIONAL SALES INC (PA)
11617 State Route 97 (12760-5603)
PHONE................................845 887-4840
Steven M Antler, *President*
▲ **EMP:** 55
SALES (est): 7.6MM **Privately Held**
WEB: www.dedeco.com
SIC: 3291 3843 Abrasive products; dental equipment & supplies

---

Long Island City
Queens County

(G-7140)
21ST CENTURY OPTICS INC (DH)
Also Called: S&G Optical
4700 33rd St Ste 1r (11101-2401)
PHONE................................347 527-1079
Ralph Woythaler, *President*
Bernard Woythaler, *Vice Pres*
Michael Woythaler, *Vice Pres*
Al Brown, *Cust Mgr*
Morris Cohen, *Manager*
EMP: 28 **EST:** 1967
SQ FT: 22,000
SALES (est): 6MM
SALES (corp-wide): 1.4MM **Privately Held**
WEB: www.21stcenturyoptics.com
SIC: 3851 5048 3827 Ophthalmic goods; ophthalmic goods; lenses, ophthalmic; lenses, optical: all types except ophthalmic
HQ: Essilor Laboratories Of America Holding Co., Inc.
13555 N Stemmons Fwy
Dallas TX 75234
214 496-4141

(G-7141)
A W R GROUP INC
3715 Hunters Point Ave (11101-1913)
PHONE................................718 729-0412
Mark Schinderman, *President*
EMP: 5
SALES (est): 1.1MM **Privately Held**
SIC: 2385 7699 Waterproof outerwear; antique repair & restoration, except furniture, automobiles

(G-7142)
AAAA YORK INC
Also Called: York Ladders
3720 12th St (11101-6009)
PHONE................................718 784-6666
Kenneth Buettner, *President*
▲ **EMP:** 10
SQ FT: 5,000
SALES (est): 1.3MM **Privately Held**
SIC: 3531 Construction machinery

(G-7143)
ABBOT & ABBOT BOX CORP
Also Called: Abbot & Abbot Packing Service
3711 10th St (11101-6043)
PHONE................................888 930-5972
Stuart Gleiber, *President*
Douglas Gleiber, *Vice Pres*
EMP: 17 **EST:** 1888
SQ FT: 40,000
SALES (est): 3.3MM **Privately Held**
WEB: www.abbotbox.com
SIC: 2441 2448 2449 3412 Boxes, wood; pallets, wood; skids, wood; wood containers; metal barrels, drums & pails; folding paperboard boxes

(G-7144)
ABLE STEEL EQUIPMENT CO INC
5002 23rd St (11101-4595)
PHONE................................718 361-9240
Bonnie S Tarkenton, *President*
Ed Morgan, *Treasurer*
EMP: 15 **EST:** 1935
SQ FT: 30,000
SALES (est): 1.6MM **Privately Held**
WEB: www.ablesteelequipment.com
SIC: 2542 1799 2531 2522 Cabinets: show, display or storage: except wood; partitions for floor attachment, prefabricated: except wood; shelving, office & store: except wood; demountable partition installation; public building & related furniture; office furniture, except wood

(G-7145)
ACTION TECHNOLOGIES INC
Also Called: Active Business Systems
3809 33rd St Apt 1 (11101-2230)
PHONE................................718 278-1000
Francine Amendola, *President*
EMP: 5
SALES (est): 232.9K **Privately Held**
SIC: 3579 Canceling machinery, post office

(G-7146)
ADVERTISING LITHOGRAPHERS
2812 41st Ave (11101-3706)
PHONE................................212 966-7771
Randolph Hafter, *President*
Robert Hafter, *Vice Pres*
EMP: 10
SQ FT: 11,250
SALES (est): 1.3MM **Privately Held**
SIC: 2752 Commercial printing, offset

(G-7147)
AIR LOUVER & DAMPER INC (PA)
2121 44th Rd (11101-5010)
PHONE................................718 392-3232
Joseph Chalpin, *President*
EMP: 12
SQ FT: 20,000
SALES (est): 2.4MM **Privately Held**
SIC: 3822 3444 Damper operators: pneumatic, thermostatic, electric; metal ventilating equipment

(G-7148)
ALFRED MAINZER INC (PA)
2708 40th Ave (11101-3725)
PHONE................................718 392-4200
Ronald Mainzer, *President*
Barry Mainzer, *Vice Pres*
Brad Packer, *Treasurer*
Sari Mainzer, *Admin Sec*
▼ **EMP:** 50 **EST:** 1938
SQ FT: 40,000
SALES (est): 4MM **Privately Held**
WEB: www.alfredmainzer.com
SIC: 2741 Miscellaneous publishing

▲ = Import ▼=Export
◆ =Import/Export

(G-7149)
ALL CITY SWITCHBOARD CORP
3541 11th St (11106-5013)
PHONE...................718 956-7244
Peter Tsimoyianis, *President*
Efstratios Kountouris, *Treasurer*
EMP: 26
SALES (est): 8.9MM **Privately Held**
WEB: www.allcityswbd.com
SIC: 3613 Switchgear & switchboard apparatus

(G-7150)
ALLSTATEBANNERSCOM CORPORATION
Also Called: Allstate Banners
3511 9th St (11106-5103)
PHONE...................718 300-1256
Panagiotis Panagi, *President*
Alexander Phioukas, *Vice Pres*
EMP: 9
SQ FT: 2,000
SALES (est): 1.5MM **Privately Held**
SIC: 2752 Commercial printing, offset

(G-7151)
ALP STONE INC
2520 50th Ave Fl 2 (11101-4421)
PHONE...................718 706-6166
Yunus Bickici, *President*
Hakton Bor, *Vice Pres*
▲ **EMP:** 15
SALES: 4MM **Privately Held**
WEB: www.alpstone.com
SIC: 3272 1743 Stone, cast concrete; tile installation, ceramic

(G-7152)
ALPHA PACKAGING INDUSTRIES INC
2004 33rd St (11105-2010)
PHONE...................718 267-4115
David Zaret, *President*
Steven Zaret, *Corp Secy*
Michael Zaret, *Vice Pres*
EMP: 35
SQ FT: 25,000
SALES (est): 12MM **Privately Held**
SIC: 2657 Folding paperboard boxes

(G-7153)
ALUMIL FABRICATION INC
4401 21st St Ste 203 (11101-5009)
PHONE...................845 469-2874
Kyt Bazenikas, *Ch of Bd*
John Engelmann, *Inv Control Mgr*
▲ **EMP:** 17
SALES (est): 3.6MM **Privately Held**
SIC: 3442 Screens, window, metal

(G-7154)
AMBRAS FINE JEWELRY INC
Also Called: Ambras Fjc
3100 47th Ave Unit 3 (11101-3010)
PHONE...................718 784-5252
Morris Dweck, *Ch of Bd*
EMP: 50
SQ FT: 9,000
SALES (est): 5.3MM **Privately Held**
SIC: 3911 Jewelry, precious metal

(G-7155)
AMCI LTD
3302 48th Ave (11101-2418)
PHONE...................718 937-5858
Justo Lorenzotti, *President*
Luis Lorenzotti, *Vice Pres*
▲ **EMP:** 60
SQ FT: 25,000
SALES (est): 5.9MM **Privately Held**
SIC: 2499 Picture frame molding, finished; picture & mirror frames, wood

(G-7156)
AMERICAN WAX COMPANY INC
Also Called: American Cleaning Solutions
3930 Review Ave (11101-2020)
P.O. Box 1943 (11101-0943)
PHONE...................718 392-8080
Alan Winik, *CEO*
Ronald Ingber, *President*
EMP: 50
SQ FT: 65,000

SALES (est): 10.8MM **Privately Held**
WEB: www.cleaning-solutions.com
SIC: 2842 Cleaning or polishing preparations

(G-7157)
AMERICAN WOODS & VENEERS WORKS
4735 27th St (11101-4410)
PHONE...................718 937-2195
Chingyu Peng, *President*
Dianna Serro, *Manager*
EMP: 30
SQ FT: 11,000
SALES (est): 4.7MM **Privately Held**
SIC: 2499 Furniture inlays (veneers); veneer work, inlaid

(G-7158)
ANIMA MUNDI HERBALS LLC
Also Called: Rainforest Apothecary
2323 Borden Ave (11101-4508)
PHONE...................415 279-5727
Adriana Ayales, *CEO*
EMP: 6
SQ FT: 1,000
SALES (est): 556K **Privately Held**
SIC: 2834 Vitamin, nutrient & hematinic preparations for human use

(G-7159)
ANTHONY LAWRENCE OF NEW YORK
Also Called: Belfair Draperies
3233 47th Ave (11101-2426)
PHONE...................212 206-8820
Joseph Calagna, *Ch of Bd*
Anthony Lawrence, *Owner*
EMP: 20
SALES (est): 3.1MM **Privately Held**
WEB: www.anthonylawrence.com
SIC: 2391 7641 2511 Draperies, plastic & textile; from purchased materials; reupholstery; wood household furniture

(G-7160)
APPLE ENTERPRISES INC
Also Called: Apple Digital Printing
1308 43rd Ave (11101-6833)
PHONE...................718 361-2200
Howard N Sturm, *CEO*
Howard Sturm, *CEO*
Adam Sturm, *President*
EMP: 30 **EST:** 1995
SALES (est): 5.7MM **Privately Held**
WEB: www.applevisualgraphics.com
SIC: 2759 7389 Commercial printing; advertising, promotional & trade show services

(G-7161)
APPLIED SAFETY LLC
4349 10th St Ste 311 (11101-6941)
PHONE...................718 608-6292
Jose Hernandez,
EMP: 8
SALES: 200K **Privately Held**
SIC: 3564 Blowers & fans

(G-7162)
ARC REMANUFACTURING INC
1940 42nd St (11105-1113)
PHONE...................718 728-0701
William P Hayes, *President*
John Hayes, *Site Mgr*
▲ **EMP:** 60
SQ FT: 150,000
SALES (est): 9.5MM **Privately Held**
WEB: www.arcparts.com
SIC: 3714 Motor vehicle engines & parts; power steering equipment, motor vehicle; windshield wiper systems, motor vehicle; motor vehicle brake systems & parts

(G-7163)
ARCHAELOGY MAGAZINE
3636 33rd St Ste 301 (11106-2329)
PHONE...................718 472-3050
Phyliss Katz, *President*
EMP: 20
SALES (est): 1.4MM **Privately Held**
WEB: www.archaeology.org
SIC: 2721 Magazines: publishing & printing

(G-7164)
ARGO ENVELOPE CORP
4310 21st St (11101-5002)
PHONE...................718 729-2700
Lawrence Chait, *Vice Pres*
Eric Chait, *Vice Pres*
EMP: 60 **EST:** 1946
SQ FT: 50,000
SALES (est): 6.3MM **Privately Held**
SIC: 2759 2752 Envelopes: printing; commercial printing, lithographic

(G-7165)
ARGO GENERAL MACHINE WORK INC
3816 11th St (11101-6114)
PHONE...................718 392-4605
Frank Scaduto, *President*
Ignazio Scaduto, *Vice Pres*
EMP: 7
SQ FT: 2,400
SALES (est): 883K **Privately Held**
SIC: 3599 Machine shop, jobbing & repair

(G-7166)
ARGO LITHOGRAPHERS INC
4310 21st St (11101-5002)
PHONE...................718 729-2700
Lawrence Chait, *President*
Eric Chait, *Vice Pres*
EMP: 25
SQ FT: 5,000
SALES: 4MM **Privately Held**
WEB: www.argoenvelope.com
SIC: 2752 5112 5111 2789 Commercial printing, offset; stationery & office supplies; printing & writing paper; bookbinding & related work; commercial printing

(G-7167)
ASCO CASTINGS INC (PA)
3100 47th Ave Ste G (11101-3013)
PHONE...................212 719-9800
Barry Smith, *General Mgr*
EMP: 6
SQ FT: 4,000
SALES (est): 1MM **Privately Held**
WEB: www.ascocasting.com
SIC: 3915 Jewelers' castings

(G-7168)
ASTRON CANDLE MANUFACTURING CO
1125 30th Ave (11102-4098)
PHONE...................718 728-3330
Menelaos G Tzelios, *President*
◆ **EMP:** 7
SQ FT: 7,000
SALES (est): 733.7K **Privately Held**
SIC: 3999 Candles

(G-7169)
ASTUCCI US LTD
4369 9th St (11101-6907)
PHONE...................718 752-9700
EMP: 18 **Privately Held**
SIC: 3172 Mfg Personal Leather Goods
PA: Astucci, U.S., Ltd.
385 5th Ave Rm 1100
New York NY 10016

(G-7170)
ASUR JEWELRY INC
4709 30th St Ste 403 (11101-3400)
PHONE...................718 472-1687
Aydin Barka, *President*
EMP: 6
SQ FT: 2,500
SALES: 700K **Privately Held**
SIC: 3915 Jewelers' castings

(G-7171)
ATLANTIC PRECIOUS METAL CAST
4132 27th St (11101-3825)
PHONE...................718 937-7100
Ricky Barbieri, *Principal*
EMP: 9
SALES (est): 630K **Privately Held**
SIC: 3911 Jewelry, precious metal

(G-7172)
AUGUST STUDIOS
Also Called: Augusta Studios
4008 22nd St Fl 3 (11101-4826)
PHONE...................718 706-6487
August Helbling, *Owner*
EMP: 8
SALES (est): 390K **Privately Held**
SIC: 2512 7641 Upholstered household furniture; upholstery work

(G-7173)
B & B SHEET METAL INC
2540 50th Ave (11101-4421)
PHONE...................718 433-2501
Robert Baschnagel, *President*
Robert Baschnagel III, *President*
Janice Sausto, *Planning*
◆ **EMP:** 50
SALES (est): 10.4MM **Privately Held**
SIC: 3444 Sheet metal specialties, not stamped

(G-7174)
BANGLA PATRIKA INC
3806 31st St 2 (11101-2719)
PHONE...................718 482-9923
Mahabubur Rahman, *President*
EMP: 9
SQ FT: 1,250
SALES: 32K **Privately Held**
SIC: 2711 Newspapers

(G-7175)
BARGOLD STORAGE SYSTEMS LLC
4141 38th St (11101-1708)
PHONE...................718 247-7000
Gerald Goldman, *Mng Member*
Alan Goldman, *Mng Member*
Jordan Goldman, *Mng Member*
Joshua Goldman, *Mng Member*
EMP: 40
SQ FT: 3,000
SALES (est): 8.6MM **Privately Held**
WEB: www.bargoldstorage.com
SIC: 3444 1796 Sheet metalwork; installing building equipment

(G-7176)
BENLEE ENTERPRISES LLC
Also Called: Luvente
3100 47th Ave Ste 2130 (11101-3010)
PHONE...................212 730-7330
Josh Dabakarov, *Principal*
Daniel Dabakarov,
EMP: 13
SALES (est): 1MM **Privately Held**
SIC: 3911 Jewelry, precious metal

(G-7177)
BIMBO BAKERIES USA INC
4011 34th Ave (11101-1105)
PHONE...................718 545-0291
Al Larocca, *Branch Mgr*
EMP: 5 **Privately Held**
SIC: 2051 Bread, cake & related products
HQ: Bimbo Bakeries Usa, Inc
255 Business Center Dr # 200
Horsham PA 19044
215 347-5500

(G-7178)
BIRCH GUYS LLC
Also Called: Birch Coffee
4035 23rd St (11101-4818)
P.O. Box 287507, New York (10128-0026)
PHONE...................917 763-0751
Paul Schlader,
EMP: 8
SALES (est): 435.6K **Privately Held**
SIC: 2095 Roasted coffee

(G-7179)
BLATT SEARLE & COMPANY LTD (PA)
4121 28th St (11101-3757)
PHONE...................212 730-7717
Searle Blatt, *President*
Alice Blatt, *Exec VP*
▲ **EMP:** 20

SALES (est): 4.3MM **Privately Held**
WEB: www.momao.com
SIC: 2337 Suits: women's, misses' & juniors'; skirts, separate: women's, misses' & juniors'; women's & misses' capes & jackets

(G-7180)
BLEECKER PASTRY TARTUFO INC
3722 13th St (11101-6025)
PHONE.................................718 937-9830
Fax: 718 392-5965
EMP: 7
SQ FT: 7,500
SALES (est): 400K **Privately Held**
SIC: 2024 5451 Mfg Ice Cream/Frozen Desert Ret Dairy Products

(G-7181)
BRIDGE PRINTING INC
4710 32nd Pl Fl 2 (11101-2415)
PHONE.................................212 243-5390
Fax: 718 361-9123
EMP: 5
SQ FT: 8,000
SALES: 1MM **Privately Held**
SIC: 2752 Lithographic Commercial Printing

(G-7182)
CABINET SHAPES CORP
3721 12th St (11101-6008)
PHONE.................................718 784-6255
Fax: 718 392-4282
EMP: 15
SALES: 1.2MM **Privately Held**
SIC: 2434 2499 1751 Mfg Wood Kitchen Cabinets Mfg Wood Products Carpentry Contractor

(G-7183)
CAMA GRAPHICS INC
Also Called: Altum Press
3200 Skillman Ave Ste B (11101-2308)
PHONE.................................718 707-9747
Anthony Cappuccio, *President*
EMP: 12
SQ FT: 4,800
SALES (est): 830K **Privately Held**
WEB: www.camagraphics.com
SIC: 2759 Commercial printing

(G-7184)
CASSINELLI FOOD PRODUCTS INC
3112 23rd Ave (11105-2407)
PHONE.................................718 274-4881
Anthony Bonfigli, *President*
Nella Costella, *Treasurer*
EMP: 6 EST: 1973
SQ FT: 3,000
SALES: 700K **Privately Held**
SIC: 2098 5411 Macaroni & spaghetti; delicatessens

(G-7185)
CIVIL SVC RTRED EMPLOYEES ASSN
Also Called: Csrea
3427 Steinway St Ste 1 (11101-8602)
PHONE.................................718 937-0290
Kjell Kjellberg, *Editor*
EMP: 12
SALES (est): 560K **Privately Held**
SIC: 2721 Magazines: publishing & printing

(G-7186)
CLADDAGH ELECTRONICS LTD
1032 47th Rd (11101-5514)
PHONE.................................718 784-0571
William J Casey, *President*
Angelo Mottola, *Vice Pres*
EMP: 20
SQ FT: 3,000
SALES (est): 3.4MM **Privately Held**
WEB: www.claddaghelectronics.com
SIC: 3613 5065 Panelboards & distribution boards, electric; electronic parts & equipment

(G-7187)
CNC MANUFACTURING CORP
Also Called: Gt Machine & Tool
3214 49th St (11103-1403)
PHONE.................................718 728-6800
Dean Theotos, *President*
EMP: 25
SALES (est): 154.6K **Privately Held**
SIC: 3599 Machine shop, jobbing & repair

(G-7188)
COCKTAIL CRATE LLC
2323 Borden Ave (11101-4508)
PHONE.................................718 316-2033
Alex Boyd, *CEO*
EMP: 5
SALES (est): 723.9K **Privately Held**
SIC: 2085 2087 Cocktails, alcoholic; cocktail mixes, nonalcoholic
HQ: Tcwc, Llc
201 E Fourteenth St
Traverse City MI 49684
231 922-8292

(G-7189)
COE DISPLAYS INC
4301 22nd St Ste 603 (11101-5031)
P.O. Box 3203, Fort Lee NJ (07024-9203)
PHONE.................................718 937-5658
Joel Sgroe, *CEO*
Masimo Russo, *Co-Owner*
EMP: 5 EST: 1960
SQ FT: 10,000
SALES (est): 691.6K **Privately Held**
SIC: 2752 3993 Commercial printing, offset; signs & advertising specialties; automotive & apparel trimmings

(G-7190)
COLOR INDUSTRIES LLC
3002 48th Ave Ste H (11101-3401)
PHONE.................................718 392-8301
Edward Tikkanen, *Mng Member*
EMP: 8
SALES (est): 1MM **Privately Held**
SIC: 2754 Commercial printing, gravure

(G-7191)
CONTRACTORS SHEET METAL LLC
3406 Skillman Ave (11101-2315)
PHONE.................................718 786-2505
Frank Bindel, *President*
Robert Cortez, *Treasurer*
EMP: 120
SALES (est): 19.6MM **Privately Held**
SIC: 3444 Sheet metalwork

(G-7192)
COOPERFRIEDMAN ELC SUP CO INC
2219 41st Ave (11101-4835)
PHONE.................................718 269-4906
EMP: 7
SALES (corp-wide): 11.7MM **Privately Held**
SIC: 3699 1731 Electrical equipment & supplies; electrical work
HQ: Cooperfriedman Electric Supply Co., Inc.
1 Matrix Dr
Monroe Township NJ 08831
732 747-2233

(G-7193)
COSMOS COMMUNICATIONS INC
1105 44th Dr (11101-7027)
PHONE.................................718 482-1800
Jack Weiss, *Ch of Bd*
Arnold Weiss, *President*
Gerald Weiss, *Corp Secy*
Jeff King, *Exec VP*
Richard Quarto, *Vice Pres*
EMP: 105 EST: 1933
SQ FT: 54,000
SALES (est): 26.7MM **Privately Held**
WEB: www.cosmosinc.net
SIC: 2752 2791 2789 Commercial printing, offset; typesetting; bookbinding & related work

(G-7194)
CRISADA INC
3913 23rd St (11101-4816)
PHONE.................................718 729-9730
Chris Kole, *President*
EMP: 5
SALES: 1.2MM **Privately Held**
WEB: www.crisada.com
SIC: 2335 2311 Gowns, formal; tailored suits & formal jackets

(G-7195)
CUSTOM CAS INC
2631 1st St (11102-4124)
PHONE.................................718 726-3575
Yiota Yerolemuo, *President*
Tasos Yerolemuo, *Vice Pres*
EMP: 20
SQ FT: 10,000
SALES (est): 2.4MM **Privately Held**
WEB: www.customcas.com
SIC: 2434 Wood kitchen cabinets

(G-7196)
CW METALS INC
3421 Greenpoint Ave (11101-2013)
PHONE.................................917 416-7906
Caesar Witek, *President*
EMP: 20
SALES: 1MM **Privately Held**
SIC: 3444 Sheet metalwork

(G-7197)
D3 REPRO GROUP INC
3825 Greenpoint Ave (11101-1911)
PHONE.................................347 507-1075
Yisseth I Sanchez, *President*
EMP: 8 EST: 2011
SALES (est): 33.5K **Privately Held**
SIC: 2759 Commercial printing

(G-7198)
DAVID FLATT FURNITURE LTD
3842 Review Ave Ste 2 (11101-2045)
PHONE.................................718 937-7944
David Flatt, *President*
▲ **EMP:** 10
SQ FT: 11,000
SALES (est): 943.2K **Privately Held**
SIC: 2541 Display fixtures, wood

(G-7199)
DEPENDABLE LITHOGRAPHERS INC
3200 Skillman Ave (11101-2309)
PHONE.................................718 472-4200
Fax: 718 472-5260
EMP: 15
SQ FT: 15,000
SALES (est): 1.5MM **Privately Held**
SIC: 2752 2789 Lithographic Commercial Printing Bookbinding/Related Work

(G-7200)
DEPP GLASS INC
4140 38th St (11101-1709)
PHONE.................................718 784-8500
Wesley R Depp, *President*
Judy Depp, *Admin Sec*
▲ **EMP:** 12 EST: 1923
SQ FT: 14,000
SALES (est): 1.7MM **Privately Held**
WEB: www.deppglass.com
SIC: 3229 3231 Lamp parts & shades, glass; mirrored glass

(G-7201)
DI FIORE AND SONS CUSTOM WDWKG
4202 Astoria Blvd (11103-2504)
PHONE.................................718 278-1663
Santino Di Fiore, *President*
Maria T Di Fiore, *Vice Pres*
EMP: 5
SQ FT: 8,000
SALES (est): 596.4K **Privately Held**
SIC: 2434 5712 5031 2499 Wood kitchen cabinets; cabinet work, custom; kitchen cabinets; decorative wood & woodwork; kitchen & bathroom remodeling; single-family home remodeling, additions & repairs

(G-7202)
DIMENSION DEVELOPMENT CORP
3630 37th St Fl 1 (11101-1606)
PHONE.................................718 361-8825
Wiston A Williams, *President*
EMP: 9
SALES (est): 256K **Privately Held**
SIC: 1389 Testing, measuring, surveying & analysis services

(G-7203)
DRILLCO EQUIPMENT CO INC
3452 11th St (11106-5012)
PHONE.................................718 777-5986
Gus Neos, *Treasurer*
Angelo Neos, *Treasurer*
▲ **EMP:** 25
SALES (est): 4.6MM **Privately Held**
SIC: 3532 Drills, bits & similar equipment

(G-7204)
DRILLCO NATIONAL GROUP INC (PA)
2432 44th St (11103-2002)
P.O. Box 2182 (11102-0182)
PHONE.................................718 726-9801
Patrick Lacey, *President*
Jim Wieder, *Corp Secy*
Nicholas Lacey, *Vice Pres*
EMP: 36
SALES (est): 5.9MM **Privately Held**
SIC: 3531 Drags, road (construction & road maintenance equipment)

(G-7205)
DURA ENGRAVING CORPORATION
Also Called: Dura Architectural Signage
4815 32nd Pl (11101-2538)
PHONE.................................718 706-6400
Eva Forst, *CEO*
Ark Forst, *President*
Daniel Forst, *Accounts Exec*
EMP: 25 EST: 1941
SQ FT: 20,000
SALES: 2MM **Privately Held**
WEB: www.duracorp.com
SIC: 3993 Signs, not made in custom sign painting shops; name plates: except engraved, etched, etc.: metal

(G-7206)
DURAL DOOR COMPANY INC
3128 Greenpoint Ave (11101-2006)
PHONE.................................718 729-1333
Peter Macari, *President*
Louis Vella, *Vice Pres*
EMP: 13 EST: 1945
SQ FT: 2,500
SALES: 1.2MM **Privately Held**
SIC: 3534 3442 Elevators & equipment; metal doors, sash & trim

(G-7207)
DWM INTERNATIONAL INC
Also Called: Society Awards
37-18 Nthrn Blvd Ste 516 (11101)
PHONE.................................646 290-7448
David Moritz, *President*
▲ **EMP:** 15
SQ FT: 3,000
SALES (est): 1.2MM **Privately Held**
SIC: 3914 7336 Trophies; art design services

(G-7208)
E & T PLASTIC MFG CO INC (PA)
Also Called: E&T Plastics
4545 37th St (11101-1801)
PHONE.................................718 729-6226
Gary Thal, *President*
Shahid Bacchus, *Controller*
Michael D'Antonio, *Credit Mgr*
Thomas Hollingsworth, *Accounts Exec*
Daniel Sanchez, *Sales Staff*
◆ **EMP:** 40 EST: 1946
SQ FT: 15,000
SALES: 75MM **Privately Held**
SIC: 3089 Extruded finished plastic products; plastic processing

(G-7209)
EDISON PRICE LIGHTING INC (PA)
Also Called: Epl
4150 22nd St (11101-4815)
PHONE.................................718 685-0700
Emma Price, *President*
Gregory Mortman, *Vice Pres*
Richard Shaver, *Vice Pres*
Joel R Siegel, *Vice Pres*
James D Vizzini, *Vice Pres*
▲ EMP: 120 EST: 1952
SQ FT: 40,000
SALES (est): 27MM **Privately Held**
SIC: 3646 Commercial indusl & institutional electric lighting fixtures

(G-7210)
EDISON PRICE LIGHTING INC
4105 21st St (11101-6102)
PHONE.................................718 685-0700
Fulgencio Bengochea, *Branch Mgr*
EMP: 80
SALES (est): 8.6MM
SALES (corp-wide): 27MM **Privately Held**
SIC: 3646 5063 Commercial indusl & institutional electric lighting fixtures; electrical apparatus & equipment
PA: Edison Price Lighting, Inc.
4150 22nd St
Long Island City NY 11101
718 685-0700

(G-7211)
EFAM ENTERPRISES LLC
Also Called: Finestar
3731 29th St (11101-2611)
PHONE.................................718 204-1760
Toll Free:.................................888 -
Jeff Aronowitz, *Accounting Mgr*
Shai Bivas, *Mng Member*
EMP: 20
SQ FT: 12,000
SALES (est): 2.7MM **Privately Held**
SIC: 3861 5045 7699 Toners, prepared photographic (not made in chemical plants); computers, peripherals & software; printing trades machinery & equipment repair

(G-7212)
EFRON DESIGNS LTD
2121 41st Ave Ste 5b (11101-4828)
PHONE.................................718 482-8440
Daniel Efron, *President*
Jill Efron, *Vice Pres*
EMP: 8
SALES (est): 1MM **Privately Held**
SIC: 3911 Jewelry apparel

(G-7213)
ELENIS NYC INC (PA)
Also Called: Eleni's Cookies
4725 34th St Ste 305 (11101-2442)
PHONE.................................718 361-8136
Eleni Gianopulos, *CEO*
Randall Gianopulos, *President*
Matthew Gilson, *Controller*
▲ EMP: 32
SQ FT: 4,000
SALES (est): 4MM **Privately Held**
SIC: 2052 Cookies

(G-7214)
ENDEAVOR PRINTING LLC
3704 29th St (11101-2612)
PHONE.................................718 570-2720
Brian Baltes,
EMP: 5
SQ FT: 2,000
SALES: 650K **Privately Held**
SIC: 2752 Commercial printing, lithographic

(G-7215)
ESENSE LLC
4402 23rd St Ste 114 (11101-5027)
PHONE.................................718 887-9779
Brad Beckerman, *Managing Prtnr*
▲ EMP: 10
SALES (est): 1.3MM **Privately Held**
SIC: 2087 Extracts, flavoring

(G-7216)
EUROPADISK LLC
2402 Queens Plz S (11101-4602)
PHONE.................................718 407-7300
James P Shelton, *President*
Vince Sbarra, *CFO*
EMP: 50
SQ FT: 75,000
SALES: 6MM **Privately Held**
SIC: 3652 Phonograph record blanks; magnetic tape (audio): prerecorded; compact laser discs, prerecorded

(G-7217)
EXHIBIT CORPORATION AMERICA
Also Called: Exhibit Portables
4623 Crane St Ste 3 (11101)
PHONE.................................718 937-2600
Gregory Abbate, *President*
Ronald A Abbate Jr, *Chairman*
Lorraine Pasieka, *Treasurer*
Giannina Abbate, *Admin Sec*
EMP: 30 EST: 1965
SQ FT: 50,000
SALES: 100K **Privately Held**
SIC: 3993 7389 2522 2521 Signs & advertising specialties; interior designer; office furniture, except wood; wood office furniture

(G-7218)
EXPERT MACHINE SERVICES INC
3944a 28th St (11101-3729)
PHONE.................................718 786-1200
Stuart Fischer, *President*
EMP: 5
SALES (est): 500.6K **Privately Held**
SIC: 3599 Machine shop, jobbing & repair

(G-7219)
EXPERT METAL SLITTERS CORP
3740 12th St (11101-6009)
PHONE.................................718 361-2735
Kent Derossi, *President*
▲ EMP: 6
SQ FT: 22,000
SALES (est): 1.3MM **Privately Held**
SIC: 3549 Cutting & slitting machinery

(G-7220)
FALCON PERSPECTIVES INC
28 Vernon Blvd Ste 45 (11101)
PHONE.................................718 706-9168
Elizabeth Toma, *President*
Frank Marrazzo, *Manager*
EMP: 8
SQ FT: 14,000
SALES (est): 1MM **Privately Held**
SIC: 3498 Coils, pipe: fabricated from purchased pipe

(G-7221)
FASHION RIBBON CO INC (PA)
Also Called: Pascale Madonna
3401 38th Ave (11101-2223)
PHONE.................................718 482-0100
William Rosenzweig, *Ch of Bd*
Jeffrey Rosenzweig, *President*
Donald Rubin, *President*
▲ EMP: 35 EST: 1949
SQ FT: 28,000
SALES (est): 1.6MM **Privately Held**
WEB: www.fashionribbon.com
SIC: 2241 Ribbons

(G-7222)
FELDMAN MANUFACTURING CORP
3010 41st Ave Ste 3fl (11101-2814)
PHONE.................................718 433-1700
Richard Feldman, *President*
▲ EMP: 93
SALES (est): 5.4MM **Privately Held**
WEB: www.ebathingsuit.com
SIC: 2339 Bathing suits: women's, misses' & juniors'

(G-7223)
FIREFIGHTERS JOURNAL
2420 Jackson Ave (11101-4323)
PHONE.................................718 391-0283
EMP: 25

SALES (est): 513.7K **Privately Held**
SIC: 2711 Newspapers-Publishing/Printing

(G-7224)
FIRST DISPLAYS INC
2415 43rd Ave Fl 2 (11101-4623)
PHONE.................................347 642-5972
Kai K Wong, *Ch of Bd*
Philip Wong, *President*
▲ EMP: 10
SALES (est): 276.6K **Privately Held**
SIC: 2752 Commercial printing, lithographic

(G-7225)
FISONIC CORP
4402 23rd St (11101-5000)
PHONE.................................212 732-3777
Robert Kremer, *CEO*
EMP: 8
SQ FT: 4,000 **Privately Held**
SIC: 3561 3433 Industrial pumps & parts; heating equipment, except electric
PA: Fisonic Corp
31-00 47th Ave Ste 106
New York NY 10023

(G-7226)
FOO YUAN FOOD PRODUCTS CO INC
2301 Borden Ave (11101-4517)
PHONE.................................212 925-2840
George Chuang, *President*
▲ EMP: 9 EST: 1979
SQ FT: 1,200
SALES (est): 805.2K **Privately Held**
SIC: 2092 Fish, fresh: prepared

(G-7227)
GAILER STAMPING DIECUTTING LLC
3718 Nthrn Blvd 324 Fl 3 (11101)
PHONE.................................212 243-5662
Dennis Dourgarian, *Manager*
EMP: 12 EST: 2000
SQ FT: 12,000
SALES: 2MM **Privately Held**
SIC: 2759 3554 Embossing on paper; die cutting & stamping machinery, paper converting

(G-7228)
GALAS FRAMING SERVICES
4224 Orchard St Fl 4 (11101-2936)
PHONE.................................718 706-0007
Fax: 718 706-0731
EMP: 15
SQ FT: 10,000
SALES: 750K **Privately Held**
SIC: 2499 5023 7699 Mfg Wood Products Whol Homefurnishings Repair Services

(G-7229)
GALMER LTD
Also Called: Galmer Silversmiths
4301 21st St Ste 130b (11101-5082)
PHONE.................................718 392-4609
Michael Izrael, *Ch of Bd*
EMP: 9
SQ FT: 10,000
SALES (est): 770K **Privately Held**
SIC: 3499 3471 Novelties & giftware, including trophies; plating of metals or formed products

(G-7230)
GEM METAL SPINNING & STAMPING
517 47th Rd (11101-5592)
PHONE.................................718 729-7014
Stephen Sloop, *President*
EMP: 5
SQ FT: 12,500
SALES: 175K **Privately Held**
SIC: 3469 Spinning metal for the trade; stamping metal for the trade

(G-7231)
GN PRINTING
4216 34th Ave (11101-1110)
PHONE.................................718 784-1713
Tony Barsamin, *President*
EMP: 20
SALES (est): 933K **Privately Held**
SIC: 2752 Commercial printing, offset

(G-7232)
GRADUAL LLC
1040 46th Ave Fl 2 (11101-5217)
PHONE.................................347 293-0974
Russell Greenberg, *Mng Member*
EMP: 10
SALES (est): 500.4K **Privately Held**
SIC: 3579 Time clocks & time recording devices

(G-7233)
GRAPHICS 247 CORP
4402 23rd St Ste 113 (11101-5027)
PHONE.................................718 729-2470
George Ibanez, *President*
EMP: 7
SALES (est): 625.5K **Privately Held**
WEB: www.graphics247.com
SIC: 2759 Publication printing

(G-7234)
GRAPHICS SERVICE BUREAU INC (PA)
Also Called: Gsb Digital
3030 47th Ave Ste 535 (11101-3492)
PHONE.................................212 684-3600
Stephan Steiner, *President*
Troy E Steiner, *Vice Pres*
Samantha Weiss, *Accounts Exec*
Jessica Andersen, *Business Anlyst*
Evan Andersen, *Manager*
EMP: 12
SQ FT: 5,000
SALES (est): 11.3MM **Privately Held**
WEB: www.gsbinc.net
SIC: 2759 Commercial printing

(G-7235)
GREAT WALL CORP
4727 36th St (11101-1823)
PHONE.................................212 704-4372
Ping Nen Lin, *Ch of Bd*
George Lin, *President*
▲ EMP: 120
SQ FT: 86,000
SALES (est): 9.6MM **Privately Held**
SIC: 2339 Athletic clothing: women's, misses' & juniors'

(G-7236)
GUARANTEED PRINTING SVC CO INC
4710 33rd St (11101-2408)
PHONE.................................212 929-2410
Bob Cohen, *President*
EMP: 20 EST: 1931
SQ FT: 3,000
SALES: 3MM **Privately Held**
SIC: 2752 Commercial printing, offset

(G-7237)
H K TECHNOLOGIES INC
4332 22nd St Ste 405 (11101-5079)
PHONE.................................718 255-1898
Rie Fechita, *Ch of Bd*
EMP: 4
SQ FT: 800
SALES (est): 1.1MM **Privately Held**
WEB: www.hktechnologies.com
SIC: 3674 Semiconductors & related devices

(G-7238)
HANNA ALTINIS CO INC
3601 48th Ave (11101-1815)
PHONE.................................718 706-1134
Kenny Altinis, *President*
John Acello, *Accountant*
EMP: 50
SQ FT: 10,000
SALES (est): 4.9MM **Privately Held**
WEB: www.altunis.us
SIC: 3911 Jewelry, precious metal

(G-7239)
HEALTHY BRAND OIL CORP (PA)
5215 11th St Ste A (11101-5830)
PHONE.................................718 937-0806
Bradly Green, *Chairman*
Jason Thomas, *Vice Pres*
▲ EMP: 20
SQ FT: 1,000
SALES (est): 81MM **Privately Held**
SIC: 2079 Cooking oils, except corn: vegetable refined

(G-7240)

HERBERT JAFFE INC
4011 Skillman Ave (11104-3203)
P.O. Box 4189 (11104-0189)
PHONE...................................718 392-1956
Herbert Jaffe, *President*
Henny Jaffe, *Treasurer*
EMP: 5
SQ FT: 5,000
SALES: 350K **Privately Held**
SIC: 3559 Sewing machines & attachments, industrial

(G-7241)

HERBERT WOLF CORP
3658 37th St Ste 3 (11101-1651)
PHONE...................................718 392-2424
Eric Wolf, *President*
EMP: 5 EST: 1947
SQ FT: 3,200
SALES: 552K **Privately Held**
SIC: 3534 3599 Elevators & equipment; grinding castings for the trade

(G-7242)

HERSCO-ORTHOTIC LABS CORP
Also Called: Hersco-Arch Products
3928 Crescent St (11101-3802)
PHONE...................................718 391-0416
James Kennedy, *President*
Cathal Kennedy, *Executive*
EMP: 20 EST: 1939
SQ FT: 3,000
SALES (est): 1.5MM **Privately Held**
WEB: www.hersco.com
SIC: 3842 Orthopedic appliances; foot appliances, orthopedic

(G-7243)

HOLA PUBLISHING CO
Also Called: Spanish Tele Dirctry Hola 912
2932 Northern Blvd (11101-4013)
PHONE...................................718 424-3129
Hernando Solano, *President*
EMP: 5
SALES: 190K **Privately Held**
SIC: 2741 Directories, telephone: publishing only, not printed on site

(G-7244)

HUMBOLDT WOODWORKING
3836 11th St (11101-6114)
PHONE...................................718 707-0022
Moshe Granit, *CEO*
EMP: 5
SALES (est): 507.5K **Privately Held**
SIC: 2431 Millwork

(G-7245)

I 2 PRINT INC
3819 24th St (11101-3619)
PHONE...................................718 937-8800
Shulan Leong, *President*
EMP: 10
SALES (est): 1.8MM **Privately Held**
WEB: www.i2print.com
SIC: 2752 Commercial printing, offset

(G-7246)

IMPORT-EXPORT CORPORATION
Also Called: Wilda
3814 30th St (11101-2792)
PHONE...................................718 707-0880
William Wu, *President*
▲ EMP: 15
SQ FT: 2,500
SALES: 7.5MM **Privately Held**
SIC: 3199 Equestrian related leather articles

(G-7247)

IN TOON AMKOR FASHIONS INC
Also Called: Galaxy Knitting Mills
4809 34th St (11101-2515)
PHONE...................................718 937-4546
EMP: 30 EST: 1985
SQ FT: 50,000
SALES (est): 1.9MM **Privately Held**
SIC: 2254 Mfg Underwear

(G-7248)

INNOVATIVE INDUSTRIES LLC
4322 22nd St Ste 205 (11101-5004)
P.O. Box 92, Westernville (13486-0092)
PHONE...................................718 784-7300
EMP: 7
SALES (est): 854.5K **Privately Held**
SIC: 3999 Barber & beauty shop equipment

(G-7249)

INTERIORS-PFT INC
Also Called: Props For Today
3200 Skillman Ave Fl 3 (11101-2308)
PHONE...................................212 244-9600
Dyann Klein, *President*
EMP: 48
SALES (est): 4.8MM **Privately Held**
SIC: 2599 Factory furniture & fixtures

(G-7250)

J C CONTINENTAL INC
Also Called: Continental Jewelry
3100 47th Ave (11101-3013)
PHONE...................................212 643-2051
Tibor Lebovich, *President*
Alexander Berger, *Treasurer*
▲ EMP: 5
SQ FT: 1,000
SALES (est): 57.2K **Privately Held**
SIC: 3911 Jewelry, precious metal

(G-7251)

J J CREATIONS INC
4742 37th St (11101-1804)
PHONE...................................718 392-2828
John Thor, *President*
EMP: 50
SALES: 22MM **Privately Held**
WEB: www.jjcreations.com
SIC: 3911 3961 Costume jewelry; earrings, precious metal

(G-7252)

JADO SEWING MACHINES INC
4008 22nd St (11101-4826)
PHONE...................................718 784-2314
Alexander Saks, *President*
EMP: 20
SQ FT: 14,000
SALES: 2.5MM **Privately Held**
WEB: www.jadosewingmachine.com
SIC: 3639 Sewing machines & attachments, domestic

(G-7253)

JIM HENSON COMPANY INC
Also Called: Jim Henson Productions
3718 Northern Blvd # 400 (11101-1636)
PHONE...................................212 794-2400
Howard Sharp, *Branch Mgr*
EMP: 50
SALES (corp-wide): 8.5MM **Privately Held**
WEB: www.farscape.com
SIC: 2399 Emblems, badges & insignia
PA: The Jim Henson Company Inc
    1416 N La Brea Ave
    Los Angeles CA 90028
    323 856-6680

(G-7254)

JOHN GAILER INC
3718 Northern Blvd Ste 3 (11101-1631)
PHONE...................................212 243-5662
Steven Dourgarian, *President*
Dennis Dourgarian, *Vice Pres*
EMP: 30
SALES (est): 2.2MM **Privately Held**
WEB: www.gailer.com
SIC: 3999 3111 Gold stamping, except books; die-cutting of leather

(G-7255)

JOHN R ROBINSON INC
3805 30th St (11101-2716)
PHONE...................................718 786-6088
Frank V Cunningham, *President*
Sharon Racette, *Vice Pres*
EMP: 20
SQ FT: 5,000
SALES (est): 4MM **Privately Held**
SIC: 3443 Heat exchangers, condensers & components

(G-7256)

JULIAN FREIRICH COMPANY INC (PA)
4601 5th St (11101-6282)
PHONE...................................718 361-9111
Paul Dardiens, *President*
Jeff Freirich, *President*
Jerry Freirich, *Chairman*
Digna Freirich, *Admin Sec*
EMP: 30 EST: 1923
SQ FT: 25,000
SALES (est): 4.8MM **Privately Held**
WEB: www.freirich.com
SIC: 2013 Prepared beef products from purchased beef; corned beef from purchased meat; pastrami from purchased meat; roast beef from purchased meat

(G-7257)

JURIST COMPANY INC
1105 44th Dr (11101-5107)
PHONE...................................212 243-8008
Joseph Jurist, *President*
David Shushansky, *Exec VP*
EMP: 7
SQ FT: 13,000
SALES (est): 1.4MM **Privately Held**
WEB: www.juristprinting.com
SIC: 2752 Commercial printing, offset

(G-7258)

JUSTA COMPANY
3464 9th St (11106-5102)
PHONE...................................718 932-6139
Janechai Sayananon, *Owner*
EMP: 8
SQ FT: 4,000
SALES: 900K **Privately Held**
WEB: www.justacompany.com
SIC: 3873 5199 Watches, clocks, watchcases & parts; gifts & novelties

(G-7259)

JUSTIN ASHLEY DESIGNS INC
4301 21st St Ste 212a (11101-5049)
PHONE...................................718 707-0200
Scott Barcvi, *President*
▲ EMP: 6
SALES (est): 540K **Privately Held**
SIC: 3911 Jewelry, precious metal

(G-7260)

KAITERY FURS LTD
2529 49th St (11103-1120)
PHONE...................................718 204-1396
Jimmy Kaitery, *President*
◆ EMP: 6 EST: 1970
SQ FT: 7,500
SALES (est): 837.3K **Privately Held**
SIC: 2371 Hats, fur; apparel, fur

(G-7261)

KARR GRAPHICS CORP
2219 41st Ave Ste 2a (11101-4807)
PHONE...................................212 645-6000
Larry Karr, *President*
Myron Karr, *Vice Pres*
EMP: 20
SQ FT: 25,000
SALES (est): 2.9MM **Privately Held**
SIC: 2752 2759 2796 2754 Commercial printing, lithographic; thermography; platemaking services; stationery: gravure printing

(G-7262)

KERNS MANUFACTURING CORP (PA)
3714 29th St (11101-2690)
PHONE...................................718 784-4044
Simon Srybnik, *Ch of Bd*
Louis Srybnik, *President*
Julius Srybnik, *Admin Sec*
▲ EMP: 125
SQ FT: 60,000
SALES (est): 19MM **Privately Held**
WEB: www.kernsmfg.com
SIC: 3469 3724 3812 3714 Electronic enclosures, stamped or pressed metal; aircraft engines & engine parts; search & navigation equipment; motor vehicle parts & accessories

(G-7263)

KOENIG IRON WORKS INC
814 37th Ave (11101-6011)
PHONE...................................718 433-0900
Barry Leistner, *President*
Norman Rosenbaum, *Vice Pres*
Mike Bock, *Project Mgr*
Peter Vermazen, *Project Mgr*
Paul Piwnicki, *Director*
EMP: 50
SQ FT: 35,000
SALES (est): 12.3MM **Privately Held**
WEB: www.koenigironworks.com
SIC: 3441 3446 Fabricated structural metal; ornamental metalwork

(G-7264)

KONG KEE FOOD CORP
4831 Van Dam St (11101-3101)
PHONE...................................718 937-2746
Ip Kong, *President*
▲ EMP: 45
SQ FT: 18,000
SALES (est): 5.8MM **Privately Held**
SIC: 2026 5141 Fermented & cultured milk products; groceries, general line

(G-7265)

KOREA CENTRAL DAILY NEWS INC (HQ)
4331 36th St (11101-1703)
PHONE...................................718 361-7700
Byoungsoo Sohn, *CEO*
Seok J Kim, *General Mgr*
Seuk Lee, *Vice Pres*
Sangmook Lee, *CFO*
Hyung J Phang, *Manager*
▲ EMP: 58
SQ FT: 10,000
SALES (est): 8.9MM **Privately Held**
SIC: 2711 Newspapers, publishing & printing

(G-7266)

KOREA TIMES NEW YORK INC (HQ)
3710 Skillman Ave (11101-1731)
PHONE...................................718 784-4526
Jae Min Chang, *CEO*
Hak Shin, *President*
▲ EMP: 80 EST: 1967
SQ FT: 16,000
SALES (est): 14.4MM
SALES (corp-wide): 85.3MM **Privately Held**
SIC: 2711 Newspapers: publishing only, not printed on site; newspapers, publishing & printing
PA: The Korea Times Los Angeles Inc
    3731 Wilshire Blvd
    Los Angeles CA 90010
    323 692-2000

(G-7267)

L & L OVERHEAD GARAGE DOORS (PA)
3125 45th St (11103-1620)
PHONE...................................718 721-2518
Louis Lauri Jr, *President*
EMP: 9
SQ FT: 5,000
SALES (est): 783.8K **Privately Held**
SIC: 3442 5211 Garage doors, overhead: metal; garage doors, sale & installation

(G-7268)

LARKIN ANYA LTD
4310 23rd St Ste 2b (11101-5020)
PHONE...................................718 361-1827
Anya Larkin, *President*
EMP: 9 EST: 1981
SQ FT: 4,000
SALES (est): 1.7MM **Privately Held**
WEB: www.anyalarkin.com
SIC: 2679 Wallpaper

(G-7269)

LARTE DEL GELATO GRUPPO INC
3100 47th Ave (11101-3013)
PHONE...................................718 383-6600
Francesco Realmuto, *Principal*
▲ EMP: 10

SALES (est): 1MM **Privately Held**
SIC: **2024** 2053 Ice cream & frozen desserts; cakes, bakery: frozen

(G-7270)
LESIEUR CRISTAL INC
1034 44th Dr Fl 2 (11101-7001)
PHONE....................................646 604-4314
Nizar Azarkane, *Managing Dir*
EMP: 5
SALES (est): 139.9K **Privately Held**
SIC: **2079** Olive oil

(G-7271)
LIC BREWERY LLC
Also Called: Lic Beer Project
3928 23rd St (11101-4817)
PHONE....................................917 832-6840
EMP: 5
SALES (est): 83K **Privately Held**
SIC: **2082** Brewers' grain

(G-7272)
LIFFEY SHEET METAL CORP
4555 36th St (11101-1821)
PHONE....................................347 381-1134
Michael Freeman, *Principal*
Francisco Piscitelly, *Principal*
Priscilla Freeman, *Shareholder*
Bridgette Piscitelli, *Shareholder*
EMP: 14
SALES (est): 2.7MM **Privately Held**
SIC: **3444** 1711 Ducts, sheet metal; ventilation & duct work contractor

(G-7273)
LINCO PRINTING INC
5022 23rd St (11101-4502)
PHONE....................................718 937-5141
Yu-Ou Lin, *President*
Sandy Lin, *Vice Pres*
Tammy Lee, *Manager*
Ivy Zhuo, *Clerk*
EMP: 40 EST: 1975
SQ FT: 34,000
SALES: 4.6MM **Privately Held**
WEB: www.lincoprinting.com
SIC: **2759** Letterpress printing

(G-7274)
LINEAR LIGHTING CORPORATION
3130 Hunters Point Ave (11101-3132)
PHONE....................................718 361-7552
Stanley Deutsch, *President*
Larry Deutsch, *Principal*
Lois Shorr, *Human Res Mgr*
Michael Deutsch, *VP Sales*
Fred Jona, *Manager*
▲ EMP: 150
SQ FT: 85,000
SALES (est): 27.1MM **Privately Held**
WEB: www.linearlighting.com
SIC: **3646** 5063 Commercial indusl & institutional electric lighting fixtures; electrical apparatus & equipment

(G-7275)
LIQUID KNITS INC
3200 Skillman Ave Fl 2 (11101-2308)
PHONE....................................718 706-6600
Jeffrey Schechter, *President*
▲ EMP: 18
SQ FT: 35,000
SALES (est): 2.7MM **Privately Held**
WEB: www.liquidknits.com
SIC: **2339** Women's & misses' athletic clothing & sportswear

(G-7276)
LITELAB CORP
540 54th Ave (11101-5925)
PHONE....................................718 361-6829
Rafael Ramirez, *Manager*
Edgar Alvarado, *Supervisor*
EMP: 6
SALES (corp-wide): 37.6MM **Privately Held**
WEB: www.litelab.com
SIC: **3646** Commercial indusl & institutional electric lighting fixtures
PA: Litelab Corp.
    251 Elm St
    Buffalo NY 14203
    716 856-4300

(G-7277)
LMC 49TH INC (DH)
Also Called: La Maison Du Chocolat
4707 30th Pl (11101-3105)
PHONE....................................718 361-9161
Armand Bongrain, *Ch of Bd*
▲ EMP: 35
SALES (est): 425.4K
SALES (corp-wide): 6.3B **Privately Held**
SIC: **2066** Chocolate; baking chocolate; chocolate bars, solid
HQ: La Maison Du Chocolat
    65 Avenue De Segur
    Paris 7e Arrondissement 75007
    142 273-944

(G-7278)
LOCKWOOD TRADE JOURNAL CO INC
Also Called: Tea & Coffee Trade Journal
3743 Crescent St Ste 2 (11101-3568)
PHONE....................................212 391-2060
George E Lockwood Jr, *President*
Frederick Lockwood, *Publisher*
Ted Hoyt, *Editor*
Robert Lockwood Sr, *Vice Pres*
▲ EMP: 20 EST: 1872
SQ FT: 4,000
SALES (est): 1.9MM **Privately Held**
WEB: www.lockwoodpublications.com
SIC: **2721** Trade journals: publishing & printing

(G-7279)
LONG ISLAND BRAND BEVS LLC
3788 Review Ave (11101-2052)
PHONE....................................855 542-2832
Philip Thomas, *CEO*
EMP: 100
SQ FT: 25,000
SALES (est): 22.1MM
SALES (corp-wide): 4.4MM **Privately Held**
SIC: **2086** Iced tea & fruit drinks, bottled & canned
PA: Long Blockchain Corp.
    12 Dubon Ct Ste 1
    Farmingdale NY 11735
    855 542-2832

(G-7280)
LUCINAS GOURMET FOOD INC
3646 37th St (11101-1606)
PHONE....................................646 835-9784
Desmond Morais, *President*
Pauline Morais, *Vice Pres*
EMP: 6
SQ FT: 500
SALES: 18.5K **Privately Held**
SIC: **2035** Pickles, sauces & salad dressings

(G-7281)
LUKAS LIGHTING INC
4020 22nd St Ste 11 (11101-4814)
PHONE....................................800 841-4011
Craig Corona, *CEO*
Ida Gold, *Purch Mgr*
John Martin, *Design Engr*
Angela Rendon, *Sales Mgr*
▲ EMP: 30
SALES (est): 7.1MM **Privately Held**
SIC: **3646** Commercial indusl & institutional electric lighting fixtures

(G-7282)
LUXERDAME CO INC
4315 Queens St Ste A (11101-2923)
PHONE....................................718 752-9800
EMP: 20 EST: 1933
SALES (est): 1.4MM **Privately Held**
SIC: **2341** 2342 Mfg Women's/Youth Underwear Mfg Bras/Girdles

(G-7283)
M A R A METALS LTD
2520 40th Ave (11101-3810)
PHONE....................................718 786-7868
Andreas Fiorentino, *President*
Andreas Vassiliou, *Vice Pres*
EMP: 6
SQ FT: 600
SALES (est): 500K **Privately Held**
SIC: **3911** Jewelry, precious metal

(G-7284)
MAC CRETE CORPORATION
Also Called: Mac Donuts of New York
3412 10th St (11106-5108)
PHONE....................................718 932-1803
Georga Papadopoulos, *President*
EMP: 10
SALES (est): 1.6MM **Privately Held**
SIC: **2051** 5149 Cakes, pies & pastries; bakery products

(G-7285)
MANA PRODUCTS INC (PA)
Also Called: Your Name Professional Brand
3202 Queens Blvd Fl 6 (11101-2341)
PHONE....................................718 361-2550
Nikos Mouyiaris, *Chairman*
Susannah Carney, *Vice Pres*
David Chan, *Vice Pres*
Edward Ewankov, *Vice Pres*
George Lambridis, *Vice Pres*
◆ EMP: 276
SALES (est): 284.9MM **Privately Held**
WEB: www.manaproducts.com
SIC: **2844** 5122 Cosmetic preparations; cosmetics

(G-7286)
MANA PRODUCTS INC
Esthetic Research Group
3202 Queens Blvd Fl 6 (11101-2341)
PHONE....................................718 361-5204
Necos Mouyiaris, *Branch Mgr*
EMP: 500
SALES (corp-wide): 284.9MM **Privately Held**
SIC: **2844** Cosmetic preparations
PA: Mana Products, Inc.
    3202 Queens Blvd Fl 6
    Long Island City NY 11101
    718 361-2550

(G-7287)
MANE ENTERPRISES INC
4929 30th Pl (11101-3116)
PHONE....................................718 472-4955
Bill Mountain, *CEO*
Nicholas Sackett, *President*
John Mountain, *Vice Pres*
▲ EMP: 55
SQ FT: 12,000
SALES (est): 5.4MM **Privately Held**
SIC: **2323** Men's & boys' neckwear

(G-7288)
MANHATTAN COOLING TOWERS INC
1142 46th Rd Ste 2 (11101-6293)
PHONE....................................212 279-1045
Richard Silver, *President*
EMP: 15
SQ FT: 10,400
SALES (est): 1.8MM **Privately Held**
SIC: **3443** Cooling towers, metal plate

(G-7289)
MANHATTAN DISPLAY INC
1215 Jackson Ave Ste B (11101-5551)
PHONE....................................718 392-1365
John Petursson, *President*
EMP: 6
SQ FT: 1,500
SALES (est): 697.4K **Privately Held**
WEB: www.manhattandisplay.com
SIC: **2542** 5046 Office & store showcases & display fixtures; store fixtures & display equipment

(G-7290)
MASTERCRAFT MANUFACTURING CO
3715 11th St (11101-6006)
PHONE....................................718 729-5620
Peter Borsits, *President*
EMP: 5 EST: 1960
SALES (est): 310K **Privately Held**
SIC: **3993** Advertising novelties

(G-7291)
MATOV INDUSTRIES INC
Also Called: Roxter Lighting
1011 40th Ave (11101-6105)
PHONE....................................718 392-5060
Alan Hochster, *President*
EMP: 20

SQ FT: 15,000
SALES (est): 3.4MM **Privately Held**
SIC: **3645** 3469 3646 5063 Residential lighting fixtures; metal stampings; commercial indusl & institutional electric lighting fixtures; lighting fixtures

(G-7292)
MECHOSHADE SYSTEMS INC (DH)
4203 35th St (11101-2301)
PHONE....................................718 729-2020
Jan Berman, *President*
Michael Haltrecht, *Business Mgr*
Carlos Herrera, *Business Mgr*
Glen Berman, *Exec VP*
Glen Burmin, *Vice Pres*
◆ EMP: 200
SQ FT: 45,000
SALES (est): 106.7MM
SALES (corp-wide): 3B **Privately Held**
WEB: www.soleilshades.com
SIC: **2591** Window shades
HQ: Springs Window Fashions, Llc
    7549 Graber Rd
    Middleton WI 53562
    608 836-1011

(G-7293)
MEDITERREAN DYRO COMPANY
1102 38th Ave (11101-6041)
PHONE....................................718 786-4888
Jimmy Austin, *President*
Amalia Malamis, *Principal*
▲ EMP: 40
SALES (est): 2.1MM **Privately Held**
SIC: **2099** Food preparations

(G-7294)
METRO DUCT SYSTEMS INC
1219 Astoria Blvd Apt 2 (11102-4478)
PHONE....................................718 278-4294
Orson Arroyo, *President*
EMP: 11
SALES (est): 1.2MM **Privately Held**
SIC: **3444** 1711 Sheet metalwork; mechanical contractor

(G-7295)
METRO GROUP INC (PA)
Also Called: Metro Grouping
5023 23rd St (11101-4501)
PHONE....................................718 729-7200
Bernard Bradpiece, *CEO*
Robert H Seidman, *President*
Reynaldo Benitez, *Engineer*
Gary Ho, *Engineer*
Jabree Brooks, *CFO*
EMP: 74 EST: 1925
SQ FT: 15,000
SALES (est): 21.4MM **Privately Held**
WEB: www.metrogroupinc.com
SIC: **3589** 1389 Water treatment equipment, industrial; chemically treating wells

(G-7296)
MICHAEL FELDMAN INC
3010 41st Ave Ste 3 (11101-2817)
PHONE....................................718 433-1700
Richard Feldman, *President*
Grace Feldman, *Treasurer*
EMP: 95 EST: 1964
SQ FT: 20,000
SALES (est): 6.6MM **Privately Held**
WEB: www.permanentfoliage.com
SIC: **2339** Bathing suits: women's, misses' & juniors'

(G-7297)
MISSION CRANE SERVICE INC (PA)
4700 33rd St (11101-2419)
PHONE....................................718 937-3333
David Chazen, *President*
EMP: 60
SQ FT: 30,000
SALES (est): 4.5MM **Privately Held**
SIC: **3999** 7993 Coin-operated amusement machines; game machines

(G-7298)
MODUTANK INC
4104 35th Ave (11101-1410)
PHONE....................................718 392-1112
John Reed Margulis, *President*
Thomas G Carren, *Vice Pres*

EMP: 10
SQ FT: 15,000
SALES (est): 2.6MM **Privately Held**
WEB: www.modutank.com
SIC: 3443 Tanks, lined: metal plate

(G-7299)
MONGRU NECKWEAR INC
1010 44th Ave Fl 2 (11101-7032)
PHONE..............................718 706-0406
Ramdihal Mongru, *President*
EMP: 40
SQ FT: 10,580
SALES (est): 4.4MM **Privately Held**
SIC: 2253 2323 5136 Neckties, knit;
men's & boys' neckwear; neckwear,
men's & boys'

(G-7300)
MUTUAL SALES CORP
Also Called: Mutual Harware
545 49th Ave (11101-5610)
PHONE..............................718 361-8373
Mary Piotrowski, *President*
Vincent Marmallardi, *Vice Pres*
Maria Stewart, *Treasurer*
Maret Asaro, *Shareholder*
Michele Gay, *Shareholder*
▲ **EMP:** 23
SQ FT: 10,000
SALES: 8.4MM **Privately Held**
SIC: 2391 7922 5131 Curtains &
draperies; equipment rental, theatrical;
textiles, woven

(G-7301)
MZB ACCESSORIES LLC
2976 Northern Blvd Fl 4 (11101-2829)
PHONE..............................718 472-7500
AMI Alterin, *Mng Member*
▲ **EMP:** 100
SALES (est): 18MM
SALES (corp-wide): 55.4MM **Privately Held**
SIC: 2844 Toilet preparations; cosmetic
preparations; deodorants, personal; lo-
tions, shaving
PA: M.Z. Berger & Co. Inc.
353 Lexington Ave Fl 14
New York NY 10016
646 690-1085

(G-7302)
N A ALUMIL CORPORATION
Also Called: Alumil NA Fabrication
4401 21st St Ste 203 (11101-5009)
PHONE..............................718 355-9393
Kyprianos Bazehika, *Ch of Bd*
John McElroy, *Vice Pres*
▲ **EMP:** 8
SALES (est): 2.7MM **Privately Held**
SIC: 3355 Aluminum rolling & drawing
PA: Alumil Aluminium Industry S.A.
Industrial Area, Stavrochori, P.O. Box
37
Kilkis 61100

(G-7303)
NATIONAL HERALD INC
Also Called: Greek Nat Hrald Dily Nwsppr In
3710 30th St (11101-2614)
PHONE..............................718 784-5255
Anthony H Diamataris, *President*
Vasilis Magalios, *Editor*
Victoria Diamataris, *Corp Secy*
Andy Dabilis, *Manager*
▲ **EMP:** 35 **EST:** 1915
SQ FT: 4,200
SALES (est): 2.6MM **Privately Held**
WEB: www.nationalherald.com
SIC: 2711 Newspapers: publishing only,
not printed on site

(G-7304)
NAZIM IZZAK INC
Also Called: N I Boutique
4402 23rd St Ste 517 (11101-5072)
PHONE..............................212 920-5546
Nazim I Guity, *President*
EMP: 6
SQ FT: 2,800
SALES (est): 494.4K **Privately Held**
SIC: 2231 5632 Apparel & outerwear
broadwoven fabrics; apparel accessories

(G-7305)
NECESSARY OBJECTS LTD (PA)
3030 47th Ave Fl 6 (11101-3433)
PHONE..............................212 334-9888
Ady Gluck Frankel, *Ch of Bd*
Bill Kauffman, *CFO*
▲ **EMP:** 50
SALES (est): 12.6MM **Privately Held**
WEB: www.necessaryobjects.com
SIC: 2335 2339 2331 Women's, juniors' &
misses' dresses; slacks: women's,
misses' & juniors'; blouses, women's &
juniors': made from purchased material

(G-7306)
NEW CLASSIC INC
4143 37th St (11101-1723)
PHONE..............................718 609-1100
Simon Yiu, *President*
Rachel Yiu, *Vice Pres*
▲ **EMP:** 14
SQ FT: 20,000
SALES (est): 1.5MM **Privately Held**
WEB: www.newclassic.net
SIC: 2387 5136 5137 Apparel belts; ap-
parel belts, men's & boys'; apparel belts,
women's & children's

(G-7307)
NEW HEYDENRYK LLC
Also Called: House of Heydenryk, The
3727 10th St (11101-6004)
PHONE..............................212 206-9611
Charles Schreiber, *President*
David Mandel, *Chairman*
Rigmor Heydenryk, *Admin Sec*
EMP: 18
SALES (est): 2.4MM **Privately Held**
WEB: www.heydenryk.com
SIC: 2499 Picture & mirror frames, wood

(G-7308)
NEW SENSOR CORPORATION (PA)
Also Called: ELECTRO-HARMONIX
5501 2nd St (11101-5908)
PHONE..............................718 937-8300
Michael Matthews, *President*
◆ **EMP:** 61
SQ FT: 89,886
SALES: 29.9MM **Privately Held**
WEB: www.newsensor.com
SIC: 3931 3671 5065 Musical instru-
ments, electric & electronic; vacuum
tubes; electronic parts & equipment

(G-7309)
NEW YORK BINDING CO INC
2121 41st Ave Ste A (11101-4833)
PHONE..............................718 729-2454
Roger Levin, *President*
Linda Van Dine, *Manager*
EMP: 40
SQ FT: 15,000
SALES (est): 4.5MM **Privately Held**
WEB: www.newyorkbindingco.com
SIC: 2241 2396 Bindings, textile; trim-
mings, textile; automotive & apparel trim-
mings

(G-7310)
NOVELTY CRYSTAL CORP (PA)
3015 48th Ave (11101-3419)
PHONE..............................718 458-6700
Rivka Michaeli, *President*
Ed Coslett, *COO*
Asher Michaeli, *Exec VP*
Joseph Michaeli, *Vice Pres*
Daniel Weatherly, *Plant Mgr*
▲ **EMP:** 100 **EST:** 1961
SQ FT: 50,000
SALES (est): 15.8MM **Privately Held**
WEB: www.noveltycrystal.com
SIC: 3089 3421 Plastic kitchenware, table-
ware & houseware; kitchenware, plastic;
cutlery

(G-7311)
NY IRON INC
3131 48th Ave Ste 2 (11101-3022)
PHONE..............................718 302-9000
Todd Devito, *Ch of Bd*
EMP: 15

SALES (est): 955.7K **Privately Held**
SIC: 7692 Welding repair

(G-7312)
NYC VINYL SCREEN PRINTING INC
4436 21st St (11101-5113)
PHONE..............................718 784-1360
Daniel Montefusco, *President*
EMP: 24
SALES (corp-wide): 1.4MM **Privately Held**
SIC: 2759 Commercial printing
PA: Nyc Vinyl Screen Printing Inc.
204 Lawrence Hill Rd
Cold Spring Harbor NY 11724
718 784-1360

(G-7313)
ODEGARD INC
3030 47th Ave Ste 700 (11101-3492)
PHONE..............................212 545-0069
John Nihoul, *Manager*
EMP: 12
SALES (corp-wide): 7.4MM **Privately Held**
WEB: www.odegardinc.com
SIC: 2273 Carpets & rugs
PA: Odegard, Inc.
200 Lexington Ave Rm 1206
New York NY 10016
212 545-0205

(G-7314)
OUGRA INC
3100 47th Ave Unit 4 (11101-3068)
PHONE..............................646 342-4575
Phillip Soliman, *President*
EMP: 4
SALES: 2MM **Privately Held**
SIC: 7372 Business oriented computer
software

(G-7315)
P C RFRS RADIOLOGY
Also Called: Radiology Film Reading Svcs
3630 37th St Frnt (11101-1606)
PHONE..............................212 586-5700
Joseph Gottesman, *President*
Joseph J Gottesman, *Med Doctor*
EMP: 8
SQ FT: 1,000
SALES (est): 874.1K **Privately Held**
WEB: www.radiologyreadings.com
SIC: 3577 Film reader devices

(G-7316)
P-RYTON CORP
Also Called: Skin Dynamic
504 50th Ave (11101-5712)
PHONE..............................718 937-7052
Joseph Palumbo Jr, *President*
Sergio Palumbo, *Vice Pres*
Joseph Palumbo Sr, *Shareholder*
Linda Palumbo, *Admin Sec*
▲ **EMP:** 11
SQ FT: 6,000
SALES (est): 1.9MM **Privately Held**
WEB: www.p-ryton.com
SIC: 3841 Surgical & medical instruments

(G-7317)
PACIFIC POLY PRODUCT CORP
3934 Crescent St (11101-3802)
PHONE..............................718 786-7129
Henry Ly, *President*
▲ **EMP:** 10 **EST:** 1982
SQ FT: 10,000
SALES: 1MM **Privately Held**
SIC: 2673 Plastic bags: made from pur-
chased materials; garment bags (plastic
film): made from purchased materials

(G-7318)
PADDY LEE FASHIONS INC
4709 36th St Fl 2 (11101-1839)
PHONE..............................718 786-6020
Ralph Covelli Jr, *CEO*
John Covelli, *Exec VP*
EMP: 15 **EST:** 1955
SQ FT: 46,000
SALES (est): 3MM **Privately Held**
WEB: www.paddylee.com
SIC: 2339 2331 Slacks: women's, misses'
& juniors'; blouses, women's & juniors':
made from purchased material

(G-7319)
PARKMATIC CAR PRKG SYSTEMS LLC (PA)
47-10 A 32nd Pl (11101)
PHONE..............................516 224-7700
Max Wassef, *President*
Elza Wassef, *Vice Pres*
EMP: 3 **EST:** 2016
SQ FT: 2,000
SALES: 3.5MM **Privately Held**
SIC: 3559 1799 Parking facility equipment
& supplies; parking facility equipment in-
stallation

(G-7320)
PARSONS-MEARES LTD
2107 41st Ave Ste 1l (11101-4802)
PHONE..............................212 242-3378
James Mears, *President*
Sally Ann Parsons, *Vice Pres*
EMP: 56
SQ FT: 12,000
SALES (est): 4.7MM **Privately Held**
WEB: www.parsons-meares.com
SIC: 2389 Theatrical costumes

(G-7321)
PASS EM-ENTRIES INC (PA)
3914 Crescent St (11101-3802)
PHONE..............................718 392-0100
Joseph Stegmayer, *President*
John La Salle, *Vice Pres*
EMP: 18
SALES (est): 1.1MM **Privately Held**
SIC: 2395 Pleating & stitching

(G-7322)
PEACHTREE ENTERPRISES INC
2219 41st Ave Ste 4a (11101-4807)
PHONE..............................212 989-3445
Robert Sussman, *President*
Jeffrey Alpert, *Vice Pres*
Bart Sussman, *Treasurer*
EMP: 38 **EST:** 1976
SALES (est): 6.4MM **Privately Held**
WEB: www.peachtree-printingnyc.com
SIC: 2752 Commercial printing, offset

(G-7323)
PELICAN BAY LTD
Also Called: Ravioli Store, The
3901 22nd St (11101-4809)
PHONE..............................718 729-9300
Donna Nasoff, *Principal*
Michael Nasoff, *Principal*
EMP: 12
SALES (est): 990K **Privately Held**
SIC: 2099 Food preparations

(G-7324)
PENN & FLETCHER INC
2107 41st Ave Fl 5 (11101-4802)
PHONE..............................212 239-6868
Ernie Smith, *President*
EMP: 15
SQ FT: 4,500
SALES (est): 1.1MM **Privately Held**
SIC: 2395 5131 Embroidery products, ex-
cept schiffli machine; lace fabrics; trim-
mings, apparel

(G-7325)
PHEONIX CUSTOM FURNITURE LTD
2107 41st Ave Fl 2 (11101-4802)
PHONE..............................212 727-2648
John J Clarke, *Principal*
Vito D'Alessandro, *Vice Pres*
EMP: 20
SQ FT: 10,000
SALES: 2MM **Privately Held**
SIC: 2512 2521 Upholstered household
furniture; wood office furniture

(G-7326)
PILOT PRODUCTS INC
2413 46th St (11103-1007)
P.O. Box 3221 (11103-0221)
PHONE..............................718 728-2141
Carolyn J Hebel, *President*
Herbert Hebel, *President*
Elizabeth Hammell, *Vice Pres*
EMP: 13
SQ FT: 17,000

▲ = Import ▼ =Export
◆ =Import/Export

SALES (est): 1.9MM **Privately Held**
SIC: 3061 Mechanical rubber goods

(G-7327)
PLATINUM SALES PROMOTION INC
Also Called: The Spirited Shipper
3514a Crescent St (11106-3920)
PHONE.................................718 361-0200
Bruce Cappels, *President*
▲ EMP: 7
SQ FT: 12,000
SALES (est): 1.4MM **Privately Held**
WEB: www.spiritedshipper.com
SIC: 3993 4225 8743 4213 Displays & cutouts, window & lobby; general warehousing; sales promotion; trucking, except local

(G-7328)
PRIME ELECTRIC MOTORS INC
4850 33rd St (11101-2514)
P.O. Box 1374 (11101-0374)
PHONE.................................718 784-1124
Gul Zaman, *President*
EMP: 9
SALES (est): 820K **Privately Held**
SIC: 7694 Electric motor repair

(G-7329)
PRIMO COAT CORP
Also Called: Ciccarelli Custom Taylor
4315 Queens St Fl 3 (11101-2947)
PHONE.................................718 349-2070
Rocco Ciccarelli, *President*
EMP: 35 EST: 1963
SQ FT: 13,500
SALES: 1MM **Privately Held**
SIC: 2311 2337 2339 2325 Suits, men's & boys': made from purchased materials; suits: women's, misses' & juniors'; women's & misses' outerwear; men's & boys' trousers & slacks

(G-7330)
PUBLICIS HEALTH LLC
Also Called: Verilogue
2701 Queens Plz N (11101-4020)
PHONE.................................212 771-5500
Alexandra Von Plato, *Mng Member*
EMP: 50
SALES (est): 2.5MM **Privately Held**
SIC: 2741 Miscellaneous publishing

(G-7331)
PULSAR TECHNOLOGY SYSTEMS INC
2720 42nd Rd (11101-4112)
PHONE.................................718 361-9292
Rudolph Robinson, *President*
Joann Pitcher, *Manager*
EMP: 9
SQ FT: 3,750
SALES: 1.3MM **Privately Held**
WEB: www.taxi-meters.com
SIC: 3825 Test equipment for electronic & electrical circuits; meters: electric, pocket, portable, panelboard, etc.

(G-7332)
PURA FRUTA LLC
2323 Borden Ave (11101-4508)
PHONE.................................415 279-5727
Mark Fridman, *Prdtn Mgr*
Adriana Ayales,
EMP: 12
SALES (est): 1.3MM **Privately Held**
SIC: 2037 Fruit juices

(G-7333)
QPBC INC
1306 38th Ave (11101-6034)
PHONE.................................718 685-1900
Kenneth Maurer, *Ch of Bd*
EMP: 40 EST: 2014
SQ FT: 20,000
SALES (est): 4.2MM **Privately Held**
SIC: 3465 5013 Body parts, automobile: stamped metal; automotive supplies & parts

(G-7334)
QUADLOGIC CONTROLS CORPORATION
Also Called: Qlc
3300 Northern Blvd Fl 2 (11101-2215)
PHONE.................................212 930-9300
Sayre Swarztrauber, *Ch of Bd*
Doron Shafrir, *President*
Phil Fram, *Vice Pres*
Newman Fruitwala, *Production*
Stanley Lo, *Engineer*
▲ EMP: 75
SQ FT: 36,000
SALES (est): 17MM **Privately Held**
SIC: 3825 7389 Electrical energy measuring equipment; meters: electric, pocket, portable, panelboard, etc.; meter readers, remote

(G-7335)
QUALITY CASTINGS INC
3100 47th Ave Ste 2120b (11101-3023)
PHONE.................................732 409-3203
Carl Morfino, *President*
EMP: 50
SQ FT: 3,200
SALES (est): 7.2MM **Privately Held**
WEB: www.qualitycasting.com
SIC: 3369 3324 Castings, except die-castings, precision; steel investment foundries

(G-7336)
QUALITY IMPRESSIONS INC
4334 32nd Pl Ste 3 (11101-2313)
PHONE.................................646 613-0002
Brennan Ganga, *President*
EMP: 6
SALES: 600K **Privately Held**
SIC: 2759 Commercial printing

(G-7337)
QUALITY OFFSET LLC
4750 30th St (11101-3404)
PHONE.................................347 342-4660
Steve Wong,
EMP: 7
SQ FT: 2,000
SALES (est): 752.8K **Privately Held**
SIC: 2759 Commercial printing

(G-7338)
RAGOZIN DATA
Also Called: Sheets, The
4402 11th St Ste 613 (11101-5184)
PHONE.................................212 674-3123
Len Ragozin, *Owner*
EMP: 20
SQ FT: 2,000
SALES (est): 1.4MM **Privately Held**
WEB: www.thesheets.com
SIC: 2721 Magazines: publishing & printing

(G-7339)
RAPID FAN & BLOWER INC
2314 39th Ave (11101-3612)
PHONE.................................718 786-2060
George J Rogner Jr, *President*
George Rogner, *Purchasing*
EMP: 10 EST: 1956
SQ FT: 15,000
SALES (est): 2.1MM **Privately Held**
WEB: www.rapidfan.com
SIC: 3564 5084 Blowing fans: industrial or commercial; turbo-blowers, industrial; industrial machinery & equipment

(G-7340)
RAVIOLI STORE INC
4344 21st St (11101-5002)
PHONE.................................718 729-9300
Michael Nasoss, *Manager*
EMP: 5
SALES (est): 500K **Privately Held**
WEB: www.raviolistore.com
SIC: 2098 5411 Macaroni & spaghetti; grocery stores

(G-7341)
RELIANCE MACHINING INC
4335 Vernon Blvd (11101-6911)
PHONE.................................718 784-0314
Lloyd Larsen, *President*
EMP: 30
SQ FT: 15,000

SALES: 3MM **Privately Held**
SIC: 3599 Machine shop, jobbing & repair

(G-7342)
RENCO MANUFACTURING INC
1040 45th Ave Fl 2 (11101-7094)
PHONE.................................718 392-8877
AVI Shaul, *President*
EMP: 32
SQ FT: 15,000
SALES: 660K **Privately Held**
SIC: 3915 Jewelers' findings & materials

(G-7343)
ROBERT MILLER ASSOCIATES LLC
2219 41st Ave Ste 505 (11101-4841)
PHONE.................................718 392-1640
Robert Miller, *Mng Member*
EMP: 15
SALES: 1MM **Privately Held**
SIC: 2389 Men's miscellaneous accessories

(G-7344)
ROLLHAUS SEATING PRODUCTS INC
4310 21st St (11101-5002)
PHONE.................................718 729-9111
Michael Rollhaus, *President*
EMP: 13 EST: 1945
SQ FT: 28,000
SALES (est): 1.8MM **Privately Held**
WEB: www.seatingproducts.com
SIC: 2599 Restaurant furniture, wood or metal; bar furniture

(G-7345)
RONBAR LABORATORIES INC
5202 Van Dam St (11101-3221)
PHONE.................................718 937-6755
Sheldon Borgen, *President*
Barry Borgen, *Vice Pres*
EMP: 11
SQ FT: 12,000
SALES: 2MM **Privately Held**
SIC: 2841 7699 Detergents, synthetic organic or inorganic alkaline; restaurant equipment repair

(G-7346)
RONER INC (PA)
3553 24th St (11106-4416)
P.O. Box 6077 (11106-0077)
PHONE.................................718 392-6020
Ron Meltsner, *President*
Eric Spar, *Vice Pres*
Henry Meltsner, *Treasurer*
Harold Spar, *Admin Sec*
▲ EMP: 5 EST: 1959
SQ FT: 20,000
SALES (est): 14.7MM **Privately Held**
SIC: 3842 5047 Hearing aids; medical & hospital equipment

(G-7347)
RONER INC
1433 31st Ave (11106-4536)
PHONE.................................718 392-6020
Marge Weber, *Branch Mgr*
EMP: 150
SALES (corp-wide): 14.7MM **Privately Held**
SIC: 3842 Hearing aids
PA: Roner, Inc.
3553 24th St
Long Island City NY 11106
718 392-6020

(G-7348)
RUBINSTEIN JEWELRY MFG CO
3100 47th Ave (11101-3013)
PHONE.................................718 784-8650
Fax: 718 784-8893
EMP: 12 EST: 1956
SQ FT: 5,000
SALES (est): 74.5K **Privately Held**
SIC: 3911 Mfg Gold Jewelry

(G-7349)
S & B FASHION INC
4315 Queens St Ste B (11101-2923)
PHONE.................................718 482-1386
Tony Song, *President*
▲ EMP: 5 EST: 2000

SALES (est): 279.4K **Privately Held**
SIC: 2389 Apparel & accessories

(G-7350)
S BROOME AND CO INC
Also Called: Samuel Broome Uniform ACC
3300 47th Ave Fl 1 (11101-2428)
PHONE.................................718 663-6800
Michael Broome, *President*
Daniel Broome, *Vice Pres*
Brigid Rumpf, *Vice Pres*
David Schaffer, *Treasurer*
ARI Wilker, *MIS Dir*
▲ EMP: 80 EST: 1917
SQ FT: 27,000
SALES (est): 7.8MM **Privately Held**
WEB: www.sbroome.com
SIC: 2339 2323 Neckwear & ties: women's, misses' & juniors'; men's & boys' neckwear

(G-7351)
SADOWSKY GUITARS LTD
2107 41st Ave Fl 4 (11101-4802)
PHONE.................................718 433-1990
Roger Sadowsky, *President*
Robin Phillips, *Shareholder*
▲ EMP: 10
SQ FT: 4,100
SALES: 1.3MM **Privately Held**
WEB: www.sadowsky.com
SIC: 3931 7699 String instruments & parts; musical instrument repair services

(G-7352)
SCOTTI GRAPHICS INC
3200 Skillman Ave Fl 1 (11101-2308)
PHONE.................................212 367-9602
Richard J Scotti, *President*
EMP: 50
SQ FT: 8,000
SALES (est): 6.4MM **Privately Held**
WEB: www.scottigraphics.com
SIC: 2752 2791 2759 Commercial printing, offset; typesetting; letterpress printing

(G-7353)
SCREEN TEAM INC
3402c Review Ave (11101-3242)
PHONE.................................718 786-2424
Richard Grubman, *President*
EMP: 10
SQ FT: 10,000
SALES: 1.5MM **Privately Held**
WEB: www.screenteam.com
SIC: 3552 Silk screens for textile industry

(G-7354)
SELECT JEWELRY INC
4728 37th St Fl 3 (11101-1809)
PHONE.................................718 784-3626
Nissim Seliktar, *Ch of Bd*
Ronny Seliktar, *President*
▲ EMP: 60
SQ FT: 40,000
SALES (est): 14.5MM **Privately Held**
SIC: 3911 5094 Jewelry, precious metal; jewelry

(G-7355)
SERVICE ADVERTISING GROUP INC
Also Called: Western Queens Gazette
4216 34th Ave (11101-1110)
PHONE.................................718 361-6161
Tony Barsamian, *President*
EMP: 15
SQ FT: 2,118
SALES (est): 870.8K **Privately Held**
WEB: www.qgazette.com
SIC: 2711 2741 7311 7313 Newspapers, publishing & printing; shopping news: publishing only, not printed on site; advertising agencies; newspaper advertising representative

(G-7356)
SHAPEWAYS INC
3002 48th Ave Ste 2 (11101-3401)
PHONE.................................646 470-3576
Gregory Kress, *CEO*
EMP: 7
SALES (est): 730.2K
SALES (corp-wide): 36.4MM **Privately Held**
SIC: 2759 Commercial printing

PA: Shapeways, Inc.
44 W 28th St Fl 12
New York NY 10001
914 356-5816

(G-7357)
SIMS GROUP USA HOLDINGS CORP
Sims Metal
3027 Greenpoint Ave (11101-2009)
PHONE..........................718 786-6031
Thomas Ferretti, *Opers-Prdtn-Mfg*
EMP: 66 **Privately Held**
SIC: 3312 3341 Stainless steel; secondary nonferrous metals
HQ: Sims Group Usa Holdings Corp
16 W 22nd St Fl 10
New York NY 10010
212 604-0710

(G-7358)
SIXTHSCENTS PAPER PRODUCTS LTD
Also Called: Sixthscents Products
37-18 Nthrn Blvd Ste 418 (11101)
PHONE..........................212 627-5066
Kristine Ferrara, *CEO*
Warren Pugach, *President*
EMP: 8 **EST:** 2009
SQ FT: 2,000
SALES: 450K **Privately Held**
SIC: 2844 Perfumes & colognes

(G-7359)
SIZZAL LLC
Also Called: Influence Graphics
1105 44th Rd Fl 2 (11101)
PHONE..........................212 354-6123
Al Weiss, *Mng Member*
Ron Sizemore,
EMP: 28
SALES (est): 3.1MM **Privately Held**
SIC: 2752 Commercial printing, offset

(G-7360)
SLYDE INC
474 48th Ave Apt 18a (11109-5711)
PHONE..........................917 331-2114
Jason Peltz, *CEO*
Edward Ludvigsen, *Principal*
Kai Blache, *CFO*
EMP: 15
SALES (est): 587.4K **Privately Held**
SIC: 7372 7389 Prepackaged software;

(G-7361)
SPANJER CORP
Also Called: Spanjer Signs
3856 11th St (11101-6114)
PHONE..........................347 448-8033
Steve Silverberg, *President*
Alissa Silverberg, *Vice Pres*
Rose Silverberg, *Admin Sec*
EMP: 6 **EST:** 1908
SQ FT: 5,000
SALES: 446K **Privately Held**
SIC: 3993 Signs, not made in custom sign painting shops

(G-7362)
STALLION INC (PA)
3620 34th St (11106-1902)
PHONE..........................718 706-0111
John Georgiades, *Ch of Bd*
Ioannis Georgiades, *President*
James Charles, *CFO*
Kyne Kim, *Director*
Achilleas Georgiades, *Admin Sec*
▲ **EMP:** 26
SQ FT: 30,000
SALES (est): 37.5MM **Privately Held**
SIC: 2371 5621 Coats, fur; ready-to-wear apparel, women's

(G-7363)
STAMP RITE TOOL & DIE INC
4311 35th St (11101-2303)
PHONE..........................718 752-0334
EMP: 5
SQ FT: 1,000
SALES: 200K **Privately Held**
SIC: 3544 Manufacturer Of Tools

(G-7364)
STANDARD MOTOR PRODUCTS INC (PA)
3718 Northern Blvd # 600 (11101-1637)
PHONE..........................718 392-0200
Lawrence I Sills, *Ch of Bd*
Eric P Sills, *President*
Tom Latimer, *General Mgr*
James J Burke, *COO*
Nicholas Corrado, *Counsel*
◆ **EMP:** 500 **EST:** 1919
SQ FT: 75,800
SALES: 1B **Publicly Held**
WEB: www.smpcorp.com
SIC: 3714 3694 3585 3564 Motor vehicle engines & parts; fuel systems & parts, motor vehicle; air conditioner parts, motor vehicle; motor vehicle electrical equipment; ignition systems, high frequency; harness wiring sets, internal combustion engines; battery cable wiring sets for internal combustion engines; compressors for refrigeration & air conditioning equipment; parts for heating, cooling & refrigerating equipment; air conditioning equipment, complete; blowers & fans; rubber & plastics hose & beltings

(G-7365)
STANLEY CREATIONS INC
Also Called: Sgg
3100 47th Ave Ste 4105 (11101-3068)
PHONE..........................718 361-6100
David Lowy, *Branch Mgr*
EMP: 111
SALES (corp-wide): 14.4MM **Privately Held**
SIC: 3911 Jewelry, precious metal
PA: Stanley Creations, Inc.
1414 Willow Ave
Elkins Park PA 19027
215 635-6200

(G-7366)
STARCRAFT PRESS INC
4402 11th St Ste 311 (11101-5150)
PHONE..........................718 383-6700
Robert Glickman, *President*
Jeff Glickman, *Vice Pres*
EMP: 8
SALES (est): 1.1MM **Privately Held**
SIC: 2759 Letterpress printing

(G-7367)
STEINWAY INC (DH)
Also Called: Steinway Hall
1 Steinway Pl (11105-1033)
PHONE..........................718 721-2600
Ronald Losby, *CEO*
Kyle R Kirkland, *Exec VP*
Gary Girouard, *Manager*
Chad Frye, *Retailers*
▲ **EMP:** 575
SQ FT: 449,000
SALES (est): 132.5MM
SALES (corp-wide): 239.6MM **Privately Held**
WEB: www.steinway.com
SIC: 3931 5736 Pianos, all types: vertical, grand, spinet, player, etc.; pianos

(G-7368)
STEINWAY AND SONS (DH)
1 Steinway Pl (11105-1033)
PHONE..........................718 721-2600
Ronald Losby, *President*
Kyle R Kirkland, *President*
Dana D Messina, *Exec VP*
John Disalvo, *Vice Pres*
Todd Sanders, *Vice Pres*
◆ **EMP:** 107
SQ FT: 450,000
SALES (est): 102MM
SALES (corp-wide): 239.6MM **Privately Held**
WEB: www.steinwaypiano.net
SIC: 3931 5736 Pianos, all types: vertical, grand, spinet, player, etc.; pianos

(G-7369)
STELLAR PRINTING INC
3838 9th St (11101-6110)
PHONE..........................718 361-1600
Dirk Anthonis, *President*
Fred Newton, *President*
EMP: 100

SQ FT: 35,000
SALES (est): 15.7MM
SALES (corp-wide): 598.4MM **Privately Held**
WEB: www.americasnewspaper.com
SIC: 2759 Newspapers: printing
HQ: News World Communications, Inc.
3600 New York Ave Ne
Washington DC 20002
202 636-3000

(G-7370)
STEVEN MADDEN LTD (PA)
Also Called: Steve Madden
5216 Barnett Ave (11104-1018)
PHONE..........................718 446-1800
Edward R Rosenfeld, *Ch of Bd*
Michael Paradise, *Exec VP*
Karla Frieders, *Chief Mktg Ofcr*
▲ **EMP:** 265
SQ FT: 90,000
SALES: 1.6B **Publicly Held**
WEB: www.mypinecastle.com
SIC: 3143 3144 3149 5632 Men's footwear, except athletic; women's footwear, except athletic; children's footwear, except athletic; handbags; apparel accessories

(G-7371)
STONE & TERRAZZO WORLD INC
5132 35th St (11101-3257)
PHONE..........................718 361-6899
Konstadinos Hagias, *President*
Mary Hagias, *Admin Sec*
EMP: 5
SQ FT: 3,500
SALES (est): 540.8K **Privately Held**
SIC: 3281 5032 Curbing, granite or stone; marble building stone

(G-7372)
STUART-DEAN CO INC
4350 10th St (11101-6910)
PHONE..........................718 472-1326
Kristen Rice, *Branch Mgr*
EMP: 13
SALES (corp-wide): 65.4MM **Privately Held**
SIC: 3479 1741 1752 Etching & engraving; stone masonry; wood floor installation & refinishing
PA: Stuart-Dean Co. Inc.
450 Fashion Ave Ste 3800
New York NY 10123
212 273-6900

(G-7373)
SUBSTRATE LLC
539 46th Ave (11101-5214)
PHONE..........................212 913-9600
James Wegner, *Partner*
EMP: 24 **EST:** 2016
SALES (est): 225.6K **Privately Held**
SIC: 3993 Displays & cutouts, window & lobby

(G-7374)
SUMMIT AEROSPACE INC
4301 21st St Ste 203 (11101-5039)
PHONE..........................718 433-1326
Moon K Lee, *President*
EMP: 7
SQ FT: 4,000
SALES (est): 1.2MM **Privately Held**
SIC: 3369 Aerospace castings, nonferrous: except aluminum

(G-7375)
SUPERIOR METALS & PROCESSING
Also Called: Super Stud Building Products
801 26th Ave (11102)
PHONE..........................718 545-7500
Raymond Frobosilo, *President*
John Conneely, *Info Tech Mgr*
▲ **EMP:** 6
SQ FT: 20,500
SALES (est): 340K **Privately Held**
SIC: 3479 Sherardizing of metals or metal products

(G-7376)
SUSSMAN-AUTOMATIC CORPORATION (PA)
Also Called: Mr Steam
4320 34th St (11101-2321)
PHONE..........................718 937-4500
Michael Pinkus, *President*
Artie Perlman, *Materials Mgr*
Patrick Baumgardner, *Buyer*
Tony Diresta, *VP Finance*
Timothy Mullally, *Sales Staff*
▲ **EMP:** 80 **EST:** 1944
SQ FT: 60,000
SALES (est): 30MM **Privately Held**
WEB: www.sussmanelectricboilers.com
SIC: 3569 Generators: steam, liquid oxygen or nitrogen

(G-7377)
SWIMWAYS CORP
3030 47th Ave Ste 680 (11101-3438)
PHONE..........................757 460-1156
David Arias, *President*
Anthony Vittone, *Vice Pres*
Monica Jones, *Sales Staff*
Darrin Bryan, *Manager*
◆ **EMP:** 149
SALES (est): 45.7MM
SALES (corp-wide): 1.6B **Privately Held**
WEB: www.swimways.com
SIC: 3089 3949 3944 Plastic boats & other marine equipment; sporting & athletic goods; games, toys & children's vehicles
PA: Spin Master Corp
225 King St W Suite 200
Toronto ON M5V 3
416 364-6002

(G-7378)
TAYLOR COMMUNICATIONS INC
Also Called: Vectra Visual
3200 Skillman Ave Fl 3 (11101-2308)
PHONE..........................718 361-1000
EMP: 6
SALES (corp-wide): 3.5B **Privately Held**
SIC: 2752 Lithographic Commercial Printing
HQ: Taylor Communications, Inc.
4205 S 96th St
Omaha NE 56003
402 898-6422

(G-7379)
TEMPTU INC
522 46th Ave Ste B (11101-5204)
PHONE..........................718 937-9503
Steven Gary, *Manager*
EMP: 5
SALES (corp-wide): 5.6MM **Privately Held**
WEB: www.temptu.com
SIC: 2844 Cosmetic preparations
PA: Temptu Inc.
26 W 17th St Rm 302
New York NY 10011
212 675-4000

(G-7380)
THEODOSIOU INC
Also Called: G T Machine & Tool
3214 49th St (11103-1403)
PHONE..........................718 728-6800
Dean Theodos, *President*
Harry Theodos, *President*
Vj Sukhu, *Manager*
EMP: 8 **EST:** 1971
SQ FT: 7,500
SALES (est): 1.6MM **Privately Held**
WEB: www.gtmachine.com
SIC: 3599 Machine shop, jobbing & repair

(G-7381)
THOMAS C WILSON LLC
Also Called: Thomas C Wilson
2111 44th Ave (11101-5007)
PHONE..........................718 729-3360
Stephen Hanley, *Ch of Bd*
David Hanley, *Opers Mgr*
Sugelis Gonzalez, *Supervisor*
Veronica Mendez, *Receptionist*
▼ **EMP:** 42 **EST:** 2009
SQ FT: 45,600
SALES (est): 12.6MM **Privately Held**
WEB: www.tcwilson.com
SIC: 3546 Power-driven handtools

▲ = Import ▼=Export
◆ =Import/Export

(G-7382)
THOMSON PRESS (INDIA)
LIMITED
Also Called: Living Media
4 Court Sq Ste 3 (11101-4351)
PHONE.................646 318-0369
Anup Uniyal, *Branch Mgr*
EMP: 5 **Privately Held**
SIC: 2752 Commercial printing, lithographic
HQ: Thomson Press India Limited
18/35, Thomson Press Building,
Faridabad HR 12100
129 228-6887

(G-7383)
TOTAL SOLUTION GRAPHICS
INC
2511 49th Ave (11101-4429)
PHONE.................718 706-1540
EMP: 3
SALES: 3MM **Privately Held**
SIC: 2759 Commercial Printing

(G-7384)
TOWERIQ INC (PA)
Also Called: Namsnet
37-18 Nthrn Blvd Ste 421 (11101)
PHONE.................844 626-7638
Connor Crowley, *CEO*
Douglas Baena, *Vice Pres*
EMP: 18
SQ FT: 11,000
SALES (est): 1.5MM **Privately Held**
SIC: 3669 Fire alarm apparatus, electric

(G-7385)
TOWNE HOUSE RESTORATIONS
INC
4309 Vernon Blvd (11101-6831)
PHONE.................718 497-9200
Ivan Cerina, *Principal*
EMP: 5 **EST:** 2011
SALES (est): 681.9K **Privately Held**
SIC: 3272 Concrete products

(G-7386)
TRANE US INC
4518 Court Sq Ste 100 (11101-4341)
PHONE.................718 721-8844
Doug Michael, *General Mgr*
Randy Krampe, *District Mgr*
Bob Wilcox, *Area Mgr*
Dave Palty, *Business Mgr*
Laura Rygielski, *Vice Pres*
EMP: 70 **Privately Held**
SIC: 3585 Refrigeration & heating equipment
HQ: Trane U.S. Inc.
3600 Pammel Creek Rd
La Crosse WI 54601
608 787-2000

(G-7387)
UNIQUE MBL GRAN ORGNZTION
CORP
3831 9th St (11101-6109)
PHONE.................718 482-0440
John Manassakis, *President*
▲ **EMP:** 5
SALES (est): 436.5K **Privately Held**
SIC: 3281 Marble, building: cut & shaped; granite, cut & shaped

(G-7388)
UNITED SHEET METAL CORP
4602 28th St (11101)
PHONE.................718 482-1197
Joseph Grgas, *President*
Siraj Bora, *Vice Pres*
Bhadresh Shah, *Vice Pres*
EMP: 50
SQ FT: 4,000
SALES (est): 4.7MM **Privately Held**
SIC: 3444 Ducts, sheet metal

(G-7389)
UNIVERSAL DESIGNS INC
3517 31st St (11106-2320)
PHONE.................718 721-1111
Panos Adamopoulos, *President*
Silvia Adamopoulos, *Vice Pres*
EMP: 6
SQ FT: 8,000

SALES: 700K **Privately Held**
SIC: 2511 2521 2541 5712 Wood household furniture; wood office furniture; wood partitions & fixtures; unfinished furniture

(G-7390)
US CONCRETE INC
Also Called: Nycon Supply
4717 27th St (11101-4410)
PHONE.................718 433-0111
Arthur G Reis, *Branch Mgr*
EMP: 30
SALES (corp-wide): 1.5B **Publicly Held**
SIC: 3273 Ready-mixed concrete
PA: U.S. Concrete, Inc.
331 N Main St
Euless TX 76039
817 835-4105

(G-7391)
VANDAM INC
1111 44th Rd Fl 403 (11101-5115)
PHONE.................212 929-0416
Stephan Muth Vandam, *President*
Jessy Cerda, *Opers Staff*
Jon Tyillian, *Research*
Bruce Ellerstein, *Director*
▲ **EMP:** 12
SQ FT: 2,500
SALES: 2MM **Privately Held**
SIC: 2741 2731 6794 Maps: publishing only, not printed on site; books: publishing only; patent buying, licensing, leasing

(G-7392)
VANILLA SKY LLC
3318 Broadway (11106-1806)
PHONE.................347 738-4195
EMP: 5
SALES (est): 276.8K **Privately Held**
SIC: 2024 Ice cream & ice milk

(G-7393)
VENUE GRAPHICS SUPPLY INC
1120 46th Rd (11101-5322)
PHONE.................718 361-1690
EMP: 13
SQ FT: 10,000
SALES: 1.2MM **Privately Held**
SIC: 2899 Mfr Industrial Chemical Solutions

(G-7394)
VERNON WINE & LIQUOR INC
5006 Vernon Blvd (11101-5702)
PHONE.................718 784-5096
Adrian Bettencourt, *Manager*
EMP: 5
SALES (est): 275.4K **Privately Held**
SIC: 2082 Malt liquors

(G-7395)
VERSAILLES DRAPERY
UPHOLSTERY
4709 30th St Ste 200 (11101-3400)
PHONE.................212 533-2059
Jorge Loayza, *President*
Ricardo Loayza, *Treasurer*
EMP: 11
SQ FT: 20,000
SALES: 1MM **Privately Held**
SIC: 2512 5714 2211 Upholstered household furniture; draperies; draperies & drapery fabrics, cotton

(G-7396)
VITOBOB FURNITURE INC
3879 13th St (11101-6119)
PHONE.................516 676-1696
Robert Longo, *President*
Michele Longo, *Admin Sec*
EMP: 5
SQ FT: 5,000
SALES (est): 490K **Privately Held**
SIC: 2426 Frames for upholstered furniture, wood

(G-7397)
WALNUT PRINTING INC (PA)
2812 41st Ave (11101-3706)
PHONE.................718 707-0100
Gerald Paul Pont, *President*
EMP: 5
SQ FT: 3,500

SALES (est): 401.6K **Privately Held**
WEB: www.walnutprinting.com
SIC: 2752 Commercial printing, offset

(G-7398)
WARREN PRINTING INC
3718 Northern Blvd # 418 (11101-1636)
PHONE.................212 627-5000
Warren Pugach, *President*
Priscilla Pugach, *Corp Secy*
Seymour Pugach, *Vice Pres*
John Rubbinaccio, *Opers Staff*
EMP: 10
SQ FT: 7,500
SALES (est): 1.8MM **Privately Held**
SIC: 2752 Commercial printing, offset

(G-7399)
WATCHCRAFT INC
2214 40th Ave Ste 4 (11101-4830)
PHONE.................347 531-0382
Eduardo Milieris, *President*
▲ **EMP:** 5
SALES (est): 742.5K **Privately Held**
SIC: 3873 5094 Watches, clocks, watchcases & parts; clocks, watches & parts

(G-7400)
WESTMORE LITHO CORP
Also Called: Westmore Litho Printing Co
4017 22nd St (11101-4834)
PHONE.................718 361-9403
EMP: 8
SQ FT: 10,000
SALES (est): 901.9K **Privately Held**
SIC: 2752 Commercial Printing Lithographic

(G-7401)
WILLIAM E WILLIAM VALVE
CORP
3852 Review Ave (11101-2019)
PHONE.................718 392-1660
Sherman Richard, *CEO*
Nicholas Sherman, *Vice Pres*
EMP: 20
SALES: 4MM **Privately Held**
SIC: 3494 Valves & pipe fittings

(G-7402)
WILLIAM E WILLIAMS VALVE
CORP
3850 Review Ave (11101-2019)
P.O. Box 1190 (11101-0190)
PHONE.................718 392-1660
Richard Sherman, *President*
Roy Psoncak, *Manager*
Glen Werthmuller, *Manager*
◆ **EMP:** 23
SQ FT: 60,000
SALES (est): 5.6MM **Privately Held**
SIC: 3494 3491 Valves & pipe fittings; industrial valves

(G-7403)
WILLIAM H JACKSON COMPANY
3629 23rd St (11106-4405)
PHONE.................718 784-4482
Eric Nelson, *Manager*
EMP: 7
SQ FT: 4,800
SALES (corp-wide): 1.5MM **Privately Held**
WEB: www.bumrails.com
SIC: 3429 Fireplace equipment, hardware: andirons, grates, screens
PA: William H Jackson Company
18 E 17th St Frnt 1
New York NY 10003
212 753-9400

(G-7404)
WINNER PRESS INC
4331 33rd St 1 (11101-2316)
PHONE.................718 937-7715
Hermi Fu, *President*
Ya Tang Fu, *Principal*
Marissa Santiago, *Admin Sec*
EMP: 25
SQ FT: 20,000
SALES (est): 3MM **Privately Held**
WEB: www.winnerpress.com
SIC: 2752 Commercial printing, offset

(G-7405)
WINSON SURNAMER INC
4402 11th St Ste 601 (11101-5149)
PHONE.................718 729-8787
Gary Levinson, *President*
Lawrence Levinson, *Treasurer*
Robert Levinson, *Admin Sec*
EMP: 5 **EST:** 1932
SQ FT: 40,000
SALES (est): 702.1K **Privately Held**
SIC: 2752 Commercial printing, offset

(G-7406)
WONTON FOOD INC
5210 37th St (11101-2001)
PHONE.................718 784-8178
Foo Kam Wong, *Manager*
EMP: 20
SQ FT: 5,320
SALES (corp-wide): 80.3MM **Privately Held**
WEB: www.wontonfood.com
SIC: 2099 2052 Noodles, fried (Chinese); cracker meal & crumbs
PA: Wonton Food Inc.
220 Moore St 222
Brooklyn NY 11206
718 628-6868

(G-7407)
WOO AUDIO INC
2219 41st Ave Ste 502 (11101-4841)
PHONE.................917 324-5284
Jack Wu, *President*
▲ **EMP:** 13 **EST:** 2010
SALES (est): 1.6MM **Privately Held**
SIC: 3651 Household audio & video equipment

(G-7408)
X BRAND EDITIONS
4020 22nd St Ste 1 (11101-4814)
PHONE.................718 482-7646
Robert Blanton, *President*
EMP: 8 **EST:** 2010
SALES (est): 1.1MM **Privately Held**
SIC: 3577 Printers & plotters

(G-7409)
XANIA LABS INC
3202 Queens Blvd Fl 6 (11101-2332)
PHONE.................718 361-2550
Nikos Mouyiaris, *President*
EMP: 5
SALES (est): 411.1K
SALES (corp-wide): 284.9MM **Privately Held**
SIC: 2844 5122 Cosmetic preparations; cosmetics
PA: Mana Products, Inc.
3202 Queens Blvd Fl 6
Long Island City NY 11101
718 361-2550

(G-7410)
YORK INTERNATIONAL
CORPORATION
1130 45th Rd (11101-5832)
PHONE.................718 389-4152
Ben Cohen, *Branch Mgr*
EMP: 94 **Privately Held**
SIC: 3585 Refrigeration & heating equipment
HQ: York International Corporation
631 S Richland Ave
York PA 17403
717 771-7890

(G-7411)
YORK LADDER INC
3720 12th St (11101-6098)
PHONE.................718 784-6666
Kenneth J Buettner, *President*
Daniel Buettner, *General Mgr*
David Caro, *Manager*
Tammy Wood, *Admin Asst*
▲ **EMP:** 10
SALES (est): 891K **Privately Held**
SIC: 2499 Ladders & stepladders, wood

(G-7412)
ZELMAN & FRIEDMAN JWLY MFG CO
4722 37th St (11101-1804)
P.O. Box 547, Woodbury (11797-0547)
PHONE....................................718 349-3400
Irwin Friedman, *President*
Morris Zelman, *Treasurer*
Gary Zelman, *Asst Treas*
Alan Zelman, *Shareholder*
EMP: 25 **EST:** 1951
SQ FT: 5,000
SALES (est): 2.3MM **Privately Held**
SIC: 3911 Jewelry, precious metal

(G-7413)
ZENITH COLOR COMM GROUP INC (PA)
4710 33rd St (11101-2408)
PHONE....................................212 989-4400
Peter D Savitt, *President*
EMP: 20
SALES (est): 4MM **Privately Held**
SIC: 2711 Commercial printing & newspaper publishing combined

---

Lowville
Lewis County

(G-7414)
CLIMAX PACKAGING INC
7840 State Route 26 (13367-2926)
PHONE....................................315 376-8000
Patrick Purdy, *President*
Mary Wuest, *CFO*
EMP: 105
SQ FT: 110,000
SALES (est): 14.1MM **Privately Held**
WEB: www.stjpkg.com
SIC: 3993 2657 Signs & advertising specialties; folding paperboard boxes

(G-7415)
FARNEY LUMBER CORPORATION
7194 Brewery Rd (13367-2524)
PHONE....................................315 346-6013
Duane Farney, *President*
Terry Farney, *Vice Pres*
Todd Farney, *Vice Pres*
Karen Farney, *Admin Sec*
EMP: 17
SQ FT: 20,000
SALES: 2MM **Privately Held**
SIC: 2421 Sawmills & planing mills, general

(G-7416)
KRAFT HEINZ FOODS COMPANY
7388 Utica Blvd (13367-9503)
PHONE....................................315 376-6575
Gary Schantz, *Production*
Tim Regan, *Branch Mgr*
EMP: 335
SQ FT: 460
SALES (corp-wide): 26.2B **Publicly Held**
WEB: www.kraftfoods.com
SIC: 2022 Cheese, natural & processed
HQ: Kraft Heinz Foods Company
1 Ppg Pl Fl 34
Pittsburgh PA 15222
412 456-5700

(G-7417)
LOWVILLE FARMERS COOP INC
5500 Shady Ave (13367-1698)
PHONE....................................315 376-6587
John Williams, *President*
Mark Karelus, *Vice Pres*
Tim Smithling, *CFO*
Stanley Szalch, *Treasurer*
Glen Beller, *Admin Sec*
EMP: 37
SQ FT: 20,000
SALES: 10MM **Privately Held**
SIC: 2048 5999 5251 5211 Prepared feeds; feed & farm supply; hardware; lumber products

(G-7418)
LOWVILLE NEWSPAPER CORPORATION
Also Called: Journal and Republican
7840 State Route 26 (13367-2926)
P.O. Box 33 (13367-0033)
PHONE....................................315 376-3525
Cindy Aucter, *Business Mgr*
Jeremiah Papineau, *Manager*
Adam Atkinson, *Manager*
EMP: 7
SALES (est): 452.3K
SALES (corp-wide): 32MM **Privately Held**
WEB: www.ogd.com
SIC: 2711 Commercial printing & newspaper publishing combined; newspapers, publishing & printing
PA: Johnson Newspaper Corporation
260 Washington St
Watertown NY
315 782-1000

(G-7419)
NEENAH NORTHEAST LLC
5492 Bostwick St (13367)
PHONE....................................315 376-3571
Larry Kieffer, *Branch Mgr*
EMP: 179
SALES (corp-wide): 1B **Publicly Held**
WEB: www.fibermark.com
SIC: 2672 Coated & laminated paper
HQ: Neenah Northeast, Llc
70 Front St
West Springfield MA 01089
413 533-0699

(G-7420)
QUBICAAMF WORLDWIDE LLC
Also Called: Pins and Lanes
7412 Utica Blvd (13367-9572)
PHONE....................................315 376-6541
Wayne White, *General Mgr*
EMP: 150
SALES (corp-wide): 24.7MM **Privately Held**
SIC: 3949 Bowling pins
HQ: Qubicaamf Worldwide, Llc
8100 Amf Dr
Mechanicsville VA 23111
804 569-1000

(G-7421)
ROYAL CUSTOM CABINETS
6149 Patty St (13367-4206)
PHONE....................................315 376-6042
David Lapp, *Owner*
EMP: 8
SALES (est): 760K **Privately Held**
SIC: 2434 Wood kitchen cabinets

(G-7422)
TUG HILL VINEYARDS
4051 Yancey Rd (13367-4710)
PHONE....................................315 376-4336
Susan Maring, *Owner*
Michael Maring, *Co-Owner*
EMP: 5 **EST:** 1981
SQ FT: 3,500
SALES (est): 359.8K **Privately Held**
SIC: 2084 Wines

Lynbrook
Nassau County

(G-7423)
ADVANCE BIOFACTURES CORP
35 Wilbur St (11563-2358)
PHONE....................................516 593-7000
Edwin Wegman, *President*
Thomas Wegman, *Senior VP*
Larry Dobross, *Admin Sec*
EMP: 20 **EST:** 1957
SQ FT: 15,000
SALES (est): 1.4MM
SALES (corp-wide): 27.4MM **Publicly Held**
WEB: www.biospecifics.com
SIC: 2836 8731 Biological products, except diagnostic; biological research

PA: Biospecifics Technologies Corp.
35 Wilbur St
Lynbrook NY 11563
516 593-7000

(G-7424)
ALL METRO EMRGNCY RESPONSE SYS
50 Broadway (11563-2519)
PHONE....................................516 750-9100
Irving Edwards, *President*
Seth Shapiro, *General Mgr*
Dean Janil, *Managing Dir*
Angela Davis, *Business Mgr*
Jim Watson, *Exec VP*
EMP: 6
SALES (est): 460K **Privately Held**
WEB: www.amerslifeline.com
SIC: 3669 Emergency alarms

(G-7425)
ALLOY MACHINE & TOOL CO INC
169 Vincent Ave (11563-2607)
PHONE....................................516 593-3445
Paul R Will, *President*
Gary Will, *Vice Pres*
EMP: 8 **EST:** 1967
SQ FT: 8,000
SALES: 900K **Privately Held**
SIC: 3679 Electronic circuits

(G-7426)
BEL TRANSFORMER INC (HQ)
Also Called: Signal Transformer
128 Atlantic Ave (11563-3477)
P.O. Box 36129, Newark NJ (07188-6106)
PHONE....................................516 239-5777
Daniel Bernstein, *President*
▲ **EMP:** 60
SALES: 17MM
SALES (corp-wide): 548.1MM **Publicly Held**
WEB: www.signaltransformer.com
SIC: 3677 Electronic coils, transformers & other inductors
PA: Bel Fuse Inc.
206 Van Vorst St
Jersey City NJ 07302
201 432-0463

(G-7427)
BIMBO BAKERIES USA INC
669 Sunrise Hwy Spc 4 (11563-3246)
PHONE....................................516 887-1024
George Weston, *Branch Mgr*
EMP: 18 **Privately Held**
SIC: 2051 Bakery: wholesale or wholesale/retail combined
HQ: Bimbo Bakeries Usa, Inc
255 Business Center Dr # 200
Horsham PA 19044
215 347-5500

(G-7428)
BIOSPECIFICS TECHNOLOGIES CORP (PA)
35 Wilbur St (11563-2358)
PHONE....................................516 593-7000
Kevin Buchi, *CEO*
Jennifer Chao, *Ch of Bd*
Ron Law, *Senior VP*
James Goris, *Controller*
Pat Caldwell, *Officer*
▲ **EMP:** 5
SALES: 27.4MM **Publicly Held**
WEB: www.biospecifics.com
SIC: 2834 Pharmaceutical preparations

(G-7429)
CASCADE TECHNICAL SERVICES LLC (DH)
30 N Prospect Ave (11563-1313)
PHONE....................................516 596-6300
Tim Smith, *CEO*
Gary Crueger, *Vice Pres*
Tyler Kopet, *CFO*
EMP: 17
SQ FT: 6,400
SALES: 5.3MM
SALES (corp-wide): 915.2MM **Privately Held**
SIC: 3822 Auto controls regulating residntl & coml environmt & applncs

(G-7430)
DOAR INC
170 Earle Ave (11563-2642)
PHONE....................................516 872-8140
Paul Neale, *Manager*
EMP: 8
SALES (corp-wide): 17.8MM **Privately Held**
WEB: www.doar.com
SIC: 3571 3575 7371 5045 Electronic computers; computer terminals; custom computer programming services; computer peripheral equipment; computer software; motion picture equipment; business consulting
PA: Doar, Inc.
1370 Broadway Fl 15l
New York NY 10018
212 235-2700

(G-7431)
FLAGSHIP ONE INC
19 Wilbur St (11563-2360)
PHONE....................................516 766-2223
EMP: 12
SALES (est): 1.9MM **Privately Held**
SIC: 3714 Motor vehicle parts & accessories

(G-7432)
JANEL CORPORATION (PA)
303 Merrick Rd Ste 400 (11563-2521)
PHONE....................................516 256-8143
Brendan J Killackey, *President*
Brian Lally, *Manager*
EMP: 2
SQ FT: 6,800
SALES: 67.5MM **Publicly Held**
WEB: www.janelgroup.net
SIC: 3556 4731 Cutting, chopping, grinding, mixing & similar machinery; freight forwarding

(G-7433)
LABGRAFIX PRINTING INC
43 Rocklyn Ave Unit B (11563-2752)
PHONE....................................516 280-8300
Lev Galkin, *President*
EMP: 6 **EST:** 2010
SALES: 1MM **Privately Held**
SIC: 3861 7384 Photographic equipment & supplies; photographic services

(G-7434)
ND LABS INC
Also Called: Nutritional Designs
202 Merrick Rd (11563-2622)
PHONE....................................516 612-4900
Beth Beller, *Ch of Bd*
Diane Altos, *President*
EMP: 10
SQ FT: 10,000
SALES (est): 1.7MM **Privately Held**
WEB: www.ndlabs.com
SIC: 2834 Vitamin, nutrient & hematinic preparations for human use

(G-7435)
PRO PRINTING
Also Called: PIP Printing
359 Merrick Rd (11563-2517)
PHONE....................................516 561-9700
Raymond Kenney Sr, *Partner*
Raymond Kenney Jr, *Partner*
EMP: 5
SQ FT: 1,000
SALES (est): 370K **Privately Held**
SIC: 2752 2791 2789 Commercial printing, offset; typesetting; bookbinding & related work

(G-7436)
RAYDON PRECISION BEARING CO
75 Merrick Rd (11563-2713)
P.O. Box 679 (11563-0679)
PHONE....................................516 887-2582
Dominick Pinto, *President*
Barbara Pinto, *Treasurer*
EMP: 6 **EST:** 1965
SQ FT: 1,000
SALES (est): 972.4K **Privately Held**
SIC: 3562 5085 Ball & roller bearings; bearings

(G-7437)
RUSSELL INDUSTRIES INC
Also Called: Conco Division
40 Horton Ave (11563-2333)
P.O. Box 807 (11563-0807)
PHONE..................................516 536-5000
Adam Russell, *President*
▲ **EMP:** 7 **EST:** 1965
SQ FT: 20,000
SALES (est): 1.4MM **Privately Held**
SIC: 3679 3675 Antennas, receiving; electronic capacitors

(G-7438)
SIGNS OF SUCCESS LTD
247 Merrick Rd Ste 101 (11563-2641)
PHONE..................................516 295-6000
Steven Cohen, *President*
EMP: 17
SQ FT: 4,500
SALES: 700K **Privately Held**
WEB: www.signs-of-success.com
SIC: 3993 Signs, not made in custom sign painting shops

(G-7439)
STATIC COATINGS INC
344 Hendrickson Ave (11563-1026)
PHONE..................................646 296-0754
EMP: 5
SALES (corp-wide): 733K **Privately Held**
SIC: 3479 Coating of metals & formed products
PA: Static Coatings Inc.
3585 Lawson Blvd Unit B
Oceanside NY 11572
516 764-0040

(G-7440)
SWIFT FULFILLMENT SERVICES
290 Broadway (11563-3293)
PHONE..................................516 593-1198
Barbara Fiegas, *President*
Preston D Theiber, *Vice Pres*
EMP: 7
SQ FT: 5,000
SALES: 999K **Privately Held**
SIC: 2721 5192 Periodicals: publishing only; books

(G-7441)
TOP FORTUNE USA LTD
100 Atlantic Ave Ste 2 (11563-3471)
PHONE..................................516 608-2694
Elan Oved, *CEO*
▲ **EMP:** 6
SALES: 1,000K **Privately Held**
SIC: 2385 Waterproof outerwear

(G-7442)
VALLEY STREAM SPORTING GDS INC
Also Called: Arrowear Athletic Apparel
325 Hendrickson Ave (11563-1055)
PHONE..................................516 593-7800
EMP: 25
SQ FT: 16,000
SALES (est): 3.3MM **Privately Held**
SIC: 2329 2262 Mfg Men's/Boy's Clothing Manmade Fiber & Silk Finishing Plant

(G-7443)
ZEBRA ENVIRONMENTAL CORP (PA)
30 N Prospect Ave (11563-1398)
PHONE..................................516 596-6300
Fax: 516 596-4422
EMP: 17
SQ FT: 6,400
SALES (est): 5.2MM **Privately Held**
SIC: 3822 Mfg Environmental Controls

Lyndonville
Orleans County

(G-7444)
ANDROS BOWMAN PRODUCTS LLC
151 West Ave (14098-9744)
PHONE..................................540 217-4100
Jon Corscer, *Branch Mgr*
EMP: 5 **Privately Held**

SIC: 2033 2099 Fruits: packaged in cans, jars, etc.; food preparations
HQ: Bowman Andros Products, Llc
10119 Old Valley Pike
Mount Jackson VA 22842
540 217-4100

(G-7445)
MIZKAN AMERICA INC
Also Called: Nakano Foods
247 West Ave (14098-9744)
PHONE..................................585 765-9171
Steven Gardepe, *Principal*
Steve Gardepe, *Plant Mgr*
Dave Carpenter, *Safety Mgr*
Steve Fortunato, *Purch Agent*
EMP: 70
SQ FT: 82,000 **Privately Held**
SIC: 2033 2099 2035 Fruit juices: packaged in cans, jars, etc.; food preparations; pickles, sauces & salad dressings
HQ: Mizkan America, Inc.
1661 Feehanville Dr # 200
Mount Prospect IL 60056
847 590-0059

(G-7446)
SHORELINE FRUIT LLC
Also Called: Atwater Foods
10190 Route 18 (14098-9785)
PHONE..................................585 765-2639
Fax: 585 765-9443
EMP: 70
SALES (corp-wide): 43.3MM **Privately Held**
SIC: 2034 Processor Of Fruit Products
PA: Shoreline Fruit, Llc
10850 E Traverse Hwy # 4001
Traverse City MI 49684
231 941-4336

Lyons
Wayne County

(G-7447)
CASWELL INC
7696 State Route 31 (14489-9116)
PHONE..................................315 946-1213
Lance Caswell, *President*
Carol Caswell, *Vice Pres*
Mike Caswell, *Shareholder*
◆ **EMP:** 10
SQ FT: 8,000
SALES (est): 2MM **Privately Held**
WEB: www.caswellplating.net
SIC: 3559 5169 Electroplating machinery & equipment; chemicals & allied products

(G-7448)
CONNEX GRINDING & MACHINING
65 Clyde Rd (14489-9364)
PHONE..................................315 946-4340
Carlton J Collins Jr, *President*
Barbara A Collins, *Treasurer*
EMP: 5 **EST:** 1979
SQ FT: 2,400
SALES (est): 503.8K **Privately Held**
SIC: 3541 Grinding machines, metalworking

(G-7449)
DELOKA LLC
150 Dunn Rd (14489-9772)
PHONE..................................315 946-6910
Scott Lord,
Dercy Gordner, *Admin Asst*
Mike Kunes,
Roger Westerman,
EMP: 5
SQ FT: 21,000
SALES (est): 730.3K **Privately Held**
WEB: www.deloka.com
SIC: 3479 Coating of metals & formed products

(G-7450)
LAGASSE WORKS INC
5 Old State Route 31 (14489-9214)
PHONE..................................315 946-9202
Daniel Lagasse, *President*
Dan Lagasse, *Manager*
▲ **EMP:** 6

SQ FT: 10,000
SALES (est): 1.4MM **Privately Held**
WEB: www.lagasseworks.com
SIC: 7692 3599 Welding repair; machine shop, jobbing & repair

(G-7451)
PENN CAN EQUIPMENT CORPORATION
Also Called: Penn Can Asphalt Materials
300 Cole Rd (14489-9602)
PHONE..................................315 378-0337
EMP: 7
SALES (corp-wide): 1.1MM **Privately Held**
SIC: 3531 Mfg Construction Machinery
PA: Penn Can Equipment Corporation
555 State Fair Blvd
Syracuse NY
315 637-3168

(G-7452)
SILGAN CONTAINERS MFG CORP
8673 Lyons Marengo Rd (14489-9726)
PHONE..................................315 946-4826
Tom Kaczynski, *Manager*
EMP: 150
SALES (corp-wide): 4.4B **Publicly Held**
WEB: www.silgancontainers.com
SIC: 3411 Food containers, metal
HQ: Silgan Containers Manufacturing Corporation
21600 Oxnard St Ste 1600
Woodland Hills CA 91367

(G-7453)
TIM CRETIN LOGGING & SAWMILL
3607 Wayne Center Rd (14489-9321)
PHONE..................................315 946-4476
Tim Cretin, *President*
EMP: 11
SQ FT: 1,961
SALES: 2MM **Privately Held**
SIC: 2411 Logging

(G-7454)
WESLOR INDUSTRIES INC
Also Called: Weslor Enterprises
924 Sohn Alloway Rd (14489-9786)
PHONE..................................315 871-4405
Scott Lord, *President*
Roger Westerman, *Treasurer*
EMP: 26
SQ FT: 10,000
SALES: 864.9K **Privately Held**
WEB: www.weslor.com
SIC: 3443 3444 3449 1799 Fabricated plate work (boiler shop); sheet metalwork; miscellaneous metalwork; welding on site

---

Lyons Falls
Lewis County

(G-7455)
OTIS PRODUCTS INC (PA)
Also Called: Otis Technology
6987 Laura St (13368-1802)
P.O. Box 582 (13368-0582)
PHONE..................................315 348-4300
Doreen Garrett, *CEO*
Larry Williams, *VP Mfg*
Nancy Devereaux, *Senior Buyer*
Steven Buxton, *Engineer*
Bob Ryan, *Engineer*
▲ **EMP:** 122
SQ FT: 12,000
SALES (est): 20.7MM **Privately Held**
WEB: www.otisgun.com
SIC: 3949 Shooting equipment & supplies, general

(G-7456)
TWIN RIVERS PAPER COMPANY LLC
Lyonsdale Rd (13368)
PHONE..................................315 348-8491
Dave Lee, *Superintendent*
Clifford Lavoie, *Maint Spvr*
Brian Thibeault, *Production*
Dennis Gigliotti, *Branch Mgr*

Wendi Gorczyca, *Admin Asst*
EMP: 37
SQ FT: 67,484 **Privately Held**
WEB: www.burrowspaper.com
SIC: 2621 Tissue paper
PA: Twin Rivers Paper Company Llc
82 Bridge Ave
Madawaska ME 04756

Macedon
Wayne County

(G-7457)
A&M MODEL MAKERS LLC
1675 Wayneport Rd Ste 1 (14502-8770)
PHONE..................................626 813-9661
Derek Backus,
EMP: 6
SALES: 350K **Privately Held**
SIC: 3999 Manufacturing industries

(G-7458)
ANKOM DEVELOPMENT LLC
2052 Oneil Rd (14502-8953)
PHONE..................................315 986-1937
Andrew Komarek,
EMP: 5 **EST:** 2006
SALES (est): 625.9K **Privately Held**
SIC: 3534 Elevators & moving stairways

(G-7459)
ANKOM TECHNOLOGY CORP
2052 Oneil Rd (14502-8953)
PHONE..................................315 986-8090
Andrew Komarek, *President*
Christopher Kelley, *Vice Pres*
Ronald Komarek, *Vice Pres*
Shawn Ritchie, *Vice Pres*
Tom Bopp, *Production*
EMP: 30
SQ FT: 50,000
SALES (est): 6.7MM **Privately Held**
WEB: www.ankom.com
SIC: 3821 5049 Laboratory equipment: fume hoods, distillation racks, etc.; laboratory equipment, except medical or dental

(G-7460)
AUBURN BEARING & MFG INC
4 State Route 350 (14502-9177)
PHONE..................................315 986-7600
Peter Schroth, *CEO*
Barbara McMillan, *Manager*
EMP: 8
SQ FT: 1,280
SALES (est): 977.3K **Privately Held**
SIC: 3599 8711 3562 5085 Custom machinery; machine shop, jobbing & repair; engineering services; ball & roller bearings; bearings, bushings, wheels & gears

(G-7461)
BALDWIN RICHARDSON FOODS CO
3268 Blue Heron Dr (14502-9337)
PHONE..................................315 986-2727
Matthew Mahoney, *Business Anlyst*
Diane Vorndran, *Manager*
EMP: 283 **Privately Held**
SIC: 2035 2099 2087 Pickles, sauces & salad dressings; mustard, prepared (wet); food preparations; extracts, flavoring
PA: Baldwin Richardson Foods Company
1 Tower Ln Ste 2390
Oakbrook Terrace IL 60181

(G-7462)
BERRY GLOBAL INC
112 Main St (14502-8996)
PHONE..................................315 986-2161
Richard Leone, *Branch Mgr*
EMP: 200 **Publicly Held**
WEB: www.6sens.com
SIC: 3089 3081 2673 Bottle caps, molded plastic; unsupported plastics film & sheet; bags: plastic, laminated & coated
HQ: Berry Global, Inc.
101 Oakley St
Evansville IN 47710
812 424-2904

(G-7463)
BERRY PLASTICS CORPORATION
200 Main St (14502-8977)
PHONE..................................315 986-6270
EMP: 400
SALES (corp-wide): 4.8B **Publicly Held**
SIC: 3081 3086 2671 Mfg Unsupported Plastic Film/Sheet Mfg Plastic Foam Products Mfg Packaging Paper/Film
HQ: Berry Plastics Corporation
101 Oakley St
Evansville IN 47710
812 424-2904

(G-7464)
CLAD INDUSTRIES LLC
1704 Wayneport Rd Ste 1 (14502-9181)
PHONE..................................585 413-4359
Alan Brown,
EMP: 7
SQ FT: 1,200
SALES (est): 1.5MM **Privately Held**
SIC: 3499 Fire- or burglary-resistive products

(G-7465)
FB SALE LLC
1688 Wayneport Rd (14502-8765)
PHONE..................................315 986-9999
Marc Fleischer,
EMP: 8 EST: 1974
SQ FT: 42,000
SALES (est): 1MM **Privately Held**
WEB: www.fleischersbagels.com
SIC: 2051 Bagels, fresh or frozen

(G-7466)
KTK THERMAL TECHNOLOGIES INC
1657 E Park Dr (14502-8892)
PHONE..................................585 678-9025
Kevin Kreger, President
Jim Palmatier, QC Mgr
Gary Turkovich, Controller
Michael Kulzer, VP Sales
Don Cimino, Sales Staff
◆ EMP: 45
SQ FT: 35,000
SALES: 6.5MM **Privately Held**
SIC: 3823 Thermal conductivity instruments, industrial process type

(G-7467)
LAWSON M WHITING INC
15 State Route 350 (14502-9177)
PHONE..................................315 986-3064
Jay D Whiting, President
Lawson M Whiting, Shareholder
EMP: 8 EST: 1973
SQ FT: 14,000
SALES (est): 1.1MM **Privately Held**
WEB: www.rockcrusher.com
SIC: 3532 Crushing, pulverizing & screening equipment

(G-7468)
PENTA-TECH COATED PRODUCTS LLC
1610 Commons Pkwy (14502-9190)
PHONE..................................315 986-4098
Robert Debruin, Branch Mgr
EMP: 12
SALES (est): 2.5MM
SALES (corp-wide): 6.3MM **Privately Held**
WEB: www.ptcp.net
SIC: 2671 Packaging paper & plastics film, coated & laminated
PA: Penta-Tech Coated Products Llc
58 Main Rd N
Hampden ME 04444
207 862-3105

(G-7469)
PLIANT LLC
200 Main St (14502-8977)
PHONE..................................315 986-6286
Wendy Barnes, Human Resources
Kim Kirby, Manager
EMP: 400

SALES (est): 48.5MM **Publicly Held**
SIC: 3081 3086 2671 Unsupported plastics film & sheet; plastics foam products; packaging paper & plastics film, coated & laminated
HQ: Berry Global, Inc.
101 Oakley St
Evansville IN 47710
812 424-2904

(G-7470)
SHORT JJ ASSOCIATES INC (PA)
1645 Wayneport Rd (14502-9110)
P.O. Box 183, Fairport (14450-0183)
PHONE..................................315 986-3511
John Short Jr, President
John J Short Jr, President
Peter J Short, CFO
EMP: 11
SQ FT: 12,500
SALES: 750K **Privately Held**
WEB: www.jjshort.com
SIC: 3069 Molded rubber products

(G-7471)
WATER TECHNOLOGIES INC (PA)
Also Called: Columbia
1635 Commons Pkwy (14502-9191)
PHONE..................................315 986-0000
Joe Cupido, President
Bruce Dan, Vice Pres
▲ EMP: 5
SALES (est): 6.1MM **Privately Held**
SIC: 3589 Water filters & softeners, household type

Machias
Cattaraugus County

(G-7472)
MACHIAS FURNITURE FACTORY INC (PA)
3638 Route 242 (14101-9727)
PHONE..................................716 353-8687
Charles I Horning, President
Cindy Horning, Vice Pres
EMP: 9
SQ FT: 25,000
SALES (est): 473.1K **Privately Held**
SIC: 2511 Wood desks, bookcases & magazine racks

Mahopac
Putnam County

(G-7473)
ADVANCED TCHNCAL SOLUTIONS INC
Also Called: Ats
8 Lupi Plz (10541-3766)
P.O. Box 28, Yorktown Heights (10598-0028)
PHONE..................................914 214-8230
Joe Yaniv, President
David Wright, VP Opers
▲ EMP: 10
SQ FT: 2,000
SALES (est): 5MM **Privately Held**
SIC: 3569 5049 Lubrication equipment, industrial; engineers' equipment & supplies

(G-7474)
MICHAEL BENALT INC
100 Buckshollow Rd (10541-3756)
PHONE..................................845 628-1008
Michael Benalt, President
Kevin Grieger, Sales Executive
Gary Lewis, Office Mgr
EMP: 25 EST: 1975
SQ FT: 37,000
SALES (est): 665.5K **Privately Held**
WEB: www.michaelbenaltinc.com
SIC: 3559 Pharmaceutical machinery

(G-7475)
MORTECH INDUSTRIES INC
961 Route 6 (10541-1796)
P.O. Box 962 (10541-0962)
PHONE..................................845 628-6138
Anthony Morando, President
EMP: 8 EST: 1945
SQ FT: 12,000
SALES: 1.5MM **Privately Held**
SIC: 3541 5999 Grinding, polishing, buffing, lapping & honing machines; buffing & polishing machines; cleaning equipment & supplies

(G-7476)
NORTHEAST DOULAS
23 Hilltop Dr (10541-2815)
PHONE..................................845 621-0654
Debbie Aglietti, Principal
EMP: 5
SALES (est): 667K **Privately Held**
SIC: 2835 Pregnancy test kits

(G-7477)
RICHS STTCHES EMB SCREENPRINT
407 Route 6 (10541-3783)
PHONE..................................845 621-2175
Rich Schnetzinger, Owner
EMP: 5
SALES: 210K **Privately Held**
SIC: 2759 Screen printing

(G-7478)
RMD HOLDING INC
Also Called: X-Press Printing & Office Sup
593 Route 6 (10541-1682)
PHONE..................................845 628-0030
Richard De Cola, President
Marie De Cola, Vice Pres
EMP: 8
SQ FT: 2,500
SALES (est): 1.1MM **Privately Held**
SIC: 2752 5943 2791 2789 Commercial printing, offset; office forms & supplies; typesetting; bookbinding & related work

(G-7479)
STEERING COLUMNS GALORE INC
8 Vine Rd (10541-5429)
PHONE..................................845 278-5762
William Lanza, President
Rick Lanza, Vice Pres
EMP: 5
SALES: 414K **Privately Held**
WEB: www.columnsgalore.com
SIC: 3714 Steering mechanisms, motor vehicle

(G-7480)
WALSH & SONS MACHINE INC
15 Secor Rd Ste 5 (10541-2078)
PHONE..................................845 526-0301
Frank Walsh, President
EMP: 6 EST: 1997
SALES (est): 652.7K **Privately Held**
SIC: 3599 Machine shop, jobbing & repair

Malone
Franklin County

(G-7481)
ADIRONDACK ICE & AIR INC
Also Called: Adirondex
26 Railroad St (12953-1014)
PHONE..................................518 483-4340
James McKee, Ch of Bd
Tim Boyea, Vice Pres
Molly Mc Kee, Admin Sec
EMP: 14 EST: 1968
SQ FT: 4,800
SALES (est): 1.6MM **Privately Held**
SIC: 2097 4222 5499 7389 Manufactured ice; storage, frozen or refrigerated goods; water: distilled mineral or spring; coffee service

(G-7482)
ADIRONDACK POWER SPORTS
5378 State Route 37 (12953-4114)
P.O. Box 390 (12953-0390)
PHONE..................................518 481-6269
John Waters, General Mgr
EMP: 8
SQ FT: 5,000
SALES (est): 905.7K **Privately Held**
SIC: 3799 5012 Recreational vehicles; recreation vehicles, all-terrain

(G-7483)
ASEPT PAK INC
64 West St (12953-1118)
PHONE..................................518 651-2026
Gary L Hanley, Ch of Bd
EMP: 23 EST: 2004
SALES (est): 5.4MM **Privately Held**
SIC: 2833 Organic medicinal chemicals: bulk, uncompounded

(G-7484)
COCA-COLA BOTTLING COMPANY
15 Ida Pkwy (12953)
PHONE..................................518 483-0422
Ron Lavalley, Branch Mgr
EMP: 28 **Privately Held**
SIC: 2086 Bottled & canned soft drinks
HQ: Coca-Cola Beverages Northeast, Inc.
1 Executive Park Dr # 330
Bedford NH 03110
603 627-7871

(G-7485)
FASPRINT
20 Finney Blvd (12953-1039)
P.O. Box 832 (12953-0832)
PHONE..................................518 483-4631
Tammi M Dupont, Owner
EMP: 6
SQ FT: 2,000
SALES (est): 705.7K **Privately Held**
SIC: 2752 Commercial printing, offset

(G-7486)
JOHNSON NEWSPAPER CORPORATION
Also Called: Malone News
469 E Main St Ste 2 (12953-2128)
PHONE..................................518 483-4700
Betsy McGivney, Auditor
Chuck Kelly, Manager
EMP: 20
SALES (corp-wide): 32MM **Privately Held**
WEB: www.ogd.com
SIC: 2711 Newspapers: publishing only, not printed on site
PA: Johnson Newspaper Corporation
260 Washington St
Watertown NY
315 782-1000

(G-7487)
LOMIR INC
Also Called: Lomir Biomedical Inc
213 W Main St (12953-9577)
P.O. Box 778 (12953-0778)
PHONE..................................518 483-7697
Teresa Price, CEO
Teresa Woodger, President
Karen Coles, General Mgr
Mr Tom Long, Chairman
EMP: 16
SQ FT: 10,000
SALES (est): 1.8MM
SALES (corp-wide): 6.9MM **Privately Held**
WEB: www.lomir.com
SIC: 3821 Laboratory equipment: fume hoods, distillation racks, etc.
PA: Lomir Biomedical Inc
95 Rue Huot
Notre-Dame-De-L'Ile-Perrot QC J7V 7
514 425-3604

(G-7488)
MALONE INDUSTRIAL PRESS INC
10 Stevens St (12953-1634)
P.O. Box 267 (12953-0267)
PHONE..................................518 483-5880
Bernard Desnoyers, President

EMP: 6 EST: 1939
SQ FT: 3,000
SALES: 725K Privately Held
SIC: 2752 5111 Commercial print-
ing, offset; printing paper; letterpress
printing

(G-7489)
SCOTTS FEED INC
Also Called: Collins Pet & Garden Center
245 Elm St (12953-1541)
PHONE.................................518 483-3110
Scott Collins, President
EMP: 23
SQ FT: 6,000
SALES (est): 4.9MM Privately Held
SIC: 2048 5191 Prepared feeds; animal
feeds

(G-7490)
SEAWAY MATS INC
Also Called: Sea Mats
252 Park St (12953-1234)
P.O. Box 407 (12953-0407)
PHONE.................................518 483-2560
Roy Hamilton, CEO
Diane Hamilton, Vice Pres
EMP: 7 EST: 1972
SALES (est): 851.3K
SALES (corp-wide): 5.4MM Privately
Held
SIC: 3069 3949 3089 2391 Mats or mat-
ting, rubber; nets: badminton, volleyball,
tennis, etc.; composition stone, plastic;
doors, folding: plastic or plastic coated
fabric; curtains & draperies
PA: Seaway Plastics Ltd
270 Boul Saint-Joseph
Lachine QC H8S 2
514 637-2323

(G-7491)
SIGNS INC
2 Boyer Ave (12953-1628)
P.O. Box 185 (12953-0185)
PHONE.................................518 483-4759
Judy Sousie, President
Shannon Niles, Treasurer
EMP: 5
SALES (est): 444.7K Privately Held
SIC: 3993 Signs & advertising specialties

(G-7492)
TITUS MOUNTAIN SAND & GRAV
LLC
17 Junction Rd (12953-4217)
P.O. Box 390 (12953-0390)
PHONE.................................518 483-3740
William Hewitt, Mng Member
EMP: 6
SALES (est): 920.8K Privately Held
SIC: 1442 Construction sand & gravel

(G-7493)
UPSTONE MATERIALS INC
Also Called: Malone Concrete Products Div
359 Elm St (12953)
P.O. Box 457, North Bangor (12966-0457)
PHONE.................................518 483-2671
Jim Odis, Manager
EMP: 6
SALES (corp-wide): 83.5MM Privately
Held
WEB: www.graymont-ab.com
SIC: 3273 Ready-mixed concrete
HQ: Upstone Materials Inc.
111 Quarry Rd
Plattsburgh NY 12901
518 561-5321

Malta
Saratoga County

(G-7494)
AIR LIQUIDE ELECTRONICS
400 Stonebreak Ext (12020-4400)
PHONE.................................518 605-4936
Peter Rabbeni, Vice Pres
Anil Kumar, Engineer
Nick Tan, Engineer
Young Park, Sales Staff
Negesse Gutema, Program Mgr
▲ EMP: 9 EST: 2013

SALES (est): 1.2MM Privately Held
SIC: 3674 Semiconductors & related devices

(G-7495)
GLOBALFOUNDRIES US INC
400 Stone Break Rd Ext (12020)
PHONE.................................518 305-9013
Alice McGrath, Principal
Norm Armour, Vice Pres
Bill Barrett, Vice Pres
Craig Luhrmann, Vice Pres
Ronnie Nutt, Opers Staff
EMP: 94 Privately Held
SIC: 3369 3572 Nonferrous foundries;
computer disk & drum drives & compo-
nents
HQ: Globalfoundries U.S. Inc.
2600 Great America Way
Santa Clara CA 95054

(G-7496)
GOLUB CORPORATION
Also Called: Price Chopper Pharmacy 184
3 Hemphill Pl Ste 116 (12020-4419)
PHONE.................................518 899-6063
Rob Russell, Branch Mgr
EMP: 31
SALES (corp-wide): 3.6B Privately Held
SIC: 3751 Motorcycles & related parts
PA: The Golub Corporation
461 Nott St
Schenectady NY 12308
518 355-5000

(G-7497)
TOKYO ELECTRON AMERICA
INC
2 Bayberry Dr (12020-6352)
PHONE.................................518 289-3100
EMP: 6 Privately Held
SIC: 3674 Semiconductors & related de-
vices
HQ: Tokyo Electron America, Inc.
2400 Grove Blvd
Austin TX 78741
512 424-1000

(G-7498)
WIRED COFFEE AND BAGEL
INC
Rr 9 (12020)
PHONE.................................518 506-3194
Matthew J Michele, President
EMP: 12
SALES (est): 1MM Privately Held
SIC: 3556 5812 Roasting machinery: cof-
fee, peanut, etc.; lunchrooms & cafeterias

Mamaroneck
Westchester County

(G-7499)
BRANDS WITHIN REACH LLC
141 Halstead Ave Ste 201 (10543-2652)
PHONE.................................847 720-9090
Olivier Sonnois, Mng Member
▲ EMP: 24
SQ FT: 2,500
SALES (est): 4.6MM
SALES (corp-wide): 52.1MM Publicly
Held
SIC: 2086 Bottled & canned soft drinks
PA: New Age Beverages Corporation
2420 17th St Ste 220
Denver CO 80202
303 566-3030

(G-7500)
CARPET FABRICATIONS INTL
628 Waverly Ave Ste 1 (10543-2259)
PHONE.................................914 381-6060
Thomas L Budetti, President
Edward Soto, Vice Pres
▲ EMP: 23
SQ FT: 15,000
SALES (est): 2.3MM Privately Held
SIC: 2273 5023 Carpets & rugs; floor cov-
erings

(G-7501)
CATHOLIC NEWS PUBLISHING
CO
Also Called: School Guide Publications
420 Railroad Way (10543-2257)
PHONE.................................914 632-7771
Myles A Ridder, President
Joseph Ridder, Treasurer
EMP: 15 EST: 1886
SQ FT: 5,500
SALES: 3MM Privately Held
WEB: www.schoolguides.com
SIC: 2741 7372 Directories: publishing
only, not printed on site; publishers' com-
puter software

(G-7502)
CB MINERALS LLC
875 Mamaroneck Ave (10543-1900)
PHONE.................................914 777-3330
Andy Shpiz, Mng Member
EMP: 19 EST: 2017
SALES (est): 4MM Privately Held
SIC: 2819 1481 Industrial inorganic chem-
icals; nonmetallic mineral services

(G-7503)
CHOCOLATIONS LLC
607 E Boston Post Rd (10543-3742)
PHONE.................................914 777-3600
Maria Valente,
EMP: 5
SALES: 200K Privately Held
SIC: 2064 Candy & other confectionery
products

(G-7504)
COLDSTREAM GROUP INC (PA)
Also Called: Nessen Lighting, The
420 Railroad Way (10543-2257)
P.O. Box 187 (10543-0187)
PHONE.................................914 698-5959
Bob Henderson, President
Ralph Izzi, Controller
▲ EMP: 19
SALES (est): 7MM Privately Held
SIC: 3646 Commercial indusl & institu-
tional electric lighting fixtures

(G-7505)
CORIUM CORPORATION (PA)
Also Called: Cromwell Group
147 Palmer Ave (10543-3632)
PHONE.................................914 381-0100
Thomas Fleisch, President
Rick Derr, Treasurer
Mike Lougee, VP Sales
Peter Sieminski, Sales Staff
▲ EMP: 18
SALES (est): 5.6MM Privately Held
WEB: www.coriumcorp.com
SIC: 3111 Leather tanning & finishing

(G-7506)
CROMWELL LEATHER
COMPANY INC
Also Called: Cromwellgroup
147 Palmer Ave (10543-3632)
PHONE.................................914 381-0100
Tom Fleisch, President
Erik Eisler, Principal
Margaret Zulkowsky, Vice Pres
Evan Fleisch, Sales Staff
▲ EMP: 14
SQ FT: 5,000
SALES (est): 2.4MM Privately Held
WEB: www.cromwellgroup.com
SIC: 3111 Leather tanning & finishing

(G-7507)
CULIN/COLELLA INC
632 Center Ave (10543-2206)
PHONE.................................914 698-7727
Raynsford Culin, President
Janice Colella Culin, Corp Secy
EMP: 9 EST: 1975
SQ FT: 10,000
SALES: 1.1MM Privately Held
WEB: www.culincolella.com
SIC: 2519 2521 Household furniture, ex-
cept wood or metal: upholstered; cabi-
nets, office: wood

(G-7508)
DIVISION DEN-BAR
ENTERPRISES
Also Called: Arborn Printing & Graphics
745 W Boston Post Rd (10543-3320)
PHONE.................................914 381-2220
Barry Arborn, President
Denise Arborn, Vice Pres
EMP: 5
SQ FT: 1,000
SALES: 650K Privately Held
SIC: 2759 2789 Commercial printing;
bookbinding & related work

(G-7509)
ENCORE RETAIL SYSTEMS INC
(PA)
180 E Prospect Ave (10543-3709)
PHONE.................................718 385-3443
Louis Fusaro, President
Stephen Cain, Vice Pres
EMP: 10
SQ FT: 10,000
SALES (est): 1.9MM Privately Held
SIC: 2499 2541 Display forms, boot &
shoes; wood partitions & fixtures

(G-7510)
FAMILY PUBLISHING GROUP
INC
Also Called: New York Familypublications
141 Halstead Ave (10543-2607)
PHONE.................................914 381-7474
Fax: 914 381-7672
EMP: 20
SQ FT: 1,200
SALES (est): 1.8MM Privately Held
SIC: 2721 2731 Periodicals-
Publishing/Printing Books-
Publishing/Printing

(G-7511)
GANNETT STLLITE INFO NTWRK
LLC
Also Called: Gannett Suburban Newspapers
700 Waverly Ave (10543-2262)
PHONE.................................914 381-3400
Larry James, Manager
EMP: 16
SQ FT: 6,000
SALES (corp-wide): 2.9B Publicly Held
WEB: www.usatoday.com
SIC: 2711 Newspapers, publishing & print-
ing
HQ: Gannett Satellite Information Network,
Llc
7950 Jones Branch Dr
Mc Lean VA 22102
703 854-6000

(G-7512)
INFLATION SYSTEMS INC
500 Ogden Ave (10543-2227)
PHONE.................................914 381-8070
Sandra Goldman, President
Robert Goldman, Vice Pres
EMP: 20
SQ FT: 7,500
SALES (est): 3.4MM Privately Held
SIC: 3069 Valves, hard rubber; hard rubber
& molded rubber products

(G-7513)
MARINE & INDUS HYDRAULICS
INC
329 Center Ave (10543-2304)
PHONE.................................914 698-2036
John J Wright, President
Brooks G Wright, Vice Pres
▲ EMP: 10
SQ FT: 10,000
SALES (est): 2.1MM Privately Held
SIC: 3625 Actuators, industrial

(G-7514)
MARVAL INDUSTRIES INC
Also Called: M I I
315 Hoyt Ave (10543-1899)
PHONE.................................914 381-2400
Alan Zimmerman, CEO
Thomas Zimmerman, Ch of Bd
Emil Kocur, Vice Pres
Logan Osberg, Opers Mgr
Manuela Blossy, Controller

▲ EMP: 70 EST: 1956
SQ FT: 54,000
SALES (est): 39.6MM **Privately Held**
WEB: www.marvalindustries.com
SIC: **2869** 5162 3089 3087 Industrial organic chemicals; plastics materials; thermoformed finished plastic products; custom compound purchased resins

(G-7515)
MDJ SALES ASSOCIATES INC
27 Doris Rd (10543-1009)
PHONE..................................914 420-5897
Michael Aaronson, *CEO*
EMP: 5
SALES: 750K **Privately Held**
SIC: **2253** Knit outerwear mills

(G-7516)
ON THE JOB EMBROIDERY & AP
154 E Boston Post Rd # 1 (10543-3736)
PHONE..................................914 381-3556
Michael Federici, *President*
Joseph Bilotto, *Vice Pres*
EMP: 5
SALES (est): 320K **Privately Held**
SIC: **2395** Embroidery products, except schiffli machine

(G-7517)
ORTHO RITE INC
434 Waverly Ave (10543-2266)
PHONE..................................914 235-9100
Gregory Sands, *President*
EMP: 28
SQ FT: 4,000
SALES: 3.2MM **Privately Held**
WEB: www.ortho-rite.com
SIC: **3842** Suspensories

(G-7518)
PALETERIA FERNANDEZ INC
350 Mamaroneck Ave (10543-2608)
PHONE..................................914 315-1598
Ignacio Fernandez, *CEO*
EMP: 12 **Privately Held**
SIC: **2024** Ice cream, bulk
PA: Paleteria Fernandez Inc.
    33 N Main St
    Port Chester NY 10573

(G-7519)
PICONE MEAT SPECIALTIES LTD
Also Called: Picone's Sausage
180 Jefferson Ave (10543-1912)
PHONE..................................914 381-3002
Frank Picone, *President*
Anthony Picone, *Vice Pres*
EMP: 8
SQ FT: 6,600
SALES (est): 2.4MM **Privately Held**
SIC: **2013** Sausages & other prepared meats

(G-7520)
POLKADOT USA INC
33 Country Rd (10543-1108)
PHONE..................................914 835-3697
Debra Schoenau, *President*
Howard Friedman, *Vice Pres*
EMP: 2
SQ FT: 6,000
SALES: 2MM **Privately Held**
WEB: www.polkadotusa.com
SIC: **2396** Apparel & other linings, except millinery

(G-7521)
RICHARD ENGDAL BAKING CORP
Also Called: Hudson Valley Baking Co
421 Waverly Ave (10543-2233)
PHONE..................................914 777-9600
Richard Cuozzo, *President*
EMP: 10
SQ FT: 4,000
SALES (est): 1.1MM **Privately Held**
SIC: **2051** Bakery: wholesale or wholesale/retail combined

(G-7522)
ROBERT E DERECKTOR INC
Also Called: Derecktor Shipyards
311 E Boston Post Rd (10543-3738)
PHONE..................................914 698-0962
Eric P Derecktor, *Ch of Bd*
E Paul Derecktor, *Ch of Bd*
Erin Federspiel, *Project Mgr*
Peter Skwarek, *Purch Dir*
Mark Russell, *Manager*
▲ EMP: 80 EST: 1947
SQ FT: 64,000
SALES (est): 15.5MM **Privately Held**
SIC: **3731** 4493 7699 3444 Ferryboats, building & repairing; boat yards, storage & incidental repair; boat repair; sheet metalwork; fabricated structural metal; fishing boats: lobster, crab, oyster, etc.: small

(G-7523)
SHORE LINE MONOGRAMMING INC
Also Called: Shore Line Momogramming & EMB
115 Hoyt Ave (10543-1891)
PHONE..................................914 698-8000
John Moller, *President*
Andrew Moller, *President*
EMP: 5
SQ FT: 18,000
SALES (est): 1.3MM **Privately Held**
SIC: **2759** 5941 Screen printing; sporting goods & bicycle shops

(G-7524)
TERRABILT INC
619 Center Ave (10543-2207)
PHONE..................................914 341-1500
Donald Meeker, *President*
EMP: 6 EST: 2011
SALES: 400K **Privately Held**
SIC: **3993** 7336 Signs, not made in custom sign painting shops; commercial art & graphic design

(G-7525)
TOM & JERRY PRINTCRAFT FORMS (PA)
960 Mamaroneck Ave (10543-1631)
P.O. Box 743 (10543-0743)
PHONE..................................914 777-7468
Thomas La Guidice, *President*
Phil Caragine, *Treasurer*
Robert Langerfeld, *Manager*
EMP: 25
SQ FT: 5,000
SALES (est): 3.9MM **Privately Held**
WEB: www.printcraftny.com
SIC: **2752** 2791 2789 Commercial printing, offset; typesetting; bookbinding & related work

(G-7526)
TRIDENT VALVE ACTUATOR CO
329 Center Ave (10543-2304)
PHONE..................................914 698-2650
John Wright, *Principal*
Kathleen Wright, *Treasurer*
EMP: 12
SQ FT: 10,000
SALES (est): 1.1MM **Privately Held**
SIC: **3625** 5085 Actuators, industrial; valves & fittings

Manchester
Ontario County

(G-7527)
ELITE MACHINE INC
3 Merrick Cir (14504-9740)
P.O. Box 8 (14504-0008)
PHONE..................................585 289-4733
Steve Hawkins, *President*
EMP: 5
SQ FT: 5,304
SALES (est): 451K **Privately Held**
SIC: **3599** Machine shop, jobbing & repair

(G-7528)
ROCHESTER INSULATED GLASS INC
73 Merrick Cir (14504-9740)
P.O. Box 168 (14504-0168)
PHONE..................................585 289-3611
Richard S Wolk, *President*
Gretchen Wolk, *Corp Secy*
Tyler Wolk, *Vice Pres*
Ashlee Bechtold, *Sales Staff*
Jennifer Luecke, *Sales Staff*
◆ EMP: 55
SALES (est): 11.9MM **Privately Held**
WEB: www.rochesterinsulatedglass.com
SIC: **3231** Insulating glass: made from purchased glass; safety glass: made from purchased glass

(G-7529)
SIDCO FILTER CORPORATION
58 North Ave (14504-9769)
PHONE..................................585 289-3100
Sidney T Cutt, *Ch of Bd*
Andrea Fitzgerald, *President*
Bill Florance, *Sales Dir*
EMP: 27
SQ FT: 20,000
SALES (est): 5.8MM **Privately Held**
WEB: www.sidcofilter.com
SIC: **3569** Filters, general line: industrial

Manhasset
Nassau County

(G-7530)
ADVANCED PROSTHETICS ORTHOTICS
Also Called: Joyce Center
50 Maple Pl (11030-1927)
PHONE..................................516 365-7225
Michael A Joyce, *President*
Cheryl Caruso, *Manager*
EMP: 10
SALES (est): 1.5MM **Privately Held**
SIC: **3842** Prosthetic appliances; orthopedic appliances

(G-7531)
CABINETRY BY TBR INC
1492 Northern Blvd (11030-3006)
PHONE..................................516 365-8500
Basiliki Ypsilantis, *Principal*
EMP: 8
SALES (est): 760.3K **Privately Held**
SIC: **2434** Wood kitchen cabinets

(G-7532)
CALIBRATED INSTRUMENTS INC
306 Aerie Ct (11030-4053)
PHONE..................................914 741-5700
John B Shroyer, *President*
▲ EMP: 10 EST: 1954
SALES (est): 1.6MM **Privately Held**
SIC: **3823** On-stream gas/liquid analysis instruments, industrial

(G-7533)
DOHNSCO INC
19 Gracewood Dr (11030-3931)
PHONE..................................516 773-4800
EMP: 5
SQ FT: 2,100
SALES (est): 310K **Privately Held**
SIC: **2741** 7379 Misc Publishing Computer Related Services

(G-7534)
FRAME SHOPPE & ART GALLERY
Also Called: Frame Shoppe & Gallery
447 Plandome Rd (11030-1942)
PHONE..................................516 365-6014
Demitri Kazianis, *Partner*
Trapani Art, *Partner*
EMP: 6
SALES (est): 429.6K **Privately Held**
SIC: **2499** 3499 7699 5999 Picture frame molding, finished; picture frames, metal; picture framing, custom; art dealers; gift shop

(G-7535)
GOLF DIRECTORIES USA INC
39 Orchard St Ste 7 (11030-1969)
PHONE..................................516 365-5351
Ray Cyrgalis, *President*
EMP: 5
SQ FT: 1,000
SALES (est): 274.8K **Privately Held**
SIC: **2741** Telephone & other directory publishing

(G-7536)
KRUG PRECISION INC
42 Webster Ave (11030-1922)
PHONE..................................516 944-9350
Michael Krug, *President*
Rosemarie Krug, *Corp Secy*
EMP: 9
SALES (est): 1.2MM **Privately Held**
SIC: **3599** Machine shop, jobbing & repair

(G-7537)
MARTIN FLYER INCORPORATED
29 Woodcliff Ct (11030-4411)
PHONE..................................212 840-8899
Gary Flyer, *President*
Mahipal Singhvi, *COO*
Sandeep Chhaparwal, *CFO*
▲ EMP: 27
SQ FT: 8,000
SALES (est): 9.9MM **Privately Held**
WEB: www.martinflyer.com
SIC: **3911** Jewelry, precious metal

(G-7538)
MDR PRINTING CORP
Also Called: Minuteman Press
125 Plandome Rd (11030-2331)
PHONE..................................516 627-3221
Les Forrai, *President*
Michael Forrai, *Vice Pres*
EMP: 5 EST: 1980
SQ FT: 1,200
SALES (est): 673.7K **Privately Held**
WEB: www.manhassetminuteman.com
SIC: **2752** Commercial printing, lithographic

(G-7539)
NATIONAL SECURITY SYSTEMS INC
511 Manhasset Woods Rd (11030-1663)
PHONE..................................516 627-2222
Jay Baron, *President*
John W Walter, *Chairman*
William T Walter, *Vice Pres*
Joan Walter, *Admin Sec*
EMP: 26
SQ FT: 3,200
SALES: 34.6MM **Privately Held**
WEB: www.plazaconstruction.com
SIC: **3699** Security control equipment & systems

(G-7540)
PRISCILLA QUART CO FIRTS
160 Plandome Rd Ste 2 (11030-2334)
PHONE..................................516 365-2755
EMP: 6
SALES (est): 278.8K **Privately Held**
SIC: **3131** Quarters

(G-7541)
SUPERIOR FURS INC
1697 Northern Blvd (11030-3026)
PHONE..................................516 365-4123
Tom Djoganopoulos, *President*
EMP: 13
SQ FT: 1,000
SALES (est): 1.1MM **Privately Held**
SIC: **2371** 5632 Apparel, fur; furriers

(G-7542)
TEA LIFE LLC
73 Plandome Rd (11030-2330)
PHONE..................................516 365-7711
Linda Villano,
EMP: 8
SQ FT: 3,000
SALES (est): 284.7K **Privately Held**
SIC: **2099** Tea blending

▲ = Import ▼=Export
◆ =Import/Export

Manlius
Onondaga County

(G-7543)
BASILEUS COMPANY LLC
8104 Cazenovia Rd (13104-6700)
PHONE...............................315 963-3516
Gerald E Wilson, *Mng Member*
◆ EMP: 10
SQ FT: 2,215
SALES (est): 940K **Privately Held**
SIC: 2211 Apparel & outerwear fabrics, cotton

(G-7544)
CARPENTER MANUFACTURING CO
110 Fairgrounds Dr (13104-2481)
P.O. Box 188 (13104-0188)
PHONE...............................315 682-9176
Thomas Carpenter, *President*
Susan C Sorensen, *Vice Pres*
Kenneth Carpenter, *Shareholder*
EMP: 20 EST: 1955
SQ FT: 14,500
SALES (est): 4.5MM **Privately Held**
WEB: www.carpentermfg.com
SIC: 3549 Wiredrawing & fabricating machinery & equipment, ex. die; cutting & slitting machinery

(G-7545)
CREATIVE YARD DESIGNS INC
8329 Us Route 20 (13104-9536)
PHONE...............................315 706-6143
Ron King, *Manager*
EMP: 5
SALES (est): 377.6K **Privately Held**
SIC: 3271 Blocks, concrete: landscape or retaining wall

(G-7546)
FILTER TECH INC (PA)
113 Fairgrounds Dr (13104-2497)
P.O. Box 527 (13104-0527)
PHONE...............................315 682-8815
Joseph F Scalise, *President*
Ahmad El-Hindi, *Principal*
Joseph El-Hindi, *Vice Pres*
Elizabeth Elhindi, *Vice Pres*
Mehdi Meghezzi, *Electrical Engi*
▲ EMP: 59
SQ FT: 10,000
SALES (est): 12.2MM **Privately Held**
WEB: www.filtertech.com
SIC: 3569 Filters, general line: industrial; lubricating systems, centralized

(G-7547)
GLOBAL INSTRUMENTATION LLC
8104 Cazenovia Rd Ste 2/3 (13104-6700)
PHONE...............................315 682-0272
James Demaso, *Mng Member*
Scott Meyers,
Craig Sellers,
EMP: 10
SALES (est): 1.9MM **Privately Held**
WEB: www.globalinstrumentation.com
SIC: 3845 Ultrasonic scanning devices, medical

(G-7548)
L& JG STICKLEY INCORPORATED (PA)
1 Stickley Dr (13104-2485)
P.O. Box 480 (13104-0480)
PHONE...............................315 682-5500
Aminy I Audi, *Ch of Bd*
Edward Audi, *President*
Paul Mercer, *General Mgr*
Robert Russell, *General Mgr*
James Torres, *General Mgr*
▲ EMP: 900 EST: 1895
SQ FT: 400,000
SALES (est): 251.4MM **Privately Held**
WEB: www.stickley.com
SIC: 2511 2519 Wood household furniture; household furniture, except wood or metal: upholstered

(G-7549)
MAYBERRY SHOE COMPANY INC
Also Called: Kangaroo Crossing
131 W Seneca St Ste B (13104-2444)
PHONE...............................315 692-4086
Bruce Mayberry, *President*
EMP: 5
SQ FT: 500
SALES (est): 776K **Privately Held**
SIC: 3149 2329 2339 Athletic shoes, except rubber or plastic; men's & boys' athletic uniforms; uniforms, athletic: women's, misses' & juniors'

(G-7550)
VOSS SIGNS LLC
112 Fairgrounds Dr Ste 2 (13104-2437)
P.O. Box 553 (13104-0553)
PHONE...............................315 682-6418
James Menter, *CFO*
Peter Rowlingson, *Accounting Mgr*
Jeff Woodworth, *VP Mktg*
Thomas Tenerovicz, *Mktg Dir*
Nicholas Diamond, *Marketing Mgr*
EMP: 25
SQ FT: 31,000
SALES (est): 3.8MM **Privately Held**
WEB: www.vosssigns.com
SIC: 2759 3993 2791 Screen printing; signs & advertising specialties; typesetting

Manorville
Suffolk County

(G-7551)
B&K PRECISION CORPORATION
31 Oakwood Dr (11949-1211)
PHONE...............................631 369-2665
Ray Kreiger, *Branch Mgr*
EMP: 5 **Privately Held**
WEB: www.bkprecision.com
SIC: 3559 Automotive related machinery
PA: B&K Precision Corporation
22820 Savi Ranch Pkwy
Yorba Linda CA 92887

(G-7552)
COVERGRIP CORPORATION
16 Douglas Ln (11949-2016)
P.O. Box 304, Holderness NH (03245-0304)
PHONE...............................855 268-3747
John Barry, *President*
▲ EMP: 5 EST: 2011
SALES (est): 800K **Privately Held**
WEB: www.covergrip.com
SIC: 2394 Canvas covers & drop cloths

(G-7553)
SAS INDUSTRIES INC
939 Wading River Manor Rd (11949)
P.O. Box 245 (11949-0245)
PHONE...............................631 727-1441
Steve Steckis, *President*
Mark Derr, *Sales Staff*
Debbie Steckis, *Manager*
Mitchell Steckis, *Info Tech Mgr*
Melissa Lampman, *Administration*
▲ EMP: 15 EST: 1973
SQ FT: 10,000
SALES (est): 3.3MM **Privately Held**
WEB: www.sasindustries.com
SIC: 3053 5085 Gaskets, all materials; industrial supplies

(G-7554)
SPLICE TECHNOLOGIES INC
625 North St (11949-2055)
P.O. Box 644 (11949-0644)
PHONE...............................631 924-8108
Robert P Auteri, *President*
Nannette M Auteri, *Admin Sec*
▼ EMP: 8
SQ FT: 2,000
SALES (est): 1.2MM **Privately Held**
WEB: www.splicetechnologies.com
SIC: 3661 Fiber optics communications equipment

(G-7555)
VULCAN IRON WORKS INC
190 Weeks Ave (11949-2034)
PHONE...............................631 395-6846
Carl Forster, *President*
EMP: 4 EST: 1926
SQ FT: 1,800
SALES (est): 2MM **Privately Held**
WEB: www.vulcanironworks.com
SIC: 3441 Fabricated structural metal

Marathon
Cortland County

(G-7556)
AUTOMATED BIOMASS SYSTEMS LLC
2235 Clarks Corners Rd (13803-1528)
PHONE...............................607 849-7800
Timmins Karl Matthieu, *Principal*
Matthew Dubitzky, *Marketing Staff*
EMP: 18
SALES (est): 5.1MM **Privately Held**
SIC: 3535 Conveyors & conveying equipment

(G-7557)
GALLERY OF MACHINES LLC
Also Called: DH Machine Tool Services
20 Front St (13803-7705)
P.O. Box 460 (13803-0460)
PHONE...............................607 849-6028
Derrick Hartman,
EMP: 4
SQ FT: 46,000
SALES: 1MM **Privately Held**
WEB: www.galleryofmachines.com
SIC: 3541 Machine tools, metal cutting type

(G-7558)
KURTZ TRUCK EQUIPMENT INC
1085 Mcgraw Marathon Rd (13803-2806)
PHONE...............................607 849-3468
Mellisa Slack, *President*
Steve Powers, *Sales Staff*
Ralph Smithling, *Executive*
EMP: 18 EST: 1960
SQ FT: 4,000
SALES (est): 3.8MM **Privately Held**
SIC: 3713 3599 3714 Specialty motor vehicle bodies; machine shop, jobbing & repair; propane conversion equipment, motor vehicle

(G-7559)
MARATHON BOAT GROUP INC
1 Grumman Way (13803-3030)
P.O. Box 549 (13803-0549)
PHONE...............................607 849-3211
Doug Potter, *President*
Greg Harvey, *Corp Secy*
▼ EMP: 15
SQ FT: 24,050
SALES (est): 1.3MM **Privately Held**
WEB: www.marathonboat.com
SIC: 3732 5551 Motorized boat, building & repairing; canoes, building & repairing; boat dealers

Marcellus
Onondaga County

(G-7560)
ARMSTRONG TRANSMITTER CORP
4835 N Street Rd (13108-9715)
PHONE...............................315 673-1269
Sinan Mimaroglu, *President*
Ron Haines, *General Mgr*
▲ EMP: 10
SQ FT: 40,000
SALES (est): 1.2MM **Privately Held**
WEB: www.armstrongtx.com
SIC: 3663 Transmitting apparatus, radio or television

(G-7561)
CHOCOLATE PIZZA COMPANY INC
3774 Lee Mulroy Rd (13108-9814)
PHONE...............................315 673-4098
Ryan Novak, *Ch of Bd*
EMP: 18
SQ FT: 7,000
SALES (est): 3MM **Privately Held**
WEB: www.chocolatepizza.com
SIC: 2066 2064 5149 Chocolate candy, solid; chocolate candy, except solid chocolate; chocolate

(G-7562)
QUIKRETE COMPANIES LLC
4993 Limeledge Rd Ste 560 (13108-9798)
PHONE...............................315 673-2020
Greg Breen, *Branch Mgr*
EMP: 20 **Privately Held**
SIC: 3272 Concrete products
HQ: The Quikrete Companies Llc
5 Concourse Pkwy Ste 1900
Atlanta GA 30328
404 634-9100

(G-7563)
SMITH SAND & GRAVEL INC
4782 Shepard Rd (13108-9745)
P.O. Box 166 (13108-0166)
PHONE...............................315 673-4124
David J Smith, *Ch of Bd*
Chelsea Smith, *Office Mgr*
EMP: 9
SALES (est): 1.6MM **Privately Held**
SIC: 1442 Common sand mining

Marcy
Oneida County

(G-7564)
DEANS PAVING INC
6002 Cavanaugh Rd (13403-2411)
PHONE...............................315 736-7601
James J Dean, *Principal*
EMP: 6
SALES: 700K **Privately Held**
WEB: www.deanspaving.com
SIC: 2951 4959 0782 7521 Asphalt paving mixtures & blocks; sweeping service: road, airport, parking lot, etc.; snowplowing; lawn services; parking lots

(G-7565)
PRAXAIR DISTRIBUTION INC
9432 State Route 49 (13403-2342)
PHONE...............................315 735-6153
Ron Marson, *Manager*
EMP: 11 **Privately Held**
SIC: 2813 Oxygen, compressed or liquefied; nitrogen; acetylene
HQ: Praxair Distribution, Inc.
10 Riverview Dr
Danbury CT 06810
203 837-2000

Margaretville
Delaware County

(G-7566)
HUBBELL INC
46124 State Highway 30 # 2 (12455-3111)
P.O. Box 664 (12455-0664)
PHONE...............................845 586-2707
Joseph Rudd Hubbell, *President*
EMP: 21
SQ FT: 5,000
SALES (est): 3.6MM **Privately Held**
SIC: 3643 Current-carrying wiring devices

(G-7567)
ROBERT GREENBURG (PA)
Cross Rd (12455)
PHONE...............................845 586-2226
Robert Greenburg, *President*
Robert Kane, *Vice Pres*
Al Bates, *Manager*
EMP: 5
SQ FT: 2,000

G
E
O
G
R
A
P
H
I
C

SALES (est): 898.5K **Privately Held**
SIC: 2851 Epoxy coatings; polyurethane coatings

Marion
Wayne County

(G-7568)
DUNLAP MACHINE LLC
4205 Sunset Dr (14505-9556)
PHONE..................................315 926-1013
Roger Dunlap, *Mng Member*
EMP: 12
SQ FT: 5,000
SALES (est): 355K **Privately Held**
SIC: 3599 3541 3542 Machine shop, jobbing & repair; machine tools, metal cutting type; machine tools, metal forming type

(G-7569)
GREEN VALLEY FOODS LLC
3736 S Main St (14505-9751)
PHONE..................................315 926-4280
Kraig H Kayser,
Timothy Benjamin,
Paul Palmby,
Jeffrey Van Riper,
EMP: 7
SQ FT: 348,000
SALES (est): 291.3K
SALES (corp-wide): 1.2B **Publicly Held**
SIC: 2033 Vegetables: packaged in cans, jars, etc.; fruits: packaged in cans, jars, etc.
PA: Seneca Foods Corporation
3736 S Main St
Marion NY 14505
315 926-8100

(G-7570)
HADLEYS FAB-WELD INC
4202 Sunset Dr (14505-9538)
PHONE..................................315 926-5101
Alan Hadley, *President*
Adriana Hadley, *Vice Pres*
EMP: 9
SQ FT: 5,800
SALES (est): 1.1MM **Privately Held**
WEB: www.hadleyfabweld.com
SIC: 7692 Welding repair

(G-7571)
J & G MACHINE & TOOL CO INC
4510 Smith Rd (14505-9509)
PHONE..................................315 310-7130
Gary Prutsman, *President*
Jody Prutsman, *Office Admin*
EMP: 14
SQ FT: 15,000
SALES: 1.5MM **Privately Held**
SIC: 3599 Machine shop, jobbing & repair

(G-7572)
PARKER-HANNIFIN CORPORATION
Also Called: Engineered Polymer Systems Div
3967 Buffalo St (14505-9616)
P.O. Box 6 (14505-0006)
PHONE..................................315 926-4211
Robson Veruti, *Manager*
EMP: 30
SALES (corp-wide): 14.3B **Publicly Held**
WEB: www.parker.com
SIC: 2821 Plastics materials & resins
PA: Parker-Hannifin Corporation
6035 Parkland Blvd
Cleveland OH 44124
216 896-3000

(G-7573)
PETER C HERMAN INC
5395 Skinner Rd (14505-9406)
P.O. Box 45 (14505-0045)
PHONE..................................315 926-4100
Matthew Herman, *President*
Joseph Herman, *Vice Pres*
EMP: 50
SQ FT: 2,000
SALES (est): 7MM **Privately Held**
SIC: 2448 Pallets, wood

(G-7574)
SENECA FOODS CORPORATION (PA)
3736 S Main St (14505-9751)
PHONE..................................315 926-8100
Arthur S Wolcott, *Ch of Bd*
Kraig H Kayser, *President*
Jerry Zaske, *General Mgr*
Paul L Palmby, *COO*
Paul Palmby, *COO*
◆ **EMP:** 50
SQ FT: 348,000
SALES: 1.2B **Publicly Held**
SIC: 2033 2037 Vegetables: packaged in cans, jars, etc.; fruits: packaged in cans, jars, etc.; vegetables, quick frozen & cold pack, excl. potato products; fruits, quick frozen & cold pack (frozen); fruit juices, frozen

(G-7575)
SENECA FOODS CORPORATION
Also Called: Vegetable Operations
3732 S Main St (14505-9751)
P.O. Box 996 (14505)
PHONE..................................315 926-4277
Dan Janke, *Manager*
Ben Scherwitz, *Admin Sec*
EMP: 18
SALES (corp-wide): 1.2B **Publicly Held**
SIC: 2099 Food preparations
PA: Seneca Foods Corporation
3736 S Main St
Marion NY 14505
315 926-8100

(G-7576)
TEC GLASS & INST LLC
Also Called: Thomas R Schul TEC GL & Inst
4211 Sunset Dr (14505-9556)
PHONE..................................315 926-7639
Thomas Schul, *Mng Member*
Hope Schul,
EMP: 7
SQ FT: 3,000
SALES: 150K **Privately Held**
WEB: www.tecglass.biz
SIC: 3231 5049 Laboratory glassware; laboratory equipment, except medical or dental

(G-7577)
VERNS MACHINE CO INC
4929 Steel Point Rd (14505-9552)
PHONE..................................315 926-4223
Al Visingard, *President*
EMP: 28 **EST:** 1975
SQ FT: 8,000
SALES (est): 3.6MM **Privately Held**
SIC: 3541 3599 3451 Machine tools, metal cutting type; machine & other job shop work; screw machine products

(G-7578)
WESSIE MACHINE INC
5229 Steel Point Rd (14505-9534)
PHONE..................................315 926-4060
Alan Wessie, *President*
EMP: 7
SALES (est): 1.1MM **Privately Held**
SIC: 3469 Machine parts, stamped or pressed metal

Marlboro
Ulster County

(G-7579)
CIGAR BOX STUDIOS INC
24 Riverview Dr (12542-5310)
PHONE..................................845 236-9283
Gary Rausenberger, *President*
Christian Patrick, *Project Mgr*
Rob Macdonald, *Purch Mgr*
Sterling Ponder, *Purch Mgr*
Liana Shea, *Director*
▲ **EMP:** 14 **EST:** 1999
SQ FT: 20,000
SALES (est): 3.6MM **Privately Held**
WEB: www.cigarboxstudios.com
SIC: 3443 Fabricated plate work (boiler shop)

(G-7580)
MAGNETIC AIDS INC
1160 Route 9w (12542-5401)
P.O. Box 2502, Newburgh (12550-0610)
PHONE..................................845 863-1400
Joe Formoso, *President*
▲ **EMP:** 8 **EST:** 1958
SALES: 550K **Privately Held**
WEB: www.magneticaids.com
SIC: 3499 Magnets, permanent: metallic

(G-7581)
MAPLE TREE KITCHEN & BATH INC
1108 Route 9w (12542-5401)
PHONE..................................845 236-3660
Joseph Bohunicky, *Principal*
EMP: 14
SALES (est): 1.8MM **Privately Held**
SIC: 2434 Wood kitchen cabinets

(G-7582)
ROYAL WINE CORPORATION
Also Called: Royal Kedem Wine
1519 Route 9w (12542-5420)
PHONE..................................845 236-4000
Michael Herzog, *Branch Mgr*
Tara-Joy Coupart, *Manager*
EMP: 15
SALES (corp-wide): 44MM **Privately Held**
SIC: 2084 5182 Wines; wine; liquor
PA: Royal Wine Corporation
63 Lefante Dr
Bayonne NJ 07002
718 384-2400

Masonville
Delaware County

(G-7583)
AXTELL BRADTKE LUMBER CO
113 Beals Pond Rd (13804-2031)
PHONE..................................607 265-3850
Stuart Axtell, *Partner*
EMP: 6
SALES (est): 554.1K **Privately Held**
SIC: 2421 5211 Sawmills & planing mills, general; lumber products

(G-7584)
MASONVILLE STONE INCORPORATED
12999 State Highway 8 (13804-2119)
PHONE..................................607 265-3597
David Barnes, *President*
Douglas Barnes, *Vice Pres*
EMP: 8
SQ FT: 7,800
SALES (est): 1MM **Privately Held**
SIC: 3281 Cut stone & stone products

Maspeth
Queens County

(G-7585)
AGL INDUSTRIES INC
5912 57th St (11378-3112)
PHONE..................................718 326-7597
Frank Lofaso, *President*
EMP: 50 **EST:** 2012
SQ FT: 4,500
SALES (est): 13.8MM **Privately Held**
SIC: 3449 Bars, concrete reinforcing: fabricated steel

(G-7586)
ALL-CITY METAL INC
5435 46th St (11378-1035)
PHONE..................................718 937-3975
Frank J Buccola, *Ch of Bd*
Roni Lifshitz, *Vice Pres*
Carlene Buccola, *Controller*
John Majowka, *Controller*
Mark Pukhovich, *Manager*
EMP: 40
SQ FT: 2,000
SALES (est): 11MM **Privately Held**
SIC: 3441 1711 Fabricated structural metal; mechanical contractor

(G-7587)
ALLE PROCESSING CORP
Also Called: Amazing Meals
5620 59th St (11378-2314)
PHONE..................................718 894-2000
Sam Hollander, *Ch of Bd*
Albert Weinstock, *President*
Yoel Greenfeld, *Exec VP*
Ehud Bassis, *Vice Pres*
Zevi Wienstock, *Purch Mgr*
▲ **EMP:** 250 **EST:** 1954
SQ FT: 75,000
SALES (est): 51.9MM **Privately Held**
WEB: www.alleprocessing.com
SIC: 2015 2038 2013 Poultry slaughtering & processing; dinners, frozen & packaged; prepared beef products from purchased beef

(G-7588)
AMAX PRINTING INC
6417 Grand Ave (11378-2421)
PHONE..................................718 384-8600
Anton Chan, *President*
Fanny Fang, *Vice Pres*
EMP: 15
SQ FT: 8,000
SALES (est): 2.3MM **Privately Held**
WEB: www.amaxprinting.com
SIC: 2759 2752 Letterpress printing; commercial printing, lithographic

(G-7589)
AMERICA NY RI WANG FD GROUP CO
5885 58th Ave (11378-2721)
PHONE..................................631 231-8999
Lian You Ye, *President*
EMP: 12
SALES (corp-wide): 10MM **Privately Held**
SIC: 2038 Ethnic foods, frozen
PA: America New York Ri Wang Food Group Co. Ltd
30 Inez Dr
Bay Shore NY 11706
631 231-8999

(G-7590)
ANDIKE MILLWORK INC (PA)
Also Called: A & M Home Improvement
5818 64th St Fl 2 (11378-2817)
PHONE..................................718 894-1796
Andrew La Russa, *President*
Mike Machalski, *Vice Pres*
EMP: 3
SQ FT: 6,500
SALES (est): 1MM **Privately Held**
WEB: www.amhomeimprovement.com
SIC: 2434 5211 2499 1521 Wood kitchen cabinets; millwork & lumber; decorative wood & woodwork; single-family home remodeling, additions & repairs

(G-7591)
APEXX OMNI-GRAPHICS INC
5829 64th St (11378-2836)
PHONE..................................718 326-3330
Larry A Peters, *Ch of Bd*
Patricio Corella, *VP Mfg*
Luis Arroyo, *Info Tech Mgr*
EMP: 55 **EST:** 1963
SQ FT: 40,000
SALES (est): 10.3MM **Privately Held**
WEB: www.apexxog.com
SIC: 3555 2656 3861 3089 Plates, offset; plates, paper: made from purchased material; plates, photographic (sensitized); plates, plastic; labels, paper: made from purchased material; packaging paper & plastics film, coated & laminated

(G-7592)
ARISTA COFFEE INC
5901 55th St (11378-3103)
PHONE..................................347 531-0813
Stephen Vouvoudakis, *Ch of Bd*
EMP: 15
SALES (est): 665.7K **Privately Held**
SIC: 3589 2095 Coffee brewing equipment; roasted coffee

(G-7593)
ASN INC
Also Called: Tri Star
6020 59th Pl Ste 2 (11378-3349)
PHONE................................718 894-0800
Albert Nawroth, *Ch of Bd*
Rudy Bove, *Vice Pres*
EMP: 40
SALES (est): 1.5MM **Privately Held**
SIC: 2759 2752 Commercial printing;
commercial printing, lithographic

(G-7594)
AUCAPINA CABINETS INC
5737 57th Dr (11378-2229)
PHONE................................718 609-9054
EMP: 8
SALES (est): 134.8K **Privately Held**
SIC: 2434 Mfg Wood Kitchen Cabinets

(G-7595)
BG BINDERY INC
5877 57th St (11378-3125)
PHONE................................631 767-4242
Barbara Michael, *CEO*
EMP: 5 EST: 2011
SALES (est): 593.6K **Privately Held**
SIC: 2789 Bookbinding & related work

(G-7596)
BIG GEYSER INC (PA)
5765 48th St (11378-2015)
PHONE................................718 821-2200
Lewis Hershkowitz, *CEO*
Irving Hershkowitz, *President*
Harold Baron, *Principal*
Jerry Reda, *COO*
Carl Galio, *Vice Pres*
▲ EMP: 200
SQ FT: 125,000
SALES (est): 103.7MM **Privately Held**
WEB: www.biggeyser.com
SIC: 2086 Bottled & canned soft drinks

(G-7597)
BIMBO BAKERIES USA INC
Also Called: Stroehmann Bakeries 33
5754 Page Pl (11378-2236)
PHONE................................718 463-6300
Steven Hartley, *Branch Mgr*
EMP: 117 **Privately Held**
SIC: 2051 5149 Bread, all types (white,
wheat, rye, etc): fresh or frozen; groceries
& related products
HQ: Bimbo Bakeries Usa, Inc
255 Business Center Dr # 200
Horsham PA 19044
215 347-5500

(G-7598)
**CANADA DRY BOTTLING CO NY
LP**
5035 56th Rd (11378-1109)
PHONE................................718 786-8550
Paul Cicicillini, *Manager*
EMP: 100
SALES (corp-wide): 51.4MM **Privately
Held**
SIC: 2086 Bottled & canned soft drinks
PA: Canada Dry Bottling Company Of New
York, L.P.
11202 15th Ave
College Point NY 11356
718 358-2000

(G-7599)
**COCA-COLA BTLG CO OF NY
INC**
5840 Borden Ave (11378-1106)
PHONE................................718 416-7575
Sharon Smith, *Manager*
EMP: 20
SALES (corp-wide): 31.8B **Publicly Held**
SIC: 2086 Bottled & canned soft drinks
HQ: The Coca-Cola Bottling Company Of
New York Inc
2500 Windy Ridge Pkwy Se
Atlanta GA 30339
770 989-3000

(G-7600)
**CRAFT CUSTOM WOODWORK
CO INC**
5949 56th Ave (11378-2324)
PHONE................................718 821-2162

Yakov Roitman, *President*
▼ EMP: 10
SQ FT: 3,500
SALES: 600K **Privately Held**
SIC: 2434 2521 Wood kitchen cabinets;
cabinets, office: wood

(G-7601)
**CRAFTSMEN WOODWORKERS
LTD**
5865 Maspeth Ave (11378-2728)
PHONE................................718 326-3350
Joseph Finocchiaro, *Principal*
EMP: 25
SQ FT: 13,000
SALES (est): 3.8MM **Privately Held**
WEB: www.craftsmenwoodworkers.com
SIC: 2431 Millwork

(G-7602)
CREATIVE IMAGES & APPLIQUE
Also Called: Cyber Swag Merchandise of NY
5208 Grand Ave Ste 2 (11378-3032)
PHONE................................718 821-8700
Bob Andreoli, *President*
Roger Clark, *Vice Pres*
EMP: 63
SQ FT: 14,500
SALES (est): 7.1MM **Privately Held**
SIC: 2396 Screen printing on fabric articles

(G-7603)
D & G SHEET METAL CO INC
5400 Grand Ave (11378-3006)
PHONE................................718 326-9111
Frank Doka, *President*
EMP: 12
SQ FT: 12,400
SALES (est): 1.3MM **Privately Held**
SIC: 3444 Sheet metalwork

(G-7604)
DAL-TILE CORPORATION
5840 55th Dr (11378-1152)
PHONE................................718 894-9574
Gary Guarascio, *Manager*
EMP: 6
SALES (corp-wide): 9.9B **Publicly Held**
WEB: www.mohawk.com
SIC: 2824 5032 Organic fibers, noncellu-
losic; ceramic wall & floor tile
HQ: Dal-Tile Corporation
7834 C F Hawn Fwy
Dallas TX 75217
214 398-1411

(G-7605)
**DAYLIGHT TECHNOLOGY USA
INC**
5971 59th St (11378-3229)
PHONE................................973 255-8100
Reawei Lee, *President*
▲ EMP: 5 EST: 2013
SQ FT: 2,000
SALES (est): 1.8MM **Privately Held**
SIC: 3229 Bulbs for electric lights

(G-7606)
**DIAMOND CORING & CUTTING
INC**
5919 55th St (11378-3103)
PHONE................................718 381-4545
David Obbink, *President*
EMP: 5
SALES: 80K **Privately Held**
SIC: 3531 Construction machinery

(G-7607)
DSI GROUP INC
Also Called: Ovation Instore
5713 49th St (11378-2020)
PHONE................................800 553-2202
Benjamin S Weshler, *Ch of Bd*
Mindy Kaufman, *COO*
Jonathan Palmer, *Vice Pres*
Joe Miklos, *Technical Mgr*
Oleg Chaban, *Engineer*
▲ EMP: 200
SQ FT: 130,000
SALES (est): 42MM **Privately Held**
SIC: 3993 Displays & cutouts, window &
lobby

(G-7608)
DURA FOAM INC
6302 59th Ave (11378-2808)
PHONE................................718 894-2488
Antony Fontana, *President*
EMP: 35 EST: 1977
SQ FT: 50,000
SALES (est): 4.2MM **Privately Held**
SIC: 3086 Plastics foam products

(G-7609)
**EAST CAST ENVLOPE
GRAPHICS LLC**
5615 55th Dr (11378-1108)
PHONE................................718 326-2424
Leslie Stern, *President*
Alfred Wilkowski, *COO*
Fred Wilkowski, *Vice Pres*
Patrick Nunziante, *CFO*
EMP: 41
SQ FT: 78,000
SALES: 8MM **Privately Held**
WEB: www.interstate-envelope.com
SIC: 2677 Envelopes

(G-7610)
**EAST COAST INTL TIRE GROUP
INC**
5746 Flushing Ave (11378-3136)
PHONE................................718 386-9088
Qixin Zhang, *CEO*
EMP: 9
SALES (est): 124.7K **Privately Held**
SIC: 3011 Tires & inner tubes

(G-7611)
EAST COAST INTL TIRE INC
5746 Flushing Ave Bldg C (11378-3136)
PHONE................................718 386-9088
EMP: 10
SALES (est): 1.2MM
SALES (corp-wide): 13.6MM **Privately
Held**
SIC: 3011 Tires & inner tubes
PA: Qingdao Taining Industry Co., Ltd.
No.247, 308 National Highway, Hai'er
Industrial Zone, Laoshan Di
Qingdao 26610
532 886-0033

(G-7612)
**ELDORADO COFFEE
ROASTERS LTD**
Also Called: Eldorado Coffee Distributors
5675 49th St (11378-2012)
PHONE................................718 418-4100
Segundo Martin, *President*
Grace Alongi, *Business Mgr*
Andres Martin, *Vice Pres*
Juan Martin, *Vice Pres*
Albert Valdes, *Vice Pres*
▲ EMP: 80 EST: 1980
SQ FT: 54,000
SALES (est): 18.3MM **Privately Held**
WEB: www.eldoradocoffee.com
SIC: 2095 Coffee extracts; coffee roasting
(except by wholesale grocers)

(G-7613)
EXTREME SPICES INC (PA)
Also Called: Sanaa Spices
5634 56th St Ste 36 (11378-1132)
PHONE................................917 496-4081
Marc Salih, *President*
▲ EMP: 2
SQ FT: 8,000
SALES (est): 1.3MM **Privately Held**
SIC: 2099 Spices, including grinding

(G-7614)
FALLON INC
5930 56th Rd (11378-2330)
PHONE................................718 326-7226
Steven Rosenblatt, *President*
EMP: 20
SQ FT: 27,000
SALES (est): 1.6MM **Privately Held**
WEB: www.structuralprocessing.com
SIC: 3471 Anodizing (plating) of metals or
formed products

(G-7615)
FINAL DIMENSION INC
57-401 59th St Fl 1 Flr 1 (11378)
PHONE................................718 786-0100

Labros Magoutas, *President*
EMP: 5
SQ FT: 3,000
SALES: 500K **Privately Held**
SIC: 2511 Wood household furniture

(G-7616)
**FORMOSA POLYMER
CORPORATION**
5641 55th Ave (11378-1104)
PHONE................................718 326-1769
Su Sheng Shyoung, *Ch of Bd*
▲ EMP: 6
SALES (est): 891.4K **Privately Held**
SIC: 2822 Ethylene-propylene rubbers,
EPDM polymers

(G-7617)
FRANKS CUSHIONS INC
6302 59th Ave (11378-2808)
PHONE................................718 848-1216
Anthony Fontana, *President*
Maryann Fontana, *Bookkeeper*
▲ EMP: 15 EST: 1930
SQ FT: 10,000
SALES (est): 1.3MM **Privately Held**
WEB: www.frankscushions.com
SIC: 2392 Cushions & pillows

(G-7618)
**GOTHIC CABINET CRAFT INC
(PA)**
5877 57th St (11378-3125)
PHONE................................347 881-1420
Theo Zaharopoulos, *President*
Greg Vassilakos, *Vice Pres*
EMP: 80
SQ FT: 100,000
SALES (est): 12.6MM **Privately Held**
WEB: www.gothiccabinetcraft.com
SIC: 2522 5712 2521 Cabinets, office: ex-
cept wood; furniture stores; cabinets, of-
fice: wood

(G-7619)
**GRAND MERIDIAN PRINTING
INC**
Also Called: GM Printing
5877 57th St (11378-3125)
PHONE................................718 937-3888
K Y Chow, *President*
Carol Chiu, *Vice Pres*
EMP: 20
SALES (est): 3.1MM **Privately Held**
SIC: 2752 2759 Commercial printing, off-
set; commercial printing

(G-7620)
**GREAT AMERICAN DESSERT CO
LLC**
5842 Maurice Ave (11378)
PHONE................................718 894-3494
Mike Goodman,
EMP: 55 EST: 1998
SALES (est): 7.6MM **Privately Held**
SIC: 2051 Cakes, bakery: except frozen

(G-7621)
GYM STORE INC
Also Called: GYM STORE.COM
5889 57th St (11378-3125)
PHONE................................718 366-7804
Christopher Kelly, *President*
▼ EMP: 5
SQ FT: 10,000
SALES: 2MM **Privately Held**
SIC: 3949 Exercise equipment

(G-7622)
HI-TECH METALS INC
5920 56th Ave (11378-2325)
PHONE................................718 894-1212
Manny Tzilzelis, *President*
Menelaos Tzilvelis, *President*
Chris Christodoulou, *Vice Pres*
Jim Sculco, *Vice Pres*
Jay Valentino, *Department Mgr*
EMP: 50
SQ FT: 10,000
SALES (est): 14.9MM **Privately Held**
WEB: www.hi-techmetals.com
SIC: 3446 Architectural metalwork

GEOGRAPHIC

(G-7623)
JACK LUCKNER STEEL SHELVING CO
Also Called: Kart
5454 43rd St (11378-1028)
P.O. Box 780005 (11378-0005)
PHONE...................................718 363-0500
Burton J Gold, *President*
EMP: 75 **EST:** 1947
SQ FT: 12,000
SALES (est): 6.9MM
SALES (corp-wide): 21.7MM **Privately Held**
WEB: www.karpinc.com
SIC: 2542 Shelving, office & store: except wood
PA: Karp Associates Inc.
　　260 Spagnoli Rd
　　Melville NY 11747
　　631 768-8300

(G-7624)
JAG LIGHTING
6105 56th Dr (11378-2407)
PHONE...................................917 226-3575
Jerzy Golonka, *Principal*
EMP: 5
SALES (est): 379.9K **Privately Held**
SIC: 3648 Lighting equipment

(G-7625)
KARP OVERSEAS CORPORATION
5454 43rd St (11378-1028)
PHONE...................................718 784-2105
Burton J Gold, *President*
EMP: 40
SQ FT: 30,000
SALES: 500K
SALES (corp-wide): 21.7MM **Privately Held**
WEB: www.karpinc.com
SIC: 3965 8742 Straight pins: steel or brass; sales (including sales management) consultant
PA: Karp Associates Inc.
　　260 Spagnoli Rd
　　Melville NY 11747
　　631 768-8300

(G-7626)
MASPETH PRESS INC
6620 Grand Ave (11378-2531)
PHONE...................................718 429-2363
Frederick F Strobel, *President*
Frederick J Strobel, *President*
Linda Strobel, *Vice Pres*
EMP: 5
SQ FT: 2,000
SALES (est): 698.6K **Privately Held**
SIC: 2759 Letterpress printing

(G-7627)
MASPETH WELDING INC
5930 54th St (11378-3004)
PHONE...................................718 497-5430
Jeffrey Anschlowar, *Ch of Bd*
Vera Galvez, *Opers Staff*
Robert Parisi, *CFO*
Evelyn Agnoli, *VP Finance*
Val Chua, *Manager*
EMP: 40 **EST:** 1977
SQ FT: 48,000
SALES (est): 11.9MM **Privately Held**
WEB: www.maspethwelding.com
SIC: 3441 7692 Fabricated structural metal; welding repair

(G-7628)
MAXSUN CORPORATION (PA)
Also Called: Maxsun Furnishings
5711 49th St (11378-2020)
PHONE...................................718 418-6800
Johnny Song Lin, *Ch of Bd*
Ernest Garcia, *Accounts Mgr*
Stephen Lin, *Manager*
▲ **EMP:** 17
SALES (est): 867.1K **Privately Held**
SIC: 2599 5719 Restaurant furniture, wood or metal; bar furniture; bar, restaurant & cafeteria furniture; lighting fixtures

(G-7629)
NELSON AIR DEVICE CORPORATION
Also Called: C W Sheet Metal
4628 54th Ave (11378-1012)
PHONE...................................718 729-3801
Nelson Blitz Jr, *President*
Thomas Howard, *COO*
Michael Doff, *Vice Pres*
Peter Unrath, *Vice Pres*
Dominic Gerardi, *Project Mgr*
EMP: 200 **EST:** 1938
SQ FT: 20,000
SALES (est): 80.7MM **Privately Held**
WEB: www.nadcw.com
SIC: 3444 1711 Ducts, sheet metal; heating & air conditioning contractors

(G-7630)
NORAMPAC NEW YORK CITY INC
5515 Grand Ave (11378-3113)
PHONE...................................718 340-2100
Marc Andre Depin, *Ch of Bd*
Phil Suffoletto, *General Mgr*
Harry Garton, *Sales Staff*
Marc Meyer, *Sales Staff*
Donna Abbo, *Executive*
EMP: 160 **EST:** 1906
SQ FT: 340,000
SALES (est): 34.8MM
SALES (corp-wide): 3.5B **Privately Held**
SIC: 2653 3993 2675 Boxes, corrugated: made from purchased materials; display items, corrugated: made from purchased materials; signs & advertising specialties; die-cut paper & board
PA: Cascades Inc
　　404 Boul Marie-Victorin
　　Kingsey Falls QC J0A 1
　　819 363-5100

(G-7631)
NY TEMPERING LLC
6021 Flushing Ave (11378-3220)
PHONE...................................718 326-8989
Tim LI, *Manager*
▲ **EMP:** 5 **EST:** 2012
SALES (est): 838.7K **Privately Held**
SIC: 3272 Concrete products

(G-7632)
OWAYNE ENTERPRISES INC
4901 Maspeth Ave (11378-2219)
PHONE...................................718 326-2200
Owen M Mester, *President*
Wayne Wattenberg, *Vice Pres*
EMP: 38
SQ FT: 30,000
SALES (est): 7.1MM **Privately Held**
SIC: 2051 Cakes, pies & pastries; cakes, bakery: except frozen

(G-7633)
P & F INDUSTRIES OF NY CORP
Also Called: P and F Machine Industries
6006 55th Dr (11378-2351)
PHONE...................................718 894-3501
Frank Passantino, *President*
▲ **EMP:** 6
SQ FT: 7,000
SALES (est): 796.2K **Privately Held**
SIC: 3599 Machine shop, jobbing & repair

(G-7634)
PATCO TAPES INC
Also Called: Patco Group
5927 56th St (11378-3395)
PHONE...................................718 497-1527
Michael Rosenberg, *Corp Secy*
Joel Rosenberg, *Vice Pres*
EMP: 8 **EST:** 1973
SQ FT: 30,000
SALES (est): 2.5MM **Privately Held**
WEB: www.patcogroup.com
SIC: 2672 2671 5199 Gummed tape, cloth or paper base: from purchased materials; paper coated or laminated for packaging; packaging materials

(G-7635)
PURVI ENTERPRISES INCORPORATED
Also Called: Sinnara
5556 44th St (11378-2024)
PHONE...................................347 808-9448
Harshi Patel, *President*
▲ **EMP:** 7
SALES (est): 616.1K **Privately Held**
SIC: 3556 Dehydrating equipment, food processing

(G-7636)
QUEENS LDGR/GRENPOINT STAR INC
6960 Grand Ave Fl 2 (11378-1828)
P.O. Box 780376 (11378-0376)
PHONE...................................718 639-7000
Walter Sanchez, *President*
Tammy Sanchez, *General Mgr*
EMP: 15
SALES (est): 587.6K **Privately Held**
SIC: 2711 Newspapers, publishing & printing

(G-7637)
RISA MANAGEMENT CORP
Also Called: Risa's
5501 43rd St Fl 3 (11378-2023)
PHONE...................................718 361-2606
D Savi Prashad, *CEO*
▲ **EMP:** 25
SQ FT: 50,000
SALES (est): 8.2MM **Privately Held**
WEB: www.risacorp.com
SIC: 3449 3441 Miscellaneous metalwork; fabricated structural metal

(G-7638)
T&B BAKERY CORP
5870 56th St (11378-3106)
PHONE...................................646 642-4300
Tomasz Eider, *President*
EMP: 6
SQ FT: 6,000
SALES: 2.8MM **Privately Held**
SIC: 2051 Bakery products, partially cooked (except frozen)

(G-7639)
TRI-STAR OFFSET CORP
6020 59th Pl Ste 3 (11378-3349)
PHONE...................................718 894-5555
Brian Nawroth, *CEO*
Al Nawroth, *President*
Mark Serwetz, *Vice Pres*
Curtis Williams, *Accounts Mgr*
Paul Teller, *Accounts Exec*
EMP: 25 **EST:** 1977
SALES (est): 5.1MM **Privately Held**
SIC: 2752 Commercial printing, offset

(G-7640)
US ALLEGRO INC
5430 44th St (11378-1034)
PHONE...................................347 408-6601
Yuriy Bogutskiy, *President*
Marty McMahon, *Vice Pres*
EMP: 30
SQ FT: 10,000
SALES: 4MM **Privately Held**
SIC: 1442 Construction sand & gravel

(G-7641)
VALENTINE PACKAGING CORP
6020 59th Pl Ste 7 (11378-3349)
PHONE...................................718 418-6000
Daniel Suchow, *Vice Pres*
Richard Suchow, *Vice Pres*
Steven Suchow, *Vice Pres*
EMP: 18 **EST:** 1953
SQ FT: 25,000
SALES (est): 4.9MM **Privately Held**
SIC: 2653 7389 Sheets, corrugated: made from purchased materials; packaging & labeling services

---

Massapequa
Nassau County

(G-7642)
A & M APPEL DISTRIBUTING INC
500 N Atlanta Ave (11758-2000)
PHONE...................................516 735-1172
Michael Appel, *Principal*
EMP: 6
SALES (est): 352.4K **Privately Held**
SIC: 2051 5149 Bakery: wholesale or wholesale/retail combined; bakery products

(G-7643)
ACRAN SPILL CONTAINMENT INC (PA)
898 N Broadway Ste 1 (11758-2307)
PHONE...................................631 841-2300
John Deangelo, *President*
EMP: 11
SALES (est): 1.7MM **Privately Held**
SIC: 2655 Containers, liquid tight fiber: from purchased material

(G-7644)
ADAMS INTERIOR FABRICATIONS
8 Iroquois Pl (11758-7622)
PHONE...................................631 249-8282
Anthony E Adams, *President*
EMP: 11
SALES (est): 1.4MM **Privately Held**
SIC: 2431 2499 Millwork; decorative wood & woodwork

(G-7645)
CANOPY BOOKS LLC (PA)
28 N Wisconsin Ave 2-1 (11758-1705)
PHONE...................................516 354-4888
Clifford Brechner, *CEO*
EMP: 4
SALES (est): 1.7MM **Privately Held**
SIC: 2731 Book publishing

(G-7646)
CORPORATE LOSS PREVEN
38 Brooklyn Ave (11758-4815)
PHONE...................................516 409-0002
Joseph Clabby, *Branch Mgr*
EMP: 5
SALES (corp-wide): 11MM **Privately Held**
SIC: 2395 Art needlework: made from purchased materials
PA: Corporate Loss Prevention Associates, Inc.
　　151 Cargo Area A 2nd Fl R
　　Jamaica NY 11430
　　516 409-0003

(G-7647)
PLURA BROADCAST INC (PA)
67 Grand Ave (11758-4947)
PHONE...................................516 997-5675
Ray Kalo, *Owner*
Gary Whitten, *Administration*
EMP: 7
SALES (est): 3MM **Privately Held**
SIC: 3679 Liquid crystal displays (LCD)

(G-7648)
PRINT IT HERE
185 Jerusalem Ave (11758-3308)
PHONE...................................516 308-7785
Shari Levine, *CEO*
EMP: 5
SALES (est): 342K **Privately Held**
SIC: 2752 Commercial printing, lithographic

(G-7649)
R KLEIN JEWELRY CO INC
Also Called: Klein & Company
39 Brockmeyer Dr (11758-7804)
PHONE...................................516 482-3260
Richard Klein, *President*
EMP: 55
SQ FT: 30,000
SALES (est): 4.7MM **Privately Held**
WEB: www.kleinjewelry.com
SIC: 3911 Jewelry, precious metal

(G-7650)
S SCHARF INC
278 N Richmond Ave (11758-3231)
PHONE...................516 541-9552
Irwin Scharf, *President*
Jesse Scharf, *Treasurer*
EMP: 13 **EST:** 1935
SQ FT: 5,000
SALES (est): 1.2MM **Privately Held**
SIC: 3911 Jewelry, precious metal

(G-7651)
SUNRISE JEWELERS OF NY INC
1220 Sunrise Hwy (11758)
PHONE...................516 541-1302
EMP: 8
SALES (est): 930K **Privately Held**
SIC: 3911 Mfg Precious Metal Jewelry

(G-7652)
SWIRLS TWIRLS INCORPORATED
4116 Sunrise Hwy (11758-5301)
PHONE...................516 541-9400
EMP: 5 **EST:** 2011
SALES (est): 252.6K **Privately Held**
SIC: 2026 Yogurt

(G-7653)
WOODS KNIFE CORPORATION
19 Brooklyn Ave (11758-4855)
PHONE...................516 798-4972
James S Woods, *President*
Ann Woods, *Vice Pres*
EMP: 24
SQ FT: 2,600
SALES (est): 2.4MM **Privately Held**
SIC: 3423 3421 Knives, agricultural or industrial; cutlery

Massapequa Park
Nassau County

(G-7654)
CUSTOM MIX INC
31 Clark Blvd (11762-2609)
PHONE...................516 797-7090
Matthew Lott, *Principal*
EMP: 9
SALES (est): 933.8K **Privately Held**
SIC: 3273 Ready-mixed concrete

(G-7655)
GENERAL DIE AND DIE CUTNG INC
11 Finch Ct (11762-3915)
PHONE...................516 665-3584
Peter Vallone Sr, *CEO*
Peter Vallone Jr, *President*
Louann Vallone Pepi, *Vice Pres*
Richard Vallone, *Treasurer*
▲ **EMP:** 55 **EST:** 1961
SQ FT: 30,000
SALES (est): 52.4K **Privately Held**
WEB: www.gendiecut.com
SIC: 2653 2675 3544 Display items, corrugated: made from purchased materials; boxes, corrugated: made from purchased materials; corrugated boxes, partitions, display items, sheets & pad; die-cut paper & board; special dies, tools, jigs & fixtures

(G-7656)
IMAGE SALES & MARKETING INC
106 Thornwood Rd (11762-4023)
PHONE...................516 238-7023
Francine Walk, *President*
Steven Walk, *Vice Pres*
EMP: 2
SQ FT: 3,000
SALES: 4MM **Privately Held**
WEB: www.imagesalesny.com
SIC: 2752 Commercial printing, lithographic

(G-7657)
INNOVATIVE SYSTEMS OF NEW YORK
201 Rose St (11762-1022)
PHONE...................516 541-7410
Joseph Esposito, *President*

EMP: 5
SALES (est): 310.1K **Privately Held**
SIC: 3577 7373 7378 Computer peripheral equipment; computer integrated systems design; computer maintenance & repair

(G-7658)
M F L B INC
Also Called: S D S of Long Island
38 Eastgate Rd (11762-1939)
PHONE...................631 254-8300
Frank Baubille, *Vice Pres*
Michael Cafiero, *Admin Sec*
EMP: 13
SALES: 450K **Privately Held**
WEB: www.mflb.com
SIC: 3677 Electronic coils, transformers & other inductors

(G-7659)
MASSAPEQUA POST
Also Called: Acj Communications
1045b Park Blvd (11762-2764)
PHONE...................516 798-5100
Alfred James, *President*
Carolyn James, *Vice Pres*
EMP: 21
SALES (est): 475.6K **Privately Held**
WEB: www.massapequapost.com
SIC: 2711 Newspapers: publishing only, not printed on site

(G-7660)
PRINT COTTAGE LLC
1138 Lakeshore Dr (11762-2056)
PHONE...................516 369-1749
James Altadonna, *Mng Member*
EMP: 10
SQ FT: 1,000
SALES: 4MM **Privately Held**
SIC: 2752 Commercial printing, lithographic

(G-7661)
TVI IMPORTS LLC
178 Abbey St (11762-3430)
PHONE...................631 793-3077
Anthony Tisi, *Mng Member*
▲ **EMP:** 6
SQ FT: 2,500
SALES: 19MM **Privately Held**
SIC: 3089 Flower pots, plastic

(G-7662)
WORLD BUSINESS MEDIA LLC
Also Called: Gsn Government Security News
4770 Sunrise Hwy Ste 105 (11762-2911)
PHONE...................212 344-0759
EMP: 12
SQ FT: 2,000
SALES: 2MM **Privately Held**
SIC: 2721 7313 7382 Periodicals-Publishing/Printing Advertising Representative Security Systems Services

---

Massena
St. Lawrence County

(G-7663)
ALCOA CORPORATION
45 County Route 42 (13662-4249)
P.O. Box 5278 (13662-5278)
PHONE...................412 315-2900
EMP: 480
SALES (corp-wide): 13.4B **Publicly Held**
SIC: 3355 Aluminum rolling & drawing
PA: Alcoa Corporation
201 Isabella St Ste 500
Pittsburgh PA 15212
412 315-2900

(G-7664)
ALCOA USA CORP
45 County Route 42 (13662-4249)
PHONE...................315 764-4011
EMP: 6
SALES (corp-wide): 13.4B **Publicly Held**
SIC: 3334 Primary aluminum
HQ: Alcoa Usa Corp.
201 Isabella St Ste 500
Pittsburgh PA 15212
212 518-5400

(G-7665)
ALCOA USA CORP
1814 State Highway 131 (13662-4210)
P.O. Box 5278 (13662-5278)
PHONE...................315 764-4106
Thomas Carter, *Supervisor*
Nathan P Rufa, *Technical Staff*
EMP: 32
SALES (corp-wide): 13.4B **Publicly Held**
SIC: 3334 Primary aluminum
HQ: Alcoa Usa Corp.
201 Isabella St Ste 500
Pittsburgh PA 15212
212 518-5400

(G-7666)
ARCONIC INC
45 County Route 42 (13662-4249)
PHONE...................315 764-4011
Bryan Murphy, *Manager*
EMP: 7
SALES (corp-wide): 14B **Publicly Held**
SIC: 3355 3353 3354 3463 Aluminum rolling & drawing; aluminum sheet & strip; aluminum extruded products; aluminum forgings
PA: Arconic Inc.
201 Isabella St Ste 200
New York NY 15212
412 553-1950

(G-7667)
CURRAN RENEWABLE ENERGY LLC
20 Commerce Dr (13662-2576)
PHONE...................315 769-2000
Kelli Curran, *Marketing Mgr*
Patrick Curran, *Mng Member*
▲ **EMP:** 30
SALES: 19.1MM **Privately Held**
SIC: 2421 Sawmills & planing mills, general

(G-7668)
KINGSTON PHARMA LLC
Also Called: Kingston Pharmaceuticals
5 County Route 42 (13662-1569)
PHONE...................315 705-4019
Venkat Kakani, *CEO*
Sridhar Thyagarajan, *Controller*
EMP: 82
SQ FT: 32,778
SALES (est): 2.9MM **Privately Held**
SIC: 2834 Druggists' preparations (pharmaceuticals)

(G-7669)
MUSTARD TIN
6100 Saint Lawrence Ctr (13662-3214)
PHONE...................315 769-8409
EMP: 5 **EST:** 2012
SALES (est): 318.7K **Privately Held**
SIC: 3356 Tin

(G-7670)
RYANS MOBILE WELDING SVC LLC
59 Bishop Ave (13662-1530)
PHONE...................315 769-5699
Ryan Rotonde, *Principal*
EMP: 8 **EST:** 2017
SALES (est): 88.7K **Privately Held**
SIC: 7692 Welding repair

(G-7671)
SEAWAY TIMBER HARVESTING INC (PA)
15121 State Highway 37 (13662-6194)
PHONE...................315 769-5970
Patrick Curran, *President*
Tim Curran, *Vice Pres*
Lee Curran, *Admin Sec*
EMP: 59
SQ FT: 15,000
SALES (est): 11.9MM **Privately Held**
SIC: 2411 4789 Logging; log loading & unloading

(G-7672)
STUBBS PRINTING INC
271 E Orvis St Ste B (13662-2352)
P.O. Box 110 (13662-0110)
PHONE...................315 769-8641
Karen Stubbs, *President*
Robert T Stubbs, *Vice Pres*

EMP: 5
SQ FT: 2,000
SALES (est): 390K **Privately Held**
SIC: 2752 Commercial printing, offset

(G-7673)
UPSTONE MATERIALS INC
Also Called: Massena Ready Mix
539 S Main St (13662-2537)
P.O. Box 825, Plattsburgh (12901)
PHONE...................315 764-0251
James Otis, *District Mgr*
EMP: 5
SQ FT: 9,608
SALES (corp-wide): 83.5MM **Privately Held**
WEB: www.graymont-ab.com
SIC: 3273 Ready-mixed concrete
HQ: Upstone Materials Inc.
111 Quarry Rd
Plattsburgh NY 12901
518 561-5321

Mastic
Suffolk County

(G-7674)
EAST END SIGN DESIGN INC
1425 Montauk Hwy (11950-2916)
PHONE...................631 399-2574
Joseph Colucci, *President*
John Dugan, *Manager*
Mike Powell, *Manager*
EMP: 5
SALES (est): 580.6K **Privately Held**
SIC: 3993 Signs, not made in custom sign painting shops

Mastic Beach
Suffolk County

(G-7675)
VINCENT GENOVESE
Also Called: Long Island Radiant Heat
19 Woodmere Dr (11951-2016)
PHONE...................631 281-8170
Vincent Genovese, *Owner*
EMP: 6
SALES (est): 674.5K **Privately Held**
SIC: 3634 5074 8711 1711 Heating units, electric (radiant heat): baseboard or wall; heating equipment & panels, solar; heating & ventilation engineering; heating & air conditioning contractors; industrial furnaces & ovens; heating equipment, except electric

---

Mattituck
Suffolk County

(G-7676)
AMEREON LTD
800 Wickham Ave (11952-1684)
P.O. Box 1200 (11952-0921)
PHONE...................631 298-5100
Joanna Paulsen, *President*
John Clauss, *Vice Pres*
EMP: 5
SQ FT: 30,000
SALES (est): 594.3K **Privately Held**
WEB: www.amereon.com
SIC: 2731 Books: publishing only

(G-7677)
LIEB CELLARS LLC
Also Called: Lieb Cellars Tasting Room
35 Cox Neck Rd (11952-1458)
P.O. Box 907, Cutchogue (11935-0907)
PHONE...................631 298-1942
Gary Madden, *General Mgr*
Dana Kowalsick, *Marketing Staff*
EMP: 20
SALES (est): 1.2MM **Privately Held**
WEB: www.liebcellars.com
SIC: 2084 Wines
PA: Lieb Cellars Llc
13050 Oregon Rd
Cutchogue NY 11935

(G-7678)
PREMIUM WINE GROUP LLC
35 Cox Neck Rd (11952-1458)
PHONE....................................631 298-1900
Russell Hearn, *Principal*
John Leo, *Principal*
▲ EMP: 22 EST: 2001
SALES (est): 3.5MM **Privately Held**
WEB: www.premiumwinegroup.com
SIC: 2084 Wines

(G-7679)
SHINN WINERY LLC
Also Called: Shinn Vineyard
2000 Oregon Rd (11952-1762)
PHONE....................................631 804-0367
Andi Parks, *Exec VP*
Barbara Shinn,
▲ EMP: 7
SALES (est): 660K **Privately Held**
SIC: 2084 Wines

(G-7680)
TIMES REVIEW NEWSPAPER CORP
Also Called: News Review, The
7780 Main Rd (11952-1539)
P.O. Box 1500 (11952-0901)
PHONE....................................631 354-8031
Troy Gustavson, *President*
Decia Fates, *Editor*
Laura Huber, *Editor*
Sonja Derr, *Sales Staff*
Kim Gersic, *Sales Associate*
EMP: 33 EST: 1857
SQ FT: 6,000
SALES (est): 3MM **Privately Held**
WEB: www.timesreview.com
SIC: 2711 2791 Newspapers: publishing only, not printed on site; typesetting

Mayfield
Fulton County

(G-7681)
BART OSTRANDER TRCKG LOG CORP
1556 State Highway 30 (12117-3755)
PHONE....................................518 661-6535
Bart D Ostrander, *President*
Evette Ostrander, *Admin Sec*
EMP: 9
SALES (est): 1.2MM **Privately Held**
SIC: 2411 4789 7389 Logging; log loading & unloading; business services

Mayville
Chautauqua County

(G-7682)
EMPIRE DEVLEOPMENT
5889 Magnolia Stedman Rd (14757-9420)
PHONE....................................716 789-2097
Micah Meredith, *Principal*
EMP: 8 EST: 2007
SALES (est): 996.7K **Privately Held**
SIC: 3423 Jewelers' hand tools

(G-7683)
KLEINFELDER JOHN
Also Called: Chautauqua Iron Works
5239 W Lake Rd (14757-9507)
PHONE....................................716 753-3163
John Kleinfelder, *Owner*
EMP: 5
SQ FT: 990
SALES (est): 467.8K **Privately Held**
SIC: 3441 3446 5947 4491 Fabricated structural metal; ornamental metalwork; artcraft & carvings; docks, incl. buildings & facilities: operation & maintenance; boat lifts; welding on site

(G-7684)
RANGE RSURCES - APPALACHIA LLC
Also Called: Lomak Petroleum
100 E Chautauqua St (14757-1040)
P.O. Box 187 (14757-0187)
PHONE....................................716 753-3385
Doug Stebbins, *Manager*
EMP: 30
SALES (corp-wide): 3.2B **Publicly Held**
WEB: www.gl-energy.com
SIC: 1382 Oil & gas exploration services
HQ: Range Resources - Appalachia, Llc.
3000 Town Center Blvd
Canonsburg PA 15317
724 743-6700

(G-7685)
STEDMAN ENERGY INC
4411 Canterbury Dr (14757-9610)
P.O. Box 1006, Chautauqua (14722-1006)
PHONE....................................716 789-3018
Kevin E McChesney, *President*
EMP: 7
SALES: 100K **Privately Held**
SIC: 1311 Crude petroleum production; natural gas production

Mc Connellsville
Oneida County

(G-7686)
HARDEN FURNITURE LLC (PA)
8550 Mill Pond Way (13401-1844)
PHONE....................................315 675-3600
Gregory Harden, *CEO*
Andrew Clark, *Vice Pres*
Pete Raynford, *Vice Pres*
J G N Schafer, *Engineer*
Roxanne Seymore, *Human Res Mgr*
▲ EMP: 183
SQ FT: 400,000
SALES: 19.7MM **Privately Held**
WEB: www.cnywinter.com
SIC: 2512 2521 5021 2511 Upholstered household furniture; living room furniture: upholstered on wood frames; wood office furniture; desks, office: wood; bookcases, office: wood; furniture; dining room furniture: wood

Mc Graw
Cortland County

(G-7687)
COUTURE TIMBER HARVESTING
2760 Phelps Rd (13101-9561)
P.O. Box 66, Cortland (13045-0066)
PHONE....................................607 836-4719
EMP: 7
SALES (est): 653.5K **Privately Held**
SIC: 2411 Logging

(G-7688)
HIGGINS SUPPLY COMPANY INC
Also Called: Higgins Supl Co
18-25 South St (13101)
PHONE....................................607 836-6474
Terri Maxson, *Ch of Bd*
Cathy Gregg, *President*
Glenn Doran, *Vice Pres*
Terri L Gutchess, *Vice Pres*
EMP: 65 EST: 1921
SQ FT: 30,000
SALES (est): 9.4MM **Privately Held**
SIC: 3842 2342 Orthopedic appliances; corset accessories: clasps, stays, etc.

(G-7689)
MCGRAW WOOD PRODUCTS LLC (PA)
1 Charles St (13101-9190)
P.O. Box 652 (13101-0652)
PHONE....................................607 836-6465
Harold J Ousby III, *Mng Member*
EMP: 30 EST: 2006
SQ FT: 100,000
SALES (est): 5.1MM **Privately Held**
WEB: www.mcgrawwoodproducts.com
SIC: 2511 2499 2441 2434 Silverware chests: wood; decorative wood & woodwork; nailed wood boxes & shook; wood kitchen cabinets

Mechanicville
Saratoga County

(G-7690)
ALABU INC
Also Called: Alabu Skin Care
30 Graves Rd (12118-3218)
PHONE....................................518 665-0411
Mary Claire, *President*
Dean Mayes, *President*
EMP: 7
SALES (est): 1.1MM **Privately Held**
WEB: www.alabu.com
SIC: 2844 Toilet preparations

(G-7691)
ALONZO FIRE WORKS DISPLAY INC (PA)
12 County Route 75 (12118-3357)
PHONE....................................518 664-9994
Jeff Alonzo, *President*
▲ EMP: 8
SALES (est): 654K **Privately Held**
WEB: www.alonzofireworks.com
SIC: 2899 7999 Fireworks; fireworks display service

(G-7692)
GLAXOSMITHKLINE LLC
108 Woodfield Blvd (12118-3038)
PHONE....................................518 852-9637
EMP: 27
SALES (corp-wide): 39.5B **Privately Held**
SIC: 2834 Pharmaceutical preparations
HQ: Glaxosmithkline Llc
5 Crescent Dr
Philadelphia PA 19112
215 751-4000

(G-7693)
POLYSET COMPANY INC
65 Hudson Ave (12118)
P.O. Box 111 (12118-0111)
PHONE....................................518 664-6000
Niladri Ghoshal, *President*
April Mullen, *Purchasing*
Rajat Ghoshal, *Treasurer*
Kevin McGrath, *Manager*
Lisa Lawliss, *Supervisor*
▲ EMP: 37
SQ FT: 40,000
SALES (est): 16.3MM **Privately Held**
WEB: www.polyset.com
SIC: 2819 3087 2952 2891 Industrial inorganic chemicals; custom compound purchased resins; coating compounds, tar; adhesives & sealants

(G-7694)
RALOID TOOL CO INC
Hc 146 (12118)
P.O. Box 551 (12118-0551)
PHONE....................................518 664-4261
Ronald Brownell, *President*
David Brownell, *Vice Pres*
Stephen Shafts, *Project Mgr*
EMP: 19 EST: 1945
SQ FT: 23,200
SALES (est): 3.5MM **Privately Held**
WEB: www.raloidtool.com
SIC: 3544 3542 Special dies & tools; die casting & extruding machines

(G-7695)
ST SILICONES INC
95 N Central Ave (12118-1543)
PHONE....................................518 664-0745
David A Scagnelli, *President*
EMP: 5
SQ FT: 3,500
SALES: 500K **Privately Held**
WEB: www.st-silicones.com
SIC: 1446 Silica mining

(G-7696)
VOICES FOR ALL LLC
29 Moreland Dr (12118-3630)
PHONE....................................518 261-1664
Paul Benedetti,
Stan Denis,
EMP: 8
SALES (est): 858.1K **Privately Held**
SIC: 3679 Voice controls

Medford
Suffolk County

(G-7697)
ACCUVEIN INC
3243 Route 112 Ste 2 (11763-1438)
P.O. Box 1303, Huntington (11743-0657)
PHONE....................................816 997-9400
Ron Goldman, *Ch of Bd*
David Beahm, *Area Mgr*
Daniel Delaney, *COO*
Heidi Siegel, *COO*
Mike Munzer, *Vice Pres*
EMP: 53
SQ FT: 5,000
SALES (est): 11MM **Privately Held**
SIC: 3829 Thermometers, including digital: clinical

(G-7698)
B & R INDUSTRIES INC
Also Called: Manifold Center, The
12 Commercial Blvd (11763-1523)
PHONE....................................631 736-2275
Christian P Burian, *President*
EMP: 12
SQ FT: 64,000
SALES (est): 2.2MM **Privately Held**
WEB: www.bnrindustries.com
SIC: 3599 Machine shop, jobbing & repair

(G-7699)
BLAIR INDUSTRIES INC (PA)
3671 Horseblock Rd (11763-2240)
PHONE....................................631 924-6600
William R Lehmann Jr, *Ch of Bd*
John Andrucci, *QC Dir*
▲ EMP: 50
SQ FT: 8,000
SALES (est): 7.9MM **Privately Held**
WEB: www.blair-hsm.com
SIC: 3728 Aircraft landing assemblies & brakes

(G-7700)
BOILERMATIC WELDING INDS INC (PA)
17 Peconic Ave (11763-3295)
PHONE....................................631 654-1341
Shasho Pole, *Ch of Bd*
Lee Fritze, *Vice Pres*
John Wojnowski, *Vice Pres*
Anthony Sala, *Safety Dir*
Tom Slattery, *Project Mgr*
EMP: 34
SQ FT: 3,200
SALES: 20.2MM **Privately Held**
WEB: www.boilermatic.com
SIC: 7692 Welding repair

(G-7701)
CHEMBIO DIAGNOSTIC SYSTEMS INC
3661 Horseblock Rd Ste A (11763-2244)
PHONE....................................631 924-1135
Javan Esfandiari, *Senior VP*
Tom Ippolito, *Vice Pres*
Paul Lambotte, *Vice Pres*
Michael Steele, *Vice Pres*
Richard Larkin, *CFO*
▲ EMP: 105
SQ FT: 14,000
SALES (est): 27.2MM
SALES (corp-wide): 33.4MM **Publicly Held**
WEB: www.chembio.com
SIC: 2835 In vitro & in vivo diagnostic substances
PA: Chembio Diagnostics, Inc.
3661 Horseblock Rd Ste C
Medford NY 11763
631 924-1135

(G-7702)
CHEMBIO DIAGNOSTICS INC (PA)
3661 Horseblock Rd Ste C (11763-2225)
PHONE....................................631 924-1135
John J Sperzel III, *CEO*
Katherine L Davis, *Ch of Bd*
Sharon Klugewicz, *President*

David Gyorke, *COO*
Javan Esfandiari, *Exec VP*
▲ **EMP:** 54
SQ FT: 39,660
SALES: 33.4MM **Publicly Held**
WEB: www.chembio.com
SIC: 2834 Pharmaceutical preparations

(G-7703)
CHROMA COMMUNICATIONS INC
2030 Route 112 (11763-3644)
P.O. Box 340, Bohemia (11716-0340)
PHONE..................................631 289-8871
Peter Gulyas, *President*
EMP: 5
SALES (est): 310K **Privately Held**
SIC: 2759 Commercial printing

(G-7704)
CLARKE HESS COMMUNICATION RES
3243 Route 112 Ste 1 (11763-1438)
PHONE..................................631 698-3350
Kenneth Salz, *President*
Doante Alessi, *Vice Pres*
EMP: 8
SQ FT: 4,500
SALES (est): 1.6MM **Privately Held**
WEB: www.clarke-hess.com
SIC: 3825 Test equipment for electronic & electrical circuits

(G-7705)
DATA FLOW INC
6 Balsam Dr (11763-4304)
PHONE..................................631 436-9200
Timothy Stead, *President*
Joseph Crook, *Vice Pres*
EMP: 8
SQ FT: 8,500
SALES: 1.7MM **Privately Held**
WEB: www.printtomail.com
SIC: 2759 Business forms: printing

(G-7706)
ENECON CORPORATION (PA)
Also Called: High Prfmce Plymr Cmposits Div
6 Platinum Ct (11763-2251)
PHONE..................................516 349-0022
Edward Krensel, *CEO*
Andrew A Janczak, *President*
Michael Tedesco, *Exec VP*
Matt Goldberg, *Vice Pres*
Robert L Kneuer, *Vice Pres*
◆ **EMP:** 65
SQ FT: 30,000
SALES: 11.9MM **Privately Held**
WEB: www.enecon.com
SIC: 2851 Coating, air curing

(G-7707)
ENEFLUX ARMTEK MAGNETICS INC (HQ)
6 Platinum Ct (11763-2251)
PHONE..................................516 576-3434
Tony Mantella, *President*
Edward Krensel, *Treasurer*
Deann Dambrosio, *Accounts Mgr*
▲ **EMP:** 4 **EST:** 1997
SQ FT: 20,000
SALES: 3MM
SALES (corp-wide): 11.9MM **Privately Held**
WEB: www.eamagnetics.com
SIC: 3264 Magnets, permanent: ceramic or ferrite
PA: Enecon Corporation
6 Platinum Ct
Medford NY 11763
516 349-0022

(G-7708)
GLOBAL TISSUE GROUP INC (PA)
870 Expressway Dr S (11763-2027)
PHONE..................................631 924-3019
Meir Elnekaveh, *CEO*
Freydoun Elhekaveh, *Ch of Bd*
David Shaoul, *President*
Philip Shaoul, *COO*
Phil Higgins, *Purch Mgr*
◆ **EMP:** 50
SQ FT: 90,000

SALES (est): 13.6MM **Privately Held**
WEB: www.gtgtissue.com
SIC: 2679 Paper products, converted

(G-7709)
H B MILLWORK INC (PA)
500 Long Island Ave (11763-2510)
PHONE..................................631 289-8086
Timothy Hollowell, *President*
Michael Hollowell, *Vice Pres*
EMP: 21
SQ FT: 6,000
SALES (est): 2.8MM **Privately Held**
WEB: www.hbmillwork.com
SIC: 2431 2436 2426 Millwork; softwood veneer & plywood; hardwood dimension & flooring mills

(G-7710)
HAMPTON ART LLC
19 Scouting Blvd (11763-2220)
PHONE..................................631 924-1335
Ronald T Gallagher,
Kevin T Gallagher,
Ron Gallagher,
Steven G Gallagher,
▲ **EMP:** 44
SQ FT: 13,500
SALES: 5.6MM **Privately Held**
WEB: www.hamptonart.com
SIC: 3069 3953 Stationers' rubber sundries; marking devices

(G-7711)
HAMPTON TECHNOLOGIES LLC
19 Scouting Blvd (11763-2220)
PHONE..................................631 924-1335
Ron Gallagher,
Ronald Gallagher, *Administration*
Kevin Gallagher,
Steven Gallagher,
▲ **EMP:** 30
SQ FT: 13,500
SALES (est): 6.1MM **Privately Held**
WEB: www.hamptonsecurity.com
SIC: 3699 Security devices

(G-7712)
HSM MACHINE WORKS INC (PA)
Also Called: Blair-Hsm
3671 Horseblock Rd (11763-2295)
PHONE..................................631 924-6600
William R Lehmann Jr, *Ch of Bd*
Kevin Dembinski, *President*
Bill Lehmann, *President*
Scott Wigley, *General Mgr*
Rex Betita, *QC Mgr*
▲ **EMP:** 39 **EST:** 1951
SQ FT: 30,000
SALES (est): 8.2MM **Privately Held**
SIC: 3599 3728 Machine shop, jobbing & repair; aircraft parts & equipment

(G-7713)
ISLAND CUSTOM STAIRS INC
23 Scouting Blvd Unit C (11763-2245)
PHONE..................................631 205-5335
Christopher L Brett, *President*
Carol Hodosky, *Treasurer*
EMP: 7
SQ FT: 5,800
SALES: 900K **Privately Held**
SIC: 3534 Elevators & moving stairways

(G-7714)
JACOBI TOOL & DIE MFG INC
Also Called: Jacobi Industries
131 Middle Island Rd (11763-1517)
P.O. Box 50 (11763-0050)
PHONE..................................631 736-5394
Roger Jacobi, *Principal*
EMP: 6
SQ FT: 10,000
SALES (est): 907.4K **Privately Held**
WEB: www.jacobiindustries.com
SIC: 3599 Machine shop, jobbing & repair

(G-7715)
K DYMOND INDUSTRIES INC
16 Commercial Blvd (11763-1523)
PHONE..................................631 828-0826
EMP: 11
SALES (est): 1.3MM **Privately Held**
SIC: 3999 Manufacturing industries

(G-7716)
L VII RESILIENT LLC
108 Cherry Ln (11763-4022)
PHONE..................................631 987-5819
John Scelsi, *Mng Member*
EMP: 12 **EST:** 2012
SALES (est): 1MM **Privately Held**
SIC: 2676 7389 Tampons, sanitary: made from purchased paper;

(G-7717)
LIVING DOORS INC
22 Scouting Blvd Ste 3 (11763-2260)
P.O. Box 95, Yaphank (11980-0095)
PHONE..................................631 924-5393
Don Plante, *President*
EMP: 10
SQ FT: 4,000
SALES: 700K **Privately Held**
WEB: www.livingdoors.com
SIC: 2431 Millwork

(G-7718)
MACROLINK INC
25 Industrial Blvd Ste 1 (11763-2243)
PHONE..................................631 924-8200
Mark Cordivari, *CEO*
EMP: 50 **EST:** 1975
SQ FT: 30,000
SALES (est): 15.5MM
SALES (corp-wide): 66.5B **Publicly Held**
WEB: www.macrolink.com
SIC: 3823 3577 Computer interface equipment for industrial process control; computer peripheral equipment
HQ: B/E Aerospace, Inc.
1400 Corporate Center Way
Wellington FL 33414
561 791-5000

(G-7719)
MICRO CONTRACT MANUFACTURING
27 Scouting Blvd Unit E (11763-2286)
PHONE..................................631 738-7874
Michael L Matula, *President*
Thomas Degasperi, *President*
Josephine Matula, *Corp Secy*
EMP: 90
SQ FT: 12,000
SALES (est): 16MM **Privately Held**
WEB: www.microcontractmfg.com
SIC: 3674 Semiconductors & related devices

(G-7720)
MTK ELECTRONICS INC
1 National Blvd (11763-2252)
PHONE..................................631 924-7666
David Radford, *President*
John Nicosia, *CIO*
▲ **EMP:** 35
SQ FT: 15,000
SALES (est): 8.1MM **Privately Held**
WEB: www.mtkelec.com
SIC: 3677 3675 Filtration devices, electronic; electronic capacitors

(G-7721)
PHYMETRIX INC
28 Scouting Blvd Ste C (11763-2250)
PHONE..................................631 627-3950
Bedros Bedrossian, *President*
Ani Omer, *Vice Pres*
Deborah Bedrossian, *VP Mktg*
EMP: 9
SQ FT: 10,000
SALES: 3MM **Privately Held**
SIC: 3826 8734 Moisture analyzers; calibration & certification

(G-7722)
POSIMECH INC
15 Scouting Blvd Unit 3 (11763-2254)
PHONE..................................631 924-5959
Steven R Fazio, *President*
Steven Fazio, *President*
Dan George, *VP Mfg*
▼ **EMP:** 22
SQ FT: 12,236
SALES (est): 3.6MM **Privately Held**
WEB: www.posimech.com
SIC: 3599 3728 Machine shop, jobbing & repair; aircraft assemblies, subassemblies & parts

(G-7723)
SAYEDA MANUFACTURING CORP
20 Scouting Blvd (11763-2221)
PHONE..................................631 345-2525
Ali Khan, *President*
EMP: 10
SQ FT: 5,000
SALES (est): 1.2MM **Privately Held**
WEB: www.sayeda.com
SIC: 3999 Barber & beauty shop equipment

(G-7724)
STAR READY-MIX INC
172 Peconic Ave (11763-3244)
P.O. Box 371 (11763-0371)
PHONE..................................631 289-8787
Thomas W Hess, *CEO*
Joseph A Di Silva, *President*
Frank Otero, *Vice Pres*
EMP: 13
SQ FT: 1,000
SALES (est): 2.2MM **Privately Held**
SIC: 3273 Ready-mixed concrete

(G-7725)
TINT WORLD
3165 Route 112 (11763-1407)
PHONE..................................631 458-1999
Timothy Kjaer, *Principal*
EMP: 5
SALES (est): 484.7K **Privately Held**
SIC: 3089 5013 Automotive parts, plastic; automotive supplies & parts

(G-7726)
WAVERLY IRON CORP
25 Commercial Blvd (11763-1531)
PHONE..................................631 732-2800
Anthony Pizzichemi, *President*
Frank Niemann, *Vice Pres*
Joseph Pizzichemi, *Project Mgr*
EMP: 21
SQ FT: 7,000
SALES (est): 4.8MM **Privately Held**
WEB: www.waverlyiron.com
SIC: 3446 Architectural metalwork

Medina
Orleans County

(G-7727)
ASSOCIATED BRANDS INC
4001 Salt Works Rd (14103-9578)
PHONE..................................585 798-3475
Scott Greenwood, *President*
James Akers, *Vice Pres*
Peter Kapferer, *Vice Pres*
Paul Kerr, *Opers Mgr*
Derek Briffett, *CFO*
◆ **EMP:** 266
SQ FT: 340,000
SALES (est): 52.8MM
SALES (corp-wide): 5.8B **Publicly Held**
WEB: www.associatedbrands.com
SIC: 2034 2043 2066 2099 Fruits, dried or dehydrated, except freeze-dried; vegetables, dried or dehydrated (except freeze-dried); cereal breakfast foods; chocolate & cocoa products; food preparations
PA: Treehouse Foods, Inc.
2021 Spring Rd Ste 600
Oak Brook IL 60523
708 483-1300

(G-7728)
BARNES METAL FINISHING INC
3932 Salt Works Rd (14103-9546)
P.O. Box 517 (14103-0517)
PHONE..................................585 798-4817
Wilfred Barnes, *President*
Darrel Barnes, *Vice Pres*
EMP: 14
SQ FT: 6,000
SALES: 800K **Privately Held**
SIC: 3471 Polishing, metals or formed products

GEOGRAPHIC

(G-7729)
BAXTER HEALTHCARE CORPORATION
711 Park Ave (14103-1078)
PHONE.....................................800 356-3454
Christopher Peticca, *Accounts Mgr*
Nelson Tatterson, *Branch Mgr*
James Kelly, *Director*
EMP: 380
SALES (corp-wide): 11.1B **Publicly Held**
SIC: 2834 Pharmaceutical preparations
HQ: Baxter Healthcare Corporation
1 Baxter Pkwy
Deerfield IL 60015
224 948-2000

(G-7730)
BMP AMERICA INC (HQ)
Also Called: B M P
11625 Maple Ridge Rd (14103-9710)
PHONE.....................................585 798-0950
Edward D Andrew, *CEO*
Peter Milicia, *President*
Peter Rodrigue, *Business Mgr*
Jason Gillard, *Vice Pres*
Alan Lebold, *Vice Pres*
▲ EMP: 112
SQ FT: 40,000
SALES (est): 24.5MM
SALES (corp-wide): 122.4MM **Privately Held**
SIC: 3555 Sticks, printers'
PA: Andrew Industries Limited
Walton House
Accrington LANCS BB5 5
128 277-8022

(G-7731)
BRUNNER INTERNATIONAL INC
3959 Bates Rd (14103-9705)
P.O. Box 111 (14103-0111)
PHONE.....................................585 798-6000
Peter Brunner, *Ch of Bd*
Brian Peyatt, *Production*
Roy Wagner, *Senior Engr*
Kim Balcerzak, *Bookkeeper*
Katie Friedl, *Auditor*
▲ EMP: 122
SALES (est): 35.7MM **Privately Held**
SIC: 3713 Truck bodies & parts

(G-7732)
CNHI LLC
Also Called: Medina Journal Register
541-543 Main St (14103)
PHONE.....................................585 798-1400
Mark Francis, *Publisher*
EMP: 38
SQ FT: 14,301 **Privately Held**
WEB: www.clintonnc.com
SIC: 2711 Newspapers, publishing & printing
HQ: Cnhi, Llc
445 Dexter Ave
Montgomery AL 36104

(G-7733)
D & W ENTERPRISES LLC
10775 W Shelby Rd (14103-9584)
PHONE.....................................585 590-6727
Darrel Barnes,
EMP: 17
SALES (est): 960K **Privately Held**
SIC: 3471 Finishing, metals or formed products

(G-7734)
F & H METAL FINISHING CO INC
Also Called: Fearby Enterprises
700 Genesee St (14103-1504)
P.O. Box 486 (14103-0486)
PHONE.....................................585 798-2151
Timothy Fearby, *President*
Patricia Caleb, *Corp Secy*
Kim Stevens, *Vice Pres*
Patti Caleb, *Treasurer*
EMP: 18
SQ FT: 10,000
SALES: 800K **Privately Held**
SIC: 3479 3471 Enameling, including porcelain, of metal products; lacquering of metal products; varnishing of metal products; painting of metal products; cleaning, polishing & finishing; buffing for the trade; finishing, metals or formed products; polishing, metals or formed products

(G-7735)
GANNETT STLLITE INFO NTWRK INC
Also Called: Greater Niagara Newspaper
413 Main St (14103-1416)
PHONE.....................................585 798-1400
Dan Caswell, *Director*
EMP: 88
SALES (corp-wide): 2.9B **Publicly Held**
WEB: www.usatoday.com
SIC: 2711 Newspapers, publishing & printing
HQ: Gannett Satellite Information Network, Llc
7950 Jones Branch Dr
Mc Lean VA 22102
703 854-6000

(G-7736)
GEOPUMP INC
213 State St (14103-1337)
PHONE.....................................585 798-6666
James Mirand, *President*
Paul Fox, *Vice Pres*
EMP: 5
SQ FT: 1,500
SALES (est): 650.2K **Privately Held**
WEB: www.geopump.com
SIC: 3561 Pumps, domestic: water or sump

(G-7737)
HANSON AGGREGATES EAST LLC
Glenwood Ave (14103)
PHONE.....................................585 798-0762
EMP: 15
SALES (corp-wide): 18.7B **Privately Held**
SIC: 3273 Mfg Ready-Mixed Concrete
HQ: Hanson Aggregates East Llc
2300 Gateway Centre Blvd
Morrisville NC 27560
919 380-2500

(G-7738)
HINSPERGERS POLY INDUSTRIES
430 W Oak Orchard St (14103-1551)
PHONE.....................................585 798-6625
Bill Thompson, *Sales Mgr*
Greg Budd, *Manager*
EMP: 27
SALES (corp-wide): 10.9MM **Privately Held**
WEB: www.hinspergers.com
SIC: 3949 Swimming pools, plastic
PA: Hinspergers Poly Industries Ltd
645 Needham Lane
Mississauga ON L5A 1
905 272-0144

(G-7739)
LEONARD OAKES ESTATE WINERY
10609 Ridge Rd (14103-9431)
PHONE.....................................585 318-4418
Wendy Wilson, *Principal*
EMP: 5
SALES (est): 346.4K **Privately Held**
SIC: 2084 Wines

(G-7740)
MEDINA MILLWORKS LLC
10694 Ridge Rd (14103-9406)
PHONE.....................................585 798-2969
Matt Graber,
Jerome Graber,
Philip Graber,
Steven Graber,
EMP: 8
SQ FT: 960
SALES (est): 1MM **Privately Held**
WEB: www.medinamillworks.com
SIC: 2431 Millwork

(G-7741)
MILLERS BULK FOOD AND BAKERY
10858 Ridge Rd (14103-9432)
PHONE.....................................585 798-9700
Steven Miller, *Principal*
EMP: 8

SALES (est): 744.2K **Privately Held**
SIC: 2051 Bakery: wholesale or wholesale/retail combined

(G-7742)
MIZKAN AMERICA INC
Also Called: Nakano Foods
711 Park Ave (14103-1078)
PHONE.....................................585 798-5720
Craig Smith, *President*
EMP: 18 **Privately Held**
SIC: 2099 2035 Vinegar; dressings, salad: raw & cooked (except dry mixes)
HQ: Mizkan America, Inc.
1661 Feehanville Dr # 200
Mount Prospect IL 60056
847 590-0059

(G-7743)
PRIDE PAK INC
11531 Maple Ridge Rd (14103-9765)
PHONE.....................................905 828-2149
Steve Carr, *CEO*
Mauro Lorusso, *Vice Pres*
EMP: 75 EST: 2015
SALES (est): 12.2MM **Privately Held**
SIC: 2099 Salads, fresh or refrigerated

(G-7744)
QUORUM GROUP LLC
Also Called: Takeform Archtectural Graphics
11601 Maple Ridge Rd (14103-9710)
PHONE.....................................585 798-8888
William Hungerford, *President*
Skip Dahlmann, *Regional Mgr*
Tom Hungerford, *Vice Pres*
Gary Fleckenstein, *Senior Engr*
Darren Campbell, *CFO*
EMP: 52
SQ FT: 35,000
SALES: 6.3MM **Privately Held**
WEB: www.takeform.net
SIC: 3993 Signs, not made in custom sign painting shops

(G-7745)
S B WHISTLER & SONS INC
11023 W Center Street Ext (14103-9557)
P.O. Box 270 (14103-0270)
PHONE.....................................585 798-3000
Brendan Whistler, *Owner*
Larry Massey, *CFO*
Sandra Whistler, *Consultant*
EMP: 42
SQ FT: 25,000
SALES (est): 13.9MM **Privately Held**
WEB: www.phinneytool.com
SIC: 3544 Special dies & tools

(G-7746)
SHELBY CRUSHED STONE INC
10830 Blair Rd (14103-9590)
PHONE.....................................585 798-4501
Thomas S Biamonte, *CEO*
April Biamonte, *Controller*
EMP: 32
SALES (est): 2.8MM **Privately Held**
SIC: 1429 1442 1422 Sandstone, crushed & broken-quarrying; gravel mining; crushed & broken limestone

(G-7747)
SIGMA INTL GEN MED APPRTUS LLC
711 Park Ave (14103-1078)
PHONE.....................................585 798-3901
Nelson Tatterson, *President*
Cory Pawlaczyk, *Buyer*
Linda Burke, *Manager*
Roger Hungerford,
Gary Colister,
▼ EMP: 500
SQ FT: 40,000
SALES (est): 219.5MM
SALES (corp-wide): 11.1B **Publicly Held**
WEB: www.sigmapumps.com
SIC: 3841 IV transfusion apparatus
PA: Baxter International Inc.
1 Baxter Pkwy
Deerfield IL 60015
224 948-2000

(G-7748)
VIVUS TECHNOLOGIES LLC
591 Mahar St (14103-1612)
PHONE.....................................585 798-6658

David Cooper,
EMP: 10
SQ FT: 20,000
SALES (est): 245.8K **Privately Held**
SIC: 3821 Autoclaves, laboratory

(G-7749)
WESTERN NEW YORK ENERGY LLC
4141 Bates Rd (14103-9706)
P.O. Box 191 (14103-0191)
PHONE.....................................585 798-9693
Timothy Winters, *Controller*
Sara Flansburg, *Accountant*
Michelle Kingdollar, *Accountant*
Mike Langdon, *Manager*
Leslie Blake, *Executive*
EMP: 40
SALES (est): 17.6MM **Privately Held**
WEB: www.wnyenergy.com
SIC: 2869 Ethanolamines

Medusa
Albany County

(G-7750)
DEGENNARO FUEL SERVICE LLC
242 County Route 357 (12120-2005)
PHONE.....................................518 239-6350
Million Ow, *Owner*
EMP: 10
SALES (est): 647.9K **Privately Held**
SIC: 2869 Fuels

Melville
Suffolk County

(G-7751)
110 SAND COMPANY (PA)
136 Spagnoli Rd (11747-3502)
PHONE.....................................631 694-2822
Chester Broman, *Partner*
EMP: 50
SQ FT: 20,000
SALES (est): 5.8MM **Privately Held**
SIC: 1442 Construction sand & gravel

(G-7752)
18 ROCKS LLC (HQ)
Also Called: Love Charm Clothing
102 Marcus Dr (11747-4212)
PHONE.....................................631 465-9990
Michael Schatten, *Mng Member*
Richard Copler,
EMP: 21 EST: 2011
SQ FT: 3,000
SALES: 20MM
SALES (corp-wide): 1.2MM **Privately Held**
SIC: 2339 Women's & misses' athletic clothing & sportswear

(G-7753)
A K ALLEN CO INC
Also Called: Allen Air
1860 Walt Whitman Rd # 900 (11747-3098)
PHONE.....................................516 747-5450
Ronald Buttner, *President*
Tim Byrnes, *General Mgr*
Steve Werlinitsch, *Plant Mgr*
Sylvia C Allen, *Treasurer*
Linda Johansen, *Financial Exec*
▲ EMP: 120 EST: 1945
SQ FT: 150,000
SALES (est): 15.7MM **Privately Held**
SIC: 3679 3443 3822 3593 Electronic circuits; cylinders, pressure: metal plate; pneumatic relays, air-conditioning type; fluid power cylinders & actuators; valves & pipe fittings; fluid power valves & hose fittings

(G-7754)
ACTION ENVELOPE & PRTG CO INC
Also Called: Action Envelopes.com
105 Maxess Rd Ste S215 (11747-3859)
PHONE.....................................631 225-3900

▲ = Import ▼=Export
◆ =Import/Export

Sharon Newman, *President*
Roger Rampergas, *Warehouse Mgr*
Amy Buhler, *Opers Staff*
Bonnie Boynton, *QC Mgr*
Ian Lewis, *Mktg Coord*
EMP: 10
SALES (est): 2MM **Privately Held**
WEB: www.actionenvelope.com
SIC: 2759 Commercial printing

(G-7755)
ADVANTAGE PLUS DIAGNOSTICS INC
200 Broadhollow Rd (11747-4846)
PHONE.................................631 393-5044
Jason Damianio, *President*
Anthony Rollo, *Admin Sec*
EMP: 5
SALES (est): 304.1K **Privately Held**
SIC: 3841 Diagnostic apparatus, medical

(G-7756)
AERO-VISION TECHNOLOGIES INC (PA)
7 Round Tree Dr (11747-3314)
PHONE.................................631 643-8349
Donald P Burkhardt, *President*
EMP: 8
SQ FT: 6,200
SALES (est): 2MM **Privately Held**
WEB: www.aero-vision.com
SIC: 3577 Computer peripheral equipment

(G-7757)
AIP PUBLISHING LLC
1305 Walt Whitman Rd # 300
(11747-4300)
PHONE.................................516 576-2200
John Haynes, *CEO*
Roy Levenson, *CFO*
EMP: 125 **EST:** 2013
SALES: 48.9MM
SALES (corp-wide): 70.4MM **Privately Held**
SIC: 2731 Books: publishing only
PA: American Institute Of Physics Incorporated
1 Physics Ellipse
College Park MD 20740
301 209-3100

(G-7758)
AIR TECHNIQUES INC (HQ)
1295 Walt Whitman Rd (11747-3062)
PHONE.................................516 433-7676
Christoph Roeer, *CEO*
Lou Guellnitz, *Vice Pres*
Robert Nordquist, *Vice Pres*
Tony Muscarella, *Facilities Mgr*
Bob Barnett, *Warehouse Mgr*
▲ **EMP:** 326
SQ FT: 92,000
SALES (est): 52MM
SALES (corp-wide): 294.1MM **Privately Held**
WEB: www.airtechniques.com
SIC: 3861 3563 3821 3844 Photographic processing equipment & chemicals; air & gas compressors including vacuum pumps; laboratory equipment: fume hoods, distillation racks, etc.; X-ray apparatus & tubes; dental equipment & supplies; pumps & pumping equipment
PA: DUrr Dental Se
Hopfigheimer Str. 17
Bietigheim-Bissingen 74321
714 270-50

(G-7759)
ALLURE EYEWEAR LLC
Also Called: Calvin Klein Eyewear
35 Hub Dr (11747-3517)
PHONE.................................631 755-2121
Larry Roth, *Partner*
EMP: 5
SALES (corp-wide): 3.2MM **Privately Held**
SIC: 3851 Eyeglasses, lenses & frames
PA: Allure Eyewear L.L.C.
265 Spagnoli Rd
Melville NY 11747
631 350-1003

(G-7760)
AMERICAN INSTITUTE PHYSICS INC
Hntngton Qad Ste 1n1-2 (11747)
PHONE.................................516 576-2410
Doris Lewis, *Branch Mgr*
EMP: 250
SALES (corp-wide): 70.4MM **Privately Held**
SIC: 2721 2731 8733 Trade journals: publishing only, not printed on site; books: publishing only; noncommercial research organizations
PA: American Institute Of Physics Incorporated
1 Physics Ellipse
College Park MD 20740
301 209-3100

(G-7761)
AN GROUP INC
17 Scott Dr (11747-1013)
P.O. Box 895 (11747-0895)
PHONE.................................631 549-4090
Steve Hopfenmuller, *President*
Steven Hopfenmuller, *President*
Jill Hopfenmuller, *Vice Pres*
EMP: 5
SALES (est): 283.2K **Privately Held**
WEB: www.smbiz.com
SIC: 2741 Business service newsletters: publishing & printing

(G-7762)
BANNER TRANSMISSION & ENG CO
Also Called: Banner Transmissions
4 Cabriolet Ln (11747-1922)
PHONE.................................516 221-9459
Cliffforddwin Hettinger, *President*
Christopher B Sweeny, *Admin Sec*
EMP: 10
SQ FT: 4,500
SALES (est): 1.2MM **Privately Held**
WEB: www.bannertransmission.com
SIC: 3714 7539 Transmissions, motor vehicle; automotive repair shops

(G-7763)
BZ MEDIA LLC
Also Called: SD Times
225 Broadhollow Rd 211e (11747-4807)
PHONE.................................631 421-4158
Ted Bahr, *President*
H Ted Bahr, *President*
Alan L Zeichick, *Exec VP*
Stacy Burris, *Vice Pres*
Caroline Seiter, *Opers Staff*
EMP: 18 **EST:** 1999
SQ FT: 4,000
SALES: 5.5MM **Privately Held**
WEB: www.bzmedia.com
SIC: 2721 Magazines: publishing & printing

(G-7764)
CANADA DRY BOTTLING CO NY LP
Also Called: Canada Dry Bottling Co of NY
135 Baylis Rd (11747-3899)
PHONE.................................631 694-7575
Michael Ricdardi, *Sales/Mktg Mgr*
EMP: 40
SALES (corp-wide): 51.4MM **Privately Held**
SIC: 2086 Bottled & canned soft drinks
PA: Canada Dry Bottling Company Of New York, L.P.
11202 15th Ave
College Point NY 11356
718 358-2000

(G-7765)
CAPY MACHINE SHOP INC (PA)
114 Spagnoli Rd (11747-3502)
PHONE.................................631 694-6916
Salvatore Capacchione, *CEO*
Rosemary Capacchione, *Shareholder*
▲ **EMP:** 40
SQ FT: 7,500
SALES (est): 10.7MM **Privately Held**
SIC: 3599 Machine shop, jobbing & repair

(G-7766)
CHROMAGRAPHICS PRESS INC
3 Martha Dr (11747-1906)
PHONE.................................631 367-6160
Frank Cuoco, *President*
Irene Cuoco, *Vice Pres*
Thomas Cuoco, *Vice Pres*
EMP: 5
SALES (est): 480K **Privately Held**
WEB: www.chromagraphicspress.com
SIC: 2752 8748 Commercial printing, lithographic; business consulting

(G-7767)
CHYRONHEGO CORPORATION (HQ)
5 Hub Dr (11747-3523)
PHONE.................................631 845-2000
Ariel Garcia, *CEO*
Johan Apel, *Chairman*
Neil Foster, *COO*
Rickard Ohrn, *COO*
Dae Yung Choe, *Vice Pres*
EMP: 95
SQ FT: 47,000
SALES (est): 37.3MM **Privately Held**
WEB: www.chyron.com
SIC: 3663 Radio & TV communications equipment

(G-7768)
COMAX AROMATICS CORPORATION
130 Baylis Rd (11747-3808)
PHONE.................................631 249-0505
Peter J Calabretta, *President*
Norman Katz, *Vice Pres*
Francis J Keppel, *Admin Sec*
EMP: 50
SQ FT: 40,000
SALES (est): 4.1MM **Privately Held**
SIC: 2869 Flavors or flavoring materials, synthetic

(G-7769)
COMAX MANUFACTURING CORP (PA)
Also Called: Comax Flavors
130 Baylis Rd (11747-3808)
PHONE.................................631 249-0505
Peter J Calabretta Jr, *Ch of Bd*
Catherine Armstrong, *Vice Pres*
Paul Calabretta, *Vice Pres*
Jake Cohen, *Accounts Exec*
Laura Ferrante, *Director*
◆ **EMP:** 55
SQ FT: 40,000
SALES (est): 11.4MM **Privately Held**
SIC: 2087 Flavoring extracts & syrups

(G-7770)
COMTECH PST CORP (HQ)
105 Baylis Rd (11747-3833)
PHONE.................................631 777-8900
Dr Stan Sloane, *CEO*
Tony E Scuderi, *VP Opers*
Wayne Mirabella, *Export Mgr*
Joseph Romano, *Mfg Spvr*
Jim Kane, *QC Mgr*
▲ **EMP:** 120
SQ FT: 46,000
SALES (est): 262.9MM
SALES (corp-wide): 671.8MM **Publicly Held**
WEB: www.comtechpst.com
SIC: 3663 3825 Microwave communication equipment; amplifiers, RF power & IF; test equipment for electronic & electric measurement
PA: Comtech Telecommunications Corp.
68 S Service Rd Ste 230
Melville NY 11747
631 962-7000

(G-7771)
COMTECH TELECOM CORP (PA)
68 S Service Rd Ste 230 (11747-2350)
PHONE.................................631 962-7000
Fred Kornberg, *Ch of Bd*
Dick Burt, *President*
Michael D Porcelain, *COO*
Kent Hellebust, *Vice Pres*
Michael Hrybenko, *Vice Pres*
◆ **EMP:** 156 **EST:** 1967
SQ FT: 9,600

SALES: 671.8MM **Publicly Held**
WEB: www.comtechtel.com
SIC: 3663 Microwave communication equipment; amplifiers, RF power & IF; mobile communication equipment

(G-7772)
CROWN NOVELTY WORKS INC
42 Elkland Rd (11747-3302)
PHONE.................................631 253-0949
EMP: 7 **EST:** 1909
SQ FT: 10,000
SALES: 1.2MM **Privately Held**
SIC: 3364 Mfg Lead Curtain Weights

(G-7773)
DADDARIO & COMPANY INC
99 Marcus Dr (11747-4209)
PHONE.................................631 439-3300
EMP: 67
SALES (corp-wide): 180MM **Privately Held**
SIC: 3931 String instruments & parts
PA: D'addario & Company, Inc.
595 Smith St
Farmingdale NY 11735
631 439-3300

(G-7774)
DESIGNER EPOXY FINISHES INC
445 Broadhollow Rd Ste 25 (11747-3645)
PHONE.................................646 943-6044
Justin Palladino, *President*
EMP: 6 **EST:** 2007
SALES (est): 890.7K **Privately Held**
SIC: 2851 1752 Epoxy coatings; floor laying & floor work

(G-7775)
DISTINCTION MAGAZINE INC
Also Called: Island Publications
235 Pinelawn Rd (11747-4226)
PHONE.................................631 843-3522
Madelyn Roberts, *CEO*
Patrice Golde, *President*
EMP: 25
SALES (est): 2.4MM **Privately Held**
SIC: 2721 Magazines: publishing & printing

(G-7776)
DORIS PANOS DESIGNS LTD
130 Old East Neck Rd (11747-3209)
PHONE.................................631 245-0580
Doris Panos, *President*
EMP: 6
SQ FT: 250
SALES (est): 710K **Privately Held**
SIC: 3911 Jewelry, precious metal

(G-7777)
E-Z-EM INC (DH)
155 Pinelawn Rd Ste 230n (11747-3249)
PHONE.................................609 524-2864
Vittorio Puppo, *CEO*
◆ **EMP:** 32
SALES (est): 11MM **Privately Held**
WEB: www.ezem.com
SIC: 2835 3841 In vitro & in vivo diagnostic substances; diagnostic apparatus, medical

(G-7778)
EQUAL OPPRTNITY PBLCATIONS INC
Also Called: Careers and The Disabled
445 Broadhollow Rd # 425 (11747-3669)
PHONE.................................631 421-9421
John R Miller III, *Ch of Bd*
Barbara Loehr, *Editor*
Maryellen Treubert, *Business Mgr*
Tamara Flaun, *Exec VP*
Kay Miller, *Exec VP*
EMP: 12
SQ FT: 3,000
SALES (est): 2.1MM **Privately Held**
WEB: www.eop.com
SIC: 2721 7361 Magazines: publishing & printing; employment agencies

(G-7779)
ESTEE LAUDER COMPANIES INC
80 Ruland Rd Ste 3 (11747-4211)
PHONE.................................631 694-2601
EMP: 74 **Publicly Held**

SIC: 2844 Toilet preparations
PA: The Estee Lauder Companies Inc
　　767 5th Ave Fl 1
　　New York NY 10153

(G-7780)
ESTEE LAUDER COMPANIES INC
7 Corporate Center Dr　(11747-3115)
PHONE.....................212 572-4200
Daja Rogers, *COO*
Timothy Iris, *Vice Pres*
Heather Klurfeld, *Vice Pres*
Nicole Masson, *Vice Pres*
Tricia Nichols, *Vice Pres*
EMP: 504　Publicly Held
WEB: www.elcompanies.com
SIC: 2844 Toilet preparations
PA: The Estee Lauder Companies Inc
　　767 5th Ave Fl 1
　　New York NY 10153

(G-7781)
ESTEE LAUDER INC
125 Pinelawn Rd　(11747-3135)
PHONE.....................631 531-1000
Gavin Kaplan, *Vice Pres*
Louis Schapiro, *Vice Pres*
David P Yacko, *Vice Pres*
Brian Patrick, *Engineer*
Gary Vanderover, *Engineer*
EMP: 100　Publicly Held
WEB: www.esteelauder.com
SIC: 2844 5999 5122 Perfumes &
colognes; toiletries, cosmetics & per-
fumes; cosmetics; perfumes & colognes;
drugs, proprietaries & sundries
HQ: Estee Lauder Inc.
　　767 5th Ave Fl 1
　　New York NY 10153
　　212 572-4200

(G-7782)
FILMPAK EXTRUSION LLC
125 Spagnoli Rd　(11747-3518)
PHONE.....................631 293-6767
Peter Levy, *President*
EMP: 60
SQ FT: 100,000
SALES: 20MM　Privately Held
SIC: 2673 Plastic bags: made from pur-
chased materials

(G-7783)
FOLDER FACTORY INC
Also Called: Folders.com
105 Maxess Rd　(11747-3851)
PHONE.....................540 477-3852
Mark Gentile, *President*
William David Gentile, *Vice Pres*
EMP: 16　EST: 1973
SALES: 2.6MM　Privately Held
WEB: www.folder.com
SIC: 2752 2759 2782 2396 Commercial
printing, offset; commercial printing;
blankbooks & looseleaf binders; automo-
tive & apparel trimmings

(G-7784)
FONAR CORPORATION (PA)
110 Marcus Dr　(11747-4292)
PHONE.....................631 694-2929
Raymond V Damadian, *Ch of Bd*
Timothy R Damadian, *President*
Luciano B Bonanni, *COO*
Claudette J V Chan, *Admin Sec*
EMP: 127
SQ FT: 78,000
SALES: 87.1MM　Publicly Held
WEB: www.fonar.com
SIC: 3845 8741 Electromedical equip-
ment; management services

(G-7785)
FOUGERA PHARMACEUTICALS INC (DH)
Also Called: Pharmaderm
60 Baylis Rd　(11747-3838)
P.O. Box 2006　(11747-0103)
PHONE.....................631 454-7677
Brian A Markison, *CEO*
Donald Degolyer, *Ch of Bd*
Jeff Bailey, *COO*
Chris Klein, *Senior VP*
George Schwab, *Vice Pres*
▲ **EMP: 250　EST: 1963**

SQ FT: 190,000
SALES (est): 284.3MM
SALES (corp-wide): 51.9B　Privately Held
WEB: www.altanapharma-us.com
SIC: 2834 2851 2821 3479 Druggists'
preparations (pharmaceuticals); ointments; paints & paint additives; plasti-
cizer/additive based plastic materials;
painting, coating & hot dipping; measuring
& controlling devices
HQ: Sandoz Inc.
　　100 College Rd W
　　Princeton NJ 08540
　　609 627-8500

(G-7786)
GPC INTERNATIONAL INC (PA)
510 Broadhollow Rd # 205　(11747-3606)
PHONE.....................631 752-9600
Steven Roth, *President*
Don Fleisheiar, *CFO*
EMP: 117
SQ FT: 2,500
SALES (est): 13MM　Privately Held
SIC: 3861 Graphic arts plates, sensitized

(G-7787)
GRAPHIC IMAGE ASSOCIATES LLC
305 Spagnoli Rd　(11747-3506)
PHONE.....................631 249-9600
EMP: 100
SQ FT: 8,500
SALES (est): 8.5MM　Privately Held
SIC: 3111 Leather Tanning/Finishing

(G-7788)
GUIDANCE GROUP INC (PA)
Also Called: Child's Work-Child's Play
1 Huntington Quad 1n03　(11747-4466)
PHONE.....................631 756-4618
Jon D Werz, *CEO*
Edward Werz, *Publisher*
EMP: 12
SALES (est): 782.3K　Privately Held
SIC: 2711 Newspapers, publishing & print-
ing

(G-7789)
HENRY SCHEIN FINCL SVCS LLC (HQ)
Also Called: Henry Schein International Inc
135 Duryea Rd　(11747-3834)
PHONE.....................631 843-5500
Stanley Bergman, *CEO*
Steven Paladino, *CFO*
EMP: 9
SALES (est): 966.7K
SALES (corp-wide): 13.2B　Publicly Held
SIC: 3843 Dental equipment & supplies
PA: Henry Schein, Inc.
　　135 Duryea Rd
　　Melville NY 11747
　　631 843-5500

(G-7790)
HONEYWELL INTERNATIONAL INC
2 Corporate Center Dr # 100　(11747-3269)
P.O. Box 1353　(11747-0353)
PHONE.....................516 577-2661
Jim Dodd, *Manager*
Ray Matthews, *Supervisor*
EMP: 21
SALES (corp-wide): 41.8B　Publicly Held
WEB: www.honeywell.com
SIC: 3724 Aircraft engines & engine parts
PA: Honeywell International Inc.
　　300 S Tryon St
　　Charlotte NC 28202
　　973 455-2000

(G-7791)
HONEYWELL INTERNATIONAL INC
2 Corporate Center Dr # 100　(11747-3269)
PHONE.....................516 577-2000
Jim Dodd, *Exec Dir*
EMP: 21
SALES (corp-wide): 41.8B　Publicly Held
SIC: 3724 Aircraft engines & engine parts
PA: Honeywell International Inc.
　　300 S Tryon St
　　Charlotte NC 28202
　　973 455-2000

(G-7792)
HONEYWELL INTERNATIONAL INC
263 Old Country Rd　(11747-2712)
P.O. Box 22324, Brooklyn　(11202-2324)
PHONE.....................212 964-5111
EMP: 657
SALES (corp-wide): 38.5B　Publicly Held
SIC: 3724 Aircraft Engines And Engine
Parts
PA: Honeywell International Inc.
　　115 Tabor Rd
　　Morris Plains NJ 28202
　　973 455-2000

(G-7793)
HONEYWELL INTERNATIONAL INC
2 Corporate Center Dr # 100　(11747-3269)
PHONE.....................516 577-2000
Ron Rothman, *President*
EMP: 400
SALES (corp-wide): 41.8B　Publicly Held
WEB: www.honeywell.com
SIC: 3724 Aircraft engines & engine parts
PA: Honeywell International Inc.
　　300 S Tryon St
　　Charlotte NC 28202
　　973 455-2000

(G-7794)
INTELLICHECK INC (PA)
535 Broadhollow Rd B51　(11747-3720)
PHONE.....................516 992-1900
Bill White, *CEO*
Michael D Malone, *Ch of Bd*
Russell T Embry, *Senior VP*
Frank Lubin, *VP Engrg*
Dan Caramore, *Sales Associate*
EMP: 29
SQ FT: 9,233
SALES: 4.4MM　Publicly Held
WEB: www.intellicheck.com
SIC: 3699 Security devices

(G-7795)
INTERDGITAL COMMUNICATIONS LLC
2 Huntington Quad Ste 4s　(11747-4508)
PHONE.....................631 622-4000
Gary Lomp, *Manager*
EMP: 125
SALES (corp-wide): 307.4MM　Publicly Held
WEB: www.interdigital.com
SIC: 3661 8731 Telephone & telegraph
apparatus; commercial physical research
HQ: Interdigital Communications, Inc.
　　200 Bellevue Pkwy Ste 300
　　Wilmington DE 19809
　　610 878-7800

(G-7796)
INTERNATIONAL METALS TRDG LLC
25 Melville Park Rd # 114　(11747-3175)
PHONE.....................866 923-0182
Ian Parker, *CEO*
Joseph Kalinowski, *Principal*
Bret Bedges, *COO*
EMP: 5　EST: 2013
SALES: 20MM　Privately Held
SIC: 3441 Building components, structural
steel

(G-7797)
ISINE INC (PA)
105 Maxess Rd Ste 124　(11747-3821)
PHONE.....................631 913-4400
Jeffrey Remmers, *President*
Louis J Morales, *Chairman*
John Masterson, *CFO*
Gary Stevens, *Shareholder*
▲ **EMP: 23**
SQ FT: 3,000
SALES (est): 3.2MM　Privately Held
WEB: www.isine.com
SIC: 3672 3674 Printed circuit boards;
semiconductors & related devices

(G-7798)
KARP ASSOCIATES INC (PA)
Also Called: Adjustable Shelving
260 Spagnoli Rd　(11747-3505)
PHONE.....................631 768-8300

Adam Gold, *Chairman*
Robert Makaw, *Vice Pres*
▲ **EMP: 95　EST: 1956**
SALES (est): 21.7MM　Privately Held
WEB: www.karpinc.com
SIC: 3442 2541 Metal doors; shelving, of-
fice & store, wood

(G-7799)
KNICKERBOCKER PARTITION CORP (PA)
260 Spagnoli Rd　(11747-3505)
P.O. Box 690, Freeport　(11520-0690)
PHONE.....................516 546-0550
Stewart Markbreiter, *President*
Mark Reiss, *VP Opers*
Andrew Kennedy, *Treasurer*
Brian Lynch, *Sales Mgr*
Ken Kuprian, *Manager*
▲ **EMP: 115**
SQ FT: 60,000
SALES (est): 15.9MM　Privately Held
WEB: www.knickerbockerpartition.com
SIC: 2542 Partitions for floor attachment,
prefabricated: except wood

(G-7800)
LEVITON MANUFACTURING CO INC (PA)
201 N Service Rd　(11747-3138)
P.O. Box 10600　(11747-0056)
PHONE.....................631 812-6000
Stephen Sokolow, *Vice Ch Bd*
Donald J Hendler, *President*
Bruno Filio, *President*
Daryoush Larizadeh, *President*
Robert Becker, *Vice Pres*
◆ **EMP: 450　EST: 1906**
SALES (est): 1.4B　Privately Held
WEB: www.leviton.com
SIC: 3613 3357 3674 3694 Fuses, elec-
tric; nonferrous wiredrawing & insulating;
building wire & cable, nonferrous; diodes,
solid state (germanium, silicon, etc.); tran-
sistors; engine electrical equipment; elec-
tronic connectors; caps & plugs, electric:
attachment

(G-7801)
LSI COMPUTER SYSTEMS
1235 Walt Whitman Rd　(11747-3086)
PHONE.....................631 271-0400
Alfred Musto, *CEO*
Attila Tetik, *President*
Alvin Kaplan, *Corp Secy*
Burt Cohen, *Vice Pres*
Peter Visconti, *VP Sales*
▲ **EMP: 35　EST: 1969**
SQ FT: 13,500
SALES (est): 4.6MM　Privately Held
WEB: www.lsicsi.com
SIC: 3674 Integrated circuits, semiconduc-
tor networks, etc.; metal oxide silicon
(MOS) devices

(G-7802)
MEDPOD INC
324 S Service Rd Ste 112　(11747-3272)
PHONE.....................631 863-8090
Jack Tawil, *Ch of Bd*
EMP: 7
SALES (est): 815.5K　Privately Held
SIC: 3826 Laser scientific & engineering
instruments; spectroscopic & other optical
properties measuring equipment; chrono-
scopes

(G-7803)
MELWOOD PARTNERS INC
102 Marcus Dr　(11747-4212)
PHONE.....................631 923-0134
Brian Wasserman, *Ch of Bd*
Richard Cotler, *Partner*
EMP: 15
SQ FT: 6,000
SALES: 10MM　Privately Held
SIC: 2211 Apparel & outerwear fabrics,
cotton

(G-7804)
MEYCO PRODUCTS INC (PA)
1225 Walt Whitman Rd　(11747-3093)
PHONE.....................631 421-9800
David W Weissner, *CEO*
John Ciniglio, *President*
Donnie Griffin, *Vice Pres*

▲ = Import　▼ =Export
◆ =Import/Export

Patricia K Weissner, *Admin Sec*
▼ EMP: 30 EST: 1898
SQ FT: 70,000
SALES (est): 21.5MM **Privately Held**
WEB: www.meycoproducts.com
SIC: 2394 Liners & covers, fabric: made from purchased materials

(G-7805)
MILITARY PARTS EXCHANGE LLC
Also Called: M P X
145 Pinelawn Rd Ste 240n (11747-3161)
PHONE............................631 243-1700
EMP: 15 **Privately Held**
SIC: 3728 Aircraft parts & equipment
PA: Military Parts Exchange Llc
   701 Nw 57th Pl
   Fort Lauderdale FL 33309

(G-7806)
MITSUBISHI ELC PWR PDTS INC
55 Marcus Dr (11747-4209)
PHONE............................516 962-2813
Paul Bell, *Manager*
Michael Lauro, *Supervisor*
Botti Michael, *IT Specialist*
EMP: 7 **Privately Held**
SIC: 3699 1731 Electrical equipment & supplies; electrical work
HQ: Mitsubishi Electric Power Products, Inc.
   530 Keystone Dr
   Warrendale PA 15086
   724 772-2555

(G-7807)
NATURAL ORGANICS LABS INC
Also Called: Universal Proteins
548 Broadhollow Rd (11747-3708)
PHONE............................631 957-5600
Gerald Kessler, *President*
Nancy Devera, *Research*
Nirmit Trivedi, *Info Tech Mgr*
EMP: 500
SALES (est): 63.5MM **Privately Held**
SIC: 2834 2087 Vitamin preparations; flavoring extracts & syrups

(G-7808)
NEWSDAY LLC (PA)
Also Called: Newsday Media Group
6 Corporate Center Dr (11747-3845)
PHONE............................631 843-4050
Patrick Dolan, *President*
Karen Bailis, *Editor*
Diane Daniels, *Editor*
Andy Edelstein, *Editor*
Don Hudson, *Editor*
EMP: 400 EST: 1940
SALES (est): 245.2MM **Privately Held**
SIC: 2711 Commercial printing & newspaper publishing combined; newspapers, publishing & printing

(G-7809)
NEWSDAY LLC
25 Deshon Dr (11747-4221)
PHONE............................631 843-3135
Raymond Jansen, *Branch Mgr*
EMP: 150
SALES (corp-wide): 245.2MM **Privately Held**
SIC: 2711 Newspapers, publishing & printing
PA: Newsday Llc
   6 Corporate Center Dr
   Melville NY 11747
   631 843-4050

(G-7810)
NIKON INSTRUMENTS INC (DH)
1300 Walt Whitman Rd Fl 2 (11747-3064)
PHONE............................631 547-4200
Yoshinobu Ishikawa, *Ch of Bd*
Toshiaki Nagano, *President*
Michael Gallo, *General Mgr*
Ichiro Terato, *Exec VP*
James Hamlin, *Vice Pres*
◆ EMP: 91
SALES (est): 40.5MM **Privately Held**
WEB: www.nikonusa.com
SIC: 3826 Analytical instruments

(G-7811)
OLYMPIC SOFTWARE & CONSULTING
290 Broadhollow Rd 130e (11747-4852)
PHONE............................631 351-0655
Chris McLean, *Owner*
EMP: 7 EST: 2001
SALES (est): 596.9K **Privately Held**
SIC: 7372 Prepackaged software

(G-7812)
OPUS TECHNOLOGY CORPORATION (PA)
10 Gwynne Rd (11747-1414)
PHONE............................631 271-1883
James Startin, *President*
EMP: 10
SALES (est): 950.8K **Privately Held**
SIC: 3679 Electronic circuits

(G-7813)
P & F INDUSTRIES INC (PA)
Also Called: P&F
445 Broadhollow Rd # 100 (11747-3615)
PHONE............................631 694-9800
Richard A Horowitz, *Ch of Bd*
Joseph A Molino Jr, *COO*
Howard Brownstein, *Bd of Directors*
Jeffrey D Franklin, *Bd of Directors*
Richard Randall, *Bd of Directors*
◆ EMP: 38 EST: 1963
SQ FT: 5,000
SALES: 65MM **Publicly Held**
WEB: www.pfina.com
SIC: 3429 3714 3546 Manufactured hardware (general); filters: oil, fuel & air, motor vehicle; grinders, portable: electric or pneumatic

(G-7814)
PARK AEROSPACE CORP (PA)
48 S Service Rd (11747-2335)
PHONE............................631 465-3600
Brian E Shore, *Ch of Bd*
Christopher T Mastrogiacomo, *President*
Mark Esquivel, *COO*
Stephen E Gilhuley, *Exec VP*
Mark A Esquivel, *Senior VP*
▲ EMP: 98
SQ FT: 8,000
SALES: 51.1MM **Publicly Held**
WEB: www.parkelectro.com
SIC: 3672 3674 Printed circuit boards; microcircuits, integrated (semiconductor)

(G-7815)
PERMIT FASHION GROUP INC
111 Forster Pl (11747-8128)
PHONE............................212 912-0988
Zhouping Zheng, *CEO*
▲ EMP: 8 EST: 2012
SALES (est): 1.2MM **Privately Held**
SIC: 2331 2337 2339 Blouses, women's & juniors': made from purchased material; skirts, separate: women's, misses' & juniors'; jackets & vests, except fur & leather: women's; slacks: women's, misses' & juniors'

(G-7816)
POLY-PAK INDUSTRIES INC (PA)
Also Called: Colorpak
125 Spagnoli Rd (11747-3518)
PHONE............................800 969-1933
Peter Levy, *Ch of Bd*
Leonard Levy, *Chairman*
Doug Kiesel, *Vice Pres*
Rose Matty, *Vice Pres*
Cheryl Bree, *Production*
◆ EMP: 280
SQ FT: 150,000
SALES (est): 67.8MM **Privately Held**
WEB: www.poly-pak.com
SIC: 2673 2677 Plastic bags: made from purchased materials; envelopes

(G-7817)
PRECISION PHARMA SERVICES INC
155 Duryea Rd (11747-3894)
PHONE............................631 752-7314
Jim Moose, *President*
June Heck, *CFO*
EMP: 125
SQ FT: 100,000

SALES (est): 24.5MM **Privately Held**
WEB: www.precisionpharma.com
SIC: 2834 Pharmaceutical preparations

(G-7818)
PUBLISHERS CLEARING HOUSE LLC
265 Spagnoli Rd Ste 1 (11747-3508)
PHONE............................516 249-4063
EMP: 31
SALES (corp-wide): 132.8MM **Privately Held**
SIC: 2741 Miscellaneous publishing
PA: Publishers Clearing House Llc
   300 Jericho Quadrangle # 300
   Jericho NY 11753
   516 883-5432

(G-7819)
RINGLEAD INC
200 Broadhollow Rd # 400 (11747-4806)
PHONE............................310 906-0545
Jaime Muirhead, *Vice Pres*
Alex Kazansky, *Opers Dir*
Brian Vitale, *CFO*
Tyler McNeil, *Controller*
Rachel Chinapen, *Marketing Staff*
EMP: 10
SALES (est): 393K **Privately Held**
SIC: 7372 Business oriented computer software

(G-7820)
ROSS COMMUNICATIONS ASSOCIATES
200 Broadhollow Rd # 207 (11747-4846)
PHONE............................631 393-5089
Robert Ross, *President*
Jodie Ross, *Vice Pres*
EMP: 10
SALES (est): 4.8MM **Privately Held**
SIC: 2721 Magazines: publishing & printing

(G-7821)
SCOUTNEWS LLC
Also Called: Health Day
150 Broadhollow Rd # 302 (11747-4901)
PHONE............................203 855-1400
George Giokas,
Barry Hoffman,
David Rouatt,
Andrew Sherman,
EMP: 10 EST: 2001
SALES (est): 802.8K **Privately Held**
WEB: www.healthday.com
SIC: 2721 Magazines: publishing & printing

(G-7822)
SIEMENS PRODUCT LIFE MGMT SFTW
Also Called: Analysis & Design Aplicat Co
60 Broadhollow Rd (11747-2504)
PHONE............................631 549-2300
Annabella Grozescu, *Engineer*
Somee Lee, *Engineer*
Christian Huber, *Accounts Mgr*
Matt McCullum, *Accounts Exec*
Keri Maher, *Manager*
EMP: 319
SALES (corp-wide): 95B **Privately Held**
SIC: 7372 Prepackaged software
HQ: Siemens Industry Software Inc.
   5800 Granite Pkwy Ste 600
   Plano TX 75024
   972 987-3000

(G-7823)
SIMPLY AMAZING ENTERPRISES INC
68 S Service Rd Ste 1 (11747-2354)
PHONE............................631 503-6452
EMP: 7 EST: 2014
SALES: 390K **Privately Held**
SIC: 2842 Mfg Polish/Sanitation Goods

(G-7824)
STAR COMMUNITY PUBLISHING
Also Called: Shoppers Weekly Newspapers
6 Corporate Center Dr (11747-3845)
PHONE............................631 843-4050
Michael Gates, *VP Sales*
EMP: 194

SALES: 45MM
SALES (corp-wide): 245.2MM **Privately Held**
WEB: www.tribune.com
SIC: 2711 Newspapers, publishing & printing
PA: Newsday Llc
   6 Corporate Center Dr
   Melville NY 11747
   631 843-4050

(G-7825)
SUPER MILLWORK INC
125 Spagnoli Rd (11747-3518)
PHONE............................631 293-5025
Dov Fulop, *Principal*
EMP: 9
SALES (corp-wide): 827.6K **Privately Held**
SIC: 2431 Doors, wood
PA: Super Millwork Inc
   330 S Service Rd
   Melville NY

(G-7826)
SUTTON PLACE SOFTWARE INC
13 Tappen Dr (11747-1019)
PHONE............................631 421-1737
Steve J Sutton, *President*
EMP: 5 EST: 1982
SALES (est): 290.2K **Privately Held**
SIC: 7372 Prepackaged software

(G-7827)
SYSTEMS TRADING INC
48 S Svc Rd Ste LI90 (11747)
PHONE............................718 261-8900
Harold Schwartz, *Ch of Bd*
EMP: 7
SQ FT: 1,650
SALES: 8MM **Privately Held**
WEB: www.btn.net
SIC: 7372 7377 Prepackaged software; computer rental & leasing

(G-7828)
TAYLOR COMMUNICATIONS INC
155 Pinelawn Rd Ste 120s (11747-3252)
PHONE............................937 221-1303
Bob Paradise, *Branch Mgr*
Dave Ohlemacher, *Technology*
EMP: 10
SALES (corp-wide): 2.8B **Privately Held**
WEB: www.stdreg.com
SIC: 2761 Manifold business forms
HQ: Taylor Communications, Inc.
   1725 Roe Crest Dr
   North Mankato MN 56003
   507 625-2828

(G-7829)
TECH SOFTWARE LLC
Also Called: BEC Acquisition Co
270 Spagnoli Rd Ste 102 (11747-3515)
PHONE............................516 986-3050
Lea Hollowell, *Consultant*
Walden Leverich,
EMP: 6
SALES (est): 413.8K **Privately Held**
SIC: 7372 Business oriented computer software

(G-7830)
TEL TECH INTERNATIONAL
200 Broadhollow Rd # 207 (11747-4846)
PHONE............................516 393-5174
Donald Wuerfl, *Manager*
EMP: 40
SALES (est): 1.1MM **Privately Held**
SIC: 7372 Prepackaged software

(G-7831)
TOPTEC PRODUCTS LLC
1225 Walt Whitman Rd (11747-3010)
PHONE............................631 421-9800
John Ciniglio, *President*
EMP: 14
SALES (est): 1.5MM **Privately Held**
SIC: 2394 Tents: made from purchased materials

(G-7832)
VERINT AMERICAS INC (HQ)
175 Broadhollow Rd # 100 (11747-4911)
PHONE............................631 962-9334
Timothy Galvin, *Manager*

Nita Rodriguez, *Director*
EMP: 14 **EST:** 2016
SALES: 2MM **Publicly Held**
SIC: 7372 Prepackaged software

(G-7833)
VERINT SEC INTELLIGENCE INC
Also Called: Vsii
175 Broadhollow Rd # 100 (11747-4911)
PHONE..............................631 962-9300
Dan Bodner, *CEO*
EMP: 100
SQ FT: 49,000
SALES: 50MM **Publicly Held**
SIC: 7372 Prepackaged software
PA: Verint Systems Inc.
 175 Broadhollow Rd # 100
 Melville NY 11747

(G-7834)
VERINT SYSTEMS INC (PA)
175 Broadhollow Rd # 100 (11747-4910)
PHONE..............................631 962-9600
Dan Bodner, *Ch of Bd*
Zwicka Ben-Zion, *Managing Dir*
Kevin Kurimsky, *Vice Pres*
Michael Landtroop, *Vice Pres*
Craig Levin, *Vice Pres*
EMP: 125
SQ FT: 49,000
SALES: 1.2B **Publicly Held**
WEB: www.verintsystems.com
SIC: 7372 7382 7373 Prepackaged software; security systems services; systems software development services

---

Memphis
Onondaga County

(G-7835)
MATTESSICH IRON LLC
1484 New State Route 31 (13112-8719)
PHONE..............................315 409-8496
Michael Mattessich, *Principal*
Danielle Mattessich, *Vice Pres*
EMP: 5 **EST:** 2010
SQ FT: 4,000
SALES: 500K **Privately Held**
SIC: 3462 Iron & steel forgings

Menands
Albany County

(G-7836)
A M & J DIGITAL
800 N Pearl St Ste 5 (12204-1893)
PHONE..............................518 434-2579
Alan Brand, *Accounts Mgr*
Nell Fodera, *Accounts Mgr*
Lori Squadere,
Beth Cipperly, *Graphic Designe*
EMP: 8
SALES (est): 1.1MM **Privately Held**
SIC: 2752 Commercial printing, lithographic

(G-7837)
ACKROYD METAL FABRICATORS INC
966 Broadway Ste 2 (12204-2521)
PHONE..............................518 434-1281
Paul Zabinski, *President*
EMP: 12
SQ FT: 40,000
SALES: 1.5MM **Privately Held**
SIC: 3441 Fabricated structural metal

(G-7838)
ALBANY INTERNATIONAL CORP
Appleton Wire Division
1373 Broadway (12204-2697)
PHONE..............................518 445-2230
Tony Ferguson, *President*
Darrin Curley, *Vice Pres*
Cliff Smith, *Vice Pres*
John Siewerdt, *Production*
Steven Maye, *Opers-Prdtn-Mfg*
EMP: 150

SALES (corp-wide): 982.4MM **Publicly Held**
WEB: www.albint.com
SIC: 2621 2296 Paper mills; tire cord & fabrics
PA: Albany International Corp.
 216 Airport Dr
 Rochester NH 03867
 603 330-5850

(G-7839)
ALBANY INTERNATIONAL CORP
Dryer Fabrics Division
1373 Broadway (12204-2697)
P.O. Box 1907, Albany (12201-1907)
PHONE..............................518 447-6400
Al Drinkwater, *Manager*
EMP: 100
SALES (corp-wide): 982.4MM **Publicly Held**
WEB: www.albint.com
SIC: 2672 Cloth lined paper: made from purchased paper
PA: Albany International Corp.
 216 Airport Dr
 Rochester NH 03867
 603 330-5850

(G-7840)
ARCADIA MFG GROUP INC
1032 Broadway (12204-2506)
PHONE..............................518 434-6213
William T Sumner, *Ch of Bd*
EMP: 6
SALES (corp-wide): 10.8MM **Privately Held**
SIC: 3498 3446 3444 3999 Fabricated pipe & fittings; ornamental metalwork; sheet metalwork; cigar lighters, except precious metal
PA: Arcadia Manufacturing Group, Inc.
 80 Cohoes Ave
 Green Island NY 12183
 518 434-6213

(G-7841)
BLASCH PRECISION CERAMICS INC (PA)
580 Broadway Ste 1 (12204-2896)
PHONE..............................518 436-1263
Robert A Baker, *Ch of Bd*
David W Bobrek, *Ch of Bd*
John Parrish, *Exec VP*
Edwin Collins, *Vice Pres*
William Johnson, *Vice Pres*
▲ **EMP:** 98
SALES: 18MM **Privately Held**
WEB: www.powermaterials.com
SIC: 3297 Graphite refractories: carbon bond or ceramic bond

(G-7842)
DYNASTY CHEMICAL CORP
444 N Pearl St (12204-1511)
PHONE..............................518 463-1146
Jane Waldman, *President*
Mel R Waldman, *Vice Pres*
Michael Waldman, *Manager*
Mike Waldman, *Manager*
▲ **EMP:** 48
SQ FT: 109,000
SALES (est): 14.8MM **Privately Held**
SIC: 2819 5169 Industrial inorganic chemicals; industrial chemicals

(G-7843)
GEROME TECHNOLOGIES INC
85 Broadway Ste 1 (12204-2791)
PHONE..............................518 463-1324
Mark Smisloff, *President*
Francis Novko, *Opers Mgr*
Justyna Zieba, *Design Engr*
Brian Treffert, *Manager*
▲ **EMP:** 54
SQ FT: 54,000
SALES (est): 17.7MM **Privately Held**
SIC: 3644 3699 7539 Insulators & insulation materials, electrical; electrical equipment & supplies; electrical services

(G-7844)
MCALLISTERS PRECISION WLDG INC
Also Called: Precision Co.
47 Broadway (12204-2767)
PHONE..............................518 221-3455

April McCallister, *President*
Jason McCallister, *Vice Pres*
EMP: 15
SQ FT: 12,000
SALES (est): 1.2MM **Privately Held**
SIC: 3446 3548 Fences or posts, ornamental iron or steel; welding & cutting apparatus & accessories

(G-7845)
MCCARTHY TIRE SVC CO NY INC
Also Called: McCarthy Tire and Auto Ctr
980 Broadway (12204-2504)
PHONE..............................518 449-5185
Rick Beckman, *Principal*
EMP: 15
SQ FT: 7,140
SALES (corp-wide): 339.7MM **Privately Held**
SIC: 3011 Automobile tires, pneumatic
HQ: McCarthy Tire Service Company Of New York, Inc.
 340 Kidder St
 Wilkes Barre PA 18702

(G-7846)
MIDLAND FARMS INC (PA)
375 Broadway (12204-2708)
PHONE..............................518 436-7038
Demetrios E Haseotes, *CEO*
Brittany Flood, *Cust Mgr*
Lane Williams, *Manager*
EMP: 51
SALES (est): 14.5MM **Privately Held**
WEB: www.midlandfarms.com
SIC: 2026 Milk processing (pasteurizing, homogenizing, bottling)

(G-7847)
NEW YORK LEGAL PUBLISHING
120 Broadway Ste 1a (12204-2722)
PHONE..............................518 459-1100
Ernest Barvoets, *President*
Edward M Neiles Jr, *Vice Pres*
Suzanne Barvoets, *Sales Staff*
EMP: 7
SALES: 1.2MM **Privately Held**
WEB: www.nylp.com
SIC: 2741 2759 2731 Miscellaneous publishing; commercial printing; book publishing

(G-7848)
SIMMONS MACHINE TOOL CORP (PA)
Also Called: Nsh
1700 Broadway (12204-2701)
PHONE..............................518 462-5431
John O Naumann, *CEO*
Hans J Naumann, *Ch of Bd*
David William Davis, *President*
Daniel T Menoncin, *Project Mgr*
Scott Mitchell, *Project Mgr*
▲ **EMP:** 104
SQ FT: 145,000
SALES (est): 19.4MM **Privately Held**
WEB: www.smtgroup.com
SIC: 3541 5084 Machine tools, metal cutting type; industrial machinery & equipment

(G-7849)
T LEMME MECHANICAL INC
Selby & Smith
1074 Broadway (12204-2507)
PHONE..............................518 436-4136
Bill Mattfeld, *Opers Mgr*
EMP: 40 **Privately Held**
SIC: 3444 Sheet metalwork
PA: T. Lemme Mechanical, Inc.
 67 Erie Blvd
 Menands NY 12204

(G-7850)
WELDING GUYS LLC
Also Called: Welding Guy, The
47 Broadway Bldg C (12204-2767)
PHONE..............................518 898-8323
Derrick White,
Antonio Garcia,
EMP: 6
SQ FT: 7,000
SALES: 200K **Privately Held**
SIC: 7692 Welding repair

Mendon
Monroe County

(G-7851)
N Y B P INC
Also Called: New York Blood Pressure
1355 Pittsford Mendon Rd (14506-9733)
P.O. Box 471 (14506-0471)
PHONE..............................585 624-2541
Gregory J Sarkis, *President*
EMP: 3
SALES: 1MM **Privately Held**
SIC: 3841 Blood pressure apparatus

(G-7852)
SAXBY IMPLEMENT CORP (PA)
Also Called: Kubota Authorized Dealer
180 Mendon Victor Rd (14506)
P.O. Box 333 (14506-0333)
PHONE..............................585 624-2938
Marvin E Hogan, *President*
Teri H Maxwell, *Vice Pres*
Randall Hogan, *Treasurer*
Joanne Hogan, *Admin Sec*
EMP: 10
SQ FT: 9,400
SALES (est): 1.2MM **Privately Held**
SIC: 3524 5083 Lawn & garden tractors & equipment; farm & garden machinery

---

Merrick
Nassau County

(G-7853)
CREATIVE MAGAZINE INC
31 Merrick Ave Ste 60 (11566-3499)
PHONE..............................516 378-0800
David Flasterstein, *President*
EMP: 5 **EST:** 2008
SALES (est): 83.6K **Privately Held**
SIC: 2721 Periodicals: publishing only

(G-7854)
D G M GRAPHICS INC
Also Called: Printing Emporium
55 Merrick Ave (11566-3415)
P.O. Box 121 (11566-0121)
PHONE..............................516 223-2220
Douglas G Mills, *President*
EMP: 11 **EST:** 1984
SQ FT: 3,300
SALES (est): 1.1MM **Privately Held**
WEB: www.printingemporium.com
SIC: 2752 2791 2789 2759 Photo-offset printing; typesetting; bookbinding & related work; commercial printing

(G-7855)
FIRST BRANDS LLC
25 Merrick Ave Ste 2 (11566-3416)
PHONE..............................646 432-4366
Albert Kassin, *Mng Member*
EMP: 25 **EST:** 2018
SALES: 10MM **Privately Held**
SIC: 3942 3944 2369 2371 Dolls & stuffed toys; games, toys & children's vehicles; headwear: girls', children's & infants'; hats, fur
PA: Best Brands Consumer Products, Inc.
 20 W 33rd St Fl 5
 New York NY 10001
 212 684-7456

(G-7856)
FUEL SOUL
188 Merrick Rd (11566-4532)
PHONE..............................516 379-0810
Gregory Fine, *CEO*
EMP: 5
SALES (est): 392.7K **Privately Held**
SIC: 2869 Fuels

(G-7857)
JON LYN INK INC
Also Called: Minuteman Press
255 Sunrise Hwy Ste 1 (11566-3700)
PHONE..............................516 546-2312
John Jutt, *President*
EMP: 6
SQ FT: 1,200

▲ = Import ▼=Export
◆ =Import/Export

SALES (est): 889K **Privately Held**
SIC: 2752 7334 2759 2791 Commercial printing, lithographic; photocopying & duplicating services; invitation & stationery printing & engraving; typesetting; bookbinding & related work

(G-7858)
L I C SCREEN PRINTING INC
2949 Joyce Ln (11566-5209)
PHONE.................................516 546-7289
Edward Rosenblum, *President*
EMP: 25
SQ FT: 15,000
SALES (est): 1.8MM **Privately Held**
WEB: www.licscreenprinting.com
SIC: 2759 3089 3993 2396 Screen printing; plastic processing; signs & advertising specialties; automotive & apparel trimmings

(G-7859)
LEADER PRINTING INC
Also Called: Print-O-Rama Copy Center
2272 Babylon Tpke (11566-3829)
PHONE.................................516 546-1544
Steve Leads, *President*
EMP: 10 **EST:** 1969
SALES (est): 737.7K **Privately Held**
SIC: 2752 7334 Photo-offset printing; photocopying & duplicating services

(G-7860)
LEGAL STRATEGIES INC
1795 Harvard Ave (11566-4413)
PHONE.................................516 377-3940
Steven Mitchell Sack, *President*
EMP: 7
SALES (est): 519.4K **Privately Held**
SIC: 2731 Book publishing

(G-7861)
MEGA SOURCING INC (PA)
Also Called: Mega Apparel International
1929 Edward Ln (11566-4922)
PHONE.................................646 682-0304
Mandy Sciortino, *President*
▲ **EMP:** 2 **EST:** 2006
SQ FT: 3,800
SALES: 7MM **Privately Held**
SIC: 2331 2321 5621 5611 Women's & misses' blouses & shirts; men's & boys' furnishings; women's clothing stores; ready-to-wear apparel, women's; men's & boys' clothing stores

(G-7862)
NORTHEAST WINDOWS USA INC
1 Kees Pl (11566-3642)
P.O. Box 159 (11566-0159)
PHONE.................................516 378-6577
Jill Kaiserman, *President*
Jeffrey Kaiserman, *Vice Pres*
Phil Reid, *Sales Executive*
▲ **EMP:** 48
SQ FT: 35,000
SALES: 8MM **Privately Held**
SIC: 3089 Windows, plastic

(G-7863)
PRESTIGE ENVELOPE & LITHOGRAPH
Also Called: Prestige Litho & Graphics
1745 Merrick Ave Ste 2 (11566-2700)
PHONE.................................631 521-7043
Gary Gingo, *CEO*
Angel Irimia, *President*
Joe Nieves, *Admin Sec*
EMP: 12
SQ FT: 30,000
SALES (est): 2.1MM **Privately Held**
WEB: www.prestigelg.com
SIC: 2752 2791 2789 7389 Commercial printing, offset; typesetting; bookbinding & related work; printing broker; envelopes

(G-7864)
QUALITY LINEALS USA INC (PA)
Also Called: Quality Fence
1 Kees Pl (11566-3642)
P.O. Box 159 (11566-0159)
PHONE.................................516 378-6577
Jill Kaiserman, *President*
Jeffrey Kaiserman, *Vice Pres*
EMP: 55

SALES: 16MM **Privately Held**
SIC: 3089 Billfold inserts, plastic

(G-7865)
WORLDWIDE TICKET CRAFT
1390 Jerusalem Ave (11566-1305)
PHONE.................................516 538-6200
Eric Colts, *President*
EMP: 60
SALES (est): 4.4MM **Privately Held**
WEB: www.ticketcraft.com
SIC: 2752 2791 2759 Tickets, lithographed; typesetting; commercial printing

Mexico
Oswego County

(G-7866)
GRANDMA BROWNS BEANS INC
5837 Scenic Ave (13114)
P.O. Box 230 (13114-0230)
PHONE.................................315 963-7221
Sandra L Brown, *President*
EMP: 15 **EST:** 1938
SQ FT: 35,000
SALES: 19.7K **Privately Held**
SIC: 2032 Canned specialties

Middle Granville
Washington County

(G-7867)
EVERGREEN SLATE COMPANY INC
2027 County Route 23 (12849)
P.O. Box 248, Granville (12832-0248)
PHONE.................................518 642-2530
Fred Whitridge, *President*
Shannon Humphrey, *General Mgr*
Ray Loomis, *Vice Pres*
Fogo Lisa, *Controller*
Jan Edwards, *Sales Staff*
◆ **EMP:** 70 **EST:** 1916
SQ FT: 1,000
SALES (est): 10.3MM **Privately Held**
WEB: www.evergreenslate.com
SIC: 3281 Slate products

(G-7868)
HILLTOP SLATE INC
Rr 22 Box A (12849)
P.O. Box 201 (12849-0201)
PHONE.................................518 642-1453
David Thomas, *President*
▲ **EMP:** 30 **EST:** 1948
SQ FT: 50,000
SALES (est): 3.4MM **Privately Held**
WEB: www.hilltopslate.com
SIC: 3281 Cut stone & stone products

(G-7869)
K-D STONE INC
Rr 22 (12849)
P.O. Box 138 (12849-0138)
PHONE.................................518 642-2082
Nelson Dunster, *President*
Kimberly Dunster, *Vice Pres*
EMP: 12
SALES (est): 1.6MM **Privately Held**
SIC: 2952 Roof cement: asphalt, fibrous or plastic

(G-7870)
SHELDON SLATE PRODUCTS CO INC
Fox Rd (12849)
P.O. Box 199 (12849-0199)
PHONE.................................518 642-1280
John Tatko Jr, *President*
EMP: 50 **EST:** 1924
SQ FT: 1,200
SALES (est): 5.3MM **Privately Held**
SIC: 3281 2952 2951 Slate products; asphalt felts & coatings; asphalt paving mixtures & blocks

(G-7871)
VERMONT MULTICOLOR SLATE
146 State Route 22a (12849-5431)
P.O. Box 202 (12849-0202)
PHONE.................................518 642-2400
William Enny, *President*
Renold Tang, *CFO*
EMP: 9
SQ FT: 10,000
SALES (est): 447.1K **Privately Held**
SIC: 1411 Slate, dimension-quarrying

Middle Grove
Saratoga County

(G-7872)
CUCCIO-ZANETTI INC
Also Called: Zanetti Millwork
455 Middle Grove Rd (12850-1107)
PHONE.................................518 587-1363
John Zanetti, *President*
EMP: 8
SQ FT: 9,000
SALES (est): 1.1MM **Privately Held**
SIC: 2431 Doors, wood

Middle Island
Suffolk County

(G-7873)
AFCO PRECAST SALES CORP
Also Called: Old Castle Precast
114 Rocky Point Rd (11953-1216)
PHONE.................................631 924-7114
Richard Affenita, *Ch of Bd*
Peter Kaplin, *President*
▲ **EMP:** 75
SQ FT: 1,560
SALES (est): 10.7MM **Privately Held**
SIC: 3272 5211 Concrete products, precast; masonry materials & supplies

(G-7874)
ALLEY CAT SIGNS INC
506 Middle Country Rd (11953-2521)
PHONE.................................631 924-7446
Albert Borsella, *President*
EMP: 12
SALES (est): 1.3MM **Privately Held**
SIC: 3993 1799 5999 Electric signs; sign installation & maintenance; awnings

(G-7875)
MID ENTERPRISE INC
809 Middle Country Rd (11953-2511)
PHONE.................................631 924-3933
Shahid Ali Khan, *Principal*
EMP: 5
SALES (est): 541.5K **Privately Held**
SIC: 3578 Automatic teller machines (ATM)

Middle Village
Queens County

(G-7876)
ACCURATE SPECIALTY METAL FABRI
6420 Admiral Ave (11379-1614)
PHONE.................................718 418-6895
Ronald Palmerick, *Ch of Bd*
Sebastian Loaysa, *General Mgr*
Al Webb, *Vice Pres*
EMP: 35
SQ FT: 30,000
SALES (est): 7.2MM
SALES (corp-wide): 51.2MM **Privately Held**
WEB: www.asm-mech.com
SIC: 3444 Ducts, sheet metal
PA: Aabco Sheet Metal Co., Inc.
47 40 Metropolitan Ave
Ridgewood NY 11385
718 821-1166

(G-7877)
AGLIKA TRADE LLC
5905 74th St (11379-5216)
PHONE.................................727 424-1944

Maya Petkova,
EMP: 10
SALES (est): 599.5K **Privately Held**
SIC: 3552 Textile machinery

(G-7878)
GOLDMONT ENTERPRISES INC
Also Called: Superior Model Form Co
7603 Caldwell Ave (11379-5233)
PHONE.................................212 947-3633
Vito Montalto, *President*
EMP: 15 **EST:** 1940
SQ FT: 7,000
SALES: 1MM **Privately Held**
WEB: www.superiormodel.com
SIC: 3999 Forms: display, dress & show

(G-7879)
J M R PLASTICS CORPORATION
5847 78th St (11379-5305)
PHONE.................................718 898-9825
John Daidone, *President*
Selina Daidone, *Corp Secy*
EMP: 8
SQ FT: 10,000
SALES: 2MM **Privately Held**
SIC: 3089 Plastic kitchenware, tableware & houseware; plastic processing

(G-7880)
JONATHAN DAVID PUBLISHERS INC
6822 Eliot Ave (11379-1131)
PHONE.................................718 456-8611
Alfred J Kolatch, *President*
Thelma Kolatch, *Corp Secy*
Marvin Sekler, *Exec VP*
Carol Zelezny, *Accounting Mgr*
▲ **EMP:** 10 **EST:** 1949
SQ FT: 2,400
SALES (est): 860K **Privately Held**
WEB: www.jdbooks.com
SIC: 2731 Books: publishing only

(G-7881)
JUNIPER ELBOW CO INC (PA)
Also Called: Juniper Industries
7215 Metropolitan Ave (11379-2198)
P.O. Box 148 (11379-0148)
PHONE.................................718 326-2546
Jesse L Wiener, *CEO*
Celia Wiener, *Vice Pres*
Elliot Wiener, *Vice Pres*
▲ **EMP:** 185 **EST:** 1929
SQ FT: 100,000
SALES (est): 24.8MM **Privately Held**
WEB: www.juniperind.com
SIC: 3444 3498 3433 3312 Elbows, for air ducts, stovepipes, etc.: sheet metal; ventilators, sheet metal; metal ventilating equipment; fabricated pipe & fittings; heating equipment, except electric; blast furnaces & steel mills

(G-7882)
JUNIPER INDUSTRIES FLORIDA INC
7215 Metropolitan Ave (11379-2107)
PHONE.................................718 326-2546
▲ **EMP:** 5
SALES (est): 384.6K **Privately Held**
SIC: 3498 Mfg Fabricated Pipe/Fittings

(G-7883)
PATDAN FUEL CORPORATION
7803 68th Rd (11379-2836)
PHONE.................................718 326-3668
EMP: 6
SALES (est): 743.4K **Privately Held**
SIC: 2869 Fuels

(G-7884)
SILVER BELL BAKING CO
6406 Admiral Ave (11379-1614)
PHONE.................................718 335-9539
Dalia Radziunas, *Owner*
EMP: 8
SQ FT: 6,000
SALES (est): 361.4K **Privately Held**
SIC: 2051 Bread, cake & related products

(G-7885)
WETHERALL CONTRACTING NY INC
8312 Penelope Ave Ste 101 (11379-2321)
PHONE..................................718 894-7011
Bryan Wetherall, *President*
EMP: 5
SALES (est): 695.2K **Privately Held**
SIC: 2323 Men's & boys' neckwear

Middleburgh
Schoharie County

(G-7886)
DR REDDYS LABORATORIES NY INC
1974 State Route 145 (12122-5315)
PHONE..................................518 827-7702
Alok Sonig, *President*
Swaninathan Chandrasekaran, *Corp Secy*
Sunil Kumar Chebrolu, *Finance*
Gv Prasad, *Director*
Satish Reddy, *Director*
EMP: 30
SALES (est): 3MM **Privately Held**
SIC: 2834 Pharmaceutical preparations
HQ: Dr. Reddy's Laboratories, Inc.
    107 College Rd E Ste 100
    Princeton NJ 08540

Middleport
Niagara County

(G-7887)
BIRCH MACHINE & TOOL INC
80 Telegraph Rd (14105-9638)
PHONE..................................716 735-9802
Jerry Stadelman, *President*
Mary Stadelman, *Vice Pres*
EMP: 7
SQ FT: 1,500
SALES (est): 605K **Privately Held**
SIC: 3599 Machine shop, jobbing & repair

(G-7888)
FMC CORPORATION
Also Called: F M C Aricultural Chem Group
100 Niagara St (14105-1398)
PHONE..................................716 735-3761
Stewart Throop, *Plant Mgr*
Jessica Morton, *Sales Mgr*
Roger L Krough, *Branch Mgr*
EMP: 50
SALES (corp-wide): 4.7B **Publicly Held**
WEB: www.fmc.com
SIC: 2879 2819 Agricultural chemicals; industrial inorganic chemicals
PA: Fmc Corporation
    2929 Walnut St
    Philadelphia PA 19104
    215 299-6000

(G-7889)
PERFORMANCE MFG INC
80 Telegraph Rd (14105-9638)
PHONE..................................716 735-3500
Jody P Herriven, *President*
Tim Worth, *Vice Pres*
EMP: 15
SALES (est): 2.2MM **Privately Held**
WEB: www.pmikartparts.com
SIC: 3599 Machine shop, jobbing & repair

(G-7890)
SIGMAMOTOR INC
3 N Main St (14105-1005)
P.O. Box 298 (14105-0298)
PHONE..................................716 735-3115
Donald Heschke, *President*
Shari Heschke, *Corp Secy*
EMP: 22 EST: 1951
SQ FT: 6,500
SALES: 6MM **Privately Held**
SIC: 3599 3494 Machine shop, jobbing & repair; valves & pipe fittings

Middletown
Orange County

(G-7891)
209 DISCOUNT OIL
10 Sands Station Rd (10940-4415)
PHONE..................................845 386-2090
Steve Cortese, *Principal*
EMP: 20
SALES (est): 1.6MM **Privately Held**
SIC: 2911 Oils, fuel

(G-7892)
ADVANCED ENTERPRISES INC
Also Called: Wonder Products
366 Highland Ave Ext (10940-4454)
PHONE..................................845 342-1009
Eugene Polanish, *President*
Christian Al, *Principal*
▲ EMP: 10
SQ FT: 100
SALES (est): 1.5MM **Privately Held**
SIC: 3842 Cotton & cotton applicators

(G-7893)
ARCHITECTURAL ENHANCEMENTS INC
135 Crotty Rd (10941-4070)
P.O. Box 4680 (10941-8680)
PHONE..................................845 343-9663
Philip Cohen, *President*
Chaim Cohen, *Exec VP*
EMP: 10 EST: 1962
SQ FT: 31,000
SALES (est): 1.5MM **Privately Held**
SIC: 2431 Millwork

(G-7894)
BALL METAL BEVERAGE CONT CORP
Also Called: Ball Metal Beverage Cont Div
95 Ballard Rd (10941-3013)
PHONE..................................845 692-3800
Terree Angerame, *Principal*
Robert Chapin, *Principal*
Noreen Dellay, *Principal*
Mike Molarski, *Warehouse Mgr*
Michael Malarski, *Buyer*
EMP: 175
SALES (corp-wide): 11.6B **Publicly Held**
SIC: 3411 Aluminum cans
HQ: Ball Metal Beverage Container Corp.
    9300 W 108th Cir
    Westminster CO 80021

(G-7895)
BRAGA WOODWORKS
19 Montgomery St (10940-5115)
PHONE..................................845 342-4636
Leo Braga, *Owner*
EMP: 5
SALES (est): 410.6K **Privately Held**
SIC: 2431 Millwork

(G-7896)
BRAIDED OAK SPIRITS LLC
12 Roberts St (10940-5007)
PHONE..................................845 381-1525
Peter J Matos,
Peter Matos,
EMP: 17 EST: 2012
SALES: 5.2MM **Privately Held**
SIC: 2085 Distilled & blended liquors

(G-7897)
BUILDERS FIRSTSOURCE INC
30 Golf Links Rd (10940-2624)
PHONE..................................860 528-2293
Mark Lefsyk, *General Mgr*
EMP: 45
SALES (corp-wide): 7.7B **Publicly Held**
SIC: 2421 Building & structural materials, wood
PA: Builders Firstsource, Inc.
    2001 Bryan St Ste 1600
    Dallas TX 75201
    214 880-3500

(G-7898)
CHROMALLOY GAS TURBINE LLC
Also Called: Chromalloy Middletown
105 Tower Dr (10941-2034)
PHONE..................................845 692-8912
Matt Wilson, *Branch Mgr*
EMP: 28
SALES (corp-wide): 2.4B **Publicly Held**
WEB: www.chromalloysatx.com
SIC: 3479 3724 Painting, coating & hot dipping; aircraft engines & engine parts
HQ: Chromalloy Gas Turbine Llc
    3999 Rca Blvd
    Palm Beach Gardens FL 33410
    561 935-3571

(G-7899)
CLASSIC HOSIERY INC
33 Mulberry St Ste 4 (10940-6359)
PHONE..................................845 342-6661
Tuvia Brach, *President*
▲ EMP: 35 EST: 1980
SQ FT: 18,000
SALES (est): 4.8MM **Privately Held**
SIC: 2251 Panty hose

(G-7900)
COMMERCIAL COMMUNICATIONS LLC
Also Called: Msdivisions
14 Montgomery St (10940-5116)
PHONE..................................845 343-9078
Steven Rosenblatt, *President*
EMP: 6
SALES (est): 881.8K **Privately Held**
WEB: www.msdspring.com
SIC: 3495 Wire springs

(G-7901)
COUNTY DRAPERIES INC
64 Genung St (10940-5317)
PHONE..................................845 342-9009
Sara Markowitz, *CEO*
Carl Markowitz, *President*
David Markowitz, *Vice Pres*
Maka Medina, *Purchasing*
Chuck Greenspan, *Natl Sales Mgr*
◆ EMP: 45
SQ FT: 50,000
SALES (est): 9.5MM **Privately Held**
WEB: www.drape.com
SIC: 2391 2392 Draperies, plastic & textile: from purchased materials; bedspreads & bed sets: made from purchased materials

(G-7902)
CROWN CORK & SEAL USA INC
21 Industrial Pl (10940)
PHONE..................................845 343-9586
EMP: 118
SALES (corp-wide): 11.1B **Publicly Held**
WEB: www.crowncork.com
SIC: 3411 Metal cans
HQ: Crown Cork & Seal Usa, Inc.
    770 Township Line Rd # 100
    Yardley PA 19067
    215 698-5100

(G-7903)
D & W DESIGN INC
62 Industrial Pl (10940-3609)
PHONE..................................845 343-3366
Mariam Weiss, *President*
David Weiss, *Vice Pres*
Simon Kraus, *Manager*
Mike Toplamos, *Admin Sec*
▲ EMP: 29
SQ FT: 50,000
SALES: 3MM **Privately Held**
WEB: www.dustinwdesign.com
SIC: 2511 2514 5712 Wood household furniture; metal household furniture; furniture stores

(G-7904)
DELFORD INDUSTRIES INC
82 Washington St 84 (10940-4268)
P.O. Box 863 (10940-0863)
PHONE..................................845 342-3901
Robert L Reach Jr, *President*
Eric McCaffrey, *Opers Staff*
Tracy Hendricks, *Executive*
EMP: 80 EST: 1983
SQ FT: 55,000
SALES: 2MM **Privately Held**
WEB: www.delford-industries.com
SIC: 3061 Mechanical rubber goods

(G-7905)
E TETZ & SONS INC (PA)
130 Crotty Rd (10941-4059)
PHONE..................................845 692-4486
Edward Tetz Jr, *Ch of Bd*
Denise Tetz, *Admin Sec*
EMP: 55 EST: 1979
SQ FT: 3,000
SALES (est): 22.8MM **Privately Held**
WEB: www.etetz-sons.com
SIC: 3273 1442 Ready-mixed concrete; construction sand & gravel

(G-7906)
EAD CASES
43 Smith St (10940-3710)
P.O. Box 957 (10940-0957)
PHONE..................................845 343-2111
Julio Diaz, *President*
EMP: 10
SALES (est): 975.1K **Privately Held**
SIC: 3161 Cases, carrying

(G-7907)
EQUILIBRIUM BREWERY LLC
22 Henry St (10940-5709)
PHONE..................................201 245-0292
Ricardo Petroni, *CEO*
Peter Oates, *COO*
EMP: 5
SQ FT: 6,800
SALES (est): 700K **Privately Held**
SIC: 2082 Malt beverages

(G-7908)
FAIRBANKS MFG LLC
79 Industrial Pl (10940-3608)
PHONE..................................845 341-0002
Michael Ruppel, *CFO*
Zeke Alenick, *Mng Member*
▲ EMP: 145 EST: 2011
SQ FT: 100,000
SALES (est): 34.5MM **Privately Held**
SIC: 2064 Candy & other confectionery products

(G-7909)
FUEL DATA SYSTEMS INC
772 Greenville Tpke (10940-7125)
PHONE..................................800 447-7870
Steve Michalek, *President*
EMP: 6 EST: 1989
SALES (est): 457.1K **Privately Held**
WEB: www.fueldatasystems.com
SIC: 7372 7371 Prepackaged software; custom computer programming services

(G-7910)
GENPAK INDUSTRIES INC
26 Republic Plz (10940-6543)
PHONE..................................518 798-9511
Jim Riley, *President*
Edward Rider, *Vice Pres*
Jenny Wang, *Vice Pres*
Shajan Koshy, *VP Opers*
Trent Alford, *Plant Mgr*
EMP: 50
SALES (est): 10.3MM
SALES (corp-wide): 19B **Privately Held**
SIC: 2657 Food containers, folding: made from purchased material
HQ: Great Pacific Enterprises (U.S.) Inc.
    10601 Westlake Dr
    Charlotte NC 28273
    980 256-7729

(G-7911)
GENPAK LLC
Republic Plz (10940)
PHONE..................................845 343-7971
Betty Hager, *Opers-Prdtn-Mfg*
EMP: 200
SQ FT: 150,000
SALES (corp-wide): 19B **Privately Held**
WEB: www.genpak.com
SIC: 3089 5046 Plastic processing; commercial cooking & food service equipment
HQ: Genpak Llc
    10601 Westlake Dr
    Charlotte NC 28273
    980 256-7729

▲ = Import ▼=Export
◆ =Import/Export

GEOGRAPHIC

(G-7912)
GERITREX LLC
40 Commercial Ave (10941-1444)
PHONE.....................................914 668-4003
Boyd Relac, *President*
Tim Sawyer, *Chairman*
John Francis, *Exec VP*
David Gershen, *CFO*
▲ EMP: 40
SQ FT: 47,500
SALES (est): 14.8MM **Privately Held**
WEB: www.geritrex.com
SIC: 2834 Pharmaceutical preparations

(G-7913)
GOLUB CORPORATION
Also Called: Price Chopper Pharmacy
511 Schutt Road Ext (10940-2569)
PHONE.....................................845 344-0327
EMP: 21
SALES (corp-wide): 3.6B **Privately Held**
SIC: 3751 Motorcycles & related parts
PA: The Golub Corporation
461 Nott St
Schenectady NY 12308
518 355-5000

(G-7914)
HONEYWELL INTERNATIONAL INC
13 Bedford Ave (10940-6401)
PHONE.....................................845 342-4400
EMP: 673
SALES (corp-wide): 41.8B **Publicly Held**
SIC: 3724 Aircraft engines & engine parts
PA: Honeywell International Inc.
300 S Tryon St
Charlotte NC 28202
973 455-2000

(G-7915)
LOCAL MEDIA GROUP INC
Orange County Publications
40 Mulberry St (10940-6302)
P.O. Box 2046 (10940-0558)
PHONE.....................................845 341-1100
Marc Davis, *Editor*
Erik Gliedman, *Editor*
Beth Kalet, *Editor*
Eric Stutz, *Editor*
Gregory Taylor, *Vice Pres*
EMP: 290
SALES (corp-wide): 1.5B **Privately Held**
WEB: www.ottaway.com
SIC: 2711 Newspapers: publishing only, not printed on site
HQ: Local Media Group, Inc.
40 Mulberry St
Middletown NY 10940
845 341-1100

(G-7916)
LOCAL MEDIA GROUP INC (DH)
40 Mulberry St (10940-6302)
P.O. Box 580 (10940-0580)
PHONE.....................................845 341-1100
John Wilcox, *President*
Patrick Purcell, *Chairman*
William T Kennedy, *COO*
Kurt Lozier, *Senior VP*
Patricia Gatto, *Vice Pres*
EMP: 50 EST: 1936
SQ FT: 10,000
SALES (est): 527.2MM **Privately Held**
WEB: www.ottaway.com
SIC: 2711 7313 Newspapers: publishing only, not printed on site; newspaper advertising representative
HQ: Local Media Group Holdings, Llc
175 Sullys Trl Ste 300
Pittsford NY 14534
585 598-0030

(G-7917)
LOCAL MEDIA GROUP INC
Also Called: Times Herald-Record
60 Brookline Ave (10940)
PHONE.....................................845 341-1100
Donna Kessler, *Editor*
Andy Mark, *Branch Mgr*
EMP: 68
SALES (corp-wide): 1.5B **Privately Held**
WEB: www.ottaway.com
SIC: 2711 Commercial printing & newspaper publishing combined

HQ: Local Media Group, Inc.
40 Mulberry St
Middletown NY 10940
845 341-1100

(G-7918)
MANDARIN SOY SAUCE INC
Also Called: Wan Ja Shan
4 Sands Station Rd (10940-4415)
PHONE.....................................845 343-1505
Michael Wu, *Ch of Bd*
▲ EMP: 25 EST: 1974
SQ FT: 85,000
SALES (est): 4.1MM **Privately Held**
WEB: www.wanjashan.com
SIC: 2035 5149 Seasonings & sauces, except tomato & dry; soy sauce; groceries & related products
PA: Wan Ja Shan Brewery Co., Ltd.
5f-6, 9, Dehui St.,
Taipei City TAP 10461

(G-7919)
MEDLINE INDUSTRIES INC
3301 Route 6 (10940-6992)
PHONE.....................................845 344-3301
Bob Catalano, *District Mgr*
Tom Schroeder, *Vice Pres*
Kerry Fischer, *Opers Mgr*
Andrew Pease, *Engineer*
Jim Digiacomo, *VP Sales*
EMP: 276
SALES (corp-wide): 5.7B **Privately Held**
SIC: 3842 3841 2326 2392 Surgical appliances & supplies; surgical & medical instruments; men's & boys' work clothing; household furnishings; surgical fabrics, cotton; scrub cloths; surgical equipment & supplies; hospital equipment & supplies; hospital furniture
PA: Medline Industries, Inc.
3 Lakes Dr
Northfield IL 60093
847 949-5500

(G-7920)
MIDDLETOWN PRESS (PA)
20 W Main St 26 (10940-5716)
PHONE.....................................845 343-1895
Jo Cover, *Owner*
EMP: 5
SQ FT: 2,800
SALES (est): 401.6K **Privately Held**
WEB: www.mtprintandpromote.com
SIC: 2752 7311 7336 5199 Commercial printing, offset; advertising agencies; graphic arts & related design; advertising specialties; commercial printing

(G-7921)
MIX N MAC LLC
280 Route 211 E (10940-3109)
PHONE.....................................845 381-5536
EMP: 5 EST: 2011
SALES (est): 413.6K **Privately Held**
SIC: 3273 Ready-mixed concrete

(G-7922)
MONROE CABLE COMPANY INC
14 Commercial Ave (10941-1444)
PHONE.....................................845 692-2800
Isaac Wieder, *President*
Michael Mayfield, *Vice Pres*
▲ EMP: 104 EST: 1978
SQ FT: 95,000
SALES (est): 39.3MM **Privately Held**
SIC: 3357 Shipboard cable, nonferrous; coaxial cable, nonferrous

(G-7923)
NEW DYNAMICS CORPORATION
15 Fortune Rd W (10941-1625)
PHONE.....................................845 692-0022
James Destefano, *President*
Walter Pawlowski, *Vice Pres*
EMP: 20
SQ FT: 35,000
SALES: 5MM **Privately Held**
WEB: www.newdynamics.net
SIC: 3842 5963 7349 Ear plugs; food services, direct sales; janitorial service, contract basis

(G-7924)
NEW YORK CUTTING & GUMMING CO
265 Ballard Rd (10941-3034)
PHONE.....................................212 563-4146
Jack Siegel, *President*
Richard Deteresa, *Principal*
Robert Siegel, *Vice Pres*
EMP: 45 EST: 1914
SQ FT: 44,000
SALES (est): 4.2MM **Privately Held**
SIC: 3089 2295 2675 2672 Laminating of plastic; laminating of fabrics; die-cut paper & board; coated & laminated paper

(G-7925)
OTTAWAY NEWSPAPERS INC
40 Mulberry St (10940-6302)
PHONE.....................................845 343-2181
Zeke Fleet, *Publisher*
Joe Vanderhoof, *Principal*
Catherine Paffenroth, *Vice Pres*
Kelly Walsh, *Accounts Exec*
Ken Ficara, *Sales Staff*
EMP: 9 EST: 2010
SALES (est): 597.5K **Privately Held**
SIC: 2711 Newspapers, publishing & printing

(G-7926)
PILLER POWER SYSTEMS INC (DH)
45 Wes Warren Dr (10941-1772)
PHONE.....................................845 695-6658
Dean Richards, *President*
Mark Nuelle, *Vice Pres*
Charles Daling, *Project Mgr*
Kathleen Wiley, *Purch Mgr*
Eric Forman, *Engineer*
▲ EMP: 40
SQ FT: 20,000
SALES: 65MM
SALES (corp-wide): 971.2MM **Privately Held**
WEB: www.piller.com
SIC: 3699 3612 Electrical equipment & supplies; transformers, except electric
HQ: Piller Group Gmbh
Abgunst 24
Osterode Am Harz 37520
552 231-10

(G-7927)
PRESIDENT CONT GROUP II LLC
Also Called: Manufacturing Facility
290 Ballard Rd (10941-3035)
PHONE.....................................845 516-1600
Brian Sizer, *Prdtn Mgr*
Richard Goldberg, *Mng Member*
EMP: 28
SALES (est): 7.8MM
SALES (corp-wide): 203.8MM **Privately Held**
SIC: 2653 Boxes, corrugated: made from purchased materials; sheets, corrugated: made from purchased materials; display items, corrugated: made from purchased materials
PA: President Container Group Ii, Llc
200 W Commercial Ave
Moonachie NJ 07074
201 933-7500

(G-7928)
PRINCETON UPHOLSTERY CO INC (PA)
Also Called: Bright Chair Co
51 Railroad Ave (10940-5117)
P.O. Box 269 (10940-0269)
PHONE.....................................845 343-2196
Stan Gottlieb, *Ch of Bd*
Roxanne Beacon, *Human Res Mgr*
Jody Gottlieb, *Admin Sec*
◆ EMP: 100
SQ FT: 100,000
SALES (est): 12.6MM **Privately Held**
WEB: www.brightchair.com
SIC: 2521 2512 Wood office furniture; upholstered household furniture

(G-7929)
RIJ PHARMACEUTICAL CORPORATION
40 Commercial Ave (10941-1444)
PHONE.....................................845 692-5799

Hassan Zaidi, *CEO*
Brij Gupta, *President*
EMP: 20
SQ FT: 52,000
SALES (est): 5.3MM **Privately Held**
WEB: www.rijpharm.com
SIC: 2834 Pharmaceutical preparations

(G-7930)
RIMS LIKE NEW INC
507 Union School Rd (10941-5018)
PHONE.....................................845 537-0396
Manuel P Heredia Jr, *Owner*
EMP: 10
SALES (est): 630K **Privately Held**
SIC: 3479 Painting of metal products

(G-7931)
S R & R INDUSTRIES INC
45 Enterprise Pl (10941-2043)
PHONE.....................................845 692-8329
Paul Rosanelli, *President*
EMP: 6
SQ FT: 10,000
SALES: 450K **Privately Held**
SIC: 3531 3462 3599 Rollers, sheepsfoot & vibratory; gears, forged steel; machine shop, jobbing & repair

(G-7932)
STAFFORD LABS ORTHOTICS/PROSTH
189 Monhagen Ave (10940-6020)
P.O. Box 1004, Goshen (10924-8004)
PHONE.....................................845 692-5227
Kimberly Thompson, *President*
EMP: 15
SALES (est): 1.1MM **Privately Held**
WEB: www.staffordlabsoandp.com
SIC: 3842 Limbs, artificial

(G-7933)
STERLING MOLDED PRODUCTS INC
9-17 Oliver Ave (10940-6095)
PHONE.....................................845 344-4546
Stephen Crescimanno, *Ch of Bd*
▲ EMP: 40
SALES (est): 7.2MM **Privately Held**
SIC: 3089 Injection molded finished plastic products

(G-7934)
SURVING STUDIOS
17 Millsburg Rd (10940-8497)
PHONE.....................................845 355-1430
Natalie Surving, *Owner*
EMP: 10
SALES (est): 1.2MM **Privately Held**
SIC: 3469 8999 Tile, floor or wall: stamped metal; sculptor's studio

(G-7935)
TPI INDUSTRIES LLC (HQ)
265 Ballard Rd (10941-3034)
PHONE.....................................845 692-2820
John Bowe, *President*
▲ EMP: 42 EST: 1978
SQ FT: 50,000
SALES (est): 82.1MM
SALES (corp-wide): 185.1MM **Privately Held**
WEB: www.darlexx.com
SIC: 2295 Laminating of fabrics
PA: Shawmut Llc
208 Manley St
West Bridgewater MA 02379
508 588-3300

(G-7936)
TRIAD PRINTING INC
Also Called: Chester Printing Service
7 Prospect St (10940-4809)
PHONE.....................................845 343-2722
Joseph Stewart, *President*
Ralph Carr, *Corp Secy*
EMP: 5
SALES (est): 861.6K **Privately Held**
SIC: 2752 Commercial printing, offset

(G-7937)
WANJASHAN INTERNATIONAL LLC
4 Sands Station Rd (10940-4415)
PHONE.....................................845 343-1505

Michael Wu, *President*
◆ **EMP:** 17
SALES (est): 2.9MM **Privately Held**
SIC: 2035 Soy sauce

(G-7938)
**WATEC AMERICA
CORPORATION**
720 Route 17m Ste 4 (10940-4350)
PHONE....................702 434-6111
Chia L Liu, *President*
EMP: 50
SALES (est): 4.3MM **Privately Held**
SIC: 3861 Cameras & related equipment

(G-7939)
ZENITH AUTOPARTS CORP
20 Industrial Pl (10940-3609)
P.O. Box 906 (10940-0906)
PHONE....................845 344-1382
Moses Goldstein, *President*
Joel Goldstein, *Vice Pres*
▲ **EMP:** 25
SQ FT: 38,000
SALES: 5MM **Privately Held**
SIC: 3694 Ignition systems, high frequency

Middleville
Herkimer County

(G-7940)
E J WILLIS COMPANY INC
37 N Main St (13406)
P.O. Box 437 (13406-0410)
PHONE....................315 891-7602
Evelyn Reile, *President*
EMP: 15
SQ FT: 75,000
SALES (est): 1.1MM **Privately Held**
SIC: 3599 Machine shop, jobbing & repair

Millbrook
Dutchess County

(G-7941)
ALICIA ADAMS ALPACA INC
3262 Franklin Ave (12545-5918)
P.O. Box 1455 (12545-1455)
PHONE....................845 868-3366
Alicaia Adams, *Ch of Bd*
Daniel Adams, *Principal*
▲ **EMP:** 8
SALES (est): 700.2K **Privately Held**
SIC: 2231 2337 Alpacas, mohair: woven;
women's & misses' capes & jackets

(G-7942)
GORDON S ANDERSON MFG CO
215 N Mabbettsville Rd (12545-5358)
P.O. Box 1459 (12545-1459)
PHONE....................845 677-3304
Stewart Anderson, *President*
Christine Horihan, *Vice Pres*
EMP: 7 **EST:** 1946
SQ FT: 7,000
SALES (est): 505.6K **Privately Held**
SIC: 3648 3559 Lighting equipment; phar-
maceutical machinery

(G-7943)
**MICRO SYSTEMS SPECIALISTS
INC**
Also Called: Mssi
3280 Franklin Ave Fl 2 (12545-5975)
P.O. Box 347 (12545-0347)
PHONE....................845 677-6150
Catherine Culkin, *President*
Dawn Roeller, *Vice Pres*
Eileen Sunderland, *Treasurer*
Judy Bruning, *Admin Sec*
EMP: 5
SQ FT: 2,000
SALES (est): 431K **Privately Held**
SIC: 7372 Business oriented computer
software

(G-7944)
MILLBROOK WINERY INC
Also Called: Millbrook Vineyard
26 Wing Rd (12545-5017)
PHONE....................845 677-8383
John Dyson, *President*
John Graziano, *Vice Pres*
▲ **EMP:** 12
SQ FT: 960
SALES (est): 1.7MM **Privately Held**
WEB: www.millbrookwine.com
SIC: 2084 Wines

Miller Place
Suffolk County

(G-7945)
MILLER PLACE PRINTING INC
451 Route 25a Unit 11 (11764-2500)
PHONE....................631 473-1158
Leah G Casey, *Ch of Bd*
EMP: 9
SALES (est): 1.1MM **Privately Held**
SIC: 2759 2752 Laser printing; business
form & card printing, lithographic

Millerton
Dutchess County

(G-7946)
**ASSOCIATED LIGHTNING ROD
CO**
6020 Route 22 (12546-4537)
P.O. Box 529 (12546-0529)
PHONE....................845 373-8309
Robert J Cooper, *President*
EMP: 18
SALES (est): 3.3MM **Privately Held**
WEB: www.alrci.com
SIC: 3643 Current-carrying wiring devices

(G-7947)
**HARNEY & SONS TEA CORP
(PA)**
5723 Route 22 (12546-4521)
PHONE....................518 789-2100
Michael Harney, *Vice Pres*
Naomi Santana, *Opers Mgr*
Elvira Cardenas, *Purchasing*
Jim Mester, *Controller*
Caitlin O'Brien, *Sales Dir*
◆ **EMP:** 150
SQ FT: 90,000
SALES (est): 44.8MM **Privately Held**
WEB: www.harney.com
SIC: 2099 5149 5499 Tea blending; tea;
tea

(G-7948)
ILLINOIS TOOL WORKS INC
5979 N Elm Ave (12546-4525)
PHONE....................860 435-2574
EMP: 89
SALES (corp-wide): 14.7B **Publicly Held**
SIC: 3089 Injection molding of plastics
PA: Illinois Tool Works Inc.
155 Harlem Ave
Glenview IL 60025
847 724-7500

(G-7949)
ITW DELTAR
5979 N Elm Ave (12546-4525)
PHONE....................860 435-2574
EMP: 6 **EST:** 2012
SALES (est): 673.6K **Privately Held**
SIC: 3089 Plastics products

Millport
Chemung County

(G-7950)
BLUE MANUFACTURING CO INC
3852 Watkins Rd (14864-9782)
PHONE....................607 796-2463
Teresa K Liston, *President*
Marlene Liston, *Vice Pres*

EMP: 6
SQ FT: 4,800
SALES (est): 733K **Privately Held**
WEB: www.bluemoonmanufacturing.com
SIC: 3599 Grease cups, metal

Milton
Ulster County

(G-7951)
**PRAGMATICS TECHNOLOGY
INC**
14 Old Indian Trl (12547-5114)
PHONE....................845 795-5071
Chris Mack, *President*
EMP: 8 **EST:** 2000
SQ FT: 700
SALES (est): 1.4MM **Privately Held**
WEB: www.pragmaticstech.com
SIC: 3825 Semiconductor test equipment

(G-7952)
SONO-TEK CORPORATION (PA)
2012 Route 9w Stop 3 (12547-5034)
PHONE....................845 795-2020
Christopher L Coccio, *Ch of Bd*
R Stephen Harshbarger, *President*
Brian Booth, *Regional Mgr*
Bennett D Bruntil, *Vice Pres*
Chris Cichetti, *Vice Pres*
▲ **EMP:** 64 **EST:** 1975
SQ FT: 50,000
SALES (est): 11.6MM **Publicly Held**
WEB: www.sprayfluxing.com
SIC: 3499 Nozzles, spray: aerosol, paint or
insecticide

(G-7953)
SUNDANCE INDUSTRIES INC
36 Greentree Ln (12547-5437)
PHONE....................845 795-5809
Alden Link, *President*
Carol Link, *Treasurer*
EMP: 5
SQ FT: 10,000
SALES: 1.5MM **Privately Held**
WEB: www.sundanceind.com
SIC: 3634 Juice extractors, electric

Mineola
Nassau County

(G-7954)
A & M STEEL STAMPS INC
55 Windsor Ave (11501-1923)
PHONE....................516 741-6223
Paul Argendorf, *President*
EMP: 5
SQ FT: 2,000
SALES: 500K **Privately Held**
SIC: 3953 Embossing seals & hand
stamps

(G-7955)
AERO TRADES MFG CORP
65 Jericho Tpke (11501-2991)
PHONE....................516 746-3360
Jeffrey E Love, *President*
John Niebuhr, *Vice Pres*
EMP: 33 **EST:** 1931
SQ FT: 60,000
SALES (est): 6.6MM **Privately Held**
WEB: www.aerotrades.com
SIC: 3728 3444 Aircraft assemblies, sub-
assemblies & parts; sheet metalwork

(G-7956)
AERODUCT INC
134 Herricks Rd (11501-2205)
PHONE....................516 248-9550
Alvin Soffler, *President*
Blanche Soffler, *Corp Secy*
Glen Soffler, *Vice Pres*
Glenn Soffler, *Vice Pres*
EMP: 20 **EST:** 1967
SQ FT: 3,500
SALES (est): 2.6MM **Privately Held**
WEB: www.aeroduct.com
SIC: 3444 1711 Sheet metalwork; ventila-
tion & duct work contractor

(G-7957)
AGRECOLOR INC (PA)
400 Sagamore Ave (11501-1987)
PHONE....................516 741-8700
Anthony Greco, *President*
Doreen Greco, *Corp Secy*
EMP: 18
SQ FT: 15,000
SALES (est): 2.4MM **Privately Held**
WEB: www.agrecolor.com
SIC: 2752 2791 2789 Commercial print-
ing, offset; typesetting; bookbinding & re-
lated work

(G-7958)
**AQUIFER DRILLING & TESTING
INC (HQ)**
Also Called: A D T
75 E 2nd St (11501-3503)
PHONE....................516 616-6026
H Leonard Rexrode Jr, *Ch of Bd*
▲ **EMP:** 60
SQ FT: 22,000
SALES (est): 24MM **Privately Held**
SIC: 1382 7375 1711 Geological explo-
ration, oil & gas field; information retrieval
services; plumbing contractors
PA: Cascade Drilling, L.P.
9406 Massillon Rd
Dundee OH 44624
330 359-0079

(G-7959)
ARISTA INNOVATIONS INC
Also Called: Arista Printing
131 Liberty Ave (11501-3510)
PHONE....................516 746-2262
Edward Sikorski, *President*
Eleanor Sikorski, *Corp Secy*
Leonard Sikorski, *Vice Pres*
Raymond Sikorski, *Vice Pres*
EMP: 30
SQ FT: 25,000
SALES (est): 3.8MM **Privately Held**
WEB: www.aristaprinters.com
SIC: 2752 2791 2789 2759 Commercial
printing, offset; typesetting; bookbinding &
related work; commercial printing

(G-7960)
BEARDSLEE REALTY
290 E Jericho Tpke (11501-2197)
PHONE....................516 747-5557
Kan McDowbll, *Manager*
EMP: 6
SALES (corp-wide): 757.3K **Privately
Held**
SIC: 2326 6519 Industrial garments,
men's & boys'; real property lessors
PA: Beardslee Realty
27 To 22 Jackson Ave
Long Island City NY 11101
718 784-4100

(G-7961)
BIMBO BAKERIES USA INC
12 E Jericho Tpke (11501-3141)
PHONE....................516 877-2850
EMP: 25
SALES (corp-wide): 13.7B **Privately Held**
SIC: 2051 Mfg Bread/Related Products
HQ: Bimbo Bakeries Usa, Inc
255 Business Center Dr # 200
Horsham PA 19044
215 347-5500

(G-7962)
BLC TEXTILES INC
330 Old Country Rd # 201 (11501-4187)
PHONE....................844 500-7900
Mark Lichter, *CEO*
Caroline Martin, *Sales Staff*
EMP: 26
SALES: 2.5MM **Privately Held**
SIC: 2299 Towels & towelings, linen &
linen-and-cotton mixtures

(G-7963)
**CANVAS PRODUCTS COMPANY
INC**
234 Herricks Rd (11501-2208)
PHONE....................516 742-1058
Edwin E Youngstrom, *President*
EMP: 10
SQ FT: 1,500

SALES (est): 1MM **Privately Held**
SIC: 2394 Awnings, fabric: made from purchased materials

(G-7964)
CAROL PERETZ
Also Called: Carol Peretz Workshop
49 Windsor Ave Ste 103 (11501-1933)
PHONE.....................516 248-6300
Carol Peretz, *Owner*
EMP: 18
SQ FT: 4,000
SALES (est): 1.1MM **Privately Held**
WEB: www.carolpretz.com
SIC: 2335 Dresses, paper: cut & sewn

(G-7965)
CAST-ALL CORPORATION
229 Liberty Ave (11501-3575)
P.O. Box 271 (11501-0271)
PHONE.....................516 741-4025
Jack Mandell, *President*
Rose Mandell, *Corp Secy*
Chaim Mandell, *Vice Pres*
Theodore Mandell, *Vice Pres*
EMP: 50 EST: 1962
SALES (est): 7.2MM **Privately Held**
WEB: www.cast-all.com
SIC: 3089 3364 3369 Injection molding of plastics; zinc & zinc-base alloy die-castings; manufactured hardware (general); nonferrous foundries

(G-7966)
COMPETICION MOWER REPAIR
75 Windsor Ave (11501-1983)
PHONE.....................516 280-6584
Christopher Sideris, *Owner*
EMP: 5
SALES (est): 495.7K **Privately Held**
SIC: 7692 Welding repair

(G-7967)
D & A SAND & GRAVEL INC
Also Called: D&A Trans Mix
335 Sagamore Ave Ste 1 (11501-1947)
PHONE.....................516 248-9444
Dominick Persico, *President*
Emilio Persico, *Vice Pres*
EMP: 7
SQ FT: 20,000
SALES (est): 2.1MM **Privately Held**
WEB: www.mix-with-us.com
SIC: 1442 Construction sand & gravel

(G-7968)
DCL FURNITURE MANUFACTURING
96 Windsor Ave (11501-1922)
PHONE.....................516 248-2683
Domingos Lopes, *President*
Carlos Lopes, *Manager*
EMP: 20
SQ FT: 2,000
SALES (est): 2.2MM **Privately Held**
WEB: www.dclfurniture.com
SIC: 2511 2522 2521 Wood household furniture; office furniture, except wood; wood office furniture

(G-7969)
DONMAR PRINTING CO
90 2nd St Ste 2 (11501-3060)
PHONE.....................516 280-2239
Sanford Scharf, *President*
EMP: 10
SALES (est): 251.8K **Privately Held**
SIC: 2752 Commercial printing, offset

(G-7970)
ELIAS ARTMETAL INC
70 E 2nd St (11501-3505)
P.O. Box 1872 (11501-0909)
PHONE.....................516 873-7501
Constantine Elias, *President*
Ruth Elias, *Vice Pres*
EMP: 19
SQ FT: 9,000
SALES: 1MM **Privately Held**
WEB: www.eliasartmetal.com
SIC: 3499 Picture frames, metal; novelties & specialties, metal

(G-7971)
ENVIRONMENTAL TEMP SYSTEMS LLC
Also Called: Ets
111 Roosevelt Ave Ste C (11501-3056)
P.O. Box 701 (11501-0701)
PHONE.....................516 640-5818
Wayman Lee, *Mng Member*
Kwon Chan,
Joseph D'Alessio,
EMP: 5
SALES: 1.2MM **Privately Held**
SIC: 3585 Refrigeration & heating equipment

(G-7972)
EPS IRON WORKS INC
38 Windsor Ave Ste 101 (11501-1932)
PHONE.....................516 294-5840
Edward Strocchia, *President*
Philip Strocchia, *Vice Pres*
EMP: 8
SQ FT: 2,000
SALES (est): 1.7MM **Privately Held**
SIC: 3441 Fabricated structural metal

(G-7973)
EXTREME AUTO ACCESSORIES CORP (PA)
Also Called: Rennen International
235 Liberty Ave (11501-3513)
PHONE.....................718 978-6722
Takang Lee, *Ch of Bd*
Weizrung Lee, *COO*
Rich Sha, *Vice Pres*
▲ EMP: 15
SQ FT: 15,000
SALES (est): 4.1MM **Privately Held**
WEB: www.renneninternational.com
SIC: 3714 5013 Wheel rims, motor vehicle; automotive supplies

(G-7974)
F J REMEY CO INC
121 Willis Ave (11501-2612)
P.O. Box 589 (11501-0589)
PHONE.....................516 741-5112
Richard A Haas, *President*
EMP: 40
SQ FT: 20,000
SALES (est): 5.7MM **Privately Held**
WEB: www.fjremey.com
SIC: 2752 5112 Commercial printing, offset; stationery

(G-7975)
FATWIRE CORPORATION
Also Called: Oracle
330 Old Country Rd # 303 (11501-4143)
PHONE.....................516 247-4500
Dorian Daley, *CEO*
Safra A Catz, *President*
Mark V Hurd, *President*
Mark Overton, *President*
Jeffrey O Henley, *Chairman*
EMP: 29
SQ FT: 17,400
SALES (est): 9.6MM
SALES (corp-wide): 39.5B **Publicly Held**
WEB: www.fatwire.com
SIC: 7372 Prepackaged software
PA: Oracle Corporation
   500 Oracle Pkwy
   Redwood City CA 94065
   650 506-7000

(G-7976)
GENERAL LED CORP
206 E Jericho Tpke (11501-2034)
PHONE.....................516 280-2854
George Geffen, *President*
EMP: 6
SALES (est): 251.5K **Privately Held**
SIC: 3648 Lighting equipment

(G-7977)
GEOTECHNICAL DRILLING INC
Also Called: Environmental Closures
75 E 2nd St (11501-3503)
PHONE.....................516 616-6055
H L Rexrode Jr, *Ch of Bd*
William Poupis, *Vice Pres*
EMP: 85
SQ FT: 1,250

SALES (est): 3.2MM **Privately Held**
SIC: 1381 Drilling oil & gas wells

(G-7978)
H KLEIN & SONS INC
95 Searing Ave Ste 2 (11501-3046)
P.O. Box 349 (11501-0349)
PHONE.....................516 746-0163
Douglas Klein, *President*
Peter Klein, *Admin Sec*
EMP: 26 EST: 1902
SQ FT: 15,000
SALES (est): 4.7MM **Privately Held**
SIC: 3444 1761 Sheet metalwork; roofing contractor; sheet metalwork

(G-7979)
H RINDUSTRIES
393 Jericho Tpke (11501-1200)
PHONE.....................516 487-3825
EMP: 5 EST: 2012
SALES (est): 324K **Privately Held**
SIC: 3088 Plastics plumbing fixtures

(G-7980)
HYGRADE FUEL INC
260 Columbus Pkwy (11501-3137)
PHONE.....................516 741-0723
R Grieco, *Principal*
EMP: 5
SALES (est): 490.2K **Privately Held**
SIC: 2911 Oils, fuel

(G-7981)
ISLAND MARKETING CORP
95 Searing Ave Ste 2 (11501-3046)
PHONE.....................516 739-0500
Frank Scarangella, *President*
EMP: 5
SALES: 400K **Privately Held**
SIC: 2879 8742 Insecticides, agricultural or household; sales (including sales management) consultant

(G-7982)
ISLAND ORDNANCE SYSTEMS LLC
267 E Jericho Tpke Ste 2 (11501-2100)
PHONE.....................516 746-2100
Amnon Parizat, *President*
Frank Anselmo, *Business Mgr*
Linda Aguilo, *CFO*
Anne Parizat, *Treasurer*
Laurie Quigley, *Executive*
▼ EMP: 13
SQ FT: 3,000
SALES (est): 2.6MM **Privately Held**
WEB: www.islandgroup.com
SIC: 3489 5099 5169 Ordnance & accessories; firearms & ammunition, except sporting; explosives

(G-7983)
ISLAND PYROCHEMICAL INDS CORP (PA)
267 E Jericho Tpke Ste 2 (11501-2100)
PHONE.....................516 746-2100
Amnon Parizat, *President*
Robert Massey, *Business Mgr*
Claudia Orjuela, *Vice Pres*
Anne Parizat, *Vice Pres*
Nathalie Parizat, *Manager*
◆ EMP: 215 EST: 1982
SQ FT: 6,000
SALES (est): 37.9MM **Privately Held**
WEB: www.worldvoi.com
SIC: 3081 2899 5169 Film base, cellulose acetate or nitrocellulose plastic; pyrotechnic ammunition: flares, signals, rockets, etc.; chemicals & allied products

(G-7984)
KHK USA INC
259 Elm Pl Ste 2 (11501-2960)
PHONE.....................516 248-3850
Toshiharu Kohara, *President*
Naoji Kohara, *Corp Secy*
Helen Kho, *Med Doctor*
Jenny Kho, *Representative*
EMP: 5 EST: 2015
SQ FT: 5,000
SALES: 1MM **Privately Held**
SIC: 3566 5084 5085 Gears, power transmission, except automotive; industrial machinery & equipment; gears

(G-7985)
LI COMMUNITY NEWSPAPERS INC
132 E 2nd St (11501-3533)
PHONE.....................516 747-8282
Angela Anton, *Publisher*
EMP: 5
SALES (est): 260.6K **Privately Held**
SIC: 2711 Commercial printing & newspaper publishing combined; newspapers, publishing & printing

(G-7986)
LIBERTY PIPE INCORPORATED
128 Liberty Ave (11501-3509)
PHONE.....................516 747-2472
John Kritis, *President*
EMP: 5
SALES (est): 516.5K **Privately Held**
SIC: 3317 Steel pipe & tubes

(G-7987)
LONG ISLAND CMNTY NWSPPERS INC (PA)
Also Called: Anton Community Newspapers
132 E 2nd St (11501-3522)
PHONE.....................516 482-4490
Angela Anton, *President*
EMP: 99
SALES (est): 7.4MM **Privately Held**
WEB: www.antonnews.com
SIC: 2711 7313 Commercial printing & newspaper publishing combined; newspaper advertising representative

(G-7988)
MAXIM HYGIENE PRODUCTS INC (PA)
Also Called: Organic Peak
121 E Jericho Tpke (11501-2031)
PHONE.....................516 621-3323
Kenneth Alvandi, *Ch of Bd*
Diana Hernandez, *Vice Pres*
▲ EMP: 16
SALES (est): 1.7MM **Privately Held**
SIC: 2676 Feminine hygiene paper products

(G-7989)
MEDIPOINT INC
Also Called: Medipoint International,
72 E 2nd St (11501-3591)
PHONE.....................516 294-8822
Peter Gollobin, *President*
EMP: 12
SQ FT: 7,200
SALES (est): 1.7MM **Privately Held**
SIC: 3841 Surgical instruments & apparatus; medical instruments & equipment, blood & bone work

(G-7990)
NASSAU CHROMIUM PLATING CO INC
122 2nd St (11501-3054)
PHONE.....................516 746-6666
George Waring, *President*
Shirley Waring, *Corp Secy*
EMP: 45 EST: 1929
SQ FT: 10,000
SALES (est): 4.6MM **Privately Held**
WEB: www.nassaufdrant.com
SIC: 3471 Plating of metals or formed products

(G-7991)
NORTH SHORE FARMS TWO LTD
330 E Jericho Tpke (11501-2111)
PHONE.....................516 280-6880
Jose Juan, *Store Mgr*
EMP: 8
SALES (est): 325.1K **Privately Held**
SIC: 2099 Food preparations

(G-7992)
NORTHEAST HARDWARE SPECIALTIES
393 Jericho Tpke Ste 103 (11501-1213)
PHONE.....................516 487-6868
Wayne A Reed Jr, *Owner*
EMP: 10
SALES: 174.6K **Privately Held**
SIC: 3599 Industrial machinery

(G-7993)
NORWOOD SCREW MACHINE PARTS
200 E 2nd St Ste 2 (11501-3519)
PHONE...................................516 481-6644
Gary Prchal, *President*
EMP: 10
SQ FT: 10,000
SALES: 1.5MM **Privately Held**
WEB: www.norwoodscrewmachine.com
SIC: 3451 Screw machine products

(G-7994)
NOVITA FABRICS FURNISHING CORP
207 Elm Pl Ste 2 (11501-2948)
PHONE...................................516 299-4500
David Rahimi, *President*
EMP: 12 EST: 2014
SQ FT: 12,000
SALES: 2.5MM **Privately Held**
SIC: 2299 Linen fabrics

(G-7995)
RA NEWHOUSE INC (PA)
110 Liberty Ave (11501-3509)
P.O. Box 791 (11501-0791)
PHONE...................................516 248-6670
Richard A Newhouse Jr, *President*
EMP: 60
SQ FT: 20,000
SALES (est): 7.5MM **Privately Held**
SIC: 2389 Uniforms & vestments; academic vestments (caps & gowns)

(G-7996)
RAYTECH CORP ASBESTOS PERSONAL
190 Willis Ave (11501-2672)
PHONE...................................516 747-0300
Richard A Lippe, *Mng Trustee*
Richard Lippe, *Mng Trustee*
EMP: 1710
SALES (est): 98.9MM **Privately Held**
SIC: 3499 Friction material, made from powdered metal

(G-7997)
REIS D FURNITURE MFG
327 Sagamore Ave Ste 2 (11501-1944)
PHONE...................................516 248-5676
Domingos Reis, *President*
Candida C Reis, *Corp Secy*
▼ EMP: 45
SQ FT: 15,000
SALES (est): 6.3MM **Privately Held**
WEB: www.mineolachamber.com
SIC: 2511 Wood household furniture

(G-7998)
RUBBER STAMPS INC
174 Herricks Rd (11501-2206)
PHONE...................................212 675-1180
Robert A Kowalsky, *President*
Abel Kowalsky, *Vice Pres*
Dorothy Kowalsky, *Admin Sec*
EMP: 25
SALES (est): 3MM **Privately Held**
WEB: www.rubberstampsinc.com
SIC: 3953 3555 2791 3069 Postmark stamps, hand: rubber or metal; printing plates; typographic composition, for the printing trade; stationers' rubber sundries

(G-7999)
S & V CUSTOM FURNITURE MFG
75 Windsor Ave Unit E (11501-1935)
PHONE...................................516 746-8299
Carlos Silva, *President*
George Valente, *Treasurer*
EMP: 10
SQ FT: 2,800
SALES (est): 1.2MM **Privately Held**
SIC: 2434 Wood kitchen cabinets

(G-8000)
SCHAEFER MACHINE CO INC
100 Hudson St (11501-3581)
PHONE...................................516 248-6880
Peter G Walter, *President*
Paul Rubilotta, *Vice Pres*
Paul Walter, *Vice Pres*
EMP: 22 EST: 1907
SQ FT: 15,000

SALES (est): 2.8MM **Privately Held**
WEB: www.schaeferco.com
SIC: 3542 3452 Machine tools, metal forming type; bolts, nuts, rivets & washers

(G-8001)
STANDARD DIVERSIFIED INC (PA)
155 Mineola Blvd (11501-3920)
PHONE...................................302 248-1100
Gregory H A Baxter, *Ch of Bd*
Edward J Sweeney, *CFO*
Bradford A Tobin, *Admin Sec*
EMP: 48
SQ FT: 18,176
SALES: 365.7MM **Publicly Held**
WEB: www.sdix.com
SIC: 2131 Chewing tobacco; smoking tobacco

(G-8002)
VISUAL ID SOURCE INC
65 E 2nd St (11501-3503)
PHONE...................................516 307-9759
Fayaz Khalfan, *Ch of Bd*
Adam ID, *Director*
EMP: 15
SQ FT: 20,000
SALES (est): 1.5MM **Privately Held**
SIC: 3993 Signs & advertising specialties

(G-8003)
WESTBURY TIMES
Also Called: Three Village Times
132 E 2nd St (11501-3522)
PHONE...................................516 747-8282
Angela Anton, *Owner*
EMP: 75
SALES (est): 1.7MM **Privately Held**
WEB: www.westburytimes.com
SIC: 2711 Newspapers, publishing & printing

Mineville
Essex County

(G-8004)
ESSEX INDUSTRIES
17 Pilfershire Rd (12956-1092)
P.O. Box 374 (12956-0374)
PHONE...................................518 942-6671
John Anello, *Manager*
EMP: 8
SALES (est): 849.4K **Privately Held**
SIC: 3999 Manufacturing industries

(G-8005)
PRE-TECH PLASTICS INC
3085 Plank Rd (12956-1050)
P.O. Box 370 (12956-0370)
PHONE...................................518 942-5950
Mike Cave, *Branch Mgr*
EMP: 30
SALES (corp-wide): 11.9MM **Privately Held**
WEB: www.pretechplastics.com
SIC: 3599 Machine shop, jobbing & repair
PA: Pre-Tech Plastics, Inc.
   209 Blair Park Rd
   Williston VT 05495
   802 879-9441

Mohawk
Herkimer County

(G-8006)
MARY F MORSE
Also Called: Kwik Kut Manufacturing Co
125 Columbia St Ste 1 (13407-1527)
P.O. Box 116 (13407-0116)
PHONE...................................315 866-2741
Mary Morse, *Owner*
EMP: 8
SQ FT: 3,600
SALES (est): 888.1K **Privately Held**
WEB: www.kwik-kut.com
SIC: 3556 Choppers, commercial, food

(G-8007)
R D R INDUSTRIES INC
146 W Main St (13407-1085)
PHONE...................................315 866-5020
Mark Rushton, *President*
EMP: 17
SQ FT: 22,000
SALES (est): 2.9MM **Privately Held**
SIC: 3444 Metal housings, enclosures, casings & other containers

---

Mohegan Lake
Westchester County

(G-8008)
BARONE OFFSET PRINTING CORP
89 Lake Ridge Cv (10547-1222)
PHONE...................................212 989-5500
Sandra Barone, *President*
EMP: 5
SALES (est): 541.3K **Privately Held**
WEB: www.baronepress.com
SIC: 2752 Commercial printing, offset

(G-8009)
CCS NORTH AMERICA LLC
Also Called: Collaborative Coffee Source
1360 Sunny Ridge Rd (10547-1430)
PHONE...................................312 834-2165
Robyn Randle, *Opers Staff*
Robert Thoresen, *Mng Member*
EMP: 5
SALES (est): 156.4K **Privately Held**
SIC: 2095 Roasted coffee

(G-8010)
ICON ENTERPRISES INTL INC
Also Called: Icon-TV
2653 Stony St (10547-2009)
PHONE...................................718 752-9764
Claudio Laraia, *President*
Moe Belin, *Vice Pres*
▲ EMP: 23
SQ FT: 7,000
SALES (est): 4.2MM **Privately Held**
WEB: www.icon-tv.org
SIC: 3663 Satellites, communications; television monitors; radio broadcasting & communications equipment; television broadcasting & communications equipment

(G-8011)
SHOPPING CENTER WINE & LIQUOR
Also Called: Kimbri Liquor
3008 E Main St (10547)
PHONE...................................914 528-1600
Cathereen Lebleu, *Owner*
EMP: 5
SALES (est): 176.1K **Privately Held**
SIC: 2086 Bottled & canned soft drinks

Moira
Franklin County

(G-8012)
MOIRA NEW HOPE FOOD PANTRY
2341 County Route 5 (12957)
PHONE...................................518 529-6524
Joanne Deno, *Director*
EMP: 20
SALES (est): 1MM **Privately Held**
SIC: 2099 Food preparations

Monroe
Orange County

(G-8013)
6TH AVE GOURMET INC
51 Forest Rd Unit 116 (10950-2948)
PHONE...................................845 782-9067
Clara Perl, *President*
EMP: 8
SQ FT: 4,000

SALES (est): 678.7K **Privately Held**
SIC: 2092 Fresh or frozen packaged fish

(G-8014)
ASSOCIATED DRAPERY & EQUIPMENT
Also Called: Novelty Scenic Studios Inc
3 Kosnitz Dr Unit 111 (10950-1163)
PHONE...................................516 671-5245
Feivel Weiss, *Principal*
Howard Kessler, *Corp Secy*
Leslie Kessler, *Vice Pres*
EMP: 10 EST: 1968
SQ FT: 19,000
SALES (est): 783.1K
SALES (corp-wide): 1.1MM **Privately Held**
SIC: 2391 Curtains & draperies
PA: Novelty Scenic Studios Inc
   3 Kosnitz Dr Unit 111
   Monroe NY
   516 671-5940

(G-8015)
B & H ELECTRONICS CORP
308 Museum Village Rd (10950-1638)
PHONE...................................845 782-5000
Harvey Horowitz, *President*
Bernard Horowitz, *Vice Pres*
EMP: 25
SQ FT: 7,300
SALES (est): 2.3MM **Privately Held**
WEB: www.bhelectronicscorp.com
SIC: 3663 8734 3651 3699 Amplifiers, RF power & IF; testing laboratories; household audio & video equipment; electrical equipment & supplies

(G-8016)
BLOOMING GROVE STAIR CO (PA)
1 Stair Way (10950-1642)
PHONE...................................845 783-4245
Glen Durant, *President*
Serena Aglaff, *Co-Owner*
EMP: 8
SALES (est): 782.3K **Privately Held**
SIC: 2431 Stair railings, wood

(G-8017)
C T A DIGITAL INC (PA)
Also Called: Sol Markowitz
326 State Route 208 (10950-2874)
PHONE...................................845 513-0433
Joseph Markowitz, *Ch of Bd*
Leo Markowitz, *President*
Eli Tritel, *Financial Exec*
Al Hoffman, *Director*
▲ EMP: 25
SALES (est): 14K **Privately Held**
WEB: www.ctadigital.com
SIC: 3944 Video game machines, except coin-operated

(G-8018)
CHECK-O-MATIC INC
13 D A Weider Blvd # 101 (10950-6685)
P.O. Box 2141 (10949-7141)
PHONE...................................845 781-7675
Chaim Ellenbogen, *President*
EMP: 7
SQ FT: 2,500
SALES (est): 1.3MM **Privately Held**
WEB: www.checkomatic.com
SIC: 2759 Publication printing

(G-8019)
DER BLATT INC
6 Taitch Ct Unit 112 (10950-2195)
PHONE...................................845 783-1148
Aron Muller, *Principal*
EMP: 11
SALES: 1.6MM **Privately Held**
SIC: 2711 Newspapers, publishing & printing

(G-8020)
FIVE STAR CREATIONS INC
4 Preshburg Blvd Unit 302 (10950-2968)
PHONE...................................845 783-1187
Baruch Weiss, *President*
EMP: 20
SQ FT: 1,500
SALES (est): 1.7MM **Privately Held**
SIC: 3961 3999 3911 Costume jewelry; bric-a-brac; jewelry, precious metal

---

(G-8021)
G & M CLEARVIEW INC
Also Called: Clearview Glass & Mirror
112 Spring St (10950-3679)
PHONE...................................845 781-4877
Chaim Weisberg, *President*
EMP: 6
SALES (est): 436.7K **Privately Held**
SIC: 3231 Mirrored glass

(G-8022)
HOUSE OF STONE INC
1015 State Route 17m (10950-1626)
PHONE...................................845 782-7271
Raymond Krok Sr, *President*
EMP: 6
SALES (est): 695.6K **Privately Held**
SIC: 3281 Granite, cut & shaped

(G-8023)
HOUSE UR HOME INC
6 Teverya Way Unit 103 (10950-5494)
PHONE...................................347 585-3308
Chayim Rosenfeld, *President*
EMP: 6
SALES: 6MM **Privately Held**
SIC: 2452 5023 5719 5943 Modular
homes, prefabricated, wood; decorative
home furnishings & supplies; wicker, rattan or reed home furnishings; office forms
& supplies; wood office furniture; office &
public building furniture

(G-8024)
JW CONSULTING INC
Also Called: KJ MEAT DIRECT
20 Chevron Rd Unit 201 (10950-7432)
PHONE...................................845 325-7070
Joel Weiss, *President*
EMP: 2 EST: 1987
SQ FT: 1,000
SALES: 4MM **Privately Held**
SIC: 2015 Poultry slaughtering & process-
ing

(G-8025)
LASER PRINTER CHECKS CORP
7 Vayoel Moshe Ct # 101 (10950-6387)
PHONE...................................845 782-5837
Solomon Klagsbrun, *President*
▼ EMP: 6
SALES (est): 696.5K **Privately Held**
SIC: 2752 Commercial printing, litho-
graphic

(G-8026)
MARKOWITZ JEWELRY CO INC
53 Forest Rd Ste 104 (10950-2903)
PHONE...................................845 774-1175
Isaac Markowitz, *President*
Baruch Markowitz, *Vice Pres*
EMP: 30
SQ FT: 10,000
SALES (est): 4.4MM **Privately Held**
WEB: www.markowitzjewelry.com
SIC: 3911 Jewelry, precious metal

(G-8027)
MEDEK LABORATORIES INC
63 First Ave (10950-2063)
PHONE...................................845 943-4988
Isaac Schwartz, *COO*
EMP: 27
SALES (est): 1.3MM **Privately Held**
SIC: 2834 Solutions, pharmaceutical

(G-8028)
MONROE STAIR PRODUCTS INC
(PA)
1 Stair Way (10950-1642)
PHONE...................................845 783-4245
Glen T Durant, *President*
Jesse J Kehoe, *Vice Pres*
Paul Graham, *Treasurer*
EMP: 29
SQ FT: 21,500
SALES (est): 3MM **Privately Held**
WEB: www.bloominggrovestair.com
SIC: 2431 Staircases & stairs, wood

(G-8029)
PRIMA SATCHEL INC
51 Forest Rd Ste 302 (10950-2938)
PHONE...................................929 367-7770
Joachim Feldman, *President*

EMP: 6
SQ FT: 2,000
SALES: 500K **Privately Held**
SIC: 2393 Textile bags

(G-8030)
REB LYBSS INC
44 Virginia Ave (10950-2214)
PHONE...................................845 238-5633
Mendel Rosenberg, *President*
EMP: 4
SALES (est): 3MM **Privately Held**
SIC: 2844 Toilet preparations

(G-8031)
STOP ENTERTAINMENT INC
408 Rye Hill Rd (10950-4509)
PHONE...................................212 242-7867
EMP: 15
SQ FT: 1,500
SALES (est): 1.1MM **Privately Held**
SIC: 2732 7311 Book Printing Advertising
Agency

(G-8032)
TRI COUNTY CUSTOM VACUUM
653 State Route 17m (10950-3309)
PHONE...................................845 774-7595
Mike Zahra, *Partner*
EMP: 5
SALES: 200K **Privately Held**
SIC: 3635 Household vacuum cleaners

Monsey
Rockland County

(G-8033)
A&B CONSERVATION LLC
12 Maple Leaf Rd (10952-3030)
PHONE...................................845 282-7272
Baruch Tabak, *General Mgr*
Dovber Tabak, *Manager*
Judah Rominek,
EMP: 7
SQ FT: 1,000
SALES (est): 499.6K **Privately Held**
SIC: 3295 Pumice, ground or otherwise
treated

(G-8034)
AMERTAC HOLDINGS INC (PA)
25 Robert Pitt Dr (10952-3365)
PHONE...................................610 336-1330
Charles Peifer, *Ch of Bd*
John Cooper, *President*
Peter Hermann, *Vice Pres*
EMP: 6
SALES (est): 29.7MM **Privately Held**
SIC: 3699 3429 5063 5072 Electrical
equipment & supplies; manufactured
hardware (general); metal fasteners; elec-
trical apparatus & equipment; hardware;
tacks

(G-8035)
ARONOWITZ METAL WORKS
5 Edwin Ln (10952-3102)
PHONE...................................845 356-1660
Avigdor Aronowitz, *Owner*
Sal Hurst CPA, *Accountant*
EMP: 5
SQ FT: 2,900
SALES (est): 293.7K **Privately Held**
SIC: 2522 Office furniture, except wood

(G-8036)
ATLANTIC SPECIALTY CO INC
20 Jeffrey Pl (10952-2703)
PHONE...................................845 356-2502
Mark Srulowitz, *President*
Seung Lee, *Treasurer*
EMP: 20 EST: 1908
SQ FT: 5,000
SALES (est): 2MM **Privately Held**
SIC: 3161 3172 Luggage; key cases

(G-8037)
DVASH FOODS INC
2 Brewer Rd (10952-4001)
PHONE...................................845 578-1959
Mel Gertner, *President*
▲ EMP: 10 EST: 2008

SALES (est): 2.4MM **Privately Held**
SIC: 2038 Frozen specialties

(G-8038)
FIRESIDE HOLDINGS LLC
59 Route 59 (10952-3536)
PHONE...................................718 564-4335
Marcia Levine, *President*
EMP: 5
SALES (est): 371.2K **Privately Held**
SIC: 2032 Mexican foods: packaged in
cans, jars, etc.

(G-8039)
MAGCREST PACKAGING INC
Also Called: Wally Packaging
5 Highview Rd (10952-2943)
PHONE...................................845 425-0451
Aaron Rubinson, *President*
Gitty Rubinson, *Vice Pres*
◆ EMP: 6
SALES (est): 1.3MM **Privately Held**
WEB: www.magcrest.com
SIC: 2673 7389 Plastic bags: made from
purchased materials;

(G-8040)
MAVIANO CORP
21 Robert Pitt Dr Ste 207 (10952-5305)
PHONE...................................845 494-2598
Brenda Falk, *President*
EMP: 7
SALES (est): 549.3K **Privately Held**
SIC: 2821 Plastics materials & resins

(G-8041)
NAVY PLUM LLC
47 Plum Rd (10952-1525)
PHONE...................................845 641-7441
Jonathan Joseph,
▲ EMP: 3
SQ FT: 2,500
SALES: 40MM **Privately Held**
SIC: 2299 5199 Fabrics: linen, jute, hemp,
ramie; yarn: flax, jute, hemp & ramie; fab-
rics, yarns & knit goods

(G-8042)
NYAHB INC
161 Route 59 Ste 101 (10952-7817)
P.O. Box 448, Spring Valley (10977-0448)
PHONE...................................845 352-5300
Alexander D Kranz, *President*
Evette Kranz, *Vice Pres*
Tara J Collazo, *Director*
Gary Bondi, *Shareholder*
▲ EMP: 3
SALES (est): 1.5MM **Privately Held**
WEB: www.galex.net
SIC: 3354 Aluminum extruded products

(G-8043)
PLASTICWARE LLC (PA)
13 Wilsher Dr (10952-2328)
PHONE...................................845 267-0790
Sam Meth, *Mng Member*
EMP: 16
SQ FT: 10,000
SALES (est): 6.3MM **Privately Held**
SIC: 3089 Plastic containers, except foam

(G-8044)
PRINT IT INC
59 Route 59 Ste 141 (10952-3543)
PHONE...................................845 371-2227
EMP: 8
SALES (est): 179.8K **Privately Held**
SIC: 2752 Commercial printing, litho-
graphic

(G-8045)
S B MANUFACTURING LLC
161 Route 59 (10952-7819)
PHONE...................................845 352-3700
Michael Bloch, *President*
Ralph Heidings, *CFO*
EMP: 14
SALES (est): 1.9MM **Privately Held**
SIC: 3999 Barber & beauty shop equip-
ment

(G-8046)
SAFE-DENT ENTERPRISES LLC
4 Orchard Hill Dr (10952-1503)
PHONE...................................845 362-0141
Hedy Worch, *Mng Member*

EMP: 5
SQ FT: 20,000
SALES (est): 442K **Privately Held**
SIC: 3843 Dental materials

(G-8047)
SAMZONG INC
46 Main St Ste 258 (10952-3055)
PHONE...................................718 475-1843
Lazer Maikowitz, *President*
▲ EMP: 4
SQ FT: 5,000
SALES: 5MM **Privately Held**
SIC: 3496 5051 Cable, uninsulated wire;
made from purchased wire; cable, wire

(G-8048)
SB MOLDS LLC
161 Route 59 Ste 203a (10952-7817)
PHONE...................................845 352-3700
Michael Bloch, *Mng Member*
EMP: 80
SALES (est): 3.3MM **Privately Held**
SIC: 3544 Industrial molds

(G-8049)
**SUNRISE SNACKS ROCKLAND
INC (PA)**
3 Sunrise Dr (10952)
PHONE...................................845 352-2676
Moshe A Singer, *President*
Rivka Singer, *Sales Staff*
EMP: 15 EST: 2008
SQ FT: 22,000
SALES: 1.4MM **Privately Held**
SIC: 2099 Popcorn, packaged: except al-
ready popped

(G-8050)
SUPERIOR INTERIORS NY CORP
25 Robert Pitt Dr Ste 208 (10952-3366)
PHONE...................................845 274-7600
Rafael Rosenberg, *President*
EMP: 10
SALES: 2MM **Privately Held**
SIC: 2493 Building board & wallboard, ex-
cept gypsum

(G-8051)
TA CHEN INTERNATIONAL INC
Also Called: Galax
17 Main St Ste 217 (10952-3707)
PHONE...................................845 352-5300
Alex Kranz, *Branch Mgr*
EMP: 10 **Privately Held**
SIC: 3452 5051 Bolts, nuts, rivets & wash-
ers; steel
HQ: Ta Chen International, Inc.
5855 Obispo Ave
Long Beach CA 90805
562 808-8000

(G-8052)
TAMI GREAT FOOD CORP
22 Briarcliff Dr (10952-2503)
PHONE...................................845 352-7901
David Rosenberg, *President*
Martin Rosenberg, *President*
Renee Rosenberg, *Vice Pres*
EMP: 8
SQ FT: 6,000
SALES (est): 585.6K **Privately Held**
SIC: 2037 2038 Vegetables, quick frozen
& cold pack, excl. potato products; frozen
specialties

(G-8053)
TELE-PAK INC
Also Called: Card Printing.us
421 Route 59 Ste 7 (10952-2847)
P.O. Box 430 (10952-0430)
PHONE...................................845 426-2300
Jack Steinmetz, *Ch of Bd*
Al Zowada, *Production*
Abraham Joseph, *Accountant*
Isaac Adler, *Sales Dir*
◆ EMP: 38
SQ FT: 7,000
SALES: 8MM **Privately Held**
WEB: www.tele-pak.com
SIC: 2754 2759 2752 7929 Commercial
printing, gravure; commercial printing;
cards, lithographed; entertainers & enter-
tainment groups

Montauk
Suffolk County

(G-8054)
JESSE JOECKEL
Also Called: Whalebone Creative
65 Tuthill Rd (11954-5460)
PHONE....................................631 668-2772
EMP: 5
SQ FT: 600
SALES (est): 385.5K Privately Held
SIC: 2339 Women's & misses' outerwear

(G-8055)
MONTAUK BREWING COMPANY INC
62 S Erie Ave (11954-5370)
P.O. Box 1079 (11954-0802)
PHONE....................................631 668-8471
Vaughan Cutillo, Vice Pres
EMP: 10
SALES (est): 25.9K Privately Held
SIC: 2082 Beer (alcoholic beverage)

(G-8056)
MONTAUK INLET SEAFOOD INC
E Lake Dr Ste 540-541 (11954)
P.O. Box 2148 (11954-0905)
PHONE....................................631 668-3419
Charles S Weimar, President
David Aripocth, Owner
Kevin Maguire, Owner
William Grimm, Vice Pres
Richard Jones, Treasurer
EMP: 3
SQ FT: 5,000
SALES (est): 1MM Privately Held
SIC: 2092 5146 5983 Fish, fresh: prepared; fish, fresh; fuel oil dealers

(G-8057)
NYEMAC INC
Also Called: On Montauk
Paradise Ln (11954)
P.O. Box 2087 (11954-0903)
PHONE....................................631 668-1303
Joseph Nye, President
Carol Macdonald-Nye, President
EMP: 8 EST: 1990
SQ FT: 1,200
SALES (est): 690K Privately Held
SIC: 2721 4813 Magazines: publishing only, not printed on site;

Montgomery
Orange County

(G-8058)
CALLANAN INDUSTRIES INC
215 Montgomery Rd (12549-2814)
P.O. Box 505, Maybrook (12543-0505)
PHONE....................................845 457-3158
Charlie Tady, Opers Mgr
Kevin Schuler, Manager
EMP: 25
SALES (corp-wide): 30.6B Privately Held
WEB: www.callanan.com
SIC: 2951 5032 2952 Asphalt & asphaltic paving mixtures (not from refineries); stone, crushed or broken; asphalt felts & coatings
HQ: Callanan Industries, Inc.
8 Southwoods Blvd Ste 4
Albany NY 12211
518 374-2222

(G-8059)
CARLISLE CONSTRUCTION MTLS LLC
9 Hudson Crossing Dr (12549-2854)
PHONE....................................386 753-0786
Scott Pearson, Manager
EMP: 65
SALES (corp-wide): 4.4B Publicly Held
WEB: www.hpanels.com
SIC: 3086 Insulation or cushioning material, foamed plastic
HQ: Carlisle Construction Materials, Llc
1285 Ritner Hwy
Carlisle PA 17013

(G-8060)
GLAXOSMITHKLINE LLC
3 Tyler St (12549-1609)
PHONE....................................845 341-7590
EMP: 26
SALES (corp-wide): 39.5B Privately Held
SIC: 2834 Pharmaceutical preparations
HQ: Glaxosmithkline Llc
5 Crescent Dr
Philadelphia PA 19112
215 751-4000

(G-8061)
GROSSO MATERIALS INC
90 Collabar Rd (12549-1805)
PHONE....................................845 361-5211
Allan Grosso, President
EMP: 10
SQ FT: 300
SALES (est): 1.7MM Privately Held
SIC: 1459 5261 5032 Shale (common) quarrying; top soil; stone, crushed or broken

(G-8062)
NORTHEAST CNSTR INDS INC
Also Called: Nci Panel Systems
657 Rte 17 K S St Ste 2 (12549)
PHONE....................................845 565-1000
Robert Schroeder, President
EMP: 10 EST: 1999
SQ FT: 12,000
SALES: 630K Privately Held
SIC: 3316 Cold finishing of steel shapes

(G-8063)
OHANA METAL & IRON WORKS INC
60 Miller Rd (12549-2424)
PHONE....................................845 344-7520
Jacob Ohana, President
EMP: 19
SQ FT: 6,000
SALES: 4.5MM Privately Held
SIC: 2431 Millwork

(G-8064)
ORANGE COUNTY IRONWORKS LLC
36 Maybrook Rd (12549-2815)
PHONE....................................845 769-3000
Matthew Haaksma, Project Mgr
Danny North, Project Mgr
Steve Michael, Prdtn Mgr
Daniel Teutul, Mng Member
Shawn Quill, Prgrmr
EMP: 44
SQ FT: 65,000
SALES: 61.3MM Privately Held
SIC: 3449 3441 1541 Miscellaneous metalwork; fabricated structural metal; industrial buildings, new construction

(G-8065)
QUICK ROLL LEAF MFG CO INC (PA)
118 Bracken Rd (12549-2600)
P.O. Box 53, Middletown (10940-0053)
PHONE....................................845 457-1500
Charles E Quick, Ch of Bd
Edward Quick Jr, President
William Crowley, Vice Pres
Solena Quick-Porras, Manager
EMP: 48 EST: 1964
SQ FT: 80,000
SALES (est): 33.8MM Privately Held
SIC: 3497 Metal foil & leaf

(G-8066)
REUTER PALLET PKG SYS INC
272 Neelytown Rd (12549-2840)
PHONE....................................845 457-9937
Joseph A Carfizzi Sr, President
George Reuter Jr, Vice Pres
EMP: 9
SQ FT: 10,000
SALES (est): 920.4K Privately Held
SIC: 2448 2441 Wood pallets & skids; nailed wood boxes & shook

(G-8067)
TILCON NEW YORK INC
Also Called: Maybrook Asphalt
215 Montgomery Rd (12549-2814)
PHONE....................................845 457-3158
Ciaran Brennan, Principal
Andrew Galletta, Transportation
EMP: 63
SALES (corp-wide): 30.6B Privately Held
SIC: 1429 Dolomitic marble, crushed & broken-quarrying
HQ: Tilcon New York Inc.
9 Entin Rd
Parsippany NJ 07054
973 366-7741

(G-8068)
VALAD ELECTRIC HEATING CORP
65 Leonards Dr (12549-2643)
PHONE....................................888 509-4927
Arthur Cecchini, Ch of Bd
Lauren Cecchini, Corp Secy
Arthur Cecchini Jr, Vice Pres
Lauren Cecchini Janes, Treasurer
EMP: 12 EST: 1941
SQ FT: 35,000
SALES (est): 3.3MM Privately Held
WEB: www.valadelectric.com
SIC: 3634 Heaters, space electric; electric household cooking appliances

Monticello
Sullivan County

(G-8069)
BLOOMING GROVE STAIR CO
309 E Broadway (12701-8839)
PHONE....................................845 791-4016
Glen Durant, Principal
EMP: 7 Privately Held
SIC: 2431 Stair railings, wood
PA: Blooming Grove Stair Co
1 Stair Way
Monroe NY 10950

(G-8070)
LOCAL MEDIA GROUP INC
Also Called: Times Herald-Record
479 Broadway (12701-1756)
PHONE....................................845 794-3712
EMP: 10
SALES (corp-wide): 610.2MM Publicly Held
SIC: 2711 Newspapers-Publishing/Printing
HQ: Local Media Group, Inc.
40 Mulberry St
Middletown NY 10940
845 294-8181

(G-8071)
MONROE STAIR PRODUCTS INC
309 E Broadway (12701-8839)
PHONE....................................845 791-4016
Glen Durant, Manager
EMP: 5
SALES (corp-wide): 3MM Privately Held
WEB: www.bloominggrovestair.com
SIC: 2431 Staircases & stairs, wood
PA: Monroe Stair Products Inc.
1 Stair Way
Monroe NY 10950
845 783-4245

(G-8072)
PATRICK ROHAN
Also Called: Wadadda.com
9 Green St (12701-1307)
PHONE....................................718 781-2573
Rohan Patrick, Owner
EMP: 5
SALES (est): 211.9K Privately Held
SIC: 2396 2759 7336 7389 Printing & embossing on plastics fabric articles; woodcuts for use in printing illustrations, posters, etc.; commercial art & graphic design; commercial art & illustration;

(G-8073)
WYDE LUMBER
419 State Route 17b (12701-3525)
PHONE....................................845 513-5571
Wallace Madnick, Owner
EMP: 11
SALES (est): 760K Privately Held
SIC: 2421 Lumber: rough, sawed or planed

Montour Falls
Schuyler County

(G-8074)
CHICONE BUILDERS LLC
Chicone Cabinetmakers
302 W South St (14865-9743)
PHONE....................................607 535-6540
David H Chicone,
EMP: 5 Privately Held
SIC: 2521 2434 Cabinets, office: wood; wood kitchen cabinets
PA: Chicone Builders Llc
302 W South St
Montour Falls NY 14865

(G-8075)
MALINA MANAGEMENT COMPANY INC
Also Called: Castel Grisch Winery
3620 County Road 16 (14865-9708)
PHONE....................................607 535-9614
Thomas Malina, President
Barbara A Malina, Treasurer
Scott Wachter, Admin Sec
EMP: 22
SQ FT: 1,250
SALES (est): 2.6MM Privately Held
SIC: 2084 5812 7011 Wines; eating places; bed & breakfast inn

(G-8076)
ROBERT M BROWN
Also Called: Malone Welding
150 Mill St (14865-9734)
PHONE....................................607 426-6250
Robert M Brown, Owner
EMP: 11
SALES (est): 368.3K Privately Held
WEB: www.empiregp.com
SIC: 7692 Welding repair

(G-8077)
TAYLOR PRECISION MACHINING
3921 Dug Rd (14865-9722)
P.O. Box 396 (14865-0396)
PHONE....................................607 535-3101
Mickey Taylor, Owner
EMP: 7
SQ FT: 1,056
SALES (est): 1MM Privately Held
SIC: 3599 Machine shop, jobbing & repair

Montrose
Westchester County

(G-8078)
QUALITY CIRCLE PRODUCTS INC
2108 Albany Post Rd (10548-1431)
P.O. Box 36 (10548-0036)
PHONE....................................914 736-6600
Gary Flaum, President
Anthony Cenname, Exec VP
▲ EMP: 70
SQ FT: 32,500
SALES (est): 14.3MM Privately Held
WEB: www.qualitycircle.com
SIC: 2679 2671 Labels, paper: made from purchased material; tags, paper (unprinted): made from purchased paper; packaging paper & plastics film, coated & laminated

Mooers
Clinton County

(G-8079)
ACME ENGINEERING PRODUCTS INC
2330 State Route 11 (12958-3725)
PHONE....................................518 236-5659
G S Presser, President
Robert Presser, Vice Pres
Julie Hawa, Finance
EMP: 25

▲ = Import ▼=Export
◆ =Import/Export

SALES (est): 4MM **Privately Held**
WEB: www.acmeprod.com
SIC: **3564** 8711 3569 Air cleaning systems; engineering services; filters

Mooers Forks
Clinton County

(G-8080)
NORTHERN TIER CNC INC (PA)
733 Woods Falls Rd (12959)
PHONE..................................518 236-4702
Jerry Meseck, *President*
Jamie Meseck, *Treasurer*
EMP: 9
SQ FT: 4,000
SALES: 1.2MM **Privately Held**
SIC: **3599** Custom machinery

Moravia
Cayuga County

(G-8081)
BROOKSIDE LUMBER INC
4191 Duryea St (13118-2500)
PHONE..................................315 497-0937
William Millier, *President*
Katherine Millier, *Shareholder*
EMP: 17
SQ FT: 10,000
SALES (est): 2.4MM **Privately Held**
SIC: **2421** Lumber: rough, sawed or planed

(G-8082)
CROSS FILTRATION LTD LBLTY CO
87 W Cayuga St (13118-3000)
P.O. Box 1082 (13118-1082)
PHONE..................................315 412-1539
Joanne Cross, *Mng Member*
◆ EMP: 10
SALES (est): 396.6K **Privately Held**
SIC: **3569** Filters, general line: industrial

(G-8083)
REPUBLICAN REGISTRAR INC
Also Called: Community Newspapers
6 Central St (13118-3609)
P.O. Box 591 (13118-0591)
PHONE..................................315 497-1551
Bernard McGuerty III, *President*
EMP: 8
SALES (est): 582.3K **Privately Held**
SIC: **2711** Newspapers

Morris
Otsego County

(G-8084)
H W NAYLOR CO INC
121 Main St (13808-6920)
P.O. Box 190 (13808-0190)
PHONE..................................607 263-5145
David Lucas, *President*
Jennifer Wynn, *Sales Staff*
▲ EMP: 12 EST: 1926
SQ FT: 10,000
SALES (est): 1.3MM **Privately Held**
WEB: www.drnaylor.com
SIC: **2834** Veterinary pharmaceutical preparations

Morrisville
Madison County

(G-8085)
COPESETIC INC
62 E Main St (13408-7731)
P.O. Box 1119 (13408-1119)
PHONE..................................315 684-7780
Eric Beyer, *President*
Anthony Lee, *Vice Pres*
David Lee, *VP Opers*
Shannon Cook, *Office Mgr*
EMP: 15

SQ FT: 10,000
SALES: 1.7MM **Privately Held**
WEB: www.copeseticinc.com
SIC: **3999** Models, except toy

Mount Kisco
Westchester County

(G-8086)
ACCEL PRINTING & GRAPHICS
128 Radio Circle Dr Ste 2 (10549-2640)
P.O. Box 185, Somers (10589-0185)
PHONE..................................914 241-3369
Bill Harden, *President*
Anna Harden, *Vice Pres*
EMP: 7
SQ FT: 2,200
SALES: 625K **Privately Held**
WEB: www.accelprinting.com
SIC: **2759** 2399 Commercial printing; banners, pennants & flags

(G-8087)
AHAE PRESS INC
100 S Bedford Rd Ste 340 (10549-3444)
PHONE..................................914 471-8671
Hyuk Kee Yoo, *Ch of Bd*
Michael Ham, *Bd of Directors*
EMP: 8 EST: 2011
SALES (est): 176.3K **Privately Held**
SIC: **2741** Miscellaneous publishing

(G-8088)
BROOKS WOODWORKING INC
15 Kensico Dr (10549-1012)
PHONE..................................914 666-2029
Richard Brooks, *President*
▲ EMP: 14
SQ FT: 5,000
SALES: 1.1MM **Privately Held**
SIC: **2499** Decorative wood & woodwork

(G-8089)
CURTIS INSTRUMENTS INC (PA)
Also Called: Curtis PMC Division
200 Kisco Ave (10549-1400)
PHONE..................................914 666-2971
Stuart Marwell, *Ch of Bd*
Eugene Finger, *President*
Wang Jinghui, *General Mgr*
Randy Miller, *Business Mgr*
Bob Baker, *Vice Pres*
▲ EMP: 150 EST: 1960
SQ FT: 35,000
SALES (est): 301.5MM **Privately Held**
SIC: **3825** 3824 3629 Elapsed time meters, electronic; speed indicators & recorders, vehicle; electronic generation equipment

(G-8090)
D C I PLASMA CENTER INC (PA)
71 S Bedford Rd (10549-3407)
PHONE..................................914 241-1646
Martin Silver, *President*
Perry Ciarrletta, *Treasurer*
EMP: 3
SQ FT: 700
SALES (est): 1.9MM **Privately Held**
SIC: **2836** Plasmas

(G-8091)
DATALINK COMPUTER PRODUCTS
165 E Main St 175 (10549-2923)
PHONE..................................914 666-2358
EMP: 10
SALES: 2.4MM **Privately Held**
SIC: **3572** 7374 Mfg Computer Storage Devices Data Processing/Preparation

(G-8092)
ENTERMARKET
280 N Bedford Rd Ste 305 (10549-1148)
PHONE..................................914 437-7268
Jeff Tong, *Owner*
EMP: 5
SALES (est): 608.2K **Privately Held**
WEB: www.entermarket.com
SIC: **2752** Commercial printing, lithographic

(G-8093)
IAT INTERACTIVE LLC
Also Called: It's About Time
333 N Bedford Rd Ste 110 (10549-1161)
P.O. Box 7862, Greenwich CT (06836-7862)
PHONE..................................914 273-2233
Thomas Laster, *Shareholder*
Laurie Kreindler, *Shareholder*
EMP: 37
SQ FT: 574,600
SALES (est): 3.4MM **Privately Held**
SIC: **2731** Textbooks: publishing & printing

(G-8094)
JEROME LEVY FORECASTING CENTER
Also Called: Industry Forecast
69 S Moger Ave Ste 202 (10549-2222)
PHONE..................................914 244-8617
David Levy, *Principal*
EMP: 5
SALES (est): 384.4K **Privately Held**
SIC: **2721** Periodicals

(G-8095)
JT ROSELLE LIGHTING & SUP INC
333 N Bedford Rd Ste 120 (10549-1158)
PHONE..................................914 666-3700
EMP: 14
SALES (est): 3.1MM **Privately Held**
SIC: **3648** Lighting equipment

(G-8096)
KIDZ TOYZ INC
280 N Bedford Rd Ste 203 (10549-1147)
PHONE..................................914 261-4453
Scott Spiegel, *President*
EMP: 2
SALES: 2MM **Privately Held**
SIC: **3944** Electronic games & toys

(G-8097)
KOHLBERG SPORTS GROUP INC (HQ)
111 Radio Circle Dr (10549-2609)
PHONE..................................914 241-7430
Walter W Farley,
EMP: 5
SALES (est): 1.1MM
SALES (corp-wide): 7.9B **Privately Held**
SIC: **3949** Hockey equipment & supplies, general
PA: Kohlberg & Co., L.L.C.
111 Radio Circle Dr
Mount Kisco NY 10549
914 241-7430

(G-8098)
LAURTOM INC
Also Called: It's About Time Publishing
333 N Bedford Rd Ste 100 (10549-1160)
PHONE..................................914 273-2233
Laurie Kreindler, *CEO*
Cheryl Deese, *Vice Pres*
Sal Marottoli, *Vice Pres*
John Nordland, *Director*
Dana Turner, *Director*
EMP: 35
SQ FT: 4,000
SALES (est): 3.8MM
SALES (corp-wide): 1.1B **Privately Held**
WEB: www.its-about-time.com
SIC: **2721** Periodicals
HQ: Herff Jones, Llc
4501 W 62nd St
Indianapolis IN 46268
800 419-5462

(G-8099)
NATIONWIDE COILS INC (PA)
24 Foxwood Cir (10549-1127)
PHONE..................................914 277-7396
Ross Stephens, *President*
Stephen Barzelatto, *Vice Pres*
Andre Ostacoli, *Opers Staff*
▼ EMP: 4
SQ FT: 1,000
SALES (est): 1.3MM **Privately Held**
WEB: www.nationwidecoils.com
SIC: **3585** Refrigeration & heating equipment

(G-8100)
NORCORP INC
Also Called: NORTHERN WESTCHESTER HOSPITAL
400 E Main St (10549-3417)
PHONE..................................914 666-1310
Joel Seligman, *President*
John Partenza, *Treasurer*
EMP: 27
SALES: 186.1K
SALES (corp-wide): 280.3MM **Privately Held**
SIC: **2326** 8062 Medical & hospital uniforms, men's; general medical & surgical hospitals
PA: Northern Westchester Hospital Association
400 E Main St
Mount Kisco NY 10549
914 666-1200

(G-8101)
ORBIT INDUSTRIES LLC
116 Radio Circle Dr # 302 (10549-2631)
PHONE..................................914 244-1500
Marc Shur,
John Katz,
EMP: 14
SALES (est): 2.7MM **Privately Held**
SIC: **2258** Lace & lace products

(G-8102)
PLASTIC & RECONSTRUCTIVE SVCS
Also Called: Spa Sciara
333 N Bedford Rd (10549-1158)
PHONE..................................914 584-5605
Sharon Dechiara, *President*
EMP: 5 EST: 2010
SQ FT: 1,800
SALES: 1.2MM **Privately Held**
SIC: **2844** Cosmetic preparations

(G-8103)
R L C ELECTRONICS INC
83 Radio Circle Dr (10549-2622)
PHONE..................................914 241-1334
Charles Alan Borck, *CEO*
Doug Borck, *President*
Sal Bentivenga, *Principal*
Peter Jeffery, *Sales Dir*
EMP: 65 EST: 1959
SQ FT: 20,000
SALES (est): 12.8MM **Privately Held**
WEB: www.rlcelectronics.com
SIC: **3679** Electronic circuits; microwave components

(G-8104)
RDI INC (PA)
Also Called: Rdi Electronics
333 N Bedford Rd Ste 135 (10549-1160)
PHONE..................................914 773-1000
James Diamond, *Ch of Bd*
Barry Miller, *President*
John Horl, *CFO*
David Del Monte, *Controller*
Ed Westring, *Natl Sales Mgr*
▲ EMP: 18
SQ FT: 10,000
SALES (est): 38.9MM **Privately Held**
WEB: www.rdiusa.com
SIC: **3679** 3678 3677 3577 Electronic circuits; electronic connectors; electronic coils, transformers & other inductors; computer peripheral equipment; nonferrous wiredrawing & insulating

(G-8105)
RPB DISTRIBUTORS LLC
Also Called: Protec Friction Supply
45 Kensico Dr (10549-1025)
PHONE..................................914 244-3600
Roy Landesberg, *President*
Parker Silzer, *Vice Pres*
▲ EMP: 8
SALES (est): 1.2MM **Privately Held**
WEB: www.protecfriction.com
SIC: **3714** 5084 5013 Motor vehicle brake systems & parts; industrial machine parts; clutches

(G-8106)
WESTCHESTER SIGNS INC
Also Called: Sign-A-Rama
145 Kisco Ave (10549-1418)
PHONE..............................914 666-7446
Karl Theile, *President*
EMP: 5
SALES (est): 339.2K Privately Held
SIC: 3993 Signs & advertising specialties

(G-8107)
XELEUM LIGHTING LLC
333 N Bedford Rd Ste 135 (10549-1160)
PHONE..............................954 617-8170
Jon Cooper, *Branch Mgr*
EMP: 11 Privately Held
SIC: 3646 Commercial indusl & institu-
tional electric lighting fixtures
HQ: Xeleum Lighting, Llc
3430 Quantum Blvd
Boynton Beach FL 33426
954 617-8170

(G-8108)
**ZIERICK MANUFACTURING
CORP (PA)**
131 Radio Circle Dr (10549-2623)
PHONE..............................800 882-8020
Gretchen Zierick, *President*
Russell Zierick, *President*
Frank Lynster, *Plant Mgr*
Fred Ackerman, *QC Dir*
Bill Searles, *Engineer*
▲ EMP: 80 EST: 1919
SQ FT: 47,500
SALES (est): 12.5MM Privately Held
WEB: www.zierick.com
SIC: 3643 3452 3644 3694 Connectors &
terminals for electrical devices; solderless
connectors (electric wiring devices); nuts,
metal; noncurrent-carrying wiring serv-
ices; terminal boards; ignition apparatus,
internal combustion engines; machinery
castings, nonferrous: ex. alum., copper,
die, etc.

(G-8109)
ZUMBACH ELECTRONICS CORP
Also Called: Elvo
140 Kisco Ave (10549-1412)
PHONE..............................914 241-7080
Bruno Zumbach, *Ch of Bd*
Rainer Zumbach, *President*
Sven Naegeli, *Vice Pres*
James Fox, *Project Mgr*
Sigrid Fuchs, *Controller*
▲ EMP: 55
SQ FT: 15,000
SALES (est): 10.9MM Privately Held
SIC: 3825 Instruments to measure electric-
ity

Mount Marion
Ulster County

(G-8110)
LAIRD TELEMEDIA
2000 Sterling Rd (12456)
PHONE..............................845 339-9555
Mark Braunstein, *CEO*
Vincent Bruno, *Vice Pres*
EMP: 110
SALES (est): 8.5MM Privately Held
WEB: www.lairdtelemedia.com
SIC: 3651 7812 Household audio & video
equipment; motion picture & video pro-
duction

(G-8111)
METHODS TOOLING & MFG INC
635 Glasco Tpke (12456)
P.O. Box 400 (12456-0400)
PHONE..............................845 246-7100
Keith Michaels, *President*
Michael Allen, *Vice Pres*
John Orourke, *Manager*
EMP: 31 EST: 1967
SQ FT: 30,000

SALES (est): 5.2MM Privately Held
WEB: www.methodstooling.com
SIC: 3545 3444 3648 2514 Tools & accessories for machine tools; sheet metalwork; stage lighting equipment; kitchen
cabinets: metal; fabricated plate work
(boiler shop); wood kitchen cabinets

(G-8112)
**NORTHEAST SOLITE
CORPORATION**
962 Kings Hwy (12456)
P.O. Box 437 (12456-0437)
PHONE..............................845 246-2177
Gary Green, *Branch Mgr*
EMP: 40
SALES (corp-wide): 16.2MM Privately
Held
WEB: www.nesolite.com
SIC: 3295 1442 3281 Minerals, ground or
treated; construction sand & gravel; slate
products
PA: Northeast Solite Corporation
1135 Kings Hwy
Saugerties NY 12477
845 246-2646

Mount Morris
Livingston County

(G-8113)
ELAM MATERIALS INC
1 Conlon Ave (14510-1038)
P.O. Box 337 (14510-0337)
PHONE..............................585 658-2248
David Spallina, *President*
EMP: 12
SALES (est): 1.7MM Privately Held
SIC: 3273 Ready-mixed concrete

(G-8114)
MT MORRIS SHOPPER INC
85 N Main St (14510-1023)
PHONE..............................585 658-3520
Jerry W Rolison, *President*
Evelyn C Rolison, *Corp Secy*
EMP: 6
SQ FT: 1,800
SALES (est): 559.5K Privately Held
WEB: www.mtmorrisshopper.com
SIC: 2741 Guides: publishing only, not
printed on site; shopping news: publishing
only, not printed on site

Mount Sinai
Suffolk County

(G-8115)
KENDALL CIRCUITS INC
5507-10 Nesconset Hwy 105 (11766)
PHONE..............................631 473-3636
Danielle Seaford, *President*
EMP: 37
SALES (est): 4.7MM Privately Held
WEB: www.wordcircuits.com
SIC: 3672 Circuit boards, television & radio
printed

(G-8116)
OSPREY BOAT
96 Mount Sinai Ave (11766-2311)
P.O. Box 331, Port Jefferson (11777-0331)
PHONE..............................631 331-4153
Amanda Cash, *Owner*
EMP: 5 EST: 2010
SALES (est): 448.2K Privately Held
SIC: 2399 Fishing nets

(G-8117)
TRANSPORTGISTICS INC
28 N Country Rd Ste 103 (11766-1518)
PHONE..............................631 567-4100
Alan Miller, *President*
Robert Munro, *COO*
Stewart Miller, *Senior VP*
Kerry Loudenback, *Vice Pres*
EMP: 12 EST: 2001
SQ FT: 3,000

SALES (est): 2.3MM Privately Held
WEB: www.transportgistics.com
SIC: 7372 Business oriented computer
software

Mount Upton
Chenango County

(G-8118)
LILAC QUARRIES LLC
1702 State Highway 8 (13809-4103)
PHONE..............................607 867-4016
Russell Heath,
EMP: 6
SALES (est): 245.9K Privately Held
SIC: 1422 Crushed & broken limestone

Mount Vernon
Westchester County

(G-8119)
AARON GROUP LLC
Also Called: Diamond Dimensions
115 S Macquesten Pkwy (10550-1724)
PHONE..............................718 392-5454
Robert Kempler, *President*
Richard Katz, *COO*
Harry Schnitzer, *Sales Staff*
Jeff Steinberg, *Sales Staff*
Cindy Chen, *Manager*
EMP: 100
SALES (est): 9MM
SALES (corp-wide): 225.3B Publicly
Held
WEB: www.saaron.com
SIC: 3911 5094 5944 Jewelry, precious
metal; jewelry; jewelry, precious stones &
precious metals
HQ: Richline Group, Inc.
1385 Broadway Fl 14
New York NY 10018

(G-8120)
ABALON PRECISION MFG CORP
717 S 3rd Ave (10550-4905)
PHONE..............................914 665-7700
Norman Orenstein, *President*
EMP: 30 EST: 1945
SQ FT: 9,000
SALES (est): 5.5MM Privately Held
SIC: 3441 Fabricated structural metal

(G-8121)
**ACCURATE METAL WEATHER
STRIP**
725 S Fulton Ave (10550-5086)
PHONE..............................914 668-6042
Fred O Kammerer, *President*
Ronald R Kammerer, *Corp Secy*
EMP: 7 EST: 1898
SQ FT: 15,000
SALES: 17.5MM Privately Held
SIC: 3442 3449 Weather strip, metal; mis-
cellaneous metalwork

(G-8122)
ALBERT AUGUSTINE LTD
161 S Macquesten Pkwy (10550-1724)
PHONE..............................718 913-9635
Stephen Griesgraber, *President*
EMP: 55 EST: 1945
SQ FT: 10,500
SALES (est): 648.1K Privately Held
WEB: www.albertaugustine.com
SIC: 3931 5736 Strings, musical instru-
ment; musical instrument stores

(G-8123)
BALL CHAIN MFG CO INC (PA)
Also Called: BCM
741 S Fulton Ave (10550-5085)
PHONE..............................914 664-7500
Valentine Taubner Jr, *President*
Valentine J Taubner III, *Vice Pres*
Steven Kapush, *Safety Mgr*
James Taubner, *Treasurer*
Susan Glaser, *Controller*
▲ EMP: 90 EST: 1938
SQ FT: 35,000

SALES (est): 12.1MM Privately Held
WEB: www.ballchain.com
SIC: 3462 Gear & chain forgings

(G-8124)
BEACON ADHESIVES INC
Also Called: Beacon Chemical
125 S Macquesten Pkwy (10550-1724)
PHONE..............................914 699-3400
Milton Meshirer, *CEO*
David Meshirer, *President*
Debbie Meshirer-Wojcik, *Vice Pres*
Barbara Meshirer, *Treasurer*
Gina Lagano, *Sales Associate*
◆ EMP: 30
SQ FT: 20,000
SALES (est): 7.3MM Privately Held
WEB: www.beacon1.com
SIC: 2891 Adhesives

(G-8125)
**BRIDGE METAL INDUSTRIES
LLC**
717 S 3rd Ave (10550-4905)
PHONE..............................914 663-9200
Alan Cowen, *Mng Member*
▲ EMP: 130
SQ FT: 8,000
SALES (est): 16.4MM Privately Held
SIC: 2542 Partitions & fixtures, except
wood

(G-8126)
**BRONX WSTCHESTER
TEMPERING INC**
160 S Macquesten Pkwy (10550-1705)
PHONE..............................914 663-9400
Miles Kiho, *President*
▲ EMP: 26
SALES (est): 4.4MM Privately Held
SIC: 3229 Art, decorative & novelty glass-
ware

(G-8127)
CANAL ASPHALT INC
645 S Columbus Ave (10550-4730)
PHONE..............................914 667-8500
August M Nigro, *President*
EMP: 10
SALES (est): 2.9MM Privately Held
SIC: 2951 Asphalt paving mixtures &
blocks

(G-8128)
CASTOLEUM CORPORATION
240 E 7th St (10550-4615)
P.O. Box 41, Yonkers (10710-0041)
PHONE..............................914 664-5877
S V Goldrich, *President*
Eric Bryan, *General Mgr*
Leslie Schwebel, *Corp Secy*
Steve Neil, *Vice Pres*
Mark House, *Government*
EMP: 15
SQ FT: 25,000
SALES (est): 2.8MM Privately Held
WEB: www.sterifab.com
SIC: 2992 2842 5169 Lubricating oils &
greases; disinfectants, household or in-
dustrial plant; coal tar products, primary &
intermediate; gum & wood chemicals

(G-8129)
**CHESTER WEST COUNTY
PRESS**
29 W 4th St (10550-4108)
P.O. Box 152, White Plains (10602-0152)
PHONE..............................914 684-0006
EMP: 6 EST: 1959
SALES (est): 280.2K Privately Held
SIC: 2711 Newspapers-Publishing/Printing

(G-8130)
CINE MAGNETICS INC
F R Chemical Division
524 S Columbus Ave (10550-4712)
PHONE..............................914 667-6707
EMP: 25
SALES (corp-wide): 18.9MM Privately
Held
SIC: 3861 Mfg Processing Chemicals For
X-Ray & Micrographics

▲ = Import ▼=Export
◆ =Import/Export

PA: Cine Magnetics, Inc.
9 W Broad St Ste 250
Stamford CT 06902
914 273-7600

(G-8131)
CLASSIC MEDALLICS INC
520 S Fulton Ave (10550-5010)
PHONE..................................718 392-5410
Gerald Singer, *President*
Mario Singer, *Vice Pres*
Doris Uhler, *Purchasing*
Lucy Walsh, *Sales Staff*
Kevin Fink, *Office Mgr*
▲ EMP: 50 EST: 1941
SALES (est): 9.7MM Privately Held
SIC: 3499 5094 Trophies, metal, except
silver; jewelry

(G-8132)
COLD MIX MANUFACTURING CORP
65 Edison Ave (10550-5003)
PHONE..................................718 463-1444
Dario Amicucci, *President*
Laura Trotta,
EMP: 17
SQ FT: 2,000
SALES (est): 4.5MM Privately Held
SIC: 2951 Asphalt paving mixtures &
blocks

(G-8133)
CON-TEES CUSTOM PRINTING LTD
Also Called: Print Masters
514 Union Ave (10550-4536)
P.O. Box 3020 (10553-3020)
PHONE..................................914 664-0251
Michael Conti, *Ch of Bd*
Joseph Conti, *President*
Joseph J Conti, *Manager*
EMP: 6
SQ FT: 10,000
SALES (est): 914.9K Privately Held
WEB: www.contees.com
SIC: 2759 Screen printing

(G-8134)
COVENTRY MANUFACTURING CO INC (PA)
115 E 3rd St (10550-3606)
P.O. Box 1160 (10551-1160)
PHONE..................................914 668-2212
Myron S Gorel, *President*
Edward R Gorel, *Vice Pres*
Phyllis Gorel, *Admin Sec*
EMP: 32 EST: 1953
SQ FT: 26,000
SALES (est): 4.1MM Privately Held
WEB: www.trulytubular.com
SIC: 3498 3317 3312 Tube fabricating
(contract bending & shaping); steel pipe &
tubes; blast furnaces & steel mills

(G-8135)
CROWN DIE CASTING CORP
268 W Lincoln Ave (10550-2509)
PHONE..................................914 667-5400
Sam Strober, *President*
Bill Gutwein, *Vice Pres*
EMP: 28
SQ FT: 17,000
SALES (est): 6MM Privately Held
WEB: www.crowndiecasting.com
SIC: 3364 3643 3444 3369 Nonferrous
die-castings except aluminum; connec-
tors, electric cord; sheet metalwork; non-
ferrous foundries; aluminum foundries;
aluminum die-castings

(G-8136)
CROWN SIGN SYSTEMS INC
2 South St (10550-1708)
PHONE..................................914 375-2118
Michelle Strum, *President*
Carolyn Cohen, *Office Mgr*
▲ EMP: 11
SALES (est): 1.9MM Privately Held
SIC: 3993 Signs, not made in custom sign
painting shops

(G-8137)
DAB-O-MATIC CORP (PA)
896 S Columbus Ave (10550-5074)
P.O. Box 3839 (10553-3839)
PHONE..................................914 699-7070
Gerard Magaletti, *Ch of Bd*
James P Bell, *President*
Scott Bell, *Vice Pres*
James Bell, *Manager*
Daphne Maurrasse, *Manager*
EMP: 67
SQ FT: 29,000
SALES: 11.9MM Privately Held
WEB: www.dabomatic.com
SIC: 3953 Pads, inking & stamping

(G-8138)
DRG NEW YORK HOLDINGS CORP (PA)
700 S Fulton Ave (10550-5014)
PHONE..................................914 668-9000
Montague Wolfson, *Ch of Bd*
Stephen Bardfield, *Corp Secy*
◆ EMP: 100
SQ FT: 40,000
SALES (est): 15.2MM Privately Held
WEB: www.wolfsoncasing.com
SIC: 2011 5149 Meat packing plants;
sausage casings

(G-8139)
DUNCAN & SON CARPENTRY INC
1 W Prospect Ave (10550-2008)
PHONE..................................914 664-4311
EMP: 21
SQ FT: 10,000
SALES (est): 2.2MM Privately Held
SIC: 2431 Carpentry Contractor

(G-8140)
DUNLEA WHL GL & MIRROR INC
Also Called: J&T Macquesten Realty
147 S Macquesten Pkwy (10550-1724)
PHONE..................................914 664-5277
Timothy Dunlea, *President*
John Arminio, *Vice Pres*
Alex Puranbuda, *Vice Pres*
EMP: 6
SQ FT: 7,000
SALES (est): 837.3K Privately Held
SIC: 3231 Insulating glass: made from pur-
chased glass

(G-8141)
FINA CABINET CORP
20 N Macquesten Pkwy (10550-1841)
PHONE..................................718 409-2900
Annette Alberti, *President*
John Albertti, *Vice Pres*
EMP: 5
SALES (est): 764.8K Privately Held
SIC: 2521 2434 2541 Cabinets, office:
wood; wood kitchen cabinets; wood parti-
tions & fixtures

(G-8142)
GERITREX HOLDINGS INC (PA)
144 E Kingsbridge Rd (10550-4909)
PHONE..................................914 668-4003
Mitch Blashinsky, *CEO*
EMP: 4
SALES (est): 1.5MM Privately Held
SIC: 2834 6719 Pharmaceutical prepara-
tions; investment holding companies, ex-
cept banks

(G-8143)
GIAGNI ENTERPRISES LLC
Also Called: Qmi
550 S Columbus Ave (10550-4712)
PHONE..................................914 699-6500
Vincent Giagni, *Mng Member*
EMP: 5
SALES (est): 582.9K Privately Held
SIC: 3432 Faucets & spigots, metal & plas-
tic

(G-8144)
GRACE RYAN & MAGNUS MLLWK LLC
17 N Bleeker St (10550-1801)
PHONE..................................914 665-0902
Joseph Grace, *Mng Member*
Thor Magnus,

Eamonn Ryan,
EMP: 70
SQ FT: 10,000
SALES (est): 7.4MM Privately Held
SIC: 2431 Millwork

(G-8145)
GRANITE TOPS INC
716 S Columbus Ave (10550-4717)
PHONE..................................914 699-2909
Christopher Sanzaro, *President*
EMP: 40
SQ FT: 11,000
SALES (est): 3.2MM Privately Held
SIC: 3281 Granite, cut & shaped

(G-8146)
H & S EDIBLE PRODUCTS CORP
119 Fulton Ln (10550-4607)
PHONE..................................914 413-3489
Mari P Sweeney, *President*
Peter J Rowan, *Vice Pres*
EMP: 30 EST: 1965
SQ FT: 13,000
SALES (est): 3.2MM Privately Held
SIC: 2099 2051 Bread crumbs, not made
in bakeries; bread, cake & related prod-
ucts

(G-8147)
HAMLET PRODUCTS INC
221 N Macquesten Pkwy # 1 (10550-1081)
PHONE..................................914 665-0307
Russ Hamlet, *President*
Marlo Barreto, *Vice Pres*
Randy Hamlet, *Vice Pres*
▲ EMP: 12
SQ FT: 12,000
SALES (est): 1.7MM Privately Held
WEB: www.hamletproducts.com
SIC: 2542 3089 5046 2541 Fixtures,
store: except wood; cases, plastic; com-
mercial equipment; wood partitions & fix-
tures

(G-8148)
HI SPEED ENVELOPE CO INC
560 S 3rd Ave Ste 1 (10550-4568)
PHONE..................................718 617-1600
Charles Romeo, *President*
Mary Romeo-Springman, *Corp Secy*
Anthony Romeo, *Director*
Fortunato C Romeo, *Director*
Jim Romeo, *Director*
EMP: 16 EST: 1939
SQ FT: 26,000
SALES (est): 1.9MM Privately Held
WEB: www.hispeedprinting.com
SIC: 2752 2759 Commercial printing, off-
set; letterpress printing

(G-8149)
HI-TECH CNC MACHINING CORP
13 Elm Ave (10550-2305)
PHONE..................................914 668-5090
Karl Hormann, *President*
Karl Hormann Jr, *Vice Pres*
EMP: 5 EST: 1970
SQ FT: 7,000
SALES: 1.2MM Privately Held
SIC: 3599 Machine shop, jobbing & repair

(G-8150)
ICE AIR LLC
80 Hartford Ave (10553-1327)
PHONE..................................914 668-4700
Anthony Gili, *Project Mgr*
Rafael Perez, *Opers Mgr*
Fredric Nadel,
▲ EMP: 12
SQ FT: 26,000
SALES (est): 7.5MM Privately Held
SIC: 3585 Air conditioning units, complete:
domestic or industrial

(G-8151)
INTERNATIONAL MERCH SVCS INC
336 S Fulton Ave Fl 1 (10553-1748)
PHONE..................................914 699-4000
Johnny Peralta, *President*
EMP: 5
SALES (est): 683.1K Privately Held
SIC: 3578 Automatic teller machines (ATM)

(G-8152)
ISO PLASTICS CORP
160 E 1st St (10550-3435)
PHONE..................................914 663-8300
Raul Silva, *President*
Jim Coughlin, *Vice Pres*
Fred Squitire, *Treasurer*
▲ EMP: 65 EST: 1996
SQ FT: 43,000
SALES (est): 11.1MM Privately Held
WEB: www.isoplastics.com
SIC: 3089 3599 Molding primary plastic;
machine & other job shop work

(G-8153)
J-K PROSTHETICS & ORTHOTICS
699 N Macquesten Pkwy (10552-2121)
PHONE..................................914 699-2077
Jack Caputo, *President*
Kathleen Caputo, *Corp Secy*
EMP: 22 EST: 1974
SALES (est): 3MM Privately Held
WEB: www.trishare.com
SIC: 3842 Limbs, artificial; prosthetic appli-
ances

(G-8154)
K & B STAMPING CO INC
Also Called: K & B Signs
29 Mount Vernon Ave (10550-2492)
PHONE..................................914 664-8555
Albert Aghabekian, *President*
Elaine Dechiara, *Manager*
EMP: 7 EST: 1946
SQ FT: 4,500
SALES (est): 1MM Privately Held
WEB: www.kbsign.com
SIC: 2759 3993 Plateless engraving;
screen printing; neon signs; displays &
cutouts, window & lobby

(G-8155)
KEY DIGITAL SYSTEMS INC
521 E 3rd St (10553-1606)
PHONE..................................914 667-9700
Mikhail Tsingberg, *President*
Michael Lakhter, *VP Sales*
Scott Pecchia, *Sales Staff*
Masha Lakhter, *VP Mktg*
Abdel Boujoual, *Manager*
▲ EMP: 20
SQ FT: 24,000
SALES: 6.2MM Privately Held
WEB: www.keydigital.com
SIC: 3651 Household audio & video equip-
ment

(G-8156)
KINGSTON BUILDING PRODUCTS LLC
Also Called: Century Awning Concepts
11 Brookdale Pl Ste 101 (10550-3505)
PHONE..................................914 665-0707
John Kingston, *President*
EMP: 9
SALES (est): 403.7K Privately Held
SIC: 2394 Canvas awnings & canopies;
shades, canvas: made from purchased
materials

(G-8157)
LEONARDO PRINTING CORP
Also Called: Leonardo Prntng
529 E 3rd St (10553-1606)
PHONE..................................914 664-7890
Frank Leonardo Jr, *President*
Mark Leonardo, *Vice Pres*
Steven Leonardo, *Admin Sec*
EMP: 5 EST: 1947
SALES (est): 621.9K Privately Held
SIC: 2752 Commercial printing, offset

(G-8158)
LGN MATERIALS & SOLUTIONS
149 Esplanade (10553-1116)
PHONE..................................888 414-0005
Maria Nonni, *President*
EMP: 12
SALES (est): 414.1K Privately Held
SIC: 2796 Steel line engraving for the
printing trade

(G-8159)
LUMINATTA INC
Also Called: Apollo Lighting and Hasco Ltg
717 S 3rd Ave (10550-4905)
PHONE....................................914 664-3600
EMP: 8 EST: 1947
SQ FT: 14,000
SALES (est): 1.5MM Privately Held
SIC: 3646 Mfg Commercial Lighting Fixtures

(G-8160)
M&F STRINGING LLC
2 Cortlandt St (10550-2723)
PHONE....................................914 664-1600
Kenneth Jacobs, Mng Member
EMP: 20 EST: 1953
SQ FT: 8,000
SALES (est): 2MM Privately Held
WEB: www.mfstringing.com
SIC: 2631 Cardboard, tagboard & strawboard

(G-8161)
METAL MAN RESTORATION
254 E 3rd St Fl 1 (10553-5115)
PHONE....................................914 662-4218
Anthony Bugliomo, Principal
EMP: 10
SALES (est): 770K Privately Held
SIC: 3471 Plating of metals or formed products

(G-8162)
MITCHELL ELECTRONICS CORP
85 W Grand St (10552-2108)
PHONE....................................914 699-3800
Nancy Lerner, President
Jonathan Lerner, Corp Secy
EMP: 25 EST: 1956
SQ FT: 5,000
SALES: 2.5MM Privately Held
WEB: www.mitchellxfmr.com
SIC: 3677 3612 Electronic coils, transformers & other inductors; specialty transformers

(G-8163)
MOUNT VERNON IRON WORKS INC
130 Miller Pl (10550-4706)
P.O. Box 3009 (10553-3009)
PHONE....................................914 668-7064
Joeseph Lividini, President
Peter M Lividini, Vice Pres
Grace Lividini, Treasurer
EMP: 7 EST: 1945
SQ FT: 2,000
SALES (est): 1.4MM Privately Held
SIC: 3441 Expansion joints (structural shapes), iron or steel

(G-8164)
MUNN WORKS LLC
150 N Macquesten Pkwy (10550-1836)
PHONE....................................914 665-6100
Max Munn, Mng Member
◆ EMP: 23
SALES: 4.7MM Privately Held
SIC: 3231 3211 Framed mirrors; antique glass

(G-8165)
NOBLE PINE PRODUCTS CO INC
240 E 7th St (10550-4615)
P.O. Box 41, Yonkers (10710-0041)
PHONE....................................914 664-5877
Sylvia Goldrich, President
Leslie Schwebel, Corp Secy
Steven Goldrich, Vice Pres
Steve Neil, Vice Pres
EMP: 12
SQ FT: 12,000
SALES (est): 2.2MM Privately Held
SIC: 2842 2879 Disinfectants, household or industrial plant; insecticides, agricultural or household

(G-8166)
NSI INDUSTRIES LLC
Tork Division
50 S Macquesten Pkwy (10550-1741)
P.O. Box 2725, Huntersville NC (28070-2725)
PHONE....................................800 841-2505

R Sam Shankar, Division Pres
EMP: 200 Privately Held
WEB: www.nsipolaris.com
SIC: 3674 3625 Light sensitive devices; switches, electric power
PA: Nsi Industries, Llc
9730 Northcross Center Ct
Huntersville NC 28078

(G-8167)
OWN INSTRUMENT INC
250 E 7th St (10550-4615)
PHONE....................................914 668-6546
Gerald Chapins, President
Jerry Chapins, Owner
Patricia Chapins, Treasurer
EMP: 13 EST: 1957
SQ FT: 5,000
SALES (est): 2.1MM Privately Held
WEB: www.owninstrument.com
SIC: 3492 Fluid power valves & hose fittings

(G-8168)
PCI INDUSTRIES CORP
550 Franklin Ave (10550-4516)
PHONE....................................914 662-2700
Richard Persico, President
EMP: 22
SALES (est): 3.5MM Privately Held
SIC: 3999 Barber & beauty shop equipment

(G-8169)
PEPSI-COLA BOTTLING CO NY INC
601 S Fulton Ave (10550-5094)
PHONE....................................914 699-2600
Mike Freeman, Sales Executive
Jim Perry, Technology
EMP: 11
SALES (corp-wide): 64.6B Publicly Held
SIC: 2086 Carbonated soft drinks, bottled & canned
HQ: Pepsi-Cola Bottling Company Of New York, Inc.
11202 15th Ave
College Point NY 11356
718 392-1000

(G-8170)
PERFECT SHOULDER COMPANY INC
2 Cortlandt St (10550-2723)
PHONE....................................914 699-8100
Harold Greenberg, President
▲ EMP: 25 EST: 1938
SQ FT: 35,000
SALES (est): 2.8MM Privately Held
SIC: 2396 Pads, shoulder: for coats, suits, etc.

(G-8171)
PRECISION COSMETICS MFG CO
519 S 5th Ave Ste 6 (10550-4476)
PHONE....................................914 667-1200
Aubrey Fenton Sr, President
Aubrey Fenton Jr, Treasurer
EMP: 5
SQ FT: 5,000
SALES: 50K Privately Held
SIC: 2844 Lipsticks

(G-8172)
PREMIER BRANDS AMERICA INC
120 Pearl St (10550-1725)
PHONE....................................718 325-3000
Pat Obrien, COO
EMP: 25
SALES (est): 4.5MM
SALES (corp-wide): 35.9MM Privately Held
SIC: 2842 2865 Shoe polish or cleaner; polishing preparations & related products; cyclic crudes & intermediates
PA: Premier Brands Of America Inc.
170 Hamilton Ave Ste 201
White Plains NY 10601
914 667-6200

(G-8173)
PRO-LINE SOLUTIONS INC
Also Called: Pry Care Products
18 Sargent Pl (10550-4727)
P.O. Box 651, Bronx (10465-0617)
PHONE....................................914 664-0002
Alex Lodato, President
EMP: 7
SQ FT: 10,000
SALES (est): 957.1K Privately Held
SIC: 2841 Soap & other detergents

(G-8174)
PROACTIVE MEDICAL PRODUCTS LLC
270 Washington St (10553-1017)
PHONE....................................845 205-6004
Mordecai Light, President
Brian Goldstein, VP Sales
▲ EMP: 8 EST: 2012
SQ FT: 20,000
SALES: 7MM Privately Held
SIC: 3841 Diagnostic apparatus, medical

(G-8175)
R I R COMMUNICATIONS SYSTEMS
20 Nuvern Ave (10550-4819)
PHONE....................................718 706-9957
EMP: 20
SALES (corp-wide): 1.8MM Privately Held
SIC: 3661 Mfg Voice & Data Communications
PA: R I R Communications Systems Inc
20 Nuvern Ave
Mount Vernon NY 10550
718 706-9957

(G-8176)
R V H ESTATES INC
138 Mount Vernon Ave (10550-1719)
PHONE....................................914 664-9888
Robert Belluzzi, President
Vincent Belluzzi, Vice Pres
EMP: 6
SALES: 390K Privately Held
SIC: 2599 Bar, restaurant & cafeteria furniture

(G-8177)
RELIABLE ELEC MT VERNON INC
519 S 5th Ave (10550-4498)
PHONE....................................914 668-4440
Jay Friedman, President
EMP: 23
SQ FT: 8,000
SALES: 75K Privately Held
WEB: www.reliableelectronics.net
SIC: 3577 Computer peripheral equipment

(G-8178)
ROHLFS STINED LEADED GL STUDIO
783 S 3rd Ave (10550-4946)
PHONE....................................914 699-4848
Peter A Rohlf, CEO
Gregory Rohlf, Vice Pres
EMP: 25
SQ FT: 10,000
SALES (est): 3.1MM Privately Held
WEB: www.rohlfstudio.com
SIC: 3231 3442 Stained glass: made from purchased glass; leaded glass; casements, aluminum

(G-8179)
SECS INC
550 S Columbus Ave (10550-4712)
PHONE....................................914 667-5600
Vincent Giagni, Ch of Bd
Leonora Giagni, Ch of Bd
Stephen Giagni, President
▲ EMP: 20
SQ FT: 15,000
SALES (est): 6.4MM Privately Held
WEB: www.prosecs.com
SIC: 3462 Gears, forged steel

(G-8180)
SIGMUND COHN CORP
121 S Columbus Ave (10553-1324)
PHONE....................................914 664-5300
Thomas Cohn, President

George Pilke, CFO
▲ EMP: 55 EST: 1901
SQ FT: 72,000
SALES (est): 12.7MM Privately Held
SIC: 3496 3339 3315 3356 Miscellaneous fabricated wire products; primary nonferrous metals; steel wire & related products; precious metals

(G-8181)
TAPE SYSTEMS INC
630 S Columbus Ave (10550-4734)
P.O. Box 8612, Pelham (10803-8612)
PHONE....................................914 668-3700
Aniello Scotti, President
▲ EMP: 10
SQ FT: 30,000
SALES (est): 2.2MM Privately Held
SIC: 3842 Adhesive tape & plasters, medicated or non-medicated

(G-8182)
TENNYSON MACHINE CO INC
535 S 5th Ave (10550-4483)
PHONE....................................914 668-5468
Lawrence A Castiglia, President
Larry Castiglia, MIS Mgr
EMP: 16 EST: 1961
SQ FT: 10,000
SALES (est): 1.2MM Privately Held
SIC: 3599 Machine shop, jobbing & repair

(G-8183)
TORK INC (PA)
50 S Macquesten Pkwy (10550-1741)
P.O. Box 2725, Huntersville NC (28070-2725)
PHONE....................................914 664-3542
Victoria White, Ch of Bd
R Sam Shankar, President
Leonard Caponigro, Vice Pres
Nicholas Murlo, Vice Pres
Joel Berson, Admin Sec
▲ EMP: 100
SQ FT: 40,000
SALES (est): 10.2MM Privately Held
WEB: www.tork.com
SIC: 3674 3625 Light sensitive devices; switches, electric power

(G-8184)
TORRE PRODUCTS CO INC
10 Beach St (10550-1702)
PHONE....................................212 925-8989
Liberty F Raho, President
Peter N Raho, Treasurer
Peter Raho, Treasurer
Philip Raho, Admin Sec
EMP: 9
SALES (est): 1MM Privately Held
SIC: 2899 2087 Essential oils; flavoring extracts & syrups

(G-8185)
TRAC REGULATORS INC
160 S Terrace Ave (10550-2408)
PHONE....................................914 699-9352
Adelmo Costantini, President
Cynthia La Sorsa, Corp Secy
Tom Notaro, Vice Pres
George Witzel, Shareholder
EMP: 20
SQ FT: 10,000
SALES (est): 3.4MM Privately Held
SIC: 3613 3491 Regulators, power; industrial valves

(G-8186)
TRI STAR LABEL INC
630 S Columbus Ave (10550-4734)
PHONE....................................914 237-4800
Dan Mesisco, President
Neil Scotti, Vice Pres
▲ EMP: 7
SQ FT: 8,000
SALES: 900K Privately Held
SIC: 2759 Labels & seals: printing

(G-8187)
TRI-TECHNOLOGIES INC
40 Hartford Ave (10553-5119)
PHONE....................................914 699-2001
David Hirsch, CEO
Dennis Di Donato, President
▲ EMP: 48
SQ FT: 25,000

SALES (est): 10.2MM **Privately Held**
SIC: 3484 3451 3444 3469 Small arms; screw machine products; sheet metalwork; metal stampings

(G-8188)
TRULY TUBULAR FITTING CORP
115 E 3rd St (10550-3606)
P.O. Box 1160 (10551-1160)
PHONE..................................914 664-8686
Myron S Gorel, *President*
Edward Gorel, *Vice Pres*
Phyllis Gorel, *Admin Sec*
EMP: 19
SQ FT: 26,000
SALES (est): 880K
SALES (corp-wide): 4.1MM **Privately Held**
WEB: www.trulytubular.com
SIC: 3498 Fabricated pipe & fittings
PA: Coventry Manufacturing Company, Inc.
115 E 3rd St
Mount Vernon NY 10550
914 668-2212

(G-8189)
TURBOFIL PACKAGING MCHS LLC
30 Beach St (10550-1702)
PHONE..................................914 239-3878
Eli Uriel, *Branch Mgr*
Deborah Smook, *Mng Member*
Elaine Epps, *Director*
▲ EMP: 10
SQ FT: 7,000
SALES (est): 2.2MM **Privately Held**
WEB: www.turbofil.com
SIC: 3565 Packing & wrapping machinery

(G-8190)
UFS INDUSTRIES INC
Also Called: Sally Sherman Foods
300 N Macquesten Pkwy (10550-1008)
PHONE..................................914 664-6262
Thomas Recine, *President*
Felix Endico, *COO*
Vincent Lombardo, *Facilities Mgr*
Sherine Robinson, *Assistant*
EMP: 100 EST: 1930
SQ FT: 50,000
SALES (est): 29.4MM **Privately Held**
SIC: 2099 Cole slaw, in bulk

(G-8191)
UNITED IRON INC
6 Roslyn Pl (10550-4540)
PHONE..................................914 667-5700
Randall Rifelli, *President*
Matt Affek, *Project Mgr*
Mickey Lee, *Project Mgr*
Cecil Bernard, *Safety Mgr*
Luigi Saturnino, *Purch Mgr*
EMP: 30 EST: 1922
SQ FT: 27,000
SALES (est): 7.3MM **Privately Held**
SIC: 3449 3441 3446 Miscellaneous metalwork; fabricated structural metal; architectural metalwork

(G-8192)
YOUR WAY CUSTOM CABINETS INC
20 N Macquesten Pkwy (10550-1841)
PHONE..................................914 371-1870
Annette Alberti, *President*
EMP: 7
SALES (est): 915.7K **Privately Held**
SIC: 2434 Wood kitchen cabinets

Mountainville
Orange County

(G-8193)
GLUTEN FREE BAKE SHOP INC
Also Called: Katz Gluten Free
19 Industry Dr (10953)
P.O. Box 58, Monroe (10949-0058)
PHONE..................................845 782-5307
Rachel Jacobowitz, *President*
Mordche Jacobowitz, *Vice Pres*
▼ EMP: 50
SQ FT: 13,000

SALES (est): 9.3MM **Privately Held**
SIC: 2051 Bakery: wholesale or wholesale/retail combined

(G-8194)
JP FILLING INC
20 Industry Dr (10953)
PHONE..................................845 534-4793
Joel Polatsek, *President*
▲ EMP: 65
SQ FT: 3,000
SALES (est): 3.2MM **Privately Held**
SIC: 2844 Perfumes & colognes

Munnsville
Madison County

(G-8195)
CUSTOM WOODCRAFT LLC
2525 Perry Schumaker Rd (13409-3620)
PHONE..................................315 843-4234
Daniel Stoltzfus,
EMP: 12
SQ FT: 11,000
SALES (est): 1.3MM **Privately Held**
SIC: 2434 5712 2511 Wood kitchen cabinets; cabinet work, custom; wood household furniture

Nanuet
Rockland County

(G-8196)
BRIGADOON SOFTWARE INC (PA)
119 Rockland Ctr 250 (10954-2956)
PHONE..................................845 624-0909
Terrance Kawles, *President*
Martin Moran, *Vice Pres*
Frank Jones, *Sls & Mktg Exec*
Tim Albright, *VP Sales*
EMP: 2
SALES (est): 1.4MM **Privately Held**
WEB: www.brigadoonsoftware.com
SIC: 7372 Prepackaged software

(G-8197)
BRUNO & CANIO LTD
130 Blauvelt Rd (10954-3602)
PHONE..................................845 624-3060
EMP: 37
SQ FT: 6,500
SALES: 1MM **Privately Held**
SIC: 2325 2337 Contract Manufacturer Men's Separate Trousers & Women's Skirts

(G-8198)
CITIZEN PUBLISHING CORP
Also Called: Rockland County Times
119 Main St Ste 2 (10954-2883)
PHONE..................................845 627-1414
Armand Miele, *Manager*
EMP: 10
SALES (est): 477.5K **Privately Held**
WEB: www.rocklandcountytimes.com
SIC: 2711 Newspapers, publishing & printing

(G-8199)
CROWN MILL WORK CORP
33 Murray Hill Dr (10954-5941)
PHONE..................................845 371-2200
Benzion Lebovits, *Ch of Bd*
EMP: 5
SQ FT: 15,500
SALES (est): 1.2MM **Privately Held**
SIC: 2431 Millwork

(G-8200)
JAR METALS INC
50 2nd Ave (10954-4405)
PHONE..................................845 425-8901
Andrew Gallina, *President*
John Shepitka, *Vice Pres*
EMP: 15
SQ FT: 10,000
SALES (est): 322.1K **Privately Held**
SIC: 3444 5085 Sheet metalwork; industrial supplies

(G-8201)
JESCAR ENTERPRISES INC
Also Called: Mazerna USA
213 Airport Executive Par (10954-5252)
PHONE..................................845 352-5850
Jeff Silver, *President*
Jeff L Silver, *President*
Tilo Franz, *Managing Dir*
▲ EMP: 5
SQ FT: 3,100
SALES (est): 1MM **Privately Held**
WEB: www.jescar.com
SIC: 2842 Automobile polish

(G-8202)
MINUTEMAN PRESS INC
121 W Nyack Rd Ste 3 (10954-2962)
PHONE..................................845 623-2277
Brian H Gunn, *President*
EMP: 5
SQ FT: 2,000
SALES (est): 611.9K **Privately Held**
SIC: 2752 Commercial printing, lithographic

(G-8203)
PHILIPP FELDHEIM INC (PA)
Also Called: Feldheim Publishers
208 Airport Executive Par (10954-5262)
PHONE..................................845 356-2282
Yitzchak Feldheim, *President*
Elia Hollander, *Managing Dir*
Mirian Mendlowitz, *Treasurer*
Suzanne Brandt, *Sales Mgr*
▲ EMP: 9 EST: 1939
SALES (est): 607.3K **Privately Held**
WEB: www.feldheim.com
SIC: 2731 Books: publishing only

(G-8204)
WENDYS AUTO EXPRESS INC
121 Main St (10954-2967)
PHONE..................................845 624-6100
Wendy Winnick, *President*
Cindy Cherny, *Manager*
EMP: 6
SALES (est): 523.1K **Privately Held**
SIC: 3711 Chassis, motor vehicle

(G-8205)
WR SMITH & SONS INC
121 W Nyack Rd (10954-2939)
P.O. Box 225, West Nyack (10994-0225)
PHONE..................................845 620-9400
William Smith, *Principal*
EMP: 7
SQ FT: 1,500
SALES (est): 914.6K **Privately Held**
SIC: 2821 3469 Plastics materials & resins; metal stampings

Naples
Ontario County

(G-8206)
BAKER LOGGING & FIREWOOD
8781 Grlnghuse Atlanta Rd (14512-9247)
PHONE..................................585 374-5733
Richard Baker, *Owner*
EMP: 9
SALES (est): 489.5K **Privately Held**
SIC: 2411 Logging camps & contractors

(G-8207)
L & D ACQUISITION LLC
1 Lake Niagara Ln (14512-9770)
PHONE..................................585 531-9000
Doug Hazlitt, *Principal*
EMP: 16
SALES (est): 1MM **Privately Held**
SIC: 2084 Wines

(G-8208)
LAKE COUNTRY WOODWORKERS LTD
12 Clark St (14512-9535)
P.O. Box 400 (14512-0400)
PHONE..................................585 374-6353
Donna Fargo, *President*
Karen Wood, *President*
Chris Cooney, *Project Mgr*
Brad Reigelsperger, *Engineer*
Sarah Wood, *Admin Asst*

▲ EMP: 40 EST: 1976
SQ FT: 30,000
SALES (est): 6.1MM **Privately Held**
WEB: www.lcww.com
SIC: 2521 Wood office furniture

(G-8209)
NAPLES VLY MRGERS ACQSTONS LLC
Also Called: Angelic Gourmet
154 N Main St (14512-9156)
P.O. Box 39 (14512-0039)
PHONE..................................585 490-1339
Donna Nichols, *Mng Member*
▼ EMP: 9
SQ FT: 6,000
SALES: 500K **Privately Held**
SIC: 2064 Cake ornaments, confectionery

Narrowsburg
Sullivan County

(G-8210)
NARROWSBURG FEED & GRAIN CO
Also Called: Honor Brand Feeds
Fifth And Main St (12764)
P.O. Box 185 (12764-0185)
PHONE..................................845 252-3936
Raymond Villeneuve, *President*
Roy G Morris, *General Mgr*
Patrick C Brown, *Treasurer*
EMP: 16 EST: 1970
SQ FT: 20,000
SALES (est): 2.1MM **Privately Held**
WEB: www.narrowsburg.org
SIC: 2048 Poultry feeds

(G-8211)
STUART COMMUNICATIONS INC
Also Called: The River Reporter
93 Erie Ave (12764-6423)
P.O. Box 150 (12764-0150)
PHONE..................................845 252-7414
Laura Stuart, *President*
Tanya Hubbert, *Sales Mgr*
EMP: 13
SALES (est): 967.2K **Privately Held**
WEB: www.riverreporter.com
SIC: 2711 Newspapers, publishing & printing

Nassau
Rensselaer County

(G-8212)
CAPITAL SAWMILL SERVICE
4119 Us Highway 20 (12123-1904)
PHONE..................................518 479-0729
Steven Daniels,
Teresa Eddy,
EMP: 9
SALES (est): 907.8K **Privately Held**
WEB: www.capitalsawmill.com
SIC: 2421 Sawmills & planing mills, general

(G-8213)
COPELAND COATING COMPANY INC
3600 Us Highway 20 (12123-1934)
P.O. Box 595 (12123-0595)
PHONE..................................518 766-2932
John R Copeland, *Ch of Bd*
Steven W Hinding, *Vice Pres*
Rick Kment, *Purch Agent*
Matthew Mitchell, *CFO*
Lawrence G Copeland, *Shareholder*
▲ EMP: 15 EST: 1945
SQ FT: 10,000
SALES (est): 4.3MM **Privately Held**
WEB: www.copelandcoating.com
SIC: 3272 Paving materials, prefabricated concrete

GEOGRAPHIC

Nedrow
Onondaga County

(G-8214)
BOWEN PRODUCTS CORPORATION
5084 S Onondaga Rd (13120-9702)
PHONE...............................315 498-4481
Charles D Smith, *President*
Louise M Smith, *Vice Pres*
EMP: 9 EST: 1896
SQ FT: 18,000
SALES (est): 1.1MM **Privately Held**
SIC: 3469 3569 Metal stampings; lubricating equipment

(G-8215)
INNOVATIVE SIGNAGE SYSTEMS INC
6321 S Salina St (13120-1026)
PHONE...............................315 469-7783
Larry Loeb, *President*
EMP: 15 EST: 1978
SQ FT: 11,000
SALES (est): 2MM **Privately Held**
WEB: www.signagesystems.com
SIC: 3993 Signs & advertising specialties

(G-8216)
ONONDAGA NATION
Onondaga Nation Factory
3951 State Route 11 (13120-8655)
PHONE...............................315 469-3230
Duane Williams, *Branch Mgr*
EMP: 8 **Privately Held**
SIC: 2111 Cigarettes
PA: Onondaga Nation
4040 Route 11
Nedrow NY 13120
315 469-0302

(G-8217)
W F SAUNDERS & SONS INC (PA)
5126 S Onondaga Rd (13120-9789)
P.O. Box A (13120-0129)
PHONE...............................315 469-3217
Sherman V Saunders Jr, *President*
Michael Saunders, *Treasurer*
EMP: 15 EST: 1891
SQ FT: 5,000
SALES (est): 7.7MM **Privately Held**
SIC: 3273 3281 Ready-mixed concrete; cut stone & stone products

Nesconset
Suffolk County

(G-8218)
HUM LIMITED LIABILITY CORP
70 Deer Valley Dr (11767-1568)
PHONE...............................631 525-2174
Richard Blumenfeld, *Principal*
EMP: 6
SALES (est): 185.1K **Privately Held**
SIC: 2051 7389 Bakery: wholesale or wholesale/retail combined;

(G-8219)
KEY HIGH VACUUM PRODUCTS INC
36 Southern Blvd (11767-1097)
PHONE...............................631 584-5959
Anthony Kozyrski, *President*
Elizabeth Kozyrski, *Corp Secy*
▲ EMP: 30
SQ FT: 15,000
SALES (est): 5.7MM **Privately Held**
WEB: www.keyhigh.com
SIC: 3589 3494 3492 3429 Vacuum cleaners & sweepers, electric: industrial; valves & pipe fittings; fluid power valves & hose fittings; manufactured hardware (general)

(G-8220)
PERFECT POLY INC
1 Gina Ct (11767-2058)
PHONE...............................631 265-0539

Malke Gelbstein, *President*
EMP: 20
SALES (est): 3.5MM **Privately Held**
SIC: 2821 Polyesters

New Berlin
Chenango County

(G-8221)
CHOBANI LLC
669 County Road 25 (13411-4403)
PHONE...............................607 847-6181
Mia Stone, *Business Mgr*
Grace Simmons, *Vice Pres*
Cagdas Sirin, *Vice Pres*
Dwayne Henderson, *Project Mgr*
Hector Yzquierdo, *Opers Mgr*
EMP: 8
SALES (corp-wide): 249.2MM **Privately Held**
SIC: 2026 Yogurt
HQ: Chobani, Llc
147 State Highway 320
Norwich NY 13815

(G-8222)
GOLDEN ARTIST COLORS INC
188 Bell Rd (13411-3616)
PHONE...............................607 847-6154
Lu Dick, *CEO*
Mark Golden, *Ch of Bd*
Barbara J Schindler, *President*
Dean Hubbard, *Purchasing*
Vaikunt Raghavan, *Engineer*
◆ EMP: 125
SQ FT: 60,000
SALES (est): 30.6MM **Privately Held**
WEB: www.goldenpaint.com
SIC: 3952 Paints, except gold & bronze: artists'; paints, gold or bronze: artists'

New City
Rockland County

(G-8223)
A TRADITION OF EXCELLENCE INC
85b Maple Ave (10956)
PHONE...............................845 638-4595
Tom Sullivan, *President*
John Cusick, *Vice Pres*
EMP: 5
SALES (est): 499.1K **Privately Held**
SIC: 2759 Screen printing

(G-8224)
DARK STAR LITHOGRAPH CORP
9 Perth Ln (10956-5808)
P.O. Box 9074, Bardonia (10954-9074)
PHONE...............................845 634-3780
Richard Suben, *President*
EMP: 5
SALES (est): 628.4K **Privately Held**
SIC: 2752 Commercial printing, offset

(G-8225)
DOCTOROW COMMUNICATIONS INC
Also Called: Home Lighting & Accessories
180 Phillips Hill Rd # 5 (10956-4132)
P.O. Box 293 (10956-0293)
PHONE...............................845 708-5166
Jeffrey Doctorow, *President*
EMP: 12
SALES (est): 1.5MM **Privately Held**
WEB: www.contractlighting.net
SIC: 2721 Magazines: publishing only, not printed on site

(G-8226)
EASTERN INDUSTRIAL STEEL CORP (PA)
4 Fringe Ct (10956-6802)
P.O. Box 132, Blauvelt (10913-0132)
PHONE...............................845 639-9749
Peter Lacombe, *President*
EMP: 15

SALES: 1MM **Privately Held**
WEB: www.easternindustrialsteel.com
SIC: 3325 3089 Steel foundries; extruded finished plastic products

(G-8227)
MSI INC
329 Strawtown Rd (10956-6634)
PHONE...............................845 639-6683
Murray Steinfink, *President*
EMP: 10
SALES (est): 804.7K **Privately Held**
SIC: 3081 Unsupported plastics film & sheet

(G-8228)
PENNYSAVER GROUP INC
Also Called: Tri State Media Group
39 S Main St Ste 1 (10956-3563)
PHONE...............................845 627-3600
Stacie Boering, *Manager*
EMP: 15
SALES (corp-wide): 7.6MM **Privately Held**
WEB: www.nysaver.com
SIC: 2711 Newspapers, publishing & printing
PA: Pennysaver Group Inc.
510 Fifth Ave
Pelham NY
914 592-5222

(G-8229)
REGAL SCREEN PRINTING INTL
Also Called: Shirt Shack
515 Route 304 Ste 1a (10956-3037)
PHONE...............................845 356-8181
Stan Mesnick, *President*
Barbara Mesnick, *Vice Pres*
EMP: 6
SALES (est): 809.2K **Privately Held**
SIC: 2759 Screen printing

(G-8230)
SHINING CREATIONS INC
Also Called: Strawtown Jewerly
40 S Main St Ste 1 (10956-3533)
PHONE...............................845 358-4911
Ellen Arkin, *President*
Glenn Arkin, *Vice Pres*
EMP: 5
SALES: 200K **Privately Held**
SIC: 3911 5944 Jewelry mountings & trimmings; jewelry, precious stones & precious metals

(G-8231)
YELLOW PAGES INC (PA)
222 N Main St (10956-5302)
PHONE...............................845 639-6060
Robert Gazzetta, *Ch of Bd*
EMP: 4
SALES (est): 6.6MM **Privately Held**
WEB: www.ypinc.net
SIC: 2741 Telephone & other directory publishing

New Hampton
Orange County

(G-8232)
BALCHEM CORPORATION (PA)
52 Sunrise Park Rd (10958-4703)
P.O. Box 600 (10958-0600)
PHONE...............................845 326-5600
Theodore L Harris, *Ch of Bd*
Ria Dake, *General Mgr*
David F Ludwig, *Vice Pres*
Scott Mason, *Vice Pres*
Irene Saavedra, *Technical Mgr*
◆ EMP: 277 EST: 1967
SQ FT: 20,000
SALES: 643.6MM **Publicly Held**
WEB: www.balchem.com
SIC: 2899 2869 Chemical preparations; methyl alcohol, synthetic methanol

(G-8233)
BCP INGREDIENTS INC (HQ)
52 Sunrise Park Rd (10958-4703)
PHONE...............................845 326-5600
Dino A Rossi, *Ch of Bd*
Richard Bendure, *COO*

John E Kuehner, *Vice Pres*
David F Ludwig, *Vice Pres*
Dana Putnam, *Vice Pres*
▼ EMP: 54
SALES (est): 18.2MM
SALES (corp-wide): 643.6MM **Publicly Held**
SIC: 2899 Chemical preparations
PA: Balchem Corporation
52 Sunrise Park Rd
New Hampton NY 10958
845 326-5600

(G-8234)
DICKS CONCRETE CO INC (PA)
1053 County Route 37 (10958-4811)
PHONE...............................845 374-5966
Richard Penaluna Jr, *President*
Barbara Penaluna, *Vice Pres*
Jan Dodd, *CFO*
EMP: 40
SQ FT: 5,000
SALES (est): 11.5MM **Privately Held**
WEB: www.dicksconcrete.com
SIC: 1442 5032 3273 3271 Sand mining; gravel mining; cement; ready-mixed concrete; concrete block & brick

(G-8235)
EAST COAST SPRING MIX INC
211 Lynch Ave (10958-4504)
PHONE...............................845 355-1215
Richard Minkus Jr, *President*
EMP: 7
SALES (est): 885.2K **Privately Held**
SIC: 3273 Ready-mixed concrete

New Hartford
Oneida County

(G-8236)
B & D ENTERPRISES UTICA INC (PA)
Also Called: Hemstrought's Bakeries
2 Campion Rd Ste 7 (13413-1647)
PHONE...............................315 735-3311
Thomas R Batters, *President*
Michael J Denz, *Vice Pres*
Mary Denz, *Treasurer*
Paul Remizowski, *Shareholder*
EMP: 75
SQ FT: 20,000
SALES (est): 9.8MM **Privately Held**
SIC: 2051 5461 5149 Bakery: wholesale or wholesale/retail combined; bakeries; bakery products

(G-8237)
BILLY BEEZ USA LLC
1 Sangertown Sq Ste 107 (13413-1519)
PHONE...............................315 235-3121
EMP: 8
SALES (corp-wide): 16.7MM **Privately Held**
SIC: 3949 Playground equipment
PA: Billy Beez Usa, Llc
3 W 35th St Fl 3 # 3
New York NY 10001
646 606-2249

(G-8238)
DARTCOM INCORPORATED
Also Called: Dart Communications
2 Oxford Xing Ste 1 (13413-3246)
PHONE...............................315 790-5456
Michael Baldwin, *President*
Ken Drake, *Software Engr*
Don Lawrence, *Software Dev*
Nicholas Baldwin, *Associate*
Nick Baldwin, *Associate*
EMP: 4
SQ FT: 7,500
SALES (est): 1.3MM **Privately Held**
WEB: www.dart.com
SIC: 7372 Business oriented computer software

(G-8239)
ELM GRAPHICS INC
9694 Mallory Rd (13413-3618)
PHONE...............................315 737-5984
Stanley Lebiednik, *President*
Gerald Eischen, *Vice Pres*

EMP: 5
SQ FT: 1,200
SALES (est): 532.6K **Privately Held**
SIC: 2759 Commercial printing

(G-8240)
FASTER-FORM CORP
Also Called: Lifesake Division
1 Faster Form Cir Ste 1 # 1 (13413-9564)
P.O. Box 704 (13413-0704)
PHONE..................................800 327-3676
J C Waszkiewicz III, *President*
Lawrence P Ulrich, *Vice Pres*
J C Waszkiewicz II, *Treasurer*
▲ EMP: 85 EST: 1959
SQ FT: 200,000
SALES (est): 7.9MM **Privately Held**
WEB: www.vincenzaflowers.com
SIC: 3999 3993 Flowers, artificial & pre-
served; bric-a-brac; displays, paint
process

(G-8241)
LOCKHEED MARTIN CORPORATION
8373 Seneca Tpke (13413-4957)
PHONE..................................315 793-5800
John Vitellaro, *Engineer*
Richard Kahler, *Manager*
Wayne Jenne, *Admin Asst*
Charles Huntington,
EMP: 80 **Publicly Held**
WEB: www.lockheedmartin.com
SIC: 3721 7371 Aircraft; custom computer
programming services
PA: Lockheed Martin Corporation
6801 Rockledge Dr
Bethesda MD 20817

(G-8242)
PAR TECHNOLOGY CORPORATION (PA)
8383 Seneca Tpke Ste 2 (13413-4991)
PHONE..................................315 738-0600
Savneet Singh, *President*
Jim Gelose, *Opers Staff*
Bryan A Menar, *CFO*
Melanie Biss, *Marketing Staff*
Mark Eldred, *Manager*
EMP: 99 EST: 1968
SQ FT: 180,200
SALES: 201.2MM **Publicly Held**
WEB: www.partech.com
SIC: 7372 7382 Prepackaged software;
confinement surveillance systems mainte-
nance & monitoring

(G-8243)
PARTECH INC (HQ)
8383 Seneca Tpke Ste 2 (13413-4991)
PHONE..................................315 738-0600
Ronald J Casciano, *CEO*
Karen E Sammon, *President*
Charles Constantino, *Director*
Gregory Cortese, *Admin Sec*
▲ EMP: 250
SQ FT: 99,400
SALES (est): 92MM
SALES (corp-wide): 201.2MM **Publicly Held**
SIC: 3571 Mainframe computers
PA: Par Technology Corporation
8383 Seneca Tpke Ste 2
New Hartford NY 13413
315 738-0600

(G-8244)
RIVERHAWK COMPANY LP
Also Called: Indikon Company
215 Clinton Rd (13413-5306)
PHONE..................................315 624-7171
Allen Williams, *Manager*
EMP: 32 **Privately Held**
WEB: www.indikon.com
SIC: 3823 3829 3674 Industrial process
measurement equipment; measuring &
controlling devices; semiconductors & re-
lated devices
PA: Riverhawk Company L.P.
215 Clinton Rd
New Hartford NY 13413

(G-8245)
SAES SMART MATERIALS INC
Also Called: Saes Memry
4355 Middle Settlement Rd (13413-5317)
PHONE..................................315 266-2026
Richard Lafond, *CEO*
Giorgio Vergani, *Ch of Bd*
John Schosser, *CFO*
Steve Dayton, *Treasurer*
▲ EMP: 27
SALES (est): 7MM
SALES (corp-wide): 60.2MM **Privately Held**
SIC: 3339 Titanium metal, sponge & gran-
ules
PA: Saes Getters Spa
Viale Italia 77
Lainate MI 20020
029 317-81

(G-8246)
SPECIAL METALS CORPORATION
4317 Middle Settlement Rd (13413-5392)
PHONE..................................315 798-2900
Rusty Fortner, *Production*
Kelly Bonner, *Buyer*
Charlie C Dickey, *Engineer*
Sharon G Dunn, *Marketing Staff*
Tammy Williams, *Technician*
EMP: 300
SALES (corp-wide): 225.3B **Publicly Held**
SIC: 3356 Nickel & nickel alloy: rolling,
drawing or extruding
HQ: Special Metals Corporation
4832 Richmond Rd Ste 100
Warrensville Heights OH 44128
216 755-3030

(G-8247)
TOWN OF HARTFORD
Also Called: Hartford Town Park System
Rr 12 (13413)
PHONE..................................315 724-0654
John Cunningham, *Director*
EMP: 7 **Privately Held**
SIC: 2531 9111 Picnic tables or benches,
park; mayors' offices
PA: Town Of Hartford
165 Cr 23
Hartford NY 12838
518 632-5255

(G-8248)
WESTROCK CP LLC
45 Campion Rd (13413-1601)
PHONE..................................770 448-2193
William Ross, *Manager*
EMP: 147
SALES (corp-wide): 16.2B **Publicly Held**
SIC: 2653 Boxes, corrugated: made from
purchased materials
HQ: Westrock Cp, Llc
1000 Abernathy Rd
Atlanta GA 30328

```
New Hyde Park
Nassau County
```

(G-8249)
ALLIED BOLT PRODUCTS LLC
3000 Marcus Ave Ste 3e09 (11042-1041)
PHONE..................................516 512-7600
Glen Malin, *Mng Member*
EMP: 26
SALES (est): 2.4MM
SALES (corp-wide): 14.4MM **Privately Held**
SIC: 3452 Bolts, nuts, rivets & washers
PA: Allied Bolt, Inc.
3000 Marcus Ave Ste 3e09
New Hyde Park NY 11042
516 512-7600

(G-8250)
APPLE COMMUTER INC
54 Lake Dr (11040-1125)
PHONE..................................917 299-0066
EMP: 6
SALES (est): 689.5K **Privately Held**
SIC: 3571 Mfg Electronic Computers

(G-8251)
ARNOUSE DIGITAL DEVICES CORP
Also Called: Biodigital
1983 Marcus Ave Ste 104 (11042-2002)
PHONE..................................516 673-4444
Michael Arnouse, *President*
Daniel Dellick, *COO*
Rich Tackels, *Vice Pres*
Roland Feibert, *Engineer*
Frank Marano, *CFO*
EMP: 62
SQ FT: 4,963
SALES (est): 6.2MM **Privately Held**
SIC: 3571 Electronic computers

(G-8252)
ATLANTIC ER INC
180 Atlantic Ave (11040-5028)
P.O. Box 6077, Astoria (11106-0077)
PHONE..................................516 294-3200
Ronald Meltsner, *President*
Eric Spar, *Vice Pres*
Harold Spar, *Treasurer*
Henry Meltsner, *Admin Sec*
▲ EMP: 50 EST: 1946
SQ FT: 20,000
SALES (est): 7.9MM **Privately Held**
WEB: www.halhen.com
SIC: 3842 Hearing aids

(G-8253)
BARC USA INC
5 Delaware Dr Ste 2 (11042-1100)
PHONE..................................516 719-1052
Joseph Jonckheere, *CEO*
Dirk Allaert, *Technology*
▲ EMP: 34
SQ FT: 17,500
SALES (est): 12.3MM
SALES (corp-wide): 919.2MM **Privately Held**
WEB: www.barclab.com
SIC: 2834 Pharmaceutical preparations
HQ: Bio Analytical Research Corporation
Industriepark-Zwijnaarde 3
Gent 9052
932 923-26

(G-8254)
BILLANTI CASTING CO INC
Also Called: Billanti Jewelry Casting
299 S 11th St (11040-5558)
P.O. Box 1117 (11040-7117)
PHONE..................................516 775-4800
EMP: 30 EST: 1955
SALES (est): 4.3MM **Privately Held**
SIC: 3911 3339 Mfg Precious Metal Jew-
elry Primary Nonferrous Metal Producer

(G-8255)
CAMBRIDGE MANUFACTURING LLC
1700 Jericho Tpke (11040-4742)
PHONE..................................516 326-1350
Peter Negri,
EMP: 8
SALES (est): 1.1MM **Privately Held**
SIC: 3826 Laser scientific & engineering
instruments

(G-8256)
CHEMICOLLOID LABORATORIES INC
55 Herricks Rd (11040-5317)
P.O. Box 14094, Hauppauge (11788-0789)
PHONE..................................516 747-2666
Geo Ryder, *President*
▲ EMP: 19 EST: 1920
SQ FT: 10,000
SALES (est): 2.9MM **Privately Held**
SIC: 3556 2099 Dairy & milk machinery;
emulsifiers, food

(G-8257)
COLORS IN OPTICS LTD
Also Called: Ic Optics
120 Broadway G (11040-5301)
PHONE..................................718 845-0300
Gabe Tusk, *Branch Mgr*
EMP: 80
SQ FT: 10,000
SALES (corp-wide): 13.6MM **Privately Held**
SIC: 3851 Eyeglasses, lenses & frames

PA: Colors In Optics, Ltd.
366 5th Ave Rm 804
New York NY
212 465-1200

(G-8258)
COMPUCOLOR ASSOCIATES INC
2200 Marcus Ave Ste C (11042-1043)
PHONE..................................516 358-0000
Thomas Weitzmann, *President*
Mark Rosner, *Admin Sec*
▲ EMP: 45
SQ FT: 22,000
SALES (est): 4.9MM **Privately Held**
WEB: www.compucolor.com
SIC: 2752 Commercial printing, offset

(G-8259)
CONTINENTAL QUILTING CO INC
3000 Marcus Ave Ste 3e6 (11042-1006)
PHONE..................................718 499-9100
Alfred G Sayegh, *President*
Stephen Sayegh, *Vice Pres*
▲ EMP: 50 EST: 1919
SQ FT: 40,000
SALES (est): 4.5MM **Privately Held**
SIC: 2392 Mattress pads; mattress protec-
tors, except rubber; comforters & quilts:
made from purchased materials

(G-8260)
CORA MATERIALS CORP
Also Called: Cora Matrls
30 Nassau Terminal Rd (11040-4928)
PHONE..................................516 488-6300
Robert Raths, *President*
Christine Goldfuss, *Marketing Mgr*
Elissa Raths, *Admin Sec*
EMP: 10
SQ FT: 10,000
SALES (est): 1.5MM **Privately Held**
WEB: www.corarefining.com
SIC: 3341 Secondary nonferrous metals

(G-8261)
DESIGNATRONICS INCORPORATED
Also Called: Stock Drive Products Div
55 Denton Ave S (11040-4901)
PHONE..................................516 328-3300
Anthony Pagliughi, *Principal*
EMP: 296
SALES (corp-wide): 90.2MM **Privately Held**
WEB: www.designatronics.com
SIC: 3625 3621 3568 3566 Motor con-
trols & accessories; motors & generators;
power transmission equipment; speed
changers, drives & gears; manufactured
hardware (general); tire cord & fabrics
PA: Designatronics Incorporated
250 Duffy Ave Unit A
Hicksville NY 11801
516 328-3300

(G-8262)
DISPLAY TECHNOLOGIES LLC (DH)
1111 Marcus Ave Ste M68 (11042-2041)
PHONE..................................718 321-3100
Marshall Goldberg, *President*
Bruce Gommermann, *Vice Pres*
Jon Noce, *Vice Pres*
Diogo Pereira, *Vice Pres*
Anthony Puglisi, *CFO*
▲ EMP: 53
SQ FT: 30,000
SALES: 76.1MM
SALES (corp-wide): 225.3B **Publicly Held**
WEB: www.display-technologies.com
SIC: 2542 Fixtures: display, office or store:
except wood

(G-8263)
EASTERN FINDING CORP
116 County Courthouse Rd (11040-5342)
PHONE..................................516 747-6640
Paul Posner, *President*
Anthony Millaci, *Partner*
Sylvia Posner, *Treasurer*
▲ EMP: 10
SQ FT: 5,000

SALES (est): 1.3MM **Privately Held**
WEB: www.easternfindings.com
SIC: 3366 Brass foundry

(G-8264)
ELECTRIC SWTCHBARD SLTIONS LLC
270 Park Ave (11040-5318)
PHONE..................................718 643-1105
Jerry Dicunzolo,
EMP: 8 EST: 2006
SQ FT: 25,000
SALES (est): 1.5MM
SALES (corp-wide): 57MM **Privately Held**
SIC: 3613 Switchboards & parts, power
PA: Power-Flo Technologies, Inc.
270 Park Ave
New Hyde Park NY 11040
516 812-6800

(G-8265)
ELI LILLY AND COMPANY
Also Called: Elanco Animal Health
1979 Marcus Ave (11042-1076)
PHONE..................................516 622-2244
Agam Upadhyay, *Vice Pres*
James Sweeny, *Manager*
Bob Allen, *Manager*
Francesca Migliore, *Analyst*
EMP: 14
SALES (corp-wide): 24.5B **Publicly Held**
WEB: www.lilly.com
SIC: 2834 Pharmaceutical preparations
PA: Eli Lilly And Company
Lilly Corporate Ctr
Indianapolis IN 46285
317 276-2000

(G-8266)
EN FOIL LLC
1 Hollow Ln Ste 200 (11042-1215)
PHONE..................................516 466-9500
Stephen Paladino, *Treasurer*
EMP: 6
SALES: 19MM **Privately Held**
SIC: 3353 Foil, aluminum

(G-8267)
EON LABS INC (DH)
1999 Marcus Ave Ste 300 (11042-1020)
PHONE..................................516 478-9700
Thomas Strungmann, *Ch of Bd*
Bernhard Hampl, *President*
Pranab Bhattacharyya, *Vice Pres*
Sadie Ciganek, *Vice Pres*
William F Holt, *Vice Pres*
EMP: 19
SQ FT: 25,000
SALES (est): 29.9MM
SALES (corp-wide): 51.9B **Privately Held**
WEB: www.sandoz.com
SIC: 2834 Pharmaceutical preparations
HQ: Sandoz Inc.
100 College Rd W
Princeton NJ 08540
609 627-8500

(G-8268)
FAR EAST INDUSTRIES INC (PA)
118 Stephan Marc Ln (11040-1811)
PHONE..................................718 687-2482
Yong Xiang Cui, *Ch of Bd*
EMP: 4
SQ FT: 1,200
SALES (est): 6.5MM **Privately Held**
SIC: 2326 Men's & boys' work clothing

(G-8269)
FERGUSON ENTERPRISES INC
Also Called: Pollardwater
200 Atlantic Ave (11040-5057)
PHONE..................................800 437-1146
Thomas Towler, *General Mgr*
EMP: 30
SALES (est): 1.3MM **Privately Held**
SIC: 3589 Sewage & water treatment
equipment

(G-8270)
GENERAL FIBRE PRODUCTS CORP
170 Nassau Terminal Rd (11040-4940)
PHONE..................................516 358-7500
Stuart Shrode, *CEO*
James Miller, *President*

Michael Petti, *Vice Pres*
Frank Anthony, *Plant Mgr*
Ruth Cartegena, *QC Mgr*
◆ EMP: 70
SQ FT: 52,000
SALES (est): 21.2MM **Privately Held**
WEB: www.generalfibre.com
SIC: 2653 2671 2675 2679 Boxes, corrugated: made from purchased materials;
packaging paper & plastics film, coated &
laminated; die-cut paper & board; corrugated paper: made from purchased material

(G-8271)
HAIN BLUEPRINT INC
1111 Marcus Ave Ste 100 (11042-2033)
PHONE..................................212 414-5741
EMP: 17
SALES (est): 5.1MM **Publicly Held**
SIC: 2037 Fruit juices
PA: The Hain Celestial Group Inc
1111 Marcus Ave Ste 100
New Hyde Park NY 11042

(G-8272)
HAIN CELESTIAL GROUP INC (PA)
1111 Marcus Ave Ste 100 (11042-2033)
PHONE..................................516 587-5000
John Carroll, *CEO*
Gary W Tickle, *CEO*
Mark L Schiller, *President*
Connor McKim, *Business Mgr*
Mark Osinoff, *Business Mgr*
◆ EMP: 130
SQ FT: 86,000
SALES: 2.3B **Publicly Held**
WEB: www.hain-celestial.com
SIC: 2023 2034 2096 2086 Dried & powdered milk & milk products; dried milk
preparations; dietary supplements, dairy
& non-dairy based; vegetable flour, meal
& powder; potato chips & similar snacks;
iced tea & fruit drinks, bottled & canned;
toilet preparations

(G-8273)
HASCO COMPONETS
906 Jericho Tpke (11040-4604)
PHONE..................................516 328-9292
Tom Marcus, *President*
▲ EMP: 20
SALES: 11MM **Privately Held**
SIC: 3625 Relays, for electronic use

(G-8274)
HONEYWELL INTERNATIONAL INC
5 Dakota Dr Ste 120 (11042-1109)
PHONE..................................516 302-9401
Noel Acevedo, *Branch Mgr*
EMP: 7
SALES (corp-wide): 41.8B **Publicly Held**
WEB: www.honeywell.com
SIC: 3724 Aircraft engines & engine parts
PA: Honeywell International Inc.
300 S Tryon St
Charlotte NC 28202
973 455-2000

(G-8275)
INTERNTNAL BUS CMMNCATIONS INC (PA)
Also Called: IBC/ Worldwide
1981 Marcus Ave Ste C105 (11042-2028)
PHONE..................................516 352-4505
Norman Kay, *President*
Philip Schoonmaker, *Exec VP*
Rachel Samaroo, *Director*
▲ EMP: 25
SQ FT: 53,000
SALES (est): 23.4MM **Privately Held**
WEB: www.ibcshell.com
SIC: 3086 2679 Packaging & shipping materials, foamed plastic; pressed fiber &
molded pulp products except food products

(G-8276)
IVER PRINTING INC
124 N 12th St (11040-4265)
PHONE..................................718 275-2070
William Iverson, *President*
Ann Iverson, *Vice Pres*

Martin Iverson, *Treasurer*
John Iverson, *Admin Sec*
EMP: 5 EST: 1979
SQ FT: 900
SALES: 400K **Privately Held**
WEB: www.iverprinting.com
SIC: 2752 Commercial printing, offset

(G-8277)
JOSEPH STRUHL CO INC
Also Called: Super Moderna/Magic Master
195 Atlantic Ave (11040-5027)
PHONE..................................516 741-3660
Clifford Struhl, *President*
Harriet Struhl, *Corp Secy*
Joseph Struhl, *Vice Pres*
EMP: 14
SQ FT: 13,000
SALES (est): 1.9MM **Privately Held**
WEB: www.magicmaster.com
SIC: 3993 Displays & cutouts, window &
lobby

(G-8278)
JSM VINYL PRODUCTS INC
44 Orchid Ln (11040-1918)
PHONE..................................516 775-4520
Fax: 516 239-2879
EMP: 15
SQ FT: 26,000
SALES: 4MM **Privately Held**
SIC: 3089 Mfg Plastic Products

(G-8279)
LAFAYETTE MIRROR & GLASS CO
2300 Marcus Ave (11042-1058)
PHONE..................................718 768-0660
Micheal Chuisano, *President*
Ben Ajeti, *Purchasing*
Anthony Garaufis, *Technology*
▲ EMP: 7 EST: 1910
SQ FT: 7,000
SALES (est): 881.2K **Privately Held**
SIC: 3211 3231 1793 Plate glass, polished & rough; mirrored glass; glass &
glazing work

(G-8280)
LIQUID MANAGEMENT PARTNERS LLC
3000 Marcus Ave Ste 1w9 (11042-1027)
PHONE..................................516 775-5050
Michael H Lam,
▲ EMP: 11
SQ FT: 3,000
SALES (est): 2.1MM **Privately Held**
SIC: 2086 5182 Carbonated beverages,
nonalcoholic: bottled & canned; wine &
distilled beverages

(G-8281)
MARLOU GARMENTS INC
2115 Jericho Tpke (11040-4703)
P.O. Box 407, West Hempstead (11552-0407)
PHONE..................................516 739-7100
Louis De Angelo, *Ch of Bd*
Rose De Angelo, *Admin Sec*
▲ EMP: 15 EST: 1952
SQ FT: 19,200
SALES (est): 1.4MM **Privately Held**
WEB: www.marlou.com
SIC: 2337 Uniforms, except athletic:
women's, misses' & juniors'

(G-8282)
MASON CONTRACT PRODUCTS LLC
85 Denton Ave (11040-4002)
P.O. Box 609, Port Washington (11050-0609)
PHONE..................................516 328-6900
Leonard Horowitz,
Lisa Horowitz,
▼ EMP: 80
SQ FT: 100,000
SALES (est): 5.9MM **Privately Held**
SIC: 2391 2211 Curtains & draperies; bedspreads, cotton

(G-8283)
NATURAL E CREATIVE LLC
Also Called: Be The Media
1110 Jericho Tpke (11040-4606)
PHONE..................................516 488-1143
Mathison Scott, *Manager*
David Mathison,
Eric Mathison,
Peter Mathison,
EMP: 11
SALES (est): 75K **Privately Held**
WEB: www.bethemedia.com
SIC: 2731 Books: publishing & printing

(G-8284)
NEW YORK PACKAGING CORP
Also Called: Redi-Bag USA
135 Fulton Ave (11040-5305)
P.O. Box 1039 (11040-7039)
PHONE..................................516 746-0600
Jeffrey Rabiea, *President*
▲ EMP: 90
SQ FT: 50,000
SALES (est): 25MM **Privately Held**
WEB: www.newyorkpackaging.com
SIC: 2673 Plastic bags: made from purchased materials

(G-8285)
NEW YORK RAVIOLI PASTA CO INC
12 Denton Ave S (11040-4904)
PHONE..................................516 270-2852
David Creo, *President*
Paul Moncada, *Corp Secy*
Joseph Zinerco, *Opers Mgr*
EMP: 20
SQ FT: 20,000
SALES (est): 3.6MM **Privately Held**
WEB: www.nyravioli.com
SIC: 2099 5499 5149 Packaged combination products: pasta, rice & potato; gourmet food stores; pasta & rice

(G-8286)
OCALA GROUP LLC
1981 Marcus Ave Ste 227 (11042-1055)
PHONE..................................516 233-2750
◆ EMP: 17
SALES (est): 2.6MM **Privately Held**
SIC: 3841 3089 Surgical & medical instruments; plastic kitchenware, tableware &
houseware

(G-8287)
OVERNIGHT MOUNTINGS INC
1400 Plaza Ave (11040-4921)
PHONE..................................516 865-3000
Morris Adwar, *CEO*
Jeffery Adwar, *President*
Matthew Roth, *Vice Pres*
David Adwar, *Sales Dir*
EMP: 55
SQ FT: 550,000
SALES (est): 7.7MM **Privately Held**
WEB: www.overnightmountings.com
SIC: 3911 Jewelry, precious metal

(G-8288)
P J D PUBLICATIONS LTD
1315 Jericho Tpke (11040-4613)
P.O. Box 966, Westbury (11590-0966)
PHONE..................................516 626-0650
Siva Sankar, *CEO*
Douglas Sankar, *Vice Pres*
Jason Sankar, *Vice Pres*
Priscilla Wong,
EMP: 5
SALES (est): 330K **Privately Held**
WEB: www.pjdonline.com
SIC: 2731 5045 Books: publishing only;
computers, peripherals & software

(G-8289)
QUALITY READY MIX INC
1824 Gilford Ave (11040-4031)
PHONE..................................516 437-0100
Eugene Messina, *President*
EMP: 15
SALES (est): 2.3MM **Privately Held**
SIC: 3273 Ready-mixed concrete

▲ = Import ▼=Export
◆ =Import/Export

(G-8290)
QUANTUM LOGIC CORP
91 5th Ave (11040-5005)
PHONE....................516 746-1380
EMP: 9 EST: 2002
SALES (est): 1.1MM Privately Held
SIC: 3572 Mfg Computer Storage Devices

(G-8291)
SATCO CASTINGS SERVICE INC
Also Called: Plaza Braceltte Mounting
1400 Plaza Ave (11040-4921)
P.O. Box 1068 (11040-1068)
PHONE....................516 354-1500
Steven Feld, President
EMP: 45
SQ FT: 18,000
SALES (est): 7MM Privately Held
WEB: www.satcocasting.com
SIC: 3915 3911 Jewelers' castings; jewelry, precious metal

(G-8292)
SHELL CONTAINERS INC
1981 Marcus Ave Ste C105 (11042-2028)
PHONE....................516 352-4505
Norman Kay, President
Philip Schoonmaker, Vice Pres
▲ EMP: 20
SQ FT: 19,000
SALES (est): 2.5MM
SALES (corp-wide): 23.4MM Privately Held
WEB: www.shellcontainers.com
SIC: 3086 2679 Packaging & shipping materials, foamed plastic; building, insulating & packaging paperboard
PA: International Business Communications, Inc.
1981 Marcus Ave Ste C105
New Hyde Park NY 11042
516 352-4505

(G-8293)
SNOW CRAFT CO INC
200 Fulton Ave (11040-5306)
P.O. Box 829 (11040-0829)
PHONE....................516 739-1399
Kirk Guyton, President
Robert Farina, Vice Pres
William Hess, Admin Sec
EMP: 28 EST: 1954
SQ FT: 22,500
SALES (est): 3.8MM Privately Held
SIC: 3086 Packaging & shipping materials, foamed plastic

(G-8294)
SONOMED INC
Also Called: Sonomed Escalon
1979 Marcus Ave Ste C105 (11042-1002)
PHONE....................516 354-0900
Barry Durante, President
Ronald Hueneke, COO
EMP: 30
SQ FT: 11,000
SALES (est): 5.7MM
SALES (corp-wide): 9.6MM Privately Held
WEB: www.sonomedinc.com
SIC: 3845 3841 Electromedical equipment; ophthalmic instruments & apparatus
PA: Escalon Medical Corp.
435 Devon Park Dr Ste 100
Wayne PA 19087
610 688-6830

(G-8295)
SPECIAL CIRCLE INC
123 Shelter Rock Rd (11040-1328)
PHONE....................516 595-9988
Lawrence Lin, Principal
Kathleen Loftus, Co-Owner
Phoebe Lin, COO
Selena Zhang, COO
Darren Yang, Chief Engr
EMP: 12
SALES (est): 281.6K Privately Held
SIC: 7372 7389 Educational computer software;

(G-8296)
TEXAS HOME SECURITY INC (PA)
Also Called: Medallion Security Door & Win
50 Rose Pl (11040-5311)
PHONE....................516 747-2100
Gregory E Falgoust, President
Brian S Falgoust, Vice Pres
Alexis Cohen, Assistant
EMP: 50
SALES (est): 6.5MM Privately Held
WEB: www.medaliondoors.com
SIC: 3442 1521 Storm doors or windows, metal; general remodeling, single-family houses

(G-8297)
THREE GEMS INC
Also Called: Sign-A-Rama
2201 Hillside Ave (11040-2714)
PHONE....................516 248-0388
Sal Italiano, President
Jane Italiano, Vice Pres
EMP: 5
SQ FT: 1,200
SALES (est): 544.6K Privately Held
WEB: www.threegems.com
SIC: 3993 Signs & advertising specialties

(G-8298)
UBM LLC (HQ)
Also Called: Ubm Tech
1983 Marcus Ave Ste 250 (11042-2000)
PHONE....................516 562-7800
Scott D Schulman, CEO
Marco Pardi, Managing Dir
Simon Carless, Exec VP
Kathleen Connolly, Exec VP
Kelley Damore, Exec VP
EMP: 60
SQ FT: 230,000
SALES (est): 257.3MM
SALES (corp-wide): 1.3B Privately Held
WEB: www.cmp.com
SIC: 2721 2711 7319 7389 Periodicals: publishing only; newspapers; media buying service; decoration service for special events
PA: Ubm Plc
240 Blackfriars Road
London SE1 8
207 921-5000

(G-8299)
UNITED METAL INDUSTRIES INC
1008 3rd Ave (11040-5529)
PHONE....................516 354-6800
Richard M Meyers, President
Robert S Meyers, Vice Pres
▲ EMP: 8 EST: 1912
SQ FT: 8,000
SALES (est): 1MM Privately Held
WEB: www.unitedmetal.net
SIC: 3429 Clamps & couplings, hose

(G-8300)
UNITED STTES BRNZE SIGN OF FLA
811 2nd Ave (11040-4869)
PHONE....................516 352-5155
George Barbeosch, President
Alan Kasten, Vice Pres
EMP: 25 EST: 1927
SQ FT: 10,000
SALES (est): 2.6MM Privately Held
WEB: www.usbronze.com
SIC: 3993 3953 Signs & advertising specialties; marking devices

(G-8301)
UNIVERSAL READY MIX INC
197 Atlantic Ave (11040-5048)
PHONE....................516 746-4535
Guilio Viti, President
Anthony Logiudice, Vice Pres
Rocco Viti, Admin Sec
EMP: 5 EST: 1997
SALES (est): 877.9K Privately Held
WEB: www.universalreadymix.com
SIC: 2951 Asphalt paving mixtures & blocks

(G-8302)
USE ACQUISITION LLC
Also Called: US Energy Group
270 Park Ave (11040-5318)
PHONE....................516 812-6800
Gregory Dinome, Engineer
Gerald Dicunzolo,
EMP: 10
SALES (est): 1.4MM Privately Held
SIC: 3822 Temperature controls, automatic

(G-8303)
WINDOWTEX INC
Also Called: Wt Shade
77 2nd Ave (11040-5030)
PHONE....................877 294-3580
Joseph J Daniels, President
Dara Centonze, Business Mgr
Chuck Raible, Vice Pres
David Lin, Opers Mgr
Fang Lin, Design Engr
EMP: 12
SALES (est): 146.9K Privately Held
SIC: 2591 Window shade rollers & fittings

New Lebanon
Columbia County

(G-8304)
WASTEQUIP MANUFACTURING CO LLC
Also Called: Wastequip - Consolidated
1079 Route 20 (12125-3206)
PHONE....................800 235-0734
Paul Fitzgerald, Branch Mgr
EMP: 33 Privately Held
WEB: www.rayfo.com
SIC: 3443 Dumpsters, garbage
HQ: Wastequip Manufacturing Company Llc
6525 Morrison Blvd # 300
Charlotte NC 28211

New Paltz
Ulster County

(G-8305)
BIMBO BAKERIES USA INC
Also Called: Freihofer's Bakery Outlet
27 N Putt Corners Rd (12561-3408)
PHONE....................845 255-4345
Mike Croce, Manager
EMP: 10
SQ FT: 21,413 Privately Held
SIC: 2051 Bread, cake & related products
HQ: Bimbo Bakeries Usa, Inc
255 Business Center Dr # 200
Horsham PA 19044
215 347-5500

(G-8306)
GILDED OTTER BREWING CO
3 Main St (12561-1742)
P.O. Box 57 (12561-0057)
PHONE....................845 256-1700
Rick Rauch, President
EMP: 70 EST: 1996
SQ FT: 10,000
SALES (est): 6.8MM Privately Held
WEB: www.gildedotter.com
SIC: 2082 5812 Beer (alcoholic beverage); eating places

(G-8307)
KEITH LEWIS STUDIO INC
64 Jewels Ct (12561-2670)
PHONE....................845 339-5629
EMP: 9
SALES (est): 412.5K Privately Held
SIC: 3911 5094 Jewelry, precious metal; jewelry

(G-8308)
KEVCO INDUSTRIES
Also Called: Engineering Educational Eqp Co
6 Millbrook Rd (12561-1315)
PHONE....................845 255-7407
Peter C Bowers, Owner
Pete Bower, MIS Staff
EMP: 7

SALES (est): 488.1K Privately Held
WEB: www.eeeco.com
SIC: 3999 Education aids, devices & supplies

(G-8309)
LYOPHILIZATION SYSTEMS INC
14 Hickory Hill Rd (12561-3104)
PHONE....................845 338-0456
Marc Thompson, President
EMP: 5
SQ FT: 6,000
SALES (est): 540K Privately Held
WEB: www.lyogroup.com
SIC: 3556 Food products machinery

(G-8310)
PDQ SHIPPING SERVICES
Also Called: PDQ Printing
8 New Paltz Plz 299 (12561-1616)
PHONE....................845 255-5500
Craig Shinkles, Owner
EMP: 8
SALES (est): 340K Privately Held
SIC: 2759 7331 Promotional printing; mailing service

(G-8311)
TOTAL WEBCASTING INC
8 Bruce St (12561-2101)
P.O. Box 665 (12561-0665)
PHONE....................845 883-0909
Robert Feldman, President
EMP: 6
SQ FT: 3,000
SALES: 700K Privately Held
SIC: 2741

(G-8312)
ULSTER COUNTY IRON WORKS LLC
64 N Putt Corners Rd (12561-3405)
PHONE....................845 255-0003
EMP: 8
SQ FT: 5,000
SALES (est): 825K Privately Held
SIC: 3499 Mfg Misc Fabricated Metal Products

(G-8313)
ULSTER PUBLISHING CO INC
Also Called: New Paltz Times
29 S Chestnut St Ste 101 (12561-1949)
P.O. Box 3329, Kingston (12402-3329)
PHONE....................845 255-7005
Debbie Alexsa, Principal
EMP: 10
SALES (corp-wide): 3.4MM Privately Held
WEB: www.ulsterpublishing.com
SIC: 2711 Newspapers: publishing only, not printed on site
PA: Ulster Publishing Co Inc
322 Wall St Fl 1
Kingston NY 12401
845 334-8205

(G-8314)
VIKING INDUSTRIES INC
89 S Ohioville Rd (12561-4012)
P.O. Box 249 (12561-0249)
PHONE....................845 883-6325
Richard Croce, President
Rich Croce, Vice Pres
Michael Cozzolino, Plant Mgr
Mark Nowak, Controller
Teri Apuzzo, Cust Mgr
EMP: 55
SQ FT: 50,000
SALES (est): 12.3MM Privately Held
WEB: www.vikingindustries.net
SIC: 2657 Folding paperboard boxes

New Rochelle
Westchester County

(G-8315)
A & T IRON WORKS INC
25 Cliff St (10801-6803)
PHONE....................914 632-8992
Gessie Tassone, President
▲ EMP: 28
SQ FT: 20,000

SALES (est): 5.6MM **Privately Held**
WEB: www.atironworks.com
SIC: 3446 5211 3441 Architectural metal-
work; fencing; fabricated structural metal

(G-8316)
ABSOLUTE COATINGS INC
38 Portman Rd (10801-2103)
PHONE..................................914 636-0700
Brian A Demkowicz, *Principal*
EMP: 35
SQ FT: 40,000
SALES (est): 1.4MM
SALES (corp-wide): 48.4MM **Privately
Held**
SIC: 2851 Polyurethane coatings
PA: Valentus Specialty Chemicals, Inc.
1999 Elizabeth St
North Brunswick NJ 08902
732 821-3200

(G-8317)
ALEXANDRA FERGUSON LLC
180 Davenport Ave (10805-2105)
PHONE..................................718 788-7768
Alexandra Ferguson, *Mng Member*
EMP: 8
SALES (est): 641.2K **Privately Held**
SIC: 2392 Cushions & pillows

(G-8318)
ALICIAS BAKERY INC
498 Main St Ste A (10801-6326)
PHONE..................................914 235-4689
Alicia Zapien, *President*
EMP: 5
SALES (est): 458.2K **Privately Held**
SIC: 2051 Doughnuts, except frozen

(G-8319)
ALLIED CONVERTERS INC
64 Drake Ave (10805-1598)
P.O. Box 548 (10802-0548)
PHONE..................................914 235-1585
Richard E Ellenbogen, *President*
Wilma J Ellenbogen, *Corp Secy*
▲ EMP: 30 EST: 1954
SQ FT: 50,000
SALES (est): 6.7MM **Privately Held**
WEB: www.garb-o-liner.com
SIC: 2673 2671 2679 Plastic bags: made
from purchased materials; plastic film,
coated or laminated for packaging; paper-
board products, converted

(G-8320)
**BENCHMARK EDUCATION CO
LLC (PA)**
145 Huguenot St Fl 8 (10801-5233)
PHONE..................................914 637-7200
Wainright Samuel, *President*
Susan Rivers, *Senior VP*
Carlos Huertas, *Warehouse Mgr*
Delphine Iroakazi, *Purchasing*
Barbara Andrews, *Finance*
▲ EMP: 75
SALES (est): 18.7MM **Privately Held**
WEB: www.benchmarkeducation.com
SIC: 2731 Book publishing

(G-8321)
BREAD FACTORY LLC
30 Grove Ave (10801-6207)
PHONE..................................914 637-8150
Jean Yves Lebris, *Partner*
Anthony Orza, *Partner*
EMP: 24 EST: 2000
SQ FT: 10,000
SALES (est): 2.7MM **Privately Held**
SIC: 2051 Bakery: wholesale or whole-
sale/retail combined

(G-8322)
BRIDGE RECORDS INC
200 Clinton Ave (10801-1525)
PHONE..................................914 654-9270
David Starobin, *President*
Becky Starobin, *Vice Pres*
Allegra Starobin, *Associate Dir*
EMP: 5
SQ FT: 2,000
SALES (est): 709.1K **Privately Held**
SIC: 3652 Master records or tapes, prepa-
ration of

(G-8323)
CASTEK INC (HQ)
20 Jones St (10801-6000)
PHONE..................................914 636-1000
Arthur M Dinitz, *President*
Mike Stento, *Vice Pres*
Robert J Welsh, *Treasurer*
▲ EMP: 3
SQ FT: 42,000
SALES (est): 3.1MM
SALES (corp-wide): 7.4MM **Privately
Held**
WEB: www.castek.net
SIC: 3272 Concrete products, precast
PA: Transpo Industries, Inc.
20 Jones St Ste 3
New Rochelle NY 10801
914 636-1000

(G-8324)
CERAMICA VARM (PA)
Also Called: Ceramica V. A. R. M.
479 5th Ave (10801-2212)
PHONE..................................914 381-6215
Fax: 914 381-3785
EMP: 9
SQ FT: 4,000
SALES: 7.5MM **Privately Held**
SIC: 3263 Mfg Of Ceramic Earthenware-
Italy

(G-8325)
**CUFFS PLANNING & MODELS
LTD**
317 Beechmont Dr (10804-4601)
PHONE..................................914 632-1883
David K Combs, *President*
David Combs, *President*
Sandra Kirkendall, *Vice Pres*
EMP: 8
SALES (est): 520K **Privately Held**
WEB: www.cuffs88.com
SIC: 7372 Business oriented computer
software

(G-8326)
DERAFFELE MFG CO INC
2525 Palmer Ave Ste 4 (10801-4476)
PHONE..................................914 636-6850
Philip De Raffele Jr, *President*
Stephen De Raffele, *Treasurer*
Joseph De Raffele, *Admin Sec*
EMP: 25 EST: 1933
SQ FT: 30,000
SALES (est): 5.2MM **Privately Held**
SIC: 3448 Buildings, portable: prefabri-
cated metal

(G-8327)
DISPLAY PRODUCERS INC
40 Winding Brook Rd (10804-2008)
PHONE..................................718 904-1200
Joseph A Laurite, *President*
Arthur E Landi, *President*
Richard Tevere, *Corp Secy*
▲ EMP: 250
SQ FT: 150,000
SALES (est): 22.5MM **Privately Held**
WEB: www.displayproducersinc.com
SIC: 3993 Displays & cutouts, window &
lobby

(G-8328)
ENTERPRISE TECH GROUP INC
3 Church St (10801-6301)
PHONE..................................914 588-0327
Liza Zaneri, *President*
EMP: 12
SALES: 950K **Privately Held**
SIC: 7372 Prepackaged software

(G-8329)
**ERIC S TURNER & COMPANY
INC**
Also Called: Turner Plating
3335 Centre Ave (10801)
PHONE..................................914 235-7114
Kenneth Turner, *President*
William Vernon Turner, *Vice Pres*
EMP: 12 EST: 1931
SQ FT: 10,000

SALES: 900K **Privately Held**
WEB: www.turnerplating.com
SIC: 3471 2851 Electroplating of metals or
formed products; finishing, metals or
formed products; polishing, metals or
formed products; paints & allied products

(G-8330)
**FORMCRAFT DISPLAY
PRODUCTS**
42 Beverly Rd (10804-1703)
PHONE..................................914 632-1410
George Bartoli, *President*
Joanne Bartoli, *Vice Pres*
EMP: 5
SQ FT: 5,000
SALES (est): 330K **Privately Held**
SIC: 3229 Christmas tree ornaments, from
glass produced on-site

(G-8331)
FORREST ENGRAVING CO INC
Also Called: Forrest Engravg
92 1st St (10801-6121)
P.O. Box 1240, Carmel (10512-8240)
PHONE..................................845 228-0200
Tom Giordano, *President*
EMP: 11
SQ FT: 3,000
SALES (est): 1MM **Privately Held**
SIC: 3993 Signs & advertising specialties

(G-8332)
**FRADAN MANUFACTURING
CORP**
499 5th Ave (10801-2212)
PHONE..................................914 632-3653
Frank De Bartolo, *President*
EMP: 15
SQ FT: 12,000
SALES (est): 2MM **Privately Held**
SIC: 3524 Lawn & garden equipment

(G-8333)
GANNETT CO INC
Also Called: Bronxville Review
92 North Ave (10801-7413)
PHONE..................................914 278-9315
Jerry McKinstry, *Principal*
EMP: 20
SALES (corp-wide): 2.9B **Publicly Held**
WEB: www.gannett.com
SIC: 2711 Newspapers, publishing & print-
ing
PA: Gannett Co., Inc.
7950 Jones Branch Dr
Mc Lean VA 22102
703 854-6000

(G-8334)
GARB-O-LINER INC
64 Drake Ave (10805-1598)
P.O. Box 548 (10802-0548)
PHONE..................................914 235-1585
Richard Ellenbogen, *President*
Richard E Ellenbogen, *President*
Wilma Ellenbogen, *Treasurer*
EMP: 7 EST: 1986
SALES (est): 1MM **Privately Held**
SIC: 2673 5113 Trash bags (plastic film):
made from purchased materials; bags,
paper & disposable plastic

(G-8335)
GEN PUBLISHING INC
Also Called: Genetic Engineering News
140 Huguenot St Fl 3 (10801-5215)
PHONE..................................914 834-3880
Mary Ann Liebert, *President*
Alex Philippidis, *Editor*
Rob Reis, *Production*
Kwafo Anoff, *Marketing Staff*
Victoria Palusevic, *Marketing Staff*
EMP: 99
SALES: 950K **Privately Held**
WEB: www.genengnews.com
SIC: 2741 Miscellaneous publishing

(G-8336)
**HAGEDORN COMMUNICATIONS
INC (PA)**
Also Called: Co-Op City News
662 Main St Ste 1 (10801-7145)
P.O. Box 680 (10802-0680)
PHONE..................................914 636-7400

Christopher Hagedorn, *President*
▲ EMP: 70
SQ FT: 20,000
SALES (est): 10MM **Privately Held**
WEB: www.rew-online.com
SIC: 2711 Newspapers: publishing only,
not printed on site

(G-8337)
HAITIAN TIMES INC
80 Lakeside Dr (10801-3130)
P.O. Box 21628, Brooklyn (11202-1628)
PHONE..................................718 230-8700
Garry P Pierre, *President*
EMP: 5
SQ FT: 1,200
SALES (est): 347K **Privately Held**
WEB: www.haitiantimes.com
SIC: 2711 Newspapers

(G-8338)
HALPERN TOOL CORP (PA)
Also Called: Vernon Devices
111 Plain Ave (10801-2206)
PHONE..................................914 633-0038
David Newmark, *President*
Marlene Werner, *Vice Pres*
EMP: 5
SQ FT: 12,500
SALES (est): 1.6MM **Privately Held**
SIC: 3541 5084 Machine tools, metal cut-
ting type; industrial machinery & equip-
ment

(G-8339)
**HARBOR ELC FABRICATION
TLS INC**
Also Called: Hefti
29 Portman Rd (10801-2104)
PHONE..................................914 636-4400
Jerry Schiff, *President*
EMP: 25
SALES (est): 5.2MM **Privately Held**
SIC: 3444 Metal housings, enclosures,
casings & other containers

(G-8340)
HB ATHLETIC INC (PA)
Also Called: Globe-Tex
56 Harrison St Ste 305 (10801-6561)
PHONE..................................914 560-8422
Robert Hurvitz, *Ch of Bd*
Stuart Hurvitz, *President*
Jaymee Kahn, *Legal Staff*
▲ EMP: 15
SQ FT: 4,500
SALES (est): 1.6MM **Privately Held**
SIC: 2339 2389 Athletic clothing:
women's, misses' & juniors'; uniforms,
athletic: women's, misses' & juniors';
women's & misses' athletic clothing &
sportswear; disposable garments & ac-
cessories

(G-8341)
HIGHLANDER REALTY INC
Also Called: Seaboard Electronics
70 Church St (10805-3204)
PHONE..................................914 235-8073
Jerrold Hacker, *President*
Dorothy Hacker, *Treasurer*
EMP: 35
SQ FT: 15,000
SALES (est): 3.9MM **Privately Held**
WEB: www.highlanderrealty.com
SIC: 3699 Security devices

(G-8342)
HOMEGROWN FOR GOOD LLC
29 Beechwood Ave (10801-6818)
PHONE..................................857 540-6361
Timothy Gibb, *CEO*
Thomas Gibb,
EMP: 10
SALES (est): 1.5MM **Privately Held**
SIC: 3021 Rubber & plastics footwear

(G-8343)
IVY CLASSIC INDUSTRIES INC
40 Plain Ave (10801-2205)
PHONE..................................914 632-8200
Anthony Schwartz, *President*
Greg Schwartz, *Vice Pres*
Justin Schwartz, *Vice Pres*
Stanley Schwartz, *Treasurer*
◆ EMP: 30

SQ FT: 30,000
SALES (est): 4.7MM **Privately Held**
SIC: 3423 3546 3547 Hand & edge tools;
power-driven handtools; rolling mill machinery

(G-8344)
J P INSTALLATIONS WAREHOUSE
29 Portman Rd (10801-2104)
PHONE..............................914 576-3188
John Pompi, *President*
EMP: 10
SALES (est): 1.1MM **Privately Held**
SIC: 2599 Factory furniture & fixtures

(G-8345)
JOHNS RAVIOLI COMPANY INC
15 Drake Ave (10805-1506)
PHONE..............................914 576-7030
Robert Guarnero, *President*
Lee Key, *Bookkeeper*
▲ EMP: 15 EST: 1950
SQ FT: 8,800
SALES (est): 2.5MM **Privately Held**
SIC: 2099 5499 Pasta, uncooked: packaged with other ingredients; gourmet food stores

(G-8346)
KORING BROS INC
30 Pine St (10801-6906)
PHONE..............................888 233-1292
EMP: 4
SQ FT: 5,000
SALES (est): 2MM **Privately Held**
SIC: 2399 Mfg Fabricated Textile Products

(G-8347)
MARY ANN LIEBERT INC
140 Huguenot St Fl 3 (10801-5215)
PHONE..............................914 740-2100
Mary Ann Liebert, *President*
Gerry Williams, *Partner*
Durland Fish PH, *Editor*
Ruth Maysonet, *Vice Pres*
Jennifer Basso, *Sales Executive*
EMP: 70
SQ FT: 4,500
SALES (est): 11.7MM **Privately Held**
WEB: www.mmsonline.com
SIC: 2721 2731 2741 Trade journals: publishing only, not printed on site; books: publishing only; miscellaneous publishing

(G-8348)
PAINT OVER RUST PRODUCTS INC
Also Called: Last N Last
38 Portman Rd (10801-2103)
PHONE..............................914 636-0700
David Sherman, *CEO*
◆ EMP: 35 EST: 1923
SQ FT: 40,000
SALES (est): 14.5MM **Privately Held**
WEB: www.absolutecoatings.com
SIC: 2851 Polyurethane coatings; varnishes

(G-8349)
PLASTIC WORKS
26 Garden St (10801-4204)
P.O. Box 51, Crompond (10517-0051)
PHONE..............................914 576-2050
David J Jeskie, *Owner*
EMP: 8 EST: 1978
SALES (est): 800K **Privately Held**
SIC: 3089 Molding primary plastic; plastic processing

(G-8350)
PREMCO INC
11 Beechwood Ave (10801-6818)
P.O. Box 266 (10802-0266)
PHONE..............................914 636-7095
Harold Jacobs, *Ch of Bd*
EMP: 18
SQ FT: 22,000
SALES (est): 4.1MM **Privately Held**
SIC: 3621 7694 Motors & generators; motor repair services

(G-8351)
RAM TRANSFORMER TECHNOLOGIES
11 Beechwood Ave (10801-6818)
P.O. Box 266 (10802-0266)
PHONE..............................914 632-3988
Harold Jacobs, *President*
EMP: 10
SQ FT: 7,600
SALES (est): 990K **Privately Held**
SIC: 3612 Transformers, except electric

(G-8352)
REINO MANUFACTURING CO INC
34 Circuit Rd (10805-1930)
PHONE..............................914 636-8990
Florence Reino, *President*
Linda Reino, *Corp Secy*
Anthony J Reino, *Med Doctor*
EMP: 10 EST: 1945
SALES (est): 554.3K **Privately Held**
SIC: 3961 Costume jewelry

(G-8353)
REPUBLIC CONSTRUCTION CO INC
305 North Ave (10801-4169)
PHONE..............................914 235-3654
Joeseph Pogostin, *President*
EMP: 6 EST: 1985
SALES (est): 480.9K **Privately Held**
SIC: 1442 Construction sand & gravel

(G-8354)
SHANGHAI HARMONY AP INTL LLC
3 Wykagyl Ter (10804-3206)
PHONE..............................646 569-5680
Robert Wang, *Mng Member*
EMP: 21
SALES (est): 763.3K **Privately Held**
SIC: 2326 2339 Men's & boys' work clothing; women's & misses' athletic clothing & sportswear

(G-8355)
TOWSE PUBLISHING CO
Also Called: Furniture World
1333 North Ave Ste A (10804-2149)
PHONE..............................914 235-3095
Russell Bienenstock, *President*
Joe Capillo, *Editor*
Mark Testa, *Sales Staff*
Barbara Bienenstock, *Director*
EMP: 11
SALES: 1MM **Privately Held**
WEB: www.furnitureworldmagazine.com
SIC: 2721 Magazines: publishing & printing

(G-8356)
TRANSPO INDUSTRIES INC (PA)
20 Jones St Ste 3 (10801-6098)
PHONE..............................914 636-1000
Arthur M Dinitz, *Ch of Bd*
Michael S Stenko, *President*
Charles Dann, *Regl Sales Mgr*
Kathy Mallon, *Executive Asst*
Lewis Kruger, *Admin Sec*
▲ EMP: 38
SQ FT: 33,000
SALES (est): 7.4MM **Privately Held**
WEB: www.transpo.com
SIC: 3089 3272 2821 Plastic hardware & building products; hardware, plastic; concrete products, precast; plastics materials & resins

```
New Windsor
Orange County
```

(G-8357)
A & R CONCRETE PRODUCTS LLC
7 Ruscitti Rd (12553-6205)
PHONE..............................845 562-0640
Jay Nannini, *President*
EMP: 25
SALES (est): 2MM **Privately Held**
SIC: 3272 Concrete products, precast

(G-8358)
AIGNER LABEL HOLDER CORP
Also Called: Aigner Index,
218 Mac Arthur Ave (12553-7011)
PHONE..............................845 562-4510
Mark Aigner, *President*
Lisa Arestin, *Accounts Mgr*
Lisa Cirig, *Sales Staff*
▲ EMP: 11 EST: 1930
SALES (est): 2.5MM **Privately Held**
WEB: www.aignerindex.com
SIC: 2679 Paper products, converted

(G-8359)
AMERICAN FELT & FILTER CO INC
Also Called: Affco
361 Walsh Ave (12553-6727)
PHONE..............................845 561-3560
Wilson H Pryne, *Ch of Bd*
▲ EMP: 60
SQ FT: 230,000
SALES (est): 25.1MM **Privately Held**
WEB: www.affco.com
SIC: 3569 Filters, general line: industrial

(G-8360)
BELSITO COMMUNICATIONS INC
Also Called: 1st Responder Newspaper
1 Ardmore St (12553-8303)
PHONE..............................845 534-9700
Joseph P Belsito, *President*
Jim Stankiewicz, *General Mgr*
Nicole Roby, *Office Admin*
EMP: 12 EST: 1997
SQ FT: 2,000
SALES (est): 1MM **Privately Held**
SIC: 2711 7374 Newspapers: publishing only, not printed on site; computer graphics service

(G-8361)
BLEND SMOOTHIE BAR
25 Creamery Dr (12553-8011)
PHONE..............................845 568-7366
EMP: 6
SALES (est): 371.6K **Privately Held**
SIC: 2037 Frozen fruits & vegetables

(G-8362)
CAFE SPICE GCT INC
Also Called: Zaika Flavors of India
677 Little Britain Rd (12553-6152)
PHONE..............................845 863-0910
Sushil Malhotra, *CEO*
Laxmi Malhotra, *COO*
Payal Malhotra, *Vice Pres*
Sameer Malhotra, *Vice Pres*
Kurt Schaller, *Purchasing*
EMP: 200
SALES (est): 47.2MM **Privately Held**
SIC: 2099 Food preparations

(G-8363)
CLASSIC TOOL DESIGN INC
31 Walnut St (12553-7021)
PHONE..............................845 562-8700
Ralph Edwards, *President*
Marge Edwards, *Vice Pres*
EMP: 20
SQ FT: 22,000
SALES (est): 1.2MM **Privately Held**
WEB: www.ctd4ac.com
SIC: 3423 Mechanics' hand tools

(G-8364)
COCA-COLA BTLG CO OF NY INC
10 Heampstead Rd (12553-5501)
PHONE..............................845 562-3037
John Lacey, *Manager*
EMP: 15
SQ FT: 15,000
SALES (corp-wide): 31.8B **Publicly Held**
SIC: 2086 Bottled & canned soft drinks
HQ: The Coca-Cola Bottling Company Of New York Inc
2500 Windy Ridge Pkwy Se
Atlanta GA 30339
770 989-3000

(G-8365)
DOCUWARE CORPORATION (DH)
4 Crotty Ln Ste 200 (12553-4778)
PHONE..............................845 563-9045
Gregory J Schloemer, *President*
Jim Roberts, *President*
Steve Behm, *Vice Pres*
Brian Love, *Vice Pres*
Stefan Schindler, *Vice Pres*
▲ EMP: 73 EST: 2000
SQ FT: 2,800
SALES (est): 13.8MM **Privately Held**
WEB: www.docuware.com
SIC: 7372 Prepackaged software
HQ: Docuware Gmbh
Therese-Giehse-Platz 2
Germering 82110
898 944-330

(G-8366)
E W SMITH PUBLISHING CO INC
Also Called: Sentinel, The
36 Meriline Ave (12553-6520)
P.O. Box 405, Vails Gate (12584-0405)
PHONE..............................845 562-1218
Everett W Smith, *Ch of Bd*
Michael Smith, *Vice Pres*
Steven Smith, *Vice Pres*
EMP: 11
SALES (est): 882.5K **Privately Held**
WEB: www.ewsmithpublishing.com
SIC: 2711 2752 Commercial printing & newspaper publishing combined; commercial printing, lithographic

(G-8367)
FIFTY DOOR PARTNERS LLC (PA)
Also Called: AJW Architectural Products
509 Temple Hill Rd (12553-5532)
P.O. Box 10189, Newburgh (12552-0189)
PHONE..............................845 562-3332
John Nichols, *Principal*
Sean McFarlane, *Vice Pres*
Amber Curti, *Supervisor*
Christopher Hansen,
Richard Lewenson,
▲ EMP: 20
SALES (est): 5.2MM **Privately Held**
SIC: 2541 2542 Cabinets, lockers & shelving; partitions & fixtures, except wood; office & store showcases & display fixtures

(G-8368)
GAMMA PRODUCTS INC
Also Called: A & J Washroom Accessories
509 Temple Hill Rd (12553-5532)
P.O. Box 10189, Newburgh (12552-0189)
PHONE..............................845 562-3332
Anthony Granuzzo, *Ch of Bd*
Richard Rebusmen, *President*
Jayne F Granuzzo, *Exec VP*
Sean McFarlane, *Accounting Mgr*
Dean El-Refaei, *Accounting Mgr*
▲ EMP: 70
SQ FT: 50,000
SALES (est): 10.8MM **Privately Held**
WEB: www.ajwashroom.com
SIC: 3261 Bathroom accessories/fittings, vitreous china or earthenware

(G-8369)
HI-TECH PACKG WORLD-WIDE LLC
110 Corporate Dr (12553-6952)
P.O. Box 4232 (12553-0232)
PHONE..............................845 947-1912
Robert Trimble, *Owner*
EMP: 2
SQ FT: 10,000
SALES (est): 1.1MM **Privately Held**
SIC: 2759 Commercial printing

(G-8370)
JUST WOOD PALLETS INC
78 Vails Gate Heights Dr (12553-8514)
PHONE..............................718 644-7013
Carlos Garcia, *Principal*
EMP: 8 EST: 2010
SALES (est): 980.5K **Privately Held**
SIC: 2448 Pallets, wood & wood with metal

(G-8371)
LARCENT ENTERPRISES INC
Also Called: Angie Washroom
509 Temple Hill Rd (12553-5532)
P.O. Box 4569 (12553-0569)
PHONE...........................845 562-3332
Anthony J Granuzzo, Ch of Bd
▲ EMP: 50
SALES (est): 6.4MM Privately Held
SIC: 3261 Bathroom accessories/fittings,
vitreous china or earthenware

(G-8372)
**METAL CONTAINER
CORPORATION**
1000 Breunig Rd (12553-8438)
PHONE...........................845 567-1500
Mark Stafford, Branch Mgr
EMP: 200
SALES (corp-wide): 1.5B Privately Held
SIC: 3411 Metal cans
HQ: Metal Container Corporation
3636 S Geyer Rd Ste 100
Saint Louis MO 63127
314 577-2000

(G-8373)
NEA NATURALS INC
815 Blooming Grove Tpke # 505
(12553-8134)
PHONE...........................845 522-8042
Jill Vozza, President
EMP: 6
SALES: 50K Privately Held
SIC: 2844 5122 Face creams or lotions;
toiletries

(G-8374)
**NEW WINDSOR WASTE WATER
PLANT**
145 Caesars Ln (12553-7742)
P.O. Box 4653 (12553-0653)
PHONE...........................845 561-2550
John Egitto, Manager
EMP: 10
SALES (est): 778.8K Privately Held
SIC: 3589 Water treatment equipment, in-
dustrial

(G-8375)
**NEWBURGH DISTRIBUTION
CORP (PA)**
463 Temple Hill Rd (12553-5527)
PHONE...........................845 561-6330
Donald Harkness, President
Sharon Harkness, Vice Pres
▲ EMP: 3
SALES (est): 42.8MM Privately Held
WEB: www.baricosmetics.com
SIC: 2844 Cosmetic preparations

(G-8376)
NEWLINE PRODUCTS INC
509 Temple Hill Rd (12553-5532)
PHONE...........................972 881-3318
Kevin Wang, CEO
Chris Bradford, President
William Bowers, CFO
▲ EMP: 195
SQ FT: 30,000
SALES (est): 15MM Privately Held
WEB: www.newlineproduct.com
SIC: 3993 Displays & cutouts, window &
lobby

(G-8377)
PATTERSON MATERIALS CORP
322 Walsh Ave (12553-6748)
P.O. Box 800, Wingdale (12594-0800)
PHONE...........................845 832-6000
John Peckham, Manager
EMP: 20
SQ FT: 6,171
SALES (corp-wide): 171.1MM Privately
Held
SIC: 1422 Crushed & broken limestone
HQ: Patterson Materials Corp
20 Haarlem Ave
White Plains NY 10603
914 949-2000

(G-8378)
**PRODUCTION RESOURCE
GROUP LLC**
539 Temple Hill Rd (12553-5533)
PHONE...........................845 567-5700
Jerry Harris, President
Richard Mc Donald, Business Mgr
EMP: 50 Privately Held
SIC: 3999 7922 Theatrical scenery; equip-
ment rental, theatrical
PA: Production Resource Group Llc
200 Business Park Dr # 109
Armonk NY 10504

(G-8379)
PVH CORP
Also Called: Van Heusen
1073 State Route 94 (12553-6821)
PHONE...........................845 561-0233
Lenore Dunn, Branch Mgr
EMP: 9
SALES (corp-wide): 9.6B Publicly Held
SIC: 2321 Men's & boys' dress shirts
PA: Pvh Corp.
200 Madison Ave Bsmt 1
New York NY 10016
212 381-3500

(G-8380)
REGE INC
110 Corporate Dr (12553-6952)
P.O. Box 4417 (12553-0417)
PHONE...........................845 565-7772
Cheskel Smilowitz, CEO
Ramon Echevarria, President
▲ EMP: 18
SQ FT: 30,000
SALES (est): 5.6MM Privately Held
WEB: www.polyworksinc.com
SIC: 2673 Plastic bags: made from pur-
chased materials

(G-8381)
SALKO KITCHENS INC
256 Walsh Ave (12553-5752)
PHONE...........................845 565-4420
Aron Sandel, President
▲ EMP: 19
SALES: 1.5MM Privately Held
WEB: www.salkokitchens.com
SIC: 2434 Wood kitchen cabinets

(G-8382)
SCREEN GEMS INC
41 Windsor Hwy (12553-6225)
PHONE...........................845 561-0036
Carl Friedwall, President
EMP: 5
SQ FT: 3,600
SALES (est): 786.9K Privately Held
WEB: www.screengemsny.com
SIC: 2262 2395 Screen printing: man-
made fiber & silk broadwoven fabrics; em-
broidery & art needlework

(G-8383)
SIMCHA CANDLE CO INC
244 Mac Arthur Ave (12553-7011)
P.O. Box 309, Monroe (10949-0309)
PHONE...........................845 783-0406
Samuel Marcus, President
▲ EMP: 6
SQ FT: 15,000
SALES (est): 620.2K Privately Held
WEB: www.simchacandle.com
SIC: 3999 Candles

(G-8384)
TILCON NEW YORK INC
Also Called: Newburgh Asphalt
50 Ruscitti Rd (12553-6204)
PHONE...........................845 562-3240
Jerry Fletcher, Branch Mgr
EMP: 5
SALES (corp-wide): 30.6B Privately Held
WEB: www.tilconny.com
SIC: 2951 Asphalt paving mixtures &
blocks
HQ: Tilcon New York Inc.
9 Entin Rd
Parsippany NJ 07054
973 366-7741

(G-8385)
USA ILLUMINATION INC
Also Called: Usai
1126 River Rd (12553-6728)
PHONE...........................845 565-8500
Bonnie Littman, Principal
Tim Milton, Vice Pres
Donald Wray, VP Engrg
Gervines Orelus, Engineer
Oriana Starr, Engineer
▲ EMP: 35
SQ FT: 40,000
SALES (est): 16.5MM Privately Held
WEB: www.usaillumination.com
SIC: 3648 Public lighting fixtures

(G-8386)
VERLA INTERNATIONAL LTD
463 Temple Hill Rd (12553-5527)
PHONE...........................845 561-2440
Mario F Maffei, President
Robert R Roth, Vice Pres
▲ EMP: 400
SQ FT: 60,000
SALES (est): 107.7MM Privately Held
SIC: 2844 Cosmetic preparations

New York
New York County

(G-8387)
1 800 POSTCARDS INC
Also Called: Circle Press
149 W 27th St Fl 3 (10001-6279)
PHONE...........................212 741-1070
David Moyal, CEO
Twelve Watts, Executive
Kathy Boegh, Graphic Designe
EMP: 60
SALES (est): 10.5MM Privately Held
SIC: 2752 Commercial printing, litho-
graphic

(G-8388)
1 ATELIER LLC
347 W 36th St Rm 303 (10018-6565)
PHONE...........................917 916-2968
Stephanie Sarka, CEO
EMP: 8 EST: 2014
SALES (est): 275.5K Privately Held
SIC: 2339 5632 7389 Women's & misses'
accessories; women's accessory & spe-
cialty stores; design services

(G-8389)
1510 ASSOCIATES LLC
1500 Lexington Ave (10029-7349)
PHONE...........................212 828-8720
EMP: 6
SALES (est): 498.4K Privately Held
SIC: 2211 Cotton Broadwoven Fabric Mill

(G-8390)
180S LLC (HQ)
1 Liberty Plz Rm 3500 (10006-1421)
PHONE...........................410 534-6320
Helen Rockey, CEO
Lester C Lee, CEO
Brian Le Gette, President
Shelley Foland, Vice Pres
Flor Andres, CFO
▲ EMP: 40
SQ FT: 45,000
SALES (est): 4.7MM
SALES (corp-wide): 2.4MM Privately
Held
SIC: 2253 Scarves & mufflers, knit
PA: 180s, Inc.
700 S Caroline St
New York NY 10006
410 534-6320

(G-8391)
2 1 2 POSTCARDS INC
121 Varick St Frnt B (10013-1408)
PHONE...........................212 767-8227
Jiff Wed Work, Manager
EMP: 25
SALES (est): 2.9MM Privately Held
SIC: 2759 2752 Commercial printing;
commercial printing, lithographic

(G-8392)
2 X 4 INC
180 Varick St Rm 1610 (10014-5861)
PHONE...........................212 647-1170
Georgie Stout, President
Michael Rock, Partner
Gala Delmont-Benatar, Project Mgr
Dan Dittrich, Production
Susan Seller, Treasurer
EMP: 22
SQ FT: 2,000
SALES (est): 3.7MM Privately Held
WEB: www.2x4.org
SIC: 2752 Commercial printing, litho-
graphic

(G-8393)
212 BIZ LLC (PA)
1410 Broadway Rm 3203 (10018-9315)
PHONE...........................212 391-4444
Ira Levinas,
▲ EMP: 9 EST: 2007
SALES: 12MM Privately Held
SIC: 3161 Clothing & apparel carrying
cases

(G-8394)
212 MEDIA LLC
460 Park Ave S Fl 4 (10016-7561)
PHONE...........................212 710-3092
Rishi Malhotra, Managing Prtnr
Inesha Singh, Sales Mgr
Neal Shenoy, Mng Member
Brian Litvack, Director
▲ EMP: 40
SALES (est): 2.9MM Privately Held
WEB: www.212media.com
SIC: 2741 Miscellaneous publishing

(G-8395)
**21ST CENTURY FOX AMERICA
INC**
1211 Aveof The Am Lowr C3 (10036)
PHONE...........................212 782-8000
Carolyn Lawler, President
Heidi Gray, Principal
Joe Abel, District Mgr
Patsy Barton, Area Mgr
Anne Crank, Area Mgr
EMP: 8
SALES (corp-wide): 90.2B Publicly Held
SIC: 2711 Newspapers, publishing & print-
ing
HQ: 21st Century Fox America, Inc.
1211 Ave Of The Americas
New York NY 10036
212 852-7000

(G-8396)
**21ST CENTURY FOX AMERICA
INC (DH)**
1211 Ave Of The Americas (10036-8701)
PHONE...........................212 852-7000
James Murdoch, CEO
John Nallen, CFO
Michael Quick, Manager
Meagan Malley, Admin Asst
EMP: 60
SQ FT: 40,000
SALES (est): 1.7B
SALES (corp-wide): 90.2B Publicly Held
SIC: 2752 4833 7812 2721 Promotional
printing, lithographic; television broad-
casting stations; motion picture produc-
tion & distribution; magazines: publishing
only, not printed on site
HQ: Twenty-First Century Fox, Inc.
1211 Avenue Of The Americ
New York NY 10036
212 852-7000

(G-8397)
**21ST CENTURY FOX AMERICA
INC**
Mirabella Magazine
200 Madison Ave Fl 8 (10016-3908)
PHONE...........................212 447-4600
Grace Mirabella, Director
EMP: 85
SALES (corp-wide): 90.2B Publicly Held
SIC: 2721 Periodicals
HQ: 21st Century Fox America, Inc.
1211 Ave Of The Americas
New York NY 10036
212 852-7000

▲ = Import ▼=Export
◆ =Import/Export

(G-8398)
2K INC
622 Broadway Fl 6 (10012-2600)
PHONE...................................646 536-3007
Strauss Zelnick, *CEO*
Lainie Goldstein, *CFO*
EMP: 6 EST: 2013
SALES (est): 392.7K **Publicly Held**
SIC: 7372 Prepackaged software
PA: Take-Two Interactive Software, Inc.
110 W 44th St
New York NY 10036

(G-8399)
30DC INC (PA)
80 Broad St Fl 5 (10004-2257)
PHONE...................................212 962-4400
Henry Pinskier, *Ch of Bd*
Theodore A Greenberg, *CFO*
EMP: 11
SALES: 738.1K **Privately Held**
SIC: 7372 Prepackaged software

(G-8400)
30DC INC
80 Broad St Fl 5 (10004-2257)
PHONE...................................212 962-4400
Teodore A Greenbird, *CFO*
Greg Laborde, *Director*
EMP: 12
SQ FT: 3,000
SALES: 1MM **Privately Held**
SIC: 7372 Application computer software

(G-8401)
31 PHILLIP LIM LLC (PA)
225 Liberty St Fl 33 (10281-1089)
PHONE...................................212 354-6540
Xuan Wen Zhou, *Mng Member*
Melissa Lee,
Phillip Lim,
▲ **EMP:** 40
SQ FT: 2,000
SALES (est): 8.5MM **Privately Held**
WEB: www.31philliplim.com
SIC: 2339 Sportswear, women's

(G-8402)
3835 LEBRON REST EQP & SUP INC (PA)
Also Called: Lebron Equipment Supply
3835 9th Ave (10034-3740)
PHONE...................................212 942-8258
Catalina Lebron, *Ch of Bd*
Manuel Lebron, *President*
Edward Perez, *Director*
EMP: 20
SQ FT: 400
SALES (est): 2.9MM **Privately Held**
SIC: 3679 Power supplies, all types: static

(G-8403)
4BUMPERS LLC
285 New Wstmnster End Ave (10023)
PHONE...................................212 721-9600
Jeffrey Levine,
Alan Levine,
EMP: 10
SALES (est): 596.8K **Privately Held**
SIC: 3714 Bumpers & bumperettes, motor
vehicle

(G-8404)
5 STAR APPAREL LLC
Also Called: Enyce
31 W 34th St Fl 7 (10001-3031)
PHONE...................................212 563-1233
Albert Pardo, *Division Mgr*
EMP: 6
SALES (corp-wide): 65.2MM **Privately
Held**
SIC: 2326 Men's & boys' work clothing
HQ: 5 Star Apparel L.L.C.
31 W 34th St Fl 4
New York NY 10001
212 563-1233

(G-8405)
525 AMERICA LLC (PA)
1411 Broadway Fl 15 (10018-3471)
PHONE...................................212 921-5688
EMP: 7
SALES: 9.3MM **Privately Held**
SIC: 2339 Women's & misses' outerwear

(G-8406)
6 SHORE ROAD LLC
54 Thompson St Fl 5 (10012-4308)
PHONE...................................212 274-9666
Pooja Kharbanda, *Mng Member*
EMP: 5 EST: 2007
SALES (est): 279.4K **Privately Held**
SIC: 2369 5621 Bathing suits &
swimwear: girls', children's & infants';
women's clothing stores

(G-8407)
6TH AVENUE SHOWCASE INC
Also Called: Tempo Paris
241 W 37th St Frnt 2 (10018-6797)
PHONE...................................212 382-0400
Shawn Assil, *President*
▲ **EMP:** 6
SQ FT: 5,300
SALES (est): 1.1MM **Privately Held**
SIC: 2339 Women's & misses' outerwear

(G-8408)
79 METRO LTD (PA)
265 W 37th St Rm 205 (10018-5031)
PHONE...................................212 944-4030
Nancy Bossio Hutnick, *President*
EMP: 1
SQ FT: 8,500
SALES (est): 1.1MM **Privately Held**
SIC: 2337 2253 2331 Women's & misses'
suits & coats; sweaters & sweater coats,
knit; blouses, women's & juniors': made
from purchased material

(G-8409)
99CENT WORLD AND VARIETY CORP
4242 Broadway (10033-3708)
PHONE...................................212 740-0010
EMP: 5
SALES (est): 294.3K **Privately Held**
SIC: 3643 Mfg Conductive Wiring Devices

(G-8410)
A & M LLC
Also Called: H and B Digital
29 W 46th St (10036-4104)
PHONE...................................212 354-1341
Tony Aama, *Mng Member*
EMP: 6
SQ FT: 3,000
SALES (est): 7MM **Privately Held**
SIC: 3634 Electric housewares & fans

(G-8411)
A & M ROSENTHAL ENTPS INC (PA)
Also Called: Dessy Creations
8 W 38th St Fl 4 (10018-0154)
PHONE...................................646 638-9600
Alan Dessy, *President*
Maryanne Walter, *Production*
Ronnie Dey, *Purchasing*
Vivian G Diamond, *Treasurer*
Nancy Vargas, *Supervisor*
◆ **EMP:** 45 EST: 1963
SQ FT: 18,400
SALES (est): 5.4MM **Privately Held**
SIC: 2335 Wedding gowns & dresses

(G-8412)
A & V CASTINGS INC
257 W 39th St Fl 16w (10018-3106)
PHONE...................................212 997-0042
Alex Kvitko, *President*
EMP: 8
SALES: 1MM **Privately Held**
SIC: 3325 3911 Alloy steel castings, ex-
cept investment; jewelry, precious metal

(G-8413)
A AND J APPAREL CORP
Also Called: Forwear
209 W 38th St Rm 1207 (10018-4498)
PHONE...................................212 398-8899
Mahin Azizian, *President*
EMP: 9
SALES (est): 1.1MM **Privately Held**
SIC: 2211 Apparel & outerwear fabrics,
cotton

(G-8414)
A ESTEBAN & COMPANY INC (PA)
132 W 36th St Rm 1000 (10018-8819)
PHONE...................................212 989-7000
Alphonso C Esteban, *Ch of Bd*
Greta Esteban, *Technology*
Bob Gannon, *Technology*
Tom Gregory, *Software Engr*
Daniel Esteban, *Admin Sec*
▲ **EMP:** 25
SALES (est): 5.6MM **Privately Held**
WEB: www.esteban.com
SIC: 2752 7334 Commercial printing, off-
set; blueprinting service

(G-8415)
A FLEISIG PAPER BOX CORP
1751 2nd Ave Apt 10a (10128-5377)
PHONE...................................212 226-7490
Robert Fleisig, *President*
EMP: 10 EST: 1999
SALES: 1MM **Privately Held**
WEB: www.afleisig.com
SIC: 2652 Setup paperboard boxes

(G-8416)
A GRAPHIC PRINTING INC
49 Market St Frnt 2 (10002-7229)
PHONE...................................212 233-9696
M Siam, *President*
▲ **EMP:** 7
SALES (est): 596.6K **Privately Held**
SIC: 2759 Commercial printing

(G-8417)
A GUIDEPOSTS CHURCH CORP
16 E 34th St Fl 21 (10016-4328)
PHONE...................................212 251-8100
Dorothy Labell, *Marketing Mgr*
William McGlynn, *Marketing Staff*
Adam Hunter, *Manager*
Sabra Ciancanelli, *Manager*
Celeste McCauley, *Senior Editor*
EMP: 180
SALES (est): 12.3MM
SALES (corp-wide): 31.6MM **Privately
Held**
SIC: 2721 Magazines: publishing only, not
printed on site
PA: A Guideposts Church Corp
39 Old Ridgebury Rd # 27
Danbury CT 06810
203 749-0203

(G-8418)
A JAFFE INC
Also Called: Sandberg & Sikorski
592 5th Ave Fl 3 (10036-4707)
PHONE...................................212 843-7464
Mihir Bhansali, *CEO*
Samuel Sandberg, *Chairman*
Angelique Crown, *VP Sales*
Salvin Dixon, *Accounts Exec*
Katelyn Lea, *Accounts Exec*
EMP: 175
SQ FT: 30,000
SALES (est): 28.4MM **Privately Held**
WEB: www.ajaffe.com
SIC: 3911 Jewelry, precious metal

(G-8419)
A THOUSAND CRANES INC
Also Called: Knitty City
208 W 79th St Apt 2 (10024-6269)
PHONE...................................212 724-9596
Pearl Chin, *President*
Arvin Chin, *Vice Pres*
EMP: 10
SALES (est): 1MM **Privately Held**
WEB: www.knittycity.com
SIC: 2299 Yarns, specialty & novelty

(G-8420)
A TO Z MEDIA INC (PA)
243 W 30th St Fl 6 (10001-2812)
PHONE...................................212 260-0237
Sarah Robertson, *CEO*
Scott Pollack, *President*
Stacy Karp, *VP Prdtn*
Barbara Coates, *Bookkeeper*
Jamie Wagner, *Advt Staff*
▲ **EMP:** 20

SALES (est): 8.3MM **Privately Held**
WEB: www.atozmedia.com
SIC: 3652 7389 Compact laser discs, prerecorded; magnetic tape (audio): prerecorded; design services

(G-8421)
A2IA CORP
24 W 40th St Fl 3 (10018-1856)
PHONE...................................917 237-0390
Jean-Louis Fages, *President*
Olivier Baret, *Senior VP*
Nikolai Gorski, *Research*
Thomas Retornaz, *Research*
Jeremy Benattar, *Sales Dir*
EMP: 8
SALES (est): 1.2MM **Privately Held**
SIC: 7372 Prepackaged software
PA: Analyse Image Intelli Artific
37 Au 39
Paris 8e Arrondissement 75008

(G-8422)
A3 APPAREL LLC
1407 Broadway Rm 716a (10018-5293)
PHONE...................................888 403-9669
Peter Regondo, *CEO*
EMP: 7 EST: 2014
SQ FT: 1,200
SALES: 8MM **Privately Held**
SIC: 2211 Apparel & outerwear fabrics,
cotton

(G-8423)
AAA AMERCN FLAG DCTG CO INC
36 W 37th St Rm 409 (10018-7452)
PHONE...................................212 279-3524
Ian Flamm, *President*
Marian Watson, *Vice Pres*
EMP: 4
SQ FT: 2,500
SALES: 1MM **Privately Held**
SIC: 2399 Flags, fabric; banners, made
from fabric

(G-8424)
ABACUS LABS INC
14 E 38th St Fl 9 (10016-0632)
PHONE...................................917 426-6642
Omar Qari, *President*
Stephanie Walsh, *Vice Pres*
Josh Halickman, *CTO*
Ted Power, *Officer*
EMP: 30
SALES (est): 156.4K
SALES (corp-wide): 16.3MM **Privately
Held**
SIC: 7372 Business oriented computer
software
PA: Certify, Inc.
20 York St Ste 201
Portland ME 04101
207 773-6100

(G-8425)
ABALENE DECORATING SERVICES
315 W 39th St Rm 611 (10018-4035)
PHONE...................................718 782-2000
Moseha Goldman, *President*
Kalmen Weiss, *President*
Miriam Weiss, *Vice Pres*
EMP: 21
SQ FT: 18,000
SALES (est): 1.8MM **Privately Held**
SIC: 2591 2391 7216 Drapery hardware
& blinds & shades; curtains & draperies;
curtain cleaning & repair

(G-8426)
ABBEVILLE PRESS INC
Also Called: Abbeville Publishing Group
116 W 23rd St Fl 5 (10011-2599)
PHONE...................................212 366-5585
Robert E Abrams, *Ch of Bd*
Nadine Winns, *Marketing Mgr*
Ada Rodriguez, *Director*
Dorothy Gutterman, *Admin Sec*
▲ **EMP:** 33
SALES (est): 3.3MM **Privately Held**
WEB: www.abbeville.com
SIC: 2731 Book publishing

(G-8427)
ABC PEANUT BUTTER LLC
295 Madison Ave Ste 1618 (10017-6434)
PHONE.....................212 661-6886
H J Warden, *Mng Member*
EMP: 355
SALES (est): 23.4MM **Privately Held**
SIC: 2099 Peanut butter

(G-8428)
ABEL NOSER SOLUTIONS LLC
1 Battery Park Plz # 601 (10004-1446)
PHONE.....................646 432-4000
Ted Morgan, *CEO*
Peter Weiler, *President*
EMP: 20
SALES: 4MM
SALES (corp-wide): 1.2MM **Privately Held**
SIC: 7372 Business oriented computer software
PA: Abel Noser Holdings, L.L.C.
24 Whitehall St Fl 6 Flr 6
New York NY 10004
646 432-4000

(G-8429)
ABEONA THERAPEUTICS INC (PA)
1330 Avenue Of Americas (10019)
PHONE.....................646 813-4712
Jo Siffert, *CEO*
Steven H Rouhandeh, *Ch of Bd*
Timothy J Miller, *President*
Jeffrey B Davis, *COO*
Victor Paulus, *Senior VP*
EMP: 42 EST: 1974
SQ FT: 5,730
SALES: 3MM **Publicly Held**
WEB: www.ampex.com
SIC: 2834 Pharmaceutical preparations

(G-8430)
ABKCO MUSIC & RECORDS INC (PA)
85 5th Ave Fl 11 (10003-3019)
PHONE.....................212 399-0300
Allen Klein, *President*
Alan E Horowitz, *Vice Pres*
Peter J Howard, *Vice Pres*
Peter Howard, *Vice Pres*
Iris W Keitel, *Vice Pres*
EMP: 20 EST: 1961
SQ FT: 11,000
SALES (est): 8MM **Privately Held**
SIC: 3652 6794 2741 7922 Phonograph records, prerecorded; magnetic tape (audio): prerecorded; compact laser discs, prerecorded; copyright buying & licensing; music, sheet: publishing only, not printed on site; legitimate live theater producers; motion picture production

(G-8431)
ABKCO MUSIC INC (HQ)
85 5th Ave Fl 11 (10003-3019)
PHONE.....................212 399-0300
Allen Klein, *President*
EMP: 10 EST: 1970
SQ FT: 12,000
SALES (est): 1.6MM
SALES (corp-wide): 8MM **Privately Held**
SIC: 2741 Miscellaneous publishing
PA: Abkco Music & Records Inc.
85 5th Ave Fl 11
New York NY 10003
212 399-0300

(G-8432)
ABLETON INC
36 W Colo Blvd Ste 300 (10013)
PHONE.....................646 723-4586
Mads Lindgren, *Principal*
Larry S Siegel, *Exec VP*
Shawn Moore, *Senior VP*
Kathy Deshazor, *Vice Pres*
Akila Mahesh, *Vice Pres*
EMP: 8
SALES (est): 423.4K **Privately Held**
SIC: 7372 Prepackaged software

(G-8433)
ABP INTERNATIONAL INC
Also Called: Electronic Tech Briefs
1466 Broadway Ste 910 (10036-7309)
PHONE.....................212 490-3999
Bill Schnirring, *Ch of Bd*
Joseph Pramberger, *President*
Domenic Mucchetti, *COO*
John Murray, *Vice Pres*
Adam Santiago, *Prdtn Mgr*
EMP: 40 EST: 1975
SQ FT: 11,000
SALES (est): 5.1MM **Privately Held**
WEB: www.emhartcontest.com
SIC: 2721 Magazines: publishing only, not printed on site

(G-8434)
ABRAHAM JWLY DESIGNERS & MFRS
71 W 47th St Ste 905 (10036-2865)
PHONE.....................212 944-1149
Can Akdemir, *Partner*
Ibrahim Akdemir, *Partner*
Iskender Akdemir, *Partner*
EMP: 16
SALES (est): 1.6MM **Privately Held**
SIC: 3911 Jewelry, precious metal

(G-8435)
ABRIMIAN BROS CORP
48 W 48th St Ste 805 (10036-1713)
PHONE.....................212 382-1106
Marty Abrimian, *President*
EMP: 10
SALES (est): 860.2K **Privately Held**
SIC: 3911 Jewelry, precious metal

(G-8436)
ABSOLUTE COLOR CORPORATION
109 W 27th St Frnt 2 (10001-6208)
PHONE.....................212 868-0404
Daniel Shil, *President*
Peter Gordon, *Vice Pres*
EMP: 8
SQ FT: 2,500
SALES (est): 1MM **Privately Held**
WEB: www.absolutcolor.com
SIC: 2796 2741 Color separations for printing; miscellaneous publishing

(G-8437)
ACADEMY OF POLITICAL SCIENCE
Also Called: POLITICAL SCIENCE QUARTERLY
475 Riverside Dr Ste 1274 (10115-1298)
PHONE.....................212 870-2500
Demetrios Caraley, *President*
Virgil Conway, *Principal*
Loren Kando, *Manager*
EMP: 6
SQ FT: 2,309
SALES: 1MM **Privately Held**
WEB: www.psqonline.org
SIC: 2721 Periodicals: publishing only

(G-8438)
ACAI OF AMERICA INC
225 W 34th St Fl 9 (10122-0901)
PHONE.....................862 205-9334
Will Anderson, *Principal*
EMP: 8
SALES (est): 1MM **Privately Held**
SIC: 3556 Juice extractors, fruit & vegetable: commercial type

(G-8439)
ACCELIFY SOLUTIONS LLC
16 W 36th St Rm 902 (10018-9748)
PHONE.....................888 922-2354
Alex Brecher, *CEO*
Joe Jacobs, *President*
David Thomas, *VP Bus Dvlpt*
Leonid Shum, *CTO*
EMP: 25
SQ FT: 3,000
SALES (est): 2.7MM **Privately Held**
SIC: 7372 Educational computer software

(G-8440)
ACCESS INTELLIGENCE LLC
Also Called: Pbi Media Inc.
249 W 17th St (10011-5390)
PHONE.....................212 204-4269
John French, *President*
Andrea Persily, *COO*
EMP: 950
SALES (est): 35.7MM
SALES (corp-wide): 77.7MM **Privately Held**
SIC: 2721 Trade journals: publishing only, not printed on site
PA: Access Intelligence Llc
9211 Corporate Blvd Fl 4
Rockville MD 20850
301 354-2000

(G-8441)
ACCESSORY PLAYS LLC
29 W 36th St (10018-7907)
PHONE.....................212 564-7301
Richard Dauplaise, *President*
EMP: 50
SQ FT: 5,000
SALES (est): 1.5MM **Privately Held**
SIC: 3961 Costume jewelry, ex. precious metal & semiprecious stones

(G-8442)
ACCESSORY STREET LLC
1370 Broadway (10018-7302)
PHONE.....................212 686-8990
Andrew Pizzo,
Mitchell Grossman,
▲ EMP: 12
SALES (est): 685.8K **Privately Held**
SIC: 2339 Women's & misses' outerwear

(G-8443)
ACCESSRIES DIRECT INTL USA INC
1450 Broadway Fl 22 (10018-2222)
PHONE.....................646 448-8200
Alberto Rosenthal, *CEO*
Rody Moreira, *President*
▲ EMP: 23
SALES (est): 12.1MM **Privately Held**
SIC: 2389 2331 2339 5137 Men's miscellaneous accessories; women's & misses' blouses & shirts; women's & misses' accessories; handbags

(G-8444)
ACCUTRAK INC
432 Washington St Ste 113 (10013)
PHONE.....................212 925-5330
Eli Camhi, *President*
Stanford Silverman, *Vice Pres*
EMP: 15
SALES (est): 1MM **Privately Held**
SIC: 3812 Electronic detection systems (aeronautical)

(G-8445)
ACE BANNER & FLAG COMPANY
Also Called: Ace Banner Flag & Graphics
115 W 28th St Apt 3r (10001-6140)
PHONE.....................212 620-9111
Carl Calo, *President*
Elizabeth Calo, *Treasurer*
Leah Segarra, *Manager*
EMP: 12 EST: 1916
SALES (est): 1MM **Privately Held**
WEB: www.acebanner.com
SIC: 2399 Banners, made from fabric; flags, fabric

(G-8446)
ACE DIAMOND CORP
30 W 47th St Ste 808r (10036-8665)
PHONE.....................212 730-8231
Herman Witriol, *President*
Margaret Witriol, *Treasurer*
EMP: 3 EST: 1975
SALES: 1MM **Privately Held**
SIC: 3915 5094 Diamond cutting & polishing; jewelry & precious stones; diamonds (gems)

(G-8447)
ACF INDUSTRIES HOLDING LLC (DH)
767 5th Ave (10153-0023)
PHONE.....................212 702-4363
Keith Cozza, *CEO*
Carl C Icahn, *President*
Richard T Buonato, *Vice Pres*
EMP: 2
SALES (est): 197.7MM
SALES (corp-wide): 955MM **Privately Held**
SIC: 3743 4741 4789 6799 Freight cars & equipment; tank freight cars & car equipment; railroad equipment, except locomotives; rental of railroad cars; railroad car repair; security speculators for own account
HQ: Highcrest Investors Llc
445 Hamilton Ave Ste 1210
New York NY 10153
212 702-4323

(G-8448)
ACKER & LI MILLS CORPORATION
44 W 62nd St Apt 3b (10023-7009)
PHONE.....................212 307-7247
Daniel Feder, *President*
▲ EMP: 5
SALES: 2MM **Privately Held**
SIC: 2231 Broadwoven fabric mills, wool

(G-8449)
ACOLYTE TECHNOLOGIES CORP
44 E 32nd St Rm 901 (10016-5508)
PHONE.....................212 629-3239
Marvin Figenbaum, *CEO*
Salvatore Guerrieri, *President*
Abel Gonzalez, *Sales Staff*
▲ EMP: 13
SALES (est): 1.8MM **Privately Held**
SIC: 3674 Light emitting diodes

(G-8450)
ACS CUSTOM USA LLC
Also Called: Advanced Comm Solutions Ltd
520 W 25th St (10001-5502)
PHONE.....................646 559-5642
Adam Rhodes, *Director*
EMP: 8
SALES (est): 752.1K **Privately Held**
SIC: 3842 Surgical appliances & supplies
PA: Advanced Communication Solutions Limited
Unit 22 - 23
Banbury OXON
129 526-6665

(G-8451)
ACTINIUM PHARMACEUTICALS INC (PA)
275 Madison Ave Ste 702 (10016-1154)
PHONE.....................646 677-3870
Sandesh Seth, *Ch of Bd*
Cynthia Pussinen, *Exec VP*
Nitya Ray, *Exec VP*
Robert N Daly, *Vice Pres*
Qing Liang, *Vice Pres*
EMP: 23 EST: 1997
SALES (est): 2.8MM **Publicly Held**
SIC: 2834 8069 Pharmaceutical preparations; cancer hospital

(G-8452)
ADA GEMS CORP
Also Called: Mordechai Collection
10 W 47th St Ste 707 (10036-3301)
PHONE.....................212 719-0100
Daniel Mor, *Treasurer*
▲ EMP: 5
SALES (est): 457.3K **Privately Held**
SIC: 3172 Cases, jewelry

(G-8453)
ADAM SCOTT DESIGNS INC
118 E 25th St Fl 11 (10010-2966)
PHONE.....................212 420-8866
Steven Dubler, *President*
◆ EMP: 20
SQ FT: 8,000

▲ = Import ▼=Export
◆ =Import/Export

SALES (est): 3.7MM **Privately Held**
WEB: www.scottadamdesigns.com
SIC: 3111 3161 3069 5199 Accessory products, leather; upholstery leather; luggage; bags, rubber or rubberized fabric; bags, textile; polyvinyl chloride resins (PVC); umbrellas, men's & boys'; hats, men's & boys'; robes, men's & boys'; men's & boys' outerwear

(G-8454)
ADAMOR INC
Also Called: Izi Creations
17 E 48th St Rm 901 (10017-1010)
PHONE..........................212 688-8885
Izidor Kamhi, *President*
EMP: 7
SALES (est): 1.1MM **Privately Held**
WEB: www.adamor.com
SIC: 3911 Jewelry, precious metal

(G-8455)
ADC DOLLS INC
112 W 34th St Ste 1207 (10120-0101)
PHONE..........................212 244-4500
Herbert E Brown, *Ch of Bd*
Gale Jarvis, *President*
Rob Porell, *CFO*
Noam Welfer, *Director*
William J Beckett, *Admin Sec*
◆ **EMP:** 163
SQ FT: 90,000
SALES (est): 11.5MM **Privately Held**
WEB: www.alexdoll.com
SIC: 3942 Dolls, except stuffed toy animals

(G-8456)
ADESSO INC (PA)
353 W 39th St Fl 2 (10018-1645)
PHONE..........................212 736-4440
Lee Schaak, *President*
Barney Wenograd, *Vice Pres*
Cherolyn L Shawe-Stratton, *Credit Staff*
Paul Berk, *VP Sales*
Lia Barbery, *Sales Staff*
◆ **EMP:** 32
SQ FT: 5,000
SALES (est): 5.2MM **Privately Held**
SIC: 3645 Floor lamps; table lamps

(G-8457)
ADFIN SOLUTIONS INC
25 W 31st St Fl 4 (10001-4413)
PHONE..........................650 464-0742
Milosz Tanski, *CTO*
EMP: 15 **EST:** 2011
SALES (est): 1.1MM **Privately Held**
SIC: 7372 Business oriented computer software

(G-8458)
ADG JEWELS LLC
15 W 47th St Ste 600 (10036-5708)
PHONE..........................212 888-1890
Raju Chanani, *Director*
EMP: 15
SALES (est): 956.6K **Privately Held**
SIC: 3911 5094 Jewelry, precious metal; jewelry & precious stones; precious metals

(G-8459)
ADGORITHMICS INC (PA)
260 Madison Ave Fl 8 (10016-2418)
PHONE..........................646 277-8728
Michael Kim, *CEO*
EMP: 5
SALES (est): 1.9MM **Privately Held**
SIC: 7372 Business oriented computer software

(G-8460)
ADITIANY INC
37 W 39th St Rm 1100 (10018-0579)
PHONE..........................212 997-8440
Nita K Shah, *President*
EMP: 2
SALES: 1.5MM **Privately Held**
SIC: 2395 Embroidery products, except schiffli machine

(G-8461)
ADOBE INC
8 W 40th St Fl 8 # 8 (10018-2275)
PHONE..........................212 471-0904
Bruce Chizen, *Manager*

EMP: 32
SALES (corp-wide): 9B **Publicly Held**
WEB: www.adobe.com
SIC: 7372 Prepackaged software
PA: Adobe Inc.
345 Park Ave
San Jose CA 95110
408 536-6000

(G-8462)
ADOBE SYSTEMS INC
1540 Broadway Fl 17 (10036-4039)
PHONE..........................212 471-0904
Fax: 212 471-0990
EMP: 20
SALES (est): 1.9MM **Privately Held**
SIC: 7372 Prepackaged Software Services

(G-8463)
ADOBE SYSTEMS INCORPORATED
Also Called: Behance
100 5th Ave Fl 5 (10011-6903)
PHONE..........................212 592-1400
Scott Belsky, *Branch Mgr*
Levi Van Veluw,
EMP: 250
SALES (corp-wide): 9B **Publicly Held**
SIC: 7372 Prepackaged software
PA: Adobe Inc.
345 Park Ave
San Jose CA 95110
408 536-6000

(G-8464)
ADRIENNE LANDAU DESIGNS INC
519 8th Ave Fl 21 (10018-4573)
PHONE..........................212 695-8362
Adrienne Landau, *CEO*
EMP: 15
SQ FT: 12,000
SALES (est): 1.7MM **Privately Held**
WEB: www.adriennelandau.com
SIC: 2337 Capes, except fur or rubber: women's, misses' & juniors'

(G-8465)
ADSTREAM AMERICA LLC (DH)
345 7th Ave Fl 6 (10001-5053)
PHONE..........................212 804-8498
Mark Smith, *General Mgr*
Michael Palmer, *Mng Member*
EMP: 20
SALES (est): 4.8MM **Privately Held**
SIC: 3993 Advertising artwork

(G-8466)
ADTECH US INC
770 Broadway Fl 4 (10003-9558)
PHONE..........................212 402-4840
Will Schmahl, *Vice Pres*
Peter Meyer, *Vice Pres*
EMP: 125
SALES (est): 5.2MM
SALES (corp-wide): 130.8B **Publicly Held**
SIC: 7372 Prepackaged software
HQ: Verizon Media Germany Gmbh
Theresienhohe 12
Munchen 80339
892 319-70

(G-8467)
ADVANCE APPAREL INTL INC
265 W 37th St Rm 906 (10018-5728)
PHONE..........................212 944-0984
Charles Hu, *President*
Eugene Hu, *Vice Pres*
▲ **EMP:** 5
SALES (est): 655.6K **Privately Held**
SIC: 2311 Men's & boys' suits & coats

(G-8468)
ADVANCE FINANCE GROUP LLC
101 Park Ave Frnt (10178-0399)
PHONE..........................212 630-5900
Tom Summer, *CFO*
Christina Cruz, *Senior Mgr*
Barbara Lupo, *Director*
Richard Marerro, *Director*
EMP: 100
SALES (est): 768.3K **Privately Held**
SIC: 2759 8721 Publication printing; auditing services

(G-8469)
ADVANCE MAGAZINE PUBLS INC
1 World Trade Ctr (10007-0089)
PHONE..........................212 286-8582
Mira Ilie, *Business Mgr*
EMP: 5
SALES (corp-wide): 5.5B **Privately Held**
SIC: 2721 Magazines: publishing & printing
HQ: Advance Magazine Publishers Inc.
1 World Trade Ctr Fl 43
New York NY 10007
212 286-2860

(G-8470)
ADVANCE MAGAZINE PUBLS INC (HQ)
Also Called: Conde Nast Publications
1 World Trade Ctr Fl 43 (10007-0090)
PHONE..........................212 286-2860
S I Newhouse Jr, *Ch of Bd*
Charles Townsend, *President*
Grace Coddington, *Principal*
Mayte Allende, *Editor*
Michael Allin, *Editor*
▲ **EMP:** 2200
SALES (est): 1B
SALES (corp-wide): 5.5B **Privately Held**
WEB: www.condenast.com
SIC: 2721 Magazines: publishing & printing
PA: Advance Publications, Inc.
1 World Trade Ctr Fl 43
New York NY 10007
718 981-1234

(G-8471)
ADVANCE MAGAZINE PUBLS INC
Also Called: Conde Nast Publications Div
1 World Trade Ctr Fl 20 (10007-0090)
PHONE..........................212 790-4422
Anna Matasyan, *Associate Dir*
EMP: 64
SALES (corp-wide): 5.5B **Privately Held**
WEB: www.condenast.com
SIC: 2721 Magazines: publishing & printing
HQ: Advance Magazine Publishers Inc.
1 World Trade Ctr Fl 43
New York NY 10007
212 286-2860

(G-8472)
ADVANCE MAGAZINE PUBLS INC
1166 Ave Of The Amrcs 1 (10036-2708)
PHONE..........................212 286-2860
Michael Wagner, *Opers Staff*
Kim Fasting-Berg, *Marketing Staff*
Alexandra Walsh, *Branch Mgr*
Christine Shugrue, *CIO*
Joe Simon, *CTO*
EMP: 64
SALES (corp-wide): 5.5B **Privately Held**
WEB: www.condenast.com
SIC: 2721 Magazines: publishing & printing
HQ: Advance Magazine Publishers Inc.
1 World Trade Ctr Fl 43
New York NY 10007
212 286-2860

(G-8473)
ADVANCE MAGAZINE PUBLS INC
Parade Publications
711 3rd Ave Rm 700 (10017-9210)
PHONE..........................212 450-7000
EMP: 195
SALES (corp-wide): 5.6B **Privately Held**
SIC: 2721 2711 Periodicals- Publishing/Printing Newspapers-Publishing/Printing
HQ: Advance Magazine Publishers Inc.
1 World Trade Ctr Fl 43
New York NY 10007
212 286-2860

(G-8474)
ADVANCE MAGAZINE PUBLS INC
Also Called: Vogue China
750 3rd Ave Frnt G (10017-2728)
PHONE..........................212 697-0126
David Orlin, *Vice Pres*
Alexandra Wolfe, *Branch Mgr*

Giulio Capua, *Executive*
Bob Pick, *Executive*
EMP: 64
SALES (corp-wide): 5.5B **Privately Held**
SIC: 2721 Magazines: publishing & printing
HQ: Advance Magazine Publishers Inc.
1 World Trade Ctr Fl 43
New York NY 10007
212 286-2860

(G-8475)
ADVANCE PUBLICATIONS INC (PA)
Also Called: Staten Island Advance
1 World Trade Ctr Fl 43 (10007-0090)
PHONE..........................718 981-1234
Samuel I Newhouse III, *President*
Michael A Newhouse, *President*
Steven O Newhouse, *President*
Caroline Harrison, *Publisher*
Joe Douglas, *General Mgr*
▲ **EMP:** 100 **EST:** 1924
SQ FT: 40,000
SALES (est): 5.5B **Privately Held**
WEB: www.advance.net
SIC: 2711 2731 2721 2791 Newspapers, publishing & printing; book publishing; magazines: publishing & printing; typesetting; commercial printing, lithographic

(G-8476)
ADVANCED BIOMEDICAL TECH INC
350 5th Ave Fl 59 (10118-5999)
PHONE..........................718 766-7898
Chiming Yu, *President*
EMP: 5
SALES (est): 161.7K **Privately Held**
SIC: 1081 8731 Metal mining exploration & development services; commercial physical research

(G-8477)
ADVANCED BUSINESS GROUP INC
Also Called: Abgprint
266 W 37th St Fl 15 (10018-6615)
PHONE..........................212 398-1010
Michael J Mulligan, *President*
EMP: 15
SQ FT: 7,000
SALES (est): 2.7MM **Privately Held**
SIC: 2752 Commercial printing, lithographic

(G-8478)
ADVANCED COPY CENTER INC
213 W 35th St Ste 501 (10001-0214)
PHONE..........................212 388-1001
Peter Lee, *President*
EMP: 8
SALES (est): 955.8K **Privately Held**
SIC: 2752 Commercial printing, lithographic

(G-8479)
ADVANCED DIGITAL PRINTING LLC
65 W 36th St Fl 11 (10018-7936)
PHONE..........................718 649-1500
Aaron Menche, *Mng Member*
EMP: 35 **EST:** 2005
SQ FT: 85,000
SALES (est): 3.7MM **Privately Held**
SIC: 2752 Commercial printing, lithographic

(G-8480)
ADVANCED FASHIONS TECHNOLOGY
110 W 40th St Rm 1100 (10018-8529)
PHONE..........................212 221-0606
EMP: 8
SALES (est): 580K **Privately Held**
SIC: 2211 Cotton Broadwoven Fabric Mill

(G-8481)
ADVANCED PRINTING NEW YORK INC
263 W 38th St (10018-4483)
PHONE..........................212 840-8108
Carlos Cruz, *President*
EMP: 8

SALES (est): 1.1MM **Privately Held**
WEB: www.apnyc.com
SIC: 2752 Commercial printing, offset

(G-8482)
ADVANCED RESPONSE
CORPORATION
345 W 58th St Apt 11a (10019-1140)
P.O. Box 2213 (10019)
PHONE..........................212 459-0887
Inge Rothenberg, *President*
P G Woog, *Owner*
Lionel Woog, *Director*
▲ EMP: 5
SALES (est): 555.4K **Privately Held**
WEB: www.broxo.com
SIC: 3634 Massage machines, electric, ex-
cept for beauty/barber shops

(G-8483)
ADVANTAGE QUICK PRINT INC
Also Called: Hampshire Lithographers
30 E 33rd St Frnt B (10016-5337)
PHONE..........................212 989-5644
Stuart Menkes, *President*
▲ EMP: 6
SQ FT: 6,000
SALES: 350K **Privately Held**
SIC: 2752 Commercial printing, offset

(G-8484)
ADVD HEART PHYS & SURGS
130 E 77th St Fl 4 (10075-1851)
PHONE..........................212 434-3000
Michael Gorman, *Principal*
EMP: 10
SALES (est): 613.4K **Privately Held**
SIC: 3845 Surgical support systems: heart-
lung machine, exc. iron lung

(G-8485)
ADVENTURE PUBLISHING
GROUP
307 7th Ave Rm 1601 (10001-6042)
PHONE..........................212 575-4510
Laurie Schacht, *President*
EMP: 20
SALES (est): 2.6MM **Privately Held**
WEB: www.adventurepub.com
SIC: 2721 Magazines: publishing only, not
printed on site

(G-8486)
ADVERTISER PERCEPTIONS
INC
1120 Ave Of The Americas (10036-6700)
PHONE..........................212 626-6683
Ken Pearl, *Principal*
Sarah Bolton, *Vice Pres*
Andy Sippel, *Vice Pres*
Karen Cramp, *Research*
EMP: 9
SALES (est): 50.8K **Privately Held**
SIC: 2711 Newspapers

(G-8487)
AEGIS OIL LIMITED VENTURES
LLC
14 Wall St Fl 20 (10005-2123)
PHONE..........................646 233-4900
James Freiman, *Manager*
EMP: 11
SALES (est): 558.3K
SALES (corp-wide): 955.3K **Privately**
Held
SIC: 1382 Oil & gas exploration services
PA: Aegis Oil Limited Ventures Llc
100 Crescent Ct Ste 700
Dallas TX 75201
214 431-5201

(G-8488)
AES ELECTRONICS INC
135 E 54th St Apt 10j (10022-4511)
PHONE..........................212 371-8120
Abraham E Schenfeld, *President*
Ruth Schenfeld, *Treasurer*
EMP: 7
SQ FT: 1,200
SALES (est): 430K **Privately Held**
SIC: 3633 5065 Household laundry equip-
ment; communication equipment

(G-8489)
AETHERA LLC
Also Called: John and Kiras
256 W 12th St (10014-1912)
PHONE..........................215 324-9222
Christopher Dal Piaz, *Mng Member*
EMP: 25
SALES (est): 809.2K **Privately Held**
SIC: 2066 2026 5149 5441 Chocolate;
milk, chocolate; chocolate; candy, nut &
confectionery stores

(G-8490)
AFFORDABLE LUXURY GROUP
INC
Also Called: Aimee Kestenberg
10 W 33rd St Rm 615 (10001-3348)
PHONE..........................631 523-9266
Adam Protass, *COO*
▲ EMP: 9
SALES (est): 237.9K **Privately Held**
SIC: 3171 Women's handbags & purses

(G-8491)
AFFYMAX INC
600 5th Ave 2 (10020-2302)
PHONE..........................650 812-8700
John A Orwin, *Ch of Bd*
Jonathan M Couchman, *President*
Mark G Thompson, *CFO*
▲ EMP: 6
SQ FT: 1,500
SALES (est): 1MM **Privately Held**
WEB: www.affymax.com
SIC: 2834 Pharmaceutical preparations

(G-8492)
AG NEOVO PROFESSIONAL INC
Also Called: Agn Professional
156 5th Ave Ste 434 (10010-7002)
PHONE..........................212 647-9080
Minson Chen, *President*
EMP: 10
SQ FT: 1,900
SALES (est): 1.3MM **Privately Held**
WEB: www.agnpro.com
SIC: 3575 Computer terminals

(G-8493)
AGI BROOKS PRODUCTION CO
INC (PA)
7 E 14th St Apt 615 (10003-3130)
PHONE..........................212 268-1533
Agi Brooks, *President*
Don Mc Lean, *Vice Pres*
EMP: 11
SQ FT: 5,000
SALES (est): 1.4MM **Privately Held**
WEB: www.agibrooks.com
SIC: 2337 2331 2335 Suits: women's,
misses' & juniors'; blouses, women's &
juniors': made from purchased material;
women's, juniors' & misses' dresses

(G-8494)
AGILENT TECHNOLOGIES INC
399 Park Ave (10022-4614)
PHONE..........................877 424-4536
EMP: 2498
SALES (corp-wide): 4.9B **Publicly Held**
SIC: 3825 Instruments to measure electric-
ity
PA: Agilent Technologies, Inc.
5301 Stevens Creek Blvd
Santa Clara CA 95051
408 345-8886

(G-8495)
AGNOVOS HEALTHCARE LLC
140 Broadway Fl 46 (10005-1155)
PHONE..........................646 502-5860
David Mackey, *CFO*
EMP: 10
SALES (est): 1.2MM
SALES (corp-wide): 9.3MM **Privately**
Held
SIC: 3842 Implants, surgical
PA: Agnovos Healthcare Usa, Llc
7301 Calhoun Pl Ste 100
Rockville MD 20855
240 753-6500

(G-8496)
AGUILAR AMPLIFICATION LLC
599 Broadway Fl 7 (10012-3371)
PHONE..........................212 431-9109
Dave Avenius, *CEO*
David Boonshoft, *CEO*
Alexander Aguilar, *President*
Marco Passarelli, *Marketing Mgr*
Dale Titus, *Marketing Staff*
▲ EMP: 10
SQ FT: 10,000
SALES (est): 1.9MM **Privately Held**
WEB: www.aguilaramp.com
SIC: 3651 Amplifiers: radio, public address
or musical instrument

(G-8497)
AHHMIGO LLC
120 Cent Park S Rm 7c (10019)
PHONE..........................212 315-1818
Yaacob Dabah, *Manager*
EMP: 12
SALES (est): 820K **Privately Held**
SIC: 2099 Food preparations

(G-8498)
AHQ LLC
Also Called: Accessory Headquarters
25 W 39th St Fl 3 (10018-4106)
PHONE..........................212 328-1560
Abe Chehebar, *Mng Member*
▲ EMP: 40 EST: 2012
SALES: 20MM **Privately Held**
SIC: 3171 Women's handbags & purses

(G-8499)
AI ENTERTAINMENT HOLDINGS
LLC (HQ)
730 5th Ave Fl 20 (10019-4105)
PHONE..........................212 247-6400
Lincoln Benet, *President*
EMP: 15
SALES (est): 3.5B **Privately Held**
SIC: 2731 Book music: publishing & print-
ing

(G-8500)
AI MEDIA GROUP INC
1359 Broadway Fl 5 (10018-7747)
PHONE..........................212 660-2400
Andy Fenster, *CEO*
John Bernbach, *Ch of Bd*
Sergio Alvarez, *COO*
Steve Evans, *COO*
Krista Lewis, *Marketing Staff*
EMP: 16
SQ FT: 2,500
SALES (est): 9.6MM **Privately Held**
SIC: 2741

(G-8501)
AIMSUN INC
Also Called: Tss-Transport Simulation
20 W 22nd St Ste 612 (10010-6067)
PHONE..........................917 267-8534
Alex Gerodimos, *President*
Jordi Casas, *Research*
Murat Aycin, *Sr Project Mgr*
Nadia Feddo, *Officer*
Josep Aymami, *Regional*
EMP: 5
SALES (est): 485.1K
SALES (corp-wide): 95B **Privately Held**
SIC: 7372 Application computer software
HQ: Aimsun S.L.
Ronda Universitat, 22 - B At
Barcelona 08007

(G-8502)
AIP MC HOLDINGS LLC (PA)
330 Madison Ave Fl 28 (10017-5018)
PHONE..........................212 627-2360
Nikhil Bodade, *Partner*
Danny Davis, *Partner*
Rich Dennis, *Partner*
Justin Fish, *Partner*
Ryan Hodgson, *Partner*
EMP: 5
SALES (est): 95MM **Privately Held**
SIC: 3399 Aluminum atomized powder;
brads: aluminum, brass or other nonfer-
rous metal or wire; metal fasteners; sta-
ples, nonferrous metal or wire

(G-8503)
AIR SKATE & AIR JUMP CORP
1385 Broadway (10018-6001)
PHONE..........................212 967-1201
Patrick Denihan, *Branch Mgr*
EMP: 5
SALES (corp-wide): 6.2MM **Privately**
Held
SIC: 3143 5139 Men's footwear, except
athletic; footwear, athletic
PA: Air Skate & Air Jump Corp.
2208 E 5th St
Brooklyn NY 11223
212 967-1201

(G-8504)
ALADDIN MANUFACTURING
CORP
295 5th Ave Ste 1412 (10016-7124)
PHONE..........................212 561-8715
Dennis Fein, *Manager*
EMP: 187
SALES (corp-wide): 9.9B **Publicly Held**
SIC: 2273 Carpets & rugs
HQ: Aladdin Manufacturing Corporation
160 S Industrial Blvd
Calhoun GA 30701
706 629-7721

(G-8505)
ALART INC
578 5th Ave Unit 33 (10036-4836)
PHONE..........................212 840-1508
Alan Becer, *President*
Arthur Becer, *Vice Pres*
Vivian Becer, *Treasurer*
EMP: 3
SALES: 2MM **Privately Held**
SIC: 3911 3281 Jewelry, precious metal;
cut stone & stone products

(G-8506)
ALBALUZ FILMS LLC
954 Lexington Ave (10021-5055)
PHONE..........................347 613-2321
Carols Plasencia, *CEO*
EMP: 1
SALES: 1MM **Privately Held**
SIC: 3312 Blast furnaces & steel mills

(G-8507)
ALBEA COSMETICS AMERICA
INC (DH)
595 Madison Ave Fl 10 (10022-1955)
PHONE..........................212 371-5100
Jean P Imbert, *President*
◆ EMP: 25
SALES (est): 252.9MM **Privately Held**
SIC: 3089 3911 5162 5051 Plastic con-
tainers, except foam; precious metal
cases; plastics products; metals service
centers & offices
HQ: Albea Services
Zac Des Barbanniers Le Signac
Gennevilliers 92230
181 932-000

(G-8508)
ALCHEMY SIMYA INC
Also Called: Birthstone Enterprises
161 Avnue Of The Americas (10013-1205)
PHONE..........................646 230-1122
Feonia Tilly, *President*
EMP: 30 EST: 2004
SALES (est): 2.3MM **Privately Held**
SIC: 3911 Jewelry, precious metal

(G-8509)
ALCOHOLICS ANONYMOUS
GRAPEVINE (PA)
475 Riverside Dr Ste 1264 (10115-0052)
PHONE..........................212 870-3400
Robin Bromley, *CEO*
Arnold Bros, *Ch of Bd*
John Skillton, *Treasurer*
Eugene O' Brien, *Controller*
▲ EMP: 15
SQ FT: 4,000
SALES: 2.9MM **Privately Held**
SIC: 2721 Periodicals: publishing only

(G-8510)
ALE VIOLA LLC
Also Called: Ippolita
259 W 30th St Fl 9-10 (10001-2809)
PHONE..................................212 868-3808
Ippolita Rostagno, *President*
Diego McDonald, *COO*
John Siedel, *Senior VP*
◆ EMP: 100
SQ FT: 15,000
SALES (est): 99.3K **Privately Held**
SIC: 3911 Jewelry apparel

(G-8511)
ALEN SANDS YORK
ASSOCIATES LTD
Also Called: Stellar Alliance
236 W 26th St Rm 801 (10001-6882)
PHONE..................................212 563-6305
Alen S York, *President*
Joshua Rosen, *Vice Pres*
▲ EMP: 10
SALES (est): 790K **Privately Held**
SIC: 2392 Comforters & quilts: made from
purchased materials

(G-8512)
ALEX SEPKUS INC
42 W 48th St Ste 501 (10036-1701)
PHONE..................................212 391-8466
Alex Sepkus, *President*
Jeffrey D Feero, *Vice Pres*
EMP: 13
SALES (est): 1.7MM **Privately Held**
SIC: 3911 Bracelets, precious metal

(G-8513)
ALEXANDER PRIMAK JEWELRY
INC
Also Called: Platina
529 5th Ave Fl 15 (10017-4674)
PHONE..................................212 398-0287
Alexander Primak, *President*
Joe Del Mauro, *Sales Mgr*
EMP: 59
SQ FT: 8,000
SALES: 11.3MM **Privately Held**
WEB: www.platinacasting.com
SIC: 3911 Jewelry, precious metal

(G-8514)
ALEXANDER WANG
INCORPORATED (PA)
386 Broadway Fl 3 (10013-6021)
PHONE..................................212 532-3103
Aimie Wang, *CEO*
Gerard Amato, *Vice Pres*
Thomas Hong, *Vice Pres*
Stephanie Harrison, *Opers Staff*
Ian Edwards, *Pub Rel Mgr*
▲ EMP: 80
SALES (est): 48.2MM **Privately Held**
SIC: 2331 2329 Blouses, women's & jun-
iors': made from purchased material; shirt
& slack suits: men's, youths' & boys'

(G-8515)
ALFRED DUNNER INC (PA)
Also Called: Skye's The Limit
1333 Broadway Fl 11 (10018-1064)
PHONE..................................212 478-4300
Peter Aresty, *President*
Joseph Aresty, *Chairman*
Jerome Aresty, *Vice Pres*
Ray Barrick, *CFO*
Teresa Madrazo, *Credit Mgr*
▲ EMP: 275 EST: 1946
SQ FT: 10,000
SALES (est): 70.3MM **Privately Held**
WEB: www.alfreddunner.com
SIC: 2337 2331 2339 Skirts, separate:
women's, misses' & juniors'; jackets &
vests, except fur & leather; women's, T-
shirts & tops, women's: made from pur-
chased materials; slacks: women's,
misses' & juniors'; shorts (outerwear):
women's, misses' & juniors'

(G-8516)
ALLAN JOHN COMPANY
611 5th Ave Fl 7 (10022-6813)
PHONE..................................212 940-2210
John Allan Meing, *CEO*
Clare Ludvigsen, *CFO*
Richard Macary, *Treasurer*

▲ EMP: 10
SALES (est): 706K
SALES (corp-wide): 1.6MM **Privately**
Held
WEB: www.johnallans.com
SIC: 2844 Toilet preparations
PA: The John Allan Company Llc
46 E 46th St
New York NY

(G-8517)
ALLIED BRONZE CORP (DEL
CORP)
32 Avenue Of The Americas (10013-2473)
PHONE..................................646 421-6400
Herbert Koenig, *President*
Susan Mc Cormick, *Manager*
▲ EMP: 40
SQ FT: 55,000
SALES (est): 4.1MM **Privately Held**
WEB: www.alliedbronze.com
SIC: 3446 Ornamental metalwork

(G-8518)
ALLIED REPRODUCTIONS INC
70 W 36th St Rm 500 (10018-8050)
PHONE..................................212 255-2472
Peter Bird, *President*
EMP: 20
SALES (est): 2MM **Privately Held**
SIC: 2752 Commercial printing, offset

(G-8519)
ALLISON CHE FASHION INC (PA)
1400 Broadway Lbby 5 (10018-5300)
PHONE..................................212 391-1433
Barbara Weiner, *President*
Edith Fisher, *Treasurer*
EMP: 12
SALES (est): 957.8K **Privately Held**
SIC: 2335 Women's, juniors' & misses'
dresses

(G-8520)
ALLSTAR CASTING
CORPORATION
240 W 37th St Frnt 7 (10018-5091)
PHONE..................................212 563-0909
EMP: 40
SQ FT: 2,200
SALES (est): 2.5MM **Privately Held**
SIC: 3915 3369 Mfg Jewelers' Materials
Nonferrous Metal Foundry

(G-8521)
ALLURE JEWELRY AND ACC
LLC (PA)
15 W 36th St Fl 12 (10018-7113)
P.O. Box 41305, Plymouth MN (55441-
0305)
PHONE..................................646 226-8057
Amy Bohaty,
Arlene Tourville,
◆ EMP: 11
SQ FT: 5,000
SALES (est): 3.2MM **Privately Held**
SIC: 3961 Costume jewelry

(G-8522)
ALLWORTH COMMUNICATIONS
INC
Also Called: Allworth Press
10 E 23rd St Ste 510 (10010-4459)
PHONE..................................212 777-8395
Tad Crawford, *President*
▲ EMP: 12
SALES (est): 1.4MM **Privately Held**
WEB: www.allworth.com
SIC: 2731 Textbooks: publishing only, not
printed on site

(G-8523)
ALLY NYC CORP
230 W 39th St Rm 525 (10018-4933)
PHONE..................................212 447-7277
Jenny Chen, *President*
EMP: 7
SQ FT: 25,000
SALES: 15MM **Privately Held**
SIC: 2339 Women's & misses' outerwear

(G-8524)
ALM MEDIA LLC (HQ)
Also Called: New York Law Journal
150 E 42nd St (10017-5612)
PHONE..................................212 457-9400
Bill Carter, *CEO*
Mark Fried, *President*
Adam Dunn, *Publisher*
Joshua Orenstein, *General Mgr*
Jim Pivirotto, *General Mgr*
EMP: 350
SQ FT: 31,000
SALES (est): 181.8MM
SALES (corp-wide): 181.8MM **Privately**
Held
WEB: www.alm.com
SIC: 2721 2711 2741 2731 Magazines:
publishing only, not printed on site; news-
papers: publishing only, not printed on
site; newsletter publishing; book publish-
ing; trade show arrangement
PA: Alm Media Holdings, Inc.
120 Broadway Fl 5
New York NY 10271
212 457-9400

(G-8525)
ALM MEDIA HOLDINGS INC (PA)
120 Broadway Fl 5 (10271-1100)
PHONE..................................212 457-9400
William L Pollak, *President*
Andrew Neblett, *President*
Jeff Fried, *Publisher*
Evan Kessler, *Publisher*
Sherry Costello, *General Mgr*
EMP: 400
SQ FT: 31,000
SALES (est): 181.8MM **Privately Held**
SIC: 2721 2711 2741 2731 Magazines:
publishing only, not printed on site; news-
papers: publishing only, not printed on
site; newsletter publishing; book publish-
ing; trade show arrangement

(G-8526)
ALPHA MEDIA GROUP INC (PA)
415 Madison Ave Fl 4 (10017-7945)
PHONE..................................212 302-2626
Kent Brownridge, *CEO*
Felix Dennis, *Ch of Bd*
Stephen Duggan, *COO*
Robert Bartner, *Shareholder*
Peter Godfrey, *Shareholder*
▲ EMP: 300
SALES (est): 36MM **Privately Held**
WEB: www.stuffmagazine.com
SIC: 2721 Magazines: publishing & printing

(G-8527)
ALPHONSE LDUC - RBERT KING
INC
Also Called: Robert King Music
180 Madison Ave 24 (10016-5267)
PHONE..................................508 238-8118
Francois Leduc, *Principal*
EMP: 6
SALES (est): 367.3K **Privately Held**
SIC: 2741 Music book & sheet music pub-
lishing

(G-8528)
ALPINA COLOR GRAPHICS INC
27 Cliff St Rm 502 (10038-2840)
PHONE..................................212 285-2700
Harish Sawhney, *President*
EMP: 7
SALES: 800K **Privately Held**
WEB: www.alpinaonline.com
SIC: 2752 Commercial printing, offset

(G-8529)
ALPINA COPYWORLD INC (PA)
Also Called: Alpina Digital
134 E 28th St (10016-8299)
PHONE..................................212 683-3511
Harish Sawhney, *CEO*
Naveen Sawhney, *President*
EMP: 15
SQ FT: 7,000
SALES: 6MM **Privately Held**
WEB: www.alpina.net
SIC: 2759 2752 Commercial printing;
commercial printing, lithographic

(G-8530)
ALPINE BUSINESS GROUP INC
(PA)
Also Called: Alpine Creative Group
30 E 33rd St Frnt A (10016-5337)
PHONE..................................212 989-4198
Steve Paster, *President*
Laura Leigh, *Vice Pres*
Rebecca Baker, *Graphic Designe*
Kelly Szymanowski, *Graphic Designe*
EMP: 10
SALES (est): 1.6MM **Privately Held**
WEB: www.alpinecreativegroup.com
SIC: 2759 2752 Invitations: printing; com-
mercial printing, lithographic

(G-8531)
ALPINE CREATIONS LTD
Also Called: TS Manufactoring
17 E 48th St Fl 6 (10017-1010)
PHONE..................................212 308-9353
Samy Sanar, *President*
Zack Sanar, *Vice Pres*
▲ EMP: 6
SQ FT: 2,000
SALES (est): 731.9K **Privately Held**
WEB: www.alpineweddingbands.com
SIC: 3911 Jewelry, precious metal

(G-8532)
ALTR INC
16 W 46th St Fl 12 (10036-4503)
PHONE..................................212 575-0077
Amish Shah, *President*
Neha Shah, *COO*
◆ EMP: 23
SQ FT: 9,000
SALES (est): 1.2MM **Privately Held**
SIC: 3911 Jewelry, precious metal

(G-8533)
ALVINA VLENTA COUTURE
COLLECTN
525 Fashion Ave Rm 1703 (10018-4935)
PHONE..................................212 921-7058
Joe Murphy, *President*
Jim Hjelm, *Principal*
Joe O'Grady, *Admin Sec*
EMP: 10
SALES (est): 802.4K
SALES (corp-wide): 11.7MM **Publicly**
Held
WEB: www.jimhelmcouture.com
SIC: 2335 Wedding gowns & dresses
PA: Jlm Couture, Inc.
225 W 37th St Fl 14
New York NY 10018
212 921-7058

(G-8534)
ALVINA VLENTA COUTURE
COLLECTN
225 W 37th St (10018-5703)
PHONE..................................212 921-7058
Joe Murphy, *President*
Jim Hjelm, *Principal*
Daniel McMillan, *Principal*
Victoria McMillan, *Principal*
Joe O'Grady, *Admin Sec*
EMP: 18
SALES (est): 3MM
SALES (corp-wide): 11.7MM **Publicly**
Held
SIC: 2335 5131 Wedding gowns &
dresses; bridal supplies
PA: Jlm Couture, Inc.
225 W 37th St Fl 14
New York NY 10018
212 921-7058

(G-8535)
ALYK INC
Also Called: Lola
150 W 22nd St Fl 5 (10011-6559)
PHONE..................................866 232-0970
Jordana Kier, *CEO*
Alexandra Friedman, *President*
Stacy Corona, *Opers Staff*
▲ EMP: 34
SALES: 15MM **Privately Held**
SIC: 2676 Tampons, sanitary: made from
purchased paper

(G-8536)
AMARANTUS BSCENCE HOLDINGS INC (PA)
110 Wall St (10005-3801)
PHONE..........................917 686-5317
Gerald E Commissiong, *President*
Barney Monte, *COO*
Elise Brownell, *Senior VP*
John W Commissiong, *Security Dir*
Brian E Harvey, *Advisor*
EMP: 12
SALES (est): 3.4MM **Publicly Held**
SIC: 2834 3829 Pharmaceutical preparations; medical diagnostic systems, nuclear

(G-8537)
AMCOM SOFTWARE INC
256 W 38th St Fl 8 (10018-9123)
PHONE..........................212 951-7600
EMP: 5
SALES (corp-wide): 169.4MM **Publicly Held**
WEB: www.amcomsoft.com
SIC: 7372 7371 Application computer software; computer software development & applications
HQ: Amcom Software, Inc.
10400 Yellow Circle Dr # 100
Eden Prairie MN 55343
952 230-5200

(G-8538)
AMENITY ANALYTICS INC
387 Park Ave S Fl 9 (10016-8810)
PHONE..........................646 786-8316
Nathaniel Storch, *President*
EMP: 24
SALES: 600K **Privately Held**
SIC: 7372 Prepackaged software

(G-8539)
AMEREX CORPORATION
512 7th Ave Fl 9 (10018-0861)
PHONE..........................212 221-3151
Renee McGovern, *Manager*
EMP: 7
SALES (corp-wide): 1.2B **Privately Held**
WEB: www.amerex-fire.com
SIC: 2331 Blouses, women's & juniors': made from purchased material
HQ: Amerex Corporation
7595 Gadsden Hwy
Trussville AL 35173
205 655-3271

(G-8540)
AMERICA CAPITAL ENERGY CORP
Also Called: Acec
405 Lexington Ave Fl 65 (10174-6301)
P.O. Box 849 (10163-0849)
PHONE..........................212 983-8316
Min Zhaing, *Ch of Bd*
Zhilin Feng, *President*
EMP: 5
SQ FT: 7,299
SALES (est): 440.3K
SALES (corp-wide): 1.9MM **Privately Held**
SIC: 1382 Oil & gas exploration services
PA: Zhongrong Group
18/F, 1088, South Rd., Pudong
Shanghai 20012
215 877-8299

(G-8541)
AMERICA HEALTH CORP
708 3rd Ave Ste 600 (10017-4201)
PHONE..........................800 860-1868
Jeff Law, *President*
EMP: 5 **EST:** 2017
SALES (est): 139.9K **Privately Held**
SIC: 2023 Dietary supplements, dairy & non-dairy based

(G-8542)
AMERICA PRESS INC (PA)
Also Called: National Catholic Wkly Review
1212 Ave Of The Americas (10036-3314)
PHONE..........................212 581-4640
Thomas Reese, *President*
Kojiro Iwamoto, *Manager*
EMP: 34 **EST:** 1909
SQ FT: 36,674

SALES (est): 4.3MM **Privately Held**
SIC: 2741 Miscellaneous publishing

(G-8543)
AMERICAN AGORA FOUNDATION INC
Also Called: Laphams Quarterly
116 E 16th St Fl 8 (10003-2158)
PHONE..........................212 590-6870
Lewis H Lapham, *President*
EMP: 30
SALES (est): 4.3MM **Privately Held**
SIC: 2721 Periodicals

(G-8544)
AMERICAN APPAREL TRADING CORP (PA)
Also Called: Vertical Apparel
209 W 38th St Rm 1004 (10018-0391)
PHONE..........................212 764-5990
Peter Marsella, *President*
Ellen Barry, *Vice Pres*
EMP: 3
SALES (est): 1.4MM **Privately Held**
SIC: 2339 Sportswear, women's

(G-8545)
AMERICAN BPTST CHRCHES MTRO NY
Flemister Housing Services
527 W 22nd St (10011-1179)
PHONE..........................212 870-3195
James D Stallings, *Principal*
EMP: 8
SALES (corp-wide): 838.5K **Privately Held**
WEB: www.abcmny.org
SIC: 2531 Church furniture
PA: American Baptist Churches Of Metropolitan New York
475 Riverside Dr Ste 432
New York NY 10115
212 870-3195

(G-8546)
AMERICAN CAT CLUB LLC
148 Madison Ave Fl 8 (10016-6777)
PHONE..........................212 779-1140
Isaac Kassin,
Soul Kassin,
EMP: 5
SALES (est): 139.9K **Privately Held**
SIC: 2047 Cat food

(G-8547)
AMERICAN CLASSIC KITCHENS INC
150 E 58th St Ste 900 (10155-0992)
PHONE..........................212 838-9308
Anna Mesaikos, *President*
EMP: 7
SALES (est): 934.8K **Privately Held**
WEB: www.americanclassickitchens.com
SIC: 2434 Wood kitchen cabinets

(G-8548)
AMERICAN COMFORT DIRECT LLC
708 3rd Ave Fl 6 (10017-4119)
PHONE..........................201 364-8309
Benzvi Cohen, *CEO*
Timothy Enarson, *Vice Pres*
EMP: 25
SALES (est): 1.7MM **Privately Held**
SIC: 3433 3634 3635 3589 Space heaters, except electric; electric household fans, heaters & humidifiers; household vacuum cleaners; carpet sweepers, except household electric vacuum sweepers; automotive air conditioners;

(G-8549)
AMERICAN DSPLAY DIE CTTERS INC
121 Varick St Rm 301 (10013-1408)
PHONE..........................212 645-1274
Juan Leon, *President*
Christa Leon, *Treasurer*
EMP: 30
SQ FT: 20,000
SALES (est): 269.4K **Privately Held**
SIC: 2675 3544 Die-cut paper & board; dies & die holders for metal cutting, forming, die casting

(G-8550)
AMERICAN GRAPHIC DESIGN AWARDS
Also Called: Graphic Design U S A
89 5th Ave Ste 901 (10003-3046)
PHONE..........................212 696-4380
Gordon Kaye, *CEO*
EMP: 5
SALES (est): 430K **Privately Held**
WEB: www.graphicdesignusa.com
SIC: 2721 Magazines: publishing & printing

(G-8551)
AMERICAN HOME MFG LLC (HQ)
302 5th Ave Fl 5 (10001-3604)
PHONE..........................212 643-0680
Nathan Accad, *President*
Isaac Ades, *COO*
Benjamin Akkad, *Vice Pres*
◆ **EMP:** 3 **EST:** 2014
SALES (est): 3.7MM
SALES (corp-wide): 76.1MM **Privately Held**
SIC: 2299 Pillow fillings: curled hair, cotton waste, moss, hemp tow
PA: Idea Nuova Inc.
302 5th Ave Fl 5
New York NY 10001
212 643-0680

(G-8552)
AMERICAN INST CHEM ENGNERS INC (PA)
Also Called: Aiche
120 Wall St Fl 23 (10005-5991)
PHONE..........................646 495-1355
William Grieco, *CEO*
Kevin Chin, *COO*
Rich Sarnie, *Project Dir*
Cody Hirashima, *Engineer*
Lucia Matthew, *Controller*
▲ **EMP:** 75
SQ FT: 18,400
SALES: 34.3MM **Privately Held**
WEB: www.naache.net
SIC: 2721 8621 2731 Magazines: publishing only, not printed on site; engineering association; book publishing

(G-8553)
AMERICAN JEWISH COMMITTEE
Also Called: Commentary Magazine
561 Fashion Ave Fl 16 (10018-1816)
PHONE..........................212 891-1400
Davi Birnstein, *Manager*
Michael Winograd, *Asst Director*
EMP: 8
SALES (corp-wide): 69.8MM **Privately Held**
WEB: www.projectinterchange.org
SIC: 2721 Magazines: publishing only, not printed on site
PA: American Jewish Committee
165 E 56th St
New York NY 10022
212 751-4000

(G-8554)
AMERICAN JEWISH CONGRESS INC (PA)
Also Called: A J Congress
825 3rd Ave Fl 181800 (10022-7519)
PHONE..........................212 879-4500
Neil Goldstein, *Director*
EMP: 20 **EST:** 1918
SQ FT: 9,000
SALES (est): 2.7MM **Privately Held**
SIC: 2721 8661 Magazines: publishing & printing; religious organizations

(G-8555)
AMERICAN JUICE COMPANY LLC
224 W 35th St Fl 11 (10001-2533)
PHONE..........................347 620-0252
Chris Wirth,
EMP: 7 **EST:** 2013
SQ FT: 400
SALES (est): 856.1K **Privately Held**
SIC: 2087 Cocktail mixes, nonalcoholic

(G-8556)
AMERICAN MINERALS INC (DH)
Also Called: Prince Minerals
21 W 46th St Fl 14 (10036-4119)
PHONE..........................646 747-4222
Willson Ropp, *President*
Steve Chapman, *Maint Spvr*
Roderik Alewijnse, *CFO*
Kevin St Germaine, *CFO*
Rob Lannerd, *Controller*
◆ **EMP:** 15 **EST:** 1963
SQ FT: 3,000
SALES (est): 38.5MM
SALES (corp-wide): 369K **Privately Held**
WEB: www.princeminerals.com
SIC: 1446 Silica mining; silica sand mining
HQ: Prince Minerals Llc
15311 Vantage Pkwy W
Houston TX 77032
646 747-4222

(G-8557)
AMERICAN ORIGINALS CORPORATION (PA)
Also Called: Gotham Diamonds
1156 Avenue Of The Americ (10036-2784)
PHONE..........................212 836-4155
Saumil Parikh, *President*
EMP: 9
SALES (est): 680.6K **Privately Held**
SIC: 3911 5094 Jewelry, precious metal; jewelry

(G-8558)
AMERICAN SOCIETY OF COMPOSERS (PA)
Also Called: Ascap
250 W 57th St Ste 1300 (10107-1300)
PHONE..........................212 621-6000
Elizabeth Matthews, *CEO*
Paul Williams, *Ch of Bd*
Robert Cannone, *President*
CIA Toscanini, *President*
Janine Small, *Partner*
EMP: 277 **EST:** 2012
SALES (est): 155.7MM **Privately Held**
WEB: www.ascap.com
SIC: 2741 Miscellaneous publishing

(G-8559)
AMERICAN SPRAY-ON CORP
5 Hanover Sq Fl 5 # 5 (10004-2757)
PHONE..........................212 929-2100
Steven Alessio, *President*
Steve Alessio, *President*
Marvin Sweet, *Chairman*
John M Alessio, *COO*
Micheal Boone, *Treasurer*
EMP: 30
SALES (est): 4.5MM **Privately Held**
SIC: 2396 2262 Automotive & apparel trimmings; fire resistance finishing: manmade & silk broadwoven

(G-8560)
AMERICO GROUP INC
498 7th Ave Fl 8 (10018-6944)
PHONE..........................212 563-2700
Tom Miller, *Manager*
EMP: 32 **Privately Held**
SIC: 2321 Men's & boys' dress shirts
PA: Americo Group Inc.
1411 Broadway Fl 2
New York NY 10018

(G-8561)
AMERICO GROUP INC (PA)
Also Called: Joseph's Cloak
1411 Broadway Fl 2 (10018-3420)
PHONE..........................212 563-2700
Eli Harari, *Ch of Bd*
Susan Feigenson, *Vice Pres*
Marc Lieber, *Vice Pres*
Alex Bessmertny, *QA Dir*
Joel Weisinger, *CFO*
◆ **EMP:** 43
SQ FT: 30,000
SALES (est): 9.8MM **Privately Held**
WEB: www.josephscloak.com
SIC: 2321 Men's & boys' dress shirts

(G-8562)
AMERIKOM GROUP INC
247 W 30th St Rm 6w (10001-2808)
PHONE..........................212 675-1329

Yaron Ben-Horin, *COO*
Nitsan Ben-Horin, *Vice Pres*
EMP: 80
SQ FT: 50,000
SALES (est): 10MM **Privately Held**
WEB: www.amerikom.com
SIC: 2759 Commercial printing

(G-8563)
AMG JV LLC (HQ)
Also Called: AMG Global NY & Enchante
ACC
15 W 34th St Fl 8 (10001-3076)
PHONE..............................212 602-1818
Aharon Franco, *President*
◆ **EMP:** 5
SQ FT: 5,000
SALES (est): 1.6MM
SALES (corp-wide): 61.5MM **Privately
Held**
SIC: 3261 Bathroom accessories/fittings,
vitreous china or earthenware
PA: Enchante Accessories Inc.
16 E 34th St Fl 16 # 16
New York NY 10016
212 725-7879

(G-8564)
AMNEWS CORPORATION
2340 Frdrck Duglass Blvd (10027)
PHONE..............................212 932-7400
Elinor Tatum, *CEO*
EMP: 27 EST: 2003
SALES: 36.9K **Privately Held**
WEB: www.amsterdamnews.com
SIC: 2711 Newspapers, publishing & print-
ing

(G-8565)
**AMOSEASTERN APPAREL INC
(PA)**
251 W 39th St Fl 12 (10018-3121)
PHONE..............................212 730-6350
Yanling Zhang, *CEO*
Hung Mao Liu, *CFO*
▲ **EMP:** 17
SALES (est): 2.1MM **Privately Held**
SIC: 2396 Apparel & other linings, except
millinery

(G-8566)
**AMPEX CASTING
CORPORATION**
23 W 47th St Unit 3 (10036-2826)
PHONE..............................212 719-1318
Joseph Ipek, *President*
EMP: 19
SQ FT: 3,000
SALES (est): 2.2MM **Privately Held**
SIC: 3915 Jewelers' castings

(G-8567)
AMPLIENCE INC
234 5th Ave Fl 2 (10001-7607)
PHONE..............................917 410-7189
James Brooke, *CEO*
Brian K Walker, *Security Dir*
Michael Jones, *Risk Mgmt Dir*
EMP: 7
SALES (est): 244.2K
SALES (corp-wide): 186.7K **Privately
Held**
SIC: 7372 Business oriented computer
software
PA: Icc Managed Services Limited
2 Sandbeck Lane
Wetherby
845 302-1922

(G-8568)
**AMSCO SCHOOL
PUBLICATIONS INC**
315 Hudson St Fl 5 (10013-1009)
PHONE..............................212 886-6500
Henry Brun, *President*
Irene Rubin, *Vice Pres*
Laurence Beller, *Treasurer*
Iris L Beller, *Admin Sec*
▼ **EMP:** 80 EST: 1935
SQ FT: 20,000
SALES (est): 6.9MM **Privately Held**
WEB: www.amscopub.com
SIC: 2731 Textbooks: publishing only, not
printed on site

(G-8569)
AMSTEAD PRESS CORP
225 W 37th St Fl 16 (10018-6637)
PHONE..............................347 416-2373
EMP: 5
SALES: 125K **Privately Held**
SIC: 2759 Commercial Printing

(G-8570)
**ANACOR PHARMACEUTICALS
INC (HQ)**
235 E 42nd St (10017-5703)
PHONE..............................212 733-2323
Douglas E Giordano, *President*
Margaret M Madden, *Vice Pres*
EMP: 21
SALES: 82.3MM
SALES (corp-wide): 53.6B **Publicly Held**
WEB: www.anacor.com
SIC: 2834 Pharmaceutical preparations
PA: Pfizer Inc.
235 E 42nd St
New York NY 10017
212 733-2323

(G-8571)
ANAGE INC
530 Fashion Ave Frnt 5 (10018-4878)
PHONE..............................212 944-6533
Kenneth Berkowitz, *President*
Fred Heiser, *Vice Pres*
▲ **EMP:** 15
SALES (est): 1.1MM **Privately Held**
SIC: 2371 Jackets, fur

(G-8572)
ANALYSTS IN MEDIA (AIM) INC
55 Broad St Fl 9 (10004-2001)
PHONE..............................212 488-1777
Garry M Chocky, *Controller*
EMP: 50
SALES (est): 4.8MM **Privately Held**
SIC: 2721 Magazines: publishing only, not
printed on site

(G-8573)
ANANDAMALI INC
35 N Moore St (10013-5711)
PHONE..............................212 343-8964
Cheryl Hazan, *President*
EMP: 10
SQ FT: 2,900
SALES (est): 800K **Privately Held**
SIC: 2519 Garden furniture, except wood,
metal, stone or concrete

(G-8574)
**ANASTASIA FURS
INTERNATIONAL (PA)**
Also Called: Alexandros
345 7th Ave Fl 20 (10001-5034)
PHONE..............................212 868-9241
Anastasia Dimitriades, *President*
Tommy Dimitriades, *Vice Pres*
Alex Dimitriades, *Admin Sec*
EMP: 10
SALES (est): 889.6K **Privately Held**
SIC: 2371 5632 7219 Fur goods; furriers;
fur garment cleaning, repairing & storage

(G-8575)
**ANAVEX LIFE SCIENCES CORP
(PA)**
51 W 52nd St Fl 7 (10019-6163)
PHONE..............................844 689-3939
Christopher Missling, *President*
Sandra Boenisch, *CFO*
EMP: 13 EST: 2004
SALES (est): 283.9K **Publicly Held**
SIC: 2834 8731 Pharmaceutical prepara-
tions; biotechnical research, commercial

(G-8576)
ANDES GOLD CORPORATION
405 Lexington Ave (10174-0002)
PHONE..............................212 541-2495
Alejandro Diaz, *CEO*
EMP: 95
SALES (est): 2.3MM
SALES (corp-wide): 9MM **Privately Held**
SIC: 1041 Gold ores mining
PA: New World Gold Corporation
350 Camino Gardens Blvd
Boca Raton FL 33432
561 962-4139

(G-8577)
ANDIGO NEW MEDIA INC
150 W 25th St Rm 900 (10001-7458)
PHONE..............................212 727-8445
Andrew Schulkind, *President*
EMP: 5
SALES (est): 508.1K **Privately Held**
WEB: www.andigo.com
SIC: 7372 Business oriented computer
software

(G-8578)
ANDREA STRONGWATER
Also Called: A Strongwater Designs
465 W End Ave (10024-4926)
PHONE..............................212 873-0905
Andrea Strongwater, *Owner*
EMP: 5
SALES (est): 225.9K **Privately Held**
SIC: 2253 Knit outerwear mills

(G-8579)
**ANDREAS PROTEIN CAKERY
INC**
229 E 85th St Unit 332 (10028-9614)
PHONE..............................646 801-9826
Andra Marchese, *Principal*
EMP: 5
SALES (est): 345.9K **Privately Held**
SIC: 2051 Bakery: wholesale or whole-
sale/retail combined

(G-8580)
ANDREW M SCHWARTZ LLC
Also Called: Sam NY
71 Gansevoort St Ste 2a (10014-1411)
PHONE..............................212 391-7070
Andrew M Schwartz, *Mng Member*
Suzanne Schwartz,
▲ **EMP:** 9
SALES (est): 1.1MM **Privately Held**
SIC: 2386 Coats & jackets, leather &
sheep-lined

(G-8581)
ANDY & EVAN INDUSTRIES INC
Also Called: Andy & Evan Shirt Co., The
1071 Ave Of The Amer # 804 (10018-3749)
PHONE..............................212 967-7908
Evan Hakalir, *President*
Isaac Maleh, *Exec VP*
A Jonathan Perl, *Vice Pres*
Rebecca Mamula, *Opers Staff*
Ariella Veitlin, *Bookkeeper*
◆ **EMP:** 9
SALES: 4MM **Privately Held**
SIC: 2361 2321 Girls' & children's
dresses, blouses & shirts; men's & boys'
furnishings

(G-8582)
ANGEL TEXTILES INC
519 8th Ave Fl 21 (10018-4573)
P.O. Box 1169, New Paltz (12561-7169)
PHONE..............................212 532-0900
Michael Nist, *CEO*
Helen Prior, *Principal*
EMP: 8
SQ FT: 1,000
SALES (est): 1.2MM **Privately Held**
WEB: www.angelnyc.com
SIC: 3552 2396 Silk screens for textile in-
dustry; automotive & apparel trimmings

(G-8583)
**ANGEL-MADE IN HEAVEN INC
(PA)**
525 Fashion Ave Rm 1710 (10018-0440)
PHONE..............................212 869-5678
Morris Dahan, *President*
▲ **EMP:** 12
SQ FT: 1,000
SALES (est): 1.3MM **Privately Held**
WEB: www.angelmih.com
SIC: 2339 Sportswear, women's

(G-8584)
ANGIOGENEX INC (PA)
Also Called: (A DEVELOPMENT STAGE
COMPANY)
425 Madison Ave Ste 902 (10017-1110)
PHONE..............................347 468-6799
William A Garland PHD, *CEO*
Richard A Salvador PHD, *President*
Robert Benezra PHD, *Chief*

Michael M Strage, *Vice Pres*
EMP: 5
SQ FT: 700
SALES (est): 561.5K **Publicly Held**
SIC: 2834 Pharmaceutical preparations

(G-8585)
ANHEUSER-BUSCH LLC
250 Park Ave Fl 2 (10177-0299)
PHONE..............................212 573-8800
Carlos Brito, *Branch Mgr*
EMP: 162
SALES (corp-wide): 1.5B **Privately Held**
SIC: 2082 Beer (alcoholic beverage)
HQ: Anheuser-Busch, Llc
1 Busch Pl
Saint Louis MO 63118
800 342-5283

(G-8586)
**ANHEUSER-BUSCH INBEV FIN
INC**
250 Park Ave (10177-0001)
PHONE..............................212 573-8800
Carlos Brito, *CEO*
Kevin Fahrenkrog, *General Mgr*
Lucas Lira, *VP Legal*
Sandro Leite, *Vice Pres*
Benoit Loore, *Vice Pres*
EMP: 10
SALES (est): 1.1MM **Privately Held**
SIC: 2082 Beer (alcoholic beverage)

(G-8587)
**ANHEUSER-BUSCH INBEV SVCS
LLC**
250 Park Ave Fl 2 (10177-0299)
PHONE..............................314 765-4729
EMP: 7
SALES (est): 664.8K **Privately Held**
SIC: 2082 Beer (alcoholic beverage)

(G-8588)
**ANHEUSR-BSCH COML
STRATEGY LLC**
125 W 24th St (10011-1901)
PHONE..............................347 429-1082
EMP: 10 EST: 2016
SALES (est): 128.6K
SALES (corp-wide): 1.5B **Privately Held**
SIC: 2085 Distilled & blended liquors
HQ: Anheuser-Busch Inbev Worldwide Inc.
1 Busch Pl
Saint Louis MO 63118

(G-8589)
ANIMA GROUP LLC
Also Called: 1884 Collection
435 E 79th St Ph H (10075-1079)
PHONE..............................917 913-2053
Alberto Petochi,
▲ **EMP:** 7
SALES (est): 967.4K **Privately Held**
SIC: 3911 Jewelry, precious metal

(G-8590)
ANIMAL FAIR MEDIA INC
545 8th Ave Rm 401 (10018-4341)
PHONE..............................212 629-0392
Wendy Diamond, *President*
EMP: 12
SQ FT: 1,200
SALES (est): 1.2MM **Privately Held**
WEB: www.animalfair.com
SIC: 2721 Magazines: publishing only, not
printed on site

(G-8591)
ANJU SYLOGENT LLC (HQ)
251 W 19th St (10011-4039)
PHONE..............................480 326-2358
Rebecca Barr, *Finance*
Elizabeth Whinnie, *Officer*
EMP: 15
SALES (est): 369.3K
SALES (corp-wide): 28.2MM **Privately
Held**
SIC: 7372 Prepackaged software
PA: Anju Software, Inc.
4500 S Lkshore Dr Ste 620
Tempe AZ 85282
630 246-2527

G
E
O
G
R
A
P
H
I
C

(G-8592)
ANNA B INC
55 Great Jones St Apt 6 (10012-1140)
PHONE.................................516 680-6609
Anna Blumenfeld, *President*
EMP: 5
SALES: 250K **Privately Held**
SIC: 2335 Bridal & formal gowns

(G-8593)
ANNA SUI CORP (PA)
484 Broome St (10013-2253)
PHONE.................................212 941-8406
Anna Sui, *Ch of Bd*
Bob Sui, *President*
Wen Liao, *Production*
Gladys Goldsmith, *Controller*
Amy Dougherty, *Sales Staff*
▲ EMP: 40
SQ FT: 3,000
SALES (est): 5.5MM **Privately Held**
WEB: www.annasui.com
SIC: 2331 2339 2335 2337 Blouses,
women's & juniors': made from purchased
material; women's & misses' athletic
clothing & sportswear; slacks: women's,
misses' & juniors'; women's, juniors' &
misses' dresses; skirts, separate:
women's, misses' & juniors'; jackets &
vests, except fur & leather: women's

(G-8594)
ANNUALS PUBLISHING CO INC
Also Called: Madison Square Press
10 E 23rd St Ste 510 (10010-4459)
PHONE.................................212 505-0950
Fax: 212 979-2207
EMP: 3
SQ FT: 1,000
SALES: 1.5MM **Privately Held**
SIC: 2731 Books-Publishing/Printing

(G-8595)
ANSWER PRINTING INC
Also Called: Answer Company, The
505 8th Ave Rm 1101 (10018-4540)
P.O. Box 3442 (10163-3442)
PHONE.................................212 922-2922
Larry Dunne, *President*
Jeni Gabler, *Accountant*
Sonia Crichton, *Bookkeeper*
Billy Rodriguez, *Sales Staff*
Brian Dunne, *Marketing Staff*
EMP: 15
SQ FT: 3,800
SALES: 6MM **Privately Held**
WEB: www.answerprinting.com
SIC: 2741 2752 Business service newslet-
ters: publishing & printing; commercial
printing, lithographic

(G-8596)
ANTERIOS INC
60 E 42nd St Ste 1160 (10165-6206)
PHONE.................................212 303-1683
Jon Edelson MD, *President*
Fabian Tenenbaum, *CFO*
Klaus Theobald MD, *Osteopathy*
EMP: 6
SALES (est): 870.6K **Privately Held**
SIC: 2834 Pharmaceutical preparations
PA: Allergan Public Limited Company
Clonshaugh Business And Technology
Park
Dublin

(G-8597)
ANTHONY L & S LLC (PA)
Also Called: Anthony L&S Footwear Group
499 Fashion Ave Fl 19s (10018-6853)
PHONE.................................212 386-7245
Joy Krooks, *Manager*
Anthony Loconte,
◆ EMP: 35
SALES (est): 5.5MM **Privately Held**
WEB: www.anthonyls.com
SIC: 3021 5139 Rubber & plastics
footwear; shoes

(G-8598)
ANTIMONY NEW YORK LLC
120 E 34th St Apt 7g (10016-4625)
PHONE.................................917 232-1836
Jason Shelowitz,
Rachel Shelowitz,
EMP: 2 EST: 2017

SALES: 5MM **Privately Held**
SIC: 2844 Toilet preparations

(G-8599)
**ANTWERP DIAMOND
DISTRIBUTORS**
581 5th Ave Fl 5 (10017-8824)
PHONE.................................212 319-3300
Phyllis Lisker, *President*
EMP: 15 EST: 1955
SQ FT: 4,000
SALES (est): 1.5MM **Privately Held**
WEB: www.antwerpdistributors.com
SIC: 3915 5094 Diamond cutting & polish-
ing; diamonds (gems)

(G-8600)
ANTWERP SALES INTL INC
Also Called: A.S.I. Fancies Ltd
576 5th Ave (10036-4807)
PHONE.................................212 354-6515
Norbert May, *President*
Danny Klugman, *Vice Pres*
EMP: 18
SQ FT: 3,500
SALES (est): 2.9MM **Privately Held**
SIC: 3915 Diamond cutting & polishing

(G-8601)
APEC PAPER INDUSTRIES LTD
Also Called: American Printing & Envelope
189 W 89th St Apt 5w (10024-1962)
PHONE.................................212 730-0088
Justin Koplin, *President*
EMP: 5 EST: 1935
SQ FT: 900
SALES: 2.4MM **Privately Held**
SIC: 2677 5112 Envelopes; envelopes

(G-8602)
APEX TEXICON INC (PA)
295 Madison Ave (10017-6434)
P.O. Box 960670, Inwood (11096-0670)
PHONE.................................516 239-4400
Edward Schlussel, *President*
John Kurz, *Vice Pres*
David Kurz, *Treasurer*
EMP: 24 EST: 1943
SQ FT: 9,000
SALES: 1.7MM **Privately Held**
SIC: 2221 2258 2257 Broadwoven fabric
mills, manmade; net & netting products;
tricot fabrics; weft knit fabric mills

(G-8603)
APICELLA JEWELERS INC
40 W 39th St Fl 4 (10018-2142)
PHONE.................................212 840-2024
John Apicella, *President*
Anthony Apicella, *Vice Pres*
EMP: 30 EST: 1946
SQ FT: 2,500
SALES (est): 3.1MM **Privately Held**
SIC: 3911 Jewelry, precious metal

(G-8604)
APOLLO APPAREL GROUP LLC
Also Called: Apollo Jeans
1407 Brdway Ste 2000-200 (10018)
PHONE.................................212 398-6585
Salim Mann, *Mng Member*
▲ EMP: 10
SALES (est): 2MM **Privately Held**
SIC: 2211 2389 Jean fabrics; men's mis-
cellaneous accessories

(G-8605)
**APOLLO INVESTMENT FUND VII
LP**
9 W 57th St Fl 43 (10019-2700)
PHONE.................................212 515-3200
Martin Kelly, *CFO*
Leon Black,
Laurence Berg,
EMP: 7
SALES (est): 741.7K **Privately Held**
SIC: 2731 Books: publishing & printing

(G-8606)
APPARATUS STUDIO (PA)
122 W 30th St Fl 4 (10001-4009)
PHONE.................................646 527-9732
Tara Carroll, *Vice Pres*
Nick Grinder, *Sales Dir*
Vanessa Fatton, *Sales Mgr*

Ariel Clay, *Accounts Mgr*
Bryan Knotts, *Accounts Mgr*
▲ EMP: 27
SQ FT: 12,000
SALES (est): 5MM **Privately Held**
SIC: 3646 Commercial indusl & institu-
tional electric lighting fixtures

(G-8607)
APPAREL GROUP LTD
Thyme
35 W 36th St Rm 10w (10018-7652)
PHONE.................................212 328-1200
Thomas Bietrich, *President*
EMP: 40 **Privately Held**
SIC: 2331 Women's & misses' blouses &
shirts
HQ: The Apparel Group Ltd
883 Trinity Dr
Lewisville TX 75056
214 469-3300

(G-8608)
APPAREL PRODUCTION INC
270 W 39th St Rm 1701 (10018-0330)
PHONE.................................212 278-8362
Theodore Sadaka, *President*
▲ EMP: 50
SALES (est): 570.3K **Privately Held**
SIC: 3949 Sporting & athletic goods

(G-8609)
APPFIGURES INC
133 Chrystie St Fl 3 (10002-2810)
PHONE.................................212 343-7900
Eliahu Michaeli, *President*
Alex Weiss, *Accounts Mgr*
Errol Markland, *Web Dvlpr*
Jorge Vargas, *Administration*
EMP: 14
SALES (est): 925.8K **Privately Held**
SIC: 7372 Business oriented computer
software

(G-8610)
APPGUARD INC (HQ)
141 W 36th St Rm 17 (10018-9489)
PHONE.................................703 786-8884
Jon Loew, *CEO*
Brody Ehrlich, *Vice Pres*
Maitland Muse, *Vice Pres*
Mike Shelton, *Marketing Staff*
Fatih Comlekoglu, *CTO*
EMP: 11
SALES: 6MM **Privately Held**
SIC: 7372 Prepackaged software

(G-8611)
**APPLICATION SECURITY INC
(DH)**
55 Broad St Rm 10a (10004-2509)
PHONE.................................212 912-4100
Jack Hembrough, *President*
Peter Schwartz, *CFO*
Andrew Herlands, *Sales Staff*
Mark Trinidad, *Mktg Dir*
EMP: 75
SALES: 1.6MM
SALES (corp-wide): 13MM **Privately
Held**
WEB: www.appsecinc.com
SIC: 7372 Business oriented computer
software
HQ: Trustwave Holdings, Inc.
70 W Madison St Ste 600
Chicago IL 60602
312 750-0950

(G-8612)
APRIL PRINTING CO INC
1201 Broadway Ste 710 (10001-5894)
PHONE.................................212 685-7455
Brad April, *President*
Muriel April, *Vice Pres*
Ariel April, *Creative Dir*
EMP: 6
SQ FT: 2,500
SALES (est): 1.1MM **Privately Held**
WEB: www.aprilprinting.com
SIC: 2752 Commercial printing, litho-
graphic

(G-8613)
**APS AMERICAN POLYMERS
SVCS INC**
104 W 40th St Rm 500 (10018-3770)
PHONE.................................212 362-7711
Gustavo Sampaio De Souza, *CEO*
◆ EMP: 2 EST: 2017
SQ FT: 300
SALES: 4MM **Privately Held**
SIC: 2821 Polyethylene resins; polypropy-
lene resins; polystyrene resins

(G-8614)
AR & AR JEWELRY INC
31 W 47th St Fl 15 (10036-2808)
PHONE.................................212 764-7916
Aras Tirtirian, *President*
Aras Tirtir, *Vice Pres*
▲ EMP: 40
SALES (est): 5.4MM **Privately Held**
SIC: 3911 Jewelry, precious metal

(G-8615)
AR PUBLISHING COMPANY INC
55 Broad St Rm 20b (10004-2589)
PHONE.................................212 482-0303
Helen Brusilovsky, *President*
EMP: 10
SALES (est): 479.6K **Privately Held**
WEB: www.vnsnews.com
SIC: 2711 Newspapers, publishing & print-
ing

(G-8616)
ARABELLA TEXTILES LLC
Also Called: Deborah Connolly & Associates
303 5th Ave Rm 1402 (10016-6601)
PHONE.................................212 679-0611
Deborah Connolly, *Mng Member*
▲ EMP: 5
SALES (est): 464.3K **Privately Held**
WEB: www.deborahconnolly.com
SIC: 2299 Batting, wadding, padding & fill-
ings

(G-8617)
ARATANA THERAPEUTICS INC
35 W 35th St Fl 11 (10001-2205)
PHONE.................................212 827-0020
Michele Gallucci, *Branch Mgr*
EMP: 6
SALES (corp-wide): 3B **Publicly Held**
SIC: 2834 Pharmaceutical preparations
HQ: Aratana Therapeutics, Inc.
11400 Tomahawk Creek Pkwy # 340
Leawood KS 66211
913 353-1000

(G-8618)
ARCHITECTS NEWSPAPER LLC
Also Called: Bd Projects
21 Murray St Fl 5 (10007-2244)
PHONE.................................212 966-0630
Dionne Darling, *Publisher*
Matthew Messner, *Editor*
John Stoughton, *Editor*
Sue Baker, *Sales Staff*
Sandy Huynh, *Marketing Staff*
EMP: 12
SALES (est): 840K **Privately Held**
WEB: www.archpaper.com
SIC: 2711 Newspapers: publishing only,
not printed on site

(G-8619)
**ARCHITECTURAL TEXTILES
USA INC**
Also Called: Architex International
36 E 23rd St Ste F (10010-4409)
PHONE.................................212 213-6972
EMP: 35
SALES (corp-wide): 65.1MM **Privately
Held**
WEB: www.architex-ljh.com
SIC: 2299 5087 Broadwoven fabrics:
linen, jute, hemp & ramie; service estab-
lishment equipment
PA: Architectural Textiles U.S.A., Inc.
3333 Commercial Ave
Northbrook IL 60062
847 205-1333

(G-8620)
AREA INC
Also Called: Area Warehouse
58 E 11th St Fl 2 (10003-6019)
PHONE...................................212 924-7084
Anki Spets, *President*
▲ EMP: 9
SQ FT: 6,000
SALES (est): 1MM **Privately Held**
WEB: www.lundstrom-id.com
SIC: 2392 Household furnishings

(G-8621)
ARGEE AMERICA INC
Also Called: Argee Sportswear
1410 Broadway Rm 1204 (10018-9352)
PHONE...................................212 768-9840
Roshan L Gera, *President*
Shyama Gera, *Vice Pres*
▲ EMP: 8
SALES (est): 1.4MM **Privately Held**
SIC: 2339 5137 Sportswear, women's;
sportswear, women's & children's

(G-8622)
ARGOSY COMPOSITE
ADVANCED MATE
225 W 34th St Ste 1106 (10122-1106)
PHONE...................................212 268-0003
Richard Rocco, *Mng Member*
Rich Rocco,
EMP: 12
SALES (est): 791.3K **Privately Held**
SIC: 3299 Ceramic fiber

(G-8623)
ARIELA AND ASSOCIATES INTL
LLC (PA)
1359 Broadway Fl 21 (10018-7824)
PHONE...................................212 683-4131
Ariela Balk, *President*
Mendel Balk, *COO*
Ed Mendoza, *Vice Pres*
Suzanne Kasper, *Production*
Lauren Riker, *Design Engr*
▲ EMP: 140
SQ FT: 27,741
SALES (est): 28.8MM **Privately Held**
WEB: www.ariela-alpha.com
SIC: 2341 Women's & children's undergarments

(G-8624)
ARLEE HOME FASHIONS INC
(PA)
Also Called: Arlee Group
36 E 31st St Rm 800 (10016-6917)
PHONE...................................212 689-0020
David Frankel, *CEO*
Sean Frankel, *Exec VP*
Marsha Caparelli, *Vice Pres*
Alan Mandell, *CFO*
▲ EMP: 60 EST: 1976
SQ FT: 15,805
SALES (est): 167.7MM **Privately Held**
SIC: 2392 Pillows, bed: made from purchased materials; chair covers & pads:
made from purchased materials

(G-8625)
ARRAY MARKETING GROUP
INC (HQ)
200 Madison Ave Ste 2121 (10016-4000)
PHONE...................................212 750-3367
Tom Hendren, *CEO*
Mike Caron, *Vice Pres*
Kevin Pattrick, *CFO*
▲ EMP: 21
SALES (est): 5.4MM
SALES (corp-wide): 211.6MM **Privately Held**
WEB: www.arraymarketing.com
SIC: 2541 Store & office display cases &
fixtures
PA: Array Canada Inc
45 Progress Ave
Scarborough ON M1P 2
416 299-4865

(G-8626)
ARSENAL HOLDINGS LLC (PA)
885 3rd Ave Rm 2403 (10022-4834)
PHONE...................................212 398-9139
Mike Healy, *Mng Member*
EMP: 7

SALES (est): 81.4MM **Privately Held**
SIC: 3812 Acceleration indicators & systems components, aerospace

(G-8627)
ART ASIAPACIFIC PUBLISHING
LLC
410 W 24th St Apt 14a (10011-1356)
PHONE...................................212 255-6003
Elaine Ng,
EMP: 8 EST: 2005
SALES: 800K **Privately Held**
SIC: 2741 Miscellaneous publishing

(G-8628)
ART INDUSTRIES OF NEW YORK
601 W 26th St Rm 1425 (10001-1160)
PHONE...................................212 633-9200
Steve Kaitz, *President*
Neal H Klein, *Vice Pres*
EMP: 50
SQ FT: 80,000
SALES (est): 6.4MM **Privately Held**
WEB: www.salinesolutions.com
SIC: 2675 Die-cut paper & board

(G-8629)
ART PEOPLE INC
594 Broadway Rm 1102 (10012-3289)
PHONE...................................212 431-4865
Gary Golkin, *President*
Carrie Golkin, *Treasurer*
EMP: 8
SQ FT: 10,000
SALES (est): 798.4K **Privately Held**
SIC: 2221 Wall covering fabrics, manmade
fiber & silk; upholstery fabrics, manmade
fiber & silk

(G-8630)
ART RESOURCES TRANSFER
INC
526 W 26th St Rm 614 (10001-5522)
PHONE...................................212 255-2919
Yael Meridan Schori, *President*
Bill Bartman, *Exec Dir*
Jennifer Seass, *Director*
▲ EMP: 5
SQ FT: 4,000
SALES: 786.8K **Privately Held**
WEB: www.artretran.com
SIC: 2791 Typesetting

(G-8631)
ART SCROLL PRINTING CORP
230 W 41st St Bsmt 1 (10036-7207)
PHONE...................................212 929-2413
Elliot Schwartz, *President*
EMP: 13
SALES (est): 1.8MM **Privately Held**
SIC: 2752 Commercial printing, offset

(G-8632)
ART-TEC JEWELRY DESIGNS
LTD (PA)
48 W 48th St Ste 401 (10036-1727)
PHONE...................................212 719-2941
Edward Zylka, *President*
EMP: 20
SQ FT: 5,000
SALES (est): 4.1MM **Privately Held**
SIC: 3911 Jewelry, precious metal

(G-8633)
ARTEAST LLC
Also Called: Zadig and Voltaire
453 Broome St (10013-2650)
PHONE...................................646 859-6020
Ascher Saddah, *Mng Member*
▲ EMP: 25
SALES (est): 3.1MM **Privately Held**
SIC: 2335 7389 5137 Women's, juniors' &
misses' dresses; apparel designers, commercial; women's & children's clothing
HQ: Zv France
11 Avenue D Iena
Paris 16e Arrondissement 75116
971 366-023

(G-8634)
ARTICULATE GLOBAL INC
244 5th Ave Ste 2960 (10001-7604)
P.O. Box 123747, Dallas TX (75312-3747)
PHONE...................................800 861-4880
Adam Schwartz, *CEO*

Lucy Suros, *President*
Megan C Niedenthal, *Opers Staff*
Christine Hendrickson, *QA Dir*
Magnus Nirell, *QC Mgr*
EMP: 200
SQ FT: 20,000
SALES (est): 22.5MM **Privately Held**
WEB: www.articulate.com
SIC: 7372 Business oriented computer
software

(G-8635)
ARTIFEX PRESS LLC
260 W 35th St Ph (10001-2528)
PHONE...................................212 414-1482
David Groz, *President*
Tiffany Bell, *Editor*
Carina Evangelista, *Editor*
Taro Masushio, *Research*
Ashley Levine, *Manager*
EMP: 15
SALES (est): 609.8K **Privately Held**
SIC: 2721 Periodicals: publishing & printing

(G-8636)
ARTISTIC FRAME CORP (PA)
979 3rd Ave Ste 1705 (10022-3804)
PHONE...................................212 289-2100
David Stevens, *President*
◆ EMP: 110
SQ FT: 400,000
SALES (est): 97.5MM **Privately Held**
SIC: 2426 5021 Frames for upholstered
furniture, wood; office furniture

(G-8637)
ARTISTIC RIBBON NOVELTY CO
INC
22 W 21st St Fl 3 (10010-6948)
P.O. Box 126, Hillsdale NJ (07642-0126)
PHONE...................................212 255-4224
Kenneth Hanz, *President*
Kenneth Handz, *President*
Steve Eigner, *Corp Secy*
▲ EMP: 20 EST: 1928
SQ FT: 15,000
SALES (est): 2.7MM **Privately Held**
WEB: www.artisticribbon.com
SIC: 2396 5131 Ribbons & bows, cut &
sewed; sewing supplies & notions; ribbons

(G-8638)
ARTISTIC TYPOGRAPHY CORP
(PA)
Also Called: Artistic Group, The
151 W 30th St Fl 8 (10001-4026)
PHONE...................................212 463-8880
Paul J Weinstein, *President*
▲ EMP: 15 EST: 1959
SQ FT: 7,500
SALES (est): 2.1MM **Privately Held**
WEB: www.tagimage.com
SIC: 2759 2791 Commercial printing; typographic composition, for the printing
trade

(G-8639)
ARTNEWS LTD (PA)
Also Called: Artnewsletter
475 5th Ave Fl 24 (10017-7202)
PHONE...................................212 398-1690
Peter M Brant, *Principal*
Victoria Hopper, *Opers Staff*
Nicole De George, *Assistant*
Jeff Mac Donald, *Assistant*
▲ EMP: 18 EST: 1902
SALES (est): 2.9MM **Privately Held**
WEB: www.artnews.com
SIC: 2721 Magazines: publishing & printing

(G-8640)
ARTSCROLL PRINTING CORP
(PA)
53 W 23rd St Fl 4 (10010-4239)
PHONE...................................212 929-2413
Elliot Schwartz, *President*
David Schwartz, *Corp Secy*
EMP: 22

SALES (est): 4.3MM **Privately Held**
SIC: 2759 2791 2752 7336 Screen printing; thermography; typesetting; commercial printing, lithographic; commercial art
& graphic design; signs & advertising specialties

(G-8641)
ARUBA NETWORKS INC
556 W 22nd St (10011-1108)
PHONE...................................732 343-1305
Jay Hatch, *Vice Pres*
Dietmar Holderle, *Vice Pres*
Lee Crum, *Opers Dir*
Peter Kersten, *Opers Dir*
David Burke, *Opers Staff*
EMP: 5
SALES (corp-wide): 30.8B **Publicly Held**
SIC: 3577 Computer peripheral equipment
HQ: Aruba Networks, Inc.
3333 Scott Blvd
Santa Clara CA 95054
408 227-4500

(G-8642)
ARUVIL INTERNATIONAL INC
(PA)
185 Madison Ave Rm 1701 (10016-7711)
PHONE...................................212 447-5020
Vilas Kulkarni, *President*
Russell Jenkins, *Vice Pres*
Evette Rivera, *Office Mgr*
▲ EMP: 5
SQ FT: 2,800
SALES (est): 7.8MM **Privately Held**
WEB: www.aruvil.com
SIC: 3315 Fence gates posts & fittings:
steel

(G-8643)
ASAHI SHIMBUN AMERICA INC
620 8th Ave (10018-1618)
PHONE...................................212 398-0257
Erika Toh, *Principal*
Ko Tanaka, *Administration*
Yoshiaki Kasuga, *Professor*
EMP: 15
SALES (est): 1.1MM **Privately Held**
SIC: 2711 Newspapers, publishing & printing

(G-8644)
ASENCE INC
65 Broadway Fl 7 (10006-2536)
PHONE...................................347 335-2606
Fax: 212 430-6501
EMP: 21
SALES: 3MM **Privately Held**
SIC: 2834 Pharmaceutical Preparations

(G-8645)
ASHKO GROUP LLC
Also Called: Wholesale
10 W 33rd St Rm 1019 (10001-3306)
PHONE...................................212 594-6050
Jack Ashkenazi, *President*
Charles Ashkenazi, *COO*
David Braha, *CFO*
Nympha Prijdekker, *Network Analyst*
▲ EMP: 18
SQ FT: 1,500
SALES (est): 3.5MM **Privately Held**
SIC: 2252 5139 Socks; footwear

(G-8646)
ASI SIGN SYSTEMS INC
192 Lexington Ave Rm 1002 (10016-6823)
PHONE...................................646 742-1320
EMP: 7
SALES (corp-wide): 20.7MM **Privately Held**
SIC: 3993 Signs & advertising specialties
PA: Asi Sign Systems, Inc.
8181 Jetstar Dr Ste 110
Irving TX 75063
214 352-9140

(G-8647)
ASIAN GLOBAL TRADING CORP
1407 Broadway Rm 2310 (10018-2665)
PHONE...................................718 786-0998
Chau Pei Hsu, *President*
▲ EMP: 8
SALES (est): 1MM **Privately Held**
SIC: 2253 Knit outerwear mills

(G-8648)
ASITE LLC
245 W 29th St Rm 1601 (10001-5216)
PHONE.............................203 545-3089
Gordon Ashworth, *Principal*
EMP: 60
SALES (est): 2.4MM
SALES (corp-wide): 10.7MM **Privately Held**
SIC: 7372 Prepackaged software
HQ: Asite Solutions Limited
1 Mark Square
London EC2A

(G-8649)
ASM USA INC
73 Spring St Rm 309 (10012-5801)
PHONE.............................212 925-2906
EMP: 13
SALES (est): 1.1MM
SALES (corp-wide): 141.2K **Privately Held**
SIC: 3444 5051 Sheet metal specialties, not stamped; steel
HQ: Approche Sur Mesure (A.S.M.)
63 Rue Edouard Vaillant
Levallois-Perret 92300
963 613-342

(G-8650)
ASP BLADE INTRMDATE HLDNGS INC
299 Park Ave Fl 34 (10171-3805)
PHONE.............................212 476-8000
Loren S Easton, *President*
EMP: 4400
SALES (est): 329.7K **Privately Held**
SIC: 3531 3523 6719 Construction machinery; forestry related equipment; farm machinery & equipment; cutters & blowers, ensilage; tractors, farm; investment holding companies, except banks

(G-8651)
ASPEN RESEARCH GROUP LTD
17 State St Fl 15 (10004-1532)
PHONE.............................212 425-9588
Mike Neff, *Manager*
EMP: 7 **Privately Held**
SIC: 7372 Business oriented computer software
PA: Aspen Research Group Ltd
802 Grand Ave Ste 120
Glenwood Springs CO 81601

(G-8652)
ASPEX INCORPORATED
161 Hudson St Apt 1a (10013-2145)
PHONE.............................212 966-0410
Gerald Henrici, *President*
James M Herriman, *Principal*
John Strohbeen, *Principal*
Sonia Ortiz, *Office Admin*
EMP: 20
SALES (est): 3.9MM **Privately Held**
SIC: 3823 3829 Computer interface equipment for industrial process control; measuring & controlling devices

(G-8653)
ASSESSMENT TECHNOLOGIES INC
1350 Ave Of The Americas (10019-4702)
PHONE.............................646 530-8666
Michael Hirsh, *President*
Manish Eros, *Technology*
Deepak Suri, *Officer*
EMP: 5
SALES (est): 254.1K **Privately Held**
SIC: 7372 Educational computer software

(G-8654)
ASSOCIATION FOR CMPT MCHY INC (PA)
Also Called: A C M
1601 Broadway Fl 10 (10019-7434)
P.O. Box 30777 (10087-0777)
PHONE.............................212 869-7440
Vicki Hanson, *CEO*
Vicki L Hanson, *CEO*
Cherry M Pancake, *President*
Achi Dosanjh, *Editor*
Yannis Ioannidis, *Corp Secy*
EMP: 72
SQ FT: 30,000

SALES: 70.1MM **Privately Held**
SIC: 2721 8621 Periodicals: publishing only; scientific membership association

(G-8655)
ASSOULINE PUBLISHING INC (PA)
3 Park Ave Ste 2702 (10016-5905)
PHONE.............................212 989-6769
Prosper Assouline, *President*
Yaffa Assouline, *Vice Pres*
Eduard De Lange, *Vice Pres*
Stephanie Labeille, *Vice Pres*
Nicole Ziomek, *Sales Staff*
◆ EMP: 12
SQ FT: 3,000
SALES (est): 3.1MM **Privately Held**
WEB: www.assouline.com
SIC: 2731 Book publishing

(G-8656)
ASTON LEATHER INC
153 W 27th St Ste 406 (10001-6258)
PHONE.............................212 481-2760
Metin Adam, *Ch of Bd*
▲ EMP: 6
SALES (est): 600K **Privately Held**
SIC: 3111 Leather tanning & finishing

(G-8657)
ASTOR ACCESSORIES LLC
1370 Broadway Rm 650 (10018-7370)
PHONE.............................212 695-6146
Abe Gabbay,
EMP: 5
SALES: 500K **Privately Held**
SIC: 2389 Apparel & accessories

(G-8658)
ASTUCCI US LTD (PA)
385 5th Ave Rm 1100 (10016-3340)
PHONE.............................212 725-3171
Dan Benmoshe, *President*
Hanna Levy, *Vice Pres*
▲ EMP: 8
SQ FT: 3,000
SALES: 15MM **Privately Held**
SIC: 3172 Cases, jewelry; cases, glasses

(G-8659)
AT&T CORP
Also Called: Sherwin Commerce
767 5th Ave Fl 12a (10153-0023)
PHONE.............................212 317-7048
Debra Surrette, *Manager*
EMP: 15
SALES (corp-wide): 170.7B **Publicly Held**
WEB: www.swbell.com
SIC: 7372 Prepackaged software
HQ: At&t Corp.
1 At&T Way
Bedminster NJ 07921
800 403-3302

(G-8660)
ATC PLASTICS LLC
Also Called: Heller Performance Polymers
555 Madison Ave Fl 5 (10022-3410)
PHONE.............................212 375-2515
Herbert Heller, *President*
EMP: 34
SALES (corp-wide): 8.2MM **Privately Held**
SIC: 3087 3643 2851 2821 Custom compound purchased resins; current-carrying wiring devices; paints & allied products; plastics materials & resins
PA: Atc Plastics, Llc
450 E 96th St Ste 500
Indianapolis IN 46240
317 469-7552

(G-8661)
ATELIERS TAMALET CORP
Also Called: Les Ateliers Tamalet
349 5th Ave (10016-5019)
PHONE.............................929 325-7976
David Benayoun, *President*
EMP: 20
SALES (est): 724.2K **Privately Held**
SIC: 3911 Jewelry apparel

(G-8662)
ATERET LLC
22 W 48th St (10036-1803)
PHONE.............................212 819-0777
Khodahbaksh Levy,
Samuel Levy,
EMP: 5
SALES (est): 410K **Privately Held**
WEB: www.ateret.com
SIC: 3911 Jewelry, precious metal

(G-8663)
ATERRA EXPLORATION LLC
230 W 56th St Apt 53d (10019-0077)
PHONE.............................212 315-0030
David G Sepiashvili, *President*
▲ EMP: 20
SALES (est): 893.1K **Privately Held**
SIC: 1382 Geological exploration, oil & gas field

(G-8664)
ATHALON SPORTGEAR INC
10 W 33rd St Rm 1012 (10001-3317)
PHONE.............................212 268-8070
Andrew Nitkin, *Ch of Bd*
Robert Goldener, *President*
Brian E Sullen, *Manager*
Brian Sullen, *Manager*
Mike McLoughlin, *Director*
▲ EMP: 7
SALES (est): 1.1MM **Privately Held**
WEB: www.athalonskyvalet.com
SIC: 3949 Bags, golf

(G-8665)
ATHLON SPT COMMUNICATIONS INC
60 E 42nd St Ste 820 (10165-0820)
PHONE.............................212 478-1910
Tracey Altman, *President*
Monique Kakar, *Vice Pres*
Dave Barber, *Relations*
EMP: 11
SALES (est): 1.2MM
SALES (corp-wide): 31.1MM **Privately Held**
SIC: 2721 Magazines: publishing only, not printed on site
PA: Athlon Sports Communications, Inc.
2451 Atrium Way Ste 320
Nashville TN 37214
615 327-0747

(G-8666)
ATLANTIC MONTHLY GROUP INC
Also Called: Atlantic, The
60 Madison Ave (10010-1600)
PHONE.............................202 266-7000
Katie Storrs, *Principal*
EMP: 25
SALES (corp-wide): 11.9MM **Privately Held**
WEB: www.theatlantic.com
SIC: 2721 Magazines: publishing only, not printed on site
PA: The Atlantic Monthly Group Inc
600 New Hampshire Ave Nw # 4
Washington DC 20037
202 266-7000

(G-8667)
ATLANTIC RECORDING CORP (DH)
Also Called: Atlantic Records
1633 Broadway Lowr 2c1 (10019-6708)
PHONE.............................212 707-2000
Craig Kauman, *Ch of Bd*
Ahmet M Ertegun, *Ch of Bd*
Julie Geenwald, *President*
Greg Kallman, *President*
Paul Sinclair, *Exec VP*
EMP: 325
SQ FT: 133,000
SALES (est): 87.1MM **Privately Held**
WEB: www.ledzep.com
SIC: 3652 Compact laser discs, prerecorded; master records or tapes, preparation of; phonograph record blanks
HQ: Warner Music Group Corp.
1633 Broadway Fl 11
New York NY 10019
212 275-2000

(G-8668)
ATLANTIC TROPHY CO INC
866 Avenue Of The America (10001-4168)
PHONE.............................212 684-6020
Arthur Schneider, *President*
EMP: 6
SQ FT: 1,000
SALES (est): 764.8K **Privately Held**
SIC: 3914 Trophies, silver; trophies, nickel silver; trophies, pewter; trophies, plated (all metals)

(G-8669)
ATLAS & COMPANY LLC
355 Lexington Ave Fl 6 (10017-6603)
PHONE.............................212 234-3100
James Atlas, *President*
David Barker, *Manager*
Peter Desrochers, *Manager*
Ulla Schnell, *Director*
EMP: 6
SALES (est): 500K **Privately Held**
SIC: 2731 Book publishing

(G-8670)
ATLAS MUSIC PUBLISHING LLC (PA)
6 E 39th St Ste 1104 (10016-0116)
PHONE.............................646 502-5170
Richard Stumpf, *CEO*
EMP: 9
SQ FT: 3,000
SALES (est): 941K **Privately Held**
SIC: 2741 Music books: publishing & printing; music, sheet: publishing only, not printed on site

(G-8671)
ATLAS PRINT SOLUTIONS INC
589 8th Ave Fl 4 (10018-3092)
PHONE.............................212 949-8775
Patrick Fardella, *Prdtn Mgr*
Mike Sorrentino, *Opers Staff*
Maureen Hoban, *Accounting Mgr*
Kathleen Tan, *Finance*
Gregg Morgan, *Accounts Exec*
EMP: 28
SALES (est): 4.4MM **Privately Held**
SIC: 2752 Commercial printing, offset

(G-8672)
ATLAS RECYCLING LLC
Also Called: Pep Realty
25 Howard St Fl 2 (10013-3164)
PHONE.............................212 925-3280
John Pasquale, *CEO*
J Pasqual, *General Mgr*
Luke Lee, *Office Mgr*
EMP: 5
SALES (est): 446.3K **Privately Held**
SIC: 2621 Paper mills

(G-8673)
ATR JEWELRY INC
71 W 47th St Ste 402 (10036-2819)
PHONE.............................212 819-0075
Aron Aranbaev, *President*
EMP: 10
SALES (est): 1.1MM **Privately Held**
WEB: www.atrjewelry.com
SIC: 3911 5944 Jewelry, precious metal; jewelry, precious stones & precious metals

(G-8674)
ATTACHMATE CORPORATION
1 Penn Plz Fl 36 (10119-3699)
PHONE.............................646 704-0042
John Sena, *Branch Mgr*
EMP: 6 **Privately Held**
SIC: 7372 Prepackaged software
HQ: Attachmate Corporation
705 5th Ave S Ste 1000
Seattle WA 98104
206 217-7100

(G-8675)
ATTENDS HEALTHCARE INC
200 Park Ave (10166-0005)
PHONE.............................212 338-5100
Michael Fagan, *CEO*
EMP: 651
SALES (est): 29.7MM
SALES (corp-wide): 5.1B **Privately Held**
SIC: 2676 Sanitary paper products

PA: Domtar Corporation
395 Boul De Maisonneuve O Bureau
200
Montreal QC H3A 1
514 848-5555

(G-8676)
ATTITUDES FOOTWEAR INC
1040 1st Ave Ste 232 (10022-2991)
PHONE.................................212 754-9113
Paul Mayer, *President*
Levy Jeff, *Exec VP*
Jeff Levy, *Vice Pres*
EMP: 3
SALES (est): 2MM **Privately Held**
SIC: 3144 Dress shoes, women's

(G-8677)
AUGURY INC
263 W 38th St Fl 16 (10018-0483)
PHONE.................................866 432-0976
Saar Yoskovitz, *CEO*
Eric Epstein, *Opers Staff*
Brian Charles, *Accounts Exec*
Brian Cherhoniak, *Sales Staff*
Trey Morris, *Marketing Mgr*
EMP: 24
SALES: 512.6K **Privately Held**
SIC: 7372 Business oriented computer
software

(G-8678)
AUGUST SILK INC (PA)
499 7th Ave Fl 5s (10018-6868)
PHONE.................................212 643-2400
Benedict Chen, *Ch of Bd*
Fritz Penwell, *President*
Pete Frankfort, *VP Prdtn*
May Lau, *Engineer*
Lauren Korolowicz, *Design Engr*
▲ **EMP:** 23
SQ FT: 83,000
SALES (est): 30MM **Privately Held**
SIC: 2321 2331 2335 2392 Men's &
boys' furnishings; women's & misses'
blouses & shirts; women's, juniors' &
misses' dresses; household furnishings

(G-8679)
AUGUST SILK INC
H F G Design
499 7th Ave Fl 5s (10018-6868)
PHONE.................................212 643-2400
Fritz Penwell, *President*
EMP: 7 **Privately Held**
SIC: 2321 2331 2335 2392 Men's &
boys' furnishings; women's & misses'
blouses & shirts; women's, juniors' &
misses' dresses; household furnishings
PA: August Silk Inc.
499 7th Ave Fl 5s
New York NY 10018

(G-8680)
AUTHENTIC BRANDS GROUP LLC (PA)
Also Called: Jones New York
1411 Broadway Fl 4 (10018-3460)
PHONE.................................212 760-2410
James Salter, *CEO*
Nicholas Woodhouse, *President*
Bridgette Fitzpatrick, *Counsel*
Jarrod Weber, *Exec VP*
Kenneth Ohashi, *Senior VP*
EMP: 150
SALES (est): 1.2B **Privately Held**
SIC: 2339 2384 5137 5611 Women's &
misses' accessories; robes & dressing
gowns; bathrobes, men's & women's:
made from purchased materials; women's
& children's lingerie & undergarments;
clothing, sportswear, men's & boys'; fran-
chises, selling or licensing

(G-8681)
AUTOKINITON US HOLDINGS INC (PA)
485 Lexington Ave Fl 31 (10017-2641)
PHONE.................................212 338-5100
Scott Jones, *President*
EMP: 5
SALES (est): 2.2B **Privately Held**
SIC: 3465 Body parts, automobile:
stamped metal

(G-8682)
AUTOMOTIVE ACCESSORIES GROUP
505 8th Ave Rm 12a05 (10018-6581)
PHONE.................................212 736-8100
Allan J Marrus, *President*
Stephen Delman, *Admin Sec*
EMP: 300
SALES (est): 16.1MM **Privately Held**
SIC: 3714 Steering mechanisms, motor ve-
hicle

(G-8683)
AUVEN THERAPEUTICS MGT LP
1325 Avenue Of The Americ (10019-6583)
PHONE.................................212 616-4000
Peter B Corr, *General Ptnr*
Stephen Evans-Freke, *General Ptnr*
EMP: 10
SALES (est): 1.6MM **Privately Held**
SIC: 2834 Pharmaceutical preparations

(G-8684)
AV THERAPEUTICS INC
Also Called: A V T
20 E 68th St Ste 204 (10065-5836)
PHONE.................................917 497-5523
Robert Pollock, *President*
Jan Geliebter, *Admin Sec*
EMP: 25 **EST:** 2007
SALES (est): 1.8MM **Privately Held**
SIC: 2836 Vaccines

(G-8685)
AVALANCHE STUDIOS NEW YORK INC
536 Broadway (10012-3915)
PHONE.................................212 993-6447
David Grijns, *Ch of Bd*
EMP: 60
SALES (est): 5.3MM
SALES (corp-wide): 1.8B **Privately Held**
SIC: 7372 Home entertainment computer
software
HQ: Fatalist Holdings Ab

Stockholm
844 276-70

(G-8686)
AVALIN LLC
221 W 37th St Fl 3 (10018-5782)
PHONE.................................212 842-2286
Zoheir Aghravi, *President*
Matt Cohen, *Vice Pres*
Kendle Linfoot, *Vice Pres*
▲ **EMP:** 14
SQ FT: 10,000
SALES (est): 1.6MM **Privately Held**
WEB: www.avalinknits.com
SIC: 2339 Women's & misses' athletic
clothing & sportswear

(G-8687)
AVANTI PRESS INC
6 W 18th St Ste 6l (10011-4630)
PHONE.................................212 414-1025
Frederic Ruffner III, *Branch Mgr*
EMP: 25
SALES (corp-wide): 14.2MM **Privately
Held**
SIC: 2771 Greeting cards
PA: Avanti Press, Inc.
155 W Congress St Ste 200
Detroit MI 48226
800 228-2684

(G-8688)
AVAYA SERVICES INC
2 Penn Plz Rm 702 (10121-1000)
PHONE.................................866 462-8292
EMP: 7
SALES (est): 468.9K **Publicly Held**
SIC: 3661 Telephones & telephone appara-
tus
HQ: Avaya Inc.
4655 Great America Pkwy
Santa Clara CA 95054
908 953-6000

(G-8689)
AVENUE THERAPEUTICS INC
2 Gansevoort St Fl 9 (10014-1667)
PHONE.................................781 652-4500
Lindsay A Rosenwald, *Ch of Bd*

Lucy Lu, *President*
Joseph Vazzano, *CFO*
Scott A Reines, *Chief Mktg Ofcr*
EMP: 6
SALES (est): 1.1MM **Privately Held**
SIC: 2834 Pharmaceutical preparations

(G-8690)
AVERY DENNISON CORPORATION
218 W 40th St Fl 8 (10018-1758)
PHONE.................................626 304-2000
Sasha Smith, *Accounts Mgr*
Peter Gunshon, *Manager*
EMP: 115
SALES (corp-wide): 7.1B **Publicly Held**
SIC: 2672 Adhesive backed films, foams &
foils
PA: Avery Dennison Corporation
207 N Goode Ave
Glendale CA 91203
626 304-2000

(G-8691)
AVI-SPL EMPLOYEE
8 W 38th St Rm 1101 (10018-6244)
PHONE.................................212 840-4801
EMP: 350
SALES (corp-wide): 596.9MM **Privately
Held**
SIC: 3669 3861 3663 3651 Mfg Commu-
nications Equip Mfg Photo Equip/Supplies
Mfg Radio/Tv Comm Equip Mfg Home
Audio/Video Eqp Whol Photo Equip/Sup-
ply
HQ: Avi-Spl Employee Emergency Relief
Fund, Inc.
6301 Benjamin Rd Ste 101
Tampa FL 33634
813 884-7168

(G-8692)
AVID TECHNOLOGY INC
90 Park Ave (10016-1301)
PHONE.................................212 983-2424
Adam Taylor, *Branch Mgr*
EMP: 22
SALES (corp-wide): 413.2MM **Publicly
Held**
WEB: www.avid.com
SIC: 3861 Editing equipment, motion pic-
ture: viewers, splicers, etc.
PA: Avid Technology, Inc.
75 Network Dr
Burlington MA 01803
978 640-6789

(G-8693)
AVITTO LEATHER GOODS INC
424 W Broadway Frnt A (10012-3796)
PHONE.................................212 219-7501
AVI Sharifi, *President*
EMP: 7
SALES (est): 560K **Privately Held**
SIC: 2211 Shoe fabrics

(G-8694)
AVM SOFTWARE INC (HQ)
Also Called: Paltalk
122 E 42nd St Rm 2600 (10168-2699)
P.O. Box 3454 (10008-3454)
PHONE.................................646 381-2468
Jason Katz, *CEO*
Wilson Kriegel, *President*
EMP: 17
SQ FT: 5,000
SALES (est): 5MM **Publicly Held**
WEB: www.mpath.com
SIC: 7372 Prepackaged software

(G-8695)
AVS GEM STONE CORP
48 W 48th St Ste 1010 (10036-1713)
PHONE.................................212 944-6380
Antonio Santos, *President*
EMP: 5
SALES (est): 305.5K **Privately Held**
SIC: 1499 Gemstone & industrial diamond
mining

(G-8696)
AWARD PUBLISHING LIMITED
40 W 55th St Apt 9b (10019-5376)
PHONE.................................212 246-0405
Iris Dodge, *Principal*
EMP: 9

SALES (est): 601.8K **Privately Held**
SIC: 2741 Miscellaneous publishing

(G-8697)
AXIM BIOTECHNOLOGIES INC
5 Rockefeller Plz Fl 20 Flr 20 (10111)
PHONE.................................212 751-0001
John W Huemoeller II, *CEO*
George E Anastassov, *Ch of Bd*
Robert Malasek, *CFO*
Philip A Van Damme, *Chief Mktg Ofcr*
Lekhram Changoer, *CTO*
EMP: 10 **EST:** 2010
SALES: 195.6K **Privately Held**
SIC: 2834 Pharmaceutical preparations

(G-8698)
AXIS NA LLC (PA)
Also Called: Axis Denim
70 W 40th St Fl 11 (10018-2619)
PHONE.................................212 302-1959
Ling Kwok,
Leigh Martin,
▲ **EMP:** 10
SALES (est): 1.1MM **Privately Held**
SIC: 2211 Denims

(G-8699)
AYEHU INC
1441 Broadway (10018-1905)
PHONE.................................408 930-5823
EMP: 5
SALES (corp-wide): 3.4MM **Privately
Held**
SIC: 7372 Business oriented computer
software
HQ: Ayehu Inc.
99 Almaden Blvd Fl 6
San Jose CA 95113
800 652-5601

(G-8700)
AZ YASHIR BAPAZ INC
Also Called: A Yashir Bapa
134 W 37th St (10018-6911)
PHONE.................................212 947-7357
Rasael Yaghoubian, *President*
EMP: 5
SALES (est): 630K **Privately Held**
SIC: 2339 Sportswear, women's

(G-8701)
AZIBI LTD
Also Called: Luna Luz
152 W 36th St Rm 403 (10018-8764)
PHONE.................................212 869-6550
Michael Samuels, *President*
EMP: 10
SALES (est): 1.3MM **Privately Held**
WEB: www.azibi.com
SIC: 3949 Sporting & athletic goods

(G-8702)
B & F ARCHITECTURAL SUPPORT GR
Also Called: Advance Construction Group
450 7th Ave Ste 307 (10123-0307)
PHONE.................................212 279-6488
Stewart Ratzker, *President*
EMP: 30
SALES (est): 2.2MM **Privately Held**
SIC: 2851 8712 3299 Paints & allied
products; architectural services; ornamen-
tal & architectural plaster work

(G-8703)
B & R PROMOTIONAL PRODUCTS
Also Called: Beal Blocks
34 W 120th St Apt 1 (10027-6478)
PHONE.................................212 563-0040
Gary Bimblick, *President*
Miriam Del Valle, *Admin Sec*
EMP: 6 **EST:** 1963
SQ FT: 5,000
SALES (est): 743.4K **Privately Held**
SIC: 3299 3999 Plaques: clay, plaster or
papier mache; plaques, picture, lami-
nated; badges, metal: policemen, firemen,
etc.

(G-8704)
B K JEWELRY CONTRACTOR INC
71 W 47th St Fl 11 (10036-2819)
PHONE............................212 398-9093
Jacob Solomon, *President*
Rachel Solomon, *Admin Sec*
EMP: 20
SQ FT: 5,000
SALES: 1MM **Privately Held**
SIC: 3911 Jewelry, precious metal

(G-8705)
B SMITH FURS INC
224 W 30th St Rm 402 (10001-0406)
PHONE............................212 967-5290
Gary Smith, *President*
Michael Hennessey, *Vice Pres*
Hennessey International, *Shareholder*
EMP: 10
SQ FT: 4,000
SALES (est): 980K **Privately Held**
SIC: 2371 Fur goods

(G-8706)
B TWEEN LLC
Also Called: Btween US
1412 Broadway Rm 1400 (10018-9836)
PHONE............................212 819-9040
Robert Terzi,
Jack Terzi,
Rochelle Terzi,
▲ **EMP:** 12
SQ FT: 3,000
SALES (est): 1.5MM **Privately Held**
SIC: 2339 Women's & misses' athletic clothing & sportswear

(G-8707)
B&B SPORTS NUTRITION LLC
Also Called: Bro Laboratories
244 W 72nd St Unit Phr (10023-2807)
PHONE............................520 869-5434
Brian Smith, *Mng Member*
Brandon Carter, *Mng Member*
EMP: 8
SALES: 900K **Privately Held**
SIC: 2023 Dietary supplements, dairy & non-dairy based

(G-8708)
B-REEL FILMS INC
401 Broadway Fl 24 (10013-3007)
PHONE............................917 388-3836
Anders Wahlquist, *President*
Fredrik Heinig, *Managing Dir*
Louise Holst, *Accountant*
Karen Yang, *Accountant*
Rasheedat Azeez, *Human Resources*
EMP: 24
SALES (est): 5.2MM **Privately Held**
SIC: 3571 Computers, digital, analog or hybrid

(G-8709)
B601 V2 INC
315 5th Ave Rm 903 (10016-6588)
PHONE............................646 391-6431
Steven Cohn, *CEO*
Petrina Holoszyc, *Opers Mgr*
Julie Ross, *Accounts Exec*
Ophir Prusak, *VP Mktg*
EMP: 6
SALES (est): 141.8K **Privately Held**
SIC: 7372 Business oriented computer software

(G-8710)
BABY SIGNATURE INC (PA)
Also Called: Dainty Home
251 5th Ave Fl 2l (10016-6515)
PHONE............................212 686-1700
Hassib Baghdadi, *President*
◆ **EMP:** 1
SQ FT: 5,000
SALES: 5MM **Privately Held**
SIC: 2391 2392 5023 Curtains & draperies; placemats, plastic or textile; shower curtains: made from purchased materials; curtains

(G-8711)
BABYFAIR INC
Also Called: Diversify Apparel
34 W 33rd St Rm 818 (10001-3304)
PHONE............................212 736-7989
Maurice Shamah, *Ch of Bd*
Ralph Shamah, *Vice Pres*
◆ **EMP:** 35 EST:** 1971
SQ FT: 8,000
SALES (est): 5.2MM **Privately Held**
WEB: www.babyfair.com
SIC: 2369 Play suits: girls', children's & infants'; rompers: infants'

(G-8712)
BACKTECH INC
2 Peter Cooper Rd Apt Mf (10010-6733)
PHONE............................973 279-0838
Eier Rystedt, *President*
EMP: 2
SALES: 1MM **Privately Held**
SIC: 3842 Surgical appliances & supplies

(G-8713)
BADGLEY MISCHKA LICENSING LLC
Also Called: Jsc Design
133 W 52nd St 5 (10019-6003)
PHONE............................212 921-1585
Lara Piropato, *Exec VP*
Kim Siu, *Exec VP*
Rob Caldwell, *Vice Pres*
Neil Cole, *Mng Member*
Taryn Kristal, *Executive*
EMP: 29
SALES (est): 3.1MM
SALES (corp-wide): 187.6MM **Publicly Held**
WEB: www.badgleymischka.com
SIC: 2326 Men's & boys' work clothing
PA: Iconix Brand Group, Inc.
1450 Broadway Fl 3
New York NY 10018
212 730-0030

(G-8714)
BAFFLER FOUNDATION INC
19 W 21st St Rm 1001 (10010-6845)
PHONE............................203 362-8147
John Summers, *President*
George Scialabba, *Treasurer*
Daniel Noah Moses, *Director*
EMP: 3
SALES: 1.6MM **Privately Held**
SIC: 2759 Publication printing

(G-8715)
BAG ARTS LTD
20 W 36th St Rm 5l (10018-9811)
PHONE............................212 684-7020
Steve Zagha, *President*
Isaac Cohen, *Vice Pres*
◆ **EMP:** 7
SQ FT: 7,000
SALES (est): 1.1MM **Privately Held**
WEB: www.bagarts.com
SIC: 3053 Packing materials

(G-8716)
BAG ARTS THE ART PACKAGING LLC
20 W 36th St Fl 5 (10018-8005)
PHONE............................212 684-7020
Steve Zagha, *President*
▲ **EMP:** 8
SQ FT: 7,000
SALES (est): 663.6K **Privately Held**
SIC: 2673 2674 Food storage & trash bags (plastic); grocers' bags: made from purchased materials

(G-8717)
BAG BAZAAR LTD
Metro Accessories
1 E 33rd St Fl 6 (10016-5099)
PHONE............................212 689-3508
Joey Shames, *Branch Mgr*
EMP: 25
SALES (corp-wide): 43.1MM **Privately Held**
WEB: www.aeny.com
SIC: 2339 Women's & misses' accessories

PA: Bag Bazaar Ltd.
1 E 33rd St Fl 6
New York NY 10016
212 689-3508

(G-8718)
BAGZNYC CORP
Also Called: Kids
19 W 34th St Rm 318 (10001-0055)
PHONE............................212 643-8202
Jeff Goldstein, *President*
Larry Zakarin, *Vice Pres*
▲ **EMP:** 18
SQ FT: 5,300
SALES (est): 1.2MM **Privately Held**
SIC: 2339 3171 Women's & misses' outerwear; women's handbags & purses

(G-8719)
BAIKAL INC (PA)
341 W 38th St Fl 3 (10018-9694)
PHONE............................212 239-4650
Josef Itskovich, *President*
▲ **EMP:** 70
SQ FT: 5,000
SALES (est): 5MM **Privately Held**
WEB: www.baikal.com
SIC: 3171 Handbags, women's

(G-8720)
BAINBRIDGE & KNIGHT LLC
801 2nd Ave Fl 19 (10017-8618)
PHONE............................212 986-5100
Carl Ruderman, *President*
Steven Schwartz, *Mng Member*
EMP: 50
SQ FT: 12,000
SALES (est): 5.2MM **Privately Held**
SIC: 2099 Food preparations

(G-8721)
BALAJEE ENTERPRISES INC
Also Called: Digitech Printers
150 W 30th St Frnt 2 (10001-4161)
PHONE............................212 629-6150
Shul Khalfan, *President*
EMP: 8
SQ FT: 2,500
SALES (est): 1MM **Privately Held**
WEB: www.digitechprinters.com
SIC: 2759 Commercial printing

(G-8722)
BALANCED TECH CORP
Also Called: New Balance Underwear
37 W 37th St Fl 10 (10018-6354)
PHONE............................212 768-8330
Ezra Jack Cattan, *Ch of Bd*
Judah Cattan, *President*
▲ **EMP:** 20
SALES (est): 1.2MM **Privately Held**
WEB: www.newbalanceunderwear.com
SIC: 2254 Underwear, knit

(G-8723)
BALTICARE INC (PA)
501 Fashion Ave Rm 414 (10018-8608)
PHONE............................646 380-9470
Al Rivera, *Engineer*
Hugh D Reitmeyer, *Director*
EMP: 10 EST:** 2007
SALES (est): 2.6MM **Privately Held**
SIC: 3585 Air conditioning units, complete: domestic or industrial

(G-8724)
BAM SALES LLC (PA)
1407 Broadway Rm 2018 (10018-2863)
PHONE............................212 781-3000
Marc Moyal,
Alan Cohen,
Scott Danziger,
Nicole Hausman,
Robert Klein,
EMP: 3
SALES (est): 1.2MM **Privately Held**
SIC: 2339 Women's & misses' athletic clothing & sportswear

(G-8725)
BARBARA MATERA LTD
890 Broadway Fl 5 (10003-1211)
PHONE............................212 475-5006
Jared Aswegan, *President*
Larry Feinman, *CFO*
EMP: 100 EST:** 1967

SQ FT: 8,500
SALES (est): 5.5MM **Privately Held**
SIC: 2389 Theatrical costumes

(G-8726)
BARBER BROTHERS JEWELRY MFG
Also Called: B & B Jewelry Mfg Co
580 5th Ave Ste 725 (10036-4724)
PHONE............................212 819-0666
Abraham Barber, *President*
Simon Barber, *Vice Pres*
EMP: 15 EST:** 1963
SQ FT: 2,200
SALES (est): 1.5MM **Privately Held**
SIC: 3911 Jewelry, precious metal

(G-8727)
BARDWIL INDUSTRIES INC (PA)
Also Called: Bardwil Linens
4 Bryant Park Fl 4 Flr 4 (10018)
PHONE............................212 944-1870
George Bardwil, *CEO*
Margaret Bellido, *Accounts Exec*
▲ **EMP:** 185 EST:** 1906
SQ FT: 12,000
SALES (est): 20.4MM **Privately Held**
WEB: www.beyondmarketing.com
SIC: 2392 2241 Napkins, fabric & nonwoven: made from purchased materials; placemats, plastic or textile; tablecloths: made from purchased materials; chair covers & pads: made from purchased materials; trimmings, textile

(G-8728)
BARE BEAUTY LASER HAIR REMOVAL
5 E 57th St Fl 18 (10022-2553)
PHONE............................718 278-2273
Debbie Patadopoulas, *Owner*
EMP: 6
SALES (est): 71.5K **Privately Held**
SIC: 3699 Laser systems & equipment

(G-8729)
BARI ENGINEERING CORP
240 Bowery (10012-3501)
PHONE............................212 966-2080
Frank Bari, *President*
EMP: 24
SQ FT: 51,000
SALES (est): 2.8MM **Privately Held**
WEB: www.bariequipment.com
SIC: 3556 5046 Food products machinery; restaurant equipment & supplies

(G-8730)
BARI-JAY FASHIONS INC (PA)
230 W 38th St Fl 12 (10018-5729)
PHONE............................212 921-1551
Bruce Cohen, *President*
EMP: 20 EST:** 1961
SQ FT: 20,000
SALES (est): 5.4MM **Privately Held**
WEB: www.barijay.com
SIC: 2335 Gowns, formal; wedding gowns & dresses

(G-8731)
BAROKA CREATIONS INC
36 W 47th St Ste 1402 (10036-8601)
P.O. Box 290744, Brooklyn (11229-0744)
PHONE............................212 768-0527
Rami Bareket, *President*
Nftali Rockah, *Vice Pres*
EMP: 7
SQ FT: 11,000
SALES: 4MM **Privately Held**
WEB: www.baroka.com
SIC: 3911 3915 Jewelry, precious metal; diamond cutting & polishing

(G-8732)
BARRAGE
401 W 47th St Frnt A (10036-2306)
PHONE............................212 586-9390
Tom Johnson, *Owner*
EMP: 20
SALES (est): 2.2MM **Privately Held**
WEB: www.barrage.com
SIC: 3639 Major kitchen appliances, except refrigerators & stoves

(G-8733)
BARRERA JOSE & MARIA CO LTD
29 W 36th St Fl 8 (10018-7668)
PHONE....................212 239-1994
Jose Barrera, *Owner*
Maria Barrera, *Co-Owner*
EMP: 28
SQ FT: 3,000
SALES (est): 2.1MM **Privately Held**
SIC: 2387 3961 Apparel belts; costume jewelry, ex. precious metal & semi-precious stones

(G-8734)
BARRY INDUSTRIES INC
Also Called: Barry Supply Co Div
36 W 17th St Frnt 1 (10011-5731)
PHONE....................212 242-5200
Barry Weinberger, *President*
William Wein, *Manager*
EMP: 15
SQ FT: 4,000
SALES (est): 1.1MM **Privately Held**
SIC: 3429 5072 Manufactured hardware (general); hardware

(G-8735)
BARTHOLOMEW MAZZA LTD INC
22 W 48th St Ste 805 (10036-1803)
P.O. Box 231444 (10023-0025)
PHONE....................212 935-4530
Hugo Mazza, *President*
Diane Mazza, *Treasurer*
EMP: 50
SQ FT: 4,000
SALES (est): 5.5MM **Privately Held**
WEB: www.mazzabartholomew.com
SIC: 3911 Jewelry, precious metal

(G-8736)
BASIL S KADHIM
Also Called: Eton International
280 Madison Ave Rm 912 (10016-0801)
PHONE....................888 520-5192
Basil S Kadhim, *Owner*
Julie A Seward, *Manager*
EMP: 8
SQ FT: 1,000
SALES (est): 994.3K **Privately Held**
WEB: www.etoninternational.com
SIC: 3663 5045 7382 5047 Television broadcasting & communications equipment; computers, peripherals & software; protective devices, security; medical equipment & supplies

(G-8737)
BASILOFF LLC
179 Bennett Ave Apt 7f (10040-4059)
PHONE....................646 671-0353
Dmitri Vassiliev, *President*
EMP: 6 **EST:** 2014
SALES (est): 330K **Privately Held**
SIC: 2261 Sponging cotton broadwoven cloth for the trade

(G-8738)
BASIN HOLDINGS LLC (PA)
200 Park Ave Fl 58b (10166-5899)
PHONE....................212 695-7376
John Fitzgibbons, *CEO*
Gail Coleman, *Exec VP*
Rick Pierce, *Finance Mgr*
Hadley Hosea, *VP Human Res*
Steve Waters, *Marketing Staff*
EMP: 21 **EST:** 2011
SALES (est): 127.8MM **Privately Held**
SIC: 3533 Oil & gas field machinery

(G-8739)
BASTIDE INC
300 Park Ave Fl 12 (10022-7419)
PHONE....................646 356-0460
Olivier Moingeon, *CEO*
Prisca Rabe, *Associate*
EMP: 54
SALES (est): 3.2MM **Privately Held**
SIC: 2844 5999 Toilet preparations; perfumes, natural or synthetic; toiletries, cosmetics & perfumes

(G-8740)
BAUBLE BAR INC
16 Madison Sq W Fl 5 (10010-1630)
PHONE....................646 846-2044
Amy Jain, *CEO*
Rotimi Akinyemiju, *COO*
Miriam Gassel, *VP Merchandise*
James Chu, *Manager*
Amy Turcios, *Associate*
▲ **EMP:** 45
SALES (est): 17.7MM **Privately Held**
SIC: 3172 Cases, jewelry

(G-8741)
BAUSCH & LOMB HOLDINGS INC (DH)
450 Lexington Ave (10017-3904)
PHONE....................585 338-6000
Brent L Saunders, *CEO*
Gerald M Ostrov, *Ch of Bd*
Stacey Williams, *Vice Pres*
Noel Bateman, *Project Mgr*
Janice Dody, *Marketing Staff*
EMP: 9
SALES (est): 2.4B
SALES (corp-wide): 8.3B **Privately Held**
SIC: 3851 2834 Ophthalmic goods; pharmaceutical preparations
HQ: Bausch Health Americas, Inc.
400 Somerset Corp Blvd
Bridgewater NJ 08807
908 927-1400

(G-8742)
BAZAAR
300 W 57th St Fl 25 (10019-3741)
PHONE....................212 903-5497
Linda Crowley, *Principal*
▲ **EMP:** 5
SALES (est): 250.6K **Privately Held**
SIC: 2721 Magazines: publishing & printing

(G-8743)
BDG MEDIA INC (PA)
Also Called: Bustle Digital Group
315 Park Ave S Fl 12 (10010-3625)
PHONE....................917 551-6510
Bryan Goldberg, *CEO*
Elizabeth Webbe Lunny, *Exec VP*
Kate Robinson, *Vice Pres*
Jessica Tarlov, *Research*
Michael Hart, *Engineer*
EMP: 50
SQ FT: 51,000
SALES (est): 38.9MM **Privately Held**
SIC: 2741

(G-8744)
BECCA INC
Also Called: Becca Cosmetics
142 W 36th St Fl 15 (10018-8785)
PHONE....................646 568-6250
▲ **EMP:** 100 **EST:** 2001
SALES (est): 4.1MM **Publicly Held**
SIC: 2844 Mfg Toilet Preparations
PA: The Estee Lauder Companies Inc
767 5th Ave Fl 1
New York NY 10153

(G-8745)
BEDFORD FREEMAN & WORTH (DH)
Also Called: Scientific American Library
1 New York Plz Ste 4500 (10004-1562)
PHONE....................212 576-9400
Elizabeth A Widdicombe, *Senior VP*
Simon Horrer, *Vice Pres*
Lawrence Jankovic, *CFO*
Michael Ross, *Treasurer*
Mike Howard, *Sales Mgr*
EMP: 192
SQ FT: 36,000
SALES (est): 78.6MM
SALES (corp-wide): 1.6B **Privately Held**
WEB: www.bfwpub.com
SIC: 2759 2732 2721 2731 Commercial printing; book printing; periodicals; textbooks: publishing only, not printed on site

(G-8746)
BEDFORD FREEMAN & WORTH
Also Called: Saint Martins Press
1 New York Plz Ste 4500 (10004-1562)
PHONE....................212 375-7000
Joan Feinberg, *President*

Adam Whitehurst, *Editor*
Patricia Suss, *Administration*
EMP: 70
SALES (est): 1.6B **Privately Held**
WEB: www.bfwpub.com
SIC: 2731 Textbooks: publishing only, not printed on site
HQ: Bedford, Freeman & Worth Publishing Group, Llc
1 New York Plz Ste 4500
New York NY 10004
212 576-9400

(G-8747)
BEDFORD COMMUNICATIONS INC
1410 Broadway Frnt 2 (10018-9302)
PHONE....................212 807-8220
Edward D Brown, *President*
EMP: 30
SALES (est): 3.9MM **Privately Held**
WEB: www.bedfordcommunications.com
SIC: 2721 Magazines: publishing only, not printed on site

(G-8748)
BEDROCK COMMUNICATIONS
Also Called: Facilities
55 E 59th St Fl 20 (10022-1181)
PHONE....................212 532-4150
Susan Wexner, *President*
Michael Caffin, *Publisher*
Michael Casffin, *Vice Pres*
George Seli, *Director*
EMP: 5
SALES (est): 434.6K **Privately Held**
WEB: www.facilitiesonline.com
SIC: 2731 Book publishing

(G-8749)
BEDROCK INDUSTRIES (PA)
45 Rockefeller Plz 2950a (10111-0100)
PHONE....................202 400-0839
Alan Kestenbaum, *CEO*
David Cheney, *President*
EMP: 7
SALES (est): 3MM **Privately Held**
SIC: 1081 Metal mining exploration & development services

(G-8750)
BEILA GROUP INC
Also Called: City Hats
285 Mott St (10012-3430)
PHONE....................212 260-1948
Alexandra Tiouleneva, *CEO*
EMP: 12
SALES (est): 1MM **Privately Held**
SIC: 3942 Hats, doll

(G-8751)
BELLATAIRE DIAMONDS INC
19 W 44th St Fl 15 (10036-6101)
PHONE....................212 687-8881
Bill Moryto, *CFO*
Charles A Meyer, *Exec Dir*
EMP: 10
SALES (est): 761.3K **Privately Held**
WEB: www.bellatairediamonds.com
SIC: 3911 Jewelry, precious metal

(G-8752)
BELLEROPHON PUBLICATIONS INC
Also Called: Metropolis Magazine
205 Lexington Ave Fl 17 (10016-6022)
PHONE....................212 627-9977
Horace Havemeyer III, *President*
Helene Silverman, *Editor*
Miguel Sosa, *Accountant*
Chelsea Bremer, *Sales Staff*
Tamara Stout, *Adv Dir*
EMP: 35
SQ FT: 4,000
SALES (est): 4.6MM **Privately Held**
WEB: www.metropolismag.com
SIC: 2721 Magazines: publishing only, not printed on site

(G-8753)
BELUGA INC (PA)
Also Called: Adjmi Apparel Group
463 7th Ave Fl 4 (10018-8725)
PHONE....................212 594-5511
Eric Adjmi, *Ch of Bd*
Mark Adjmi, *Vice Pres*

Gerard Agoglia, *CFO*
Joey Dwek, *Info Tech Mgr*
Tony Ching, *IT/INT Sup*
▲ **EMP:** 40
SQ FT: 15,000
SALES (est): 6.8MM **Privately Held**
WEB: www.beluga.com
SIC: 2329 Men's & boys' sportswear & athletic clothing

(G-8754)
BEN WACHTER ASSOCIATES INC (PA)
Also Called: B W A
36 W 44th St Ste 700 (10036-8105)
PHONE....................212 736-4064
Andrew Lerner, *President*
Hilda McDuff, *Exec VP*
Mauricio Caballero, *VP Mfg*
Nuno Lacerda, *Director*
▲ **EMP:** 5
SALES (est): 2.4MM **Privately Held**
SIC: 2331 5199 2321 Women's & misses' blouses & shirts; fabrics, yarns & knit goods; cotton yarns; men's & boys' furnishings

(G-8755)
BENARTEX LLC
132 W 36th St Rm 401 (10018-8837)
PHONE....................212 840-3250
Susan Neill, *Vice Pres*
David Lochner, *Mng Member*
Susan Kemler, *Manager*
Jessica Marano, *Graphic Designe*
▲ **EMP:** 25
SQ FT: 7,000
SALES (est): 4MM **Privately Held**
WEB: www.benartex.com
SIC: 2211 Apparel & outerwear fabrics, cotton

(G-8756)
BENCHMARK GRAPHICS LTD
9 E 37th St Fl 5 (10016-2894)
PHONE....................212 683-1711
Fax: 212 889-1927
EMP: 15
SQ FT: 5,000
SALES (est): 1.8MM **Privately Held**
SIC: 2752 Lithographic Commercial Printing

(G-8757)
BENETTON TRADING USA INC (PA)
601 5th Ave Fl 4 (10017-8258)
P.O. Box 6020, Somerset NJ (08875-6020)
PHONE....................212 593-0290
ARI Hoffman, *Principal*
◆ **EMP:** 7
SALES (est): 985.6K **Privately Held**
SIC: 2329 Men's & boys' sportswear & athletic clothing

(G-8758)
BENSON INDUSTRIES INC
192 Lexington Ave Rm 502 (10016-6912)
PHONE....................212 779-3230
John Frank, *Manager*
EMP: 10
SALES (corp-wide): 225.3B **Publicly Held**
SIC: 3231 1793 5031 Products of purchased glass; glass & glazing work; lumber, plywood & millwork
HQ: Benson Industries, Inc.
1650 Nw Naito Pkwy # 250
Portland OR 97209
503 226-7611

(G-8759)
BENTLEY MANUFACTURING INC (PA)
10 W 33rd St Rm 220 (10001-3306)
PHONE....................212 714-1800
Victor Braha, *President*
Ralph Braha, *CFO*
Eli Braha, *Admin Sec*
◆ **EMP:** 7
SQ FT: 5,200
SALES (est): 2.2MM **Privately Held**
SIC: 2676 Diapers, paper (disposable): made from purchased paper; napkins, sanitary: made from purchased paper

(G-8760)
BERNARD CHAUS INC (HQ)
530 7th Ave Fl 18　(10018-4855)
PHONE....................................212 354-1280
Ariel Chaus, *CEO*
Judith Leech, *Vice Pres*
Larisa Mikhaylov, *Vice Pres*
William P Runge, *CFO*
Jackie Muldowney, *VP Merchandise*
▲ **EMP:** 76
SQ FT: 33,000
SALES (est): 58.5MM **Privately Held**
SIC: 2339 2331 Sportswear, women's;
　slacks: women's, misses' & juniors';
　shorts (outerwear): women's, misses' &
　juniors'; women's & misses' blouses &
　shirts
PA: Jl Parc Llc
　　9015 Queens Blvd
　　Rego Park NY 11374
　　718 271-0703

(G-8761)
BERNARD CHAUS INC
Also Called: Cynthia Steffe
515 7th Ave Ste 18　(10018-5902)
PHONE....................................646 562-4700
Tina Cardell, *Branch Mgr*
EMP: 200
SALES (corp-wide): 58.5MM **Privately
Held**
SIC: 2339 2331 Sportswear, women's;
　slacks: women's, misses' & juniors';
　shorts (outerwear): women's, misses' &
　juniors'; women's & misses' blouses &
　shirts
HQ: Bernard Chaus, Inc.
　　530 7th Ave Fl 18
　　New York NY 10018
　　212 354-1280

(G-8762)
BERNETTE APPAREL LLC
42 W 39th St Fl 2　(10018-3895)
PHONE....................................212 279-5526
Adam Siskind,
Jeff Siskind,
EMP: 16
SQ FT: 7,000
SALES (est): 1.1MM **Privately Held**
WEB: www.btexusa.com
SIC: 2329 Sweaters & sweater jackets:
　men's & boys'

(G-8763)
**BERNHARD ARNOLD &
COMPANY INC (PA)**
551 5th Ave Fl 3　(10176-2800)
PHONE....................................212 907-1500
Jennifer Odwyer, *Partner*
David Rotem, *Exec VP*
Howard Brecher, *Vice Pres*
Frances Alvarez, *Vice Pres*
Allison Ames, *Vice Pres*
EMP: 3
SQ FT: 70,000
SALES: 36MM **Publicly Held**
WEB: www.valueline.com
SIC: 2721 6282 Periodicals: publishing
　only; investment advice

(G-8764)
BERTELSMANN INC (DH)
1745 Broadway Fl 20　(10019-4651)
PHONE....................................212 782-1000
Jaroslaw Gabor, *CEO*
Thomas Rabe, *Ch of Bd*
Joshua Kraus, *President*
Karin Schlautmann, *Exec VP*
Carol Cunningham, *Vice Pres*
▲ **EMP:** 30
SALES (est): 1.7B
SALES (corp-wide): 75.3MM **Privately
Held**
WEB: www.bertelsmann.com
SIC: 2731 2721 7819 3652 Books: pub-
　lishing & printing; magazines: publishing
　& printing; trade journals: publishing &
　printing; video tape or disk reproduction;
　compact laser discs, prerecorded; com-
　mercial & industrial building operation
HQ: Bertelsmann Se & Co. Kgaa
　　Carl-Bertelsmann-Str. 270
　　Gutersloh 33335
　　524 180-0

(G-8765)
**BERTELSMANN PUBG GROUP
INC (DH)**
1540 Broadway Fl 24　(10036-4039)
PHONE....................................212 782-1000
Thomas Middelhoff, *CEO*
Robert J Sorrentino, *CEO*
Hans-Martin Sorge, *Ch of Bd*
Peter Olson, *President*
Bernhard U Derlath, *Treasurer*
EMP: 1000
SQ FT: 710,000
SALES (est): 89.8MM
SALES (corp-wide): 75.3MM **Privately
Held**
SIC: 2731 2721 Books: publishing only;
　magazines: publishing only, not printed on
　site
HQ: Bertelsmann, Inc.
　　1745 Broadway Fl 20
　　New York NY 10019
　　212 782-1000

(G-8766)
**BEST BRANDS CONSUMER
PDTS INC (PA)**
20 W 33rd St Fl 5　(10001-3305)
PHONE....................................212 684-7456
Alber Kassin, *President*
Albert Kassin, *President*
David Green, *VP Opers*
Yocasta Pena, *Export Mgr*
▲ **EMP:** 8
SQ FT: 26,000
SALES (est): 10MM **Privately Held**
SIC: 2369 2371 Headwear: girls', chil-
　dren's & infants'; hats, fur

(G-8767)
**BESTYPE DIGITAL IMAGING
LLC**
285 W Broadway Frnt A　(10013-2246)
PHONE....................................212 966-6886
John W Lam, *Mng Member*
Chick Lam,
EMP: 10
SQ FT: 3,000
SALES: 1MM **Privately Held**
SIC: 2759 Commercial printing

(G-8768)
**BETH KOBLINER COMPANY
LLC**
1995 Broadway Ste 1800　(10023-5857)
PHONE....................................212 501-8407
Beth Kobliner,
EMP: 5
SALES (est): 274.6K **Privately Held**
SIC: 2711 Newspapers, publishing & print-
　ing

(G-8769)
BETH WARD STUDIOS LLC
133 W 25th St Rm 8e　(10001-7281)
PHONE....................................646 922-7575
Beth Ward, *Mng Member*
EMP: 10
SALES: 3.4MM **Privately Held**
SIC: 3961 Costume jewelry

(G-8770)
BETSY & ADAM LTD (PA)
525 Fashion Ave Fl 21　(10018-4921)
PHONE....................................212 302-3750
Martin Sklar, *President*
▲ **EMP:** 50
SALES (est): 14.8MM **Privately Held**
WEB: www.betsyandadam.com
SIC: 2253 Dresses & skirts

(G-8771)
BETTERTEX INC
Also Called: Bettertex Interiors
450 Broadway　(10013-5822)
PHONE....................................212 431-3373
Raymond Nakash, *President*
EMP: 15 **EST:** 2008
SALES (est): 1.5MM **Privately Held**
SIC: 2391 7641 Curtains & draperies; up-
　holstery work

(G-8772)
**BEVERAGE MEDIA GROUP INC
(PA)**
152 Madison Ave Rm 600　(10016-5471)
PHONE....................................212 571-3232
Mike Roth, *President*
Annie Douglass, *Vice Pres*
Debbie Winslow, *Controller*
Anya Sagee, *Sales Staff*
Kristen Wolfe, *Manager*
▲ **EMP:** 25
SQ FT: 13,300
SALES (est): 1.8MM **Privately Held**
WEB: www.bevmedia.com
SIC: 2721 Magazines: publishing only, not
　printed on site

(G-8773)
BEYOND LOOM INC (PA)
Also Called: Franetta
262 W 38th St Rm 203　(10018-5881)
P.O. Box 105　(10150-0105)
PHONE....................................212 575-3100
Joanne Satin, *President*
▲ **EMP:** 6 **EST:** 1991
SQ FT: 4,000
SALES (est): 607.3K **Privately Held**
WEB: www.beyondtheloom.com
SIC: 2211 2221 2231 Cotton broad
　woven goods; silk broadwoven fabrics;
　fabric finishing: wool, mohair or similar
　fibers

(G-8774)
BEYONDLY INC
Also Called: Everplans
20 W 20th St Ste 1004　(10011-9252)
PHONE....................................646 658-3665
Abby Schneiderman, *President*
Adam Seifer, *President*
EMP: 22
SQ FT: 1,700
SALES (est): 1.3MM **Privately Held**
SIC: 7372 Business oriented computer
　software

(G-8775)
BEYONDSPRING INC
28 Liberty St Fl 39　(10005-1451)
PHONE....................................646 305-6387
Lan Huang, *Ch of Bd*
James R Tonra, *Senior VP*
Edward Dongheng Liu, *CFO*
Ramon W Mohanlal, *Chief Mktg Ofcr*
G Kenneth Lloyd, *Security Dir*
EMP: 52
SQ FT: 7,238
SALES (est): 2.5MM **Privately Held**
SIC: 2834 Pharmaceutical preparations

(G-8776)
**BEYONDSPRING
PHRMCEUTICALS INC**
28 Liberty St Fl 39　(10005-1451)
PHONE....................................646 305-6387
Lan Huang, *CEO*
G Kenneth Lloyd, *COO*
Steven D Reich, *Vice Pres*
Robert Dickey IV, *CFO*
Gloria Lee, *Chief Mktg Ofcr*
EMP: 11
SALES (est): 1.2MM **Privately Held**
SIC: 2834 Pharmaceutical preparations

(G-8777)
BH BRAND INC
Also Called: Silly Feet
10 W 33rd St Rm 218　(10001-3306)
PHONE....................................212 239-1635
Kenny Harari, *CEO*
Morris Harari, *President*
▲ **EMP:** 25
SQ FT: 4,500
SALES (est): 10.8MM **Privately Held**
SIC: 3143 3144 5139 Men's footwear, ex-
　cept athletic; women's footwear, except
　athletic; footwear

(G-8778)
BH MULTI COM CORP (PA)
Also Called: Effy
15 W 46th St Fl 6　(10036-4196)
PHONE....................................212 944-0020
Effy Hematian, *CEO*
Fatolah Hematian, *Ch of Bd*

David Bassalalli, *Corp Secy*
Hertsel Akhavan, *Vice Pres*
▲ **EMP:** 47
SQ FT: 6,000
SALES (est): 5.2MM **Privately Held**
WEB: www.bhmulti.com
SIC: 3911 Jewelry, precious metal

(G-8779)
BIANCA GROUP LTD
244 W 39th St Fl 4　(10018-4413)
PHONE....................................212 768-3011
Ricardo Garcia, *President*
EMP: 5
SQ FT: 2,200
SALES: 200K **Privately Held**
SIC: 3953 3543 Marking devices; indus-
　trial patterns

(G-8780)
BIBO INTERNATIONAL LLC
130 Water St Apt 4g　(10005-1614)
P.O. Box 492, Newport RI　(02840-0492)
PHONE....................................617 304-2242
Mark Lester, *Mng Member*
EMP: 18 **EST:** 2011
SALES: 1.6MM **Privately Held**
SIC: 2084 Wines, brandy & brandy spirits

(G-8781)
BICKER INC
Also Called: Holiday House Publishing
50 Broad St Ste 301　(10004-2826)
PHONE....................................212 688-0085
John H Briggs Jr, *President*
Kate Briggs, *Vice Pres*
Mary Cash, *Vice Pres*
Lisa Lee, *Production*
▲ **EMP:** 15 **EST:** 1935
SQ FT: 2,000
SALES (est): 2.3MM **Privately Held**
WEB: www.holidayhouse.com
SIC: 2731 Books: publishing only

(G-8782)
BIDPRESS LLC
659 Washington St Apt 5r　(10014-2874)
P.O. Box 351, Asheville NC　(28802-0351)
PHONE....................................267 973-8876
Anthony Wavering, *CEO*
EMP: 5 **EST:** 2013
SQ FT: 1,000
SALES (est): 189.8K **Privately Held**
SIC: 2759 Screen printing

(G-8783)
BIELKA INC
141 E 56th St Apt 6f　(10022-2713)
PHONE....................................212 980-6841
Robert Bruce Bielka, *President*
Regina Suzanne Eros, *Vice Pres*
EMP: 5
SQ FT: 1,200
SALES (est): 453.6K **Privately Held**
WEB: www.bielkajewelry.com
SIC: 3911 Jewelry, precious metal

(G-8784)
**BIG APPLE ELEVTR SRV &
CONSULT**
247 W 30th St　(10001-2824)
PHONE....................................212 279-0700
Jaclyn Hanning, *CEO*
Joseph Hanning, *President*
EMP: 8
SALES (est): 454.4K **Privately Held**
SIC: 3534 Elevators & equipment

(G-8785)
BIG APPLE SIGN CORP (PA)
Also Called: BIG APPLE VISUAL GROUP
247 W 35th St Rm 400　(10001-1925)
PHONE....................................212 629-3650
Amir Khalfan, *Ch of Bd*
Richi Shah, *CFO*
Zeenath Fatima, *Accounts Exec*
Shamie Seeraj, *Manager*
Maria B Varga, *Consultant*
▲ **EMP:** 93
SQ FT: 40,000
SALES: 18.2MM **Privately Held**
WEB: www.bigapplegroup.com
SIC: 2399 2759 3993 Banners, made
　from fabric; commercial printing; signs,
　not made in custom sign painting shops;
　displays & cutouts, window & lobby

▲ = Import ▼=Export
◆ =Import/Export

(G-8786)
BIG FISH ENTERTAINMENT LLC
5 Times Sq Fl 9 (10036-6531)
PHONE..................646 797-4955
Anthony Crisano, *Production*
Daniel Cesareo, *Mng Member*
EMP: 200
SALES: 25.7MM **Privately Held**
SIC: 3663 Studio equipment, radio & television broadcasting

(G-8787)
BIG IDEA BRANDS LLC
Also Called: Flow Society
1410 Broadway Frnt 4 (10018-9343)
PHONE..................212 938-0270
Mark Elenowitz, *CEO*
Anthony Ottimo, *President*
Brian Frank, *Principal*
Carlos Vazquez, *COO*
Larry Fihma, *Senior VP*
▲ EMP: 10
SQ FT: 4,000
SALES (est): 857.6K **Privately Held**
SIC: 2329 Athletic (warmup, sweat & jogging) suits: men's & boys'

(G-8788)
BIG WHITE WALL HOLDING INC
41 E 11th St Fl 11 (10003-4602)
PHONE..................917 281-2649
Tina Trenkler, *CEO*
EMP: 15 EST: 2013
SQ FT: 1,200
SALES: 250K
SALES (corp-wide): 29.1K **Privately Held**
SIC: 7372 Application computer software
HQ: Bigwhitewall Limited
36-38 Whitefriars Street
London EC4Y

(G-8789)
BIGNAY INC
315 E 86th St Apt 21ge (10028-4867)
PHONE..................786 346-1673
Lucas Toledo, *CEO*
Gabriel Nudel, *COO*
Eric Sevillia, *CFO*
Emanuel Ravera, *CTO*
EMP: 8 EST: 2014
SALES (est): 924K **Privately Held**
SIC: 3751 5571 5941 Bicycles & related parts; bicycles, motorized; bicycle & bicycle parts

(G-8790)
BILCO INDUSTRIES INC
214 W 39th St Rm 301 (10018-8311)
PHONE..................917 783-5008
Billy Chen, *President*
Jerry Lau, *Vice Pres*
EMP: 16 EST: 2013
SALES: 30MM **Privately Held**
SIC: 2329 2339 5136 5137 Men's & boys' sportswear & athletic clothing; women's & misses' athletic clothing & sportswear; men's & boys' sportswear & work clothing; work clothing, men's & boys'; women's & children's clothing

(G-8791)
BILLION TOWER INTL LLC
Also Called: Machine Clothing Company
989 6th Ave Fl 8 (10018-0871)
PHONE..................212 220-0608
Joeson Ko Cho Shun,
▲ EMP: 15
SQ FT: 4,500
SALES: 122MM **Privately Held**
SIC: 2326 5136 Men's & boys' work clothing; men's & boys' clothing

(G-8792)
BILLION TOWER USA LLC
989 Avenue Of The America (10018-0871)
PHONE..................212 220-0608
Joeson Cho Shun Ko,
EMP: 5
SALES: 5MM **Privately Held**
SIC: 2329 Men's & boys' sportswear & athletic clothing

(G-8793)
BILLY BEEZ USA LLC (PA)
3 W 35th St Fl 3 # 3 (10001-2237)
PHONE..................646 606-2249

Ron Palerico, *General Mgr*
Mark Bain, *Sales Staff*
EMP: 17
SALES (est): 16.7MM **Privately Held**
SIC: 3949 5137 7999 Playground equipment; women's & children's dresses, suits, skirts & blouses; amusement ride

(G-8794)
BILLYKIRK
16a Orchard St (10002-6110)
PHONE..................212 217-0679
EMP: 8
SALES (est): 406.2K **Privately Held**
SIC: 3199 Leather garments
PA: Billykirk
150 Bay St Fl 3
Jersey City NJ 07302

(G-8795)
BINO PRODUCTS LLC
236 5th Ave Fl 8 (10001-7989)
PHONE..................212 886-6899
Joseph L Sutton, *CEO*
EMP: 50
SALES (est): 4.2MM **Privately Held**
SIC: 3634 Housewares, excluding cooking appliances & utensils

(G-8796)
BIOCONTINUUM GROUP INC
116 Chambers St (10007-1336)
PHONE..................212 406-1060
John M Dimor, *President*
EMP: 5
SQ FT: 1,200
SALES (est): 290K **Privately Held**
WEB: www.bioc.net
SIC: 3999 Education aids, devices & supplies

(G-8797)
BIOFEEDBACK INSTRUMENT CORP
Also Called: Allied Products
255 W 98th St Apt 3d (10025-5596)
PHONE..................212 222-5665
Philip Brotman, *President*
▲ EMP: 8
SQ FT: 1,000
SALES: 800K **Privately Held**
WEB: www.biof.com
SIC: 3845 5045 5734 Electromedical apparatus; computers, peripherals & software; computer peripheral equipment; computer & software stores

(G-8798)
BIOLITEC INC
110 E 42nd St Rm 1800 (10017-5648)
PHONE..................413 525-0600
Wolfgang Neuberger, *CEO*
EMP: 50
SQ FT: 16,000
SALES (est): 5.1MM
SALES (corp-wide): 1.8MM **Privately Held**
WEB: www.biolitec-us.com
SIC: 3229 Fiber optics strands
HQ: Biolitec Biomedical Technology Gmbh
Otto-Schott-Str. 15
Jena 07745
364 151-9530

(G-8799)
BIOMUP USA INC
412 W 15th St Ste 1000 (10011-7054)
PHONE..................800 436-6266
Patrice Ferrand, *Chairman*
Jean-Paul Alves, *CFO*
EMP: 6
SALES (est): 338.3K
SALES (corp-wide): 1.9MM **Privately Held**
SIC: 2836 Biological products, except diagnostic
PA: Biom' Up
8 Allee Irene Joliot Curie
Saint-Priest 69800
486 573-610

(G-8800)
BIRDSIGNS INC
16 W 19th St Apt 3e (10011-4336)
PHONE..................201 388-7613
Zvetan Dragulev, *CEO*

EMP: 5
SALES (est): 117.2K **Privately Held**
SIC: 7372 7389 Application computer software;

(G-8801)
BIRNBAUM & BULLOCK LTD
151 W 25th St Rm 2a (10001-7262)
PHONE..................212 242-2914
Robert Bullock, *CEO*
Steven Birnbaum, *President*
EMP: 8
SQ FT: 1,500
SALES (est): 1.1MM **Privately Held**
SIC: 2335 Wedding gowns & dresses

(G-8802)
BISLEY INC
Also Called: Bisley North America
1140 Broadway Rm 902 (10001-7504)
PHONE..................212 675-3055
Garth Fielding, *Managing Dir*
▲ EMP: 6
SALES (est): 389.8K **Privately Held**
SIC: 2522 Office furniture, except wood

(G-8803)
BISTATE OIL MANAGEMENT CORP
10 E 40th St Rm 2710 (10016-0301)
PHONE..................212 935-4110
Richard D Siegal, *President*
Maria Scibelli, *Principal*
Paul H Howard, *Vice Pres*
EMP: 10
SQ FT: 4,500
SALES (est): 2.8MM **Privately Held**
SIC: 1382 Oil & gas exploration services

(G-8804)
BIZBASH MEDIA INC (PA)
Also Called: Bizbash Masterplanner
115 W 27th St Fl 8 (10001-6217)
PHONE..................646 638-3602
David Adler, *CEO*
Richard Aaron, *President*
Carrie Sims, *Publisher*
Michele Laufik, *Editor*
Jean-Claude Chaouloff, *Vice Pres*
EMP: 55
SQ FT: 5,000
SALES (est): 11.9MM **Privately Held**
WEB: www.bizbash.com
SIC: 2759 2721 Advertising literature: printing; periodicals: publishing & printing

(G-8805)
BJ MAGAZINES INC
200 Varick St (10014-4810)
PHONE..................212 367-9705
Renu Hooda, *President*
EMP: 5
SALES (est): 530K **Privately Held**
SIC: 2721 Periodicals

(G-8806)
BLACK BOOK PHOTOGRAPHY INC
Also Called: Black Book, The
740 Broadway Ste 202 (10003-9518)
PHONE..................212 979-6700
Ted Rubin, *President*
Mike Compton, *Vice Pres*
Jared Kalfus, *Vice Pres*
Brandy Duckworth, *Opers Spvr*
Kelly Landress, *Sales Staff*
▲ EMP: 19 EST: 1970
SALES (est): 1.3MM
SALES (corp-wide): 3.3MM **Privately Held**
WEB: www.modernholdings.com
SIC: 2741 Directories: publishing only, not printed on site
PA: Modern Holding Company
601 Lexington Ave Rm 5900
New York NY

(G-8807)
BLACKBOOK MEDIA CORP
32 Union Sq E Ste 4l (10003-3209)
PHONE..................212 334-1800
Robert Hoff, *CEO*
Joseph Landry, *President*
EMP: 21
SQ FT: 1,500

SALES (est): 2.4MM **Privately Held**
SIC: 2721 Magazines: publishing & printing

(G-8808)
BLADES
659 Broadway (10012-2302)
PHONE..................212 477-1059
Myrick Bryan, *Buyer*
George Pohntes, *Manager*
Marvin Williams, *Manager*
▼ EMP: 10
SALES (est): 783.8K **Privately Held**
SIC: 3949 Skateboards

(G-8809)
BLANCHE P FIELD LLC
155 E 56th St Ph (10022-2718)
PHONE..................212 355-6616
Blanche Field, *President*
EMP: 25 EST: 1942
SQ FT: 3,000
SALES (est): 1.5MM **Privately Held**
SIC: 3999 5932 Shades, lamp or candle; antiques

(G-8810)
BLINC GROUP LLC
40 Fulton St Fl 6 (10038-1850)
PHONE..................212 879-2329
Arnaud Dumas De Rauly, *CEO*
EMP: 13
SALES (est): 1.4MM **Privately Held**
SIC: 3999

(G-8811)
BLISS FOODS INC
Also Called: Yorganic
275 Greenwich St Frnt 2 (10007-3824)
PHONE..................212 732-8888
Sung Kim, *President*
Shawn Reilly, *Vice Pres*
EMP: 5
SALES (est): 466.3K **Privately Held**
SIC: 2026 Yogurt

(G-8812)
BLISS FOODS INC
Also Called: Yorganic
275 Greenwich St Frnt 2 (10007-3824)
PHONE..................212 732-8888
EMP: 11 **Privately Held**
SIC: 2026 Mfg Fluid Milk

(G-8813)
BLISS-POSTON THE SECOND WIND
928 Broadway Ste 403 (10010-8151)
PHONE..................212 481-1055
Marcia Poston, *Vice Pres*
John Bliss, *Exec Dir*
EMP: 6
SALES (est): 522.9K **Privately Held**
SIC: 2011 Lard from carcasses slaughtered on site

(G-8814)
BLOOMSBURG CARPET INDS INC
Also Called: Silver Creek Carpet
11 E 26th St Frnt (10010-1431)
PHONE..................212 688-7447
Thomas J Habib, *Branch Mgr*
EMP: 6
SALES (corp-wide): 45MM **Privately Held**
SIC: 2273 Carpets & rugs
PA: Bloomsburg Carpet Industries, Inc.
4999 Columbia Blvd
Bloomsburg PA 17815
800 233-8773

(G-8815)
BLOOMSBURY PUBLISHING INC
Also Called: Bloomsbury USA
1385 Brdwy Fl 5 Flr 5 (10018)
PHONE..................212 419-5300
Nigel Newton, *President*
Doug White, *Principal*
Katie Gallof, *Editor*
Melissa Kavonic, *Editor*
Matthew Kopel, *Editor*
◆ EMP: 100

SALES (est): 14.8MM
SALES (corp-wide): 209.8MM **Privately Held**
WEB: www.bloomsburyusa.com
SIC: 2731 Book publishing
PA: Bloomsbury Publishing Plc
　　31 Bedford Avenue
　　London WC1B
　　207 631-5600

(G-8816)
BLU SAND LLC
26 Broadway Fl 8 (10004-1744)
PHONE.............................212 564-1147
Eddie Shomer, *Vice Pres*
Morris Sitt,
▲ **EMP:** 9
SALES (est): 1.1MM **Privately Held**
WEB: www.blusand.com
SIC: 2211 Towels & toweling, cotton

(G-8817)
BLUE AND WHITE PUBLISHING INC
Also Called: Bwog
425 Riverside Dr Apt 3c (10025-7724)
PHONE.............................215 431-3339
Jake Hershman, *CEO*
EMP: 10 **EST:** 2013
SALES (est): 504.7K **Privately Held**
SIC: 2711 Newspapers: publishing only, not printed on site

(G-8818)
BLUE DUCK TRADING LTD
463 7th Ave Rm 806 (10018-8712)
PHONE.............................212 268-3122
Barry Novick, *President*
▲ **EMP:** 8
SQ FT: 4,500
SALES: 3MM **Privately Held**
WEB: www.blueduckshearling.com
SIC: 2339 2311 Women's & misses' jackets & coats, except sportswear; coats, tailored, men's & boys': from purchased materials

(G-8819)
BLUE HORIZON MEDIA INC (PA)
11 Park Pl Rm 1508 (10007-2816)
PHONE.............................212 661-7878
Geoffrey D Lurie, *COO*
David Bernstein, *CFO*
EMP: 16
SQ FT: 16,000
SALES (est): 2.8MM **Privately Held**
WEB: www.bluehrzn.com
SIC: 2721 Magazines: publishing only, not printed on site

(G-8820)
BLUE TEE CORP (PA)
387 Park Ave S Fl 5 (10016-1495)
PHONE.............................212 598-0880
David P Alldian, *Ch of Bd*
William M Kelly, *President*
Annette Marino D'Arienzo, *Exec Dir*
◆ **EMP:** 7
SQ FT: 2,500
SALES (est): 124.4MM **Privately Held**
SIC: 3533 3589 5093 3715 Water well drilling equipment; garbage disposers & compactors, commercial; ferrous metal scrap & waste; semitrailers for truck tractors; water quality monitoring & control systems; structural shapes, iron or steel

(G-8821)
BLUE WOLF GROUP LLC (HQ)
11 E 26th St Fl 21 (10010-1413)
PHONE.............................866 455-9653
Tim Anderson, *Principal*
Eric Berridge, *Mng Member*
Michael Kirven,
EMP: 100
SQ FT: 5,000
SALES: 80.4MM
SALES (corp-wide): 79.5B **Publicly Held**
WEB: www.bluewolfgroup.com
SIC: 7372 Business oriented computer software
PA: International Business Machines Corporation
　　1 New Orchard Rd Ste 1 # 1
　　Armonk NY 10504
　　914 499-1900

(G-8822)
BLUESOHO (PA)
160 Varick St Fl 2 (10013-1251)
PHONE.............................646 805-2583
Jennifer Bergin, *Managing Prtnr*
Tom Galbreath, *Managing Prtnr*
John Puterbaugh, *Managing Prtnr*
Stephanie Stanton, *Managing Prtnr*
David Zuaiter, *General Mgr*
EMP: 10
SALES (est): 2.4MM **Privately Held**
SIC: 2752 Commercial printing, offset

(G-8823)
BLUM & FINK INC
Also Called: Fleurette
158 W 29th St Fl 12 (10001-5300)
PHONE.............................212 695-2606
Stanley Blum, *President*
▲ **EMP:** 12 **EST:** 1961
SQ FT: 10,000
SALES (est): 1.7MM **Privately Held**
SIC: 2371 5137 Fur coats & other fur apparel; fur clothing, women's & children's

(G-8824)
BMG RIGHTS MANAGEMENT (US) LLC (DH)
Also Called: Bmg Chrysalis
1 Park Ave Ste 1800 (10016-5804)
PHONE.............................212 561-3000
Hartwig Masuch, *CEO*
Jon Cohen, *Exec VP*
Claribel Caraballo, *Vice Pres*
Pamela Lillig, *Vice Pres*
Cyndi Lynott, *Vice Pres*
EMP: 20
SALES (est): 3.6MM
SALES (corp-wide): 75.3MM **Privately Held**
SIC: 2731 Books: publishing only
HQ: Bertelsmann Se & Co. Kgaa
　　Carl-Bertelsmann-Str. 270
　　Gutersloh 33335
　　524 180-0

(G-8825)
BNNS CO INC
71 W 47th St Ste 600-601 (10036-2866)
PHONE.............................212 302-1844
Nick Barhnakov, *President*
Simon Nikhamin, *Vice Pres*
EMP: 8
SALES (est): 510K **Privately Held**
WEB: www.bnnsco.com
SIC: 3961 Costume jewelry

(G-8826)
BNP MEDIA INC
350 5th Ave Fl 60 (10118-6001)
PHONE.............................646 849-7100
Matt McLiverty, *Sales Staff*
Domenika Eklem, *Marketing Staff*
EMP: 68
SALES (corp-wide): 156.9MM **Privately Held**
SIC: 2721 Trade journals: publishing only, not printed on site
PA: Bnp Media, Inc.
　　2401 W Big Beaver Rd # 700
　　Troy MI 48084
　　248 362-3700

(G-8827)
BOARDMAN SIMONS PUBLISHING (PA)
Also Called: Davidson Publishing
88 Pine St 23 (10005-1809)
PHONE.............................212 620-7200
Arthur J McGinnis Jr, *President*
EMP: 40
SALES (est): 9MM **Privately Held**
WEB: www.sbpub.com
SIC: 2721 2731 8249 Periodicals: publishing only; books: publishing only; correspondence school

(G-8828)
BOCKS INC
Also Called: Cleancult
195 Chrystie St Rm 502h (10002-1224)
PHONE.............................833 437-3363
Ryan Lupberger, *CEO*
Zachary Bedrosian, *CTO*
EMP: 10

SQ FT: 1,000
SALES: 3.6MM **Privately Held**
SIC: 2841 Soap & other detergents

(G-8829)
BOEING COMPANY
304 Park Ave S (10010-4301)
PHONE.............................201 259-9400
Donald Boeing, *Branch Mgr*
EMP: 897
SALES (corp-wide): 101.1B **Publicly Held**
SIC: 3721 Airplanes, fixed or rotary wing
PA: The Boeing Company
　　100 N Riverside Plz
　　Chicago IL 60606
　　312 544-2000

(G-8830)
BOEING DIGITAL SOLUTIONS INC
444 Park Ave S Fl 10 (10016-7321)
PHONE.............................212 478-1200
EMP: 5
SALES (corp-wide): 101.1B **Publicly Held**
SIC: 7372 Publishers' computer software
HQ: Boeing Digital Solutions, Inc
　　55 Inverness Dr E
　　Englewood CO 80112
　　303 799-9090

(G-8831)
BOLLMAN HAT COMPANY
Also Called: Betmar
411 5th Ave Fl 2 (10016-2276)
PHONE.............................212 981-9836
Sean Leon, *Mktg Dir*
Alice Gallant, *Manager*
Paula Calvert, *Creative Dir*
EMP: 6
SALES (corp-wide): 291.8MM **Privately Held**
WEB: www.bollmanhats.com
SIC: 2353 Hats, caps & millinery
PA: Bollman Hat Company
　　110 E Main St
　　Adamstown PA 19501
　　717 484-4361

(G-8832)
BOMBAS LLC
37 E 18th St Fl 4 (10003-2001)
PHONE.............................800 314-0980
Morgan Cummings, *Manager*
Andrew Heath,
EMP: 7 **EST:** 2013
SALES (est): 635.7K **Privately Held**
SIC: 2252 Anklets & socks; socks

(G-8833)
BOMBER LLC (PA)
Also Called: Bomber Ski
681 5th Ave Ph 13 (10022-4326)
PHONE.............................212 980-2442
Robert Cooper, *CEO*
Ryan Giunta, *Chief Mktg Ofcr*
EMP: 5
SALES (est): 392.4K **Privately Held**
SIC: 3949 Snow skis

(G-8834)
BONELLI FOODS LLC
139 Fulton St Rm 314 (10038-2537)
PHONE.............................212 346-0942
Tommaso Asaro, *Mng Member*
▲ **EMP:** 1
SQ FT: 1,000
SALES: 1.4MM **Privately Held**
SIC: 2079 Olive oil

(G-8835)
BOOM LLC
Also Called: Boom Creative Development
800 3rd Ave Fl 2 (10022-7683)
PHONE.............................646 218-0752
Art Degaetano, *President*
Glenn Marks, *COO*
Rick Barr, *Vice Pres*
Shef Worboys, *IT/INT Sup*
◆ **EMP:** 35
SQ FT: 12,000
SALES: 5.8MM **Privately Held**
WEB: www.boomllc.com
SIC: 3999 5122 Atomizers, toiletry; cosmetics, perfumes & hair products

(G-8836)
BOOSEY AND HAWKES INC (PA)
229 W 28th St 11 (10001-5915)
PHONE.............................212 358-5300
Steven Lankenau, *Vice Pres*
Paul Vernon, *CTO*
Hannah Waddell, *Executive*
▲ **EMP:** 20
SALES (est): 3MM **Privately Held**
WEB: www.christopherrouse.com
SIC: 2741 7389 Music book & sheet music publishing; music copying service; music distribution systems

(G-8837)
BORGHESE INC (PA)
Also Called: Princess Marcella Borghese
3 E 54th St Fl 20 (10022-3130)
PHONE.............................212 659-5318
Christopher Stephen West, *President*
Frank Palladino, *CFO*
Michael Tugetman, *Treasurer*
Maria Monastersky, *Manager*
◆ **EMP:** 25
SQ FT: 10,000
SALES (est): 7.1MM **Privately Held**
WEB: www.chateauxdemeures.com
SIC: 2844 5961 Toilet preparations; cosmetics & perfumes, mail order

(G-8838)
BOTKIER NY LLC
19 W 34th St Fl 7 (10001-0055)
PHONE.............................212 343-2782
David Seamon,
EMP: 8
SALES (est): 604.8K **Privately Held**
SIC: 2339 Women's & misses' accessories
PA: Trebbianno, Llc
　　19 W 34th St Fl 7
　　New York NY 10001

(G-8839)
BOUCHERON JOAILLERIE USA INC
Also Called: Parfums Boucheron Jewelry
460 Park Ave Fl 12 (10022-1906)
PHONE.............................212 715-7330
Thomas Indermuhle, *Ch of Bd*
EMP: 8
SALES (est): 571.7K
SALES (corp-wide): 258.7MM **Privately Held**
SIC: 3423 3915 Jewelers' hand tools; jewelers' findings & materials
HQ: Boucheron Holding
　　26 Place Vendome
　　Paris 1er Arrondissement 75001
　　142 444-244

(G-8840)
BOULEVARD ARTS INC
1133 Broadway Ste 1523 (10010-7927)
PHONE.............................917 968-8693
Elizabeth Reede, *CEO*
Chelsea Menzies, *Vice Pres*
Robert Knowles, *Surgery Dir*
EMP: 6 **EST:** 2013
SALES: 300K **Privately Held**
SIC: 7372 Home entertainment computer software

(G-8841)
BOURNE MUSIC PUBLISHERS
Also Called: Bourne Co
35 W 45th St Fl 2 (10036-4918)
PHONE.............................212 391-4300
Mary Elizabeth Bourne, *Owner*
EMP: 19
SQ FT: 6,500
SALES (est): 943.2K **Privately Held**
WEB: www.bournemusic.com
SIC: 2741 Music, sheet: publishing only, not printed on site

(G-8842)
BOYLAN BOTTLING CO INC
6 E 43rd St Fl 18 (10017-4657)
PHONE.............................800 289-7978
Ronald C Fiorina, *President*
Mark Fiorina, *Vice Pres*
▲ **EMP:** 30 **EST:** 1891
SQ FT: 25,000

SALES (est): 6.3MM **Privately Held**
WEB: www.boylanbottling.com
SIC: 2086 2087 Soft drinks: packaged in cans, bottles, etc.; beverage bases, concentrates, syrups, powders & mixes

(G-8843)
BPE STUDIO INC
270 W 38th St Rm 702 (10018-1520)
PHONE..................................212 868-9896
Dan Ping Zhang, *President*
EMP: 5
SALES (est): 410K **Privately Held**
SIC: 2396 Linings, apparel: made from purchased materials

(G-8844)
BRADLEY MARKETING GROUP INC
1431 Broadway Fl 12 (10018-1912)
PHONE..................................212 967-6100
James Lemmo, *Principal*
Edward Brucia, *Vice Pres*
Kathy Reccardi, *Vice Pres*
Adam Perry, *VP Sales*
Jackie Sneyers, *Executive Asst*
EMP: 6
SALES (corp-wide): 20.1MM **Privately Held**
WEB: www.bradleymg.com
SIC: 2759 Commercial printing
PA: Bradley Marketing Group, Inc.
170 Wilbur Pl Ste 700
Bohemia NY 11716
631 231-9200

(G-8845)
BRAINPOP LLC
Also Called: Brainpop Group
71 W 23rd St Fl 17 (10010-4183)
PHONE..................................212 574-6017
Raffi Kahana, *Senior VP*
Mike Watanabe, *Senior VP*
Daniel Donohue, *Vice Pres*
Demian Johnson, *Vice Pres*
Avraham Kadar, *Mng Member*
EMP: 50
SALES (est): 6.6MM **Privately Held**
SIC: 7372 Educational computer software

(G-8846)
BRAL NADER FINE JEWELRY INC
576 5th Ave (10036-4807)
PHONE..................................800 493-1222
EMP: 5
SALES: 3MM **Privately Held**
SIC: 3911 Mfg Fine Jewelry

(G-8847)
BRANNKEY INC (PA)
Also Called: Honora
1385 Broadway Fl 14 (10018-6017)
PHONE..................................212 371-1515
Joel Schechter, *Ch of Bd*
Roberta Schechter, *Vice Pres*
Michael Scheerer, *Marketing Staff*
▲ EMP: 52 EST: 1969
SQ FT: 6,500
SALES (est): 10.6MM **Privately Held**
WEB: www.honora.com
SIC: 3911 Jewelry, precious metal

(G-8848)
BRASILANS PRESS PBLCATIONS INC
60 W 46th St Rm 302 (10036)
P.O. Box 985 (10185-0985)
PHONE..................................212 764-6161
EMP: 40
SALES (est): 2.1MM **Privately Held**
SIC: 2711 Newspapers-Publishing/Printing

(G-8849)
BRAZE INC
330 W 34th St Fl 18 (10001-2406)
PHONE..................................504 327-7269
William Magnuson, *CEO*
Myles Kleeger, *President*
Gareth Ballard, *Vice Pres*
Warrick Godfrey, *Vice Pres*
Oliver Bell, *Treasurer*
EMP: 55 EST: 2011
SALES: 28.3MM **Privately Held**
SIC: 7372 Application computer software

(G-8850)
BREATHER PRODUCTS US INC (PA)
455 Broadway Fl 3 (10013-2575)
PHONE..................................800 471-8704
Julien Smith, *CEO*
Caterina Rizzi, *Vice Pres*
Gianna Doukas, *Opers Staff*
Walter Mangandi, *Opers Staff*
EMP: 33 EST: 2013
SALES (est): 4.2MM **Privately Held**
SIC: 2521 Wood office furniture

(G-8851)
BRIGANTINE INC
225 W 37th St (10018-5703)
PHONE..................................212 354-8550
Isidore Friedman, *Ch of Bd*
Mark Friedman, *President*
Paul Friedman, *President*
William Fuchs, *Treasurer*
EMP: 5
SQ FT: 10,000
SALES (est): 635.1K
SALES (corp-wide): 8MM **Privately Held**
WEB: www.brigantine.com
SIC: 2329 2339 Men's & boys' leather, wool & down-filled outerwear; women's & misses' jackets & coats, except sportswear
PA: S. Rothschild & Co., Inc.
1407 Broadway Fl 10
New York NY 10018
212 354-8550

(G-8852)
BRIGHT KIDS NYC INC
177 E 87th St 402 (10128-2226)
PHONE..................................917 539-4575
Bige Doruk, *CEO*
Taylor Kelly, *Director*
▲ EMP: 40 EST: 2009
SALES: 0 **Privately Held**
SIC: 2731 8299 8748 Textbooks: publishing & printing; tutoring school; testing service, educational or personnel

(G-8853)
BRIGHTIDEA INCORPORATED
1040 Ave Of The Ameri 18a (10018-3877)
PHONE..................................212 594-4500
Matthew Greeley, *CEO*
EMP: 97
SALES (corp-wide): 8.6MM **Privately Held**
SIC: 7372 Prepackaged software
PA: Brightidea Incorporated
25 Pacific Ave
San Francisco CA
415 814-3817

(G-8854)
BRILLIANT JEWELERS/MJJ INC
Also Called: Mjj Brilliant
902 Broadway Fl 18 (10010-6038)
PHONE..................................212 353-2326
Nicolay Yakubovich, *Ch of Bd*
Robert Schwartz, *COO*
Jason Yakubovich, *Opers Staff*
Abdul Kampani, *CFO*
Mihir Patel, *Finance Mgr*
EMP: 120
SALES (est): 17.7MM **Privately Held**
WEB: www.mjjbrilliant.com
SIC: 3911 Jewelry, precious metal

(G-8855)
BRISTOL SEAMLESS RING CORP
209 W 86th St Apt 817 (10024-3337)
PHONE..................................212 874-2645
Irving Skydell, *President*
EMP: 16 EST: 1910
SALES (est): 173.1K **Privately Held**
SIC: 3911 Jewelry, precious metal

(G-8856)
BRISTOL-MYERS SQUIBB COMPANY (PA)
430 E 29th St Fl 14 (10016-8367)
PHONE..................................212 546-4000
Giovanni Caforio, *CEO*
Sandra Leung, *Exec VP*
Thomas J Lynch, *Exec VP*
Paul Biondi, *Senior VP*

Adam Dubow, *Senior VP*
EMP: 1200 EST: 1887
SALES: 22.5B **Publicly Held**
WEB: www.bms.com
SIC: 2834 Pharmaceutical preparations

(G-8857)
BRISTOL-MYERS SQUIBB INTL CORP (HQ)
430 E 29th St (10016-8367)
PHONE..................................212 546-4000
Peter R Dolan, *Ch of Bd*
EMP: 29
SALES (est): 12.4MM
SALES (corp-wide): 22.5B **Publicly Held**
WEB: www.bms.com
SIC: 2834 Pharmaceutical preparations
PA: Bristol-Myers Squibb Company
430 E 29th St Fl 14
New York NY 10016
212 546-4000

(G-8858)
BROADCAST MANAGER INC
Also Called: Promosuite
65 Broadway Ste 602 (10006-2519)
PHONE..................................212 509-1200
Rocco Macri, *CEO*
Christopher Bungo, *President*
Craig Zimmerman, *President*
Rachel Field, *VP Sales*
Andrew Smith, *Manager*
EMP: 8
SALES (est): 890K **Privately Held**
WEB: www.broadcastmanager.org
SIC: 3651 Amplifiers: radio, public address or musical instrument

(G-8859)
BROADWAY TECHNOLOGY LLC (PA)
28 Liberty St Fl 50 (10005-1498)
PHONE..................................646 912-6450
Jonathan Fieldman, *COO*
Andy Browning, *Vice Pres*
Mary Loeffler, *Vice Pres*
Sheyenne Brown, *Opers-Prdtn-Mfg*
Preston Mesick, *Accounts Mgr*
EMP: 20
SALES: 1MM **Privately Held**
WEB: www.broadwaytechnology.com
SIC: 7372 Business oriented computer software

(G-8860)
BROKEN THREADS INC
147 W 35th St Ste 1401 (10001-8213)
PHONE..................................212 730-4351
Rohan Shah, *Ch of Bd*
▲ EMP: 2 EST: 2007
SQ FT: 500
SALES (est): 4.1MM **Privately Held**
SIC: 2329 Men's & boys' sportswear & athletic clothing

(G-8861)
BROOKE MAYA INC
124 W 36th St Fl 7 (10018-8845)
PHONE..................................212 268-2626
Allen Hakimian, *President*
◆ EMP: 35
SQ FT: 11,000
SALES (est): 3MM **Privately Held**
SIC: 2361 Dresses: girls', children's & infants'

(G-8862)
BROWN PUBLISHING NETWORK INC
122 E 42nd St Rm 2810 (10168-2893)
PHONE..................................212 682-3330
Marie Brown, *Branch Mgr*
EMP: 5
SALES (corp-wide): 7.2MM **Privately Held**
WEB: www.brownpubnet.com
SIC: 2731 Textbooks: publishing only, not printed on site
PA: Brown Publishing Network, Inc.
10 City Sq Ste 3
Charlestown MA 02129
781 547-7600

(G-8863)
BROWNSTONE PUBLISHERS INC
149 5th Ave Fl 10 (10010-6832)
PHONE..................................212 473-8200
John Striker, *President*
Peter Campfield, *Exec VP*
Andrew Shapiro, *Vice Pres*
Janet Urbina, *CFO*
Sean Richter, *Human Res Mgr*
EMP: 46
SQ FT: 10,000
SALES (est): 3.4MM **Privately Held**
SIC: 2721 2741 Periodicals: publishing only; miscellaneous publishing

(G-8864)
BRUMIS IMPORTS INC
Also Called: Core Home
42 W 39th St Fl 4 (10018-3841)
PHONE..................................646 845-6000
Alan Bram, *President*
Steven Bram, *Vice Pres*
Yana Shum, *Controller*
Leslie Sheroda, *Sales Staff*
Taggart Shannon, *Director*
▲ EMP: 60
SALES (est): 328MM **Privately Held**
SIC: 3634 Housewares, excluding cooking appliances & utensils

(G-8865)
BSO ENERGY CORP
125 Park Ave Ste 2507 (10017-5529)
PHONE..................................212 520-1827
Sergio S Correa, *President*
Roberto A Santos, *Director*
EMP: 10
SALES (est): 1.3MM **Privately Held**
SIC: 2821 Thermoplastic materials

(G-8866)
BULKLEY DUNTON (DH)
1 Penn Plz Ste 2814 (10119-2814)
PHONE..................................212 863-1800
Doehner George, *President*
Joseph Debellis, *Vice Pres*
Jo Oliver, *Vice Pres*
Sally Golczewski, *Accounts Mgr*
Westbrook Pegler, *Sales Staff*
EMP: 34
SALES (est): 44.7MM
SALES (corp-wide): 8.7B **Publicly Held**
SIC: 2741 Miscellaneous publishing
HQ: Veritiv Operating Company
1000 Abernathy Rd Bldg 4
Atlanta GA 30328
770 391-8200

(G-8867)
BULL STREET LLC
Also Called: Supdates
19 W 69th St Apt 201 (10023-4750)
PHONE..................................212 495-9855
Jared Gettinger,
EMP: 5
SALES (est): 266K **Privately Held**
SIC: 7372 Application computer software

(G-8868)
BUREAU OF NATIONAL AFFAIRS INC
25 W 43rd St Ste 1007 (10036-7410)
PHONE..................................212 687-4530
John Herzfeld, *Manager*
EMP: 23
SALES (corp-wide): 1.8B **Privately Held**
SIC: 2711 Newspapers
HQ: The Bureau Of National Affairs Inc
1801 S Bell St Ste Cn110
Arlington VA 22202
703 341-3000

(G-8869)
BURLEN CORP
6 E 32nd St Fl 10 (10016-5415)
PHONE..................................212 684-0052
Steve Klein, *President*
EMP: 12
SALES (corp-wide): 389.2MM **Privately Held**
SIC: 2342 Girdles & panty girdles

HQ: Burlen Corp.
1904 Mccormick Dr
Tifton GA 31793
229 382-4100

(G-8870)
BURNS ARCHIVE PHTGRAPHIC DISTR
140 E 38th St Frnt 1 (10016-2686)
PHONE..................................212 889-1938
Stanley Burns MD, *Owner*
▼ EMP: 4
SQ FT: 4,000
SALES (est): 1MM **Privately Held**
WEB: www.burnsarchive.com
SIC: 2731 8099 Book publishing; medical photography & art

(G-8871)
BUSINESS EXPERT PRESS LLC
222 E 46th St Rm 203 (10017-2906)
PHONE..................................212 661-8810
Scott Isenberg, *Executive*
Michael Dupler,
EMP: 15
SALES (est): 6.7K **Privately Held**
SIC: 2741 Miscellaneous publishing

(G-8872)
BUSINESS INTEGRITY INC (DH)
79 Madison Ave Fl 2 (10016-7805)
PHONE..................................718 238-2008
Tim Allen, *President*
Thomas Mule, *COO*
Mark Winders, *Vice Pres*
EMP: 6
SQ FT: 3,000
SALES (est): 805.5K **Privately Held**
WEB: www.business-integrity.com
SIC: 7372 Business oriented computer software

(G-8873)
BUSINESS JOURNALS
1166 Ave Of The America (10036-2708)
PHONE..................................212 790-5100
Keith Edwards, *Manager*
EMP: 11
SALES (corp-wide): 1.3B **Privately Held**
SIC: 2711 Newspapers
HQ: The Business Journals
120 W Morehead St Ste 420
Charlotte NC 28202
704 371-3248

(G-8874)
BUTTONS & TRIMCOM INC
519 8th Ave Rm 26 (10018-5275)
PHONE..................................212 868-1971
Peter Frankel, *President*
Susan Frankel, *Vice Pres*
EMP: 13
SQ FT: 2,200
SALES (est): 1.5MM **Privately Held**
SIC: 3965 3089 3499 Buttons & parts; buckles & buckle parts; novelties, plastic; novelties & specialties, metal

(G-8875)
BUZZOOLE INC
450 Park Ave S Fl 3 (10016-7320)
PHONE..................................347 964-0120
Fabrizio Perrone, *CEO*
EMP: 7
SALES (est): 193.9K **Privately Held**
SIC: 2741

(G-8876)
BY ROBERT JAMES
74 Orchard St (10002-4515)
PHONE..................................212 253-2121
Robert Loomis, *Principal*
EMP: 5
SALES (est): 658.9K **Privately Held**
SIC: 2329 5611 Men's & boys' clothing; men's & boys' clothing stores

(G-8877)
BYELOCORP SCIENTIFIC INC (PA)
76 Perry St (10014-3238)
PHONE..................................212 785-2580
Lowell A Mintz, *Ch of Bd*
William Begell, *President*
Kathleen Kent, *Vice Pres*

EMP: 27
SALES (est): 1.6MM **Privately Held**
SIC: 3491 3443 Industrial valves; industrial vessels, tanks & containers

(G-8878)
BYER CALIFORNIA
1407 Broadway Rm 807 (10018-5149)
PHONE..................................212 944-8989
Martin Bernstein, *Manager*
EMP: 7
SALES (corp-wide): 347.6MM **Privately Held**
WEB: www.byer.com
SIC: 3842 Surgical appliances & supplies
PA: Byer California
66 Potrero Ave
San Francisco CA 94103
415 626-7844

(G-8879)
BYLINER INC
27 W 24th St Ste 202 (10010-3299)
PHONE..................................415 680-3608
John Tayman, *CEO*
Deanna Brown, *President*
Theodore Barnett, *COO*
EMP: 20 EST: 2010
SALES (est): 1.4MM **Privately Held**
SIC: 2731 2741 Book publishing;

(G-8880)
BYTE CONSULTING INC
295 Madison Ave Fl 35 (10017-6414)
PHONE..................................646 500-8606
Rak Chugh, *President*
Shridhar Kumar, *Controller*
Dan Costin, *Director*
Thomas Loop, *Bd of Directors*
Kai Chuang, *Executive Asst*
EMP: 8
SALES (est): 943.6K **Privately Held**
WEB: www.byteconsulting.com
SIC: 7372 Prepackaged software

(G-8881)
C O P R A INC
Also Called: Copra
215 E Broadway Apt 2r (10002-5518)
PHONE..................................917 224-1727
Benjamin Minges, *President*
EMP: 5
SQ FT: 1,900
SALES (est): 153.8K **Privately Held**
SIC: 2037 Frozen fruits & vegetables

(G-8882)
CA INC (HQ)
520 Madison Ave (10022-4213)
PHONE..................................800 225-5224
Michael P Gregoire, *CEO*
Joseph Walther, *Principal*
Chantal Martinez, *Counsel*
Anthony Radesca, *Senior VP*
Barbara Baldwin, *Vice Pres*
EMP: 1500 EST: 1974
SALES: 4.2B
SALES (corp-wide): 20.8B **Publicly Held**
WEB: www.cai.com
SIC: 7372 8742 Business oriented computer software; application computer software; management consulting services
PA: Broadcom Inc.
1320 Ridder Park Dr
San Jose CA 95131
408 433-8000

(G-8883)
CABBA PRINTING INCORPORATED
Also Called: Copyright Reprographics
133 E 55th St (10022-3502)
P.O. Box 3444 (10163-3444)
PHONE..................................212 319-4747
Carol L Schor, *President*
William F Bloxham, *Admin Sec*
EMP: 5
SQ FT: 590
SALES (est): 528K **Privately Held**
WEB: www.copyrightreprographics.com
SIC: 2752 Commercial printing, offset

(G-8884)
CABRIOLE DESIGNS INC
315 E 91st St Ste 3 (10128-5938)
PHONE..................................212 593-4528

Louis Tonna, *President*
EMP: 6
SALES (est): 476.2K **Privately Held**
WEB: www.cabrioledesign.com
SIC: 2391 Curtains & draperies

(G-8885)
CACHET INDUSTRIES INC
463 Fashion Ave Rm 601 (10018-8720)
PHONE..................................212 944-2188
David Darouvar, *President*
Mark Naim, *Admin Sec*
▲ EMP: 30
SQ FT: 12,000
SALES (est): 4.8MM **Privately Held**
SIC: 2335 Wedding gowns & dresses

(G-8886)
CAI INC (PA)
Also Called: Copen International Limited
430 E 56th St (10022-4171)
PHONE..................................212 819-0008
Carin Trundle, *CEO*
Barry Emmanuel, *President*
◆ EMP: 4
SQ FT: 2,300
SALES (est): 2.3MM **Privately Held**
WEB: www.midsouthmfg.com
SIC: 2211 2396 Pocketing twill, cotton; waistbands, trouser

(G-8887)
CAI DESIGN INC
240 W 37th St Rm 303 (10018-2419)
PHONE..................................212 401-9973
Yiming Cai, *Partner*
Yisei Cai, *Partner*
▲ EMP: 14
SALES (est): 554.9K **Privately Held**
SIC: 2339 Sportswear, women's

(G-8888)
CAITHNESS EQUITIES CORPORATION (PA)
Also Called: Shepherds Flat
565 5th Ave Fl 29 (10017-2478)
PHONE..................................212 599-2112
James D Bishop Jr, *Ch of Bd*
James C Sullivan, *Senior VP*
Christopher T Mc Callion, *Vice Pres*
Gail Conboy, *Admin Sec*
EMP: 23
SALES (est): 38.8MM **Privately Held**
WEB: www.caithnessenergy.com
SIC: 3491 4911 4961 6162 Compressed gas cylinder valves; generation, electric power; steam supply systems, including geothermal; mortgage bankers

(G-8889)
CALIFORNIA PETRO TRNSPT CORP
114 W 47th St (10036-1510)
PHONE..................................212 302-5151
Frank Bilotta, *President*
EMP: 2
SALES (est): 1.9MM **Privately Held**
SIC: 2911 Petroleum refining

(G-8890)
CALIFORNIA US HOLDINGS INC
417 5th Ave Lbby 7th (10016-3380)
PHONE..................................212 726-6500
Bruno Bonnell, *President*
EMP: 564
SQ FT: 90,000
SALES (est): 28.4MM
SALES (corp-wide): 3.2MM **Privately Held**
SIC: 7372 5045 Prepackaged software; computers, peripherals & software
PA: Atari Sa
Atari
Paris 9e Arrondissement 75009
972 335-791

(G-8891)
CALIGOR RX INC
1226 Lexington Ave Frnt 1 (10028-1446)
PHONE..................................212 988-0590
Tammy Bishop, *CEO*
EMP: 29 EST: 2011
SALES (est): 6MM **Privately Held**
SIC: 2834 Pharmaceutical preparations

(G-8892)
CALLAWAY ARTS & ENTRMT INC
41 Union Sq W Ste 1101 (10003-3253)
PHONE..................................646 465-4667
John Lee, *CEO*
Nicholas Callaway, *President*
EMP: 11
SALES (est): 679.9K **Privately Held**
SIC: 2731 Books: publishing & printing

(G-8893)
CALLAWAY DIGITAL ARTS INC
41 Union Sq W Ste 1101 (10003-3253)
PHONE..................................212 675-3050
Rex Ishibashi, *CEO*
John Lee, *President*
Nicholas Callaway, *Officer*
EMP: 30
SALES (est): 1.8MM **Privately Held**
SIC: 7372 Application computer software

(G-8894)
CALVIN KLEIN INC
654 Madison Ave (10065-8445)
PHONE..................................212 292-9000
Fax: 212 292-9001
EMP: 50
SALES (corp-wide): 8.2B **Publicly Held**
SIC: 3161 Mfg Luggage
HQ: Calvin Klein, Inc.
205 W 39th St Lbby 2
New York NY 10018
212 719-2600

(G-8895)
CALYPSO TECHNOLOGY INC
99 Park Ave (10016-1601)
PHONE..................................212 905-0735
Thomas M Hans, *Sales Mgr*
Sarah Ristine, *Sales Staff*
Ken Byrne, *Manager*
Robert Dennis, *Manager*
John Blake, *Sr Software Eng*
EMP: 25
SALES (corp-wide): 177.9K **Privately Held**
WEB: www.calypso.com
SIC: 7372 Prepackaged software
HQ: Calypso Technology, Inc.
595 Market St Ste 700
San Francisco CA 94105
415 817-2400

(G-8896)
CAMBRIDGE INFO GROUP INC (PA)
Also Called: C I G
888 7th Ave Ste 1701 (10106-1799)
PHONE..................................301 961-6700
Andrew M Snyder, *CEO*
Robert Snyder, *Chairman*
Michael K Chung, *COO*
Barbara Inkellis, *Senior VP*
Larisa Avner Trainor, *Senior VP*
EMP: 12
SQ FT: 24,000
SALES (est): 345.3MM **Privately Held**
WEB: www.csa.com
SIC: 2741 Technical manual & paper publishing

(G-8897)
CAMBRIDGE UNIVERSITY PRESS
165 Broadway Fl 20 (10006-1435)
PHONE..................................212 337-5000
Pamela Cooper, *Sales Staff*
Stephanie Kaelin, *Sales Staff*
Jeffrey Zingle, *Sales Staff*
Tania Saiz, *Mktg Dir*
Jessica Frisenda, *Marketing Mgr*
EMP: 80
SALES (corp-wide): 430.8MM **Privately Held**
SIC: 2731 2721 4226 Books: publishing only; periodicals; special warehousing & storage
PA: Cambridge University Press
University Printing House
Cambridge CAMBS CB2 8
122 335-8331

(G-8898)
CAMINUS CORPORATION (DH)
340 Madison Ave Fl 8 (10173-0899)
PHONE....................212 515-3600
John A Andrus, *President*
EMP: 65 EST: 1999
SALES (est): 11.7MM
SALES (corp-wide): 8.4B **Publicly Held**
SIC: 7372 7379 Business oriented computer software; computer related consulting services
HQ: Fis Data Systems Inc.
200 Campus Dr
Collegeville PA 19426
484 582-2000

(G-8899)
CAMPBELL ALLIANCE GROUP INC
335 Madison Ave Fl 17 (10017-4677)
PHONE....................212 377-2740
EMP: 24 EST: 1997
SQ FT: 50
SALES (est): 3MM **Privately Held**
SIC: 2834 Mfg Pharmaceutical Preparations

(G-8900)
CANADA GOOSE INC
601 W 26th St Rm 1745 (10001-1141)
PHONE....................888 276-6297
EMP: 5
SALES (corp-wide): 18.7MM **Privately Held**
SIC: 2339 Uniforms, athletic: women's, misses' & juniors'
PA: Canada Goose Inc
250 Bowie Ave
Toronto ON M6E 4
416 780-9850

(G-8901)
CANALI USA INC (DH)
415 W 13th St Fl 2 (10014-1114)
PHONE....................212 767-0205
Paolo Canali, *CEO*
Georgio Canali, *Vice Pres*
David Granados, *Director*
▲ EMP: 41
SALES (est): 2.1MM **Privately Held**
SIC: 2311 Suits, men's & boys': made from purchased materials
HQ: Canali Spa
Via Lombardia 17
Sovico 20845
039 201-4226

(G-8902)
CANDEX SOLUTIONS INC
420 Lexington Ave Rm 300 (10170-0399)
PHONE....................215 650-3214
Jeremy Lappin, *CEO*
Mark Steinke, *President*
Marianna Suckova, *Vice Pres*
Shani Vaza, *Vice Pres*
EMP: 5
SALES: 843.6K **Privately Held**
SIC: 7372 Business oriented computer software

(G-8903)
CANDLESTICKS INC
112 W 34th St Fl 18 (10120-0911)
PHONE....................212 947-8900
▲ EMP: 10
SQ FT: 5,500
SALES (est): 1.2MM **Privately Held**
SIC: 2341 2369 2339 2322 Mfg Clothing

(G-8904)
CANE SUGAR LLC
Also Called: Cane Simple
950 3rd Ave Ste 2200 (10022-2773)
PHONE....................212 329-2695
Reid Chase, *Mng Member*
EMP: 6
SALES: 230K **Privately Held**
SIC: 2062 Cane syrup from purchased raw sugar

(G-8905)
CANOPY CANOPY CANOPY INC
Also Called: Triple Canopy
264 Canal St Ste 3w (10013-3592)
PHONE....................347 529-5182

Peter Russo, *President*
Bidita Choudhury, *Editor*
Momo Ishiguro, *Asst Director*
EMP: 10
SALES: 1.1MM **Privately Held**
SIC: 2721 Periodicals: publishing & printing

(G-8906)
CANT LIVE WITHOUT IT LLC
Also Called: S'Well Bottle
28 W 23rd St Fl 5 (10010-5259)
PHONE....................844 517-9355
Sarah Kauss, *CEO*
Lance Mayer, *Sales Staff*
Lara Garvilla, *Executive Asst*
▲ EMP: 100
SQ FT: 25,000
SALES (est): 36.8MM **Privately Held**
SIC: 3429 Vacuum bottles or jugs

(G-8907)
CANTON NOODLE CORPORATION
101 Mott St (10013-5093)
PHONE....................212 226-3276
James Eng, *Principal*
EMP: 8 EST: 1951
SQ FT: 4,000
SALES (est): 600K **Privately Held**
SIC: 2098 Noodles (e.g. egg, plain & water), dry

(G-8908)
CANYON PUBLISHING INC
55 John St Ste 6 (10038-3752)
PHONE....................212 334-0227
EMP: 10
SALES (est): 880K **Privately Held**
SIC: 2752 Publishing Firm

(G-8909)
CAP USA JERSEYMAN HARLEM INC (PA)
112 W 125th St (10027)
PHONE....................212 222-7942
Sung R Park, *Ch of Bd*
EMP: 5
SALES (est): 401.6K **Privately Held**
SIC: 2257 Jersey cloth

(G-8910)
CAPCO WAI SHING LLC
132 W 36th St Rm 509 (10018-8843)
PHONE....................212 268-1976
Jim Capuano, *Mng Member*
EMP: 8
SALES (est): 921.4K **Privately Held**
SIC: 3089 Clothes hangers, plastic

(G-8911)
CAPITAL E FINANCIAL GROUP
Also Called: Victoire Latam Asset MGT LLC
598 Madison Ave Fl 9 (10022-1668)
PHONE....................212 319-6550
Nadim Razzouck, *Chairman*
EMP: 10
SALES (est): 1.2MM **Privately Held**
SIC: 3524 6799 Hedge trimmers, electric; venture capital companies

(G-8912)
CAPITAL GOLD CORPORATION (PA)
601 Lexington Ave Fl 36 (10022-4611)
PHONE....................212 668-0842
▲ EMP: 8
SALES (est): 15.1MM **Privately Held**
SIC: 1041 1499 Gold And Mineral Exploration

(G-8913)
CAPITAL PARTNERS LLC
390 Park Ave 13th (10022-4608)
PHONE....................212 935-4990
John J Veronis, *Mng Member*
Bert Abrams, *Consultant*
Randolph Lehman, *MIS Dir*
Jeff Stevenson,
EMP: 100 EST: 1996
SALES (est): 532.6K **Privately Held**
SIC: 2721 Magazines: publishing only, not printed on site

(G-8914)
CAPITAL PROGRAMS INC
Also Called: CPI
420 Lexington Ave Lbby 6 (10170-0024)
PHONE....................212 842-4640
Sabi Kanaan, *CEO*
EMP: 7
SQ FT: 1,000
SALES (est): 590K **Privately Held**
SIC: 7372 Application computer software

(G-8915)
CARAVAN INTERNATIONAL CORP
641 Lexington Ave Fl 13 (10022-4503)
PHONE....................212 223-7190
Ursula Cernuschi, *President*
Dennis Friedman, *Vice Pres*
EMP: 6 EST: 1963
SQ FT: 32,000
SALES: 2.5MM **Privately Held**
WEB: www.caravan-ny.com
SIC: 3728 5065 Aircraft parts & equipment; communication equipment

(G-8916)
CARIBBEAN FASHION GROUP INC
Also Called: Cfg Group
1410 Broadway Rm 3202 (10018-9314)
PHONE....................212 706-8851
Andy Tie, *President*
Marc Friedland, *President*
▲ EMP: 8
SQ FT: 1,200
SALES: 10MM **Privately Held**
SIC: 2329 2339 5621 Men's & boys' sportswear & athletic clothing; athletic (warmup, sweat & jogging) suits: men's & boys'; down-filled clothing: men's & boys'; women's & misses' athletic clothing & sportswear; athletic clothing: women's, misses' & juniors'; maternity clothing; women's clothing stores

(G-8917)
CARL FISCHER LLC (PA)
48 Wall St 28 (10005-2903)
PHONE....................212 777-0900
Hayden Connor, *CEO*
Denise Eaton, *Editor*
Casey Yu, *Controller*
Rachel L'Heureux, *Sales Staff*
Alison Wofford, *Marketing Mgr*
EMP: 20 EST: 1872
SALES (est): 2.9MM **Privately Held**
WEB: www.carlfischer.com
SIC: 2741 5736 5099 5199 Music, sheet: publishing & printing; musical instrument stores; sheet music; musical instruments parts & accessories; sheet music

(G-8918)
CARLO MONTE DESIGNS INC
17 E 48th St Fl 8 (10017-1010)
PHONE....................212 935-5611
Karnik Garipian, *President*
Haci Garipian, *President*
EMP: 6
SQ FT: 2,400
SALES: 2.5MM **Privately Held**
WEB: www.montecarlodesigns.com
SIC: 3911 Jewelry, precious metal

(G-8919)
CARODA INC
254 W 35th St (10001-2504)
PHONE....................212 630-9986
Ida Leigh M Law, *CEO*
EMP: 30 EST: 2009
SALES (est): 1.2MM **Privately Held**
SIC: 2329 Athletic (warmup, sweat & jogging) suits: men's & boys'

(G-8920)
CAROL FOR EVA GRAHAM INC
366 5th Ave Rm 815 (10001-2211)
PHONE....................212 889-8686
Carol Graham, *President*
Eva C Graham, *Vice Pres*
EMP: 12
SQ FT: 10,000
SALES (est): 2.2MM **Privately Held**
SIC: 3961 Costume jewelry, ex. precious metal & semiprecious stones

(G-8921)
CAROL GROUP LTD
Also Called: Habitat Magazine
150 W 30th St Rm 902 (10001-4125)
PHONE....................212 505-2030
Carol Ott, *President*
Paul Ukena, *Partner*
Ivis Fundichely, *Opers Mgr*
EMP: 7
SQ FT: 1,000
SALES: 891K **Privately Held**
WEB: www.habitatmag.com
SIC: 2721 Magazines: publishing only, not printed on site

(G-8922)
CAROLINA AMATO INC
350 7th Ave Rm 501 (10001-1944)
PHONE....................212 768-9095
Carolina Amato, *President*
▲ EMP: 6
SALES: 1.5MM **Privately Held**
WEB: www.carolinaamato.com
SIC: 2339 Women's & misses' accessories

(G-8923)
CAROLINA HERRERA LTD (HQ)
501 Fashion Ave Fl 17 (10018-5911)
PHONE....................212 944-5757
Claudia Thomas, *President*
Lisa Arnold, *Vice Pres*
Laura Sorensen, *Vice Pres*
Wes Gordon, *Creative Dir*
▼ EMP: 45
SALES (est): 19.3MM
SALES (corp-wide): 165.4K **Privately Held**
WEB: www.carolinaherrera.com
SIC: 2337 2339 Skirts, separate: women's, misses' & juniors'; women's & misses' outerwear
PA: Equipamientos Puig Sl
Calle Lardero, 3 - Bj
Logrono
941 202-026

(G-8924)
CARRERA CASTING CORP
64 W 48th St Fl 2 (10036-1708)
PHONE....................212 382-3296
Eric Schwartz, *Ch of Bd*
Owen Schwartz, *President*
Joel Weiss, *Vice Pres*
Jovie Chorzepa, *Executive*
EMP: 160
SQ FT: 8,000
SALES (est): 41.9MM **Privately Held**
WEB: www.carreracasting.net
SIC: 3915 3369 Jewelers' castings; non-ferrous foundries

(G-8925)
CARRY HOT INC
Also Called: Carry Hot USA
545 W 45th St Rm 501 (10036-3409)
PHONE....................212 279-7535
Sanford Plotkin, *President*
EMP: 20
SALES (est): 1.2MM **Privately Held**
WEB: www.carryhot.com
SIC: 2393 5113 5085 Bags & containers, except sleeping bags: textile; sanitary food containers; commercial containers

(G-8926)
CARVART GLASS INC (PA)
1441 Broadway Fl 28 (10018-1905)
PHONE....................212 675-0030
Antoly Geyman, *President*
Edward Geyman, *Vice Pres*
Mark Scelfo, *Vice Pres*
Oskar Shulman, *Project Mgr*
Sharon Sauli, *Sales Associate*
EMP: 25
SQ FT: 17,000
SALES (est): 5.6MM **Privately Held**
WEB: www.carvart.com
SIC: 3231 Art glass: made from purchased glass

(G-8927)
CARVIN FRENCH JEWELERS INC
515 Madison Ave Rm 5c (10022-5439)
PHONE....................212 755-6474
Andre Chervin, *President*

Grafinka Chunov, *Controller*
EMP: 20 **EST:** 1954
SQ FT: 4,000
SALES (est): 2.1MM **Privately Held**
SIC: 3911 3961 Jewelry, precious metal; costume jewelry

(G-8928)
CAS BIOSCIENCES LLC
1501 Broadway Fl 12 (10036-5505)
PHONE....................844 227-2467
Steven Seltzer,
EMP: 250
SQ FT: 1,000
SALES (est): 16.2MM **Privately Held**
SIC: 2834 Pharmaceutical preparations

(G-8929)
CASSINI PARFUMS LTD
3 W 57th St Fl 8 (10019-3407)
PHONE....................212 753-7540
EMP: 8
SQ FT: 8,000
SALES (est): 797.6K **Privately Held**
SIC: 2844 Mfg Fragrances

(G-8930)
CASTLE BRANDS INC (PA)
122 E 42nd St Rm 5000 (10168-4700)
PHONE....................646 356-0200
Mark E Andrews III, *Ch of Bd*
Richard J Lampen, *President*
Amanda Schuster, *Partner*
John S Glover, *COO*
Alejandra Pena, *Senior VP*
▲ **EMP:** 46
SQ FT: 5,000
SALES: 95.8MM **Privately Held**
WEB: www.castlebrandsinc.com
SIC: 2085 2082 Rum (alcoholic beverage); scotch whiskey; vodka (alcoholic beverage); malt liquors

(G-8931)
CASTLE CONNOLLY MEDICAL LTD
42 W 24th St Fl 2 (10010-3201)
PHONE....................212 367-8400
John J Connolly, *President*
William Liss-Levinson, *Opers Staff*
Jean Morgan, *Research*
Nicki Hughes, *Comms Mgr*
Magda Spyridakis, *Office Mgr*
EMP: 25
SQ FT: 500
SALES (est): 3.4MM
SALES (corp-wide): 1.2B **Publicly Held**
WEB: www.eldercareliving.com
SIC: 2731 Books: publishing only
HQ: Everyday Health, Inc.
345 Hudson St Rm 1600
New York NY 10014
646 728-9500

(G-8932)
CASUALS ETC INC
Also Called: E T C
16 E 52nd St Fl 4 (10022-5306)
PHONE....................212 838-1319
William Rondina, *President*
Steven Steinberg, *CFO*
EMP: 100
SALES (est): 5MM **Privately Held**
SIC: 2339 5137 Women's & misses' athletic clothing & sportswear; sportswear, women's & children's

(G-8933)
CATALYST GROUP INC
Also Called: Catalyst Group Design
345 7th Ave Rm 1100 (10001-5165)
PHONE....................212 243-7777
Nicholas Gould, *CEO*
Jon Mysel, *President*
Peter Hughes, *Admin Sec*
EMP: 6
SQ FT: 2,000
SALES (est): 774.6K **Privately Held**
WEB: www.catalystgroupdesign.com
SIC: 7372 Application computer software

(G-8934)
CATAPULT
1140 Broadway Rm 704 (10001-7504)
PHONE....................323 839-6204
Russell Hunter, *Principal*

EMP: 5
SALES (est): 135.2K **Privately Held**
SIC: 3599 Catapults

(G-8935)
CATAPULT LLC (PA)
1140 Broadway Rm 704 (10001-7504)
PHONE....................303 717-0334
Leigh Newman, *Editor*
Elizabeth Koch,
EMP: 4 **EST:** 2009
SALES (est): 1MM **Privately Held**
SIC: 2741 Miscellaneous publishing

(G-8936)
CATCH VENTURES INC
30 W 63rd St Apt 14o (10023-7173)
PHONE....................347 620-4351
Scott Graulich, *President*
EMP: 10
SALES (est): 252.5K **Privately Held**
SIC: 7372 7389 Application computer software;

(G-8937)
CATHAY HOME INC (PA)
230 5th Ave Ste 215 (10001-7914)
PHONE....................212 213-0988
Zhiming Qian, *Ch of Bd*
◆ **EMP:** 23
SQ FT: 10,000
SALES (est): 40MM **Privately Held**
SIC: 2392 Blankets, comforters & beddings

(G-8938)
CATHERINE STEIN DESIGNS INC
411 5th Ave Rm 600 (10016-2270)
PHONE....................212 840-1188
Catherine Stein, *President*
Sharon Goldberg, *Vice Pres*
EMP: 30
SQ FT: 10,000
SALES (est): 2MM **Privately Held**
WEB: www.csteindesigns.com
SIC: 3961 Costume jewelry, ex. precious metal & semiprecious stones

(G-8939)
CAVA SPILIADIS USA
200 W 57th St Ste 908 (10019-3211)
PHONE....................212 247-8214
Martha Tsapanos, *Principal*
▲ **EMP:** 20 **EST:** 2007
SALES (est): 225.9K **Privately Held**
SIC: 2084 Wines

(G-8940)
CCT INC
Also Called: Committee For Color & Trends
60 Madison Ave Ste 1209 (10010-1635)
P.O. Box 1621 (10159-1621)
PHONE....................212 532-3355
Ellen Campuzano, *President*
EMP: 6
SQ FT: 1,500
SALES (est): 492.7K **Privately Held**
SIC: 2732 Books: printing only

(G-8941)
CEGID CORPORATION
274 Madison Ave Rm 1404 (10016-0720)
PHONE....................212 757-9038
Mario Daddino, *Sales Staff*
Michael Wong, *Sales Executive*
Arnaud Coste, *Manager*
Brian Archibald, *Manager*
EMP: 16
SALES (est): 2MM
SALES (corp-wide): 177.9K **Privately Held**
SIC: 7372 Word processing computer software
HQ: Cegid Group
52 Quai Paul Sedallian
Lyon 9e Arrondissement 69009
426 295-051

(G-8942)
CELLECTIS INC
430 E 29th St Ste 810 (10016-8367)
PHONE....................347 809-5980
Stefan Scherer, *Senior VP*
Ariane Hamaide, *Vice Pres*
Simon Harnest, *Vice Pres*
Sonal Temburni, *Research*

Mathieu Simon, *Chief Mktg Ofcr*
EMP: 11
SALES (est): 1.8MM
SALES (corp-wide): 16.8MM **Publicly Held**
SIC: 2834 Pharmaceutical preparations
PA: Cellectis
8 Rue De La Croix Jarry
Paris 13e Arrondissement 75013
181 691-600

(G-8943)
CELONIS INC
114 W 41st St Fl 16 (10036-7308)
PHONE....................973 652-8821
Colin Barnett, *Sales Executive*
Mike Ross, *Executive*
EMP: 6 **EST:** 2016
SALES (est): 438.3K
SALES (corp-wide): 9.4MM **Privately Held**
SIC: 7372 Prepackaged software
PA: Celonis Se
Theresienstr. 6
Munchen 80333
894 161-5967

(G-8944)
CEMENTEX LATEX CORP
121 Varick St Frnt 2 (10013-1408)
PHONE....................212 741-1770
Arthur Gononsky, *President*
Susan Gononsky, *Corp Secy*
Jeff Gonosky, *Vice Pres*
▼ **EMP:** 10 **EST:** 1936
SQ FT: 12,000
SALES (est): 850K **Privately Held**
WEB: www.cementex.com
SIC: 3089 3069 5084 Plastic hardware & building products; reclaimed rubber & specialty rubber compounds; machine tools & accessories

(G-8945)
CEMEX CEMENT INC
590 Madison Ave Fl 41 (10022-2524)
PHONE....................212 317-6000
Javier Garcia, *President*
EMP: 78 **Privately Held**
SIC: 3273 Ready-mixed concrete
HQ: Cemex Cement, Inc.
10100 Katy Fwy Ste 300
Houston TX 77043
713 650-6200

(G-8946)
CEMOI INC (PA)
5 Penn Plz Ste 2325 (10001-1810)
PHONE....................212 583-4920
Thierry Beaujeon, *CEO*
▲ **EMP:** 2
SALES (est): 4.3MM **Privately Held**
SIC: 2066 Chocolate bars, solid

(G-8947)
CENIBRA INC
1251 Ave Of The Americas (10020-1104)
PHONE....................212 818-8242
Yoshida Kazuhiro, *President*
▲ **EMP:** 6
SALES: 1B **Privately Held**
SIC: 2611 5159 Pulp mills; bristles

(G-8948)
CENTENNIAL MEDIA LLC
10th Floor 40 Worth St Flr 10 (10013)
PHONE....................646 527-7320
Sebastian Raatz, *Partner*
Benjamin Harris, *Partner*
▼ **EMP:** 15 **EST:** 2017
SALES: 12MM **Privately Held**
SIC: 2721 Magazines: publishing only, not printed on site

(G-8949)
CENTINEL SPINE LLC (PA)
505 Park Ave Fl 14 (10022-1106)
PHONE....................212 583-9700
John J Viscogliosi, *CEO*
Michael Will, *President*
Daniel Levy, *VP Sales*
EMP: 5
SALES (est): 4.6MM **Privately Held**
SIC: 3842 Surgical appliances & supplies

(G-8950)
CENTRAL APPAREL GROUP LTD
Also Called: Central Park Active Wear
16 W 36th St Rm 1202 (10018-9751)
PHONE....................212 868-6505
Shalom Asher, *CEO*
Steve Goldfarb, *President*
◆ **EMP:** 18
SQ FT: 900
SALES (est): 10MM **Privately Held**
SIC: 2339 5621 Sportswear, women's; women's sportswear

(G-8951)
CENTRAL CNFRNCE OF AMRCN RBBIS
355 Lexington Ave Fl 18 (10017-6615)
PHONE....................212 972-3636
Jonathan A Stein, *President*
Hara Person, *Publisher*
Sonja Pilz, *Editor*
Walter Jacob, *Vice Pres*
Laurie Kurzynowski, *Opers Staff*
▲ **EMP:** 16
SALES (est): 2.5MM **Privately Held**
WEB: www.ccarnet.org
SIC: 2731 Books: publishing only; pamphlets: publishing only, not printed on site

(G-8952)
CENTRAL MILLS INC
Also Called: Freeze Divisional Centl Mills
1400 Broadway Rm 1605 (10018-5200)
PHONE....................212 764-9011
Solomon Shalam, *Branch Mgr*
EMP: 110
SALES (est): 16.8MM
SALES (corp-wide): 79.1MM **Privately Held**
SIC: 2329 2339 2253 Men's & boys' sportswear & athletic clothing; women's & misses' outerwear; T-shirts & tops, knit
PA: Central Mills, Inc.
473 Ridge Rd
Dayton NJ 08810
732 329-2009

(G-8953)
CENTRAL TEXTILES INC
Also Called: Cotswolt Industries
10 E 40th St Rm 3410 (10016-0301)
PHONE....................212 213-8740
James McKinnon, *Manager*
EMP: 15
SALES (corp-wide): 48.7MM **Privately Held**
WEB: www.ctextiles.com
SIC: 2261 2262 Finishing plants, cotton; finishing plants, manmade fiber & silk fabrics
PA: Central Textiles, Inc.
237 Mill Ave
Central SC 29630
864 639-2491

(G-8954)
CENTRIC BRANDS INC
77 Mercer St (10012-4460)
PHONE....................212 925-5727
Jenniferstend Hawkins, *VP Mktg*
EMP: 5
SALES (corp-wide): 596.6MM **Publicly Held**
SIC: 2337 Women's & misses' suits & skirts
PA: Centric Brands Inc.
350 5th Ave Fl 6
New York NY 10118
646 582-6000

(G-8955)
CENTRIC BRANDS INC (PA)
350 5th Ave Fl 6 (10118-0700)
PHONE....................646 582-6000
Jason Rabin, *CEO*
William Sweedler, *Ch of Bd*
Andrew Tarshis, *Exec VP*
Anurup S Pruthi, *CFO*
EMP: 80
SQ FT: 305,000

SALES: 596.6MM **Publicly Held**
WEB: www.innovogroup.com
SIC: 2339 2311 2325 3111 Jeans:
women's, misses' & juniors'; men's &
boys' suits & coats; jeans: men's, youths'
& boys'; accessory products, leather;
handbag leather; shoe leather; apparel
belts; women's & misses' suits & skirts

(G-8956)
CENTRIC DENIM USA LLC (HQ)
Also Called: Buffalo Jeans
350 5th Ave Fl 6 (10118-0700)
PHONE.............................646 839-7000
Bruce Philip Rockowitz,
EMP: 1
SALES (est): 2.4MM
SALES (corp-wide): 596.6MM **Publicly Held**
SIC: 2325 2339 5651 Jeans: men's,
youths' & boys'; jeans: women's, misses'
& juniors'; jeans stores
PA: Centric Brands Inc.
350 5th Ave Fl 6
New York NY 10118
646 582-6000

(G-8957)
CENTRIC SOCKS LLC
350 5th Ave Lbby 9 (10118-0109)
PHONE.............................646 839-7000
Dow Famulak, *Mng Member*
EMP: 25
SALES (est): 1.6MM
SALES (corp-wide): 596.6MM **Publicly Held**
SIC: 2252 Socks
PA: Centric Brands Inc.
350 5th Ave Fl 6
New York NY 10118
646 582-6000

(G-8958)
CENTRIC WEST LLC (HQ)
Also Called: Joes Jeans
350 5th Ave Fl 5 (10118-0110)
PHONE.............................646 839-7000
Suzy Biszantz, *CEO*
Elena Pickett, *Senior VP*
Jessica Volpe, *Manager*
EMP: 110
SQ FT: 150,000
SALES (est): 34MM
SALES (corp-wide): 596.6MM **Publicly Held**
SIC: 2339 Jeans: women's, misses' & juniors'
PA: Centric Brands Inc.
350 5th Ave Fl 6
New York NY 10118
646 582-6000

(G-8959)
CENTRO INC
841 Broadway Fl 6 (10003-4704)
P.O. Box 13464, Chicago IL (60613-0464)
PHONE.............................212 791-9450
Kelly Wenzel, *Chief Mktg Ofcr*
EMP: 259
SALES (corp-wide): 23.6MM **Privately Held**
SIC: 3089 Plastic processing
PA: Centro, Inc.
11 E Madison St Ste 600
Chicago IL 60602
312 423-1565

(G-8960)
CENTURY GRAND INC
Also Called: Century Pharmacy Three
302 Grand St (10002-4465)
PHONE.............................212 925-3838
Steven T Ho, *Principal*
EMP: 10
SALES (est): 1.3MM **Privately Held**
SIC: 2834 Druggists' preparations (pharmaceuticals)

(G-8961)
CEO CAST INC
211 E 43rd St Rm 400 (10017-8620)
PHONE.............................212 732-4300
Kenneth Sgro, *President*
Jim Fallon, *Managing Prtnr*
EMP: 18
SQ FT: 25,000

SALES (est): 1.3MM **Privately Held**
WEB: www.ceocast.com
SIC: 2741 Business service newsletters:
publishing & printing

(G-8962)
CEROS INC (PA)
40 W 25th St Fl 12 (10010-2759)
PHONE.............................347 744-9250
Simon Burg, *CEO*
Mark Healy, *Chief*
Matthew Wellschlager, *Vice Pres*
Noelle Tassey, *Opers Staff*
Aaron Wood, *QA Dir*
EMP: 30 EST: 2007
SALES (est): 7.8MM **Privately Held**
SIC: 7372 Publishers' computer software

(G-8963)
CEYLAN & CO LLC
24 W 46th St Apt 3 (10036-4505)
PHONE.............................646 858-3022
Furkan Ceylan,
EMP: 6
SALES (est): 478.8K **Privately Held**
SIC: 3999 5961 Manufacturing industries;

(G-8964)
CFO PUBLISHING LLC (PA)
50 Broad St Frnt (10004-2354)
PHONE.............................212 459-3004
Alan Glass, *CEO*
Richard Rivera, *President*
Sean Allocca, *Editor*
EMP: 42
SQ FT: 7,500
SALES (est): 7.8MM **Privately Held**
SIC: 2721 Magazines: publishing only, not
printed on site

(G-8965)
CGI TECHNOLOGIES SOLUTIONS INC
655 3rd Ave Ste 700 (10017-9124)
PHONE.............................212 682-7411
Don O'Brien, *Principal*
EMP: 15
SALES (corp-wide): 8.8B **Privately Held**
SIC: 7372 5045 7379 Prepackaged software; computer software; computer related consulting services
HQ: Cgi Technologies And Solutions Inc.
11325 Random Hills Rd
Fairfax VA 22030
703 267-8000

(G-8966)
CHAIN STORE AGE MAGAZINE
425 Park Ave (10022-3506)
PHONE.............................212 756-5000
EMP: 5
SQ FT: 30,000
SALES (est): 402.6K
SALES (corp-wide): 122.5MM **Privately Held**
SIC: 2731 Book Publisher
PA: Lebhar-Friedman, Inc.
150 W 30th St Fl 19
New York NY 33610
212 756-5000

(G-8967)
CHAINDOM ENTERPRISES INC
48 W 48th St Ste 200 (10036-1779)
PHONE.............................212 719-4778
Fikri Akdemir, *President*
Steve Pinkin, *Treasurer*
EMP: 6
SQ FT: 2,500
SALES (est): 533.5K **Privately Held**
SIC: 3911 Jewelry, precious metal

(G-8968)
CHAM COLD BREW LLC
300 Park Ave Fl 12 (10022-7419)
PHONE.............................646 926-0206
Niko Nikolaou, *CEO*
Georgia Masouras, *CFO*
EMP: 5
SALES (est): 124.5K **Privately Held**
SIC: 2086 5149 Iced tea & fruit drinks,
bottled & canned; coffee & tea

(G-8969)
CHAMPION ZIPPER CORP
Also Called: Sew True
447 W 36th St Fl 2 (10018-6300)
PHONE.............................212 239-0414
Steven Silberberg, *President*
Chris Roldan, *Principal*
EMP: 6
SQ FT: 5,000
SALES: 1.3MM **Privately Held**
WEB: www.sewtrue.com
SIC: 3965 2241 Zipper; trimmings, textile

(G-8970)
CHANSE PETROLEUM CORPORATION (PA)
828 5th Ave Apt 1f (10065-7272)
PHONE.............................212 682-3789
Kai Chang, *President*
EMP: 3 EST: 1972
SQ FT: 1,000
SALES (est): 1.6MM **Privately Held**
SIC: 1311 Crude petroleum production;
natural gas production

(G-8971)
CHARING CROSS MUSIC INC
3 Columbus Cir Ste 1720 (10019-8708)
PHONE.............................212 541-7571
Paul Simon, *President*
EMP: 6
SQ FT: 1,000
SALES (est): 410K **Privately Held**
SIC: 2741 Music, sheet: publishing only,
not printed on site

(G-8972)
CHARIS & MAE INC
31 W 34th St Fl 8 (10001-3030)
PHONE.............................212 641-0816
Yi Shan Su, *President*
EMP: 5
SALES (est): 239.4K **Privately Held**
SIC: 3911 Jewelry, precious metal

(G-8973)
CHARLES HENRICKS INC
Also Called: Starkey & Henricks
70 W 36th St Rm 500 (10018-8050)
PHONE.............................212 243-5800
Peter Bird, *President*
EMP: 15
SALES (est): 1.6MM **Privately Held**
SIC: 2796 Gravure printing plates or cylinders, preparation of

(G-8974)
CHARLES KRYPELL INC
22 W 48th St Ste 801-803 (10036-1819)
PHONE.............................212 752-3313
Charles Krypell, *President*
Debbie Krypell, *Vice Pres*
Judy Loew, *Accounts Exec*
Janinne Mugnolo, *Manager*
Marianna Randone, *Manager*
EMP: 20 EST: 1989
SALES (est): 499.5K **Privately Held**
WEB: www.charleskrypell.com
SIC: 3911 Jewelry, precious metal

(G-8975)
CHARLES P ROGERS BRASS BEDS (PA)
Also Called: Charles P Rogers Brass Ir Bed
26 W 17th St (10011-5710)
PHONE.............................212 675-4400
Linda Klein, *President*
David Klein, *Vice Pres*
Steven Wilson, *Sales Staff*
Jeannine Tuttle, *Manager*
Chung Wan, *Master*
◆ EMP: 15 EST: 1979
SQ FT: 9,000
SALES (est): 3.9MM **Privately Held**
SIC: 2514 5712 5961 Beds, including
folding & cabinet, household: metal; beds
& accessories; furniture & furnishings,
mail order

(G-8976)
CHARMING FASHION INC
247 W 38th St Rm 1400 (10018-0230)
PHONE.............................212 730-2872
Charles Kim, *President*
EMP: 5

SALES (est): 261K **Privately Held**
SIC: 2211 Apparel & outerwear fabrics,
cotton

(G-8977)
CHARTER VENTURES LLC
135 W 36th St Rm 1800 (10018-6951)
PHONE.............................212 868-0222
Jennifer Lai,
Howard Cohen,
▲ EMP: 10 EST: 2000
SQ FT: 4,838
SALES (est): 1.5MM **Privately Held**
SIC: 2253 Sweaters & sweater coats, knit
PA: Charter Ventures Limited
6a/F Chiap Luen Indl Bldg
Kwai Chung NT

(G-8978)
CHECK GROUP LLC
1385 Broadway Fl 16 (10018-6041)
PHONE.............................212 221-4700
Lawrence Jemal,
Richard Tan, *Admin Sec*
▲ EMP: 100 EST: 1999
SALES (est): 6.8MM **Privately Held**
WEB: www.checkgroup.com
SIC: 2311 2321 2322 2325 Men's &
boys' suits & coats; men's & boys' furnishings; underwear, men's & boys': made
from purchased materials; men's & boys'
trousers & slacks

(G-8979)
CHECKPOINT THERAPEUTICS INC
2 Gansevoort St Fl 9 (10014-1667)
PHONE.............................781 652-4500
Michael S Weiss, *Ch of Bd*
James F Oliviero III, *President*
William Garrett Gray, *CFO*
Scott Boilen, *Bd of Directors*
Barry Salzman, *Bd of Directors*
EMP: 7
SALES: 3.5MM **Publicly Held**
SIC: 2834 8731 Pharmaceutical preparations; biotechnical research, commercial
PA: Fortress Biotech, Inc.
2 Gansevoort St Fl 9
New York NY 10014

(G-8980)
CHELSEA PLASTICS INC
200 Lexington Ave Rm 914 (10016-6255)
PHONE.............................212 924-4530
George Frechter, *President*
EMP: 12
SQ FT: 7,000
SALES (est): 1.5MM **Privately Held**
WEB: www.chelseaplastics.com
SIC: 3082 Unsupported plastics profile
shapes

(G-8981)
CHERI MON BABY LLC
1412 Broadway Rm 1608 (10018-9270)
PHONE.............................212 354-5511
Ralph Kassin, *President*
▲ EMP: 6
SQ FT: 1,500
SALES (est): 605.9K **Privately Held**
SIC: 2361 Girls' & children's blouses &
shirts

(G-8982)
CHERRY LANE MAGAZINE LLC
1745 Broadway 19 (10019-4640)
PHONE.............................212 561-3000
Peter Primont, *Mng Member*
EMP: 80
SQ FT: 30,000
SALES (est): 4.9MM **Privately Held**
SIC: 2741 Miscellaneous publishing

(G-8983)
CHESKY RECORDS INC
1650 Broadway Ste 900 (10019-6965)
PHONE.............................212 586-7799
Norman Chesky, *President*
David Chesky, *Vice Pres*
Jeff Lanier, *Manager*
EMP: 12
SQ FT: 6,000
SALES (est): 1.2MM **Privately Held**
SIC: 3652 Phonograph record blanks;
compact laser discs, prerecorded

(G-8984)
CHF INDUSTRIES INC (PA)
1 Park Ave Fl 9 (10016-5803)
P.O. Box 410727, Charlotte NC (28241-0727)
PHONE...................212 951-7800
Frank Foley, *President*
Spencer Foley, *Vice Pres*
Don Harwood, *CFO*
Ryan Cox, *Marketing Staff*
◆ EMP: 30
SQ FT: 50,000
SALES (est): 90.2MM **Privately Held**
SIC: 2221 5023 Bedding, manmade or silk fabric; window covering parts & accessories; linens & towels

(G-8985)
CHIA USA LLC
Also Called: Chia Company
379 W Broadway (10012-5121)
PHONE...................212 226-7512
John Foss, *CEO*
April Helliwell, *COO*
EMP: 1 EST: 2014
SQ FT: 3,000
SALES (est): 18MM
SALES (corp-wide): 26MM **Privately Held**
SIC: 2043 5153 Cereal breakfast foods; grains; barley
PA: Chia Inc.
379 W Broadway
New York NY 10012
212 226-7512

(G-8986)
CHILD NUTRITION PROG DEPT ED
1011 1st Ave Fl 6 (10022-4112)
PHONE...................212 371-1000
Thomas Smith, *President*
Christine Plantamura, *Admin Asst*
EMP: 99
SALES (est): 3.6MM **Privately Held**
SIC: 2099 Food preparations

(G-8987)
CHINA DAILY DISTRIBUTION CORP (HQ)
1500 Broadway Ste 2800 (10036-4097)
PHONE...................212 537-8888
Larry Lee, *CEO*
Leshuo Dong, *General Mgr*
Kenny Zheng, *Graphic Designe*
EMP: 20
SALES (est): 1.1MM
SALES (corp-wide): 110.3MM **Privately Held**
SIC: 2711 Newspapers
PA: China Daily
No.15, Huixin East Street, Chaoyang District
Beijing 10002
106 499-5969

(G-8988)
CHINA HUAREN ORGANIC PDTS INC
100 Wall St Fl 15 (10005-3701)
PHONE...................212 232-0120
Cao Yushu, *CEO*
▲ EMP: 3
SALES: 7.4MM **Privately Held**
WEB: www.ultradatasystems.com
SIC: 2099 2844 Food preparations; toilet preparations

(G-8989)
CHINA INDUSTRIAL STEEL INC
110 Wall St Fl 11 (10005-3834)
PHONE...................646 328-1502
Shenghong Liu, *Principal*
EMP: 2
SALES: 649.3MM **Privately Held**
SIC: 3312 Blast furnaces & steel mills

(G-8990)
CHINA LITHIUM TECHNOLOGIES (PA)
15 W 39th St Fl 14 (10018-0626)
PHONE...................212 391-2688
EMP: 9
SQ FT: 215

SALES: 15.7MM **Privately Held**
SIC: 3691 3629 Mfg Storage Batteries Mfg Electrical Industrial Apparatus

(G-8991)
CHINA N E PETRO HOLDINGS LTD
445 Park Ave (10022-2606)
PHONE...................212 307-3568
Jingfu LI, *CEO*
Shaohui Chen, *CFO*
EMP: 715
SALES: 99.5MM **Privately Held**
WEB: www.cnepetroleum.com
SIC: 1311 Crude petroleum production

(G-8992)
CHINA NEWSWEEK CORPORATION
15 E 40th St Fl 11 (10016-0463)
PHONE...................212 481-2510
WEI Xiang Peng, *Ch of Bd*
Fred Teng, *Exec Dir*
EMP: 10
SALES (est): 440K **Privately Held**
SIC: 2711 Newspapers

(G-8993)
CHINA TING FSHION GROUP USA LL (HQ)
525 7th Ave Rm 1606 (10018-0401)
PHONE...................212 716-1600
Ren Shen, *President*
▲ EMP: 7
SALES (est): 8.5MM
SALES (corp-wide): 12.4MM **Privately Held**
SIC: 2269 2335 2339 Linen fabrics: dyeing, finishing & printing; dresses: paper; cut & sewn; ensemble dresses: women's, misses' & juniors'; women's & misses' outerwear
PA: Zhejiang Huading Group Co., Ltd.
No.56, Beisha East Road, Yuhang District
Hangzhou 31119
571 862-5900

(G-8994)
CHOBANI LLC
200 Lafayette St Fl 6 (10012-4079)
PHONE...................646 998-3800
Paul Zollinger, *Exec VP*
Matthew Graziose, *Project Mgr*
Sunitha Dayaram, *Director*
Kevin Jennette, *Director*
EMP: 19
SALES (corp-wide): 249.2MM **Privately Held**
SIC: 2026 Yogurt
HQ: Chobani, Llc
147 State Highway 320
Norwich NY 13815

(G-8995)
CHOCNYC LLC
4996 Broadway (10034-1635)
PHONE...................917 804-4848
Jemal Edwards, *Principal*
Brad Jon Doles, *Principal*
Dewayne Jemal Edwards, *Principal*
EMP: 6
SALES (est): 246.3K **Privately Held**
SIC: 2051 Cakes, bakery: except frozen

(G-8996)
CHOCOLAT MODERNE LLC
27 W 20th St Ste 904 (10011-3725)
PHONE...................212 229-4797
Joan Coukos, *Mng Member*
▲ EMP: 5
SQ FT: 950
SALES (est): 250K **Privately Held**
WEB: www.chocolatmoderne.com
SIC: 2064 5145 5961 Candy & other confectionery products; candy; mail order house

(G-8997)
CHRISTIAN CASEY LLC (PA)
Also Called: Sean John
1440 Broadway Frnt 3 (10018-2301)
PHONE...................212 500-2200
Dawn Robertson,
Sean John,

▲ EMP: 40
SQ FT: 5,000
SALES (est): 20.3MM **Privately Held**
SIC: 2325 2322 2321 2311 Men's & boys' trousers & slacks; men's & boys' underwear & nightwear; men's & boys' furnishings; men's & boys' suits & coats

(G-8998)
CHRISTIAN CASEY LLC
Also Called: Sean John Clothing
1440 Broadway Frnt 3 (10018-2301)
PHONE...................212 500-2200
Kevin Lowney, *Branch Mgr*
EMP: 37
SALES (corp-wide): 20.3MM **Privately Held**
SIC: 2325 2322 2321 2311 Men's & boys' trousers & slacks; men's & boys' underwear & nightwear; men's & boys' furnishings; men's & boys' suits & coats
PA: Christian Casey Llc
1440 Broadway Frnt 3
New York NY 10018
212 500-2200

(G-8999)
CHRISTIAN DIOR PERFUMES LLC (DH)
19 E 57th St (10022-2506)
PHONE...................212 931-2200
Pamela Baxter, *CEO*
Scott Johnson, *COO*
Joanna Grillo, *Vice Pres*
Diana Miles, *Vice Pres*
Pertrand Tesra, *Vice Pres*
◆ EMP: 35 EST: 2003
SALES: 34.2MM
SALES (corp-wide): 361.7MM **Privately Held**
WEB: www.saniflo.com
SIC: 2844 3999 Perfumes, natural or synthetic; cosmetic preparations; atomizers, toiletry
HQ: Parfums Christian Dior
33 Avenue Hoche
Paris 8e Arrondissement 75008
149 538-500

(G-9000)
CHRISTIAN SIRIANO HOLDINGS LLC
5 W 54th St (10019-5404)
PHONE...................212 695-5494
Christian Siriano, *Managing Dir*
EMP: 9
SQ FT: 3,000
SALES (est): 1.2MM **Privately Held**
SIC: 2335 Women's, juniors' & misses' dresses

(G-9001)
CHRISTINA SALES INC
1441 Broadway (10018-1905)
PHONE...................212 391-0710
Joey Schwebel, *President*
▲ EMP: 10
SQ FT: 5,000
SALES (est): 1.2MM **Privately Held**
SIC: 2339 5137 Bathing suits: women's, misses' & juniors'; swimsuits: women's, children's & infants'

(G-9002)
CHRISTOPHER DESIGNS INC
50 W 47th St Ste 1507 (10036-8687)
PHONE...................212 382-1013
Christopher Slowinski, *President*
Colleen Manger, *Vice Pres*
Ewa Slowinski, *Vice Pres*
Donna Piotrowski, *Controller*
Ursula Piekut, *Mktg Dir*
▲ EMP: 27
SQ FT: 3,800
SALES (est): 4MM **Privately Held**
WEB: www.christopherdesigns.com
SIC: 3915 3911 Jewelers' materials & lapidary work; jewelry, precious metal

(G-9003)
CHRISTOS INC
318 W 39th St Fl 12 (10018-1484)
PHONE...................212 921-0025
Christos Yiannakou, *President*
Michael Decuollo, *Vice Pres*
▲ EMP: 37

SQ FT: 7,500
SALES (est): 2.4MM **Privately Held**
WEB: www.christosbridal.com
SIC: 2335 Wedding gowns & dresses

(G-9004)
CHURCH PUBLISHING INCORPORATED (HQ)
Also Called: Morehouse Publishing
445 5th Ave Frnt 1 (10016-0133)
PHONE...................212 592-1800
Alan F Blanchard, *President*
Mark Dazzo, *Vice Pres*
▼ EMP: 8
SALES (est): 1MM
SALES (corp-wide): 371.4MM **Privately Held**
WEB: www.preparingforsunday.com
SIC: 2731 Books: publishing only
PA: Church Pension Group Services Corporation
19 E 34th St
New York NY 10016
212 592-1800

(G-9005)
CINCH TECHNOLOGIES INC
7 World Trade Ctr (10007-2140)
PHONE...................212 266-0022
Maya Komerov, *CEO*
Patrick Hainault, *Vice Pres*
Camille McGratty, *Vice Pres*
EMP: 6 EST: 2017
SALES: 100K **Privately Held**
SIC: 7372 Prepackaged software

(G-9006)
CINDERELLA PRESS LTD
327 Canal St 3 (10013-2513)
PHONE...................212 431-3130
Robert Cenedella, *President*
Peter Nashel, *Mktg Dir*
EMP: 6
SALES (est): 548.5K **Privately Held**
SIC: 2731 Books: publishing only

(G-9007)
CINE DESIGN GROUP LLC
Also Called: Cinedeck
15 Park Row Lbby L (10038-2321)
PHONE...................646 747-0734
Charles Dautremont,
EMP: 8
SQ FT: 5,000
SALES (est): 737.2K **Privately Held**
SIC: 3575 Cathode ray tube (CRT), computer terminal

(G-9008)
CINEDIGM SOFTWARE
45 W 36th St Fl 7 (10018-7634)
PHONE...................212 206-9001
Dan Sherlock, *President*
Jill Calcaterra, *Principal*
Jane Davis, *Counsel*
Erick Opeka, *Exec VP*
Diane Anselmo, *Vice Pres*
EMP: 5
SALES (est): 303.4K **Privately Held**
SIC: 7372 Prepackaged software

(G-9009)
CINER MANUFACTURING CO INC
20 W 37th St Fl 10 (10018-7484)
PHONE...................212 947-3770
David Hill, *President*
Patricia Ciner Hill, *Vice Pres*
EMP: 28
SQ FT: 6,000
SALES (est): 3.7MM **Privately Held**
SIC: 3961 Costume jewelry, ex. precious metal & semiprecious stones

(G-9010)
CIRCLE PEAK CAPITAL MGT LLC (PA)
1325 Ave Of The Americas (10019-6026)
PHONE...................646 230-8812
R Adam Smith, *CEO*
James H Clippard, *Principal*
Holbrook M Forusz, *Principal*
Jay T Kinn, *Vice Pres*
Lynn Menschenfreund, *Vice Pres*
▲ EMP: 30

SALES (est): 733.8MM **Privately Held**
SIC: 2053 6799 Pies, bakery: frozen; venture capital companies

(G-9011)
CIRCLE PRESS INC (PA)
Also Called: Press Room New York Division
121 Varick St Fl 4 (10013-1451)
PHONE..................................212 924-4277
Richard T Springer, *President*
Lawrence Lembo, *Vice Pres*
Benjamin Caringal, *Treasurer*
EMP: 51
SQ FT: 30,000
SALES (est): 4.5MM **Privately Held**
SIC: 2752 2796 Commercial printing, lithographic; platemaking services

(G-9012)
CISCO SYSTEMS INC
1 Penn Plz Ste 3306 (10119-3306)
PHONE..................................212 714-4000
Carl Demarco, *Partner*
Moshe Roznitsky, *Partner*
Christopher Augenstein, *Regional Mgr*
Adam Pasieka, *Regional Mgr*
Jonathan Carmel, *Business Mgr*
EMP: 250
SALES (corp-wide): 51.9B **Publicly Held**
WEB: www.cisco.com
SIC: 3577 7373 Data conversion equipment, media-to-media: computer; computer integrated systems design
PA: Cisco Systems, Inc.
170 W Tasman Dr
San Jose CA 95134
408 526-4000

(G-9013)
CIT AEROSPACE LLC
11 W 42nd St (10036-8002)
PHONE..................................212 461-5200
EMP: 6
SALES (est): 113.3K **Privately Held**
SIC: 3812 Search & navigation equipment
PA: Hkac Holdings (Ireland) Limited
5th Floor
Dun Laoghaire

(G-9014)
CITIGROUP INC
388 Greenwich St (10013-2362)
PHONE..................................212 816-6000
Michael Carpenter, *CEO*
ARI Glazer, *President*
Barbara Tasiounis, *President*
Gerrit Parker, *Managing Prtnr*
Tapodyuti Bose, *Managing Dir*
EMP: 97
SALES (corp-wide): 72.8B **Publicly Held**
SIC: 2621 Parchment, securites & bank note papers
PA: Citigroup Inc.
388 Greenwich St
New York NY 10013
212 559-1000

(G-9015)
CITISOURCE INDUSTRIES INC
244 5th Ave Ste 229 (10001-7604)
PHONE..................................212 683-1033
◆ EMP: 30
SALES (est): 3.9MM **Privately Held**
SIC: 2231 5131 Wool Broadwoven Fabric Mill Whol Piece Goods/Notions

(G-9016)
CITY AND STATE NY LLC
Also Called: Think Tank
61 Broadway Rm 1315 (10006-2721)
PHONE..................................212 268-0442
Tom Allon, *CEO*
Lissa Blake, *Publisher*
Jim Katocin, *Vice Pres*
Dawn M Rubino, *Manager*
Guillaume Federighi, *Director*
EMP: 27 EST: 2012
SALES (est): 1.3MM **Privately Held**
SIC: 2721 Magazines: publishing & printing

(G-9017)
CITY CASTING CORP
151 W 46th St Fl 5 (10036-8512)
PHONE..................................212 938-0511
Luis Ontiveros, *CEO*
EMP: 7

SALES (est): 1MM **Privately Held**
SIC: 3369 White metal castings (lead, tin, antimony), except die

(G-9018)
CITY SPORTS INC
64 W 48th St Frnt B (10036-1708)
PHONE..................................212 730-2009
EMP: 6
SALES (corp-wide): 135.8MM **Privately Held**
SIC: 3949 Mfg Sporting/Athletic Goods
PA: City Sports, Inc.
77 N Washington St # 500
Boston MA 02114
617 391-9100

(G-9019)
CITY SPORTS IMAGING INC
20 E 46th St Rm 200 (10017-9287)
PHONE..................................212 481-3600
Lawrence Silverberg, *President*
EMP: 20
SALES (est): 1.2MM **Privately Held**
SIC: 3845 Magnetic resonance imaging device, nuclear

(G-9020)
CITYSCAPE OB/GYN PLLC
38 E 32nd St Fl 4 (10016-5567)
PHONE..................................212 683-3595
Heidi S Rosenberg, *Principal*
EMP: 6
SALES (est): 2.7MM **Privately Held**
SIC: 3842 Gynecological supplies & appliances

(G-9021)
CITYWIRE LLC
Also Called: Citywire Americas
1350 Ave Of The Am Frnt 4 (10019)
PHONE..................................646 503-2216
Atholl Simpson, *Editor*
Marissa Lewis, *Mng Member*
Raj Dhaliwal, *Manager*
EMP: 13
SALES (est): 1.5MM
SALES (corp-wide): 47.9MM **Privately Held**
SIC: 2711 Newspapers
HQ: Citywire Financial Publishers Ltd
87 Vauxhall Walk
London SE11
207 840-2250

(G-9022)
CJ JEWELRY INC
2 W 47th St Ste 1106 (10036-3318)
PHONE..................................212 719-2464
Chaim Fischman, *President*
▲ EMP: 12
SALES (est): 1.3MM **Privately Held**
WEB: www.cjjewelry.com
SIC: 3911 Jewelry apparel

(G-9023)
CLASSIC BUSINESS SOLUTIONS
42 W 38th St Rm 1204 (10018-0054)
PHONE..................................212 563-9100
David Beck, *President*
Tara Jarick, *Art Dir*
▲ EMP: 5
SALES (est): 789.8K **Privately Held**
WEB: www.classicbusinesssolutions.com
SIC: 2752 Commercial printing, lithographic

(G-9024)
CLASSIC DESIGNER WORKSHOP INC
265 W 37th St Rm 703 (10018-5929)
PHONE..................................212 730-8480
Keith Lin, *General Mgr*
EMP: 8
SALES (est): 631.2K **Privately Held**
SIC: 2326 2341 Industrial garments, men's & boys'; women's & children's undergarments

(G-9025)
CLASSIC FLAVORS FRAGRANCES INC
878 W End Ave Apt 12b (10025-4957)
PHONE..................................212 777-0004

George Ivolin, *CEO*
EMP: 6
SQ FT: 750
SALES (est): 836K **Privately Held**
SIC: 2869 2899 5122 5169 Flavors or flavoring materials, synthetic; perfumes, flavorings & food additives; chemical preparations; essential oils; cosmetics, perfumes & hair products; aromatic chemicals; chemical additives; essential oils

(G-9026)
CLASSIC SOFA LTD
130 E 63rd St Ph B (10065-7340)
PHONE..................................212 620-0485
Jeffrey Stone, *President*
Maurice Stone, *Shareholder*
▲ EMP: 55
SQ FT: 15,000
SALES (est): 6.2MM **Privately Held**
SIC: 2512 5712 Couches, sofas & davenports: upholstered on wood frames; furniture stores

(G-9027)
CLASSPASS INC (PA)
275 7th Ave Fl 11 (10001-6708)
PHONE..................................888 493-5953
Payal Kadakia, *President*
Chloe Ross, *Vice Pres*
Rochelle Williams, *Opers Staff*
Jorge Gonzalez, *Engineer*
Doug McKay, *Engineer*
EMP: 29
SALES (est): 8.2MM **Privately Held**
SIC: 2741

(G-9028)
CLASSROOM INC
123 William St 1201 (10038-3804)
PHONE..................................212 545-8400
Lisa Holton, *President*
EMP: 25
SALES: 5MM **Privately Held**
SIC: 7372 7379 Educational computer software; computer related consulting services

(G-9029)
CLAYTON DUBILIER & RICE FUN (PA)
375 Park Ave Fl 18 (10152-0144)
PHONE..................................212 407-5200
Joseph L Rice III, *Ch of Bd*
Donald J Gogel, *President*
Eileen Smith, *Administration*
▲ EMP: 50 EST: 1985
SALES: 3.1MM **Privately Held**
SIC: 3825 3661 3812 3577 Test equipment for electronic & electric measurement; digital test equipment, electronic & electrical circuits; telephone & telegraph apparatus; switching equipment, telephone; headsets, telephone; search & navigation equipment; computer peripheral equipment; computer terminals; prepackaged software

(G-9030)
CLEAN BEAUTY COLLECTIVE INC
Also Called: Fusion Brands America Inc.
45 W 45th St Fl 2 (10036-4607)
PHONE..................................212 269-1387
Gregory Black, *President*
Euranie Battiste, *Manager*
EMP: 25
SQ FT: 8,500
SALES (est): 18MM
SALES (corp-wide): 27.6MM **Privately Held**
WEB: www.fusionbrandscorp.com
SIC: 2844 5122 Cosmetic preparations; cosmetics
PA: Fusion Brands Inc
40 St Clair Ave W Suite 200
Toronto ON M4V 1
800 261-9110

(G-9031)
CLEVER GOATS MEDIA LLC
40 Exchange Pl Ste 1602 (10005-2727)
PHONE..................................917 512-0340
Lionel Crear,
EMP: 5

SALES (est): 312.6K **Privately Held**
SIC: 7372 Home entertainment computer software

(G-9032)
CLINIQUE LABORATORIES LLC (DH)
Also Called: Clinique Laboratories, Inc.
767 5th Ave Fl 41 (10153-0023)
PHONE..................................212 572-4200
Daniel J Brestle, *CEO*
William P Lauder, *Ch of Bd*
Mary Armas, *Vice Pres*
Anthony Battaglia, *Vice Pres*
Elizabeth Dinardo, *Vice Pres*
▲ EMP: 2
SQ FT: 20,000.
SALES (est): 2.4MM **Publicly Held**
WEB: www.clinique.com
SIC: 2844 5122 Cosmetic preparations; cosmetics
HQ: Estee Lauder Inc.
767 5th Ave Fl 1
New York NY 10153
212 572-4200

(G-9033)
CLINIQUE SERVICES INC (DH)
767 5th Ave Fl Conc6 (10153-0003)
PHONE..................................212 572-4200
Lynne Greene, *Ch of Bd*
William P Lauder, *President*
Jessica Rotnicki, *Managing Dir*
Gregory Polcer, *Exec VP*
Goullin Arnaud, *Vice Pres*
EMP: 9
SALES (est): 2.4MM **Publicly Held**
SIC: 2844 Cosmetic preparations
HQ: Clinique Laboratories, Llc
767 5th Ave Fl 41
New York NY 10153
212 572-4200

(G-9034)
CLO-SHURE INTL INC (PA)
224 W 35th St Ste 1000 (10001-2533)
PHONE..................................212 268-5029
Cory Liner, *Principal*
▲ EMP: 8
SALES (est): 832.6K **Privately Held**
SIC: 3965 Fasteners, buttons, needles & pins

(G-9035)
CLOPAY AMES TRUE TEMPER (HQ)
712 5th Ave (10019-4108)
PHONE..................................212 957-5096
Ronald J Kramer, *CEO*
Mark Schrage, *Finance Mgr*
EMP: 11
SALES (est): 437.1MM
SALES (corp-wide): 1.9B **Publicly Held**
SIC: 3423 3799 3524 Garden & farm tools, including shovels; shovels, spades (hand tools); wheelbarrows; lawn & garden equipment
PA: Griffon Corporation
712 5th Ave Fl 18
New York NY 10019
212 957-5000

(G-9036)
CLOUD PRINTING
66 W Broadway Frnt E (10007-2113)
PHONE..................................212 775-0888
Vivian Lin, *Owner*
EMP: 7
SALES (est): 148.6K **Privately Held**
SIC: 2752 Commercial printing, lithographic

(G-9037)
CLOUDSENSE INC
295 Madison Ave Fl 39 (10017-6341)
PHONE..................................917 880-6195
Jonathan Douglas, *Exec VP*
Julian Hodges, *Engineer*
David Hawkes, *Sales Engr*
Chris Parsons, *Sales Staff*
Chris Tyndorf, *Sales Staff*
EMP: 6
SALES (est): 674.3K
SALES (corp-wide): 9.1MM **Privately Held**
SIC: 7372 Prepackaged software

HQ: Cloudsense Ltd
Moray House
London W1W 7
207 580-6685

(G-9038)
CLP HOLDINGS LLC (PA)
575 Madison Ave Ste 1006 (10022-8511)
P.O. Box 20627 (10021-0072)
PHONE......................917 846-5094
Cesar Pereira, *Mng Member*
EMP: 6
SQ FT: 1,500
SALES (est): 105MM **Privately Held**
SIC: 2672 Coated & laminated paper

(G-9039)
CLP PB LLC (PA)
Also Called: Perseus Books Group
1290 Ave Of The Amrcas (10104-0101)
PHONE......................212 340-8100
Joe Mangan, *COO*
Charles Gallagher, *CFO*
Sonya Harris, *Sales Staff*
David Steinberger,
◆ EMP: 40
SQ FT: 16,800
SALES (est): 140.4MM **Privately Held**
WEB: www.perseusbooks.com
SIC: 2721 Comic books: publishing only,
not printed on site

(G-9040)
CLYDE DUNEIER INC (PA)
415 Madison Ave Fl 6 (10017-7929)
PHONE......................212 398-1122
Dana Duneier, *CEO*
Mark Duneier, *President*
Clyde Duneier, *Treasurer*
▲ EMP: 100
SQ FT: 12,000
SALES (est): 13.6MM **Privately Held**
SIC: 3911 5094 Pearl jewelry, natural or
cultured; jewelry & precious stones

(G-9041)
CMNTY CORPORATION
228 E 45th St Rm 9e (10017-3337)
PHONE......................646 712-9949
Zach Katagiri, *Principal*
EMP: 5
SALES (est): 407.6K **Privately Held**
SIC: 7372 Prepackaged software

(G-9042)
CMX MEDIA LLC
Also Called: Complex Magazine
1271 Av Of The Americas (10020-1300)
PHONE......................917 793-5831
Rich Antoniello, *CEO*
Scott Cherkin, *Exec VP*
Moksha Fitzgibbons, *Exec VP*
Aleksey Baksheyev, *Vice Pres*
Edgar Hernandez, *Vice Pres*
▲ EMP: 20
SALES (est): 4.7MM **Privately Held**
WEB: www.complex.com
SIC: 2721 Magazines: publishing & printing

(G-9043)
COACH SERVICES INC (HQ)
10 Hudson Yards (10001-2157)
PHONE......................212 594-1850
Gebhard Rainer, *President*
David Enright, *Senior VP*
Jane F Nielsen, *CFO*
Todd Kahn, *Admin Sec*
◆ EMP: 41
SALES (est): 9.6MM
SALES (corp-wide): 6B **Publicly Held**
SIC: 3171 Handbags, women's
PA: Tapestry, Inc.
10 Hudson Yards
New York NY 10001
212 594-1850

(G-9044)
COALITION ON POSITIVE HEALTH
1751 Park Ave Fl 4 (10035-2809)
PHONE......................212 633-2500
Gloria Searson, *Director*
EMP: 14
SALES: 591K **Privately Held**
SIC: 7372 Educational computer software

(G-9045)
COBICO PRODUCTIONS INC
344 E 50th St Apt 1b (10022-7963)
PHONE......................347 417-5883
Jacob Babchuk, *President*
EMP: 5
SALES (est): 34K **Privately Held**
SIC: 2752 7335 Commercial printing, litho-
graphic; commercial photography

(G-9046)
COCKPIT USA INC
15 W 39th St Fl 12 (10018-0628)
PHONE......................212 575-1616
Jacky Clyman, *Branch Mgr*
EMP: 12
SALES (corp-wide): 10.5MM **Privately Held**
WEB: www.avirex.com
SIC: 2386 5136 5611 5961 Coats & jack-
ets, leather & sheep-lined; sportswear,
men's & boys'; clothing, sportswear,
men's & boys'; clothing, mail order (ex-
cept women's)
PA: Cockpit Usa, Inc.
15 W 39th St Fl 12
New York NY 10018
212 575-1616

(G-9047)
CODA MEDIA INC
Also Called: Coda Story
108 W 39th St Rm 1000 (10018-8267)
PHONE......................917 478-2565
Greenberg Ilan, *Principal*
EMP: 5 EST: 2016
SALES (est): 171.1K **Privately Held**
SIC: 2721 Magazines: publishing only, not
printed on site

(G-9048)
CODESTERS INC
900 Broadway Ste 903 (10003-1223)
PHONE......................646 232-1025
Gordon Smith, *CEO*
Manesh Patel, *Treasurer*
Kimberly Sauter, *Manager*
Juan Farfan, *Web Dvlpr*
Kate Sullivan, *Teacher*
EMP: 8
SQ FT: 4,500
SALES: 600K **Privately Held**
SIC: 2731 8299 Textbooks: publishing &
printing; schools & educational service

(G-9049)
COGNOTION INC
1407 Broadway Fl 24 (10018-5101)
PHONE......................347 692-0640
Joanna Schneier, *CEO*
Jonathan Dariyanani, *President*
Michael Goldberg, *CFO*
EMP: 4
SQ FT: 1,000
SALES: 8MM **Privately Held**
SIC: 7372 Educational computer software

(G-9050)
COLGAT-PLMOLIVE CENTL AMER INC (HQ)
300 Park Ave (10022-7402)
PHONE......................212 310-2000
Ian Cook, *Ch of Bd*
EMP: 10
SALES (est): 8MM
SALES (corp-wide): 15.5B **Publicly Held**
SIC: 2844 Toothpastes or powders, denti-
frices
PA: Colgate-Palmolive Company
300 Park Ave Fl 3
New York NY 10022
212 310-2000

(G-9051)
COLGATE-PALMOLIVE COMPANY (PA)
300 Park Ave Fl 3 (10022-7499)
PHONE......................212 310-2000
Ian Cook, *Ch of Bd*
Noel R Wallace, *President*
John J Huston, *Senior VP*
Philip G Shotts, *Vice Pres*
Henning I Jakobsen, *CFO*
◆ EMP: 3000

SALES: 15.5B **Publicly Held**
WEB: www.colgate.com
SIC: 2844 3991 2841 2842 Toothpastes
or powders, dentifrices; mouthwashes;
deodorants, personal; shaving preparations; toothbrushes, except electric; soap
& other detergents; detergents, synthetic
organic or inorganic alkaline; dishwashing
compounds; soap: granulated, liquid,
cake, flaked or chip; specialty cleaning,
polishes & sanitation goods; fabric softeners; bleaches, household: dry or liquid;
dog & cat food

(G-9052)
COLGATE-PALMOLIVE NJ INC
300 Park Ave Fl 8 (10022-7499)
PHONE......................212 310-2000
Bill Shanahan, *President*
EMP: 20
SALES (est): 3.1MM
SALES (corp-wide): 15.5B **Publicly Held**
WEB: www.colgate.com
SIC: 2841 Soap & other detergents
PA: Colgate-Palmolive Company
300 Park Ave Fl 3
New York NY 10022
212 310-2000

(G-9053)
COLLECTION XIIX LTD (PA)
1370 Broadway Fl 17 (10018-7764)
PHONE......................212 686-8990
Andrew Pizzo, *President*
Ron D'Angelo, *Vice Pres*
Ralph Bergman, *CFO*
Rae Li Piec, *Bookkeeper*
Amanda Schellaci, *Info Tech Mgr*
▲ EMP: 10
SQ FT: 14,000
SALES (est): 22.9MM **Privately Held**
WEB: www.collection18.com
SIC: 2339 Women's & misses' accessories

(G-9054)
COLONY HOLDINGS INTL LLC
131 W 35th St Fl 6 (10001-2111)
PHONE......................212 868-2800
Douglas Chan, *CEO*
EMP: 10
SALES: 950K **Privately Held**
SIC: 2321 Men's & boys' furnishings

(G-9055)
COLOR UNLIMITED INC
244 5th Ave Frnt (10001-7604)
PHONE......................212 802-7547
Henri Boll, *Principal*
EMP: 5
SQ FT: 1,200
SALES: 100K **Privately Held**
WEB: www.go2museum.com
SIC: 2741 Art copy: publishing & printing

(G-9056)
COLORFAST
121 Varick St Fl 9 (10013-1408)
PHONE......................212 929-2440
John R Arbucci, *President*
Ira Schwidel, *Vice Pres*
EMP: 15
SALES (est): 1MM **Privately Held**
WEB: www.vividcolorinternational.com
SIC: 2752 Commercial printing, offset

(G-9057)
COLORTEX INC
1202 Lexington Ave 115 (10028-1439)
P.O. Box 115 (10028-0015)
PHONE......................212 564-2000
Steven Usdan, *President*
▲ EMP: 5
SQ FT: 10,000
SALES (est): 412.8K **Privately Held**
SIC: 2281 5199 Yarn spinning mills; yarns

(G-9058)
COLUMBIA DAILY SPECTATOR
2875 Broadway Ste 303 (10025-7846)
PHONE......................212 854-9550
Rana Hilal, *Production*
April Wong, *Controller*
Thomas Carlyle, *Controller*
Han Zhang, *Sales Mgr*
Rachit Mohan, *Sales Associate*
EMP: 20

SALES: 287.6K **Privately Held**
WEB: www.columbiaspectator.com
SIC: 2711 Newspapers, publishing & print-
ing

(G-9059)
COLUMBIA RECORDS INC
25 Madison Ave Fl 19 (10010-8601)
PHONE......................212 833-8000
Ron Perry, *CEO*
Azim Rashid, *Senior VP*
John Strazza, *Vice Pres*
EMP: 14
SALES (est): 1.8MM **Privately Held**
SIC: 3652 Pre-recorded records & tapes
HQ: Sony Music Entertainment, Inc.
25 Madison Ave Fl 19
New York NY 10010
212 833-8000

(G-9060)
COLUMBIA UNIVERSITY PRESS (HQ)
61 W 62nd St Fl 3 (10023-7015)
PHONE......................212 459-0600
Gregory Lara, *Info Tech Dir*
Jennifer Crewe, *Director*
Rebecca Castillo, *Meeting Planner*
▲ EMP: 23
SQ FT: 31,500
SALES: 9.4MM
SALES (corp-wide): 2.8B **Privately Held**
SIC: 2731 Books: publishing only; pam-
phlets: publishing only, not printed on site
PA: The Trustees Of Columbia University In
The City Of New York
116th And Bdwy Way
New York NY 10027
212 854-9970

(G-9061)
COLUMBIA UNIVERSITY PRESS
61 W 62nd St Fl 3 (10023-7015)
PHONE......................212 459-0600
EMP: 37
SALES (corp-wide): 2.8B **Privately Held**
SIC: 2731 Books: publishing only
HQ: Columbia University Press
61 W 62nd St Fl 3
New York NY 10023
212 459-0600

(G-9062)
COLUMBIA UNIVERSITY PRESS
61 W 62nd St Fl 3 (10023-7015)
PHONE......................212 459-0600
Angela Ajayi, *Branch Mgr*
EMP: 50
SALES (corp-wide): 2.8B **Privately Held**
SIC: 2731 5192 Books: publishing only;
pamphlets: publishing only, not printed on
site; books
HQ: Columbia University Press
61 W 62nd St Fl 3
New York NY 10023
212 459-0600

(G-9063)
COLUMBUS TRADING CORP
Also Called: Columbus Accessories
120 W 31st St Rm 600 (10001-3407)
PHONE......................212 564-1780
Chin C S Kim, *President*
▲ EMP: 15
SALES (est): 1.4MM **Privately Held**
SIC: 3961 Costume jewelry

(G-9064)
COMELY INTERNATIONAL TRDG INC
303 5th Ave Rm 1903 (10016-6658)
PHONE......................212 683-1240
Qinghe Liu, *President*
Xu Sue Wang, *Vice Pres*
▲ EMP: 5
SQ FT: 1,800
SALES (est): 2.4MM **Privately Held**
WEB: www.comelyinternational.com
SIC: 2519 Furniture, household: glass,
fiberglass & plastic

(G-9065)
COMINT APPAREL GROUP LLC
Also Called: Sebby Clothing
463 7th Ave Fl 4 (10018-8725)
P.O. Box 630, Englewood NJ (07631-0630)
PHONE..............................212 947-7474
Carlos Donzis, *Mng Member*
Graciela Donzis,
▲ EMP: 35
SQ FT: 4,000
SALES (est): 3.6MM **Privately Held**
WEB: www.comintapparel.com
SIC: 2339 Women's & misses' outerwear

(G-9066)
COMMENTARY INC
165 E 56th St Fl 16 (10022-2709)
PHONE..............................212 891-1400
Davi Birnstein, *Publisher*
EMP: 10
SALES: 2.2MM **Privately Held**
SIC: 2721 Magazines: publishing & printing

(G-9067)
COMMERCIAL GASKETS NEW YORK
247 W 38th St Rm 409 (10018-1047)
PHONE..............................212 244-8130
Stewart Shabman, *Principal*
EMP: 11
SALES (est): 1.3MM **Privately Held**
SIC: 3053 Packing, metallic

(G-9068)
COMMONWEAL FOUNDATION INC
Also Called: Commonweal Magazine
475 Riverside Dr Rm 405 (10115-0433)
PHONE..............................212 662-4200
Thomas Baker, *President*
James Hannan, *Vice Pres*
Steven Aubrey, *Manager*
Matthew Sitman, *Assoc Editor*
Tiina Aleman, *Art Dir*
EMP: 10 EST: 1924
SALES: 2MM **Privately Held**
WEB: www.catholicsinpublicsquare.org
SIC: 2721 Magazines: publishing only, not printed on site

(G-9069)
COMMONWEALTH TOY NOVELTY INC (PA)
875 6th Ave Rm 910 (10001-3578)
PHONE..............................212 242-4070
Steven Greenfield, *Ch of Bd*
Lee Schneider, *President*
Saami Siddiqui, *Merchandise Mgr*
Greg Hogue, *Manager*
Jaime Latzman, *Director*
◆ EMP: 52 EST: 1934
SQ FT: 16,000
SALES (est): 8.4MM **Privately Held**
SIC: 3942 Stuffed toys, including animals

(G-9070)
COMMUNITY MEDIA LLC
Also Called: Downtown Express Newspaper
515 Canal St Fl 1 (10013-1330)
PHONE..............................212 229-1890
John Sutter,
EMP: 20
SALES (est): 1MM **Privately Held**
WEB: www.communitymediallc.com
SIC: 2711 2752 Newspapers, publishing & printing; commercial printing, lithographic

(G-9071)
COMPAR MANUFACTURING CORP
308 Dyckman St (10034-5351)
PHONE..............................212 304-2777
Alex Neuburger, *President*
Steven Neuburger, *Vice Pres*
EMP: 50
SALES (est): 3.2MM
SALES (corp-wide): 9.8MM **Privately Held**
SIC: 3496 3469 Miscellaneous fabricated wire products; metal stampings
PA: Magic Novelty Co., Inc.
308 Dyckman St
New York NY 10034
212 304-2777

(G-9072)
COMPELLD INC
57 Reade St Apt 10f (10007-1709)
PHONE..............................917 494-4462
Shruti Joshi, *President*
EMP: 7
SALES: 50K **Privately Held**
SIC: 7372 8748 Application computer software; business consulting

(G-9073)
COMPLETE PUBLISHING SOLUTIONS
Also Called: CPS Creative
350 W 51st St Apt 13b (10019-6445)
PHONE..............................212 242-7321
James Hohl, *Mng Member*
EMP: 5
SQ FT: 900
SALES (est): 337.6K **Privately Held**
WEB: www.cpspress.com
SIC: 2741 Miscellaneous publishing

(G-9074)
COMPLEX MEDIA INC (PA)
229 W 43rd St Fl 10 (10036-3982)
PHONE..............................917 793-5831
Richard Antoniello, *President*
Ederson Alves, *Vice Pres*
Brian Kelley, *Admin Sec*
Fred Miketa, *Merchandising*
EMP: 45
SALES (est): 122.5MM **Privately Held**
SIC: 2721 Magazines: publishing & printing

(G-9075)
CONCEALED BASEBOARD HTG CO LLC
48 Wall St Ste 1100 (10005-2907)
PHONE..............................212 378-6710
Roger Thomas, *Mng Member*
EMP: 10
SQ FT: 500
SALES (est): 586.8K **Privately Held**
SIC: 3567 Heating units & devices, industrial: electric

(G-9076)
CONCEPTS NYC INC
Also Called: Concept Nyc
25 W 39th St Lbby A (10018-4199)
PHONE..............................212 244-1033
Joseph Bibi, *President*
Elliott J Bibi, *Vice Pres*
Reuben J Bibi, *Vice Pres*
▲ EMP: 25
SALES (est): 4.3MM **Privately Held**
SIC: 2221 Apparel & outerwear fabric, manmade fiber or silk

(G-9077)
CONCORD JEWELRY MFG CO LLC
Also Called: Concord Jwlry Mfrs
64 W 48th St Ste 1004 (10036-1708)
PHONE..............................212 719-4030
Ann Seregi, *President*
EMP: 25 EST: 1951
SALES (est): 1.8MM **Privately Held**
SIC: 3911 Jewelry, precious metal

(G-9078)
CONCORDE APPAREL COMPANY LLC (PA)
55 W 39th St Fl 11 (10018-3803)
PHONE..............................212 307-7848
Lee Wattenburg,
Paul Wattenburg,
▲ EMP: 5
SALES: 20.7MM **Privately Held**
SIC: 2311 Men's & boys' suits & coats

(G-9079)
CONDE NAST ENTERTAINMENT LLC
Also Called: Teen Vogue
1 World Trade Ctr (10007-0089)
PHONE..............................212 286-2860
Robert Sauerberg Jr, *President*
Susan Plagemann, *Publisher*
Edward Barsamian, *Editor*
Shakeil Greeley, *Editor*
Emma Morrison, *Editor*
EMP: 2615 EST: 2013

SALES (est): 228.8MM
SALES (corp-wide): 5.5B **Privately Held**
SIC: 2721 Magazines: publishing & printing
PA: Advance Publications, Inc.
1 World Trade Ctr Fl 43
New York NY 10007
718 981-1234

(G-9080)
CONDECO SOFTWARE INC
1350 Broadway Rm 1712 (10018-0900)
PHONE..............................408 508-7330
Martin Brooker, *COO*
Gary Bull, *COO*
Ian Cole, *CFO*
Lynda Lowe, *Chief Mktg Ofcr*
Paul Goodridge, *Exec Dir*
EMP: 25
SALES (corp-wide): 41.3MM **Privately Held**
SIC: 7372 Business oriented computer software
HQ: Condeco Software, Inc.
2105 S Bascom Ave Ste 150
Campbell CA 95008
917 677-7600

(G-9081)
CONFERENCE BOARD INC (PA)
845 3rd Ave Fl 2 (10022-6600)
PHONE..............................212 759-0900
Jonathan Spector, *President*
Francisco G Rodr Guez, *Trustee*
James H Slamp, *Exec VP*
Marion Feigenbaum, *Vice Pres*
Rebecca Ray, *Vice Pres*
EMP: 180
SQ FT: 49,750
SALES: 25.4MM **Privately Held**
WEB: www.conference-board.org
SIC: 2721 8299 Periodicals: publishing only; educational service, nondegree granting: continuing educ.

(G-9082)
CONFIANT INC
72 Madison Ave Fl 2 (10016-8731)
PHONE..............................646 397-4198
Louis-David Mangin, *CEO*
Amit Dodeja, *COO*
EMP: 12
SALES (est): 306K **Privately Held**
SIC: 7372 Business oriented computer software

(G-9083)
CONGRESS FOR JEWISH CULTURE
Also Called: DI ZUKUNFT
1133 Broadway Ste 1019 (10010-7996)
P.O. Box 1590 (10159-1590)
PHONE..............................212 505-8040
Barnett Zumoff, *President*
Shane Baker, *Exec Dir*
EMP: 5
SQ FT: 800
SALES: 94.8K **Privately Held**
SIC: 2731 2721 7922 Book music: publishing only, not printed on site; periodicals: publishing only; theatrical producers & services; theatrical producers

(G-9084)
CONNECTIVA SYSTEMS INC (PA)
19 W 44th St Ste 611 (10036-5900)
PHONE..............................646 722-8741
AVI Basu, *President*
EMP: 18
SALES (est): 24.1MM **Privately Held**
WEB: www.connectivasystems.com
SIC: 3695 Computer software tape & disks: blank, rigid & floppy

(G-9085)
CONSOLIDATED CHILDRENS AP INC (HQ)
Also Called: Bonjour For Kids
100 W 33rd St Ste 1105 (10001-2990)
PHONE..............................212 239-8615
Mark Adjmi, *President*
Jack Adjmi, *Chairman*
Joy Mahana, *Treasurer*
Jeffrey Longua, *Director*
▲ EMP: 3

SALES (est): 6.9MM
SALES (corp-wide): 27.1MM **Privately Held**
SIC: 2361 Dresses: girls', children's & infants'
PA: Adjmi Apparel Group Llc
463 7th Ave
New York NY 10018
212 239-8615

(G-9086)
CONSOLIDATED COLOR PRESS INC
307 7th Ave Rm 904 (10001-6049)
PHONE..............................212 929-8197
William D Sommers Jr, *President*
Richard M Sommers, *Vice Pres*
Richard Sommers, *Vice Pres*
EMP: 12
SALES (est): 1.5MM **Privately Held**
SIC: 2752 2791 Commercial printing, offset; typesetting

(G-9087)
CONSOLIDATED LOOSE LEAF INC (PA)
989 Avnue Of The Americas (10018-5410)
PHONE..............................212 924-5800
Sol Kleinman, *President*
Martin Schneider, *Corp Secy*
EMP: 45
SQ FT: 32,000
SALES (est): 3MM **Privately Held**
SIC: 2782 Looseleaf binders & devices; library binders, looseleaf

(G-9088)
CONSTELLATION BRANDS SMO LLC
111 8th Ave (10011-5201)
PHONE..............................585 396-7161
EMP: 5
SALES (est): 250.5K
SALES (corp-wide): 8.1B **Publicly Held**
SIC: 2084 Wines, brandy & brandy spirits
PA: Constellation Brands, Inc.
207 High Point Dr # 100
Victor NY 14564
585 678-7100

(G-9089)
CONTACTIVE INC
137 Varick St Ste 605 (10013-1105)
PHONE..............................646 476-9059
Inaki Berenguer, *CEO*
Julio Viera, *President*
EMP: 50
SALES (est): 2.2MM
SALES (corp-wide): 122.9MM **Privately Held**
SIC: 7372 Application computer software
PA: Fuze, Inc.
2 Copley Pl Ste 700
Boston MA 02116
800 890-1553

(G-9090)
CONTINUITY PUBLISHING INC
15 W 39th St Fl 9 (10018-0631)
PHONE..............................212 869-4170
Neil Adams, *President*
Kristine Adams, *Vice Pres*
Marilyn Adams, *Vice Pres*
EMP: 12
SQ FT: 4,000
SALES (est): 750K **Privately Held**
SIC: 2721 Comic books: publishing only, not printed on site

(G-9091)
CONTINUITY SOFTWARE INC
5 Penn Plz Fl 23 (10001-1810)
PHONE..............................646 216-8628
Gil Hecht, *CEO*
Giza Venture Fund, *Shareholder*
EMP: 40
SALES (est): 2.1MM **Privately Held**
SIC: 7372 Business oriented computer software

(G-9092)
CONTINUUM INTL PUBG GROUP INC
15 W 26th St Fl 8 (10010-1065)
PHONE..............................646 649-4215

G E O G R A P H I C

Fax: 212 953-9554
EMP: 12
SALES (corp-wide): 173.2MM **Privately Held**
SIC: 2731 Book Publishers
HQ: The Continuum International Publishing Group Inc
175 5th Ave Lbby 5
New York NY

(G-9093)
CONVENIENCE STORE NEWS
770 Broadway Fl 5 (10003-9554)
PHONE..................................214 217-7800
Maureen Arzato, *Principal*
EMP: 5
SALES (est): 309.3K **Privately Held**
WEB: www.csnews.com
SIC: 2721 Magazines: publishing & printing

(G-9094)
CONVERSION LABS INC (PA)
800 3rd Ave Ste 2800 (10022-7604)
PHONE..................................866 351-5907
John R Strawn Jr, *Ch of Bd*
Justin Schreiber, *President*
Robert Kalkstein, *CFO*
Joseph Ditrolio, *Chief Mktg Ofcr*
Stefan Galluppi, *Officer*
EMP: 11 **EST:** 1987
SALES: 8.3MM **Publicly Held**
SIC: 2833 Medicinals & botanicals

(G-9095)
COOKIES INC
Also Called: Carnival
143 Madison Ave Fl 6 (10016-6705)
PHONE..................................917 261-4981
Charles Dweck, *President*
Mitch Melamed, *Director*
▲ **EMP:** 575
SALES (est): 28.3MM **Privately Held**
SIC: 2353 5947 Hats, trimmed: women's, misses' & children's; gift, novelty & souvenir shop

(G-9096)
COOKS INTL LTD LBLTY CO
7 World Trade Ctr Fl 46 (10007-2337)
PHONE..................................212 741-4407
Henry Mandil,
◆ **EMP:** 5
SQ FT: 1,500
SALES (est): 270K **Privately Held**
SIC: 2999 3567 Fuel briquettes or boulets: made with petroleum binder; metal melting furnaces, industrial: electric

(G-9097)
COPEN UNITED LLC
37 W 39th St Fl 6 (10018-3886)
PHONE..................................212 819-0008
Haim Hoenig, *CEO*
◆ **EMP:** 9 **EST:** 2012
SALES (est): 928.5K **Privately Held**
SIC: 2299 Ramie yarn, thread, roving & textiles
PA: Selecta International Limited
Rm 11-13 16/F One Midtown
Tsuen Wan NT

(G-9098)
COPIA INTERACTIVE LLC
105 Madison Ave (10016-7418)
PHONE..................................212 481-0520
Michael Schluter, *Partner*
Nathan Cayzer, *Senior VP*
Seth Kaufman, *Vice Pres*
EMP: 16
SALES (est): 1.1MM **Privately Held**
SIC: 2711 Newspapers, publishing & printing

(G-9099)
COPY ROOM INC
885 3rd Ave Lowr 2ll (10022-4804)
PHONE..................................212 371-8600
George Dispigno, *President*
EMP: 12
SQ FT: 4,000
SALES (est): 2.5MM **Privately Held**
WEB: www.nydmv.com
SIC: 2759 2789 7389 Commercial printing; magazines, binding; laminating service

(G-9100)
COPY4LES INC
146 W 29th St Rm 9w (10001-8207)
PHONE..................................212 487-9778
Davesham Walter Panagoda, *CEO*
EMP: 11
SALES (est): 2.1MM **Privately Held**
SIC: 3555 Copy holders, printers'

(G-9101)
CORBERTEX LLC
1412 Broadway Rm 1100 (10018-3320)
PHONE..................................212 971-0008
Howard Corber,
EMP: 5
SALES (est): 310K **Privately Held**
SIC: 3552 Textile machinery

(G-9102)
CORDIS SOLUTIONS INC
Also Called: Excelerateds2p
380 Lexington Ave Fl 17 (10168-1799)
PHONE..................................917 909-2002
Ramesh Varsani, *President*
Conor Mullanie, *Vice Pres*
Rob Verity, *Sales Staff*
Ramesh Bobbala, *Consultant*
Cynthia Goco-Nakar, *Director*
EMP: 10
SALES (est): 370.2K **Privately Held**
SIC: 7372 Application computer software
PA: Cordis Solutions Limited
Unit 15, North Circular Business Park
London
845 625-0425

(G-9103)
COREMET TRADING INC
160 Brdwy Ste 1107 (10038)
PHONE..................................212 964-3600
Leo Horowitz, *Ch of Bd*
M Elliott Czermak, *Vice Pres*
Warren Katzman, *Treasurer*
◆ **EMP:** 5
SQ FT: 800
SALES (est): 1.1MM **Privately Held**
SIC: 1081 Metal mining exploration & development services

(G-9104)
CORINNE MCCORMACK INC
7 W 36th St Fl 9 (10018-7158)
PHONE..................................212 868-7919
Corinne McCormack, *President*
▲ **EMP:** 10
SALES (est): 1.1MM
SALES (corp-wide): 1.4MM **Privately Held**
WEB: www.corinnemccormack.com
SIC: 3851 Eyeglasses, lenses & frames
HQ: Fgx International Inc.
500 George Washington Hwy
Smithfield RI 02917
401 231-3800

(G-9105)
CORNING INCORPORATED
767 5th Ave Ste 2301 (10153-0012)
PHONE..................................646 521-9600
Karen Nelson, *Branch Mgr*
EMP: 5
SALES (corp-wide): 11.2B **Publicly Held**
WEB: www.corning.com
SIC: 3229 Pressed & blown glass
PA: Corning Incorporated
1 Riverfront Plz
Corning NY 14831
607 974-9000

(G-9106)
COSMOPOLITAN MAGAZINE
300 W 57th St Fl 38 (10019-3299)
PHONE..................................212 649-2000
EMP: 5
SALES (est): 350.5K **Privately Held**
SIC: 2721 Magazines: publishing only, not printed on site

(G-9107)
COTY INC (PA)
350 5th Ave (10118-0110)
PHONE..................................212 389-7300
Pierre Laubies, *CEO*
Edgar Huber, *President*
Sylvie Moreau, *President*
Giovanni Pieraccioni, *COO*

Pierre-Andre Terisse, *CFO*
◆ **EMP:** 60
SALES: 8.6B **Publicly Held**
WEB: www.cotyshop.com
SIC: 2844 Toilet preparations

(G-9108)
COTY US LLC (HQ)
Also Called: Private Portfolio
350 5th Ave (10118-0110)
PHONE..................................212 389-7000
Bart Becht, *CEO*
Patrice De Talhout, *Exec VP*
Camillo Pane, *Exec VP*
Mario Reis, *Exec VP*
Jules Kaufman, *Senior VP*
◆ **EMP:** 130
SALES (est): 442.6MM **Publicly Held**
WEB: www.cotyinc.com
SIC: 2844 Perfumes & colognes; cosmetic preparations

(G-9109)
COUNTER EVOLUTION
37 W 17th St (10011-5503)
PHONE..................................212 647-7505
Jim Malone, *Owner*
Madelyn Riddleberger, *Manager*
EMP: 6
SALES (est): 808.5K **Privately Held**
SIC: 3131 Counters

(G-9110)
COUNTESS CORPORATION
Also Called: Terani Couture
225 W 37th St Fl 12 (10018-5726)
PHONE..................................212 869-7070
Daryoush Peter Tehrant, *President*
Matt Schwartz, *COO*
Derek Voyticki, *Cust Mgr*
Joyce Hatoum, *Accounts Exec*
Benny Saghian, *Rector*
▲ **EMP:** 8
SQ FT: 10,000
SALES (est): 1.7MM **Privately Held**
SIC: 2337 Women's & misses' suits & coats

(G-9111)
COUNTESS MARA INC
120 W 45th St Fl 37 (10036-4195)
PHONE..................................212 768-7300
Ross Gershkowitz, *President*
EMP: 6
SQ FT: 3,000
SALES: 358.6K
SALES (corp-wide): 153.3MM **Privately Held**
WEB: www.randacorp.com
SIC: 2323 Neckties, men's & boys': made from purchased materials
HQ: Randa Corporation
417 5th Ave Fl 11
New York NY 10016
212 768-8800

(G-9112)
COUTURE INC
16 W 37th St Frnt 1 (10018-7404)
PHONE..................................212 921-1166
Catherine Ansel, *Principal*
▲ **EMP:** 5 **EST:** 2007
SALES (est): 470K **Privately Held**
SIC: 2335 Wedding gowns & dresses

(G-9113)
COVE POINT HOLDINGS LLC (PA)
60 E 42nd St Rm 3210 (10165-0056)
PHONE..................................212 599-3388
William C Morris, *Chairman*
EMP: 20
SALES: 26.5K **Privately Held**
SIC: 2671 2672 Paper coated or laminated for packaging; adhesive papers, labels or tapes: from purchased material

(G-9114)
CPT USA LLC (PA)
Also Called: Captain USA
15 W 39th St Fl 12 (10018-0628)
PHONE..................................212 575-1616
Jeffrey Clyman,
▲ **EMP:** 27
SQ FT: 4,200

SALES (est): 2.4MM **Privately Held**
SIC: 2371 Apparel, fur

(G-9115)
CRABTREE PUBLISHING INC
350 5th Ave Ste 3304 (10118-3304)
PHONE..................................212 496-5040
John Siemens, *Branch Mgr*
EMP: 27
SALES (corp-wide): 4MM **Privately Held**
WEB: www.crabtreebooks.com
SIC: 2731 Books: publishing & printing
PA: Crabtree Publishing Company Limited
616 Welland Ave
St Catharines ON L2M 5
905 682-5221

(G-9116)
CRAFT CLERICAL CLOTHES INC
Also Called: Craft Robe Co.
247 W 37th St Rm 1700 (10018-5051)
PHONE..................................212 764-6122
Marvin Goldman, *President*
EMP: 8
SQ FT: 3,000
SALES: 1MM **Privately Held**
SIC: 2389 5699 Uniforms & vestments; academic vestments (caps & gowns); clergymen's vestments; uniforms; caps & gowns (academic vestments); clergy vestments

(G-9117)
CRAFTATLANTIC LLC
Also Called: Craft Atlantic
115 Greenwich Ave (10014-1915)
PHONE..................................646 726-4205
Pierre Mordacq, *Mng Member*
EMP: 13
SALES (est): 1.2MM **Privately Held**
SIC: 2329 Knickers, dress (separate): men's & boys'

(G-9118)
CRAIN COMMUNICATIONS INC
Business Insurance
685 3rd Ave (10017-4024)
PHONE..................................212 210-0100
Martin Ross, *Principal*
Erin Smith, *Sales Staff*
Nicole Margaritonda, *Manager*
Christina Nelson, *Manager*
Matt Ackermann, *Director*
EMP: 200
SALES (corp-wide): 225MM **Privately Held**
WEB: www.crainsnewyork.com
SIC: 2721 7812 Magazines: publishing only, not printed on site; motion picture & video production
PA: Crain Communications, Inc.
1155 Gratiot Ave
Detroit MI 48207
313 446-6000

(G-9119)
CREATIVE FORMS INC
80 Varick St Apt 10a (10013-1945)
P.O. Box 1485 (10013-0878)
PHONE..................................212 431-7540
Donald Macpherson, *President*
EMP: 5
SALES (est): 450K **Privately Held**
SIC: 2752 Commercial printing, offset

(G-9120)
CREATIVE PRINTING CORP
Also Called: Creative Prntng
70 W 36th St Rm 500 (10018-8050)
PHONE..................................212 226-3870
Mark Jackson, *President*
Candice Jackson, *Corp Secy*
Dave Bird, *Vice Pres*
Doug Bird, *Vice Pres*
EMP: 7
SQ FT: 6,000
SALES (est): 560K **Privately Held**
WEB: www.starkey-henricks.com
SIC: 2752 Commercial printing, offset

(G-9121)
CREATIVE TOOLS & SUPPLY INC
Also Called: All Craft Jewelry Supply
135 W 29th St Rm 205 (10001-5191)
PHONE..................................212 279-7077

Tevel Herbstman, *President*
▲ EMP: 9
SQ FT: 2,000
SALES (est): 1.3MM **Privately Held**
SIC: 3915 Jewelers' materials & lapidary work

(G-9122)
CREDIT UNION JOURNAL INC
Also Called: Source Media
1 State St Fl 26 (10004-1561)
PHONE................................212 803-8200
Aaron Passman, *Editor*
Michael Scarchilli, *Chief*
Sean Kron, *CFO*
David Evans, *Ch Credit Ofcr*
Tracy John, *Accountant*
EMP: 5
SALES (est): 575.2K **Privately Held**
WEB: www.cujournal.com
SIC: 2721 Magazines: publishing & printing

(G-9123)
CROWLEY TAR PRODUCTS CO INC (PA)
305 Madison Ave Ste 1035 (10165-1036)
PHONE................................212 682-1200
William A Callaman, *CEO*
William Jennings, *Principal*
▲ EMP: 7
SQ FT: 10,000
SALES (est): 3.2MM **Privately Held**
WEB: www.crowleychemical.com
SIC: 2865 Cyclic crudes, coal tar; tar

(G-9124)
CROWN JEWELERS INTL INC
168 7th Ave S (10014-2727)
PHONE................................212 420-7800
Neryo Shimunov, *Ch of Bd*
EMP: 5
SALES (est): 494.9K **Privately Held**
SIC: 3911 5094 Jewelry, precious metal; jewelry

(G-9125)
CRUNCHED INC
41 E 11th St (10003-4602)
PHONE................................415 484-9909
Sean Black, *CEO*
Roger Billerey-Mosier, *Engineer*
EMP: 7
SALES (est): 340.3K
SALES (corp-wide): 303.2MM **Privately Held**
SIC: 7372 Business oriented computer software
HQ: Clearslide, Inc.
45 Fremont St Fl 32
San Francisco CA 94105
877 360-3366

(G-9126)
CRUZIN MANAGEMENT INC (DH)
401 Park Ave S Fl 7 (10016-8808)
PHONE................................212 641-8700
Jay S Maltby, *President*
Thomas A Valdes, *Exec VP*
D Chris Mitchell, *Senior VP*
Ousik Yu, *Senior VP*
Ezra Shashoua, *CFO*
▼ EMP: 50
SQ FT: 250,000
SALES (est): 31.4MM
SALES (corp-wide): 182.4MM **Privately Held**
WEB: www.cruzanrum.com
SIC: 2085 2084 5182 Rum (alcoholic beverage); brandy; liquor
HQ: The Absolut Spirits Company Inc
250 Park Ave 17
New York NY 10177
914 848-4800

(G-9127)
CSCO LLC
1407 Broadway Rm 1503 (10018-5100)
PHONE................................212 375-6180
David Apperman, *President*
Salomon Murciano, *Vice Pres*
Penelope Savinon, *Admin Sec*
▲ EMP: 22 EST: 2014
SALES (est): 600.3K **Privately Held**
SIC: 2335 Women's, juniors' & misses' dresses

(G-9128)
CTS LLC
Also Called: Costello Tagliapietra
211 E 18th St Apt 4d (10003-3624)
PHONE................................212 278-0058
Aby Saltiel,
Jeffrey Costello,
Regino Nieves,
Robert Tagliapietra,
EMP: 5
SQ FT: 5,000
SALES (est): 382.4K **Privately Held**
SIC: 2335 Women's, juniors' & misses' dresses

(G-9129)
CUBIC TRNSP SYSTEMS INC
245 W 17th St Fl 8 (10011-5373)
PHONE................................212 255-1810
Richard Trenery, *Branch Mgr*
EMP: 15
SALES (corp-wide): 1.2B **Publicly Held**
SIC: 3829 3714 3581 Fare registers for street cars, buses, etc.; motor vehicle parts & accessories; automatic vending machines
HQ: Cubic Transportation Systems, Inc.
5650 Kearny Mesa Rd
San Diego CA 92111
858 268-3100

(G-9130)
CUEBID TECHNOLOGIES INC (PA)
40 Exchange Pl Ste 1602 (10005-2727)
PHONE................................302 380-3910
Eyal Ben Gal, *Principal*
EMP: 3
SALES (est): 4.3MM **Privately Held**
SIC: 3671 Electron tubes

(G-9131)
CULT RECORDS LLC
263 Bowery Apt 3 (10002-5656)
PHONE................................718 395-2077
Julian Casablancas, *Co-Owner*
EMP: 5
SALES (est): 261.4K **Privately Held**
SIC: 3652 Pre-recorded records & tapes

(G-9132)
CULTUREIQ INC (PA)
7 Penn Plz Ste 1112 (10001-3390)
PHONE................................212 755-8633
Gregory Besner, *CEO*
Paul Maass, *Sales Associate*
Alex Hart, *Officer*
Rob Beres, *Sr Consultant*
EMP: 50
SQ FT: 4,500
SALES (est): 4.4MM **Privately Held**
SIC: 7372 Prepackaged software

(G-9133)
CUREATR INC
222 Broadway Fl 20 (10038-2510)
PHONE................................212 203-3927
Richard Resnick, *CEO*
James Bradley, *Ch of Bd*
Mary Stuyvesant, *President*
Oleksiy Khomenko, *COO*
Julia Pulzone, *CFO*
EMP: 25 EST: 2011
SQ FT: 300
SALES (est): 1.4MM **Privately Held**
SIC: 7372 Business oriented computer software

(G-9134)
CUREMDCOM INC
120 Broadway Fl 35 (10271-3599)
PHONE................................212 509-6200
Bilal Hashmat, *CEO*
Kamal Hashmat, *Ch of Bd*
James Austin, *Controller*
Nick Wilcox, *Finance*
Naela Hashmat, *Human Res Dir*
EMP: 25
SQ FT: 12,100
SALES: 14MM **Privately Held**
WEB: www.curemd.com
SIC: 7372 8082 8621 Prepackaged software; home health care services; health association

(G-9135)
CUSTOM SPORTS LAB INC
Also Called: U S Orthotic Center
515 Madison Ave Rm 1204 (10022-5484)
PHONE................................212 832-1648
Jeff Rich, *President*
EMP: 5
SALES: 500K **Privately Held**
SIC: 3149 3842 8734 Athletic shoes, except rubber or plastic; orthopedic appliances; product testing laboratory, safety or performance

(G-9136)
CUSTOMIZE ELITE SOCKS LLC
156 2nd Ave Apt 2c (10003-5759)
PHONE................................212 533-8551
Roger Cheng, *Principal*
EMP: 5
SALES (est): 463.6K **Privately Held**
SIC: 2252 Socks

(G-9137)
CUSTOMSHOW INC
216 E 45th St Fl 17 (10017-3304)
PHONE................................800 255-5303
Paul Shapiro, *CEO*
George Chevalier, *Ch of Bd*
Greg Gordon, *CTO*
EMP: 8
SQ FT: 3,000
SALES (est): 353.8K **Privately Held**
SIC: 7372 Application computer software

(G-9138)
CW FASTENERS & ZIPPERS CORP
142 W 36th St Fl 5 (10018-8796)
PHONE................................212 594-3203
Suk Chun Wong, *Principal*
EMP: 13
SALES (est): 1.5MM **Privately Held**
SIC: 3965 Fasteners; zipper

(G-9139)
CY FASHION CORP
525 7th Ave Rm 811 (10018-0988)
PHONE................................212 730-8600
Irene Cho, *CEO*
Barkin Eren, *President*
EMP: 3
SQ FT: 1,100
SALES: 2MM **Privately Held**
SIC: 2211 Apparel & outerwear fabrics, cotton

(G-9140)
CYBERLIMIT INC
257 W 38th St Fl 6 (10018-4457)
PHONE................................212 840-9597
David MEI, *President*
EMP: 10
SQ FT: 2,000
SALES: 210K **Privately Held**
SIC: 2331 2321 Women's & misses' blouses & shirts; men's & boys' furnishings

(G-9141)
CYGNET STUDIO INC
319 W 118th St 1b (10026-1027)
PHONE................................646 450-4550
Daniel Ehrenard, *General Mgr*
EMP: 12
SALES (est): 937.2K **Privately Held**
SIC: 2389 Costumes

(G-9142)
CYNTHIA ROWLEY INC (PA)
376 Bleecker St (10014-3210)
PHONE................................212 242-3803
Cynthia Rowley, *Ch of Bd*
Robert Shaw, *CFO*
Lisa Rosario, *Sales Mgr*
Kim Fiorentino, *Director*
Nicole Loher, *Director*
▲ EMP: 12
SQ FT: 7,000
SALES (est): 1.9MM **Privately Held**
SIC: 2331 2335 2339 Women's & misses' blouses & shirts; women's, juniors' & misses' dresses; women's & misses' outerwear; women's & misses' accessories; women's & misses' athletic clothing & sportswear

(G-9143)
CYPRESS BIOSCIENCE INC
110 E 59th St Fl 33 (10022-1315)
PHONE................................858 452-2323
Jay D Kranzler PHD, *Ch of Bd*
Sabrina Martucci Johnson, *COO*
Sharon Kay Cochran, *Manager*
R Michael Gendreau PHD, *Officer*
Srinivas G RAO PHD, *Officer*
EMP: 16
SQ FT: 5,700
SALES (est): 3.3MM **Privately Held**
WEB: www.cypressbio.com
SIC: 2836 Biological products, except diagnostic

(G-9144)
D & A OFFSET SERVICES INC
185 Varick St Ste 3 (10014-4607)
PHONE................................212 924-0612
Al D'Elia, *President*
Henny D'Elia, *Corp Secy*
Carmine D'Elia, *Vice Pres*
Vincent D'Elia, *Vice Pres*
EMP: 14
SQ FT: 11,000
SALES (est): 1.4MM **Privately Held**
SIC: 2796 Engraving platemaking services

(G-9145)
D & D WINDOW TECH INC (PA)
979 3rd Ave Lbby 132 (10022-1298)
PHONE................................212 308-2822
Amos Regev, *President*
EMP: 5
SQ FT: 250
SALES (est): 401.6K **Privately Held**
SIC: 2591 5023 Window blinds; window shades; venetian blinds; vertical blinds; window shades

(G-9146)
D M J CASTING INC
62 W 47th St Ste 508 (10036-3270)
PHONE................................212 719-1951
David Green, *President*
EMP: 5
SALES: 310K **Privately Held**
SIC: 3911 Jewelry, precious metal

(G-9147)
D R S INC (PA)
Also Called: Dason Company Div
64 W 48th St Ste 1302 (10036-1708)
PHONE................................212 819-0237
Peter Susser, *President*
Joseph Borella, *Vice Pres*
Robert Galiardo, *Manager*
▲ EMP: 30 EST: 1946
SQ FT: 4,000
SALES (est): 2.5MM **Privately Held**
WEB: www.drsny.com
SIC: 3911 5094 Rings, finger: precious metal; jewelers' findings

(G-9148)
D R S WATCH MATERIALS
64 W 48th St Ste 1302 (10036-1708)
PHONE................................212 819-0470
Joseph Borella, *Vice Pres*
EMP: 40 EST: 1980
SALES (est): 1.7MM **Privately Held**
SIC: 3915 Jewel preparing: instruments, tools, watches & jewelry

(G-9149)
D3 LED LLC
Also Called: D3 NY
566 7th Ave Rm 504 (10018-1866)
PHONE................................917 757-9671
George Pappas, *Mng Member*
EMP: 22 **Privately Held**
SIC: 3999 Advertising display products
PA: D3 Led, Llc
11370 Sunrise Park Dr
Rancho Cordova CA 95742

(G-9150)
DABBY-REID LTD
347 W 36th St Rm 701 (10018-7225)
PHONE................................212 356-0040
Ida Reid, *President*
EMP: 15

G
E
O
G
R
A
P
H
I
C

SALES: 165.6K **Privately Held**
SIC: 3961 5094 Costume jewelry, ex. precious metal & semiprecious stones; jewelry & precious stones

(G-9151)
DAHESHIST PUBLISHING CO LTD
1775 Broadway 501 (10019-1903)
PHONE......................212 581-8360
Mervat Zahid, *President*
EMP: 10
SQ FT: 2,500
SALES (est): 867.9K **Privately Held**
WEB: www.daheshheritage.org
SIC: 2731 Books: publishing only

(G-9152)
DAILY BEAST COMPANY LLC (HQ)
7 Hanover Sq (10004-2616)
PHONE......................212 445-4600
Tara F Chan, *Editor*
Laura Davis, *Editor*
Jessica Durham, *Editor*
Hank Gilman, *Editor*
Paul Naughton, *Editor*
▲ **EMP:** 34 **EST:** 1936
SQ FT: 203,000
SALES (est): 61.5MM
SALES (corp-wide): 4.2B **Publicly Held**
WEB: www.newsweek.com
SIC: 2721 Magazines: publishing only, not printed on site
PA: Iac/Interactivecorp
555 W 18th St
New York NY 10011
212 314-7300

(G-9153)
DAILY MUSE INC (PA)
Also Called: Muse, The
1375 Broadway Fl 20 (10018-7020)
PHONE......................646 357-3201
Jens Fischer, *Principal*
Alex Cavoulacos, *Principal*
Dan Kelske, *Accounts Mgr*
Andrea Siegel, *Accounts Mgr*
Kerry Fusco, *Accounts Exec*
EMP: 38
SALES (est): 12MM **Privately Held**
SIC: 2711 Newspapers, publishing & printing

(G-9154)
DAILY NEWS LP (DH)
Also Called: New York Daily News
4 New York Plz Fl 6 (10004-2828)
PHONE......................212 210-2100
William D Holiber, *President*
Marc Kramer, *General Ptnr*
Grant Whitmore, *Exec VP*
Renny Raymundo, *Director*
Dennis Smith, *Director*
▲ **EMP:** 600
SQ FT: 150,000
SALES (est): 331.9MM
SALES (corp-wide): 1B **Publicly Held**
WEB: www.nydailynews.com
SIC: 2711 Commercial printing & newspaper publishing combined
HQ: Trx Pubco, Llc
435 N Michigan Ave
Chicago IL 60611
312 222-9100

(G-9155)
DAILY RACING FORM INC (HQ)
708 3rd Ave Fl 12 (10017-4129)
PHONE......................212 366-7600
Steven Crist, *President*
Vic Denicola, *Chief*
Irwin Cohen, *Vice Pres*
Charles Hayward, *Vice Pres*
Michael Kravchenko, *Vice Pres*
▼ **EMP:** 140 **EST:** 1894
SQ FT: 34,000
SALES (est): 45.2MM
SALES (corp-wide): 263.8MM **Privately Held**
WEB: www.drf.com
SIC: 2711 Newspapers, publishing & printing

PA: Arlington Capital Partners, L.P.
5425 Wisconsin Ave # 200
Chevy Chase MD 20815
202 337-7500

(G-9156)
DAILY RACING FORM LLC
75 Broad St (10004-2415)
PHONE......................212 514-2180
Dan Illman, *Editor*
Mandy Minger, *VP Mktg*
EMP: 12
SALES (corp-wide): 263.8MM **Privately Held**
SIC: 2711 Newspapers, publishing & printing
HQ: Daily Racing Form Llc
708 3rd Ave Fl 12
New York NY 10017
212 366-7600

(G-9157)
DAILY WORLD PRESS INC
Also Called: Daily Sun New York
228 E 45th St Rm 700 (10017-3336)
PHONE......................212 922-9201
Yoshida Gin, *President*
EMP: 10
SALES (est): 591.9K **Privately Held**
SIC: 2711 Commercial printing & newspaper publishing combined; newspapers, publishing & printing

(G-9158)
DAILYCANDY INC
584 Broadway Rm 510 (10012-5244)
PHONE......................646 230-8719
Danielle Levy, *Ch of Bd*
Catherine Levene, *COO*
Peter A Sheinbaum, *COO*
EMP: 23
SQ FT: 6,100
SALES (est): 2.4MM **Privately Held**
WEB: www.dailycandy.com
SIC: 2741 Miscellaneous publishing

(G-9159)
DAKOTT LLC
244 Madison Ave Ste 211 (10016-2817)
PHONE......................888 805-6795
Michael Etedgi, *CEO*
Joshua Martin, *Exec VP*
Vera A Etedgi, *CFO*
▲ **EMP:** 5
SQ FT: 2,500
SALES (est): 1MM **Privately Held**
SIC: 3944 Scooters, children's

(G-9160)
DAMPITS INTERNATIONAL INC
425 W 57th St (10019-1764)
P.O. Box 493 (10019)
PHONE......................212 581-3047
David Hollander, *President*
Tair Hollander, *Vice Pres*
EMP: 5 **EST:** 1966
SALES (est): 480K **Privately Held**
SIC: 3634 Humidifiers, electric: household

(G-9161)
DANA MICHELE LLC
3 E 84th St (10028-0447)
PHONE......................917 757-7777
Dana Schiavo, *President*
EMP: 1
SQ FT: 5,000
SALES (est): 2MM **Privately Held**
SIC: 3942 3944 2339 Dolls & stuffed toys; games, toys & children's vehicles; women's & misses' outerwear

(G-9162)
DANAHER CORPORATION
445 E 14th St Apt 3f (10009-2805)
PHONE......................516 443-9432
EMP: 186
SALES (corp-wide): 19.8B **Publicly Held**
SIC: 3823 Water quality monitoring & control systems
PA: Danaher Corporation
2200 Penn Ave Nw Ste 800w
Washington DC 20037
202 828-0850

(G-9163)
DANDELION ENERGY INC
335 Madison Ave Fl 4 (10017-4675)
PHONE......................603 781-2663
Kathleen Hannun, *CEO*
Rajeev Quazi, *President*
EMP: 12
SALES (est): 589.2K **Privately Held**
SIC: 3433 Heating equipment, except electric

(G-9164)
DANHIER CO LLC
Also Called: Christophe Danhier
380 Rector Pl Apt 3d (10280-1442)
PHONE......................212 563-7683
Christophe Danhier,
EMP: 14
SQ FT: 1,200
SALES (est): 1.5MM **Privately Held**
WEB: www.danhier.com
SIC: 3915 Jewelers' materials & lapidary work

(G-9165)
DANI II INC (PA)
1 River Pl Apt 2410 (10036-4381)
PHONE......................212 869-5999
Kirat Singh, *CEO*
Chris Mohr, *Regl Sales Mgr*
▲ **EMP:** 14
SALES (est): 1.2MM **Privately Held**
SIC: 2339 Women's & misses' outerwear

(G-9166)
DANICE STORES INC
305 W 125th St (10027-3620)
PHONE......................212 665-0389
Barry Group, *Manager*
EMP: 12
SALES (corp-wide): 53.9MM **Privately Held**
SIC: 2339 5137 Sportswear, women's; sportswear, women's & children's
PA: Danice Stores, Inc.
525 Fashion Ave Rm 507
New York NY 10018
212 776-1001

(G-9167)
DANIEL M FRIEDMAN & ASSOC INC
19w W 34th St Fl 4 (10001)
PHONE......................212 695-5545
Daniel M Friedman, *President*
▲ **EMP:** 30
SQ FT: 5,000
SALES (est): 4.7MM **Publicly Held**
WEB: www.dmfassociates.com
SIC: 2387 Apparel belts
PA: Steven Madden, Ltd.
5216 Barnett Ave
Long Island City NY 11104

(G-9168)
DANNY MACAROONS INC
2191 3rd Ave Ste 3 (10035-3520)
PHONE......................260 622-8463
Daniel Cohen, *President*
EMP: 6 **EST:** 2010
SALES (est): 512.4K **Privately Held**
SIC: 2052 Cookies & crackers

(G-9169)
DANRAY TEXTILES CORP (PA)
Also Called: Dantex Trimming & Textile Co
270 W 39th St Fl 5 (10018-4409)
PHONE......................212 354-5213
Daniel Bergstein, *President*
Danny Bergstein, *Branch Mgr*
▲ **EMP:** 13
SQ FT: 2,000
SALES (est): 915.3K **Privately Held**
SIC: 2241 Trimmings, textile

(G-9170)
DARKPULSE INC (PA)
350 5th Ave Fl 59 (10118-5999)
PHONE......................800 436-1436
Dennis M Oleary, *Ch of Bd*
Thomas A Cellucci, *Co-CEO*
Stephen Goodman, *CFO*
David Singer, *Chief Mktg Ofcr*
Mark Banash, *CTO*
EMP: 5

SALES (est): 568.7K **Publicly Held**
WEB: www.kleverkart.com
SIC: 3822 3829 Thermostats & other environmental sensors; thermometers & temperature sensors; temperature sensors, except industrial process & aircraft

(G-9171)
DASH PRINTING INC
153 W 27th St (10001-6203)
PHONE......................212 643-8534
David Ashendorf, *President*
Rachel Feiner, *Exec VP*
EMP: 5
SQ FT: 1,100
SALES (est): 457.1K **Privately Held**
WEB: www.dashprinting.com
SIC: 2759 Commercial printing

(G-9172)
DASHLANE INC
44 W 18th St Fl 4 (10011-4645)
PHONE......................212 596-7510
Emmanuel Schalit, *CEO*
Alexandre Barreira, *President*
Alexis Fogel, *Vice Pres*
Guillaume Maron, *Vice Pres*
David Lapter, *CFO*
EMP: 45
SALES (est): 4.7MM **Privately Held**
SIC: 7372 Prepackaged software

(G-9173)
DATA IMPLEMENTATION INC
5 E 22nd St Apt 14t (10010-5325)
PHONE......................212 979-2015
Gerald A Goldstein, *President*
William F Hahn, *Vice Pres*
Diana Goldstein, *Treasurer*
Debra Hahn, *Admin Sec*
EMP: 5
SALES (est): 410K **Privately Held**
SIC: 7372 Prepackaged software

(G-9174)
DATADOG INC (PA)
620 8th Ave Fl 45 (10018-1741)
PHONE......................866 329-4466
Olivier Pomel, *CEO*
Alexis Le-Quoc, *President*
Rob Dinuzzo, *Vice Pres*
Diana Preziosi, *Opers Staff*
David Obstler, *CFO*
EMP: 101
SQ FT: 97,000
SALES: 198MM **Publicly Held**
SIC: 7372 Prepackaged software; publishers' computer software

(G-9175)
DATAMAX INTERNATIONAL INC
Also Called: Data Max
132 Nassau St Rm 511 (10038-2433)
PHONE......................212 693-0933
Saul Wasser, *CEO*
Max Wasser, *Treasurer*
Richard Dawkins, *Executive Asst*
▲ **EMP:** 45
SQ FT: 15,000
SALES (est): 4.2MM **Privately Held**
WEB: www.datamaxplanners.com
SIC: 2782 3172 Checkbooks; diaries; personal leather goods

(G-9176)
DAVES ELECTRIC MOTORS & PUMPS
282 E 7th St Apt 1 (10009-6027)
PHONE......................212 982-2930
Yefim Vinokur, *President*
EMP: 5
SQ FT: 5,600
SALES (est): 769.9K **Privately Held**
SIC: 7694 7699 Electric motor repair; pumps & pumping equipment repair

(G-9177)
DAVID & YOUNG CO INC
366 5th Ave Rm 707 (10001-2211)
PHONE......................212 594-6034
John Yoo, *President*
EMP: 6 **EST:** 2005
SALES (est): 494.7K **Privately Held**
SIC: 2389 Apparel & accessories

(G-9178)
DAVID FRIEDMAN CHAIN CO INC
Also Called: David Friedman and Sons
10 E 38th St Fl 6 (10016-0014)
PHONE..................................212 684-1760
Peter Banyasz, *President*
Matthew Friedman, *Vice Pres*
EMP: 15 **EST:** 1913
SQ FT: 5,000
SALES (est): 1.4MM **Privately Held**
SIC: 3911 Jewelry, precious metal

(G-9179)
DAVID ISSEKS & SONS INC
298 Broome St (10002-3704)
PHONE..................................212 966-8694
David Hackhauser, *President*
Joyce Hockhauser, *Exec VP*
EMP: 22
SQ FT: 5,000
SALES (est): 1.6MM **Privately Held**
SIC: 3443 7699 2449 Water tanks, metal
plate; tank repair; wood containers

(G-9180)
DAVID KING LINEN INC
295 5th Ave Ste 1202 (10016-7110)
PHONE..................................718 241-7298
Abraham Aosi, *Ch of Bd*
▲ **EMP:** 15
SQ FT: 8,000
SALES (est): 1.8MM **Privately Held**
SIC: 2299 5023 Linen fabrics; linens &
towels

(G-9181)
DAVID PEYSER SPORTSWEAR INC
Also Called: 30 Degrees Weatherproof
4 Bryant Park Fl 12 Flr 12 (10018)
PHONE..................................212 695-7716
Eliot Peyser, *Branch Mgr*
EMP: 40
SALES (corp-wide): 88MM **Privately Held**
WEB: www.mvsport.com
SIC: 2329 5651 Men's & boys' sportswear
& athletic clothing; unisex clothing stores
PA: David Peyser Sportswear, Inc.
90 Spence St
Bay Shore NY 11706
631 231-7788

(G-9182)
DAVID S DIAMONDS INC
546 5th Ave Fl 7 (10036-5000)
PHONE..................................212 921-8029
David So, *Principal*
Joan So, *Vice Pres*
▲ **EMP:** 15
SQ FT: 350
SALES (est): 2.5MM **Privately Held**
WEB: www.davidsdiamonds.com
SIC: 3911 5944 Jewelry, precious metal;
jewelry, precious stones & precious met-
als

(G-9183)
DAVID SUTHERLAND SHOWROOMS - N (PA)
D&D Building 979 3rd (10022)
PHONE..................................212 871-9717
Thomas William, *Principal*
EMP: 5
SALES (est): 366.1K **Privately Held**
SIC: 2511 Wood household furniture

(G-9184)
DAVID WEEKS STUDIO
38 Walker St Frnt 1 (10013-3589)
PHONE..................................212 966-3433
David Weeks, *President*
Abbey Rich, *Production*
Carlos Salgado, *Manager*
▲ **EMP:** 18
SALES (est): 2.5MM **Privately Held**
SIC: 3645 5719 Residential lighting fix-
tures; lighting fixtures

(G-9185)
DAVID WEISZ & SONS USA LLC
20 W 47th St Ste 601 (10036-3268)
PHONE..................................212 840-4747
David Weisz, *Mng Member*
EMP: 8

SALES (est): 1.2MM **Privately Held**
SIC: 3911 5094 Jewelry, precious metal;
diamonds (gems)

(G-9186)
DAVID YURMAN ENTERPRISES LLC (PA)
Also Called: Yurman Retail
24 Vestry St (10013-1903)
PHONE..................................212 896-1550
Gabriella Forte, *CEO*
Ava Farshidi, *Counsel*
Tom Orourke, *Vice Pres*
Ifora Tshikalu, *Opers Staff*
Jean Baudet, *Research*
◆ **EMP:** 300
SQ FT: 75,000
SALES (est): 215.1MM **Privately Held**
SIC: 3911 Jewelry, precious metal

(G-9187)
DAVID YURMAN RETAIL LLC
712 Madison Ave (10065-7207)
PHONE..................................877 226-1400
EMP: 7
SALES (est): 881.6K
SALES (corp-wide): 275MM **Privately Held**
SIC: 3911 Mfg Precious Metal Jewelry
PA: David Yurman Enterprises Llc
24 Vestry St
New York NY 10013
212 896-1550

(G-9188)
DAVLER MEDIA GROUP LLC (PA)
213 W 35th St Rm 1201 (10001-1916)
PHONE..................................212 315-0800
Bethany Braun, *Editor*
Rosalind Muggeridge, *Editor*
Janet Barbash, *Vice Pres*
Sheri Lapidus, *Vice Pres*
Tony Diaz, *Prdtn Dir*
EMP: 30
SALES (est): 4.8MM **Privately Held**
WEB: www.davlermedia.com
SIC: 2721 Magazines: publishing & printing

(G-9189)
DAVOS BRANDS LLC
381 Park Ave S Rm 1015 (10016-8827)
PHONE..................................212 779-1911
Andrew Chrisomaois, *CEO*
Blake Bond, *COO*
Richard Fein, *Vice Pres*
Sean Hartnell, *Vice Pres*
Kenrik Mannion, *Vice Pres*
◆ **EMP:** 10
SALES (est): 311.7K **Privately Held**
SIC: 2084 Neutral spirits, fruit

(G-9190)
DAXOR CORPORATION (PA)
350 5th Ave Ste 4740 (10118-0002)
PHONE..................................212 330-8500
Michael Feldschuh, *Ch of Bd*
Guido Manzo, *Vice Pres*
Soren Thompson, *VP Bus Dvlpt*
Robert J Michel, *CFO*
John Wilkens, *CFO*
EMP: 12
SALES (est): 1.7MM **Publicly Held**
WEB: www.daxor.com
SIC: 3841 8099 Surgical & medical instru-
ments; sperm bank; blood bank

(G-9191)
DE MATTEIS FOOD CORP
5 W 19th St Fl 10 (10011-4281)
PHONE..................................646 629-8554
Gabriella De Matteis, *President*
Luca Nava, *Vice Pres*
EMP: 5
SQ FT: 1,000
SALES (est): 153.8K
SALES (corp-wide): 1.3MM **Privately Held**
SIC: 2099 Pasta, uncooked: packaged with
other ingredients
HQ: De Matteis Agroalimentare Spa
Zona Industriale Valle Ufita
Flumeri AV 83040
082 542-12

(G-9192)
DE MEO BROTHERS INC (PA)
Also Called: De Meo Brothers Hair
129 W 29th St Fl 5 (10001-5294)
PHONE..................................212 268-1400
Gabriel Klugmann, *President*
▲ **EMP:** 7
SQ FT: 6,000
SALES (est): 928.8K **Privately Held**
SIC: 3999 6221 Hair & hair-based prod-
ucts; commodity traders, contracts

(G-9193)
DEBMAR-MERCURY
75 Rockefeller Plz # 1600 (10019-6908)
PHONE..................................212 669-5025
Ira Bernstein, *President*
Stephanie Eno, *Vice Pres*
Bonck Karen, *Vice Pres*
Damon Zaleski, *VP Sales*
Peggy Woop, *Administration*
EMP: 9
SALES (est): 721.7K **Privately Held**
SIC: 2836 Culture media

(G-9194)
DEEPHAVEN DATA LABS LLC (PA)
79 Madison Ave (10016-7802)
PHONE..................................855 828-8445
Pete Goddard, *CEO*
Ryan Caudy, *CTO*
EMP: 2
SALES (est): 1.1MM **Privately Held**
SIC: 7372 Application computer software

(G-9195)
DEFINITION PRESS INC
141 Greene St (10012-3201)
PHONE..................................212 777-4490
Margot Carpenter, *Exec Dir*
Ellen Reiss, *Director*
EMP: 10 **EST:** 1954
SQ FT: 2,210
SALES (est): 780K **Privately Held**
WEB: www.definitionpress.com
SIC: 2731 Books: publishing only

(G-9196)
DEFRAN SYSTEMS INC
1 Penn Plz Ste 1700 (10119-1700)
PHONE..................................212 727-8342
Fran L Turso, *President*
Ron Aceto, *Vice Pres*
Deborah Huyer, *Vice Pres*
Greg Travis, *Vice Pres*
Art Khanlian, *CIO*
EMP: 35
SALES (est): 2.2MM
SALES (corp-wide): 222.5MM **Privately Held**
WEB: www.defran.com
SIC: 7372 7371 Prepackaged software;
custom computer programming services
HQ: Netsmart Technologies, Inc.
4950 College Blvd
Overland Park KS 66211

(G-9197)
DELCATH SYSTEMS INC (PA)
1633 Broadway Fl 22c (10019-6708)
PHONE..................................212 489-2100
Jennifer K Simpson, *President*
John Purpura, *Exec VP*
Barbra C Keck, *CFO*
EMP: 46
SQ FT: 6,877
SALES (est): 3.4MM **Privately Held**
WEB: www.delcath.com
SIC: 3841 2834 Surgical & medical instru-
ments; catheters; pharmaceutical prepa-
rations

(G-9198)
DELL COMMUNICATIONS INC
Also Called: Dell Graphics
109 W 27th St Frnt 2 (10001-6208)
PHONE..................................212 989-3434
Steve Dell, *President*
David Frattura, *Vice Pres*
EMP: 5
SQ FT: 5,000
SALES (est): 784.8K **Privately Held**
WEB: www.dellgraphics.com
SIC: 2752 Commercial printing, offset

(G-9199)
DELTA GALIL USA INC
6 E 32nd St Fl 9 (10016-5415)
PHONE..................................212 710-6440
EMP: 6
SALES (corp-wide): 389.2MM **Privately Held**
SIC: 2341 Women's & children's undergar-
ments; women's & children's nightwear
HQ: Delta Galil Usa Inc.
1 Harmon Plz Fl 5
Secaucus NJ 07094
201 902-0055

(G-9200)
DEMOS MEDICAL PUBLISHING LLC
11 W 42nd St Ste 15c (10036-8002)
PHONE..................................516 889-1791
Phyllis Gold, *President*
EMP: 10
SQ FT: 1,600
SALES (est): 970K **Privately Held**
WEB: www.demosmedpub.com
SIC: 2731 2721 Books: publishing only;
trade journals: publishing only, not printed
on site

(G-9201)
DENIM KING DEPOT LLC
1350 6th Ave Ste 1004 (10019-4702)
PHONE..................................917 477-0550
Ben Dovid, *Mng Member*
EMP: 40
SALES (est): 1MM **Privately Held**
SIC: 2325 2339 Men's & boys' jeans &
dungarees; jeans: women's, misses' &
juniors'

(G-9202)
DENIZ INFORMATION SYSTEMS
Also Called: Dis
208 E 51st St Ste 129 (10022-6557)
P.O. Box 841 (10150-0841)
PHONE..................................212 750-5199
Haluk Deniz, *Ch of Bd*
Nihat Ozkaya, *VP Opers*
Karen Emer, *VP Mktg*
EMP: 9
SQ FT: 600
SALES (est): 527.2K **Privately Held**
SIC: 7372 5045 Prepackaged software;
computers, peripherals & software

(G-9203)
DENNIS BASSO COUTURE INC
Also Called: Dennis Basso Furs
825 Madison Ave (10065-5042)
PHONE..................................212 794-4500
Dennis Basso, *President*
▲ **EMP:** 12
SALES (est): 1.2MM **Privately Held**
SIC: 2371 Fur goods

(G-9204)
DENNIS PUBLISHING INC
Also Called: Week Publications, The
55 W 39th St Fl 5 (10018-3850)
P.O. Box 111 (10018-0002)
PHONE..................................646 717-9500
Steven Kotok, *CEO*
Loren Talbot, *Editor*
Chris Mitchell, *Opers Mgr*
Reisa Feigenbaum, *Manager*
Kathy Magennis, *Manager*
EMP: 100
SALES (est): 24MM
SALES (corp-wide): 373.4K **Privately Held**
SIC: 2721 Magazines: publishing only, not
printed on site
HQ: Dennis Publishing Limited
31-32 Alfred Place
London WC1E
203 890-3890

(G-9205)
DESIGN ARCHIVES INC
1460 Broadway (10036-7329)
PHONE..................................212 768-0617
Veena Advani, *President*
EMP: 5
SQ FT: 2,000
SALES (est): 411.5K **Privately Held**
SIC: 2395 5137 Embroidery & art needle-
work; women's & children's clothing

(G-9206)
DESIGN LITHOGRAPHERS INC
519 8th Ave Ste 3 (10018-6506)
PHONE..................212 645-8900
Daniel Green, *President*
Dan Green, *Officer*
EMP: 12
SALES (est): 1.1MM **Privately Held**
WEB: www.designlitho.com
SIC: 2752 Commercial printing, offset

(G-9207)
DESIGN SOURCE BY LG INC
115 Bowery Frnt 1 (10002-4933)
PHONE..................212 274-0022
Leo Greisman, *CEO*
▲ EMP: 23 EST: 1968
SQ FT: 1,000
SALES (est): 3MM **Privately Held**
SIC: 3423 Plumbers' hand tools

(G-9208)
DESIGNLOGOCOM INC
Also Called: Impressions Prtg & Graphics
15 W 37th St Lbby A (10018-5317)
PHONE..................212 564-0200
Arif Jacksi, *Chairman*
EMP: 6
SALES (est): 825.8K **Privately Held**
WEB: www.designlogo.com
SIC: 2752 Commercial printing, litho-
graphic

(G-9209)
DESIGNWAY LTD
27 E 21st St Fl 7 (10010-6249)
PHONE..................212 254-2220
Joan Morgan, *President*
EMP: 6
SALES: 1MM **Privately Held**
SIC: 2211 5712 Draperies & drapery fab-
rics, cotton; custom made furniture, ex-
cept cabinets

(G-9210)
DETNY FOOTWEAR INC
Also Called: Shane & Shawn
1 River Pl Apt 1224 (10036-4369)
PHONE..................212 423-1040
Shane Ward, *CEO*
Shawn J Ward, *President*
▲ EMP: 8
SQ FT: 1,800
SALES: 1MM **Privately Held**
WEB: www.detny.com
SIC: 3143 3144 3021 Men's footwear, ex-
cept athletic; women's footwear, except
athletic; rubber & plastics footwear

(G-9211)
DETOUR APPAREL INC (PA)
Also Called: Chula Girls
530 7th Ave Rm 608 (10018-4888)
PHONE..................212 221-3265
Lisa Medina, *President*
EMP: 46 EST: 2003
SQ FT: 3,000
SALES (est): 1.9MM **Privately Held**
SIC: 2369 Jackets: girls', children's & in-
fants'

(G-9212)
DEVA CONCEPTS LLC
Also Called: Devacurl
75 Spring St Fl 8 (10012-4071)
PHONE..................212 343-0344
Robert Schaeffler, *CEO*
Mark Ellis, *CFO*
Samantha Mellone, *Relations*
EMP: 50
SALES (est): 7.4MM **Privately Held**
SIC: 3999 Atomizers, toiletry

(G-9213)
DEW GRAPHICS INC
Also Called: Dew Graphics
519 8th Ave Fl 18 (10018-4577)
PHONE..................212 727-8820
Elaine Weisbrot, *President*
Don Weisbrot, *Vice Pres*
EMP: 35
SQ FT: 17,000
SALES (est): 2.9MM **Privately Held**
SIC: 2759 Screen printing

(G-9214)
DEZAWY LLC
Also Called: Thewritedeal
55 W 116th St Ste 327 (10026-2508)
PHONE..................917 436-8820
Yves Sorokobi, *Mng Member*
EMP: 6
SALES: 70K **Privately Held**
SIC: 2741 7389 Miscellaneous publishing;

(G-9215)
DFA NEW YORK LLC
318 W 39th St Fl 10 (10018-1486)
PHONE..................212 523-0021
Alan Madoff, *Mng Member*
Jeff Zwiebel,
▲ EMP: 21
SALES (est): 2.5MM **Privately Held**
SIC: 2339 Women's & misses' accessories

(G-9216)
DIA
535 W 22nd St Fl 4 (10011-1119)
PHONE..................212 675-4097
Nathalie De Gunzburg, *Principal*
EMP: 1
SALES (est): 13.3MM **Privately Held**
SIC: 2675 Die-cut paper & board

(G-9217)
DIALASE INC
36 W 47th St Ste 709 (10036-8601)
PHONE..................212 575-8833
Isace Landerer, *President*
EMP: 5
SQ FT: 1,200
SALES (est): 330K **Privately Held**
SIC: 3915 Diamond cutting & polishing

(G-9218)
DIAMEX INC
580 5th Ave Ste 625 (10036-4725)
PHONE..................212 575-8145
David Steinmetz, *President*
Ronald Vanderlinden, *Vice Pres*
EMP: 5
SQ FT: 1,200
SALES (est): 590.4K **Privately Held**
SIC: 3915 5094 Diamond cutting & polish-
ing; diamonds (gems)

(G-9219)
**DIAMOND CONSTELLATION
CORP**
37 W 47th St Ste 506 (10036-2809)
P.O. Box 650466, Fresh Meadows (11365-
0466)
PHONE..................212 819-0324
Fax: 212 944-9245
EMP: 6 EST: 1959
SQ FT: 2,500
SALES (est): 470K **Privately Held**
SIC: 3915 5094 Diamond Cutting & Whol
Of Precious Diamonds

(G-9220)
**DIAMOND DISTRIBUTORS INC
(PA)**
608 5th Ave Fl 10 (10020-2303)
PHONE..................212 921-9188
EMP: 7
SALES (est): 1.6MM **Privately Held**
SIC: 3911 Jewelry, precious metal

(G-9221)
DIAMOND INSCRIPTION TECH
36 W 47th St Ste 1008 (10036-8601)
PHONE..................646 366-7944
Jacob Dresdner, *Owner*
EMP: 10
SALES (est): 921.9K **Privately Held**
WEB: www.dresdiam.com
SIC: 2759 Laser printing

(G-9222)
DIAMOND SEAFOODS INC
366 Amsterdam Ave Ste 234 (10024-6746)
PHONE..................503 351-3240
Wendy Schwartz, *President*
Wendi Schwartz, *President*
Jonathan Schwartz, *Vice Pres*
▲ EMP: 5 EST: 1998
SQ FT: 500

SALES (est): 25MM **Privately Held**
SIC: 2091 Seafood products: packaged in
cans, jars, etc.

(G-9223)
DIANOS KATHRYN DESIGNS
150 W 55th St (10019-5586)
PHONE..................212 267-1584
Kathryn Dianos, *Owner*
EMP: 5
SALES (est): 308.8K **Privately Held**
SIC: 2339 7389 Women's & misses' ath-
letic clothing & sportswear; apparel de-
signers, commercial

(G-9224)
DIGIDAY MEDIA LLC
1 Liberty Plz Fl 9 (10006-1451)
PHONE..................646 419-4357
Newton J Friese, *CEO*
Brian Morrissey, *President*
Nancy Picker, *Exec VP*
Elaine Mershon, *Vice Pres*
Andrea Sontz, *Vice Pres*
EMP: 40
SALES (est): 708.5K **Privately Held**
SIC: 3695 Magnetic & optical recording
media

(G-9225)
DIGIFAB SYSTEMS INC
1412 Broadway Ste 2100 (10018-9228)
PHONE..................212 944-9882
Avedik Izmirlian, *Branch Mgr*
EMP: 5
SALES (est): 387.8K **Privately Held**
SIC: 3663 Digital encoders
PA: Digifab Systems, Inc.
5015 Pacific Blvd
Vernon CA 90058

(G-9226)
**DIGITAL COLOR CONCEPTS
INC (PA)**
Also Called: D C C
30 W 21st St Fl 5 (10010-6961)
PHONE..................212 989-4888
Stephen Pandolfi, *CEO*
Kevin Finn, *Exec VP*
Donald Terwilliger, *Exec VP*
Bret Hesler, *Vice Pres*
Doug Simmons, *Vice Pres*
EMP: 24
SQ FT: 15,000
SALES (est): 15.7MM **Privately Held**
WEB: www.dccnyc.com
SIC: 2752 2791 Commercial printing, litho-
graphic; photocomposition, for the printing
trade

(G-9227)
DIGITAL EVOLUTION INC (PA)
200 N End Ave Apt 20e (10282-7018)
PHONE..................212 732-2722
Eric Pulier, *CEO*
Dominic Giordano, *President*
Nicholas Giordano, *Vice Pres*
Frank Covella, *IT/INT Sup*
Kelly Faller, *Director*
EMP: 23 EST: 2000
SQ FT: 5,000
SALES (est): 3.6MM **Privately Held**
WEB: www.digitalevolution.com
SIC: 2759 7336 7384 Commercial print-
ing; commercial art & graphic design;
graphic arts & related design; photofinish
laboratories; photograph developing & re-
touching

(G-9228)
**DILIGENT BOARD MEMBER
SVCS LLC**
310 5th Ave Fl 7 (10001-3605)
PHONE..................212 741-8181
Warren Allen, *Counsel*
Bryan Zwahlen, *Vice Pres*
CHI Chan, *Opers Staff*
Matthew Evangelisti, *Engineer*
John Desimone, *Senior Engr*
EMP: 20
SQ FT: 8,000
SALES (est): 1.4MM **Privately Held**
SIC: 7372 Prepackaged software

(G-9229)
DILIGENT CORPORATION (DH)
111 W 33rd St 16 (10001-2904)
P.O. Box 419829, Boston MA (02241-9829)
PHONE..................212 741-8181
Brian Stafford, *President*
Warren Allen, *Counsel*
Michael Flickman, *Exec VP*
Jeff Hilk, *Exec VP*
Thomas N Tartaro, *Exec VP*
EMP: 148
SALES (est): 100.9MM **Privately Held**
SIC: 7372 Business oriented computer
software

(G-9230)
DIMODA DESIGNS INC
48 W 48th St Ste 403 (10036-1713)
PHONE..................212 355-8166
Karabet Koroglu, *CEO*
Hayk Ogulluk, *President*
Garo Koroglu, *Vice Pres*
EMP: 25
SALES (est): 1.9MM **Privately Held**
WEB: www.dimoda.com
SIC: 3911 Jewelry, precious metal

(G-9231)
**DIRECT MKTG EDCTL
FNDATION INC**
Also Called: Dmef/Edge
1333 Broadway Rm 301 (10018-1170)
PHONE..................212 790-1512
Terri L Bartlett, *President*
John Taborosi, *COO*
Linda High, *Exec VP*
Marie Adolphe, *Vice Pres*
Gina Scala, *Vice Pres*
EMP: 8
SALES: 1.3MM **Privately Held**
WEB: www.the-dmef.com
SIC: 2721 Trade journals: publishing only,
not printed on site

(G-9232)
DIRECT PRINT INC (PA)
77 E 125th St (10035-1622)
PHONE..................212 987-6003
Kevin Williams, *President*
EMP: 9
SALES (est): 1.9MM **Privately Held**
SIC: 2752 Commercial printing, litho-
graphic

(G-9233)
**DIRTY LEMON BEVERAGES LLC
(PA)**
95 Grand St Apt 5 (10013-5902)
PHONE..................877 897-7784
Zak Normantin, *CEO*
EMP: 9
SALES (est): 2MM **Privately Held**
SIC: 2086 Lemonade: packaged in cans,
bottles, etc.

(G-9234)
DISCOVER CASTING INC
17 W 45th St (10036-4907)
PHONE..................212 398-5050
Luis Perlaza, *President*
Yanneth Perlaza, *Vice Pres*
EMP: 5
SQ FT: 1,900
SALES (est): 3.4MM **Privately Held**
SIC: 3911 2752 Jewelry, precious metal;
commercial printing, lithographic

(G-9235)
DISCOVER MEDIA LLC
Also Called: Discover Magazine
90 5th Ave Ste 1100 (10011-2051)
PHONE..................212 624-4800
EMP: 35
SQ FT: 11,500
SALES (est): 3.2MM **Privately Held**
SIC: 2721 Periodicals Printing & Publishing

(G-9236)
DISPATCH GRAPHICS INC
Also Called: Dispatch Letter Service
344 W 38th St Fl 4r (10018-8432)
PHONE..................212 307-5943
Paul A Grech, *President*
Stephen Grech, *Exec VP*
EMP: 10

▲ = Import ▼=Export
◆ =Import/Export

SQ FT: 8,000
SALES (est): 1.2MM **Privately Held**
SIC: 2752 7331 2791 2789 Commercial printing, offset; mailing service; typesetting; bookbinding & related work

(G-9237)
DISPLAY SHOP INC (PA)
261 Madison Ave Fl 9 (10016-2311)
PHONE..................................646 202-9494
Manuel Rodrigues, *Owner*
EMP: 13
SALES (est): 4.2MM **Privately Held**
SIC: 2542 Fixtures: display, office or store: except wood

(G-9238)
DISSENT MAGAZINE
120 Wall St Fl 31 (10005-4007)
PHONE..................................212 316-3120
Michael Walder, *President*
EMP: 10
SALES (est): 789.6K **Privately Held**
SIC: 2721 Magazines: publishing only, not printed on site

(G-9239)
DISTINCTIVE PRINTING INC
225 W 37th St Fl 16 (10018-6637)
PHONE..................................212 727-3000
Fax: 212 727-3004
EMP: 6
SQ FT: 5,000
SALES (est): 866.2K **Privately Held**
SIC: 2752 Lithographic Commercial Printing

(G-9240)
DISTRIBIO USA LLC
Also Called: Biologique Recherche
261 5th Ave Rm 2000 (10016-7701)
PHONE..................................212 989-6077
Philippe Allouche,
EMP: 5
SALES (est): 1MM **Privately Held**
WEB: www.biologiquerecherche.com
SIC: 2844 Face creams or lotions

(G-9241)
DK PUBLISHING
345 Hudson St (10014-4502)
PHONE..................................212 366-2000
Tom Korman, *Vice Pres*
Ashlee Silver, *Personnel*
Stephanie Kull, *Sales Staff*
Gary June, *Branch Mgr*
▲ **EMP:** 18
SALES (corp-wide): 75.3MM **Privately Held**
SIC: 2741 Miscellaneous publishing
HQ: Dorling Kindersley Limited
Shell Mex House
London WC2R
207 010-3000

(G-9242)
DNP ELECTRONICS AMERICA LLC
Also Called: Deal
335 Madison Ave Fl 3 (10017-4616)
PHONE..................................212 503-1060
Masaru Suzuki, *President*
Kaoru Kando, *CFO*
▲ **EMP:** 60
SALES (est): 6.4MM **Privately Held**
SIC: 3861 Screens, projection
HQ: Dnp Corporation Usa
335 Madison Ave Fl 3
New York NY 10017

(G-9243)
DO OVER LLC
1410 Broadway Rm 301 (10018-9377)
PHONE..................................212 302-2336
Joseph Zaccai,
EMP: 5
SALES (est): 177.6K **Privately Held**
SIC: 2211 Apparel & outerwear fabrics, cotton

(G-9244)
DOCUMENT JOURNAL INC
264 Canal St (10013-3529)
PHONE..................................646 586-3099
▲ **EMP:** 9

SALES (est): 439.5K **Privately Held**
SIC: 2711 Newspapers, publishing & printing

(G-9245)
DOLBY LABORATORIES INC
1350 6th Ave Fl 28 (10019-4702)
PHONE..................................212 767-1700
Bill Allen, *Manager*
EMP: 15
SALES (corp-wide): 1.1B **Publicly Held**
WEB: www.dolby.com
SIC: 3861 Motion picture film
PA: Dolby Laboratories, Inc.
1275 Market St
San Francisco CA 94103
415 558-0200

(G-9246)
DOLPHIN DATA CAPTURE LLC
45 Rockefeller Plz # 2000 (10111-0100)
PHONE..................................516 429-5663
EMP: 5
SALES (est): 600.2K **Privately Held**
SIC: 3577 Computer peripheral equipment

(G-9247)
DONALD BRUHNKE
Also Called: Chicago Watermark Company
455 W 37th St Apt 1018 (10018-4785)
PHONE..................................212 600-1260
Donald Bruhnke, *Owner*
EMP: 10
SQ FT: 1,200
SALES: 1MM **Privately Held**
SIC: 2759 Commercial printing

(G-9248)
DONNA DISTEFANO LTD (PA)
37 W 20th St Ste 1106 (10011-3713)
PHONE..................................212 594-3757
Donna Distefano, *President*
EMP: 9
SALES (est): 820.8K **Privately Held**
SIC: 3911 Jewelry, precious metal

(G-9249)
DONNA KARAN INTERNATIONAL INC (HQ)
240 W 40th St (10018-1533)
PHONE..................................212 789-1500
Patricia F Kalberer, *CFO*
◆ **EMP:** 10 **EST:** 1996
SQ FT: 80,000
SALES (est): 387.7MM
SALES (corp-wide): 3B **Publicly Held**
WEB: www.donnakaran.com
SIC: 2335 2337 2331 2339 Women's, juniors' & misses' dresses; jackets & vests, except fur & leather: women's; skirts, separate: women's, misses' & juniors'; suits: women's, misses' & juniors'; blouses, women's & juniors': made from purchased material; shirts, women's & juniors': made from purchased materials; women's, misses' & juniors' outerwear; slacks: women's, misses' & juniors'; jeans: women's, misses' & juniors'; athletic clothing: women's, misses' & juniors'; men's & boys' furnishings; slacks, dress: men's, youths' & boys'; jeans: men's, youths' & boys'
PA: G-Iii Apparel Group, Ltd.
512 7th Ave Fl 35
New York NY 10018
212 403-0500

(G-9250)
DONNA KARAN INTERNATIONAL INC
240 W 40th St Bsmt (10018-1533)
PHONE..................................212 768-5800
Fred Wilson, *Manager*
EMP: 8
SALES (corp-wide): 3B **Publicly Held**
WEB: www.donnakaran.com
SIC: 2335 2337 2331 2339 Women's, juniors' & misses' dresses; jackets & vests, except fur & leather: women's; blouses, women's & juniors': made from purchased material; women's & misses' outerwear; men's & boys' furnishings; slacks, dress: men's, youths' & boys'

HQ: Donna Karan International Inc.
240 W 40th St
New York NY 10018
212 789-1500

(G-9251)
DONNA MORGAN LLC
Also Called: Ali Ro
225 W 37th St (10018-5703)
PHONE..................................212 575-2550
Mary Brownstein, *Production*
Kathleen Mc Feeters,
Donna Annunziata,
Milton Cahn,
Larry Lefkowitz,
EMP: 25
SALES (est): 3.6MM **Privately Held**
WEB: www.donnamorgan.com
SIC: 3161 Clothing & apparel carrying cases

(G-9252)
DONNELLEY FINANCIAL LLC
Also Called: Bowne Business Solutions
555 5th Ave Fl 4 (10017-9271)
PHONE..................................212 351-9000
Susan Fenwick, *Vice Pres*
EMP: 60
SALES (corp-wide): 963MM **Publicly Held**
SIC: 2752 Commercial printing, lithographic
HQ: Donnelley Financial, Llc
35 W Wacker Dr
Chicago IL 60601
844 866-4337

(G-9253)
DONORWALL INC
125 Maiden Ln Rm 205 (10038-5099)
P.O. Box 1005 (10272-1005)
PHONE..................................212 766-9670
Barry Silverberg, *President*
EMP: 16
SALES (est): 1.3MM **Privately Held**
WEB: www.donorwall.com
SIC: 3999 Plaques, picture, laminated

(G-9254)
DORAL APPAREL GROUP INC
498 Fashion Ave Fl 10 (10018-6957)
PHONE..................................917 208-5652
Martin Ehrlich, *President*
EMP: 9
SQ FT: 5,000
SALES (est): 902.5K **Privately Held**
SIC: 2339 2326 Women's & misses' athletic clothing & sportswear; men's & boys' work clothing

(G-9255)
DOREMUS FP LLC
228 E 45th St Fl 10 (10017-3331)
PHONE..................................212 366-3800
Dave Wade, *President*
Edmond Sorg, *CFO*
EMP: 47
SQ FT: 13,800
SALES (est): 6.9MM **Privately Held**
WEB: www.doremusfp.com
SIC: 2759 Financial note & certificate printing & engraving

(G-9256)
DOUBLE TAKE FASHIONS INC
1407 Broadway Rm 712 (10018-5293)
PHONE..................................718 832-9000
Michael Mizrahi, *President*
Jeanette Mizrahi, *Vice Pres*
Daniel Marchese, *Manager*
EMP: 15
SQ FT: 5,000
SALES (est): 1.6MM **Privately Held**
WEB: www.doubletakefashions.com
SIC: 2339 Sportswear, women's

(G-9257)
DOVER GLOBAL HOLDINGS INC (HQ)
280 Park Ave (10017-1274)
PHONE..................................212 922-1640
Robert A Livingston, *President*
Richard Lochridge, *Bd of Directors*
Mary Winston, *Bd of Directors*
Annette Della Penna, *Analyst*
◆ **EMP:** 18

SALES (est): 3.6MM
SALES (corp-wide): 6.9B **Publicly Held**
SIC: 3531 3542 3565 3534 Construction machinery; machine tools, metal forming type; packaging machinery; elevators & moving stairways
PA: Dover Corporation
3005 Highland Pkwy # 200
Downers Grove IL 60515
630 541-1540

(G-9258)
DOW JONES & COMPANY INC (HQ)
1211 Avenue Of The Americ (10036-8711)
P.O. Box 300, Princeton NJ (08543-0300)
PHONE..................................609 627-2999
William Lewis, *CEO*
Edwin Finn Jr, *President*
Mark Pope, *Managing Dir*
Guido Schenk, *Managing Dir*
John Bussey, *Editor*
▲ **EMP:** 500 **EST:** 1882
SALES (est): 1.7B
SALES (corp-wide): 10B **Publicly Held**
SIC: 2711 2721 Newspapers, publishing & printing; magazines: publishing & printing
PA: News Corporation
1211 Avenue Of The Americ
New York NY 10036
212 416-3400

(G-9259)
DOW JONES & COMPANY INC
1211 Avenue Of The Americ (10036-8711)
PHONE..................................212 597-5983
John Kennelly, *Sales Dir*
Edwin Finn, *Branch Mgr*
EMP: 46
SALES (corp-wide): 10B **Publicly Held**
SIC: 2711 2721 6289 7383 Newspapers, publishing & printing; magazines: publishing only, not printed on site; statistical reports (periodicals): publishing & printing; financial reporting; stock quotation service; news reporting services for newspapers & periodicals; business oriented computer software
HQ: Dow Jones & Company, Inc.
1211 Avenue Of The Americ
New York NY 10036
609 627-2999

(G-9260)
DOW JONES AER COMPANY INC
1211 Av Of The Am Lwr C3r (10036)
PHONE..................................212 416-2000
Teresa Vozzo, *General Mgr*
Jennifer Hayek, *Business Mgr*
Larry Hoffman, *Exec VP*
Patrick Purcell, *Exec VP*
Rick Butare, *Vice Pres*
EMP: 701
SALES (est): 125.7MM
SALES (corp-wide): 10B **Publicly Held**
WEB: www.opinionjournal.com
SIC: 2721 Periodicals
HQ: Dow Jones & Company, Inc.
1211 Avenue Of The Americ
New York NY 10036
609 627-2999

(G-9261)
DOWA INTERNATIONAL CORP
370 Lexington Ave Rm 1002 (10017-6586)
PHONE..................................212 697-3217
Junichi Nagao, *President*
Akihisa Yamaguchi, *Marketing Mgr*
EMP: 13 **Privately Held**
WEB: www.dicny.com
SIC: 1241 8732 Coal mining services; research services, except laboratory
PA: Dowa Holdings Co.,Ltd.
4-14-1, Sotokanda
Chiyoda-Ku TKY 101-0

(G-9262)
DOWNTOWN INTERIORS INC
250 Hudson St Lbby 1 (10013-1413)
PHONE..................................212 337-0230
Hertzel Abraham, *President*
Nicole Rowars, *Bookkeeper*
EMP: 12
SQ FT: 3,600

SALES (est): 1MM **Privately Held**
SIC: 3553 Furniture makers' machinery, woodworking

(G-9263)
DOWNTOWN MEDIA GROUP LLC
Also Called: Tokion Magazine
12 W 27th St Ste 1000 (10001-6903)
PHONE................................646 723-4510
Larry Rosenblum,
Isam Walji,
EMP: 15
SALES (est): 1.4MM **Privately Held**
SIC: 2721 Periodicals

(G-9264)
DR JAYSCOM
853 Broadway Ste 1900 (10003-4703)
PHONE................................888 437-5297
▼ **EMP:** 9
SALES (est): 1.1MM **Privately Held**
SIC: 2339 Women's & misses' athletic clothing & sportswear

(G-9265)
DRAGON TRADING INC
Also Called: DRAGON STEEL PRODUCTS
211 E 70th St Apt 20d (10021-5209)
PHONE................................212 717-1496
James Steindecker, *President*
Chen Tan, *Manager*
◆ **EMP:** 9
SQ FT: 800
SALES: 15.8MM **Privately Held**
SIC: 3315 3731 3321 3462 Cable, steel: insulated or armored; marine rigging; cast iron pipe & fittings; chains, forged steel

(G-9266)
DRAPER ASSOCIATES INCORPORATED
121 Varick St Rm 203 (10013-1455)
P.O. Box 393 (10014-0393)
PHONE................................212 255-2727
Joseph Disomma, *President*
EMP: 15
SQ FT: 1,200
SALES (est): 179K **Privately Held**
WEB: www.draperassociates.com
SIC: 2741 2791 Miscellaneous publishing; typesetting

(G-9267)
DREAMWAVE LLC
34 W 33rd St Fl 2 (10001-3304)
PHONE................................212 594-4250
George Saade, *Controller*
Jakey Dweck, *VP Sales*
David Grazi, *Mng Member*
▲ **EMP:** 26
SQ FT: 13,000
SALES (est): 2.7MM **Privately Held**
SIC: 2389 Men's miscellaneous accessories

(G-9268)
DRESDIAM INC
Also Called: Jacob Dresdner Co
36 W 47th St Ste 1008 (10036-8601)
PHONE................................212 819-2217
Jacob Dresdner, *President*
EMP: 40
SQ FT: 3,000
SALES (est): 3.5MM **Privately Held**
SIC: 3915 Diamond cutting & polishing

(G-9269)
DRESSY TESSY INC (PA)
Also Called: Dt Industry
1410 Broadway Rm 502 (10018-9373)
PHONE................................212 869-0750
Kitty Koo, *President*
▲ **EMP:** 9
SQ FT: 5,000
SALES (est): 702.6K **Privately Held**
SIC: 2253 Knit outerwear mills

(G-9270)
DREW PHILIPS CORP (PA)
Also Called: Supply & Demand
231 W 39th St (10018-1070)
PHONE................................212 354-0095
Andrew Cohen, *President*
▲ **EMP:** 15

SALES (est): 2.1MM **Privately Held**
WEB: www.supplydemand.com
SIC: 2339 Sportswear, women's

(G-9271)
DREYFUS ASHBY INC (HQ)
630 3rd Ave Fl 15 (10017-6939)
PHONE................................212 818-0770
Chris Ryan, *President*
Micheal Katz, *President*
Kate McGuire, *Regional Mgr*
Daniel Schmalen, *Vice Pres*
Patrick Sere, *Vice Pres*
▲ **EMP:** 34
SQ FT: 3,000
SALES (est): 3.1MM
SALES (corp-wide): 47.6MM **Privately Held**
WEB: www.dreyfusashby.com
SIC: 3646 2084 3645 Commercial indusl & institutional electric lighting fixtures; wines, brandy & brandy spirits; lamp & light shades
PA: Sa Maison Joseph Drouhin
7 Rue D Enfer
Beaune 21200
380 246-888

(G-9272)
DROPCAR OPERATING COMPANY INC (HQ)
1412 Broadway Ste 2100 (10018-9228)
PHONE................................646 342-1595
Michael Richardson, *CEO*
Jon Collins, *President*
Paul Commons, *CFO*
EMP: 7
SALES (est): 457.4K
SALES (corp-wide): 6MM **Publicly Held**
SIC: 7372 Business oriented computer software
PA: Dropcar, Inc.
1412 Broadway Fl 21
New York NY 10018
646 342-1595

(G-9273)
DRUMMOND FRAMING INC
38 W 21st St Fl 10 (10010-6969)
PHONE................................212 647-1701
Donald Delli Paoli, *Owner*
Mariko Frost, *Office Mgr*
EMP: 14 **EST:** 1975
SQ FT: 2,300
SALES (est): 2MM **Privately Held**
WEB: www.drummondframing.com
SIC: 2499 Picture frame molding, finished

(G-9274)
DTI FINANCIAL INC
Also Called: Dga Energy
1148 5th Ave Ste 1b (10128-0807)
PHONE................................212 661-7673
Dee Gulati, *President*
Michael Groski, *Controller*
EMP: 50
SQ FT: 10,000
SALES (est): 273.8K **Privately Held**
SIC: 1389 Grading oil & gas well foundations

(G-9275)
DU MONDE TRADING INC
Also Called: Up Country
1407 Brrdwy Rm 1905 (10018)
PHONE................................212 944-1306
Donald Eatz, *President*
Dale Trienekens, *COO*
▲ **EMP:** 50
SQ FT: 4,500
SALES (est): 6.5MM **Privately Held**
SIC: 2339 2326 Women's & misses' jackets & coats, except sportswear; men's & boys' work clothing

(G-9276)
DUCDUC LLC (PA)
Also Called: Ducduc Nyc
200 Lexington Ave Rm 715 (10016-6101)
PHONE................................212 226-1868
Lelia Holynskyj, *Opers Mgr*
Philip Eidles, *Mng Member*
Brady Wilcox, *Officer*
EMP: 15
SALES (est): 2.7MM **Privately Held**
SIC: 2511 Children's wood furniture

(G-9277)
DUCK RIVER TEXTILES INC (PA)
295 5th Ave (10016-7103)
PHONE................................212 679-2980
Eili Alhakim, *President*
Raymond Cohen, *COO*
Oury Alhakim, *Vice Pres*
Joel Bren, *Vice Pres*
◆ **EMP:** 18 **EST:** 1997
SQ FT: 50,000
SALES (est): 3.6MM **Privately Held**
WEB: www.duckrivertextile.com
SIC: 2269 Linen fabrics: dyeing, finishing & printing

(G-9278)
DUCON TECHNOLOGIES INC (PA)
5 Penn Plz (10001-1810)
PHONE................................631 694-1700
Aron Govil, *Chairman*
William Papa, *Chairman*
Renato Delarama, *Vice Pres*
Bob Gupta, *Vice Pres*
Dan Uhr, *Technical Mgr*
◆ **EMP:** 471
SQ FT: 35,000
SALES (est): 431.5MM **Privately Held**
WEB: www.ducon.com
SIC: 3537 3564 1629 1623 Industrial trucks & tractors; blowers & fans; power plant construction; communication line & transmission tower construction; road construction & maintenance machinery

(G-9279)
DUNE INC
200 Lexington Ave Rm 200 # 200 (10016-6103)
PHONE................................212 925-6171
Richard Shemtov, *President*
Aaron Shemtov, *Vice Pres*
▲ **EMP:** 5
SQ FT: 12,000
SALES (est): 794.6K **Privately Held**
WEB: www.dune-ny.com
SIC: 2511 Wood household furniture

(G-9280)
DURAN JEWELRY INC
36 W 47th St Ste 1205 (10036-8637)
PHONE................................212 431-1959
Erol Civi, *President*
Arlet Tknezi, *Manager*
▲ **EMP:** 6
SQ FT: 1,000
SALES (est): 460K **Privately Held**
SIC: 3911 Jewelry, precious metal

(G-9281)
DURATA THERAPEUTICS INC
7 Times Sq Ste 3502 (10036-6540)
PHONE................................646 871-6400
Paul R Edick, *CEO*
Richard U De Schutter, *Ch of Bd*
Corey N Fishman, *COO*
Michael Dunne, *Officer*
John P Shannon, *Officer*
EMP: 5
SQ FT: 9,000
SALES (est): 386.3K **Privately Held**
SIC: 2834 8731 Antibiotics, packaged; commercial physical research

(G-9282)
DUXIANA DUX BED
235 E 58th St (10022-1201)
PHONE................................212 755-2600
Bo Gustafsson, *Principal*
EMP: 6
SALES (est): 529K **Privately Held**
SIC: 2515 5712 5719 Mattresses & bedsprings; beds & accessories; beddings & linens

(G-9283)
DVF STUDIO LLC (PA)
Also Called: Diane Von Furstenberg The Shop
440 W 14th St (10014-1004)
PHONE................................212 741-6607
Aprilyn Villafana, *Area Mgr*
Robert McCormick, *COO*
Krista Grega, *Vice Pres*
Joe Reedy, *Vice Pres*
Irene Wu, *Vice Pres*

▲ **EMP:** 75
SALES (est): 23.1MM **Privately Held**
WEB: www.dvf.com
SIC: 3199 2389 5621 Leather garments; disposable garments & accessories; women's specialty clothing stores

(G-9284)
DVF STUDIO LLC (PA)
252 W 37th St Fl 14 (10018-6636)
PHONE................................646 576-8009
Anna Vinnikova, *Finance Asst*
EMP: 7
SALES (est): 2.7MM **Privately Held**
SIC: 3199 2389 5621 Leather garments; disposable garments & accessories; women's specialty clothing stores

(G-9285)
DWELL LIFE INC
Also Called: Dwell Store The
60 Broad St Fl 24 (10004-2342)
PHONE................................212 382-2010
Regina Flynn, *Office Mgr*
EMP: 25
SALES (corp-wide): 20MM **Privately Held**
SIC: 2741 Miscellaneous publishing
PA: Dwell Life, Inc.
595 Pacific Ave 4
San Francisco CA 94133
415 373-5100

(G-9286)
DWNLD INC
601394 Broadway Fl 6 Flr 6 (10013)
PHONE................................484 483-6572
Aj Framk, *CEO*
Alexandra Keating, *CEO*
EMP: 28
SALES (est): 663.9K **Privately Held**
SIC: 7372 Application computer software

(G-9287)
DYENAMIX INC
359 Broadway Frnt 2 (10013-3932)
PHONE................................212 941-6642
Raylene Marasco, *President*
EMP: 7
SALES: 250K **Privately Held**
SIC: 2261 2262 2752 Dyeing cotton broadwoven fabrics; screen printing of cotton broadwoven fabrics; screen printing: manmade fiber & silk broadwoven fabrics; commercial printing, lithographic

(G-9288)
DYNAMICA INC
930 5th Ave Apt 3f (10021-2680)
PHONE................................212 818-1900
Daniel Schwartz, *President*
▲ **EMP:** 10
SALES (est): 1.1MM **Privately Held**
SIC: 3821 Laboratory apparatus & furniture

(G-9289)
E C PUBLICATIONS INC
1700 Broadway Fl 5 (10019-5905)
PHONE................................212 728-1844
Paul Levitz, *President*
Dorothy Crouch, *Vice Pres*
Peter Bagnolini, *CFO*
EMP: 12 **EST:** 1942
SALES (est): 939.7K
SALES (corp-wide): 170.7B **Publicly Held**
SIC: 2721 Magazines: publishing only, not printed on site
HQ: Warner Communications Llc
1 Time Warner Ctr
New York NY 10019
212 484-8000

(G-9290)
E P SEWING PLEATING INC
327 W 36th St Frnt 2 (10018-6405)
PHONE................................212 967-2575
EMP: 20 **EST:** 1998
SALES (est): 820K **Privately Held**
SIC: 2342 Mfg Bras/Girdles

(G-9291)
E SCHREIBER INC
580 5th Ave Fl 32a (10036-4716)
PHONE................................212 382-0280
Norbert Steinmetz, *President*

Ben Moller, *Vice Pres*
▲ **EMP:** 22
SQ FT: 5,000
SALES (est): 2MM **Privately Held**
WEB: www.eschreiber.com
SIC: 3915 5094 Diamond cutting & polishing; diamonds (gems)

(G-9292)
E W WILLIAMS PUBLICATIONS
Also Called: LDB Interior Textiles
370 Lexington Ave Rm 1409 (10017-6583)
PHONE.....................212 661-1516
Aleksandra Ilnicki, *Editor*
Philippa Hochschild, *Manager*
EMP: 9
SALES (corp-wide): 42.3MM **Privately Held**
WEB: www.williamspublications.com
SIC: 2721 2731 Magazines: publishing only, not printed on site; textbooks: publishing only, not printed on site
HQ: E W Williams Publications
2125 Center Ave Ste 305
Fort Lee NJ 07024

(G-9293)
E&I PRINTING
145 W 55th St Apt 12a (10019-5354)
PHONE.....................212 206-0506
Eric Eisenberg, *President*
EMP: 15
SALES (est): 5MM **Privately Held**
WEB: www.eiprints.com
SIC: 2759 Commercial printing

(G-9294)
E-PLAY BRANDS LLC
25 W 39th St Lbby A (10018-4199)
PHONE.....................212 563-2646
Joseph Esses,
EMP: 6
SALES (est): 288.5K **Privately Held**
SIC: 2361 2369 Shirts: girls', children's & infants'; dresses: girls', children's & infants'; coat & legging sets: girls' & children's

(G-9295)
E-WON INDUSTRIAL CO INC
Also Called: New York Trading Co
625 Main St Apt 1532 (10044-0036)
PHONE.....................212 750-9610
▲ **EMP:** 37
SQ FT: 1,000
SALES (est): 4MM **Privately Held**
SIC: 3965 Mfg Buttons

(G-9296)
EAGLE ART PUBLISHING INC
475 Park Ave S Rm 2800 (10016-6901)
PHONE.....................212 685-7411
Samuel J Lurie, *President*
EMP: 5
SALES (est): 330K **Privately Held**
SIC: 2731 Book publishing

(G-9297)
EAGLE LACE DYEING CORP
335 W 35th St Fl 2 (10001-1726)
PHONE.....................212 947-2712
Leonard Shally, *President*
EMP: 10
SALES (est): 620K **Privately Held**
SIC: 2258 2396 Dyeing & finishing lace goods & warp knit fabric; automotive & apparel trimmings

(G-9298)
EAGLES NEST HOLDINGS LLC (PA)
Also Called: Sabin Robbins
455 E 86th St (10028-6400)
PHONE.....................513 874-5270
Wayne Penrod,
Joseph Hardiman,
EMP: 32
SQ FT: 6,000
SALES (est): 13.3MM **Privately Held**
SIC: 2679 Paper products, converted

(G-9299)
EARL G GRAVES PUBG CO INC (HQ)
Also Called: Black Enterprise
260 Madison Ave Ste 11 (10016-2413)
PHONE.....................212 242-8000
Earl G Graves Sr, *CEO*
Earl Butch Graves Jr, *CEO*
Jacques Jiha, *Principal*
Dirk J Caldwell, *Senior VP*
Angela Mitchell, *Vice Pres*
EMP: 83
SQ FT: 22,000
SALES (est): 7.8MM
SALES (corp-wide): 20.2MM **Privately Held**
SIC: 2721 Magazines: publishing only, not printed on site
PA: Earl G. Graves, Ltd.
260 Madison Ave Ste 11
New York NY 10016
212 242-8000

(G-9300)
EARRING KING JEWELRY MFG INC
62 W 47th St Ste 1202 (10036-3230)
PHONE.....................718 544-7947
Kowk Mok, *President*
Jane Mok, *Vice Pres*
EMP: 7
SALES (est): 630K **Privately Held**
SIC: 3911 Jewelry, precious metal

(G-9301)
EARTH ENTERPRISES INC
Also Called: Green Earth Enterprise
250 W 40th St Fl 15 (10018-4601)
PHONE.....................212 741-3999
Susan Hort, *President*
Usman Shaikh, *Business Mgr*
Michael Hort, *Vice Pres*
Micheal Hort, *Vice Pres*
Oscar Rivera, *QC Mgr*
EMP: 25
SQ FT: 40,000
SALES (est): 7.5MM **Privately Held**
SIC: 2752 Commercial printing, offset

(G-9302)
EAST COAST ORTHOIC & PROS COR
3927 Broadway (10032-1538)
PHONE.....................212 923-2161
Lawrence Benenati, *Branch Mgr*
EMP: 14
SALES (corp-wide): 12.7MM **Privately Held**
SIC: 3842 Orthopedic appliances
PA: East Coast Orthotic & Prosthetic Corp.
75 Burt Dr
Deer Park NY 11729
516 248-5566

(G-9303)
EAST MEET EAST INC
32 W 39th St Fl 4 (10018-2166)
PHONE.....................646 481-0033
Mariko Tokioka, *Ch of Bd*
Kunal Thadani, *Manager*
Kentaro Ejima, *Admin Sec*
EMP: 7 **EST:** 2014
SALES (est): 299.1K **Privately Held**
SIC: 2741

(G-9304)
EASTERN JEWELRY MFG CO INC
48 W 48th St Ste 707 (10036-1714)
PHONE.....................212 840-0001
Soloman Witriol, *President*
EMP: 50
SQ FT: 16,000
SALES (est): 3.4MM **Privately Held**
SIC: 3911 Jewelry apparel; bracelets, precious metal; earrings, precious metal; rosaries or other small religious articles, precious metal

(G-9305)
EASTERN SILK MILLS INC
148 W 37th St Fl 3 (10018-6987)
PHONE.....................212 730-1300
Andy Ryu, *Controller*
EMP: 9

SALES (corp-wide): 4.4MM **Privately Held**
SIC: 2262 2221 Dyeing: manmade fiber & silk broadwoven fabrics; broadwoven fabric mills, manmade
PA: Eastern Silk Mills Inc.
212 Catherine St
Elizabeth NJ

(G-9306)
EASTERN STRATEGIC MATERIALS
45 Rockefeller Plz # 2000 (10111-0100)
PHONE.....................212 332-1619
Kai Wong, *President*
Matthew Harris, *Vice Pres*
EMP: 41
SALES (est): 4MM **Privately Held**
SIC: 3365 3812 3822 Aerospace castings, aluminum; defense systems & equipment; space vehicle guidance systems & equipment; energy cutoff controls, residential or commercial types

(G-9307)
EASTNETS AMERICAS CORP
450 7th Ave Ste 1509 (10123-1509)
PHONE.....................212 631-0666
Hazem Mulhim, *President*
Andrea Sessler, *Officer*
EMP: 10
SALES (est): 1.4MM **Privately Held**
SIC: 7372 Business oriented computer software

(G-9308)
EATALY NET USA LLC (PA)
2 W 24th St (10010)
PHONE.....................212 897-2895
Sal Claps, *Director*
EMP: 8
SALES (est): 6.6MM **Privately Held**
SIC: 2032 Italian foods: packaged in cans, jars, etc.

(G-9309)
EB ACQUISITIONS LLC
444 Madison Ave Ste 501 (10022-6974)
PHONE.....................212 355-3310
Nachum Stein,
EMP: 100
SALES (est): 5.7MM **Privately Held**
SIC: 3643 3315 Connectors, electric cord; wire & fabricated wire products

(G-9310)
EB COUTURE LTD
Also Called: Elie Balleh Couture
110 W 34th St Rm 1002 (10001-2128)
PHONE.....................212 912-0190
Mari Mineh, *Post Master*
▲ **EMP:** 20
SALES (est): 179.8K **Privately Held**
SIC: 2389 2329 5137 Apparel for handicapped; knickers, dress (separate): men's & boys'; women's & children's clothing

(G-9311)
EBNER PUBLISHING INTERNATIONAL
Also Called: Watchtime Magazine
37 W 26th St Rm 412 (10010-1077)
PHONE.....................646 742-0740
Wolfgang Blum, *President*
Sara Orlando, *Adv Dir*
Rosangela Alonzo, *Office Mgr*
Steve Brown, *Office Mgr*
Mark Bernardo, *Manager*
EMP: 5
SALES (est): 45.7K **Privately Held**
WEB: www.watchtime.com
SIC: 2721 Magazines: publishing & printing

(G-9312)
EBREVIA INC
12 E 49th St Fl 11 (10017-1012)
PHONE.....................203 870-3000
Ned Gannon, *President*
Adam Nguyen, *Senior VP*
Jacob Mundt, *CTO*
EMP: 20
SQ FT: 30,000

SALES (est): 5.6MM
SALES (corp-wide): 963MM **Publicly Held**
SIC: 7372 Business oriented computer software
PA: Donnelley Financial Solutions, Inc.
35 W Wacker Dr
Chicago IL 60601
844 866-4337

(G-9313)
ECCELLA CORPORATION
75 Broad St Rm 2900 (10004-2475)
PHONE.....................718 612-0451
Meitav Harpaz, *CEO*
Gil Rosen, *President*
Christopher Evans, *Manager*
Aaron Gendle, *Sr Consultant*
EMP: 8
SQ FT: 2,960
SALES (est): 509.1K
SALES (corp-wide): 33.3K **Privately Held**
SIC: 7372 7389 Business oriented computer software;
PA: Ngdata
Sluisweg 2, Internal Postal Box 10
Gent
933 882-20

(G-9314)
ECCLESIASTICAL COMMUNICATIONS
Also Called: Catholic New York
1011 1st Ave Fl 6 (10022-4112)
PHONE.....................212 688-2399
Bishop Robert A Brucato, *President*
John Woods, *Manager*
Matthew Schiller, *Manager*
Robert Schu, *Executive*
EMP: 13
SALES (est): 750K **Privately Held**
SIC: 2711 Newspapers: publishing only, not printed on site

(G-9315)
ECHO GROUP INC
62 W 39th St Ste 1005 (10018-3818)
PHONE.....................917 608-7440
Fax: 212 382-2490
EMP: 15
SALES (est): 980K **Privately Held**
SIC: 3911 Mfg Precious Metal Jewelry

(G-9316)
ECLECTIC CNTRACT FURN INDS INC
450 Fashion Ave Ste 2710 (10123-2710)
PHONE.....................212 967-5504
Alex Marc, *President*
▲ **EMP:** 14
SQ FT: 1,000
SALES (est): 2MM **Privately Held**
WEB: www.eclecticcontract.com
SIC: 2511 Wood household furniture

(G-9317)
ECLIPSE COLLECTION JEWELERS (PA)
6 E 45th St Rm 1206 (10017-2439)
PHONE.....................212 764-6883
Vatcag Aghjayan, *President*
EMP: 8
SALES (est): 1MM **Privately Held**
SIC: 3911 Jewelry, precious metal

(G-9318)
ECONOMIST INTELLIGENCE UNIT NA
750 3rd Ave Fl 5 (10017-2723)
PHONE.....................212 554-0600
Chris Stibbs, *Ch of Bd*
David Cox, *Senior VP*
Paul Rossi, *Senior VP*
EMP: 68
SQ FT: 18,000
SALES (est): 11.8MM
SALES (corp-wide): 448.5MM **Privately Held**
WEB: www.eiu.com
SIC: 2721 8732 Periodicals: publishing only; business analysis

HQ: The Economist Newspaper Group Incorporated
750 3rd Ave Fl 5
New York NY 10017
212 541-0500

(G-9319)
**ECONOMIST NEWSPAPER NA
INC (DH)**
Also Called: Economist Magazine, The
750 3rd Ave Fl 5 (10017-2723)
PHONE....................212 554-0676
Chris Stibbs, *CEO*
Leo Mirani, *Editor*
Samantha Weinberg, *Editor*
Paul Rossi, *Exec VP*
Jessica Martinson, *Opers Staff*
EMP: 22
SQ FT: 28,900
SALES (est): 17.7MM
SALES (corp-wide): 448.5MM **Privately
Held**
SIC: 2711 5192 Newspapers; magazines
HQ: The Economist Newspaper Group In-
corporated
750 3rd Ave Fl 5
New York NY 10017
212 541-0500

(G-9320)
EDESIA WORLD WIDE LLC
1485 5th Ave (10035-2772)
PHONE....................646 705-3505
Sabbia Auriti,
Antonia Ricco,
EMP: 2
SALES: 2MM **Privately Held**
SIC: 2032 7389 Italian foods: packaged in
cans, jars, etc.;

(G-9321)
**EDITIONS DE PRFUMS
MADISON LLC (HQ)**
654 Madison Ave Rm 1609 (10065-8430)
PHONE....................646 666-0527
Frederic Malle, *General Mgr*
EMP: 9
SALES (est): 1.5MM **Publicly Held**
SIC: 2844 Perfumes & colognes

(G-9322)
**EDRINGTON GROUP USA LLC
(PA)**
27 W 23rd St Fl 4 (10010-4216)
PHONE....................212 352-6000
Herb Kopf, *Regional Mgr*
Michael Misiorski, *COO*
Jim Brennan, *Vice Pres*
Michael Kastin, *Vice Pres*
Chris Spalding, *Vice Pres*
EMP: 31
SALES (est): 12.3MM **Privately Held**
SIC: 2084 Wines, brandy & brandy spirits

(G-9323)
EDSIM LEATHER CO INC (PA)
131 W 35th St Fl 14 (10001-2111)
PHONE....................212 695-8500
Simone Kamali, *President*
Edmond Kamali, *Vice Pres*
Edmond R Kamali, *Vice Pres*
Joel Kamali, *Sales Mgr*
Daniel Kamali, *Senior Mgr*
▲ EMP: 20 EST: 1981
SQ FT: 7,000
SALES: 37MM **Privately Held**
WEB: www.hinet.net
SIC: 3111 Leather tanning & finishing

(G-9324)
EDUCATIONAL NETWORKS INC
104 W 40th St Rm 1810 (10018-3758)
PHONE....................866 526-0200
Franziska Hoelzke, *Project Mgr*
Robert Corbi, *Sales Staff*
Erica Amalfitano, *Marketing Staff*
Oliver Diaz-Neda, *Marketing Staff*
Liz Milivio, *Office Mgr*
EMP: 7
SALES (corp-wide): 3MM **Privately Held**
SIC: 7372 Educational computer software
PA: Educational Networks, Inc
901 Ponce De Leon Blvd # 508
Coral Gables FL 33134
866 526-0200

(G-9325)
EEBOO CORPORATION
170 W 74th St Apt 102 (10023-2351)
PHONE....................212 222-0823
Maria Galison, *President*
Alex Nunes, *Sales Staff*
Samantha Singleton, *Admin Asst*
▲ EMP: 14
SQ FT: 1,000
SALES (est): 2.4MM **Privately Held**
WEB: www.eeboo.com
SIC: 3944 Board games, puzzles & mod-
els, except electronic; puzzles

(G-9326)
**EFRONT FINANCIAL
SOLUTIONS INC**
Also Called: E-Front
11 E 44th St Rm 1502 (10017-0054)
PHONE....................212 220-0660
Eric Bernstein, *COO*
Kevin Colelli, *Project Mgr*
Alan Guo, *Engineer*
Brett Angwin, *Sales Dir*
Melanie McLean, *Accounts Mgr*
EMP: 25
SALES (corp-wide): 29.9MM **Privately
Held**
SIC: 7372 Business oriented computer
software
HQ: E-Front
2 4
Paris 16e Arrondissement 75116
149 964-060

(G-9327)
EFT ANALYTICS INC (HQ)
350 5th Ave Ste 4810 (10118-4810)
PHONE....................212 290-2300
Brent Youngers, *President*
Craig Ennis, *CTO*
EMP: 8
SALES (est): 1.1MM
SALES (corp-wide): 40.6B **Privately Held**
SIC: 7372 Application computer software
PA: Koch Industries, Inc.
4111 E 37th St N
Wichita KS 67220
316 828-5500

(G-9328)
EGMONT US INC
443 Park Ave S Rm 806 (10016-7322)
PHONE....................212 685-0102
▲ EMP: 8
SALES (est): 615K
SALES (corp-wide): 1.6B **Privately Held**
SIC: 2731 Books-Publishing/Printing
HQ: Egmont Uk Limited
The Yellow Building
London EC3R
203 220-0400

(G-9329)
EIDOSMEDIA INC
14 Wall St Ste 6c (10005-2170)
PHONE....................646 795-2100
Steven Ball, *CEO*
EMP: 22
SALES (est): 2.8MM **Privately Held**
SIC: 2721 Periodicals: publishing & print-
ing
HQ: Eidosmedia Spa
Corso Vercelli 40
Milano MI 20145
023 673-2000

(G-9330)
**EILEENS SPECIAL
CHEESECAKE**
17 Cleveland Pl Frnt A (10012-4052)
PHONE....................212 966-5585
Eileen Avezzano, *President*
EMP: 6 EST: 1975
SQ FT: 600
SALES (est): 310K **Privately Held**
WEB: www.eileenscheesecake.com
SIC: 2051 Bakery: wholesale or whole-
sale/retail combined; cakes, bakery: ex-
cept frozen

(G-9331)
EL-LA DESIGN INC
Also Called: My Apparel
209 W 38th St Rm 901 (10018-4558)
PHONE....................212 382-1080
Elaine Lai, *President*
EMP: 5
SALES (est): 590K **Privately Held**
SIC: 2339 Sportswear, women's

(G-9332)
ELANA LADEROS LTD
Also Called: Joanna Mastroianni
230 W 38th St Fl 15 (10018-9026)
PHONE....................212 764-0840
Joanna Mastroianni, *President*
EMP: 10
SQ FT: 3,500
SALES (est): 1.6MM **Privately Held**
WEB: www.joannamastroianni.com
SIC: 2335 Wedding gowns & dresses

(G-9333)
ELDEEN CLOTHING INC
250 W 39th St (10018-4414)
PHONE....................212 719-9190
Spenser Alpern, *CEO*
EMP: 5 EST: 2014 **Privately Held**
SIC: 2231 Apparel & outerwear broadwo-
ven fabrics

(G-9334)
**ELECTRIC LIGHTING AGENCIES
(PA)**
Also Called: Ela
36 W 25th St Fl 6 (10010-2757)
PHONE....................212 645-4580
EMP: 22
SALES (est): 3.8MM **Privately Held**
SIC: 3646 Mfg Commercial Lighting Fix-
tures

(G-9335)
ELECTRONIC ARTS INC
1515 Broadway Rm 3601 (10036-8901)
PHONE....................212 672-0722
Barbara Gallacher, *Vice Pres*
EMP: 7
SALES (corp-wide): 4.9B **Publicly Held**
WEB: www.ea.com
SIC: 7372 Prepackaged software
PA: Electronic Arts Inc.
209 Redwood Shores Pkwy
Redwood City CA 94065
650 628-1500

(G-9336)
ELEGANT HEADWEAR CO INC
Also Called: ABG Accessories
10 W 33rd St Rm 1122 (10001-3306)
PHONE....................212 695-8520
Phyllis Oristanio, *Accounts Mgr*
Michael Brett, *Branch Mgr*
Kimberly Arezzi, *Manager*
EMP: 8
SALES (corp-wide): 34.3MM **Privately
Held**
WEB: www.elegantheadwear.com
SIC: 2253 T-shirts & tops, knit
PA: Elegant Headwear Co. Inc.
1000 Jefferson Ave
Elizabeth NJ 07201
908 558-1200

(G-9337)
**ELEGANT JEWELERS MFG CO
INC**
31 W 47th St Ste 301 (10036-2888)
PHONE....................212 869-4951
Sandy Petropoulos, *President*
Nick Seretis, *Vice Pres*
EMP: 12
SQ FT: 1,500
SALES (est): 1.1MM **Privately Held**
WEB: www.elegantsilverjewellery.net
SIC: 3911 Jewelry, precious metal

(G-9338)
ELEVONDATA LABS INC
1350 Ave Of The Amrcs 2nd (10019-4702)
PHONE....................470 222-5438
Rohit Tandon, *CEO*
EMP: 50
SALES: 4MM **Privately Held**
SIC: 7372 Prepackaged software

(G-9339)
ELIE TAHARI LTD
501 5th Ave Fl 2 (10017-7825)
PHONE....................212 763-2000
Elie Tahari, *Principal*
EMP: 8
SALES (corp-wide): 171.9MM **Privately
Held**
SIC: 2331 2339 2337 5621 Blouses,
women's & juniors': made from purchased
material; slacks: women's, misses' & juniors'; suits: women's, misses' & juniors';
jackets & vests, except fur & leather:
women's; women's clothing stores; men's
& boys' clothing stores
PA: Elie Tahari Ltd.
16 Bleeker St
Millburn NJ 07041
973 671-6300

(G-9340)
ELIE TAHARI LTD
1114 Ave Of The Americas (10036-7703)
PHONE....................212 763-2000
Jackie Buffon, *Vice Pres*
Arthur S Levine, *Branch Mgr*
Peter Marra, *Manager*
Alex Tai, *Web Dvlpr*
EMP: 60
SALES (corp-wide): 171.9MM **Privately
Held**
SIC: 2331 2337 Blouses, women's & jun-
iors': made from purchased material; uni-
forms, except athletic: women's, misses'
& juniors'
PA: Elie Tahari Ltd.
16 Bleeker St
Millburn NJ 07041
973 671-6300

(G-9341)
ELIE TAHARI LTD
510 5th Ave Lbby A (10036-7507)
PHONE....................973 671-6300
Lisanne Kolligs, *President*
Jane Coppola, *Vice Pres*
Susan Kellogg, *Manager*
EMP: 75
SALES (corp-wide): 171.9MM **Privately
Held**
SIC: 2337 Suits: women's, misses' & jun-
iors'
PA: Elie Tahari Ltd.
16 Bleeker St
Millburn NJ 07041
973 671-6300

(G-9342)
**ELIS BREAD (ELI ZABAR) INC
(PA)**
403 E 91st St (10128-6800)
PHONE....................212 772-2011
Eli Zabar, *President*
Robert Shaloff, *VP Opers*
German Calle, *Manager*
EMP: 10
SALES (est): 15.8MM **Privately Held**
WEB: www.elisbread.com
SIC: 2045 Bread & bread type roll mixes:
from purchased flour

(G-9343)
ELITE DAILY INC
53 W 23rd St Fl 12 (10010-4313)
PHONE....................212 402-9097
Martin Clarke, *President*
EMP: 15
SALES (est): 14.4MM **Privately Held**
SIC: 2741

(G-9344)
ELITE GLASS FABRICATION LLC
14 Wall St Ste 3a (10005-2119)
PHONE....................201 333-8100
Jason Zoracki,
EMP: 350
SALES (est): 482.2K **Privately Held**
SIC: 3211 Flat glass

(G-9345)
ELITE PARFUMS LTD (HQ)
551 5th Ave Rm 1500 (10176-1599)
PHONE....................212 983-2640
Jean Madar, *President*
Philippe Benacin, *President*
Bruce Elbelia, *Exec VP*

Wayne C Hamerling, *Exec VP*
Russell Greenberg, *CFO*
▲ **EMP:** 57
SQ FT: 12,000
SALES (est): 4MM
SALES (corp-wide): 675.5MM **Publicly Held**
SIC: 2844 5122 Toilet preparations; perfumes; toiletries
PA: Inter Parfums, Inc.
551 5th Ave
New York NY 10176
212 983-2640

(G-9346)
ELITE TRAVELER LLC
441 Lexington Ave Fl 3 (10017-3950)
PHONE....................................646 430-7900
Kat Czarnecki, *Business Mgr*
Eishah Sulaiman, *Business Mgr*
Lorraine Cousland, *Senior VP*
Lorraine Chu, *Production*
Samantha Coles, *Manager*
EMP: 11
SALES (est): 806.6K **Privately Held**
SIC: 2721 Magazines: publishing & printing

(G-9347)
ELIZABETH FILLMORE LLC
27 W 20th St Ste 705 (10011-3727)
PHONE....................................212 647-0863
Thomas Allen, *Vice Pres*
Elizabeth Fillmore,
EMP: 7
SQ FT: 1,900
SALES (est): 900.6K **Privately Held**
WEB: www.elizabethfillmorebridal.com
SIC: 2335 Wedding gowns & dresses

(G-9348)
ELIZABETH GILLETT LTD
Also Called: Elizabeth Gillett Designs
260 W 36th St Rm 802 (10018-8992)
PHONE....................................212 629-7993
Elizabeth Gillett, *President*
Tarafawn Marek, *Exec VP*
◆ **EMP:** 6
SQ FT: 1,500
SALES (est): 2.2MM **Privately Held**
WEB: www.egillett.com
SIC: 2339 Scarves, hoods, headbands, etc.: women's

(G-9349)
ELLIOT MANN NYC INC
324 E 9th St Frnt A (10003-7929)
PHONE....................................212 260-0658
Lisa Paul, *Principal*
EMP: 6
SALES (est): 838.9K **Privately Held**
SIC: 2339 Women's & misses' accessories

(G-9350)
ELMGANG ENTERPRISES I INC
Also Called: Espostos Fnest Qlty Ssage Pdts
354 W 38th St Frnt (10018-2954)
PHONE....................................212 868-4142
David Samuels, *President*
EMP: 10
SQ FT: 5,000
SALES (est): 1.6MM **Privately Held**
WEB: www.espositosausage.com
SIC: 2013 5147 Sausages & related products, from purchased meat; meats & meat products

(G-9351)
ELODINA INC
222 Broadway Fl 19 (10038-2550)
PHONE....................................646 402-5202
EMP: 5
SALES (est): 156K **Privately Held**
SIC: 7372 Business oriented computer software

(G-9352)
ELSEVIER INC (DH)
230 Park Ave Fl 8 (10169-0123)
PHONE....................................212 989-5800
Ron Mobed, *CEO*
Hajo Oltmanns, *President*
Andrew Berin, *Publisher*
Mj Janse, *Editor*
Jane Rylcy, *Editor*
◆ **EMP:** 277 **EST:** 1962
SQ FT: 65,000

SALES (est): 224.6MM
SALES (corp-wide): 9.6B **Privately Held**
WEB: www.elsevierfoundation.org
SIC: 2741 Technical manuals: publishing only, not printed on site
HQ: Elsevier B.V.
Radarweg 29
Amsterdam
204 853-911

(G-9353)
ELUMINOCITY US INC
80 Pine St Fl 24 (10005-1732)
PHONE....................................651 528-1165
Sebastian Jagsch, *CEO*
Robert Rizzo, *Opers Staff*
EMP: 2 **EST:** 2015
SQ FT: 200
SALES (est): 1.8MM **Privately Held**
SIC: 3648 3694 3629 Street lighting fixtures; battery charging generators, automobile & aircraft; battery chargers, rectifying or nonrotating

(G-9354)
ELY BEACH SOLAR LLC
5030 Broadway Ste 819 (10034-1670)
PHONE....................................718 796-9400
Alison Karmel, *Vice Pres*
EMP: 7
SALES (est): 642.4K **Privately Held**
SIC: 3674 Solar cells

(G-9355)
EMA JEWELRY INC
246 W 38th St Fl 6 (10018-5854)
PHONE....................................212 575-8989
Michael Weiss, *CEO*
Edward Weiss, *Vice Pres*
Alex Weiss, *Treasurer*
Elena Grinberg, *Accountant*
Jonathan Weiss, *Manager*
▼ **EMP:** 65
SQ FT: 7,500
SALES (est): 8.9MM **Privately Held**
WEB: www.emajewelry.com
SIC: 3911 3961 Jewelry, precious metal; costume jewelry

(G-9356)
EMBASSY APPAREL INC
37 W 37th St Fl 10 (10018-6354)
PHONE....................................212 768-8330
Ezra Cattan, *President*
Jack Cattan, *Vice Pres*
Judah Cattan, *Vice Pres*
EMP: 18
SQ FT: 10,000
SALES (est): 950.8K **Privately Held**
SIC: 2331 5136 5137 Women's & misses' blouses & shirts; men's & boys' furnishings; women's & children's accessories

(G-9357)
EMBER MEDIA CORPORATION
224 W 35th St 1502 (10001-2507)
PHONE....................................212 695-1919
Clayton A Banks, *President*
Andi Fehr, *Vice Pres*
EMP: 10
SQ FT: 2,500
SALES (est): 920K **Privately Held**
WEB: www.embermedia.com
SIC: 3695 Magnetic & optical recording media

(G-9358)
EMBLAZE SYSTEMS INC (HQ)
Also Called: Geo Publishing
424 Madison Ave Fl 16 (10017-1137)
PHONE....................................212 371-1100
Bruce Edwards, *President*
Joe Budenholzer, *President*
Brad Grob, *Vice Pres*
Lydia Edward, *Treasurer*
Marc Honorof, *Admin Sec*
EMP: 120
SQ FT: 7,000
SALES (est): 7MM **Privately Held**
SIC: 7372 Prepackaged software
PA: B.S.D Crown Ltd
7 Begin Menachem Rd
Ramat Gan
374 017-70

(G-9359)
EMC CORPORATION
2 Penn Plz Fl 24 (10121-2600)
PHONE....................................212 564-6866
Tony Picciuti, *Engineer*
Sean Williford, *Senior Engr*
Christopher Lattanzio, *Accounts Exec*
Julieann Lalina, *Manager*
Chris Byrne, *Manager*
EMP: 200
SALES (corp-wide): 90.6B **Publicly Held**
WEB: www.emc.com
SIC: 3572 Computer storage devices
HQ: Emc Corporation
176 South St
Hopkinton MA 01748
508 435-1000

(G-9360)
EMCO ELECTRIC SERVICES LLC
526 W 26th St Rm 1012 (10001-5541)
PHONE....................................212 420-9766
Meziar Ghavidel, *Mng Member*
Mehr Mansuri, *Mng Member*
EMP: 5 **EST:** 2013
SALES (est): 170K **Privately Held**
SIC: 3699 1731 Electrical equipment & supplies; electronic controls installation

(G-9361)
EMERSON ELECTRIC CO
1250 Broadway Ste 2300 (10001-3726)
PHONE....................................212 244-2490
Jennifer Nichols, *Principal*
EMP: 23
SALES (corp-wide): 17.4B **Publicly Held**
WEB: www.gotoemerson.com
SIC: 3823 Industrial instrmnts msrmnt display/control process variable
PA: Emerson Electric Co.
8000 West Florissant Ave
Saint Louis MO 63136
314 553-2000

(G-9362)
EMPIRICAL RESOLUTION INC
Also Called: Quill.org
41 E 11th St Fl 11 (10003-4602)
PHONE....................................510 671-0222
Peter Gault, *Exec Dir*
Hannah Monk, *Director*
EMP: 15
SALES (est): 1.6MM **Privately Held**
SIC: 7372 Educational computer software

(G-9363)
EMSARU USA CORP
Also Called: Hampshire Jewels
608 5th Ave Ste 500 (10020-2303)
PHONE....................................212 459-9355
Harry Molhan, *President*
EMP: 5
SALES (est): 430K **Privately Held**
SIC: 3911 Jewelry, precious metal

(G-9364)
EMSIG MANUFACTURING CORP (PA)
263 W 38th St Fl 5 (10018-0291)
PHONE....................................718 784-7717
Lawrence Jacobs, *President*
John Lerner, *Vice Pres*
Arthur Klein, *Admin Sec*
◆ **EMP:** 15 **EST:** 1965
SQ FT: 19,000
SALES (est): 24.7MM **Privately Held**
SIC: 3965 Buttons & parts

(G-9365)
EMUSICCOM INC
215 Lexington Ave Fl 18 (10016-6023)
PHONE....................................212 201-9240
Peter Chapman, *CEO*
Daniel Stein, *Ch of Bd*
David Packman, *President*
Emusic News, *Vice Pres*
Martin Hammond, *Cust Svc Dir*
EMP: 75
SALES (est): 10.7MM **Privately Held**
WEB: www.emusic.com
SIC: 3652 Pre-recorded records & tapes

(G-9366)
EMX DIGITAL LLC (PA)
Also Called: Breal Time
261 Madison Ave Fl 4 (10016-3906)
PHONE....................................212 792-6810
Louis Ashner, *Vice Pres*
Nicholas Colletti, *Technical Mgr*
Brian Weigel, *Mng Member*
Michael Grosinger, *Director*
Maria Laino, *Director*
EMP: 7 **EST:** 2016
SALES (est): 6.8MM **Privately Held**
SIC: 7372 Business oriented computer software

(G-9367)
ENCHANTE LITES LLC (HQ)
Also Called: AMG Global
15 W 34th St Fl 8 (10001-3076)
PHONE....................................212 602-1818
Ezra Erani, *President*
Abraham Weinberger, *CFO*
Aharon Franco,
▲ **EMP:** 8
SALES (est): 2.5MM
SALES (corp-wide): 61.5MM **Privately Held**
SIC: 3648 Decorative area lighting fixtures
PA: Enchante Accessories Inc.
16 E 34th St Fl 16 # 16
New York NY 10016
212 725-7879

(G-9368)
ENCYSIVE PHARMACEUTICALS INC (HQ)
235 E 42nd St (10017-5703)
PHONE....................................212 733-2323
John M Pietruski, *Ch of Bd*
Bruce D Given, *President*
Richard A F Dixon, *Senior VP*
Paul S Manierre, *Vice Pres*
Thierry A Plouvier, *Opers Staff*
▲ **EMP:** 35
SQ FT: 40,730
SALES (est): 13.9MM
SALES (corp-wide): 53.6B **Publicly Held**
SIC: 2834 8733 Pharmaceutical preparations; medical research
PA: Pfizer Inc.
235 E 42nd St
New York NY 10017
212 733-2323

(G-9369)
ENDAVA INC (HQ)
757 3rd Ave Ste 1901 (10017-2048)
PHONE....................................212 920-7240
Dan Sullivan, *President*
Paul Chapman, *Sales Staff*
Andrew Rowland, *Sales Staff*
Nicholas Zakrzewski, *Marketing Staff*
Steve Meigh, *Sr Project Mgr*
EMP: 13
SQ FT: 2,000
SALES (est): 24.3MM
SALES (corp-wide): 364.6MM **Privately Held**
SIC: 7372 7371 7375 Business oriented computer software; custom computer programming services; on-line data base information retrieval
PA: Endava Plc
125 Old Broad Street
London EC2N
207 367-1000

(G-9370)
ENDOVOR INC
1330 1st Ave Apt 1119 (10021-4792)
PHONE....................................214 679-7385
Derek Carroll, *CEO*
EMP: 5
SALES (est): 198.4K **Privately Held**
SIC: 3841 Surgical & medical instruments

(G-9371)
ENDOVOR LLC
525 E 68th St A1027 (10065-4870)
PHONE....................................214 679-7385
Derek Carroll, *Opers Staff*
EMP: 8
SALES (est): 293.5K **Privately Held**
SIC: 3841 Surgical & medical instruments

(G-9372)
ENDURANCE LLC
530 7th Ave Rm 902 (10018-4874)
PHONE....................................212 719-2500
Athanasios Nastos,
Renjie Luo,
Daidai Ni,
Qiwen Zhao,
▲ EMP: 20
SALES (est): 1.9MM Privately Held
SIC: 2329 Men's & boys' sportswear & athletic clothing

(G-9373)
ENDURART INC
Also Called: Quality Embedments Mfg Co
132 Nassau St Rm 1100 (10038-2430)
PHONE....................................212 473-7000
Stuart Levine, President
EMP: 30
SQ FT: 18,000
SALES (est): 2.4MM Privately Held
SIC: 3914 2821 Trophies; plastics materials & resins

(G-9374)
ENERGY BRANDS INC (HQ)
Also Called: Glaceau
260 Madison Ave Fl 10 (10016-2417)
PHONE....................................212 545-6000
J Darius Bikoff, CEO
Michael Repole, President
Carol Dollard, COO
Michael Venuti, CFO
▼ EMP: 45
SQ FT: 15,000
SALES (est): 27.1MM
SALES (corp-wide): 31.8B Publicly Held
WEB: www.energybrands.com
SIC: 2086 Soft drinks: packaged in cans, bottles, etc.
PA: The Coca-Cola Company
1 Coca Cola Plz Nw
Atlanta GA 30313
404 676-2121

(G-9375)
ENERGY INTELLIGENCE GROUP INC (PA)
270 Madison Ave Fl 19 (10016-0601)
PHONE....................................212 532-1112
David Kirsch, Managing Dir
Stephanie Cooke, Editor
Tom Haywood, Editor
Jill Junnola, Editor
John Schaik, Editor
EMP: 30
SQ FT: 7,000
SALES (est): 12MM Privately Held
SIC: 2741 Newsletter publishing

(G-9376)
ENERTIV INC
320 W 37th St Ste 1500 (10018-4232)
PHONE....................................646 350-3525
Connell McGill, Ch of Bd
Alan Chen, Sales Staff
Comly Wilson, Marketing Staff
EMP: 6
SALES (est): 1MM Privately Held
SIC: 3825 Instruments to measure electricity

(G-9377)
ENGELACK GEM CORPORATION
36 W 47th St Ste 601 (10036-8636)
PHONE....................................212 719-3094
Imre England, President
Herman Ackerman, Vice Pres
EMP: 2
SALES: 1MM Privately Held
SIC: 3915 Lapidary work & diamond cutting & polishing

(G-9378)
ENGLISH COMPUTER CONSULTING
Also Called: Englishcomp
404 5th Ave Fl 3 (10018-7510)
PHONE....................................212 764-1717
Jim English, President
EMP: 6 EST: 1997

SALES (est): 480.2K Privately Held
WEB: www.englishcomp.com
SIC: 7372 Prepackaged software

(G-9379)
ENHANCE A COLOUR CORP
211 E 43rd St Rm 700 (10017-4821)
PHONE....................................212 490-3620
EMP: 43
SALES (corp-wide): 9.8MM Privately Held
SIC: 2741 Misc Publishing
PA: Enhance A Colour Corp.
15 Old Newtown Rd
Danbury CT 06810
203 748-5111

(G-9380)
ENLIGHTEN AIR INC
23 E 81st St Apt 10 (10028-0225)
P.O. Box 3111, Sag Harbor (11963-0405)
PHONE....................................917 656-1248
William O'Boyle, CEO
EMP: 5
SALES: 392MM Privately Held
SIC: 3728 Target drones

(G-9381)
ENPLAS AMERICA INC
299 Park Ave Fl 41a (10171-3808)
PHONE....................................646 892-7811
EMP: 9
SALES (est): 1.1MM Privately Held
SIC: 3714 5065 3827 Gears, motor vehicle; semiconductor devices; lenses, optical: all types except ophthalmic
PA: Enplas Corporation
2-30-1, Namiki
Kawaguchi STM 332-0

(G-9382)
ENTERPRISE PRESS INC
627 Greenwich St (10014-3327)
PHONE....................................212 741-2111
Robert Hort, Ch of Bd
Benjamin Hort, President
Michael Rabinowitz, President
Michael Hort, Principal
Andrew Hort, Treasurer
EMP: 145 EST: 1915
SQ FT: 85,000
SALES (est): 12.5MM Privately Held
SIC: 2759 2752 Commercial printing; commercial printing, lithographic

(G-9383)
ENTREPRENEUR MEDIA INC
462 Fashion Ave Fl 11 (10018-7433)
PHONE....................................646 502-5463
Vanessa Campos, Marketing Staff
Justin Koenigsderger, Branch Mgr
Jennifer Dorsey, Director
EMP: 15
SALES (corp-wide): 16.4MM Privately Held
SIC: 2721 Magazines: publishing & printing
PA: Entrepreneur Media, Inc.
18061 Fitch
Irvine CA 92614
949 261-2325

(G-9384)
ENUMERAL BIOMEDICAL CORP
1370 Broadway Fl 5 (10018-7350)
PHONE....................................347 227-4787
Arthur H Tinkelenberg, CEO
Kevin Sarney, Vice Pres
EMP: 6
SALES (est): 1.3MM
SALES (corp-wide): 2.6MM Privately Held
SIC: 2834 Pharmaceutical preparations
PA: Enumeral Biomedical Holdings, Inc.
200 Cambridge St
Cambridge MA 02141
617 945-9146

(G-9385)
ENVY PUBLISHING GROUP INC
Also Called: N V Magazine
118 E 25th St Bsmt Ll (10010-2915)
PHONE....................................212 253-9874
Kyle Donovan, CEO
Maria Gordian, President
Christopher Chaney, Adv Dir
EMP: 6

SQ FT: 3,000
SALES: 500K Privately Held
WEB: www.nvmagazine.com
SIC: 2721 6282 Periodicals; investment advice

(G-9386)
EOS PRODUCTS LLC
19 W 44th St Ste 811 (10036-5901)
PHONE....................................212 929-6367
Jonathan Teller, CEO
Sarah Slover, President
▼ EMP: 75
SQ FT: 10,948
SALES (est): 22.6MM
SALES (corp-wide): 22.8MM Privately Held
WEB: www.20-10.com
SIC: 2844 Toilet preparations
PA: The Kind Group Llc
19 W 44th St Ste 811
New York NY 10036
212 645-0800

(G-9387)
EPIC BEAUTY CO LLC
929 Park Ave 5 (10028-0211)
PHONE....................................212 327-3059
Annette McCoy, Mng Member
Maggie G Wedemeyer,
EMP: 2
SQ FT: 500
SALES (est): 1MM Privately Held
SIC: 2844 7991 Cosmetic preparations; spas

(G-9388)
EPOST INTERNATIONAL INC
483 10th Ave (10018-1118)
PHONE....................................212 352-9390
Justine Brown, President
EMP: 5
SALES: 1MM Privately Held
SIC: 2741

(G-9389)
EQUILEND HOLDINGS LLC (PA)
225 Liberty St Fl 10 (10281-1049)
PHONE....................................212 901-2200
Brian Lamb, CEO
Sally Chu, Vice Pres
Alexa Lemstra, Vice Pres
Manoj Mangla, Vice Pres
Louis Rayman, Vice Pres
EMP: 30
SQ FT: 5,500
SALES (est): 8.6MM Privately Held
WEB: www.equilend.com
SIC: 7372 Business oriented computer software

(G-9390)
EQUIPMENT APPAREL LLC
19 W 34th St Fl 8 (10001-3006)
PHONE....................................212 502-1890
Gila Dweck,
▲ EMP: 100
SALES (est): 7.7MM Privately Held
SIC: 2211 Apparel & outerwear fabrics, cotton

(G-9391)
EQUIVITAL INC
19 W 34th St Rm 1018 (10001-3006)
PHONE....................................646 513-4169
Anmol Sood, CEO
Anand Vasudev, Vice Pres
EMP: 22
SALES (est): 1.7MM Privately Held
SIC: 3845 Patient monitoring apparatus

(G-9392)
ER BUTLER & CO INC (PA)
55 Prince St Frnt A (10012-3472)
P.O. Box 272 (10012-0005)
PHONE....................................212 925-3565
Edward R Butler, CEO
Cynthia Laplaige, Project Mgr
Monika Wilson, Project Mgr
Troy Mann, Engineer
Kiki Clark, Manager
▲ EMP: 25
SQ FT: 11,000

SALES (est): 5.2MM Privately Held
WEB: www.erbutler.com
SIC: 3429 5072 8742 7699 Manufactured hardware (general); builders' hardware; industry specialist consultants; miscellaneous building item repair services; plumbing fixture fittings & trim; residential lighting fixtures

(G-9393)
ERIC WINTERLING INC
Also Called: Winterling, Eric Costumes
20 W 20th St Fl 5 (10011-9257)
PHONE....................................212 629-7686
Eric Winterling, President
EMP: 50
SALES (est): 4.8MM Privately Held
SIC: 2389 Costumes

(G-9394)
ERICKSON BEAMON LTD
498 Fashion Ave Rm 2406 (10018-6798)
PHONE....................................212 643-4810
Karen Foster Erickson, President
Eric Erickson, Vice Pres
EMP: 15
SQ FT: 7,500
SALES (est): 2MM Privately Held
WEB: www.ericksonbeamon.com
SIC: 3961 Costume jewelry, ex. precious metal & semiprecious stones

(G-9395)
ERIKA T SCHWARTZ MD PC
724 5th Ave Fl 10 (10019-4106)
PHONE....................................212 873-3420
Erika T Schwartz, President
Joshua Trutt, Vice Pres
EMP: 6
SALES (est): 1.2MM Privately Held
SIC: 2834 8011 Hormone preparations; specialized medical practitioners, except internal

(G-9396)
ESCHEN PROSTHETIC & ORTHOTIC L
510 E 73rd St Ste 201 (10021-4010)
PHONE....................................212 606-1262
Andrew Meyers, President
EMP: 20
SQ FT: 6,000
SALES (est): 2.7MM Privately Held
SIC: 3842 Braces, orthopedic; prosthetic appliances

(G-9397)
ESI CASES & ACCESSORIES INC
44 E 32nd St Rm 601 (10016-5557)
PHONE....................................212 883-8838
Elliot Azoulay, Ch of Bd
Karen Kuchta, Vice Pres
▲ EMP: 38 EST: 1993
SQ FT: 10,000
SALES (est): 10.3MM Privately Held
WEB: www.esicellular.com
SIC: 3661 Telephone & telegraph apparatus

(G-9398)
ESSAR AMERICAS
277 Park Ave 47th (10172-0003)
PHONE....................................212 292-2600
EMP: 5
SALES (est): 348.8K Privately Held
SIC: 1389 Oil & gas field services

(G-9399)
ESSAR STEEL MINNESOTA LLC (PA)
150 E 52nd St Fl 27 (10022-6017)
PHONE....................................212 292-2600
Carola Almonte, Administration
▲ EMP: 17
SALES (est): 7.7MM Privately Held
SIC: 1011 Iron ore mining

(G-9400)
ESSENCE VENTURES LLC
225 Liberty St Fl 9 (10281-1088)
PHONE....................................212 522-1212
Ed Lewis, CEO
EMP: 165

▲ = Import ▼=Export
◆ =Import/Export

SALES (est): 3.3MM **Privately Held**
SIC: 2721 Magazines: publishing only, not printed on site

(G-9401)
ESSENTIAL PUBLICATIONS US LLC
Also Called: Essential Homme Magazine
14 E 4th St Rm 604 (10012-1141)
PHONE..................................646 707-0898
Algis Puidokas, *Principal*
Terry Lu, *Chief*
EMP: 5 EST: 2009
SALES (est): 255.6K **Privately Held**
SIC: 2721 Magazines: publishing & printing

(G-9402)
ESSENTIAL RIBBONS INC
53 W 36th St Rm 405 (10018-7623)
PHONE..................................212 967-4173
Jie Lin, *Ch of Bd*
▲ EMP: 7
SALES (est): 620.2K **Privately Held**
SIC: 2241 Ribbons

(G-9403)
ESSEQUATTRO USA INC
1 Little West 12th St (10014-1302)
PHONE..................................917 862-0005
Giovanni De Santis, *Principal*
EMP: 6
SALES (est): 553.7K **Privately Held**
SIC: 2426 Carvings, furniture: wood

(G-9404)
ESSEX MANUFACTURING INC
Also Called: Baum Essex
350 5th Ave Ste 2400 (10118-0128)
P.O. Box 190, Washington GA (30673-0190)
PHONE..................................212 239-0080
William Baum, *CEO*
Myron Baum, *Ch of Bd*
Charles J Baum, *President*
Peter Baum, *COO*
Angelika Halka, *Executive*
◆ EMP: 75 EST: 1961
SQ FT: 85,300
SALES (est): 9.3MM **Privately Held**
SIC: 3999 3171 2385 Umbrellas, canes & parts; women's handbags & purses; raincoats, except vulcanized rubber: purchased materials

(G-9405)
ESSIE COSMETICS LTD
575 5th Ave (10017-2422)
PHONE..................................212 818-1500
Esther Weingarten, *President*
Blanche Weingarten, *Treasurer*
◆ EMP: 75
SQ FT: 25,000
SALES (est): 15.4MM
SALES (corp-wide): 4.4B **Privately Held**
WEB: www.essie.com
SIC: 2844 5122 Manicure preparations; toilet preparations; cosmetics
HQ: L'oreal Usa, Inc.
10 Hudson Yards
New York NY 10001
212 818-1500

(G-9406)
ESTEE LAUDER COMPANIES INC
9 W 22nd St (10010-5101)
PHONE..................................917 606-3240
EMP: 504 **Publicly Held**
SIC: 2844 Toilet preparations
PA: The Estee Lauder Companies Inc
767 5th Ave Fl 1
New York NY 10153

(G-9407)
ESTEE LAUDER COMPANIES INC
110 E 59th St Fl 37 (10022-1600)
PHONE..................................212 572-4200
Marielle Hemschot, *Executive*
EMP: 21 **Publicly Held**
SIC: 2844 Cosmetic preparations
PA: The Estee Lauder Companies Inc
767 5th Ave Fl 1
New York NY 10153

(G-9408)
ESTEE LAUDER COMPANIES INC
655 Madison Ave Fl 15 (10065-8043)
PHONE..................................212 756-4800
Denise Dicanio, *Director*
Gina Kim, *Director*
Shanna Weinblatt, *Director*
EMP: 7 **Publicly Held**
SIC: 2844 Cosmetic preparations
PA: The Estee Lauder Companies Inc
767 5th Ave Fl 1
New York NY 10153

(G-9409)
ESTEE LAUDER COMPANIES INC
28 W 23rd St (10010-5204)
PHONE..................................646 762-7718
Ann Nedell, *Director*
EMP: 14 **Publicly Held**
SIC: 2844 Toilet preparations
PA: The Estee Lauder Companies Inc
767 5th Ave Fl 1
New York NY 10153

(G-9410)
ESTEE LAUDER COMPANIES INC (PA)
767 5th Ave Fl 1 (10153-0003)
PHONE..................................212 572-4200
William P Lauder, *Ch of Bd*
John Demsey, *President*
Fabrizio Freda, *President*
Carl Haney, *Exec VP*
Sara E Moss, *Exec VP*
◆ EMP: 1000
SALES (est): 14.8B **Publicly Held**
WEB: www.elcompanies.com
SIC: 2844 Cosmetic preparations

(G-9411)
ESTEE LAUDER COMPANIES INC
65 Bleecker St Frnt 1 (10012-2420)
PHONE..................................646 602-7590
EMP: 504 **Publicly Held**
SIC: 2844 Toilet preparations
PA: The Estee Lauder Companies Inc
767 5th Ave Fl 1
New York NY 10153

(G-9412)
ETERNAL FORTUNE FASHION LLC (PA)
Also Called: Profile Nyc
135 W 36th St Fl 3 (10018-6900)
PHONE..................................212 965-5322
Teresa Tian, *Controller*
Roy Zou, *Mng Member*
Candice Wong,
◆ EMP: 1
SQ FT: 5,600
SALES (est): 1.9MM **Privately Held**
SIC: 2329 Men's & boys' sportswear & athletic clothing

(G-9413)
ETNA PRODUCTS CO INC (PA)
99 Madison Ave Fl 11 (10016-7419)
PHONE..................................212 989-7591
Raymond Trinh, *Ch of Bd*
Jeffrey Snyder, *Ch of Bd*
Paula Snyder, *Admin Sec*
▲ EMP: 19 EST: 1957
SQ FT: 15,000
SALES (est): 3.4MM **Privately Held**
WEB: www.etna.com
SIC: 3089 5021 Plastic kitchenware, tableware & houseware; furniture

(G-9414)
ETNA TOOL & DIE CORPORATION
42 Bond St Frnt A (10012-2476)
PHONE..................................212 475-4350
Keranus Galuppo, *President*
James Galuppo, *Admin Sec*
EMP: 12 EST: 1946
SQ FT: 14,000

SALES (est): 1.3MM **Privately Held**
WEB: www.etnatoolanddie.com
SIC: 3599 3544 7692 Machine shop, jobbing & repair; special dies & tools; welding repair

(G-9415)
ETON INSTITUTE
1 Rockefeller Plz Fl 11 (10020-2073)
PHONE..................................855 334-3688
EMP: 10
SALES (est): 710K **Privately Held**
SIC: 3999 Mfg Misc Products

(G-9416)
EU DESIGN LLC
73 Spring St Rm 506 (10012-5802)
PHONE..................................212 420-7788
Roberto Berardi, *President*
Leonardo Caraffini, *Business Mgr*
Alyssa Miller, *Accounts Mgr*
Yelena Vilman, *Manager*
Susan Wong, *Manager*
▲ EMP: 7 EST: 1999
SALES (est): 948K **Privately Held**
WEB: www.eu-design.com
SIC: 3965 3961 5131 Buttons & parts; costume jewelry; piece goods & other fabrics; ribbons
PA: Eu Design, Hk Limited
Rm 301-302 3/F Tins Enterprises Ctr
Cheung Sha Wan KLN

(G-9417)
EUGENE BIRO CORP
581 5th Ave Fl 3 (10017-8826)
PHONE..................................212 997-0146
Eugene Biro, *President*
Ety Biro, *Vice Pres*
Jack Ko, *Info Tech Dir*
EMP: 30 EST: 1975
SQ FT: 15,000
SALES (est): 3.9MM **Privately Held**
WEB: www.eugenebiro.com
SIC: 3915 5094 Diamond cutting & polishing; diamonds (gems)

(G-9418)
EUPHORBIA PRODUCTIONS LTD
632 Broadway Fl 9 (10012-2614)
PHONE..................................212 533-1700
Philip Glass, *President*
Kurt Munkaisi, *Officer*
EMP: 6
SALES (est): 483K **Privately Held**
WEB: www.euphorbia.com
SIC: 2741 7389 Music books: publishing only, not printed on site; music recording producer

(G-9419)
EURO BANDS INC
247 W 37th St Ste 700 (10018-5706)
PHONE..................................212 719-9777
Zbigniew Jarosh, *President*
EMP: 16
SALES: 500K **Privately Held**
WEB: www.e-bands.net
SIC: 3911 Jewelry, precious metal

(G-9420)
EUROCO COSTUMES INC
306 W 38th St Rm 1600 (10018-3324)
PHONE..................................212 629-9665
Janet Bloor, *President*
▼ EMP: 9
SALES (est): 1MM **Privately Held**
SIC: 2389 Theatrical costumes

(G-9421)
EUROPROJECTS INTL INC
Also Called: Adotta America
152 W 25th St Fl 8b (10001-7402)
PHONE..................................917 262-0795
Luigi Zannier, *President*
EMP: 11
SALES (corp-wide): 13MM **Privately Held**
SIC: 3211 Structural glass
PA: Europrojects Int'l Inc
500 Nordhoff Pl Ste 5
Englewood NJ 07631
201 408-5215

(G-9422)
EV-BOX NORTH AMERICA INC
335 Madison Ave Fl 4 (10017-4675)
PHONE..................................646 930-6305
Nicholas Lalli, *Director*
EMP: 5
SQ FT: 12,000
SALES (est): 237.6K **Privately Held**
SIC: 3694 Automotive electrical equipment

(G-9423)
EVADO FILIP
159 Bleecker St (10012-1457)
PHONE..................................917 774-8666
Craig Gainsboro, *CFO*
EMP: 12
SQ FT: 2,000
SALES (est): 819.2K **Privately Held**
SIC: 3663

(G-9424)
EVERBLOCK SYSTEMS LLC (PA)
790 Madison Ave Rm 506 (10065-6124)
PHONE..................................844 422-5625
Arnon Rosan, *Mng Member*
EMP: 7 EST: 2015
SALES: 4.8MM **Privately Held**
SIC: 3271 3251 3299 3089 Blocks, concrete: landscape or retaining wall; structural brick & blocks; blocks & brick, sand lime; injection molded finished plastic products

(G-9425)
EVERCORE PARTNERS SVCS E LLC
55 E 52nd St (10055-0002)
PHONE..................................212 857-3100
James Park, *Managing Dir*
Greg Sefanov, *Managing Dir*
Victor Chan, *Vice Pres*
Aaron Eisenberg, *Vice Pres*
James Lilly, *Vice Pres*
EMP: 2214
SALES (est): 132.9MM **Publicly Held**
SIC: 2711 Newspapers, publishing & printing
PA: Evercore Inc.
55 E 52nd St Fl 36
New York NY 10055

(G-9426)
EVEREST BBN INC
42 Broadway Ste 1736 (10004-3853)
PHONE..................................212 268-7979
EMP: 11 EST: 2011
SALES (est): 1.7MM **Privately Held**
SIC: 3825 Mfg Electrical Measuring Instruments

(G-9427)
EVERLAST SPORTS MFG CORP (DH)
42 W 39th St (10018-3809)
PHONE..................................212 239-0990
Neil Morton, *CEO*
▲ EMP: 41 EST: 1945
SQ FT: 300,000
SALES (est): 11.6MM **Privately Held**
SIC: 3949 5091 Sporting & athletic goods; sporting & recreation goods

(G-9428)
EVERLAST WORLDWIDE INC (DH)
42 W 39th St Fl 3 (10018-3832)
PHONE..................................212 239-0990
Beth Rasmussen, *Vice Pres*
Jay Senzatimore, *Vice Pres*
Mark Hunter, *CFO*
Edward Ban, *Controller*
Shannon Keith, *Finance Mgr*
▲ EMP: 40
SQ FT: 12,087
SALES: 70MM **Privately Held**
SIC: 3949 8049 3144 3149 Boxing equipment & supplies, general; nutritionist; women's footwear, except athletic; children's footwear, except athletic

(G-9429)
EVERSTONE INDUSTRIES LLC
242 W 122nd St Apt 4b (10027-5468)
PHONE..................................347 777-8150

GEOGRAPHIC

Everstone Adams, *Principal*
EMP: 25
SALES (est): 686K **Privately Held**
SIC: 3999 Manufacturing industries

(G-9430)
EVOCATE MEDIA LLC
100 W 139th St Apt 34a (10030-2217)
PHONE..................................646 361-3014
Parveez Syed, *Mng Member*
EMP: 10
SALES: 0 **Privately Held**
SIC: 7372 7389 Application computer software;

(G-9431)
EVOKE NEUROSCIENCE INC
11 W 25th St Fl 10 (10010-2054)
PHONE..................................917 261-6096
David Hagedorn, *CEO*
James Thompson, *Principal*
EMP: 13
SQ FT: 2,000
SALES: 140MM **Privately Held**
SIC: 3845 Electromedical equipment

(G-9432)
EVOLUTION SPIRITS INC
Also Called: Monkey Rum
401 Park Ave S (10016-8808)
PHONE..................................917 543-7880
Ian Crystal, *President*
David Goodacre, *Officer*
EMP: 7
SALES (est): 589.8K **Privately Held**
SIC: 2085 Rum (alcoholic beverage)

(G-9433)
EWATCHFACTORY CORP (PA)
Also Called: Pacific Concepts
390 5th Ave Rm 910 (10018-8111)
PHONE..................................212 564-8318
Remi Chabrat, *CEO*
Jaffy Ng, *Accountant*
Moritz Neuhaeuser, *Marketing Staff*
Vanessa Ramirez, *Manager*
Barbara A Rizzo, *Manager*
▲ **EMP:** 5
SQ FT: 1,200
SALES (est): 531.9K **Privately Held**
WEB: www.watchfactory.com
SIC: 3873 Watches, clocks, watchcases & parts

(G-9434)
EX EL ENTERPRISES LTD
630 Fort Washington Ave (10040-3900)
PHONE..................................212 489-4500
Henry Lehman, *President*
EMP: 11
SQ FT: 1,900
SALES (est): 960K **Privately Held**
WEB: www.ex-el.com
SIC: 7372 7373 Prepackaged software; systems software development services

(G-9435)
EX-CELL HOME FASHIONS INC (DH)
1333 Broadway Fl 8 (10018-1064)
P.O. Box 1879, Goldsboro NC (27533-1879)
PHONE..................................919 735-7111
Joe Granger, *CEO*
Andrew Skobe, *CFO*
Margaritta Topielski, *CTO*
Dan K Martin, *Admin Sec*
◆ **EMP:** 200 **EST:** 1932
SALES (est): 40.1MM **Privately Held**
WEB: www.ecshs.com
SIC: 2392 Cushions & pillows; tablecloths & table settings; shower curtains: made from purchased materials
HQ: Glenoit Llc
1500 N Carolina St
Goldsboro NC 27530
919 735-7111

(G-9436)
EX-IT MEDICAL DEVICES INC
1330 Ave Of The Americas (10019-5400)
PHONE..................................212 653-0637
Shlomo Shopen, *CEO*
EMP: 3
SALES: 10MM **Privately Held**
SIC: 2844 Cosmetic preparations

(G-9437)
EXACT SOLUTIONS INC
139 Fulton St Rm 511 (10038-2535)
PHONE..................................212 707-8627
Hardev Deindsa, *President*
Lubna Shaikh, *Human Res Mgr*
Narvinder Matharu, *Sales Engr*
Ruchir Garg, *CTO*
EMP: 11
SALES (est): 1MM **Privately Held**
WEB: www.exact-solutions.com
SIC: 7372 Business oriented computer software

(G-9438)
EXC HOLDINGS I CORP (HQ)
666 5th Ave Fl 36 (10103-3102)
PHONE..................................212 644-5900
Andreas Kramvis, *Ch of Bd*
Brian Hoesterey, *President*
Barbara L Burns, *Vice Pres*
Paul Igoe, *Vice Pres*
Vinay Kumar, *Vice Pres*
EMP: 6500
SALES (est): 1.2B **Privately Held**
SIC: 3674 3827 3648 3679 Semiconductor diodes & rectifiers; optical instruments & apparatus; outdoor lighting equipment; electronic circuits
PA: Exc Holdings Lp
666 5th Ave Fl 36
New York NY 10103
212 644-5900

(G-9439)
EXC HOLDINGS II CORP (DH)
666 5th Ave Fl 36 (10103-3102)
PHONE..................................212 644-5900
Andrea Kramvis, *Ch of Bd*
Brian Hoesterey, *President*
Barbara L Burns, *Vice Pres*
Paul Igoe, *Vice Pres*
Vinay Kumar, *Vice Pres*
EMP: 6500
SALES (est): 1.2B **Privately Held**
SIC: 3674 3827 3648 3679 Semiconductor diodes & rectifiers; optical instruments & apparatus; outdoor lighting equipment; electronic circuits
HQ: Exc Holdings I Corp.
666 5th Ave Fl 36
New York NY 10103
212 644-5900

(G-9440)
EXC HOLDINGS LP (PA)
666 5th Ave Fl 36 (10103-3102)
PHONE..................................212 644-5900
Exc Holding GP Corp, *General Ptnr*
EMP: 2
SALES (est): 1.2B **Privately Held**
SIC: 3674 3827 3648 3679 Semiconductor diodes & rectifiers; optical instruments & apparatus; outdoor lighting equipment; electronic circuits

(G-9441)
EXCEL GRAPHICS SERVICES INC
519 8th Ave Fl 18 (10018-4577)
PHONE..................................212 929-2183
Joseph Risola, *President*
Anthony Fazio III, *Vice Pres*
EMP: 12 **EST:** 1997
SQ FT: 16,500
SALES (est): 1.7MM **Privately Held**
SIC: 2752 Commercial printing, offset

(G-9442)
EXCEL TECHNOLOGY INC
780 3rd Ave (10017-2024)
PHONE..................................212 355-3400
Donald Hill, *CEO*
EMP: 15 **Publicly Held**
WEB: www.exceltechinc.com
SIC: 3845 Electromedical equipment
HQ: Excel Technology, Inc.
125 Middlesex Tpke
Bedford MA 01730
781 266-5700

(G-9443)
EXCELLED SHEEPSKIN & LEA COAT (PA)
Also Called: RG Apparel Group
1359 Broadway Fl 9 (10018-7190)
P.O. Box 659, Carteret NJ (07008-0659)
PHONE..................................212 594-5843
William Goldman, *President*
Myron Goldman, *Chairman*
Rachel Cooper, *Vice Pres*
Michael Holzberg, *Vice Pres*
Mike Holzberg, *Vice Pres*
▲ **EMP:** 12 **EST:** 1927
SQ FT: 50,000
SALES (est): 65.5MM **Privately Held**
WEB: www.leathercoatsetc.com
SIC: 2386 3172 2337 2311 Coats & jackets, leather & sheep-lined; personal leather goods; women's & misses' suits & coats; men's & boys' suits & coats

(G-9444)
EXCELSIOR GRAPHICS INC
485 Madison Ave Fl 13 (10022-5803)
PHONE..................................212 730-6200
Harold Siegel, *President*
EMP: 5
SQ FT: 8,000
SALES (est): 450K **Privately Held**
SIC: 2752 Commercial printing, offset

(G-9445)
EXECUTIVE SIGN CORPORATION
347 W 36th St Rm 902 (10018-6491)
PHONE..................................212 397-4050
Isaac Goldman, *President*
Kelle Hankins, *Vice Pres*
EMP: 6
SQ FT: 1,800
SALES: 600K **Privately Held**
SIC: 3993 Signs, not made in custom sign painting shops

(G-9446)
EXOTIC PRINT AND PAPER INC
Also Called: Arthur Invitation
15 E 13th St (10003-4405)
PHONE..................................212 807-0465
Arfa Rejaei, *Ch of Bd*
Arthur Rajaei, *President*
EMP: 11
SQ FT: 1,800
SALES (est): 1.1MM **Privately Held**
SIC: 2759 5947 Commercial printing; gift shop

(G-9447)
EXPERIMENT LLC
260 5th Ave Fl 3 (10001-6408)
PHONE..................................212 889-1659
Matthew Lore,
Peter Burri,
▲ **EMP:** 5
SALES (est): 517.5K **Privately Held**
SIC: 2732 Book printing

(G-9448)
EXPERIMENT PUBLISHING LLC
220 E 23rd St Ste 600 (10010-4658)
PHONE..................................212 889-1273
Matthew Lore, *Mng Member*
Batya Rosenblum, *Assoc Editor*
▲ **EMP:** 9
SALES (est): 902.6K **Privately Held**
SIC: 2741 Miscellaneous publishing

(G-9449)
EXPRESS CHECKOUT LLC
110 E 1st St Apt 20 (10009-7977)
PHONE..................................646 512-2068
William Hogben,
EMP: 6
SQ FT: 300
SALES (est): 313.4K **Privately Held**
SIC: 7372 Application computer software

(G-9450)
EXTREME GROUP HOLDINGS LLC (DH)
25 Madison Ave Fl 19 (10010-8601)
PHONE..................................212 833-8000
▲ **EMP:** 13
SALES (est): 1.9MM **Privately Held**
SIC: 3652 Pre-recorded records & tapes

HQ: Sony/Atv Music Publishing Llc
25 Madison Ave Fl 24
New York NY 10010
212 833-7730

(G-9451)
EYELOCK CORPORATION
321 W 44th St Ste 702 (10036-5468)
PHONE..................................855 393-5625
Amy Romeo, *CFO*
Chris Ream, *Security Dir*
EMP: 19
SALES: 3.8MM
SALES (corp-wide): 446.8MM **Publicly Held**
SIC: 3699 Security control equipment & systems
HQ: Eyelock Llc
321 W 44th St Ste 702
New York NY 10036
855 393-5625

(G-9452)
EYELOCK LLC (HQ)
321 W 44th St Ste 702 (10036-5468)
PHONE..................................855 393-5625
Jeff Carter, *CEO*
Sarvesh Makthal, *President*
Michael Petrov, *VP Engrg*
Anthony Antolino,
Samuel Carter,
EMP: 10 **EST:** 2015
SALES (est): 10.2MM
SALES (corp-wide): 446.8MM **Publicly Held**
SIC: 3699 Security control equipment & systems
PA: Voxx International Corporation
2351 J Lawson Blvd
Orlando FL 32824
800 645-7750

(G-9453)
EYENOVIA INC
295 Madison Ave Fl 24 (10017-6354)
PHONE..................................917 289-1117
Fredric N Eshelman, *Ch of Bd*
Jennifer Clasby, *Vice Pres*
Luke Clauson, *Vice Pres*
John Gandolfo, *CFO*
Tsontcho Ianchulev, *Chief Mktg Ofcr*
EMP: 24
SQ FT: 3,800
SALES (est): 879.4K **Privately Held**
SIC: 2834 8731 Pharmaceutical preparations; biological research

(G-9454)
F & J DESIGNS INC
Also Called: Thalian
526 Fashion Ave Fl 8 (10018-4822)
PHONE..................................212 302-8755
▲ **EMP:** 9
SQ FT: 5,000
SALES (est): 1.3MM **Privately Held**
SIC: 2339 5137 Mfg Women's/Misses' Outerwear Whol Women's/Child's Clothing

(G-9455)
F P H COMMUNICATIONS
225 Broadway Ste 2008 (10007-3737)
PHONE..................................212 528-1728
Steve Young, *President*
EMP: 2
SQ FT: 2,100
SALES: 3.5MM **Privately Held**
SIC: 2731 Book publishing

(G-9456)
F&M ORNAMENTAL DESIGNS LLC
Also Called: Desiron
200 Lexington Ave Rm 1316 (10016-6201)
PHONE..................................908 241-7776
Frank J Carfaro, *Mng Member*
▲ **EMP:** 45
SALES (est): 4.6MM **Privately Held**
SIC: 2514 Metal household furniture

(G-9457)
F-O-R SOFTWARE LLC
Also Called: Two-Four Software
757 3rd Ave Fl 20 (10017-2046)
PHONE..................................212 231-9506
Steve Davis, *Branch Mgr*

▲ = Import ▼=Export
◆ =Import/Export

EMP: 15
SALES (corp-wide): 3.1MM **Privately Held**
SIC: 7372 Prepackaged software
PA: F-O-R Software Llc
    10 Bank St Ste 880
    White Plains NY 10606
    914 220-8800

(G-9458)
F5 NETWORKS INC
600 Lexington Ave Fl 5 (10022-7634)
PHONE..................................888 882-7535
James Reardon, *Principal*
EMP: 6 **Publicly Held**
SIC: 2752 Commercial printing, litho-
    graphic
PA: F5 Networks, Inc.
    801 5th Ave
    Seattle WA 98104

(G-9459)
FABBIAN USA CORP
307 W 38th St Rm 1103 (10018-2946)
PHONE..................................973 882-3824
Vincenzo Tersigni, *Vice Pres*
▲ EMP: 6
SQ FT: 33,000
SALES (est): 953.5K **Privately Held**
SIC: 3648 Lighting equipment

(G-9460)
FACSIMILE CMMNCATIONS INDS INC (PA)
Also Called: Atlantic Business Products
134 W 26th St Fl 3 (10001-6803)
PHONE..................................212 741-6400
Larry Weiss, *Ch of Bd*
Bill Green, *Vice Pres*
Jonathan Elson, *Project Mgr*
Adam Wall, *Opers Staff*
Russ Klein, *CFO*
EMP: 75
SQ FT: 12,000
SALES (est): 45.8MM **Privately Held**
WEB: www.tomorrowsoffice.com
SIC: 3861 3571 Photocopy machines;
    computers, digital, analog or hybrid

(G-9461)
FADER INC
71 W 23rd St Ste 1300 (10010-3540)
PHONE..................................212 741-7100
Jon Cohen, *President*
EMP: 14
SALES (est): 1.4MM **Privately Held**
SIC: 2721 Magazines: publishing only, not
    printed on site

(G-9462)
FAHRENHEIT NY INC
315 W 39th St Rm 803 (10018-1492)
PHONE..................................212 354-6554
Connie Bates, *President*
Christine Bates, *Admin Sec*
EMP: 7
SQ FT: 2,200
SALES (est): 908.9K **Privately Held**
SIC: 3199 3172 Leather belting & strap-
    ping; personal leather goods

(G-9463)
FAIRCHILD PUBLICATIONS INC (DH)
Also Called: Womens Wear Daily
475 5th Ave (10017-6220)
PHONE..................................212 630-4000
Charles H Townsend, *President*
Richard Baylef, *President*
Michael Coady, *President*
Lee W Lik, *Managing Dir*
Zack Blomquist, *Editor*
▲ EMP: 600
SQ FT: 150,000
SALES (est): 146.8MM
SALES (corp-wide): 5.5B **Privately Held**
WEB: www.fairchildbooks.com
SIC: 2721 2711 2731 Periodicals; news-
    papers; book publishing
HQ: Advance Magazine Publishers Inc.
    1 World Trade Ctr Fl 43
    New York NY 10007
    212 286-2860

(G-9464)
FAIRCHILD PUBLISHING LLC
4 Times Sq Fl 17 (10036-6625)
PHONE..................................212 286-3897
EMP: 8
SALES (est): 803K **Privately Held**
SIC: 2721 Periodicals

(G-9465)
FAIRMOUNT PRESS
70 W 36th St Rm 500 (10018-8050)
PHONE..................................212 255-2300
Peter Bird, *President*
EMP: 6
SALES (est): 510.1K **Privately Held**
SIC: 2759 7334 Letterpress printing; pho-
    tocopying & duplicating services

(G-9466)
FAM CREATIONS
7 W 45th St Ste 1404 (10036-4905)
PHONE..................................212 869-4833
EMP: 20
SALES (est): 1.6MM **Privately Held**
SIC: 3911 Jewelry Manufacturer

(G-9467)
FAMILY PUBLICATIONS LTD
325 W 38th St Rm 804 (10018-9623)
PHONE..................................212 947-2177
Gail Granet-Velez, *President*
EMP: 12
SALES (est): 1.2MM **Privately Held**
WEB: www.familypublications.com
SIC: 2741 7999 Guides: publishing only,
    not printed on site; exposition operation

(G-9468)
FANCY FLAMINGO LLC
450 W 17th St Apt 528 (10011-5846)
PHONE..................................516 209-7306
Sanchali Sundaram, *CEO*
Senthil Sundaram, *COO*
EMP: 6 EST: 2011
SALES (est): 407.5K **Privately Held**
SIC: 2086 Bottled & canned soft drinks

(G-9469)
FANSHAWE FOODS LLC
5 Columbus Cir (10019-1412)
PHONE..................................212 757-3130
Lee Zalben, *President*
EMP: 10
SALES (est): 564.3K **Privately Held**
SIC: 2099 5149 Food preparations; spe-
    cialty food items

(G-9470)
FANTASIA INTERNATIONAL LLC ✪
1384 Broadway Ste 1101 (10018-6108)
PHONE..................................212 869-0432
John Kaye, *President*
Johnathan Honig, *Vice Pres*
Susan Doneson, *Admin Sec*
EMP: 3 EST: 2019
SALES: 20MM **Privately Held**
SIC: 3589 Commercial cooking & food-
    warming equipment

(G-9471)
FANTASIA JEWELRY INC
42 W 39th St Fl 14 (10018-2082)
PHONE..................................212 921-9590
Sebastian De Serio, *President*
Joseph De Serio, *Vice Pres*
Edward Deserio, *Treasurer*
EMP: 42
SQ FT: 7,000
SALES (est): 3.2MM **Privately Held**
WEB: www.fantasiajewelry.com
SIC: 3961 3911 Costume jewelry, ex. pre-
    cious metal & semiprecious stones; jew-
    elry, precious metal

(G-9472)
FANTASY SPORTS MEDIA GROUP INC
Also Called: Fantasy Sports Network
27 W 20th St Ste 900 (10011-3725)
PHONE..................................416 917-6002
Leonard Asper, *President*
EMP: 20
SALES: 2.5MM **Privately Held**
SIC: 2741 Miscellaneous publishing

(G-9473)
FARMERS DOG INC
214 Sullivan St Fl 5 (10012-1354)
PHONE..................................646 780-7957
EMP: 5
SALES (est): 233.9K **Privately Held**
SIC: 2047 Dog food

(G-9474)
FASHION ACCENTS LLC
365 5th Ave Rm 802 (10001-2231)
PHONE..................................401 331-6626
EMP: 13
SALES (corp-wide): 3.4MM **Privately Held**
SIC: 3961 Earrings, except precious metal
PA: Fashion Accents, Llc
    100 Nashua St
    Providence RI 02904
    401 331-6626

(G-9475)
FASHION AVE SWEATER KNITS LLC
525 7th Ave Fl 4 (10018-4940)
PHONE..................................212 302-8282
Melvyn Weiss, *President*
Laura Amodeo,
Edward Barman,
Roland Hollandworth,
EMP: 109
SQ FT: 18,000
SALES (est): 5.8MM **Privately Held**
SIC: 2339 Service apparel, washable:
    women's

(G-9476)
FASHION AVENUE KNITS INC
Also Called: Its Our Time
1400 Broadway Rm 2401 (10018-5300)
PHONE..................................718 456-9000
Mel Weiss, *Manager*
EMP: 10
SALES (est): 1MM
SALES (corp-wide): 50.9MM **Privately Held**
WEB: www.fashionavenueknits.com
SIC: 2253 Knit outerwear mills
PA: Fashion Avenue Knits Inc.
    525 7th Ave Fl 4
    New York NY 10018
    718 456-9000

(G-9477)
FASHION CALENDAR INTERNATIONAL
153 E 87th St Apt 6a (10128-2705)
PHONE..................................212 289-0420
Ruth Finley, *Owner*
EMP: 7 EST: 1939
SALES (est): 665.9K **Privately Held**
WEB: www.fashioncalendar.net
SIC: 2721 Periodicals

(G-9478)
FASHIONDEX INC
153 W 27th St Ste 701 (10001-6255)
PHONE..................................914 271-6121
Andrea Kennedy, *President*
Max Andrews, *Vice Pres*
▲ EMP: 6
SALES: 150K **Privately Held**
WEB: www.fashiondex.com
SIC: 2741 5192 Telephone & other direc-
    tory publishing; books, periodicals &
    newspapers

(G-9479)
FAVIANA INTERNATIONAL INC (PA)
320 W 37th St Fl 10 (10018-4675)
PHONE..................................212 594-4422
Parviz Pourmoradi, *President*
Omid Pourmoradi, *Vice Pres*
Diego Ledezma, *Production*
Shala Pourmoradi, *Treasurer*
▲ EMP: 31
SQ FT: 32,000
SALES: 7.8MM **Privately Held**
WEB: www.faviana.com
SIC: 2335 Women's, juniors' & misses'
    dresses

(G-9480)
FEDERAL ENVELOPE INC
22 W 32nd St (10001-3807)
PHONE..................................212 243-8380
Fax: 212 691-8076
EMP: 10 EST: 1953
SQ FT: 10,000
SALES (est): 730K **Privately Held**
SIC: 2759 2752 Printer Of Printing En-
    velopes Letterpress & An Offset Printing
    Service

(G-9481)
FEDERAL PUMP CORPORATION
250 E 73rd St Apt 18c (10021-4314)
PHONE..................................718 451-2000
Christopher Murtagh, *President*
Tony Tsang, *Engineer*
Brooke Kanarek, *Sales Staff*
▲ EMP: 45 EST: 1935
SQ FT: 53,000
SALES (est): 18.3MM
SALES (corp-wide): 5.4MM **Privately Held**
SIC: 3561 Industrial pumps & parts
PA: Pumpman Holdings, Llc
    600 Madison Ave
    New York NY 10022
    626 939-0300

(G-9482)
FELDMAN COMPANY INC
Also Called: Ango Home
241 W 37th St Rm 1001 (10018-7072)
PHONE..................................212 966-1303
Alfred Feldman, *President*
Hershel Feldman, *Vice Pres*
Eli Jeidel, *Vice Pres*
Tammy Lehman, *Executive*
▲ EMP: 13
SQ FT: 6,000
SALES (est): 2.5MM **Privately Held**
WEB: www.feldmanco.com
SIC: 2299 5023 Fabrics: linen, jute, hemp,
    ramie; home furnishings

(G-9483)
FEMINIST PRESS INC
365 5th Ave Ste 5406 (10016-4309)
PHONE..................................212 817-7915
Yamberlie Tavarez, *Development*
Howard Kritz, *Personnel*
Hannah Goodwin, *Admin Mgr*
Jamia Wilson, *Exec Dir*
B Altman, *Exec Dir*
EMP: 8
SQ FT: 2,000
SALES: 878.4K **Privately Held**
SIC: 2731 Book publishing

(G-9484)
FERRARA BAKERY & CAFE INC (PA)
195 Grand St (10013-3717)
PHONE..................................212 226-6150
Ernest Lepore, *Ch of Bd*
Peter Lepore, *President*
Josie Olah, *General Mgr*
Jose Torres, *General Mgr*
Anthony Sessa, *Opers Staff*
▲ EMP: 110 EST: 1892
SALES (est): 15.2MM **Privately Held**
WEB: www.ferraracafe.com
SIC: 2051 5461 Cakes, bakery: except
    frozen; pastries, e.g. danish: except
    frozen; bakeries; cakes; pastries

(G-9485)
FERRIS USA LLC
18 W 108th St Apt 4a (10025-8918)
PHONE..................................617 895-8102
Taylor Conlin, *Mng Member*
EMP: 8
SALES: 150K **Privately Held**
SIC: 2326 2329 5621 Men's & boys' work
    clothing; men's & boys' sportswear & ath-
    letic clothing; field jackets, military; ready-
    to-wear apparel, women's

(G-9486)
FEVERTREE USA INC
37 W 26th St Ph (10010-1049)
PHONE..................................718 852-5577
Charles Gibb, *CEO*
EMP: 10

SALES (est): 26.5MM
SALES (corp-wide): 305MM **Privately Held**
SIC: 2086 Carbonated beverages, nonalcoholic: bottled & canned
HQ: Fevertree Limited
186-188 Shepherds Bush Road
London W6 7N

(G-9487)
FIBER-SEAL OF NEW YORK INC (PA)
979 3rd Ave Ste 903 (10022-3802)
PHONE...................................212 888-5580
Steven Mittman, *President*
Roberta Mittman, *Corp Secy*
▲ EMP: 5 EST: 1954
SALES (est): 9.8MM **Privately Held**
WEB: www.lewismittman.com
SIC: 2512 2511 Upholstered household furniture; wood bedroom furniture

(G-9488)
FIBRE CASE & NOVELTY CO INC (PA)
270 Lafayette St Ste 1510 (10012-3377)
PHONE...................................212 254-6060
Elliot Kozer, *President*
Richard Rubin, *Treasurer*
EMP: 4 EST: 1956
SALES (est): 2.4MM **Privately Held**
SIC: 3161 Sample cases; trunks

(G-9489)
FIDELUS TECHNOLOGIES LLC
240 W 35th St Fl 6 (10001-2506)
PHONE...................................212 616-7800
Ron Rosansky, *President*
David Buckenheimer, *Exec VP*
Don Harloff, *Vice Pres*
Jerry Love, *Vice Pres*
Nancee Pronsati, *Vice Pres*
EMP: 51
SQ FT: 25,000
SALES (est): 16.3MM **Privately Held**
WEB: www.fidelus.com
SIC: 7372 Prepackaged software

(G-9490)
FIDESA US CORPORATION
17 State St Unit 122 (10004-1501)
PHONE...................................212 269-9000
Robert Thompson, *Principal*
Frank Miglionico, *Vice Pres*
Nevin Patton, *Vice Pres*
Brian Tang, *Vice Pres*
Scott O'Brien, *Project Mgr*
EMP: 400
SALES (est): 26.9MM
SALES (corp-wide): 566.1MM **Privately Held**
WEB: www.royalbluefinancial.com
SIC: 7372 7371 Prepackaged software; custom computer programming services
HQ: Fidessa Group Holdings Limited
2nd Floor, Concourse 2
Belfast
289 046-3000

(G-9491)
FIERCE FUN TOYS LLC
100 Riverside Dr Ste 2 (10024-4822)
P.O. Box 905 (10024-0546)
PHONE...................................646 322-7172
Angela Larson, *Mng Member*
EMP: 7
SALES (est): 447.2K **Privately Held**
SIC: 3942 5092 Stuffed toys, including animals; toys & hobby goods & supplies

(G-9492)
FIESTA JEWELRY CORPORATION (PA)
Also Called: F2nyc
8 W 38th St Rm 801 (10018-0890)
PHONE...................................212 564-6847
Carlos Hatch, *President*
EMP: 3
SALES (est): 1MM **Privately Held**
SIC: 3911 Jewelry, precious metal

(G-9493)
FINDMINE INC
33 E 33rd St Rm 807 (10016-5370)
PHONE...................................925 787-6181

Michelle Bacharach, *CEO*
Devon Safran, *Vice Pres*
EMP: 15 EST: 2014
SALES (est): 335.7K **Privately Held**
SIC: 7372 Business oriented computer software

(G-9494)
FINE CUT DIAMONDS CORPORATION
50 W 47th St Ste 1101 (10036-8687)
PHONE...................................212 575-8780
Michael Deutsch, *President*
EMP: 5 EST: 1967
SALES (est): 413.3K **Privately Held**
SIC: 3915 5094 Diamond cutting & polishing; diamonds (gems)

(G-9495)
FINE SHEER INDUSTRIES INC (PA)
350 5th Ave Ste 4710 (10118-4710)
PHONE...................................212 594-4224
Grace Franco, *President*
Isaac Franco, *President*
David Franco, *Info Tech Dir*
▲ EMP: 18
SQ FT: 6,000
SALES (est): 275.1K **Privately Held**
SIC: 2252 2251 2369 Socks; panty hose; leggings: girls', children's & infants'

(G-9496)
FINE SOUNDS GROUP INC (PA)
Also Called: World of McIntosh
214 Lafayette St (10012-4079)
PHONE...................................212 364-0219
Charles Randall, *CEO*
Mauro Grange, *Ch of Bd*
Giovanni Palacardo, *CFO*
EMP: 12
SALES (est): 23.4MM **Privately Held**
SIC: 3679 Recording heads, speech & musical equipment; recording & playback heads, magnetic; recording & playback apparatus, including phonograph

(G-9497)
FIREMAXX SYSTEMS CORP
307 7th Ave Rm 507 (10001-6079)
PHONE...................................212 645-7414
Donald Fischer, *Principal*
EMP: 23
SQ FT: 1,200
SALES: 3.3MM **Privately Held**
SIC: 3669 Fire detection systems, electric

(G-9498)
FIRST CHOICE NEWS INC
639 1/2 Broadway (10012)
PHONE...................................212 477-2044
Raffie Hadibhai, *Ch of Bd*
EMP: 6
SALES (est): 229K **Privately Held**
SIC: 2711 5311 Newspapers, publishing & printing; department stores, discount

(G-9499)
FIRST GAMES PUBLR NETWRK INC
Also Called: 1gpn
420 Lexington Ave Rm 412 (10170-0499)
PHONE...................................212 983-0501
EMP: 100
SALES: 1,000K **Privately Held**
SIC: 2741 Developer & Publisher Mmog

(G-9500)
FIRST IMAGE DESIGN CORP
98 Cuttrmill Rd Ste 231 (10036)
PHONE...................................212 221-8282
David Hematian, *Ch of Bd*
Kathy Kamali, *Principal*
EMP: 20
SQ FT: 3,000
SALES (est): 2MM **Privately Held**
WEB: www.firstimage.net
SIC: 3911 Jewelry, precious metal

(G-9501)
FIRST LOVE FASHIONS LLC
1407 Broadway Rm 2010 (10018-2718)
PHONE...................................212 256-1089
Joseph Hamadani, *President*
EMP: 10

SALES (est): 1.2MM **Privately Held**
SIC: 2339 Women's & misses' athletic clothing & sportswear

(G-9502)
FIRST2PRINT INC
494 8th Ave Fl 12 (10001-2578)
PHONE...................................212 868-6886
Neil Brasleau, *CEO*
EMP: 7 EST: 2000
SALES (est): 937.2K **Privately Held**
WEB: www.first2print.com
SIC: 2759 Screen printing

(G-9503)
FISCHER DIAMONDS INC
580 5th Ave Ste 613 (10036-4725)
PHONE...................................212 869-1990
Jeffrey H Fisher, *President*
EMP: 10
SALES (est): 1MM **Privately Held**
WEB: www.fischerdiamonds.com
SIC: 3915 Lapidary work & diamond cutting & polishing

(G-9504)
FISCHLER DIAMONDS INC
580 5th Ave Ste 3100 (10036-4701)
PHONE...................................212 921-8196
Serge Fischler, *Ch of Bd*
Marcella Fischler, *Vice Pres*
▲ EMP: 5
SALES (est): 518.7K **Privately Held**
WEB: www.fischlerdiamonds.com
SIC: 3915 5094 Diamond cutting & polishing; diamonds (gems)

(G-9505)
FISCHLER HOCKEY SERVICE
200 W 109th St Apt C5 (10025-2252)
PHONE...................................212 749-4152
EMP: 10
SALES (est): 438.9K **Privately Held**
SIC: 2741 Misc Publishing

(G-9506)
FISH & CROWN LTD (PA)
42 W 39th St (10018-3809)
PHONE...................................212 707-9603
Bergljot Wathne, *President*
Thorunn Wathne, *Corp Secy*
Soffia Wathne, *Vice Pres*
Thomas Faivre, *CFO*
◆ EMP: 100
SQ FT: 14,350
SALES (est): 8.9MM **Privately Held**
WEB: www.wathne.com
SIC: 3161 3999 Luggage; novelties, bric-a-brac & hobby kits

(G-9507)
FISONIC CORP (PA)
Also Called: Fisonic Technology
31-00 47th Ave Ste 106 (10023)
PHONE...................................716 763-0295
Robert Kremer, *CEO*
Professor Vladimir Fisenko, *Ch of Bd*
Joe Hoose, *President*
▲ EMP: 10
SQ FT: 1,000
SALES: 1.8MM **Privately Held**
WEB: www.fisonic.com
SIC: 3561 3433 Pumps & pumping equipment; heating equipment, except electric

(G-9508)
FIVE STAR PRTG & MAILING SVCS
225 W 37th St Fl 16 (10018-6637)
PHONE...................................212 929-0300
Judith Magnus, *President*
Steven Magnus, *Vice Pres*
▲ EMP: 13
SQ FT: 4,800
SALES: 2MM **Privately Held**
SIC: 2752 7331 3993 Commercial printing, offset; mailing service; signs & advertising specialties

(G-9509)
FLAVORS HOLDINGS INC (DH)
35 E 62nd St (10065-8014)
PHONE...................................212 572-8677
Albert Mazone, *CEO*
EMP: 10 EST: 2015

SALES (est): 188.1MM **Privately Held**
SIC: 2869 6712 Sweeteners, synthetic; bank holding companies
HQ: Macandrews & Forbes Inc.
38 E 63rd St
New York NY 10065
212 688-9000

(G-9510)
FLIK INTERNATIONAL/COMPASS
450 Lexington Ave (10017-3904)
PHONE...................................212 450-4750
Chris Sarell, *Director*
EMP: 50
SALES (est): 3.4MM **Privately Held**
SIC: 2099 Food preparations

(G-9511)
FLYCELL INC
80 Pine St Fl 29 (10005-1714)
PHONE...................................212 400-1212
Cristian Carnevale, *CEO*
Gita Chandra, *Controller*
Michele Berardi, *Network Mgr*
EMP: 57
SQ FT: 2,000
SALES (est): 5.9MM
SALES (corp-wide): 1.7MM **Privately Held**
WEB: www.flycell.com
SIC: 3663 Mobile communication equipment
PA: Acotel Group Spa
Via Della Valle Dei Fontanili 29/37
Roma RM 00168
066 114-1000

(G-9512)
FLYNNS INC (PA)
Also Called: Flynn's Xerox
115 W 30th St (10001-4010)
PHONE...................................212 339-8700
Martin Lerner, *Ch of Bd*
Arthur Cantor, *President*
Brian Cantor, *Vice Pres*
Eric Roberts, *Sales Staff*
▲ EMP: 35
SQ FT: 4,200
SALES (est): 6.1MM **Privately Held**
WEB: www.lorraineflynn.com
SIC: 2752 5943 Commercial printing, lithographic; stationery stores

(G-9513)
FOLEON INC
228 E 45th St Rm 9e (10017-3337)
PHONE...................................347 727-6809
Jacob Willemsen, *President*
Daan Reijnders, *Principal*
EMP: 11
SALES (est): 526.4K **Privately Held**
SIC: 2721 Magazines: publishing & printing

(G-9514)
FOLIA WATER INC
175 Varick St (10014-4604)
PHONE...................................412 802-5083
Jonathan Levine, *CEO*
Theresa Dankovich, *Ch of Bd*
Juliet Martinez, *Principal*
Cantwell Carson, *COO*
John Rossmiller, *CFO*
EMP: 8 EST: 2016
SALES (est): 422.6K **Privately Held**
SIC: 2679 8731 Filter paper: made from purchased material; biological research

(G-9515)
FOREVER GROWN DIAMONDS INC
20 W 47th St Ste 1006 (10036-3303)
PHONE...................................917 261-4511
Kinish Shah, *President*
◆ EMP: 2
SQ FT: 480
SALES: 3MM **Privately Held**
SIC: 3915 5094 Diamond cutting & polishing; diamonds (gems)

(G-9516)
FORMART CORP
Also Called: Bellini Collections
312 5th Ave Fl 6 (10001-3603)
PHONE...................................212 819-1819
Sheung MEI Liu, *President*
EMP: 12

▲ = Import ▼=Export
◆ =Import/Export

SQ FT: 2,100
SALES (est): 1.7MM **Privately Held**
WEB: www.cancerpins.com
SIC: 3171 5094 5137 3961 Purses,
women's; jewelry; watches & parts;
purses; costume jewelry

(G-9517)
FORTRESS BIOTECH INC (PA)
2 Gansevoort St Fl 9 (10014-1667)
PHONE..........................781 652-4500
Lindsay A Rosenwald, *Ch of Bd*
Eric K Rowinsky, *Ch of Bd*
George Avgerinos, *Senior VP*
Robyn M Hunter, *CFO*
Dov Klein, *Bd of Directors*
EMP: 31
SALES: 26.8MM **Publicly Held**
SIC: 2834 Pharmaceutical preparations

(G-9518)
FORTUNE MEDIA USA CORPORATION
225 Liberty St (10281-1048)
PHONE..........................212 522-1212
Alan Murray, *CEO*
EMP: 125
SALES (est): 2.6MM **Privately Held**
SIC: 2721 Magazines: publishing & printing

(G-9519)
FOUNDATION CENTER INC (PA)
1 Financial Sq Fl 24 (10005-3076)
PHONE..........................212 620-4230
Bradford K Smith, *President*
Nancy Albilal, *Vice Pres*
Monisha De Quadros, *Vice Pres*
Deedee Dickey, *Vice Pres*
Loretta Ferrari, *Vice Pres*
▲ **EMP:** 125
SQ FT: 150,000
SALES: 24.1MM **Privately Held**
WEB: www.fdncenter.net
SIC: 2741 8231 Directories: publishing
only, not printed on site; libraries

(G-9520)
FOUNDTION FOR A MNDFUL SOC INC (PA)
228 Park Ave S (10003-1502)
PHONE..........................902 431-8062
Andrew Karr, *Treasurer*
Ken Swick, *Controller*
James Gimian, *Exec Dir*
EMP: 5
SALES: 2.5MM **Privately Held**
SIC: 2721 Magazines: publishing & printing

(G-9521)
FOUR M STUDIOS
125 Park Ave Fl 20 (10017-8545)
PHONE..........................212 557-6600
Andrea Gingold, *Branch Mgr*
EMP: 250
SALES (corp-wide): 3.1B **Publicly Held**
WEB: www.meredith.com
SIC: 2721 Magazines: publishing & printing
PA: Meredith Corporation
1716 Locust St
Des Moines IA 50309
515 284-3000

(G-9522)
FOUR M STUDIOS
Also Called: Meredith Corporate Solutions
805 3rd Ave Fl 22 (10022-7541)
PHONE..........................212 499-2000
Laura Johnson, *Editor*
Tyler Hub, *Business Mgr*
Leslie Rohr, *Business Mgr*
Nancy Elias, *Research*
Kim Leconey, *Research*
EMP: 17
SALES (corp-wide): 3.1B **Publicly Held**
WEB: www.meredith.com
SIC: 2721 Magazines: publishing only, not
printed on site
PA: Meredith Corporation
1716 Locust St
Des Moines IA 50309
515 284-3000

(G-9523)
FOUR M STUDIOS
Also Called: Meredith Hispanic Ventures
805 3rd Ave Fl 29 (10022-7593)
PHONE..........................515 284-2157
Cheryl Corbin, *Advt Staff*
Mike Lovell, *Branch Mgr*
EMP: 96
SALES (corp-wide): 3.1B **Publicly Held**
SIC: 2721 2731 Magazines: publishing &
printing; books: publishing only
PA: Meredith Corporation
1716 Locust St
Des Moines IA 50309
515 284-3000

(G-9524)
FOURTYS NY INC
231 W 39th St Rm 806 (10018-0734)
PHONE..........................212 382-0301
Dawn Mayo, *President*
EMP: 10
SQ FT: 4,000
SALES: 900K **Privately Held**
SIC: 2331 Women's & misses' blouses &
shirts

(G-9525)
FOWNES BROTHERS & CO INC (PA)
16 E 34th St Fl 5 (10016-4370)
PHONE..........................800 345-6837
Thomas Gluckman, *Ch of Bd*
Chris Giattino, *Exec VP*
Helmuth Dosch, *Vice Pres*
Bruna Maney, *Vice Pres*
Howard Samuels, *Vice Pres*
◆ **EMP:** 50 **EST:** 1887
SQ FT: 18,000
SALES (est): 66.2MM **Privately Held**
SIC: 3151 2381 5136 5137 Gloves,
leather: dress or semidress; gloves,
woven or knit: made from purchased ma-
terials; gloves, men's & boys'; gloves,
women's & children's; gloves, sport & ath-
letic: boxing, handball, etc.

(G-9526)
FOX UNLIMITED INC
345 7th Ave Rm 2b (10001-5058)
PHONE..........................212 736-3071
Marvin Levenson, *President*
Brittany Levenson, *Assistant*
EMP: 5
SQ FT: 4,000
SALES (est): 689K **Privately Held**
WEB: www.foxunlimited.com
SIC: 2371 Apparel, fur

(G-9527)
FOXHILL PRESS INC
37 E 7th St Ste 2 (10003-8027)
PHONE..........................212 995-9620
▲ **EMP:** 20
SQ FT: 1,600
SALES (est): 1.1MM
SALES (corp-wide): 35.2MM **Privately Held**
SIC: 2731 Books-Publishing/Printing
PA: Mcevoy Properties Llc
85 2nd St Fl 6
San Francisco CA 94107

(G-9528)
FRANCEPRESS LLC (PA)
115 E 57th St Fl 11 (10022-2120)
PHONE..........................646 202-9828
Louis Kyle, *Mng Member*
▲ **EMP:** 14
SQ FT: 1,800
SALES (est): 597.4K **Privately Held**
SIC: 2711 Newspapers, publishing & print-
ing

(G-9529)
FRANCIS EMORY FITCH INC (HQ)
Also Called: Fitch Group
229 W 28th St (10001-5915)
PHONE..........................212 619-3800
William Contessa, *CEO*
Joe Barrett, *Exec VP*
Geoffrey Tomashoff, *Production*
Frank Riina, *Supervisor*
EMP: 23 **EST:** 1886

SQ FT: 25,000
SALES (est): 2.8MM **Privately Held**
WEB: www.fitchgroup.com
SIC: 2721 2752 Periodicals: publishing
only; commercial printing, offset
PA: Topside Advisors, Llc
84 Rockledge Rd
Bronxville NY 10708
212 619-3800

(G-9530)
FRANCO APPAREL GROUP INC
Also Called: Franco Apparel Group Team
1407 Broadway (10018-5100)
PHONE..........................212 967-7272
Ike Franco, *Ch of Bd*
▲ **EMP:** 100
SQ FT: 15,000
SALES (est): 8.9MM **Privately Held**
WEB: www.francoapparel.com
SIC: 2369 Girls' & children's outerwear

(G-9531)
FRANK BILLANTI CASTING CO INC
42 W 38th St Rm 204 (10018-6220)
PHONE..........................212 221-0440
Frank L Billanti, *President*
Kristin N Billanti, *Principal*
Katherine O Billanti, *Vice Pres*
Frank Billanti, *Administration*
Frank J Billanti, *Administration*
EMP: 16
SALES: 1MM **Privately Held**
SIC: 3915 Jewelers' castings

(G-9532)
FRANK BLANCATO INC
64 W 48th St Fl 16 (10036-1708)
PHONE..........................212 768-1495
Frank Blancato, *President*
EMP: 10
SALES (est): 4MM **Privately Held**
WEB: www.fblancato.com
SIC: 3911 Jewelry, precious metal

(G-9533)
FRANKLIN REPORT LLC
201 E 69th St Apt 14j (10021-5470)
PHONE..........................212 639-9100
Elizabeth Franklin, *Owner*
Beverly Hevron, *Representative*
EMP: 8
SALES (est): 600K **Privately Held**
WEB: www.franklinreport.com
SIC: 2731 Book publishing

(G-9534)
FREEDOM RAINS INC
Also Called: Northern Goose Polar Project
230 W 39th St Fl 7 (10018-4977)
PHONE..........................646 710-4512
Bobby Reiger, *CEO*
Steven Zellman, *President*
Nick Grazione, *COO*
▲ **EMP:** 8
SQ FT: 3,500
SALES: 12MM **Privately Held**
SIC: 2253 Jackets, knit; sweaters &
sweater coats, knit

(G-9535)
FRENCH ACCNT RUGS & TAPESTRIES
36 E 31st St Frnt B (10016-6821)
PHONE..........................212 686-6097
Kevin Rahmanan, *President*
▲ **EMP:** 6
SQ FT: 10,000
SALES (est): 774.6K **Privately Held**
WEB: www.farugs.com
SIC: 2211 Upholstery, tapestry & wall cov-
erings: cotton; casement cloth, cotton;
tapestry fabrics, cotton

(G-9536)
FRENCH ATMOSPHERE INC (PA)
Also Called: Urban Rose
421 7th Ave 525 (10001-2002)
PHONE..........................516 371-9100
Lawrence Kessler, *President*
Benjamin Kessler, *Vice Pres*
▲ **EMP:** 15
SQ FT: 1,350
SALES (est): 1MM **Privately Held**
SIC: 2339 Sportswear, women's

(G-9537)
FRENCH MORNING LLC
27 W 20th St Ste 800 (10011-3726)
PHONE..........................646 290-7463
Emmanuel Saint-Martin, *President*
David Treussard, *Managing Prtnr*
EMP: 6
SQ FT: 1,200
SALES (est): 258.9K **Privately Held**
SIC: 2711 Newspapers: publishing only,
not printed on site

(G-9538)
FRENCH PUBLISHERS AGENCY INC
Also Called: Le Bureau Du Livre Francais
853 Broadway Ste 1509 (10003-4715)
PHONE..........................212 254-4540
Frances Black, *Branch Mgr*
EMP: 5
SALES (est): 452.7K
SALES (corp-wide): 2MM **Privately Held**
SIC: 2731 Books: publishing only
PA: Bureau Int De L Edition Fr
115 Boulevard Saint Germain
Paris 75006
144 411-313

(G-9539)
FRESH PRINTS LLC
134 E 70th St (10021-5035)
PHONE..........................917 826-2752
Jacob Goodman,
Josh Arbit,
EMP: 40
SALES (est): 2MM **Privately Held**
SIC: 2759 7389 Screen printing;

(G-9540)
FRESHLY INC (PA)
Also Called: F3 Foods
115 E 23rd St Fl 7 (10010-4561)
PHONE..........................844 373-7459
Michael Wystrach, *CEO*
Mayur Gupta, *Chief Mktg Ofcr*
Segal Ben, *Manager*
Harrison Borges, *Software Engr*
Carter Comstock, *Admin Sec*
EMP: 31 **EST:** 2015
SALES (est): 102.6MM **Privately Held**
SIC: 2099 Ready-to-eat meals, salads &
sandwiches

(G-9541)
FRIDGE MAGAZINE INC
108 W 39th St Fl 4 (10018-3614)
PHONE..........................212 997-7673
Jonathon Levine, *President*
EMP: 5
SALES (est): 410K **Privately Held**
WEB: www.fridgemagazine.com
SIC: 2721 Magazines: publishing only, not
printed on site

(G-9542)
FROEBE GROUP LLC
154 W 27th St Rm 4 (10001-6215)
PHONE..........................646 649-2150
Thomas Daughhetee, *Production*
Troy Froebe, *Mng Member*
EMP: 8
SALES: 800K **Privately Held**
SIC: 2741 Business service newsletters:
publishing & printing

(G-9543)
FROZEN FOOD DIGEST INC
Also Called: Quick Frzen Foods Annual Prcss
271 Madison Ave Ste 805 (10016-1005)
PHONE..........................212 557-8600
Saul Beck, *President*
Audrey Beck, *Publisher*
Anna Beck, *Vice Pres*
▲ **EMP:** 6
SALES (est): 510K **Privately Held**
SIC: 2721 Magazines: publishing only, not
printed on site

(G-9544)
FRP APPAREL GROUP LLC
110 W 40th St Fl 26 (10018-3626)
PHONE..........................212 695-8000
Johann Cooke,
Edwin Herman,
▲ **EMP:** 9

SALES (est): 620K **Privately Held**
SIC: 2221 Upholstery, tapestry & wall covering fabrics

(G-9545)
FRUIT ST HLTH PUB BENEFT CORP
85 Broad St Fl 18 (10004-2783)
PHONE................................347 960-6400
Laurence Girard, *CEO*
Christopher Meatto, *CFO*
Asif Ali, *VP Sales*
EMP: 5
SALES (est): 401.3K **Privately Held**
SIC: 7372 Prepackaged software

(G-9546)
FSR BEAUTY LTD
411 5th Ave Rm 804 (10016-2264)
PHONE................................212 447-0036
Jerrold Rauchwerger, *President*
Maxine Rauchwerger, *Vice Pres*
Falen Rauchwerger, *Marketing Staff*
▲ **EMP:** 6
SQ FT: 1,300
SALES (est): 752.4K **Privately Held**
SIC: 2844 Face creams or lotions; lipsticks

(G-9547)
FT PUBLICATIONS INC (HQ)
Also Called: Financial Times, The
330 Hudson St (10013-1046)
PHONE................................212 641-6500
Loredana Beg, *Ch of Bd*
David Bell, *President*
Ciaran Larkin, *Editor*
Bridget Welch, *Editor*
Mirela Xhota, *Accounts Mgr*
▲ **EMP:** 80
SQ FT: 40,000
SALES (est): 18.4MM **Privately Held**
SIC: 2711 Newspapers, publishing & printing

(G-9548)
FT PUBLICATIONS INC
Also Called: Financial Times Newspaper
330 Hudson St (10013-1046)
PHONE................................212 641-2420
EMP: 46 **Privately Held**
SIC: 2711 Newspapers: publishing only, not printed on site
HQ: F.T. Publications Inc.
330 Hudson St
New York NY 10013
212 641-6500

(G-9549)
FUDA GROUP (USA) CORPORATION
48 Wall St Fl 11 (10005-2887)
PHONE................................646 751-7488
Benjamin Wu, *CEO*
Robert Rash,
EMP: 7
SALES (est): 299.2K **Privately Held**
SIC: 1041 Gold recovery from tailings

(G-9550)
FULCRUM PROMOTIONS & PRTG LLC
Also Called: Fulcrum Promos
135 W 41st St (10036-7303)
PHONE................................203 909-6362
Gia-Marie Vacca, *Partner*
Vincent Miceli,
Anthony Monaco,
EMP: 4 **EST:** 2010
SQ FT: 700
SALES: 1MM **Privately Held**
SIC: 2759 7389 Promotional printing; advertising, promotional & trade show services

(G-9551)
FULL CIRCLE HOME LLC
131 W 35th St Fl 8 (10001-2111)
PHONE................................212 432-0001
Tal Chitayat, *CEO*
David Chitayat, *Managing Dir*
▲ **EMP:** 9
SALES: 1.5MM **Privately Held**
SIC: 3991 5199 Brooms & brushes; gifts & novelties

(G-9552)
FUN MEDIA INC
1001 Ave Of The Americas (10018-5460)
PHONE................................646 472-0135
Joseph Giarraputo, *President*
A Basodan, *Principal*
P Panerai, *Chairman*
Francesco Librio, *Admin Sec*
EMP: 25
SQ FT: 7,500
SALES (est): 2.6MM
SALES (corp-wide): 6.3MM **Privately Held**
WEB: www.classeditori.com
SIC: 2721 7319 Magazines: publishing only, not printed on site; transit advertising services
PA: Class Editori Spa
Via Marco Burigozzo 5
Milano MI 20122
025 821-91

(G-9553)
FUNG WONG BAKERY INC
Also Called: Fung Wong Bakery Shop
30 Mott St Frnt (10013-5037)
PHONE................................212 267-4037
EMP: 20
SQ FT: 600
SALES (est): 1.7MM **Privately Held**
SIC: 2051 Mfg Bread/Related Products

(G-9554)
FUSION PRO PERFORMANCE LTD
Also Called: Ki Pro Performance
16 W 36th St Rm 1205 (10018-9754)
PHONE................................917 833-0761
Steven Goldfarb, *President*
EMP: 16 **EST:** 2014
SQ FT: 2,000
SALES (est): 11.8MM **Privately Held**
SIC: 2339 Athletic clothing: women's, misses' & juniors'

(G-9555)
FUTURE MEDIA GROUP INC
1 World Trade Ctr Fl 39 (10007-0090)
PHONE................................646 854-1375
Marc Lotenberg, *Principal*
Miles Bingham, *Principal*
Eric Crown, *Principal*
EMP: 70
SALES (est): 1.6MM **Privately Held**
SIC: 2721 Magazines: publishing only, not printed on site

(G-9556)
FX INC
Also Called: Facilities Exchange
1 Penn Plz Ste 6238 (10119-0002)
PHONE................................212 244-2240
Martin Friedman, *President*
Charles Valva, *Corp Secy*
EMP: 18
SQ FT: 15,000
SALES (est): 1.5MM **Privately Held**
SIC: 2522 7641 1799 5712 Office furniture, except wood; furniture refinishing; counter top installation; office furniture

(G-9557)
G & P PRINTING INC
142 Baxter St (10013-3605)
PHONE................................212 274-8092
Stanley Chen, *President*
EMP: 5 **EST:** 1998
SALES (est): 477.7K **Privately Held**
WEB: www.gpprinting.com
SIC: 2752 Commercial printing, offset

(G-9558)
G I CERTIFIED INC
623 W 51st St (10019-5008)
PHONE................................212 397-1945
Michael Borrico, *Ch of Bd*
C Russonello, *Director*
Charlie Rucinelli, *Director*
EMP: 6
SALES: 500K **Privately Held**
WEB: www.certifiedny.com
SIC: 3993 Signs & advertising specialties

(G-9559)
G SCHIRMER INC (HQ)
Also Called: Music Sales
180 Madison Ave Ste 2400 (10016-5241)
PHONE................................212 254-2100
Barrie Edwards, *President*
John Castaldo, *Controller*
Greg Legaz, *Librarian*
Jessica Hobbs, *Manager*
Andrew Stein-Zeller, *Manager*
▲ **EMP:** 4
SALES (est): 5.5MM
SALES (corp-wide): 13.9MM **Privately Held**
WEB: www.schirmer.com
SIC: 2741 7929 Music books: publishing only, not printed on site; entertainers & entertainment groups
PA: Music Sales Corporation
180 Madison Ave Ste 2400
New York NY 10016
212 254-2100

(G-9560)
G-III APPAREL GROUP LTD (PA)
512 7th Ave Fl 35 (10018-0832)
PHONE................................212 403-0500
Morris Goldfarb, *Ch of Bd*
Sammy Aaron, *President*
Wayne S Miller, *COO*
Jeffrey Goldfarb, *Exec VP*
Neal S Nackman, *CFO*
▲ **EMP:** 277
SQ FT: 313,000
SALES: 3B **Publicly Held**
WEB: www.g-iii.com
SIC: 2337 2339 2311 2329 Women's & misses' suits & coats; women's & misses' outerwear; men's & boys' suits & coats; coats, overcoats & vests; jackets (suede, leatherette, etc.), sport: men's & boys'; garments, leather; coats & jackets, leather & sheep-lined; pants, leather; men's & boys' clothing

(G-9561)
G-III APPAREL GROUP LTD
Jessica Howard
512 Fashion Ave Fl 35 (10018-0832)
PHONE................................212 403-0500
Karol Gass, *Branch Mgr*
EMP: 50
SALES (corp-wide): 3B **Publicly Held**
SIC: 2335 Women's, juniors' & misses' dresses
PA: G-Iii Apparel Group, Ltd.
512 7th Ave Fl 35
New York NY 10018
212 403-0500

(G-9562)
G-III APPAREL GROUP LTD
Jl Colebrook Cloth Div
512 7th Ave Fl 35 (10018-0832)
PHONE................................212 840-7272
EMP: 10
SALES (corp-wide): 2.8B **Publicly Held**
SIC: 2311 Mfg Men's/Boy's Suits/Coats
PA: G-Iii Apparel Group, Ltd.
512 7th Ave Fl 35
New York NY 10018
212 403-0500

(G-9563)
G-III LEATHER FASHIONS INC
Also Called: G-III Apparel Group
512 7th Ave Fl 35 (10018-0832)
PHONE................................212 403-0500
EMP: 20
SALES (corp-wide): 3B **Publicly Held**
SIC: 2386 2337 2339 Leather & sheep-lined clothing; women's & misses' suits & coats; women's & misses' outerwear
HQ: G-Iii Leather Fashions, Inc.
512 Fashion Ave Fl 35
New York NY 10018
212 403-0500

(G-9564)
G18 CORPORATION
250 W 93rd St Apt 9h (10025-7394)
PHONE................................212 869-0010
Laurence Goldfarb, *President*
EMP: 2

(G-9565)
GABRIELLE ANDRA
305 W 21st St (10011-3073)
PHONE................................212 366-9624
Andra Gabrielle, *Owner*
EMP: 5
SALES (est): 220K **Privately Held**
SIC: 2331 Blouses, women's & juniors': made from purchased material

(G-9566)
GALISON PUBLISHING LLC
Also Called: Mudpuppy
70 W 36th St Fl 11 (10018-1249)
PHONE................................212 354-8840
Bill Miller, *CEO*
Jennifer Schroder, *Vice Pres*
Clairissa McLaurin, *Production*
Sam Minnitti, *CFO*
Malin Johnsson, *Marketing Staff*
▲ **EMP:** 20
SQ FT: 7,500
SALES (est): 2.5MM
SALES (corp-wide): 29.9MM **Privately Held**
SIC: 2741 Miscellaneous publishing
PA: The Mcevoy Group Llc
680 2nd St
San Francisco CA 94107
415 537-4200

(G-9567)
GALLERY 57 DENTAL
24 W 57th St Ste 701 (10019-3949)
PHONE................................212 246-8700
Andrew Koenigsberg DDS, *Principal*
Stefani Brannon, *Office Mgr*
EMP: 20
SALES (est): 2.2MM **Privately Held**
SIC: 3843 Enamels, dentists'

(G-9568)
GALT INDUSTRIES INC
121 E 71st St Frnt A (10021-4275)
PHONE................................212 758-0770
George T Votis, *Ch of Bd*
▲ **EMP:** 9
SQ FT: 2,000
SALES (est): 1.3MM **Privately Held**
SIC: 3089 Injection molding of plastics

(G-9569)
GAME TIME LLC
1407 Broadway Rm 400 (10018-3843)
PHONE................................914 557-9662
Adam Pennington, *Mng Member*
Patrick McGeough,
▲ **EMP:** 17 **EST:** 1999
SQ FT: 30,000
SALES (est): 3.5MM **Privately Held**
SIC: 3873 Watches, clocks, watchcases & parts

(G-9570)
GAMECLUB INC
46 W 65th St Apt 1a (10023-6621)
PHONE................................415 359-5742
Daniel Sherman, *CEO*
EMP: 2
SALES: 1MM **Privately Held**
SIC: 7372 Prepackaged software

(G-9571)
GAMES FOR CHANGE INC
205 E 42nd St Fl 20 (10017-5706)
PHONE................................212 242-4922
Susanna Pollack, *President*
Sara Cornish, *Project Dir*
Ling Lu, *Controller*
Meghan Ventura, *Manager*
Asif Khan, *Director*
EMP: 1 **EST:** 2004
SALES: 1.3MM **Privately Held**
SIC: 7372 Prepackaged software

(G-9572)
GAPPA TEXTILES INC
295 5th Ave Ste 1021 (10016-7105)
PHONE................................212 481-7100
Suat Engin Sezer, *Ch of Bd*
Mahmud Topal, *President*
Boran Batur, *Vice Pres*

SALES: 7MM **Privately Held**
SIC: 2337 Women's & misses' suits & coats

Ebru Yildiz, *Analyst*
▲ **EMP:** 8
SALES (est): 830.3K
SALES (corp-wide): 3.3B **Privately Held**
WEB: www.gappausa.com
SIC: 2299 Fabrics: linen, jute, hemp, ramie
PA: Calik Holding Anonim Sirketi
No:163 Esentepe Buyukdere Caddesi
Istanbul (Europe) 34394
212 306-5000

(G-9573)
GARAN INCORPORATED (HQ)
200 Madison Ave Fl 4 (10016-3905)
PHONE....................212 563-1292
Seymour Lichtenstein, *CEO*
Jerald Kamiel, *President*
Marvin S Robinson, *Vice Pres*
David M Fligel, *CFO*
◆ **EMP:** 120 **EST:** 1957
SQ FT: 38,500
SALES (est): 601.3MM
SALES (corp-wide): 225.3B **Publicly Held**
WEB: www.garanimals.com
SIC: 2361 2369 2331 2339 T-shirts & tops: girls', children's & infants'; slacks: girls' & children's; T-shirts & tops, women's: made from purchased materials; shirts, women's & juniors': made from purchased materials; jeans: women's, misses' & juniors'; men's & boys' furnishings; sport shirts, men's & boys': from purchased materials
PA: Berkshire Hathaway Inc.
3555 Farnam St Ste 1140
Omaha NE 68131
402 346-1400

(G-9574)
GARAN MANUFACTURING CORP (DH)
200 Madison Ave Fl 4 (10016-3905)
PHONE....................212 563-2000
Seymour Lichtenstein, *CEO*
Ron Dutta, *President*
Jerald Kamiel, *President*
David M Fligel, *Vice Pres*
▼ **EMP:** 1
SALES (est): 21.2MM
SALES (corp-wide): 225.3B **Publicly Held**
SIC: 2361 2369 2331 2339 T-shirts & tops: girls', children's & infants'; slacks: girls' & children's; T-shirts & tops, women's: made from purchased materials; shirts, women's & juniors': made from purchased materials; jeans: women's, misses' & juniors'; men's & boys' furnishings; sport shirts, men's & boys': from purchased materials
HQ: Garan, Incorporated
200 Madison Ave Fl 4
New York NY 10016
212 563-1292

(G-9575)
GARYS LOFT
28 W 36th St (10018-1284)
PHONE....................212 244-0970
Roger Wingfield, *Manager*
EMP: 6
SALES (est): 764K **Privately Held**
SIC: 3861 Photographic equipment & supplies

(G-9576)
GB GROUP INC
Umpire State Bldg 1808 (10021)
PHONE....................212 594-3748
Howard Zhanz, *President*
EMP: 8
SALES (est): 548.4K **Privately Held**
WEB: www.crystalsland.com
SIC: 3699 Laser systems & equipment

(G-9577)
GBG NATIONAL BRANDS GROUP LLC
350 5th Ave Lbby 9 (10118-0109)
PHONE....................646 839-7000
Bruce Philip Rockowitz, *CEO*
Dow Peter Famulak, *President*
Ronald Ventricelli, *CFO*
Jason Andrew Rabin, *Chief Mktg Ofcr*
EMP: 6

SALES (est): 402.9K **Privately Held**
SIC: 2321 Men's & boys' furnishings
HQ: Fung Holdings (1937) Limited
4,11/F Lifung Twr
Lai Chi Kok KLN

(G-9578)
GBG USA INC
350 5th Ave Fl 7 (10118-0701)
PHONE....................646 839-7083
EMP: 93 **Privately Held**
SIC: 2387 Apparel belts
HQ: Gbg Usa Inc.
350 5th Ave Lbby 11
New York NY 10118
646 839-7000

(G-9579)
GBG USA INC
Lf USA Accessories
261 W 35th St Fl 15 (10001-1902)
PHONE....................212 615-3400
Steven Kahn, *Branch Mgr*
EMP: 50 **Privately Held**
SIC: 2387 Apparel belts
HQ: Gbg Usa Inc.
350 5th Ave Lbby 11
New York NY 10118
646 839-7000

(G-9580)
GCE INTERNATIONAL INC (PA)
Also Called: Great China Empire
1385 Broadway Fl 21 (10018-6022)
PHONE....................212 704-4800
Donald Oberfield, *President*
Peter Markson, *Chairman*
Brad Gero, *VP Opers*
Martin J Kelly, *Treasurer*
Susan McNeill, *Manager*
▲ **EMP:** 100 **EST:** 1920
SQ FT: 40,000
SALES (est): 191MM **Privately Held**
WEB: www.parisaccessories.com
SIC: 2253 2389 2331 5137 Hats & headwear, knit; scarves & mufflers, knit; handkerchiefs, except paper; T-shirts & tops, women's: made from purchased materials; blouses, women's & juniors': made from purchased material; scarves, women's & children's; gloves, women's & children's; scarves, men's & boys'; gloves, men's & boys'

(G-9581)
GCE INTERNATIONAL INC
Also Called: Baar & Beards
350 5th Ave Ste 616 (10118-0110)
PHONE....................212 868-0500
Martin Kelly, *Manager*
EMP: 12
SALES (corp-wide): 191MM **Privately Held**
WEB: www.parisaccessories.com
SIC: 2353 2361 2381 Hats, caps & millinery; girls' & children's dresses, blouses & shirts; fabric dress & work gloves
PA: Gce International, Inc.
1385 Broadway Fl 21
New York NY 10118
212 704-4800

(G-9582)
GCE INTERNATIONAL INC
Also Called: Capital Mercury Shirtmakers Co
1359 Broadway Rm 2000 (10018-7841)
PHONE....................773 263-1210
Peter Markson, *CEO*
EMP: 60
SALES (corp-wide): 191MM **Privately Held**
WEB: www.parisaccessories.com
SIC: 2321 Men's & boys' dress shirts
PA: Gce International, Inc.
1385 Broadway Fl 21
New York NY 10118
212 704-4800

(G-9583)
GDS PUBLISHING INC
40 Wall St Fl 5 (10005-1472)
PHONE....................212 796-2000
Dave Cullinane, *Principal*
EMP: 14

SALES (est): 1.3MM
SALES (corp-wide): 34.7MM **Privately Held**
SIC: 2741
HQ: Gds Publishing Limited
Queen Square House
Bristol BS1 4
117 921-4000

(G-9584)
GE HEALTHCARE FINCL SVCS INC
299 Park Ave Fl 3 (10171-0022)
PHONE....................212 713-2000
Batcrio Buyo, *Branch Mgr*
EMP: 5 **Publicly Held**
SIC: 2759 Commercial printing
HQ: Ge Healthcare Financial Services, Inc.
500 W Monroe St Fl 19
Chicago IL 60661
312 697-3999

(G-9585)
GELIKO LLC
1601 3rd Ave Apt 16a (10128-3455)
PHONE....................212 876-5620
Zach Rubin, *Mng Member*
▲ **EMP:** 20
SALES (est): 2.6MM **Privately Held**
SIC: 2899 Gelatin

(G-9586)
GEMPRINT CORPORATION
580 5th Ave Bsmt LI05 (10036-4726)
PHONE....................212 997-0007
Angelo Palmieri, *President*
EMP: 20
SQ FT: 5,500
SALES (est): 1.1MM **Privately Held**
SIC: 3826 Laser scientific & engineering instruments

(G-9587)
GEMVETO JEWELRY COMPANY INC
18 E 48th St Rm 501 (10017-1014)
PHONE....................212 755-2522
Jean Vitau, *President*
Irene Vitau, *Corp Secy*
EMP: 20
SQ FT: 3,500
SALES (est): 2.6MM **Privately Held**
WEB: www.gems-online.org
SIC: 3911 Jewelry, precious metal

(G-9588)
GENERAL ART COMPANY INC
Also Called: General Art Framing
14 E 38th St Fl 6 (10016-0636)
PHONE....................212 255-1298
Jen Chan, *President*
EMP: 10
SQ FT: 4,000
SALES (est): 1MM **Privately Held**
SIC: 2499 5023 Picture frame molding, finished; frames & framing, picture & mirror

(G-9589)
GENERAL LED HOLDINGS LLC
Also Called: Acolyte Industries
19 W 36th St Fl 6 (10018-7943)
PHONE....................212 629-6830
EMP: 15
SALES (corp-wide): 970.6K **Privately Held**
SIC: 3674 Light emitting diodes
PA: General Led Holdings, Llc
1074 Arion Cir Ste 116
San Antonio TX 78216
210 360-1444

(G-9590)
GENERAL MEDIA STRATEGIES INC
Also Called: African American Observer
521 5th Ave Fl 17 (10175-1799)
PHONE....................212 586-4141
Steve Mallory, *President*
Daniel Gossels, *Managing Dir*
EMP: 8 **EST:** 2001
SALES: 250K **Privately Held**
SIC: 2711 Newspapers

(G-9591)
GENERAL SPORTWEAR COMPANY INC (PA)
230 W 38th St Fl 4 (10018-9085)
P.O. Box 588, Ellenville (12428-0588)
PHONE....................212 764-5820
Herbert Rosenstock, *Ch of Bd*
Jeffrey Rosenstock, *President*
David Rosenstock, *Corp Secy*
Brad Chananie, *VP Sales*
Robin Starkey, *Sales Staff*
◆ **EMP:** 120 **EST:** 1927
SQ FT: 20,000
SALES (est): 25.7MM **Privately Held**
WEB: www.generalsportwear.com
SIC: 2361 2369 2329 T-shirts & tops: girls', children's & infants'; jeans: girls', children's & infants'; men's & boys' sportswear & athletic clothing

(G-9592)
GENESIS MANNEQUINS USA II INC
413 W 14th St Ste 209 (10014-1091)
PHONE....................212 505-6600
Joseph Klinow, *President*
▲ **EMP:** 5
SQ FT: 3,500
SALES (est): 2.3MM **Privately Held**
SIC: 3999 Mannequins

(G-9593)
GENEVA HEALTHCARE LLC (HQ)
3 Columbus Cir Fl 15 (10019-8716)
PHONE....................646 665-2044
Yuri Sudhakar, *CEO*
Jeff Marchese, *COO*
Earl Bray, *CFO*
Debra Halligan, *Ch Nursing Ofcr*
Manish Wadhwa, *Officer*
EMP: 2
SALES (est): 3.3MM
SALES (corp-wide): 399.4MM **Publicly Held**
SIC: 3845 Electromedical equipment
PA: Biotelemetry, Inc.
1000 Cedar Hollow Rd # 10
Malvern PA 19355
610 729-7000

(G-9594)
GENEVA WATCH COMPANY INC (DH)
1407 Broadway Rm 400 (10018-3843)
PHONE....................212 221-1177
▲ **EMP:** 20
SQ FT: 15,000
SALES (est): 6.1MM
SALES (corp-wide): 98.7K **Privately Held**
SIC: 3873 Mfg Watches/Clocks/Parts
HQ: Awc Liquidating Co.
1407 Broadway Rm 400
New York NY 10018
212 221-1177

(G-9595)
GENIE INSTANT PRINTING CO INC
Also Called: Genie Instant Printing Center
37 W 43rd St (10036-7403)
PHONE....................212 575-8258
Sal Cohen, *President*
Ronnie Cohen, *Vice Pres*
EMP: 10
SALES (est): 1MM **Privately Held**
SIC: 2759 2752 Commercial printing; photo-offset printing

(G-9596)
GENZYME CORPORATION
Also Called: Genzyme Genetics
521 W 57th St Fl 5 (10019-2916)
PHONE....................212 698-0300
Dale Lawrence, *Business Mgr*
Jim Luisi, *Human Res Dir*
Robert Barclay, *Manager*
Michael B Broscius, *Pathologist*
Moacyr Da Silva, *Director*
EMP: 67 **Privately Held**
SIC: 2834 Pharmaceutical preparations
HQ: Genzyme Corporation
50 Binney St
Cambridge MA 02142
617 252-7500

(G-9597)
GEOFFREY BEENE INC
37 W 57th St Frnt 2 (10019-3410)
PHONE..................................212 371-5570
Geoffrey Beene, *President*
G Thompson Hutton, *President*
Russell Nardozza, *COO*
Mara Hutton, *Executive*
EMP: 20
SALES: 1.6MM **Privately Held**
WEB: www.geoffreybeene.com
SIC: 2335 2337 2331 2339 Women's,
   juniors' & misses' dresses; skirts, sepa-
   rate: women's, misses' & juniors'; jackets
   & vests, except fur & leather: women's;
   blouses, women's & juniors': made from
   purchased material; slacks: women's,
   misses' & juniors'

(G-9598)
**GEON PERFORMANCE
SOLUTIONS LLC**
430 Park Ave Fl 18 (10022-3568)
PHONE..................................888 910-0536
Jared Kramer, *Manager*
EMP: 40 **Privately Held**
SIC: 2822 Ethylene-propylene rubbers,
   EPDM polymers
HQ: Geon Performance Solutions, Llc
   33587 Walker Rd
   Avon Lake OH 44012
   888 910-0536

(G-9599)
GEONEX INTERNATIONAL CORP
200 Park Ave S Ste 920 (10003-1509)
PHONE..................................212 473-4555
George Nikiforov, *President*
EMP: 6
SQ FT: 1,000
SALES (est): 720K **Privately Held**
SIC: 2435 Hardwood plywood, prefinished

(G-9600)
GEORGE KNITTING MILLS CORP
116 W 23rd St Fl 4 (10011-2410)
PHONE..................................212 242-3300
Lawrence Aibel, *President*
Richard Aibel, *Vice Pres*
EMP: 5 EST: 1958
SQ FT: 10,000
SALES (est): 738.7K **Privately Held**
SIC: 2258 Pile fabrics, warp or flat knit

(G-9601)
GEORGE LEDERMAN INC
515 Madison Ave Rm 1218 (10022-5452)
PHONE..................................212 753-4556
Serge Lederman, *President*
Adrienne Lederman, *Vice Pres*
Janine Lederman, *Admin Sec*
EMP: 5
SQ FT: 800
SALES (est): 567.7K **Privately Held**
WEB: www.glederman.com
SIC: 3911 Jewelry, precious metal

(G-9602)
**GEORGY CREATIVE FASHIONS
INC**
Also Called: Georgie Kaye
249 W 29th St (10001-5211)
PHONE..................................212 279-4885
George Kambouris, *President*
EMP: 6
SQ FT: 3,000
SALES (est): 484.9K **Privately Held**
SIC: 2371 5136 5137 2386 Fur goods;
   fur clothing, men's & boys'; fur clothing,
   women's & children's; garments, leather

(G-9603)
GERLI & CO INC
Also Called: American Silk Mills
41 Madison Ave Ste 4101 (10010-2203)
PHONE..................................212 213-1919
Robin L Slough, *President*
Cynthia Douthit, *Vice Pres*
John M Sullivan Jr, *Vice Pres*
Russell Sokolas, *Plant Mgr*
James Harowicz, *CFO*
◆ EMP: 270
SQ FT: 7,500

SALES (est): 22.8MM **Privately Held**
SIC: 2211 2221 Cotton broad woven
   goods; broadwoven fabric mills, manmade; rayon broadwoven fabrics; silk
   broadwoven fabrics

(G-9604)
GERSON & GERSON INC (PA)
100 W 33rd St Ste 911 (10001-2913)
PHONE..................................212 244-6775
Matthew Gerson, *Ch of Bd*
Ian Hitman, *Vice Pres*
Larry Jones, *Prdtn Mgr*
Shelley Striar, *Prdtn Mgr*
Anita Shih, *Production*
◆ EMP: 120 EST: 1935
SQ FT: 13,000
SALES (est): 21.2MM **Privately Held**
WEB: www.gersonandgerson.com
SIC: 2369 2361 Girls' & children's outer-
   wear; dresses: girls', children's & infants'

(G-9605)
GFB FASHIONS LTD
Also Called: Jonathan Michael Coats
463 Fashion Ave Rm 1502 (10018-7596)
PHONE..................................212 239-9230
Paul Cohen, *President*
▲ EMP: 12
SALES (est): 1.1MM **Privately Held**
SIC: 2339 Women's & misses' jackets &
   coats, except sportswear

(G-9606)
GG DESIGN AND PRINTING
93 Henry St Frnt 1 (10002-7035)
PHONE..................................718 321-3220
Allan Yin, *President*
▲ EMP: 9
SQ FT: 3,500
SALES: 1MM **Privately Held**
SIC: 2791 7336 Typesetting; graphic arts
   & related design

(G-9607)
GH BASS & CO (DH)
512 7th Ave Fl 28 (10018-0845)
PHONE..................................646 768-4600
John Gietl, *President*
▲ EMP: 50 EST: 1987
SALES (est): 78.7MM
SALES (corp-wide): 3B **Publicly Held**
WEB: www.ghbass.com
SIC: 3144 3143 3149 5661 Women's
   footwear, except athletic; men's footwear,
   except athletic; children's footwear, ex-
   cept athletic; shoe stores

(G-9608)
GIFTS SOFTWARE INC
360 Lexington Ave Rm 601 (10017-6562)
PHONE..................................904 438-6000
Jawaid M Khan, *CEO*
EMP: 35
SQ FT: 10,000
SALES (est): 1.2MM
SALES (corp-wide): 8.4B **Publicly Held**
WEB: www.giftssoft.com
SIC: 7372 Business oriented computer
   software
PA: Fidelity National Information Services,
   Inc.
   601 Riverside Ave
   Jacksonville FL 32204
   904 438-6000

(G-9609)
GILDAN APPAREL USA INC (DH)
Also Called: Anvil Knitwear, Inc.
48 W 38th St Fl 8 (10018-0043)
PHONE..................................212 476-0341
Anthony Corsano, *Ch of Bd*
Jacob Hollander, *Exec VP*
▲ EMP: 65
SALES (est): 534.1MM
SALES (corp-wide): 2.9B **Privately Held**
WEB: www.anvilknitwear.com
SIC: 2253 2331 Knit outerwear mills;
   women's & misses' blouses & shirts

(G-9610)
GILIBERTO DESIGNS INC
142 W 36th St Fl 8 (10018-8792)
PHONE..................................212 695-0216
Rosario Giliberto Jr, *President*
Anthony Giliberto, *CFO*

EMP: 23
SQ FT: 6,500
SALES: 2.3MM **Privately Held**
WEB: www.gilibertodesigns.com
SIC: 2311 5611 Men's & boys' suits &
   coats; clothing accessories: men's &
   boys'

(G-9611)
GILMORES SOUND ADVICE INC
599 11th Ave Fl 5 (10036-2110)
PHONE..................................212 265-4445
Edward Gilmore, *President*
Tamara M Gilmore,
EMP: 12
SALES (est): 1.6MM **Privately Held**
SIC: 3651 Audio electronic systems

(G-9612)
GINA GROUP LLC
Also Called: Gina Hosiery
10 W 33rd St Ph 3 (10001-3317)
PHONE..................................212 947-2445
Charles Ashear, *Opers Mgr*
Paul Kubie, *VP Bus Dvlpt*
Edmond Harary, *CFO*
Eddie Spigel, *Accounts Exec*
Tanya Moya, *Sales Staff*
◆ EMP: 35
SQ FT: 10,500
SALES (est): 8.8MM **Privately Held**
WEB: www.ginagroup.com
SIC: 2251 2252 Women's hosiery, except
   socks; socks

(G-9613)
GIOVANE LTD
Also Called: Giovane Piranesi
592 5th Ave Ste L (10036-4707)
PHONE..................................212 332-7373
Sami Hajibay, *President*
Mishel H H Piranesi, *Vice Pres*
EMP: 22
SQ FT: 8,500
SALES (est): 3.2MM **Privately Held**
SIC: 3911 Jewelry, precious metal

(G-9614)
GIOVANNI BAKERY CORP
Also Called: Trio French Bakery
476 9th Ave (10018-5603)
P.O. Box 50057, Staten Island (10305-
0057)
PHONE..................................212 695-4296
EMP: 13 EST: 1953
SALES (est): 40.3K **Privately Held**
SIC: 2051 5461 Bread, all types (white,
   wheat, rye, etc): fresh or frozen; rolls,
   bread type: fresh or frozen; bread

(G-9615)
GIVAUDAN FRAGRANCES CORP
40 W 57th St Fl 11 (10019-4001)
PHONE..................................212 649-8800
Brian Kwok, *Business Mgr*
Larry Giardelli, *Warehouse Mgr*
Haley Rutkowski, *Buyer*
Lauren Bitet, *Accounts Exec*
Cindy Jones, *Business Anlyst*
EMP: 130
SALES (corp-wide): 5.5B **Privately Held**
SIC: 2869 Perfume materials, synthetic;
   flavors or flavoring materials, synthetic
HQ: Givaudan Fragrances Corporation
   1199 Edison Dr Ste 1-2
   Cincinnati OH 45216
   513 948-3428

(G-9616)
GIVI INC
16 W 56th St Fl 4 (10019-3872)
PHONE..................................212 586-5029
Mario Fabris, *President*
EMP: 12
SALES (est): 1.3MM **Privately Held**
SIC: 3111 5661 3999 Bag leather; shoe
   stores; atomizers, toiletry
HQ: Givi Holding Srl
   Piazza Luigi Einaudi 4
   Milano MI
   027 600-8529

(G-9617)
GLACEE SKINCARE LLC
611 W 136th St Apt 4 (10031-8137)
PHONE..................................212 690-7632

Jose De La Cruz,
EMP: 6 EST: 2015
SALES: 280.4K **Privately Held**
SIC: 2844 Lotions, shaving; cosmetic
   preparations

(G-9618)
GLAMOUR MAGAZINE
4 Times Sq Fl 16 (10036-6625)
PHONE..................................212 286-2860
Maggie Mann, *Editor*
Wendy Naugle, *Editor*
Bill Wackermann, *Vice Pres*
Ashley Curry-Taliento, *Director*
Emily Mahaney, *Director*
EMP: 5
SALES (est): 425.1K **Privately Held**
SIC: 2721 Magazines: publishing & printing

(G-9619)
GLASSVIEW LLC (PA)
25 E 67th St Ph A (10065-5871)
PHONE..................................646 844-4922
Alyssa Rodia, *Business Mgr*
Patrick Kirby, *Vice Pres*
James Brooks, *Mng Member*
Mike Parent, *Exec Dir*
Michael Goefron, *Security Dir*
EMP: 40
SALES: 51MM **Privately Held**
SIC: 2741 Miscellaneous publishing

(G-9620)
**GLENN HOROWITZ
BOOKSELLER INC**
20 W 55th St Ph (10019-0026)
PHONE..................................212 691-9100
Glenn Horowitz, *President*
EMP: 9
SALES (est): 1.2MM **Privately Held**
SIC: 2759 5932 Publication printing; rare
   books

(G-9621)
GLITCH INC
75 Broad St Ste 1904 (10004-2415)
PHONE..................................866 364-2733
Joel Spolsky, *CEO*
◆ EMP: 5
SALES (est): 1.1MM **Privately Held**
WEB: www.fogcreek.com
SIC: 7372 7371 Prepackaged software;
   custom computer programming services

(G-9622)
GLOBAL ALLIANCE FOR TB
40 Wall St Fl 24 (10005-1338)
PHONE..................................212 227-7540
Melvin K Spigelman, *President*
Maarten Van Cleeff, *President*
Robert C Lorette, *Senior VP*
Kathleen Schostack, *Vice Pres*
Bradley Jensen, *Finance*
EMP: 27
SQ FT: 8,500
SALES: 53MM **Privately Held**
WEB: www.tballiance.org
SIC: 2834 Druggists' preparations (phar-
   maceuticals)

(G-9623)
**GLOBAL ALUMINA SERVICES
CO**
277 Park Ave Fl 40 (10172-2902)
PHONE..................................212 309-8060
EMP: 500
SQ FT: 15,400
SALES (est): 25.8MM
SALES (corp-wide): 26MM **Privately
Held**
SIC: 3297 Mfg Nonclay Refractories
PA: Global Alumina Corporation
   277 Park Ave Fl 40
   New York NY
   212 351-0000

(G-9624)
**GLOBAL APPLCTIONS
SOLUTION LLC**
125 Park Ave Fl 25 (10017-5550)
PHONE..................................212 741-9595
EMP: 8
SALES: 125.1K **Privately Held**
SIC: 7372 7379 Prepackaged Software
   Services Computer Related Services

▲ = Import ▼=Export
◆ =Import/Export

(G-9625)
GLOBAL FINANCE MAGAZINE
Also Called: Global Finance Magazine.
7 E 20th St (10003-1106)
PHONE..........................212 524-3223
Josepy Giarraputo, *Principal*
Dulce Chicon, *Vice Pres*
EMP: 5
SALES (est): 705.1K **Privately Held**
WEB: www.gfmag.com
SIC: 2721 Periodicals

(G-9626)
GLOBAL FINANCE MEDIA INC
Also Called: Global Finance Magazine.
7 E 20th St Fl 2 (10003-1106)
PHONE..........................212 447-7900
Andrew Spindler, *CEO*
EMP: 12
SALES (est): 1.3MM **Privately Held**
SIC: 2721 5192 Periodicals; magazines

(G-9627)
GLOBAL FIRE CORPORATION
244 5th Ave Ste 2238 (10001-7604)
PHONE..........................888 320-1799
Daniel Olszanski, *President*
◆ EMP: 21
SALES: 4.8MM **Privately Held**
WEB: www.globalfirecorp.com
SIC: 3711 Fire department vehicles (motor vehicles), assembly of

(G-9628)
GLOBAL GEM CORPORATION
Also Called: Global Creations
425 Madison Ave Rm 400 (10017-1141)
PHONE..........................212 350-9936
Moosa Ebrahimian, *President*
Robert Ebrahimian, *Vice Pres*
Steve Ebrahimian, *Manager*
EMP: 5
SQ FT: 1,100
SALES (est): 400K **Privately Held**
WEB: www.globalcreations.com
SIC: 3911 5094 Jewelry, precious metal; diamonds (gems)

(G-9629)
GLOBAL GOLD INC (PA)
500 7th Ave Fl 17a (10018-4708)
PHONE..........................212 239-4657
John Bang, *CEO*
Bruce Fisher, *President*
Jeffrey Fischer, *Vice Pres*
Jeff Fisher, *Vice Pres*
Richard Fleet, *Vice Pres*
▲ EMP: 15
SALES (est): 7.3MM **Privately Held**
SIC: 2337 Women's & misses' suits & coats

(G-9630)
GLOBAL GRIND DIGITAL
512 Fashion Ave Fl 42 (10018-4603)
PHONE..........................212 840-9399
Osman Eralt, *CEO*
Tricia Clarke-Stone, *Principal*
Kelsey Paine, *Assoc Editor*
EMP: 30
SALES (est): 2MM **Privately Held**
SIC: 2741 Miscellaneous publishing

(G-9631)
GLOBAL PLASTICS LLC
21 Downing St Frnt 1 (10014-0836)
PHONE..........................800 417-4605
EMP: 33 **Privately Held**
SIC: 2821 Plastics materials & resins
PA: Global Plastics, Llc
99 Middle St Ste 1
Manchester NH 03101

(G-9632)
GLOBAL RESOURCES SG INC
Also Called: Milli Home
267 5th Ave Rm 506 (10016-7503)
PHONE..........................212 686-1411
▲ EMP: 12
SQ FT: 800
SALES (est): 1.5MM **Privately Held**
SIC: 2299 3635 Mfg Textile Goods Mfg Home Vacuum Cleaners

(G-9633)
GLORIA APPAREL INC
500 Fashion Ave 8 (10018-4502)
PHONE..........................212 947-0869
Young H Lee, *President*
◆ EMP: 10
SQ FT: 3,500
SALES (est): 36MM **Privately Held**
WEB: www.gloria-texteis.com
SIC: 2339 Women's & misses' outerwear

(G-9634)
GLUCK ORGELBAU INC
170 Park Row Apt 20a (10038-1156)
PHONE..........................212 233-2684
Sebastian M Gluck, *President*
Albert Jensenmoulton, *General Mgr*
Joseph Disalle, *Technician*
EMP: 5 EST: 1985
SALES (est): 370K **Privately Held**
SIC: 3931 Organs, all types: pipe, reed, hand, electronic, etc.

(G-9635)
GNCC CAPITAL INC (PA)
244 5th Ave Ste 2525 (10001-7604)
PHONE..........................702 951-9793
Nicolaas Edward Blom, *President*
EMP: 5
SALES (est): 1.7MM **Privately Held**
SIC: 1041 Gold ores

(G-9636)
GODIVA CHOCOLATIER INC (DH)
333 W 34th St Fl 6 (10001-2566)
PHONE..........................212 984-5900
Jim Goldman, *President*
Olivier De Mendez, *President*
Manoj Loya, *President*
James Ricciardi, *Vice Pres*
Chris Choi, *Opers Staff*
▲ EMP: 35
SQ FT: 15,000
SALES (est): 793.9MM
SALES (corp-wide): 355.8K **Privately Held**
WEB: www.godiva.com
SIC: 2066 5149 5441 2064 Chocolate candy, solid; chocolate; candy; candy & other confectionery products
HQ: Yildiz Holding Anonim Sirketi
No:6/1 Kisikli Mahallesi
Istanbul (Anatolia) 34692
216 524-2900

(G-9637)
GOGO JEANS INC
1407 Broadway Rm 1801 (10018-2875)
PHONE..........................212 944-2391
David Katach, *CEO*
▲ EMP: 4
SQ FT: 1,500
SALES: 10MM **Privately Held**
SIC: 2339 Jeans: women's, misses' & juniors'

(G-9638)
GOLDARAMA COMPANY INC
Also Called: Silvertique Fine Jewelry
56 W 45th St Ste 1504 (10036-4206)
PHONE..........................212 730-7299
Ernie Golan, *President*
Hagay Golan, *Vice Pres*
EMP: 7
SALES (est): 660K **Privately Held**
SIC: 3911 Jewelry, precious metal

(G-9639)
GOLDBERGER COMPANY LLC (PA)
Also Called: Goldberger International
36 W 25th St Fl 17 (10010-2706)
PHONE..........................212 924-1194
Jeffrey Holtzman, *Mng Member*
Lawrence Doppelt,
Michael Pietrafesa,
▲ EMP: 16 EST: 1916
SQ FT: 10,000
SALES: 2MM **Privately Held**
WEB: www.goldbergerdoll.com
SIC: 3942 Dolls & doll clothing; stuffed toys, including animals

(G-9640)
GOLDEN ARGOSY LLC (PA)
225 W 34th St 1106 (10122-1106)
PHONE..........................212 268-0003
Paul Marks, *CEO*
Richard Rocco, *President*
EMP: 2
SALES (est): 120MM **Privately Held**
SIC: 3353 5199 Aluminum sheet, plate & foil; foil, aluminum: household

(G-9641)
GOLDEN EAGLE MARKETING LLC
244 5th Ave (10001-7604)
PHONE..........................212 726-1242
Monika Sylvester,
EMP: 5 EST: 2009
SALES (est): 217.8K **Privately Held**
SIC: 2741

(G-9642)
GOLDEN INTEGRITY INC
Also Called: B K Integrity
37 W 47th St Ste 1601 (10036-3069)
PHONE..........................212 764-6753
Darek Schwartz, *President*
Khris Kornezi, *Vice Pres*
EMP: 20
SALES: 150K **Privately Held**
WEB: www.goldenintegrity.com
SIC: 3911 5944 Jewel settings & mountings, precious metal; jewelry stores

(G-9643)
GOLDSTAR LIGHTING LLC
1407 Broadway Fl 30 (10018-2480)
PHONE..........................646 543-6811
EMP: 18
SQ FT: 18,000
SALES (est): 1.3MM **Privately Held**
SIC: 3641 Mfg Electric Lamps

(G-9644)
GOOD HOME CO INC
132 W 24th St (10011-1981)
PHONE..........................212 352-1509
Christine Dimmick, *President*
Arni Halling, *Exec VP*
EMP: 6
SQ FT: 1,800
SALES (est): 1.2MM **Privately Held**
WEB: www.thegoodhomecompany.com
SIC: 2844 Oral preparations

(G-9645)
GOOD SHOW SPORTWEAR INC
Also Called: Good Show Sportswear
132 Mulberry St 3 (10013-5551)
PHONE..........................212 334-8751
Danny Tsui, *Owner*
EMP: 11
SALES (est): 350K **Privately Held**
SIC: 3949 Sporting & athletic goods

(G-9646)
GORGA FEHREN FINE JEWELRY LLC
Also Called: Eva Fehren
153 E 88th St (10128-2270)
PHONE..........................646 861-3595
Ann Gorga, *CEO*
EMP: 6
SALES: 0 **Privately Held**
SIC: 3911 7389 Jewelry, precious metal;

(G-9647)
GOTHAM ENERGY 360 LLC
48 Wall St Fl 5 (10005-2911)
PHONE..........................917 338-1023
Jennifer Kearney, *Mng Member*
Debbie Rosenfeld, *Analyst*
EMP: 10 EST: 2008
SALES (est): 546.5K **Privately Held**
SIC: 1389 8748 Oil consultants; energy conservation consultant

(G-9648)
GOTHAM VETERINARY CENTER PC
700 Columbus Ave Frnt 5 (10025-6662)
PHONE..........................212 222-1900
Bonnie Brown, *President*
EMP: 20

SALES (est): 4MM **Privately Held**
SIC: 2835 Veterinary diagnostic substances

(G-9649)
GOTTLIEB & SONS INC
Also Called: Gottlieb Jewelery Mfg
21 W 47th St Fl 4 (10036-2825)
PHONE..........................212 575-1907
Allen Gottlieb, *Owner*
EMP: 25
SALES (corp-wide): 7.8MM **Privately Held**
WEB: www.gottlieb-sons.com
SIC: 3911 Jewelry, precious metal
PA: Gottlieb & Sons, Inc.
1100 Superior Ave E # 2050
Cleveland OH 44114
216 771-4785

(G-9650)
GOYARD INC (HQ)
Also Called: Goyard US
20 E 63rd St (10065-7210)
PHONE..........................212 813-0005
Deborah Ruiz, *Manager*
EMP: 6
SALES (est): 2.1MM
SALES (corp-wide): 55.2MM **Privately Held**
SIC: 3161 5137 Wardrobe bags (luggage); handbags
PA: Goyard St Honore
16 Place Vendome
Paris 1er Arrondissement 75001
142 601-881

(G-9651)
GOYARD MIAMI LLC (DH)
Also Called: Maison Goyard
20 E 63rd St (10065-7210)
PHONE..........................212 813-0005
Deborah Ruiz,
EMP: 6 EST: 2015
SALES (est): 1MM
SALES (corp-wide): 55.2MM **Privately Held**
SIC: 3161 5137 Wardrobe bags (luggage); handbags
HQ: Goyard, Inc.
20 E 63rd St
New York NY 10065
212 813-0005

(G-9652)
GOYARD NM BEVERLY HILLS LLC
20 E 63rd St (10065-7210)
PHONE..........................212 355-3872
▲ EMP: 6 EST: 2014
SALES (est): 750K **Privately Held**
SIC: 3161 Luggage

(G-9653)
GQ MAGAZINE
4 Times Sq Fl 9 (10036-6518)
PHONE..........................212 286-2860
Charles Townsend, *CEO*
Lisa Cohen, *Editor*
Tom Florio, *Vice Pres*
Peter Hunsinger, *Vice Pres*
Will Welch, *Assoc Editor*
EMP: 8
SALES (est): 570K **Privately Held**
SIC: 2731 Book publishing

(G-9654)
GRADIAN HEALTH SYSTEMS INC
915 Broadway Ste 1001 (10010-8268)
PHONE..........................212 537-0340
Stephen M Rudy, *CEO*
Stephen Rudy, *CEO*
Erica Frenkel, *Vice Pres*
Adam Lewis, *Marketing Staff*
EMP: 7
SQ FT: 3,400
SALES (est): 786.5K **Privately Held**
SIC: 3841 Anesthesia apparatus

(G-9655)
GRAFCONECT CORP
575 8th Ave Rm 1902 (10018-3023)
PHONE..........................212 714-1795
Carl Odhner, *President*
Matthew Lento, *VP Opers*

Maggie Yeoh, *Manager*
EMP: 6 **EST:** 2012
SQ FT: 2,000
SALES: 1.9MM **Privately Held**
SIC: 2752 Commercial printing, lithographic

(G-9656)
GRAMERCY DESIGNS INC
Also Called: Trench
287 Park Ave S Fl 2 (10010-5413)
PHONE..........................201 919-8570
Kenneth Rogala, *President*
EMP: 3
SQ FT: 1,250
SALES: 1.1MM **Privately Held**
SIC: 2353 5136 5137 Hats, caps & millinery; men's & boys' hats, scarves & gloves; hats: women's, children's & infants'

(G-9657)
GRAMERCY JEWELRY MFG CORP
35 W 45th St Fl 5 (10036-4903)
PHONE..........................212 268-0461
Danny Lai, *President*
Peter Law, *Vice Pres*
▲ **EMP:** 50
SQ FT: 13,000
SALES (est): 6.8MM **Privately Held**
WEB: www.gramercyjewelry.com
SIC: 3911 Jewelry apparel

(G-9658)
GRAND CENTRAL PUBLISHING (DH)
1290 Ave Of The Americas (10104-0101)
PHONE..........................212 364-1200
David Young, *Ch of Bd*
Beth Ford, *Principal*
Lawrence Kirshbaum, *Principal*
Jennifer Espaillat, *Sales Staff*
Jessica Bromberg, *Manager*
EMP: 240 **EST:** 1960
SQ FT: 140,000
SALES (est): 33.4MM
SALES (corp-wide): 68.6MM **Privately Held**
WEB: www.biggamesmallworld.com
SIC: 2731 Books: publishing only
HQ: Hachette Book Group, Inc.
　　1290 Ave Of The Americas
　　New York NY 10104
　　800 759-0190

(G-9659)
GRAND MAES CNTRY NATURALS LLC
340 E 93rd St Apt 30h (10128-5556)
PHONE..........................212 348-8171
Barry Berman, *Mng Member*
EMP: 5
SALES (est): 574.4K **Privately Held**
SIC: 2048 Canned pet food (except dog & cat); dry pet food (except dog & cat); frozen pet food (except dog & cat)

(G-9660)
GRAND SLAM HOLDINGS LLC (DH)
Also Called: Blackstone Group
345 Park Ave Bsmt Lb4 (10154-0004)
PHONE..........................212 583-5000
Stephen A Schwarzman, *CEO*
EMP: 31
SALES (est): 531.6MM
SALES (corp-wide): 6.8B **Publicly Held**
WEB: www.backstone-gro.com
SIC: 3842 Surgical appliances & supplies; implants, surgical

(G-9661)
GRANDEUR CREATIONS INC
146 W 29th St Rm 9e (10001-8207)
PHONE..........................212 643-1277
Jal Billimoria, *President*
Meherukh Billimoria, *Treasurer*
EMP: 6
SQ FT: 2,450
SALES (est): 531.2K **Privately Held**
WEB: www.grandeurcreations.com
SIC: 3911 Rings, finger: precious metal; bracelets, precious metal

(G-9662)
GRANTOO LLC
60 Broad St Ste 3502 (10004-2356)
PHONE..........................646 356-0460
Tamer Ossama Hassanein, *Vice Pres*
EMP: 5
SALES (est): 205.7K **Privately Held**
SIC: 7372 Application computer software

(G-9663)
GRANTS FINANCIAL PUBLISHING
Also Called: Grant's Interest Rate Observer
233 Broadway Fl 24 (10279-2502)
PHONE..........................212 809-7994
James Grant, *President*
John Dalberto, *Sales Staff*
John McCarthy, *Art Dir*
Evan Lorenz, *Analyst*
Harrison Waddill, *Analyst*
EMP: 10
SALES (est): 1.6MM **Privately Held**
WEB: www.grantspub.com
SIC: 2741 Miscellaneous publishing

(G-9664)
GRAPHIC LAB INC
228 E 45th St Fl 4 (10017-3303)
PHONE..........................212 682-1815
Richard Campisi, *President*
Carmine Campisi Jr, *Vice Pres*
Robert Campisi, *Treasurer*
Jeannette Duran, *Controller*
Albert Mahoney, *Accounts Exec*
EMP: 34
SQ FT: 7,600
SALES (est): 5MM **Privately Held**
WEB: www.gocdp.com
SIC: 2752 Commercial printing, lithographic

(G-9665)
GRAPHICS FOR INDUSTRY INC
Also Called: Graphic For Industry
307 W 36th St Fl 10 (10018-6474)
PHONE..........................212 889-6202
Mark Palmer, *President*
Jesse Navas, *Director*
EMP: 10 **EST:** 1973
SQ FT: 5,000
SALES (est): 1MM **Privately Held**
SIC: 2759 Screen printing

(G-9666)
GRAPHIS INC
389 5th Ave Rm 1105 (10016-3350)
PHONE..........................212 532-9387
B Martin Pedersen, *President*
Arna Pedersen, *Manager*
▲ **EMP:** 10
SQ FT: 5,000
SALES (est): 1.5MM **Privately Held**
WEB: www.graphis.com
SIC: 2721 2731 Magazines: publishing only, not printed on site; books: publishing only

(G-9667)
GRAVITY EAST VILLAGE INC
515 E 5th St (10009-6703)
PHONE..........................212 388-9788
Michael J Perrine, *Chairman*
EMP: 7
SALES (est): 746.1K **Privately Held**
SIC: 3845 Colonascopes, electromedical

(G-9668)
GRAYERS AMERICA INC
304 Bleecker St Frnt 1 (10014-3400)
PHONE..........................310 953-2742
Peter Georgiou, *CEO*
EMP: 10
SALES (est): 1.1MM **Privately Held**
SIC: 2321 Men's & boys' furnishings

(G-9669)
GREAT LIFE ELIXIRS LLC
244 5th Ave Unit F177 (10001-7604)
PHONE..........................332 204-1953
EMP: 51
SALES (est): 1.9MM **Privately Held**
SIC: 2833 Medicinals & botanicals

(G-9670)
GREAT UNIVERSAL CORP
Also Called: ATW Group
1441 Broadway Ste 6066 (10018-1905)
PHONE..........................917 302-0065
Grace Lu, *President*
◆ **EMP:** 20
SQ FT: 1,000
SALES (est): 8.1MM **Privately Held**
SIC: 2361 2321 Girls' & children's dresses, blouses & shirts; men's & boys' dress shirts

(G-9671)
GREEN BEACON SOLUTIONS LLC
875 Ave Of The Amer Fl 20 (10001-3565)
PHONE..........................617 485-5000
Tom Burger, *Branch Mgr*
EMP: 6
SALES (corp-wide): 7.6MM **Privately Held**
SIC: 2542 Postal lock boxes, mail racks & related products
PA: Green Beacon Solutions, Llc
　　875 Avenue Of The America
　　New York NY 10001
　　617 485-5000

(G-9672)
GREEN GIRL PRTG & MSGNR INC
44 W 39th St (10018-3802)
PHONE..........................212 575-0357
Alice Harford, *President*
EMP: 6
SALES (est): 579.9K **Privately Held**
SIC: 2752 Commercial printing, lithographic

(G-9673)
GREENBEADS LLC
Also Called: Emily and Ashley
220 E 72nd St Apt 17d (10021-4531)
PHONE..........................212 327-2765
Emily Green, *Partner*
Ashley Green, *Partner*
EMP: 5
SALES (est): 350K **Privately Held**
WEB: www.greenbeads.com
SIC: 3961 Costume jewelry

(G-9674)
GRESHAM TECHNOLOGIES (US) INC
11 Park Pl Fl 3 (10007-2858)
PHONE..........................646 943-5955
Ian Manocha, *CEO*
Tom Mullan, *CFO*
EMP: 15
SALES: 5MM
SALES (corp-wide): 24.7MM **Privately Held**
SIC: 7372 Application computer software
PA: Gresham Technologies Plc
　　Aldermary House
　　London EC4N
　　207 653-0200

(G-9675)
GREY STATE APPAREL LLC
305 7th Ave Rm 13a (10001-6154)
PHONE..........................212 255-4216
Saima Chowdhury, *CEO*
EMP: 23 **EST:** 2015
SALES (est): 848.1K **Privately Held**
SIC: 2331 Women's & misses' blouses & shirts

(G-9676)
GRIFFON CORPORATION (PA)
712 5th Ave Fl 18 (10019-4108)
PHONE..........................212 957-5000
Ronald J Kramer, *CEO*
Harvey R Blau, *Ch of Bd*
Robert F Mehmel, *President*
Douglas Wetmore, *Exec VP*
Seth L Kaplan, *Senior VP*
◆ **EMP:** 20 **EST:** 1959
SQ FT: 20,000
SALES: 1.9B **Publicly Held**
WEB: www.griffoncorp.com
SIC: 3442 2431 1751 1799 Garage doors, overhead: metal; garage doors, overhead: wood; garage door, installation or erection; home/office interiors finishing; furnishing & remodeling; prefabricated fireplace installation; laminated plastics plate & sheet; laminated plastic sheets; radio & TV communications equipment

(G-9677)
GRILLBOT LLC
401 E 81st St Ste Ph-A (10028-5811)
PHONE..........................646 258-5639
Ethan Woods, *Vice Pres*
Shawn Dickerson, *Creative Dir*
EMP: 5
SALES (est): 845.2K **Privately Held**
SIC: 2842 Cleaning or polishing preparations

(G-9678)
GRIND
1216 Broadway Fl 2 (10001-4482)
PHONE..........................646 558-3250
EMP: 7
SALES (est): 749.1K **Privately Held**
SIC: 3599 Mfg Industrial Machinery

(G-9679)
GRINNELL DESIGNS LTD
260 W 39th St Rm 302 (10018-4434)
PHONE..........................212 391-5277
Francis De Ocampo, *President*
Larry Holliday, *Vice Pres*
Patricia Hudson, *Vice Pres*
EMP: 20
SQ FT: 4,000
SALES (est): 2.4MM **Privately Held**
WEB: www.grinnelldesigns.com
SIC: 3911 Jewelry, precious metal

(G-9680)
GRIT ENERGY SERVICES INC (PA)
100 Wall St Fl 11 (10005-3763)
PHONE..........................212 701-4500
Steven Baffico, *CEO*
Jerry Baftian, *COO*
Jennifer Wilson, *CFO*
EMP: 5 **EST:** 2017
SALES (est): 1.3MM **Privately Held**
SIC: 1389 Oil field services

(G-9681)
GROHE AMERICA INC
160 5th Ave Fl 4 (10010-7065)
PHONE..........................212 206-8820
Ivana Molzen MBA, *Manager*
EMP: 8
SALES (corp-wide): 177.9K **Privately Held**
SIC: 2499 Laundry products, wood
HQ: Grohe America, Inc.
　　200 N Gary Ave Ste G
　　Roselle IL 60172
　　630 582-7711

(G-9682)
GROLIER INTERNATIONAL INC (HQ)
557 Broadway (10012-3962)
PHONE..........................212 343-6100
Lisa Tarsi, *Principal*
EMP: 4
SALES (est): 2.3MM
SALES (corp-wide): 1.6B **Publicly Held**
SIC: 2731 Book publishing
PA: Scholastic Corporation
　　557 Broadway Lbby 1
　　New York NY 10012
　　212 343-6100

(G-9683)
GROM COLUMBUS LLC
1796 Broadway (10019-1400)
PHONE..........................212 974-3444
Eran Keren, *Principal*
▲ **EMP:** 6 **EST:** 2010
SALES: 412.3K
SALES (corp-wide): 58.3B **Privately Held**
SIC: 2024 Ice cream, bulk

PA: Unilever N.V.
Weena 455
Rotterdam
102 174-000

(G-9684)
GROUP COMMERCE INC (PA)
902 Broadway Fl 6 (10010-6039)
PHONE..................................646 346-0598
Jonty Kelt, *CEO*
David Lebow, *President*
EMP: 11
SALES (est): 2.5MM **Privately Held**
SIC: 7372 Prepackaged software

(G-9685)
GROUPE 16SUR20 LLC (PA)
Also Called: Seize Sur Vingt
198 Bowery (10012-4203)
P.O. Box 2280, Lenox MA (01240-5280)
PHONE..................................212 625-1620
James Jurney Jr, *Mng Member*
EMP: 15
SQ FT: 2,000
SALES (est): 1.6MM **Privately Held**
SIC: 2329 2321 2325 Men's & boys'
sportswear & athletic clothing; men's &
boys' furnishings; men's & boys' trousers
& slacks

(G-9686)
GROWNBEANS INC
110 Bank St Apt 2j (10014-2164)
PHONE..................................212 989-3486
Karen Groner, *President*
EMP: 5
SQ FT: 2,400
SALES (est): 412.3K **Privately Held**
SIC: 3172 Personal leather goods

(G-9687)
GRUNER + JAHR PRTG & PUBG CO
Also Called: New York Times Co Mag Group
110 5th Ave Fl 7 (10011-5632)
PHONE..................................212 463-1000
John Heins, *Manager*
EMP: 160
SALES (corp-wide): 644.8MM **Privately Held**
WEB: www.gjusa.com
SIC: 2721 7311 Magazines: publishing
only, not printed on site; advertising agencies
PA: Gruner + Jahr Usa Group, Inc.
1745 Broadway Fl 16
New York NY 10019
866 323-9336

(G-9688)
GRUNER + JAHR USA GROUP INC (PA)
Also Called: Gruner Jahr USA Publishing Div
1745 Broadway Fl 16 (10019-4640)
PHONE..................................866 323-9336
Mike Amundson, *President*
Gregg Black, *Exec VP*
Larry Hawkey, *Exec VP*
Dan Nitz, *Exec VP*
◆ EMP: 500
SQ FT: 173,000
SALES (est): 644.8MM **Privately Held**
WEB: www.gjusa.com
SIC: 2721 2754 Periodicals: publishing &
printing; magazines: publishing & printing;
commercial printing, gravure

(G-9689)
GRUNT APPAREL INC
105 Duane St Apt 7c (10007-3603)
PHONE..................................646 878-6171
Wendy Cheung, *President*
Bill Ng, *Vice Pres*
▲ EMP: 7
SQ FT: 1,000
SALES: 500K **Privately Held**
SIC: 2321 5611 5136 Men's & boys'
sports & polo shirts; men's & boys' clothing stores; caps; men's & boys'

(G-9690)
GSCP EMAX ACQUISITION LLC
85 Broad St (10004-2434)
PHONE..................................212 902-1000
Henry M Paulson Jr, *CEO*
EMP: 5

SALES (est): 408.9K **Privately Held**
SIC: 3442 Metal doors, sash & trim

(G-9691)
GUARDIAN NEWS & MEDIA LLC
61 Broadway Rm 1425 (10006-2719)
PHONE..................................917 900-4663
John Winskowicz, *Director*
Eamonn Store,
EMP: 48
SALES (est): 3.9MM
SALES (corp-wide): 288.8MM **Privately Held**
SIC: 2711 Newspapers, publishing & printing
HQ: Guardian News & Media Limited
Kings Place
London N1 9G
203 353-2000

(G-9692)
GUERNICA INC
Also Called: Guernica Magazine
157 Columbus Ave Ste 424 (10023-6082)
PHONE..................................646 327-7138
Phineas Lambert, *Publisher*
Joel Whitney, *Principal*
Lorraine Adams, *Principal*
Michael Archer, *Principal*
Elizabeth Onusko, *Principal*
EMP: 15
SALES: 20K **Privately Held**
SIC: 2721 Magazines: publishing only, not
printed on site

(G-9693)
GUEST INFORMAT LLC
Also Called: Quick Guide
110 E 42nd St Rm 1714 (10017-5611)
PHONE..................................212 557-3010
Lisa Nusynowitz, *Principal*
EMP: 13 **Privately Held**
SIC: 2741 Miscellaneous publishing
HQ: Guest Informat, L.L.C.
21200 Erwin St
Woodland Hills CA
818 716-7484

(G-9694)
GUEST OF A GUEST INC
113 Jane St (10014-1700)
PHONE..................................212 206-0397
Victoria Eisner, *CEO*
Christie Grimm, *Mktg Dir*
Mackenzie Johnson, *Marketing Staff*
Romina Rosenow, *Manager*
EMP: 6 EST: 2013
SALES (est): 262.9K **Privately Held**
SIC: 2711 Newspapers: publishing only,
not printed on site

(G-9695)
GUILD DIAMOND PRODUCTS INC (PA)
1212 Avenue Of The Americ (10036-1602)
PHONE..................................212 871-0007
Jacques H Elion, *President*
Douglas Panker, *Corp Secy*
▲ EMP: 13
SQ FT: 7,000
SALES (est): 1.4MM **Privately Held**
SIC: 3911 3915 Jewelry, precious metal;
diamond cutting & polishing

(G-9696)
GUILFORD PUBLICATIONS INC
Also Called: Guilford Press
7 Penn Plz Ste 1200 (10001-1020)
PHONE..................................212 431-9800
Robert Matloff, *President*
Anna Nelson, *Editor*
Seymour Weingarten, *Corp Secy*
Clarke Puja, *Vice Pres*
Katya Edwards, *Production*
EMP: 75 EST: 1973
SQ FT: 10,000
SALES (est): 8.6MM **Privately Held**
WEB: www.guilford.com
SIC: 2741 2731 2721 7812 Miscellaneous publishing; books: publishing only;
trade journals: publishing & printing;
audio-visual program production

(G-9697)
GUILFORD PUBLICATIONS INC
Also Called: Guilford Press
370 7th Ave Ste 1200 (10001-1020)
PHONE..................................800 365-7006
Robert Matloff, *President*
Martin Coleman, *Editor*
Carolyn Graham, *Editor*
Laura Patchkofsky, *Editor*
Vernita Hurston, *Credit Mgr*
EMP: 7
SALES (est): 66.5K **Privately Held**
SIC: 2741 2731 Miscellaneous publishing;
book publishing

(G-9698)
GUMUCHIAN FILS LTD
16 E 52nd St Ste 701 (10022-5307)
PHONE..................................212 588-7084
Irma Gumuchdjian, *President*
Patricia Jones, *Vice Pres*
Myriam Schreiber, *Vice Pres*
Andre Gumuchdjian, *Treasurer*
EMP: 15 EST: 1979
SQ FT: 1,700
SALES (est): 2.1MM **Privately Held**
WEB: www.gumuchianfils.com
SIC: 3911 5094 Jewelry, precious metal;
precious stones (gems)

(G-9699)
GUOSA LIFE SCIENCES INC
708 3rd Ave Fl 6 (10017-4119)
PHONE..................................718 813-7806
Charles Oviawe, *Principal*
Edema Oviawe,
EMP: 12 EST: 2012
SALES (est): 887.1K **Privately Held**
SIC: 2834 8999 Solutions, pharmaceutical; tablets, pharmaceutical; scientific
consulting

(G-9700)
GW ACQUISITION LLC
Also Called: G&W Industries
1370 Broadway Rm 1100 (10018-7774)
PHONE..................................212 736-4848
Michael Marinoff, *Principal*
Alyssa Ramjattan, *Associate*
▲ EMP: 34
SALES: 100MM **Privately Held**
SIC: 2361 2369 Girls' & children's blouses
& shirts; girls' & children's outerwear

(G-9701)
H BEST LTD
Moret Time
1411 Broadway Fl 8 (10018-3565)
PHONE..................................212 354-2400
Morris Chabott, *Director*
EMP: 10 **Privately Held**
SIC: 3873 Watches, clocks, watchcases &
parts
PA: H. Best, Ltd.
1411 Broadway Fl 8
New York NY 10018

(G-9702)
H C KIONKA & CO INC
Also Called: Kimberley Diamond
15 Maiden Ln Ste 908 (10038-5118)
PHONE..................................212 227-3155
Mark Levy, *President*
Mark Baum, *Vice Pres*
Elizabeth Ozog-Osewski, *Accounting Mgr*
EMP: 13
SQ FT: 2,500
SALES (est): 8MM **Privately Held**
WEB: www.kimberleydiamond.com
SIC: 3911 Jewelry apparel

(G-9703)
H GROUP LLC
Also Called: H Group, The
462 7th Ave Fl 9 (10018-7436)
PHONE..................................212 719-5500
Joe Dahan,
EMP: 15 EST: 2004
SALES (est): 231.2K **Privately Held**
SIC: 2211 Apparel & outerwear fabrics,
cotton

(G-9704)
HACHETTE BOOK GROUP INC (DH)
1290 Ave Of The Americas (10104-0101)
PHONE..................................800 759-0190
David Young, *Ch of Bd*
Benjamin Greenberg, *Editor*
Kurt Hassler, *Editor*
Amy Pierpont, *Chief*
Kenneth Michaels, *COO*
◆ EMP: 350
SALES (est): 454MM
SALES (corp-wide): 68.6MM **Privately Held**
SIC: 2731 5192 Books: publishing only;
books, periodicals & newspapers
HQ: Hachette Livre
Istra Gecri Hachette Jeunesse
Vanves 92170
964 407-244

(G-9705)
HACHETTE BOOK GROUP USA
237 Park Ave (10017-3140)
PHONE..................................212 364-1200
Michael Galvin, *Vice Pres*
Mark Kent, *Vice Pres*
Stephen Mubarek, *Vice Pres*
Kimi Owens, *Train & Dev Mgr*
Tishana Knight, *Sales Mgr*
EMP: 20
SALES (est): 1.1MM **Privately Held**
SIC: 2731 Books: publishing only

(G-9706)
HADDAD BROS INC (PA)
Also Called: Madonna
28 W 36th St Rm 1026 (10018-1290)
PHONE..................................212 563-2117
Alan Haddad, *President*
Mac Haddad, *Chairman*
◆ EMP: 12
SQ FT: 3,500
SALES (est): 6.4MM **Privately Held**
WEB: www.haddadbros.com
SIC: 2361 2321 Girls' & children's
dresses, blouses & shirts; men's & boys'
furnishings

(G-9707)
HADDAD HOSIERY LLC
34 W 33rd St Rm 401 (10001-3342)
PHONE..................................212 251-0022
Jack Haddad, *President*
▲ EMP: 5 EST: 2000
SALES (est): 431.3K **Privately Held**
SIC: 2252 Hosiery

(G-9708)
HAGEDORN COMMUNICATIONS INC
20 W 22nd St Ste 906 (10010-5862)
PHONE..................................914 636-7400
Chris Vivion, *Manager*
EMP: 5
SALES (corp-wide): 10MM **Privately Held**
WEB: www.fouke.com
SIC: 2711 2741 Newspapers; miscellaneous publishing
PA: Hagedorn Communications, Inc.
662 Main St Ste 1
New Rochelle NY 10801
914 636-7400

(G-9709)
HAILO NETWORK USA INC
568 Broadway Fl 11 (10012-3374)
PHONE..................................646 561-8552
EMP: 5 EST: 2012
SALES (est): 470K **Privately Held**
SIC: 7372 Prepackaged Software Services

(G-9710)
HALABIEH GROUP INC
Also Called: Suslo
209 W 38th St Fl 5 (10018-4405)
PHONE..................................347 987-8263
Eli Halabieh, *President*
EMP: 10
SQ FT: 2,200
SALES: 5MM **Privately Held**
SIC: 2329 2325 5136 Shirt & slack suits:
men's, youths' & boys'; jeans: men's,
youths' & boys'; men's & boys' clothing

(G-9711)
HALEYS COMET SEAFOOD CORP
605 3rd Ave Fl 34 (10158-3499)
PHONE.....................................212 571-1828
Robert Leone, *President*
EMP: 45
SALES: 1.5MM **Privately Held**
SIC: 2211 Long cloth, cotton

(G-9712)
HALMODE APPAREL INC
Also Called: Halmode Petite Div
1400 Brdwy 11th & Fl 16 (10018)
PHONE.....................................212 819-9114
Jay Diamond, *CEO*
Bea Myerson, *Exec VP*
Michael M Saunders, *Vice Pres*
▲ **EMP:** 600
SQ FT: 240,000
SALES (est): 34.9MM
SALES (corp-wide): 594MM **Privately Held**
SIC: 2339 2335 5137 Sportswear, women's; uniforms, athletic: women's, misses' & juniors'; maternity clothing; women's, juniors' & misses' dresses; women's & children's clothing
PA: Kellwood Company, Llc
600 Kellwood Pkwy Ste 110
Chesterfield MO 63017
314 576-3100

(G-9713)
HALO ASSOCIATES
289 Bleecker St Fl 5 (10014-4106)
PHONE.....................................212 691-9549
EMP: 6
SQ FT: 7,000
SALES: 500K **Privately Held**
SIC: 3299 8999 Art Related Services

(G-9714)
HAMIL AMERICA INC
42 W 39th St Fl 15 (10018-2081)
PHONE.....................................212 244-2645
Jerry Miller, *President*
▲ **EMP:** 16
SALES (est): 1.4MM
SALES (corp-wide): 39.8MM **Privately Held**
WEB: www.algo.com
SIC: 2253 Knit outerwear mills
PA: Groupe Algo Inc
5555 Rue Cypihot
Saint-Laurent QC H4S 1
514 388-8888

(G-9715)
HAMMERMAN BROS INC
Also Called: H2 At Hammerman
50 W 57th St Fl 12 (10019-3914)
PHONE.....................................212 956-2800
Brett Hammerman, *President*
Darcy Hammerman, *Vice Pres*
EMP: 9
SQ FT: 10,000
SALES (est): 1.7MM **Privately Held**
WEB: www.hammermanbrothers.com
SIC: 3911 3873 Bracelets, precious metal; earrings, precious metal; necklaces, precious metal; rings, finger: precious metal; watches, clocks, watchcases & parts

(G-9716)
HAMPSHIRE SUB II INC (HQ)
114 W 41st St Fl 5 (10036-7308)
PHONE.....................................631 321-0923
Martin Axman, *President*
Mark Abramson, *VP Sales*
◆ **EMP:** 70
SQ FT: 7,000
SALES (est): 8.4MM
SALES (corp-wide): 91.4MM **Publicly Held**
WEB: www.item-eyes.com
SIC: 2337 2339 5137 Skirts, separate: women's, misses' & juniors'; jackets & vests, except fur & leather: women's; slacks: women's, misses' & juniors'; women's & children's clothing
PA: Hampshire Group, Limited
1924 Pearman Dairy Rd
Anderson SC 29625
212 540-5666

(G-9717)
HAMPTON PRESS INCORPORATED
307 7th Ave Rm 506 (10001-6079)
PHONE.....................................646 638-3800
Barbara Bernstein, *Owner*
EMP: 9
SALES (est): 689.9K **Privately Held**
SIC: 2741 Miscellaneous publishing

(G-9718)
HANDCRAFT MANUFACTURING CORP (PA)
34 W 33rd St Rm 401 (10001-3342)
PHONE.....................................212 251-0022
Isaac Mizrahi, *President*
Ed Cordero, *Opers Staff*
Myla Mirasol, *Production*
Marshall Mizrahi, *Treasurer*
Jennifer Leite, *Asst Controller*
▲ **EMP:** 150
SQ FT: 11,000
SALES (est): 17.1MM **Privately Held**
WEB: www.handcraftmfg.com
SIC: 2341 Women's & children's undergarments

(G-9719)
HANDSOME DANS LLC (PA)
186 1st Ave (10009-4002)
PHONE.....................................917 965-2499
EMP: 5 EST: 2012
SALES (est): 1.5MM **Privately Held**
SIC: 2064 Candy & other confectionery products

(G-9720)
HANDY & HARMAN LTD (DH)
Also Called: Hnh
590 Madison Ave Rm 3202 (10022-8536)
PHONE.....................................212 520-2300
Jack L Howard, *CEO*
Warren G Lichtenstein, *Ch of Bd*
William T Fejes Jr, *Senior VP*
James F McCabe Jr, *Senior VP*
Douglas B Woodworth, *CFO*
▼ **EMP:** 799
SALES: 828.3MM
SALES (corp-wide): 1.5B **Publicly Held**
WEB: www.whxcorp.com
SIC: 3339 3011 3312 Precious metals; tire & inner tube materials & related products; wire products, steel or iron
HQ: Sph Group Holdings Llc
590 Madison Ave Fl 32
New York NY 10022
212 520-2300

(G-9721)
HANESBRANDS INC
260 Madison Ave Fl 6 (10016-2406)
PHONE.....................................212 576-9300
Kimberly Sorrano, *Office Mgr*
Marla Boggs, *Manager*
EMP: 9
SALES (corp-wide): 6.8B **Publicly Held**
WEB: www.hanesbrands.com
SIC: 2211 5699 Apparel & outerwear fabrics, cotton; sports apparel
PA: Hanesbrands Inc.
1000 E Hanes Mill Rd
Winston Salem NC 27105
336 519-8080

(G-9722)
HANIA BY ANYA COLE LLC
16 W 56th St Fl 4 (10019-3872)
PHONE.....................................212 302-3550
Anya Cole, *Mng Member*
Julie Conroy, *Creative Dir*
EMP: 8
SALES (est): 1MM **Privately Held**
SIC: 2253 Knit outerwear mills

(G-9723)
HANSA USA LLC
18 E 48th St (10017-1014)
PHONE.....................................646 412-6407
Andrew Fox, *Mng Member*
Eric Hu, *Director*
▲ **EMP:** 20
SALES (est): 3.7MM **Privately Held**
SIC: 3911 Jewelry, precious metal

(G-9724)
HANSAE CO LTD
501 Fashion Ave Rm 208 (10018-8611)
PHONE.....................................212 354-6690
Aesun Kim, *Mng Member*
EMP: 10
SALES: 958.3K
SALES (corp-wide): 1.1B **Privately Held**
SIC: 2329 2331 Men's & boys' sportswear & athletic clothing; T-shirts & tops, women's: made from purchased materials
PA: Hansae Co., Ltd.
5/F Jeongwoo Bldg.
Seoul 07238
822 377-9077

(G-9725)
HARD TEN CLOTHING INC
231 W 39th St Rm 606 (10018-0745)
PHONE.....................................212 302-1321
Jesse Battino, *Principal*
EMP: 5
SALES: 5MM **Privately Held**
SIC: 2361 5136 Shirts: girls', children's & infants'; shirts, men's & boys'

(G-9726)
HARPERCOLLINS
195 Broadway (10007-3100)
PHONE.....................................212 207-7000
Brian Murray, *President*
Katherine Nintzel, *Editor*
Clarissa Wong, *Editor*
Diane Bailey, *Senior VP*
Tod Shuttleworth, *Senior VP*
EMP: 12 EST: 2012
SALES (est): 204.3K
SALES (corp-wide): 10B **Publicly Held**
SIC: 2731 Books: publishing only
PA: News Corporation
1211 Avenue Of The Americ
New York NY 10036
212 416-3400

(G-9727)
HARPERCOLLINS PUBLISHERS LLC (HQ)
Also Called: William Morrow Publishing
195 Broadway (10007-3100)
PHONE.....................................212 207-7000
Brian Murray, *CEO*
David Steinberger, *President*
Craig Swinwood, *Publisher*
Jordan Brown, *Editor*
Robin Oconnor, *Editor*
▲ **EMP:** 600 EST: 1817
SQ FT: 260,000
SALES (est): 695.1MM
SALES (corp-wide): 10B **Publicly Held**
WEB: www.harpercollins.com
SIC: 2731 Books: publishing only
PA: News Corporation
1211 Avenue Of The Americ
New York NY 10036
212 416-3400

(G-9728)
HARPERCOLLINS PUBLISHERS LLC
Harlequin & Silhouette Books
233 Broadway Rm 1001 (10279-1099)
PHONE.....................................212 553-4200
Eisbell Swift, *Branch Mgr*
EMP: 43
SALES (corp-wide): 10B **Publicly Held**
SIC: 2731 Book publishing
HQ: Harpercollins Publishers L.L.C.
195 Broadway
New York NY 10007
212 207-7000

(G-9729)
HARPERS MAGAZINE FOUNDATION
666 Broadway Fl 11 (10012-2394)
PHONE.....................................212 420-5720
John Macarthur, *President*
John R Mc Arthur, *President*
Jocelyn Giannini, *Vice Pres*
Peter D Kendall, *Vice Pres*
Peter Kendall, *Vice Pres*
EMP: 28 EST: 1982
SQ FT: 7,800

SALES: 6.6MM **Privately Held**
SIC: 2721 Magazines: publishing only, not printed on site

(G-9730)
HARRISON SPORTSWEAR INC
Also Called: Eric Signature
260 W 39th St Fl 7 (10018-4410)
PHONE.....................................212 391-1051
Eric Makofsky, *President*
Lemuel Shiuh, *Vice Pres*
Xie Ai Yi, *Vice Pres*
▲ **EMP:** 12
SQ FT: 3,000
SALES (est): 1.4MM **Privately Held**
WEB: www.randykemper.com
SIC: 2337 Pantsuits: women's, misses' & juniors'; skirts, separate: women's, misses' & juniors'; jackets & vests, except fur & leather: women's

(G-9731)
HARRY N ABRAMS INCORPORATED
Also Called: Stewart Tobori & Chang Div
195 Broadway Fl 9 (10007-3122)
PHONE.....................................212 206-7715
Herve De La Martiniere, *Ch of Bd*
Michael Jacobs, *Ch of Bd*
Shawna Mullen, *Publisher*
Tamar Brazis, *Editor*
Laura Dozier, *Editor*
▲ **EMP:** 94 EST: 1949
SQ FT: 30,000
SALES (est): 35.1MM
SALES (corp-wide): 5.2MM **Privately Held**
WEB: www.hnabooks.com
SIC: 2731 Books: publishing only
PA: La Martiniere Groupe
Martiniere Media Participations Mpp L
Paris 75019

(G-9732)
HARRY WINSTON INC (DH)
717 5th Ave Fl 9 (10022-8132)
PHONE.....................................212 399-1000
Nayla Hayek, *CEO*
Raymond Simpson, *Exec VP*
Stephen Bolcar, *Vice Pres*
Tom Dixon, *Vice Pres*
Gwen Halsted-Horne, *Vice Pres*
▲ **EMP:** 110 EST: 1932
SQ FT: 18,000
SALES (est): 61.1MM
SALES (corp-wide): 8.5B **Privately Held**
SIC: 3911 5944 Jewelry, precious metal; jewelry, precious stones & precious metals; watches
HQ: Hw Holdings, Inc.
718 5th Ave
New York NY 10019
212 399-1000

(G-9733)
HARRYS INC (PA)
Also Called: Harry's Razor Company
75 Varick St Fl 9 (10013-1917)
PHONE.....................................888 212-6855
Andy Katz-Mayfield, *CEO*
Jeffrey Raider, *Corp Secy*
Stefan Knoll, *Vice Pres*
Christine Pfleckl, *Vice Pres*
Ryan Dougherty, *Prdtn Mgr*
▲ **EMP:** 87
SALES (est): 24.9MM **Privately Held**
SIC: 3634 Razors, electric

(G-9734)
HART ENERGY PUBLISHING LLLP
110 William St Fl 18 (10038-3954)
PHONE.....................................212 621-4621
EMP: 5
SALES (corp-wide): 49.3MM **Privately Held**
SIC: 2721 2741 Magaziine/Newsletter Publisher
PA: Hart Energy Llc
1616 S Voss Rd Ste 1000
Houston TX 77057
713 993-9320

(G-9735)

HASKELL JEWELS LTD (PA)
390 5th Ave Fl 2 (10018-8162)
PHONE...................................212 764-3332
Linda Fialkoss, *Principal*
▲ EMP: 50
SALES (est): 3.4MM **Privately Held**
SIC: 3911 Jewelry, precious metal

(G-9736)

HAUTE BY BLAIR STANLEY LLC
330 E 38th St Apt 23e (10016-2780)
PHONE...................................212 557-7868
EMP: 5
SQ FT: 1,000
SALES: 375K **Privately Held**
SIC: 2335 Mfg Women's/Misses' Dresses

(G-9737)

HAYMARKET GROUP LTD
Also Called: Chocolatier Magazine
12 W 37th St 9 (10018-7480)
PHONE...................................212 239-0855
Fax: 212 967-4184
EMP: 12
SQ FT: 3,000
SALES (est): 950K **Privately Held**
SIC: 2721 Magazine Publishers

(G-9738)

HAYMARKET MEDIA INC (DH)
Also Called: Prweek/Prescribing Reference
275 7th Ave Fl 10 (10001-6756)
PHONE...................................646 638-6000
Kevin Costello, *CEO*
Amey Bordikar, *President*
Dominic Barone, *Publisher*
Chad Holloway, *Publisher*
Rachael Prasher, *Managing Dir*
▲ EMP: 130
SQ FT: 27,000
SALES (est): 80.5MM
SALES (corp-wide): 219.2MM **Privately Held**
SIC: 2721 Magazines: publishing only, not printed on site

(G-9739)

HAYNES ROBERTS INC
601 W 26th St Rm 1655 (10001-1151)
PHONE...................................212 989-1901
Timothy Haynes, *Owner*
▲ EMP: 15
SALES (est): 1.9MM **Privately Held**
SIC: 3679 Electronic components

(G-9740)

HC CONTRACTING INC
Also Called: Ferrara Manufacturing Company
318 W 39th St Fl 4 (10018-1493)
PHONE...................................212 643-9292
Carolyn Ferrara, *President*
Joseph Ferrara, *Vice Pres*
Tracy Logan, *Engineer*
Cameron McKee, *Project Engr*
Kyle Bohannon, *Manager*
◆ EMP: 60 EST: 1987
SQ FT: 25,000
SALES: 5MM **Privately Held**
WEB: www.ferraramfg.com
SIC: 2339 2326 Service apparel, washable: women's; service apparel (baker, barber, lab, etc.), washable: men's

(G-9741)

HEALTHIX INC (PA)
40 Worth St Fl 5 (10013-2955)
PHONE...................................877 695-4749
Todd Rogow, *President*
Lloyd Lederkramer, *Business Mgr*
Adam Becker, *Vice Pres*
Vivienne Destefano, *Vice Pres*
Thomas Moore, *Vice Pres*
EMP: 15
SALES: 12.1MM **Privately Held**
SIC: 7372 Prepackaged software

(G-9742)

HEARST BUSINESS PUBLISHING INC
Also Called: Diversion Magazine
888 7th Ave Fl 2 (10106-0001)
PHONE...................................212 969-7500
Cathy Cavender, *Principal*
EMP: 16

SALES (corp-wide): 8.3B **Privately Held**
SIC: 2721 Magazines: publishing only, not printed on site
HQ: Hearst Business Publishing, Inc.
300 W 57th St Fl 2
New York NY 10019
704 348-8614

(G-9743)

HEARST COMMUNICATIONS INC (DH)
Also Called: San Francisco Chronicle
300 W 57th St (10019-3741)
PHONE...................................212 649-2000
Steven R Swartz, *CEO*
Mark E Aldam, *President*
Allison Chin, *Editor*
Jennifer Condon, *Editor*
Kari Costas, *Editor*
▲ EMP: 1100
SQ FT: 100,000
SALES (est): 327.2MM
SALES (corp-wide): 8.3B **Privately Held**
WEB: www.telegram.com
SIC: 2711 Newspapers, publishing & printing
HQ: Hearst Holdings Inc
300 W 57th St
New York NY 10019
212 649-2000

(G-9744)

HEARST COMMUNICATIONS INC
828 9th Ave (10019-5587)
PHONE...................................212 247-1014
EMP: 7
SALES (corp-wide): 8.3B **Privately Held**
SIC: 2711 Newspapers, publishing & printing
HQ: Hearst Communications, Inc.
300 W 57th St
New York NY 10019
212 649-2000

(G-9745)

HEARST COMMUNICATIONS INC (DH)
Also Called: Hearst Interactive Media
300 W 57th St (10019-3741)
PHONE...................................212 649-2000
Steven R Swartz, *CEO*
Mark E Aldam, *President*
Roberta Kowalishin, *President*
George R Hearst Jr, *Chairman*
Michael C Labonia, *Exec VP*
EMP: 113
SALES (est): 27.6MM
SALES (corp-wide): 8.3B **Privately Held**
SIC: 2721 Magazines: publishing only, not printed on site
HQ: Hearst Holdings Inc
300 W 57th St
New York NY 10019
212 649-2000

(G-9746)

HEARST CORPORATION
Seventeen Magazine
300 W 57th St Fl 29 (10019-3741)
PHONE...................................212 649-3100
Noelle Devoe, *Editor*
Jen Abidor, *Assoc Editor*
Jessica Musumeci, *Director*
EMP: 50
SALES (corp-wide): 8.3B **Privately Held**
SIC: 2721 Magazines: publishing only, not printed on site
PA: The Hearst Corporation
300 W 57th St Fl 42
New York NY 10019
212 649-2000

(G-9747)

HEARST CORPORATION
Also Called: Oprah Magazine
224 W 57th St Frnt 1 (10019-3212)
PHONE...................................212 903-5366
Amy Gross, *Principal*
Leigh Haber, *Manager*
EMP: 35
SALES (corp-wide): 8.3B **Privately Held**
WEB: www.hearstcorp.com
SIC: 2721 Magazines: publishing & printing

PA: The Hearst Corporation
300 W 57th St Fl 42
New York NY 10019
212 649-2000

(G-9748)

HEARST CORPORATION
Also Called: Elle Magazine
1633 Broadway Fl 44 (10019-6708)
PHONE...................................212 767-5800
Laurie Abraham, *Principal*
Karen Marx, *Exec Dir*
Amanda Fitzsimons, *Senior Editor*
Kate Metcalfe, *Internal Med*
EMP: 300
SALES (corp-wide): 8.3B **Privately Held**
WEB: www.popphoto.com
SIC: 2721 Magazines: publishing only, not printed on site
PA: The Hearst Corporation
300 W 57th St Fl 42
New York NY 10019
212 649-2000

(G-9749)

HEARST CORPORATION
Also Called: Popular Mechanics
810 7th Ave (10019-5818)
PHONE...................................516 382-4580
Keesha Crooks, *General Mgr*
Joe Oldham, *Branch Mgr*
Holly Frick, *Director*
Janice Limon, *Executive*
EMP: 60
SALES (corp-wide): 8.3B **Privately Held**
WEB: www.hearstcorp.com
SIC: 2721 Magazines: publishing only, not printed on site
PA: The Hearst Corporation
300 W 57th St Fl 42
New York NY 10019
212 649-2000

(G-9750)

HEARST CORPORATION
Also Called: Esquire Magazine
300 W 57th St Fl 21 (10019-3741)
PHONE...................................212 649-4271
Jack Essig, *Vice Pres*
Natasha Zarinsky, *Marketing Staff*
EMP: 70
SALES (corp-wide): 8.3B **Privately Held**
SIC: 2721 Magazines: publishing only, not printed on site
PA: The Hearst Corporation
300 W 57th St Fl 42
New York NY 10019
212 649-2000

(G-9751)

HEARST CORPORATION
Also Called: Seventeen Magazine
1440 Broadway Fl 13 (10018-2301)
PHONE...................................212 204-4300
Howard Grier, *Publisher*
Sabrina Weill, *Editor*
EMP: 100
SALES (corp-wide): 8.3B **Privately Held**
WEB: www.hearstcorp.com
SIC: 2721 Magazines: publishing & printing
PA: The Hearst Corporation
300 W 57th St Fl 42
New York NY 10019
212 649-2000

(G-9752)

HEARST CORPORATION
Also Called: Harper's Bazaar
1700 Broadway (10019-5905)
PHONE...................................212 903-5000
Victoria Pedersen, *Editor*
Carol Smith, *Vice Pres*
Christopher Hertwig, *Prdtn Mgr*
Jim Taylor, *Manager*
Anthony Arnold, *Manager*
EMP: 65
SALES (corp-wide): 8.3B **Privately Held**
WEB: www.hearstcorp.com
SIC: 2721 Magazines: publishing & printing
PA: The Hearst Corporation
300 W 57th St Fl 42
New York NY 10019
212 649-2000

(G-9753)

HEARST CORPORATION
Also Called: Country Living
300 W 57th St Fl 32 (10019-3741)
PHONE...................................212 649-3204
Rachel Barrett, *Chief*
Nancy Soriano, *Manager*
EMP: 100
SALES (corp-wide): 8.3B **Privately Held**
WEB: www.hearstcorp.com
SIC: 2721 Magazines: publishing only, not printed on site
PA: The Hearst Corporation
300 W 57th St Fl 42
New York NY 10019
212 649-2000

(G-9754)

HEARST CORPORATION
Hearst Magazines International
300 W 57th St Fl 42 (10019-3790)
PHONE...................................212 649-2275
Vicki Wellington, *Branch Mgr*
Alexander Karpodinis, *Technical Staff*
EMP: 50
SALES (corp-wide): 8.3B **Privately Held**
SIC: 2721 2731 2711 Magazines: publishing only, not printed on site; books: publishing only; newspapers, publishing & printing; newspapers: publishing only, not printed on site
PA: The Hearst Corporation
300 W 57th St Fl 42
New York NY 10019
212 649-2000

(G-9755)

HEARST DIGITAL STUDIOS INC
Also Called: Hearst Entertainment
300 W 57th St Fl 18 (10019-3741)
PHONE...................................212 969-7552
Neeraj Khemlani, *Ch of Bd*
Mike Bachmann, *CFO*
EMP: 40
SQ FT: 2,500
SALES (est): 1.2MM **Privately Held**
SIC: 2741 7371 ; computer software development & applications

(G-9756)

HEARST HOLDINGS INC (HQ)
300 W 57th St (10019-3741)
PHONE...................................212 649-2000
George R Hearst Jr, *Ch of Bd*
Cathleen P Black, *Senior VP*
John G Conomikes, *Senior VP*
George B Irish, *Senior VP*
Raymond E Joslin, *Senior VP*
▲ EMP: 10
SALES (est): 683MM
SALES (corp-wide): 8.3B **Privately Held**
SIC: 2721 4841 Magazines: publishing only, not printed on site; cable television services
PA: The Hearst Corporation
300 W 57th St Fl 42
New York NY 10019
212 649-2000

(G-9757)

HEART OF TEA
419 Lafayette St Fl 2f (10003-7033)
PHONE...................................917 725-3164
Gerami Masoud, *CEO*
EMP: 10 EST: 2014
SALES (est): 1.1MM **Privately Held**
SIC: 2086 Iced tea & fruit drinks, bottled & canned

(G-9758)

HEARTS OF PALM LLC
Also Called: Ruby Road
1411 Broadway Fl 23 (10018-3471)
PHONE...................................212 944-6660
Peter Aresty,
EMP: 45 **Privately Held**
SIC: 2339 Women's & misses' athletic clothing & sportswear
PA: Hearts Of Palm, Llc
1411 Broadway Fl 25
New York NY 10018

(G-9759)
HEARTS OF PALM LLC (PA)
Also Called: Ruby Road
1411 Broadway Fl 25 (10018-3496)
PHONE..........................212 944-6660
Raymond Barrick, *CFO*
Peter Aresty,
EMP: 55
SQ FT: 25,000
SALES (est): 8.3MM **Privately Held**
SIC: 2339 Women's & misses' athletic clothing & sportswear

(G-9760)
HEAT USA II LLC
35 E 21st St (10010-6212)
PHONE..........................212 564-4328
Mark Kohan, *Director*
EMP: 23
SALES (corp-wide): 3.4MM **Privately Held**
SIC: 2911 Oils, fuel
PA: Heat Usa Ii Llc
11902 23rd Ave
College Point NY 11356
212 254-4328

(G-9761)
HEDAYA HOME FASHIONS INC (PA)
295 5th Ave Ste 1503 (10016-7126)
PHONE..........................212 889-1111
Joseph Hedaya, *Ch of Bd*
Nathan Hedaya, *President*
▲ **EMP:** 110
SQ FT: 50,000
SALES (est): 12.3MM **Privately Held**
SIC: 2392 2339 5131 Placemats, plastic or textile; towels, fabric & nonwoven: made from purchased materials; aprons, except rubber or plastic: women's, misses', juniors'; piece goods & notions

(G-9762)
HEED LLC
462 Fashion Ave Fl 5 (10018-7852)
PHONE..........................646 708-7111
EMP: 25
SALES (est): 1.3MM **Privately Held**
SIC: 2741

(G-9763)
HELIUM MEDIA INC
Also Called: Heleo.com
165 Duane St Apt 7b (10013-3348)
PHONE..........................917 596-4081
Rufus Griscom, *CEO*
EMP: 5
SALES (est): 173.7K **Privately Held**
SIC: 2741 Miscellaneous publishing

(G-9764)
HELVETICA PRESS INCORPORATED
Also Called: Vendome Press
244 5th Ave (10001-7604)
PHONE..........................212 737-1857
Mark Magowan, *President*
Alexis Gregory, *Chairman*
▲ **EMP:** 5
SQ FT: 3,000
SALES: 31.4K **Privately Held**
WEB: www.vendomepress.com
SIC: 2741 Miscellaneous publishing

(G-9765)
HENRY DUNAY DESIGNS INC
10 W 46th St Ste 1200 (10036-9312)
PHONE..........................212 768-9700
Henry Dunay, *President*
EMP: 30
SQ FT: 6,000
SALES (est): 3.8MM **Privately Held**
WEB: www.henrydunay.com
SIC: 3911 5944 Jewelry, precious metal; jewelry stores

(G-9766)
HENRY HOLT AND COMPANY LLC
Also Called: Owl Books Div
175 5th Ave Ste 400 (10010-7726)
PHONE..........................646 307-5095
Kenn Russell, *Editor*
Maggie Richards, *Vice Pres*

Jason Reigal, *Prdtn Mgr*
Jason Liebman, *Mktg Dir*
Caroline Zancan, *Assoc Editor*
◆ **EMP:** 80
SQ FT: 30,000
SALES (est): 10.9MM
SALES (corp-wide): 1.6B **Privately Held**
WEB: www.henryholt.com
SIC: 2731 Books: publishing only
HQ: Macmillan Holdings, Llc
120 Broadway Fl 22
New York NY 10271

(G-9767)
HERALD PUBLISHING COMPANY LLC
4 Times Sq Fl 23 (10036-6518)
PHONE..........................315 470-2022
EMP: 6 **EST:** 2013
SALES (est): 281.8K **Privately Held**
SIC: 2711 Newspapers, publishing & printing

(G-9768)
HERMAN KAY COMPANY LTD
Also Called: Michael Kors
463 7th Ave Fl 12 (10018-7499)
PHONE..........................212 239-2025
Richard Kringstein, *Ch of Bd*
Barry Kringstein, *President*
Samantha Fawcett, *Vice Pres*
▼ **EMP:** 250 **EST:** 2009
SALES (est): 18.3MM
SALES (corp-wide): 183.5MM **Privately Held**
SIC: 2337 2339 2329 Women's & misses' suits & coats; women's & misses' outerwear; men's & boys' leather, wool & down-filled outerwear
PA: Mystic Inc.
463 7th Ave Fl 12
New York NY 10018
212 239-2025

(G-9769)
HERMAN MILLER INC
1177 Ave Of The Amrcs 1 (10036-2789)
PHONE..........................212 753-3022
George Greco, *Manager*
EMP: 40
SALES (corp-wide): 2.5B **Publicly Held**
WEB: www.hermanmiller.com
SIC: 2522 Office furniture, except wood
PA: Herman Miller, Inc.
855 E Main Ave
Zeeland MI 49464
616 654-3000

(G-9770)
HERSHEL HOROWITZ CORP
50 W 47th St Ste 2011 (10036-8687)
PHONE..........................212 719-1710
Leibish Horowitz, *President*
Rachel Horowitz, *Treasurer*
Chaya Dachner, *Admin Sec*
EMP: 7
SQ FT: 1,300
SALES (est): 2.3MM **Privately Held**
SIC: 3915 Diamond cutting & polishing

(G-9771)
HESS CORPORATION (PA)
1185 Avenue Of The Americ (10036-2607)
PHONE..........................212 997-8500
John B Hess, *CEO*
James H Quigley, *Ch of Bd*
David Duke, *Partner*
Tammy Goshorn, *Business Mgr*
Gregory P Hill, *COO*
▲ **EMP:** 254 **EST:** 1920
SALES: 6.4B **Publicly Held**
WEB: www.hess.com
SIC: 1311 2911 5171 5541 Crude petroleum production; natural gas production; petroleum refining; petroleum bulk stations; petroleum terminals; filling stations; gasoline; transmission, electric power

(G-9772)
HESS ENERGY EXPLORATION LTD (HQ)
1185 Ave Of The Americas (10036-2601)
PHONE..........................732 750-6500
Kevin B Wilcox, *Vice Pres*
Timothy B Goodell, *Vice Pres*
John P Reilly, *Vice Pres*

EMP: 3
SALES (est): 2.2MM
SALES (corp-wide): 6.4B **Publicly Held**
SIC: 1382 1311 Oil & gas exploration services; crude petroleum & natural gas production
PA: Hess Corporation
1185 Avenue Of The Americ
New York NY 10036
212 997-8500

(G-9773)
HESS EXPLRTION PROD HLDNGS LTD (DH)
1185 Ave Of The Americas (10036-2601)
PHONE..........................732 750-6000
John P Rielly, *Vice Pres*
Kevin B Wilcox, *Vice Pres*
EMP: 3
SALES (est): 1.2MM
SALES (corp-wide): 6.4B **Publicly Held**
SIC: 1382 1311 Oil & gas exploration services; crude petroleum & natural gas production
HQ: Hess Energy Exploration Limited
1185 Ave Of The Americas
New York NY 10036
732 750-6500

(G-9774)
HESS OIL VIRGIN ISLAND CORP
1185 Ave Of The Amer 39 (10036-2603)
PHONE..........................212 997-8500
John Hess, *Ch of Bd*
EMP: 3000
SALES (est): 228.8MM
SALES (corp-wide): 6.4B **Publicly Held**
WEB: www.hess.com
SIC: 2911 Petroleum refining
PA: Hess Corporation
1185 Avenue Of The Americ
New York NY 10036
212 997-8500

(G-9775)
HESS PIPELINE CORPORATION
1185 Ave Of The Amer 39 (10036-2603)
PHONE..........................212 997-8500
John Hess, *CEO*
Timothy B Goodell, *Principal*
EMP: 197
SALES (est): 22.5MM
SALES (corp-wide): 6.4B **Publicly Held**
WEB: www.hess.com
SIC: 1311 2911 Crude petroleum production; natural gas production; petroleum refining
PA: Hess Corporation
1185 Avenue Of The Americ
New York NY 10036
212 997-8500

(G-9776)
HESS TIOGA GAS PLANT LLC
1185 Ave Of The Americas (10036-2601)
PHONE..........................212 997-8500
Jonathan C Stein, *Principal*
Theresa Hayden, *Credit Mgr*
John Hess,
EMP: 226 **EST:** 2012
SALES (est): 894.9K **Privately Held**
SIC: 1311 Crude petroleum production

(G-9777)
HF MFG CORP (PA)
Also Called: Happy Fella
1460 Broadway (10036-7329)
P.O. Box 318, Hewlett (11557-0318)
PHONE..........................212 594-9142
Bruce Tucker, *President*
Michael Tucker, *Vice Pres*
◆ **EMP:** 60 **EST:** 1963
SQ FT: 2,000
SALES (est): 6.1MM **Privately Held**
WEB: www.hfmfgcorp.com
SIC: 2329 Men's & boys' sportswear & athletic clothing

(G-9778)
HFC PRESTIGE INTL US LLC
350 5th Ave (10118-0110)
PHONE..........................212 389-7800
Patrice De Talhouet,
Kevin Monaco,
EMP: 3000 **EST:** 2015

SALES (est): 1B **Publicly Held**
SIC: 2844 2676 3421 2842 Toilet preparations; towels, napkins & tissue paper products; razor blades & razors; specialty cleaning preparations; soap: granulated, liquid, cake, flaked or chip
PA: Coty Inc.
350 5th Ave
New York NY 10118

(G-9779)
HH LIQUIDATING CORP
Also Called: Zinc Corporation America Div
110 E 59th St Fl 34 (10022-1308)
PHONE..........................646 282-2500
William E Flaherty, *Ch of Bd*
EMP: 843
SALES (est): 86MM **Privately Held**
SIC: 3624 2999 3356 3339 Carbon & graphite products; electrodes, thermal & electrolytic uses: carbon, graphite; carbon specialties for electrical use; coke, calcined petroleum: made from purchased materials; coke (not from refineries), petroleum; lead & zinc; zinc refining (primary), including slabs & dust

(G-9780)
HIGH ALCHEMY LLC
584 Broadway Rm 1008 (10012-5239)
PHONE..........................212 224-9600
Brandon Geiling, *Manager*
EMP: 10
SALES (est): 957.2K **Privately Held**
SIC: 2211 Apparel & outerwear fabrics, cotton

(G-9781)
HIGH POINT DESIGN LLC
1411 Broadway Fl 8 (10018-3565)
PHONE..........................212 354-2400
Mark Lopiparo, *CFO*
Daniel Chrem, *Sales Staff*
▲ **EMP:** 15
SQ FT: 20,000
SALES (est): 1.9MM **Privately Held**
SIC: 2252 Hosiery

(G-9782)
HIGH QUALITY VIDEO INC (PA)
12 W 27th St Fl 7 (10001-6903)
PHONE..........................212 686-9534
Hirofumy Imoto, *President*
EMP: 10
SALES (est): 1.1MM **Privately Held**
SIC: 3652 Pre-recorded records & tapes

(G-9783)
HIGHCREST INVESTORS LLC (HQ)
445 Hamilton Ave Ste 1210 (10153)
PHONE..........................212 702-4323
Carl C Icahn, *Ch of Bd*
EMP: 80
SQ FT: 25,000
SALES (est): 219.6MM
SALES (corp-wide): 955MM **Privately Held**
SIC: 3743 4741 4789 4813 Freight cars & equipment; rental of railroad cars; railroad car repair; local telephone communications; long distance telephone communications;
PA: Starfire Holding Corporation
767 5th Ave Fl 47
New York NY 10153
914 614-7000

(G-9784)
HIGHLINE MEDIA LLC
375 Park Ave (10152-3804)
PHONE..........................859 692-2100
Andrew Goodenough, *President*
Thomas Flynn, *CFO*
EMP: 250
SALES (est): 7.4MM **Privately Held**
WEB: www.highlinemedia.com
SIC: 2731 2711 2721 2741 Books: publishing only; pamphlets: publishing only, not printed on site; newspapers: publishing only, not printed on site; periodicals: publishing only; directories: publishing only, not printed on site

▲ = Import ▼=Export
◆ =Import/Export

PA: Summit Business Media Holding Company
4157 Olympic Blvd Ste 225
Erlanger KY 41018

(G-9785)
HILLARY MERCHANT INC
2 Wall St Ste 807 (10005-2001)
PHONE..................................646 575-9242
Zhaoxiong Zhang, *President*
EMP: 8 **EST:** 2012
SQ FT: 500
SALES: 1MM **Privately Held**
SIC: 2326 5621 Men's & boys' work clothing; ready-to-wear apparel, women's

(G-9786)
HILLS PET PRODUCTS INC (DH)
300 Park Ave (10022-7402)
PHONE..................................212 310-2000
N Thompson, *Principal*
EMP: 5
SALES (est): 7.1MM
SALES (corp-wide): 15.5B **Publicly Held**
SIC: 2047 Dog & cat food
HQ: Hill's Pet Nutrition, Inc.
400 Sw 8th Ave Ste 101
Topeka KS 66603
800 255-0449

(G-9787)
HIMATSINGKA AMERICA INC (DH)
261 5th Ave Rm 1400 (10016-7707)
PHONE..................................212 824-2949
Julie McKenzie, *CEO*
Steve Zaffos, *President*
Ashutosh Halbe, *CFO*
◆ **EMP:** 24 **EST:** 1998
SQ FT: 26,500
SALES (est): 328MM
SALES (corp-wide): 225.9MM **Privately Held**
WEB: www.dwholdings.com
SIC: 2392 5719 Bedspreads & bed sets: made from purchased materials; towels

(G-9788)
HIMATSINGKA AMERICA INC
Also Called: Global Textile
261 5th Ave Rm 501 (10016-0036)
PHONE..................................212 252-0802
EMP: 20
SALES (corp-wide): 225.9MM **Privately Held**
WEB: www.divatex.com
SIC: 2221 Silk broadwoven fabrics
HQ: Himatsingka America Inc.
261 5th Ave Rm 1400
New York NY 10016
212 824-2949

(G-9789)
HIMATSINGKA HOLDINGS NA INC (HQ)
261 5th Ave Rm 1400 (10016-7707)
PHONE..................................212 824-2949
Amitabh Himatsingka, *Ch of Bd*
Shrikant Himatsingka, *President*
Ajoy Kumar Himatsingka, *Principal*
Dinesh Kumar Himatsingka, *Principal*
Rajiv Khaitan, *Chairman*
▲ **EMP:** 1
SALES (est): 328MM
SALES (corp-wide): 225.9MM **Privately Held**
SIC: 2221 Silk broadwoven fabrics
PA: Himatsingka Seide Limited
10/24, Kumarakrupa Road,
Bengaluru KA 56000
802 237-8000

(G-9790)
HINGE INC
508 Laguardia Pl (10012-2693)
PHONE..................................214 576-9352
Justin McLeod, *President*
Jared Sine, *Admin Sec*
EMP: 14
SALES (est): 1.3MM
SALES (corp-wide): 4.2B **Publicly Held**
SIC: 7372 Application computer software
HQ: The Match Group Inc
8750 N Cntl Expy Ste 1400
Dallas TX 75231
214 576-9352

(G-9791)
HIPPO INTERNATIONAL LLC
333 W 86th St Apt 1207 (10024-3150)
PHONE..................................617 230-0599
Lian Liu, *Principal*
EMP: 5
SALES (est): 620.3K **Privately Held**
SIC: 3674 Microprocessors

(G-9792)
HIPPOCRENE BOOKS INC (PA)
171 Madison Ave Rm 1605 (10016-5113)
PHONE..................................212 685-4371
George Blagowidow, *President*
▲ **EMP:** 6
SQ FT: 1,200
SALES (est): 908.5K **Privately Held**
WEB: www.hippocrenebooks.com
SIC: 2731 Textbooks: publishing only, not printed on site

(G-9793)
HIS PRODUCTIONS USA INC
Also Called: Kingstreet Sounds
15 Broad St Apt 3030 (10005-1992)
PHONE..................................212 594-3737
Hisanao Ishioka, *President*
EMP: 7
SALES (est): 1.1MM **Privately Held**
WEB: www.kingstreetsounds.com
SIC: 3652 5084 Pre-recorded records & tapes; recording instruments & accessories

(G-9794)
HISTORIC TW INC (DH)
75 Rockefeller Plz (10019-6908)
PHONE..................................212 484-8000
RE Turner, *Vice Ch Bd*
Richard D Parsons, *President*
Christopher P Bogart, *Exec VP*
Carl F Dill Jr, *Vice Pres*
Joseph Ripp, *CFO*
▲ **EMP:** 38
SQ FT: 451,000
SALES (est): 2.7B
SALES (corp-wide): 170.7B **Publicly Held**
SIC: 3652 6794 2741 7812 Compact laser discs, prerecorded; magnetic tape (audio): prerecorded; music licensing to radio stations; performance rights, publishing & licensing; music royalties, sheet & record; music, sheet: publishing only, not printed on site; music books: publishing only, not printed on site; motion picture production & distribution; television film production; motion picture production & distribution, television; video tape production; cable television services; magazines: publishing only, not printed on site

(G-9795)
HJN INC (PA)
Also Called: Bentones Enterprises
16 W 46th St Fl 9 (10036-4503)
PHONE..................................212 398-9564
Joel Namdar, *CEO*
▲ **EMP:** 15
SALES (est): 1.9MM **Privately Held**
SIC: 3911 Rings, finger: precious metal

(G-9796)
HK METAL TRADING LTD
450 Fashion Ave Ste 2300 (10123-2300)
PHONE..................................212 868-3333
Kenny Chen, *Partner*
▼ **EMP:** 6
SQ FT: 350
SALES: 3MM **Privately Held**
SIC: 3399 Metal powders, pastes & flakes

(G-9797)
HKS PRINTING COMPANY INC
Also Called: Official Press, The
115 E 27th St (10016-8945)
PHONE..................................212 675-2529
Inhyung You, *President*
Sue You, *Corp Secy*
EMP: 10
SALES (est): 940K **Privately Held**
SIC: 2752 2791 Lithographing on metal; typesetting

(G-9798)
HNI CORPORATION
200 Lexington Ave Rm 1112 (10016-6219)
PHONE..................................212 683-2232
Tom Talon, *President*
EMP: 226
SALES (corp-wide): 2.2B **Publicly Held**
WEB: www.honi.com
SIC: 2521 Wood office furniture
PA: Hni Corporation
600 E 2nd St
Muscatine IA 52761
563 272-7400

(G-9799)
HOFFMANN-LA ROCHE INC
430 E 29th St (10016-8367)
PHONE..................................973 890-2291
Eileen Kelly, *Branch Mgr*
Alexa Georginow, *Agent*
EMP: 6
SALES (corp-wide): 57.2B **Privately Held**
SIC: 2834 Pharmaceutical preparations
HQ: Hoffmann-La Roche Inc.
150 Clove Rd Ste 88th
Little Falls NJ 07424
973 890-2268

(G-9800)
HOGAN FLAVORS & FRAGRANCES
Also Called: Hogan Fragrances International
130 E 18th St Frnt (10003-2416)
PHONE..................................212 598-4310
Ray Hogan, *Ch of Bd*
Cory Warner, *Vice Pres*
Sean Hogan, *VP Sales*
EMP: 35
SQ FT: 3,000
SALES (est): 4.3MM **Privately Held**
WEB: www.hoganff.com
SIC: 2844 Perfumes & colognes

(G-9801)
HOLBROOKE INC
Also Called: Holbrooke By Sberry
444 E 20th St Apt 1b (10009-8142)
PHONE..................................646 397-4674
EMP: 5
SALES (est): 309.8K **Privately Held**
SIC: 3961 Costume jewelry

(G-9802)
HOLDENS SCREEN SUPPLY CORP
121 Varick St (10013-1408)
PHONE..................................212 627-2727
Arthur J Gononsky, *President*
EMP: 8
SALES (est): 352.4K **Privately Held**
SIC: 2752 Commercial printing, lithographic

(G-9803)
HOLLAND & SHERRY INC (PA)
Also Called: Holland & Sherry Intr Design
330 E 59th St Ph (10022-1537)
PHONE..................................212 542-8410
Sergio Casalena, *Ch of Bd*
Bryan Dicker, *President*
Daniel Waldron, *Vice Pres*
Tracy Lau, *Accountant*
Helaine Samuels, *Human Res Mgr*
▲ **EMP:** 29
SQ FT: 4,700
SALES (est): 18.9MM **Privately Held**
WEB: www.hollandandsherry.com
SIC: 2395 7389 2519 5021 Embroidery & art needlework; design services; garden furniture, except wood, metal, stone or concrete; furniture

(G-9804)
HOLLANDER HM FSHONS HLDNGS LLC
440 Park Ave S Fl 10 (10016-8012)
PHONE..................................212 575-0400
Jeff Hollander, *President*
EMP: 10
SALES (corp-wide): 1B **Privately Held**
WEB: www.hollander.com
SIC: 2392 Pillows, bed: made from purchased materials

HQ: Hollander Home Fashions Holdings, Llc
6501 Congress Ave Ste 300
Boca Raton FL 33487
212 302-6571

(G-9805)
HOLLANDER SLEEP PRODUCTS LLC
440 Park Ave S (10016-8012)
PHONE..................................212 575-0400
Donald Kelly, *Branch Mgr*
EMP: 79
SALES (corp-wide): 1B **Privately Held**
SIC: 2392 Cushions & pillows
HQ: Hollander Sleep Products, Llc
901 W Yamato Rd Ste 250
Boca Raton FL 33431
561 997-6900

(G-9806)
HOLMES GROUP THE INC
271 W 47th St Apt 23a (10036-1447)
PHONE..................................212 333-2300
Paul Holmes, *President*
Greg Druey, *President*
EMP: 6
SALES (est): 610.8K **Privately Held**
WEB: www.holmesreport.com
SIC: 2741 8748 Miscellaneous publishing; business consulting

(G-9807)
HOME FASHIONS INTL LLC (PA)
295 5th Ave Ste 1520 (10016-7126)
PHONE..................................212 689-3579
Tom Goldstein, *Controller*
David Li, *Mng Member*
▲ **EMP:** 39
SQ FT: 3,600
SALES: 19MM **Privately Held**
SIC: 2392 Pillows, bed: made from purchased materials

(G-9808)
HOME FASHIONS INTL LLC
Also Called: Hfi
295 5th Ave Ste 1520 (10016-7126)
PHONE..................................212 684-0091
Tom Goldtsein, *Controller*
EMP: 15
SALES (corp-wide): 19MM **Privately Held**
SIC: 2392 Pillows, bed: made from purchased materials
PA: Home Fashions International, Llc
295 5th Ave Ste 1520
New York NY 10016
212 689-3579

(G-9809)
HOOEK PRODUKTION INC
307 7th Ave Rm 1204 (10001-6061)
PHONE..................................212 367-9111
Joseph Primiano, *President*
▲ **EMP:** 7
SALES (est): 1.1MM **Privately Held**
SIC: 2752 Commercial printing, lithographic

(G-9810)
HOOKIPA PHARMA INC
350 5th Ave Ste 7240 (10118-7200)
PHONE..................................431 890-6360
Jorn Aldag, *CEO*
Jan Van De Winkel, *Ch of Bd*
Anders Lilja, *Senior VP*
Klaus Orlinger, *Senior VP*
Reinhard Kandera, *CFO*
EMP: 78
SALES (est): 822.6K **Privately Held**
SIC: 2834 Pharmaceutical preparations

(G-9811)
HOPE INTERNATIONAL PRODUCTIONS
315 W 57th St Apt 6h (10019-3145)
P.O. Box 237078 (10023-0029)
PHONE..................................212 247-3188
David King, *Ch of Bd*
Hope King, *President*
EMP: 18
SQ FT: 1,800

SALES (est): 1.3MM **Privately Held**
SIC: 3652 3651 5099 1531 Phonograph records, prerecorded; magnetic tape (audio): prerecorded; video cassette recorders/players & accessories; phonograph records; tapes & cassettes, prerecorded; video cassettes, accessories & supplies; operative builders

(G-9812)
HORIZON FLOORS I LLC
11 Broadway Lbby 5 (10004-1330)
PHONE...............................212 509-9686
Alex Shaoulpour, *President*
EMP: 1
SALES (est): 4MM **Privately Held**
SIC: 2426 Hardwood dimension & flooring mills

(G-9813)
HORO CREATIONS LLC
Also Called: Designs By Hc
71 W 47th St Ste 404 (10036-2865)
PHONE...............................212 719-4818
Suresh Krishnani, *President*
Vinay Krishnani,
EMP: 6
SALES (est): 618.8K **Privately Held**
SIC: 3911 Jewelry, precious metal

(G-9814)
HOSEL & ACKERSON INC (PA)
570 Fashion Ave Rm 805 (10018-1603)
PHONE...............................212 575-1490
Monte Braverman, *President*
EMP: 8 EST: 1944
SALES (est): 553.2K **Privately Held**
SIC: 2258 2395 2269 Lace, knit; embroidery products, except schiffli machine; finishing plants

(G-9815)
HOSPITALITY GRAPHIC SYSTEMS
500 10th Ave (10018-1180)
PHONE...............................212 563-9334
EMP: 11
SALES (est): 1.1MM **Privately Held**
SIC: 3993 Mfg Signs/Advertising Specialties

(G-9816)
HOSPITALITY GRAPHICS INC
545 8th Ave Rm 401 (10018-4341)
PHONE...............................212 643-6700
Louis Melito, *President*
Marshall Silverman, *Treasurer*
EMP: 9
SQ FT: 3,500
SALES (est): 1.5MM **Privately Held**
WEB: www.hginyc.com
SIC: 2752 Commercial printing, offset

(G-9817)
HOSPITALITY INC
247 W 35th St Fl 4 (10001-1925)
PHONE...............................212 268-1930
Howard Pitler, *President*
EMP: 22
SALES (est): 1.1MM **Privately Held**
SIC: 2759 6513 Commercial printing; apartment building operators

(G-9818)
HOT SOX COMPANY INCORPORATED (PA)
Also Called: Polo Ralph Lauren Hosiery Div
95 Madison Ave Fl 15 (10016-7801)
PHONE...............................212 957-2000
Gary Wolkowitz, *President*
Mark Gordon, *Senior VP*
Sarah Wolkowitz, *Treasurer*
Josephine Cordero, *Controller*
Verdell Hankins, *Manager*
◆ **EMP:** 85
SQ FT: 18,000
SALES (est): 8.7MM **Privately Held**
SIC: 2252 2251 Men's, boys' & girls' hosiery; women's hosiery, except socks

(G-9819)
HOUGHTON MIFFLIN HARCOURT CO
Also Called: Hmh
3 Park Ave Fl 18 (10016-5902)
PHONE...............................212 420-5800
EMP: 5
SALES (corp-wide): 1.3B **Publicly Held**
SIC: 3999 2731 Education aids, devices & supplies; book publishing
PA: Houghton Mifflin Harcourt Company
125 High St Ste 900
Boston MA 02110
617 351-5000

(G-9820)
HOUGHTON MIFFLIN HARCOURT PUBG
Also Called: Houghton Mifflin Clarion Books
3 Park Ave Fl 18 (10016-5902)
PHONE...............................212 420-5800
Ann Healy, *Manager*
EMP: 40
SALES (corp-wide): 1.3B **Publicly Held**
WEB: www.hmco.com
SIC: 2731 Textbooks: publishing only, not printed on site
HQ: Houghton Mifflin Harcourt Publishing Company
125 High St Ste 900
Boston MA 02110
617 351-5000

(G-9821)
HOULES USA INC
979 3rd Ave Ste 1200 (10022-1234)
PHONE...............................212 935-3900
Philippe Dasilva, *Manager*
EMP: 5
SALES (corp-wide): 1.3MM **Privately Held**
WEB: www.houlesusa.com
SIC: 3911 Trimmings for canes, umbrellas, etc.: precious metal
HQ: Houles Usa Inc
8687 Melrose Ave Ste B617
West Hollywood CA 90069
310 652-6171

(G-9822)
HOUND & GATOS PET FOODS CORP
14 Wall St Fl 20 (10005-2123)
P.O. Box 11750, Atlanta GA (30355-1750)
PHONE...............................212 618-1917
Will Post, *President*
EMP: 8
SQ FT: 25,000
SALES: 1.4MM **Privately Held**
WEB: www.houndgatos.com
SIC: 2047 Dog & cat food

(G-9823)
HOURGLASS INTERACTIVE LLC
1 Union Sq S Apt 20j (10003-4192)
PHONE...............................954 254-2853
David Scott, *Mng Member*
EMP: 12 EST: 2016
SALES: 150K **Privately Held**
SIC: 7372 7389 Prepackaged software;

(G-9824)
HOUSE OF PORTFOLIOS CO INC (PA)
37 W 26th St Rm 305 (10010-1047)
PHONE...............................212 206-7323
Thomas Lombardo, *President*
EMP: 22
SQ FT: 900
SALES (est): 2.8MM **Privately Held**
WEB: www.houseofportfolios.com
SIC: 3172 5948 Personal leather goods; leather goods, except luggage & shoes

(G-9825)
HOUSE OF PORTFOLIOS CO INC
48 W 21st St (10010-6907)
PHONE...............................212 206-7323
Thomas Lombardo, *Branch Mgr*
EMP: 17 **Privately Held**
WEB: www.houseofportfolios.com
SIC: 3172 Personal leather goods
PA: The House Of Portfolios Co Inc
37 W 26th St Rm 305
New York NY 10010

(G-9826)
HOUSE PEARL FASHIONS (US) LTD
1410 Broadway Rm 1501 (10018-9834)
PHONE...............................212 840-3183
Mehesh Seth, *President*
EMP: 10
SQ FT: 4,000
SALES (corp-wide): 118.5MM **Privately Held**
SIC: 2329 2339 Coats (oiled fabric, leatherette, etc.): men's & boys'; women's & misses' outerwear; women's & misses' accessories
HQ: House Of Pearl Fashions (Us) Ltd.
300-2 D&E Rr 17
Lodi NJ 07644

(G-9827)
HOVEE INC
722 Saint Nicholas Ave (10031-4002)
PHONE...............................646 249-6200
Paul Kogan, *CEO*
EMP: 10
SALES (est): 593.6K **Privately Held**
SIC: 7372 7389 Business oriented computer software;

(G-9828)
HP INC
556 W 22nd St Fl 8 (10011-1108)
PHONE...............................650 857-1501
David Pepe, *Business Mgr*
Jason Wadleigh, *Senior Engr*
Claudia Lewis, *Manager*
Cynthia Lin, *Manager*
Nitin Kaulavkar, *Info Tech Mgr*
EMP: 9
SALES (corp-wide): 58.4B **Publicly Held**
SIC: 3571 Personal computers (microcomputers)
PA: Hp, Inc.
1501 Page Mill Rd
Palo Alto CA 94304
650 857-1501

(G-9829)
HPE CLOTHING CORPORATION
Also Called: H P E
60 Broad St Ste 3502 (10004-2356)
PHONE...............................946 356-0474
Nicholas Harris, *President*
EMP: 10
SQ FT: 500
SALES: 989K **Privately Held**
SIC: 2329 Athletic (warmup, sweat & jogging) suits: men's & boys'
PA: Human Performance Engineering Limited
10 Barley Mow Passage
London

(G-9830)
HS HOMEWORX LLC
18 E 74th St Fl 5 (10021-2612)
PHONE...............................646 870-0406
Yvonne Franco, *Controller*
Harry Slatkin, *Mng Member*
EMP: 5
SALES (est): 391.4K **Privately Held**
SIC: 3999 7389 Candles;

(G-9831)
HUDSON ENVELOPE CORPORATION (PA)
Also Called: Jam Paper
135 3rd Ave (10003-2543)
PHONE...............................212 473-6666
Michael Jacobs, *President*
Janet Jacobs, *Vice Pres*
Kyle Lerner, *CFO*
Craig Hoberman, *Manager*
▲ **EMP:** 25
SQ FT: 7,000
SALES (est): 4.4MM **Privately Held**
SIC: 2752 2759 Commercial printing, offset; envelopes: printing

(G-9832)
HUDSON GROUP (HG) INC
250 Greenwich St (10007-2140)
PHONE...............................212 971-6800
EMP: 6

SALES (corp-wide): 8.7B **Privately Held**
SIC: 2711 Newspapers, publishing & printing
HQ: Hudson Group (Hg), Inc.
1 Meadowlands Plz
East Rutherford NJ 07073

(G-9833)
HUDSON PARK PRESS INC
232 Madison Ave Rm 1400 (10016-2918)
P.O. Box 774, Pine Plains (12567-0774)
PHONE...............................212 929-8898
Gilman Park, *Ch of Bd*
▲ **EMP:** 5
SALES (est): 398.4K **Privately Held**
SIC: 2752 2731 Publication printing, lithographic; books: publishing only

(G-9834)
HUDSON PRINTING CO INC
747 3rd Ave Lbby 3 (10017-2810)
PHONE...............................718 937-8600
Robert Bergman, *President*
Alan Bergman, *Admin Sec*
EMP: 25 EST: 1923
SQ FT: 33,000
SALES (est): 3.1MM **Privately Held**
WEB: www.hudsonprints.com
SIC: 2752 2789 Commercial printing, offset; bookbinding & related work

(G-9835)
HUGO BOSS USA INC (HQ)
55 Water St Fl 48 (10041-3204)
PHONE...............................212 940-0600
Andre Maeder, *CEO*
Anthony Lucia, *President*
Mark Brashear, *Managing Dir*
JD Perez, *Area Mgr*
Gerd Von Podewils, *Senior VP*
◆ **EMP:** 75
SQ FT: 100,000
SALES (est): 280.2MM
SALES (corp-wide): 3.2B **Privately Held**
WEB: www.hugobossusa.com
SIC: 2311 2325 2337 5136 Men's & boys' suits & coats; men's & boys' trousers & slacks; women's & misses' suits & coats; women's, misses' & juniors'; skirts, separate: women's, misses' & juniors'; jackets & vests, except fur & leather: women's; men's & boys' suits & trousers; men's & boys' sportswear & work clothing; men's & boys' outerwear; men's & boys' clothing stores; franchises, selling or licensing
PA: Hugo Boss Ag
Dieselstr. 12
Metzingen 72555
712 394-0

(G-9836)
HUMAN CONDITION SAFETY INC
61 Broadway Fl 31 (10006-2803)
PHONE...............................646 867-0644
Alexander R Baugh, *Ch of Bd*
Greg Wolyniec, *President*
Robert Price, *CFO*
Gary Foreman, *CTO*
EMP: 10
SALES (est): 1.7MM **Privately Held**
SIC: 7372 5099 Prepackaged software; safety equipment & supplies

(G-9837)
HUMAN LIFE FOUNDATION INC
271 Madison Ave Ste 1005 (10016-1006)
PHONE...............................212 685-5210
Maria McFadden, *President*
Faith McFadden, *Vice Pres*
Ann Conlon, *Admin Sec*
EMP: 5 EST: 1974
SQ FT: 500
SALES: 459.2K **Privately Held**
WEB: www.humanlifereview.com
SIC: 2721 8399 8733 Periodicals: publishing only; social service information exchange; noncommercial research organizations

(G-9838)
HUMANA PRESS INC
233 Spring St Fl 6 (10013-1522)
PHONE...............................212 460-1500
Thomas Lanigan, *President*
Julia Lanigan, *Vice Pres*

▲ = Import ▼=Export
◆ =Import/Export

▲ **EMP:** 40
SQ FT: 8,500
SALES (est): 2.1MM
SALES (corp-wide): 1.6B **Privately Held**
WEB: www.humanapr.com
SIC: 2741 2731 2721 Technical papers: publishing only, not printed on site; book clubs: publishing only, not printed on site; trade journals: publishing only, not printed on site
HQ: Springer Science + Business Media, Llc
233 Spring St Fl 6
New York NY 10013
212 460-1500

(G-9839)
HUMANSCALE CORPORATION (PA)
1114 Avenue Of The Americ (10036-7703)
PHONE.................................212 725-4749
Robert King, *CEO*
Heather Fennimore, *President*
Elliot Balis, *District Mgr*
Steve McManama, *District Mgr*
Jeffrey Johnson, *Business Mgr*
◆ **EMP:** 32
SQ FT: 10,000
SALES (est): 142.2MM **Privately Held**
SIC: 3577 2521 Computer peripheral equipment; wood office furniture

(G-9840)
HUMOR RAINBOW INC
Also Called: Okcupid
555 W 18th St (10011-2822)
PHONE.................................646 402-9113
Michael Maxim, *President*
Elliot Gwynn, *Software Engr*
EMP: 43
SALES (est): 2MM
SALES (corp-wide): 4.2B **Publicly Held**
SIC: 2741 Miscellaneous publishing
PA: Iac/Interactivecorp
555 W 18th St
New York NY 10011
212 314-7300

(G-9841)
HW HOLDINGS INC (DH)
718 5th Ave (10019-4102)
PHONE.................................212 399-1000
Nayla Hayek, *CEO*
EMP: 4
SALES (est): 61.3MM
SALES (corp-wide): 8.5B **Privately Held**
SIC: 3911 5944 6719 Jewelry, precious metal; jewelry, precious stones & precious metals; watches; investment holding companies, except banks
HQ: The Swatch Group Far East Distribution Ltd
Seevorstadt 6
Biel-Bienne BE 2502
323 436-811

(G-9842)
HYDROGEN TECHNOLOGY CORP
915 Broadway Ste 801 (10010-7139)
PHONE.................................800 315-9554
Matthew Kane, *Vice Pres*
EMP: 27 **EST:** 2017
SALES: 3MM **Privately Held**
SIC: 7372 Application computer software

(G-9843)
HYPERLAW INC
17 W 70th St Apt 4 (10023-4544)
PHONE.................................212 873-6982
Alan D Sugarman, *President*
EMP: 10
SALES (est): 830K **Privately Held**
WEB: www.hyperlaw.com
SIC: 7372 Publishers' computer software

(G-9844)
HYPOXICO INC
50 Lexington Ave Ste 249 (10010-2935)
PHONE.................................212 972-1009
Gary Kotliar, *President*
Yulia Soukhanova, *Vice Pres*
Brian Oe Strike, *Vice Pres*
Dylan Bowman, *Sales Staff*
▲ **EMP:** 6
SQ FT: 3,000

SALES (est): 500K **Privately Held**
WEB: www.hypoxico.com
SIC: 3949 Exercise equipment

(G-9845)
I LOVE ACCESSORIES INC
10 W 33rd St Rm 210 (10001-3326)
PHONE.................................212 239-1875
Daren Malles, *President*
▲ **EMP:** 5
SQ FT: 1,200
SALES: 5MM **Privately Held**
SIC: 3961 Costume jewelry

(G-9846)
I N K T INC
250 W 54th St Fl 9 (10019-5597)
PHONE.................................212 957-2700
Gary Winnick, *CEO*
Scott Jacobson, *COO*
Bill Passer, *Acting CFO*
Ed Ickowski, *Senior VP*
Jim Vickers, *Senior VP*
▲ **EMP:** 10
SALES (est): 1.6MM **Privately Held**
WEB: www.t-ink.com
SIC: 2759 5085 Commercial printing; ink, printers'

(G-9847)
I S C A CORP (PA)
Also Called: Elliot Lauren
512 7th Ave Fl 7 (10018-0862)
PHONE.................................212 719-5123
Elliot Grosovsky, *Ch of Bd*
Laura French, *Director*
▲ **EMP:** 16
SQ FT: 4,200
SALES (est): 4.7MM **Privately Held**
SIC: 2335 Women's, juniors' & misses' dresses

(G-9848)
I SHALOM & CO INC
411 5th Ave Fl 4 (10016-2272)
PHONE.................................212 532-7911
Isaac Shalom, *Ch of Bd*
Albert Bhojwani, *Traffic Mgr*
A Koven, *Traffic Mgr*
Valerie Shalom, *Treasurer*
Edward Kurzawa, *Controller*
EMP: 150 **EST:** 1919
SQ FT: 9,000
SALES (est): 20.4K **Privately Held**
SIC: 2389 2339 Men's miscellaneous accessories; women's & misses' accessories

(G-9849)
I SPIEWAK & SONS INC
225 W 37th St Fl 15l (10018-6667)
PHONE.................................212 695-1620
Roy J Spiewak, *Ch of Bd*
▲ **EMP:** 35 **EST:** 1904
SQ FT: 10,000
SALES (est): 6.5MM **Privately Held**
SIC: 2329 Men's & boys' leather, wool & down-filled outerwear; field jackets, military; down-filled clothing: men's & boys'

(G-9850)
IAC SEARCH LLC (HQ)
555 W 18th St (10011-2822)
PHONE.................................212 314-7300
Barry Diller, *Chairman*
Trish Lounsbury, *Senior VP*
Paul Scribano, *Vice Pres*
David Sullivan, *Consultant*
Cesar Villarreal, *Supervisor*
EMP: 37
SALES (est): 6.6MM
SALES (corp-wide): 4.2B **Publicly Held**
SIC: 7372 7375 Prepackaged software; information retrieval services; on-line data base information retrieval
PA: Iac/Interactivecorp
555 W 18th St
New York NY 10011
212 314-7300

(G-9851)
IAC/INTERACTIVECORP (PA)
555 W 18th St (10011-2822)
PHONE.................................212 314-7300
Joseph Levin, *CEO*
Barry Diller, *Ch of Bd*

Victor A Kaufman, *Vice Ch Bd*
Lloyd Grove, *Editor*
Martha Mercer, *Editor*
EMP: 3300
SQ FT: 202,500
SALES: 4.2B **Publicly Held**
WEB: www.usanetworks.com
SIC: 7372 7375 5961 Prepackaged software; information retrieval services; on-line data base information retrieval; catalog & mail-order houses

(G-9852)
IBIO INC
600 Madison Ave Ste 1601 (10022-1737)
PHONE.................................302 355-0650
Robert B Kay, *Ch of Bd*
Robert L Erwin, *President*
Wayne Fitzmaurice, *Vice Pres*
James P Mullaney, *CFO*
Terence Ryan, *Security Dir*
EMP: 43 **EST:** 2008
SALES: 2MM **Privately Held**
SIC: 2834 Pharmaceutical preparations

(G-9853)
IBRANDS INTERNATIONAL LLC
230 W 39th St (10018-4411)
PHONE.................................212 354-1330
Marc Garson, *Chairman*
EMP: 16 **EST:** 2014
SQ FT: 4,200
SALES (est): 585.6K **Privately Held**
SIC: 2321 Polo shirts, men's & boys': made from purchased materials

(G-9854)
ICARUS ENTERPRISES INC
568 Broadway Fl 11 (10012-3374)
PHONE.................................917 969-4461
Nicholas Hubbard, *President*
EMP: 5
SALES: 500K **Privately Held**
SIC: 2721 Magazines: publishing & printing

(G-9855)
ICER SPORTS LLC
1385 Broadway Fl 16 (10018-6041)
PHONE.................................212 221-4700
Iven Sandler, *Mng Member*
EMP: 5
SALES (est): 480K **Privately Held**
SIC: 2329 2331 Men's & boys' sportswear & athletic clothing; women's & misses' blouses & shirts

(G-9856)
IDALIA SOLAR TECHNOLOGIES LLC
270 Lafayette St Ste 1402 (10012-3364)
PHONE.................................212 792-3913
Marc Dee,
Eric Laufer,
EMP: 9
SQ FT: 2,500
SALES: 500K **Privately Held**
SIC: 3674 Solar cells

(G-9857)
IDEAL CREATIONS INC
10 W 33rd St Rm 708 (10001-3306)
PHONE.................................212 563-5928
Moses Grunbaum, *President*
▲ **EMP:** 20
SALES (est): 1.4MM **Privately Held**
WEB: www.idealcreations.net
SIC: 2369 5136 Headwear: girls', children's & infants'; hats, men's & boys'

(G-9858)
IDEAL FASTENER CORPORATION
Also Called: Ideal Accessories
246 W 38th St Rm 502 (10018-9074)
PHONE.................................212 244-0260
Ralph Gut, *President*
Steven Gut, *Director*
EMP: 95
SALES (corp-wide): 46MM **Privately Held**
WEB: www.idealfastener.com
SIC: 3965 Fasteners, buttons, needles & pins

PA: Ideal Fastener Corporation
603 W Industry Dr
Oxford NC 27565
919 693-3115

(G-9859)
IEP ENERGY HOLDING LLC
767 5th Ave Ste 4600 (10153-0023)
PHONE.................................212 702-4300
EMP: 2746
SALES (est): 109.8K
SALES (corp-wide): 11.7B **Publicly Held**
SIC: 2911 Petroleum refining
HQ: Icahn Enterprises Holdings L.P.
767 5th Ave Fl 17
New York NY 10153
212 702-4300

(G-9860)
IFG CORP
1372 Brdwy 12ae 12 Ae (10018)
PHONE.................................212 629-9600
EMP: 159
SALES (corp-wide): 36.9MM **Privately Held**
SIC: 2329 2339 Athletic (warmup, sweat & jogging) suits: men's & boys'; athletic clothing: women's, misses' & juniors'
PA: Ifg Corp.
463 7th Ave Fl 5
New York NY 10018
212 629-9600

(G-9861)
IFG CORP
463 7th Ave Fl 4 (10018-8725)
PHONE.................................212 239-8615
Ronald Adjmi, *President*
EMP: 5
SALES (corp-wide): 36.9MM **Privately Held**
SIC: 2329 Athletic (warmup, sweat & jogging) suits: men's & boys'
PA: Ifg Corp.
463 7th Ave Fl 5
New York NY 10018
212 629-9600

(G-9862)
IHI INC (HQ)
150 E 52nd St Fl 24 (10022-6246)
PHONE.................................212 599-8100
Masato Kawaguchi, *CEO*
◆ **EMP:** 27
SALES (est): 372.3MM **Privately Held**
WEB: www.ihiinc.ihi.co.jp
SIC: 3812 1731 Acceleration indicators & systems components, aerospace; energy management controls

(G-9863)
IKEDDI ENTERPRISES INC (PA)
1407 Brdwy Ste 1600 (10018)
PHONE.................................212 302-7644
Raymond Salem, *Ch of Bd*
David Salem, *Vice Pres*
Eddie Salem, *Production*
Bruce Cotter, *CFO*
Marcy Marcus, *Accounts Exec*
◆ **EMP:** 18
SQ FT: 28,000
SALES (est): 3.9MM **Privately Held**
SIC: 2339 Sportswear, women's

(G-9864)
IKEDDI ENTERPRISES INC
1407 Broadway Rm 1805 (10018-2764)
PHONE.................................212 302-7644
Raymond Salem, *Manager*
EMP: 6 **Privately Held**
SIC: 2339 Sportswear, women's
PA: Ikeddi Enterprises Inc.
1407 Brdwy Ste 1600
New York NY 10018

(G-9865)
ILES FORMULA INC (PA)
40 Harrison St Apt 17h (10013-2722)
PHONE.................................315 834-2478
Jeacques Masi, *CEO*
Wendy Iles, *President*
EMP: 6 **EST:** 2013
SALES: 700K **Privately Held**
SIC: 2844 Toilet preparations

(G-9866)
IMEK MEDIA LLC
32 Broadway Ste 511 (10004-1665)
PHONE....................................212 422-9000
Kemi Osukoya,
EMP: 20 **EST:** 2012
SALES (est): 1.5MM **Privately Held**
SIC: 2721 Magazines: publishing only, not printed on site

(G-9867)
IMENA JEWELRY MANUFACTURER INC
2 W 45th St Ste 1000 (10036-4252)
PHONE....................................212 827-0073
Paul Yan, *President*
Cindy Yan, *Office Mgr*
EMP: 15
SALES (est): 1.7MM **Privately Held**
SIC: 3911 Jewelry, precious metal

(G-9868)
IMG THE DAILY
432 W 45th St Fl 5 (10036-3503)
PHONE....................................212 541-5640
George Maier, *Principal*
EMP: 5
SALES (est): 345.5K **Privately Held**
SIC: 2711 Newspapers, publishing & printing

(G-9869)
IMPERIAL-HARVARD LABEL CO
Also Called: Harvard Woven Label
236 W 40th St Fl 3 (10018-1692)
PHONE....................................212 736-8420
Ira I Altfeder, *President*
Larry Saputo, *Treasurer*
EMP: 10
SQ FT: 3,000
SALES (est): 1.2MM **Privately Held**
SIC: 2241 Labels, woven

(G-9870)
IMPERIUM PARTNERS GROUP LLC (PA)
509 Madison Ave (10022-5501)
PHONE....................................212 433-1360
Maurice Hryshko, *Accountant*
John Michaelson,
EMP: 135
SALES (est): 14.4MM **Privately Held**
SIC: 3674 Microcircuits, integrated (semiconductor)

(G-9871)
IMPRESSIONS INC
36 W 37th St Rm 400 (10018-7497)
PHONE....................................212 594-5954
John Baise, *Principal*
EMP: 5
SALES (est): 659K **Privately Held**
SIC: 2721 Magazines: publishing only, not printed on site

(G-9872)
IMPRINT BRANDED CONTENT LLC
34 W 27th St Rm 501 (10001-6996)
PHONE....................................212 888-8073
Andy Seibert, *Mng Member*
EMP: 7
SALES (est): 378.3K **Privately Held**
SIC: 2759 Imprinting
PA: Sullivan & Company Marketing Collateral, Inc.
450 W 14th St Fl 12
New York NY

(G-9873)
IN MOCEAN GROUP LLC (PA)
463 Fashion Ave Fl 21 (10018-7595)
PHONE....................................212 944-0317
Angelina Simone, *Vice Pres*
Joy Pescaru, *Production*
Sal Azzinnari, *CFO*
Monica Astalus, *Human Resources*
Anthony Francese, *VP Sales*
◆ **EMP:** 95
SQ FT: 12,000
SALES (est): 15.2MM **Privately Held**
SIC: 2369 Bathing suits & swimwear: girls', children's & infants'

(G-9874)
IN-STEP MARKETING INC (PA)
Also Called: Z Card North America
39 Broadway Fl 32 (10006-3047)
PHONE....................................212 797-3450
Tim Kunhardt, *President*
EMP: 15
SQ FT: 6,600
SALES (est): 2.9MM **Privately Held**
WEB: www.zcardna.com
SIC: 2752 5199 8742 Promotional printing, lithographic; advertising specialties; marketing consulting services

(G-9875)
INCON GEMS INC
Also Called: Jeypore Group
2 W 46th St Ste 603 (10036-4561)
PHONE....................................212 221-8560
Raju Gupta, *President*
EMP: 15
SQ FT: 2,000
SALES (est): 1.6MM **Privately Held**
SIC: 3911 5094 Jewelry, precious metal; precious stones (gems)

(G-9876)
INCRO MARKETING USA CORP (PA)
157 Columbus Ave (10023-6082)
PHONE....................................917 365-5552
Rachel Braha, *President*
EMP: 1
SALES: 1MM **Privately Held**
SIC: 2091 8742 Canned & cured fish & seafoods; marketing consulting services

(G-9877)
INCYCLE SOFTWARE CORP (PA)
1120 Ave Of The Americas (10036-6700)
PHONE....................................212 626-2608
Martin Rajotte, *President*
Julie Beaulieu, *CFO*
EMP: 10
SALES (est): 1.5MM **Privately Held**
SIC: 7372 Application computer software

(G-9878)
INDEGY INC
1460 Broadway (10036-7329)
PHONE....................................866 801-5394
Barak Perelman, *CEO*
Todd Warwick, *Vice Pres*
Greg Bunting, *Regl Sales Mgr*
Joe Scotto, *Chief Mktg Ofcr*
EMP: 30
SALES (est): 933K **Privately Held**
SIC: 7372 7382 Prepackaged software; security systems services

(G-9879)
INDEX MAGAZINE
526 W 26th St Rm 920 (10001-5540)
PHONE....................................212 243-1428
Peter Halley, *Owner*
EMP: 6
SALES (est): 300K **Privately Held**
WEB: www.indexmagazine.com
SIC: 2721 Magazines: publishing & printing

(G-9880)
INDIA ABROAD PUBLICATIONS INC
102 Madison Ave Frnt B (10016-7592)
PHONE....................................212 929-1727
Ajit Balakrishnan, *President*
Geeta Singh, *Sales Executive*
EMP: 59
SQ FT: 6,500
SALES (est): 4.5MM **Privately Held**
SIC: 2711 Newspapers: publishing only, not printed on site

(G-9881)
INDIGO HOME INC
230 5th Ave Ste 1916 (10001-7730)
PHONE....................................212 684-4146
Taniya Kapoor, *Ch of Bd*
◆ **EMP:** 6 **EST:** 2004
SALES (est): 798K **Privately Held**
WEB: www.indigohome.com
SIC: 2392 Blankets, comforters & beddings

(G-9882)
INDONESIAN IMPORTS INC (PA)
Also Called: Elliot Lucca
339 5th Ave Fl 2 (10016-5016)
PHONE....................................855 725-5656
Mark A Talucchi, *CEO*
◆ **EMP:** 60
SQ FT: 52,000
SALES (est): 8MM **Privately Held**
WEB: www.elliottlucca.com
SIC: 3911 5961 Earrings, precious metal; jewelry, mail order

(G-9883)
INDULGE DESSERTS HOLDINGS LLC (PA)
666 5th Ave Fl 27 (10103-0001)
PHONE....................................212 231-8600
Andy Unanue, *Mng Member*
EMP: 2
SALES (est): 2.4MM **Privately Held**
SIC: 2051 2024 Cakes, pies & pastries; dairy based frozen desserts

(G-9884)
INFINITY AUGMENTED REALITY INC
228 Park Ave S 61130 (10003-1502)
PHONE....................................917 677-2084
Motti Kushnir, *CEO*
Moshe Hogeg, *Ch of Bd*
Enon Landenberg, *President*
Ortal Zanzuri, *CFO*
EMP: 6
SALES (est): 179.5K **Privately Held**
SIC: 7372 Prepackaged software; custom computer programming services; computer software development & applications

(G-9885)
INFIRMARY NYC
1720 2nd Ave (10128-4411)
P.O. Box 286389 (10128-0004)
PHONE....................................504 606-6280
James Cottingham, *Principal*
EMP: 5
SALES (est): 148.1K **Privately Held**
SIC: 2085 Cordials & premixed alcoholic cocktails

(G-9886)
INFOBASE HOLDINGS INC (HQ)
Also Called: Learn360
132 W 31st St Fl 17 (10001-3406)
PHONE....................................212 967-8800
Mark D McDonnell, *President*
David Giuffre, *Editor*
Kayla Harrington, *Editor*
Jonathan Leith, *Editor*
Matthew Spearman, *Editor*
▲ **EMP:** 54 **EST:** 1940
SALES (est): 15.3MM
SALES (corp-wide): 16.2MM **Privately Held**
WEB: www.factsonfile.com
SIC: 2731 7372 Books: publishing only; prepackaged software
PA: Infobase Publishing Company
132 W 31st St Fl 17
New York NY 10001
212 967-8800

(G-9887)
INFOBASE PUBLISHING COMPANY (PA)
Also Called: Films Media Group
132 W 31st St Fl 17 (10001-3406)
PHONE....................................212 967-8800
Mark D McDonnell, *Ch of Bd*
Julia Unigovski, *Editor*
Zina Scarpulla, *Marketing Staff*
Domenic Durante, *Manager*
Trevor Smith, *IT/INT Sup*
EMP: 1
SALES (est): 16.2MM **Privately Held**
SIC: 2731 7372 Books: publishing only; prepackaged software

(G-9888)
INFORMA BUSINESS MEDIA INC (HQ)
Also Called: Penton Information Services
605 3rd Ave (10158-0180)
PHONE....................................212 204-4200
Patrick Martell, *CEO*
Margaret McCartney, *General Mgr*
Roger Randall, *General Mgr*
Jennifer Chun, *Principal*
Mary Hall, *Principal*
EMP: 179 **EST:** 1989
SQ FT: 83,000
SALES (est): 251.1MM
SALES (corp-wide): 3B **Privately Held**
WEB: www.primediabusiness.com
SIC: 2721 Magazines: publishing only, not printed on site
PA: Informa Plc
5 Howick Place
London SW1P
207 017-7483

(G-9889)
INFORMA MEDIA INC (DH)
Also Called: Penton Media - Aviation Week
605 3rd Ave Fl 22 (10158-0007)
PHONE....................................212 204-4200
David Kieselstein, *Ch of Bd*
Sandi Brown, *President*
Paul Miller, *President*
Francine Brasseur, *Publisher*
Geoff Belz, *Principal*
▲ **EMP:** 500 **EST:** 1976
SQ FT: 189,000
SALES (est): 182.2MM
SALES (corp-wide): 3B **Privately Held**
WEB: www.penton.com
SIC: 2721 7389 7313 7375 Magazines: publishing only, not printed on site; periodicals: publishing & printing; magazines: publishing & printing; advertising, promotional & trade show services; printed media advertising representatives; on-line data base information retrieval
HQ: Informa Business Media, Inc.
605 3rd Ave
New York NY 10158
212 204-4200

(G-9890)
INFORMA MEDIA INC
Also Called: Used Equipment Directory
1166 Ave Of The Americas (10036-2708)
PHONE....................................212 204-4200
James Mack, *Principal*
EMP: 9
SALES (corp-wide): 3B **Privately Held**
WEB: www.penton.com
SIC: 2721 Magazines: publishing & printing
HQ: Informa Media, Inc.
605 3rd Ave Fl 22
New York NY 10158
212 204-4200

(G-9891)
INFORMA SOLUTIONS INC
Also Called: Analytics Intell
45 Rockefeller Plz # 2000 (10111-0100)
PHONE....................................516 543-3733
David Bissainthe, *President*
EMP: 48 **EST:** 2015
SQ FT: 200
SALES (est): 1.1MM **Privately Held**
SIC: 7372 7373 7374 Prepackaged software; computer integrated systems design; data processing & preparation; data processing service

(G-9892)
INFORMA UK LTD
Lloyd's List Intelligence
52 Vanderbilt Ave Fl 7 (10017-3846)
PHONE....................................646 957-8966
EMP: 6
SALES (corp-wide): 3B **Privately Held**
SIC: 2711 Newspapers
HQ: Informa Uk Limited
5 Howick Place
London SW1P
207 017-6242

(G-9893)
INFORMATICA LLC
810 7th Ave Ste 1100c (10019-7597)
PHONE....................................212 845-7650
Michael Warthen, *Sales Staff*
Alistair Duguid, *Manager*
Ron Reichenbach, *Manager*
EMP: 11 **Privately Held**
SIC: 7372 Prepackaged software

PA: Informatica Llc
2100 Seaport Blvd
Redwood City CA 94063

(G-9894)
INFORMERLY INC
35 Essex St (10002-4712)
PHONE..................................646 238-7137
Ranjan Roy, *CEO*
Emily Moss, *President*
EMP: 5
SALES (est): 270K **Privately Held**
SIC: 7372 Prepackaged software

(G-9895)
INKKAS LLC
38 E 29th St Rm 6r (10016-7963)
PHONE..................................646 845-9803
Daniel Ben-Mun, *Mng Member*
EMP: 6
SALES (est): 698K **Privately Held**
SIC: 3021 Canvas shoes, rubber soled

(G-9896)
INNOFUN DIGITAL ENTRMT LLC
19 W 34th St Rm 1018 (10001-3006)
PHONE..................................347 708-0078
Wang Shiqiang, *CEO*
EMP: 15
SALES: 500K **Privately Held**
SIC: 7372 Application computer software

(G-9897)
INNOVATIVE DESIGNS LLC
141 W 36th St Fl 8 (10018-6980)
PHONE..................................212 695-0892
Douglas Haber, *Mng Member*
Ashley McMullan, *Director*
▲ **EMP:** 34
SQ FT: 8,000
SALES (est): 54MM **Privately Held**
SIC: 2678 3944 Stationery products; craft
& hobby kits & sets

(G-9898)
INNROAD INC
519 8th Ave Fl 15 (10018-4765)
PHONE..................................631 458-1437
Murat Ozsu, *CEO*
Ahmet Can, *Vice Pres*
Caitlin Terry, *Manager*
Harmeet Oberoi, *Master*
Christopher Frometa, *Advisor*
EMP: 30 **EST:** 2000
SALES: 1.5MM **Privately Held**
SIC: 7372 Business oriented computer
software
PA: Innroad Software Development Serv-
ices Private Limited
B Wing, 1st Floor Software Building 2
Hyderabad TS 50008

(G-9899)
INO-TEX LLC
135 W 36th St Fl 6 (10018-9482)
PHONE..................................212 400-2205
Yongjun Yu, *Director*
EMP: 6
SALES (est): 406K
SALES (corp-wide): 600.5MM **Privately
Held**
SIC: 2299 Batts & batting: cotton mill
waste & related material; ramie yarn,
thread, roving & textiles
PA: Jiangsu Lianfa Textile Co., Ltd.
No.88, Henglian Road, Chengdong
Town, Hai'an County
Nantong 22660
513 888-6906

(G-9900)
INORI JEWELS
580 5th Ave (10036-4701)
PHONE..................................347 703-5078
Guy Israeli, *Owner*
EMP: 10 **EST:** 2014
SALES (est): 748.5K **Privately Held**
SIC: 3911 Jewelry, precious metal

(G-9901)
INPROTOPIA CORPORATION
401 W 110th St Apt 2001 (10025-2445)
PHONE..................................917 338-7501
Souyun Lee, *CEO*
WEI-Yeh Lee, *Exec VP*
EMP: 11 **EST:** 2011

SALES (est): 616.4K **Privately Held**
SIC: 7372 7373 7371 Business oriented
computer software; systems software development services; computer software
systems analysis & design, custom

(G-9902)
**INSIGHT VENTURE PARTNERS
IV**
1114 Avenue Of The Americ (10036-7703)
PHONE..................................212 230-9200
Alex Crisses, *Partner*
EMP: 150
SALES (est): 120.2K **Privately Held**
SIC: 7372 Prepackaged software

(G-9903)
**INSPIRED ENTERTAINMENT INC
(PA)**
250 W 57th St Ste 2223 (10107-0013)
PHONE..................................646 565-3861
Luke L Alvarez, *CEO*
A Lorne Weil, *Ch of Bd*
Brooks Pierce, *President*
Daniel B Silvers, *Exec VP*
Stewart F B Baker, *CFO*
EMP: 19
SALES: 141.3MM **Publicly Held**
SIC: 7372 7993 7999 Prepackaged soft-
ware; arcades; gambling & lottery serv-
ices

(G-9904)
INSTANT STREAM INC
Also Called: Stream Police
1271 Ave Of The Americas (10020-1300)
PHONE..................................917 438-7182
Michael Daly III, *CEO*
EMP: 32
SALES (est): 2.3MM **Privately Held**
SIC: 2752 Commercial printing, litho-
graphic

(G-9905)
**INSTITUTE OF ELECTRICAL AND
EL**
Ieee Communications Society
3 Park Ave Fl 17 (10016-5902)
PHONE..................................212 705-8900
Christina Zarrello, *Editor*
David Bell, *Commander*
Paul McMenamin, *Vice Pres*
David Singer, *Vice Pres*
John Sivo, *Project Mgr*
EMP: 25
SALES (corp-wide): 494.3MM **Privately
Held**
SIC: 2721 Trade journals: publishing &
printing
PA: The Institute Of Electrical And Electron-
ics Engineers Incorporated
445 Hoes Ln
Piscataway NJ 08854
212 419-7900

(G-9906)
INT TRADING USA LLC
261 W 35th St Ste 1100 (10001-1900)
PHONE..................................212 760-2338
Sung Pak,
▲ **EMP:** 230 **EST:** 2004
SALES (est): 33.5MM **Privately Held**
SIC: 2325 2339 Men's & boys' trousers &
slacks; women's & misses' outerwear

(G-9907)
**INTEGRATED COPYRIGHT
GROUP**
Also Called: Evergreen
1745 Broadway 19 (10019-4640)
PHONE..................................615 329-3999
John Barker, *President*
EMP: 22
SALES (est): 1.4MM **Privately Held**
SIC: 2741 Music, sheet: publishing only,
not printed on site

(G-9908)
**INTEGRATED GRAPHICS INC
(PA)**
Also Called: I C S
7 W 36th St Fl 12 (10018-7154)
PHONE..................................212 592-5600
James Kearns, *President*
Jay Beber, *Vice Pres*

EMP: 5
SALES (est): 3.3MM **Privately Held**
WEB: www.integratedgraphics.com
SIC: 2759 8748 Commercial printing; busi-
ness consulting

(G-9909)
**INTELLIGNC THE FTR CMPTNG
NWSL**
Also Called: Intelligence Newsletter
360 Central Park W (10025-6541)
P.O. Box 20008 (10025-1510)
PHONE..................................212 222-1123
Edward Rosenfeld, *Owner*
EMP: 10
SALES (est): 445.4K **Privately Held**
WEB: www.eintelligence.com
SIC: 2721 Magazines: publishing only, not
printed on site

(G-9910)
INTELLITRAVEL MEDIA INC (DH)
530 Fashion Ave Rm 201 (10018-4821)
PHONE..................................646 695-6700
Nancy Telliho, *Ch of Bd*
Harold Shain, *President*
EMP: 8
SALES (est): 782.3K
SALES (corp-wide): 4.2B **Publicly Held**
SIC: 2721 Magazines: publishing only, not
printed on site
HQ: The Daily Beast Company Llc
7 Hanover Sq
New York NY 10004
212 445-4600

(G-9911)
INTER PARFUMS INC (PA)
551 5th Ave (10176-0001)
PHONE..................................212 983-2640
Jean Madar, *Ch of Bd*
Philippe Benacin, *President*
Debbie Nuzzo, *Vice Pres*
Russell Greenberg, *CFO*
Philippe Santi, *CFO*
▲ **EMP:** 68
SQ FT: 16,800
SALES: 675.5MM **Publicly Held**
WEB: www.interparfumsinc.com
SIC: 2844 Cosmetic preparations; per-
fumes & colognes

(G-9912)
INTER PARFUMS USA LLC
551 5th Ave Rm 1500 (10176-1599)
PHONE..................................212 983-2640
Jean Madar, *Ch of Bd*
Russell Greenberg, *CFO*
EMP: 7
SALES (est): 595.7K
SALES (corp-wide): 675.5MM **Publicly
Held**
SIC: 2844 Concentrates, perfume
PA: Inter Parfums, Inc.
551 5th Ave
New York NY 10176
212 983-2640

(G-9913)
INTERBRAND LLC
1 W 37th St Fl 9 (10018-5354)
PHONE..................................212 840-9595
Bob McMeekin, *President*
EMP: 9
SALES (corp-wide): 6MM **Privately Held**
WEB: www.interbrandllc.com
SIC: 2321 Men's & boys' furnishings
PA: Interbrand Llc
225 Dupont St Ste 2
Plainview NY 11803
516 349-5884

(G-9914)
**INTERCEPT
PHARMACEUTICALS INC (PA)**
10 Hudson Yards Fl 37 (10001-2160)
PHONE..................................646 747-1000
Mark Pruzanski, *President*
Christian Weyer, *Exec VP*
Richard Kim, *Senior VP*
Lisa Defrancesco, *Vice Pres*
Sandip S Kapadia, *CFO*
EMP: 72
SQ FT: 45,500
SALES: 179.8MM **Publicly Held**
SIC: 2834 Pharmaceutical preparations

(G-9915)
INTERFACEFLOR LLC
330 5th Ave Fl 12 (10001-3213)
PHONE..................................212 686-8284
Pete Waldron, *Manager*
EMP: 25
SALES (corp-wide): 1.1B **Publicly Held**
WEB: www.ca.interfaceinc.com
SIC: 2273 Finishers of tufted carpets &
rugs
HQ: Interfaceflor, Llc
1503 Orchard Hill Rd
Lagrange GA 30240
706 882-1891

(G-9916)
**INTERHELLENIC PUBLISHING
INC**
Also Called: Estiator
421 7th Ave Ste 810 (10001-2002)
PHONE..................................212 967-5016
Peter Makrias, *President*
EMP: 7
SQ FT: 1,500
SALES: 1.2MM **Privately Held**
WEB: www.estiator.com
SIC: 2721 Magazines: publishing only, not
printed on site

(G-9917)
**INTERNATIONAL AIDS VCCNE
INTTV (PA)**
125 Broad St Fl 9th (10004-2400)
PHONE..................................212 847-1111
Alex Godwin Coutinho, *Ch of Bd*
Margaret McGlynn, *President*
Thomas P Monath, *Partner*
David N Cook, *COO*
Lynn Doren, *Senior VP*
EMP: 95
SQ FT: 32,000
SALES: 72.3MM **Privately Held**
WEB: www.iavi.org
SIC: 2836 8731 Vaccines; commercial
physical research

(G-9918)
**INTERNATIONAL DATA GROUP
INC**
Also Called: Idg Technetwork
117 E 55th St Ste 204 (10022-3502)
PHONE..................................212 331-7883
EMP: 30
SALES (corp-wide): 3.5B **Privately Held**
SIC: 2721 8732 Periodicals-Publish-
ing/Printing Commercial Nonphysical Re-
search Business Services
PA: International Data Group, Inc.
1 Exeter Plz Fl 15
Boston MA 02116
617 534-1200

(G-9919)
**INTERNATIONAL DIRECT
GROUP INC**
Also Called: Idg
525 7th Ave Rm 208 (10018-5280)
PHONE..................................212 921-9036
Haynes Holding, *CEO*
Toby Williams, *General Mgr*
Joel Ratner, *Exec VP*
Wesley Matthews, *CFO*
Elysia Tietjen, *Accounts Exec*
◆ **EMP:** 30
SALES (est): 5.3MM **Privately Held**
WEB: www.internationaldg.com
SIC: 2331 7389 Blouses, women's & jun-
iors': made from purchased material; de-
sign services

(G-9920)
**INTERNATIONAL INSPIRATIONS
LLC (PA)**
358 5th Ave Rm 501 (10001-2228)
PHONE..................................212 465-8500
Saul Shaya Reiter, *CEO*
◆ **EMP:** 46
SQ FT: 1,000
SALES (est): 7.8MM **Privately Held**
SIC: 3961 Costume jewelry

(PA)=Parent Co (HQ)=Headquarters (DH)=Div Headquarters
✿ = New Business established in last 2 years
2020 Harris
New York Manufacturers Directory
377

G E O G R A P H I C

(G-9921)
INTERNATIONAL MGT NETWRK
445 Park Ave Fl 9 (10022-8606)
PHONE..................................646 401-0032
Jeff Krantz, *President*
EMP: 15
SALES: 950K **Privately Held**
SIC: 7372 Prepackaged software

(G-9922)
INTERNATIONAL OFFICE
Also Called: Ioc
110 Greene St Ste 1206 (10012-4319)
PHONE..................................212 334-4617
Marcello Pepori, *President*
Pratima Raichur, *Director*
▲ **EMP:** 5
SALES (est): 249.2K **Privately Held**
SIC: 2522 Office furniture, except wood
PA: International Office Concept Spa
Via Dell'artigianato 12
Giussano MB 20833

(G-9923)
INTERNATIONL STUDIOS INC
108 W 39th St Rm 1300 (10018-3614)
PHONE..................................212 819-1616
Alan S Ginsberg, *President*
EMP: 5
SALES (est): 360K **Privately Held**
SIC: 2211 Apparel & outerwear fabrics, cotton

(G-9924)
INTERNTNAL FLVORS FRGRNCES INC (PA)
Also Called: Iff
521 W 57th St (10019-2929)
PHONE..................................212 765-5500
Andreas Fibig, *Ch of Bd*
Anne Chwat, *Exec VP*
Francisco Fortanet, *Exec VP*
Gregory Yep, *Exec VP*
Bob Anderson, *Vice Pres*
EMP: 180
SALES: 3.9B **Publicly Held**
WEB: www.iff.com
SIC: 2869 2844 2087 Flavors or flavoring materials, synthetic; perfume materials, synthetic; toilet preparations; flavoring extracts & syrups

(G-9925)
INTERTEX USA INC
Also Called: B C America
131 W 35th St Fl 10 (10001-2111)
PHONE..................................212 279-3601
Yong Lee, *President*
Jesse Lee, *Software Dev*
EMP: 15
SQ FT: 6,500
SALES (est): 1MM **Privately Held**
SIC: 2221 2262 Specialty broadwoven fabrics, including twisted weaves; screen printing: manmade fiber & silk broadwoven fabrics

(G-9926)
INTERVIEW NEW YORK
77 Bleecker St (10012-1547)
PHONE..................................857 928-4120
Russell Cameron, *Principal*
EMP: 5
SALES (est): 219.5K **Privately Held**
SIC: 2721 Magazines: publishing only, not printed on site

(G-9927)
INTEVA PRODUCTS LLC
30 Rockefeller Plz (10112-0015)
PHONE..................................248 655-8886
Lon Offenbacher, *Branch Mgr*
EMP: 300
SALES (corp-wide): 4.1B **Privately Held**
SIC: 3089 Injection molding of plastics
HQ: Inteva Products, Llc
1401 Crooks Rd
Troy MI 48084

(G-9928)
INTIMATECO LLC
Also Called: Inteco Intimates
463 7th Ave Rm 602 (10018-8719)
PHONE..................................212 239-4411
Gaby Sutton,

Eli Levy,
◆ **EMP:** 8 **EST:** 2008
SALES (est): 3.9MM **Privately Held**
SIC: 2341 Women's & children's underwear

(G-9929)
INTRA-CELLULAR THERAPIES INC (PA)
430 E 29th St Ste 900 (10016-8367)
PHONE..................................646 440-9333
Sharon Mates, *Ch of Bd*
John A Bardi, *Senior VP*
Robert E Davis, *Senior VP*
Michael I Halstead, *Senior VP*
Kimberly E Vanover, *Senior VP*
▲ **EMP:** 49
SQ FT: 32,287
SALES (est): 982.6K **Publicly Held**
WEB: www.intracellulartherapies.com
SIC: 2834 8732 Pharmaceutical preparations; research services, except laboratory

(G-9930)
INTRALINKS HOLDINGS INC (HQ)
685 3rd Ave Fl 9 (10017-4151)
PHONE..................................212 543-7700
Leif Oleary, *CEO*
Wayne Berkowitz, *Senior VP*
Daren Glenister, *Vice Pres*
Kevin Merchant, *Vice Pres*
Peter Robinson, *Vice Pres*
EMP: 27
SALES (est): 201.3MM
SALES (corp-wide): 3.4B **Publicly Held**
SIC: 7372 7382 Prepackaged software; security systems services
PA: Ss&C Technologies Holdings, Inc.
80 Lamberton Rd
Windsor CT 06095
860 298-4500

(G-9931)
INTRAWORLDS INC
222 Broadway Fl 19 (10038-2550)
PHONE..................................631 602-5333
Stephan Herrlich, *President*
EMP: 5
SALES (est): 117.2K **Privately Held**
SIC: 7372 Application computer software

(G-9932)
INTSTRUX LLC
Also Called: Pixacore
15 W 39th St Fl 13 (10018-0627)
PHONE..................................646 688-2782
Sanjiv Mody, *President*
Daniel McNally, *Exec VP*
Thom Graves, *Vice Pres*
Anisha Mody, *Vice Pres*
Charles Hecht, *Marketing Staff*
EMP: 25
SQ FT: 7,500
SALES: 6.5MM **Privately Held**
SIC: 2834 Digitalis pharmaceutical preparations

(G-9933)
INTUITION PUBLISHING LIMITED
40 E 34th St Rm 1101 (10016-4501)
PHONE..................................212 838-7115
David Harrison, *Manager*
Francis McKeagney, *Officer*
Monica Janajri, *Advisor*
EMP: 7
SALES (corp-wide): 35.1MM **Privately Held**
SIC: 2741 Miscellaneous publishing
PA: Intuition Publishing Limited
Ifsc House
Dublin D01 R
160 543-00

(G-9934)
INTURN
22 W 19th St Ste 5l (10011-4204)
PHONE..................................212 639-9675
Ronen Lazar, *CEO*
Tony D'Annibale, *Senior VP*
Courtney Montgomery, *Vice Pres*
Brian Rogers, *Vice Pres*
Lisa Chiswick, *Buyer*
EMP: 6

SALES (est): 544.2K **Privately Held**
SIC: 7372 Business oriented computer software

(G-9935)
INVESTMENTNEWS LLC
685 3rd Ave (10017-4024)
PHONE..................................212 210-0100
Christine Shaw, *CEO*
Sarah Haase, *Manager*
Pablo Turcios, *Director*
Scott Valenzano, *Director*
EMP: 50
SALES (est): 2.5MM **Privately Held**
WEB: www.investmentnews.net
SIC: 2711 Newspapers, publishing & printing

(G-9936)
INVESTORS BUSINESS DAILY INC
140 E 45th St Ste 19b (10017-7143)
PHONE..................................212 626-7676
Janice Janendo, *Branch Mgr*
EMP: 18
SALES (corp-wide): 231.5MM **Privately Held**
WEB: www.investors.com
SIC: 2711 6282 Newspapers, publishing & printing; investment advice
HQ: Investor's Business Daily, Inc.
12655 Beatrice St
Los Angeles CA 90066
310 448-6000

(G-9937)
INVISION INC (HQ)
25 W 43rd St Ste 609 (10036-7422)
PHONE..................................212 557-5554
Steve Marshall, *CEO*
Maura Clancy, *Partner*
Teresa Taveras, *Partner*
David Fraga, *COO*
Kami Ragsdale, *COO*
EMP: 5
SALES (est): 1.2MM
SALES (corp-wide): 92.5MM **Privately Held**
SIC: 7372 Prepackaged software
PA: Mediaocean Llc
45 W 18th St
New York NY 10011
212 633-8100

(G-9938)
IPC/RAZOR LLC (PA)
277 Park Ave Fl 39 (10172-2901)
PHONE..................................212 551-4500
Douglas Korn, *Mng Member*
Douglas R Korn, *Mng Member*
EMP: 60 **EST:** 2010
SALES (est): 64.4MM **Privately Held**
SIC: 3541 Machine tools, metal cutting type

(G-9939)
IR MEDIA GROUP (USA) INC
25 Broadway Fl 9 (10004-1058)
PHONE..................................212 425-9649
Ian Richman, *Ch of Bd*
Ben Ashwell, *Editor*
Candice Monts-Petit, *Editor*
Andrea Pion, *Sales Staff*
Brigitte Toledano, *Sales Staff*
EMP: 30 **EST:** 1995
SALES (est): 1.7MM
SALES (corp-wide): 4MM **Privately Held**
WEB: www.irmag.com
SIC: 2731 Books: publishing only
HQ: Cross-Border Publishing (London) Limited
111-113 Great Titchfield Street
London

(G-9940)
IRIDESSE INC
600 Madison Ave Fl 5 (10022-1615)
PHONE..................................212 230-6000
Patrick B Dorsey, *President*
Judith A Baldissard, *Principal*
Michael W Connolly, *Principal*
James N Fernandez, *Principal*
Robert L Cepek, *Chairman*
EMP: 15
SALES (est): 1.9MM **Privately Held**
SIC: 3911 Necklaces, precious metal

(G-9941)
IRISH AMERICA INC
Also Called: Irish America Magazine
875 Americas Rm 2100 (10001-3586)
PHONE..................................212 725-2993
Niall O'Dowd, *Publisher*
Brendon Maclua, *Shareholder*
EMP: 20
SQ FT: 3,000
SALES (est): 1.9MM **Privately Held**
WEB: www.smurfitkappa.com
SIC: 2721 Magazines: publishing only, not printed on site
HQ: Smurfit Kappa Packaging Limited
Beech Hill
Dublin 4

(G-9942)
IRISH ECHO NEWSPAPER CORP
165 Madison Ave Rm 302 (10016-5431)
PHONE..................................212 482-4818
Peter Quinn, *Ch of Bd*
Tracey Quilligan, *Manager*
EMP: 19 **EST:** 1928
SQ FT: 3,000
SALES (est): 1.3MM **Privately Held**
WEB: www.irishecho.com
SIC: 2711 Newspapers: publishing only, not printed on site

(G-9943)
IRISH TRIBUNE INC
Also Called: Irish Voice Newspaper
875 Avenue Of The Amerrm2 Rm 2100 (10001)
PHONE..................................212 684-3366
Niell O'Dowd, *President*
Robert S Bennett, *Partner*
Sean E Crowley, *Partner*
Ann Marie Zito, *Opers Mgr*
EMP: 14
SALES (est): 744K **Privately Held**
WEB: www.smurfitkappa.com
SIC: 2711 Newspapers, publishing & printing
HQ: Smurfit Kappa Packaging Limited
Beech Hill
Dublin 4

(G-9944)
IRV INC
Also Called: Warshaw Jacobson Group
475 Park Ave S Fl 11 (10016-6901)
PHONE..................................212 334-4507
Steve Warshaw, *President*
Sal Mercadante, *President*
Jay Warshaw, *Vice Pres*
Charly Walter, *Marketing Mgr*
EMP: 23
SALES (est): 1.2MM **Privately Held**
SIC: 7372 7371 Prepackaged software; custom computer programming services

(G-9945)
ISFEL CO INC (PA)
Also Called: Top Stuff
110 W 34th St Rm 1101 (10001-2115)
PHONE..................................212 736-6216
Joseph Feldman, *President*
◆ **EMP:** 8 **EST:** 1948
SQ FT: 2,000
SALES (est): 3.1MM **Privately Held**
WEB: www.topstuff.com
SIC: 2369 Girls' & children's outerwear

(G-9946)
ISONICS CORPORATION
535 8th Ave Fl 3 (10018-4305)
PHONE..................................212 356-7400
EMP: 4
SALES: 22.1MM **Privately Held**
SIC: 2819 3674 Mfg Industrial Inorganic Chemicals Mfg Semiconductors/Related Devices

(G-9947)
ITC MFG GROUP INC
109 W 38th St Rm 701 (10018-3673)
PHONE..................................212 684-3696
Anthony Dadika, *President*
Irwin Jaeger, *Vice Pres*
EMP: 10
SQ FT: 6,000

▲ = Import ▼=Export
◆ =Import/Export

SALES (est): 1.4MM **Privately Held**
SIC: 2241 3965 2759 Labels, woven; fasteners, buttons, needles & pins; tags: printing

(G-9948)
ITOCHU PROMINENT USA LLC
1411 Broadway Fl 7 (10018-3401)
PHONE.................................212 827-5715
Takeshi Ogura, *President*
Tim Vecchione, *Vice Pres*
Thomas Poggioli, *CFO*
▲ **EMP:** 200
SQ FT: 1,500
SALES (est): 33.8MM **Privately Held**
WEB: www.itochu.com
SIC: 2326 2337 Men's & boys' work clothing; women's & misses' suits & skirts
HQ: Itochu International Inc.
1251 Ave Of The Amrcas 51
New York NY 10020
212 818-8000

(G-9949)
IVERIC BIO INC (PA)
1 Penn Plz Fl 35 (10119-3601)
PHONE.................................212 845-8200
David R Guyer, *Ch of Bd*
Glenn P Sblendorio, *President*
Keith Westby, *COO*
Henric Bjarke, *Vice Pres*
Allison Luo, *Vice Pres*
EMP: 30
SQ FT: 13,500
SALES (est): 50.9MM **Publicly Held**
SIC: 2834 Pharmaceutical preparations

(G-9950)
IZQUIERDO STUDIOS LTD
122 W 30th St (10001-4009)
PHONE.................................212 807-9757
Martin Izquierdo, *President*
EMP: 13
SALES (est): 1.1MM **Privately Held**
SIC: 2389 Theatrical costumes

(G-9951)
IZUN PHARMACEUTICALS CORP (PA)
1 Rockefeller Plz Fl 11 (10020-2073)
PHONE.................................212 618-6357
William Levine, *CEO*
Ronald Stern, *President*
Leslie Kraus, *CFO*
EMP: 13
SALES (est): 1.2MM **Privately Held**
WEB: www.izunpharma.com
SIC: 2834 Pharmaceutical preparations

(G-9952)
J & H CREATIONS INC
19 W 36th St Fl 3 (10018-7103)
PHONE.................................212 465-0962
Jay Baek, *President*
▲ **EMP:** 20
SQ FT: 2,000
SALES (est): 2.6MM **Privately Held**
WEB: www.jhcreation.com
SIC: 3961 5094 Costume jewelry, ex. precious metal & semiprecious stones; jewelry

(G-9953)
J & M TEXTILE CO INC
505 8th Ave Rm 701 (10018-4552)
PHONE.................................212 268-8000
▲ **EMP:** 11
SQ FT: 7,000
SALES (est): 1.1MM **Privately Held**
SIC: 2241 5131 Narrow Fabric Mill Whol Piece Goods/Notions

(G-9954)
J & X PRODUCTION INC
327 W 36th St 7f (10018-6405)
PHONE.................................718 200-1228
Guo Jun Lin, *President*
EMP: 10
SALES (est): 127K **Privately Held**
SIC: 2311 Men's & boys' suits & coats

(G-9955)
J EDLIN INTERIORS LTD
122 W 27th St Fl 2 (10001-6274)
PHONE.................................212 243-2111
Jeffrey Edlin, *President*

Joyse Edlin, *Vice Pres*
▲ **EMP:** 10
SALES (est): 1MM **Privately Held**
WEB: www.reisner.net
SIC: 2391 Curtains & draperies

(G-9956)
J PERCY FOR MRVIN RCHARDS LTD (HQ)
512 Fashion Ave (10018-4603)
PHONE.................................212 944-5300
Morris Goldfarb, *Ch of Bd*
Sammy Aaron, *President*
Andrew Reid, *Vice Pres*
Allan Inger, *CFO*
Lee Lipton, *Admin Sec*
◆ **EMP:** 40
SQ FT: 12,000
SALES (corp-wide): 4.4MM
SALES (corp-wide): 3B **Publicly Held**
SIC: 2386 2371 2337 2339 Coats & jackets, leather & sheep-lined; fur coats & other fur apparel; women's & misses' suits & coats; women's & misses' jackets & coats, except sportswear
PA: G-lii Apparel Group, Ltd.
512 7th Ave Fl 35
New York NY 10018
212 403-0500

(G-9957)
J R GOLD DESIGNS LTD
555 5th Ave Fl 19 (10017-2416)
PHONE.................................212 922-9292
Rami Uziel, *President*
Rina Uziel, *Principal*
EMP: 10
SQ FT: 2,500
SALES: 10MM **Privately Held**
WEB: www.rinalimor.com
SIC: 3911 5094 Jewelry, precious metal; jewelry

(G-9958)
J R NITES (PA)
1400 Broadway Fl 6 (10018-0728)
PHONE.................................212 354-9670
John Klein, *Principal*
EMP: 8
SALES (est): 1MM **Privately Held**
SIC: 2335 Women's, juniors' & misses' dresses

(G-9959)
J9 TECHNOLOGIES INC
25 Broadway Fl 9 (10004-1058)
PHONE.................................412 586-5038
Alan Wasserberger, *President*
Robert C Roach, *CTO*
EMP: 20
SALES (est): 2.7MM **Privately Held**
SIC: 7372 Operating systems computer software

(G-9960)
JAC USA INC
45 Broadway Ste 1810 (10006-3710)
PHONE.................................212 841-7430
Kazunari Okuda, *Ch of Bd*
Sinji Naka, *President*
EMP: 5
SQ FT: 1,400
SALES (est): 3.1MM **Privately Held**
WEB: www.jacusa.com
SIC: 3728 Aircraft parts & equipment
PA: Japan Aerospace Corporation
1-1-1, Minamiaoyama
Minato-Ku TKY 107-0

(G-9961)
JACKS AND JOKERS 52 LLC
215 E 68th St Apt 5o (10065-5720)
PHONE.................................917 740-2595
Scot Lerner,
EMP: 5
SALES (est): 631.3K **Privately Held**
SIC: 2321 Blouses, boys': made from purchased materials

(G-9962)
JACKSON DAKOTA INC (PA)
979 3rd Ave Ste 503 (10022-1393)
PHONE.................................212 838-9444
Dakota Jackson, *President*
Gwyneth Perrott, *Manager*
▲ **EMP:** 2

SQ FT: 5,500
SALES (est): 5.4MM **Privately Held**
WEB: www.dakotajackson.com
SIC: 2512 Upholstered household furniture

(G-9963)
JACLYN LLC (HQ)
500 7th Ave (10018-4502)
PHONE.................................201 909-6000
Robert Chestnov, *President*
Anthony Christon, *CFO*
▲ **EMP:** 75
SQ FT: 16,000
SALES (est): 38MM
SALES (corp-wide): 34.6MM **Privately Held**
WEB: www.jaclyninc.com
SIC: 3199 3111 2824 3172 Equestrian related leather articles; bag leather; vinyl fibers; cosmetic bags
PA: Jaclyn Holdings Parent Llc
197 W Spring Valley Ave
Maywood NJ 07607
201 909-6000

(G-9964)
JACMEL JEWELRY INC (PA)
1385 Broadway Fl 8 (10018-2102)
PHONE.................................718 349-4300
Jack Rahmey, *President*
Morris Dweck, *Vice Pres*
Scott Thomson, *Vice Pres*
Evan Barkley, *Treasurer*
Randy Leder, *Accounts Exec*
▲ **EMP:** 134 **EST:** 1977
SQ FT: 60,000
SALES (est): 90MM **Privately Held**
WEB: www.jacmel.com
SIC: 3911 Medals, precious or semiprecious metal

(G-9965)
JACOB HIDARY FOUNDATION INC
10 W 33rd St Rm 900 (10001-3317)
PHONE.................................212 736-6540
Abe Hidary, *President*
Jack A Hidary, *Vice Pres*
EMP: 10
SALES: 123.4K **Privately Held**
SIC: 2329 Men's & boys' sportswear & athletic clothing

(G-9966)
JACOBS & COHEN INC
Also Called: Sun Source
255 W 36th St Fl 9 (10018-7583)
PHONE.................................212 714-2702
Benjamin Cohen, *Ch of Bd*
Edward Jacobs, *President*
EMP: 25
SALES (est): 20.4K **Privately Held**
WEB: www.sunsourcejewelry.com
SIC: 3911 Jewelry, precious metal

(G-9967)
JAG FOOTWEAR ACC & RET CORP
1411 Broadway Fl 20 (10018-3471)
PHONE.................................800 999-1877
EMP: 6000 **Privately Held**
SIC: 3171 5661 5632 5139 Women's handbags & purses; handbags, women's; purses, women's; shoe stores; women's shoes; women's boots; apparel accessories; handbags; footwear; boots, canvas or leather: women's
HQ: Jag Footwear, Accessories And Retail Corporation
411 W Putnam Ave Fl 3
Greenwich CT 06830
239 301-3001

(G-9968)
JAGUAR CASTING CO INC
100 United Nations Plz 38a (10017-1713)
PHONE.................................212 869-0197
Puzant Khatchadourian, *President*
Jean Khatchadourian, *Vice Pres*
EMP: 25 **EST:** 1966
SQ FT: 5,000
SALES (est): 2.9MM **Privately Held**
SIC: 3915 3911 Jewelers' castings; jewelry, precious metal

(G-9969)
JAGUAR JEWELRY CASTING NY INC
48 W 48th St Ste 500 (10036-1713)
PHONE.................................212 768-4848
Hovig Kajajian, *President*
Kevork Vekerejian, *Owner*
Jack Hallak, *Vice Pres*
Jospeh Nakashian, *Info Tech Mgr*
EMP: 9
SQ FT: 2,500
SALES: 2MM **Privately Held**
SIC: 3911 Jewelry apparel

(G-9970)
JAKOB SCHLAEPFER INC
37 W 26th St Rm 208 (10010-1150)
PHONE.................................212 221-2323
Peter Anderegg, *President*
Shkendie Kaziu, *Vice Pres*
EMP: 3
SQ FT: 1,000
SALES (est): 1.3MM **Privately Held**
WEB: www.jakobschlaepfer.com
SIC: 2221 2241 Broadwoven fabric mills, manmade; trimmings, textile

(G-9971)
JAMES MORGAN PUBLISHING (PA)
5 Penn Plz Ste 2300 (10001-1821)
PHONE.................................212 655-5470
David L Hancock, *Chairman*
Cindy Sauer, *Vice Pres*
Nickcole Watkins, *Marketing Mgr*
Bethany Marshall, *Asst Director*
Aubrey Kosa, *Author*
EMP: 1
SALES (est): 2MM **Privately Held**
SIC: 2731 Books: publishing & printing

(G-9972)
JAMES THOMPSON & COMPANY INC (PA)
463 7th Ave Rm 1603 (10018-7421)
PHONE.................................212 686-4242
Nicholas Griseto, *President*
Barry Garr, *Vice Pres*
Terry Schultz, *Manager*
▲ **EMP:** 42 **EST:** 1860
SALES (est): 13MM **Privately Held**
WEB: www.jamesthompson.com
SIC: 2299 Burlap, jute

(G-9973)
JANE BOHAN INC
611 Broadway (10012-2608)
PHONE.................................212 529-6090
Jane Bohan, *President*
Laura Bothfeld, *Vice Pres*
▲ **EMP:** 6
SQ FT: 300
SALES: 970K **Privately Held**
SIC: 3911 Jewelry, precious metal

(G-9974)
JANES DESIGNER YRN PTTRNS INC
Also Called: Jane Knitting Kit
1745 Broadway Ste 1750 (10019-4640)
PHONE.................................347 260-3071
Jane Klein, *Principal*
EMP: 6
SQ FT: 50
SALES: 6K **Privately Held**
SIC: 2282 5949 Knitting yarn: twisting, winding or spooling; sewing, needlework & piece goods

(G-9975)
JANICE MOSES REPRESENTS
99 Battery Pl Apt 10d (10280-1324)
PHONE.................................212 898-4898
Janice Moses, *Principal*
EMP: 5
SALES (est): 354.1K **Privately Held**
SIC: 2672 Coated paper, except photographic, carbon or abrasive

(G-9976)
JAPAN PRINTING & GRAPHICS INC
48 Wall St Fl 5 (10005-2911)
PHONE.................................212 406-2905

Hiroshi Ono, *President*
Shinjiro Kokawa, *Production*
EMP: 7
SALES (est): 500K **Privately Held**
WEB: www.japanprint.com
SIC: 2759 2752 Commercial printing;
commercial printing, lithographic

(G-9977)
JARVIK HEART INC
333 W 52nd St Ste 700 (10019-6238)
PHONE................................212 397-3911
Robert Jarvik MD, *President*
Kamal Gandhi, *Vice Pres*
Catherine Andrus, *Engineer*
Latha Kavala, *Engineer*
Robert Scharp, *Engineer*
EMP: 36
SALES (est): 6.7MM **Privately Held**
WEB: www.jarvikheart.com
SIC: 3845 Surgical support systems: heart-
lung machine, exc. iron lung

(G-9978)
JASANI DESIGNS USA INC
28 W 44th St Ste 1014 (10036-7431)
PHONE................................212 257-6465
Ameya S Joshi, *President*
Grace Kosovitch, *Controller*
Mary Soriano, *Office Admin*
EMP: 8
SALES (est): 2.1MM **Privately Held**
SIC: 3911 Jewelry, precious metal
PA: Jasani
Hw - 6010, 6th Floor,
Mumbai MH 40005

(G-9979)
JAX COCO USA LLC
5 Penn Plz Ste 2300 (10001-1821)
PHONE................................347 688-8198
John Craig, *COO*
Greg Ritter, *Sales Staff*
Joel McMinn, *Regional*
▲ **EMP:** 5 **EST:** 2013
SALES: 300K **Privately Held**
SIC: 2076 Coconut oil

(G-9980)
**JAY STRONGWATER HOLDINGS
LLC (HQ)**
12 W 21st St Fl 11 (10010-7097)
PHONE................................646 657-0558
John J Ling, *CEO*
Brenda Jordan, *Accounts Exec*
▲ **EMP:** 1000
SALES (est): 126.5MM
SALES (corp-wide): 200.2MM **Privately
Held**
SIC: 3499 3911 3471 3229 Picture
frames, metal; jewelry, precious metal;
decorative plating & finishing of formed
products; glassware, art or decorative
PA: Rauch Industries, Inc.
3800a Little Mountain Rd
Gastonia NC 28056
704 867-5333

(G-9981)
JAYA APPAREL GROUP LLC
1384 Broadway Fl 18 (10018-6122)
PHONE................................212 764-4980
Don Lewis, *Branch Mgr*
EMP: 20
SALES (corp-wide): 23.8MM **Privately
Held**
SIC: 2339 Women's & misses' athletic
clothing & sportswear
PA: Jaya Apparel Group Llc
5175 S Soto St
Vernon CA 90058
323 584-3500

(G-9982)
JAYDEN STAR LLC
385 5th Ave Rm 507 (10016-3346)
PHONE................................212 686-0400
Maurice Mandelbaum, *Vice Pres*
Jason Mandelbaum, *Mng Member*
Steven Tam, *Info Tech Dir*
EMP: 30
SQ FT: 5,000
SALES (est): 1.7MM **Privately Held**
SIC: 3911 5094 Jewelry apparel; jewelry &
precious stones

(G-9983)
JAYMAR JEWELRY CO INC
69 5th Ave Apt 8d (10003-3008)
PHONE................................212 564-4788
Jayson Levy, *President*
EMP: 5
SQ FT: 3,000
SALES (est): 551.2K **Privately Held**
SIC: 3961 Costume jewelry, ex. precious
metal & semiprecious stones

(G-9984)
JBS LIMITED
1400 Broadway Rm 1703 (10018-0671)
PHONE................................212 764-4600
Shari Levine, *President*
EMP: 24
SQ FT: 10,000 **Privately Held**
SIC: 2335 5621 Bridal & formal gowns;
women's specialty clothing stores
PA: J.B.S., Limited
1375 Broadway Fl 4
New York NY 10018

(G-9985)
JBS LIMITED (PA)
Also Called: Pisarro Nights
1375 Broadway Fl 4 (10018-7001)
PHONE................................212 221-8403
Shari Levine, *Ch of Bd*
Mike Mann, *President*
◆ **EMP:** 30
SALES (est): 5MM **Privately Held**
SIC: 2335 Bridal & formal gowns

(G-9986)
JC CALIFORNIA INC
359 Broadway Fl 3 (10013-3932)
PHONE................................212 334-4380
Hayati Banastey, *President*
EMP: 5
SALES (est): 186.2K **Privately Held**
SIC: 2389 Apparel & accessories

(G-9987)
JC CRYSTAL INC
260 W 35th St Fl 10 (10001-2528)
PHONE................................212 594-0858
Jimmy Ping Chong Loh, *President*
▲ **EMP:** 50
SQ FT: 5,000
SALES: 5.8MM **Privately Held**
SIC: 3911 Jewelry apparel

(G-9988)
**JCDECAUX MALLSCAPE LLC
(DH)**
350 5th Ave Fl 73 (10118-7401)
PHONE................................646 834-1200
Bernard Pariost,
Jean-Luc Decaux,
EMP: 14
SALES (est): 1.9MM
SALES (corp-wide): 9.5MM **Privately
Held**
SIC: 2531 Benches for public buildings
HQ: Jcdecaux North America, Inc.
350 5th Ave Fl 73
New York NY 10118
646 834-1200

(G-9989)
JDS GRAPHICS INC
Also Called: Jds Graphics
226 W 37th St Fl 10 (10018-9016)
PHONE................................973 330-3300
Debra Yuran, *President*
Sheryl Heller, *Vice Pres*
Jeffery Kirschenbaum, *Vice Pres*
EMP: 12
SQ FT: 2,500
SALES (est): 1.1MM **Privately Held**
WEB: www.jdsgraphics.com
SIC: 2752 Commercial printing, offset

(G-9990)
**JEAN PHILIPPE FRAGRANCES
LLC**
551 5th Ave Rm 1500 (10176-1599)
PHONE................................212 983-2640
Jean Madar,
Russell Greenberg,
◆ **EMP:** 57
SQ FT: 7,000

SALES (est): 9.9MM
SALES (corp-wide): 675.5MM **Publicly
Held**
WEB: www.interparfumsinc.com
SIC: 2844 Perfumes & colognes
PA: Inter Parfums, Inc.
551 5th Ave
New York NY 10176
212 983-2640

(G-9991)
JEANJER LLC
Also Called: Just For Men Div
1400 Broadway Fl 15 (10018-5300)
PHONE................................212 944-1330
Joe Nakash, *President*
AVI Naakash, *Vice Pres*
Ralph Nakash, *Treasurer*
Charles Flores, *Sales Staff*
John Banevicius 6463838123, *Manager*
▲ **EMP:** 3000
SALES (est): 105.7MM **Privately Held**
SIC: 2331 2337 2339 2369 Blouses,
women's & juniors': made from purchased
material; suits: women's, misses' & jun-
iors'; slacks: women's, misses' & juniors';
girls' & children's outerwear

(G-9992)
JEFF COOPER INC
15 W 47th St Ste 1602 (10036-5703)
PHONE................................516 333-8200
Jeff Cooper, *President*
Laurie Cooper, *Vice Pres*
David Cooper, *Manager*
EMP: 12 **EST:** 1978
SALES (est): 1.8MM **Privately Held**
WEB: www.jcplatinum.com
SIC: 3911 Rings, finger: precious metal

(G-9993)
JEMCAP SERVICING LLC
360 Madison Ave Rm 1902 (10017-7158)
PHONE................................212 213-9353
Marsh Peter, *Principal*
EMP: 5 **EST:** 2015
SALES (est): 278.6K **Privately Held**
SIC: 1389 Roustabout service

(G-9994)
**JENALEX CREATIVE
MARKETING INC**
116 E 57th St Fl 3 (10022-2613)
PHONE................................212 935-2266
Alexandra Grondahl, *President*
Ludwig J Cserhat, *Corp Secy*
▲ **EMP:** 7
SQ FT: 2,000
SALES (est): 800.2K **Privately Held**
WEB: www.jenalex.com
SIC: 3999 Boutiquing: decorating gift items
with sequins, fruit, etc.

(G-9995)
JERRY SORBARA FURS INC
39 W 32nd St Rm 1400 (10001-3841)
PHONE................................212 594-3897
Jerry Sorbara, *President*
Sal Sorbara, *Vice Pres*
Catherine Wilson, *Treasurer*
EMP: 11 **EST:** 1975
SQ FT: 4,500
SALES: 2MM **Privately Held**
SIC: 2371 Apparel, fur

(G-9996)
JEWELS BY STAR LTD
Also Called: JB Star
555 5th Ave Fl 7 (10017-9267)
PHONE................................212 308-3490
Yehuda Fouzailoff, *President*
Yehuda Feodailoff, *President*
Rafael Fouzailoff, *Vice Pres*
EMP: 20
SQ FT: 2,000
SALES (est): 2.6MM **Privately Held**
WEB: www.jewelsbystar.com
SIC: 3911 Jewelry, precious metal

(G-9997)
JEWELTEX MFG CORP
48 W 48th St Ste 507 (10036-1713)
PHONE................................212 921-8188
Barry Rosenfeld, *President*
Joe Itzkowitx, *Admin Sec*
EMP: 13

SQ FT: 1,500
SALES (est): 2.3MM **Privately Held**
SIC: 3911 Jewelry, precious metal

(G-9998)
JEWISH WEEK INC (PA)
1501 Broadway Ste 505 (10036-5504)
PHONE................................212 921-7822
Rich Waloff, *Publisher*
Gary Rosenblatt, *Principal*
Robert Goldblum, *Editor*
Stephanie Leone, *Accounts Exec*
Ani Vuolo, *Sales Executive*
EMP: 35 **EST:** 1970
SQ FT: 6,000
SALES: 7MM **Privately Held**
WEB: www.thejewishweek.com
SIC: 2711 Newspapers: publishing only,
not printed on site

(G-9999)
**JFE ENGINEERING
CORPORATION**
350 Park Ave Fl 27th (10022-6022)
PHONE................................212 310-9320
Hedenori Tawaza, *Branch Mgr*
EMP: 10 **Privately Held**
SIC: 3312 Sheet or strip, steel, hot-rolled
PA: Jfe Engineering Corporation
1-8-1, Marunouchi
Chiyoda-Ku TKY 100-0

(G-10000)
JFE STEEL AMERICA INC (HQ)
600 3rd Ave Fl 12 (10016-1921)
PHONE................................212 310-9320
Kaoru Okamoto, *President*
Ann Fronimakas, *Admin Sec*
EMP: 7
SALES (est): 2.1MM **Privately Held**
SIC: 3312 Sheet or strip, steel, hot-rolled

(G-10001)
JFS INC (HQ)
Also Called: Joe Fresh
531 W 26th St Unit 531 # 531
(10001-5514)
PHONE................................646 264-1200
Mario Grauso, *President*
Doris Josovitz, *Manager*
EMP: 21 **EST:** 2010
SALES (est): 3.3MM
SALES (corp-wide): 35.4B **Privately Held**
SIC: 2253 T-shirts & tops, knit
PA: Loblaw Companies Limited
1 Presidents Choice Cir
Brampton ON L6Y 5
905 459-2500

(G-10002)
JGX LLC
1407 Broadway Rm 1416 (10018-2842)
PHONE................................212 575-1244
Nouri Jaradeh, *Vice Pres*
Jack Grazi, *Vice Pres*
EMP: 5
SQ FT: 3,000
SALES (est): 95.7K **Privately Held**
SIC: 2369 Leggings: girls', children's & in-
fants'

(G-10003)
**JILL FAGIN ENTERPRISES INC
(PA)**
Also Called: Jillery
39 E 12th St Apt 612 (10003-4621)
PHONE................................212 674-9383
Jill Fagin, *President*
EMP: 8
SALES: 670K **Privately Held**
SIC: 3961 3262 Costume jewelry; vitreous
china table & kitchenware

(G-10004)
JIM WACHTLER INC
1212 Avenue Of The (10036)
PHONE................................212 755-4367
James Wachtler, *President*
EMP: 3
SALES: 3MM **Privately Held**
SIC: 3915 5094 5944 Gems, real & imita-
tion: preparation for settings; diamond
cutting & polishing; precious stones
(gems); jewelry, precious stones & pre-
cious metals

▲ = Import ▼=Export
◆ =Import/Export

(G-10005)
JIMEALE INCORPORATED
130 Church St Ste 163 (10007-2226)
P.O. Box 841, Southport CT (06890-0841)
PHONE..................................917 686-5383
▲ EMP: 6
SALES (est): 692.9K Privately Held
SIC: 2389 Mfg Accessories

(G-10006)
JIMMY CRYSTAL NEW YORK CO LTD
47 W 37th St Fl 3 (10018-6294)
PHONE..................................212 594-0858
Ping Chong Loh, Ch of Bd
Alice Chui, Vice Pres
▲ EMP: 32
SQ FT: 13,500
SALES (est): 3.4MM Privately Held
SIC: 3231 3911 Watch crystals, glass;
jewelry, precious metal

(G-10007)
JIRANIMO INDUSTRIES LTD
Also Called: Long Paige
49a W 37th St (10018-6202)
PHONE..................................212 921-5106
Parviz Shirian, President
Aaron Ostad, President
Adam Ostad, Vice Pres
Shamouiel Ostad, Treasurer
▲ EMP: 12
SQ FT: 17,500
SALES (est): 1.3MM Privately Held
SIC: 2335 Women's, juniors' & misses'
dresses

(G-10008)
JJ BASICS LLC (PA)
1400 Broadway 14 (10018-5300)
PHONE..................................212 768-4779
Steven Bensadigh, President
Vivien Zhao, Vice Pres
Subhash Parikh, Controller
Randi Gefen, VP Sales
Jhislaine Diaz, Manager
▲ EMP: 21
SALES (est): 2.2MM Privately Held
SIC: 2253 Sweaters & sweater coats, knit

(G-10009)
JJ FANTASIA INC
38 W 32nd St (10001-3816)
PHONE..................................212 868-1198
Cheng Hsuan Wu, Ch of Bd
EMP: 7
SALES (est): 630.1K Privately Held
SIC: 3961 Jewelry apparel, non-precious
metals

(G-10010)
JM MANUFACTURER INC
241 W 37th St Rm 924 (10018-6970)
PHONE..................................212 869-0626
Liuchu Jia, Principal
EMP: 3
SQ FT: 700
SALES (est): 4.1MM Privately Held
SIC: 2221 Apparel & outerwear fabric,
manmade fiber or silk

(G-10011)
JM STUDIO INC
247 W 35th St Fl 3 (10001-1926)
PHONE..................................646 546-5514
Yim Lan Dong, CEO
▲ EMP: 15
SQ FT: 6,000
SALES (est): 1.7MM Privately Held
SIC: 2389 5699 Uniforms & vestments;
sports apparel

(G-10012)
JOAN BOYCE LTD (PA)
19 W 44th St Ste 417 (10036-5900)
PHONE..................................212 867-7474
Joan Boyce, President
Allen Boyce, Vice Pres
EMP: 4
SQ FT: 1,100
SALES: 7MM Privately Held
WEB: www.joanboyce.com
SIC: 3911 5944 Jewelry, precious metal;
jewelry stores

(G-10013)
JOBSON MEDICAL INFORMATION LLC (DH)
395 Hudson St Fl 3 (10014-7455)
PHONE..................................212 274-7000
Michael Tansey, CEO
Michael J Bender, Partner
Addie Blackburn, Publisher
Tom Lamond, Publisher
Donna Gindy, COO
▲ EMP: 120 EST: 1958
SALES (est): 72.7MM
SALES (corp-wide): 705MM Privately
Held
WEB: www.revoptom.com
SIC: 2721 2741 Magazines: publishing &
printing; miscellaneous publishing
HQ: Jobson Medical Information Holdings
Llc
440 9th Ave Fl 14
New York NY 10001
212 274-7000

(G-10014)
JOE BENBASSET INC (PA)
213 W 35th St Fl 11 (10001-0208)
PHONE..................................212 594-8440
Murray Benbasset, President
◆ EMP: 25 EST: 1948
SQ FT: 10,000
SALES (est): 5.5MM Privately Held
SIC: 2339 Sportswear, women's

(G-10015)
JOED PRESS
242 W 36th St Fl 8 (10018-7542)
PHONE..................................212 243-3620
Angela Vann, General Mgr
EMP: 5 EST: 2010
SALES (est): 268.1K Privately Held
SIC: 2759 Commercial printing

(G-10016)
JOHN KOCHIS CUSTOM DESIGNS
237 W 35th St Ste 502 (10001-1905)
PHONE..................................212 244-6046
John Kochis, Owner
EMP: 7
SALES: 300K Privately Held
SIC: 2311 Tailored suits & formal jackets

(G-10017)
JOHN KRISTIANSEN NEW YORK INC
665 Broadway Frnt (10012-2300)
PHONE..................................212 388-1097
John Kristiansen, President
EMP: 10
SALES (est): 953.1K Privately Held
SIC: 2389 Costumes

(G-10018)
JOHN N FEHLINGER CO INC (PA)
20 Vesey St Rm 1000 (10007-4225)
PHONE..................................212 233-5656
Kevin Arcuri, President
John Capuano, Treasurer
Ruth Hoffman, Asst Treas
James Talerico, Manager
Sheree Pelmen, Admin Sec
▲ EMP: 15 EST: 1945
SQ FT: 4,000
SALES (est): 5MM Privately Held
WEB: www.fehlingerco.com
SIC: 3491 3561 5084 5085 Steam traps;
pumps & pumping equipment; industrial
pumps & parts; industrial machinery &
equipment; water pumps (industrial);
valves & fittings

(G-10019)
JOHN SZOKE GRAPHICS INC
Also Called: John Szoke Editions
24 W 57th St Ste 304 (10019-3918)
PHONE..................................212 219-8300
John Szoke, President
▲ EMP: 8
SQ FT: 10,000
SALES (est): 520K Privately Held
WEB: www.johnszokeeditions.com
SIC: 2741 Miscellaneous publishing

(G-10020)
JOLIBE ATELIER LLC
325 W 38th St Studio (10018)
PHONE..................................917 319-5908
Joel Diaz, President
EMP: 10 EST: 2007
SALES: 1.7MM Privately Held
SIC: 2389 Men's miscellaneous acces-
sories

(G-10021)
JON TERI SPORTS INC (PA)
241 W 37th St Frnt 2 (10018-6797)
PHONE..................................212 398-0657
Rickie Freeman, President
Leora Platt, Sales Staff
▲ EMP: 35 EST: 1981
SQ FT: 6,000
SALES (est): 4.5MM Privately Held
SIC: 2335 2337 Women's, juniors' &
misses' dresses; suits: women's, misses'
& juniors'

(G-10022)
JONATHAN MEIZLER LLC
Also Called: Title of Work
57 Orchard St (10002-5414)
PHONE..................................212 213-2977
Jonathan Meizler, Mng Member
EMP: 7
SQ FT: 1,500
SALES (est): 418K Privately Held
SIC: 2389 Men's miscellaneous acces-
sories

(G-10023)
JONATHAN MICHAEL COAT CORP
463 Fashion Ave Rm 1502 (10018-7596)
PHONE..................................212 239-9230
Bruce Heart, President
Nathan Printz, Corp Secy
▲ EMP: 7
SQ FT: 1,500
SALES (est): 840.5K Privately Held
SIC: 2339 Women's & misses' jackets &
coats, except sportswear

(G-10024)
JORDACHE ENTERPRISES INC
Fubu Jeans By Je Sport Co Div
1400 Broadway Rm 1415 (10018-5336)
PHONE..................................212 944-1330
Ezri Sirveb, Branch Mgr
EMP: 100
SALES (corp-wide): 1.3B Privately Held
WEB: www.jordache.com
SIC: 2339 2325 2369 2331 Slacks:
women's, misses' & juniors'; men's &
boys' trousers & slacks; slacks: girls' &
children's; jackets: girls', children's & infants'; shirts, women's & juniors': made
from purchased materials; men's & boys'
furnishings; shirts: girls', children's & infants'
PA: Jordache Enterprises Inc.
1400 Broadway Rm 1400 # 1400
New York NY 10018
212 643-8400

(G-10025)
JORDACHE ENTERPRISES INC (PA)
1400 Broadway Rm 1400 # 1400
(10018-5336)
PHONE..................................212 643-8400
Joe Nakash, CEO
Ralph Nakash, Corp Secy
Linda Cammarano, Vice Pres
Shaul Cohen, Vice Pres
Matt Debnar, Vice Pres
◆ EMP: 145
SALES (est): 1.3B Privately Held
WEB: www.jordache.com
SIC: 2339 2325 2369 2331 Slacks:
women's, misses' & juniors'; men's &
boys' trousers & slacks; slacks: girls' &
children's; jackets: girls', children's & in-
fants'; shirts, women's & juniors': made
from purchased materials; men's & boys'
furnishings; shirts: girls', children's & in-
fants'

(G-10026)
JOSEPH (UK) INC
1061 Madison Ave Grnd (10028-0239)
PHONE..................................212 570-0077
Hiroaki Sumi, Ch of Bd
Louis Loketch, Principal
EMP: 5
SALES (est): 527.5K Privately Held
SIC: 2329 5621 5651 Men's & boys'
sportswear & athletic clothing; women's
clothing stores; jeans stores

(G-10027)
JOSEPH INDUSTRIES INC (PA)
Also Called: Color Fx
1410 Broadway Rm 1201 (10018-9348)
PHONE..................................212 764-0010
Prakash Joseph, President
Alex Goldberg, Vice Pres
Peter Goldberger, CTO
▲ EMP: 50
SALES (est): 5.6MM Privately Held
SIC: 2389 Men's miscellaneous acces-
sories

(G-10028)
JOSEPH TREU SUCCESSORS INC
104 W 27th St Rm 5b (10001-0242)
PHONE..................................212 691-7026
Harvey Schreibman, President
Arlene Schreibman, Corp Secy
EMP: 5
SQ FT: 3,000
SALES: 700K Privately Held
SIC: 3953 Embossing seals & hand
stamps

(G-10029)
JOSIE ACCESSORIES INC
Also Called: Elrene Home Fashions
261 5th Ave Fl 10 (10016-7701)
PHONE..................................212 889-6376
Bryan Siegel, Ch of Bd
Craig Siegel, Vice Pres
Richard Orent, CFO
◆ EMP: 90 EST: 1945
SQ FT: 20,000
SALES (est): 11.4MM Privately Held
SIC: 2392 Tablecloths: made from pur-
chased materials; placemats, plastic or
textile

(G-10030)
JOTALY INC
Also Called: Andin International Inc.
1385 Broadway Fl 12 (10018-6118)
PHONE..................................212 886-6000
Ofer Azrielant, Ch of Bd
John C Esposito, Vice Pres
Isaac E Drucker, Asst Sec
▲ EMP: 750
SQ FT: 48,000
SALES (est): 87.8MM
SALES (corp-wide): 225.3B Publicly
Held
WEB: www.andin.com
SIC: 3911 Jewelry, precious metal
HQ: Richline Group, Inc.
1385 Broadway Fl 14
New York NY 10018

(G-10031)
JOVANI FASHION LTD
1370 Broadway Fl 4 (10018-7786)
PHONE..................................212 279-0222
Saul Maslavi, President
Abraham Maslavi, Vice Pres
▲ EMP: 30
SQ FT: 8,000
SALES (est): 3.8MM Privately Held
WEB: www.jovani.com
SIC: 2335 Gowns, formal

(G-10032)
JPL DESIGNS LTD
343 E 30th St Apt 3k (10016-6409)
PHONE..................................212 689-7096
John Leveroni, Ch of Bd
EMP: 8
SALES (est): 686.9K Privately Held
SIC: 3449 Miscellaneous metalwork

(G-10033)
JR LICENSING LLC
Also Called: Judith Ripka Fine Jewelry
1333 Broadway Fl 10 (10018-1064)
PHONE....................................212 244-1230
Judith Ripka, *Mng Member*
EMP: 9
SALES (est): 2.9MM
SALES (corp-wide): 35.4MM **Publicly Held**
SIC: 3911 5094 5944 Jewelry apparel; jewelry; jewelry stores
PA: Xcel Brands, Inc.
1333 Broadway Fl 10
New York NY 10018
347 727-2474

(G-10034)
JRG APPAREL GROUP COMPANY LTD (DH)
Also Called: Indigo Rein
1407 Broadway Rm 817 (10018-3287)
PHONE....................................212 997-0900
Jay Gorman, *Ch of Bd*
▲ EMP: 24
SQ FT: 3,300
SALES (est): 21.8MM
SALES (corp-wide): 128.3K **Privately Held**
SIC: 2211 Denims
HQ: Cherry Group Co., Ltd.
25f,Cherry Mansion, No.2, Nanjing Rd.,Shinan District
Qingdao 26607
532 857-9716

(G-10035)
JS BLANK & CO INC
112 Madison Ave Fl 7 (10016-7484)
PHONE....................................212 689-4835
Joseph S Blank, *CEO*
Barbara Blank, *Vice Pres*
EMP: 25
SQ FT: 7,500
SALES (est): 2.6MM **Privately Held**
SIC: 2323 Men's & boys' neckwear

(G-10036)
JSA JEWELRY INC
38 W 48th St Ste 801 (10036-1805)
PHONE....................................212 764-4504
Norayr Mayisoglu, *President*
EMP: 10
SALES (est): 905.1K **Privately Held**
SIC: 3911 Jewelry, precious metal

(G-10037)
JUDYS GROUP INC
226 W 37th St Fl 7 (10018-0659)
PHONE....................................212 921-0515
Howard Schlossberg, *President*
Michelle Pepper, *CFO*
▲ EMP: 50
SQ FT: 11,000
SALES (est): 10.5MM **Privately Held**
WEB: www.judysgroup.com
SIC: 2337 2339 2335 Suits: women's, misses' & juniors'; athletic clothing: women's, misses' & juniors'; women's, juniors' & misses' dresses

(G-10038)
JULIUS KLEIN GROUP
580 5th Ave Ste 500 (10036-4727)
PHONE....................................212 719-1811
Julius Klein, *Owner*
Moshe Klein, *Sales Dir*
Sidney Mandel, *Sales Executive*
Gidon Presser, *CTO*
▲ EMP: 50
SALES (est): 4.4MM **Privately Held**
SIC: 3915 Diamond cutting & polishing

(G-10039)
JULIUS LOWY FRAME RESTORING CO
232 E 59th St 4fn (10022-1464)
PHONE....................................212 861-8585
Lawrence A Shar, *President*
Patty Tan, *Human Resources*
EMP: 35
SQ FT: 20,000
SALES (est): 4.2MM **Privately Held**
WEB: www.lowyonline.com
SIC: 2499 8999 Picture frame molding, finished; art restoration

(G-10040)
JUMP DESIGN GROUP INC (PA)
Also Called: Jump Design Group, The
1400 Broadway Fl 2 (10018-1075)
PHONE....................................212 869-3300
Glenn Schlossberg, *CEO*
Terry Friedman, *President*
Peter Gabbe, *Principal*
Jodie Mendoza, *Vice Pres*
Joann Abellar, *Project Mgr*
▲ EMP: 110
SQ FT: 18,000
SALES (est): 35MM **Privately Held**
WEB: www.jumpapparel.com
SIC: 2335 Women's, juniors' & misses' dresses

(G-10041)
JUMPROPE INC
121 W 27th St Ste 1204 (10001-6261)
PHONE....................................347 927-5867
Jesse Olsen, *CEO*
Justin Meyer, *COO*
Nathan Patton, *Engineer*
EMP: 9
SQ FT: 500
SALES (est): 507.5K **Privately Held**
SIC: 7372 Educational computer software

(G-10042)
JUNE JACOBS LABS LLC
460 Park Ave Fl 16 (10022-1829)
PHONE....................................212 471-4830
Tiffany Cavallaro, *Vice Pres*
Priya Panchal, *Purchasing*
Tamara Ramos, *Marketing Staff*
Violet Lee, *Director*
Marvin Sternlicht,
EMP: 64
SALES (corp-wide): 16.4MM **Privately Held**
SIC: 2844 Cosmetic preparations
PA: June Jacobs Labs, Llc
46 Graphic Pl
Moonachie NJ 07074
201 329-9100

(G-10043)
JUPITER CREATIONS INC
252 W 38th St Rm 603 (10018-9234)
PHONE....................................917 493-9393
Michael Katina, *President*
▲ EMP: 2
SALES (est): 3MM **Privately Held**
SIC: 3942 3944 Dolls & stuffed toys; airplanes, toy

(G-10044)
JUST BOTTOMS & TOPS INC (PA)
Also Called: Hot Cashews
1412 Broadway Rm 1808 (10018-9228)
PHONE....................................212 564-3202
Mickey Mait, *President*
Sanders Acker, *Vice Pres*
Mitch Levy, *Vice Pres*
Aaron Feder, *Treasurer*
Jerry Hymowitz, *Admin Sec*
EMP: 10
SQ FT: 3,900
SALES (est): 915.3K **Privately Held**
SIC: 2329 2339 Sweaters & sweater jackets: men's & boys'; women's & misses' outerwear

(G-10045)
JUST BRASS INC
215 W 90th St Apt 9a (10024-1224)
PHONE....................................212 724-5447
Ronald Zabinski, *President*
EMP: 5
SALES: 150K **Privately Held**
SIC: 3172 5136 2321 Personal leather goods; shirts, men's & boys'; men's & boys' furnishings

(G-10046)
JUST GOODS INC
311 W 43rd St Fl 12 (10036-6004)
PHONE....................................855 282-5878
Ira Laufer, *CEO*

Dan Danai, *CFO*
EMP: 14 EST: 2013
SALES: 976K **Privately Held**
SIC: 2086 Water, pasteurized: packaged in cans, bottles, etc.

(G-10047)
JUSTPERFECTMSP LTD
48 W 48th St Ste 401 (10036-1727)
PHONE....................................877 201-0005
Edward Zylka, *President*
Shirley Glumer, *Exec VP*
Ewa Zylka, *Director*
▲ EMP: 45 EST: 1994
SQ FT: 5,000
SALES (est): 1.9MM **Privately Held**
SIC: 3911 5094 Jewelry, precious metal; jewelry & precious stones
PA: Art-Tec Jewelry Designs Ltd
48 W 48th St Ste 401
New York NY 10036

(G-10048)
JUSTYNA KAMINSKA NY INC
1261 Broadway Rm 406 (10001-3631)
PHONE....................................917 423-5527
J Kaminska Cabbad, *President*
Justyna Kaminska Cabbad, *President*
▲ EMP: 1
SQ FT: 800
SALES: 1MM **Privately Held**
SIC: 3911 Jewelry, precious metal

(G-10049)
JUVLY AESTHETICS INC
18 E 41st St Rm 406 (10017-6269)
PHONE....................................614 686-3627
Justin Harper, *Principal*
Erin Sutley,
EMP: 100
SALES (est): 3.4MM **Privately Held**
SIC: 3845 Laser systems & equipment, medical

(G-10050)
JVL VENTURES LLC
Also Called: Softcard
230 Park Ave Rm 2829 (10169-2801)
PHONE....................................212 365-7555
Michael Abbott, *CEO*
EMP: 100
SQ FT: 9,000
SALES (est): 16.4MM **Privately Held**
SIC: 7372 Application computer software

(G-10051)
K ROAD POWER MANAGEMENT LLC (PA)
330 Madison Ave Fl 25 (10017-5022)
PHONE....................................212 351-0535
William Kriegel, *CEO*
Carl Weatherley-White, *CFO*
Gerrit Nicholas, *Director*
EMP: 9
SALES (est): 1.2MM **Privately Held**
SIC: 3612 Transformers, except electric

(G-10052)
K T P DESIGN CO INC
118 E 28th St Rm 707 (10016-8448)
PHONE....................................212 481-6613
Patrick Walsh, *President*
▼ EMP: 15 EST: 1998
SALES: 1.6MM **Privately Held**
WEB: www.customtie.com
SIC: 2339 Neckwear & ties: women's, misses' & juniors'

(G-10053)
K2 INTERNATIONAL CORP
22 W 32nd St Fl 9 (10001-0902)
PHONE....................................212 947-1734
John Hyun Kim, *President*
▲ EMP: 5
SQ FT: 7,000
SALES (est): 390K **Privately Held**
SIC: 3961 Costume jewelry

(G-10054)
KAAZING CORPORATION
250 Park Ave Fl 7 (10177-0799)
PHONE....................................212 572-4859
Vikram Mehta, *Branch Mgr*
EMP: 29 **Privately Held**
SIC: 7372 Business oriented computer software

PA: Kaazing Corporation
2107 N 1st St Ste 660
San Jose CA 95131

(G-10055)
KADMON CORPORATION LLC (PA)
450 E 29th St Fl 5 (10016-8367)
PHONE....................................212 308-6000
Harlan Waksal, *CEO*
Samuel D Waksal, *Chairman*
Larry Cohen, *Exec VP*
John Ryan, *Exec VP*
Zhenping Zhu, *Exec VP*
EMP: 10
SALES (est): 26.2MM **Privately Held**
SIC: 2834 Pharmaceutical preparations

(G-10056)
KADMON HOLDINGS INC
450 E 29th St (10016-8367)
PHONE....................................212 308-6000
Tasos G Konidaris, *Ch of Bd*
Bart M Schwartz, *Ch of Bd*
Harlan W Waksal, *President*
Sanjay Aggarwal, *Vice Pres*
Steven Meehan, *CFO*
EMP: 58
SALES: 1.4MM **Privately Held**
SIC: 2836 2834 Biological products, except diagnostic; pharmaceutical preparations

(G-10057)
KAHN-LUCAS-LANCASTER INC
112 W 34th St Ste 600 (10120-0700)
PHONE....................................212 239-2407
EMP: 80
SALES (corp-wide): 44.5MM **Privately Held**
SIC: 2369 Mfg Girl/Youth Outerwear
PA: Kahn-Lucas-Lancaster, Inc.
306 Primrose Ln
Mountville PA 17554
717 537-4140

(G-10058)
KALEIDOSCOPE IMAGING INC
251 W 39th St Fl 4 (10018-3143)
PHONE....................................212 631-9947
Garo Ksparian, *Partner*
EMP: 30
SALES (est): 4.7MM
SALES (corp-wide): 13MM **Privately Held**
SIC: 2752 Commercial printing, lithographic
PA: Kaleidoscope Imaging, Inc.
700 N Sacramento Blvd # 265
Chicago IL 60612
773 722-9300

(G-10059)
KALEKO BROS
62 W 47th St Ste 1504 (10036-3249)
PHONE....................................212 819-0100
Jerome Kaleko, *Partner*
EMP: 5 EST: 1948
SQ FT: 2,000
SALES (est): 304.2K **Privately Held**
SIC: 3915 Diamond cutting & polishing

(G-10060)
KALIKOW BROTHERS LP
34 W 33rd St Fl 4n (10001-3304)
PHONE....................................212 643-0315
Marc Kalikow, *President*
Paul Levine, *Vice Pres*
EMP: 30 EST: 1929
SQ FT: 8,000
SALES (est): 1.8MM
SALES (corp-wide): 596.6MM **Publicly Held**
WEB: www.fishmantobin.com
SIC: 2325 Trousers, dress (separate): men's, youths' & boys'
HQ: F&T Apparel Llc
4000 Chemical Rd Ste 500
Plymouth Meeting PA 19462
646 839-7000

GEOGRAPHIC

(G-10061)
KALLEN CORP
Also Called: Capstone Printing
99 Hudson St (10013-2815)
P.O. Box 516 (10014-0516)
PHONE.................................212 242-1470
Alan Finkelstein, *President*
EMP: 5
SQ FT: 3,000
SALES (est): 849.4K **Privately Held**
SIC: 2759 Commercial printing

(G-10062)
KALTEX AMERICA INC
350 5th Ave Ste 7100 (10118-7120)
PHONE.................................212 971-0575
Hebe Schecter, *CEO*
Rafael M Kalach, *Ch of Bd*
Jennifer Mason, *CFO*
EMP: 18 EST: 1987
SQ FT: 1,000
SALES (est): 161MM **Privately Held**
SIC: 2339 2325 Jeans: women's, misses'
& juniors'; jeans: men's, youths' & boys'
HQ: Kaltex North America, Inc.
350 5th Ave Ste 7100
New York NY 10118
212 894-3200

(G-10063)
KALTEX NORTH AMERICA INC
(HQ)
350 5th Ave Ste 7100 (10118-7120)
PHONE.................................212 894-3200
Rafael Kalach, *Ch of Bd*
Moises Kalach, *Senior VP*
▲ EMP: 10
SALES (est): 192.6MM **Privately Held**
WEB: www.kaltexhome.com
SIC: 2392 Comforters & quilts: made from
purchased materials

(G-10064)
KAMWO MERIDIAN HERBS LLC
211 Grand St (10013-4223)
PHONE.................................212 966-6370
Thomas N Leung,
EMP: 48
SALES (est): 1.7MM **Privately Held**
SIC: 2833 Drugs & herbs: grading, grinding
& milling

(G-10065)
KANE-M INC
Also Called: Morito/Kane-M
135 W 29th St Rm 1003 (10001-5162)
PHONE.................................973 777-2797
EMP: 7
SQ FT: 10,000
SALES (est): 490.9K **Privately Held**
SIC: 3965 Fasteners, buttons, needles &
pins
PA: Morito Co., Ltd.
4-2-4, Minamihonmachi, Chuo-Ku
Osaka OSK 541-0

(G-10066)
KANEKA AMERICA LLC
546 5th Ave Fl 21 (10036-5000)
PHONE.................................212 705-4340
Masahiko Miyauchi, *Engineer*
Yasushi Kawasumi, *Controller*
Kazuo Kuruma,
EMP: 73 EST: 1972
SALES (est): 10.9MM **Privately Held**
WEB: www.kanecaron.com
SIC: 2295 2834 2099 3089 Resin or
plastic coated fabrics; pharmaceutical
preparations; food preparations; synthetic
resin finished products; chemical prepara-
tions
HQ: Kaneka Americas Holding, Inc.
6250 Underwood Rd
Pasadena TX 77507
281 474-7084

(G-10067)
KAPLAN INC
Kaplan Interactive
444 Madison Ave Ste 803 (10022-6903)
PHONE.................................212 752-1840
EMP: 35
SALES (corp-wide): 2.5B **Publicly Held**
SIC: 2731 Software Book Publishers

HQ: Kaplan, Inc.
750 3rd Ave Fl 7
New York NY 10017
212 492-5800

(G-10068)
KAPRIELIAN ENTERPRISES INC
Also Called: Concord Settings
207 W 25th St Fl 8 (10001-7158)
PHONE.................................212 645-6623
Hratch Kaprielian, *President*
▲ EMP: 70
SQ FT: 6,000
SALES (est): 9.7MM **Privately Held**
WEB: www.kaprielian.com
SIC: 3911 3915 Jewel settings & mount-
ings, precious metal; jewelers' materials &
lapidary work

(G-10069)
KARBRA COMPANY
460 Park Ave Rm 401 (10022-1848)
PHONE.................................212 736-9300
Sing Ming Liu, *Partner*
Carole Roth, *Partner*
Peter Roth, *Partner*
Fiam Ildiko Roth, *Vice Pres*
George Barna, *MIS Dir*
EMP: 140 EST: 1940
SQ FT: 10,000
SALES (est): 11.5MM **Privately Held**
WEB: www.karbra.com
SIC: 3915 3911 3369 3341 Jewelers'
castings; jewelry, precious metal; nonfer-
rous foundries; secondary nonferrous
metals

(G-10070)
KARTELL US INC
39 Greene St (10013-2605)
PHONE.................................212 966-6665
◆ EMP: 6
SALES (est): 130.3K **Privately Held**
SIC: 2392 Household furnishings

(G-10071)
KAS-RAY INDUSTRIES INC
Also Called: Kay-Ray Industries
122 W 26th St (10001-6804)
PHONE.................................212 620-3144
Tony Petrizzo, *President*
EMP: 10
SQ FT: 10,000
SALES (est): 1.9MM **Privately Held**
WEB: www.kasray.com
SIC: 2752 5112 5021 Commercial print-
ing, offset; stationery & office supplies; of-
fice furniture

(G-10072)
KASEYA US LLC (PA)
26 W 17th St Fl 9 (10011-5710)
PHONE.................................415 694-5700
Fred Voccola, *Mng Member*
Isaac Itenberg,
EMP: 15
SALES (est): 7.5MM **Privately Held**
SIC: 7372 Prepackaged software

(G-10073)
KASISTO INC
43 W 24th St Fl 8 (10010-3205)
PHONE.................................917 734-4750
Zor Gorelov, *CEO*
William Mark, *Principal*
Jeffrey Seltzer, *Principal*
Rich Ciapala, *Senior VP*
Marcus Toh, *Senior VP*
EMP: 40 EST: 2013
SQ FT: 150
SALES (est): 528.1K **Privately Held**
SIC: 7372 Business oriented computer
software

(G-10074)
KASPER GROUP LLC (HQ)
1412 Broadway Fl 5 (10018-3330)
PHONE.................................212 354-4311
EMP: 15
SALES (est): 1.7MM
SALES (corp-wide): 244.7MM **Privately
Held**
SIC: 2339 Mfg Women's/Misses' Outer-
wear

PA: Jones Holdings Llc
1411 Brdwy
New York NY
215 785-4000

(G-10075)
KASPER GROUP LLC (DH)
1412 Broadway Fl 5 (10018-3330)
PHONE.................................212 354-4311
Gregg I Marks, *CEO*
Irene Koumendouros, *President*
Daniel Fishman, *COO*
Nikki Palma, *Exec VP*
◆ EMP: 250
SALES (est): 88.9MM
SALES (corp-wide): 1.7B **Privately Held**
SIC: 2335 Women's, juniors' & misses'
dresses
HQ: Premier Brands Group Holdings Llc
1441 Broadway
New York NY 10018
215 785-4000

(G-10076)
KATE SPADE HOLDINGS LLC
(HQ)
Also Called: Kate Spade & Company LLC
2 Park Ave Fl 8 (10016-5613)
PHONE.................................212 354-4900
George M Carrara, *President*
Timothy F Michno, *Senior VP*
Linda Yanussi, *Senior VP*
Agnieszka Mizerska, *Opers Mgr*
Morgan Booker, *Production*
◆ EMP: 420
SQ FT: 135,000
SALES (est): 1.3B
SALES (corp-wide): 6B **Publicly Held**
WEB: www.lizclaiborne.com
SIC: 2331 5651 5136 5137 Women's &
misses' blouses & shirts; family clothing
stores; unisex clothing stores; men's &
boys' clothing; women's & children's
clothing; catalog & mail-order houses
PA: Tapestry, Inc.
10 Hudson Yards
New York NY 10001
212 594-1850

(G-10077)
KATES PAPERIE LTD
188 Lafayette St Frnt A (10013-3200)
PHONE.................................212 966-3904
Leonard Flax, *Manager*
▲ EMP: 6
SALES (est): 330K **Privately Held**
SIC: 2759 Announcements: engraved

(G-10078)
KATHMANDO VALLEY
PRESERVATION
Also Called: H THEOPHILE
36 W 25th St Fl 17 (10010-2706)
PHONE.................................212 727-0074
Erich Theophile, *Owner*
EMP: 10
SALES (est): 491.4K **Privately Held**
SIC: 3851 Temples & fronts, ophthalmic

(G-10079)
KAUFMAN BROTHERS
PRINTING
327 W 36th St Rm 403 (10018-6971)
PHONE.................................212 563-1854
Harvey Kaufman, *Mng Member*
Oliver Henderson, *Manager*
EMP: 5
SQ FT: 2,000
SALES (est): 1.8MM **Privately Held**
SIC: 2752 2759 2789 Commercial print-
ing, offset; letterpress printing; bookbind-
ing & related work

(G-10080)
KAWASHO FOODS USA INC
45 Broadway Fl 18 (10006-3007)
PHONE.................................212 841-7400
Tatsuya Ito, *President*
EMP: 11
SALES: 52MM **Privately Held**
SIC: 2032 Canned specialties
HQ: Kawasho Foods Corporation
2-7-1, Otemachi
Chiyoda-Ku TKY 100-0

(G-10081)
KAY SEE DENTAL MFG CO
777 Avenue Of The (10001)
PHONE.................................816 842-2817
Yachiyo Smith, *President*
Hiro Iwata, *Vice Pres*
Clark Y Smith, *Vice Pres*
Ken Lerner, *Property Mgr*
EMP: 12 EST: 1947
SQ FT: 15,000
SALES (est): 1.4MM **Privately Held**
WEB: www.hydrocast.com
SIC: 3843 Dental equipment; dental mate-
rials

(G-10082)
KAYMIL PRINTING COMPANY
INC
Also Called: Kaymil Ticket Company
140 W 30th St Frnt (10001-4005)
PHONE.................................212 594-3718
Richwar Warner, *President*
Manny Serrano, *Prdtn Mgr*
EMP: 5 EST: 1961
SQ FT: 6,000
SALES (est): 248.2K **Privately Held**
WEB: www.kaymil.com
SIC: 2759 2752 Letterpress printing;
screen printing; offset & photolithographic
printing

(G-10083)
KAYO OF CALIFORNIA
525 Fashion Ave Rm 309 (10018-0485)
PHONE.................................212 354-6336
Janis Dardick, *Vice Pres*
Steven Berman, *Manager*
EMP: 5
SALES (corp-wide): 8.4MM **Privately
Held**
WEB: www.kayo.com
SIC: 2337 2339 Skirts, separate:
women's, misses' & juniors'; sportswear,
women's; shorts (outerwear): women's,
misses' & juniors'; slacks: women's,
misses' & juniors'
PA: Kayo Of California
161 W 39th St
Los Angeles CA 90037
323 233-6107

(G-10084)
KBL HEALTHCARE LP
757 3rd Ave Fl 20 (10017-2046)
PHONE.................................212 319-5555
Dr Marlene Krauss, *Manager*
EMP: 8
SALES (est): 619.9K **Privately Held**
SIC: 2834 Pharmaceutical preparations

(G-10085)
KBS COMMUNICATIONS LLC
Also Called: Mystery Scene Magazine
331 W 57th St Ste 148 (10019-3101)
PHONE.................................212 765-7124
Kathleen M Stine, *Mng Member*
Brian Skupin,
EMP: 12
SALES (est): 950.6K **Privately Held**
WEB: www.mysteryscenemag.com
SIC: 2721 Magazines: publishing & printing

(G-10086)
KCP HOLDCO INC (PA)
603 W 50th St (10019-7029)
PHONE.................................212 265-1500
Paul Blum, *CEO*
Bruce Cohen, *Vice Pres*
Chris Yoham, *Vice Pres*
Patricia Khoury, *Opers Mgr*
Janine Rhodes, *Cust Mgr*
EMP: 15
SALES (est): 465.8MM **Privately Held**
SIC: 3143 3171 5661 5632 Men's
footwear, except athletic; handbags,
women's; purses, women's; shoe stores;
women's boots; men's shoes; women's
accessory & specialty stores; apparel ac-
cessories; costume jewelry; handbags;
men's & boys' clothing stores

(G-10087)
KEARNEY-NATIONAL INC (HQ)
Also Called: Coto Technology
565 5th Ave Fl 4 (10017-2424)
PHONE.................................212 661-4600

Robert R Dyson, *Ch of Bd*
Marc Feldman, *Vice Pres*
John Fitzsimons, *Admin Sec*
◆ **EMP:** 10 **EST:** 1988
SALES (est): 196.1MM
SALES (corp-wide): 482MM **Privately Held**
WEB: www.cotorelay.com
SIC: 3679 3694 3714 3625 Electronic switches; engine electrical equipment; fuel systems & parts, motor vehicle; relays & industrial controls
PA: The Dyson-Kissner-Moran Corporation
　2515 South Rd Ste 5
　Poughkeepsie NY 12601
　212 661-4600

(G-10088)
KELLY GRACE CORP (PA)
Also Called: Danny & Nicole
49 W 37th St Fl 10 (10018-0180)
PHONE..........................212 704-9603
Jamshid Zar, *Ch of Bd*
Daniel Zar, *President*
Esshagh Zar, *Vice Pres*
Korosh Zar, *Vice Pres*
▲ **EMP:** 110
SQ FT: 16,000
SALES (est): 15.3MM **Privately Held**
WEB: www.dannyandnicole.com
SIC: 2335 Wedding gowns & dresses

(G-10089)
KENNETH COLE PRODUCTIONS INC (HQ)
603 W 50th St (10019-7051)
PHONE..........................212 265-1500
Marc Schneider, *CEO*
Mia Dellosso-Caputo, *President*
Chris Nakatani, *President*
Joshua Schulman, *President*
Scott Williamson, *President*
▲ **EMP:** 264
SQ FT: 119,000
SALES (est): 465.6MM
SALES (corp-wide): 465.8MM **Privately Held**
WEB: www.kennethcole.com
SIC: 3143 3144 3171 5661 Men's footwear, except athletic; women's footwear, except athletic; handbags, women's; purses, women's; shoe stores; women's boots; men's shoes; women's accessory & specialty stores; apparel accessories; costume jewelry; handbags; men's & boys' clothing stores
PA: Kcp Holdco, Inc.
　603 W 50th St
　New York NY 10019
　212 265-1500

(G-10090)
KENNETH J LANE INC
20 W 37th St Fl 9 (10018-7367)
PHONE..........................212 868-1780
Kenneth J Lane, *President*
EMP: 15
SQ FT: 5,500
SALES (est): 1.6MM **Privately Held**
SIC: 3961 Jewelry apparel, non-precious metals

(G-10091)
KENSINGTON & SONS LLC
Also Called: Sir Kensington's
270 Lafayette St Ste 200 (10012-3376)
PHONE..........................646 430-8298
Sami Freeman, *Division Mgr*
Zachary Gazzaniga, *COO*
Monisha Khushalani, *VP Finance*
Emily Grant, *Marketing Staff*
Megan Vimini, *Marketing Staff*
EMP: 30
SALES (est): 2.1MM **Privately Held**
SIC: 2035 2033 5149 Mayonnaise; mustard, prepared (wet); catsup: packaged in cans, jars, etc.; condiments

(G-10092)
KENSINGTON PUBLISHING CORP
Also Called: Zebra Books
119 W 40th St Fl 21 (10018-2522)
PHONE..........................212 407-1500
Steven Zacharius, *CEO*
Laurie Parkin, *Vice Pres*

Robin Cook, *Production*
M Elley, *Production*
Ross Plotkin, *Production*
EMP: 81
SQ FT: 25,000
SALES (est): 10.5MM **Privately Held**
WEB: www.kensingtonbooks.com
SIC: 2731 5192 Books: publishing only; books

(G-10093)
KENT ASSOCIATES INC
99 Battery Pl Apt 11p (10280-1324)
PHONE..........................212 675-0722
Herman Lederfarb, *President*
EMP: 8 **EST:** 1947
SQ FT: 4,000
SALES (est): 870K **Privately Held**
SIC: 2752 Commercial printing, offset

(G-10094)
KENT CHEMICAL CORPORATION
460 Park Ave Fl 7 (10022-1841)
PHONE..........................212 521-1700
John Farber, *Ch of Bd*
John Oram, *President*
Susan Aibinder, *Treasurer*
Maya Farber, *Director*
Paul Sailick, *Admin Sec*
◆ **EMP:** 25 **EST:** 1983
SQ FT: 15,000
SALES (est): 3.9MM
SALES (corp-wide): 1.7B **Privately Held**
SIC: 2821 2869 2911 2899 Polyvinyl chloride resins (PVC); flavors or flavoring materials, synthetic; perfume materials, synthetic; paraffin wax; fire retardant chemicals; unsupported plastics film & sheet; solutions, pharmaceutical
PA: Icc Industries Inc.
　460 Park Ave Fl 7
　New York NY 10022
　212 521-1700

(G-10095)
KEY BRAND ENTERTAINMENT INC
104 Franklin St (10013-2923)
PHONE..........................212 966-5400
EMP: 121
SALES (corp-wide): 473K **Privately Held**
SIC: 2752 Lithographic Commercial Printing
PA: Key Brand Entertainment, Inc.
　1619 Broadway Fl 9
　New York NY 10019
　917 421-5400

(G-10096)
KIDS DISCOVER LLC
192 Lexington Ave Rm 1003 (10016-6913)
PHONE..........................212 677-4457
Theodore Levine, *Mng Member*
EMP: 6
SALES (est): 256.1K **Privately Held**
SIC: 2721 Magazines: publishing only, not printed on site

(G-10097)
KIDZ CONCEPTS LLC
Also Called: One Step Up Kids
1412 Broadway Fl 3 (10018-3372)
PHONE..........................212 398-1110
Harry Adjmi,
Irwin Gindi,
◆ **EMP:** 52
SQ FT: 15,000
SALES (est): 10.4MM **Privately Held**
WEB: www.kidzconcepts.com
SIC: 2389 5137 Costumes; women's & children's sportswear & swimsuits

(G-10098)
KIDZ WORLD INC
Also Called: High Energy U. S. A.
226 W 37th St Fl 12 (10018-9850)
PHONE..........................212 563-4949
Vittorio Dana, *President*
Victor Hara, *Vice Pres*
▲ **EMP:** 15
SQ FT: 2,172
SALES (est): 165.1K **Privately Held**
SIC: 2329 Men's & boys' sportswear & athletic clothing

(G-10099)
KIK US INC
Also Called: Kinecosystem
161 Bowery Apt 6 (10002-2846)
PHONE..........................519 505-7616
Edward Livingston, *CEO*
Peter Heinke, *CFO*
Brandon Brunet, *Controller*
EMP: 12
SALES: 500K
SALES (corp-wide): 18MM **Privately Held**
SIC: 7372 Application computer software
PA: Kik Interactive Inc.
　420 Weber St N Suite I
　Waterloo ON
　226 868-0056

(G-10100)
KIM EUGENIA INC
347 W 36th St Rm 502 (10018-7262)
PHONE..........................212 674-1345
Eugenia Kim, *President*
▲ **EMP:** 8
SQ FT: 1,400
SALES (est): 1.6MM **Privately Held**
WEB: www.eugeniakim.com
SIC: 2353 Hats, caps & millinery

(G-10101)
KIM SEYBERT INC (PA)
37 W 37th St Fl 9 (10018-6219)
PHONE..........................212 564-7850
Kim Seybert, *President*
◆ **EMP:** 16
SQ FT: 10,000
SALES: 5MM **Privately Held**
WEB: www.kimseybert.com
SIC: 2392 Household furnishings

(G-10102)
KIMBALL OFFICE INC
215 Park Ave S Fl 3 (10003-1616)
PHONE..........................212 753-6161
Michael Donahue, *Vice Pres*
Thomas P Mitchell, *Manager*
EMP: 30
SALES (corp-wide): 768MM **Publicly Held**
SIC: 2521 Wood office furniture
HQ: Kimball Office Inc.
　1600 Royal St
　Jasper IN 47546

(G-10103)
KIMBERLY-CLARK CORPORATION
1285 Ave Of The Americas (10019-6031)
PHONE..........................212 554-4252
Guy Zbonack, *Principal*
EMP: 83
SALES (corp-wide): 18.4B **Publicly Held**
WEB: www.kimberly-clark.com
SIC: 2621 2676 Sanitary tissue paper; infant & baby paper products
PA: Kimberly-Clark Corporation
　351 Phelps Dr
　Irving TX 75038
　972 281-1200

(G-10104)
KIND GROUP LLC (PA)
19 W 44th St Ste 811 (10036-5901)
PHONE..........................212 645-0800
Jonathan Teller, *Mng Member*
EMP: 2
SQ FT: 3,000
SALES (est): 22.8MM **Privately Held**
WEB: www.20-10.com
SIC: 2844 Toilet preparations

(G-10105)
KINDLING INC
440 Park Ave S Fl 14 (10016-8012)
PHONE..........................212 400-6296
Timothy Meaney, *CEO*
Daniel Summa, *President*
Richard Ziade, *Admin Sec*
EMP: 17
SALES (est): 1MM **Privately Held**
SIC: 7372 Business oriented computer software

(G-10106)
KINETIC MARKETING INC
1133 Broadway Ste 221 (10010-8197)
PHONE..........................212 620-0600
Charles Y Beyda, *Vice Pres*
▲ **EMP:** 7
SQ FT: 2,000
SALES (est): 901K **Privately Held**
WEB: www.kineticmarketing.net
SIC: 3699 5065 Household electrical equipment; electronic parts & equipment

(G-10107)
KING DISPLAYS INC
333 W 52nd St (10019-6238)
PHONE..........................212 629-8455
Wayne Sapper, *President*
Julie Rivkin, *Accountant*
EMP: 14
SQ FT: 7,500
SALES (est): 1.8MM **Privately Held**
WEB: www.kingdisplays.com
SIC: 3999 3993 Theatrical scenery; displays & cutouts, window & lobby

(G-10108)
KINGBOARD HOLDINGS LIMITED
120 Broadway Fl 32 (10271-3299)
PHONE..........................705 844-1993
EMP: 600
SALES (est): 12.1MM **Privately Held**
SIC: 3672 7371 Printed circuit boards; computer software development & applications

(G-10109)
KINGOLD JEWELRY INC (PA)
888c 8th Ave 106 (10019-8511)
PHONE..........................212 509-1700
Zhihong Jia, *Ch of Bd*
Bin Liu, *CFO*
EMP: 11
SALES: 2.4B **Publicly Held**
WEB: www.desonco.com
SIC: 3911 5944 Jewelry, precious metal; jewel settings & mountings, precious metal; silverware

(G-10110)
KITCHECO INC
50 W 34th St Apt 16b7 (10001-3088)
PHONE..........................917 388-7479
Jason Lee, *Director*
EMP: 5
SALES: 100K **Privately Held**
SIC: 7372 2741 Application computer software;

(G-10111)
KITON BUILDING CORP
4 E 54th St (10022-4203)
PHONE..........................212 486-3224
Antonio De Matteis, *Ch of Bd*
Ciro Paone, *President*
EMP: 20
SQ FT: 18,077
SALES (est): 2MM **Privately Held**
SIC: 2389 Costumes

(G-10112)
KKR MILLENNIUM GP LLC
9 W 57th St Ste 4150 (10019-2701)
PHONE..........................212 750-8300
Lawrence J Rogers, *President*
EMP: 4850
SALES (est): 930.7MM **Publicly Held**
SIC: 2515 Mattresses, innerspring or box spring
PA: Kkr & Co. Inc.
　9 W 57th St Ste 4200
　New York NY 10019

(G-10113)
KKR NTRAL RSOURCES FUND I-A LP
9 W 57th St Ste 4200 (10019-2707)
PHONE..........................212 750-8300
David J Sorkin, *General Counsel*
EMP: 6
SALES (est): 25.1MM **Publicly Held**
SIC: 1382 Oil & gas exploration services
PA: Kkr & Co. Inc.
　9 W 57th St Ste 4200
　New York NY 10019

▲ = Import ▼=Export
◆ =Import/Export

(G-10114)
KLAUBER BROTHERS INC (PA)
253 W 35th St Fl 11 (10001-1907)
PHONE..................................212 686-2531
Roger Klauber, *President*
Mark Klauber, *Vice Pres*
Andy Larivee, *Prdtn Mgr*
Gordon Klauber, *Treasurer*
Mario Larosa, *Controller*
▲ **EMP:** 35 **EST:** 1942
SQ FT: 11,000
SALES: 133K **Privately Held**
WEB: www.klauberlace.com
SIC: 2258 5131 Lace, knit; warp & flat knit
products; textile converters

(G-10115)
KLUTZ (HQ)
Also Called: Klutz Store
568 Broadway Rm 503 (10012-3264)
PHONE..................................650 687-2600
Richard Robinson, *CEO*
of Purch, *CEO*
Dewitt Durham, *Vice Pres*
▲ **EMP:** 23 **EST:** 1978
SALES (est): 9.1MM
SALES (corp-wide): 1.6B **Publicly Held**
WEB: www.klutz.com
SIC: 2731 Books: publishing & printing
PA: Scholastic Corporation
557 Broadway Lbby 1
New York NY 10012
212 343-6100

(G-10116)
KNIT ILLUSTRATED INC
247 W 37th St Frnt 3 (10018-5130)
PHONE..................................212 268-9054
Peter Tam, *President*
▲ **EMP:** 20
SALES: 2MM **Privately Held**
WEB: www.knitillustrated.com
SIC: 2253 Sweaters & sweater coats, knit

(G-10117)
KNOA SOFTWARE INC (PA)
41 E 11th St Fl 11 (10003-4602)
PHONE..................................212 807-9608
Brian Berns, *CEO*
Yee Ping Wu, *President*
Jerry Dolinsky, *Exec VP*
Philip Lui, *Vice Pres*
Simon Adell, *CFO*
▲ **EMP:** 35
SQ FT: 12,500
SALES (est): 3.3MM **Privately Held**
WEB: www.knoa.com
SIC: 7372 Prepackaged software

(G-10118)
KNOLL INC
Also Called: Knoll Textile
1330 Ave Of The A (10019)
PHONE..................................212 343-4124
Caroline Mattar, *Sales Staff*
Cara Mead, *Sales Staff*
Amy Dara, *Manager*
Germaine Bosquez, *Manager*
EMP: 100 **Publicly Held**
WEB: www.knoll.com
SIC: 2521 2522 2511 Wood office furni-
ture; panel systems & partitions, office:
except wood; wood household furniture
PA: Knoll, Inc.
1235 Water St
East Greenville PA 18041

(G-10119)
**KOBALT MUSIC PUBG AMER
INC (HQ)**
2 Gansevoort St Fl 6 (10014-1667)
PHONE..................................212 247-6204
Willard Ahdritz, *CEO*
Ron Cerrito, *General Mgr*
Sandeep Das, *General Mgr*
Pete Dodge, *General Mgr*
Sue Drew, *General Mgr*
EMP: 70
SALES (est): 23.6MM
SALES (corp-wide): 402.1MM **Privately
Held**
WEB: www.kobaltmusic.com
SIC: 2731 Book music: publishing & print-
ing

PA: Kobalt Music Group Limited
1 Cousin Lane
London EC4R
207 401-5500

(G-10120)
**KOBE STEEL USA HOLDINGS
INC (HQ)**
535 Madison Ave Fl 5 (10022-4214)
PHONE..................................212 751-9400
Hiroya Kawasaki, *President*
Mike Wilson, *Purch Mgr*
◆ **EMP:** 8
SQ FT: 5,697
SALES (est): 232.7MM **Privately Held**
WEB: www.kobelco.com
SIC: 3542 3089 Extruding machines (ma-
chine tools), metal; injection molding of
plastics

(G-10121)
KOCH SUPPLY & TRADING LP
350 5th Ave Ste 4810 (10118-4810)
PHONE..................................212 319-4895
EMP: 5
SALES (corp-wide): 40.6B **Privately Held**
SIC: 2911 Petroleum refining
HQ: Koch Supply & Trading, Lp
4111 E 37th St N
Wichita KS 67220
316 828-5500

(G-10122)
KODANSHA USA INC
451 Park Ave S Fl 7 (10016-7390)
PHONE..................................917 322-6200
Sawako Noma, *Ch of Bd*
Yoichi Kiyata, *Sr Exec VP*
▲ **EMP:** 9
SQ FT: 7,000
SALES (est): 3.6MM **Privately Held**
SIC: 2731 5192 Books: publishing only;
books

(G-10123)
KOKIN INC
270 W 38th St Rm 1500 (10018-1588)
PHONE..................................212 643-8225
Steven Kokin, *President*
Audrey Kokin, *Corp Secy*
Gary Kokin, *Vice Pres*
▲ **EMP:** 30
SALES (est): 3.6MM **Privately Held**
SIC: 2353 2341 Hats, caps & millinery;
women's & children's nightwear

(G-10124)
KOMAR LAYERING LLC (HQ)
Also Called: O'Bryan Bros
16 E 34th St Fl 10 (10016-4360)
PHONE..................................212 725-1500
Charlie Komar, *President*
David Komar, *Principal*
Moira Shields, *Vice Pres*
Allen R Bartine, *CFO*
Shelley Sosnoff, *Director*
▲ **EMP:** 40
SQ FT: 13,000
SALES: 11MM
SALES (corp-wide): 260MM **Privately
Held**
WEB: www.cuddlduds.com
SIC: 2341 Nightgowns & negligees:
women's & children's; pajamas & bed-
jackets: women's & children's; slips:
women's, misses', children's & infants';
panties: women's, misses', children's &
infants'
PA: Charles Komar & Sons, Inc.
90 Hudson St Fl 9
Jersey City NJ 07302
212 725-1500

(G-10125)
KOMAR LUXURY BRANDS
16 E 34th St Fl 10 (10016-4360)
PHONE..................................646 472-0060
Charles Komar, *President*
▲ **EMP:** 8

SALES (est): 887.6K
SALES (corp-wide): 260MM **Privately
Held**
SIC: 2341 2384 5137 2329 Women's &
children's nightwear; robes & dressing
gowns; nightwear: women's, children's &
infants'; sweaters & sweater jackets:
men's & boys'
PA: Charles Komar & Sons, Inc.
90 Hudson St Fl 9
Jersey City NJ 07302
212 725-1500

(G-10126)
**KOPPERS CHOCLAT SPECIALTY
INC**
501 Madison Ave Rm 402 (10022-5635)
PHONE..................................917 834-2290
Lorie Alexander, *Principal*
Adriana Tejada, *Technology*
EMP: 7
SALES (est): 576.7K **Privately Held**
SIC: 2064 Candy & other confectionery
products

(G-10127)
KORANGY PUBLISHING INC (PA)
Also Called: Real Deal, The
450 W 31st St Fl 4 (10001-4613)
PHONE..................................212 260-1332
Amir Korangy, *CEO*
James Kleimann, *Editor*
Hannah Miet, *Editor*
Derek Smith, *Project Mgr*
John Harrison, *CFO*
EMP: 120
SALES (est): 15.5MM **Privately Held**
SIC: 2741 Miscellaneous publishing

(G-10128)
KORIN INC
233 Broadway Rm 1801 (10279-0810)
PHONE..................................212 587-7021
Saori Kawano, *President*
John Wong, *CFO*
Mitsuko Muramatsu, *Sales Staff*
Elaine LI, *Marketing Staff*
Mari Sugai, *Marketing Staff*
◆ **EMP:** 43
SQ FT: 8,000
SALES (est): 6.8MM **Privately Held**
WEB: www.korin.com
SIC: 3262 3263 3421 3589 Vitreous
china table & kitchenware; commercial
tableware or kitchen articles, fine earthen-
ware; cutlery; commercial cooking & food-
warming equipment; barbecues, grills &
braziers (outdoor cooking)

(G-10129)
KOSSARS ON GRAND LLC
367 Grand St (10002-3951)
PHONE..................................212 473-4810
Evan Giniger, *CEO*
EMP: 10
SALES (est): 728.3K **Privately Held**
SIC: 2051 Rolls, bread type: fresh or
frozen

(G-10130)
KOTEL IMPORTERS INC
22 W 48th St Ste 607 (10036-1803)
PHONE..................................212 245-6200
Raphel Dagan, *President*
EMP: 12
SQ FT: 1,200
SALES (est): 1.1MM **Privately Held**
SIC: 1499 Gemstone & industrial diamond
mining

(G-10131)
**KOWA AMERICAN
CORPORATION (DH)**
55 E 59th St Fl 19 (10022-1112)
PHONE..................................212 303-7800
Reid C Anthony, *Ch of Bd*
Takashi Mamemura, *Ch of Bd*
Ron Cimmino, *Business Mgr*
Kanako Fujimoto, *Accounting Mgr*
Jenny Hsieh,
◆ **EMP:** 20
SQ FT: 6,400
SALES (est): 4.5MM **Privately Held**
SIC: 2819 5032 5131 Industrial inorganic
chemicals; tile, clay or other ceramic, ex-
cluding refractory; textiles, woven

(G-10132)
**KOZINN+SONS MERCHANT
TAILORS**
Also Called: Saint Laurie
150 W 55th St Frnt 3 (10019-5586)
PHONE..................................212 643-1916
Andrew Kozinn, *CEO*
▲ **EMP:** 26
SQ FT: 7,500
SALES (est): 3.3MM **Privately Held**
WEB: www.saintlaurie.com
SIC: 2311 2337 5611 5621 Suits, men's
& boys': made from purchased materials;
suits: women's, misses' & juniors'; suits,
men's; women's clothing stores

(G-10133)
**KPS CAPITAL PARTNERS LP
(PA)**
485 Lexington Ave Fl 31 (10017-2641)
PHONE..................................212 338-5100
Michael G Psaros, *Managing Prtnr*
Jay Bernstein, *Partner*
Raquel Palmer, *Partner*
David Shapiro, *Partner*
Talia Campbell, *Associate*
◆ **EMP:** 40
SQ FT: 6,000
SALES (est): 1.9B **Privately Held**
SIC: 3541 6722 3545 5084 Machine
tools, metal cutting type; management in-
vestment, open-end; machine tool acces-
sories; industrial machinery & equipment

(G-10134)
KRAINZ CREATIONS INC
589 5th Ave (10017-1923)
PHONE..................................212 583-1555
Roland Krainz, *President*
Frank Gannon, *Foreman/Supr*
Paola Parra, *Manager*
Cristina Cicero, *Assistant*
EMP: 35
SALES (est): 3.6MM **Privately Held**
SIC: 3911 Jewelry, precious metal

(G-10135)
KRAMAN IRON WORKS INC
410 E 10th St (10009-4203)
PHONE..................................212 460-8400
Richard Kraman, *President*
EMP: 11 **EST:** 1913
SQ FT: 3,600
SALES: 1.6MM **Privately Held**
SIC: 3449 Miscellaneous metalwork

(G-10136)
KRASNER GROUP INC (PA)
40 W 37th St Ph A (10018-7415)
PHONE..................................212 268-4100
Al Cerbo, *Vice Pres*
Barry Ort, *Vice Pres*
David Pardington, *CFO*
▼ **EMP:** 1
SQ FT: 4,500
SALES (est): 8.2MM **Privately Held**
SIC: 3911 2339 2331 2335 Jewelry, pre-
cious metal; women's & misses' acces-
sories; women's & misses' blouses &
shirts; women's, juniors' & misses'
dresses

(G-10137)
KRAUS & SONS INC
355 S End Ave Apt 10j (10280-1056)
PHONE..................................212 620-0408
Paul Schneider, *President*
Mildred Schneider, *Treasurer*
EMP: 15 **EST:** 1886
SQ FT: 5,000
SALES (est): 1.6MM **Privately Held**
WEB: www.krausbanners.com
SIC: 2399 3993 2394 3965 Banners,
made from fabric; signs & advertising
specialties; tents: made from purchased
materials; buttons & parts

(G-10138)
**KRAUS ORGANIZATION LIMITED
(PA)**
Also Called: Bernan Associates
181 Hudson St Ste 2a (10013-1812)
PHONE..................................212 686-5411
Frank Cermak, *President*
Herbert Gstalder, *Chairman*

Steven Gstalder, *Vice Pres*
EMP: 80
SALES (est): 8.2MM **Privately Held**
WEB: www.krausorgltd.com
SIC: 2741 7383 7389 Miscellaneous publishing; news pictures, gathering & distributing; photographic library service

(G-10139)
KRAVITZ DESIGN INC (PA)
13 Crosby St Rm 401 (10013-3145)
PHONE..................212 625-1644
Lenny Kravitz, *Ch of Bd*
Richard Feldstein, *Admin Sec*
▲ **EMP:** 8
SALES (est): 1.1MM **Privately Held**
SIC: 2732 Books: printing only

(G-10140)
KRUX DIGITAL INC
155 Ave Of The Amer Fl 12 (10013-1507)
PHONE..................646 476-6261
Tom Chavez, *President*
David Huang, *Opers Staff*
EMP: 15
SALES (corp-wide): 13.2B **Publicly Held**
SIC: 7372 Business oriented computer software
HQ: Krux Digital, Inc.
　　50 Fremont St Ste 300
　　San Francisco CA 94105
　　888 415-5789

(G-10141)
KRYON SYSTEMS INC
135 E 57th St (10022-2050)
PHONE..................800 618-4318
Harel Tayeb, *CEO*
Dalia Holzman, *Director*
EMP: 110 **EST:** 2011
SALES (est): 175K **Privately Held**
SIC: 7372 Business oriented computer software

(G-10142)
KSE SPORTSMAN MEDIA INC (PA)
1040 Ave Of The Americas (10018-3703)
PHONE..................212 852-6600
David Koff, *CEO*
Peter Kern, *Chairman*
Jeff Paro, *Chairman*
Michael Carney, *Vice Pres*
Andy Goldstein, *CFO*
EMP: 59
SALES (est): 38.6MM **Privately Held**
SIC: 2326 5045 Industrial garments, men's & boys'; computer software

(G-10143)
KSK INTERNATIONAL INC (PA)
Also Called: Easel
450 Park Ave Ste 2703 (10022-2668)
PHONE..................212 354-7770
Neil Weiss, *CEO*
EMP: 25
SQ FT: 10,335
SALES (est): 1.8MM **Privately Held**
SIC: 2331 2339 Women's & misses' blouses & shirts; women's & misses' accessories

(G-10144)
KT GROUP INC
13 W 36th St Fl 3 (10018-7139)
PHONE..................212 760-2500
Eugene Huh, *President*
Yujin Huh, *Chairman*
▲ **EMP:** 8
SALES (est): 954K **Privately Held**
SIC: 2321 Sport shirts, men's & boys': from purchased materials

(G-10145)
KURT GAUM INC
Also Called: Soper Designs
580 5th Ave Ste 303 (10036-4724)
PHONE..................212 719-2836
Blake Soper, *President*
Peter Boutsas, *Vice Pres*
EMP: 13 **EST:** 1954
SQ FT: 1,250
SALES (est): 1.6MM **Privately Held**
WEB: www.kurtgaum.com
SIC: 3911 Jewelry, precious metal

(G-10146)
KYBOD GROUP LLC
Also Called: Sriracha2go
305 E 40th St Apt 5k (10016-2017)
PHONE..................408 306-1657
Kyle Lewis,
Farbod Deylamian,
EMP: 2
SALES: 1.5MM **Privately Held**
SIC: 3085 Plastics bottles

(G-10147)
KYLE EDITING LLC
48 W 25th St Fl 5 (10010-2767)
PHONE..................212 675-3464
Jackie Sparks, *Business Mgr*
Sarah Farrand, *Producer*
Nate Taylor, *Director*
Tina Mintus,
EMP: 9 **EST:** 2010
SALES (est): 1MM **Privately Held**
WEB: www.kyleedit.com
SIC: 3861 Editing equipment, motion picture: viewers, splicers, etc.

(G-10148)
L & M OPTICAL DISC LLC
Also Called: L & M West
65 W 36th St Fl 11 (10018-7936)
PHONE..................718 649-3500
Aaron Menche,
▲ **EMP:** 100
SALES (est): 12.7MM **Privately Held**
WEB: www.dxbind.com
SIC: 3695 Optical disks & tape, blank

(G-10149)
L A BURDICK CHOCOLATES
5 E 20th St (10003-1103)
PHONE..................212 796-0143
Larry Burdick, *Branch Mgr*
EMP: 5
SALES (est): 269.6K **Privately Held**
SIC: 2064 Candy & other confectionery products
PA: Bb Walpole Liquidation Nh, Inc.
　　47 Main St Unit 1
　　Walpole NH 03608

(G-10150)
L D WEISS INC (PA)
Also Called: Bandaroos
320 E 42nd St Apt 3106 (10017-5990)
P.O. Box 14, Skaneateles (13152-0014)
PHONE..................212 697-3023
Lawrence D Weiss, *President*
Katharine Weiss, *Vice Pres*
Katie Weiss, *CFO*
John Weiss, *Admin Sec*
▲ **EMP:** 6
SQ FT: 3,000
SALES (est): 448.4K **Privately Held**
WEB: www.linescale.com
SIC: 2339 2389 8742 Women's & misses' accessories; men's miscellaneous accessories; new products & services consultants

(G-10151)
L F FASHION ORIENT INTL CO LTD
32 W 40th St Apt 2l (10018-3839)
PHONE..................917 667-3398
Lisa Li, *President*
▲ **EMP:** 5
SALES (est): 350.1K **Privately Held**
SIC: 2311 2335 Men's & boys' suits & coats; women's, juniors' & misses' dresses

(G-10152)
L-3 CMMNCTONS NTRONIX HOLDINGS
600 3rd Ave Fl 34 (10016-1901)
PHONE..................212 697-1111
Michael T Strianese, *President*
Steven M Post, *Senior VP*
Ralph G D'Ambrosio, *CFO*
EMP: 65
SALES (est): 17.9MM
SALES (corp-wide): 6.8B **Publicly Held**
SIC: 3625 3699 8711 Marine & navy auxiliary controls; underwater sound equipment; marine engineering

HQ: L3 Technologies, Inc.
　　600 3rd Ave Fl 34
　　New York NY 10016
　　212 697-1111

(G-10153)
L3 FOREIGN HOLDINGS INC (DH)
Also Called: L3 Communication
600 3rd Ave Fl 32 (10016-1901)
PHONE..................212 697-1111
Jim Parker, *President*
Brian Pope, *President*
Larry Riddle, *President*
Elissa Seidenglanz, *President*
Michael T Strianese, *Principal*
▲ **EMP:** 119
SALES (est): 83.9MM
SALES (corp-wide): 6.8B **Publicly Held**
SIC: 3663 3669 3679 3812 Telemetering equipment, electronic; receiver-transmitter units (transceiver); amplifiers, RF power & IF; signaling apparatus, electric; intercommunication systems, electric; microwave components; search & navigation equipment; guided missile & space vehicle parts & auxiliary equipment
HQ: L3 Technologies, Inc.
　　600 3rd Ave Fl 34
　　New York NY 10016
　　212 697-1111

(G-10154)
L3 TECHNOLOGIES INC (HQ)
600 3rd Ave Fl 34 (10016-1901)
PHONE..................212 697-1111
Christopher Kubasik, *President*
EMP: 277 **EST:** 1997
SALES: 10.2B
SALES (corp-wide): 6.8B **Publicly Held**
SIC: 3669 3663 3769 3679 Signaling apparatus, electric; intercommunication systems, electric; telemetering equipment, electronic; receiver-transmitter units (transceiver); amplifiers, RF power & IF; guided missile & space vehicle parts & auxiliary equipment; microwave components; search & navigation equipment; aircraft control systems, electronic
PA: L3harris Technologies, Inc.
　　1025 W Nasa Blvd
　　Melbourne FL 32919
　　321 727-9100

(G-10155)
LA COLA 1 INC
529 W 42nd St Apt 5b (10036-6228)
PHONE..................917 509-6669
Thomas Dugal, *Principal*
George Doerre, *Manager*
Elissa Williams, *Info Tech Mgr*
EMP: 5
SALES (est): 270.6K **Privately Held**
SIC: 2086 Soft drinks: packaged in cans, bottles, etc.

(G-10156)
LA CREMERIA
178 Mulberry St (10012-4556)
PHONE..................212 226-6758
Alessandro Tiodesam, *Managing Prtnr*
Elena Tiodesam, *Partner*
EMP: 6
SALES (est): 258.3K **Privately Held**
SIC: 2024 Ice cream, bulk

(G-10157)
LA FINA DESIGN INC
42 W 38th St Rm 1200 (10018-6212)
PHONE..................212 689-6725
Chol Choi, *President*
Peter Choi, *President*
▲ **EMP:** 7
SALES (est): 952.7K **Privately Held**
SIC: 3911 Jewelry, precious metal

(G-10158)
LA LAME INC
Also Called: La Lame Importers
215 W 40th St Fl 5 (10018-1602)
PHONE..................212 921-9770
Benjamin Schneer, *CEO*
Edward Schneer, *President*
Glen Schneer, *Principal*
▲ **EMP:** 8 **EST:** 1958
SQ FT: 7,500

SALES (est): 1.3MM **Privately Held**
WEB: www.lalame.com
SIC: 2299 2241 2282 2221 Yarns, specialty & novelty; fabrics: linen, jute, hemp, ramie; braids, textile; embroidery yarn; twisting, winding or spooling; spandex broadwoven fabrics; brocade, cotton; textile converters

(G-10159)
LABEL SOURCE INC
321 W 35th St (10001-1739)
PHONE..................212 244-1403
Stuart Rosen, *President*
EMP: 6
SQ FT: 2,000
SALES (est): 1.2MM **Privately Held**
SIC: 2241 Labels, woven

(G-10160)
LABELS INTER-GLOBAL INC
Also Called: Labels I-G
109 W 38th St Rm 701 (10018-3673)
PHONE..................212 398-0006
Steve Ziangos, *President*
Rosena Rasheed, *Technology*
Steve Sellinger, *Technology*
Eric Pit, *Executive*
▲ **EMP:** 14
SQ FT: 3,400
SALES (est): 2.2MM **Privately Held**
WEB: www.labelsig.com
SIC: 2759 5112 2241 Labels & seals: printing; stationery & office supplies; labels, woven

(G-10161)
LABELTEX MILLS INC
1430 Broadway Rm 1510 (10018-3368)
PHONE..................212 279-6165
Raphaela Penn, *Vice Pres*
Ian Kantor, *Manager*
EMP: 7 **Privately Held**
WEB: www.labeltexmills.com
SIC: 2241 Narrow fabric mills
PA: Labeltex Mills, Inc.
　　6100 Wilmington Ave
　　Los Angeles CA 90001

(G-10162)
LADY ESTER LINGERIE CORP
Also Called: Sliperfection
33 E 33rd St Rm 800 (10016-5335)
PHONE..................212 689-1729
Robert T Sadock, *CEO*
M William Sadock, *President*
Karen L Sadock, *Exec VP*
Greg Strahn, *CFO*
EMP: 45 **EST:** 1929
SQ FT: 15,000
SALES (est): 4.4MM **Privately Held**
SIC: 2384 2341 Robes & dressing gowns; chemises, camisoles & teddies: women's & children's

(G-10163)
LAFAYETTE PUB INC
Also Called: Temple Bar
332 Lafayette St (10012-2739)
PHONE..................212 925-4242
George Schwartz, *President*
EMP: 25
SALES (est): 1.4MM **Privately Held**
WEB: www.templebarnyc.com
SIC: 2599 5813 Bar, restaurant & cafeteria furniture; drinking places

(G-10164)
LAGARDERE NORTH AMERICA INC (DH)
60 E 42nd St Ste 1940 (10165-6201)
PHONE..................212 477-7373
David Leckey, *Senior VP*
Anne Billaz, *Vice Pres*
Richard Rabinowitz, *Vice Pres*
Thierry Auger, *Technology*
EMP: 21
SALES (est): 161.8MM
SALES (corp-wide): 68.6MM **Privately Held**
SIC: 2721 Magazines: publishing only, not printed on site
HQ: Lagardere Media
　　4 Rue De Presbourg
　　Paris
　　140 691-600

(G-10165)
LAI APPAREL DESIGN INC
Also Called: Ella Design
209 W 38th St Rm 901 (10018-4558)
PHONE................................212 382-1075
Elaine Lai, *President*
▲ EMP: 21
SQ FT: 7,000
SALES (est): 3.5MM Privately Held
SIC: 2339 Women's & misses' athletic
clothing & sportswear

(G-10166)
LALI JEWELRY INC
Also Called: Lali Jewels
50 W 47th St Ste 1610 (10036-8734)
PHONE................................212 944-2277
Arun Bassalali, *President*
Adam Bassalali, *Vice Pres*
▲ EMP: 4 EST: 2015
SQ FT: 1,000
SALES: 3MM Privately Held
SIC: 3911 5094 Pearl jewelry, natural or
cultured; jewelry & precious stones

(G-10167)
LALIQUE NORTH AMERICA INC
Also Called: Lalique Boutique
609 Madison Ave (10022-1901)
PHONE................................212 355-6550
Marya Samawi, *Branch Mgr*
EMP: 20
SALES (corp-wide): 156.1MM Privately
Held
SIC: 3231 5719 Watch crystals, glass;
kitchenware
HQ: Lalique North America, Inc.
133 5th Ave Fl 3
New York NY 10003
212 355-8536

(G-10168)
LAND N SEA INC (PA)
1440 Broadway Frnt 3 (10018-2301)
PHONE................................212 444-6000
Robert Sobel, *Ch of Bd*
Kirk Gellin, *Ch of Bd*
Lyle Phillips, *General Mgr*
Fred Mandato, *Vice Pres*
Heather Smith, *Opers Mgr*
◆ EMP: 100 EST: 1958
SALES (est): 56.1MM Privately Held
SIC: 2361 2331 2369 2339 Blouses:
girls', children's & infants'; blouses,
women's & juniors': made from purchased
material; girls' & children's outerwear;
women's & misses' outerwear; family
clothing stores

(G-10169)
LANDLORD GUARD INC
1 Maiden Ln Fl 7 (10038-5168)
PHONE................................212 695-6505
Christine Mathis, *President*
Evelyn Hernandez, *Analyst*
Christina Wang, *Analyst*
EMP: 10
SALES (est): 780K Privately Held
SIC: 2759 Advertising literature: printing

(G-10170)
**LANDMARK SIGNS ELEC MAINT
CORP (PA)**
1501 Broadway Ste 501 (10036-5501)
PHONE................................212 262-3699
Anthony Calvano, *President*
Christina Faulkner, *Office Mgr*
Joseph Matriss, *Director*
EMP: 18
SALES (est): 2.8MM Privately Held
SIC: 3993 Signs & advertising specialties

(G-10171)
**LANDMARK SIGNS ELEC MAINT
CORP**
1 Times Sq Frnt (10036-6560)
PHONE................................212 354-7551
EMP: 17
SALES (corp-wide): 2.8MM Privately
Held
SIC: 3993 Signs & advertising specialties

PA: Landmark Signs & Electrical Maintenance Corporation
1501 Broadway Ste 501
New York NY 10036
212 262-3699

(G-10172)
LANGUAGE AND GRAPHICS INC
350 W 57th St Apt 14i (10019-3762)
PHONE................................212 315-5266
Margaret Keppler, *President*
Patricia Encinosa, *Vice Pres*
Michael Keppler, *Treasurer*
EMP: 5
SALES (est): 317.1K Privately Held
SIC: 2741 7389 Miscellaneous publishing;
translation services

(G-10173)
LAREGENCE INC
34 W 27th St Fl 2 (10001-6901)
PHONE................................212 736-2548
Jay Perlstein, *President*
Kathy Jones, *Treasurer*
Lily Lau, *Office Mgr*
▼ EMP: 20
SALES (est): 2.6MM Privately Held
SIC: 2221 2391 Upholstery, tapestry &
wall covering fabrics; curtains & draperies

(G-10174)
LARTE DEL GELATO INC
75 9th Ave Frnt 38 (10011-4730)
PHONE................................212 366-0570
Francisco Realmuto, *Owner*
▲ EMP: 9
SALES (est): 755.5K Privately Held
SIC: 2052 2099 Cones, ice cream; jelly,
corncob (gelatin)

(G-10175)
LASER & ELECTRON BEAM INC
77 7th Ave Apt 3h (10011-6612)
PHONE................................603 626-6080
EMP: 6
SQ FT: 4,800
SALES (est): 65.9K Privately Held
SIC: 3599 8734 8711 Operates As A Ma-
chine Shop Testing Laboratory & Consult-
ing Service For Hi-Tech Equipment

(G-10176)
LATCHABLE INC
450 W 33rd St Fl 12 (10001-2610)
PHONE................................917 338-3915
Luke Schoenfelder, *CEO*
EMP: 200 EST: 2014
SALES (est): 355.7K Privately Held
SIC: 7372 Business oriented computer
software

(G-10177)
**LATINA MEDIA VENTURES LLC
(PA)**
114 E 25th St Fl 11 (10010-2979)
PHONE................................212 642-0200
Edward Lewis, *Ch of Bd*
Peter Glusker, *Mng Member*
Molly Ashby,
Christy Haubegger,
Cynthia R Lewis,
▲ EMP: 46
SALES (est): 14.2MM Privately Held
WEB: www.latinapromotions.com
SIC: 2721 Magazines: publishing & printing

(G-10178)
LAUFER WIND GROUP LLC
270 Lafayette St Ste 1402 (10012-3364)
PHONE................................212 792-3912
Eric Laufer, *Mng Member*
EMP: 15
SALES (est): 2.5MM Privately Held
SIC: 3812 Radar systems & equipment

(G-10179)
LAZARE KAPLAN INTL INC (PA)
580 5th Ave Ste 701 (10036-4726)
PHONE................................212 972-9700
Maurice Tempelsman, *Ch of Bd*
Leon Tempelsman, *Vice Chairman*
William H Moryto, *CFO*
Marcee Feinberg, *VP Mktg*
▲ EMP: 56 EST: 1903

SALES (est): 9.3MM Privately Held
WEB: www.lazarediamonds.com
SIC: 3915 Diamond cutting & polishing

(G-10180)
LE BOOK PUBLISHING INC (HQ)
580 Broadway Rm 912 (10012-3297)
PHONE................................212 334-5252
Veronique Kolasa, *President*
Michael Kazam, *Vice Pres*
▲ EMP: 9
SALES (est): 1.1MM Privately Held
WEB: www.lebook.com
SIC: 2731 Books: publishing only

(G-10181)
LEA & VIOLA INC
525 Fashion Ave Rm 1401 (10018-4914)
PHONE................................646 918-6866
Minji Kim, *President*
EMP: 6
SQ FT: 4,000
SALES (est): 810K Privately Held
SIC: 2331 Women's & misses' blouses &
shirts

(G-10182)
**LEADERSHIP CONNECT INC
(PA)**
1407 Broadway Rm 318 (10018-3853)
PHONE................................212 627-4140
Michael Crosby, *CEO*
Sanja Klima, *Vice Pres*
Shai Tzach, *Vice Pres*
Jackie Johnson, *Cust Mgr*
Brian Combs, *Sales Staff*
EMP: 70
SQ FT: 11,400
SALES (est): 11.2MM Privately Held
SIC: 2721 2741 Periodicals: publishing
only; directories: publishing only, not
printed on site

(G-10183)
LEADERTEX INTL INC
Also Called: Leadertex Group
135 W 36th St Fl 12 (10018-6981)
PHONE................................212 563-2242
Joseph Delijani, *Ch of Bd*
▲ EMP: 20
SALES (est): 1.7MM Privately Held
SIC: 2252 Men's, boys' & girls' hosiery

(G-10184)
**LEANNE MARSHALL DESIGNS
INC**
39 W 38th St Fl 12 (10018-1952)
PHONE................................646 918-6349
Leanne Marshall, *CEO*
EMP: 10
SALES (est): 770.4K Privately Held
SIC: 2335 Bridal & formal gowns

(G-10185)
LEARNINGEXPRESS LLC
224 W 29th St Fl 3 (10001-5204)
PHONE................................646 274-6454
Barry Lippman, *CEO*
Kheil McIntyre, *COO*
Ilsa Halpern, *Vice Pres*
Steve Nolan, *Vice Pres*
Janine Swenson, *Marketing Staff*
EMP: 35
SALES (est): 5.7MM Privately Held
WEB: www.learningexpressllc.com
SIC: 2731 Book publishing

(G-10186)
**LEATHER HUB WORLDWIDE
LLC**
264 W 40th St Fl 17 (10018-1512)
PHONE................................310 386-2247
Jaggi Singh,
EMP: 250
SALES (est): 3MM Privately Held
SIC: 3111 Industrial leather products

(G-10187)
LEBLON HOLDINGS LLC
33 Irving Pl Fl 3 (10003-2332)
PHONE................................212 741-2675
Jim Myers, *CFO*
Steven Luttmann,
▲ EMP: 35
SQ FT: 3,000

SALES (est): 3.8MM Privately Held
SIC: 2085 Rum (alcoholic beverage)
PA: Bacardi Limited
65 Pitts Bay Road
Hamilton

(G-10188)
LEBLON LLC
266 W 26th St Ste 801 (10001-6722)
PHONE................................786 281-5672
Thomas Bonney, *CFO*
Steve Luttmann, *Mng Member*
Gerrard Schweitzer,
▲ EMP: 40
SALES (est): 2.9MM Privately Held
SIC: 2085 Distilled & blended liquors

(G-10189)
**LEE & LOW BOOKS
INCORPORATED**
Also Called: Bebop Books
95 Madison Ave Rm 1205 (10016-7808)
PHONE................................212 779-4400
Thomas Low, *President*
Jessica Echeverria, *Editor*
Jennifer Fox, *Editor*
Craig Low, *Vice Pres*
Louise May, *Vice Pres*
▲ EMP: 14
SQ FT: 4,500
SALES (est): 1.7MM Privately Held
WEB: www.leeandlow.com
SIC: 2731 Books: publishing only

(G-10190)
**LEE WORLD INDUSTRIES LLC
(PA)**
150 Broadway Ste 1608 (10038-4381)
PHONE................................212 265-8866
James Lee, *CEO*
Lisa Lee, *Vice Pres*
▲ EMP: 13
SQ FT: 14,500
SALES: 4MM Privately Held
WEB: www.leeworld.com
SIC: 3714 Motor vehicle parts & acces-
sories

(G-10191)
**LEE YUEN FUNG TRADING CO
INC (PA)**
125 W 29th St Fl 5 (10001-5780)
PHONE................................212 594-9595
Moon Tong Fok, *President*
EMP: 14
SQ FT: 4,000
SALES: 8MM Privately Held
SIC: 2833 5149 Drugs & herbs: grading,
grinding & milling; seasonings, sauces &
extracts

(G-10192)
**LEFRAK ENTERTAINMENT CO
LTD**
Also Called: L M R
40 W 57th St Fl 4 (10019-4001)
PHONE................................212 586-3600
Samuel J Lefrak, *Ch of Bd*
Richard S Lefrak, *Vice Ch Bd*
Herbert Moelis, *President*
EMP: 9
SALES (est): 660K Privately Held
SIC: 2741 3652 Music book & sheet music
publishing; pre-recorded records & tapes

(G-10193)
**LEHMANN PRINTING COMPANY
INC**
247 W 37th St Rm 2a (10018-5706)
PHONE................................212 929-2395
David Lehmann, *President*
Ruth Lehmann, *Manager*
EMP: 5
SQ FT: 10,000
SALES (est): 763.5K Privately Held
WEB: www.lehmannprinting.com
SIC: 2752 Commercial printing, offset

(G-10194)
LEMETRIC HAIR CENTERS INC
124 E 40th St Rm 601 (10016-1769)
PHONE................................212 986-5620
Elline Surianello, *President*
Marvin Blender, *Vice Pres*
EMP: 15

SALES (est): 1.2MM **Privately Held**
WEB: www.lemetric.com
SIC: 3999 7231 Hairpin mountings; beauty shops

(G-10195)
LENDING TRIMMING CO INC
179 Christopher St (10014-2815)
PHONE....................212 242-7502
John Benis, *President*
William Jarblum, *Admin Sec*
EMP: 80 **EST:** 1944
SQ FT: 7,000
SALES (est): 4.6MM **Privately Held**
SIC: 2396 Trimming, fabric

(G-10196)
LENG UNIVERSAL INC
Also Called: Emoji
530 7th Ave Rm 1101 (10018-4868)
PHONE....................212 398-6800
EMP: 12
SQ FT: 3,800
SALES (est): 1.2MM **Privately Held**
SIC: 2369 2339 2325 Mfg Girl/Youth Outerwear Mfg Women's/Misses' Outerwear Mfg Men's/Boy's Trousers

(G-10197)
LENORE MARSHALL INC
231 W 29th St Frnt 1 (10001-5209)
PHONE....................212 947-5945
Leo Marshall, *President*
John Petkanas, *President*
▲ **EMP:** 5 **EST:** 1957
SALES (est): 390K **Privately Held**
SIC: 2353 Millinery

(G-10198)
LEO D BERNSTEIN & SONS INC (PA)
Also Called: Bernstein Display
151 W 25th St Frnt 1 (10001-7204)
PHONE....................212 337-9578
Roger Friedman, *Ch of Bd*
Anthony Tripoli, *President*
Edmund Bernstein, *Chairman*
Mitchell Bernstein, *COO*
Doreen McMzi, *Sales Staff*
▲ **EMP:** 20 **EST:** 1965
SQ FT: 192,000
SALES (est): 18.8MM **Privately Held**
WEB: www.bernsteindisplay.com
SIC: 3999 2541 5046 7389 Forms: display, dress & show; store & office display cases & fixtures; store fixtures; store equipment; design services

(G-10199)
LEO INGWER INC
62 W 47th St Ste 1004 (10036-3286)
PHONE....................212 719-1342
Kenneth Ingwer, *President*
Danielle I Cohen, *Vice Pres*
Rochelle Ingwer-Levine, *Vice Pres*
Matt Selig, *VP Sales*
Ashley Ingwer, *Sales Staff*
EMP: 42 **EST:** 1941
SQ FT: 3,500
SALES (est): 5.8MM **Privately Held**
WEB: www.leoingwer.com
SIC: 3911 Mountings, gold or silver; pens, leather goods, etc.

(G-10200)
LEO PAPER INC
286 5th Ave Fl 6 (10001-4512)
PHONE....................917 305-0708
Bijan Pakzada, *President*
EMP: 7
SALES (est): 426.5K **Privately Held**
SIC: 2759 Commercial printing

(G-10201)
LEO SCHACHTER & CO INC
529 5th Ave (10017-4608)
PHONE....................212 688-2000
Michael Metz, *CEO*
Joe Green, *Exec VP*
EMP: 100
SALES (est): 3.6MM **Privately Held**
SIC: 3911 5094 Jewelry apparel; diamonds (gems)

(G-10202)
LEO SCHACHTER DIAMONDS LLC
Also Called: Leo Diamond, The
50 W 47th St Ste 2100 (10036-8687)
PHONE....................212 688-2000
Lenny Kramer, *Sales Staff*
Elliot Tannenbaum, *Mng Member*
Michael Steinmetz, *Manager*
Mimi Fishman, *Network Mgr*
Eric Austein,
EMP: 100 **EST:** 1981
SQ FT: 11,335
SALES (est): 15.4MM
SALES (corp-wide): 10.2MM **Privately Held**
WEB: www.leoschachter.com
SIC: 3915 5094 Jewelers' materials & lapidary work; jewelry & precious stones
PA: Leo Schachter Diamonds Ltd
54 Bezalel
Ramat Gan 52521
357 662-23

(G-10203)
LEON MEGE INC
Also Called: Art of Platinum, The
151 W 46th St Ste 901 (10036-8512)
PHONE....................212 768-3868
Leon Mege, *Owner*
EMP: 12
SQ FT: 4,500
SALES (est): 810.5K **Privately Held**
WEB: www.artofplatinum.com
SIC: 3911 Jewelry, precious metal

(G-10204)
LESLIE STUART CO INC
Also Called: Donna Degan
149 W 36th St Fl 8 (10018-9474)
PHONE....................212 629-4551
Gene Fobarty, *President*
Donna Degan, *Vice Pres*
Eli Jeidel, *Vice Pres*
Eugene Fogarty, *Director*
▲ **EMP:** 17
SQ FT: 4,000
SALES (est): 2.2MM **Privately Held**
WEB: www.donnadegnan.com
SIC: 2339 Women's & misses' athletic clothing & sportswear

(G-10205)
LEVI SHABTAI
1 W 47th St (10036-4785)
PHONE....................212 302-7393
Levi Shabtai, *Owner*
EMP: 5
SALES (est): 208.6K **Privately Held**
SIC: 3915 Diamond cutting & polishing

(G-10206)
LEVY GROUP INC (PA)
Also Called: Liz Claiborne Coats
1333 Broadway Fl 9 (10018-1064)
PHONE....................212 398-0707
Donald Levy, *President*
Lawrence Levy, *Vice Pres*
Larry Leeder, *VP Sales*
Max Norman, *Manager*
Gary Seagobind, *MIS Dir*
▲ **EMP:** 150 **EST:** 1995
SQ FT: 27,000
SALES (est): 80.5MM **Privately Held**
WEB: www.oasisfarm.com
SIC: 2385 2337 Raincoats, except vulcanized rubber: purchased materials; jackets & vests, except fur & leather: women's

(G-10207)
LF OUTERWEAR LLC
463 7th Ave Fl 12 (10018-7499)
PHONE....................212 239-2025
Richard Kringstein,
Barry Kringstein,
▲ **EMP:** 80
SALES (est): 3.4MM **Privately Held**
SIC: 2337 Women's & misses' suits & coats

(G-10208)
LF SOURCING (MILLWORK) LLC
1359 Broadway Fl 18 (10018-7839)
PHONE....................212 827-3352
▲ **EMP:** 6 **EST:** 2011

SALES (est): 145.9K **Privately Held**
SIC: 2369 Headwear: girls', children's & infants'
HQ: Li & Fung Limited
11/F Llifung Twr
Lai Chi Kok KLN

(G-10209)
LIBERTY APPAREL COMPANY INC (PA)
1407 Broadway Rm 1500 (10018-2836)
PHONE....................718 625-4000
Hagai Laniado, *President*
Albert Negri, *Principal*
Bryan Lattmen, *Vice Pres*
Jeffrey Wine, *CFO*
▲ **EMP:** 50
SQ FT: 38,000
SALES (est): 4MM **Privately Held**
WEB: www.libertyapparel.com
SIC: 2331 2339 2369 Women's & misses' blouses & shirts; women's & misses' outerwear; girls' & children's outerwear

(G-10210)
LICENDERS (PA)
939 8th Ave (10019-4264)
PHONE....................212 759-5200
Adie Horowitz, *Principal*
EMP: 9 **EST:** 2010
SALES (est): 1.2MM **Privately Held**
SIC: 3647 5087 Headlights (fixtures), vehicular; service establishment equipment

(G-10211)
LIFE EARTH COMPANY
200 W 113th St Apt 2d (10026-3303)
PHONE....................310 751-0627
Reginald Askew, *CEO*
EMP: 2
SALES: 7.5MM **Privately Held**
SIC: 2013 2086 Frozen meats from purchased meat; soft drinks: packaged in cans, bottles, etc.

(G-10212)
LIFE ON EARTH INC (PA)
575 Lexington Ave Fl 4 (10022-6146)
PHONE....................646 844-9897
Fernando Oswaldo Leonzo, *Ch of Bd*
John Romagosa, *President*
Robert Gunther, *COO*
Randy Berholtz, *Exec VP*
EMP: 16 **EST:** 2013
SALES: 1MM **Publicly Held**
SIC: 2087 Beverage bases

(G-10213)
LIFE STYLE DESIGN GROUP
Also Called: Sag Harbor
1441 Broadway Fl 7 (10018-1905)
PHONE....................212 391-8666
EMP: 35 **EST:** 1975
SQ FT: 12,000
SALES (est): 2.6MM
SALES (corp-wide): 594MM **Privately Held**
WEB: www.kellwoodco.com
SIC: 2339 Sportswear, women's
PA: Kellwood Company, Llc
600 Kellwood Pkwy Ste 110
Chesterfield MO 63017
314 576-3100

(G-10214)
LIFESTYLE DESIGN USA LTD
Also Called: Cyber Knit
315 W 39th St Rm 1400 (10018-4063)
PHONE....................212 279-9400
Daniel Honig, *President*
Janine Girardi, *Director*
▲ **EMP:** 6
SQ FT: 1,000
SALES (est): 1.1MM **Privately Held**
SIC: 2257 Dyeing & finishing circular knit fabrics

(G-10215)
LIFTFORWARD INC (PA)
180 Maiden Ln Fl 10 (10038-5178)
PHONE....................917 693-4993
Jeffrey Rogers, *President*
Barbara Steinberg, *Controller*
Anthony Galan, *Underwriter*
Geoff Miller, *Exec Dir*
Paul Wright, *Director*

EMP: 20
SALES: 25MM **Privately Held**
SIC: 7372 Business oriented computer software

(G-10216)
LIGHT HOUSE HILL MARKETING
Also Called: Signatures Group
38 W 39th St Fl 4l (10018-2150)
PHONE....................212 354-1338
Donald Schmidt, *President*
▲ **EMP:** 16
SQ FT: 2,900
SALES (est): 1.7MM **Privately Held**
WEB: www.signaturespromo.com
SIC: 2231 Apparel & outerwear broadwoven fabrics

(G-10217)
LIGHT INC
530 Fashion Ave Rm 1002 (10018-4869)
PHONE....................212 629-3255
Alice Sim, *President*
▲ **EMP:** 6 **EST:** 1993
SALES (est): 881.5K **Privately Held**
WEB: www.light.com
SIC: 2339 Women's & misses' outerwear

(G-10218)
LIGHTBULB PRESS INC
39 W 28th St (10001-4203)
PHONE....................212 485-8800
Kenneth Morris, *Ch of Bd*
Delphine Leymarie, *Office Mgr*
Kara Wilson, *Director*
EMP: 30
SQ FT: 7,500
SALES (est): 2.7MM **Privately Held**
WEB: www.lightbulbpress.net
SIC: 2741 Miscellaneous publishing

(G-10219)
LIGHTHOUSE COMPONENTS
14 Wall St (10005-2101)
PHONE....................917 993-6820
Maurice Gaete, *CEO*
EMP: 25
SALES (est): 944.2K **Privately Held**
SIC: 3679 Electronic components

(G-10220)
LILY & TAYLOR INC
Also Called: Lilly Collection
247 W 37th St Frnt 6 (10018-5042)
PHONE....................212 564-5459
Sohail Elyaszadeh, *President*
Morris Elyaszadeh, *Manager*
▲ **EMP:** 15
SQ FT: 3,500
SALES: 6MM **Privately Held**
WEB: www.lilyandtaylor.com
SIC: 2335 2337 Gowns, formal; suits: women's, misses' & juniors'; slacks: women's, misses' & juniors'

(G-10221)
LINDER NEW YORK LLC
195 Chrystie St Rm 900 (10002-1230)
PHONE....................646 678-5819
Sam Linder, *Mng Member*
EMP: 10 **EST:** 2007
SALES (est): 1.2MM **Privately Held**
SIC: 2329 2389 Athletic (warmup, sweat & jogging) suits: men's & boys'; men's miscellaneous accessories

(G-10222)
LINTEX LINENS INC
295 5th Ave Ste 1703 (10016-7130)
PHONE....................212 679-8046
Kurt Hamburger, *President*
Rae Ellen Blum, *Vice Pres*
◆ **EMP:** 500
SQ FT: 6,000
SALES (est): 36.4MM **Privately Held**
SIC: 2299 5023 Fabrics: linen, jute, hemp, ramie; linens, table

(G-10223)
LIONEL HABAS ASSOCIATES INC
1601 3rd Ave Apt 22d (10128-0028)
PHONE....................212 860-8454
EMP: 10
SQ FT: 200

▲ = Import ▼=Export
◆ =Import/Export

SALES (est): 840K **Privately Held**
SIC: 2652 Mfg Setup Paperboard Boxes

(G-10224)
LIPPINCOTT MASSIE MCQUILKIN L
27 W 20th St Ste 305 (10011-3731)
PHONE.............................212 352-2055
Rob McQuilkin, *Mng Member*
Laney Becker, *Agent*
Clare Mao, *Assistant*
EMP: 10
SALES (est): 896.1K **Privately Held**
SIC: 2731 Books: publishing only

(G-10225)
LIST & BEISLER GMBH
311 W 43rd St Fl 12 (10036-6004)
PHONE.............................646 866-6960
Samuel Grigg, *Director*
EMP: 30
SALES (est): 942.1K **Privately Held**
SIC: 2095 Roasted coffee

(G-10226)
LITERARY CLASSICS OF US
Also Called: Library of America
14 E 60th St Ste 1101 (10022-7115)
PHONE.............................212 308-3360
Cheryl Hurley, *President*
Geoffrey Obrien, *Chief*
Daniel Baker, *CFO*
Benjamin Ordover, *Treasurer*
Lily TSE, *Accountant*
▲ EMP: 16
SQ FT: 4,000
SALES: 6MM **Privately Held**
SIC: 2731 2732 Books: publishing only; book printing

(G-10227)
LITHOMATIC BUSINESS FORMS INC
233 W 18th St Frnt A (10011-4570)
PHONE.............................212 255-6700
Irwin Ostrega, *President*
EMP: 3 EST: 1971
SQ FT: 5,000
SALES: 1.5MM **Privately Held**
SIC: 2752 Commercial printing, offset

(G-10228)
LITTLE BEE BOOKS INC
Also Called: Bonnier Publishing Usa, Inc.
251 Park Ave S Fl 12 (10010-7302)
PHONE.............................212 321-0237
Shimul Tolia, *President*
Sonali Fry, *Publisher*
Thomas Morgan, *Finance Dir*
Charlie Ilgunas, *Assistant*
▲ EMP: 40
SQ FT: 4,000
SALES (est): 1.6MM
SALES (corp-wide): 2.9B **Privately Held**
SIC: 2731 Books: publishing only
HQ: Bonnier Ab
    Kungsgatan 49
    Stockholm 111 2
    873 640-00

(G-10229)
LITTLE ERIC SHOES ON MADISON
1118 Madison Ave (10028-0406)
PHONE.............................212 717-1513
Robert Pansinkoff, *President*
Robert Pasinkoff, *President*
EMP: 6
SALES (est): 904.7K **Privately Held**
SIC: 3021 Canvas shoes, rubber soled

(G-10230)
LITTLE WOLF CABINET SHOP INC
1583 1st Ave Frnt 1 (10028-4273)
PHONE.............................212 734-1116
John Wolf, *President*
Maureen Fritsch, *Corp Secy*
John Fritsch, *Vice Pres*
EMP: 20
SQ FT: 2,500
SALES (est): 2.8MM **Privately Held**
SIC: 2511 5712 Wood household furniture; furniture stores

(G-10231)
LITTLEBITS ELECTRONICS INC (HQ)
601 W 26th St Rm M274 (10001-1129)
PHONE.............................917 464-4577
Paul Berberian, *CEO*
EMP: 52
SQ FT: 18,000
SALES (est): 12.4MM **Privately Held**
SIC: 3944 Electronic toys

(G-10232)
LIVE UP TOP INC
1460 Broadway (10036-7329)
PHONE.............................866 333-1332
Frank Barletta,
EMP: 15
SALES (est): 169.6K **Privately Held**
SIC: 7372 7389 Business oriented computer software;

(G-10233)
LIVE VOTE II INC
105 W 86th St 322 (10024-3412)
PHONE.............................646 343-9053
EMP: 5 EST: 2017
SALES (est): 142.2K **Privately Held**
SIC: 7372 7371 Prepackaged Software Services Custom Computer Programing

(G-10234)
LIVERIGHT PUBLISHING CORP
Also Called: Norton, Ww & Company,
500 5th Ave Fl 6 (10110-0501)
PHONE.............................212 354-5500
Drake McSeely, *President*
Victor Schmalzer, *General Mgr*
John G Benedict, *Vice Pres*
Star Lawrence, *Vice Pres*
Philip Marino, *Marketing Staff*
EMP: 9
SQ FT: 3,000
SALES (est): 888.2K
SALES (corp-wide): 180.7MM **Privately Held**
WEB: www.wwnorton.com
SIC: 2731 Books: publishing only
PA: W. W. Norton & Company, Inc.
    500 5th Ave Fl 5
    New York NY 10110
    212 354-5500

(G-10235)
LIVETILES CORP (PA)
137 W 25th St Fl 6 (10001-7232)
PHONE.............................917 472-7887
Owen Brandt, *Vice Pres*
Daniel Goss, *Vice Pres*
Jonathan Green, *Finance Dir*
Jed Khan, *Sales Staff*
EMP: 18
SQ FT: 100
SALES (est): 3.8MM **Privately Held**
SIC: 7372 Business oriented computer software

(G-10236)
LLC MAJOR MAJOR
1407 Broadway Fl 10 (10018-3271)
PHONE.............................212 354-8550
Claudia Polon, *Credit Staff*
EMP: 50
SALES (est): 1.2MM **Privately Held**
SIC: 2326 Men's & boys' work clothing

(G-10237)
LMC 49TH INC
Also Called: La Maison Du Chocolat
1018 Madison Ave (10075-0113)
PHONE.............................212 744-7117
Joel Matos, *Manager*
EMP: 15
SALES (corp-wide): 6.3B **Privately Held**
SIC: 2066 Chocolate
HQ: Lmc 49th, Inc.
    4707 30th Pl
    Long Island City NY 11101
    718 361-9161

(G-10238)
LMR GROUP INC
463 7th Ave Fl 4 (10018-8725)
PHONE.............................212 730-9221
Linlin Fang, *Principal*
Robi Hagooli, *Principal*

Steven Stuppler, *Director*
EMP: 5 EST: 2016
SALES (est): 247.8K **Privately Held**
SIC: 2335 Women's, juniors' & misses' dresses

(G-10239)
LOAR GROUP INC (PA)
450 Lexington Ave Fl 31 (10017-3925)
PHONE.............................212 210-9348
Dirkson Charles, *CEO*
Jim Mullen, *President*
Glenn Dalessandro, *CFO*
EMP: 144
SALES (est): 23.6MM **Privately Held**
SIC: 3728 Aircraft parts & equipment

(G-10240)
LOCATIONS MAGAZINE
124 E 79th St (10075-0353)
PHONE.............................212 288-4745
Joel Scher, *Owner*
EMP: 5
SALES (est): 290K **Privately Held**
SIC: 2721 Magazines: publishing only, not printed on site

(G-10241)
LOCKHEED MARTIN CORPORATION
420 Lexington Ave Rm 2601 (10170-2602)
PHONE.............................212 953-1510
Ellen Strauss, *Manager*
Victoria Davila, *Manager*
EMP: 8 **Publicly Held**
WEB: www.lockheedmartin.com
SIC: 3812 Search & navigation equipment
PA: Lockheed Martin Corporation
    6801 Rockledge Dr
    Bethesda MD 20817

(G-10242)
LOCKHEED MARTIN CORPORATION
600 3rd Ave Fl 35 (10016-2001)
PHONE.............................212 697-1105
Larry Ramie, *Engineer*
Lisa McMeekin, *Branch Mgr*
EMP: 85 **Publicly Held**
WEB: www.lockheedmartin.com
SIC: 3812 Search & navigation equipment
PA: Lockheed Martin Corporation
    6801 Rockledge Dr
    Bethesda MD 20817

(G-10243)
LOGO
1515 Broadway (10036-8901)
PHONE.............................212 846-2568
Felix Colon, *Manager*
EMP: 6 EST: 2008
SALES (est): 498.2K **Privately Held**
SIC: 2869 Fuels

(G-10244)
LOIS KITCHEN LLC
206 Avenue A Apt 2a (10009-3405)
PHONE.............................216 308-9335
Nora O'Malley,
EMP: 5
SALES (est): 165.7K **Privately Held**
SIC: 3999 Manufacturing industries

(G-10245)
LOKAI HOLDINGS LLC
180 Varick St Rm 504 (10014-5423)
PHONE.............................646 979-3474
Steven Izen, *CEO*
Jessica Harrington, *Opers Staff*
Andrew Actman, *CFO*
Elyse McAvoy, *Accounts Exec*
Corinne Mesa, *Accounts Exec*
▲ EMP: 10
SALES: 13MM **Privately Held**
SIC: 3911 5199 Bracelets, precious metal; general merchandise, non-durable

(G-10246)
LOLLYTOGS LTD (PA)
Also Called: Lt Apparel Group
100 W 33rd St Ste 1012 (10001-2984)
PHONE.............................212 502-6000
Richard Sutton, *CEO*
Morris Sutton, *President*
Judy Reiley, *Vice Pres*

Joseph Sutton, *Vice Pres*
Jeffrey Sutton, *Treasurer*
◆ EMP: 80 EST: 1958
SQ FT: 40,000
SALES (est): 2.6MM **Privately Held**
SIC: 2369 5137 Girls' & children's outerwear; sportswear, women's & children's

(G-10247)
LONDON THEATER NEWS LTD
12 E 86th St Apt 620 (10028-0511)
PHONE.............................212 517-8608
Roger Harris, *President*
EMP: 19
SALES (est): 130K **Privately Held**
SIC: 2741 7922 Newsletter publishing; ticket agency, theatrical

(G-10248)
LONGEVITY BRANDS LLC
Also Called: Swim USA
250 W 39th St Rm 405 (10018-4630)
PHONE.............................212 231-7877
EMP: 5
SALES (est): 379.2K **Privately Held**
SIC: 2329 2369 Bathing suits & swimwear: men's & boys'; bathing suits & swimwear: girls', children's & infants'

(G-10249)
LONGO NEW YORK INC
444 W 17th St (10011-5893)
P.O. Box 511, Wharton NJ (07885-0511)
PHONE.............................212 929-7128
EMP: 10
SALES (est): 530.5K **Privately Held**
SIC: 7694 Armature Rewinding

(G-10250)
LONGTAIL STUDIOS INC
180 Varick St Rm 820 (10014-5419)
PHONE.............................646 443-8146
Gerard Guillemot, *President*
Claude Guillemot, *Vice Pres*
Michelle Guillemot, *Vice Pres*
Yves Guillemot, *Vice Pres*
Ho-Kin MA, *Technology*
EMP: 26
SQ FT: 4,000
SALES (est): 3.3MM **Privately Held**
WEB: www.longtailstudios.com
SIC: 3695 Computer software tape & disks: blank, rigid & floppy

(G-10251)
LOOK BY M INC
838 Avenue Of The America (10001-4194)
PHONE.............................212 213-4019
Youjung Kim, *President*
▲ EMP: 5
SALES (est): 398.4K **Privately Held**
SIC: 2252 Tights & leg warmers

(G-10252)
LOOKBOOKS MEDIA INC
208 W 30th St Rm 802 (10001-0883)
PHONE.............................646 737-3360
Emmanuel Serrano, *VP Finance*
Johanna Fulache, *Accounts Mgr*
Adam Helfgott, *CTO*
EMP: 15
SALES (est): 1.1MM **Privately Held**
SIC: 7372 Application computer software

(G-10253)
LOOM CONCEPTS LLC
767 Lexington Ave Rm 405 (10065-8553)
PHONE.............................212 813-9586
▲ EMP: 2
SQ FT: 500
SALES: 1.8MM **Privately Held**
SIC: 2273 Mfg Carpets/Rugs

(G-10254)
LOOMSTATE LLC
270 Bowery Fl 3 (10012-3674)
PHONE.............................212 219-2300
Annie Graziani, *General Mgr*
Leron Garriques, *Accounting Mgr*
Art Ryan, *Mng Member*
Orlando Medina,
Kevin Ryan,
▲ EMP: 25
SALES (est): 3.7MM **Privately Held**
SIC: 2231 Weaving mill, broadwoven fabrics: wool or similar fabric

(G-10255)
LORAL SPACE & COMMNCTNS HOLDNG
600 5th Ave Fl 16 (10020-2324)
PHONE.....................212 697-1105
EMP: 30
SALES (est): 1.6MM **Publicly Held**
SIC: 3663 Satellites, communications
HQ: Loral Spacecom Corporation
　　565 5th Ave Fl 19
　　New York NY 10017
　　212 697-1105

(G-10256)
LORAL SPACE COMMUNICATIONS INC (PA)
600 5th Ave Fl 16 (10020-2324)
PHONE.....................212 697-1105
Mark H Rachesky, *Ch of Bd*
Michael B Targoff, *Vice Ch Bd*
AVI Katz, *President*
Michael Targoff, *Vice Chairman*
Maude Brunschwig, *Vice Pres*
EMP: 22
SQ FT: 9,000
SALES (est): 870MM **Publicly Held**
WEB: www.ssloral.com
SIC: 3663 4899 Satellites, communications; satellite earth stations; data communication services

(G-10257)
LORAL SPACECOM CORPORATION (HQ)
565 5th Ave Fl 19 (10017-2431)
PHONE.....................212 697-1105
Michael Targoff, *CEO*
Harvey Rein, *Vice Pres*
Randy Simons, *Opers Mgr*
Richard Mastoloni, *Treasurer*
John Stack, *Asst Treas*
EMP: 30
SALES: 869.4MM **Publicly Held**
WEB: www.hq.loral.com
SIC: 3663 Satellites, communications

(G-10258)
LOREAL USA INC
Biotherm
575 5th Ave Bsmt (10017-2422)
PHONE.....................212 818-1500
Felicia Borzelino, *President*
Matt Fluck, *President*
Lou Giallella, *President*
Janice Wolk, *General Mgr*
Robert J Cassou, *Senior VP*
EMP: 470
SALES (corp-wide): 4.4B **Privately Held**
WEB: www.loralparisusa.com
SIC: 2844 Hair preparations, including shampoos; cosmetic preparations; perfumes & colognes
HQ: L'oreal Usa, Inc.
　　10 Hudson Yards
　　New York NY 10001
　　212 818-1500

(G-10259)
LOREAL USA INC
435 Hudson St (10014-3941)
PHONE.....................917 606-9554
EMP: 373
SALES (corp-wide): 4.4B **Privately Held**
WEB: www.loralparisusa.com
SIC: 2844 5122 Toilet preparations; cosmetics, perfumes & hair products
HQ: L'oreal Usa, Inc.
　　10 Hudson Yards
　　New York NY 10001
　　212 818-1500

(G-10260)
LOREAL USA INC
10 Hudson Yards Fl 27 (10001-2159)
PHONE.....................212 389-4201
Karen Czajkowski, *Branch Mgr*
EMP: 30
SALES (corp-wide): 4.4B **Privately Held**
WEB: www.loralparisusa.com
SIC: 2844 Depilatories (cosmetic); shampoos, rinses, conditioners: hair; face creams or lotions; hair coloring preparations

HQ: L'oreal Usa, Inc.
　　10 Hudson Yards
　　New York NY 10001
　　212 818-1500

(G-10261)
LOREAL USA INC
1485 5th Ave (10035-2772)
PHONE.....................646 658-5477
Hal Dally, *Vice Pres*
Candy Gebhart, *Vice Pres*
Roxanne Barretto, *Marketing Staff*
Bill Lynch, *Info Tech Dir*
Martin Aubut, *Director*
EMP: 274
SALES (corp-wide): 4.4B **Privately Held**
SIC: 2844 Toilet preparations
HQ: L'oreal Usa, Inc.
　　10 Hudson Yards
　　New York NY 10001
　　212 818-1500

(G-10262)
LOREAL USA PRODUCTS INC (DH)
10 Hudson Yards (10001-2157)
P.O. Box 701050, Salt Lake City UT (84170-1050)
PHONE.....................212 818-1500
Frederic Roze, *President*
Elizabeth Richardson, *President*
Rebecca Caruso, *Exec VP*
Jessica Hauff, *Senior VP*
Kevin Mason, *Vice Pres*
▲ EMP: 5
SALES (est): 10.9MM
SALES (corp-wide): 4.4B **Privately Held**
SIC: 2844 Hair coloring preparations; shaving preparations; cosmetic preparations; toilet preparations
HQ: L'oreal Usa, Inc.
　　10 Hudson Yards
　　New York NY 10001
　　212 818-1500

(G-10263)
LORELEI ORTHOTICS PROSTHETICS
30 E 40th St Rm 905 (10016-1231)
PHONE.....................212 727-2011
Brian Kilcommons, *President*
Alene Chase, *Vice Pres*
EMP: 6
SQ FT: 5,000
SALES (est): 839.6K **Privately Held**
SIC: 3842 Braces, orthopedic; prosthetic appliances

(G-10264)
LORNAMEAD INC (DH)
1359 Broadway Fl 17 (10018-7117)
PHONE.....................716 874-7190
Randy Sloan, *CEO*
Brian Bradley, *Exec VP*
Jeff Lokken, *Vice Pres*
James Carney, *VP Opers*
Alex Stugis, *Opers Mgr*
◆ EMP: 90
SQ FT: 66,000
SALES (est): 19MM **Privately Held**
WEB: www.lornameadna.com
SIC: 2844 3843 Cosmetic preparations; compounds, dental

(G-10265)
LOS ANGLES TMES CMMNCTIONS LLC
711 3rd Ave (10017-4014)
PHONE.....................212 692-7170
Bonnie Sherer-Herrera, *Vice Pres*
Bob Hanna, *Branch Mgr*
EMP: 19
SALES (corp-wide): 846.2MM **Privately Held**
SIC: 2711 Newspapers
PA: Los Angeles Times Communications, Llc
　　2300 E Imperial Hwy
　　El Segundo CA 90245
　　213 237-5000

(G-10266)
LOS ANGLES TMES CMMNCTIONS LLC
780 3rd Ave Fl 40 (10017-2024)
PHONE.....................212 418-9600
Virginia Moncada, *Manager*
EMP: 35
SALES (corp-wide): 846.2MM **Privately Held**
SIC: 2711 Newspapers, publishing & printing
PA: Los Angeles Times Communications, Llc
　　2300 E Imperial Hwy
　　El Segundo CA 90245
　　213 237-5000

(G-10267)
LOST WORLDS INC
920 Riverside Dr Apt 68 (10032-5468)
PHONE.....................212 923-3423
Stuart Clurman, *President*
EMP: 9
SALES (est): 670K **Privately Held**
SIC: 2386 5699 Coats & jackets, leather & sheep-lined; leather garments

(G-10268)
LOTTA LUV BEAUTY LLC
1359 Broadway Fl 17 (10018-7117)
PHONE.....................646 786-2847
Elizabeth Alli,
▲ EMP: 10
SQ FT: 20,000
SALES (est): 1MM **Privately Held**
SIC: 2834 5122 Lip balms; cosmetics
PA: Li & Fung Limited
　　C/O Appleby
　　Hamilton

(G-10269)
LOU SALLY FASHIONS CORP (HQ)
Also Called: S L Fashions Group
1400 Broadway Fl 6 (10018-0728)
PHONE.....................212 354-9670
Mitchell Grabow, *President*
▲ EMP: 29
SQ FT: 5,500
SALES: 35MM
SALES (corp-wide): 42.9MM **Privately Held**
SIC: 2335 Women's, juniors' & misses' dresses
PA: Alex Apparel Group, Inc.
　　1407 Broadway Rm 1500
　　New York NY 10018
　　212 730-1533

(G-10270)
LOU SALLY FASHIONS CORP
1400 Broadway Frnt 3 (10018-5367)
PHONE.....................212 354-1283
Tony Porni, *Vice Pres*
EMP: 40
SALES (corp-wide): 42.9MM **Privately Held**
SIC: 2335 Women's, juniors' & misses' dresses
HQ: Lou Sally Fashions Corp
　　1400 Broadway Fl 6
　　New York NY 10018
　　212 354-9670

(G-10271)
LOUIS VUITTON NORTH AMER INC
1000 3rd Ave (10022-1230)
PHONE.....................212 644-2574
Michael Chavez, *Store Mgr*
Laura Knaub, *Store Mgr*
Annette Payne, *Store Mgr*
Alix Hamilton, *Advt Staff*
Melina Gordon, *Branch Mgr*
EMP: 9
SALES (corp-wide): 361.7MM **Privately Held**
SIC: 2711 Newspapers, publishing & printing
HQ: Louis Vuitton North America, Inc.
　　1 E 57th St
　　New York NY 10022
　　212 758-8877

(G-10272)
LOUNGEHOUSE LLC
34 W 33rd St Fl 11 (10001-3325)
PHONE.....................646 524-2965
Irving Safdieh, *Mng Member*
EMP: 20
SQ FT: 10,000
SALES (est): 942.4K **Privately Held**
SIC: 2341 5632 5651 Nightgowns & negligees: women's & children's; women's accessory & specialty stores; family clothing stores

(G-10273)
LOVEE DOLL & TOY CO INC
39 W 38th St Rm 4w (10018-5540)
PHONE.....................212 242-1545
Sam Horowitz, *President*
▲ EMP: 5 EST: 1962
SQ FT: 40,000
SALES (est): 896.2K **Privately Held**
SIC: 3942 Dolls, except stuffed toy animals

(G-10274)
LR ACQUISITION LLC
1407 Broadway Rm 1207 (10018-2899)
PHONE.....................212 301-8765
Sammy Catton, *CEO*
Harry Catton, *CFO*
EMP: 10 EST: 2017
SALES: 1.1MM **Privately Held**
SIC: 2252 Hosiery

(G-10275)
LR PARIS LLC (PA)
345 7th Ave Fl 19th (10001-5006)
PHONE.....................845 709-8013
Claire Souchet, *General Mgr*
Charles Dolige, *Mng Member*
Delaney Poon, *Manager*
Mariemma Dolige,
▲ EMP: 19
SALES (est): 1.4MM **Privately Held**
WEB: www.lrparis.com
SIC: 2389 3499 5947 5137 Masquerade costumes; giftware, brass goods; gift, novelty & souvenir shop; scarves, women's & children's; cloth cutting, bolting or winding; fabrics: linen, jute, hemp, ramie

(G-10276)
LS POWER EQUITY PARTNERS LP (PA)
1700 Broadway Fl 35 (10019-5905)
PHONE.....................212 615-3456
Mike Segal, *Ch of Bd*
Mark Brennan, *Exec VP*
Shimon Edelstein, *Exec VP*
John King, *Exec VP*
David Nanus, *Exec VP*
EMP: 1
SALES (est): 110.4MM **Privately Held**
WEB: www.ziccardi.com
SIC: 3568 1796 Power transmission equipment; power generating equipment installation

(G-10277)
LT2 LLC
Also Called: Letigre
250 Park Ave S Fl 10 (10003-1402)
PHONE.....................212 684-1510
Ryan O'Sullivan,
EMP: 25
SQ FT: 1,500
SALES: 25MM **Privately Held**
WEB: www.lt2.com
SIC: 2321 2331 Men's & boys' furnishings; women's & misses' blouses & shirts

(G-10278)
LTB MEDIA (USA) INC
Also Called: Louise Blouin Media
77 Water St Ste 702 (10005-4416)
PHONE.....................212 447-9555
Louise B Macbain, *President*
Anne-Laure Schuler, *Vice Pres*
Rochelle Stolzenberg, *Sales Dir*
EMP: 100
SQ FT: 16,000
SALES (est): 9.2MM **Privately Held**
SIC: 2721 Magazines: publishing & printing

▲ = Import ▼=Export
◆ =Import/Export

(G-10279)
LUCKY MAGAZINE
4 Times Sq Fl 22 (10036-6518)
PHONE.................212 286-6220
EMP: 15
SALES (est): 1.2MM Privately Held
SIC: 2721 Periodicals-Publishing/Printing

(G-10280)
LUCKY PEACH LLC
60 E 11th St Fl 5 (10003-6009)
PHONE.................212 228-0031
Narie Chung, Finance
Susan Wright,
EMP: 7
SALES (est): 762.6K Privately Held
SIC: 2741 Miscellaneous publishing

(G-10281)
LUDLOW MUSIC INC
266 W 37th St Fl 17 (10018-6655)
PHONE.................212 594-9795
Larry Richmond, President
Allen Brackerman, General Mgr
Bernard Gartler, Vice Pres
EMP: 14 EST: 1949
SALES (est): 655.3K Privately Held
SIC: 2741 Music, sheet: publishing only,
not printed on site

(G-10282)
**LUKOIL AMERICAS
CORPORATION (HQ)**
505 5th Ave Fl 9 (10017-4921)
PHONE.................212 421-4141
Robert Ferluga, CEO
Vadim Guzman, Ch of Bd
EMP: 125 EST: 1997
SALES (est): 140.9MM
SALES (corp-wide): 4B Privately Held
SIC: 1311 Crude petroleum & natural gas
PA: Lukoil, Pao
D. 11 Bulvar Sretenski
Moscow 10100
495 627-4999

(G-10283)
LULUVISE INC
229 W 116th St Apt 5a (10026-2799)
PHONE.................914 309-7812
Kewhyun Kelly-Yuoh, CFO
EMP: 25 EST: 2011
SQ FT: 1,000
SALES (est): 1.4MM Privately Held
SIC: 7372 Application computer software

(G-10284)
LUNZER INC
305 E 86th St (10028-4702)
PHONE.................201 794-2800
Jay K R Lunzer, CEO
EMP: 7
SQ FT: 10,000
SALES (est): 625.9K Privately Held
SIC: 3291 Abrasive products

(G-10285)
LUXCORE NETWORKS INC (PA)
14 Wall St Fl 20 (10005-2123)
PHONE.................212 618-1724
Gerald Ramdeen, CEO
Richard B Black, COO
Nick Lefkaditis, Vice Pres
Dr Marcus W Shute, Vice Pres
Tamer Yacoub, Vice Pres
EMP: 13
SALES (est): 2.7MM Privately Held
SIC: 3661 Telephones & telephone apparatus

(G-10286)
**LUXE IMAGINE CONSULTING
LLC**
261 W 35th St Ste 404 (10001-1906)
PHONE.................212 273-9770
EMP: 5
SALES (est): 270K Privately Held
SIC: 2329 2339 Mfg Mens Children &
Women's Apparel

(G-10287)
LVL XIII BRANDS INC
315 W 39th St Rm 1201 (10018-3928)
PHONE.................646 530-2795
Antonio Brown, CEO

EMP: 10
SQ FT: 600
SALES: 962K Privately Held
SIC: 2311 Men's & boys' suits & coats

(G-10288)
LYNN BRANDS LLC
230 W 38th St Fl 12 (10018-9052)
PHONE.................212 921-5495
Sean Wang,
EMP: 50
SALES (est): 1MM Privately Held
SIC: 2331 Women's & misses' blouses &
shirts

(G-10289)
LYNN BRANDS LLC
729 Seventh Ave (10019-6831)
PHONE.................626 376-8948
Shawn Wang, Mng Member
EMP: 40
SALES (est): 906.5K Privately Held
SIC: 2326 Men's & boys' work clothing

(G-10290)
LYTELINE LLC
175 Varick St Fl 8 (10014-7408)
P.O. Box 36527, Los Angeles CA (90036-
0527)
PHONE.................657 333-5983
M McAdams, Mng Member
EMP: 7
SALES (est): 611.9K Privately Held
SIC: 2833 5961 Vitamins, natural or syn-
thetic: bulk, uncompounded;

(G-10291)
M & S QUALITY CO LTD
26 W 47th St Ste 502 (10036-8603)
PHONE.................212 302-8757
Michael Saks, President
EMP: 10
SALES (est): 969.5K Privately Held
SIC: 3911 Jewelry, precious metal

(G-10292)
M & S SCHMALBERG INC
242 W 36th St Rm 700 (10018-8965)
PHONE.................212 244-2090
Warren Brand, President
Deborah Brand, Vice Pres
EMP: 10 EST: 1947
SQ FT: 2,500
SALES (est): 700K Privately Held
SIC: 3999 5992 Flowers, artificial & pre-
served; florists

(G-10293)
M G NEW YORK INC
14 E 60th St Ste 400 (10022-7146)
PHONE.................212 371-5566
Marlyse Gros, President
▲ EMP: 10
SQ FT: 1,665
SALES (est): 25.9MM Privately Held
SIC: 3172 Cosmetic bags

(G-10294)
**M H MANUFACTURING
INCORPORATED**
50 W 47th St (10036-8621)
P.O. Box 1743 (10163-1743)
PHONE.................212 461-6900
Judah Poupko, Vice Pres
David Habif, Sr Associate
EMP: 9
SALES (est): 1.2MM Privately Held
WEB: www.mhdco.com
SIC: 3911 Pins (jewelry), precious metal

(G-10295)
M HESKIA COMPANY INC
98 Cutter Rd Ste 125 (10036)
PHONE.................212 768-1845
EMP: 5
SALES (est): 450K Privately Held
SIC: 3911 Mfg Jewelry

(G-10296)
M HIDARY & CO INC
10 W 33rd St Rm 900 (10001-3317)
PHONE.................212 736-6540
Margie Valverde, Managing Dir
Morris Hidary, Chairman
Joanne Lee, Prdtn Mgr

Joan Malcolm, Production
David Hidary, Treasurer
◆ EMP: 100 EST: 1948
SQ FT: 20,000
SALES (est): 18.2MM Privately Held
SIC: 2369 2311 2325 2329 Girls' & children's outerwear; men's & boys' suits &
coats; men's & boys' trousers & slacks;
men's & boys' sportswear & athletic clothing; men's & boys' clothing; women's &
children's clothing

(G-10297)
M I T POLY-CART CORP
211 Central Park W (10024-6020)
PHONE.................212 724-7290
Dan Moss, President
Isaac Rinkewich, Vice Pres
Tova Moss, Treasurer
EMP: 5
SQ FT: 1,000
SALES (est): 300K Privately Held
WEB: www.mitpolycart.com
SIC: 3089 Plastic containers, except foam

(G-10298)
M L DESIGN INC (PA)
77 Ludlow St Frnt 1 (10002-3898)
PHONE.................212 233-0213
Tommy Lam, President
▲ EMP: 5
SALES (est): 713.4K Privately Held
SIC: 2752 Commercial printing, offset

(G-10299)
M S B INTERNATIONAL LTD (PA)
Also Called: Nyc Design Co
1412 Broadway Rm 1210 (10018-9228)
PHONE.................212 302-5551
Maia Chait, President
Robert Guttenberg, President
Sunny Leigh, Vice Pres
▲ EMP: 15
SALES (est): 2.6MM Privately Held
SIC: 2331 2321 2325 Women's & misses'
blouses & shirts; men's & boys' furnish-
ings; men's & boys' trousers & slacks

(G-10300)
M S RIVIERA INC
Also Called: Rfg
42 W 48th St Fl 4 (10036-1706)
PHONE.................212 391-0206
Michael Palmeri, President
Steven Donadio, Opers Mgr
EMP: 21
SALES (est): 1.2MM Privately Held
SIC: 3911 Jewelry, precious metal

(G-10301)
**M SHANKEN COMMUNICATIONS
INC (PA)**
825 8th Ave Fl 33 (10019-8872)
PHONE.................212 684-4224
Marvin R Shanken, Ch of Bd
Michael Moaba, Vice Ch Bd
Owen Dugan, Editor
Gordon Mott, Editor
David Savona, Editor
EMP: 125
SQ FT: 15,000
SALES (est): 26.6MM Privately Held
SIC: 2721 Magazines: publishing & printing

(G-10302)
**M2 FASHION GROUP HOLDINGS
INC**
Also Called: M2 Apparel
153 E 87th St Apt 10d (10128-2708)
PHONE.................917 208-2948
Ming Lee Wilcox, President
EMP: 6
SQ FT: 1,000
SALES (est): 2MM Privately Held
SIC: 2389 Apparel for handicapped

(G-10303)
**MAC FADDEN HOLDINGS INC
(PA)**
Also Called: Sterling McFadden
333 7th Ave Fl 11 (10001-5824)
PHONE.................212 979-4805
Peter J Callahan, Ch of Bd
Michael J Boylan, President
Anna Blanco, Vice Pres

EMP: 35
SQ FT: 11,000
SALES (est): 9.3MM Privately Held
WEB: www.macfad.com
SIC: 2721 1382 Magazines: publishing
only, not printed on site; oil & gas explo-
ration services

(G-10304)
MAC SWED INC
20 W 36th St Rm 5l (10018-9811)
PHONE.................212 684-7730
Marc Shams, President
▲ EMP: 15
SQ FT: 15,000
SALES (est): 539.6K Privately Held
SIC: 3949 Bowling equipment & supplies

(G-10305)
**MACANDREWS & FORBES INC
(PA)**
35 E 62nd St (10065-8014)
PHONE.................212 572-8600
Ronald O Perelman, CEO
Paul M Meister, President
Barry F Schwartz, Vice Chairman
George Davis, Exec VP
Debra Perelman, Exec VP
◆ EMP: 230
SQ FT: 12,000
SALES (est): 14.1B Privately Held
WEB: www.macandrewsandforbes.com
SIC: 2711 Newspapers, publishing & print-
ing

(G-10306)
**MACFADDEN CMMNCTIONS
GROUP LLC**
Also Called: HSN
333 7th Ave Fl 11 (10001-5824)
PHONE.................212 979-4800
Peter Callahan, Managing Prtnr
Jess Schesser, Partner
Brian Moy, Business Mgr
Dennis Respol, Mfg Staff
Jean Yannes, Accounting Mgr
▲ EMP: 105
SQ FT: 33,000
SALES (est): 14MM Privately Held
SIC: 2721 Magazines: publishing only, not
printed on site

(G-10307)
**MACMILLAN COLLEGE PUBG
CO INC**
866 3rd Ave Frnt 2 (10022-6221)
PHONE.................212 702-2000
John Bender, Manager
EMP: 10 Privately Held
SIC: 2731 Book publishing
HQ: Springer Nature (Uk) Limited
20 New Wharf Road
London
207 014-6085

(G-10308)
MACMILLAN HOLDINGS LLC
1 New York Plz Ste 4500 (10004-1562)
PHONE.................212 576-9428
Fritz Foy, Principal
EMP: 12
SALES (corp-wide): 1.6B Privately Held
SIC: 2721 Magazines: publishing only, not
printed on site
HQ: Macmillan Holdings, Llc
120 Broadway Fl 22
New York NY 10271

(G-10309)
MACMILLAN PUBLISHERS INC
175 5th Ave Ste 400 (10010-7726)
PHONE.................646 307-5151
John Sargent, CEO
Kim Cardascia, Editor
Monique Patterson, Editor
Daniela Rapp, Editor
Marc Resnick, Editor
▲ EMP: 1200
SALES (est): 108.4MM Privately Held
SIC: 2731 5192 Books: publishing only;
books
HQ: Springer Nature (Uk) Limited
20 New Wharf Road
London
207 014-6085

(G-10310)
MACMILLAN PUBLISHING GROUP LLC (DH)
Also Called: Palagrave Macmillan
175 5th Ave (10010-7703)
PHONE..................................212 674-5145
Sally Richardson, *President*
Marta Fleming, *Publisher*
Nichole Argyres, *Editor*
Hope Dellon, *Editor*
Michael Homler, *Editor*
◆ EMP: 361
SQ FT: 81,000
SALES (est): 107.3MM
SALES (corp-wide): 1.6B Privately Held
WEB: www.stmartins.com
SIC: 2731 5192 Books: publishing only;
    books

(G-10311)
MADAME ALEXANDER DOLL 2018 LLC
600 3rd Ave Fl 2 (10016-1919)
PHONE..................................917 576-8381
Noam Welfer, *Vice Pres*
Yuen Kwan Cheung, *Manager*
EMP: 6 EST: 2018
SQ FT: 500
SALES (est): 203.3K Privately Held
SIC: 3942 Dolls, except stuffed toy animals

(G-10312)
MADAME ALEXANDER DOLL CO LLC
112 W 34th St Ste 1410 (10120-1201)
PHONE..................................212 244-4500
Adolfo Reynoso, *Branch Mgr*
EMP: 100
SALES (corp-wide): 44.5MM Privately Held
SIC: 3942 Dolls, except stuffed toy animals
HQ: Madame Alexander Doll Company, Llc
    306 Primrose Ln
    Mountville PA 17554
    717 537-4140

(G-10313)
MADE FRESH DAILY
226 Front St (10038-2009)
PHONE..................................212 285-2253
Jackie Moran, *Manager*
EMP: 7
SALES (est): 373.7K Privately Held
SIC: 2711 Newspapers, publishing & printing

(G-10314)
MADHAT INC
149 Sullivan St Apt 3e (10012-3041)
PHONE..................................518 947-0732
Jude Anasta, *CEO*
EMP: 5 EST: 2015
SALES (est): 149.4K Privately Held
SIC: 7372 Application computer software

(G-10315)
MADISON LIFESTYLE NY LLC (PA)
1412 Broadway Rm 1610 (10018-9270)
PHONE..................................212 725-4002
Adriana Cerrato, *General Mgr*
Moshe Levy,
EMP: 3
SQ FT: 1,800
SALES: 11MM Privately Held
SIC: 3089 5023 Plastic kitchenware, table-
    ware & houseware; kitchenware; glass-
    ware

(G-10316)
MADOFF ENERGY III LLC
319 Lafayette St (10012-2711)
PHONE..................................212 744-1918
Andy Madoff, *Mng Member*
EMP: 8
SQ FT: 3,000
SALES: 29.4K Privately Held
SIC: 1382 Oil & gas exploration services

(G-10317)
MAESA LLC (HQ)
Also Called: Maesa Engineering Beauty
40 Worth St Rm 705 (10013-2994)
PHONE..................................212 674-5555
David Hutchinson, *Vice Pres*

Rachana Shah, *Vice Pres*
Jeffrey Klein, *CFO*
Mikaela Maxwell, *Marketing Staff*
Suzy Losardo, *Director*
◆ EMP: 50
SQ FT: 2,500
SALES: 85.4MM
SALES (corp-wide): 43.7MM Privately Held
WEB: www.zorbitresources.com
SIC: 2844 Toilet preparations
PA: Maesa
    15 Rue Pasteur
    Levallois-Perret 92300
    141 055-555

(G-10318)
MAFCO CONSOLIDATED GROUP INC (HQ)
35 E 62nd St (10065-8014)
PHONE..................................212 572-8600
Ronald O Perelman, *Ch of Bd*
EMP: 10
SALES (est): 287.7MM Privately Held
SIC: 2121 2131 2869 Cigars; smoking to-
    bacco; flavors or flavoring materials, syn-
    thetic

(G-10319)
MAG BRANDS LLC
Also Called: Babydoll
463 7th Ave Fl 4 (10018-8725)
PHONE..................................212 629-9600
Raymond A Dayan, *CEO*
Gerard Agoglia, *CFO*
Michael Nagurka, *Controller*
Mark Adjmi,
▲ EMP: 55
SALES (est): 6.4MM Privately Held
SIC: 2339 Service apparel, washable:
    women's

(G-10320)
MAGAZINE I SPECTRUM E
Also Called: I Triple E Spectrum
3 Park Ave Fl 17 (10016-5902)
PHONE..................................212 419-7555
James Vick, *Principal*
EMP: 38 EST: 2001
SALES (est): 1.6MM Privately Held
SIC: 2721 Periodicals

(G-10321)
MAGEBA USA LLC
575 Lexington Ave Fl 4 (10022-6146)
PHONE..................................212 317-1991
Thomas Spuler, *CEO*
Jim Hatch, *President*
Gianni Moor, *COO*
James Hatch, *Vice Pres*
Chet Harrigan, *Manager*
▲ EMP: 20 EST: 2011
SALES (est): 12.2MM Privately Held
SIC: 3441 3562 Expansion joints (struc-
    tural shapes), iron or steel; ball bearings
    & parts

(G-10322)
MAGER & GOUGELMAN INC (PA)
345 E 37th St Rm 316 (10016-3256)
PHONE..................................212 661-3939
Henry P Gougelman, *President*
EMP: 7
SALES (est): 855.4K Privately Held
WEB: www.artificial-eyes.com
SIC: 3851 Eyes, glass & plastic

(G-10323)
MAGGY LONDON INTERNATIONAL LTD (PA)
Also Called: Maggy London Blouse Div
225 W 37th St Fl 7 (10018-6721)
PHONE..................................212 944-7199
Larry Lefkowitz, *Ch of Bd*
Milton Cahn, *Chairman*
Devin Fitzpatrick, *Vice Pres*
Bill Newberry, *Buyer*
Lynda Massey, *Finance Asst*
◆ EMP: 65
SQ FT: 18,000
SALES (est): 50.6MM Privately Held
SIC: 2331 Women's & misses' blouses &
    shirts

(G-10324)
MAGIC BRANDS INTERNATIONAL LLC
31 W 34th St Rm 401 (10001-3036)
PHONE..................................212 563-4999
Edward J Falack,
Albert Pardo,
▲ EMP: 10
SALES (est): 1.1MM Privately Held
SIC: 2211 Apparel & outerwear fabrics,
    cotton

(G-10325)
MAGIC NOVELTY CO INC (PA)
308 Dyckman St (10034-5397)
PHONE..................................212 304-2777
Alex Neuburger, *President*
David Neuburger, *Vice Pres*
Steven Neuburger, *Vice Pres*
Wendy Torres, *Controller*
Diana Gurevich, *Manager*
▲ EMP: 50 EST: 1940
SQ FT: 40,000
SALES (est): 9.8MM Privately Held
SIC: 3961 5094 3915 3469 Costume
    jewelry, ex. precious metal & semi-
    precious stones; jewelry; jewelers' materi-
    als & lapidary work; metal stampings;
    miscellaneous fabricated wire products

(G-10326)
MAGIC NUMBERS INC
Also Called: Glitter
29 Little West 12th St (10014-1393)
PHONE..................................646 839-8578
EMP: 5 EST: 2015
SQ FT: 16,000
SALES (est): 280K Privately Held
SIC: 7372 Prepackaged Software Services

(G-10327)
MAGIC SOFTWARE INC
1 Penn Plz Ste 2412 (10119-2402)
PHONE..................................646 827-9788
Akhtar Kamdar, *CEO*
Adarsh Mehra, *CFO*
Nagesh Mehra, *Exec Dir*
EMP: 13
SALES (est): 438K Privately Held
SIC: 7372 Prepackaged software

(G-10328)
MAGIC TANK LLC
80 Maiden Ln Rm 2204 (10038-4815)
PHONE..................................877 646-2442
Steve Distritzky, *President*
EMP: 3
SQ FT: 8,000
SALES: 5MM Privately Held
SIC: 2865 Cyclic organic crudes

(G-10329)
MAGIC TOUCH ICEWARES INTL
220 E 72nd St Apt 11g (10021-4527)
PHONE..................................212 794-2852
Susan Gitelson, *President*
◆ EMP: 6
SQ FT: 3,000
SALES (est): 824.7K Privately Held
SIC: 3069 5049 Laboratory sundries:
    cases, covers, funnels, cups, etc.; labora-
    tory equipment, except medical or dental

(G-10330)
MAGNUM CREATION INC
23 W 47th St Fl 5 (10036-2826)
PHONE..................................212 869-2600
Nathan Cohen, *President*
Mira Cohen, *Vice Pres*
EMP: 13
SQ FT: 5,500
SALES (est): 1.5MM Privately Held
SIC: 3911 Jewelry, precious metal

(G-10331)
MAIDENFORM LLC
260 Madison Ave Fl 6 (10016-2406)
PHONE..................................201 436-9200
Eileen Mahoney, *Exec VP*
Kevin Urban, *Exec VP*
Tiffin Jernstedt, *Senior VP*
Nica Canto, *Vice Pres*
Tarrah Forte, *Vice Pres*
EMP: 10

SALES (corp-wide): 6.8B Publicly Held
WEB: www.maidenform.com
SIC: 2259 2254 Girdles & other foundation
    garments, knit; knit underwear mills
HQ: Maidenform Llc
    1000 E Hanes Mill Rd
    Winston Salem NC 27105
    336 519-8080

(G-10332)
MAILERS-PBLSHER WLFARE TR FUND
1501 Broadway (10036-5601)
PHONE..................................212 869-5986
EMP: 1
SALES (est): 1.8MM Privately Held
SIC: 2741 Miscellaneous publishing

(G-10333)
MAIYET INC (PA)
16 Crosby St Apt Corp (10013-3108)
PHONE..................................212 343-9999
Paul Van Zyl, *Ch of Bd*
EMP: 5
SALES (est): 1MM
SALES (corp-wide): 1.1MM Privately Held
SIC: 2329 2339 Men's & boys' leather,
    wool & down-filled outerwear; women's &
    misses' outerwear

(G-10334)
MAJESTIC RAYON CORPORATION
54 W 21st St Rm 1005 (10010-7327)
PHONE..................................212 929-6443
Lawrence Aibel, *President*
Richard Aibel, *Vice Pres*
Anthony Castro, *CFO*
▲ EMP: 25 EST: 1930
SALES (est): 3.6MM Privately Held
SIC: 2282 2269 Twisting yarn; winding
    yarn; finishing plants

(G-10335)
MAJESTY BRANDS LLC
469 7th Ave Rm 1301 (10018-7616)
PHONE..................................212 283-3400
Jack Safdeye, *CEO*
▲ EMP: 5
SALES (est): 221.4K Privately Held
SIC: 2252 Socks

(G-10336)
MALIN + GOETZ INC (PA)
330 7th Ave Ste 2100 (10001-5236)
PHONE..................................212 244-7771
Matthew Malin, *Ch of Bd*
Andrew Goetz, *President*
Amanda Michaud, *Marketing Mgr*
Erik Erk, *Manager*
Ashima Jain, *Director*
EMP: 12
SQ FT: 600
SALES (est): 2.6MM Privately Held
WEB: www.malinandgoetz.com
SIC: 2844 5999 Cosmetic preparations;
    cosmetics

(G-10337)
MALLORY & CHURCH LLC
552 Fashion Ave Rm 202 (10018-3247)
PHONE..................................212 868-7888
Paul Weiss, *Mng Member*
EMP: 9
SALES (est): 22.2K Privately Held
SIC: 2323 Neckties, men's & boys': made
    from purchased materials

(G-10338)
MALOUF COLETTE INC
27 E 28th St (10016-7921)
PHONE..................................212 941-9588
Colette Malouf, *President*
Lee Tam, *Prdtn Mgr*
April Klavins, *Finance*
EMP: 14
SALES (est): 1.9MM Privately Held
WEB: www.colettemalouf.com
SIC: 3999 Hair & hair-based products

(G-10339)
MAN OF WORLD
25 W 39th St Fl 5 (10018-4075)
PHONE..................................212 915-0017

Alan Maleh, *Principal*
EMP: 5
SALES (est): 847.3K **Privately Held**
SIC: 2836 Culture media

(G-10340)
MANCHU NEW YORK INC
530 Fashion Ave Rm 1906 (10018-4853)
PHONE..................................212 921-5050
▲ EMP: 8
SQ FT: 5,100
SALES (est): 705.4K **Privately Held**
SIC: 2361 2339 2311 Manufacturer's Rep Of Garment Manufacturer

(G-10341)
MANCHU TIMES FASHION INC
530 Sventh Ave Ste 1906 (10018)
PHONE..................................212 921-5050
Michael Durbin, *CEO*
Jay Goldman, *Administration*
▲ EMP: 8 EST: 2014
SQ FT: 2,300
SALES (est): 831.5K **Privately Held**
SIC: 2339 Women's & misses' outerwear
PA: Manchu Times Fashion Limited
Rm 1102-1103 Ginza Plz
Mongkok KLN

(G-10342)
MANHATTAN CABINETS INC
1349 2nd Ave (10021-4504)
PHONE..................................212 548-2436
Zaheer Akber, *President*
EMP: 3
SQ FT: 1,300
SALES (est): 1.7MM **Privately Held**
SIC: 2514 1751 Kitchen cabinets: metal; cabinet building & installation

(G-10343)
MANHATTAN EASTSIDE DEV CORP
Also Called: Eastside Orthotics Prosthetics
622 W 168th St Ste Vc333 (10032-3720)
PHONE..................................212 305-3275
Matt D Flynn, *CEO*
Matt Flynn, *President*
EMP: 10 EST: 2011
SALES (est): 537.6K **Privately Held**
SIC: 3841 Medical instruments & equipment, blood & bone work

(G-10344)
MANHATTAN MEDIA LLC (PA)
Also Called: Avenue Magazine
535 5th Ave Fl 23 (10017-3678)
PHONE..................................212 268-8600
Joanne Harras, *CEO*
Thomas Allon, *President*
Toni-Ann Douglas, *Sales Staff*
Laura Cassella, *Director*
Mark Gilbertson, *Admin Sec*
EMP: 19
SQ FT: 7,500
SALES (est): 10.9MM **Privately Held**
SIC: 2711 2721 Newspapers: publishing only, not printed on site; magazines: publishing only, not printed on site

(G-10345)
MANHATTAN SCIENTIFICS INC (PA)
405 Lexington Ave Fl 26 (10174-2699)
PHONE..................................212 541-2405
Emmanuel Tsoupanarias, *Ch of Bd*
Leonard Friedman, *Admin Sec*
EMP: 11
SQ FT: 300
SALES: 142K **Publicly Held**
SIC: 3699 Electrical equipment & supplies

(G-10346)
MANHATTAN TIMES INC
5030 Broadway Ste 801 (10034-1666)
PHONE..................................212 569-5800
Mike Fitelson, *Publisher*
Luis Miranda, *Chairman*
EMP: 15
SALES (est): 662.1K **Privately Held**
SIC: 2711 Newspapers: publishing only, not printed on site

(G-10347)
MANN PUBLICATIONS INC
450 Fashion Ave Ste 2306 (10123-2306)
PHONE..................................212 840-6266
Jeffrey Mann, *President*
Alex Harrell, *Assoc Editor*
Mahzabeen Alam, *Admin Asst*
EMP: 20
SQ FT: 4,000
SALES (est): 2.5MM **Privately Held**
SIC: 2721 Magazines: publishing only, not printed on site

(G-10348)
MANNESMANN CORPORATION
601 Lexington Ave Fl 56 (10022-4611)
PHONE..................................212 258-4000
Peter Prinz Wittgenstein, *President*
Dr Manfred Becker, *Exec VP*
Joseph E Innamorati, *Vice Pres*
Olaf Klinger, *Treasurer*
▲ EMP: 100
SALES (est): 20.6MM
SALES (corp-wide): 95B **Privately Held**
SIC: 3536 3544 3511 3547 Hoists; cranes, industrial plant; cranes, overhead traveling; special dies, tools, jigs & fixtures; industrial molds; turbo-generators; hydraulic turbines; rolling mill machinery; steel rolling machinery; pumps & pumping equipment; internal combustion engines
HQ: Siemens Corporation
300 New Jersey Ave Nw # 10
Washington DC 20001
202 434-4800

(G-10349)
MANNY GRUNBERG INC
62 W 47th St Ste 703 (10036-3185)
PHONE..................................212 302-6173
EMP: 33 EST: 1952
SQ FT: 2,000
SALES (est): 2.4MM **Privately Held**
SIC: 3911 Mfg Precious Jewelry

(G-10350)
MANRICO USA INC
Also Called: Manrico Cashmere
922 Madison Ave (10021-3576)
PHONE..................................212 794-4200
Virgile Verellen, *Branch Mgr*
EMP: 5
SALES (corp-wide): 8.2MM **Privately Held**
SIC: 2253 Sweaters & sweater coats, knit
PA: Manrico Usa, Inc.
922 Madison Ave
New York NY 10021
212 794-4200

(G-10351)
MANRICO USA INC (PA)
922 Madison Ave (10021-3576)
PHONE..................................212 794-4200
Manrico Calzoni, *President*
Virgile Verellen, *Branch Mgr*
Cecilia Montanucci, *Executive*
▲ EMP: 5
SQ FT: 750
SALES (est): 8.2MM **Privately Held**
SIC: 2299 Upholstery filling, textile

(G-10352)
MANSFIELD PRESS INC
599 11th Ave Fl 3 (10036-2110)
PHONE..................................212 265-5411
Stanley J Friedman, *President*
Marc Friedman, *Exec VP*
Frank J Ephraim, *Vice Pres*
EMP: 15 EST: 1935
SALES (est): 1.9MM **Privately Held**
SIC: 2752 Lithographing on metal

(G-10353)
MANSUETO VENTURES LLC
Also Called: Fast Company Magazine
7 World Trade Ctr Fl 29 (10007-2174)
PHONE..................................212 389-5300
Jennifer Henkus, *Publisher*
Jane Hazel, *Principal*
Joe Angio, *Editor*
Abigail Baron, *Editor*
Leigh Buchanan, *Editor*
EMP: 225

SALES (est): 60.9MM **Privately Held**
SIC: 2721 Magazines: publishing only, not printed on site

(G-10354)
MARCASIANO INC
296 Elizabeth St Apt 2f (10012-3590)
PHONE..................................212 614-9412
Mary Jane Marcasiano, *President*
EMP: 5 EST: 1977
SQ FT: 3,000
SALES (est): 501.4K **Privately Held**
SIC: 2339 Sportswear, women's

(G-10355)
MARCO HI-TECH JV LLC (PA)
475 Park Ave S Fl 10 (10016-6930)
PHONE..................................212 798-8100
Reuben Seltzer,
David Garner,
Alan Kestenbaum,
Mark Levitt,
▲ EMP: 8
SQ FT: 4,000
SALES (est): 1.4MM **Privately Held**
WEB: www.marcohi-tech.com
SIC: 2834 Vitamin, nutrient & hematinic preparations for human use

(G-10356)
MARCO INDUSTRIES LTD (PA)
475 Park Ave S 10f (10016-6901)
PHONE..................................212 798-8100
Mike Barinholtz, *President*
Kenya Fernandez, *Office Mgr*
EMP: 4
SALES (est): 5.9MM **Privately Held**
SIC: 3339 Platinum group metal refining (primary)

(G-10357)
MARCONI INTL USA CO LTD
214 W 39th St Rm 703 (10018-5566)
PHONE..................................212 391-2626
Lilian Ching, *President*
▲ EMP: 9
SQ FT: 2,500
SALES (est): 1.3MM **Privately Held**
SIC: 2339 Women's & misses' athletic clothing & sportswear

(G-10358)
MARCUS GOLDMAN INC
Also Called: Run It Systems
37 W 39th St Rm 1201 (10018-0577)
PHONE..................................212 431-0707
Robert Marcus, *President*
Walter Crespin, *Technical Mgr*
Tamar Markowitz, *Marketing Staff*
Roger Fried, *Technical Staff*
Orren Grushkin, *Admin Sec*
EMP: 14
SQ FT: 5,000
SALES (est): 1.7MM **Privately Held**
WEB: www.runit.com
SIC: 7372 Application computer software

(G-10359)
MARI STRINGS INC
14 W 71st St (10023-4209)
PHONE..................................212 799-6781
Daniel Mari, *President*
▲ EMP: 15
SQ FT: 1,600
SALES (est): 400K **Privately Held**
SIC: 3931 Strings, musical instrument

(G-10360)
MARIE CLAIRE USA
Also Called: Marie Claire Magazine
300 W 57th St Fl 34 (10019-1497)
PHONE..................................212 841-8493
Nancy Berger, *Vice Pres*
Christine Kistner, *Vice Pres*
Chris Moore, *Research*
▲ EMP: 100
SALES (est): 924.1K **Privately Held**
SIC: 2721 Magazines: publishing & printing

(G-10361)
MARINA JEWELRY CO INC
Also Called: Jn Marina
42 W 48th St Ste 804 (10036-1712)
PHONE..................................212 354-5027
Joseph Fontana, *President*
Anthony Barona, *Partner*

EMP: 6
SQ FT: 1,200
SALES (est): 540K **Privately Held**
WEB: www.marina-jewellery.com
SIC: 3911 3339 Jewelry, precious metal; primary nonferrous metals

(G-10362)
MARITIME ACTIVITY REPORTS (PA)
118 E 25th St Fl 2 (10010-2994)
PHONE..................................212 477-6700
John C O'Malley, *Vice Pres*
Esther Rothenberger, *Opers Mgr*
Jocelyn Redfern, *Marketing Mgr*
EMP: 28
SQ FT: 2,500
SALES (est): 1.8MM **Privately Held**
SIC: 2721 Magazines: publishing only, not printed on site

(G-10363)
MARK KING JEWELRY INC
62 W 47th St Ste 310r (10036-3245)
PHONE..................................212 921-0746
Mark Beznicki, *President*
EMP: 8
SQ FT: 1,000
SALES (est): 1MM **Privately Held**
SIC: 3911 5094 Jewelry, precious metal; jewelry & precious stones

(G-10364)
MARK LEVINE
Also Called: Kids Discover
149 5th Ave Fl 10 (10010-6832)
PHONE..................................212 677-4457
Mark Levine, *Owner*
▲ EMP: 11
SQ FT: 2,500
SALES (est): 810K **Privately Held**
SIC: 2721 Magazines: publishing only, not printed on site

(G-10365)
MARK NELSON DESIGNS LLC
174 5th Ave Ste 501 (10010-6050)
PHONE..................................646 422-7020
Mark Nelson, *Mng Member*
▲ EMP: 10
SALES (est): 1.4MM **Privately Held**
SIC: 2273 Rugs, hand & machine made

(G-10366)
MARK ROBINSON INC
18 E 48th St Rm 1102 (10017-1059)
PHONE..................................212 223-3515
Mark Robinson, *President*
EMP: 9
SQ FT: 200
SALES (est): 1.5MM **Privately Held**
WEB: www.markrobinson.net
SIC: 3911 Jewelry, precious metal

(G-10367)
MARKET FACTORY INC
45 W 27th St Frnt 1 (10001-6916)
PHONE..................................212 625-9988
James Sinclair, *CEO*
Darren Jer, *COO*
Julia Mantel, *Project Mgr*
Aron Szanto, *Engineer*
Tom Guilfoyle, *Sales Staff*
EMP: 19
SQ FT: 3,000
SALES (est): 5.3MM **Privately Held**
SIC: 7372 Business oriented computer software

(G-10368)
MARKET LOGIC SOFTWARE INC
80 Pine St Fl 24 (10005-1732)
PHONE..................................646 405-1041
Kay Iversen, *Director*
EMP: 19
SALES (est): 182.1K **Privately Held**
SIC: 7372 Prepackaged software

(G-10369)
MARKET PARTNERS INTERNATIONAL
Also Called: Publishing Trends
232 Madison Ave Rm 1400 (10016-2918)
PHONE..................................212 447-0855
Lorraine Shanley, *President*

GEOGRAPHIC

Constance Sayre, *Director*
EMP: 5
SQ FT: 1,300
SALES (est) 379.1K **Privately Held**
WEB:
www.marketpartnersinternational.com
SIC: 2741 Miscellaneous publishing

(G-10370)
MARKETING ACTION
XECUTIVES INC
50 W 96th St Apt 7b (10025-6529)
PHONE...................212 971-9155
Karen Korman, *President*
Barry Steinman, *Vice Pres*
EMP: 5
SALES: 2MM **Privately Held**
WEB: www.mactionx.com
SIC: 2241 Trimmings, textile

(G-10371)
MARKETRESEARCHCOM INC
641 Ave Of The America (10011-2014)
PHONE...................212 807-2600
Rocco Distefano, *Branch Mgr*
EMP: 15
SALES (corp-wide): 33.4MM **Privately**
Held
WEB: www.marketresearch.com
SIC: 2741 Miscellaneous publishing
PA: Marketresearch.Com, Inc.
6116 Executive Blvd # 501
Rockville MD 20852
240 747-3000

(G-10372)
MARLEY SPOON INC
Also Called: Martha & Marley Spoon
601 W 26th St Rm 900 (10001-1143)
PHONE...................866 228-4513
Fabian Siegel, *President*
Anjali Grover, *Managing Dir*
EMP: 140
SALES (est): 1.2MM
SALES (corp-wide): 8.3MM **Privately**
Held
SIC: 3411 8742 Food & beverage containers; food & beverage consultant
PA: Marley Spoon Ag
Paul-Lincke-Ufer 39/-40
Berlin
302 084-8051

(G-10373)
MARRETTI USA INC
101 Ave Of The Amrcas 9th (10013-1941)
PHONE...................212 255-5565
Marzia Marzi, *President*
EMP: 8 **EST:** 2008
SQ FT: 600
SALES (est): 565.3K **Privately Held**
SIC: 2431 5021 Staircases, stairs & railings; furniture

(G-10374)
MARTHA STEWART LIVING (HQ)
601 W 26th St Rm 900 (10001-1143)
PHONE...................212 827-8000
Daniel W Dienst, *CEO*
Jacqueline Landaeta, *President*
Ann Casey Bukawyn, *Exec VP*
Shelley S Nandkeolyar, *Exec VP*
Allison Jacques, *Senior VP*
▲ **EMP:** 120
SQ FT: 176,550
SALES (est): 212.1MM
SALES (corp-wide): 169.9MM **Publicly**
Held
WEB: www.marthastewart.com
SIC: 2721 2731 4813 7812 Magazines:
publishing only, not printed on site; book
publishing; ; motion picture production &
distribution, television
PA: Sequential Brands Group, Inc.
601 W 26th St Fl 9
New York NY 10001
646 564-2577

(G-10375)
MARTHA STEWART LIVING
OMNI LLC
20 W 43rd St (10036-7400)
PHONE...................212 827-8000
Robin Marino, *CEO*
Anthony Luscia, *Editor*
Kevin Sharkey, *Director*

Jeffrey W Ubben, *Bd of Directors*
Rachel Stewart, *Merchandising*
▲ **EMP:** 350 **EST:** 1997
SALES (est): 25.3MM
SALES (corp-wide): 169.9MM **Publicly**
Held
WEB: www.msliving.com
SIC: 2721 Magazines: publishing only, not
printed on site
HQ: Martha Stewart Living Omnimedia, Inc.
601 W 26th St Rm 900
New York NY 10001
212 827-8000

(G-10376)
MARVELLISSIMA INTL LTD
333 E 46th St Apt 20a (10017-7431)
PHONE...................212 682-7306
Marvel Perilla, *President*
Shanez Kollnescher, *Vice Pres*
Ellen Stutzer, *Vice Pres*
Abba Kyari, *Shareholder*
Lola Osunsade, *Shareholder*
EMP: 6
SALES (est): 615.2K **Privately Held**
SIC: 2844 5122 Toilet preparations; cosmetics

(G-10377)
MARY BRIGHT INC
269 E 10th St Apt 7 (10009-4849)
PHONE...................212 677-1970
David Paskin, *President*
Mary Bright, *President*
EMP: 6
SALES: 367K **Privately Held**
WEB: www.marybright.com
SIC: 2258 Curtains & curtain fabrics, lace

(G-10378)
MAS CUTTING INC
257 W 39th St Rm 11e (10018-3228)
PHONE...................212 869-0826
Kitman MA, *President*
EMP: 6
SALES (est): 350K **Privately Held**
SIC: 2396 Apparel findings & trimmings

(G-10379)
MASQUERADE LLC
Also Called: Holloween Adventures
104 4th Ave (10003-5232)
PHONE...................212 673-4546
Tony Bianchi, *Manager*
EMP: 16
SQ FT: 20,000
SALES (corp-wide): 8MM **Privately Held**
WEB: www.halloweenadventure.com
SIC: 2389 Masquerade costumes
PA: Masquerade, Llc
104 4th Ave
New York NY 10003
516 732-7242

(G-10380)
MATA FASHIONS LLC
222 W 37th St Fl 4 (10018-9158)
PHONE...................917 716-7894
Maria Maglaras, *Treasurer*
Dona Elias,
EMP: 2 **EST:** 2014
SQ FT: 1,200
SALES: 1MM **Privately Held**
SIC: 2384 Dressing gowns, men's &
women's: from purchased materials

(G-10381)
MATACI INC
Also Called: Lazo Setter Company
247 W 35th St Fl 15 (10001-1915)
PHONE...................212 502-1899
Adrianna Chico, *President*
▲ **EMP:** 60
SALES (est): 6.2MM **Privately Held**
SIC: 3961 Costume jewelry

(G-10382)
MATEL LLC
90 Park Ave Fl 18 (10016-1322)
PHONE...................646 825-6760
Samuel Susz, *Editor*
Eliana Cruz, *Senior Mgr*
April Hamilton, *Senior Mgr*
EMP: 5

SALES (est): 365.8K **Privately Held**
SIC: 3944 Games, toys & children's vehicles

(G-10383)
MATERNE NORTH AMERICA
CORP (DH)
Also Called: Gogo Squeez
20 W 22nd St Fl 12 (10010-5843)
PHONE...................212 675-7881
Michel Larroche, *CEO*
William Graham, *President*
Carole Larson, *CFO*
◆ **EMP:** 277
SALES: 162K
SALES (corp-wide): 7.4MM **Privately**
Held
SIC: 2035 5145 Pickles, sauces & salad
dressings; snack foods
HQ: Materne
45 Chemin Des Peupliers
Dardilly 69570
478 663-232

(G-10384)
MATHISEN VENTURES INC
Also Called: Cruise Industry News
441 Lexington Ave Rm 809 (10017-3935)
PHONE...................212 986-1025
Oivind Mathisen, *President*
Abby Forlander, *Advt Staff*
EMP: 6
SALES (est): 628.9K **Privately Held**
WEB: www.cruiseindustrynews.com
SIC: 2731 2721 2741 Book publishing;
periodicals: publishing only; magazines:
publishing only, not printed on site;
newsletter publishing

(G-10385)
MATRIXCARE INC
Also Called: Sigmacare
575 8th Ave Fl 15 (10018-3175)
PHONE...................518 583-6400
EMP: 7
SALES (corp-wide): 61.8MM **Privately**
Held
SIC: 7372 7371 Prepackaged software;
custom computer programming services
HQ: Matrixcare, Inc.
10900 Hampshire Ave S # 100
Bloomington MN 55438
952 995-9800

(G-10386)
MAURICE MAX INC
Also Called: Roxanne Assoulin
49 W 27th St Fl 5 (10001-6936)
PHONE...................212 334-6573
Roxanne Assoulin, *President*
Meyer Assoulin, *Vice Pres*
EMP: 34
SALES (est): 5.6MM **Privately Held**
WEB: www.leeangel.com
SIC: 3961 Costume jewelry

(G-10387)
MAVEN MARKETING LLC (PA)
Also Called: Golf Odyssey
349 5th Ave Fl 8 (10016-5019)
PHONE...................615 510-3248
Justin Tapper, *CEO*
Ryan Klockner, *President*
Dean Strickler, *Exec Dir*
Wayne Caparas,
EMP: 7 **EST:** 2008
SALES (est): 3.2MM **Privately Held**
SIC: 7372 7371 8742 Educational computer software; software programming applications; marketing consulting services

(G-10388)
MAVERIK LACROSSE LLC
535 W 24th St Fl 5 (10011-1140)
PHONE...................516 213-3050
John Gagliardi,
▲ **EMP:** 5022
SALES (est): 373.4K
SALES (corp-wide): 7.9B **Privately Held**
SIC: 3949 Lacrosse equipment & supplies,
general
HQ: Kohlberg Sports Group, Inc.
111 Radio Circle Dr
Mount Kisco NY 10549

(G-10389)
MAX HEADER
Also Called: Palogloss Fashions
12 Pinehurst Ave Apt 1h (10033-6412)
PHONE...................680 888-9786
Header Max, *Owner*
◆ **EMP:** 48
SALES (est): 1.4MM **Privately Held**
SIC: 2519 3911 Furniture, household:
glass, fiberglass & plastic; jewelry, precious metal

(G-10390)
MAX BRENNER UNION SQUARE
LLC
841 Broadway (10003-4704)
PHONE...................646 467-8803
Ever M Elivo, *Principal*
▲ **EMP:** 5
SALES (est): 585.6K **Privately Held**
SIC: 2066 Chocolate bars, solid

(G-10391)
MAX KAHAN INC
20 W 47th St Ste 300 (10036-3303)
PHONE...................212 575-4646
Max Kahan, *President*
David Gluck, *Vice Pres*
Abraham Grossman, *Treasurer*
EMP: 10
SQ FT: 3,000
SALES (est): 980K **Privately Held**
SIC: 3915 Jewelers' materials & lapidary
work

(G-10392)
MAYBELLINE INC
575 5th Ave Fl Mezz (10017-2422)
PHONE...................212 885-1310
Robert N Hiatt, *Ch of Bd*
John R Wendt, *President*
Gerald C Beddall, *President*
Jack J Bucher, *President*
Daniel J Coffey Jr, *President*
EMP: 4118 **EST:** 1915
SALES (est): 72.6K
SALES (corp-wide): 4.4B **Privately Held**
WEB: www.maybelline.com
SIC: 2841 2844 Soap: granulated, liquid,
cake, flaked or chip; cosmetic preparations
HQ: L'oreal Usa, Inc.
10 Hudson Yards
New York NY 10001
212 818-1500

(G-10393)
MAZ SYSTEMS INC (PA)
109 W 27th St Fl 7 (10001-6208)
PHONE...................855 629-3444
Paul Canetti, *CEO*
Michael Ram, *President*
Paul Shouvik, *President*
Shikha Arora, *Principal*
Simon Baumer, *Principal*
EMP: 10
SALES (est): 2.9MM **Privately Held**
SIC: 7372 Publishers' computer software

(G-10394)
MBNY LLC (PA)
260 5th Ave Fl 9 (10001-6408)
PHONE...................646 467-8810
Yaniv Shtanger, *Mng Member*
EMP: 10
SALES (est): 1.2MM **Privately Held**
SIC: 2066 Chocolate bars, solid

(G-10395)
MC SQUARED NYC INC
Also Called: Mancum Graphics
121 Varick St Frnt B (10013-1408)
PHONE...................212 947-2260
Robert Copjec, *President*
EMP: 10 **EST:** 2011
SQ FT: 2,000
SALES (est): 1.7MM **Privately Held**
SIC: 2752 Commercial printing, offset

(G-10396)
MCCALL PATTERN COMPANY (HQ)
Also Called: Butterck McCall Vogue Pattern
120 Broadway Fl 34 (10271-3499)
P.O. Box 3755, Manhattan KS (66505-8502)
PHONE..............................212 465-6800
Frank J Rizzo, *Ch of Bd*
Robin Davies, *President*
Kathleen Klausner, *Senior VP*
Nancy Dicocco, *Vice Pres*
Gail Hamilton, *Vice Pres*
▲ EMP: 200
SQ FT: 62,600
SALES (est): 47MM
SALES (corp-wide): 382.2MM **Publicly Held**
WEB: www.mccallpattern.com
SIC: 2335 Dresses, paper: cut & sewn; ensemble dresses: women's, misses' & juniors'
PA: Css Industries, Inc.
450 Plymouth Rd Ste 300
Plymouth Meeting PA 19462
610 729-3959

(G-10397)
MCGRAW-HILL EDUCATION INC (PA)
2 Penn Plz Fl 20 (10121-2100)
PHONE..............................646 766-2000
Lloyd Waterhouse, *CEO*
Chadwick Schockemoehl, *District Mgr*
Alfred Essa, *Vice Pres*
Deborah Flanagan, *Vice Pres*
Lisa Gilgen, *Vice Pres*
EMP: 63
SALES (est): 20.4MM **Privately Held**
SIC: 2731 Books: publishing only

(G-10398)
MCGRAW-HILL GLOBL EDCATN HLDNG (PA)
Also Called: McGraw Hill Education
2 Penn Plz Fl 20 (10121-2100)
P.O. Box 182605, Columbus OH (43218-2605)
PHONE..............................800 338-3987
Lloyd Waterhouse, *President*
Heath Morrison, *President*
William Okun, *President*
Sally Shankland, *President*
David Patterson, *Managing Dir*
EMP: 89
SALES (est): 1.3B **Privately Held**
SIC: 2731 Book publishing

(G-10399)
MCGRAW-HILL SCHOOL EDUCATION H (HQ)
2 Penn Plz Fl 20 (10121-2100)
PHONE..............................646 766-2000
David Levin, *President*
Teresa Martin-Retortillo, *Senior VP*
David B Stafford, *Senior VP*
Maryellen Valaitis, *Senior VP*
Patrick Milano, *CFO*
EMP: 500
SALES: 750MM
SALES (corp-wide): 1.3B **Privately Held**
SIC: 2731 Books: publishing only
PA: Mcgraw-Hill Global Education Holdings, Llc
2 Penn Plz Fl 20
New York NY 10121
800 338-3987

(G-10400)
MCGRAW-HILL SCHOOL EDUCATN LLC
2 Penn Plz Fl 20 (10121-2100)
PHONE..............................646 766-2060
David Levin, *President*
Teresa Martin-Retortillo, *Senior VP*
Maryellen Valaitis, *Senior VP*
Patrick Milano, *CFO*
David Wright, *CIO*
EMP: 599 EST: 2013
SALES (est): 94.6MM
SALES (corp-wide): 1.3B **Privately Held**
SIC: 2731 Books: publishing & printing

HQ: Mcgraw-Hill School Education Holdings, Llc
2 Penn Plz Fl 20
New York NY 10121
646 766-2000

(G-10401)
MCM PRODUCTS USA INC (PA)
681 5th Ave Fl 10 (10022-4306)
PHONE..............................646 756-4090
Michael R Callahan, *CEO*
Paolo Fontanelli, *CEO*
Sung-Joo Kim, *Ch of Bd*
Patrick Valeo, *President*
EMP: 50 EST: 2007
SALES (est): 26.2MM **Privately Held**
SIC: 3171 3149 3199 Women's handbags & purses; athletic shoes, except rubber or plastic; belt laces, leather

(G-10402)
MCMAHON GROUP LLC (PA)
Also Called: McMahon Publishing Group
545 W 45th St (10036-3409)
PHONE..............................212 957-5300
Raymond E McMahon, *CEO*
Van N Velle, *President*
Kristin Jannacone, *Editor*
Frank Tagarello, *Vice Pres*
Rose Anne McMahon, *Treasurer*
EMP: 72
SALES: 16.3MM **Privately Held**
SIC: 2721 Trade journals: publishing only, not printed on site

(G-10403)
MCPC INC
Also Called: McArdle Solutions
731 Lexington Ave (10022-1331)
PHONE..............................212 583-6000
Lisa Arsenault, *President*
Donald Thomas, *Vice Pres*
EMP: 100 EST: 1947
SQ FT: 350,000
SALES: 7MM
SALES (corp-wide): 1.8B **Privately Held**
WEB: www.mcardleprinting.com
SIC: 2752 Commercial printing, offset
HQ: The Bureau Of National Affairs Inc
1801 S Bell St Ste Cn110
Arlington VA 22202
703 341-3000

(G-10404)
MDI HOLDINGS LLC
Also Called: C/O Court Sq Capitl Partners
399 Park Ave Fl 14 (10022-4614)
PHONE..............................212 559-1127
Joseph M Silvestri, *President*
EMP: 2900
SALES (est): 187.9MM **Privately Held**
SIC: 2842 2874 2992 2752 Cleaning or polishing preparations; phosphates; lubricating oils; offset & photolithographic printing; printers & plotters; plating compounds

(G-10405)
ME & RO INC
241 Elizabeth St Frnt A (10012-3544)
PHONE..............................212 431-8744
Robin Renzi, *CEO*
Charmayne Swickle, *Opers Staff*
EMP: 9
SQ FT: 4,000
SALES (est): 2.3MM **Privately Held**
WEB: www.meandrojewelry.com
SIC: 3911 3915 Jewelry, precious metal; jewelers' materials & lapidary work

(G-10406)
MEALPLAN CORP
203 E 4th St Apt 6 (10009-7281)
PHONE..............................909 706-8398
Kevin Carter, *President*
Daniel Mao, *Vice Pres*
Vinh Thai, *Treasurer*
Helal Saleh, *Sales Mgr*
Michelle Chen, *Admin Sec*
EMP: 5
SALES (est): 141.8K **Privately Held**
SIC: 7372 Prepackaged software

(G-10407)
MED REVIEWS LLC
1370 Broadway Fl 5 (10018-7350)
PHONE..............................212 239-5860
EMP: 27 EST: 1998
SQ FT: 10,000
SALES (est): 3.6MM **Privately Held**
SIC: 2721 Publishers Of Medical Journals

(G-10408)
MEDALLION ASSOCIATES INC
37 W 20th St Fl 4 (10011-3791)
PHONE..............................212 929-9130
Donna Peters, *Principal*
▲ EMP: 50
SALES (est): 5.3MM **Privately Held**
WEB: www.medallionltd.com
SIC: 2752 2759 2791 Commercial printing, offset; promotional printing; typesetting

(G-10409)
MEDAPTIVE HEALTH INC
235 W 22nd St Apt 7d (10011-2747)
PHONE..............................646 541-7389
Clay Williams, *CEO*
EMP: 6
SALES (est): 73.7K **Privately Held**
SIC: 7372 Application computer software

(G-10410)
MEDIA PRESS CORP
55 John St 520 (10038-3752)
PHONE..............................212 791-6347
EMP: 20
SALES (est): 1MM **Privately Held**
SIC: 2721 Periodicals-Publishing/Printing

(G-10411)
MEDIA TRANSCRIPTS INC
41 W 83rd St Apt 2b (10024-5247)
PHONE..............................212 362-1481
Pat King, *President*
Pat Podell, *Administration*
▲ EMP: 24
SALES (est): 1.7MM **Privately Held**
WEB: www.mediatranscripts.com
SIC: 2741 Miscellaneous publishing

(G-10412)
MEDIA TRUST LLC (PA)
404 Park Ave S Fl 2 (10016-8404)
PHONE..............................212 802-1162
Peter Bordes, *CEO*
Keith Cohn, *President*
Trevor Thomas, *Officer*
EMP: 5
SALES (est): 4MM **Privately Held**
SIC: 2741 7311 ; advertising agencies

(G-10413)
MEDIAMORPH INC (HQ)
205 Lexington Ave Fl 7 (10016-6020)
PHONE..............................212 643-0762
Rob Gardos, *CEO*
Bill Woods, *Exec VP*
Trevor Dolan, *Vice Pres*
Lloyd Jacobs, *Vice Pres*
Rupesh Kanthan, *Vice Pres*
EMP: 8 EST: 2007
SALES (est): 1.2MM
SALES (corp-wide): 1.9MM **Privately Held**
SIC: 7372 Prepackaged software
PA: Whip Networks, Inc.
1841 Centinela Ave
Santa Monica CA 90404
310 998-1976

(G-10414)
MEDIAPLANET PUBLISHING HSE INC (DH)
350 7th Ave Fl 18 (10001-1931)
PHONE..............................646 922-1400
Luciana Olson, *President*
Timothy Rossi, *Finance*
EMP: 35
SALES (est): 9.4MM **Privately Held**
SIC: 2731 Book publishing

(G-10415)
MEDIAPOST COMMUNICATIONS LLC
1460 Broadway Fl 12 (10036-7306)
PHONE..............................212 204-2000
Ken Fadner, *CEO*
Jeff Loechner, *President*
Phyllis Fine, *Editor*
Sean Hargrave, *Editor*
Steve McClellan, *Editor*
EMP: 50
SALES (est): 5.3MM **Privately Held**
WEB: www.mediapost.com
SIC: 7372 Publishers' computer software

(G-10416)
MEDICAL DAILY INC
7 Hanover Sq Fl 6 (10004-2702)
PHONE..............................646 867-7100
Johnathan Davis, *President*
Dong-Chan Kim, *Principal*
Etienne Uzac, *Treasurer*
EMP: 30
SALES (est): 1.7MM **Privately Held**
SIC: 2741

(G-10417)
MEDIDATA SOLUTIONS INC (DH)
350 Hudson St Fl 9 (10014-4535)
PHONE..............................212 918-1800
Tarek A Sherif, *Ch of Bd*
Glen M De Vries, *President*
Michael L Capone, *COO*
Sastry Chilukuri, *Exec VP*
Jill Larsen, *Exec VP*
EMP: 432
SQ FT: 137,535
SALES: 635.7MM
SALES (corp-wide): 1.8B **Privately Held**
WEB: www.mdsol.com
SIC: 7372 Application computer software
HQ: Dassault Systemes Americas Corp.
175 Wyman St
Waltham MA 02451
781 810-3000

(G-10418)
MEDIKIDZ USA INC
Also Called: Jumo
205 Lexington Ave Rm 1601 (10016-6022)
PHONE..............................646 895-9319
Kevin Aniskovich, *CEO*
Kate Hersov, *Founder*
Mitzie Garland, *CFO*
EMP: 7 EST: 2013
SQ FT: 1,000
SALES (est): 2.9MM **Privately Held**
SIC: 2721 2731 Comic books: publishing & printing; books: publishing only

(G-10419)
MEDIUS SOFTWARE INC
Also Called: Medius North America
12 E 49th St Fl 11 (10017-1012)
PHONE..............................877 295-0058
EMP: 17
SALES (est): 205.4K **Privately Held**
SIC: 7372 Prepackaged Software Services

(G-10420)
MEDSCALE PLUS LLC
152 W 57th St Fl 52 (10019-3484)
PHONE..............................212 218-4070
Charles Gassenheimer, *CEO*
EMP: 8
SALES (est): 186.1K **Privately Held**
SIC: 7372 Application computer software

(G-10421)
MEE ACCESSORIES LLC (PA)
Also Called: Mark Ecko Enterprises
475 10th Ave Fl 9 (10018-9718)
PHONE..............................917 262-1000
Mark Ecko, *CEO*
Seth Gerszberg, *President*
Jeff Jones, *Vice Pres*
Greg Lucci, *Vice Pres*
▲ EMP: 350
SQ FT: 30,000
SALES (est): 30.2MM **Privately Held**
WEB: www.phys-sci.com
SIC: 2329 5136 5621 5611 Men's & boys' sportswear & athletic clothing; sportswear, men's & boys'; women's clothing stores; men's & boys' clothing stores

(G-10422)
MEEGENIUS INC
151 W 25th St Fl 3 (10001-7228)
P.O. Box 287434 (10128-0024)
PHONE...............................212 283-7285
David K Park, *CEO*
EMP: 5
SALES: 60K **Privately Held**
SIC: 2731 Book publishing

(G-10423)
MEGA POWER SPORTS CORPORATION
1123 Broadway Ph (10010-2084)
PHONE...............................212 627-3380
EMP: 6 EST: 1995
SALES (est): 360K **Privately Held**
SIC: 2353 5136 5137 Mfg & Whol Hats

(G-10424)
MEIRAGTX HOLDINGS PLC (PA)
430 E 29th St Fl 10 (10016-8367)
PHONE...............................646 490-2965
Keith R Harris, *Ch of Bd*
Alexandria Forbes, *President*
Richard Giroux, *COO*
Stuart Naylor, *Officer*
Bruce Gottlieb, *Admin Sec*
EMP: 25
SQ FT: 5,887
SALES (est): 10.2MM **Publicly Held**
SIC: 2836 Biological products, except diagnostic

(G-10425)
MEIYUME USA INC
Also Called: Jackel International
1359 Broadway Fl 17 (10018-7117)
PHONE...............................646 927-2370
Gerard Raymond, *President*
Sebastien Williams, *Sales Executive*
April Wasnick, *Manager*
Scott Pestyner, *Admin Sec*
◆ EMP: 30
SQ FT: 11,800
SALES (est): 11.4MM **Privately Held**
WEB: www.jackelus.com
SIC: 2844 Cosmetic preparations

(G-10426)
MEKANISM INC
250 Hudson St Rm 200 (10013-1458)
PHONE...............................212 226-2772
Lissa Pinkas, *Business Mgr*
Laura Peguero, *Branch Mgr*
EMP: 40
SALES (corp-wide): 13.2MM **Privately Held**
SIC: 3993 Signs & advertising specialties
PA: Mekanism, Inc.
640 2nd St Fl 3
San Francisco CA 94107
415 908-4000

(G-10427)
MEL BERNIE AND COMPANY INC
Also Called: 1928 Jewelry Co
384 5th Ave Fl 4 (10018-8140)
PHONE...............................212 889-8570
Mel Bernie, *President*
EMP: 5
SALES (corp-wide): 55.6MM **Privately Held**
WEB: www.1928.com
SIC: 3961 Costume jewelry
PA: Mel Bernie And Company, Inc.
3000 W Empire Ave
Burbank CA 91504
818 841-1928

(G-10428)
MELCHER MEDIA INC
124 W 13th St (10011-7802)
PHONE...............................212 727-2322
Charles Melcher, *President*
Karl Daum, *Editor*
Daniel Valle, *Assistant VP*
Kurt Andrews, *Vice Pres*
Bonnie Eldon, *VP Opers*
▲ EMP: 11
SQ FT: 1,500

SALES (est): 1.8MM **Privately Held**
WEB: www.melcher.com
SIC: 2731 2789 Books: publishing only; bookbinding & related work

(G-10429)
MEMO AMERICA INC
60 Broad St Ste 3502 (10004-2356)
PHONE...............................646 356-0460
John Molloy, *President*
Dean Laskowski, *Vice Pres*
EMP: 25
SALES: 1MM **Privately Held**
SIC: 2844 Perfumes & colognes

(G-10430)
MEMORY MD INC (PA)
205 E 42nd St Fl 14 (10017-5752)
PHONE...............................917 318-0215
Boris Goldstein, *Ch of Bd*
Yuriy Shirokikh, *CFO*
EMP: 5
SALES (est): 583.8K **Privately Held**
SIC: 3841 5047 Diagnostic apparatus, medical; diagnostic equipment, medical

(G-10431)
MENS JOURNAL LLC
1290 Ave Of The Americas (10104-0295)
PHONE...............................212 484-1616
Greg Emmanuel, *Ch Credit Ofcr*
John Gruber, *Executive*
Jay Gallagher, *Risk Mgmt Dir*
EMP: 1214
SALES (est): 6.6MM
SALES (corp-wide): 363MM **Privately Held**
SIC: 2741 Miscellaneous publishing
PA: Worldwide Media Services Group Inc.
1350 E Newprt Ctr Dr 20
Deerfield Beach FL 33442
561 989-1342

(G-10432)
MER GEMS CORP
Also Called: Romir Enterprises
62 W 47th St Ste 614 (10036-3201)
PHONE...............................212 714-9129
Roshel Mirzakanzov, *President*
Nelly Mirzakanzov, *Vice Pres*
◆ EMP: 5 EST: 1998
SQ FT: 800
SALES: 1MM **Privately Held**
SIC: 3911 5094 Jewelry, precious metal; jewelry & precious stones

(G-10433)
MERGENT INC
444 Madison Ave Ste 502 (10022-6976)
PHONE...............................212 413-7700
Jonathan Worral, *CEO*
Mike Winn, *Managing Dir*
Greg Collins, *Vice Pres*
Charles E Miller Jr, *CFO*
Karlyn Johnston, *Marketing Staff*
EMP: 300
SALES (est): 16.5MM **Privately Held**
SIC: 2721 Magazines: publishing only, not printed on site

(G-10434)
MERIDIAN ADHESIVES GROUP LLC (PA)
100 Park Ave Fl 31 (10017-5584)
PHONE...............................212 771-1717
Dan Pelton, *CEO*
EMP: 3
SALES (est): 45.6MM **Privately Held**
SIC: 2891 Adhesives & sealants

(G-10435)
MERRILL COMMUNICATIONS LLC
1345 Ave Of The Amrcs 1 (10105-0199)
PHONE...............................212 620-5600
EMP: 7
SALES (corp-wide): 566.6MM **Privately Held**
SIC: 2759 Commercial printing
HQ: Merrill Communications Llc
1 Merrill Cir
Saint Paul MN 55108
651 646-4501

(G-10436)
MERRILL CORPORATION
25 W 45th St Ste 900 (10036-4902)
PHONE...............................917 934-7300
Peter Jordan, *Branch Mgr*
EMP: 87
SALES (corp-wide): 566.6MM **Privately Held**
WEB: www.merrillcorp.com
SIC: 2759 Commercial printing
PA: Merrill Corporation
1 Merrill Cir
Saint Paul MN 55108
651 646-4501

(G-10437)
MERRILL CORPORATION
1345 Ave Of The Ave Fl 17 Flr 17 (10105)
PHONE...............................212 620-5600
Tony Anzivino, *Vice Pres*
Susan Kindya, *Sales Dir*
Mike James, *Manager*
Simone Solivan, *Business Dir*
Maureen Harris, *Executive*
EMP: 100
SALES (corp-wide): 566.6MM **Privately Held**
WEB: www.merrillcorp.com
SIC: 2741 Miscellaneous publishing
PA: Merrill Corporation
1 Merrill Cir
Saint Paul MN 55108
651 646-4501

(G-10438)
MERRILL NEW YORK COMPANY INC
Also Called: Merrill Communications
246 W 54th St (10019-5502)
PHONE...............................212 229-6500
Tod Albright, *President*
EMP: 200
SALES (est): 11.9MM
SALES (corp-wide): 566.6MM **Privately Held**
WEB: www.merrillcorp.com
SIC: 2759 2752 Financial note & certificate printing & engraving; commercial printing, lithographic
PA: Merrill Corporation
1 Merrill Cir
Saint Paul MN 55108
651 646-4501

(G-10439)
MERYL DIAMOND LTD (PA)
Also Called: M D L
1375 Broadway Fl 9 (10018-7052)
PHONE...............................212 730-0333
Meryl Diamond, *President*
Kim Reinle, *Financial Exec*
▲ EMP: 60
SQ FT: 13,000
SALES (est): 101.1MM **Privately Held**
SIC: 2339 2389 Sportswear, women's; men's miscellaneous accessories

(G-10440)
MESH LLC
350 5th Ave Lbby 9 (10118-0109)
PHONE...............................646 839-7000
Richard Darling,
▲ EMP: 30
SALES (est): 1.6MM **Privately Held**
SIC: 2326 Men's & boys' work clothing
HQ: Gbg Usa Inc.
350 5th Ave Lbby 11
New York NY 10118
646 839-7000

(G-10441)
MESOBLAST INC
505 5th Ave Fl 3 (10017-4910)
PHONE...............................212 880-2060
Silviu Itescu, *CEO*
Daniel Devine, *Vice Pres*
Christopher James, *Vice Pres*
Juliana Benito, *Research*
Suhujey Lopez, *Research*
EMP: 8
SALES (est): 4.5MM **Privately Held**
SIC: 2834 Drugs acting on the cardiovascular system, except diagnostic
PA: Mesoblast Limited
55 Collins St
Melbourne VIC 3000

(G-10442)
MESSEX GROUP INC
244 5th Ave Ste D256 (10001-7604)
PHONE...............................646 229-2582
Tom Carmody, *President*
Diana Popescu, *Vice Pres*
EMP: 4 EST: 2011
SQ FT: 1,000
SALES: 2MM **Privately Held**
SIC: 2325 Men's & boys' jeans & dungarees

(G-10443)
METALSIGMA USA INC
350 5th Ave (10118-0110)
PHONE...............................212 731-4346
Carlo Geddo, *President*
EMP: 3
SQ FT: 400
SALES: 8MM
SALES (corp-wide): 37.6MM **Privately Held**
SIC: 3449 Curtain wall, metal
PA: Metalsigma Tunesi Spa
Via Vicinale Galdina S.P. 34
Arluno MI 20010
029 015-762

(G-10444)
METRO CREATIVE GRAPHICS INC (PA)
519 8th Ave Fl 18 (10018-4577)
PHONE...............................212 947-5100
Robert Zimmerman, *CEO*
Andrew Shapiro, *Ch of Bd*
Darrell Davis, *Vice Pres*
Benjamin Sandoval, *Controller*
Robert Forrest, *Art Dir*
EMP: 38
SQ FT: 22,000
SALES (est): 6.4MM **Privately Held**
WEB: www.metroeditorialservices.com
SIC: 2731 2759 Books: publishing & printing; screen printing

(G-10445)
METRO FUEL LLC
800 3rd Ave Fl 28 (10022-7604)
PHONE...............................212 836-9608
EMP: 207 EST: 2010
SALES (est): 523.6K
SALES (corp-wide): 1.6B **Publicly Held**
SIC: 2869 Fuels
PA: Outfront Media Inc.
405 Lexington Ave Fl 17
New York NY 10174
212 297-6400

(G-10446)
METROSOURCE PUBLISHING INC
498 Fashion Ave Fl 10 (10018-6957)
PHONE...............................212 691-5127
Rob Davis, *President*
Chris Rivera, *Manager*
EMP: 12
SALES (est): 1.3MM
SALES (corp-wide): 4.8MM **Privately Held**
SIC: 2721 Magazines: publishing & printing; magazines: publishing only, not printed on site
PA: Davler Media Group Llc
213 W 35th St Rm 1201
New York NY 10001
212 315-0800

(G-10447)
MG IMAGING
229 W 28th St Rm 300 (10001-5915)
PHONE...............................212 704-4073
Mario Gambuzza, *President*
EMP: 5
SALES (est): 773.3K **Privately Held**
SIC: 3577 Printers & plotters

(G-10448)
MGK GROUP INC
Also Called: Lamontage
979 3rd Ave Ste 1811 (10022-3804)
PHONE...............................212 989-2732
Liora Manne, *President*
Erica Daniels, *Manager*
EMP: 30
SQ FT: 10,000

SALES (est): 4MM **Privately Held**
WEB: www.lamontage.com
SIC: **2273** 2211 2221 2392 Rugs, hand &
machine made; upholstery fabrics, cotton;
tapestry fabrics, cotton; wall covering fabrics, manmade fiber & silk; household furnishings; textile bags; nonwoven fabrics

(G-10449)
MHG STUDIO INC
175 Rivington St Frnt 2 (10002-2517)
PHONE.................................212 674-7610
Michele Glick, *President*
Victor Guarneri, *Vice Pres*
EMP: 3
SALES: 1MM **Privately Held**
WEB: www.mhgstudio.com
SIC: **3172** Personal leather goods

(G-10450)
MIAMI MEDIA LLC (HQ)
72 Madison Ave Fl 11 (10016-8731)
PHONE.................................212 268-8600
Thomas Allon, *Mng Member*
EMP: 12
SALES (est): 1.5MM
SALES (corp-wide): 10.9MM **Privately
Held**
SIC: **2711** 2721 Newspapers: publishing
only, not printed on site; magazines: pub-
lishing only, not printed on site
PA: Manhattan Media, Llc
535 5th Ave Fl 23
New York NY 10017
212 268-8600

(G-10451)
MICHAEL ANDREWS LLC
Also Called: Michael Andrews Bespoke
680 Broadway Fl Mezz (10012-2322)
PHONE.................................212 677-1755
Michael Mantegna, *CEO*
Cory Sylvester, *VP Opers*
▲ EMP: 16
SALES (est): 933.8K **Privately Held**
SIC: **2311** 5611 Suits, men's & boys':
made from purchased materials; men's &
boys' clothing stores

(G-10452)
MICHAEL BONDANZA INC
10 E 38th St Fl 6 (10016-0619)
PHONE.................................212 869-0043
Michael Bondanza, *President*
Geri Bondanza, *Vice Pres*
EMP: 26
SQ FT: 2,500
SALES (est): 3.3MM **Privately Held**
WEB: www.bondanza.com
SIC: **3911** 5094 Jewelry, precious metal;
jewelry

(G-10453)
MICHAEL KARP MUSIC INC
Also Called: 39th Street Music-Div
59 W 71st St Apt 7a (10023-4115)
PHONE.................................212 840-3285
Michael Karp, *President*
EMP: 6
SQ FT: 5,500
SALES (est): 490K **Privately Held**
WEB: www.michaelkarpmusic.com
SIC: **2741** 7389 Music, sheet: publishing
only, not printed on site; music & broad-
casting services

(G-10454)
MICHAELIAN & KOHLBERG INC
225 E 59th St (10022-1403)
PHONE.................................212 431-9009
EMP: 9
SALES (corp-wide): 4.2MM **Privately
Held**
SIC: **2273** Mfg Carpets/Rugs
PA: Michaelian & Kohlberg, Inc.
5216 Brevard Rd
Horse Shoe NC 28742
828 891-8511

(G-10455)
**MICKELBERRY
COMMUNICATIONS INC (PA)**
405 Park Ave (10022-4405)
PHONE.................................212 832-0303
James C Marlas, *Ch of Bd*
Gregory J Garville, *President*

Nigel Morgan, *CFO*
Al Wester, *Creative Dir*
EMP: 8
SQ FT: 4,000
SALES (est): 46.5MM **Privately Held**
WEB: www.mickelberry.com
SIC: **2752** 7311 Commercial printing, litho-
graphic; advertising agencies

(G-10456)
MICRO PUBLISHING INC
Also Called: Micropage
71 W 23rd St Lbby A (10010-3521)
PHONE.................................212 533-9180
EMP: 5
SQ FT: 9,000
SALES: 3MM **Privately Held**
SIC: **2731** 2796 Book-Publishing/Printing
Platemaking Services

(G-10457)
**MICRO SEMICDTR
RESEARCHES LLC (PA)**
310 W 52nd St Apt 12b (10019-6292)
PHONE.................................646 863-6070
Seiji Yamashita, *Principal*
▲ EMP: 4
SALES (est): 1.7MM **Privately Held**
SIC: **3674** 8748 Semiconductors & related
devices; test development & evaluation
service

(G-10458)
MICROMEM TECHNOLOGIES
245 Park Ave Fl 24 (10167-2699)
PHONE.................................212 672-1806
Steven Van Fleet, *Principal*
EMP: 10
SALES (est): 545.8K **Privately Held**
SIC: **3674** Semiconductors & related de-
vices

(G-10459)
MICROSOFT CORPORATION
11 Times Sq Fl 9 (10036-6619)
PHONE.................................212 245-2100
Scott Velechko, *Business Mgr*
Caryn Weiss, *Accounts Mgr*
Seth Amera, *Sales Staff*
David Lochridge, *Sales Staff*
Joanne Steinhart, *Manager*
EMP: 10
SALES (corp-wide): 125.8B **Publicly
Held**
WEB: www.microsoft.com
SIC: **7372** Application computer software
PA: Microsoft Corporation
1 Microsoft Way
Redmond WA 98052
425 882-8080

(G-10460)
**MICROSTRATEGY
INCORPORATED**
5 Penn Plz Ste 901 (10001-1837)
PHONE.................................888 537-8135
John Larkin, *CEO*
EMP: 15
SALES (corp-wide): 497.6MM **Publicly
Held**
WEB: www.microstrategy.com
SIC: **7372** Application computer software
PA: Microstrategy Incorporated
1850 Towers Crescent Plz # 700
Tysons Corner VA 22182
703 848-8600

(G-10461)
**MIDAS MDICI GROUP HOLDINGS
INC (PA)**
445 Park Ave Frnt 5 (10022-8603)
PHONE.................................212 792-0920
Nana Baffour, *Ch of Bd*
Johnson M Kachidza, *President*
Robert F McCarthy, *Exec VP*
Frank Asante-Kissi, *Officer*
EMP: 4
SALES (est): 80.7MM **Privately Held**
SIC: **7372** Prepackaged software

(G-10462)
MIDURA JEWELS INC
36 W 47th St Ste 809i (10036-8601)
PHONE.................................213 265-8090
EMP: 2 EST: 2013

SALES: 1MM **Privately Held**
SIC: **3911** 5094 5944 Mfg Precious Metal
Jewelry Whol Jewelry/Precious Stones
Ret Jewelry

(G-10463)
MIKAEL AGHAL LLC
49 W 38th St Fl 4 (10018-1913)
PHONE.................................212 596-4010
Michael Hakimi,
Albert Aghalarian,
◆ EMP: 11
SQ FT: 5,000
SALES (est): 786K **Privately Held**
WEB: www.mikaelaghal.com
SIC: **2339** Athletic clothing: women's,
misses' & juniors'; women's & misses'
athletic clothing & sportswear

(G-10464)
MIKAM GRAPHICS LLC
1440 Broadway Fl 22 (10018-3041)
PHONE.................................212 684-9393
Donald Pesce, *Vice Pres*
Jeff Getelman, *Mng Member*
EMP: 100
SQ FT: 5,000
SALES (est): 9MM
SALES (corp-wide): 1.1B **Publicly Held**
WEB: www.mikam.com
SIC: **2752** Commercial printing, offset
PA: Innerworkings, Inc.
203 N Lasalle St Ste 1800
Chicago IL 60601
312 642-3700

(G-10465)
MILAAYA INC
Also Called: Milaaya Embroideries
147 W 35th St Ste 602 (10001-0118)
PHONE.................................212 764-6386
Gayatri Khanna, *President*
EMP: 4
SALES: 1.2MM **Privately Held**
SIC: **2395** Embroidery products, except
schiffli machine

(G-10466)
**MILLENNIUM MEDICAL
PUBLISHING**
611 Broadway Rm 310 (10012-2654)
PHONE.................................212 995-2211
Steve Kurlander, *CEO*
EMP: 18
SQ FT: 3,000
SALES: 6MM **Privately Held**
SIC: **2741** Miscellaneous publishing

(G-10467)
**MILLENNIUM PRODUCTIONS
INC**
Also Called: Alice & Trixie
265 W 37th St 11 (10018-5707)
PHONE.................................212 944-6203
Andrew Oshrin, *President*
Lynn Harechmak, *Bookkeeper*
Samantha Grossinger, *Accounts Exec*
Malise Collins, *Sales Staff*
▲ EMP: 12
SQ FT: 2,000
SALES (est): 1.3MM **Privately Held**
WEB: www.aliceandtrixie.com
SIC: **2335** 2339 Housedresses; sports-
wear, women's

(G-10468)
MILLER & BERKOWITZ LTD
345 7th Ave Fl 20 (10001-5034)
PHONE.................................212 244-5459
Nathan Berkowitz, *President*
EMP: 13 EST: 1949
SQ FT: 13,500
SALES (est): 780K **Privately Held**
SIC: **2371** Fur goods

(G-10469)
MILLER & VEIT INC
22 W 48th St Ste 703 (10036-1820)
PHONE.................................212 247-2275
Edward Ludel, *President*
Edward E Ludel, *Vice Pres*
Barbara Ludel, *Admin Sec*
EMP: 10
SQ FT: 1,566

SALES (est): 1MM **Privately Held**
SIC: **3915** 5094 Diamond cutting & polishing; diamonds (gems)

(G-10470)
**MILTON MERL & ASSOCIATES
INC**
647 W 174th St Bsmt B (10033-7716)
PHONE.................................212 634-9292
Milton Merl, *President*
Bob Langelius, *Engineer*
Charles Houghton, *Creative Dir*
▲ EMP: 5
SQ FT: 2,000
SALES (est): 725.2K **Privately Held**
WEB: www.miltonmerl.com
SIC: **2542** Partitions & fixtures, except
wood

(G-10471)
MILTONS OF NEW YORK INC
110 W 40th St Rm 1001 (10018-8535)
PHONE.................................212 997-3359
Kerman Minbatiwalla, *President*
Shalini Amersey, *Vice Pres*
EMP: 6
SQ FT: 600
SALES (est): 1.1MM **Privately Held**
WEB: www.miltonsny.com
SIC: **2339** 2321 2325 2369 Women's &
misses' outerwear; men's & boys' furnish-
ings; men's & boys' trousers & slacks;
girls' & children's outerwear

(G-10472)
MIMEOCOM INC (PA)
3 Park Ave Fl 22 (10016-5909)
P.O. Box 654018, Dallas TX (75265-4018)
PHONE.................................212 847-3000
Adam Slutsky, *CEO*
John Delbridge, *COO*
Nicole P Haughey, *COO*
Mike Barker, *Vice Pres*
Adam Bellusci, *Vice Pres*
EMP: 277
SQ FT: 145,000
SALES (est): 189MM **Privately Held**
WEB: www.mimeo.com
SIC: **2759** Commercial printing

(G-10473)
MIMI SO INTERNATIONAL LLC
Also Called: Mimi So New York
22 W 48th St Ste 902 (10036-1803)
PHONE.................................212 300-8600
Molly Conlin, *Marketing Mgr*
Karissa Basile, *Marketing Staff*
Mimi So, *Mng Member*
Stephanie Preville, *Director*
EMP: 20
SALES (est): 3.3MM **Privately Held**
SIC: **3911** 5944 5094 Jewelry, precious
metal; jewelry stores; jewelry

(G-10474)
MIN HO DESIGNS INC
425 Madison Ave Rm 1703 (10017-1150)
PHONE.................................212 838-3667
Fax: 212 838-3689
EMP: 9
SQ FT: 1,600
SALES (est): 740K **Privately Held**
SIC: **3911** Mfg Jewelry

(G-10475)
MINDFUL FOODS INC
Also Called: Soozy's Grain-Free
246 5th Ave Fl 3 (10001-7608)
PHONE.................................646 708-0454
Mason Sexton, *President*
EMP: 3
SALES: 1MM **Privately Held**
SIC: **2052** Bakery products, dry

(G-10476)
**MINERALS TECHNOLOGIES INC
(PA)**
622 3rd Ave Rm 3800 (10017-6729)
PHONE.................................212 878-1800
Douglas T Dietrich, *CEO*
Duane R Dunham, *Ch of Bd*
Thomas J Meek, *Senior VP*
Michael A Cipolla, *Vice Pres*
Matthew E Garth, *CFO*
▲ EMP: 50

SALES: 1.8B **Publicly Held**
WEB: www.mineralstech.com
SIC: 2819 3274 1411 3281 Calcium compounds & salts, inorganic; quicklime; limestone & marble dimension stone; limestone, cut & shaped; limestone; minerals, ground or otherwise treated

(G-10477)
MING PAO (NEW YORK) INC
265 Canal St Ste 403 (10013-6010)
PHONE...............................212 334-2220
EMP: 10
SALES (corp-wide): 429.1MM **Privately Held**
SIC: 2711 Printing & Circulation Of Newspaper
HQ: Ming Pao (New York), Inc
4331 33rd St
Long Island City NY

(G-10478)
MINK MART INC
345 7th Ave Fl 9 (10001-5049)
PHONE...............................212 868-2785
George J Haralabatos, *President*
EMP: 7 EST: 1960
SQ FT: 7,200
SALES (est): 680K **Privately Held**
SIC: 2371 Apparel, fur

(G-10479)
MINY GROUP INC
148 Lafayette St Fl 2 (10013-3115)
PHONE...............................212 925-6722
Shun Yen Siu, *President*
Harvey Lock, *Vice Pres*
Deirdre Quinn, *Vice Pres*
Anita Wong, *Vice Pres*
EMP: 70
SALES (est): 3.1MM **Privately Held**
SIC: 2337 Women's & misses' suits & coats

(G-10480)
MINYANVILLE MEDIA INC
708 3rd Ave Fl 6 (10017-4119)
PHONE...............................212 991-6200
Todd Harrison, *CEO*
Kevin Wassong, *President*
Bradford Campeau-Laurion, *CTO*
EMP: 23
SQ FT: 6,000
SALES (est): 1.5MM **Privately Held**
SIC: 2741 Miscellaneous publishing

(G-10481)
MISS GROUP (PA)
1410 Broadway Rm 703 (10018-9365)
PHONE...............................212 391-2535
▲ EMP: 9
SALES (est): 5MM **Privately Held**
SIC: 2329 Mens And Boys Clothing, Nec, Nsk

(G-10482)
MISS SPORTSWEAR INC (PA)
Also Called: Miss Group, The
1410 Broadway Rm 703 (10018-9365)
PHONE...............................212 391-2535
Moses Fallas, *Ch of Bd*
Alan Fallas, *Vice Pres*
▲ EMP: 3
SQ FT: 8,000
SALES (est): 19MM **Privately Held**
SIC: 2339 Women's & misses' athletic clothing & sportswear

(G-10483)
MISTDODA INC (DH)
Also Called: Croscill Home Fashions
261 5th Ave Fl 25 (10016-7601)
PHONE...............................919 735-7111
Douglas Kahn, *CEO*
Marc Navarre, *President*
Joe Granger, *Vice Pres*
Ken Hedrick, *Vice Pres*
Clifford F Campbell, *CFO*
▲ EMP: 50 EST: 1925
SQ FT: 35,000
SALES (est): 77.7MM
SALES (corp-wide): 4.1B **Privately Held**
WEB: www.croscill.com
SIC: 2391 5023 Curtains & draperies; decorative home furnishings & supplies

(G-10484)
MITSUBISHI CHEMICAL AMER INC (HQ)
Also Called: Composite Materials Division
655 3rd Ave Fl 15 (10017-9135)
PHONE...............................212 223-3043
John Canfield, *President*
Nicholas Oliva, *General Counsel*
Stephen Rose, *Legal Staff*
◆ EMP: 41
SALES (est): 236.3MM **Privately Held**
SIC: 3355 3444 3443 2893 Aluminum rolling & drawing; sheet metalwork; fabricated plate work (boiler shop); printing ink

(G-10485)
MKSF INC
Also Called: Marc Kaufman Furs
212 W 30th St (10001-4901)
PHONE...............................212 563-3877
Marc Kaufman, *CEO*
EMP: 10
SALES (est): 479K **Privately Held**
SIC: 2371 Fur coats & other fur apparel

(G-10486)
MMJ APPAREL LLC
1407 Broadway Fl 10 (10018-3271)
PHONE...............................212 354-8550
Mark Friedman, *President*
Daniel Torczyner, *CFO*
Claudia Polon, *Credit Staff*
EMP: 50
SQ FT: 7,500
SALES: 20MM **Privately Held**
SIC: 2335 Women's, juniors' & misses' dresses

(G-10487)
MOBO SYSTEMS INC
Also Called: Go Mobo
26 Broadway Fl 24 (10004-1840)
PHONE...............................212 260-0895
Noah H Glass, *CEO*
Matt Tucker, *COO*
Matthew Tucker, *COO*
Marty Hahnfeld, *Vice Pres*
Scott Lamb, *Vice Pres*
EMP: 86
SQ FT: 400
SALES (est): 13.2MM **Privately Held**
SIC: 7372 Business oriented computer software

(G-10488)
MODERN LANGUAGE ASSN AMER INC
Also Called: M L A
85 Broad St Fl 5 (10004-1789)
PHONE...............................646 576-5000
Margaret W Ferguson, *President*
Cameron Bardrick, *Editor*
Margit Longbrake, *Editor*
Emma Marciano, *Editor*
Kwame Anthony Appiah, *Vice Pres*
EMP: 110 EST: 1883
SQ FT: 37,500
SALES: 16.3MM **Privately Held**
SIC: 2731 8641 Books: publishing only; educator's association

(G-10489)
MODO RETAIL LLC
Also Called: Modo Eyewear
252 Mott St (10012-3436)
PHONE...............................212 965-4900
Sue Ng, *Controller*
Alex Lenaro,
EMP: 40
SALES (est): 3.2MM **Privately Held**
SIC: 3851 Spectacles

(G-10490)
MODULEX NEW YORK INC
Also Called: Asi Sign Systems
192 Lexington Ave Rm 1002 (10016-6823)
PHONE...............................646 742-1320
Selwyn Josset, *President*
John Jackson, *Sales Staff*
Lauren Corrigan, *Office Mgr*
EMP: 8
SQ FT: 2,200
SALES: 2.1MM **Privately Held**
SIC: 3993 Signs, not made in custom sign painting shops

(G-10491)
MODULIGHTOR INC
246 E 58th St (10022-2011)
PHONE...............................212 371-0336
Ernest Wagner, *President*
▲ EMP: 12
SQ FT: 7,000
SALES (est): 1.5MM **Privately Held**
WEB: www.Modulightor.com
SIC: 3646 3645 Commercial indusl & institutional electric lighting fixtures; residential lighting fixtures

(G-10492)
MOELIS CAPITAL PARTNERS LLC (PA)
399 Park Ave Fl 5 (10022-4416)
PHONE...............................212 883-3800
Kurt Larsen,
Barbara Hill,
James Johnston,
Andy Kieffer,
Joel Killion,
EMP: 477
SALES (est): 199.1MM **Privately Held**
SIC: 3728 4581 Fuselage assembly, aircraft; aircraft upholstery repair

(G-10493)
MOHAWK GROUP HOLDINGS INC (PA)
37 E 18th St Fl 7 (10003-2001)
PHONE...............................347 676-1681
Yaniv Sarig, *President*
Peter Datos, *COO*
Fabrice Hamaide, *CFO*
Roi Zahut, *CTO*
Joseph A Risico, *General Counsel*
EMP: 4
SQ FT: 5,200
SALES: 73.2MM **Publicly Held**
SIC: 3639 3585 Major kitchen appliances, except refrigerators & stoves; dehumidifiers electric, except portable; air conditioning units, complete: domestic or industrial

(G-10494)
MOLABS INC
32 Little West 12th St (10014-1303)
PHONE...............................310 721-6828
James Payne, *CEO*
EMP: 6 EST: 2015
SALES (est): 163.7K **Privately Held**
SIC: 7372 Application computer software

(G-10495)
MOM DAD PUBLISHING INC
Also Called: C/O Pdell Ndell Fine Winberger
59 Maiden Ln Fl 27 (10038-4647)
PHONE...............................646 476-9170
Bert Padell, *President*
EMP: 30
SALES (est): 2.4MM **Privately Held**
SIC: 2741 Music, sheet: publishing only, not printed on site

(G-10496)
MOMOFUKU 171 FIRST AVENUE LLC
171 1st Ave (10003-2949)
PHONE...............................212 777-7773
Marguerite Zabar Mariscal, *CEO*
Ryan Schuler, *General Mgr*
David Chang, *Mng Member*
Nicole Hakli, *Manager*
Matthew Rudofker, *Director*
EMP: 52 EST: 2007
SALES (est): 6.2MM **Privately Held**
SIC: 2098 Noodles (e.g. egg, plain & water), dry

(G-10497)
MONACELLI PRESS LLC
6 W 18th St Ste 2c (10011-4633)
PHONE...............................212 229-9925
Gianfranco Monacelli, *President*
Michael Vagnetti, *Prdtn Dir*
Susan Enochs, *Pub Rel Dir*
Sarah Herda, *Marketing Staff*
Jaime Noven, *Marketing Staff*
▲ EMP: 8
SALES (est): 809.8K **Privately Held**
WEB: www.monacellipress.com
SIC: 2731 Books: publishing only

(G-10498)
MONDO PUBLISHING INC (PA)
980 Avenue Of The America (10018-7810)
PHONE...............................212 268-3560
Mark Vineis, *President*
Ellen Ungaro, *Editor*
Sallye Drinkard, *Prdtn Mgr*
Charles Arasi, *Manager*
◆ EMP: 16
SALES (est): 1.9MM **Privately Held**
WEB: www.mondopub.com
SIC: 2731 Books: publishing only

(G-10499)
MONELLE JEWELRY
608 5th Ave Ste 504 (10020-2303)
PHONE...............................212 977-9535
Avis Swed, *Owner*
EMP: 3
SQ FT: 600
SALES: 1.1MM **Privately Held**
WEB: www.monellejewelry.com
SIC: 3911 Jewelry, precious metal

(G-10500)
MONGODB INC (PA)
1633 Broadway Fl 38 (10019-6763)
PHONE...............................646 727-4092
Tom Killalea, *Ch of Bd*
Dev Ittycheria, *President*
Michael Gordon, *COO*
Seong Park, *Vice Pres*
Angelo Olivera, *Engineer*
EMP: 148 EST: 2007
SQ FT: 106,230
SALES: 267MM **Publicly Held**
SIC: 7372 Prepackaged software

(G-10501)
MONTHLY GIFT INC
Also Called: Montly Gift
401 Park Ave S (10016-8808)
PHONE...............................888 444-9661
Lisamarie Scotti, *Vice Pres*
EMP: 6
SQ FT: 350
SALES (est): 500K **Privately Held**
SIC: 2676 Sanitary paper products

(G-10502)
MORELLE PRODUCTS LTD
Also Called: Philippe Adec Paris
211 E 18th St Apt 4d (10003-3624)
PHONE...............................212 391-8070
EMP: 17
SQ FT: 13,500
SALES (est): 1.4MM **Privately Held**
SIC: 2339 5137 Mfg Women's/Misses' Outerwear Whol Women's/Child's Clothing

(G-10503)
MORGIK METAL DESIGNS
145 Hudson St Frnt 4 (10013-2122)
P.O. Box 213, Elmwood Park NJ (07407-0213)
PHONE...............................212 463-0304
Larry Kaufman, *President*
Joe Kaufman, *Admin Sec*
EMP: 18
SQ FT: 4,000
SALES (est): 2.5MM **Privately Held**
WEB: www.morgik.com
SIC: 3446 1761 3429 Architectural metalwork; architectural sheet metal work; furniture builders' & other household hardware

(G-10504)
MORRIS BROTHERS SIGN SVC INC
37 W 20th St Ste 708 (10011-3717)
PHONE...............................212 675-9130
Peter V Bellantone, *President*
Michael Bellantone, *Opers Staff*
EMP: 3
SQ FT: 2,000
SALES: 1MM **Privately Held**
WEB: www.morrisbrotherssigns.com
SIC: 3993 Signs & advertising specialties

(G-10505)
MOSBY HOLDINGS CORP (DH)
125 Park Ave (10017-5529)
PHONE...............................212 309-8100

Ron Mobed, *President*
EMP: 6
SALES (est): 82.3MM
SALES (corp-wide): 9.6B **Privately Held**
SIC: 2741 8999 Technical manuals: publishing only, not printed on site; writing for publication
HQ: Relx Inc.
230 Park Ave Ste 700
New York NY 10169
212 309-8100

(G-10506)
MOSCHOS FURS INC
345 7th Ave Rm 1501 (10001-5042)
PHONE..................................212 244-0255
George Moschos, *President*
Patricia Moschos, *Corp Secy*
EMP: 5
SQ FT: 4,000
SALES (est): 350K **Privately Held**
SIC: 2371 Fur coats & other fur apparel

(G-10507)
MOSCOT WHOLESALE CORP (PA)
69 W 14th St Fl 2 (10011-7417)
PHONE..................................212 647-1550
Dr Harvey Moscot, *President*
Jennifer Scott, *Vice Pres*
Kenny Moscot, *Shareholder*
Judith MEI,
▲ **EMP:** 6
SQ FT: 2,000
SALES (est): 511.7K **Privately Held**
SIC: 3851 5049 Frames, lenses & parts, eyeglass & spectacle; optical goods

(G-10508)
MOTEMA MUSIC LLC
8 W 127th St Apt 2 (10027-3949)
PHONE..................................212 860-6969
Wade Bordick, *General Mgr*
Haley Brawner, *Marketing Staff*
Jana Herzen,
EMP: 7
SQ FT: 600
SALES: 700K **Privately Held**
SIC: 2782 5735 Record albums; records

(G-10509)
MOUNTAIN AND ISLES LLC
525 7th Ave Fl 22 (10018-0428)
PHONE..................................212 354-1890
Marie Huftel,
Victor Rousso,
EMP: 11
SALES (est): 533K **Privately Held**
SIC: 2389 Men's miscellaneous accessories

(G-10510)
MP STUDIO INC
147 W 35th St Ste 1603 (10001-2100)
PHONE..................................212 302-5666
EMP: 5 **EST:** 2013
SALES (est): 300K **Privately Held**
SIC: 2337 Mfg Women's/Misses' Suits/Coats

(G-10511)
MPDRAW LLC
109 Ludlow St (10002-3240)
PHONE..................................212 228-8383
EMP: 25 **EST:** 2009
SALES (est): 1.6MM **Privately Held**
SIC: 3421 Table & food cutlery, including butchers'

(G-10512)
MPDW INC (PA)
158 W 29th St Fl 12 (10001-5300)
PHONE..................................925 631-6878
Sharon Huebschwerlen, *CEO*
▲ **EMP:** 7
SQ FT: 7,000
SALES (est): 952.9K **Privately Held**
WEB: www.mycrapac.com
SIC: 2385 Raincoats, except vulcanized rubber: purchased materials

(G-10513)
MRINALINI INC
Also Called: M & R Design
469 7th Ave Rm 1254 (10018-7605)
PHONE..................................646 510-2747

Mrinalini Kumari, *President*
EMP: 6
SALES (est): 41.4K **Privately Held**
SIC: 2395 Embroidery & art needlework

(G-10514)
MRS JOHN L STRONG & CO LLC
Also Called: Strong Ventures
699 Madison Ave Fl 5 (10065-8039)
PHONE..................................212 838-3775
Joe Lewis, *President*
Nanette Brown,
EMP: 14
SALES (est): 1.5MM **Privately Held**
WEB: www.mrsstrong.com
SIC: 2754 Stationery: gravure printing

(G-10515)
MRT TEXTILE INC
350 5th Ave (10118-0110)
PHONE..................................800 674-1073
Ibrahim Eyidemir, *President*
David Davitoglu, *Vice Pres*
Vincent Timpone, *Vice Pres*
Eli Marcus, *Marketing Staff*
EMP: 3
SQ FT: 7,000
SALES: 4MM **Privately Held**
SIC: 2341 5137 Chemises, camisoles & teddies: women's & children's; women's & children's lingerie & undergarments

(G-10516)
MTM PUBLISHING INC
435 W 23rd St Apt 8c (10011-1437)
P.O. Box 304, High Falls (12440-0304)
PHONE..................................212 242-6930
Valerie Tomaselli, *President*
EMP: 6
SALES (est): 516.7K **Privately Held**
SIC: 2741 Miscellaneous publishing

(G-10517)
MUD PUDDLE BOOKS INC
36 W 25th St Fl 5 (10010-2718)
PHONE..................................212 647-9168
Gregory Boehm, *President*
▲ **EMP:** 5
SQ FT: 3,000
SALES (est): 603K **Privately Held**
WEB: www.mudpuddlebooks.com
SIC: 2731 Books: publishing only

(G-10518)
MULITEX USA INC
215 W 40th St Fl 7 (10018-1575)
PHONE..................................212 398-0440
Harry Mohinani, *CEO*
Sivaprakasham Rajakkal, *President*
Vijay Mohinani, *Director*
▲ **EMP:** 6
SQ FT: 2,000
SALES: 7.1MM **Privately Held**
WEB: www.mulitex.com
SIC: 2321 2325 2331 Men's & boys' furnishings; men's & boys' trousers & slacks; women's & misses' blouses & shirts
PA: Mulitex (Exports) Limited
9/F Angel Twr
Lai Chi Kok KLN

(G-10519)
MULTI PACKAGING SOLUTIONS INC (DH)
885 3rd Ave Fl 28 (10022-4834)
P.O. Box 26127, Lansing MI (48909-6127)
PHONE..................................646 885-0005
Marc Shore, *CEO*
Kevin Kain, *President*
Dennis Kaltman, *President*
Betsy Meschke, *Business Mgr*
Rick Smith, *Exec VP*
◆ **EMP:** 20
SALES: 964.9MM
SALES (corp-wide): 16.2B **Publicly Held**
WEB: www.ivyhill-wms.com
SIC: 2731 2761 3089 5092 Books: publishing & printing; continuous forms, office & business; identification cards, plastic; arts & crafts equipment & supplies; packaging paper & plastics film, coated & laminated; screen printing

HQ: Multi Packaging Solutions International Limited
885 3rd Ave Fl 28
New York NY 10022
646 885-0005

(G-10520)
MULTI PACKG SOLUTIONS INTL LTD (DH)
885 3rd Ave Fl 28 (10022-4834)
PHONE..................................646 885-0005
Marc Shore, *President*
Dennis Kaltman, *Exec VP*
Rick Smith, *Exec VP*
Mark Wenham, *Exec VP*
Tim Whitfield, *Exec VP*
EMP: 31 **EST:** 2005
SQ FT: 9,772
SALES: 1.6B
SALES (corp-wide): 16.2B **Publicly Held**
SIC: 2657 Folding paperboard boxes
HQ: Wrkco Inc.
1000 Abernathy Rd
Atlanta GA 30328
770 448-2193

(G-10521)
MUSIC SALES CORPORATION (PA)
Also Called: Acorn
180 Madison Ave Ste 2400 (10016-5241)
PHONE..................................212 254-2100
Barrie Edwards, *President*
Susan Feder, *Vice Pres*
Robert Wise, *Vice Pres*
John Castaldo, *Controller*
Rene Flores, *Sales Mgr*
▲ **EMP:** 6
SQ FT: 6,800
SALES (est): 13.9MM **Privately Held**
WEB: www.msc-catalog.com
SIC: 2741 Music books: publishing only, not printed on site; music, sheet: publishing only, not printed on site

(G-10522)
MUSTANG BIO INC
2 Gansevoort St Fl 9 (10014-1667)
PHONE..................................781 652-4500
Michael S Weiss, *Ch of Bd*
Manuel Litchman, *President*
Brian Achenbach, *Senior VP*
Neil Herskowitz, *Bd of Directors*
EMP: 38
SALES (est): 292.8K **Publicly Held**
SIC: 2834 Pharmaceutical preparations
PA: Fortress Biotech, Inc.
2 Gansevoort St Fl 9
New York NY 10014

(G-10523)
MX SOLAR USA LLC
100 Wall St Ste 1000 (10005-3727)
PHONE..................................732 356-7300
◆ **EMP:** 150
SALES (est): 10.1MM **Privately Held**
SIC: 3433 Mfg Heating Equipment-Non-electric

(G-10524)
MY MOST FAVORITE FOOD
247 W 72nd St Frnt 1 (10023-2723)
PHONE..................................212 580-5130
Scott A Magram, *Principal*
EMP: 5
SALES (est): 271.8K **Privately Held**
SIC: 2052 2024 Bakery products, dry; ices, flavored (frozen dessert)

(G-10525)
MYERS GROUP LLC (PA)
Also Called: Sogimex
257 W 38th St (10018-4457)
PHONE..................................973 761-6414
Jay Myers,
◆ **EMP:** 9
SQ FT: 3,200
SALES (est): 87MM **Privately Held**
SIC: 3111 Tanneries, leather

(G-10526)
MYLAN HEALTH MANAGEMENT LLC
405 Lexington Ave (10174-0002)
PHONE..................................917 262-2950

Adele Gulfo, *Principal*
EMP: 9 **EST:** 2016
SALES (est): 1MM **Privately Held**
SIC: 2834 Pharmaceutical preparations

(G-10527)
MYMEE INC
101 Avenue Of Flr 3 (10013)
PHONE..................................917 476-4122
Mette Dyhrberg, *President*
Daniel Rothman, *COO*
EMP: 10
SALES (est): 372.3K **Privately Held**
SIC: 7372 Prepackaged software

(G-10528)
MYSTIC INC (PA)
Also Called: Herman Kay
463 7th Ave Fl 12 (10018-7499)
PHONE..................................212 239-2025
Richard Kringstein, *President*
Barry Kringstein, *Vice Pres*
Kim Reid, *VP Sales*
▲ **EMP:** 108
SQ FT: 35,000
SALES: 183.5MM **Privately Held**
WEB: www.mystic.com
SIC: 2339 Women's & misses' outerwear

(G-10529)
N Y WINSTONS INC
Also Called: Eko-Blu
5 W 86th St Apt 9e (10024-3664)
PHONE..................................212 665-3166
Lauren Swoszowski, *CEO*
EMP: 5
SALES (est): 212.9K **Privately Held**
SIC: 2086 Bottled & canned soft drinks

(G-10530)
NAGLE FUEL CORPORATION
Also Called: BP
265 Nagle Ave (10034-3573)
PHONE..................................212 304-4618
Johnny Arais, *Manager*
EMP: 6
SALES (est): 344.1K **Privately Held**
SIC: 2869 Fuels

(G-10531)
NAKED BRAND GROUP INC
225 5th Ave Apt 2d (10010-1133)
PHONE..................................212 851-8050
Carole Hochman, *CEO*
EMP: 6
SALES: 2.8MM **Publicly Held**
SIC: 2342 5137 Bras, girdles & allied garments; lingerie
PA: Naked Brand Group Limited
Alexandria Creative Park Building 7b 2
Huntley St
Alexandria NSW 2015

(G-10532)
NANZ CUSTOM HARDWARE INC (PA)
Also Called: Nanz Company, The
20 Vandam St Fl 5l (10013-1277)
PHONE..................................212 367-7000
Carl Sorenson, *CEO*
Samual Michaelson, *COO*
Steve Nanz, *COO*
Itzhak Bishburg, *Project Mgr*
Gregory Morales, *Prdtn Mgr*
◆ **EMP:** 35
SQ FT: 7,500
SALES (est): 24.1MM **Privately Held**
WEB: www.nanz.com
SIC: 3429 5031 Door opening & closing devices, except electrical; building materials, interior

(G-10533)
NAPEAN LLC
Also Called: Luxury Daily
401 Broadway Ste 1408 (10013-3022)
PHONE..................................917 968-6757
Sophie Doran, *Chief*
Mir Maqbool Alam Khan,
EMP: 8
SALES (est): 850K **Privately Held**
SIC: 2741

(G-10534)
NASCO PRINTING CORPORATION
121 Varick St Rm 201 (10013-1408)
PHONE..............................212 229-2462
Reid Goldman, *President*
EMP: 5
SQ FT: 1,500
SALES (est): 449.6K **Privately Held**
WEB: www.nascoprint.com
SIC: 2752 Commercial printing, lithographic

(G-10535)
NASSERATI INC
Also Called: Lotus Thread
225 W 39th St Fl 6 (10018-3103)
PHONE..............................212 947-8100
Nasser Mokhtarzadeh, *CEO*
Maribel Diaz, *President*
▲ EMP: 7 EST: 2011
SQ FT: 5,000
SALES: 1.8MM **Privately Held**
SIC: 2335 Bridal & formal gowns

(G-10536)
NAT NAST COMPANY INC (PA)
1370 Broadway Rm 900 (10018-7309)
PHONE..............................212 575-1186
Sonny Haddad, *President*
Lawrence Deparis, *President*
▲ EMP: 22
SALES (est): 1.5MM **Privately Held**
WEB: www.natnast.com
SIC: 2321 Blouses, boys': made from purchased materials

(G-10537)
NATHAN LOVE LLC
407 Broome St Rm 6r (10013-3213)
PHONE..............................212 925-7111
Joe Burrascano,
EMP: 10
SALES: 1.6MM **Privately Held**
SIC: 3931 Musical instruments

(G-10538)
NATION COMPANY LLC
Also Called: Nation, The
520 8th Ave Rm 2100 (10018-4164)
PHONE..............................212 209-5400
Scott Klein, *President*
Ricky D'Ambrose, *Editor*
Sky Barsch, *Adv Dir*
Teresa Stack, *Mng Member*
Debra Eliezer, *Program Mgr*
EMP: 30 EST: 1865
SQ FT: 11,000
SALES (est): 5.6MM **Privately Held**
SIC: 2721 Magazines: publishing only, not printed on site

(G-10539)
NATION MAGAZINE
33 Irving Pl Fl 8 (10003-2307)
PHONE..............................212 209-5400
Victor Navasky, *Publisher*
EMP: 40 EST: 2008
SALES (est): 572.3K **Privately Held**
SIC: 2721 Magazines: publishing only, not printed on site

(G-10540)
NATIONAL ADVERTISING & PRTG
231 W 29th St Rm 1408 (10001-5589)
P.O. Box 1775 (10001)
PHONE..............................212 629-7650
Scott Damashek, *President*
Tiffany Moy, *Partner*
EMP: 5
SALES (est): 701.7K **Privately Held**
SIC: 3993 2679 Advertising novelties; novelties, paper: made from purchased material

(G-10541)
NATIONAL CONTRACT INDUSTRIES
Also Called: Nci
510 E 86th St Apt 16b (10028-7508)
P.O. Box 671 (10028-0044)
PHONE..............................212 249-0045
Maxwell J Moss, *President*
EMP: 5

SQ FT: 1,000
SALES (est): 1.5MM **Privately Held**
WEB: www.ncionline.com
SIC: 2221 Wall covering fabrics, manmade fiber & silk

(G-10542)
NATIONAL FLAG & DISPLAY CO INC (PA)
30 E 21st St Apt 2b (10010-7217)
PHONE..............................212 228-6600
Howard J Siegel, *President*
Alan R Siegel, *Vice Pres*
Alan Siegel, *Vice Pres*
▲ EMP: 20
SQ FT: 8,500
SALES (est): 7.4MM **Privately Held**
WEB: www.nationalflag.com
SIC: 2399 Flags, fabric

(G-10543)
NATIONAL GGRAPHIC PARTNERS LLC
485 Lexington Ave Fl 3 (10017-2651)
PHONE..............................212 656-0726
Amori Langstaff, *Director*
EMP: 5
SALES (est): 324.4K **Privately Held**
SIC: 2721 Magazines: publishing & printing

(G-10544)
NATIONAL REPRODUCTIONS INC
229 W 28th St Fl 9 (10001-5915)
PHONE..............................212 619-3800
George Pavoides, *CEO*
John K Fitch III, *President*
EMP: 30 EST: 1946
SQ FT: 5,000
SALES (est): 2.6MM
SALES (corp-wide): 2.8MM **Privately Held**
WEB: www.fitchgroup.com
SIC: 2752 7334 Photo-offset printing; photocopying & duplicating services
HQ: Francis Emory Fitch Inc
229 W 28th St
New York NY 10001
212 619-3800

(G-10545)
NATIONAL REVIEW INC (PA)
Also Called: NATIONAL REVIEW ONLINE
19 W 44th St Ste 1701 (10036-6101)
PHONE..............................212 679-7330
Thomas L Rhodes, *President*
Molly Powell, *Editor*
James Kilbridge, *CFO*
Rose Demaio, *Treasurer*
Lynn Gibson, *Manager*
EMP: 30 EST: 1955
SQ FT: 17,000
SALES: 5.6MM **Privately Held**
WEB: www.nationalreview.com
SIC: 2721 Magazines: publishing only, not printed on site; periodicals: publishing only

(G-10546)
NATIONAL SPINNING CO INC
Also Called: Caron Distribution Center
1212 Ave Of The Americ St (10036-1602)
PHONE..............................212 382-6400
Todd Browder, *Principal*
Sherri Thomas, *Credit Staff*
EMP: 25
SALES (corp-wide): 198.2MM **Privately Held**
WEB: www.natspin.com
SIC: 2281 2269 5199 Yarn spinning mills; finishing plants; yarns
PA: National Spinning Co., Inc.
1481 W 2nd St Ste 103
Washington NC 27889
252 975-7111

(G-10547)
NATIONAL TIME RECORDING EQP CO
64 Reade St Fl 2 (10007-1870)
PHONE..............................212 227-3310
Stanley A Akivis, *President*
Richard Akivis, *Vice Pres*
Ethel Akivis, *Treasurer*
EMP: 10 EST: 1932

SQ FT: 10,000
SALES: 1,000K **Privately Held**
WEB: www.national-pinkpages.com
SIC: 3579 7629 3873 3625 Dating & numbering devices; business machine repair, electric; watches, clocks, watch-cases & parts; relays & industrial controls

(G-10548)
NATIONAL TOBACCO COMPANY LP
Also Called: North Atlantic Trading Co
257 Park Ave S Fl 7 (10010-7304)
PHONE..............................212 253-8185
Thomas Holmes, *Chairman*
EMP: 10
SALES (corp-wide): 365.7MM **Publicly Held**
SIC: 2131 Chewing tobacco
HQ: National Tobacco Company, L.P.
5201 Interchange Way
Louisville KY 40229
800 579-0975

(G-10549)
NATIVE TEXTILES INC (PA)
411 5th Ave Rm 901 (10016-2260)
PHONE..............................212 951-5100
John Gunyan, *President*
Carl Andersen, *Vice Pres*
EMP: 6
SQ FT: 7,000
SALES (est): 12.1MM **Privately Held**
SIC: 2253 2254 Knit outerwear mills; knit underwear mills

(G-10550)
NATORI COMPANY INCORPORATED (PA)
180 Madison Ave Fl 18 (10016-5267)
PHONE..............................212 532-7796
Josie Natori, *Ch of Bd*
Pamela Stengel, *Opers Staff*
Shilvy Yee, *Buyer*
Judith O'Donnell, *Engineer*
Eileen Montellese, *CFO*
▲ EMP: 60
SQ FT: 10,500
SALES (est): 38.5MM **Privately Held**
SIC: 2384 2341 Bathrobes, men's & women's: made from purchased materials; women's & children's nightwear

(G-10551)
NATORI COMPANY INCORPORATED
Also Called: Natori Company, The
180 Madison Ave Fl 19 (10016-5267)
PHONE..............................212 532-7796
Efren Lota, *Manager*
EMP: 40
SALES (corp-wide): 38.5MM **Privately Held**
SIC: 2341 Women's & children's underwear
PA: The Natori Company Incorporated
180 Madison Ave Fl 18
New York NY 10016
212 532-7796

(G-10552)
NATURAL MATTERS INC
300 W 12th St (10014-1939)
PHONE..............................212 337-3077
John J Castro, *Ch of Bd*
EMP: 6
SALES (est): 370.4K **Privately Held**
SIC: 2099 Food preparations

(G-10553)
NATURE PUBLISHING CO
345 Park Ave S (10010-1707)
PHONE..............................212 726-9200
Heather Dunphy, *Marketing Mgr*
David Bagshaw, *Manager*
Wanda Puo, *Manager*
John Vallecillo, *Manager*
Michael Francisco, *Assoc Editor*
EMP: 5
SALES (est): 136.5K **Privately Held**
SIC: 2741 Miscellaneous publishing

(G-10554)
NAUTILUS CONTROLS CORP
99 Madison Ave Fl 5 (10016-7419)
PHONE..............................917 676-7005
EMP: 6
SALES (est): 586.9K **Privately Held**
SIC: 3823 Industrial instrmnts msrmnt display/control process variable

(G-10555)
NAUTILUSTHINK INC
360 W 36th St Apt 7s (10018-6496)
PHONE..............................646 239-6858
John Steele, *President*
Liz Peterson, *Manager*
EMP: 7 EST: 2014
SALES: 1.3MM **Privately Held**
SIC: 2721 Magazines: publishing & printing

(G-10556)
NAVAS DESIGNS INC
200 E 58th St Apt 17b (10022-2035)
PHONE..............................818 988-9050
EMP: 25
SQ FT: 4,000
SALES: 1.7MM **Privately Held**
SIC: 2211 Cotton Broadwoven Fabric Mill

(G-10557)
NAVATAR GROUP INC (HQ)
90 Broad St Ste 1703 (10004-2373)
PHONE..............................212 863-9655
Alok Misra, *President*
Ketan Khandkar, *Vice Pres*
Allan Siegert, *VP Sales*
Laura Llano, *Accounts Mgr*
Christopher Joyce, *Accounts Exec*
EMP: 40
SALES (est): 12.7MM **Privately Held**
WEB: www.navatargroup.com
SIC: 7372 Business oriented computer software

(G-10558)
NBM PUBLISHING INC
Also Called: Nantier Ball Minoustchine Pubg
160 Brdway Ste 700 E Wing (10038)
PHONE..............................646 559-4681
Terry Nantier, *President*
Mart Minoustchine, *Vice Pres*
Chris Beall, *Admin Sec*
▲ EMP: 5
SQ FT: 1,200
SALES: 600K **Privately Held**
WEB: www.nbmpub.com
SIC: 2731 Books: publishing only

(G-10559)
NC AUDIENCE EXCHANGE LLC
1211 Ave Of The Americas (10036-8701)
PHONE..............................212 416-3400
EMP: 15
SALES (est): 301K
SALES (corp-wide): 10B **Publicly Held**
SIC: 2731 2711 Book publishing; newspapers, publishing & printing
PA: News Corporation
1211 Avenue Of The Americ
New York NY 10036
212 416-3400

(G-10560)
NCM PUBLISHERS INC
200 Varick St Rm 608 (10014-7486)
PHONE..............................212 691-9100
Michael Zerneck, *President*
EMP: 8
SQ FT: 10,000
SALES: 1MM **Privately Held**
SIC: 2721 7812 Trade journals: publishing only, not printed on site; video tape production

(G-10561)
NEIL SAVALIA INC
15 W 47th St Ste 903 (10036-5715)
PHONE..............................212 869-0123
Neil Savalia, *President*
EMP: 10
SQ FT: 1,000
SALES: 2MM **Privately Held**
SIC: 3911 5944 5094 Jewelry, precious metal; jewelry stores; jewelry & precious stones

▲ = Import ▼=Export
◆ =Import/Export

(G-10562)
NEMARIS INC
475 Park Ave S Fl 11 (10016-6901)
PHONE....................................646 794-8648
Frank Schwab, *CEO*
Stephen Schwab, *COO*
Virginie Lafage, *Info Tech Mgr*
EMP: 20
SALES (est): 1.3MM Privately Held
SIC: 7372 Educational computer software

(G-10563)
NEON
1400 Broadway Rm 300 (10018-1078)
PHONE....................................212 727-5628
Roni Grill, *Vice Pres*
Sabrina Prince, *Vice Pres*
Julie Tripi, *Vice Pres*
Sherman Yee, *Vice Pres*
Carl Weber, *Prdtn Mgr*
EMP: 11 EST: 2010
SALES (est): 2MM Privately Held
SIC: 2813 Neon

(G-10564)
NERVVE TECHNOLOGIES INC (PA)
450 Park Ave Fl 30 (10022-2637)
PHONE....................................716 800-2250
Thomas Slowe, *CEO*
Jose Cecin, *COO*
Jacob Goellner, *CTO*
EMP: 22
SALES (est): 3.7MM Privately Held
SIC: 7372 8711 Application computer software; electrical or electronic engineering

(G-10565)
NES JEWELRY INC (PA)
Also Called: Nes Costume
10 W 33rd St Fl 9 (10001-3306)
PHONE....................................212 502-0025
Nemo Gindi, *President*
Jack Yedid, *Vice Pres*
Kenia Ceballos, *Prdtn Mgr*
Steve Gottlieb, *VP Sales*
Laurie Haines, *VP Sales*
▲ EMP: 70
SQ FT: 14,000
SALES (est): 31.1MM Privately Held
SIC: 3961 Costume jewelry

(G-10566)
NESHER PRINTING INC
30 E 33rd St Frnt A (10016-5337)
PHONE....................................212 760-2521
Sheldon Wrotslavsky, *President*
EMP: 6 EST: 1971
SQ FT: 3,500
SALES: 1MM Privately Held
WEB: www.nesherprinting.com
SIC: 2752 Commercial printing, offset

(G-10567)
NESS LEGWEAR LLC
1407 Broadway Rm 2010 (10018-2718)
PHONE....................................212 335-0777
David Antebi, *Principal*
▲ EMP: 1
SQ FT: 600
SALES: 2.5MM Privately Held
SIC: 2252 Socks

(G-10568)
NESTLE USA INC
Also Called: Perugina Div
520 Madison Ave (10022-4213)
PHONE....................................212 688-2490
Rosa Dimaggio, *Manager*
EMP: 139
SALES (corp-wide): 92B Privately Held
WEB: www.nestleusa.com
SIC: 2023 Evaporated milk
HQ: Nestle Usa, Inc.
1812 N Moore St Ste 118
Rosslyn VA 22209
818 549-6000

(G-10569)
NETOLOGIC INC
Also Called: Investars
17 State St Fl 38 (10004-1537)
PHONE....................................212 269-3796
Kei Kianpoor, *CEO*
John Eagleton, *President*

Lars Heimsath, *Marketing Staff*
Anna Aunon, *Office Mgr*
William Eagleton,
EMP: 45
SQ FT: 1,900
SALES (est): 3.1MM Privately Held
WEB: www.aidworks.com
SIC: 7372 Prepackaged software

(G-10570)
NETSUITE INC
8 W 40th St Fl 8 # 8 (10018-2275)
PHONE....................................646 652-5700
Zachary Nelson, *CEO*
EMP: 9
SALES (corp-wide): 39.5B Publicly Held
SIC: 7372 Prepackaged software
HQ: Netsuite Inc.
2955 Campus Dr Ste 100
San Mateo CA 94403
650 627-1000

(G-10571)
NETWORK INFRSTRUCTURE TECH INC
Also Called: N I T
90 John St Fl 7 (10038-3202)
PHONE....................................212 404-7340
Lior Blik, *President*
Craig Calafiore, *Exec VP*
Garry Chocky, *Finance*
Sharon Schedra, *Human Res Dir*
Brian Crowley, *Manager*
EMP: 2
SQ FT: 3,900
SALES (est): 5.3MM
SALES (corp-wide): 9MM Privately Held
WEB: www.nitconnect.com
SIC: 7372 Business oriented computer software
PA: Exzac, Inc.
Harborside Financial Ctr
Jersey City NJ 07311
201 204-5300

(G-10572)
NEUMANN JUTTA NEW YORK INC
355 E 4th St (10009-8513)
PHONE....................................212 982-7048
Jutta Neumann, *President*
▲ EMP: 10
SQ FT: 750
SALES: 800K Privately Held
SIC: 3143 3144 3172 Sandals, men's; sandals, women's; personal leather goods

(G-10573)
NEUROSTEER INC
375 S End Ave Apt 26c (10280-1080)
PHONE....................................401 837-0351
Nathan Intrator, *CEO*
Paul Weinberg, *CFO*
Ariel Hazi, *Director*
EMP: 12
SALES (est): 482.9K Privately Held
SIC: 3845 Electromedical equipment

(G-10574)
NEUROTROPE INC
1185 Ave Of The Amrcas Fl (10036-2601)
PHONE....................................973 242-0005
Charles S Ryan, *CEO*
Joshua N Silverman, *Ch of Bd*
William S Singer, *Vice Ch Bd*
Daniel L Alkon, *President*
Robert Weinstein, *CFO*
EMP: 5 EST: 2011
SALES (est): 433.6K Privately Held
SIC: 2834 8731 Pharmaceutical preparations; biological research

(G-10575)
NEVERWARE INC (PA)
112 W 27th St Ste 201 (10001-6242)
PHONE....................................516 302-3223
Jonathan Hefter, *CEO*
Andrew Bauer, *COO*
Emily Esposito, *Accounts Mgr*
Ted Brandston, *Software Dev*
David Sayles, *Director*
EMP: 12 EST: 2011
SQ FT: 2,000

SALES (est): 2.9MM Privately Held
SIC: 7372 Business oriented computer software

(G-10576)
NEW AUDIO LLC
Also Called: Master & Dynamics
132 W 31st St Rm 701 (10001-3478)
PHONE....................................212 213-6060
Jonathan Levine, *CEO*
John Anderew, *Sales Staff*
Viggo Olsen, *Officer*
▲ EMP: 30
SQ FT: 10,000
SALES: 6MM Privately Held
SIC: 3651 Microphones

(G-10577)
NEW AVON LLC (HQ)
1 Liberty Plz Fl 25 (10006-1430)
PHONE....................................212 282-6000
Betty Palm, *President*
Anjana Srivastava, *President*
Steven Bosson, *Mng Member*
Ginny Edwars,
Helene F Rutledge,
EMP: 268
SQ FT: 100,000
SALES (est): 1.1B Privately Held
SIC: 2844 5122 5999 Cosmetic preparations; cosmetics; cosmetics

(G-10578)
NEW DEAL PRINTING CORP (PA)
Also Called: Altro Business Forms Div
420 E 55th St Apt Grdp (10022-5149)
PHONE....................................718 729-5800
David Ruzal, *President*
Doreen Beynders, *Corp Secy*
▲ EMP: 20
SALES (est): 9MM Privately Held
WEB: www.narcainus.com
SIC: 2759 Commercial printing

(G-10579)
NEW DIRECTIONS PUBLISHING
80 8th Ave Fl 19 (10011-7146)
PHONE....................................212 255-0230
Peggy Fox, *President*
Christopher Wait, *Editor*
Declan Spring, *Senior Editor*
EMP: 10 EST: 1936
SQ FT: 2,800
SALES (est): 1.2MM Privately Held
WEB: www.ndpublishing.com
SIC: 2731 Books: publishing only

(G-10580)
NEW ENERGY SYSTEMS GROUP
116 W 23rd St Fl 5 (10011-2599)
PHONE....................................917 573-0302
Weihe Yu, *Ch of Bd*
Jufeng Chen, *CFO*
EMP: 214
SALES (est): 10.4MM Privately Held
SIC: 3691 3433 Storage batteries; solar heaters & collectors; space heaters, except electric

(G-10581)
NEW ENGLAND ORTHOTIC & PROST
235 E 38th St (10016-2896)
PHONE....................................212 682-9313
Ryan Murphy, *Manager*
EMP: 5
SALES (corp-wide): 28.1MM Privately Held
WEB: www.neops.com
SIC: 3842 Limbs, artificial; prosthetic appliances
PA: New England Orthotic And Prosthetic Systems, Llc
16 Commercial St
Branford CT 06405
203 483-8488

(G-10582)
NEW GENERATION LIGHTING INC
144 Bowery Frnt 1 (10013-4288)
PHONE....................................212 966-0328
Tony Chu, *Manager*
EMP: 10

SALES (est): 880K Privately Held
WEB: www.newgenerationlighting.com
SIC: 3645 Residential lighting fixtures

(G-10583)
NEW GOLDSTAR 1 PRINTING CORP
63 Orchard St (10002-5414)
PHONE....................................212 343-3909
Xue Hua Xie, *President*
EMP: 8
SALES (est): 502.6K Privately Held
SIC: 2752 Commercial printing, lithographic

(G-10584)
NEW HAMPTON CREATIONS INC
237 W 35th St Ste 502 (10001-1905)
PHONE....................................212 244-7474
Victor Hoffman, *President*
David P Hoffman, *Corp Secy*
EMP: 5
SQ FT: 1,000
SALES (est): 522.3K Privately Held
WEB: www.nyshose.com
SIC: 2252 Socks

(G-10585)
NEW HOPE MEDIA LLC
Also Called: Additude Magazine
108 W 39th St Rm 805 (10018-8277)
PHONE....................................646 366-0830
Mark Gleason, *COO*
Susan Caughman,
EMP: 6
SALES (est): 630.3K Privately Held
SIC: 2721 Magazines: publishing & printing

(G-10586)
NEW MEDIA INVESTMENT GROUP INC (PA)
1345 Avenue Of The Americ (10105-0014)
PHONE....................................212 479-3160
Michael E Reed, *Ch of Bd*
EMP: 300
SALES: 1.5B Privately Held
SIC: 2711 7373 Newspapers, publishing & printing; systems integration services

(G-10587)
NEW MOUNTAIN CAPITAL LLC (PA)
787 7th Ave Fl 49 (10019-6018)
PHONE....................................212 720-0300
Steven B Klinsky, *CEO*
David Coquillette, *Managing Dir*
Sunil Mishra, *Managing Dir*
Thomas Morgan, *Managing Dir*
Andre Moura, *Managing Dir*
EMP: 98
SALES (est): 2B Privately Held
SIC: 2819 Industrial inorganic chemicals

(G-10588)
NEW PRESS
120 Wall St Fl 31 (10005-4007)
PHONE....................................212 629-8802
Ellen Adler, *Publisher*
Emily Albarillo, *Production*
Hasan Fogle, *Accounting Mgr*
Paris Williams, *Accounts Mgr*
Josh Itkin, *Sales Staff*
EMP: 20
SQ FT: 3,500
SALES: 5.1MM Privately Held
WEB: www.thenewpress.com
SIC: 2731 Book publishing

(G-10589)
NEW REPUBLIC
1 Union Sq W Fl 6 (10003-3303)
PHONE....................................212 989-8200
EMP: 5 EST: 2015
SALES (est): 371K Privately Held
SIC: 2711 Newspapers, publishing & printing

(G-10590)
NEW STYLE SIGNS LIMITED INC
171 Madison Ave Rm 204 (10016-5110)
PHONE....................................212 242-7848
Joseph Fleischer, *President*
Ilan Aboody, *Sales Staff*
Anna Vershinskaya, *Manager*
EMP: 10

SALES (est): 1.3MM **Privately Held**
SIC: 3993 Displays & cutouts, window & lobby; signs, not made in custom sign painting shops

(G-10591)
NEW TRIAD FOR COLLABORATIVE
205 W 86th St Apt 911 (10024-3344)
PHONE..................................212 873-9610
EMP: 24
SALES (est): 90.1K **Privately Held**
SIC: 7372 Prepackaged software

(G-10592)
NEW YORK ACCESSORY GROUP INC (PA)
411 5th Ave Fl 4 (10016-2272)
PHONE..................................212 532-7911
Isaac Shallom, *CEO*
Joseph Tawil, *President*
Leslie Shalom, *COO*
Bill Paganini, *CFO*
▲ EMP: 50
SALES (est): 10.7MM **Privately Held**
SIC: 2389 2339 Men's miscellaneous accessories; women's & misses' accessories

(G-10593)
NEW YORK CVL SRVC EMPLYS PBLSH
Also Called: Chief, The
277 Broadway Ste 1506 (10007-2008)
PHONE..................................212 962-2690
Edward Prial, *President*
EMP: 12
SALES (est): 828.7K **Privately Held**
SIC: 2711 Newspapers: publishing only, not printed on site

(G-10594)
NEW YORK DAILY NEWS
4 New York Plz Fl 6 (10004-2473)
PHONE..................................212 248-2100
Nikhil Rele, *Principal*
EMP: 5
SALES (est): 371.8K **Privately Held**
SIC: 2711 Newspapers, publishing & printing

(G-10595)
NEW YORK ELEGANCE ENTPS INC
385 5th Ave Rm 709 (10016-3344)
PHONE..................................212 685-3088
Wing CHI Chung, *President*
▲ EMP: 15
SQ FT: 2,000
SALES (est): 1.3MM **Privately Held**
SIC: 2342 Brassieres

(G-10596)
NEW YORK ENRGY SYNTHETICS INC
375 Park Ave Ste 2607 (10152-2600)
PHONE..................................212 634-4787
EMP: 6
SALES (est): 450K **Privately Held**
SIC: 3825 3229 Mfg Electrical Measuring Instruments Mfg Pressed/Blown Glass

(G-10597)
NEW YORK FINDINGS CORP
70 Bowery Unit 8 (10013-4607)
PHONE..................................212 925-5745
Cheryl Kerber, *President*
Mel Kerber, *Treasurer*
EMP: 15 EST: 1953
SQ FT: 3,000
SALES (est): 1.5MM **Privately Held**
WEB: www.newyorkfindings.com
SIC: 3915 5094 Jewelers' findings & materials; jewelers' findings

(G-10598)
NEW YORK FSHION WEEK GUIDE LLC
387 Park Ave S Fl 5 (10016-8810)
PHONE..................................646 757-9119
Lanzer Robinson,
EMP: 15
SALES (est): 453.4K **Privately Held**
SIC: 2721 Magazines: publishing & printing

(G-10599)
NEW YORK MEDIA LLC (PA)
75 Varick St Ste 1404 (10013-1917)
PHONE..................................212 508-0700
Michael Silberman, *General Mgr*
Tara Abell, *Editor*
Gillian Duffy, *Editor*
Steve Fishman, *Editor*
Kathleen Hou, *Editor*
EMP: 109
SQ FT: 73,000
SALES (est): 71.4MM **Privately Held**
SIC: 2721 Magazines: publishing only, not printed on site

(G-10600)
NEW YORK MOVES MAGAZINE LLC
393 Broadway Fl 2 (10013-3532)
P.O. Box 4097 (10163-4097)
PHONE..................................212 396-2394
Richard Ellison, *Chief*
Mamoonah Yaqub, *Mng Member*
EMP: 10
SALES (est): 59K **Privately Held**
SIC: 2721 Magazines: publishing only, not printed on site

(G-10601)
NEW YORK PRESS INC
72 Madison Ave Fl 11 (10016-8731)
PHONE..................................212 268-8600
Russ Smith, *President*
EMP: 50
SQ FT: 10,000
SALES (est): 3.8MM **Privately Held**
WEB: www.nypress.com
SIC: 2711 Newspapers, publishing & printing

(G-10602)
NEW YORK SPRING WATER INC
517 W 36th St (10018-1100)
PHONE..................................212 777-4649
Richard Zakka, *President*
▲ EMP: 28
SQ FT: 200,000
SALES (est): 37.5K **Privately Held**
SIC: 2086 Mineral water, carbonated: packaged in cans, bottles, etc.

(G-10603)
NEW YORK SWEATER COMPANY INC
141 W 36th St Rm 17 (10018-9489)
PHONE..................................845 629-9533
Leonard Keff, *President*
EMP: 30
SALES (est): 2.1MM **Privately Held**
SIC: 2253 Sweaters & sweater coats, knit

(G-10604)
NEW YORK TIMES COMPANY (PA)
620 8th Ave Bsmt 1 (10018-1604)
PHONE..................................212 556-1234
Arthur Sulzberger Jr, *Ch of Bd*
Mark Thompson, *President*
Sharon Pian Chan, *President*
Alida Becker, *Editor*
Susan Chira, *Editor*
EMP: 277
SQ FT: 828,000
SALES: 1.7B **Publicly Held**
WEB: www.nytco.com
SIC: 2711 4832 4833 7383 Newspapers, publishing & printing; radio broadcasting stations; television broadcasting stations; news feature syndicate; information retrieval services

(G-10605)
NEW YORK TIMES COMPANY
Also Called: Timesdigest
620 8th Ave Bsmt 1 (10018-1604)
PHONE..................................212 556-1200
Tom Brady, *Branch Mgr*
EMP: 7
SALES (corp-wide): 1.7B **Publicly Held**
SIC: 2741 Miscellaneous publishing
PA: The New York Times Company
620 8th Ave Bsmt 1
New York NY 10018
212 556-1234

(G-10606)
NEW YORK TIMES COMPANY
Also Called: Times Center, The
620 8th Ave Bsmt 1 (10018-1604)
PHONE..................................212 556-4300
Melanie Masserant, *Branch Mgr*
EMP: 12
SALES (corp-wide): 1.7B **Publicly Held**
SIC: 2711 Newspapers, publishing & printing
PA: The New York Times Company
620 8th Ave Bsmt 1
New York NY 10018
212 556-1234

(G-10607)
NEW YORK UNIVERSITY
Also Called: Washington Square News
7 E 12th St Ste 800 (10003-4475)
PHONE..................................212 998-4300
David Cosgrove, *General Mgr*
Jasmina Husovic, *Facilities Mgr*
Geetha Gopalan, *Research*
Avdar San, *Research*
Richard Rosner, *Med Doctor*
EMP: 25
SQ FT: 7,410
SALES (corp-wide): 8.5B **Privately Held**
WEB: www.nyu.edu
SIC: 2711 8221 Newspapers, publishing & printing; university
PA: New York University
70 Washington Sq S
New York NY 10012

(G-10608)
NEW YORK1 NEWS OPERATIONS
75 9th Ave Frnt 6 (10011-7033)
PHONE..................................212 379-3311
Steve Paulus, *CEO*
EMP: 12
SALES (est): 724.1K **Privately Held**
SIC: 2711 Newspapers, publishing & printing

(G-10609)
NEWBAY MEDIA LLC (HQ)
28 E 28th St Fl 12 (10016-7959)
PHONE..................................212 378-0400
Steve Palm, *CEO*
Seth Barton, *Editor*
Adam Goldstein, *Exec VP*
Carmel King, *Exec VP*
Paul Mastronardi, *CFO*
EMP: 75
SALES (est): 64.2MM
SALES (corp-wide): 158.8MM **Privately Held**
WEB: www.nbmedia.com
SIC: 2741 Miscellaneous publishing
PA: Future Plc
Quay House
Bath BA1 1
122 544-2244

(G-10610)
NEWPORT GRAPHICS INC
121 Varick St Rm 302 (10013-1408)
PHONE..................................212 924-2600
John Di Somma, *President*
Michael Paulmasano, *Vice Pres*
EMP: 30 EST: 1971
SQ FT: 10,000
SALES (est): 3MM **Privately Held**
WEB: www.newportgraphics.com
SIC: 2752 2789 Commercial printing, offset; bookbinding & related work

(G-10611)
NEWS COMMUNICATIONS INC (PA)
501 Madison Ave Fl 23 (10022-5608)
PHONE..................................212 689-2500
James A Finkelstein, *Ch of Bd*
Jerry A Finkelstein, *Ch of Bd*
E Paul Leishman, *CFO*
EMP: 11
SQ FT: 2,900
SALES (est): 8.9MM **Privately Held**
WEB: www.thehill.com
SIC: 2711 Newspapers: publishing only, not printed on site

(G-10612)
NEWS CORPORATION (PA)
1211 Avenue Of The Americ (10036-8705)
PHONE..................................212 416-3400
Robert J Thomson, *CEO*
K Rupert Murdoch, *Ch of Bd*
Lachlan K Murdoch, *Ch of Bd*
Maria Delgado, *Area Mgr*
Roseann Green, *Area Mgr*
EMP: 224
SALES: 10B **Publicly Held**
SIC: 2731 7375 2711 Book publishing; on-line data base information retrieval; newspapers, publishing & printing

(G-10613)
NEWS INDIA USA LLC
Also Called: News India Times
37 W 20th St Ste 1109 (10011-3749)
PHONE..................................212 675-7515
Shomik Chaudhuri, *Adv Dir*
Dr Sudhir Parikh,
EMP: 8
SALES (est): 600K **Privately Held**
SIC: 2711 Commercial printing & newspaper publishing combined

(G-10614)
NEWS INDIA USA INC
Also Called: News India Times
37 W 20th St Ste 1109 (10011-3749)
PHONE..................................212 675-7515
Veena Merchant, *President*
Prakash Parekh, *Mktg Dir*
Vikram Chatwal, *Director*
EMP: 15
SQ FT: 6,000
SALES (est): 720K **Privately Held**
SIC: 2711 2731 2791 Newspapers, publishing & printing; books: publishing & printing; typesetting

(G-10615)
NEWS/SPRTS MICROWAVE RENTL INC
Also Called: NSM Surveillance
415 Madison Ave Fl 11 (10017-7930)
PHONE..................................619 670-0572
Andrew R Berdy, *President*
Carlos Arnero, *COO*
EMP: 35
SQ FT: 10,000
SALES (est): 5MM **Privately Held**
WEB: www.nsmsurveillance.com
SIC: 3699 Security devices; security control equipment & systems
PA: Solutionpoint International, Inc.
415 Madison Ave Fl 11
New York NY 10017

(G-10616)
NEWSWEEK LLC
7 Hanover Sq Fl 5 (10004-2636)
PHONE..................................646 867-7100
Etienne Uzac, *President*
Nicholas Loffredo, *Editor*
EMP: 7 EST: 2013
SALES (est): 101.4K **Privately Held**
SIC: 2711 Newspapers, publishing & printing

(G-10617)
NEWSWEEK MEDIA GROUP INC (PA)
Also Called: International Business Times
7 Hanover Sq Fl 5 (10004-2636)
PHONE..................................646 867-7100
Etienne Uzac, *President*
Alan Press, *President*
Shaun Hekking, *Vice Pres*
Mitchell Caplan, *Chief Mktg Ofcr*
James Green, *Risk Mgmt Dir*
EMP: 60
SQ FT: 50,000
SALES (est): 30.9MM **Privately Held**
SIC: 2711 Newspapers, publishing & printing

(G-10618)
NEXT BIG SOUND INC
125 Park Ave Fl 19 (10017-8545)
PHONE..................................646 657-9837
Alex White, *CEO*
David Hoffman, *Founder*
Samir Rayani, *Founder*

Yu-Ting Lin, *VP Finance*
Jay Troop, *Analyst*
EMP: 6 **EST:** 2008
SALES (est) 1MM **Privately Held**
SIC: 3695 Magnetic & optical recording
media

(G-10619)
NEXT POTENTIAL LLC
Also Called: Nextpotential
278 E 10th St Apt 5b (10009-4868)
PHONE..................................401 742-5190
Jack Blanchette, *President*
John Blanchette, *Principal*
EMP: 6
SALES (est): 466.8K **Privately Held**
SIC: 2819 Catalysts, chemical

(G-10620)
NFE MANAGEMENT LLC
1345 Avenue Of The Americ (10105-4599)
PHONE..................................212 798-6100
Joseph Adams Jr, *President*
Demetrios Tserpelis, *Principal*
Kenneth Nicholson, *COO*
Cameron Macdougall, *Admin Sec*
Rosario Lualhati, *Administration*
EMP: 15
SQ FT: 2,038,200
SALES (est): 1MM **Privately Held**
SIC: 1321 Natural gas liquids

(G-10621)
**NICHE MEDIA HOLDINGS LLC
(HQ)**
Also Called: Greengale Publishing
257 Park Ave S Fl 5 (10010-7304)
PHONE..................................702 990-2500
Kim Armenta, *Publisher*
Lauren Epstein, *Editor*
Maria Blondeaux, *COO*
Jonathan Kushnir, *CFO*
Kenny Chen, *Manager*
EMP: 26
SALES (est): 27.9MM
SALES (corp-wide): 41MM **Privately
Held**
SIC: 2721 Magazines: publishing & printing
PA: Dickey Publishing, Inc.
3280 Peachtree Rd Ne S
Atlanta GA 30305
404 949-0700

(G-10622)
NICHOLAS KIRKWOOD LLC (PA)
598 Madison Ave (10022-1610)
PHONE..................................646 559-5239
Marell Battle, *Manager*
EMP: 11
SALES (est): 1.1MM **Privately Held**
SIC: 3144 3143 Women's footwear, ex-
cept athletic; men's footwear, except ath-
letic

(G-10623)
NICK LUGO INC
Also Called: La Voz Hispana
159 E 116th St Fl 2 (10029-1399)
PHONE..................................212 348-2100
Nick Lugo, *President*
EMP: 12
SALES (est): 483.7K **Privately Held**
SIC: 2711 Newspapers, publishing & print-
ing

(G-10624)
**NICKELODEON MAGAZINES INC
(HQ)**
1633 Broadway Fl 7 (10019-7637)
PHONE..................................212 541-1949
Herb Scannell, *President*
Jeff Dunn, *COO*
Dan Sullivan, *Senior VP*
Michele Opam, *Director*
EMP: 3
SALES (est): 4.2MM
SALES (corp-wide): 12.9B **Publicly Held**
SIC: 2721 Magazines: publishing only, not
printed on site
PA: Viacom Inc.
1515 Broadway
New York NY 10036
212 258-6000

(G-10625)
NICOLO RAINERI
Also Called: Nicolo Raineri Jeweler
82 Bowery (10013-4656)
PHONE..................................212 925-6128
Nicolo Raineri, *Owner*
▲ **EMP:** 6
SQ FT: 3,000
SALES (est): 623.4K **Privately Held**
WEB: www.rainerijewelers.com
SIC: 3911 5944 Jewelry, precious metal;
jewelry, precious stones & precious met-
als

(G-10626)
NIGHTINGALE FOOD ENTPS INC
2306 1st Ave (10035-4304)
PHONE..................................347 577-1630
Constantinos Kotjias, *Ch of Bd*
▼ **EMP:** 4
SALES: 1.5MM **Privately Held**
SIC: 2051 Bread, cake & related products

(G-10627)
NIKKEI AMERICA INC (HQ)
1325 Avenue Of The Americ (10019-6055)
PHONE..................................212 261-6200
Hisao Tonedachi, *President*
Hiro Aki Honda, *Exec VP*
Kiyoshi Noma, *Vice Pres*
Yihsuan Wu, *Asst Mgr*
EMP: 40
SQ FT: 33,000
SALES (est): 6.9MM **Privately Held**
WEB: www.nikkeius.com
SIC: 2711 Newspapers, publishing & print-
ing

(G-10628)
**NIKKEI AMERICA HOLDINGS
INC (HQ)**
1325 Ave Of The Usa (10019)
PHONE..................................212 261-6200
Kiyoshi Hasegawa, *President*
Fumiko Tanaka, *Vice Pres*
Nikkei Yamamoto, *Vice Pres*
EMP: 60
SQ FT: 33,000
SALES: 27MM **Privately Held**
WEB: www.nikkei.com
SIC: 2711 Newspapers, publishing & print-
ing

(G-10629)
NIMBLETV INC
450 Fashion Ave Fl 43 (10123-4399)
PHONE..................................646 502-7010
Anand Subramanian, *CEO*
Peter Von Schlossberg, *President*
Paul George, *CTO*
EMP: 12
SALES (est): 831.1K
SALES (corp-wide): 143.8MM **Publicly
Held**
SIC: 2741
PA: Synacor, Inc.
40 La Riviere Dr Ste 300
Buffalo NY 14202
716 853-1362

(G-10630)
NINE WEST HOLDINGS INC
1411 Broadway Fl 15 (10018-3471)
PHONE..................................212 391-5000
EMP: 6
SALES (corp-wide): 2.2B **Privately Held**
SIC: 2335 Retail Womens Apparel
HQ: Nine West Holdings, Inc.
180 Rittenhouse Cir
Bristol PA 18018
215 785-4000

(G-10631)
NINTH WAVE INC
115 Broadway Rm 1705 (10006-1615)
PHONE..................................212 401-6381
George Anderson, *CEO*
EMP: 25
SALES (est): 456.2K **Privately Held**
SIC: 7372 Business oriented computer
software

(G-10632)
NLR COUNTER TOPS LLC
902 E 92nd St (10128)
PHONE..................................347 295-0410
AVI Harel, *Mng Member*
EMP: 5
SALES (est): 467.8K **Privately Held**
SIC: 2541 5211 Counter & sink
tops; counter tops; countersinks

(G-10633)
NO LONGER EMPTY INC
122 W 27th St Fl 10 (10001-6227)
PHONE..................................202 413-4262
Ashley Browne, *Bookkeeper*
Carol Stakenas, *Exec Dir*
Naomi Ringskog, *Exec Dir*
EMP: 6 **EST:** 2012
SALES: 680.6K **Privately Held**
SIC: 3812 Aircraft/aerospace flight instru-
ments & guidance systems

(G-10634)
NOAH ENTERPRISES LTD (PA)
520 8th Ave Lbby 2 (10018-6590)
PHONE..................................212 736-2888
Sam Noah, *President*
▲ **EMP:** 20
SQ FT: 12,000
SALES (est): 1.3MM **Privately Held**
WEB: www.noahenterprises.com
SIC: 2339 5137 Sportswear, women's;
sportswear, women's & children's

(G-10635)
NOCHAIRS INC
325 W 38th St Rm 310 (10018-9664)
PHONE..................................917 748-8731
Anthony Lilore, *President*
Celeste Lilore, *Vice Pres*
EMP: 2
SQ FT: 1,100
SALES: 1MM **Privately Held**
SIC: 2211 2259 5199 Bags & bagging,
cotton; bags & bagging, knit; bags, textile

(G-10636)
NOETIC PARTNERS INC
445 Park Ave Frnt 1 (10022-8600)
PHONE..................................212 836-4351
Justin Magruder, *President*
EMP: 15
SQ FT: 300
SALES: 2.7MM **Privately Held**
SIC: 7372 5734 Business oriented com-
puter software; software, business & non-
game

(G-10637)
NOIR JEWELRY LLC
358 5th Ave Rm 501 (10001-2228)
PHONE..................................212 465-8500
Shaya Reiter, *CEO*
EMP: 6
SQ FT: 10,000
SALES (est): 522.2K
SALES (corp-wide): 7.8MM **Privately
Held**
SIC: 3961 Costume jewelry
PA: International Inspirations, Llc
358 5th Ave Rm 501
New York NY 10001
212 465-8500

(G-10638)
NOOK MEDIA LLC
122 5th Ave (10011-5605)
PHONE..................................212 633-3300
Michael P Huseby, *CEO*
EMP: 5
SALES (est): 290.1K
SALES (corp-wide): 3.5B **Privately Held**
SIC: 7372 Application computer software
HQ: Barnes & Noble, Inc.
122 5th Ave Fl 2
New York NY 10011
212 633-3300

(G-10639)
NORDIC PRESS INC
243 E 34th St (10016-4852)
PHONE..................................212 686-3356
Denis Mets, *President*
Siri Uriko, *Manager*
Anne Karu, *Administration*
EMP: 5

SALES (est): 210K **Privately Held**
WEB: www.metronome.com
SIC: 2711 Newspapers: publishing only,
not printed on site

(G-10640)
NORFALCO LLC
330 Madison Ave Fl 7 (10017-5040)
PHONE..................................416 775-1431
Paul Shaw, *President*
◆ **EMP:** 10
SALES (est): 119.8MM
SALES (corp-wide): 205.4B **Privately
Held**
SIC: 2819 Sulfuric acid, oleum
HQ: Glencore Ltd.
330 Madison Ave Ste 700
New York NY 10017
646 949-2500

(G-10641)
**NORTH AMERICAN GRAPHICS
INC**
150 Varick St Rm 303 (10013-1218)
PHONE..................................212 725-2200
Arthur Ascher, *President*
EMP: 10
SQ FT: 2,500
SALES (est): 1.2MM **Privately Held**
SIC: 2759 7336 Commercial printing;
graphic arts & related design

(G-10642)
NORTH AMERICAN MILLS INC
Also Called: Chams
1370 Broadway Rm 1101 (10018-7826)
PHONE..................................212 695-6146
▲ **EMP:** 15
SQ FT: 6,600
SALES (est): 1MM **Privately Held**
SIC: 2329 Mfg Men's/Boy's Clothing

(G-10643)
NORTH SIX INC
159 Bleecker St Frnt A (10012-1457)
PHONE..................................212 463-7227
Oliver Hicks, *President*
EMP: 12
SALES (est): 10.5MM **Privately Held**
SIC: 2759 7812 Commercial printing; mo-
tion picture & video production

(G-10644)
NORTHPOINT DIGITAL LLC
1540 Broadway Fl 41 (10036-4039)
PHONE..................................212 819-1700
Jeffrey Penner, *Partner*
Andree Engelhardt, *Business Mgr*
Edwin Pacheco, *Human Res Mgr*
Elizabeth Brackett, *Mktg Coord*
Arwin Holmes, *Sr Project Mgr*
EMP: 8 **EST:** 2015
SALES (est): 191.4K **Privately Held**
SIC: 3571 Computers, digital, analog or
hybrid

(G-10645)
**NORTHPOINT TRADING INC
(PA)**
347 5th Ave (10016-5010)
PHONE..................................212 481-8001
Abe Kassin, *President*
Isaac Kassin, *Vice Pres*
Jacob Kassin, *Regl Sales Mgr*
◆ **EMP:** 10
SQ FT: 4,000
SALES (est): 20.8MM **Privately Held**
SIC: 2273 2211 2392 6512 Carpets &
rugs; handkerchief fabrics, cotton; blan-
kets, comforters & beddings; shopping
center, property operation only

(G-10646)
NORTHWELL HEALTH INC
Also Called: Center For Comprehensive Care
30 7th Ave (10011-6629)
PHONE..................................646 665-6000
Joseph Nuccio, *Technical Staff*
Rebecca Mazurkiewicz, *Director*
Sherri Sandel, *Director*
Rob Nockowitz, *Surgery Dir*
EMP: 673 **Privately Held**
SIC: 3585 Refrigeration & heating equip-
ment

PA: Northwell Health, Inc.
2000 Marcus Ave
New Hyde Park NY 11042

(G-10647)
NORTONLIFELOCK INC
Also Called: Symantec
1 Penn Plz Ste 5420 (10119-5420)
PHONE..................646 487-6000
Ken Lowe, *Manager*
EMP: 65
SALES (corp-wide): 4.7B **Publicly Held**
WEB: www.symantec.com
SIC: 7372 Prepackaged software
PA: Nortonlifelock Inc.
60 E Rio Salado Pkwy # 1
Tempe AZ 85281
650 527-8000

(G-10648)
NOVA INC
362 5th Ave Ste 1001 (10001-2251)
PHONE..................212 967-1139
Vinod Jain, *CEO*
Berry Nooj, *President*
▲ **EMP:** 8
SQ FT: 1,300
SALES (est): 680.5K **Privately Held**
SIC: 2752 7389 Offset & photolithographic
printing; automobile recovery service

(G-10649)
NOVARTIS PHARMACEUTICALS CORP
230 Park Ave (10169-0005)
PHONE..................888 669-6682
Therese Johnsen, *Accounts Mgr*
Ruthel Watson, *Accounts Mgr*
Tina Sluga, *Marketing Staff*
Jaclyn Feeley, *Branch Mgr*
EMP: 5
SALES (corp-wide): 51.9B **Privately Held**
SIC: 2834 Pharmaceutical preparations
HQ: Novartis Pharmaceuticals Corporation
1 Health Plz
East Hanover NJ 07936
862 778-8300

(G-10650)
NOVEN PHARMACEUTICALS INC
350 5th Ave Ste 3700 (10118-3799)
PHONE..................212 682-4420
Jeffrey F Eisenberg, *CEO*
EMP: 32
SQ FT: 25,000 **Privately Held**
SIC: 2834 Pharmaceutical preparations
HQ: Noven Pharmaceuticals, Inc.
11960 Sw 144th St
Miami FL 33186
305 964-3393

(G-10651)
NR FRAGRANCES & COSMETICS INC
1220 Broadway Rm 700 (10001-4312)
PHONE..................212 686-4006
Khalid Raja, *President*
EMP: 2
SALES (est): 3.8MM **Privately Held**
SIC: 2844 Concentrates, perfume

(G-10652)
NSGV INC
Also Called: American Heritage Magazine
90 5th Ave (10011-7629)
PHONE..................212 367-3100
Malcolm S Forbes Jr, *Ch of Bd*
EMP: 50
SALES (corp-wide): 181.1MM **Privately Held**
WEB: www.forbes.com
SIC: 2721 Magazines: publishing only,
printed on site
HQ: Nsgv Inc.
499 Washington Blvd Fl 9
Jersey City NJ 07310
212 620-2200

(G-10653)
NUCARE PHARMACY INC
Also Called: Nucare Pharmacy & Surgical
1789 1st Ave (10128-6901)
PHONE..................212 426-9300
Harry Wivietsky, *President*

Russell Shvartsshteyn, *Vice Pres*
Kenny Wivietsky, *Manager*
EMP: 14
SQ FT: 2,100
SALES (est): 3MM **Privately Held**
WEB: www.mynucare.com
SIC: 3842 5912 Surgical appliances &
supplies; drug stores & proprietary stores

(G-10654)
NUCARE PHARMACY WEST LLC
Also Called: Nucare Pharmacy & Surgical
250 9th Ave (10001-6602)
PHONE..................212 462-2525
Robert Marchini, *Mng Member*
Rob Marchini, *Mng Member*
Russell Shavartsshtyn,
Harry Wivietsky,
EMP: 11
SALES (est): 1.5MM **Privately Held**
WEB: www.mynucare.com
SIC: 3842 5912 Surgical appliances &
supplies; drug stores & proprietary stores

(G-10655)
NUMERIX LLC (PA)
99 Park Ave Fl 5 (10016-1360)
PHONE..................212 302-2220
Steven R O'Hanlon, *CEO*
Gregory Whitten, *Chairman*
EMP: 90
SQ FT: 31,650
SALES: 67.3MM **Privately Held**
SIC: 7372 Business oriented computer
software

(G-10656)
NUTRACEUTICAL WELLNESS INC
Also Called: Nutrafol
136 Madison Ave Fl 10 (10016-6790)
PHONE..................888 454-3320
Giorgos Tsetis, *CEO*
Roland Peralta, *President*
EMP: 8
SQ FT: 1,000
SALES (est): 990K **Privately Held**
SIC: 2834 Vitamin preparations

(G-10657)
NUTRAQUEEN LLC
138 E 34th St Apt 2f (10016-4773)
PHONE..................347 368-6568
Silvia Demeter, *CEO*
EMP: 12
SALES (est): 909.2K **Privately Held**
WEB: www.nutraqueen.com
SIC: 2833 Vitamins, natural or synthetic:
bulk, uncompounded

(G-10658)
NUTRIFAST LLC
244 5th Ave Ste W249 (10001-7604)
PHONE..................347 671-3181
Andres Ballares,
EMP: 10 **EST:** 2013
SALES (est): 548.4K **Privately Held**
SIC: 2024 Ice cream & frozen desserts

(G-10659)
NY DENIM INC
1407 Broadway Rm 1021 (10018-3256)
PHONE..................212 764-6668
EMP: 10
SALES (est): 720K **Privately Held**
SIC: 2253 Knit Outerwear Mills

(G-10660)
NYC DISTRICT COUNCIL UBCJA
395 Hudson St Lbby 3 (10014-7450)
PHONE..................212 366-7500
Michael Forde, *Principal*
EMP: 2
SALES (est): 27.9MM **Privately Held**
SIC: 3423 Carpenters' hand tools, except
saws: levels, chisels, etc.

(G-10661)
NYC IDOL APPAREL INC
214 W 39th St Rm 807 (10018-4455)
PHONE..................212 997-9797
David Shaaya, *President*
▲ **EMP:** 4 **EST:** 2008
SQ FT: 700

SALES: 2MM **Privately Held**
SIC: 2329 2337 Down-filled clothing:
men's & boys'; skirts, separate: women's,
misses' & juniors'

(G-10662)
NYC KNITWEAR INC
525 Fashion Ave Rm 701 (10018-0473)
PHONE..................212 840-1313
Jian Guo, *Chairman*
▲ **EMP:** 22
SQ FT: 13,000
SALES (est): 2.4MM **Privately Held**
SIC: 2331 Women's & misses' blouses &
shirts

(G-10663)
NYLON LLC
Also Called: Nylon Magazine
110 Greene St Ste 607 (10012-3838)
PHONE..................212 226-6454
Dana Fields, *Exec VP*
Candice Adams, *CFO*
Stephanie Lopez, *Asst Controller*
Carolin Fernandez, *Accountant*
Nicole Degregoris, *Marketing Staff*
EMP: 20
SALES (est): 3.7MM **Privately Held**
WEB: www.nylonmag.com
SIC: 2721 Magazines: publishing only, not
printed on site

(G-10664)
NYLON MEDIA INC (PA)
Also Called: Nylonshop
110 Greene St Ste 607 (10012-3838)
PHONE..................212 226-6454
Paul Greenberg, *CEO*
Marc Luzzatto, *Ch of Bd*
Jamie Elden, *President*
Carrie S Reynolds, *President*
James Condon, *CFO*
EMP: 16
SALES (est): 5.8MM **Privately Held**
SIC: 2721 Magazines: publishing & printing

(G-10665)
NYMAN JEWELRY INC (PA)
66 W 9th St (10011-8972)
PHONE..................212 944-1976
Corc Aydin, *President*
EMP: 6
SQ FT: 2,000
SALES (est): 558.2K **Privately Held**
SIC: 3915 5944 Gems, real & imitation:
preparation for settings; jewelry stores

(G-10666)
NYP HOLDINGS INC (DH)
Also Called: New York Post
1211 Ave Of The Americas (10036-8790)
PHONE..................212 997-9272
K Rupert Murdoch, *President*
▲ **EMP:** 486
SALES (est): 153MM
SALES (corp-wide): 10B **Publicly Held**
WEB: www.nypost.com
SIC: 2711 Commercial printing & newspa-
per publishing combined
HQ: News Preferred Holdings Inc
20 Westport Rd
Wilton CT 06897
203 563-6483

(G-10667)
NYREV INC
Also Called: New York Review of Books
435 Hudson St Rm 300 (10014-3949)
P.O. Box 9310, Big Sandy TX (75755-
3316)
PHONE..................212 757-8070
Rae S Hederman, *Ch of Bd*
Nicholas During, *Manager*
Lucy McKeon, *Assoc Editor*
EMP: 35 **EST:** 1970
SQ FT: 12,000
SALES: 82.6K **Privately Held**
WEB: www.nybooks.com
SIC: 2721 Magazines: publishing only, not
printed on site

(G-10668)
NYS NYU-CNTR INTL COOPERATION
418 Lafayette St (10003-6947)
PHONE..................212 998-3680

Chris Jones, *Director*
Noah Gall, *Assistant*
EMP: 30
SALES (est): 1.6MM **Privately Held**
SIC: 2759 Publication printing

(G-10669)
NYT CAPITAL LLC (HQ)
620 8th Ave (10018-1618)
PHONE..................212 556-1234
Dave Frank, *Vice Pres*
EMP: 18
SALES: 43.2K
SALES (corp-wide): 1.7B **Publicly Held**
SIC: 2711 5192 5963 7322 Newspapers,
publishing & printing; commercial printing
& newspaper publishing combined; newspapers; newspapers, home delivery, not
by printers or publishers; collection
agency, except real estate; credit reporting services
PA: The New York Times Company
620 8th Ave Bsmt 1
New York NY 10018
212 556-1234

(G-10670)
NYTIMES CORPORATE
620 8th Ave Fl 17 (10018-1618)
PHONE..................212 556-1234
Ben Schott, *Principal*
Marcus Payadue, *Editor*
Jane Perlez, *Editor*
Jennifer Steinhauer, *Chief*
Bruni Frank, *Producer*
EMP: 6 **EST:** 2009
SALES (est): 265.8K **Privately Held**
SIC: 2711 Newspapers, publishing & print-
ing

(G-10671)
O VAL NICK MUSIC CO INC
254 W 72nd St Apt 1a (10023-2851)
PHONE..................212 873-2179
Nicholas Ashford, *President*
EMP: 5
SALES (est): 231.8K **Privately Held**
SIC: 2741 Miscellaneous publishing

(G-10672)
OAKHURST PARTNERS LLC
Also Called: Amicale Cashmere
148 Madison Ave Fl 13 (10016-6772)
PHONE..................212 502-3220
Matthew Pfeufer, *CFO*
Kathy Surgenor, *VP Merchandise*
Boris Shlomm, *Mng Member*
Kami Kennedy, *Manager*
Abby Martinez, *Merchandising*
▲ **EMP:** 5
SQ FT: 5,000
SALES (est): 822.1K **Privately Held**
SIC: 2231 Apparel & outerwear broadwo-
ven fabrics

(G-10673)
OATLY INC
220 E 42nd St Rm 409a (10017-5833)
PHONE..................646 625-4633
Toni Petersson, *President*
Mike Messersmith, *General Mgr*
Andrew Blankemeyer, *Finance*
EMP: 25
SALES (est): 421K
SALES (corp-wide): 115.2MM **Privately Held**
SIC: 2026 Milk drinks, flavored
HQ: Oatly Ab
Stora Varvsgatan 6a
Malmo 211 1
418 475-500

(G-10674)
OBSERVER MEDIA LLC
1 Whitehall St Fl 7 (10004-2129)
PHONE..................212 755-2400
Reiss Robyn, *Publisher*
Joseph Meyer, *Principal*
Dan Entin, *Vice Pres*
Lauren Russell, *Marketing Mgr*
EMP: 22
SALES (est): 1.5MM **Privately Held**
SIC: 2711 Newspapers, publishing & print-
ing

▲ = Import ▼=Export
◆ =Import/Export

(G-10675)
OCCIDENTAL ENERGY MKTG INC
1230 Av Of The Amrcs 80 (10020-1513)
PHONE..................212 632-4950
Francis Sheridan, *Manager*
EMP: 5
SALES (corp-wide): 18.9B **Publicly Held**
SIC: 1382 Oil & gas exploration services
HQ: Occidental Energy Marketing, Inc.
 5 Greenway Plz Ste 110
 Houston TX 77046
 713 215-7000

(G-10676)
OCEAN WAVES SWIM LLC
19 W 34th St Fl 11 (10001-3075)
PHONE..................212 967-4481
Eli Seruya,
Lisa Bailey,
▲ EMP: 7
SQ FT: 1,600
SALES (est): 465.7K **Privately Held**
SIC: 2339 Bathing suits: women's, misses' & juniors'

(G-10677)
OCI USA INC (PA)
660 Madison Ave Fl 19 (10065-8415)
PHONE..................646 589-6180
Kevin Struve, *President*
▲ EMP: 8 EST: 2013
SALES (est): 2MM **Privately Held**
SIC: 2873 2861 Ammonium nitrate, ammonium sulfate; methanol, natural (wood alcohol)

(G-10678)
OCIP HOLDING LLC
660 Madison Ave Fl 19 (10065-8415)
PHONE..................646 589-6180
Kevin Struve, *Manager*
EMP: 4 EST: 2014
SALES (est): 343.3MM **Privately Held**
SIC: 2861 2873 Methanol, natural (wood alcohol); ammonium nitrate, ammonium sulfate

(G-10679)
OCTAVE MUSIC GROUP INC (DH)
850 3rd Ave Ste 15th (10022-6222)
PHONE..................212 991-6540
Ross Honey, *President*
EMP: 2
SALES (est): 65MM
SALES (corp-wide): 96.7MM **Privately Held**
SIC: 3651 Household audio & video equipment

(G-10680)
ODY ACCESSORIES INC
1239 Broadway (10001-4311)
PHONE..................212 239-0580
Michael Weiss, *President*
▲ EMP: 27
SQ FT: 12,000
SALES (est): 3.6MM **Privately Held**
SIC: 2339 Women's & misses' accessories

(G-10681)
ODYSSEY MAG PUBG GROUP INC
4 New York Plz (10004-2413)
PHONE..................212 545-4800
David J Pecker, *Principal*
EMP: 140
SALES (est): 2.5MM
SALES (corp-wide): 363MM **Privately Held**
SIC: 2721 Magazines: publishing & printing
PA: Worldwide Media Services Group Inc.
 1350 E Newprt Ctr Dr 20
 Deerfield Beach FL 33442
 561 989-1342

(G-10682)
OKEY ENTERPRISES INC
347 5th Ave Rm 1005 (10016-5033)
PHONE..................212 213-2640
Felek Ozdemir Sitkiye, *Principal*
EMP: 9
SALES (est): 967K **Privately Held**
SIC: 2759 Screen printing

(G-10683)
OKRA ENERGY LLC
99 Jane St Apt 5d (10014-7230)
PHONE..................206 495-7574
Louis Ravenet, *CEO*
Andrea Ravenet, *COO*
Donald Gongaware, *CTO*
EMP: 8
SALES (est): 1MM **Privately Held**
SIC: 1321 Natural gas liquids

(G-10684)
OLB GROUP INC
200 Park Ave Ste 1700 (10166-0005)
PHONE..................212 278-0900
Ronny Yakov, *President*
EMP: 1
SALES: 9MM **Privately Held**
SIC: 7372 Business oriented computer software

(G-10685)
OLDCASTLE BUILDING ENVELOPE
1350 Ave Of The Americas (10019-4702)
PHONE..................212 957-5400
Melissa Wood, *Assistant*
EMP: 12 EST: 2014
SALES (est): 4.7MM
SALES (corp-wide): 30.6B **Privately Held**
SIC: 3231 Products of purchased glass
PA: Crh Public Limited Company
 Stonemasons Way
 Dublin D16 K
 140 410-00

(G-10686)
OLYMPIC JEWELRY INC
62 W 47th St Ste 810 (10036-4179)
PHONE..................212 768-7004
Roberto Ganz, *President*
Mike Genuth, *Vice Pres*
EMP: 4
SALES (est): 1.2MM **Privately Held**
SIC: 3873 5094 Watches, clocks, watchcases & parts; clocks, watches & parts

(G-10687)
OMRIX BIOPHARMACEUTICALS INC
1 Rckfller Ctr Ste 2322 (10020)
PHONE..................908 218-0707
Robert Taub, *CEO*
Larry Ellberger, *Ch of Bd*
Nissim Mashiach, *President*
V Marc Droppert, *Exec VP*
Nanci Prado, *Vice Pres*
EMP: 212
SQ FT: 8,945
SALES (est): 13.7MM
SALES (corp-wide): 81.5B **Publicly Held**
WEB: www.omrix.com
SIC: 2836 Biological products, except diagnostic
HQ: Ethicon Inc.
 Us Route 22
 Somerville NJ 08876
 732 524-0400

(G-10688)
OMX (US) INC
Also Called: Nasdaq Omx
140 Broadway Fl 25 (10005-1142)
PHONE..................646 428-2800
Roland Tibell, *President*
David Hirschfeld, *Managing Dir*
Thomas Fay, *Vice Pres*
Andrew Lacatena, *Opers Staff*
Alden Frelinghuysen, *Sales Staff*
EMP: 1500
SQ FT: 50,000
SALES (est): 58.4MM **Privately Held**
SIC: 7372 Application computer software

(G-10689)
ON DEMAND BOOKS LLC
939 Lexington Ave (10065-5771)
PHONE..................212 966-2222
Dane Neller,
Herbert Krippner,
EMP: 5
SALES (est): 923.8K **Privately Held**
WEB: www.ondemandbooks.com
SIC: 7372 Publishers' computer software

(G-10690)
ONE JEANSWEAR GROUP LLC (DH)
Also Called: Jones Jeanswear Group
1441 Broadway Fl 11 (10018-1905)
PHONE..................212 575-2571
Jack N Gross, *CEO*
Stella Hagen, *Vice Pres*
Jennie Inge, *Human Res Mgr*
Janine Liss, *Department Mgr*
Patricia Logerfo, *Executive Asst*
▲ EMP: 300
SALES (est): 71.4MM
SALES (corp-wide): 1.7B **Privately Held**
WEB: www.jny.com
SIC: 2339 2325 Jeans: women's, misses' & juniors'; men's & boys' jeans & dungarees
HQ: Premier Brands Group Holdings Llc
 1441 Broadway
 New York NY 10018
 215 785-4000

(G-10691)
ONE STEP UP LTD (PA)
Also Called: Osu NJ Distribution
1412 Broadway Fl 3 (10018-3372)
PHONE..................212 398-1110
Harry Adjmi, *President*
Tom Wentley, *Vice Pres*
Sandy Gewercman, *CFO*
◆ EMP: 93
SALES (est): 30.9MM **Privately Held**
SIC: 2339 2329 Women's & misses' athletic clothing & sportswear; men's & boys' sportswear & athletic clothing

(G-10692)
ONE-BLUE LLC
1350 Broadway Rm 1406 (10018-0926)
PHONE..................212 223-4380
Roel Kramer, *CEO*
Dan Berman, *CFO*
Tom Chen, *CFO*
William Lenihan, *Director*
Jack Slobod, *General Counsel*
EMP: 7
SALES (est): 676.5K **Privately Held**
SIC: 7372 Application computer software

(G-10693)
ONIA LLC (PA)
Also Called: Onia Com
10 E 40th St Fl 37 (10016-0301)
PHONE..................646 701-0008
Theresa Falcone, *VP Finance*
Jake Post, *Sales Staff*
Yasmin Hekmat, *Pub Rel Dir*
Carl Cunow, *Mng Member*
Nathan Romano, *Mng Member*
◆ EMP: 20
SQ FT: 1,200
SALES (est): 2.9MM **Privately Held**
SIC: 2389 5136 5137 5139 Men's miscellaneous accessories; men's & boys' clothing; women's & children's clothing; shoes

(G-10694)
ONLY HEARTS LTD (PA)
134 W 37th St Fl 9 (10018-6946)
PHONE..................212 268-0886
Jonathan Stewart, *President*
Tina Vito, *Opers Staff*
Carol Ottavino, *Bookkeeper*
Helena Stuart, *VP Sales*
Lisa Freemont, *Manager*
EMP: 43
SQ FT: 4,000
SALES (est): 4.8MM **Privately Held**
SIC: 2341 5137 2339 Women's & children's underwear; women's & children's clothing; lingerie; women's & children's accessories; women's & misses' outerwear

(G-10695)
ONYX SOLAR GROUP LLC
79 Madison Ave Fl 8 (10016-7810)
PHONE..................917 951-9732
David Mann, *Principal*
Diego Cuevas, *Vice Pres*
▲ EMP: 9
SALES (est): 1MM **Privately Held**
SIC: 3674 Photovoltaic devices, solid state

(G-10696)
OOVA INC
152 W 57th St (10019-3386)
PHONE..................215 880-3125
Aparna Divaraniya, *CEO*
Jerome Scelza, *CTO*
EMP: 8
SALES (est): 442.7K **Privately Held**
SIC: 2834 7372 Medicines, capsuled or ampuled; application computer software

(G-10697)
OPENFIN INC
80 Broad St Fl 35 (10004-2216)
PHONE..................917 450-8822
Mazy Dar, *CEO*
Adam Toms, *CEO*
Fred Doerr, *President*
Omer Lifshitz, *Vice Pres*
Alexandra Boyle, *Sales Dir*
EMP: 9
SQ FT: 1,500
SALES (est): 1MM **Privately Held**
SIC: 7372 7371 Prepackaged software; custom computer programming services

(G-10698)
OPENROAD INTEGRATED MEDIA INC
180 Maiden Ln Ste 2803 (10038-4988)
PHONE..................212 691-0900
Paul Slavin, *CEO*
Jane Friedman, *Ch of Bd*
Sarah Mangiola, *Editor*
Laura Ferguson, *Senior VP*
Jennifer Jackson, *Vice Pres*
EMP: 23
SALES (est): 2.8MM **Privately Held**
SIC: 2741 Miscellaneous publishing

(G-10699)
OPERATIVE MEDIA INC (DH)
6 E 32nd St Fl 3 (10016-5415)
PHONE..................212 994-8930
Lorne Brown, *President*
Michael Leo, *Principal*
Ronnie Bell, *Vice Pres*
Alexa Cupo, *Opers Mgr*
Kristina Kiki Burton, *Opers Staff*
EMP: 79
SALES (est): 49.4MM **Privately Held**
WEB: www.operative.com
SIC: 7372 Business oriented computer software
HQ: Sintec Media Ltd
 21 Hefetzdi Nachum
 Jerusalem 95484
 265 151-22

(G-10700)
OPPOSUITS USA INC
228 E 45th St Rm 9e (10017-3337)
PHONE..................917 438-8878
Jelle Van Der Zwet, *President*
Manon Lisbet, *CFO*
EMP: 25
SALES: 6MM **Privately Held**
SIC: 2311 2337 Men's & boys' suits & coats; women's & misses' suits & skirts

(G-10701)
ORACLE CORPORATION
120 Park Ave Fl 26 (10017-5511)
PHONE..................212 508-7700
Lawrence Lavine, *Managing Dir*
Ben Marini, *Vice Pres*
Martin Zabielski, *Vice Pres*
Joe Laferlita, *Engineer*
Art Staple, *Accounts Exec*
EMP: 250
SALES (corp-wide): 39.5B **Publicly Held**
WEB: www.forcecapital.com
SIC: 7372 Business oriented computer software
PA: Oracle Corporation
 500 Oracle Pkwy
 Redwood City CA 94065
 650 506-7000

(G-10702)
ORANGENIUS INC
79 Madison Ave Fl 4 (10016-7805)
PHONE..................631 742-0648
Grace Cho, *CEO*
Kate Flanagan, *Opers Staff*
Robert Schlackman, *CTO*

EMP: 16 **EST:** 2015
SALES (est): 607.5K **Privately Held**
SIC: 7372 Business oriented computer software

(G-10703)
ORBIS BRYNMORE LITHOGRAPHICS
1735 2nd Ave Frnt 1 (10128-3516)
PHONE..................212 987-2100
Ceasar Romero, *President*
Anna Romero, *Admin Sec*
EMP: 8 **EST:** 1932
SALES (est): 1.1MM **Privately Held**
SIC: 2752 Commercial printing, offset

(G-10704)
ORCAM INC
16 Madison Sq W Fl 11 (10010-1629)
PHONE..................800 713-3741
Rhys Filmer, *President*
Rami Yehuda, *Vice Pres*
Eliav Rodman, *Marketing Staff*
Eytan Kiselstain, *Manager*
Chana Turner, *Software Engr*
EMP: 10
SALES (est): 685.5K **Privately Held**
SIC: 3842 Technical aids for the handicapped

(G-10705)
ORCHARD APP INC
101 5th Ave Fl 4 (10003-1008)
PHONE..................888 217-2718
Jonathan Kelfer, *CTO*
EMP: 26
SALES (corp-wide): 3.7MM **Privately Held**
SIC: 7372 Prepackaged software
PA: Orchard App, Inc.
53 W 21st St 2
New York NY
888 217-2718

(G-10706)
ORCHARD APPAREL GROUP LTD
212 W 35th St Fl 7 (10001-2508)
PHONE..................212 268-8701
Robert Fox, *President*
EMP: 5
SALES (est): 349.1K
SALES (corp-wide): 52.9MM **Privately Held**
WEB: www.robertfox.com
SIC: 2331 Blouses, women's & juniors': made from purchased material
PA: Robert Fox Inc.
79 Main St
Mineola NY 11501
516 294-2678

(G-10707)
ORCHARD PLATFORM ADVISORS LLC
55 W 21st St Fl 2 (10010-6813)
PHONE..................888 217-2718
Christine Ponder, *Opers Staff*
Bram Cohen, *Accountant*
Adam Rochkind, *Director*
Ethan Schwarzbach, *Director*
EMP: 26
SALES (est): 1.2MM **Privately Held**
SIC: 7372 Prepackaged software

(G-10708)
ORCHID MANUFACTURING CO INC
Also Called: Jessica Michelle
77 W 55th St Apt 4k (10019-4920)
PHONE..................212 840-5700
Michael Laufer, *Ch of Bd*
Michael H Laufer, *President*
Richard Weiss, *Controller*
EMP: 10 **EST:** 1983
SALES (est): 980K **Privately Held**
SIC: 2331 Women's & misses' blouses & shirts

(G-10709)
ORDERGROOVE INC
75 Broad St Fl 23 (10004-2487)
PHONE..................866 253-1261
Greg Alvo, *CEO*
Andrew Magne, *Partner*

Erin Rucker, *COO*
Dave Frechette, *Senior VP*
Stephanie Chan, *Vice Pres*
EMP: 28 **EST:** 2011
SALES (est): 3.5MM **Privately Held**
SIC: 7372 Business oriented computer software

(G-10710)
ORENS DAILY ROAST INC (PA)
12 E 46th St Fl 6 (10017-2418)
PHONE..................212 348-5400
Oren Bloostein, *President*
▲ **EMP:** 7
SQ FT: 400
SALES (est): 14.1MM **Privately Held**
SIC: 2095 5149 5499 Instant coffee; coffee, green or roasted; coffee

(G-10711)
ORPHEO USA CORP
353 Lexington Ave Lbby 1 (10016-0977)
PHONE..................212 464-8255
Alain Eisenstein, *CEO*
EMP: 5
SALES (est): 739.1K **Privately Held**
SIC: 3695 7371 Audio range tape, blank; computer software development & applications

(G-10712)
ORTHO MEDICAL PRODUCTS (PA)
315 E 83rd St (10028-4301)
P.O. Box 847617, Dallas TX (75284-7617)
PHONE..................212 879-3700
Jane Wilde, *President*
EMP: 22 **EST:** 1944
SQ FT: 7,500
SALES (est): 2.3MM **Privately Held**
SIC: 3841 3842 5999 Surgical & medical instruments; orthopedic appliances; orthopedic & prosthesis applications

(G-10713)
OS33 INC
16 W 22nd St Fl 6 (10010-5969)
PHONE..................708 336-3466
Jacob Kazakevich, *President*
Aron Derstine, *Vice Pres*
Gabor Kelemen, *Vice Pres*
Arthur Podgayetskiy, *Engineer*
Edwin Velasquez, *Info Tech Mgr*
EMP: 6
SALES (est): 3.9MM **Privately Held**
SIC: 7372 7371 Business oriented computer software; computer software development; computer software development & applications; computer software systems analysis & design, custom
PA: Os33 Services Corp.
120 Wood Ave S Ste 505
Iselin NJ 08830
866 796-0310

(G-10714)
OSCAR HEYMAN & BROS INC (PA)
501 Madison Ave Fl 15 (10022-5676)
PHONE..................212 593-0400
Marvin Heyman, *President*
Adam Heyman, *Vice Pres*
Thomas Heyman, *Treasurer*
Whitney Wenk, *Sales Staff*
Lewis Heyman, *Admin Sec*
EMP: 50 **EST:** 1912
SQ FT: 12,000
SALES (est): 7MM **Privately Held**
WEB: www.oscarheyman.com
SIC: 3911 Jewelry, precious metal

(G-10715)
OSPREY PUBLISHING INC
1385 Broadway Fl 5 (10018-6050)
PHONE..................212 419-5300
Rebecca Smart, *Principal*
▲ **EMP:** 9
SALES (est): 569.8K **Privately Held**
SIC: 2731 Book publishing

(G-10716)
OTHER PRESS LLC
267 5th Ave Fl 6 (10016-7508)
PHONE..................212 414-0054
Judith Gurewich, *CEO*
Bill Foo, *CFO*

Terrie A Akers, *Manager*
Yvonne Cardenas, *Manager*
Jessica Greer, *Director*
EMP: 8
SALES (est): 1.2MM **Privately Held**
WEB: www.otherpress.com
SIC: 2731 Books: publishing only

(G-10717)
OTIS ELEVATOR COMPANY
1 Penn Plz Frnt 6 (10119-0200)
PHONE..................917 339-9600
Jerry Ewell, *Branch Mgr*
Ben Petruzella, *Manager*
EMP: 33
SALES (corp-wide): 66.5B **Publicly Held**
SIC: 3534 1796 7699 Elevators & equipment; escalators, passenger & freight; walkways, moving; installing building equipment; elevator installation & conversion; miscellaneous building item repair services; elevators: inspection, service & repair
HQ: Otis Elevator Company
1 Carrier Pl
Farmington CT 06032
860 674-3000

(G-10718)
OUTDOOR SPORTSMAN GROUP
1040 6th Ave Rm 12 (10018-0933)
PHONE..................323 791-7190
Jody Howard, *Prdtn Mgr*
Jenny Kaeb, *Production*
Franca Manini, *Purchasing*
James McConville, *Sales Staff*
Brian Sullivan, *Marketing Staff*
EMP: 5
SALES (est): 324.8K **Privately Held**
SIC: 2721 Magazines: publishing only, not printed on site

(G-10719)
OVED MENS LLC
31 W 34th St Fl 4 (10001-3036)
PHONE..................212 563-4999
Isaac Oved, *Principal*
EMP: 20
SALES (est): 2MM **Privately Held**
SIC: 2321 Men's & boys' sports & polo shirts

(G-10720)
OVERTURE MEDIA INC
411 Lafayette St Ste 638 (10003-7032)
PHONE..................917 446-7455
Jared Weiss, *CEO*
EMP: 7 **EST:** 2014
SQ FT: 153
SALES (est): 345.4K **Privately Held**
SIC: 7372 Prepackaged software

(G-10721)
OVID THERAPEUTICS INC
1460 Broadway Fl 4 (10036-7328)
PHONE..................646 661-7661
Jeremy M Levin, *Ch of Bd*
Dirk Haasner, *Senior VP*
Thomas Perone, *Senior VP*
Michael Ciraolo, *Vice Pres*
Leslie Leahy, *Vice Pres*
EMP: 43
SALES (est): 8.6MM **Privately Held**
SIC: 2834 Pharmaceutical preparations

(G-10722)
OWENS TABLE MIXERS LLC
250 Mercer St Apt C616 (10012-6123)
PHONE..................650 303-7342
Tyler Holland, *CEO*
EMP: 5
SALES (est): 359.2K **Privately Held**
SIC: 2086 Bottled & canned soft drinks

(G-10723)
OXFORD BOOK COMPANY INC
9 Pine St (10005-4701)
PHONE..................212 227-2120
William Dinger, *President*
Paulina Baczewski, *Human Resources*
EMP: 150

SALES (est): 5.2MM
SALES (corp-wide): 58.3MM **Privately Held**
WEB: www.sadlier.com
SIC: 2731 Textbooks: publishing only, not printed on site
PA: William H. Sadlier, Inc.
9 Pine St
New York NY 10005
212 233-3646

(G-10724)
OXFORD CLEANERS
847 Lexington Ave Frnt (10065-6636)
PHONE..................212 734-0006
Joong Lee, *Owner*
EMP: 5
SALES (est): 280K **Privately Held**
SIC: 3589 7215 Commercial cleaning equipment; coin-operated laundries & cleaning

(G-10725)
OXFORD INDUSTRIES INC
Also Called: Lanier Clothes
600 5th Ave Fl 12 (10020-2325)
PHONE..................212 247-7712
Michael Parker, *Vice Pres*
Tracy Hunt, *Accounting Mgr*
Greg Love, *VP Sales*
Alan Rubin, *Branch Mgr*
Elissa Golub, *Admin Asst*
EMP: 25
SALES (corp-wide): 1.1B **Publicly Held**
SIC: 2329 Athletic (warmup, sweat & jogging) suits: men's & boys'
PA: Oxford Industries, Inc.
999 Peachtree St Ne # 688
Atlanta GA 30309
404 659-2424

(G-10726)
OXFORD INDUSTRIES INC
25 W 39th St (10018-3805)
PHONE..................212 840-2288
Fran Hicks, *Manager*
EMP: 14
SALES (corp-wide): 1.1B **Publicly Held**
WEB: www.oxm.com
SIC: 2321 Men's & boys' furnishings
PA: Oxford Industries, Inc.
999 Peachtree St Ne # 688
Atlanta GA 30309
404 659-2424

(G-10727)
OXFORD UNIVERSITY PRESS LLC (HQ)
Also Called: Oxford University Press USA
198 Madison Ave Fl 8 (10016-4308)
PHONE..................212 726-6000
Niko Pfund, *President*
Laura Pearson, *General Mgr*
Theo Calderara, *Editor*
Susan Ferber, *Editor*
Jeremy Lewis, *Editor*
◆ **EMP:** 265 **EST:** 1973
SQ FT: 145,000
SALES (est): 144.2MM
SALES (corp-wide): 1.5B **Privately Held**
SIC: 2731 5961 Books: publishing only; book & record clubs
PA: Oxford University
University Offices
Oxford OXON OX1 2
186 527-0000

(G-10728)
OXFORD UNIVERSITY PRESS LLC
Chancellor Masters & Scholrs
198 Madison Ave Fl 8 (10016-4308)
PHONE..................212 726-6000
Giles Kerr, *Finance*
EMP: 8
SALES (corp-wide): 1.5B **Privately Held**
SIC: 2731 5961 Book publishing; book & record clubs
HQ: Oxford University Press, Llc
198 Madison Ave Fl 8
New York NY 10016
212 726-6000

(G-10729)
OXO INTERNATIONAL INC
601 W 26th St Rm 950 (10001-1178)
PHONE..................212 242-3333
Alex Lee, *President*
Thomas Hanson, *Engineer*
Zachary Kowalski, *Engineer*
Tracy Cheuerman, *CFO*
Edward Ahn, *Accounting Mgr*
◆ EMP: 110
SALES (est): 15.4MM **Privately Held**
SIC: 3631 3469 5099 Household cooking equipment; household cooking & kitchen utensils, metal; baby carriages, strollers & related products
PA: Helen Of Troy Limited
C/O Conyers, Dill & Pearman
Hamilton HM 11

(G-10730)
OZMODYL LTD
Also Called: Soho and Tribeca Map
233 Broadway Rm 707 (10279-0705)
PHONE..................212 226-0622
EMP: 5
SALES (est): 550K **Privately Held**
SIC: 2731 Publish A Map And Guide Book Of The Soho And Tribeca Area

(G-10731)
P & I SPORTSWEAR INC
384 5th Ave (10018-8103)
PHONE..................718 934-4587
Ignacio Bursztyn, *President*
Flora Bursztyn, *Vice Pres*
EMP: 5
SALES: 1.2MM **Privately Held**
SIC: 2339 2329 Sportswear, women's; men's & boys' sportswear & athletic clothing

(G-10732)
P & W PRESS INC
20 W 22nd St Ste 710 (10010-5877)
PHONE..................646 486-3417
Philip Foxman, *President*
Keith Foxman, *Vice Pres*
EMP: 20
SQ FT: 3,000
SALES (est): 2.7MM **Privately Held**
WEB: www.pwpress.com
SIC: 2752 2759 Commercial printing, offset; letterpress printing

(G-10733)
P E GUERIN (PA)
23 Jane St (10014-1999)
PHONE..................212 243-5270
Andrew F Ward, *President*
Martin Grubman, *General Mgr*
Katie Sandy, *Creative Dir*
Terrell Elders, *Executive*
Ryan Ward, *Associate*
◆ EMP: 69 EST: 1857
SALES (est): 6.5MM **Privately Held**
WEB: www.peguerin.com
SIC: 3429 5072 3432 5074 Door locks, bolts & checks; builders' hardware; plumbing fixture fittings & trim; plumbing fittings & supplies; drapery hardware & blinds & shades; window covering parts & accessories

(G-10734)
P&C GROUP INC (PA)
Also Called: P & C Insurance Systems
111 Broadway Rm 1703 (10006-1914)
PHONE..................212 425-9200
Michael Loizou, *President*
Georgette Loizou, *Exec VP*
EMP: 15
SQ FT: 4,500
SALES: 3MM **Privately Held**
WEB: www.pandcis.com
SIC: 7372 Application computer software

(G-10735)
PACE EDITIONS INC (PA)
Also Called: Pace Prints
32 E 57th St Fl 3 (10022-8573)
PHONE..................212 421-3237
Richard H Solomon, *President*
Sylvie Harris, *Manager*
Donald Traver, *Director*
Alicia Scalera, *Advisor*
EMP: 21

SQ FT: 10,000
SALES (est): 2.3MM **Privately Held**
WEB: www.paceprints.com
SIC: 2741 7999 Art copy & poster publishing; art gallery, commercial

(G-10736)
PACE EDITIONS INC
44 W 18th St Fl 5 (10011-4644)
PHONE..................212 643-6353
Richard Soloman, *President*
EMP: 5
SALES (corp-wide): 2.3MM **Privately Held**
WEB: www.paceprints.com
SIC: 2752 2759 2741 Commercial printing, lithographic; commercial printing; miscellaneous publishing
PA: Pace Editions, Inc.
32 E 57th St Fl 3
New York NY 10022
212 421-3237

(G-10737)
PACHANGA INC
Also Called: Fika
824 10th Ave (10019-5040)
PHONE..................212 832-0022
Lars Akerlund, *Ch of Bd*
EMP: 13 EST: 2013
SALES (est): 2MM **Privately Held**
SIC: 2064 Candy & other confectionery products

(G-10738)
PACIFIC ALLIANCE USA INC
350 5th Ave Lbby 9 (10118-0109)
PHONE..................336 500-8184
Bruce P Rockowitz, *Branch Mgr*
EMP: 6 **Privately Held**
SIC: 2339 Women's & misses' outerwear
HQ: Pacific Alliance Usa, Inc.
1450 Broadway Fl 21
New York NY 10018

(G-10739)
PACIFIC ALLIANCE USA INC (DH)
1450 Broadway Fl 21 (10018-2221)
PHONE..................646 839-7000
Bruce Philip Rockowitz, *CEO*
Dow Famulak, *President*
Richard Darling, *Principal*
Ron Ventricelli, *COO*
▲ EMP: 66
SALES (est): 25.4MM **Privately Held**
SIC: 2339 Women's & misses' outerwear
HQ: Gbg Usa Inc.
350 5th Ave Lbby 11
New York NY 10118
646 839-7000

(G-10740)
PACK AMERICA CORP (HQ)
108 W 39th St Fl 16 (10018-8255)
PHONE..................212 508-6666
Hisao Ueda, *President*
Haruyuki Kochi, *Vice Pres*
Rory Dunwoody, *Sales Mgr*
▲ EMP: 4
SQ FT: 3,100
SALES (est): 6.5MM **Privately Held**
WEB: www.packdash.com
SIC: 2673 2679 Plastic bags: made from purchased materials; paper products, converted

(G-10741)
PALETOT LTD
Also Called: Patricia Underwood
499 Fashion Ave Rm 25s (10018-6847)
PHONE..................212 268-3774
Judy Hummel, *President*
Patricia Underwood, *Chairman*
EMP: 11
SQ FT: 1,500
SALES (est): 986.1K **Privately Held**
SIC: 2353 Hats & caps; millinery

(G-10742)
PALGRAVE MACMILLAN LTD
175 5th Ave Frnt 4 (10010-7728)
PHONE..................646 307-5028
Michelle Chen, *Editor*
Andy Williams, *Opers Dir*
Marit Vagstad, *Director*

▲ EMP: 9
SALES (est): 929.4K **Privately Held**
WEB: www.palgrave-usa.com
SIC: 2731 Books: publishing only
HQ: Springer Nature Limited
Cromwell Place
Basingstoke HANTS RG24
125 632-9242

(G-10743)
PALLADIA INC
105 W 17th St (10011-5432)
PHONE..................212 206-3669
Corinne Workman, *Manager*
EMP: 116
SALES (corp-wide): 36.6MM **Privately Held**
SIC: 3421 Table & food cutlery, including butchers'
PA: Palladia, Inc.
305 7th Ave Fl 10
New York NY 10001

(G-10744)
PAN AMERICAN LEATHERS INC (PA)
347 W 36th St Rm 1204 (10018-6480)
PHONE..................978 741-4150
Mark Mendal, *President*
▲ EMP: 3
SQ FT: 3,000
SALES (est): 1.4MM **Privately Held**
WEB: www.panamleathers.com
SIC: 3111 5199 Finishing of leather; leather goods, except footwear, gloves, luggage, belting

(G-10745)
PANDA PLATES INC (PA)
Also Called: Yumble Kids
1450 Broadway Fl 40 (10018-2240)
PHONE..................888 997-6623
Joanna Parker, *President*
EMP: 5
SALES (est): 1.7MM **Privately Held**
SIC: 2099 Ready-to-eat meals, salads & sandwiches

(G-10746)
PANGEA BRANDS LLC (PA)
6 W 20th St Fl 3 (10011-9270)
PHONE..................617 638-0001
Joshua Fink, *Mng Member*
Michael London,
Dan Miller,
▲ EMP: 6
SQ FT: 5,000
SALES (est): 1.7MM **Privately Held**
SIC: 2396 Apparel & other linings, except millinery

(G-10747)
PAPA BUBBLE
380 Broome St Frnt A (10013-3799)
PHONE..................212 966-2599
EMP: 7
SALES (est): 496.8K **Privately Held**
SIC: 2064 Mfg Candy/Confectionery

(G-10748)
PAPER BOX CORP
Also Called: Aaaaaa Creative Designs
1751 2nd Ave Apt 10a (10128-5377)
PHONE..................212 226-7490
Robert Fleisig, *President*
EMP: 70
SALES (est): 6.1MM **Privately Held**
SIC: 2631 2657 Folding boxboard; setup boxboard; folding paperboard boxes

(G-10749)
PAPER MAGIC GROUP INC
345 7th Ave Fl 6 (10001-5053)
PHONE..................631 521-3682
Nathan Caldwell, *Manager*
EMP: 450
SALES (corp-wide): 382.2MM **Publicly Held**
WEB: www.papermagic.com
SIC: 2771 2678 Greeting cards; stationery products
HQ: Paper Magic Group Inc.
54 Glenmra Ntl Blvd
Moosic PA 18507
570 961-3863

(G-10750)
PAPER PUBLISHING COMPANY INC
Also Called: Paper Magazine
15 E 32nd St (10016-5423)
PHONE..................212 226-4405
David Hershkovits, *President*
Kim Hastreiter, *Treasurer*
EMP: 27
SQ FT: 3,000
SALES (est): 3.5MM **Privately Held**
WEB: www.papermag.com
SIC: 2721 Magazines: publishing only, not printed on site

(G-10751)
PAPERCUTZ INC
Also Called: Paper Comics
160 Broadway Rm 700e (10038-4241)
PHONE..................646 559-4681
Terry Nantier, *President*
Jim Salicrup, *Vice Pres*
Jeffrey Whitman, *Production*
Sven Larsen, *VP Mktg*
◆ EMP: 5
SALES (est): 2MM **Privately Held**
SIC: 2731 Books: publishing only

(G-10752)
PARACE BIONICS LLC
100 Park Ave Rm 1600 (10017-5538)
PHONE..................877 727-2231
Vandette Carter, *Mng Member*
EMP: 5
SALES (est): 345.8K **Privately Held**
SIC: 3841 Surgical & medical instruments

(G-10753)
PARACHUTE PUBLISHING LLC
322 8th Ave Ste 702 (10001-6791)
PHONE..................212 337-6743
Joan Waricha,
Jane Stine,
▲ EMP: 30
SALES (est): 2.9MM **Privately Held**
WEB: www.parachuteproperties.com
SIC: 2731 Books: publishing only

(G-10754)
PARADE PUBLICATIONS INC (DH)
Also Called: Parade Magazine
711 3rd Ave (10017-4014)
PHONE..................212 450-7000
Carlo Vittorini, *CEO*
Susan Ollinick, *President*
Michelle LI, *Supervisor*
EMP: 37
SALES (est): 5.9MM
SALES (corp-wide): 5.5B **Privately Held**
SIC: 2721 Magazines: publishing only, not printed on site
HQ: The Herald Newspapers Company Inc
220 S Warren St
Syracuse NY 13202
315 470-0011

(G-10755)
PARADIGM SPINE LLC
505 Park Ave Fl 14 (10022-1106)
PHONE..................888 273-9897
Marc Viscigliosi, *CEO*
Gutmar Eisen, *President*
Gerry Marini, *President*
Steven Amelio, *CFO*
Hallett Mathews, *Chief Mktg Ofcr*
EMP: 23
SQ FT: 1,500
SALES (est): 8.4MM
SALES (corp-wide): 2.9MM **Privately Held**
SIC: 3842 Implants, surgical
PA: Rti Surgical Holdings, Inc.
520 Lake Cook Rd Ste 315
Deerfield IL 60015
386 418-8888

(G-10756)
PARAMOUNT TEXTILES INC
34 Walker St (10013-3514)
PHONE..................212 966-1040
Steven Katz, *CEO*
Estate J Katz, *President*
Ronald Katz, *Vice Pres*
Alan Katz, *Admin Sec*

EMP: 10 **EST:** 1940
SQ FT: 15,000
SALES (est): 1.2MM **Privately Held**
WEB: www.paramounttextile.com
SIC: 2392 5023 5047 Household furnishings; linens & towels; linens, table; surgical equipment & supplies

(G-10757)
PARENTS GUIDE NETWORK CORP
Also Called: P G Media
419 Park Ave S Rm 505 (10016-8410)
PHONE.....................212 213-8840
Steve Elgort, *President*
Michael Landau, *Managing Dir*
Margaret Baldauf, *Art Dir*
Susanne Kimball, *Art Dir*
Howard Baum, *Executive*
EMP: 25
SALES (est): 2.4MM **Privately Held**
WEB: www.parentguidenews.com
SIC: 2721 8351 Magazines: publishing only, not printed on site; child day care services

(G-10758)
PARETEUM CORPORATION (PA)
1185 Ave Of The Amrcas Fl (10036-2601)
PHONE.....................212 984-1096
Robert H Turner, *Ch of Bd*
Daphna Stein, *Exec VP*
Laura W Thomas, *CFO*
Victor Bozzo, *Ch Credit Ofcr*
EMP: 27
SALES: 13.5MM **Publicly Held**
SIC: 7372 Prepackaged software

(G-10759)
PARIJAT JEWELS INC
36 W 47th St Ste 809i (10036-8601)
PHONE.....................212 302-2549
Ramesh Vaje, *President*
EMP: 7
SALES (est): 2.5MM **Privately Held**
SIC: 3911 Jewelry, precious metal

(G-10760)
PARIS REVIEW FOUNDATION INC
544 W 27th St Fl 3 (10001-5537)
PHONE.....................212 343-1333
Robert T McDonell, *Ch of Bd*
Jessica Calderon, *General Mgr*
Emily Cole-Kelly, *Principal*
Jeffery Gleaves, *Manager*
Nicole Rudick, *Manager*
EMP: 7
SALES: 1.9MM **Privately Held**
SIC: 2721 Periodicals

(G-10761)
PARIS WEDDING CENTER CORP
45 E Broadway Fl 2 (10002-6804)
PHONE.....................212 267-8088
Yuki Lin, *Branch Mgr*
EMP: 26
SALES (corp-wide): 888.6K **Privately Held**
SIC: 2335 Wedding gowns & dresses
PA: Paris Wedding Center Corp.
42-53 42 55 Main St
Flushing NY 11355
347 368-4085

(G-10762)
PARK ASSIST LLC
57 W 38th St Fl 11 (10018-1296)
PHONE.....................646 666-7525
Jeremy Lewis, *General Mgr*
Gaby Eini, *Opers Mgr*
Brett Johnson, *Engineer*
Sally Loftin, *Accountant*
Nicholas Minutelli, *Financial Analy*
▲ **EMP:** 70
SALES (est): 1.4MM **Privately Held**
WEB: www.parkassist.com
SIC: 3559 Parking facility equipment & supplies

(G-10763)
PARK WEST JEWELERY INC
565 W End Ave Apt 8b (10024-2734)
PHONE.....................646 329-6145
Dale Bearman, *President*
EMP: 6

SQ FT: 900
SALES (est): 490K **Privately Held**
SIC: 3911 Jewelry apparel

(G-10764)
PARKER WARBY RETAIL INC (PA)
Also Called: Warby Parker Eyewear
161 Ave Of The Amrcs Fl 6 (10013-1205)
PHONE.....................646 517-5223
Neil Blumenthal, *CEO*
Dave Gilboa, *CEO*
Andy Hunt, *Partner*
Rhiannon Duvall, *Sales Staff*
Owen Meehan, *Sales Staff*
▲ **EMP:** 55
SALES (est): 25.2MM **Privately Held**
SIC: 3851 5995 Eyeglasses, lenses & frames; optical goods stores

(G-10765)
PARLOR LABS INC
Also Called: Ponder
515 W 19th St (10011-2872)
PHONE.....................866 801-7323
Alexander Selkirk, *President*
EMP: 5
SALES (est): 236K **Privately Held**
SIC: 7372 8748 Educational computer software; systems engineering consultant, ex. computer or professional

(G-10766)
PASABAHCE USA
41 Madison Ave Fl 7 (10010-2202)
PHONE.....................212 683-1600
Martin Anderson, *Director*
▲ **EMP:** 4
SALES (est): 25MM **Privately Held**
SIC: 3229 Art, decorative & novelty glassware

(G-10767)
PASSPORT BRANDS INC (PA)
240 Madison Ave Fl 8 (10016-2878)
PHONE.....................646 459-2625
Robert S Stec, *CEO*
Robert Arnot, *President*
Ernest K Jacquet, *Director*
◆ **EMP:** 35
SQ FT: 13,500
SALES (est): 6.5MM **Publicly Held**
WEB: www.icisaacs.com
SIC: 2325 2339 Jeans: men's, youths' & boys'; slacks, dress: men's, youths' & boys'; shorts (outerwear): men's, youths' & boys'; jeans: women's, misses' & juniors'; slacks: women's, misses' & juniors'; shorts (outerwear): women's, misses' & juniors'

(G-10768)
PAT & ROSE DRESS INC
327 W 36th St Rm 3a (10018-7014)
PHONE.....................212 279-1357
Rosalia Panebianco, *President*
Pat Capolupo, *Manager*
EMP: 60
SQ FT: 5,000
SALES (est): 3.6MM **Privately Held**
SIC: 2335 2331 2337 2339 Women's, juniors' & misses' dresses; blouses, women's & juniors': made from purchased material; skirts, separate: women's, misses' & juniors'; women's & misses' outerwear; men's & boys' trousers & slacks; men's & boys' suits & coats

(G-10769)
PATMIAN LLC
655 Madison Ave Fl 24 (10065-8043)
PHONE.....................212 758-0770
George Botis, *Chairman*
EMP: 350
SALES (est): 19.9MM **Privately Held**
SIC: 3089 3544 Plastic processing; special dies, tools, jigs & fixtures

(G-10770)
PAUL DAVID ENTERPRISES INC
19 W 34th St Rm 1018 (10001-3006)
PHONE.....................646 667-5530
Daniel Korolev, *Vice Pres*
EMP: 9 **EST:** 2013
SALES (est): 356.2K **Privately Held**
SIC: 2431 Jalousies, glass, wood frame

(G-10771)
PAULA DORF COSMETICS INC
850 7th Ave Ste 801 (10019-5446)
PHONE.....................212 582-0073
Sandy Dekovnick, *CEO*
Sandy De Kovnick, *CEO*
Paula Dorf, *President*
▲ **EMP:** 30
SALES (est): 4.2MM **Privately Held**
WEB: www.pauladorf.com
SIC: 2844 5122 Toilet preparations; cosmetics, perfumes & hair products

(G-10772)
PAULA VARSALONA LTD
552 Fashion Ave Rm 602 (10018-3239)
PHONE.....................212 570-9100
Paula Varsalona, *President*
Sam Kim, *Director*
Terje Vist, *Creative Dir*
EMP: 15
SQ FT: 5,000
SALES (est): 1.3MM **Privately Held**
WEB: www.paulavarsalona.com
SIC: 2335 2396 Wedding gowns & dresses; veils & veiling: bridal, funeral, etc.

(G-10773)
PAULSON & CO INC (PA)
1133 Ave Of The Americas (10036-6710)
PHONE.....................212 956-2221
John Paulson, *President*
Michael Waldorf, *Managing Dir*
Rufus Coes, *COO*
Justin Beeber, *Senior VP*
Andrew Hoine, *Senior VP*
◆ **EMP:** 105
SALES (est): 239.6MM **Privately Held**
WEB: www.paulsonco.com
SIC: 3931 Musical instruments; pianos, all types: vertical, grand, spinet, player, etc.; string instruments & parts; woodwind instruments & parts

(G-10774)
PAVANA USA INC
10 W 33rd St Rm 408 (10001-3306)
PHONE.....................646 833-8811
Avisha Uttamchandani, *President*
Marie Paran, *Sales Staff*
▲ **EMP:** 5
SALES (est): 951.4K **Privately Held**
SIC: 3873 Watches, clocks, watchcases & parts

(G-10775)
PAVMED INC
60 E 42nd St Fl 46 (10165-0043)
PHONE.....................212 949-4319
Lishan Aklog, *Ch of Bd*
Michael J Glennon, *Vice Ch Bd*
Dennis M McGrath, *CFO*
Brian J Deguzman, *Chief Mktg Ofcr*
EMP: 5
SALES (est): 842.7K **Privately Held**
SIC: 3841 Surgical & medical instruments

(G-10776)
PEANUT BUTTER & CO INC
119 W 57th St Ste 300 (10019-2302)
P.O. Box 2000 (10101-2000)
PHONE.....................212 757-3130
Lee E Zalben, *President*
Linda Grimard-Bender, *Natl Sales Mgr*
▲ **EMP:** 25
SALES (est): 5.5MM **Privately Held**
WEB: www.ilovepeanutbutter.com
SIC: 2099 Peanut butter

(G-10777)
PEARL ERWIN INC (PA)
389 5th Ave Rm 1100 (10016-3350)
PHONE.....................212 889-7410
Erwin Pearl, *President*
Michael Elswit, *Vice Pres*
Peter Indiveri, *CFO*
Joel Weinstein, *CFO*
Raquel Garcia, *Manager*
EMP: 30 **EST:** 1954
SALES (est): 33.8MM **Privately Held**
SIC: 3961 3911 Costume jewelry; jewelry, precious metal

(G-10778)
PEARL RIVER TEXTILES INC
57 W 38th St Rm 1202 (10018-5510)
PHONE.....................212 629-5490
Kenneth Farah, *President*
▲ **EMP:** 7
SALES (est): 51.2K **Privately Held**
SIC: 2341 5131 Women's & children's nightwear; piece goods & other fabrics

(G-10779)
PEARSON EDUCATION INC
1185 Avenue Of The Americ (10036-2601)
PHONE.....................212 782-3337
Roth Wilkofsky, *President*
EMP: 16
SALES (corp-wide): 5.3B **Privately Held**
WEB: www.phgenit.com
SIC: 2731 Book publishing
HQ: Pearson Education, Inc.
221 River St
Hoboken NJ 07030
201 236-7000

(G-10780)
PEARSON EDUCATION INC
375 Hudson St (10014-3658)
PHONE.....................212 366-2000
Tom Altier, *Branch Mgr*
EMP: 27
SALES (corp-wide): 5.3B **Privately Held**
WEB: www.phgenit.com
SIC: 2731 Book publishing
HQ: Pearson Education, Inc.
221 River St
Hoboken NJ 07030
201 236-7000

(G-10781)
PEARSON EDUCATION HOLDINGS INC (HQ)
330 Hudson St Fl 9 (10013-1046)
PHONE.....................201 236-6716
Will Ethridge, *President*
Bill Triant, *President*
Michelle West, *Editor*
Barbara Byrne, *Vice Chairman*
Michael Benjamin, *Vice Pres*
▲ **EMP:** 2000 **EST:** 1998
SQ FT: 475,000
SALES (est): 5.3B
SALES (corp-wide): 5.3B **Privately Held**
WEB: www.pearsoned.com
SIC: 2731 Textbooks: publishing & printing
PA: Pearson Plc
Shell Mex House
London WC2R
207 010-2000

(G-10782)
PEARSON INC (HQ)
1330 Hudson St (10013)
PHONE.....................212 641-2400
John Fallon, *CEO*
Boone Novy, *Principal*
Matthew Wie, *Principal*
Coleen Morrison, *Editor*
Glen Moreno, *Chairman*
◆ **EMP:** 58
SALES (est): 2.2B
SALES (corp-wide): 5.3B **Privately Held**
SIC: 2711 2731 Newspapers; books: publishing & printing; textbooks: publishing & printing
PA: Pearson Plc
Shell Mex House
London WC2R
207 010-2000

(G-10783)
PEARSON LONGMAN LLC
51 Madison Ave Fl 27 (10010-1609)
PHONE.....................917 981-2200
Roth Wilkofsky, *Manager*
EMP: 120
SALES (corp-wide): 5.3B **Privately Held**
SIC: 2731 Books: publishing & printing
HQ: Pearson Longman Llc
10 Bank St Ste 1030
White Plains NY 10606
212 641-2400

▲ = Import ▼=Export
◆ =Import/Export

(G-10784)
PEEK A BOO USA INC
Also Called: Beaba USA
555 8th Ave Rm 403 (10018-4383)
PHONE..................................201 533-8700
Lisa Speransky, *CEO*
▲ EMP: 5
SQ FT: 1,200
SALES (est): 756.4K
SALES (corp-wide): 37.1MM **Privately
Held**
SIC: 3089 3634 Plastic kitchenware, table-
ware & houseware; electric household
cooking appliances
PA: Beaba
37 Rue De Liege
Paris 8e Arrondissement 75008

(G-10785)
**PEER INTERNATIONAL CORP
(HQ)**
Also Called: 3239603400 La Head Quarters
152 W 57th St Fl 10 (10019-3340)
PHONE..................................212 265-3910
Ralph Peer II, *President*
Elizabeth W Peer, *Vice Pres*
Cecile Russo, *Vice Pres*
Kathryn Spanberger, *Vice Pres*
Todd Vunderink, *Vice Pres*
▲ EMP: 30
SALES (est): 2.8MM
SALES (corp-wide): 9.7MM **Privately
Held**
SIC: 2741 Music books: publishing only,
not printed on site
PA: Southern Music Publishing Co., Inc.
810 7th Ave Fl 36
New York NY 10019
212 265-3910

(G-10786)
**PEER-SOUTHERN
PRODUCTIONS INC (HQ)**
152 W 57th St Fl 10 (10019-3340)
PHONE..................................212 265-3910
Ralph Peer II, *President*
Marilyn La Vine, *Admin Sec*
EMP: 30 EST: 1961
SALES (est): 1.8MM
SALES (corp-wide): 9.7MM **Privately
Held**
SIC: 3652 Master records or tapes, prepa-
ration of
PA: Southern Music Publishing Co., Inc.
810 7th Ave Fl 36
New York NY 10019
212 265-3910

(G-10787)
PEERMUSIC III LTD (PA)
152 W 57th St Fl 10 (10019-3340)
PHONE..................................212 265-3910
EMP: 13 EST: 1994
SALES (est): 5.5MM **Privately Held**
SIC: 2741 Music books: publishing only,
not printed on site

(G-10788)
PEERMUSIC LTD (HQ)
152 W 57th St Fl 10 (10019-3340)
PHONE..................................212 265-3910
Ralph Peer II, *President*
Elizabeth W Peer, *Vice Pres*
Cecile Russo, *Vice Pres*
Katheryn Spanberger, *Vice Pres*
EMP: 12
SALES (est): 3.1MM
SALES (corp-wide): 9.7MM **Privately
Held**
WEB: www.digitalpressure.com
SIC: 2741 7922 Music books: publishing
only, not printed on site; theatrical produc-
ers & services
PA: Southern Music Publishing Co., Inc.
810 7th Ave Fl 36
New York NY 10019
212 265-3910

(G-10789)
PEGASUS BOOKS NY LTD
148 W 37th St Fl 13 (10018-6976)
PHONE..................................646 343-9502
EMP: 5
SALES: 500K **Privately Held**
SIC: 2731 Book publishing

(G-10790)
PEGASYSTEMS INC
1120 Ave Of The Americas (10036-6700)
PHONE..................................212 626-6550
Beth Saperstein, *Branch Mgr*
EMP: 25
SALES (corp-wide): 891.5MM **Publicly
Held**
WEB: www.pega.com
SIC: 7372 7379 Business oriented com-
puter software; computer related consult-
ing services
PA: Pegasystems Inc.
1 Rogers St
Cambridge MA 02142
617 374-9600

(G-10791)
PENGUIN PUTNAM INC
375 Hudson St Bsmt 1 (10014-3672)
P.O. Box 20998, Floral Park (11002-0998)
PHONE..................................212 366-2000
John Fagan, *CEO*
▲ EMP: 9
SALES (est): 1.2MM **Privately Held**
SIC: 2731 Books: publishing only

(G-10792)
PENGUIN RANDOM HOUSE LLC
1540 Broadway (10036-4039)
PHONE..................................212 782-1000
Markus Dohle, *CEO*
Paul Buckley, *Vice Pres*
Henrik Pahls, *Vice Pres*
Michael Rowsey, *Vice Pres*
Mara Davis, *Project Mgr*
EMP: 25
SALES (corp-wide): 75.3MM **Privately
Held**
SIC: 2731 Books: publishing only
HQ: Penguin Random House Llc
1745 Broadway Frnt 1
New York NY 10019
212 782-9000

(G-10793)
**PENGUIN RANDOM HOUSE LLC
(DH)**
1745 Broadway Frnt 1 (10019-4644)
PHONE..................................212 782-9000
Markus Dohle, *CEO*
Madeline McIntosh, *President*
Avideh Bashirrad, *Publisher*
Casey McIntyre, *Publisher*
Judith Curr, *Exec VP*
▲ EMP: 277
SALES (est): 1.5B
SALES (corp-wide): 75.3MM **Privately
Held**
SIC: 2731 Books: publishing only
HQ: Bertelsmann Se & Co. Kgaa
Carl-Bertelsmann-Str. 270
Gutersloh 33335
524 180-0

(G-10794)
PENGUIN RANDOM HOUSE LLC
1745 Broadway Frnt 3 (10019-4641)
PHONE..................................212 572-6162
Markus Dohle, *CEO*
EMP: 513
SALES (corp-wide): 75.3MM **Privately
Held**
SIC: 2731 5942 Books: publishing only;
book stores
HQ: Penguin Random House Llc
1745 Broadway Frnt 1
New York NY 10019
212 782-9000

(G-10795)
**PENHOUSE MEDIA GROUP INC
(PA)**
11 Penn Plz Fl 12 (10001-2027)
PHONE..................................212 702-6000
John Prebich, *President*
Claude Bertin, *Exec VP*
Nina Guccione, *Exec VP*
Hope Brick, *Vice Pres*
Larry Sutter, *Admin Sec*
▲ EMP: 150

SALES (est): 11.5MM **Privately Held**
SIC: 2721 5999 6512 6794 Magazines:
publishing only, not printed on site; art
dealers; commercial & industrial building
operation; copyright buying & licensing

(G-10796)
PENSIONS & INVESTMENTS
Also Called: P&I, Pper P I Daily P I People
711 3rd Ave (10017-4014)
PHONE..................................212 210-0763
William T Bisson Jr, *Principal*
EMP: 43
SALES (est): 3.7MM **Privately Held**
SIC: 2721 Magazines: publishing & printing

(G-10797)
PEPE CREATIONS INC
2 W 45th St Ste 1003 (10036-4212)
PHONE..................................212 391-1514
Frank Gomez, *President*
EMP: 12
SALES (est): 1.5MM **Privately Held**
WEB: www.pepecreations.com
SIC: 3961 Costume jewelry

(G-10798)
PEPSICO INC
350 Hudson St (10014-4504)
PHONE..................................914 253-2000
Jennifer Edwards, *Accountant*
Indranie Balkaran, *Senior Mgr*
Dawn Cloutier, *Senior Mgr*
Eric Potter, *Senior Mgr*
Eric G Harnischfeger, *Director*
EMP: 5
SALES (corp-wide): 64.6B **Publicly Held**
SIC: 2086 Carbonated soft drinks, bottled
& canned
PA: Pepsico, Inc.
700 Anderson Hill Rd
Purchase NY 10577
914 253-2000

(G-10799)
**PEPSICO DESIGN &
INNOVATION**
350 Hudson St (10014-4504)
PHONE..................................917 405-9307
EMP: 5 EST: 2017
SALES (est): 272.3K **Privately Held**
SIC: 2086 Carbonated soft drinks, bottled
& canned

(G-10800)
PER ANNUM INC
555 8th Ave Rm 202 (10018-4386)
PHONE..................................212 647-8700
Alicia Settle, *President*
Tom Settle, *Corp Secy*
▲ EMP: 25
SQ FT: 14,000
SALES (est): 2MM **Privately Held**
WEB: www.perannum.com
SIC: 2741 Miscellaneous publishing

(G-10801)
PEREGRINE INDUSTRIES INC
40 Wall St (10005-1304)
PHONE..................................631 838-2870
Richard Rubin, *CEO*
Amir Uziel, *Director*
EMP: 5
SALES (est): 404.5K
SALES (corp-wide): 601.1K **Privately
Held**
SIC: 3569 Filters
PA: Dolomite Holdings Ltd
8 Hamanofim
Herzliya 46725
722 220-930

(G-10802)
PEREIRA & ODELL LLC
5 Crosby St Rm 5h (10013-3154)
PHONE..................................212 897-1000
Cory Berger, *Director*
Rory Hill, *Director*
EMP: 8
SALES (est): 890.6K
SALES (corp-wide): 21.8MM **Privately
Held**
SIC: 3993 Advertising artwork

PA: Pereira & O'dell Llc
215 2nd St Ste 100
San Francisco CA 94105
415 284-9916

(G-10803)
**PERFUMERS WORKSHOP INTL
LTD (PA)**
350 7th Ave Rm 802 (10001-1941)
PHONE..................................212 644-8950
Donald G Bauchner, *President*
Steven Levenson, *Exec VP*
▲ EMP: 8
SQ FT: 1,800
SALES (est): 1MM **Privately Held**
SIC: 2844 Perfumes & colognes

(G-10804)
PERIMONDO LLC
331 W 84th St Apt 2 (10024-4215)
P.O. Box 200 (10024-0200)
PHONE..................................212 749-0721
Matthias Rebmann, *Mng Member*
Revecca Horowitz, *Mng Member*
▲ EMP: 6
SALES (est): 1.1MM **Privately Held**
SIC: 2074 Lecithin, cottonseed

(G-10805)
PERMA GLOW LTD INC
48 W 48th St Ste 301 (10036-1713)
PHONE..................................212 575-9677
Richard Scandaglia, *President*
Joseph Scandaglia, *Vice Pres*
▲ EMP: 15
SQ FT: 2,000
SALES: 400K **Privately Held**
SIC: 3915 Jewel cutting, drilling, polishing,
recutting or setting

(G-10806)
**PERMANENT OBSERVER
MISSION**
320 E 51st St (10022-7803)
PHONE..................................212 883-0140
Iyad Ameen Madani, *Principal*
EMP: 5 EST: 2016
SALES (est): 124.6K **Privately Held**
SIC: 2711 Newspapers, publishing & print-
ing

(G-10807)
**PERRY ELLIS INTERNATIONAL
INC**
1126 Avenue Of The Americ (10036)
PHONE..................................212 536-5400
Maria Folyk-Kushneir, *Senior VP*
John Griffin, *Branch Mgr*
EMP: 12
SALES (corp-wide): 874.8MM **Privately
Held**
SIC: 2321 2325 6794 Men's & boys'
sports & polo shirts; men's & boys'
trousers & slacks; trousers, dress (sepa-
rate): men's, youths' & boys'; shorts (out-
erwear): men's, youths' & boys';
franchises, selling or licensing
HQ: Perry Ellis International Inc
3000 Nw 107th Ave
Doral FL 33172
305 592-2830

(G-10808)
**PERRY ELLIS INTERNATIONAL
INC**
42 W 39th St Fl 4 (10018-3841)
PHONE..................................212 536-5499
Kevin Kiley, *Branch Mgr*
EMP: 9
SALES (corp-wide): 874.8MM **Privately
Held**
WEB: www.cubabera.com
SIC: 2321 Men's & boys' sports & polo
shirts
HQ: Perry Ellis International Inc
3000 Nw 107th Ave
Doral FL 33172
305 592-2830

(G-10809)
**PERRY ELLIS MENSWEAR LLC
(DH)**
Also Called: Perry Ellis America
1120 Avenue Of The Americ (10036-6700)
PHONE..................................212 221-7500

Doug Jakubowski, *Ch of Bd*
Awadhesh K Sinha, *COO*
Linda Nash Merker, *VP Human Res*
◆ **EMP:** 150 **EST:** 1893
SQ FT: 27,000
SALES (est): 106.3MM
SALES (corp-wide): 874.8MM **Privately Held**
WEB: www.perryellis.com
SIC: 2325 5611 2321 2387 Slacks, dress: men's, youths' & boys'; jeans: men's, youths' & boys'; men's & boys' clothing stores; men's & boys' furnishings; apparel belts; suspenders; neckties; men's & boys' made from purchased materials
HQ: Perry Ellis International Inc
3000 Nw 107th Ave
Doral FL 33172
305 592-2830

(G-10810)
PERRY STREET SOFTWARE INC
489 5th Ave Rm 29a (10017-6137)
PHONE..................415 935-1429
John Skandros, *President*
Eric Silverberg, *Admin Sec*
EMP: 5 **EST:** 2011
SALES (est): 391.4K **Privately Held**
SIC: 7372 Prepackaged software

(G-10811)
PESSELNIK & COHEN INC
82 Bowery Unit 10 (10013-4656)
PHONE..................212 925-0287
Salvatore Diadema, *President*
Stephen De Angelo, *Admin Sec*
EMP: 7
SALES (est): 550K **Privately Held**
SIC: 3911 5094 Jewelry, precious metal; jewelry; watches & parts

(G-10812)
PET PROTEINS LLC
347 W 36th St Rm 1204 (10018-6480)
PHONE..................888 293-1029
Steven Mendal,
Jayme Mendal,
Mark Mendal,
◆ **EMP:** 7
SQ FT: 500
SALES: 1MM **Privately Held**
SIC: 2047 Dog & cat food

(G-10813)
PETER ATMAN INC
6 E 45th St Rm 1100 (10017-2475)
PHONE..................212 644-8882
Peter Philipakos, *Ch of Bd*
Peter Phillips, *President*
Peter Dressel, *Prgrmr*
EMP: 10 **EST:** 1977
SALES (est): 1.3MM **Privately Held**
WEB: www.peteratman.com
SIC: 3911 5944 Jewelry, precious metal; jewelry, precious stones & precious metals

(G-10814)
PETER LANG PUBLISHING INC (HQ)
29 Broadway Rm 1800 (10006-3221)
PHONE..................212 647-7700
Christopher Myers, *Director*
Netthoevel Simone, *Director*
Laura Diegel, *Assistant*
EMP: 12
SQ FT: 8,000
SALES (est): 1.3MM
SALES (corp-wide): 274.9K **Privately Held**
WEB: www.peterlangusa.com
SIC: 2731 Textbooks: publishing only, not printed on site
PA: The Peter Lang Trust For Underprivileged Children
Lyday Close
Stroud GLOS
145 230-1123

(G-10815)
PETER MAYER PUBLISHERS INC
Also Called: Overlook Press, The
195 Broadway Fl 9 (10007-3122)
PHONE..................212 673-2210

Peter Mayer, *President*
George Davidson, *Production*
Michael Goldsmith, *Analyst*
▲ **EMP:** 13
SALES: 1MM **Privately Held**
WEB: www.overlookpress.com
SIC: 2731 Books: publishing only

(G-10816)
PETER THOMAS ROTH LABS LLC (PA)
Also Called: Naturally Serious
460 Park Ave Fl 16 (10022-1829)
PHONE..................212 581-5800
June Jacobs,
Peter Roth,
▲ **EMP:** 40
SQ FT: 5,500
SALES (est): 28.2MM **Privately Held**
SIC: 2844 Cosmetic preparations

(G-10817)
PETNET SOLUTIONS INC
660 1st Ave Rm 140 (10016-3295)
PHONE..................865 218-2000
Barry Scott, *CEO*
EMP: 6
SALES (corp-wide): 95B **Privately Held**
SIC: 2835 In vitro & in vivo diagnostic substances
HQ: Petnet Solutions, Inc.
810 Innovation Dr
Knoxville TN 37932
865 218-2000

(G-10818)
PETRO RIVER OIL CORP (PA)
205 E 42nd St Fl 14 (10017-5752)
PHONE..................469 828-3900
Scot Cohen, *Ch of Bd*
Stephen Brunner, *President*
David Briones, *CFO*
EMP: 4
SALES: 1.6MM **Publicly Held**
SIC: 1311 Crude petroleum & natural gas

(G-10819)
PEXIP INC (DH)
240 W 35th St Ste 400 (10001-2568)
PHONE..................703 338-3544
Adam Marlin, *Vice Pres*
Richard Coder, *Vice Pres*
Joseph Seah, *Technical Mgr*
Bryan Jurries, *Human Res Mgr*
Kjell Anderson, *Sales Dir*
EMP: 12 **EST:** 2012
SALES (est): 4.9MM
SALES (corp-wide): 6MM **Privately Held**
SIC: 7372 Application computer software
HQ: Pexip As
Lilleakerveien 2a
Oslo 0283
220 188-00

(G-10820)
PFIZER HCP CORPORATION (HQ)
235 E 42nd St (10017-5703)
PHONE..................212 733-2323
Ian C Read, *CEO*
Lisa Samuels, *Counsel*
Rady Johnson, *Exec VP*
Freda C Lewis-Hall, *Exec VP*
Carl Wilbanks, *Senior VP*
▲ **EMP:** 12
SALES (est): 4.4MM
SALES (corp-wide): 53.6B **Publicly Held**
WEB: www.pfizer.com
SIC: 2834 Pharmaceutical preparations
PA: Pfizer Inc.
235 E 42nd St
New York NY 10017
212 733-2323

(G-10821)
PFIZER INC (PA)
235 E 42nd St (10017-5703)
PHONE..................212 733-2323
Albert Bourla, *CEO*
Ian C Read, *Ch of Bd*
Douglas M Lankler, *Exec VP*
Dawn Rogers, *Exec VP*
Douglas Giordano, *Senior VP*
EMP: 2500 **EST:** 1942

SALES: 53.6B **Publicly Held**
WEB: www.pfizer.com
SIC: 2833 2834 Antibiotics; drugs acting on the cardiovascular system, except diagnostic

(G-10822)
PFIZER INC
150 E 42nd St Fl 38 (10017-5612)
PHONE..................937 746-3603
Daniel Reardon, *Principal*
Lorraine Hook, *District Mgr*
Markus Green, *Counsel*
John Hong, *Counsel*
Karen Staff, *Counsel*
EMP: 214
SALES (corp-wide): 53.6B **Publicly Held**
SIC: 2834 Pharmaceutical preparations
PA: Pfizer Inc.
235 E 42nd St
New York NY 10017
212 733-2323

(G-10823)
PFIZER INC
150 E 42nd St Bsmt 2 (10017-5612)
PHONE..................212 733-6276
Ira Stoler, *Manager*
Rafael Rivera, *Manager*
EMP: 70
SALES (corp-wide): 53.6B **Publicly Held**
WEB: www.pfizer.com
SIC: 2834 Pharmaceutical preparations
PA: Pfizer Inc.
235 E 42nd St
New York NY 10017
212 733-2323

(G-10824)
PFIZER OVERSEAS LLC
235 E 42nd St (10017-5703)
PHONE..................212 733-2323
Ian C Read, *Ch of Bd*
Mikael Dolsten, *President*
Frank D'Amelio, *Exec VP*
Chuck Hill, *Exec VP*
Rady Johnson, *Exec VP*
EMP: 8
SALES (est): 484.5K
SALES (corp-wide): 53.6B **Publicly Held**
SIC: 2834 2833 Pharmaceutical preparations; antibiotics
PA: Pfizer Inc.
235 E 42nd St
New York NY 10017
212 733-2323

(G-10825)
PHAIDON PRESS INC
65 Bleecker St Fl 8 (10012-2420)
PHONE..................212 652-5400
Keith Fox, *CEO*
Bridget McCarthy, *Editor*
Deborah Aaronson, *Vice Pres*
Andrew Price, *Vice Pres*
Chris Conti, *Sales Staff*
▲ **EMP:** 20
SALES (est): 2.6MM
SALES (corp-wide): 35.5MM **Privately Held**
SIC: 2731 Books: publishing only
HQ: Phaidon Press Limited
18 Regents Wharf All Saints Street
London
207 843-1000

(G-10826)
PHILADELPHIA COATINGS LLC
780 3rd Ave Fl 22 (10017-2024)
PHONE..................917 929-4738
Stefanos Kasselakis, *CEO*
EMP: 15
SALES (est): 666.2K **Privately Held**
SIC: 2851 Paints & allied products

(G-10827)
PHILIP MORRIS GLOBL BRANDS INC (HQ)
120 Park Ave Fl 6 (10017-5592)
PHONE..................917 663-2000
EMP: 4
SALES (est): 36.3MM
SALES (corp-wide): 79.8B **Publicly Held**
SIC: 2111 Cigarettes

PA: Philip Morris International Inc.
120 Park Ave Fl 6
New York NY 10017
917 663-2000

(G-10828)
PHILIP MORRIS INTL INC (PA)
120 Park Ave Fl 6 (10017-5592)
PHONE..................917 663-2000
Andre Calantzopoulos, *CEO*
Jacek Olczak, *COO*
Massimo Andolina, *Senior VP*
Werner Barth, *Senior VP*
Charles Bendotti, *Senior VP*
EMP: 98
SALES: 79.8B **Publicly Held**
SIC: 2111 Cigarettes

(G-10829)
PHILLIPS-VAN HEUSEN EUROPE
Also Called: Pvh Europe
200 Madison Ave Bsmt 1 (10016-3913)
PHONE..................212 381-3500
Ellen Constantinides, *President*
John Neely, *Vice Pres*
Warren Gerber, *Finance*
EMP: 12
SALES: 20MM
SALES (corp-wide): 9.6B **Publicly Held**
SIC: 2321 2331 2253 3143 Men's & boys' dress shirts; blouses, women's & juniors': made from purchased material; sweaters & sweater coats, knit; men's footwear, except athletic; ready-to-wear apparel, women's; men's & boys' clothing stores
PA: Pvh Corp.
200 Madison Ave Bsmt 1
New York NY 10016
212 381-3500

(G-10830)
PHOENIX USA LLC
315 W 33rd St Apt 30h (10001-2795)
PHONE..................646 351-6598
Roger Garcia,
▲ **EMP:** 2
SALES (est): 4.5MM **Privately Held**
SIC: 2211 7389 Apparel & outerwear fabrics, cotton;

(G-10831)
PHOENIX VENTURE FUND LLC
70 E 55th St Fl 10 (10022-3334)
PHONE..................212 759-1909
Philip S Sassower, *Ch of Bd*
EMP: 21
SALES (est): 1.8MM **Privately Held**
SIC: 3577 Computer peripheral equipment

(G-10832)
PHYSICALMIND INSTITUTE
84 Wooster St Ste 605 (10012-4363)
PHONE..................212 343-2150
Joan Breibart, *General Mgr*
▲ **EMP:** 10
SALES (est): 1MM **Privately Held**
SIC: 3949 7812 8621 Exercise equipment; video tape production; professional membership organizations

(G-10833)
PIAGGIO GROUP AMERICAS INC
257 Park Ave S Fl 4 (10010-7304)
PHONE..................212 380-4400
Diego Graffi, *CEO*
Mario Di Maria, *President*
Erik Larson, *Technical Staff*
Cesare Bargellini, *Advisor*
◆ **EMP:** 35
SALES (est): 8MM **Privately Held**
WEB: www.piaggiousa.com
SIC: 3751 Motor scooters & parts
PA: Immsi Spa
Piazza Vilfredo Pareto 3
Mantova MN 46100

(G-10834)
PIANO SOFTWARE INC (PA)
1 World Trade Ctr Ste 46d (10007-0092)
PHONE..................646 350-1999
Kweli Washington, *COO*
Chris Barnett, *Engineer*
Alex Franta, *CFO*
Allison Munro, *Chief Mktg Ofcr*

▲ = Import ▼=Export
◆ =Import/Export

EMP: 23
SALES (est): 10MM **Privately Held**
SIC: 7372 Application computer software

(G-10835)
PICADOR USA
175 5th Ave (10010-7703)
PHONE.................................646 307-5629
Frances Coady, *Vice Pres*
EMP: 12
SALES (est): 767.1K **Privately Held**
SALES (corp-wide): 1.6B **Privately Held**
SIC: 2731 Books: publishing only
HQ: Macmillan Holdings, Llc
120 Broadway Fl 22
New York NY 10271

(G-10836)
PICTOURE INC
110 Wall St (10005-3801)
PHONE.................................212 641-0098
Lamese Bakhsh, *CEO*
EMP: 5
SALES (est): 130.5K **Privately Held**
SIC: 2741

(G-10837)
PIDYON CONTROLS INC (PA)
141 W 24th St Apt 4 (10011-1958)
PHONE.................................212 683-9523
Yochi Cohen, *CEO*
EMP: 16
SQ FT: 10,000
SALES: 10MM **Privately Held**
SIC: 3944 Child restraint seats, automotive

(G-10838)
PIEMONTE HOME MADE RAVIOLI CO
190 Grand St (10013-3712)
PHONE.................................212 226-0475
Mario Bertorelli, *President*
EMP: 6
SALES (corp-wide): 1.7MM **Privately Held**
WEB: www.piemonteravioli.com
SIC: 2098 Noodles (e.g. egg, plain & water), dry
PA: Piemonte Home Made Ravioli Co, Inc
3436 65th St
Woodside NY 11377
718 429-1972

(G-10839)
PILOT INC (PA)
421 W 24th St Apt 4c (10011-1244)
PHONE.................................212 951-1133
Ben Brooks, *President*
EMP: 8
SALES (est): 483K **Privately Held**
SIC: 7372 7389 Business oriented computer software;

(G-10840)
PILOT INC
110 E 25th St (10010-2913)
PHONE.................................212 951-1133
Ben Brooks, *Manager*
EMP: 8
SALES (corp-wide): 483K **Privately Held**
SIC: 7372 7389 Business oriented computer software;
PA: Pilot, Inc.
421 W 24th St Apt 4c
New York NY 10011
212 951-1133

(G-10841)
PIN PHARMA INC
55 Broadway Ste 315 (10006-3008)
PHONE.................................212 543-2583
Hestaline Reynolds, *Principal*
Sophie Hanscom, *Research*
EMP: 9
SALES (est): 983.7K **Privately Held**
SIC: 3452 Pins

(G-10842)
PINGMD INC
136 Madison Ave Fl 6 (10016-6795)
PHONE.................................212 632-2665
Lawrence Sosnow, *Ch of Bd*
Susan Driscoll, *President*
Aditi Deeg, *Vice Pres*
Joshua Pokotilow, *VP Engrg*
EMP: 6 EST: 2009

SALES (est): 498.5K **Privately Held**
SIC: 7372 Application computer software

(G-10843)
PINK INC
23 E 10th St Apt 1b (10003-6114)
PHONE.................................212 352-8282
Debra Roth, *President*
EMP: 22
SQ FT: 2,000
SALES: 1.6MM **Privately Held**
WEB: www.pinkinc.org
SIC: 2395 Quilted fabrics or cloth

(G-10844)
PINK CRUSH LLC
1410 Broadway Rm 1002 (10018-9359)
PHONE.................................718 788-6978
Rori Nadrich, *President*
Raymond Kassin, *Vice Pres*
EMP: 4
SQ FT: 1,800
SALES: 2MM **Privately Held**
SIC: 2369 Girls' & children's outerwear

(G-10845)
PINS N NEEDLES
1045 Lexington Ave Apt 2n (10021-3254)
PHONE.................................212 535-6222
Rachel Low, *CEO*
EMP: 10
SALES (est): 1.1MM **Privately Held**
SIC: 3452 Pins

(G-10846)
PITNEY BOWES INC
637 W 27th St Fl 8 (10001-1019)
PHONE.................................212 564-7548
Joe Mackin, *Branch Mgr*
EMP: 35
SALES (corp-wide): 3.5B **Publicly Held**
SIC: 3579 7359 Postage meters; business machine & electronic equipment rental services
PA: Pitney Bowes Inc.
3001 Summer St Ste 3
Stamford CT 06905
203 356-5000

(G-10847)
PITNEY BOWES INC
90 Park Ave Rm 1110 (10016-1301)
PHONE.................................203 356-5000
Michael Levitan, *Principal*
Rajeeb Mohapatra, *Senior VP*
Bill Borrelle, *Vice Pres*
Tony Esposito, *Engineer*
Maria Hagan, *Engineer*
EMP: 35
SALES (corp-wide): 3.5B **Publicly Held**
SIC: 3579 7359 Postage meters; business machine & electronic equipment rental services
PA: Pitney Bowes Inc.
3001 Summer St Ste 3
Stamford CT 06905
203 356-5000

(G-10848)
PIWIK PRO LLC
222 Broadway Fl 19 (10038-2550)
PHONE.................................888 444-0049
Maiciej Zawadski, *CEO*
EMP: 30
SALES (est): 987.2K **Privately Held**
SIC: 7372 Application computer software

(G-10849)
PKG GROUP
560 Broadway Rm 406 (10012-3938)
PHONE.................................212 965-0112
Mallory Wood, *Accounts Exec*
Edward Csaszar, *Manager*
EMP: 7
SALES (est): 679.7K **Privately Held**
SIC: 2631 Container, packaging & boxboard

(G-10850)
PLACE VENDOME HOLDING CO INC
Also Called: R & F Marketing
230 5th Ave Ste 1112 (10001-7829)
PHONE.................................212 696-0765
Rhonda Finkelstein, *Ch of Bd*
Arnold Finkelstein, *President*

◆ EMP: 110
SALES (est): 17.6MM **Privately Held**
WEB: www.rfmarketing.com
SIC: 2392 Pillows, bed: made from purchased materials

(G-10851)
PLANET GOLD CLOTHING CO INC
Also Called: Yummy Fabric
500 Fashion Ave Fl 17a (10018-4708)
PHONE.................................646 432-5100
Bruce Fischer, *Ch of Bd*
David Chen, *Vice Pres*
Tolia Merson, *VP Opers*
Kani Siu, *Prdtn Mgr*
▲ EMP: 150
SALES (est): 19.4MM **Privately Held**
SIC: 2339 5137 Sportswear, women's; sportswear, women's & children's

(G-10852)
PLASCOLINE INC
275 Madison Ave Fl 14th (10016-1101)
PHONE.................................917 410-5754
EMP: 18
SQ FT: 2,000
SALES: 7MM **Privately Held**
SIC: 3089 Mfg Plastic Products

(G-10853)
PLAYBILL INCORPORATED (PA)
729 7th Ave Fl 4 (10019-6827)
PHONE.................................212 557-5757
Philip S Birsh, *President*
Jolie Schaffzin, *Publisher*
Arthur T Birsh, *Chairman*
Mark Peikert, *Chief*
Joan Alleman-Birsh, *Exec VP*
EMP: 20 EST: 1882
SQ FT: 4,500
SALES (est): 20.3MM **Privately Held**
SIC: 2721 Magazines: publishing & printing

(G-10854)
PLEASURE CHEST SALES LTD
156 7th Ave S (10014-2727)
PHONE.................................212 242-2158
Brian Robinson, *President*
EMP: 10
SALES (est): 83.8K **Privately Held**
WEB: www.pleasurewipes.com
SIC: 3089 Novelties, plastic

(G-10855)
PLECTICA LLC
25 Broadway Fl 9 (10004-1058)
PHONE.................................646 941-8822
Adam Riggs, *Partner*
Derek Cabrera, *Partner*
Laura Cabrera, *Partner*
EMP: 14
SQ FT: 300
SALES (est): 260.2K **Privately Held**
SIC: 7372 Application computer software

(G-10856)
PLEXI CRAFT QUALITY PRODUCTS
200 Lexington Ave Rm 914 (10016-6255)
PHONE.................................212 924-3244
George Frechter, *President*
EMP: 15
SQ FT: 10,000
SALES (est): 2.4MM **Privately Held**
WEB: www.plexi-craft.com
SIC: 2511 Wood household furniture

(G-10857)
PLUGG LLC
Also Called: Coliseum
1410 Broadway Frnt 2 (10018-9302)
PHONE.................................212 840-6655
John Kiplani, *Branch Mgr*
EMP: 10
SALES (est): 1.2MM
SALES (corp-wide): 6MM **Privately Held**
WEB: www.coliseum.com
SIC: 2331 2335 2339 Women's & misses' blouses & shirts; women's, juniors' & misses' dresses; slacks: women's, misses' & juniors'

PA: Plugg Llc
250 Moonachie Rd Ste 204
Moonachie NJ 07074
201 662-8200

(G-10858)
PMI GLOBAL SERVICES INC
120 Park Ave Fl 6 (10017-5579)
PHONE.................................917 663-2000
James R Mortensen, *President*
Julia Hoeng, *Director*
Alice Vaskova, *Director*
EMP: 23
SALES (est): 4.8MM
SALES (corp-wide): 79.8B **Publicly Held**
SIC: 2111 Cigarettes
PA: Philip Morris International Inc.
120 Park Ave Fl 6
New York NY 10017
917 663-2000

(G-10859)
PODRAVKA INTERNATIONAL USA
420 Lexington Ave Rm 2034 (10170-0012)
PHONE.................................212 661-0125
Domagoj Kero, *President*
Milka Jacvic, *Administration*
▲ EMP: 12
SALES (est): 1.9MM **Privately Held**
SIC: 3631 Barbecues, grills & braziers (outdoor cooking)

(G-10860)
POETS HOUSE INC
10 River Ter (10282-1240)
PHONE.................................212 431-7920
Frank Platt, *Vice Pres*
Martin Gomez, *Treasurer*
Jane Preston, *Exec Dir*
Fredric Hugue, *Admin Sec*
EMP: 14 EST: 1985
SALES: 1.6MM **Privately Held**
SIC: 2731 8231 Book publishing; libraries

(G-10861)
POLLACK GRAPHICS INC
601 W 26th St Ste M204 (10001-1101)
PHONE.................................212 727-8400
Glenn Pollack, *President*
EMP: 5
SQ FT: 1,600
SALES (est): 450K **Privately Held**
SIC: 2752 Commercial printing, offset

(G-10862)
POLYCOM INC
1 Penn Plz Fl 48 (10119-4899)
P.O. Box 26137 (10087-6137)
PHONE.................................212 372-6960
John Poole, *Vice Pres*
Glenn Grieshaber, *Sales Dir*
Damian Aliseo, *Sales Mgr*
Dina Becchina, *Accounts Mgr*
Tom Gagliardi, *Accounts Exec*
EMP: 38
SALES (corp-wide): 1.6B **Publicly Held**
WEB: www.polycom.com
SIC: 3661 Telephones & telephone apparatus
HQ: Polycom, Inc.
345 Encinal St
Santa Cruz CA 95060
831 426-5858

(G-10863)
POLYMER SLUTIONS GROUP FIN LLC (PA)
100 Park Ave Fl 31 (10017-5584)
PHONE.................................212 771-1717
Mike Ivany, *CEO*
EMP: 5 EST: 2015
SALES (est): 68.8MM **Privately Held**
SIC: 2869 Industrial organic chemicals

(G-10864)
POM INDUSTRIES LLC
251 W 39th St Fl 2 (10018-3122)
PHONE.................................800 695-4791
Nicholas Caruso, *Mng Member*
Alexander Caruso,
EMP: 4
SQ FT: 3,000
SALES: 1MM **Privately Held**
SIC: 3999 Self-defense sprays

(G-10865)
POPNYC 1 LLC
Also Called: Pop Nyc
75 Saint Nicholas Pl 2e (10032-8036)
PHONE......................................646 684-4600
Gina Panella, *Mng Member*
Joseph Peraino,
▲ EMP: 5
SQ FT: 1,000
SALES: 2MM **Privately Held**
SIC: 2339 Women's & misses' accessories

(G-10866)
POPPIN INC
16 Madison Sq W Fl 3 (10010-1630)
PHONE......................................212 391-7200
Randy Nicolau, *CEO*
Sara Olds, *Area Mgr*
Andrew Benoit, *COO*
Jeremy Westin, *Exec VP*
Jimmy Abbott, *Vice Pres*
▲ EMP: 52 EST: 2009
SALES (est): 19.3MM **Privately Held**
SIC: 2521 2522 Cabinets, office: wood; tables, office: wood; chairs, office: padded or plain, except wood

(G-10867)
PORTFOLIO DECISIONWARE INC
235 W 48th St (10036-1404)
PHONE......................................212 947-1326
Jeff Hewitt, *President*
Dennis Piccininni, *COO*
Phil Wolf, *Senior VP*
Paul Samarel, *Officer*
EMP: 30
SALES (est): 1.9MM **Privately Held**
SIC: 7372 Prepackaged software

(G-10868)
PORTFOLIO MEDIA INC
Also Called: Law360
111 W 19th St Fl 5 (10011-4166)
PHONE......................................646 783-7100
Scott Roberts, *CEO*
EMP: 200
SQ FT: 46,000
SALES (est): 19.5MM
SALES (corp-wide): 9.6B **Privately Held**
WEB: www.portfoliomedia.com
SIC: 2741 Business service newsletters: publishing & printing
HQ: Relx Inc.
230 Park Ave Ste 700
New York NY 10169
212 309-8100

(G-10869)
PORTWARE LLC (HQ)
233 Broadway Fl 24 (10279-2502)
PHONE......................................212 425-5233
Alfred Eskandar, *CEO*
Scott Depetris, *President*
Jason La, *Engineer*
Darek Loter, *Accounts Mgr*
Adam Steinhaus, *Manager*
EMP: 66
SALES (est): 14.5MM
SALES (corp-wide): 1.4B **Publicly Held**
SIC: 7372 Prepackaged software
PA: Factset Research Systems Inc.
601 Merritt 7
Norwalk CT 06851
203 810-1000

(G-10870)
POSITIVE PRINT LITHO OFFSET
121 Varick St Rm 204 (10013-1408)
PHONE......................................212 431-4850
Garry Koppel, *President*
EMP: 8
SQ FT: 2,000
SALES (est): 1MM **Privately Held**
SIC: 2752 Commercial printing, offset

(G-10871)
POST ROAD
101 E 16th St Apt 4b (10003-2150)
PHONE......................................203 545-2122
David Ryan, *President*
Karim Demirdache, *Managing Prtnr*
John Todd, *Managing Prtnr*
EMP: 14

SALES (est): 833.3K **Privately Held**
SIC: 2752 7371 Publication printing, lithographic; computer software development & applications

(G-10872)
POWA TECHNOLOGIES INC
1 Bryant Park Ste 39 (10036-6747)
PHONE......................................347 344-7848
EMP: 40
SQ FT: 10,000
SALES (est): 3.8MM
SALES (corp-wide): 328.1K **Privately Held**
SIC: 7372 3578 Prepackaged Software Services Mfg Calculating Equipment
HQ: Powa Technologies Group Plc
Heron Tower 35th Floor
London EC2N

(G-10873)
PRC LIQUIDATING COMPANY
Also Called: New York Running Co
10 Columbus Cir (10019-1158)
PHONE......................................212 823-9626
Eugene Mitchell, *Bd of Directors*
EMP: 30
SALES (corp-wide): 6B **Privately Held**
SIC: 3949 Sporting & athletic goods
HQ: Prc Liquidating Company
632 Overhill Rd
Ardmore PA 19003
610 649-1876

(G-10874)
PRECISION APPAREL MFG LLC
3 Hanover Sq Apt 14g (10004-2623)
PHONE......................................201 805-2664
Ram Narayanan, *President*
EMP: 2
SQ FT: 2,000
SALES: 10MM **Privately Held**
SIC: 2253 T-shirts & tops, knit

(G-10875)
PRECISION INTERNATIONAL CO INC
Also Called: Cenere
201 E 28th St 9n (10016-8538)
PHONE......................................212 268-9090
Michelle Kim, *President*
James Cioffi, *Sales Staff*
▲ EMP: 6
SQ FT: 4,200
SALES (est): 754.9K **Privately Held**
SIC: 3873 5094 Watches, clocks, watchcases & parts; jewelry & precious stones

(G-10876)
PREMIER BRNDS GROUP HLDNGS LLC (HQ)
Also Called: One Jeanswear Group, LLC
1441 Broadway (10018-1905)
PHONE......................................215 785-4000
Ralph A Schipani, *President*
Dominic Petrozzi, *Opers Staff*
Joseph T Donnalley, *Treasurer*
Wendy Gove, *Manager*
◆ EMP: 277 EST: 1997
SALES (est): 1.7B **Privately Held**
SIC: 2337 Women's & misses' suits & coats
PA: Jasper Parent, Llc
9 W 57th St Ste 3100
New York NY 10019
212 796-8500

(G-10877)
PREMIER BRNDS GROUP HLDNGS LLC
Jones New York
1411 Broadway (10018-3496)
PHONE......................................212 642-3860
Gail Onorato, *Principal*
EMP: 6
SALES (corp-wide): 1.7B **Privately Held**
WEB: www.jny.com
SIC: 2339 Sportswear, women's
HQ: Premier Brands Group Holdings Llc
1441 Broadway
New York NY 10018
215 785-4000

(G-10878)
PREMIER BRNDS GROUP HLDNGS LLC
Also Called: Jones New York
1441 Broadway Fl 20 (10018-1905)
PHONE......................................212 575-2571
Jack Gross, *Branch Mgr*
EMP: 7
SALES (corp-wide): 1.7B **Privately Held**
WEB: www.jny.com
SIC: 2329 2339 Men's & boys' sportswear & athletic clothing; women's & misses' athletic clothing & sportswear
HQ: Premier Brands Group Holdings Llc
1441 Broadway
New York NY 10018
215 785-4000

(G-10879)
PREMIER BRNDS GROUP HLDNGS LLC
Also Called: Jones New York
575 Fashion Ave Frnt 1 (10018-1886)
PHONE......................................212 642-3860
Charles Hostepler, *President*
Lisa Garson, *Branch Mgr*
EMP: 22
SALES (corp-wide): 1.7B **Privately Held**
WEB: www.jny.com
SIC: 2339 Sportswear, women's
HQ: Premier Brands Group Holdings Llc
1441 Broadway
New York NY 10018
215 785-4000

(G-10880)
PREMIUM 5 KIDS LLC
Also Called: AG Kids
31 W 34th St (10001-3009)
PHONE......................................212 563-4999
Lucille Pagano, *Vice Pres*
Albert Pardo,
EMP: 15
SALES (est): 526K **Privately Held**
SIC: 2211 Apparel & outerwear fabrics, cotton

(G-10881)
PRESCRIBING REFERENCE INC
275 7th Ave Fl 10 (10001-6756)
PHONE......................................646 638-6000
William Pecover, *Ch of Bd*
Lee Maniscalco, *President*
Ian Griggs, *Editor*
Steve Barrett, *Vice Pres*
Michael Kriak, *CFO*
EMP: 85
SQ FT: 18,000
SALES (est): 3.5MM
SALES (corp-wide): 219.2MM **Privately Held**
SIC: 2721 Magazines: publishing only, not printed on site
HQ: Haymarket Media, Inc.
275 7th Ave Fl 10
New York NY 10001
646 638-6000

(G-10882)
PRESCRIPTIVES INC (DH)
Also Called: Estee Lauder
767 5th Ave (10153-0023)
PHONE......................................212 572-4400
Pamela Baxter, *President*
EMP: 7
SALES (est): 1.2MM **Publicly Held**
WEB: www.prescriptives.com
SIC: 2844 Toilet preparations
HQ: Estee Lauder Inc.
767 5th Ave Fl 1
New York NY 10153
212 572-4200

(G-10883)
PRESS GLASS NA INC (PA)
1345 Ave Of The Flr 2 (10105)
PHONE......................................212 631-3044
EMP: 3
SALES (est): 17.8MM **Privately Held**
SIC: 3231 Insulating glass: made from purchased glass; art glass: made from purchased glass

(G-10884)
PRESTEL PUBLISHING LLC
900 Broadway Ste 603 (10003-1237)
PHONE......................................212 995-2720
Stephen Hulburt, *Vice Pres*
▲ EMP: 8
SQ FT: 1,620
SALES (est): 1MM
SALES (corp-wide): 75.3MM **Privately Held**
SIC: 2731 Books: publishing only
HQ: Verlagsgruppe Random House Gmbh
Neumarkter Str. 28
Munchen 81673
894 136-0

(G-10885)
PRESTIGE GLOBAL NY SLS CORP
42 W 38th St Rm 802 (10018-0064)
PHONE......................................212 776-4322
Linda Tencek, *President*
EMP: 7 EST: 2015
SALES (est): 298.2K **Privately Held**
SIC: 2329 Riding clothes:, men's, youths' & boys'

(G-10886)
PREVAIL THERAPEUTICS INC
430 E 29th St Ste 940 (10016-8367)
PHONE......................................917 336-9310
Francois Nader, *Ch of Bd*
Asa Abeliovich, *President*
Brett Kaplan, *CFO*
Jeffrey Sevigny, *Chief Mktg Ofcr*
Yong Dai, *CTO*
EMP: 43
SQ FT: 17,526
SALES (est): 11.1MM **Privately Held**
SIC: 2836 Biological products, except diagnostic

(G-10887)
PRICING ENGINE INC
175 Varick St Fl 4 (10014-7412)
P.O. Box 221 (10276-0221)
PHONE......................................917 549-3289
Jeremy Kagan, *CEO*
Yagmur Coker, *CTO*
EMP: 10
SALES (est): 268.4K **Privately Held**
SIC: 7372 Business oriented computer software

(G-10888)
PRIDE & JOYS INC
Also Called: OLIVEA MATHEWS
1400 Broadway Rm 503 (10018-1044)
PHONE......................................212 594-9820
Eli Rousso, *Ch of Bd*
Rochelle Reis, *Corp Secy*
Neil Rousso, *Vice Pres*
EMP: 15
SQ FT: 4,000
SALES: 7.4MM **Privately Held**
SIC: 2339 2329 Sportswear, women's; knickers, dress (separate): men's & boys'

(G-10889)
PRIMARY WAVE PUBLISHING LLC
116 E 16th St Fl 9 (10003-2123)
PHONE......................................212 661-6990
Seth Faber, *Partner*
Justin Shukat, *Partner*
Robert Dippold, *VP Sls/Mktg*
Erica Emerson, *Controller*
Ramon Villa, *VP Finance*
EMP: 45
SALES (est): 1.1MM **Privately Held**
SIC: 2741 Miscellaneous publishing

(G-10890)
PRIME PACK LLC
Also Called: Prime Pharmaceutical
303 5th Ave Rm 1007 (10016-6681)
PHONE......................................732 253-7734
Sreedara Nagarajan, *Mng Member*
Amrita Gupta,
Lakshmi Nagarajan,
▲ EMP: 10
SQ FT: 13,598
SALES (est): 1.2MM **Privately Held**
SIC: 2834 Pharmaceutical preparations

▲ = Import ▼ =Export
◆ =Import/Export

(G-10891)
PRIME VIEW USA INC
36 W 44th St Ste 812 (10036-8105)
PHONE..................212 730-4905
Shay Giuili, *CEO*
▲ EMP: 5
SALES: 2MM **Privately Held**
SIC: 3663 Television broadcasting & communications equipment

(G-10892)
PRINCESS MUSIC PUBLISHING CO
1650 Broadway Ste 701 (10019-6966)
PHONE..................212 586-0240
Hal Webman, *Owner*
EMP: 20
SALES (est): 1MM **Privately Held**
SIC: 2741 Music books: publishing & printing

(G-10893)
PRINCIPIA PARTNERS LLC
140 Broadway Fl 46 (10005-1155)
PHONE..................212 480-2270
Sean Togher, *Exec VP*
Theresa Adams, *Mng Member*
Suzanne Brower, *Sr Software Eng*
Brian Donnally,
Woodward Hoffman,
EMP: 55
SALES (est): 4.9MM **Privately Held**
WEB: www.ppllc.com
SIC: 7372 8742 Business oriented computer software; financial consultant

(G-10894)
PRINT CITY CORP
165 W 29th St (10001-5101)
PHONE..................212 487-9778
Anna Wadolowska-Panagoda, *Ch of Bd*
Walter Panagoda, *President*
Buck Benik, *Executive*
EMP: 16
SALES (est): 545K **Privately Held**
SIC: 2759 Commercial printing

(G-10895)
PRINT MANAGEMENT GROUP INC
31 W 34th St Fl 7 (10001-3031)
PHONE..................212 213-1555
John Scalli, *President*
Toni Santaniello, *Prdtn Mgr*
Adriane Caproni, *Art Dir*
EMP: 7
SALES (est): 1.6MM **Privately Held**
SIC: 2752 Commercial printing, lithographic

(G-10896)
PRINT MEDIA INC
350 7th Ave Fl 12 (10001-1937)
PHONE..................212 563-4040
Jordan H Wachtell, *Ch of Bd*
▲ EMP: 100
SQ FT: 2,000
SALES (est): 11MM **Privately Held**
SIC: 2752 Commercial printing, offset

(G-10897)
PRINTECH BUSINESS SYSTEMS INC
519 8th Ave Fl 3 (10018-4594)
PHONE..................212 290-2542
Frank Passantino, *President*
Marc Zaransky, *Vice Pres*
Sue Teraghty, *Office Mgr*
EMP: 18
SQ FT: 15,000
SALES (est): 3.2MM **Privately Held**
WEB: www.printechny.com
SIC: 2789 2752 7374 2759 Binding only: books, pamphlets, magazines, etc.; commercial printing, lithographic; commercial printing, offset; optical scanning data service; promotional printing

(G-10898)
PRINTFACILITY INC
225 Broadway Fl 3 (10007-3904)
PHONE..................212 349-4009
Farah Khan, *CEO*
EMP: 8
SQ FT: 2,000

SALES (est): 670K **Privately Held**
WEB: www.printfacility.com
SIC: 2759 Commercial printing

(G-10899)
PRINTINGHOUSE PRESS LTD
10 E 39th St Rm 700 (10016-0111)
PHONE..................212 719-0990
Myron Schonfeld, *Chairman*
Sean Leary, *Production*
EMP: 6
SALES (est): 1MM **Privately Held**
WEB: www.phpny.com
SIC: 2752 Commercial printing, offset

(G-10900)
PRO DRONES USA LLC
115 E 57th St Fl 11 (10022-2120)
PHONE..................718 530-3558
Vivien Heriard Dubreuil,
EMP: 12 EST: 2015
SALES (est): 649.2K **Privately Held**
SIC: 3721 Aircraft

(G-10901)
PRO PUBLICA INC
155 Ave Of The Americas (10013-1507)
PHONE..................212 514-5250
Richard Tofel, *President*
Tim Golden, *Editor*
Stephanie Little, *Vice Pres*
Ragan Rhyne, *Vice Pres*
Barbara Zinkant, *Finance*
EMP: 52
SALES: 14.5MM **Privately Held**
SIC: 2741

(G-10902)
PROCTER & GAMBLE COMPANY
120 W 45th St Fl 3 (10036-4041)
PHONE..................646 885-4201
Brandon Lane, *Treasurer*
Nancy Medici, *Branch Mgr*
EMP: 150
SALES (corp-wide): 67.6B **Publicly Held**
SIC: 2844 Deodorants, personal
PA: The Procter & Gamble Company
1 Procter And Gamble Plz
Cincinnati OH 45202
513 983-1100

(G-10903)
PRODUCT DEVELOPMENT INTL LLC
Also Called: Pdi Fashion
215 W 40th St Fl 8 (10018-1575)
PHONE..................212 279-6170
Donald L Foss, *Mng Member*
Eric Chu,
▲ EMP: 9
SQ FT: 5,000
SALES (est): 1.1MM **Privately Held**
SIC: 2335 Women's, juniors' & misses' dresses

(G-10904)
PROFESSNAL SPT PBLICATIONS INC (PA)
Also Called: Touchdown
519 8th Ave (10018-6506)
PHONE..................212 697-1460
Mitchell Zeifman, *President*
Robert McIntosh, *Editor*
Martin Lewis, *Exec VP*
Marisa Kravitz, *Vice Pres*
James Scotti, *Vice Pres*
EMP: 70
SALES (est): 22.6MM **Privately Held**
WEB: www.pspsports.com
SIC: 2721 7941 Magazines: publishing only, not printed on site; sports promotion

(G-10905)
PROGENICS PHARMACEUTICALS INC (PA)
1 World Trade Ctr Fl 47 (10007-0089)
PHONE..................646 975-2500
Mark R Baker, *CEO*
Peter J Crowley, *Ch of Bd*
Benedict Osorio, *COO*
Vivien Wong, *Exec VP*
Bryce Tenbarge, *Senior VP*
EMP: 79
SQ FT: 26,000

SALES: 15.6MM **Publicly Held**
WEB: www.progenics.com
SIC: 2834 Pharmaceutical preparations

(G-10906)
PROGRESSIVE FIBRE PRODUCTS CO
160 Broadway Rm 1105 (10038-4212)
PHONE..................212 566-2720
Elliot Kozer, *President*
EMP: 40
SALES (est): 3.7MM **Privately Held**
WEB: www.fibrecase.com
SIC: 3161 Sample cases

(G-10907)
PROLINK INDUSTRIES INC
1407 Broadway Rm 3605 (10018-2364)
PHONE..................212 354-5690
▲ EMP: 10
SALES (est): 1.1MM **Privately Held**
SIC: 2389 Mfg Apparel/Accessories

(G-10908)
PROMENADE MAGAZINES INC
246 W 38th St F10 (10018-5805)
PHONE..................212 888-3500
Mellisa White, *CEO*
James White Sr, *President*
James White Jr, *Vice Pres*
Eva Jordan, *Bookkeeper*
EMP: 12 EST: 1934
SALES (est): 600K **Privately Held**
SIC: 2721 Magazines: publishing only, not printed on site

(G-10909)
PROMOTIONAL SALES BOOKS LLC
30 W 26th St Frnt (10010-2011)
PHONE..................212 675-0364
EMP: 5
SQ FT: 2,500
SALES (est): 410K **Privately Held**
SIC: 2732 Publisher

(G-10910)
PROMPT BINDERY CO INC
350 W 38th St (10018-5206)
PHONE..................212 675-5181
EMP: 12 EST: 1946
SQ FT: 5,800
SALES (est): 687.6K **Privately Held**
SIC: 2789 Bookbinding/Related Work

(G-10911)
PRONOVIAS USA INC
45 E 58th St (10022-1617)
PHONE..................212 897-6393
Alberto Palatchi, *Ch of Bd*
Joseluis Perez Herrero, *President*
Jordi Morral, *Exec VP*
Nicole Vega, *Manager*
▲ EMP: 30
SALES (est): 4MM
SALES (corp-wide): 28.7MM **Privately Held**
WEB: www.pronoviasusa.com
SIC: 2335 Gowns, formal
PA: Galma Grupo Corporativo S.L.
Calle Lagasca, 99 - Esc B 2 Plt 8 B 2 A
Madrid 28006
938 135-286

(G-10912)
PRONTO JEWELRY INC
23 W 47th St (10036-2826)
PHONE..................212 719-9455
Misak Terjinian, *President*
EMP: 23
SALES (est): 1.8MM **Privately Held**
SIC: 3911 Jewelry, precious metal

(G-10913)
PROOF 7 LTD
149 W 27th St Fl 4 (10001-6279)
PHONE..................212 680-1843
Joshua Cooper, *President*
Laurence Chandler, *Vice Pres*
Kadeem Buckham, *Production*
EMP: 10
SQ FT: 3,000

SALES (est): 1.2MM **Privately Held**
SIC: 2759 7336 7299 Card printing & engraving, except greeting; advertising literature: printing; catalogs: printing; announcements: engraved; graphic arts & related design; party planning service

(G-10914)
PROPER CLOTH LLC
495 Broadway Fl 6 (10012-4457)
PHONE..................646 964-4221
Joseph Skerritt, *Mng Member*
EMP: 8
SQ FT: 3,000
SALES (est): 942.6K **Privately Held**
SIC: 2311 Men's & boys' suits & coats

(G-10915)
PROPS DISPLAYS & INTERIORS
Also Called: Pdi
132 W 18th St (10011-5403)
PHONE..................212 620-3840
Stephen Sebbane, *President*
Wendy Isaacson, *President*
EMP: 15
SALES (est): 1.3MM **Privately Held**
SIC: 3993 3999 2431 Displays, paint process; stage hardware & equipment, except lighting; interior & ornamental woodwork & trim

(G-10916)
PROSPECT NEWS INC
6 Maiden Ln Fl 9 (10038-5134)
PHONE..................212 374-2800
Bernard Dankowski, *President*
Zhaniece Springer, *Admin Asst*
EMP: 13 EST: 2007
SALES (est): 545.4K **Privately Held**
SIC: 2711 Newspapers, publishing & printing

(G-10917)
PRYM FASHION AMERICAS LLC (DH)
Also Called: Sher Plastics
470 7th Ave (10018-7600)
PHONE..................212 760-9660
Richard Sher, *Mng Member*
Greg Adler, *Administration*
Cindy Sher,
EMP: 52
SALES (est): 1.4MM
SALES (corp-wide): 177.9K **Privately Held**
SIC: 3965 5131 Fasteners, buttons, needles & pins; piece goods & notions
HQ: Prym Fashion Gmbh
Zweifaller Str. 130
Stolberg (Rhld.) 52224
240 214-05

(G-10918)
PS38 LLC
Also Called: Public School
209 W 38th St Fl 5 (10018-4405)
PHONE..................212 302-1108
EMP: 7 EST: 2012
SALES (est): 301.2K **Privately Held**
SIC: 2311 2337 Men's & boys' suits & coats; suits: women's, misses' & juniors'

(G-10919)
PSYCHONOMIC SOCIETY INC
233 Spring St Fl 7 (10013-1522)
PHONE..................512 381-1494
EMP: 26
SQ FT: 6,000
SALES: 954.7K **Privately Held**
SIC: 2721 2789 2752 Periodical-Publish/Print Bookbinding/Related Work Lithographic Coml Print

(G-10920)
PTI-PACIFIC INC
16 W 32nd St Rm 306 (10001-0306)
PHONE..................212 414-8495
Simon Chong, *President*
▲ EMP: 5 EST: 2009
SALES (est): 9MM **Privately Held**
SIC: 2329 2339 2369 Men's & boys' athletic uniforms; women's & misses' outerwear; girls' & children's outerwear

(G-10921)
PTS FINANCIAL TECHNOLOGY LLC
1001 Ave Of The Americas (10018-5460)
PHONE..................................844 825-7634
Farid Naib, *CEO*
EMP: 40 **EST:** 1999
SALES (est): 1MM **Privately Held**
SIC: 7372 Application computer software

(G-10922)
PUBLIC RELATIONS SOC AMER INC (PA)
Also Called: PRSA
120 Wall St Fl 21 (10005-4024)
PHONE..................................212 460-1400
Joseph P Truncale, *CEO*
William Murray, *President*
Jeffrey P Julin, *Principal*
Errol Cockfield, *Vice Pres*
Jane Law, *Comms Mgr*
EMP: 50
SQ FT: 22,000
SALES: 12MM **Privately Held**
WEB: www.newyorkcity.com
SIC: 2721 8621 Trade journals: publishing only, not printed on site; professional membership organizations

(G-10923)
PUBLISHING GROUP AMERICA INC
Also Called: American Profile Magazine
60 E 42nd St Ste 1146 (10165-1146)
PHONE..................................646 658-0550
Peggy Bosco, *Branch Mgr*
EMP: 18
SALES (corp-wide): 5.8MM **Privately Held**
WEB: www.pubgroupofamerica.com
SIC: 2711 Newspapers: publishing only, not printed on site
PA: Publishing Group Of America, Inc.
　1200 Clinton St Ste 219
　Nashville TN 37203
　615 468-6000

(G-10924)
PUBLISHING SYNTHESIS LTD
39 Crosby St Apt 2n (10013-3254)
PHONE..................................212 219-0135
Otto H Barz, *Partner*
George Ernsberger, *Manager*
EMP: 6 **EST:** 1975
SQ FT: 1,000
SALES (est): 420K **Privately Held**
WEB: www.pubsyn.com
SIC: 2791 Typesetting

(G-10925)
PUGLISI & CO
800 3rd Ave Ste 902 (10022-7768)
PHONE..................................212 300-2285
Jeff Puglisi, *Branch Mgr*
EMP: 41
SALES (corp-wide): 2.9MM **Privately Held**
SIC: 1231 Anthracite mining
PA: Puglisi & Co.
　399 Park Ave Fl 37
　New York NY
　212 832-1110

(G-10926)
PUIG USA INC (HQ)
183 Madison Ave Fl 19 (10016-4501)
PHONE..................................917 208-3219
Marc Puig, *President*
Iliana Mauri, *Assistant VP*
Sergio Sainz, *Vice Pres*
Kathy Campos, *Director*
▲ **EMP:** 15
SALES (est): 2.3MM
SALES (corp-wide): 432.3MM **Privately Held**
SIC: 2844 Toilet preparations
PA: Puig Sl
　Plaza Europa, 46 - 48
　L'hospitalet De Llobregat 08902
　934 007-000

(G-10927)
PURE GREEN HOLDINGS INC
121 Nassau St (10038-2496)
PHONE..................................917 209-8811

Heather Levy, *Principal*
EMP: 10
SALES (est): 283.4K **Privately Held**
SIC: 2037 Fruit juices

(G-10928)
PURE TRADE US INC
347 5th Ave Rm 604 (10016-5031)
PHONE..................................212 256-1600
Stefane Ladous, *CEO*
▲ **EMP:** 40
SALES (est): 3.5MM **Privately Held**
SIC: 2652 3171 Setup paperboard boxes; women's handbags & purses

(G-10929)
PUREBASE NETWORKS INC
37 Wall St Apt 9a (10005-2019)
PHONE..................................646 670-8964
Steven Ridder, *CEO*
EMP: 8
SALES (est): 204.7K **Privately Held**
SIC: 7372 Business oriented computer software

(G-10930)
PURELY MAPLE LLC
902 Broadway Fl 6 (10010-6039)
P.O. Box 20784 (10025-1523)
PHONE..................................203 997-9309
ARI Tolwin, *CEO*
EMP: 15 **EST:** 2013
SALES (est): 936.4K **Privately Held**
SIC: 2086 Fruit drinks (less than 100% juice): packaged in cans, etc.

(G-10931)
PUREOLOGY RESEARCH LLC
565 5th Ave (10017-2413)
PHONE..................................212 984-4360
Pat Parenty, *General Mgr*
EMP: 18
SALES (est): 1.5MM
SALES (corp-wide): 4.4B **Privately Held**
WEB: www.pureology.com
SIC: 2844 Hair preparations, including shampoos
HQ: L'oreal Usa, Inc.
　10 Hudson Yards
　New York NY 10001
　212 818-1500

(G-10932)
PUTNAM ROLLING LADDER CO INC (PA)
32 Howard St (10013-3112)
P.O. Box 111, Hoboken NJ (07030-0111)
PHONE..................................212 226-5147
Warren R Monsees, *President*
K Laura Monsees, *Director*
Gregg Monsees, *Admin Sec*
▲ **EMP:** 15 **EST:** 1897
SQ FT: 45,000
SALES (est): 3.4MM **Privately Held**
WEB: www.putnamrollingladder.com
SIC: 2499 5084 Ladders, wood; woodworking machinery

(G-10933)
PVH CORP (PA)
200 Madison Ave Bsmt 1 (10016-3913)
P.O. Box 64945, Saint Paul MN (55164-0945)
PHONE..................................212 381-3500
Cheryl Abel-Hodges, *CEO*
Francis K Duane, *CEO*
Daniel Grieder, *CEO*
Emanuel Chirico, *Ch of Bd*
Stefan Larsson, *President*
◆ **EMP:** 100 **EST:** 1881
SQ FT: 209,000
SALES: 9.6B **Publicly Held**
WEB: www.pvh.com
SIC: 2321 2331 2253 3143 Men's & boys' dress shirts; sport shirts, men's & boys': from purchased materials; blouses, women's & juniors': made from purchased material; shirts, women's & juniors': made from purchased materials; sweaters & sweater coats, knit; shirts (outerwear), knit; men's footwear, except athletic; ready-to-wear apparel, women's; men's & boys' clothing stores

(G-10934)
PVH CORP
Also Called: Tommy Hilfiger
285 Madison Ave Fl 2 (10017-6437)
PHONE..................................212 549-6000
Laurent Albouy, *Managing Dir*
Leeron Quiroga, *District Mgr*
Betsy Grass, *Exec VP*
Jennifer Puetzer, *Exec VP*
Bradley Burchfield, *Vice Pres*
EMP: 6
SALES (corp-wide): 9.6B **Publicly Held**
SIC: 2321 2331 2253 3143 Men's & boys' dress shirts; sport shirts, men's & boys': from purchased materials; blouses, women's & juniors': made from purchased material; shirts, women's & juniors': made from purchased materials; sweaters & sweater coats, knit; shirts (outerwear), knit; men's footwear, except athletic; ready-to-wear apparel, women's; men's & boys' clothing stores
PA: Pvh Corp.
　200 Madison Ave Bsmt 1
　New York NY 10016
　212 381-3500

(G-10935)
PVH CORP
Van Heusen
200 Madison Ave Bsmt 1 (10016-3913)
PHONE..................................212 381-3800
Eric Lichtmess, *Vice Pres*
Kevin Burd, *Opers Staff*
Kristen Nakashian, *VP Sales*
Ken Duane, *Branch Mgr*
Alfred Bianchi, *Manager*
EMP: 7
SALES (corp-wide): 9.6B **Publicly Held**
WEB: www.pvh.com
SIC: 2329 2339 Men's & boys' sportswear & athletic clothing; sportswear, women's
PA: Pvh Corp.
　200 Madison Ave Bsmt 1
　New York NY 10016
　212 381-3500

(G-10936)
PVH CORP
Also Called: Van Heusen
404 5th Ave Fl 4 (10018-7566)
PHONE..................................212 502-6300
Allain Russo, *President*
EMP: 60
SALES (corp-wide): 9.6B **Publicly Held**
WEB: www.pvh.com
SIC: 2339 Women's & misses' outerwear
PA: Pvh Corp.
　200 Madison Ave Bsmt 1
　New York NY 10016
　212 381-3500

(G-10937)
PVH CORP
Also Called: Van Heusen
205 W 39th St Fl 4 (10018-3102)
PHONE..................................212 719-2600
Lauren Kinder, *Vice Pres*
Nick Cucci, *Opers Staff*
Ulrich Urimm, *Branch Mgr*
David Esser, *Manager*
Zev Krauss, *Manager*
EMP: 9
SALES (corp-wide): 9.6B **Publicly Held**
SIC: 2321 2331 Men's & boys' dress shirts; sport shirts, men's & boys': from purchased materials; blouses, women's & juniors': made from purchased material; shirts, women's & juniors': made from purchased materials
PA: Pvh Corp.
　200 Madison Ave Bsmt 1
　New York NY 10016
　212 381-3500

(G-10938)
PVI SOLAR INC
599 11th Ave Bby (10036-2110)
PHONE..................................212 280-2100
Paul Mladineo, *Managing Dir*
Ted Hasenstaub, *Exec VP*
Ed Shenker, *Exec VP*
EMP: 8

SALES (est): 642.1K **Privately Held**
SIC: 3674 3679 Integrated circuits, semiconductor networks, etc.; electronic loads & power supplies

(G-10939)
PWXYZ LLC
Also Called: Publishers Weekly
71 W 23rd St Ste 1608 (10010-4186)
PHONE..................................212 377-5500
George W Slowik Jr, *President*
Isaac Meisner, *General Mgr*
Andrew Albanese, *Editor*
Annie Coreno, *Editor*
Diane Patrick, *Editor*
EMP: 50
SALES (est): 952.8K **Privately Held**
SIC: 2741 Miscellaneous publishing

(G-10940)
Q COMMUNICATIONS INC
Also Called: Passport Magazine
247 W 35th St Rm 1200 (10001-1917)
PHONE..................................212 594-6520
Don Tuthill, *President*
Dan Bocchino, *Production*
Robert Adams, *Treasurer*
EMP: 7
SALES (est): 890K **Privately Held**
WEB: www.passportmagazine.net
SIC: 2721 Magazines: publishing only, not printed on site

(G-10941)
Q ED CREATIONS
Also Called: Savoritefactory
2 W 46th St Ste 1408 (10036-4502)
PHONE..................................212 391-1155
Ariel Assaf, *Owner*
Daniel Assaf, *Co-Owner*
◆ **EMP:** 1
SQ FT: 1,400
SALES: 3.7MM **Privately Held**
SIC: 3911 5094 Jewelry, precious metal; jewelry

(G-10942)
Q SQUARED DESIGN LLC
1133 Broadway Ste 1424 (10010-7941)
P.O. Box 1550, Sanibel FL (33957-1550)
PHONE..................................212 686-8860
Karen Scanlon, *COO*
Nancy Mosny, *Mng Member*
Rudolf Mosny,
▲ **EMP:** 25 **EST:** 2008
SALES (est): 2.9MM **Privately Held**
SIC: 3089 2392 Tableware, plastic; household furnishings

(G-10943)
QHI GROUP INCORPORATED
40 Wall St Ste 2866 (10005-1304)
PHONE..................................646 512-5727
Steven Quinn, *President*
EMP: 5 **EST:** 2010
SALES (est): 658.5K **Privately Held**
SIC: 3829 Thermometers & temperature sensors

(G-10944)
QLOGIX ENTERTAINMENT LLC
600 W 113th St 7b4 (10025-7952)
PHONE..................................215 459-6315
Shyno Mathew, *CEO*
Jennifer Appawu, *President*
EMP: 5
SALES (est): 125.8K **Privately Held**
SIC: 7372 7371 Educational computer software; custom computer programming services

(G-10945)
QMETIS INC
57 W 57th St Fl 4 (10019-2827)
PHONE..................................212 500-5000
Jack Fitzgibbons, *President*
EMP: 7
SALES (est): 334K **Privately Held**
SIC: 7372 Business oriented computer software

(G-10946)
QTALK PUBLISHING LLC
1 E Broadway Fl 4 (10038-1113)
PHONE..................................877 549-1841
Maurice Hazan, *Principal*

EMP: 7
SALES (est): 193.9K **Privately Held**
SIC: 2741 Miscellaneous publishing

(G-10947)
QUAD/GRAPHICS INC
3 Times Sq (10036-6564)
PHONE...................212 672-1300
Elizabeth Fowler-Oisson, *Sales Mgr*
Lawrence Kennedy, *Sales Staff*
Steve Stoma, *Manager*
EMP: 120
SALES (corp-wide): 4.1B **Publicly Held**
SIC: 2752 Commercial printing, offset
PA: Quad/Graphics Inc.
N61w23044 Harrys Way
Sussex WI 53089
414 566-6000

(G-10948)
QUAD/GRAPHICS INC
60 5th Ave Lowr Level (10011-8868)
PHONE...................212 206-5535
EMP: 509
SALES (corp-wide): 4.1B **Publicly Held**
SIC: 2752 Commercial printing, offset
PA: Quad/Graphics Inc.
N61w23044 Harrys Way
Sussex WI 53089
414 566-6000

(G-10949)
QUAD/GRAPHICS INC
375 Hudson St (10014-3658)
PHONE...................212 741-1001
Mike Horton, *Branch Mgr*
EMP: 509
SALES (corp-wide): 4.1B **Publicly Held**
SIC: 2752 Commercial printing, offset
PA: Quad/Graphics Inc.
N61w23044 Harrys Way
Sussex WI 53089
414 566-6000

(G-10950)
QUALITY PATTERNS INC
246 W 38th St Fl 9 (10018-9076)
PHONE...................212 704-0355
Mario Lipari, *President*
Joe Lipari, *Vice Pres*
EMP: 70
SQ FT: 14,000
SALES (est): 5.8MM **Privately Held**
WEB: www.qualitypatterns.com
SIC: 2335 2741 Women's, juniors' &
misses' dresses; miscellaneous publishing

(G-10951)
QUANTIFY ENERGY LLC
3 Columbus Cir Fl 15 (10019-8716)
PHONE...................917 268-1234
Sumanth Reddy, *Mng Member*
Avraj Sandhu,
EMP: 2
SALES (est): 15MM **Privately Held**
SIC: 3699 Electrical equipment & supplies

(G-10952)
QUARTET FINANCIAL SYSTEMS INC (PA)
1412 Broadway Rm 2300 (10018-9240)
PHONE...................845 358-6071
Kathleen Perrotte, *President*
Olivier Billiard, *Manager*
Julien BEC, *Manager*
Josh Lambert, *Software Dev*
David Cassonnet, *Director*
EMP: 15
SALES: 5.9MM **Privately Held**
SIC: 7372 Prepackaged software

(G-10953)
QUARTO GROUP INC (HQ)
276 5th Ave Rm 205 (10001-8308)
PHONE...................212 779-0700
Lawrence Orbach, *Chairman*
Maryke Neher, *Production*
Carolyn Bresh, *CFO*
Kate Kirby, *Director*
▲ EMP: 30
SALES (est): 48MM
SALES (corp-wide): 149.2MM **Privately Held**
WEB: www.quarto.com
SIC: 2731 Books: publishing only

PA: Quarto Group Inc(The)
The Old Brewery
London N7 9B
207 700-6700

(G-10954)
QUARTZ MEDIA LLC
675 6th Ave Ste 410 (10010-5100)
PHONE...................646 539-6604
Yinka Adegoke, *Editor*
Meredith Bennett-Smith, *Editor*
Sona Rai, *Comms Dir*
Oliver Staley, *Manager*
Liz Rioux-Christian, *Director*
EMP: 50
SALES (est): 6.6MM **Privately Held**
SIC: 2721 Magazines: publishing only, not
printed on site

(G-10955)
QUEST BEAD & CAST INC
Also Called: Quest Beads
49 W 37th St Fl 16 (10018-6226)
PHONE...................212 354-1737
Marcelle Rosenstrauch, *President*
▼ EMP: 8
SQ FT: 2,000
SALES (est): 510K **Privately Held**
WEB: www.questbeads.com
SIC: 3914 Pewter ware

(G-10956)
QUEST MEDIA LLC
Also Called: Quest Magazine
920 3rd Ave Fl 6 (10022-3627)
PHONE...................646 840-3404
Tykischa Jacobs, *Production*
Christopher Meigher,
EMP: 19
SQ FT: 9,000
SALES (est): 2.6MM **Privately Held**
SIC: 2721 Magazines: publishing only, not
printed on site

(G-10957)
QUILTED KOALA LTD
1384 Broadway Ste 15 (10018-6108)
PHONE...................800 223-5678
Stephanie Oppenheim, *CEO*
David Weinstein, *President*
EMP: 11
SALES (est): 148.2K **Privately Held**
SIC: 3171 5137 5632 Women's handbags
& purses; handbags; handbags

(G-10958)
QUINN AND CO OF NY LTD
48 W 38th St Ph (10018-6248)
PHONE...................212 868-1900
Florence Quinn, *President*
Morgan Painvin, *Exec VP*
John Frazier, *Officer*
EMP: 70
SALES: 10MM **Privately Held**
SIC: 2084 5141 7011 4724 Wines,
brandy & brandy spirits; food brokers; re-
sort hotel; travel agencies

(G-10959)
QUOGUE CAPITAL LLC
1285 Ave Of The Ave Fl 35 Flr 35 (10019)
PHONE...................212 554-4475
Wayne Rothbaum, *Mng Member*
EMP: 5 EST: 2001
SALES (est): 406.8K **Privately Held**
SIC: 2834 Pharmaceutical preparations

(G-10960)
QUOTABLE CARDS INC
611 Broadway Rm 615 (10012-2650)
PHONE...................212 420-7552
Gillian Simon, *CEO*
Lauren Dopkin, *Sales Mgr*
Carol Monte, *Director*
Kris Ohlsen, *Director*
▲ EMP: 6
SALES (est): 500K **Privately Held**
WEB: www.quotablecards.com
SIC: 2771 2782 Greeting cards; memo-
randum books, printed

(G-10961)
QUOVO INC (PA)
54 W 21st St Frnt 1 (10010-7319)
PHONE...................212 643-0695
Lowell Putnam, *CEO*

David Kaplowitz, *Vice Pres*
John Whitfield, *VP Engrg*
John Wellington, *Sales Dir*
Hayden Pirkle, *Marketing Staff*
EMP: 20
SALES (est): 3.9MM **Privately Held**
SIC: 7372 Application computer software

(G-10962)
QWORLDSTAR INC
200 Park Ave S Fl 8 (10003-1526)
PHONE...................212 768-4500
EMP: 8 EST: 2013
SALES (est): 470.7K **Privately Held**
SIC: 2741 Internet Publishing And Broad-
casting

(G-10963)
R & M GRAPHICS OF NEW YORK
121 Varick St Fl 9 (10013-1408)
PHONE...................212 929-0294
Mario Balzano, *President*
Ron Balzano, *Vice Pres*
EMP: 15 EST: 1991
SQ FT: 10,000
SALES: 1.5MM **Privately Held**
SIC: 2759 Commercial printing

(G-10964)
R & M INDUSTRIES INC
111 Broadway Rm 1112 (10006-1933)
PHONE...................212 366-6414
Erik Van Kreuninger, *CEO*
Metje Saffir, *Principal*
Robert Van Kreuninger, *Vice Pres*
▲ EMP: 14
SQ FT: 198,000
SALES (est): 995.9K **Privately Held**
SIC: 2392 Pillows, bed: made from pur-
chased materials; tablecloths: made from
purchased materials

(G-10965)
R & M RICHARDS INC (PA)
10 Times Sq Fl 4 (10018-1879)
PHONE...................212 921-8820
Mario Déllanno, *CEO*
Richard Dellanno, *President*
Robert Dellanno, *Vice Pres*
Robert Dellano, *Vice Pres*
Stephanie Louis, *Production*
▲ EMP: 106
SQ FT: 19,000
SALES (est): 26.8MM **Privately Held**
WEB: www.rmrich.com
SIC: 2337 2335 Women's & misses' suits
& skirts; women's, juniors' & misses'
dresses

(G-10966)
R & R GROSBARD INC
1156 Avenue Of The Amrcs (10036-2702)
PHONE...................212 575-0077
Robert Grosbard, *Ch of Bd*
Amish Shah, *COO*
Glendy Harinarain, *Controller*
EMP: 30
SALES (est): 3.3MM **Privately Held**
SIC: 3911 Jewelry apparel

(G-10967)
R R DONNELLEY & SONS COMPANY
Also Called: Studio 26
250 W 26th St Rm 402 (10001-6737)
PHONE...................646 755-8125
Mike James, *Manager*
EMP: 8
SALES (corp-wide): 6.8B **Publicly Held**
WEB: www.rrdonnelley.com
SIC: 2759 Commercial printing
PA: R. R. Donnelley & Sons Company
35 W Wacker Dr
Chicago IL 60601
312 326-8000

(G-10968)
R-PAC INTERNATIONAL CORP (PA)
132 W 36th St Fl 7 (10018-8825)
PHONE...................212 465-1818
Daniel Teitelbaum, *CEO*
Michael Teitelbaum, *President*
Cheryl Depalma, *Vice Pres*
Peter D Amico, *CFO*
Marian Brass, *Admin Asst*

◆ EMP: 40
SQ FT: 15,000
SALES (est): 8.9MM **Privately Held**
SIC: 2241 Labels, woven

(G-10969)
R-S RESTAURANT EQP MFG CORP (PA)
Also Called: Preferred Wholesale
272 Bowery (10012-3674)
PHONE...................212 925-0335
Chekee Ho, *President*
▲ EMP: 10
SQ FT: 2,500
SALES (est): 1.8MM **Privately Held**
SIC: 3589 5046 Commercial cooking &
foodwarming equipment; restaurant
equipment & supplies

(G-10970)
RADICLE FARM LLC
Also Called: Radicle Farm Company
394 Broadway Fl 5 (10013-6023)
P.O. Box 7361, Newark NJ (07107-0361)
PHONE...................315 226-3294
Christopher Washington, *CEO*
Jenna Blumenfeld, *Principal*
Tony Gibbons, *Principal*
Silvia Huerta, *Principal*
James Livengood, *Principal*
EMP: 5
SALES (est): 183K **Privately Held**
SIC: 2099 Salads, fresh or refrigerated

(G-10971)
RAG & BONE INDUSTRIES LLC (PA)
425 W 13th St Fl 3 (10014-1123)
PHONE...................212 278-8214
Kay Wright, *General Mgr*
Vanessa Abreu, *Vice Pres*
Greg Hubbert, *Vice Pres*
Lucia Contreras, *Store Mgr*
INA Bartkus, *Prdtn Mgr*
▲ EMP: 70
SALES (est): 42MM **Privately Held**
SIC: 2326 Men's & boys' work clothing

(G-10972)
RAILWORKS TRANSIT SYSTEMS INC (DH)
5 Penn Plz (10001-1810)
PHONE...................212 502-7900
Jeffrey M Levy, *President*
Daniel Brown, *Principal*
Gene Cellini, *Senior VP*
John August, *Vice Pres*
Geane Jospeh Celoini, *Vice Pres*
EMP: 19
SALES (est): 70.3MM
SALES (corp-wide): 1.4B **Privately Held**
SIC: 3531 Railway track equipment
HQ: Railworks Corporation
5 Penn Plz
New York NY 10001
212 502-7900

(G-10973)
RAINFOREST INC
Also Called: Rft
54 W 40th St (10018-2602)
PHONE...................212 575-7620
Jack Wu, *Ch of Bd*
Daisy Wu, *CFO*
▲ EMP: 10
SQ FT: 11,850
SALES (est): 2.7MM **Privately Held**
SIC: 2329 8742 6794 Men's & boys'
leather, wool & down-filled outerwear;
down-filled clothing: men's & boys'; jack-
ets (suede, leatherette, etc.), sport: men's
& boys'; marketing consulting services;
patent owners & lessors

(G-10974)
RALEIGH & DRAKE PBC (PA)
110 E 25th St Fl 3 (10010-2913)
PHONE...................212 625-8212
Patrick Sarkissian, *CEO*
Gilad Goren,
EMP: 7
SALES (est): 1.9MM **Privately Held**
SIC: 7372 Application computer software

(G-10975)
RALPH LAUREN CORPORATION (PA)
650 Madison Ave Fl C1 (10022-1070)
PHONE..................................212 318-7000
Ralph Lauren, *Ch of Bd*
David Lauren, *Vice Ch Bd*
Patrice Louvet, *President*
Valerie Hermann, *President*
Jane Hamilton Nielsen, *COO*
◆ EMP: 500 EST: 1967
SQ FT: 270,000
SALES: 6.3B **Publicly Held**
WEB: www.polo.com
SIC: **2325** 2321 2253 2323 Men's & boys' trousers & slacks; men's & boys' dress shirts; men's & boys' sports & polo shirts; shirts (outerwear), knit; sweaters & sweater coats, knit; ties, handsewn: made from purchased materials; topcoats, men's & boys': made from purchased materials; men's & boys' sportswear & athletic clothing; sweaters & sweater jackets: men's & boys'

(G-10976)
RAMSBURY PROPERTY US INC (DH)
Also Called: Benetton Services
601 5th Ave Fl 4 (10017-8258)
P.O. Box 6020, Somerset NJ (08875-6020)
PHONE..................................212 223-6250
Carlo Tunioli, *Vice Pres*
Diane Mravcak, *Vice Pres*
▲ EMP: 13
SQ FT: 10,000
SALES (est): 4.4MM
SALES (corp-wide): 863.3K **Privately Held**
SIC: **2329** 2339 5651 8742 Men's & boys' sportswear & athletic clothing; sportswear, women's; family clothing stores; marketing consulting services

(G-10977)
RAMSEY SOLUTIONS LLC
228 Park Ave S Ste 29075 (10003-1502)
PHONE..................................888 329-1055
Travis Ramsey, *CEO*
Carlos Ali, *COO*
Aldo Fernandez, *CTO*
EMP: 12
SALES (est): 88K
SALES (corp-wide): 2.2MM **Privately Held**
SIC: **7372** Prepackaged software
PA: A5 Corp.
6800 Koll Center Pkwy # 16
Pleasanton CA 94566
408 512-1583

(G-10978)
RAMY BROOK LLC
231 W 39th St Rm 720 (10018-1089)
PHONE..................................212 744-2789
Ira Rosenfeld, *COO*
George Moody, *Opers Mgr*
Nellie Roch, *Opers Mgr*
Richie Bucello, *Store Mgr*
Justine Brisacone, *Accounts Exec*
▲ EMP: 30
SQ FT: 5,000
SALES (est): 4.9MM **Privately Held**
SIC: **2331** Women's & misses' blouses & shirts

(G-10979)
RANDA ACCESSORIES LEA GDS LLC
417 5th Ave Fl 11 (10016-2238)
PHONE..................................212 354-5100
John Hastings, *Branch Mgr*
EMP: 100
SALES (corp-wide): 153.3MM **Privately Held**
SIC: **2387** 3161 3172 2389 Apparel belts; attache cases; briefcases; suitcases; wallets; suspenders; neckties, men's & boys': made from purchased materials
PA: Randa Accessories Leather Goods Llc
5600 N River Rd Ste 500
Rosemont IL 60018
847 292-8300

(G-10980)
RANDALL LOEFFLER INC
588 Broadway Rm 1203 (10012-5237)
PHONE..................................212 226-8787
Brian Murphy, *CEO*
Amanda Thomas, *COO*
Jessica L Randall, *Creative Dir*
▲ EMP: 30
SQ FT: 2,500
SALES (est): 5.6MM **Privately Held**
SIC: **3131** 7371 5699 Boot & shoe accessories; computer software development & applications; designers, apparel

(G-10981)
RASCO GRAPHICS INC
519 8th Ave Fl 18 (10018-4577)
PHONE..................................212 206-0447
Howard Frank, *President*
EMP: 6
SQ FT: 2,000
SALES (est): 570K **Privately Held**
SIC: **2752** Commercial printing, offset

(G-10982)
RASNA THERAPEUTICS INC
420 Lexington Ave # 2525 (10170-0002)
PHONE..................................646 396-4087
Kunwar Shailubhai, *CEO*
Alessandro Padova, *Ch of Bd*
James Tripp, *COO*
Tiziano Lazzaretti, *CFO*
EMP: 5
SQ FT: 3,011
SALES (est): 406.4K **Privately Held**
SIC: **2834** Pharmaceutical preparations

(G-10983)
RAVEN NEW YORK LLC
450 W 15th St (10011-7097)
PHONE..................................212 584-9690
Fax: 212 466-1808
▲ EMP: 6
SQ FT: 2,500
SALES (est): 710K **Privately Held**
SIC: **2331** 2335 Womens And Misses Blouses And Shirts, Nsk

(G-10984)
RAXON FABRICS CORP (HQ)
261 5th Ave (10016-7701)
PHONE..................................212 532-6816
Joe Berasi, *President*
Ruud Averson, *President*
Harry Ellis, *Vice Pres*
Claus Maenzsiebje, *Treasurer*
▲ EMP: 13 EST: 1947
SQ FT: 7,400
SALES (est): 4.8MM **Privately Held**
WEB: www.raxon.com
SIC: **2262** Silk broadwoven fabric finishing
PA: Vescom B.V.
V Diepenheim Scheltusln 32
Leusden
334 944-010

(G-10985)
RAY GRIFFITHS INC
303 5th Ave Rm 1901 (10016-6658)
PHONE..................................212 689-7209
Ray Griffiths, *Principal*
Kirsten Geary, *Marketing Staff*
EMP: 7
SALES (est): 457.8K **Privately Held**
SIC: **1499** Gem stones (natural) mining

(G-10986)
RAY MEDICA INC
505 Park Ave Ste 1400 (10022-9315)
PHONE..................................952 885-0500
Mary Fuller, *CFO*
EMP: 45
SALES (est): 1.9MM **Privately Held**
SIC: **3845** Electromedical equipment

(G-10987)
RAY THETA INC
31 W 34th St Fl 7 (10001-3031)
PHONE..................................646 757-4956
Mark Gazit, *CEO*
Erica Dardon, *Office Mgr*
Joel Kandy, *Business Dir*
EMP: 7
SALES (est): 45K **Privately Held**
SIC: **7372** Business oriented computer software

PA: Theta Ray Ltd
8 Hanagar
Hod Hasharon
722 287-777

(G-10988)
RAYDOOR INC
134 W 29th St Rm 909 (10001-5304)
PHONE..................................212 421-0641
Luke Sigel, *President*
Justin Brownell, *Project Mgr*
Theodore Fotopoulos, *Opers Mgr*
Catherine Isalguez, *Marketing Staff*
EMP: 6
SALES (est): 1MM **Privately Held**
WEB: www.raydoor.com
SIC: **3442** Metal doors, sash & trim

(G-10989)
RB DIAMOND INC
22 W 48th St Ste 904 (10036-1803)
PHONE..................................212 398-4560
Rafael Inoyatov, *Principal*
EMP: 5
SALES (est): 396.3K **Privately Held**
SIC: **3356** Gold & gold alloy bars, sheets, strip, etc.

(G-10990)
RDA HOLDING CO (PA)
Also Called: Rittlewood Holding Co
750 3rd Ave (10017-2703)
PHONE..................................914 238-1000
Harvey Golub, *CEO*
Fredric G Reynolds, *Ch of Bd*
Bonnie Kintzer, *President*
Randall Curran, *Chairman*
Albert L Perruzza, *Exec VP*
EMP: 24
SQ FT: 445,193
SALES (est): 1.1B **Privately Held**
SIC: **2721** 2731 5961 2741 Periodicals; book publishing; catalog & mail-order houses; miscellaneous publishing

(G-10991)
RDD PHARMA INC
3 Columbus Cir Fl 15 (10019-8716)
PHONE..................................302 319-9970
John Temperato, *CEO*
Mark Sirgo, *Ch of Bd*
Nir Barak, *Principal*
Arie Giniger, *Bd of Directors*
EMP: 5
SQ FT: 150
SALES (est): 280.1K **Privately Held**
SIC: **3841** Surgical & medical instruments

(G-10992)
REACTIVECORE LLC
79 Madison Ave Fl 8 (10016-7810)
PHONE..................................631 944-1618
Kenny Klepper, *CEO*
EMP: 5
SALES (est): 180.8K **Privately Held**
SIC: **7372** 7379 Business oriented computer software; computer related consulting services

(G-10993)
READERS DIGEST ASSN INCTHE
16 E 34th St Fl 14 (10016-4360)
PHONE..................................414 423-0100
Skip Dietz, *Mktg Dir*
Diane Jones, *Branch Mgr*
EMP: 16 **Privately Held**
WEB: www.rd.com
SIC: **2721** Magazines: publishing only, not printed on site
HQ: Trusted Media Brands, Inc.
750 3rd Ave Fl 3
New York NY 10017
914 238-1000

(G-10994)
REAL ESTATE MEDIA INC
120 Broadway Fl 5 (10271-1100)
PHONE..................................212 929-6976
EMP: 45
SALES (est): 3.9MM **Privately Held**
SIC: **2721** Periodicals-Publishing/Printing

(G-10995)
REALITY ANALYTICS INC (PA)
Also Called: Reality Ai
157 Columbus Ave (10023-6082)
PHONE..................................347 363-2200
Stuart Feffer, *CEO*
Jeff Sieracki, *CTO*
EMP: 3
SALES (est): 2MM **Privately Held**
SIC: **7372** Business oriented computer software

(G-10996)
REASON SOFTWARE COMPANY INC
228 Park Ave S Unit 74122 (10003-1502)
PHONE..................................646 664-1038
Andrew Newman, *CEO*
EMP: 10
SQ FT: 2,000
SALES (est): 324.8K **Privately Held**
SIC: **7372** Operating systems computer software

(G-10997)
REDBOOK MAGAZINE
224 W 57th St Lbby Fl22 (10019-3212)
PHONE..................................212 649-3331
Daniel Zucchi, *Principal*
EMP: 12
SALES (est): 1.4MM **Privately Held**
SIC: **2721** 7313 Magazines: publishing & printing; radio, television, publisher representatives

(G-10998)
REDKEN 5TH AVENUE NYC LLC
575 5th Ave Fl 23 (10017-2430)
PHONE..................................212 818-1500
Carolyn O'Connor, *Assistant VP*
Karen Zipp, *Vice Pres*
Anup Trivedi, *Research*
Kevin Bauman, *Controller*
Suzie Manofsky, *Marketing Staff*
▼ EMP: 134 EST: 1995
SALES (est): 18.1MM
SALES (corp-wide): 4.4B **Privately Held**
WEB: www.redken.com
SIC: **2844** Cosmetic preparations
HQ: L'oreal Usa, Inc.
10 Hudson Yards
New York NY 10001
212 818-1500

(G-10999)
REENTRY GAMES INC
215 E 5th St (10003-8563)
PHONE..................................646 421-0080
Andrew Kutruff, *President*
EMP: 5
SALES (est): 235.3K **Privately Held**
SIC: **7372** Home entertainment computer software

(G-11000)
REFINERY 29 INC (PA)
225 Broadway Fl 23 (10007-3728)
PHONE..................................212 966-3112
Philippe Von Borries, *Principal*
Christene Barberich, *Principal*
Piera Gelardi, *Principal*
Melissa Goidel, *Principal*
Justin Stesano, *Principal*
EMP: 88
SALES (est): 5.4MM **Privately Held**
SIC: **2741** Miscellaneous publishing

(G-11001)
REGAL EMBLEM CO INC
250 W Broadway Fl 2 (10013-2431)
P.O. Box 230695 (10023-0012)
PHONE..................................212 925-8833
Judith Nadelson, *President*
Michael Bottino, *Vice Pres*
EMP: 15 EST: 1931
SQ FT: 5,000
SALES (est): 1.7MM **Privately Held**
SIC: **2399** Emblems, badges & insignia: from purchased materials

(G-11002)
REINHOLD BROTHERS INC
799 Park Ave (10021-3275)
PHONE..................................212 867-8310
John Reinhold, *President*

▲ = Import ▼ =Export
◆ =Import/Export

EMP: 20
SALES (est): 1.5MM **Privately Held**
SIC: **3911** 5944 Jewel settings & mountings, precious metal; pearl jewelry, natural or cultured; jewelry, precious stones & precious metals

(G-11003)
RELIANT SECURITY
450 Fashion Ave Ste 503 (10123-0591)
PHONE.................................917 338-2200
Richard Newman, *CEO*
Mark Weiner, *Principal*
Sam Akiba, *Executive*
EMP: 23
SALES (est): 2.8MM **Privately Held**
SIC: **7372** Prepackaged software

(G-11004)
RELMADA THERAPEUTICS INC
750 3rd Ave Fl 9 (10017-2718)
PHONE.................................646 677-3853
Sergio Traversa, *CEO*
Danny KAO, *Senior VP*
Ottavio Vitolo, *Senior VP*
Gina Diguglielmo, *Vice Pres*
Michael D Becker, *CFO*
EMP: 20 EST: 2007
SALES (est): 2.5MM **Privately Held**
SIC: **2834** Pharmaceutical preparations

(G-11005)
RELX INC (DH)
Also Called: Reed Business Information
230 Park Ave Ste 700 (10169-0005)
PHONE.................................212 309-8100
Mark Kelsey, *CEO*
Maura Donovan, *Vice Pres*
Henry Z Horbaczewski, *Vice Pres*
Robin Sundaram, *Vice Pres*
Stephen Collier, *Engineer*
◆ EMP: 40
SQ FT: 30,000
SALES (est): 5.6B
SALES (corp-wide): 9.6B **Privately Held**
WEB: www.lexis-nexis.com
SIC: **2721** 2731 7389 7374 Trade journals: publishing only, not printed on site; books: publishing only; trade show arrangement; data processing & preparation; systems analysis or design

(G-11006)
RELX INC
249 W 17th St (10011-5390)
PHONE.................................212 463-6644
Cheryl Miller, *Manager*
EMP: 35
SALES (corp-wide): 9.6B **Privately Held**
WEB: www.lexis-nexis.com
SIC: **2721** Magazines: publishing only, not printed on site
HQ: Relx Inc.
230 Park Ave Ste 700
New York NY 10169
212 309-8100

(G-11007)
RELX INC
655 6th Ave (10010-5107)
PHONE.................................212 633-3900
Russell White, *President*
EMP: 260
SALES (corp-wide): 9.6B **Privately Held**
WEB: www.lexis-nexis.com
SIC: **2721** Periodicals
HQ: Relx Inc.
230 Park Ave Ste 700
New York NY 10169
212 309-8100

(G-11008)
REMAINS LIGHTING
130 W 28th St Frnt 1 (10001-6151)
PHONE.................................212 675-8051
David Calligeros, *Owner*
Jimmy Kaston, *General Mgr*
Hayley Mace, *Sales Staff*
Lauren Reed, *Sales Staff*
Alice Kriz, *Marketing Staff*
EMP: 20
SQ FT: 1,500
SALES (est): 2.5MM **Privately Held**
SIC: **3646** 3645 Commercial indusl & institutional electric lighting fixtures; residential lighting fixtures

(G-11009)
REMCODA   LLC
230 W 39th St Fl 10 (10018-4927)
PHONE.................................212 354-1330
Marc Garson,
EMP: 6
SALES (est): 294.3K **Privately Held**
SIC: **2992** Oils & greases, blending & compounding

(G-11010)
RENAISSANCE BIJOU LTD
20 W 47th St Ste 18 (10036-3303)
PHONE.................................212 869-1969
Elias Theodoropoulos, *President*
EMP: 8
SQ FT: 3,000
SALES (est): 680K **Privately Held**
SIC: **3911** Jewelry, precious metal

(G-11011)
RENAISSNCE CRPT TAPESTRIES INC
Also Called: Renaissance Global
200 Lexington Ave Rm 1006 (10016-6255)
PHONE.................................212 696-0080
Jan Soleimani, *President*
Jeffrey Soleimani, *Vice Pres*
Bergi Andonian, *Admin Sec*
▲ EMP: 12
SQ FT: 7,000
SALES (est): 1.5MM **Privately Held**
SIC: **2273** 2211 Rugs, hand & machine made; tapestry fabrics, cotton

(G-11012)
RENCO GROUP INC (PA)
Also Called: Renco Group of Companies, Inc.
1 Rockefeller Plz Fl 29 (10020-2021)
PHONE.................................212 541-6000
Ira Leon Rennert, *President*
ARI Rennert, *Chairman*
Marvin Koenig, *Exec VP*
John Binko, *Vice Pres*
Roger L Fay, *Vice Pres*
◆ EMP: 4
SQ FT: 10,000
SALES (est): 4.1B **Privately Held**
WEB: www.rencogroup.net
SIC: **3312** 3316 2514 2511 Sheet or strip, steel, cold-rolled: own hot-rolled; corrugating iron & steel, cold-rolled; metal kitchen & dining room furniture; wood household furniture; kitchen & dining room furniture; handbags, women's; cages, wire

(G-11013)
RENEGADE NATION LTD
434 Ave Of The Amer Fl 6 (10011-8411)
PHONE.................................212 868-9000
Jerry Eisner, *Principal*
Christopher Dixon, *CFO*
Gloria Winter, *Office Mgr*
Louis Arzonico, *Art Dir*
EMP: 15 EST: 1993
SQ FT: 4,400
SALES (est): 1.9MM **Privately Held**
WEB: www.renegadenation.com
SIC: **2782** Record albums

(G-11014)
RENEGADE NATION ONLINE LLC
434 Ave Of The Americas # 6 (10011-8411)
PHONE.................................212 868-9000
Jerome Eisner, *Accountant*
EMP: 8
SQ FT: 2,400
SALES (est): 265K **Privately Held**
SIC: **2741**

(G-11015)
REPERTOIRE INTERNATIONAL DE LI
Also Called: RILM
365 5th Ave Fl 3 (10016-4309)
PHONE.................................212 817-1990
Yun Fan, *Editor*
Maria Rose, *Editor*
Lori Rothstein, *Editor*
Rachael Brungard, *Assoc Editor*
Barbara Mackenzie, *Director*
EMP: 25

SALES: 3.7MM **Privately Held**
SIC: **2731** 2741 Book publishing; miscellaneous publishing

(G-11016)
REPUBLIC CLOTHING CORPORATION
Also Called: Republic Clothing Group
1411 Broadway Fl 37 (10018-3413)
PHONE.................................212 719-3000
Steven M Sall, *Ch of Bd*
Michael Warner, *President*
Henry McGuire, *Vice Pres*
Walker Choi, *CIO*
Betty Yeung, *Technical Staff*
▲ EMP: 30
SQ FT: 7,500
SALES (est): 10.5MM **Privately Held**
SIC: **2339** Women's & misses' outerwear

(G-11017)
REPUBLIC CLOTHING GROUP INC
1411 Broadway Fl 37 (10018-3413)
PHONE.................................212 719-3000
Michael Warner, *President*
Steven M Sall, *Chairman*
Jerry Kau, *Opers Mgr*
EMP: 150
SQ FT: 7,500
SALES (est): 3.3MM **Privately Held**
SIC: **2339** Aprons, except rubber or plastic: women's, misses', juniors'

(G-11018)
RESERVOIR MEDIA MANAGEMENT INC (PA)
75 Varick St Fl 9a (10013-1917)
PHONE.................................212 675-0541
Golnar Khosrowshahi, *CEO*
Rell Lafargue, *COO*
Donna Caseine, *Vice Pres*
Jeff McGrath, *Vice Pres*
Faith Newman, *Vice Pres*
EMP: 12
SALES: 1.2MM **Privately Held**
SIC: **2741** Music book & sheet music publishing

(G-11019)
RESONANT LEGAL MEDIA LLC (PA)
Also Called: Trialgraphix
1 Penn Plz Ste 1514 (10119-1514)
PHONE.................................800 781-3591
Richard S Pennell, *CEO*
Steven Stolberg, *President*
Luis E Otero, *Vice Pres*
Patrick Paulin, *Vice Pres*
Ana Miguel, *Admin Sec*
EMP: 90
SQ FT: 35,000
SALES (est): 28.2MM **Privately Held**
SIC: **2752** 7336 3993 2761 Commercial printing, offset; graphic arts & related design; signs & advertising specialties; manifold business forms

(G-11020)
RESOURCE PTRLM&PTROCHMCL INTL
3 Columbus Cir Fl 15 (10019-8716)
PHONE.................................212 537-3856
Damon Lee, *Ch of Bd*
Daunette Lee, *Vice Pres*
Akpan Ekpo, *Director*
EMP: 20
SALES (est): 423.4K **Privately Held**
SIC: **1311** Crude petroleum production

(G-11021)
RESTAURANT 570 8TH AVENUE LLC
Also Called: Wok To Walk
213 W 40th St Fl 3 (10018-1627)
PHONE.................................646 722-8191
Aviv Schwietzer,
EMP: 15
SALES (est): 1.5MM **Privately Held**
SIC: **2599** Food wagons, restaurant

(G-11022)
RESTORSEA LLC
641 Lexington Ave Fl 27 (10022-4503)
PHONE.................................212 828-8878
EMP: 7 EST: 2012
SALES (est): 1.2MM **Privately Held**
SIC: **2844** Mfg Toilet Preparations

(G-11023)
RETINA LABS (USA) INC
165 Broadway Ste 2301 (10006-1428)
PHONE.................................866 344-2692
Richard Pridham, *CEO*
EMP: 10
SALES (est): 221.8K **Privately Held**
SIC: **7372** Business oriented computer software

(G-11024)
RETROPHIN LLC
777 3rd Ave Fl 22 (10017-1401)
PHONE.................................646 564-3680
Martin Shkreli, *CEO*
Julio Gagne, *Vice Pres*
Richard Pagliery, *Vice Pres*
Christopher Porter, *Vice Pres*
Sally O'Hollaren, *Mktg Dir*
EMP: 8
SALES (est): 832.1K **Privately Held**
SIC: **2834** Pharmaceutical preparations

(G-11025)
REVIVAL SASH & DOOR LLC (PA)
135 E 57th St Bldg 15125 (10022-2050)
PHONE.................................973 500-4242
Mike Canizales, *Mng Member*
EMP: 6 EST: 2017
SALES (est): 2.1MM **Privately Held**
SIC: **3442** Sash, door or window: metal

(G-11026)
REVLON INC (PA)
1 New York Plz Fl 49 (10004-1961)
PHONE.................................212 527-4000
Debra G Perelman, *President*
Jon Levin, *General Mgr*
Sylvia Potter, *Business Mgr*
Iris Rauseo, *Business Mgr*
Carlos Barreto, *Vice Pres*
▲ EMP: 277
SQ FT: 153,000
SALES: 2.5B **Publicly Held**
WEB: www.revlon.com
SIC: **2844** Toilet preparations; cosmetic preparations; perfumes & colognes; hair preparations, including shampoos

(G-11027)
REVLON CONSUMER PRODUCTS CORP (HQ)
1 New York Plz (10004-1901)
PHONE.................................212 527-4000
Ronald O Perelman, *Ch of Bd*
Gianni Pieraccioni, *COO*
Kiki Gregware, *Vice Pres*
Juan R Figuereo, *CFO*
Johanna Chandler, *Credit Staff*
▲ EMP: 277
SQ FT: 91,000
SALES: 2.5B **Publicly Held**
SIC: **3421** 2844 Clippers, fingernail & toenail; scissors, hand; cosmetic preparations

(G-11028)
REVMAN INTERNATIONAL INC (DH)
Also Called: Revman Distribution Center
350 5th Ave Fl 70 (10118-7000)
PHONE.................................212 894-3100
Richard Roman, *President*
Normand Savaria, *Senior VP*
Hebe Schetcher, *CFO*
Peter Roman, *Sales Staff*
Cynthia Beck, *Manager*
◆ EMP: 40
SQ FT: 20,000
SALES (est): 31.6MM **Privately Held**
WEB: www.revman.com
SIC: **2391** 2392 Draperies, plastic & textile: from purchased materials; comforters & quilts: made from purchased materials

HQ: Kaltex North America, Inc.
350 5th Ave Ste 7100
New York NY 10118
212 894-3200

(G-11029)
REVOL USA LLC
41 Madison Ave Ste 1904 (10010-2337)
PHONE...........................678 456-8671
Raphael Palomo, *Mng Member*
▲ EMP: 10
SALES (est): 1.1MM
SALES (corp-wide): 2.4MM **Privately Held**
SIC: 3469 Porcelain enameled products & utensils
HQ: Revol Porcelaine Sa
3 Rue Hector Revol
Saint-Uze 26240
475 039-981

(G-11030)
REVOLUTIONWEAR INC
1745 Broadway Fl 17 (10019-4642)
PHONE...........................617 669-9191
Mathias Ingvarsson, *President*
▲ EMP: 5
SALES (est): 368.2K **Privately Held**
SIC: 2322 Men's & boys' underwear & nightwear

(G-11031)
REYNOLDS METALS COMPANY LLC (HQ)
390 Park Ave (10022-4608)
PHONE...........................212 518-5400
Tomas Mar Sigurdsson, *President*
Francesco Bassoli, *Vice Pres*
Robert Bear, *Vice Pres*
Amador Cardenas, *Vice Pres*
John Kenna, *Vice Pres*
◆ EMP: 1 EST: 1928
SALES (est): 1.3B
SALES (corp-wide): 13.4B **Publicly Held**
SIC: 3411 Aluminum cans
PA: Alcoa Corporation
201 Isabella St Ste 500
Pittsburgh PA 15212
412 315-2900

(G-11032)
RFP LLC
Also Called: Bridal Guide
228 E 45th St Fl 11 (10017-3345)
PHONE...........................212 838-7733
Barry Rosenbloom, *Partner*
Yelena Malinovskaya, *Partner*
Mike Rosenbloom, *Partner*
Jeff Hendlin, *Publisher*
Naima Difranco, *Editor*
EMP: 35
SQ FT: 11,000
SALES (est): 5.3MM **Privately Held**
WEB: www.bridalguide.com
SIC: 2721 4724 Magazines: publishing only, not printed on site; travel agencies

(G-11033)
RG BARRY CORPORATION
Also Called: Dearfoams Div
9 E 37th St Fl 11 (10016-2822)
PHONE...........................212 244-3145
Howard Eisenberg, *Manager*
EMP: 10
SALES (corp-wide): 94.2MM **Privately Held**
WEB: www.rgbarry.com
SIC: 3142 House slippers
HQ: R. G. Barry Corporation
13405 Yarmouth Rd Nw
Pickerington OH 43147
614 864-6400

(G-11034)
RG GLASS CREATIONS INC
Also Called: R G Glass
1441 Broadway Ste 28 (10018-1905)
PHONE...........................212 675-0030
Edward Geyman, *President*
Joseph Laporta, *Controller*
Maria Roman, *Administration*
EMP: 38
SALES (est): 7.8MM **Privately Held**
SIC: 3211 Construction glass

(G-11035)
RHODA LEE INC
77 W 55th St Apt 4k (10019-4920)
PHONE...........................212 840-5700
Michael Laufer, *President*
Henry Alcalay, *Vice Pres*
Audrey Laufer, *Vice Pres*
▲ EMP: 75 EST: 1947
SQ FT: 11,000
SALES (est): 6.2MM **Privately Held**
SIC: 2331 2337 2339 Blouses, women's & juniors': made from purchased material; skirts, separate: women's, misses' & juniors'; slacks: women's, misses' & juniors'

(G-11036)
RIBZ LLC
1407 Broadway Rm 1402 (10018-2838)
PHONE...........................212 764-9595
EMP: 5
SALES (est): 330K **Privately Held**
SIC: 2389 Mfg Apparel/Accessories

(G-11037)
RICHEMONT NORTH AMERICA INC
Also Called: Iwc New York Btq
535 Madison Ave (10022-4214)
PHONE...........................212 355-7052
Schellmoser Andrea, *Branch Mgr*
EMP: 5
SALES (corp-wide): 15.7B **Privately Held**
SIC: 3873 Watches, clocks, watchcases & parts
HQ: Richemont North America, Inc.
645 5th Ave Fl 5
New York NY 10022
212 891-2440

(G-11038)
RICHEMONT NORTH AMERICA INC
Also Called: Vacheron New York Btq
729 Madison Ave (10065-8003)
PHONE...........................212 644-9500
EMP: 5
SALES (corp-wide): 15.7B **Privately Held**
SIC: 3873 Watches, clocks, watchcases & parts
HQ: Richemont North America, Inc.
645 5th Ave Fl 5
New York NY 10022
212 891-2440

(G-11039)
RICHLINE GROUP INC
Eclipse Design Div
245 W 29th St Rm 900 (10001-5396)
PHONE...........................212 643-2908
Eric Frid, *Branch Mgr*
EMP: 45
SALES (corp-wide): 225.3B **Publicly Held**
WEB: www.aurafin.net
SIC: 3911 Earrings, precious metal
HQ: Richline Group, Inc.
1385 Broadway Fl 14
New York NY 10018

(G-11040)
RICHLINE GROUP INC
1385 Broadway Fl 12 (10018-6118)
PHONE...........................212 764-8454
EMP: 194
SALES (corp-wide): 194.6B **Publicly Held**
SIC: 3911 5094 Mfg Precious Metal Jewelry Whol Jewelry/Precious Stones
HQ: Richline Group, Inc.
1385 Broadway Fl 12
New York NY 10018
212 886-6000

(G-11041)
RICHLINE GROUP INC
Also Called: Aurafin Oroamerica
1385 Broadway Fl 12 (10018-6118)
PHONE...........................914 699-0000
EMP: 177
SALES (corp-wide): 194.6B **Publicly Held**
SIC: 3911 Mfg Precious Metal Jewelry

HQ: Richline Group, Inc.
1385 Broadway Fl 12
New York NY 10018
212 886-6000

(G-11042)
RICHLOOM FABRICS CORP (PA)
261 5th Ave Fl 12 (10016-7794)
PHONE...........................212 685-5400
James Richman, *Ch of Bd*
Fred M Richman, *President*
Ralph Geller, *Vice Pres*
Marvin Karp, *CFO*
Sidney J Silverman, *Admin Sec*
◆ EMP: 10
SQ FT: 12,000
SALES (est): 33.4MM **Privately Held**
SIC: 2391 5131 2392 Curtains & draperies; drapery material, woven; household furnishings

(G-11043)
RICHLOOM FABRICS GROUP INC (PA)
Also Called: Berkshire Weaving
261 5th Ave Fl 12 (10016-7794)
PHONE...........................212 685-5400
Great Neck Richman, *CEO*
James Richman, *Ch of Bd*
Sean Prouty, *Vice Pres*
Rich Wold, *Finance Dir*
Patrizia Fox, *Manager*
▲ EMP: 5
SQ FT: 1,500
SALES (est): 1.8MM **Privately Held**
SIC: 2392 2391 Blankets, comforters & beddings; curtains & draperies

(G-11044)
RIMOWA INC (PA)
Also Called: Rimowa Distribution
598 Madison Ave Fl 8 (10022-1670)
PHONE...........................214 360-4268
Jason Schmidt, *Regional Mgr*
Robert Cochrant, *Exec VP*
Wilson Frias, *Asst Mgr*
Thomas Overton, *Associate*
▲ EMP: 13
SALES (est): 2MM **Privately Held**
SIC: 3161 Clothing & apparel carrying cases

(G-11045)
RINGS WIRE INC
Also Called: Rome Fastener
246 W 38th St Rm 501 (10018-9089)
PHONE...........................212 741-9779
Dr Stanley Reiter, *President*
EMP: 5
SALES (corp-wide): 2.4MM **Privately Held**
SIC: 3965 Fasteners, snap; buckles & buckle parts
PA: Rings Wire Inc
257 Depot Rd
Milford CT 06460
203 874-6719

(G-11046)
RIRI USA INC
350 5th Ave Ste 6700 (10118-6704)
PHONE...........................212 268-3866
L Benjamin Howell II, *Ch of Bd*
▲ EMP: 6
SQ FT: 5,000
SALES (est): 553.9K
SALES (corp-wide): 66.9MM **Privately Held**
SIC: 3965 Zipper
HQ: Riri Sa
Via Della Regione Veneto 3
Padova PD 35127
049 899-6611

(G-11047)
RISION INC
306 E 78th St Apt 1b (10075-2243)
PHONE...........................212 987-2628
Kate Cornick, *CEO*
Earle Harper, *COO*
Ryan O'Donnell, *Vice Pres*
EMP: 7 EST: 2015
SALES (est): 299.7K **Privately Held**
SIC: 7372 7389 Business oriented computer software;

(G-11048)
RISK SOCIETY MANAGEMENT PUBG
Also Called: Risk Management Magazine
655 3rd Ave Fl 2 (10017-9130)
PHONE...........................212 286-9364
Jack Hampton, *Exec Dir*
EMP: 43
SALES (est): 1.7MM
SALES (corp-wide): 15.3MM **Privately Held**
SIC: 2721 Magazines: publishing only, not printed on site
PA: Risk And Insurance Management Society, Inc.
1407 Broadway Fl 29
New York NY 10018
212 655-6030

(G-11049)
RITCHIE CORP
263 W 38th St Fl 13 (10018-0280)
PHONE...........................212 768-0083
Lynn Ritchie, *President*
▲ EMP: 16 EST: 1990
SQ FT: 3,000
SALES (est): 1.4MM **Privately Held**
WEB: www.lynn-ritchie.com
SIC: 2339 Sportswear, women's

(G-11050)
RIVIERA SUN INC
Also Called: Vilebrequin
512 Fashion Ave Fl 30 (10018-0839)
PHONE...........................212 546-9220
Stacey Bell, *Store Mgr*
Jessica Odwazny, *Opers Staff*
Sabrina Ruggeri, *Accountant*
Estefania Garcia-Correa, *Accounts Exec*
Joshua Josevski, *Marketing Mgr*
EMP: 7
SALES (corp-wide): 1.4MM **Privately Held**
SIC: 2253 Bathing suits & swimwear, knit
PA: Riviera Sun Inc
512 7th Ave Fl 30
New York NY 10018
212 546-9220

(G-11051)
RIZZOLI INTL PUBLICATIONS INC (DH)
300 Park Ave S Fl 4 (10010-5399)
PHONE...........................212 387-3400
Antonio Polito, *President*
Chris Pangborn, *General Mgr*
Gloria Ahn, *Editor*
Ron Broadhurst, *Editor*
Charles Myer, *Vice Pres*
▲ EMP: 40
SALES (est): 14.8MM
SALES (corp-wide): 432.7K **Privately Held**
WEB: www.rizzoliusa.com
SIC: 2731 5192 5942 5961 Books: publishing only; books; book stores; books, mail order (except book clubs)
HQ: Rizzoli Education Spa
Via Arnoldo Mondadori 1
Segrate MI 20090
028 470-71

(G-11052)
RIZZOLI INTL PUBLICATIONS INC
Also Called: Universe Publishing
300 Park Ave S Fl 3 (10010-5399)
PHONE...........................212 387-3572
Antonio Polito, *President*
EMP: 15
SALES (corp-wide): 432.7K **Privately Held**
SIC: 2731 Book publishing
HQ: Rizzoli International Publications, Inc.
300 Park Ave S Fl 4
New York NY 10010
212 387-3400

(G-11053)
RIZZOLI INTL PUBLICATIONS INC
Also Called: Amica Magazine
300 Park Ave Frnt 4 (10022-7404)
PHONE...........................212 308-2000
Imma Vaccaro, *Manager*

EMP: 12
SALES (corp-wide): 432.7K **Privately Held**
SIC: 2741 Miscellaneous publishing
HQ: Rizzoli International Publications, Inc.
300 Park Ave S Fl 4
New York NY 10010
212 387-3400

(G-11054)
RJM2 LTD
241 W 37th St Rm 926 (10018-6963)
PHONE..........................212 944-1660
Richard Weinsieder, *President*
Meryl Weinsieder, *Vice Pres*
▲ **EMP:** 5
SALES (est): 487.2K **Privately Held**
WEB: www.rjm2ltd.com
SIC: 2389 Men's miscellaneous accessories

(G-11055)
RLE INDUSTRIES LLC
Also Called: Robert Lighting & Energy
1175 York Ave Apt 15e (10065-7175)
PHONE..........................973 276-1444
Scott Koenig, *CEO*
Louis A Bani, *President*
Marvin Koenig, *Chairman*
◆ **EMP:** 35
SQ FT: 20,000
SALES (est): 13.2MM **Privately Held**
WEB: www.rleindustries.com
SIC: 3646 8748 Ornamental lighting fixtures, commercial; energy conservation consultant

(G-11056)
RND ENTERPRISES INC
Also Called: Next Magazine
446 W 33rd St (10001-2601)
PHONE..........................212 627-0165
David Moyal, *President*
EMP: 4
SALES (est): 1MM **Privately Held**
SIC: 2721 Magazines: publishing & printing

(G-11057)
RND FOOD SERVICE INC
88 W Broadway (10007-1195)
PHONE..........................917 291-0061
Thomas Nowakowski, *President*
EMP: 10
SALES: 165K **Privately Held**
SIC: 2051 Bakery: wholesale or wholesale/retail combined

(G-11058)
ROADRUNNER RECORDS INC (PA)
1290 Ave Of The Americas (10104-0101)
PHONE..........................212 274-7500
Jones Nachsin, *President*
Jason Martin, *Vice Pres*
Austin Stephens, *Director*
Phil Kaso, *Regional*
EMP: 46
SQ FT: 8,000
SALES (est): 6.3MM **Privately Held**
WEB: www.roadrunnerrecords.com
SIC: 3652 Magnetic tape (audio): prerecorded

(G-11059)
ROBELL RESEARCH INC
Also Called: Supersmile
655 Madison Ave Fl 24 (10065-8043)
PHONE..........................212 755-6577
Irwin Smigel, *CEO*
Lucia Smigel, *President*
Joel Levy, *COO*
Phil Mussman, *Sales Dir*
▲ **EMP:** 8
SALES (est): 1.9MM **Privately Held**
SIC: 2844 5122 Oral preparations; mouthwashes; toiletries

(G-11060)
ROBERT DANES DANES INC (PA)
481 Greenwich St Apt 5b (10013-1398)
PHONE..........................212 226-1351
Rachel Danes, *President*
Robert Danes, *Treasurer*
EMP: 4
SQ FT: 1,500

SALES: 1.6MM **Privately Held**
WEB: www.robertdanes.com
SIC: 2331 Women's & misses' blouses & shirts

(G-11061)
ROBERT J DELUCA ASSOCIATES
Also Called: Rjd Associates
260 Riverside Dr Apt 8a (10025-5259)
PHONE..........................845 357-3212
Robert J Deluca, *President*
Donna Novarro, *Opers Staff*
EMP: 1 **EST:** 1996
SQ FT: 500
SALES (est): 1.8MM **Privately Held**
SIC: 3399 Iron ore recovery from open hearth slag

(G-11062)
ROBERTO COIN INC (PA)
579 5th Ave Fl 17 (10017-8760)
PHONE..........................212 486-4545
Anthony Peter Webster, *Ch of Bd*
Nicole Villa, *Store Mgr*
▼ **EMP:** 13
SQ FT: 3,500
SALES (est): 2.9MM **Privately Held**
WEB: www.robertocoin.com
SIC: 3911 Jewelry, precious metal

(G-11063)
ROBESPIERRE INC
Also Called: Nanette Lepore Showroom
214 W 39th St Ph Ste 602 (10018-4404)
PHONE..........................212 764-8810
Megan Darling, *Manager*
EMP: 8
SALES (corp-wide): 15.9MM **Privately Held**
WEB: www.nanettelepore.com
SIC: 2339 Sportswear, women's
PA: Robespierre, Inc.
225 W 35th St Ste 801
New York NY 10001
212 594-0012

(G-11064)
ROBIN STANLEY INC
Also Called: Pearltek
1212 Avenue Of The Americ (10036-1602)
PHONE..........................212 871-0007
Stanley Robin, *President*
EMP: 6 **EST:** 1975
SALES (est): 510K **Privately Held**
SIC: 3911 Pearl jewelry, natural or cultured

(G-11065)
ROBLY DIGITAL MARKETING LLC
93 Leonard St Apt 6 (10013-3459)
PHONE..........................917 238-0730
Adam Robinson, *Mng Member*
EMP: 40
SALES (est): 966.9K **Privately Held**
SIC: 7372 Prepackaged software

(G-11066)
ROCCO BORMIOLI GLASS CO INC (PA)
41 Madison Ave Ste 1603 (10010-2236)
PHONE..........................212 719-0606
Davide Sereni, *Ch of Bd*
Rocco Bormioli, *President*
Michael Marchitto, *Opers Staff*
Maurizio Amari, *Treasurer*
▲ **EMP:** 30 **EST:** 1978
SALES (est): 4.3MM **Privately Held**
SIC: 3221 Glass containers

(G-11067)
ROCHE TCRC INC
420 E 29th St Fl 15 Flr 15 (10016)
PHONE..........................800 626-3553
Judith Dunn, *CEO*
EMP: 7
SALES (est): 824.2K
SALES (corp-wide): 57.2B **Privately Held**
SIC: 2834 Pharmaceutical preparations
PA: Roche Holding Ag
Grenzacherstrasse 124
Basel BS 4058
616 881-111

(G-11068)
ROCKET PHARMACEUTICALS INC (PA)
350 5th Ave Ste 7530 (10118-7501)
PHONE..........................646 440-9100
Roderick Wong, *Ch of Bd*
Gaurav Shah, *President*
Kinnari Patel, *COO*
Kamran Alam, *Senior VP*
Deirdre Odonnell, *Opers Mgr*
EMP: 20
SQ FT: 4,400
SALES (est): 2.9MM **Publicly Held**
WEB: www.inotekcorp.com
SIC: 2834 Pharmaceutical preparations

(G-11069)
ROCKPORT PA LLC (PA)
505 5th Ave Fl 26 (10017-4910)
PHONE..........................212 482-8580
Leo Budin, *Manager*
Manoj Abraham, *Technical Staff*
William Trepp,
EMP: 10
SALES (est): 2.2MM **Privately Held**
SIC: 7372 Prepackaged software

(G-11070)
RODEM INCORPORATED
Also Called: Galian Handbags
120 W 29th St Frnt A (10001-5596)
PHONE..........................212 779-7122
John Woo, *General Mgr*
▲ **EMP:** 10
SALES (est): 765.6K **Privately Held**
SIC: 3171 Women's handbags & purses

(G-11071)
ROFFE ACCESSORIES INC
833 Broadway Apt 4 (10003-4700)
PHONE..........................212 213-1440
Murray Roffe, *Ch of Bd*
James Barr, *Vice Pres*
Alison Hauser, *Vice Pres*
Mark Ptak, *Vice Pres*
Laura Bach, *VP Sales*
▲ **EMP:** 30
SQ FT: 50,000
SALES (est): 3.8MM **Privately Held**
SIC: 2321 2323 5136 Men's & boys' furnishings; men's & boys' neckwear; neckwear, men's & boys'

(G-11072)
ROGAN LLC
330 Bowery (10012-2414)
PHONE..........................212 680-1407
Kevin Ryan, *Branch Mgr*
EMP: 5
SALES (corp-wide): 2.4MM **Privately Held**
WEB: www.roganandcompany.com
SIC: 2335 Women's, juniors' & misses' dresses
PA: Rogan, Llc
270 Bowery 3
New York NY 10012
646 496-9339

(G-11073)
ROGAN LLC (PA)
270 Bowery 3 (10012-3674)
PHONE..........................646 496-9339
Kylea Vignovich, *Prdtn Mgr*
Natalie Marshall, *Sales Executive*
Kristina Papilion, *Sales Executive*
Rogan Gregory, *Creative Dir*
Cole Prottas, *Executive*
▲ **EMP:** 25
SALES (est): 2.4MM **Privately Held**
WEB: www.roganandcompany.com
SIC: 2335 Women's, juniors' & misses' dresses

(G-11074)
ROGER & SONS INC
268 Bowery Frnt 6 (10012-3992)
PHONE..........................212 226-4734
Carl Saitta, *Ch of Bd*
Anthony Saitta, *Ch of Bd*
Maria Saitta, *President*
Joe Cirone, *Vice Pres*
EMP: 8
SQ FT: 15,000

SALES (est): 2.1MM **Privately Held**
SIC: 3589 5046 5719 Commercial cooking & foodwarming equipment; restaurant equipment & supplies; kitchenware

(G-11075)
ROGERS GROUP INC
Also Called: Ferrara Manufacturing
318 W 39th St Fl 4 (10018-1493)
PHONE..........................212 643-9292
Joe Ferrara, *Ch of Bd*
Carolyn Ferrara, *President*
Joseph Ferrara, *Vice Pres*
Chris Byers, *Project Mgr*
Kimberly Lockhart, *QC Mgr*
EMP: 50
SQ FT: 25,000
SALES (est): 4MM **Privately Held**
SIC: 2369 2339 Girls' & children's outerwear; women's & misses' outerwear

(G-11076)
ROLI USA INC
100 5th Ave (10011-6903)
PHONE..........................412 600-4840
Patrick Jacob, *Exec VP*
Elizabeth Frascoia, *Opers Staff*
Danny Siger, *Manager*
EMP: 15 **EST:** 2015
SALES (est): 689.4K **Privately Held**
SIC: 3931 Musical instruments

(G-11077)
ROLLING STONE MAGAZINE
1290 Ave Of The Amer Fl 2 (10104-0295)
PHONE..........................212 484-1616
R Brownridge, *Principal*
John Gruber, *Controller*
Demetra Balodimas, *Accounts Mgr*
EMP: 9
SALES (est): 749.3K **Privately Held**
WEB: www.rollingstone.com
SIC: 2741 2721 Miscellaneous publishing; periodicals

(G-11078)
ROMA INDUSTRIES LLC
12 W 37th St Fl 10 (10018-7379)
PHONE..........................212 268-0723
Paul Aglietti, *Vice Pres*
Kristin Franz, *Manager*
Howard Baum, *Director*
EMP: 8
SALES (corp-wide): 44.1MM **Privately Held**
WEB: www.watchstraps.com
SIC: 3172 Watch straps, except metal
PA: Roma Industries Llc
12821 Starkey Rd Ste 4500
Largo FL 33773
727 545-9009

(G-11079)
ROMANCE & CO INC
2 W 47th St Ste 1111 (10036)
PHONE..........................212 382-0337
Uriel Kaykov, *CEO*
EMP: 6
SALES (est): 305.4K **Privately Held**
SIC: 1499 5094 Diamond mining, industrial; diamonds (gems)

(G-11080)
RONNI NICOLE GROUP LLC
1400 Broadway Rm 2102 (10018-0649)
PHONE..........................212 764-1000
Ronnie Russell, *President*
Ouida Oliver, *Vice Pres*
Ale Barbera, *Production*
Andy Hilowitz, *VP Human Res*
Cheryl Jeffries, *Sales Mgr*
◆ **EMP:** 35
SQ FT: 2,500
SALES (est): 4.1MM **Privately Held**
SIC: 2335 Women's, juniors' & misses' dresses

(G-11081)
ROO INC
Also Called: Aura
41 E 11th St Fl 11 (10003-4602)
PHONE..........................212 905-6100
Maximus Yaney, *President*
EMP: 14

SALES (est): 10MM **Privately Held**
SIC: 3699 Security control equipment & systems

(G-11082)
ROSEMONT PRESS INCORPORATED (PA)
253 Church St Apt 2 (10013-3438)
PHONE..................212 239-4770
James J Reardon, *Ch of Bd*
Tom Ryan, *Vice Pres*
Patricia Reardon, *Manager*
▲ EMP: 48 EST: 1963
SQ FT: 12,800
SALES (est): 8.2MM **Privately Held**
WEB: www.rosemontpress.com
SIC: 2752 2789 Commercial printing, offset; bookbinding & related work

(G-11083)
ROSEN MANDELL & IMMERMAN INC
Also Called: Rmi Printing
121 Varick St Rm 301 (10013-1408)
PHONE..................212 691-2277
Steve Visoky, *President*
EMP: 24
SQ FT: 3,500
SALES (est): 2.8MM **Privately Held**
WEB: www.rmiprinting.com
SIC: 2789 2752 Bookbinding & related work; commercial printing, lithographic

(G-11084)
ROSEN PUBLISHING GROUP INC
29 E 21st St Fl 2 (10010-6256)
P.O. Box 29278 (10087-9278)
PHONE..................212 777-3017
Roger C Rosen, *President*
Holly Cefrey, *Editor*
Gina Hayn, *Vice Pres*
Christopher Brand, *Mktg Dir*
Bruce Richards, *Marketing Staff*
▲ EMP: 150
SQ FT: 12,000
SALES (est): 40.9MM **Privately Held**
WEB: www.rosenpublishing.com
SIC: 2731 Books: publishing only

(G-11085)
ROSETTI HANDBAGS AND ACC (DH)
350 5th Ave Lbby 9 (10118-0109)
PHONE..................646 839-7945
Jane Thompson, *President*
▲ EMP: 45
SQ FT: 4,000
SALES (est): 7MM **Privately Held**
SIC: 2389 Men's miscellaneous accessories
HQ: Gbg Usa Inc.
350 5th Ave Lbby 11
New York NY 10118
646 839-7000

(G-11086)
ROSY BLUE INC (HQ)
529 5th Ave Fl 12 (10017-4676)
PHONE..................212 687-8838
Aashish Jhaveri, *Ch of Bd*
Dipu Mehta, *Ch of Bd*
Shyam Jagirdar, *Vice Pres*
EMP: 35
SQ FT: 9,000
SALES (est): 4.8MM
SALES (corp-wide): 177.9K **Privately Held**
WEB: www.rosyblue.com
SIC: 3911 5094 Jewelry, precious metal; diamonds (gems)

(G-11087)
ROUGH DRAFT PUBLISHING LLC
Also Called: Proof Magazine
1916 Old Chelsea Sta (10113)
PHONE..................212 741-4773
Stephen Davis,
EMP: 15
SALES (est): 1.1MM **Privately Held**
SIC: 2721 Magazines: publishing only, not printed on site

(G-11088)
ROUGH GUIDES US LTD
345 Hudson St Fl 4 (10014-4536)
PHONE..................212 414-3635
Martin Dunford, *Exec Dir*
▲ EMP: 75 EST: 1982
SALES (est): 3.9MM **Privately Held**
WEB: www.roughguides.com
SIC: 2741 Miscellaneous publishing

(G-11089)
ROYAL MIRACLE CORP
2 W 46th St Ste 909 (10036-4502)
PHONE..................212 921-5797
Edmond Elyassian, *President*
EMP: 30
SQ FT: 5,000
SALES (est): 20.2MM **Privately Held**
WEB: www.royalmiracle.com
SIC: 3911 Jewelry, precious metal

(G-11090)
ROYAL NEWS CORP
Also Called: Royal Media Group
8 W 38th St Rm 901 (10018-6239)
PHONE..................212 564-8972
Jonathan Hornblass, *President*
Molly Stewart, *Vice Pres*
Rakib Mohiuddin, *Controller*
Jason Rosen, *Sales Staff*
Skylar Taylor, *Marketing Staff*
EMP: 12
SQ FT: 2,000
SALES (est): 1.2MM **Privately Held**
WEB: www.momentic.com
SIC: 2711 Newspapers, publishing & printing

(G-11091)
ROYAL PROMOTION GROUP INC
Also Called: Rpg
119 W 57th St Ste 906 (10019-2401)
PHONE..................212 246-3780
Bruce E Teitelbaum, *CEO*
Ellen L Friedman, *Exec VP*
Andrea Millner, *Exec VP*
Eric Williams, *Exec VP*
Ajay Khanna, *CFO*
▲ EMP: 60
SQ FT: 20,000
SALES (est): 9.8MM **Privately Held**
WEB: www.royalpromo.com
SIC: 3993 Displays & cutouts, window & lobby

(G-11092)
ROYALTY NETWORK INC (PA)
224 W 30th St Rm 1007 (10001-1077)
PHONE..................212 967-4300
Frank Liwall, *President*
Renato Olivari, *Senior VP*
Daniel Abowd, *Vice Pres*
Lawson Higgins, *Vice Pres*
EMP: 8
SQ FT: 2,500
SALES (est): 739.8K **Privately Held**
WEB: www.roynet.com
SIC: 2741 Patterns, paper: publishing & printing

(G-11093)
RP55 INC
230 W 39th St Fl 7 (10018-4977)
PHONE..................212 840-4035
Ron Poisson, *Manager*
EMP: 6
SALES (corp-wide): 9.1MM **Privately Held**
SIC: 2329 Men's & boys' sportswear & athletic clothing
PA: Rp55, Inc.
520 Viking Dr
Virginia Beach VA 23452
757 428-0300

(G-11094)
RSL MEDIA LLC
Also Called: New York Enterprise Report
1001 Ave Of The Ave Fl 11 Flr 11 (10018)
PHONE..................212 307-6760
Robert Lebin,
EMP: 9

SALES (est): 1MM **Privately Held**
SIC: 2721 2741 Magazines: publishing only, not printed on site; miscellaneous publishing

(G-11095)
RTR BAG & CO LTD
127 W 26th St Rm 301 (10001-6979)
PHONE..................212 620-0011
Ron Raznick, *President*
▲ EMP: 6
SALES (est): 553.7K **Privately Held**
SIC: 2673 2674 Plastic bags: made from purchased materials; shopping bags: made from purchased materials

(G-11096)
RUBY NEWCO LLC
1211 Ave Of The Americas (10036-8701)
PHONE..................212 852-7000
Keith Rupert Murdoch, *CEO*
EMP: 6
SALES (est): 228.2K
SALES (corp-wide): 10B **Publicly Held**
SIC: 2711 2721 6289 Newspapers, publishing & printing; magazines: publishing only, not printed on site; statistical reports (periodicals): publishing & printing; financial reporting; stock quotation service
HQ: News Preferred Holdings Inc
20 Westport Rd
Wilton CT 06897
203 563-6483

(G-11097)
RUDOLF FRIEDMAN INC
42 W 48th St Ste 1102 (10036-1701)
PHONE..................212 869-5070
Alexander Nadaner, *President*
Fay Nadaner, *Treasurer*
Celena Hecht, *Admin Sec*
EMP: 12 EST: 1946
SQ FT: 1,200
SALES (est): 940K **Privately Held**
WEB: www.rudolffriedmann.com
SIC: 3911 Jewelry, precious metal

(G-11098)
RUMSON ACQUISITION LLC
Also Called: Stephen Dweck
1385 Broadway Fl 9 (10018-6001)
PHONE..................718 349-4300
Jack Rahmey, *President*
EMP: 18
SQ FT: 4,500
SALES: 3MM **Privately Held**
SIC: 3911 Jewelry, precious metal

(G-11099)
RUNS INC
14 Wall St Fl 203420 (10005-2101)
PHONE..................212 618-1201
EMP: 50
SALES (est): 787.2K **Privately Held**
SIC: 7372 Prepackaged Software Services

(G-11100)
RUSSIAN STANDARD VODKA USA INC (PA)
Also Called: Roust USA
232 Madison Ave Fl 16 (10016-2909)
PHONE..................212 679-1894
Leonid Yangarber, *CEO*
Marianna Kosheleva, *CEO*
Michael Stoner, *President*
Steve Ballard, *Division Mgr*
Giulio Bertozzi, *General Mgr*
◆ EMP: 5
SALES (est): 1.6MM **Privately Held**
SIC: 2085 Vodka (alcoholic beverage)

(G-11101)
RVC ENTERPRISES LLC (PA)
Also Called: Dereon/24 K Style
1384 Broadway Fl 17 (10018-0508)
P.O. Box 607 (10150-0607)
PHONE..................212 391-4600
Victor Azrak, *Mng Member*
Charles Azrak,
Reuben Azrak,
▲ EMP: 29
SALES (est): 8.3MM **Privately Held**
SIC: 2339 Women's & misses' outerwear

(G-11102)
RYAN GEMS INC
20 E 46th St Rm 500 (10017-9284)
PHONE..................212 697-0149
Edison Akhavan, *President*
Khin Chit, *Accounts Mgr*
▲ EMP: 38
SQ FT: 4,500
SALES (est): 9MM **Privately Held**
WEB: www.ryangems.com
SIC: 3911 Jewelry, precious metal

(G-11103)
RYLAND PETERS & SMALL INC
341 E 116th St (10029-1502)
PHONE..................646 791-5410
David Peters, *President*
▲ EMP: 6
SALES (est): 586.9K **Privately Held**
WEB: www.rylandpeters.com
SIC: 2731 Books: publishing only

(G-11104)
S & C BRIDAL LLC (PA)
1407 Broadway Fl 41 (10018-2348)
PHONE..................212 789-7000
Stanley Cayre,
Amin Cayre,
Hank Shalom,
▲ EMP: 12
SQ FT: 10,000
SALES (est): 5.2MM **Privately Held**
WEB: www.usangels.com
SIC: 2361 5641 Girls' & children's dresses, blouses & shirts; children's wear

(G-11105)
S & C BRIDALS LLC
Also Called: US Angels
1407 Broadway Fl 41 (10018-2348)
PHONE..................213 624-4477
David Gardner, *Branch Mgr*
EMP: 8
SALES (corp-wide): 5.2MM **Privately Held**
SIC: 2361 5641 Girls' & children's dresses, blouses & shirts; children's wear
PA: S & C Bridal Llc
1407 Broadway Fl 41
New York NY 10018
212 789-7000

(G-11106)
S & S MANUFACTURING CO INC (PA)
1375 Broadway Fl 2 (10018-7073)
PHONE..................212 444-6000
Kirk Gellin, *Co-President*
Robert Sobel, *Co-President*
Robert Frederick, *Vice Pres*
▲ EMP: 75
SQ FT: 21,000
SALES (est): 5.7MM **Privately Held**
SIC: 2331 2339 Blouses, women's & juniors': made from purchased material; sportswear, women's

(G-11107)
S C MAGAZINE
275 7th Ave Fl 10 (10001-6756)
PHONE..................646 638-6018
Amit Yoran, *Principal*
Richard Scalise, *Manager*
Oliver McAteer, *Assoc Editor*
▲ EMP: 7 EST: 2010
SALES (est): 444.9K **Privately Held**
SIC: 2721 Magazines: publishing only, not printed on site

(G-11108)
S G I
40 E 52nd St Frnt A (10022-5911)
PHONE..................917 386-0385
Richard L Miller, *Principal*
EMP: 5
SALES (est): 401.4K **Privately Held**
SIC: 3577 Computer peripheral equipment

(G-11109)
S P BOOKS INC
99 Spring St Fl 3 (10012-3929)
PHONE..................212 431-5011
Pearson Allen, *President*
EMP: 6

SALES: 1.5MM **Privately Held**
WEB: www.spibooks.com
SIC: 2731 5192 Book publishing; books

(G-11110)
S ROTHSCHILD & CO INC (PA)
Also Called: RCM Design Division
1407 Broadway Fl 10 (10018-3271)
PHONE..................................212 354-8550
Isidore Friedman, *CEO*
Mark Friedman, *President*
William Mitchell, *CFO*
◆ EMP: 110 EST: 1881
SQ FT: 50,000
SALES (est): 8MM **Privately Held**
SIC: 2369 Girls' & children's outerwear

(G-11111)
SAAD COLLECTION INC (PA)
1165 Broadway Ste 305 (10001-7450)
PHONE..................................212 937-0341
Farzana Younus, *President*
EMP: 9
SALES (est): 1.3MM **Privately Held**
SIC: 2321 2331 Men's & boys' furnishings;
women's & misses' blouses & shirts

(G-11112)
**SABIN ROBBINS PAPER
COMPANY**
455 E 86th St (10028-6400)
PHONE..................................513 874-5270
Thomas Roberts, *President*
EMP: 30
SALES (est): 10.4MM **Privately Held**
SIC: 2621 Building paper, sheathing

(G-11113)
**SACKS AND COMPANY NEW
YORK (PA)**
119 W 57th St Ste 512 (10019-2302)
PHONE..................................212 741-1000
Carla Sacks, *President*
Ethan Stuber, *Personnel Assit*
EMP: 9
SALES (est): 849.8K **Privately Held**
SIC: 2741 Miscellaneous publishing

(G-11114)
SAFE SKIES LLC (PA)
Also Called: TSA Luggage Locks
954 3rd Ave Ste 504 (10022-2013)
PHONE..................................888 632-5027
David Tropp, *Mng Member*
▲ EMP: 9
SQ FT: 70,000
SALES (est): 106.4MM **Privately Held**
SIC: 3429 Locks or lock sets

(G-11115)
SAGE AUDIO VIDEO TECH LLC
53 W 36th St Rm 605 (10018-7991)
PHONE..................................212 213-1523
EMP: 42
SALES (est): 1.3MM **Privately Held**
SIC: 3651 Household audio & video equip-
ment

(G-11116)
SAKONNET TECHNOLOGY LLC
11 E 44th St Fl 1000 (10017-0058)
PHONE..................................212 849-9267
Alarik Myrin, *Partner*
Melanie Penachio, *Vice Pres*
EMP: 30
SALES (est): 2.5MM **Privately Held**
WEB: www.sknt.com
SIC: 7372 Business oriented computer
software

(G-11117)
SALE 121 CORP
1324 Lexington Ave # 111 (10128-1145)
PHONE..................................240 855-8988
Mohammad Naz, *Branch Mgr*
EMP: 99
SALES (corp-wide): 3.5MM **Privately
Held**
SIC: 3572 8748 7371 7373 Disk drives,
computer; systems engineering consult-
ant, ex. computer or professional; com-
puter software development; systems
software development services

PA: Sale 121 Corp
1467 68th Ave
Sacramento CA 95822
888 233-7667

(G-11118)
SALES HACKER INC
505 E 14th St Apt 5h (10009-2904)
P.O. Box 503, Armonk (10504-0503)
PHONE..................................516 660-2836
Max Altschuler, *CEO*
EMP: 6
SALES (est): 139K
SALES (corp-wide): 4.3MM **Privately
Held**
SIC: 7372 8742 Business oriented com-
puter software; marketing consulting serv-
ices
PA: Outreach Corporation
333 Elliott Ave W Ste 500
Seattle WA 98119
206 235-3672

(G-11119)
**SALES TAX ASSET RCEIVABLE
CORP**
255 Greenwich St Fl 6 (10007-2422)
PHONE..................................212 788-5874
Allan Anders, *President*
Jay Olson, *Treasurer*
EMP: 3
SALES: 170.4MM **Privately Held**
SIC: 3953 Embossing seals, corporate &
official

(G-11120)
SALMCO JEWELRY CORP
Also Called: Bay Sales Company
22 W 32nd St Fl 16 (10001-1698)
PHONE..................................212 695-8792
Errol Salm, *President*
Morton Salm, *Principal*
Lance Salm, *Manager*
▲ EMP: 17
SQ FT: 6,000
SALES (est): 2.6MM **Privately Held**
WEB: www.baysalesinc.com
SIC: 3961 Costume jewelry, ex. precious
metal & semiprecious stones

(G-11121)
SALONCLICK LLC
Also Called: Min New York
117 Crosby St (10012-3301)
PHONE..................................718 643-6793
Chad Muranczyk,
EMP: 12
SQ FT: 2,000
SALES (est): 2MM **Privately Held**
SIC: 2844 Hair coloring preparations; hair
preparations, including shampoos

(G-11122)
**SALSA PROFESSIONAL
APPAREL LLC**
Also Called: Giclee Unique Apparel
1441 Broadway Fl 3 (10018-1905)
PHONE..................................212 575-6565
Gigi De Jesus-Frerichs,
▲ EMP: 5
SQ FT: 980
SALES (est): 5MM **Privately Held**
SIC: 3842 2339 2326 2311 Clothing, fire
resistant & protective; service apparel,
washable: women's; work apparel, except
uniforms; service apparel (baker, barber,
lab, etc.), washable: men's; work uniforms; firemen's uniforms: made from purchased materials; military uniforms, men's
& youths': purchased materials; men's &
boys' uniforms

(G-11123)
SALUTEM GROUP LLC
44 Wall St Fl 12 (10005-2433)
PHONE..................................347 620-2640
Mikhail Abarshalin, *Principal*
EMP: 7
SALES (est): 660.5K **Privately Held**
SIC: 2834 Pharmaceutical preparations

(G-11124)
SAM SALEM & SON LLC
302 5th Ave Fl 4 (10001-3604)
PHONE..................................212 695-6020
Amit Nanda, *Vice Pres*

Jesse Salem, *Mng Member*
Sam Salem,
Carey Sutton,
◆ EMP: 13
SQ FT: 1,800
SALES (est): 4.1MM **Privately Held**
SIC: 2299 Linen fabrics

(G-11125)
SAMOSS GROUP LTD (PA)
Also Called: Samuel H Moss
213 W 35th St Rm 1301 (10001-0206)
PHONE..................................212 239-6677
Julius Hirsch, *President*
Ranning Marks, *Vice Pres*
Humberto Estrada, *Manager*
EMP: 30
SQ FT: 9,000
SALES (est): 1.7MM **Privately Held**
WEB: www.thesamossgrp.com
SIC: 3953 Marking devices

(G-11126)
SAMUEL FRENCH INC (PA)
235 Park Ave S Fl 5 (10003-1405)
PHONE..................................212 206-8990
Nathan Collins, *Ch of Bd*
Charles Nostrand, *President*
Zachary Orts, *Chief*
Merle Cosgrove, *Vice Pres*
Richard Spana, *Treasurer*
EMP: 45 EST: 1830
SQ FT: 17,000
SALES (est): 6.7MM **Privately Held**
WEB: www.samuelfrench.com
SIC: 2731 5942 5192 Books: publishing &
printing; book stores; books

(G-11127)
SAMUEL SCHULMAN FURS INC
Also Called: Alexandre Furs
150 W 30th St Fl 13 (10001-4185)
PHONE..................................212 736-5550
Edwin L Schulman, *President*
Larry Schulman, *Vice Pres*
Stanley R Schulman, *Treasurer*
EMP: 25 EST: 1940
SQ FT: 12,000
SALES (est): 1.4MM **Privately Held**
SIC: 2371 Fur coats & other fur apparel;
jackets, fur

(G-11128)
SAN ESTERS CORPORATION
Also Called: W A American
55 E 59th St Fl 1900a (10022-1706)
PHONE..................................212 223-0020
Yoshiro Inoue, *President*
EMP: 15
SALES (est): 3MM **Privately Held**
WEB: www.sanester.com
SIC: 2869 Amines, acids, salts, esters

(G-11129)
SANCTUARY BRANDS LLC (PA)
Also Called: Tailorbyrd
70 W 40th St Fl 5 (10018-2626)
PHONE..................................212 704-4014
Larry Stemerman, *CEO*
Traci Young, *President*
◆ EMP: 18
SQ FT: 100
SALES: 100MM **Privately Held**
SIC: 2329 5136 5611 Riding clothes:,
men's, youths' & boys'; men's & boys'
clothing; men's & boys' clothing stores

(G-11130)
SANDBOX BRANDS INC
26 W 17th St Lbby (10011-5710)
PHONE..................................212 647-8877
David Barber, *President*
Tom Hubben, *Vice Pres*
EMP: 7 EST: 1997
SALES: 490K **Privately Held**
WEB: www.sandboxbrands.com
SIC: 3944 Games, toys & children's vehi-
cles

(G-11131)
SANDOW MEDIA LLC
101 Park Ave Fl 4 (10178-0300)
PHONE..................................646 805-0200
Brandon Sherrod, *Opers Staff*
Joshua Hash, *Senior Engr*
Jacqueline Nelson, *VP Bus Dvlpt*

Nicole Wieder, *Marketing Staff*
William Kirkland, *Branch Mgr*
EMP: 10
SALES (corp-wide): 86.3MM **Privately
Held**
SIC: 2721 Magazines: publishing only, not
printed on site
PA: Sandow Media, Llc
3651 Fau Blvd Ste 200
Boca Raton FL 33431
561 961-7700

(G-11132)
**SANGUINE GAS EXPLORATION
LLC**
152 W 57th St Fl 4100 (10019-3322)
PHONE..................................212 582-8555
Randy Nelson, *Branch Mgr*
EMP: 26
SALES (corp-wide): 104.3MM **Privately
Held**
SIC: 1382 Oil & gas exploration services
PA: Sanguine Gas Exploration, L.L.C.
110 W 7th St Ste 2700
Tulsa OK 74119
918 494-6070

(G-11133)
SANOY INC
Also Called: Bonnie J
19 W 36th St Fl 11 (10018-7699)
PHONE..................................212 695-6384
Larry Jonas, *President*
Bonnie Jonas, *Vice Pres*
EMP: 28
SQ FT: 5,000
SALES (est): 4.1MM **Privately Held**
SIC: 3911 3961 Jewelry, precious metal;
costume jewelry

(G-11134)
SANTEE PRINT WORKS (PA)
58 W 40th St Fl 11 (10018-2638)
PHONE..................................212 997-1570
Martin Barocas, *Chairman*
Leon Barocas, *Vice Pres*
Gregg Fabrizio, *Plant Supt*
Kent Taylor, *Prdtn Mgr*
Jerry Blackmon, *Comptroller*
▲ EMP: 500 EST: 1949
SQ FT: 1,500,000
SALES (est): 102MM **Privately Held**
WEB: www.classiccottons.com
SIC: 2261 Screen printing of cotton broad-
woven fabrics; printing of cotton broadwo-
ven fabrics

(G-11135)
SAPPHIRE SYSTEMS INC (HQ)
405 Lexington Ave Fl 49 (10174-0002)
PHONE..................................212 905-0100
Clare Howard, *Business Mgr*
Gregory Smith, *Business Mgr*
Uys Moller, *Vice Pres*
Donna Jones, *Project Mgr*
Heather Linder, *Project Mgr*
EMP: 10
SALES (est): 1.5MM
SALES (corp-wide): 47.1MM **Privately
Held**
SIC: 7372 Business oriented computer
software
PA: Sapphire Systems Limited
32 London Bridge Street
London SE1 9
207 648-2022

(G-11136)
**SARATOGA LIGHTING
HOLDINGS LLC (PA)**
535 Madison Ave Fl 4 (10022-4291)
PHONE..................................212 906-7800
Christian L Oberbeck,
Damon H Ball,
Richard A Petrocelli,
▲ EMP: 3
SALES (est): 62.2MM **Privately Held**
SIC: 3641 3645 3646 3648 Electric
lamps & parts for generalized applica-
tions; residential lighting fixtures; com-
mercial indusl & institutional electric
lighting fixtures; lighting equipment

(G-11137)
SARGENT MANUFACTURING INC
120 E 124th St (10035-1933)
P.O. Box 740607, Bronx (10474-9425)
PHONE................................212 722-7000
Richard Oswald, *President*
Robert Oswald, *Vice Pres*
Daniel Glynn, *Technician*
EMP: 2
SQ FT: 5,000
SALES: 1.4MM
SALES (corp-wide): 3.4MM **Privately Held**
SIC: 3443 Chutes & troughs
PA: H. C. Oswald Supply Co., Inc.
725 Whittier St
Bronx NY 10474
718 620-1400

(G-11138)
SARGENTO FOODS INC
498 7th Ave (10018-6798)
PHONE................................920 893-8484
EMP: 108
SALES (corp-wide): 1.8B **Privately Held**
SIC: 2022 Natural cheese; processed cheese
PA: Sargento Foods Inc.
1 Persnickety Pl
Plymouth WI 53073
920 893-8484

(G-11139)
SARINA ACCESSORIES LLC
469 Fashion Ave Rm 1301 (10018-7616)
PHONE................................212 239-8106
Marc Faham, *Mng Member*
▲ EMP: 12
SALES (est): 2.5MM **Privately Held**
SIC: 3961 2339 3873 Costume jewelry; scarves, hoods, headbands, etc.; women's; watches, clocks, watchcases & parts

(G-11140)
SATELLITE INCORPORATED
43 W 46th St Ste 503 (10036-4121)
PHONE................................212 221-6687
Paula S Cruz, *General Mgr*
EMP: 5
SALES (est): 316.3K **Privately Held**
SIC: 3911 Jewelry, precious metal

(G-11141)
SAVEUR MAGAZINE
304 Park Ave S Fl 8 (10010-4310)
PHONE................................212 219-7400
Max Falkowitz, *Editor*
Coleman Andrews, *Manager*
Kat Craddock, *Manager*
EMP: 32
SALES (est): 2MM **Privately Held**
SIC: 2721 Magazines: publishing & printing

(G-11142)
SAVWATT USA INC (PA)
475 Park Ave S Fl 30 (10016-6901)
PHONE................................646 478-2676
Michael Haug, *CEO*
Isaac H Sutton, *Ch of Bd*
EMP: 8
SQ FT: 2,000
SALES (est): 715.8K **Publicly Held**
SIC: 3646 3645 Commercial indusl & institutional electric lighting fixtures; residential lighting fixtures

(G-11143)
SB CORPORATION
114 W 41st St Fl 4 (10036-7308)
PHONE................................212 822-3166
Rob Cohen, *Principal*
▼ EMP: 5
SALES (est): 360K **Privately Held**
SIC: 2329 Men's & boys' sportswear & athletic clothing

(G-11144)
SB NEW YORK INC (HQ)
Also Called: Metro New York
120 Broadway (10271-0002)
PHONE................................212 457-7790
Oskar Bjorner, *CFO*
Michele Earl, *Accounting Dir*

Audrey Harmaty, *Human Res Dir*
Jennifer Fisher, *Manager*
Wesley Alves, *Info Tech Dir*
EMP: 57
SALES (est): 10.2MM **Privately Held**
WEB: www.metronewyork.com
SIC: 2711 Newspapers, publishing & printing

(G-11145)
SC BUILDING SOLUTIONS LLC
53 W 23rd St Fl 12 (10010-4313)
PHONE................................800 564-1152
Ross Goldenberg,
Jason Griffith,
EMP: 80
SALES: 2.6MM **Privately Held**
SIC: 7372 8742 Application computer software; real estate consultant

(G-11146)
SC SUPPLY CHAIN MANAGEMENT LLC
Also Called: SCM
90 Broad St Ste 1504 (10004-2276)
PHONE................................212 344-3322
Anan Bishara, *Mng Member*
▲ EMP: 6
SQ FT: 2,600
SALES: 900K **Privately Held**
SIC: 3569 Filters

(G-11147)
SCALAMANDRE SILKS INC (PA)
979 3rd Ave Ste 202 (10022-1294)
PHONE................................212 980-3888
▲ EMP: 65 EST: 1927
SALES (est): 62.1MM **Privately Held**
SIC: 2221 2241 5131 2273 Manmad Brdwv Fabric Mill Narrow Fabric Mill Whol Piece Goods/Notions

(G-11148)
SCH DPX CORPORATION
22 W 21st St Ste 700 (10010-6982)
PHONE................................917 405-5377
Joe Schoenfelder, *President*
EMP: 7
SALES (est): 510K **Privately Held**
WEB: www.schoenfelder.com
SIC: 2369 Girls' & children's outerwear

(G-11149)
SCHALLER MANUFACTURING CORP (PA)
Also Called: Schaller & Weber
1654 2nd Ave Apt 2n (10028-3109)
PHONE................................718 721-5480
Ralph Schaller, *Ch of Bd*
Marianne Schaller, *Vice Pres*
Harald Nagel, *Manager*
Jesse Denes, *Director*
Jeremy Schaller, *Director*
EMP: 70 EST: 1937
SQ FT: 16,000
SALES (est): 8.8MM **Privately Held**
WEB: www.schallerweber.com
SIC: 2013 5421 Prepared pork products from purchased pork; meat & fish markets

(G-11150)
SCHALLER MANUFACTURING CORP
Also Called: Schaller & Webber
1654 2nd Ave Apt 2n (10028-3109)
PHONE................................212 879-3047
Chris Cunningham, *Manager*
EMP: 12
SALES: 1.1MM
SALES (corp-wide): 8.8MM **Privately Held**
WEB: www.schallerweber.com
SIC: 2013 Sausages & other prepared meats
PA: Schaller Manufacturing Corp.
1654 2nd Ave Apt 2n
New York NY 10028
718 721-5480

(G-11151)
SCHINDLER ELEVATOR CORPORATION
620 12th Ave Fl 4 (10036-1016)
PHONE................................212 708-1000
Jack Walsh, *Manager*

Karissa Basile, *Manager*
Michael Zelencic, *Supervisor*
EMP: 250
SALES (corp-wide): 10.9B **Privately Held**
WEB: www.us.schindler.com
SIC: 3534 1796 Elevators & equipment; installing building equipment
HQ: Schindler Elevator Corporation
20 Whippany Rd
Morristown NJ 07960
973 397-6500

(G-11152)
SCHINDLER ELEVATOR CORPORATION
1211 6th Ave Ste 2950 (10036-8705)
PHONE................................800 225-3123
James Iannaccone, *Manager*
EMP: 30
SALES (corp-wide): 10.9B **Privately Held**
WEB: www.us.schindler.com
SIC: 3534 1796 Elevators & equipment; elevator installation & conversion
HQ: Schindler Elevator Corporation
20 Whippany Rd
Morristown NJ 07960
973 397-6500

(G-11153)
SCHNEEMAN STUDIO LIMITED
330 W 38th St Rm 505 (10018-8639)
PHONE................................212 244-3330
John Schneeman, *President*
EMP: 5
SQ FT: 2,000
SALES: 500K **Privately Held**
SIC: 2389 Theatrical costumes

(G-11154)
SCHNEIDER AMALCO INC
600 3rd Ave Fl 2 (10016-1919)
PHONE................................917 470-9674
Thomas Schneider, *CEO*
EMP: 10
SQ FT: 3,500
SALES (est): 515.8K **Privately Held**
SIC: 1381 1389 6792 Drilling oil & gas wells; oil field services; oil royalty traders; oil leases, buying & selling on own account

(G-11155)
SCHNEIDER ELC SYSTEMS USA INC
7 E 8th St (10003-5901)
PHONE................................214 527-3099
EMP: 10
SALES (corp-wide): 177.9K **Privately Held**
SIC: 3823 Flow instruments, industrial process type
HQ: Schneider Electric Systems Usa, Inc.
38 Neponset Ave
Foxboro MA 02035
508 543-8750

(G-11156)
SCHNEIDER ELECTRIC IT CORP
Also Called: APC-Mge
520 8th Ave Rm 2103 (10018-6507)
PHONE................................646 335-0216
Brian Goffe, *Engineer*
George Chappas, *Manager*
EMP: 10
SALES (corp-wide): 177.9K **Privately Held**
WEB: www.apcc.com
SIC: 3612 Power & distribution transformers
HQ: Schneider Electric It Corporation
132 Fairgrounds Rd
West Kingston RI 02892
401 789-5735

(G-11157)
SCHNEIDER ELECTRIC USA INC
112 W 34th St Ste 908 (10120-0999)
PHONE................................646 335-0220
James Montemarano, *Principal*
James Labzda, *Accounts Exec*
EMP: 136
SALES (corp-wide): 177.9K **Privately Held**
SIC: 3613 Switchgear & switchboard apparatus

HQ: Schneider Electric Usa, Inc.
201 Wshington St Ste 2700
Boston MA 02108
978 975-9600

(G-11158)
SCHNEIDER MILLS INC
Also Called: Wilkesboro Road
1430 Broadway Rm 1202 (10018-3390)
P.O. Box 519, Taylorsville NC (28681-0519)
PHONE................................828 632-0801
Kim Cline, *Business Mgr*
Tim Little, *Opers Staff*
Curt Parker, *QC Mgr*
Mark Mincieli, *Research*
Emmett Pruett, *Manager*
EMP: 250
SALES (est): 37.6MM
SALES (corp-wide): 54.9MM **Privately Held**
SIC: 2211 2221 Broadwoven fabric mills, cotton; broadwoven fabric mills, manmade
PA: Schneider Mills, Inc.
1170 Nc Highway 16 N
Taylorsville NC 28681
828 632-8181

(G-11159)
SCHOEN TRIMMING & CORD CO INC
151 W 25th St Fl 10 (10001-7250)
PHONE................................212 255-3949
Martin Silver, *President*
▲ EMP: 17
SQ FT: 6,000
SALES: 2.5MM **Privately Held**
SIC: 2241 Cords, fabric

(G-11160)
SCHOLASTIC CORPORATION (PA)
557 Broadway Lbby 1 (10012-3999)
PHONE................................212 343-6100
Richard Robinson, *Ch of Bd*
Suzanne Bilyeu, *Editor*
Katie Brickner, *Editor*
Emily Teresa, *Editor*
Michael Haggen, *Ch Acad Ofcr*
▲ EMP: 9
SQ FT: 500,000
SALES: 1.6B **Publicly Held**
WEB: www.scholastic.com
SIC: 2731 2721 7372 7812 Books: publishing only; textbooks: publishing only, not printed on site; magazines: publishing only, not printed on site; educational computer software; non-theatrical motion picture production, television; video production; motion picture production; copyright buying & licensing; advertising agencies

(G-11161)
SCHOLASTIC INC (HQ)
Also Called: Scholastic U.S.A.
557 Broadway Lbby 1 (10012-3999)
PHONE................................212 343-6100
Richard Robinson, *Ch of Bd*
Ken Killen, *General Mgr*
Janice Behrens, *Editor*
Eric Black, *Editor*
Judy Goldberg, *Editor*
◆ EMP: 2000 EST: 1920
SQ FT: 300,000
SALES (est): 1.5B
SALES (corp-wide): 1.6B **Publicly Held**
WEB: www.scholasticdealer.com
SIC: 2731 2721 7372 7812 Books: publishing only; textbooks: publishing only, not printed on site; magazines: publishing only, not printed on site; statistical reports (periodicals): publishing only; educational computer software; video production; television film production; motion picture production & distribution
PA: Scholastic Corporation
557 Broadway Lbby 1
New York NY 10012
212 343-6100

▲ = Import ▼=Export
◆ =Import/Export

(G-11162)
SCHOLASTIC INC
Also Called: Scholastic Copy Center
120 Mercer St (10012-3806)
PHONE....................212 343-6100
Anthony Giammanco, *Editor*
Noah Rosenfield, *Software Dev*
Greg Barnett, *Administration*
EMP: 25
SALES (corp-wide): 1.6B **Publicly Held**
WEB: www.scholasticdealer.com
SIC: 2731 Book publishing
HQ: Scholastic Inc.
557 Broadway Lbby 1
New York NY 10012
212 343-6100

(G-11163)
SCHOLASTIC INC
568 Broadway Rm 809 (10012-3253)
PHONE....................212 343-7100
Seth Radwell, *Branch Mgr*
EMP: 100
SALES (corp-wide): 1.6B **Publicly Held**
WEB: www.scholasticdealer.com
SIC: 2741 Business service newsletters:
publishing & printing
HQ: Scholastic Inc.
557 Broadway Lbby 1
New York NY 10012
212 343-6100

(G-11164)
SCHOOLNET INC (DH)
525 Fashion Ave Fl 4 (10018-4940)
PHONE....................646 496-9000
Jonathan D Harber, *CEO*
Mark Chernis, *President*
Susan Aspey, *Vice Pres*
Andy Brenner, *Vice Pres*
Marsha Spanswick, *Project Mgr*
EMP: 116
SQ FT: 11,500
SALES (est): 10.7MM
SALES (corp-wide): 5.3B **Privately Held**
WEB: www.schoolnet.com
SIC: 7372 7373 Educational computer
software; systems software development
services
HQ: Pearson Education, Inc.
221 River St
Hoboken NJ 07030
201 236-7000

(G-11165)
SCI BORE INC
70 Irving Pl Apt 5c (10003-2218)
PHONE....................212 674-7128
Robert Olsen, *Partner*
Nadiya D Jinnah, *Partner*
EMP: 7
SALES (est): 550K **Privately Held**
SIC: 3496 Miscellaneous fabricated wire
products

(G-11166)
SCIENTIFIC PLASTICS INC
243 W 30th St Fl 8 (10001-2812)
PHONE....................212 967-1199
Steven Stegman, *President*
Jeffrey Stegman, *Vice Pres*
EMP: 12 EST: 1940
SALES (est): 1.1MM **Privately Held**
WEB: www.scientificplastics.com
SIC: 3842 Surgical appliances & supplies

(G-11167)
SCITERRA LLC
244 5th Ave Ste L280 (10001-7604)
PHONE....................646 883-3724
EMP: 5
SALES: 200K **Privately Held**
SIC: 7372 Prepackaged Software Services

(G-11168)
SCOOPS R US INCORPORATED
1514 Broadway (10036-4002)
PHONE....................212 730-7959
EMP: 8
SALES (est): 652.9K **Privately Held**
SIC: 2024 Mfg Ice Cream/Frozen Desert

(G-11169)
SCOTT SILVERSTEIN LLC
242 W 38th St (10018-5804)
PHONE....................212 781-1818

Scott Silverstein, *Mng Member*
EMP: 8 EST: 2016
SALES (est): 628K **Privately Held**
SIC: 3144 Dress shoes, women's

(G-11170)
**SCREEN GEMS-EMI MUSIC INC
(DH)**
Also Called: EMI Music Publishing
150 5th Ave Fl 7 (10011-4372)
PHONE....................212 786-8000
Martin Bandier, *CEO*
Santiago Men Ndez-Pidal, *Managing Dir*
Joanne Boris, *Exec VP*
Tom Inett, *Director*
EMP: 60
SQ FT: 45,000
SALES (est): 47.6MM **Privately Held**
SIC: 2741 Music, sheet: publishing only,
not printed on site

(G-11171)
SCROLL MEDIA INC
235 W 102nd St Apt 14i (10025-8432)
PHONE....................617 395-8904
Samir Patil, *President*
EMP: 5 EST: 2013
SALES (est): 660K **Privately Held**
SIC: 3577 Data conversion equipment,
media-to-media: computer

(G-11172)
**SEABAY MEDIA HOLDINGS LLC
(PA)**
Also Called: Metro Nespaper
120 Broadway Fl 6 (10271-0034)
PHONE....................212 457-7790
Pelle Tornberg, *CEO*
Lexy Torzilli, *Accounts Exec*
EMP: 1
SALES (est): 14.4MM **Privately Held**
SIC: 2711 2741 Newspapers, publishing &
printing; miscellaneous publishing

(G-11173)
SEAN JOHN CLOTHING INC
1710 Broadway Frnt 1 (10019-5254)
PHONE....................212 500-2200
Sean John, *Manager*
EMP: 30 **Privately Held**
SIC: 2325 Men's & boys' trousers & slacks
PA: Sean John Clothing, Inc.
1440 Broadway Frnt 3
New York NY 10018

(G-11174)
**SEAN JOHN CLOTHING INC
(PA)**
1440 Broadway Frnt 3 (10018-2301)
PHONE....................212 500-2200
Jeff Tweedy, *President*
Sean John, *Manager*
EMP: 23
SALES (est): 6.4MM **Privately Held**
SIC: 2325 Men's & boys' trousers & slacks

(G-11175)
**SECRET CELEBRITY LICENSING
LLC**
1431 Broadway Fl 10 (10018-1910)
PHONE....................212 812-9277
Kathryn Sio, *Mng Member*
EMP: 5
SALES (est): 930.2K **Privately Held**
SIC: 3648 5023 Decorative area lighting
fixtures; decorative home furnishings &
supplies

(G-11176)
SECURED SERVICES INC (PA)
110 William St Fl 14 (10038-3901)
PHONE....................866 419-3900
King T Moore, *President*
EMP: 4
SALES (est): 3.2MM **Privately Held**
WEB: www.secured-services.com
SIC: 7372 Prepackaged software

(G-11177)
SECURITY LETTER
166 E 96th St Apt 3b (10128-2512)
PHONE....................212 348-1553
Robert McCrie, *Owner*
EMP: 5 EST: 1970

SALES (est): 270K **Privately Held**
SIC: 2721 8742 Trade journals: publishing
only, not printed on site; business consultant

(G-11178)
**SEEDLNGS LF SCNCE
VENTURES LLC**
230 E 15th St Apt 1a (10003-3941)
PHONE....................917 913-8511
Keith Rubin, *CEO*
Ken Solovay, *
EMP: 7
SALES (est): 541.3K **Privately Held**
SIC: 3841 Surgical & medical instruments

(G-11179)
SEELOS CORPORATION
300 Park Ave (10022-7402)
PHONE....................646 998-6475
Richard Pascoe, *CEO*
Mary Naggs, *Vice Pres*
Kelly Deck, *Exec Dir*
Brian Dorsey, *Officer*
Neil Morton, *Officer*
EMP: 5
SALES (est): 134.4K
SALES (corp-wide): 1.8MM **Publicly Held**
SIC: 2834 Pharmaceutical preparations
PA: Seelos Therapeutics, Inc.
300 Park Ave Fl 12
New York NY 10022
646 998-6475

(G-11180)
**SEELOS THERAPEUTICS INC
(PA)**
Also Called: Apricus
300 Park Ave Fl 12 (10022-7419)
PHONE....................646 998-6475
Richard W Pascoe, *CEO*
Kleanthis G Xanthopoulos, *Ch of Bd*
Brian T Dorsey, *Senior VP*
Neil Morton, *Senior VP*
Brian Dorsey, *Vice Pres*
EMP: 11
SQ FT: 9,000
SALES (est): 1.8MM **Publicly Held**
WEB: www.nexmed.com
SIC: 2834 Pharmaceutical preparations

(G-11181)
SEFAIRA INC
135 E 57th St Fl 6 (10022-2185)
PHONE....................855 733-2472
Mads Jensen, *CEO*
Nick Obrien, *Counsel*
Hugh McEvoy, *Vice Pres*
Stephen Grist, *CFO*
Scott Stelzer, *Accounts Mgr*
EMP: 35
SALES (est): 2.6MM
SALES (corp-wide): 57.1K **Privately Held**
SIC: 7372 Business oriented computer
software
HQ: Trimble Europe B.V.
Meerheide 45
Eersel 5521
497 532-421

(G-11182)
SEGOVIA TECHNOLOGY CO
33 Irving Pl Fl 7 (10003-2332)
PHONE....................212 868-4412
Michael Faye, *CEO*
Liana Paris, *Manager*
EMP: 10
SQ FT: 1,500
SALES (est): 696.7K **Privately Held**
SIC: 7372 Prepackaged software

(G-11183)
SEIDLIN CONSULTING
580 W End Ave (10024-1723)
PHONE....................212 496-2043
Mindell Seidlin, *Owner*
EMP: 1
SALES: 1MM **Privately Held**
SIC: 2834 Pharmaceutical preparations

(G-11184)
SEKAS INTERNATIONAL LTD
345 7th Ave Fl 9 (10001-5049)
PHONE....................212 629-6095
Nicholas Sekas, *President*
Athina Orthodoxou, *Vice Pres*

EMP: 10
SQ FT: 2,500
SALES (est): 2.5MM **Privately Held**
SIC: 2371 Fur goods

(G-11185)
**SELECT INDUSTRIES NEW
YORK INC**
450 Fashion Ave Ste 3002 (10123-3002)
PHONE....................800 723-5333
Jerry Friedman, *Principal*
Luann Abbatiello, *District Mgr*
Jonathan Beyer, *Counsel*
Eunice Jackson, *Counsel*
Goldie Weixel, *Counsel*
▲ EMP: 13 EST: 2011
SALES (est): 2.2MM **Privately Held**
SIC: 3999 Manufacturing industries

(G-11186)
**SELECT INFORMATION
EXCHANGE**
175 W 79th St 3a (10024-6450)
PHONE....................212 496-6435
George H Wein, *Owner*
Alex Wein, *Manager*
Dan Lam, *Prgrmr*
EMP: 18
SQ FT: 2,200
SALES (est): 1.1MM **Privately Held**
WEB: www.siecom.com
SIC: 2741 7331 Catalogs: publishing only,
not printed on site; mailing list compilers

(G-11187)
**SELECTIVE BEAUTY
CORPORATION**
315 Bleecker St 109 (10014-3427)
PHONE....................585 336-7600
Sylvie Ganter, *President*
Andrew Hershey, *Director*
▲ EMP: 10
SALES (est): 798K **Privately Held**
WEB: www.selective-beauty.com
SIC: 2844 Perfumes & colognes

(G-11188)
**SELLAS LIFE SCIENCES GROUP
INC (PA)**
15 W 38th St Fl 10 (10018-5501)
PHONE....................917 438-4353
Jane Wasman, *Ch of Bd*
Angelos M Stergiou, *President*
Barbara A Wood, *Exec VP*
Gene Mack, *CFO*
Nicholas J Sarlis, *Chief Mktg Ofcr*
EMP: 11
SQ FT: 3,700
SALES (est): 2.6MM **Publicly Held**
SIC: 2834 Pharmaceutical preparations

(G-11189)
SEMI-LINEAR INC
1123 Broadway Ste 718 (10010-2097)
PHONE....................212 243-2108
Linda Holliday, *CEO*
Joel Smernoff, *COO*
Michael Kostadinovich, *CFO*
Peta Savva, *Marketing Staff*
EMP: 5
SALES (est): 526.6K **Privately Held**
SIC: 3599 Industrial machinery

(G-11190)
SENIOR BRANDS LLC
347 5th Ave Rm 506 (10016-5007)
PHONE....................212 213-5100
Dan Rosow, *Mng Member*
EMP: 9 EST: 2017
SALES (est): 1MM **Privately Held**
SIC: 3089 Plastic kitchenware, tableware &
houseware

(G-11191)
**SENSATIONAL COLLECTION INC
(PA)**
1410 Broadway Rm 505 (10018-9372)
PHONE....................212 840-7388
Azar Kada, *Owner*
Jeff Matalon, *VP Sales*
▲ EMP: 3
SQ FT: 5,600

SALES (est): 3.8MM **Privately Held**
SIC: 2339 5137 Women's & misses' athletic clothing & sportswear; women's & children's sportswear & swimsuits

(G-11192)
SENSUAL INC
Also Called: Icy Hot Lingerie
463 7th Ave Rm 1101 (10018-8704)
PHONE..............................212 869-1450
Sami Souid, *CEO*
EMP: 20
SQ FT: 4,000
SALES (est): 2MM
SALES (corp-wide): 2.4MM **Privately Held**
SIC: 2342 Bras, girdles & allied garments
PA: Usa Apparel Group Inc
463 7th Ave Rm 1101
New York NY 10018
212 869-1450

(G-11193)
SERIESONE INC
860 Broadway Fl 5 (10003-1228)
PHONE..............................212 385-1552
EMP: 6
SALES (corp-wide): 306.1K **Privately Held**
SIC: 7372 Prepackaged software
PA: Seriesone Inc.
175 Sw 7th St Ste 1800
Miami FL 33130
786 473-6400

(G-11194)
SERRAVIEW AMERICA INC
2 Wall St Fl 10 (10005-2004)
PHONE..............................800 903-3716
Stephen Macnee, *CEO*
Ian Morley, *Principal*
EMP: 70
SQ FT: 1,000
SALES (est): 1.3MM **Privately Held**
SIC: 7372 Business oriented computer software

(G-11195)
SERVICENOW INC
60 E 42nd St Ste 1230 (10165-1203)
PHONE..............................914 318-1168
Tom Moore, *Branch Mgr*
EMP: 10
SALES (corp-wide): 2.6B **Publicly Held**
SIC: 7372 Business oriented computer software
PA: Servicenow, Inc.
2225 Lawson Ln
Santa Clara CA 95054
408 501-8550

(G-11196)
SEVEN STORIES PRESS INC
140 Watts St (10013-1738)
PHONE..............................212 226-8760
Daniel Simon, *President*
Dan Simon, *Publisher*
Rebecca Stefoff, *Publisher*
Elizabeth Delong, *Editor*
Dennis Loo, *COO*
▲ **EMP:** 7
SQ FT: 2,500
SALES (est): 1.1MM **Privately Held**
WEB: www.sevenstories.com
SIC: 2731 Books: publishing only

(G-11197)
SG NYC LLC
28 W 27th St Fl 12 (10001-7075)
PHONE..............................310 210-1837
Daniel Chiu, *Managing Prtnr*
Stephanie Garcia, *Managing Prtnr*
EMP: 20
SQ FT: 4,000
SALES (est): 4.2MM **Privately Held**
SIC: 2335 Women's, juniors' & misses' dresses

(G-11198)
SGD NORTH AMERICA
900 3rd Ave Fl 4 (10022-4998)
PHONE..............................212 753-4200
Peter Acerra, *President*
Scott Beals, *Accounts Mgr*
▲ **EMP:** 33 **EST:** 2007

SALES (est): 3.5MM **Privately Held**
SIC: 3221 Glass containers

(G-11199)
SGD PHARMA PACKAGING INC
900 3rd Ave Fl 4 (10022-4998)
PHONE..............................212 223-7100
Nadir Lahneur, *President*
EMP: 10
SQ FT: 2,500
SALES (est): 147.6K
SALES (corp-wide): 2.6B **Privately Held**
SIC: 3221 Glass containers
HQ: Sgd S.A.
14 B Terrasse Bellini
Puteaux 92800
140 903-600

(G-11200)
SHADAL LLC
Also Called: Sermoneta Gloves
609 Madison Ave Ste 611 (10022-1901)
PHONE..............................212 319-5946
Aldo Sermonetta, *Manager*
EMP: 6
SALES (est): 18.1K **Privately Held**
SIC: 3111 Glove leather

(G-11201)
SHADOWTV INC
630 9th Ave Ste 202 (10036-4752)
PHONE..............................212 445-2540
Joachim Kim, *President*
Tracy Fred, *Bookkeeper*
Daniela Gorelov, *Marketing Staff*
EMP: 6
SALES (est): 855K **Privately Held**
WEB: www.shadowtv.com
SIC: 3575 Computer terminals, monitors & components

(G-11202)
SHAH DIAMONDS INC
Also Called: Venus
22 W 48th St Ste 600 (10036-1820)
PHONE..............................212 888-9393
Natwar Shah, *President*
Harshit Shah, *Sales Staff*
Helen Hemsley, *Executive*
Gita Shah, *Admin Sec*
▲ **EMP:** 19
SQ FT: 4,000
SALES (est): 3.2MM **Privately Held**
WEB: www.hoc.com
SIC: 3911 3915 5094 Jewelry, precious metal; diamond cutting & polishing; jewelry; diamonds (gems)

(G-11203)
SHAHIN DESIGNS LTD
766 Madison Ave Fl 3 (10065-6563)
PHONE..............................212 737-7225
Samouhi Shahin, *President*
EMP: 5
SALES (est): 390K **Privately Held**
SIC: 2211 Apparel & outerwear fabrics, cotton

(G-11204)
SHAKE INC
175 Varick St Fl 4 (10014-7412)
PHONE..............................650 544-5479
Abraham Geiger, *CEO*
Oscar Garza, *Software Engr*
EMP: 13 **EST:** 2012
SQ FT: 1,000
SALES (est): 936.8K **Privately Held**
SIC: 7372 Business oriented computer software

(G-11205)
SHANU GEMS INC
1212 Ave Of The Americas (10036-1602)
P.O. Box 680, New City (10956-0680)
PHONE..............................212 921-4470
Pramod Agrawal, *President*
Manensha Agrawal, *Vice Pres*
EMP: 10
SALES (est): 840K **Privately Held**
WEB: www.shanugems.com
SIC: 3911 5094 Jewelry, precious metal; jewelry

(G-11206)
SHAPEWAYS INC (PA)
44 W 28th St Fl 12 (10001-4212)
PHONE..............................914 356-5816
Gregory Kress, *CEO*
Peter Weijmarshausen, *CEO*
Marleen Vogelaar, *COO*
Bucco Asma, *Engineer*
William Davis, *Engineer*
EMP: 188
SALES (est): 36.4MM **Privately Held**
SIC: 2759 Commercial printing

(G-11207)
SHAPIRO BERNSTEIN & CO INC
488 Madison Ave Fl 1201 (10022-5708)
PHONE..............................212 588-0878
Micheal Brettler, *President*
Eric Beall, *Vice Pres*
Alexa Cabellon, *Manager*
Laura Sodders, *Consultant*
▲ **EMP:** 12
SALES (est): 850K **Privately Held**
WEB: www.shapirobernstein.com
SIC: 2741 Music, sheet: publishing only, not printed on site

(G-11208)
SHAREDBOOK INC
110 William St Fl 30 (10038-3901)
PHONE..............................646 442-8840
Caroline Vanderlip, *CEO*
Josef Hollander, *President*
EMP: 30
SQ FT: 8,000
SALES (est): 397.5K **Privately Held**
WEB: www.sharedbook.com
SIC: 2741 5942 Miscellaneous publishing; book stores

(G-11209)
SHAWMUT WOODWORKING & SUP INC
Also Called: Shawmutdesign and Construction
3 E 54th St Fl 8 (10022-3141)
PHONE..............................212 920-8900
Aymen Daghfous, *Project Mgr*
Michael Zajac, *Accountant*
Michael Simon, *Branch Mgr*
Joseph Boyle, *Sr Project Mgr*
Tracy Aronoff, *Manager*
EMP: 151
SALES (corp-wide): 1.1B **Privately Held**
WEB: www.shawmut.com
SIC: 2431 Millwork
PA: Shawmut Woodworking & Supply, Inc.
560 Harrison Ave Ste 200
Boston MA 02118
617 622-7000

(G-11210)
SHELLEY PROMOTIONS INC
87 5th Ave (10003)
PHONE..............................212 924-4987
James Scott Shelley, *President*
EMP: 5
SALES (est): 370K **Privately Held**
SIC: 3861 Photographic film, plate & paper holders

(G-11211)
SHENGKUN NORTH AMERICA INC
262 W 38th St Rm 903 (10018-9173)
PHONE..............................212 217-2460
Wen Ming MA, *CEO*
Mia Kang, *Project Mgr*
EMP: 10 **EST:** 2015
SQ FT: 1,200
SALES: 3.2MM **Privately Held**
SIC: 2221 5131 5949 Textile mills, broadwoven: silk & manmade, also glass; textiles, woven; fabric stores piece goods

(G-11212)
SHERWOOD GROUP INC
166 E 96th St Apt 5a (10128-2533)
PHONE..............................240 731-8573
Howard Schwartz, *President*
▲ **EMP:** 7
SQ FT: 1,000

SALES (est): 1.1MM **Privately Held**
SIC: 2759 3999 2399 5199 Promotional printing; advertising display products; flags, fabric; advertising specialties

(G-11213)
SHIELD PRESS INC
9 Lispenard St Fl 1 (10013-2290)
PHONE..............................212 431-7489
Bryan Shield, *President*
Stephen Shield, *Treasurer*
Ellen Shield, *Admin Sec*
EMP: 6 **EST:** 1940
SQ FT: 1,500
SALES: 750K **Privately Held**
SIC: 2752 7389 Commercial printing, offset; printers' services: folding, collating

(G-11214)
SHIMADA SHOJI (HK) LIMITED
165 W 46th St Ste 709 (10036-2519)
PHONE..............................212 268-0465
Toshio Shimada, *Branch Mgr*
EMP: 8 **Privately Held**
SIC: 3965 Buttons & parts
HQ: Shimada Shoji (H.K.) Limited
Rm 507-511 5/F Cheung Sha Wan Plz Twr 1
Cheung Sha Wan KLN

(G-11215)
SHINDO USA INC
162 W 36th St (10018-6901)
PHONE..............................212 868-9311
Tadashi Shindo, *CEO*
Shingo Nagai, *Principal*
Junichiro Tanaka, *Regl Sales Mgr*
Masako Yasuda, *Wholesale*
Meg Mitra, *Sales Staff*
EMP: 7
SALES (est): 429.3K **Privately Held**
SIC: 2211 Stretch fabrics, cotton

(G-11216)
SHIRA ACCESSORIES LTD
28 W 36th St Fl 6 (10018-8006)
PHONE..............................212 594-4455
Barry Shapiro, *President*
EMP: 15
SQ FT: 2,000
SALES (est): 1.8MM **Privately Held**
SIC: 3961 Costume jewelry

(G-11217)
SHIRO LIMITED
928 Broadway Ste 806 (10010-8128)
PHONE..............................212 780-0007
Gary Mandel, *President*
▲ **EMP:** 5
SQ FT: 2,000
SALES (est): 390.8K **Privately Held**
SIC: 3911 Jewelry, precious metal

(G-11218)
SHISEIDO AMERICAS CORPORATION (HQ)
Also Called: Shiseido Cosmetics
900 3rd Ave Fl 15 (10022-4792)
PHONE..............................212 805-2300
Marc Rey, *President*
Edward W Klause, *Vice Pres*
Tatsuya Toda, *Vice Pres*
Giannine Camplani, *Human Resources*
Deanna Johnston, *CIO*
◆ **EMP:** 7
SQ FT: 108,000
SALES (est): 484.3MM **Privately Held**
SIC: 2844 5122 Cosmetic preparations; toilet preparations; cosmetics; toilet preparations

(G-11219)
SHRINEETA PHARMACY
1749 Amsterdam Ave Frnt (10031-4618)
PHONE..............................212 234-7959
Robby Annamaneni, *Principal*
EMP: 5
SALES (est): 731.3K **Privately Held**
SIC: 2834 Pharmaceutical preparations

(G-11220)
SHRINEETA PHARMACY INC
Also Called: Amsterdam Pharmacy
1743 Amsterdam Ave (10031-4614)
PHONE..............................212 234-7959
Sreenivasa R Gade, *Ch of Bd*

Ravinder Annamaneni, *Director*
EMP: 21
SQ FT: 1,600
SALES (est): 7.2MM **Privately Held**
SIC: 2834 Pharmaceutical preparations

(G-11221)
SHYAM AHUJA LIMITED
201 E 56th St Frnt A (10022-3724)
PHONE..................................212 644-5910
Azmina Merali, *Branch Mgr*
EMP: 7
SALES (corp-wide): 965.8K **Privately Held**
WEB: www.shyamahujahome.com
SIC: 2391 2273 3999 Curtains & draperies; carpets & rugs; atomizers, toiletry
PA: Shyam Ahuja Private Limited
A - 6 Poonam Appartment
Mumbai MH 40001
222 492-0424

(G-11222)
SHYK INTERNATIONAL CORP
258 Riverside Dr Apt 7b (10025-6160)
PHONE..................................212 663-3302
Steven Kline, *President*
EMP: 2
SQ FT: 2,500
SALES: 75MM **Privately Held**
SIC: 3651 Home entertainment equipment, electronic

(G-11223)
SIDE HUSTLE MUSIC GROUP LLC
600 3rd Ave Fl 2 (10016-1919)
PHONE..................................800 219-4003
Fabian Cummings, *Prgrmr*
EMP: 10
SQ FT: 10,000
SALES (est): 1.7MM **Privately Held**
WEB: www.sidehustlemusicgroup.com
SIC: 3652 Pre-recorded records & tapes

(G-11224)
SIEGEL & STOCKMAN INC
126 W 25th St Frnt 1 (10001-7413)
PHONE..................................212 633-1508
Chris Israel, *President*
Tess Tobias, *Comptroller*
▲ EMP: 5
SALES (est): 374.2K **Privately Held**
SIC: 3999 Mannequins

(G-11225)
SIEMENS AG
1 Penn Plz (10119-0002)
PHONE..................................212 946-2440
Shawn Connington, *Opers Mgr*
Bob Costa, *Engineer*
Jerry Fitzgerald, *Finance*
EMP: 9
SALES (corp-wide): 881.6K **Privately Held**
SIC: 3661 Telephones & telephone apparatus
PA: Siemens Ag
432 N Franklin St
Syracuse NY

(G-11226)
SIEMENS CORPORATION
527 Madison Ave Fl 8 (10022-4376)
PHONE..................................202 434-7800
Erik Valerio, *Project Mgr*
Kaival Patel, *Opers Mgr*
Craig Henry, *Engineer*
Brad Culp, *Sales Executive*
Guido Hartmann, *Info Tech Mgr*
EMP: 10
SALES (corp-wide): 95B **Privately Held**
SIC: 3661 3843 3844 3612 Telephones & telephone apparatus; electric lamps; radiographic X-ray apparatus & tubes; distribution transformers, electric; voltage regulators, transmission & distribution; nonferrous wiredrawing & insulating
HQ: Siemens Corporation
300 New Jersey Ave Nw # 10
Washington DC 20001
202 434-4800

(G-11227)
SIEMENS MOBILITY INC (HQ)
1 Penn Plz Ste 1100 (10119-1101)
PHONE..................................212 672-4000
Marc Buncher, *President*
EMP: 10
SALES (est): 318.1MM
SALES (corp-wide): 95B **Privately Held**
SIC: 3711 3743 Motor vehicles & car bodies; railway motor cars
PA: Siemens Ag
Werner-Von-Siemens-Str. 1
Munchen 80333
896 360-0

(G-11228)
SIEMENS USA HOLDINGS INC
527 Madison Ave Fl 8 (10022-4376)
PHONE..................................212 258-4000
George C Nolan, *President*
Jim W White, *General Mgr*
Joan Conner, *Area Mgr*
Michael Wallace, *Counsel*
Shirley Smedley, *Vice Pres*
EMP: 300
SALES (est): 40MM
SALES (corp-wide): 95B **Privately Held**
SIC: 3612 3844 3641 3357 Distribution transformers, electric; voltage regulators, transmission & distribution; radiographic X-ray apparatus & tubes; electric lamps; nonferrous wiredrawing & insulating; telephones & telephone apparatus
PA: Siemens Ag
Werner-Von-Siemens-Str. 1
Munchen 80333
896 360-0

(G-11229)
SIFONYA INC
Also Called: Cego Custom Shirts
303 Park Ave S Frnt 2 (10010-3677)
PHONE..................................212 620-4512
Carl Goldberg, *President*
EMP: 6
SQ FT: 300
SALES: 600K **Privately Held**
WEB: www.cego.com
SIC: 2321 5131 Men's & boys' furnishings; piece goods & other fabrics

(G-11230)
SIGA TECHNOLOGIES INC (PA)
31 E 62nd St (10065-8014)
PHONE..................................212 672-9100
Phillip L Gomez, *CEO*
Eric A Rose, *Ch of Bd*
Dennis E Hruby, *Vice Pres*
Herb Vloedman, *Vice Pres*
Daniel Luckshire, *CFO*
EMP: 37
SQ FT: 3,200
SALES: 477MM **Publicly Held**
WEB: www.siga.com
SIC: 2834 2836 Pharmaceutical preparations; vaccines & other immunizing products

(G-11231)
SIGMA WORLDWIDE LLC (PA)
65 W 83rd St Apt 5 (10024-5237)
PHONE..................................646 217-0629
Jeffrey Muti, *CEO*
Peter Devries, *Opers Staff*
Kenneth Tang, *Manager*
EMP: 8
SALES: 15MM **Privately Held**
SIC: 3161 5099 3089 Cases, carrying; cases, carrying; cases, plastic

(G-11232)
SIGN CENTER INC
Also Called: Sign Company, The
127 W 26th St Rm 401 (10001-6870)
PHONE..................................212 967-2113
Mark Dressman, *President*
James Kelly, *Vice Pres*
EMP: 10
SALES (est): 807.9K **Privately Held**
SIC: 3993 Signs, not made in custom sign painting shops; displays & cutouts, window & lobby

(G-11233)
SIGN COMPANY
Also Called: Sjm Interface
15 W 39th St Fl 7 (10018-0633)
PHONE..................................212 967-2113
EMP: 9
SALES (est): 544.6K **Privately Held**
SIC: 3993 5812 Mfg Signs/Advertising Specialties Eating Place

(G-11234)
SIGNA CHEMISTRY INC (PA)
400 Madison Ave Fl 21 (10017-8901)
PHONE..................................212 933-4101
Michael Lefenfeld, *President*
Michael Alt, *Vice Pres*
Paul Krumrine, *Research*
Dennis Ramprashad, *Controller*
David Field, *Executive*
EMP: 14
SQ FT: 7,000
SALES (est): 7.6MM **Privately Held**
WEB: www.signachem.com
SIC: 2819 3511 Catalysts, chemical; hydraulic turbine generator set units, complete

(G-11235)
SIGNATURE DIAMOND ENTPS LLC
15 W 47th St Ste 203 (10036-5708)
PHONE..................................212 869-5115
Jeremy S Hill,
EMP: 40
SQ FT: 3,000
SALES (est): 3.2MM **Privately Held**
SIC: 1499 Diamond mining, industrial

(G-11236)
SIGNEXPO ENTERPRISES INC (PA)
Also Called: Sign Expo
127 W 26th St Rm 401 (10001-6870)
PHONE..................................212 925-8585
Offer Sharaby, *CEO*
Frayda Sharaby, *Ch of Bd*
Michelle Shapiro, *General Mgr*
Edgar Guttzeit, *Marketing Mgr*
EMP: 14
SALES (est): 1.5MM **Privately Held**
SIC: 3993 Signs & advertising specialties

(G-11237)
SIGNIFY NORTH AMERICA CORP
267 5th Ave (10016-7503)
PHONE..................................646 265-7170
Jeffrey Cassis, *CEO*
EMP: 190
SALES (corp-wide): 7.2B **Privately Held**
SIC: 3646 Commercial indusl & institutional electric lighting fixtures
HQ: Signify North America Corporation
200 Franklin Square Dr
Somerset NJ 08873
732 563-3000

(G-11238)
SIGNPOST INC
127 W 26th St Fl 2 (10001-6881)
PHONE..................................877 334-2837
Stuart Wall, *CEO*
Joy Stukel, *Sales Staff*
Lauren Smith, *Sales Executive*
Brandon Obregon, *Marketing Staff*
Kelly Henley, *Consultant*
EMP: 250
SALES (est): 2.5MM **Privately Held**
SIC: 7372 Application computer software

(G-11239)
SILVATRIM CORP
Also Called: Silvatrim Corporation America
324 W 22nd St (10011-3252)
PHONE..................................212 675-0933
William Shanok, *President*
Daniel Shanock, *Vice Pres*
Frederick Shanok, *Vice Pres*
Victor Shanok, *Treasurer*
EMP: 120 EST: 1931
SQ FT: 120,000
SALES (est): 8MM **Privately Held**
SIC: 3089 Plastic processing; molding primary plastic

(G-11240)
SILVERLIGHT DIGITAL LLC
15 E 32nd St Fl 3 (10016-5570)
PHONE..................................646 650-5330
Lori Goldberg, *CEO*
Michael Ackerman, *Business Mgr*
Benjamin Friedman, *Vice Pres*
Anthony Frisina, *Vice Pres*
David Sapinski, *Account Dir*
EMP: 5
SALES (est): 289K **Privately Held**
SIC: 3663 7319 Digital encoders; media buying service

(G-11241)
SIMILARWEB INC
35 E 21st St Fl 9 (10010-6268)
P.O. Box 307, West Nyack (10994-0307)
PHONE..................................347 685-5422
Jason Schwartz, *CFO*
Paloma Bernard, *Manager*
Alyson Breidbart, *Manager*
Moshe Alexander, *Consultant*
Laura Himmelstein, *Consultant*
EMP: 18
SALES (est): 567.4K **Privately Held**
SIC: 7372 Prepackaged software

(G-11242)
SIMKA DIAMOND CORP
580 5th Ave Ste 523 (10036-4724)
PHONE..................................212 921-4420
Philip Katz, *President*
Isaac Friedman, *Vice Pres*
Surie Friedman, *Admin Sec*
Raizel Katz, *Admin Sec*
EMP: 15
SALES (est): 1.4MM **Privately Held**
WEB: www.simkadiamond.com
SIC: 3911 Jewelry, precious metal

(G-11243)
SIMMONS-BOARDMAN PUBG CORP (HQ)
55 Broad St Fl 26 (10004-2580)
PHONE..................................212 620-7200
Arthur J Mc Ginnis Jr, *President*
Carol Franklin, *Manager*
EMP: 3 EST: 1928
SQ FT: 10,000
SALES (est): 9MM **Privately Held**
WEB: www.marinelog.com
SIC: 2721 2731 8249 Magazines: publishing only, not printed on site; book music: publishing only, not printed on site; correspondence school

(G-11244)
SIMON & SCHUSTER INC
Pocket Books
1230 Ave Of The Americas (10020-1586)
PHONE..................................212 698-7000
Jonathan Karp, *Publisher*
Carolyn Kroll Reidy, *Branch Mgr*
EMP: 51
SALES (corp-wide): 25.9B **Publicly Held**
SIC: 2731 Books: publishing only
HQ: Simon & Schuster, Inc.
1230 Ave Of The Americas
New York NY 10020
212 698-7000

(G-11245)
SIMON & SIMON LLC
Also Called: Magic Maestro Music
1745 Broadway Fl 17 (10019-4642)
PHONE..................................202 419-0490
Bonnie Simon, *Mng Member*
Stephen Simon,
EMP: 5
SALES: 10K **Privately Held**
SIC: 2782 Record albums

(G-11246)
SIMON SCHUSTER DIGITAL SLS INC
51 W 52d St (10019)
PHONE..................................212 698-4391
Carolyn Reidy, *Chairman*
Robert Riger, *Vice Pres*
Laura Roode, *Director*
EMP: 53
SALES (est): 3.2MM
SALES (corp-wide): 25.9B **Publicly Held**
SIC: 2731 Book publishing

HQ: Simon & Schuster, Inc.
1230 Ave Of The Americas
New York NY 10020
212 698-7000

(G-11247)
SIMPLY ACTIVE COSMETICS INC
433 W 21st St Apt 2c (10011-2909)
PHONE..............................646 554-6421
Ron Robinson, *CEO*
EMP: 1
SQ FT: 1,000
SALES: 3MM **Privately Held**
SIC: 2844 Cosmetic preparations

(G-11248)
SING TAO NEWSPAPERS NY LTD (PA)
Also Called: Sing Tao Daily
188 Lafayette St (10013-3200)
PHONE..............................212 699-3800
Robin Mui, *CEO*
Rick Ho, *General Mgr*
Alice Lee, *Corp Secy*
James Duan, *Info Tech Mgr*
▲ EMP: 20
SALES: 22.5MM **Privately Held**
WEB: www.nysingtao.com
SIC: 2711 2741 Newspapers: publishing only, not printed on site; miscellaneous publishing

(G-11249)
SING TRIX
118 W 22nd St Fl 3 (10011-2416)
P.O. Box 200 (10029-0200)
PHONE..............................212 352-1500
Al Roque, *Principal*
John Devecka, *Vice Pres*
Eric Berkowitz, *Mng Member*
EMP: 10
SALES (est): 962.8K **Privately Held**
SIC: 3651 Home entertainment equipment, electronic

(G-11250)
SINO PRINTING INC
30 Allen St Frnt A (10002-5363)
PHONE..............................212 334-6896
Craig Marsden, *Principal*
◆ EMP: 15
SALES (est): 1.1MM **Privately Held**
SIC: 2759 Screen printing

(G-11251)
SISKIND GROUP INC
1385 Broadway Fl 24 (10018-6009)
PHONE..............................212 840-0880
Jon Siskind, *President*
Richard L Siskind, *Vice Pres*
EMP: 15
SALES (est): 2.5MM **Privately Held**
SIC: 2329 2339 Men's & boys' sportswear & athletic clothing; sportswear, women's

(G-11252)
SISTER SISTER INC (PA)
463 7th Ave Fl 4 (10018-8725)
PHONE..............................212 629-9600
Jack Adjmi, *Ch of Bd*
Joseph Dwek, *President*
Joseph Dweck, *President*
Mark Adjmi, *Vice Pres*
Terry Dwek, *Vice Pres*
▲ EMP: 6
SQ FT: 15,000
SALES (est): 4.9MM **Privately Held**
SIC: 2369 2329 Headwear: girls', children's & infants'; men's & boys' sportswear & athletic clothing

(G-11253)
SIZMEK DSP INC
Also Called: Rocket Fuel
401 Park Ave S Fl 5 (10016-8808)
PHONE..............................212 594-8888
Peter Sulick, *Manager*
EMP: 17
SALES (corp-wide): 463.4MM **Privately Held**
SIC: 3993 Advertising artwork
HQ: Sizmek Dsp, Inc.
2000 Seaport Blvd Ste 400
Redwood City CA 94063

(G-11254)
SK CAPITAL PARTNERS II LP (PA)
430 Park Ave Fl 18 (10022-3568)
PHONE..............................212 826-2700
Stephen Dincelli, *Managing Dir*
Jared Kramer, *Vice Pres*
Barry Siadat,
EMP: 19
SALES (est): 992.8MM **Privately Held**
SIC: 2821 2299 Nylon resins; batting, wadding, padding & fillings

(G-11255)
SK TITAN HOLDINGS LLC (HQ)
400 Park Ave (10022-4406)
PHONE..............................212 826-2700
Barry Siadat, *Mng Member*
EMP: 6 EST: 2009
SALES (est): 1.2B
SALES (corp-wide): 992.8MM **Privately Held**
SIC: 2821 2299 Nylon resins; batting, wadding, padding & fillings
PA: Sk Capital Partners Ii, L.P.
430 Park Ave Fl 18
New York NY 10022
212 826-2700

(G-11256)
SKAFFLES GROUP LLC
1400 Broadway Fl 26 (10018-5396)
PHONE..............................212 944-9494
Steven Shwekey, *Mng Member*
EMP: 18 **Privately Held**
SIC: 3999 Pet supplies
PA: Skaffles Group Limited Liability Company
139 Ocean Ave
Lakewood NJ 08701

(G-11257)
SKETCH STUDIO TRADING INC
218 W 37th St Rm 600 (10018-9039)
PHONE..............................212 244-2875
ARI Merabi, *President*
Isaac Merabi, *Manager*
EMP: 3
SALES (est): 8.1MM **Privately Held**
SIC: 2384 Bathrobes, men's & women's: made from purchased materials

(G-11258)
SKILLS ALLIANCE INC
135 W 29th St Rm 201 (10001-5104)
PHONE..............................646 492-5300
Joseph Wolf CPA, *Principal*
EMP: 8
SALES (est): 896.2K **Privately Held**
SIC: 2834 Pharmaceutical preparations

(G-11259)
SKIP HOP INC
50 W 23rd St Fl 10 (10010-5270)
PHONE..............................646 902-9874
Michael Damant, *CEO*
Michael Damiant, *CEO*
Ellen Damiant, *COO*
Janet Villano, *Vice Pres*
Michael Fox, *CFO*
◆ EMP: 40
SALES (est): 25.2MM
SALES (corp-wide): 3.4B **Publicly Held**
WEB: www.skiphop.com
SIC: 2361 3942 2676 Girls' & children's dresses, blouses & shirts; stuffed toys, including animals; infant & baby paper products
HQ: Skip Hop Holdings, Inc.
50 W 23rd St Fl 10
New York NY 10010
212 868-9850

(G-11260)
SKIP HOP HOLDINGS INC (HQ)
50 W 23rd St Fl 10 (10010-5270)
PHONE..............................212 868-9850
Michael Diamant, *CEO*
EMP: 3
SALES (est): 25.2MM
SALES (corp-wide): 3.4B **Publicly Held**
SIC: 2361 3942 2676 6719 Girls' & children's dresses, blouses & shirts; stuffed toys, including animals; infant & baby paper products; investment holding companies, except banks

PA: Carter's, Inc.
3438 Peachtree Rd Ne # 18
Atlanta GA 30326
678 791-1000

(G-11261)
SKIVA INTERNATIONAL INC (PA)
Also Called: Trentset Originals
1407 Broadway Frnt 5 (10018-2342)
PHONE..............................212 736-9520
Albert Chehebar, *Ch of Bd*
Isaac Chehebar, *Vice Pres*
Chuck Frei, *CFO*
Morris Manopla, *Sales Staff*
◆ EMP: 34
SALES (est): 18.8MM **Privately Held**
SIC: 2389 5137 Men's miscellaneous accessories; women's & children's accessories

(G-11262)
SKY ART MEDIA INC
Also Called: Whitewall Magazine
132 Bowery Apt 2f (10013-4297)
PHONE..............................917 355-9022
Michael Klug, *President*
Ashley A Clairmont, *Mktg Dir*
Margaux Cerruti, *Manager*
EMP: 7
SALES (est): 902.8K **Privately Held**
SIC: 2721 Magazines: publishing & printing

(G-11263)
SKY FRAME & ART INC
Also Called: Pop A2z
141 W 28th St Fl 12 (10001-6115)
PHONE..............................212 925-7856
Robert Benrimon, *President*
Sheila Benrimon, *Vice Pres*
EMP: 45
SQ FT: 7,000
SALES (est): 5.5MM **Privately Held**
SIC: 2499 Picture frame molding, finished

(G-11264)
SKYHORSE PUBLISHING INC (PA)
Also Called: All Worth Press
307 W 36th St Fl 11 (10018-6592)
PHONE..............................212 643-6816
Tony Lyons, *President*
Terry Buck, *Editor*
Chelsey Emmelhainz, *Editor*
Julie Ganz, *Editor*
Olga Greco, *Editor*
▲ EMP: 50
SALES: 35MM **Privately Held**
WEB: www.skyhorsepublishing.com
SIC: 2731 Books: publishing only

(G-11265)
SKYLER BRAND VENTURES LLC
150 W 56th St Apt 5301 (10019-3839)
PHONE..............................646 979-5904
Betsy Schmalz Ferguson, *President*
Paul Wahlgren, *Managing Dir*
Konstantinos M Lahanas, *Vice Pres*
Jules Zecchino, *Officer*
EMP: 5 EST: 2013
SALES: 1MM **Privately Held**
SIC: 3841 Skin grafting equipment

(G-11266)
SKYSTEM LLC
100 W 92nd St Apt 20d (10025-7504)
PHONE..............................877 778-3320
Shagun Malhotra, *CEO*
EMP: 5
SALES (est): 251.4K **Privately Held**
SIC: 7372 Business oriented computer software

(G-11267)
SLEEPABLE SOFAS LTD
Also Called: Lodi Down & Feather
600 3rd Ave Fl 15 (10016-1928)
PHONE..............................973 546-4502
Donna De Matteo, *President*
EMP: 80
SQ FT: 28,000

SALES (est): 12.2MM
SALES (corp-wide): 15.4MM **Privately Held**
WEB: www.sleepablesofas.com
SIC: 2515 2512 2392 Sofa beds (convertible sofas); wood upholstered chairs & couches; household furnishings; comforters & quilts: made from purchased materials
PA: Carlyle Custom Convertibles Ltd
6 Empire Blvd
Moonachie NJ 07074
973 546-4502

(G-11268)
SLEEPWEAR HOLDINGS INC
Also Called: Knothe Apparel Group
1372 Broadway Fl 18 (10018-6107)
PHONE..............................516 466-4738
Brian Minkoff, *CEO*
Richard N Bern, *Ch of Bd*
Maria Zoccoli, *President*
Richard Bern, *CFO*
Ken Le, *Manager*
▲ EMP: 125
SQ FT: 11,500
SALES (est): 89.8K **Privately Held**
WEB: www.knothe.com
SIC: 2322 2341 Nightwear, men's & boys': from purchased materials; pajamas & bedjackets: women's & children's

(G-11269)
SLIDEBEAN INCORPORATED
25 Broadway (10004-1010)
PHONE..............................866 365-0588
Jose Cayasso, *CEO*
EMP: 15
SALES: 500K **Privately Held**
SIC: 7372 Prepackaged software

(G-11270)
SM NEWS PLUS INCORPORATED
346 E 59th St Frnt 1 (10022-1527)
PHONE..............................212 888-0153
M Faraq, *President*
EMP: 5
SALES (est): 170.8K **Privately Held**
SIC: 2711 Newspapers

(G-11271)
SMART & STRONG LLC
Also Called: Poz Publishing
212 W 35th St Fl 8 (10001-2508)
PHONE..............................212 938-2051
Brad Peebles, *Partner*
Regan Hofmann, *Publisher*
Sean O'Brien Strub, *Founder*
Dennis Daniel, *Finance Dir*
EMP: 25
SALES (est): 2.6MM **Privately Held**
WEB: www.poz.com
SIC: 2721 Magazines: publishing only, not printed on site

(G-11272)
SMART SPACE PRODUCTS LLC (PA)
244 5th Ave Ste 2487 (10001-7604)
PHONE..............................877 777-2441
Adam Rozen, *Mng Member*
EMP: 5
SQ FT: 1,200
SALES: 1MM **Privately Held**
SIC: 2599 5712 Hotel furniture; furniture stores

(G-11273)
SMILE SPECIALISTS
236 E 36th St (10016-3777)
PHONE..............................877 337-6135
Marvin Lagstein, *Principal*
EMP: 9 EST: 2013
SALES (est): 1.3MM **Privately Held**
SIC: 3843 Cutting instruments, dental

(G-11274)
SMITH & WATSON
200 Lexington Ave Rm 805 (10016-6111)
PHONE..............................212 686-6444
Robert Ryan, *President*
John P Ryan, *Chairman*
Barbara R Pilcher, *Vice Pres*
▲ EMP: 20 EST: 1907
SQ FT: 8,000

▲ = Import ▼=Export
◆ =Import/Export

SALES: 2MM **Privately Held**
WEB: www.smith-watson.com
SIC: 2512 Upholstered household furniture

(G-11275)
SMM - NORTH AMERICA TRADE CORP
Also Called: Sims Metal Management
16 W 22nd St Fl 10 (10010-5967)
PHONE.................................212 604-0710
Robert A Kelman, *President*
Michael S Collins, *Vice Pres*
EMP: 5
SALES (est): 1.2MM **Privately Held**
SIC: 3291 Grit, steel

(G-11276)
SMOOTH INDUSTRIES INCORPORATED
1411 Broadway Rm 3000 (10018-3496)
PHONE.................................212 869-1080
Celeste Chan, *President*
▲ EMP: 25
SQ FT: 7,000
SALES (est): 1.9MM **Privately Held**
WEB: www.smoothny.com
SIC: 2339 Women's & misses' outerwear

(G-11277)
SMOOTH MAGAZINE
55 John St Ste 800 (10038-3752)
PHONE.................................212 925-1150
Sandra Vasceannie, *President*
EMP: 10
SALES (est): 724K **Privately Held**
SIC: 2721 Magazines: publishing only, not printed on site

(G-11278)
SNEAKER NEWS INC
41 Elizabeth St Ste 301 (10013-4637)
PHONE.................................347 687-1588
Yu-Ming Wu, *President*
EMP: 9
SALES: 1.8MM **Privately Held**
SIC: 2741 Shopping news: publishing only, not printed on site

(G-11279)
SNEAKERS SOFTWARE INC
Also Called: Dvmax
519 8th Ave Rm 812 (10018-4588)
PHONE.................................800 877-9221
Paul R Greenman, *CEO*
Larry White, *Engineer*
Kathie Stecher, *Office Mgr*
EMP: 18
SQ FT: 800
SALES: 3MM **Privately Held**
WEB: www.DVMAX.com
SIC: 7372 Prepackaged software

(G-11280)
SNOWMAN
350 5th Ave Fl 59 (10118-5999)
PHONE.................................212 239-8818
Baekkyu Suh, *Mng Member*
EMP: 6
SALES (est): 578.9K **Privately Held**
SIC: 2339 Sportswear, women's

(G-11281)
SOCIAL REGISTER ASSOCIATION
14 Wall St Ste 3f (10005-2141)
PHONE.................................646 612-7314
Matthew Campbell, *President*
EMP: 18 EST: 1971
SALES (est): 92.8K **Privately Held**
WEB: www.socialregisterassociation.com
SIC: 2731 Books: publishing only

(G-11282)
SOCIALED INC
335 Madison Ave Rm 5f2 (10017-4781)
PHONE.................................516 297-2172
Patrick Sullivan, *CEO*
EMP: 6
SALES (est): 135.3K **Privately Held**
SIC: 7372 Educational computer software

(G-11283)
SOCIETY FOR THE STUDY
Also Called: PARABOLA
20 W 20th St Fl 2 (10011-9260)
PHONE.................................212 822-8806
Steven Schiff, *President*
Jeff Zaleski, *Publisher*
EMP: 7
SQ FT: 1,500
SALES: 558.4K **Privately Held**
SIC: 2721 2731 5942 Magazines: publishing only, not printed on site; video tapes, prerecorded; audio tapes, prerecorded; book stores

(G-11284)
SOFT SHEEN PRODUCTS INC (DH)
10 Hudson Yards Fl 27 (10001-2159)
PHONE.................................212 818-1500
Patricia Cumberland, *President*
Said Dabbagh, *President*
Alejandro Lopez, *General Mgr*
Candace Matthews, *Principal*
Simpson Julette, *Assistant VP*
◆ EMP: 1 EST: 1964
SALES (est): 3.6MM
SALES (corp-wide): 4.4B **Privately Held**
WEB: www.softsheen-carson.com
SIC: 2844 Shampoos, rinses, conditioners: hair
HQ: L'oreal Usa, Inc.
10 Hudson Yards
New York NY 10001
212 818-1500

(G-11285)
SOHO APPAREL LTD
Also Called: Flirtatious
525 7th Ave Fl 6 (10018-4960)
PHONE.................................212 840-1109
Nikou Achouri, *President*
Jeffrey Stein, *Exec VP*
EMP: 5
SQ FT: 3,140
SALES (est): 527.6K **Privately Held**
SIC: 2331 5137 Women's & misses' blouses & shirts; women's & children's clothing

(G-11286)
SOHO PRESS INC
79 Madison Ave Fl 8 (10016-7810)
PHONE.................................212 260-1900
Juris Jurjevics, *President*
Laura Hruska, *Vice Pres*
Meredith Barnes, *Manager*
Rachel Kowal, *Manager*
EMP: 5
SALES (est): 724K **Privately Held**
WEB: www.sohopress.com
SIC: 2731 5942 Books: publishing only; book stores

(G-11287)
SOL SAVRANSKY DIAMONDS INC
25 W 43rd St Ste 802 (10036-7428)
PHONE.................................212 730-4700
Eli Savransky, *CEO*
Craig Chinsky, *Vice Pres*
Hanna Epstein, *Admin Sec*
◆ EMP: 14
SQ FT: 5,000
SALES (est): 2.4MM **Privately Held**
WEB: www.savransky.com
SIC: 3911 5094 Jewelry, precious metal; jewelry

(G-11288)
SOLABIA USA INC
28 W 44th St (10036-7406)
PHONE.................................212 847-2397
Michael J Conti, *President*
▲ EMP: 7
SQ FT: 1,100
SALES (est): 6.6MM **Privately Held**
SIC: 2844 Cosmetic preparations

(G-11289)
SOLARPATH INC
Also Called: Solarpath Sun Solutions
415 Madison Ave Fl 14 (10017-7935)
PHONE.................................201 490-4499
Ori Aldubi, *CEO*

Amir Warshazsky, *President*
EMP: 6
SQ FT: 5,000
SALES (est): 900.6K **Privately Held**
SIC: 3646 Commercial indusl & institutional electric lighting fixtures

(G-11290)
SOLSTARS INC
Also Called: Solstarny
575 Madison Ave Ste 1006 (10022-8511)
PHONE.................................212 605-0430
Haim Hassin, *President*
◆ EMP: 7
SALES (est): 706.4K **Privately Held**
SIC: 2084 Wine cellars, bonded: engaged in blending wines

(G-11291)
SOLSTISS INC
561 Fashion Ave Fl 16 (10018-1816)
PHONE.................................212 719-9194
Francois Damide, *President*
Sandrine Bernard, *Exec VP*
Ahsan Masood, *Controller*
Sara Harris, *Marketing Mgr*
EMP: 6
SQ FT: 3,500
SALES (est): 624.7K **Privately Held**
SIC: 2241 2258 Silk narrow fabrics; lace & lace products

(G-11292)
SOLUDOS LLC
520 Broadway Fl 5 (10012-4436)
PHONE.................................212 219-1101
Brigid Foster, *COO*
Catherine Leavitt, *Vice Pres*
Ardit Keqi, *Accountant*
Meredith Hamilton, *Accounts Exec*
Alexis Pena, *Director*
▲ EMP: 13 EST: 2010
SALES (est): 1.9MM **Privately Held**
SIC: 3021 7389 Shoes, rubber or plastic molded to fabric; shoe designers

(G-11293)
SOLUTIA BUSINESS ENTPS INC
111 8th Ave (10011-5201)
PHONE.................................314 674-1000
Timothy J Spihlman, *Ch of Bd*
EMP: 15
SALES (est): 1MM **Publicly Held**
SIC: 2824 Organic fibers, noncellulosic
HQ: Solutia Inc.
575 Maryville Centre Dr
Saint Louis MO 63141
423 229-2000

(G-11294)
SONY BROADBAND ENTERTAINMENT (DH)
550 Madison Ave Fl 6 (10022-3211)
PHONE.................................212 833-6800
Howard Stringer, *Ch of Bd*
Nobuyuki Idei, *Vice Chairman*
Robert Wiesenthal, *CFO*
Arnulfo Gonzalez, *Info Tech Dir*
▲ EMP: 12
SQ FT: 20,000
SALES (est): 904.8MM **Privately Held**
SIC: 3652 7812 5734 7832 Pre-recorded records & tapes; motion picture production & distribution; motion picture production & distribution, television; software, computer games; motion picture theaters, except drive-in; video discs & tapes, prerecorded
HQ: Sony Corporation Of America
25 Madison Ave Fl 27
New York NY 10010
212 833-8000

(G-11295)
SONY CORPORATION OF AMERICA (HQ)
Also Called: Sony Music Entertainment
25 Madison Ave Fl 27 (10010-8601)
PHONE.................................212 833-8000
Kazuo Hirai, *Ch of Bd*
Kimberly Manfre, *Exec VP*
Nicole Seligman, *Exec VP*
Mary Jo V Green, *Senior VP*
Steven E Kober, *Senior VP*
◆ EMP: 250
SQ FT: 20,000

SALES (est): 8B **Privately Held**
WEB: www.sony.com
SIC: 3695 3652 3651 3577 Optical disks & tape, blank; compact laser discs, prerecorded; household audio & video equipment; computer peripheral equipment; computer storage devices

(G-11296)
SONY DADC US INC
Also Called: Sony Style
550 Madison Ave (10022-3211)
PHONE.................................212 833-8800
Anand Mathur, *General Mgr*
John Fukunaga, *Counsel*
Toru Katsumoto, *Sr Exec VP*
Gregory Boone, *Exec VP*
Jim Underwood, *Exec VP*
EMP: 386 **Privately Held**
SIC: 3695 Optical disks & tape, blank
HQ: Sony Dadc Us Inc.
1800 N Fruitridge Ave
Terre Haute IN 47804
812 462-8100

(G-11297)
SONY MUSIC ENTERTAINMENT
Also Called: Sony Music Holdings
25 Madison Ave Fl 19 (10010-8601)
PHONE.................................212 833-8000
Thomas Mottola, *CEO*
Frommer Jennifer, *Vice Pres*
Jenny Miskov, *Manager*
Ivy Tsai, *Sr Software Eng*
EMP: 2000 **Privately Held**
WEB: www.sonymusic.com
SIC: 3652 Pre-recorded records & tapes
HQ: Sony Music Entertainment, Inc.
25 Madison Ave Fl 19
New York NY 10010
212 833-8000

(G-11298)
SONY MUSIC ENTERTAINMENT INC (DH)
Also Called: Sony Wonder
25 Madison Ave Fl 19 (10010-8601)
PHONE.................................212 833-8000
Hartwig Masuch, *CEO*
Robert Sorrentino, *Ch of Bd*
Tim Bowen, *Principal*
Kevin Kelleher, *Principal*
Andrew Lack, *Principal*
▲ EMP: 2000
SQ FT: 500,000
SALES (est): 909.3MM **Privately Held**
WEB: www.sonymusic.com
SIC: 3652 5064 Pre-recorded records & tapes; electrical appliances, television & radio
HQ: Sony Broadband Entertainment Corp
550 Madison Ave Fl 6
New York NY 10022
212 833-6800

(G-11299)
SONY MUSIC HOLDINGS INC (DH)
Also Called: Sony Music Entertainment
25 Madison Ave Fl 26 (10010-8601)
PHONE.................................212 833-8000
Douglas P Morris, *CEO*
Steven E Kober, *President*
Charles Goldstuck, *President*
Richard Griffiths, *President*
Robert Jamieson, *President*
◆ EMP: 800
SQ FT: 300,000
SALES (est): 509.3MM **Privately Held**
WEB: www.bmgentertainment.com
SIC: 3652 5099 2741 Pre-recorded records & tapes; phonograph records; tapes & cassettes, prerecorded; compact discs; miscellaneous publishing
HQ: Sony Corporation Of America
25 Madison Ave Fl 27
New York NY 10010
212 833-8000

(G-11300)
SONY/ATV MUSIC PUBLISHING LLC (DH)
25 Madison Ave Fl 24 (10010-8601)
PHONE.................................212 833-7730
Martin N Bandier, *CEO*
Jorge Mejia, *President*

Kaz Ambe, *Exec VP*
Stuart Bondell, *Exec VP*
Peter Brodsky, *Exec VP*
▲ EMP: 20 EST: 1995
SALES (est): 14.6MM **Privately Held**
SIC: 2741 Music book & sheet music publishing
HQ: Sony Corporation Of America
25 Madison Ave Fl 27
New York NY 10010
212 833-8000

(G-11301)
SOS CHEFS NEW YORK INC
104 Avenue B Apt 1 (10009-6286)
P.O. Box 517 (10021-0011)
PHONE....................212 505-5813
Atef Boulaabi, *President*
▲ EMP: 5
SALES (est): 591.3K **Privately Held**
WEB: www.sos-chefs.com
SIC: 2099 Seasonings & spices

(G-11302)
SOS INTERNATIONAL LLC
426 W Broadway Apt 6a (10012-3773)
PHONE....................212 742-2410
Samantha O'Neil, *Manager*
Doug Meyer, *Director*
EMP: 353
SALES (corp-wide): 93.7MM **Privately Held**
SIC: 3724 Aircraft engines & engine parts
PA: Sos International Llc
1881 Campus Commons Dr # 500
Reston VA 20191
703 391-9680

(G-11303)
SOTERIX MEDICAL INC
Also Called: Soterix Medical Technologies
237 W 35th St Ste 1401 (10001-1950)
PHONE....................888 990-8327
Lucas Parra, *President*
Pragya Bista, *Manager*
▲ EMP: 12
SALES (est): 655.5K **Privately Held**
SIC: 3845 Electromedical equipment

(G-11304)
SOURCE MEDIA LLC (HQ)
1 State St Fl 27 (10004-1561)
PHONE....................212 803-8200
Gemma Postlethwaite, *CEO*
Victor Kuo, *General Mgr*
Dean Anason, *Editor*
Suleman Din, *Editor*
Christopher Wood Online E, *Editor*
▲ EMP: 191
SQ FT: 60,000
SALES (est): 174.8MM
SALES (corp-wide): 194.2MM **Privately Held**
WEB: www.sourcemedia.com/
SIC: 2721 Magazines: publishing & printing

(G-11305)
SOUTH BRIDGE PRESS INC
122 W 26th St Fl 3 (10001-6804)
PHONE....................212 233-4047
Mitch Nochlin, *President*
EMP: 8
SALES (est): 946.9K **Privately Held**
SIC: 2752 Commercial printing, offset

(G-11306)
SOUTINE INC
104 W 70th St Frnt 1 (10023-4454)
PHONE....................212 496-1450
Madge Rosenberg, *President*
Barry Rosenberg, *Vice Pres*
EMP: 6
SQ FT: 600
SALES (est): 497.2K **Privately Held**
WEB: www.soutine.com
SIC: 2051 5812 Bakery: wholesale or wholesale/retail combined; caterers

(G-11307)
SOVEREIGN BRANDS LLC (PA)
383 W Broadway Apt 5 (10012-4377)
PHONE....................212 343-8366
Brett R Berish, *CEO*
Brett Berish, *Managing Prtnr*
Brandon Jones, *Area Mgr*
Amelia Salafrio, *Area Mgr*

Scott Cohen, *VP Opers*
◆ EMP: 6
SQ FT: 1,800
SALES (est): 1.7MM **Privately Held**
WEB: www.sovereignbrands.com
SIC: 2085 Distilled & blended liquors

(G-11308)
SPARK CREATIONS INC
10 W 46th St Fl 9 (10036-4515)
PHONE....................212 575-8385
Eli Aviram, *President*
Benjamin Aviram, *Vice Pres*
▲ EMP: 17
SQ FT: 4,000
SALES (est): 1.8MM **Privately Held**
WEB: www.sparkcreations.com
SIC: 3911 Jewelry, precious metal

(G-11309)
SPARTA COMMERCIAL SERVICES INC (PA)
555 5th Ave Fl 14 (10017-9257)
PHONE....................212 239-2666
Anthony L Havens, *Ch of Bd*
Anthony Havens, *COO*
Richard P Trotter, *COO*
Anthony Adler, *Exec VP*
Sandra L Ahman, *Vice Pres*
EMP: 11
SQ FT: 3,000
SALES (est): 604.8K **Publicly Held**
WEB: www.spartacommercial.com
SIC: 7372 7375 Prepackaged software; on-line data base information retrieval

(G-11310)
SPARTACIST PUBLISHING CO
48 Warren St (10007-1017)
P.O. Box 1377 (10116-1377)
PHONE....................212 732-7860
Elizabeth R Gordis, *CEO*
James M Robertson, *President*
Meghan Kilduff, *Vice Pres*
A Robinson Hunt, *Treasurer*
EMP: 20
SALES (est): 1.8MM **Privately Held**
SIC: 2731 2711 Pamphlets: publishing only, not printed on site; newspapers: publishing only, not printed on site

(G-11311)
SPARTAN BRANDS INC (PA)
451 Park Ave S Fl 5 (10016-7390)
PHONE....................212 340-0320
Gary Grey, *President*
Eli Motovich, *CFO*
Tara Mattera, *Marketing Staff*
◆ EMP: 12 EST: 1946
SQ FT: 2,500
SALES (est): 12.9MM **Privately Held**
WEB: www.spartanbrands.com
SIC: 3999 Hair & hair-based products

(G-11312)
SPECIALNEEDSWARE INC
Also Called: Oneder
1 Irving Pl Apt V9c (10003-9713)
PHONE....................646 278-9959
Jonathan Izak, *CEO*
Stuart Carapola, *Manager*
EMP: 14 EST: 2014
SQ FT: 2,200
SALES (est): 1.1MM **Privately Held**
SIC: 7372 Educational computer software

(G-11313)
SPECIALTY SIGNS CO INC
15 W 39th St Fl 7 (10018-0633)
PHONE....................212 243-8521
Marc Frankel, *President*
EMP: 13 EST: 1971
SQ FT: 6,000
SALES (est): 850K **Privately Held**
SIC: 3993 Signs & advertising specialties

(G-11314)
SPECILTY BUS MCHS HOLDINGS LLC
260 W 35th St Fl 11 (10001-2528)
PHONE....................212 587-9600
Steven Schaps, *Mng Member*
EMP: 26
SALES (est): 3.6MM **Privately Held**
SIC: 3555 Printing trades machinery

(G-11315)
SPECTRUM APPAREL INC
463 Fashion Ave Fl 12 (10018-7499)
PHONE....................212 239-2025
Richard Kringstein, *President*
EMP: 85
SALES (est): 5.7MM **Privately Held**
SIC: 2339 Women's & misses' jackets & coats, except sportswear

(G-11316)
SPECTRUM PRTG LITHOGRAPHY INC
Also Called: Earth Spectrum
505 8th Ave Rm 1802 (10018-4707)
PHONE....................212 255-3131
Peter Mandelkern, *President*
Karen Targrove, *Vice Pres*
EMP: 26
SQ FT: 5,000
SALES (est): 2.3MM **Privately Held**
SIC: 2752 2789 2759 2675 Color lithography; bookbinding & related work; commercial printing; die-cut paper & board

(G-11317)
SPEKTRIX INC
115 W 30th St Rm 501 (10001-4071)
PHONE....................646 741-5110
Molly Johnson, *Project Mgr*
David Ciano, *Accounts Exec*
Hailey Colwell, *Marketing Staff*
Rebecca Kahn, *Mng Member*
EMP: 6
SQ FT: 1,200
SALES (est): 163.7K **Privately Held**
SIC: 7372 Publishers' computer software

(G-11318)
SPENCER AB INC
265 W 37th St Rm 2388 (10018-5757)
PHONE....................646 831-3728
Tommy Tsui, *President*
Joel Glentz, *VP Sales*
EMP: 7
SALES (est): 1.5MM **Privately Held**
SIC: 2335 2331 Women's, juniors' & misses' dresses; women's & misses' blouses & shirts

(G-11319)
SPEYSIDE FOUNDRY HOLDINGS LLC (PA)
430 E 86th St (10028-6441)
PHONE....................212 994-0308
Kevin Daugherty, *CEO*
EMP: 2
SALES (est): 24.3MM **Privately Held**
SIC: 3325 3543 3369 3321 Alloy steel castings, except investment; industrial patterns; nonferrous foundries; gray iron castings; ductile iron castings

(G-11320)
SPF HOLDINGS II LLC
9 W 57th St Ste 4200 (10019-2707)
PHONE....................212 750-8300
Dave West, *President*
EMP: 9
SALES (est): 2.1B
SALES (corp-wide): 7.8B **Publicly Held**
SIC: 2033 5149 6719 2099 Fruits & fruit products in cans, jars, etc.; vegetables & vegetable products in cans, jars, etc.; tomato products: packaged in cans, jars, etc.; canned goods: fruit, vegetables, seafood, meats, etc.; pet foods; personal holding companies, except banks; syrups; frosting, ready-to-use; sandwiches, assembled & packaged: for wholesale market; peanut butter
PA: The J M Smucker Company
1 Strawberry Ln
Orrville OH 44667
330 682-3000

(G-11321)
SPH GROUP HOLDINGS LLC (HQ)
590 Madison Ave Fl 32 (10022-2524)
PHONE....................212 520-2300
Jack L Howard, *CEO*
EMP: 14 EST: 2013

SALES (est): 828.3MM
SALES (corp-wide): 1.5B **Publicly Held**
SIC: 3339 3011 3312 Precious metals; tire & inner tube materials & related products; wire products, steel or iron
PA: Steel Partners Holdings L.P.
590 Madison Ave Rm 3202
New York NY 10022
212 520-2300

(G-11322)
SPHERE CABLES & CHIPS INC (PA)
121 Fulton St Fl 4 (10038-2737)
PHONE....................212 619-3132
Michael Nastashkin, *CEO*
EMP: 34
SQ FT: 5,500
SALES (est): 5.4MM **Privately Held**
WEB: www.cablesandchipsinc.com
SIC: 2298 3644 5734 5063 Cable, fiber; switch boxes, electric; computer peripheral equipment; electronic wire & cable; connectors, electronic; local area network (LAN) systems integrator

(G-11323)
SPIN MAGAZINE MEDIA
276 5th Ave Rm 800 (10001-4509)
PHONE....................212 231-7400
Nion McEvoy, *CEO*
Jack Jensen, *President*
Tom Fernald, *Vice Pres*
EMP: 20
SALES (est): 218.2K
SALES (corp-wide): 3.2MM **Privately Held**
WEB: www.spinmag.com
SIC: 2721 Magazines: publishing only, not printed on site
PA: Buzz Media Inc.
6464 W Sunset Blvd # 650
Los Angeles CA 90028
213 252-8999

(G-11324)
SPIRIT MUSIC GROUP INC (HQ)
235 W 23rd St Fl 4 (10011-2371)
PHONE....................212 533-7672
Mark Fried, *President*
David Renzer, *Chairman*
Joe Borrino, *COO*
Sultana Kraja, *Manager*
James Cheney, *Director*
EMP: 20
SALES (est): 1.9MM **Publicly Held**
WEB: www.spiritmusicgroup.com
SIC: 2741 Music books: publishing & printing

(G-11325)
SPLACER INC
33 W 17th St Fl 6 (10011-5511)
PHONE....................646 853-9789
ADI Biran, *CEO*
Gabi Peles, *COO*
EMP: 6
SALES (est): 350K **Privately Held**
SIC: 7372 Application computer software

(G-11326)
SPORTS ILLUSTRATED FOR KIDS
1271 Ave Of The Americas (10020-1300)
PHONE....................212 522-1212
Don Logan, *CEO*
Joe Ripp, *Principal*
Chris Chambers, *Editor*
Mj Day, *Editor*
Paul Fichtenbaum, *Editor*
▲ EMP: 50
SALES (est): 5.5MM
SALES (corp-wide): 3.1B **Publicly Held**
WEB: www.siphoto.com
SIC: 2721 Magazines: publishing only, not printed on site
HQ: Ti Gotham Inc.
225 Liberty St
New York NY 10281
212 522-1212

(G-11327)
SPORTS PBLICATIONS PROD NY LLC
708 3rd Ave Fl 12 (10017-4129)
PHONE..................................212 366-7700
Brent Diamond,
EMP: 80
SALES (est): 2.3MM **Privately Held**
SIC: 2711 Newspapers, publishing & printing

(G-11328)
SPORTS PRODUCTS AMERICA LLC
Popsicle Playwear
34 W 33rd St Fl 2 (10001-3304)
PHONE..................................212 594-5511
Alan Kahn, Export Mgr
Richard Adjmi, Sales Associate
EMP: 50
SALES (corp-wide): 27.1MM **Privately Held**
SIC: 2361 Girls' & children's blouses & shirts
HQ: Sports Products Of America Llc
463 7th Ave
New York NY 10018
212 629-9600

(G-11329)
SPORTS REPORTER INC
527 3rd Ave Ste 327 (10016-4168)
PHONE..................................212 737-2750
Lindsay Hamilton, President
EMP: 6
SALES (est): 280K **Privately Held**
WEB: www.sportsreporter.com
SIC: 2711 Newspapers, publishing & printing

(G-11330)
SPORTSGRID INC
404 5th Ave Fl 3 (10018-7510)
PHONE..................................646 849-4085
Jeremy Stein, CEO
Alexander Dubin, Shareholder
Louis Maione, Shareholder
EMP: 10
SALES: 1MM **Privately Held**
SIC: 2741

(G-11331)
SPRAY MORET LLC
Also Called: Sprayground
1411 Broadway Fl 8 (10018-3565)
PHONE..................................917 213-9592
David Ben-David,
▲ **EMP:** 5
SALES (est): 117.2K **Privately Held**
SIC: 2393 Canvas bags

(G-11332)
SPRING INC
41 E 11th St Fl 11 (10003-4602)
PHONE..................................646 732-0323
Ofer Leidner, President
EMP: 6
SALES (est): 468.2K **Privately Held**
SIC: 7372 Application computer software

(G-11333)
SPRINGER ADIS US LLC (DH)
233 Spring St Fl 6 (10013-1522)
PHONE..................................212 460-1500
Derk Haank, CEO
Neil Levine, Editor
Dahlia Fisch, Assoc Editor
Eddie Bates, Technical Staff
EMP: 17
SALES (est): 3MM
SALES (corp-wide): 1.6B **Privately Held**
SIC: 2721 2731 Trade journals: publishing only, not printed on site; magazines: publishing only, not printed on site; books: publishing only
HQ: Springer Science + Business Media, Llc
233 Spring St Fl 6
New York NY 10013
212 460-1500

(G-11334)
SPRINGER HEALTHCARE LLC
233 Spring St (10013-1522)
PHONE..................................212 460-1500

Christina Leber, Credit Mgr
Rick Werdann, Branch Mgr
EMP: 25
SALES (corp-wide): 1.6B **Privately Held**
SIC: 2721 Trade journals: publishing only, not printed on site
HQ: Springer Nature Three Gmbh
Heidelberger Platz 3
Berlin 14197
308 278-70

(G-11335)
SPRINGER NATURE
Also Called: Kluwer Academic Publishers
233 Spring St (10013-1522)
PHONE..................................212 460-1500
Doris Drechsler, President
Rick Werdann, General Mgr
Welmoed Spahr, Managing Dir
Priyanka Ganesh, Editor
William Helms, Editor
▲ **EMP:** 66
SALES (est): 6.1MM **Privately Held**
SIC: 2731 Book publishing

(G-11336)
SPRINGER NATURE AMERICA INC (DH)
Also Called: Nature Publishing Group
1 New York Plz Ste 4500 (10004-1562)
PHONE..................................212 726-9200
Frank Vrancken Peeters, CEO
Matt Hansen, Publisher
Myles Axton, Editor
Sunya Bhutta, Editor
Pearson Helen, Editor
▼ **EMP:** 380
SQ FT: 66,000
SALES: 300MM **Privately Held**
WEB: www.nature.com
SIC: 2741 Miscellaneous publishing
HQ: Springer Nature Limited
Cromwell Place
Basingstoke HANTS RG24
125 632-9242

(G-11337)
SPRINGER NATURE CUST SERV CENT
Also Called: Springer Customer Svc Ctr LLC
233 Spring St (10013-1522)
PHONE..................................212 460-1500
Edward Woods, CFO
EMP: 400
SQ FT: 80,000
SALES (est): 28.6MM
SALES (corp-wide): 1.6B **Privately Held**
SIC: 2731 Book publishing
HQ: Springer Nature Customer Service Center Gmbh
Tiergartenstr. 15-17
Heidelberg 69121
622 134-50

(G-11338)
SPRINGER PUBLISHING CO LLC
11 W 42nd St Ste 15a (10036-8007)
PHONE..................................212 431-4370
Ursula Springer, President
Frank Costanzo, Vice Pres
Jason Roth, Vice Pres
Pascal Schwarzer, Vice Pres
Christina Morgan, Production
EMP: 38 **EST:** 1950
SQ FT: 9,000
SALES (est): 7.6MM **Privately Held**
WEB: www.springerpub.com
SIC: 2731 2721 Books: publishing only; trade journals: publishing only, not printed on site

(G-11339)
SPRINGER SCNCE + BUS MEDIA LLC (DH)
Also Called: Springer Business Media
233 Spring St Fl 6 (10013-1522)
PHONE..................................212 460-1500
Miguel Quesada, General Mgr
Jesus Gonzalez, Principal
Mayra Castro, Editor
Katherine Chabalko, Editor
Ron Doering, Editor
◆ **EMP:** 62 **EST:** 1964
SQ FT: 40,000

SALES (est): 83.1MM
SALES (corp-wide): 1.6B **Privately Held**
WEB: www.telospub.com
SIC: 2721 2731 Trade journals: publishing only, not printed on site; books: publishing only
HQ: Springer Nature Three Gmbh
Heidelberger Platz 3
Berlin 14197
308 278-70

(G-11340)
SPUTNICK 84 LLC
Also Called: Out of Print
1745 Broadway Frnt 3 (10019-4641)
PHONE..................................844 667-7468
Todd Lawton, Principal
Jeffrey Leblanc, Principal
EMP: 7
SALES (est): 658.2K
SALES (corp-wide): 75.3MM **Privately Held**
SIC: 2752 Commercial printing, lithographic
HQ: Penguin Random House Llc
1745 Broadway Frnt 1
New York NY 10019
212 782-9000

(G-11341)
SRP APPAREL GROUP INC
525 7th Ave Rm 1808 (10018-5274)
PHONE..................................212 764-4810
Scott Pianin, President
▲ **EMP:** 5
SALES (est): 905.3K **Privately Held**
SIC: 2339 Women's & misses' outerwear

(G-11342)
SSA TRADING LTD
226 W 37th St Fl 6l (10018-9020)
PHONE..................................646 465-9500
Gary Cohen, President
Robert Klein, CFO
Marc Klein, Treasurer
EMP: 12
SQ FT: 5,000
SALES (est): 1.4MM **Privately Held**
SIC: 2339 Sportswear, women's

(G-11343)
SSG FASHIONS LTD
27 E 37th St Frnt 1 (10016-3004)
PHONE..................................212 221-0933
William Seng, President
▲ **EMP:** 6
SQ FT: 3,000
SALES (est): 966.2K **Privately Held**
WEB: www.ssgfashions.com
SIC: 2339 2335 Sportswear, women's; women's, juniors' & misses' dresses

(G-11344)
STANDARD ANALYTICS IO INC
7 World Trade Ctr 46th (10007-2140)
PHONE..................................917 882-5422
Tiffany Bogich, COO
EMP: 6
SALES (est): 219.1K **Privately Held**
SIC: 2721 2741 7371 7374 Periodicals; ; computer software development; data processing & preparation; distribution channels consultant

(G-11345)
STANDARD INDUSTRIES INC
9 W 57th St Fl 30 (10019-2701)
PHONE..................................212 821-1600
David Millstone, CEO
David Winter, Co-CEO
Clayton McGratty, Vice Pres
EMP: 18
SALES (est): 3.1MM **Privately Held**
SIC: 3272 Building materials, except block or brick: concrete

(G-11346)
STANDARD SCREEN SUPPLY CORP (PA)
Also Called: Active Process Supply
121 Varick St Rm 200 (10013-1408)
PHONE..................................212 627-2727
Arthur Gononsky, President
Susan Gononsky, Treasurer
◆ **EMP:** 21 **EST:** 1951

SALES (est): 3.1MM **Privately Held**
WEB: www.standardscreen.com
SIC: 2893 Screen process ink

(G-11347)
STANMARK JEWELRY INC
64 W 48th St Ste 1303 (10036-1708)
PHONE..................................212 730-2557
Stanley Krukowski, President
EMP: 6
SQ FT: 10,000
SALES (est): 510K **Privately Held**
WEB: www.stanmark.com
SIC: 3911 5944 Jewelry, precious metal; jewelry stores

(G-11348)
STAR CHILDRENS DRESS CO INC (PA)
Also Called: Rare Editions
1250 Broadway Fl 18 (10001-3749)
PHONE..................................212 279-1524
Edward Rosen, Ch of Bd
Dominique Carter, Production
Joann Wynn, Consultant
Ken Dippold, Info Tech Mgr
◆ **EMP:** 60
SQ FT: 12,000
SALES (est): 38.6MM **Privately Held**
WEB: www.rareeditions.com
SIC: 2361 Dresses: girls', children's & infants'

(G-11349)
STAR WIRE MESH FABRICATORS
518 E 119th St (10035-4432)
P.O. Box 678 (10035-0678)
PHONE..................................212 831-4133
Alex Pavur, President
Anistasia Pavur, Treasurer
EMP: 5
SQ FT: 2,500
SALES (est): 510K **Privately Held**
WEB: www.starwiremesh.com
SIC: 3496 Screening, woven wire: made from purchased wire; mesh, made from purchased wire

(G-11350)
STARFIRE HOLDING CORPORATION (PA)
767 5th Ave Fl 47 (10153-0023)
PHONE..................................914 614-7000
Carl Celian Icahn, Ch of Bd
Keith Cozza, Vice Pres
EMP: 50
SALES (est): 955MM **Privately Held**
SIC: 3743 4741 4789 Freight cars & equipment; rental of railroad cars; railroad car repair

(G-11351)
STARLITE MEDIA LLC (PA)
118 E 28th St Rm 601 (10016-8447)
PHONE..................................212 909-7700
Harold Lueken, CEO
Rick Fulginiti, Manager
Thomas Mule, CIO
Tim Daly,
Karen Jolicoeur,
EMP: 30
SQ FT: 1,000
SALES: 3.7MM **Privately Held**
WEB: www.starlitemedia.com
SIC: 3993 Signs & advertising specialties

(G-11352)
STEEL PARTNERS HOLDINGS LP (PA)
590 Madison Ave Rm 3202 (10022-8536)
PHONE..................................212 520-2300
Jack L Howard, President
Douglas B Woodworth, CFO
EMP: 59
SQ FT: 15,660
SALES: 1.5B **Publicly Held**
SIC: 3479 3497 1381 6141 Etching & engraving; copper foil; gold foil or leaf; nickel foil; silver foil or leaf; drilling oil & gas wells; consumer finance companies

(G-11353)
STEEZYS LLC
80 8th Ave 202 (10011-5126)
PHONE..................................646 276-5333
Robert Lebowitz, *Mng Member*
Edina Sultanik,
EMP: 7
SALES (est): 592.2K **Privately Held**
SIC: 3961 Costume jewelry, ex. precious
　metal & semiprecious stones

(G-11354)
STEFAN FURS INC
150 W 30th St Fl 15 (10001-4138)
PHONE..................................212 594-2788
Alex Amanatides, *President*
EMP: 5
SQ FT: 800
SALES (est): 382.1K **Privately Held**
SIC: 2371 Fur goods

(G-11355)
**STEINWAY MUSICAL INSTRS
INC (HQ)**
1133 Avenue Of The Americ (10036-6710)
PHONE..................................781 894-9770
Michael T Sweeney, *President*
Ron Losby, *President*
John Stoner Jr, *President*
Donna M Lucente, *Vice Pres*
Dennis M Hanson, *Treasurer*
◆ EMP: 37
SALES (est): 237.4MM
SALES (corp-wide): 239.6MM **Privately
Held**
WEB: www.steinwaymusical.com
SIC: 3931 Musical instruments; pianos, all
　types: vertical, grand, spinet, player, etc.;
　string instruments & parts; woodwind in-
　struments & parts
PA: Paulson & Co. Inc.
　1133 Ave Of The Americas
　New York NY 10036
　212 956-2221

(G-11356)
**STEMLINE THERAPEUTICS INC
(PA)**
750 Lexington Ave Fl 11 (10022-9817)
PHONE..................................646 502-2311
Ivan Bergstein, *Ch of Bd*
Kenneth Hoberman, *COO*
David G Gionco, *CFO*
Craig Paulsen, *Manager*
Megan Sardone, *Manager*
EMP: 37
SALES: 500K **Publicly Held**
WEB: www.stemline.com
SIC: 2834 Pharmaceutical preparations

(G-11357)
STENSUL INC (PA)
150 W 25th St Fl 3 (10001-7404)
PHONE..................................212 380-8620
Noah Dinkin, *CEO*
Gabriel Sosa, *Vice Pres*
Jonathan Travin, *Vice Pres*
Michael Zusel, *Consultant*
EMP: 6
SQ FT: 5,500
SALES (est): 3.6MM **Privately Held**
SIC: 7372 Prepackaged software

(G-11358)
**STEPHAN & COMPANY ACC LTD
(PA)**
251 W 19th St Apt 1f (10011-4043)
PHONE..................................212 481-3888
Stephan Rubin, *President*
▲ EMP: 20
SALES (est): 1.7MM **Privately Held**
WEB: www.stephanco.com
SIC: 3961 Costume jewelry, ex. precious
　metal & semiprecious stones

(G-11359)
**STEPHEN SINGER PATTERN CO
INC**
Also Called: Popular Pattern
340 W 39th St Fl 4 (10018-1345)
PHONE..................................212 947-2902
Stephen Singer, *President*
EMP: 12
SQ FT: 7,000

SALES (est): 1.9MM **Privately Held**
SIC: 2621 2741 Pattern tissue; miscella-
　neous publishing

(G-11360)
STERLING SOUND INC
88 10th Ave Frnt 6 (10011-4745)
PHONE..................................212 604-9433
Murat Aktar, *President*
Stephanie Geny-Bikialo, *Project Mgr*
Mark Glaser, *Project Mgr*
Phillip Sztenderowicz, *Engineer*
Sara Chaudhari, *Asst Controller*
EMP: 30
SALES (est): 4.7MM **Privately Held**
SIC: 3652 Master records or tapes, prepa-
　ration of

(G-11361)
**STEVENS BANDES GRAPHICS
CORP**
333 Hudson St Fl 3 (10013-1006)
PHONE..................................212 675-1128
Stephen Kilduff, *President*
Kevin Roach, *Admin Sec*
EMP: 10
SQ FT: 2,500
SALES: 1.5MM **Privately Held**
WEB: www.stevensbandes.com
SIC: 2752 Commercial printing, offset

(G-11362)
STEVES ORIGINAL FURS INC
345 7th Ave Fl 9 (10001-5049)
PHONE..................................212 967-8007
Steve Panaretos, *President*
Aspasia Panaretos, *Admin Sec*
EMP: 20
SALES (est): 2MM **Privately Held**
WEB: www.stevesoriginalfurs.com
SIC: 2371 Fur finishers & liners for the fur
　goods trade

(G-11363)
STICKY SOCKS LLC
200 W 60th St Apt 7g (10023-8504)
PHONE..................................212 541-5927
Eva Di Nardo, *President*
EMP: 5
SALES (est): 309K **Privately Held**
SIC: 2252 Socks

(G-11364)
STITCH & COUTURE INC (PA)
Also Called: Lela Rose
224 W 30th St Fl 14 (10001-1493)
PHONE..................................212 947-9204
Lela Rose, *CEO*
Chanelle Smith, *Production*
Caroline Faulkner, *Accounts Exec*
Caitlin Costello, *Sales Staff*
Tricia Starr, *Pub Rel Staff*
EMP: 30
SQ FT: 3,000
SALES (est): 8MM **Privately Held**
WEB: www.lelarose.com
SIC: 2331 2335 Blouses, women's & jun-
　iors': made from purchased material;
　shirts, women's & juniors': made from
　purchased materials; bridal & formal
　gowns

(G-11365)
**STONE HOUSE ASSOCIATES
INC**
37 W 47th St Ste 910 (10036-2809)
PHONE..................................212 221-7447
Elaine Wong, *President*
EMP: 5
SALES: 450K **Privately Held**
WEB: www.theidea-network.com
SIC: 3911 Jewelry, precious metal

(G-11366)
STONESONG PRESS LLC
270 W 39th St Rm 201 (10018-0137)
PHONE..................................212 929-4600
Emmanuelle Morgen, *Principal*
Judy Linden, *Exec VP*
Alyssa Jennette, *Production*
Alison Fargis, *Mng Member*
Leila Campoli, *Agent*
EMP: 6 EST: 1978
SALES (est): 450K **Privately Held**
SIC: 2731 Book publishing

(G-11367)
STONY APPAREL CORP
Also Called: Eye Shadow
1407 Broadway Rm 3300 (10018-2395)
PHONE..................................212 391-0022
Shaun Jackson, *Manager*
EMP: 5
SIC: 2339 Women's & misses' athletic
　clothing & sportswear
PA: Stony Apparel Corp.
　1500 S Evergreen Ave
　Los Angeles CA 90023

(G-11368)
**STRAIGHT ARROW PUBLISHING
CO**
Also Called: Mens Journal
1290 Ave Of The Amer Fl 2 (10104-0298)
PHONE..................................212 484-1616
John Gruber, *CFO*
EMP: 200
SALES (est): 12.2MM
SALES (corp-wide): 62.6MM **Privately
Held**
WEB: www.mensjournal.com
SIC: 2741 Miscellaneous publishing
PA: Wenner Media Llc
　1290 Ave Of The Amer Fl 2
　New York NY 10104
　212 484-1616

(G-11369)
STRATCONGLOBAL INC
685 3rd Ave Fl 4 (10017-8408)
PHONE..................................212 989-2355
Joanna Peters, *Principal*
EMP: 5
SALES (est): 215.4K **Privately Held**
SIC: 2711 Newspapers

(G-11370)
STREET SMART DESIGNS INC
29 W 35th St Fl 6 (10001-2299)
PHONE..................................646 865-0056
Richard H Bienen, *Ch of Bd*
▲ EMP: 6
SALES (est): 977.6K **Privately Held**
WEB: www.streetsmartdesigns.com
SIC: 3111 5137 Handbag leather; hand-
　bags

(G-11371)
STREET SMARTS VR INC
116 Nassau St Ste 523 (10038-2402)
PHONE..................................413 438-7787
George Lamb, *Principal*
Oliver Noteware, *Principal*
EMP: 6 EST: 2017
SALES (est): 628.2K **Privately Held**
SIC: 7372 Prepackaged software

(G-11372)
STREETCRED NYC LLC
1006 6th Ave Fl 3 (10018-0283)
PHONE..................................646 675-0073
Tomislav Markovski, *CEO*
EMP: 5
SALES: 950K **Privately Held**
SIC: 7372 7389 Application computer soft-
　ware;

(G-11373)
STRIATA INC
48 Wall St Ste 1100 (10005-2903)
PHONE..................................212 918-4677
Michael Wright, *President*
Garin Toren, *COO*
Renee Hart, *Project Mgr*
Jacqui Michelson, *CFO*
Samantha Duran, *Accounts Mgr*
EMP: 85
SQ FT: 6,000
SALES (est): 6.3MM **Privately Held**
WEB: www.striata.com
SIC: 7372 Application computer software

(G-11374)
STRIDER GLOBAL LLC
261 W 28th St Apt 6a (10001-5936)
PHONE..................................212 726-1302
EMP: 5
SALES: 100K **Privately Held**
SIC: 3648 Mfg Lighting Equipment

(G-11375)
**STRUCTURED RETAIL
PRODUCTS**
Also Called: SRP
225 Park Ave S Fl 8 (10003-1604)
PHONE..................................212 224-3692
Sunny Singh, *Principal*
Joe Burris, *Principal*
EMP: 5
SQ FT: 60,000
SALES (est): 233.8K
SALES (corp-wide): 497.5MM **Privately
Held**
SIC: 7372 Business oriented computer
　software
HQ: Euromoney Global Limited
　8 Bouverie Street
　London EC4Y
　207 779-8888

(G-11376)
STRUCTUREDWEB INC
20 W 20th St Ste 402 (10011-9258)
PHONE..................................201 325-3110
Daniel Nissan, *President*
Yotam Hadass, *Vice Pres*
Kali Brockunier, *Marketing Mgr*
Rodrigo Bazua, *Marketing Staff*
Gerard Suppa, *Manager*
EMP: 40
SQ FT: 7,500
SALES (est): 5.1MM **Privately Held**
WEB: www.structuredweb.com
SIC: 7372 7371 Business oriented com-
　puter software; computer software devel-
　opment; software programming
　applications

(G-11377)
STUDIO 22 PRINT
20 Park Ave (10016-3840)
PHONE..................................212 679-2656
E J Rosenberger, *Principal*
EMP: 8
SALES (est): 786.5K **Privately Held**
SIC: 2752 Commercial printing, litho-
　graphic

(G-11378)
**STUDIO ASSOCIATES OF NEW
YORK**
242 W 30th St Rm 604 (10001-4913)
P.O. Box 4306 (10163-4306)
PHONE..................................212 268-1163
Edward Jenner, *President*
Joseph Perilla, *Corp Secy*
EMP: 6
SALES (est): 450K **Privately Held**
WEB: www.sanylaser.com
SIC: 3299 Architectural sculptures: gyp-
　sum, clay, papier mache, etc.

(G-11379)
**STUDIO ONE LEATHER DESIGN
INC**
270 W 39th St Rm 505 (10018-0334)
PHONE..................................212 760-1701
Arthur Coines, *President*
Ken Sackheim, *Editor*
EMP: 12
SQ FT: 2,500
SALES (est): 3.5MM **Privately Held**
SIC: 2386 3543 3111 Garments, leather;
　foundry patternmaking; leather tanning &
　finishing

(G-11380)
STUFF MAGAZINE
1040 Ave Of The Amrcas (10018-3703)
PHONE..................................212 302-2626
Steven Collvin, *President*
EMP: 5
SALES (est): 500K **Privately Held**
SIC: 2721 Magazines: publishing & printing

(G-11381)
STYLECLICK INC (HQ)
810 7th Ave Fl 18 (10019-5879)
PHONE..................................212 329-0300
Lisa Brown, *CEO*
Robert Halper, *Exec VP*
Bruce Goldstein, *Exec VP*
Barry W Hall, *CFO*
EMP: 52

SALES (est): 3.6MM
SALES (corp-wide): 4.2B **Publicly Held**
WEB: www.styleclick.com
SIC: 7372 Business oriented computer
software
PA: Iac/Interactivecorp
555 W 18th St
New York NY 10011
212 314-7300

(G-11382)
STYLISTIC PRESS INC
99 Battery Pl Apt 11p (10280-1324)
PHONE.....................................212 675-0797
Jeff Lederfarb, *President*
EMP: 15
SQ FT: 2,500
SALES (est): 1.4MM **Privately Held**
SIC: 2752 Commercial printing, offset

(G-11383)
SUBE INC
Also Called: Satya Jewelry
146 W 29th St Rm 4e (10001-0057)
PHONE.....................................212 243-6930
Satya Scainetti, *President*
Faneeza Allie, *CFO*
Faneeza Allie-Cruz, *CFO*
Jenna Palazzo, *Sales Staff*
Ron Sosely, *Director*
◆ EMP: 30
SQ FT: 6,000
SALES: 4.6MM **Privately Held**
WEB: www.satyajewelry.com
SIC: 3911 Jewelry, precious metal

(G-11384)
SUCCESS APPAREL LLC
19 W 34th St Fl 7 (10001-0055)
PHONE.....................................212 502-1890
Gila Goodman, *Branch Mgr*
EMP: 59
SALES (corp-wide): 9.7MM **Privately
Held**
SIC: 2211 Apparel & outerwear fabrics,
cotton
PA: Success Apparel Llc
521 Park Ave Apt 10a
New York NY 10065

(G-11385)
**SUGAR FOODS CORPORATION
(PA)**
950 3rd Ave Fl 21 (10022-2786)
PHONE.....................................212 753-6900
Donald G Tober, *Ch of Bd*
Marty Wilson, *President*
Stephen Odell, *President*
Myron Stein, *Vice Pres*
Jack Vivinetto, *CFO*
◆ EMP: 34
SQ FT: 10,000
SALES (est): 286.3MM **Privately Held**
WEB: www.sugarfoods.com
SIC: 2869 2023 2099 2068 Sweeteners,
synthetic; cream substitutes; sugar; sea-
sonings & spices; packaged combination
products: pasta, rice & potato; bread
crumbs, not made in bakeries; salted &
roasted nuts & seeds; packaging & label-
ing services

(G-11386)
**SULLIVAN ST BKY - HLLS KIT
INC**
533 W 47th St (10036-7903)
PHONE.....................................212 265-5580
James Lahey, *Principal*
▲ EMP: 29
SALES (est): 4.4MM **Privately Held**
SIC: 2051 Bread, cake & related products

(G-11387)
SUMA INDUSTRIES INC
345 E 52nd St Apt 9d (10022-6344)
PHONE.....................................646 436-5202
Arthur Forst, *President*
Bob Katz, *Exec VP*
Robert Katz, *Exec VP*
Christopher Patterson, *Vice Pres*
EMP: 5
SALES (est): 420K **Privately Held**
WEB: www.sumaindustries.com
SIC: 3993 Signs, not made in custom sign
painting shops

(G-11388)
SUMER GOLD LTD
33 W 46th St Fl 4 (10036-4103)
PHONE.....................................212 354-8677
Juan Merchan, *President*
Suzanna Merchan, *Treasurer*
EMP: 6
SQ FT: 700
SALES (est): 634.5K **Privately Held**
SIC: 3911 Jewelry, precious metal

(G-11389)
**SUMITOMO ELC USA HOLDINGS
INC (HQ)**
600 5th Ave Fl 18 (10020-2320)
PHONE.....................................212 490-6610
Yoshitomo Kasui, *President*
Shuji Nosaka, *Treasurer*
▲ EMP: 8
SALES: 46MM **Privately Held**
WEB: www.engsin.com
SIC: 3674 Semiconductors & related de-
vices

(G-11390)
**SUMMIT FINCL DISCLOSURE
LLC**
216 E 45th St Fl 15 (10017-3304)
PHONE.....................................212 913-0510
James W Palmiter, *Owner*
Kenneth M McClure, *Owner*
Scott Damico, *COO*
EMP: 40
SQ FT: 15,000
SALES (est): 8MM
SALES (corp-wide): 4.3B **Publicly Held**
SIC: 2621 Printing paper
PA: Broadridge Financial Solutions, Inc.
5 Dakota Dr Ste 300
New Hyde Park NY 11042
516 472-5400

(G-11391)
**SUMMIT PROFESSIONAL
NETWORKS**
469 Fashion Ave Fl 10 (10018-7640)
PHONE.....................................212 557-7480
Joyce Coots, *Education*
EMP: 60
SALES (corp-wide): 181.8MM **Privately
Held**
SIC: 2721 Magazines: publishing & printing
HQ: Summit Professional Networks
4157 Olympic Blvd Ste 225
Erlanger KY 41018
859 692-2100

(G-11392)
SUNA BROS INC
10 W 46th St Fl 5 (10036-4515)
PHONE.....................................212 869-5670
Aron Suna, *President*
Jonathan Suna, *Admin Sec*
EMP: 30 EST: 1934
SQ FT: 5,000
SALES (est): 4.2MM **Privately Held**
WEB: www.sunabros.com
SIC: 3911 5944 Jewelry, precious metal;
jewelry stores

(G-11393)
**SUNHAM HOME FASHIONS LLC
(PA)**
136 Madison Ave Fl 16 (10016-6786)
PHONE.....................................212 695-1218
Howard Yung, *CEO*
Jane Bognacki, *President*
Arthur Coubanou, *COO*
Jason LI, *Purch Mgr*
Stephanie Hannon, *Purchasing*
◆ EMP: 58
SQ FT: 15,000
SALES (est): 32.8MM **Privately Held**
WEB: www.sunham.com
SIC: 2392 Blankets, comforters & beddings

(G-11394)
**SUNSHINE DIAMOND CUTTER
INC**
38 W 48th St Ste 905 (10036-1805)
PHONE.....................................212 221-1028
Manglaben Dhanani, *President*
EMP: 7

SALES (est): 532.4K **Privately Held**
SIC: 3915 Lapidary work & diamond cutting & polishing

(G-11395)
**SUNWIN GLOBAL INDUSTRY
INC**
295 5th Ave Ste 515 (10016-7103)
PHONE.....................................646 370-6196
Sophie Cheng, *President*
EMP: 5
SQ FT: 850
SALES: 423.6K
SALES (corp-wide): 125.1MM **Privately
Held**
SIC: 2258 5137 Lace & warp knit fabric
mills; baby goods; apparel belts, women's
& children's
PA: Shanghai Sunwin Investment Holding
Group Co., Ltd.
Rm. 04, 3/F, Building 11, 688 Lane,
Hengnan Rd., Minhang Dist.
Shanghai 20111
216 036-0260

(G-11396)
SUPER-TRIM INC
30 W 24th St Fl 4 (10010-3558)
PHONE.....................................212 255-2370
Daniel Noy, *President*
EMP: 20
SQ FT: 5,000
SALES (est): 1.1MM **Privately Held**
WEB: www.supertrim.com
SIC: 2258 5131 Lace & lace products;
lace fabrics

(G-11397)
SUPERMEDIA LLC
Also Called: Verizon
2 Penn Plz Fl 22 (10121-2296)
PHONE.....................................212 513-9700
Jeanne Ryans, *Manager*
EMP: 100
SALES (corp-wide): 1.6B **Privately Held**
WEB: www.verizon.superpages.com
SIC: 2741 8741 Directories: publishing
only, not printed on site; administrative
management
HQ: Supermedia Llc
2200 W Airfield Dr
Dfw Airport TX 75261
972 453-7000

(G-11398)
SURE FIT INC
58 W 40th St Rm 2a (10018-2658)
PHONE.....................................212 395-9340
EMP: 25 **Privately Held**
SIC: 2392 Mfg Household Furnishings
HQ: Sure Fit Home Products, Llc
8000 Quarry Rd Ste C
Alburtis PA 18011
610 264-7000

(G-11399)
SUREPURE INC
405 Lexington Ave Fl 25 (10174-0002)
PHONE.....................................917 368-8480
Guy Kebble, *President*
Stephen Robinson, *CFO*
EMP: 6
SALES: 1.2MM **Privately Held**
SIC: 3559 Chemical machinery & equip-
ment; refinery, chemical processing &
similar machinery

(G-11400)
SURFACE MAGAZINE
Also Called: Surface Publishing
134 W 26th St Frnt 1 (10001-6803)
PHONE.....................................646 805-0200
Richard Klein, *Owner*
Lance Crapo, *Principal*
Adriana Gelves, *Adv Dir*
EMP: 25
SALES (est): 1.9MM **Privately Held**
SIC: 2721 Periodicals

(G-11401)
SURFACE MEDIA LLC
1 World Trade Ctr Fl 32 (10007-0090)
PHONE.....................................212 229-1500
David Basulto, *Principal*
Laurie Sadove, *Controller*
EMP: 5

SALES (est): 358.7K **Privately Held**
SIC: 2721 Magazines: publishing & printing

(G-11402)
SUSSEX PUBLISHERS LLC (PA)
Also Called: Psychology Today
115 E 23rd St Fl 9 (10010-4559)
PHONE.....................................212 260-7210
John P Colman, *President*
EMP: 20
SQ FT: 7,400
SALES (est): 2.7MM **Privately Held**
WEB: www.blues-buster.com
SIC: 2721 Magazines: publishing & printing

(G-11403)
SWANK INC
90 Park Ave Rm 1302 (10016-1395)
PHONE.....................................212 867-2600
John A Tulin, *Ch of Bd*
Eric P Luft, *President*
Paul Duckett, *Senior VP*
James E Tulin, *Senior VP*
Christophe Wolf, *Senior VP*
▲ EMP: 256 EST: 1936
SQ FT: 242,000
SALES (est): 388.2K
SALES (corp-wide): 153.3MM **Privately
Held**
WEB: www.swankaccessories.com
SIC: 2389 5611 Men's miscellaneous ac-
cessories; clothing accessories: men's &
boys'
PA: Randa Accessories Leather Goods Llc
5600 N River Rd Ste 500
Rosemont IL 60018
847 292-8300

(G-11404)
**SWAPS MONITOR
PUBLICATIONS INC**
29 Broadway Rm 1510 (10006-3226)
PHONE.....................................212 742-8550
Paul Spraos, *President*
EMP: 10
SALES (est): 1.1MM **Privately Held**
WEB: www.financialcalendar.com
SIC: 2721 6282 Periodicals; investment
advice

(G-11405)
**SWAROVSKI NORTH AMERICA
LTD**
1 Penn Plz Frnt 4 (10119-0202)
PHONE.....................................212 695-1502
EMP: 7
SALES (corp-wide): 4.7B **Privately Held**
SIC: 3961 Costume jewelry
HQ: Swarovski North America Limited
1 Kenney Dr
Cranston RI 02920
401 463-6400

(G-11406)
SWATFAME INC
530 Fashion Ave Rm 1204 (10018-4862)
PHONE.....................................212 944-8022
Marcy Olin, *Branch Mgr*
EMP: 6
SALES (corp-wide): 185.4MM **Privately
Held**
WEB: www.swatfame.com
SIC: 2339 2369 Women's & misses' ath-
letic clothing & sportswear; girls' & chil-
dren's outerwear
PA: Swat.Fame, Inc.
16425 Gale Ave
City Of Industry CA 91745
626 961-7928

(G-11407)
SWEET MOUTH INC
244 5th Ave Ste L243 (10001-7604)
PHONE.....................................800 433-7758
Lucas Dawson, *President*
EMP: 20
SQ FT: 2,000
SALES (est): 720.6K **Privately Held**
SIC: 2731 Book publishing

(G-11408)
SWELL LLC
28 W 23rd St Fl 5 (10010-5259)
PHONE.....................................646 738-8981
Sarah Kauss, *President*
Josh Dean, *Chief Mktg Ofcr*

EMP: 14
SALES (est): 2MM **Privately Held**
SIC: 3993 Signs & advertising specialties

(G-11409)
SYMPHONY TALENT LLC (PA)
19 W 34th St Rm 1000 (10001-3006)
PHONE................................212 999-9000
Roopesh Nair, *CEO*
Ryan Kellogg, *Vice Pres*
Vangie Sison, *Vice Pres*
Carl Calarco, *CFO*
Ty Johnson, *Manager*
EMP: 75 **EST:** 2007
SALES: 50MM **Privately Held**
SIC: 7372 7361 Business oriented computer software; employment agencies

(G-11410)
SYMRISE INC
505 Park Ave Fl 15 (10022-9333)
PHONE................................646 459-5000
Brooke Aboozia, *Vice Pres*
Keri Affronti, *Vice Pres*
Sara Garofalo, *Research*
Elaine Tiang, *Marketing Staff*
Achim Daub, *Branch Mgr*
EMP: 25
SALES (corp-wide): 3.6B **Privately Held**
WEB: www.symriseinc.com
SIC: 2869 Perfume materials, synthetic; flavors or flavoring materials, synthetic
HQ: Symrise Inc.
　891 Busse Rd
　Elk Grove Village IL 60007
　201 288-3200

(G-11411)
SYNCED INC
120 Walker St Ste 4 (10013-4117)
PHONE................................917 565-5591
Andrew Ferenci, *CEO*
Scott Paladini, *COO*
Michael Paladini, *Risk Mgmt Dir*
EMP: 5
SALES: 5MM **Privately Held**
SIC: 7372 Application computer software

(G-11412)
SYNCO TECHNOLOGIES INC
54 W 21st St Rm 602 (10010-7347)
P.O. Box 976 (10113-0976)
PHONE................................212 255-2031
John Rau, *President*
Terry Cook, *Vice Pres*
EMP: 6
SQ FT: 1,250
SALES: 1MM **Privately Held**
WEB: www.syncotec.com
SIC: 7372 Prepackaged software

(G-11413)
SYNERGY PHARMACEUTICALS INC (HQ)
420 Lexington Ave Rm 2500 (10170-0020)
PHONE................................212 227-8611
EMP: 6
SQ FT: 1,750
SALES (est): 992.3K **Publicly Held**
SIC: 2836 8731 Mfg Biological Products Commercial Physical Research

(G-11414)
T & M PLATING INC
357 W 36th St Fl 7 (10018-6455)
PHONE................................212 967-1110
Joseph AMI, *President*
EMP: 30 **EST:** 1935
SQ FT: 24,000
SALES (est): 3.2MM **Privately Held**
SIC: 3471 Electroplating of metals or formed products

(G-11415)
T & R KNITTING MILLS INC
1410 Broadway Rm 401 (10018-9374)
PHONE................................212 840-8665
Rocco Marini, *Branch Mgr*
EMP: 16
SALES (corp-wide): 20MM **Privately Held**
SIC: 2253 Knit outerwear mills
PA: T & R Knitting Mills Inc.
　8000 Cooper Ave Ste 6
　Glendale NY 11385
　718 497-4017

(G-11416)
T L DIAMOND & COMPANY INC (PA)
Also Called: Eagle Zinc Co Div
116 E 68th St Apt 5a (10065-5995)
PHONE................................212 249-6660
Theodore L Diamond, *President*
C W Diamond, *Corp Secy*
EMP: 9 **EST:** 1950
SQ FT: 5,000
SALES (est): 6.7MM **Privately Held**
SIC: 3356 Lead & zinc

(G-11417)
T M W DIAMONDS MFG CO (PA)
15 W 47th St Ste 302 (10036-3442)
PHONE................................212 869-8444
Leibis Morgenstern, *President*
Jonah Morgenstern, *Vice Pres*
EMP: 9
SALES: 1.5MM **Privately Held**
SIC: 3915 5094 Diamond cutting & polishing; diamonds (gems)

(G-11418)
T O DEY SERVICE CORP
Also Called: To Dey
151 W 46th St Fl 3 (10036-8512)
PHONE................................212 683-6300
Rose Bifulco, *President*
Thomas Bifulco, *Vice Pres*
Ciro Bifulco, *Treasurer*
EMP: 16
SQ FT: 6,700
SALES: 1.7MM **Privately Held**
SIC: 3144 3143 Orthopedic shoes, women's; men's footwear, except athletic

(G-11419)
T O GRONLUND COMPANY INC
200 Lexington Ave Rm 1515 (10016-6112)
PHONE................................212 679-3535
Robert L Gronlund, *President*
Brooks Grounlund, *Corp Secy*
EMP: 18
SQ FT: 3,600
SALES (est): 2.1MM **Privately Held**
SIC: 2599 Cabinets, factory

(G-11420)
T V TRADE MEDIA INC
Also Called: TV Executive
216 E 75th St Apt 1w (10021-2921)
PHONE................................212 288-3933
Dom Serafini, *President*
EMP: 12
SQ FT: 2,000
SALES (est): 890K **Privately Held**
SIC: 2721 Magazines: publishing & printing

(G-11421)
TAAZU INC
14 Wall St Fl 203420 (10005-2101)
PHONE................................212 618-1201
Giri Devanur, *CEO*
Artit Wangperawong, *CTO*
EMP: 20 **EST:** 2018
SALES (est): 660.5K **Privately Held**
SIC: 7372 5961 Application computer software;

(G-11422)
TABRISSE COLLECTIONS INC
Also Called: Oberon
1412 Broadway (10018-9228)
PHONE................................212 921-1014
Mark Naim, *President*
Ebi Shaer, *Vice Pres*
Sam Naim, *Treasurer*
EMP: 10
SQ FT: 5,500
SALES (est): 644.5K **Privately Held**
SIC: 2335 Women's, juniors' & misses' dresses

(G-11423)
TACTICA INTERNATIONAL INC (PA)
11 W 42nd St (10036-8002)
PHONE................................212 575-0500
Prem Ramchandani, *President*
Kurt Streams, *CFO*
AVI Sivan, *Director*
Paul Greenfield, *Admin Sec*
▲ **EMP:** 28

SQ FT: 11,500
SALES (est): 3MM **Privately Held**
SIC: 3634 3999 Electric housewares & fans; hair & hair-based products

(G-11424)
TAHARI ASL LLC
Also Called: Tahari Arthur S Levine
525 Fashion Ave Rm 701 (10018-0473)
PHONE................................212 763-2800
Lester Schreiber, *Manager*
EMP: 309
SALES (corp-wide): 85.1MM **Privately Held**
SIC: 2331 2335 2339 Blouses, women's & juniors': made from purchased material; women's, juniors' & misses' dresses; slacks: women's, misses' & juniors'
PA: Tahari A.S.L. Llc
　16 Bleeker St
　Millburn NJ 07041
　888 734-7459

(G-11425)
TAILORED SPORTSMAN LLC
Also Called: Ogulnick Uniforms
230 W 38th St Fl 6 (10018-9058)
PHONE................................646 366-8733
Van Isaacs,
▲ **EMP:** 12
SALES (est): 1.8MM **Privately Held**
WEB: www.thetailoredsportsman.com
SIC: 2339 Neckwear & ties: women's, misses' & juniors'; riding habits: women's, misses' & juniors'

(G-11426)
TALISMAN INDUSTRIES LLC
237 Flatbush Ave Apt 3 (10007)
PHONE................................908 433-7116
Gregory Kremler,
EMP: 5
SALES (est): 179.9K **Privately Held**
SIC: 3999 Manufacturing industries

(G-11427)
TAMBETTI INC
48 W 48th St Ste 501 (10036-1713)
PHONE................................212 751-9584
Dvora Horvitz, *President*
Joseph Segal, *Corp Secy*
EMP: 6
SQ FT: 1,612
SALES (est): 340K **Privately Held**
SIC: 3911 Jewelry, precious metal

(G-11428)
TAMSEN Z LLC
350 Park Ave Fl 4 (10022-6067)
PHONE................................212 292-6412
Tamsen Ziff, *Mng Member*
EMP: 5
SALES (est): 348.3K **Privately Held**
SIC: 3911 Jewelry, precious metal

(G-11429)
TANAGRO JEWELRY CORP
36 W 44th St Ste 1101 (10036-8104)
PHONE................................212 753-2817
Pietro Dibenedetto, *President*
Antonio Dibenedetto, *Vice Pres*
EMP: 20
SQ FT: 2,200
SALES: 4.3MM **Privately Held**
WEB: www.tanagro.com
SIC: 3911 Jewelry, precious metal

(G-11430)
TANGO PUBLISHING CORPORATION
101 W 79th St Apt 2g (10024-6478)
PHONE................................646 773-3060
Andrea Miller, *President*
Sanjay Bhatnagar, *CTO*
EMP: 27
SALES: 3.8MM **Privately Held**
SIC: 2741 Miscellaneous publishing

(G-11431)
TAO GROUP LLC
355 W 16th St (10011-5902)
PHONE................................646 625-4818
EMP: 7
SALES (est): 145.6K **Privately Held**
SIC: 2599 5963 Food wagons, restaurant; beverage services, direct sales

(G-11432)
TAP2PLAY LLC
110 W 40th St Rm 1902 (10018-3699)
PHONE................................914 960-6232
Ilya Nikolayev, *CEO*
EMP: 5 **EST:** 2017
SALES (est): 128.9K **Privately Held**
SIC: 7372 Prepackaged software

(G-11433)
TAPESTRY INC
515 W 33rd St (10001-1302)
PHONE................................212 615-2082
EMP: 9
SALES (corp-wide): 6B **Publicly Held**
SIC: 3171 Handbags, women's
PA: Tapestry, Inc.
　10 Hudson Yards
　New York NY 10001
　212 594-1850

(G-11434)
TAPESTRY INC (PA)
10 Hudson Yards (10001-2157)
PHONE................................212 594-1850
Jide Zeitlin, *Ch of Bd*
Dominic Cioffoletti, *Vice Pres*
Kevin Dozier, *Vice Pres*
Dave Enright, *Vice Pres*
Glenn King, *Vice Pres*
◆ **EMP:** 277
SQ FT: 695,000
SALES: 6B **Publicly Held**
WEB: www.coach.com
SIC: 3172 2387 3143 3144 Personal leather goods; apparel belts; men's footwear, except athletic; women's footwear, except athletic; handbags, women's

(G-11435)
TAPINATOR INC (PA)
110 W 40th St Rm 1902 (10018-3699)
PHONE................................914 930-6232
Ilya Nikolayev, *Ch of Bd*
Andrew Merkatz, *President*
Brian Chan, *Admin Sec*
EMP: 7
SQ FT: 1,000
SALES: 2.8MM **Publicly Held**
SIC: 7372 Prepackaged software; application computer software

(G-11436)
TARSIER LTD
1365 York Ave Apt 23e (10021-4036)
PHONE................................646 880-8680
Isaac H Sutton, *Ch of Bd*
EMP: 106
SALES (est): 8.1MM **Privately Held**
SIC: 3645 3674 3648 Residential lighting fixtures; light emitting diodes; public lighting fixtures

(G-11437)
TAYLOR & FRANCIS GROUP LLC
52 Vanderbilt Ave Fl 11 (10017-3839)
PHONE................................212 216-7800
Len Cornacchia, *Principal*
Hilary Lafoe, *Editor*
Colleen Franciscus, *Production*
Marie McVeigh, *Production*
Dave Miniaci, *Production*
EMP: 133
SALES (corp-wide): 3B **Privately Held**
SIC: 2741 Miscellaneous publishing
HQ: Taylor & Francis Group, Llc
　6000 Broken Sound Pkwy Nw # 300
　Boca Raton FL 33487
　561 994-0555

(G-11438)
TBHL INTERNATIONAL LLC
Also Called: Globe-Tex Apparal
252 W 38th St Fl 11 (10018-5806)
PHONE................................212 799-2007
Stuart Hurvitz, *Principal*
Robert Hurvitz,
Joel Limenes,
EMP: 10 **EST:** 1995
SQ FT: 1,400
SALES (est): 1MM **Privately Held**
SIC: 2329 2339 Men's & boys' sportswear & athletic clothing; women's & misses' outerwear

(G-11439)
TC TRANSCONTINENTAL USA INC
Also Called: Transcontinental Ross-Ellis
67 Irving Pl Fl 2 (10003-2202)
PHONE..................................818 993-4767
Nina Sheldon, *Director*
EMP: 6
SALES (corp-wide): 1.6B **Privately Held**
SIC: 2759 Commercial printing
HQ: Tc Transcontinental U.S.A. Inc.
8550 Balboa Blvd Ste 240
Northridge CA 91325
818 993-4767

(G-11440)
TDG OPERATIONS LLC
200 Lexington Ave Rm 1314 (10016-6201)
PHONE..................................212 779-4300
Mark Nestler, *Owner*
EMP: 9
SALES (corp-wide): 405MM **Publicly Held**
SIC: 2273 Carpets & rugs
HQ: Tdg Operations, Llc
716 Bill Myles Dr
Saraland AL 36571
251 675-9080

(G-11441)
TE NEUES PUBLISHING CO LP (PA)
350 7th Ave Rm 301 (10001-1957)
PHONE..................................212 627-9090
Hendrik Te Neues, *Managing Prtnr*
Sebastian Te Neues, *Partner*
Allison Stern, *Vice Pres*
◆ EMP: 11
SQ FT: 5,000
SALES (est): 1.3MM **Privately Held**
WEB: www.teneues-usa.com
SIC: 2741 5192 Miscellaneous publishing; books

(G-11442)
TEACHERGAMING LLC
809 W 181st St 231 (10033-4516)
PHONE..................................866 644-9323
Joel Levin, *Principal*
Santeri Koivisto, *Principal*
Jannika Aalto, *COO*
EMP: 12 EST: 2012
SQ FT: 200
SALES (est): 309.8K **Privately Held**
SIC: 7372 Educational computer software

(G-11443)
TEACHLEY LLC
25 Broadway Fl 13 (10004-1081)
PHONE..................................347 552-1272
Rachael Labrecque, *Partner*
Kara Carpenter, *Partner*
Dana Pagar, *Partner*
EMP: 6
SALES (est): 480.2K **Privately Held**
SIC: 7372 Educational computer software

(G-11444)
TECH TIMES LLC
61 Broadway Ste A (10006-2713)
PHONE..................................646 599-7201
Johnathan Davis,
EMP: 5
SALES (est): 214.3K **Privately Held**
SIC: 2711 Newspapers, publishing & printing

(G-11445)
TECHGRASS
77 Water St (10005-4401)
PHONE..................................646 719-2000
Susan Aexander, *Mng Member*
EMP: 10
SALES (est): 580.6K **Privately Held**
SIC: 3999 Grasses, artificial & preserved

(G-11446)
TECHNOLOGY DESKING INC
39 Broadway Rm 1640 (10006-3057)
PHONE..................................212 257-6998
Lee Markwick, *President*
▲ EMP: 26
SQ FT: 6,100
SALES: 4.1MM **Privately Held**
SIC: 2521 Wood office furniture

(G-11447)
TECSYS US INC (HQ)
1001 Ave Of The Amricas 4 (10018-5476)
PHONE..................................800 922-8649
David Malcom Brereton, *Ch of Bd*
Peter Brereton, *President*
Andrew Brereton, *Corp Secy*
J Mark Brereton, *Vice Pres*
EMP: 6
SQ FT: 1,600
SALES: 7.1MM
SALES (corp-wide): 56.9MM **Privately Held**
SIC: 7372 Prepackaged software
PA: Tecsys Inc
1 Place Alexis Nihon Bureau 800
Montreal QC H3Z 3
514 866-0001

(G-11448)
TECTONIC FLOORING USA LLC
1140 1st Ave Frnt 1 (10065-7961)
PHONE..................................212 686-2700
Mondo Pallon,
Rupert Dowd,
▲ EMP: 4
SQ FT: 2,100
SALES: 7MM **Privately Held**
SIC: 2426 Flooring, hardwood

(G-11449)
TELEPHONE SALES & SERVICE CO (PA)
132 W Broadway (10013-3396)
PHONE..................................212 233-8505
William Bradley, *President*
Neil Bradley, *Vice Pres*
EMP: 23
SQ FT: 4,000
SALES (est): 3MM **Privately Held**
SIC: 3612 1731 Transmission & distribution voltage regulators; sound equipment specialization

(G-11450)
TELESCA-HEYMAN INC
304 E 94th St 6 (10128-5688)
PHONE..................................212 534-3442
Mario Dire, *President*
Remo Dire, *Vice Pres*
EMP: 15 EST: 1958
SQ FT: 14,500
SALES (est): 805.2K **Privately Held**
SIC: 2541 7641 Cabinets, except refrigerated: show, display, etc.: wood; furniture refinishing; antique furniture repair & restoration

(G-11451)
TELMAR INFORMATION SERVICES (PA)
711 3rd Ave Rm 1500 (10017-9201)
PHONE..................................212 725-3000
Stanley Federman, *Ch of Bd*
Corey V Panno, *President*
Corey Panno, *President*
Susan Lanzetta, *Exec VP*
EMP: 30
SQ FT: 4,400
SALES (est): 17.3MM **Privately Held**
WEB: www.telmar.com
SIC: 7372 Business oriented computer software

(G-11452)
TEMPLE ST CLAIR LLC
594 Broadway Rm 306 (10012-3234)
PHONE..................................212 219-8664
Kimberly Rainone, *Vice Pres*
Frank Trent, *CFO*
Katie Fisher, *Sales Staff*
Melanie Oswald, *Marketing Staff*
Temple St Clair, *Mng Member*
▲ EMP: 27
SALES: 13MM **Privately Held**
SIC: 3911 Jewelry, precious metal

(G-11453)
TERRA ENRGY RESOURCE TECH INC (PA)
99 Park Ave Ph A (10016-1340)
PHONE..................................212 286-9197
Dmitry Vilbaum, *CEO*
Alexandre Agaian PHD, *Ch of Bd*
EMP: 10

SALES (est): 3.3MM **Publicly Held**
WEB: www.terrainsight.com
SIC: 1389 Testing, measuring, surveying & analysis services

(G-11454)
TERRANUA US CORP
535 5th Ave Fl 4 (10017-8020)
PHONE..................................212 852-9028
Brian Fahey, *CEO*
EMP: 16
SALES (est): 2.3MM **Privately Held**
SIC: 7372 Prepackaged software
HQ: Mycomplianceoffice Limited
Unit 2c
Dublin

(G-11455)
TESLA MOTORS INC
10 Columbus Cir Ste 102d (10019-1215)
PHONE..................................212 206-1204
EMP: 663
SALES (corp-wide): 4B **Publicly Held**
SIC: 3711 3714 Mfg Motor Vehicle/Car Bodies & Components
PA: Tesla Motors, Inc.
3500 Deer Creek Rd
Palo Alto CA 94304
650 681-5000

(G-11456)
TEXPORT FABRICS CORP
Also Called: Rose-Ann Division
495 Broadway Fl 7 (10012-4457)
PHONE..................................212 226-6066
Sonia Essebag, *President*
▲ EMP: 10
SQ FT: 48,000
SALES (est): 1.1MM **Privately Held**
SIC: 2335 Women's, juniors' & misses' dresses

(G-11457)
TG THERAPEUTICS INC
2 Gansevoort St Fl 9 (10014-1667)
PHONE..................................212 554-4484
Michael S Weiss, *Ch of Bd*
Peter Sportelli, *COO*
Robert Niecestro, *Exec VP*
Amy Cavers, *Vice Pres*
Deedee Cornelius, *Research*
EMP: 64
SALES: 152K **Privately Held**
WEB: www.manhattanpharma.com
SIC: 2834 Pharmaceutical preparations

(G-11458)
TGP FLYING CLOUD HOLDINGS LLC
565 5th Ave Fl 27 (10017-2478)
PHONE..................................646 829-3900
James Pagano, *Principal*
Ashlynn Smith, *Principal*
EMP: 25
SALES: 500K **Privately Held**
SIC: 3511 Turbines & turbine generator sets

(G-11459)
THE DESIGN GROUP INC
Also Called: J.hoaglund
240 Madison Ave Fl 8 (10016-2878)
PHONE..................................212 681-1548
Robert Rosen, *President*
Daniel Cohen, *Chairman*
▲ EMP: 10
SALES: 3MM **Privately Held**
SIC: 2339 Women's & misses' outerwear

(G-11460)
THEHUFFINGTONPOSTCOM INC (DH)
Also Called: Huffington Post, The
770 Broadway Fl 4 (10003-9558)
PHONE..................................212 245-7844
Eric Hippeau, *CEO*
Jolie Doggett, *Editor*
Grace Maalouf, *Editor*
Chris McGonigal, *Editor*
Kate Palmer, *Editor*
EMP: 31
SALES (est): 4.4MM
SALES (corp-wide): 130.8B **Publicly Held**
SIC: 2741

(G-11461)
THEIRAPP LLC
Also Called: Apprise Mobile
950 3rd Ave Ste 190 (10022-2705)
PHONE..................................212 896-1255
Ben Gholian, *Partner*
Doug Pierce, *COO*
Jeffrey Corbin, *Mng Member*
EMP: 35
SALES (est): 2.1MM
SALES (corp-wide): 5.5MM **Privately Held**
SIC: 7372 Application computer software
PA: Kanan, Corbin, Schupak & Aronow, Inc.
420 5th Ave Rm 300
New York NY 10018
212 682-6300

(G-11462)
THEORY LLC
1114 Avenue Of The Americ (10036-7703)
PHONE..................................212 762-2300
Pamela Meany, *Human Res Dir*
Andrew Rosen, *Manager*
EMP: 100 **Privately Held**
SIC: 2337 Suits: women's, misses' & juniors'
HQ: Theory Llc
38 Gansevoort St
New York NY 10014
212 300-0800

(G-11463)
THEORY LLC
1157 Madison Ave (10028-0409)
PHONE..................................212 879-0265
Sylke Cunha, *Branch Mgr*
EMP: 7 **Privately Held**
SIC: 2337 Suits: women's, misses' & juniors'
HQ: Theory Llc
38 Gansevoort St
New York NY 10014
212 300-0800

(G-11464)
THESKIMM INC
50 W 23rd St Ste 501 (10010-5278)
PHONE..................................646 213-4754
Carly Zakin, *CEO*
EMP: 15
SQ FT: 1,500
SALES (est): 1.4MM **Privately Held**
SIC: 2741

(G-11465)
THESTREET INC (HQ)
14 Wall St Fl 15 (10005-2139)
PHONE..................................212 321-5000
David Callaway, *President*
Jeffrey Davis, *President*
Margaret De Luna, *President*
Rachelle Zorn, *President*
Eric Lundberg, *CFO*
EMP: 69
SALES: 53MM
SALES (corp-wide): 77K **Publicly Held**
WEB: www.thestreet.com
SIC: 2711 2721 Newspapers: publishing only, not printed on site; periodicals: publishing only
PA: Themaven, Inc.
1500 4th Ave Ste 200
Seattle WA 98101
775 600-2765

(G-11466)
THING DAEMON INC
Also Called: Fancy
57 Bond St Frnt A (10012-2483)
PHONE..................................917 746-9895
Joseph Einhorn, *CEO*
Jack Einhorn, *President*
Michael Silverman, *COO*
Kevin Siewert, *Vice Pres*
Andrew Tuch, *Vice Pres*
EMP: 25 EST: 2010
SALES (est): 4MM **Privately Held**
SIC: 7372 Application computer software

(G-11467)
THOMAS GROUP INC
Also Called: Thomas Group, The
131 Varick St Rm 1016 (10013-1417)
PHONE..................................212 947-6400
Jamie H Tomashoff, *President*

GEOGRAPHIC

EMP: 10
SQ FT: 18,000
SALES (est): 2.2MM **Privately Held**
WEB: www.thethomasgroup.com
SIC: 2752 2791 2789 Commercial print-
ing, offset; typesetting; bookbinding & re-
lated work

(G-11468)
**THOMAS PUBLISHING
COMPANY LLC (PA)**
Also Called: Thomas Enterprise Solutions
5 Penn Plz Fl 8 (10001-1860)
PHONE..............................212 695-0500
Jos E Andrade, *Ch of Bd*
Tony Uphoff, *President*
Sandra Hanzlik, *Partner*
Heather Holst-Knudsen, *Publisher*
Tom Greco, *Vice Pres*
EMP: 300 EST: 1898
SALES (est): 185.1MM **Privately Held**
WEB: www.inboundlogistics.com
SIC: 2741 2721 7374 7331 Directories:
publishing only, not printed on site; cata-
logs: publishing only, not printed on site;
trade journals: publishing only, not printed
on site; data processing service; direct
mail advertising services

(G-11469)
**THOMAS PUBLISHING
COMPANY LLC**
5 Penn Plz Fl 9 (10001-1860)
PHONE..............................212 695-0500
EMP: 70
SALES (corp-wide): 167MM **Privately
Held**
SIC: 2741 Misc Publishing
PA: Thomas Publishing Company Llc
5 Penn Plz Fl 9
New York NY 10001
212 695-0500

(G-11470)
**THOMAS PUBLISHING
COMPANY LLC**
Also Called: Magazine Group
5 Penn Plz Fl 8 (10001-1860)
PHONE..............................212 695-0500
Ralph Richardson, *Manager*
EMP: 9
SALES (corp-wide): 185.1MM **Privately
Held**
WEB: www.inboundlogistics.com
SIC: 2721 Magazines: publishing only, not
printed on site
PA: Thomas Publishing Company Llc
5 Penn Plz Fl 8
New York NY 10001
212 695-0500

(G-11471)
**THOMAS PUBLISHING
COMPANY LLC**
Managing Automation Magazine
5 Penn Plz Fl 8 (10001-1860)
PHONE..............................212 695-0500
Margret Bresto, *Manager*
EMP: 9
SALES (corp-wide): 185.1MM **Privately
Held**
WEB: www.inboundlogistics.com
SIC: 2721 Magazines: publishing & printing
PA: Thomas Publishing Company Llc
5 Penn Plz Fl 8
New York NY 10001
212 695-0500

(G-11472)
THOMAS SASSON CO INC
555 5th Ave Rm 1900 (10017-9250)
PHONE..............................212 697-4998
Jeffery Thomas, *President*
Lois Dianne Sasson, *Vice Pres*
EMP: 2
SQ FT: 1,000
SALES: 1MM **Privately Held**
SIC: 3911 Jewelry apparel

(G-11473)
THOMPSON FERRIER LLC
230 5th Ave Ste 1004 (10001-7834)
PHONE..............................212 244-2212
Raffi Arslanian,
Pauline Dana,

▲ EMP: 9 EST: 2011
SQ FT: 2,000
SALES (est): 1.2MM **Privately Held**
SIC: 3999 2844 Candles; concentrates,
perfume

(G-11474)
**THOMSON REUTERS
CORPORATION**
500 Pearl St (10007-1316)
PHONE..............................212 393-9461
Gail Appleson, *Principal*
EMP: 15
SALES (corp-wide): 10.6B **Publicly Held**
SIC: 2741 Miscellaneous publishing
HQ: Thomson Reuters Corporation
3 Times Sq
New York NY 10036
646 223-4000

(G-11475)
**THOMSON REUTERS
CORPORATION (DH)**
3 Times Sq (10036-6564)
PHONE..............................646 223-4000
James C Smith, *President*
Piotr Marczewski, *President*
Charlotte Rushton, *President*
Lisa Gregory, *Editor*
Brian Peccarelli, *COO*
▲ EMP: 1192 EST: 1977
SALES: 5.5B
SALES (corp-wide): 10.6B **Publicly Held**
WEB: www.thomsonreuters.com
SIC: 2741 8111 7372 7383 Miscella-
neous publishing; legal services; prepack-
aged software; news syndicates
HQ: Woodbridge Company Limited, The
65 Queen St W Suite 2400
Toronto ON M5H 2
416 364-8700

(G-11476)
THORNWILLOW PRESS LTD
57 W 58th St Ste 11e (10019-1630)
P.O. Box 1202 (10028-0048)
PHONE..............................212 980-0738
Luke Pontifell, *President*
EMP: 3
SALES: 1MM **Privately Held**
WEB: www.thornwillow.com
SIC: 2731 5942 Book publishing; book
stores

(G-11477)
THREAD LLC (PA)
26 W 17th St Rm 301 (10011-5730)
PHONE..............................212 414-8844
Beth Blake,
Melissa Akey,
▲ EMP: 5
SALES (est): 482.1K **Privately Held**
WEB: www.threaddesign.com
SIC: 2335 Bridal & formal gowns

(G-11478)
**THREE FIVE III-V MATERIALS
INC**
19 W 21st St Rm 203 (10010-6866)
PHONE..............................212 213-8290
Thomas Guan, *President*
EMP: 10
SALES (est): 919.2K **Privately Held**
SIC: 3679 Electronic loads & power sup-
plies

(G-11479)
TI GOTHAM INC
Sports Illustrated Magazine
1271 Ave Of The Americas (10020-1300)
PHONE..............................212 522-1212
Dick Raskopf, *Publisher*
Jorg Stratmann, *Publisher*
John Cantarella, *General Mgr*
Bradford Wallick, *Principal*
Robert Horning, *Editor*
EMP: 37
SALES (corp-wide): 3.1B **Publicly Held**
SIC: 2721 2731 Magazines: publishing &
printing; book publishing
HQ: Ti Gotham Inc.
225 Liberty St
New York NY 10281
212 522-1212

(G-11480)
TI GOTHAM INC
Also Called: Fortune Magazine
135 W 50th St (10020-1201)
P.O. Box 5979 (10087-5979)
PHONE..............................212 522-1633
Jessic Dodell-Feder, *Editor*
Jan Krawczyk, *Train & Dev Mgr*
Anthony Brown, *Manager*
Jason Sheeler, *Director*
EMP: 20
SALES (corp-wide): 3.1B **Publicly Held**
SIC: 2721 Magazines: publishing only, not
printed on site
HQ: Ti Gotham Inc.
225 Liberty St
New York NY 10281
212 522-1212

(G-11481)
TI GOTHAM INC (HQ)
Also Called: Time Inc.
225 Liberty St (10281-1048)
P.O. Box 231035 (10023-0018)
PHONE..............................212 522-1212
Joseph Ceryanec, *President*
Joan Carter, *Publisher*
Armando Correa, *Editor*
Chelsea White, *Editor*
Joel Baboolal, *Business Mgr*
◆ EMP: 2800
SQ FT: 696,000
SALES (est): 2.7B
SALES (corp-wide): 3.1B **Publicly Held**
WEB: www.timeinc.com
SIC: 2721 Magazines: publishing only, not
printed on site
PA: Meredith Corporation
1716 Locust St
Des Moines IA 50309
515 284-3000

(G-11482)
TI GOTHAM INC
Time/Fortune Money Group
1271 Ave Of The Amer Sb7 (10020-1302)
PHONE..............................212 522-0361
Ann Moore, *CEO*
Greg Daugherty, *Education*
EMP: 28
SALES (corp-wide): 3.1B **Publicly Held**
SIC: 2721 Magazines: publishing only, not
printed on site
HQ: Ti Gotham Inc.
225 Liberty St
New York NY 10281
212 522-1212

(G-11483)
TIBCO SOFTWARE INC
120 W 45th St Fl 18 (10036-4041)
PHONE..............................646 495-2600
M Williams, *Branch Mgr*
EMP: 9
SALES (corp-wide): 885.6MM **Privately
Held**
SIC: 7372 Prepackaged software
HQ: Tibco Software Inc.
3307 Hillview Ave
Palo Alto CA 94304

(G-11484)
TIE KING INC
Jimmy's Sales
42 W 38th St Rm 1200 (10018-6212)
PHONE..............................212 714-9611
Jimmy Azizo, *President*
EMP: 5
SALES (corp-wide): 5.5MM **Privately
Held**
WEB: www.thetieking.com
SIC: 2323 Ties, handsewn: made from pur-
chased materials
PA: The Tie King Inc
243 44th St
Brooklyn NY 11232
718 768-8484

(G-11485)
TIGER 21 LLC
1995 Broadway Fl 6 (10023-5882)
PHONE..............................212 360-1700
Michael Sonnenfeldt, *Principal*
Harley Frank, *Vice Pres*
Abby George, *VP Opers*
Marian Stier, *Officer*

EMP: 7
SALES (est): 1.7MM **Privately Held**
SIC: 2273 Carpets & rugs

(G-11486)
TIGER J LLC
1430 Broadway Rm 1900 (10018-3308)
PHONE..............................212 465-9300
Jeffrey Steinberg, *Ch of Bd*
Mark Locks, *President*
Arnold Brodsky, *CFO*
Guillaume Poupart, *Director*
▲ EMP: 49
SQ FT: 15,600
SALES (est): 32MM **Privately Held**
WEB: www.terrytiger.com
SIC: 2337 2339 Jackets & vests, except
fur & leather: women's; women's &
misses' suits & skirts; skirts, separate:
women's, misses' & juniors'; sportswear,
women's

(G-11487)
TIKA MOBILE INC (PA)
Also Called: Tikamobile
902 Broadway Fl 6 (10010-6039)
PHONE..............................646 650-5545
Anthony Bowden, *Principal*
Manish Sharma, *Principal*
Cliona Barry, *Analyst*
EMP: 7
SQ FT: 500
SALES (est): 1.5MM **Privately Held**
SIC: 7372 Business oriented computer
software

(G-11488)
**TILLSONBURG COMPANY USA
INC**
37 W 39th St Rm 1101 (10018-3894)
PHONE..............................267 994-8096
Tony Cooper, *CEO*
Ramaswamy Arakoni, *Ch of Bd*
Sandy Jabaly, *Director*
Alex Lam, *Director*
Jai Waney, *Director*
▲ EMP: 50
SQ FT: 3,000
SALES (est): 5MM **Privately Held**
SIC: 2339 2329 Women's & misses' ath-
letic clothing & sportswear; men's & boys'
sportswear & athletic clothing
PA: Tillsonburg Company Limited
18/F Corporation Sq
Kowloon Bay KLN

(G-11489)
**TIME HOME ENTERTAINMENT
INC**
1271 Ave Of The Americas (10020-1300)
PHONE..............................212 522-1212
Jim Childs, *Publisher*
EMP: 32
SALES (est): 2.4MM
SALES (corp-wide): 3.1B **Publicly Held**
SIC: 2731 Book publishing
HQ: Ti Gotham Inc.
225 Liberty St
New York NY 10281
212 522-1212

(G-11490)
**TIME INC AFFLUENT MEDIA
GROUP (DH)**
Also Called: Travel Leisure Magazine
1120 Ave Of The Americas (10036-6700)
PHONE..............................212 382-5600
Ted Kelly, *President*
EMP: 5
SALES (est): 461.2K
SALES (corp-wide): 3.1B **Publicly Held**
SIC: 2721 7389 Magazines: publishing
only, not printed on site; subscription ful-
fillment services: magazine, newspaper,
etc.
HQ: Southern Progress Corporation
2100 Lakeshore Dr
Birmingham AL 35209
205 445-6000

(G-11491)
TIME OUT AMERICA LLC
Also Called: Time Out New York
1540 Broadway Fl 42 (10036-4039)
PHONE..............................646 432-3000

Morgan Olsen, *Editor*
Jaclyn Rivas, *Editor*
Amoi Alawoya, *Human Res Mgr*
ARI Romeo, *Sales Staff*
Benjamin Levine, *Sales Executive*
EMP: 200 **EST:** 2011
SALES (est): 5.9MM
SALES (corp-wide): 62.6MM **Privately Held**
SIC: 2721 Magazines: publishing & printing
PA: Time Out Group Plc
77 Wicklow Street
London WC1X
207 813-3000

(G-11492)
TIME OUT NEW YORK PARTNERS LP
475 10th Ave Fl 12 (10018-1175)
PHONE....................................646 432-3000
Alison Tocci, *President*
Tony Elliott, *Partner*
Marisa Fari A, *Publisher*
Michael Freidson, *Principal*
Justin Etheridge, *Exec VP*
▲ **EMP:** 91
SALES (est): 17.8MM
SALES (corp-wide): 62.6MM **Privately Held**
SIC: 2721 Periodicals
HQ: Time Out Digital Limited
4th Floor
London
207 813-3000

(G-11493)
TIME TO KNOW INC
655 3rd Ave Fl 21 (10017-5621)
PHONE....................................212 230-1210
Yonit Tzadok, *CFO*
Jamie Iesner, *Director*
Lawrence Malkin, *Director*
EMP: 9
SALES (est): 851.5K **Privately Held**
SIC: 7372 Educational computer software

(G-11494)
TIME WARNER COMPANIES INC (DH)
1 Time Warner Ctr Bsmt B (10019-6010)
PHONE....................................212 484-8000
Jeff Bewkes, *Ch of Bd*
Robert Seiden, *Managing Dir*
Erin Garbarino, *Counsel*
Souad Ghosn-Saab, *Counsel*
Julie Kim, *Counsel*
EMP: 96
SQ FT: 451,000
SALES (est): 68.3MM
SALES (corp-wide): 170.7B **Publicly Held**
SIC: 3652 6794 2741 7812 Compact laser discs, prerecorded; magnetic tape (audio): prerecorded; music licensing to radio stations; performance rights, publishing & licensing; music royalties, sheet & record; music, sheet: publishing only, not printed on site; music books: publishing only, not printed on site; motion picture production & distribution; television film production; motion picture production & distribution, television; video tape production; cable television services; magazines: publishing only, not printed on site

(G-11495)
TIMELESS FASHIONS LLC
100 United Nations Plz 28e (10017-1753)
PHONE....................................212 730-9328
Navin Mahtani, *Mng Member*
Ravi Datwani,
▲ **EMP:** 7
SQ FT: 2,900
SALES (est): 10MM **Privately Held**
SIC: 2389 Apparel for handicapped

(G-11496)
TIMES SQUARE STUDIOS LTD
Also Called: ABC Television Network
1500 Broadway Fl 2 (10036-4055)
PHONE....................................212 930-7720
Ruth Anne Alsop, *Senior VP*
Jeff Hartnett, *Manager*
EMP: 200

SALES (est): 30.6MM
SALES (corp-wide): 90.2B **Publicly Held**
WEB: www.go.com
SIC: 3663 Studio equipment, radio & television broadcasting
HQ: Twdc Enterprises 18 Corp.
500 S Buena Vista St
Burbank CA 91521

(G-11497)
TIMING GROUP LLC
237 W 37th St Ste 1100 (10018-6770)
P.O. Box 275, Tallman (10982-0275)
PHONE....................................646 878-2600
AVI Schwebel, *Mng Member*
Alan Friedman,
▲ **EMP:** 15
SALES (est): 1.7MM **Privately Held**
SIC: 3021 Rubber & plastics footwear

(G-11498)
TIO FOODS LLC
Also Called: Tio Gazpacho
120 E 23rd St Fl 5 (10010-4519)
PHONE....................................917 946-1160
Austin V Allan, *CEO*
Adam Pasquale, *Treasurer*
Amy Marpman, *Director*
EMP: 10 **EST:** 2013
SQ FT: 150
SALES (est): 605K **Privately Held**
SIC: 2038 Soups, frozen
HQ: Tipp Distributors, Inc.
500 W Overland Ave # 300
El Paso TX 79901
915 594-1618

(G-11499)
TITAN CONTROLS INC
122 W 27th St Fl 5 (10001-6227)
PHONE....................................516 358-2407
Paul Deronde, *President*
Gary Sefcheck, *Vice Pres*
EMP: 11
SQ FT: 2,000
SALES (est): 820K **Privately Held**
WEB: www.titancontrols.com
SIC: 3829 Temperature sensors, except industrial process & aircraft

(G-11500)
TIZIANA THERAPEUTICS INC
420 Lexington Ave # 2525 (10170-0002)
PHONE....................................646 396-4970
Kunwar Shailubhai, *Principal*
EMP: 8
SALES (est): 281.7K **Privately Held**
SIC: 2835 Microbiology & virology diagnostic products
PA: Tiziana Life Sciences Plc
3rd Floor, 11-12 St. James's Square
London
207 495-2379

(G-11501)
TLC-LC INC (PA)
115 E 57th St Bsmt (10022-2049)
PHONE....................................212 756-8900
Loida Nicolas Lewis, *Ch of Bd*
Reynaldo P Glover, *President*
▲ **EMP:** 27
SQ FT: 2,500
SALES (est): 62.1MM **Privately Held**
SIC: 2024 2096 5149 5411 Ice cream & ice milk; potato chips & similar snacks; beverages, except coffee & tea; grocery stores

(G-11502)
TM MUSIC INC
Also Called: Casablanca Records
9 E 63rd St Apt 2-3 (10065-7236)
PHONE....................................212 471-4000
Thomas Mottola, *President*
EMP: 10
SQ FT: 12,000
SALES (est): 5MM **Privately Held**
SIC: 2782 Record albums

(G-11503)
TMS STRUCTURES INC
1745 Broadway Fl 17 (10019-4642)
PHONE....................................646 740-7646
Gilbert Roy, *CEO*
EMP: 150

SALES (est): 4.6MM **Privately Held**
SIC: 3441 Fabricated structural metal

(G-11504)
TOHO COMPANY LIMITED
1501 Broadway Ste 2005 (10036-5600)
PHONE....................................212 391-9058
Darryl Pitt, *Manager*
EMP: 6 **Privately Held**
SIC: 3999 Stringing beads
PA: Toho Co.,Ltd.
5-9, Koyochonishi, Higashinada-Ku
Kobe HYO 658-0

(G-11505)
TOHO SHOJI (NEW YORK) INC
990 Avenue Of The America (10018-5419)
PHONE....................................212 868-7466
T Mishide, *President*
▲ **EMP:** 15
SALES (est): 1.2MM **Privately Held**
SIC: 3961 Costume jewelry
PA: Toho Shoji Co., Ltd.
5-29-8, Asakusabashi
Taito-Ku TKY 111-0

(G-11506)
TOLTEC FABRICS INC
437 5th Ave Fl 10 (10016-2205)
PHONE....................................212 706-9310
Barbara Nymark, *President*
EMP: 155
SQ FT: 6,000
SALES (est): 8.2MM
SALES (corp-wide): 300K **Privately Held**
WEB: www.interfacefabricsgroup.com
SIC: 2221 2262 Broadwoven fabric mills, manmade; decorative finishing of manmade broadwoven fabrics
HQ: Duvaltex (Us), Inc.
9 Oak St
Guilford ME 04443
207 873-3331

(G-11507)
TOM & LINDA PLATT INC
55 W 39th St Rm 1701 (10018-0540)
PHONE....................................212 221-7208
Linda Platt, *President*
Tom Platt, *Treasurer*
Andrew Scott, *Sales Staff*
EMP: 13
SALES (est): 1.3MM **Privately Held**
WEB: www.tomandlindaplatt.com
SIC: 2335 Women's, juniors' & misses' dresses

(G-11508)
TOM DOHERTY ASSOCIATES INC
Also Called: Tor Books
175 5th Ave Frnt 1 (10010-7704)
PHONE....................................212 388-0100
Tom Doherty, *President*
Devi Pillai, *Publisher*
Roy Gainsburg, *Exec VP*
Philip Schwartz, *Exec VP*
Eileen Lawrence, *Exec Dir*
EMP: 44
SQ FT: 7,000
SALES (est): 8.2MM
SALES (corp-wide): 1.6B **Privately Held**
WEB: www.stmartins.com
SIC: 2731 Books: publishing only
HQ: Macmillan Holdings, Llc
120 Broadway Fl 22
New York NY 10271

(G-11509)
TOM JAMES COMPANY
717 5th Ave (10022-8101)
PHONE....................................212 593-0204
George Mattos, *Branch Mgr*
EMP: 10
SALES (corp-wide): 492.1MM **Privately Held**
WEB: www.englishamericanco.com
SIC: 2311 Suits, men's & boys': made from purchased materials
PA: Tom James Company
263 Seaboard Ln
Franklin TN 37067
615 771-1122

(G-11510)
TOMAS MAIER
956 Madison Ave Frnt 1 (10021-2635)
PHONE....................................212 988-8686
Tomas Maier, *Owner*
EMP: 6
SALES (est): 562.1K **Privately Held**
SIC: 2253 Bathing suits & swimwear, knit; jerseys, knit

(G-11511)
TOMMY BOY ENTERTAINMENT LLC
220 E 23rd St Ste 509 (10010-4665)
PHONE....................................212 388-8300
Linda Williams, *Controller*
Thomas Silverman,
EMP: 12
SALES (est): 1.7MM **Privately Held**
WEB: www.tommyboy.com
SIC: 2782 Record albums

(G-11512)
TOMMY JOHN INC
100 Broadway Ste 1101 (10005-4504)
PHONE....................................800 708-3490
Thomas J Patterson, *President*
John Wu, *COO*
Al Valdes, *Vice Pres*
Wendy Lam, *Production*
Sam Giligich, *Business Anlyst*
▲ **EMP:** 50
SQ FT: 17,500
SALES (est): 18.3MM **Privately Held**
SIC: 2322 Men's & boys' underwear & nightwear

(G-11513)
TONIX PHARMACEUTICALS INC (HQ)
509 Madison Ave Rm 1608 (10022-5534)
PHONE....................................917 288-8908
Seth Lederman, *President*
EMP: 6
SALES (est): 791.4K **Publicly Held**
SIC: 2834 Pharmaceutical preparations

(G-11514)
TONIX PHRMCEUTICALS HOLDG CORP (PA)
509 Madison Ave Rm 1608 (10022-5534)
PHONE....................................212 980-9155
Seth Lederman, *Ch of Bd*
Jessica Morris, *COO*
Bradley Saenger, *CFO*
Gregory Sullivan, *Chief Mktg Ofcr*
Patrick Grace, *Bd of Directors*
EMP: 7
SQ FT: 2,658
SALES (est): 1.5MM **Publicly Held**
SIC: 2834 Pharmaceutical preparations

(G-11515)
TOPPAN MERRILL USA INC (DH)
747 3rd Ave Fl 7 (10017-2821)
PHONE....................................212 596-7747
Jeff Riback, *President*
Glen Buchbaum, *Senior VP*
Edward Vaccaro, *Vice Pres*
EMP: 107
SALES (est): 31.3MM **Privately Held**
SIC: 2759 8732 Commercial printing; merger, acquisition & reorganization research
HQ: Toppan Leefung Pte. Ltd.
1 Kim Seng Promenade
Singapore 23799
682 696-00

(G-11516)
TORAY HOLDING (USA) INC (HQ)
461 5th Ave Fl 9 (10017-7730)
PHONE....................................212 697-8150
Akihiro Nikkaku, *President*
Yasuke Orito, *Principal*
◆ **EMP:** 50
SALES (est): 516.3MM **Privately Held**
SIC: 2821 Plastics materials & resins

(G-11517)
TORAY INDUSTRIES INC
600 3rd Ave Fl 5 (10016-1919)
PHONE....................................212 697-8150
Yvette Kosar, *Branch Mgr*

EMP: 8 **Privately Held**
WEB: www.toray.co.jp
SIC: 2221 2821 3089 3081 Broadwoven fabric mills, manmade; plastics materials & resins; plastic processing; unsupported plastics film & sheet
PA: Toray Industries,Inc.
　2-1-1, Nihombashimuromachi
　Chuo-Ku TKY 103-0

(G-11518)
TOSHIBA AMER INFO SYSTEMS INC (DH)
1251 Ave Of The Amrcas St (10020-1104)
P.O. Box 19724, Irvine CA (92623-9724)
PHONE..........................949 583-3000
Mark Simons, *CEO*
Ted Flati, *Vice Pres*
◆ **EMP:** 257
SQ FT: 446,000
SALES (est): 258.6MM **Privately Held**
WEB: www.toshiba-components.com
SIC: 3571 3577 3572 3661 Electronic computers; computer peripheral equipment; disk drives, computer; telephones & telephone apparatus; facsimile equipment; computers, peripherals & software
HQ: Toshiba America Inc
　1251 Ave Of Ameri
　New York NY 10020
　212 596-0600

(G-11519)
TOSHIBA AMERICA INC (HQ)
1251 Ave Of Ameri (10020)
PHONE..........................212 596-0600
Hideo Ito, *CEO*
Takeshi Okatomi, *Ch of Bd*
Hiromitsu Igarashi, *President*
Hisashi Izumi, *President*
Toru Uchiike, *President*
◆ **EMP:** 28
SALES (est): 4.1B **Privately Held**
SIC: 3651 3631 5064 5075 Television receiving sets; video cassette recorders/players & accessories; microwave ovens, including portable; household; video cassette recorders & accessories; high fidelity equipment; compressors, air conditioning; personal computers (microcomputers); multiplex equipment, telephone & telegraph

(G-11520)
TOTAL CONCEPT GRAPHIC INC
519 8th Ave Rm 805a (10018-5182)
PHONE..........................212 229-2626
Joe Ferrara, *President*
John Chessa, *Vice Pres*
EMP: 4
SQ FT: 500
SALES: 2MM **Privately Held**
SIC: 2752 Commercial printing, offset

(G-11521)
TOTO USA INC
20 W 22nd St Frnt 2 (10010-5887)
PHONE..........................917 237-0665
Kazuo Sako, *Principal*
Lori Peterson, *Human Res Mgr*
EMP: 5 **Privately Held**
SIC: 3432 Plumbing fixture fittings & trim
HQ: Toto U.S.A., Inc.
　1155 Southern Rd
　Morrow GA 30260

(G-11522)
TOUCHCARE P LLC
135 Madison Ave Fl 5 (10016-6759)
PHONE..........................646 824-5373
Joel Kristoferson, *CEO*
EMP: 17
SALES (est): 883.1K **Privately Held**
SIC: 7372 Business oriented computer software

(G-11523)
TOUCHTUNES MUSIC CORPORATION (HQ)
Also Called: Touch Tunes
850 3rd Ave Ste 15c (10022-7263)
PHONE..........................847 419-3300
Charles Goldstuck, *CEO*
Ross Honey, *President*
Marc Felsen, *Senior VP*
Vicki Saunders, *Senior VP*

Pam Schoenfeld, *Senior VP*
EMP: 60
SALES (est): 73.5MM
SALES (corp-wide): 96.7MM **Privately Held**
SIC: 3651 Household audio & video equipment; audio electronic systems
PA: Searchlight Capital Partners, L.P.
　745 5th Ave Fl 27
　New York NY 10151
　212 293-3730

(G-11524)
TOWNLEY INC
Also Called: Townley Cosmetics
10 W 33rd St Rm 418 (10001-3324)
PHONE..........................212 779-0544
Abraham Safdieh, *President*
Joe Gindi, *Vice Pres*
Felena Jagarnauth, *Vice Pres*
▲ **EMP:** 30
SQ FT: 9,000
SALES (est): 5.6MM **Privately Held**
SIC: 3915 Jewelers' materials & lapidary work

(G-11525)
TOYMAX INC (DH)
Also Called: Candy Planet Division
200 5th Ave (10010-3302)
PHONE..........................212 633-6611
David Ki Kwan Chu, *Ch of Bd*
Steven Lebensfeld, *President*
Carmine Russo, *COO*
Harvey Goldberg, *Exec VP*
Kenneth Price, *Senior VP*
EMP: 8
SQ FT: 30,000
SALES (est): 3.6MM **Publicly Held**
WEB: www.toymax.com
SIC: 3944 5092 Games, toys & children's vehicles; toys

(G-11526)
TR APPAREL LLC (HQ)
Also Called: Row, The
609 Greenwich St Fl 3 (10014-3610)
PHONE..........................646 358-3888
Francois Kress, *President*
Ashley Olsen, *Owner*
Mary Kate Olsen, *Owner*
Catherine Dueck, *Vice Pres*
Kimberly Kennedy, *Opers Staff*
EMP: 9
SALES (est): 11.6MM
SALES (corp-wide): 10.7MM **Privately Held**
WEB: www.therow.com
SIC: 2389 5632 Academic vestments (caps & gowns); women's accessory & specialty stores
PA: Dualstar Entertainment Group Llc
　609 Greenwich St Fl 3
　New York NY 10014
　646 770-9333

(G-11527)
TR DESIGNS INC
Also Called: Tracy Reese
260 W 39th St Fl 19 (10018-0360)
PHONE..........................212 398-9300
ADI Kandel, *President*
Tracy Reese, *Principal*
Om Batheja, *Vice Pres*
▲ **EMP:** 32
SQ FT: 11,000
SALES (est): 4.1MM **Privately Held**
SIC: 2339 Sportswear, women's

(G-11528)
TRADDLE LLC
165 Broadway (10006-1404)
PHONE..........................646 330-0436
Prateek Chopra, *CEO*
EMP: 1
SALES: 1MM **Privately Held**
SIC: 7372 Business oriented computer software
PA: Traddle Intertrade Private Limited
　D 3, Farishta Complex,
　Raipur CT 49200

(G-11529)
TRADEBLOCK INC
156 5th Ave Fl 7 (10010-7706)
PHONE..........................212 231-8353

EMP: 1000
SALES: 200MM **Privately Held**
SIC: 7372 Application computer software

(G-11530)
TRADING SERVICES INTERNATIONAL
Also Called: Tsi Technologies
133 W 72nd St Rm 601 (10023-3236)
PHONE..........................212 501-0142
Joel Darr, *President*
Judy Darr, *Vice Pres*
▲ **EMP:** 14
SQ FT: 2,000
SALES (est): 24MM **Privately Held**
WEB: www.tsitec.com
SIC: 3679 5013 Electronic circuits; motor vehicle supplies & new parts

(G-11531)
TRAFALGAR COMPANY LLC (HQ)
417 5th Ave Fl 11 (10016-2238)
PHONE..........................212 768-8800
Jeffrey Spiegel, *Mng Member*
John Hastings,
▲ **EMP:** 5 **EST:** 2003
SQ FT: 6,500
SALES (est): 640.2K
SALES (corp-wide): 153.3MM **Privately Held**
WEB: www.ghurka.com
SIC: 2387 3172 3161 2389 Apparel belts; wallets; attache cases; briefcases; suitcases; suspenders
PA: Randa Accessories Leather Goods Llc
　5600 N River Rd Ste 500
　Rosemont IL 60018
　847 292-8300

(G-11532)
TRANS-HIGH CORPORATION
250 W 57th St Ste 920 (10107-0003)
PHONE..........................212 387-0500
EMP: 22 **EST:** 2013
SALES (est): 2.6MM **Privately Held**
SIC: 2721 Periodicals-Publishing/Printing

(G-11533)
TRANS-LUX CORPORATION (HQ)
135 E 57th St Unit 100 (10022-2172)
PHONE..........................800 243-5544
Salvatore J Zizza, *Ch of Bd*
Alberto Shaio, *President*
Todd Dupee, *Senior VP*
Alexandro Gomez, *Senior VP*
John Hammock, *Chief Mktg Ofcr*
▲ **EMP:** 66
SALES: 14.4MM **Publicly Held**
WEB: www.trans-lux.com
SIC: 3993 Electric signs
PA: Unilumin North America Inc.
　254 W 31st St
　New York NY 10001
　732 904-2037

(G-11534)
TRASH AND VAUDEVILLE INC
96 E 7th St Frnt A (10009-8042)
PHONE..........................212 777-1727
Diana Otoole, *Manager*
EMP: 6
SALES (corp-wide): 1MM **Privately Held**
SIC: 2389 Men's miscellaneous accessories
PA: Trash And Vaudeville, Inc.
　5200 W Side Ave
　North Bergen NJ 07047
　201 520-0420

(G-11535)
TREAAU INC
60 E 120th St Fl 2 (10035-3571)
PHONE..........................703 731-0196
Tahira White, *Principal*
Marcus Scott, *Principal*
EMP: 6
SALES (est): 340K **Privately Held**
SIC: 7372 7389 Application computer software;

(G-11536)
TREND POT INC
40 Exchange Pl Ste 1902 (10005-2711)
PHONE..........................212 431-9970
Tetsuji Shintani, *Ch of Bd*
▲ **EMP:** 25
SQ FT: 2,000
SALES: 2.5MM **Privately Held**
WEB: www.trendpot.com
SIC: 2721 Periodicals

(G-11537)
TRENDSFORMERS LTD LIABILITY CO
Also Called: Trensdformers
150 W 56th St Apt 6406 (10019-3848)
PHONE..........................888 700-2423
David Klar, *
EMP: 4
SQ FT: 5,000
SALES: 2MM **Privately Held**
SIC: 3999 8748 Atomizers, toiletry; business consulting

(G-11538)
TRI-FORCE SALES LLC
767 3rd Ave Rm 35b (10017-2082)
PHONE..........................732 261-5507
Robert Bracebic, *President*
Scp Crusader LLC, *Principal*
Matthew Marone, *Vice Pres*
Hemang Mehta, *Vice Pres*
▼ **EMP:** 24
SQ FT: 5,500
SALES: 12MM **Privately Held**
SIC: 3999 8742 Models, except toy; marketing consulting services

(G-11539)
TRI-PLEX PACKAGING CORPORATION
307 5th Ave Fl 7 (10016-6574)
PHONE..........................212 481-6070
Ken Golden, *President*
Barry Walsh, *Opers Staff*
Adam Caraher, *Director*
▲ **EMP:** 26
SALES: 10MM **Privately Held**
WEB: www.lieberman-nyc.com
SIC: 3999 2671 Advertising display products; paper coated or laminated for packaging

(G-11540)
TRI-STATE BRICK & STONE NY INC (PA)
333 7th Ave Fl 5 (10001-5829)
PHONE..........................212 366-0300
Robert Turzilli, *President*
Michael Falcone, *Vice Pres*
Vincent Falcone, *Vice Pres*
Louis J Formica, *Vice Pres*
▲ **EMP:** 60
SQ FT: 6,500
SALES (est): 26.8MM **Privately Held**
SIC: 2421 5031 Building & structural materials, wood; building materials, exterior

(G-11541)
TRI-STATE ENVELOPE CORPORATION
1 W 34th St Rm 704 (10001-3024)
PHONE..........................212 736-3110
Jeff Loden, *Opers Staff*
Fe Cruz, *Accounting Mgr*
John Swenson, *Branch Mgr*
James Macmannis, *Manager*
Frank Carlo, *Info Tech Dir*
EMP: 15
SALES (corp-wide): 125.6MM **Privately Held**
WEB: www.tristateenvelope.com
SIC: 2759 Commercial printing
PA: Tri-State Envelope Corporation
　20th Market St
　Ashland PA 17921
　570 875-0433

(G-11542)
TRIANON COLLECTION INC
Also Called: Seaman Schepps
16 W 46th St Fl 10 (10036-4503)
PHONE..........................212 921-9450
Anthony Hopenka JM, *CEO*
Joseph Bauer, *President*

Manwant Walia, *Manager*
▲ **EMP:** 24
SQ FT: 3,390
SALES (est): 3.3MM **Privately Held**
WEB: www.trianonnet.com
SIC: 3911 Jewelry, precious metal
PA: Banisa Corporation
21860 Masters Cir
Estero FL 33928
239 949-2309

(G-11543)
TRIBUNE ENTERTAINMENT CO DEL
220 E 42nd St Fl 26 (10017-5806)
PHONE.....................203 866-2204
EMP: 40
SALES (corp-wide): 2.7B **Publicly Held**
SIC: 2711 2741 4833 Newspapers, publishing & printing; miscellaneous publishing; television broadcasting stations
HQ: Tribune Entertainment Company (Del)
435 N Michigan Ave Fl 19
Chicago IL 60611
312 222-4441

(G-11544)
TRICYCLE FOUNDATION INC
89 5th Ave Ste 301 (10003-3020)
PHONE.....................800 873-9871
Alyssa Snow, *Controller*
Joellen Sommer, *Controller*
Phil Ryan, *Webmaster*
James Shaheen, *Exec Dir*
EMP: 9
SQ FT: 2,500
SALES: 2.1MM **Privately Held**
SIC: 2711 Newspapers: publishing only, not printed on site

(G-11545)
TRIMASTER/HTECH HOLDING LLC (HQ)
590 Madison Ave Fl 27 (10022-2544)
PHONE.....................212 257-6772
EMP: 4
SALES (est): 18.7MM **Privately Held**
SIC: 3544 3545 Special dies, tools, jigs & fixtures; precision tools, machinists'

(G-11546)
TRIMFIT INC (PA)
Also Called: Trimfit Global
463 7th Ave Rm 1501 (10018-7596)
PHONE.....................215 245-1122
Martin Kramer, *Ch of Bd*
Arnold A Kramer, *President*
▲ **EMP:** 40 **EST:** 1921
SQ FT: 12,000
SALES (est): 45.8MM **Privately Held**
WEB: www.trimfit.com
SIC: 2252 2251 Socks; tights & leg warmers; women's hosiery, except socks

(G-11547)
TRIMWORLD INC
247 W 37th St Rm 11e (10018-5064)
PHONE.....................212 354-8973
Louis Nunez, *President*
Mark Menis, *Vice Pres*
EMP: 10
SQ FT: 1,000
SALES (est): 911.4K **Privately Held**
SIC: 2395 Embroidery & art needlework

(G-11548)
TRIUMPH APPAREL CORPORATION (PA)
530 Fashion Ave Ste M1 (10018-4878)
PHONE.....................212 302-2606
Carol Hockman, *President*
Donald Schupak, *Principal*
John A Sarto, *CFO*
Henry Mortimer, *Director*
◆ **EMP:** 42
SALES (est): 78.8MM **Privately Held**
WEB: www.danskin.com
SIC: 2331 Women's & misses' blouses & shirts

(G-11549)
TRIUMPH LEARNING LLC (DH)
Also Called: Options Publishing
212 W 35th St Fl 2 (10001-2508)
PHONE.....................212 652-0200

Rick Noble, *President*
Thomas Emrick, *President*
Brad Peters, *President*
Michael Morley, *Publisher*
Jack Beers, *Vice Pres*
▲ **EMP:** 50 **EST:** 1963
SALES (est): 23.1MM
SALES (corp-wide): 83.8MM **Privately Held**
SIC: 2741 Miscellaneous publishing

(G-11550)
TRUEEX LLC
162 5th Ave Ste 900 (10010-5972)
PHONE.....................646 786-8526
Sunil Hirani, *CEO*
Karen O'Connor, *COO*
Karen L O'Connor, *COO*
David Hayman, *Opers Dir*
Tu-Lien Nguyen, *Project Dir*
EMP: 48
SALES (est): 462.1K **Privately Held**
SIC: 7372 Business oriented computer software

(G-11551)
TRUNK & TROLLEY LLC
15 W 34th St (10001-3015)
PHONE.....................212 947-9001
Sammy Sitt,
Steven Russo,
▲ **EMP:** 5
SQ FT: 25,000
SALES (est): 290K **Privately Held**
SIC: 3161 Luggage

(G-11552)
TRUST OF COLUM UNIVE IN THE CI
Also Called: Columbia Univ Publications
2929 Broadway Fl 3 (10025-7819)
PHONE.....................212 854-2793
Sandy Kaufman, *Director*
EMP: 19
SALES (corp-wide): 2.8B **Privately Held**
WEB: www.columbia.edu
SIC: 2754 8221 Labels: gravure printing; letter, circular & form: gravure printing; university
PA: The Trustees Of Columbia University In The City Of New York
116th And Bdwy Way
New York NY 10027
212 854-9970

(G-11553)
TRUSTED MEDIA BRANDS INC (HQ)
Also Called: Reader's Digest
750 3rd Ave Fl 3 (10017-2723)
PHONE.....................914 238-1000
Randall Curran, *Ch of Bd*
Bonnie Kintzer, *President*
Howard Halligan, *COO*
Brian Kennedy, *COO*
Phyllis Gebhardt, *Senior VP*
◆ **EMP:** 1100 **EST:** 1922
SQ FT: 445,193
SALES (est): 1.1B **Privately Held**
WEB: www.rd.com
SIC: 2721 2731 5961 2741 Magazines: publishing only, not printed on site; books: publishing only; books, mail order (except book clubs); record &/or tape (music or video) club, mail order; miscellaneous publishing

(G-11554)
TRYP TIMES SQUARE
234 W 48th St (10036-1540)
PHONE.....................212 246-8800
EMP: 6
SALES (est): 122.7K **Privately Held**
SIC: 2711 Newspapers

(G-11555)
TSAR USA LLC
99 Madison Ave Fl 5 (10016-7419)
PHONE.....................646 415-7968
Lucy Tupu, *General Mgr*
David Sharpley, *Mng Member*
▲ **EMP:** 12 **EST:** 2011
SALES (est): 1.4MM **Privately Held**
SIC: 2273 Carpets, hand & machine made

PA: Dakee Australia Pty. Ltd.
3 Wellington St
St Kilda VIC 3182

(G-11556)
TTG LLC
Also Called: Titan Technology Group
115 W 30th St Rm 209 (10001-4218)
PHONE.....................917 777-0959
Mark Liebmam, *Mng Member*
Mark Liebman, *Info Tech Dir*
Danny Keren,
EMP: 9
SQ FT: 1,600
SALES (est): 968.9K **Privately Held**
WEB: www.titantechgroup.com
SIC: 7372 Prepackaged software

(G-11557)
TUCANO USA INC
77 Bleecker St Apt C212 (10012-1586)
PHONE.....................212 966-9211
Franco Luini, *President*
Sergio Musati, *Exec VP*
◆ **EMP:** 6
SQ FT: 1,200
SALES (est): 4.8MM **Privately Held**
SIC: 3199 Leather garments

(G-11558)
TUDOR ELECTRICAL SUPPLY CO INC
137 W 24th St (10011-1901)
PHONE.....................212 867-7550
Jay Wittner, *President*
Steve Kramer, *Vice Pres*
EMP: 8
SQ FT: 8,500
SALES (est): 1.4MM **Privately Held**
SIC: 3645 5063 Residential lighting fixtures; electrical supplies

(G-11559)
TURN ON PRODUCTS INC (PA)
Also Called: Almost Famous Clothing
48 W 37th St Fl 5 (10018-7321)
PHONE.....................212 764-2121
Peter Kossoy, *President*
Adam Kossoy, *Vice Pres*
Robert Regina, *Vice Pres*
Marc Wasserman, *CFO*
▲ **EMP:** 80
SQ FT: 20,000
SALES (est): 65.8MM **Privately Held**
WEB: www.youniqueclothing.com
SIC: 2339 2331 Sportswear, women's; women's & misses' blouses & shirts

(G-11560)
TURN ON PRODUCTS INC
Also Called: Younique Clothing
525 7th Ave Rm 1403 (10018-4967)
PHONE.....................212 764-4545
Peter Kossoy, *President*
EMP: 12
SALES (corp-wide): 65.8MM **Privately Held**
WEB: www.youniqueclothing.com
SIC: 2331 2339 2337 2335 Blouses, women's & juniors': made from purchased material; slacks: women's, misses' & juniors'; skirts, separate: women's, misses' & juniors'; women's, juniors' & misses' dresses
PA: Turn On Products Inc.
48 W 37th St Fl 5
New York NY 10018
212 764-2121

(G-11561)
TV GUIDE MAGAZINE LLC (HQ)
50 Rockefeller Plz Fl 14 (10020-1617)
PHONE.....................800 866-1400
David J Fishman, *CEO*
Michell Lindquist, *CFO*
Mark Gudewitz, *Manager*
Michael Clayton,
Mark Fernberg,
EMP: 5
SALES (est): 97.2MM
SALES (corp-wide): 99.5MM **Privately Held**
SIC: 2721 Magazines: publishing & printing

PA: Ntvb Media, Inc.
213 Park Dr
Troy MI 48083
248 583-4190

(G-11562)
TV GUIDE MAGAZINE GROUP INC (DH)
1211 Ave Of The Americas (10036-8701)
PHONE.....................212 852-7500
John Loughlin, *CEO*
Michael Clayton, *Vice Pres*
Richard Steele, *CFO*
▲ **EMP:** 100
SQ FT: 40,000
SALES (est): 10.1MM
SALES (corp-wide): 99.5MM **Privately Held**
SIC: 2721 Magazines: publishing only, not printed on site; television schedules: publishing only, not printed on site

(G-11563)
TWCC PRODUCT AND SALES
122 5th Ave (10011-5605)
PHONE.....................212 614-9364
Katrina Hanritty, *Vice Pres*
EMP: 50
SALES (est): 2.7MM **Privately Held**
SIC: 2389 7389 Apparel & accessories; design services

(G-11564)
TWIST INTIMATE GROUP LLC (PA)
Also Called: Twist Intimate Apparel
35 W 35th St Rm 903 (10001-2238)
PHONE.....................212 695-5990
Jack Sardar, *Sales Staff*
Jack Saldar, *Mng Member*
David Sutone,
◆ **EMP:** 7
SQ FT: 5,000
SALES (est): 1.1MM **Privately Held**
SIC: 2322 Underwear, men's & boys': made from purchased materials

(G-11565)
TWO PALMS PRESS INC
476 Broadway Ste 3f (10013-2641)
PHONE.....................212 965-8598
David Lasry, *President*
Abelan Lasry, *Co-Owner*
EMP: 10
SALES: 950K **Privately Held**
WEB: www.twopalmspress.com
SIC: 2741 Miscellaneous publishing

(G-11566)
TWO WORLDS ARTS LTD (PA)
122 W 18th St (10011-5403)
PHONE.....................212 929-2210
Jean Chau, *President*
Frank Chau, *Vice Pres*
EMP: 6
SQ FT: 5,000
SALES (est): 931.1K **Privately Held**
SIC: 3645 2519 5099 5021 Table lamps; household furniture, except wood or metal: upholstered; antiques; household furniture

(G-11567)
TWP AMERICA INC (DH)
Also Called: Tien Wah Press
299 Broadway Ste 720 (10007-1987)
PHONE.....................212 274-8090
Regina Ang, *Human Res Mgr*
Yoichi Sanada, *Director*
◆ **EMP:** 7
SQ FT: 4,500
SALES (est): 559.7K **Privately Held**
WEB: www.twpny.com
SIC: 2732 Books: printing only
HQ: Tien Wah Press (Pte.) Limited
25 New Industrial Road
Singapore 53621
646 662-22

(G-11568)
TYME GLOBAL TECHNOLOGIES LLC
Also Called: Hotelexpert
60 W 66th St Apt 15a (10023-6288)
PHONE.....................212 796-1950

Ryan Levin, *Principal*
David Cristescu, *CFO*
EMP: 21
SALES (est): 481.3K **Privately Held**
SIC: 7372 Business oriented computer software

(G-11569)
TYME TECHNOLOGIES INC (PA)
17 State St Fl 7 (10004-1585)
PHONE..................................212 461-2315
Steve Hoffman, *CEO*
Ben R Taylor, *President*
Michele Korfin, *Ch Credit Ofcr*
Giuseppe Del Priore, *Chief Mktg Ofcr*
David Carberry, *Director*
EMP: 11
SQ FT: 4,752
SALES (est): 2.1MM **Publicly Held**
SIC: 2834 Pharmaceutical preparations

(G-11570)
U INVITE LIMITED
17 State St Ste 4000 (10004-1508)
PHONE..................................212 739-0620
EMP: 9
SALES: 100K **Privately Held**
SIC: 2752 Business form & card printing, lithographic

(G-11571)
U S JAPAN PUBLICATION NY INC
147 W 35th St Ste 1705 (10001-2100)
PHONE..................................212 252-8833
Nobuo Ijichi, *Ch of Bd*
Naoki Hishida, *Art Dir*
▲ **EMP:** 7
SQ FT: 2,500
SALES (est): 760K **Privately Held**
SIC: 2721 Magazines: publishing only, not printed on site

(G-11572)
U SERVE BRANDS INC
Also Called: Insomnia Cookies On The Hill
345 7th Ave Rm 501 (10001-5054)
PHONE..................................877 632-6654
Seth Berkowitz, *Chairman*
EMP: 13
SALES (est): 1.4MM **Privately Held**
SIC: 2052 Pretzels

(G-11573)
UBEES INC
575 5th Ave 21 (10017-2422)
PHONE..................................916 505-8470
Arnaud Lacourt, *Principal*
Laurence Bouju, *Principal*
JC Morisseau, *Principal*
EMP: 12
SALES (est): 329.6K **Privately Held**
SIC: 3999 Smokers, bee (beekeepers' supplies)

(G-11574)
UBM INC
605 3rd Ave Fl 22 (10158-0007)
PHONE..................................212 600-3000
David Levin, *CEO*
Tim Wilson, *Editor*
Christopher Fischer, *Business Mgr*
Bryan Jones, *Business Mgr*
Greg McDonald, *Business Mgr*
EMP: 3500
SALES (est): 228.8MM
SALES (corp-wide): 1.3B **Privately Held**
WEB: www.unm.com
SIC: 2721 2711 8732 2741 Periodicals; newspapers; commercial nonphysical research; business research service; business service newsletters: publishing & printing
PA: Ubm Plc
　　240 Blackfriars Road
　　London SE1 8
　　207 921-5000

(G-11575)
UBM LLC
Also Called: Cmp Media
605 3rd Ave Fl 22 (10158-0007)
PHONE..................................516 562-5000
Jim Donahue, *Editor*
Paul Travis, *Editor*
Marcy Holeton, *Vice Pres*

Aaron Murawski, *Vice Pres*
Diana Richard, *Vice Pres*
EMP: 10
SALES (corp-wide): 1.3B **Privately Held**
WEB: www.cmp.com
SIC: 2711 2721 Commercial printing & newspaper publishing combined; magazines: publishing & printing
HQ: Ubm, Llc
　　1983 Marcus Ave Ste 250
　　New Hyde Park NY 11042
　　516 562-7800

(G-11576)
UFO CONTEMPORARY INC
42 W 38th St Rm 1204 (10018-0054)
P.O. Box 20505 (10017-0005)
PHONE..................................212 226-5400
Lorna Brody, *President*
▲ **EMP:** 10
SALES (est): 1.1MM **Privately Held**
WEB: www.ufojeans.com
SIC: 2389 Men's miscellaneous accessories

(G-11577)
UFX HOLDING I CORPORATION (HQ)
55 E 52nd St Fl 35 (10055-0002)
PHONE..................................212 644-5900
Vincent MAI, *Principal*
▲ **EMP:** 1
SALES (est): 61.3MM
SALES (corp-wide): 3B **Privately Held**
SIC: 3299 Ceramic fiber
PA: Aea Investors Lp
　　666 5th Ave Fl 36
　　New York NY 10103
　　212 644-5900

(G-11578)
UFX HOLDING II CORPORATION (DH)
55 E 52nd St Fl 35 (10055-0002)
PHONE..................................212 644-5900
Vincent MAI, *Principal*
EMP: 1
SALES (est): 61.3MM
SALES (corp-wide): 3B **Privately Held**
SIC: 3299 Ceramic fiber

(G-11579)
ULLINK INC (DH)
11 Times Sq Ste 31d (10036-6622)
PHONE..................................646 565-6675
Torben Munch, *President*
Michael Savettiere, *Managing Dir*
Nicolas Rodriguez, *Project Mgr*
Narendhar Vemulapalli, *Project Mgr*
Richard Curcio, *Senior Engr*
EMP: 10
SALES (est): 11.1MM
SALES (corp-wide): 177.9K **Privately Held**
SIC: 7372 Business oriented computer software
HQ: Itiviti Usa Holding Inc.
　　190 S La Salle St # 1200
　　Chicago IL 60603
　　312 327-8555

(G-11580)
UNACAST INC (PA)
245 5th Ave Rm 1101 (10016-8720)
PHONE..................................917 670-7852
Thomas Walle, *CEO*
Kjartan Slette, *COO*
Eyal Alon, *Vice Pres*
Tomas Jansson, *Vice Pres*
Linn Jordet Nygaard, *Vice Pres*
EMP: 8 **EST:** 2016
SALES (est): 1.6MM **Privately Held**
SIC: 7372 7371 Application computer software; computer software development

(G-11581)
UNDERLINE COMMUNICATIONS LLC
12 W 27th St Fl 14 (10001-6903)
PHONE..................................212 994-4340
Kate Whitenight, *Partner*
Joshua McFarren, *Director*
Ashley Paterson, *Art Dir*
Susan Berman Drews,
Susan Myers,

EMP: 10
SALES (est): 1.3MM **Privately Held**
WEB: www.underlinecom.com
SIC: 2741 Miscellaneous publishing

(G-11582)
UNI JEWELRY INC
48 W 48th St Ste 1401 (10036-1718)
PHONE..................................212 398-1818
Frank Lee, *President*
▲ **EMP:** 7
SQ FT: 1,000
SALES (est): 540K **Privately Held**
SIC: 3911 5094 Jewelry, precious metal; jewelry

(G-11583)
UNIFIED INC IED
35 W 36th St (10018-7906)
PHONE..................................646 370-4650
EMP: 10
SALES (est): 500K **Privately Held**
SIC: 2389 Mfg Apparel/Accessories

(G-11584)
UNIFIED MEDIA INC
180 Madison Ave (10016-5267)
PHONE..................................917 595-2710
Sheldon Owen, *CEO*
Brian Benenhaley, *Vice Pres*
Barry Hott, *Manager*
James Errico, *Senior Mgr*
EMP: 17
SALES (est): 1.1MM **Privately Held**
SIC: 2711 Newspapers, publishing & printing

(G-11585)
UNIFOR INC
149 5th Ave Ste 3r (10010-6899)
PHONE..................................212 673-3434
Gianfranco Marinelli, *President*
Angela Dispensa, *COO*
▲ **EMP:** 19
SALES (est): 3MM **Privately Held**
SIC: 2531 Public building & related furniture

(G-11586)
UNIFORMED FIRE OFFICER ASSOIAT
125 Maiden Ln (10038-4912)
PHONE..................................212 293-9300
Richard D Brower, *President*
John Corr, *Vice Pres*
James M Slevin, *Admin Sec*
EMP: 17
SQ FT: 1,500
SALES: 7.6MM **Privately Held**
SIC: 1389 Fire fighting, oil & gas field

(G-11587)
UNIFRAX HOLDING CO (DH)
55 E 52nd St Fl 35 (10055-0002)
PHONE..................................212 644-5900
Vincent MAI, *Principal*
EMP: 1
SALES (est): 61.3MM
SALES (corp-wide): 3B **Privately Held**
SIC: 3299 Ceramic fiber

(G-11588)
UNILEVER UNITED STATES INC
390 Park Ave (10022-4608)
PHONE..................................212 546-0200
Christine Dealbuquerque, *Marketing Staff*
Christine Wright, *Marketing Staff*
David Mallon, *Manager*
Joseph Everard, *Senior Mgr*
Kathy Hefferle, *Senior Mgr*
EMP: 10
SALES (corp-wide): 58.3B **Privately Held**
SIC: 2086 2024 2038 2844 Bottled & canned soft drinks; ice cream & frozen desserts; frozen specialties; toilet preparations; toothpastes or powders, dentifrices; hair preparations, including shampoos; cosmetic preparations; detergents, synthetic organic or inorganic alkaline; dishwashing compounds; soap: granulated, liquid, cake, flaked or chip; dressings, salad: raw & cooked (except dry mixes)

HQ: Unilever United States, Inc.
　　700 Sylvan Ave
　　Englewood Cliffs NJ 07632
　　201 735-9661

(G-11589)
UNILEVER UNITED STATES INC
Also Called: Elizabeth Arden
663 5th Ave Fl 8 (10022-5328)
PHONE..................................212 546-0200
Teresa McKee, *Manager*
EMP: 250
SALES (corp-wide): 58.3B **Privately Held**
WEB: www.unilever.com
SIC: 2086 2024 2038 2844 Bottled & canned soft drinks; ice cream & frozen desserts; frozen specialties; toilet preparations; toothpastes or powders, dentifrices; hair preparations, including shampoos; cosmetic preparations; detergents, synthetic organic or inorganic alkaline; dishwashing compounds; soap: granulated, liquid, cake, flaked or chip; dressings, salad: raw & cooked (except dry mixes)
HQ: Unilever United States, Inc.
　　700 Sylvan Ave
　　Englewood Cliffs NJ 07632
　　201 735-9661

(G-11590)
UNILUMIN NORTH AMERICA INC (PA)
254 W 31st St (10001-2813)
PHONE..................................732 904-2037
Alberto Shaio, *President*
EMP: 2
SALES (est): 14.4MM **Publicly Held**
SIC: 3993 Electric signs

(G-11591)
UNIMEX CORPORATION (PA)
54 E 64th St (10065-7306)
PHONE..................................800 886-0390
Arthur L Carter, *Ch of Bd*
Tom Scheinman, *President*
William Heidrich, *General Ptnr*
Vincent A Bohn Jr, *Vice Pres*
Brian G Kempner, *Vice Pres*
EMP: 100
SQ FT: 10,000
SALES (est): 40.6MM **Privately Held**
SIC: 3495 Wire springs

(G-11592)
UNIPHARM INC
350 5th Ave Ste 6701 (10118-6708)
PHONE..................................212 594-3260
Victor Sapritsky, *President*
Robert D Sires, *President*
Chris Adamo, *General Mgr*
Ricardo De, *COO*
Elena Prokhorova, *Opers Mgr*
▼ **EMP:** 100
SALES (est): 30.1MM **Privately Held**
WEB: www.unipharmus.com
SIC: 2834 5122 Vitamin preparations; vitamins & minerals

(G-11593)
UNIQLO USA LLC
546 Broadway (10012-3912)
PHONE..................................877 486-4756
Andrew Rosen, *Mng Member*
▲ **EMP:** 17
SALES (est): 1.9MM **Privately Held**
SIC: 2329 2337 5621 Sweaters & sweater jackets: men's & boys'; women's & misses' capes & jackets; women's clothing stores
PA: Fast Retailing Co., Ltd.
　　9-7-1, Akasaka
　　Minato-Ku TKY 107-0

(G-11594)
UNIQUE DESIGNS INC
521 5th Ave Rm 820 (10175-0800)
PHONE..................................212 575-7701
Tejas Shah, *CEO*
Ben Yep, *President*
Chai Lin, *Vice Pres*
Karen Lin, *Controller*
EMP: 19
SQ FT: 1,000

SALES (est): 147.5MM **Privately Held**
WEB: www.uniquedesigns.com
SIC: 3911 Jewelry, precious metal

(G-11595)
UNIQUE PETZ LLC
10 W 33rd St Rm 220 (10001-3306)
PHONE..................212 714-1800
Adam Ash, *President*
▲ **EMP:** 25
SALES (est): 20MM **Privately Held**
SIC: 3999 Pet supplies

(G-11596)
UNISYSTEMS INC (PA)
Also Called: Modern Publishing
155 E 55th St Apt 203 (10022-4051)
PHONE..................212 826-0850
Larry Steinberg, *Ch of Bd*
Andrew Steinberg, *President*
Warren Cohen, *Exec VP*
▲ **EMP:** 34
SQ FT: 8,200
SALES (est): 3.6MM **Privately Held**
WEB: www.modernpublishing.com
SIC: 2731 Books: publishing only

(G-11597)
UNITED BROTHERS JEWELRY INC
Also Called: U B J
48 W 48th St Ste 700 (10036-1703)
PHONE..................212 921-2558
Gabriel Nisanov, *CEO*
Roman Nisanov, *Vice Pres*
Israel Nisanov, *Treasurer*
Israel Maximof, *Admin Sec*
EMP: 20
SQ FT: 6,000
SALES (est): 4.2MM **Privately Held**
SIC: 3911 Jewelry, precious metal

(G-11598)
UNITED KNITWEAR INTERNATIONAL (PA)
379 W Broadway Fl 3 (10012-5122)
PHONE..................212 354-2920
Carlos Hausner, *President*
▲ **EMP:** 3 EST: 1969
SALES (est): 4.8MM **Privately Held**
WEB: www.unitedknitwear.com
SIC: 2253 5136 5137 Sweaters & sweater coats, knit; men's & boys' clothing; women's & children's clothing

(G-11599)
UNITED RETAIL II
Also Called: Happy Sock
436 W Broadway (10012-3752)
PHONE..................212 966-9692
EMP: 6 EST: 2013
SALES (est): 400.9K **Privately Held**
SIC: 2252 Socks

(G-11600)
UNITED RUBBER SUPPLY CO INC
54 Warren St (10007-1078)
PHONE..................212 233-6650
Bob Zone, *Branch Mgr*
EMP: 5
SALES (corp-wide): 2.1MM **Privately Held**
SIC: 3069 Medical & laboratory rubber sundries & related products
PA: United Rubber Supply Co Inc
9b Commercial St
Hicksville NY 11801
516 822-7999

(G-11601)
UNITED STRUCTURE SOLUTION INC
240 W 65th St Apt 26c (10023-6412)
PHONE..................347 227-7526
Ying Lu, *President*
EMP: 15 EST: 2010
SALES: 2MM **Privately Held**
SIC: 3441 Fabricated structural metal

(G-11602)
UNITED SYNGGUE CNSRVTIVE JDISM (PA)
3080 Broadway (10027-4650)
PHONE..................212 533-7800

Rabbi Steven Wernick, *CEO*
Rabbi Jerome Epstein, *Exec VP*
Rose McMahon, *Finance*
Sara Wienclaw, *Med Doctor*
Pamela Flores, *Manager*
▲ **EMP:** 50
SALES (est): 16.8MM **Privately Held**
WEB: www.uscj.org
SIC: 2731 8661 Books: publishing only; religious organizations

(G-11603)
UNITONE COMMUNICATION SYSTEMS
220 E 23rd St Ste 411 (10010-4659)
PHONE..................212 777-9090
Lucien Bohbot, *President*
Preya Khusial, *Vice Pres*
EMP: 6
SALES (est): 983.4K **Privately Held**
WEB: www.unitonecom.com
SIC: 3669 7622 Burglar alarm apparatus, electric; fire alarm apparatus, electric; intercommunication systems, electric; communication equipment repair

(G-11604)
UNIVERSAL CMMNCATIONS OF MIAMI
Also Called: Elite Traveler Magazine
801 2nd Ave Lbby (10017-4706)
PHONE..................212 986-5100
Geoffrey Lurie, *CEO*
Carl Reuderman, *Ch of Bd*
Douglas Gollan, *President*
Mikki Dorsey, *Exec VP*
Daniel Wade, *Exec VP*
EMP: 125
SALES (est): 10.7MM **Privately Held**
SIC: 2721 Magazines: publishing & printing

(G-11605)
UNIVERSAL EDITION INC
Also Called: Ue Music
331 W 57th St Ste 380 (10019-3101)
PHONE..................917 213-2177
Robert Thompson, *President*
▲ **EMP:** 65
SQ FT: 5,000
SALES: 8MM **Privately Held**
WEB: www.roxannapanufnik.com
SIC: 2741 Music books: publishing & printing

(G-11606)
UNIVERSAL ELLIOT CORP
327 W 36th St Rm 700 (10018-6929)
PHONE..................212 736-8877
Mike Gadh, *President*
Ush Gadh, *Vice Pres*
Gurpal Gadh, *Admin Sec*
EMP: 9
SALES (est): 605K **Privately Held**
SIC: 2387 Apparel belts

(G-11607)
UNIVERSAL LUXURY BRANDS INC (PA)
452 W Broadway (10012-3141)
PHONE..................646 248-5700
Kobi Gutman, *CEO*
Victoria Coulter, *Controller*
EMP: 7
SALES (est): 2.6MM **Privately Held**
SIC: 3951 Fountain pens & fountain pen desk sets

(G-11608)
UNIVERSAL MUS GROUP HLDNGS INC (DH)
1755 Broadway Fl 6 (10019-3743)
PHONE..................212 333-8000
Alain Levy, *Principal*
▲ **EMP:** 24

SALES (est): 45.4MM
SALES (corp-wide): 78.1MM **Privately Held**
SIC: 3652 5099 6794 8742 Magnetic tape (audio): prerecorded; master records or tapes, preparation of; phonograph records, prerecorded; compact discs; phonograph records; tapes & cassettes, prerecorded; video cassettes, accessories & supplies; copyright buying & licensing; music licensing & royalties; business consultant; men's & boys' clothing; women's & children's clothing
HQ: Universal Music Group, Inc.
2220 Colorado Ave
Santa Monica CA 90404
310 865-4000

(G-11609)
UNIVERSAL MUSIC GROUP INC
825 8th Ave Fl C2b (10019-7472)
PHONE..................212 333-8237
Kyle Owen, *General Mgr*
Bill Evans, *Regional Mgr*
Marshall Carr, *Vice Pres*
Jennifer Hirsch-Davis, *Vice Pres*
Ping Hu, *Vice Pres*
EMP: 11
SALES (corp-wide): 78.1MM **Privately Held**
SIC: 3652 Pre-recorded records & tapes
HQ: Universal Music Group, Inc.
2220 Colorado Ave
Santa Monica CA 90404
310 865-4000

(G-11610)
UNQORK INC
85 5th Ave Fl 6 (10003-3019)
PHONE..................844 486-7675
Gary Hoberman, *CEO*
Ted Ranft, *Risk Mgmt Dir*
EMP: 25
SQ FT: 10,000
SALES (est): 607.2K **Privately Held**
SIC: 7372 Business oriented computer software

(G-11611)
UNTITLED MEDIA
Also Called: Indira Cesarine
45 Lispenard St Apt 1w (10013-2530)
PHONE..................212 780-0960
Indira Cesarine, *President*
EMP: 45
SALES (est): 3.1MM **Privately Held**
SIC: 2721 7335 Magazines: publishing only, not printed on site; commercial photography

(G-11612)
UNTUCKIT LLC (PA)
110 Greene St Ste 400 (10012-3832)
PHONE..................347 524-9111
Chris Riccobono, *CEO*
Brent Paulsen, *Managing Dir*
Aaron Sanandres, *Co-CEO*
Alex McGeoch, *Manager*
Joy Holmes, *Office Admin*
▲ **EMP:** 56
SALES (est): 85MM **Privately Held**
SIC: 2326 2339 Men's & boys' work clothing; athletic clothing: women's, misses' & juniors'

(G-11613)
UNTUCKIT LLC
379 W Broadway Fl 2 (10012-5125)
PHONE..................646 724-1857
EMP: 132
SALES (corp-wide): 85MM **Privately Held**
SIC: 2326 2339 Men's & boys' work clothing; athletic clothing: women's, misses' & juniors'
PA: Untuckit, Llc
110 Greene St Ste 400
New York NY 10012
347 524-9111

(G-11614)
UPTOWN MEDIA GROUP LLC
113 E 125th St Frnt 1 (10035-1661)
PHONE..................212 360-5073
EMP: 36

SALES (est): 4MM **Privately Held**
SIC: 2721 Publishing & Printing Magazines

(G-11615)
URBAN APPAREL GROUP INC
226 W 37th St Fl 6l (10018-9020)
PHONE..................212 947-7009
Karen Camporeale, *President*
Noreen Camporeale, *Vice Pres*
Dave Dulinski, *CFO*
David A Dulinski, *CFO*
Larry Shapiro, *Director*
◆ **EMP:** 37
SQ FT: 9,000
SALES (est): 4.1MM **Privately Held**
WEB: www.urbanapparel.com
SIC: 2339 Sportswear, women's

(G-11616)
URBAN MAPPING INC
Also Called: Umi
295 Madison Ave Rm 1010 (10017-6340)
PHONE..................415 946-8170
Ian White, *President*
John Marshall, *CTO*
Amy Ocasio, *Admin Sec*
EMP: 11
SALES (est): 1.1MM **Privately Held**
WEB: www.urbanmapping.com
SIC: 2741 Atlas, map & guide publishing

(G-11617)
URBAN TEXTILES INC
Also Called: Forest Uniforms
254 W 35th St Unit 13 (10001-2517)
PHONE..................212 777-1900
Michael Schackett, *President*
Maria Pino, *Accounting Mgr*
▲ **EMP:** 10
SQ FT: 5,000
SALES (est): 1.5MM **Privately Held**
SIC: 2311 Men's & boys' uniforms

(G-11618)
URBANDADDY INC
900 Broadway Ste 1003 (10003-1215)
P.O. Box 1050 (10276-1050)
PHONE..................212 929-7905
Lance Broumand, *CEO*
Lebaron Meyer, *Vice Pres*
Erica Wertheim, *Sales Staff*
Bailey Edwards, *Manager*
Taylor Tobin, *Assoc Editor*
EMP: 14
SALES (est): 3.2MM **Privately Held**
SIC: 2721 Magazines: publishing & printing

(G-11619)
UROGEN LTD
689 5th Ave Fl 14 (10022-3148)
PHONE..................646 768-9780
EMP: 5
SALES (est): 694.1K **Privately Held**
SIC: 2834 Pharmaceutical preparations

(G-11620)
UROGEN PHARMA INC
499 Park Ave Ste 1200 (10022-1240)
PHONE..................646 506-4663
Elizabeth Barrett, *Principal*
Stephen Mullennix, *Principal*
Peter Pfreundschuh, *Principal*
EMP: 14
SALES (est): 2.6MM **Privately Held**
SIC: 2834 Pharmaceutical preparations

(G-11621)
URTHWORX INC
320 W 106th St Apt 2f (10025-3470)
PHONE..................646 373-7535
Michael Fox, *CEO*
EMP: 5 EST: 2014
SALES (est): 304.8K **Privately Held**
SIC: 7372 7389 Home entertainment computer software;

(G-11622)
US CHINA MAGAZINE
200 W 95th St Apt 21 (10025-6315)
PHONE..................212 663-4333
Zhong Vhan, *President*
Angila Chan, *Vice Pres*
Andrew Jee, *Director*
EMP: 25 EST: 1994
SALES: 500K **Privately Held**
SIC: 2721 Periodicals

(G-11623)
US DESIGN GROUP LTD
Also Called: Request Jeans
1385 Broadway Rm 1905 (10018-6001)
PHONE................................212 354-4070
Frank Jbara, *President*
Frank Jebara, *President*
Assad Charles Jebara, *Vice Pres*
Imad Jebara, *Admin Sec*
▲ EMP: 18
SQ FT: 10,000
SALES (est): 1.2MM **Privately Held**
SIC: 2211 Apparel & outerwear fabrics,
cotton

(G-11624)
US DIAGNOSTICS INC
Also Called: Vertaloc
711 3rd Ave Rm 1502 (10017-9200)
PHONE................................866 216-5308
Edward Letko, *President*
▲ EMP: 20
SALES (est): 3.2MM **Privately Held**
SIC: 2835 In vitro & in vivo diagnostic sub-
stances

(G-11625)
**US HOME TEXTILES GROUP
LLC**
1400 Broadway Fl 18 (10018-5300)
PHONE................................212 768-3030
▲ EMP: 6
SALES (est): 570K **Privately Held**
SIC: 2221 Manmade Broadwoven Fabric
Mill

(G-11626)
**US NEWS & WORLD REPORT
INC (PA)**
120 5th Ave Fl 7 (10011-5637)
PHONE................................212 716-6800
Mortimer B Zuckerman, *CEO*
Dino Colucci, *Partner*
Heide Fasnacht, *Partner*
Andrew Graber, *Partner*
Jodie Jacobson, *Partner*
▲ EMP: 150
SQ FT: 100,000
SALES (est): 101.1MM **Privately Held**
WEB: www.usnews.com
SIC: 2721 Magazines: publishing & printing

(G-11627)
US SPACE LLC
1212 Avenue Of The (10036)
PHONE................................646 278-0371
Craig Weston, *President*
Ed Wright, *Vice Pres*
Mark Piegza, *CFO*
EMP: 9
SALES (est): 1.3MM **Privately Held**
SIC: 3663 Radio & TV communications
equipment

(G-11628)
US WEEKLY LLC
1290 Ave Of The Americas (10104-0295)
PHONE................................212 484-1616
David J Pecker, *CEO*
Elizabeth Abts, *Editor*
Emily Longeretta, *Editor*
Sharon Tharp, *Editor*
Vanessa Grimaldi, *Fire Chief*
EMP: 75
SQ FT: 15,000
SALES (est): 9.3MM
SALES (corp-wide): 363MM **Privately
Held**
WEB: www.usweekly.com
SIC: 2721 Magazines: publishing only, not
printed on site
PA: Worldwide Media Services Group Inc.
　　1350 E Newprt Ctr Dr 20
　　Deerfield Beach FL 33442
　　561 989-1342

(G-11629)
USA FURS BY GEORGE INC
212 W 30th St (10001-4901)
PHONE................................212 643-1415
George Chrisomalides, *President*
Johanna Chrisomalides, *Vice Pres*
EMP: 4
SQ FT: 2,500

SALES: 1MM **Privately Held**
SIC: 2371 Fur goods

(G-11630)
**USA TODAY INTERNATIONAL
CORP**
535 Madison Ave Fl 27 (10022-4216)
PHONE................................703 854-3400
David Mazzarella, *Manager*
EMP: 7
SALES (corp-wide): 2.9B **Publicly Held**
SIC: 2711 Newspapers, publishing & print-
ing
HQ: Usa Today International Corp
　　7950 Jones Branch Dr
　　Mc Lean VA 22102

(G-11631)
USPA ACCESSORIES LLC
Also Called: Concept One Accessories
1411 Broadway Fl 7 (10018-3401)
PHONE................................212 868-2590
Margaret Close, *Vice Pres*
Kim White, *Vice Pres*
Peter Vorrias, *Prdtn Mgr*
Angeline Gomez, *Production*
Ann Perez, *Production*
▲ EMP: 150
SQ FT: 38,000
SALES (est): 21.2MM **Privately Held**
SIC: 2339 Women's & misses' accessories

(G-11632)
USQ GROUP LLC
222 Broadway Fl 19 (10038-2550)
PHONE................................212 777-7751
Shanto Goswami, *CEO*
EMP: 5
SALES (est): 198.3K **Privately Held**
SIC: 7372 Application computer software;
home entertainment computer software

(G-11633)
**VALENTIN & KALICH JWLY MFG
LTD**
Also Called: Valentin Magro
42 W 48th St Ste 903 (10036-1712)
PHONE................................212 575-9044
Valente Magro, *President*
Terry Magro, *Vice Pres*
EMP: 24
SALES (est): 3.1MM **Privately Held**
SIC: 3911 Jewelry, precious metal

(G-11634)
**VALENTINE JEWELRY MFG CO
INC**
31 W 47th St Ste 602 (10036-2833)
PHONE................................212 382-0606
Emil Feiger, *President*
EMP: 20 **EST:** 1969
SQ FT: 2,000
SALES (est): 1.9MM **Privately Held**
SIC: 3911 Jewelry, precious metal

(G-11635)
VALIANT ENTERTAINMENT LLC
350 7th Ave Rm 300 (10001-1957)
PHONE................................212 972-0361
Russell Brown, *President*
Lysa Hawkins, *Editor*
Warren Simons, *Editor*
Peter Stern, *Opers Mgr*
Connor Hill, *Opers Staff*
EMP: 20
SQ FT: 4,000
SALES: 5MM
SALES (corp-wide): 1.8MM **Privately
Held**
SIC: 2721 Comic books: publishing only,
not printed on site
HQ: Dmg Entertainment, Inc.
　　9290 Civic Center Dr
　　Beverly Hills CA 90210
　　310 275-3750

(G-11636)
VALMONT INC (PA)
1 W 34th St Rm 303 (10001-3011)
PHONE................................212 685-1653
Nicholas Vales, *President*
Nicholas Vale, *President*
Nick Vale, *VP Opers*
▲ EMP: 15 **EST:** 1944
SQ FT: 1,000

SALES (est): 3.1MM
SALES (corp-wide): 3.3MM **Privately
Held**
SIC: 2342 5961 Brassieres; catalog &
mail-order houses

(G-11637)
VALUE LINE INC (HQ)
551 5th Ave Fl 3 (10176-2800)
PHONE................................212 907-1500
Howard A Brecher, *Ch of Bd*
Stephen R Anastasio, *CFO*
Mary Bernstein, *Accountant*
Bobby Darlington, *Accounts Mgr*
Stephen Davis, *Director*
EMP: 57
SQ FT: 24,726
SALES: 35.8MM
SALES (corp-wide): 36MM **Publicly Held**
SIC: 2721 6282 2741 Magazines: pub-
lishing only, not printed on site; invest-
ment advisory service; miscellaneous
publishing
PA: Bernhard Arnold & Company Inc
　　551 5th Ave Fl 3
　　New York NY 10176
　　212 907-1500

(G-11638)
VALUE LINE PUBLISHING LLC
551 5th Ave Fl 3 (10176-2800)
PHONE................................201 842-8054
Howard Brether, *CEO*
EMP: 175
SQ FT: 80,000
SALES (est): 36.7MM
SALES (corp-wide): 36MM **Publicly Held**
SIC: 2721 Periodicals: publishing only
HQ: Value Line, Inc.
　　551 5th Ave Fl 3
　　New York NY 10176
　　212 907-1500

(G-11639)
**VANDER HEYDEN
WOODWORKING**
Also Called: Tapestries Etc
151 W 25th St Fl 8 (10001-7204)
PHONE................................212 242-0525
Marcia Vander Heyden, *President*
EMP: 6
SQ FT: 3,000
SALES (est): 480K **Privately Held**
WEB: www.metookids.com
SIC: 2431 0742 Interior & ornamental
woodwork & trim; veterinary services,
specialties

(G-11640)
VANITY FAIR
285 Fulton St (10007-0089)
PHONE................................212 286-7919
Radhika Jones, *Principal*
Graydon Carter, *Chief*
◆ EMP: 15
SALES (est): 1.7MM **Privately Held**
WEB: www.vf.com
SIC: 2721 Magazines: publishing & printing

(G-11641)
VANITY FAIR BRANDS LP
25 W 39th St (10018-3805)
PHONE................................212 548-1548
Pat Lager, *Manager*
EMP: 250
SALES (corp-wide): 225.3B **Publicly
Held**
SIC: 2341 Nightgowns & negligees:
women's & children's
HQ: Vanity Fair Brands, Lp
　　1 Fruit Of The Loom Dr
　　Bowling Green KY 42103
　　270 781-6400

(G-11642)
VANITY ROOM INC
Also Called: Four Star
230 W 39th St Rm 900 (10018-4438)
PHONE................................212 921-7154
Geneva Goldsmith, *President*
EMP: 10
SALES (est): 2.8MM **Privately Held**
SIC: 2331 2335 Women's & misses'
blouses & shirts; women's, juniors' &
misses' dresses

(G-11643)
VARIABLE GRAPHICS LLC
15 W 36th St Rm 601 (10018-7122)
PHONE................................212 691-2323
Keneth Ratskin, *Mng Member*
Arthur Raskin,
Kenneth Ratskin,
▲ EMP: 6
SALES (est): 851.2K **Privately Held**
WEB: www.variablegraphics.com
SIC: 2752 Commercial printing, offset

(G-11644)
VARICK STREET LITHO INC
149 W 27th St Fl 4 (10001-6279)
PHONE................................646 843-0800
EMP: 6
SALES (est): 718.9K **Privately Held**
SIC: 2759 Commercial printing

(G-11645)
VARNISH SOFTWARE INC
85 Broad St Fl 18 (10004-2783)
PHONE................................201 857-2832
Lars Larsson, *President*
Daniel Jacobs, *Sales Mgr*
Dan Jacobs, *Sales Staff*
EMP: 5
SALES (est): 146.4K **Privately Held**
SIC: 7372 Business oriented computer
software

(G-11646)
VARONIS SYSTEMS INC (PA)
1250 Broadway Fl 29 (10001-3720)
PHONE................................877 292-8787
Yakov Faitelson, *Ch of Bd*
Guy Melamed, *COO*
David Bass, *Exec VP*
James O'Boyle, *Senior VP*
Gilad Raz, *Vice Pres*
EMP: 148
SQ FT: 46,000
SALES: 270.2MM **Publicly Held**
SIC: 7372 Prepackaged software; busi-
ness oriented computer software

(G-11647)
VARSITY MONITOR LLC
50 5th Ave Fl 3 Flr 3 (10011)
PHONE................................212 691-6292
Sam Carnahan, *Managing Prtnr*
Farrah Carnahan, *Managing Dir*
EMP: 9
SALES (est): 470K **Privately Held**
SIC: 7372 Business oriented computer
software

(G-11648)
VASQUEZ TITO
Also Called: Tito Moldmaker Co
36 W 47th St Ste 206 (10036-8636)
PHONE................................212 944-0441
Tito Vasquez, *Owner*
EMP: 10
SALES (est): 868.9K **Privately Held**
SIC: 2822 Silicone rubbers

(G-11649)
VAUGHAN DESIGNS INC (HQ)
979 3rd Ave Ste 1511 (10022-3804)
PHONE................................212 319-7070
Michael Vaughan, *President*
▲ EMP: 13
SQ FT: 1,700
SALES (est): 1.9MM
SALES (corp-wide): 19.8MM **Privately
Held**
WEB: www.vaughandesigns.com
SIC: 3645 5021 Residential lighting fix-
tures; tables, occasional
PA: Vaughan Limited
　　Unit 1 Chelsea Harbour Design Cen-
　　tre, Chelsea Harbour
　　London SW10
　　207 349-4600

(G-11650)
VAULTCOM INC (PA)
Also Called: Vault.com, Vault Media
132 W 31st St Rm 1501 (10001-3406)
PHONE................................212 366-4212
Eric Ober, *President*
Matt Moody, *Editor*
Laurie Pasiuk, *Editor*
Phil Stott, *Editor*

▲ = Import ▼=Export
◆ =Import/Export

Samer Hamadeh, *Chairman*
EMP: 33 **EST:** 1992
SALES (est): 5.7MM **Privately Held**
WEB: www.vaultmatch.com
SIC: 2731 7361 Books: publishing only;
employment agencies

(G-11651)
VECTOR GROUP LTD
712 5th Ave (10019-4108)
PHONE..............................212 409-2800
Ellen Jorgenson, *Manager*
EMP: 244
SALES (corp-wide): 1.8B **Publicly Held**
SIC: 2111 Cigarettes
PA: Vector Group Ltd.
4400 Biscayne Blvd Fl 10
Miami FL 33137
305 579-8000

(G-11652)
VEEA INC
Also Called: Veeapay
164 E 83rd St (10028-1901)
PHONE..............................212 535-6050
EMP: 15 **EST:** 2014
SALES (est): 2.7MM **Privately Held**
SIC: 3823 Computer interface equipment
for industrial process control

(G-11653)
VEGA COFFEE INC
325 N End Ave Apt 4b (10282-1027)
PHONE..............................415 881-7969
William Deluca, *Co-Owner*
Noushin Ketabi, *Co-Owner*
Robert Terenzi, *Co-Owner*
EMP: 5
SALES (est): 204.8K **Privately Held**
SIC: 2095 Roasted coffee

(G-11654)
VENDOME GROUP LLC
237 W 35th St Fl 16 (10001-1905)
PHONE..............................646 795-3899
Jane Butler, *CEO*
Mark Fried, *President*
Maria Safina, *General Mgr*
Julie Miller, *Chief*
Ron Lowy, *Vice Pres*
EMP: 89
SALES (est): 11.8MM **Privately Held**
SIC: 2741 Miscellaneous publishing

(G-11655)
VENTRUS BIOSCIENCES INC
99 Hudson St (10013-2815)
PHONE..............................646 706-5208
John Gunderson, *Counsel*
Diane Hague, *Controller*
Melissa Fiacco, *Accounting Mgr*
Steve Reynolds, *Finance*
Ray Kauffman, *Director*
EMP: 8 **EST:** 2017
SALES (est): 743.6K **Privately Held**
SIC: 2834 Pharmaceutical preparations

(G-11656)
VENTURA ENTERPRISE CO INC
512 Fashion Ave Fl 38 (10018-0827)
PHONE..............................212 391-0170
Saul Tawil, *Ch of Bd*
Shelley Rindner, *Exec VP*
Henry Dweck, *Vice Pres*
Phil Horowitz, *VP Sales*
Anne King, *Director*
▲ **EMP:** 40
SQ FT: 8,000
SALES (est): 4.3MM **Privately Held**
SIC: 2326 2331 Men's & boys' work cloth-
ing; women's & misses' blouses & shirts

(G-11657)
VERA WANG GROUP LLC (PA)
Also Called: V E W
15 E 26th St Fl 4 (10010-1536)
PHONE..............................212 575-6400
Vera W Becker, *Ch of Bd*
Kali Argianas, *General Mgr*
Steve Mendonca, *Marketing Mgr*
▲ **EMP:** 190 **EST:** 2004
SQ FT: 14,000

SALES (est): 43MM **Privately Held**
WEB: www.verawang.com
SIC: 2335 5621 Bridal & formal gowns;
wedding gowns & dresses; gowns, formal; bridal shops; dress shops

(G-11658)
VERANDA PUBLICATIONS INC
Also Called: Veranda Magazine
300 W 57th St Fl 28 (10019-5288)
PHONE..............................212 903-5206
Lisa Newsom, *President*
Victor Maze, *Editor*
Brian Woodcock, *Editor*
Ellen McGauley, *Manager*
Ashley Leath, *Assistant*
EMP: 8
SALES (corp-wide): 8.3B **Privately Held**
WEB: www.hearstcorp.com
SIC: 2721 Magazines: publishing only, not
printed on site
PA: The Hearst Corporation
300 W 57th St Fl 42
New York NY 10019
212 649-2000

(G-11659)
VERATEX INC (PA)
534 W 42nd St Apt 8 (10036-6221)
P.O. Box 682 (10108-0682)
PHONE..............................212 683-9300
Claude Simon, *President*
John Simon, *Vice Pres*
▲ **EMP:** 10
SQ FT: 2,500
SALES (est): 1.8MM **Privately Held**
SIC: 2258 Tricot fabrics

(G-11660)
VERDONETTE INC
270 W 39th St Fl 5 (10018-4409)
PHONE..............................212 719-2003
EMP: 5
SALES (est): 310K **Privately Held**
SIC: 2395 Pleating/Stitching Services

(G-11661)
VERILED INC
100 Church St Ste 871 (10007-2601)
PHONE..............................877 521-5520
Michael Handerhan, *CEO*
◆ **EMP:** 6
SQ FT: 2,000
SALES: 2.4MM **Privately Held**
SIC: 3674 Light emitting diodes

(G-11662)
VERRAGIO LTD (PA)
132 W 36th St Bsmt (10018-6903)
PHONE..............................212 868-8181
Barry Nisguretsky, *President*
Nick Ozkan, *Vice Pres*
Alicia Thompson, *Vice Pres*
Jeff Sullivan, *Natl Sales Mgr*
Tab Judd, *Regl Sales Mgr*
▲ **EMP:** 20
SQ FT: 8,000
SALES (est): 3.5MM **Privately Held**
WEB: www.verragio.com
SIC: 3911 Jewelry, precious metal

(G-11663)
VERRIS INC
99 Wall St Unit 236 (10005-4301)
PHONE..............................201 565-1648
John Paris, *CEO*
Scott Berchin, *Senior VP*
EMP: 2
SALES: 2MM **Privately Held**
SIC: 7372 7389 Prepackaged software;

(G-11664)
VERSAILLES INDUSTRIES LLC
485 Fashion Ave Rm 500 (10018-6804)
PHONE..............................212 792-9615
Freddy Hamra, *Mng Member*
▲ **EMP:** 6
SALES (est): 579.6K **Privately Held**
SIC: 2329 Riding clothes:, men's, youths' &
boys'

(G-11665)
VERSO CORPORATION
370 Lexington Ave Rm 802 (10017-6510)
PHONE..............................212 599-2700

Gerhard Nussbaumer, *Principal*
EMP: 400 **Publicly Held**
SIC: 2621 3554 Paper mills; paper indus-
tries machinery
PA: Verso Corporation
8540 Gander Creek Dr
Miamisburg OH 45342

(G-11666)
VERTANA GROUP LLC (PA)
Also Called: Killer Motor Sports
450 Lexington Ave Fl 4 (10017-3912)
PHONE..............................646 430-8226
Emmanuel Tesone, *President*
EMP: 5 **EST:** 2012
SALES (est): 2.5MM **Privately Held**
SIC: 7372 Prepackaged software

(G-11667)
**VERTICAL RESEARCH
PARTNERS LLC**
52 Vanderbilt Ave Rm 200 (10017-3860)
PHONE..............................212 257-6499
EMP: 18
SALES (corp-wide): 4.4MM **Privately
Held**
SIC: 2591 Drapery Hardware And Blinds
And Shades
PA: Vertical Research Partners Llc
1 Landmark Sq Fl 4
Stamford CT 06901
203 276-5680

(G-11668)
VETROELITE INC
115 W 30th St Rm 402 (10001-4179)
PHONE..............................925 724-7900
Daniele Feletto, *Ch of Bd*
Daniele Cortesi, *Natl Sales Mgr*
▲ **EMP:** 6
SALES (est): 547.1K **Privately Held**
SIC: 3565 Packing & wrapping machinery

(G-11669)
VETTA JEWELRY INC (PA)
Also Called: Spring Street Design Group
989 Avenue Of The America (10018-0875)
PHONE..............................212 564-8250
Edwin Peissis, *Ch of Bd*
Mary Walsh, *President*
▲ **EMP:** 20
SALES (est): 4MM **Privately Held**
WEB: www.cosmotronics.com
SIC: 3961 Costume jewelry

(G-11670)
VEXOS INC (HQ)
60 E 42nd St Ste 1250 (10165-1299)
PHONE..............................855 711-3227
Paul Jona, *President*
Brad Koury, *General Mgr*
Cyril Fernandes, *Senior VP*
Kaspars Fricbergs, *Senior VP*
Stephanie Martin, *Senior VP*
EMP: 10
SALES (est): 150MM **Privately Held**
SIC: 3672 Printed circuit boards

(G-11671)
VF SERVICES LLC
25 W 39th St (10018-3805)
P.O. Box 4307 (10163-4307)
PHONE..............................212 575-7820
EMP: 5
SALES (corp-wide): 13.8MM **Publicly
Held**
SIC: 2211 Apparel & outerwear fabrics,
cotton
HQ: Vf Services, Llc
105 Corporate Center Blvd
Greensboro NC 27408
336 424-6000

(G-11672)
VGG HOLDING LLC
590 Madison Ave Fl 41 (10022-2524)
PHONE..............................212 415-6700
EMP: 5
SALES (est): 587.8K **Privately Held**
SIC: 3674 Semiconductors & related de-
vices

(G-11673)
VHX CORPORATION
555 W 18th St (10011-2822)
PHONE..............................347 689-1446

Jamie Wilkinson, *CEO*
Kevin Sheurs, *CTO*
EMP: 13 **EST:** 2013
SALES (est): 1MM
SALES (corp-wide): 4.2B **Publicly Held**
SIC: 7372 Application computer software
PA: Iac/Interactivecorp
555 W 18th St
New York NY 10011
212 314-7300

(G-11674)
**VIA AMERICA FINE JEWELRY
INC**
578 5th Ave Unit 26 (10036-4836)
PHONE..............................212 302-1218
Mary Yogurtcu, *President*
Sadik Yogurtco, *Vice Pres*
Harutyn Temurco, *Admin Sec*
EMP: 5
SQ FT: 3,000
SALES (est): 420K **Privately Held**
SIC: 3915 Jewelers' materials & lapidary
work

(G-11675)
VIBE MEDIA GROUP LLC
Also Called: Vibe Magazine
120 Wall St Fl 21 (10005-4024)
P.O. Box 618180, Chicago IL (60661-8171)
PHONE..............................212 448-7300
Desire Thompson, *Editor*
Danyel Smith, *Vice Pres*
Gary R Lewis, *Officer*
Steve Aaron,
EMP: 65
SALES (est): 3.5MM **Privately Held**
SIC: 2721 Magazines: publishing & printing

(G-11676)
**VICKERS STOCK RESEARCH
CORP**
61 Broadway Rm 1910 (10006-2761)
PHONE..............................212 425-7500
Fern Dorsey, *President*
EMP: 40
SQ FT: 5,000
SALES (est): 2.7MM
SALES (corp-wide): 14.3MM **Privately
Held**
WEB: www.vickers-stock.com
SIC: 2721 Periodicals
PA: Argus Research Company
61 Broadway Rm 1910
New York NY 10006
212 425-7500

(G-11677)
VICTORIA ALBI INTERNATIONAL
Also Called: Makari
1178 Broadway Fl 5 (10001-5404)
PHONE..............................212 689-2600
Raquel Aini, *CEO*
▲ **EMP:** 10
SALES (est): 1.7MM **Privately Held**
SIC: 2844 Cosmetic preparations

(G-11678)
VICTORY GARDEN
31 Carmine St Frnt A (10014-4427)
PHONE..............................212 206-7273
Sophia Brittain, *Owner*
EMP: 7 **EST:** 2011
SALES (est): 423.8K **Privately Held**
SIC: 2024 Ice cream, bulk

(G-11679)
VIDAL CANDIES USA INC
845 3rd Ave Fl 6 (10022-6630)
PHONE..............................609 781-8169
John Curiel, *Sales Mgr*
Mitchell Bernstein, *Sales Staff*
◆ **EMP:** 9
SALES (est): 988.2K
SALES (corp-wide): 129.1MM **Privately
Held**
SIC: 2064 Candy & other confectionery
products
PA: Vidal Golosinas Sa
Avenida Gutierrez Mellado, S/N
Molina De Segura 30500
968 647-100

G
E
O
G
R
A
P
H
I
C

(G-11680)
VIEW COLLECTIONS INC
265 W 37th St Rm 5w (10018-5750)
PHONE.....................................212 944-4030
David Shavolian, *President*
Nathan Shavolian, *Chairman*
EMP: 12
SQ FT: 6,000
SALES (est): 1.2MM **Privately Held**
SIC: 2337 Suits: women's, misses' & jun-
iors'

(G-11681)
VIEWFINDER INC
Also Called: First View
101 W 23rd St Ste 2303 (10011-2490)
PHONE.....................................212 831-0939
Donald Asbey, *President*
Marcio Moraes, *Vice Pres*
EMP: 5 EST: 1995
SALES (est): 574.9K **Privately Held**
WEB: www.firstview.com
SIC: 2741 Miscellaneous publishing

(G-11682)
VIGO INDUSTRIES LLC (PA)
138 W 25th St Fl 3 (10001-7471)
PHONE.....................................866 591-7792
Leonid Valdberg, *Mng Member*
◆ EMP: 32
SALES (est): 6.8MM **Privately Held**
SIC: 3431 3469 Bathroom fixtures, includ-
ing sinks; kitchen fixtures & equipment:
metal, except cast aluminum

(G-11683)
VIKTOR GOLD ENTERPRISE CORP
58 W 47th St Unit 36 (10036-8610)
PHONE.....................................212 768-8885
Boris Yakutilov, *Principal*
EMP: 3 EST: 1996
SALES: 1MM **Privately Held**
SIC: 3911 Jewelry, precious metal

(G-11684)
VILLEROY & BOCH USA INC
41 Madison Ave Ste 1801 (10010-2226)
PHONE.....................................212 213-8149
Alison Hudak, *Manager*
EMP: 11
SALES (corp-wide): 976.6MM **Privately Held**
SIC: 3089 Plastic kitchenware, tableware &
houseware
HQ: Villeroy & Boch Usa, Inc.
3a S Middlesex Ave
Monroe Township NJ 08831
800 536-2284

(G-11685)
VINOUS GROUP LLC
Also Called: Delectable
54 W 40th St (10018-2602)
PHONE.....................................917 275-5184
EMP: 6 EST: 2016
SQ FT: 100
SALES (est): 170.5K **Privately Held**
SIC: 2741 Internet Publishing And Broad-
casting

(G-11686)
VIRGIL MOUNTAIN INC (PA)
1 E 28th St Fl 4 (10016-7432)
PHONE.....................................212 378-0007
Stephen Dignam, *President*
Edmund Mandrala, *Corp Secy*
Gerard Glenn, *Vice Pres*
▲ EMP: 8
SQ FT: 5,000
SALES (est): 1MM **Privately Held**
SIC: 2752 Commercial printing, litho-
graphic

(G-11687)
VIRIDIS LEARNING INC
2 Gold St Apt 4005 (10038-4862)
PHONE.....................................347 420-9181
Felix Ortiz, *CEO*
Felix W Ortiz III, *Principal*
Alex Carstens, *COO*
EMP: 6
SALES (est): 33.2K **Privately Held**
SIC: 7372 Prepackaged software

(G-11688)
VIROPRO INC
49 W 38th St Fl 11 (10018-1933)
PHONE.....................................650 300-5190
Bruce A Cohen, *Ch of Bd*
Joseph J Vallner, *President*
Scott M Brown, *Security Dir*
EMP: 34
SALES (est): 1.8MM **Privately Held**
SIC: 2834 Pharmaceutical preparations

(G-11689)
VIRTUAL FACILITY INC
39 W 37th St Fl 17 (10018-0192)
PHONE.....................................646 891-4861
Mark Prewett, *CEO*
EMP: 10
SALES (est): 221.8K **Privately Held**
SIC: 7372 Business oriented computer
software

(G-11690)
VIRTUAL FRAMEWORKS INC (PA)
115 5th Ave Frnt 2 (10003-1004)
PHONE.....................................646 690-8207
Tomer Benami, *Vice Pres*
EMP: 9
SALES (est): 2.3MM **Privately Held**
SIC: 7372 Application computer software

(G-11691)
VIRTUAL SUPER LLC
116 E 27th St Fl 3 (10016-8942)
PHONE.....................................212 685-6400
Joshua Smith,
EMP: 5
SALES: 50K **Privately Held**
SIC: 3822 Building services monitoring
controls, automatic

(G-11692)
VISION LOGIC INC
300 Park Ave Fl 12 (10022-7419)
PHONE.....................................212 729-4606
Lou Bivona, *President*
John Walsh, *Principal*
Graham Conran, *COO*
Rick Urban, *Vice Pres*
EMP: 5 EST: 2016
SALES: 500K **Privately Held**
SIC: 7372 7373 Application computer soft-
ware; value-added resellers, computer
systems

(G-11693)
VISIONAIRE PUBLISHING LLC
Also Called: V Magazine
30 W 24th St (10010-3207)
PHONE.....................................646 434-6091
Donald Hearn, *Prdtn Dir*
Lars Petersen, *Director*
Stephen Gan,
Cecilia Dean,
James Kaliardos,
▲ EMP: 20
SALES (est): 3.1MM **Privately Held**
WEB: www.visionaireworld.com
SIC: 2721 Magazines: publishing only, not
printed on site

(G-11694)
VITAFEDE (PA)
25 W 26th St Fl 5 (10010-1039)
PHONE.....................................646 869-4003
Mitch Naidrich, *Principal*
▲ EMP: 11
SALES (est): 3.9MM **Privately Held**
SIC: 3961 Bracelets, except precious
metal

(G-11695)
VITALIS LLC
902 Broadway Fl 6 (10010-6039)
PHONE.....................................646 831-7338
Joseph Habboushe,
EMP: 5 EST: 2012
SALES (est): 58.7K **Privately Held**
SIC: 2834 Pharmaceutical preparations

(G-11696)
VITALIZE LABS LLC
Also Called: Eboost
134 Spring St Ste 502 (10012-3886)
PHONE.....................................212 966-6130

Malijian Sjam, *CFO*
John McDonald,
Josh Taekman,
EMP: 5
SQ FT: 1,000
SALES: 3MM **Privately Held**
SIC: 2833 Vitamins, natural or synthetic:
bulk, uncompounded

(G-11697)
VITIPRINTS LLC
630 9th Ave Ste 208 (10036-4752)
PHONE.....................................646 591-4343
Amy Reese,
Andrew Ferber,
EMP: 5
SALES: 1MM **Privately Held**
SIC: 2844 Oral preparations

(G-11698)
VITRA INC (DH)
95 Madison Ave Frnt 1 (10016-7801)
PHONE.....................................212 463-5700
Rolf Fehlbaum, *CEO*
Melissa Shelton, *President*
Gabriel Colon-Amador, *Sales Staff*
Noriko Hayashi, *Sales Staff*
Claudette Marasigan, *Manager*
◆ EMP: 16
SALES (est): 16.9MM
SALES (corp-wide): 177.9MM **Privately
Held**
SIC: 2522 Chairs, office: padded or plain,
except wood
HQ: Vitra Collections Ag
Klunenfeldstrasse 22
Muttenz BL 4132
418 111-327

(G-11699)
VIZBEE INC
120 E 23rd St Fl 5 (10010-4519)
PHONE.....................................650 787-1424
Darren Feher, *CEO*
Prashanth Pappu, *Principal*
EMP: 8
SALES (est): 200K **Privately Held**
SIC: 7372 7371 Home entertainment com-
puter software; computer software sys-
tems analysis & design, custom

(G-11700)
VIZIO MEDICAL DEVICES LLC
200 Chambers St Apt 28a (10007-1350)
PHONE.....................................646 845-7382
EMP: 10
SALES (est): 600K **Privately Held**
SIC: 3841 Mfg Surgical/Medical Instru-
ments

(G-11701)
VNOVOM SVETE
55 Broad St Fl 20 (10004-2589)
PHONE.....................................212 302-9480
Helen Brusilovski, *Principal*
EMP: 9
SALES (est): 318.5K **Privately Held**
SIC: 2711 Commercial printing & newspa-
per publishing combined

(G-11702)
VOGEL APPLIED TECHNOLOGIES
Also Called: Brainwave Toys-New York
36 E 12th St Fl 7 (10003-4604)
PHONE.....................................212 677-3136
David Vogel, *President*
EMP: 1
SQ FT: 500
SALES: 1MM **Privately Held**
WEB: www.brainwavetoys.com
SIC: 3944 Games, toys & children's vehi-
cles

(G-11703)
VOGUE TOO PLTING STITCHING EMB
265 W 37th St Fl 14 (10018-5707)
PHONE.....................................212 354-1022
Larry Geffner, *President*
EMP: 13 EST: 2001
SALES (est): 1.1MM **Privately Held**
SIC: 2395 Pleating & tucking, for the trade

(G-11704)
VON MUSULIN PATRICIA
148 W 24th St Fl 10 (10011-1951)
PHONE.....................................212 206-8345
Patricia Von Musulin, *President*
EMP: 8
SALES (est): 610K **Privately Held**
SIC: 3911 3961 Jewelry, precious metal;
jewelry apparel, non-precious metals

(G-11705)
VON POK & CHANG NEW YORK INC
4 E 43rd St 7 (10017-4607)
PHONE.....................................212 599-0556
Omega Chang, *President*
▲ EMP: 6
SQ FT: 1,000
SALES (est): 4.8MM **Privately Held**
WEB: www.vonpok.com
SIC: 3993 Advertising novelties

(G-11706)
VONDOM LLC
979 3rd Ave Ste 1532 (10022-3806)
PHONE.....................................212 207-3252
Olga Tomas, *CFO*
Antonio Esteve,
▲ EMP: 4
SALES: 1.6MM **Privately Held**
SIC: 2519 Furniture, household: glass,
fiberglass & plastic

(G-11707)
VOSS USA INC
236 W 30th St Rm 900 (10001-0900)
PHONE.....................................212 995-2255
Jack Baelsito, *CEO*
Antoinette Borromeo, *Regional Mgr*
Joe Bayern, *COO*
Patrick Larkin, *Vice Pres*
Mark Zettle, *Vice Pres*
◆ EMP: 150
SQ FT: 1,000
SALES (est): 36MM
SALES (corp-wide): 177.9K **Privately
Held**
SIC: 3561 Pumps & pumping equipment
HQ: Voss Of Norway As
Vatnestrom Industriomr 5
Vatnestrom 4730

(G-11708)
VSM INVESTORS LLC (PA)
245 Park Ave Fl 41 (10167-0002)
PHONE.....................................212 351-1600
◆ EMP: 1 EST: 2000
SALES (est): 402.8MM **Privately Held**
SIC: 3842 2599 2515 Wheelchairs; per-
sonal safety equipment; respirators; hos-
pital beds; hospital furniture, except beds;
mattresses & foundations

(G-11709)
VUNIVERSE INC
575 5th Ave Fl 17 (10017-2422)
PHONE.....................................212 206-1041
Evelyn Brady-Watters, *CEO*
EMP: 5
SALES: 398.9K **Privately Held**
SIC: 7372 Application computer software

(G-11710)
VVS INTERNATIONAL INC
2 W 46th St (10036-4811)
PHONE.....................................212 302-5410
EMP: 5
SALES (est): 252.8K **Privately Held**
SIC: 2834 Pharmaceutical preparations

(G-11711)
VYERA PHARMACEUTICALS LLC
600 3rd Ave Fl 10 (10016-1923)
PHONE.....................................646 356-5577
Kevin Mulleady, *CEO*
Eliseo Salinas, *President*
Howard L Dorfman, *Senior VP*
Nicholas Pelliccione, *Vice Pres*
Michael Harrison, *CFO*
EMP: 25

▲ = Import ▼=Export
◆ =Import/Export

SALES (est): 10.1MM
SALES (corp-wide): 1.2MM **Privately Held**
SIC: 2836 5122 Biological products, except diagnostic; pharmaceuticals
PA: Phoenixus Ag
Haldenstrasse 5
Baar ZG 6340
417 602-424

(G-11712)
W B BOW TIE CORP
Also Called: Bentley Cravats
521 W 26th St Fl 6 (10001-5531)
PHONE..................................212 683-6130
Walter Schick, *President*
Marion Schick, *Admin Sec*
EMP: 10 EST: 1948
SQ FT: 10,000
SALES (est): 514.9K **Privately Held**
SIC: 2323 Neckties, men's & boys': made from purchased materials

(G-11713)
W W NORTON & COMPANY INC (PA)
500 5th Ave Fl 5 (10110-0054)
PHONE..................................212 354-5500
W Drake McFeely, *President*
Catherine J Abelman, *Editor*
Beth Ammerman, *Editor*
Danielle R Belfiore, *Editor*
Katherine Brayton, *Editor*
◆ EMP: 130 EST: 1923
SQ FT: 30,000
SALES (est): 180.7MM **Privately Held**
WEB: www.wwnorton.com
SIC: 2731 5192 Textbooks: publishing only, not printed on site; books: publishing only; books

(G-11714)
W W NORTON & COMPANY INC
Countryman Press, The
500 5th Ave Lbby 1 (10110-0105)
PHONE..................................212 354-5500
Ann Treistman, *Branch Mgr*
EMP: 8
SALES (corp-wide): 180.7MM **Privately Held**
SIC: 2731 Book publishing
PA: W. W. Norton & Company, Inc.
500 5th Ave Fl 5
New York NY 10110
212 354-5500

(G-11715)
WACOAL AMERICA INC
Also Called: Dkny Underwear
136 Madison Ave Fl 15 (10016-6787)
PHONE..................................212 743-9600
Rich Murray, *Branch Mgr*
EMP: 30 **Privately Held**
WEB: www.wacoal-america.com
SIC: 2342 Bras, girdles & allied garments
HQ: Wacoal America, Inc.
1 Wacoal Plz
Lyndhurst NJ 07071
201 933-8400

(G-11716)
WALDMAN PUBLISHING CORPORATION (PA)
570 Fashion Ave Rm 800 (10018-1603)
P.O. Box 1587 (10028-0013)
PHONE..................................212 730-9590
Rachel Waldman, *Ch of Bd*
▲ EMP: 10
SQ FT: 3,200
SALES (est): 2.4MM **Privately Held**
SIC: 2731 Textbooks: publishing only, not printed on site

(G-11717)
WALL STREET REPORTER MAGAZINE
419 Lafayette St Fl 2 (10003-7033)
PHONE..................................212 363-2600
Jack Marks, *President*
Alan Wolski, *Treasurer*
EMP: 62 EST: 1993
SQ FT: 9,000
SALES (est): 4MM **Privately Held**
WEB: www.wallstreetreporter.com
SIC: 2721 Magazines: publishing & printing

(G-11718)
WALLACE REFINERS INC
15 W 47th St Ste 808 (10036-5703)
PHONE..................................212 391-2649
EMP: 5
SQ FT: 1,500
SALES (est): 510K **Privately Held**
SIC: 3339 5094 Refine Buys And Wholesales Precious Metals

(G-11719)
WARM
181 Mott St Frnt 1 (10012-4581)
PHONE..................................212 925-1200
Rob Magnotta, *Principal*
EMP: 10 EST: 2014
SALES (est): 427K **Privately Held**
SIC: 2253 Warm weather knit outerwear, including beachwear

(G-11720)
WARNACO GROUP INC (HQ)
501 Fashion Ave (10018-5903)
PHONE..................................212 287-8000
Helen McCluskey, *CEO*
James B Gerson, *President*
Joanne Kaye, *President*
Martha Olson, *President*
Michael Prendergast, *President*
◆ EMP: 30
SALES (est): 779.2MM
SALES (corp-wide): 9.6B **Publicly Held**
SIC: 2322 2329 2339 2369 Underwear, men's & boys': made from purchased materials; men's & boys' sportswear & athletic clothing; women's & misses' outerwear; bathing suits: women's, misses' & juniors'; beachwear: women's, misses' & juniors'; children's bathing suits & beachwear; bras, girdles & allied garments; brassieres; girdles & panty girdles; panties: women's, misses', children's & infants'; women's & children's nightwear
PA: Pvh Corp.
200 Madison Ave Bsmt 1
New York NY 10016
212 381-3500

(G-11721)
WARNACO INC (DH)
Also Called: Warner S
501 Fashion Ave Fl 14 (10018-5942)
PHONE..................................212 287-8000
Joseph R Gromek, *Ch of Bd*
Charles R Perrin, *Ch of Bd*
Helen McCluskey, *President*
Les Hall, *President*
Larry Rutkowski, *Exec VP*
◆ EMP: 300 EST: 1874
SQ FT: 25,000
SALES (est): 362.7MM
SALES (corp-wide): 9.6B **Publicly Held**
WEB: www.warnaco.com
SIC: 2341 2321 2329 2322 Panties: women's, misses', children's & infants'; women's & children's nightwear; men's & boys' dress shirts; men's & boys' sportswear & athletic clothing; underwear, men's & boys': made from purchased materials; men's & boys' neckwear; brassieres
HQ: The Warnaco Group Inc
501 Fashion Ave
New York NY 10018
212 287-8000

(G-11722)
WARNER MUSIC GROUP CORP (DH)
1633 Broadway Fl 11 (10019-7637)
PHONE..................................212 275-2000
Stu Bergen, *CEO*
Stephen Cooper, *CEO*
Cameron Strang, *CEO*
Michael Lynton, *Ch of Bd*
Kevin Gore, *President*
EMP: 230
SALES: 4B **Privately Held**
SIC: 3652 6794 Pre-recorded records & tapes; music licensing & royalties

(G-11723)
WARNER MUSIC INC (DH)
1633 Broadway Fl 11 (10019-7637)
PHONE..................................212 275-2000
Paul Rene' Albertini, *President*

Howie Singer, *President*
Pat Creed, *General Mgr*
John Delaney, *COO*
David H Johnson, *Exec VP*
▼ EMP: 100
SQ FT: 333,500
SALES (est): 657.6MM **Privately Held**
SIC: 2741 3652 Music, sheet: publishing & printing; phonograph records, prerecorded
HQ: Wmg Acquisition Corp.
1633 Broadway Fl 7
New York NY 10019
212 275-2000

(G-11724)
WARREN CORPORATION (DH)
711 5th Ave Fl 11 (10022-3113)
PHONE..................................917 379-3434
Pier Guerci, *President*
Guy Birkhead, *Senior VP*
Lisa Cornish, *Vice Pres*
Kate Schlosstein, *Marketing Staff*
Richard Anderman, *Admin Sec*
◆ EMP: 180 EST: 1853
SQ FT: 330,000
SALES (est): 24.8MM
SALES (corp-wide): 361.7MM **Privately Held**
WEB: www.warrencorp.com
SIC: 2231 Overcoatings: wool, mohair or similar fibers; suitings: wool, mohair or similar fibers
HQ: Loro Piana Spa
Corso Pietro Rolandi 10
Quarona VC 13017
016 320-1111

(G-11725)
WARREN ENERGY SERVICES LLC
1114 Ave Of The Americas (10036-7703)
PHONE..................................212 697-9660
James A Watt,
EMP: 10
SQ FT: 4,200
SALES (est): 409.7K **Publicly Held**
SIC: 1382 Oil & gas exploration services
PA: Warren Resources, Inc.
5420 Lbj Fwy Ste 600
Dallas TX 75240

(G-11726)
WASTECORP PUMPS LLC (PA)
345 W 85th St Apt 23 (10024-3834)
P.O. Box 70, Grand Island (14072-0070)
PHONE..................................888 829-2783
Dan Starr,
◆ EMP: 10
SQ FT: 2,000,000
SALES (est): 1.3MM **Privately Held**
SIC: 3561 Pumps & pumping equipment

(G-11727)
WATCH JOURNAL LLC
110 E 25th St Fl 4 (10010-2913)
PHONE..................................212 229-1500
Marc Lotenberg,
EMP: 6
SALES (est): 1.7MM **Privately Held**
SIC: 2721 Magazines: publishing & printing

(G-11728)
WATCHANISH LLC
1 Rockefeller Plz Fl 11 (10020-2073)
PHONE..................................917 558-0404
Anish Bhatt, *Principal*
EMP: 10
SALES (est): 249.7K **Privately Held**
SIC: 2741 Miscellaneous publishing

(G-11729)
WATER ENERGY SYSTEMS LLC
1 Maiden Ln (10038-4015)
PHONE..................................844 822-7665
EMP: 8 EST: 2015
SALES (est): 431K **Privately Held**
SIC: 3589 Mfg Service Industry Machinery

(G-11730)
WATERBURY GARMENT LLC
Also Called: Jackie's Girls
16 E 34th St Fl 10 (10016-4360)
PHONE..................................212 725-1500
Daniel Livingston, *President*
Harry Gaffney, *CFO*

▲ EMP: 30 EST: 1921
SQ FT: 19,000
SALES (est): 1.6MM
SALES (corp-wide): 260MM **Privately Held**
WEB: www.waterburygarment.com
SIC: 2341 2369 2322 Women's & children's nightwear; children's robes & housecoats; men's & boys' underwear & nightwear
HQ: Komar Kids, L.L.C.
90 Hudson St
Jersey City NJ 07302
212 725-1500

(G-11731)
WATSON ADVENTURES LLC
330 W 38th St Rm 407 (10018-8307)
PHONE..................................212 564-8293
Daniel Maranon, *Principal*
Laura Lovejoy, *Accounts Mgr*
Tara Melvin, *Accounts Mgr*
Maggie Murphy, *Accounts Mgr*
Corin Coyle, *Sales Staff*
EMP: 6
SALES (est): 550.2K **Privately Held**
SIC: 3949 Sporting & athletic goods

(G-11732)
WAY OUT TOYS INC
230 5th Ave Ste 800 (10001-7851)
PHONE..................................212 689-9094
Eddie Mishan, *President*
Al Mishan, *Vice Pres*
Jeffrey Mishan, *Vice Pres*
Steven Mishan, *Vice Pres*
EMP: 6
SALES (est): 660K **Privately Held**
SIC: 3944 5092 Games, toys & children's vehicles; toys & games

(G-11733)
WE WORK
1 Little West 12th St (10014-1302)
PHONE..................................877 673-6628
Leah Weiss,
EMP: 8
SALES (est): 499.6K **Privately Held**
SIC: 2011 Meat packing plants

(G-11734)
WEA INTERNATIONAL INC (DH)
75 Rockefeller Plz (10019-6908)
PHONE..................................212 275-1300
Tom Shaheen, *President*
Keith Bruce, *Senior VP*
EMP: 100
SQ FT: 3,500
SALES (est): 127.9MM **Privately Held**
SIC: 3652 Master records or tapes, preparation of

(G-11735)
WEEKLY BUSINESS NEWS CORP
274 Madison Ave Rm 1101 (10016-0700)
PHONE..................................212 689-5888
Yoshiaki Takahashi, *President*
EMP: 6
SALES (est): 222.5K **Privately Held**
SIC: 2711 Newspapers, publishing & printing

(G-11736)
WEIDER PUBLICATIONS LLC
Also Called: A M I
1 Park Ave Fl 10 (10016-5818)
PHONE..................................212 545-4800
Lisa Wheeler, *Editor*
Beverly Levy, *Branch Mgr*
Chris Tarrow, *Manager*
Madeline Fabbro, *Graphic Designe*
EMP: 200
SALES (corp-wide): 363MM **Privately Held**
WEB: www.fitnessonline.com
SIC: 2721 Magazines: publishing only, not printed on site
HQ: Weider Publications, Llc
3699 Wilshire Blvd # 1220
Los Angeles CA 90010

(G-11737)
WEISCO INC
246 W 38th St Fl 6 (10018-5854)
PHONE..................................212 575-8989

Alex Weiss, *President*
Edward Weiss, *Vice Pres*
Peter Weiss, *Treasurer*
EMP: 15
SQ FT: 7,000
SALES (est): 1.5MM **Privately Held**
WEB: www.weisco.com
SIC: 3911 Jewelry, precious metal

(G-11738)
WELCOME RAIN PUBLISHERS LLC
Also Called: South Brooklyn Book Company
230 5th Ave (10001-7704)
PHONE................................212 686-1909
John Weber,
EMP: 2
SALES: 1.5MM **Privately Held**
SIC: 2741 Miscellaneous publishing

(G-11739)
WELDING CHAPTER OF NEW YORK
44 W 28th St Fl 12 (10001-4212)
PHONE................................212 481-1496
Ray Hopkins, *President*
EMP: 5
SALES (est): 417.6K **Privately Held**
SIC: 7692 Welding repair

(G-11740)
WELLQUEST INTERNATIONAL INC (PA)
230 5th Ave Ste 800 (10001-7851)
PHONE................................212 689-9094
Eddie Mishan, *President*
Al Mishan, *Vice Pres*
Isaac Mishan, *Vice Pres*
Morris Mishan, *Vice Pres*
▲ **EMP:** 6
SQ FT: 2,000
SALES (est): 847.4K **Privately Held**
WEB: www.wellquestinternational.com
SIC: 2833 5122 Vitamins, natural or synthetic: bulk, uncompounded; vitamins & minerals

(G-11741)
WELLSPRING CORP (PA)
54a Ludlow St (10002-5410)
PHONE................................212 529-5454
Yon K Lai, *Ch of Bd*
Danny Lai, *President*
EMP: 5
SQ FT: 1,000
SALES (est): 741.4K **Privately Held**
WEB: www.wellspringcorp.com
SIC: 2064 5149 Candy & other confectionery products; groceries & related products; chocolate; mineral or spring water bottling; crackers, cookies & bakery products

(G-11742)
WELLSPRING OMNI HOLDINGS CORP
390 Park Ave (10022-4608)
PHONE................................212 318-9800
William F Dawson Jr, *President*
Joshua C Cascade, *Corp Secy*
EMP: 950
SALES (est): 12.1MM **Privately Held**
SIC: 1382 1389 7349 Seismograph surveys; lease tanks, oil field: erecting, cleaning & repairing; cleaning service, industrial or commercial

(G-11743)
WENNER MEDIA LLC (PA)
Also Called: Rolling Stone
1290 Ave Of The Amer Fl 2 (10104-0295)
P.O. Box 30895 (10087-0895)
PHONE................................212 484-1616
Hugh Scogin, *CEO*
Christopher Barber, *President*
Dana L Fields, *Publisher*
Steven Schwartz, *Chairman*
Katey Distefano, *COO*
▲ **EMP:** 250
SQ FT: 75,000
SALES (est): 62.6MM **Privately Held**
SIC: 2721 Magazines: publishing only, not printed on site

(G-11744)
WEST INTERNET TRADING COMPANY
Also Called: Idonethis
47 Great Jones St Fl 5 (10012-1196)
PHONE................................415 484-5848
EMP: 6
SALES (est): 320K **Privately Held**
SIC: 7372 Prepackaged Software Services

(G-11745)
WESTMAN ATELIER LLC
135 Central Park W 10s (10023-2413)
PHONE................................917 297-0842
Pamela Yueh, *CFO*
Gucci Westman, *Mng Member*
David Neville,
EMP: 9
SQ FT: 2,000
SALES: 1.4MM **Privately Held**
SIC: 2844 Cosmetic preparations

(G-11746)
WESTPOINT HOME LLC (HQ)
777 3rd Ave Fl 7 (10017-1307)
PHONE................................212 930-2000
Abrar Hussain, *General Mgr*
McNulty Elizabeth, *Exec VP*
Jud Lusk, *Vice Pres*
Glenda Guerri, *VP Bus Dvlpt*
Douglas Wind, *Accounting Mgr*
◆ **EMP:** 800
SALES (est): 697.7MM
SALES (corp-wide): 11.7B **Publicly Held**
SIC: 2221 2211 Bedding, manmade or silk fabric; sheets, bedding & table cloths: cotton
PA: Icahn Enterprises L.P.
767 5th Ave Ste 4700
New York NY 10153
212 702-4300

(G-11747)
WESTPOINT INTERNATIONAL INC
28 E 28th St Bsmt 2 (10016-7939)
PHONE................................212 930-2000
Joseph Pennacchio, *CEO*
EMP: 6000
SALES (est): 310.7K
SALES (corp-wide): 11.7B **Publicly Held**
SIC: 2211 Broadwoven fabric mills, cotton
PA: Icahn Enterprises L.P.
767 5th Ave Ste 4700
New York NY 10153
212 702-4300

(G-11748)
WESTROCK MWV LLC
299 Park Ave Fl 13 (10171-3800)
PHONE................................212 688-5000
Luke John, *Trustee*
Jeff Jensen, *Vice Pres*
Tony Milikin, *Vice Pres*
John Cherry, *Sales Staff*
John A Luke, *Branch Mgr*
EMP: 227
SALES (corp-wide): 16.2B **Publicly Held**
WEB: www.meadwestvaco.com
SIC: 2631 2671 2678 2677 Linerboard; packaging paper & plastics film, coated & laminated; stationery products; envelopes; gum & wood chemicals
HQ: Westrock Mwv, Llc
501 S 5th St
Richmond VA 23219
804 444-1000

(G-11749)
WHENTECH LLC (PA)
55 E 52nd St Fl 40 (10055-0055)
PHONE................................212 571-0042
David Wender,
EMP: 11
SALES (est): 3.1MM **Privately Held**
WEB: www.whentech.com
SIC: 7372 Business oriented computer software

(G-11750)
WHISPR GROUP INC
6 Saint Johns Ln (10013-2115)
PHONE................................212 924-3979
Joakim Leijon, *President*
EMP: 13 **EST:** 2009

SQ FT: 4,000
SALES (est): 1MM **Privately Held**
SIC: 3993 5199 7389 7311 Advertising artwork; advertising specialties; ; advertising consultant

(G-11751)
WHITEBOARD VENTURES INC
Also Called: Xpand
315 W 36th St Fl 10 (10018-6527)
PHONE................................855 972-6346
Deb Bardhan, *CEO*
Kalyan Anumula, *President*
EMP: 16
SALES (est): 51.6K **Privately Held**
SIC: 7372 Application computer software

(G-11752)
WHITTALL & SHON (PA)
1201 Broadway Ste 904a (10001-5656)
PHONE................................212 594-2626
Elliot Whittall, *President*
Richard Shon, *Vice Pres*
EMP: 3
SALES (est): 14.2MM **Privately Held**
SIC: 2353 2321 Hats: cloth, straw & felt; millinery; men's & boys' furnishings

(G-11753)
WICKED SPOON INC
127 W 24th St Fl 6 (10011-1943)
PHONE................................646 335-2890
Alex Rozhitsky, *President*
EMP: 11
SALES: 750K **Privately Held**
SIC: 2024 Ice cream & frozen desserts

(G-11754)
WIDMER TIME RECORDER COMPANY
27 Park Pl Rm 219 (10007-2526)
PHONE................................212 227-0405
Robert Widmer, *President*
EMP: 10
SALES (corp-wide): 7.7MM **Privately Held**
WEB: www.widmertime.com
SIC: 3579 Time clocks & time recording devices
PA: Widmer Time Recorder Company Inc
228 Park St
Hackensack NJ 07601
201 489-3810

(G-11755)
WILLCO FINE ART LTD
145 Nassau St Apt 9c (10038-1514)
PHONE................................718 935-9567
William Wolod, *President*
EMP: 10
SALES: 700K **Privately Held**
SIC: 2759 Commercial printing

(G-11756)
WILLIAM GOLDBERG DIAMOND CORP
589 5th Ave Fl 14 (10017-7293)
PHONE................................212 980-4343
Saul Goldberg, *Ch of Bd*
Benjamin Goldberg, *President*
Eve Goldberg, *Vice Pres*
Lili Goldberg, *CFO*
EMP: 20 **EST:** 1954
SQ FT: 6,000
SALES (est): 5.5MM **Privately Held**
SIC: 3915 3911 5094 Diamond cutting & polishing; jewelry, precious metal; jewelry & precious stones

(G-11757)
WILLIAM H SADLIER INC (PA)
9 Pine St (10005-4701)
PHONE................................212 233-3646
Frank S Dinger, *Ch of Bd*
Ray Fagan, *President*
William S Dinger, *President*
Suzan Larroquette, *Division Mgr*
Perla Bonilla, *Regional Mgr*
◆ **EMP:** 111 **EST:** 1928
SQ FT: 56,000
SALES (est): 59.3MM
SALES (corp-wide): 58.3MM **Privately Held**
WEB: www.sadlier.com
SIC: 2731 Books: publishing only

(G-11758)
WILLIAM H SHAPIRO
Also Called: Shapiro Wlliam NY Univ Med Ctr
530 1st Ave Ste 3e (10016-6402)
PHONE................................212 263-7037
William H Shapiro, *Owner*
EMP: 5 **EST:** 1999
SALES (est): 424.9K **Privately Held**
SIC: 3842 Hearing aids

(G-11759)
WILLIAM SOMERVILLE MAINTENANCE
129 E 124th St (10035-1934)
PHONE................................212 534-4600
Merna Miller, *President*
EMP: 68
SQ FT: 40,000
SALES (est): 5.2MM **Privately Held**
SIC: 2511 Wood household furniture

(G-11760)
WILLIAMS-SONOMA STORES INC
Also Called: Williams-Sonoma Store 154
110 7th Ave (10011-1801)
PHONE................................212 633-2203
Donnie Cassell, *Manager*
EMP: 13
SALES (corp-wide): 5.6B **Publicly Held**
SIC: 3263 Cookware, fine earthenware
HQ: Williams-Sonoma Stores, Inc.
3250 Van Ness Ave
San Francisco CA 94109
415 421-7900

(G-11761)
WILLIS MC DONALD CO INC
44 W 62nd St Ph A (10023-7039)
PHONE................................212 366-1526
Jerry Dennehy, *President*
EMP: 15
SQ FT: 10,000
SALES: 1.3MM **Privately Held**
SIC: 2759 2732 Periodicals: printing; pamphlets: printing only, not published on site

(G-11762)
WILMAX USA LLC
315 5th Ave Rm 505 (10016-6592)
PHONE................................917 388-2790
Maksym Kyrylov,
EMP: 15
SQ FT: 1,500
SALES (est): 1MM **Privately Held**
SIC: 3469 Cooking ware, porcelain enameled

(G-11763)
WINDIAM USA INC
580 5th Ave Ste 2907 (10036-4724)
PHONE................................212 542-0949
Sacha Zaidman, *CEO*
EMP: 6
SALES (est): 19.3K **Privately Held**
SIC: 3915 Diamond cutting & polishing

(G-11764)
WINE & SPIRITS MAGAZINE INC (PA)
2 W 32nd St Ste 601 (10001-3834)
PHONE................................212 695-4660
Joshua Greene, *President*
Marcy Crimmins, *Vice Pres*
Roy Schneider, *Finance Dir*
EMP: 6
SQ FT: 2,300
SALES (est): 1.1MM **Privately Held**
WEB: www.wineandspiritsmagazine.com
SIC: 2721 Magazines: publishing only, not printed on site

(G-11765)
WING HEUNG NOODLE INC
144 Baxter St (10013-3605)
PHONE................................212 966-7496
Ng Shoong Kwong, *Ch of Bd*
EMP: 13
SQ FT: 2,000
SALES (est): 910K **Privately Held**
WEB: www.chicago-chinatown.com
SIC: 2098 Noodles (e.g. egg, plain & water), dry

(G-11766)
WING KEI NOODLE INC
102 Canal St (10002-6004)
PHONE....................212 226-1644
Yik Pui Kong, *Ch of Bd*
EMP: 17
SQ FT: 1,200
SALES (est): 1.5MM **Privately Held**
SIC: 2098 Macaroni products (e.g. alphabets, rings & shells), dry

(G-11767)
WINK INC
606 W 28th St Fl 6 (10001-1108)
PHONE....................212 389-1382
EMP: 45 EST: 2013
SALES (est): 2.2MM
SALES (corp-wide): 19.5MM **Privately Held**
SIC: 7372 5961 Prepackaged Software Services Ret Mail-Order House
PA: Quirky, Inc.
606 W 28th St Fl 7
New York NY 10001
212 389-4759

(G-11768)
WINK LABS INC (DH)
606 W 28th St Fl 7 (10001-1177)
PHONE....................844 946-5277
EMP: 30
SQ FT: 6,000
SALES (est): 15.7MM
SALES (corp-wide): 26.2B **Privately Held**
SIC: 7372 Application computer software

(G-11769)
WINSIGHT LLC
90 Broad St Ste 402 (10004-3312)
PHONE....................646 708-7309
Sarah Lockyer, *Vice Pres*
EMP: 7
SALES (est): 473K
SALES (corp-wide): 15.9MM **Privately Held**
SIC: 2721 Periodicals
HQ: Winsight, Llc
300 S Riverside Plz # 1600
Chicago IL 60606
312 876-0004

(G-11770)
WIZQ INC
307 5th Ave Fl 8 (10016-6573)
PHONE....................586 381-9048
Marcus Kay, *CEO*
Wing Tung LI, *Controller*
EMP: 10 EST: 2011
SQ FT: 3,000
SALES (est): 358.3K **Privately Held**
SIC: 7372 Prepackaged software

(G-11771)
WMG ACQUISITION CORP (DH)
1633 Broadway Fl 7 (10019-7637)
PHONE....................212 275-2000
Stephen F Cooper, *President*
Mark Ansorge, *Exec VP*
Paul M Robinson, *Exec VP*
Will Tanous, *Exec VP*
Steven Macri, *CFO*
EMP: 14
SALES (est): 714.2MM **Privately Held**
SIC: 2782 2741 7929 Record albums; music books: publishing & printing; music, sheet: publishing & printing; musical entertainers
HQ: Warner Music Group Corp.
1633 Broadway Fl 11
New York NY 10019
212 275-2000

(G-11772)
WOBBLEWORKS INC (PA)
Also Called: 3doodler
89 5th Ave Ste 602 (10003-3020)
PHONE....................718 618-9904
Maxwell Bogue, *CEO*
Daniel Cowen, *COO*
Peter Dilworth, *CTO*
EMP: 21
SALES (est): 2.8MM **Privately Held**
SIC: 3944 Electronic toys

(G-11773)
WOCHIT INC (PA)
12 E 33rd St Fl 4 (10016-5090)
PHONE....................212 979-8343
Dror Ginzberg, *CEO*
Ron Maayan, *Ch Acad Ofcr*
Drew Berkowitz, *Vice Pres*
Elizabeth Hellman, *Vice Pres*
Ran Yakir, *Vice Pres*
EMP: 9
SALES (est): 3.7MM **Privately Held**
SIC: 7372 7812 Business oriented computer software; publishers' computer software; video production

(G-11774)
WOLTERS KLUWER US INC
28 Liberty St Fl 26 (10005-1514)
PHONE....................212 894-8920
Grant Barrick, *Vice Pres*
Jennifer Brogan, *Vice Pres*
Linda Buan, *Vice Pres*
Cheri Palmer, *Vice Pres*
Gary Mrozek, *Opers Mgr*
EMP: 12
SALES (corp-wide): 4.8B **Privately Held**
SIC: 2731 Books: publishing only
HQ: Wolters Kluwer United States Inc.
2700 Lake Cook Rd
Riverwoods IL 60015
847 580-5000

(G-11775)
WOMENS E NEWS INC
6 Barclay St Fl 6 # 6 (10007-2721)
PHONE....................212 244-1720
Rita Henley Jensen, *President*
Angie Alvarado, *Director*
Lori Sokol, *Assistant*
EMP: 7
SALES (est): 840.9K **Privately Held**
WEB: www.womensenews.org
SIC: 2721 Magazines: publishing only, not printed on site

(G-11776)
WONTON FOOD INC
183 E Broadway (10002-5503)
PHONE....................212 677-8865
Chan Wai, *Principal*
EMP: 15
SALES (corp-wide): 80.3MM **Privately Held**
WEB: www.wontonfood.com
SIC: 2099 2098 Noodles, fried (Chinese); noodles (e.g. egg, plain & water), dry
PA: Wonton Food Inc.
220 Moore St 222
Brooklyn NY 11206
718 628-6868

(G-11777)
WOOLMARK AMERICAS INC
Also Called: Woolmark Company, The
110 E 25th St Fl 3 (10010-2913)
PHONE....................347 767-3160
Velma George, *Principal*
Lucas Tyson, *Manager*
EMP: 1
SALES (est): 2.6MM **Privately Held**
SIC: 2231 Cloth, wool: mending
PA: Australian Wool Innovation Limited
L 6 68 Harrington St
The Rocks NSW 2000

(G-11778)
WORKING MOTHER MEDIA INC
Also Called: Diversity Best Practices
2 Park Ave Fl 27 (10016-9303)
PHONE....................212 351-6400
Carol Evans, *President*
Joan Labarge, *Publisher*
Jacqueline Labrocca, *Opers Dir*
Krista Carothers, *Research*
Karen Dahms, *Research*
EMP: 51 EST: 2001
SQ FT: 15,000
SALES (est): 5.1MM
SALES (corp-wide): 2.9B **Privately Held**
WEB: www.workingmother.com
SIC: 2721 4813 Magazines: publishing only, not printed on site;
HQ: Bonnier Corporation
460 N Orlando Ave Ste 200
Winter Park FL 32789

(G-11779)
WORKMAN PUBLISHING CO INC (PA)
Also Called: Algonquin Books Chapel Hl Div
225 Varick St Fl 9 (10014-4381)
PHONE....................212 254-5900
Dan Reynolds, *CEO*
Deborah Balmuth, *Publisher*
Kate Karol, *Editor*
Mary Oneill, *Editor*
Jessica Rozler, *Editor*
◆ EMP: 200
SQ FT: 57,000
SALES (est): 92.7MM **Privately Held**
WEB: www.pageaday.com
SIC: 2731 Books: publishing only

(G-11780)
WORKMAN PUBLISHING CO INC
Artisan House Div
708 Broadway Fl 6 (10003-9508)
PHONE....................212 254-5900
Richard Petry, *Controller*
EMP: 150
SALES (corp-wide): 92.7MM **Privately Held**
WEB: www.pageaday.com
SIC: 2731 Books: publishing only
PA: Workman Publishing Co. Inc.
225 Varick St Fl 9
New York NY 10014
212 254-5900

(G-11781)
WORLD GUIDE PUBLISHING
1271 Ave Of The Americas (10020-1300)
PHONE....................800 331-7840
Tina Threston, *CEO*
EMP: 40
SQ FT: 600
SALES (est): 1.5MM **Privately Held**
SIC: 2721 Magazines: publishing only, not printed on site

(G-11782)
WORLD MARITIME NEWS
118 E 25th St Fl 2 (10010-2977)
PHONE....................212 477-6700
John Omalley, *President*
John Murray, *Vice Pres*
EMP: 5 EST: 2013
SALES (est): 260.6K **Privately Held**
SIC: 3731 Shipbuilding & repairing

(G-11783)
WORLDS BEST COOKIE DOUGH INC
164 Bleecker St (10012-1408)
PHONE....................347 592-3422
Shameo Sufin, *CEO*
EMP: 7
SALES: 1MM **Privately Held**
SIC: 2051 7371 Bakery: wholesale or wholesale/retail combined; computer software development & applications

(G-11784)
WORLDWIDE MEDIA SVCS GROUP INC
Also Called: AMI
4 New York Plz (10004-2413)
PHONE....................212 545-4800
David Pecker, *CEO*
Robin Chang, *Vice Pres*
Dean Durbin, *CFO*
Dara Markus, *Advt Staff*
EMP: 311
SALES (corp-wide): 363MM **Privately Held**
SIC: 2741 2711 Miscellaneous publishing; newspapers: publishing only, not printed on site
PA: Worldwide Media Services Group Inc.
1350 E Newprt Ctr Dr 20
Deerfield Beach FL 33442
561 989-1342

(G-11785)
WORTH COLLECTION LTD (PA)
Also Called: W By Worth
520 8th Ave Rm 2301 (10018-4108)
PHONE....................212 268-0312
Susan Gustafson, *CEO*
Kathy Bonner, *Exec VP*
Haroute Panossian, *Controller*
Jane Woods, *Sales Associate*
Jamie Emhoff, *Consultant*
▲ EMP: 50
SQ FT: 8,000
SALES (est): 56.3MM **Privately Held**
WEB: www.worthny.com
SIC: 2335 Women's, juniors' & misses' dresses

(G-11786)
WORTH IMPORTS LLC
93 Worth St Ste 201 (10013-8200)
PHONE....................212 398-5410
Rj Bhasin, *Mng Member*
EMP: 1
SALES: 2MM **Privately Held**
SIC: 2329 Men's & boys' sportswear & athletic clothing

(G-11787)
WORTH PUBLISHERS INC
1 New York Plz Ste 4500 (10004-1562)
PHONE....................212 475-6000
Elizabeth Widdicombe, *President*
Karen Johnson, *Publisher*
Christine Cardone, *Editor*
Marc Edwards, *Sales Staff*
Sarah Berger, *Assoc Editor*
EMP: 110 EST: 1966
SQ FT: 14,000
SALES (est): 23.6MM
SALES (corp-wide): 1.6B **Privately Held**
WEB: www.hpbuny.com
SIC: 2731 Textbooks: publishing only, not printed on site
HQ: Macmillan Holdings, Llc
120 Broadway Fl 22
New York NY 10271

(G-11788)
WORZALLA PUBLISHING COMPANY
222 W 37th St Fl 10 (10018-9001)
PHONE....................212 967-7909
Lynn Carroll, *Branch Mgr*
EMP: 190
SALES (corp-wide): 141.9MM **Privately Held**
SIC: 2732 Book printing
PA: Worzalla Inc
3535 Jefferson St
Stevens Point WI 54481
715 344-9600

(G-11789)
WP COMPANY LLC
Also Called: Washington Post Advg Sls Ofc
395 Hudson St Lbby 1 (10014-3669)
PHONE....................212 445-5050
Rick Tippett, *Director*
EMP: 5 **Privately Held**
SIC: 2711 Newspapers, publishing & printing
HQ: Wp Company Llc
1301 K St Nw
Washington DC 20071

(G-11790)
WP LAVORI USA INC (DH)
597 Broadway Fl 2 (10012-3211)
PHONE....................212 244-6074
Cristina Calori, *President*
Ethem Gungor, *Vice Pres*
▲ EMP: 5
SALES (est): 1.2MM **Privately Held**
SIC: 2311 5136 Men's & boys' suits & coats; men's & boys' clothing

(G-11791)
WR DESIGN CORP
Also Called: Wr9000
230 W 39th St Fl 5f (10018-4933)
PHONE....................212 354-9000
Sunny Lam, *President*
EMP: 20
SALES: 8.4MM **Privately Held**
SIC: 2253 Sweaters & sweater coats, knit

(G-11792)
WSN INC
Also Called: World Screen News
1123 Broadway Ste 1207 (10010-2007)
PHONE....................212 924-7620
Ricardo Guise, *President*
Mansha Daswani, *Publisher*
Nathalie Jaspar, *Vice Pres*

Kristin Brzoznowski, *Assoc Editor*
Victor Cuevas, *Director*
EMP: 6
SQ FT: 500
SALES (est): 540K **Privately Held**
WEB: www.worldscreen.com
SIC: 2721 Magazines: publishing only, not printed on site

(G-11793)
WYETH LLC (HQ)
235 E 42nd St (10017-5703)
PHONE.....................212 733-2323
Ian Reid, *CEO*
Etienne N Attar, *President*
Richard R Deluca, *President*
Michael Kamarck, *President*
Joseph Mahady, *President*
◆ **EMP:** 850 EST: 1926
SALES (est): 4.5B
SALES (corp-wide): 53.6B **Publicly Held**
WEB: www.wyeth.com
SIC: 2836 2834 Biological products, except diagnostic; allergens, allergenic extracts; vaccines; veterinary biological products; analgesics; cough medicines; veterinary pharmaceutical preparations
PA: Pfizer Inc.
235 E 42nd St
New York NY 10017
212 733-2323

(G-11794)
X FUNCTION INC (PA)
45 W 89th St Apt 4a (10024-2078)
PHONE.....................212 231-0092
Frank E Barnes III, *CEO*
Michelle Lanken, *CFO*
EMP: 21
SALES: 4.5MM **Publicly Held**
SIC: 7372 7371 Prepackaged software; custom computer programming services

(G-11795)
X MYLES MAR INC
Also Called: Marx Myles Graphic Services
875 Ave Of The Am Rm 1715 (10001)
PHONE.....................212 683-2015
Arthur Marx, *President*
Sheldon Marx, *Vice Pres*
EMP: 40
SALES (est): 6MM **Privately Held**
WEB: www.marxmyles.com
SIC: 2759 2791 2789 2752 Commercial printing; typesetting; bookbinding & related work; commercial printing, lithographic

(G-11796)
X VISION INC
209 W 38th St Rm 1003 (10018-4754)
PHONE.....................917 412-3570
Judith Kim, *President*
Will Huang, *Co-Founder*
EMP: 8
SALES (est): 178.8K **Privately Held**
SIC: 2339 5136 5651 Women's & misses' athletic clothing & sportswear; men's & boys' sportswear & work clothing; family clothing stores; unisex clothing stores

(G-11797)
XANADU
150 W 30th St Rm 702 (10001-4155)
PHONE.....................212 465-0580
Gus Xanthoudakis, *Owner*
EMP: 5
SQ FT: 5,000
SALES: 750K **Privately Held**
SIC: 2371 Apparel, fur

(G-11798)
XING LIN USA INTL CORP
1410 Broadway Rm 3201 (10018-9313)
PHONE.....................212 947-4846
Wen Y Wu, *President*
Richard Jacobs, *General Mgr*
▲ **EMP:** 5
SQ FT: 900
SALES: 6.5MM **Privately Held**
SIC: 2211 Denims

(G-11799)
XINYA INTERNATIONAL TRADING CO
Also Called: Polly Treating
115 W 30th St Rm 1109 (10001-4056)
PHONE.....................212 216-9681
Peng Sen Liu, *President*
EMP: 6 EST: 1996
SALES: 700K **Privately Held**
SIC: 2387 3851 Apparel belts; glasses, sun or glare

(G-11800)
XL GRAPHICS INC
121 Varick St Rm 300 (10013-1408)
PHONE.....................212 929-8700
Jeff Baltimore, *Ch of Bd*
EMP: 5
SQ FT: 4,000
SALES (est): 610.9K **Privately Held**
SIC: 2759 Commercial printing

(G-11801)
XOMOX JEWELRY INC
151 W 46th St Fl 15 (10036-8512)
PHONE.....................212 944-8428
Mark Bugnacki, *President*
EMP: 7
SQ FT: 1,200
SALES (est): 850K **Privately Held**
WEB: www.xomoxjewelry.com
SIC: 3911 Jewelry, precious metal

(G-11802)
XSTELOS HOLDINGS INC
630 5th Ave Ste 2600 (10111-2697)
PHONE.....................212 729-4962
Jonathan M Couchman, *President*
EMP: 3
SALES (est): 28.7MM **Privately Held**
SIC: 2834 Pharmaceutical preparations

(G-11803)
Y-MABS THERAPEUTICS INC (PA)
230 Park Ave Rm 3350 (10169-3302)
PHONE.....................917 817-2992
Claus Juan Moller San Pedro, *CEO*
Thomas Gad, *Ch of Bd*
Joris Wiel Jan Wilms, *COO*
Torben Lund-Hansen, *Senior VP*
Bo Kruse, *CFO*
EMP: 17
SQ FT: 4,312
SALES (est): 3.9MM **Publicly Held**
SIC: 2834 Pharmaceutical preparations

(G-11804)
YACOUBIAN JEWELERS INC
2 W 45th St Ste 1104 (10036-4248)
PHONE.....................212 302-6729
Mike Yacoubian, *President*
EMP: 30
SALES (est): 2.7MM **Privately Held**
SIC: 3961 Costume jewelry

(G-11805)
YALE ROBBINS INC
Also Called: Manhattan Map Co
205 Lexington Ave Fl 12 (10016-6022)
PHONE.....................212 683-5700
Yale Robbins, *President*
Henry Robbins, *Vice Pres*
Ian Goodwin, *Research*
Victor Marcos, *Research*
Courtney Reilly, *Sales Staff*
EMP: 60
SQ FT: 4,000
SALES (est): 8.9MM **Privately Held**
WEB: www.yalerobbins.com
SIC: 2721 8742 6531 Periodicals: publishing & printing; business consultant; real estate brokers & agents

(G-11806)
YAM TV LLC
144 W 23rd St Apt 8e (10011-9403)
PHONE.....................917 932-5418
Matan Koren,
EMP: 2
SALES: 5MM **Privately Held**
SIC: 2741 7819 Miscellaneous publishing; services allied to motion pictures

(G-11807)
YARNZ INTERNATIONAL INC
260 W 36th St Rm 201 (10018-7524)
PHONE.....................212 868-5883
Mujadid Shah, *Chairman*
▲ **EMP:** 6 EST: 2000
SALES (est): 691K **Privately Held**
WEB: www.yarnz.com
SIC: 2231 Apparel & outerwear broadwoven fabrics

(G-11808)
YEOHLEE INC
12 W 29th St (10001-4516)
PHONE.....................212 631-8099
Yeohlee Teng, *President*
Arthur Laurel, *Manager*
EMP: 13 EST: 1975
SQ FT: 6,000
SALES (est): 1.5MM **Privately Held**
WEB: www.yeohlee.com
SIC: 2331 2335 2337 Women's & misses' blouses & shirts; women's, juniors' & misses' dresses; women's & misses' suits & coats

(G-11809)
YIGAL-AZROUEL INC (PA)
500 7th Ave Fl 8 (10018-4502)
PHONE.....................212 302-1194
Yigal Azrouel, *President*
Flora Cervantes, *Principal*
Danielle B Smotrich, *Executive Asst*
EMP: 30
SALES (est): 3.4MM **Privately Held**
WEB: www.yigal-azrouel.com
SIC: 2369 2339 Girls' & children's outerwear; women's & misses' outerwear

(G-11810)
YIWEN USA INC
60 E 42nd St Ste 1030 (10165-1030)
P.O. Box 857 (10116-0857)
PHONE.....................212 370-0828
You Chang, *President*
EMP: 10
SALES (est): 1MM
SALES (corp-wide): 1.2MM **Privately Held**
SIC: 2899 Chemical preparations
PA: Dalian Yiwen New Materials Technology Development Co., Ltd.
Industrial Park, Ganhe Village, Paotai Town, Puwan New Area
Dalian 11600

(G-11811)
YOMIURI INTERNATIONAL INC
747 3rd Ave Fl 28 (10017-2832)
PHONE.....................212 752-2196
Michiro Okamoto, *Principal*
EMP: 7
SALES (est): 693.8K **Privately Held**
SIC: 3714 Motor vehicle parts & accessories
HQ: Yomiuri Shimbun, The
1-7-1, Otemachi
Chiyoda-Ku TKY 100-0

(G-11812)
YOU AND ME LEGWEAR LLC
10 W 33rd St Rm 300 (10001-3306)
PHONE.....................212 279-9292
Albert Cohen,
▲ **EMP:** 18
SQ FT: 5,000
SALES (est): 6.7MM **Privately Held**
SIC: 2252 Hosiery

(G-11813)
YS PUBLISHING CO INC
228 E 45th St Rm 700 (10017-3336)
PHONE.....................212 682-9360
Hitoshi Yoshida, *President*
Eri Sano, *Editor*
Ayako Ueda, *Editor*
Shintaro Torii, *Exec VP*
Miyuki Hanakoshi, *Accountant*
▲ **EMP:** 9
SALES (est): 1.1MM **Privately Held**
WEB: www.us-benricho.com
SIC: 2731 Books: publishing only

(G-11814)
Z-PLY CORP
Also Called: Texray
213 W 35th St Ste 5w (10001)
PHONE.....................212 398-7011
Timothy Chung, *Ch of Bd*
J J Hou, *Exec VP*
Sam Chang, *CFO*
▲ **EMP:** 40
SQ FT: 5,000
SALES (est): 5.1MM **Privately Held**
WEB: www.z-ply.com
SIC: 2339 2369 Women's & misses' athletic clothing & sportswear; girls' & children's outerwear

(G-11815)
ZAK JEWELRY TOOLS INC
55 W 47th St Fl 2 (10036-2812)
PHONE.....................212 768-8122
Roman Zak, *President*
Robert Zak, *Vice Pres*
◆ **EMP:** 14
SQ FT: 7,500
SALES (est): 1.8MM **Privately Held**
SIC: 3915 5251 Jewel preparing: instruments, tools, watches & jewelry; tools

(G-11816)
ZAR GROUP LLC (PA)
Also Called: Zar Apparel Group
1450 Broadway Fl 17 (10018-2217)
PHONE.....................212 944-2510
Bobby Zar, *CEO*
Bruce Bond, *President*
Mansour Zar, *Chairman*
Michael Namdar, *Director*
▼ **EMP:** 11
SALES: 100MM **Privately Held**
SIC: 2339 Women's & misses' outerwear

(G-11817)
ZAZOOM LLC (PA)
Also Called: Zazoom Media Group
1 Exchange Plz Ste 801 (10006-3008)
PHONE.....................212 321-2100
Tim Minton, *CEO*
Steve Charlier, *Vice Pres*
Troy Frisby, *Producer*
Sean Dowling, *Associate*
EMP: 17
SALES (est): 1.6MM **Privately Held**
SIC: 2741

(G-11818)
ZEDGE INC
22 Cortlandt St Fl 11 (10007-3171)
PHONE.....................330 577-3424
Michael Jonas, *CEO*
Howard S Jonas, *Vice Ch Bd*
Jonathan Reich, *COO*
Todd Feldman, *Director*
Eric Peltier, *Director*
EMP: 64
SQ FT: 500
SALES: 10.8MM **Privately Held**
SIC: 7372 Prepackaged software

(G-11819)
ZEEBA JEWELRY MFG INC
Also Called: Zeeba Jewelry Manufacturing
36 W 47th St Ste 902a (10036-8641)
PHONE.....................212 997-1009
Fred Navi, *President*
Ray Lavi, *Vice Pres*
EMP: 3
SQ FT: 2,000
SALES: 1MM **Privately Held**
SIC: 3911 Jewelry, precious metal

(G-11820)
ZENITH ENERGY US LOGISTICS (PA)
725 5th Ave Fl 19 (10022-2519)
PHONE.....................212 993-1280
Jeff Armstrong, *CEO*
EMP: 1
SALES (est): 9.8MM **Privately Held**
SIC: 1311 Crude petroleum & natural gas

(G-11821)
ZETEK CORPORATION
Also Called: Zeteck
13 E 37th St Ste 701 (10016-2841)
PHONE.....................212 668-1485

Bertrand Dorfman, *President*
Raymond McKee, *Opers Staff*
Bertand Dorfman, *IT/INT Sup*
EMP: 10
SQ FT: 1,500
SALES (est): 1.1MM **Privately Held**
WEB: www.zetek.com
SIC: 3663 3669 7622 7629 Radio & TV communications equipment; fire detection systems, electric; communication equipment repair; electrical equipment repair services

(G-11822)
ZG APPAREL GROUP LLC
1450 Broadway Fl 17 (10018-2217)
PHONE.................................212 944-2510
Mansour Zar,
Babak Zar,
◆ **EMP:** 40 **EST:** 2014
SQ FT: 20,000
SALES (est): 17.7MM **Privately Held**
SIC: 2339 Women's & misses' athletic clothing & sportswear; athletic clothing: women's, misses' & juniors'

(G-11823)
ZIA POWER INC
116 E 27th St (10016-8942)
PHONE.................................845 661-8388
Nathaniel Thompkins, *President*
EMP: 36
SQ FT: 2,000
SALES (est): 1.4MM **Privately Held**
SIC: 2339 Women's & misses' outerwear

(G-11824)
ZIFF DAVIS PUBLISHING LLC (DH)
Also Called: Ziff-Davis Publishing
28 E 28th St Fl 10 (10016-7939)
PHONE.................................212 503-3500
Stephen Burch, *Partner*
Michelle Dwyer, *Partner*
Geoff Inns, *Managing Dir*
Brian Stewart, *Managing Dir*
Tom McGrade, *Exec VP*
▲ **EMP:** 100
SQ FT: 310,000
SALES (est): 94.3MM
SALES (corp-wide): 1.2B **Publicly Held**
WEB: www.zdnet.com
SIC: 2721 2731 7371 Periodicals; book publishing; custom computer programming services

(G-11825)
ZINEPAK LLC
349 5th Ave (10016-5019)
PHONE.................................212 706-8621
Brittney Hodak, *Mng Member*
Brittany Hodak, *Mng Member*
Carly Prakapas, *Sr Project Mgr*
EMP: 10
SALES: 2.9MM **Privately Held**
SIC: 2731 Book publishing

(G-11826)
ZIRCONIA CREATIONS INTL
134 W 29th St Rm 801 (10001-0107)
PHONE.................................212 239-3730
Michael Halpert, *President*
Yisha Weber, *Vice Pres*
EMP: 8
SQ FT: 3,000
SALES (est): 1.1MM **Privately Held**
SIC: 3915 Jewelers' materials & lapidary work

(G-11827)
ZITOMER LLC
969 Madison Ave Fl 1 (10021-2763)
PHONE.................................212 737-5560
Thanh Tran, *Principal*
▲ **EMP:** 9
SALES (est): 1.5MM **Privately Held**
SIC: 2834 Solutions, pharmaceutical

(G-11828)
ZOGRAPHOS DESIGNS LTD
300 E 33rd St Apt 9m (10016-9412)
PHONE.................................212 545-0227
Nicos Zographos, *President*
EMP: 8
SQ FT: 2,250

SALES (est): 961.6K **Privately Held**
WEB: www.zographos.com
SIC: 2521 2522 Wood office furniture; office furniture, except wood

(G-11829)
ZOOMIFIER CORPORATION
216 E 45th St Fl 17 (10017-3304)
PHONE.................................800 255-5303
Chetan Saiya, *CEO*
EMP: 100
SALES (corp-wide): 13.9MM **Privately Held**
SIC: 7372 Business oriented computer software
PA: Zoomifier Corporation
870 Market St Ste 919
San Francisco CA 94102
800 255-5303

(G-11830)
ZORLU USA INC (PA)
295 5th Ave Ste 503 (10016-7103)
PHONE.................................212 689-4622
Filiz Ozpicak, *Vice Pres*
Alihan Altunbas, *Finance Mgr*
Liana Morvillo, *Manager*
Salih Poyraz, *Manager*
▲ **EMP:** 60
SALES (est): 9.5MM **Privately Held**
WEB: www.zorluusa.com
SIC: 2221 5131 Textile mills, broadwoven: silk & manmade, also glass; textiles, woven

New York Mills
Oneida County

(G-11831)
DI HIGHWAY SIGN STRUCTURE CORP
40 Greenman Ave (13417-1004)
P.O. Box 123 (13417-0123)
PHONE.................................315 736-8312
Steven Mulvihill, *General Mgr*
Jane Mulvihill, *Principal*
Dean Knapp, *Engineer*
Noreen Sheridan, *Controller*
EMP: 40
SQ FT: 35,000
SALES (est): 12.8MM **Privately Held**
SIC: 3499 Metal household articles; trophies, metal, except silver

(G-11832)
FOUNTAINHEAD GROUP INC (PA)
Also Called: Burgess Products Division
23 Garden St (13417-1318)
PHONE.................................315 736-0037
John F Romano, *CEO*
John O'Toole, *President*
Jackie Romano, *Vice Pres*
Linda E Romano, *Vice Pres*
James Siepiola, *Vice Pres*
◆ **EMP:** 150 **EST:** 1973
SQ FT: 40,000
SALES (est): 34.9MM **Privately Held**
WEB: www.thefountainheadgroup.com
SIC: 3563 3523 3569 Spraying outfits: metals, paints & chemicals (compressor); sprayers & spraying machines, agricultural; fertilizing, spraying, dusting & irrigation machinery; firefighting apparatus

(G-11833)
FOUNTAINHEAD GROUP INC
Bridgeview Aerosol
3 Graden St (13417)
PHONE.................................708 598-7100
Jack Young, *COO*
EMP: 170
SALES (corp-wide): 34.9MM **Privately Held**
SIC: 3563 2813 Spraying outfits: metals, paints & chemicals (compressor); aerosols
PA: The Fountainhead Group Inc
23 Garden St
New York Mills NY 13417
315 736-0037

(G-11834)
HERMOSA CORP
102 Main St (13417-1103)
P.O. Box 274 (13417-0274)
PHONE.................................315 768-4320
Steven Mulvihill, *President*
Michael Sheridan Pe, *Vice Pres*
Daniel M Hubbell, *Shareholder*
Peter M Hubbell, *Shareholder*
EMP: 20
SQ FT: 40,000
SALES (est): 3.4MM **Privately Held**
WEB: www.hermosacorp.com
SIC: 3993 Signs, not made in custom sign painting shops

(G-11835)
MOHAWK VALLEY KNT MCHY CO INC
561 Main St (13417-1431)
PHONE.................................315 736-3038
Thomas P Firsching, *President*
EMP: 19
SQ FT: 40,000
SALES (est): 3.4MM **Privately Held**
SIC: 3552 Textile machinery

(G-11836)
QUALITY MACHINING SERVICE INC
70 Sauquoit St (13417-1018)
PHONE.................................315 736-5774
Tom Ostrander, *President*
EMP: 5
SQ FT: 3,000
SALES (est): 150K **Privately Held**
SIC: 3599 Machine shop, jobbing & repair

Newark
Wayne County

(G-11837)
ADDEX INC
251 Murray St (14513-1216)
PHONE.................................781 344-5800
Rudiger Von Kraus, *President*
Robert E Cree, *Exec VP*
Bill Randolph, *Executive*
Mary Cree, *Executive Asst*
▲ **EMP:** 5
SQ FT: 10,000
SALES (est): 1.6MM **Privately Held**
WEB: www.addexinc.com
SIC: 3559 Plastics working machinery

(G-11838)
C&C AUTOMATICS INC
127 W Shore Blvd (14513-1259)
PHONE.................................315 331-1436
Craig T Parsons, *President*
Craig Halstead, *Vice Pres*
EMP: 20
SQ FT: 9,000
SALES (est): 2.1MM **Privately Held**
WEB: www.ccautomatics.com
SIC: 3451 Screw machine products

(G-11839)
CELMET CO
105 Norton St (14513-1218)
P.O. Box 271 (14513-0271)
PHONE.................................585 647-1760
Jeffrey T Schlarbaum, *Principal*
EMP: 5
SALES (est): 624.5K **Privately Held**
SIC: 3679 Electronic circuits

(G-11840)
HALLAGAN MANUFACTURING CO INC
500 Hoffman St (14513-1858)
P.O. Box 268 (14513-0268)
PHONE.................................315 331-4640
Charles W Hallagan, *Ch of Bd*
Stephen Hallagan, *President*
Walter Hallagan, *Vice Pres*
EMP: 80
SQ FT: 97,000
SALES (est): 10.3MM **Privately Held**
SIC: 2512 Living room furniture: upholstered on wood frames

(G-11841)
IEC ELECTRONICS CORP (PA)
105 Norton St (14513-1298)
PHONE.................................315 331-7742
Jeremy R Nowak, *Ch of Bd*
Jeffrey T Schlarbaum, *President*
Jens Hauvn, *Senior VP*
Eric Wright, *Engineer*
Thomas L Barbato, *CFO*
▲ **EMP:** 277
SQ FT: 235,000
SALES: 116.9MM **Publicly Held**
WEB: www.iec-electronics.com
SIC: 3672 3679 Printed circuit boards; electronic circuits

(G-11842)
IEC ELECTRONICS WIRE CABLE INC
105 Norton St (14513-1218)
P.O. Box 271 (14513-0271)
PHONE.................................585 924-9010
Jeffrey T Schlarbaum, *President*
Donald S Doody, *Vice Pres*
Vincent Leo, *CFO*
EMP: 100
SQ FT: 19,000
SALES (est): 12.1MM
SALES (corp-wide): 116.9MM **Publicly Held**
WEB: www.val-u-tech.com
SIC: 3679 Electronic circuits
PA: Iec Electronics Corp.
105 Norton St
Newark NY 14513
315 331-7742

(G-11843)
LEGENDARY AUTO INTERIORS LTD
121 W Shore Blvd (14513-1259)
PHONE.................................315 331-1212
Martin J Beckenbach, *Ch of Bd*
▲ **EMP:** 40
SQ FT: 12,000
SALES (est): 5.5MM **Privately Held**
WEB: www.legendaryautointeriors.com
SIC: 2396 5013 5531 3429 Automotive trimmings, fabric; automotive trim; automotive accessories; manufactured hardware (general); leather tanning & finishing; nonwoven fabrics

(G-11844)
MACO BAG CORPORATION
412 Van Buren St (14513-9205)
PHONE.................................315 226-1000
J Scott Miller, *Ch of Bd*
Craig Miller, *President*
Susan Miller, *Corp Secy*
Bob Finley, *Safety Dir*
Doug Kirchhoff, *Opers Staff*
▲ **EMP:** 140 **EST:** 1929
SQ FT: 60,000
SALES (est): 38MM **Privately Held**
WEB: www.macobag.com
SIC: 3081 2673 Plastic film & sheet; plastic & pliofilm bags

(G-11845)
MCDOWELL RESEARCH CO INC (HQ)
2000 Technology Pkwy (14513-2175)
PHONE.................................315 332-7100
John D Kavazanjian, *President*
Julius Cirin, *Vice Pres*
Ty Christiaansen, *Mfg Staff*
Edward Knauf, *Marketing Staff*
Mike Adkins, *Executive*
▲ **EMP:** 100
SQ FT: 54,000
SALES (est): 126MM
SALES (corp-wide): 87.1MM **Publicly Held**
WEB: www.mrc-power.com
SIC: 3669 Intercommunication systems, electric
PA: Ultralife Corporation
2000 Technology Pkwy
Newark NY 14513
315 332-7100

(G-11846)
MICRO-TECH MACHINE INC
301 W Shore Blvd (14513-1261)
PHONE................................315 331-6671
Michael R Davis, *President*
Amy Davis, *CFO*
EMP: 44
SQ FT: 13,000
SALES (est): 7.4MM **Privately Held**
WEB: www.microtechmachine.com
SIC: 3599 Machine shop, jobbing & repair

(G-11847)
MOOSEBERRY SOAP CO LLC
513 W Union St Ste B (14513-1365)
PHONE................................315 332-8913
Mary Bartolotta, *Mng Member*
EMP: 7 EST: 2011
SQ FT: 5,000
SALES (est): 890.6K **Privately Held**
SIC: 2841 Soap: granulated, liquid, cake,
flaked or chip

(G-11848)
**NORTH AMERICAN FILTER
CORP (PA)**
Also Called: Nafco
200 W Shore Blvd (14513-1258)
PHONE................................800 265-8943
Steve Taylor, *President*
Ann Stokes, *Buyer*
John Henry, *Sales Staff*
▼ EMP: 74
SQ FT: 75,000
SALES (est): 14.3MM **Privately Held**
WEB: www.nafcoinc.com
SIC: 3569 3564 Filters, general line: in-
dustrial; blowers & fans

(G-11849)
**P V C MOLDING
TECHNOLOGIES**
122 W Shore Blvd (14513-1258)
PHONE................................315 331-1212
Martin Beckenbach, *President*
EMP: 12
SQ FT: 14,198
SALES (est): 1MM **Privately Held**
SIC: 3089 Molding primary plastic

(G-11850)
**PROGRESSIVE GRAPHICS &
PRTG**
415 West Ave (14513-2026)
P.O. Box 492 (14513-0492)
PHONE................................315 331-3635
Robert Kelly, *President*
Dennis Chasse, *Vice Pres*
EMP: 6
SALES (est): 505.7K **Privately Held**
SIC: 2752 2791 2789 Commercial print-
ing, offset; typesetting; bookbinding & re-
lated work

(G-11851)
**SMITH METAL WORKS NEWARK
INC**
1000 E Union St (14513-1643)
PHONE................................315 331-1651
Wayne F Smith, *President*
Janice Smith, *Treasurer*
Gail Rosann Tack, *Human Res Mgr*
EMP: 27 EST: 1942
SQ FT: 5,000
SALES (est): 7.5MM **Privately Held**
WEB: www.smithspreaders.com
SIC: 3714 3599 Sanders, motor vehicle
safety; machine shop, jobbing & repair;
custom machinery

(G-11852)
SPINCO METAL PRODUCTS INC
1 Country Club Dr (14513-1250)
PHONE................................315 331-6285
C Robert Straubing Jr, *Ch of Bd*
John Bulger, *Admin Sec*
▲ EMP: 80
SQ FT: 48,000
SALES (est): 22.9MM **Privately Held**
WEB: www.spincometal.com
SIC: 3498 Tube fabricating (contract bend-
ing & shaping)

(G-11853)
SUPERGEN PRODUCTS LLC
320 Hoffman St (14513-1830)
PHONE................................315 573-7887
Paul Cole, *Mng Member*
EMP: 9
SALES (est): 140K **Privately Held**
SIC: 3621 Motors & generators

(G-11854)
ULTRALIFE CORPORATION (PA)
2000 Technology Pkwy (14513-2175)
PHONE................................315 332-7100
Bradford T Whitmore, *Ch of Bd*
Michael D Popielec, *President*
Elton Sim, *Regional Mgr*
Mike Crumpler, *Vice Pres*
Jim Rasmussen, *Vice Pres*
▲ EMP: 272
SQ FT: 250,000
SALES (est): 87.1MM **Publicly Held**
WEB: www.ulbi.com
SIC: 3679 3691 Electronic loads & power
supplies; harness assemblies for elec-
tronic use: wire or cable; parametric am-
plifiers; alkaline cell storage batteries

(G-11855)
**UPSTATE REFRACTORY SVCS
INC**
100 Erie Blvd (14513-1163)
PHONE................................315 331-2955
David Wetmore, *President*
Diane Wetmore, *Vice Pres*
Marcie Traugh, *Safety Mgr*
Bryan Wetmore, *Warehouse Mgr*
Mike Parker, *Sales Staff*
EMP: 29
SQ FT: 18,000
SALES (est): 5.5MM **Privately Held**
WEB: www.upstaterefractoryservices.com
SIC: 3255 5085 Clay refractories; refrac-
tory material

(G-11856)
VAN LAEKEN RICHARD
Also Called: Harris Machine
2680 Parker Rd (14513-9750)
PHONE................................315 331-0289
Richard Van Laeken, *Owner*
EMP: 5 EST: 1995
SQ FT: 2,600
SALES (est): 450K **Privately Held**
SIC: 3599 Machine shop, jobbing & repair

Newburgh
Orange County

(G-11857)
**AFFORDBLE GRAN CBNTRY
OUTL INC**
Also Called: Granite Shop
179 S Plank Rd (12550-3037)
PHONE................................845 564-0500
John Quiles, *President*
Pete Nieto, *Admin Sec*
EMP: 10
SALES (est): 1.5MM **Privately Held**
SIC: 2434 Wood kitchen cabinets

(G-11858)
**ARCTIC GLACIER NEWBURGH
INC (DH)**
225 Lake St (12550-5242)
PHONE................................845 561-0549
Robert Nagy, *President*
Keith McMahon, *Vice Pres*
Hugh Adams, *Admin Sec*
EMP: 15
SQ FT: 40,000
SALES (est): 3.8MM
SALES (corp-wide): 2.4B **Publicly Held**
SIC: 2097 Manufactured ice
HQ: Agi Ccaa Inc
625 Henry Ave
Winnipeg MB R3A 0
204 772-2473

(G-11859)
BIG SHINE WORLDWIDE INC
Also Called: Big Shine Energy
300 Corporate Blvd (12550-6402)
PHONE................................845 444-5255
Dong IL Lee, *CEO*
Bong Hee Lee Kim, *Admin Sec*
EMP: 6
SALES (est): 30MM **Privately Held**
SIC: 3646 Commercial indusl & institu-
tional electric lighting fixtures

(G-11860)
BIMBO BAKERIES USA INC
98 Scobie Dr (12550-3257)
PHONE................................845 568-0943
EMP: 53 **Privately Held**
SIC: 2051 Bakery: wholesale or whole-
sale/retail combined
HQ: Bimbo Bakeries Usa, Inc
255 Business Center Dr # 200
Horsham PA 19044
215 347-5500

(G-11861)
**COMMODORE CHOCOLATIER
USA INC**
482 Broadway (12550-5333)
P.O. Box 2657 (12550-0880)
PHONE................................845 561-3960
John Courtsunis, *President*
EMP: 10 EST: 1935
SQ FT: 5,000
SALES: 1MM **Privately Held**
SIC: 2066 5149 5441 Chocolate; choco-
late; candy

(G-11862)
CONSOLIDATED SPRING LLC
Also Called: Atlas Industries
11 Spring St (12550-5511)
PHONE................................845 391-8855
EMP: 10
SALES (est): 821.9K **Privately Held**
SIC: 3999 Manufacturing industries

(G-11863)
E & O MARI INC
Also Called: La Bella Strings
256 Broadway (12550-5487)
P.O. Box 869 (12551-0869)
PHONE................................845 562-4400
Richard Cocco Jr, *President*
Eric Cocco, *Vice Pres*
Lorenza Cocco, *Director*
▲ EMP: 89 EST: 1915
SQ FT: 29,000
SALES (est): 12.8MM **Privately Held**
SIC: 3931 Strings, musical instrument

(G-11864)
**EMPIRE BUSINESS FORMS INC
(PA)**
Also Called: Forms For You Division
128 S Robinson Ave 2 (12550-5822)
P.O. Box 3480, Poughkeepsie (12603-
0480)
PHONE................................845 562-7780
John Vincent Rice, *President*
Louise Rice, *Corp Secy*
EMP: 12
SQ FT: 10,000
SALES (est): 2MM **Privately Held**
SIC: 2759 5112 Business forms: printing;
business forms

(G-11865)
**FRAGRANCE ACQUISITIONS
LLC**
Also Called: Preferred Fragrance
1900 Corporate Blvd (12550-6412)
PHONE................................845 534-9172
Glenn Palmer, *Partner*
Miguel Prian, *Sales Staff*
▲ EMP: 70 EST: 2011
SALES (est): 11.2MM **Privately Held**
SIC: 2844 Perfumes & colognes

(G-11866)
GASOFT EQUIPMENT INC
231 Dubois St (12550-3410)
PHONE................................845 863-1010
Tony M Colandrea, *President*
Nick Gurlakis, *Vice Pres*
◆ EMP: 14

SQ FT: 5,000
SALES: 5.6MM **Privately Held**
SIC: 3577 5045 Computer peripheral
equipment; computers, peripherals & software

(G-11867)
GLASBAU HAHN AMERICA LLC
15 Little Brook Ln Ste 2 (12550-1687)
PHONE................................845 566-3331
Jamie Ponton, *Principal*
Cathy Lima, *Manager*
▲ EMP: 5
SALES (est): 390K **Privately Held**
SIC: 2542 Counters or counter display
cases: except wood

(G-11868)
**HUDSON VALLEY BLACK
PRESS**
343 Broadway (12550-5301)
P.O. Box 2160 (12550-0332)
PHONE................................845 562-1313
Charles Stewart, *President*
John Callahan, *Accounts Exec*
EMP: 7
SQ FT: 4,000
SALES (est): 378.6K **Privately Held**
SIC: 2711 Newspapers: publishing only,
not printed on site

(G-11869)
**HUDSON VALLEY OFFICE FURN
INC**
7 Wisner Ave (12550-5133)
PHONE................................845 565-6673
Tom Chickery, *Owner*
EMP: 8
SALES (corp-wide): 2MM **Privately Held**
WEB: www.thewowguys.com
SIC: 2522 Office furniture, except wood
PA: Hudson Valley Office Furniture, Inc.
375 Main St
Poughkeepsie NY 12601
845 471-7910

(G-11870)
**HUDSON VALLEY PAPER
WORKS INC**
8 Lander St 15 (12550-4938)
PHONE................................845 569-8883
Luke Pontifell, *President*
▲ EMP: 15
SALES (est): 1.2MM **Privately Held**
SIC: 2732 Book printing

(G-11871)
**HUDSON VALLEY STEEL
PRODUCTS**
5231 Route 9w (12550-1483)
PHONE................................845 565-2270
Bradley Bloomer, *Administration*
EMP: 5
SALES (est): 361.7K **Privately Held**
SIC: 3312 Hot-rolled iron & steel products

(G-11872)
LA ESCONDIDA INC
129 Lake St (12550-5242)
PHONE................................845 562-1387
Andres Garcia, *President*
Emigdio Carrera, *Vice Pres*
EMP: 8
SQ FT: 2,000
SALES (est): 850.5K **Privately Held**
WEB: www.laescondida.com
SIC: 2099 Tortillas, fresh or refrigerated

(G-11873)
MIXTURE SCREEN PRINTING
1607 Route 300 100 (12550-1738)
PHONE................................845 561-2857
Christopher D Fahrbach, *Owner*
EMP: 8
SALES (est): 515.6K **Privately Held**
SIC: 2759 3993 5099 Screen printing;
signs & advertising specialties; signs, ex-
cept electric

(G-11874)
MOKAI MANUFACTURING INC
13 Jeanne Dr (12550-1788)
PHONE................................845 566-8287
Rick Murray, *President*
Justin Bruyn, *Design Engr*

▲ = Import ▼=Export
◆ =Import/Export

EMP: 6
SALES (est): 1MM Privately Held
WEB: www.mokai.com
SIC: 3732 Boat building & repairing

(G-11875)
MONDELEZ GLOBAL LLC
Also Called: Nabisco
800 Corporate Blvd (12550-6407)
PHONE..................................845 567-4701
Patrick Sherman, General Mgr
EMP: 6 Publicly Held
SIC: 2022 Cheese, natural & processed
HQ: Mondelez Global Llc
3 N Pkwy Ste 300
Deerfield IL 60015
847 943-4000

(G-11876)
NEWBURGH BREWING
COMPANY LLC
88 S Colden St (12550-5640)
Rural Route 72, Salisbury Mills (12577)
PHONE..................................845 569-2337
Paul Halayko, COO
EMP: 14 EST: 2012
SALES (est): 2.2MM Privately Held
SIC: 2082 Beer (alcoholic beverage)

(G-11877)
NEWBURGH ENVELOPE CORP
1720 Route 300 (12550-8930)
PHONE..................................845 566-4211
Carl Stillwaggon, President
Stuart Stillwaggon, Vice Pres
EMP: 7
SQ FT: 1,800
SALES (est): 640K Privately Held
SIC: 2752 Commercial printing, offset

(G-11878)
ORANGE COUNTY CHOPPERS
INC
Also Called: O C Choppers
14 Crossroads Ct (12550-5064)
PHONE..................................845 522-5200
Paul Teutul Sr, President
Rosie Meyers, VP Bus Dvlpt
EMP: 6
SALES: 1MM Privately Held
SIC: 3751 Motorcycles & related parts

(G-11879)
ORANGE DIE CUTTING CORP
Also Called: Orange Packaging
1 Favoriti Ave (12550-4015)
P.O. Box 2295 (12550-0441)
PHONE..................................845 562-0900
Anthony Esposito Sr, Ch of Bd
Anthony Esposito Jr, President
Hector Torres, General Mgr
▲ EMP: 120 EST: 1950
SQ FT: 40,000
SALES (est): 27.7MM Privately Held
SIC: 2653 Corrugated & solid fiber boxes

(G-11880)
ORNAMETAL INC
216 S William St (12550-5845)
PHONE..................................845 562-5151
Richard Cohen, Owner
EMP: 5
SALES (est): 387K Privately Held
SIC: 3446 Stairs, staircases, stair treads:
prefabricated metal

(G-11881)
PECKHAM MATERIALS CORP
322 Walsh Ave (12553-6748)
P.O. Box 4074, New Windsor (12553-0074)
PHONE..................................845 562-5370
EMP: 5
SALES (corp-wide): 171.1MM Privately
Held
SIC: 2951 Asphalt & asphaltic paving mix-
tures (not from refineries)
HQ: Peckham Materials Corp
20 Haarlem Ave Ste 200
White Plains NY 10603
914 686-2045

(G-11882)
PEPSI-COLA NEWBURGH BTLG
INC
Also Called: Pepsico
1 Pepsi Way (12550-3921)
PHONE..................................845 562-5400
Charles T Tenney Jr, President
John Croce, Division Mgr
Laureen Fee, General Mgr
Tom Strahle, COO
Carson Baker, Opers Staff
EMP: 150 EST: 1939
SALES (est): 28.9MM Privately Held
SIC: 2086 Carbonated soft drinks, bottled
& canned

(G-11883)
PRISMATIC DYEING & FINSHG
INC
40 Wisner Ave (12550-5132)
P.O. Box 2456 (12550-0732)
PHONE..................................845 561-1800
Gary Innocenti, President
Deborah Emerick, Manager
EMP: 60 EST: 1997
SQ FT: 110,000
SALES (est): 10.2MM Privately Held
WEB: www.prismaticdyeing.com
SIC: 2861 2269 2262 2261 Dyeing mate-
rials, natural; finishing plants; finishing
plants, manmade fiber & silk fabrics; fin-
ishing plants, cotton

(G-11884)
PROKOSCH AND SONN SHEET
METAL
772 South St (12550-4149)
PHONE..................................845 562-4211
Alfred Prokosch Jr, Ch of Bd
Annunciata Prokosch, President
John F Prokosch, Vice Pres
EMP: 21
SQ FT: 2,400
SALES (est): 4.1MM Privately Held
SIC: 3444 1711 Sheet metal specialties,
not stamped; heating & air conditioning
contractors

(G-11885)
PROSTHETIC REHABILITATION
CTR (PA)
2 Winding Ln (12550-2223)
PHONE..................................845 565-8255
Andrew Carubia, President
Carol Hatcher, Admin Sec
EMP: 8
SALES (est): 1.2MM Privately Held
SIC: 3842 5999 Limbs, artificial; artificial
limbs

(G-11886)
SANDY LITTMAN INC
Also Called: American Glass Light
420 N Montgomery St (12550-3680)
PHONE..................................845 562-1112
Sandy Littman, President
John Soltes, Manager
▲ EMP: 5
SQ FT: 800
SALES (est): 1MM Privately Held
WEB: www.americanglasslight.com
SIC: 3646 3645 Chandeliers, commercial;
chandeliers, residential

(G-11887)
STEELWAYS INC
Also Called: Steelways Shipyard
401 S Water St (12553-6038)
PHONE..................................845 562-0860
David Plotkins, Ch of Bd
Brian Plotkins, Exec VP
Steve Laker, CFO
EMP: 29
SQ FT: 15,000
SALES (est): 6.8MM Privately Held
WEB: www.steelwaysinc.com
SIC: 3731 3443 Commercial cargo ships,
building & repairing; tanks, standard or
custom fabricated: metal plate
PA: Steelways Holdings Group, Inc.
401 S Water St
Newburgh NY 12553

(G-11888)
TAKEOUT PRINTING LLC
610 Broadway Ste 222 (12550-5130)
PHONE..................................845 564-2609
Michael A D'Agostino, Mng Member
EMP: 5
SALES: 1K Privately Held
SIC: 2759 8742 Commercial printing; mar-
keting consulting services

(G-11889)
TELECHEMISCHE INC
222 Dupont Ave (12550-4060)
PHONE..................................845 561-3237
Mary Mallavarapu, Ch of Bd
Leo Mallavarapu PHD, President
Anita Soares, Admin Sec
EMP: 6
SALES: 100K Privately Held
WEB: www.telechemische.en.ecplaza.net
SIC: 2821 2869 Plastics materials &
resins; industrial organic chemicals

(G-11890)
UNICO SPECIAL PRODUCTS INC
25 Renwick St (12550-6029)
PHONE..................................845 562-9255
Joseph Guarneri Jr, President
Edward Guarneri, Corp Secy
Michael Guarneri, Vice Pres
▲ EMP: 50
SQ FT: 44,000
SALES: 250K Privately Held
SIC: 3083 Plastic finished products, lami-
nated

(G-11891)
UNIVERSAL THIN FILM LAB
CORP
232 N Plank Rd (12550-1775)
PHONE..................................845 562-0601
Carmelo Comito, President
Alison Comito, Treasurer
Vanity Escoto, Office Mgr
EMP: 7 EST: 1997
SQ FT: 3,000
SALES: 1MM Privately Held
SIC: 3559 Optical lens machinery

(G-11892)
URETHANE TECHNOLOGY CO
INC
Also Called: U T C
59 Temple Ave (12550-5117)
PHONE..................................845 561-5500
Beate Regenauer, President
Andreus Ragenaeur, Vice Pres
Bolker Rageneaur, Vice Pres
Thomas Regenauer, Vice Pres
▼ EMP: 12
SQ FT: 20,000
SALES: 14MM Privately Held
SIC: 2821 Plastics materials & resins

(G-11893)
WALLKILL VALLEY
PUBLICATIONS
Also Called: Wallkill Valley Times
300 Stony Brook Ct Ste B (12550-6535)
PHONE..................................845 561-0170
Carl Aiello, President
EMP: 20
SQ FT: 1,500
SALES (est): 1.1MM Privately Held
WEB: www.tcnewspapers.com
SIC: 2711 2791 2752 2721 Newspapers:
publishing only, not printed on site; type-
setting; commercial printing, lithographic;
periodicals

Newfane
Niagara County

(G-11894)
KSM GROUP LTD
2905 Beebe Rd (14108-9655)
PHONE..................................716 751-6006
Daniel King, President
Judith M King, Vice Pres
EMP: 5
SQ FT: 18,000

SALES (est): 430K Privately Held
WEB: www.ksmgroup.org
SIC: 3444 Sheet metalwork

(G-11895)
SAVACO INC
2905 Beebe Rd (14108-9655)
PHONE..................................716 751-9455
Judith King, President
EMP: 7
SQ FT: 18,000
SALES: 500K Privately Held
WEB: www.savacoinc.com
SIC: 3444 Sheet metalwork

(G-11896)
VANTE INC
Also Called: Plasticweld Systems
3600 Coomer Rd (14108-9651)
PHONE..................................716 778-7691
Brian Strini, CEO
Norman Strobel, President
▲ EMP: 10
SQ FT: 4,800
SALES (est): 1.9MM Privately Held
WEB: www.plasticweldsystems.com
SIC: 3841 3548 Catheters; welding appa-
ratus
HQ: Machine Solutions, Inc.
2951 W Shamrell Blvd # 107
Flagstaff AZ 86005
928 556-3109

Newfield
Tompkins County

(G-11897)
OMNI TURBINE PARTS LLC
12 Seely Hill Rd (14867-9756)
PHONE..................................607 564-9922
Mark Doelling,
EMP: 10
SALES (est): 1.3MM Privately Held
SIC: 3599 Machine shop, jobbing & repair

Newport
Herkimer County

(G-11898)
FULLER TOOL INCORPORATED
225 Platform Rd (13416-2217)
PHONE..................................315 891-3183
Rodney Fuller, CEO
EMP: 10
SQ FT: 2,800
SALES: 500K Privately Held
WEB: www.fullertool.com
SIC: 3312 3544 Tool & die steel & alloys;
special dies, tools, jigs & fixtures

(G-11899)
REYNOLDS DRAPERY SERVICE
INC
Also Called: Country Coin-Op
7440 Main St (13416-7707)
P.O. Box 470 (13416-0470)
PHONE..................................315 845-8632
Richard Reynolds, President
Michael Moody, Vice Pres
EMP: 10 EST: 1964
SQ FT: 6,500
SALES (est): 1MM Privately Held
SIC: 2391 5023 5714 7216 Draperies,
plastic & textile: from purchased materi-
als; draperies; draperies; curtain cleaning
& repair; fire resistance finishing of cotton
broadwoven fabrics; laundry, coin-oper-
ated

Niagara Falls
Niagara County

(G-11900)
AAVID NIAGARA LLC (DH)
3315 Haseley Dr (14304-1460)
PHONE..................................716 297-0652
Barry Heckman, CEO
Alan Wong, President

Scott Mowry, *Vice Pres*
Jill Couture, *Controller*
Robert Corvino,
▲ **EMP:** 50
SQ FT: 45,000
SALES (est): 28.8MM
SALES (corp-wide): 915.2MM **Privately Held**
WEB: www.niagarathermal.com
SIC: 3443 5084 Heat exchangers, condensers & components; heat exchange equipment, industrial
HQ: Aavid Thermalloy, Llc
　1 Aavid Cir
　Laconia NH 03246
　603 528-3400

(G-11901)
ADVANTAGE MACHINING INC
6421 Wendt Dr (14304-1100)
PHONE....................716 731-6418
Scott Ranney, *President*
EMP: 10
SALES (est): 1.1MM **Privately Held**
SIC: 3599 Machine shop, jobbing & repair

(G-11902)
AM RETAIL GROUP INC
Also Called: Dkny
1900 Military Rd (14304-1737)
PHONE....................716 297-0752
Elizabeth Carroll, *Branch Mgr*
EMP: 157
SALES (corp-wide): 3B **Publicly Held**
SIC: 2335 Women's, juniors' & misses' dresses
HQ: Am Retail Group, Inc.
　7401 Boone Ave N
　Brooklyn Park MN 55428

(G-11903)
AMERICARB INC
6100 Niagara Falls Blvd (14304-1534)
PHONE....................419 281-5800
Matt Reineke, *President*
Leland P Reineke, *Chairman*
Ajit Sane, *Vice Pres*
Tim Barrett, *CFO*
Brian Guido, *VP Sales*
▲ **EMP:** 75
SQ FT: 140,000
SALES (est): 18.5MM **Privately Held**
SIC: 3624 Carbon & graphite products

(G-11904)
AMERICARB INTERNATIONAL CORP
6100 Niagara Falls Blvd (14304-1534)
PHONE....................419 281-5800
Matt Reineke, *CEO*
Lee Reineke, *Chairman*
Brian Guido, *Vice Pres*
Rick Mellino, *Vice Pres*
Eugene Cabonor, *CFO*
EMP: 7 EST: 2010
SALES (est): 635K **Privately Held**
SIC: 3624 Carbon & graphite products

(G-11905)
AMTEK RESEARCH LLC
1711 Cudaback Ave # 3865 (14303-1709)
PHONE....................416 400-2906
Ajay Misra, *Branch Mgr*
EMP: 23
SALES (corp-wide): 134.6K **Privately Held**
SIC: 2819 2899 Industrial inorganic chemicals; fuel tank or engine cleaning chemicals
PA: Amtek Research, Llc
　705 Killarney Dr Nw
　Huntsville AL

(G-11906)
ANGUS CHEMICAL COMPANY
Also Called: Angus Buffers & Biochemicals
2236 Liberty Dr (14304-3756)
PHONE....................716 283-1434
Mark Deuble, *Manager*
EMP: 23
SALES (corp-wide): 5.8B **Privately Held**
SIC: 2836 Culture media
HQ: Angus Chemical Company
　1500 E Lake Cook Rd
　Buffalo Grove IL 60089
　847 215-8600

(G-11907)
APOLLO STEEL CORPORATION
4800 Tomson Ave (14304-2150)
PHONE....................716 283-8758
George J Merkling III, *President*
EMP: 16
SQ FT: 15,000
SALES (est): 5.7MM **Privately Held**
SIC: 3441 Bridge sections, prefabricated highway; bridge sections, prefabricated railway; expansion joints (structural shapes), iron or steel; floor jacks, metal

(G-11908)
BIKE SHOPCOM LLC
2045 Niagara Falls Blvd (14304-1675)
PHONE....................716 236-7500
Bryan Riley, *CEO*
EMP: 3
SQ FT: 2,000
SALES: 2MM **Privately Held**
SIC: 3751 Bicycles & related parts

(G-11909)
BRAUN HORTICULTURE INC
3302 Highland Ave (14305-2013)
P.O. Box 260 (14305-0260)
PHONE....................716 282-6101
Peter Braun, *President*
▲ **EMP:** 7
SQ FT: 31,500
SALES (est): 1.3MM **Privately Held**
WEB: www.braungroup.com
SIC: 3315 Baskets, steel wire
HQ: Braun Nursery Limited
　2004 Glancaster Rd
　Mount Hope ON L0R 1
　905 648-1911

(G-11910)
BRODA MACHINE CO INC
8745 Packard Rd (14304-1497)
PHONE....................716 297-3221
Matthew Broda, *President*
Thomas J Broda, *President*
Lillian Broda, *Corp Secy*
Mark Broda, *Vice Pres*
Jeff Kilroy, *Plant Mgr*
EMP: 13
SQ FT: 10,000
SALES (est): 3.6MM **Privately Held**
WEB: www.brodamachine.com
SIC: 3599 Machine shop, jobbing & repair

(G-11911)
CALSPAN CORPORATION
Also Called: Calspan Flight Research Center
2041 Niagara Falls Blvd (14304-1617)
PHONE....................716 236-1040
Paul Nafziger, *Branch Mgr*
EMP: 11
SALES (corp-wide): 78.4MM **Privately Held**
WEB: www.windtunnel.com
SIC: 3721 Research & development on aircraft by the manufacturer
HQ: Calspan Corporation
　4455 Genesee St
　Buffalo NY 14225
　716 631-6955

(G-11912)
CASCADES NEW YORK INC
4001 Packard Rd (14303-2202)
PHONE....................716 285-3681
Toni Lionetti, *General Mgr*
Chris Debinski, *Production*
Shawn Vanin, *Purch Agent*
Mary Malone, *Manager*
EMP: 115
SALES (corp-wide): 3.5B **Privately Held**
SIC: 2621 Paper mills
HQ: Cascades New York Inc.
　1845 Emerson St
　Rochester NY 14606
　585 527-8110

(G-11913)
CCT (US) INC
2221 Niagara Falls Blvd # 5 (14304-5709)
PHONE....................716 297-7509
Yves Therrien, *President*
Jacques Chevrette, *Admin Sec*
▲ **EMP:** 15
SQ FT: 20,000

SALES (est): 595.4K
SALES (corp-wide): 11MM **Privately Held**
SIC: 2679 Building, insulating & packaging paper; building, insulating & packaging paperboard
PA: Papiers C.C.T. Inc
　830 Rue Saint-Viateur
　Berthierville QC J0K 1
　450 836-3846

(G-11914)
CENTRE DE CONFORMITE ICC INC
2150 Liberty Dr Ste 1 (14304-3780)
PHONE....................716 283-0002
Shirley Coles, *Office Mgr*
EMP: 28
SALES (corp-wide): 36.3MM **Privately Held**
SIC: 2673 Bags: plastic, laminated & coated
PA: Centre De Conformite Icc Inc
　88 Av Lindsay
　Dorval QC H9P 2
　514 636-8146

(G-11915)
CNHI LLC
Also Called: Tonanwanda News
473 3rd St Ste 201 (14301-1500)
PHONE....................716 693-1000
Wayne Lowman, *Branch Mgr*
EMP: 100
SQ FT: 21,892 **Privately Held**
WEB: www.clintonnc.com
SIC: 2711 Newspapers: publishing only, not printed on site
HQ: Cnhi, Llc
　445 Dexter Ave
　Montgomery AL 36104

(G-11916)
CNHI LLC
Also Called: Niagara Gazette
473 3rd St Ste 201 (14301-1500)
PHONE....................716 282-2311
Steve Braver, *Principal*
Cheryl Phillips, *Director*
EMP: 55
SQ FT: 21,534 **Privately Held**
WEB: www.clintonnc.com
SIC: 2711 2741 Newspapers: publishing only, not printed on site; miscellaneous publishing
HQ: Cnhi, Llc
　445 Dexter Ave
　Montgomery AL 36104

(G-11917)
COSTANZOS WELDING INC (PA)
Also Called: Cataract Steel Industries
22nd Allen St (14302)
P.O. Box 862 (14302-0862)
PHONE....................716 282-0845
Scott Costanzo, *President*
Thomas Costanzo, *Vice Pres*
Jim Willett, *Manager*
▼ **EMP:** 49
SQ FT: 100,000
SALES (est): 8MM **Privately Held**
WEB: www.cataractsteel.com
SIC: 3443 Heat exchangers, plate type

(G-11918)
CRYSTAL CERES INDUSTRIES INC
2250 Liberty Dr (14304-3756)
PHONE....................716 283-0445
Michael Lynch, *Vice Pres*
▲ **EMP:** 58
SALES (est): 8.2MM **Privately Held**
WEB: www.cerescrystal.com
SIC: 1481 7631 Nonmetallic mineral services; diamond setter

(G-11919)
CSI INTERNATIONAL INC
1001 Main St (14301-1111)
PHONE....................800 441-2895
Steven Brown, *President*
Jorge Garcia, *Area Mgr*
Walter Conklin, *Site Mgr*
Maria Vatri, *Controller*
Kathleen Butera, *Human Res Mgr*
▲ **EMP:** 40
SQ FT: 37,000

SALES (est): 6.8MM **Privately Held**
SIC: 3911 3914 5947 Jewelry, precious metal; trophies, plated (all metals); gift shop

(G-11920)
DELFINGEN US-NEW YORK INC
Also Called: Sofanou
2221 Niagara Falls Blvd # 12 (14304-5709)
PHONE....................716 215-0300
Bernard Streit, *President*
Olivier Mathieu, *General Mgr*
David Streit, *Vice Pres*
Erica Stamboulian, *Engineer*
Mark Blanke, *Treasurer*
▲ **EMP:** 25
SALES (est): 7.2MM
SALES (corp-wide): 3.1MM **Privately Held**
SIC: 3643 Caps & plugs, electric: attachment
HQ: Delfingen Us, Inc.
　3985 W Hamlin Rd
　Rochester Hills MI 48309

(G-11921)
DUREZ CORPORATION
5000 Packard Rd (14304-1510)
PHONE....................716 286-0100
John W Fisher, *CEO*
EMP: 15 **Privately Held**
SIC: 2865 2821 Cyclic crudes & intermediates; plastics materials & resins
HQ: Durez Corporation
　46820 Magellan Dr Ste C
　Novi MI 48377
　248 313-7000

(G-11922)
EASTERN MACHINE AND ELECTRIC
1041 Niagara Ave (14305-2639)
PHONE....................716 284-8271
Louis Destino, *President*
Daniel Destino, *Corp Secy*
EMP: 6 EST: 1957
SQ FT: 7,200
SALES (est): 514.2K **Privately Held**
SIC: 3599 Machine shop, jobbing & repair

(G-11923)
EMPIRE EMERGENCY APPARATUS INC
3995 Lockport Rd (14305-2317)
PHONE....................716 348-3473
Michael J McLaughlin, *CEO*
EMP: 28
SALES (est): 5.4MM **Privately Held**
SIC: 3711 3714 Cars, armored, assembly of; fire department vehicles (motor vehicles), assembly of; motor vehicle parts & accessories

(G-11924)
ENSIL TECHNICAL SERVICES INC
1901 Maryland Ave (14305-1722)
PHONE....................716 282-1020
Farsad Kiani, *President*
Louis Koikas, *Principal*
EMP: 50
SALES (est): 7MM **Privately Held**
SIC: 3672 Printed circuit boards

(G-11925)
EUROTEX INC
Also Called: Eurotex North America
4600 Witmer Rd (14305-1217)
PHONE....................716 205-8861
Sasha Mitic, *President*
▲ **EMP:** 12
SALES (est): 1.3MM **Privately Held**
SIC: 2295 Coated fabrics, not rubberized

(G-11926)
FELICETTI CONCRETE PRODUCTS
4129 Hyde Park Blvd (14305-1711)
PHONE....................716 284-5740
Gene Felicetti, *Corp Secy*
Henry Felicetti, *Vice Pres*
Frank M Felicetti, *Shareholder*
Phillip Felicetti, *Shareholder*
Richard B Felicetti, *Shareholder*
EMP: 7

▲ = Import　▼=Export
◆ =Import/Export

SQ FT: 1,750
SALES (est): 1.2MM **Privately Held**
SIC: 3271 Blocks, concrete or cinder: standard; brick, concrete

(G-11927)
FELTON MACHINE CO INC
2221 Niagara Falls Blvd (14304-5709)
P.O. Box 239 (14304-0239)
PHONE................................716 215-9001
Robert J Schroeder, *President*
Jeff Gorney, *Mfg Staff*
Bridget M Schroeder, *Treasurer*
Mike Schroder, *Info Tech Mgr*
EMP: 38
SQ FT: 42,000
SALES (est): 6.3MM **Privately Held**
WEB: www.feltonmachine.com
SIC: 3599 Machine shop, jobbing & repair

(G-11928)
FERRO ELECTRONICS MATERIALS
4511 Hyde Park Blvd (14305-1215)
PHONE................................716 278-9400
Lyndon La Brake, *Branch Mgr*
EMP: 180
SALES (corp-wide): 1.6B **Publicly Held**
SIC: 3264 2819 Porcelain electrical supplies; industrial inorganic chemicals
HQ: Ferro Electronics Materials Inc
1789 Transelco Dr
Penn Yan NY 14527
315 536-3357

(G-11929)
FLAME CONTROL COATINGS LLC
4120 Hyde Park Blvd (14305-1793)
PHONE................................716 282-1399
Tim Lockhart, *Marketing Mgr*
Jeff Fallon,
Jonathan Hatch,
▼ **EMP:** 26 **EST:** 1976
SQ FT: 26,000
SALES (est): 7.3MM **Privately Held**
WEB: www.flamecontrol.com
SIC: 2899 Fire retardant chemicals

(G-11930)
FROSS INDUSTRIES INC
Also Called: Niagara Development & Mfg Div
3315 Haseley Dr (14304-1460)
PHONE................................716 297-0652
Silvio Derubeis, *President*
Robert Schultz, *Vice Pres*
Donald H Smith, *Treasurer*
Gordon Smith, *Admin Sec*
EMP: 50 **EST:** 1981
SQ FT: 16,000
SALES (est): 6.2MM **Privately Held**
SIC: 3443 3599 Heat exchangers, plate type; machine shop, jobbing & repair

(G-11931)
GLOBE METALLURGICAL INC
Also Called: Globe Specialty Metals
3807 Highland Ave (14305-1723)
PHONE................................716 804-0862
Grace Huang, *Controller*
Paul Kwapiszeski, *Branch Mgr*
Jeffery Circle, *Technology*
EMP: 90
SALES (corp-wide): 2.2B **Privately Held**
WEB: www.globemetallurgical.com
SIC: 3339 3313 Silicon refining (primary, over 99% pure); ferromanganese, not made in blast furnaces
HQ: Globe Metallurgical Inc.
Co Rd 32
Waterford OH 45786
740 984-2361

(G-11932)
GRAPHICOMM INC
Also Called: Insty-Prints
7703 Niagara Falls Blvd (14304-1739)
P.O. Box 543, Grand Island (14072-0543)
PHONE................................716 283-0830
John Jones, *President*
Jill Welsby, *Graphic Designe*
EMP: 5
SQ FT: 2,200

SALES (est): 640K **Privately Held**
SIC: 2752 7334 2791 2789 Commercial printing, lithographic; photocopying & duplicating services; typesetting; bookbinding & related work

(G-11933)
GREENPAC MILL LLC (DH)
4400 Royal Ave (14303-2128)
PHONE................................716 299-0560
Murray Hewitt, *General Mgr*
Craig Eddy, *Opers Mgr*
Michael Lengyel, *Engineer*
Luc Nadeau,
▲ **EMP:** 110 **EST:** 2010
SALES (est): 47.6MM
SALES (corp-wide): 3.5B **Privately Held**
SIC: 2631 Linerboard
HQ: Cascades New York Inc.
1845 Emerson St
Rochester NY 14606
585 527-8110

(G-11934)
GUESS INC
1826 Military Rd Spc 113 (14304-1772)
PHONE................................716 298-3561
Danielle Guetta, *Manager*
EMP: 25
SALES (corp-wide): 2.6B **Publicly Held**
WEB: www.guess.com
SIC: 2325 Men's & boys' jeans & dungarees
PA: Guess , Inc.
1444 S Alameda St
Los Angeles CA 90021
213 765-3100

(G-11935)
HELMEL ENGINEERING PDTS INC
6520 Lockport Rd (14305-3512)
PHONE................................716 297-8644
Erwin Helmel, *President*
Dora Helmel, *Admin Sec*
Robert Kerns, *Technician*
▲ **EMP:** 22
SQ FT: 23,000
SALES: 2.7MM **Privately Held**
WEB: www.helmel.com
SIC: 3829 Measuring & controlling devices

(G-11936)
IMBIBITIVE TECH AMER CORP
Also Called: Imbtec America
1623 Military Rd Ste 1011 (14304-1745)
PHONE................................888 843-2323
John Brinkman, *President*
Bruno Iafrate, *Vice Pres*
EMP: 5
SALES: 254K
SALES (corp-wide): 4.5MM **Privately Held**
SIC: 2821 5162 Plastics materials & resins; plastics materials & basic shapes
PA: Imbibitive Technologies Corporation
1623 Military Rd Ste 1011
Niagara Falls NY 14304
888 843-2323

(G-11937)
IMBIBITIVE TECHNOLOGIES CORP (PA)
1623 Military Rd Ste 1011 (14304-1745)
PHONE................................888 843-2323
John Brinkman, *President*
Richard Hall, *Vice Pres*
Nick Flor, *CFO*
Richard Halinda, *Treasurer*
EMP: 4
SALES (est): 4.5MM **Privately Held**
SIC: 2821 5162 Plastics materials & resins; plastics materials & basic shapes

(G-11938)
IMERYS FSED MNRL NGARA FLS INC
3455 Hyde Park Blvd (14305-2201)
PHONE................................716 286-1234
EMP: 5
SALES (corp-wide): 3MM **Privately Held**
SIC: 3291 Abrasive products

HQ: Imerys Fused Minerals Niagara Falls, Inc.
2000 College Ave
Niagara Falls NY 14305

(G-11939)
IMERYS FSED MNRL NGARA FLS INC
4901 Hyde Park Blvd (14305-1224)
P.O. Box 1438 (14302-1438)
PHONE................................716 286-1250
Dave Gratz, *Manager*
EMP: 9
SALES (corp-wide): 3MM **Privately Held**
SIC: 3291 Abrasive products
HQ: Imerys Fused Minerals Niagara Falls, Inc.
2000 College Ave
Niagara Falls NY 14305

(G-11940)
IMERYS FSED MNRL NGARA FLS INC (DH)
2000 College Ave (14305-1734)
P.O. Box 1438 (14302-1438)
PHONE................................716 286-1250
Christian Pfeifer, *CEO*
◆ **EMP:** 35
SQ FT: 4,950
SALES: 8.1MM
SALES (corp-wide): 3MM **Privately Held**
SIC: 3291 Abrasive products
HQ: Imerys Usa, Inc.
100 Mansell Ct E Ste 300
Roswell GA 30076
770 645-3300

(G-11941)
INDUSTRIAL SERVICES OF WNY
7221 Niagara Falls Blvd (14304-1715)
PHONE................................716 799-7788
Georgena Dinieri, *Owner*
EMP: 5
SALES (est): 239K **Privately Held**
SIC: 3599 Machine & other job shop work

(G-11942)
J D CALATO MANUFACTURING CO (PA)
Also Called: Regal Tip
4501 Hyde Park Blvd (14305-1215)
PHONE................................716 285-3546
Carol Calato, *CEO*
Joseph D Calato, *CEO*
Catherine Calato, *Vice Pres*
EMP: 35 **EST:** 1961
SQ FT: 17,000
SALES (est): 4.1MM **Privately Held**
WEB: www.calato.com
SIC: 3931 Guitars & parts, electric & non-electric; drums, parts & accessories (musical instruments)

(G-11943)
JOHNNIE RYAN CO INC
3084 Niagara St (14303-2030)
PHONE................................716 282-1606
Paul Janik, *Vice Pres*
EMP: 15
SQ FT: 10,000
SALES (est): 2.1MM **Privately Held**
WEB: www.johnnieryan.com
SIC: 2086 Soft drinks: packaged in cans, bottles, etc.

(G-11944)
KINTEX INC
Also Called: Niagara Thermo Products
3315 Haseley Dr (14304-1460)
PHONE................................716 297-0652
Barry Heckman, *Owner*
Donald Hall, *Engineer*
EMP: 90
SALES (est): 6.3MM **Privately Held**
SIC: 3443 Heat exchangers, condensers & components

(G-11945)
L A R ELECTRONICS CORP
2733 Niagara St (14303-2027)
PHONE................................716 285-0555
Lawrence Kutner, *President*
EMP: 7 **EST:** 1980
SQ FT: 3,500

SALES: 150K **Privately Held**
WEB: www.laraudio.com
SIC: 3651 5065 1731 Speaker systems; sound equipment, electronic; sound equipment specialization

(G-11946)
LIDDELL CORPORATION
4600 Witmer Ind Est 5 (14305-1364)
PHONE................................716 297-8557
Lon Flick, *President*
EMP: 14
SALES: 1.3MM **Privately Held**
WEB: www.nicel.com
SIC: 2844 Cosmetic preparations

(G-11947)
LIQUID INDUSTRIES INC
7219 New Jersey Ave (14305)
PHONE................................716 628-2999
Hamish Shaw, *President*
EMP: 6
SALES (est): 694.3K **Privately Held**
SIC: 3589 Car washing machinery

(G-11948)
LOCKHEED MARTIN CORPORATION
2221 Niagara Falls Blvd (14304-5709)
PHONE................................716 297-1000
Mike Davis, *Safety Mgr*
Donald Kellner, *QC Mgr*
Jonathan D Mack, *Engineer*
Matthew McGrath, *Manager*
James Archibald, *Executive*
EMP: 40 **Publicly Held**
WEB: www.lockheedmartin.com
SIC: 3721 3812 3769 Motorized aircraft; search & navigation equipment; guided missile & space vehicle parts & auxiliary equipment
PA: Lockheed Martin Corporation
6801 Rockledge Dr
Bethesda MD 20817

(G-11949)
MARIPHARM LABORATORIES
2045 Niagara Falls Blvd (14304-1675)
PHONE................................716 984-6520
Christopher Dean, *Owner*
EMP: 10
SALES (est): 564.9K **Privately Held**
SIC: 3821 Laboratory apparatus & furniture

(G-11950)
METAL PRODUCTS INTL LLC
7510 Porter Rd Ste 4 (14304-1692)
PHONE................................716 215-1930
Thomas Fleckestien,
Kenneth Koedinger,
▲ **EMP:** 5
SALES: 12MM **Privately Held**
WEB: www.metalproducts.com
SIC: 3449 Miscellaneous metalwork

(G-11951)
METRO MATTRESS CORP
2212 Military Rd (14304-1760)
PHONE................................716 205-2300
Randy Pegan, *Branch Mgr*
EMP: 28
SALES (corp-wide): 42MM **Privately Held**
SIC: 2515 5712 5719 Mattresses & bedsprings; beds & accessories; beddings & linens
PA: Metro Mattress Corp.
3545 John Glenn Blvd
Syracuse NY 13209
315 218-1200

(G-11952)
MOOG INC
Also Called: Moog - Isp
6686 Walmore Rd (14304-1638)
PHONE................................716 731-6300
Donna Lough, *Accountant*
Jerry Fritz, *Branch Mgr*
Thomas Donnelly, *Manager*
Cheryl Gray, *Manager*
Randy Fahs, *Contract Law*
EMP: 100
SALES (corp-wide): 2.9B **Publicly Held**
SIC: 2819 Industrial inorganic chemicals

PA: Moog Inc.
400 Jamison Rd
Elma NY 14059
716 805-2604

(G-11953)
NATIONAL MAINT CONTG CORP
Also Called: Nmcc
5600 Niagara Falls Blvd (14304-1532)
P.O. Box 258 (14304-0258)
PHONE....................................716 285-1583
Samuel D Lehr, *President*
EMP: 54
SALES: 5MM **Privately Held**
SIC: 3499 Welding tips, heat resistant:
metal

(G-11954)
NIAGARA SAMPLE BOOK CO INC
1717 Mackenna Ave (14303-1715)
PHONE....................................716 284-6151
Joseph P Pinzotti, *President*
Marsha A Pinzotti, *Vice Pres*
Mary B Pinzotti, *Treasurer*
Marcella Pinzotti, *Admin Sec*
EMP: 15 **EST:** 1945
SQ FT: 20,000
SALES (est): 1.3MM **Privately Held**
WEB: www.niagarasample.com
SIC: 2782 2759 Sample books; commer-
cial printing

(G-11955)
NIKE INC
1886 Military Rd (14304-1772)
PHONE....................................716 298-5615
EMP: 7
SALES (corp-wide): 39.1B **Publicly Held**
SIC: 3021 Rubber & plastics footwear
PA: Nike, Inc.
1 Sw Bowerman Dr
Beaverton OR 97005
503 671-6453

(G-11956)
NORTH AMERICAN HOGANAS INC
5950 Packard Rd (14304-1584)
P.O. Box 310 (14304-0310)
PHONE....................................716 285-3451
Avinash Gore, *President*
Terry Heinrich, *Corp Secy*
George Gillespie, *Vice Pres*
Nagarjuna Nandivada, *Vice Pres*
Roberta Fraser, *Office Mgr*
◆ **EMP:** 41
SALES (est): 14MM
SALES (corp-wide): 1.1B **Privately Held**
SIC: 2819 Iron (ferric/ferrous) compounds
or salts
HQ: North American Hoganas Holdings,
Inc.
111 Hoganas Way
Hollsopple PA 15935
814 479-2551

(G-11957)
NORTHKNIGHT LOGISTICS INC
7724 Buffalo Ave (14304-4134)
PHONE....................................716 283-3090
John Rendle, *CEO*
◆ **EMP:** 15 **EST:** 2007
SQ FT: 14,000
SALES (est): 2MM **Privately Held**
SIC: 3429 Builders' hardware

(G-11958)
NUTTALL GEAR L L C (HQ)
Also Called: Delroyd Worm Gear
2221 Niagara Falls Blvd # 17 (14304-5709)
PHONE....................................716 298-4100
Michael Hurt, *CEO*
Scott Jimbroni, *General Mgr*
Denis Hadden, *QC Mgr*
Paul Doricko, *Sales Mgr*
John Proven, *Sales Mgr*
▲ **EMP:** 45
SQ FT: 107,000
SALES (est): 15MM
SALES (corp-wide): 1.1B **Publicly Held**
WEB: www.nuttallgear.com
SIC: 3566 Gears, power transmission, ex-
cept automotive

PA: Altra Industrial Motion Corp.
300 Granite St Ste 201
Braintree MA 02184
781 917-0600

(G-11959)
OCCIDENTAL CHEMICAL CORP
4700 Buffalo Ave (14304-3821)
P.O. Box 344 (14302-0344)
PHONE....................................716 278-7795
Joseph Guzzetta, *Engineer*
Tom Feeney, *Branch Mgr*
Nancy McDonell, *Administration*
EMP: 35
SALES (corp-wide): 18.9B **Publicly Held**
WEB: www.oxychem.com
SIC: 2812 Alkalies & chlorine
HQ: Occidental Chemical Corporation
14555 Dallas Pkwy Ste 400
Dallas TX 75254
972 404-3800

(G-11960)
OCCIDENTAL CHEMICAL CORP
56 Street & Energy Blvd (14302)
P.O. Box 344 (14302-0344)
PHONE....................................716 278-7794
Herb Jones, *General Mgr*
EMP: 200
SALES (corp-wide): 18.9B **Publicly Held**
SIC: 2874 2812 Phosphatic fertilizers;
chlorine, compressed or liquefied
HQ: Occidental Chemical Corporation
14555 Dallas Pkwy Ste 400
Dallas TX 75254
972 404-3800

(G-11961)
OLIN CHLOR ALKALI LOGISTICS
Also Called: Chlor Alkali Products & Vinyls
2400 Buffalo Ave (14303-1959)
P.O. Box 748 (14302-0748)
PHONE....................................716 278-6411
Marc Audet, *Plant Mgr*
Donna Dye-Sholk, *Finance Mgr*
Tom Tirabassi, *Manager*
Rick Mac Donell, *Administration*
EMP: 150
SALES (corp-wide): 6.9B **Publicly Held**
WEB: www.olin.com
SIC: 2812 2842 Alkalies & chlorine; spe-
cialty cleaning, polishes & sanitation
goods
HQ: Olin Chlor Alkali Logistics Inc
490 Stuart Rd Ne
Cleveland TN 37312
423 336-4850

(G-11962)
OXAIR LTD
8320 Quarry Rd (14304-1068)
P.O. Box 4039 (14304-8039)
PHONE....................................716 298-8288
Flavio Zeni, *President*
◆ **EMP:** 5
SQ FT: 10,000
SALES (est): 886.4K **Privately Held**
WEB: www.oxair.com
SIC: 2813 Oxygen, compressed or lique-
fied

(G-11963)
PARMED PHARMACEUTICALS LLC (HQ)
4220 Hyde Park Blvd (14305-1798)
PHONE....................................716 773-1113
Michael C Kaufmann, *CEO*
Dominick Palmo, *Exec VP*
Daniel H Movens, *Senior VP*
James W Hillman, *Vice Pres*
Jim Hillman, *Vice Pres*
▲ **EMP:** 90
SQ FT: 30,000
SALES (est): 11.9MM
SALES (corp-wide): 145.5B **Publicly
Held**
WEB: www.parmed.com
SIC: 2834 Pharmaceutical preparations
PA: Cardinal Health, Inc.
7000 Cardinal Pl
Dublin OH 43017
614 757-5000

(G-11964)
PENETRADAR CORPORATION
2509 Niagara Falls Blvd (14304-4518)
PHONE....................................716 731-2629
Anthony J Alongi, *President*
Carol Eames, *CIO*
EMP: 15
SQ FT: 15,000
SALES (est): 2.1MM **Privately Held**
WEB: www.penetradar.com
SIC: 3812 Radar systems & equipment

(G-11965)
PLIOTRON COMPANY AMERICA LLC
4650 Witmer Indus Est (14305-1360)
PHONE....................................716 298-4457
Robert Leiiahton, *Plant Mgr*
Albert E Matthews,
Linda Matthews,
EMP: 5 **EST:** 1962
SQ FT: 8,125
SALES (est): 363K **Privately Held**
WEB: www.pliotron.com
SIC: 3564 Filters, air: furnaces, air condi-
tioning equipment, etc.

(G-11966)
PRAXAIR INC
4501 Royal Ave (14303-2121)
PHONE....................................716 286-4600
Brian McKie, *Branch Mgr*
Jerad Stager, *Manager*
Patrick McJury, *Database Admin*
Kevin Vaughn, *Technician*
EMP: 50 **Privately Held**
SIC: 2813 Industrial gases
HQ: Praxair, Inc.
10 Riverview Dr
Danbury CT 06810
203 837-2000

(G-11967)
PRECIOUS PLATE INC
2124 Liberty Dr (14304-3799)
PHONE....................................716 283-0690
David R Hurst, *President*
William Copping, *Vice Pres*
Scott Law, *Vice Pres*
David Miller, *Vice Pres*
Ken Russell, *Safety Mgr*
▲ **EMP:** 75
SQ FT: 65,000
SALES (est): 16.8MM **Privately Held**
SIC: 3471 Electroplating of metals or
formed products

(G-11968)
PRECISION ELCTRO MNRL PMCO INC
150 Portage Rd (14303-1535)
P.O. Box 8 (14302-0008)
PHONE....................................716 284-2484
EMP: 25
SQ FT: 40,000
SALES (est): 2MM **Privately Held**
SIC: 2819 3291 1446 Mfg Industrial Inor-
ganic Chemicals Mfg Abrasive Products
Industrial Sand Mining

(G-11969)
PRECISION PROCESS INC (PA)
2111 Liberty Dr (14304-3744)
PHONE....................................716 731-1587
David Hurst, *CEO*
Bill Copping, *Vice Pres*
Joe Hoyt, *VP Finance*
David Miller, *VP Sales*
John Bondi, *Sales Mgr*
▲ **EMP:** 83
SQ FT: 65,000
SALES (est): 17.3MM **Privately Held**
WEB: www.precisionprocess.com
SIC: 3559 Electroplating machinery &
equipment

(G-11970)
RAINBOW AWNING CO INC
Also Called: Awnings By Rainbow
9025 Niagara Falls Blvd (14304-1974)
PHONE....................................716 297-3939
Stephen A Ruest, *President*
Joan H Dittbrenner, *Treasurer*
EMP: 6
SQ FT: 6,000

SALES (est): 81.2K **Privately Held**
WEB: www.rainbowawning.com
SIC: 3444 5999 1799 1521 Awnings,
sheet metal; awnings; screening contractor: window, door, etc.; patio & deck construction & repair

(G-11971)
RANNEY PRECISION
Also Called: Ranney Precision Machining
6421 Wendt Dr (14304-1100)
PHONE....................................716 731-6418
David Ranney, *Owner*
Joanne Ranney, *Co-Owner*
EMP: 17
SQ FT: 10,000
SALES (est): 1.6MM **Privately Held**
WEB: www.ranneyprecision.com
SIC: 3451 Screw machine products

(G-11972)
RELIANCE FLUID TECH LLC
3943 Buffalo Ave (14303-2136)
PHONE....................................716 332-0988
John Garguiolo, *President*
EMP: 47
SALES: 45MM **Privately Held**
SIC: 2899 Corrosion preventive lubricant

(G-11973)
RICHARDSON MOLDING LLC
Also Called: Niagara Falls Plant
3123 Highland Ave (14305-2051)
PHONE....................................716 282-1261
John Signore, *Manager*
EMP: 80
SALES (corp-wide): 106.7MM **Privately
Held**
WEB: www.tulipcorp.com
SIC: 3089 Injection molding of plastics
HQ: Richardson Molding Incorporated
2405 Norcross Dr
Columbus IN 47201
812 342-0139

(G-11974)
RT MACHINED SPECIALTIES
2221 Niagara Falls Blvd (14304-5709)
PHONE....................................716 731-2055
Rebecca Christie, *President*
EMP: 5
SALES: 300K **Privately Held**
SIC: 3599 Machine shop, jobbing & repair

(G-11975)
RUS INDUSTRIES INC
3255 Lockport Rd (14305-2398)
PHONE....................................716 284-7828
Alice G Carlson, *Ch of Bd*
James A Ryding, *Vice Pres*
Greg Robinson, *VP Sales*
Pat Johnson, *Manager*
Erik Carlson, *Shareholder*
▲ **EMP:** 32
SQ FT: 29,000
SALES (est): 4.8MM **Privately Held**
WEB: www.rusindustries.com
SIC: 3441 3661 Fabricated structural
metal; communication headgear, tele-
phone

(G-11976)
SAINT GOBAIN GRAINS & POWDERS
6600 Walmore Rd (14304-1638)
PHONE....................................716 731-8200
Tom Vincent, *Principal*
▲ **EMP:** 1000
SALES (est): 74.7MM
SALES (corp-wide): 215.9MM **Privately
Held**
SIC: 3269 2891 3221 Laboratory & indus-
trial pottery; chemical porcelain; adhe-
sives; adhesives, plastic; cement, except
linoleum & tile; epoxy adhesives; food
containers, glass
HQ: Saint-Gobain Corporation
20 Moores Rd
Malvern PA 19355

(G-11977)
SAINT-GBAIN ADVNCED CRMICS LLC (HQ)
Also Called: Structural Ceramics Division
23 Acheson Dr (14303-1555)
PHONE....................................716 278-6066

Ron Lambright, *CEO*
Jean Louis Beffa, *Ch of Bd*
Curtis Schmit, *General Mgr*
Diana Tierney, *Human Res Mgr*
▲ **EMP:** 150
SQ FT: 1,064
SALES (est): 29.2MM
SALES (corp-wide): 215.9MM **Privately Held**
WEB: www.hexoloy.com
SIC: 3269 Laboratory & industrial pottery
PA: Compagnie De Saint-Gobain
Les Miroirs La Defense 3
Courbevoie 92400
140 880-316

(G-11978)
SAINT-GOBAIN DYNAMICS INC
Also Called: Structural Ceramics Group
23 Acheson Dr (14303-1555)
PHONE..............................716 278-6007
Curtis M Schmit, *President*
EMP: 10
SALES (est): 1MM **Privately Held**
SIC: 3297 Nonclay refractories

(G-11979)
SAINT-GOBAIN STRL CERAMICS
23 Acheson Dr (14303-1555)
PHONE..............................716 278-6233
John T Crowe, *CEO*
◆ **EMP:** 1714
SALES (est): 139.8MM
SALES (corp-wide): 215.9MM **Privately Held**
SIC: 3255 Brick, clay refractory
HQ: Saint-Gobain Corporation
20 Moores Rd
Malvern PA 19355

(G-11980)
SHIPMAN PRINTING INDS INC (PA)
Also Called: Shipman Print Solutions
2424 Niagara Falls Blvd (14304-4562)
P.O. Box 357 (14304-0357)
PHONE..............................716 504-7700
Gary Blum, *Ch of Bd*
Richard Faiola, *Exec VP*
Randy Duncan, *Vice Pres*
Michael Fiore, *Vice Pres*
EMP: 22 **EST:** 1905
SQ FT: 20,000
SALES (est): 3MM **Privately Held**
WEB: www.shipmanprint.com
SIC: 2752 2789 2759 Commercial printing, offset; bookbinding & related work; envelopes; printing

(G-11981)
SILIPOS HOLDING LLC (PA)
7049 Williams Rd (14304-3731)
PHONE..............................716 283-0700
Richard Margolis, *President*
Thomas Bickelman, *QC Mgr*
◆ **EMP:** 7 **EST:** 2015
SQ FT: 35,000
SALES (est): 34.6MM **Privately Held**
SIC: 3842 Surgical appliances & supplies

(G-11982)
STEPHENSON CUSTOM CASE COMPANY
Also Called: Portequip Work Stations
1623 Military Rd (14304-1745)
PHONE..............................905 542-8762
John Stephenson, *Owner*
EMP: 30
SALES: 950K **Privately Held**
SIC: 3949 Sporting & athletic goods

(G-11983)
SWISSMAR INC
6391 Walmore Rd (14304-1613)
PHONE..............................905 764-1121
Daniel Oehy, *President*
George Hobson, *VP Finance*
EMP: 8 **EST:** 1990
SQ FT: 15,000
SALES (est): 917.4K **Privately Held**
SIC: 3262 5719 China cookware; housewares

(G-11984)
TAM CERAMICS GROUP OF NY LLC
4511 Hyde Park Blvd (14305-1298)
PHONE..............................716 278-9400
George Bilkey, *President*
Mike Chu,
EMP: 62
SQ FT: 3,750
SALES: 30MM **Privately Held**
SIC: 3399 Powder, metal

(G-11985)
TAM CERAMICS LLC
4511 Hyde Park Blvd (14305-1298)
PHONE..............................716 278-9480
Robert Difranco, *Purchasing*
Paul Bernard, *QC Mgr*
Brad McLeod, *Engineer*
Chris Merry, *Controller*
George H Bilkey IV, *Mng Member*
▲ **EMP:** 52
SQ FT: 373,593
SALES (est): 18.1MM **Privately Held**
SIC: 2899 Chemical preparations
PA: All American Holdings, Llc
3714 W End Ave
Nashville TN 37205

(G-11986)
TECMOTIV (USA) INC
1500 James Ave (14305-1222)
PHONE..............................716 282-1211
Arthur Hayden, *President*
Gary Sheedy, *President*
◆ **EMP:** 42
SQ FT: 27,000
SALES (est): 9.8MM **Privately Held**
WEB: www.tecmotiv.com
SIC: 3795 7699 Specialized tank components, military; tank repair

(G-11987)
UNIFRAX CORPORATION
2351 Whirlpool St (14305-2413)
PHONE..............................716 278-3800
Paul Boymel, *Vice Pres*
Michael Kirchner, *Vice Pres*
Paul Viola, *Vice Pres*
Diane Tearce, *Purch Agent*
Adam Cadin, *Engineer*
EMP: 34
SALES (est): 5MM **Privately Held**
SIC: 3296 Mineral wool insulation products

(G-11988)
US DRIVES INC
2221 Niagara Falls Blvd # 41 (14304-5709)
P.O. Box 281 (14304-0281)
PHONE..............................716 731-1606
Kader Laroussi, *President*
Dick Torbenson, *President*
James S Grisante, *Vice Pres*
Paul Wizner, *VP Prdtn*
Theodore G Nuding, *VP Finance*
EMP: 60
SQ FT: 70,000
SALES (est): 9.6MM **Privately Held**
WEB: www.usdrivesinc.com
SIC: 3625 Motor controls, electric

(G-11989)
VIOLA CABINET CORPORATION
Also Called: Viola Construction
4205 Hyde Park Blvd (14305-1709)
PHONE..............................716 284-6327
Pat Viola, *President*
EMP: 6
SQ FT: 3,500
SALES: 1MM **Privately Held**
SIC: 2434 Wood kitchen cabinets

(G-11990)
VISHAY THIN FILM LLC
2160 Liberty Dr (14304-3727)
PHONE..............................716 283-4025
Dr Felix Zandman, *President*
Rachel Corulli, *Purch Mgr*
Robert A Freece, *Treasurer*
William Spires, *Admin Sec*
▲ **EMP:** 154
SQ FT: 33,000

SALES (est): 23.9MM
SALES (corp-wide): 3B **Publicly Held**
SIC: 3676 3861 3577 Electronic resistors; photographic equipment & supplies; computer peripheral equipment
HQ: Dale Vishay Electronics Llc
1122 23rd St
Columbus NE 68601
605 665-9301

(G-11991)
WASHINGTOM MILLS ELEC MNRLS (HQ)
1801 Buffalo Ave (14303-1528)
P.O. Box 423 (14302-0423)
PHONE..............................716 278-6600
Don McLeod, *President*
Anne Williams, *Exec VP*
Donald McLeod, *Vice Pres*
Jef Perry, *Plant Mgr*
Marie Hinds, *Safety Mgr*
◆ **EMP:** 100
SALES (est): 28.2MM
SALES (corp-wide): 175.7MM **Privately Held**
WEB: www.washingtonmills.com
SIC: 3291 2819 Abrasive grains; industrial inorganic chemicals
PA: Washington Mills Group, Inc.
20 N Main St
North Grafton MA 01536
508 839-6511

(G-11992)
YORKVILLE SOUND INC
4625 Witmer Indus Est (14305-1390)
PHONE..............................716 297-2920
Steven Long, *Owner*
Jack Long, *Founder*
Kathy Haney, *Warehouse Mgr*
Betty Vandenbosch, *Credit Staff*
Steve Hendee, *Sales Staff*
▲ **EMP:** 7
SALES (est): 1.3MM **Privately Held**
SIC: 3651 Audio electronic systems

Nichols
Tioga County

(G-11993)
WOODS MACHINE AND TOOL LLC
150 Howell St (13812-2146)
PHONE..............................607 699-3253
Ricky E Woods,
Michael Woods,
Richard Woods,
EMP: 16
SQ FT: 2,400
SALES (est): 1.4MM **Privately Held**
SIC: 3599 Machine shop, jobbing & repair

Niskayuna
Schenectady County

(G-11994)
ADC ACQUISITION COMPANY
Also Called: Automated Dynamics
2 Commerce Park Rd (12309-3545)
PHONE..............................518 377-6471
Robert Langone, *President*
Gabriel Benarroch, *Business Mgr*
Robert Becker, *Opers Staff*
Dave Hauber, *Engineer*
Mike Urbanski, *Enginr/R&D Asst*
▼ **EMP:** 34
SQ FT: 30,000
SALES: 5.7MM
SALES (corp-wide): 3.7B **Privately Held**
WEB: www.automateddynamics.com
SIC: 3083 Thermoplastic laminates: rods, tubes, plates & sheet
HQ: Trelleborg Coated Systems Us, Inc.
715 Railroad Ave
Rutherfordton NC 28139
828 286-9126

(G-11995)
GE GLOBAL RESEARCH
1 Research Cir (12309-1027)
PHONE..............................518 387-5000

Victor R Abate, *Senior VP*
Lawrence Kool, *Vice Pres*
James Biaglow, *Safety Mgr*
Todd Curtis, *Engineer*
Hullas Sehgal, *Engineer*
EMP: 1200 **EST:** 2016
SALES (est): 329.5K
SALES (corp-wide): 121.6B **Publicly Held**
SIC: 3511 8742 Turbines & turbine generator sets; industrial consultant
PA: General Electric Company
41 Farnsworth St
Boston MA 02210
617 443-3000

(G-11996)
GENERAL ELECTRIC COMPANY
2690 Balltown Rd Bldg 600 (12309-1004)
PHONE..............................518 385-7620
Doug Wood, *Branch Mgr*
EMP: 50
SALES (corp-wide): 121.6B **Publicly Held**
SIC: 3511 3612 3724 Steam turbines; gas turbines, mechanical drive; autotransformers, electric (power transformers); research & development on aircraft engines & parts
PA: General Electric Company
41 Farnsworth St
Boston MA 02210
617 443-3000

Norfolk
St. Lawrence County

(G-11997)
APC PAPER COMPANY INC
100 Remington Ave (13667-4136)
P.O. Box 756 (13667-0756)
PHONE..............................315 384-4225
Al Ames, *Manager*
EMP: 55 **Privately Held**
WEB: www.apcpaper.com
SIC: 2621 4953 2674 2611 Kraft paper; refuse systems; bags: uncoated paper & multiwall; pulp mills
PA: Apc Paper Company, Inc.
130 Sullivan St
Claremont NH 03743

(G-11998)
CRANESVILLE BLOCK CO INC
Also Called: Cranesville Concrete
8405 State Highway 56 (13667-4221)
PHONE..............................315 384-4000
Randy Braul, *Manager*
EMP: 6
SALES (corp-wide): 45MM **Privately Held**
SIC: 3273 5211 Ready-mixed concrete; masonry materials & supplies
PA: Cranesville Block Co., Inc.
1250 Riverfront Ctr
Amsterdam NY 12010
518 684-6154

(G-11999)
LENCORE ACOUSTICS CORP
1 S Main St (13667-3111)
P.O. Box 616 (13667-0616)
PHONE..............................315 384-9114
Brian Leonard, *Branch Mgr*
EMP: 10
SALES (corp-wide): 6.1MM **Privately Held**
WEB: www.lencore.com
SIC: 3296 Acoustical board & tile, mineral wool
PA: Lencore Acoustics Corp.
1 Crossways Park Dr W
Woodbury NY 11797
516 682-9292

(G-12000)
NORTHERN MACHINING INC
2a N Main St (13667-4154)
PHONE..............................315 384-3189
Ted Ashley, *President*
Kathie Ashley, *Vice Pres*
EMP: 10
SQ FT: 7,000

SALES: 1.1MM **Privately Held**
WEB: www.northernmachininginc.com
SIC: 3599 Machine shop, jobbing & repair

North Babylon
Suffolk County

(G-12001)
GO BLUE TECHNOLOGIES LTD
325 August Rd (11703-1014)
PHONE..................................631 404-6285
Carlo Drago, *CEO*
EMP: 1
SALES: 1MM **Privately Held**
SIC: 3624 3842 Carbon & graphite products; gas masks

(G-12002)
QUALITY FUEL 1 CORPORATION
Also Called: BP
1235 Deer Park Ave (11703-3112)
PHONE..................................631 392-4090
EMP: 5
SALES (est): 598.3K **Privately Held**
SIC: 2869 Fuels

North Baldwin
Nassau County

(G-12003)
CHRONICLES SYSTEMS INC
840 Newton Ave (11510-2825)
PHONE..................................516 992-2553
Newton Charles, *President*
EMP: 5
SQ FT: 100
SALES: 60K **Privately Held**
SIC: 7372 Prepackaged software

(G-12004)
DURA SPEC INC
Also Called: Jamaica Electroplating
1239 Village Ct (11510-1138)
PHONE..................................718 526-3053
Fax: 718 657-8867
EMP: 18
SQ FT: 5,000
SALES (est): 1.5MM **Privately Held**
SIC: 3471 Electroplating Of Metals

(G-12005)
GENESIS MACHINING CORP
725 Brooklyn Ave (11510-2708)
PHONE..................................516 377-1197
Michael A Chin, *President*
EMP: 12
SQ FT: 4,000
SALES (est): 1.9MM **Privately Held**
SIC: 3599 Machine shop, jobbing & repair

(G-12006)
HUBRAY INC
Also Called: Stu-Art Supplies
2045 Grand Ave (11510-2915)
PHONE..................................800 645-2855
Lisa Hubley, *President*
Andrew Ray, *Vice Pres*
EMP: 12
SQ FT: 10,000
SALES: 1MM **Privately Held**
WEB: www.stu-artsupplies.com
SIC: 2675 2499 5961 Panels, cardboard, die-cut: made from purchased materials; picture & mirror frames, wood; mail order house

(G-12007)
SANDY DUFTLER DESIGNS LTD
775 Brooklyn Ave Ste 105 (11510-2948)
PHONE..................................516 379-3084
Irwin Duftler, *CEO*
Sandra Duftler, *Ch of Bd*
Gregg Duftler, *President*
EMP: 12
SALES (est): 1.2MM **Privately Held**
SIC: 2387 Apparel belts

(G-12008)
SPLIT SYSTEMS CORP (PA)
Also Called: Johnson Contrls Authorized Dlr
1593 Grand Ave (11510-1849)
PHONE..................................516 223-5511
Charles Solon, *President*
Mike Solon, *Vice Pres*
EMP: 21
SALES (est): 1.5MM **Privately Held**
SIC: 3585 5075 Air conditioning equipment, complete; refrigeration equipment, complete; warm air heating & air conditioning

(G-12009)
SWIRL BLISS LLC
1777 Grand Ave (11510-2429)
PHONE..................................516 867-9475
Jeanette Reed,
EMP: 5 EST: 2013
SALES (est): 331.9K **Privately Held**
SIC: 2024 Yogurt desserts, frozen

(G-12010)
V C N GROUP LTD INC
1 Clifton St (11510-2114)
PHONE..................................516 223-4812
Florence Abate, *President*
Vincent Abate, *Vice Pres*
Anthony Abate, *Admin Sec*
EMP: 5
SQ FT: 500
SALES (est): 523.6K **Privately Held**
SIC: 2752 Advertising posters, lithographed

(G-12011)
VORTEX VENTURES INC
857 Newton Ave (11510-2826)
PHONE..................................516 946-8345
Kevin Walters, *President*
EMP: 5
SALES (est): 193.4K **Privately Held**
SIC: 7372 7389 Publishers' computer software;

(G-12012)
W & B MAZZA & SONS INC
Also Called: Mazza Co, The
2145 Marion Pl (11510-2921)
PHONE..................................516 379-4130
William Mazza Sr, *President*
William Mazza Jr, *Treasurer*
Steven Mazza, *VP Mktg*
Jeffrey Mazza, *Admin Sec*
EMP: 28
SQ FT: 8,000
SALES (est): 3MM **Privately Held**
WEB: www.mazzajewelry.com
SIC: 3911 Rings, finger: precious metal

North Bellmore
Nassau County

(G-12013)
21ST CENTURY FINISHES INC
1353 Newbridge Rd Unit A (11710-1661)
P.O. Box 471, Bellmore (11710-0471)
PHONE..................................516 221-7000
Al Doerbecker, *President*
EMP: 15
SALES (est): 1.4MM **Privately Held**
SIC: 3471 Plating of metals or formed products

(G-12014)
CAPITOL RESTORATION CORP
2473 Belmond Ave (11710-1205)
PHONE..................................516 783-1425
Seeme Rizvi, *President*
EMP: 6
SALES (est): 672.2K **Privately Held**
SIC: 3297 1771 1521 Brick refractories; concrete repair; new construction, single-family houses

(G-12015)
CHANGDU TECHNOLOGY (USA) CO
1417 Horseshoe Dr (11710-2458)
PHONE..................................917 340-1976
Chunlan Wang, *President*
Kevin Qiu, *Manager*

EMP: 15
SALES: 1MM **Privately Held**
SIC: 2731 Book publishing

(G-12016)
COSTANZA READY MIX INC
1345 Newbridge Rd (11710-1629)
PHONE..................................516 783-4444
Frank Costanza, *President*
EMP: 5
SALES (est): 540.3K **Privately Held**
SIC: 3273 Ready-mixed concrete

(G-12017)
CUPCAKE CONTESSAS CORPORATION
1242 Julia Ln (11710-1925)
PHONE..................................516 307-1222
Laura Andreacchi, *Chairman*
EMP: 6
SALES (est): 412K **Privately Held**
SIC: 2051 Cakes, bakery: except frozen

(G-12018)
CUSTOM DISPLAY MANUFACTURE
1686 Logan St (11710-2528)
PHONE..................................516 783-6491
Paul Kassbaum, *President*
EMP: 5
SQ FT: 8,000
SALES (est): 440K **Privately Held**
SIC: 2511 3993 Chairs, household, except upholstered: wood; signs & advertising specialties

(G-12019)
GEORGE BASCH CO INC
1554 Peapond Rd (11710-2925)
P.O. Box 188, Freeport (11520-0188)
PHONE..................................516 378-8100
Laurie Basch-Levy, *President*
Mildred Basch, *Treasurer*
Rhonda Ax, *Admin Sec*
EMP: 10 EST: 1929
SQ FT: 6,800
SALES (est): 1MM **Privately Held**
WEB: www.nevrdull.com
SIC: 2842 Cleaning or polishing preparations

(G-12020)
KP INDUSTRIES INC
Also Called: K P Signs
2481 Charles Ct Ste 1 (11710-2761)
P.O. Box 1000, Bethpage (11714-0019)
PHONE..................................516 679-3161
EMP: 11 EST: 1997
SQ FT: 3,600
SALES (est): 1.5MM **Privately Held**
SIC: 3993 Mfg Signs & Advertising Specialties

North Chili
Monroe County

(G-12021)
ALBERT GATES INC
3434 Union St (14514-9731)
PHONE..................................585 594-9401
Andrew J Laniak, *Ch of Bd*
Robert J Brinkman, *President*
Dan Ferries, *General Mgr*
James Adams, *Vice Pres*
Erica Mayes, *Human Resources*
EMP: 75
SQ FT: 26,000
SALES: 17.4MM
SALES (corp-wide): 99.2MM **Privately Held**
WEB: www.gatesalbert.com
SIC: 3451 Screw machine products
PA: Brinkman International Group, Inc.
167 Ames St
Rochester NY 14611
585 429-5000

(G-12022)
P TOOL & DIE CO INC
3535 Union St (14514-9709)
P.O. Box 369 (14514-0369)
PHONE..................................585 889-1340
Michael J Sucese, *President*

John Hall, *Project Mgr*
EMP: 22
SQ FT: 18,000
SALES (est): 4.6MM **Privately Held**
SIC: 3544 Special dies & tools

North Collins
Erie County

(G-12023)
AMERICAN WIRE TIE INC (PA)
2073 Franklin St (14111-9636)
P.O. Box 696 (14111-0696)
PHONE..................................716 337-2412
James W Smith, *President*
Leslie Oleary, *Sales Staff*
Amelia Jarzynski, *Sales Associate*
Gregory C Mumbach, *Admin Sec*
▲ EMP: 30
SQ FT: 54,000
SALES (est): 12.4MM **Privately Held**
WEB: www.americanwiretie.com
SIC: 3599 3496 3315 2631 Ties, form: metal; miscellaneous fabricated wire products; steel wire & related products; paperboard mills

(G-12024)
CRESCENT MARKETING INC (PA)
Also Called: Crescent Manufacturing
10285 Eagle Dr (14111)
P.O. Box 1500 (14111-1500)
PHONE..................................716 337-0145
Richard Frazer Jr, *President*
Rick Taber, *Plant Mgr*
Karen Frazer, *CFO*
▲ EMP: 123
SQ FT: 110,000
SALES (est): 36.6MM **Privately Held**
SIC: 2842 Specialty cleaning preparations

(G-12025)
E & D SPECIALTY STANDS INC
2081 Franklin St (14111-9636)
P.O. Box 700 (14111-0700)
PHONE..................................716 337-0161
David A Metzger, *President*
Gerald Paul Sullivan, *Purch Mgr*
Dean Metzger, *CFO*
Charlene Heppel, *Controller*
John Williams, *Sales Mgr*
EMP: 50 EST: 1956
SQ FT: 85,000
SALES (est): 9MM **Privately Held**
WEB: www.edstands.com
SIC: 2531 Bleacher seating, portable

(G-12026)
NITRO MANUFACTURING LLC
440 Shirley Rd (14111)
PHONE..................................716 646-9900
Christine Frascella, *Mng Member*
Tim Frascella,
William Frascella,
Dave Kota,
EMP: 5
SALES (est): 630.1K **Privately Held**
SIC: 3599 Machine shop, jobbing & repair

(G-12027)
NITRO WHEELS INC
4440 Shirley Rd (14111-9783)
PHONE..................................716 337-0709
Louis Frascella, *Principal*
EMP: 10
SALES (est): 1MM **Privately Held**
SIC: 3312 Wheels, locomotive & car: iron & steel

(G-12028)
RENALDOS SALES & SERVICE CTR
1770 Milestrip Rd (14111-9753)
P.O. Box 820 (14111-0820)
PHONE..................................716 337-3760
James V Renaldo, *President*
Joan E Renaldo, *Vice Pres*
EMP: 8
SQ FT: 3,800

SALES: 4.8MM **Privately Held**
SIC: **3523** 3713 Trailers & wagons, farm; planting machines, agricultural; truck bodies (motor vehicles)

(G-12029)
TIMBERBUILT INC
10821 Schaffstall Dr (14111)
P.O. Box 940 (14111-0940)
PHONE..............................716 337-0012
George Klemens, *President*
Kathryn Armbruster, *Office Mgr*
EMP: 10
SQ FT: 10,200
SALES (est): 1.4MM **Privately Held**
WEB: www.timberbuilt.com
SIC: **2452** Log cabins, prefabricated, wood

(G-12030)
WINTERS RAILROAD SERVICE INC
11309 Sisson Hwy (14111-9729)
PHONE..............................716 337-2668
David Winter, *President*
Michael Winter, *Corp Secy*
EMP: 6
SQ FT: 15,000
SALES: 530K **Privately Held**
SIC: **3423** 3441 Hand & edge tools; fabricated structural metal

North Creek
Warren County

(G-12031)
CREATIVE STAGE LIGHTING CO INC
Also Called: C S L
149 State Route 28n (12853-2707)
P.O. Box 567 (12853-0567)
PHONE..............................518 251-3302
George B Studnicky III, *President*
Julie Allen, *Purch Agent*
Jason Lemery, *CFO*
Ashley Oconnor, *Sales Staff*
Lily Studnicky, *Admin Sec*
◆ **EMP:** 43
SQ FT: 32,000
SALES: 8MM **Privately Held**
WEB: www.creativestagelighting.com
SIC: **3648** 5063 7922 Lighting equipment; lighting fixtures, commercial & industrial; lighting, theatrical

North Java
Wyoming County

(G-12032)
SELECT INTERIOR DOOR LTD
Also Called: Select Door
2074 Perry Rd (14113-9722)
P.O. Box 178 (14113-0178)
PHONE..............................585 535-9900
John Angelbeck, *President*
John Bochiechio, *Prdtn Mgr*
Maureen Ronan, *CFO*
EMP: 40
SQ FT: 25,000
SALES (est): 5.7MM **Privately Held**
WEB: www.sidl.com
SIC: **2431** 3231 Doors, wood; products of purchased glass

North Lawrence
St. Lawrence County

(G-12033)
UPSTATE NIAGARA COOP INC
Also Called: North Country Dairy
22 County Route 52 (12967-9539)
PHONE..............................315 389-5111
Tim Gominiack, *Branch Mgr*
EMP: 59
SALES (corp-wide): 903.7MM **Privately Held**
SIC: **2026** Milk & cream, except fermented, cultured & flavored

PA: Upstate Niagara Cooperative, Inc.
25 Anderson Rd
Buffalo NY 14225
716 892-3156

North Rose
Wayne County

(G-12034)
FLEISCHMANNS VINEGAR CO INC
Also Called: Fleischman Vinegar
4754 State Route 414 (14516-9704)
PHONE..............................315 587-4414
John Wilson, *Manager*
EMP: 20 **Privately Held**
WEB: www.breadworld.com
SIC: **2099** Vinegar
HQ: Fleischmann's Vinegar Company, Inc.
12604 Hiddencreek Way A
Cerritos CA 90703
562 483-4619

(G-12035)
GARGRAVES TRACKAGE CORPORATION
Also Called: Gardner The Train Doctor
8967 Ridge Rd (14516-9753)
PHONE..............................315 483-6577
Michael Roder, *President*
Thomas Roder, *Vice Pres*
EMP: 6
SQ FT: 5,000
SALES: 500K **Privately Held**
WEB: www.gargraves.com
SIC: **3944** 5945 Trains & equipment, toy: electric & mechanical; hobby, toy & game shops

(G-12036)
OLMSTEAD MACHINE INC
10399 Warehouse Ave (14516-9537)
P.O. Box 331 (14516-0331)
PHONE..............................315 587-9864
Dale Liechti, *President*
EMP: 10
SQ FT: 10,000
SALES (est): 1.5MM **Privately Held**
SIC: **3599** Machine shop, jobbing & repair

North Salem
Westchester County

(G-12037)
TOTAL ENERGY FABRICATION CORP
2 Hardscrabble Rd (10560-1014)
PHONE..............................580 363-1500
Robert Armentano, *CEO*
Gary Harvey, *Principal*
Frank Kovacs, *Principal*
▲ **EMP:** 6
SALES (est): 1.3MM **Privately Held**
SIC: **3491** Pressure valves & regulators, industrial

North Syracuse
Onondaga County

(G-12038)
CLEANROOM SYSTEMS INC
7000 Performance Dr (13212-3439)
PHONE..............................315 452-7400
Larry Wetzel, *President*
Bruce Meissner, *Engineer*
Deb Emery, *CFO*
Michael Wetzel, *Human Resources*
EMP: 41
SQ FT: 48,378
SALES (est): 211.1K
SALES (corp-wide): 9.1MM **Privately Held**
WEB: www.cleanroomsystems.com
SIC: **3585** Refrigeration equipment, complete

PA: Air Innovations, Inc.
7000 Performance Dr
North Syracuse NY 13212
315 452-7400

(G-12039)
DISPLAYS BY RIOUX INC
6090 E Taft Rd (13212-3303)
PHONE..............................315 458-3639
EMP: 7
SQ FT: 12,200
SALES (est): 875.2K **Privately Held**
SIC: **3083** 3089 Mfg Laminated Plastic Plate/Sheet Mfg Plastic Products

(G-12040)
DL MANUFACTURING INC
340 Gateway Park Dr (13212-3758)
PHONE..............................315 432-8977
Donald L Metz, *Ch of Bd*
EMP: 30
SQ FT: 22,000
SALES: 12MM **Privately Held**
WEB: www.dlmanufacturing.com
SIC: **3537** 5084 5031 5075 Loading docks: portable, adjustable & hydraulic; industrial machinery & equipment; doors; ventilating equipment & supplies

(G-12041)
G A BRAUN INC (PA)
79 General Irwin Blvd (13212-5279)
P.O. Box 3029, Syracuse (13220-3029)
PHONE..............................315 475-3123
JB Werner, *Ch of Bd*
Joe Gudenburr, *President*
David Welsh, *General Mgr*
David Clark, *Vice Pres*
Vito Petrera, *Plant Mgr*
▲ **EMP:** 150
SQ FT: 75,000
SALES (est): 45.7MM **Privately Held**
WEB: www.gabraun.com
SIC: **3582** 5087 Washing machines, laundry: commercial, incl. coin-operated; laundry equipment & supplies

(G-12042)
GAYLORD BROS INC
Also Called: Gaylord Archival
7282 William Barry Blvd (13212-3347)
P.O. Box 4901, Syracuse (13221-4901)
PHONE..............................315 457-5070
R Keith George, *CEO*
Keith George, *President*
Joseph Faiola, *Finance*
Paul Randall, *Sales Mgr*
Mary Rake, *Cust Mgr*
▼ **EMP:** 65
SQ FT: 80,000
SALES (est): 17.9MM
SALES (corp-wide): 115.2MM **Privately Held**
WEB: www.gaylord.com
SIC: **2679** 2657 2542 Adding machine rolls, paper: made from purchased material; folding paperboard boxes; fixtures: display, office or store: except wood
PA: Demco, Inc.
4810 Forest Run Rd
Madison WI 53704
800 356-1200

(G-12043)
GEDDES BAKERY CO INC
421 S Main St (13212-2800)
PHONE..............................315 437-8084
Vasilios Pappas, *President*
Michele Cousineau, *Sales Mgr*
EMP: 24
SQ FT: 5,600
SALES (est): 3.3MM **Privately Held**
WEB: www.geddesbakery.com
SIC: **2051** 5461 Bakery: wholesale or wholesale/retail combined; bakeries

(G-12044)
GRYPHON SENSORS LLC
5801 E Taft Rd (13212-3291)
PHONE..............................315 452-8882
Anthony Albanese, *President*
Michael Pecoraro, *Engineer*
EMP: 15
SQ FT: 1,000

SALES: 2.9MM **Privately Held**
SIC: **3812** Antennas, radar or communications

(G-12045)
ICM CONTROLS CORP
7313 William Barry Blvd (13212-3384)
PHONE..............................315 233-5266
Hassan B Kadah, *Ch of Bd*
Andrew Kadah, *President*
Laurie Kadah, *Treasurer*
▲ **EMP:** 18
SALES (est): 3.2MM
SALES (corp-wide): 50MM **Privately Held**
SIC: **3625** Electric controls & control accessories, industrial
PA: International Controls & Measurements Corp.
7313 William Barry Blvd
North Syracuse NY 13212
315 233-5266

(G-12046)
INTERNTNAL CNTRLS MSRMNTS CORP (PA)
Also Called: ICM
7313 William Barry Blvd (13212-3384)
PHONE..............................315 233-5266
Hassan B Kadah, *Ch of Bd*
Andrew Kadah, *President*
Laurie Kadah, *Treasurer*
▲ **EMP:** 194
SQ FT: 85,000
SALES: 50MM **Privately Held**
WEB: www.icmcontrols.com
SIC: **3625** Electric controls & control accessories, industrial

(G-12047)
JADAK TECHNOLOGIES INC
7279 William Barry Blvd (13212-3349)
PHONE..............................315 701-0678
Janie Goddard, *President*
Jennifer Cruse, *Purch Mgr*
Jennifer Salisbury, *Buyer*
James Bowden, *QC Mgr*
Colleen Hurley, *QC Mgr*
EMP: 165
SALES (est): 28.3MM **Publicly Held**
WEB: www.jadaktech.com
SIC: **3577** Bar code (magnetic ink) printers
HQ: Novanta Corporation
125 Middlesex Tpke
Bedford MA 01730
781 266-5700

(G-12048)
NORTHERN READY MIX LLC (HQ)
6131 E Taft Rd (13212-2525)
P.O. Box 420, Fulton (13069-0420)
PHONE..............................315 336-7900
Joseph F Riccelli, *CEO*
Richard J Riccelli Sr, *President*
EMP: 15
SALES (est): 5.2MM **Privately Held**
WEB: www.northerncompanies.com
SIC: **3273** Ready-mixed concrete

(G-12049)
SRC VENTURES INC (HQ)
7502 Round Pond Rd (13212-2558)
PHONE..............................315 452-8000
Paul Tremont, *Chairman*
Mary Pat Hartnett, *Admin Sec*
EMP: 161
SALES (est): 4MM
SALES (corp-wide): 141.4MM **Privately Held**
SIC: **3812** Antennas, radar or communications
PA: Src, Inc.
7502 Round Pond Rd
North Syracuse NY 13212
315 452-8000

North Tonawanda
Niagara County

(G-12050)
369 RIVER ROAD INC
369 River Rd (14120-7108)
PHONE................................716 694-5001
Michael Deakin, *President*
EMP: 25
SQ FT: 25,000
SALES (est): 1MM **Privately Held**
SIC: 3496 Miscellaneous fabricated wire products

(G-12051)
AMERI-CUT TOOL GRINDING INC
Also Called: Superior Tool Company
1020 Oliver St (14120-2710)
PHONE................................716 692-3900
Todd Brosius Jr, *President*
EMP: 5
SQ FT: 10,000
SALES: 500K **Privately Held**
WEB: www.superiortoolllc.com
SIC: 3545 Cutting tools for machine tools

(G-12052)
AN-COR INDUSTRIAL PLASTICS INC
900 Niagara Falls Blvd (14120-2096)
PHONE................................716 695-3141
Merrill W Arthur, *President*
Norman Hirschey, *Engineer*
Kevin Sweeney, *Design Engr*
Paul Biondi, *CFO*
Ronald Hughes, *Sales Mgr*
EMP: 83
SQ FT: 96,000
SALES (est): 22.9MM **Privately Held**
WEB: www.an-cor.com
SIC: 3089 3088 Plastic & fiberglass tanks; plastics plumbing fixtures

(G-12053)
ARMSTRONG PUMPS INC
93 East Ave (14120-6594)
PHONE................................716 693-8813
J A C Armstrong, *CEO*
Bruce Van Nus, *Managing Dir*
Niall Murphy, *Opers Staff*
Robert Pettitt, *Engineer*
Cathy Yanulevich, *Accountant*
◆ **EMP:** 100 **EST:** 1966
SQ FT: 150,000
SALES (est): 48.6MM
SALES (corp-wide): 561.7MM **Privately Held**
WEB: www.armstrongpumps.com
SIC: 3561 Industrial pumps & parts
PA: S. A. Armstrong Limited
23 Bertrand Ave
Scarborough ON M1L 2
416 755-2291

(G-12054)
ASCENSION INDUSTRIES INC (PA)
1254 Erie Ave (14120-3036)
PHONE................................716 693-9381
Jack Kopczynski Jr, *Ch of Bd*
Donald Naab, *President*
Jim Brodzik, *Foreman/Supr*
Paul Keefe, *Buyer*
Daniel Meyers, *Engineer*
▲ **EMP:** 120 **EST:** 2000
SQ FT: 140,000
SALES (est): 27.3MM **Privately Held**
WEB: www.asmfab.com
SIC: 3544 3541 3444 Special dies, tools, jigs & fixtures; machine tools, metal cutting type; sheet metalwork

(G-12055)
AUDUBON MACHINERY CORPORATION (PA)
Also Called: Oxygen Generating Systems Intl
814 Wurlitzer Dr (14120-3042)
PHONE................................716 564-5165
Joseph M McMahon, *President*
Robert Schlehr, *Vice Pres*
Timothy Blach, *CFO*
◆ **EMP:** 60
SQ FT: 40,000
SALES (est): 24.4MM **Privately Held**
WEB: www.ogsi.com
SIC: 3569 Gas producers, generators & other gas related equipment

(G-12056)
BAKER TOOL & DIE
48 Industrial Dr (14120-3244)
PHONE................................716 694-2025
Jon C Olstad, *President*
EMP: 8
SALES (est): 690K **Privately Held**
SIC: 3312 Blast furnaces & steel mills

(G-12057)
BAKER TOOL & DIE & DIE
48 Industrial Dr (14120-3244)
PHONE................................716 694-2025
Jon C Olstad, *President*
EMP: 6
SQ FT: 6,000
SALES (est): 480K **Privately Held**
SIC: 3312 Tool & die steel

(G-12058)
BATTENFELD GREASE OIL CORP NY
1174 Erie Ave (14120-3036)
P.O. Box 728 (14120-0728)
PHONE................................716 695-2100
Barbara A Bellanti, *Ch of Bd*
John A Bellanti, *President*
▲ **EMP:** 39
SALES (est): 11.8MM **Privately Held**
SIC: 2992 Oils & greases, blending & compounding

(G-12059)
BROADWAY KNITTING MILLS INC
1333 Strad Ave Ste 216 (14120-3061)
PHONE................................716 692-4421
Craig Boyce, *President*
Russell Boyce, *Vice Pres*
Susan Boyce, *Treasurer*
Molly Boyce, *Admin Sec*
EMP: 5 **EST:** 1932
SQ FT: 8,400
SALES (est): 210K **Privately Held**
WEB: www.broadwayknitting.com
SIC: 2329 5611 2326 Jackets (suede, leatherette, etc.), sport: men's & boys'; clothing accessories: men's & boys'; men's & boys' work clothing

(G-12060)
BUFFALO ABRASIVES INC (HQ)
960 Erie Ave (14120-3503)
PHONE................................716 693-3856
Jeffrey J Binkley, *CEO*
Tim Wagner, *Vice Pres*
Frank Pawlik, *Safety Mgr*
Sally Bradley, *Technical Staff*
Dave Herman, *Maintence Staff*
▲ **EMP:** 45
SQ FT: 65,000
SALES (est): 11.9MM **Privately Held**
WEB: www.buffaloabrasives.com
SIC: 3291 Abrasive products

(G-12061)
CALGON CARBON CORPORATION
830 River Rd (14120-6557)
PHONE................................716 531-9113
EMP: 9
SALES (est): 1.2MM **Privately Held**
SIC: 2819 Charcoal (carbon), activated

(G-12062)
COMMERCIAL FABRICS INC
908 Niagara Falls Blvd (14120-2019)
PHONE................................716 694-0641
Michel Senecal, *President*
James Senecal, *Corp Secy*
EMP: 15
SQ FT: 30,000
SALES (est): 1.7MM **Privately Held**
WEB: www.commercialfabrics.com
SIC: 3999 Hot tub & spa covers

(G-12063)
CONFER PLASTICS INC
97 Witmer Rd (14120-2421)
PHONE................................800 635-3213
Douglas C Confer, *President*
Bob Confer, *Vice Pres*
Cliff Hoover, *QC Mgr*
Frank Fedele, *CFO*
Mike Confer, *Human Res Dir*
◆ **EMP:** 130 **EST:** 1973
SQ FT: 100,000
SALES (est): 37.1MM **Privately Held**
WEB: www.conferladders.com
SIC: 3089 Blow molded finished plastic products

(G-12064)
COOPERSURGICAL INC
825 Wurlitzer Dr (14120-3041)
PHONE................................716 693-6230
Jennifer Gates, *Branch Mgr*
EMP: 17
SALES (corp-wide): 2.5B **Publicly Held**
WEB: www.barrlabs.com
SIC: 2834 Pharmaceutical preparations
HQ: Coopersurgical, Inc.
95 Corporate Dr
Trumbull CT 06611

(G-12065)
DMIC INC
Also Called: Delaware Manufacturing Inds
3776 Commerce Ct (14120-2024)
PHONE................................716 743-4360
Chuck Wolski, *Principal*
EMP: 9
SALES (est): 1.3MM **Privately Held**
SIC: 3492 3714 Fluid power valves for aircraft; motor vehicle parts & accessories

(G-12066)
EXPEDIENT HEAT TREATING CORP
61 Dale Dr (14120-4201)
PHONE................................716 433-1177
Paul Waild, *President*
EMP: 5 **EST:** 1979
SQ FT: 2,000
SALES (est): 400K **Privately Held**
SIC: 3398 Metal heat treating

(G-12067)
FEI PRODUCTS LLC (PA)
825 Wurlitzer Dr (14120-3041)
PHONE................................716 693-6230
Charles S Craig, *President*
Paul Wasielewski, *Opers Staff*
EMP: 35
SQ FT: 23,500
SALES (est): 5.2MM **Privately Held**
SIC: 3089 Plastic processing

(G-12068)
FREY CONCRETE INC
Also Called: Frey Sand & Gravel
3949 Frest Pk Way Ste 400 (14120)
PHONE................................716 213-5832
Martin L Segarra, *President*
EMP: 9
SALES (est): 1MM **Privately Held**
SIC: 3273 Ready-mixed concrete

(G-12069)
GARDEI INDUSTRIES LLC (PA)
Also Called: F K Williams Division
1087 Erie Ave (14120-3532)
PHONE................................716 693-7100
Lori Ferraraccio, *Mng Member*
Jordon Lizy,
▲ **EMP:** 17 **EST:** 1936
SQ FT: 25,000
SALES (est): 1.6MM **Privately Held**
WEB: www.gardei.net
SIC: 2679 3545 Paper products, converted; machine tool accessories

(G-12070)
GLI-DEX SALES CORP
Also Called: Glidden Machine & Tool
855 Wurlitzer Dr (14120-3041)
PHONE................................716 692-6501
James Gerace, *President*
Robert Gerace, *Vice Pres*
Marcia Gerace, *Treasurer*
EMP: 35 **EST:** 1946
SQ FT: 12,000
SALES (est): 2.5MM **Privately Held**
WEB: www.glidex.biz
SIC: 3599 Machine shop, jobbing & repair

(G-12071)
GRIFFIN CHEMICAL COMPANY LLC
Also Called: W.O.w Brand Products
889 Erie Ave Ste 1 (14120-3533)
PHONE................................716 693-2465
Gregory Robinson, *Mng Member*
Bernard Zysman,
EMP: 9
SQ FT: 15,000
SALES: 500K **Privately Held**
SIC: 2842 Specialty cleaning preparations

(G-12072)
ISLAND STREET LUMBER CO INC
11 Felton St (14120-6503)
PHONE................................716 692-4127
James Le Blanc, *President*
Joan Le Blanc, *Vice Pres*
EMP: 5
SQ FT: 11,500
SALES (est): 641.1K **Privately Held**
SIC: 2431 5211 Millwork; millwork & lumber

(G-12073)
ISOLATION SYSTEMS INC
889 Erie Ave Ste 1 (14120-3533)
PHONE................................716 694-6390
Ted Arts, *President*
Theodore Arts, *Sales Staff*
EMP: 10
SQ FT: 98,000
SALES (est): 2.3MM **Privately Held**
WEB: www.isolation-systems.com
SIC: 3564 Filters, air: furnaces, air conditioning equipment, etc.

(G-12074)
J RETTENMAIER USA LP
50 Bridge St (14120-6842)
PHONE................................716 693-4040
EMP: 51
SALES (corp-wide): 355.8K **Privately Held**
SIC: 2823 2299 Cellulosic manmade fibers; flock (recovered textile fibers)
HQ: J. Rettenmaier Usa Lp
16369 Us Highway 131 S
Schoolcraft MI 49087
269 679-2340

(G-12075)
J RETTENMAIER USA LP
4 Detroit St (14120)
PHONE................................716 693-4009
Jit Ang, *Exec VP*
Jerry Bianchi, *Manager*
EMP: 58
SALES (corp-wide): 355.8K **Privately Held**
WEB: www.ifcfiber.com
SIC: 2023 2299 2823 Dry, condensed, evaporated dairy products; flock (recovered textile fibers); cellulosic manmade fibers
HQ: J. Rettenmaier Usa Lp
16369 Us Highway 131 S
Schoolcraft MI 49087
269 679-2340

(G-12076)
L & S METALS INC
111 Witmer Rd (14120-2443)
PHONE................................716 692-6865
Gary Schade, *President*
EMP: 23
SQ FT: 17,000
SALES (est): 4MM **Privately Held**
WEB: www.ls-metals.com
SIC: 3599 7692 Machine shop, jobbing & repair; welding repair

(G-12077)
LISTON MANUFACTURING INC
421 Payne Ave (14120-6987)
P.O. Box 178 (14120-0178)
PHONE................................716 695-2111
Theodore Pyrak, *Ch of Bd*
Joseph Laduca, *Vice Pres*

Russell Laduca, *Vice Pres*
Charles E Pyrak, *Treasurer*
Edward Pyrak, *Treasurer*
EMP: 50 **EST:** 1954
SQ FT: 60,000
SALES (est): 10.7MM **Privately Held**
WEB: www.listonmfg.com
SIC: 3568 Bearings, bushings & blocks

(G-12078)
MODU-CRAFT INC
337 Payne Ave (14120-7236)
PHONE..................................716 694-0709
Kenneth Babka, *President*
EMP: 7
SALES (corp-wide): 1MM **Privately Held**
SIC: 2599 3821 Factory furniture & fixtures; laboratory furniture
PA: Modu-Craft Inc
      276 Creekside Dr
      Tonawanda NY 14150
      716 694-0709

(G-12079)
NIAGARA SHEETS LLC
7393 Shawnee Rd (14120-1325)
PHONE..................................716 692-1129
John Bolender, *President*
Skip Polowy, *Vice Pres*
Jeff Gebauer, *Prdtn Mgr*
Mona Macfarlane, *HR Admin*
James Proefrock, *Database Admin*
▲ **EMP:** 75 **EST:** 2007
SALES (est): 35MM
SALES (corp-wide): 148.3MM **Privately Held**
SIC: 2653 Boxes, corrugated: made from purchased materials
PA: Jamestown Container Corp
      14 Deming Dr
      Falconer NY 14733
      716 665-4623

(G-12080)
OCCIDENTAL CHEMICAL CORP
3780 Commerce Ct Ste 600 (14120-2025)
PHONE..................................716 694-3827
Rose Zenturin, *General Mgr*
EMP: 5
SALES (corp-wide): 18.9B **Publicly Held**
WEB: www.oxychem.com
SIC: 2812 Alkalies & chlorine
HQ: Occidental Chemical Corporation
      14555 Dallas Pkwy Ste 400
      Dallas TX 75254
      972 404-3800

(G-12081)
PELLETS LLC
63 Industrial Dr Ste 3 (14120-3248)
PHONE..................................716 693-1750
Mike Deakin, *President*
Kevin Walters, *Technical Staff*
Kathy Reitz, *Admin Sec*
Kevin Deakin,
▲ **EMP:** 6 **EST:** 1948
SQ FT: 7,500
SALES (est): 938.3K
SALES (corp-wide): 2.6MM **Privately Held**
WEB: www.pelletsllc.com
SIC: 3291 Abrasive metal & steel products
PA: Val-Kro, Inc.
      369 River Rd
      North Tonawanda NY
      716 694-5001

(G-12082)
PIONEER PRINTERS INC
Also Called: Gardei Manufacturing
1087 Erie Ave (14120-3532)
PHONE..................................716 693-7100
Carl Hoover, *CEO*
EMP: 16
SQ FT: 7,000
SALES (est): 2.7MM **Privately Held**
WEB: www.pioneerprinters.com
SIC: 2752 Commercial printing, offset

(G-12083)
PROTOTYPE MANUFACTURING CORP
836 Wurlitzer Dr (14120-3042)
P.O. Box 136 (14120-0136)
PHONE..................................716 695-1700
Richard A Christie, *President*

Timothy G Christie, *Vice Pres*
EMP: 10
SQ FT: 8,000
SALES (est): 1.6MM **Privately Held**
SIC: 3599 Machine shop, jobbing & repair

(G-12084)
RAVE INC
940 River Rd (14120-6555)
PHONE..................................716 695-1110
Albert Bluemle, *President*
EMP: 64
SALES (est): 5.2MM **Privately Held**
SIC: 3999 Education aids, devices & supplies

(G-12085)
RECORD ADVERTISER
435 River Rd (14120-6809)
P.O. Box 668 (14120-0668)
PHONE..................................716 693-1000
Wayne Lowman, *President*
EMP: 40
SALES (est): 1.1MM **Privately Held**
SIC: 2711 Newspapers

(G-12086)
RILEY GEAR CORPORATION
61 Felton St (14120-6598)
PHONE..................................716 694-0900
William Taylor, *Sales Staff*
Donn Neffke, *Manager*
Dan Steinhauser, *Manager*
EMP: 20
SALES (est): 3.5MM
SALES (corp-wide): 28.5MM **Privately Held**
WEB: www.rileygear.com
SIC: 3462 Gears, forged steel
PA: Riley Gear Corporation
      1 Precision Dr
      Saint Augustine FL 32092
      904 829-5652

(G-12087)
RIVERFRONT COSTUME DESIGN
Also Called: A D M
200 River Rd (14120-5708)
PHONE..................................716 693-2501
Paul Tucker, *President*
Barbara Tucker, *Vice Pres*
EMP: 9
SQ FT: 12,500
SALES (est): 1MM **Privately Held**
SIC: 2521 2522 Cabinets, office: wood; cabinets, office: except wood

(G-12088)
ROEMAC INDUSTRIAL SALES INC
Also Called: Buffalo Snowmelter
27 Fredericka St (14120-6590)
PHONE..................................716 692-7332
Mitchell Roemer, *President*
Greg Roemer, *Corp Secy*
Nicholas B Roemer, *Vice Pres*
EMP: 9 **EST:** 1947
SQ FT: 7,000
SALES (est): 900K **Privately Held**
WEB: www.roemac.com
SIC: 3443 3585 Fabricated plate work (boiler shop); evaporative condensers, heat transfer equipment

(G-12089)
ROGER L URBAN INC (PA)
Also Called: Platter's Chocolates
908 Niagara Falls Blvd # 107 (14120-2021)
PHONE..................................716 693-5391
Joseph Urban, *President*
Sherry Di Guiseppe, *Vice Pres*
Sherry Guiseppe, *Comms Dir*
Michael Urban, *Shareholder*
EMP: 21
SQ FT: 11,000
SALES (est): 2.7MM **Privately Held**
WEB: www.platterschocolate.com
SIC: 2066 5441 5145 2064 Chocolate candy, solid; candy; confectionery; candy & other confectionery products

(G-12090)
SHANNON GLOBAL ENRGY SOLUTIONS
Also Called: Insultech
75 Main St (14120-5903)
P.O. Box 199 (14120-0199)
PHONE..................................716 693-7954
Frank Kovacs, *President*
Chad Snopkowski, *Project Mgr*
Robert Weir, *Admin Sec*
▼ **EMP:** 58
SQ FT: 20,000
SALES (est): 7.4MM **Privately Held**
WEB: www.corian-countertop.com
SIC: 2299 Insulating felts

(G-12091)
SOLID SURFACE ACRYLICS LLC
800 Walck Rd Ste 14 (14120-3500)
PHONE..................................716 743-1870
Tom Brown, *Sales Mgr*
Jack Tillotsom,
Merrill Arthur,
EMP: 16
SQ FT: 76,000
SALES (est): 3.8MM **Privately Held**
WEB: www.ssacrylics.com
SIC: 2824 Acrylic fibers

(G-12092)
STRASSBURG MEDICAL LLC
525 Wheatfield St (14120-7034)
P.O. Box 1213, Lockport (14095-1213)
PHONE..................................800 452-0631
David Strassburg,
Amanda Bunn,
Terry A Strassburg,
EMP: 4
SALES (est): 1.3MM **Privately Held**
WEB: www.thesock.com
SIC: 2252 Socks

(G-12093)
T-S-K ELECTRONICS INC
908 Niagara Falls Blvd # 201 (14120-2021)
PHONE..................................716 693-3916
Kevin Kedzierski, *President*
Michael Kedzierski, *Vice Pres*
EMP: 5 **EST:** 1958
SQ FT: 15,000
SALES (est): 727.7K **Privately Held**
SIC: 3679 Electronic circuits

(G-12094)
TABER ACQUISITION CORP
Also Called: Taber Industries
455 Bryant St (14120-7043)
PHONE..................................716 694-4000
Daniel Slawson, *Ch of Bd*
Lori Anderson, *Vice Pres*
Danny Thaler, *Production*
Marty Slawson, *VP Engrg*
Mary Keenan, *QC Mgr*
EMP: 60
SQ FT: 72,000
SALES (est): 18.5MM **Privately Held**
WEB: www.taberindustries.com
SIC: 3823 Pressure measurement instruments, industrial

(G-12095)
TAYLOR DEVICES INC (PA)
90 Taylor Dr (14120-6894)
P.O. Box 748 (14120-0748)
PHONE..................................716 694-0800
Timothy J Sopko, *CEO*
Alan R Klembczyk, *President*
Richard G Hill, *Vice Pres*
Dave Mooney, *QC Mgr*
Sean Frye, *Engineer*
▲ **EMP:** 110 **EST:** 1955
SALES (est): 33.6MM **Publicly Held**
WEB: www.taylordevices.com
SIC: 3569 Industrial shock absorbers

(G-12096)
TRINITY TOOLS INC
261 Main St (14120-7106)
PHONE..................................716 694-1111
Mitchell Banas, *President*
Chris Wein, *Vice Pres*
Michael Ostrowski, *Admin Sec*
EMP: 20
SQ FT: 18,000

SALES (est): 2.2MM **Privately Held**
WEB: www.trinitytoolrentals.com
SIC: 3544 3545 Special dies & tools; jigs & fixtures; gauges (machine tool accessories)

(G-12097)
UNITED MATERIALS LLC (PA)
3949 Frest Pk Way Ste 400 (14120)
PHONE..................................716 683-1432
Ross Eckert, *Ch of Bd*
Peter Romano, *President*
Roger Ball, *CFO*
EMP: 57
SQ FT: 15,000
SALES (est): 17.3MM **Privately Held**
SIC: 3273 Ready-mixed concrete

(G-12098)
WESTROCK CP LLC
51 Robinson St (14120-6805)
PHONE..................................716 694-1000
Mark Savre, *Manager*
EMP: 165
SALES (corp-wide): 16.2B **Publicly Held**
WEB: www.sto.com
SIC: 2653 3412 Boxes, corrugated: made from purchased materials; metal barrels, drums & pails
HQ: Westrock Cp, Llc
      1000 Abernathy Rd
      Atlanta GA 30328

Northport
Suffolk County

(G-12099)
BIO-CHEM BARRIER SYSTEMS LLC
11 W Scudder Pl (11768-3040)
PHONE..................................631 261-2682
Patricia J Maloney,
Raymond Maloney,
EMP: 8
SQ FT: 1,200
SALES: 1.6MM **Privately Held**
WEB: www.bio-chembarriersystemllc.com
SIC: 3842 Personal safety equipment

(G-12100)
CADDELL BURNS MANUFACTURING CO
247 Asharoken Ave (11768-1120)
PHONE..................................631 757-1772
Vincent Burns, *President*
Caryl Burns, *Vice Pres*
EMP: 20
SQ FT: 14,000
SALES (est): 2.6MM **Privately Held**
WEB: www.caddell-burns.com
SIC: 3677 3612 Coil windings, electronic; transformers, except electric

(G-12101)
CHASE CORPORATION
Also Called: Chase Partners
7 Harbour Point Dr (11768-1556)
PHONE..................................631 827-0476
EMP: 11
SALES (corp-wide): 281.3MM **Publicly Held**
SIC: 3644 Noncurrent-carrying wiring services
PA: Chase Corporation
      295 University Ave
      Westwood MA 02090
      781 332-0700

(G-12102)
CYPRESS SEMICONDUCTOR CORP
Also Called: Sales Office
34 Rowley Dr (11768-3246)
PHONE..................................631 261-1358
Carl Finke, *Branch Mgr*
EMP: 14
SALES (corp-wide): 2.4B **Publicly Held**
WEB: www.cypress.com
SIC: 3674 5065 Semiconductors & related devices; electronic parts & equipment

G
E
O
G
R
A
P
H
I
C

PA: Cypress Semiconductor Corporation
198 Champion Ct
San Jose CA 95134
408 943-2600

(G-12103)
ENTREPRENEUR VENTURES INC
652 Bread Chese Hollow Rd (11768-2327)
PHONE................................631 261-1111
Alan Lipari, *Principal*
EMP: 7
SALES (est): 582.3K **Privately Held**
SIC: 2092 Fresh or frozen packaged fish

(G-12104)
FRANKLIN PACKAGING INC (PA)
96 Sea Cove Rd (11768-1847)
PHONE................................631 582-8900
Steven Lincon, *CEO*
Joan Lincoln, *Treasurer*
EMP: 6
SQ FT: 1,500
SALES: 800K **Privately Held**
SIC: 2759 Labels & seals: printing

(G-12105)
HUNTINGTON WOODWORKING INC
Also Called: Mica World
4 Fox Hollow Ridings Ct (11768-2241)
PHONE................................631 271-7897
Anthony Perico Jr, *President*
Marie Perico, *Vice Pres*
EMP: 5
SALES (est): 772.5K **Privately Held**
WEB: www.mica-world.com
SIC: 2434 Wood kitchen cabinets

(G-12106)
KEEP HEALTHY INC
1019 Fort Salonga Rd (11768-2270)
PHONE................................631 651-9090
Ronald Sowa, *President*
EMP: 12 **EST:** 2014
SALES (est): 550K **Privately Held**
SIC: 2064 Breakfast bars

(G-12107)
LEDAN INC
Also Called: Ledan Design Group
6 Annetta Ave (11768-1802)
PHONE................................631 239-1226
Daniel Leo Sr, *CEO*
Steven Leo, *President*
Dan Leo Jr, *Vice Pres*
EMP: 25 **EST:** 1955
SQ FT: 20,000
SALES (est): 3.1MM **Privately Held**
WEB: www.ledan.com
SIC: 2542 Office & store showcases & display fixtures

(G-12108)
LIK LLC
6 Bluff Point Rd (11768-1516)
PHONE................................516 848-5135
Laura Kampa, *President*
EMP: 10
SALES (est): 761.8K **Privately Held**
SIC: 3669 Communications equipment

(G-12109)
MARKETING GROUP INTERNATIONAL
Also Called: Mgi
1 Stargazer Ct (11768-1054)
PHONE................................631 754-8095
Bruce Chautin, *Partner*
Linda Kupcewicz, *Partner*
▲ **EMP:** 7
SALES (est): 1.1MM **Privately Held**
SIC: 2679 Paper products, converted

(G-12110)
NIKISH SOFTWARE CORP
12 Whispering Fields Dr (11768-2866)
PHONE................................631 754-1618
Kishin Bharwani, *President*
Nitsha Bharwani, *Vice Pres*
EMP: 6

SALES (est): 566.6K **Privately Held**
WEB: www.nikish.com
SIC: 7372 Business oriented computer software

(G-12111)
WACF ENTERPRISE INC
275 Asharoken Ave (11768-1120)
PHONE................................631 745-5841
Richard Orofino, *Owner*
EMP: 50
SQ FT: 4,000
SALES (est): 5.2MM **Privately Held**
SIC: 2833 Botanical products, medicinal: ground, graded or milled

(G-12112)
X-GEN PHARMACEUTICALS INC
4 York Ct (11768-3346)
P.O. Box 150 (11768-0150)
PHONE................................631 261-8188
Susan Badia, *Branch Mgr*
EMP: 30
SALES (corp-wide): 3.9MM **Privately Held**
SIC: 2834 Pharmaceutical preparations
PA: X-Gen Pharmaceuticals, Inc.
300 Daniel Zenker Dr
Big Flats NY 14814
607 562-2700

Northville
Fulton County

(G-12113)
BEST TINSMITH SUPPLY INC
4 Zetta Dr (12134-5322)
PHONE................................518 863-2541
John Crawford Jr, *President*
Claudia Hutchins, *Treasurer*
EMP: 5
SQ FT: 6,000
SALES: 507.1K **Privately Held**
SIC: 3444 Sheet metalwork

Norwich
Chenango County

(G-12114)
BYTHEWAY PUBLISHING SERVICES
365 Follett Hill Rd (13815-3378)
PHONE................................607 334-8365
Betty Bytheway, *Owner*
Lori Holland, *Office Mgr*
EMP: 17
SALES (est): 1.4MM **Privately Held**
WEB: www.bytheway.com
SIC: 2791 Typesetting

(G-12115)
CHENANGO CONCRETE CORP
Also Called: Boeing Medcl Trtmnt Mltry Arcr
County Rd 32 E River Rd (13815)
P.O. Box 270 (13815-0270)
PHONE................................607 334-2545
Mike Dwyer, *Director*
EMP: 10
SQ FT: 3,264
SALES (corp-wide): 5.9MM **Privately Held**
SIC: 3271 Concrete block & brick
PA: Chenango Concrete Corp.
145 Podpadic Rd
Richmondville NY 12149
518 294-9964

(G-12116)
CHENANGO UNION PRINTING INC
15 American Ave (13815-1834)
P.O. Box 149 (13815-0149)
PHONE................................607 334-2112
Andrew Phelps, *President*
David Phelps, *Shareholder*
Pam Phelps, *Admin Sec*
EMP: 8

SALES (est): 1.2MM **Privately Held**
WEB: www.chenangounion.com
SIC: 2759 2752 Letterpress printing; commercial printing, offset

(G-12117)
CHENTRONICS LLC
50 Ohara Dr (13815-2029)
PHONE................................607 334-5531
John Killean, *President*
▲ **EMP:** 22
SALES (est): 4.5MM
SALES (corp-wide): 40.6B **Privately Held**
WEB: www.chentronics.com
SIC: 3433 Heating equipment, except electric
PA: Koch Industries, Inc.
4111 E 37th St N
Wichita KS 67220
316 828-5500

(G-12118)
CHOBANI LLC (HQ)
147 State Highway 320 (13815-3561)
PHONE................................607 337-1246
Hamdi Ulukaya, *CEO*
Peter McGuinness, *President*
Robert Gelo, *Division Mgr*
Tim Brown, *COO*
Obrien Kyle, *Exec VP*
◆ **EMP:** 120
SQ FT: 60,000
SALES (est): 935.4MM
SALES (corp-wide): 249.2MM **Privately Held**
SIC: 2026 Yogurt
PA: Chobani Global Holdings, Llc
147 State Highway 320
Norwich NY 13815
607 847-6181

(G-12119)
CHOBANI IDAHO LLC
147 State Highway 320 (13815-3561)
PHONE................................208 432-2248
Jose Trelles, *Manager*
Emily Acee, *Administration*
EMP: 7
SALES (est): 110.5K
SALES (corp-wide): 249.2MM **Privately Held**
SIC: 2024 Dairy based frozen desserts
HQ: Chobani, Llc
147 State Highway 320
Norwich NY 13815

(G-12120)
DAN WESSON CORP
Also Called: Cz USA Dwf Dan Wesson Firearm
65 Borden Ave (13815-1179)
PHONE................................607 336-1174
Robert W Serva, *President*
EMP: 18
SQ FT: 24,000
SALES (est): 1.4MM **Privately Held**
WEB: www.danwessonfirearms.com
SIC: 3484 Small arms

(G-12121)
ELECTRON COIL INC
Also Called: Eci
141 Barr Rd (13815)
P.O. Box 71 (13815-0071)
PHONE................................607 336-7414
Douglas Marchant, *CEO*
John Barnett, *General Mgr*
Richard Marchant, *Vice Pres*
Paula McCall, *Purch Agent*
Elaine Marchant, *Admin Sec*
EMP: 55
SQ FT: 10,000
SALES (est): 10.7MM **Privately Held**
WEB: www.electroncoil.com
SIC: 3621 3612 3675 3677 Coils, for electric motors or generators; power & distribution transformers; electronic capacitors; electronic coils, transformers & other inductors

(G-12122)
GOLUB CORPORATION
Also Called: Price Chopper Pharmacy
5631 State Highway 12 (13815-3205)
PHONE................................607 336-2588
Vincent Mainella, *Branch Mgr*

Myles Johnson, *Manager*
EMP: 23
SALES (corp-wide): 3.6B **Privately Held**
SIC: 3751 Motorcycles & related parts
PA: The Golub Corporation
461 Nott St
Schenectady NY 12308
518 355-5000

(G-12123)
KERRY BFNCTNAL INGREDIENTS INC (DH)
Also Called: Kerry Bio-Science
158 State Highway 320 (13815-3561)
PHONE................................608 363-1200
Stan McCarthy, *CEO*
Michael O'Neill, *President*
Gerry Behan, *Chairman*
◆ **EMP:** 95
SQ FT: 127,353
SALES (est): 22.2MM **Privately Held**
SIC: 2079 2023 2099 Edible fats & oils; dry, condensed, evaporated dairy products; seasonings: dry mixes
HQ: Kerry Inc.
3400 Millington Rd
Beloit WI 53511
608 363-1200

(G-12124)
LABEL GALLERY INC
1 Lee Ave 11 (13815-1108)
PHONE................................607 334-3244
Christopher Ulatowski, *President*
Anna Ulatowski, *Vice Pres*
EMP: 30
SQ FT: 15,000
SALES (est): 6.5MM **Privately Held**
WEB: www.labelgallery.net
SIC: 2672 2752 Labels (unprinted), gummed: made from purchased materials; commercial printing, lithographic

(G-12125)
NORWICH PHARMACEUTICALS INC
Also Called: Norwich Pharma Services
6826 State Highway 12 (13815-3335)
PHONE................................607 335-3000
Chris Calhoun, *President*
Darren Alkins, *President*
Lisa Graver, *Exec VP*
Allen Bergeron, *Research*
Kevin Bain, *CFO*
▲ **EMP:** 375
SQ FT: 375,000
SALES (est): 73.2MM **Privately Held**
SIC: 2834 Pharmaceutical preparations
PA: Alvogen Group, Inc.
44 Whippany Rd Ste 300
Morristown NJ 07960

(G-12126)
PRECISION BUILT TOPS LLC
89 Borden Ave (13815-1179)
PHONE................................607 336-5417
Steven Serafan, *President*
EMP: 6
SALES (est): 696.7K **Privately Held**
WEB: www.precisionbuilttops.com
SIC: 2434 Wood kitchen cabinets

(G-12127)
PRIME TOOL & DIE LLC
6277 County Road 32 (13815-3560)
P.O. Box 83 (13815-0083)
PHONE................................607 334-5435
George H Prime Jr, *Mng Member*
EMP: 6
SALES: 400K **Privately Held**
SIC: 3544 Jigs & fixtures

(G-12128)
SUN PRINTING INCORPORATED
57 Borden Ave 65 (13815-1148)
P.O. Box 151 (13815-0151)
PHONE................................607 337-3034
Bradford R Dick, *Principal*
EMP: 29 **EST:** 2001
SALES (est): 2.5MM **Privately Held**
SIC: 2752 Commercial printing, lithographic

▲ = Import ▼=Export
◆ =Import/Export

(G-12129)
TOMAHAWK WELDING SVCS & INSPTN
30 Midland Dr Apt W16 (13815-1945)
P.O. Box 5 (13815-0005)
PHONE..................................903 249-4451
Chad Arnold, *Principal*
EMP: 8
SALES (est): 88.7K **Privately Held**
SIC: 7692 Welding repair

(G-12130)
UNISON INDUSTRIES LLC
5345 State Highway 12 (13815-1246)
P.O. Box 310 (13815-0310)
PHONE..................................607 335-5000
Jim Markham, *Engineer*
Mike Terzo, *Engineer*
Gary Cummings, *Manager*
Chris Cuozzo, *Maintence Staff*
EMP: 350
SALES (corp-wide): 121.6B **Publicly Held**
WEB: www.unisonindustries.com
SIC: 3679 3769 Electronic circuits; guided missile & space vehicle parts & auxiliary equipment
HQ: Unison Industries, Llc
7575 Baymeadows Way
Jacksonville FL 32256
904 739-4000

Norwood
St. Lawrence County

(G-12131)
BARRETT PAVING MATERIALS INC
Also Called: Norwood Quar Btmnous Con Plnts
Rr 56 (13668)
P.O. Box 203 (13668-0203)
PHONE..................................315 353-6611
David R Wright, *Superintendent*
EMP: 25
SALES (corp-wide): 83.5MM **Privately Held**
WEB: www.barrettpaving.com
SIC: 2951 5032 1611 2952 Concrete, bituminous; paving materials; surfacing & paving; asphalt felts & coatings
HQ: Barrett Paving Materials Inc.
3 Becker Farm Rd Ste 307
Roseland NJ 07068
973 533-1001

(G-12132)
POTTERS INDUSTRIES LLC
56 Reynolds Rd (13668-4131)
PHONE..................................315 265-4920
Andy Gray, *Manager*
EMP: 40
SALES (corp-wide): 1.6B **Publicly Held**
WEB: www.flexolite.com
SIC: 3231 Reflector glass beads, for highway signs or reflectors
HQ: Potters Industries, Llc
300 Lindenwood Dr
Malvern PA 19355
610 651-4700

Nunda
Livingston County

(G-12133)
ONCE AGAIN NUT BUTTER COLLECTV (PA)
12 S State St (14517)
P.O. Box 429 (14517-0429)
PHONE..................................585 468-2535
Robert Gelser, *President*
Brandon Underwood, *Purchasing*
Lawrence Filipski, *CFO*
Gary Hersey, *Sales Staff*
Robert Collins, *Manager*
▲ **EMP:** 64
SQ FT: 20,000

SALES: 55.9MM **Privately Held**
WEB: www.onceagainnutbutter.com
SIC: 2099 Peanut butter; almond pastes; honey, strained & bottled

(G-12134)
SEATING INC
60 N State St (14517)
P.O. Box 898 (14517-0898)
PHONE..................................800 468-2475
Judy Hart, *President*
Doug Hart, *Vice Pres*
EMP: 31
SQ FT: 65,000
SALES (est): 3.7MM **Privately Held**
WEB: www.seatinginc.com
SIC: 2522 2531 Office chairs, benches & stools, except wood; public building & related furniture

Nyack
Rockland County

(G-12135)
AMS STAR STRUCTURES INC
453 S Broadway (10960-4807)
PHONE..................................914 584-0898
Wade Petty, *President*
Robert Schroeder, *Principal*
EMP: 2
SALES: 1MM **Privately Held**
SIC: 2394 Tents: made from purchased materials

(G-12136)
BECTON DICKINSON AND COMPANY
Also Called: Bd Initiative-Hlthcare Wrkr SA
1 Main St Apt 3307 (10960-3236)
PHONE..................................845 353-3371
Jill Garnette, *Manager*
EMP: 379
SALES (corp-wide): 15.9B **Publicly Held**
SIC: 3841 Diagnostic apparatus, medical
PA: Becton, Dickinson And Company
1 Becton Dr
Franklin Lakes NJ 07417
201 847-6800

(G-12137)
BERRY INDUSTRIAL GROUP INC (PA)
30 Main St (10960-3202)
PHONE..................................845 353-8338
Debra Berry, *CEO*
Peter Berry, *President*
Lori Lichtig, *General Mgr*
Lenny Kochuba, *Sales Mgr*
Faye McFarlane, *Executive Asst*
EMP: 5
SQ FT: 1,800
SALES (est): 1.2MM **Privately Held**
WEB: www.berryindustrial.com
SIC: 2448 5031 Pallets, wood; lumber: rough, dressed & finished

(G-12138)
CHARLES PERRELLA INC
78 S Broadway (10960-6802)
P.O. Box 775 (10960-0775)
PHONE..................................845 348-4777
Marie Somos, *President*
Richard Townsend, *Corp Secy*
Phyllis Townsend, *Vice Pres*
EMP: 20
SQ FT: 7,500
SALES (est): 1.4MM **Privately Held**
WEB: www.perrellainc.com
SIC: 3911 5944 Jewelry, precious metal; jewelry stores

(G-12139)
CONCEPT PRINTING INC
Also Called: Concept Printing and Promotion
40 Lydecker St (10960-2104)
PHONE..................................845 353-4040
Kerry Gaughan Monahan, *President*
Kelley Dionne, *Vice Pres*
▲ **EMP:** 4
SALES: 1.3MM **Privately Held**
WEB: www.conceptprintinginc.com
SIC: 2752 5199 Commercial printing, offset; advertising specialties

(G-12140)
DESIGNPLEX LLC
107 Cedar Hill Ave (10960-3705)
PHONE..................................845 358-6647
Loren Bloom, *President*
EMP: 5
SQ FT: 1,500
SALES: 200K **Privately Held**
WEB: www.designplex.org
SIC: 3993 Signs & advertising specialties

(G-12141)
DIRECTORY MAJOR MALLS INC
20 N Broadway Ste 2 (10960-2644)
P.O. Box 837 (10960-0837)
PHONE..................................845 348-7000
Tama J Shor, *President*
EMP: 8
SALES (est): 794.1K **Privately Held**
WEB: www.directoryofmajormalls.com
SIC: 2741 6531 Atlases: publishing only, not printed on site; real estate agents & managers

(G-12142)
EASTERN PRECISION MFG
76 S Franklin St 78 (10960-3734)
PHONE..................................845 358-1951
Harold Hill, *President*
EMP: 6 **EST:** 1973
SQ FT: 600
SALES (est): 410.3K **Privately Held**
SIC: 3569 Firefighting apparatus

(G-12143)
EDROY PRODUCTS CO INC
245 N Midland Ave (10960-1949)
P.O. Box 998 (10960-0998)
PHONE..................................845 358-6600
Steven Stoltze, *President*
EMP: 7 **EST:** 1937
SQ FT: 4,700
SALES: 606.2K **Privately Held**
WEB: www.edroyproducts.com
SIC: 3827 Optical instruments & lenses

(G-12144)
GLOBAL BRANDS INC
1031 Route 9w S (10960-4907)
PHONE..................................845 358-1212
Ralph Ferrante, *CEO*
Herbert M Paul, *President*
EMP: 8
SQ FT: 1,250
SALES (est): 802.1K **Privately Held**
SIC: 2086 Mineral water, carbonated: packaged in cans, bottles, etc.

(G-12145)
LUGO NUTRITION INC
51 N Broadway Ste 2 (10960-2639)
PHONE..................................302 573-2503
Richard Lugo, *President*
Nicholas Lugo, *Vice Pres*
Karen Logu, *CFO*
EMP: 6
SALES (est): 348.4K **Privately Held**
SIC: 2099 Food preparations

(G-12146)
TANDY LEATHER FACTORY INC
298 Main St (10960-2418)
PHONE..................................845 480-3588
Kelly Perini, *Manager*
EMP: 5
SALES (corp-wide): 83.1MM **Publicly Held**
SIC: 3111 5199 5948 Accessory products, leather; lace leather; leather, leather goods & furs; leather goods, except luggage & shoes
PA: Tandy Leather Factory, Inc.
1900 Se Loop 820
Fort Worth TX 76140
817 872-3200

(G-12147)
TEKA PRECISION INC
251 Mountainview Ave (10960-1700)
PHONE..................................845 753-1900
Helen Roderick, *President*
EMP: 7
SQ FT: 1,500

SALES (est): 660K **Privately Held**
SIC: 3496 3541 3495 3452 Miscellaneous fabricated wire products; machine tools, metal cutting type; wire springs; bolts, nuts, rivets & washers

(G-12148)
WIRELESS COMMUNICATIONS INC
4 Chemong Ct (10960-2307)
PHONE..................................845 353-5921
Robert H Colten, *Owner*
EMP: 5
SALES (est): 317.7K **Privately Held**
SIC: 3663 Radio broadcasting & communications equipment

Oakdale
Suffolk County

(G-12149)
CJ COMPONENT PRODUCTS LLC
624 Tower Mews (11769-2449)
PHONE..................................631 567-3733
David Howe, *CEO*
Amy Indence, *Accountant*
▼ **EMP:** 5
SQ FT: 880
SALES (est): 770.5K **Privately Held**
WEB: www.cjcomponents.com
SIC: 3663 Radio & TV communications equipment

(G-12150)
DARK STORM INDUSTRIES LLC
4116 Sunrise Hwy (11769-1013)
PHONE..................................631 967-3170
Ed Newman, *Managing Prtnr*
EMP: 7
SALES (est): 450.1K **Privately Held**
SIC: 3484 Guns (firearms) or gun parts, 30 mm. & below

(G-12151)
GALAXY SOFTWARE LLC
927 Montauk Hwy Unit 229 (11769-3011)
P.O. Box 229 (11769-0229)
PHONE..................................631 244-8405
Andrew Cohen, *Sales Executive*
Cathline Cohen,
EMP: 8
SALES (est): 727.3K **Privately Held**
WEB: www.galaxy-software.com
SIC: 7372 7371 Application computer software; software programming applications

(G-12152)
GSA UPSTATE NY (PA)
755 Montauk Hwy (11769-1801)
PHONE..................................631 244-5744
John Beaver, *CEO*
Chris Biava, *Engineer*
EMP: 2
SQ FT: 1,000
SALES (est): 4.8MM **Privately Held**
WEB: www.gsasales.com
SIC: 3699 Electrical equipment & supplies

(G-12153)
MODERN ITLN BKY OF W BABYLON
301 Locust Ave (11769-1652)
PHONE..................................631 589-7300
James Turco, *Principal*
Jerry Yllanes, *Persnl Mgr*
Frank Dibenedetto, *Natl Sales Mgr*
EMP: 170
SQ FT: 54,000
SALES (est): 43.9MM **Privately Held**
WEB: www.modernbakedprod.com
SIC: 2051 5142 5149 Bread, all types (white, wheat, rye, etc): fresh or frozen; bakery products, frozen; bakery products

(G-12154)
MORELAND HOSE & BELTING CORP
4118 Sunrise Hwy (11769-1013)
PHONE..................................631 563-7071
William Delmore, *Manager*
EMP: 8

SALES (est): 1MM
SALES (corp-wide): 6.4MM **Privately Held**
WEB: www.morelandhose.com
SIC: 3052 Hose, pneumatic: rubber or rubberized fabric
PA: Moreland Hose & Belting Corp
135 Adams Ave
Hempstead NY 11550
516 485-9898

(G-12155)
SPECIALTY FABRICATORS
4120 Sunrise Hwy (11769-1079)
PHONE..................631 433-0258
Charlie Aguilera, *Principal*
EMP: 10
SALES (est): 1.3MM **Privately Held**
SIC: 3399 Primary metal products

(G-12156)
STEEL-BRITE LTD
Also Called: September Associates
2 Dawn Dr (11769-1624)
PHONE..................631 589-4044
Marilyn Cohen, *President*
Susan McCarthy, *Managing Dir*
EMP: 10
SQ FT: 2,500
SALES (est): 770K **Privately Held**
SIC: 3993 5072 Displays & cutouts, window & lobby; hardware

Oakfield
Genesee County

(G-12157)
KEEBLER COMPANY
2999 Judge Rd (14125-9771)
PHONE..................585 948-8010
Ed Watson, *Manager*
EMP: 17
SALES (corp-wide): 13.5B **Publicly Held**
WEB: www.keebler.com
SIC: 2052 Cookies
HQ: Keebler Company
1 Kellogg Sq
Battle Creek MI 49017
269 961-2000

(G-12158)
UNITED STATES GYPSUM COMPANY
2750 Maple Ave (14125-9722)
PHONE..................585 948-5221
James Perry, *Plant Mgr*
Ray Tamblin, *Plant Engr*
Gregg Diefenbacher, *Branch Mgr*
Mike Pedro, *Manager*
Jeff Rupp, *Director*
EMP: 123
SALES (corp-wide): 8.2B **Privately Held**
WEB: www.usg.com
SIC: 3275 Gypsum products
HQ: United States Gypsum Company
550 W Adams St Ste 1300
Chicago IL 60661
312 606-4000

Oakland Gardens
Queens County

(G-12159)
ANANDSAR INC
Also Called: Ateaz Organic Coffe & Tea
5616 201st St (11364-1624)
PHONE..................551 556-5555
Aman Singh, *Principal*
Gary Kahlon, *COO*
Samrina Kahlon, *CFO*
EMP: 26
SALES: 600K **Privately Held**
SIC: 2099 2095 5149 5499 Tea blending; coffee, ground: mixed with grain or chicory; coffee & tea; coffee

(G-12160)
SLIMS BAGELS UNLIMITED INC (PA)
22118 Horace Harding Expy (11364-2390)
P.O. Box 640206 (11364-0206)
PHONE..................718 229-1140
Joseph Dvir, *President*
David Katz, *Vice Pres*
EMP: 27
SQ FT: 5,000
SALES (est): 1.5MM **Privately Held**
SIC: 2051 5641 Bakery: wholesale or wholesale/retail combined; children's & infants' wear stores

Oaks Corners
Ontario County

(G-12161)
ELDERLEE INCORPORATED (HQ)
729 Cross Rd (14518)
P.O. Box 10 (14518-0010)
PHONE..................315 789-6670
Basil A Shorb III, *Ch of Bd*
William J Shorb, *President*
David Dejohn, *Vice Pres*
Robert Rook, *Vice Pres*
Paul R Strain, *Vice Pres*
EMP: 120
SQ FT: 240,000
SALES (est): 45.5MM
SALES (corp-wide): 78.7MM **Privately Held**
WEB: www.elderlee.com
SIC: 3312 1611 3444 3993 Iron & steel: galvanized, pipes, plates, sheets, etc.; guardrail construction, highways; guard rails, highway: sheet metal; signs & advertising specialties; concrete products
PA: Reh Holdings, Inc
150 S Sumner St
York PA 17404
717 843-0021

(G-12162)
HANSON AGGREGATES PA LLC
2026 County Rd Ste 6 (14518)
PHONE..................315 789-6202
Kenny Thurston, *Opers-Prdtn-Mfg*
EMP: 25
SALES (corp-wide): 20.6B **Privately Held**
SIC: 1442 3281 1422 Gravel mining; stone, quarrying & processing of own stone products; crushed & broken limestone
HQ: Hanson Aggregates Pennsylvania, Llc
7660 Imperial Way
Allentown PA 18195
610 366-4626

Oceanside
Nassau County

(G-12163)
3KRF LLC
3516 Hargale Rd (11572-5820)
PHONE..................516 208-6824
Timothy Hopper, *Managing Prtnr*
Mark Gruenspecht, *Mng Member*
EMP: 5
SALES (est): 410K **Privately Held**
SIC: 3699 Electrical welding equipment

(G-12164)
ADF ACCESSORIES INC
Also Called: Todaysgentleman.com
3539 Lawson Blvd (11572-4993)
PHONE..................516 450-5755
Jack Fischman, *President*
Chanie Manheimer, *Vice Pres*
▲ **EMP:** 5
SALES (est): 628.9K **Privately Held**
WEB: www.todaysgentleman.com
SIC: 2389 Men's miscellaneous accessories

(G-12165)
AHW PRINTING CORP
Also Called: PIP Printing
2920 Long Beach Rd (11572-3114)
PHONE..................516 536-3600
Alan Waldman, *President*
Harriet Waldman, *Treasurer*
EMP: 11
SQ FT: 1,900
SALES (est): 1.8MM **Privately Held**
SIC: 2752 Commercial printing, offset

(G-12166)
ASTRODYNE INC
18 Neil Ct (11572-5816)
P.O. Box 354, Rockville Centre (11571-0354)
PHONE..................516 536-5755
David J Salwen, *CEO*
Ira M Salwen, *President*
Barbara Salwen, *Admin Sec*
EMP: 6
SQ FT: 5,000
SALES (est): 931.1K **Privately Held**
SIC: 3861 5045 5734 Photographic equipment & supplies; computers, peripherals & software; computer software; computer & software stores; computer software & accessories

(G-12167)
CHUDNOW MANUFACTURING CO INC
3055 New St (11572-2743)
PHONE..................516 593-4222
Richard B Cohen, *President*
EMP: 45 **EST:** 1934
SQ FT: 28,000
SALES: 5MM **Privately Held**
SIC: 3585 Soda fountain & beverage dispensing equipment & parts; soda fountains, parts & accessories

(G-12168)
D & M CUSTOM CABINETS INC
2994 Long Beach Rd (11572-3205)
P.O. Box 37 (11572-0037)
PHONE..................516 678-2818
Fax: 516 678-0042
EMP: 12
SQ FT: 7,500
SALES (est): 1.3MM **Privately Held**
SIC: 2434 Mfg Wood Kitchen Cabinet Doors

(G-12169)
DDC TECHNOLOGIES INC
311 Woods Ave Unit B (11572-2152)
PHONE..................516 594-1533
Dimitri Donskoy, *President*
Nickolay Shrago, *Engineer*
Alex Chernovets, *Marketing Mgr*
Donskoy Dmitry, *Manager*
EMP: 5
SALES (est): 872.9K **Privately Held**
WEB: www.ddctech.com
SIC: 3845 Laser systems & equipment, medical

(G-12170)
EAST COAST MOLDERS INC
3001 New St Ste F (11572-2747)
PHONE..................516 240-6000
EMP: 225
SQ FT: 7,000
SALES (est): 9.5MM **Privately Held**
SIC: 2342 Mfg Bras/Girdles

(G-12171)
EXPRESS BUILDING SUPPLY INC
Also Called: Wholesale Window Warehouse
3550 Lawson Blvd (11572-4908)
PHONE..................516 608-0379
Robert Freedman, *President*
EMP: 25 **EST:** 1996
SQ FT: 9,000
SALES (est): 2.5MM **Privately Held**
SIC: 3211 5031 5211 Window glass, clear & colored; windows; windows, storm: wood or metal

(G-12172)
FIRST MANUFACTURING CO INC (HQ)
Also Called: FMC Fashion Division
3800 Oceanside Rd W (11572-5904)
PHONE..................516 763-0400
Ajmal Cheema, *Ch of Bd*
Mushtaq Cheema, *President*
Amir Mukhtar, *Production*
Jorge Espinal, *Sales Mgr*
Pat Curran, *Manager*
▲ **EMP:** 36
SQ FT: 80,000
SALES (est): 8.4MM
SALES (corp-wide): 32.6MM **Privately Held**
SIC: 3199 3172 Leather garments; personal leather goods
PA: Leather Field (Pvt) Limited.
Cheema Square, Capital Road
Sialkot
523 556-272

(G-12173)
FIVE BORO DOORS MOULDINGS INC
3569 Maple Ct (11572-4821)
PHONE..................718 865-9371
Usher Krasne, *Principal*
EMP: 9
SALES (est): 173.4K **Privately Held**
SIC: 3442 Metal doors, sash & trim

(G-12174)
HENNIG CUSTOM WOODWORK CORP
Also Called: Hennig Custom Woodworking
2497 Long Beach Rd (11572-1321)
PHONE..................516 536-3460
James Hennig, *President*
EMP: 5
SALES: 500K **Privately Held**
SIC: 2421 7389 5031 2499 Furniture dimension stock, softwood; laminating service; kitchen cabinets; decorative wood & woodwork; cabinet & finish carpentry

(G-12175)
HERGO ERGONOMIC SUPPORT SYST (PA)
3530 Lawson Blvd (11572-4908)
PHONE..................888 222-7270
Eli E Hertz, *CEO*
Barry J Goldsammler, *Senior VP*
Albert Hirschson, *Senior VP*
I Marilyn Hertz, *Vice Pres*
Kristen Speranza-Diamond, *Vice Pres*
◆ **EMP:** 40
SQ FT: 42,000
SALES (est): 5.8MM **Privately Held**
WEB: www.hergo.com
SIC: 3577 3699 3444 2542 Computer peripheral equipment; electrical equipment & supplies; sheet metalwork; partitions & fixtures, except wood; office furniture, except wood

(G-12176)
IP MED INC
3571 Hargale Rd (11572-5821)
PHONE..................516 766-3800
Judah Isaacs, *President*
EMP: 7
SALES (est): 346K **Privately Held**
SIC: 2836 3841 2834 5122 Bacterial vaccines; inhalators, surgical & medical; proprietary drug products; drugs & drug proprietaries

(G-12177)
JQ WOODWORKING INC
3085 New St (11572-2743)
PHONE..................516 766-3424
John Quinn, *Ch of Bd*
EMP: 5
SQ FT: 10,000
SALES: 1MM **Privately Held**
SIC: 3259 1751 Architectural clay products; cabinet & finish carpentry

(G-12178)
KANTEK INC
Also Called: Spectrum
3460a Hampton Rd (11572-4803)
PHONE..................516 594-4600

▲ = Import ▼=Export
◆ =Import/Export

Herman Kappel, *President*
AVI Kappel, *General Mgr*
Nancy Pollack,
▲ EMP: 30
SQ FT: 25,000
SALES (est): 12.1MM **Privately Held**
WEB: www.kantek.com
SIC: 3577 5045 Computer peripheral
equipment; computers, peripherals & software

(G-12179)
L N D INCORPORATED
Also Called: Lnd
3230 Lawson Blvd (11572-3796)
PHONE....................................516 678-6141
Peter T Neyland, *President*
Bill Ayers, *Vice Pres*
Spencer B Neyland, *Vice Pres*
Robert Sears, *Purch Dir*
Robert Sierzputowski, *Purch Mgr*
EMP: 45 EST: 1964
SQ FT: 14,000
SALES (est): 10.7MM **Privately Held**
WEB: www.lndinc.com
SIC: 3829 Nuclear radiation & testing apparatus

(G-12180)
LOVE BRIGHT JEWELRY INC
Also Called: Lovebrightjewelry.com
3446 Frederick St (11572-4713)
PHONE....................................516 620-2509
Bhupen Kapadia, *President*
EMP: 25
SQ FT: 2,000
SALES (est): 1.4MM **Privately Held**
SIC: 3911 5094 5944 Jewelry apparel;
jewelry; jewelry stores

(G-12181)
MARK PERI INTERNATIONAL
3516 Hargale Rd (11572-5820)
PHONE....................................516 208-6824
Mark Gruenspecht, *Director*
EMP: 10
SALES (est): 797.8K **Privately Held**
SIC: 3663 Radio & TV communications
equipment

(G-12182)
MARKPERICOM
3516 Hargale Rd (11572-5820)
PHONE....................................516 208-6824
Mark Gruenstpecht, *President*
EMP: 9
SALES (est): 711.8K **Privately Held**
SIC: 3569 General industrial machinery

(G-12183)
ONLY NATURAL INC
Also Called: Bio Nutrition
3580 Oceanside Rd Unit 5 (11572-5825)
PHONE....................................516 897-7001
Robert Lomacchio, *President*
Ryan Lomacchio, *Vice Pres*
◆ EMP: 15
SQ FT: 3,600
SALES (est): 2.6MM **Privately Held**
WEB: www.onlynaturalinc.com
SIC: 2833 5499 Vitamins, natural or synthetic: bulk, uncompounded; health & dietetic food stores

(G-12184)
PIER-TECH INC
7 Hampton Rd (11572-4838)
PHONE....................................516 442-5420
Robert Sackaris, *Ch of Bd*
EMP: 42
SALES (est): 8.8MM **Privately Held**
SIC: 3531 Construction machinery

(G-12185)
POETRY MAILING LIST MARSH HAWK
2823 Rockaway Ave (11572-1018)
P.O. Box 206, East Rockaway (11518-0206)
PHONE....................................516 766-1891
Jane Augustine, *President*
EMP: 5
SALES: 45.4K **Privately Held**
SIC: 2731 Book publishing

(G-12186)
RADIANT PRO LTD
245 Merrick Rd (11572-1428)
PHONE....................................516 763-5678
John Cioento, *Owner*
EMP: 7
SALES (est): 719.8K **Privately Held**
SIC: 3567 Radiant heating systems, industrial process

(G-12187)
ROSE TRUNK MFG CO INC
3935 Sally Ln (11572-5934)
PHONE....................................516 766-6686
Melvin Lapidus, *President*
Mark Lapidus, *Vice Pres*
◆ EMP: 15 EST: 1945
SQ FT: 15,000
SALES (est): 1.8MM **Privately Held**
WEB: www.rosetrunk.com
SIC: 3161 Trunks

(G-12188)
ROYAL MARBLE & GRANITE INC
3295 Royal Ave (11572-3625)
PHONE....................................516 536-5900
Richard Tafuri, *President*
Anthony Tafuri, *Vice Pres*
▲ EMP: 8
SQ FT: 8,000
SALES (est): 893.4K **Privately Held**
SIC: 3281 3272 Granite, cut & shaped; art
marble, concrete

(G-12189)
SEA WAVES INC (PA)
2425 Long Beach Rd (11572-1320)
PHONE....................................516 766-4201
Brian Corhan, *President*
Harold Corhan, *Vice Pres*
▲ EMP: 5
SQ FT: 2,000
SALES (est): 660.1K **Privately Held**
SIC: 2339 Bathing suits: women's, misses'
& juniors'; beachwear: women's, misses'
& juniors'

(G-12190)
SIGELOCK SYSTEMS LLC (PA)
3205 Lawson Blvd (11572-3703)
PHONE....................................888 744-3562
George Sigelakis, *President*
Scott Horak, *Exec VP*
Ira Wender, *Senior VP*
Larry Davis, *Vice Pres*
Michelle Sigelakis, *Vice Pres*
EMP: 4
SALES (est): 1.1MM **Privately Held**
SIC: 3569 4971 Firefighting apparatus &
related equipment; water distribution or
supply systems for irrigation

(G-12191)
STATIC COATINGS INC (PA)
3585 Lawson Blvd Unit B (11572-4993)
PHONE....................................516 764-0040
EMP: 5
SALES (est): 733K **Privately Held**
SIC: 3479 Metal coating & allied service

(G-12192)
STRONG GROUP INC
222 Atlantic Ave Unit B (11572-2045)
PHONE....................................516 766-6300
EMP: 8
SALES (est): 605K **Privately Held**
SIC: 2311 Manufacture Police Equipment

(G-12193)
STYLES MANUFACTURING CORP
3571 Hargale Rd (11572-5821)
PHONE....................................516 763-5303
Louis Fuchs, *President*
Ron Keyes, *Vice Pres*
▲ EMP: 5
SALES (est): 5MM **Privately Held**
SIC: 3315 Hangers (garment), wire

(G-12194)
TAG FLANGE & MACHINING INC
3375 Royal Ave (11572-4812)
PHONE....................................516 536-1300
Theodore A Gallucci III, *President*
Sean F Gallucci, *Vice Pres*

EMP: 6
SQ FT: 10,000
SALES (est): 500K **Privately Held**
SIC: 3498 Fabricated pipe & fittings

(G-12195)
UNITED THREAD MILLS CORP (PA)
3530 Lawson Blvd Gf (11572-4908)
P.O. Box 766, Rockville Centre (11571-0766)
PHONE....................................516 536-3900
Ira Henkus, *President*
▼ EMP: 6 EST: 1948
SQ FT: 66,000
SALES (est): 54.2MM **Privately Held**
SIC: 2284 2281 Thread mills; yarn spinning mills

(G-12196)
VENEER ONE INC
3415 Hampton Rd (11572-4835)
PHONE....................................516 536-6480
Victor Giaime, *Ch of Bd*
Arnold Lanzillotta, *President*
Steve Horan, *Admin Sec*
▲ EMP: 28
SQ FT: 19,000
SALES (est): 4.5MM **Privately Held**
WEB: www.veneer1.com
SIC: 2435 Hardwood veneer & plywood

(G-12197)
VIANA SIGNS CORP
3520 Lawson Blvd (11572-4908)
PHONE....................................516 887-2000
Leo Viana, *President*
EMP: 10
SALES (est): 1MM **Privately Held**
SIC: 3993 Signs & advertising specialties

(G-12198)
WOOD INNOVATIONS OF SUFFOLK
100 Daly Blvd Apt 3218 (11572-6041)
PHONE....................................631 698-2345
Gino Genna, *President*
Mary Weiss, *Treasurer*
EMP: 6
SALES (est): 891.4K **Privately Held**
WEB: www.woodin.com
SIC: 2431 2499 5712 1799 Interior & ornamental woodwork & trim; exterior & ornamental woodwork & trim; decorative
wood & woodwork; outdoor & garden furniture; fence construction

(G-12199)
YALE TROUSER CORPORATION
Also Called: Smokey Joes
3670 Oceanside Rd W Ste 6 (11572-5961)
PHONE....................................516 255-0700
Arnold Bloom, *President*
Gary Bloom, *Vice Pres*
EMP: 10 EST: 1950
SALES (est): 1.1MM **Privately Held**
WEB: www.yaletrouser.com
SIC: 2325 2321 Slacks, dress: men's,
youths' & boys'; trousers, dress (separate): men's, youths' & boys'; men's &
boys' furnishings

Odessa
Schuyler County

(G-12200)
FINGER LAKES CHEESE TRAIL
4970 County Road 14 (14869-9730)
PHONE....................................607 857-5726
Carmella Hoffman, *Treasurer*
EMP: 13
SALES (est): 718.6K **Privately Held**
SIC: 2026 Fluid milk

Ogdensburg
St. Lawrence County

(G-12201)
ALGONQUIN POWER
19 Mill St (13669-1304)
PHONE....................................315 393-5595
Walter Bracy, *Manager*
EMP: 7
SALES (est): 886.8K **Privately Held**
SIC: 3634 Electric housewares & fans

(G-12202)
ANSEN CORPORATION
100 Chimney Point Dr (13669-2206)
PHONE....................................315 393-3573
James Kingman, *CEO*
Jerry W Slusser, *President*
Kenneth Emter, *Corp Secy*
Jason W Slusser, *Director*
▲ EMP: 3
SQ FT: 72,000
SALES (est): 42.9MM
SALES (corp-wide): 38MM **Privately Held**
WEB: www.ansencorp.com
SIC: 3672 Printed circuit boards
PA: Mbpj Corporation
420 E Bayfront Pkwy
Erie PA 16507
814 461-9120

(G-12203)
CANARM LTD
808 Commerce Park Dr (13669-2208)
PHONE....................................800 267-4427
David Beatty, *CEO*
James Cooper, *President*
▲ EMP: 2
SQ FT: 1,500
SALES: 75MM
SALES (corp-wide): 174MM **Privately Held**
SIC: 3564 3645 3646 5064 Blowing fans:
industrial or commercial; exhaust fans: industrial or commercial; ventilating fans:
industrial or commercial; residential lighting fixtures; commercial indusl & institutional electric lighting fixtures; fans,
household: electric; fans, industrial; lighting fixtures, commercial & industrial; lighting fixtures, residential
PA: Canarm Ltd
2157 Parkedale Ave
Brockville ON K6V 0
613 342-5424

(G-12204)
DEFELSKO CORPORATION
800 Proctor Ave (13669-2205)
PHONE....................................315 393-4450
Frank Koch, *President*
David Beamish, *Chairman*
Linda K Beamish, *Vice Pres*
Linda Beamish, *Vice Pres*
Michael Beamish, *Engineer*
◆ EMP: 60
SQ FT: 15,000
SALES (est): 17.5MM **Privately Held**
WEB: www.defelsko.com
SIC: 3823 3829 Industrial instrmnts
msrmnt display/control process variable;
measuring & controlling devices

(G-12205)
HANSON AGGREGATES PA LLC
701 Cedar St (13669-3000)
P.O. Box 250 (13669-0250)
PHONE....................................315 393-3743
Daniel O'Connor, *Manager*
EMP: 14
SQ FT: 2,196
SALES (corp-wide): 20.6B **Privately Held**
SIC: 1429 1422 Grits mining (crushed
stone); limestones, ground
HQ: Hanson Aggregates Pennsylvania, Llc
7660 Imperial Way
Allentown PA 18195
610 366-4626

GEOGRAPHIC

(G-12206)
HOOSIER MAGNETICS INC
110 Denny St (13669-1797)
PHONE....................................315 323-5832
B Thomas Shirk, *President*
Mary Alice Shirk, *Admin Sec*
◆ **EMP:** 50 **EST:** 1988
SQ FT: 30,000
SALES (est): 8.7MM **Privately Held**
WEB: www.hoosiermagnetics.com
SIC: 3264 Ferrite & ferrite parts

(G-12207)
LAWTONS ELECTRIC MOTOR SERVICE
Also Called: Lawton Electric Co
148 Cemetery Rd (13669-4179)
PHONE....................................315 393-2728
Bernard Lawton, *Partner*
Timothy Lawton, *Partner*
EMP: 7 **EST:** 1968
SALES: 500K **Privately Held**
SIC: 7694 Electric motor repair

(G-12208)
MAXAM NORTH AMERICA INC
3 Cemetary Dr (13669-4528)
PHONE....................................315 322-8651
EMP: 5
SALES (corp-wide): 48.6MM **Privately Held**
SIC: 2892 5169 Explosives; explosives
HQ: Maxam North America, Inc.
　　433 Las Colinas Blvd E # 900
　　Irving TX 75039
　　801 233-6000

(G-12209)
MED-ENG LLC
103 Tulloch Dr (13669-2215)
PHONE....................................315 713-0130
Scott Obrien, *CEO*
Dennis Morris, *President*
EMP: 40
SALES (est): 3.5MM
SALES (corp-wide): 1B **Privately Held**
WEB: www.allen-vanguard.com
SIC: 2311 Military uniforms, men's & youths': purchased materials
HQ: Safariland, Llc
　　13386 International Pkwy
　　Jacksonville FL 32218
　　904 741-5400

(G-12210)
QUEENAIRE TECHNOLOGIES INC
9483 State Highway 37 (13669-4467)
PHONE....................................315 393-5454
Susan Duffy, *President*
Paul McGrath, *Opers Dir*
Nicole M Duffy, *CFO*
Tom Coplen, *Sales Staff*
▼ **EMP:** 6
SQ FT: 6,600
SALES (est): 1.3MM **Privately Held**
SIC: 3559 Ozone machines

(G-12211)
T-BASE COMMUNICATIONS USA INC
806 Commerce Park Dr (13669-2208)
PHONE....................................315 713-0013
Sharylyn Ayotte, *President*
EMP: 40
SALES (est): 3.2MM **Privately Held**
SIC: 2759 Commercial printing

(G-12212)
TULMAR MANUFACTURING INC
101 Tulloch Dr (13669-2215)
PHONE....................................315 393-7191
Manna Doyle, *President*
EMP: 8
SQ FT: 7,700
SALES: 900K
SALES (corp-wide): 14.3MM **Privately Held**
SIC: 2399 Military insignia, textile
PA: Tulmar Safety Systems Inc
　　1123 Cameron St
　　Hawkesbury ON K6A 2
　　613 632-1282

Old Bethpage
Nassau County

(G-12213)
ALJO PRECISION PRODUCTS INC
205 Bethpge Sweet Holw (11804-1309)
PHONE....................................516 420-4419
John Adelmann, *President*
Albert Adelmann, *Vice Pres*
Michael Mattern, *Vice Pres*
Tyrone Faas, *Info Tech Mgr*
EMP: 35 **EST:** 1953
SQ FT: 24,000
SALES (est): 5MM **Privately Held**
WEB: www.aljogefa.com
SIC: 3599 Machine shop, jobbing & repair

(G-12214)
ALJO-GEFA PRECISION MFG LLC
205 Bethpage Sweet Holw (11804-1309)
PHONE....................................516 420-4419
John Addleman, *Partner*
Tyrone Faas, *General Mgr*
Albert Adelmann, *Vice Pres*
Robert Zerebak, *Vice Pres*
Gregory Nasta, *QC Mgr*
EMP: 33 **EST:** 1999
SQ FT: 26,000
SALES (est): 5.9MM **Privately Held**
SIC: 3599 Machine shop, jobbing & repair

(G-12215)
BARSON COMPOSITES CORPORATION (PA)
Also Called: Hitemco
160 Bethpage Sweet (11804)
PHONE....................................516 752-7882
Terrell Barnard, *CEO*
Edwin Garofalo, *COO*
Walter Brandsema, *Mfg Staff*
Dana Barnard, *CFO*
Christine Montaperto, *Accountant*
EMP: 50
SQ FT: 32,500
SALES (est): 14.4MM **Privately Held**
WEB: www.hitemco.com
SIC: 3479 2899 2851 Coating of metals & formed products; chemical preparations; paints & allied products

(G-12216)
GEFA INSTRUMENT CORP
205 Bethpage Sweet (11804)
PHONE....................................516 420-4419
Gunther Faas, *President*
Tyrone Faas, *Treasurer*
Collette Faas, *Shareholder*
EMP: 12 **EST:** 1966
SQ FT: 10,000
SALES (est): 1.2MM **Privately Held**
SIC: 3599 Machine shop, jobbing & repair

(G-12217)
HITEMCO MED APPLICATIONS INC
Also Called: Hi-Med
160 Sweet Hollow Rd (11804-1315)
PHONE....................................516 752-7882
Edwin Garofalo, *President*
John Legeros, *Director*
Bruce McCormick, *Director*
EMP: 134
SQ FT: 5,000
SALES (est): 13.1MM
SALES (corp-wide): 14.4MM **Privately Held**
WEB: www.hitemco.com
SIC: 3479 Painting, coating & hot dipping
PA: Barson Composites Corporation
　　160 Bethpage Sweet
　　Old Bethpage NY 11804
　　516 752-7882

(G-12218)
INTELLIGEN POWER SYSTEMS LLC
301 Winding Rd (11804-1322)
PHONE....................................212 750-0373
David H Lesser,
Stephen Bellone,
EMP: 8
SALES (est): 990K **Privately Held**
SIC: 3621 Power generators

(G-12219)
SEVILLE CENTRAL MIX CORP
495 Wining Rd (11804)
PHONE....................................516 293-6190
Peter Buck, *Branch Mgr*
EMP: 60
SALES (corp-wide): 7.8MM **Privately Held**
WEB: www.sevillecentralmix.com
SIC: 3273 3531 Ready-mixed concrete; concrete plants
PA: Seville Central Mix Corp.
　　157 Albany Ave
　　Freeport NY 11520
　　516 868-3000

(G-12220)
STASI INDUSTRIES INC
501 Winding Rd (11804-1336)
PHONE....................................516 334-2742
Crescenzo Stasi, *President*
EMP: 6
SALES (est): 209.4K **Privately Held**
SIC: 3999 Manufacturing industries

Old Forge
Herkimer County

(G-12221)
ADIRONDACK OUTDOOR CENTER LLC (PA)
2839 State Route 28 (13420-7905)
P.O. Box 1146 (13420-1146)
PHONE....................................315 369-2300
John Nemjo,
EMP: 8
SALES (est): 2.3MM **Privately Held**
SIC: 3949 5091 Camping equipment & supplies; camping equipment & supplies

---

Old Westbury
Nassau County

(G-12222)
CATHY DANIELS LTD (PA)
Also Called: Ecco Bay Sportswear
11 Orchard Ln (11568-1047)
PHONE....................................212 354-8000
Herb Chestler, *Ch of Bd*
Steven Chestler, *President*
Elizabeth Go, *Controller*
Jerry Passaretti, *Sales Executive*
◆ **EMP:** 50
SALES (est): 5.6MM **Privately Held**
WEB: www.cathydaniels.com
SIC: 2339 Sportswear, women's

Olean
Cattaraugus County

(G-12223)
AVX CORPORATION
Also Called: Olean Advanced Products
1695 Seneca Ave (14760-9532)
PHONE....................................716 372-6611
EMP: 95
SALES (corp-wide): 14.8B **Publicly Held**
SIC: 3675 5065 Mfg Electronic Capacitors Whol Electronic Parts/Equipment
HQ: Avx Corporation
　　1 Avx Blvd
　　Fountain Inn SC 29644
　　864 967-2150

(G-12224)
BILLINGS SHEET METAL INC
1002 S Union St (14760-3974)
PHONE....................................716 372-6165
James Billings, *President*
Jason Billings, *Project Mgr*
Debbie Billings, *Treasurer*
EMP: 6
SQ FT: 4,800
SALES: 800K **Privately Held**
WEB: www.billingssheetmetal.com
SIC: 3444 Sheet metalwork

(G-12225)
BIMBO BAKERIES USA INC
Also Called: Stroehmann Bakeries 56
111 N 2nd St (14760-2501)
PHONE....................................716 372-8444
Ted Lipeowski, *Branch Mgr*
EMP: 140 **Privately Held**
SIC: 2051 Bakery: wholesale or whole-sale/retail combined
HQ: Bimbo Bakeries Usa, Inc
　　255 Business Center Dr # 200
　　Horsham PA 19044
　　215 347-5500

(G-12226)
BRADFORD PUBLICATIONS INC
Also Called: Times Herald, The
639 W Norton Dr (14760-1402)
PHONE....................................716 373-2500
Lori Coffman, *Manager*
EMP: 130
SQ FT: 22,300 **Privately Held**
WEB: www.oleantimesherald.com
SIC: 2711 7313 Newspapers, publishing & printing; newspaper advertising representative
HQ: Bradford Publishing Company
　　43 Main St
　　Bradford PA 16701
　　814 368-3173

(G-12227)
CAPSTREAM TECHNOLOGIES LLC
1204 Vine St (14760-1271)
PHONE....................................716 945-7100
Joseph Caruso, *General Mgr*
Michael Krysick,
EMP: 6
SALES (est): 990.7K **Privately Held**
SIC: 3669 Intercommunication systems, electric

(G-12228)
CITY OF OLEAN
Also Called: Olean Waste Water Treatment
174 S 19th St (14760-3326)
PHONE....................................716 376-5694
Jeremy Meerdink, *Manager*
EMP: 9
SQ FT: 1,080 **Privately Held**
SIC: 3589 9111 Water treatment equipment, industrial; mayors' offices
PA: City Of Olean
　　101 E State St Ste 1
　　Olean NY 14760
　　716 376-5683

(G-12229)
CONCRETE MIXER SUPPLYCOM INC (PA)
1721 Cornell Dr (14760-9753)
PHONE....................................716 375-5565
Audrey D Pavia, *President*
◆ **EMP:** 9
SQ FT: 3,000
SALES (est): 1.6MM **Privately Held**
SIC: 3713 Truck bodies & parts

(G-12230)
COOPER POWER SYSTEMS LLC
1648 Dugan Rd (14760-9527)
PHONE....................................716 375-7100
Mark Schubel, *Branch Mgr*
EMP: 300 **Privately Held**
WEB: www.cooperpower.com
SIC: 3612 3699 3674 3643 Transformers, except electric; electrical equipment & supplies; semiconductors & related devices; current-carrying wiring devices; switchgear & switchboard apparatus
HQ: Cooper Power Systems, Llc
　　2300 Badger Dr
　　Waukesha WI 53188
　　262 896-2400

(G-12231)
CYTEC INDUSTRIES INC
Also Called: Cytec Solvay Group
1405 Buffalo St (14760-1197)
PHONE..................................716 372-9650
David Lilley, *Branch Mgr*
Mary Isaman, *Info Tech Mgr*
Maureen Dearmitt, *Technology*
Rick Jordan, *Technical Staff*
EMP: 66
SALES (corp-wide): 12.8MM **Privately Held**
SIC: 2899 2821 2672 2851 Water treating compounds; plastics materials & resins; adhesive backed films, foams & foils; paints & allied products; cellulosic manmade fibers
HQ: Cytec Industries Inc.
4500 Mcginnis Ferry Rd
Alpharetta GA 30005

(G-12232)
DRESSER-RAND GROUP INC
500 Paul Clark Dr (14760-9560)
PHONE..................................716 375-3000
Michael Jeannerette, *Project Mgr*
Mike Johnson, *Facilities Mgr*
Job Barboza, *Engineer*
Steve Bielecki, *Engineer*
Scott Macwilliams, *Engineer*
EMP: 66
SALES (corp-wide): 95B **Privately Held**
SIC: 3563 3511 Air & gas compressors; turbines & turbine generator sets
HQ: Dresser-Rand Group Inc.
15375 Memorial Dr Ste 600
Houston TX 77079
713 354-6100

(G-12233)
DYNAMIC SEALING TECH INC
Also Called: Scott Rotary Seals
301 W Franklin St (14760-1211)
PHONE..................................716 376-0708
Jeffrey Meister, *Branch Mgr*
EMP: 8
SQ FT: 15,000
SALES (corp-wide): 12.5MM **Privately Held**
SIC: 3492 Control valves, fluid power: hydraulic & pneumatic
PA: Dynamic Sealing Technologies, Inc.
13829 Jay St Nw
Andover MN 55304
763 786-3758

(G-12234)
DZ9 POWER LLC
408 Wayne St (14760-2462)
P.O. Box 862 (14760-0862)
PHONE..................................877 533-5530
Brian Benka, *President*
EMP: 7 EST: 2015
SALES (est): 358.3K **Privately Held**
SIC: 3499 Target drones, for use by ships: metal

(G-12235)
ELANTAS PDG INC
1405 Buffalo St (14760-1139)
PHONE..................................716 372-9650
EMP: 9
SALES (corp-wide): 385.1K **Privately Held**
SIC: 2851 Lacquers, varnishes, enamels & other coatings
HQ: Elantas Pdg, Inc.
5200 N 2nd St
Saint Louis MO 63147
314 621-5700

(G-12236)
G & H WOOD PRODUCTS LLC
Also Called: Pallets Plus
2427 N Union Street Ext (14760-1529)
PHONE..................................716 372-0341
Terrance Grant,
EMP: 10
SQ FT: 4,343
SALES (est): 1.2MM **Privately Held**
SIC: 2448 Pallets, wood

(G-12237)
KAMERYS WHOLESALE MEATS INC
322 E Riverside Dr (14760-3964)
PHONE..................................716 372-6756
David A Kamery, *President*
EMP: 6
SALES (est): 572.6K **Privately Held**
SIC: 2011 5147 Meat packing plants; meats, fresh

(G-12238)
L AMERICAN LTD
Also Called: Swatt Baking Co
222 Homer St (14760-1132)
PHONE..................................716 372-9480
Leonard Anzivine, *President*
Lee Anzivine, *Vice Pres*
EMP: 16
SQ FT: 9,400
SALES (est): 2MM **Privately Held**
WEB: www.lamerican.com
SIC: 2051 5461 Bread, all types (white, wheat, rye, etc): fresh or frozen; rolls, bread type: fresh or frozen; bakeries

(G-12239)
NES BEARING COMPANY INC
1601 Johnson St (14760-1127)
PHONE..................................716 372-6532
Christopher Napoleon, *President*
Melissa Curran, *Opers Mgr*
Jim Hardy, *QC Mgr*
Jeremy Martin, *Engineer*
Elijah Bell, *Design Engr*
▲ EMP: 48
SALES (est): 13.6MM **Privately Held**
WEB: www.nesbearings.com
SIC: 3562 8711 Ball bearings & parts; sanitary engineers

(G-12240)
PIERCE STEEL FABRICATORS
430 N 7th St (14760-2330)
P.O. Box 504 (14760-0504)
PHONE..................................716 372-7652
Michael Derose, *President*
Daniel Derose, *Vice Pres*
Larry Hinman, *Sales Staff*
EMP: 11
SQ FT: 20,000
SALES (est): 2.6MM **Privately Held**
WEB: www.piercesteel.com
SIC: 3441 Fabricated structural metal

(G-12241)
SOLEPOXY INC
211 W Franklin St (14760-1211)
PHONE..................................716 372-6300
Jeff Belt, *Ch of Bd*
Kaitlyn Penston, *Manager*
Art Burkhart, *Director*
◆ EMP: 55 EST: 2010
SQ FT: 250,000
SALES (est): 14.1MM **Privately Held**
SIC: 2821 Plastics materials & resins

(G-12242)
SOMAR NORTH AMERICA CORP
211 W Franklin St (14760-1211)
PHONE..................................716 458-0742
Takayuki Kawano, *President*
Kanan Wright, *Accountant*
EMP: 5 EST: 2017
SALES (est): 360.8K **Privately Held**
SIC: 3089 Plastic containers, except foam

(G-12243)
TOTAL PIPING SOLUTIONS INC
1760 Haskell Rd (14760-9756)
P.O. Box 525 (14760-0525)
PHONE..................................716 372-0160
Daryl Piontek, *President*
Mark Langenhan, *President*
▲ EMP: 10
SQ FT: 35,000
SALES (est): 2.4MM **Privately Held**
WEB: www.tps.us
SIC: 3498 Fabricated pipe & fittings

Oneida
Madison County

(G-12244)
GOLUB CORPORATION
Also Called: Price Chopper Pharmacy
142 Genesee St (13421-2704)
PHONE..................................315 363-0679
Nena Crowne, *Branch Mgr*
EMP: 21
SALES (corp-wide): 3.6B **Privately Held**
SIC: 3751 Motorcycles & related parts
PA: The Golub Corporation
461 Nott St
Schenectady NY 12308
518 355-5000

(G-12245)
HARTMAN ENTERPRISES INC
455 Elizabeth St (13421-2438)
P.O. Box 360 (13421-0360)
PHONE..................................315 363-7300
Robert E Sweet Jr, *CEO*
Bob Sweep, *President*
EMP: 55
SQ FT: 18,000
SALES (est): 10.2MM **Privately Held**
WEB: www.hartmanenterprisesinc.com
SIC: 3599 7692 Machine shop, jobbing & repair; welding repair

(G-12246)
HP HOOD LLC
252 Genesee St (13421-2709)
P.O. Box 491 (13421-0491)
PHONE..................................315 363-3870
James Davis, *Purch Mgr*
Steve Pelky, *Manager*
EMP: 200
SALES (corp-wide): 2.2B **Privately Held**
WEB: www.hphood.com
SIC: 2026 5143 Fluid milk; dairy products, except dried or canned
PA: Hp Hood Llc
6 Kimball Ln Ste 400
Lynnfield MA 01940
617 887-8441

(G-12247)
M M WELDING
558 Lenox Ave (13421-1522)
PHONE..................................315 363-3980
Michael Marley, *Owner*
Denice Marley, *Partner*
EMP: 20
SALES (est): 428.9K **Privately Held**
SIC: 7692 Welding repair

(G-12248)
NUTECH BIOSCIENCES INC
537 Fitch St (13421-1515)
PHONE..................................315 505-6500
Pratap Reddy, *President*
EMP: 15
SQ FT: 2,000
SALES: 2MM **Privately Held**
SIC: 3295 Minerals, ground or otherwise treated

(G-12249)
ONEIDA INTERNATIONAL INC
163-181 Kenwood Ave (13421)
PHONE..................................315 361-3000
Terry G Westbrook, *President*
EMP: 6
SALES (est): 301.7K
SALES (corp-wide): 654.7MM **Privately Held**
WEB: www.oneida.net
SIC: 3262 3231 3914 3421 Vitreous china table & kitchenware; ornamental glass: cut, engraved or otherwise decorated; silverware & plated ware; cutlery
HQ: Oneida Ltd.
163 Kenwood Ave Ste 181
Oneida NY 13421
315 361-3000

(G-12250)
ONEIDA MOLDED PLASTICS LLC (PA)
104 S Warner St (13421-1510)
PHONE..................................315 363-7980

Barry Uber, *Ch of Bd*
Frank Gillette, *Engineer*
David McManmon, *Engineer*
Kevin McGreevy, *VP Bus Dvlpt*
Pam Laube, *Accounting Mgr*
▲ EMP: 130 EST: 2006
SQ FT: 82,000
SALES (est): 34.3MM **Privately Held**
WEB: oneidamoldedplastics.com
SIC: 3089 Injection molding of plastics

(G-12251)
ONEIDA PUBLICATIONS INC
Also Called: Oneida Dispatch
730 Lenox Ave (13421-1513)
PHONE..................................315 363-5100
Phil Austin, *CEO*
Kyle Mennig, *Editor*
Bradley Markowski, *Sales Staff*
Janice Collins, *Advt Staff*
EMP: 40 EST: 1851
SQ FT: 10,000
SALES (est): 2.1MM **Privately Held**
SIC: 2711 Newspapers, publishing & printing

(G-12252)
ONEIDA SILVERSMITHS INC
163 Kenwood Ave 181 (13421-2829)
PHONE..................................315 361-3000
James E Joseph, *Ch of Bd*
EMP: 7
SALES (est): 705.1K
SALES (corp-wide): 654.7MM **Privately Held**
WEB: www.oneida.net
SIC: 3262 3231 3914 3421 Vitreous china table & kitchenware; ornamental glass: cut, engraved or otherwise decorated; silverware & plated ware; cutlery
HQ: Oneida Ltd.
163 Kenwood Ave Ste 181
Oneida NY 13421
315 361-3000

(G-12253)
PATHFINDER 103 INC
229 Park Ave (13421-2021)
PHONE..................................315 363-4260
Larry Manser, *President*
EMP: 8
SALES (est): 961.4K **Privately Held**
SIC: 3589 Sewer cleaning equipment, power

(G-12254)
SHIRL-LYNN OF NEW YORK (PA)
266 Wilson St (13421)
PHONE..................................315 363-5898
Shirley Thurston, *Partner*
Mary Blau, *Partner*
EMP: 12
SQ FT: 4,300
SALES: 1MM **Privately Held**
SIC: 2339 5699 5632 Women's & misses' athletic clothing & sportswear; bathing suits: women's, misses' & juniors'; bathing suits; sports apparel; costumes, masquerade or theatrical; dancewear

(G-12255)
V & J GRAPHICS INC
153 Phelps St (13421-1708)
PHONE..................................315 363-1933
Vernon Waters, *President*
Janice Waters, *Treasurer*
Sandy Harrison,
EMP: 8
SQ FT: 4,960
SALES (est): 989.5K **Privately Held**
SIC: 2752 Commercial printing, offset

Oneonta
Otsego County

(G-12256)
AMERICAN BLADE MFG LLC (PA)
Also Called: G C Casting
138 Roundhouse Rd (13820-1200)
PHONE..................................607 432-4518
Raymond Harvey,
EMP: 12 EST: 1946

SQ FT: 1,500
SALES (est): 1.3MM **Privately Held**
WEB: www.charleslay.com
SIC: 3365 3366 Aluminum foundries;
bronze foundry

(G-12257)
ARNAN DEVELOPMENT CORP
(PA)
Also Called: Pickett Building Materials
6459 State Highway 23 (13820-6542)
PHONE..............................607 432-8391
Robert A Harlem Jr, *Ch of Bd*
Rebecca Lloyd, *Vice Pres*
Brant Conover, *Sales Staff*
Gavin Ralston, *Sales Staff*
Oneonta Orcutt, *Manager*
EMP: 52
SQ FT: 40,000
SALES: 14.9MM **Privately Held**
WEB: www.oneontablock.com
SIC: 3271 3272 5082 5211 Architectural
concrete: block, split, fluted, screen, etc.;
concrete products; septic tanks, concrete;
masonry equipment & supplies; lumber &
other building materials; management
services

(G-12258)
ASTROCOM ELECTRONICS INC
115 Dk Lifgren Dr (13820-3682)
PHONE..............................607 432-1930
Terry D Lifgren, *President*
Doug Lifgren, *COO*
Dan Berard, *Vice Pres*
Betty Catapano, *Engineer*
Ed May, *Info Tech Mgr*
▲ **EMP:** 93 **EST:** 1961
SQ FT: 65,000
SALES (est): 16.1MM **Privately Held**
WEB: www.astrocom-electronics.com
SIC: 3661 Autotransformers for telephone
switchboards

(G-12259)
BK ASSOCIATES INTL INC
127 Commerce Rd (13820-3539)
P.O. Box 1238 (13820-5238)
PHONE..............................607 432-1499
Paul Karabinis, *President*
Steve Palmer, *General Mgr*
Eugene Bettiol Sr, *Treasurer*
EMP: 15
SQ FT: 20,000
SALES (est): 2.4MM **Privately Held**
SIC: 2095 Coffee roasting (except by
wholesale grocers)

(G-12260)
BROOKS BOTTLING CO LLC
5560 State Highway 7 (13820-3699)
PHONE..............................607 432-1782
Ryan Brooks, *Mng Member*
EMP: 10
SALES (est): 1.4MM **Privately Held**
SIC: 3565 Bottling machinery: filling, cap-
ping, labeling

(G-12261)
BURT RIGID BOX INC
58 Browne St (13820-1092)
PHONE..............................607 433-2510
EMP: 52
SQ FT: 77,280
SALES (est): 4.9MM
SALES (corp-wide): 19.6MM **Privately
Held**
WEB: www.burtbox.com
SIC: 2653 2657 2652 Boxes, solid fiber:
made from purchased materials; folding
paperboard boxes; setup paperboard
boxes
PA: Burt Rigid Box, Inc.
58 Browne St
Oneonta NY 13820
607 433-2510

(G-12262)
BURT RIGID BOX INC (PA)
58 Browne St (13820-1092)
P.O. Box 1883, Buffalo (14225-8883)
PHONE..............................607 433-2510
W Russell Hurd, *President*
William Howard, *Vice Pres*
Marissa Hager, *Project Mgr*
Greg Ward, *Opers Mgr*

William Miller, *CIO*
▲ **EMP:** 10
SQ FT: 500,000
SALES (est): 19.6MM **Privately Held**
WEB: www.burtbox.com
SIC: 2631 Folding boxboard; setup
boxboard

(G-12263)
CITY OF ONEONTA
Also Called: Oneonta City Wtr Trtmnt Plant
110 East St (13820-1304)
PHONE..............................607 433-3470
Stanley Shaffer, *Manager*
EMP: 5 **Privately Held**
SIC: 3589 9111 Water treatment equip-
ment, industrial; mayors' offices
PA: City Of Oneonta
258 Main St Ste 1
Oneonta NY 13820
607 432-6450

(G-12264)
CO-OPTICS AMERICA LAB INC
Also Called: Co-Optics Groups, The
297 River Street Svc Rd Service (13820)
PHONE..............................607 432-0557
Paul Strenn, *President*
Israel Soto, *Vice Pres*
EMP: 20
SQ FT: 3,300
SALES (est): 3MM **Privately Held**
WEB: www.co-optics.com
SIC: 3851 3229 Lenses, ophthalmic;
pressed & blown glass

(G-12265)
COBLESKILL STONE
PRODUCTS INC
Also Called: Oneonta Asphalt
57 Ceperley Ave (13820)
P.O. Box 1366 (13820-5366)
PHONE..............................607 432-8321
Lennie Goodspeed, *Branch Mgr*
EMP: 10
SQ FT: 1,353
SALES (corp-wide): 126.7MM **Privately
Held**
WEB: www.cobleskillstone.com
SIC: 2951 Asphalt & asphaltic paving mix-
tures (not from refineries)
PA: Cobleskill Stone Products, Inc.
112 Rock Rd
Cobleskill NY 12043
518 234-0221

(G-12266)
COMMERCIAL DISPLAY DESIGN
LLC
58 Browne St (13820-1061)
PHONE..............................607 336-7353
W Russell Hurd,
Thomas G Naughton,
Gregory C Yungbluth,
EMP: 15
SALES (est): 110K
SALES (corp-wide): 19.6MM **Privately
Held**
SIC: 2521 Cabinets; office: wood
PA: Burt Rigid Box, Inc.
58 Browne St
Oneonta NY 13820
607 433-2510

(G-12267)
COMMUNITY NEWSPAPER
GROUP LLC
Daily Star, The
102 Chestnut St (13820-2584)
P.O. Box 250 (13820-0250)
PHONE..............................607 432-1000
Fred Scheller, *Branch Mgr*
EMP: 20 **Privately Held**
WEB: www.clintonnc.com
SIC: 2711 2752 Newspapers: publishing
only, not printed on site; commercial print-
ing, lithographic
HQ: Community Newspaper Group, Llc
3500 Colonnade Pkwy # 600
Birmingham AL 35243

(G-12268)
COOPERSTOWN BREWING CO
LLC
41 Browne St (13820-1472)
P.O. Box 276, Milford (13807-0276)
PHONE..............................607 286-9330
Dennis Haeley, *Partner*
Jewel Hall, *Partner*
Stanley Hall, *Partner*
EMP: 5
SQ FT: 5,000
SALES (est): 437.1K **Privately Held**
WEB: www.cooperstownbrewing.com
SIC: 2082 Beer (alcoholic beverage)

(G-12269)
CORNING INCORPORATED
275 River St (13820-2299)
PHONE..............................607 433-3100
Edward Smith, *Production*
Darrell Garner, *Engineer*
Teri Mauk, *Enginr/R&D Mgr*
EMP: 25
SQ FT: 20,106
SALES (corp-wide): 11.2B **Publicly Held**
WEB: www.corning.com
SIC: 3229 Pressed & blown glass
PA: Corning Incorporated
1 Riverfront Plz
Corning NY 14831
607 974-9000

(G-12270)
CREATIVE ORTHOTICS &
PROSTHET
Also Called: Hanger Clinic
37 Associate Dr (13820-2266)
PHONE..............................607 431-2526
Chris German, *Manager*
EMP: 7
SALES (corp-wide): 1B **Publicly Held**
WEB: www.creativeoandp.com
SIC: 3842 Orthopedic appliances
HQ: Creative Orthotics & Prosthetics, Inc.
1300 College Ave Ste 1
Elmira NY 14901
607 734-7215

(G-12271)
FOTIS ONEONTA ITALIAN
BAKERY
42 River St (13820-4320)
PHONE..............................607 432-3871
James Tomaino, *Owner*
EMP: 6
SALES (est): 508.7K **Privately Held**
SIC: 2051 Bakery: wholesale or whole-
sale/retail combined

(G-12272)
HANGER INC
37 Associate Dr (13820-2266)
PHONE..............................607 431-2526
EMP: 15
SALES (corp-wide): 1B **Publicly Held**
SIC: 3842 Surgical appliances & supplies
PA: Hanger, Inc.
10910 Domain Dr Ste 300
Austin TX 78758
512 777-3800

(G-12273)
LUTZ FEED CO INC
80 Lower River St (13820-2375)
PHONE..............................607 432-7984
Steven Lutz, *President*
Douglas Whittacker, *Vice Pres*
Robert Lutz, *Treasurer*
EMP: 28 **EST:** 1958
SQ FT: 15,264
SALES (est): 10.5MM **Privately Held**
SIC: 2048 Prepared feeds

(G-12274)
MAM MOLDING INC
147 River St (13820-2239)
PHONE..............................607 433-2121
Siro Vergari, *Principal*
EMP: 5
SALES (est): 460.8K **Privately Held**
SIC: 3089 Injection molding of plastics

(G-12275)
MEDICAL COACHES
INCORPORATED
399 County Highway 58 (13820-3422)
P.O. Box 129 (13820-0129)
PHONE..............................607 432-1333
Chad Smith, *President*
Kathy Caffery, *Purch Agent*
Tony Quinones, *Engineer*
Ben Miller, *Design Engr*
Jim Bazan, *Controller*
◆ **EMP:** 50 **EST:** 1952
SQ FT: 100,000
SALES: 7.8MM **Privately Held**
WEB: www.medcoach.com
SIC: 3711 Automobile assembly, including
specialty automobiles

(G-12276)
MOLD-A-MATIC CORPORATION
Also Called: Mamco
147 River St (13820-2276)
PHONE..............................607 433-2121
Siro Vergari, *Ch of Bd*
Mark Vergari, *Vice Pres*
▲ **EMP:** 45 **EST:** 1964
SQ FT: 31,000
SALES: 4MM **Privately Held**
WEB: www.mamcomolding.com
SIC: 3549 3089 Assembly machines, in-
cluding robotic; plastic processing

(G-12277)
NORTH AMERICAN SUPPLY LLC
(PA)
62 Roundhouse Rd (13820-1286)
PHONE..............................607 432-1480
Charles R Lay,
EMP: 6
SALES (est): 1.3MM **Privately Held**
SIC: 3531 Snow plow attachments

(G-12278)
ONEONTA FENCE
2 Washburn St (13820-2721)
PHONE..............................607 433-6707
EMP: 6
SALES (est): 506.7K **Privately Held**
SIC: 3089 3315 Fences, gates & acces-
sories: plastic; fence gates posts & fit-
tings: steel

(G-12279)
OTSEGO READY MIX INC
2 Wells Ave (13820-2723)
PHONE..............................607 432-3400
Robert Harlem Jr, *President*
EMP: 16
SQ FT: 8,000
SALES: 3.9MM **Privately Held**
SIC: 3273 Ready-mixed concrete

(G-12280)
PONY FARM PRESS &
GRAPHICS
Also Called: Village Print Room
330 Pony Farm Rd (13820-3591)
PHONE..............................607 432-9020
Edward May, *President*
EMP: 7
SQ FT: 12,000
SALES (est): 594.5K **Privately Held**
WEB: www.ponyfarmpress.com
SIC: 2759 Commercial printing

(G-12281)
RJ MILLWORKERS INC
12 Lewis St (13820-2652)
PHONE..............................607 433-0525
Randy J Morley, *President*
Ellen Morley, *Vice Pres*
Christy Parish, *Opers Mgr*
EMP: 20
SALES (est): 3.7MM **Privately Held**
WEB: www.rjmillworkers.com
SIC: 2431 Doors, wood

(G-12282)
T S PINK CORP
Also Called: TS Pink
139 Pony Farm Rd (13820-3537)
PHONE..............................607 432-1100
Todd Pink, *President*
Bruce Hirabayashi, *COO*
Diana Colone, *Vice Pres*

▲ EMP: 16
SQ FT: 15,000
SALES (est): 2.6MM Privately Held
WEB: www.tspink.com
SIC: 2841 Textile soap

Ontario
Wayne County

(G-12283)
APTI PRO SYSTEMS 2000 INC
6368 Dean Pkwy (14519-8970)
PHONE..................................585 265-0160
Michael Bechtold, Ch of Bd
Matt Carlson, CFO
▲ EMP: 90
SQ FT: 15,000
SALES (est): 344.1K
SALES (corp-wide): 23.8MM Privately
Held
WEB: www.websterny.com
SIC: 3471 3827 Polishing, metals or
formed products; lens grinding equip-
ment, except ophthalmic
PA: Vi Manufacturing, Inc.
164 Orchard St
Webster NY 14580
585 872-5650

(G-12284)
ARIEL OPTICS INC
261 David Pkwy (14519-8955)
PHONE..................................585 265-4820
Frederick Koch, President
EMP: 8
SALES (est): 525K Privately Held
WEB: www.arieloptics.com
SIC: 3827 Prisms, optical

(G-12285)
AVALANCHE FABRICATION INC
6314 Dean Pkwy (14519-9011)
PHONE..................................585 545-4000
Paul Duerr, President
Thad Spaulding, Vice Pres
EMP: 14 EST: 1998
SQ FT: 5,500
SALES: 1.1MM Privately Held
WEB: www.afinc.biz
SIC: 3444 Sheet metal specialties, not
stamped

(G-12286)
CS AUTOMATION INC
Also Called: C S Welding
518 Berg Rd (14519-9376)
PHONE..................................315 524-5123
Craig Schieven, Principal
EMP: 10
SALES (est): 480K Privately Held
SIC: 7692 7389 8742 Welding repair; in-
spection & testing services; automation &
robotics consultant

(G-12287)
DATA CONTROL INC
277 David Pkwy (14519-8955)
PHONE..................................585 265-2980
Lori Ferguson, President
EMP: 4
SQ FT: 12,712
SALES: 1MM Privately Held
WEB: www.datacontrolinc.com
SIC: 2542 Fixtures: display, office or store:
except wood

(G-12288)
**DJ ACQUISITION MANAGEMENT
CORP (PA)**
Also Called: Weco Metal Products
6364 Dean Pkwy (14519-8970)
PHONE..................................585 265-3000
Donald Cornwell, President
John R Gillan, Vice Pres
▲ EMP: 75
SQ FT: 55,000
SALES (est): 13.7MM Privately Held
WEB: www.wecometal.com
SIC: 3444 Sheet metalwork

(G-12289)
**FRED A NUDD CORPORATION
(PA)**
1743 State Route 104 (14519-8935)
P.O. Box 577 (14519-0577)
PHONE..................................315 524-2531
Thomas Nudd, President
Frederick Nudd, Vice Pres
Lance Palmisano, Project Mgr
Lyle Nudd, Marketing Staff
EMP: 32
SQ FT: 40,000
SALES (est): 5.6MM Privately Held
WEB: www.nuddtowers.com
SIC: 3444 3441 1799 1622 Sheet metal-
work; tower sections, radio & television
transmission; antenna installation; bridge,
tunnel & elevated highway

(G-12290)
HARBEC INC
358 Timothy Ln (14519-9012)
PHONE..................................585 265-0010
Robert Bechtold, President
John Hoefen, Production
Keith Harbec, Engineer
Doug McKnight, Engineer
Amy Bechtold, Manager
EMP: 100
SQ FT: 15,000
SALES (est): 24MM Privately Held
WEB: www.harbec.com
SIC: 3089 Injection molded finished plastic
products; injection molding of plastics

(G-12291)
**INTEGRITY TOOL
INCORPORATED**
6485 Furnace Rd (14519-8920)
PHONE..................................315 524-4409
Mike Freidler, President
EMP: 13 EST: 1996
SQ FT: 6,000
SALES (est): 2MM Privately Held
SIC: 3599 Machine shop, jobbing & repair

(G-12292)
L&B FABRICATORS LLC
6285 Dean Prwy (14519)
PHONE..................................585 265-2731
EMP: 10
SALES (est): 1.5MM Privately Held
SIC: 3441 3444 3312 Fabricated struc-
tural metal; sheet metalwork; blast fur-
naces & steel mills

(G-12293)
LAKE IMMUNOGENICS INC
348 Berg Rd (14519-9374)
PHONE..................................585 265-1973
James Bowman, President
Barbara Bowman, Vice Pres
Ginger Sullivan, Manager
EMP: 15
SQ FT: 8,000
SALES (est): 3.1MM Privately Held
WEB: www.lakeimmunogenics.com
SIC: 2836 Plasmas; veterinary biological
products

(G-12294)
NORTHERN BIODIESEL INC
317 State Route 104 (14519-8958)
PHONE..................................585 545-4534
Jason Masters, Ch of Bd
Robert Bethold, Vice Pres
EMP: 5
SALES (est): 690K Privately Held
WEB: www.northernbiodiesel.com
SIC: 2911 Diesel fuels

(G-12295)
OPTIMAX SYSTEMS INC (PA)
6367 Dean Pkwy (14519-8939)
PHONE..................................585 265-1020
Michael P Mandina, Ch of Bd
Richard Plympton, Vice Pres
John Rohrbaugh, Facilities Mgr
Andrew Haefner, Mfg Staff
Betsy Lake, Production
EMP: 120
SQ FT: 40,000

SALES (est): 32.2MM Privately Held
WEB: www.optimaxsi.com
SIC: 3827 Lenses, optical: all types except
ophthalmic; prisms, optical

(G-12296)
OPTIPRO SYSTEMS LLC
6368 Dean Pkwy (14519-8970)
PHONE..................................585 265-0160
Mike Bechtold, Mng Member
◆ EMP: 54
SQ FT: 50,000
SALES (est): 13.3MM
SALES (corp-wide): 10.5MM Privately
Held
WEB: www.optipro.com
SIC: 3559 3827 Optical lens machinery;
optical instruments & lenses
PA: Brightside 09 Inc.
6368 Dean Pkwy
Ontario NY 14519
585 265-0160

(G-12297)
PHOTON GEAR INC
245 David Pkwy (14519-8955)
P.O. Box 495 (14519-0495)
PHONE..................................585 265-3360
Gary Blough, President
EMP: 11
SQ FT: 5,400
SALES (est): 2.2MM Privately Held
WEB: www.photongear.com
SIC: 3827 8711 Optical elements & as-
semblies, except ophthalmic; engineering
services

(G-12298)
R C KOLSTAD WATER CORP
73 Lake Rd (14519-9311)
PHONE..................................585 216-2230
William Kolstad, President
EMP: 5 EST: 1999
SALES: 2MM Privately Held
SIC: 3589 Water treatment equipment, in-
dustrial

(G-12299)
RANGER DESIGN US INC
6377 Dean Pkwy (14519-8939)
PHONE..................................800 565-5321
Derek Cowie, President
Randal Cowie, Chairman
Marcus Pilgrim, Business Mgr
Braden Harper, Vice Pres
Katie Stearns, Human Resources
▲ EMP: 20
SQ FT: 80,000
SALES (est): 3.6MM Privately Held
SIC: 3711 Motor vehicles & car bodies

(G-12300)
**ROCHESTER INDUSTRIAL CTRL
INC (PA)**
6400 Furnace Rd (14519-9744)
PHONE..................................315 524-4555
Anthony J Mastrodonato, CEO
Robin Cook, QC Mgr
Tammy Johnson, QC Mgr
Peter Farrell, Engineer
Zachary Pond, Engineer
▲ EMP: 99
SQ FT: 23,600
SALES: 10MM Privately Held
SIC: 3625 3679 3672 Relays & industrial
controls; electronic circuits; printed circuit
boards

(G-12301)
**ROCHESTER INDUSTRIAL CTRL
INC**
Also Called: R I C
6345 Furnace Rd (14519-9744)
PHONE..................................315 524-4555
Eric Albert, President
EMP: 100
SQ FT: 8,050
SALES (corp-wide): 10MM Privately
Held
SIC: 3679 Electronic circuits
PA: Rochester Industrial Control, Inc.
6400 Furnace Rd
Ontario NY 14519
315 524-4555

(G-12302)
**SCIENTIFIC POLYMER
PRODUCTS**
6265 Dean Pkwy (14519-8997)
PHONE..................................585 265-0413
Bret Vanzo, Ch of Bd
EMP: 5
SQ FT: 10,000
SALES (est): 1.2MM Privately Held
WEB: www.scientificpolymer.com
SIC: 2819 Industrial inorganic chemicals

(G-12303)
SMITH INTERNATIONAL INC
Also Called: Smith Service Corps
1915 Lake Rd (14519-9792)
PHONE..................................585 265-2330
Drew Smith, Principal
EMP: 12 Publicly Held
WEB: www.smith-intl.com
SIC: 3533 Oil & gas field machinery
HQ: Smith International, Inc.
1310 Rankin Rd
Houston TX 77073
281 443-3370

Orangeburg
Rockland County

(G-12304)
**AALBORG INSTRS & CONTRLS
INC**
20 Corporate Dr (10962-2616)
PHONE..................................845 398-3160
T J Baan, CEO
Aleksandr Benis, Electrical Engi
Christine Pomponio, Human Res Mgr
Michael Muir, Sales Executive
Diane Reed, Executive
EMP: 54
SQ FT: 33,000
SALES (est): 11.4MM Privately Held
WEB: www.aalborg.com
SIC: 3823 3824 3577 3494 Primary ele-
ments for process flow measurement;
fluid meters & counting devices; computer
peripheral equipment; valves & pipe fit-
tings; fluid power valves & hose fittings

(G-12305)
API INDUSTRIES INC (PA)
Also Called: Aluf Plastics Division
2 Glenshaw St (10962-1207)
PHONE..................................845 365-2200
Susan Rosenberg, CEO
Reuven Rosenberg, President
David Anderson, Vice Pres
Tom Cross, Vice Pres
Greg Kampschroer, Vice Pres
◆ EMP: 310
SQ FT: 300,000
SALES (est): 149.1MM Privately Held
SIC: 2673 3081 Plastic bags: made from
purchased materials; unsupported plas-
tics film & sheet

(G-12306)
API INDUSTRIES INC
Base Plastics
2 Glenshaw St (10962-1207)
PHONE..................................845 365-2200
Susan Rosenberg, CEO
EMP: 125
SALES (corp-wide): 149.1MM Privately
Held
SIC: 2673 3081 Plastic bags: made from
purchased materials; unsupported plas-
tics film & sheet
PA: Api Industries, Inc.
2 Glenshaw St
Orangeburg NY 10962
845 365-2200

(G-12307)
ARON STREIT INC
Also Called: Streit Matzoh Co
171 Route 303 (10962-2209)
PHONE..................................212 475-7000
Aron S Yagoda, Ch of Bd
Alan Adler, Vice Pres
Matthew Dinatale, Warehouse Mgr
Michael Tepper, Purchasing
Laura Burke, VP Sales

GEOGRAPHIC

▲ EMP: 45
SQ FT: 100,000
SALES (est): 7.9MM **Privately Held**
WEB: www.streitsmatzos.com
SIC: 2052 5149 Matzos; bakery products

(G-12308)
CEROVENE INC
10 Corporate Dr (10962-2614)
PHONE..................................845 359-1101
Manish Shah, *President*
EMP: 10 **Privately Held**
SIC: 2834 Pharmaceutical preparations
PA: Cerovene Inc.
　612 Corporate Way Ste 10
　Valley Cottage NY 10989

(G-12309)
CHROMALLOY AMERICAN LLC
(DH)
330 Blaisdell Rd (10962-2510)
PHONE..................................845 230-7355
Armand F Lauzon Jr, *CEO*
EMP: 24 EST: 1986
SALES (est): 26.2MM
SALES (corp-wide): 2.4B **Publicly Held**
SIC: 3724 7699 Aircraft engines & engine
　parts; engine repair & replacement, non-
　automotive
HQ: Chromalloy Gas Turbine Llc
　3999 Rca Blvd
　Palm Beach Gardens FL 33410
　561 935-3571

(G-12310)
CHROMALLOY GAS TURBINE
LLC
Also Called: Chromalloy New York
330 Blaisdell Rd (10962-2510)
PHONE..................................845 359-2462
Anthony Licciardi, *President*
Dennis Walsh, *President*
Zixi Huang, *Engineer*
Anthony Lombardi, *Controller*
Cathy Vazquez, *Human Res Mgr*
EMP: 200
SALES (corp-wide): 2.4B **Publicly Held**
WEB: www.chromalloysatx.com
SIC: 3724 Aircraft engines & engine parts
HQ: Chromalloy Gas Turbine Llc
　3999 Rca Blvd
　Palm Beach Gardens FL 33410
　561 935-3571

(G-12311)
CRESTRON ELECTRONICS INC
Also Called: Creston Electronics
88 Ramland Rd S (10962-2622)
PHONE..................................201 894-0670
Peggie Devaney, *Project Mgr*
Atul Baxi, *Engineer*
Esteban Gonzalez, *Engineer*
Daniel Previti, *Engineer*
Luis Rubio, *Project Engr*
EMP: 100
SALES (corp-wide): 626.7MM **Privately
Held**
SIC: 3714 3625 Motor vehicle parts & ac-
　cessories; relays & industrial controls
PA: Crestron Electronics, Inc.
　15 Volvo Dr
　Rockleigh NJ 07647
　201 767-3400

(G-12312)
DHS SYSTEMS LLC (HQ)
560 Route 303 Ste 206 (10962-1329)
PHONE..................................845 359-6066
Samuel R Marrone, *CEO*
A Jon Prusmack, *President*
Chuck Gregory, *Vice Pres*
Brian Mindich, *Mfg Dir*
Mike Davis, *Human Res Mgr*
▲ EMP: 15
SQ FT: 75,000
SALES: 80MM **Privately Held**
WEB: www.drash.com
SIC: 2394 Tents: made from purchased
　materials

(G-12313)
EMMI USA INC
100 Dutch Hill Rd Ste 220 (10962-2198)
PHONE..................................845 268-9990
Steven Millard, *President*
Paul Schilt, *President*

Mattaias Kinz, *Chairman*
Carol Nicolay, *Sales Staff*
▲ EMP: 19
SQ FT: 12,000
SALES (est): 3.7MM
SALES (corp-wide): 251.6MM **Privately
Held**
WEB: www.emmiusa.com
SIC: 2096 Cheese curls & puffs
HQ: Emmi International Ag
　Landenbergstrasse 1
　Luzern LU 6005
　412 272-727

(G-12314)
ESSILOR LABORATORIES AMER
INC
Also Called: Nova Optical
165 Route 303 (10962-2209)
PHONE..................................845 365-6700
EMP: 50
SALES (corp-wide): 100.9MM **Privately
Held**
SIC: 3851 Mfg Ophthalmic Goods
HQ: Essilor Laboratories Of America, Inc.
　13515 N Stemmons Fwy
　Dallas TX 75234
　972 241-4141

(G-12315)
EUROMED INC
25 Corporate Dr (10962-2615)
PHONE..................................845 359-4039
Richard Wildnauer, *Ch of Bd*
Thomas E Gardner, *President*
Stephen Powell, *COO*
Brian Coughlin, *Vice Pres*
Ravi Ramjit, *Vice Pres*
◆ EMP: 95
SQ FT: 42,000
SALES (est): 22.8MM
SALES (corp-wide): 401.1MM **Privately
Held**
WEB: www.euromedinc.com
SIC: 3842 Bandages & dressings
PA: Scapa Group Public Limited Company
　994 Manchester Road
　Ashton-Under-Lyne LANCS OL7 0
　161 301-7400

(G-12316)
FERRO MACHINE CO INC
70 S Greenbush Rd (10962-1323)
PHONE..................................845 398-3641
John Ferrogari, *President*
Susan Ferrogari, *Vice Pres*
EMP: 5
SQ FT: 4,500
SALES (est): 490K **Privately Held**
SIC: 3599 Machine shop, jobbing & repair

(G-12317)
GUARDIAN BOOTH LLC (PA)
527 Route 303 (10962-1303)
PHONE..................................844 992-6684
Abraham Taub, *Owner*
▲ EMP: 10
SALES (est): 2.1MM **Privately Held**
SIC: 3448 Docks: prefabricated metal

(G-12318)
GUARDIAN BOOTH LLC
527 Ny 303 (10962)
PHONE..................................844 992-6684
Abraham Taub, *Branch Mgr*
EMP: 10
SALES (corp-wide): 2.1MM **Privately
Held**
SIC: 3448 Docks: prefabricated metal
PA: Guardian Booth Llc
　527 Route 303
　Orangeburg NY 10962
　844 992-6684

(G-12319)
INERTIA SWITCH INC
70 S Greenbush Rd (10962-1323)
PHONE..................................845 359-8300
Ruth Fischer, *President*
Brian Digirolamo, *Chief Engr*
Nadine Nodhturft, *Controller*
EMP: 25 EST: 1959
SQ FT: 9,500

SALES (est): 5.4MM **Privately Held**
WEB: www.inertiaswitch.com
SIC: 3625 3812 3643 3613 Control cir-
　cuit devices, magnet & solid state; accel-
　eration indicators & systems components,
　aerospace; current-carrying wiring de-
　vices; switchgear & switchboard appara-
　tus

(G-12320)
INNOVATIVE PLASTICS CORP
(PA)
400 Route 303 (10962-1340)
PHONE..................................845 359-7500
Judith Hershaft, *Ch of Bd*
Stephen Hershaft, *Vice Pres*
Andy Fraga, *Prdtn Mgr*
Mike Parejo, *Purch Agent*
Peter Streitman, *CFO*
▼ EMP: 150 EST: 1982
SQ FT: 100,000
SALES: 40.4MM **Privately Held**
WEB: www.innovative-plastics.com
SIC: 3089 Injection molding of plastics;
　thermoformed finished plastic products;
　molding primary plastic

(G-12321)
INSTRUMENTATION
LABORATORY CO
526 Route 303 (10962-1309)
PHONE..................................845 680-0028
Doug Ward, *General Mgr*
Steve Hartenfels, *Materials Mgr*
Randy Vlasak, *Facilities Mgr*
Stephanie Annessi, *Engineer*
Jose Borges, *Engineer*
EMP: 180
SQ FT: 54,883
SALES (corp-wide): 115.1MM **Privately
Held**
WEB: www.ilww.com
SIC: 2836 3842 3821 2899 Blood deriva-
　tives; surgical appliances & supplies; lab-
　oratory apparatus & furniture; chemical
　preparations
HQ: Instrumentation Laboratory Company
　180 Hartwell Rd
　Bedford MA 01730
　781 861-0710

(G-12322)
LTS INC
37 Ramland Rd 2 (10962-2606)
PHONE..................................845 494-2940
Hirak Aarmaker, *President*
Slava Kogan, *Treasurer*
▲ EMP: 12
SQ FT: 1,400
SALES (est): 1.5MM **Privately Held**
WEB: www.ltschem.com
SIC: 2865 Chemical indicators

(G-12323)
MACHIDA INCORPORATED
Also Called: Vision-Sciences
40 Ramland Rd S Ste 1 (10962-2698)
PHONE..................................845 365-0600
Ron Hadani, *CEO*
Mark Landman, *Vice Pres*
Ranbir Johar, *Mfg Spvr*
Yoav M Cohen, *CFO*
Christian Escobar, *Chief Mktg Ofcr*
EMP: 7
SQ FT: 10,000
SALES (est): 1.9MM
SALES (corp-wide): 56.3MM **Privately
Held**
WEB: www.visionsciences.com
SIC: 3827 Boroscopes
HQ: Cogentix Medical, Inc.
　5420 Feltl Rd
　Minnetonka MN 55343

(G-12324)
NICE-PAK PRODUCTS INC (PA)
2 Nice Pak Park (10962-1376)
PHONE..................................845 365-1700
Robert Julius, *President*
John Culligan, *President*
Jon Kupperman, *President*
Zachary Julius, *Exec VP*
William E Dwan, *Senior VP*
◆ EMP: 400
SQ FT: 168,000

SALES (est): 378.5MM **Privately Held**
WEB: www.nicepak.com
SIC: 2621 7389 2676 Towels, tissues &
　napkins: paper & stock; sanitary tissue
　paper; packaging & labeling services;
　sanitary paper products

(G-12325)
PICCINI INDUSTRIES LTD
37 Ramland Rd (10962-2606)
PHONE..................................845 365-0614
John Piccininni, *Ch of Bd*
EMP: 30
SQ FT: 23,000
SALES (est): 3.2MM **Privately Held**
WEB: www.piccini.net
SIC: 2421 2522 2521 2511 Sawmills &
　planing mills, general; office furniture, ex-
　cept wood; wood office furniture; wood
　household furniture; wood kitchen cabi-
　nets; millwork

(G-12326)
PRAXAIR INC
542 Route 303 (10962-1309)
PHONE..................................845 359-4200
Mark Murphy, *President*
Darryl Draper, *Purch Mgr*
Paul Gilman, *Info Tech Dir*
EMP: 150 **Privately Held**
SIC: 2813 Industrial gases
HQ: Praxair, Inc.
　10 Riverview Dr
　Danbury CT 06810
　203 837-2000

(G-12327)
PRAXAIR SURFACE TECH INC
560 Route 303 (10962-1329)
PHONE..................................845 398-8322
David Strauff, *Manager*
EMP: 160 **Privately Held**
SIC: 3471 Plating & polishing
HQ: Praxair Surface Technologies, Inc.
　1500 Polco St
　Indianapolis IN 46222
　317 240-2500

(G-12328)
PRODUCTO ELECTRIC CORP
Also Called: Peco Conduit Fittings
11 Kings Hwy (10962-1897)
PHONE..................................845 359-4900
Arthur Lemay, *President*
John Fischer, *Vice Pres*
◆ EMP: 30 EST: 1935
SQ FT: 54,000
SALES (est): 5.1MM **Privately Held**
WEB: www.pecoelect.com
SIC: 3644 Electric conduits & fittings

(G-12329)
PROFESSNAL DSPOSABLES
INTL INC (PA)
2 Nice Pak Park (10962-1317)
PHONE..................................800 999-6423
Robert P Julius, *President*
William E Dwan, *Senior VP*
◆ EMP: 50
SALES (est): 192.5MM **Privately Held**
SIC: 2676 7389 2621 Sanitary paper
　products; packaging & labeling services;
　towels, tissues & napkins: paper & stock;
　sanitary tissue paper

(G-12330)
RUSKIN COMPANY
Also Called: Diversified Air Products Sales
1 Corporate Dr (10962-2615)
PHONE..................................845 767-4100
EMP: 8 **Privately Held**
SIC: 3822 Damper operators: pneumatic,
　thermostatic, electric
HQ: Ruskin Company
　3900 Doctor Greaves Rd
　Grandview MO 64030
　816 761-7476

(G-12331)
SENSORMATIC ELECTRONICS
LLC
10 Corporate Dr (10962-2614)
PHONE..................................845 365-3125
Per-Olof Loof, *President*
EMP: 15 **Privately Held**
WEB: www.sensormatic.com

2020 Harris
New York Manufacturers Directory

▲ = Import ▼=Export
◆ =Import/Export

SIC: **3812** Detection apparatus: electronic/magnetic field, light/heat
HQ: Sensormatic Electronics, Llc
6600 Congress Ave
Boca Raton FL 33487
561 912-6000

(G-12332)
SEQUA CORPORATION
330 Blaisdell Rd (10962-2510)
PHONE..................................201 343-1122
John Lansdale, *President*
Donna Costello, *Controller*
Gary Palomba, *Director*
EMP: 50
SQ FT: 367,000
SALES (corp-wide): 2.4B **Publicly Held**
WEB: www.sequa.com
SIC: **3479** Coating of metals & formed products
HQ: Sequa Corporation
3999 Rca Blvd
Palm Beach Gardens FL 33410
561 935-3571

(G-12333)
ZACKS ENTERPRISES INC
Also Called: Zagwear
33 Corporate Dr (10962-2615)
PHONE..................................800 366-4924
Toby Zacks, *CEO*
Judd Karofsky, *President*
Lenny Polakoff, *Exec VP*
Bob Hay, *Senior VP*
Nate Jacobs, *Senior VP*
▲ EMP: 50
SQ FT: 48,000
SALES (est): 14.1MM **Privately Held**
SIC: **2759 8742** Screen printing; marketing consulting services

---

Orchard Park
Erie County

(G-12334)
A LUNT DESIGN INC
5755 Big Tree Rd (14127-4115)
P.O. Box 247 (14127-0247)
PHONE..................................716 662-0781
Audrey Lunt, *President*
Thomas Lunt, *Vice Pres*
Robert Kresse, *Shareholder*
▲ EMP: 16
SQ FT: 15,000
SALES (est): 1.4MM **Privately Held**
WEB: www.alunt.com
SIC: **2389** Disposable garments & accessories

(G-12335)
A TITAN INSTRUMENTS INC
10 Centere Dr (14127)
PHONE..................................716 667-9211
Michael Tuber, *President*
Chirstopher Mahle, *Vice Pres*
Kevin Ernst, *Opers Staff*
Marcus Simmons, *Sales Mgr*
Jaclyn Schiller, *Marketing Staff*
▲ EMP: 15
SQ FT: 3,000
SALES (est): 3.1MM **Privately Held**
WEB: www.atitan.com
SIC: **3841** Surgical & medical instruments

(G-12336)
ACCIPITER RADAR CORPORATION
40 Centre Dr Ste 3 (14127-4100)
PHONE..................................716 508-4432
Tim Nohara, *President*
Darryl Nohara, *Vice Pres*
Gerry Key, *Sales Staff*
Josey V Melick, *Sales Staff*
EMP: 5
SALES (est): 560K **Privately Held**
SIC: **3812** Search & navigation equipment
HQ: Accipiter Radar Technologies Inc
576 Hwy 20
Fenwick ON L0S 1
905 228-6888

(G-12337)
ADVAN-TECH MANUFACTURING INC
3645 California Rd (14127-1715)
PHONE..................................716 667-1500
Peter Munschauer, *President*
Mathew Weierheiser, *QC Mgr*
Denise Dietz, *Manager*
Tim Smith, *Consultant*
EMP: 23
SQ FT: 7,750
SALES (est): 3.7MM **Privately Held**
SIC: **3599** Machine shop, jobbing & repair

(G-12338)
AURORA INDUS MACHINING INC
3380 N Benzing Rd (14127-1538)
PHONE..................................716 826-7911
Robert T Hesse, *President*
Mary C Hesse, *Vice Pres*
John Breen, *Treasurer*
EMP: 25
SQ FT: 20,000
SALES (est): 4.5MM
SALES (corp-wide): 39.8MM **Privately Held**
WEB: www.auroraheatexchangers.com
SIC: **3443** Heat exchangers, condensers & components; vessels, process or storage (from boiler shops); metal plate
PA: Hesse Industrial Sales, Inc.
3370 N Benzing Rd
Orchard Park NY 14127
716 827-4951

(G-12339)
BOS-HATTEN INC
Also Called: Ipe
50 Cobham Dr (14127-4121)
PHONE..................................716 662-7030
EMP: 10
SQ FT: 5,500
SALES (est): 747.9K
SALES (corp-wide): 345MM **Publicly Held**
SIC: **3443** Mfg Fabricated Plate Work
HQ: Peerless Mfg. Co.
14651 Dallas Pkwy Ste 500
Dallas TX 75254
214 357-6181

(G-12340)
BOSTON VALLEY POTTERY INC (PA)
Also Called: Boston Valley Terra Cotta
6860 S Abbott Rd (14127-4707)
PHONE..................................716 649-7490
John B Krouse, *Principal*
Gretchen E Krouse, *Vice Pres*
Richard O Krouse, *Vice Pres*
William D Krouse, *Vice Pres*
Gary Jamoni, *Safety Mgr*
▲ EMP: 135
SQ FT: 95,300
SALES (est): 21.2MM **Privately Held**
SIC: **3259** Architectural terra cotta; roofing tile, clay

(G-12341)
BUCKLEY QC FASTENERS INC
3874 California Rd (14127-2262)
PHONE..................................716 662-1490
Ruth M Kohl, *General Mgr*
Mark Furjanic, *Controller*
Kris Furjanic, *Sales Staff*
EMP: 32
SQ FT: 11,000
SALES (est): 4MM **Privately Held**
SIC: **3452** Nuts, metal; bolts, metal; screws, metal

(G-12342)
BUFFALO CIRCUITS INC
105 Mid County Dr (14127-1773)
PHONE..................................716 662-2113
Peter Messina Jr, *President*
Liz Bever, *Manager*
EMP: 7
SQ FT: 4,920
SALES (est): 1MM **Privately Held**
SIC: **3672 7336** Circuit boards, television & radio printed; silk screen design

(G-12343)
BURGESS-MANNING INC (DH)
Also Called: Skimovex USA
50 Cobham Dr (14127-4121)
PHONE..................................716 662-6540
Warner G Martin, *Ch of Bd*
Robert Sherman, *President*
Anthony Paliwoda, *VP Finance*
Shirley Martin, *Admin Sec*
▲ EMP: 60
SQ FT: 5,500
SALES (est): 19.4MM
SALES (corp-wide): 337.3MM **Publicly Held**
WEB: www.burgessmanning.com
SIC: **3625** Noise control equipment
HQ: Peerless Mfg. Co.
14651 Dallas Pkwy Ste 500
Dallas TX 75254
214 357-6181

(G-12344)
CARBON ACTIVATED CORPORATION
336 Stonehenge Dr (14127-2841)
PHONE..................................716 662-2005
Chris Allen, *Branch Mgr*
EMP: 8 **Privately Held**
WEB: www.carbonactivatedcorp.com
SIC: **2819** Charcoal (carbon), activated
PA: Carbon Activated Corporation
2250 S Central Ave
Compton CA 90220

(G-12345)
COBHAM HOLDINGS INC (DH)
Also Called: Cobham Holdings US Inc.
10 Cobham Dr (14127-4121)
PHONE..................................716 662-0006
Betty Bible, *President*
Bob Murphy, *Principal*
Lucas Mesmer, *Design Engr*
EMP: 18
SALES (est): 900.2MM
SALES (corp-wide): 2.3B **Privately Held**
SIC: **3679 3812** Microwave components; acceleration indicators & systems components, aerospace

(G-12346)
COBHAM MANAGEMENT SERVICES INC
Also Called: Cobham Mission Systems Div
10 Centre Dr (14127-2280)
PHONE..................................716 662-0006
Scott Weiner, *CEO*
Barbara Walters, *Buyer*
Michael Lobaugh, *Engineer*
Mike Rapp, *Engineer*
Brett Stroke, *Engineer*
◆ EMP: 2650
SALES (est): 228.8MM
SALES (corp-wide): 2.3B **Privately Held**
SIC: **3812** Search & navigation equipment
HQ: Cobham Holdings Inc.
10 Cobham Dr
Orchard Park NY 14127
716 662-0006

(G-12347)
COBHAM MISSION SYSTEMS (HQ)
10 Centre Dr (14127-2280)
PHONE..................................716 662-0006
Kenneth Kota, *Ch of Bd*
Kelly Coffield, *President*
Kenneth A Kota, *General Mgr*
Chuck Connelly, *Safety Dir*
Paul Crvelin, *Plant Mgr*
EMP: 277
SALES (est): 228.8MM
SALES (corp-wide): 2.3B **Privately Held**
SIC: **3812** Search & navigation equipment
PA: Cobham Plc
Brook Road
Wimborne BH21
120 288-2020

(G-12348)
CONTECH ENGNERED SOLUTIONS LLC
34 Birdsong Pkwy (14127-3067)
PHONE..................................716 870-9091
Gene Majchrzack, *Principal*
EMP: 12 **Privately Held**
SIC: **3443** Fabricated plate work (boiler shop)
HQ: Contech Engineered Solutions Llc
9025 Centre Pointe Dr # 400
West Chester OH 45069
513 645-7000

(G-12349)
CURBELL MEDICAL PRODUCTS INC
20 Centre Dr (14127-4102)
PHONE..................................716 667-2520
Tracy Rogers, *Sales Staff*
Mary Deibel, *Marketing Staff*
Dave Zavah, *Branch Mgr*
Don Gleason, *Supervisor*
EMP: 12
SALES (corp-wide): 216.5MM **Privately Held**
SIC: **3669** Intercommunication systems, electric
HQ: Curbell Medical Products, Inc.
7 Cobham Dr
Orchard Park NY 14127

(G-12350)
CURBELL MEDICAL PRODUCTS INC (HQ)
7 Cobham Dr (14127-4180)
PHONE..................................716 667-2520
Thomas E Leone, *Ch of Bd*
Christine L Sabuda, *Vice Ch Bd*
Doug Rockwood, *Exec VP*
Don Gibson, *Vice Pres*
Thomas Cecala, *Mfg Staff*
▲ EMP: 152
SALES: 50.5MM
SALES (corp-wide): 216.5MM **Privately Held**
WEB: www.curbell.com
SIC: **3669** Intercommunication systems, electric
PA: Curbell, Inc.
7 Cobham Dr
Orchard Park NY 14127
716 667-3377

(G-12351)
DESMI-AFTI INC
227 Thorn Ave Bldg C (14127-2600)
P.O. Box 575 (14127-0575)
PHONE..................................716 662-0632
Peter Lane, *President*
Andy Nash, *Business Mgr*
▼ EMP: 20
SQ FT: 26,131
SALES (est): 5MM **Privately Held**
WEB: www.afti.com
SIC: **3533 3535** Oil field machinery & equipment; belt conveyor systems, general industrial use

(G-12352)
FLOW-SAFE INC
3865 Taylor Rd (14127-2297)
PHONE..................................716 662-2585
Warner Martin, *Ch of Bd*
Kevin Martin, *President*
John Ostroot, *Engineer*
Sharon Ruggiero, *
▲ EMP: 40
SQ FT: 25,000
SALES (est): 8.5MM **Privately Held**
SIC: **3491 5074** Industrial valves; plumbing & heating valves

(G-12353)
GAYMAR INDUSTRIES INC
10 Centre Dr (14127-2280)
PHONE..................................800 828-7341
Bradford L Saar, *CEO*
Kent J Davies, *Principal*
▲ EMP: 350 EST: 1956
SQ FT: 110,000
SALES (est): 45.1MM
SALES (corp-wide): 13.6B **Publicly Held**
WEB: www.gaymar.com
SIC: **3841** Surgical & medical instruments
PA: Stryker Corporation
2825 Airview Blvd
Portage MI 49002
269 385-2600

(G-12354)
IMPACT JOURNALS LLC
Also Called: Publishing Medical Journals
6666 E Quaker St Ste 1 (14127-2547)
PHONE..........................800 922-0957
Zoya Demidenko, *Mng Member*
Brian Bittman, *Software Dev*
EMP: 8
SALES: 100K **Privately Held**
SIC: 2721 Periodicals: publishing & printing

(G-12355)
ITT CORP
7 Centre Dr (14127-2281)
PHONE..........................716 662-1900
Michael Siino, *President*
Scott Shular, *Opers Staff*
Shelly Even, *Buyer*
Justin Reese, *Buyer*
Christopher Amara, *Sales Staff*
EMP: 20
SALES (est): 3.2MM **Privately Held**
SIC: 3625 Control equipment, electric

(G-12356)
ITT ENIDINE INC (DH)
Also Called: Enivate - Aerospace Division
7 Centre Dr (14127-2281)
PHONE..........................716 662-1900
Dennise Ramos, *CEO*
Munish Nanda, *Ch of Bd*
Dennis Schully, *President*
David Snowberger, *Business Mgr*
Dan Claycomb, *Plant Mgr*
▲ EMP: 275
SQ FT: 85,000
SALES (est): 116.4MM
SALES (corp-wide): 2.7B **Publicly Held**
WEB: www.enidine.com
SIC: 3724 3714 3593 Aircraft engines & engine parts; motor vehicle parts & accessories; fluid power cylinders & actuators
HQ: Itt Llc
1133 Westchester Ave N-100
White Plains NY 10604
914 641-2000

(G-12357)
J H BUSCHER INC
227 Thorn Ave Ste 30 (14127-2671)
PHONE..........................716 667-2003
John H Buscher, *President*
Margaret G Buscher, *Vice Pres*
EMP: 5
SQ FT: 3,000
SALES: 700K **Privately Held**
WEB: www.jhbi.com
SIC: 3491 Industrial valves

(G-12358)
JARACZ JR JOSEPH PAUL
64 Ferndale Dr (14127-1644)
PHONE..........................716 533-1377
Joseph Paul Jaracz Jr, *Owner*
Kyle Gooding, *CFO*
EMP: 8
SALES (est): 293.5K **Privately Held**
SIC: 3845 3841 Electromedical equipment; surgical & medical instruments

(G-12359)
KELSON PRODUCTS INC
3300 N Benzing Rd (14127-1538)
PHONE..........................716 825-2585
Joseph P Merz, *President*
EMP: 7
SQ FT: 10,864
SALES: 700K **Privately Held**
WEB: www.kelsonproducts.com
SIC: 3069 Rubberized fabrics

(G-12360)
KINEDYNE INC
Also Called: Engineered Lifting Tech
3566 S Benzing Rd (14127-1703)
PHONE..........................716 667-6833
William Hanes, *President*
EMP: 18
SQ FT: 17,000
SALES (est): 4.3MM **Privately Held**
SIC: 3531 Cranes

(G-12361)
LAKE REGION MEDICAL INC
3902 California Rd (14127-2275)
P.O. Box 637 (14127-0637)
PHONE..........................716 662-5025
Joe Burck, *Project Mgr*
Michael Ekstrum, *Opers Staff*
Dee Leahy, *Buyer*
Himal Kafle, *Engineer*
Rogelio Velazquez, *Engineer*
EMP: 110
SALES (corp-wide): 1.2B **Publicly Held**
SIC: 3841 Surgical instruments & apparatus; medical instruments & equipment; blood & bone work
HQ: Lake Region Medical, Inc.
100 Fordham Rd Ste 3
Wilmington MA 01887

(G-12362)
LD MCCAULEY LLC
3875 California Rd (14127-2239)
PHONE..........................716 662-6744
Durham McCauley, *President*
Peter McCauley, *Vice Pres*
David Powers, *Vice Pres*
EMP: 120
SALES (est): 15.5MM **Privately Held**
SIC: 3452 Bolts, nuts, rivets & washers

(G-12363)
MANZELLA KNITTING
3345 N Benzing Rd (14127-1539)
PHONE..........................716 825-0808
Ed Masanovic, *Owner*
▲ EMP: 7
SALES (est): 608.3K **Privately Held**
SIC: 2381 Gloves, work: woven or knit, made from purchased materials

(G-12364)
MARATHON ROOFING PRODUCTS INC
3310 N Benzing Rd (14127-1538)
PHONE..........................716 685-3340
Tod Cislo, *President*
Tim Krawczyk, *Sales Staff*
Erik Piechowicz, *Sales Staff*
Ann Mitchell, *Associate*
◆ EMP: 10
SQ FT: 30,000
SALES (est): 3MM **Privately Held**
WEB: www.marathondrains.com
SIC: 2952 5033 Roofing materials; roofing & siding materials

(G-12365)
MEDSOURCE TECHNOLOGIES LLC
3902 California Rd (14127-2275)
PHONE..........................716 662-5025
Jim Clark, *Manager*
EMP: 100
SALES (corp-wide): 1.2B **Publicly Held**
WEB: www.medsourcetech.com
SIC: 3841 Surgical & medical instruments
HQ: Medsource Technologies, Llc
100 Fordham Rd Ste 1
Wilmington MA 01887
978 570-6900

(G-12366)
MENTHOLATUM COMPANY (DH)
707 Sterling Dr (14127-1587)
PHONE..........................716 677-2500
Akiyoshi Yoshida PHD, *CEO*
Kunio Yamada, *President*
Francis Chan, *Vice Pres*
Meryl Reis, *Vice Pres*
Michael Lonczak, *Project Mgr*
◆ EMP: 34 EST: 1889
SQ FT: 102,000
SALES (est): 51.7MM **Privately Held**
WEB: www.mentholatum.com
SIC: 2844 2834 Toilet preparations; analgesics
HQ: Rohto Usa Inc
707 Sterling Dr
Orchard Park NY 14127
716 677-2500

(G-12367)
MRP SUPPORTS LLC
3310 N Benzing Rd (14127-1538)
PHONE..........................716 332-7673

Tod Cislo, *Mng Member*
▲ EMP: 16
SQ FT: 37,000
SALES: 1.3MM **Privately Held**
SIC: 2541 Pedestals & statuary, wood

(G-12368)
NITRAM ENERGY INC
Also Called: Alco Products Div
50 Cobham Dr (14127-4121)
PHONE..........................716 662-6540
Peter J Burlage, *CEO*
Robert Sherman, *President*
Shirley Martin, *Admin Sec*
EMP: 50 EST: 1979
SQ FT: 5,500
SALES (est): 4.5MM
SALES (corp-wide): 337.3MM **Publicly Held**
SIC: 3625 3443 Control equipment, electric; heat exchangers: coolers (after, inter), condensers, etc.
HQ: Peerless Mfg. Co.
14651 Dallas Pkwy Ste 500
Dallas TX 75254
214 357-6181

(G-12369)
P M PLASTICS INC
1 Bank St Ste 1 # 1 (14127-2997)
PHONE..........................716 662-1255
Paul Sparks, *President*
Mark Zybert, *Treasurer*
EMP: 25
SQ FT: 46,000
SALES: 3.5MM **Privately Held**
SIC: 3089 Injection molding of plastics

(G-12370)
PANAGRAPHICS INC
Also Called: Polish American Journal
30 Quail Run (14127-4611)
P.O. Box 198, Bowmansville (14026-0198)
PHONE..........................716 312-8088
Mark A Cohan, *President*
Christopher Misztal, *Vice Pres*
Caroline Szczepanski, *Treasurer*
EMP: 5
SQ FT: 1,200
SALES (est): 462K **Privately Held**
SIC: 2791 2711 Typesetting; newspapers

(G-12371)
PARATUS INDUSTRIES INC
6659 E Quaker St (14127-2503)
PHONE..........................716 826-2000
Stephen Idziur, *President*
Thomas Zimmermann, *Vice Pres*
EMP: 30
SQ FT: 20,000
SALES (est): 4.8MM **Privately Held**
WEB: www.paratusindustries.com
SIC: 3999 Barber & beauty shop equipment

(G-12372)
POLYMER CONVERSIONS INC
5732 Big Tree Rd (14127-4196)
PHONE..........................716 662-8550
Jack E Bertsch, *CEO*
Benjamin Harp, *COO*
John Welton, *Vice Pres*
Wells Crawley, *Engineer*
Steve Hoch, *Engineer*
EMP: 70
SQ FT: 35,000
SALES (est): 18.7MM **Privately Held**
WEB: www.polymerconversions.com
SIC: 3089 Molding primary plastic; injection molding of plastics

(G-12373)
PRECISION ABRASIVES CORP
3176 Abbott Rd (14127-1069)
PHONE..........................716 826-5833
Kevin Wyckoff, *President*
Pam Vogel, *Exec VP*
Jeff Kraatz, *Plant Mgr*
Craig Young, *Prdtn Mgr*
Stacey Coyne, *Purch Mgr*
▲ EMP: 50
SQ FT: 25,000
SALES (est): 6.9MM
SALES (corp-wide): 11MM **Privately Held**
WEB: www.wesand.com
SIC: 3291 Coated abrasive products

PA: Sopark Corp.
3300 S Park Ave
Buffalo NY 14218
716 822-0434

(G-12374)
PUMPCRETE CORPORATION
7126 Ellicott Rd (14127-3438)
PHONE..........................716 667-7867
George Culp, *President*
Melissa Williams, *General Ptnr*
Lisa Pickard, *Manager*
EMP: 8
SQ FT: 3,500
SALES: 1.8MM **Privately Held**
SIC: 3561 Pumps & pumping equipment

(G-12375)
QUAKER MILLWORK & LUMBER INC
77 S Davis St (14127-2684)
PHONE..........................716 662-3388
Robert J Raber, *President*
EMP: 40
SQ FT: 36,000
SALES (est): 6.7MM **Privately Held**
WEB: www.quakermills.com
SIC: 2431 Doors & door parts & trim, wood

(G-12376)
QUALITY INDUSTRIAL SERVICES
Also Called: Bws Specialty Fabrication
75 Bank St (14127-2908)
PHONE..........................716 667-7703
John E Sisson, *CEO*
EMP: 14
SQ FT: 52,800
SALES (est): 2.9MM **Privately Held**
SIC: 3496 7692 Miscellaneous fabricated wire products; welding repair

(G-12377)
STI-CO INDUSTRIES INC
11 Cobham Dr Ste A (14127-4187)
PHONE..........................716 662-2680
Antoinette Kaiser, *CEO*
Antoinette P Kaiser, *CEO*
Kyle Sawiat, *President*
Michael King, *Production*
Andy Drews, *Technical Staff*
EMP: 48
SQ FT: 10,000
SALES (est): 12.2MM **Privately Held**
WEB: www.sti-co.com
SIC: 3663 Antennas, transmitting & communications

(G-12378)
TAYLOR METALWORKS INC
3925 California Rd (14127-2276)
PHONE..........................716 662-3113
Peter G Taylor, *President*
Jason Taylor, *Vice Pres*
EMP: 110
SQ FT: 37,000
SALES (est): 21.8MM **Privately Held**
WEB: www.taylorcnc.com
SIC: 3451 3365 Screw machine products; aluminum & aluminum-based alloy castings

(G-12379)
TRANSPORT NATIONAL DEV INC (PA)
Also Called: North American Carbide
5720 Ellis Rd (14127-2223)
PHONE..........................716 662-0270
Robert A Gralke, *President*
Robert Gralke Jr, *Sales Mgr*
Cindy Donnelly, *Manager*
Marsha Gralke, *Admin Sec*
EMP: 50
SQ FT: 30,000
SALES (est): 15.7MM **Privately Held**
SIC: 3541 Machine tools, metal cutting type

(G-12380)
TRANSPORT NATIONAL DEV INC
Also Called: North American Carbide of NY
5720 Ellis Rd (14127-2223)
PHONE..........................716 662-0270
Robert Gralke, *Enginr/R&D Mgr*

▲ = Import ▼=Export
◆ =Import/Export

EMP: 50
SALES (corp-wide): 15.7MM **Privately Held**
SIC: 2819 3545 Carbides; machine tool accessories
PA: Transport National Development, Inc.
5720 Ellis Rd
Orchard Park NY 14127
716 662-0270

(G-12381)
UNITED MATERIALS LLC
Also Called: Frey Concrete Incoporated
75 Bank St (14127-2908)
PHONE..................................716 662-0564
EMP: 6
SALES (corp-wide): 19.2MM **Privately Held**
SIC: 3273 1442 Mfg Ready-Mixed Concrete Construction Sand/Gravel
PA: United Materials, L.L.C.
3949 Frest Pk Way Ste 400
North Tonawanda NY 14120
716 683-1432

(G-12382)
VIBRATION & NOISE ENGRG CORP
Also Called: Vanec
3374 N Benzing Rd (14127-1538)
PHONE..................................716 827-4959
Art Cagney, *President*
Thomas Love, *President*
EMP: 3
SQ FT: 2,000
SALES (est): 1.6MM **Privately Held**
WEB: www.vanec.com
SIC: 3625 5084 Noise control equipment; industrial machinery & equipment

(G-12383)
WATERHOUSE PUBLICATIONS INC
Also Called: Ink Well Press
3770 Transit Rd (14127-2053)
PHONE..................................716 662-4200
Robert Rozeski, *President*
EMP: 30
SALES: 3.4MM **Privately Held**
SIC: 2759 2791 2752 Commercial printing; typesetting; commercial printing, lithographic

Oriskany
Oneida County

(G-12384)
BONIDE PRODUCTS LLC
6301 Sutliff Rd (13424-4326)
PHONE..................................315 736-8231
James J Wurz, *CEO*
Edward Turz, *Vice Pres*
Dwight Hammond, *Sales Staff*
Ron Harnist, *Sales Staff*
Mia Keske, *Sales Staff*
▲ **EMP:** 2
SQ FT: 27,000
SALES (est): 48.2MM
SALES (corp-wide): 64.2B **Privately Held**
WEB: www.bonideproducts.com
SIC: 2899 Chemical preparations
HQ: Control Solutions, Inc.
5903 Genoa Red Bluff Rd
Pasadena TX 77507
281 892-2500

(G-12385)
CALDWELL BENNETT INC
Also Called: C B I
6152 County Seat Rd (13424-4308)
P.O. Box 610, Rome (13442-0610)
PHONE..................................315 337-8540
Douglas Brazinski, *President*
Brian Brazinski, *Vice Pres*
Brian Brazinski, *Vice Pres*
Joan Brazinski, *Vice Pres*
Paul Brazinski, *Vice Pres*
EMP: 45
SQ FT: 40,000
SALES (est): 9.1MM **Privately Held**
WEB: www.cbicables.com
SIC: 3357 Communication wire

(G-12386)
COVENTYA INC (DH)
132 Clear Rd (13424-4300)
PHONE..................................216 351-1500
Lon Thrasher, *Ch of Bd*
Mark Andrus, *Business Mgr*
Andrew Pinkelman, *Purch Mgr*
Adam Ricco, *Research*
Alex Roggia, *Technology*
◆ **EMP:** 70 **EST:** 1967
SQ FT: 51,000
SALES (est): 13.5MM
SALES (corp-wide): 25.2MM **Privately Held**
WEB: www.taskem.com
SIC: 2899 Water treating compounds
HQ: Coventya
7 Rue Du Cdt D Estienne D Orves
Villeneuve-La-Garenne 92390
142 042-975

(G-12387)
COVENTYA INC
132 Clear Rd (13424-4300)
PHONE..................................315 768-6635
EMP: 11
SALES (corp-wide): 25.2MM **Privately Held**
WEB: www.sirius-tech.com
SIC: 2899 Plating compounds
HQ: Coventya, Inc.
132 Clear Rd
Oriskany NY 13424
216 351-1500

(G-12388)
CPP - STEEL TREATERS
100 Furnace St (13424-4816)
PHONE..................................315 736-3081
Joseph Weber, *President*
Jennifer Landry, *Manager*
David Stopera, *Manager*
EMP: 29 **EST:** 1957
SQ FT: 4,000
SALES (est): 5.7MM
SALES (corp-wide): 6.9B **Privately Held**
SIC: 3398 Metal heat treating
HQ: Cpp-Syracuse, Inc.
901 E Genesee St
Chittenango NY 13037
315 687-0014

(G-12389)
DAIMLER BUSES NORTH AMER INC
165 Base Rd (13424)
P.O. Box 748 (13424-0748)
PHONE..................................315 768-8101
Bernd Voigt, *Ch of Bd*
Andreas Strecker, *President*
Harry Rendel, *CFO*
▲ **EMP:** 560
SQ FT: 40,000
SALES (est): 68.3MM
SALES (corp-wide): 191.6B **Privately Held**
WEB: www.orionbus.com
SIC: 3713 3711 Truck & bus bodies; motor buses, except trackless trolleys, assembly of
HQ: Daimler Trucks North America Llc
4555 N Channel Ave
Portland OR 97217
503 745-8000

(G-12390)
FIBER INSTRUMENT SALES INC (PA)
Also Called: F I S
161 Clear Rd (13424-4339)
PHONE..................................315 736-2206
Frank Giotto, *President*
Susan Grabinsky, *President*
Alison Stanulevich, *Counsel*
Kirk Donley, *Senior VP*
Valerie Sitler, *Senior VP*
◆ **EMP:** 220
SQ FT: 90,000
SALES (est): 108.1MM **Privately Held**
WEB: www.fisfiber.com
SIC: 3661 3643 2298 3699 Fiber optics communications equipment; connectors & terminals for electrical devices; cable, fiber; security devices

(G-12391)
GOLD MEDAL PACKING INC
8301 Old River Rd (13424)
P.O. Box 652 (13424-0652)
PHONE..................................315 337-1911
Joseph Rocco Jr, *President*
Nancy Stilwell, *Controller*
Liz Shapano, *Admin Sec*
EMP: 60
SQ FT: 10,000
SALES (est): 8.5MM **Privately Held**
WEB: www.goldmedalpacking.com
SIC: 2011 Meat packing plants

(G-12392)
INDUSTRIAL OIL TANK SERVICE
120 Dry Rd (13424-4311)
PHONE..................................315 736-6080
John E Hitchings Jr, *President*
John E Hitchings Sr, *Admin Sec*
EMP: 10
SQ FT: 11,580
SALES (est): 1.8MM **Privately Held**
SIC: 2992 Re-refining lubricating oils & greases

(G-12393)
ORISKANY ARMS INC
175 Clear Rd (13424-4301)
PHONE..................................315 737-2196
Frank Giotto, *CEO*
Jim Rabbia, *President*
EMP: 13
SQ FT: 10,000
SALES (est): 4MM **Privately Held**
SIC: 3484 Guns (firearms) or gun parts, 30 mm. & below

(G-12394)
SEIFERT GRAPHICS INC
Also Called: Seifert Transit Graphics
6133 Judd Rd (13424-4220)
PHONE..................................315 736-2744
Karen M Seifert, *President*
Sara Barden, *Production*
Emmett Seifert, *Accounts Exec*
EMP: 15
SQ FT: 20,000
SALES (est): 3.4MM **Privately Held**
WEB: www.seifertgraphics.com
SIC: 3993 Signs & advertising specialties

(G-12395)
SQUARE ONE COATING SYSTEMS LLC
170 Base Rd (13424-4204)
PHONE..................................315 790-5921
Jody McRedmond, *Manager*
EMP: 9 **EST:** 2013
SALES (est): 1.1MM **Privately Held**
SIC: 3471 Plating & polishing

(G-12396)
SUIT-KOTE CORPORATION
Also Called: Central Asphalt
191 Dry Rd (13424-4312)
PHONE..................................315 735-8501
Lee Wall, *Branch Mgr*
EMP: 13
SALES (corp-wide): 272.8MM **Privately Held**
WEB: www.suit-kote.com
SIC: 2951 Asphalt paving mixtures & blocks
PA: Suit-Kote Corporation
1911 Lorings Crossing Rd
Cortland NY 13045
607 753-1100

(G-12397)
SUMAX CYCLE PRODUCTS INC
122 Clear Rd (13424-4300)
PHONE..................................315 768-1058
Linda Van Scoten, *President*
Kirk Van Scotten, *Vice Pres*
EMP: 16
SQ FT: 11,000
SALES: 611.4K **Privately Held**
WEB: www.sumax.com
SIC: 3751 Motorcycles & related parts; motorcycle accessories

(G-12398)
TERAHERTZ TECHNOLOGIES INC
Also Called: T T I
169 Clear Rd (13424-4301)
PHONE..................................315 736-3642
Michael Mazzatti, *President*
EMP: 6
SQ FT: 28,000
SALES: 1.8MM **Privately Held**
WEB: www.terahertztechnologies.com
SIC: 3661 8742 8731 Fiber optics communications equipment; industrial & labor consulting services; electronic research

(G-12399)
TLC-THE LIGHT CONNECTION INC
132 Base Rd (13424-4204)
PHONE..................................315 736-7384
Brian Mohar, *President*
Brain Mohar, *President*
Fritz Barns, *Principal*
Doug Rouse, *Principal*
Keith Vanderzell, *Principal*
EMP: 70
SQ FT: 19,500
SALES (est): 19.5MM
SALES (corp-wide): 108.1MM **Privately Held**
WEB: www.thelightconnection.com
SIC: 3357 Fiber optic cable (insulated)
PA: Fiber Instrument Sales, Inc.
161 Clear Rd
Oriskany NY 13424
315 736-2206

Oriskany Falls
Oneida County

(G-12400)
HANSON AGGREGATES PA LLC
1780 State Route 12b (13425)
P.O. Box 368 (13425-0368)
PHONE..................................315 821-7222
Donald Henings, *Manager*
EMP: 15
SALES (corp-wide): 20.6B **Privately Held**
SIC: 1442 1429 1422 Common sand mining; grits mining (crushed stone); crushed & broken limestone
HQ: Hanson Aggregates Pennsylvania, Llc
7660 Imperial Way
Allentown PA 18195
610 366-4626

(G-12401)
ZIELINSKIS ASPHALT INC
4989 State Route 12b (13425-4541)
PHONE..................................315 306-4057
Kevin J Zielinski, *Principal*
EMP: 12
SALES (est): 2.4MM **Privately Held**
SIC: 2951 Asphalt paving mixtures & blocks

Ossining
Westchester County

(G-12402)
CATARACT HOSE CO
Also Called: Cataract Hose Co No 2
6 Waller Ave (10562-4711)
PHONE..................................914 941-9019
Louie Diloreto, *President*
EMP: 40
SALES (est): 2.7MM **Privately Held**
SIC: 3052 Fire hose, rubber

(G-12403)
CLEAR CAST TECHNOLOGIES INC (PA)
99 N Water St (10562-3255)
PHONE..................................914 945-0848
Peter Goldstein, *President*
Jerry Brown, *COO*
Chris Beigie, *Vice Pres*
Janice McAlevy, *Sales Staff*
Lynn Waltenbaugh, *Sales Staff*
▲ **EMP:** 30

SQ FT: 28,000
SALES (est): 5.2MM **Privately Held**
WEB: www.clearcasttech.com
SIC: 3083 Plastic finished products, laminated

(G-12404)
METALLIZED CARBON CORPORATION (PA)
Also Called: Metcar Products
19 S Water St (10562-4633)
PHONE................................914 941-3738
Matt Brennan, *Ch of Bd*
Manuel Debarros, *Prdtn Mgr*
Jeri Lacari, *Buyer*
Theresa Maniscalco, *Buyer*
Chris Dipaolo, *Engineer*
EMP: 140 **EST:** 1945
SQ FT: 50,000
SALES (est): 32.6MM **Privately Held**
WEB: www.carbongraphite.net
SIC: 3624 3568 Electric carbons; carbon specialties for electrical use; fibers, carbon & graphite; power transmission equipment

(G-12405)
OSSINING BAKERY LMP INC
50 N Highland Ave (10562-3432)
PHONE................................914 941-2654
Tony Martins, *President*
EMP: 7 **EST:** 1973
SQ FT: 3,000
SALES: 490K **Privately Held**
SIC: 2051 Bread, cake & related products

(G-12406)
OSSINING VILLAGE OF INC
Also Called: Indian Water Treatment Plant
25 Fowler Ave (10562-1919)
P.O. Box 1166 (10562-0996)
PHONE................................914 202-9668
George Gibson, *Chief*
EMP: 5 **Privately Held**
SIC: 3589 Water treatment equipment, industrial
PA: Ossining, Village Of Inc
16 Croton Ave Ste 2
Ossining NY 10562
914 941-3554

(G-12407)
PAN AMERICAN ROLLER INC
5 Broad Ave (10562-4601)
P.O. Box 1225 (10562-0057)
PHONE................................914 762-8700
Gertrude Wolf, *Corp Secy*
Michael Wolf, *Vice Pres*
EMP: 10
SQ FT: 15,000
SALES: 1MM **Privately Held**
SIC: 3991 Paint rollers

Oswego
Oswego County

(G-12408)
BATTERY RESEARCH AND TSTG INC
1313 County Route 1 (13126-5999)
PHONE................................315 342-2373
Patricia I Demar, *CEO*
Petter Demar, *Vice Pres*
Dennis Barber, *Natl Sales Mgr*
EMP: 10
SQ FT: 3,600
SALES: 2MM **Privately Held**
WEB: www.batteryresearch.com
SIC: 3691 Storage batteries

(G-12409)
DOTTO WAGNER
Also Called: Local News
185 E Seneca St (13126-1600)
P.O. Box 276 (13126-0276)
PHONE................................315 342-8020
Wagner Dotto, *Owner*
EMP: 6
SALES (est): 723.7K **Privately Held**
WEB: www.cnyfall.com
SIC: 2721 Magazines: publishing only, not printed on site

(G-12410)
ENERGY NUCLEAR OPERATIONS
Also Called: Chemistry Department
268 Lake Rd (13126-6325)
P.O. Box 110, Lycoming (13093-0110)
PHONE................................315 342-0055
Ted Sullivan, *Vice Pres*
EMP: 30
SALES (est): 8.6MM **Privately Held**
SIC: 3443 Nuclear reactors, military or industrial

(G-12411)
HEALTHWAY PRODUCTS COMPANY
249a Mitchell St (13126-1279)
PHONE................................315 207-1410
William O'Hara, *President*
Michael Daly, *Vice Pres*
EMP: 25
SQ FT: 33,000
SALES (est): 3.8MM **Privately Held**
SIC: 3564 3585 Blowers & fans; refrigeration & heating equipment

(G-12412)
INDUSTRIAL PRECISION PDTS INC
350 Mitchell St (13126-1270)
PHONE................................315 343-4421
William J Gallagher, *Chairman*
EMP: 20 **EST:** 1951
SQ FT: 26,000
SALES: 1.7MM **Privately Held**
WEB: www.indprecision.com
SIC: 3599 Machine shop, jobbing & repair; custom machinery

(G-12413)
LAZAREK INC
209 Erie St (13126)
P.O. Box 1006 (13126-0506)
PHONE................................315 343-1242
Walter Lazarek Jr, *President*
Stanley Lazarek, *Admin Sec*
EMP: 5 **EST:** 1936
SQ FT: 950
SALES (est): 661K **Privately Held**
SIC: 3273 5032 1442 Ready-mixed concrete; concrete & cinder block; construction sand mining; gravel mining

(G-12414)
MITCHELL PRTG & MAILING INC (PA)
1 Burkle St (13126-3261)
P.O. Box 815 (13126-0815)
PHONE................................315 343-3531
John Henry, *President*
Kathleen Henry, *Vice Pres*
EMP: 10 **EST:** 1930
SQ FT: 2,112
SALES: 400K **Privately Held**
WEB: www.mpcny.com
SIC: 2752 Commercial printing, offset

(G-12415)
NORTHLAND FILTER INTL LLC
249a Mitchell St (13126-1279)
PHONE................................315 207-1410
Dennis Hollenbeck, *Plant Mgr*
Gilles Morin,
◆ **EMP:** 20
SALES (est): 4.4MM **Privately Held**
WEB: www.northlandfilter.com
SIC: 3564 Filters, air: furnaces, air conditioning equipment, etc.

(G-12416)
NOVELIS CORPORATION
448 County Route 1a (13126-5962)
P.O. Box 28 (13126-0028)
PHONE................................315 342-1036
Thomas Walpole, *Engineer*
EMP: 300
SALES (corp-wide): 6.3B **Privately Held**
SIC: 3353 Aluminum sheet, plate & foil
HQ: Novelis Corporation
3560 Lenox Rd Ne Ste 2000
Atlanta GA 30326
404 760-4000

(G-12417)
NOVELIS CORPORATION
72 Alcan W Entrance Rd (13126)
P.O. Box 28 (13126-0028)
PHONE................................315 349-0121
Jack Morrison, *Principal*
EMP: 300
SALES (corp-wide): 6.3B **Privately Held**
SIC: 3353 Aluminum sheet, plate & foil
HQ: Novelis Corporation
3560 Lenox Rd Ne Ste 2000
Atlanta GA 30326
404 760-4000

(G-12418)
NOVELIS INC
448 County Route 1a (13126-5963)
PHONE................................315 349-0121
Steve Fisher, *CEO*
Philip Robert Martens, *Ch of Bd*
Martin Beech, *Opers Staff*
Craig Formoza, *Mfg Staff*
Michael Herron, *Purch Mgr*
▲ **EMP:** 25
SALES: 3.4MM **Privately Held**
SIC: 3355 Aluminum ingot

(G-12419)
PATRICK KRAFT (PA)
Also Called: Kraftees
262 W Seneca St (13126-1820)
PHONE................................315 343-9376
Patrick Kraft, *Owner*
Chris McRae, *Marketing Staff*
EMP: 6
SQ FT: 1,500
SALES (est): 921K **Privately Held**
WEB: www.kraftees.com
SIC: 2759 5942 Screen printing; college book stores

(G-12420)
SAMPLE NEWS GROUP LLC
Also Called: Palladium Times
140 W 1st St (13126-1514)
PHONE................................315 343-3800
John Spalding, *Manager*
EMP: 55
SQ FT: 9,620
SALES (est): 3.5MM
SALES (corp-wide): 8MM **Privately Held**
WEB: www.gatehousemedia.com
SIC: 2711 2752 Newspapers, publishing & printing; commercial printing, lithographic
PA: Sample News Group, L.L.C.
28 W South St
Corry PA 16407
814 665-8291

(G-12421)
SPEEDWAY PRESS INC (HQ)
Also Called: Mitchell's Speedway Press
1 Burkle St (13126-3271)
P.O. Box 2006 (13126-0606)
PHONE................................315 343-3531
George Caruso Jr, *President*
Romeo Caruso, *Corp Secy*
Douglas Caruso, *Vice Pres*
Kathy Henry, *VP Sales*
Carol Haynes, *Graphic Designe*
EMP: 9
SQ FT: 9,000
SALES (est): 360K
SALES (corp-wide): 400K **Privately Held**
WEB: www.speedwaypress.com
SIC: 2752 Commercial printing, offset
PA: Mitchell Printing & Mailing, Inc.
1 Burkle St
Oswego NY 13126
315 343-3531

(G-12422)
STONES HOMEMADE CANDIES INC
23 W Seneca St (13126-1540)
PHONE................................315 343-8401
Margaret Stanchowicz, *President*
Margaret Stachowicz, *President*
EMP: 7 **EST:** 1946
SALES (est): 703.6K **Privately Held**
SIC: 2064 Candy & other confectionery products

Ovid
Seneca County

(G-12423)
CROSSWINDS FARM & CREAMERY
6762 Log City Rd (14521-9789)
PHONE................................607 327-0363
Sarah B Vanorden, *Owner*
EMP: 5
SALES (est): 236.8K **Privately Held**
SIC: 2022 5451 Natural cheese; dairy products stores

(G-12424)
HOSMER INC
Also Called: Hosmer's Winery
6999 State Route 89 (14521-9569)
PHONE................................888 467-9463
Cameron Hosmer, *President*
Maren Hosmer, *Vice Pres*
EMP: 15
SALES: 500K **Privately Held**
WEB: www.hosmerwinery.com
SIC: 2084 Wines

(G-12425)
SENECA COUNTY AREA SHOPPER
1885 State Route 96a (14521-9712)
PHONE................................607 532-4333
Joan E Hendrix, *Principal*
EMP: 6
SALES (est): 290.3K **Privately Held**
SIC: 2711 Commercial printing & newspaper publishing combined; newspapers, publishing & printing

(G-12426)
SHELDRAKE POINT VINEYARD LLC
Also Called: Sheldrake Point Winery
7448 County Road 153 (14521-9564)
PHONE................................607 532-8967
Robert Madill, *General Mgr*
Christine Maguire, *Manager*
EMP: 10
SQ FT: 4,063
SALES: 800K **Privately Held**
SIC: 2084 Wines

(G-12427)
THIRSTY OWL WINE COMPANY INC
6861 State Route 89 (14521-9599)
PHONE................................607 869-5805
Jonathan C Cupp, *President*
John Cupp, *President*
EMP: 7
SALES (est): 781.4K **Privately Held**
WEB: www.thirstyowl.com
SIC: 2084 Wines

Owego
Tioga County

(G-12428)
APPLIED TECHNOLOGY MFG CORP
71 Temple St (13827-1338)
P.O. Box 189 (13827-0189)
PHONE................................607 687-2200
Stephen M Lounsberry III, *President*
Peter C Lounsberry, *Vice Pres*
Steven Bean, *Production*
Steve Bean, *Manager*
EMP: 30 **EST:** 1927
SQ FT: 25,000
SALES (est): 7.9MM **Privately Held**
WEB: www.appliedtechmfg.com
SIC: 3531 3599 Railway track equipment; railroad related equipment; machine & other job shop work

(G-12429)
C & C READY-MIX CORPORATION
3818 Rt 17 C (13827)
P.O. Box 174 (13827-0174)
PHONE.................................607 687-1690
Andy Cerretani, *Enginr/R&D Mgr*
EMP: 10
SALES (corp-wide): 5.3MM **Privately Held**
WEB: www.ccreadymix.com
SIC: 3273 2951 Ready-mixed concrete; asphalt paving mixtures & blocks
PA: C & C Ready-Mix Corporation
3112 Vestal Rd
Vestal NY 13850
607 797-5108

(G-12430)
INDUSTRIAL PAINT SERVICES CORP
60 W Main St 62 (13827-1537)
PHONE.................................607 687-0107
Jean Chapman, *President*
EMP: 17
SQ FT: 20,000
SALES (est): 1.7MM **Privately Held**
WEB: www.ipsowego.com
SIC: 3479 Painting of metal products

(G-12431)
KYOCERA PRECISION TOOLS INC
Also Called: New York Division
1436 Taylor Rd (13827-1833)
PHONE.................................607 687-0012
Stephen Hansen, *Branch Mgr*
EMP: 14 **Publicly Held**
WEB: www.tycom.com
SIC: 3541 Machine tools, metal cutting type
HQ: Kyocera Precision Tools, Inc
102 Industrial Park Rd
Hendersonville NC 28792
800 823-7284

(G-12432)
LAKE VIEW GRAPHICS INC
2771 Waits Rd Ste 101 (13827-6308)
PHONE.................................607 687-7033
David Springsteen, *President*
EMP: 5
SQ FT: 720
SALES: 9MM **Privately Held**
WEB: www.lakeviewselections.com
SIC: 2752 Commercial printing, offset

(G-12433)
LOCKHEED MARTIN CORPORATION
1801 State Route 17 (13827)
PHONE.................................607 751-2000
Bryan Ruskavich, *Mktg Dir*
Joseph Trench, *Manager*
Lroy Newton, *Software Engr*
EMP: 1261 **Publicly Held**
WEB: www.lockheedmartin.com
SIC: 3812 3761 Search & navigation equipment; guided missiles & space vehicles
PA: Lockheed Martin Corporation
6801 Rockledge Dr
Bethesda MD 20817

(G-12434)
NATIONAL PAPER CONVERTING INC
207 Corporate Dr (13827-3249)
PHONE.................................607 687-6049
Eric Kretzmer, *President*
Michael Kretzmer, *Vice Pres*
EMP: 5
SQ FT: 8,000
SALES (est): 921.3K **Privately Held**
WEB: www.nationaladh.com
SIC: 2621 5199 Absorbent paper; packaging materials

(G-12435)
NORWESCO INC
263 Corporate Dr (13827-3249)
PHONE.................................607 687-8081
Rich Barto, *Director*
EMP: 11

SALES (corp-wide): 44.1MM **Privately Held**
WEB: www.ncmmolding.com
SIC: 3089 Plastic & fiberglass tanks
PA: Norwesco, Inc.
4365 Steiner St
Saint Bonifacius MN 55375
952 446-1945

(G-12436)
OWEGO PENNYSAVER PRESS INC
181 Front St (13827-1520)
P.O. Box 149 (13827-0149)
PHONE.................................607 687-2434
George V Lynett, *President*
Wendy Post, *Editor*
EMP: 10
SALES (est): 560.9K
SALES (corp-wide): 12.3MM **Privately Held**
WEB: www.sundayreview.com
SIC: 2711 Newspapers, publishing & printing
PA: Towanda Printing Co Inc
116 N Main St
Towanda PA 18848
570 265-2151

(G-12437)
SANMINA CORPORATION
1200 Taylor Rd (13827-1292)
PHONE.................................607 689-5000
Dennis Young, *President*
Brian Barber, *Purch Mgr*
Jannell Taylor, *Engineer*
Theresa Nugent, *Human Res Mgr*
Mark Gable, *Branch Mgr*
EMP: 500 **Publicly Held**
WEB: www.sanmina.com
SIC: 3672 Circuit boards, television & radio printed
PA: Sanmina Corporation
2700 N 1st St
San Jose CA 95134

(G-12438)
TIOGA COUNTY COURIER
59 Church St (13827-1439)
PHONE.................................607 687-0108
Mary Jones, *Owner*
EMP: 5
SALES (est): 204.6K **Privately Held**
SIC: 2711 Newspapers: publishing only, not printed on site

(G-12439)
WAGNER MILLWORK INC
Also Called: Wagner Lumber
4060 Gaskill Rd (13827-4741)
PHONE.................................607 687-5362
Steven Schaeffer, *Vice Pres*
Renee Lindloff, *Safety Mgr*
Steve Houseknecht, *Sales Staff*
▼ **EMP:** 70
SQ FT: 60,000
SALES (est): 17.4MM **Privately Held**
WEB: www.wagnerlumber.com
SIC: 2421 2431 2426 Sawmills & planing mills, general; millwork; hardwood dimension & flooring mills

(G-12440)
WHOLESALE MULCH & SAWDUST INC
Also Called: Tioga County Waste Wood Recycl
3711 Waverly Rd (13827-2860)
PHONE.................................607 687-2637
Philip Nestor, *President*
Cynthia Nestor, *Vice Pres*
EMP: 5
SQ FT: 1,624
SALES (est): 460K **Privately Held**
SIC: 2499 Mulch or sawdust products, wood

Oxford
Chenango County

(G-12441)
AUTOMECHA INTERNATIONAL LTD (PA)
48 S Canal St (13830-4318)
P.O. Box 660 (13830-0660)
PHONE.................................607 843-2235
Kenneth E St John, *President*
Kevin Gates, *Controller*
Mike Sawyer, *Manager*
Sonjia Strobach, *Admin Sec*
EMP: 28
SQ FT: 23,000
SALES (est): 4.5MM **Privately Held**
WEB: www.asmarc.com
SIC: 3579 5044 3565 3554 Addressing machines, plates & plate embossers; address labeling machines; mailing, letter handling & addressing machines; office equipment; packaging machinery; paper industries machinery

(G-12442)
RAPID REPRODUCTIONS LLC
4511 State Hwy 12 (13830)
P.O. Box 598 (13830-0598)
PHONE.................................607 843-2221
Bryant Latourette,
EMP: 8 EST: 1977
SQ FT: 11,000
SALES: 680K **Privately Held**
SIC: 2752 Commercial printing, offset

Oyster Bay
Nassau County

(G-12443)
AMERICAN TRANS-COIL CORP
Also Called: A T C
69 Hamilton Ave Ste 3 (11771-1573)
P.O. Box 629 (11771-0629)
PHONE.................................516 922-9640
Mark Masin, *President*
William Rogers, *Principal*
EMP: 15 EST: 1960
SQ FT: 5,000
SALES (est): 2.2MM **Privately Held**
WEB: www.atc-us.com
SIC: 3677 Electronic coils, transformers & other inductors

(G-12444)
APOTHECUS PHARMACEUTICAL CORP (PA)
220 Townsend Sq (11771-2339)
PHONE.................................516 624-8200
Thomas Leon, *Ch of Bd*
Daniel Leon, *President*
Jonathan Leon, *Vice Pres*
Paul Gabel, *VP Opers*
Michael Lesser, *CFO*
EMP: 14
SQ FT: 7,000
SALES (est): 4.6MM **Privately Held**
WEB: www.apothecus.com
SIC: 2834 5122 Pharmaceutical preparations; proprietary (patent) medicines

(G-12445)
CIRCO FILE CORP
69 Hamilton Ave Ste 1 (11771-1573)
PHONE.................................516 922-1848
Thomas Carrella, *President*
Ralph Carrella, *Shareholder*
EMP: 7 EST: 1955
SQ FT: 2,000
SALES (est): 1MM **Privately Held**
WEB: www.circofile.com
SIC: 3545 Cutting tools for machine tools

(G-12446)
COMANDER TERMINALS LLC
1 Commander Sq (11771-1536)
PHONE.................................516 922-7600
Abrham Prznaski, *President*
EMP: 14
SALES (est): 1.6MM **Privately Held**
SIC: 2843 Oils & greases

(G-12447)
ENGINEERING MAINT PDTS INC
Also Called: Hippo Industries
250 Berry Hill Rd (11771-3121)
P.O. Box 548 (11771-0548)
PHONE.................................516 624-9774
Ansuya Dave, *President*
Peter Dave, *Vice Pres*
Shashidhar H Dave, *Vice Pres*
EMP: 14
SQ FT: 4,000
SALES (est): 3.6MM **Privately Held**
SIC: 2899 5169 Corrosion preventive lubricant; anti-corrosion products

(G-12448)
IMREX LLC (PA)
55 Sandy Hill Rd (11771-3110)
P.O. Box 154 (11771-0154)
PHONE.................................516 479-3675
Jacob Armon, *Mng Member*
Harry Armon,
Alan J Weiss,
EMP: 350 EST: 1997
SQ FT: 32,000
SALES (est): 44.1MM **Privately Held**
WEB: www.imrex.com
SIC: 3679 Electronic circuits

(G-12449)
MILL-MAX MFG CORP
190 Pine Hollow Rd (11771-4711)
P.O. Box 300 (11771-0300)
PHONE.................................516 922-6000
Roger L Bahnik, *Ch of Bd*
James W Litke, *President*
Claude A Bahnik, *Vice Pres*
Bradley E Kuczinski, *Vice Pres*
Brad Kuczinski, *VP Mfg*
▲ **EMP:** 190 EST: 1971
SQ FT: 135,000
SALES: 71.5MM **Privately Held**
WEB: www.mil-max.com
SIC: 3678 5065 Electronic connectors; electronic parts & equipment

(G-12450)
MIRODDI IMAGING INC (PA)
Also Called: M Squared Graphics
27 Centre View Dr (11771-2815)
PHONE.................................516 624-6898
Cherrise Miroddi, *Ch of Bd*
EMP: 2
SQ FT: 8,000
SALES (est): 1MM **Privately Held**
WEB: www.msquaredgraphics.com
SIC: 2796 Gravure printing plates or cylinders, preparation of

(G-12451)
MYX BEVERAGE LLC
Also Called: Myx Fusions
39 E Main St Unit 101 (11771-2407)
PHONE.................................585 978-3542
Peter Reaske,
Nicki Minaj,
▼ **EMP:** 13
SQ FT: 600
SALES (est): 12MM **Privately Held**
SIC: 2087 Beverage bases

(G-12452)
OYSTER BAY BREWING COMPANY
36 Audrey Ave (11771-1548)
PHONE.................................516 802-5546
Gabriel Haim, *Ch of Bd*
EMP: 11 EST: 2012
SQ FT: 6,000
SALES: 1MM **Privately Held**
SIC: 2082 Beer (alcoholic beverage)

(G-12453)
OYSTER BAY PUBLICATIONS LLC
146 Cove Rd (11771-3315)
P.O. Box 63 (11771-0063)
PHONE.................................516 922-1300
Darlene Bello, *Office Mgr*
Eugene Zaphiris,
EMP: 5
SALES (est): 53.2K **Privately Held**
SIC: 2741 Miscellaneous publishing

(G-12454)
PRINTERY
Also Called: Printing House of W S Miller
43 W Main St (11771-2215)
PHONE..................................516 922-3250
William Miller, *President*
Mary Abbene, *Vice Pres*
EMP: 5 EST: 1973
SALES (est): 533.5K **Privately Held**
SIC: 2759 2791 Card printing & engraving,
   except greeting; typesetting

(G-12455)
PURE GREEN LLC
439 Centre Island Rd (11771-5012)
PHONE..................................800 306-9122
Brigitte Stetson, *Principal*
EMP: 5 EST: 2007
SALES (est): 888.9K **Privately Held**
SIC: 2842 Specialty cleaning, polishes &
   sanitation goods

(G-12456)
R F GIARDINA CO
200 Lexington Ave Apt 3a (11771-2114)
P.O. Box 562 (11771-0562)
PHONE..................................516 922-1364
Robert Giardina, *President*
EMP: 10
SALES (est): 833K **Privately Held**
WEB: www.rfgco.com
SIC: 3944 Craft & hobby kits & sets

Ozone Park
Queens County

(G-12457)
ABIGAL PRESS INC
9735 133rd Ave (11417-2119)
P.O. Box 170704 (11417-0704)
PHONE..................................718 641-5350
Salvatore Stratis, *CEO*
Jeff Gaines, *President*
Jeffrey Gaines, *President*
Lois Berl, *Vice Pres*
Michael O'Connor, *CFO*
◆ EMP: 98 EST: 1956
SQ FT: 30,000
SALES (est): 13.9MM **Privately Held**
WEB: www.abigal.com
SIC: 2759 Card printing & engraving, ex-
   cept greeting

(G-12458)
**CENTRE INTERIORS WDWKG
CO INC**
10001 103rd Ave (11417-1712)
PHONE..................................718 323-1343
Alex Lee, *President*
EMP: 20
SALES (est): 3.5MM **Privately Held**
SIC: 2521 Wood office desks & tables

(G-12459)
COIL CRAFT INC (PA)
10324 99th St (11417-1639)
PHONE..................................718 369-1210
Roy Henry, *President*
Rohal Henry, *COO*
EMP: 5
SQ FT: 4,300
SALES (est): 900K **Privately Held**
SIC: 3585 Heating equipment, complete

(G-12460)
**ELEVATOR VENTURES
CORPORATION**
Also Called: Ver-Tech Elevator
9720 99th St (11416-2602)
PHONE..................................212 375-1900
Don Gelestino, *Owner*
Ken Margherini, *VP Bus Dvlpt*
Dylan Blades, *Sales Staff*
EMP: 99
SALES (est): 10.2MM **Privately Held**
SIC: 3534 Elevators & moving stairways

(G-12461)
FASTENER DIMENSIONS INC
9403 104th St (11416-1723)
PHONE..................................718 847-6321
Darryl A Hinkle, *President*

EMP: 35
SQ FT: 24,000
SALES (est): 3.2MM **Privately Held**
WEB: www.fastdim.com
SIC: 3429 5085 5088 3452 Aircraft hard-
   ware; fasteners, industrial: nuts, bolts,
   screws, etc.; aircraft equipment & sup-
   plies; bolts, nuts, rivets & washers

(G-12462)
FOOD GEMS LTD
8423 Rockaway Blvd (11416-1249)
PHONE..................................718 296-7788
Bradley Stroll, *President*
Frank Kurt, *Vice Pres*
EMP: 24
SQ FT: 10,000
SALES (est): 2.7MM **Privately Held**
WEB: www.foodgems.com
SIC: 2051 5812 Bakery: wholesale or
   wholesale/retail combined; eating places

(G-12463)
**JOLDESON ONE AEROSPACE
INDS**
Also Called: Joldeson One Aerospace Inds
10002 103rd Ave (11417-1713)
PHONE..................................718 848-7396
Ecatarina Joldeson, *President*
George Joldeson, *Vice Pres*
Richard Joldeson, *Admin Sec*
EMP: 93
SALES: 8.5MM **Privately Held**
SIC: 3728 3496 3812 3643 Aircraft parts
   & equipment; woven wire products;
   search & navigation equipment; current-
   carrying wiring devices; conveyors & con-
   veying equipment; partitions & fixtures,
   except wood

(G-12464)
JULIA KNIT INC
8050 Pitkin Ave (11417-1211)
PHONE..................................718 848-1900
Avraham Lip, *President*
▲ EMP: 6
SALES (est): 1.3MM **Privately Held**
SIC: 2253 Sweaters & sweater coats, knit

(G-12465)
KW DISTRIBUTORS GROUP INC
Also Called: Kw Kitchen Design
9018 Liberty Ave (11417-1350)
PHONE..................................718 843-3500
Vito Altesi, *President*
Daniel Altesi, *Corp Secy*
Riccardo Altesi, *Vice Pres*
▲ EMP: 10
SQ FT: 3,600
SALES (est): 1MM **Privately Held**
SIC: 2434 Wood kitchen cabinets

(G-12466)
PREMIER KNITS LTD
9735 133rd Ave (11417-2119)
PHONE..................................718 323-8264
Panta Ardeljan, *President*
Petar Ardeljan Jr, *Vice Pres*
EMP: 10
SQ FT: 35,000
SALES (est): 610K **Privately Held**
WEB: www.premierknits.com
SIC: 2253 5199 Sweaters & sweater
   coats, knit; knit goods

(G-12467)
ROBERT COHEN
Also Called: Allied Orthopedics
10540 Rockaway Blvd Ste A (11417-2304)
PHONE..................................718 789-0996
Robert F Cohen, *Owner*
EMP: 6
SQ FT: 4,000
SALES (est): 587.9K **Privately Held**
SIC: 3842 Limbs, artificial; braces, ortho-
   pedic

(G-12468)
WALL TOOL & TAPE CORP
Also Called: Wall Tool Manufacturing
8111 101st Ave (11416-2008)
P.O. Box 20637, Floral Park (11002-0637)
PHONE..................................718 641-6813
EMP: 20
SQ FT: 12,000

SALES (est): 3.2MM **Privately Held**
SIC: 3423 Mfg Hand/Edge Tools

(G-12469)
**WORKSMAN TRADING CORP
(PA)**
Also Called: Worksman Cycles
9415 100th St (11416-1707)
P.O. Box 170732 (11417-0732)
PHONE..................................718 322-2000
Jeffrey A Mishkin, *President*
Wayne Sosin, *President*
Brian Mishkin, *Vice Pres*
◆ EMP: 2 EST: 1898
SQ FT: 100,000
SALES (est): 6.9MM **Privately Held**
SIC: 3751 5962 5091 5941 Motorcycles,
   bicycles & parts; merchandising machine
   operators; bicycle equipment & supplies;
   bicycle & bicycle parts

(G-12470)
ZONE FABRICATORS INC
10780 101st St (11417-2609)
PHONE..................................718 272-0200
Peter Scaminaci, *President*
Frances Hultin, *Vice Pres*
EMP: 16
SQ FT: 8,000
SALES (est): 2.1MM **Privately Held**
WEB: www.zonefabinc.com
SIC: 3089 3443 Plastic processing; metal
   parts

Painted Post
Steuben County

(G-12471)
AUTOMATED CELLS & EQP INC
9699 Enterprise Dr (14870-9166)
PHONE..................................607 936-1341
James Morris, *President*
Mike Joyce, *Project Mgr*
Pete Dehaan, *Engineer*
Jonathan Deroner, *Engineer*
Joshua Hathaway, *Engineer*
EMP: 38
SQ FT: 27,000
SALES (est): 10.9MM **Privately Held**
WEB: www.autocells.com
SIC: 3569 5084 Robots, assembly line: in-
   dustrial & commercial; robots, industrial

(G-12472)
CORNING INCORPORATED
905 Addison Rd (14870-9726)
PHONE..................................607 974-1274
Dipak Chowdhury, *Division VP*
Jeffrey Schmidt, *Counsel*
Terri Mauk, *Plant Mgr*
Marianne Park, *Project Mgr*
Ji Wang, *Project Mgr*
EMP: 50
SALES (corp-wide): 11.2B **Publicly Held**
WEB: www.corning.com
SIC: 3229 3264 Glass fiber products;
   porcelain electrical supplies
PA: Corning Incorporated
   1 Riverfront Plz
   Corning NY 14831
   607 974-9000

(G-12473)
CORNING INCORPORATED
890 Addison Rd (14870-9726)
PHONE..................................607 974-9000
Norman Neumayer, *Project Mgr*
Chad Keefer, *Opers Staff*
Bruce Hostrander, *Engineer*
Hideki Masaki, *Engineer*
Fran Merrill, *Engineer*
EMP: 900
SALES (corp-wide): 11.2B **Publicly Held**
WEB: www.corning.com
SIC: 3357 3661 3211 3229 Fiber optic
   cable (insulated); telephone & telegraph
   apparatus; flat glass; pressed & blown
   glass; semiconductors & related devices;
   analytical instruments
PA: Corning Incorporated
   1 Riverfront Plz
   Corning NY 14831
   607 974-9000

(G-12474)
**DRESSER-RAND (DELAWARE)
LLC (DH)**
100 E Chemung St (14870-1377)
PHONE..................................607 937-2011
Anthony Gioffredi,
EMP: 1
SALES (est): 15MM
SALES (corp-wide): 95B **Privately Held**
SIC: 3563 Air & gas compressors
HQ: Dresser-Rand Company
   500 Paul Clark Dr
   Olean NY 14760
   716 375-3000

(G-12475)
**SCHULER-HAAS ELECTRIC
CORP**
598 Ritas Way (14870-8546)
PHONE..................................607 936-3514
Mark Bruzzi, *Project Mgr*
EMP: 7
SALES (est): 778.5K
SALES (corp-wide): 21MM **Privately
Held**
SIC: 3699 1731 Electrical equipment &
   supplies; electrical work
PA: Schuler-Haas Electric Corp.
   240 Commerce Dr
   Rochester NY 14623
   585 325-1060

(G-12476)
SIRIANNI HARDWOODS INC
912 Addison Rd (14870-9729)
PHONE..................................607 962-4688
James Sirianni, *COO*
Tom Armentano, *Purch Agent*
Mary Sirianni, *Treasurer*
EMP: 24
SQ FT: 69,024
SALES (est): 3.5MM **Privately Held**
WEB: www.siriannihardwoods.com
SIC: 2421 Sawmills & planing mills, gen-
   eral

Palatine Bridge
Montgomery County

(G-12477)
LEE NEWSPAPERS INC
6113 State Highway 5 (13428-2809)
P.O. Box 121 (13428-0121)
PHONE..................................518 673-3237
Fred Lee, *Principal*
EMP: 13
SALES (est): 888.1K **Privately Held**
SIC: 2711 Newspapers, publishing & print-
   ing

(G-12478)
LEE PUBLICATIONS INC (PA)
Also Called: Waste Management
6113 State Highway 5 (13428-2809)
P.O. Box 121 (13428-0121)
PHONE..................................518 673-3237
Fred Lee, *President*
Joan Kark-Wren, *Editor*
Janet Lee Button, *Treasurer*
Lyndsay Bock, *Human Res Mgr*
Dave Dornburgh, *Sales Staff*
EMP: 99
SQ FT: 25,000
SALES (est): 11.9MM **Privately Held**
WEB: www.leepub.com
SIC: 2711 Newspapers, publishing & print-
   ing

Palenville
Greene County

(G-12479)
**NATIONAL PARACHUTE
INDUSTRIES**
Also Called: National Parachute Industry
78 White Rd Extensio (12463)
P.O. Box 245 (12463-0245)
PHONE..................................908 782-1646
Larry Krueger, *President*
Jeanette Krueger, *Admin Sec*

EMP: 20 EST: 1976
SQ FT: 6,000
SALES (est): 1.2MM **Privately Held**
SIC: 2399 Parachutes

(G-12480)
PRECISION TOOL AND MFG
314 Pennsylvania Ave (12463-2615)
P.O. Box 160 (12463-0160)
PHONE..................................518 678-3130
Alan Schneck, *President*
EMP: 27
SALES (est): 3.2MM **Privately Held**
SIC: 3599 Machine shop, jobbing & repair

Palisades
Rockland County

(G-12481)
HISTORY PUBLISHING COMPANY LLC
173 Route 9w (10964-1616)
P.O. Box 700 (10964-0700)
PHONE..................................845 398-8161
Don Bracken, *Mng Member*
EMP: 6
SALES (est): 462.2K **Privately Held**
WEB: www.historypublishingco.com
SIC: 2741 Posters: publishing only, not printed on site

(G-12482)
SKAE POWER SOLUTIONS LLC (PA)
348 Route 9w (10964-1200)
P.O. Box 615 (10964-0615)
PHONE..................................845 365-9103
Jack Hoagland, *Project Mgr*
Malachy McPartland, *Project Mgr*
Jason Ketcham, *Engineer*
Anthony Russo, *Engineer*
Tim Sullivan, *Engineer*
EMP: 30
SQ FT: 6,000
SALES (est): 7.9MM **Privately Held**
WEB: www.skaepower.com
SIC: 3699 8711 Electrical equipment & supplies; consulting engineer

(G-12483)
TRI VALLEY IRON INC
700 Oak Tree Rd (10964-1533)
P.O. Box 234 (10964-0234)
PHONE..................................845 365-1013
Nancy Bucciarelli, *President*
James McCarthy, *Vice Pres*
EMP: 15
SALES: 1.5MM **Privately Held**
SIC: 3312 Bars, iron: made in steel mills

(G-12484)
VELL COMPANY INC
700 Oak Tree Rd (10964-1533)
P.O. Box 622 (10964-0622)
PHONE..................................845 365-1013
Larry Bucciarelli, *Principal*
EMP: 8
SALES (est): 1MM **Privately Held**
SIC: 3312 Bars & bar shapes, steel, hot-rolled

Palmyra
Wayne County

(G-12485)
FARADYNE MOTORS LLC
Also Called: Juan Motors
2077 Division St (14522-9211)
PHONE..................................315 331-5985
Mellisa Kidd, *Mng Member*
Juan Lugo, *Mng Member*
Colin R Sabol, *Director*
▲ EMP: 14
SQ FT: 28,000
SALES (est): 4.2MM **Publicly Held**
WEB: www.faradynemotors.com
SIC: 3621 Motors, electric
PA: Xylem Inc.
1 International Dr
Rye Brook NY 10573

(G-12486)
FINZER HOLDING LLC
Also Called: Finzer Roller New York
2085 Division St (14522-9211)
PHONE..................................315 597-1147
David Finzer, *President*
Kevin Byer, *Plant Mgr*
Brian La Due, *Executive*
EMP: 27
SALES (corp-wide): 12.7MM **Privately Held**
SIC: 3069 3061 Roll coverings, rubber; mechanical rubber goods
PA: Finzer Holding Llc
129 Rawls Rd
Des Plaines IL 60018
847 390-6200

(G-12487)
GARLOCK SEALING TECH LLC
1666 Division St (14522-9350)
PHONE..................................315 597-4811
Paul Baldetti, *Manager*
EMP: 950
SALES (corp-wide): 1.5B **Publicly Held**
SIC: 3053 Gaskets & sealing devices
HQ: Garlock Sealing Technologies Llc
1666 Division St
Palmyra NY 14522
315 597-4811

(G-12488)
GENTNER PRECISION COMPONENTS
406 Stafford Rd (14522-9426)
PHONE..................................315 597-5734
Richard Genter, *President*
John E Gentner Jr, *Principal*
EMP: 5
SALES (est): 438.4K **Privately Held**
SIC: 3599 Machine shop, jobbing & repair

(G-12489)
JRLON INC
4344 Fox Rd (14522-9423)
P.O. Box 244 (14522-0244)
PHONE..................................315 597-4067
James F Redmond, *President*
Lindsey Redmond, *Corp Secy*
Brandon Redmond, *Vice Pres*
Jerry Sprague, *Engineer*
Douglas Camp, *Sales Staff*
▲ EMP: 80 EST: 1981
SQ FT: 60,000
SALES (est): 18.1MM **Privately Held**
WEB: www.jrlon.com
SIC: 2821 3566 3479 3462 Molding compounds, plastics; gears, power transmission, except automotive; painting, coating & hot dipping; iron & steel forgings; paints & allied products

(G-12490)
LABCO OF PALMYRA INC
904 Canandaigua Rd (14522-9701)
P.O. Box 216 (14522-0216)
PHONE..................................315 597-5202
Gary Laberge, *President*
Lynette McTigue, *Vice Pres*
Sharyl Digiovanni, *Treasurer*
Marybeth Laberge, *Admin Sec*
EMP: 12
SQ FT: 7,800
SALES (est): 1.7MM **Privately Held**
WEB: www.labco-ny.com
SIC: 3599 Machine shop, jobbing & repair

(G-12491)
MODERN COATING AND RESEARCH
Also Called: Modern Coating & Research
400 E Main St (14522-1132)
PHONE..................................315 597-3517
Michael McManus, *President*
EMP: 11
SALES (corp-wide): 700K **Privately Held**
SIC: 3479 Etching & engraving
PA: Modern Coating And Research
400 E Main St
Palmyra NY 14522
315 597-3517

(G-12492)
MODERN COATING AND RESEARCH (PA)
400 E Main St (14522-1132)
PHONE..................................315 597-3517
James Deagman, *President*
Jae Chatfield, *Manager*
James Hollingsworth, *Shareholder*
EMP: 11
SQ FT: 26,000
SALES: 700K **Privately Held**
WEB: www.moderncoatings.com
SIC: 3479 Coating of metals & formed products

(G-12493)
PAUL T FREUND CORPORATION (PA)
216 Park Dr (14522-1114)
P.O. Box 475 (14522-0475)
PHONE..................................315 597-4873
Dennis Baron, *President*
Paul T Freund Jr, *Corp Secy*
Thomas Farnham, *Vice Pres*
▲ EMP: 85
SQ FT: 126,000
SALES (est): 7.2MM **Privately Held**
WEB: www.freundcarton.com
SIC: 2652 Filing boxes, paperboard: made from purchased materials

(G-12494)
V TECHNICAL TEXTILES INC
Also Called: Shieldex Trading-US
4502 State Route 31 (14522-9740)
PHONE..................................315 597-1674
Jeannie Hoge, *President*
EMP: 1
SQ FT: 1,000
SALES: 3.6MM **Privately Held**
SIC: 2221 2295 2284 2335 Broadwoven fabric mills, manmade; coated fabrics, not rubberized; thread mills; dresses, paper: cut & sewn; industrial sewing thread; hosiery kits, sewing & mending

Parish
Oswego County

(G-12495)
BIOSPHERIX LTD
Also Called: Biospherix Medical
25 Union St (13131)
PHONE..................................315 387-3414
Rich Ruffos, *Research*
Ray Gould, *Sales Mgr*
Andrew McKenzie, *Sales Staff*
Kevin Murray, *Sales Staff*
Erin Power, *Technical Staff*
EMP: 50
SQ FT: 30,000
SALES (est): 10.6MM **Privately Held**
WEB: www.biospherix.com
SIC: 3821 Laboratory equipment: fume hoods, distillation racks, etc.

Patchogue
Suffolk County

(G-12496)
BAKERY INNOVATIVE TECH CORP
139 N Ocean Ave (11772-2018)
PHONE..................................631 758-3081
Robert White, *President*
EMP: 15
SQ FT: 8,000
SALES: 1.5MM **Privately Held**
WEB: www.bit-corp.com
SIC: 3625 Motor control accessories, including overload relays

(G-12497)
BAYSHORE ELECTRIC MOTORS
Also Called: Bayshore Motors
33 Suffolk Ave (11772-1651)
PHONE..................................631 475-1397
Paul Phillips, *Owner*
EMP: 5

SALES (est): 220.1K **Privately Held**
SIC: 7694 Electric motor repair

(G-12498)
CLASSIC LABELS INC
217 River Ave (11772-3312)
PHONE..................................631 467-2300
John Orta, *President*
EMP: 21
SQ FT: 29,000
SALES (est): 2MM **Privately Held**
WEB: www.classiclabels.com
SIC: 2759 2891 2672 2671 Labels & seals: printing; adhesives & sealants; coated & laminated paper; packaging paper & plastics film, coated & laminated

(G-12499)
DEPOT LABEL COMPANY INC
Also Called: Colonial Label
217 River Ave (11772-3312)
PHONE..................................631 467-2952
Mike Juliano, *President*
EMP: 8
SALES (est): 1.9MM **Privately Held**
SIC: 2679 5013 2671 2241 Tags & labels, paper; automotive supplies & parts; packaging paper & plastics film, coated & laminated; narrow fabric mills

(G-12500)
EQUICHECK LLC
20 Medford Ave Ste 7 (11772-1220)
PHONE..................................631 987-6356
Warren Rothstein, *Owner*
Rob Visalli, *Case Mgr*
EMP: 5
SALES (est): 300K **Privately Held**
WEB: www.equicheck.com
SIC: 3851 Lens coating, ophthalmic

(G-12501)
G & M DEGE INC
147 West Ave (11772-3526)
PHONE..................................631 475-1450
Nick Gallipoli, *President*
Angela Gallipoli, *Vice Pres*
EMP: 14
SALES (est): 3.2MM **Privately Held**
SIC: 2851 Removers & cleaners

(G-12502)
HOPTRON BREWTIQUE
22 W Main St Ste 11 (11772-3007)
PHONE..................................631 438-0296
Amanda Danielsen, *Owner*
EMP: 8
SALES (est): 578.5K **Privately Held**
SIC: 2082 5182 Beer (alcoholic beverage); wine coolers, alcoholic

(G-12503)
JABO AGRICULTURAL INC
9 Northwood Ln (11772-2228)
PHONE..................................631 475-1800
Robert Muchnick, *CEO*
Jacob Gurewich, *President*
EMP: 5
SQ FT: 1,000
SALES (est): 226.8K **Privately Held**
SIC: 2452 Farm & agricultural buildings, prefabricated wood

(G-12504)
JOHN LOR PUBLISHING LTD
Also Called: Islip Bulletin
20 Medford Ave Ste 1 (11772-1220)
P.O. Box 780 (11772-0780)
PHONE..................................631 475-1000
EMP: 20 EST: 1950
SALES (est): 981.7K **Privately Held**
WEB: www.islipbulletin.net
SIC: 2711 Newspapers: publishing only, not printed on site

(G-12505)
KEVIN FREEMAN
Also Called: Rf Inter Science Co
414 S Service Rd Ste 119 (11772-2254)
PHONE..................................631 447-5321
Kevin Freeman, *President*
EMP: 5
SALES (est): 399.6K **Privately Held**
SIC: 3827 Optical instruments & apparatus

GEOGRAPHIC

(G-12506)
L3 TECHNOLOGIES INC
L3 Communications Narda - Atm
49 Rider Ave (11772-3915)
PHONE..................................631 289-0363
Bill Dunleavy, *Purch Mgr*
Geoffrey Smith, *Branch Mgr*
Dirk Aubram, *Info Tech Mgr*
EMP: 50
SALES (corp-wide): 6.8B **Publicly Held**
SIC: 3679 Microwave components
HQ: L3 Technologies, Inc.
　600 3rd Ave Fl 34
　New York NY 10016
　212 697-1111

(G-12507)
NEW LIVING INC
99 Waverly Ave Apt 6d (11772-1922)
P.O. Box 1519, Stony Brook (11790-0909)
PHONE..................................631 751-8819
Christine Harvey, *Principal*
EMP: 8
SALES (est): 293.7K **Privately Held**
SIC: 2711 Newspapers, publishing & print-
ing

(G-12508)
PARIS ART LABEL CO INC
217 River Ave (11772-3312)
PHONE..................................631 467-2300
Ronald P Tarantino, *Ch of Bd*
▲ EMP: 100 EST: 1925
SQ FT: 20,000
SALES (est): 17.2MM
SALES (corp-wide): 16.2B **Publicly Held**
WEB: www.parisartlabel.com
SIC: 2759 Commercial printing
HQ: Multi Packaging Solutions International
　Limited
　885 3rd Ave Fl 28
　New York NY 10022
　646 885-0005

(G-12509)
PATCHOGUE ADVANCE INC
Also Called: Long Island Advance
20 Medford Ave Ste 1 (11772-1220)
PHONE..................................631 475-1000
John T Tuthill III, *President*
Lorelei T Tuthill, *Admin Sec*
EMP: 35 EST: 1821
SQ FT: 7,000
SALES (est): 1.8MM **Privately Held**
WEB: www.longislandadvance.net
SIC: 2711 Newspapers: publishing only,
not printed on site

(G-12510)
PRINCETON LABEL &
PACKAGING
217 River Ave (11772-3312)
PHONE..................................609 490-0800
Donald J Guli, *President*
Tony Mannino, *Officer*
EMP: 35
SQ FT: 7,800
SALES (est): 5.8MM **Privately Held**
WEB: www.princetonlabel.com
SIC: 2672 7389 Labels (unprinted),
gummed: made from purchased materi-
als; packaging & labeling services

(G-12511)
RELIABLE WELDING &
FABRICATION
214 W Main St (11772-3004)
PHONE..................................631 758-2637
EMP: 7
SALES (est): 490K **Privately Held**
SIC: 7692 5051 5021 1799 Welding Re-
pair Metals Service Center Whol Furniture
Special Trade Contractor

(G-12512)
SUFFOLK MCHY & PWR TL
CORP (PA)
Also Called: Gschwind Group
12 Waverly Ave (11772-1902)
PHONE..................................631 289-7153
Arthur F Gschwind Sr, *President*
Debbie Freyre, *General Mgr*
Tom Davies, *Director*
▼ EMP: 3 EST: 1977
SQ FT: 4,000

SALES (est): 1.2MM **Privately Held**
WEB: www.timberwolf1.com
SIC: 3425 Saw blades & handsaws

(G-12513)
T & SMOOTHIE INC
499 N Service Rd Ste 83 (11772-2290)
PHONE..................................631 804-6653
Tiffany Wirth, *Principal*
EMP: 6
SALES (est): 316.5K **Privately Held**
SIC: 2037 Frozen fruits & vegetables

(G-12514)
YOMAN MADEO FANO
1 S Ocean Ave (11772-3738)
PHONE..................................631 438-0246
EMP: 5 **Privately Held**
SIC: 2759 Business forms: printing
PA: Yoman Madeo Fano
　299 Broadway Ste 810
　New York NY 10007

Patterson
Putnam County

(G-12515)
DICAMILLO MARBLE AND
GRANITE
20 Jon Barrett Rd (12563-2164)
PHONE..................................845 878-0078
Fax: 845 878-2250
EMP: 20 EST: 1991
SALES (est): 1.6MM **Privately Held**
SIC: 3281 Mfg Cut Stone/Products

(G-12516)
EAST HUDSON WATERSHED
CORP
2 Route 164 (12563-2813)
PHONE..................................845 319-6349
Peter Parsons, *President*
EMP: 5
SQ FT: 1,000
SALES (est): 2.7MM **Privately Held**
SIC: 3822 Auto controls regulating residntl
& coml environmt & applncs

(G-12517)
GOLDEN GROUP
INTERNATIONAL LTD
305 Quaker Rd (12563-2191)
P.O. Box 407, Brewster (10509-0407)
PHONE..................................845 440-1025
Jacqueline Transue, *President*
Kevin Hanna, *Info Tech Mgr*
EMP: 6
SALES (est): 530K **Privately Held**
SIC: 2673 5113 3444 5199 Trash bags
(plastic film): made from purchased mate-
rials; food storage & trash bags (plastic);
bags, paper & disposable plastic; bins,
prefabricated sheet metal; art goods &
supplies

(G-12518)
JRS PHARMA LP (DH)
2981 Route 22 Ste 1 (12563-2359)
PHONE..................................845 878-8300
Josef Rettenmaier, *Partner*
J Rettenmaier America, *Partner*
Josef Otto Rettenmaier, *Partner*
J Rettenmaier Holding USA, *Partner*
Antony Gerardi, *Safety Mgr*
◆ EMP: 48
SQ FT: 46,000
SALES (est): 22.6MM
SALES (corp-wide): 355.8K **Privately**
Held
SIC: 2834 Druggists' preparations (phar-
maceuticals)
HQ: Jrs Pharma Gmbh & Co. Kg
　Holzmuhle 1
　Rosenberg 73494
　796 715-2312

(G-12519)
REELEX PACKAGING
SOLUTIONS INC
39 Jon Barrett Rd (12563-2165)
PHONE..................................845 878-7878
Thomas R Copp, *President*

Frank Kotzur, *Vice Pres*
Ronald Zajac, *Vice Pres*
Crystal Newman, *Purchasing*
Gregory Kotzur, *Engineer*
▲ EMP: 40
SQ FT: 50,000
SALES (est): 9.2MM **Privately Held**
SIC: 3549 6794 Metalworking machinery;
patent buying, licensing, leasing
PA: Da Capo Al Fine Ltd
　81 Stone Crop Ln
　Cold Spring NY 10516
　845 265-2011

(G-12520)
SPANISH ARTISAN WINE
GROUP LLC
Also Called: Spanish Artisan Wine Group Ltd
370 Cushman Rd (12563-2638)
PHONE..................................914 414-6982
Gerry Dawes, *Principal*
Gerald Dawes, *Mng Member*
EMP: 5
SALES (est): 1MM **Privately Held**
SIC: 2084 5182 7389 Wines; neutral spir-
its; brokers, business: buying & selling
business enterprises

(G-12521)
TAUMEL METALFORMING CORP
Also Called: Taumel Assembly Systems
25 Jon Barrett Rd (12563-2165)
PHONE..................................845 878-3100
Ernest Bodmer, *President*
Tony A Huber, *Vice Pres*
Werner Stutz, *Vice Pres*
Peter Bodmer, *Treasurer*
EMP: 8
SQ FT: 10,000
SALES (est): 839.7K **Privately Held**
WEB: www.taumel.com
SIC: 3542 Machine tools, metal forming
type

(G-12522)
WERLATONE INC
17 Jon Barrett Rd (12563-2165)
P.O. Box 47, Brewster (10509-0047)
PHONE..................................845 278-2220
Glen C Werlau, *Ch of Bd*
Austin Kile, *Corp Secy*
Eric Kowalik, *Mfg Spvr*
Werner Schuster, *Mfg Spvr*
Giny Coleman, *Purchasing*
EMP: 38 EST: 1965
SQ FT: 7,000
SALES (est): 7.5MM **Privately Held**
WEB: www.werlatone.com
SIC: 3679 Microwave components; elec-
tronic circuits

Pavilion
Genesee County

(G-12523)
HANSON AGGREGATES NEW
YORK LLC
6895 Ellicott Street Rd (14525-9614)
PHONE..................................585 638-5841
Daniel M Meehan, *Principal*
Craig Green, *Opers Staff*
Kelly Kinney, *Office Mgr*
EMP: 15
SALES (corp-wide): 20.6B **Privately Held**
SIC: 3273 Ready-mixed concrete
HQ: Hanson Aggregates New York Llc
　8505 Freport Pkwy Ste 500
　Irving TX 75063

(G-12524)
WNY CHEESE ENTERPRISE
LLC
Also Called: Craigs Station Cheese
1842 Craig Rd (14525-9200)
PHONE..................................585 243-6516
Gordon Lafferty, *General Mgr*
EMP: 20
SALES (est): 739K
SALES (corp-wide): 13.6B **Privately Held**
SIC: 2022 Cheese, natural & processed

PA: Dairy Farmers Of America, Inc.
　1405 N 98th St
　Kansas City KS 66111
　816 801-6455

(G-12525)
WNY ENTERPRISE LLC
1840 Craig Rd (14525-9200)
PHONE..................................585 243-6514
Brian Paris, *General Mgr*
EMP: 20
SALES (est): 6.6MM
SALES (corp-wide): 13.6B **Privately Held**
SIC: 2026 Milk processing (pasteurizing,
homogenizing, bottling)
PA: Dairy Farmers Of America, Inc.
　1405 N 98th St
　Kansas City KS 66111
　816 801-6455

Pawling
Dutchess County

(G-12526)
JOE PIETRYKA INCORPORATED
(PA)
85 Charles Colman Blvd (12564-1160)
PHONE..................................845 855-1201
Joseph W Pietryka, *Ch of Bd*
EMP: 49
SQ FT: 65,000
SALES (est): 13.1MM **Privately Held**
WEB: www.dwconcepts.net
SIC: 3089 Injection molded finished plastic
products

(G-12527)
PAWLING ENGINEERED PDTS
INC
157 Charles Colman Blvd (12564-1121)
PHONE..................................845 855-1000
Craig Busby, *President*
John Rickert, *Vice Pres*
EMP: 120
SQ FT: 250,000
SALES (est): 10.4MM **Privately Held**
SIC: 3061 3089 Mechanical rubber goods;
extruded finished plastic products

(G-12528)
PIETRYKA PLASTICS LLC
85 Charles Colman Blvd (12564-1160)
PHONE..................................845 855-1201
Diana Tomassetti,
EMP: 30
SALES (est): 5.2MM **Privately Held**
SIC: 3089 Injection molded finished plastic
products

Pearl River
Rockland County

(G-12529)
C B MANAGEMENT SERVICES
INC
Also Called: Beitals Aquarium Sales & Svc
73 S Pearl St (10965-2235)
PHONE..................................845 735-2300
Craig Beital, *President*
Creig Beital, *President*
EMP: 13
SQ FT: 5,000
SALES (est): 970K **Privately Held**
WEB: www.cbmanagementservices.com
SIC: 3231 5999 7389 Aquariums & reflec-
tors, glass; aquarium supplies; aquarium
design & maintenance

(G-12530)
FIVE STAR MILLWORK LLC
6 E Dexter Plz (10965-2360)
PHONE..................................845 920-0247
Marco Santos,
Dario Fonseca,
Tiago Fonseca,
EMP: 12
SQ FT: 15,000
SALES (est): 2MM **Privately Held**
SIC: 2431 Millwork

(G-12531)
FUJITSU NTWRK CMMNICATIONS INC
2 Blue Hill Plz Ste 1609 (10965-3115)
PHONE..................................845 731-2000
Bob Demarco, *Manager*
EMP: 18 **Privately Held**
WEB: www.fnc.fujitsu.com
SIC: 3661 8731 3663 Fiber optics communications equipment; commercial physical research; radio & TV communications equipment
HQ: Fujitsu Network Communications, Inc.
   2801 Telecom Pkwy
   Richardson TX 75082

(G-12532)
HUDSON TECHNOLOGIES COMPANY (HQ)
1 Blue Hill Plz Ste 1541 (10965-3110)
PHONE..................................845 735-6000
Kevin Zugibe, *Ch of Bd*
Briann Coleman, *President*
Stephen Mandracchia, *Vice Pres*
EMP: 48
SQ FT: 4,500
SALES: 48.6MM **Publicly Held**
SIC: 2869 Fluorinated hydrocarbon gases

(G-12533)
HUNTER DOUGLAS INC (DH)
1 Blue Hill Plz Ste 1569 (10965-6101)
PHONE..................................845 664-7000
Ralph Sonnenberg, *Ch of Bd*
Marvin B Hopkins, *President*
David H Sonnenberg, *President*
Marko H Sonnenberg, *President*
Ajit Mehra, *Exec VP*
◆ **EMP:** 100
SQ FT: 32,000
SALES (est): 2.4B **Privately Held**
WEB: www.hunterdouglas.com
SIC: 2591 3444 5084 Window blinds; window shades; venetian blinds; sheet metalwork; industrial machinery & equipment
HQ: Hunter Douglas N.V.
   Piekstraat 2
   Rotterdam 3071
   104 869-911

(G-12534)
HUNTS POINT CLEAN ENERGY LLC
Also Called: Hpce
401 N Middletown Rd (10965-1298)
PHONE..................................203 451-5143
Alfredo Forte,
Steven Switzen,
EMP: 6
SQ FT: 63,000
SALES (est): 267.4K **Privately Held**
SIC: 2869 Methyl alcohol, synthetic methanol

(G-12535)
JANE BAKES INC
40 S Main St (10965-2425)
PHONE..................................845 920-1100
Jane Carroll, *Principal*
EMP: 5
SALES (est): 150K **Privately Held**
SIC: 2051 Bakery: wholesale or wholesale/retail combined

(G-12536)
KRAFT HAT MANUFACTURERS INC
7 Veterans Pkwy (10965-1328)
PHONE..................................845 735-6200
Israel Rosenzweig, *President*
Steven Rosenzweig, *Corp Secy*
Lawrence Rosenzweig, *Vice Pres*
▲ **EMP:** 100
SQ FT: 34,000
SALES (est): 9.4MM **Privately Held**
WEB: www.krafthat.com
SIC: 2353 Hats & caps; millinery

(G-12537)
LEVOLOR INC (DH)
1 Blue Hill Plz (10965-3104)
PHONE..................................845 664-7000
Marvin B Hopkins, *President*
▲ **EMP:** 300

SALES (est): 47.8MM **Privately Held**
SIC: 2591 Window blinds; blinds vertical
HQ: Hunter Douglas Inc.
   1 Blue Hill Plz Ste 1569
   Pearl River NY 10965
   845 664-7000

(G-12538)
PROTEIN SCIENCES CORPORATION
401 N Middletown Rd (10965-1298)
PHONE..................................203 686-0800
Bill Edsall, *Project Mgr*
Manon M J Cox, *Branch Mgr*
Joseph Revello, *Director*
EMP: 10 **Privately Held**
SIC: 2834 Pharmaceutical preparations
HQ: Protein Sciences Corporation
   1000 Research Pkwy
   Meriden CT 06450
   203 686-0800

(G-12539)
QUALITY GRAPHICS TRI STATE
171 Center St (10965-1630)
PHONE..................................845 735-2523
Phyllis Schweizer, *President*
Bruce Schweizer, *Vice Pres*
EMP: 5
SALES (est): 788.6K **Privately Held**
SIC: 2752 Commercial printing, offset

(G-12540)
RK PHARMA INC (PA)
401 N Middletown Rd (10965-1298)
PHONE..................................646 884-3765
George Roby Thomas, *CEO*
Ravishanker Kovi, *Chairman*
Michael Chang, *Director*
EMP: 3
SQ FT: 90,000
SALES (est): 2MM **Privately Held**
SIC: 2834 Pharmaceutical preparations

(G-12541)
SKIN PRINTS INC
63 Walter St (10965-1723)
PHONE..................................845 920-8756
Diane Kaufman, *President*
EMP: 3
SQ FT: 10,000
SALES (est): 1.2MM **Privately Held**
SIC: 2269 Finishing plants

(G-12542)
UTILITY ENGINEERING CO
40 Walter St (10965-1795)
PHONE..................................845 735-8900
George Huston, *President*
EMP: 10
SQ FT: 7,400
SALES (est): 620K **Privately Held**
WEB: www.utilitydisplays.com
SIC: 3496 Miscellaneous fabricated wire products

(G-12543)
WYETH HOLDINGS LLC
Also Called: Wyeth Pharmaceutical Division
401 N Middletown Rd (10965-1298)
PHONE..................................845 602-5000
David Zisa, *Principal*
James S Morrissey, *Project Leader*
EMP: 100
SALES (corp-wide): 53.6B **Publicly Held**
SIC: 2834 2836 3842 3841 Pharmaceutical preparations; biological products, except diagnostic; surgical appliances & supplies; surgical & medical instruments; ophthalmic goods; chemical preparations
HQ: Wyeth Holdings Llc
   5 Giralda Farms
   Madison NJ 07940

(G-12544)
XENIAL INC
Also Called: Pcamerica
1 Blue Hill Plz Ste 16 (10965-3100)
PHONE..................................845 920-0800
David J Gosman, *CEO*
EMP: 21
SALES (corp-wide): 3.3B **Publicly Held**
SIC: 7372 Business oriented computer software

HQ: Xenial, Inc.
   3420 Toringdon Way # 400
   Charlotte NC 28277
   770 829-8640

Peconic
Suffolk County

(G-12545)
DORSET FARMS INC
Also Called: Lenz
38355 Main Rd (11958)
P.O. Box 28 (11958-0028)
PHONE..................................631 734-6010
Peter Carroll, *President*
▲ **EMP:** 10
SALES (est): 1MM **Privately Held**
SIC: 2084 Wines

(G-12546)
J PETROCELLI WINE CELLARS LLC
Also Called: Raphael
39390 Route 25 (11958-1501)
P.O. Box 17 (11958-0017)
PHONE..................................631 765-1100
Chip Cheek, *Sales Mgr*
Jack Petrocelli, *Mng Member*
Diandra Petrocellii, *Manager*
▲ **EMP:** 25
SALES: 450K **Privately Held**
SIC: 2084 5921 Wines; wine

(G-12547)
PINDAR VINEYARDS LLC
37645 Route 25 (11958-1514)
P.O. Box 332 (11958-0332)
PHONE..................................631 734-6200
Herdotes Damianos, *Mng Member*
Rose Faiella, *Planning Mgr*
EMP: 20
SQ FT: 5,000
SALES (est): 2.2MM **Privately Held**
WEB: www.pindar.net
SIC: 2084 Wines

Peekskill
Westchester County

(G-12548)
BASF CORPORATION
1057 Lower South St (10566-5302)
PHONE..................................914 737-2554
Margaret Yee, *Counsel*
Kristen Priolo, *Engineer*
Daniel S Gulley, *Branch Mgr*
Donna Duarte, *Admin Asst*
EMP: 344
SALES (corp-wide): 71.7B **Privately Held**
WEB: www.basf.com
SIC: 2869 Industrial organic chemicals
HQ: Basf Corporation
   100 Park Ave
   Florham Park NJ 07932
   973 245-6000

(G-12549)
CANDLES BY FOSTER
810 South St (10566-3431)
P.O. Box 89 (10566-0089)
PHONE..................................914 739-9226
Donald Foster, *Owner*
EMP: 6
SQ FT: 6,500
SALES (est): 355.5K **Privately Held**
SIC: 3999 5999 Candles; candle shops

(G-12550)
ELEVATOR ACCESSORIES MFG
Also Called: Paxton Metal Craft Division
1035 Howard St 37 (10566-2819)
P.O. Box 430 (10566-0430)
PHONE..................................914 739-7004
Alan Messing, *President*
John Johnson, *Vice Pres*
Vicki Messing, *Admin Sec*
EMP: 12
SALES (est): 2.2MM **Privately Held**
SIC: 3534 3441 3446 3444 Elevators & equipment; fabricated structural metal; architectural metalwork; sheet metalwork

(G-12551)
GIULIANTE MACHINE TOOL INC
12 John Walsh Blvd (10566-5323)
PHONE..................................914 835-0008
Martha Giuliante, *President*
Armando Giuliante, *Vice Pres*
Marcelo Giuliante, *Vice Pres*
EMP: 25
SQ FT: 27,000
SALES (est): 4.9MM **Privately Held**
WEB: www.gmtgear.com
SIC: 3599 Machine shop, jobbing & repair

(G-12552)
HAT FACTORY FURNITURE CO
Also Called: Hudson Cabinetry Design
1000 N Division St Ste 8 (10566-1830)
PHONE..................................914 788-6288
Douglas Bialor, *Owner*
EMP: 6
SALES (est): 119.7K **Privately Held**
SIC: 3553 Cabinet makers' machinery

(G-12553)
HUDSON MIRROR LLC
Also Called: Mirrorlite Superscript
710 Washington St (10566-5418)
PHONE..................................914 930-8906
Dwayne Reith, *Vice Pres*
Gary Reith,
EMP: 25
SQ FT: 2,000
SALES (est): 4MM **Privately Held**
SIC: 3827 Mirrors, optical

(G-12554)
OMC2 LLC
1000 N Division St Ste 15 (10566-1830)
PHONE..................................415 580-0262
Danielle Applestone,
EMP: 7 **EST:** 2017
SALES (est): 845.3K **Privately Held**
SIC: 3541 Milling machines

(G-12555)
RESCUESTUFF INC
962 Washington St (10566-5816)
PHONE..................................718 318-7570
Greg Grimaldi, *President*
Seth Porter, *CFO*
EMP: 5
SQ FT: 2,000
SALES (est): 250K **Privately Held**
WEB: www.rescuestuff.net
SIC: 2395 2262 Embroidery products, except schiffli machine; screen printing: manmade fiber & silk broadwoven fabrics

(G-12556)
RMS PACKAGING INC
Also Called: Aurora Sef
1050 Lower South St (10566-5313)
PHONE..................................914 205-2070
Sheldon Rosenberg, *President*
▲ **EMP:** 16
SALES (est): 4.4MM **Privately Held**
SIC: 2671 Plastic film, coated or laminated for packaging

(G-12557)
SD CHRISTIE ASSOCIATES INC
424 Central Ave Ste 5 (10566-2056)
P.O. Box 5158, Cary NC (27512-5158)
PHONE..................................914 734-1800
Thomas Christie, *President*
EMP: 5
SALES (est): 503.9K **Privately Held**
SIC: 3069 5085 Molded rubber products; mattress protectors, rubber; fasteners, industrial: nuts, bolts, screws, etc.; rubber goods, mechanical

(G-12558)
VIVID RGB LIGHTING LLC
824 Main St Ste 1 (10566-2052)
PHONE..................................718 635-0817
Brian Fassett, *Managing Dir*
EMP: 7
SQ FT: 3,000
SALES (est): 770.9K **Privately Held**
SIC: 3648 Lighting equipment

(G-12559)
W DESIGNE INC
Also Called: Wood Design
5 John Walsh Blvd (10566-5307)
PHONE................................914 736-1058
Alex Bernabo, *President*
▲ EMP: 20
SQ FT: 25,000
SALES (est): 3.1MM **Privately Held**
SIC: 2434 2517 Wood kitchen cabinets;
   wood television & radio cabinets

(G-12560)
WALTER G LEGGE COMPANY INC
Also Called: Legge System
444 Central Av (10566-2003)
P.O. Box 591 (10566-0591)
PHONE................................914 737-5040
Elizabeth Bauer, *President*
Jane Fejes, *Manager*
▲ EMP: 9 EST: 1936
SQ FT: 10,000
SALES (est): 1.7MM **Privately Held**
WEB: www.leggesystems.com
SIC: 2842 3272 3679 Sanitation prepara-
   tions, disinfectants & deodorants; tile, pre-
   cast terrazzo or concrete; power supplies,
   all types: static

(G-12561)
WESTCHESTER TECHNOLOGIES INC
8 John Walsh Blvd Ste 311 (10566-5347)
PHONE................................914 736-1034
Roger Prahl, *CEO*
EMP: 23
SQ FT: 4,000
SALES: 4.1MM **Privately Held**
WEB: www.microoptics.com
SIC: 3827 Optical instruments & apparatus

(G-12562)
WESTYPO PRINTERS INC
540 Harrison Ave (10566-2318)
P.O. Box 190 (10566-0190)
PHONE................................914 737-7394
Mike Mc Guggart, *President*
Teri Mc Gugart, *Treasurer*
EMP: 6 EST: 1964
SQ FT: 8,000
SALES (est): 544.5K **Privately Held**
SIC: 2752 2759 Commercial printing, off-
   set; commercial printing

(G-12563)
WHITE PLAINS COAT APRON CO INC
Also Called: White Plains Linen
4 John Walsh Blvd (10566-5323)
PHONE................................914 736-2610
Allan Botchman, *Ch of Bd*
Bruce Botchman, *President*
Keith Botchman, *Vice Pres*
Len Labonia, *Vice Pres*
Thomas Moscati, *VP Sales*
EMP: 7
SQ FT: 30,000
SALES (est): 2.3MM **Privately Held**
SIC: 2389 7213 Uniforms & vestments;
   apron supply

Pelham
Westchester County

(G-12564)
ARCHIE COMIC PUBLICATIONS INC
Also Called: Archie Comics Publishers
629 Fifth Ave Ste 100 (10803-3714)
PHONE................................914 381-5155
Michael Silberkleit, *Chairman*
Steve Mooar, *Vice Pres*
Stephen Oswald, *Train & Dev Mgr*
EMP: 75 EST: 1939
SQ FT: 10,000
SALES (est): 13.3MM **Privately Held**
WEB: www.archiecomics.com
SIC: 2721 Comic books: publishing only,
   not printed on site

(G-12565)
BANK-MILLER CO INC
333 Fifth Ave (10803-1203)
PHONE................................914 227-9357
Steven Bank, *President*
▲ EMP: 20
SQ FT: 5,500
SALES (est): 2.6MM **Privately Held**
WEB: www.bankmiller.com
SIC: 2259 2339 5131 Convertors, knit
   goods; women's & misses' outerwear;
   textile converters

(G-12566)
IMPERIA MASONRY SUPPLY CORP (PA)
57 Canal Rd (10803-2706)
PHONE................................914 738-0900
Joseph Imperia, *President*
Lisa Carabello, *Admin Sec*
▲ EMP: 32 EST: 1927
SQ FT: 8,400
SALES (est): 3.2MM **Privately Held**
WEB: www.imperiabros.com
SIC: 3271 5031 5032 5211 Blocks, con-
   crete or cinder: standard; lumber, plywood
   & millwork; brick, stone & related material;
   brick, except refractory; stone, crushed or
   broken; lumber & other building materials;
   lumber products; brick; masonry materials
   & supplies

(G-12567)
MANACRAFT PRECISION INC
945 Spring Rd (10803-2714)
PHONE................................914 654-0967
Richard Osterer, *President*
EMP: 10 EST: 1946
SQ FT: 3,000
SALES (est): 1.2MM **Privately Held**
SIC: 3451 Screw machine products

(G-12568)
SHORELINE PUBLISHING INC
629 Fifth Ave Ste B01 (10803-3708)
PHONE................................914 738-7869
Edward Shapiro, *President*
EMP: 7
SQ FT: 1,000
SALES (est): 941.3K **Privately Held**
WEB: www.shorelinepub.com
SIC: 2721 2752 Magazines: publishing
   only, not printed on site; commercial print-
   ing, offset

Penfield
Monroe County

(G-12569)
ALUMI-TECH LLC
1640 Harris Rd (14526-1816)
PHONE................................585 663-7010
James Putnam,
EMP: 8
SQ FT: 2,500
SALES (est): 815.7K **Privately Held**
WEB: www.saddlestackers.com
SIC: 7692 Welding repair

(G-12570)
DOLOMITE PRODUCTS COMPANY INC
746 Whalen Rd (14526-1022)
PHONE................................585 586-2568
Pat Tooley, *Branch Mgr*
EMP: 20
SQ FT: 2,280
SALES (corp-wide): 30.6B **Privately Held**
WEB: www.dolomitegroup.com
SIC: 1429 Trap rock, crushed & broken-
   quarrying
HQ: Dolomite Products Company Inc.
   1150 Penfield Rd
   Rochester NY 14625
   315 524-1998

(G-12571)
NIFTY BAR GRINDING & CUTTING
450 Whitney Rd (14526-2326)
PHONE................................585 381-0450
John Raimondi, *President*

EMP: 23 EST: 1967
SQ FT: 24,000
SALES (est): 5MM **Privately Held**
WEB: www.niftybar.com
SIC: 3541 Machine tools, metal cutting
   type

(G-12572)
RANGE REPAIR WAREHOUSE
421 Penbrooke Dr Ste 2 (14526-2045)
PHONE................................585 235-0980
Paul V Ciminelli, *Owner*
EMP: 5
SALES (est): 274.5K **Privately Held**
SIC: 3499 Fabricated metal products

(G-12573)
ROBINSON TOOLS LLC
Also Called: Garco
477 Whitney Rd (14526-2328)
PHONE................................585 586-5432
James D Keppel, *President*
Philip Decaire, *Manager*
EMP: 7
SQ FT: 5,000
SALES (est): 650K **Privately Held**
WEB: www.robinsontools.com
SIC: 3423 Hand & edge tools

(G-12574)
SCHNEIDER ELECTRIC USA INC
441 Penbrooke Dr Ste 9 (14526-2046)
PHONE................................585 377-1313
Brian Hoffman, *Manager*
Marina Velazquez, *Manager*
EMP: 11
SALES (corp-wide): 177.9K **Privately Held**
WEB: www.squared.com
SIC: 3612 Transformers, except electric
HQ: Schneider Electric Usa, Inc.
   201 Wshington St Ste 2700
   Boston MA 02108
   978 975-9600

(G-12575)
THERMO FISHER SCIENTIFIC INC
1935 Penfield Rd (14526-1434)
PHONE................................585 899-7780
EMP: 47
SALES (corp-wide): 24.3B **Publicly Held**
SIC: 3826 Analytical instruments
PA: Thermo Fisher Scientific Inc.
   168 3rd Ave
   Waltham MA 02451
   781 622-1000

(G-12576)
VIEWSPORT INTERNATIONAL INC
11 Feathery Cir (14526-2816)
PHONE................................585 259-1562
Benjamin Wood, *President*
EMP: 3
SALES (est): 5.7MM **Privately Held**
SIC: 2396 7389 Screen printing on fabric
   articles;

Penn Yan
Yates County

(G-12577)
ANTHONY ROAD WINE CO INC
1020 Anthony Rd (14527-9632)
PHONE................................315 536-2182
John Martini, *President*
Ann Martini, *Vice Pres*
Elizabeth Castner, *Manager*
EMP: 15
SQ FT: 3,800
SALES (est): 1.8MM **Privately Held**
WEB: www.anthonyroadwine.com
SIC: 2084 Wines

(G-12578)
BIRKETT MILLS (PA)
163 Main St Ste 2 (14527-1284)
PHONE................................315 536-3311
Wayne W Wagner, *President*
Jeffrey S Gifford, *Exec VP*
Brian McFetridge, *CFO*
Wayne Agner, *Relations*

◆ EMP: 5 EST: 1797
SQ FT: 12,018
SALES (est): 7.8MM **Privately Held**
WEB: www.thebirkettmills.com
SIC: 2041 5999 5261 Flour & other grain
   mill products; farm equipment & supplies;
   nurseries & garden centers; lawn & gar-
   den supplies

(G-12579)
BIRKETT MILLS
163 Main St Ste 3 (14527-1284)
PHONE................................315 536-4112
Jeff Gifford, *Manager*
EMP: 32
SQ FT: 60,455
SALES (corp-wide): 7.8MM **Privately Held**
WEB: www.thebirkettmills.com
SIC: 2041 Flour & other grain mill products
PA: The Birkett Mills
   163 Main St Ste 2
   Penn Yan NY 14527
   315 536-3311

(G-12580)
CHRONICLE EXPRESS
138 Main St (14527-1299)
PHONE................................315 536-4422
George Barnes, *President*
Irene Vanderlinder, *Sales/Mktg Mgr*
EMP: 15
SALES (est): 704K **Privately Held**
WEB: www.chronicleexpress.com
SIC: 2711 5994 Newspapers, publishing &
   printing; news dealers & newsstands

(G-12581)
DAVID F DE MARCO
Also Called: De Marco Vineyards
929 Davy Rd (14527-9644)
P.O. Box 551 (14527-0551)
PHONE................................315 536-0882
David F De Marco, *Owner*
EMP: 5
SQ FT: 4,500
SALES: 240K **Privately Held**
WEB: www.daviddemarco.com
SIC: 2084 Wines

(G-12582)
FERRO CORPORATION
1789 Transelco Dr (14527-9752)
PHONE................................315 536-3357
Hector Ortino, *Branch Mgr*
EMP: 200
SALES (corp-wide): 1.6B **Publicly Held**
WEB: www.ferro.com
SIC: 2819 Industrial inorganic chemicals
PA: Ferro Corporation
   6060 Parkland Blvd # 250
   Mayfield Heights OH 44124
   216 875-5600

(G-12583)
FERRO ELECTRONICS MATERIALS (HQ)
Also Called: Ferro Electronic Mtl Systems
1789 Transelco Dr (14527-9752)
PHONE................................315 536-3357
Lyn Labrake, *Manager*
◆ EMP: 2
SALES (est): 15.3MM
SALES (corp-wide): 1.6B **Publicly Held**
SIC: 3264 Porcelain electrical supplies
PA: Ferro Corporation
   6060 Parkland Blvd # 250
   Mayfield Heights OH 44124
   216 875-5600

(G-12584)
FOX RUN VINEYARDS INC
670 State Route 14 (14527-9622)
PHONE................................315 536-4616
Scott Osbourne, *President*
Ruth Osborn, *Vice Pres*
Kelli Shaffner, *Marketing Staff*
EMP: 12
SQ FT: 8,000
SALES (est): 3.7MM **Privately Held**
WEB: www.foxrunvineyards.com
SIC: 2084 Wines

▲ = Import ▼=Export
◆ =Import/Export

(G-12585)
HANSON AGGREGATES EAST LLC
131 Garfield Ave (14527-1655)
P.O. Box 168 (14527-0168)
PHONE..................................315 536-9391
Kenny Thurston, *Manager*
EMP: 6
SALES (corp-wide): 20.6B **Privately Held**
WEB: www.hansonaggeast.com
SIC: 1442 Common sand mining
HQ: Hanson Aggregates East Llc
    3131 Rdu Center Dr
    Morrisville NC 27560
    919 380-2500

(G-12586)
HOFFMAN & HOFFMAN
Also Called: Rooster Hill Vineyards
489 State Route 54 (14527-9595)
P.O. Box 11 (14527-0011)
PHONE..................................315 536-4773
David W Hoffman, *Partner*
Amy E Hoffman, *Partner*
Amy Hoffman, *CFO*
EMP: 7
SALES (est): 574.1K **Privately Held**
WEB: www.roosterhill.com
SIC: 2084 Wines

(G-12587)
IVAN HORNING
Also Called: Horning Greenhouses
848 State Route 14a (14527-9189)
PHONE..................................315 536-3028
Ivan Horning, *Owner*
Mason Horning, *Asst Mgr*
EMP: 6
SALES: 450K **Privately Held**
SIC: 2499 0181 Decorative wood & wood-
    work; flowers: grown under cover (e.g.
    greenhouse production)

(G-12588)
JASPER TRANSPORT LLC
1680 Flat St (14527-9024)
P.O. Box 441 (14527-0441)
PHONE..................................315 729-5760
Ross Newcomb,
EMP: 6
SALES (est): 570K **Privately Held**
SIC: 3537 Trucks, tractors, loaders, carri-
    ers & similar equipment

(G-12589)
KAN PAK LLC
105 Horizon Park Dr (14527-8764)
PHONE..................................620 440-2319
EMP: 6
SALES (corp-wide): 1.3B **Privately Held**
SIC: 2024 Ice cream & frozen desserts
HQ: Kan. Pak, Llc
    151 S Whittier Rd
    Wichita KS 67207
    620 442-6820

(G-12590)
PREJEAN WINERY INC
2634 State Route 14 (14527-9735)
PHONE..................................315 536-7524
Elizabeth Prejean, *President*
Thomas Prejean, *Vice Pres*
EMP: 11
SQ FT: 6,000
SALES (est): 1.2MM **Privately Held**
WEB: www.prejeanwinery.com
SIC: 2084 Wines

(G-12591)
RED TAIL RIDGE INC
Also Called: Red Tail Ridge Winery
846 State Route 14 (14527-9622)
PHONE..................................315 536-4580
Mike Schnelle, *President*
Nancy Irelan, *Principal*
EMP: 15
SALES (est): 485.2K **Privately Held**
SIC: 2084 Wines

(G-12592)
RIBBLE LUMBER INC
249 1/2 Lake St (14527-1812)
PHONE..................................315 536-6221
Roger C Ribble, *President*
Roger A Ribble Sr, *Corp Secy*

EMP: 5
SALES (est): 360K **Privately Held**
SIC: 2434 1794 4212 Wood kitchen cabi-
    nets; excavation work; dump truck
    haulage

(G-12593)
ROTO SALT COMPANY INC
118 Monell St (14527-1404)
PHONE..................................315 536-3742
Brett M Oakes, *President*
Susan Ettinger, *Vice Pres*
Ann Olney, *Office Mgr*
EMP: 32
SQ FT: 20,000
SALES (est): 7.8MM **Privately Held**
SIC: 2899 3281 Salt; building stone prod-
    ucts

(G-12594)
SILGAN PLASTICS LLC
40 Powell Ln (14527-1072)
PHONE..................................315 536-5690
Joseph Pollhein, *Manager*
Stacy Fisher, *Manager*
Jon Panceria, *Manager*
Amanda Sprague, *Administration*
EMP: 250
SQ FT: 100,000
SALES (corp-wide): 4.4B **Publicly Held**
WEB: www.silganplastics.com
SIC: 3089 Plastic containers, except foam
HQ: Silgan Plastics Llc
    14515 North Outer 40 Rd # 210
    Chesterfield MO 63017
    800 274-5426

Perry
Wyoming County

(G-12595)
AMERICAN CLSSIC OUTFITTERS INC
Also Called: Liebe NY
200 Main St N Ste 1 (14530-1215)
PHONE..................................585 237-6111
Jim Liebe, *Mng Member*
EMP: 95
SQ FT: 200,000
SALES (est): 6.6MM **Privately Held**
WEB: www.americanclassicoutfitters.com
SIC: 2329 Men's & boys' athletic uniforms

(G-12596)
CREATIVE FOOD INGREDIENTS INC
Also Called: CFI
1 Lincoln Ave (14530-1605)
PHONE..................................585 237-2213
Andrew W O'Flaherty, *CEO*
Debra Bevans, *Human Res Dir*
◆ EMP: 140
SALES (est): 25.4MM **Privately Held**
SIC: 2052 Bakery products, dry

(G-12597)
EAST HILL CREAMERY LLC
346 Main St S (14530-9551)
PHONE..................................585 237-3622
Gary Burley, *Mng Member*
EMP: 6
SALES (est): 203.6K **Privately Held**
SIC: 2022 Cheese spreads, dips, pastes &
    other cheese products

(G-12598)
J N WHITE ASSOCIATES INC
Also Called: J.N. White Designs
129 N Center St (14530-9701)
P.O. Box 219 (14530-0219)
PHONE..................................585 237-5191
Randy White, *President*
Ken Boss, *Vice Pres*
Mary Patrick-Grabows, *Vice Pres*
John Steff, *Vice Pres*
Susan C White, *Vice Pres*
EMP: 95
SQ FT: 25,000
SALES (est): 17.5MM **Privately Held**
WEB: www.jnwhitedesigns.com
SIC: 2759 7389 Screen printing; printed
    circuitry graphic layout

(G-12599)
SIGN LANGUAGE INC
Also Called: Sign Language Custom WD
Signs
6491 State Route 20a (14530-9758)
PHONE..................................585 237-2620
Dave Caito, *President*
Jeff Fitch, *Corp Secy*
Mike Fitch, *Exec VP*
EMP: 8
SQ FT: 3,000
SALES (est): 1.2MM **Privately Held**
WEB: www.signlanguageinc.com
SIC: 3993 Signs, not made in custom sign
    painting shops

Petersburg
Rensselaer County

(G-12600)
TONOGA INC (PA)
Also Called: Taconic
95-136 Coonbrook Rd (12138)
P.O. Box 69 (12138-0069)
PHONE..................................518 658-3202
Andrew G Russell, *Chairman*
Lawrence Carroll, *Exec VP*
Sharon Goodermote, *Vice Pres*
Manfred Huschka, *Vice Pres*
Douglas Merrill, *Vice Pres*
▲ EMP: 180 EST: 1961
SQ FT: 150,000
SALES (est): 117.3MM **Privately Held**
WEB: www.taconic-afd.com
SIC: 2295 3629 Resin or plastic coated
    fabrics; electronic generation equipment

Phelps
Ontario County

(G-12601)
AMERICAN CRMIC PROCESS RES LLC
835 Mcivor Rd (14532-9535)
P.O. Box 213 (14532-0213)
PHONE..................................315 828-6268
Jesse Sheckler,
EMP: 6
SQ FT: 18,670
SALES (est): 259.3K **Privately Held**
SIC: 3299 Nonmetallic mineral products

(G-12602)
BENEMY WELDING & FABRICATION
8 Pleasant Ave (14532-1100)
PHONE..................................315 548-8500
Dave Suhr, *President*
Christine Suhr, *Vice Pres*
EMP: 6
SQ FT: 1,852
SALES (est): 675.2K **Privately Held**
SIC: 7692 Welding repair

(G-12603)
DORGAN WELDING SERVICE
1378 White Rd (14532-9502)
PHONE..................................315 462-9030
Bob Dorgan, *Owner*
EMP: 5
SQ FT: 7,000
SALES: 450K **Privately Held**
SIC: 7692 1799 Welding repair; welding
    on site

(G-12604)
HANSON AGGREGATES EAST LLC
392 State Route 96 (14532-9531)
PHONE..................................315 548-4913
Mike Cool, *Manager*
EMP: 26
SQ FT: 6,756
SALES (corp-wide): 20.6B **Privately Held**
SIC: 3273 1442 Ready-mixed concrete;
    construction sand & gravel
HQ: Hanson Aggregates East Llc
    3131 Rdu Center Dr
    Morrisville NC 27560
    919 380-2500

(G-12605)
MAGNUS PRECISION MFG INC
1912 State Route 96 (14532-9705)
PHONE..................................315 548-8032
Thomas Shepard, *Principal*
Magnus Precision, *VP Mfg*
Phil Zimmerman, *Mfg Spvr*
Steve Strauss, *Purch Agent*
Eric Galens, *QC Mgr*
EMP: 68
SQ FT: 55,000
SALES (est): 13.6MM
SALES (corp-wide): 61MM **Privately Held**
WEB: www.magnuscnc.com
SIC: 3625 3544 Relays & industrial con-
    trols; special dies & tools
PA: Floturn, Inc.
    4236 Thunderbird Ln
    West Chester OH 45014
    513 860-8040

(G-12606)
PHELPS CEMENT PRODUCTS INC
5 S Newark St (14532-9708)
P.O. Box 40 (14532-0040)
PHONE..................................315 548-9415
Gerald Haers, *Ch of Bd*
Michael Haers, *President*
Gerry Haers, *Admin Sec*
EMP: 23
SQ FT: 4,000
SALES (est): 4.9MM **Privately Held**
WEB: www.phelpscement.com
SIC: 3271 5211 5032 Blocks, concrete or
    cinder: standard; lumber & other building
    materials; brick, stone & related material

(G-12607)
SENECA CERAMICS CORP
835 Mcivor Rd (14532-9535)
P.O. Box 213 (14532-0213)
PHONE..................................315 781-0100
Chad Scheckler, *President*
Howard Hersey, *Treasurer*
Larisa Scheckler, *Admin Sec*
EMP: 6
SALES (est): 300K **Privately Held**
SIC: 3469 Utensils, household: porcelain
    enameled

(G-12608)
SHEPPARD GRAIN ENTERPRISES LLC
1615 Maryland Rd (14532-9507)
PHONE..................................315 548-9271
Steve Sheppard, *Mng Member*
◆ EMP: 35
SQ FT: 3,600
SALES (est): 40MM **Privately Held**
SIC: 2041 Flour & other grain mill products

(G-12609)
TRIPLETT MACHINE INC
1374 Phelps Junction Rd (14532-9747)
PHONE..................................315 548-3198
Douglas A Triplett Jr, *CEO*
Greg Triplett, *Plant Mgr*
Jeffrey Triplett, *Treasurer*
Douglas Triplett Sr, *Shareholder*
EMP: 65
SQ FT: 30,000
SALES (est): 14.9MM **Privately Held**
WEB: www.triplettmachine.com
SIC: 3599 Machine shop, jobbing & repair

(G-12610)
VALVETECH INC
1391 Phelps Junction Rd (14532-9747)
P.O. Box 118 (14532-0118)
PHONE..................................315 548-4551
Michael Mullally, *President*
Jeff Merkel, *Opers Mgr*
Michelle Smith, *Purch Mgr*
Jeff Pullano, *Chief Engr*
Joseph Acquista, *Engineer*
EMP: 35
SQ FT: 1,000
SALES (est): 7.3MM
SALES (corp-wide): 165.6MM **Privately Held**
WEB: www.valvetech.net
SIC: 3592 Valves, aircraft

PA: G.W. Lisk Company, Inc.
2 South St
Clifton Springs NY 14432
315 462-2611

(G-12611)
Z-AXIS INC
Also Called: Boundless Technologies
1916 State Route 96 (14532-9705)
PHONE...............................315 548-5000
Michael Allen, *President*
▲ **EMP:** 72
SQ FT: 30,000
SALES (est): 16.5MM **Privately Held**
WEB: www.zaxis.net
SIC: 3699 3577 3845 Electrical equipment & supplies; computer peripheral equipment; electromedical equipment

Philadelphia
Jefferson County

(G-12612)
NATURES WAREHOUSE
55 Main St (13673-4189)
P.O. Box 221, Kidron OH (44636-0221)
PHONE...............................800 215-4372
Cari L Laudon, *Partner*
Daniel Laudon, *Partner*
EMP: 10
SALES (est): 1.3MM **Privately Held**
SIC: 2899 2841 5499 Essential oils; soap & other detergents; vitamin food stores

Philmont
Columbia County

(G-12613)
FALLS MANUFACTURING INC
(PA)
95 Main St (12565)
P.O. Box 798 (12565-0798)
PHONE...............................518 672-7189
Frederick A Meyer, *President*
EMP: 8
SQ FT: 4,800
SALES (est): 2.3MM **Privately Held**
SIC: 2381 2339 Fabric dress & work gloves; women's & misses' outerwear

(G-12614)
PVC CONTAINER
CORPORATION
Also Called: Nova Pack
370 Stevers Crossing Rd (12565)
PHONE...............................518 672-7721
Edna Hover, *Manager*
EMP: 160
SALES (corp-wide): 141MM **Privately Held**
WEB: www.airopak.com
SIC: 3085 3089 Plastics bottles; molding primary plastic
HQ: Pvc Container Corporation
15450 South Outer 40 Rd # 120
Chesterfield MO 63017

Phoenix
Oswego County

(G-12615)
AMERICAN MATERIAL
PROCESSING
126 Bankrupt Rd (13135-2193)
P.O. Box 12 (13135-0012)
PHONE...............................315 318-0017
Lawson Whiting, *President*
Matthew Eddy, *COO*
Jason McKinney, *Vice Pres*
EMP: 11 **EST:** 2013
SQ FT: 800

SALES (est): 1.3MM **Privately Held**
SIC: 3532 3569 5082 3535 Crushing, pulverizing & screening equipment; feeders, ore & aggregate; ice crushers (machinery); crushing, pulverizing & screening machinery; belt conveyor systems, general industrial use; bulk handling conveyor systems

(G-12616)
LOCK 1 DISTILLING COMPANY
LLC
17 Culvert St (13135)
PHONE...............................315 934-4376
Stephen Dates, *Mng Member*
Brendan Backus,
Kevin Dates,
EMP: 5
SQ FT: 7,000
SALES: 150K **Privately Held**
SIC: 2082 Beer (alcoholic beverage)

(G-12617)
MAJESTIC MOLD & TOOL INC
177 Volney St (13135-3116)
PHONE...............................315 695-2079
Timothy King, *President*
Dennis Lyons, *Vice Pres*
Stephen Corsette, *Treasurer*
Pam Najdul, *Manager*
EMP: 16
SQ FT: 8,000
SALES (est): 3.6MM **Privately Held**
WEB: www.majesticmold.com
SIC: 2821 Molding compounds, plastics

(G-12618)
NUTRATECH LABS INC
406 State Route 264 (13135-2124)
PHONE...............................315 695-2256
Philip R Stone, *Ch of Bd*
EMP: 5 **EST:** 2017
SALES (est): 676.5K **Privately Held**
SIC: 2834 Pharmaceutical preparations

(G-12619)
PHOENIX WELDING & FABG INC
Also Called: Phoenix Material Handling
10 County Route 6 (13135-2118)
PHONE...............................315 695-2223
Brian D Dates, *Ch of Bd*
Dan Schmitt, *Controller*
Tom Pierson, *Supervisor*
EMP: 5
SQ FT: 2,500
SALES (est): 970.3K **Privately Held**
SIC: 7692 Welding repair

(G-12620)
PWF ENTERPRISE LLC
19 County Route 6 B (13135-2117)
PHONE...............................315 695-2223
Dan Schmitt, *Controller*
Brenden Backus, *Mng Member*
Kevin Doontes, *Mng Member*
Tom Pierson, *Info Tech Dir*
EMP: 10
SALES (est): 1.7MM **Privately Held**
SIC: 3441 2899 Fabricated structural metal; fluxes: brazing, soldering, galvanizing & welding

(G-12621)
SOUTHERN GRAPHIC SYSTEMS
LLC
Also Called: SGS
67 County Route 59 (13135-2116)
PHONE...............................315 695-7079
Ginny Paparo, *Manager*
Jennifer Shutts, *Technology*
Vic Baranowski,
EMP: 27
SALES (corp-wide): 272.7MM **Privately Held**
SIC: 3555 Printing trades machinery
HQ: Southern Graphic Systems, Llc
626 W Main St Ste 500
Louisville KY 40202
502 637-5443

Piermont
Rockland County

(G-12622)
ROCKLAND COLLOID CORP
(PA)
Also Called: Rockaloid
44 Franklin St (10968-1010)
P.O. Box 3120, Oregon City OR (97045-0306)
PHONE...............................845 359-5559
Robert Cone, *President*
Robert Cone Jr, *Vice Pres*
Francis Cooper, *Treasurer*
EMP: 5 **EST:** 1966
SQ FT: 3,000
SALES (est): 697.4K **Privately Held**
WEB: www.rockloid.com
SIC: 3861 5043 Photographic equipment & supplies; photographic equipment & supplies

Piffard
Livingston County

(G-12623)
ARKEMA INC
Also Called: Genesee Plant
3289 Genesee St (14533-9745)
P.O. Box 188, Geneseo (14454-0188)
PHONE...............................585 243-6359
Martin Foess, *Branch Mgr*
Eileen Maher, *Manager*
Valeria Kazarinova, *Analyst*
Nick Walker, *Representative*
EMP: 170
SALES (corp-wide): 98.4MM **Privately Held**
SIC: 2869 2819 Industrial organic chemicals; industrial inorganic chemicals
HQ: Arkema Inc.
900 First Ave
King Of Prussia PA 19406
610 205-7000

(G-12624)
EXXELIA-RAF TABTRONICS
LLC
2854 Genesee St (14533-9749)
P.O. Box 128, Geneseo (14454-0128)
PHONE...............................585 243-4331
James Charles Tabbi, *Manager*
EMP: 43
SALES (corp-wide): 16MM **Privately Held**
SIC: 3677 3643 3612 Electronic transformers; coil windings, electronic; current-carrying wiring devices; transformers, except electric
PA: Exxelia-Raf Tabtronics, Llc
1221 N Us Highway 17 92
Longwood FL 32750
386 736-1698

Pine Bush
Orange County

(G-12625)
MOBILE MEDIA INC (PA)
24 Center St (12566-6004)
P.O. Box 177 (12566-0177)
PHONE...............................845 744-8080
Lance Pennington, *Principal*
Nancy Pennington, *Vice Pres*
Matt Skradski, *Natl Sales Mgr*
▲ **EMP:** 45
SQ FT: 31,000
SALES (est): 10.9MM **Privately Held**
WEB: www.rolleasy.com
SIC: 2542 Partitions & fixtures, except wood

(G-12626)
P & B WOODWORKING INC
2415 State Route 52 (12566-7041)
P.O. Box 225 (12566-0225)
PHONE...............................845 744-2508
Jake Donnell, *President*

Steven Reinhardt, *Vice Pres*
EMP: 10
SQ FT: 11,000
SALES: 1.1MM **Privately Held**
SIC: 2431 Millwork

Pine City
Chemung County

(G-12627)
DALRYMPLE GRAV & CONTG
CO INC (HQ)
2105 S Broadway (14871-9700)
PHONE...............................607 739-0391
David J Dalrymple, *Ch of Bd*
Robert H Dalrymple, *President*
Edward C Dalrymple Jr, *Vice Pres*
Don Benjamin, *Plant Mgr*
Jason Strawser, *Sales Executive*
EMP: 18 **EST:** 1890
SQ FT: 10,000
SALES (est): 49.5MM
SALES (corp-wide): 105.6MM **Privately Held**
SIC: 1442 3273 Construction sand & gravel; ready-mixed concrete
PA: Dalrymple Holding Corp
2105 S Broadway
Pine City NY 14871
607 737-6200

(G-12628)
DALRYMPLE HOLDING CORP
(PA)
2105 S Broadway (14871-9700)
PHONE...............................607 737-6200
David J Dalrymple, *President*
Edward C Dalrymple Jr, *Vice Pres*
Sue Knighton, *Director*
Robert H Dalrymple, *Admin Sec*
EMP: 20
SQ FT: 5,000
SALES (est): 105.6MM **Privately Held**
SIC: 3273 1611 1442 1622 Ready-mixed concrete; highway & street construction; construction sand & gravel; bridge construction; stone, quarrying & processing of own stone products

(G-12629)
SENECA STONE CORPORATION
(HQ)
2105 S Broadway (14871-9700)
PHONE...............................607 737-6200
David J Dalrymple, *President*
Edward C Dalrymple Jr, *Vice Pres*
Robert H Dalrymple, *Vice Pres*
Edward C Dalrymple Sr, *Treasurer*
Sandy Strong, *Accounts Mgr*
EMP: 4
SQ FT: 800
SALES (est): 1.7MM
SALES (corp-wide): 105.6MM **Privately Held**
SIC: 3281 1771 1442 Cut stone & stone products; concrete work; construction sand & gravel
PA: Dalrymple Holding Corp
2105 S Broadway
Pine City NY 14871
607 737-6200

Pine Island
Orange County

(G-12630)
REELCOLOGY INC
39 Transport Ln (10969-1223)
P.O. Box 305 (10969-0305)
PHONE...............................845 258-1880
Kenneth H Smith, *President*
EMP: 15
SQ FT: 7,000
SALES (est): 1.8MM **Privately Held**
SIC: 3496 3499 Cable, uninsulated wire: made from purchased wire; reels, cable: metal

(G-12631)
SABILA CORP (PA)
480 Liberty Corners Rd (10969-1918)
P.O. Box 691 (10969-0691)
PHONE....................................845 981-7128
Kenan Porter, *CEO*
▲ EMP: 9 EST: 2010
SALES (est): 7.1MM **Privately Held**
SIC: 2087 Concentrates, drink

Pine Plains
Dutchess County

(G-12632)
ABRA MEDIA INC
Also Called: Live Oak Media
2773 W Church St (12567-5421)
P.O. Box 652 (12567-0652)
PHONE....................................518 398-1010
Arnold Cardillo, *President*
Debra Cardillo, *Admin Sec*
EMP: 6
SALES (est): 480K **Privately Held**
WEB: www.liveoakmedia.com
SIC: 2741 7812 Miscellaneous publishing;
audio-visual program production

(G-12633)
DUTCH SPIRITS LLC
Also Called: Dutch's Spirits
98 Ryan Rd (12567-5022)
PHONE....................................518 398-1022
Ariel Schlein, *Mng Member*
John Adams,
Ronit Schlein,
▲ EMP: 17
SQ FT: 7,424,000
SALES: 250K **Privately Held**
SIC: 2084 5999 2085 Neutral spirits, fruit;
alcoholic beverage making equipment &
supplies; cocktails, alcoholic

Pine Valley
Chemung County

(G-12634)
AMES COMPANIES INC
114 Smith Rd (14872)
P.O. Box 126 (14872-0126)
PHONE....................................607 739-4544
John Stoner, *Owner*
Mark Schrage, *Manager*
EMP: 20
SQ FT: 13,235
SALES (corp-wide): 1.5B **Publicly Held**
WEB: www.ames.com
SIC: 3423 Hand & edge tools
HQ: The Ames Companies Inc
465 Railroad Ave
Camp Hill PA 17011
717 737-1500

Pittsford
Monroe County

(G-12635)
AD PUBLICATIONS INC
8 Greenwood Park (14534-2912)
PHONE....................................585 248-2888
Donald Stahl, *President*
Cheryl Stahl, *Vice Pres*
Patricia Stahl, *Admin Sec*
EMP: 10
SQ FT: 450
SALES (est): 786.8K **Privately Held**
SIC: 2759 Coupons: printing

(G-12636)
**AMERICAN-SWISS PRODUCTS
CO INC**
1987 W Jefferson Rd (14534-1041)
PHONE....................................585 292-1720
Rebecca J Luce, *President*
Zahl Cama, *QC Mgr*
Lori Durfee, *Human Res Mgr*
Becky Luce, *Director*
EMP: 6
SQ FT: 7,000

SALES (est): 1.2MM **Privately Held**
WEB: www.americanswiss.com
SIC: 3451 Screw machine products

(G-12637)
**BRIGHT LINE ETING SLUTIONS
LLC**
41 Lake Lacoma Dr (14534-3954)
PHONE....................................585 245-2956
Julia Harold,
EMP: 26
SALES: 6MM **Privately Held**
SIC: 2741

(G-12638)
EASTMAN KODAK COMPANY
1818 W Jefferson Rd (14534-1033)
PHONE....................................585 722-9695
Dawn Schweitze, *Principal*
EMP: 67
SALES (corp-wide): 1.3B **Publicly Held**
SIC: 3861 Film, sensitized motion picture,
X-ray, still camera, etc.
PA: Eastman Kodak Company
343 State St
Rochester NY 14650
585 724-4000

(G-12639)
EMPHASCIENCE
115 Sullys Trl Ste 6 (14534-4571)
PHONE....................................585 348-9415
EMP: 6
SALES (est): 698.5K **Privately Held**
SIC: 2834 Pharmaceutical preparations

(G-12640)
FLUOROLOGIC INC
33 Bishops Ct (14534-2882)
PHONE....................................585 248-2796
Laura Weller-Brophy, *CEO*
EMP: 7
SALES (est): 407K **Privately Held**
SIC: 3841 Surgical & medical instruments

(G-12641)
GATEHOUSE MEDIA LLC (HQ)
175 Sullys Trl Fl 3 (14534-4560)
PHONE....................................585 598-0030
Kirk Davis, *CEO*
Rick Daniels, *President*
Peter Newton, *President*
Paul Ameden, *Principal*
Brad Dennison, *Senior VP*
▲ EMP: 277
SQ FT: 15,000
SALES (est): 714.7MM
SALES (corp-wide): 1.5B **Privately Held**
WEB: www.gatehousemedia.com
SIC: 2711 7311 2759 Newspapers, pub-
lishing & printing; advertising agencies;
commercial printing
PA: New Media Investment Group Inc.
1345 Avenue Of The Americ
New York NY 10105
212 479-3160

(G-12642)
**GATEHUSE MEDIA PA
HOLDINGS INC (HQ)**
175 Sullys Trl Fl 3 (14534-4560)
PHONE....................................585 598-0030
Kirk Davis, *CEO*
EMP: 41
SALES (est): 11.2MM
SALES (corp-wide): 1.5B **Privately Held**
SIC: 2711 Commercial printing & newspa-
per publishing combined
PA: New Media Investment Group Inc.
1345 Avenue Of The Americ
New York NY 10105
212 479-3160

(G-12643)
IMAGINANT INC
Also Called: Jsr Ultrasonics Division
3800 Monroe Ave Ste 29 (14534-1330)
PHONE....................................585 264-0480
Todd Jackson, *CEO*
Samuel Rosenberg, *President*
Robert Hibbard, *Corp Secy*
Sam Rosenberg, *Program Mgr*
Stephen Smith, *Program Mgr*
EMP: 32
SQ FT: 10,000

SALES (est): 5.9MM **Privately Held**
WEB: www.jsrultrasonics.com
SIC: 3829 Measuring & controlling devices

(G-12644)
INFIMED INC
15 Fisher Rd (14534-9544)
PHONE....................................585 383-1710
EMP: 7
SALES (corp-wide): 8.3MM **Privately
Held**
SIC: 3845 Mfg Electromedical Equipment
PA: Infimed, Inc.
121 Metropolitan Park Dr
Liverpool NY 13088
315 453-4545

(G-12645)
KERNOW NORTH AMERICA
5 Park Forest Dr (14534-3557)
PHONE....................................585 586-3590
EMP: 11
SALES (est): 1.1MM **Privately Held**
SIC: 3089 Mfg Plastic Products

(G-12646)
LIFE JUICE BRANDS LLC
115 Brook Rd (14534-1144)
PHONE....................................585 944-7982
Peter Schulick, *CEO*
EMP: 4
SQ FT: 1,400
SALES: 1.7MM **Privately Held**
SIC: 2033 Vegetable juices: packaged in
cans, jars, etc.

(G-12647)
**LOCAL MEDIA GROUP
HOLDINGS LLC (DH)**
175 Sullys Trl Ste 300 (14534-4560)
PHONE....................................585 598-0030
Kirk Davis, *CEO*
EMP: 3
SALES (est): 527.2MM
SALES (corp-wide): 1.5B **Privately Held**
SIC: 2711 Commercial printing & newspa-
per publishing combined
HQ: Gatehouse Media, Llc
175 Sullys Trl Fl 3
Pittsford NY 14534
585 598-0030

(G-12648)
**MAGNUM SHIELDING
CORPORATION**
3800 Monroe Ave Ste 14f (14534-1330)
P.O. Box 827 (14534-0827)
PHONE....................................585 381-9957
Scott Hurwitz, *President*
Kara Ray, *Buyer*
Chad Conklin, *Purchasing*
Sue Myer, *Office Mgr*
Chris Hughson, *Technology*
▲ EMP: 50
SQ FT: 15,000
SALES (est): 9.1MM **Privately Held**
WEB: www.magnumshielding.com
SIC: 3694 Ignition apparatus & distributors

(G-12649)
MARDEK LLC
73 N Wilmarth Rd (14534-9775)
P.O. Box 134, North Hero VT (05474-0134)
PHONE....................................585 735-9333
Charles Dekar, *President*
Nick Dekar, *President*
Kathy Taylor, *Cust Mgr*
▲ EMP: 5
SALES: 2MM **Privately Held**
SIC: 3312 Rods, iron & steel: made in steel
mills

(G-12650)
MASTERLIBRARYCOM LLC
1160 Pittsford Victor Rd J (14534-3825)
PHONE....................................585 270-6676
Mark Winterstein, *Mktg Dir*
Thomas Rauscher, *Mng Member*
Dawn Rauscher, *Mng Member*
Dan Grassel, *Director*
EMP: 10
SQ FT: 1,500
SALES (est): 77.7K **Privately Held**
SIC: 7372 Application computer software

(G-12651)
**MATYS HEALTHY PRODUCTS
LLC**
140 Office Pkwy (14534-1758)
P.O. Box 88 (14534-0088)
PHONE....................................585 218-0507
Carolyn Harrington,
Robert Harrington,
Thomas Harrington,
EMP: 8
SALES (est): 549.6K **Privately Held**
SIC: 2833 5499 Medicinal chemicals;
health & dietetic food stores

(G-12652)
MILLERCOORS LLC
1000 Pittsford Victor Rd (14534-3822)
PHONE....................................585 385-0670
Dennis Perreault, *Branch Mgr*
EMP: 25
SALES (corp-wide): 10.7B **Publicly Held**
SIC: 2082 Beer (alcoholic beverage)
HQ: Millercoors Llc
250 S Wacker Dr Ste 800
Chicago IL 60606
312 496-2700

(G-12653)
OPTICS TECHNOLOGY INC
3800 Monroe Ave Ste 3 (14534-1330)
PHONE....................................585 586-0950
John Warda, *President*
EMP: 4
SQ FT: 6,000
SALES (est): 1.1MM **Privately Held**
WEB: www.opticstechnology.com
SIC: 3827 3599 Lenses, optical: all types
except ophthalmic; lens mounts; optical
elements & assemblies, except oph-
thalmic; machine & other job shop work;
machine shop, jobbing & repair

(G-12654)
PA PELLETS LLC (HQ)
1 Fischers Rd Ste 160 (14534)
PHONE....................................814 848-9970
Dan Wetzel, *Principal*
Jeremy Watson, *Plant Mgr*
▼ EMP: 13 EST: 2010
SALES (est): 2.7MM
SALES (corp-wide): 22.1MM **Privately
Held**
SIC: 2421 Fuelwood, from mill waste
PA: Biomaxx, Llc
1160 Pittsford Victor Rd F
Pittsford NY 14534
585 596-8324

(G-12655)
PACTIV LLC
1169 Pittsford Victor Rd (14534-3809)
P.O. Box 5032, Lake Forest IL (60045-
5032)
PHONE....................................585 248-1213
EMP: 50
SALES (corp-wide): 14.1MM **Privately
Held**
WEB: www.pactiv.com
SIC: 2653 2631 Corrugated & solid fiber
boxes; container board
HQ: Pactiv Llc
1900 W Field Ct
Lake Forest IL 60045
847 482-2000

(G-12656)
ROCKWELL AUTOMATION INC
1000 Pittsford Victor Rd # 17 (14534-3822)
PHONE....................................585 487-2700
Laurie Borshard, *Opers Staff*
Scott Turling, *Manager*
Brian Blaisdell, *Manager*
EMP: 27 **Publicly Held**
SIC: 3625 Relays & industrial controls
PA: Rockwell Automation, Inc.
1201 S 2nd St
Milwaukee WI 53204

(G-12657)
UNITED TECHNOLOGIES CORP
Lenel
1212 Pittsford Victor Rd (14534-3820)
PHONE....................................866 788-5095
John Merlino, *Director*
EMP: 500

SALES (corp-wide): 66.5B Publicly Held
SIC: 3699 Electrical equipment & supplies
PA: United Technologies Corporation
10 Farm Springs Rd
Farmington CT 06032
860 728-7000

(G-12658)
XELIC INCORPORATED
1250 Pittsford Victor Rd # 370
(14534-9541)
PHONE.................585 415-2764
Mark Gibson, *President*
Doug Bush, *Vice Pres*
Jamie Boeheim, *Design Engr*
Kenny Chung, *Design Engr*
Mark Grabosky, *Treasurer*
EMP: 18
SQ FT: 2,400
SALES: 3MM Privately Held
WEB: www.xelic.com
SIC: 3825 Integrated circuit testers

Plainview
Nassau County

(G-12659)
AEROFLEX HOLDING CORP
35 S Service Rd (11803-4117)
P.O. Box 6022 (11803-0622)
PHONE.................516 694-6700
Leonard Borow, *President*
John Buyko, *Exec VP*
Andrew F Kaminsky, *Senior VP*
Edward Wactlar, *Senior VP*
John Adamovich Jr, *CFO*
▼ EMP: 2700
SQ FT: 90,000
SALES (est): 189MM
SALES (corp-wide): 2.3B Privately Held
SIC: 3674 Semiconductors & related devices
HQ: Cobham Holdings Inc.
10 Cobham Dr
Orchard Park NY 14127
716 662-0006

(G-12660)
AEROFLEX INCORPORATED (HQ)
Also Called: Cobham Semiconductor Solutions
35 S Service Rd (11803-4117)
P.O. Box 6022 (11803-0622)
PHONE.................516 694-6700
Robert B McKeon, *Ch of Bd*
Leonard J Borow, *President*
John Buyko, *Exec VP*
Russell Storrs, *Materials Mgr*
Brent Engelbert, *Buyer*
▲ EMP: 450
SQ FT: 69,000
SALES (est): 456.4MM
SALES (corp-wide): 2.3B Privately Held
WEB: www.aeroflex.com
SIC: 3812 3621 3677 3674 Acceleration indicators & systems components, aerospace; torque motors, electric; electronic coils, transformers & other inductors; microcircuits, integrated (semiconductor); mesh, made from purchased wire; optical instruments & apparatus
PA: Cobham Plc
Brook Road
Wimborne BH21
120 288-2020

(G-12661)
ALCATEL-LUCENT USA INC
1 Fairchild Ct Ste 340 (11803-1720)
PHONE.................516 349-4900
EMP: 58
SALES (corp-wide): 25.8B Privately Held
SIC: 3661 Telephone & telegraph apparatus
HQ: Nokia Of America Corporation
600 Mountain Ave Ste 700
New Providence NJ 07974

(G-12662)
AMERICAN CASTING AND MFG CORP (PA)
51 Commercial St (11803-2490)
PHONE.................800 342-0333
Norman Wenk III, *President*
H L Christian Wenk IV, *Corp Secy*
Don Wenk, *Vice Pres*
Joseph Wenk, *Vice Pres*
Jim Wenk, *VP Mktg*
◆ EMP: 70 EST: 1916
SQ FT: 40,000
SALES: 15.5MM Privately Held
WEB: www.americancasting.com
SIC: 3089 3364 2759 5085 Injection molding of plastics; lead die-castings; labels & seals: printing; seals, industrial

(G-12663)
AMERICAN CASTING AND MFG CORP
65 S Terminal Dr (11803-2310)
PHONE.................516 349-7010
Norman Wenk, *Branch Mgr*
EMP: 5
SALES (corp-wide): 15.5MM Privately Held
WEB: www.americancasting.com
SIC: 3089 3364 3429 Injection molding of plastics; lead die-castings; manufactured hardware (general)
PA: American Casting And Manufacturing Corporation
51 Commercial St
Plainview NY 11803
800 342-0333

(G-12664)
AUDIO VIDEO INVASION INC
Also Called: AVI
53 Werman Ct (11803-4507)
PHONE.................516 345-2636
Panos Anassis, *Principal*
Mary Antonacci, *Office Mgr*
EMP: 15
SALES (est): 1.9MM Privately Held
SIC: 3651 5999 Household audio & video equipment; audio-visual equipment & supplies

(G-12665)
AUFHAUSER CORPORATION (PA)
39 West Mall (11803-4209)
PHONE.................516 694-8696
Keith Aufhauser, *President*
Edgar Torres, *Business Mgr*
Peter Wan, *Vice Pres*
PI Tsang Wu, *Vice Pres*
Fred Wu, *Treasurer*
▲ EMP: 18
SQ FT: 28,000
SALES: 50MM Privately Held
WEB: www.aufhauser.net
SIC: 3356 5051 2899 Welding rods; solder: wire, bar, acid core, & rosin core; metals service centers & offices; fluxes: brazing, soldering, galvanizing & welding

(G-12666)
AUFHAUSER MANUFACTURING CORP
Also Called: Aufhauser Corp Canada
39 West Mall (11803-4209)
PHONE.................516 694-8696
R Keith Aufhauser, *President*
Wu PI Tsang, *Vice Pres*
Fred Wu, *Treasurer*
EMP: 20
SQ FT: 25,000
SALES: 25MM Privately Held
WEB: www.brazing.com
SIC: 3356 Welding rods

(G-12667)
CENTROID INC
111 E Ames Ct Unit 1 (11803-2311)
PHONE.................516 349-0070
Gerald I Starr, *Ch of Bd*
Marc A Starr, *President*
Nancy Budd, *Purch Agent*
Cindy Howard, *Engineer*
Peggy Carey, *Office Mgr*
EMP: 23 EST: 1965
SQ FT: 8,000

SALES (est): 4.5MM Privately Held
WEB: www.centroidinc.com
SIC: 3679 Electronic circuits

(G-12668)
CHERRY LANE LITHOGRAPHING CORP
15 E Bethpage Rd Unit A (11803-4217)
PHONE.................516 293-9294
William Citterbart Jr, *President*
Joann Citterbart, *Corp Secy*
William Citterbart III, *Vice Pres*
Jo-Ann Citterbart, *Legal Staff*
EMP: 48 EST: 1962
SQ FT: 54,000
SALES (est): 9.1MM Privately Held
WEB: www.cherrylanelitho.com
SIC: 2752 Commercial printing, offset

(G-12669)
COBHAM LONG ISLAND INC (DH)
35 S Service Rd (11803-4117)
P.O. Box 6022 (11803-0622)
PHONE.................516 694-6700
Jill Kale, *CEO*
Leonard Borow, *Ch of Bd*
Carl Caruso, *Senior VP*
Kevin J Finnegan, *Vice Pres*
Rob Sichenzia, *Vice Pres*
EMP: 422
SQ FT: 69,000
SALES (est): 151.4MM
SALES (corp-wide): 2.3B Privately Held
SIC: 3679 3621 3674 3827 Electronic circuits; motors, electric; microcircuits, integrated (semiconductor); optical instruments & lenses

(G-12670)
COINMACH SERVICE CORP
303 Sunnyside Blvd # 70 (11803-1598)
PHONE.................516 349-8555
Robert M Doyle, *Ch of Bd*
Carol A Siebuhr, *President*
Adrian Verquer, *President*
Joe McCarley, *Database Admin*
EMP: 805
SQ FT: 11,600
SALES (est): 94.4MM
SALES (corp-wide): 361.2MM Privately Held
SIC: 3633 5087 Household laundry equipment; laundry equipment & supplies
HQ: Spin Holdco Inc.
303 Sunnyside Blvd # 70
Plainview NY 11803

(G-12671)
COLONIAL GROUP LLC
150 Express St Ste 2 (11803-2421)
PHONE.................516 349-8010
Pierre Lavi,
EMP: 25
SALES (est): 1.9MM Privately Held
SIC: 3724 Aircraft engines & engine parts

(G-12672)
CONRAD BLASIUS EQUIPMENT CO
Also Called: Cbe/New York
199 Newtown Rd (11803-4308)
PHONE.................516 753-1200
Richard Fiordelisi Sr, *President*
Richard C Fiordelisi Jr, *President*
EMP: 6
SQ FT: 10,000
SALES (est): 630K Privately Held
SIC: 3599 3291 2842 5084 Tubing, flexible metallic; coated abrasive products; metal polish; industrial machinery & equipment

(G-12673)
CONTROLLED CASTINGS CORP
31 Commercial Ct (11803-2403)
PHONE.................516 349-1718
EMP: 30 EST: 1961
SQ FT: 32,500
SALES (est): 3.8MM Privately Held
SIC: 3369 Nonferrous Metal Foundry

(G-12674)
CORAL CAST LLC
31 Commercial Ct (11803-2403)
PHONE.................516 349-1300
Joseph Marden,
EMP: 21
SALES (est): 3.5MM Privately Held
SIC: 3272 Precast terrazo or concrete products

(G-12675)
CORE SWX LLC
91b Commercial St (11803-2401)
PHONE.................516 595-7488
Jenson Seepersad, *Finance*
Ross Kanarek, *Mng Member*
EMP: 12
SALES: 5MM Privately Held
SIC: 3861 Cameras & related equipment

(G-12676)
COX & COMPANY INC
1664 Old Country Rd (11803-5013)
PHONE.................212 366-0200
John Smith, *Ch of Bd*
Thomas Ferguson, *Senior VP*
Laszlo Salamon, *Plant Mgr*
Kevin Pierce, *Buyer*
Theresa Pierce, *Purchasing*
▲ EMP: 185 EST: 1944
SQ FT: 90,000
SALES (est): 52.3MM Privately Held
SIC: 3625 3743 3822 3812 Relays & industrial controls; railroad equipment; auto controls regulating residntl & coml environmt & applncs; search & navigation equipment; current-carrying wiring devices; aircraft parts & equipment; deicing equipment, aircraft

(G-12677)
CSC SW HOLDCO INC (HQ)
Also Called: CSC Serviceworks, Inc.
303 Sunnyside Blvd # 70 (11803-1597)
PHONE.................516 349-8555
Mark Hjelle, *CEO*
Gary Stuart, *Accountant*
Brian Bass, *Sales Staff*
Kelli Bodinizzo, *Sales Staff*
Nicholas Kotsidis, *Sales Staff*
EMP: 92
SALES (est): 264.5MM
SALES (corp-wide): 361.2MM Privately Held
SIC: 3633 5087 Household laundry equipment; laundry equipment & supplies
PA: Csc Serviceworks Holdings, Inc.
303 Sunnyside Blvd # 70
Plainview NY 11803
516 349-8555

(G-12678)
DERM-BURO INC (PA)
Also Called: G-Forces
229 Newtown Rd (11803-4309)
PHONE.................516 694-8300
Frank Guthart, *President*
Mark Guthart, *Exec VP*
EMP: 46
SQ FT: 1,100
SALES (est): 4.3MM Privately Held
WEB: www.gforces.com
SIC: 3841 5122 5047 3842 Surgical & medical instruments; pharmaceuticals; instruments, surgical & medical; surgical appliances & supplies

(G-12679)
DIE-MATIC PRODUCTS LLC
130 Express St (11803-2477)
PHONE.................516 433-7900
Arnold Klein, *President*
Evelyn Martinez, *Controller*
Dan Farber, *Info Tech Mgr*
Sheldon Fox,
Barry Blazer,
EMP: 30 EST: 1944
SQ FT: 30,000
SALES (est): 5.2MM Privately Held
WEB: www.diematicproducts.com
SIC: 3469 Stamping metal for the trade

(G-12680)
EASTERNCCTV (USA) LLC (PA)
50 Commercial St (11803-2426)
PHONE.................516 870-3779

Xianjie Xiong, *President*
Shawn Stewart, *Mfg Staff*
Jimmy Theblitz, *Accounts Mgr*
Yenting Huang, *Marketing Staff*
Erick Milicich, *Manager*
EMP: 15
SALES (est): 12.9MM **Privately Held**
SIC: 3861 Cameras & related equipment

(G-12681)
EBY ELECTRO INC
210 Express St (11803-2423)
PHONE....................516 576-7777
Mitchell Solomon, *President*
John Mancini, *COO*
Mike Davis, *Vice Pres*
Hector Santiago, *Production*
Margo Schein, *Purch Mgr*
▲ **EMP:** 28
SQ FT: 20,000
SALES (est): 5.7MM **Privately Held**
WEB: www.ebyelectro.com
SIC: 3678 Electronic connectors

(G-12682)
ECONOMETRIC SOFTWARE INC
15 Gloria Pl (11803-6314)
PHONE....................516 938-5254
William H Greene, *President*
EMP: 5
SALES (est): 380.9K **Privately Held**
WEB: www.limdep.com
SIC: 7372 Prepackaged software

(G-12683)
EMDA INC
81 Westbury Ave (11803-3627)
PHONE....................631 243-6363
Alan Steinbok, *President*
EMP: 10
SALES: 1MM **Privately Held**
WEB: www.emdainc.com
SIC: 3861 Photographic equipment & supplies

(G-12684)
EVANS & PAUL LLC
140 Dupont St (11803-1603)
PHONE....................516 576-0800
Jeffrey Evans, *Mng Member*
EMP: 50
SQ FT: 30,000
SALES: 5.1MM **Privately Held**
SIC: 2599 2542 1799 Hospital furniture, except beds; fixtures, office: except wood; office furniture installation

(G-12685)
FIBRE MATERIALS CORP
40 Dupont St (11803-1679)
PHONE....................516 349-1660
Glenn Fellows, *CEO*
Brian Grossberg, *President*
▲ **EMP:** 27 **EST:** 1963
SQ FT: 34,000
SALES (est): 4.6MM **Privately Held**
WEB: www.fibrematerials.com
SIC: 3089 5162 Washers, plastic; plastics materials & basic shapes

(G-12686)
FULL MOTION BEVERAGE INC (PA)
998 Old Country Rd (11803-4928)
PHONE....................631 585-1100
Peter Frazzetto, *CEO*
Vincent Butta, *President*
Chris Mollica, *President*
Paul Dua, *Vice Pres*
Tim Mayette, *CFO*
EMP: 6
SALES: 396.4K **Publicly Held**
WEB: www.web2corp.com
SIC: 2869 Alcohols, non-beverage

(G-12687)
HOSHIZAKI NRTHEASTERN DIST CTR
150 Dupont St Ste 100 (11803-1603)
PHONE....................516 605-1411
Toshio Mase, *President*
Mitsuhiro Nomura, *CFO*
Artic Rade, *Admin Sec*
▲ **EMP:** 6

SALES (est): 1.1MM **Privately Held**
WEB: www.hoshizaki.com
SIC: 3585 Ice making machinery
HQ: Hoshizaki America, Inc.
618 Highway 74 S
Peachtree City GA 30269
770 487-2331

(G-12688)
HOWARD J MOORE COMPANY INC
Also Called: Morco
210 Terminal Dr Ste B (11803-2322)
PHONE....................631 351-8467
Eric Moore, *President*
Harris Moore, *Plant Mgr*
Spencer Moore, *Sales Mgr*
EMP: 28 **EST:** 1945
SQ FT: 17,000
SALES (est): 5.5MM **Privately Held**
WEB: www.morcofab.com
SIC: 3082 2679 Unsupported plastics profile shapes; building, insulating & packaging paper

(G-12689)
INDUSTRIAL RAW MATERIALS LLC
Also Called: Industrial Wax
39 West Mall (11803-4209)
PHONE....................212 688-8080
Keith Aufhauser, *Mng Member*
▲ **EMP:** 19
SQ FT: 6,000
SALES (est): 4.2MM
SALES (corp-wide): 50MM **Privately Held**
WEB: www.industrialwax.com
SIC: 2911 5172 Paraffin wax; petroleum products
PA: Aufhauser Corporation
39 West Mall
Plainview NY 11803
516 694-8696

(G-12690)
INTELLIDYNE LLC
303 Sunnyside Blvd # 75 (11803-1597)
PHONE....................516 676-0777
Les Bober, *Business Mgr*
David Siegel, *Vice Pres*
Carla Guerra, *Sales Staff*
Jack Hammer, *Mng Member*
Kristine Wagner, *Manager*
EMP: 17
SQ FT: 4,500
SALES (est): 3.5MM **Privately Held**
WEB: www.intellidynellc.com
SIC: 3822 Temperature controls, automatic

(G-12691)
INTERPARTS INTERNATIONAL INC (PA)
190 Express St (11803-2405)
P.O. Box 855 (11803-0855)
PHONE....................516 576-2000
Hung Da Yang, *President*
▲ **EMP:** 20
SQ FT: 40,000
SALES (est): 2.3MM **Privately Held**
SIC: 3714 5013 3566 Motor vehicle brake systems & parts; automotive brakes; speed changers, drives & gears

(G-12692)
JEM CONTAINER CORP
151 Fairchild Ave Ste 1 (11803-1716)
P.O. Box 456, Farmingdale (11735-0456)
PHONE....................800 521-0145
Ohn C Mc Laughlin, *Ch of Bd*
EMP: 10
SALES (est): 1.4MM **Privately Held**
SIC: 3086 Packaging & shipping materials, foamed plastic

(G-12693)
KAREY KASSL CORP
Also Called: Karey Products
180 Terminal Dr (11803-2324)
PHONE....................516 349-8484
Gary J Kassl, *CEO*
Ronald Kassl, *President*
▲ **EMP:** 30
SQ FT: 40,000

SALES (est): 2.5MM **Privately Held**
SIC: 3442 Storm doors or windows, metal

(G-12694)
KENSTAN LOCK & HARDWARE CO INC
Also Called: Kenstan Lock Co.
101 Commercial St Ste 100 (11803-2408)
PHONE....................631 423-1977
Hans E R Bosch, *President*
Oscar Bosch, *Executive*
Santiago Mesonero, *Representative*
▲ **EMP:** 38 **EST:** 1964
SQ FT: 10,000
SALES (est): 8.4MM **Privately Held**
WEB: www.kenstan.com
SIC: 3429 Cabinet hardware

(G-12695)
KIMDU CORPORATION
1662 Old Country Rd # 9 (11803-7000)
P.O. Box 9 (11803-0009)
PHONE....................516 723-1339
Gary Speiser, *President*
EMP: 20 **EST:** 2013
SQ FT: 10,000
SALES (est): 1.6MM **Privately Held**
SIC: 3812 Aircraft control systems, electronic

(G-12696)
LIFETIME CHIMNEY SUPPLY LLC
171 E Ames Ct (11803-2332)
PHONE....................516 576-8144
Abraham J Finkler, *President*
Deborah Grandison, *General Mgr*
Dennis Martinez, *Vice Pres*
Joshua Lang, *Director*
▲ **EMP:** 5
SQ FT: 6,000
SALES (est): 1.2MM **Privately Held**
WEB: www.lifetimechimneysupply.com
SIC: 3443 5023 Liners, industrial: metal plate; kitchenware

(G-12697)
LITTLE BIRD CHOCOLATES INC
Also Called: Little Bird Kitchen
25 Fairchild Ave Ste 200 (11803-1724)
PHONE....................646 620-6395
Sara Meyer, *President*
Corey Meyer, *Owner*
EMP: 9
SALES (est): 696.5K **Privately Held**
SIC: 2064 Candy & other confectionery products

(G-12698)
MACHINE COMPONENTS CORP
70 Newtown Rd (11803-4382)
PHONE....................516 694-7222
Joseph Kaplan, *President*
Miriam Kaplan, *President*
Jay Kaplan, *Corp Secy*
EMP: 25 **EST:** 1959
SQ FT: 10,000
SALES (est): 5MM **Privately Held**
WEB: www.machinecomp.com
SIC: 3568 3625 Clutches, except vehicular; switches, electronic applications

(G-12699)
MARCEL FINISHING CORP
4 David Ct (11803-6009)
PHONE....................718 381-2889
Marcel Brenka, *President*
Floarea Brenka, *Admin Sec*
EMP: 30
SQ FT: 7,000
SALES (est): 1.9MM **Privately Held**
SIC: 2269 2261 2262 Finishing plants; finishing plants, cotton; finishing plants, manmade fiber & silk fabrics

(G-12700)
METAL TEK PRODUCTS
100 Express St (11803-2405)
PHONE....................516 586-4514
Chris Loften, *Principal*
EMP: 8
SALES (est): 347.6K **Privately Held**
SIC: 3444 Sheet metal specialties, not stamped

(G-12701)
METROFAB PIPE INCORPORATED
15 Fairchild Ct (11803-1701)
PHONE....................516 349-7373
Elizabeth Ficken, *President*
Joe Magliato, *Vice Pres*
EMP: 10
SALES (est): 2.6MM **Privately Held**
SIC: 3462 3443 Flange, valve & pipe fitting forgings, ferrous; pipe, standpipe & culverts

(G-12702)
MGD BRANDS INC
Also Called: Finesse Accessories
30 Commercial Ct (11803-2415)
PHONE....................516 545-0150
Arthur Damast, *CEO*
Scott Damast, *Vice Pres*
▲ **EMP:** 50
SALES (est): 25MM **Privately Held**
WEB: www.finessenovelty.com
SIC: 3911 3999 5094 5131 Jewelry, precious metal; hair & hair-based products; jewelry; hair accessories; ribbons; novelties

(G-12703)
N & G OF AMERICA INC
28 W Lane Dr (11803-5436)
PHONE....................516 428-3414
Najmi Hussain, *President*
EMP: 12
SALES: 500K **Privately Held**
SIC: 3571 Electronic computers

(G-12704)
NASH PRINTING INC
Also Called: Sir Speedy
101 Dupont St Ste 2 (11803-1612)
PHONE....................516 935-4567
Noor Baqueri, *President*
Ali Baqueri, *Vice Pres*
Hussain Baqueri, *CFO*
EMP: 10
SQ FT: 4,500
SALES (est): 1.9MM **Privately Held**
SIC: 2752 Commercial printing, lithographic

(G-12705)
NUCLEAR DIAGNOSTIC PDTS NY INC
130 Commercial St (11803-2414)
PHONE....................516 575-4201
Wayne Wong, *Ch of Bd*
EMP: 7
SALES (est): 986.7K **Privately Held**
SIC: 3829 Medical diagnostic systems, nuclear

(G-12706)
P D R INC
Also Called: Sir Speedy
101 Dupont St (11803-1608)
PHONE....................516 829-5300
Pat Riccardi, *President*
EMP: 8
SQ FT: 4,500
SALES (est): 1.1MM **Privately Held**
SIC: 2752 2791 Commercial printing, lithographic; typesetting

(G-12707)
PETER DIGIOIA
Also Called: Medsurg Direct
7 Sherwood Dr (11803-3218)
PHONE....................516 644-5517
Peter Digioia, *Owner*
EMP: 5
SALES (est): 424.1K **Privately Held**
SIC: 3841 5047 Surgical & medical instruments; medical equipment & supplies

(G-12708)
PORT EVERGLADES MACHINE WORKS
Also Called: P E Machine Works
57 Colgate Dr (11803-1803)
PHONE....................516 367-2280
Steven Bellask, *President*
John Schaefer, *Vice Pres*
EMP: 10
SQ FT: 10,000

SALES (est): 966K **Privately Held**
SIC: 3599 3731 Machine shop, jobbing &
repair; shipbuilding & repairing

(G-12709)
PURITY PRODUCTS INC
200 Terminal Dr (11803-2312)
PHONE....................................516 767-1967
Jahn Levin, *President*
Sabrina Levin, *Research*
Michael Iwanciw, *Engineer*
Carol Capone, *HR Admin*
Roman Yuditsky, *Technology*
▲ EMP: 61
SALES (est): 14.2MM **Privately Held**
SIC: 2834 Vitamin, nutrient & hematinic
preparations for human use

(G-12710)
ROCKWELL INDUSTRIES INTL
CORP
80 Newtown Rd (11803-4302)
PHONE....................................516 927-8300
Thomas Milone, *President*
John T Milone, *Vice Pres*
Steven Berliner, *Sales Staff*
David Puckett, *Director*
◆ EMP: 31
SQ FT: 23,000
SALES: 29.4MM **Privately Held**
WEB: www.rockwellind.com
SIC: 3812 Aircraft/aerospace flight instru-
ments & guidance systems

(G-12711)
ROMAC ELECTRONICS INC
155 E Ames Ct Unit 1 (11803-2383)
PHONE....................................516 349-7900
Jerome Bloomberg, *President*
Lee Bloomberg, *Vice Pres*
Michael Bloomberg, *Vice Pres*
Ronald Bloomberg, *Vice Pres*
William Becker, *CFO*
EMP: 49 EST: 1952
SQ FT: 42,000
SALES (est): 9.9MM **Privately Held**
WEB: www.romacelectronics.com
SIC: 3499 Shims, metal

(G-12712)
S E A SUPPLIES LTD
Also Called: S E A Supls
1670 Old Country Rd # 104 (11803-5000)
PHONE....................................516 694-6677
Martin Reynolds, *Vice Pres*
EMP: 15
SQ FT: 1,400
SALES (est): 1.5MM **Privately Held**
WEB: www.seasupplies.com
SIC: 2819 3646 Industrial inorganic chem-
icals; commercial indusl & institutional
electric lighting fixtures

(G-12713)
SAFE SEAT USA INC
1670 Old Country Rd # 116 (11803-5000)
PHONE....................................516 586-8240
Erez Barak, *President*
EMP: 10
SALES (est): 462.1K **Privately Held**
SIC: 2842 Disinfectants, household or in-
dustrial plant

(G-12714)
SMC DIODE SOLUTIONS LLC
101 Sunnyside Blvd (11803-1538)
PHONE....................................631 965-0869
Yunji Corcoran, *Mng Member*
EMP: 5
SQ FT: 5,000
SALES (est): 270.2K **Privately Held**
SIC: 3674 Diodes, solid state (germanium,
silicon, etc.)

(G-12715)
SPIN HOLDCO INC (DH)
303 Sunnyside Blvd (11803-1597)
PHONE....................................516 349-8555
Bob Doyl, *Principal*
EMP: 1
SALES (est): 136.6MM
SALES (corp-wide): 361.2MM **Privately**
Held
SIC: 3633 5087 Household laundry equip-
ment; laundry equipment & supplies

HQ: Csc Sw Holdco, Inc.
303 Sunnyside Blvd # 70
Plainview NY 11803
516 349-8555

(G-12716)
STEVAL GRAPHICS CONCEPTS
INC
Also Called: Graphic Concepts
7 Fairchild Ct Ste 200 (11803-1701)
PHONE....................................516 576-0220
Stephen Trigg, *CEO*
EMP: 12
SQ FT: 5,000
SALES (est): 760K **Privately Held**
SIC: 2752 Commercial printing, offset

(G-12717)
SUPREME SCREW PRODUCTS
INC
10 Skyline Dr Unit B (11803-2517)
PHONE....................................718 293-6600
Misha Migdal, *President*
EMP: 65 EST: 1963
SQ FT: 11,000
SALES (est): 5.2MM **Privately Held**
SIC: 3451 Screw machine products

(G-12718)
TECHNIC INC
Also Called: Advanced Technology Division
111 E Ames Ct Unit 2 (11803-2311)
PHONE....................................516 349-0700
Rob Sheddy, *Branch Mgr*
EMP: 15
SALES (corp-wide): 125.5MM **Privately**
Held
WEB: www.technic.com
SIC: 2899 3559 Metal treating com-
pounds; electroplating machinery &
equipment
PA: Technic, Inc.
47 Molter St
Cranston RI 02910
401 781-6100

(G-12719)
TRANE US INC
245 Newtown Rd Ste 500 (11803-4300)
PHONE....................................631 952-9477
Steve Wey, *District Mgr*
EMP: 20 **Privately Held**
SIC: 3585 Refrigeration & heating equip-
ment
HQ: Trane U.S. Inc.
3600 Pammel Creek Rd
La Crosse WI 54601
608 787-2000

(G-12720)
U2O USA LLC
206 Terminal Dr (11803-2312)
PHONE....................................516 813-9500
Sam Lamba, *Chairman*
Dennis Dantes, *Vice Pres*
EMP: 3
SALES (est): 6MM
SALES (corp-wide): 6.7MM **Privately**
Held
SIC: 3661 5065 Headsets, telephone; mo-
bile telephone equipment
PA: U2o Global Co.,Ltd.
Floor No.4, Floor U2o, No.385,
Huanzhu Road, Jimei District
Xiamen 36102
592 574-3713

(G-12721)
ULTRA FINE JEWELRY MFG
180 Dupont St Unit C (11803-1616)
PHONE....................................516 349-2848
Benjamin Matalon, *President*
Sandra Matalon, *Vice Pres*
▲ EMP: 20 EST: 1978
SALES (est): 2.3MM **Privately Held**
SIC: 3911 Jewelry, precious metal

(G-12722)
VASO CORPORATION (PA)
137 Commercial St Ste 200 (11803-2410)
PHONE....................................516 997-4600
Joshua Markowitz, *Ch of Bd*
David Lieberman, *Vice Ch Bd*
Jun MA, *President*
Peter C Castle, *COO*
Michael J Beecher, *CFO*

▲ EMP: 17
SQ FT: 8,700
SALES: 73.9MM **Publicly Held**
WEB: www.vasomedical.com
SIC: 3845 3841 7374 Electromedical
equipment; surgical & medical instru-
ments; data processing & preparation

(G-12723)
VASOMEDICAL SOLUTIONS INC
137 Commercial St Ste 200 (11803-2410)
PHONE....................................516 997-4600
Alex Zou, *Regional Mgr*
David Nierle, *Vice Pres*
Hong Chen, *Senior Engr*
Jai Daodat, *Accountant*
Paul Wyckoff, *Personnel*
EMP: 99
SALES (est): 23.1MM
SALES (corp-wide): 73.9MM **Publicly**
Held
SIC: 3841 Diagnostic apparatus, medical
PA: Vaso Corporation
137 Commercial St Ste 200
Plainview NY 11803
516 997-4600

(G-12724)
VEECO INSTRUMENTS INC
Also Called: Veeco Process Equipment
1 Terminal Dr (11803-2313)
PHONE....................................516 349-8300
Emmanuel Lakios, *Branch Mgr*
EMP: 150
SALES (corp-wide): 542MM **Publicly**
Held
WEB: www.veeco.com
SIC: 3612 5932 Transformers, except
electric; building materials, secondhand
PA: Veeco Instruments Inc.
1 Terminal Dr
Plainview NY 11803
516 677-0200

(G-12725)
VEECO INSTRUMENTS INC (PA)
1 Terminal Dr (11803-2313)
PHONE....................................516 677-0200
John R Peeler, *Ch of Bd*
John P Kiernan, *Senior VP*
Vince Amorosi, *Vice Pres*
Gerry Blumenstock, *Vice Pres*
Kathy Damiani, *Vice Pres*
▲ EMP: 277
SQ FT: 80,000
SALES: 542MM **Publicly Held**
WEB: www.veeco.com
SIC: 3559 Semiconductor manufacturing
machinery

(G-12726)
VEECO PROCESS EQUIPMENT
INC (HQ)
1 Terminal Dr (11803-2313)
PHONE....................................516 677-0200
John R Peeler, *CEO*
Derek Derosia, *Regional Mgr*
John Bulman, *Exec VP*
David Glass, *Exec VP*
Bill Miller, *Exec VP*
▲ EMP: 112
SQ FT: 18,000
SALES (est): 169.1MM
SALES (corp-wide): 542MM **Publicly**
Held
SIC: 3569 Assembly machines, non-metal-
working
PA: Veeco Instruments Inc.
1 Terminal Dr
Plainview NY 11803
516 677-0200

(G-12727)
VERTIV CORPORATION
79 Express St Fl 14 (11803-2419)
PHONE....................................516 349-8500
Tammy Burns, *Branch Mgr*
EMP: 8
SALES (corp-wide): 2.9B **Privately Held**
SIC: 3823 Industrial instrmnts msrmnt dis-
play/control process variable
HQ: Vertiv Corporation
1050 Dearborn Dr
Columbus OH 43085
614 888-0246

(G-12728)
WILLIAM CHARLES PRTG CO
INC
7 Fairchild Ct Ste 100 (11803-1701)
PHONE....................................516 349-0900
Chris Pellegrini, *President*
Joseph Pellegrini, *President*
Jamie Foster, *President*
Charles Pelligrini, *Principal*
Ed Simon, *Manager*
EMP: 35 EST: 1935
SQ FT: 17,000
SALES (est): 6.3MM **Privately Held**
WEB: www.williamcharlesprinting.com
SIC: 2752 2759 2789 Commercial print-
ing, offset; letterpress printing; bookbind-
ing & related work

(G-12729)
XPRESS PRINTING INC
Also Called: T L X
7 Fairchild Ct Ste 100 (11803-1701)
PHONE....................................516 605-1000
Chris Moscatl, *President*
EMP: 8
SQ FT: 60,000
SALES (est): 885K **Privately Held**
SIC: 2759 Promotional printing

(G-12730)
Y & Z PRECISION INC
Also Called: Y & Z Precision Machine Shop
155 E Ames Ct Unit 4 (11803-2300)
PHONE....................................516 349-8243
Zoltan Vays, *President*
Ryszard Dobrogowski, *Admin Sec*
EMP: 15
SQ FT: 7,400
SALES (est): 2.5MM **Privately Held**
SIC: 3671 Electron tubes

Plattsburgh
Clinton County

(G-12731)
ADIRONDACK PENNYSAVER
INC
177 Margaret St (12901-1837)
PHONE....................................518 563-0100
Corinne Rigby, *President*
Mark Rigby, *Corp Secy*
EMP: 25
SQ FT: 5,000
SALES (est): 2.5MM **Privately Held**
WEB: www.adkpennysaver.com
SIC: 2741 2759 Shopping news: publish-
ing & printing; commercial printing

(G-12732)
APGN INC
Also Called: Apg Neuros
160 Banker Rd (12901-7309)
PHONE....................................518 324-4150
Omar Hammoud, *President*
EMP: 30
SALES (corp-wide): 15.5MM **Privately**
Held
SIC: 3564 Blowing fans: industrial or com-
mercial
HQ: Apgn Inc
1270 Boul Michele-Bohec
Blainville QC J7C 5
450 939-0799

(G-12733)
AWR ENERGY INC
35 Melody Ln (12901-6414)
P.O. Box 3027 (12901-0298)
PHONE....................................585 469-7750
Steve Baiocchi, *President*
George Klemann, *Treasurer*
EMP: 10
SALES (est): 911.9K **Privately Held**
SIC: 3511 Turbines & turbine generator
sets

(G-12734)
B3CG INTERCONNECT USA INC
18 Northern Ave Ste 100 (12903-3905)
PHONE....................................518 324-4800
Stefan Baumans, *President*
Marc Brosseau, *Vice Pres*
EMP: 2

▲ = Import ▼=Export
◆ =Import/Export

SALES (est): 3.1MM
SALES (corp-wide): 518.4MM **Privately Held**
SIC: 3679 Harness assemblies for electronic use: wire or cable
HQ: B3cg Interconnect Inc
310 Boul Industriel
Saint-Eustache QC J7R 5
450 491-4040

(G-12735)
BIMBO BAKERIES USA INC
67 S Peru St (12901-3834)
PHONE..................................518 563-1320
Saith Haris, *Manager*
EMP: 17 **Privately Held**
SIC: 2051 Bread, cake & related products
HQ: Bimbo Bakeries Usa, Inc
255 Business Center Dr # 200
Horsham PA 19044
215 347-5500

(G-12736)
BIOTECH ENERGY INC
Also Called: Biotech Energy Systems
100 Clinton Point Dr (12901-6002)
PHONE..................................800 340-1387
Stan Kinsman, *CEO*
EMP: 6 EST: 2015
SALES (est): 316.4K **Privately Held**
SIC: 3433 Burners, furnaces, boilers & stokers

(G-12737)
BOMBARDIER MASS TRANSIT CORP
71 Wall St (12901-3755)
PHONE..................................518 566-0150
William Spurr, *President*
Rene Lalande, *Vice Pres*
James Tooley, *Vice Pres*
Ronald Barnes, *Materials Mgr*
Greg Fox, *Opers Staff*
▲ EMP: 380
SALES (est): 68.4MM
SALES (corp-wide): 16.2B **Privately Held**
SIC: 3743 Railroad equipment
PA: Bombardier Inc
800 Boul Rene-Levesque O 29e etage
Montreal QC H3B 1
514 861-9481

(G-12738)
BOMBARDIER TRNSP HOLDINGS USA
Also Called: Bombardier Corp Track
71 Wall St (12901-3755)
PHONE..................................518 566-5067
George Psycharis, *General Mgr*
EMP: 21
SALES (corp-wide): 16.2B **Privately Held**
SIC: 3721 Aircraft
HQ: Bombardier Transportation (Holdings)
Usa Inc.
1251 Waterfront Pl
Pittsburgh PA 15222
412 655-5700

(G-12739)
BRUSHTECH (DISC) INC
4 Matt Ave (12901-3736)
P.O. Box 1130 (12901-0068)
PHONE..................................518 563-8420
Nora Gunjian, *President*
Zaven Gunjian, *Vice Pres*
▲ EMP: 18
SQ FT: 34,000
SALES (est): 3.3MM **Privately Held**
WEB: www.brushtech.com
SIC: 3991 Brushes, household or industrial

(G-12740)
CAMSO MANUFACTURING USA LTD (DH)
1 Martina Cir (12901-7421)
PHONE..................................518 561-7528
Ivan Warmuth, *Ch of Bd*
John Farrell, *General Mgr*
John Robare, *Prdtn Mgr*
Mario Bouchard, *Treasurer*
Pierre Milot, *Director*
◆ EMP: 70

SALES (est): 17.2MM
SALES (corp-wide): 1B **Privately Held**
SIC: 3061 Oil & gas field machinery rubber goods (mechanical)
HQ: Camso Inc
2633 Rue Macpherson
Magog QC J1X 0
819 868-1500

(G-12741)
CEIT CORP
625 State Route 3 Unit 2 (12901-6530)
PHONE..................................518 825-0649
Fax: 518 825-0651
▲ EMP: 10
SQ FT: 15,000
SALES (est): 950K **Privately Held**
SIC: 3648 Mfg Lighting Equipment

(G-12742)
CINTUBE LTD
139 Distribution Way (12901-3734)
PHONE..................................518 324-3333
EMP: 11
SALES (est): 1.5MM **Privately Held**
SIC: 3399 Primary metal products

(G-12743)
COMMUNITY NEWSPAPER GROUP LLC
Also Called: Plattsburgh Press-Republican
170 Margaret St (12901-1838)
P.O. Box 459 (12901-0459)
PHONE..................................518 565-4114
Bob Parks, *Branch Mgr*
EMP: 20 **Privately Held**
WEB: www.clintonnc.com
SIC: 2711 Newspapers, publishing & printing
HQ: Community Newspaper Group, Llc
3500 Colonnade Pkwy # 600
Birmingham AL 35243

(G-12744)
DENTON PUBLICATIONS INC
Also Called: Free Trader
21 Mckinley Ave Ste 3 (12901-3800)
PHONE..................................518 561-9680
Cindy Tucker, *General Mgr*
EMP: 20
SALES (corp-wide): 6MM **Privately Held**
WEB: www.denpubs.com
SIC: 2711 2721 Commercial printing & newspaper publishing combined; periodicals
PA: Denton Publications, Inc.
14 Hand Ave
Elizabethtown NY 12932
518 873-6368

(G-12745)
DUQUETTES STEEL & STRUCTURAL F
193 Sharron Ave (12901-3833)
PHONE..................................518 563-3161
Frank Duquette, *Manager*
EMP: 23
SALES (est): 5.5MM **Privately Held**
SIC: 3441 Fabricated structural metal

(G-12746)
EURO GEAR (USA) INC
1 Cumberland Ave (12901-1833)
PHONE..................................518 578-1775
Eloise Beauche, *Branch Mgr*
EMP: 8
SALES (corp-wide): 5.4MM **Privately Held**
SIC: 3241 3599 Natural cement; machine & other job shop work
PA: Euro Gear (Usa), Inc.
1395 Brickell Ave Ste 800
Miami FL 33131
518 578-1775

(G-12747)
FEDEX GROUND PACKAGE SYS INC
82 Gateway Dr (12901-5371)
PHONE..................................800 463-3339
EMP: 7
SALES (corp-wide): 69.6B **Publicly Held**
SIC: 3086 Packaging & shipping materials, foamed plastic

HQ: Fedex Ground Package System, Inc.
1000 Fed Ex Dr
Coraopolis PA 15108
800 463-3339

(G-12748)
GEORGIA-PACIFIC LLC
327 Margaret St (12901-1719)
PHONE..................................518 561-3500
Kirk Stallsmith, *Vice Pres*
Matt Bokus, *Safety Mgr*
Tom Nix, *Supervisor*
Stefan Goralczyk, *Info Tech Mgr*
Phil Racine, *Info Tech Mgr*
EMP: 540
SQ FT: 14,464
SALES (corp-wide): 40.6B **Privately Held**
WEB: www.gp.com
SIC: 2621 2676 Paper mills; sanitary paper products
HQ: Georgia-Pacific Llc
133 Peachtree St Nw
Atlanta GA 30303
404 652-4000

(G-12749)
GRAYMONT MATERIALS INC
Also Called: Plattsburgh Quarry
111 Quarry Rd (12901-6215)
PHONE..................................518 561-5200
Todd Kempainen, *President*
John Coupal, *Superintendent*
William Trudo, *Manager*
Charlie Mitchell, *Maintence Staff*
EMP: 28
SALES (est): 922.1K **Privately Held**
SIC: 3281 2951 Stone, quarrying & processing of own stone products; asphalt paving mixtures & blocks

(G-12750)
HANET PLASTICS USA INC
139 Distribution Way (12901-3734)
PHONE..................................518 324-5850
EMP: 5
SALES (est): 370K **Privately Held**
SIC: 2821 Mfg Plastic Materials/Resins

(G-12751)
HERITAGE PRINTING CENTER
94 Margaret St (12901-2925)
PHONE..................................518 563-8240
Roger A Conant, *Partner*
Roger W Conant, *Partner*
EMP: 7 EST: 1976
SQ FT: 2,200
SALES (est): 730.2K **Privately Held**
WEB: www.heritageprint.com
SIC: 2752 Commercial printing, offset

(G-12752)
IEC HOLDEN CORPORATION
51 Distribution Way (12901-3731)
PHONE..................................518 213-3991
Robert Briscoe, *Ch of Bd*
▲ EMP: 17
SALES (est): 3.5MM **Privately Held**
SIC: 3621 Inverters, rotating: electrical

(G-12753)
INTRAPAC INTERNATIONAL CORP
4 Plant St (12901-3771)
PHONE..................................518 561-2030
Anthony Staring, *Manager*
EMP: 150
SALES (corp-wide): 153.3MM **Privately Held**
SIC: 3085 3221 Plastics bottles; glass containers
PA: Intrapac International Corporation
136 Fairview Rd Ste 320
Mooresville NC 28117
704 360-8910

(G-12754)
ISLAND MACHINE INC
86 Boynton Ave (12901-1236)
PHONE..................................518 562-1232
Marvin C Benton, *President*
Marvin Benton, *President*
Bonnie Benton, *Vice Pres*
EMP: 9
SQ FT: 2,100
SALES: 600K **Privately Held**
SIC: 3599 Machine shop, jobbing & repair

(G-12755)
JOHNS MANVILLE CORPORATION
1 Kaycee Loop Rd (12901-2010)
PHONE..................................518 565-3000
Jim Kopaska, *Plant Mgr*
Steve Kuhn, *Manager*
Brent Leclerc, *Manager*
EMP: 28
SALES (corp-wide): 225.3B **Publicly Held**
WEB: www.jm.com
SIC: 2952 Roofing materials
HQ: Johns Manville Corporation
717 17th St Ste 800
Denver CO 80202
303 978-2000

(G-12756)
KNORR BRAKE COMPANY LLC
613 State Route 3 Unit 1 (12901-6530)
PHONE..................................518 561-1387
Phil Rockwell, *Site Mgr*
EMP: 6
SALES (corp-wide): 711.6K **Privately Held**
WEB: www.knorrbrakecorp.com
SIC: 3743 Brakes, air & vacuum: railway; rapid transit cars & equipment
HQ: Knorr Brake Company Llc
1 Arthur Peck Dr
Westminster MD 21157
410 875-0900

(G-12757)
LAKESIDE CONTAINER CORP (PA)
299 Arizona Ave (12903-4429)
P.O. Box 845 (12901-0845)
PHONE..................................518 561-6150
George Bouyea, *President*
Paige Raville, *Vice Pres*
Ron Charette, *Opers Mgr*
Carol Hollenbeck, *Sales Staff*
Miki Worden, *Program Mgr*
EMP: 19 EST: 1958
SQ FT: 65,000
SALES (est): 2.2MM **Privately Held**
WEB: www.lakesidecontainer.com
SIC: 2653 Boxes, corrugated: made from purchased materials

(G-12758)
LEROUX FUELS
994 Military Tpke (12901-5926)
PHONE..................................518 563-3653
Nicholas Leroux, *Principal*
EMP: 10
SALES (est): 1.5MM **Privately Held**
SIC: 2869 Fuels

(G-12759)
MOLD-RITE PLASTICS LLC
1 Plant St (12901-3788)
P.O. Box 160 (12901-0160)
PHONE..................................518 561-1812
Dennis Houpt, *Senior VP*
Keith Kelble, *Vice Pres*
Eric Zeisloft, *Vice Pres*
John Hartman, *Prdtn Mgr*
Robbie Brooks, *Traffic Mgr*
EMP: 9 **Privately Held**
SIC: 3089 Injection molding of plastics
HQ: Mold-Rite Plastics, Llc
30 N La Salle St Ste 2425
Chicago IL 60602
518 561-1812

(G-12760)
MONAGHAN MEDICAL CORPORATION (PA)
5 Latour Ave Ste 1600 (12901-7271)
PHONE..................................518 561-7330
Gerald Slemko, *President*
Janet Smith, *Division Mgr*
Dominic Coppolo, *Vice Pres*
William Seitz, *Vice Pres*
Angele Babin, *Accountant*
▲ EMP: 52
SALES (est): 9.9MM **Privately Held**
WEB: www.monaghanmed.com
SIC: 3842 Surgical appliances & supplies

(G-12761)

NORSK TITANIUM US INC (DH)
44 Martina Cir (12901-7420)
PHONE..................................518 324-4010
Michael Canario, *CEO*
Ashar Ashary, *Vice Pres*
Bart V Aalst, *CFO*
Stephen Littauer, *CFO*
Charles Fuller, *Ch Credit Ofcr*
EMP: 43
SQ FT: 5,000
SALES (est): 3.5MM **Privately Held**
SIC: 3728 Aircraft assemblies, subassemblies & parts
HQ: Norsk Titanium Equipment As
Flyplassveien 20
Honefoss 3514
321 413-52

(G-12762)

NORTHEAST CONCRETE PDTS INC
1024 Military Tpke (12901-5959)
PHONE..................................518 563-0700
Arthur Spiegel, *President*
James L Neverett, *Senior VP*
Darren C Babbie, *Vice Pres*
Jill Friedrich, *Administration*
EMP: 15 EST: 1938
SQ FT: 31,500
SALES (est): 1.4MM **Privately Held**
WEB: www.concretebuildingsupply.com
SIC: 3272 Precast terrazo or concrete products

(G-12763)

NORTHEAST GROUP
Also Called: Strictly Business
12 Nepco Way (12903-3961)
PHONE..................................518 563-8214
Herb Carpenter, *Partner*
Mary Carpenter, *Partner*
Mike Carpenter, *Partner*
▲ EMP: 55
SALES (est): 6.6MM **Privately Held**
WEB: www.sbmonthly.com
SIC: 2721 Periodicals

(G-12764)

NORTHEAST PRTG & DIST CO INC
163 Idaho Ave (12903-3987)
PHONE..................................514 577-3545
EMP: 7
SALES (corp-wide): 5.6MM **Privately Held**
SIC: 2721 Periodicals
PA: Northeast Printing & Distribution Company, Inc.
12 Nepco Way
Plattsburgh NY 12903
518 563-8214

(G-12765)

NORTHEAST PRTG & DIST CO INC (PA)
Also Called: Northeast Group, The
12 Nepco Way (12903-3961)
PHONE..................................518 563-8214
Herb Carpenter, *President*
Marcia Vicencio, *Editor*
Mary E Carpenter, *Vice Pres*
Michael Carpenter, *Vice Pres*
Betsy Vicencio, *Vice Pres*
▲ EMP: 36
SQ FT: 115,000
SALES (est): 5.6MM **Privately Held**
WEB: www.thenortheastgroup.com
SIC: 2752 Commercial printing, offset

(G-12766)

PACTIV LLC
74 Weed St (12901-1260)
PHONE..................................518 562-6101
James Morris, *Vice Pres*
Anthony Searing, *Plant Mgr*
Cynthia Maynard, *Buyer*
Matt Labombard, *QC Mgr*
Lisa Smith, *Marketing Mgr*
EMP: 200
SQ FT: 64,904

SALES (corp-wide): 14.1MM **Privately Held**
WEB: www.pactiv.com
SIC: 2656 2657 2671 Plates, paper: made from purchased material; food containers, folding: made from purchased material; packaging paper & plastics film, coated & laminated
HQ: Pactiv Llc
1900 W Field Ct
Lake Forest IL 60045
847 482-2000

(G-12767)

PERFORMANCE DIESEL SERVICE LLC
24 Latour Ave (12901-7206)
PHONE..................................315 854-5269
Scott Roketenetz,
EMP: 12
SALES (est): 1.9MM **Privately Held**
SIC: 2911 Diesel fuels

(G-12768)

PLATTCO CORPORATION (PA)
7 White St (12901-3471)
PHONE..................................518 563-4640
Douglas J Crozierm, *Ch of Bd*
Justin Soule, *Business Mgr*
Stacie Chapman, *Purch Mgr*
Bob Bourgeois, *Natl Sales Mgr*
Danielle Ross, *Sales Mgr*
◆ EMP: 50 EST: 1897
SQ FT: 60,000
SALES (est): 12.6MM **Privately Held**
WEB: www.plattco.com
SIC: 3369 3491 3322 Machinery castings, nonferrous: ex. alum., copper, die, etc.; industrial valves; malleable iron foundries

(G-12769)

PLATTCO CORPORATION
18 White St (12901-3438)
PHONE..................................518 563-4640
Justin Soule, *Sales Staff*
Doug Crozier, *Branch Mgr*
EMP: 11
SALES (est): 1.4MM
SALES (corp-wide): 12.6MM **Privately Held**
WEB: www.plattco.com
SIC: 3369 Nonferrous foundries
PA: Plattco Corporation
7 White St
Plattsburgh NY 12901
518 563-4640

(G-12770)

PLATTSBURGH SHEET METAL INC
95 Sailly Ave (12901-1726)
PHONE..................................518 561-4930
Sandra Carlo, *President*
EMP: 5
SALES: 1MM **Privately Held**
SIC: 3444 Sheet metalwork

(G-12771)

PREVOST CAR (US) INC
260 Banker Rd (12901-7310)
PHONE..................................518 957-2052
Jason McHael, *Branch Mgr*
EMP: 150
SALES (corp-wide): 43.4B **Privately Held**
SIC: 3711 Buses, all types, assembly of
HQ: Prevost Car (Us) Inc.
7900 National Service Rd
Greensboro NC 27409
908 222-7211

(G-12772)

PRIM HALL ENTERPRISES INC
11 Spellman Rd (12901-5326)
PHONE..................................518 561-7408
John Prim, *President*
David Hall, *Vice Pres*
EMP: 12
SQ FT: 43,000
SALES (est): 1.4MM **Privately Held**
WEB: www.primhall.com
SIC: 3555 7699 3542 7389 Printing trades machinery; industrial machinery & equipment repair; machine tools, metal forming type; design, commercial & industrial

(G-12773)

R & S MACHINE CENTER INC
Also Called: R&S Machine
4398 Route 22 (12901-5851)
P.O. Box 40 (12901-0040)
PHONE..................................518 563-4016
Robert Davenport, *President*
EMP: 10
SQ FT: 7,000
SALES: 1.9MM **Privately Held**
SIC: 3599 5051 Machine shop, jobbing & repair; steel

(G-12774)

RAPA INDEPENDENT NORTH AMERICA
Also Called: Rina
124 Connecticut Rd (12903-4955)
PHONE..................................518 561-0513
Manil Whig, *President*
▲ EMP: 6
SQ FT: 5,000
SALES: 200K **Privately Held**
SIC: 2013 Sausage casings, natural

(G-12775)

SALERNO PACKAGING INC (HQ)
Also Called: Salerno Plastic Film and Bags
14 Gus Lapham Ln (12901-6534)
PHONE..................................518 563-3636
Kurt Strater, *President*
Mac Elgin, *Vice Pres*
EMP: 13
SALES (est): 37.6MM **Privately Held**
SIC: 2673 Plastic bags: made from purchased materials

(G-12776)

SEMEC CORP
20 Gateway Dr (12901-5371)
PHONE..................................518 825-0160
Mario Babin, *Manager*
Deborah Wells, *Admin Mgr*
▲ EMP: 15
SALES (est): 2.1MM **Privately Held**
SIC: 3743 Railroad equipment

(G-12777)

SKYKO INTERNATIONAL LLC
35 Gateway Dr Ste 201 (12901-5382)
P.O. Box 2778 (12901-0239)
PHONE..................................518 562-9696
Krista Schultz,
EMP: 16
SALES (est): 3MM
SALES (corp-wide): 2.8MM **Privately Held**
SIC: 3643 Power line cable
PA: Skyko International Llc
243 New Sweden Rd
Woodstock CT 06281
860 928-5170

(G-12778)

SSF PRODUCTION LLC
194 Pleasant Ridge Rd (12901-5841)
PHONE..................................518 324-3407
Frank Filbir, *Mng Member*
Tilo Hilderbrand,
▲ EMP: 10
SQ FT: 17,000
SALES (est): 1.8MM **Privately Held**
SIC: 3296 Acoustical board & tile, mineral wool

(G-12779)

STEELE TRUSS AND PANEL LLC
112 Trade Rd (12901-6259)
P.O. Box 1023, Peru (12972-1023)
PHONE..................................518 562-4663
Loretta Steele, *Mng Member*
Leslie Baker,
EMP: 9
SQ FT: 12,000
SALES: 488K **Privately Held**
SIC: 3443 Truss plates, metal

(G-12780)

STEELE TRUSS COMPANY INC
118 Trade Rd (12901-6259)
PHONE..................................518 562-4663
Robert Steele, *CEO*
Joel C Steele, *President*
Thomas E Steele Sr, *President*
Loretta Steele, *Corp Secy*

Marvin Hooper, *VP Engrg*
EMP: 25
SQ FT: 80,000
SALES: 2MM **Privately Held**
WEB: www.steeltrusses.net
SIC: 2439 1541 Trusses, wooden roof; steel building construction

(G-12781)

STERRX LLC
141 Idaho Ave (12903-3987)
PHONE..................................518 324-7879
Terry Wiley, *VP Mfg*
Jeff Babbie, *Project Mgr*
Gary Hanley,
EMP: 32
SALES (est): 8.5MM **Privately Held**
SIC: 2834 Solutions, pharmaceutical

(G-12782)

STUDLEY PRTG PUBLICATIONS INC
Also Called: Northern Explorng/Timeless T
4701 State Route 9 (12901-6036)
PHONE..................................518 563-1414
William Studley, *President*
Bridgette Studley, *Finance*
Lynn Roberts-Devins, *Accounts Exec*
Kim Mousseau, *Publications*
EMP: 18
SALES (est): 3.3MM **Privately Held**
WEB: www.studleyprinting.com
SIC: 2752 8743 Commercial printing, offset; public relations & publicity

(G-12783)

SWAROVSKI LIGHTING LTD (PA)
Also Called: Schonbek
61 Industrial Blvd (12901-1908)
PHONE..................................518 563-7500
John Simms, *CEO*
Andrew Schonbek, *President*
Brock Trombley, *Opers Mgr*
Roxanne Trombly, *Production*
Deborah Buskey, *Engineer*
◆ EMP: 240
SQ FT: 200,000
SALES (est): 56.6MM **Privately Held**
SIC: 3645 Residential lighting fixtures

(G-12784)

SWAROVSKI LIGHTING LTD
Also Called: Schonbek Shipping Bldg
1483 Military Tpke Ste B (12901-7453)
PHONE..................................518 324-6378
PR Llier, *Principal*
EMP: 400
SALES (corp-wide): 56.6MM **Privately Held**
SIC: 3645 Chandeliers, residential
PA: Swarovski Lighting, Ltd.
61 Industrial Blvd
Plattsburgh NY 12901
518 563-7500

(G-12785)

TITHERINGTON DESIGN & MFG
102 Sharron Ave Unit 1 (12901-3828)
PHONE..................................518 324-2205
Philip D Titherington, *CEO*
EMP: 11
SALES (est): 1.9MM **Privately Held**
SIC: 3089 7336 Injection molding of plastics; package design

(G-12786)

UMS MANUFACTURING LLC
194 Pleasant Ridge Rd (12901-5841)
PHONE..................................518 562-2410
Mark Schulter, *Mng Member*
Udo Schulter,
EMP: 10
SQ FT: 57,000
SALES (est): 1.2MM **Privately Held**
SIC: 2675 Waterproof cardboard: made from purchased materials

(G-12787)

UPSTONE MATERIALS INC (DH)
111 Quarry Rd (12901-6215)
PHONE..................................518 561-5321
Sylvan Gross, *President*
EMP: 57 EST: 2017
SQ FT: 5,000

SALES: 40MM
SALES (corp-wide): 83.5MM **Privately Held**
SIC: **1429** 3273 2951 Grits mining (crushed stone); ready-mixed concrete; asphalt & asphaltic paving mixtures (not from refineries)
HQ: Barrett Industries Corporation
73 Headquarters Plz
Morristown NJ 07960
973 533-1001

(G-12788)
UPSTONE MATERIALS INC
Also Called: Potsdam Stone Concrete
111 Quarry Rd (12901-6215)
PHONE..................................315 265-8036
Judy Fuhr, *Superintendent*
Dave Gordon, *Plant Mgr*
Donny Smith, *Manager*
EMP: 17
SQ FT: 3,769
SALES (corp-wide): 83.5MM **Privately Held**
WEB: www.graymont-ab.com
SIC: **3273** 5083 Ready-mixed concrete; landscaping equipment
HQ: Upstone Materials Inc.
111 Quarry Rd
Plattsburgh NY 12901
518 561-5321

(G-12789)
VALCOUR BREWING COMPANY LLC
49 Ohio Rd (12903-4409)
PHONE..................................518 324-2337
Mary Pearl, *Mng Member*
Margaret Weicher, *Mng Member*
EMP: 27
SALES: 1.2MM **Privately Held**
SIC: **2082** 5921 Malt beverages; beer (packaged)

(G-12790)
WEBER INTL PACKG CO LLC
318 Cornelia St (12901-2300)
PHONE..................................518 561-8282
K Heinz Weber, *CEO*
Michael Hanley, *Engineer*
Tihamer Monostori,
EMP: 54
SQ FT: 44,000
SALES (est): 10.2MM **Privately Held**
WEB: www.weberintl.com
SIC: **3089** Plastic containers, except foam

(G-12791)
WESTINGHOUSE A BRAKE TECH CORP
Vapor Stone Rail Systems
72 Arizona Ave (12903-4427)
PHONE..................................518 561-0044
Bob Brassee, *Manager*
EMP: 70
SALES (corp-wide): 4.3B **Publicly Held**
WEB: www.wabtecglobalservices.com
SIC: **3743** Brakes, air & vacuum: railway; locomotives & parts; freight cars & equipment; rapid transit cars & equipment
PA: Westinghouse Air Brake Technologies Corporation
30 Isabella St
Pittsburgh PA 15212
412 825-1000

(G-12792)
WOODFALLS INDUSTRIES
434 Burke Rd (12901-5214)
PHONE..................................518 236-7201
Tammy Deyo, *Owner*
EMP: 10 EST: 2010
SALES (est): 450K **Privately Held**
SIC: **3999** Manufacturing industries

(G-12793)
XBORDER ENTERTAINMENT LLC
568 State Route 3 (12901-6526)
PHONE..................................518 726-7036
Casey Spiegel, *Mng Member*
EMP: 7
SQ FT: 35,000
SALES (est): 193.4K **Privately Held**
SIC: **7372** Application computer software

Pleasant Valley
Dutchess County

(G-12794)
SIMMONS FABRICATING SVC INC
1558 Main St (12569)
P.O. Box 690 (12569-0690)
PHONE..................................845 635-3755
Robert Lalonde, *President*
Colleen Lalonde, *President*
EMP: 5
SQ FT: 5,000
SALES: 250K **Privately Held**
SIC: **3444** Sheet metalwork

Pleasantville
Westchester County

(G-12795)
CARLARA GROUP LTD
Also Called: Sir Speedy
467 Bedford Rd (10570-2928)
PHONE..................................914 769-2020
Carlos Bernard, *President*
Susana Lara, *Vice Pres*
EMP: 5
SQ FT: 3,000
SALES (est): 1MM **Privately Held**
SIC: **2752** 2791 2789 Commercial printing, lithographic; typesetting; bookbinding & related work

(G-12796)
COUNTY FABRICATORS
175 Marble Ave (10570-3421)
PHONE..................................914 741-0219
Kristina Benza, *Mng Member*
Amanda Decesare, *Director*
Laura Zapata, *Admin Dir*
Phillip R Benza,
Phillip Benza,
EMP: 18
SQ FT: 13,200
SALES: 1.5MM **Privately Held**
WEB: www.countyfabricators.com
SIC: **3441** Fabricated structural metal

(G-12797)
OPTIMIZED DEVICES INC
220 Marble Ave (10570-3465)
PHONE..................................914 769-6100
Arthur Zuch, *President*
Robert Zuch, *Vice Pres*
EMP: 13
SQ FT: 6,000
SALES (est): 2.1MM **Privately Held**
WEB: www.optdev.com
SIC: **3825** Test equipment for electronic & electric measurement

(G-12798)
READERS DGEST YUNG FMILIES INC
Readers Digest Rd (10570)
PHONE..................................914 238-1000
Thomas O Ryder, *Ch of Bd*
EMP: 25
SALES (est): 868.4K **Privately Held**
WEB: www.rd.com
SIC: **2731** Book publishing
HQ: Trusted Media Brands, Inc.
750 3rd Ave Fl 3
New York NY 10017
914 238-1000

(G-12799)
READERS DIGEST SLS & SVCS INC
Readers Digest Rd (10570)
PHONE..................................914 238-1000
Daniel Lagani, *Ch of Bd*
Gregory Coleman, *President*
Paul Gillow, *Counsel*
Mark Sirota, *Counsel*
Beth Clerc, *Vice Pres*
EMP: 156 EST: 1961
SALES (est): 20.9MM **Privately Held**
WEB: www.changeone.com
SIC: **2721** Periodicals

HQ: Trusted Media Brands, Inc.
750 3rd Ave Fl 3
New York NY 10017
914 238-1000

(G-12800)
TECHNICAL PRECISION CORP
Also Called: Tepco
1 Vanderbilt Ave (10570-2805)
PHONE..................................845 473-0548
Dave Sauter, *President*
Cynthia Sauter, *Admin Sec*
EMP: 10
SQ FT: 8,500
SALES (est): 92.1K **Privately Held**
SIC: **3599** Machine shop, jobbing & repair

Poestenkill
Rensselaer County

(G-12801)
CANTON BIO-MEDICAL INC (PA)
Also Called: Saint-Gobain Performance Plas
11 Sicho Rd (12140-3102)
PHONE..................................518 283-5963
John Bedell, *Principal*
EMP: 36
SQ FT: 36,000
SALES (est): 2.4MM **Privately Held**
SIC: **2822** Silicone rubbers

(G-12802)
DYNAMIC SYSTEMS INC (PA)
Also Called: D S I
323 Rte 355 (12140)
P.O. Box 1234 (12140-1234)
PHONE..................................518 283-5350
David Ferguson, *President*
Jean Jacon, *Vice Pres*
Kevin Borkowski, *Opers Mgr*
Emily Warren, *Materials Mgr*
Ethan Bowerman, *Production*
▲ EMP: 38 EST: 1957
SQ FT: 29,000
SALES (est): 6.3MM **Privately Held**
WEB: www.gleeble.com
SIC: **3829** Measuring & controlling devices

(G-12803)
INTER STATE LAMINATES INC
44 Main St (12140-3201)
P.O. Box 270 (12140-0270)
PHONE..................................518 283-8355
Harold Crandall, *President*
Debbie Crandall, *Admin Sec*
EMP: 46
SALES (est): 6.1MM **Privately Held**
WEB: www.isltops.com
SIC: **3083** 2541 Plastic finished products, laminated; wood partitions & fixtures

(G-12804)
SAINT-GOBAIN PRFMCE PLAS CORP
11 Sicho Rd (12140-3102)
PHONE..................................518 283-5963
Lynn Monrow, *General Mgr*
EMP: 41
SALES (corp-wide): 215.9MM **Privately Held**
SIC: **3089** Spouting, plastic & glass fiber reinforced
HQ: Saint-Gobain Performance Plastics Corporation
31500 Solon Rd
Solon OH 44139
440 836-6900

(G-12805)
VAN SLYKE BELTING LLC
606 Snyders Corners Rd (12140-2914)
PHONE..................................518 283-5479
H Van, *Principal*
EMP: 6 EST: 2001
SALES (est): 652.2K **Privately Held**
SIC: **3052** Rubber belting

Pomona
Rockland County

(G-12806)
CAMBRIDGE SECURITY SEALS LLC
1 Cambridge Plz (10970-2676)
PHONE..................................845 520-4111
Shannon McElroy, *Vice Pres*
Forrest Anderson, *Regl Sales Mgr*
Jill Nilsson, *Sales Staff*
Elisha Tropper, *Mng Member*
◆ EMP: 20
SQ FT: 25,000
SALES (est): 5.1MM **Privately Held**
SIC: **3089** Injection molding of plastics

(G-12807)
DJS NYC INC
Also Called: Deejays
3 Laura Ln (10970-2016)
PHONE..................................845 445-8618
Chaim Einhorn, *President*
Sarah Koenig, *Admin Sec*
EMP: 8
SALES: 1.6MM **Privately Held**
SIC: **3674** Solid state electronic devices

(G-12808)
SAN JAE EDUCATIONAL RESOU
9 Chamberlain Ct (10970-2837)
PHONE..................................845 364-5458
EMP: 4
SALES (est): 1MM **Privately Held**
SIC: **7372** Prepackaged Software Services

Port Byron
Cayuga County

(G-12809)
MARTENS COUNTRY KIT PDTS LLC
1323 Towpath Rd (13140)
P.O. Box 428 (13140-0428)
PHONE..................................315 776-8821
Jill Skrupa, *Sales Staff*
Timothy Martens,
▲ EMP: 10
SALES (est): 859.8K **Privately Held**
SIC: **2099** Potatoes, dried: packaged with other ingredients

(G-12810)
MAX 200 PERFORMANCE DOG EQP
2113 State Route 31 (13140-9423)
PHONE..................................315 776-9588
Irene Lamphere, *President*
Alfred Lamphere, *Vice Pres*
Joyce Scott, *Director*
EMP: 22
SQ FT: 18,000
SALES: 1.5MM **Privately Held**
WEB: www.max200.com
SIC: **3199** Dog furnishings: collars, leashes, muzzles, etc.: leather

(G-12811)
PRECISION DIECUTTING INC
1381 Spring Lake Rd (13140-3375)
PHONE..................................315 776-8465
Norma Compson, *President*
Jamie Compson, *Vice Pres*
EMP: 6
SALES: 300K **Privately Held**
SIC: **2675** Stencil board, die-cut: made from purchased materials

Port Chester
Westchester County

(G-12812)
AIR STRUCTURES AMERCN TECH INC
211 S Ridge St Ste 3 (10573-3445)
PHONE..................................914 937-4500
Donato A Fraioli, *CEO*

Rosemarie Fraioli, *Admin Sec*
▼ **EMP:** 50
SQ FT: 2,500
SALES (est): 10MM **Privately Held**
WEB: www.asati.com
SIC: 2394 Tents: made from purchased materials

(G-12813)
ALBUMX CORP
Also Called: Renanssance The Book
21 Grace Church St (10573-4911)
PHONE....................................914 939-6878
Terry Huang, *President*
Albert Huang, *Prdtn Mgr*
Victor Huang, *Human Resources*
▲ **EMP:** 80
SQ FT: 27,000
SALES (est): 7.9MM **Privately Held**
WEB: www.renaissancealbums.com
SIC: 2782 Albums

(G-12814)
ALWAYS PRINTING
149 Highland St (10573-3394)
PHONE....................................914 481-5209
Jodi McCredo, *Owner*
EMP: 5
SALES (est): 531.9K **Privately Held**
SIC: 2752 Commercial printing, offset

(G-12815)
COMPOSITE FORMS INC
7 Merritt St (10573-3502)
PHONE....................................914 937-1808
Frank J Madonia, *CEO*
Frank Madonia Jr, *President*
Frank Madonia Sr, *Director*
EMP: 10
SQ FT: 6,500
SALES (est): 930K **Privately Held**
WEB: www.sidingsolutions.com
SIC: 2752 5112 Commercial printing, offset; business forms

(G-12816)
D & M ENTERPRISES INCORPORATED
Also Called: A W S
1 Mill St Ste 2 (10573-6301)
PHONE....................................914 937-6430
Dino Alampi, *President*
Mary Alampi, *Vice Pres*
Barbara J Grote, *Admin Asst*
EMP: 8
SQ FT: 5,000
SALES: 327K **Privately Held**
SIC: 3088 3999 Hot tubs, plastic or fiberglass; hot tubs

(G-12817)
DESIGNS BY NOVELLO INC
505 N Main St (10573-3360)
PHONE....................................914 934-7711
George Bulger, *Owner*
▲ **EMP:** 5 **EST:** 1997
SALES (est): 654.3K **Privately Held**
SIC: 3449 Bars, concrete reinforcing: fabricated steel

(G-12818)
EAGLE INSTRUMENTS INC
35 Grove St (10573-4501)
PHONE....................................914 939-6843
Robert Schneider, *President*
EMP: 7
SQ FT: 4,000
SALES (est): 1MM **Privately Held**
SIC: 3599 Machine shop, jobbing & repair

(G-12819)
EHS GROUP LLC
69 Townsend St (10573-4311)
PHONE....................................914 937-6162
Steven Kennedy, *President*
Lisa Cartolano, *Corp Secy*
EMP: 8
SQ FT: 6,000
SALES (est): 1.6MM **Privately Held**
SIC: 2759 Envelopes: printing

(G-12820)
EMPIRE COFFEE COMPANY INC
106 Purdy Ave (10573-4624)
PHONE....................................914 934-1100
Steven Dunefsky, *President*

Michael Riger, *Vice Pres*
Todd Good, *VP Opers*
Robert Richter, *Admin Sec*
▲ **EMP:** 35
SQ FT: 30,000
SALES (est): 6.5MM **Privately Held**
WEB: www.empire-coffee.com
SIC: 2095 Coffee roasting (except by wholesale grocers)

(G-12821)
GMP LLC
Also Called: Graphic Management Partners
47 Purdy Ave (10573-5028)
PHONE....................................914 939-0571
Paul Humphrey, *Partner*
Jim Berger, *Vice Pres*
Paul Cherico, *Vice Pres*
Anthony Corrado, *Vice Pres*
Mike Geraghty, *Vice Pres*
EMP: 80
SQ FT: 20,000
SALES: 12.6MM **Privately Held**
SIC: 2752 Promotional printing, lithographic

(G-12822)
GOOD BREAD BAKERY
Also Called: Best Bread
33 New Broad St Ste 1 (10573-4651)
PHONE....................................914 939-3900
Michael Beldotti, *Owner*
Chris Beldotti, *Owner*
EMP: 15
SALES (est): 1.4MM **Privately Held**
SIC: 2051 Bakery: wholesale or wholesale/retail combined

(G-12823)
JJ CASSONE BAKERY INC
202 S Regent St (10573-4791)
PHONE....................................914 939-1568
Mary Lou Cassone, *President*
Dominic Ambrose, *Vice Pres*
Tony Crusco, *Vice Pres*
Jack Guarcello, *Vice Pres*
Greg Mancuso, *Vice Pres*
▲ **EMP:** 280
SQ FT: 180,000
SALES (est): 51MM **Privately Held**
WEB: www.jjcassone.com
SIC: 2051 5461 Bakery: wholesale or wholesale/retail combined; bread, all types (white, wheat, rye, etc): fresh or frozen; bakeries

(G-12824)
LANZA CORP
Also Called: Sign Design
404 Willett Ave (10573-3132)
PHONE....................................914 937-6360
Joseph Lanza, *President*
Nick Contrata, *Project Mgr*
Sue Bonci, *Office Mgr*
EMP: 9
SQ FT: 4,000
SALES (est): 1.4MM **Privately Held**
WEB: www.clicksignage.com
SIC: 2394 7389 5999 2499 Canvas awnings & canopies; sign painting & lettering shop; awnings; carved & turned wood; sign installation & maintenance; electric signs

(G-12825)
MATTHEW SHIVELY LLC
40 Merritt St (10573-3539)
PHONE....................................914 937-3531
Matthew Shively,
EMP: 7
SQ FT: 5,000
SALES (est): 439.9K **Privately Held**
SIC: 2519 Household furniture

(G-12826)
PALETERIA FERNANDEZ INC (PA)
33 N Main St (10573-4208)
PHONE....................................914 939-3694
Fernandez Paleteria, *Principal*
EMP: 9
SALES (est): 1.1MM **Privately Held**
SIC: 2024 Ice cream, bulk

(G-12827)
PARSONS & WHITTEMORE INC
4 International Dr # 300 (10573-1064)
PHONE....................................914 937-9009
Arthur L Schwartz, *President*
George F Landegger, *Chairman*
Robert H Masson, *Vice Pres*
Jose Alvelo, *Treasurer*
Frank Grasso, *Treasurer*
EMP: 367 **EST:** 1853
SQ FT: 16,650
SALES (est): 75.2MM
SALES (corp-wide): 77.8MM **Privately Held**
SIC: 2611 Pulp mills
PA: Parsons & Whittemore Enterprises Corp.
　4 International Dr # 300
　Port Chester NY 10573
　914 937-9009

(G-12828)
PARSONS WHITTEMORE ENTPS CORP (PA)
4 International Dr # 300 (10573-1064)
PHONE....................................914 937-9009
George F Landegger, *Ch of Bd*
Carl C Landegger, *Vice Ch Bd*
Steven Sweeney, *CFO*
Frank Grasso, *Treasurer*
EMP: 25
SQ FT: 16,650
SALES (est): 77.8MM **Privately Held**
SIC: 2611 Pulp mills

(G-12829)
SWISSBIT NA INC
18 Willett Ave 202 (10573-4368)
PHONE....................................914 935-1400
Anthony Cerreta, *President*
Vincenzo Esposito, *Managing Dir*
Grady Lambert, *Business Mgr*
Thomas McCormick, *Chief Engr*
Tony Cerreta, *Sales Staff*
EMP: 3
SQ FT: 2,050
SALES: 20MM
SALES (corp-wide): 392.5K **Privately Held**
WEB: www.swissbitna.com
SIC: 3674 Semiconductors & related devices
HQ: Swissbit Ag
　Industriestrasse 4-8
　Bronschhofen SG 9552
　719 130-303

(G-12830)
ULMER SALES LLC
Also Called: U K Sailmakers
10 Midland Ave Ste 1 (10573-4927)
PHONE....................................718 885-1700
Charles Ulmer, *President*
Kerry Klinler, *Vice Pres*
Rob Roy, *Representative*
EMP: 12
SQ FT: 6,500
SALES (est): 1.6MM **Privately Held**
SIC: 2394 Sails: made from purchased materials

(G-12831)
ZYLOWARE CORPORATION (PA)
Also Called: Zyloware Eyewear
8 Slater St Ste 1 (10573-4984)
PHONE....................................914 708-1200
Christopher Shyer, *President*
Robert Shyer, *Principal*
Jennifer Derryberry, *Vice Pres*
James Shyer, *Vice Pres*
Jim Galinsky, *VP Sales*
▲ **EMP:** 66
SQ FT: 21,000
SALES (est): 9.7MM **Privately Held**
WEB: www.zyloware.com
SIC: 3851 Frames & parts, eyeglass & spectacle

Port Jeff STA
Suffolk County

(G-12832)
AHMAZING BOUTIQUE INC
Also Called: Orchard Way
5225 Nesconset Hwy Ste 42 (11776-2060)
PHONE....................................631 828-1474
James McDonald,
Kristine McDonald,
EMP: 7 **EST:** 2017
SALES: 1.6MM **Privately Held**
SIC: 7372 Prepackaged software

(G-12833)
BILTRON AUTOMOTIVE PRODUCTS
509 Bicycle Path Unit Q (11776-3491)
PHONE....................................631 928-8613
Ron Stoll, *President*
▲ **EMP:** 30
SQ FT: 21,000
SALES (est): 4.7MM **Privately Held**
WEB: www.biltronauto.com
SIC: 3714 3566 3462 Steering mechanisms, motor vehicle; speed changers, drives & gears; iron & steel forgings

(G-12834)
DESIGN/OL INC
200 Wilson St Unit D2 (11776-1150)
PHONE....................................631 474-2134
William Delongis, *President*
August Oetting, *Vice Pres*
EMP: 14
SQ FT: 12,500
SALES: 2.5MM **Privately Held**
WEB: www.design-ol.com
SIC: 3728 Aircraft assemblies, subassemblies & parts

(G-12835)
NORTH SHORE HOME IMPROVER
200 Wilson St (11776-1100)
PHONE....................................631 474-2824
David Kielhurn, *CEO*
Patrick Murphy, *CIO*
EMP: 16
SALES (est): 910K **Privately Held**
WEB: www.lihomeshows.com
SIC: 2731 Books: publishing only

(G-12836)
NORTH SHORE ORTHTICS PRSTHTICS
591 Bicycle Path Ste D (11776-3421)
PHONE....................................631 928-3040
Robert Biaggi,
EMP: 7
SQ FT: 1,000
SALES (est): 895K **Privately Held**
WEB: www.nsop.com
SIC: 3842 5999 Limbs, artificial; artificial limbs

(G-12837)
OCCUNOMIX INTERNATIONAL LLC
585 Bicycle Path Ste 52 (11776-3431)
PHONE....................................631 741-1940
Richard Hauser, *Mng Member*
▲ **EMP:** 45
SQ FT: 48,500
SALES (est): 10.3MM **Privately Held**
WEB: www.occunomix.com
SIC: 3842 2311 2326 5047 Personal safety equipment; men's & boys' uniforms; men's & boys' work clothing; medical & hospital equipment

(G-12838)
STARGATE COMPUTER CORP
24 Harmony Dr (11776-3168)
P.O. Box 11161, Hauppauge (11788-0702)
PHONE....................................516 474-4799
EMP: 5
SALES (est): 400K **Privately Held**
SIC: 3571 Mfg Electronic Computers

▲ = Import ▼=Export
◆ =Import/Export

(G-12839)
TKM TECHNOLOGIES INC
623 Bicycle Path Ste 5 (11776-3444)
P.O. Box 665, Mount Sinai (11766-0665)
PHONE..............................631 474-4700
Mike Moroff, *President*
Monika Moroff, *Vice Pres*
EMP: 6
SQ FT: 1,200
SALES: 950K **Privately Held**
WEB: www.tkmtechnologies.com
SIC: 3651 8711 Household audio & video equipment; electrical or electronic engineering

---

Port Jefferson
Suffolk County

(G-12840)
CHIP IT ALL LTD
366 Sheep Pasture Rd (11777-2059)
P.O. Box 959, Port Jeff STA (11776-0812)
PHONE..............................631 473-2040
Richard Edgar, *President*
Linda Edgar, *Admin Sec*
EMP: 7
SQ FT: 720
SALES (est): 885.9K **Privately Held**
SIC: 2411 Wood chips, produced in the field

(G-12841)
LONG ISLAND GEOTECH
6 Berkshire Ct (11777-1906)
PHONE..............................631 473-1044
Micheal Verruto, *President*
EMP: 5
SALES (est): 308.6K **Privately Held**
SIC: 3272 Concrete products

(G-12842)
M H MANDELBAUM ORTHOTIC
116 Oakland Ave (11777-2172)
PHONE..............................631 473-8668
Martin H Mandelbaum, *President*
Marc Werner, *Vice Pres*
EMP: 10
SQ FT: 5,300
SALES (est): 1.3MM **Privately Held**
WEB: www.mhmoandp.com
SIC: 3842 5999 8011 Orthopedic appliances; prosthetic appliances; artificial limbs; offices & clinics of medical doctors

(G-12843)
PACE WALKERS OF AMERICA INC
Also Called: Thomas Jefferson Press
105 Washington Ave (11777-2003)
P.O. Box 843, East Setauket (11733-0653)
PHONE..............................631 444-2147
Steven Jonas, *President*
EMP: 12
SALES (est): 958.5K **Privately Held**
SIC: 2731 Book publishing

(G-12844)
WHITFORD DEVELOPMENT INC
646 Main St Ste 301 (11777-2230)
PHONE..............................631 471-7711
Fax: 631 471-0332
EMP: 11
SALES (est): 1.1MM **Privately Held**
SIC: 2789 Bookbinding/Related Work

Port Jervis
Orange County

(G-12845)
CHOCOLATE LADY LLC
14 Blue Heron Ln (12771-3377)
PHONE..............................516 532-0551
Lee Perrotta-Fityo, *President*
EMP: 5
SALES (est): 226.9K **Privately Held**
SIC: 2066 Chocolate

(G-12846)
CONIC SYSTEMS INC
11 Rebel Ln (12771-3547)
PHONE..............................845 856-4053
Vincent Genovese, *President*
◆ EMP: 10 EST: 1990
SQ FT: 12,000
SALES (est): 1.5MM **Privately Held**
WEB: www.conicsystems.com
SIC: 3625 Control equipment, electric

(G-12847)
DATATRAN LABS INC
Also Called: Nireco America
11 Rebel Ln (12771-3547)
PHONE..............................845 856-4313
Vincent Genovesse, *President*
EMP: 7 EST: 1969
SQ FT: 11,000
SALES (est): 1MM **Privately Held**
WEB: www.datatranlabs.com
SIC: 3625 3577 Industrial controls: push button, selector switches, pilot; computer peripheral equipment

(G-12848)
FLANAGANS CREATIVE DISP INC
55 Jersey Ave (12771-2514)
P.O. Box 98 (12771-0098)
PHONE..............................845 858-2542
Michael Flanagan, *President*
EMP: 35 EST: 1998
SQ FT: 30,000
SALES (est): 6.9MM **Privately Held**
SIC: 3496 Miscellaneous fabricated wire products

(G-12849)
GILLINDER BROTHERS INC
Also Called: Gillinder Glass
39 Erie St 55 (12771-2809)
P.O. Box 1007 (12771-0187)
PHONE..............................845 856-5375
Charles E Gillinder, *Ch of Bd*
Susan Gillinder, *Corp Secy*
Christopher Michael, *Engineer*
Roberta Gervasi, *Sales Staff*
▲ EMP: 70 EST: 1912
SQ FT: 120,000
SALES: 7MM **Privately Held**
WEB: www.gillinderglass.com
SIC: 3229 Pressed & blown glass

(G-12850)
HORNET GROUP INC
Also Called: Hgi Skydyne
100 River Rd (12771-2931)
PHONE..............................845 858-6400
Jay Benson, *CEO*
EMP: 70
SALES (est): 8.8MM **Privately Held**
WEB: www.hornetgroup.com
SIC: 3089 3449 7336 3412 Boxes, plastic; miscellaneous metalwork; package design; metal barrels, drums & pails; metal cans; luggage

(G-12851)
KALTEC FOOD PACKAGING INC
36 Center St 40 (12771)
PHONE..............................845 856-9888
Nick Mascarra, *CEO*
Ed Mascara, *President*
Harriet L Mascara, *Shareholder*
▲ EMP: 30
SQ FT: 20,000
SALES (est): 5MM **Privately Held**
SIC: 2052 Cookies

(G-12852)
KALTECH FOOD PACKAGING INC
3640 Center St (12771)
PHONE..............................845 856-1210
Harriet L Mascara, *CEO*
Frank Mascara, *Exec VP*
Edward Mascara, *Vice Pres*
EMP: 26
SQ FT: 70,000
SALES: 22MM **Privately Held**
SIC: 2033 Spaghetti & other pasta sauce: packaged in cans, jars, etc.

(G-12853)
KLG USA LLC
20 W King St (12771-3061)
P.O. Box 1111 (12771-0154)
PHONE..............................845 856-5311
Joseph Healey, *Ch of Bd*
Rob Edmonds, *President*
▲ EMP: 1000
SQ FT: 4,210
SALES (est): 164.9MM **Privately Held**
WEB: www.kolmar.com
SIC: 2844 7389 2834 Cosmetic preparations; packaging & labeling services; pharmaceutical preparations

(G-12854)
PARAMOUNT GRAPHIX
26 Hill St (12771-2024)
PHONE..............................845 367-5003
Daniel King, *Principal*
Cabe Flesher, *Vice Pres*
Malia Christie, *Sr Project Mgr*
EMP: 5
SALES (est): 310.2K **Privately Held**
SIC: 2499 Signboards, wood

(G-12855)
PORT JERVIS MACHINE CORP
176 1/2 Jersey Ave (12771-2612)
PHONE..............................845 856-6210
Sal Spiezio, *Manager*
EMP: 8
SALES (corp-wide): 781.7K **Privately Held**
SIC: 3599 Machine shop, jobbing & repair
PA: Port Jervis Machine Corporation
180 Jersey Ave
Port Jervis NY
845 856-3333

(G-12856)
SAMAKI INC
62 Jersey Ave (12771-2513)
P.O. Box 554, Westbrookville (12785-0554)
PHONE..............................845 858-1012
Simon Marrian, *President*
Laura Marrian, *Treasurer*
EMP: 7
SQ FT: 2,800
SALES (est): 880.8K **Privately Held**
WEB: www.samaki.com
SIC: 2091 Fish, smoked; fish, cured

(G-12857)
SKYDYNE COMPANY
100 River Rd (12771-2997)
PHONE..............................845 858-6400
Peter A Keay, *President*
Peter A Siebert, *Corp Secy*
▲ EMP: 70
SALES (est): 17MM **Privately Held**
WEB: www.skydyne.com
SIC: 2655 Containers, laminated phenolic & vulcanized fiber

(G-12858)
SWIMWEAR ANYWHERE INC
Also Called: Finals, The
21 Minisink Ave (12771-2320)
PHONE..............................845 858-4141
Nancy Piccolo, *Manager*
EMP: 40
SALES (corp-wide): 52MM **Privately Held**
SIC: 2329 2339 Bathing suits & swimwear: men's & boys'; athletic (warmup, sweat & jogging) suits: men's & boys'; bathing suits: women's, misses' & juniors'; athletic clothing: women's, misses' & juniors'
PA: Swimwear Anywhere, Inc.
85 Sherwood Ave
Farmingdale NY 11735
631 420-1400

Port Washington
Nassau County

(G-12859)
ACTIONCRAFT PRODUCTS INC
2 Manhasset Ave (11050-2008)
PHONE..............................516 883-6423
Nina Straus, *President*

EMP: 8 EST: 1951
SQ FT: 4,000
SALES (est): 381.6K **Privately Held**
WEB: www.industrialtest.com
SIC: 2759 Tags: printing

(G-12860)
ADVANCED POLYMER SOLUTIONS LLC
99 Seaview Blvd Ste 1a (11050-4632)
PHONE..............................516 621-5800
Purushoth Kesavan, *Production*
John M Ryan,
Rita M Ryan,
EMP: 9
SQ FT: 10,000
SALES (est): 1.7MM **Privately Held**
WEB: www.advancedpolymersolutions.com
SIC: 2891 8731 Adhesives & sealants; chemical laboratory, except testing

(G-12861)
ALAN F BOURGUET
63 Essex Ct (11050-4222)
PHONE..............................516 883-4315
Alan F Bourguet, *President*
EMP: 15 EST: 2001
SALES (est): 842.1K **Privately Held**
SIC: 2844 Perfumes & colognes

(G-12862)
ALMOND JEWELERS INC
Also Called: Almond Group
16 S Maryland Ave (11050-2913)
P.O. Box 471 (11050-0135)
PHONE..............................516 933-6000
Jonathan Mandelbaum, *President*
Maurice Mandelbaum, *Vice Pres*
▲ EMP: 15
SQ FT: 3,500
SALES: 100MM **Privately Held**
SIC: 3911 Jewelry, precious metal

(G-12863)
APPLE & EVE LLC (DH)
2 Seaview Blvd Ste 100 (11050-4634)
PHONE..............................516 621-1122
Gordon Crane, *President*
John Emerson, *President*
Chris McFadden, *Regional Mgr*
Robert Mortati, *Vice Pres*
David Yarmoff, *Vice Pres*
◆ EMP: 65
SQ FT: 14,000
SALES (est): 35.7MM
SALES (corp-wide): 402MM **Privately Held**
WEB: www.appleandeve.com
SIC: 2033 Fruit juices: packaged in cans, jars, etc.
HQ: Us Juice Partners, Llc
2 Seaview Blvd
Port Washington NY 11050
516 621-1122

(G-12864)
ARENA GRAPHICS INC
Also Called: Arena Sports Center
52 Main St Frnt (11050-2952)
PHONE..............................516 767-5108
Christopher J Avazis, *President*
Steven Avazis, *Vice Pres*
EMP: 9
SQ FT: 4,700
SALES (est): 1.2MM **Privately Held**
WEB: www.arenagraphics.com
SIC: 2759 5941 2395 Screen printing; sporting goods & bicycle shops; embroidery products, except schiffli machine

(G-12865)
BOMBAY KITCHEN FOODS INC
76 S Bayles Ave (11050-3729)
PHONE..............................516 767-7401
Sanjiv Mody, *President*
Ajit Mody, *Treasurer*
Sachin Mody, *Admin Sec*
▲ EMP: 15
SQ FT: 18,000
SALES: 2.5MM **Privately Held**
SIC: 2099 Food preparations

(G-12866)
CHANNEL MANUFACTURING INC (PA)
55 Channel Dr (11050-2258)
PHONE..................................516 944-6271
Jordan Klein, *President*
▲ EMP: 25 EST: 2000
SALES (est): 2.9MM Privately Held
WEB: www.channelmfg.com
SIC: 2499 3537 Food handling & processing products, wood; industrial trucks & tractors

(G-12867)
CHATEAU IMPORTS LTD
8 Maple St Ste 10 (11050-2964)
PHONE..................................516 841-6343
James Milleew, *CEO*
EMP: 5 EST: 2011
SQ FT: 500
SALES (est): 254.8K Privately Held
SIC: 2086 Carbonated beverages, nonalcoholic: bottled & canned

(G-12868)
CHOICE MAGAZINE LISTENING INC
85 Channel Dr Ste 3 (11050-2278)
PHONE..................................516 883-8280
William O'Conner, *Chairman*
Lois Miller, *Manager*
Sondra Mochson, *Director*
EMP: 7
SALES (est): 799.7K Privately Held
WEB: www.choicemagazinelistening.org
SIC: 2721 8322 Periodicals; social services for the handicapped

(G-12869)
COMPOZ A PUZZLE INC
2 Secatoag Ave (11050-2107)
PHONE..................................516 883-2311
EMP: 5
SQ FT: 4,000
SALES: 500K Privately Held
SIC: 3944 5945 Mfg Games/Toys Ret Hobbies/Toys/Games

(G-12870)
CRHMDU ISULATIONS LLC
1 Soundview Gdns Apt C (11050-2340)
PHONE..................................516 353-7749
Carlos Heredia, *Mng Member*
EMP: 3
SALES: 2MM Privately Held
SIC: 3357 7389 Fiber optic cable (insulated);

(G-12871)
DATA PALETTE INFO SVCS LLC
35 Marino Ave (11050-4207)
PHONE..................................718 433-1060
Ravi Adaia, *Technology*
Ramil Cargullo, *Software Dev*
Joel Ronis,
▲ EMP: 75
SQ FT: 35,000
SALES (est): 10.3MM Privately Held
SIC: 2759 7331 7374 7389 Laser printing; mailing service; data processing & preparation;

(G-12872)
DIAMOND BOUTIQUE
77 Main St (11050-2929)
PHONE..................................516 444-3373
Joseph Daniel, *Owner*
EMP: 6
SALES: 2.5MM Privately Held
SIC: 3915 5944 Jewel cutting, drilling, polishing, recutting or setting; jewelry stores

(G-12873)
DJ PUBLISHING INC
25 Willowdale Ave (11050-3716)
PHONE..................................516 767-2500
Vincent P Testa, *President*
EMP: 50
SALES (est): 2.8MM Privately Held
WEB: www.testabags.com
SIC: 2721 Magazines: publishing only, not printed on site

(G-12874)
DOMA MARKETING INC
28 Haven Ave Ste 226 (11050-3646)
PHONE..................................516 684-1111
Doron Katz, *Owner*
Susan Brenman, *Manager*
EMP: 5 EST: 2012
SQ FT: 2,000
SALES: 100K Privately Held
SIC: 2066 Chocolate

(G-12875)
DRIVE MEDICAL SPV LLC
Also Called: Drive Devilbiss Healthcare
99 Seaview Blvd (11050-4606)
PHONE..................................516 998-4600
Robert J Gilligan, *CEO*
David Pugh, *President*
Nick Gargano, *Vice Pres*
Pearl Goldstein, *Vice Pres*
Jim McGuiness, *Vice Pres*
EMP: 6
SALES (est): 275.3K Privately Held
SIC: 3841 Medical instruments & equipment, blood & bone work
PA: Medical Depot, Inc.
99 Seaview Blvd Ste 210
Port Washington NY 11050

(G-12876)
E GLOBAL SOLUTIONS INC
Also Called: E G S
8 Haven Ave Ste 221 (11050-3636)
P.O. Box 771 (11050-0771)
PHONE..................................516 767-5138
Anthony Straggi, *Ch of Bd*
EMP: 6
SQ FT: 9,000
SALES (est): 690K Privately Held
SIC: 3822 Auto controls regulating residntl & coml environmt & applncs

(G-12877)
ELCO MANUFACTURING CO INC (PA)
26 Ivy Way (11050-3802)
P.O. Box 1759 (11050-7759)
PHONE..................................516 767-3577
Eric Weintraub, *President*
Stanley Weintraub, *Vice Pres*
E Nash, *Admin Sec*
EMP: 19 EST: 1904
SQ FT: 10,000
SALES: 1.5MM Privately Held
WEB: www.elcomfg.com
SIC: 3172 5199 Personal leather goods; advertising specialties

(G-12878)
EQUINE IMAGING LLC (PA)
169 Middle Neck Rd (11050-1212)
PHONE..................................414 326-0665
Geoge Papaioannou, *Mng Member*
EMP: 12
SALES: 16MM Privately Held
SIC: 3826 Analytical instruments

(G-12879)
FINER TOUCH PRINTING CORP
4 Yennicock Ave (11050-2131)
PHONE..................................516 944-8000
Kenny Cummings, *President*
EMP: 10
SQ FT: 2,500
SALES: 1.1MM Privately Held
WEB: www.comiccastle.com
SIC: 2752 Commercial printing, offset

(G-12880)
FRANKLIN-DOUGLAS INC
Also Called: Omnimusic
52 Main St Side (11050-2965)
PHONE..................................516 883-0121
Douglas Wood, *President*
Patricia Wood, *Vice Pres*
Jon Anderson, *Administration*
EMP: 12 EST: 1975
SQ FT: 4,000
SALES (est): 1.1MM Privately Held
WEB: www.omnimusic.com
SIC: 2741 Music book & sheet music publishing

(G-12881)
G & C WELDING CO INC
39 Annette Dr (11050-2803)
PHONE..................................516 883-3228
Carmine Meluzio, *President*
EMP: 5
SALES (est): 179.5K Privately Held
SIC: 7692 1799 Welding repair; welding on site

(G-12882)
HAWTHORNE GARDEN COMPANY (HQ)
Also Called: Hawthorne Gardening Co.
800 Port Washington Blvd (11050-3720)
PHONE..................................516 883-6550
James Hagedorn, *CEO*
Michael C Lukemire, *COO*
Randy Coleman, *CFO*
Ivan C Smith, *Ch Credit Ofcr*
Denise S Stump, *Officer*
EMP: 14
SALES (est): 65.8MM
SALES (corp-wide): 2.6B Publicly Held
SIC: 3542 0782 7342 Machine tools, metal forming type; lawn & garden services; pest control services
PA: The Scotts Miracle-Gro Company
14111 Scottslawn Rd
Marysville OH 43040
937 644-0011

(G-12883)
HERCULES GROUP INC
27 Seaview Blvd (11050-4610)
PHONE..................................212 813-8000
Sara Amani, *President*
▲ EMP: 20
SQ FT: 2,000
SALES (est): 4.2MM Privately Held
WEB: www.herculesgroup.com
SIC: 2385 Diaper covers, waterproof: made from purchased materials

(G-12884)
HOWMEDICA OSTEONICS CORP
95 Seaview Blvd Ste 201 (11050-4633)
PHONE..................................516 484-0897
Rich Hadrain, *Manager*
EMP: 6
SALES (corp-wide): 13.6B Publicly Held
SIC: 3842 Surgical appliances & supplies
HQ: Howmedica Osteonics Corp.
325 Corporate Dr
Mahwah NJ 07430
201 831-5000

(G-12885)
HURRYWORKS LLC
990 Seaview Blvd (11050)
PHONE..................................516 998-4600
Richard Kolodny, *CEO*
EMP: 99
SQ FT: 10,000
SALES (est): 2.5MM Privately Held
SIC: 3841 Surgical & medical instruments

(G-12886)
IDENTFICATION DATA IMAGING LLC
Also Called: IDI
26 Harbor Park Dr (11050-4602)
PHONE..................................516 484-6500
Pat Screnzel,
Jeffrey Brodsky,
▼ EMP: 6
SQ FT: 1,300
SALES (est): 590.7K Privately Held
WEB: www.idius.com
SIC: 3999 Identification badges & insignia

(G-12887)
IDEOLI GROUP INC
20w Vanderventer Ave LI (11050-3700)
PHONE..................................212 705-8769
George Stroumboulis, *CEO*
Chris Hartswick,
EMP: 10
SQ FT: 2,000
SALES: 213K Privately Held
SIC: 2599 3646 Bar, restaurant & cafeteria furniture; commercial indusl & institutional electric lighting fixtures

(G-12888)
INDUSTRIAL TEST EQP CO INC
2 Manhasset Ave (11050-2008)
PHONE..................................516 883-6423
Jay Monroe, *President*
Barbara Monroe, *Admin Sec*
EMP: 20
SQ FT: 8,000
SALES: 1MM Privately Held
WEB: www.rf-pwr-amps.com
SIC: 3621 3829 2759 Generating apparatus & parts, electrical; gas detectors; tags: printing

(G-12889)
INTECH 21 INC
21 Harbor Park Dr (11050-4658)
PHONE..................................516 626-7221
George Y Bilenko, *President*
Victor Zelmanovich, *Exec VP*
Jules Leibman, *Shareholder*
▲ EMP: 12
SQ FT: 8,000
SALES (est): 1.8MM Privately Held
WEB: www.intech21.com
SIC: 3674 Computer logic modules

(G-12890)
IVY ENTERPRISES INC (HQ)
25 Harbor Park Dr (11050-4605)
PHONE..................................516 621-9779
Hee J Chang, *President*
Rick Price, *Vice Pres*
Peter Kim, *Controller*
Sara Chang, *Asst Mgr*
Tom Brancato, *Director*
▲ EMP: 500
SALES (est): 26.9MM
SALES (corp-wide): 43.1MM Privately Held
SIC: 3999 5087 Fingernails, artificial; beauty parlor equipment & supplies
PA: Kiss Nail Products, Inc.
25 Harbor Park Dr
Port Washington NY 11050
516 625-9292

(G-12891)
JAIDAN INDUSTRIES INC
Also Called: Absolute Business Products
16 Capi Ln (11050-3410)
PHONE..................................516 944-3650
Richard Sussman, *President*
Rhonda Sussman, *Human Res Mgr*
▲ EMP: 16
SALES (est): 3.5MM Privately Held
WEB: www.jaidan.com
SIC: 3442 Window & door frames; moldings & trim, except automobile: metal

(G-12892)
JESCO LIGHTING INC
15 Harbor Park Dr (11050-4604)
PHONE..................................718 366-3211
Richard Kurtz, *Chairman*
Edward MA, *Chairman*
Paulin Tham, *VP Mktg*
▲ EMP: 50
SQ FT: 70,000
SALES (est): 11.7MM Privately Held
SIC: 3646 Commercial indusl & institutional electric lighting fixtures

(G-12893)
JESCO LIGHTING GROUP LLC (PA)
15 Harbor Park Dr (11050-4604)
PHONE..................................718 366-3211
Richard Kurtz, *President*
Dmitriy Ostrovskiy, *Director*
Mark Wolff, *Director*
Maria Aziz, *Executive*
▲ EMP: 50
SQ FT: 70,000
SALES (est): 8.6MM Privately Held
SIC: 3646 Commercial indusl & institutional electric lighting fixtures

(G-12894)
JWIN ELECTRONICS CORP (PA)
Also Called: Iluv
2 Harbor Park Dr (11050-4602)
PHONE..................................516 626-7188
Justin Kim, *CEO*
Dena Kim, *Exec VP*
Kevin Lim, *CFO*

▲ = Import ▼=Export
◆ =Import/Export

◆ **EMP:** 110
SQ FT: 132,000
SALES (est) 19.5MM **Privately Held**
WEB: www.jwin.com
SIC: 3651 Television receiving sets; radio receiving sets; home entertainment equipment, electronic

(G-12895)
KITTYWALK SYSTEMS INC
10 Farmview Rd (11050-4511)
PHONE................516 627-8418
Jeff King, *CEO*
Lise King, *President*
▲ **EMP:** 2
SALES: 1MM **Privately Held**
SIC: 3999 Pet supplies

(G-12896)
KLEARBAR INC
8 Graywood Rd (11050-1516)
PHONE................516 684-9892
Mark Klein, *President*
Scott Bercu, *Admin Sec*
▲ **EMP:** 5
SALES (est) 408.2K **Privately Held**
SIC: 3585 Soda fountain & beverage dispensing equipment & parts

(G-12897)
KRAUS USA INC
12 Harbor Park Dr (11050-4649)
PHONE................800 775-0703
Russel Levi, *President*
Russell Levi, *President*
Michael Rukhlin, *Principal*
Daniel Lusby, *CFO*
Kathy Rivera, *Sales Staff*
▲ **EMP:** 10
SQ FT: 37,500
SALES (est) 2.5MM **Privately Held**
SIC: 3431 3261 Bathroom fixtures, including sinks; sinks: enameled iron, cast iron or pressed metal; sinks, vitreous china

(G-12898)
KURTSKRAFT INC
Also Called: Minuteman Press
437 Port Washington Blvd (11050-4225)
PHONE................516 944-4449
Joel Ronis, *President*
EMP: 5
SQ FT: 1,700
SALES: 1MM **Privately Held**
SIC: 2752 2759 Commercial printing, lithographic; invitation & stationery printing & engraving

(G-12899)
LIF INDUSTRIES INC (PA)
Also Called: Long Island Fireproof Door
5 Harbor Park Dr Ste 1 (11050-4698)
PHONE................516 390-6800
Vincent Gallo, *Ch of Bd*
Joseph Gallo Jr, *President*
Anthony Gallo, *Vice Pres*
Michelle Kim, *Project Mgr*
Jerry Napolionello, *Project Mgr*
EMP: 76
SQ FT: 85,000
SALES (est) 22.9MM **Privately Held**
WEB: www.lifi.net
SIC: 3442 5031 Metal doors; window & door frames; door frames, all materials

(G-12900)
LIFC CORP
101 Haven Ave (11050-3936)
PHONE................516 426-5737
Brian Kenny, *President*
EMP: 5
SALES (est) 410K **Privately Held**
SIC: 3569 5812 Firefighting apparatus & related equipment; caterers

(G-12901)
LTS NY INC
99 Seaview Blvd Ste 1b (11050-4632)
PHONE................646 558-3888
Richard Kang, *President*
Vivian Cheng, *Business Mgr*
Alice Liu, *Accounts Mgr*
Tiffany Pridanonda, *Accounts Exec*
Vincent Tran, *Executive*
EMP: 5 EST: 2015

SALES (est) 188.7K **Privately Held**
SIC: 3699 Security devices

(G-12902)
LUXOTTICA OF AMERICA INC
44 Harbor Park Dr (11050-4652)
PHONE................516 484-3800
Michael Braine, *Vice Pres*
Chris Nuzzi, *Marketing Staff*
Luca Biondolillo, *Director*
EMP: 200
SALES (corp-wide) 1.4MM **Privately Held**
SIC: 3851 5048 5099 Ophthalmic goods; frames, ophthalmic; sunglasses
HQ: Luxottica Of America Inc.
4000 Luxottica Pl
Mason OH 45040

(G-12903)
M R C INDUSTRIES INC
Also Called: Mason Medical Products
99 Seaview Blvd Ste 210 (11050-4632)
P.O. Box 609 (11050-0609)
PHONE................516 328-6900
Leonard Horowitz, *CEO*
Bernice Wien, *Treasurer*
◆ **EMP:** 200
SQ FT: 60,000
SALES (est) 22.2MM **Privately Held**
WEB: www.masonmedical.com
SIC: 2515 Mattresses & foundations

(G-12904)
MEDER TEXTILE CO INC
20 Lynn Rd (11050-4437)
PHONE................516 883-0409
Bruce T Lindemann, *President*
EMP: 4 EST: 1936
SQ FT: 500
SALES: 1MM **Privately Held**
SIC: 2211 Upholstery fabrics, cotton

(G-12905)
MEDICAL DEPOT INC (PA)
Also Called: Drive Devilbiss Healthcare
99 Seaview Blvd Ste 210 (11050-4632)
P.O. Box 842450, Boston MA (02284-2450)
PHONE................516 998-4600
Robert J Gilligan, *CEO*
Kelly Devine, *President*
Thomas Reynolds, *President*
Kurt Rudolph, *Business Mgr*
Jeff Schwartz, *Exec VP*
◆ **EMP:** 250
SQ FT: 43,159
SALES (est) 378.6MM **Privately Held**
WEB: www.drivemedical.com
SIC: 3841 Surgical & medical instruments

(G-12906)
MEDSAFE SYSTEMS INC
46 Orchard Farm Rd (11050-3338)
PHONE................516 883-8222
Bernard Shore, *President*
EMP: 6
SQ FT: 1,000
SALES: 1.2MM **Privately Held**
SIC: 3823 Telemetering instruments, industrial process type

(G-12907)
MEKATRONICS INCORPORATED
85 Channel Dr Ste 2 (11050-2248)
PHONE................516 883-6805
Jack Bendror, *President*
Bob Ferrando, *Opers Mgr*
▲ **EMP:** 24
SQ FT: 30,000
SALES (est) 4MM **Privately Held**
SIC: 3679 3555 3861 Electronic circuits; printing trades machinery; microfilm equipment: cameras, projectors, readers, etc.

(G-12908)
MUSIC & SOUND RETAILER INC
Also Called: Retailer, The
25 Willowdale Ave (11050-3716)
PHONE................516 767-2500
Vincent Testa, *President*
EMP: 28
SQ FT: 1,500
SALES (est) 1.7MM **Privately Held**
SIC: 2721 Magazines: publishing only, not printed on site

(G-12909)
N Y BIJOUX CORP
33 Sands Point Rd (11050-1625)
PHONE................212 244-9585
Hylong Kim, *President*
▲ **EMP:** 5
SALES (est) 687.9K **Privately Held**
WEB: www.nybijouxcorp.com
SIC: 3911 Jewelry, precious metal

(G-12910)
OSWALD MANUFACTURING CO INC
65 Channel Dr (11050-2216)
PHONE................516 883-8850
Fred Oswald, *President*
Angella Oswald, *Vice Pres*
▲ **EMP:** 30
SQ FT: 22,000
SALES (est) 3.9MM **Privately Held**
SIC: 3531 Construction machinery

(G-12911)
OZTECK INDUSTRIES INC
65 Channel Dr (11050-2216)
PHONE................516 883-8857
Fred Oswald, *President*
Angella Oswald, *Vice Pres*
Tiffany Shackatano, *Vice Pres*
◆ **EMP:** 40
SQ FT: 22,000
SALES (est) 10MM **Privately Held**
WEB: www.oztec.com
SIC: 3531 Vibrators for concrete construction; surfacers, concrete grinding

(G-12912)
PALL BIOMEDICAL INC
Also Called: Pall Medical
25 Harbor Park Dr (11050-4605)
PHONE................516 484-3600
Eric Kransnoff, *Principal*
Stella Rivera, *Human Res Mgr*
▲ **EMP:** 200
SALES (est) 31.5MM
SALES (corp-wide) 19.8B **Publicly Held**
WEB: www.pall.com
SIC: 3842 Surgical appliances & supplies
HQ: Pall Corporation
25 Harbor Park Dr
Port Washington NY 11050
516 484-5400

(G-12913)
PALL CORPORATION (HQ)
Also Called: Pall Aerospace
25 Harbor Park Dr (11050-4664)
PHONE................516 484-5400
Rainer Blair, *President*
Yves Baratelli, *President*
Michael Egholm, *President*
Naresh Narasimhan, *President*
Wayne Miller, *Business Mgr*
▲ **EMP:** 1200 EST: 1946
SQ FT: 25,000
SALES (est) 2.5B
SALES (corp-wide) 19.8B **Publicly Held**
WEB: www.pall.com
SIC: 3714 3569 3599 2834 Filters: oil, fuel & air, motor vehicle; filters; filters, general line: industrial; filter elements, fluid, hydraulic line; separators for steam, gas, vapor or air (machinery); air intake filters, internal combustion engine, except auto; gasoline filters, internal combustion engine, except auto; oil filters, internal combustion engine, except automotive; solutions, pharmaceutical; surgical & medical instruments; IV transfusion apparatus
PA: Danaher Corporation
2200 Penn Ave Nw Ste 800w
Washington DC 20037
202 828-0850

(G-12914)
PALL CORPORATION
Also Called: Pall Life Sciences
25 Harbor Park Dr (11050-4664)
PHONE................516 484-2818
Noelle Britton, *Vice Pres*
Paul Dittman, *Vice Pres*
Eric Janson, *Engineer*
Tore Lindstrom, *Engineer*
Paul Mendoza, *Finance*
EMP: 750

SALES (corp-wide) 19.8B **Publicly Held**
WEB: www.pall.com
SIC: 3842 Surgical appliances & supplies
HQ: Pall Corporation
25 Harbor Park Dr
Port Washington NY 11050
516 484-5400

(G-12915)
PREMIER HEART LLC
110 Main St (11050-2860)
PHONE................516 883-3383
Joseph T Shen, *Med Doctor*
Joseph Shen MD, *Mng Member*
James Mann, *Manager*
Richard Hayden,
EMP: 5
SQ FT: 3,000
SALES: 1.2MM **Privately Held**
SIC: 7372 Business oriented computer software

(G-12916)
PROFICIENT SURGICAL EQP INC
99 Seaview Blvd Ste 1c (11050-4632)
PHONE................516 487-1175
Steven Baum, *President*
Chris Fiengo, *Sales Staff*
Jason Vacca, *Sales Staff*
Michael Albano, *Sales Executive*
Alicia Mamarella, *Office Mgr*
▲ **EMP:** 6 EST: 1996
SALES (est) 710K **Privately Held**
WEB: www.proficientsurgical.com
SIC: 3842 Surgical appliances & supplies

(G-12917)
RADNOR-WALLACE (PA)
921 Port Washington Blvd # 1 (11050-2976)
PHONE................516 767-2131
Michael O'Beirne, *Director*
EMP: 5
SQ FT: 600
SALES: 500K **Privately Held**
WEB: www.radnorwallace.com
SIC: 7372 Prepackaged software

(G-12918)
ROAR BEVERAGES LLC
2 Seaview Blvd Fl 3 (11050-4634)
PHONE................631 683-5565
Roland Neffey, *CEO*
John Behling, *General Mgr*
Vincent Nesi, *COO*
Andrew Zambratto, *Vice Pres*
▼ **EMP:** 21
SALES: 7MM **Privately Held**
SIC: 2087 Concentrates, drink

(G-12919)
ROBERT BARTHOLOMEW LTD
Also Called: Magnus Sands Point Shop
15 Main St (11050-2916)
PHONE................516 767-2970
Robert C Mazza, *President*
Robert S Mazza, *President*
Donal Keogh, *President*
Laura Mazza, *Vice Pres*
EMP: 32
SQ FT: 12,000
SALES (est) 5.1MM **Privately Held**
WEB: www.robertbartholomew.com
SIC: 3911 Jewelry, precious metal

(G-12920)
SAFAVIEH INC
40 Harbor Park Dr (11050-4602)
PHONE................516 945-1900
Mohsen Yaraghi, *Ch of Bd*
EMP: 525
SALES (est) 350MM **Privately Held**
SIC: 2273 5712 Rugs, hand & machine made; furniture stores

(G-12921)
SAINT HONORE PASTRY SHOP INC
993 Port Washington Blvd (11050-2910)
PHONE................516 767-2555
Jacques Leguelaf, *President*
EMP: 5
SQ FT: 1,500

SALES (est): 270K **Privately Held**
SIC: 2051 5461 Bread, cake & related products; bakeries

(G-12922)
SANREX CORPORATION
50 Seaview Blvd Ste 2 (11050-4615)
PHONE..............................516 625-1313
Ryoji Fujimoto, *President*
▲ **EMP:** 15
SQ FT: 13,000
SALES: 13.8MM **Privately Held**
WEB: www.sanrex.com
SIC: 3674 Semiconductors & related devices
PA: Sansha Electric Manufacturing Co.,Ltd.
3-1-56, Nishiawaji, Higashiyodogawa-Ku
Osaka OSK 533-0

(G-12923)
SCHOLIUM INTERNATIONAL INC
151 Cow Neck Rd (11050-1143)
PHONE..............................516 883-8032
Arthur A Candido, *President*
Elena M Candido, *Vice Pres*
EMP: 5 **EST:** 1970
SQ FT: 1,800
SALES (est): 319.2K **Privately Held**
WEB: www.scholium.com
SIC: 2731 5192 Book publishing; books

(G-12924)
SHAKE-N-GO FASHION INC
83 Harbor Rd (11050-2535)
PHONE..............................516 944-7777
EMP: 48
SALES (corp-wide): 315.2MM **Privately Held**
SIC: 3999 Hairpin mountings
PA: Shake-N-Go Fashion, Inc.
85 Harbor Rd
Port Washington NY 11050
516 944-7777

(G-12925)
SHAKE-N-GO FASHION INC (PA)
85 Harbor Rd (11050-2535)
PHONE..............................516 944-7777
James K Kim, *Ch of Bd*
Danny Khym, *COO*
Mike Kim, *Vice Pres*
Betty Kim, *Treasurer*
Jessica Cho, *Controller*
◆ **EMP:** 200
SQ FT: 75,000
SALES (est): 315.2MM **Privately Held**
WEB: www.shake-n-gofashions.com
SIC: 3999 Hairpin mountings; wigs, including doll wigs, toupees or wiglets

(G-12926)
SHARODINE INC
18 Haven Ave Frnt 2 (11050-3642)
PHONE..............................516 767-3548
Ron Sharoni, *President*
EMP: 9
SALES (est): 1.3MM **Privately Held**
SIC: 3911 Jewelry, precious metal

(G-12927)
SOUND COMMUNICATIONS INC
25 Willowdale Ave (11050-3716)
PHONE..............................516 767-2500
Vincent Testa, *President*
Fred Gumm, *Art Dir*
EMP: 40
SALES (est): 2.2MM **Privately Held**
SIC: 2721 Magazines: publishing only, not printed on site

(G-12928)
SWITCH BEVERAGE COMPANY LLC
2 Seaview Blvd Fl 3 (11050-4634)
PHONE..............................203 202-7383
Brian Boyd, *CEO*
Maura Mottolese, *President*
EMP: 11
SQ FT: 1,200

SALES (est): 767.3K
SALES (corp-wide): 402MM **Privately Held**
WEB: www.switchbev.com
SIC: 2096 2086 Potato chips & similar snacks; carbonated beverages, nonalcoholic: bottled & canned
HQ: Apple & Eve, Llc
2 Seaview Blvd Ste 100
Port Washington NY 11050
516 621-1122

(G-12929)
TESTA COMMUNICATIONS INC
Also Called: Sound & Communication
25 Willowdale Ave (11050-3716)
PHONE..............................516 767-2500
Vincent Testa, *President*
Chris Caruso, *Editor*
Steve Thorakos, *Prdtn Mgr*
Robin Hazan, *Office Mgr*
Anthony Vargas, *Assoc Editor*
EMP: 40
SQ FT: 1,500
SALES (est): 4.2MM **Privately Held**
WEB: www.testa.com
SIC: 2721 Magazines: publishing only, not printed on site

(G-12930)
US JUICE PARTNERS LLC (DH)
Also Called: Apple
2 Seaview Blvd (11050-4614)
PHONE..............................516 621-1122
Pierre-Paul Lassonde, *Ch of Bd*
EMP: 5
SALES (est): 35.7MM
SALES (corp-wide): 402MM **Privately Held**
SIC: 2033 Fruit juices: packaged in cans, jars, etc.
HQ: Industries Lassonde Inc
755 Rue Principale
Rougemont QC J0L 1
450 469-4926

(G-12931)
WELL-MADE TOY MFG CORPORATION
146 Soundview Dr (11050-1751)
PHONE..............................718 381-4225
Fred F Catapano, *President*
▲ **EMP:** 20
SALES (est): 2.8MM **Privately Held**
WEB: www.wellmadetoy.com
SIC: 3942 Stuffed toys, including animals

Portageville
Wyoming County

(G-12932)
FILLMORE GREENHOUSES INC
11589 State Route 19a (14536-9611)
PHONE..............................585 567-2678
Mario Van Logten, *Chairman*
▲ **EMP:** 45
SALES (est): 6.6MM **Privately Held**
SIC: 3448 Greenhouses: prefabricated metal

Portland
Chautauqua County

(G-12933)
OLDE CHTQUA VNEYARDS LTD LBLTY
Also Called: Twentyone Brix Winery
6654 W Main Rd (14769-9621)
PHONE..............................716 792-2749
Kris Kane, *General Mgr*
Marion Jordan, *General Mgr*
Jay Hardenburg, *Manager*
Bryan Jordan,
Michael Jordan,
EMP: 12
SQ FT: 10,000
SALES (est): 1.3MM **Privately Held**
SIC: 2084 5921 Wines; wine

Portville
Cattaraugus County

(G-12934)
FIBERCEL PACKAGING LLC (HQ)
46 Brooklyn St (14770-9529)
P.O. Box 610 (14770-0610)
PHONE..............................716 933-8703
Bruce E Olson,
Richard Flanagan,
Gale Hastings,
Robert T Hinett,
Cheryl A Leblanc,
EMP: 28
SQ FT: 7,200
SALES (est): 10.9MM **Privately Held**
SIC: 2621 Paper mills

(G-12935)
IA CONSTRUCTION CORPORATION
Also Called: Portville Sand & Gravel Div
Rr 305 Box S (14770)
PHONE..............................716 933-8787
John Taylor, *Sales/Mktg Mgr*
William Slavin, *Manager*
EMP: 5
SQ FT: 1,800
SALES (corp-wide): 83.5MM **Privately Held**
WEB: www.iaconstruction.com
SIC: 1442 Gravel mining
HQ: Ia Construction Corporation
24 Gibb Rd
Franklin PA 16323
814 432-3184

Potsdam
St. Lawrence County

(G-12936)
DONALD SNYDER JR
Also Called: Donald Snyder Jr Logging
528 Allen Falls Rd (13676-4032)
PHONE..............................315 265-4485
EMP: 15
SALES (est): 1.1MM **Privately Held**
SIC: 2411 Logging

(G-12937)
LCDRIVES CORP
Also Called: Lc Drives
67 Main St (13676-2037)
PHONE..............................860 712-8926
Russel Marvin, *CEO*
Scott McNulty, *Vice Pres*
Nigel Shepherd, *Vice Pres*
Mark Sperry, *Vice Pres*
Rob Tremper, *CFO*
EMP: 40 **EST:** 2012
SALES (est): 2.3MM **Privately Held**
SIC: 3621 Motors & generators

(G-12938)
NORTH COUNTRY THIS WEEK INC
Also Called: Northcountrynow.com
4 Clarkson Ave (13676-1409)
P.O. Box 975 (13676-0975)
PHONE..............................315 265-1000
William C Shumway, *President*
EMP: 21
SQ FT: 2,000
SALES (est): 850K **Privately Held**
WEB: www.northcountrynow.com
SIC: 2711 Newspapers: publishing only, not printed on site

(G-12939)
POTSDAM SPECIALTY PAPER INC
Also Called: Pspi
547a Sissonville Rd (13676-3549)
PHONE..............................315 265-4000
Mike Huth, *CEO*
WEI Qun Zhang, *President*
Roxanne Kilgore, *Senior Buyer*
Joel Behm, *Technical Mgr*
Cathy Brothers, *Controller*

◆ **EMP:** 70
SQ FT: 18,400
SALES (est): 13.6MM **Privately Held**
SIC: 2621 Paper mills
PA: Seafront (Hong Kong) Company Limited
Rm B 9/F Sun Hing Steel Furniture Coml Bldg
Mongkok KLN

(G-12940)
RANDY SIXBERRY
Also Called: Great Northern Printing Co
6 Main St Ste 101 (13676-2066)
P.O. Box 270 (13676-0270)
PHONE..............................315 265-6211
Randy Sixberry, *Owner*
Ranah Matott, *Corp Secy*
EMP: 7
SQ FT: 3,800
SALES (est): 700K **Privately Held**
SIC: 2396 5699 Screen printing on fabric articles; T-shirts, custom printed

(G-12941)
SNYDER LOGGING
528 Allen Falls Rd (13676-4032)
PHONE..............................315 265-1462
Donald Snyder, *Owner*
EMP: 12
SALES (est): 605.6K **Privately Held**
SIC: 2411 Logging camps & contractors

(G-12942)
SUNFEATHER NATURAL SOAP CO INC
Also Called: Sunfeather Herbal Soap
1551 State Highway 72 (13676-4031)
PHONE..............................315 265-1776
Sandra Maine, *CEO*
EMP: 8
SQ FT: 6,000
SALES (est): 930K **Privately Held**
WEB: www.sunsoap.com
SIC: 2841 Soap & other detergents

Poughkeepsie
Dutchess County

(G-12943)
AMERICAN HORMONES INC
69 W Cedar St Ste 2 (12601-2608)
PHONE..............................845 471-7272
Salvatore J Rubino, *Principal*
Ashok Kadambi, *Principal*
Govind Gill, *Lab Dir*
EMP: 12
SALES (est): 2.6MM **Privately Held**
WEB: www.americanhormones.com
SIC: 2834 Hormone preparations

(G-12944)
APPARATUS MFG INC
13 Commerce St (12603-2608)
PHONE..............................845 471-5116
Norman Murley, *President*
Chris Murley, *Manager*
Nick Murley, *Manager*
EMP: 6
SQ FT: 7,500
SALES: 600K **Privately Held**
WEB: www.apparatusmfg.com
SIC: 3444 Sheet metal specialties, not stamped

(G-12945)
ATLANTIS ENERGY SYSTEMS INC (PA)
7 Industry St (12603-2617)
PHONE..............................845 486-4052
Frank Pao, *Principal*
Joe Morrissey, *Vice Pres*
▲ **EMP:** 10
SALES (est): 2.5MM **Privately Held**
SIC: 3674 Solar cells

(G-12946)
ATLANTIS ENERGY SYSTEMS INC
7 Industry St (12603-2617)
PHONE..............................916 438-2930
Frank Pao, *President*
Eleanor Pao, *Director*

▲ = Import ▼=Export
◆ =Import/Export

EMP: 3
SQ FT: 10,000
SALES (est): 1.4MM Privately Held
SIC: 3674 3433 Semiconductors & related
devices; solar heaters & collectors

(G-12947)
AW MACK MANUFACTURING CO INC
1098 Dutchess Tpke (12603-1150)
P.O. Box 2956 (12603-8956)
PHONE..................................845 452-4050
Albert Mack, *CEO*
John Mack, *Vice Pres*
Fred Gerth, *Foreman/Supr*
Diane Conners, *Office Mgr*
EMP: 16
SQ FT: 19,000
SALES (est): 2.3MM Privately Held
SIC: 3599 Machine shop, jobbing & repair

(G-12948)
CETEK INC
19 Commerce St (12603-2608)
PHONE..................................845 452-3510
Fayiz Hilal, *President*
John Hilal, *Vice Pres*
▲ **EMP:** 37
SQ FT: 20,000
SALES (est): 3.9MM Privately Held
SIC: 3299 3599 3444 3825 Ceramic
fiber; machine shop, jobbing & repair;
forming machine work, sheet metal; in-
struments to measure electricity; porce-
lain electrical supplies

(G-12949)
CHOCOVISION CORPORATION (PA)
331 Main St (12601-3145)
PHONE..................................845 473-8003
Aneel Potluri, *President*
Ian Lazarus, *Vice Pres*
Matt D'Amato, *Purchasing*
◆ **EMP:** 10
SALES: 3MM Privately Held
WEB: www.chocovision.com
SIC: 3599 Custom machinery

(G-12950)
CREATIVE COUNTER TOPS INC
17 Van Kleeck Dr (12601-2163)
PHONE..................................845 471-6480
Andrew Schor, *President*
EMP: 12
SALES: 600K Privately Held
SIC: 2541 Counters or counter display
cases, wood; cabinets, except refriger-
ated: show, display, etc.: wood

(G-12951)
DORSEY METROLOGY INTL INC
53 Oakley St (12601-2004)
PHONE..................................845 229-2929
Devon Luty, *President*
Peter Klepp, *President*
Mark Swenson, *Vice Pres*
Courtney Britton, *Engineer*
John Giannetti, *Engineer*
EMP: 40
SQ FT: 18,000
SALES: 6MM Privately Held
WEB: www.dorseymetrology.com
SIC: 3545 5084 3827 3699 Gauges (ma-
chine tool accessories); precision tools,
machinists'; industrial machinery & equip-
ment; optical instruments & lenses; opti-
cal comparators; electrical equipment &
supplies

(G-12952)
DYSON-KISSNER-MORAN CORP (PA)
2515 South Rd Ste 5 (12601-5474)
PHONE..................................212 661-4600
Robert R Dyson, *Ch of Bd*
Michael J Harris, *President*
Lynn J McCluskey, *Treasurer*
Steve Colantonio, *Accountant*
Christopher Dyson, *Bd of Directors*
◆ **EMP:** 30
SALES (est): 482MM Privately Held
SIC: 3433 3625 3699 Gas burners, indus-
trial; motor controls, electric; security de-
vices

(G-12953)
EAW ELECTRONIC SYSTEMS INC
900 Dutchess Tpke Ste 3 (12603-1554)
PHONE..................................845 471-5290
Victoria Winiarski, *President*
Edward Winiarski, *Vice Pres*
EMP: 7
SALES (est): 1.3MM Privately Held
WEB: www.eawelectro.com
SIC: 3568 Power transmission equipment

(G-12954)
FACES MAGAZINE INC (PA)
46 Violet Ave (12601-1521)
PHONE..................................201 843-4004
▲ **EMP:** 18
SALES (est): 3.3MM Privately Held
SIC: 2721 Teen Magazine Publisher

(G-12955)
FACES MAGAZINE INC
40 Violet Ave (12601-1521)
PHONE..................................845 454-7420
EMP: 100
SALES (corp-wide): 3.3MM Privately
Held
SIC: 2731 Books-Publishing/Printing
PA: Faces Magazine Inc
46 Violet Ave
Poughkeepsie NY 12601
201 843-4004

(G-12956)
GANNETT STLLITE INFO NTWRK LLC
Also Called: Poughkeepsie Journal
85 Civic Center Plz (12601-2498)
P.O. Box 1231 (12602-1231)
PHONE..................................845 454-2000
Barry Rothfeld, *Branch Mgr*
EMP: 250
SALES (corp-wide): 2.9B Publicly Held
WEB: www.usatoday.com
SIC: 2711 Newspapers, publishing & print-
ing
HQ: Gannett Satellite Information Network,
Llc
7950 Jones Branch Dr
Mc Lean VA 22102
703 854-6000

(G-12957)
GET REAL SURFACES INC (PA)
121 Washington St (12601-1806)
PHONE..................................845 337-4483
George Bishop, *President*
Avis Bishop, *Vice Pres*
▼ **EMP:** 33
SQ FT: 19,800
SALES (est): 6.4MM Privately Held
WEB: www.getrealsurfaces.com
SIC: 3271 3272 Architectural concrete:
block, split, fluted, screen, etc.; concrete
products

(G-12958)
GLOEDE NEON SIGNS LTD INC
97 N Clinton St (12601-2032)
PHONE..................................845 471-4366
Barbara Fitzgerald, *President*
Todd Lanthier, *Opers Mgr*
EMP: 12 EST: 1922
SQ FT: 9,500
SALES (est): 1.7MM Privately Held
WEB: www.gloedesigns.com
SIC: 3993 1799 Electric signs; neon signs;
sign installation & maintenance

(G-12959)
GREAT EASTERN COLOR LITH (PA)
46 Violet Ave (12601-1599)
PHONE..................................845 454-7420
Lawrence Perretta, *President*
Louis Perretta Jr, *Vice Pres*
EMP: 150 EST: 1949
SQ FT: 115,000
SALES (est): 15.1MM Privately Held
WEB: www.magnapublishing.com
SIC: 2752 Commercial printing, offset

(G-12960)
GW MANUFACTURING
Also Called: G W Manufacturing
46 Violet Ave (12601-1521)
PHONE..................................718 386-8078
George Stavilla, *President*
▲ **EMP:** 32
SALES (est): 5.5MM Privately Held
SIC: 2431 Millwork

(G-12961)
HATFIELD METAL FAB INC
16 Hatfield Ln (12603-6250)
PHONE..................................845 454-9078
Ann Hatfield, *Ch of Bd*
Chris Hatfield, *Vice Pres*
Christopher Hatfield, *Vice Pres*
Henry Hatfield, *Vice Pres*
EMP: 45
SQ FT: 60,000
SALES (est): 10.6MM Privately Held
WEB: www.hatfieldmetal.com
SIC: 3444 5051 3479 3499 Sheet metal
specialties, not stamped; sheets, metal;
painting, coating & hot dipping; metal
household articles

(G-12962)
HVR MSO LLC
Also Called: Radloop
2678 South Rd Ste 202 (12601-5254)
PHONE..................................833 345-6974
Richard Friedland, *Mng Member*
Justin Wadsworth,
EMP: 5
SALES: 350K Privately Held
SIC: 7372 Application computer software

(G-12963)
INTERNATIONAL BUS MCHS CORP
Also Called: IBM
2455 South Rd (12601-5463)
PHONE..................................845 433-1234
Dave Turek, *President*
Gary Napolitano, *Vice Pres*
Maureen Lo, *Purch Mgr*
Rebecca Howard, *Engineer*
Richard Kordzikowski, *Engineer*
EMP: 4500
SALES (corp-wide): 79.5B Publicly Held
WEB: www.ibm.com
SIC: 3571 Electronic computers
PA: International Business Machines Cor-
poration
1 New Orchard Rd Ste 1 # 1
Armonk NY 10504
914 499-1900

(G-12964)
JAMES L TAYLOR MFG CO (PA)
Also Called: James L. Taylor Mfg.
130 Salt Point Tpke (12603-1016)
PHONE..................................845 452-3780
Michael Burdis, *CEO*
Bradley Quick, *Vice Pres*
Emily Burdis, *Marketing Staff*
◆ **EMP:** 21 EST: 1911
SALES (est): 4MM Privately Held
WEB: www.jltclamps.com
SIC: 3553 Woodworking machinery

(G-12965)
JAMES L TAYLOR MFG CO
Also Called: Jlt Lancaster Clamps Div
130 Salt Point Tpke (12603-1016)
PHONE..................................845 452-3780
Michael Burdis, *President*
EMP: 9
SALES (corp-wide): 4MM Privately Held
WEB: www.jltclamps.com
SIC: 3553 Woodworking machinery
PA: James L. Taylor Manufacturing Co.
130 Salt Point Tpke
Poughkeepsie NY 12603
845 452-3780

(G-12966)
KOSHII MAXELUM AMERICA INC
12 Van Kleeck Dr (12601-2164)
P.O. Box 352 (12602-0352)
PHONE..................................845 471-0500
Mick Morita, *Ch of Bd*
John Macisaac, *Human Res Mgr*

Michele Niles, *Executive*
▲ **EMP:** 34
SQ FT: 60,000
SALES (est): 6.8MM Privately Held
WEB: www.kmamax.com
SIC: 3743 Railway maintenance cars
PA: Koshii & Co., Ltd.
1-2-158, Hirabayashikita, Suminoe-Ku
Osaka OSK 559-0

(G-12967)
LJMM INC
Also Called: Nilda Desserts
188 Washington St (12601-1357)
PHONE..................................845 454-5876
Linda Tritto, *President*
Jason Tritto, *Vice Pres*
EMP: 20
SQ FT: 4,000
SALES: 1.2MM Privately Held
SIC: 2051 Bakery: wholesale or whole-
sale/retail combined

(G-12968)
MACHINE TECHNOLOGY INC
104 Bushwick Rd (12603-3813)
PHONE..................................845 454-4030
Klaus Greinacher, *President*
EMP: 5
SQ FT: 3,500
SALES (est): 430K Privately Held
SIC: 3829 Measuring & controlling devices

(G-12969)
MARCO MANUFACTURING INC
55 Page Park Dr (12603-2583)
P.O. Box 3733 (12603-0733)
PHONE..................................845 485-1571
Michael Ratliff, *President*
Brian Lowe, *Opers Mgr*
Jim Burger, *Materials Mgr*
Dan Buschel, *Engineer*
Timothy McMorris, *Sales Mgr*
EMP: 40
SQ FT: 10,000
SALES (est): 9.7MM Privately Held
WEB: www.marcomanf.com
SIC: 3672 Printed circuit boards

(G-12970)
MID HDSON WKSHP FOR THE DSBLED
188 Washington St (12601-1357)
PHONE..................................845 471-3820
Robert Nellis, *President*
Richard Stark, *Vice Pres*
▲ **EMP:** 25
SQ FT: 52,000
SALES: 762.5K Privately Held
WEB: www.midhudsonworkshop.com
SIC: 3679 Electronic circuits

(G-12971)
MODERN CABINET COMPANY INC
Also Called: Kitchen Cabinet Co
17 Van Kleeck Dr (12601-2163)
PHONE..................................845 473-4900
Andrew Schor, *President*
Lisa Turner, *Vice Pres*
Maxine Schor, *Treasurer*
EMP: 45
SQ FT: 21,000
SALES (est): 6.2MM Privately Held
SIC: 2434 Wood kitchen cabinets

(G-12972)
MPI INCORPORATED (PA)
165 Smith St Stop 3 (12601-2108)
PHONE..................................845 471-7630
Bruce S Phipps, *Ch of Bd*
Michael Goudy, *Vice Pres*
Bill Nicholas, *Plant Mgr*
Chris Chmura, *Project Mgr*
Luwana James, *Mfg Staff*
▼ **EMP:** 109 EST: 1951
SQ FT: 30,000
SALES (est): 18.1MM Privately Held
WEB: www.mpi-systems.com
SIC: 3542 Pressing machines

(G-12973)
MR SMOOTHIE
207 South Ave Ste F102 (12601)
PHONE..................................845 296-1686
Robert Botllieri, *Branch Mgr*

EMP: 5
SALES (corp-wide): 765K **Privately Held**
SIC: 2087 Concentrates, drink
PA: Mr Smoothie
　　1000 Ross Park Mall Dr Vc13
　　Pittsburgh PA 15237
　　412 630-9065

(G-12974)
NEW BGNNNGS WIN DOOR DSTRS LLC
28 Willowbrook Hts (12603-5708)
PHONE..........................845 214-0698
Kevin Hickey, *Sales Executive*
Domenica Haines, *Mng Member*
EMP: 10
SALES (est): 1.2MM **Privately Held**
SIC: 3442 5031 Window & door frames; windows

(G-12975)
NILDAS DESSERTS LIMITED
188 Washington St (12601-1357)
PHONE..........................845 454-5876
James Milano, *President*
EMP: 10
SQ FT: 5,000
SALES: 500K **Privately Held**
SIC: 2051 Bakery: wholesale or wholesale/retail combined

(G-12976)
NUTRA-VET RESEARCH CORP
201 Smith St (12601-2198)
PHONE..........................845 473-1900
Robert Abady, *President*
EMP: 10 **EST:** 1971
SQ FT: 14,000
SALES (est): 822.8K **Privately Held**
SIC: 2048 Mineral feed supplements

(G-12977)
OPTIMUM APPLIED SYSTEMS INC
16 Victory Ln Ste 5 (12603-1563)
P.O. Box 3572 (12603-0572)
PHONE..........................845 471-3333
Edward Awiniarski, *President*
EMP: 19
SALES: 950K **Privately Held**
SIC: 3699 Electrical equipment & supplies

(G-12978)
PERRETTA GRAPHICS CORP
46 Violet Ave (12601-1521)
PHONE..........................845 473-0550
Lawrence Perretta, *President*
Neil Rockwell, *Publisher*
Christopher Perretta, *Vice Pres*
Louis Perretta Jr, *Vice Pres*
Timothy Perretta, *Vice Pres*
▲ **EMP:** 40
SQ FT: 115,000
SALES (est): 8.7MM **Privately Held**
SIC: 3555 Printing trades machinery

(G-12979)
ROBERT ABADY DOG FOOD CO LTD
201 Smith St (12601-2198)
PHONE..........................845 473-1900
Robert Abady, *President*
EMP: 12
SALES (est): 1.5MM **Privately Held**
SIC: 2047 Dog food; cat food

(G-12980)
ROYAL COPENHAGEN INC (PA)
63 Page Park Dr (12603-2583)
P.O. Box 610, Belmar NJ (07719-0610)
PHONE..........................845 454-4442
Nicolai Lindhardt, *President*
Karin Skipper-Ulstrup, *Marketing Mgr*
Niels Bastrup, *Creative Dir*
▲ **EMP:** 11
SQ FT: 6,000
SALES (est): 924.3K **Privately Held**
SIC: 2392 Tablecloths & table settings

(G-12981)
SCHATZ BEARING CORPORATION
10 Fairview Ave (12601-1312)
PHONE..........................845 452-6000
Dr Stephen D E Pomeroy, *CEO*

Bob Lanser, *Plant Mgr*
Dave Hotchkiss, *Engineer*
Brad Euker CPA, *Controller*
Derrick Ohlhoff, *Manager*
▲ **EMP:** 75
SQ FT: 50,000
SALES (est): 21.2MM **Privately Held**
WEB: www.schatzbearing.com
SIC: 3562 Ball bearings & parts

(G-12982)
SCIANE ENTERPRISES INC
Also Called: Emdroidme
2600 South Rd Ste 37 (12601-7004)
PHONE..........................845 452-2400
Diane Pawenski, *Ch of Bd*
EMP: 7
SALES (est): 149.8K **Privately Held**
SIC: 2395 2261 Embroidery products, except schiffli machine; screen printing of cotton broadwoven fabrics

(G-12983)
SPECTRA VISTA CORPORATION
29 Firemens Way Stop 3 (12603-6523)
PHONE..........................845 471-7007
William G Goffe, *Ch of Bd*
Tom Corl, *President*
Larry Slomer, *Senior Engr*
Ward Duffield, *Manager*
John Giogakis, *Manager*
EMP: 6
SQ FT: 2,000
SALES (est): 1MM **Privately Held**
SIC: 3826 Spectrometers

(G-12984)
STANFORDVILLE MCH & MFG CO INC (PA)
Also Called: Kent Gage & Tool Company
29 Victory Ln (12603-1562)
P.O. Box B, Stanfordville (12581-0152)
PHONE..........................845 868-2266
Neal Johnsen, *Ch of Bd*
Peter Johnsen, *Vice Pres*
Joe La Falce, *CFO*
Ann Marie Johnsen, *Treasurer*
EMP: 57
SALES (est): 9MM **Privately Held**
WEB: www.stanfordville.com
SIC: 3599 Machine shop, jobbing & repair

(G-12985)
STEBE SHCJHJFF
18 Lynbrook Rd (12603-4608)
PHONE..........................839 383-9833
EMP: 10
SALES (est): 480K **Privately Held**
SIC: 2051 Mfg Bread/Related Products

(G-12986)
SUPERIOR WLLS OF HDSON VLY INC
Also Called: Superior Walls of Hudson Vly
68 Violet Ave (12601-1521)
PHONE..........................845 485-4033
Karen Ackert, *President*
Arthur Ackert Sr, *General Mgr*
Tammi Ackert, *Treasurer*
EMP: 50
SALES (est): 5.8MM **Privately Held**
WEB: www.superiorwallshv.com
SIC: 3272 Precast terrazo or concrete products; concrete products, precast

(G-12987)
T-SHIRT FACTORY INC
Also Called: Millman's
12 Fowler Ave (12603-2403)
PHONE..........................845 454-2255
Ellin B Millman, *President*
Samuel Millman, *Admin Sec*
EMP: 10
SQ FT: 2,000
SALES (est): 1.1MM **Privately Held**
SIC: 2759 Screen printing

(G-12988)
VANTAGE MFG & ASSEMBLY LLC
Also Called: Vma
900 Dutchess Tpke (12603-1554)
P.O. Box 3623 (12603-0623)
PHONE..........................845 471-5290
Edward Winiarski, *President*

Greg Devine, *Production*
Bill Reagan, *Engineer*
Mike Sterbenz, *Finance Mgr*
EMP: 48
SALES: 19.6MM **Privately Held**
SIC: 3824 Electromechanical counters

(G-12989)
VETERINARY BIOCHEMICAL LTD
201 Smith St (12601-2110)
PHONE..........................845 473-1900
Robert Abady, *President*
EMP: 5
SQ FT: 14,000
SALES (est): 650K **Privately Held**
SIC: 2048 Feed supplements

(G-12990)
VIKING IRON WORKS INC
37 Hatfield Ln (12603-6249)
PHONE..........................845 471-5010
Richard J Kunkel, *Ch of Bd*
Richard J Kunke, *President*
Paul Kunkel, *Vice Pres*
David Kunkel, *Shareholder*
James Kunkel, *Shareholder*
EMP: 14
SQ FT: 6,000
SALES (est): 3.3MM **Privately Held**
WEB: www.vikingironworks.com
SIC: 3462 Iron & steel forgings

Pound Ridge
Westchester County

(G-12991)
BIORESEARCH INC (PA)
4 Sunset Ln (10576-2318)
PHONE..........................212 734-5315
Leonard Kirth, *President*
Preston Keller, *President*
EMP: 9
SQ FT: 7,000
SALES (est): 928.8K **Privately Held**
WEB: www.bioresearch.com
SIC: 3841 Surgical & medical instruments

(G-12992)
DYNAX CORPORATION
79 Westchester Ave (10576-1702)
P.O. Box 285 (10576-0285)
PHONE..........................914 764-0202
Eduard K Kleiner PHD, *President*
Chang Jho, *Vice Pres*
Louis McAdams, *Prdtn Mgr*
Bryan Rambo, *VP Sales*
Andrea Goldhagen, *Office Admin*
▲ **EMP:** 6
SQ FT: 3,600
SALES (est): 1.3MM **Privately Held**
WEB: www.dynaxcorp.com
SIC: 2822 2824 Fluoro rubbers; fluorocarbon fibers

(G-12993)
LLOYD PRICE ICON FOOD BRANDS
Also Called: Lawdy Miss Clawdy
95 Horseshoe Hill Rd (10576-1636)
PHONE..........................914 764-8624
Lloyd Price, *Ch of Bd*
EMP: 15
SQ FT: 2,500
SALES (est): 950K **Privately Held**
WEB: www.lawdymissclawdy.com
SIC: 2052 Cookies

Pulaski
Oswego County

(G-12994)
FELIX SCHOELLER NORTH AMER INC
179 County Route 2a (13142-2546)
P.O. Box 250 (13142-0250)
PHONE..........................315 298-8425
Michael Szidat, *Ch of Bd*
James Walsh, *Vice Pres*
Jen Weeks, *Purch Mgr*
Bill Froass, *Sales Staff*

Paul Nash, *Sales Staff*
◆ **EMP:** 75 **EST:** 1961
SQ FT: 150,000
SALES (est): 1.7MM
SALES (corp-wide): 112.1MM **Privately Held**
WEB: www.felix-schoeller.com
SIC: 2672 5113 Coated & laminated paper; industrial & personal service paper
HQ: Schoeller Beteiligungen Gmbh
　　Burg Gretesch 1
　　Osnabruck 49086
　　541 380-00

(G-12995)
FULTON BOILER WORKS INC (PA)
3981 Port St (13142-4604)
P.O. Box 257 (13142-0257)
PHONE..........................315 298-5121
Ronald B Palm, *Ch of Bd*
Josh Brown, *Project Mgr*
Patrick Mullane, *QC Mgr*
Dave Dionne, *Engineer*
Tom Tighe, *Engineer*
◆ **EMP:** 60
SQ FT: 120,000
SALES (est): 87.2MM **Privately Held**
WEB: www.fulton.com
SIC: 3443 Boilers: industrial, power, or marine

(G-12996)
FULTON BOILER WORKS INC
972 Centerville Rd (13142-2595)
PHONE..........................315 298-5121
Ronald Palm, *Manager*
EMP: 250
SALES (corp-wide): 82.1MM **Privately Held**
SIC: 3443 Fabricated plate work (boiler shop)
PA: Fulton Boiler Works, Inc.
　　3981 Port St
　　Pulaski NY 13142
　　315 298-5121

(G-12997)
FULTON CHINA LLC
3981 Port St (13142-4604)
P.O. Box 257 (13142-0257)
PHONE..........................315 298-0112
Shane Peabody, *Principal*
EMP: 6
SALES (est): 613.5K **Privately Held**
SIC: 3443 Fabricated plate work (boiler shop)

(G-12998)
FULTON HEATING SOLUTIONS INC
972 Centerville Rd (13142-2595)
P.O. Box 257 (13142-0257)
PHONE..........................315 298-5121
Ronald B Palm Jr, *Ch of Bd*
Karen Currier, *Credit Mgr*
▲ **EMP:** 55
SQ FT: 200,000
SALES (est): 5.7MM
SALES (corp-wide): 19.1MM **Privately Held**
SIC: 3433 Burners, furnaces, boilers & stokers
PA: Hangzhou Fulton Thermal Equipment Co., Ltd.
　　No.09,Street 18, Xiasha Economic And Technological Development Z
　　Hangzhou
　　571 867-2589

(G-12999)
FULTON VOLCANIC INC (PA)
Also Called: Fulton Companies
3981 Port St (13142-4604)
P.O. Box 257 (13142-0257)
PHONE..........................315 298-5121
Ronald B Palm, *Ch of Bd*
Jian Chen, *General Mgr*
Kathy Sega, *Exec VP*
Mark Hilton, *VP Mfg*
Carol Larock, *Buyer*
▼ **EMP:** 70
SQ FT: 20,000

SALES (est): 31.1MM **Privately Held**
WEB: www.volcanic-heater.com
SIC: 3433 3567 3634 Heating equipment, except electric; heating units & devices, industrial: electric; electric housewares & fans

(G-13000)
HEALTHWAY HOME PRODUCTS INC
3420 Maple Ave (13142-4502)
P.O. Box 485 (13142-0485)
PHONE..................................315 298-2904
Vincent G Lobdell Sr, *Ch of Bd*
Jason Francher, *Business Mgr*
Jeff Herberger, *Vice Pres*
Vince Lobdell Jr, *Vice Pres*
Yinyin C Blodgett, *Opers Mgr*
▲ **EMP:** 30
SQ FT: 20,000
SALES (est): 8.5MM **Privately Held**
WEB: www.healthway.com
SIC: 3564 Filters, air: furnaces, air conditioning equipment, etc.

Purchase
Westchester County

(G-13001)
APOLLO MANAGEMENT V LP
1 Manhattanville Rd # 201 (10577-2100)
PHONE..................................914 467-6510
Lourenco Goncalves, *Ch of Bd*
Leon Black, *Mng Member*
Joshua Harris, *Mng Member*
Marc Rowan, *Mng Member*
EMP: 25
SALES (est): 6MM **Publicly Held**
SIC: 3272 3354 5051 Building materials, except block or brick: concrete; aluminum extruded products; iron & steel (ferrous) products
PA: Apollo Global Management, Inc.
  9 W 57th St Fl 43
  New York NY 10019

(G-13002)
BEVERAGES FOODS & SERVICE INDS
Also Called: Pepsico
700 Anderson Hill Rd (10577-1401)
PHONE..................................914 253-2000
Steve Reinemund, *CEO*
Rebecca Davis, *General Mgr*
Nadim Nakfoor, *General Mgr*
Steve Risley, *QC Mgr*
Erica Mui, *Engineer*
EMP: 100
SALES (est): 8.6MM
SALES (corp-wide): 64.6B **Publicly Held**
WEB: www.pepsico.com
SIC: 2086 Carbonated soft drinks, bottled & canned
PA: Pepsico, Inc.
  700 Anderson Hill Rd
  Purchase NY 10577
  914 253-2000

(G-13003)
CENTRAL NAT PULP & PPR SLS INC
3 Manhattanville Rd (10577-2116)
PHONE..................................914 696-9000
Andrew Wallach, *President*
Kenneth L Wallach, *Chairman*
Tara Williams, *Business Mgr*
Rich Cohen, *Opers Staff*
Eric Delfau, *Opers Staff*
EMP: 2500
SALES (est): 92.1MM
SALES (corp-wide): 4.3B **Privately Held**
SIC: 2611 Pulp mills, mechanical & recycling processing
PA: Central National Gottesman Inc.
  3 Manhattanville Rd # 301
  Purchase NY 10577
  914 696-9000

(G-13004)
HITACHI CABLE AMERICA INC (DH)
2 Manhattanville Rd # 301 (10577-2118)
PHONE..................................914 694-9200

Toro Aoki, *CEO*
Steve Kacines, *General Mgr*
John Muller, *General Mgr*
David Fundin, *Business Mgr*
Tatsuo Kinoshita, *Corp Secy*
▲ **EMP:** 13
SQ FT: 6,000
SALES (est): 167.7MM **Privately Held**
WEB: www.hitachi-cable.com
SIC: 3052 Rubber & plastics hose & beltings
HQ: Hitachi Metals America, Ltd.
  2 Manhattanville Rd # 301
  Purchase NY 10577
  914 694-9200

(G-13005)
HITACHI METALS AMERICA LTD (HQ)
2 Manhattanville Rd # 301 (10577-2103)
PHONE..................................914 694-9200
Hideaki Takahashi, *CEO*
Tomoyasu Kubota, *Ch of Bd*
Tomoyuki Hatano, *President*
Hiroaki Nakanishi, *President*
Sachi Toita, *President*
▲ **EMP:** 45 **EST:** 1965
SQ FT: 25,000
SALES (est): 1.7B **Privately Held**
SIC: 3264 3577 3365 5051 Magnets, permanent: ceramic or ferrite; computer peripheral equipment; aluminum & aluminum-based alloy castings: steel; castings, rough: iron or steel; ductile iron castings; gray iron castings; automotive related machinery

(G-13006)
LIGHTING HOLDINGS INTL LLC (PA)
4 Manhattanville Rd (10577-2139)
PHONE..................................845 306-1850
Dionne Gadsden, *CEO*
Steve Imgham, *CEO*
William Drexles, *CFO*
◆ **EMP:** 1400
SQ FT: 1,700
SALES (est): 141.7MM **Privately Held**
WEB: www.sli-lighting.com
SIC: 3641 5719 5063 4225 Electric lamps & parts for generalized applications; lamps & lamp shades; lighting fixtures; general warehousing; current-carrying wiring devices; pressed & blown glass

(G-13007)
MAM USA CORPORATION
2700 Westchester Ave # 315 (10577-2554)
PHONE..................................914 269-2500
Jennifer Mitchell, *CEO*
Fritz Hirsch, *CEO*
Niklaus Schertenlieb, *President*
Bernd Deussen, *Vice Pres*
Stefan Roehrig, *Vice Pres*
▲ **EMP:** 10
SALES (est): 2.1MM
SALES (corp-wide): 331.2K **Privately Held**
SIC: 3069 5999 Baby pacifiers, rubber; infant furnishings & equipment
HQ: Mam Babyartikel Gesellschaft M.B.H.
  Lorenz Mandl-Gasse 50
  Wien 1160
  149 141-0

(G-13008)
PEPSI-COLA METRO BTLG CO INC
700 Anderson Hill Rd (10577-1444)
PHONE..................................914 253-2000
Robert K Biggart, *President*
Bob Dague, *Opers Staff*
Tressa Meiser, *Opers Staff*
Jon Spear, *Opers Staff*
Alexandra Reynozo, *Production*
EMP: 5
SALES (est): 2.5MM **Privately Held**
SIC: 2086 Carbonated soft drinks, bottled & canned

(G-13009)
PEPSI-COLA SALES AND DIST INC (HQ)
700 Anderson Hill Rd (10577-1444)
PHONE..................................914 253-2000
Kirk Tanner, *CEO*
Michelle Caley, *Sales Associate*
EMP: 9
SALES (est): 1MM
SALES (corp-wide): 64.6B **Publicly Held**
SIC: 2086 5149 Carbonated soft drinks, bottled & canned; beverages, except coffee & tea
PA: Pepsico, Inc.
  700 Anderson Hill Rd
  Purchase NY 10577
  914 253-2000

(G-13010)
PEPSICO INC (PA)
700 Anderson Hill Rd (10577-1444)
PHONE..................................914 253-2000
Ramon Laguarta, *Ch of Bd*
Mehmood Khan, *Exec VP*
David Yawman, *Exec VP*
Marie T Gallagher, *Senior VP*
Hugh F Johnston, *CFO*
◆ **EMP:** 1500 **EST:** 1919
SALES (est): 64.6B **Publicly Held**
WEB: www.pepsico.com
SIC: 2096 2087 2086 2037 Potato chips & similar snacks; corn chips & other corn-based snacks; potato chips & other potato-based snacks; cheese curls & puffs; flavoring extracts & syrups; syrups, drink; fruit juices: concentrated for fountain use; concentrates, drink; bottled & canned soft drinks; iced tea & fruit drinks, bottled & canned; soft drinks: packaged in cans, bottles, etc.; carbonated beverages, non-alcoholic: bottled & canned; fruit juices; cookies & crackers; cereal breakfast foods; oatmeal: prepared as cereal breakfast food

(G-13011)
PEPSICO INC
Anderson Hill Rd (10577)
PHONE..................................914 253-2000
D Wayne Calloway, *Ch of Bd*
EMP: 700
SALES (corp-wide): 64.6B **Publicly Held**
SIC: 2086 Carbonated soft drinks, bottled & canned
PA: Pepsico, Inc.
  700 Anderson Hill Rd
  Purchase NY 10577
  914 253-2000

(G-13012)
PEPSICO INC
700 Anderson Hill Rd (10577-1444)
PHONE..................................914 253-2713
Denise Passarella, *Branch Mgr*
EMP: 10
SALES (corp-wide): 64.6B **Publicly Held**
SIC: 2086 Carbonated soft drinks, bottled & canned
PA: Pepsico, Inc.
  700 Anderson Hill Rd
  Purchase NY 10577
  914 253-2000

(G-13013)
PEPSICO CAPITAL RESOURCES INC
700 Anderson Hill Rd (10577-1444)
PHONE..................................914 253-2000
Judy Germano, *Principal*
EMP: 6
SALES (est): 395.2K **Privately Held**
SIC: 2086 Bottled & canned soft drinks

(G-13014)
PEPSICO SALES INC
700 Anderson Hill Rd (10577-1444)
PHONE..................................914 253-2000
Charles F Mueller, *Principal*
EMP: 7
SALES (est): 100.4K
SALES (corp-wide): 64.6B **Publicly Held**
SIC: 2086 5149 Carbonated soft drinks, bottled & canned; beverages, except coffee & tea

PA: Pepsico, Inc.
  700 Anderson Hill Rd
  Purchase NY 10577
  914 253-2000

(G-13015)
REGAL TRADING INC
Also Called: Regal Commodities
2975 Westchester Ave # 210 (10577-2500)
PHONE..................................914 694-6100
Joseph Apuzzo Jr, *CEO*
Sid Abramowitz, *Vice Pres*
▲ **EMP:** 35
SALES (est): 5.9MM **Privately Held**
SIC: 2095 Coffee roasting (except by wholesale grocers)

Queens Village
Queens County

(G-13016)
ALL TIME PRODUCTS INC
21167 Jamaica Ave (11428-1621)
PHONE..................................718 464-1400
Junior Lindo, *President*
Vinton Lindo, *Admin Sec*
EMP: 6
SALES (est): 726K **Privately Held**
SIC: 2752 Commercial printing, offset

(G-13017)
ALLSTAR GRAPHICS LTD
22034 Jamaica Ave (11428-2141)
PHONE..................................718 740-2240
Barry Kessler, *President*
Charles Kessler, *Vice Pres*
Jeff Kessler, *Treasurer*
Al Epstein, *Admin Sec*
EMP: 20
SQ FT: 2,000
SALES (est): 1.2MM **Privately Held**
WEB: www.allstargraphics.com
SIC: 3993 Signs & advertising specialties

(G-13018)
COLGATE-PALMOLIVE COMPANY
21818 100th Ave (11429-1209)
PHONE..................................718 506-3961
EMP: 279
SALES (corp-wide): 15.5B **Publicly Held**
SIC: 2844 Toothpastes or powders, dentifrices
PA: Colgate-Palmolive Company
  300 Park Ave Fl 3
  New York NY 10022
  212 310-2000

(G-13019)
EAST END VINEYARDS LLC
Also Called: Clovis Point
21548 Jamaica Ave (11428-1716)
P.O. Box 669, Jamesport (11947-0669)
PHONE..................................718 468-0500
Hal R Ginsburg, *Mng Member*
▲ **EMP:** 7
SQ FT: 5,000
SALES: 300K **Privately Held**
SIC: 2084 Wines

(G-13020)
GRAY GLASS INC
21744 98th Ave Ste C (11429-1252)
PHONE..................................718 217-2943
Christopher A Viggiano, *Ch of Bd*
William O Bryan, *Vice Pres*
Bill Obryan, *Vice Pres*
Jim Valenti, *VP Sales*
Val Krejci, *Office Mgr*
▲ **EMP:** 49 **EST:** 1946
SQ FT: 50,000
SALES: 7.8MM **Privately Held**
WEB: www.grayglass.net
SIC: 3229 3231 Glass tubes & tubing; products of purchased glass

(G-13021)
IGNELZI INTERIORS INC
9805 217th St (11429-1234)
PHONE..................................718 464-0279
Paul Ignelzi, *President*
Hugo Pomies, *Vice Pres*
EMP: 20

SQ FT: 16,000
SALES (est): 3.1MM **Privately Held**
WEB: www.ignelziinteriors.com
SIC: 2431 2434 Woodwork, interior & ornamental; wood kitchen cabinets

(G-13022)
J3 PRINTING INC
11214 Colfax St (11429-2221)
PHONE................................516 304-6103
Robet Nelson, *Principal*
EMP: 5 EST: 2015
SALES (est): 122.8K **Privately Held**
SIC: 2752 Commercial printing, lithographic

(G-13023)
JAMAICA LAMP CORP
21220 Jamaica Ave (11428-1618)
PHONE................................718 776-5039
Irving Shernock, *President*
▲ EMP: 30 EST: 1955
SQ FT: 20,000
SALES (est): 2.6MM **Privately Held**
SIC: 3999 3645 Shades, lamp or candle; residential lighting fixtures

(G-13024)
LAMS FOODS INC
9723 218th St (11429-1251)
PHONE................................718 217-0476
Sherlock Lam, *President*
Cleveland Lam, *Vice Pres*
Shervin Lam, *Vice Pres*
▲ EMP: 17
SQ FT: 20,000
SALES (est): 3.3MM **Privately Held**
WEB: www.lamsnacks.com
SIC: 2099 Noodles, fried (Chinese)

(G-13025)
MSQ CORPORATION
21504 Hempstead Ave (11429-1222)
PHONE................................718 465-0900
Craig Zoly, *President*
EMP: 8
SALES (est): 295.6K **Privately Held**
SIC: 2024 Ice cream & ice milk

(G-13026)
SPACE AGE PLSTIC FBRCATORS INC
8522 218th St (11427-1433)
PHONE................................718 324-4062
Arthur Barsky, *President*
Joel Barsky, *Vice Pres*
EMP: 15
SALES: 2.6MM **Privately Held**
WEB: www.plastic64.com
SIC: 3089 Plastic hardware & building products; plastic processing

(G-13027)
VOLKERT PRECISION TECH INC
22240 96th Ave Ste 3 (11429-1330)
PHONE................................718 464-9500
Kenneth J Heim, *Ch of Bd*
Jerome Bloomberg, *Vice Pres*
EMP: 47
SQ FT: 50,000
SALES (est): 9.1MM **Privately Held**
WEB: www.volkertprecision.com
SIC: 3469 Stamping metal for the trade; machine parts, stamped or pressed metal

(G-13028)
XEDIT CORP
Also Called: Servo Reeler System
21831 97th Ave (11429-1232)
PHONE................................718 380-1592
Claude Karczmer, *President*
EMP: 7
SQ FT: 1,800
SALES (est): 660K **Privately Held**
WEB: www.servoreelers.com
SIC: 3679 Electronic circuits

Queensbury
Warren County

(G-13029)
ADIRONDACK PRECISION CUT STONE (PA)
536 Queensbury Ave (12804-7612)
PHONE................................518 681-3060
Kris Johnston, *Owner*
EMP: 12
SALES (est): 1.7MM **Privately Held**
SIC: 3281 Granite, cut & shaped

(G-13030)
AMSTERDAM PRINTING & LITHO INC
Resource One
428 Corinth Rd (12804-7816)
P.O. Box 267, Hagaman (12086-0267)
PHONE................................518 792-6501
Kevin Kirbey, *Manager*
EMP: 10
SQ FT: 24,000
SALES (corp-wide): 2.8B **Privately Held**
WEB: www.amsterdamprinting.com
SIC: 2752 Commercial printing, offset
HQ: Amsterdam Printing & Litho, Inc.
166 Wallins Corners Rd
Amsterdam NY 12010
518 842-6000

(G-13031)
ANGIODYNAMICS INC
603 Queensbury Ave (12804-7619)
PHONE................................518 798-1215
Jacob Galough, *QC Mgr*
Jim Culhane, *Research*
William Hamilton, *Research*
Mike Barry, *Manager*
Kate Blosser, *Manager*
EMP: 32
SALES (corp-wide): 270.6MM **Publicly Held**
SIC: 3841 Surgical & medical instruments
PA: Angiodynamics, Inc.
14 Plaza Dr
Latham NY 12110
518 795-1400

(G-13032)
ANGIODYNAMICS INC
603 Queensbury Ave (12804-7619)
PHONE................................518 975-1400
EMP: 400
SALES (corp-wide): 270.6MM **Publicly Held**
SIC: 3841 Surgical & medical instruments
PA: Angiodynamics, Inc.
14 Plaza Dr
Latham NY 12110
518 795-1400

(G-13033)
ANGIODYNAMICS INC
543 Queensbury Ave (12804-7629)
PHONE................................518 742-4430
EMP: 275
SALES (corp-wide): 270.6MM **Publicly Held**
SIC: 3841 Surgical & medical instruments
PA: Angiodynamics, Inc.
14 Plaza Dr
Latham NY 12110
518 795-1400

(G-13034)
B Q P INC
6 Collins Dr (12804-1493)
PHONE................................518 793-4999
Tom Brennen, *President*
Susan Brennen, *Vice Pres*
EMP: 8
SALES (est): 743.3K **Privately Held**
SIC: 2752 Commercial printing, offset

(G-13035)
C R BARD INC
289 Bay Rd (12804-2015)
PHONE................................518 793-2531
Chris Melton, *President*
Vincent Cafiso, *Vice Pres*
Michael Jacobs, *Terminal Mgr*
Michelle Weller, *Purch Mgr*

John Greening, *Research*
EMP: 485
SALES (corp-wide): 15.9B **Publicly Held**
SIC: 3841 Surgical & medical instruments
HQ: C. R. Bard, Inc.
1 Becton Dr
Franklin Lakes NJ 07417
908 277-8000

(G-13036)
C R BARD INC
30 Collins Dr (12804-1493)
PHONE................................518 793-2531
Frank Madia, *Branch Mgr*
EMP: 82
SALES (corp-wide): 15.9B **Publicly Held**
SIC: 3841 Surgical & medical instruments
HQ: C. R. Bard, Inc.
1 Becton Dr
Franklin Lakes NJ 07417
908 277-8000

(G-13037)
DUKE CONCRETE PRODUCTS INC
50 Duke Dr (12804-2048)
PHONE................................518 793-7743
O E S Hedbring, *Ch of Bd*
John Hedbring, *President*
Derek Lloyd, *General Mgr*
Gary Hukey, *Vice Pres*
Carl Barlow, *Sales Staff*
EMP: 25
SQ FT: 9,000
SALES (est): 4.9MM **Privately Held**
WEB: www.dukeconcrete.com
SIC: 3271 5211 5082 Blocks, concrete or cinder: standard; concrete & cinder block; masonry materials & supplies; masonry equipment & supplies
PA: The Fort Miller Service Corp
688 Wilbur Ave
Greenwich NY 12834

(G-13038)
FLOWMEDICA INC
603 Queensbury Ave (12804-7619)
PHONE................................800 772-6446
Jeff Elkins, *President*
EMP: 14
SQ FT: 6,614
SALES (est): 966.4K **Privately Held**
WEB: www.flowmedica.com
SIC: 3841 Surgical & medical instruments

(G-13039)
G F LABELS LLC
10 Ferguson Ln (12804-7641)
PHONE................................518 798-6643
Steve Badera, *General Mgr*
Jacob Vanness, *Vice Pres*
Robert Gray, *Mng Member*
Betsy Carney, *Admin Sec*
EMP: 14
SQ FT: 12,000
SALES (est): 2.9MM **Privately Held**
WEB: www.gflabels.com
SIC: 2752 5113 Commercial printing, lithographic; paperboard & products

(G-13040)
GEORGE LAKE DISTILLING COMPANY
2 Pinecroft Dr (12804-9350)
PHONE................................518 639-1025
Robin McDougall,
John McDougall,
EMP: 5
SALES (est): 343.6K **Privately Held**
SIC: 2085 Distilled & blended liquors

(G-13041)
GLENS FALLS READY MIX INC
Also Called: Crainville Block Co
112 Big Boom Rd (12804-7861)
PHONE................................518 793-1695
John Tesiero, *President*
EMP: 12
SQ FT: 195
SALES (est): 770K **Privately Held**
SIC: 3272 3273 Concrete products, precast; ready-mixed concrete

(G-13042)
HARRIS LOGGING INC
39 Mud Pond Rd (12804-7313)
PHONE................................518 792-1083
EMP: 30
SALES (est): 2.2MM **Privately Held**
SIC: 2411 Logging

(G-13043)
HJE COMPANY INC
820 Quaker Rd (12804-3811)
PHONE................................518 792-8733
Joseph Tunick Strauss, *President*
EMP: 5
SQ FT: 4,500
SALES (est): 605K **Privately Held**
SIC: 3549 3399 Metalworking machinery; powder, metal

(G-13044)
JAMES KING WOODWORKING INC
656 County Line Rd (12804-7621)
PHONE................................518 761-6091
Scott Kingsley, *President*
James Morris, *Vice Pres*
EMP: 6
SQ FT: 76,230
SALES (est): 660.4K **Privately Held**
SIC: 2431 Millwork

(G-13045)
JE MONAHAN FABRICATIONS LLC
559 Queensbury Ave 1/2 (12804-7613)
PHONE................................518 761-0414
Harold A Smith,
Joe E Monahan,
Walter R Smith,
EMP: 11
SQ FT: 25,000
SALES (est): 1.2MM **Privately Held**
SIC: 3499 Welding tips, heat resistant: metal

(G-13046)
KINGSBURY PRINTING CO INC
813 Bay Rd (12804-5906)
PHONE................................518 747-6606
Robert Bombard, *President*
EMP: 6
SALES: 600K **Privately Held**
WEB: www.kingsburyprinting.com
SIC: 2752 Commercial printing, offset

(G-13047)
KOKE INC
582 Queensbury Ave (12804-7612)
PHONE................................800 535-5303
Richard Koke, *President*
Michael Nelson, *CFO*
◆ EMP: 20 EST: 1972
SQ FT: 36,000
SALES (est): 5.3MM **Privately Held**
SIC: 3537 5084 Trucks, tractors, loaders, carriers & similar equipment; materials handling machinery

(G-13048)
M & S PRECISION MACHINE CO LLC
27 Casey Rd (12804-7627)
PHONE................................518 747-1193
Dave Mc Donald, *Mng Member*
Michael Spirowski,
▲ EMP: 10
SALES: 1.2MM **Privately Held**
SIC: 3545 3599 Machine tool accessories; machine & other job shop work

(G-13049)
MORRIS PRODUCTS INC
53 Carey Rd (12804-7880)
PHONE................................518 743-0523
Jeff Schwartz, *President*
▲ EMP: 10
SQ FT: 20,000
SALES (est): 2.5MM
SALES (corp-wide): 34.6MM **Privately Held**
WEB: www.morrisproducts.com
SIC: 3625 5063 Electric controls & control accessories, industrial; electrical construction materials

HQ: Diversitech Corporation
6650 Sugarloaf Pkwy # 100
Duluth GA 30097
678 542-3600

(G-13050)
NORTHERN DESIGN & BLDG ASSOC
Also Called: Hamilton Design Kit Homes
100 Park Rd (12804-7616)
P.O. Box 47, Hudson Falls (12839-0047)
PHONE......................518 747-2200
Richard Kent McNairy, *CEO*
Douglas Thayer, *Exec VP*
Bob Niedermeyer, *Vice Pres*
EMP: 21
SQ FT: 20,000
SALES (est): 3.1MM **Privately Held**
SIC: 2452 7389 Log cabins, prefabricated, wood; design services

(G-13051)
PECKHAM ROAD CORP
375 Bay Rd Ste 101 (12804-3013)
PHONE......................518 792-3157
John R Peckham, *President*
EMP: 30
SALES (est): 14MM **Privately Held**
SIC: 2951 Asphalt paving mixtures & blocks

(G-13052)
PRAXIS POWDER TECHNOLOGY INC
604 Queensbury Ave (12804-7618)
PHONE......................518 812-0112
Joseph A Grohowski, *President*
Piemme Jobe, *President*
Tracy Macneal, *Vice Pres*
Cris Ginn, *Research*
Loran Chapman, *Engineer*
EMP: 24
SQ FT: 8,400
SALES (est): 5.4MM **Privately Held**
SIC: 3841 Diagnostic apparatus, medical

(G-13053)
PRIME WOOD PRODUCTS
1288 Vaughn Rd (12804-7356)
PHONE......................518 792-1407
Richard Caravaggio, *Owner*
EMP: 6
SALES (est): 369K **Privately Held**
SIC: 2499 Decorative wood & woodwork

(G-13054)
RWS MANUFACTURING INC
22 Ferguson Ln (12804-7641)
PHONE......................518 361-1657
Eric Fortin, *President*
Yvin Fortin, *Vice Pres*
EMP: 5
SALES (est): 839.2K
SALES (corp-wide): 2.5MM **Privately Held**
SIC: 2429 Shavings & packaging, excelsior
PA: Litiere Royal Inc
2327 Boul Du Versant-Nord Bureau
250
Quebec QC G1N 4
418 780-3373

(G-13055)
S & H ENTERPRISES INC
Also Called: Nationwide Lifts
10b Holden Ave (12804-3316)
PHONE......................888 323-8755
Andrew Darnley, *President*
EMP: 5
SALES (est): 465.9K **Privately Held**
SIC: 3534 3999 Stair elevators, motor powered; wheelchair lifts

(G-13056)
SEELEY MACHINE INC
Also Called: Seeley Machine & Fabrication
75 Big Boom Rd (12804-7858)
PHONE......................518 798-9510
Daryl W Pechtel, *Ch of Bd*
Craig Seeley, *President*
Barbara Seeley, *Corp Secy*
Charles Seeley, *Vice Pres*
Ed Leonard, *Supervisor*
EMP: 25
SQ FT: 14,000

SALES (est): 5.1MM **Privately Held**
WEB: www.seeleymachine.com
SIC: 3599 Machine shop, jobbing & repair

(G-13057)
SINCLAIR INTERNATIONAL COMPANY (PA)
85 Boulevard (12804-3903)
PHONE......................518 798-2361
David H Sinclair Jr, *President*
Brian Phelps, *General Mgr*
Don Bolton, *Sales Staff*
Jason Viele, *Manager*
EMP: 73
SQ FT: 28,000
SALES (est): 11.3MM **Privately Held**
SIC: 3496 3554 3569 Wire cloth & woven wire products; paper industries machinery; filters

(G-13058)
THE KINGSBURY PRINTING CO INC
632 County Line Rd (12804-7621)
PHONE......................518 747-6606
Robert Bombard Jr, *Ch of Bd*
Robert L Bombard Jr, *Ch of Bd*
Janette Bombard, *Vice Pres*
EMP: 8
SQ FT: 2,070
SALES (est): 1.1MM **Privately Held**
SIC: 2752 Commercial printing, offset

(G-13059)
TRIBUNE MEDIA SERVICES INC (DH)
Also Called: TV Data
40 Media Dr (12804-4086)
PHONE......................518 792-9914
Daniel Kazan, *CEO*
John B Kelleher, *President*
Kathleen Daly, *General Mgr*
Deborah Lyon, *Consultant*
Suanne Yasko, *Asst Mgr*
EMP: 300
SQ FT: 38,000
SALES (est): 35.4MM
SALES (corp-wide): 2.7B **Publicly Held**
WEB: www.tvdata.com
SIC: 2741 Miscellaneous publishing
HQ: Tribune Media Company
515 N State St Ste 2400
Chicago IL 60654
312 222-3394

(G-13060)
WF LAKE CORP
65 Park Rd (12804-7615)
P.O. Box 4214 (12804-0214)
PHONE......................518 798-9934
Jim Meyer, *President*
John L Hodgkins III, *Corp Secy*
John Hodgkins, *Treasurer*
Kate Henderson, *Sales Staff*
Jody Meyer, *Executive*
▲ **EMP:** 25
SQ FT: 33,000
SALES (est): 5.5MM **Privately Held**
WEB: www.wflake.com
SIC: 3052 Rubber & plastics hose & belt-ings

Quogue
Suffolk County

(G-13061)
PECONIC PLASTICS INC
6062 Old Country Rd (11959)
P.O. Box 1425 (11959-1425)
PHONE......................631 653-3676
Ralph Ponto, *President*
Gerhart Ponto, *Vice Pres*
EMP: 10
SALES (est): 865.4K **Privately Held**
WEB: www.peconicplastics.com
SIC: 3089 Molding primary plastic; injection molding of plastics

---

Randolph
Cattaraugus County

(G-13062)
FENTON MOBILITY PRODUCTS INC
26 Center St (14772-1024)
PHONE......................716 484-7014
Richard I Fenton, *President*
Sean Fenton, *Vice Pres*
Scott Fenton, *CFO*
Mary Gabalski, *Consultant*
Sam Harrison, *Commercial*
EMP: 6
SQ FT: 8,500
SALES (est): 1.4MM **Privately Held**
SIC: 3444 Coal chutes, prefabricated sheet metal

(G-13063)
METALLIC LADDER MFG CORP
Also Called: Alumidock
41 S Washington St (14772-1326)
P.O. Box 68 (14772-0068)
PHONE......................716 358-6201
William Wadsworth, *President*
Christian Monroe, *Sls & Mktg Exec*
Daryl Wadsworth, *Admin Sec*
▼ **EMP:** 15
SQ FT: 12,000
SALES (est): 3.3MM **Privately Held**
WEB: www.alumidock.com
SIC: 3448 3499 Docks: prefabricated metal; ladders, portable: metal

(G-13064)
RANDOLPH DIMENSION CORPORATION
216 Main St Ste 216 (14772)
PHONE......................716 358-6901
EMP: 10 EST: 1965
SQ FT: 72,000
SALES (est): 130.2K **Privately Held**
SIC: 2426 2431 Hardwood Dimension/Floor Mill Mfg Millwork

(G-13065)
REGISTER GRAPHICS INC
220 Main St (14772-1213)
P.O. Box 98 (14772-0098)
PHONE......................716 358-2921
Robert G Beach, *President*
Tim Beach, *President*
Ann Biscup, *Superintendent*
Mark Hinman, *Corp Secy*
Jean D Beach, *Vice Pres*
EMP: 23 EST: 1865
SQ FT: 13,000
SALES (est): 3.1MM **Privately Held**
WEB: www.registergraphics.com
SIC: 2752 Commercial printing, offset

Ransomville
Niagara County

(G-13066)
J F MACHINING COMPANY INC
2382 Balmer Rd (14131-9787)
P.O. Box 249 (14131-0249)
PHONE......................716 791-3910
Joseph Fleckenstein, *President*
Kelly Fleckenstein, *Vice Pres*
EMP: 10
SQ FT: 2,000
SALES (est): 800K **Privately Held**
SIC: 3599 Machine shop, jobbing & repair

Ravena
Albany County

(G-13067)
BLEEZARDE PUBLISHING INC
Also Called: Greenville Local
164 Main St (12143-1112)
PHONE......................518 756-2030
Richard G Bleezarde, *President*
Keith Shoemaker, *Advt Staff*

Melanie Lekocevic, *Manager*
EMP: 8 EST: 1880
SQ FT: 5,400
SALES: 305K **Privately Held**
SIC: 2711 Commercial printing & newspaper publishing combined

(G-13068)
LAFARGE BUILDING MATERIALS INC
Rr (12143)
PHONE......................518 756-5000
Martin Turecky, *Manager*
EMP: 14
SALES (corp-wide): 27.6B **Privately Held**
SIC: 3241 Masonry cement
HQ: Lafarge Building Materials Inc.
8700 W Bryn Mawr Ave 300n
Chicago IL 60631
678 746-2000

(G-13069)
LAFARGE NORTH AMERICA INC
1916 Route 9 W (12143)
P.O. Box 3 (12143-0003)
PHONE......................518 756-5000
Bernie Dushane, *Maint Spvr*
Christopher Ricciardi, *Production*
Martin Turecky, *Branch Mgr*
EMP: 27
SALES (corp-wide): 27.6B **Privately Held**
WEB: www.lafargenorthamerica.com
SIC: 3273 3272 3271 1442 Ready-mixed concrete; concrete products; precast terrazo or concrete products; prestressed concrete products; cylinder pipe, prestressed or pretensioned concrete; blocks, concrete or cinder: standard; construction sand & gravel; construction sand mining; gravel mining; asphalt paving mixtures & blocks; paving mixtures; asphalt & asphaltic paving mixtures (not from refineries); portland cement
HQ: Lafarge North America Inc.
8700 W Bryn Mawr Ave
Chicago IL 60631
773 372-1000

Red Creek
Wayne County

(G-13070)
SMOOTHBORE INTERNATIONAL INC
13881 Westbury Cutoff Rd (13143)
PHONE......................315 754-8124
Jason Smith, *President*
EMP: 7
SALES (est): 782.6K **Privately Held**
SIC: 2411 Logging camps & contractors

(G-13071)
WAYUGA COMMUNITY NEWSPAPERS (PA)
Also Called: Wayuga News
6784 Main St (13143)
P.O. Box 199 (13143-0199)
PHONE......................315 754-6229
Angelo Palermo, *President*
Carol Palermo, *Vice Pres*
EMP: 22
SQ FT: 9,520
SALES (est): 2MM **Privately Held**
WEB: www.wayuga.com
SIC: 2711 2741 Newspapers, publishing & printing; miscellaneous publishing

---

Red Hook
Dutchess County

(G-13072)
CHICKEN HAWK RACING INC
54 Elizabeth St Ste 10 (12571-1722)
PHONE......................845 758-0700
David Podolsky, *President*
▲ **EMP:** 6
SALES: 850K **Privately Held**
WEB: www.chickenhawkracing.com
SIC: 3433 3751 Unit heaters, domestic; motorcycle accessories

---

(G-13073)
CORT CONTRACTING
188 W Market St (12571-2710)
PHONE..............................845 758-1190
Ralph Cort, *Owner*
EMP: 10
SALES (est): 680K **Privately Held**
WEB: www.cortcontracting.com
SIC: 2452 Prefabricated wood buildings

(G-13074)
UNIVERSAL BUILDERS SUPPLY INC
45 Ocallaghan Ln (12571-1776)
PHONE..............................845 758-8801
Dave Rice, *CFO*
EMP: 16
SALES (corp-wide): 20MM **Privately Held**
WEB: www.ubs1.com
SIC: 3357 Nonferrous wiredrawing & insulating
PA: Universal Builders Supply Inc
27 Horton Ave Ste 5
New Rochelle NY 10801
914 699-2400

(G-13075)
WITH YOU DESIGNS LLC
Also Called: With You Lockets
23a E Mkt St Red Hook (12571)
PHONE..............................800 413-0670
Troy Haley, *CEO*
EMP: 8
SALES: 1.5MM **Privately Held**
SIC: 3479 Engraving jewelry silverware, or metal

Rego Park
Queens County

(G-13076)
DIDCO INC
8570 67th Ave (11374-5225)
PHONE..............................212 997-5022
Malcolm Doyle, *President*
EMP: 12 **EST:** 2012
SALES (est): 831.8K **Privately Held**
SIC: 1499 Gemstone & industrial diamond mining

(G-13077)
J I INTRNTNAL CONTACT LENS LAB
6352 Saunders St Ste A (11374-2000)
PHONE..............................718 997-1212
Joseph Itzkowitz, *President*
EMP: 7 **EST:** 1964
SQ FT: 2,000
SALES: 750K **Privately Held**
SIC: 3851 Contact lenses

(G-13078)
JL PARC LLC (PA)
9015 Queens Blvd (11374)
PHONE..............................718 271-0703
Ariel Chaus, *CEO*
William Runge, *CFO*
Mary E Joy, *VP Human Res*
EMP: 4
SALES (est): 58.5MM **Privately Held**
SIC: 2339 2331 Sportswear, women's; women's & misses' blouses & shirts

(G-13079)
KEFA INDUSTRIES GROUP INC
9219 63rd Dr (11374-2926)
PHONE..............................718 568-9297
Keyan Xing, *Principal*
Huicong Cong, *Manager*
▲ **EMP:** 7
SALES (est): 461K **Privately Held**
SIC: 3499 Machine bases, metal

(G-13080)
METRO LUBE (PA)
9110 Metropolitan Ave (11374-5328)
PHONE..............................718 947-1167
Fernando Magalhaes, *Principal*
EMP: 5
SALES (est): 1.4MM **Privately Held**
SIC: 3589 Car washing machinery

(G-13081)
PROFESSIONAL PAVERS CORP
6605 Woodhaven Blvd Bsmt (11374-5235)
P.O. Box 790186, Middle Village (11379-0186)
PHONE..............................718 784-7853
Duarte N Lopes, *Ch of Bd*
Nunu Lopes, *President*
Joseph Foley, *Vice Pres*
▲ **EMP:** 30
SALES (est): 6.6MM **Privately Held**
SIC: 3531 Road construction & maintenance machinery

(G-13082)
SPECTACLE OPTICAL INC
9801 67th Ave Apt 7f (11374-4903)
PHONE..............................646 706-1015
Elizabeth Geheran, *CEO*
EMP: 5
SALES (est): 283.3K **Privately Held**
SIC: 3851 Spectacles

Remsen
Oneida County

(G-13083)
BUILDING NEW BRIDGES LLC
202 State Route 365 (13438-5702)
PHONE..............................315 960-1242
Luis Garcia,
EMP: 10
SALES: 450K **Privately Held**
SIC: 3444 Restaurant sheet metalwork

Rensselaer
Rensselaer County

(G-13084)
ALBANY INTERNATIONAL CORP
Press Fabrics Division
253 Troy Rd (12144-9473)
P.O. Box 1907, Albany (12201-1907)
PHONE..............................518 445-2200
Steve Sassaman, *General Mgr*
EMP: 180
SALES (corp-wide): 982.4MM **Publicly Held**
WEB: www.albint.com
SIC: 2221 2297 2241 Paper broadwoven fabrics; nonwoven fabrics; narrow fabric mills
PA: Albany International Corp.
216 Airport Dr
Rochester NH 03867
603 330-5850

(G-13085)
ALBANY MOLECULAR RESEARCH INC
Also Called: Amri Rensselaer
81 Columbia Tpke (12144-3411)
PHONE..............................518 433-7700
Thomas E D'Ambra, *Ch of Bd*
EMP: 10
SALES (corp-wide): 137.4MM **Privately Held**
SIC: 2833 Medicinals & botanicals
HQ: Albany Molecular Research, Inc.
26 Corporate Cir
Albany NY 12203

(G-13086)
ALBANY MOLECULAR RESEARCH INC
Also Called: Amri
33 Riverside Ave (12144-2951)
PHONE..............................518 512-2000
Vadim Mozhaev, *Research*
Mary Lemme, *Accountant*
Venkat Chikkala, *Human Res Mgr*
Leah Rucinski, *Accounts Mgr*
Steven R Hagen, *Branch Mgr*
EMP: 10
SALES (corp-wide): 137.4MM **Privately Held**
SIC: 2833 Medicinals & botanicals
HQ: Albany Molecular Research, Inc.
26 Corporate Cir
Albany NY 12203

(G-13087)
BASF CORPORATION
Chemicals Division
70 Riverside Ave (12144)
PHONE..............................518 465-6534
Wayne Sinclair, *Manager*
EMP: 280
SALES (corp-wide): 71.7B **Privately Held**
WEB: www.basf.com
SIC: 2869 Industrial organic chemicals
HQ: Basf Corporation
100 Park Ave
Florham Park NJ 07932
973 245-6000

(G-13088)
GREAT 4 IMAGE INC
Also Called: G4i
5 Forest Hills Blvd (12144-5831)
PHONE..............................518 424-2058
Daren Arakelian, *President*
▲ **EMP:** 26
SALES: 1MM **Privately Held**
WEB: www.g4i.com
SIC: 2311 Men's & boys' suits & coats

(G-13089)
INTEGRATED LINER TECH INC (PA)
45 Discovery Dr (12144-3466)
PHONE..............................518 621-7422
Paul Petrosino, *Ch of Bd*
James Crouch, *Vice Pres*
Corey Hagedorn, *Production*
Ken Greene, *Project Engr*
Dee Vandyke, *Accountant*
▲ **EMP:** 48
SQ FT: 30,000
SALES (est): 9.7MM **Privately Held**
WEB: www.integratedliner.com
SIC: 3821 2822 Chemical laboratory apparatus; synthetic rubber

(G-13090)
R J VALENTE GRAVEL INC
315 Partition St Ext (12144-2041)
PHONE..............................518 432-4470
Tim Banks, *Manager*
EMP: 15
SALES (est): 768.4K
SALES (corp-wide): 19.4MM **Privately Held**
SIC: 1442 Construction sand & gravel
PA: R. J. Valente Gravel, Inc.
1 Madison St
Troy NY 12180
518 432-4470

(G-13091)
REGENERON PHARMACEUTICALS INC
81 Columbia Tpke (12144-3423)
PHONE..............................518 488-6000
Dr Randall Rupp, *General Mgr*
Anita Berg, *Buyer*
Sarah Hagadorn, *Buyer*
Megan Miftari, *Buyer*
Halit Akgun, *Manager*
EMP: 40
SALES (corp-wide): 6.7B **Publicly Held**
WEB: www.regeneron.com
SIC: 2834 Pharmaceutical preparations
PA: Regeneron Pharmaceuticals Inc
777 Old Saw Mill River Rd # 10
Tarrytown NY 10591
914 847-7000

(G-13092)
STEMCULTURES LLC
1 Discovery Dr (12144-3448)
PHONE..............................518 621-0848
Jeffrey Stern, *CEO*
William Price, *COO*
Christopher Fasano, *Bd of Directors*
EMP: 7
SALES (est): 445.3K **Privately Held**
SIC: 2836 Culture media

(G-13093)
ULTRADIAN DIAGNOSTICS LLC
5 University Pl A324 (12144-3461)
PHONE..............................518 618-0046
John P Willis,
EMP: 5
SQ FT: 2,000
SALES (est): 579.3K **Privately Held**
SIC: 3845 Electromedical equipment

Retsof
Livingston County

(G-13094)
AMERICAN ROCK SALT COMPANY LLC (PA)
3846 Retsof Rd (14539)
P.O. Box 190, Mount Morris (14510-0190)
PHONE..............................585 991-6878
Gunther Buerman, *Ch of Bd*
Justin Curley, *General Mgr*
Joseph G Bucci, *Principal*
Lee McKinney, *Safety Dir*
Greg Norris, *Plant Mgr*
▲ **EMP:** 20
SALES (est): 787.2MM **Privately Held**
WEB: www.americanrocksalt.com
SIC: 1479 5169 Rock salt mining; salts, industrial

Rexford
Saratoga County

(G-13095)
MOBIUS LABS INC
37 Vischer Ferry Rd (12148-1617)
PHONE..............................518 961-2600
Frank Lipowitz, *Principal*
EMP: 5
SALES (est): 263.7K **Privately Held**
SIC: 3829 Hydrometers, except industrial process type

(G-13096)
PARRINGTON INSTRUMENTS
12 Droms Rd (12148-1401)
PHONE..............................518 373-8420
Josef Parrington, *Principal*
EMP: 5
SALES (est): 681.2K **Privately Held**
SIC: 3823 Industrial instrmnts msrmnt display/control process variable

(G-13097)
PRESTACYCLE LLC
689 Riverview Rd (12148-1427)
PHONE..............................518 588-5546
David Finlayson, *Mng Member*
▲ **EMP:** 5
SQ FT: 2,000
SALES: 1.4MM **Privately Held**
SIC: 3751 Bicycles & related parts

Rhinebeck
Dutchess County

(G-13098)
CORE GROUP DISPLAYS INC
41 Pitcher Rd (12572-1035)
PHONE..............................845 876-5109
Dan Riso, *President*
Kurt Haldin, *Director*
◆ **EMP:** 21 **EST:** 2007
SALES: 1.2MM **Privately Held**
SIC: 2542 Partitions & fixtures, except wood

(G-13099)
DUTCHESS WINES LLC
Also Called: Alison Wine & Vineyard
39 Lorraine Dr (12572-1203)
P.O. Box 619 (12572-0619)
PHONE..............................845 876-1319
Richard Lewit, *President*
EMP: 5
SALES: 280K **Privately Held**
WEB: www.alisonwine.com
SIC: 2084 Wines

(G-13100)
PDQ MANUFACTURING CO INC
29 Hilee Rd (12572-2349)
PHONE..............................845 889-3123
Scott Hutchins, *Ch of Bd*
Kristin Hutchins, *President*

▲ = Import ▼=Export
◆ =Import/Export

EMP: 45 EST: 1975
SQ FT: 40,000
SALES (est): 7.6MM **Privately Held**
WEB: www.pdqmfg.com
SIC: 3444 Sheet metal specialties, not
stamped

(G-13101)
SMITHERS TOOLS & MCH PDTS INC
Also Called: Stamp
3718 Route 9g (12572-1139)
P.O. Box 391 (12572-0391)
PHONE..................................845 876-3063
Roland Jennings, *Ch of Bd*
Gary L Hosey, *President*
Robert Nevins, *Vice Pres*
Joann Russell, *Vice Pres*
EMP: 63 EST: 1947
SQ FT: 35,000
SALES (est): 10MM **Privately Held**
WEB: www.stampinc.com
SIC: 3699 3469 7692 3599 Electrical
equipment & supplies; stamping metal for
the trade; welding repair; machine shop,
jobbing & repair

(G-13102)
UMBRO MACHINE & TOOL CO INC
3811 Route 9g (12572-1042)
PHONE..................................845 876-4669
Gerald Umbro, *President*
Claire Umbro, *Vice Pres*
Rosemary Kavanaugh, *Admin Sec*
EMP: 12 EST: 1959
SQ FT: 1,800
SALES: 1MM **Privately Held**
SIC: 3451 Screw machine products

(G-13103)
WARREN CUTLERY CORP
3584 Route 9g (12572-3309)
P.O. Box 289 (12572-0289)
PHONE..................................845 876-3444
James Zitz, *President*
Richard Von Husen, *Vice Pres*
EMP: 10
SQ FT: 3,500
SALES (est): 1.6MM **Privately Held**
WEB: www.warrencutlery.com
SIC: 3421 3291 5072 5085 Cutlery; abra-
sive products; cutlery; abrasives

(G-13104)
WATER ORACLE
41 E Market St Ste 4 (12572-1657)
P.O. Box 542, Hyde Park (12538-0542)
PHONE..................................845 876-8327
Stacey Held, *Principal*
EMP: 5 EST: 2016
SALES (est): 91K **Privately Held**
SIC: 7372 Prepackaged software

Richfield Springs
Otsego County

(G-13105)
ANDELA TOOL & MACHINE INC
Also Called: Andela Products
493 State Route 28 (13439-3739)
PHONE..................................315 858-0055
Cynthia Andela, *President*
James Andela, *Vice Pres*
▼ EMP: 8
SQ FT: 10,000
SALES (est): 1.9MM **Privately Held**
WEB: www.andelaproducts.com
SIC: 3559 Recycling machinery

(G-13106)
WELDING AND BRAZING SVCS INC
2761 County Highway 26 (13439-3049)
PHONE..................................607 397-1009
David R Parker, *President*
Kay Parker, *Vice Pres*
Carter Cook, *Manager*
EMP: 5
SALES (est): 376.9K **Privately Held**
SIC: 7692 Brazing

Richmond Hill
Queens County

(G-13107)
ALL AMERICAN STAIRS & RAILING
13023 91st Ave (11418-3320)
PHONE..................................718 441-8400
Marie Bottari, *President*
EMP: 12
SALES (est): 2.4MM **Privately Held**
SIC: 3446 Stairs, fire escapes, balconies,
railings & ladders

(G-13108)
ATLANTIC FARM & FOOD INC
11415 Atlantic Ave (11418-3139)
PHONE..................................718 441-3152
Gurcharn Singh, *Principal*
EMP: 13
SALES (est): 1.7MM **Privately Held**
SIC: 2037 8611 Frozen fruits & vegeta-
bles; growers' marketing advisory service

(G-13109)
BARALAN USA INC (DH)
Also Called: Arrowpak
12019 89th Ave (11418-3235)
PHONE..................................718 849-5768
Roland Baranes, *President*
Ellis Rudman, *Corp Secy*
Jim Slowey, *Vice Pres*
Luisa Kamelhar, *Human Res Dir*
◆ EMP: 35 EST: 1980
SQ FT: 70,000
SALES (est): 4.9MM
SALES (corp-wide): 1MM **Privately Held**
WEB: www.arrowpak.com
SIC: 3221 3089 Cosmetic jars, glass;
plastic containers, except foam
HQ: Baralan International Spa
Via Nicolo' Copernico 34
Trezzano Sul Naviglio MI 20090
024 844-961

(G-13110)
BELLE MAISON USA LTD
Also Called: Stylemaster
8950 127th St (11418-3323)
PHONE..................................718 805-0200
Elizabeth Romano, *Ch of Bd*
Ethel Romano, *Vice Pres*
◆ EMP: 30
SALES (est): 3.2MM **Privately Held**
WEB: www.stylemasterusa.com
SIC: 2392 2391 Bedspreads & bed sets:
made from purchased materials; curtains,
window: made from purchased materials

(G-13111)
CARLOS & ALEX ATELIER INC
Also Called: C & A Atelier
10010 91st Ave Fl 2 (11418-2118)
PHONE..................................718 441-8911
Carlos Queiroz, *CEO*
EMP: 24
SQ FT: 22,000
SALES (est): 2MM **Privately Held**
SIC: 2434 2511 Wood kitchen cabinets;
wood household furniture

(G-13112)
ELECTRON TOP MFG CO INC
12615 89th Ave (11418-3337)
PHONE..................................718 846-7400
Craig Strauss, *President*
Frederick W Strauss III, *Vice Pres*
Kimberly S Hess, *Treasurer*
EMP: 41 EST: 1947
SQ FT: 20,000
SALES (est): 6.4MM **Privately Held**
WEB: www.electrontop.com
SIC: 3714 Tops, motor vehicle

(G-13113)
EMPIRE STATE METAL PDTS INC
10110 Jamaica Ave (11418-2007)
PHONE..................................718 847-1617
David Millshauser, *President*
▲ EMP: 20 EST: 1946
SQ FT: 20,475

SALES: 2MM **Privately Held**
SIC: 3965 Buttons & parts; buckles &
buckle parts

(G-13114)
GAUGHAN CONSTRUCTION CORP
13034 90th Ave (11418-3309)
PHONE..................................718 850-9577
Anthony Gaughan, *President*
EMP: 5
SQ FT: 6,000
SALES (est): 731.1K **Privately Held**
SIC: 2541 Wood partitions & fixtures

(G-13115)
HILL KNITTING MILLS INC
10005 92nd Ave Ste Mgmt (11418-2910)
PHONE..................................718 846-5000
Jeff Rosen, *President*
Peter Cruciata, *Corp Secy*
EMP: 23
SQ FT: 30,000
SALES (est): 2.1MM **Privately Held**
SIC: 2257 Pile fabrics, circular knit

(G-13116)
J & E TALIT INC
13011 Atlantic Ave Fl 2 (11418-3334)
PHONE..................................718 850-1333
Eitan Talit, *President*
EMP: 8
SQ FT: 6,000
SALES (est): 1MM **Privately Held**
WEB: www.jandetalit.com
SIC: 2253 2339 T-shirts & tops, knit;
sportswear, women's

(G-13117)
J & S LICATA BROS INC
Also Called: Monteforte Bakery
8931 129th St (11418-3326)
PHONE..................................718 805-6924
Salvatore Licata, *President*
Joseph Licata, *Vice Pres*
EMP: 15
SQ FT: 8,000
SALES (est): 2.2MM **Privately Held**
SIC: 2051 Bread, cake & related products

(G-13118)
OLYMPIC ICE CREAM CO INC
Also Called: Marinos Italian Ices
12910 91st Ave (11418-3317)
PHONE..................................718 849-6200
Michael Barone Sr, *President*
Frank Barone, *Vice Pres*
▼ EMP: 35
SQ FT: 50,000
SALES: 5MM **Privately Held**
WEB: www.marinositalianices.com
SIC: 2024 Ices, flavored (frozen dessert)

(G-13119)
PREMIER PAINT ROLLER CO LLC
13111 Atlantic Ave (11418-3397)
PHONE..................................718 441-7700
Kevin Leichter, *President*
Charles Dawson, *General Mgr*
Sari Nathan, *COO*
Seth Alexander, *Financial Analy*
Paul Schmitke, *VP Sales*
◆ EMP: 100
SQ FT: 250,000
SALES (est): 11.3MM **Privately Held**
WEB: www.premierpaintroller.com
SIC: 3991 Paint rollers

(G-13120)
PREMIER PAINT ROLLER CO LLC (PA)
13111 Atlantic Ave (11418-3397)
PHONE..................................718 441-7700
Kevin Leichter, *CEO*
EMP: 11 EST: 2004
SALES (est): 2.1MM **Privately Held**
SIC: 3991 5198 Paint rollers; paint
brushes, rollers, sprayers

(G-13121)
RESEARCH CENTRE OF KABBALAH
Also Called: Kabbalah Centre
8384 115th St (11418-1303)
PHONE..................................718 805-0380
Philip Berg, *President*
Beatrice Cohen, *Treasurer*
Karen Berg, *Admin Sec*
EMP: 6
SQ FT: 40,000
SALES (est): 536.6K **Privately Held**
WEB: www.kabbalahcentre.com
SIC: 2731 Books: publishing only; pam-
phlets: publishing only, not printed on site

(G-13122)
RUBIES COSTUME COMPANY INC (PA)
12008 Jamaica Ave (11418-2521)
PHONE..................................718 846-1008
Marc P Beige, *Ch of Bd*
Joanne Rudis, *Division Mgr*
Howard Beige, *Vice Pres*
Jeffrey Cohen, *Controller*
Michael Laimo, *Sales Mgr*
◆ EMP: 400
SQ FT: 55,000
SALES (est): 366.5MM **Privately Held**
SIC: 2389 7299 Costumes; costume rental

(G-13123)
RUBIES COSTUME COMPANY INC
12017 Jamaica Ave (11418-2522)
PHONE..................................718 441-0834
Arthur Savarese, *Branch Mgr*
EMP: 148
SALES (corp-wide): 366.5MM **Privately Held**
SIC: 2389 Costumes
PA: Rubie's Costume Company, Inc.
12008 Jamaica Ave
Richmond Hill NY 11418
718 846-1008

(G-13124)
RUBIES COSTUME COMPANY INC
1 Rubie Plz (11418)
PHONE..................................718 846-1008
Rick Roche, *Vice Pres*
Ellen DOE, *Human Res Dir*
Michael Laimo, *Sales Mgr*
Erin Breig, *Sales Staff*
Richard Tinari, *Sales Staff*
EMP: 148
SALES (corp-wide): 366.5MM **Privately Held**
SIC: 2389 7299 Costumes; costume rental
PA: Rubie's Costume Company, Inc.
12008 Jamaica Ave
Richmond Hill NY 11418
718 846-1008

(G-13125)
RUBIES MASQUERADE COMPANY LLC (HQ)
1 Rubie Plz (11418)
PHONE..................................718 846-1008
Dick Roche, *Opers Staff*
Dave Defina, *Controller*
EMP: 6
SALES (est): 11.2MM
SALES (corp-wide): 366.5MM **Privately Held**
SIC: 2389 Masquerade costumes
PA: Rubie's Costume Company, Inc.
12008 Jamaica Ave
Richmond Hill NY 11418
718 846-1008

(G-13126)
SUPER EXPRESS USA PUBG CORP
8410 101st St Apt 4l (11418-1150)
PHONE..................................212 227-5800
Ana Gierzphall, *President*
Kazimierz Szosler, *Sales Mgr*
EMP: 12 EST: 2010
SALES (est): 801.2K **Privately Held**
SIC: 2741 Miscellaneous publishing

(G-13127)
TERBO LTD
Also Called: Interiors By Robert
8905 130th St (11418-3328)
PHONE......................................718 847-2860
Robert Boccard, *President*
EMP: 9
SQ FT: 3,400
SALES (est): 941.9K **Privately Held**
SIC: 2391 2392 7641 Curtains &
draperies; household furnishings; uphol-
stery work

(G-13128)
WOMENS HEALTH CARE PC
(PA)
Also Called: Park Avenue Nutrition
11311 Jamaica Ave Ste C (11418-2476)
PHONE......................................718 850-0009
Rehana Sajjad, *CEO*
EMP: 4
SALES (est): 1.1MM **Privately Held**
SIC: 3842 7991 7299 Gynecological sup-
plies & appliances; physical fitness facili-
ties; personal appearance services

Richmondville
Schoharie County

(G-13129)
CHENANGO CONCRETE CORP
(PA)
145 Podpadic Rd (12149-2205)
PHONE......................................518 294-9964
Martin Galasso, *President*
Timothy Gaffney Sr, *CFO*
Emil Galasso, *Treasurer*
Cathy Manchester, *Executive Asst*
EMP: 12
SALES (est): 5.9MM **Privately Held**
SIC: 3273 Ready-mixed concrete

(G-13130)
TRI-CITY HIGHWAY PRODUCTS
INC
145 Podpadic Rd (12149-2205)
PHONE......................................518 294-9964
Martin Galasso, *CEO*
David Black, *Chairman*
Martin A Galasso Jr, *Chairman*
Christina Brizzee, *Controller*
EMP: 23
SALES (est): 5.3MM **Privately Held**
SIC: 2951 1442 Asphalt paving mixtures &
blocks; construction sand & gravel

Ridge
Suffolk County

(G-13131)
AIRWELD INC
1740 Middle Country Rd (11961-2407)
PHONE......................................631 924-6366
John Zak, *Branch Mgr*
EMP: 5
SALES (corp-wide): 26.7MM **Privately
Held**
SIC: 7692 Welding repair
PA: Airweld, Inc.
94 Marine St
Farmingdale NY 11735
631 694-4343

(G-13132)
AMERICAN PHYSICAL SOCIETY
Also Called: Physical Review
1 Research Rd (11961-2701)
PHONE......................................631 591-4025
David Ehrenstein, *Editor*
Stephen Skolnick, *Editor*
Sarah Monk, *Opers Staff*
CHI Misal, *Accountant*
Stephan Addo, *Manager*
EMP: 95
SALES (corp-wide): 63.9MM **Privately
Held**
WEB: www.phystec.net
SIC: 2721 Trade journals: publishing only,
not printed on site

PA: American Physical Society
1 Physics Ellipse
College Park MD 20740
301 209-3200

(G-13133)
QUALITY AND ASRN TECH
CORP (PA)
Also Called: Qna Tech
18 Marginwood Dr (11961-2902)
PHONE......................................646 450-6762
Marcos Merced, *CEO*
Brad Terris, *Accounts Exec*
Rick Schliemann, *CTO*
EMP: 7
SALES: 500K **Privately Held**
SIC: 7372 7379 Business oriented com-
puter software; computer hardware re-
quirements analysis

(G-13134)
RESIDENTIAL FENCES CORP
1760 Middle Country Rd (11961-2415)
PHONE......................................631 205-9758
John Gulino, *Branch Mgr*
EMP: 30
SALES (corp-wide): 12.5MM **Privately
Held**
SIC: 3273 Ready-mixed concrete
PA: Residential Fences Corp.
1775 Middle Country Rd
Ridge NY 11961
631 924-3011

(G-13135)
WEATHER TIGHT EXTERIORS
8 Woodbrook Dr (11961-2132)
PHONE......................................631 375-5108
Rick Dandria, *Owner*
EMP: 8
SALES (est): 550K **Privately Held**
SIC: 2421 Siding (dressed lumber)

Ridgewood
Queens County

(G-13136)
333 J & M FOOD CORP
Also Called: Allsupermarkets
333 Seneca Ave (11385-1338)
PHONE......................................718 381-1493
Jose Espinal, *Ch of Bd*
EMP: 12 EST: 2011
SALES (est): 2.4MM **Privately Held**
SIC: 2674 Grocers' bags: made from pur-
chased materials

(G-13137)
AABCO SHEET METAL CO INC
(PA)
Also Called: Asm Mechanical Systems
47 40 Metropolitan Ave (11385)
PHONE......................................718 821-1166
Ronald J Palmerick, *President*
Richard Minieri, *President*
Edmund MEI, *President*
EMP: 75
SQ FT: 85,000
SALES (est): 51.2MM **Privately Held**
SIC: 3444 1711 1761 Ducts, sheet metal;
metal housings, enclosures, casings &
other containers; ventilation & duct work
contractor; sheet metalwork

(G-13138)
ABR MOLDING ANDY LLC
1624 Centre St (11385-5336)
PHONE......................................212 576-1821
Andy Skoczek, *Owner*
Elizabeth Janowska, *Office Mgr*
▲ EMP: 15
SALES (est): 2.5MM **Privately Held**
SIC: 3089 Molding primary plastic

(G-13139)
ALPINE BUILDING SUPPLY INC
4626 Metropolitan Ave (11385-1045)
PHONE......................................718 456-2522
Marcangelo Cotoia, *President*
EMP: 7
SALES (est): 94.9K **Privately Held**
SIC: 3272 Concrete products

(G-13140)
BARKER BROTHERS
INCORPORATED
1666 Summerfield St Ste 1 (11385-5748)
PHONE......................................718 456-6400
Kenneth A Doyle, *Ch of Bd*
Edwin Doyle, *Ch of Bd*
Jeffrey Simonton, *COO*
Walter Doyle, *Vice Pres*
David Thomas, *Vice Pres*
▲ EMP: 100 EST: 1911
SQ FT: 50,000
SALES (est): 16.8MM **Privately Held**
WEB: www.bardoabrasives.com
SIC: 3291 Buffing or polishing wheels,
abrasive or nonabrasive

(G-13141)
BEST ADHESIVES CO INC
4702 Metropolitan Ave (11385-1047)
PHONE......................................718 417-3800
Sholm Singer, *President*
EMP: 6
SQ FT: 10,000
SALES (est): 928.8K **Privately Held**
SIC: 2891 Adhesives

(G-13142)
BRICK & BALLERSTEIN INC
1085 Irving Ave (11385-5745)
P.O. Box 1158, Yorktown Heights (10598-
8158)
PHONE......................................718 497-1400
Robert Levinson, *Ch of Bd*
Gary Levinson, *President*
Bruce Levinson, *Vice Pres*
▲ EMP: 82
SQ FT: 54,000
SALES (est): 15.1MM **Privately Held**
WEB: www.brickandballerstein.com
SIC: 2652 Setup paperboard boxes

(G-13143)
COSCO ENTERPRISES INC
Also Called: Cosco Soap & Detergent
1930 Troutman St (11385-1020)
PHONE......................................718 383-4488
Andrew Cook, *President*
Lawrence McGreevy, *Vice Pres*
EMP: 7 EST: 1966
SQ FT: 10,000
SALES (est): 1.4MM **Privately Held**
SIC: 2841 Soap & other detergents

(G-13144)
COSCO INTERPRISES INC
Also Called: Cosco Soap and Detergent
1930 Troutman St Ste 1 (11385-1020)
PHONE......................................718 417-8995
Andrew Cook, *President*
EMP: 35
SALES (est): 7.6MM **Privately Held**
SIC: 2841 Soap & other detergents

(G-13145)
ELECTRO-OPTICAL PRODUCTS
CORP
6240 Forest Ave Fl 2 (11385-1929)
P.O. Box 650441, Fresh Meadows (11365-
0441)
PHONE......................................718 456-6000
Ziva Tuchman, *President*
EMP: 6
SQ FT: 1,600
SALES: 1MM **Privately Held**
WEB: www.eopc.com
SIC: 3829 Measuring & controlling devices

(G-13146)
GENERAL COATINGS TECH INC
(PA)
24 Woodward Ave (11385-1022)
PHONE......................................718 821-1232
Michael Ghitelman, *President*
Robert Ghitelman, *Vice Pres*
EMP: 25
SQ FT: 160,000
SALES (est): 8.9MM **Privately Held**
SIC: 2851 Paints & paint additives; var-
nishes

(G-13147)
J & C FINISHING
1067 Wyckoff Ave (11385-5751)
PHONE......................................718 456-1087

Jose Hernandez, *President*
EMP: 20
SALES: 1.2MM **Privately Held**
SIC: 2389 Apparel & accessories

(G-13148)
JULIAN A MCDERMOTT
CORPORATION
Also Called: McDermott Light & Signal
1639 Stephen St (11385-5345)
PHONE......................................718 456-3606
Vernon McDermott, *Ch of Bd*
Andrea McDermott, *Vice Pres*
Harold Meditz, *Sales Staff*
▲ EMP: 45 EST: 1943
SQ FT: 25,000
SALES: 6MM **Privately Held**
WEB: www.mcdermottlight.com
SIC: 3648 Lighting equipment

(G-13149)
L S SIGN CO INC
1030 Wyckoff Ave (11385-5355)
PHONE......................................718 469-8600
Anthony Fodera, *President*
Joseph Fodera, *Vice Pres*
Christian Tomas, *Treasurer*
EMP: 19
SQ FT: 10,000
SALES (est): 1.6MM **Privately Held**
SIC: 3993 Signs, not made in custom sign
painting shops

(G-13150)
LONG ISLAND STAMP & SEAL
CO
Also Called: L I Stamp
5431 Myrtle Ave Ste 2 (11385-3403)
P.O. Box 863990 (11386-3990)
PHONE......................................718 628-8550
Harriet Pollak, *President*
Harry Pollak, *Vice Pres*
EMP: 15
SQ FT: 4,000
SALES (est): 980K **Privately Held**
SIC: 3953 Date stamps, hand: rubber or
metal

(G-13151)
LUDWIG AND LARSEN
4655 Metro Ave Ste 201 (11385-1194)
PHONE......................................718 369-0999
EMP: 6
SALES (est): 563.6K **Privately Held**
SIC: 2542 2541 3446 3643 Office & store
showcases & display fixtures; store & office display cases & fixtures; bank fixtures, ornamental metal; lightning
arrestors & coils

(G-13152)
N Y ELLI DESIGN CORP
5001 Metropolitan Ave 1 (11385-1052)
PHONE......................................718 228-0014
Dimitra Ligas, *CEO*
▲ EMP: 15
SQ FT: 30,000
SALES: 10.1MM **Privately Held**
WEB: www.ellicorp.com
SIC: 2434 2521 2531 Wood kitchen cabi-
nets; cabinets, office: wood; public build-
ing & related furniture; library furniture

(G-13153)
NULUX INC
1717 Troutman St (11385-1034)
PHONE......................................718 383-1112
Delia Price, *President*
Frank Conti, *Vice Pres*
EMP: 33
SQ FT: 4,500
SALES (est): 6.5MM **Privately Held**
WEB: www.nulux.com
SIC: 3645 3646 Residential lighting fix-
tures; commercial indusl & institutional
electric lighting fixtures

(G-13154)
ON THE SPOT BINDING INC
4805 Metropolitan Ave (11385-1007)
P.O. Box 863104 (11386-3104)
PHONE......................................718 497-2200
Isaac Mutzen, *President*
Nathan Hirsch, *Corp Secy*
Jerry Josefson, *Vice Pres*
EMP: 26

SQ FT: 10,000
SALES (est): 2MM **Privately Held**
SIC: 2789 Binding & repair of books, magazines & pamphlets

(G-13155)
PLANET EMBROIDERY
6695 Forest Ave (11385-3839)
PHONE.................................718 381-4827
Edwin Sotto, *Owner*
EMP: 12 EST: 2010
SALES (est): 134.8K **Privately Held**
SIC: 2395 Embroidery products, except schiffli machine; embroidery & art needlework

(G-13156)
PRINT BETTER INC
5939 Myrtle Ave (11385-5657)
PHONE.................................347 348-1841
Ayman Naguib, *Ch of Bd*
▲ EMP: 7 EST: 2010
SALES (est): 587.9K **Privately Held**
SIC: 2752 Commercial printing, lithographic

(G-13157)
PUBLIMAX PRINTING CORP
6615 Traffic Ave (11385-3307)
PHONE.................................718 366-7133
Patricia Flores, *President*
▲ EMP: 6
SALES (est): 1MM **Privately Held**
WEB: www.publimaxprinting.com
SIC: 2752 Commercial printing, lithographic

(G-13158)
RIDGEWOOD TIMES PRTG & PUBG
Also Called: Times News Weekly
6071 Woodbine St Fl 1 (11385-3242)
P.O. Box 860299 (11386-0299)
PHONE.................................718 821-7500
Maureen E Walthers, *President*
EMP: 30
SQ FT: 3,500
SALES (est): 1.6MM **Privately Held**
WEB: www.timesnewsweekly.com
SIC: 2711 Commercial printing & newspaper publishing combined

(G-13159)
SCHNEIDER M SOAP & CHEMICAL CO
1930 Troutman St (11385-1020)
PHONE.................................718 389-1000
Andrew Cook, *President*
EMP: 8 EST: 1969
SQ FT: 10,000
SALES (est): 740K **Privately Held**
SIC: 2841 Soap: granulated, liquid, cake, flaked or chip

(G-13160)
SPARCLEAN MBL REFINISHING INC
6915 64th Pl (11385-5251)
PHONE.................................718 445-2351
Rafa Colman, *President*
EMP: 5
SALES (est): 305.5K **Privately Held**
SIC: 1429 Marble, crushed & broken-quarrying

(G-13161)
SPECIALISTS LTD
Also Called: Wapons Specialists
4740 Metropolitan Ave (11385-1195)
PHONE.................................212 941-7696
EMP: 11 EST: 2015
SALES (est): 1.5MM **Privately Held**
SIC: 3999 Manufacturing industries

(G-13162)
STUDIO SILVERSMITHS INC
6315 Traffic Ave (11385-2629)
PHONE.................................718 418-6785
Arnold Godinger, *Ch of Bd*
Issac Godinger, *President*
Larry Lack, *Vice Pres*
▲ EMP: 40
SQ FT: 300,000

SALES (est): 3.8MM **Privately Held**
SIC: 3914 5199 Silverware; gifts & novelties

(G-13163)
TEC - CRETE TRANSIT MIX CORP
4673 Metropolitan Ave (11385-1044)
PHONE.................................718 657-6880
Linda Gisond, *Ch of Bd*
EMP: 25
SQ FT: 20,000
SALES (est): 3.3MM **Privately Held**
SIC: 3273 Ready-mixed concrete

(G-13164)
TRADING EDGE LTD
1923 Bleecker St Apt 1r (11385-9200)
PHONE.................................347 699-7079
Michael Oniszczuk, *Purch Mgr*
EMP: 5
SALES (est): 130.5K **Privately Held**
SIC: 2741

(G-13165)
TRI-BORO SHELVING INC
1940 Flushing Ave (11385-1043)
PHONE.................................718 782-8527
Fred Demaio, *President*
Covington Stan, *Plant Mgr*
John De Maio, *Sales/Mktg Mgr*
EMP: 15
SQ FT: 11,950
SALES (corp-wide): 8.5MM **Privately Held**
WEB: www.triboroshelving.com
SIC: 2542 5046 5084 Shelving, office & store: except wood; shelving, commercial & industrial; materials handling machinery
PA: Tri-Boro Shelving, Inc.
300 Dominion Dr
Farmville VA 23901
434 315-5600

(G-13166)
VIP FOODS INC
1080 Wyckoff Ave (11385-5757)
PHONE.................................718 821-5330
Edward Fruend, *President*
Mendel Fruend, *Vice Pres*
Tobias Fruend, *Treasurer*
▲ EMP: 25 EST: 1983
SQ FT: 13,000
SALES (est): 4MM **Privately Held**
WEB: www.vipfoodsinc.com
SIC: 2099 Dessert mixes & fillings; gelatin dessert preparations

---

Rifton
Ulster County

(G-13167)
COMMUNITY PRODUCTS LLC (PA)
Also Called: COMMUNITY PLAYTHINGS AND RIFTO
101 Woodcrest Dr (12471-7200)
P.O. Box 260 (12471-0260)
PHONE.................................845 658-8799
John Rhodes, *CEO*
Eric Nelson, *Train & Dev Mgr*
Dorothea Maendel, *Admin Sec*
▲ EMP: 106
SQ FT: 5,000
SALES: 100.5MM **Privately Held**
WEB: www.communityplaythings.com
SIC: 3842 2511 3844 Orthopedic appliances; children's wood furniture; therapeutic X-ray apparatus & tubes

(G-13168)
COMMUNITY PRODUCTS LLC
2032 Route 213 St (12471-7700)
P.O. Box 903 (12471-0903)
PHONE.................................845 658-8351
Christoph Meier,
EMP: 30
SALES (corp-wide): 100.5MM **Privately Held**
SIC: 3993 Signs & advertising specialties

PA: Community Products, Llc
101 Woodcrest Dr
Rifton NY 12471
845 658-8799

Ripley
Chautauqua County

(G-13169)
CHROMA LOGIC
6651 Wiley Rd (14775-9527)
PHONE.................................716 736-2458
Jason W Peterson, *President*
Jhon Mara, *Vice Pres*
Jason Peterson, *Marketing Mgr*
EMP: 2
SQ FT: 5,000
SALES: 1.5MM **Privately Held**
SIC: 3552 Dyeing, drying & finishing machinery & equipment

(G-13170)
RIPLEY MACHINE & TOOL CO INC
9825 E Main Rd (14775-9504)
PHONE.................................716 736-3205
Andrew Reinwald, *President*
Quenti Besink, *Vice Pres*
EMP: 17 EST: 1944
SQ FT: 15,000
SALES (est): 2.6MM **Privately Held**
SIC: 3599 Machine shop, jobbing & repair

Riverhead
Suffolk County

(G-13171)
AUTO-MATE TECHNOLOGIES LLC
34 Hinda Blvd (11901-4804)
PHONE.................................631 727-8886
Kenneth Herzog,
▼ EMP: 12
SALES (est): 1.9MM **Privately Held**
WEB: www.automatetech.com
SIC: 3365 Machinery castings, aluminum

(G-13172)
BERRY SPECIALTY TAPES LLC
1852 Old Country Rd (11901-3144)
PHONE.................................631 727-6000
John Pufahl, *Vice Pres*
Robert Pufahl, *Vice Pres*
Joseph M Pufahl,
EMP: 110 EST: 2002
SALES (est): 14.2MM **Publicly Held**
SIC: 2672 Tape, pressure sensitive: made from purchased materials; coated paper, except photographic, carbon or abrasive
HQ: Berry Global, Inc.
101 Oakley St
Evansville IN 47710
812 424-2904

(G-13173)
CUSTOM WOODWORK LTD
Also Called: Heritage Wide Plank Flooring
205 Marcy Ave (11901-3029)
PHONE.................................631 727-5260
Cathaleen Lanieri, *President*
EMP: 16
SQ FT: 3,500
SALES (est): 2.9MM **Privately Held**
WEB: www.heritagewideplankflooring.com
SIC: 2426 Flooring, hardwood

(G-13174)
EASTERN WELDING INC
274 Mill Rd (11901-3145)
PHONE.................................631 727-0306
William Stubelek, *President*
Brian Stubelek, *Vice Pres*
EMP: 6
SQ FT: 10,000
SALES: 228.4K **Privately Held**
SIC: 3713 3523 3732 4226 Truck bodies (motor vehicles); farm machinery & equipment; boat building & repairing; special warehousing & storage; fabricated structural metal

(G-13175)
KAPS-ALL PACKAGING SYSTEMS
200 Mill Rd (11901-3125)
PHONE.................................631 574-8778
Kenneth Herzog, *Ch of Bd*
John Hawkins, *Purch Agent*
Michael Herzog, *Info Tech Mgr*
◆ EMP: 61
SQ FT: 60,000
SALES (est): 16.2MM **Privately Held**
WEB: www.kapsall.com
SIC: 3565 Bottling machinery: filling, capping, labeling

(G-13176)
KOPPERT CRESS USA LLC
2975 Sound Ave (11901-1114)
PHONE.................................631 779-3640
Eddie Creces, *Branch Mgr*
EMP: 20 **Privately Held**
SIC: 2099 Salads, fresh or refrigerated
PA: Koppert Cress Usa Llc
23423 County Road 48
Cutchogue NY 11935

(G-13177)
LA FORGE FRANCAISE LTD INC
100 Kroemer Ave (11901-3117)
P.O. Box 1322, Boulder UT (84716-1322)
PHONE.................................631 591-0572
Patrice Humbert, *President*
Marlyse Humbert, *Vice Pres*
EMP: 6
SQ FT: 1,000
SALES (est): 579.6K **Privately Held**
SIC: 2514 Metal household furniture

(G-13178)
LEHNEIS ORTHOTICS PROSTHETIC
518 E Main St (11901-2529)
PHONE.................................631 369-3115
EMP: 7
SALES (corp-wide): 5MM **Privately Held**
SIC: 3842 5047 5999 Mfg Surgical Appliances/Supplies Whol Medical/Hospital Equipment Ret Misc Merchandise
PA: Lehneis Orthotics & Prosthetic Associates Ltd
13 Bedells Landing Rd
Roslyn NY
516 621-7277

(G-13179)
LONG IRELAND BREWING LLC
723 Pulaski St (11901-3039)
PHONE.................................631 403-4303
Gregory Martin, *President*
EMP: 5
SALES: 668K **Privately Held**
SIC: 2082 Beer (alcoholic beverage)

(G-13180)
LONG ISLAND GREEN GUYS
26 Silverbrook Dr (11901-4269)
PHONE.................................631 664-4306
Martin Hand, *Principal*
EMP: 5
SALES (est): 473.9K **Privately Held**
SIC: 3272 Grease traps, concrete

(G-13181)
LUXFER MAGTECH INC
680 Elton St (11901-2555)
PHONE.................................631 727-8600
Brian Purves, *CEO*
Marc Lamensdorf, *President*
Deepak Madan, *Vice Pres*
Deborah Simsen, *Treasurer*
James Gardella, *Exec Dir*
EMP: 80
SALES (est): 14MM
SALES (corp-wide): 487.9MM **Privately Held**
SIC: 2899 5149 Desalter kits, sea water; oxidizers, inorganic; groceries & related products
PA: Luxfer Holdings Plc
Ancorage Gateway
Salford LANCS M50 3
161 300-0611

(G-13182)
MAHIN IMPRESSIONS INC
30 W Main St Ste 301 (11901-2806)
PHONE..........................212 871-9777
Sharon Mahin, *President*
Brian Mahin, *Treasurer*
Anthony Goodwin, *Admin Sec*
EMP: 3
SALES: 1MM **Privately Held**
WEB: www.mahinimpressions.com
SIC: 2752 Commercial printing, offset

(G-13183)
NORTH COAST OUTFITTERS LTD
1015 E Main St Ste 1 (11901-2678)
PHONE..........................631 727-5580
Charles Darling III, *President*
Maria Lafrance, *Office Mgr*
▼ EMP: 20
SQ FT: 30,000
SALES (est): 2.2MM **Privately Held**
WEB: www.charlieshorse.com
SIC: 3949 3444 3354 Sporting & athletic goods; sheet metalwork; aluminum extruded products

(G-13184)
PHOENIX WOOD WRIGHTS LTD
132 Kroemer Ave 3 (11901-3117)
PHONE..........................631 727-9691
James Gleason, *President*
EMP: 14 EST: 2007
SALES (est): 2.3MM **Privately Held**
SIC: 3553 Bandsaws, woodworking

(G-13185)
QUANTUM KNOWLEDGE LLC
356 Reeves Ave (11901-1109)
PHONE..........................631 727-6111
Alexander Pozamantir,
EMP: 7
SALES (est): 790.4K **Privately Held**
SIC: 3572 Computer storage devices

(G-13186)
RAILEX WINE SERVICES LLC (PA)
Also Called: Northwest Wine Services
889 Harrison Ave (11901-2090)
P.O. Box 936 (11901-0936)
PHONE..........................631 369-7000
James Kleist, *Vice Pres*
Joseph Leuci, *CFO*
EMP: 45
SALES (est): 12.5MM **Privately Held**
SIC: 2084 Wines

(G-13187)
ROBERT & WILLIAM INC (PA)
224 Griffing Ave (11901-3214)
PHONE..........................631 727-5780
Wil S Field, *CEO*
William Schofield Sr, *CEO*
Robert Frankel, *President*
▼ EMP: 5 EST: 1997
SQ FT: 3,200
SALES: 30.1MM **Privately Held**
WEB: www.randw.com
SIC: 2011 Meat by-products from meat slaughtered on site

(G-13188)
SCHILLER STORES INC (PA)
Also Called: Le Creuset
509 Tanger Mall Dr (11901-6405)
PHONE..........................631 208-9400
Michael Kryivski, *Executive*
EMP: 5
SALES (est): 491K **Privately Held**
SIC: 3469 Cooking ware, porcelain enameled

(G-13189)
SENTRY AUTOMATIC SPRINKLER
735 Flanders Rd (11901-3828)
PHONE..........................631 723-3095
Thomas Andracchi, *President*
EMP: 10
SALES (est): 980K **Privately Held**
SIC: 3569 Sprinkler systems, fire: automatic

(G-13190)
TIKI INDUSTRIES INC
8 Tree Haven Ln (11901-4908)
PHONE..........................516 779-3629
Kalani Aiwohi, *President*
EMP: 5
SALES (est): 261.3K **Privately Held**
SIC: 3999 1611 1622 1741 Manufacturing industries; general contractor, highway & street construction; sidewalk construction; bridge construction; masonry & other stonework; waterproofing

(G-13191)
TUTHILL CORPORATION
75 Kings Dr (11901-6202)
PHONE..........................631 727-1097
EMP: 467
SALES (corp-wide): 469.3MM **Privately Held**
SIC: 3511 Mfg Steel Turbines
PA: Tuthill Corporation
8500 S Madison St
Burr Ridge IL 60527
630 382-4900

(G-13192)
WEDEL SIGN COMPANY INC
705 W Main St (11901-2843)
PHONE..........................631 727-4577
Barry Wedel, *President*
EMP: 5
SQ FT: 2,000
SALES: 276.8K **Privately Held**
SIC: 3993 Electric signs

(G-13193)
WINE SERVICES INC
1129 Cross River Dr Ste A (11901-1703)
PHONE..........................631 722-3800
John White, *President*
John Flock, *Director*
EMP: 5
SQ FT: 21,000
SALES (est): 420.1K **Privately Held**
WEB: www.wineservices.com
SIC: 2084 Wine cellars, bonded: engaged in blending wines

Rochester
Monroe County

(G-13194)
A Q P INC
Also Called: Advanced Quickprinting
2975 Brighton Henrietta T (14623-2787)
PHONE..........................585 256-1690
James L Roach, *President*
EMP: 7
SQ FT: 3,700
SALES (est): 1MM **Privately Held**
SIC: 2752 7334 Commercial printing, offset; photocopying & duplicating services

(G-13195)
A R ARENA PRODUCTS INC
2101 Mount Read Blvd (14615-3708)
PHONE..........................585 277-1680
Anthony R Arena, *CEO*
Jeff Reeves, *Mfg Mgr*
Joseph Vaccarella, *Engineer*
Don Wilcox, *Engineer*
Steve Duchon, *Natl Sales Mgr*
▲ EMP: 20
SQ FT: 30,000
SALES (est): 7MM **Privately Held**
WEB: www.arenaproducts.com
SIC: 3089 7359 Plastic containers, except foam; shipping container leasing

(G-13196)
AAA WELDING AND FABRICATION OF
1085 Lyell Ave (14606-1935)
PHONE..........................585 254-2830
Sam Dinch, *President*
Steven Stadtmiller, *Corp Secy*
EMP: 9
SQ FT: 16,000

SALES (est): 2MM **Privately Held**
WEB: www.aaawelding.com
SIC: 3441 1623 7692 Fabricated structural metal; pipe laying construction; welding repair

(G-13197)
AARON TOOL & MOLD INC
620 Trolley Blvd (14606-4215)
PHONE..........................585 426-5100
Daniel Morgan, *President*
Ellen Morgan, *Vice Pres*
EMP: 8
SQ FT: 6,000
SALES (est): 1.1MM **Privately Held**
WEB: www.aaronmold.com
SIC: 3089 Injection molding of plastics

(G-13198)
ACAD DESIGN CORP
975 Mount Read Blvd (14606-2829)
PHONE..........................585 254-6960
Thomas Sheen, *President*
Karen Sheen, *Vice Pres*
Dan Maus, *Engineer*
EMP: 13
SQ FT: 20,000
SALES: 2MM **Privately Held**
WEB: www.acaddesigncorp.com
SIC: 3599 7389 8711 Machine & other job shop work; design services; engineering services

(G-13199)
ACCEDE MOLD & TOOL CO INC
1125 Lexington Ave (14606-2995)
PHONE..........................585 254-6490
Roger Fox, *CEO*
Alton L Fox, *President*
Nancy Fox, *Vice Pres*
Ken Doran, *Mfg Spvr*
John Nelson, *Purch Mgr*
▲ EMP: 58
SQ FT: 38,000
SALES (est): 12.4MM **Privately Held**
WEB: www.accedemold.com
SIC: 3544 3599 Forms (molds), for foundry & plastics working machinery; custom machinery

(G-13200)
ACCU COAT INC
111 Humboldt St Ste 8 (14609-7415)
PHONE..........................585 288-2330
Paul Meier-Wang, *President*
Patrick Iuliamello, *Vice Pres*
EMP: 7
SQ FT: 4,500
SALES (est): 1.2MM **Privately Held**
WEB: www.accucoatinc.com
SIC: 3827 Optical instruments & lenses

(G-13201)
ACCURATE PNT POWDR COATING INC
606 Hague St (14606-1214)
PHONE..........................585 235-1650
Christopher Ralph, *President*
Jeremy Seaver, *General Mgr*
EMP: 17
SQ FT: 40,000
SALES: 1.2MM **Privately Held**
SIC: 3479 3999 Etching & engraving; coating of metals & formed products; barber & beauty shop equipment

(G-13202)
ACCURATE TOOL & DIE LLC
1085 Lyell Ave (14606-1935)
PHONE..........................585 254-2830
Sam Dinch, *Mng Member*
Mark Drewiega,
Steve Drewiega,
Gene Lippa,
EMP: 15
SQ FT: 15,000
SALES: 1.1MM **Privately Held**
SIC: 3599 Machine shop, jobbing & repair

(G-13203)
ACME PRECISION SCREW PDTS INC
623 Glide St (14606-1345)
P.O. Box 60649 (14606-0649)
PHONE..........................585 328-2028
Rodney Czudak, *President*

EMP: 18
SQ FT: 10,000
SALES (est): 3.5MM **Privately Held**
SIC: 3451 Screw machine products

(G-13204)
ACRO INDUSTRIES INC
554 Colfax St (14606-3112)
PHONE..........................585 254-3661
Joseph A Noto, *President*
John H Gefell, *Vice Pres*
James Francisco, *Opers Mgr*
Mark Keenan, *Purch Mgr*
Duane Olin, *Engineer*
▲ EMP: 148
SQ FT: 150,000
SALES (est): 56.2MM **Privately Held**
WEB: www.acroind.com
SIC: 3444 3599 3443 3469 Culverts, flumes & pipes; amusement park equipment; fabricated plate work (boiler shop); metal stampings

(G-13205)
ACUITY POLYMERS INC
1667 Lake Ave Ste 303 (14615-3047)
PHONE..........................585 458-8409
James Bonafini, *President*
EMP: 8
SALES (est): 743.1K **Privately Held**
SIC: 3851 Contact lenses

(G-13206)
ADDISON PRECISION MFG CORP
500 Avis St (14615-3308)
P.O. Box 15393 (14615-0393)
PHONE..........................585 254-1386
Robert E Champagne, *CEO*
Rodney C Champagne, *President*
Roger C Champagne, *Vice Pres*
Eric Caudill, *Manager*
EMP: 72 EST: 1950
SQ FT: 40,000
SALES (est): 15.6MM **Privately Held**
WEB: www.addisonprec.com
SIC: 3599 Machine shop, jobbing & repair

(G-13207)
ADRIAN JULES LTD
Also Called: Adrian-Jules Custom Tailor
1392 E Ridge Rd (14621-2005)
P.O. Box 17260 (14617-0260)
PHONE..........................585 342-5886
Adriano P Roberti, *Ch of Bd*
Arnald J Roberti, *President*
Peter E Roberti, *President*
Scotti Gaylor, *Manager*
Aj Lamberson, *Manager*
▲ EMP: 80 EST: 1964
SQ FT: 14,000
SALES (est): 8MM **Privately Held**
WEB: www.adrianjules.com
SIC: 2311 5699 2325 Men's & boys' suits & coats; custom tailor; men's & boys' trousers & slacks

(G-13208)
ADVANCE CIRCUIT TECHNOLOGY INC
19 Jetview Dr (14624-4903)
PHONE..........................585 328-2000
James Morrison, *Ch of Bd*
Bob Kajfasz, *Vice Pres*
Robert Kajfasz, *Vice Pres*
Kalman Zsamboky, *Vice Pres*
Kal Zsamboky, *Sales Executive*
▲ EMP: 42 EST: 1998
SQ FT: 35,000
SALES (est): 10.5MM **Privately Held**
WEB: www.advcircuit.com
SIC: 3679 3672 Electronic circuits; printed circuit boards

(G-13209)
ADVANCED COATING SERVICE LLC
15 Hytec Cir (14606-4255)
P.O. Box 60387 (14606-0387)
PHONE..........................585 247-3970
Donald Titus, *Mng Member*
Donald E Titus Jr, *Mng Member*
EMP: 7

SALES (est): 1MM **Privately Held**
WEB: www.acscoating.com
SIC: 3479 Etching & engraving; coating of metals & formed products

(G-13210)
ADVANCED GLASS INDUSTRIES INC
Also Called: A G I
1335 Emerson St (14606-3006)
P.O. Box 60467 (14606-0467)
PHONE.................................585 458-8040
Anthony Marino, *President*
H John Fischer, *Vice Pres*
▲ EMP: 51
SQ FT: 42,000
SALES (est): 17.4MM **Privately Held**
WEB: www.agi.com
SIC: 3827 Lenses, optical: all types except ophthalmic

(G-13211)
ADVANCED MACHINE INC
439 Central Ave Ste 108 (14605-3016)
PHONE.................................585 423-8255
John Bauman, *President*
Jacqueline De Mario, *Treasurer*
Dana Byron, *Admin Sec*
EMP: 10 EST: 1999
SQ FT: 5,600
SALES (est): 1.3MM **Privately Held**
SIC: 3599 Machine shop, jobbing & repair

(G-13212)
ADVANTAGE METALWORK FINSHG LLC
1000 University Ave # 700 (14607-1286)
PHONE.................................585 454-0160
Chet Wester, *CEO*
Arthur Carroll, *Exec VP*
Dale Campbell, *Vice Pres*
Bryan Carter, *Project Engr*
EMP: 86
SALES (est): 21.4MM **Privately Held**
SIC: 3444 Sheet metalwork

(G-13213)
ADVANTECH INDUSTRIES INC
3850 Buffalo Rd (14624-1104)
PHONE.................................585 247-0701
James Gizzi, *Ch of Bd*
EMP: 115
SALES: 26.4MM **Privately Held**
WEB: www.advantechindustries.com
SIC: 3399 3444 Laminating steel; sheet metalwork

(G-13214)
ADVENT TOOL & MOLD INC
999 Ridgeway Ave (14615-3819)
PHONE.................................585 254-2000
Ken Desrosiers, *Ch of Bd*
James Murphy, *Vice Pres*
David Klafehn, *Mfg Mgr*
David Bierbrauer, *Engineer*
Joe Lenhardt, *Engineer*
▲ EMP: 103
SQ FT: 53,000
SALES (est): 22.1MM
SALES (corp-wide): 2.4B **Privately Held**
WEB: www.adventtool.com
SIC: 3089 3544 3545 Injection molding of plastics; industrial molds; tools & accessories for machine tools
HQ: Rochling Engineering Plastics Se & Co. Kg
Rochlingstr. 1
Haren (Ems) 49733
593 470-10

(G-13215)
AFP ENTERPRISES INC
100 Holleder Pkwy (14615-3800)
PHONE.................................585 254-1128
Albert F Porter, *Chairman*
▲ EMP: 112
SQ FT: 165,000
SALES (est): 30.7MM **Privately Held**
WEB: www.ajlmfg.com
SIC: 3444 Sheet metalwork

(G-13216)
ALCOA FASTENING SYSTEMS
181 Mckee Rd (14611-2011)
PHONE.................................585 368-5049
Vitaliy Rusakov, *CEO*

EMP: 8 EST: 2015
SALES (est): 672.1K **Privately Held**
SIC: 3353 Aluminum sheet & strip

(G-13217)
ALKEMY MACHINE LLC
Also Called: Aurora Machine
1600 Lexington Ave 103c (14606-3000)
PHONE.................................585 436-8730
Jonathan Amoia, *General Mgr*
Jordan Kowalczyk, *General Mgr*
EMP: 8
SALES (est): 1.7MM **Privately Held**
SIC: 3444 3599 Culverts, flumes & pipes; amusement park equipment; machine shop, jobbing & repair

(G-13218)
ALLIANCE AUTOMATION SYSTEMS
400 Trabold Rd (14624-2529)
PHONE.................................585 426-2700
Arthur Anderson, *CEO*
Stewart H Rodman, *Ch of Bd*
Jeffrey Hoffman, *CFO*
Robert Huener, *Director*
Robert T Isherwood, *Director*
▲ EMP: 125
SQ FT: 120,000
SALES (est): 15MM **Privately Held**
SIC: 3549 3569 Assembly machines, including robotic; assembly machines, non-metalworking

(G-13219)
ALLIANCE PRECISION PLAS CORP (PA)
1220 Lee Rd (14606-4252)
PHONE.................................585 426-5310
Walter C Butler Jr, *CEO*
Bradley C Scott, *President*
Clay Kearns, *Purchasing*
Diane Smalley, *Purchasing*
James Beifus, *QC Mgr*
▲ EMP: 200 EST: 1998
SQ FT: 80,000
SALES (est): 64.2MM **Privately Held**
WEB: www.allianceppc.com
SIC: 3089 3544 Injection molded finished plastic products; dies, plastics forming

(G-13220)
ALLIANCE PRECISION PLAS CORP
105 Elmore Dr (14606-3429)
PHONE.................................585 426-5310
Brad Scott, *Branch Mgr*
Robert Levesque, *Maintence Staff*
EMP: 53
SALES (corp-wide): 64.2MM **Privately Held**
SIC: 3089 3544 Injection molded finished plastic products; dies, plastics forming
PA: Alliance Precision Plastics Corporation
1220 Lee Rd
Rochester NY 14606
585 426-5310

(G-13221)
ALLIANCE-MCALPIN NY LLC
1220 Lee Rd (14606-4252)
PHONE.................................585 426-5310
Walter C Butler Jr,
EMP: 15
SALES (est): 118.4K
SALES (corp-wide): 64.2MM **Privately Held**
SIC: 3089 Injection molded finished plastic products
PA: Alliance Precision Plastics Corporation
1220 Lee Rd
Rochester NY 14606
585 426-5310

(G-13222)
ALLSTATE TOOL AND DIE INC
Also Called: Atd Precision Machining
15 Coldwater Cres (14624-2590)
PHONE.................................585 426-0400
Paul Held Sr, *President*
Paul Held Jr, *President*
Thomas Saraceni, *General Mgr*
Elizabeth Held, *Vice Pres*
Jennifer Held, *Assistant*
▲ EMP: 68 EST: 1967

SQ FT: 37,000
SALES (est): 9.7MM **Privately Held**
WEB: www.atdprecision.com
SIC: 3544 Special dies & tools

(G-13223)
ALOI SOLUTIONS LLC (PA)
Also Called: Aloi Materials Handling
140 Commerce Dr (14623-3504)
PHONE.................................585 292-0920
Jeff Gambril, *President*
Robert Manion, *Vice Pres*
Michael Rhault, *Project Engr*
Patti Heagle, *Accounts Mgr*
Dan Marshall, *Accounts Mgr*
▲ EMP: 30 EST: 1987
SQ FT: 16,500
SALES (est): 7.9MM **Privately Held**
WEB: www.aloi.com
SIC: 3599 3999 Custom machinery; atomizers, toiletry

(G-13224)
ALPHA IRON WORKS LLC
65 Goodway Dr S (14623-3018)
PHONE.................................585 424-7260
Debbie Mancini, *Engineer*
Evangelos Economides, *Mng Member*
Simon Economides, *Bd of Directors*
EMP: 16 EST: 1978
SQ FT: 13,000
SALES (est): 3.3MM **Privately Held**
WEB: www.alphairon.com
SIC: 3441 Fabricated structural metal

(G-13225)
ALTON MANUFACTURING INC
825 Lee Rd (14606-4290)
PHONE.................................585 458-2600
George Chornobil, *Ch of Bd*
Andrew Chornobil, *President*
John Sykes, *Sales Engr*
Bohdan Chornobil, *Shareholder*
Christine Sykes, *Shareholder*
EMP: 90 EST: 1966
SQ FT: 150,000
SALES (est): 16.3MM **Privately Held**
WEB: www.altonmfg.com
SIC: 3469 3544 3541 Stamping metal for the trade; special dies, tools, jigs & fixtures; machine tools, metal cutting type

(G-13226)
AMARR COMPANY
Also Called: Amarr Garage Doors
550 Mile Crssing Blvd 1 (14624)
PHONE.................................585 426-8290
Philip Bordelen, *Manager*
EMP: 10
SALES (corp-wide): 9.3B **Privately Held**
WEB: www.amarr.com
SIC: 3442 5211 Garage doors, overhead; metal; garage doors, sale & installation
HQ: Amarr Company
165 Carriage Ct
Winston Salem NC 27105
336 744-5100

(G-13227)
AMBRELL CORPORATION (HQ)
1655 Lyell Ave (14606-2311)
PHONE.................................585 889-0236
Tony Mazzullo, *President*
Girish Dahake, *Vice Pres*
Tony Lucido, *Vice Pres*
Dan King, *Project Mgr*
Marty Pryor, *Buyer*
▲ EMP: 13
SQ FT: 25,000
SALES: 21.4MM
SALES (corp-wide): 78.5MM **Publicly Held**
WEB: www.ameritherm.com
SIC: 3567 Induction heating equipment
PA: Intest Corporation
804 E Gate Dr Ste 200
Mount Laurel NJ 08054
856 505-8800

(G-13228)
AMERICAN AEROGEL CORPORATION
460 Buffalo Rd Ste 200a (14611-2026)
PHONE.................................585 328-2140
Michael Hone, *CEO*
Jay McHarg, *President*

David Abruzzese, *Vice Pres*
Jeff Sullivan, *Director*
EMP: 34
SQ FT: 40,000
SALES (est): 12.1MM **Privately Held**
WEB: www.americanaerogel.com
SIC: 3441 Fabricated structural metal

(G-13229)
AMERICAN PACKAGING CORPORATION
1555 Lyell Ave (14606-2145)
PHONE.................................585 254-2002
Peter Scottland, *President*
EMP: 7
SALES (corp-wide): 280.5MM **Privately Held**
SIC: 2673 3497 2671 Bags: plastic, laminated & coated; metal foil & leaf; paper coated or laminated for packaging
PA: American Packaging Corporation
100 Apc Way
Columbus WI 53925
920 623-2291

(G-13230)
AMERICAN PACKAGING CORPORATION
777 Driving Park Ave (14613-1591)
PHONE.................................585 254-9500
Wanda Coots, *Engineer*
Rocco Lombardo, *Engineer*
William Tornow, *Plant Engr*
Kelly O'Mealia, *Human Resources*
David Soper, *Accounts Mgr*
EMP: 112
SALES (corp-wide): 280.5MM **Privately Held**
SIC: 2673 3497 2671 2754 Bags: plastic, laminated & coated; metal foil & leaf; paper coated or laminated for packaging; rotogravure printing; bags: uncoated paper & multiwall
PA: American Packaging Corporation
100 Apc Way
Columbus WI 53925
920 623-2291

(G-13231)
AMERICAN SPECIALTY MFG CO
Also Called: Boss Sauce
272 Hudson Ave (14605-2124)
P.O. Box 31344 (14603-1344)
PHONE.................................585 544-5600
Eddie Harris, *President*
Loreta Pope, *Vice Pres*
Regina Harris, *Treasurer*
EMP: 11
SQ FT: 6,500
SALES (est): 400K **Privately Held**
SIC: 2035 Seasonings, meat sauces (except tomato & dry)

(G-13232)
AMERICAN SPORTS MEDIA LLC (PA)
2604 Elmwood Ave Ste 343 (14618-2213)
PHONE.................................585 377-9636
David Jones,
David Aultman,
Brian Spindler,
EMP: 1
SQ FT: 3,000
SALES (est): 1.2MM **Privately Held**
WEB: www.americansportsmedia.com
SIC: 2711 Newspapers: publishing only, not printed on site

(G-13233)
AMERICAN TIME MFG LTD
Also Called: American Products
1600 N Clinton Ave Ste 1 (14621-2200)
PHONE.................................585 266-5120
Clifford Charlson, *President*
Jeff Harrington, *Vice Pres*
▲ EMP: 18
SQ FT: 7,000
SALES (est): 1.9MM **Privately Held**
WEB: www.americanproducts-ny.com
SIC: 3873 Watchcases

GEOGRAPHIC

(G-13234)
AMETEK INC
Also Called: Ametek Power Instruments
255 Union St N (14605-2699)
P.O. Box 1764, Paoli PA (19301-0801)
PHONE......................................585 263-7700
Bo Bojczuk, Exec VP
Richard Murphy, Opers Staff
Paul Parsons, Opers Staff
John Wonders, QC Mgr
John Sotack, Engineer
EMP: 68
SALES (corp-wide): 4.8B Publicly Held
SIC: 3621 3823 3825 3812 Motors &
generators; industrial instrmnts msrmnt
display/control process variable; instru-
ments to measure electricity; search &
navigation equipment; electrical equip-
ment & supplies
PA: Ametek, Inc.
1100 Cassatt Rd
Berwyn PA 19312
610 647-2121

(G-13235)
ANALOG DIGITAL TECHNOLOGY LLC
Also Called: Adtech
95 Mount Read Blvd # 149 (14611-1923)
PHONE......................................585 698-1845
Tom Crumlish, President
Eric Hauptmann, Vice Pres
EMP: 9
SQ FT: 6,500
SALES (est): 1.1MM Privately Held
WEB: www.adtech-inst.com
SIC: 3699 5084 Chimes, electric; indus-
trial machinery & equipment

(G-13236)
ANDEX CORP
69 Deep Rock Rd (14624-3575)
PHONE......................................585 328-3790
Andrew J Cherre, President
EMP: 30 EST: 1962
SQ FT: 17,000
SALES (est): 6.6MM Privately Held
SIC: 2621 Filter paper

(G-13237)
ANDROS MANUFACTURING CORP
30 Hojack Park (14612-1994)
PHONE......................................585 663-5700
Russell Steenhoff, CEO
Nancy Commanda, Vice Pres
EMP: 6
SQ FT: 12,000
SALES: 700K Privately Held
WEB: www.androsmfg.com
SIC: 3451 3643 Screw machine products;
solderless connectors (electric wiring de-
vices)

(G-13238)
ANMAR ACQUISITION LLC (HQ)
35 Vantage Point Dr (14624-1142)
PHONE......................................585 352-7777
Lee Rudow, CEO
John Zimmer, CFO
EMP: 5
SALES (est): 2.5MM
SALES (corp-wide): 160.9MM Publicly
Held
SIC: 3825 Radar testing instrments, elec-
tric
PA: Transcat, Inc.
35 Vantage Point Dr
Rochester NY 14624
585 352-7777

(G-13239)
ANTAB MCH SPRFINISHING LAB INC
46 Latta Rd (14612-4708)
PHONE......................................585 865-8290
Araxie Aintablian, President
▲ EMP: 7
SALES (est): 470K Privately Held
SIC: 3599 Machine shop, jobbing & repair

(G-13240)
APPLIED COATINGS HOLDING CORP (PA)
1653 E Main St Ste 1 (14609-7000)
PHONE......................................585 482-0300
Bruno Glavich, President
Holly Gallagher, Manager
◆ EMP: 8 EST: 1998
SQ FT: 5,000
SALES (est): 5MM Privately Held
SIC: 3827 Optical elements & assemblies,
except ophthalmic

(G-13241)
APPLIED IMAGE INC
1653 E Main St Ste 1 (14609-7090)
PHONE......................................585 482-0300
Dave Doubledee, President
Glenn Jackling, General Mgr
Gregory Peck, Vice Pres
John Daly, Opers Mgr
Char Colotti, Sales Executive
EMP: 20
SQ FT: 20,000
SALES: 4.7MM
SALES (corp-wide): 5MM Privately Held
WEB: www.appliedimage.net
SIC: 3826 3827 7335 Analytical optical in-
struments; optical instruments & appara-
tus; color separation, photographic &
movie film
PA: Applied Coatings Holding Corp.
1653 E Main St Ste 1
Rochester NY 14609
585 482-0300

(G-13242)
ARBR STUDIOS LLC
35 Norman St (14613-1809)
PHONE......................................585 254-7607
Fritz Zeller, Mng Member
Jason Cudzilo,
Daniel Fallon,
EMP: 10 EST: 2012
SQ FT: 10,000
SALES: 1MM Privately Held
SIC: 2431 Woodwork, interior & ornamen-
tal

(G-13243)
ARCH CHEMICALS INC
Also Called: Lonza
100 Mckee Rd (14611-2013)
P.O. Box 30205 (14603-3205)
PHONE......................................585 436-3030
Michael Neilson, Counsel
Carol Burley, Production
Meg Kubarycz, Senior Buyer
Francien Trubia, Controller
Mary Turcotte, Human Res Mgr
EMP: 175
SALES (corp-wide): 5.5B Privately Held
WEB: www.archchemicals.com
SIC: 2819 Industrial inorganic chemicals
HQ: Arch Chemicals, Inc.
1200 Bluegrass Lakes Pkwy
Alpharetta GA 30004
678 624-5800

(G-13244)
ARCONIC FASTENING SYSTEMS
181 Mckee Rd (14611-2011)
PHONE......................................585 368-5049
Elmer L Doty, President
EMP: 11
SALES (est): 1.7MM Privately Held
SIC: 3411 Metal cans

(G-13245)
ARM ROCHESTER INC
740 Driving Park Ave I1 (14613-1534)
PHONE......................................585 354-5077
Armando Santiago, President
James Jacus, Director
Robert Vavrina, Director
EMP: 15
SALES (est): 1.9MM Privately Held
SIC: 3086 7389 Padding, foamed plastic;

(G-13246)
ARNOLD MAGNETIC TECH CORP (HQ)
Also Called: Magnetic Technology
770 Linden Ave (14625-2716)
PHONE......................................585 385-9010
Gordon H McNeil, President
Ted Baker, General Mgr
Roy Hollon, General Mgr
Michael Carney, Project Engr
Dave Goff, Project Engr
▲ EMP: 182
SQ FT: 70,000
SALES (est): 218.2MM Publicly Held
WEB: www.arnoldmagnetics.com
SIC: 3264 3499 Magnets, permanent: ce-
ramic or ferrite; magnets, permanent:
metallic

(G-13247)
ARNPRIOR RPID MFG SLUTIONS INC (PA)
2400 Mount Read Blvd # 112 (14615-2744)
PHONE......................................585 617-6301
Leonard M Levie, Ch of Bd
John Wilbur, President
Pamela Barnard, Principal
Thomas Palumbo, Principal
Carol Rath, Principal
EMP: 152
SALES (est): 26MM Privately Held
SIC: 3999 Advertising display products

(G-13248)
ARNPRIOR RPID MFG SLUTIONS INC
2400 Mount Read Blvd # 1124
(14615-2744)
PHONE......................................585 617-6301
Thomas Palumbo, Manager
EMP: 9 Privately Held
SIC: 3999 Advertising display products
PA: Arnprior Rapid Manufacturing Solu-
tions, Inc.
2400 Mount Read Blvd # 112
Rochester NY 14615

(G-13249)
ART-CRAFT OPTICAL COMPANY INC
57 Goodway Dr S (14623-3018)
PHONE......................................585 546-6640
C Thomas Eagle, President
Martin Gullen, Exec VP
Christopher Eagle, VP Opers
Donald Bennett, Finance Dir
Charles Thomas Eagle Jr, VP Mktg
EMP: 49
SQ FT: 90,000
SALES (est): 9.1MM Privately Held
WEB: www.artcraftoptical.com
SIC: 3851 Frames & parts, eyeglass &
spectacle

(G-13250)
ARYZTA LLC
Dalton Div
64 Chester St (14611-2110)
PHONE......................................585 235-8160
Connie Springfield, Manager
EMP: 13
SALES (corp-wide): 3.9B Privately Held
WEB: www.pennantfoods.com
SIC: 2041 2051 Flour & other grain mill
products; bread, cake & related products
HQ: Aryzta Llc
6080 Center Dr Ste 900
Los Angeles CA 90045
310 417-4700

(G-13251)
ARYZTA LLC
Also Called: Pennant Foods
235 Buffalo Rd (14611-1905)
PHONE......................................585 235-8160
Steven Smith, Branch Mgr
David Bonacci, Representative
EMP: 218
SALES (corp-wide): 3.9B Privately Held
WEB: www.pennantfoods.com
SIC: 2051 2052 Bread, cake & related
products; bakery products, dry
HQ: Aryzta Llc
6080 Center Dr Ste 900
Los Angeles CA 90045
310 417-4700

(G-13252)
ASCRIBE INC
383 Buell Rd (14624-3123)
PHONE......................................585 413-0298

Mark Shaw, Ch of Bd
Dean Saklis, President
EMP: 50
SALES (est): 3.6MM Privately Held
SIC: 3999 7389 3479 Atomizers, toiletry;
grinding, precision: commercial or indus-
trial; etching & engraving

(G-13253)
ASP INDUSTRIES INC
9 Evelyn St (14606-5533)
PHONE......................................585 254-9130
Suzanne M Phillips, President
Susan Allen, Controller
EMP: 20
SQ FT: 23,000
SALES (est): 2.8MM Privately Held
WEB: www.aspindustries.com
SIC: 3444 3441 Sheet metal specialties,
not stamped; fabricated structural metal

(G-13254)
AVRO INC
Also Called: Avr Optics
3635 Buffalo Rd Ste 2 (14624-1120)
PHONE......................................585 445-7588
Peter Brunt, Vice Pres
Lane Manning, Engineer
EMP: 7
SALES (est): 199.3K Privately Held
SIC: 3821 Laboratory equipment: fume
hoods, distillation racks, etc.

(G-13255)
AYCAN MEDICAL SYSTEMS LLC
693 East Ave Ste 102 (14607-2160)
PHONE......................................585 271-3078
Frank Burkhardt, Mng Member
EMP: 15 EST: 2003
SQ FT: 4,000
SALES (est): 1.8MM Privately Held
SIC: 7372 Business oriented computer
software

(G-13256)
AYDATA MANAGEMENT LLC
693 East Ave Ste 102 (14607-2160)
PHONE......................................585 271-6133
Frank Burkhardt,
Peter Brunnengraeber,
EMP: 8
SALES (est): 186.1K Privately Held
SIC: 7372 Prepackaged software

(G-13257)
BAGEL LAND
1896 Monroe Ave (14618-1918)
PHONE......................................585 442-3080
Robert Juliano, Owner
EMP: 20
SALES (est): 1.1MM Privately Held
SIC: 2051 5461 Bagels, fresh or frozen;
bakeries

(G-13258)
BAGS UNLIMITED INC
7 Canal St (14608-1910)
PHONE......................................585 436-6282
Michael Macaluso, President
Marion Oyer, General Mgr
Dave Street, General Mgr
Valerie Macaluso, Manager
Ken Seen, Manager
▲ EMP: 20
SQ FT: 90,000
SALES (est): 5MM Privately Held
WEB: www.bagsunlimited.com
SIC: 2673 2759 Plastic bags: made from
purchased materials; bags, plastic: print-
ing

(G-13259)
BAKER COMMODITIES INC
Rochester Division
2268 Browncroft Blvd (14625-1000)
PHONE......................................585 482-1880
William Schmieder, Manager
EMP: 40
SALES (corp-wide): 153.6MM Privately
Held
WEB: www.bakercommodities.com
SIC: 2077 2048 Tallow rendering, inedible;
prepared feeds

PA: Baker Commodities, Inc.
4020 Bandini Blvd
Vernon CA 90058
323 268-2801

(G-13260)
BALIVA CONCRETE PRODUCTS INC
245 Paul Rd (14624-4923)
P.O. Box 24581 (14624-0581)
PHONE.....................585 328-8442
Richard Baliva, *President*
EMP: 6 EST: 1943
SQ FT: 3,000
SALES: 750K **Privately Held**
SIC: 3272 Concrete products

(G-13261)
BAUM CHRISTINE AND JOHN CORP
Also Called: Minuteman Press
1577 W Ridge Rd (14615-2520)
PHONE.....................585 621-8910
John Baum, *President*
Christine Baum, *Vice Pres*
EMP: 9
SQ FT: 2,500
SALES (est): 1.5MM **Privately Held**
SIC: 2752 2791 2789 Commercial printing, lithographic; typesetting; bookbinding & related work

(G-13262)
BAUSCH & LOMB INCORPORATED
1 Bausch And Lomb Pl (14604-2799)
P.O. Box 25169, Lehigh Valley PA (18002-5169)
PHONE.....................585 338-6000
John Ferris, *Vice Pres*
Denis Polyn, *Vice Pres*
Ruth Sleeman, *Vice Pres*
Tracy Valorie, *Vice Pres*
William McClain, *Project Mgr*
EMP: 53
SALES (corp-wide): 8.3B **Privately Held**
SIC: 3851 Ophthalmic goods
HQ: Bausch & Lomb Incorporated
400 Somerset Corp Blvd
Bridgewater NJ 08807
585 338-6000

(G-13263)
BAUSCH & LOMB INCORPORATED
1400 N Goodman St (14609-3596)
PHONE.....................585 338-6000
Charles E Conway, *Manager*
Eugene J Romeo, *Director*
EMP: 400
SQ FT: 2,336
SALES (corp-wide): 8.3B **Privately Held**
WEB: www.bausch.com
SIC: 3851 Ophthalmic goods
HQ: Bausch & Lomb Incorporated
400 Somerset Corp Blvd
Bridgewater NJ 08807
585 338-6000

(G-13264)
BEASTONS BUDGET PRINTING INC
Also Called: Sir Speedy
1260 Scttsvlle Rd Ste 300 (14624)
PHONE.....................585 244-2721
Nancy Beaston, *President*
Shel D Beaston, *Vice Pres*
Shel Beaston, *Vice Pres*
EMP: 9
SALES (est): 1.4MM **Privately Held**
SIC: 2752 2791 2789 Commercial printing, lithographic; typesetting; bookbinding & related work

(G-13265)
BEETS LOVE PRODUCTION LLC
1150 Lee Rd Sectiona (14606-4251)
PHONE.....................585 270-2471
Simon Woods, *Project Mgr*
Dave Stocklosa, *Finance Dir*
EMP: 35
SQ FT: 98,500
SALES: 1.5MM **Privately Held**
SIC: 2063 Beet sugar

(G-13266)
BEREZA IRON WORKS INC
87 Dewey Ave (14608-1289)
PHONE.....................585 254-6311
William Goy, *President*
Irene E Gratton, *Vice Pres*
EMP: 18
SQ FT: 15,000
SALES: 4.4MM **Privately Held**
SIC: 3441 Fabricated structural metal

(G-13267)
BETTER POWER INC
508 White Spruce Blvd (14623-1613)
PHONE.....................585 475-1321
Catherine Henn, *Owner*
EMP: 6
SQ FT: 4,000
SALES (est): 1.5MM **Privately Held**
WEB: www.betterlighting.com
SIC: 3569 Gas generators

(G-13268)
BFGG INVESTORS GROUP LLC
1900 University Ave (14610-2621)
PHONE.....................585 424-3456
Chris Guider, *Mng Member*
EMP: 5
SALES (est): 530K **Privately Held**
SIC: 3081 Film base, cellulose acetate or nitrocellulose plastic

(G-13269)
BIGSKY TECHNOLOGIES LLC
1600 N Clinton Ave Ste 11 (14621-2200)
PHONE.....................585 270-5282
Cathy A Fleischer, *Mng Member*
EMP: 7
SQ FT: 2,000
SALES (est): 1.4MM **Privately Held**
SIC: 2843 Surface active agents

(G-13270)
BITTNER COMPANY LLC
Also Called: AlphaGraphics
75 Goodway Dr Ste 3 (14623-3000)
PHONE.....................585 214-1790
EMP: 13
SALES (est): 1.5MM **Privately Held**
SIC: 2752 Comm Prtg Litho

(G-13271)
BLACKBOX BIOMETRICS INC
125 Tech Park Dr Ste 1131 (14623-2438)
PHONE.....................585 329-3399
Joseph V Bridgeford, *Ch of Bd*
Scott Featherman, *Business Mgr*
Vincent Baier, *Engineer*
EMP: 22
SALES (est): 2.5MM **Privately Held**
SIC: 3999 Barber & beauty shop equipment

(G-13272)
BLOCH INDUSTRIES LLC
140 Commerce Dr (14623-3504)
PHONE.....................585 334-9600
Brian Geary, *Mng Member*
EMP: 60
SQ FT: 54,000
SALES (est): 5.2MM **Privately Held**
WEB: www.blochindustries.com
SIC: 2434 2541 2431 2521 Wood kitchen cabinets; counters or counter display cases, wood; millwork; wood office furniture

(G-13273)
BLUE CHIP MOLD INC
95 Lagrange Ave (14613-1509)
PHONE.....................585 647-1790
Paul A Engert, *President*
EMP: 13
SQ FT: 10,250
SALES: 1.3MM **Privately Held**
SIC: 3544 Industrial molds

(G-13274)
BLUE TOAD HARD CIDER
120 Mushroom Blvd (14623-3263)
PHONE.....................585 424-5508
Scott Hallock, *Managing Dir*
Todd Rath, *Co-Owner*
EMP: 20

SALES (est): 2.1MM **Privately Held**
SIC: 3556 Presses, food: cheese, beet, cider & sugarcane

(G-13275)
BMA MEDIA SERVICES INC
Also Called: Spinergy
1655 Lyell Ave (14606-2311)
PHONE.....................585 385-2060
EMP: 29 EST: 2013
SQ FT: 79,000
SALES (est): 1.7MM **Privately Held**
SIC: 3695 Mfg Magnetic/Optical Recording Media

(G-13276)
BODYCOTE THERMAL PROC INC
620 Buffalo Rd (14611-2006)
PHONE.....................585 436-7876
Tony Schaut, *Branch Mgr*
EMP: 24
SQ FT: 10,000
SALES (corp-wide): 935.8MM **Privately Held**
SIC: 3398 Metal heat treating
HQ: Bodycote Thermal Processing, Inc.
12700 Park Central Dr # 700
Dallas TX 75251
214 904-2420

(G-13277)
BOEHM SURGICAL INSTRUMENT CORP
966 Chili Ave Ste 3 (14611-2896)
PHONE.....................585 436-6584
Paul Boehm, *President*
Mary L Cooper, *Treasurer*
EMP: 11 EST: 1915
SQ FT: 13,000
SALES: 1MM **Privately Held**
SIC: 3841 3843 3429 3641 Surgical & medical instruments; dental equipment; keys, locks & related hardware; electric lamps & parts for specialized applications; medical & hospital equipment

(G-13278)
BOOK1ONE LLC
655 Driving Park Ave (14613-1566)
PHONE.....................585 458-2101
Peter Pape, *CEO*
Marc Bardeen,
EMP: 7
SALES (est): 1MM **Privately Held**
WEB: www.book1one.com
SIC: 2732 Books: printing & binding

(G-13279)
BOYDELL & BREWER INC
Also Called: Camden House
668 Mount Hope Ave (14620-2731)
PHONE.....................585 275-0419
Sue Smit, *President*
EMP: 12
SQ FT: 1,500
SALES (est): 1.3MM **Privately Held**
SIC: 2731 Book music: publishing only, not printed on site
PA: Boydell & Brewer Group Limited
Unit 4 Bridge Farm Business Park
Woodbridge

(G-13280)
BRAYLEY TOOL & MACHINE INC
1685 Lyell Ave (14606-2311)
PHONE.....................585 342-7190
Stephen Roeger, *President*
Rena Roeger, *Vice Pres*
EMP: 8
SQ FT: 6,500
SALES: 700K **Privately Held**
WEB: www.brayleytool.com
SIC: 3544 Special dies & tools

(G-13281)
BRINKMAN INTL GROUP INC (PA)
167 Ames St (14611-1701)
PHONE.....................585 429-5000
Andrew J Laniak, *CEO*
Robert Brinkman, *Ch of Bd*
Daniel Bavineau, *Mfg Staff*
Doug Larson, *Engineer*
Joe Morlino, *Engineer*

EMP: 1
SQ FT: 12,000
SALES (est): 99.2MM **Privately Held**
WEB: www.brinkmanig.com
SIC: 3545 3451 3325 3542 Thread cutting dies; screw machine products; steel foundries; machine tools, metal forming type

(G-13282)
BRINKMAN PRODUCTS INC
Also Called: Davenport
167 Ames St (14611-1701)
PHONE.....................585 235-4545
Andrew J Laniak, *President*
Andrew Laniak, *COO*
Dick Huber, *Mfg Staff*
Jim Henderson, *Plant Engr*
Greg Zenuk, *Sales Staff*
▲ EMP: 290
SQ FT: 118,000
SALES (est): 48.8MM
SALES (corp-wide): 99.2MM **Privately Held**
WEB: www.davenportmachine.com
SIC: 3541 5084 Machine tools, metal cutting type; industrial machinery & equipment
PA: Brinkman International Group, Inc.
167 Ames St
Rochester NY 14611
585 429-5000

(G-13283)
BRISTOL BOARDING INC
1149 Highland Ave (14620-1869)
PHONE.....................585 271-7860
EMP: 6 EST: 1974
SALES (est): 1.1MM **Privately Held**
SIC: 2441 5099 Mfg Shipping Cases & Whol Carrying Cases

(G-13284)
BROWN PUBLISHING LLC
323 Aldine St (14619-1207)
PHONE.....................585 484-0432
Rodney Brown, *Administration*
EMP: 7
SALES (est): 90.9K **Privately Held**
SIC: 2711 Newspapers: publishing only, not printed on site

(G-13285)
BSV METAL FINISHERS INC
Also Called: Bsv Enterprises
750 Saint Paul St (14605-1737)
PHONE.....................585 747-7070
Benjamin S Vasquez, *President*
EMP: 26
SQ FT: 13,000
SALES (est): 6.5MM **Privately Held**
SIC: 3398 Metal heat treating

(G-13286)
BURKE & BANNAYAN
2465 W Ridge Rd Ste 2 (14626-3046)
PHONE.....................585 723-1010
Vic Bannayan, *President*
EMP: 5
SQ FT: 2,480
SALES (est): 370K **Privately Held**
SIC: 3911 7631 5944 Jewelry, precious metal; jewelry repair services; jewelry stores

(G-13287)
BURKE FRGING HEAT TREATING INC
30 Sherer St (14611-1618)
PHONE.....................585 235-6060
Ronald Thompson, *Ch of Bd*
James Granville, *Vice Pres*
Martha Vanderhoof, *Treasurer*
EMP: 24
SQ FT: 58,000
SALES (est): 5.4MM **Privately Held**
SIC: 3462 3398 Iron & steel forgings; metal heat treating

(G-13288)
BURNETT PROCESS INC (HQ)
545 Colfax St (14606-3111)
PHONE.....................585 254-8080
Jack Cannon, *Ch of Bd*
▲ EMP: 1
SQ FT: 60,000

SALES (est): 5.4MM
SALES (corp-wide): 38.7MM **Privately Held**
WEB: www.burnettprocessinc.com
SIC: **3296** 3086 7699 Fiberglass insulation; plastics foam products; industrial equipment services
PA: Cannon Industries, Inc.
525 Lee Rd
Rochester NY 14606
585 254-8080

(G-13289)
BURNETT PROCESS INC
545 Colfax St (14606-3111)
PHONE..................................585 277-1623
Ronald Salayda, *Manager*
EMP: 30
SALES (corp-wide): 38.7MM **Privately Held**
WEB: www.burnettprocessinc.com
SIC: **3569** Filters
HQ: Burnett Process, Inc.
545 Colfax St
Rochester NY 14606
585 254-8080

(G-13290)
C J WINTER MACHINE TECH (HQ)
167 Ames St (14611-1701)
PHONE..................................585 429-5000
Robert Brinkman, *President*
Joe Palma, *Senior Buyer*
Paul Allart, *Engineer*
Philip Daggar, *Treasurer*
Connie Tribotte, *Personnel*
EMP: 20 EST: 1933
SQ FT: 118,000
SALES (est): 4MM
SALES (corp-wide): 99.2MM **Privately Held**
WEB: www.cjwinter.com
SIC: **3545** 3542 3325 Thread cutting dies; machine tools, metal forming type; steel foundries
PA: Brinkman International Group, Inc.
167 Ames St
Rochester NY 14611
585 429-5000

(G-13291)
C R C MANUFACTURING INC
37 Curlew St (14606-2535)
PHONE..................................585 254-8820
EMP: 10
SQ FT: 7,000
SALES (est): 1.1MM **Privately Held**
SIC: **3599** 3451 Mfg Industrial Machinery Mfg Machine Products

(G-13292)
CALIBER IMGING DIAGNOSTICS INC (PA)
50 Methodist Hill Dr # 100 (14623-4268)
PHONE..................................585 239-9800
L Michael Hone, *CEO*
William J Shea, *Ch of Bd*
William J Fox, *Vice Pres*
Joseph R Williams, *Vice Pres*
Karen Howe, *CFO*
EMP: 35
SQ FT: 20,000
SALES (est): 4MM **Publicly Held**
WEB: www.lucid-tech.com
SIC: **3827** 3845 3841 Optical instruments & lenses; electromedical equipment; surgical & medical instruments

(G-13293)
CANFIELD & TACK INC
Also Called: Dellas Graphics
925 Exchange St (14608-2802)
PHONE..................................585 235-7710
Michael Guche, *CEO*
Ray Brown, *President*
Gary Cvejic, *COO*
Chris Adams, *VP Finance*
Ron Julian, *Executive*
EMP: 85 EST: 1926
SQ FT: 45,000
SALES (est): 25.9MM **Privately Held**
WEB: www.canfieldtack.com
SIC: **2752** 4225 Commercial printing, offset; general warehousing & storage

(G-13294)
CANNON INDUSTRIES INC (PA)
525 Lee Rd (14606-4236)
PHONE..................................585 254-8080
Jack Cannon, *CEO*
Reggie Cannon, *President*
Lawrence Streaker, *Purchasing*
Kiet Tran, *Manager*
Dustin Beuerlein, *Info Tech Mgr*
▲ EMP: 97
SQ FT: 100,000
SALES (est): 38.7MM **Privately Held**
WEB: www.cannonind.com
SIC: **3444** 3469 5051 3861 Sheet metalwork; metal stampings; metals service centers & offices; photocopy machines

(G-13295)
CAPS TEAMWEAR INC
65 Milburn St (14607-2914)
PHONE..................................585 663-1750
Roy Brewer Jr, *Manager*
Mike Capuano, *Manager*
EMP: 5
SALES (est): 353K **Privately Held**
SIC: **2329** Men's & boys' sportswear & athletic clothing

(G-13296)
CARESTREAM HEALTH INC
1669 Lake Ave (14652-0001)
PHONE..................................585 627-1800
EMP: 300
SALES (corp-wide): 23.7B **Privately Held**
SIC: **3861** Photographic equipment & supplies
HQ: Carestream Health, Inc.
150 Verona St
Rochester NY 14608

(G-13297)
CARTA USA LLC
1600 Lexington Ave # 116 (14606-3061)
PHONE..................................585 436-3012
Mike Welch, *General Mgr*
Jake Carey, *Vice Pres*
▲ EMP: 20 EST: 1992
SALES (est): 511.6K
SALES (corp-wide): 149.1MM **Privately Held**
SIC: **2621** Paper mills
PA: Flower City Printing, Inc.
1725 Mount Read Blvd
Rochester NY 14606
585 663-9000

(G-13298)
CARTER STREET BAKERY INC
580 Child St (14606)
PHONE..................................585 749-7104
Takele Delnesa, *President*
EMP: 8 EST: 2015
SALES (est): 408.2K **Privately Held**
SIC: **2051** Bakery: wholesale or wholesale/retail combined

(G-13299)
CASCADES NEW YORK INC (DH)
1845 Emerson St (14606-3123)
PHONE..................................585 527-8110
Albino Metauro, *President*
Pascal Barreto, *QC Mgr*
Brian Uhler, *Technical Mgr*
EMP: 115 EST: 1998
SQ FT: 6,000
SALES (est): 1B
SALES (corp-wide): 3.5B **Privately Held**
WEB: www.metrowaste.com
SIC: **2621** Paper mills
HQ: Cascades Canada Ulc
404 Boul Marie-Victorin
Kingsey Falls QC J0A 1
819 363-5100

(G-13300)
CASUAL FRIDAY INC
1561 Lyell Ave (14606-2123)
PHONE..................................585 544-9470
Anthony Germano, *President*
Mimi Wakefield, *Sales Staff*
EMP: 12
SQ FT: 6,000
SALES (est): 1.6MM **Privately Held**
SIC: **2396** 2395 Fabric printing & stamping; embroidery products, except schiffli machine

(G-13301)
CDJ STAMPING INC
146 Halstead St Ste 123 (14610-1954)
PHONE..................................585 224-8120
Timothy Merklinger, *President*
Jason Schulmerich, *Vice Pres*
EMP: 5
SQ FT: 4,000
SALES (est): 442.8K **Privately Held**
WEB: www.cdjstamping.com
SIC: **3089** Injection molding of plastics; plastic processing

(G-13302)
CEIPAL LLC
722 Weiland Rd (14626-3957)
PHONE..................................585 351-2934
EMP: 5 EST: 2014
SQ FT: 3,000
SALES (est): 300K **Privately Held**
SIC: **7372** Prepackaged Software Services

(G-13303)
CEIPAL LLC
687 Lee Rd Ste 208a (14606-4257)
PHONE..................................585 584-1316
Sameer Penakalapati, *Mng Member*
EMP: 5
SALES (est): 257.9K **Privately Held**
SIC: **7372** Application computer software

(G-13304)
CELLEC TECHNOLOGIES INC
125 Tech Park Dr Ste 2111 (14623-2448)
PHONE..................................585 454-9166
Christopher Schauerman, *President*
Brian Landi, *Vice Pres*
Ryne Raffaelle, *Vice Pres*
Matthew Ganter, *Treasurer*
EMP: 5
SALES (est): 252.9K **Privately Held**
SIC: **3691** Storage batteries

(G-13305)
CENTERLESS TECHNOLOGY INC
45 Wells St (14611-2821)
PHONE..................................585 436-2240
Daniel Burns, *President*
Jim Ozminskowski, *Corp Secy*
Les Malovics, *Vice Pres*
EMP: 10
SQ FT: 11,000
SALES (est): 1.8MM **Privately Held**
WEB: www.centerlesstech.com
SIC: **3599** Machine & other job shop work

(G-13306)
CENTURY MOLD COMPANY INC (PA)
25 Vantage Point Dr (14624-1142)
PHONE..................................585 352-8600
Ron Ricotta, *CEO*
David Dick, *Exec VP*
Bruce Dixon, *Plant Mgr*
Richard Liberte, *Plant Mgr*
Dion Decker, *Facilities Mgr*
▲ EMP: 100
SQ FT: 80,000
SALES (est): 203.7MM **Privately Held**
WEB: www.centurymold.com
SIC: **3089** 3544 Injection molding of plastics; industrial molds

(G-13307)
CENTURY MOLD MEXICO LLC (HQ)
25 Vantage Point Dr (14624-1142)
PHONE..................................585 352-8600
Ronald Ricotta,
▲ EMP: 7
SALES (est): 49.2MM
SALES (corp-wide): 203.7MM **Privately Held**
SIC: **3089** Injection molding of plastics
PA: Century Mold Company, Inc.
25 Vantage Point Dr
Rochester NY 14624
585 352-8600

(G-13308)
CERION ENERGY INC
1 Blossom Rd (14610-1009)
PHONE..................................585 271-5630
George M Stadler, *CEO*

Landon Mertz, *Ch of Bd*
▼ EMP: 25
SALES (est): 4.5MM **Privately Held**
SIC: **2819** Industrial inorganic chemicals

(G-13309)
CERION LLC
1 Blossom Rd (14610-1009)
PHONE..................................585 271-5630
Bill Stewart, *COO*
Chris Skipper, *Vice Pres*
George M Stadler,
EMP: 15
SALES (est): 3MM **Privately Held**
SIC: **2819** Industrial inorganic chemicals

(G-13310)
CHAMPION PHOTOCHEMISTRY INC
1669 Lake Ave (14615)
PHONE..................................585 760-6444
R Fraser Mason, *Ch of Bd*
Peter Newton, *President*
◆ EMP: 65
SQ FT: 375,000
SALES (est): 10.4MM
SALES (corp-wide): 704K **Privately Held**
WEB: www.championphotochemistry.com
SIC: **3861** Photographic processing chemicals
HQ: Champion Photochemistry Limited
1760 Meyerside Dr
Mississauga ON L5T 1
905 670-7900

(G-13311)
CHAMTEK MFG INC
123 Louise St (14606-1321)
PHONE..................................585 328-4900
Donald Zenkel, *President*
Thomas Williams, *Vice Pres*
Franklin Chamberlain, *Admin Sec*
EMP: 15
SQ FT: 18,000
SALES (est): 1.6MM **Privately Held**
WEB: www.chamtek.com
SIC: **3544** 3444 Special dies & tools; sheet metalwork

(G-13312)
CHECKLIST BOARDS CORPORATION
763 Linden Ave Ste 2 (14625-2725)
PHONE..................................585 586-0152
Rick Taylor, *President*
Jim Wemett, *Vice Pres*
Gail Floros, *Executive*
EMP: 5
SALES: 500K **Privately Held**
SIC: **3993** Signs, not made in custom sign painting shops

(G-13313)
CHINA IMPRINT LLC
750 Saint Paul St (14605-1737)
PHONE..................................585 563-3391
William A Dolan II,
▲ EMP: 5
SQ FT: 20,000
SALES: 2MM **Privately Held**
SIC: **2752** Promotional printing, lithographic

(G-13314)
CHRISTI PLASTICS INC
215 Tremont St (14608-2393)
PHONE..................................585 436-8510
Earl Martin, *President*
Deborah Scally, *Treasurer*
EMP: 4
SQ FT: 10,500
SALES: 1.1MM **Privately Held**
SIC: **3089** Extruded finished plastic products

(G-13315)
CITY NEWSPAPER
250 N Goodman St Ste 1 (14607-1199)
PHONE..................................585 244-3329
Mary Towler, *Publisher*
Bill Towler, *Publisher*
Betsy Matthews, *Sales Mgr*
Becka Rafferty, *Art Dir*
Tim Macaluso, *Correspondent*
EMP: 8

▲ = Import ▼=Export
◆ =Import/Export

SALES (est): 414.3K **Privately Held**
SIC: 2711 Commercial printing & newspaper publishing combined; newspapers, publishing & printing

(G-13316)
CJK MANUFACTURING LLC
160 Commerce Dr (14623-3504)
PHONE.................................585 663-6370
Keith Woodward,
Charles Tutty,
EMP: 14
SQ FT: 20,000
SALES (est): 3.1MM **Privately Held**
WEB: www.cjkmanufacturing.com
SIC: 3089 Thermoformed finished plastic products

(G-13317)
CLARSONS CORP
Also Called: Express Press
215 Tremont St Ste 8 (14608-2366)
PHONE.................................585 235-8775
David Clar, *President*
Robert M Clar, *President*
Joan Clar, *Admin Sec*
EMP: 11 EST: 1978
SQ FT: 4,000
SALES (est): 1.5MM **Privately Held**
WEB: www.expresspress.com
SIC: 2752 2791 7334 Commercial printing, offset; typesetting; photocopying & duplicating services

(G-13318)
CLERIO VISION INC (PA)
312 Susquehanna Rd (14618-2940)
PHONE.................................617 216-7881
Mikael Totterman, *CEO*
EMP: 12
SQ FT: 2,000
SALES (est): 9.6MM **Privately Held**
SIC: 3841 Surgical lasers

(G-13319)
COAST TO COAST CIRCUITS INC
Metro Circuits
205 Lagrange Ave (14613-1562)
PHONE.................................585 254-2980
Walter Stender, *CEO*
Walt Stender, *CEO*
Cheryl Covert, *Principal*
EMP: 45
SALES (corp-wide): 13.8MM **Privately Held**
WEB: www.speedycircuits.com
SIC: 3672 Wiring boards
PA: Coast To Coast Circuits, Inc.
5331 Mcfadden Ave
Huntington Beach CA 92649
714 891-9441

(G-13320)
COATING TECHNOLOGY INC
800 Saint Paul St (14605-1032)
PHONE.................................585 546-7170
Stanley Dahle, *Ch of Bd*
Ronald L Feeley, *President*
EMP: 30
SQ FT: 40,000
SALES (est): 3.5MM
SALES (corp-wide): 17.1MM **Privately Held**
WEB: www.coatingtechnologyinc.com
SIC: 3471 Plating of metals or formed products
PA: The Metal Arts Company Inc
800 Saint Paul St
Rochester NY

(G-13321)
CONDOR ELECTRONICS CORP
295 Mount Read Blvd (14611-1931)
P.O. Box 60590 (14606-0590)
PHONE.................................585 235-1500
Wayne S Corso, *President*
Lisa Corso, *Corp Secy*
▲ EMP: 30 EST: 1967
SQ FT: 18,000
SALES (est): 4.7MM **Privately Held**
WEB: www.condorelectronics.com
SIC: 3679 Harness assemblies for electronic use: wire or cable

(G-13322)
CONE BUDDY SYSTEM INC
3495 Winton Pl Ste E290 (14623-2819)
PHONE.................................585 427-9940
Robert Sotile, *President*
EMP: 15 EST: 1994
SALES (est): 1.4MM **Privately Held**
WEB: www.buddysystemusa.com
SIC: 2052 Cones, ice cream

(G-13323)
CONNECTION MOLD INC
585 Ling Rd (14612-1936)
PHONE.................................585 458-6463
Thomas Strecker, *President*
EMP: 7
SQ FT: 6,800
SALES (est): 1MM **Privately Held**
WEB: www.connectionmold.com
SIC: 3965 Button blanks & molds

(G-13324)
CONOPCO INC
28 Mansfield St (14606-2327)
PHONE.................................585 647-8322
John Frank, *Branch Mgr*
EMP: 35
SALES (corp-wide): 58.3B **Privately Held**
SIC: 2844 Toilet preparations
HQ: Conopco, Inc.
700 Sylvan Ave
Englewood Cliffs NJ 07632
201 894-7760

(G-13325)
CONSOLIDATED CONTAINER CO LLC
Also Called: Liquitane
18 Champeney Ter (14605-2711)
PHONE.................................585 262-6470
Jerry Zaklick, *Plant Mgr*
EMP: 150
SALES (corp-wide): 14B **Publicly Held**
WEB: www.cccllc.com
SIC: 2655 2656 Fiber cans, drums & containers; sanitary food containers
HQ: Consolidated Container Company, Llc
2500 Windy Ridge Pkwy Se # 1400
Atlanta GA 30339
678 742-4600

(G-13326)
CORBETT STVES PTTERN WORKS INC
80 Lowell St (14605-1831)
PHONE.................................585 546-7109
John K Steeves Jr, *President*
Kevin Steeves, *Vice Pres*
Jorge Williams, *Engineer*
EMP: 20 EST: 1914
SQ FT: 20,000
SALES (est): 3.3MM **Privately Held**
WEB: www.corbett-steeves.com
SIC: 3365 3599 3553 3469 Machinery castings, aluminum; machine shop, jobbing & repair; pattern makers' machinery, woodworking; patterns on metal

(G-13327)
CRAFTSMAN MANUFACTURING CO IN
1279 Mount Read Blvd (14606-2817)
PHONE.................................585 426-5780
Kevin Contestabile, *President*
EMP: 5
SQ FT: 3,000
SALES: 320K **Privately Held**
SIC: 3599 Machine shop, jobbing & repair

(G-13328)
CRATER SERVICE GROUP INC
111 Humboldt St (14609-7463)
PHONE.................................585 482-7770
Craig Schinsing, *President*
EMP: 9
SQ FT: 8,000
SALES (est): 1.5MM **Privately Held**
WEB: www.rygan.com
SIC: 2752 Commercial printing, offset

(G-13329)
CRYOVAC INC
1525 Brooks Ave (14624-3545)
PHONE.................................585 436-3211
Mark Davis, *Manager*

EMP: 150
SALES (corp-wide): 4.7B **Publicly Held**
WEB: www.cryovac.com
SIC: 3087 Custom compound purchased resins
HQ: Cryovac, Llc
2415 Cascade Pointe Blvd
Charlotte NC 28208
980 430-7000

(G-13330)
CRYSTAL LINTON TECHNOLOGIES
2180 Brigh Henri Town Lin (14623)
PHONE.................................585 444-8784
Rick Webb, *COO*
Todd Barnum, *COO*
John Reese, *Engineer*
Joel Stefl, *Engineer*
Marc Waggener, *Controller*
EMP: 11 EST: 2013
SQ FT: 15,713
SALES (est): 2.6MM **Privately Held**
SIC: 3821 Furnaces, laboratory

(G-13331)
CSW INC
Also Called: Diegraphics Group
70 Pixley Industrial Pkwy (14624-2377)
PHONE.................................585 247-4010
Ann Lukasik, *General Mgr*
Jim Mootz, *Finance*
Laurie Willard, *Cust Mgr*
Ed Reynolds, *Branch Mgr*
Angela Hawk, *Manager*
EMP: 15
SALES (est): 3MM
SALES (corp-wide): 16.6MM **Privately Held**
WEB: www.citystamp.com
SIC: 3555 2796 2791 Printing plates; platemaking services; typesetting
PA: Csw, Inc.
45 Tyburski Rd
Ludlow MA 01056
413 589-1311

(G-13332)
CUMMINS-WAGNER-SIEWERT LLC (HQ)
Also Called: Kineflow Division
175 Akron St (14609-7209)
PHONE.................................585 482-9640
Doug Ardimger, *President*
Kate Interlichia, *Engineer*
Dee N Christopoulos, *Human Res Dir*
Nicholas Brown, *Sales Staff*
Bruce Collins, *Manager*
EMP: 43
SQ FT: 15,000
SALES (est): 11.7MM
SALES (corp-wide): 83.3MM **Privately Held**
WEB: www.siewertequipment.com
SIC: 3519 5084 Internal combustion engines; pumps & pumping equipment
PA: Cummins-Wagner Company, Inc.
10901 Pump House Rd
Annapolis Junction MD 20701
800 966-1277

(G-13333)
CURAEGIS TECHNOLOGIES INC (PA)
1999 Mount Read Blvd # 3 (14615-3700)
PHONE.................................585 254-1100
Richard A Kaplan, *CEO*
Gary A Siconolfi, *Ch of Bd*
Keith E Gleasman, *President*
Leigh White, *Exec VP*
Steve Urbanik, *Engineer*
EMP: 24
SQ FT: 13,650
SALES: 37K **Publicly Held**
WEB: www.torvec.com
SIC: 7372 3561 Business oriented computer software; pumps & pumping equipment

(G-13334)
CUSTOM SOUND AND VIDEO
Also Called: Casco Security
40 Rutter St (14606-1806)
PHONE.................................585 424-5000
Casimer S Plonczynski, *President*
Rosa F Ladelfa, *Business Mgr*

EMP: 20
SQ FT: 6,500
SALES (est): 2.2MM **Privately Held**
SIC: 3699 5731 7629 Security devices; radio, television & electronic stores; electronic equipment repair

(G-13335)
DAGOSTINO IRON WORKS INC
10 Deep Rock Rd (14624-3520)
PHONE.................................585 235-8850
Kenneth D'Agostino Jr, *President*
Kenneth J D'Agostino Jr, *President*
EMP: 9
SQ FT: 4,000
SALES (est): 1.3MM **Privately Held**
SIC: 3449 5051 5999 Bars, concrete reinforcing; fabricated steel; steel; alcoholic beverage making equipment & supplies

(G-13336)
DAILY RECORD (PA)
Also Called: Daily Media
16 W Main St Ste G9 (14614-1604)
PHONE.................................585 232-2035
Jim Dolan, *President*
Andrew Green, *Research*
EMP: 10
SQ FT: 36,000
SALES (est): 654K **Privately Held**
WEB: www.dailyrecord.com
SIC: 2752 2711 Commercial printing, lithographic; newspapers, publishing & printing

(G-13337)
DANISCO US INC
Also Called: Genencor Division Danisco US
3490 Winton Pl (14623-2829)
PHONE.................................585 256-5200
Robert Villas, *Manager*
EMP: 75
SALES (corp-wide): 30.6B **Publicly Held**
SIC: 2835 8731 2899 2869 In vitro & in vivo diagnostic substances; commercial physical research; chemical preparations; industrial organic chemicals
HQ: Danisco Us Inc.
925 Page Mill Rd
Palo Alto CA 94304
650 846-7500

(G-13338)
DANISCO US INC
Also Called: Genencor International
1700 Lexington Ave (14606-3140)
PHONE.................................585 277-4300
Thomas Mitchell, *Branch Mgr*
Dave Cress, *Maintence Staff*
EMP: 100
SALES (corp-wide): 30.6B **Publicly Held**
SIC: 2819 2087 Industrial inorganic chemicals; flavoring extracts & syrups
HQ: Danisco Us Inc.
925 Page Mill Rd
Palo Alto CA 94304
650 846-7500

(G-13339)
DAYTON ROGERS NEW YORK LLC
150 Fedex Way (14624-1174)
PHONE.................................585 349-4040
Ron Lowry, *CEO*
Rich Vanaernum, *General Mgr*
Thomas A Pilon, *Vice Pres*
Mark D Spiczka, *Treasurer*
Jerome Mattern, *Human Res Dir*
EMP: 60
SQ FT: 38,000
SALES (est): 8.6MM
SALES (corp-wide): 78.5MM **Privately Held**
SIC: 3469 Stamping metal for the trade
PA: Dayton Rogers Manufacturing Co.
8401 W 35w Service Dr Ne
Minneapolis MN 55449
763 717-6450

(G-13340)
DEAD RINGER LLC
2100 Brghton Hnrtta St375 (14623)
PHONE.................................585 355-4685
Kristian Meyer, *Vice Pres*
Jesse Erdle,
▲ EMP: 2 EST: 2011

SALES: 2.6MM **Privately Held**
SIC: 3423 5091 Hand & edge tools; sharpeners, sporting goods

(G-13341)
DEAL INTERNATIONAL INC
110 Halstead St Ste 1 (14610-1952)
P.O. Box 10088 (14610-0088)
PHONE..................................585 288-4444
Menish Damani, *President*
Manish Damani, *Prgrmr*
▲ EMP: 26
SQ FT: 6,000
SALES (est): 5.1MM **Privately Held**
WEB: www.diihq.com
SIC: 2891 Sealants

(G-13342)
DEES AUDIO & VISION
347 Seneca Pkwy (14613-1416)
PHONE..................................585 719-9256
EMP: 5
SALES (est): 150K **Privately Held**
SIC: 3571 Electronics/Audio/Sales

(G-13343)
DIAMOND PACKAGING HOLDINGS LLC
111 Commerce Dr (14623-3503)
PHONE..................................585 334-8030
Dave Rydell, *Vice Pres*
Keith Robinson,
EMP: 8
SALES (est): 1MM **Privately Held**
SIC: 2657 3089 Food containers, folding: made from purchased material; air mattresses, plastic

(G-13344)
DIAMOND PAPER BOX COMPANY
Also Called: Diamond Packaging
111 Commerce Dr (14623-3503)
P.O. Box 23620 (14692-3620)
PHONE..................................585 334-8030
Karla Gerrie Fichter, *CEO*
Dave Rydell, *President*
Christine Grady, *Project Mgr*
Mike Corey, *Traffic Mgr*
Andrew Gauvin, *Design Engr*
◆ EMP: 260
SQ FT: 90,000
SALES: 63MM **Privately Held**
WEB: www.diamondpkg.com
SIC: 2657 Folding paperboard boxes

(G-13345)
DIEMAX OF ROCHESTER INC
1555 Lyell Ave Ste 141 (14606-2147)
PHONE..................................585 288-3912
Richard J Oliver, *President*
Wayne Rotella, *Vice Pres*
Ryan Prue, *Treasurer*
▲ EMP: 7
SQ FT: 900
SALES (est): 998.2K **Privately Held**
WEB: www.diemax.com
SIC: 3544 Special dies & tools

(G-13346)
DIGITRONIK LABS INC
1344 University Ave # 6100 (14607-1657)
PHONE..................................585 360-0043
Shawn Mott, *President*
Chris Coon, *Vice Pres*
Stephen Mokey, *Treasurer*
David Coon, *Admin Sec*
EMP: 10
SQ FT: 3,500
SALES: 1.2MM **Privately Held**
SIC: 3823 8731 8711 7371 Controllers for process variables, all types; computer (hardware) development; engineering services; custom computer programming services

(G-13347)
DIMENSION TECHNOLOGIES INC
Also Called: D T I
315 Mount Read Blvd Ste 5 (14611-1900)
PHONE..................................585 436-3530
Arnold Lagergren, *CEO*
Arnold D Lagergren, *President*
Michael Casciano, *President*

Jesse B Eichenlaub, *Vice Pres*
EMP: 5
SQ FT: 3,400
SALES (est): 1.1MM **Privately Held**
WEB: www.dti3d.com
SIC: 3679 Liquid crystal displays (LCD)

(G-13348)
DIPAOLO BAKING CO INC
598 Plymouth Ave N (14608-1691)
PHONE..................................585 303-5013
Dominick P Massa, *President*
Stephen Woerner, *Vice Pres*
EMP: 80 EST: 1910
SQ FT: 30,000
SALES (est): 12.7MM **Privately Held**
WEB: www.dipaolobread.com
SIC: 2051 5461 Bread, all types (white, wheat, rye, etc): fresh or frozen; rolls, bread type: fresh or frozen; bakeries; bread

(G-13349)
DISTECH SYSTEMS INC (HQ)
1000 University Ave # 400 (14607-1286)
PHONE..................................585 254-7020
John J Perrotti, *CEO*
Dan Schwab, *President*
▲ EMP: 3
SQ FT: 12,900
SALES (est): 7.6MM
SALES (corp-wide): 825.5MM **Privately Held**
WEB: www.distechsystems.com
SIC: 3569 Assembly machines, non-metal-working
PA: Gleason Corporation
1000 University Ave
Rochester NY 14607
585 473-1000

(G-13350)
DIVERSIFIED ENVELOPE LTD
95 Mount Read Blvd # 103 (14611-1923)
PHONE..................................585 615-4697
Fax: 585 527-8106
EMP: 10
SQ FT: 13,000
SALES: 1MM **Privately Held**
SIC: 2759 2752 5112 Commercial Printing Lithographic/Offset Commmercial Printing Whol Stationery/Office Supplies

(G-13351)
DIXON TOOL AND MANUFACTURING
240 Burrows St (14606-2637)
PHONE..................................585 235-1352
Rober Hyder, *President*
EMP: 10
SQ FT: 5,224
SALES (est): 1.4MM **Privately Held**
SIC: 3544 Dies, steel rule

(G-13352)
DOCK HARDWARE INCORPORATED
Also Called: Rogers Enterprises
24 Seneca Ave Ste 4 (14621-2387)
P.O. Box 17266 (14617-0266)
PHONE..................................585 266-7920
Garry Rogers, *President*
EMP: 10
SALES (est): 960K **Privately Held**
WEB: www.dockhardware.com
SIC: 3545 Machine tool accessories

(G-13353)
DOCUMENT STRATEGIES LLC
185 Gibbs St (14605-2907)
P.O. Box 16065 (14616-0065)
PHONE..................................585 506-9000
James Bowen, *Principal*
Jeremy Hutchinson, *Software Dev*
EMP: 12
SALES (est): 590.5K **Privately Held**
SIC: 7372 Application computer software

(G-13354)
DOLOMITE PRODUCTS COMPANY INC (DH)
Also Called: Shadow Lake Golf & Racquet CLB
1150 Penfield Rd (14625-2202)
PHONE..................................315 524-1998

John M Odenbach Jr, *President*
John Topping, *General Mgr*
John Siel, *Chairman*
Massimo Colombai, *QC Mgr*
Gardner Odenbach, *Treasurer*
EMP: 25 EST: 1920
SQ FT: 5,000
SALES (est): 26.2MM
SALES (corp-wide): 30.6B **Privately Held**
WEB: www.dolomitegroup.com
SIC: 2951 1422 5031 8741 Paving mixtures; dolomite, crushed & broken-quarrying; building materials, exterior; building materials, interior; circuit management for motion picture theaters; golf club, membership; golf, tennis & ski shops

(G-13355)
DOUBLE HELIX OPTICS INC
260 E Main St Ste 6367 (14604-2101)
PHONE..................................917 689-6490
Leslie Kimerling, *CEO*
EMP: 6
SALES (est): 279.1K **Privately Held**
SIC: 3827 Lenses, optical: all types except ophthalmic

(G-13356)
DRAPERY INDUSTRIES INC
175 Humboldt St Ste 222 (14610-1060)
PHONE..................................585 232-2992
Mark Kosinski, *President*
David Geen, *Vice Pres*
Eric Kosinski, *Project Mgr*
Lauren Novick, *Accounts Mgr*
EMP: 14
SQ FT: 8,000
SALES (est): 1.6MM **Privately Held**
WEB: www.draperyindustries.com
SIC: 2391 2591 1799 Curtains; window: made from purchased materials; draperies, plastic & textile: from purchased materials; window blinds; home/office interiors finishing, furnishing & remodeling; drapery track installation

(G-13357)
DRT AEROSPACE LLC
500 Mile Crossing Blvd (14624-6205)
PHONE..................................585 247-5940
Gary Van Gundy, *CEO*
EMP: 8 **Privately Held**
SIC: 3545 3761 3728 Precision tools, machinists'; guided missiles & space vehicles; aircraft parts & equipment
HQ: Drt Aerospace, Llc
8694 Rite Track Way
West Chester OH 45069
937 298-7391

(G-13358)
DYNA-TECH QUALITY INC
1570 Emerson St (14606-3118)
PHONE..................................585 458-9970
Andy Masters, *President*
EMP: 5 EST: 1998
SALES (est): 362.4K **Privately Held**
SIC: 3599 Machine shop, jobbing & repair

(G-13359)
DYNAMASTERS INC
1570 Emerson St (14606-3118)
PHONE..................................585 458-9970
Andy Mastrodonato Sr, *President*
EMP: 5 EST: 2008
SALES (est): 440K **Privately Held**
SIC: 3569 Assembly machines, non-metal-working

(G-13360)
DYNAMIC DIES INC
70 Pixley Industrial Pkwy (14624-2377)
PHONE..................................585 247-4010
Fax: 585 247-7203
EMP: 14
SALES (corp-wide): 22.2MM **Privately Held**
SIC: 3544 Mfg Dies/Tools/Jigs/Fixtures
PA: Dynamic Dies, Inc.
1705 Commerce Rd
Holland OH 43528
419 865-0249

(G-13361)
EAGLE GRAPHICS INC
149 Anderson Ave (14607-1106)
PHONE..................................585 244-5006
Nancy Powell, *President*
Michael W Powell, *Vice Pres*
EMP: 9
SQ FT: 10,000
SALES (est): 1.6MM **Privately Held**
WEB: www.eaglegraphicsinc.com
SIC: 2752 Commercial printing, offset

(G-13362)
EAST PATTERN & MODEL CORP (PA)
769 Trabold Rd (14624-2547)
P.O. Box 245, North Greece (14515-0245)
PHONE..................................585 461-3240
Warren H Kellogg, *President*
Mark Landers, *General Mgr*
Lisa Smyder, *Opers Mgr*
Carl Sudore, *Purch Mgr*
Paul Dalba, *QC Mgr*
EMP: 26
SQ FT: 15,000
SALES: 3MM **Privately Held**
SIC: 3544 3089 3365 3275 Industrial molds; injection molding of plastics; aluminum foundries; gypsum products

(G-13363)
EAST PATTERN & MODEL CORP
80 Saginaw Dr (14623-3132)
PHONE..................................585 461-3240
Warren Kellogg, *President*
Paul Dalba, *QC Mgr*
EMP: 10
SALES (corp-wide): 3MM **Privately Held**
SIC: 3089 3544 3442 3365 Injection molding of plastics; special dies, tools, jigs & fixtures; metal doors, sash & trim; aluminum foundries
PA: East Pattern & Model Corp.
769 Trabold Rd
Rochester NY 14624
585 461-3240

(G-13364)
EAST RIDGE QUICK PRINT
1249 Ridgeway Ave Ste Y (14615-3761)
PHONE..................................585 266-4911
Richard San Angelo, *President*
Janice San Angelo, *Vice Pres*
EMP: 15
SQ FT: 6,000
SALES (est): 1.5MM **Privately Held**
WEB: www.eastridgequickprint.com
SIC: 2752 Commercial printing, offset

(G-13365)
EASTMAN CHEMICAL COMPANY
2255 Mount Read Blvd (14615)
PHONE..................................585 722-2905
Castle Amy, *Business Mgr*
Cedric Davis, *Engineer*
Davis Joshua, *Engineer*
James Downs, *Senior Engr*
Allman Amanda, *Corp Comm Staff*
EMP: 60
WEB: www.eastman.com
SIC: 2821 Plastics materials & resins
PA: Eastman Chemical Company
200 S Wilcox Dr
Kingsport TN 37660

(G-13366)
EASTMAN KODAK COMPANY
233 Olde Harbour Trl (14612-2936)
PHONE..................................585 722-2187
Gus Gleichauf, *Principal*
Danielle Atkins, *Vice Pres*
Steve Smith, *Sales Staff*
EMP: 65
SALES (corp-wide): 1.3B **Publicly Held**
SIC: 3861 Film, sensitized motion picture, X-ray, still camera, etc.
PA: Eastman Kodak Company
343 State St
Rochester NY 14650
585 724-4000

▲ = Import ▼=Export
◆ =Import/Export

(G-13367)
EASTMAN KODAK COMPANY (PA)
343 State St (14650-0001)
PHONE..................585 724-4000
James V Continenza, *Ch of Bd*
Tom McHugh, *General Mgr*
Patrick Duckworth, *Business Mgr*
Roger W Byrd, *Senior VP*
John O'Grady, *Senior VP*
◆ EMP: 277
SALES: 1.3B **Publicly Held**
SIC: 3861 3577 7384 Film, sensitized motion picture, X-ray, still camera, etc.; cameras, still & motion picture (all types); photographic paper & cloth, all types; computer peripheral equipment; graphic displays, except graphic terminals; optical scanning devices; photofinish laboratories

(G-13368)
EASTMAN KODAK COMPANY
1669 Lake Ave Bldg 31-4 (14652-0001)
PHONE..................585 724-5600
Tim Kiehle, *Branch Mgr*
EMP: 60
SALES (corp-wide): 1.3B **Publicly Held**
SIC: 3861 Film, sensitized motion picture, X-ray, still camera, etc.
PA: Eastman Kodak Company
343 State St
Rochester NY 14650
585 724-4000

(G-13369)
EASTMAN KODAK COMPANY
39 Kaywood Dr (14626-3753)
PHONE..................585 726-6261
Raul Santiago, *Branch Mgr*
EMP: 65
SALES (corp-wide): 1.3B **Publicly Held**
SIC: 3861 Film, sensitized motion picture, X-ray, still camera, etc.
PA: Eastman Kodak Company
343 State St
Rochester NY 14650
585 724-4000

(G-13370)
EASTMAN KODAK COMPANY
2600 Manitou Rd (14650-0001)
PHONE..................585 724-4000
EMP: 74
SALES (corp-wide): 1.3B **Publicly Held**
SIC: 3861 Film, sensitized motion picture, X-ray, still camera, etc.
PA: Eastman Kodak Company
343 State St
Rochester NY 14650
585 724-4000

(G-13371)
EASTMAN KODAK COMPANY
343 State St (14650-0001)
PHONE..................800 698-3324
Lori Perez, *Branch Mgr*
Lisa Swartz, *Director*
EMP: 15
SALES (corp-wide): 1.3B **Publicly Held**
SIC: 3861 Film, sensitized motion picture, X-ray, still camera, etc.
PA: Eastman Kodak Company
343 State St
Rochester NY 14650
585 724-4000

(G-13372)
EASTMAN KODAK COMPANY
1999 Lake Ave 6/83/RI (14650-0001)
PHONE..................585 722-4385
Mary J Hellyar, *Branch Mgr*
EMP: 99
SALES (corp-wide): 1.3B **Publicly Held**
SIC: 3861 Film, sensitized motion picture, X-ray, still camera, etc.
PA: Eastman Kodak Company
343 State St
Rochester NY 14650
585 724-4000

(G-13373)
EASTMAN KODAK COMPANY
300 Weiland Road (14650-0001)
PHONE..................585 588-5598
EMP: 78

SALES (corp-wide): 1.3B **Publicly Held**
SIC: 3861 Film, sensitized motion picture, X-ray, still camera, etc.
PA: Eastman Kodak Company
343 State St
Rochester NY 14650
585 724-4000

(G-13374)
EASTMAN KODAK COMPANY
343 State St (14650-0001)
PHONE..................585 726-7000
EMP: 130
SALES (corp-wide): 1.3B **Publicly Held**
SIC: 3861 Film, sensitized motion picture, X-ray, still camera, etc.
PA: Eastman Kodak Company
343 State St
Rochester NY 14650
585 724-4000

(G-13375)
EASTMAN KODAK COMPANY
336 Initiative Dr (14624-6217)
PHONE..................585 722-4007
Susan Shattuck, *Purch Agent*
Megan Wright, *Marketing Mgr*
Chris Larson, *Manager*
Roger Lowry, *Director*
Doreen D'Angelo, *Admin Asst*
EMP: 5
SQ FT: 14,909
SALES (corp-wide): 1.3B **Publicly Held**
SIC: 3861 Film, sensitized motion picture, X-ray, still camera, etc.
PA: Eastman Kodak Company
343 State St
Rochester NY 14650
585 724-4000

(G-13376)
EASTMAN KODAK COMPANY
100 Latona Rd Gate 340 (14652-0001)
PHONE..................585 588-3896
Jack Kosoff, *Branch Mgr*
EMP: 78
SALES (corp-wide): 1.3B **Publicly Held**
SIC: 3861 Film, sensitized motion picture, X-ray, still camera, etc.
PA: Eastman Kodak Company
343 State St
Rochester NY 14650
585 724-4000

(G-13377)
EASTMAN KODAK COMPANY
343 State St (14650-0001)
P.O. Box 15399 (14615-0399)
PHONE..................585 724-4000
EMP: 39
SALES (corp-wide): 1.3B **Publicly Held**
SIC: 3861 Photographic equipment & supplies
PA: Eastman Kodak Company
343 State St
Rochester NY 14650
585 724-4000

(G-13378)
EASTMAN PARK MICROGRAPHICS INC
100 Latona Rd Bldg 318 (14652-0001)
PHONE..................866 934-4376
William D Oates, *President*
Susanna Records, *Info Tech Mgr*
EMP: 8
SALES (est): 889.5K **Privately Held**
SIC: 3861 Film, sensitized motion picture, X-ray, still camera, etc.
PA: Eastman Park Micrographics Inc
6300 Cedar Springs Rd
Dallas TX 75235

(G-13379)
EBERHARDT ENTERPRISES INC
1325 Mount Read Blvd (14606-2819)
PHONE..................585 458-7681
Peter Eberhardt, *President*
▲ EMP: 10
SQ FT: 18,000
SALES (est): 1.4MM **Privately Held**
SIC: 3544 Special dies, tools, jigs & fixtures

(G-13380)
EIS LEGACY LLC
Also Called: Light Fabrications
40 Hytec Cir (14606-4255)
PHONE..................585 426-5330
Jim Cucinelli, *Principal*
Brian Spychalski, *Plant Mgr*
Christian Yorgure, *Research*
Jeff Rentovich, *VP Sales*
EMP: 39
SALES (corp-wide): 1.1B **Privately Held**
SIC: 2672 3842 7699 Adhesive backed films, foams & foils; adhesive papers, labels or tapes: from purchased material; adhesive tape & plasters, medicated or non-medicated; industrial equipment services
HQ: Eis Legacy, Llc
2018 Powers Ferry Rd Se # 50
Atlanta GA 30339
678 255-3600

(G-13381)
ELAB SMOKERS BOUTIQUE
4373 Lake Ave (14612-4864)
PHONE..................585 865-4513
Steve J Glover, *Partner*
Steve Glover, *Partner*
Mark Landon, *Partner*
EMP: 5
SALES (est): 621.1K **Privately Held**
SIC: 2131 5621 Chewing & smoking tobacco; boutiques

(G-13382)
ELECTRONICS & INNOVATION LTD
150 Research Blvd (14623-3436)
PHONE..................585 214-0598
Tony Harris, *President*
John Andrews, *Vice Pres*
▼ EMP: 10
SALES (est): 2MM **Privately Held**
WEB: www.electronicsandinnovation.com
SIC: 3679 Parametric amplifiers; electronic circuits

(G-13383)
ELITE TURNING & MACHINING CORP
42 Marway Cir (14624-2321)
PHONE..................585 445-8765
Paul Pettrone, *President*
Anthony Thomas, *Vice Pres*
EMP: 20
SALES (est): 2MM **Privately Held**
SIC: 3599 Machine shop, jobbing & repair

(G-13384)
ELO TOUCH SOLUTIONS INC
2245 Brdgtn Hnrtta Twn Ln (14623)
PHONE..................585 427-2802
Craig Witsoe, *CEO*
Jim Melton, *Vice Pres*
Sean Miller, *Vice Pres*
Dave Renner, *Vice Pres*
Bruno Thuillier, *Vice Pres*
▲ EMP: 21 EST: 2012
SALES (est): 4.6MM **Privately Held**
SIC: 3571 Computers, digital, analog or hybrid

(G-13385)
EMERSON & OLIVER LLC
44 Elton St (14607-1370)
PHONE..................585 775-9929
Laura Bascomb-Werth, *Principal*
EMP: 5
SALES (est): 412.5K **Privately Held**
SIC: 2339 Women's & misses' outerwear

(G-13386)
EMERSON PROCESS MGT LLLP
3559 Winton Pl Ste 1 (14623-2856)
PHONE..................585 214-8340
Brian Engle, *Area Mgr*
EMP: 15
SALES (corp-wide): 17.4B **Publicly Held**
SIC: 3823 Industrial instrmnts msrmnt display/control process variable
HQ: Emerson Process Management Lllp
1100 W Louis Henna Blvd
Round Rock TX 78681

(G-13387)
EMPIRE FABRICATORS INC
Also Called: Cusimano, Michael
95 Saginaw Dr (14623-3131)
PHONE..................585 235-3050
Michael Cusimano, *President*
Chad Cusimano, *Vice Pres*
EMP: 7
SQ FT: 10,000
SALES (est): 1.1MM **Privately Held**
WEB: www.empirefabricators.com
SIC: 2541 5084 Counter & sink tops; countersinks

(G-13388)
EMPIRE METAL FABRICATORS INC
1385 Empire Blvd Ste 3 (14609-5915)
PHONE..................585 288-2140
John Singer, *President*
EMP: 7
SQ FT: 4,000
SALES (est): 520K **Privately Held**
SIC: 3441 Fabricated structural metal

(G-13389)
ENBI INDIANA INC
1661 Lyell Ave (14606-2311)
PHONE..................585 647-1627
Tuan Doan, *Opers Mgr*
Darren Kraft, *Engineer*
Mike McMindes, *Branch Mgr*
EMP: 25
SALES (corp-wide): 38.7MM **Privately Held**
SIC: 3069 Printers' rolls & blankets: rubber or rubberized fabric
PA: Indiana Enbi Inc
1703 Mccall Dr
Shelbyville IN 46176
317 398-3267

(G-13390)
ENBI ROCHESTER INC
465 Paul Rd Ste A (14624-4779)
PHONE..................585 647-1651
James Maulicchi, *Ch of Bd*
Darren Kraft, *Engineer*
EMP: 6
SALES (est): 486.2K **Privately Held**
SIC: 3562 Ball & roller bearings

(G-13391)
ENERGY HARVESTERS LLC
Also Called: Walking Charger, The
63 Garden Dr (14609-4342)
PHONE..................617 325-9852
Lawrence Grumer, *CEO*
Sherry Handel, *COO*
EMP: 5
SALES (est): 46.6K **Privately Held**
SIC: 3629 Electrical industrial apparatus

(G-13392)
ENERGY MATERIALS CORPORATION
1999 Lk Ave B82 Ste B304 (14650-0001)
PHONE..................315 247-0880
Stephan Deluca, *CEO*
Leslie Fritzemeier, *Exec VP*
Scott Stewart, *Treasurer*
Les Fritzemeier, *Exec Dir*
EMP: 5
SALES (est): 283.4K **Privately Held**
SIC: 3674 Semiconductors & related devices

(G-13393)
ENGRAV-O-TYPE PRESS INC
Also Called: Epi Printing & Finishing
30 Bermar Park Ste 2 (14624-1541)
PHONE..................585 262-7590
Rick Speciale, *President*
Tracey Kohl, *Vice Pres*
Rick Porreca, *Prdtn Mgr*
Emile L Speciale Jr, *Treasurer*
EMP: 17
SQ FT: 12,000
SALES (est): 3.5MM **Privately Held**
WEB: www.epiprinting.com
SIC: 2752 Commercial printing, offset

(G-13394)
ENI MKS PRODUCTS GROUP
100 Highpower Rd (14623-3498)
PHONE.................................585 427-8300
Paul Eyerman, *Principal*
▲ EMP: 10
SALES (est): 1.4MM
SALES (corp-wide): 2B Publicly Held
SIC: 3823 Industrial instrmnts msrmnt display/control process variable
PA: Mks Instruments, Inc.
2 Tech Dr Ste 201
Andover MA 01810
978 645-5500

(G-13395)
ENI TECHNOLOGY INC (HQ)
100 Highpower Rd (14623-3498)
PHONE.................................585 427-8300
John R Bertucci, *CEO*
Edward Maier, *General Mgr*
Michael Laska, *Engineer*
▲ EMP: 500
SQ FT: 160,000
SALES (est): 24.9MM
SALES (corp-wide): 2B Publicly Held
WEB: www.enipower.com
SIC: 3679 3677 3663 3621 Electronic loads & power supplies; electronic coils, transformers & other inductors; radio & TV communications equipment; motors & generators
PA: Mks Instruments, Inc.
2 Tech Dr Ste 201
Andover MA 01810
978 645-5500

(G-13396)
EPP TEAM INC
Also Called: Empire Precision Plastics
500 Lee Rd Ste 400 (14606-4260)
PHONE.................................585 454-4995
Neal P Elli, *Ch of Bd*
Bob Zygulski, *COO*
Rick Wilson, *Vice Pres*
Eric Canaday, *Opers Spvr*
Raghava Gujja, *Opers Staff*
▲ EMP: 82
SQ FT: 45,000
SALES (est): 17.2MM Privately Held
WEB: www.empireprecision.com
SIC: 3089 Injection molded finished plastic products; injection molding of plastics

(G-13397)
ERDLE PERFORATING HOLDINGS INC (PA)
100 Pixley Indus Pkwy (14624-2325)
PHONE.................................585 247-4700
Frank Pfau, *President*
Thomas J Pariso, *Exec VP*
John B Gibson, *Vice Pres*
Angela M Mockbee, *Vice Pres*
Gary Smith, *Senior Buyer*
EMP: 100 EST: 1870
SQ FT: 92,000
SALES (est): 25.3MM Privately Held
SIC: 3469 Perforated metal, stamped

(G-13398)
ERNIE GREEN INDUSTRIES INC
Also Called: Eg Industries
85 Pixley Industrial Pkwy (14624-2322)
PHONE.................................585 295-8951
EMP: 100
SALES (corp-wide): 351.5MM Privately Held
SIC: 3089 Injection molding of plastics
PA: Ernie Green Industries, Inc.
2030 Dividend Dr
Columbus OH 43228
614 219-1423

(G-13399)
ERNIE GREEN INDUSTRIES INC
Also Called: Eg Industries
1667 Emerson St (14606-3119)
PHONE.................................585 647-2300
Scott McDermott, *Purch Agent*
Aaron Leighton, *Controller*
Nartign Vanmanen, *Manager*
Stan Tezyk, *Manager*
EMP: 240

SALES (corp-wide): 351.5MM Privately Held
SIC: 3089 Injection molding of plastics; blow molded finished plastic products
PA: Ernie Green Industries, Inc.
2030 Dividend Dr
Columbus OH 43228
614 219-1423

(G-13400)
ERNIE GREEN INDUSTRIES INC
Also Called: Eg Indsturies
460 Buffalo Rd Ste 220 (14611-2022)
PHONE.................................585 647-2300
Bill Cleveland, *Opers Staff*
Micah Higgins, *QC Mgr*
Diane Lannon, *Manager*
EMP: 100
SALES (corp-wide): 351.5MM Privately Held
SIC: 3089 Injection molding of plastics; blow molded finished plastic products
PA: Ernie Green Industries, Inc.
2030 Dividend Dr
Columbus OH 43228
614 219-1423

(G-13401)
ESTEBANIA ENTERPRISES INC
Also Called: Aries Precision Products
15 Mcardle St Ste A (14611-1513)
PHONE.................................585 529-9330
EMP: 7
SQ FT: 9,600
SALES (est): 1.1MM Privately Held
SIC: 3599 Mfg Industrial Machinery

(G-13402)
ET PRECISION OPTICS INC
33 Curlew St (14606-2535)
PHONE.................................585 254-2560
Thomas R Eckler, *President*
EMP: 71
SQ FT: 3,000
SALES (est): 12.6MM Privately Held
WEB: www.etprecision.com
SIC: 3599 Machine shop, jobbing & repair

(G-13403)
EXACT MACHINING & MFG
305 Commerce Dr Ste 7 (14623-3538)
PHONE.................................585 334-7090
Dan Bleier, *President*
Tim Bleier, *Corp Secy*
Jay Pryor, *Vice Pres*
EMP: 5 EST: 1998
SQ FT: 3,600
SALES (est): 638.2K Privately Held
SIC: 3599 Machine shop, jobbing & repair

(G-13404)
EXCEL MACHINE TECHNOLOGIES INC
50 Bermar Park Ste 5&6 (14624-1545)
PHONE.................................585 426-1911
Jason Boyle, *President*
Jeremy Shamp, *Vice Pres*
Anne Marie Powarzynski, *Office Mgr*
EMP: 11 EST: 2010
SALES: 8.1MM Privately Held
SIC: 3599 Machine shop, jobbing & repair

(G-13405)
EXCELSUS SOLUTIONS LLC
12 Pixley Industrial Pkwy # 40 (14624-2364)
PHONE.................................585 533-0003
Mark Laniak, *CEO*
Jason Thomas, *President*
David Laniak, *General Mgr*
John Bennett, *CFO*
Sheryl Wilcox, *Marketing Staff*
EMP: 24
SQ FT: 18,000
SALES (est): 5.4MM Privately Held
WEB: www.excelsussolutions.com
SIC: 2752 Commercial printing, lithographic

(G-13406)
EXIGO PRECISION INC
190 Murray St (14606-1126)
P.O. Box 60917 (14606-0917)
PHONE.................................585 254-5818
EMP: 7

SALES (est): 499.5K Privately Held
SIC: 3599 Mfg Industrial Machinery

(G-13407)
EXPOSITOR NEWSPAPERS INC
Also Called: Rochester Golf Week
2535 Brighton Henrietta (14623-2711)
PHONE.................................585 427-2468
Barbara Morgenstern, *President*
George Morgenstern, *Editor*
EMP: 6
SALES (est): 270K Privately Held
SIC: 2711 Newspapers: publishing only, not printed on site

(G-13408)
FARO INDUSTRIES INC
340 Lyell Ave (14606-1697)
PHONE.................................585 647-6000
Matthew Mc Conville, *President*
Lisa Abbott, *Admin Sec*
EMP: 17 EST: 1967
SQ FT: 26,000
SALES (est): 3.3MM Privately Held
WEB: www.faroindustries.com
SIC: 3089 Injection molding of plastics

(G-13409)
FIELDTEX PRODUCTS INC
3055 Brighton Henrietta (14623-2749)
PHONE.................................585 427-2940
Sanford R Abbey, *President*
Jonathan Abbey, *General Mgr*
Cynthia Helander, *Plant Mgr*
Ted Hartman, *Manager*
Linda Waters, *Director*
▲ EMP: 130
SQ FT: 40,000
SALES (est): 27.1MM Privately Held
WEB: www.e-firstaidsupplies.com
SIC: 3151 3161 Leather gloves & mittens; cases, carrying

(G-13410)
FINGER LAKES CHEMICALS INC (PA)
Also Called: Finger Lakes/Castle
420 Saint Paul St (14605-1734)
PHONE.................................585 454-4760
Ewald Blatter, *President*
Hans Blatter, *Vice Pres*
EMP: 50 EST: 1967
SQ FT: 100,000
SALES: 10MM Privately Held
WEB: www.castlepackspower.com
SIC: 2842 5169 Specialty cleaning preparations; chemicals & allied products

(G-13411)
FIRTH RIXSON INC (DH)
Also Called: Firth Rixson Monroe
181 Mckee Rd (14611-2011)
PHONE.................................585 328-1383
David C Mortimer, *CEO*
Bob Lang, *Principal*
Andrew Maskery, *Controller*
Alison Stirrup, *Controller*
Sebastien Coste, *Info Tech Dir*
▲ EMP: 80
SQ FT: 23,821
SALES (est): 111.7MM
SALES (corp-wide): 14B Publicly Held
WEB: www.firthrixson.com
SIC: 3462 Aircraft forgings, ferrous
HQ: Firth Rixson Limited
Centre Court Building
Sheffield
114 219-3000

(G-13412)
FIVE STAR TOOL CO INC
125 Elmgrove Park (14624-1359)
PHONE.................................585 328-9580
Kenneth Klalonde, *President*
Joanne Rizzitano, *Purchasing*
Mark Schaefer, *Design Engr*
Kenneth Lalonde, *VP Sales*
Stan Yates, *Sales Engr*
EMP: 23 EST: 1965
SQ FT: 9,200
SALES (est): 4MM Privately Held
SIC: 3451 3541 Screw machine products; milling machines

(G-13413)
FLINT GROUP US LLC
Also Called: Flint Ink North America Div
73 Cook Dr (14623-3509)
PHONE.................................585 458-1223
Harry Reeves, *Manager*
Rory Pelliccia, *Technician*
EMP: 26
SALES (corp-wide): 177.9K Privately Held
WEB: www.flintink.com
SIC: 2893 Printing ink
HQ: Flint Group Us Llc
17177 N Laurel Park Dr # 300
Livonia MI 48152
734 781-4600

(G-13414)
FLOUR CITY GROWLERS INC
125 Amsterdam Rd (14610-1006)
PHONE.................................585 360-8709
Robert Long, *President*
EMP: 12
SALES (est): 1.5MM Privately Held
SIC: 3231 Decorated glassware: chipped, engraved, etched, etc.

(G-13415)
FLOWER CITY PRINTING INC (PA)
1725 Mount Read Blvd (14606-2827)
P.O. Box 60680 (14606-0680)
PHONE.................................585 663-9000
George Scharr, *CEO*
Theresa Clemons, *General Mgr*
Timothy Welch, *Exec VP*
Dave Ziemba, *Plant Mgr*
Jim Calamia, *Prdtn Mgr*
EMP: 197
SQ FT: 135,000
SALES (est): 149.1MM Privately Held
WEB: www.flowercityprinting.com
SIC: 2657 2752 Folding paperboard boxes; commercial printing, offset

(G-13416)
FLOWER CITY PRINTING INC
1001 Lee Rd (14606-4243)
PHONE.................................585 512-1235
Matt Bryant, *Principal*
EMP: 5
SALES (corp-wide): 149.1MM Privately Held
SIC: 2752 Commercial printing, lithographic
PA: Flower City Printing, Inc.
1725 Mount Read Blvd
Rochester NY 14606
585 663-9000

(G-13417)
FLOWER CY TISSUE MILLS CO INC (PA)
700 Driving Park Ave (14613-1506)
P.O. Box 13497 (14613-0497)
PHONE.................................585 458-9200
William F Shafer III, *Ch of Bd*
William F Shafer IV, *Vice Pres*
Thomas Myers, *CFO*
Don Macdonald, *Sales Dir*
Philip Yawman III, *Admin Sec*
▲ EMP: 60 EST: 1906
SQ FT: 46,000
SALES (est): 16.8MM Privately Held
WEB: www.flowercitytissue.com
SIC: 2621 Wrapping paper

(G-13418)
FLUXDATA INCORPORATED
176 Anderson Ave Ste F304 (14607-1169)
PHONE.................................800 425-0176
Pano Spiliotis, *President*
Tim Hattenberger, *Vice Pres*
John Szydlo, *Vice Pres*
Lu Luo, *VP Opers*
Lawrence Taplin, *CTO*
EMP: 6
SQ FT: 4,665
SALES (est): 1.3MM
SALES (corp-wide): 1.5B Privately Held
SIC: 3861 Aerial cameras
PA: Halma Public Limited Company
Misbourne Court
Amersham BUCKS HP7 0
149 472-1111

▲ = Import ▼=Export
◆ =Import/Export

(G-13419)
FORBES PRECISION INC
100 Boxart St Ste 105 (14612-5658)
PHONE..................................585 865-7069
Michael Forbes, *Ch of Bd*
EMP: 11
SQ FT: 3,000
SALES: 1MM **Privately Held**
SIC: 3599 Machine shop, jobbing & repair

(G-13420)
FORGE METAL FINISHING INC
383 Buell Rd (14624-3123)
PHONE..................................585 730-7340
Mark Shaw, *President*
EMP: 6 **EST:** 2012
SQ FT: 10,000
SALES (est): 540.4K **Privately Held**
SIC: 3471 Anodizing (plating) of metals or
formed products

(G-13421)
FORWARD ENTERPRISES INC
Also Called: Brewer & Newell Printing
250 Cumberland St Ste 100 (14605-2847)
PHONE..................................585 235-7670
Gerald Ward, *President*
Lisa Fairchild, *General Mgr*
Dick Shellman, *General Mgr*
Melinda Ward, *Vice Pres*
Stan Phillips, *Representative*
EMP: 10 **EST:** 1921
SQ FT: 4,000
SALES (est): 1.2MM **Privately Held**
SIC: 2759 2752 Letterpress printing; com-
mercial printing, offset

(G-13422)
FRAMING TECHNOLOGY INC
137 Syke St (14611-1738)
PHONE..................................585 464-8470
Chris Hill, *President*
Jim Hartke, *Vice Pres*
Angela Webb, *Manager*
Nicole King, *Office Admin*
▲ **EMP:** 20
SALES: 2.2MM **Privately Held**
WEB: www.framingtech.com
SIC: 3441 Fabricated structural metal

(G-13423)
FRANK J MARTELLO
Also Called: Countertop Creations
1227 Maple St (14611-1545)
PHONE..................................585 235-2780
Frank J Martello, *Owner*
EMP: 6 **EST:** 1996
SQ FT: 6,000
SALES (est): 620.9K **Privately Held**
WEB: www.countertop-creations.com
SIC: 2541 Counter & sink tops

(G-13424)
FRESHOP INC
3246 Monroe Ave Ste 1 (14618-4628)
PHONE..................................585 738-6035
Brian Moyer, *CEO*
Karthik Balasubramanian, *President*
▼ **EMP:** 35
SQ FT: 20,000
SALES (est): 446.9K **Privately Held**
SIC: 7372 Application computer software

(G-13425)
FTT MEDICAL INC
Also Called: Electrosurgical Instrument Co
275 Commerce Dr (14623-3505)
PHONE..................................585 444-0980
John Longuil, *CEO*
Karlee Schramm, *Executive Asst*
EMP: 8
SQ FT: 9,000
SALES (est): 1.4MM **Privately Held**
WEB: www.electrosurgicalinstrument.com
SIC: 3841 Surgical & medical instruments

(G-13426)
FULCRUM ACOUSTIC LLC
25 Circle St Ste 104 (14607-1072)
PHONE..................................866 234-0678
Stephen Siegel, *President*
Rich Frembes,
EMP: 5
SALES (est): 1MM **Privately Held**
SIC: 3651 Household audio & video equip-
ment

(G-13427)
GADABOUT USA WHEELCHAIRS INC
892 E Ridge Rd (14621-1718)
P.O. Box 17890 (14617-0890)
PHONE..................................585 338-2110
Michael Fonte, *President*
EMP: 15
SALES (est): 853.6K **Privately Held**
SIC: 3842 Wheelchairs

(G-13428)
GANNETT CO INC
Also Called: Democrat & Chronicle
245 E Main St (14604-2103)
PHONE..................................585 232-7100
Helen Barber, *District Mgr*
William Hart, *Finance Dir*
Colleen Spiwak, *Cust Mgr*
Brian Ambor, *Branch Mgr*
Theresa Marquez, *Producer*
EMP: 76
SALES (corp-wide): 2.9B **Publicly Held**
SIC: 2711 Newspapers, publishing & print-
ing
PA: Gannett Co., Inc.
7950 Jones Branch Dr
Mc Lean VA 22102
703 854-6000

(G-13429)
GATTI TOOL & MOLD INC
997 Beahan Rd (14624-3548)
PHONE..................................585 328-1350
EMP: 12
SALES (est): 1.2MM **Privately Held**
SIC: 3544 Manufactures Molds

(G-13430)
GE MDS LLC (HQ)
Also Called: Aferge Mds
175 Science Pkwy (14620-4260)
PHONE..................................585 242-9600
Henry Garcia, *Opers Mgr*
Stephen Cyran, *Engineer*
Joseph Kodweis, *Engineer*
Anthony Tatta, *Engineer*
Thomas Hodge, *Senior Engr*
◆ **EMP:** 200
SALES (est): 26.8MM
SALES (corp-wide): 121.6B **Publicly
Held**
WEB: www.microwavedata.com
SIC: 3663 Radio & TV communications
equipment
PA: General Electric Company
41 Farnsworth St
Boston MA 02210
617 443-3000

(G-13431)
GEM MANUFACTURING INC
853 West Ave Bldg 17a (14611-2413)
PHONE..................................585 235-1670
Scott Keller, *President*
EMP: 5
SQ FT: 7,000
SALES (est): 801.6K **Privately Held**
WEB: www.gemmachine.com
SIC: 3451 Screw machine products

(G-13432)
GENENCOR INTERNATIONAL INC
3490 Winton Pl (14623-2829)
PHONE..................................585 256-5200
Walt Golembeski, *Manager*
Roger Brennecke, *Info Tech Mgr*
EMP: 9
SALES (est): 928.3K **Privately Held**
SIC: 2869 Industrial organic chemicals

(G-13433)
GENERAL PLATING LLC
850 Saint Paul St Ste 10 (14605-1065)
PHONE..................................585 423-0830
Tom Schenkel, *Partner*
Don Schenkel, *Partner*
John Schenkel, *Partner*
Richard Schenkel, *Partner*
Roger Schenkel, *Partner*
EMP: 20 **EST:** 1890
SQ FT: 35,000

SALES (est): 724.7K **Privately Held**
SIC: 3471 Electroplating of metals or
formed products

(G-13434)
GENERAL WELDING & FABG INC
60 Saginaw Dr Ste 4 (14623-3159)
PHONE..................................585 697-7660
Cheryl Lis, *Vice Pres*
EMP: 14
SALES (corp-wide): 6MM **Privately Held**
WEB: www.gwfab.com
SIC: 3713 5531 7539 Truck bodies &
parts; trailer hitches, automotive; trailer
repair
PA: General Welding & Fabricating, Inc.
991 Maple Rd
Elma NY 14059
716 652-0033

(G-13435)
GENESEE MANUFACTURING CO INC
566 Hollenbeck St (14621-2288)
PHONE..................................585 266-3201
Kevin Hite, *President*
Donald A Kohler Jr, *Vice Pres*
EMP: 9 **EST:** 1905
SQ FT: 8,000
SALES (est): 558.3K **Privately Held**
WEB: www.geneseemfg.com
SIC: 3545 5084 Cutting tools for machine
tools; industrial machinery & equipment

(G-13436)
GENESIS DIGITAL IMAGING INC
150 Verona St (14608-1733)
PHONE..................................310 305-7358
Joseph Eliafan, *President*
EMP: 9
SALES (est): 1MM
SALES (corp-wide): 23.7B **Privately Held**
WEB: www.genesisdigitalimaging.com
SIC: 3844 Radiographic X-ray apparatus &
tubes
HQ: Carestream Health, Inc.
150 Verona St
Rochester NY 14608

(G-13437)
GERMAN MACHINE & ASSEMBLY INC
226 Jay St (14608-1623)
PHONE..................................585 546-4200
Kim Beasley, *Ch of Bd*
Scott Boheen, *President*
EMP: 25
SALES (est): 3.5MM **Privately Held**
WEB: www.germanmach.com
SIC: 3469 Machine parts, stamped or
pressed metal

(G-13438)
GERMANOW-SIMON CORPORATION
Also Called: G-S Plastic Optics
408 Saint Paul St (14605-1788)
PHONE..................................585 232-1440
Andrew Germanow, *Ch of Bd*
Don Seames, *Materials Mgr*
Ginny Andrews, *Export Mgr*
Nicholas Turner, *Engineer*
Mike Spuck, *Comptroller*
◆ **EMP:** 40 **EST:** 1916
SQ FT: 125,000
SALES (est): 9.3MM **Privately Held**
WEB: www.gsoptics.com
SIC: 3089 3827 Plastic processing; optical
instruments & lenses

(G-13439)
GETINGE GROUP LOGISTICS AMERI
1777 E Henrietta Rd (14623-3133)
PHONE..................................585 475-1400
John Aymong, *President*
Jeff Carrig, *Area Mgr*
Charles Dacey, *Area Mgr*
Steve Nesburg, *Area Mgr*
Harald Castler, *Vice Pres*
▲ **EMP:** 174
SALES (est): 26.4MM
SALES (corp-wide): 6.1B **Privately Held**
SIC: 3842 Sterilizers, hospital & surgical

HQ: Getinge Ab
Lindholmspiren 7a
Goteborg 417 5
103 350-000

(G-13440)
GH INDUCTION ATMOSPHERES LLC
35 Industrial Park Cir (14624-2403)
PHONE..................................585 368-2120
Steven Skewes,
Dale Wilcox,
▲ **EMP:** 35
SQ FT: 19,000
SALES (est): 8.2MM
SALES (corp-wide): 1.6B **Publicly Held**
WEB: www.inductionatmospheres.com
SIC: 3542 Machine tools, metal forming
type
PA: Park-Ohio Holdings Corp.
6065 Parkland Blvd Ste 1
Cleveland OH 44124
440 947-2200

(G-13441)
GLASSFAB INC
257 Ormond St (14605-3024)
PHONE..................................585 262-4000
Robert Saltzman, *Ch of Bd*
Daniel Saltzman, *President*
George Dean, *Sales Staff*
Wayne Leon, *Mktg Dir*
Tom Kirk, *Manager*
▲ **EMP:** 30
SQ FT: 30,000
SALES (est): 6.3MM **Privately Held**
WEB: www.glassfab.com
SIC: 3231 Products of purchased glass

(G-13442)
GLASTEEL PARTS & SERVICES INC (DH)
1000 West Ave (14611-2442)
P.O. Box 23600 (14692-3600)
PHONE..................................585 235-1010
Gary Brewer, *President*
EMP: 50
SQ FT: 18,000
SALES (est): 9.2MM
SALES (corp-wide): 352.2K **Privately
Held**
SIC: 3229 Pressed & blown glass
HQ: Pfaudler, Inc.
1000 West Ave
Rochester NY 14611
585 235-1000

(G-13443)
GLAXOSMITHKLINE LLC
1177 Winton Rd S (14618-2240)
PHONE..................................585 738-9025
Joanne Mitchell-Mclare, *Sales Staff*
EMP: 26
SALES (corp-wide): 39.5B **Privately Held**
SIC: 2834 Pharmaceutical preparations
HQ: Glaxosmithkline Llc
5 Crescent Dr
Philadelphia PA 19112
215 751-4000

(G-13444)
GLEASON CORPORATION (PA)
1000 University Ave (14607-1286)
P.O. Box 22970 (14692-2970)
PHONE..................................585 473-1000
John J Perrotti, *President*
Karl-Heinz K Bler, *Managing Dir*
James S Gleason, *Chairman*
Stephen Rosini, *Regional Mgr*
Edward J Pelta, *Vice Pres*
◆ **EMP:** 800
SQ FT: 721,400
SALES (est): 825.5MM **Privately Held**
SIC: 3541 3829 Machine tools, metal cut-
ting type; gear cutting & finishing ma-
chines; numerically controlled metal
cutting machine tools; machine tool re-
placement & repair parts, metal cutting
types; physical property testing equip-
ment

(G-13445)
GLEASON WORKS (HQ)
1000 University Ave (14607-1286)
P.O. Box 22970 (14692-2970)
PHONE..................................585 473-1000

James S Gleason, *Ch of Bd*
John J Perrotti, *President*
Nanci Malin Peck, *Vice Pres*
Edward J Pelta, *Vice Pres*
John W Pysnack, *Vice Pres*
◆ **EMP:** 925 **EST:** 1865
SQ FT: 721,000
SALES (est): 275.5MM
SALES (corp-wide): 825.5MM **Privately Held**
WEB: www.gleason.com
SIC: 3714 3728 3566 3541 Gears, motor vehicle; gears, aircraft power transmission; gears, power transmission, except automotive; gear cutting & finishing machines; numerically controlled metal cutting machine tools; machine tool replacement & repair parts, metal cutting types; physical property testing equipment; metal stampings
PA: Gleason Corporation
1000 University Ave
Rochester NY 14607
585 473-1000

(G-13446)
GLOBAL PRECISION INDS INC
955 Millstead Way (14624-5107)
PHONE..........................585 254-0010
Mark Wheeler, *CEO*
Bob Nuccitelli, *President*
EMP: 15
SALES (est): 3.1MM **Privately Held**
WEB: www.global-precision.com
SIC: 3599 Machine shop, jobbing & repair

(G-13447)
GM COMPONENTS HOLDINGS LLC
Also Called: Gmch Rochester
1000 Lexington Ave (14606-2810)
P.O. Box 92700 (14692-8800)
PHONE..........................585 647-7000
Chuck Gifford, *Principal*
Jane Shewman, *Senior Buyer*
Charles Knapp, *Manager*
EMP: 350
SQ FT: 2,250 **Publicly Held**
SIC: 3714 Motor vehicle parts & accessories
HQ: Gm Components Holdings, Llc
300 Renaissance Ctr
Detroit MI 48243

(G-13448)
GOLD PRIDE PRESS INC
12 Pixley Industrial Pkwy # 40
(14624-2364)
PHONE..........................585 224-8800
Ted Rhodes, *Vice Pres*
EMP: 20
SQ FT: 30,000
SALES (est): 4.4MM **Privately Held**
WEB: www.goldpride.com
SIC: 2789 Trade binding services

(G-13449)
GRADIENT LENS CORPORATION
207 Tremont St Ste 1 (14608-2398)
PHONE..........................585 235-2620
Douglas Kindred, *President*
Leland Atkinson, *Vice Pres*
Imelda Griffith, *Production*
Duncan Moore, *Director*
Abbie Huchzermeier, *Technician*
EMP: 35
SQ FT: 9,500
SALES (est): 4.8MM **Privately Held**
WEB: www.gradientlens.com
SIC: 3827 Optical instruments & apparatus; interferometers

(G-13450)
GRAYWOOD COMPANIES INC
1001 Lexington Ave Ste 3 (14606-2898)
PHONE..........................585 738-8889
John M Summers, *CEO*
Eugene Baldino, *President*
Dave Krigeer, *Vice Pres*
Sam Eberhard, *Purch Mgr*
Nate Theriault, *Engineer*
▲ **EMP:** 620 **EST:** 2005
SQ FT: 36,000

SALES (est): 95.6MM **Privately Held**
SIC: 3545 3544 3398 3541 Machine tool accessories; drill bits, metalworking; taps, machine tool; reamers, machine tool; special dies, tools, jigs & fixtures; metal heat treating; boring mills

(G-13451)
GREEN AMAZON LLC
75 S Clinton Ave Ste 510 (14604)
PHONE..........................585 300-1319
Walid Nosir, *Mng Member*
EMP: 6 **EST:** 2016
SALES (est): 50K **Privately Held**
SIC: 2879 7389 Insecticides & pesticides; insecticides, agricultural or household;

(G-13452)
GSP COMPONENTS INC
1190 Brooks Ave (14624-3112)
PHONE..........................585 436-3377
Ronald J Motsay, *CEO*
Tim Lynn, *QC Mgr*
Debra Bennett, *Human Res Dir*
Eric Aldridge, *Manager*
Rick Palmer, *Director*
EMP: 62 **EST:** 1951
SQ FT: 34,000
SALES (est): 17.1MM **Privately Held**
WEB: www.gspcomponents.com
SIC: 3451 Screw machine products

(G-13453)
GUPP SIGNS INC
340 Lake Ave (14608-1077)
PHONE..........................585 244-5070
Larry Melrose, *President*
Nancy Melrose, *Vice Pres*
EMP: 5
SALES (est): 532.2K **Privately Held**
WEB: www.guppsigns.com
SIC: 3993 Signs & advertising specialties

(G-13454)
H RISCH INC
44 Saginaw Dr (14623-3132)
PHONE..........................585 442-0110
Sara Tartaglia, *CEO*
Michael Pauly, *President*
EMP: 60 **EST:** 1935
SQ FT: 15,000
SALES (est): 9.1MM **Privately Held**
WEB: www.hrisch.com
SIC: 3089 Floor coverings, plastic

(G-13455)
H S ASSEMBLY INC
570 Hollandback (14605)
PHONE..........................585 266-4287
David Marcellus, *President*
Jeff Fregoe, *Design Engr*
EMP: 5
SALES (est): 605K **Privately Held**
WEB: www.hsassembly.com
SIC: 3541 8711 Machine tools, metal cutting type; engineering services

(G-13456)
H T SPECIALTY INC
70 Bermar Park (14624-1541)
PHONE..........................585 458-4060
Russel W Thiel, *President*
Donna Thiel, *Treasurer*
EMP: 18 **EST:** 1967
SQ FT: 8,400
SALES (est): 2.2MM **Privately Held**
SIC: 3599 Machine shop, jobbing & repair

(G-13457)
HAMTRONICS INC
39 Willnick Cir (14626-4748)
PHONE..........................585 392-9430
G Francis Vogt, *President*
EMP: 7
SALES (est): 500K **Privately Held**
SIC: 3663 5961 Radio broadcasting & communications equipment; mail order house

(G-13458)
HANSON AGGREGATES PA LLC
1535 Scottsville Rd (14623-1934)
PHONE..........................585 436-3250
Jeff Kramarz, *Branch Mgr*
EMP: 15

SALES (corp-wide): 20.6B **Privately Held**
SIC: 2899 1442 Concrete curing & hardening compounds; gravel mining
HQ: Hanson Aggregates Pennsylvania, Llc
7660 Imperial Way
Allentown PA 18195
610 366-4626

(G-13459)
HARRIS CORPORATION
800 Lee Rd (14606-4248)
P.O. Box 60488 (14606-0488)
PHONE......................413 263-6200
Christopher Young, *CEO*
William Gattle, *President*
David McCaffrey, *Branch Mgr*
EMP: 509
SALES (corp-wide): 6.8B **Publicly Held**
SIC: 3669 Burglar alarm apparatus, electric
PA: L3harris Technologies, Inc.
1025 W Nasa Blvd
Melbourne FL 32919
321 727-9100

(G-13460)
HARRIS GLOBL CMMUNICATIONS INC
1350 Jefferson Rd (14623-3106)
PHONE..........................585 244-5830
Chris Young, *President*
▼ **EMP:** 1200
SALES: 1.1B
SALES (corp-wide): 6.8B **Publicly Held**
SIC: 3663 Receivers, radio communications
PA: L3harris Technologies, Inc.
1025 W Nasa Blvd
Melbourne FL 32919
321 727-9100

(G-13461)
HAWVER DISPLAY INC (PA)
140 Carter St (14621-5136)
PHONE..........................585 544-2290
Timothy Culver, *President*
Cindy Bauman, *Purch Mgr*
Dan Nistico, *Sales Executive*
EMP: 29
SQ FT: 44,000
SALES (est): 3.7MM **Privately Held**
WEB: www.hawver.com
SIC: 2542 Fixtures: display, office or store: except wood

(G-13462)
HAZLOW ELECTRONICS INC
49 Saint Bridgets Dr (14605-1899)
PHONE..........................585 325-5323
Alma Publow, *President*
Andrew Publow, *Vice Pres*
James Bunce, *Project Dir*
EMP: 25 **EST:** 1971
SQ FT: 40,000
SALES (est): 5.7MM **Privately Held**
WEB: www.hazlow.com
SIC: 3679 3672 Harness assemblies for electronic use: wire or cable; printed circuit boards

(G-13463)
HEALTH CARE ORIGINALS INC
1 Pleasant St Ste 442 (14604-1455)
PHONE..........................585 471-8215
Jared Dwarika, *Owner*
EMP: 9
SALES (est): 399.9K **Privately Held**
SIC: 3845 8731 Electromedical apparatus; medical research, commercial

(G-13464)
HELIO PRECISION PRODUCTS INC
Also Called: Hn Precision
200 Tech Park Dr (14623-2445)
PHONE..........................585 697-5434
EMP: 21
SALES (corp-wide): 31.3MM **Privately Held**
SIC: 3592 Valves, engine
PA: Helio Precision Products, Inc
601 N Skokie Hwy Ste B
Lake Bluff IL 60044
847 473-1300

(G-13465)
HIGH END PRINT SOLUTIONS INC
250 Cumberland St Ste 100 (14605-2847)
PHONE..........................585 325-5320
Gerald Ward, *President*
Lisa Fairchild, *Sales Staff*
EMP: 15
SQ FT: 18,000
SALES (est): 3MM **Privately Held**
WEB: www.stvincentpress.com
SIC: 2752 Commercial printing, offset

(G-13466)
HIGH FALLS BREWING COMPANY LLC (DH)
Also Called: North Americas Breweries
445 Saint Paul St (14605-1726)
P.O. Box 30762 (14603-0762)
PHONE..........................585 263-9318
Samuel T Hubbard Jr,
Michael C Atseff,
John Henderson,
William A Neilson,
Norman E Snyder,
◆ **EMP:** 114
SQ FT: 900,000
SALES (est): 57.5MM **Privately Held**
WEB: www.highfalls.com
SIC: 2082 Beer (alcoholic beverage); ale (alcoholic beverage)

(G-13467)
HIGH FALLS OPERATING CO LLC
445 Saint Paul St (14605-1726)
PHONE..........................585 546-1030
Kenneth Yartz, *Officer*
EMP: 800
SALES (est): 104.6MM **Privately Held**
SIC: 2082 Malt beverage products
HQ: North American Breweries, Inc.
445 Saint Paul St
Rochester NY 14605

(G-13468)
HIGH SPEED HAMMER COMPANY INC
Also Called: Assembly Equipment Division
313 Norton St (14621-3331)
PHONE..........................585 266-4287
David Marcellus, *President*
Richard Marcellus, *Corp Secy*
EMP: 15 **EST:** 1917
SQ FT: 12,000
SALES: 1MM **Privately Held**
SIC: 3542 3541 Riveting machines; machine tools, metal cutting: exotic (explosive, etc.); machine tool replacement & repair parts, metal cutting types

(G-13469)
HIS VISION INC
1260 Lyell Ave (14606-2040)
PHONE..........................585 254-0022
Patrick Ho, *President*
Wayne Ohl, *Admin Sec*
▲ **EMP:** 48 **EST:** 1941
SQ FT: 21,000
SALES: 3.5MM **Privately Held**
WEB: www.rochesteroptical.com
SIC: 3851 Frames & parts, eyeglass & spectacle

(G-13470)
HOBART CORPORATION
3495 Winton Pl (14623-2824)
PHONE..........................585 427-9000
Pat Allen, *Manager*
EMP: 50
SALES (corp-wide): 14.7B **Publicly Held**
SIC: 3589 Dishwashing machines, commercial
HQ: Hobart Llc
701 S Ridge Ave
Troy OH 45373
937 332-3000

(G-13471)
HOVER-DAVIS INC (DH)
100 Paragon Dr (14624-1129)
PHONE..........................585 352-9590
John Hover, *President*
Peter Davis, *Vice Pres*
Dave Lyndaker, *Engineer*

▲ = Import ▼=Export
◆ =Import/Export

▲ EMP: 125
SQ FT: 66,000
SALES (est): 16.1MM **Privately Held**
WEB: www.hoverdavis.com
SIC: 3549 Assembly machines, including robotic

(G-13472)
HY-TECH MOLD INC
60 Elmgrove Park (14624-1363)
PHONE.................................585 247-2450
Donald Philipp, *President*
Patricia Philipp, *Vice Pres*
Stuart Norris, *Treasurer*
EMP: 10
SQ FT: 10,000
SALES: 800K **Privately Held**
WEB: www.hy-techmold.com
SIC: 3544 Industrial molds

(G-13473)
ID SIGNSYSTEMS INC
410 Atlantic Ave (14609-7356)
PHONE.................................585 266-5750
Katrina Beatty, *CEO*
Paul Dudley, *President*
Jeff Ureles, *COO*
◆ EMP: 48
SQ FT: 15,000
SALES (est): 5.7MM **Privately Held**
WEB: www.idsignsystems.com
SIC: 3993 Electric signs

(G-13474)
IEC ELECTRONICS CORP
Celmet
1365 Emerson St (14606-3006)
PHONE.................................585 647-1760
Todd Oconnor, *Engineer*
Tom Guiliani, *Director*
EMP: 80
SALES (corp-wide): 96.4MM **Publicly Held**
SIC: 3444 Sheet metalwork
PA: Iec Electronics Corp.
105 Norton St
Newark NY 14513
315 331-7742

(G-13475)
IHEARTCOMMUNICATIONS INC
Also Called: Wham 1180 AM
100 Chestnut St Ste 1700 (14604-2418)
PHONE.................................585 454-4884
Karen Carey, *President*
Jay Leonard, *Vice Chairman*
Tony Andrulis, *Director*
EMP: 120 **Publicly Held**
SIC: 3663 4832 Radio receiver networks;
radio broadcasting stations
HQ: Iheartcommunications, Inc.
20880 Stone Oak Pkwy
San Antonio TX 78258
210 822-2828

(G-13476)
IMAGE360
Also Called: Signs Now
275 Marketplace Dr (14623-6001)
PHONE.................................585 272-1234
Julie St Germaine, *President*
Jackie Ciresi, *Treasurer*
EMP: 5
SALES (est): 712.9K **Privately Held**
WEB: www.signsnow405.com
SIC: 3993 Signs & advertising specialties

(G-13477)
IMPRESSIONS INTERNATIONAL INC
410 Alexander St Ste 2 (14607-1038)
PHONE.................................585 442-5240
Terry Gersey, *President*
Harry Gersey, *Vice Pres*
▲ EMP: 7
SQ FT: 2,500
SALES (est): 872.7K **Privately Held**
WEB: www.checkfraud.com
SIC: 3555 Printing plates

(G-13478)
INNEX INDUSTRIES INC
6 Marway Dr (14624-2349)
PHONE.................................585 247-3575
Tom Blaszczykiewicz, *President*
▼ EMP: 28

SQ FT: 20,000
SALES (est): 5.6MM **Privately Held**
WEB: www.innexind.com
SIC: 3599 Machine shop, jobbing & repair

(G-13479)
INSTANT AGAIN LLC
1277 Mount Read Blvd # 2 (14606-2850)
PHONE.................................585 436-8003
Kathy Pfeffer, *Office Mgr*
Andrew Gross III,
EMP: 20
SALES (est): 3MM **Privately Held**
WEB: www.instantagain.com
SIC: 2752 Commercial printing, lithographic

(G-13480)
INSTANT MONOGRAMMING INC
1150 University Ave Ste 5 (14607-1647)
PHONE.................................585 654-5550
Daniel Bloom, *President*
Deborah Bloom, *Corp Secy*
EMP: 7
SALES (est): 724.8K **Privately Held**
SIC: 2395 Embroidery products, except
schiffli machine; emblems, embroidered

(G-13481)
INTELLIMETAL INC
2025 Brighton Henrietta (14623-2509)
PHONE.................................585 424-3260
Kim Lazzara Zapiach, *President*
Linda Brockett, *General Mgr*
Scott Lazzara, *General Mgr*
Tony Delvecchio, *Opers Mgr*
EMP: 57
SALES (est): 14.1MM **Privately Held**
SIC: 3444 Sheet metalwork

(G-13482)
INTERNATIONAL PAPER COMPANY
200 Boxart St (14612-5646)
PHONE.................................585 663-1000
Pam Hayes, *Safety Mgr*
John McCormick, *Purch Mgr*
Les Senft, *Manager*
John Lew, *Manager*
Bob Wilson, *Clerk*
EMP: 150
SALES (corp-wide): 23.3B **Publicly Held**
WEB: www.internationalpaper.com
SIC: 2653 2671 Boxes, corrugated: made
from purchased materials; packaging
paper & plastics film, coated & laminated
PA: International Paper Company
6400 Poplar Ave
Memphis TN 38197
901 419-9000

(G-13483)
INTRINSIQ MATERIALS INC
1200 Ridgeway Ave Ste 110 (14615-3758)
P.O. Box 15532 (14615-0532)
PHONE.................................585 301-4432
Robert Cournoyer, *President*
EMP: 7 EST: 2011
SALES (est): 1MM **Privately Held**
WEB: www.intrinsiqmaterials.com
SIC: 2893 8731 Printing ink; electronic research

(G-13484)
IROQUOIS ROCK PRODUCTS INC (DH)
1150 Penfield Rd (14625-2202)
PHONE.................................585 381-7010
John Odenbach Jr, *President*
Richard E Williams, *President*
David Fingar, *Vice Pres*
Frederick J Odenbach, *Vice Pres*
Gerard Odenbach, *Vice Pres*
EMP: 10
SQ FT: 5,000
SALES (est): 2.6MM
SALES (corp-wide): 30.6B **Privately Held**
SIC: 3281 2951 3273 Stone, quarrying &
processing of own stone products; paving
mixtures; asphalt & asphaltic paving mixtures (not from refineries); road materials,
bituminous (not from refineries); ready-
mixed concrete

HQ: Dolomite Products Company Inc.
1150 Penfield Rd
Rochester NY 14625
315 524-1998

(G-13485)
J MACKENZIE LTD
234 Wallace Way (14624-6216)
P.O. Box 22678 (14692-2678)
PHONE.................................585 321-1770
James E Hammer, *President*
Christopher F Wieser, *Admin Sec*
▲ EMP: 39
SQ FT: 56,000
SALES (est): 3.5MM
SALES (corp-wide): 119.2MM **Privately Held**
WEB: www.jmackenzie.com
SIC: 2789 Paper cutting
PA: Hammer Packaging Corp.
200 Lucius Gordon Dr
West Henrietta NY 14586
585 424-3880

(G-13486)
J VOGLER ENTERPRISE LLC
15 Evelyn St (14606-5533)
P.O. Box 24361 (14624-0361)
PHONE.................................585 247-1625
James Vogler,
EMP: 10
SQ FT: 6,000
SALES (est): 1.8MM **Privately Held**
WEB: www.jvogler.com
SIC: 3541 Machine tools, metal cutting type

(G-13487)
JAM INDUSTRIES INC
Also Called: Ace Manufacturing
9 Marway Cir (14624-2320)
PHONE.................................585 458-9830
Eric L Johnson, *Ch of Bd*
Martha Moriarty, *Vice Pres*
Jeff Johnson, *Foreman/Supr*
▲ EMP: 45
SQ FT: 25,000
SALES (est): 8.9MM **Privately Held**
WEB: www.jamindustries.com
SIC: 3599 Machine shop, jobbing & repair;
machine & other job shop work

(G-13488)
JAMES CONOLLY PRINTING CO
72 Marway Cir (14624-2380)
PHONE.................................585 426-4150
Robert Conolly, *President*
Mark Assenato, *Vice Pres*
Beth Calkins, *Manager*
EMP: 21 EST: 1968
SQ FT: 13,000
SALES (est): 3.2MM **Privately Held**
SIC: 2752 2791 2789 Commercial printing, offset; typesetting; bookbinding & related work

(G-13489)
JAMESTOWN CONT OF ROCHESTER
82 Edwards Deming Dr (14606-2842)
PHONE.................................585 254-9190
Bruce Janowsky, *Ch of Bd*
Dick P Weimer, *Corp Secy*
Joseph R Palmeri, *Vice Pres*
Melissa Guenter, *Accountant*
EMP: 70
SALES (est): 22.9MM
SALES (corp-wide): 148.3MM **Privately Held**
WEB: www.jamestowncontainer.com
SIC: 2653 Boxes, corrugated: made from
purchased materials
PA: Jamestown Container Corp
14 Deming Dr
Falconer NY 14733
716 665-4623

(G-13490)
JASCO TOOLS LLC
Also Called: Arch Globl Precision Rochester
1390 Mount Read Blvd (14606-2820)
PHONE.................................585 254-7000
Kelli Micoli, *Mng Member*
EMP: 71

SALES (est): 3.4MM
SALES (corp-wide): 724.3MM **Privately Held**
SIC: 3545 Precision tools, machinists'
HQ: Arch Global Precision Llc
2600 S Telg Rd Ste 180
Bloomfield Hills MI 48302
734 266-6900

(G-13491)
JAVLYN PROCESS SYSTEMS LLC
3136 Winton Rd S Ste 102 (14623-2928)
PHONE.................................585 424-5580
Victor Tifone, *President*
EMP: 23
SQ FT: 8,000
SALES (est): 1.4MM
SALES (corp-wide): 355.8K **Privately Held**
SIC: 3569 8742 Liquid automation machinery & equipment; automation & robotics consultant; food & beverage consultant
HQ: Krones, Inc.
9600 S 58th St
Franklin WI 53132
414 409-4000

(G-13492)
JML OPTICAL INDUSTRIES LLC
Also Called: Gregg Sadwick
820 Linden Ave (14625-2710)
PHONE.................................585 248-8900
Bob Bicksler, *CEO*
Joseph Lobozzo II, *President*
Trett Sadwick, *COO*
Graldine Lynch, *Vice Pres*
Michael McCusker, *Vice Pres*
▲ EMP: 86
SQ FT: 72,000
SALES: 14.1MM **Privately Held**
SIC: 3827 Lenses, optical: all types except
ophthalmic; mirrors, optical; prisms, optical

(G-13493)
JOHNSON CONTROLS
90 Goodway Dr Ste 1 (14623-3039)
PHONE.................................585 288-6200
Kerry Maier, *Human Res Dir*
Gary Gokey, *Branch Mgr*
EMP: 74 **Privately Held**
WEB: www.simplexgrinnell.com
SIC: 3669 Emergency alarms
HQ: Johnson Controls Fire Protection Lp
6600 Congress Ave
Boca Raton FL 33487
561 988-7200

(G-13494)
JOHNSON CONTROLS INC
90 Goodway Dr Ste 1 (14623-3039)
PHONE.................................585 924-9346
Joe Knight, *Manager*
EMP: 37 **Privately Held**
SIC: 3822 Temperature controls, automatic
HQ: Johnson Controls, Inc.
5757 N Green Bay Ave
Milwaukee WI 53209
414 524-1200

(G-13495)
JOHNSON CONTROLS INC
1669 Lake Ave Bldg 333 (14652-0001)
PHONE.................................585 724-2232
Lee Arbagast, *Branch Mgr*
EMP: 120 **Privately Held**
SIC: 2531 3714 3691 3822 Seats, automobile; motor vehicle body components &
frame; instrument board assemblies,
motor vehicle; lead acid batteries (storage
batteries); building services monitoring
controls, automatic; facilities support services
HQ: Johnson Controls, Inc.
5757 N Green Bay Ave
Milwaukee WI 53209
414 524-1200

(G-13496)
JORDAN MACHINE INC
1241 Ridgeway Ave Ste I (14615-3757)
PHONE.................................585 647-3585
Thomas Lacey, *President*
Jordan Kesselring, *Vice Pres*

Christine Lacey, *CFO*
EMP: 5 **EST:** 2016
SALES (est): 223K **Privately Held**
SIC: 3599 Machine shop, jobbing & repair

(G-13497)
JS COATING SOLUTIONS INC
12 Pixley Industrial Pkwy (14624-2364)
PHONE.....................585 471-8354
Eric Johnson, *CEO*
Jeremy Seaver, *President*
EMP: 8
SQ FT: 4,500
SALES: 485.5K **Privately Held**
SIC: 3479 Painting of metal products

(G-13498)
JTEKT TORSEN NORTH AMERICA
2 Jetview Dr (14624-4904)
PHONE.....................585 464-5000
Hiroyuki Kaijima, *President*
Joseph Parisi, *Admin Sec*
▲ **EMP:** 10
SQ FT: 30,000
SALES (est): 2.2MM **Privately Held**
SIC: 3714 3711 Motor vehicle parts & accessories; motor vehicles & car bodies
HQ: Jtekt North America Corporation
    7 Research Dr Ste A
    Greenville SC 29607
    440 835-1000

(G-13499)
JUST IN TIME CNC MACHININ
13 Marway Dr (14624-2351)
PHONE.....................585 247-3850
Jim Alexander, *Principal*
EMP: 5
SALES (est): 867.4K **Privately Held**
SIC: 3599 Machine shop, jobbing & repair

(G-13500)
JUST PRESS PRINT LLC
304 Whitney St (14606-1110)
PHONE.....................585 783-1300
Raphael Coccia, *President*
EMP: 7
SALES (est): 450.4K **Privately Held**
SIC: 2752 Commercial printing, offset

(G-13501)
K BARTHELMES MFG CO INC
61 Brooklea Dr (14624-2701)
PHONE.....................585 328-8140
EMP: 15
SQ FT: 55,000
SALES (est): 1.9MM **Privately Held**
SIC: 3444 Mfg Sheet Metalwork

(G-13502)
KEVIN J KASSMAN
Also Called: Uniform Express
1408 Buffalo Rd (14624-1827)
PHONE.....................585 529-4245
Kevin J Kassman, *Owner*
EMP: 6
SQ FT: 4,500
SALES: 600K **Privately Held**
SIC: 2395 2396 Embroidery products, except schiffli machine; screen printing on fabric articles

(G-13503)
KLEE CORP
Also Called: Klees Car Wash and Detailing
340 Jefferson Rd (14623-2644)
PHONE.....................585 272-0320
Daniel Edelman, *Manager*
EMP: 7
SQ FT: 5,625
SALES (corp-wide): 21.7MM **Privately Held**
SIC: 3589 Car washing machinery
PA: Klee Corp
    38 Boulder Creek Dr
    Rush NY 14543
    585 321-1510

(G-13504)
KODAK ALARIS INC (DH)
336 Initiative Dr (14624-6217)
PHONE.....................888 242-2424
Marc Jourlait, *CEO*
Rick Costanzom, *President*
Dennis Olbrich, *President*

Nicki Zongrone, *President*
Jeff Goodman, *COOO*
◆ **EMP:** 277
SALES (est): 264.1MM **Privately Held**
SIC: 3861 Photographic equipment & supplies
HQ: Kodak Alaris Holdings Limited
    Hemel One Boundary Way
    Hemel Hempstead HERTS HP2 7
    845 757-3175

(G-13505)
KODAK GRAPHIC COMMUNICATIONS
343 State St (14650-0002)
P.O. Box 982138, El Paso TX (79998-2138)
PHONE.....................585 724-4000
Jeffrey Jacobson, *President*
EMP: 14
SALES (est): 4MM **Privately Held**
SIC: 3861 Photographic equipment & supplies

(G-13506)
KURZ AND ZOBEL INC
688 Colfax St (14606-3193)
PHONE.....................585 254-9060
Michael Zobel Jr, *President*
EMP: 8 **EST:** 1948
SQ FT: 15,000
SALES (est): 867.9K **Privately Held**
SIC: 3599 3462 Machine shop, jobbing & repair; gear & chain forgings

(G-13507)
L3HARRIS TECHNOLOGIES INC
Harris Rf Communications
1680 University Ave (14610-1839)
PHONE.....................585 244-5830
Madjid Abdi, *Principal*
Dana Mehnert, *Branch Mgr*
Tony Dal Santo, *Sr Software Eng*
EMP: 2600
SALES (corp-wide): 6.8B **Publicly Held**
SIC: 3663 Radio & TV communications equipment
PA: L3harris Technologies, Inc.
    1025 W Nasa Blvd
    Melbourne FL 32919
    321 727-9100

(G-13508)
L3HARRIS TECHNOLOGIES INC
Also Called: Harris Corporation
400 Initiative Dr (14624-6219)
P.O. Box 60488 (14606-0488)
PHONE.....................585 269-6600
William Brown, *President*
Heather Fernandez, *Accounts Mgr*
Kathryn Lloyd, *Branch Mgr*
EMP: 800
SALES (corp-wide): 6.8B **Publicly Held**
SIC: 3812 Space vehicle guidance systems & equipment
PA: L3harris Technologies, Inc.
    1025 W Nasa Blvd
    Melbourne FL 32919
    321 727-9100

(G-13509)
L3HARRIS TECHNOLOGIES INC
Also Called: Harris Corporation
800 Lee Rd Bldg 601 (14606-4248)
P.O. Box 60488 (14606-0488)
PHONE.....................585 269-5001
William Gattle, *President*
David Melcher, *President*
Richard Wambach, *Branch Mgr*
EMP: 400
SALES (corp-wide): 6.8B **Publicly Held**
SIC: 3812 Space vehicle guidance systems & equipment
PA: L3harris Technologies, Inc.
    1025 W Nasa Blvd
    Melbourne FL 32919
    321 727-9100

(G-13510)
L3HARRIS TECHNOLOGIES INC
2696 Manitou Rd Bldg 101 (14624-1173)
PHONE.....................585 269-5000
Heather Fernandez, *Accounts Mgr*
James R Kulp, *Branch Mgr*
EMP: 163

SALES (corp-wide): 6.8B **Publicly Held**
SIC: 3812 Space vehicle guidance systems & equipment
PA: L3harris Technologies, Inc.
    1025 W Nasa Blvd
    Melbourne FL 32919
    321 727-9100

(G-13511)
L3HARRIS TECHNOLOGIES INC
Also Called: Rf Communications
570 Culver Rd (14609-7442)
PHONE.....................585 244-5830
Dana Mehnert, *Vice Pres*
EMP: 20
SALES (corp-wide): 6.8B **Publicly Held**
SIC: 3661 3671 Telephone & telegraph apparatus; electron tubes
PA: L3harris Technologies, Inc.
    1025 W Nasa Blvd
    Melbourne FL 32919
    321 727-9100

(G-13512)
L3HARRIS TECHNOLOGIES INC
50 Carlson Rd (14610-1063)
PHONE.....................585 244-5830
EMP: 441
SALES (corp-wide): 6.8B **Publicly Held**
SIC: 3663 Radio & TV communications equipment
PA: L3harris Technologies, Inc.
    1025 W Nasa Blvd
    Melbourne FL 32919
    321 727-9100

(G-13513)
L3HARRIS TECHNOLOGIES INC
Also Called: Harris Rf Communications
1350 Jefferson Rd (14623-3106)
PHONE.....................585 244-5830
EMP: 441
SALES (corp-wide): 6.8B **Publicly Held**
SIC: 3663 Radio & TV communications equipment
PA: L3harris Technologies, Inc.
    1025 W Nasa Blvd
    Melbourne FL 32919
    321 727-9100

(G-13514)
LAZER INCORPORATED (PA)
Also Called: Lazer Photo Engraving
1465 Jefferson Rd Ste 110 (14623-3149)
PHONE.....................336 744-8047
Gary Staford, *President*
EMP: 50
SQ FT: 10,000
SALES (est): 3.5MM **Privately Held**
WEB: www.lazerinc.com
SIC: 2796 Color separations for printing

(G-13515)
LENS TRIPTAR CO INC
439 Monroe Ave Ste 1 (14607-3787)
PHONE.....................585 473-4470
Allen Krisiloff, *President*
EMP: 5
SQ FT: 3,300
SALES (est): 821.4K **Privately Held**
WEB: www.triptar.com
SIC: 3827 Lenses, optical: all types except ophthalmic

(G-13516)
LEXINGTON MACHINING LLC
677 Buffalo Rd (14611-2014)
PHONE.....................585 235-0880
Ken Vivlamore, *Vice Pres*
Rick Donofrio, *Controller*
Kathi Horch, *Systems Staff*
EMP: 100 **Privately Held**
SIC: 3451 Screw machine products
PA: Lexington Machining Llc
    677 Buffalo Rd
    Rochester NY 14611

(G-13517)
LEXINGTON MACHINING LLC (PA)
677 Buffalo Rd (14611-2014)
PHONE.....................585 235-0880
Michael Lubin, *Ch of Bd*
Warren Delano, *President*
Timothy Duemmel, *General Mgr*
Tom Mogavero, *Materials Mgr*

Grace Ziobrowski, *Human Res Mgr*
EMP: 174
SALES: 22.7MM **Privately Held**
WEB: www.lexingtonmachining.com
SIC: 3451 Screw machine products

(G-13518)
LIGHTFORCE TECHNOLOGY INC
1057 E Henrietta Rd (14623-2635)
P.O. Box 22853 (14692-2853)
PHONE.....................585 292-5610
Peter Hammond, *President*
Robert Houde, *Manager*
EMP: 7
SQ FT: 200
SALES: 1MM **Privately Held**
WEB: www.lightforcetech.com
SIC: 3827 Optical elements & assemblies, except ophthalmic

(G-13519)
LMD POWER OF LIGHT CORP
Also Called: Lasermaxdefense
3495 Winton Pl Ste A37 (14623-2818)
PHONE.....................585 272-5420
Susan H Walter, *President*
Will H Walter, *Exec VP*
Daniel J Maier, *CFO*
EMP: 54
SQ FT: 10,250
SALES (est): 11.2MM **Privately Held**
WEB: www.lasermax.com
SIC: 3699 3674 Laser systems & equipment; semiconductors & related devices

(G-13520)
LMT TECHNOLOGY SOLUTIONS
4 Commercial St Ste 400 (14614-1000)
PHONE.....................585 784-7470
Nate Benitez, *General Mgr*
Alma Vieru, *VP Opers*
Katelynn Smith, *Accounting Mgr*
Rich Baker, *VP Sales*
Lillian Sandvik,
EMP: 10 **EST:** 2017
SALES (est): 391.8K **Privately Held**
SIC: 7372 Prepackaged software

(G-13521)
LOAD/N/GO BEVERAGE CORP (PA)
Also Called: Fiz Beverages
355 Portland Ave (14605-1565)
PHONE.....................585 218-4019
Paul Johnson, *President*
EMP: 10 **EST:** 1964
SQ FT: 11,000
SALES (est): 1.6MM **Privately Held**
SIC: 2086 5181 5149 5921 Soft drinks: packaged in cans, bottles, etc.; beer & other fermented malt liquors; soft drinks; beer (packaged)

(G-13522)
LOGICAL OPERATIONS INC
3535 Winton Pl (14623-2803)
PHONE.....................585 350-7000
Bill Rosenthal, *President*
▲ **EMP:** 110
SALES (est): 21.5MM **Privately Held**
SIC: 2732 8249 8243 5999 Books: printing & binding; business training services; software training, computer; educational aids & electronic training materials; training materials, electronic

(G-13523)
LOUIS HEINDL & SON INC
Also Called: Heindl Printers
306 Central Ave (14605-3007)
P.O. Box 31121 (14603-1121)
PHONE.....................585 454-5080
P J Heindl, *President*
Debra Heindl, *Vice Pres*
EMP: 6 **EST:** 1873
SQ FT: 3,500
SALES: 540K **Privately Held**
SIC: 2752 2759 2791 2789 Commercial printing, offset; letterpress printing; typesetting; bookbinding & related work

(G-13524)
LUMETRICS INC
1565 Jefferson Rd Ste 420 (14623-3190)
PHONE.....................585 214-2455
John Hart, *President*

▲ = Import ▼=Export
◆ =Import/Export

Todd Blalock, *Vice Pres*
Steve Heveron-Smith, *Vice Pres*
Steve Kelly, *Vice Pres*
Jason Ness, *Purch Agent*
▼ **EMP:** 17
SQ FT: 4,416
SALES (est): 4.4MM **Privately Held**
WEB: www.lumetrics.com
SIC: 3827 Optical instruments & apparatus

(G-13525)
MACAUTO USA INC (HQ)
80 Excel Dr (14621-3470)
PHONE..................585 342-2060
J J Liao, *President*
Douglas Chang, *Treasurer*
◆ **EMP:** 30
SQ FT: 15,000
SALES (est): 5.9MM **Privately Held**
SIC: 3089 Automotive parts, plastic

(G-13526)
MACHINECRAFT INC
1645 Lyell Ave Ste 125 (14606-2331)
PHONE..................585 436-1070
Alan D Lintz, *Ch of Bd*
EMP: 25
SQ FT: 8,750
SALES (est): 2.4MM **Privately Held**
SIC: 3544 Special dies & tools

(G-13527)
MACINNES TOOL CORPORATION
1700 Hudson Ave Ste 3 (14617-5155)
PHONE..................585 467-1920
Gary Haines, *President*
Sherry Haines, *Treasurer*
Emily Haines, *Personnel*
EMP: 20 **EST:** 1953
SQ FT: 6,000
SALES (est): 2.5MM **Privately Held**
WEB: www.macto.com
SIC: 3545 5085 Cutting tools for machine tools; industrial supplies

(G-13528)
MADISON & DUNN
850 Saint Paul St Ste 29 (14605-1065)
PHONE..................585 563-7760
Christine Baliva, *Owner*
EMP: 6
SALES (est): 750.6K **Privately Held**
SIC: 2426 Flooring, hardwood

(G-13529)
MAGNA PRODUCTS CORP
777 Mount Read Blvd (14606-2129)
PHONE..................585 647-2280
Kenneth Morrow, *President*
Pat Morrow, *Vice Pres*
Laurie Kinsella, *Purchasing*
John Troy, *Supervisor*
EMP: 20
SALES (est): 4.2MM **Privately Held**
WEB: www.magnaproducts.com
SIC: 3621 3566 Servomotors, electric; drives, high speed industrial, except hydrostatic

(G-13530)
MAGNETIC TECHNOLOGIES CORP (DH)
770 Linden Ave (14625-2764)
PHONE..................585 385-9010
Gordon H McNeil, *Ch of Bd*
Dale Gulick, *Engineer*
Kathleen Palia, *Controller*
Greg Daly, *Accounting Mgr*
Lisa Goetz, *Manager*
▲ **EMP:** 60
SQ FT: 70,000
SALES (est): 10.2MM **Publicly Held**
WEB: www.arnoldmagnetics.com
SIC: 3677 Electronic coils, transformers & other inductors
HQ: Arnold Magnetic Technologies Corporation
770 Linden Ave
Rochester NY 14625
585 385-9010

(G-13531)
MANITOU CONCRETE
1260 Jefferson Rd (14623-3104)
PHONE..................585 424-6040

John Pelrier, *Manager*
EMP: 65
SQ FT: 2,536
SALES (est): 6.4MM **Privately Held**
SIC: 3273 Ready-mixed concrete

(G-13532)
MANUFACTURING RESOURCES INC
2392 Innovation Way # 4 (14624-6225)
PHONE..................631 481-0041
James Wildman, *Ch of Bd*
James Widman, *Ch of Bd*
EMP: 40 **EST:** 2002
SQ FT: 30,000
SALES (est): 805.7K **Privately Held**
WEB: www.mfgresource.com
SIC: 3444 3549 Sheet metalwork; assembly machines, including robotic

(G-13533)
MANUFACTURING SOLUTIONS INC
850 Saint Paul St Ste 11 (14605-1065)
PHONE..................585 235-3320
Oscar Wilson, *President*
EMP: 25
SQ FT: 5,000
SALES (est): 3.4MM **Privately Held**
WEB: www.mfgsolonline.com
SIC: 3699 Electrical equipment & supplies

(G-13534)
MARACLE INDUSTRIAL FINSHG CO
93 Kilbourn Rd (14618-3607)
PHONE..................585 387-9077
Thomas Maracle, *President*
Nelson Maracle, *Vice Pres*
EMP: 30 **EST:** 1960
SQ FT: 30,000
SALES (est): 3.1MM **Privately Held**
SIC: 3471 Finishing, metals or formed products

(G-13535)
MARDON TOOL & DIE CO INC
19 Lois St (14606-1801)
PHONE..................585 254-4545
Donald Fox, *President*
EMP: 13 **EST:** 1981
SQ FT: 4,000
SALES (est): 1.8MM **Privately Held**
SIC: 3599 Machine shop, jobbing & repair

(G-13536)
MAREX AQUISITION CORP
1385 Emerson St (14606-3027)
PHONE..................585 458-3940
Gary Baxter, *Ch of Bd*
John Olivieri Sr, *Ch of Bd*
Leonard Olivieri, *Vice Pres*
▲ **EMP:** 115
SQ FT: 55,000
SALES (est): 9.6MM
SALES (corp-wide): 51MM **Privately Held**
WEB: www.martecindustries.com
SIC: 3469 3444 3443 3441 Metal stampings; sheet metalwork; fabricated plate work (boiler shop); fabricated structural metal
PA: Peko Precision Products, Inc.
1400 Emerson St
Rochester NY 14606
585 647-3010

(G-13537)
MASTRO GRAPHIC ARTS INC
67 Deep Rock Rd (14624-3519)
PHONE..................585 436-7570
Rae Mastrofilippo, *Ch of Bd*
William Betteridge, *President*
Thomas Tortora, *CFO*
Nick Mastro, *Treasurer*
EMP: 34
SQ FT: 23,000
SALES (est): 8.1MM **Privately Held**
WEB: www.mastrographics.com
SIC: 2759 2754 Screen printing; rotary photogravure printing

(G-13538)
MCALPIN INDUSTRIES INC (PA)
255 Hollenbeck St (14621-3294)
PHONE..................585 266-3060
Kenneth McAlpin, *CEO*
Mike McAlpin, *Exec VP*
Chris Fronczak, *Mfg Staff*
Tony Harper, *Mfg Staff*
Sergio Oropeza, *Engineer*
▲ **EMP:** 150 **EST:** 1964
SQ FT: 140,000
SALES (est): 30.3MM **Privately Held**
WEB: www.mcalpin-ind.com
SIC: 3444 Sheet metal specialties, not stamped

(G-13539)
MCALPIN INDUSTRIES INC
Also Called: Monroe Plating Div
265 Hollenbeck St (14621-3294)
PHONE..................585 544-5335
Mike Mumm, *Branch Mgr*
EMP: 45
SQ FT: 8,000
SALES (corp-wide): 29.5MM **Privately Held**
WEB: www.mcalpin-ind.com
SIC: 3471 Finishing, metals or formed products
PA: Mcalpin Industries, Inc.
255 Hollenbeck St
Rochester NY 14621
585 266-3060

(G-13540)
MCM NATURAL STONE INC
860 Linden Ave Ste 1 (14625-2718)
PHONE..................585 586-6510
Marilyn Valle, *President*
Larissa Huge, *Sales Staff*
EMP: 12
SALES (est): 1.7MM **Privately Held**
WEB: www.mcmstone.com
SIC: 3281 5032 1423 Granite, cut & shaped; limestone, cut & shaped; granite building stone; limestone; crushed & broken granite

(G-13541)
MELIORUM TECHNOLOGIES INC
620 Park Ave 145 (14607-2943)
PHONE..................585 313-0616
Jason Rama, *President*
▼ **EMP:** 5
SALES (est): 487.3K **Privately Held**
SIC: 2821 2819 Silicone resins; aluminum oxide

(G-13542)
MERCURY PRINT PRODUCTIONS INC (PA)
2332 Innovation Way 4 (14624-6225)
PHONE..................585 458-7900
John Place, *CEO*
Christian Schamberger, *President*
Steve Adolf, *Vice Pres*
Basil Newton, *Plant Mgr*
Derek Shoales, *Project Mgr*
▲ **EMP:** 200
SQ FT: 80,000
SALES (est): 76.8MM **Privately Held**
WEB: www.mercuryprint.com
SIC: 2752 7334 2791 2789 Commercial printing, offset; photocopying & duplicating services; typesetting; bookbinding & related work

(G-13543)
METROPOLITAN GRANITE & MBL INC
860 Maple St Ste 100 (14611-1612)
PHONE..................585 342-7020
Helmettin Cakir, *President*
EMP: 5
SALES: 450K **Privately Held**
SIC: 2541 Counter & sink tops

(G-13544)
MICHAEL TODD STEVENS
Also Called: Rochester Screen Printing
95 Mount Read Blvd # 125 (14611-1923)
PHONE..................585 436-9957
Michael Stevens, *Owner*
EMP: 5

SALES (est): 317K **Privately Held**
SIC: 3953 Screens, textile printing

(G-13545)
MICRO INSTRUMENT CORP
Also Called: Automated Systems Group
1199 Emerson St (14606-3038)
P.O. Box 60619 (14606-0619)
PHONE..................585 458-3150
William Gunther, *President*
Anthony De Salvo, *President*
Jens Pfeffer, *Exec VP*
Chris Lindstrom, *Project Mgr*
Dale Niehaus, *QC Mgr*
EMP: 100 **EST:** 1944
SQ FT: 56,000
SALES (est): 25.2MM **Privately Held**
WEB: www.microinst.com
SIC: 3599 3613 7389 6552 Machine shop, jobbing & repair; control panels, electric; grinding, precision: commercial or industrial; land subdividers & developers, commercial; special dies, tools, jigs & fixtures; aluminum foundries

(G-13546)
MICRO THREADED PRODUCTS INC
325 Mount Read Blvd Ste 4 (14611-1928)
PHONE..................585 288-0080
Robert Osipovitch, *President*
EMP: 5
SALES (est): 568.8K **Privately Held**
SIC: 3451 Screw machine products

(G-13547)
MICROERA PRINTERS INC
304 Whitney St (14606-1110)
PHONE..................585 783-1300
Bruno Coccia, *Ch of Bd*
Raphael Coccia, *Vice Pres*
EMP: 22
SQ FT: 20,000
SALES (est): 3.9MM **Privately Held**
WEB: www.microera.com
SIC: 2752 Commercial printing, offset

(G-13548)
MICRON INDS ROCHESTER INC
31 Industrial Park Cir (14624-2403)
PHONE..................585 247-6130
Stephen K Schmidt, *President*
Kirk Schmidt, *Vice Pres*
Eric Schmidt, *Admin Sec*
EMP: 9
SQ FT: 20,000
SALES (est): 1.3MM **Privately Held**
WEB: www.micronindustries.com
SIC: 3544 Special dies & tools; industrial molds

(G-13549)
MILLER METAL FABRICATING INC
315 Commerce Dr (14623-3507)
PHONE..................585 359-3400
Steven Mertz, *President*
Simon Sharp, *Design Engr*
EMP: 9 **EST:** 1978
SQ FT: 10,500
SALES (est): 1.4MM **Privately Held**
SIC: 3443 3441 3545 7692 Weldments; fabricated structural metal for bridges; precision tools, machinists'; welding repair; sandblasting of building exteriors

(G-13550)
MINORITY REPORTER INC (PA)
19 Borrowdale Dr (14626-1751)
P.O. Box 26352 (14626-0352)
PHONE..................585 225-3628
Dave McCleary, *Principal*
EMP: 8
SALES (est): 625.1K **Privately Held**
SIC: 2711 Newspapers, publishing & printing

(G-13551)
MINORITY REPORTER INC
506 W Broad St (14608-1802)
PHONE..................585 301-4199
EMP: 23
SALES (corp-wide): 625.1K **Privately Held**
SIC: 2711 Newspapers, publishing & printing

PA: Minority Reporter Inc
19 Borrowdale Dr
Rochester NY 14626
585 225-3628

(G-13552)
MITCHELL MACHINE TOOL LLC
190 Murray St (14606-1126)
PHONE.....................585 254-7520
Michael Mitchell,
Maryland Mitchell,
EMP: 5
SALES (est): 363K **Privately Held**
WEB: www.mitchellmachinetool.com
SIC: 3599 Machine shop, jobbing & repair

(G-13553)
MITEL NETWORKS INC
300 State St Ste 100 (14614-1047)
PHONE.....................877 654-3573
Don Joos, *Branch Mgr*
EMP: 9
SALES (corp-wide): 1B **Privately Held**
SIC: 3661 3663 7372 Telephone & tele-
graph apparatus; radio & TV communica-
tions equipment; prepackaged software
HQ: Mitel Networks, Inc.
1146 N Alma School Rd
Mesa AZ 85201

(G-13554)
MKS INSTRUMENTS INC
100 Highpower Rd (14623-3498)
PHONE.....................585 292-7472
Vitaliy Maksimchuk, *Opers Staff*
Jim Elwert, *Buyer*
Ana Espinoza, *Buyer*
Debbie Saraceni, *Purchasing*
David Coumou, *Technical Mgr*
EMP: 20
SALES (corp-wide): 2B **Publicly Held**
WEB: www.mksinst.com
SIC: 3823 Industrial instrmnts msrmnt dis-
play/control process variable
PA: Mks Instruments, Inc.
2 Tech Dr Ste 201
Andover MA 01810
978 645-5500

(G-13555)
MKS MEDICAL ELECTRONICS
Also Called: M K S
100 Highpower Rd (14623-3498)
PHONE.....................585 292-7400
Paul M Eyerman, *General Mgr*
Yogi Chawla, *Design Engr*
EMP: 112 **EST:** 1970
SQ FT: 20,000
SALES (est): 10.3MM
SALES (corp-wide): 2B **Publicly Held**
WEB: www.mksinst.com
SIC: 3621 3663 Generating apparatus &
parts, electrical; amplifiers, RF power & IF
PA: Mks Instruments, Inc.
2 Tech Dr Ste 201
Andover MA 01810
978 645-5500

(G-13556)
MOLECULAR GLASSES INC
1667 Lake Ave Ste 278b (14615-3047)
PHONE.....................585 210-2861
Michel Molaire, *CEO*
Mark Juba, *COO*
EMP: 9 **EST:** 2015
SQ FT: 1,000
SALES (est): 338.4K **Privately Held**
SIC: 2869 High purity grade chemicals, or-
ganic

(G-13557)
MONROE CNTY CHAPTER NYSARC INC
Also Called: Arcworks
1651 Lyell Ave (14606-2309)
PHONE.....................585 698-1320
Micheal Czora, *Branch Mgr*
EMP: 5
SALES (corp-wide): 70.6MM **Privately
Held**
SIC: 3085 Plastics bottles
HQ: Monroe County Chapter, Nysarc, Inc.
2060 Brighton Henrietta
Rochester NY 14623
585 271-0660

(G-13558)
MONROE PIPING & SHTMTL LLC (PA)
Also Called: MP&sm
68 Humboldt St (14609-7496)
P.O. Box 90600 (14609-0600)
PHONE.....................585 482-0200
Dan Englert, *CEO*
Curtis Peterson, *CEO*
Mark Lohrmann, *Division Mgr*
Jeffrey Turner, *General Mgr*
Troy Peterson, *VP Admin*
EMP: 75 **EST:** 1967
SQ FT: 25,000
SALES (est): 31.3MM **Privately Held**
WEB: www.monroepiping.com
SIC: 3444 Sheet metalwork

(G-13559)
MOONEY-KEEHLEY INC
38 Saginaw Dr (14623-3175)
PHONE.....................585 271-1573
David Hedges, *President*
Kenneth Hempson, *Owner*
Elihu Hedges Jr, *Vice Pres*
Judith Gessner, *Treasurer*
Elizabeth Hedges, *Admin Sec*
EMP: 6 **EST:** 1944
SQ FT: 12,000
SALES (est): 910.3K **Privately Held**
WEB: www.mooneykeehley.com
SIC: 2752 7389 Cards, lithographed; en-
graving service
PA: 22 Winston, Inc.
22 Winston Pl
Rochester NY 14607
585 271-1573

(G-13560)
MORGOOD TOOLS INC
940 Millstead Way (14624-5108)
P.O. Box 24997 (14624-0997)
PHONE.....................585 436-8828
Virginia L Marshall, *CEO*
Doug Meier, *President*
David Pedeville, *Vice Pres*
Dana Neu, *Engineer*
Diane Soper, *CFO*
EMP: 60 **EST:** 1945
SQ FT: 30,000
SALES (est): 9MM **Privately Held**
WEB: www.morgood.com
SIC: 3545 Cutting tools for machine tools;
cams (machine tool accessories)

(G-13561)
MOSAIC MICROSYSTEMS LLC
500 Lee Rd Ste 200 (14606-4261)
PHONE.....................585 314-7441
Christine Whitman, *CEO*
Paul Ballentine, *President*
Andrew Pescoe, *Director*
EMP: 5
SQ FT: 10,000
SALES: 50K **Privately Held**
SIC: 3674 Semiconductors & related de-
vices

(G-13562)
MULLERS CIDER HOUSE LLC
1344 University Ave # 180 (14607-1656)
PHONE.....................585 287-5875
Samuel Conjerti, *Mng Member*
EMP: 5
SALES (est): 339.8K **Privately Held**
SIC: 2099 Cider, nonalcoholic

(G-13563)
MULTIPLE IMPRSSONS OF RCHESTER (PA)
Also Called: Minuteman Press
41 Chestnut St (14604-2303)
PHONE.....................585 546-1160
William Malone Sr, *President*
Jay Malone, *Corp Secy*
Brad Amedeo, *Prdtn Mgr*
EMP: 8
SQ FT: 3,600
SALES (est): 958K **Privately Held**
WEB: www.dtmmp.com
SIC: 2752 7334 2791 2789 Commercial
printing, lithographic; photocopying & du-
plicating services; typesetting; bookbind-
ing & related work

(G-13564)
MWI INC (PA)
1269 Brighton Henrietta T (14623-2485)
PHONE.....................585 424-4200
David Mc Mahon, *Ch of Bd*
Kevin Mc Mahon, *President*
Brian Mc Mahon, *COO*
Ryan Mc Mahon, *Vice Pres*
Ryan McMahon, *Vice Pres*
▲ **EMP:** 100
SQ FT: 28,000
SALES (est): 22.9MM **Privately Held**
WEB: www.mwiedm.com
SIC: 3624 Carbon & graphite products

(G-13565)
NALGE NUNC INTERNATIONAL CORP (DH)
1600 Lexington Ave # 107 (14606-3000)
PHONE.....................585 498-2661
Michaeline Reed, *Principal*
L Johansen, *Manager*
◆ **EMP:** 903
SQ FT: 275,000
SALES (est): 246.3MM
SALES (corp-wide): 24.3B **Publicly Held**
WEB: www.nuncbrand.com
SIC: 3089 3949 3821 3085 Plastic pro-
cessing; plastic & fiberglass tanks; sport-
ing & athletic goods; laboratory apparatus
& furniture; plastics bottles; laminated
plastics plate & sheet
HQ: Fisher Scientific International Llc
81 Wyman St
Waltham MA 02451
781 622-1000

(G-13566)
NATIONWIDE CIRCUITS INC
1444 Emerson St (14606-3009)
PHONE.....................585 328-0791
Alan Austin, *President*
Judith Austin, *COO*
Thomas Ericson, *Engineer*
Bob Falkenstein, *Manager*
EMP: 28 **EST:** 1971
SQ FT: 20,000
SALES (est): 3.9MM **Privately Held**
WEB: www.nciproto.com
SIC: 3672 Wiring boards

(G-13567)
NATIONWIDE PRECISION PDTS CORP
Also Called: Hn Precision-Ny
200 Tech Park Dr (14623-2445)
PHONE.....................585 272-7100
Dan Nash, *CEO*
Dan Brooks, *Vice Pres*
Rick Menaldino, *Vice Pres*
Sharon Pierce, *Vice Pres*
Paul Ainsworth, *CFO*
▲ **EMP:** 425 **EST:** 1999
SQ FT: 160,000
SALES (est): 114.7MM **Privately Held**
WEB: www.nationwideprecision.com
SIC: 3356 Nonferrous rolling & drawing

(G-13568)
NAVITAR INC
200 Commerce Dr (14623-3589)
PHONE.....................585 359-4000
Julian Goldstein, *Ch of Bd*
Chris Meetze, *Business Mgr*
Craig Fitzgerald, *Vice Pres*
Jeremy Goldstein, *Vice Pres*
Dave Weber, *Vice Pres*
▼ **EMP:** 71
SQ FT: 19,000
SALES (est): 17MM **Privately Held**
WEB: www.navitar.com
SIC: 3699 3651 3827 3674 Laser sys-
tems & equipment; household audio &
video equipment; optical instruments &
lenses; semiconductors & related de-
vices; radio & TV communications equip-
ment; pressed & blown glass

(G-13569)
NBN TECHNOLOGIES LLC
136 Wilshire Rd (14618-1221)
PHONE.....................585 355-5556
Shimon Miamon PHD,
Joseph Wodenscheck,
EMP: 6

SALES (est): 698.4K **Privately Held**
SIC: 3699 Electrical equipment & supplies

(G-13570)
NEW YORK MANUFACTURED PRODUCTS
6 Cairn St (14611-2416)
PHONE.....................585 254-9353
Salvatore Anselmo, *Partner*
Boubane Aselmo, *Partner*
EMP: 10
SALES: 2MM **Privately Held**
SIC: 3441 3499 3089 Fabricated struc-
tural metal; metal household articles; in-
jection molding of plastics

(G-13571)
NEW YORK MANUFACTURING CORP
6 Cairn St (14611-2416)
PHONE.....................585 254-9353
Salvatore Anselmo,
Bouabane Anselmo,
EMP: 6
SQ FT: 20,000
SALES (est): 975K **Privately Held**
WEB: www.newyorkmanufacturing.com
SIC: 3599 Machine shop, jobbing & repair

(G-13572)
NEW YORK MARKING DEVICES CORP
C H Morse Stamp Co
700 Clinton Ave S Ste 2 (14620-1383)
PHONE.....................585 454-5188
Joseph Stummer, *President*
Peter J Stummer, *Branch Mgr*
EMP: 6
SALES (est): 541.2K
SALES (corp-wide): 1.7MM **Privately
Held**
WEB: www.nymarking.com
SIC: 3953 Embossing seals & hand
stamps
PA: New York Marking Devices Corp
2207 Teall Ave
Syracuse NY 13206
315 463-8641

(G-13573)
NEW YORK SUGARS LLC
2301 Mount Read Blvd (14615-2743)
PHONE.....................585 500-0155
Bill Bergin, *Controller*
John Yonover,
EMP: 10
SQ FT: 15,000
SALES: 3.5MM
SALES (corp-wide): 278.1MM **Privately
Held**
SIC: 2099 2063 Sugar; liquid sugar from
sugar beets
PA: Indiana Sugars Inc
911 Virginia St
Gary IN 46402
219 886-9151

(G-13574)
NEWPORT CORPORATION
705 Saint Paul St (14605-1730)
PHONE.....................585 248-4246
Lynn Connolly, *Production*
Linda Nittolo, *Purchasing*
Dana Jensen, *Engineer*
Christophe Palmer, *Manager*
Brian Grove, *Technology*
EMP: 20
SALES (corp-wide): 2B **Publicly Held**
WEB: www.newport.com
SIC: 3821 Laboratory apparatus & furniture
HQ: Newport Corporation
1791 Deere Ave
Irvine CA 92606
949 863-3144

(G-13575)
NEWPORT ROCHESTER INC
705 Saint Paul St (14605-1730)
PHONE.....................585 262-1325
Chris Palmer, *General Mgr*
▲ **EMP:** 60
SALES (est): 19.3MM
SALES (corp-wide): 2B **Publicly Held**
WEB: www.newport.com
SIC: 3827 Gratings, diffraction

▲ = Import ▼ =Export
◆ =Import/Export

HQ: Newport Corporation
1791 Deere Ave
Irvine CA 92606
949 863-3144

(G-13576)
NEXIS 3 LLC
1681 Lyell Ave (14606-2311)
PHONE..............................585 285-4120
Steve Schoenacker,
EMP: 20
SQ FT: 65,000
SALES: 3.5MM **Privately Held**
SIC: 2434 Wood kitchen cabinets

(G-13577)
NICOFORM INC
72 Cascade Dr Ste 12 (14614-1109)
PHONE..............................585 454-5530
Berl Stein, *President*
Richard Kraynik, *Vice Pres*
John Contino, *Prdtn Mgr*
Chris Reynolds, *QC Mgr*
Joe Jachlewski, *Engineer*
▼ **EMP:** 20
SQ FT: 12,000
SALES: 2.4MM **Privately Held**
WEB: www.nicoform.com
SIC: 3544 3599 Industrial molds; bellows,
industrial: metal

(G-13578)
NORDON INC (PA)
691 Exchange St (14608-2714)
PHONE..............................585 546-6200
Terry J Donovan, *CEO*
Gabriel Campa, *Project Mgr*
Richard Sullivan, *Sales Engr*
Ernst G Timm, *Shareholder*
◆ **EMP:** 100
SQ FT: 64,000
SALES (est): 26.7MM **Privately Held**
WEB: www.nordon.org
SIC: 3089 3544 Injection molding of plas-
tics; industrial molds

(G-13579)
NORDON INC
1600 Lexington Ave 235a (14606-3000)
PHONE..............................585 546-6200
James Dickerson, *Manager*
EMP: 42
SALES (corp-wide): 26.7MM **Privately
Held**
SIC: 3089 3544 Injection molding of plas-
tics; industrial molds
PA: Nordon, Inc.
691 Exchange St
Rochester NY 14608
585 546-6200

(G-13580)
NORDON INC
711 Exchange St (14608)
PHONE..............................585 546-6200
Paul Reed, *Manager*
EMP: 24
SALES (corp-wide): 26.7MM **Privately
Held**
WEB: www.nordon.org
SIC: 3089 3544 Injection molding of plas-
tics; industrial molds
PA: Nordon, Inc.
691 Exchange St
Rochester NY 14608
585 546-6200

(G-13581)
**NORTH AMERICAN BREWERIES
INC (DH)**
Also Called: Northamerican Breweries
445 Saint Paul St (14605-1726)
PHONE..............................585 546-1030
Kris Sirchio, *CEO*
Richard Lozyniak, *Ch of Bd*
Dan Harrington, *VP Finance*
▼ **EMP:** 10
SALES (est): 333.7MM **Privately Held**
SIC: 2082 Beer (alcoholic beverage)

(G-13582)
**NORTH AMRCN BRWRIES
HLDNGS LLC (PA)**
445 Saint Paul St (14605-1726)
PHONE..............................585 546-1030
Rich Lozyniak, *CEO*

EMP: 26
SALES (est): 76.7MM **Privately Held**
SIC: 2082 Beer (alcoholic beverage)

(G-13583)
**NORTHEASTERN SEALCOAT
INC**
470 Hollenbeck St Ste 3 (14621-2287)
PHONE..............................585 544-4372
Shawn Grimes, *President*
EMP: 10
SQ FT: 4,000
SALES (est): 1.9MM **Privately Held**
SIC: 2951 2952 4959 Asphalt paving mix-
tures & blocks; asphalt felts & coatings;
snowplowing

(G-13584)
**NORTHERN AIR SYSTEMS INC
(PA)**
3605 Buffalo Rd (14624-1120)
PHONE..............................585 594-5050
Timothy Confer, *President*
Garland Beasley, *Vice Pres*
Joseph Denninger, *Vice Pres*
Nick Gangemi, *VP Sales*
EMP: 46
SQ FT: 45,000
SALES (est): 11.2MM **Privately Held**
SIC: 3585 Heating & air conditioning com-
bination units

(G-13585)
**NORTHERN AIR TECHNOLOGY
INC (PA)**
3605 Buffalo Rd (14624-1120)
PHONE..............................585 594-5050
Timothy J Confer, *President*
EMP: 7 EST: 2000
SQ FT: 1,000
SALES (est): 1.1MM **Privately Held**
SIC: 3648 Outdoor lighting equipment

(G-13586)
**NORTHERN KING LURES INC
(PA)**
167 Armstrong Rd (14616-2703)
P.O. Box 12482 (14612-0482)
PHONE..............................585 865-3373
Patsy Distaffen, *President*
EMP: 5
SALES (est): 733K **Privately Held**
WEB: www.northernkinglures.com
SIC: 3949 Lures, fishing: artificial

(G-13587)
NU WAYS INC
655 Pullman Ave (14615-3334)
PHONE..............................585 254-7510
Edward A Coleman, *President*
Richard Albert, *Treasurer*
Michael Bater, *Finance*
EMP: 6 EST: 1996
SALES (est): 1.2MM **Privately Held**
SIC: 2591 Window blinds

(G-13588)
OLDCASTLE MATERIALS INC
1260 Jefferson Rd (14623-3104)
PHONE..............................585 424-6410
John Peltier, *Manager*
Daniel Coe, *Manager*
EMP: 5
SALES (corp-wide): 30.6B **Privately Held**
WEB: www.oldcastlematerials.com
SIC: 3273 Ready-mixed concrete
HQ: Oldcastle Materials, Inc.
900 Ashwood Pkwy Ste 700
Atlanta GA 30338

(G-13589)
OLEDWORKS LLC (PA)
1645 Lyell Ave Ste 140 (14606-2331)
PHONE..............................585 287-6802
David Dejoy, *CEO*
Michael Boroson, *CTO*
Giana Phelan,
EMP: 28
SALES (est): 4MM **Privately Held**
SIC: 3641 3646 3999 3674 Electric
lamps; commercial indusl & institutional
electric lighting fixtures; barber & beauty
shop equipment; light emitting diodes

(G-13590)
OMG DESSERTS INC
1227 Ridgeway Ave Ste J (14615-3759)
PHONE..............................585 698-1561
Mary E Graham, *President*
Mary Graham, *President*
EMP: 10
SALES (est): 1MM **Privately Held**
SIC: 2099 Desserts, ready-to-mix

(G-13591)
ONTARIO PLASTICS INC
2503 Dewey Ave (14616-4728)
PHONE..............................585 663-2644
Gerard Reynolds, *President*
Jim Beifus, *Principal*
Ralph E Barnes, *Vice Pres*
▲ **EMP:** 35
SQ FT: 40,000
SALES (est): 7.8MM **Privately Held**
WEB: www.ontario-plastics.com
SIC: 3082 3089 Unsupported plastics pro-
file shapes; plastic containers, except
foam; boxes, plastic

(G-13592)
ORMEC SYSTEMS CORP (PA)
19 Linden Park (14625-2776)
PHONE..............................585 385-3520
Edward J Krasnicki, *CEO*
Chris Suflita, *Site Mgr*
Alice Burggraaff, *Accountant*
Jim Stocker, *Human Res Dir*
Thom Cymbal, *Sales Staff*
EMP: 35
SQ FT: 15,600
SALES (est): 5.7MM **Privately Held**
WEB: www.ormec.com
SIC: 3823 3672 Controllers for process
variables, all types; printed circuit boards

(G-13593)
OROLIA USA INC (DH)
1565 Jefferson Rd Ste 460 (14623-3190)
PHONE..............................585 321-5800
Elizabeth Withers, *President*
John Fischer, *Vice Pres*
Jennifer Steier, *Vice Pres*
Alexandria Dunham, *Human Res Mgr*
Darrell Johanneman, *Admin Sec*
EMP: 55 EST: 1972
SQ FT: 26,000
SALES (est): 13.8MM
SALES (corp-wide): 15.6MM **Privately
Held**
WEB: www.spectracomcorp.com
SIC: 3829 Measuring & controlling devices
HQ: Orolia Holding Sas
Batiment Drakkar 2
Valbonne 06560
492 907-040

(G-13594)
**ORTHO-CLINICAL DIAGNOSTICS
INC**
513 Technology Blvd (14626-3601)
PHONE..............................585 453-3000
Tony Higgins, *Engineer*
Keith Elphick, *Manager*
Osmaan Khan, *Manager*
Melissa Kraemer, *Manager*
Jennifer McHugh, *Manager*
EMP: 18
SALES (est): 5.4MM **Privately Held**
SIC: 2834 Pharmaceutical preparations

(G-13595)
**ORTHO-CLINICAL DIAGNOSTICS
INC**
100 Latona Rd Bldg 313 (14626)
PHONE..............................585 453-4771
EMP: 400
SALES (corp-wide): 594.4MM **Privately
Held**
SIC: 3841 Diagnostic apparatus, medical
PA: Ortho-Clinical Diagnostics, Inc.
1001 Route 202
Raritan NJ 08869
908 218-8000

(G-13596)
**ORTHO-CLINICAL DIAGNOSTICS
INC**
Also Called: Ortho/Rochester Tech
2402 Innovation Way # 3 (14624)
PHONE..............................585 453-5200
EMP: 14
SALES (corp-wide): 594.4MM **Privately
Held**
SIC: 3841 Diagnostic apparatus, medical
PA: Ortho-Clinical Diagnostics, Inc.
1001 Route 202
Raritan NJ 08869
908 218-8000

(G-13597)
**ORTHO-CLINICAL DIAGNOSTICS
INC**
1000 Lee Rd (14626)
PHONE..............................585 453-3000
EMP: 33
SALES (corp-wide): 594.4MM **Privately
Held**
WEB: www.orthoclinical.com
SIC: 2835 Blood derivative diagnostic
agents
PA: Ortho-Clinical Diagnostics, Inc.
1001 Route 202
Raritan NJ 08869
908 218-8000

(G-13598)
ORTHOGONAL
1999 Lake Ave (14650-0001)
PHONE..............................585 254-2775
John Defranco, *CEO*
Fox Holt, *Principal*
EMP: 5
SALES (est): 684.6K **Privately Held**
SIC: 3679 Liquid crystal displays (LCD)

(G-13599)
**ORTHOTICS & PROSTHETICS
DEPT**
Also Called: Strong Hospital
4901 Lac De Ville Blvd (14618-5647)
PHONE..............................585 341-9299
Rob Brown, *Manager*
EMP: 15
SALES (est): 1MM **Privately Held**
SIC: 3842 Orthopedic appliances

(G-13600)
OTEX PROTECTIVE INC
2180 Brighton Henrietta (14623-2704)
PHONE..............................585 232-7160
Jacob Weidert, *CEO*
EMP: 6
SALES (est): 735.7K **Privately Held**
SIC: 2311 Men's & boys' uniforms

(G-13601)
OVITZ CORPORATION
260 E Main St (14604-2101)
PHONE..............................585 967-2114
Joseph Rosenshein, *Principal*
Joung Yoon Kim, *Principal*
Walter Rusnak, *Principal*
Nicolas Brown, *Engrg Dir*
Nader Anvari, *Director*
EMP: 9
SALES (est): 498.7K **Privately Held**
SIC: 3841 Diagnostic apparatus, medical

(G-13602)
OZIPKO ENTERPRISES INC
Also Called: Printing Plus
125 White Spruce Blvd (14623-1607)
PHONE..............................585 424-6740
Rita Ozipko, *President*
Carl Ozipko, *Vice Pres*
Jim Ozipko, *Admin Sec*
EMP: 8
SQ FT: 3,000
SALES (est): 890K **Privately Held**
SIC: 2752 Commercial printing, offset

(G-13603)
P & H MACHINE SHOP INC
40 Industrial Park Cir (14624-2404)
PHONE..............................585 247-5500
Fax: 585 247-5572
EMP: 5
SQ FT: 3,000

SALES (est): 360K **Privately Held**
SIC: 3544 Mfg Dies/Tools/Jigs/Fixtures

(G-13604)
P & R INDUSTRIES INC (PA)
1524 N Clinton Ave (14621-2206)
PHONE..................................585 266-6725
Lawrence F Coyle, *President*
Charles Sheelar, *Vice Pres*
David Coyle, *Plant Mgr*
Robert Brawn, *Project Mgr*
Donna Stein, *Purch Agent*
EMP: 32
SQ FT: 22,000
SALES (est): 12.2MM **Privately Held**
SIC: 3544 3541 Special dies & tools; machine tools, metal cutting type

(G-13605)
P K G EQUIPMENT INCORPORATED
367 Paul Rd (14624-4925)
PHONE..................................585 436-4650
Stephen Pontarelli, *CEO*
Stephen T Pontarelli, *Ch of Bd*
Carla Pontarelli, *Vice Pres*
Eugene Jolly, *Project Mgr*
Maria Parker, *Treasurer*
EMP: 30
SQ FT: 35,000
SALES (est): 8.3MM **Privately Held**
WEB: www.pkgequipment.com
SIC: 3559 3441 Metal finishing equipment for plating, etc.; fabricated structural metal

(G-13606)
PALLET DIVISION INC
40 Silver St (14611-2208)
PHONE..................................585 328-3780
Bernie Mangold, *President*
EMP: 7
SALES (est): 1MM **Privately Held**
SIC: 2448 Pallets, wood & metal combination

(G-13607)
PALLET SERVICES INC
1681 Lyell Ave Ste 100 (14606-2334)
PHONE..................................585 647-4020
Donald Matre, *Branch Mgr*
EMP: 40
SALES (est): 3.3MM
SALES (corp-wide): 23MM **Privately Held**
SIC: 2448 Pallets, wood
PA: Pallet Services, Inc.
4055 Casillio Pkwy
Clarence NY 14031
716 873-7700

(G-13608)
PANTHER GRAPHICS INC (PA)
465 Central Ave (14605-3012)
PHONE..................................585 546-7163
Daryll A Jackson Sr, *President*
Ebony Reynolds, *President*
Daromell Jackson, *Human Res Mgr*
Rachael Hudson-Rodvik, *Office Mgr*
Vince Anzalone, *Shareholder*
▲ EMP: 38
SQ FT: 12,000
SALES (est): 55.3MM **Privately Held**
WEB: www.panthergraphics.net
SIC: 2752 Commercial printing, offset

(G-13609)
PARADISO CNSLD ENTPS LLC
Also Called: Sailorbags
1115 E Main St Unit 58 (14609-6156)
PHONE..................................585 924-3937
Neal Popper, *Sales Mgr*
Tina Paradiso, *Mng Member*
EMP: 5 EST: 2011
SALES (est): 202.4K **Privately Held**
SIC: 3171 Handbags, women's

(G-13610)
PARAGON STEEL RULE DIES INC
979 Mount Read Blvd (14606-2829)
PHONE..................................585 254-3395
Michael McDeid, *President*
Jon Rector, *Prdtn Mgr*
Teresa McDeid, *Manager*
EMP: 13
SQ FT: 13,000

SALES (est): 2.2MM **Privately Held**
WEB: www.paragonsrd.com
SIC: 3544 Dies, steel rule

(G-13611)
PARK ENTERPRISES ROCHESTER INC
226 Jay St (14608-1623)
PHONE..................................585 546-4200
Sook Cha Park, *President*
Rob Brunskill, *Principal*
Hyo Sang Park, *Principal*
Tom Sydeski, *Principal*
Sik Park, *Exec VP*
◆ EMP: 200
SQ FT: 60,000
SALES (est): 33.1MM **Privately Held**
WEB: www.parkent.com
SIC: 3545 Precision tools, machinists'

(G-13612)
PEKO PRECISION PRODUCTS INC
70 Holworthy St (14606-1313)
PHONE..................................585 301-1386
Gary Baxter, *Mktg Dir*
Sonny Sok, *Manager*
EMP: 12
SALES (corp-wide): 51MM **Privately Held**
WEB: www.pekoprecision.com
SIC: 3599 Crankshafts & camshafts, machining; machine shop, jobbing & repair
PA: Peko Precision Products, Inc.
1400 Emerson St
Rochester NY 14606
585 647-3010

(G-13613)
PENNANT INGREDIENTS INC (DH)
64 Chester St (14611-2110)
PHONE..................................585 235-8160
Simon Teel, *President*
Karel Zimmermann, *President*
EMP: 90 EST: 2015
SALES (est): 57.1MM
SALES (corp-wide): 30.1MM **Privately Held**
SIC: 2099 Seasonings & spices

(G-13614)
PEPSI-COLA METRO BTLG CO INC
400 Creative Dr (14624-6221)
PHONE..................................585 454-5220
Micheal Matney, *Manager*
Janet Kasparian, *Administration*
EMP: 115
SALES (corp-wide): 64.6B **Publicly Held**
WEB: www.joy-of-cola.com
SIC: 2086 5149 Carbonated soft drinks, bottled & canned; soft drinks
HQ: Pepsi-Cola Metropolitan Bottling Company, Inc.
1111 Westchester Ave
White Plains NY 10604
914 767-6000

(G-13615)
PERFORMANCE TECHNOLOGIES INC (DH)
3500 Winton Pl Ste 4 (14623-2860)
PHONE..................................585 256-0200
John M Slusser, *Ch of Bd*
John J Peters, *Senior VP*
J Patrick Rice, *Senior VP*
Dorrance W Lamb, *CFO*
EMP: 32
SQ FT: 32,000
SALES (est): 13.7MM
SALES (corp-wide): 618.5MM **Publicly Held**
WEB: www.pt.com
SIC: 3672 3661 3577 7373 Printed circuit boards; telephone & telegraph apparatus; computer peripheral equipment; computer integrated systems design
HQ: Sonus Networks, Inc.
4 Technology Park Dr
Westford MA 01886
978 614-8100

(G-13616)
PERI-FACTS ACADEMY
601 Elmwood Ave (14642-0001)
PHONE..................................585 275-6037
Dr James Woods, *Senior Editor*
EMP: 5
SALES (est): 273.1K **Privately Held**
SIC: 2731 Textbooks: publishing & printing

(G-13617)
PFAUDLER INC (DH)
Also Called: Pfaudler USA
1000 West Ave (14611-2442)
P.O. Box 23600 (14692-3600)
PHONE..................................585 235-1000
Micheal F Powers, *President*
Keith Quintana, *General Mgr*
Gene Sak, *Project Mgr*
Peter Grant, *Senior Buyer*
John Briner, *Engineer*
◆ EMP: 300
SQ FT: 500,000
SALES (est): 119.7MM
SALES (corp-wide): 352.2K **Privately Held**
SIC: 3559 Refinery, chemical processing & similar machinery; pharmaceutical machinery
HQ: Pfaudler Gmbh
Louis-Schuler-Str. 1
Waghausel 68753
620 285-0

(G-13618)
PFAUDLER US INC
1000 West Ave (14611-2442)
P.O. Box 23600 (14692-3600)
PHONE..................................585 235-1000
Bob Waddell, *CEO*
EMP: 200 EST: 2014
SALES (est): 32.8K
SALES (corp-wide): 352.2K **Privately Held**
SIC: 3443 Fabricated plate work (boiler shop)
HQ: Pfaudler International
Rue Edward Steichen 2
Luxembourg

(G-13619)
PH DAVID J ROSSI
50 Celtic Ln (14626-4362)
PHONE..................................585 455-1160
David Rossi, *Principal*
EMP: 5
SALES (est): 615.1K **Privately Held**
SIC: 2834 Pharmaceutical preparations

(G-13620)
PHARMADVA LLC
36 King St (14608-1922)
PHONE..................................585 469-1410
Chuck Dubois, *Vice Pres*
Joshua Eddy, *Finance Mgr*
Jonathan Sacks, *Mng Member*
Joel Reiser, *CTO*
Duane Girdner,
EMP: 6
SALES: 80K **Privately Held**
SIC: 3845 Electromedical equipment

(G-13621)
PHOENIX GRAPHICS INC
464 State St 470 (14608-1739)
PHONE..................................585 232-4040
Sal De Biase III, *President*
Mark Stavalone, *Vice Pres*
EMP: 20
SALES (est): 5.4MM **Privately Held**
WEB: www.phoenix-graphics.com
SIC: 2752 Commercial printing, offset

(G-13622)
PHOTONAMICS INC
Also Called: Elmgrove Technologies Div
558 Elmgrove Rd (14606-3348)
PHONE..................................585 247-8990
Ross Cooley, *President*
Eric Johengen, *Vice Pres*
EMP: 10 EST: 1971
SQ FT: 4,000
SALES (est): 2MM **Privately Held**
WEB: www.elmgrovetechnologies.com
SIC: 3672 Printed circuit boards

(G-13623)
PIERCE INDUSTRIES LLC
465 Paul Rd Ste A (14624-4779)
PHONE..................................585 458-0888
Dick Webb, *CEO*
Rick Schopinsky, *President*
Chris Perkins, *Office Mgr*
▲ EMP: 40
SQ FT: 60,000
SALES (est): 13.7MM
SALES (corp-wide): 38.7MM **Privately Held**
WEB: www.pierceindustries.com
SIC: 3441 Fabricated structural metal
PA: Indiana Enbi Inc
1703 Mccall Dr
Shelbyville IN 46176
317 398-3267

(G-13624)
PIERREPONT VISUAL GRAPHICS
15 Elser Ter (14611-1607)
PHONE..................................585 305-9672
Scott Zappia, *President*
Terence Zappia, *Vice Pres*
EMP: 2 EST: 1958
SQ FT: 15,000
SALES (est): 1MM **Privately Held**
WEB: www.pierrepont.com
SIC: 3993 Signs & advertising specialties

(G-13625)
PIXOS PRINT
75 Goodway Dr (14623-3000)
PHONE..................................585 500-4600
Ron Bittner, *Owner*
Mike Bittner, *Co-Owner*
Steven Patrick, *Accounts Exec*
John Green, *Manager*
Lance Eddinger, *Graphic Designe*
EMP: 6
SALES (est): 122.8K **Privately Held**
SIC: 2752 Commercial printing, offset

(G-13626)
PLUG POWER INC
1200 Ridgeway Ave Ste 123 (14615-3758)
PHONE..................................585 474-3993
EMP: 6
SALES (corp-wide): 174.6MM **Publicly Held**
SIC: 3629 3674 Electrochemical generators (fuel cells); fuel cells, solid state
PA: Plug Power Inc.
968 Albany Shaker Rd
Latham NY 12110
518 782-7100

(G-13627)
PMI INDUSTRIES LLC
350 Buell Rd (14624-3124)
PHONE..................................585 464-8050
V Sheldon Alfiero, *President*
◆ EMP: 30 EST: 1978
SQ FT: 48,500
SALES (est): 8.9MM
SALES (corp-wide): 38.3MM **Privately Held**
WEB: www.pro-moldinc.com
SIC: 3544 3089 Industrial molds; injection molded finished plastic products
PA: Bam Enterprises, Inc.
2937 Alt Blvd
Grand Island NY 14072
716 773-7634

(G-13628)
POLYMAG TEK INC
215 Tremont St Ste 2 (14608-2371)
PHONE..................................585 235-8390
Pete Byam, *President*
Jennifer Sweet, *Treasurer*
Ronald W Sweet, *Treasurer*
Joseph Rodibaugh, *Technical Staff*
James W Fischer, *Admin Sec*
EMP: 12
SALES: 2MM **Privately Held**
WEB: www.polymagtek.com
SIC: 3547 7389 5085 Rolling mill machinery; design services; mill supplies

(G-13629)
POLYMER ENGINEERED PDTS INC
23 Moonlanding Rd (14624-2505)
PHONE..................................585 426-1811
George Peroutka, *President*
EMP: 100
SQ FT: 55,000
SALES (corp-wide): 13.9MM **Privately Held**
SIC: 3089 Injection molding of plastics
PA: Polymer Engineered Products, Inc.
595 Summer St Ste 2
Stamford CT 06901
203 324-3737

(G-13630)
POSEIDON SYSTEMS LLC
200 Canal View Blvd # 300 (14623-2851)
PHONE..................................585 239-6025
Stephen Steen, *Vice Pres*
Graham Martin, *Engineer*
Alexander Pelkey, *Engineer*
Carol Marquardt, *Office Mgr*
Karen Street, *Office Mgr*
EMP: 11
SQ FT: 6,000
SALES (est): 2.2MM **Privately Held**
SIC: 3829 3823 Measuring & controlling devices; industrial instrmnts msrmnt display/control process variable; flow instruments, industrial process type; data loggers, industrial process type

(G-13631)
POWER-FLO TECHNOLOGIES INC
Also Called: Auburn Armature
62 Marway Cir (14624-2321)
PHONE..................................585 426-4607
Joe Santasia, *Manager*
EMP: 36
SALES (corp-wide): 57MM **Privately Held**
SIC: 7694 Electric motor repair
PA: Power-Flo Technologies, Inc.
270 Park Ave
New Hyde Park NY 11040
516 812-6800

(G-13632)
PPI CORP
Also Called: Ftt Manufacturing
275 Commerce Dr (14623-3505)
PHONE..................................585 880-7277
John Longuil, *President*
Darrell Gibson, *Mfg Mgr*
Mike Cianciola, *Purch Mgr*
Paul Opela, *Controller*
Janet Oliviari, *Human Resources*
EMP: 42
SALES (est): 361.2K **Privately Held**
SIC: 3541 3449 3599 3544 Numerically controlled metal cutting machine tools; miscellaneous metalwork; machine shop, jobbing & repair; special dies, tools, jigs & fixtures

(G-13633)
PPI CORP
Also Called: Ftt Mfg
275 Commerce Dr (14623-3505)
PHONE..................................585 243-0300
John Longuil, *CEO*
Paul Opela, *Vice Pres*
Mike Cianciola, *Purch Mgr*
Dan Hallquist, *CFO*
Lou Giglia, *Technical Staff*
▲ EMP: 60
SQ FT: 57,000
SALES (est): 13.5MM **Privately Held**
WEB: www.fttmfg.com
SIC: 3545 3451 5047 3541 Precision tools, machinists'; screw machine products; instruments, surgical & medical; numerically controlled metal cutting machine tools; electrical discharge machining (EDM); machinery castings, aluminum

(G-13634)
PRECISE TOOL & MFG INC
9 Coldwater Cres (14624-2512)
PHONE..................................585 247-0700
John S Gizzi, *President*
John P Gizzi, *President*

Rose A Poirier, *Corp Secy*
Gary Mastro, *Vice Pres*
▲ EMP: 100
SQ FT: 150,000
SALES (est): 22.2MM **Privately Held**
WEB: www.precisetool.com
SIC: 3541 Numerically controlled metal cutting machine tools

(G-13635)
PRECISION DESIGN SYSTEMS INC
1645 Lyell Ave Ste 136 (14606-2386)
PHONE..................................585 426-4500
William J West, *President*
Jeff Sutton, *Vice Pres*
EMP: 20
SQ FT: 18,000
SALES (est): 3MM **Privately Held**
SIC: 3829 3479 Measuring & controlling devices; name plates: engraved, etched, etc.

(G-13636)
PRECISION GRINDING & MFG CORP (PA)
Also Called: PGM
1305 Emerson St (14606-3098)
PHONE..................................585 458-4300
Michael Hockenberger, *CEO*
William C Hockenberger, *Ch of Bd*
Todd Hockenberger, *Vice Pres*
Fred Cadwell, *Mfg Staff*
Carlton Morgan, *Buyer*
▲ EMP: 126 EST: 1967
SQ FT: 62,000
SALES: 30.3MM **Privately Held**
WEB: www.pgmcorp.com
SIC: 3545 3544 Precision tools, machinists'; special dies & tools

(G-13637)
PRECISION LASER TECHNOLOGY LLC
Also Called: Plt
1001 Lexington Ave Ste 4 (14606-2847)
PHONE..................................585 458-6208
Ron Natale Jr, *Mng Member*
James Garcia,
EMP: 10
SQ FT: 7,000
SALES (est): 864.5K **Privately Held**
SIC: 7692 7699 Welding repair; cash register repair

(G-13638)
PRECISION MACHINE TECH LLC
Also Called: Spex
85 Excel Dr (14621-3471)
PHONE..................................585 467-1840
Michael Nolan, *President*
Helen Lombardo, *Vice Pres*
Scott Adams, *Purchasing*
Lisa Fess, *Manager*
▲ EMP: 60
SQ FT: 16,000
SALES: 14.3MM **Privately Held**
WEB: www.spex1.com
SIC: 3599 Machine shop, jobbing & repair

(G-13639)
PRECISION MAGNETICS LLC
770 Linden Ave (14625-2716)
PHONE..................................585 385-9010
Michael Stachura, *General Mgr*
Andrew Albers,
Terence R Loughrey,
Terence Loughrey,
▲ EMP: 50
SQ FT: 12,000
SALES (est): 5.9MM **Privately Held**
WEB: www.precisionmagnetics.com
SIC: 3499 Magnets, permanent: metallic

(G-13640)
PREMIER SIGN SYSTEMS LLC
10 Excel Dr (14621-3470)
PHONE..................................585 235-0390
Jeff Sherwood, *Owner*
James Peacock, *Principal*
EMP: 29
SALES (est): 4.5MM **Privately Held**
SIC: 3993 Electric signs

(G-13641)
PRESSTEK PRINTING
20 Balfour Dr (14621-3202)
PHONE..................................585 266-2770
Stanley E Freimuth, *CEO*
Ronald T Cardone, *Vice Pres*
Cathleen V Cavanna, *Vice Pres*
Joseph Demharter, *Vice Pres*
Arnon Dror, *Vice Pres*
EMP: 6
SALES (est): 470.1K **Privately Held**
SIC: 2752 Commercial printing, offset

(G-13642)
PRESSTEK PRINTING LLC
521 E Ridge Rd (14621-1203)
PHONE..................................585 467-8140
Dennis Collins, *President*
EMP: 10
SQ FT: 1,400
SALES (est): 459.7K **Privately Held**
SIC: 2752 2791 Commercial printing, offset; typesetting

(G-13643)
PRESSTEK PRINTING LLC
Also Called: Washburn Litho Envirgo Prtg
20 Balfour Dr (14621-3202)
P.O. Box 67211 (14617-7211)
PHONE..................................585 266-2770
Antony Disalvo, *President*
Dennis Collins, *Vice Pres*
EMP: 14
SQ FT: 6,600
SALES (est): 1.7MM **Privately Held**
SIC: 2759 2752 Commercial printing; commercial printing, lithographic

(G-13644)
PRINT ON DEMAND INITIATIVE INC
1240 Jefferson Rd (14623-3104)
PHONE..................................585 239-6044
Gaurav Govil, *President*
EMP: 19
SQ FT: 900
SALES: 118.2K **Privately Held**
SIC: 2752 Commercial printing, lithographic

(G-13645)
PRINTROC INC
620 South Ave (14620-1316)
PHONE..................................585 461-2556
Ronald Schutt, *President*
Daniel McCarthy, *Vice Pres*
Jesse McCarthy, *Director*
EMP: 12
SQ FT: 6,000
SALES (est): 1.2MM **Privately Held**
WEB: www.pinnacleprinters.com
SIC: 2752 Commercial printing, offset

(G-13646)
PRIVATE LBEL FODS RCHESTER INC
1686 Lyell Ave (14606-2312)
P.O. Box 60805 (14606-0805)
PHONE..................................585 254-9205
Bonnie Lavorato, *Ch of Bd*
Frank Lavorato III, *Vice Pres*
Russ Eliason, *CFO*
EMP: 30
SQ FT: 125,000
SALES (est): 8.3MM **Privately Held**
WEB: www.privatelabelfoods.com
SIC: 2099 Food preparations

(G-13647)
PRO-TECH WLDG FABRICATION INC
Also Called: Pro-Tech Sno Pusher
711 West Ave (14611-2412)
PHONE..................................585 436-9855
Michael P Weagley, *President*
EMP: 35
SQ FT: 30,000
SALES (est): 8.3MM **Privately Held**
SIC: 3531 7692 Snow plow attachments; welding repair

(G-13648)
PRO-VALUE DISTRIBUTION INC
1547 Lyell Ave Ste 3 (14606-2123)
PHONE..................................585 783-1461

Thomas W Mayberry, *President*
EMP: 6
SQ FT: 4,000
SALES (est): 804.4K **Privately Held**
SIC: 3714 Motor vehicle parts & accessories

(G-13649)
PRODUCT INTEGRATION & MFG INC
55 Fessenden St (14611-2815)
PHONE..................................585 436-6260
Tyrone Reaves, *Ch of Bd*
John Breedy, *Engineer*
Brenda Wilson, *Human Res Mgr*
Long Nguyen, *Manager*
EMP: 22
SQ FT: 25,000
SALES (est): 4.5MM **Privately Held**
SIC: 3444 Forming machine work, sheet metal

(G-13650)
PRODUCTION METAL CUTTING INC
1 Curlew St (14606-2535)
P.O. Box 60535 (14606-0535)
PHONE..................................585 458-7136
Leo T Glogowski, *President*
▲ EMP: 12
SQ FT: 34,000
SALES (est): 2.1MM
SALES (corp-wide): 2.4MM **Privately Held**
WEB: www.zedcomachinery.com
SIC: 3545 Machine tool accessories
PA: Zedco Machinery Inc
1 Curlew St
Rochester NY 14606
585 458-6920

(G-13651)
PSB LTD
543 Atlantic Ave Ste 2 (14609-7396)
PHONE..................................585 654-7078
Robert Armitage, *President*
EMP: 13
SQ FT: 30,000
SALES (est): 2.5MM **Privately Held**
WEB: www.psb.net
SIC: 3471 Electroplating & plating

(G-13652)
PULLMAN MFG CORPORATION
77 Commerce Dr (14623-3501)
PHONE..................................585 334-1350
Chris Biegel, *CEO*
William A Palmer, *Shareholder*
▼ EMP: 6 EST: 1886
SQ FT: 36,000
SALES (est): 1.2MM **Privately Held**
WEB: www.pullmanmfg.com
SIC: 3495 Sash balances, spring

(G-13653)
PULSAFEEDER INC (HQ)
Also Called: Engineered Products Oper Epo
2883 Brghton Hnrietta Twn (14623-2790)
PHONE..................................585 292-8000
Richard C Morgan, *Ch of Bd*
John Carter, *Ch of Bd*
Dieter Sauer, *President*
Despina Dipaola, *Buyer*
Harry Maharajh, *Engineer*
◆ EMP: 122
SQ FT: 45,000
SALES (est): 25.3MM
SALES (corp-wide): 2.4B **Publicly Held**
WEB: www.pulsa.com
SIC: 3561 3825 3823 3822 Industrial pumps & parts; measuring instruments & meters, electric; industrial instrmnts msrmnt display/control process variable; auto controls regulating residntl & coml environmt & applncs; relays & industrial controls; measuring & dispensing pumps
PA: Idex Corporation
1925 W Field Ct Ste 200
Lake Forest IL 60045
847 498-7070

(G-13654)
PYRAGON INC
95 Mount Read Blvd Ste 14 (14611-1936)
PHONE..................................585 697-0444
Thomas Crumlish, *President*

◆ **EMP:** 9
SQ FT: 3,000
SALES (est): 1.7MM **Privately Held**
WEB: www.pyragon.com
SIC: 3679 Antennas, receiving

(G-13655)
QED TECHNOLOGIES INTL INC
Also Called: Q.E.d
1040 University Ave (14607-1282)
PHONE..............................585 256-6540
Andrew Kulawiec, *CEO*
Jerry Carapella, *Engineer*
Paul Dumas, *Engineer*
Christopher Hall, *Engineer*
Chris Maloney, *Engineer*
▲ **EMP:** 45
SALES (est): 19.1MM
SALES (corp-wide): 590.1MM **Publicly Held**
WEB: www.qedmrf.com
SIC: 3827 Optical instruments & lenses
PA: Cabot Microelectronics Corporation
    870 N Commons Dr
    Aurora IL 60504
    630 375-6631

(G-13656)
QES SOLUTIONS INC (PA)
1547 Lyell Ave (14606-2123)
PHONE..............................585 783-1455
Thomas W Mayberry, *Ch of Bd*
Beb Mayberry, *President*
◆ **EMP:** 98
SQ FT: 15,000
SALES (est): 16.2MM **Privately Held**
SIC: 3559 Metal finishing equipment for plating, etc.

(G-13657)
QOS ENTERPRISES LLC
282 Hollenbeck St (14621-3235)
PHONE..............................585 454-0550
Edward McGrattan,
EMP: 7
SALES (est): 855.1K **Privately Held**
WEB: www.qosllc.com
SIC: 3471 Plating & polishing

(G-13658)
QUADRISTI LLC
275 Mount Read Blvd (14611-1924)
PHONE..............................585 279-3318
Marc Iacona,
▲ **EMP:** 11
SQ FT: 10,000
SALES: 500K
SALES (corp-wide): 52MM **Privately Held**
SIC: 3644 Electric conduits & fittings
PA: Simcona Electronics Corp
    275 Mount Read Blvd
    Rochester NY 14611
    585 328-3230

(G-13659)
QUALITY CONTRACT ASSEMBLIES
Also Called: Qca
100 Boxart St Ste 251 (14612-5656)
P.O. Box 12868 (14612-0868)
PHONE..............................585 663-9030
Richard Frank, *President*
Lynn Gongwer, *Bookkeeper*
▲ **EMP:** 12
SQ FT: 5,500
SALES (est): 1.9MM **Privately Held**
WEB: www.qcacorp.com
SIC: 3679 Electronic circuits; harness assemblies for electronic use: wire or cable

(G-13660)
QUALITY VISION INTL INC (PA)
Also Called: Optical Gaging Products Div
850 Hudson Ave (14621-4839)
PHONE..............................585 544-0450
Edward T Polidor, *CEO*
Keith Polidor, *COO*
Frank Opett, *Opers Staff*
Karl Cullati, *Electrical Engi*
David E Francati Sr, *CFO*
▲ **EMP:** 337 **EST:** 1954
SALES (est): 91.4MM **Privately Held**
SIC: 3827 Optical test & inspection equipment

(G-13661)
QUALITY VISION INTL INC
Optical Gaging Products Div
850 Hudson Ave (14621-4839)
PHONE..............................585 544-0400
R Stephen Flynn, *President*
EMP: 20
SALES (corp-wide): 91.4MM **Privately Held**
SIC: 3829 3826 Measuring & controlling devices; analytical instruments
PA: Quality Vision International Inc.
    850 Hudson Ave
    Rochester NY 14621
    585 544-0450

(G-13662)
QUALITY VISION SERVICES INC
Also Called: Quality Vision International
1175 North St (14621-4942)
PHONE..............................585 544-0450
Timothy Moriarty, *President*
George Guarino, *CFO*
▲ **EMP:** 56 **EST:** 2000
SALES (est): 11MM
SALES (corp-wide): 91.4MM **Privately Held**
SIC: 3827 8734 Optical comparators; optical test & inspection equipment; calibration & certification
PA: Quality Vision International Inc.
    850 Hudson Ave
    Rochester NY 14621
    585 544-0450

(G-13663)
QUANTUM MEDICAL IMAGING LLC
150 Verona St (14608-1733)
PHONE..............................631 567-5800
Scott Matovich, *President*
Shalom Cohen, *President*
Keith Matovich, *Vice Pres*
▲ **EMP:** 100
SQ FT: 55,000
SALES (est): 24.3MM
SALES (corp-wide): 23.7B **Privately Held**
WEB: www.qmiteam.com
SIC: 3844 5047 Radiographic X-ray apparatus & tubes; medical equipment & supplies
HQ: Carestream Health, Inc.
    150 Verona St
    Rochester NY 14608

(G-13664)
QUANTUM SAILS ROCHESTER LLC
1461 Hudson Ave (14621-1716)
PHONE..............................585 342-5200
Kristofer Werner, *President*
EMP: 5 **EST:** 2015
SALES (est): 325K **Privately Held**
SIC: 2394 7532 Convertible tops, canvas or boat: from purchased materials; sails: made from purchased materials; canvas boat seats; liners & covers, fabric: made from purchased materials; tops (canvas or plastic), installation or repair: automotive

(G-13665)
QUINTEL USA INC
1200 Ridgeway Ave Ste 132 (14615-3758)
PHONE..............................585 420-8364
Michael Liu, *Principal*
Robert Fishback, *Manager*
▲ **EMP:** 50
SALES (est): 9MM **Privately Held**
SIC: 3663 Radio & TV communications equipment

(G-13666)
R P FEDDER CORP (PA)
740 Driving Park Ave B (14613-1596)
PHONE..............................585 288-1600
Stephen Quinn, *Ch of Bd*
Joseph Vancura, *President*
Joseph Pennise, *Vice Pres*
James Engel, *Engineer*
Daryl Maciuska, *Engineer*
▲ **EMP:** 28 **EST:** 1958
SQ FT: 65,000

SALES: 15MM **Privately Held**
WEB: www.rpfedder.com
SIC: 3564 5075 2674 Filters, air: furnaces, air conditioning equipment, etc.; air filters; bags: uncoated paper & multiwall

(G-13667)
R V DOW ENTERPRISES INC
Also Called: B J Long Co
466 Central Ave (14605-3011)
PHONE..............................585 454-5862
Richard V Dow, *President*
▲ **EMP:** 17 **EST:** 1953
SQ FT: 9,000
SALES (est): 700K **Privately Held**
WEB: www.bjlong.com
SIC: 3999 Pipe cleaners

(G-13668)
RAM MACHINING LLC
1645 Lyell Ave Ste 158 (14606-2386)
P.O. Box 24685 (14624-0685)
PHONE..............................585 426-1007
Daniel L Pixley,
EMP: 5
SALES: 400K **Privately Held**
SIC: 3599 Machine shop, jobbing & repair

(G-13669)
RAPID PRECISION MACHINING INC
Also Called: Quality Plus
50 Lafayette Rd (14609-3119)
PHONE..............................585 467-0780
John Nolan, *President*
EMP: 70
SQ FT: 51,000
SALES: 6.6MM **Privately Held**
SIC: 3541 Machine tools, metal cutting type

(G-13670)
RED OAK SOFTWARE INC
3349 Monroe Ave Ste 175 (14618-5513)
PHONE..............................585 454-3170
Greg Waffen, *Branch Mgr*
EMP: 5
SALES (corp-wide): 1.3MM **Privately Held**
WEB: www.redoaksw.com
SIC: 7372 Prepackaged software
PA: Red Oak Software Inc
    115 Us Highway 46 F1000
    Mountain Lakes NJ 07046
    973 316-6064

(G-13671)
RHINO TRUNK & CASE INC
Also Called: Trunk Outlet
565 Blossom Rd Ste J (14610-1859)
PHONE..............................585 244-4553
Gregory Hurwitz, *President*
EMP: 15
SALES: 5MM **Privately Held**
WEB: www.trunkoutlet.com
SIC: 3161 Luggage

(G-13672)
RID LOM PRECISION MFG
50 Regency Oaks Blvd (14624-5901)
P.O. Box 64473 (14624-6873)
PHONE..............................585 594-8600
John D Rider, *President*
EMP: 20
SQ FT: 7,100
SALES (est): 2.9MM **Privately Held**
WEB: www.ridlom.com
SIC: 3544 Special dies & tools

(G-13673)
RIDGE CABINET & SHOWCASE INC
1545 Mount Read Blvd # 2 (14606-2848)
PHONE..............................585 663-0560
Steve Lader, *Ch of Bd*
EMP: 20
SQ FT: 6,200
SALES (est): 3.6MM **Privately Held**
SIC: 2511 Wood household furniture

(G-13674)
RIVERVIEW ASSOCIATES INC
Also Called: Riverside Automation
1040 Jay St (14611-1110)
PHONE..............................585 235-5980
John A Christopher, *Ch of Bd*
Jeff Snell, *Engineer*
Debbie Smardz, *Admin Asst*
EMP: 13
SQ FT: 20,000
SALES: 2.5MM **Privately Held**
WEB: www.riversideautomation.com
SIC: 3559 Automotive related machinery

(G-13675)
RLI SCHLGEL SPECIALTY PDTS LLC (HQ)
1555 Jefferson Rd (14623-3109)
PHONE..............................585 627-5919
Ken Pitts, *Mng Member*
Jeff Sfetko, *Manager*
EMP: 3
SALES (est): 1.4MM
SALES (corp-wide): 25.6MM **Privately Held**
SIC: 2299 2396 3069 Automotive felts; automotive trimmings, fabric; printers' rolls & blankets: rubber or rubberized fabric
PA: Right Lane Industries Llc
    350 N Orleans St 9000n
    Chicago IL 60654
    857 869-4132

(G-13676)
RMB EMBROIDERY SERVICE
176 Anderson Ave Ste F110 (14607-1169)
PHONE..............................585 271-5560
Ruta Szabo, *Partner*
Birute Collier, *Partner*
Maria Stankus, *Partner*
EMP: 7 **EST:** 1995
SQ FT: 850
SALES: 140K **Privately Held**
SIC: 2397 Schiffli machine embroideries

(G-13677)
ROBERT J FARAONE
Also Called: O Tex
1600 N Clinton Ave (14621-2200)
PHONE..............................585 232-7160
Robert J Faraone, *Owner*
EMP: 7
SALES: 500K **Privately Held**
WEB: www.otex.com
SIC: 3545 Tool holders

(G-13678)
ROCCERA LLC
771 Elmgrove Rd Bldg No2 (14624-6200)
PHONE..............................585 426-0887
Syamal Ghosh, *President*
Frank Kaduc, *Vice Pres*
Kathy Ortiz, *Office Mgr*
EMP: 18
SQ FT: 10,000
SALES (est): 2.2MM **Privately Held**
SIC: 3297 3432 3599 Heat resistant mixtures; alumina fused refractories; plumbing fixture fittings & trim; machine & other job shop work; custom machinery

(G-13679)
ROCHESTER 100 INC
40 Jefferson Rd (14623-2132)
P.O. Box 92801 (14692-8901)
PHONE..............................585 475-0200
Nicholas Sfikas, *President*
Catherine Sfikas, *Principal*
Geraldine E Warner, *Corp Secy*
William Fish, *Vice Pres*
Carleen Fien, *Admin Sec*
▲ **EMP:** 129
SQ FT: 100,000
SALES (est): 19.6MM **Privately Held**
WEB: www.rochester100.com
SIC: 2672 2677 Adhesive papers, labels or tapes: from purchased material; envelopes

(G-13680)
ROCHESTER AREA MDIA PRTNERS LL
280 State St (14614-1033)
PHONE..............................585 244-3329

Norm Silverstein,
EMP: 14
SALES (est): 258.3K **Privately Held**
SIC: 2711 Newspapers: publishing only, not printed on site

(G-13681)
ROCHESTER ASPHALT MATERIALS (DH)
1150 Penfield Rd (14625-2202)
PHONE.............................585 381-7010
John M Odenbach Jr, *President*
Gardner Odenbach, *Treasurer*
Mary Swierkos, *Admin Sec*
EMP: 8
SQ FT: 5,000
SALES (est): 12.9MM
SALES (corp-wide): 30.6B **Privately Held**
SIC: 2951 3273 Road materials, bituminous (not from refineries); ready-mixed concrete

(G-13682)
ROCHESTER ATOMATED SYSTEMS INC
40 Regency Oaks Blvd (14624-5901)
PHONE.............................585 594-3222
Jerrold Potter, *President*
Frank Denaro, *Vice Pres*
George Gamer, *Vice Pres*
EMP: 20
SQ FT: 12,000
SALES (est): 3.9MM **Privately Held**
WEB: www.rochauto.com
SIC: 3599 Machine shop, jobbing & repair; custom machinery

(G-13683)
ROCHESTER BUSINESS JOURNAL
16 W Main St Ste 341 (14614-1604)
PHONE.............................585 546-8303
Susan Holliday, *President*
Lisa Granite, *Assoc Editor*
EMP: 35
SALES (est): 2.6MM **Privately Held**
WEB: www.rbj.net
SIC: 2711 Newspapers: publishing only, not printed on site

(G-13684)
ROCHESTER CATHOLIC PRESS (PA)
Also Called: Catholic Courier
1150 Buffalo Rd (14624-1823)
P.O. Box 24379 (14624-0379)
PHONE.............................585 529-9530
Bishop S R Matano, *President*
Bishop Salvatore R Matano, *President*
Karen M Franz, *General Mgr*
William H Kedley, *Treasurer*
Rev Daniel Condon, *Admin Sec*
EMP: 16
SQ FT: 3,188
SALES (est): 1.3MM **Privately Held**
WEB: www.catholiccourier.com
SIC: 2711 Newspapers: publishing only, not printed on site

(G-13685)
ROCHESTER COCA COLA BOTTLING
Also Called: Coca-Cola
123 Upper Falls Blvd (14605-2156)
PHONE.............................585 546-3900
George Keim, *Manager*
EMP: 65
SALES (corp-wide): 31.8B **Publicly Held**
SIC: 2086 5149 Bottled & canned soft drinks; groceries & related products
HQ: Rochester Coca Cola Bottling Corp
300 Oak St
Pittston PA 18640
570 655-2874

(G-13686)
ROCHESTER COLONIAL MFG CORP (PA)
1794 Lyell Ave (14606-2316)
PHONE.............................585 254-8191
Mark S Gionta, *CEO*
Norm Dix, *President*
Steve Trotta, *Vice Pres*
Paul Gionta, *Plant Mgr*
Shane Haefele, *Project Mgr*

EMP: 100
SQ FT: 100,000
SALES (est): 14.1MM **Privately Held**
WEB: www.rochestercolonial.com
SIC: 2431 3442 3231 3444 Windows & window parts & trim, wood; metal doors, sash & trim; strengthened or reinforced glass; sheet metalwork

(G-13687)
ROCHESTER COUNTERTOP INC (PA)
Also Called: Premier Cabinet Wholesalers
3300 Monroe Ave Ste 212 (14618-4621)
PHONE.............................585 338-2260
Dean Pelletier, *President*
EMP: 10
SQ FT: 5,000
SALES (est): 861.6K **Privately Held**
WEB: www.premiercabinetwholesalers.com
SIC: 2541 1799 5031 Counter & sink tops; counter top installation; kitchen cabinets

(G-13688)
ROCHESTER DEMOCRAT & CHRONICLE
55 Exchange Blvd (14614-2001)
PHONE.............................585 232-7100
Fax: 585 258-2734
EMP: 26
SALES (est): 2.1MM **Privately Held**
SIC: 2711 Newspapers-Publishing/Printing

(G-13689)
ROCHESTER GEAR INC
213 Norman St (14613-1875)
PHONE.............................585 254-5442
Anthony J Fedor, *President*
Scott Caccamise, *Exec VP*
EMP: 37
SQ FT: 25,000
SALES (est): 6.5MM **Privately Held**
WEB: www.rochestergear.com
SIC: 3566 Gears, power transmission, except automotive

(G-13690)
ROCHESTER MIDLAND CORPORATION (PA)
155 Paragon Dr (14624-1167)
P.O. Box 64462 (14624-6862)
PHONE.............................585 336-2200
H Bradley Calkins, *CEO*
Harlan D Calkins, *Ch of Bd*
Kevin McCormick, *President*
Glenn A Paynter, *President*
Cathy Lindahl, *Co-CEO*
◆ **EMP:** 170
SQ FT: 190,000
SALES (est): 129.4MM **Privately Held**
WEB: www.rochestermidland.com
SIC: 2842 2676 2899 Specialty cleaning, polishes & sanitation goods; floor waxes; cleaning or polishing preparations; disinfectants, household or industrial plant; feminine hygiene paper products; chemical preparations

(G-13691)
ROCHESTER ORTHOPEDIC LABS (PA)
300 Airpark Dr Ste 100 (14624-5723)
PHONE.............................585 272-1060
David Forbes, *President*
Ronald McKay, *Vice Pres*
Gerald Tendall, *Vice Pres*
Eric Ober, *Admin Sec*
EMP: 8 EST: 1962
SQ FT: 12,000
SALES (est): 1.9MM **Privately Held**
WEB: www.rochesterorthopediclabs.com
SIC: 3842 Limbs, artificial; braces, elastic; braces, orthopedic

(G-13692)
ROCHESTER OVERNIGHT PLTG LLC
2 Cairn St (14611-2416)
PHONE.............................585 328-4590
Catherine Hurd, *President*
Kathy Hurd, *COO*
EMP: 60
SQ FT: 40,000

SALES (est): 5.9MM **Privately Held**
WEB: www.rochesterplatingworks.com
SIC: 3471 Plating of metals or formed products

(G-13693)
ROCHESTER PERSONAL DEFENSE LLC
115 Redwood Rd (14615-3028)
P.O. Box 67333 (14617-7333)
PHONE.............................585 406-6758
EMP: 5
SALES (est): 540.3K **Privately Held**
SIC: 3812 Defense systems & equipment

(G-13694)
ROCHESTER PHOTONICS CORP
115 Canal Landing Blvd (14626-5105)
PHONE.............................585 387-0674
Michael Morris, *CEO*
Paul Marx, *President*
EMP: 60
SQ FT: 52,000
SALES (est): 4.5MM
SALES (corp-wide): 11.2B **Publicly Held**
WEB: www.corning.com
SIC: 3827 Optical instruments & lenses
PA: Corning Incorporated
1 Riverfront Plz
Corning NY 14831
607 974-9000

(G-13695)
ROCHESTER SEAL PRO LLC
155 W Hill Est (14626-4519)
PHONE.............................585 594-3818
Joshua Piron, *President*
EMP: 5
SALES (est): 500K **Privately Held**
SIC: 2951 0781 Asphalt paving mixtures & blocks; landscape services

(G-13696)
ROCHESTER SILVER WORKS LLC
100 Latona Rd Bldg 110 (14652-0001)
P.O. Box 15397 (14615-0397)
PHONE.............................585 477-9501
Bob Surash, *Technical Mgr*
◆ **EMP:** 50
SALES (est): 13.2MM **Privately Held**
SIC: 1044 Silver ores processing

(G-13697)
ROCHESTER SILVER WORKS LLC
240 Aster St (14615)
P.O. Box 15397 (14615-0397)
PHONE.............................585 743-1610
▲ **EMP:** 9
SALES (est): 1MM **Privately Held**
SIC: 3339 Silver refining (primary)

(G-13698)
ROCHESTER STAMPINGS INC
400 Trade Ct (14624-4773)
PHONE.............................585 467-5241
L Charles Hicks, *President*
EMP: 16 EST: 1958
SQ FT: 15,000
SALES (est): 2.9MM **Privately Held**
WEB: www.rochstamp.com
SIC: 3544 3469 3452 Special dies & tools; metal stampings; bolts, nuts, rivets & washers

(G-13699)
ROCHESTER STEEL TREATING WORKS
962 E Main St (14605-2780)
PHONE.............................585 546-3348
Eugene Miller, *President*
Brian Miller, *COO*
EMP: 18
SQ FT: 13,000
SALES (est): 2MM **Privately Held**
WEB: www.rstwinc.com
SIC: 3398 Metal heat treating

(G-13700)
ROCHESTER STRUCTURAL LLC
961 Lyell Ave Bldg 5 (14606-1956)
PHONE.............................585 436-1250
David Yelle, *President*
Chad Simpson, *Project Mgr*

Kathy Hungerford, *Administration*
Brian Carmer,
EMP: 25
SQ FT: 15,000
SALES (est): 7.1MM **Privately Held**
SIC: 3312 1791 Structural shapes & pilings, steel; structural steel erection

(G-13701)
ROCHESTER TOOL AND MOLD INC
515 Lee Rd (14606-4236)
PHONE.............................585 464-9336
Al Kapoor, *President*
Paul Tolley, *Vice Pres*
EMP: 11
SQ FT: 5,600
SALES (est): 1.8MM **Privately Held**
WEB: www.rochestertoolandmold.com
SIC: 3544 3599 Industrial molds; machine shop, jobbing & repair

(G-13702)
ROECHLING MEDICAL ROCHESTER LP (HQ)
999 Ridgeway Ave (14615-3819)
PHONE.............................585 254-2000
Lewis H Carter, *President*
David Klafehn, *Mfg Mgr*
Donaven James, *QC Mgr*
Stephen Samoranski, *Engineer*
Roy Goodwin, *Project Engr*
EMP: 76
SALES (est): 25.8MM
SALES (corp-wide): 2.4B **Privately Held**
SIC: 3089 3544 3545 Injection molding of plastics; industrial molds; tools & accessories for machine tools
PA: Rochling Se & Co. Kg
Richard-Wagner-Str. 9
Mannheim 68165
621 440-20

(G-13703)
ROESSEL & CO INC
199 Lagrange Ave (14613-1593)
PHONE.............................585 458-5560
William R Laitenberger, *President*
Kathy Laitenberger, *President*
Alfred P Laitenberger, *Treasurer*
David Feavearyear, *Accounts Mgr*
Patrick Mulrooney, *Manager*
EMP: 8 EST: 1952
SQ FT: 6,000
SALES: 2MM **Privately Held**
WEB: www.roessel.com
SIC: 3823 Water quality monitoring & control systems

(G-13704)
ROHRBACH BREWING COMPANY INC
3859 Buffalo Rd (14624-1103)
PHONE.............................585 594-9800
John Urlaub, *President*
Patricia Yahn-Urlaub, *Vice Pres*
Brittany Statt, *Mktg Dir*
EMP: 60
SQ FT: 6,000
SALES (est): 5.9MM **Privately Held**
WEB: www.rohrbachs.com
SIC: 2082 Beer (alcoholic beverage)

(G-13705)
ROMOLD INC
5 Moonlanding Rd (14624-2505)
PHONE.............................585 529-4440
Louis Romano, *President*
Diane Romano, *Corp Secy*
▲ **EMP:** 16
SQ FT: 11,500
SALES (est): 1.4MM **Privately Held**
WEB: www.romold.net
SIC: 3089 Injection molding of plastics

(G-13706)
ROSEMOUNT INC
3559 Winton Pl Ste 1 (14623-2856)
PHONE.............................585 424-2460
Paul Mahoney, *Manager*
EMP: 6
SALES (corp-wide): 17.4B **Publicly Held**
WEB: www.rosemount.com
SIC: 3823 Industrial instrmnts msrmnt display/control process variable

HQ: Rosemount Inc.
8200 Market Blvd
Chanhassen MN 55317
952 906-8888

(G-13707)
ROTORK CONTROLS INC
Also Called: Jordon Controls
675 Mile Crossing Blvd (14624-6212)
PHONE..........................585 328-1550
EMP: 12
SALES (corp-wide): 893.6MM Privately
Held
SIC: 3625 Actuators, industrial
HQ: Rotork Controls Inc.
675 Mile Crossing Blvd
Rochester NY 14624
585 247-2304

(G-13708)
RPC PHOTONICS INC
330 Clay Rd (14623-3227)
PHONE..........................585 272-2840
Dr G Michael Morris, CEO
James Buckwell, Engineer
Sam Ward, Engineer
Lisa Kingsley, Controller
EMP: 19
SALES (est): 5MM Privately Held
SIC: 3827 Optical instruments & apparatus

(G-13709)
RT SOLUTIONS LLC
Also Called: Worm Power
80 Linden Oaks Ste 210 (14625-2809)
PHONE..........................585 245-3456
Thomas Herlihy, President
Shawn Ferro, Manager
EMP: 8
SQ FT: 80,000
SALES (est): 1.3MM Privately Held
SIC: 2873 8711 Nitrogenous fertilizers; en-
gineering services

(G-13710)
RUBY AUTOMATION LLC
1000 University Ave # 800 (14607-1286)
PHONE..........................585 254-8840
EMP: 80
SALES (corp-wide): 781.2MM Privately
Held
SIC: 3625 Motor controls & accessories
HQ: Ruby Automation, Llc
1 Vision Way
Bloomfield CT 06002
860 687-5000

(G-13711)
**SAFE PASSAGE
INTERNATIONAL INC**
333 Metro Park Ste F204 (14623-2632)
PHONE..........................585 292-4910
Andrew Figiel, Owner
Michael Rooksby, COO
Phong Tran, Software Dev
EMP: 14
SQ FT: 3,500
SALES: 1.2MM Privately Held
WEB: www.safe-passage.com
SIC: 7372 7371 Prepackaged software;
custom computer programming services

(G-13712)
SAMCO SCIENTIFIC LLC
75 Panorama Creek Dr (14625-2303)
PHONE..........................800 625-4327
Tuyen Nguyen, Principal
◆ EMP: 167
SQ FT: 80,000
SALES (est): 18.2MM
SALES (corp-wide): 24.3B Publicly Held
WEB: www.samcosci.com
SIC: 3085 Plastics bottles
PA: Thermo Fisher Scientific Inc.
168 3rd Ave
Waltham MA 02451
781 622-1000

(G-13713)
**SANDSTONE TECHNOLOGIES
CORP (PA)**
2117 Buffalo Rd 245 (14624-1507)
PHONE..........................585 785-5537
Timothy Williams, President
◆ EMP: 1

SALES: 1MM Privately Held
SIC: 3661 Fiber optics communications
equipment

(G-13714)
**SANDSTONE TECHNOLOGIES
CORP**
2117 Buffalo Rd Unit 245 (14624-1507)
PHONE..........................585 785-5537
Matthew Brodie, Branch Mgr
EMP: 7
SALES (corp-wide): 1MM Privately Held
SIC: 3661 Fiber optics communications
equipment
PA: Sandstone Technologies Corp.
2117 Buffalo Rd 245
Rochester NY 14624
585 785-5537

(G-13715)
SATISPIE LLC
155 Balta Dr (14623-3142)
PHONE..........................716 982-4600
Mike Pinkowski,
▲ EMP: 20
SALES (est): 5.5MM Privately Held
WEB: www.satispie.com
SIC: 2051 Cakes, pies & pastries

(G-13716)
**SAVAGE & SON INSTALLATIONS
LLC**
676 Pullman Ave (14615-3335)
P.O. Box 12647 (14612-0647)
PHONE..........................585 342-7533
Gerald Champman,
EMP: 30 EST: 2008
SALES (est): 4.1MM Privately Held
SIC: 2952 Mastic roofing composition

(G-13717)
**SCHLEGEL ELECTRONIC MTLS
INC (PA)**
1600 Lexington Ave # 236 (14606-3068)
PHONE..........................585 295-2030
Johnny C C Lo, President
Haydee Dibble, Sales Staff
EMP: 15
SQ FT: 25,000
SALES (est): 2.1MM Privately Held
SIC: 3053 Gaskets, all materials

(G-13718)
SCHLEGEL SYSTEMS INC (DH)
Also Called: S S I
1555 Jefferson Rd (14623-3109)
PHONE..........................585 427-7200
Jeff Grady, CEO
Jonathan Petromelis, Ch of Bd
Paula Toland, Accounts Mgr
▲ EMP: 200 EST: 1885
SQ FT: 150,000
SALES (est): 286.2MM
SALES (corp-wide): 759.8MM Privately
Held
WEB: www.schlegel.com
SIC: 3053 3089 3069 Gaskets, packing &
sealing devices; plastic hardware & build-
ing products; pillows, sponge rubber

(G-13719)
SCJ ASSOCIATES INC
60 Commerce Dr (14623-3502)
PHONE..........................585 359-0600
Scott Sutherland, Ch of Bd
Laurie Rosekrans, Project Mgr
Mark Sweers, Mfg Staff
Joan Holdforth, Purch Agent
Bruce Heacock, Buyer
EMP: 40
SQ FT: 15,000
SALES (est): 11.4MM Privately Held
WEB: www.scjassociates.com
SIC: 3825 Test equipment for electronic &
electric measurement

(G-13720)
SDJ MACHINE SHOP INC
1215 Mount Read Blvd # 1 (14606-2895)
PHONE..........................585 458-1236
Don Celestino, President
EMP: 11
SQ FT: 20,000

SALES (est): 1.8MM Privately Held
WEB: www.sdjmachine.com
SIC: 3599 Machine shop, jobbing & repair

(G-13721)
SEISENBACHER INC
175 Humboldt St Ste 250 (14610-1058)
PHONE..........................585 730-4960
Ken Biggins, CEO
Werner Pumhosel, Director
Lisa Testa, Admin Sec
EMP: 10 EST: 2016
SALES (est): 183K
SALES (corp-wide): 355.8K Privately
Held
SIC: 3743 Rapid transit cars & equipment
HQ: Seisenbacher Gesellschaft M.B.H.
Schwarzenberg 82
Ybbsitz 3341
501 191-00

(G-13722)
**SELBY MARKETING
ASSOCIATES INC (PA)**
Also Called: Direct 2 Market Solutions
1001 Lexington Aveste 800 (14606)
PHONE..........................585 377-0750
Richard L Selby, President
EMP: 15
SQ FT: 6,000
SALES: 3MM Privately Held
SIC: 2741 7319 Miscellaneous publishing;
media buying service

(G-13723)
SEMROK INC
Also Called: Semrock
3625 Buffalo Rd Ste 6 (14624-1179)
PHONE..........................585 594-7050
Victor Mizrahi, President
Michael Siwinski, Vice Pres
Bernadette Ayala, Mfg Staff
James Dresser, Engineer
Craig Hodgson, Engineer
EMP: 99
SQ FT: 22,000
SALES (est): 834.6K
SALES (corp-wide): 2.4B Publicly Held
WEB: www.semrock.com
SIC: 3229 Optical glass
PA: Idex Corporation
1925 W Field Ct Ste 200
Lake Forest IL 60045
847 498-7070

(G-13724)
SERI SYSTEMS INC
172 Metro Park (14623-2610)
PHONE..........................585 272-5515
Ron Lablanc, Vice Pres
Martin Sondervan, Vice Pres
Dan Wagner, Vice Pres
Robert McJury, VP Sales
EMP: 20
SQ FT: 6,000
SALES: 2MM Privately Held
SIC: 2759 Decals: printing; labels & seals:
printing; screen printing

(G-13725)
SHADE TREE GREETINGS INC
704 Clinton Ave S (14620-1454)
PHONE..........................585 442-4580
Richard Cancilla, President
EMP: 12
SALES (est): 122.9K Privately Held
SIC: 2771 2759 Greeting cards; invitation
& stationery printing & engraving

(G-13726)
**SHAMROCK PLASTIC
CORPORATION**
95 Mount Read Blvd (14611-1923)
PHONE..........................585 328-6040
Timothy Kelly, President
EMP: 5
SALES: 1.2MM Privately Held
SIC: 3089 Plastic processing

(G-13727)
**SHAMROCK PLASTICS & TOOL
INC**
95 Mount Read Blvd # 149 (14611-1933)
PHONE..........................585 328-6040
Timothy Kelly, President

EMP: 5
SQ FT: 10,000
SALES: 1.2MM Privately Held
SIC: 3089 Injection molded finished plastic
products

(G-13728)
SIEMENS INDUSTRY INC
50 Methodist Hill Dr # 1500 (14623-4269)
PHONE..........................585 797-2300
Greg Aiken, Branch Mgr
Karen Demeester, Executive
EMP: 40
SALES (corp-wide): 95B Privately Held
WEB: www.sibt.com
SIC: 3822 7629 1731 5075 Temperature
controls, automatic; electrical equipment
repair services; electrical work; warm air
heating & air conditioning; plumbing & hy-
dronic heating supplies
HQ: Siemens Industry, Inc.
1000 Deerfield Pkwy
Buffalo Grove IL 60089
847 215-1000

(G-13729)
SIGN IMPRESSIONS INC
2590 W Ridge Rd Ste 6 (14626-3041)
PHONE..........................585 723-0420
Gerald Mallaber, President
EMP: 8
SQ FT: 3,000
SALES (est): 1MM Privately Held
WEB: www.signimpressions.com
SIC: 3993 Signs, not made in custom sign
painting shops

(G-13730)
**SIGNATURE NAME PLATE CO
INC**
292 Commerce Dr (14623-3506)
PHONE..........................585 321-9960
William Monell, President
Harry T Bain Jr, Vice Pres
EMP: 7
SQ FT: 9,000
SALES (est): 784.9K Privately Held
WEB: www.signaturenp.com
SIC: 3993 Name plates: except engraved,
etched, etc.: metal

(G-13731)
**SIKORSKY AIRCRAFT
CORPORATION**
Also Called: Impact Tech A Skrsky Innvtions
300 Canal View Blvd (14623-2811)
PHONE..........................585 424-1990
James Cycon, General Mgr
EMP: 68 Publicly Held
SIC: 3721 Aircraft
HQ: Sikorsky Aircraft Corporation
6900 Main St
Stratford CT 06614

(G-13732)
SKILLSOFT CORPORATION
Also Called: Element K
500 Canal View Blvd (14623-2800)
PHONE..........................585 240-7500
Bruce Barnes, Chairman
Carrie Dailor, Sr Software Eng
EMP: 10
SALES (corp-wide): 352.2K Privately
Held
SIC: 7372 Educational computer software
HQ: Skillsoft Corporation
300 Innovative Way # 201
Nashua NH 03062
603 324-3000

(G-13733)
SLIM LINE CASE CO INC
64 Spencer St (14608-1423)
PHONE..........................585 546-3639
Bette Thomas, CEO
Andrea Coulter, President
EMP: 15
SQ FT: 14,000
SALES: 560K Privately Held
WEB: www.slimlinecase.com
SIC: 3172 Leather cases

(G-13734)
SOCIAL SCIENCE ELECTRONIC PUBG
1239 University Ave (14607-1636)
PHONE..................................585 442-8170
Greg Gordon, *President*
EMP: 16 **EST:** 1996
SALES (est): 1.2MM **Privately Held**
WEB: www.ssrn.com
SIC: 2741 8299 Miscellaneous publishing; educational services

(G-13735)
SOLID CELL INC
771 Elmgrove Rd (14624-6200)
PHONE..................................585 426-5000
Sergey Somov, *Research*
Zachary Rosen, *CFO*
EMP: 10
SALES (est): 1.9MM **Privately Held**
SIC: 3674 Semiconductors & related devices

(G-13736)
SOLID SURFACES INC
1 Townline Cir (14623-2500)
PHONE..................................585 292-5340
Gregg Sadwick, *President*
EMP: 100
SQ FT: 7,800
SALES (est): 4.5MM
SALES (corp-wide): 113.8MM **Privately Held**
WEB: www.solidsurfacesinc.net
SIC: 2541 2821 Counter & sink tops; table or counter tops, plastic laminated; plastics materials & resins
PA: Clio Holdings Llc
300 Park St Ste 380
Birmingham MI

(G-13737)
SOUND SOURCE INC
161 Norris Dr (14610-2422)
PHONE..................................585 271-5370
John Castronova, *President*
Robert Storms, *Vice Pres*
EMP: 7
SQ FT: 7,500
SALES (est): 982.4K **Privately Held**
SIC: 3931 5731 Musical instruments; consumer electronic equipment

(G-13738)
SPECTRUM CABLE CORPORATION
295 Mount Read Blvd Ste 2 (14611-1967)
PHONE..................................585 235-7714
Marc Iacona, *CEO*
Mark Philip, *President*
Simon Braitman, *Corp Secy*
EMP: 6
SQ FT: 17,000
SALES (est): 1.3MM **Privately Held**
WEB: www.spectrumcablecorp.com
SIC: 3315 1731 Wire & fabricated wire products; electrical work

(G-13739)
SPIN-RITE CORPORATION
30 Dubelbeiss Ln (14622-2402)
P.O. Box 67184 (14617-7184)
PHONE..................................585 266-5200
Gary Bohrer, *President*
EMP: 16
SQ FT: 1,400
SALES (est): 3.5MM **Privately Held**
SIC: 3312 Tool & die steel & alloys

(G-13740)
SPX CORPORATION
Kaytex
1000 Millstead Way (14624-5110)
PHONE..................................585 436-5550
Tom Fitzimmons, *Manager*
EMP: 50
SALES (corp-wide): 1.5B **Publicly Held**
SIC: 3559 Semiconductor manufacturing machinery
PA: Spx Corporation
13320a Balntyn Corp Pl
Charlotte NC 28277
980 474-3700

(G-13741)
SPX CORPORATION
SPX Flow Technology
135 Mount Read Blvd (14611-1921)
P.O. Box 31370 (14603-1370)
PHONE..................................585 436-5550
Jim Mayers, *Branch Mgr*
EMP: 480
SALES (corp-wide): 1.5B **Publicly Held**
WEB: www.spx.com
SIC: 3443 Cooling towers, metal plate
PA: Spx Corporation
13320a Balntyn Corp Pl
Charlotte NC 28277
980 474-3700

(G-13742)
SPX FLOW US LLC (HQ)
Also Called: SPX Flow Technology
135 Mount Read Blvd (14611-1921)
PHONE..................................585 436-5550
Tom Rosenthal, *Technical Staff*
Mark Kalen, *Director*
Christopher J Kearney,
EMP: 94
SALES (est): 281.5MM
SALES (corp-wide): 2B **Publicly Held**
SIC: 3824 7699 Impeller & counter driven flow meters; cash register repair
PA: Spx Flow, Inc.
13320 Balntyn Corp Pl
Charlotte NC 28277
704 752-4400

(G-13743)
STAMPER TECHNOLOGY INC
232 Wallace Way (14624-6216)
PHONE..................................585 247-8370
Bruce Ha, *President*
▲ **EMP:** 7
SQ FT: 5,000
SALES (est): 1.1MM **Privately Held**
SIC: 3695 Magnetic & optical recording media

(G-13744)
STEEL WORK INC
340 Oak St (14608-1727)
PHONE..................................585 232-1555
Tim Grove, *President*
EMP: 9
SQ FT: 7,000
SALES (est): 1.4MM **Privately Held**
WEB: www.steelwork.com
SIC: 3446 3444 Architectural metalwork; sheet metalwork

(G-13745)
STEFAN SYDOR OPTICS INC
31 Jetview Dr (14624-4903)
P.O. Box 20001 (14602-0001)
PHONE..................................585 271-7300
James Sydor, *President*
Michael Naselaris, *General Mgr*
Sam Ezzezew, *Prdtn Mgr*
Joe Tipps, *Prdtn Mgr*
Patrick Drury, *Engineer*
▼ **EMP:** 43
SQ FT: 40,000
SALES (est): 11.4MM **Privately Held**
WEB: www.sydor.com
SIC: 3827 3229 3211 Optical instruments & apparatus; pressed & blown glass; flat glass

(G-13746)
STERILIZ LLC
150 Linden Oaks Ste B (14625-2824)
PHONE..................................585 415-5411
James T Townsend,
Samuel R Trapani,
EMP: 5
SALES (est): 691.9K **Privately Held**
SIC: 3821 3842 Sterilizers; sterilizers, hospital & surgical

(G-13747)
STEVEN COFFEY PALLET S INC
3376 Edgemere Dr (14612-1128)
PHONE..................................585 261-6783
Steven Coffey, *Principal*
EMP: 8
SALES (est): 960.1K **Privately Held**
SIC: 2448 Pallets, wood & wood with metal

(G-13748)
STRAUSS EYE PROSTHETICS INC
360 White Spruce Blvd (14623-1604)
PHONE..................................585 424-1350
James V Strauss, *President*
Josie Strauss, *Admin Sec*
EMP: 5
SQ FT: 2,024
SALES (est): 310K **Privately Held**
WEB: www.strausseye.com
SIC: 3851 Eyes, glass & plastic

(G-13749)
STRIKER ORTHOPEDICS
7 Linden Park (14625-2712)
PHONE..................................585 381-1773
Thomas B Housler, *President*
Harold J Housler, *Corp Secy*
Robert A Housler, *Vice Pres*
Maricel De Leon, *Manager*
EMP: 20
SQ FT: 7,800
SALES (est): 2.6MM **Privately Held**
SIC: 3841 Surgical & medical instruments

(G-13750)
SUPERIOR TECHNOLOGY INC
200 Paragon Dr (14624-1159)
PHONE..................................585 352-6556
John P Shortino, *President*
Anthony J Shortino, *Vice Pres*
Joseph Shortino, *Vice Pres*
▲ **EMP:** 50 **EST:** 1987
SQ FT: 36,500
SALES (est): 10.3MM **Privately Held**
WEB: www.superiortech.org
SIC: 3599 Machine shop, jobbing & repair

(G-13751)
SWEETWATER ENERGY INC
500 Lee Rd Ste 200 (14606-4261)
PHONE..................................585 647-5760
Jack Baron, *CEO*
James Hvisdas, *Vice Pres*
Nina Pearlmutter, *Vice Pres*
Sarad Parekh, *CTO*
▲ **EMP:** 7
SALES (est): 1.3MM **Privately Held**
SIC: 2046 Corn sugar

(G-13752)
SWIFT MULTIGRAPHICS LLC
55 Southwood Ln (14618-4019)
PHONE..................................585 442-8000
Kenneth Stahl, *Principal*
EMP: 2
SQ FT: 200
SALES: 1MM **Privately Held**
SIC: 2759 3999 Promotional printing; advertising display products

(G-13753)
SYNERGY FLAVORS NY COMPANY LLC
Also Called: Vanlab
86 White St (14608-1435)
PHONE..................................585 232-6647
Bob Strassner, *Branch Mgr*
EMP: 9 **Privately Held**
SIC: 2087 Flavoring extracts & syrups
HQ: Synergy Flavors (Ny) Company Llc
1500 Synergy Dr
Wauconda IL 60084
585 232-6648

(G-13754)
SYNTEC TECHNOLOGIES INC
Also Called: Syntec Optics
515 Lee Rd (14606-4236)
PHONE..................................585 768-2513
Alok Kapoor, *President*
Terry Phelix, *Vice Pres*
Steve Polvinen, *Vice Pres*
Douglas Axtell, *VP Opers*
Tim Vorndran, *Opers Mgr*
EMP: 60
SQ FT: 25,000
SALES (est): 20MM **Privately Held**
WEB: www.syntecoptics.com
SIC: 3089 Injection molding of plastics

(G-13755)
T & C POWER CONVERSION INC
132 Humboldt St (14610-1046)
PHONE..................................585 482-5551
Tomasz Mokrzan, *President*
EMP: 13
SQ FT: 3,000
SALES (est): 2.5MM **Privately Held**
WEB: www.tcpowerconversion.com
SIC: 3825 Radio frequency measuring equipment

(G-13756)
T & L AUTOMATICS INC
770 Emerson St (14613-1895)
PHONE..................................585 647-3717
Thomas W Hassett, *President*
Vincent Buzzelli, *Senior VP*
David Murphy, *Vice Pres*
EMP: 120
SQ FT: 120,000
SALES (est): 23.3MM **Privately Held**
WEB: www.tandlautomatics.com
SIC: 3451 Screw machine products

(G-13757)
T L F GRAPHICS INC (PA)
Also Called: Tlf Graphics
235 Metro Park (14623-2618)
PHONE..................................585 272-5500
Ronald Leblanc, *Ch of Bd*
Dan Wagner, *Vice Pres*
Tom Crowley, *Materials Mgr*
Ray McHargue, *Safety Mgr*
Peter Tarnow, *Production*
EMP: 59
SQ FT: 12,000
SALES (est): 14.4MM **Privately Held**
SIC: 2672 2759 Tape, pressure sensitive: made from purchased materials; screen printing

(G-13758)
TAC SCREW PRODUCTS INC
170 Bennington Dr (14616-4754)
PHONE..................................585 663-5840
Julius Papp, *President*
Mark Laisure, *Vice Pres*
EMP: 10
SQ FT: 4,000
SALES (est): 1.4MM **Privately Held**
SIC: 3451 Screw machine products

(G-13759)
TCS INDUSTRIES INC
400 Trabold Rd (14624-2529)
PHONE..................................585 426-1160
Manoj Shekar, *President*
▲ **EMP:** 80
SQ FT: 110,000
SALES: 17MM **Privately Held**
WEB: www.tcsindustries.com
SIC: 3444 Sheet metalwork

(G-13760)
TE CONNECTIVITY CORPORATION
2245 Brighton Henrta Twn (14623-2705)
PHONE..................................585 785-2500
John Rowe, *Manager*
EMP: 50
SALES (corp-wide): 13.9B **Privately Held**
WEB: www.raychem.com
SIC: 3679 Electronic circuits
HQ: Te Connectivity Corporation
1050 Westlakes Dr
Berwyn PA 19312
610 893-9800

(G-13761)
TEALE MACHINE COMPANY INC
1425 University Ave (14607-1617)
P.O. Box 10340 (14610-0340)
PHONE..................................585 244-6700
Ronald E Larock, *Ch of Bd*
Aimee Ciulla, *Vice Pres*
Michael E Larock, *Vice Pres*
Aimee R Larock, *Treasurer*
Renee Hebing, *Executive Asst*
EMP: 70
SQ FT: 22,000
SALES (est): 18.1MM **Privately Held**
WEB: www.tealemachine.com
SIC: 3451 3625 Screw machine products; numerical controls

(G-13762)
TECH PARK FOOD SERVICES LLC
Also Called: Rochester Technology Park
789 Elmgrove Rd (14624-6200)
PHONE........................585 295-1250
Naresh Ramarathnan, *CFO*
EMP: 5
SALES (est): 310.9K **Privately Held**
SIC: 3721 1541 Research & development on aircraft by the manufacturer; warehouse construction

(G-13763)
TEL-TRU INC (PA)
Also Called: Tel-Tru Manufacturing Company
408 Saint Paul St (14605-1734)
PHONE........................585 295-0225
Andrew Germanow, *President*
Christopher Smock, *Vice Pres*
Tony Brancato, *Engineer*
Paul Marchand, *Engineer*
David Trump, *Technology*
EMP: 50
SALES (est): 8.9MM **Privately Held**
SIC: 3823 Temperature measurement instruments, industrial; temperature instruments: industrial process type; pressure measurement instruments, industrial

(G-13764)
THE CALDWELL MANUFACTURING CO (PA)
2605 Manitou Rd Ste 100 (14624-1199)
P.O. Box 92891 (14692-8991)
PHONE........................585 352-3790
Edward A Boucher, *CEO*
Eric W Mertz, *Ch of Bd*
James Boucher, *Ch of Bd*
Tom Fening, *Vice Pres*
Kevin Novak, *Vice Pres*
◆ EMP: 100 EST: 1888
SQ FT: 126,000
SALES (est): 66.5MM **Privately Held**
WEB: www.caldwellmfgco.com
SIC: 3495 Wire springs

(G-13765)
THERMO FISHER SCIENTIFIC INC
1999 Mnt Rd Blvd 1-3 (14615)
PHONE........................585 458-8008
Helene Diederich, *Branch Mgr*
EMP: 307
SALES (corp-wide): 24.3B **Publicly Held**
WEB: www.thermo.com
SIC: 3826 Analytical instruments
PA: Thermo Fisher Scientific Inc.
168 3rd Ave
Waltham MA 02451
781 622-1000

(G-13766)
THERMO FISHER SCIENTIFIC INC
75 Panorama Creek Dr (14625-2385)
PHONE........................585 899-7610
Barbara Dorsey, *Opers Mgr*
Matthew Rodems, *Engineer*
Raymond Mercier, *Marketing Staff*
John Foster, *Manager*
Cathy Powers, *Manager*
EMP: 900
SALES (corp-wide): 24.3B **Publicly Held**
SIC: 3826 Analytical instruments
PA: Thermo Fisher Scientific Inc.
168 3rd Ave
Waltham MA 02451
781 622-1000

(G-13767)
THREE POINT VENTURES LLC
Also Called: Skooba Design
3495 Winton Pl Ste E120 (14623-2838)
PHONE........................585 697-3444
Michael J Hess,
▲ EMP: 10
SQ FT: 20,000
SALES (est): 640K **Privately Held**
WEB: www.roadwired.com
SIC: 3161 Cases, carrying

(G-13768)
TODD WALBRIDGE
Also Called: T M Design Screen Printing
1916 Lyell Ave (14606-2306)
PHONE........................585 254-3018
Todd Walbridge, *Owner*
EMP: 7
SQ FT: 3,500
SALES (est): 732.8K **Privately Held**
WEB: www.tmdesigncorp.com
SIC: 2759 3993 2396 2395 Screen printing; signs & advertising specialties; automotive & apparel trimmings; pleating & stitching

(G-13769)
TOKENIZE INC
125 Tech Park Dr 2137b (14623-2446)
PHONE........................585 981-9919
Melanie Shapiro, *CEO*
EMP: 11 EST: 2014
SALES (est): 1.1MM **Privately Held**
SIC: 3669 8731 Intercommunication systems, electric; computer (hardware) development

(G-13770)
TOUCHSTONE TECHNOLOGY INC
350 Mile Crossing Blvd (14624-6207)
PHONE........................585 458-2690
Eric B Snavely, *Ch of Bd*
Alan Robertson, *Engineer*
Todd Sheehan, *Design Engr*
David J Meisenzahl, *CFO*
Kelly Fairchild, *Controller*
▲ EMP: 16
SQ FT: 13,000
SALES (est): 5.5MM **Privately Held**
WEB: www.touchstn.com
SIC: 3575 Computer terminals, monitors & components; keyboards, computer, office machine

(G-13771)
TRANE US INC
75 Town Centre Dr Ste I (14623-4259)
PHONE........................585 256-2500
Dan Wendo, *Branch Mgr*
EMP: 47 **Privately Held**
SIC: 3585 Refrigeration & heating equipment
HQ: Trane U.S. Inc.
3600 Pammel Creek Rd
La Crosse WI 54601
608 787-2000

(G-13772)
TRANSCAT INC (PA)
35 Vantage Point Dr (14624-1175)
PHONE........................585 352-7777
Charles P Hadeed, *Ch of Bd*
Lee D Rudow, *President*
Katie Brown, *Business Mgr*
Scott Clemo, *Business Mgr*
Peter Hadeed, *Business Mgr*
◆ EMP: 277
SQ FT: 37,300
SALES: 160.9MM **Publicly Held**
WEB: www.transmationcorp.com
SIC: 3825 7699 Instruments to measure electricity; scientific equipment repair service

(G-13773)
TRIPLEX INDUSTRIES INC
100 Boxart St Ste 27 (14612-5659)
PHONE........................585 621-6920
Christa Roesner, *President*
EMP: 10
SQ FT: 8,500
SALES (est): 1.7MM **Privately Held**
SIC: 3599 Machine shop, jobbing & repair

(G-13774)
TROYER INC
4555 Lyell Rd (14606-4316)
PHONE........................585 352-5590
William Colton, *President*
EMP: 15
SQ FT: 18,000
SALES (est): 2.2MM **Privately Held**
SIC: 3711 3714 5531 Automobile assembly, including specialty automobiles; motor vehicle parts & accessories; speed shops, including race car supplies

(G-13775)
TRUESENSE IMAGING INC
1964 Lake Ave (14615-2316)
PHONE........................585 784-5500
Chris McNiffe, *CEO*
Daniel Oconnor, *Engineer*
Rachel Kielon, *CFO*
Joe Blakely, *Sales Staff*
Stephanie Newman, *Info Tech Mgr*
EMP: 207 EST: 2011
SQ FT: 260,000
SALES (est): 26.2MM
SALES (corp-wide): 5.8B **Publicly Held**
SIC: 3861 Film, sensitized motion picture, X-ray, still camera, etc.
HQ: Semiconductor Components Industries, Llc
5005 E Mcdowell Rd
Phoenix AZ 85008
800 282-9855

(G-13776)
TRUFORM MANUFACTURING CORP
1500 N Clinton Ave (14621-2206)
PHONE........................585 458-1090
Tyrone Reaves, *Ch of Bd*
Bryan Putt, *General Mgr*
Dan Kane, *Project Mgr*
EMP: 70
SQ FT: 45,000
SALES (est): 14.3MM **Privately Held**
WEB: www.truformmfg.com
SIC: 3444 Sheet metalwork

(G-13777)
TRUTH HARDWARE CORPORATION
Also Called: Amesburytruth
1555 Jefferson Rd (14623-3109)
PHONE........................585 627-5964
James McFarlane, *Engineer*
Ken Rhodam, *Manager*
EMP: 6
SALES (corp-wide): 759.8MM **Privately Held**
SIC: 2431 3442 3429 Windows & window parts & trim, wood; metal doors, sash & trim; manufactured hardware (general)
HQ: Truth Hardware Corporation
3600 Minnesota Dr Ste 800
Edina MN 55435

(G-13778)
TURNER BELLOWS INC
Also Called: Tb
526 Child St Ste 1 (14606-1187)
PHONE........................585 235-4456
Marilyn Yeager, *CEO*
Amanda Pontaella, *Ch of Bd*
▲ EMP: 45 EST: 1971
SQ FT: 85,000
SALES (est): 8.3MM **Privately Held**
WEB: www.turnerbellows.com
SIC: 3081 3069 3861 Unsupported plastics film & sheet; foam rubber; photographic sensitized goods

(G-13779)
TURNING POINT TOOL LLC
135 Dodge St (14606-1503)
PHONE........................585 288-7380
Rob Kirby, *Opers Mgr*
Connie Pezzulo, *Office Mgr*
Frank Pezzulo,
Robert Kirby,
EMP: 6
SALES (est): 856.4K **Privately Held**
WEB: www.turningpointtool.com
SIC: 3599 Machine shop, jobbing & repair

(G-13780)
ULTRA TOOL AND MANUFACTURING
159 Lagrange Ave (14613-1511)
P.O. Box 17860 (14617-0860)
PHONE........................585 467-3700
Daniel E Herzog, *President*
James M Schmeer, *Vice Pres*
Deb Hansen, *Director*
EMP: 13
SQ FT: 4,000
SALES: 1.3MM **Privately Held**
SIC: 3599 Machine shop, jobbing & repair

(G-13781)
UNICELL BODY COMPANY INC
1319 Brighton Henrietta (14623-2408)
PHONE........................585 424-2660
Steven Bones, *Manager*
Steve Bones, *Manager*
EMP: 14
SQ FT: 7,200
SALES (corp-wide): 20MM **Privately Held**
WEB: www.unicell.com
SIC: 3713 Truck bodies (motor vehicles)
PA: Unicell Body Company, Inc
571 Howard St
Buffalo NY 14206
716 853-8628

(G-13782)
UNIFAB INC
215 Tremont St Ste 31 (14608-2370)
PHONE........................585 235-1760
Brian Malark, *President*
Bill Martin, *Vice Pres*
William S Martin, *Vice Pres*
EMP: 7
SQ FT: 2,500
SALES: 1MM **Privately Held**
SIC: 3089 Injection molding of plastics; plastic processing

(G-13783)
UNITHER MANUFACTURING LLC (DH)
755 Jefferson Rd (14623-3270)
PHONE........................585 475-9000
Kevin Haehl, *General Mgr*
▲ EMP: 250
SALES (est): 68.5MM
SALES (corp-wide): 10.6MM **Privately Held**
SIC: 2834 Pharmaceutical preparations
HQ: Unither Pharmaceuticals
Espace Industriel Nord
Amiens 80080
322 547-300

(G-13784)
UNITHER MANUFACTURING LLC
331 Clay Rd (14623-3226)
PHONE........................585 274-5430
EMP: 12
SALES (corp-wide): 10.6MM **Privately Held**
SIC: 2834 Pharmaceutical preparations
HQ: Unither Manufacturing Llc
755 Jefferson Rd
Rochester NY 14623
585 475-9000

(G-13785)
UNIVERSAL PRECISION CORP
40 Commerce Dr (14623-3502)
PHONE........................585 321-9760
Michael J Schmitt, *President*
Michael Domenico, *Vice Pres*
Jeff Hooper, *Treasurer*
Donna Domenico, *Office Mgr*
EMP: 24
SQ FT: 12,000
SALES (est): 4.3MM **Privately Held**
WEB: www.universalprecision.com
SIC: 3444 Sheet metal specialties, not stamped

(G-13786)
UNIVERSITY OF ROCHESTER
Also Called: Labortory For Laser Energetics
250 E River Rd (14623-1212)
PHONE........................585 275-3483
Robert Jungquist, *Engineer*
Tim Flannery, *Electrical Engi*
Rebecca Wadsworth, *Manager*
John Spaulding, *Admin Asst*
John Howell, *Professor*
EMP: 400
SALES (corp-wide): 2.9B **Privately Held**
WEB: www.rochester.edu
SIC: 3845 8221 Laser systems & equipment, medical; university
PA: University Of Rochester
500 Joseph C Wilson Blvd
Rochester NY 14627
585 275-2121

(G-13787)
UPSTATE CABINET COMPANY INC
32 Marway Cir (14624-2321)
PHONE..................585 429-5090
Todd Whelehan, *President*
Vincenzo Delucia, *Vice Pres*
EMP: 14
SQ FT: 30,000
SALES (est): 1.8MM **Privately Held**
WEB: www.upstatecabinet.com
SIC: 2434 5712 Wood kitchen cabinets; furniture stores

(G-13788)
UPSTATE INCRETE INCORPORATED
1029 Lyell Ave Ste A (14606-1959)
PHONE..................585 254-2010
Jeff Barlette, *Principal*
EMP: 9
SALES (est): 1.2MM **Privately Held**
SIC: 2421 Building & structural materials, wood

(G-13789)
UPSTATE NIAGARA COOP INC
Also Called: Sealtest Dairy Products
45 Fulton Ave (14608-1032)
PHONE..................585 458-1880
Michelle Coyle, *Personnel*
Rick Holz, *Manager*
Stephan Hranjec, *Manager*
EMP: 150
SQ FT: 40,000
SALES (corp-wide): 903.7MM **Privately Held**
SIC: 2026 Milk processing (pasteurizing, homogenizing, bottling)
PA: Upstate Niagara Cooperative, Inc.
25 Anderson Rd
Buffalo NY 14225
716 892-3156

(G-13790)
USAIRPORTS SERVICES INC
Also Called: US Airports Flight Support Svc
1295 Scottsville Rd (14624-5125)
PHONE..................585 527-6835
Anthony Castillo, *President*
EMP: 22
SQ FT: 23,800 **Privately Held**
WEB: www.usairportsflight.com
SIC: 3728 Refueling equipment for use in flight, airplane
PA: Usairports Services, Inc
1 Airport Way Ste 300
Rochester NY 14624

(G-13791)
VA INC
Also Called: Vincent Associates
803 Linden Ave Ste 1 (14625-2723)
PHONE..................585 385-5930
Kevin Farrell, *Ch of Bd*
Stephen Pasquarella, *Vice Pres*
Steve Pasquarella, *Vice Pres*
EMP: 25
SQ FT: 6,500
SALES (est): 4.3MM **Privately Held**
WEB: www.uniblitz.com
SIC: 3861 3827 Shutters, camera; optical instruments & lenses

(G-13792)
VACCINEX INC
1895 Mount Hope Ave (14620-4540)
PHONE..................585 271-2700
Albert D Friedberg, *Ch of Bd*
Maurice Zauderer, *President*
Raymond E Watkins, *COO*
John E Leonard, *Senior VP*
Ernest S Smith, *Senior VP*
EMP: 44
SQ FT: 31,180
SALES: 724K **Privately Held**
WEB: www.vaccinex.com
SIC: 2834 Pharmaceutical preparations

(G-13793)
VALASSIS COMMUNICATIONS INC
Also Called: Printed Deals
5 Marway Cir Ste 8 (14624-2362)
PHONE..................585 627-4138

EMP: 5 **Privately Held**
SIC: 2721 Magazines: publishing & printing
HQ: Valassis Communications, Inc.
19975 Victor Pkwy
Livonia MI 48152
734 591-3000

(G-13794)
VAN REENEN TOOL & DIE INC
350 Commerce Dr Ste 4 (14623-3547)
P.O. Box 10256 (14610-0256)
PHONE..................585 288-6000
Richard Van Reenen, *President*
Richard V Reenen, *President*
Zack V Reenen, *Managing Dir*
Amy V Reenen, *Vice Pres*
EMP: 12
SQ FT: 35,000
SALES (est): 1.8MM **Privately Held**
WEB: www.vanreenentoolanddieinc.com
SIC: 3469 3544 3599 Stamping metal for the trade; special dies, tools, jigs & fixtures; machine shop, jobbing & repair

(G-13795)
VAN THOMAS INC
Also Called: Ruggeri Manufacturing
740 Driving Park Ave G1 (14613-1594)
PHONE..................585 426-1414
Charles E Thomas, *President*
Gary Vander Mallie, *Vice Pres*
▲ **EMP:** 35
SQ FT: 37,000
SALES: 850K **Privately Held**
SIC: 3599 3544 Machine & other job shop work; special dies, tools, jigs & fixtures

(G-13796)
VETERANS OFFSET PRINTING INC
Also Called: Veteran Offset Printing
500 N Goodman St (14609-6136)
PHONE..................585 288-2900
Louie Difillippo, *President*
John Duque, *Vice Pres*
EMP: 3 **EST:** 1940
SALES: 2MM **Privately Held**
SIC: 2752 2759 Commercial printing, offset; commercial printing

(G-13797)
VIGNERI CHOCOLATE INC
810 Emerson St (14613-1804)
PHONE..................585 254-6160
Alex Vigneri, *CEO*
◆ **EMP:** 7 **EST:** 2012
SQ FT: 10,000
SALES: 500K **Privately Held**
SIC: 2064 Candy bars, including chocolate covered bars; chocolate candy, except solid chocolate

(G-13798)
W M T PUBLICATIONS INC
280 State St (14614-1033)
PHONE..................585 244-3329
Mary Anna Towler, *President*
William J Towler, *Treasurer*
EMP: 16
SALES (est): 863K **Privately Held**
SIC: 2711 Newspapers, publishing & printing

(G-13799)
WATER WISE OF AMERICA INC
75 Bermar Park Ste 5 (14624-1500)
PHONE..................585 232-1210
Michael Bromley, *President*
Anne Jefferson, *Corp Secy*
EMP: 10
SQ FT: 2,500
SALES (est): 1.6MM **Privately Held**
WEB: www.waterwiseofamerica.com
SIC: 2899 5169 Water treating compounds; chemicals & allied products

(G-13800)
WEB SEAL INC (PA)
15 Oregon St (14605-3094)
PHONE..................585 546-1320
John F Hurley, *President*
Betty A Hurley, *Treasurer*
Bonnie Kaufman, *Accounting Mgr*
Julia Magone, *Manager*
EMP: 20 **EST:** 1960
SQ FT: 13,000

SALES (est): 4.7MM **Privately Held**
WEB: www.websealinc.com
SIC: 3053 5085 Gaskets & sealing devices; seals, industrial

(G-13801)
WELCH MACHINE INC
961 Lyell Ave Bldg 1-6 (14606-1956)
PHONE..................585 647-3578
Martin Welch, *President*
EMP: 5
SQ FT: 5,000
SALES (est): 633.4K **Privately Held**
SIC: 3541 Machine tool replacement & repair parts, metal cutting types

(G-13802)
WERE FORMS INC
500 Helendale Rd Ste 190 (14609-3125)
PHONE..................585 482-4400
Kim Hostutler, *President*
EMP: 6
SQ FT: 2,000
SALES (est): 480K **Privately Held**
WEB: www.wereforms.com
SIC: 2759 Commercial printing

(G-13803)
WHIRLWIND MUSIC DISTRS INC
99 Ling Rd (14612-1965)
PHONE..................800 733-9473
Michael Laiacona, *Principal*
Debbie Noble, *Prdtn Mgr*
Holly Bryan, *Purch Agent*
Carl Cornell, *Chief Engr*
Mike Shapiro, *Engineer*
▲ **EMP:** 100
SQ FT: 28,000
SALES (est): 21.3MM **Privately Held**
WEB: www.whirlwindusa.com
SIC: 3651 3678 3663 3643 Audio electronic systems; amplifiers: radio, public address or musical instrument; public address systems; electronic connectors; radio & TV communications equipment; current-carrying wiring devices; nonferrous wiredrawing & insulating

(G-13804)
WHITESTONE DEV GROUP LLC
Also Called: Ry-Gan Printing
111 Humboldt St (14609-7463)
PHONE..................585 482-7770
Scott Wihlen, *Mng Member*
Chuck Armbruster, *Executive*
EMP: 8
SALES (est): 747.1K **Privately Held**
SIC: 2752 Commercial printing, lithographic

(G-13805)
WIKOFF COLOR CORPORATION
686 Pullman Ave (14615-3335)
PHONE..................585 458-0653
EMP: 16
SALES (corp-wide): 145.1MM **Privately Held**
SIC: 2893 Printing ink
PA: Wikoff Color Corporation
1886 Merritt Rd
Fort Mill SC 29715
803 548-2210

(G-13806)
WINDSOR TECHNOLOGY LLC
1527 Lyell Ave (14606-2121)
PHONE..................585 461-2500
Grant Randall, *President*
Chad Notebaert, *Engineer*
Mary Carlson, *Design Engr*
Thomas Bonadio,
EMP: 10
SQ FT: 40,000
SALES (est): 10MM **Privately Held**
WEB: www.windsortec.com
SIC: 3672 Printed circuit boards

(G-13807)
WOERNER INDUSTRIES INC
Also Called: Wizer Equipment
485 Hague St (14606-1296)
PHONE..................585 436-1934
Philip Collins, *President*
EMP: 40

SALES (corp-wide): 4.2MM **Privately Held**
WEB: www.lasscowizer.com
SIC: 3555 Printing trades machinery
PA: Woerner Industries, Llc
485 Hague St
Rochester NY
585 235-1991

(G-13808)
WORDINGHAM MACHINE CO INC
Also Called: Wordingham Technologies
515 Lee Rd (14606-4236)
PHONE..................585 924-2294
Alok Kapoor, *CEO*
Steven Polvinen, *General Mgr*
EMP: 45
SQ FT: 26,000
SALES (est): 9MM **Privately Held**
SIC: 3599 Machine shop, jobbing & repair

(G-13809)
WORLDWIDE ELECTRIC CORP LLC
3540 Winton Pl (14623-2858)
PHONE..................800 808-2131
Jim Taylor, *President*
Rick Simmonds, *President*
Jon Smith, *Engineer*
Jay Weismose, *Design Engr*
Mitchell Starr, *CFO*
EMP: 50
SALES (est): 2MM **Privately Held**
SIC: 3621 5063 Motors, electric; electrical supplies

(G-13810)
XACTRA TECHNOLOGIES INC
105 Mclaughlin Rd Ste F (14615-3762)
PHONE..................585 426-2030
David W Binn, *President*
EMP: 55
SQ FT: 33,000
SALES (est): 7.7MM **Privately Held**
WEB: www.prestigeprecision.com
SIC: 3545 Precision tools, machinists'

(G-13811)
XEROX CORPORATION
80 Linden Oaks (14625-2809)
PHONE..................585 264-5584
EMP: 200
SALES (corp-wide): 21.4B **Publicly Held**
SIC: 3861 Mfg Photographic Equipment/Supplies
PA: Xerox Corporation
45 Glover Ave Ste 700
Norwalk CT 06851
203 968-3000

(G-13812)
XLI MANUFACTURING LLC
55 Vanguard Pkwy (14606-3101)
PHONE..................585 436-2250
Chad Carta, *Mng Member*
EMP: 49
SQ FT: 32,000
SALES: 6MM **Privately Held**
SIC: 3451 3444 3441 Screw machine products; sheet metalwork; fabricated structural metal

(G-13813)
YELLOWPAGECITYCOM
280 Kenneth Dr Ste 300 (14623-5263)
PHONE..................585 410-6688
Kevin Fisher, *Production*
Ashley Poulton, *Production*
Arthur Ellis, *Accountant*
Brian Gilbert, *Sales Staff*
Janet Nelson, *Mktg Coord*
EMP: 18
SALES (est): 2.3MM **Privately Held**
SIC: 3993 Signs & advertising specialties

(G-13814)
ZEROVALENT NANOMETALS INC
693 East Ave Ste 103 (14607-2160)
PHONE..................585 298-8592
Joseph Fargnoli, *Principal*
EMP: 7

SALES (est): 295.4K **Privately Held**
SIC: 3339 Antimony refining (primary); cobalt refining (primary); babbitt metal (primary); beryllium metal

(G-13815)
ZIP PRODUCTS INC
565 Blossom Rd Ste E (14610-1873)
P.O. Box 10502 (14610-0502)
PHONE..................................585 482-0044
Nikolay Petukhov, *President*
EMP: 14 **EST:** 1998
SQ FT: 9,500
SALES: 800K **Privately Held**
SIC: 3599 3452 3429 Machine shop, jobbing & repair; bolts, nuts, rivets & washers; dowel pins, metal; motor vehicle hardware; aircraft & marine hardware, inc. pulleys & similar items

(G-13816)
ZWEIGLES INC
651 Plymouth Ave N (14608-1689)
PHONE..................................585 546-1740
Julie E Camardo-Steron, *Ch of Bd*
Roberta Camardo, *President*
Michael Bidzerkowny, *General Mgr*
Tina Steinmetz, *Purch Mgr*
Mike Keller, *CFO*
EMP: 55 **EST:** 1880
SQ FT: 37,000
SALES (est): 12.7MM **Privately Held**
WEB: www.zweigles.com
SIC: 2013 Sausages from purchased meat

Rock City Falls
Saratoga County

(G-13817)
COTTRELL PAPER COMPANY INC
1135 Rock City Rd (12863-1208)
P.O. Box 35 (12863-0035)
PHONE..................................518 885-1702
Jack L Cottrell, *Ch of Bd*
Ben Cottrell, *Vice Pres*
Tom Harrington, *Sales Mgr*
Darren Costanzo, *Manager*
▲ **EMP:** 36 **EST:** 1926
SQ FT: 40,000
SALES (est): 9.2MM **Privately Held**
WEB: www.cottrellpaper.com
SIC: 2621 Specialty papers; insulation siding, paper

Rock Hill
Sullivan County

(G-13818)
DEB EL FOOD PRODUCTS LLC
88 Rock Hill Dr (12775-7201)
PHONE..................................845 295-8050
Amado Gallo Jaleaf, *Branch Mgr*
EMP: 12 **Privately Held**
SIC: 2015 Egg processing
PA: Deb El Food Products Llc
520 Broad St Fl 6
Newark NJ 07102

Rock Stream
Schuyler County

(G-13819)
ROCK STREAM VINEYARDS
162 Fir Tree Point Rd (14878-9700)
PHONE..................................607 243-8322
Mark Karasz, *Owner*
EMP: 7
SALES (est): 682.6K **Privately Held**
SIC: 2084 Wines

Rock Tavern
Orange County

(G-13820)
CREATIVE DESIGN AND MCH INC
197 Stone Castle Rd (12575-5000)
PHONE..................................845 778-9001
Clifford Broderick, *CEO*
◆ **EMP:** 25
SQ FT: 24,000
SALES (est): 5.3MM **Privately Held**
SIC: 3469 Machine parts, stamped or pressed metal

(G-13821)
POLICH TALLIX INC
453 State Route 17k (12575-5011)
PHONE..................................845 567-9464
Richard Polich, *President*
Adam Demchak, *Vice Pres*
Duncan Urquhart, *CFO*
J Duncan Urquhart, *CFO*
▲ **EMP:** 63
SALES (est): 13.4MM **Privately Held**
SIC: 3369 3499 Nonferrous foundries; novelties & specialties, metal
PA: Uap Production Llc
236 W 26th St Rm 5nw
New York NY 10001
212 727-2819

Rockaway Beach
Queens County

(G-13822)
EXCEL CONVEYOR LLC
350 Beach 79th St Ste 1 (11693-2068)
PHONE..................................718 474-0001
Mitch Popescu, *COO*
Hilda Masih, *Mng Member*
EMP: 10
SALES (est): 2.5MM **Privately Held**
SIC: 3535 7699 Conveyors & conveying equipment; industrial machinery & equipment repair

(G-13823)
WAVE PUBLISHING CO INC
Also Called: Wave of Long Island, The
8808 Rockaway Beach Blvd (11693-1608)
PHONE..................................718 634-4000
Susan Locke, *President*
Carol Keenan, *Publisher*
Sanford Bernstein, *Treasurer*
Mark Healey, *Manager*
Dan Guarino, *Assoc Editor*
EMP: 15
SQ FT: 4,500
SALES: 850K **Privately Held**
SIC: 2711 8111 Newspapers: publishing only, not printed on site; legal services

Rockaway Park
Queens County

(G-13824)
EVELO INC
327 Beach 101st St (11694-2831)
PHONE..................................917 251-8743
Yevgeniy Morekovic, *President*
Boris Morekovic, *Vice Pres*
Bill Cummings, *Cust Svc Dir*
▲ **EMP:** 2
SALES: 1MM **Privately Held**
SIC: 3751 Bicycles & related parts

(G-13825)
RELIANCE MICA CO INC
336 Beach 149th St (11694-1027)
PHONE..................................718 788-0282
Peter Yanello Jr, *President*
Peter Yannello, *Manager*
▲ **EMP:** 6 **EST:** 1924
SQ FT: 10,000
SALES (est): 635.4K **Privately Held**
SIC: 3299 Mica products

Rockville Centre
Nassau County

(G-13826)
BIANCA BURGERS LLC
Also Called: Janowski Hamburger
15 S Long Beach Rd (11570-5621)
PHONE..................................516 764-9591
William Vogelsberg, *President*
EMP: 12
SALES (est): 1.4MM **Privately Held**
SIC: 2013 Sausages & other prepared meats

(G-13827)
CREATION BAUMANN USA INC
114 N Centre Ave (11570-3948)
PHONE..................................516 764-7431
George Baumann, *President*
Gloria Mastranni, *Human Res Mgr*
Harry Persaus, *Executive*
EMP: 30
SALES (est): 1.9MM **Privately Held**
SIC: 2211 2221 5949 5131 Apparel & outerwear fabrics, cotton; broadwoven fabric mills, manmade; fabric stores piece goods; piece goods & other fabrics

(G-13828)
GRAPHIC FABRICATIONS INC
Also Called: Minuteman Press
488a Sunrise Hwy (11570-5037)
PHONE..................................516 763-3222
George Dormani, *President*
EMP: 6
SQ FT: 4,000
SALES (est): 865.9K **Privately Held**
SIC: 2752 7334 2791 Commercial printing, lithographic; photocopying & duplicating services; typesetting

(G-13829)
INDUSTRIAL MCH GEAR WORKS LLC
77 Woodland Ave (11570-6015)
PHONE..................................516 695-4442
Susan Lehrman, *Mng Member*
Richard C Lehrman,
EMP: 5 **EST:** 1944
SQ FT: 4,000
SALES (est): 250K **Privately Held**
SIC: 3462 Gears, forged steel

(G-13830)
MERCURY ENVELOPE CO INC
Also Called: Mercury Envelope Printing
100 Merrick Rd Ste 204e (11570-4801)
P.O. Box 200 (11571-0200)
PHONE..................................516 678-6744
Maurice Deutsch, *Ch of Bd*
Scott Deutsch, *President*
Deutsch Maurice, *Vice Pres*
Colleen Cunningham, *CFO*
EMP: 75
SQ FT: 2,500
SALES (est): 18.8MM **Privately Held**
SIC: 2677 Envelopes

(G-13831)
MURPHS FAMOUS INC
200 Raymond St (11570-2544)
PHONE..................................516 398-0417
Steven Murphy, *CEO*
EMP: 8 **EST:** 2013
SALES: 500K **Privately Held**
SIC: 2082 5182 Malt beverages; wine & distilled beverages

(G-13832)
NAITO INTERNATIONAL CORP
100 Merrick Rd Ste 400e (11570-4882)
PHONE..................................718 309-2425
Abdallah Elouadghin, *CEO*
EMP: 10
SQ FT: 2,500
SALES (est): 50MM **Privately Held**
SIC: 3942 2339 Dolls & stuffed toys; women's & misses' accessories

(G-13833)
PRIME GARMENTS INC
66 Randall Ave (11570-3922)
PHONE..................................212 354-7294

Joseph Hamdar, *President*
▲ **EMP:** 14
SALES (est): 2.3MM **Privately Held**
SIC: 2342 Bras, girdles & allied garments

(G-13834)
PROGRESSUS COMPANY INC
100 Merrick Rd Ste 510w (11570-4825)
PHONE..................................516 255-0245
Lawrence Hutzler, *President*
Lillian Ehrenhaus, *Vice Pres*
▲ **EMP:** 10
SQ FT: 60,000
SALES (est): 1.2MM **Privately Held**
WEB: www.progressus.com
SIC: 3469 Household cooking & kitchen utensils, metal

(G-13835)
QUALITY METAL STAMPING LLC (PA)
100 Merrick Rd Ste 310w (11570-4884)
PHONE..................................516 255-9000
Robert Serling, *Owner*
EMP: 3
SQ FT: 2,000
SALES (est): 8.7MM **Privately Held**
SIC: 3469 Stamping metal for the trade

(G-13836)
SLEEP IMPROVEMENT CENTER INC
178 Sunrise Hwy Fl 2 (11570-4704)
PHONE..................................516 536-5799
Reza Naghavi, *President*
EMP: 12
SALES (est): 1MM **Privately Held**
SIC: 2515 Sleep furniture

(G-13837)
SOLVE ADVISORS INC
265 Sunrise Hwy Ste 22 (11570-4912)
PHONE..................................646 699-5041
Yevgeniy Grinberg, *President*
Gerard Nealon, *President*
EMP: 8 **EST:** 2011
SQ FT: 2,000
SALES (est): 687.2K **Privately Held**
SIC: 7372 Business oriented computer software

(G-13838)
SOUTHBAY FUEL INJECTORS
566 Merrick Rd Ste 3 (11570-5547)
PHONE..................................516 442-4707
EMP: 7
SALES (est): 721.3K **Privately Held**
SIC: 2869 Fuels

(G-13839)
TRUEFORGE GLOBAL MCHY CORP
100 Merrick Rd Ste 208e (11570-4817)
PHONE..................................516 825-7040
Ronald E Jaggie, *President*
◆ **EMP:** 3
SQ FT: 2,500
SALES (est): 9MM **Privately Held**
WEB: www.trueforge.com
SIC: 3542 Forging machinery & hammers

(G-13840)
VENDING TIMES INC
55 Maple Ave Ste 304 (11570-4267)
PHONE..................................516 442-1850
Alicia Lavay, *President*
Nicolas Montano, *Vice Pres*
Frances Lavay, *Treasurer*
EMP: 11 **EST:** 1961
SQ FT: 4,000
SALES (est): 1.1MM **Privately Held**
SIC: 2721 2741 Magazines: publishing only, not printed on site; miscellaneous publishing

▲ = Import ▼ = Export
◆ = Import/Export

Rome
Oneida County

(G-13841)

ALLIANCE PAVING MATERIALS INC
846 Lawrence St (13440-8102)
PHONE..............................315 337-0795
Kimberly Ocuto, *President*
EMP: 6
SQ FT: 4,000
SALES (est): 820K **Privately Held**
SIC: 2951 1771 Road materials, bituminous (not from refineries); driveway, parking lot & blacktop contractors

(G-13842)

BAE SYSTEMS INFO & ELEC SYS
581 Phoenix Dr (13441-4914)
PHONE..............................603 885-4321
Carlos Camacho, *Engineer*
Martiza Johnson, *Engineer*
Danny Morabito, *Accountant*
Chris Powell, *Sales Executive*
Faith Allen, *Manager*
EMP: 35
SALES (corp-wide): 21.6B **Privately Held**
SIC: 3812 Search & navigation equipment
HQ: Bae Systems Information And Electronic Systems Integration Inc.
65 Spit Brook Rd
Nashua NH 03060
603 885-4321

(G-13843)

BARTELL MACHINERY SYSTEMS LLC (DH)
6321 Elmer Hill Rd (13440-9325)
PHONE..............................315 336-7600
Pat Morocco, *President*
Christopher Fatata, *Materials Mgr*
Kelly Ashley, *Buyer*
Michael Buisman, *Engineer*
Paul Gatley, *Engineer*
◆ EMP: 150
SQ FT: 115,000
SALES (est): 31.1MM
SALES (corp-wide): 1.2B **Privately Held**
WEB: www.bartellmachinery.com
SIC: 3549 5531 Metalworking machinery; automotive & home supply stores
HQ: Pettibone L.L.C.
27501 Bella Vista Pkwy
Warrenville IL 60555
630 353-5000

(G-13844)

BAUMS CASTORINE COMPANY INC
200 Matthew St (13440)
P.O. Box 230 (13442-0230)
PHONE..............................315 336-8154
Charles F Mowry, *President*
Paul H Berger Jr, *Chairman*
Theodore Mowry, *Vice Pres*
▼ EMP: 7 EST: 1879
SQ FT: 22,000
SALES (est): 1.6MM **Privately Held**
WEB: www.baumscastorine.com
SIC: 2992 2841 Lubricating oils & greases; soap & other detergents

(G-13845)

BECK VAULT COMPANY
6648 Shank Ave (13440-9357)
PHONE..............................315 337-7590
EMP: 5 EST: 1946
SQ FT: 4,500
SALES: 500K **Privately Held**
SIC: 3272 7359 Mfg Concrete Burial Vaults & Rents Burial Equipment

(G-13846)

CATHEDRAL CORPORATION (PA)
632 Ellsworth Rd (13441-4808)
PHONE..............................315 338-0021
Marianne W Gaige, *President*
Robert Staph, *Principal*
Larry J Beasley, *Vice Pres*
Paul Harrington, *Vice Pres*

Aart Knyff, *Vice Pres*
EMP: 138
SQ FT: 58,000
SALES: 36.2MM **Privately Held**
WEB: www.cathedralcorporation.com
SIC: 2752 Commercial printing, offset

(G-13847)

COLD POINT CORPORATION
Also Called: Adirondack-Aire
7500 Cold Point Dr (13440-1852)
PHONE..............................315 339-2331
Gary F Brockett, *President*
Terry L Crawford, *Vice Pres*
▲ EMP: 30
SQ FT: 18,000
SALES (est): 5.5MM **Privately Held**
WEB: www.coldpointcorp.com
SIC: 3585 Refrigeration & heating equipment

(G-13848)

ENVIROMASTER INTERNATIONAL LLC
Also Called: E M I
5780 Success Dr (13440-1769)
P.O. Box 4729, Utica (13504-4729)
PHONE..............................315 336-3716
Joe Hughes, *Engineer*
Earl C Reed,
Timothy Reed,
▲ EMP: 100
SQ FT: 52,000
SALES (est): 11.5MM
SALES (corp-wide): 107.2MM **Privately Held**
WEB: www.ecrinternational.com
SIC: 3585 Heating & air conditioning combination units
PA: Ecr International, Inc.
2201 Dwyer Ave
Utica NY 13501
315 797-1310

(G-13849)

GOODRICH CORPORATION
104 Otis St (13441-4714)
PHONE..............................315 838-1200
Jeff Meredith, *Managing Prtnr*
Steve Croke, *Vice Pres*
Mike Duffy, *Engineer*
Russ Ertley, *Engineer*
Frank Kucerak, *Engineer*
EMP: 200
SALES (corp-wide): 66.5B **Publicly Held**
WEB: www.bfgoodrich.com
SIC: 3728 Aircraft assemblies, subassemblies & parts
HQ: Goodrich Corporation
2730 W Tyvola Rd 4
Charlotte NC 28217
704 423-7000

(G-13850)

HCI ENGINEERING
5880 Bartlett Rd (13440-1111)
PHONE..............................315 336-3450
Jim Carrol, *General Mgr*
James Carroll, *Engineer*
Staurt Hatzinder, *Manager*
EMP: 3
SALES: 1MM **Privately Held**
SIC: 3829 Measuring & controlling devices

(G-13851)

HUBBARD TOOL AND DIE CORP
Rome Indus Ctr Bldg 5 (13440)
PHONE..............................315 337-7840
Eric Hubbard, *President*
Randall Hubbard, *Treasurer*
EMP: 22 EST: 1957
SQ FT: 12,000
SALES: 3MM **Privately Held**
SIC: 3599 3545 Machine shop, jobbing & repair; precision tools, machinists'

(G-13852)

J DAVIS MANUFACTURING CO INC
Also Called: R-Tronics
222 Erie Blvd E (13440-6814)
PHONE..............................315 337-7574
Lucille Kroeger, *CEO*
Rocco Garro, *Exec VP*
EMP: 20
SQ FT: 8,000

SALES (est): 4.5MM **Privately Held**
WEB: www.r-tronics.com
SIC: 3496 Cable, uninsulated wire: made from purchased wire

(G-13853)

KRIS-TECH WIRE COMPANY INC (PA)
80 Otis St (13441-4712)
P.O. Box 4377 (13442-4377)
PHONE..............................315 339-5268
Jon C Brodock, *CEO*
Cheryl Ingersoll, *COO*
Jim Darling, *Vice Pres*
Dave Hughes, *Engineer*
Laura Lake, *Engineer*
▲ EMP: 37
SQ FT: 50,000
SALES (est): 17.3MM **Privately Held**
WEB: www.kristechwire.com
SIC: 3357 Appliance fixture wire, nonferrous

(G-13854)

LEONARD BUS SALES INC
730 Ellsworth Rd (13441-4309)
PHONE..............................607 467-3100
Mike Leonard, *President*
EMP: 6
SALES (corp-wide): 40.5MM **Privately Held**
SIC: 3711 5012 Buses, all types, assembly of; buses
PA: Leonard Bus Sales, Inc.
4 Leonard Way
Deposit NY 13754
607 467-3100

(G-13855)

MCINTOSH BOX & PALLET CO INC
200 6th St (13440-6069)
PHONE..............................315 446-9350
Dan Balitz, *Manager*
EMP: 26
SALES (corp-wide): 38.4MM **Privately Held**
WEB: www.mcintoshbox.com
SIC: 2499 2448 2441 5085 Spools, wood; wood pallets & skids; nailed wood boxes & shook; bins & containers, storage
PA: Mcintosh Box & Pallet Co., Inc.
5864 Pyle Dr
East Syracuse NY 13057
315 446-9350

(G-13856)

MGS MANUFACTURING INC (PA)
Also Called: Mgs Group, The
122 Otis St (13441-4714)
P.O. Box 4259 (13442-4259)
PHONE..............................315 337-3350
Robert Johnson, *Ch of Bd*
Scott Stephan, *COO*
William Gurecki, *Vice Pres*
Brian Johnson, *Safety Mgr*
Bob Sandore, *Engineer*
▲ EMP: 50 EST: 1957
SQ FT: 20,000
SALES (est): 18MM **Privately Held**
SIC: 3549 Wiredrawing & fabricating machinery & equipment, ex. die

(G-13857)

MSI-MOLDING SOLUTIONS INC
6247 State Route 233 (13440-1037)
PHONE..............................315 736-2412
Frank Giotto, *Ch of Bd*
Thomas Bashant, *President*
Cindy Waterman, *Production*
Wayne Panther, *Manager*
▲ EMP: 20
SALES: 2.8MM
SALES (corp-wide): 108.1MM **Privately Held**
SIC: 3089 Molding primary plastic
PA: Fiber Instrument Sales, Inc.
161 Clear Rd
Oriskany NY 13424
315 736-2206

(G-13858)

NASH METALWARE CO INC
Also Called: American Metal
200 Railroad St (13440-6951)
P.O. Box 59 (13442-0059)
PHONE..............................315 339-5794
Donald Beebe, *Manager*
EMP: 11
SALES (corp-wide): 12.5MM **Privately Held**
SIC: 3469 5719 Household cooking & kitchen utensils, metal; kitchenware
PA: Nash Metalware Co Inc
72 N 15th St
Brooklyn NY 11222
718 384-1500

(G-13859)

NCI GROUP INC
Metal Building Components Mbci
6168 State Route 233 (13440-1033)
P.O. Box 4141 (13442-4141)
PHONE..............................315 339-1245
Chuck Glady, *Branch Mgr*
EMP: 100
SALES (corp-wide): 2B **Publicly Held**
SIC: 3448 3444 3441 Buildings, portable: prefabricated metal; prefabricated metal components; sheet metalwork; fabricated structural metal
HQ: Nci Group, Inc.
10943 N Sam Huston Pkwy W
Houston TX 77064
281 897-7788

(G-13860)

NORAS CANDY SHOP
Also Called: Candy Land
321 N Doxtator St (13440-3121)
PHONE..............................315 337-4530
Spiro Haritatos, *Owner*
EMP: 14
SALES (est): 1.2MM **Privately Held**
SIC: 2064 5441 2066 Candy & other confectionery products; candy; chocolate & cocoa products

(G-13861)

NORTEK POWDER COATING LLC
5900 Success Dr (13440-1743)
PHONE..............................315 337-2339
Borin Chea, *Mng Member*
Borin Keith,
◆ EMP: 16
SALES: 3.2MM **Privately Held**
SIC: 2851 Paints & allied products

(G-13862)

OMEGA WIRE INC
900 Railroad St (13440-6900)
PHONE..............................315 337-4300
James A Spargo IV, *Manager*
EMP: 50
SQ FT: 50,980
SALES (corp-wide): 2.9B **Privately Held**
WEB: www.omegawire.com
SIC: 3366 Copper foundries
HQ: Omega Wire, Inc.
12 Masonic Ave
Camden NY 13316
315 245-3800

(G-13863)

PERATON INC
474 Phoenix Dr (13441-4911)
PHONE..............................315 838-7000
Vic Choo, *Branch Mgr*
EMP: 40
SALES (corp-wide): 1B **Privately Held**
WEB: www.ittind.com
SIC: 3625 Control equipment, electric
HQ: Peraton Inc.
12975 Worldgate Dr # 100
Herndon VA 20170
703 668-6000

(G-13864)

PROFESSIONAL TECHNOLOGY INC
Also Called: Professional Technologies
5433 Lowell Rd (13440-7815)
PHONE..............................315 337-4156
John Puleo, *President*
EMP: 5

SALES (est): 540K **Privately Held**
SIC: 3651 1731 Speaker systems; communications specialization

(G-13865)
R&S STEEL LLC
412 Canal St (13440-6835)
PHONE..............................315 281-0123
Paul Raulli, *Mng Member*
Richie T Raulli,
Thomas Raulli,
EMP: 21
SQ FT: 5,600
SALES (est): 4.3MM **Privately Held**
SIC: 3441 Building components, structural steel

(G-13866)
RAULLI IRON WORKS INC
133 Mill St (13440-6945)
PHONE..............................315 337-8070
Agostino Raulli, *President*
Mark Raulli, *Vice Pres*
EMP: 10 EST: 1938
SQ FT: 3,600
SALES: 900K **Privately Held**
WEB:
www.raulliandsonsincornamental.com
SIC: 3446 Ornamental metalwork

(G-13867)
RENMATIX INC
679 Ellsworth Rd (13441-4809)
PHONE..............................315 356-4780
EMP: 7
SALES (corp-wide): 11.7MM **Privately Held**
SIC: 2836 Biological products, except diagnostic
PA: Renmatix, Inc.
660 Allendale Rd
King Of Prussia PA 19406
484 751-4000

(G-13868)
ROME MAIN STREET ALLIANCE INC
506 N James St (13440-4216)
PHONE..............................315 271-8356
EMP: 6
SALES: 48.4K **Privately Held**
SIC: 2711 Newspapers, publishing & printing

(G-13869)
ROME SIGN & DISPLAY CO
510 Erie Blvd W (13440-4806)
PHONE..............................315 336-0550
Randall Denton, *President*
Anna Johnson, *Business Mgr*
Terrance Denton, *Vice Pres*
EMP: 7
SQ FT: 1,000
SALES (est): 917.3K **Privately Held**
SIC: 3993 Signs, not made in custom sign painting shops

(G-13870)
ROME SPECIALTY COMPANY INC
Also Called: Rosco Div
501 W Embargo St (13440-4061)
P.O. Box 109 (13442-0109)
PHONE..............................315 337-8200
Judith Kiernan, *President*
◆ EMP: 20
SQ FT: 35,000
SALES (est): 2.2MM **Privately Held**
WEB: www.roscoinc.com
SIC: 3949 Fishing equipment

(G-13871)
RTD MANUFACTURING INC
6273 State Route 233 (13440-1037)
PHONE..............................315 337-3151
Brian P Getbehead, *President*
Robert Getbehead, *Vice Pres*
Sandra Vanslyke, *Manager*
Iva S Getbehead, *Admin Sec*
EMP: 7
SQ FT: 3,500
SALES: 700K **Privately Held**
WEB: www.rtdmfg.com
SIC: 3599 3541 3531 Machine shop, jobbing & repair; boring mills; crushers, grinders & similar equipment

(G-13872)
SERWAY BROS INC (PA)
Also Called: Serway Cabinet Trends
Plant 2 Rome Indus Ctr (13440)
PHONE..............................315 337-0601
Christine N Serway, *Ch of Bd*
James Pacific, *Director*
Sophia Pelose, *Admin Sec*
EMP: 8 EST: 1946
SQ FT: 20,800
SALES (est): 1.7MM **Privately Held**
WEB: www.serway.com
SIC: 2541 5211 3648 5719 Counters or counter display cases, wood; cabinets, kitchen; lighting fixtures, except electric: residential; lighting fixtures; wood kitchen cabinets

(G-13873)
TIPS & DIES INC
505 Rome Industrial Park (13440-6948)
PHONE..............................315 337-4161
Randall Hubbard, *President*
Jim Milliman, *Engineer*
Gary Johnson, *Sales Staff*
Larry Derrick, *Technical Staff*
EMP: 12
SALES: 2.3MM **Privately Held**
WEB: www.tipsanddies.com
SIC: 3544 Special dies & tools

(G-13874)
TONYS ORNAMENTAL IR WORKS INC
6757 Martin St (13440-7106)
P.O. Box 4425 (13442-4425)
PHONE..............................315 337-3730
EMP: 20
SQ FT: 13,800
SALES (est): 3.4MM **Privately Held**
SIC: 3449 3446 Mfg Misc Structural Metalwork Mfg Architectural Metalwork

(G-13875)
UTC AEROSPACE SYSTEMS
104 Otis St (13441-4714)
PHONE..............................315 838-1200
Frank Kucerak, *Principal*
Daniel Sweet, *Materials Mgr*
Paul Delorenzo, *Engineer*
Kyle Johnson, *Engineer*
David O'Hern, *Engineer*
EMP: 24
SALES (est): 3.8MM **Privately Held**
SIC: 3728 Aircraft parts & equipment

(G-13876)
VARFLEX CORPORATION
512 W Court St (13440-4000)
P.O. Box 551 (13442-0551)
PHONE..............................315 336-4400
Daniel J Burgdorf, *President*
William L Griffin, *Vice Pres*
Charles J Schoff, *Treasurer*
Charles Schoff, *Human Res Mgr*
Larry Snow, *Manager*
▲ EMP: 150 EST: 1924
SQ FT: 144,000
SALES (est): 12.1MM **Privately Held**
WEB: www.varflex.com
SIC: 3644 Insulators & insulation materials, electrical

(G-13877)
WORTHINGTON INDUSTRIES INC
530 Henry St (13440-5639)
PHONE..............................315 336-5500
Roger Pratt, *Plant Mgr*
Jerry Tomassi, *Safety Mgr*
EMP: 72
SALES (corp-wide): 3.7B **Publicly Held**
SIC: 3316 Strip steel, cold-rolled: from purchased hot-rolled
PA: Worthington Industries, Inc.
200 W Wilson Bridge Rd
Worthington OH 43085
614 438-3210

Romulus
Seneca County

(G-13878)
COBBLESTONE FRM WINERY VINYRD
5102 State Route 89 (14541-9779)
PHONE..............................315 549-1004
Jennifer Clark, *Principal*
EMP: 10
SALES (est): 822K **Privately Held**
SIC: 2084 Wines

(G-13879)
SCHRADER MEAT MARKET
1937 Summerville Rd (14541-9800)
PHONE..............................607 869-6328
Keith Schrader, *Owner*
EMP: 19
SALES: 600K **Privately Held**
SIC: 3421 2013 Table & food cutlery, including butchers'; sausages & other prepared meats

(G-13880)
SOUTH SENECA VINYL LLC
1585 Yale Farm Rd (14541-9761)
PHONE..............................315 585-6050
Nelson Sensenig,
EMP: 9
SQ FT: 5,000
SALES (est): 1.2MM **Privately Held**
SIC: 3211 Window glass, clear & colored

(G-13881)
SWEDISH HILL VINEYARD INC
Also Called: Swedish Hill Winery
4565 State Route 414 (14541-9769)
PHONE..............................607 403-0029
David Peterson, *CEO*
Richard Peterson, *President*
Cynthia Peterson, *Vice Pres*
Tracy Harris, *Safety Mgr*
Derek Wilber, *Manager*
EMP: 70
SALES: 6MM **Privately Held**
SIC: 2084 0721 Wines; vines, cultivation of

Ronkonkoma
Suffolk County

(G-13882)
A A TECHNOLOGY INC
101 Trade Zone Dr (11779-7363)
PHONE..............................631 913-0400
Henry Tang, *CEO*
Frank Rosselli, *Vice Pres*
James Stapleton, *Vice Pres*
Chris Leone, *Info Tech Mgr*
Ray Lin,
◆ EMP: 85
SQ FT: 15,700
SALES (est): 8.6MM **Privately Held**
SIC: 3672 Printed circuit boards

(G-13883)
A FIRE INC
23 Parr Dr (11779-3019)
PHONE..............................631 897-9449
EMP: 8
SALES (est): 708.2K **Privately Held**
SIC: 3999 Manufacturing industries

(G-13884)
ACCELA INC
100 Comac St Ste 2 (11779-6928)
PHONE..............................631 563-5005
Daryl Blowes, *General Mgr*
EMP: 10 **Privately Held**
SIC: 7372 Prepackaged software
PA: Accela, Inc.
2633 Camino Ramon Ste 500
San Ramon CA 94583

(G-13885)
ACCENT LABEL & TAG CO INC (PA)
348 Woodlawn Ave (11779-5055)
PHONE..............................631 244-7066

Larry Gutman, *President*
EMP: 6
SALES (est): 592.2K **Privately Held**
WEB: www.accentlabelandtag.com
SIC: 2679 7336 Labels, paper: made from purchased material; graphic arts & related design

(G-13886)
ACE CANVAS & TENT CORP
155 Raynor Ave (11779-6666)
PHONE..............................631 981-9705
Vincent Cardillo, *Vice Pres*
▲ EMP: 10
SQ FT: 5,500
SALES (est): 1.5MM **Privately Held**
SIC: 3081 2394 7359 Vinyl film & sheet; canvas & related products; tent & tarpaulin rental

(G-13887)
ACME INDUSTRIES OF W BABYLON
125 Gary Way Ste 2 (11779-6576)
PHONE..............................631 737-5231
John Landrio, *President*
EMP: 10
SQ FT: 3,000
SALES (est): 1.8MM **Privately Held**
SIC: 3599 7389 Machine shop, jobbing & repair; grinding, precision: commercial or industrial

(G-13888)
ADAPTIVE MFG TECH INC
Also Called: Quickpouch Packaging Automtn
181 Remington Blvd (11779-6911)
PHONE..............................631 580-5400
Terence Larocca, *CEO*
Timothy Ford, *Accounts Exec*
EMP: 32
SQ FT: 18,000
SALES (est): 7.4MM **Privately Held**
WEB: www.amtautomation.com
SIC: 3542 3599 Machine tools, metal forming type; custom machinery

(G-13889)
ADVANCE MICRO POWER CORP
2190 Smithtown Ave (11779-7355)
PHONE..............................631 471-6157
Jasbir Mahajan, *President*
▲ EMP: 15
SQ FT: 14,000
SALES (est): 1.6MM **Privately Held**
SIC: 3672 Printed circuit boards

(G-13890)
ADVANCED MANUFACTURING SVC INC
100 13th Ave Ste 2 (11779-6820)
PHONE..............................631 676-5210
John Nucatola, *President*
EMP: 28
SALES (est): 6.5MM **Privately Held**
SIC: 3672 Printed circuit boards

(G-13891)
ADVANCED PHOTONICS INC
151 Trade Zone Dr (11779-7384)
PHONE..............................631 471-3693
Robert Turner, *President*
Richard Turner, *Vice Pres*
Jack Raybin, *CFO*
EMP: 14
SQ FT: 5,000
SALES: 1.4MM **Privately Held**
WEB: www.advancedphotonicsusa.com
SIC: 3699 5084 Laser systems & equipment; industrial machinery & equipment

(G-13892)
AERO-DATA METAL CRAFTERS INC
2085 5th Ave (11779-6903)
PHONE..............................631 471-7733
Robert De Luca, *President*
William Mabanta, *Vice Pres*
David Rubinstein, *Project Mgr*
Coryn Skolnick, *Project Mgr*
Chris Behr, *Purch Agent*
▼ EMP: 110
SQ FT: 100,000

▲ = Import ▼=Export
◆ =Import/Export

SALES (est): 23.1MM **Privately Held**
WEB: www.metal-crafters.com
SIC: 3444 3446 3443 3441 Sheet metal specialties, not stamped; architectural metalwork; fabricated plate work (boiler shop); fabricated structural metal; cold finishing of steel shapes

(G-13893)
AIR CRAFTERS INC
2085 5th Ave (11779-6903)
PHONE..................................631 471-7788
Robert Deluca, *President*
Michael Hennessey, *Vice Pres*
Chris Behr, *Purchasing*
William Mabanta, *Admin Sec*
EMP: 105
SQ FT: 40,000
SALES: 12MM **Privately Held**
WEB: www.air-crafters.com
SIC: 2542 5085 3625 3564 Fixtures, office: except wood; clean room supplies; relays & industrial controls; blowers & fans

(G-13894)
AIRGLE CORPORATION
711 Koehler Ave Ste 3 (11779-7410)
PHONE..................................866 501-7750
Yang Lo, *President*
Mike Anderson, *Vice Pres*
▲ **EMP:** 20 **EST:** 2006
SQ FT: 7,300
SALES (est): 202.9K **Privately Held**
SIC: 3589 3564 Water purification equipment, household type; air purification equipment

(G-13895)
AKSHAR EXTRACTS INC
59 Remington Blvd (11779-6954)
PHONE..................................631 588-9727
▲ **EMP:** 5
SQ FT: 3,000
SALES: 500K **Privately Held**
SIC: 2836 Mfg Biological Products

(G-13896)
ALKEN INDUSTRIES INC
2175 5th Ave (11779-6217)
PHONE..................................631 467-2000
Tami Senior, *President*
Anthony Landisi, *President*
Paul Neave, *General Mgr*
Emanuel Dumont, *Vice Pres*
Bridgette Senior, *Vice Pres*
EMP: 40
SQ FT: 33,000
SALES (est): 16.7MM **Privately Held**
WEB: www.alkenind.com
SIC: 3728 3441 Aircraft parts & equipment; fabricated structural metal

(G-13897)
ALL PACKAGING MCHY & SUPS CORP
90 13th Ave Unit 11 (11779-6818)
PHONE..................................631 588-7310
Albert Bolla, *President*
Joel Busel, *Vice Pres*
Samul Posner, *Vice Pres*
EMP: 10
SQ FT: 10,000
SALES: 2.7MM
SALES (corp-wide): 2.5MM **Privately Held**
WEB: www.triopackaging.com
SIC: 3565 Packaging machinery
PA: Trio Packaging Corp.
200 Trade Zone Dr Unit 1
Ronkonkoma NY 11779
631 588-0800

(G-13898)
ALLIANT TCHSYSTEMS OPRTONS LLC
77 Raynor Ave (11779-6649)
PHONE..................................631 737-6100
Robert Bakos, *Vice Pres*
EMP: 20 **Publicly Held**
WEB: www.mrcwdc.com
SIC: 3721 Research & development on aircraft by the manufacturer
HQ: Alliant Techsystems Operations Llc
4700 Nathan Ln N
Plymouth MN 55305

(G-13899)
ALLURE METAL WORKS INC
71 Hoffman Ln (11749-5007)
PHONE..................................631 588-0220
Jillian Guido, *Principal*
EMP: 10
SALES (est): 1.5MM **Privately Held**
SIC: 3444 1711 Sheet metalwork; plumbing, heating, air-conditioning contractors

(G-13900)
ALROD ASSOCIATES INC
710 Union Pkwy Ste 9 (11779-7428)
PHONE..................................631 981-2193
Evan Alrod, *President*
EMP: 10
SQ FT: 6,000
SALES (est): 1.1MM **Privately Held**
SIC: 2541 2542 5046 Store fixtures, wood; fixtures, store: except wood; store fixtures

(G-13901)
ALTAQUIP LLC
200 13th Ave Unit 6 (11779-6815)
PHONE..................................631 580-4740
EMP: 8
SALES (corp-wide): 194.6B **Publicly Held**
SIC: 3699 Mfg Electrical Equipment/Supplies
HQ: Altaquip Llc
100 Production Dr
Harrison OH 45030
513 674-6464

(G-13902)
AMERICAN BOTTLING COMPANY
Also Called: Snapple Distributors
2004 Orville Dr N (11779-7645)
PHONE..................................516 714-0002
Ray Russo, *Manager*
EMP: 19 **Publicly Held**
SIC: 2086 Bottled & canned soft drinks
HQ: The American Bottling Company
5301 Legacy Dr
Plano TX 75024

(G-13903)
AMERICAN QUALITY EMBROIDERY (PA)
740 Koehler Ave (11779-7406)
PHONE..................................631 467-3200
Robert Kalinowski, *President*
EMP: 1
SQ FT: 1,600
SALES (est): 17.8MM **Privately Held**
SIC: 2284 2395 Embroidery thread; embroidery products, except schiffli machine

(G-13904)
AMETEK INC
903 S 2nd St (11779-7201)
PHONE..................................631 467-8400
EMP: 6
SALES (corp-wide): 4.8B **Publicly Held**
SIC: 3621 Motors & generators
PA: Ametek, Inc.
1100 Cassatt Rd
Berwyn PA 19312
610 647-2121

(G-13905)
AMETEK CTS US INC (PA)
903 S 2nd St (11779-7201)
PHONE..................................631 467-8400
Mark Swanson, *President*
EMP: 25 **EST:** 1953
SQ FT: 10,600
SALES (est): 5.5MM **Privately Held**
WEB: www.ifi.com
SIC: 3663 Amplifiers, RF power & IF

(G-13906)
AMP NUTRACEUTICALS INC
2130 Pond Rd Ste H (11779-7239)
PHONE..................................631 676-5537
EMP: 6 **EST:** 2017
SALES (est): 108.9K **Privately Held**
SIC: 2834 Medicines, capsuled or ampuled

(G-13907)
AMRON ELECTRONICS INC
160 Gary Way (11779-6509)
PHONE..................................631 737-1234
Rick Foora, *CEO*
EMP: 50
SALES (est): 2.7MM **Privately Held**
SIC: 3679 Commutators, electronic

(G-13908)
APOLLO DISPLAY TECH CORP (PA)
87 Raynor Ave Ste 1 (11779-6667)
PHONE..................................631 580-4360
Bernhard Staller, *President*
Chimei Innolux, *Partner*
Joanne Sottile, *Senior VP*
Matthew Evko, *Marketing Staff*
Scott Makboulia, *Technology*
◆ **EMP:** 35
SQ FT: 15,000
SALES (est): 5.8MM **Privately Held**
WEB: www.apollodisplays.com
SIC: 3679 5065 Liquid crystal displays (LCD); electronic parts & equipment

(G-13909)
ARTISAN MACHINING INC
49 Remington Blvd (11779-6909)
PHONE..................................631 589-1416
John Caccavale, *President*
EMP: 7
SALES (est): 800K **Privately Held**
WEB: www.artisanmachining.com
SIC: 3599 Machine shop, jobbing & repair

(G-13910)
AZTEC INDUSTRIES INC
200 13th Ave Unit 5 (11779-6815)
PHONE..................................631 585-1331
Phil Del Giudice, *President*
EMP: 6
SQ FT: 2,500
SALES (est): 500K **Privately Held**
SIC: 2522 Panel systems & partitions, office: except wood

(G-13911)
B & B PRECISION COMPONENTS INC
301 Christopher St # 303 (11779-6922)
PHONE..................................631 273-3321
Lucille Bricker, *President*
EMP: 5 **EST:** 1966
SQ FT: 12,000
SALES (est): 1.6MM **Privately Held**
WEB: www.bbprecisioncomponents.com
SIC: 3728 Aircraft parts & equipment

(G-13912)
B H AIRCRAFT COMPANY INC (PA)
2230 Smithtown Ave (11779-7329)
PHONE..................................631 580-9747
Vincent E Kearns, *Ch of Bd*
Daniel Kearns, *President*
Sebastian F Digiacomo, *Principal*
Dan Fugua, *Principal*
Paul Goggi, *Principal*
EMP: 90 **EST:** 1933
SQ FT: 100,000
SALES (est): 14.7MM **Privately Held**
WEB: www.bhaircraft.com
SIC: 3724 Aircraft engines & engine parts

(G-13913)
BANNER METALCRAFT INC
300 Trade Zone Dr (11779-7345)
PHONE..................................631 563-7303
Kenneth R Bednar, *President*
Nancy E Bednar, *Corp Secy*
Richard Martin, *Foreman/Supr*
Kurt Butcher, *Engineer*
Linda Herzing, *Office Mgr*
EMP: 70
SQ FT: 32,000
SALES: 12.1MM **Privately Held**
WEB: www.bannermetalcraft.com
SIC: 3444 Sheet metal specialties, not stamped

(G-13914)
BCM ELECTRONICS MANUF SERVICES
3279 Veterans Memorial (11779-7673)
PHONE..................................631 580-9516
K Linden, *Principal*
EMP: 7
SALES (est): 1MM **Privately Held**
SIC: 3672 Printed circuit boards

(G-13915)
BECKER ELECTRONICS INC
50 Alexander Ct Ste 2 (11779-6568)
PHONE..................................631 619-9100
David M Sosnow, *CEO*
Sharon Becker, *Vice Pres*
Patrick Spagnuolo, *Treasurer*
EMP: 80
SQ FT: 14,000
SALES (est): 12MM **Privately Held**
WEB: www.beckerelectronicsinc.com
SIC: 3679 5065 Harness assemblies for electronic use: wire or cable; electronic parts & equipment

(G-13916)
BETATRONIX INC
125 Comac St (11779-6931)
PHONE..................................631 582-6740
Wayne Demmons, *Vice Pres*
Andrew Hansen, *Engineer*
▼ **EMP:** 30
SALES (est): 5.4MM **Privately Held**
SIC: 3823 Industrial instrmnts msrmnt display/control process variable

(G-13917)
BOBLEY-HARMANN CORPORATION
Also Called: Gift Valleys.com
200 Trade Zone Dr Unit 2 (11779-7359)
PHONE..................................516 433-3800
Mark Bobley, *President*
▲ **EMP:** 8
SQ FT: 500
SALES (est): 912.1K **Privately Held**
WEB: www.bobley.com
SIC: 2731 2759 Book publishing; promotional printing

(G-13918)
BROADWAY NEON SIGN CORP
Also Called: Broadway National
1900 Ocean Ave (11779-6520)
PHONE..................................908 241-4177
William Paparella, *President*
EMP: 18
SQ FT: 50,000
SALES (est): 3MM **Privately Held**
WEB: www.broadwaynational.com
SIC: 3993 3444 2431 2394 Neon signs; sheet metalwork; millwork; canvas & related products

(G-13919)
C TO C DESIGN & PRINT INC
1850 Pond Rd Unit B (11779-7210)
PHONE..................................631 885-4020
Anthony Aceto, *Ch of Bd*
EMP: 10
SALES (est): 1.3MM **Privately Held**
SIC: 2752 Commercial printing, lithographic

(G-13920)
CALCHEM CORPORATION (PA)
2001 Ocean Ave (11779-6500)
P.O. Box 4258, Huntington (11743-0777)
PHONE..................................631 423-5696
John H Chen, *President*
Molly Chen, *Exec VP*
▲ **EMP:** 7
SQ FT: 12,000
SALES (est): 1.9MM **Privately Held**
WEB: www.calchemcorp.com
SIC: 2893 Printing ink

(G-13921)
CANFIELD AEROSPACE & MAR INC
90 Remington Blvd (11779-6910)
PHONE..................................631 648-1050
EMP: 20 **EST:** 2000
SALES (est): 1.2MM **Privately Held**
SIC: 3728 Mfg Aircraft Parts/Equipment

(G-13922)
CAROLINA PRECISION PLAS LLC
Also Called: Cpp Global
115 Comac St (11779-6931)
PHONE..................................631 981-0743
EMP: 94
SALES (corp-wide): 60.9MM **Privately Held**
SIC: 3089 Injection molding of plastics
PA: Carolina Precision Plastics Llc
405 Commerce Pl
Asheboro NC 27203
336 498-2654

(G-13923)
CEDAR GRAPHICS INC
1700 Ocean Ave Ste 1 (11779-6582)
PHONE..................................631 467-1444
Robert Kashan, CEO
Dennis Ganzak, Chairman
Frank Detomasso, Manager
EMP: 57
SALES (est): 9.9MM **Privately Held**
SIC: 2752 Commercial printing, offset

(G-13924)
CEDAR WEST INC (PA)
1700 Ocean Ave Ste 1 (11779-6570)
PHONE..................................631 467-1444
Joanne D Herman, President
Michael Clark, Vice Pres
Robert Herman, Vice Pres
Gloria J Smalley, CFO
EMP: 56
SALES (est): 6.3MM **Privately Held**
WEB: www.cedarwest.com
SIC: 2752 Commercial printing, offset

(G-13925)
COPY X/PRESS LTD
Also Called: Ocean Printing
700 Union Pkwy Ste 5 (11779-7427)
PHONE..................................631 585-2200
John Harkins, President
David Milano, Vice Pres
John Berhalter, Plant Mgr
Terri Bligh, Bookkeeper
EMP: 63
SQ FT: 30,000
SALES (est): 8.8MM **Privately Held**
WEB: www.oceanprinting.com
SIC: 2759 Commercial printing

(G-13926)
CORNING RUBBER COMPANY INC
Also Called: Corning Wax
1744 Julia Goldbach Ave (11779-6413)
PHONE..................................631 738-0041
Robert Schiemel, President
Claudio Acquafredda, Vice Pres
▲ EMP: 14
SQ FT: 10,000
SALES: 1.2MM **Privately Held**
WEB: www.corningwax.com
SIC: 3843 Wax, dental

(G-13927)
CRYSTALONICS INC
2805 Veterans Mem Hwy 14 (11779-7680)
PHONE..................................631 981-6140
Paul Weinstein, President
Brian Gomes, Treasurer
Joseph Plescia, Treasurer
EMP: 12
SQ FT: 14,000
SALES (est): 1.6MM **Privately Held**
WEB: www.crystalonics.com
SIC: 3674 Hybrid integrated circuits

(G-13928)
CRYSTALONICS OF NEW YORK INC
2805 Vets Memorial (11779)
PHONE..................................631 981-6140
Paul Weinstein, President
David Weinstein, Vice Pres
EMP: 12
SQ FT: 3,000
SALES (est): 948.3K **Privately Held**
SIC: 3674 Semiconductors & related devices

(G-13929)
DAK MICA AND WOOD PRODUCTS
Also Called: Coronet Kitchen & Bath
2147 5th Ave (11779-6908)
PHONE..................................631 467-0749
David Kaplan, President
EMP: 5
SQ FT: 5,800
SALES: 1MM **Privately Held**
SIC: 2434 5031 1751 Wood kitchen cabinets; kitchen cabinets; cabinet & finish carpentry

(G-13930)
DELLA SYSTEMS INC
951 S 2nd St (11779-7203)
PHONE..................................631 580-0010
John Della Croce, President
Mike Walsh, Engineer
EMP: 14
SQ FT: 3,000
SALES (est): 2.5MM **Privately Held**
WEB: www.dellasystems.com
SIC: 3672 8711 Printed circuit boards; engineering services

(G-13931)
DYNAMIC LABORATORIES INC
Also Called: Dynamic Labs
30 Haynes Ct (11779-7220)
PHONE..................................631 231-7474
David Beauchamp, President
Steven Zwerman, Vice Pres
▲ EMP: 38
SQ FT: 18,000
SALES (est): 9.5MM **Privately Held**
SIC: 3827 5049 Optical instruments & lenses; optical goods

(G-13932)
EAST/WEST INDUSTRIES INC
Also Called: Ew
2002 Orville Dr N (11779-7661)
PHONE..................................631 981-5900
Teresa Ferraro, President
Mary Spinosa, Corp Secy
Joseph Spinosa, Vice Pres
Anthony Coker, Mfg Staff
David Guterman, Purchasing
EMP: 45
SQ FT: 38,000
SALES (est): 10.1MM **Privately Held**
WEB: www.eastwestindustries.com
SIC: 3728 2531 Seat ejector devices, aircraft; oxygen systems, aircraft; seats, aircraft

(G-13933)
EASTERN STOREFRONTS & MTLS INC
1739 Julia Goldbach Ave (11779-6412)
P.O. Box 431, Bohemia (11716-0431)
PHONE..................................631 471-7065
Timothy Dittmeier, Ch of Bd
EMP: 14
SALES (est): 2.3MM **Privately Held**
SIC: 3442 Store fronts, prefabricated, metal

(G-13934)
ELEMENTAR AMERICAS INC
119 Comac St (11779-6931)
PHONE..................................856 787-0022
Georg Schick, President
Ken Slight, Vice Pres
EMP: 9
SQ FT: 2,100
SALES (est): 2.3MM **Privately Held**
WEB: www.elementar-inc.com
SIC: 3826 Protein analyzers, laboratory type

(G-13935)
ELITE STEEL FABRICATORS INC
2165 5th Ave (11779-6908)
PHONE..................................631 285-1008
Lucky Damiao, President
EMP: 7
SALES (est): 1.3MM **Privately Held**
SIC: 3441 1791 Fabricated structural metal; structural steel erection

(G-13936)
ES BETA INC
125 Comac St (11779-6931)
PHONE..................................631 582-6740
Wayne Demmons, Vice Pres
John Karcher, Controller
EMP: 36 EST: 1966
SALES (est): 2.3MM
SALES (corp-wide): 88.3MM **Privately Held**
SIC: 3677 Electronic coils, transformers & other inductors
PA: Electro Switch Business Trust
775 Pleasant St Ste 1
Weymouth MA 02189
781 335-1195

(G-13937)
EXECUTIVE MIRROR DOORS INC
1 Comac Loop Unit 7 (11779-6816)
PHONE..................................631 234-1090
Robert Cozzie, President
Carol Cozzie, Vice Pres
EMP: 7
SQ FT: 5,400
SALES (est): 799.2K **Privately Held**
WEB: www.executivemirror.com
SIC: 3231 5211 5085 Doors, glass: made from purchased glass; door & window products; industrial supplies

(G-13938)
FIRST IMPRESSIONS FINISHING
132 Remington Blvd (11779-6912)
PHONE..................................631 467-2244
Scott Shapiro, President
Laura Shapiro, Vice Pres
EMP: 6
SQ FT: 4,000
SALES (est): 351.9K **Privately Held**
SIC: 3471 Finishing, metals or formed products

(G-13939)
FORMATIX CORP (PA)
9 Colt Ct (11779-6949)
PHONE..................................631 467-3399
Radjesh Guptar, CEO
EMP: 20
SALES (est): 2.4MM **Privately Held**
SIC: 3089 Blister or bubble formed packaging, plastic

(G-13940)
FOUR PAWS PRODUCTS LTD
3125 Vtrans Mem Hwy Ste 1 (11779-7644)
PHONE..................................631 436-7421
Allen Simon, President
Barry Askin, Vice Pres
Ray Gallagher, CFO
▲ EMP: 85 EST: 1970
SQ FT: 50,000
SALES (est): 8.5MM
SALES (corp-wide): 2.2B **Publicly Held**
WEB: www.fourpaws.com
SIC: 3999 2844 Pet supplies; toilet preparations
PA: Central Garden & Pet Company
1340 Treat Blvd Ste 600
Walnut Creek CA 94597
925 948-4000

(G-13941)
GENERAL CUTTING INC
90 13th Ave Unit 10 (11779-6818)
PHONE..................................631 580-5011
Ralph Viteritti, President
EMP: 12
SQ FT: 8,000
SALES (est): 946K **Privately Held**
SIC: 3599 Machine shop, jobbing & repair

(G-13942)
GLIPTONE MANUFACTURING INC
Also Called: Camco
1740 Julia Goldbach Ave (11779-6409)
PHONE..................................631 285-7250
Rocco Caporaso Jr, President
▲ EMP: 10
SQ FT: 6,500

SALES (est): 1.9MM **Privately Held**
WEB: www.gliptone.com
SIC: 2842 Specialty cleaning preparations; automobile polish

(G-13943)
GLOBAL ENTITY MEDIA INC
2090 5th Ave Ste 2 (11779-6958)
PHONE..................................631 580-7772
Michael J Cutino, Principal
EMP: 5
SALES (est): 600.5K **Privately Held**
SIC: 2721 Periodicals: publishing only

(G-13944)
GOT POWER INC
5 Campus Ln (11779-1924)
PHONE..................................631 767-9493
Luis Duarte, Owner
EMP: 5
SALES: 100K **Privately Held**
SIC: 3621 Motors & generators

(G-13945)
H A GUDEN COMPANY INC
99 Raynor Ave (11779-6634)
PHONE..................................631 737-2900
Paul A Guden, President
Kirby D Moyers, Vice Pres
Paul Guden, Export Mgr
Carol Gumbrecht, Manager
Kirby Moyers, Executive
▲ EMP: 25
SQ FT: 20,000
SALES: 10.2MM **Privately Held**
SIC: 3429 5072 Manufactured hardware (general); hardware

(G-13946)
HASTINGS TILE & BATH INC (PA)
711 Koehler Ave Ste 8 (11779-7410)
PHONE..................................631 285-3330
Lee Kohrman, President
Michael Homola, President
Richard Kucera, Corp Secy
John Kamuda, Technical Mgr
Ryan Homola, Sales Staff
▲ EMP: 20
SQ FT: 36,000
SALES (est): 5.4MM **Privately Held**
WEB: www.hastingstilebath.com
SIC: 3253 Ceramic wall & floor tile

(G-13947)
IMPALA PRESS LTD
931 S 2nd St (11779-7203)
PHONE..................................631 588-4262
Peter Wolf, President
EMP: 8
SQ FT: 6,000
SALES (est): 1.2MM **Privately Held**
WEB: www.impalapress.com
SIC: 2752 Commercial printing, offset

(G-13948)
INGENIOUS DESIGNS LLC
Also Called: Idl
2060 9th Ave (11779-6253)
PHONE..................................631 254-3376
Joy Mangano, Ch of Bd
Ronni Fauci, Vice Pres
◆ EMP: 110
SQ FT: 63,000
SALES (est): 30.4MM **Publicly Held**
WEB: www.ingeniousdesigns.com
SIC: 2392 5199 3089 5099 Mops, floor & dust; broom, mop & paint handles; plastic containers, except foam; containers: glass, metal or plastic
HQ: Hsn, Inc.
1 Home Shopping Netwrk Dr
Saint Petersburg FL 33729

(G-13949)
ISLAND RESEARCH AND DEV CORP
Also Called: Island Technology
200 13th Ave Unit 12 (11779-6815)
PHONE..................................631 471-7100
Robert Guy Ward, President
Raquel Girardi, Technology
EMP: 75
SQ FT: 10,000

▲ = Import ▼=Export
◆ =Import/Export

SALES (est): 9.8MM Privately Held
WEB: www.islandresearch.net
SIC: 3679 Electronic circuits

(G-13950)
J F M SHEET METAL INC
2090 Pond Rd (11779-7216)
PHONE................................631 737-8494
Joseph Magri, President
Jeff Stern, Manager
EMP: 5
SALES: 450K Privately Held
SIC: 3441 Fabricated structural metal

(G-13951)
J R S PRECISION MACHINING
40 Raynor Ave Ste 2 (11779-6623)
PHONE................................631 737-1330
Scott Sopko, President
EMP: 8
SQ FT: 2,000
SALES (est): 891.7K Privately Held
SIC: 3599 Machine shop, jobbing & repair

(G-13952)
J&T METAL INC
38 Raynor Ave Ste 3 (11779-6618)
P.O. Box 380 (11779-0380)
PHONE................................631 471-5335
Theresa A Edrehi, Ch of Bd
EMP: 8
SALES (est): 1.1MM Privately Held
SIC: 3444 Sheet metalwork

(G-13953)
JAAB PRECISION INC
180 Gary Way (11779-6509)
PHONE................................631 218-3725
Joseph W Aloi, President
Josephine Blasso, Office Mgr
EMP: 9
SALES (est): 2.3MM Privately Held
SIC: 3441 Fabricated structural metal

(G-13954)
JET REDI MIX CONCRETE INC
Also Called: J E T
2101 Pond Rd Ste 1 (11779-7213)
PHONE................................631 580-3640
Steve Jensen, President
Harold Jensen, President
EMP: 14
SQ FT: 15,000
SALES (est): 2.2MM Privately Held
WEB: www.jetredimixconcrete.com
SIC: 3273 Ready-mixed concrete

(G-13955)
JMG FUEL INC
3 Fowler Ave (11779-4105)
PHONE................................631 579-4319
Brian Gauci, Principal
EMP: 6
SALES (est): 681.1K Privately Held
SIC: 2869 Fuels

(G-13956)
KELTRON ELECTRONICS (DE CORP)
Also Called: Keltron Connector Co.
3385 Vtrans Mem Hwy Ste E (11779-7660)
PHONE................................631 567-6300
David Levison, President
▲ EMP: 15
SALES (est): 2.1MM Privately Held
WEB: www.keltronconnectors.com
SIC: 3679 Electronic circuits

(G-13957)
KETCHAM MEDICINE CABINETS
3505 Vtrans Mem Hwy Ste L (11779-7613)
PHONE................................631 615-6151
Tracey Bonham, General Mgr
Gina Lacarrubba, Vice Pres
EMP: 25
SALES: 10MM Privately Held
SIC: 3431 Bathroom fixtures, including sinks

(G-13958)
KNF CLEAN ROOM PRODUCTS CORP
1800 Ocean Ave (11779-6532)
PHONE................................631 588-7000
Philip J Carcara, Ch of Bd

Al Shouga, Plant Mgr
Chris Marx, Manager
Kathy Stuerzel, Manager
Randy Ferdinand, Director
EMP: 50
SQ FT: 22,000
SALES (est): 9.1MM Privately Held
SIC: 3699 1541 3081 5085 Electrical
equipment & supplies; pharmaceutical
manufacturing plant construction; unsup-
ported plastics film & sheet; clean room
supplies

(G-13959)
KONDOR TECHNOLOGIES INC
206 Christopher St (11779-6921)
PHONE................................631 471-8832
Nils Youngwall, President
▲ EMP: 10
SQ FT: 3,500
SALES (est): 1.8MM Privately Held
SIC: 3599 Machine shop, jobbing & repair

(G-13960)
L W S INC
125 Gary Way Ste 1 (11779-6576)
PHONE................................631 580-0472
Leon Shapiro, President
EMP: 15
SQ FT: 3,000
SALES (est): 1.4MM Privately Held
SIC: 3471 Finishing, metals or formed
products; polishing, metals or formed
products

(G-13961)
LAB CRAFTERS INC
2085 5th Ave (11779-6903)
PHONE................................631 471-7755
Bob Deluca Sr, President
Robert Deluca, Principal
Edward Fiance, Principal
William Mabanta, Vice Pres
Coryn Skolnick, Project Mgr
EMP: 25
SQ FT: 90,000
SALES (est): 6.7MM Privately Held
SIC: 3821 5049 Laboratory equipment:
fume hoods, distillation racks, etc.; labo-
ratory equipment, except medical or den-
tal

(G-13962)
LAB-AIDS INC
17 Colt Ct (11779-6949)
PHONE................................631 737-1133
Morton Frank, President
David M Frank, President
Michelle Etheridge, Marketing Mgr
Rachel Porter, Marketing Staff
▲ EMP: 49 EST: 1963
SQ FT: 41,000
SALES (est): 8.1MM Privately Held
WEB: www.lab-aid.com
SIC: 3999 Education aids, devices & sup-
plies

(G-13963)
LAKELAND INDUSTRIES INC (PA)
3555 Vtrans Mem Hwy Ste C (11779-7636)
PHONE................................631 981-9700
A John Kreft, Ch of Bd
Christopher J Ryan, President
Charles D Roberson, COO
Daniel L Edwards, Senior VP
Teri W Hunt, CFO
▼ EMP: 195
SALES: 99MM Publicly Held
WEB: www.lakeland-ind.com
SIC: 3842 2389 Personal safety equip-
ment; clothing, fire resistant & protective;
gloves, safety; disposable garments & ac-
cessories

(G-13964)
LANCO CORPORATION
Also Called: Brijon
2905 Vtrans Mem Hwy Ste 3 (11779-7655)
PHONE................................631 231-2300
Brian Landow, President
Tom Kronberger, Regional Mgr
Mike Zimmerman, COO
Irwin Landow, Vice Pres
Dan Ventola, Vice Pres
◆ EMP: 250

SQ FT: 40,000
SALES (est): 48.5MM Privately Held
WEB: www.lancopromo.com
SIC: 3993 2066 5149 2064 Signs & advertising specialties; chocolate & cocoa
products; chocolate; candy & other confectionery products

(G-13965)
LANGER BIOMECHANICS INC
2905 Vtrans Mem Hwy Ste 2 (11779-7655)
PHONE................................800 645-5520
Bruce Marrison, CEO
Jason Kraus, President
Karen Strebel, Info Tech Mgr
EMP: 71
SALES (est): 9.3MM
SALES (corp-wide): 11MM Privately Held
SIC: 3842 Braces, orthopedic
PA: Orthotic Holdings, Inc.
2905 Veterans Mem Hwy
Ronkonkoma NY 11779
416 479-8609

(G-13966)
LINK CONTROL SYSTEMS INC
16 Colt Ct (11779-6948)
P.O. Box 1177 (11779-0588)
PHONE................................631 471-3950
William F Bowden, President
EMP: 15
SQ FT: 12,000
SALES (est): 3MM Privately Held
WEB: www.linkconsys.com
SIC: 3613 Control panels, electric

(G-13967)
LONG ISLAND BUSINESS NEWS
2150 Smithtown Ave Ste 7 (11779-7348)
PHONE................................631 737-1700
Jordan Zeigler, Partner
Scott Schoen, Vice Pres
EMP: 22 EST: 1953
SQ FT: 6,000
SALES (est): 1.5MM
SALES (corp-wide): 461MM Privately
Held
WEB: www.libn.com
SIC: 2711 Newspapers, publishing & print-
ing
HQ: Dolan Llc
222 S 9th St Ste 2300
Minneapolis MN 55402

(G-13968)
MAHARLIKA HOLDINGS LLC
Also Called: Atis Colojet
111 Trade Zone Ct Unit A (11779-7367)
PHONE................................631 319-6203
Erez Shoshoni, General Mgr
▲ EMP: 14
SALES: 3MM Privately Held
SIC: 3559 Chemical machinery & equip-
ment

(G-13969)
MANTEL & MANTEL STAMPING CORP
802 S 4th St (11779-7200)
PHONE................................631 467-1916
Edward Mantel, President
EMP: 8 EST: 1977
SQ FT: 7,500
SALES: 1MM Privately Held
SIC: 3544 3469 Special dies & tools;
metal stampings

(G-13970)
MARCOVICCI-WENZ ENGINEERING
33 Comac Loop Unit 10 (11779-6856)
PHONE................................631 467-9040
Ted Wenz, President
Peter Marcovicci, Vice Pres
EMP: 6
SQ FT: 4,000
SALES (est): 877.2K Privately Held
SIC: 3714 5531 3711 Motor vehicle en-
gines & parts; speed shops, including
race car supplies; automobile assembly,
including specialty automobiles

(G-13971)
MAYFAIR MACHINE COMPANY INC
128 Remington Blvd (11779-6912)
PHONE................................631 981-6644
EMP: 6
SQ FT: 1,500
SALES (est): 610K Privately Held
SIC: 3599 Machine Shop

(G-13972)
MEHR FOIL CORP
200 13th Ave Unit 10 (11779-6815)
PHONE................................631 648-9742
Tariq Mehr, President
EMP: 6
SALES: 600K Privately Held
SIC: 3089 3365 Cups, plastic, except
foam; cooking/kitchen utensils, cast alu-
minum

(G-13973)
MICRO PHOTO ACOUSTICS INC
105 Comac St (11779-6931)
PHONE................................631 750-6035
Xiaojie Zhao, President
EMP: 5
SALES (est): 738.9K Privately Held
SIC: 3826 Laser scientific & engineering
instruments
PA: Advanced Optowave Corporation
105 Comac St
Ronkonkoma NY 11779

(G-13974)
MIN-MAX MACHINE LTD
1971 Pond Rd (11779-7244)
PHONE................................631 585-4378
Randy Neubauer, Ch of Bd
Ralph Neubauer, Vice Pres
Rodney Neubauer, Treasurer
EMP: 18
SQ FT: 18,000
SALES: 4MM Privately Held
SIC: 3728 Aircraft assemblies, subassem-
blies & parts

(G-13975)
MINUTEMEN PRECSN MCHNING TOOL
Also Called: Minutemen Precision Mch & Tl
135 Raynor Ave (11779-6666)
PHONE................................631 467-4900
Michael Castoro, Ch of Bd
Carlo J Castoro, Treasurer
Albert Costabile, Administration
Craig Hobi, Administration
Peter Rayfield, Administration
EMP: 37
SQ FT: 14,900
SALES (est): 8.1MM Privately Held
SIC: 3728 3599 Aircraft parts & equip-
ment; machine shop, jobbing & repair

(G-13976)
MNS FUEL CORP
2154 Pond Rd (11779-7216)
P.O. Box 344, East Islip (11730-0344)
PHONE................................516 735-3835
Irene F Walsh, Principal
EMP: 12
SALES (est): 2.5MM Privately Held
SIC: 2869 Fuels

(G-13977)
MULTIMATIC PRODUCTS INC
900 Marconi Ave (11779-7212)
PHONE................................800 767-7633
Hyman Jack Kipnes, President
Irving Kipnes, Treasurer
EMP: 74 EST: 1962
SQ FT: 20,000
SALES: 3MM Privately Held
WEB: www.multimaticproducts.com
SIC: 3451 3541 Screw machine products;
machine tools, metal cutting type

(G-13978)
N & L INSTRUMENTS INC
90 13th Ave Unit 1 (11779-6818)
PHONE................................631 471-4000
John Walz, President
Anthony Kearney, Treasurer
EMP: 17
SQ FT: 20,000

(PA)=Parent Co (HQ)=Headquarters (DH)=Div Headquarters
✿ = New Business established in last 2 years

2020 Harris
New York Manufacturers Directory

529

GEOGRAPHIC

SALES (est): 2MM **Privately Held**
WEB: www.namf.com
SIC: **3571** 3444 Electronic computers; sheet metalwork

(G-13979)
NATECH PLASTICS INC
85 Remington Blvd (11779-6923)
PHONE..............................631 580-3506
Gerd Nagler, *Ch of Bd*
Thomas Nagler, *President*
Carol Nagler, *Vice Pres*
Jennifer Nagler, *Manager*
Christine Murray, *Admin Asst*
EMP: 45 EST: 1998
SQ FT: 10,000
SALES (est): 10.5MM **Privately Held**
WEB: www.natechplastics.com
SIC: **3089** Injection molding of plastics

(G-13980)
NATURES BOUNTY CO
2100 Smithtown Ave (11779-7347)
PHONE..............................631 244-2021
Dorie Greenblatt, *Principal*
EMP: 90 **Publicly Held**
SIC: **2833** 5122 5499 5961 Vitamins, natural or synthetic: bulk, uncompounded; vitamins & minerals; health & dietetic food stores; vitamin food stores; health foods; pharmaceuticals, mail order
HQ: The Nature's Bounty Co
2100 Smithtown Ave
Ronkonkoma NY 11779
631 200-2000

(G-13981)
NATURES BOUNTY INC (DH)
2100 Smithtown Ave (11779-7347)
PHONE..............................631 200-2000
Dipak Golechha, *Ch of Bd*
Paul L Sturman, *President*
Steve Conboy, *CFO*
▲ EMP: 800
SQ FT: 15,000
SALES (est): 274.4MM **Publicly Held**
WEB: www.nbty.com
SIC: **2834** Vitamin preparations
HQ: The Nature's Bounty Co
2100 Smithtown Ave
Ronkonkoma NY 11779
631 200-2000

(G-13982)
NBTY MANUFACTURING LLC (DH)
2100 Smithtown Ave (11779-7347)
PHONE..............................631 567-9500
Marilyn Figueroa, *Senior VP*
Norberto Carrasquillo, *Mfg Staff*
Andrew Winkle, *Engineer*
Harvey Kamil, *Mng Member*
Geysa Gonzalez, *Manager*
◆ EMP: 47
SQ FT: 6,000,000
SALES (est): 106.5MM **Publicly Held**
SIC: **2833** 5122 Vitamins, natural or synthetic: bulk, uncompounded; vitamins & minerals
HQ: The Nature's Bounty Co
2100 Smithtown Ave
Ronkonkoma NY 11779
631 200-2000

(G-13983)
NEW AGE PRECISION TECH INC
151 Remington Blvd (11779-6911)
PHONE..............................631 471-4000
Mario Costa, *President*
EMP: 20
SQ FT: 25,000
SALES: 1MM **Privately Held**
SIC: **3599** Machine shop, jobbing & repair

(G-13984)
OAKDALE INDUSTRIAL ELEC CORP
1995 Pond Rd (11779-7259)
PHONE..............................631 737-4092
Abraham Mamoor, *President*
Allen Mamoor, *Vice Pres*
▼ EMP: 15
SQ FT: 5,000
SALES (est): 3.7MM **Privately Held**
SIC: **3679** 3672 5065 Electronic circuits; printed circuit boards; electronic parts

(G-13985)
OAKLEE INTERNATIONAL INC
Also Called: Pro-Tek Packaging Group
125 Raynor Ave (11779-6666)
PHONE..............................631 436-7900
Leo Lee, *President*
Alice Zebrowski, *Exec VP*
Donna Neumann, *Exec Dir*
EMP: 75
SALES (est): 11MM **Privately Held**
WEB: www.oaklee.com
SIC: **2672** 3081 Adhesive papers, labels or tapes: from purchased material; unsupported plastics film & sheet

(G-13986)
OMEGA HEATER COMPANY INC
2059 9th Ave (11779-6233)
PHONE..............................631 588-8820
Alfred Gaudio, *President*
▲ EMP: 60 EST: 1970
SQ FT: 30,000
SALES: 3MM **Privately Held**
WEB: www.omegaheater.com
SIC: **3433** Heating equipment, except electric

(G-13987)
OMNTEC MFG INC
1993 Pond Rd (11779-7259)
P.O. Box 30 (11779-0030)
PHONE..............................631 981-2001
Lee J Nicholson, *President*
Tom Dalessandro, *Exec VP*
Kurt Gibson, *Sales Mgr*
Doreen Metz, *Sales Mgr*
▲ EMP: 34
SQ FT: 13,600
SALES (est): 6.7MM **Privately Held**
WEB: www.omntec.com
SIC: **3625** 5065 Relays & industrial controls; electronic parts & equipment

(G-13988)
OPERATEIT INC
2805 Vtrans Mem Hwy Ste 2 (11779-7680)
PHONE..............................631 259-4777
Keith Tobias, *President*
EMP: 9
SALES (est): 511.9K **Privately Held**
SIC: **7372** Prepackaged software

(G-13989)
P R B METAL PRODUCTS INC
200 Christopher St (11779-6921)
PHONE..............................631 467-1800
Ronald Breunig, *President*
Peter Breunig, *Treasurer*
EMP: 10
SQ FT: 10,000
SALES: 1MM **Privately Held**
SIC: **3444** 3465 3469 Sheet metal specialties, not stamped; automotive stampings; metal stampings

(G-13990)
PAAL TECHNOLOGIES INC
152 Remington Blvd Ste 1 (11779-6964)
PHONE..............................631 319-6262
Latha Chandran, *Ch of Bd*
Prem Chandran, *Vice Pres*
EMP: 5
SALES: 300K **Privately Held**
WEB: www.paaltech.com
SIC: **3679** Harness assemblies for electronic use: wire or cable

(G-13991)
PARAMOUNT EQUIPMENT INC
Also Called: O P I Industries
201 Christopher St (11779-6956)
PHONE..............................631 981-4422
▲ EMP: 20
SQ FT: 10,000
SALES (est): 4.7MM **Privately Held**
SIC: **2673** 5113 Mfg Bags-Plastic/Coated Paper Whol Industrial/Service Paper

(G-13992)
PARSLEY APPAREL CORP
2153 Pond Rd (11779-7214)
PHONE..............................631 981-7,181
Ronald Colnick, *President*
EMP: 50
SQ FT: 5,000

SALES (est): 3MM **Privately Held**
SIC: **2335** Wedding gowns & dresses

(G-13993)
PAUL MICHAEL GROUP INC
Also Called: PMG
460 Hawkins Ave (11779-4248)
P.O. Box 1493 (11779-0426)
PHONE..............................631 585-5700
Vincent Gennaro, *President*
▲ EMP: 7
SQ FT: 1,500
SALES (est): 974.9K **Privately Held**
SIC: **2752** 7389 Commercial printing, offset; packaging & labeling services

(G-13994)
PHOTONICS INDUSTRIES INTL INC (PA)
1800 Ocean Ave Unit A (11779-6532)
PHONE..............................631 218-2240
Yusong Yin, *President*
▲ EMP: 95
SQ FT: 184,000
SALES: 3.5MM **Privately Held**
WEB: www.photonix.com
SIC: **3826** Analytical instruments

(G-13995)
PIC A POC ENTERPRISES INC
53 Union Ave (11779-5814)
P.O. Box 338, Holbrook (11741-0338)
PHONE..............................631 981-2094
Nicholas J Ullrich II, *President*
Marilyn Ullrich, *Principal*
EMP: 5
SQ FT: 2,000
SALES: 500K **Privately Held**
SIC: **2752** 7336 Commercial printing, offset; graphic arts & related design

(G-13996)
PRINTCORP INC
2050 Ocean Ave (11779-6536)
PHONE..............................631 696-0641
Joseph C Fazzingo Jr, *CEO*
EMP: 22 EST: 1994
SALES (est): 3.2MM **Privately Held**
SIC: **2752** Commercial printing, offset

(G-13997)
PRONTO TOOL & DIE CO INC
50 Remington Blvd (11779-6910)
PHONE..............................631 981-8920
Michael Silvestri, *President*
Donna Schecker, *Corp Secy*
Marion Silvestri, *Vice Pres*
EMP: 30 EST: 1980
SQ FT: 10,000
SALES (est): 4.5MM **Privately Held**
SIC: **3544** 3599 3469 Special dies & tools; machine & other job shop work; metal stampings

(G-13998)
QUALITY KING DISTRIBUTORS INC
201 Comac St (11779-6950)
PHONE..............................631 439-2027
Glenn H Nussdorf, *CEO*
Janine Louie, *Executive*
EMP: 135
SALES (corp-wide): 374.4MM **Privately Held**
SIC: **2844** 5122 Toilet preparations; toilet preparations
PA: Quality King Distributors, Inc.
35 Sawgrass Dr Ste 3
Bellport NY 11713
631 439-2000

(G-13999)
QUALITY ONE WIRELESS LLC
2127 Lakeland Ave Unit 2 (11779-7431)
PHONE..............................631 233-3337
John Chiorando, *CEO*
EMP: 250
SALES (corp-wide): 189MM **Privately Held**
SIC: **3661** Headsets, telephone
PA: Quality One Wireless, Llc
7651 Southland Blvd
Orlando FL 32809
407 857-3737

(G-14000)
R S T CABLE AND TAPE INC
2130 Pond Rd Ste B (11779-7239)
PHONE..............................631 981-0096
David M Rothert, *President*
William Hilder, *Vice Pres*
EMP: 8
SQ FT: 6,500
SALES (est): 2MM **Privately Held**
SIC: **3479** Painting, coating & hot dipping; coating of metals with plastic or resins

(G-14001)
RATAN RONKONKOMA
3055 Veterans Mem Hwy (11779-7612)
PHONE..............................631 588-6800
Mahesh Ratanji, *Administration*
EMP: 8 EST: 2011
SALES (est): 1MM **Privately Held**
SIC: **3421** Table & food cutlery, including butchers'

(G-14002)
RESONANCE TECHNOLOGIES INC
109 Comac St (11779-6931)
PHONE..............................631 237-4901
George Szenczy, *President*
Mark Anatov, *Director*
EMP: 35
SALES: 5MM **Privately Held**
WEB: www.res-tek.com
SIC: **3678** Electronic connectors

(G-14003)
RIGICON INC
2805 Veterans Memo (11779-7647)
PHONE..............................631 676-3376
Ahmet Melih Luleci, *President*
EMP: 7
SALES (est): 562.5K **Privately Held**
SIC: **3842** Implants, surgical

(G-14004)
ROGER LATARI
Also Called: Island Precision
30 Raynor Ave Ste 1 (11779-6628)
PHONE..............................631 580-2422
Roger Licari, *Owner*
EMP: 5
SALES (est): 330K **Privately Held**
WEB: www.rogerblench.info
SIC: **3599** Machine shop, jobbing & repair

(G-14005)
RONA PRECISION INC
Also Called: Rona Precision Mfg
142 Remington Blvd Ste 2 (11779-6960)
PHONE..............................631 737-4034
Ronald Alber, *President*
EMP: 6
SQ FT: 3,500
SALES (est): 752.4K **Privately Held**
SIC: **3599** Machine shop, jobbing & repair

(G-14006)
SENTRY TECHNOLOGY CORPORATION
Also Called: Knogo
1881 Lakeland Ave (11779-7416)
PHONE..............................631 739-2000
Peter Murdoch, *CEO*
Joane Miller, *CFO*
Elizabeth Heyder, *Admin Sec*
▲ EMP: 30
SQ FT: 20,000
SALES (est): 3.4MM **Publicly Held**
SIC: **3812** 7359 Detection apparatus: electronic/magnetic field, light/heat; electronic equipment rental, except computers
PA: Sentry Technology Corporation
1881 Lakeland Ave
Ronkonkoma NY 11779

(G-14007)
SENTRY TECHNOLOGY CORPORATION (PA)
Also Called: Sentry Funding Partnership
1881 Lakeland Ave (11779-7416)
PHONE..............................800 645-4224
Peter L Murdoch, *Ch of Bd*
Joseph Ryan, *Vice Pres*
Matt Eckert, *Senior Engr*
Joan E Miller, *CFO*
Joan Miller, *VP Finance*

▲ = Import ▼ =Export
◆ =Import/Export

▲ **EMP:** 13
SQ FT: 20,000
SALES (est): 9.6MM **Publicly Held**
SIC: 3812 3663 Detection apparatus:
electronic/magnetic field, light/heat; televi-
sion closed circuit equipment

(G-14008)
SETAUKET MANUFACTURING CO
202 Christopher St (11779-6921)
PHONE................................631 231-7272
Michael Horrigan, *President*
Linda Horrigan, *Vice Pres*
EMP: 5
SQ FT: 4,000
SALES: 500K **Privately Held**
SIC: 2833 5499 Medicinals & botanicals;
health & dietetic food stores

(G-14009)
SIMON DEFENSE INC
1 Trade Zone Dr Unit 15 (11779-7343)
PHONE................................516 217-6000
CJ Calleson, *Director*
EMP: 7 **EST:** 2014
SQ FT: 2,000
SALES (est): 409.2K **Privately Held**
SIC: 3452 Bolts, metal

(G-14010)
SOC AMERICA INC
3505 Veterans Memorial Hw (11779-7613)
PHONE................................631 472-6666
Neil Sato, *President*
Yuichi Sato, *Vice Pres*
Dawn Minichello, *Executive Asst*
EMP: 15
SQ FT: 3,200
SALES (est): 2.4MM **Privately Held**
WEB: www.san-o.com
SIC: 3613 Fuses, electric
PA: Soc Corporation
3-16-17, Takanawa
Minato-Ku TKY 108-0

(G-14011)
SPECIALTY MICROWAVE CORP
120 Raynor Ave (11779-6655)
PHONE................................631 737-1919
Stephen Faber, *President*
EMP: 18
SQ FT: 7,500
SALES (est): 3.2MM **Privately Held**
WEB: www.specialtymicrowave.com
SIC: 3663 Microwave communication
equipment

(G-14012)
SPECIALTY MODEL & MOLD INC
2231 5th Ave Ste 22 (11779-6284)
PHONE................................631 475-0840
Nicholas Ziroli Jr, *President*
EMP: 5
SALES (est): 743.9K **Privately Held**
SIC: 3544 3089 Industrial molds; thermo-
formed finished plastic products

(G-14013)
SPX CORPORATION
Also Called: SPX Precision Components
70 Raynor Ave (11779-6650)
PHONE................................631 467-2632
EMP: 50
SALES (corp-wide): 1.4B **Publicly Held**
SIC: 3443 Mfg Fabricated Plate Work
PA: Spx Corporation
13320a Balntyn Corp Pl
Charlotte NC 28277
980 474-3700

(G-14014)
ST JAMES PRINTING INC
656 Rosevale Ave (11779-3098)
PHONE................................631 981-2095
Gert Kuehnel, *President*
EMP: 5
SQ FT: 5,000
SALES (est): 300K **Privately Held**
SIC: 2759 2752 Commercial printing;
commercial printing, lithographic

(G-14015)
SURF-TECH MANUFACTURING CORP
28 Colt Ct (11779-6948)
PHONE................................631 589-1194
Richard Eggert, *President*
EMP: 12
SQ FT: 8,000
SALES (est): 2.5MM **Privately Held**
WEB: www.surftechmfg.com
SIC: 3672 5045 Printed circuit boards;
computers, peripherals & software

(G-14016)
SWITCHING POWER INC
3601 Veterans Mem Hwy (11779-7691)
PHONE................................631 981-7231
Melvin Kravitz, *President*
Carmen Midiri, *Purch Mgr*
Onder Onal, *QC Mgr*
Mark Herringer, *Engineer*
David Kravitz, *Engineer*
▲ **EMP:** 65
SQ FT: 30,000
SALES (est): 14.2MM **Privately Held**
WEB: www.switchpwr.com
SIC: 3613 5065 3643 3612 Power
switching equipment; electronic parts &
equipment; current-carrying wiring de-
vices; transformers, except electric

(G-14017)
TRANSISTOR DEVICES INC
125 Comac St (11779-6931)
PHONE................................631 471-7492
Ron Deluca, *Manager*
Jack Dorsa, *Manager*
EMP: 27
SALES (corp-wide): 216.8MM **Privately
Held**
WEB: www.transdev.com
SIC: 3625 3612 3672 3812 Switches,
electric power; power transformers, elec-
tric; printed circuit boards; search & navi-
gation equipment
PA: Transistor Devices, Inc.
36 Newburgh Rd
Hackettstown NJ 07840
908 850-5088

(G-14018)
TRUEMADE PRODUCTS INC
910 Marconi Ave (11779-7212)
PHONE................................631 981-4755
Carmen Yvonne Mender, *President*
EMP: 5
SQ FT: 4,000
SALES: 400K **Privately Held**
SIC: 3541 Machine tools, metal cutting
type

(G-14019)
U S AIR TOOL CO INC (PA)
Also Called: U S Air Tool International
60 Fleetwood Ct (11779-6907)
PHONE................................631 471-3300
Geoffrey J Percz, *Ch of Bd*
Laurence Percz, *Vice Pres*
▲ **EMP:** 25 **EST:** 1951
SQ FT: 14,000
SALES (est): 9.2MM **Privately Held**
SIC: 3423 5084 3542 Hand & edge tools;
pneumatic tools & equipment; sheet met-
alworking machines

(G-14020)
UCR STEEL GROUP LLC
90 Trade Zone Ct (11779-7369)
PHONE................................718 764-3414
Charlie Starce, *Mng Member*
EMP: 15
SQ FT: 33,000
SALES (est): 3.1MM **Privately Held**
SIC: 3444 Sheet metalwork

(G-14021)
ULTRAFLEX POWER TECHNOLOGIES
158 Remington Blvd Ste 2 (11779-6966)
PHONE................................631 467-6814
Mario Metodiev, *President*
Nedelina Metodieva, *Treasurer*
Marne Kwiatkowski, *Accounts Exec*
EMP: 5
SQ FT: 3,000

SALES (est): 571.1K **Privately Held**
SIC: 3567 Induction heating equipment

(G-14022)
ULTRAVOLT INC
1800 Ocean Ave Unit A (11779-6532)
PHONE................................631 471-4444
James Morrison, *CEO*
EMP: 100
SQ FT: 20,000
SALES (est): 21.1MM
SALES (corp-wide): 718.8MM **Publicly
Held**
WEB: www.ultravolt.com
SIC: 3679 5065 5084 Power supplies, all
types: static; electronic parts & equip-
ment; power plant machinery
PA: Advanced Energy Industries, Inc.
1625 Sharp Point Dr
Fort Collins CO 80525
970 221-4670

(G-14023)
VACUUM INSTRUMENT CORPORATION (PA)
Also Called: Vic Leak Detection
2101 9th Ave Ste A (11779-6276)
PHONE................................631 737-0900
Frederick Ewing II, *CEO*
David Uribe, *General Mgr*
John Schreiner, *Vice Pres*
Rodney Sano, *Marketing Staff*
Phyllis Smith, *Manager*
EMP: 100
SQ FT: 48,000
SALES (est): 27.9MM **Privately Held**
WEB: www.vacuuminst.com
SIC: 3823 3829 3812 Industrial instrmnts
msrmnt display/control process variable;
measuring & controlling devices; search &
navigation equipment

(G-14024)
VORMITTAG ASSOCIATES INC (PA)
Also Called: V A I
120 Comac St Ste 1 (11779-6941)
PHONE................................800 824-7776
Robert Vormittag, *President*
Russ Cereola, *Vice Pres*
Larry Murphy, *Vice Pres*
Claudio Gallina, *Project Dir*
Luke Heaton, *Project Dir*
EMP: 6
SQ FT: 15,000
SALES (est): 36.6MM **Privately Held**
WEB: www.vaihome.com
SIC: 7372 7371 5045 Prepackaged soft-
ware; computer software systems analy-
sis & design, custom; computers,
peripherals & software

(G-14025)
VOSKY PRECISION MACHINING CORP
70 Air Park Dr (11779-7360)
PHONE................................631 737-3200
Mourad Voskinarian, *President*
Andrew Voskinarian, *Foreman/Supr*
Krista Philips, *Technology*
EMP: 18
SQ FT: 11,000
SALES (est): 4.1MM **Privately Held**
WEB: www.voskyprecision.com
SIC: 3728 3469 3599 Aircraft parts &
equipment; machine parts, stamped or
pressed metal; machine shop, jobbing &
repair

(G-14026)
WENNER BREAD PRODUCTS INC (PA)
2001 Orville Dr N (11779-7661)
PHONE................................800 869-6262
Richard R Wenner, *CEO*
Lawrence L Wenner, *Senior VP*
Nelly Margolin, *Vice Pres*
Andrew Pisani, *Vice Pres*
Daniel Wenner, *Vice Pres*
▲ **EMP:** 277 **EST:** 1975
SQ FT: 140,000

SALES (est): 105.7MM **Privately Held**
WEB: www.wenner-bread.com
SIC: 2051 2053 5461 Bread, all types
(white, wheat, rye, etc): fresh or frozen;
frozen bakery products, except bread;
bakeries

(G-14027)
WENNER BREAD PRODUCTS INC
Also Called: Wenner Bakery
2001 Orville Dr N (11779-7661)
PHONE................................800 869-6262
EMP: 35
SALES (corp-wide): 105.7MM **Privately
Held**
SIC: 2051 2053 5461 5149 Bread, all
types (white, wheat, rye, etc): fresh or
frozen; frozen bakery products, except
bread; bakeries; bakery products
PA: Wenner Bread Products, Inc.
2001 Orville Dr N
Ronkonkoma NY 11779
800 869-6262

(G-14028)
WILCO INDUSTRIES INC
788 Marconi Ave (11779-7230)
P.O. Box 277 (11779-0277)
PHONE................................631 676-2593
Otto Wildmann, *President*
EMP: 9
SQ FT: 8,000
SALES (est): 970K **Privately Held**
WEB: www.wilcoindustries.com
SIC: 3728 Aircraft assemblies, subassem-
blies & parts

(G-14029)
ZETA MACHINE CORP
206 Christopher St (11779-6921)
PHONE................................631 471-8832
Frank Castelli, *President*
Carol Castelli, *Vice Pres*
EMP: 8 **EST:** 1975
SQ FT: 8,000
SALES (est): 1.1MM **Privately Held**
SIC: 3469 Machine parts, stamped or
pressed metal

Roosevelt
Nassau County

(G-14030)
AUTOSTAT CORPORATION
209 Nassau Rd 11 (11575-1756)
P.O. Box 170 (11575-0170)
PHONE................................516 379-9447
Arthur Baer, *President*
▲ **EMP:** 10 **EST:** 1955
SQ FT: 9,000
SALES (est): 1.2MM **Privately Held**
SIC: 3549 Marking machines, metalwork-
ing

(G-14031)
K F I INC
33 Debevoise Ave (11575-1711)
PHONE................................516 546-2904
Sion Elalouf, *President*
Jeff Denecke, *Opers Staff*
▲ **EMP:** 8
SALES (est): 491.7K **Privately Held**
WEB: www.euroyarns.com
SIC: 2299 Yarns, specialty & novelty

(G-14032)
SEXTET FABRICS INC
145 Babylon Tpke (11575-2122)
PHONE................................516 593-0608
Gordon Stern, *CEO*
Barbara Ross, *President*
▲ **EMP:** 12 **EST:** 1971
SALES: 5MM **Privately Held**
SIC: 2259 Convertors, knit goods

(G-14033)
SOUTH SHORE ICE CO INC
89 E Fulton Ave (11575-2212)
PHONE................................516 379-2056
Al Farina, *President*
EMP: 10
SQ FT: 4,500

GEOGRAPHIC

SALES (est): 1MM **Privately Held**
SIC: 2097 5999 5169 Manufactured ice; ice; dry ice

(G-14034)
TROPICAL DRIFTWOOD ORIGINALS
Also Called: Tdo Sandblasting
499 Nassau Rd (11575-1019)
PHONE................................516 623-0980
John O'Brien Sr, *President*
EMP: 5 EST: 1959
SQ FT: 4,000
SALES: 270K **Privately Held**
SIC: 3441 3446 3471 Fabricated structural metal; architectural metalwork; sand blasting of metal parts

Roscoe
Sullivan County

(G-14035)
PROHIBITION DISTILLERY LLC
10 Union St (12776-5210)
PHONE................................917 685-8989
Brian Facquet, *Mng Member*
Robert Mack, *Manager*
Philip Facquet Jr,
EMP: 8
SALES (est): 511.8K **Privately Held**
SIC: 2085 Distilled & blended liquors

Rosedale
Queens County

(G-14036)
LARRY KINGS CORPORATION
13708 250th St (11422-2110)
PHONE................................718 481-8741
Larry Yoen, *President*
Clara Wong, *Treasurer*
Johnny Yoen, *Shareholder*
Penny Yoen, *Admin Sec*
EMP: 6
SALES (est): 802.8K **Privately Held**
SIC: 3825 Instruments to measure electricity

(G-14037)
MASTRO CONCRETE INC
15433 Brookville Blvd (11422-3163)
PHONE................................718 528-6788
Tony Mastronardi, *President*
Mario Mastronardi, *Vice Pres*
EMP: 8
SQ FT: 10,000
SALES (est): 1.4MM **Privately Held**
SIC: 3273 Ready-mixed concrete

(G-14038)
WATER COOLING CORP
24520 Merrick Blvd (11422-1464)
P.O. Box 220056 (11422-0056)
PHONE................................718 723-6500
Elliott Miller, *President*
Jim Adelis, *Admin Sec*
EMP: 7 EST: 1939
SQ FT: 5,500
SALES (est): 1.3MM **Privately Held**
WEB: www.watcopumps.com
SIC: 3443 3561 Water tanks, metal plate; tanks, standard or custom fabricated: metal plate; pumps, domestic: water or sump; industrial pumps & parts

Roslyn
Nassau County

(G-14039)
BEACON SPCH LNGE PTHLGY PHYS
Also Called: Beacon Therapy Services
1441 Old Northern Blvd (11576-2256)
PHONE................................516 626-1635
Barbar Lehrer, *Partner*
Barbara Lehrer, *Partner*
Jonathan Lehrer, *Human Res Mgr*
EMP: 16

SQ FT: 5,500
SALES: 7MM **Privately Held**
SIC: 3841 Inhalation therapy equipment

(G-14040)
CLOUD ROCK GROUP LLC
525 Bryant Ave (11576-1146)
PHONE................................516 967-6023
Leon Hedvat, *Manager*
EMP: 5
SALES (est): 163.4K **Privately Held**
SIC: 7372 7389 Application computer software; business services

(G-14041)
CUSTOM ECO FRIENDLY LLC (PA)
Also Called: Custom Eco Friendly Bags
50 Spruce Dr (11576-2330)
PHONE................................347 227-0229
Matthew Kesten, *CEO*
Jonathan Wollman, *President*
▲ EMP: 16
SQ FT: 250
SALES: 4MM **Privately Held**
SIC: 2674 Shopping bags: made from purchased materials

(G-14042)
DYNAMIC PHOTOGRAPHY INC
Also Called: Daisy Memory Products
48 Flamingo Rd N (11576-2606)
PHONE................................516 381-2951
Robert M Deangelo Jr, *President*
Richard J Deangelo, *Vice Pres*
EMP: 5
SALES: 7MM **Privately Held**
SIC: 3674 7336 7221 Magnetic bubble memory device; commercial art & graphic design; photographer, still or video

(G-14043)
HAND CARE INC
42 Sugar Maple Dr (11576-3207)
P.O. Box 331, Albertson (11507-0331)
PHONE................................516 747-5649
Harrison Fuller, *President*
Patricia Fuller, *Admin Sec*
▲ EMP: 2
SQ FT: 15,000
SALES: 2MM **Privately Held**
WEB: www.handcare.net
SIC: 3842 Gloves, safety; adhesive tape & plasters, medicated or non-medicated

(G-14044)
NEW YORK LASER & AESTHETICKS
1025 Nthrn Blvd Ste 206 (11576)
PHONE................................516 627-7777
Ofra Grinbaum, *Owner*
EMP: 5
SALES (est): 445.8K **Privately Held**
SIC: 3845 Laser systems & equipment, medical

(G-14045)
NORTHWEST COMPANY LLC (PA)
Also Called: Wilmington Products USA
49 Bryant Ave (11576-1123)
P.O. Box 263 (11576-0263)
PHONE................................516 484-6996
Ross Auerbach, *President*
Marc Friedman, *COO*
Glenn Auerbach, *Exec VP*
Trina Grana, *Production*
Robert Jolson, *CFO*
◆ EMP: 175
SQ FT: 15,000
SALES (est): 57.3MM **Privately Held**
WEB: www.thenorthwest.com
SIC: 2211 Blankets & blanketings, cotton

(G-14046)
ROVEL MANUFACTURING CO INC
52 Wimbledon Dr (11576-3082)
PHONE................................516 365-2752
William Levor, *President*
Andrew A Levor, *Vice Pres*
EMP: 5
SQ FT: 10,000

SALES: 400K **Privately Held**
SIC: 2299 Batts & batting: cotton mill waste & related material; batting, wadding, padding & fillings

(G-14047)
WM E MARTIN AND SONS CO INC
55 Bryant Ave Ste 300 (11576-1158)
PHONE................................516 605-2444
William Martin Jr, *President*
William S Martin, *Vice Pres*
William J Martin, *Vice Pres*
Spencer Martin, *Accounting Mgr*
Blake Martin, *Director*
▲ EMP: 22 EST: 1954
SQ FT: 60,000
SALES (est): 6.8MM **Privately Held**
SIC: 2099 2034 Spices, including grinding; vegetables, dried or dehydrated (except freeze-dried)

Roslyn Heights
Nassau County

(G-14048)
CABOT COACH BUILDERS INC
Also Called: Royale Limousine Manufacturers
77 Carriage Ln (11577-2615)
PHONE................................516 625-4000
Lucy Berritto, *Manager*
EMP: 8
SALES (corp-wide): 11.1MM **Privately Held**
WEB: www.royalelimo.com
SIC: 3711 5511 Automobile assembly, including specialty automobiles; automobiles, new & used
PA: Cabot Coach Builders Inc.
    99 Newark St
    Haverhill MA 01832
    978 374-4530

(G-14049)
CUAN CORP
16 Jessica Pl (11577-1905)
PHONE................................917 579-3774
Pauline Murray, *President*
EMP: 7
SALES (est): 883.6K **Privately Held**
SIC: 2431 Millwork

(G-14050)
ERGUN INC
10 Mineola Ave Unit B (11577-1067)
PHONE................................631 721-0049
Omer Eguner, *President*
EMP: 2
SQ FT: 200
SALES: 15.9MM **Privately Held**
SIC: 2911 Oils, fuel

(G-14051)
HIGHWAY TOLL ADM LLC
66 Powerhouse Rd Ste 301 (11577-1372)
P.O. Box 30 (11577-0030)
PHONE................................516 684-9584
David Centner, *CEO*
Anggit Narotama, *Financial Analy*
▲ EMP: 15
SALES (est): 5.3MM
SALES (corp-wide): 370.1MM **Publicly Held**
SIC: 3829 Toll booths, automatic
PA: Verra Mobility Corporation
    1150 N Alma School Rd
    Mesa AZ 85201
    480 443-7000

(G-14052)
IET LABS INC (PA)
1 Expressway Plz Ste 120 (11577-2031)
PHONE................................516 334-5959
Sam Sheena, *President*
David Sheena, *Vice Pres*
Ben Sheena, *VP Sales*
▲ EMP: 12
SQ FT: 11,000
SALES (est): 5MM **Privately Held**
SIC: 3825 Test equipment for electronic & electrical circuits

(G-14053)
KIM JAE PRINTING CO INC
249 Parkside Dr (11577-2211)
PHONE................................212 691-6289
Jae Kye Kim, *President*
Yun Kim, *Vice Pres*
EMP: 5 EST: 1974
SQ FT: 6,000
SALES (est): 500K **Privately Held**
SIC: 2759 2752 Newspapers: printing; commercial printing, lithographic

(G-14054)
KINGS READY MIX INC
703 3rd Ave Fl 2 Flr 2 (11577)
PHONE................................718 853-4644
Robert Bruzzese, *CEO*
Vincent Falcone, *President*
Michael Falcone, *Corp Secy*
Michael Solomon, *CFO*
EMP: 50
SQ FT: 60,000
SALES: 7.6MM **Privately Held**
SIC: 3273 Ready-mixed concrete

(G-14055)
PIONEER WINDOW HOLDINGS INC (PA)
Also Called: Pioneer Windows Manufacturing
3 Expressway Plz Ste 221 (11577-2033)
PHONE................................516 822-7000
Vincent Amato, *Ch of Bd*
Anthony J Ross, *President*
Tony Fabbricatore, *Vice Pres*
Dennis Dolan, *Project Mgr*
Zach Katz, *Project Mgr*
EMP: 12
SALES (est): 15.3MM **Privately Held**
WEB: www.pwindows.com
SIC: 3442 Storm doors or windows, metal

(G-14056)
ROSLYN BREAD COMPANY INC
190 Mineola Ave (11577-2093)
PHONE................................516 625-1470
EMP: 35
SQ FT: 3,500
SALES: 1.1MM **Privately Held**
SIC: 2051 5149 5461 5812 Mfg Whol Ret Bread & Restaurant

(G-14057)
SOMERSET MANUFACTURERS INC
36 Glen Cove Rd (11577-1703)
PHONE................................516 626-3832
Jacob Ambalu, *President*
Esther Ambalu, *Vice Pres*
EMP: 20
SALES (est): 1.6MM **Privately Held**
SIC: 3911 Jewelry, precious metal

(G-14058)
SUNYNAMS FASHIONS LTD
Also Called: Sunny Names
170 Westwood Cir (11577-1838)
PHONE................................212 268-5200
Sunny Neman, *President*
▲ EMP: 7
SALES (est): 962.4K **Privately Held**
SIC: 2339 Women's & misses' outerwear

(G-14059)
US CONCRETE INC
Also Called: Kings Ready Mix
10 Powerhouse Rd (11577-1311)
PHONE................................718 853-4644
EMP: 50
SALES (corp-wide): 1.5B **Publicly Held**
SIC: 3273 Ready-mixed concrete
PA: U.S. Concrete, Inc.
    331 N Main St
    Euless TX 76039
    817 835-4105

▲ = Import ▼=Export
◆ =Import/Export

Rotterdam Junction
Schenectady County

(G-14060)
SI GROUP INC
Also Called: Si Group Global Manufacturing
1000 Main St (12150)
PHONE..................................518 347-4200
David Dawood, *VP Opers*
EMP: 200 **Privately Held**
SIC: 2865 Phenol, alkylated & cumene
HQ: Si Group, Inc.
2750 Balltown Rd
Schenectady NY 12309
518 347-4200

(G-14061)
SI GROUP INC
Rr 5 Box South (12150)
P.O. Box 1046, Schenectady (12301-1046)
PHONE..................................518 347-4200
Andy Barrett, *General Mgr*
EMP: 150 **Privately Held**
WEB: www.schenectadyinternational.com
SIC: 2851 Varnishes
HQ: Si Group, Inc.
2750 Balltown Rd
Schenectady NY 12309
518 347-4200

Round Lake
Saratoga County

(G-14062)
USHERS MACHINE AND TOOL CO INC
180 Ushers Rd (12151-1806)
PHONE..................................518 877-5501
Don Lincoln, *President*
Joseph Hopeck, *President*
EMP: 20
SQ FT: 5,000
SALES (est): 4.3MM
SALES (corp-wide): 3.1B **Privately Held**
WEB: www.ushersm.com
SIC: 3599 Machine shop, jobbing & repair
PA: Aalberts N.V.
Stadsplateau 18
Utrecht
303 079-300

(G-14063)
WYRESTORM TECHNOLOGIES LLC
23 Wood Rd (12151-1708)
PHONE..................................518 289-1293
Derek Hulbert, *President*
Joe Dunbar, *Manager*
Jennifer Grey,
▲ EMP: 15
SQ FT: 2,500
SALES (est): 2.9MM **Privately Held**
SIC: 3651 Household audio & video equipment
HQ: Wyrestorm Technologies Europe Limited
Unit 22 Kelvin Road Ergo Business Park
Swindon WILTS SN3 3
179 323-0343

Round Top
Greene County

(G-14064)
ROUND TOP KNIT & SCREENING
Rr 31 (12473)
P.O. Box 188 (12473-0188)
PHONE..................................518 622-3600
Manny Voss, *Owner*
Carla Panzarino, *Sales Staff*
EMP: 5
SQ FT: 6,000
SALES: 750K **Privately Held**
SIC: 2759 5651 2395 2396 Screen printing; family clothing stores; embroidery & art needlework; automotive & apparel trimmings

Rouses Point
Clinton County

(G-14065)
CHAMPLAIN PLASTICS INC
Also Called: Champlain Hanger
87 Pillsbury Rd (12979-1701)
P.O. Box 2947, Plattsburgh (12901-0269)
PHONE..................................518 297-3700
Alan L Taveroff, *Ch of Bd*
Joe Zalter, *President*
Robert Lafontaine, *Sales Staff*
▲ EMP: 85
SALES (est): 14.7MM
SALES (corp-wide): 4.9MM **Privately Held**
WEB: www.olympicpoolaccessories.com
SIC: 3089 Injection molding of plastics
PA: Canadian Buttons Limited
7020 Boul Newman
Lasalle QC H8N 3
514 363-0210

(G-14066)
PFIZER INC
Also Called: Wyeth
64 Maple St (12979-1424)
P.O. Box 127 (12979-0127)
PHONE..................................518 297-6611
William Brooks, *Branch Mgr*
EMP: 440
SALES (corp-wide): 53.6B **Publicly Held**
WEB: www.wyeth.com
SIC: 2834 Pharmaceutical preparations
PA: Pfizer Inc.
235 E 42nd St
New York NY 10017
212 733-2323

(G-14067)
POWERTEX INC (PA)
Also Called: Powertex Bulk Shipg Solutions
1 Lincoln Blvd Ste 101 (12979-1040)
PHONE..................................518 297-4000
Stephen D Podd, *President*
Karen M Lamberton, *Treasurer*
▲ EMP: 34 EST: 1977
SQ FT: 65,900
SALES (est): 8.8MM **Privately Held**
WEB: www.powertex.com
SIC: 3089 Plastic containers, except foam

(G-14068)
SANDYS DELI INC
Also Called: Last Resort, The
90 Montgomery St (12979-1018)
PHONE..................................518 297-6951
Carolyn Reid, *President*
EMP: 6 EST: 2016
SQ FT: 1,000
SALES: 145K
SALES (corp-wide): 450K **Privately Held**
SIC: 2599 Bar, restaurant & cafeteria furniture
PA: Sandy's Deli Inc
133 Lake St
Rouses Point NY 12979
518 297-6951

Rush
Monroe County

(G-14069)
CONVERGENT AUDIO TECH INC
85 High Tech Dr (14543-9623)
PHONE..................................585 359-2700
Ken Stevens, *President*
Truddy Stevens, *Vice Pres*
EMP: 5
SQ FT: 3,300
SALES (est): 832.7K **Privately Held**
SIC: 3651 Audio electronic systems

(G-14070)
EXTEK INC
7500 W Henrietta Rd (14543-9790)
PHONE..................................585 533-1672
Caroline Eastman, *Branch Mgr*
EMP: 50

SALES (corp-wide): 5.5MM **Privately Held**
WEB: www.sts.ethoxint.com
SIC: 3841 Surgical & medical instruments
PA: Extek, Inc.
370 Summit Point Dr
Henrietta NY
585 321-5000

(G-14071)
GPM ASSOCIATES LLC
Graphik Promotional Products
45 High Tech Dr Ste 100 (14543-9746)
PHONE..................................585 359-1770
John Dobbertin, *Controller*
Jim McDermott,
EMP: 6
SALES (corp-wide): 15.5MM **Privately Held**
SIC: 2393 Textile bags
PA: Gpm Associates Llc
45 High Tech Dr
Rush NY 14543
585 334-4800

(G-14072)
GPP POST-CLOSING INC
Also Called: Global Precision Products
90 High Tech Dr (14543-9746)
PHONE..................................585 334-4640
Mark Labell, *CEO*
Doug Labell, *Vice Pres*
EMP: 22
SQ FT: 250,000
SALES (est): 4.4MM **Privately Held**
WEB: www.globalppi.com
SIC: 3599 Machine shop, jobbing & repair

(G-14073)
KEUKA STUDIOS INC
1011 Rush Henrietta Townl (14543-9763)
PHONE..................................585 624-5960
Dan White, *President*
Jeanne White, *Corp Secy*
Jason White, *Opers Staff*
▼ EMP: 8
SALES (est): 1.2MM **Privately Held**
WEB: www.keuka-studios.com
SIC: 3446 Architectural metalwork

(G-14074)
SPS MEDICAL SUPPLY CORP (DH)
6789 W Henrietta Rd (14543-9797)
PHONE..................................585 359-0130
Gary Steinberg, *President*
John Hughes, *General Mgr*
Daniel Lupica, *Opers Mgr*
Mary Reed, *Finance Mgr*
Tim Brundage, *Sales Staff*
◆ EMP: 73
SQ FT: 40,000
SALES (est): 19.7MM
SALES (corp-wide): 918.1MM **Publicly Held**
WEB: www.spsmedical.com
SIC: 3842 Surgical appliances & supplies
HQ: Crosstex International, Inc.
10 Ranick Rd
Hauppauge NY 11788
631 582-6777

Rushville
Yates County

(G-14075)
RUSH MACHINERY INC
4761 State Route 364 (14544-9721)
PHONE..................................585 554-3070
William P Freese, *President*
▲ EMP: 9
SQ FT: 7,000
SALES (est): 2.1MM **Privately Held**
SIC: 3541 Centering machines

Rye
Westchester County

(G-14076)
CONSOLIDATED EDISON CO NY INC
511 Theodore Fremd Ave (10580-1432)
PHONE..................................914 933-2936
William McGrath, *Principal*
Victor Billinghurst, *Engineer*
Kimberly Moliterno, *Administration*
EMP: 19
SALES (corp-wide): 12.3B **Publicly Held**
SIC: 2869 Fuels
HQ: Consolidated Edison Company Of New York, Inc.
4 Irving Pl
New York NY 10003
212 460-4600

(G-14077)
GAZETTE PRESS INC
2 Clinton Ave (10580-1629)
PHONE..................................914 963-8300
Richard Martinelli, *CEO*
Angelo R Martinelli, *President*
Angelo Martinelli, *Chairman*
Carol Martinelli, *Treasurer*
EMP: 20
SQ FT: 10,000
SALES (est): 2.5MM **Privately Held**
SIC: 2759 2796 2791 2789 Letterpress printing; platemaking services; typesetting; bookbinding & related work; commercial printing, lithographic

(G-14078)
GB AERO ENGINE LLC
555 Theodore Fremd Ave (10580-1451)
PHONE..................................914 925-9600
Jason Anthoine, *Vice Pres*
Raynard Benvenuti,
Noah Roy,
Rob Wolf,
EMP: 390
SALES (est): 16.5MM **Privately Held**
SIC: 3724 3541 3769 Aircraft engines & engine parts; machine tools, metal cutting type; guided missile & space vehicle parts & auxiliary equipment

(G-14079)
GLOBAL GOLD CORPORATION (PA)
555 Theodore Fremd Ave C208 (10580-1451)
PHONE..................................914 925-0020
Van Z Krikorian, *Ch of Bd*
W E S Urquhart, *Vice Pres*
Jan Dulman, *CFO*
Drury J Gallagher, *Treasurer*
EMP: 12
SALES (est): 3.3MM **Publicly Held**
WEB: www.globalgoldcorp.com
SIC: 1021 1041 1094 1044 Copper ores; gold ores; uranium ore mining; silver ores

(G-14080)
HIBERT PUBLISHING LLC
222 Purchase St (10580-2101)
PHONE..................................914 381-7474
Gary Hibert, *Branch Mgr*
Tyler White, *Relations*
EMP: 5
SALES (est): 241.3K
SALES (corp-wide): 1.1MM **Privately Held**
SIC: 2741 Miscellaneous publishing
PA: Hibert Publishing Llc
7555 E Hampden Ave # 405
Denver CO 80231
303 312-1000

(G-14081)
HYDRIVE ENERGY
350 Theodore Fremd Ave (10580-1573)
PHONE..................................914 925-9100
EMP: 6
SALES (est): 451.8K **Privately Held**
SIC: 2086 Mfg Bottled/Canned Soft Drinks

(G-14082)
JUDITH N GRAHAM INC
Also Called: Pink and Palmer
64 Halls Ln　(10580-3124)
PHONE..................................914 921-5446
James Graham, *Principal*
EMP: 7
SALES (est): 537.5K　Privately Held
SIC: 2844　Toilet preparations

(G-14083)
MONEYPAPER INC
411 Theodore Fremd Ave # 132
(10580-1410)
P.O. Box 451　(10580-0451)
PHONE..................................914 925-0022
Vita Nelson, *President*
EMP: 12
SALES (est): 807.6K　Privately Held
WEB: www.giftsofstock.com
SIC: 2711　6282　Newspapers, publishing &
printing; investment advice

(G-14084)
QUOIN LLC
555 Theodore Fremd Ave B302
(10580-1451)
PHONE..................................914 967-9400
Martin Franklin, *CEO*
EMP: 1402
SALES (est): 50.7MM
SALES (corp-wide): 8.6B　Publicly Held
WEB: www.jarden.com
SIC: 3089　Plastic containers, except foam
HQ: Jarden Llc
221 River St
Hoboken NJ 07030

(G-14085)
RYE RECORD
14 Elm Pl Ste 200　(10580-2951)
PHONE..................................914 713-3213
Dolores Eyler, *Partner*
Allen Clarck, *Partner*
Robin Jovanovich, *Partner*
EMP: 8
SALES (est): 500K　Privately Held
SIC: 2721　Periodicals

(G-14086)
WESTERN OIL AND GAS JV INC
Also Called: Michael Neuman
7 Mccullough Pl　(10580-2934)
PHONE..................................914 967-4758
Michael Neuman, *President*
Richard Neuman, *Vice Pres*
EMP: 3　EST: 2008
SALES (est): 2.1MM　Privately Held
SIC: 1321　8748　1381　Natural gas liquids;
energy conservation consultant; drilling oil
& gas wells

Rye Brook
Westchester County

(G-14087)
CHROMOSENSE LLC
476 N Ridge St　(10573-1108)
PHONE..................................646 541-2302
Filip Mlekicki, *COO*
Masoud Ghandehari,
Alexey Sidyelyev,
EMP: 6
SALES (est): 95.6K　Privately Held
SIC: 3826　Analytical instruments

(G-14088)
ELIAS FRAGRANCES INC (PA)
3 Hunter Dr　(10573-1406)
PHONE..................................718 693-6400
Robert Elias, *President*
Lewis Elias, *Exec VP*
Barbara Elias, *Admin Sec*
▲ EMP: 17　EST: 1972
SQ FT: 8,000
SALES (est): 3.2MM　Privately Held
SIC: 2844　5122　Perfumes, natural or syn-
thetic; perfumes

(G-14089)
FLOW CONTROL LLC (HQ)
1 International Dr　(10573-1058)
PHONE..................................914 323-5700

Sonia Hollies, *Mng Member*
EMP: 250
SALES: 25MM　Publicly Held
SIC: 3561　Pumps, domestic: water or
sump

(G-14090)
IT WINDOWS & DOORS INC
245 Treetop Cres　(10573-1644)
PHONE..................................646 220-8398
EMP: 5
SALES (est): 407.7K　Privately Held
SIC: 3442　Screens, window, metal; storm
doors or windows, metal; window spac-
ers; sash, door or window: metal

(G-14091)
MARSHALL CAVENDISH CORP
Also Called: Benchmark Books
800 Westchester Ave N641　(10573-1360)
PHONE..................................914 332-8888
Richard Farley, *President*
Dora Woo, *Partner*
Patricia Ong, *Sales Mgr*
Thomas Corbia, *Consultant*
Anvis They, *Executive*
▲ EMP: 40
SALES (est): 3.8MM
SALES (corp-wide): 1.4B　Privately Held
WEB: www.marshallcavendish.com
SIC: 2731　Books: publishing only
HQ: Marshall Cavendish Limited
32-38 Saffron Hill
London　EC1N

(G-14092)
**MITSUI CHEMICALS AMERICA
INC (HQ)**
800 Westchester Ave N607　(10573-1354)
PHONE..................................914 253-0777
Naoto Tani, *President*
Minoru Koshibe, *General Mgr*
Ken Migita, *General Mgr*
Kenji Miyachi, *General Mgr*
Toshimitsu Narutaki, *Business Mgr*
◆ EMP: 40
SQ FT: 13,000
SALES (est): 248.9MM　Privately Held
SIC: 2865　3082　8731　5169　Cyclic crudes
& intermediates; unsupported plastics
profile shapes; computer (hardware) de-
velopment; chemical additives; loan insti-
tutions, general & industrial;
plasticizer/additive based plastic materials

(G-14093)
PROGRESSIVE PRODUCTS LLC
4 International Dr # 224　(10573-1065)
PHONE..................................914 417-6022
Jason Englander, *CEO*
Gabby Hunter, *Accounting Mgr*
Mark Zeitler,
▲ EMP: 8
SQ FT: 2,000
SALES: 10MM　Privately Held
SIC: 2842　Cleaning or polishing prepara-
tions

(G-14094)
**SNAPPLE BEVERAGE CORP
(HQ)**
900 King St　(10573-1226)
PHONE..................................914 612-4000
Larry D Young, *CEO*
Ernie Cavallo, *President*
Scott Miller, *Vice Pres*
Michael Sandes, *Vice Pres*
EMP: 70
SQ FT: 55,000
SALES (est): 54.3MM　Publicly Held
SIC: 2086　Soft drinks: packaged in cans,
bottles, etc.

(G-14095)
XYLEM INC (PA)
1 International Dr　(10573-1058)
PHONE..................................914 323-5700
Markos I Tambakeras, *Ch of Bd*
D Randall Bays, *President*
Christian Blanc, *President*
Patrick K Decker, *President*
David Flinton, *President*
EMP: 277
SQ FT: 67,000
SALES: 5.2B　Publicly Held
SIC: 3561　Pumps & pumping equipment

Sag Harbor
Suffolk County

(G-14096)
**CAM TOUCHVIEW PRODUCTS
INC**
51 Division St　(11963-3162)
P.O. Box 1980　(11963-0067)
PHONE..................................631 842-3400
Emanuel Cardinale, *President*
EMP: 15　EST: 2013
SQ FT: 4,000
SALES: 1.2MM　Privately Held
SIC: 3674　Thin film circuits

(G-14097)
COASTAL PUBLICATIONS INC
22 Division St　(11963)
P.O. Box 1620　(11963-0058)
PHONE..................................631 725-1700
Gavin Menu, *Principal*
EMP: 10
SALES (est): 663.1K　Privately Held
SIC: 2741　Miscellaneous publishing

(G-14098)
DORTRONICS SYSTEMS INC
1668 Bhmpton Sag Hbr Tpke　(11963-3706)
PHONE..................................631 725-0505
Paul R Scheerer, *CEO*
John Fitzpaprick, *President*
John Fitzpatrick, *President*
Jodi Stangler, *COO*
Mary Scheerer, *Vice Pres*
EMP: 21
SQ FT: 10,000
SALES (est): 3.9MM
SALES (corp-wide): 16.7MM　Privately
Held
WEB: www.dortronics.com
SIC: 3429　3679　3625　3089　Locks or lock
sets; electronic switches; switches, elec-
tronic applications; timing devices, elec-
tronic; plastic hardware & building
products
PA: Sag Harbor Industries, Inc.
1668 Bhmpton Sag Hbr Tpke
Sag Harbor NY 11963
631 725-0440

(G-14099)
LUBBU INC
20 Payne Ave　(11963-1204)
PHONE..................................917 693-9600
Robbie Vorhaus, *CEO*
EMP: 6
SALES: 125K　Privately Held
SIC: 7372　Application computer software

(G-14100)
SAG HARBOR EXPRESS
22 Division St　(11963)
P.O. Box 1620　(11963-0058)
PHONE..................................631 725-1700
Bryan Boyhan, *Manager*
EMP: 7
SALES (est): 543.5K　Privately Held
WEB: www.sagharboronline.com
SIC: 2741　2711　Miscellaneous publishing;
newspapers

(G-14101)
**SAG HARBOR INDUSTRIES INC
(PA)**
1668 Bhmpton Sag Hbr Tpke　(11963-3714)
PHONE..................................631 725-0440
Paul R Scheerer Jr, *Ch of Bd*
Mary Scheerer, *President*
John Fitzpatrick, *Vice Pres*
Dave Leeney, *Vice Pres*
Rhonda Baker, *Office Mgr*
EMP: 50　EST: 1946
SQ FT: 50,000
SALES (est): 16.7MM　Privately Held
WEB: www.sagharborind.com
SIC: 3621　3672　3677　5065　Coils, for
electric motors or generators; printed cir-
cuit boards; electronic coils, transformers
& other inductors; electronic parts &
equipment; transformers, except electric

(G-14102)
SECOND CHANCE PRESS INC
Also Called: Permanent Press
4170 Noyac Rd　(11963-2809)
PHONE..................................631 725-1101
Martin Shepard, *President*
Jessica Kalfaian, *Publisher*
Rania Graetz, *Editor*
Judith Shepard, *Vice Pres*
Nick Collins, *Manager*
EMP: 6
SALES: 420K　Privately Held
WEB: www.thepermanentpress.com
SIC: 2731　5942　Books: publishing only;
book stores

Sagaponack
Suffolk County

(G-14103)
**WOLFFER ESTATE VINEYARD
INC**
Also Called: Wolffer Estate Winery
139 Sagg Rd　(11962-2006)
P.O. Box 9002　(11962-9002)
PHONE..................................631 537-5106
Christian Wolffer, *President*
▲ EMP: 50
SALES (est): 9MM　Privately Held
WEB: www.wolffer.com
SIC: 2084　5813　Wines; wine bar

Saint Albans
Queens County

(G-14104)
A LESLEY DUMMETT
10415 185th St　(11412-1009)
PHONE..................................646 541-1168
Lesley A Dummett, *Owner*
EMP: 1
SALES: 10MM　Privately Held
SIC: 2731　Book publishing

(G-14105)
**HOUSE OF THE FOAMING CASE
INC**
110 08 Dunkirk St　(11412)
PHONE..................................718 454-0101
EMP: 7
SALES (est): 1MM　Privately Held
SIC: 3523　Mfg Farm Machinery/Equipment

(G-14106)
**INTEGRATED TECH SUPPORT
SVCS**
Also Called: Itss
18616 Jordan Ave　(11412-2308)
PHONE..................................718 454-2497
Gerald Cortez, *President*
Damon Kinebrew, *Sales/Mktg Dir*
EMP: 7
SQ FT: 1,000
SALES: 150K　Privately Held
SIC: 2522　Office furniture, except wood

Saint James
Suffolk County

(G-14107)
2600 ENTERPRISES INC
Also Called: The Hacker Quarterly
2 Flowerfield Ste 30　(11780-1507)
P.O. Box 848, Middle Island　(11953-0848)
PHONE..................................631 474-2677
Emmanuelle Goldstein, *Principal*
Eric Corley, *Editor*
▲ EMP: 10
SALES: 1MM　Privately Held
WEB: www.2600.net
SIC: 2721　Magazines: publishing only, not
printed on site

(G-14108)
CREATE-A-CARD INC
16 Brasswood Rd　(11780-3410)
PHONE..................................631 584-2273

Arthur Messina, *President*
Denise Laurenti, *President*
Kathy Messina, *Vice Pres*
Messina Arthur, *CTO*
EMP: 5
SQ FT: 1,200
SALES: 375K **Privately Held**
WEB: www.createacardinc.com
SIC: 2752 2759 Color lithography; post
cards, picture: lithographed; visiting cards
(including business): printing

(G-14109)
DESIGN SOLUTIONS LI INC
711 Middle Country Rd (11780-3209)
PHONE..................................631 656-8700
Mario Adragna, *Owner*
EMP: 1
SQ FT: 6,000
SALES: 4MM **Privately Held**
SIC: 3639 Major kitchen appliances, ex-
cept refrigerators & stoves

(G-14110)
**EAST COAST BUSINESS FORMS
INC**
Also Called: Accurate Business Systems
320 Lake Ave Ste 2 (11780-2255)
PHONE..................................631 231-9300
Dan Glenn, *President*
Roni O Trolio, *Prdtn Mgr*
Ed Kaufmann, *Manager*
EMP: 6
SALES (est): 1MM **Privately Held**
WEB: www.ecoastgraphics.com
SIC: 2752 Commercial printing, litho-
graphic

(G-14111)
HADFIELD INC
49 Fifty Acre Rd (11780-1304)
PHONE..................................631 981-4314
Charles Hadfield, *President*
EMP: 10
SALES (est): 1MM **Privately Held**
SIC: 7692 1799 Welding repair; welding
on site

(G-14112)
POLYMERS MERONA INC
Also Called: P M I
347 Lake Ave Ste 4 (11780-2278)
P.O. Box 515 (11780-0515)
PHONE..................................631 862-8010
Ricky E Profit, *Ch of Bd*
Barbara Profit, *Corp Secy*
Brian Montroy, *Vice Pres*
▼ **EMP:** 10
SQ FT: 4,000
SALES (est): 5.8MM **Privately Held**
WEB: www.polymers-merona.com
SIC: 2821 Plastics materials & resins

(G-14113)
**RE HANSEN INDUSTRIES INC
(PA)**
Also Called: Islandaire
500 Middle Country Rd A (11780-3236)
PHONE..................................631 471-2900
Robert Hansen Jr, *Ch of Bd*
Somya Mishra, *Engineer*
Glenn Myhr, *Engineer*
Elizabeth Cipolla, *Accountant*
Bill Cnadel, *Sales Staff*
◆ **EMP:** 118
SALES (est): 25.1MM **Privately Held**
SIC: 3585 3822 3433 5722 Air condition-
ing equipment, complete; heat pumps,
electric; auto controls regulating residntl &
coml environmt & applncs; heating equip-
ment, except electric; air conditioning
room units, self-contained; plumbing,
heating, air-conditioning contractors

(G-14114)
**SMITHTOWN CONCRETE
PRODUCTS**
441 Middle Country Rd (11780-3201)
P.O. Box 612, Smithtown (11787-0612)
PHONE..................................631 265-1815
Neil Spevak, *President*
Barbara Spevak, *Treasurer*
EMP: 16 EST: 1940

SALES: 950K **Privately Held**
WEB: www.smithtownconcrete.com
SIC: 3271 Blocks, concrete or cinder: stan-
dard

(G-14115)
TRADEWINS PUBLISHING CORP
528 Route 25a Ste A (11780-1440)
PHONE..................................631 361-6916
Steve Schmidt, *President*
Jane Schmidt, *Admin Sec*
Lanciotti Danell, *Associate*
EMP: 5
SQ FT: 1,000
SALES (est): 303.6K **Privately Held**
WEB: www.tradewinspublishing.com
SIC: 2741 Miscellaneous publishing

Saint Johnsville
Montgomery County

(G-14116)
COUNTRYSIDE TRUSS LLC
360 County Highway 151 (13452-2920)
PHONE..................................315 985-0643
Isaac Renda, *Mng Member*
EMP: 7
SALES (est): 523.6K **Privately Held**
SIC: 3448 2952 Trusses & framing: pre-
fabricated metal; roofing materials

(G-14117)
HANSON AGGREGATES PA INC
7904 St Hwy 5 (13452-3514)
PHONE..................................518 568-2444
Don Sheldon, *Manager*
EMP: 10
SALES (corp-wide): 20.6B **Privately Held**
SIC: 1442 1422 Common sand mining;
limestones, ground
HQ: Hanson Aggregates Pennsylvania, Llc
7660 Imperial Way
Allentown PA 18195
610 366-4626

(G-14118)
HELMONT MILLS INC (HQ)
15 Lion Ave (13452-1398)
PHONE..................................518 568-7913
George G Gehring Jr, *CEO*
Mark Hoover, *Finance*
EMP: 1 EST: 1992
SALES (est): 10.4MM
SALES (corp-wide): 64MM **Privately
Held**
SIC: 2258 Lace & warp knit fabric mills
PA: Gehring Tricot Corporation
68 Ransom St
Dolgeville NY 13329
315 429-8551

(G-14119)
HIGHWAY GARAGE
110 State Highway 331 (13452-2818)
PHONE..................................518 568-2837
Rich Crum, *Manager*
EMP: 7 EST: 2011
SALES (est): 412.3K **Privately Held**
SIC: 3531 Drags, road (construction &
road maintenance equipment)

(G-14120)
RC ENTPS BUS & TRCK INC
5895 State Highway 29 (13452-2413)
P.O. Box 193 (13452-0193)
PHONE..................................518 568-5753
Robert Crum, *Ch of Bd*
EMP: 6
SALES (est): 460K **Privately Held**
SIC: 7694 Motor repair services

Salamanca
Cattaraugus County

(G-14121)
ALICE PERKINS
Also Called: A & F Trucking & Excavating
148 Washington St (14779-1045)
PHONE..................................716 378-5100
Alice Perkins, *Co-Owner*
Fred Perkins, *Co-Owner*

EMP: 6
SQ FT: 3,212
SALES (est): 1.5MM **Privately Held**
SIC: 1389 4212 1411 Excavating slush
pits & cellars; dump truck haulage; granite
dimension stone

(G-14122)
MCHONE INDUSTRIES INC
110 Elm St (14779-1500)
P.O. Box 69 (14779-0069)
PHONE..................................716 945-3380
Arnold McHone, *President*
Eva McHone, *Vice Pres*
Joe Stomieroski, *Purchasing*
EMP: 75
SQ FT: 75,000
SALES (est): 17.7MM **Privately Held**
WEB: www.mchoneind.com
SIC: 3469 3317 3569 3444 Metal stamp-
ings; steel pipe & tubes; robots, assembly
line: industrial & commercial; sheet metal-
work

(G-14123)
MERITOOL LLC
4496 Route 353 (14779-9781)
P.O. Box 148 (14779-0148)
PHONE..................................716 699-6005
Brent Findlay, *Engineer*
Timm Herman, *Mng Member*
Donna Finegan,
▲ **EMP:** 28 EST: 1939
SQ FT: 29,000
SALES (est): 4.4MM **Privately Held**
WEB: www.meritool.com
SIC: 3546 Power-driven handtools

(G-14124)
MONROE TABLE COMPANY INC
255 Rochester St Ste 15 (14779-1563)
PHONE..................................716 945-7700
Douglas Kirchner, *CEO*
Orville Johnston, *President*
EMP: 12
SALES (est): 1.3MM **Privately Held**
SIC: 2599 Bar, restaurant & cafeteria furni-
ture

(G-14125)
**NORTON-SMITH HARDWOODS
INC (PA)**
Also Called: Arbor Valley Flooring
25 Morningside Ave (14779-1210)
PHONE..................................716 945-0346
Art Smith, *Co-President*
Dan Smith, *Co-President*
▼ **EMP:** 7
SQ FT: 18,000
SALES (est): 2MM **Privately Held**
SIC: 2426 Dimension, hardwood

(G-14126)
**SALAMANCA LUMBER
COMPANY INC**
59 Rochester St (14779-1508)
P.O. Box 416 (14779-0416)
PHONE..................................716 945-4810
Reinier Taapken, *President*
Rinus Vollenberg, *Vice Pres*
Tony Wenke, *Inv Control Mgr*
▼ **EMP:** 45
SQ FT: 3,000
SALES (est): 7.1MM
SALES (corp-wide): 17.1MM **Privately
Held**
WEB: www.salamancalumber.com
SIC: 2421 Kiln drying of lumber
PA: Leyenaar Taapken Lamaker Holding
B.V.
Kamerlingh Onnesweg 7
Vianen Ut 4131
347 374-844

(G-14127)
**SALAMANCA PRESS PENNY
SAVER**
Also Called: Salamanca Penny Saver
36 River St (14779-1495)
PHONE..................................716 945-1500
F David Radler, *President*
Kevin Burleson, *Principal*
Ernie Sage, *Sales/Mktg Mgr*
John H Satterwhite, *Treasurer*
EMP: 30

SALES (est): 1.7MM **Privately Held**
SIC: 2741 2759 2711 Shopping news:
publishing & printing; commercial printing;
newspapers

(G-14128)
**SENECA MANUFACTURING
COMPANY**
175 Rochester St (14779-1508)
P.O. Box 496 (14779-0496)
PHONE..................................716 945-4400
Gary Sanden, *Partner*
Travis Heron, *Partner*
▲ **EMP:** 8
SQ FT: 40,000
SALES (est): 1.7MM **Privately Held**
SIC: 2111 Cigarettes

(G-14129)
SNYDER MANUFACTURING INC
Also Called: SMI
255 Rochester St Unit 1 (14779-1563)
PHONE..................................716 945-0354
James F Snyder, *President*
Cynthia Snyder, *Corp Secy*
▲ **EMP:** 25 EST: 2000
SQ FT: 40,000
SALES (est): 4.8MM **Privately Held**
WEB: www.snyder-mfg.com
SIC: 3423 Hand & edge tools

(G-14130)
**STRATEGIES NORTH AMERICA
INC**
Also Called: Ellicottville Kitchen Eqp
150 Elm St (14779-2002)
P.O. Box 1549, Ellicottville (14731-1549)
PHONE..................................716 945-6053
John Karassik, *President*
EMP: 5
SQ FT: 4,000
SALES (est): 929.3K **Privately Held**
SIC: 3589 Dishwashing machines, com-
mercial

(G-14131)
SUN-TIMES MEDIA GROUP INC
Also Called: Salamanca Daily Reporter
36 River St (14779-1474)
P.O. Box 111 (14779-0111)
PHONE..................................716 945-1644
Kevin Burleson, *Manager*
EMP: 32
SALES (corp-wide): 4.3MM **Privately
Held**
SIC: 2711 Newspapers, publishing & print-
ing
HQ: Sun-Times Media Group, Inc.
30 N Racine Ave Ste 300
Chicago IL 60607
312 321-3000

Salem
Washington County

(G-14132)
CAROLINA EASTERN-VAIL INC
Also Called: Carol Vail
4134 State Route 22 (12865)
PHONE..................................518 854-9785
Charles Tucker, *Branch Mgr*
EMP: 25
SALES (corp-wide): 61.9MM **Privately
Held**
SIC: 2875 Fertilizers, mixing only
PA: Carolina Eastern-Vail, Inc.
831 County Rte 28
Niverville NY 12130
518 784-9166

(G-14133)
MAPLELAND FARMS LLC
647 Bunker Hill Rd (12865-1716)
PHONE..................................518 854-7669
David Campbell, *President*
Terry Campbell, *Vice Pres*
EMP: 7
SALES (est): 254.7K **Privately Held**
SIC: 2087 0191 Syrups, flavoring (except
drink); general farms, primarily crop

Salisbury Mills
Orange County

(G-14134)
CALLAHAN & NANNINI QUARRY INC
276 Clove Rd (12577-5224)
P.O. Box 164 (12577-0164)
PHONE..........................845 496-4323
Robert Nannini, *President*
Bob Nannini, *Vice Pres*
Jay Nannini, *Vice Pres*
EMP: 5
SQ FT: 3,600
SALES (est): 4.3MM **Privately Held**
SIC: 1459 5032 Shale (common) quarrying; stone, crushed or broken

Salt Point
Dutchess County

(G-14135)
WOODWORKS
2559 Route 44 (12578-8004)
PHONE..........................845 677-3960
Robert Gerch, *President*
▲ EMP: 10
SALES (est): 1.4MM **Privately Held**
SIC: 2431 5031 1751 Windows & window parts & trim, wood; doors & windows; window & door (prefabricated) installation

Sanborn
Niagara County

(G-14136)
BRIDGE COMPONENTS INC
2122 Cory Dr (14132-9338)
PHONE..........................716 731-1184
Silvio G Derubeis, *Principal*
Tyler Spears, *Agent*
EMP: 6
SALES (est): 628.8K **Privately Held**
SIC: 3399 Primary metal products

(G-14137)
BRIDGESTONE APM COMPANY
6350 Inducon Dr E (14132-9015)
PHONE..........................419 423-9552
Duke Kawai, *Manager*
EMP: 60 **Privately Held**
SIC: 3061 Automotive rubber goods (mechanical)
HQ: Bridgestone Apm Company
2030 Production Dr
Findlay OH 45840
419 423-9552

(G-14138)
BRUCE PIERCE
Also Called: Core Welding
2386 Lockport Rd (14132-9011)
P.O. Box 209 (14132-0209)
PHONE..........................716 731-9310
Bruce Pierce, *Owner*
EMP: 5
SQ FT: 4,080
SALES (est): 500K **Privately Held**
WEB: www.brucepierce.com
SIC: 3443 3599 7692 1799 Fabricated plate work (boiler shop); machine shop, jobbing & repair; welding repair; sandblasting of building exteriors

(G-14139)
BUFFALO GEAR INC
3635 Lockport Rd (14132-9704)
PHONE..........................716 731-2100
Daniel Szczygiel, *President*
Gail Nichols, *Vice Pres*
▲ EMP: 20 EST: 1962
SQ FT: 22,000
SALES (est): 4MM **Privately Held**
WEB: www.buffalogear.com
SIC: 3566 Gears, power transmission, except automotive

(G-14140)
EDWARDS VACUUM LLC (DH)
6400 Inducon Corporate Dr (14132)
PHONE..........................800 848-9800
Matthew Taylor, *CEO*
John O'Sullivan, *Ch of Bd*
Butch Paddock, *President*
Michael Allison, *Vice Pres*
Nigel Wenden, *Vice Pres*
▲ EMP: 100
SALES (est): 191.4MM
SALES (corp-wide): 10.5B **Privately Held**
SIC: 3563 Vacuum (air extraction) systems, industrial
HQ: Atlas Copco North America Llc
6 Century Dr Ste 310
Parsippany NJ 07054
973 397-3400

(G-14141)
FINGER FOOD PRODUCTS INC
6400 Inducon Dr W (14132-9019)
P.O. Box 560, Niagara Falls (14304-0560)
PHONE..........................716 297-4888
Jason Cordova, *CEO*
EMP: 48
SQ FT: 34,000
SALES (est): 7MM **Privately Held**
WEB: www.fingerfoodproducts.com
SIC: 2038 Frozen specialties

(G-14142)
GAMBLE & GAMBLE INC (PA)
Also Called: Unit Step Company
5890 West St (14132-9245)
PHONE..........................716 731-3239
Ronald H Gamble, *President*
EMP: 4
SQ FT: 2,500
SALES (est): 1.1MM **Privately Held**
SIC: 3272 Concrete products, precast

(G-14143)
INNOVATIVE CLEANING SOLUTIONS
2990 Carney Dr (14132-9305)
PHONE..........................716 731-4408
EMP: 5
SQ FT: 1,600
SALES (est): 727.2K **Privately Held**
SIC: 3559 Mfg Misc Industry Machinery

(G-14144)
KATZ GROUP AMERICAS INC (DH)
Also Called: Katz Americas
3685 Lockport Rd (14132-9404)
PHONE..........................716 995-3059
Tammy Gorzka, *President*
Dale Fischer, *Production*
Amy Minnick, *Purchasing*
Michael Dimartino, *CFO*
Cindy Mazza, *Accountant*
▲ EMP: 50
SQ FT: 70,000
SALES (est): 13.6MM
SALES (corp-wide): 924MM **Privately Held**
WEB: www.american-coaster.com
SIC: 2679 Paper products, converted
HQ: Katz Gmbh & Co. Kg
Hauptstr. 2
Weisenbach 76599
722 464-70

(G-14145)
KINSHOFER USA INC
6420 Inducon Dr W Ste G (14132-9025)
PHONE..........................716 731-4333
Martin Francois, *General Mgr*
Brendan Refalo, *Director*
◆ EMP: 24
SALES (est): 5.2MM
SALES (corp-wide): 6.1B **Privately Held**
SIC: 3531 Excavators: cable, clamshell, crane, derrick, dragline, etc.; cranes
HQ: Kinshofer Gmbh
Hauptstr. 76
Waakirchen 83666
802 188-990

(G-14146)
MYLES TOOL COMPANY INC
6300 Inducon Corporate Dr (14132-9346)
PHONE..........................716 731-1300

Myles Barraclough, *President*
Tim Barraclough, *Vice Pres*
Paul Reding, *Prdtn Mgr*
Joe Adams, *Manager*
▲ EMP: 42 EST: 1977
SQ FT: 4,500
SALES (est): 9.9MM **Privately Held**
WEB: www.mylestool.com
SIC: 3545 3541 Machine tool accessories; machine tools, metal cutting type

(G-14147)
PRECISION PLUS VACUUM PARTS
6416 Inducon Dr W (14132-9019)
PHONE..........................716 297-2039
Joe Miller, *President*
▲ EMP: 62
SQ FT: 20,000
SALES (est): 9.3MM
SALES (corp-wide): 10.5B **Privately Held**
WEB: www.precisionplus.com
SIC: 3563 Vacuum pumps, except laboratory
HQ: Edwards Vacuum Llc
6400 Inducon Corporate Dr
Sanborn NY 14132
800 848-9800

(G-14148)
PYROTEK INCORPORATED
Metaullics Systems Division
2040 Cory Dr (14132-9388)
PHONE..........................716 731-3221
George Bitler, *Principal*
Kevin Scott, *Manager*
EMP: 50
SALES (corp-wide): 565.8MM **Privately Held**
SIC: 3624 3569 3999 Carbon & graphite products; filters; chairs, hydraulic, barber & beauty shop
PA: Pyrotek Incorporated
705 W 1st Ave
Spokane WA 99201
509 926-6212

(G-14149)
SHARP PRINTING INC
3477 Lockport Rd (14132-9491)
PHONE..........................716 731-3994
Slade Sharpsteen, *President*
EMP: 7
SQ FT: 1,200
SALES (est): 1MM **Privately Held**
WEB: www.sharpprinting.com
SIC: 2752 Commercial printing, offset

(G-14150)
SHIPMAN PRINTING INDS INC
6120 Lendell Dr (14132-9455)
PHONE..........................716 504-7700
Gary E Blum, *Branch Mgr*
EMP: 12
SALES (corp-wide): 3MM **Privately Held**
SIC: 2752 Commercial printing, offset
PA: Shipman Printing Industries, Inc.
2424 Niagara Falls Blvd
Niagara Falls NY 14304
716 504-7700

(G-14151)
UNITED BIOCHEMICALS LLC
6351 Inducon Dr E (14132-9016)
PHONE..........................716 731-5161
Dr Duane Mazur, *Vice Pres*
Manuel Brocke-Benz, *Mng Member*
▲ EMP: 30
SALES (est): 9.1MM
SALES (corp-wide): 1.4B **Publicly Held**
SIC: 2869 Industrial organic chemicals
HQ: Vwr International, Llc
100 W Matsonford Rd # 1
Radnor PA 19087
610 386-1700

(G-14152)
UNITED MATERIALS LLC
2186 Cory Dr (14132-9338)
PHONE..........................716 731-2332
Lean Guilinan, *Manager*
EMP: 22
SALES (corp-wide): 17.3MM **Privately Held**
SIC: 3273 Ready-mixed concrete

PA: United Materials, L.L.C.
3949 Frest Pk Way Ste 400
North Tonawanda NY 14120
716 683-1432

(G-14153)
VOSS MANUFACTURING INC
2345 Lockport Rd (14132-9636)
PHONE..........................716 731-5062
Rita Voss Kammerer, *President*
Thomas Kammerer, *Vice Pres*
Voss Lute, *Engineer*
Ursula Voss, *Admin Sec*
◆ EMP: 73
SQ FT: 55,000
SALES (est): 24.6MM **Privately Held**
WEB: www.vossmfg.com
SIC: 3444 3599 7389 3549 Sheet metalwork; custom machinery; design, commercial & industrial; metalworking machinery

Sandy Creek
Oswego County

(G-14154)
CASTERS CUSTOM SAWING
6323 Us Route 11 (13145-2191)
PHONE..........................315 387-5104
Edith Caster, *Principal*
EMP: 8
SALES (est): 934.1K **Privately Held**
SIC: 2421 Lumber: rough, sawed or planed

Sangerfield
Oneida County

(G-14155)
CHAMPION HOME BUILDERS INC
951 Rte 12 S (13455)
P.O. Box 177 (13455-0177)
PHONE..........................315 841-4122
John Copeletti, *General Mgr*
EMP: 150
SQ FT: 115,000
SALES (corp-wide): 1.3B **Publicly Held**
WEB: www.championaz.com
SIC: 2451 Mobile homes
HQ: Champion Home Builders, Inc.
755 W Big Beaver Rd # 1000
Troy MI 48084
248 614-8200

Saranac Lake
Franklin County

(G-14156)
ADIRONDACK PUBLISHING CO INC (DH)
Also Called: Adirondack Daily Enterprise
54 Broadway (12983-1704)
P.O. Box 318 (12983-0318)
PHONE..........................518 891-2600
George Ogden Nutting, *President*
Morgan Ryan, *Editor*
Steve Bradley, *Prdtn Mgr*
Rick Burman, *Foreman/Supr*
Alec Bieber, *Manager*
EMP: 32 EST: 1904
SQ FT: 5,000
SALES (est): 2.9MM **Privately Held**
SIC: 2711 2752 Job printing & newspaper publishing combined; commercial printing, lithographic
HQ: The Ogden Newspapers Inc
1500 Main St
Wheeling WV 26003
304 233-0100

(G-14157)
COMPASS PRINTING PLUS
42 Main St (12983-1708)
P.O. Box 631, Lake Placid (12946-0631)
PHONE..........................518 523-3308
Tom Connors, *Owner*
EMP: 9

SALES (est): 1.2MM **Privately Held**
SIC: 2752 Commercial printing, offset

(G-14158)
GETTING THE WORD OUT INC
Also Called: ADIRONDACK EXPLORER
36 Church St Apt 106 (12983-1850)
PHONE.................................518 891-9352
Dick Beamish, *President*
Tracy Ormsbee, *Publisher*
Phil Brown, *Editor*
Andreas Mowka, *Director*
EMP: 5
SALES: 932K **Privately Held**
SIC: 2721 Magazines: publishing only, not
printed on site

(G-14159)
NORTHERN NEW YORK RURAL
Also Called: NORTH COUNTRY BEHAV-
IORAL HEALT
126 Kiwassa Rd (12983-2357)
P.O. Box 891 (12983-0891)
PHONE.................................518 891-9460
Robin Calkins, *Bookkeeper*
Samantha Dashnaw, *Manager*
Samantha Denshaw, *Manager*
Barry Brogan, *Director*
EMP: 5
SALES: 489.7K **Privately Held**
SIC: 3999 Education aids, devices & sup-
plies

(G-14160)
UPSTONE MATERIALS INC
909 State Route 3 (12983-5109)
PHONE.................................518 891-0236
David Gordan, *Manager*
EMP: 22
SALES (corp-wide): 83.5MM **Privately
Held**
WEB: www.graymont-ab.com
SIC: 1422 Crushed & broken limestone
HQ: Upstone Materials Inc.
111 Quarry Rd
Plattsburgh NY 12901
518 561-5321

Saratoga Springs
Saratoga County

(G-14161)
**09 FLSHY BLL/DSERT SUNRISE
LLC**
2 Smith Bridge Rd (12866-5617)
PHONE.................................518 583-6638
Lindsey Heumann CPA, *Principal*
EMP: 5
SALES (est): 326.1K **Privately Held**
SIC: 3291 Hones

(G-14162)
**ADIRONDACK SIGN COMPANY
LLC**
72 Ballston Ave (12866-4427)
PHONE.................................518 409-7446
Adam Wakulenko, *Managing Prtnr*
John Natale, *Managing Prtnr*
Carl Wheeler, *Vice Pres*
Thomas Wheeler, *Vice Pres*
Wayne Wheeler, *Vice Pres*
EMP: 10
SQ FT: 3,200
SALES: 936K **Privately Held**
SIC: 3993 1799 Signs, not made in cus-
tom sign painting shops; sign installation
& maintenance

(G-14163)
**ADIRONDACK SIGN PERFECT
INC**
72 Ballston Ave (12866-4427)
PHONE.................................518 409-7446
John Natale, *Principal*
Adam Wakulenko, *Principal*
EMP: 8 EST: 2007
SQ FT: 3,500
SALES: 740K **Privately Held**
SIC: 3993 Electric signs

(G-14164)
AGROCHEM INC
26 Freedom Way (12866-9075)
PHONE.................................518 226-4850
Robert J Demarco, *Principal*
EMP: 20
SQ FT: 38,000
SALES (est): 6.5MM **Privately Held**
WEB: www.agrocheminc.com
SIC: 2879 Agricultural chemicals

(G-14165)
**BALL METAL BEVERAGE CONT
CORP**
Also Called: Ball Metal Beverage Cont Div
11 Adams Rd (12866-9061)
PHONE.................................518 587-6030
Harold Hall, *Superintendent*
Steve Di Loreto, *Plant Mgr*
Steven Di Lorto, *Plant Mgr*
Andy Sharp, *Purch Agent*
Robert Nelson, *Engineer*
EMP: 225
SALES (corp-wide): 11.6B **Publicly Held**
SIC: 3411 Metal cans
HQ: Ball Metal Beverage Container Corp.
9300 W 108th Cir
Westminster CO 80021

(G-14166)
BIG JOHNS ADIRONDACK INC
Also Called: Big John's Beef Jerky
45 N Milton Rd (12866-6137)
PHONE.................................518 587-3680
John Ponessa, *President*
EMP: 5
SALES: 60K **Privately Held**
SIC: 2013 Snack sticks, including jerky:
from purchased meat

(G-14167)
C C INDUSTRIES INC
344 Burgoyne Rd (12866-5493)
PHONE.................................518 581-7633
Charles Carlstrom, *President*
EMP: 13
SQ FT: 9,500
SALES: 450K **Privately Held**
SIC: 2754 Imprinting, gravure

(G-14168)
**CAPITAL STONE SARATOGA
LLC**
4295 Route 50 (12866-2962)
PHONE.................................518 226-8677
Paul Sicluna,
EMP: 6
SALES (est): 581.9K **Privately Held**
SIC: 3281 Granite, cut & shaped

(G-14169)
CHEQUEDCOM INC
513 Broadway Ste 1 (12866-6730)
PHONE.................................888 412-0699
Greg Moran, *CEO*
John Tobison, *COO*
Gary Ito, *CFO*
Kevin Williams, *Security Dir*
EMP: 30 EST: 2012
SALES (est): 2.7MM
SALES (corp-wide): 12.6MM **Privately
Held**
SIC: 7372 8742 Business oriented com-
puter software; human resource consult-
ing services
PA: Chequed Holdings, Llc
513 Broadway Ste 1
Saratoga Springs NY 12866
888 412-0699

(G-14170)
COLUMBIA CABINETS LLC
489 Broadway Ste 2 (12866-6734)
PHONE.................................518 283-1700
EMP: 11
SALES (corp-wide): 1.1MM **Privately
Held**
SIC: 2434 Wood kitchen cabinets
PA: Columbia Cabinets, Llc
20 Maple Ave Ste F
Armonk NY 10504
212 972-7550

(G-14171)
ENCORE ELECTRONICS INC
4400 Route 50 (12866-2924)
PHONE.................................518 584-5354
Thomas J Barrett, *General Mgr*
Richard Leonard, *Purch Mgr*
Jim Frederick, *Sales Mgr*
Tom Moeller, *CTO*
EMP: 25
SQ FT: 15,000
SALES (est): 5.8MM **Privately Held**
WEB: www.encore-elec.com
SIC: 3824 Mechanical & electromechanical
counters & devices; electromechanical
counters

(G-14172)
**ESPEY MFG & ELECTRONICS
CORP (PA)**
233 Ballston Ave (12866-4767)
PHONE.................................518 584-4100
Howard Pinsley, *Ch of Bd*
Patrick T Enright Jr, *President*
Wayne Potter, *COO*
David Brockenbrough, *Engineer*
David A O'Neil, *CFO*
EMP: 164 EST: 1928
SQ FT: 151,000
SALES: 36.4MM **Publicly Held**
WEB: www.espey.com
SIC: 3679 Electronic circuits

(G-14173)
**ESSITY PROF HYGIENE N AMER
LLC**
Also Called: ESSITY PROFESSIONAL HY-
GIENE NORTH AMERICA LLC
49 Geyser Rd (12866-9038)
PHONE.................................518 583-2785
Tim Cutler, *Manager*
EMP: 219
SALES (corp-wide): 13.1B **Privately Held**
SIC: 2621 Paper mills
HQ: Essity Professional Hygiene North
America Llc
984 Winchester Rd
Neenah WI 54956
920 727-3770

(G-14174)
**FIRST SIGNS SARATOGA
SPRINGS**
Also Called: Fastsigns
30 Gick Rd (12866-8517)
PHONE.................................518 306-4449
EMP: 5
SALES (est): 216.2K **Privately Held**
SIC: 3993 Signs & advertising specialties

(G-14175)
FREEDOM MFG LLC
3 Duplainville Rd Apt C (12866-9074)
PHONE.................................518 584-0441
Scott Mummert, *Principal*
EMP: 14
SALES (est): 1.5MM **Privately Held**
SIC: 3999 Barber & beauty shop equip-
ment

(G-14176)
**FRIENDLY FUEL
INCORPORATED**
54 Church St (12866-2007)
PHONE.................................518 581-7036
Manjinder Grewal, *Principal*
EMP: 5
SALES (est): 491.8K **Privately Held**
SIC: 2869 Fuels

(G-14177)
GOLUB CORPORATION
3045 Route 50 (12866-2919)
PHONE.................................518 583-3697
Paul R Flately, *Manager*
EMP: 31
SALES (corp-wide): 3.6B **Privately Held**
SIC: 3751 Motorcycles & related parts
PA: The Golub Corporation
461 Nott St
Schenectady NY 12308
518 355-5000

(G-14178)
GRANT GRAPHICS LLC
Also Called: Hs Grant
610 Maple Ave (12866-5606)
PHONE.................................518 583-2818
Hoyt S Grant III, *Owner*
Rita Grant, *Business Mgr*
Andrew Defeo, *Sales Staff*
EMP: 5
SALES (est): 1.5MM **Privately Held**
SIC: 3993 Signs & advertising specialties

(G-14179)
**GREAT AMERICAN BICYCLE
LLC**
41 Geyser Rd (12866-9038)
PHONE.................................518 584-8100
Ben Serotta, *Mng Member*
EMP: 50
SQ FT: 15,000
SALES (est): 6.9MM **Privately Held**
WEB: www.serotta.com
SIC: 3751 5941 Bicycles & related parts;
frames, motorcycle & bicycle; sporting
goods & bicycle shops

(G-14180)
**GREENFIELD MANUFACTURING
INC**
25 Freedom Way (12866-9076)
PHONE.................................518 581-2368
Duane R Palmateer, *President*
▲ EMP: 11 EST: 1996
SQ FT: 40,000
SALES (est): 2.2MM **Privately Held**
WEB: www.greenfieldmfg.com
SIC: 2899 Acid resist for etching

(G-14181)
HAPPY SOFTWARE LLC
11 Federal St (12866-4111)
PHONE.................................518 584-4668
Joseph Mastrianni, *CEO*
Jennifer Terito, *Opers Mgr*
EMP: 7 EST: 1994
SQ FT: 1,500
SALES (est): 1MM
SALES (corp-wide): 121.8MM **Privately
Held**
WEB: www.happysoftware.com
SIC: 7372 Business oriented computer
software
PA: Mri Software Llc
28925 Fountain Pkwy
Solon OH 44139
800 321-8770

(G-14182)
HUNTINGTON INGALLS INC
33 Cady Hill Blvd (12866-9047)
PHONE.................................518 884-3834
Peter Wedesky, *Branch Mgr*
EMP: 50 **Publicly Held**
SIC: 3731 Shipbuilding & repairing
HQ: Huntington Ingalls Incorporated
4101 Washington Ave
Newport News VA 23607
757 380-2000

(G-14183)
INCENTIVATE HEALTH LLC
60 Railroad Pl Ste 101 (12866-3045)
PHONE.................................518 469-8491
J Lawrence Toole, *President*
Patricia Hasbrouck, *Co-Owner*
Robert Legrande II, *Co-Owner*
EMP: 5
SALES (est): 156K **Privately Held**
SIC: 7372 Application computer software

(G-14184)
JOURNAL REGISTER COMPANY
Also Called: Saratogian USA Today
20 Lake Ave (12866-2314)
PHONE.................................518 584-4242
Ashley Schaal, *Sales Staff*
Linda Feltman, *Manager*
EMP: 80
SALES (corp-wide): 697.5MM **Privately
Held**
SIC: 2711 Newspapers: publishing only,
not printed on site
PA: Journal Register Company
5 Hanover Sq Fl 25
New York NY 10004

(G-14185)
NALCO COMPANY LLC
6 Butler Pl 2 (12866-2155)
PHONE..............................518 796-1985
Joseph Fitzhenry, *Manager*
EMP: 20
SALES (corp-wide): 14.6B **Publicly Held**
WEB: www.nalco.com
SIC: 2899 5169 Chemical preparations; chemicals & allied products
HQ: Nalco Company Llc
　　1601 W Diehl Rd
　　Naperville IL 60563
　　630 305-1000

(G-14186)
NANOBIONOVUM LLC
117 Grand Ave (12866-4118)
P.O. Box 4434 (12866-8026)
PHONE..............................518 581-1171
Lance Bell, *CEO*
Glenn Kitterman, *Business Anlyst*
EMP: 10
SQ FT: 5,000
SALES (est): 708.6K **Privately Held**
SIC: 3841 Diagnostic apparatus, medical

(G-14187)
PHYTOFILTER TECHNOLOGIES INC
9 Kirby Rd Apt 19 (12866-9287)
PHONE..............................518 507-6399
Martin Mittelmark, *CEO*
EMP: 5 EST: 2010
SALES (est): 400K **Privately Held**
SIC: 3564 Air purification equipment

(G-14188)
PRIME TURBINE PARTS LLC
77 Railroad Pl (12866-2124)
PHONE..............................518 306-7306
Martin Harr,
◆ EMP: 3
SALES: 2MM **Privately Held**
SIC: 3511 Turbines & turbine generator sets

(G-14189)
QUAD/GRAPHICS INC
56 Duplainville Rd (12866-9050)
PHONE..............................518 581-4000
Dave Blais, *Vice Pres*
Tom Kazda, *Engineer*
Dan Frankowski, *Branch Mgr*
Vic Eckstein, *Manager*
Thomas S Estock, *Manager*
EMP: 900
SALES (corp-wide): 4.1B **Publicly Held**
WEB: www.qg.com
SIC: 2752 2791 2789 Commercial printing, offset; typesetting; bookbinding & related work
PA: Quad/Graphics Inc.
　　N61w23044 Harrys Way
　　Sussex WI 53089
　　414 566-6000

(G-14190)
RECORD
Also Called: Sunday Record, The
20 Lake Ave (12866-2314)
PHONE..............................518 270-1200
Chad Beatty, *President*
Fred Degesco, *President*
Genette Brookshire, *Editor*
EMP: 1
SQ FT: 35,000
SALES (est): 1.1MM
SALES (corp-wide): 697.5MM **Privately Held**
WEB: www.troyrecord.com
SIC: 2711 Commercial printing & newspaper publishing combined; newspapers, publishing & printing
PA: Journal Register Company
　　5 Hanover Sq Fl 25
　　New York NY 10004

(G-14191)
REDSPRING COMMUNICATIONS INC
125 High Rock Ave (12866-2307)
PHONE..............................518 587-0547
James Hill, *President*
EMP: 44

SQ FT: 10,500
SALES (est): 3MM **Privately Held**
WEB: www.redspring.com
SIC: 2741 Newsletter publishing; posters: publishing only, not printed on site

(G-14192)
SARATOGA CHIPS LLC
63 Putnam St Ste 202 (12866-3285)
PHONE..............................877 901-6950
James R Schneider, *President*
Joseph Boff, *Vice Pres*
Danny Jameson, *Vice Pres*
Joel I Bobrow, *Vice Pres*
Tim Kennedy, *CFO*
EMP: 7
SQ FT: 1,500
SALES: 1MM **Privately Held**
SIC: 2096 Popcorn, already popped (except candy covered)

(G-14193)
SARATOGA SPRING WATER COMPANY
11 Geyser Rd (12866-9038)
PHONE..............................518 584-6363
Adam Madkour, *CEO*
Steve Gilbank, *Principal*
Michael Lawson, *Plant Mgr*
Cindy Carpenter, *Accountant*
Shanon Green, *Human Res Mgr*
EMP: 22
SQ FT: 40,000
SALES (est): 6MM **Privately Held**
WEB: www.saratogaspringwater.com
SIC: 2086 Mineral water, carbonated: packaged in cans, bottles, etc.

(G-14194)
STRATEGIC SIGNAGE SOURCING LLC
2 Gilbert Rd (12866-9701)
PHONE..............................518 450-1093
Robert L Keyser, *President*
Kenneth W Wasson, *Vice Pres*
Carole Van Buren, *Project Mgr*
Suzanne K Nelson, *Marketing Staff*
Jeff Mangione, *Program Mgr*
EMP: 10
SALES (est): 1.1MM **Privately Held**
SIC: 3993 Electric signs

(G-14195)
WARD LAFRANCE TRUCK CORP
26 Congress St Ste 259f (12866-4168)
PHONE..............................518 893-1865
EMP: 15 EST: 1978
SALES: 12.8MM **Privately Held**
SIC: 3537 Trucks: freight, baggage, etc.: industrial, except mining

---

Saugerties
Ulster County

(G-14196)
ADIRONDACK STAIRS INC
990 Kings Hwy (12477-4373)
P.O. Box 419 (12477-0419)
PHONE..............................845 246-2525
Karl H Neumann, *President*
Mattie Anttila, *Vice Pres*
EMP: 12 EST: 1966
SALES (est): 1.3MM **Privately Held**
SIC: 2431 Staircases & stairs, wood

(G-14197)
ARISTA FLAG CORPORATION
157 W Saugerties Rd (12477-3532)
P.O. Box 319 (12477-0319)
PHONE..............................845 246-7700
Stephen Suma, *President*
Susan Suma, *Corp Secy*
Rita Mary Suma, *Vice Pres*
EMP: 12
SQ FT: 5,500
SALES (est): 1.1MM **Privately Held**
WEB: www.aristaflag.com
SIC: 2399 Banners, made from fabric; flags, fabric; pennants

(G-14198)
CERES TECHNOLOGIES INC
5 Tower Dr (12477-4386)
P.O. Box 209 (12477-0209)
PHONE..............................845 247-4701
Kevin Brady, *President*
Petra Klein, *Vice Pres*
Kali Brady, *Project Mgr*
Bryan Jones, *Project Mgr*
Robert Wilson, *Mfg Staff*
EMP: 70
SQ FT: 50,000
SALES: 21.1MM **Privately Held**
SIC: 3674 3823 3826 Semiconductors & related devices; industrial instrmnts msrmnt display/control process variable; analytical instruments

(G-14199)
CVD EQUIPMENT CORPORATION
1117 Kings Hwy (12477-4343)
PHONE..............................845 246-3631
Kevin Collions, *Manager*
EMP: 20
SALES (corp-wide): 24.3MM **Publicly Held**
WEB: www.cvdequipment.com
SIC: 3559 Sewing machines & hat & zipper making machinery
PA: Cvd Equipment Corporation
　　355 S Technology Dr
　　Central Islip NY 11722
　　631 981-7081

(G-14200)
DE LUXE PACKAGING CORP
63 North St (12477-1039)
PHONE..............................416 754-4633
Richard Goulet, *President*
EMP: 50 EST: 2003
SALES (est): 6.3MM
SALES (corp-wide): 2.9B **Privately Held**
SIC: 3497 2671 Foil containers for bakery goods & frozen foods; paper coated or laminated for packaging
HQ: Novolex Holdings, Llc
　　101 E Carolina Ave
　　Hartsville SC 29550
　　843 857-4800

(G-14201)
DELUXE PACKAGING CORP
63 North St (12477-1039)
P.O. Box 269 (12477-0269)
PHONE..............................845 246-6090
Richard Goulet, *Branch Mgr*
EMP: 19
SQ FT: 32,740
SALES (corp-wide): 2.9B **Privately Held**
WEB: www.deluxepack.com
SIC: 2676 Toilet paper: made from purchased paper
HQ: Papercon Canada Holding Corp
　　200 Av Marien
　　Montreal-Est QC H1B 4
　　514 645-4571

(G-14202)
INQUIRING MINDS INC (PA)
65 S Partition St (12477)
PHONE..............................845 246-5775
Bryan Donahue, *President*
EMP: 11 EST: 2012
SALES (est): 1.1MM **Privately Held**
SIC: 3421 Table & food cutlery, including butchers'

(G-14203)
KENBENCO INC
Also Called: Benson Steel Fabricators
437 Route 212 (12477-4620)
P.O. Box 480 (12477-0480)
PHONE..............................845 246-3066
Myron E Benson, *Owner*
EMP: 15
SQ FT: 12,000
SALES (est): 3.1MM **Privately Held**
WEB: www.bensonsteelfabricators.com
SIC: 3312 3431 Blast furnaces & steel mills; metal sanitary ware

(G-14204)
LODOLCE MACHINE CO INC
196 Malden Tpke (12477-5015)
PHONE..............................845 246-7017

Michael Lodolce, *President*
▲ EMP: 38 EST: 1963
SQ FT: 65,000
SALES (est): 7.6MM **Privately Held**
WEB: www.lodolce.com
SIC: 3599 1761 3479 Machine shop, jobbing & repair; sheet metalwork; painting, coating & hot dipping

(G-14205)
NORTHEAST SOLITE CORPORATION (PA)
1135 Kings Hwy (12477-4343)
P.O. Box 437, Mount Marion (12456-0437)
PHONE..............................845 246-2646
John W Roberts, *Ch of Bd*
Philip M Nesmith, *President*
Jessica Eng, *Senior VP*
James Gregory, *Vice Pres*
Max Kalafat, *Vice Pres*
EMP: 40
SALES (est): 16.2MM **Privately Held**
WEB: www.nesolite.com
SIC: 3295 Minerals, ground or treated

(G-14206)
ORGANIC NECTARS INC
162 Malden Tpke Bldg 5 (12477-5015)
P.O. Box 158, Malden On Hudson (12453-0158)
PHONE..............................845 246-0506
Lisa Protter, *CEO*
EMP: 5
SALES (est): 280.6K **Privately Held**
SIC: 2033 Fruit nectars: packaged in cans, jars, etc.

(G-14207)
PAPER HOUSE PRODUCTIONS INC
160 Malden Tpke Bldg 2 (12477-5015)
P.O. Box 259 (12477-0259)
PHONE..............................845 246-7261
Donald A Guidi, *CEO*
Pam Gardeski, *Vice Pres*
Pamela Gardeski, *Vice Pres*
Jon Holter, *Vice Pres*
Tara Sturm, *Production*
▲ EMP: 25
SQ FT: 16,000
SALES (est): 4.1MM **Privately Held**
WEB: www.paperhouseproductions.com
SIC: 2771 2752 5112 5945 Greeting cards; decals, lithographed; greeting cards; hobby & craft supplies

(G-14208)
PESCES BAKERY INC
Also Called: Pesce Bakery
20 Pesce Ct (12477-5054)
PHONE..............................845 246-4730
Richard Pesce, *President*
Rich Pesce, *President*
EMP: 6 EST: 1946
SQ FT: 3,000
SALES (est): 564.1K **Privately Held**
SIC: 2051 5461 Bakery: wholesale or wholesale/retail combined; bakeries

(G-14209)
PETE LEVIN MUSIC INC
598 Schoolhouse Rd (12477-3325)
PHONE..............................845 247-9211
Peter Levin, *President*
Theresa Levin, *Vice Pres*
Theresa R Levin, *Vice Pres*
EMP: 5
SALES (est): 340K **Privately Held**
WEB: www.petelevin.com
SIC: 3652 Pre-recorded records & tapes

(G-14210)
ROTHE WELDING INC
1455 Route 212 (12477-3040)
PHONE..............................845 246-3051
Dorothy L Fauci, *Chairman*
EMP: 8
SQ FT: 11,500
SALES (est): 1.8MM **Privately Held**
WEB: www.hvaccess.com
SIC: 3441 7692 Fabricated structural metal; welding repair

(G-14211)
SAUGERTIES DELICIOSO INC
3218 Route 9w (12477-5237)
PHONE..............................845 217-5072
EMP: 5
SALES (est): 194.5K **Privately Held**
SIC: 2711 Newspapers

(G-14212)
SIMULAIDS INC
16 Simulaids Dr (12477-5067)
P.O. Box 1289 (12477-8289)
PHONE..............................845 679-2475
Dean T Johnson, *CEO*
Jack McNeff, *Vice Pres*
Gus Hof, *Prdtn Mgr*
Nicole Heckler, *Buyer*
Patricia Stockman, *Human Res Mgr*
EMP: 93 EST: 1963
SQ FT: 50,000
SALES (est): 18.1MM
SALES (corp-wide): 269.1MM **Privately Held**
WEB: www.simulaids.com
SIC: 3841 7841 3699 Surgical & medical instruments; video tape rental; electrical equipment & supplies
HQ: Nasco Healthcare Inc.
901 Janesville Ave
Fort Atkinson WI 53538
920 568-5600

(G-14213)
STAINLESS DESIGN CONCEPTS LTD
Also Called: SDC
1117 Kings Hwy (12477-4343)
P.O. Box 514, Smithtown (11787-0514)
PHONE..............................845 246-3631
Len Rosenbaum, *Ch of Bd*
Kevin Twitty, *Engineer*
Glen Charles, *CFO*
Mary Sauer, *Sales Staff*
EMP: 35 EST: 1986
SQ FT: 25,000
SALES (est): 6.5MM
SALES (corp-wide): 24.3MM **Publicly Held**
WEB: www.stainlessdesign.com
SIC: 3559 Chemical machinery & equipment
PA: Cvd Equipment Corporation
355 S Technology Dr
Central Islip NY 11722
631 981-7081

(G-14214)
STUART SPECTOR DESIGNS LTD
1450 Route 212 (12477-3028)
PHONE..............................845 246-6124
Stuart Spector, *President*
Darryl Ford, *General Mgr*
▲ EMP: 9
SQ FT: 4,500
SALES: 850K **Privately Held**
WEB: www.ssdbass.com
SIC: 3931 Guitars & parts, electric & non-electric

(G-14215)
THE SMOKE HOUSE OF CATSKILLS
724 Route 212 (12477-4617)
PHONE..............................845 246-8767
Charles Rothe, *President*
EMP: 7 EST: 1952
SQ FT: 2,400
SALES (est): 266.2K **Privately Held**
SIC: 2011 5421 Meat packing plants; meat markets, including freezer provisioners

(G-14216)
WORKING FAMILY SOLUTIONS INC
359 Washington Avenue Ext (12477-5221)
P.O. Box 88, Malden On Hudson (12453-0088)
PHONE..............................845 802-6182
Danielle N Heller, *CEO*
EMP: 5
SALES (est): 360.9K **Privately Held**
SIC: 2835 Pregnancy test kits

(G-14217)
ZENITH SOLUTIONS
23 Robinson St (12477-1030)
PHONE..............................718 575-8570
P Bilello, *Principal*
Pasquale Bilello, *Principal*
EMP: 6 EST: 2001
SALES (est): 694.9K **Privately Held**
SIC: 2834 Intravenous solutions

Sauquoit
Oneida County

(G-14218)
CUSTOM STAIR & MILLWORK CO
Also Called: Kitchen Design Center
6 Gridley Pl (13456-3416)
PHONE..............................315 839-5793
John Dweyer, *President*
EMP: 9
SQ FT: 10,000
SALES (est): 750K **Privately Held**
SIC: 2431 Staircases & stairs, wood

(G-14219)
LEATHERSTOCKING MOBILE HOME PA
2089 Doolittle Rd (13456-2409)
PHONE..............................315 839-5691
Jane W Brennan, *Ch of Bd*
EMP: 5
SALES (est): 613.7K **Privately Held**
SIC: 2451 Mobile homes

Savannah
Wayne County

(G-14220)
PEARL TECHNOLOGIES INC
13297 Seneca St (13146-9663)
P.O. Box 196 (13146-0196)
PHONE..............................315 365-3742
Laurent Cros, *CEO*
Bill Gillette, *Mfg Mgr*
Gary Stover, *Purch Agent*
Amy Hoad, *Buyer*
Ray Wright, *Engineer*
EMP: 35
SQ FT: 35,000
SALES (est): 8.4MM **Privately Held**
SIC: 3559 Plastics working machinery
HQ: Gloucester Engineering Co., Inc.
11 Dory Rd
Gloucester MA 01930
978 281-1800

(G-14221)
PURE FUNCTIONAL FOODS INC
267 State Route 89 (13146-9711)
PHONE..............................315 294-0733
EMP: 20
SALES (est): 3.6MM **Privately Held**
SIC: 2099 Food preparations

Sayville
Suffolk County

(G-14222)
AQUARIUM PUMP & PIPING SYSTEMS
528 Chester Rd (11782-1808)
PHONE..............................631 567-5555
Charles Eckstein, *Owner*
EMP: 11
SQ FT: 2,500
SALES (est): 614.2K **Privately Held**
SIC: 3499 3089 Aquarium accessories, metal; aquarium accessories, plastic

(G-14223)
BRAINWORKS SOFTWARE DEV CORP (PA)
100 S Main St Ste 102 (11782-3148)
PHONE..............................631 563-5000
John Barry, *President*
EMP: 49
SQ FT: 4,000
SALES (est): 5.8MM **Privately Held**
SIC: 7372 Prepackaged software

(G-14224)
BUNGERS SURF SHOP
Also Called: Bunger Sayville
247 W Main St (11782-2522)
PHONE..............................631 244-3646
Sammy Hito, *Principal*
EMP: 8 EST: 2012
SALES (est): 481.4K **Privately Held**
SIC: 3949 Surfboards; water sports equipment

(G-14225)
ESC CONTROL ELECTRONICS LLC
Also Called: Control Elec Div Fil-Coil
98 Lincoln Ave (11782-2711)
PHONE..............................631 467-5328
Daniel Barnett, *IT/INT Sup*
Paul Alessandrini,
▲ EMP: 35
SQ FT: 2,000
SALES (est): 4.8MM **Privately Held**
SIC: 3677 3679 3841 3851 Electronic transformers; filtration devices, electronic; delay lines; surgical & medical instruments; ophthalmic goods
PA: Fil-Coil (Fc) Corp.
98 Lincoln Ave
Sayville NY 11782

(G-14226)
FIL-COIL (FC) CORP (PA)
Also Called: Custom Power System
98 Lincoln Ave (11782-2711)
PHONE..............................631 467-5328
Carrol Trust, *CEO*
Paul Alessandrini Sr, *Ch of Bd*
Batt Trust, *Vice Pres*
Michelle Reynolds, *Bookkeeper*
Lauren Banfi, *Admin Asst*
▲ EMP: 45
SQ FT: 6,000
SALES (est): 5.9MM **Privately Held**
SIC: 3677 Filtration devices, electronic

(G-14227)
FIL-COIL INTERNATIONAL LLC
98 Lincoln Ave (11782-2711)
PHONE..............................631 467-5328
Laura Ritter, *Vice Chairman*
EMP: 14
SQ FT: 1,500
SALES (est): 637.9K **Privately Held**
SIC: 3677 Transformers power supply, electronic type

(G-14228)
KKW CORP
Also Called: Koster Keunen Waxes
90 Bourne Blvd (11782-3307)
PHONE..............................631 589-5454
Richard B Koster, *Ch of Bd*
▲ EMP: 40
SQ FT: 60,000
SALES (est): 6.1MM **Privately Held**
WEB: www.paramold.com
SIC: 3999 Candles

(G-14229)
KOSTER KEUNEN WAXES LTD
90 Bourne Blvd (11782-3307)
PHONE..............................631 589-0400
Richard Koster, *President*
▲ EMP: 15
SQ FT: 45,000
SALES (est): 2MM **Privately Held**
SIC: 2911 Mineral waxes, natural

(G-14230)
OPTIKA EYES LTD
153 Main St Unit 1 (11782-2566)
PHONE..............................631 567-8852
Nancy Pacella, *President*
EMP: 8
SQ FT: 1,000
SALES (est): 610K **Privately Held**
SIC: 3851 5995 Frames, lenses & parts, eyeglass & spectacle; contact lenses; optical goods stores

(G-14231)
REDDI CAR CORP
174 Greeley Ave (11782-2396)
PHONE..............................631 589-3141
Kenneth Johnson, *President*
EMP: 7 EST: 1957
SQ FT: 5,000
SALES (est): 517.1K **Privately Held**
SIC: 2851 2899 5085 Paints & paint additives; chemical preparations; fasteners, industrial: nuts, bolts, screws, etc.

(G-14232)
WEEKS & REICHEL PRINTING INC
131 Railroad Ave (11782-2799)
PHONE..............................631 589-1443
John A Weeks, *President*
Robert Reichel, *Treasurer*
EMP: 5
SQ FT: 2,400
SALES (est): 537.1K **Privately Held**
SIC: 2759 2752 Letterpress printing; commercial printing, offset

Scarsdale
Westchester County

(G-14233)
AMERICAN EPOXY AND METAL INC
83 Cushman Rd (10583-3403)
PHONE..............................718 828-7828
Samer Daniel, *President*
Ralph Maccarino, *Vice Pres*
EMP: 8
SALES (est): 996.7K **Privately Held**
WEB: www.americanepoxy.com
SIC: 2821 2511 Epoxy resins; whatnot shelves: wood; tables, household: wood

(G-14234)
CRANIAL TECHNOLOGIES INC
495 Central Park Ave (10583-1068)
PHONE..............................914 472-0975
Tammy Jones, *Manager*
EMP: 7 **Privately Held**
SIC: 3842 Orthopedic appliances
PA: Cranial Technologies, Inc.
1395 W Auto Dr
Tempe AZ 85284

(G-14235)
EASTCO MANUFACTURING CORP
Also Called: K & S & East
38 Wilmot Cir (10583-6722)
PHONE..............................914 738-5667
Jack Koff, *President*
Philip Schwartzman, *Vice Pres*
EMP: 12
SALES (est): 2MM **Privately Held**
SIC: 3699 Electrical equipment & supplies

(G-14236)
GOTHAM CITY INDUSTRIES INC (PA)
372 Fort Hill Rd (10583-2411)
PHONE..............................914 713-3449
Barbara Chalson, *President*
Jay Chalson, *Vice Pres*
Roger Nafziger, *Director*
▲ EMP: 1
SQ FT: 17,000
SALES (est): 2.5MM **Privately Held**
WEB: www.gothamind.com
SIC: 2541 Display fixtures, wood

(G-14237)
JAPAN AMERICA LEARNING CTR INC (PA)
Also Called: Enjoy
81 Montgomery Ave (10583-5104)
P.O. Box 606, Hartsdale (10530-0606)
PHONE..............................914 723-7600
Kazuko Maeda, *President*
Norman Floerke, *Production*
EMP: 10
SQ FT: 2,000
SALES: 300K **Privately Held**
SIC: 2721 8299 Trade journals: publishing only, not printed on site; language school

G E O G R A P H I C

(G-14238)
LAND PACKAGING CORP
7 Black Birch Ln (10583-7456)
PHONE.................................914 472-5976
Lawrence Rosefeld, *President*
Lawrence Rosenfeld, *President*
EMP: 10
SQ FT: 3,000
SALES: 5MM **Privately Held**
SIC: 2653 Corrugated boxes, partitions, display items, sheets & pad

(G-14239)
NATHAN PRINTING EXPRESS INC
740 Central Park Ave (10583-2504)
PHONE.................................914 472-0914
Nathan Wong, *President*
Alex Wong, *Vice Pres*
EMP: 7
SQ FT: 1,600
SALES (est): 779.6K **Privately Held**
SIC: 2759 Screen printing

(G-14240)
PERFORMANCE SOURCING GROUP INC (PA)
109 Montgomery Ave (10583-5531)
PHONE.................................914 636-2100
S Shwartz, *President*
Sanjay Tillu, *CFO*
EMP: 40
SALES: 35MM **Privately Held**
SIC: 2392 Household furnishings

(G-14241)
S I COMMUNICATIONS INC
Also Called: Scarsdale Inquirer
8 Harwood Ct (10583-4104)
P.O. Box 418 (10583-0418)
PHONE.................................914 725-2500
Deborah White, *President*
Sandy Greene, *Editor*
Todd Sliss, *Editor*
Eileen Farrell, *Director*
EMP: 18
SALES (est): 1MM **Privately Held**
WEB: www.scarsdaleinquirer.com
SIC: 2711 Newspapers: publishing only, not printed on site

(G-14242)
SHERIDAN HOUSE INC
230 Nelson Rd (10583-5908)
PHONE.................................914 725-5431
Lothar Simon, *President*
Jeannine Simon, *Vice Pres*
▲ EMP: 5 EST: 1940
SQ FT: 4,000
SALES (est): 709.7K **Privately Held**
WEB: www.sheridanhouse.com
SIC: 2731 Book publishing

(G-14243)
ZANZANO WOODWORKING INC
91 Locust Ave (10583-6230)
PHONE.................................914 725-6025
Michael Zanzano, *Principal*
EMP: 13
SALES (est): 1.6MM **Privately Held**
SIC: 2431 Millwork

Schenectady
Schenectady County

(G-14244)
A W HAMEL STAIR MFG INC
3111 Amsterdam Rd (12302-6328)
PHONE.................................518 346-3031
Joseph Lucarelli, *President*
Scott Ressel, *General Mgr*
Donald Lucarelli, *Vice Pres*
EMP: 16
SQ FT: 30,000
SALES (est): 1.8MM **Privately Held**
SIC: 2431 Staircases & stairs, wood; stair railings, wood

(G-14245)
AMERICAN HSPTALS PATIENT GUIDE
1890 Maxon Rd Ext (12308-1140)
P.O. Box 1031 (12301-1031)
PHONE.................................518 346-1099
Robert J Kosineski Sr, *President*
EMP: 10
SALES (est): 806.5K **Privately Held**
SIC: 2741 Miscellaneous publishing

(G-14246)
AUTERRA INC
2135 Technology Dr (12308-1143)
PHONE.................................518 382-9600
Eric Burnett, *President*
Steven T Jackson, *Vice Pres*
EMP: 9 EST: 2006
SALES (est): 2MM **Privately Held**
SIC: 2819 Industrial inorganic chemicals

(G-14247)
AXLE EXPRESS
729 Broadway (12305-2703)
PHONE.................................518 347-2220
Samuel Caldarazzo, *President*
EMP: 25
SALES (est): 2.2MM **Privately Held**
SIC: 3714 Motor vehicle parts & accessories

(G-14248)
BAKE-RITE INTERNATIONAL INC
412 Warren St (12305-1116)
PHONE.................................518 395-3340
Kathryn Donovan, *President*
Brian Donavan, *Vice Pres*
Brian S Donovan, *Vice Pres*
◆ EMP: 5 EST: 1995
SALES (est): 833.2K **Privately Held**
WEB: www.bake-rite.com
SIC: 3556 Food products machinery

(G-14249)
BENCHEMARK PRINTING INC
1890 Maxon Rd Ext (12308-1149)
P.O. Box 1031 (12301-1031)
PHONE.................................518 393-1361
Robert Kosineski, *President*
Denise Hecker, *Human Resources*
Michael Ryan, *Accounts Mgr*
Joe Prock, *Accounts Exec*
Anna Beckwith, *Director*
▲ EMP: 55
SQ FT: 75,000
SALES (est): 14.7MM **Privately Held**
SIC: 2752 2791 2789 2759 Commercial printing, offset; typesetting; bookbinding & related work; commercial printing

(G-14250)
CALLANAN INDUSTRIES INC
145 Cordell Rd (12303-2701)
P.O. Box 40, Selkirk (12158-0040)
PHONE.................................518 382-5354
Bryan Francett, *General Mgr*
Steve Akers, *Plant Mgr*
Anthony Miele, *Foreman/Supr*
Nick Duncan, *Project Engr*
Pete Skelly, *Credit Mgr*
EMP: 9
SALES (corp-wide): 30.6B **Privately Held**
SIC: 3999 Barber & beauty shop equipment
HQ: Callanan Industries, Inc.
    8 Southwoods Blvd Ste 4
    Albany NY 12211
    518 374-2222

(G-14251)
CAPITAL DST PRINT & IMAGING
Also Called: Allegra Print & Imaging
2075 Central Ave (12304-4426)
PHONE.................................518 456-6773
Jim Cazavilan, *President*
EMP: 7
SQ FT: 2,500
SALES (est): 1MM **Privately Held**
WEB: www.allegraalbany.com
SIC: 2752 7334 Commercial printing, offset; photocopying & duplicating services

(G-14252)
CAPITAL STONE LLC
2241 Central Ave (12304-4379)
PHONE.................................518 382-7588
James Nass, *President*
Carmine Petti, *Manager*
EMP: 9
SQ FT: 5,000
SALES: 1MM **Privately Held**
SIC: 3281 Granite, cut & shaped

(G-14253)
CASCADE TECHNICAL SERVICES LLC
2846 Curry Rd Ste B (12303-3463)
PHONE.................................518 355-2201
Matthew Ednie, *Manager*
EMP: 5
SALES (corp-wide): 915.2MM **Privately Held**
WEB: www.teamzebra.com
SIC: 3822 Auto controls regulating residntl & coml environmt & applncs
HQ: Cascade Technical Services Llc
    30 N Prospect Ave
    Lynbrook NY 11563
    516 596-6300

(G-14254)
CASCADES NEW YORK INC
801 Corporation Park (12302-1061)
PHONE.................................518 346-6151
Marc Andre Depin, *President*
EMP: 150
SALES (corp-wide): 3.5B **Privately Held**
SIC: 2621 Paper mills
HQ: Cascades New York Inc.
    1845 Emerson St
    Rochester NY 14606
    585 527-8110

(G-14255)
CHURCH & DWIGHT CO INC
Also Called: Arm & Hammer
706 Ennis Rd (12306-7420)
PHONE.................................518 887-5109
Douglas Waddell, *Branch Mgr*
EMP: 12
SALES (corp-wide): 4.1B **Publicly Held**
WEB: www.churchdwight.com
SIC: 2812 Sodium bicarbonate
PA: Church & Dwight Co., Inc.
    500 Charles Ewing Blvd
    Ewing NJ 08628
    609 806-1200

(G-14256)
CIANFARANI ARMANDO
Also Called: Armando & Sons General Welding
114 Van Guysling Ave (12305-2709)
PHONE.................................518 393-7755
Armando Cianfarani, *Owner*
EMP: 5
SQ FT: 7,000
SALES: 1MM **Privately Held**
SIC: 3446 Architectural metalwork

(G-14257)
CLEMENTE LATHAM CONCRETE CORP
Also Called: Clemente Latham North Div
1245 Kings Rd (12303-2831)
P.O. Box 15097, Albany (12212-5097)
PHONE.................................518 374-2222
Frank A Clemente, *Ch of Bd*
Linda Hiserote, *Credit Mgr*
EMP: 100
SALES (est): 14.1MM
SALES (corp-wide): 30.6B **Privately Held**
SIC: 3273 5032 Ready-mixed concrete; brick, stone & related material
HQ: Oldcastle Materials, Inc.
    900 Ashwood Pkwy Ste 700
    Atlanta GA 30338

(G-14258)
CODINOS LIMITED INC
704 Corporation Park # 5 (12302-1091)
PHONE.................................518 372-3308
Scott Devantier, *President*
Rita Vose, *Shareholder*
EMP: 33
SQ FT: 33,000

SALES: 6.1MM **Privately Held**
SIC: 2038 Frozen specialties

(G-14259)
CON REL AUTO ELECTRIC INC
3637 Carman Rd (12303-5401)
PHONE.................................518 356-1646
Kevin Relyea, *President*
Michael Relyea, *Corp Secy*
David O'Connell, *Vice Pres*
Gloria Mc Cue, *Financial Exec*
EMP: 35
SQ FT: 9,000
SALES: 3.9MM **Privately Held**
SIC: 3621 3694 3625 Starters, for motors; alternators, automotive; relays & industrial controls

(G-14260)
DAILY GAZETTE COMPANY (PA)
2345 Maxon Rd Ext (12308-1150)
P.O. Box 1090 (12301-1090)
PHONE.................................518 374-4141
John Hume, *President*
Rosanne Cheeseman, *Publisher*
John Deaugustine, *Publisher*
Elizabeth Lind, *Vice Pres*
Ernest Grandy, *Treasurer*
EMP: 325 EST: 1894
SQ FT: 111,000
SALES (est): 73.2MM **Privately Held**
WEB: www.dailygazette.com
SIC: 2711 Commercial printing & newspaper publishing combined; newspapers, publishing & printing

(G-14261)
DSM NUTRITIONAL PRODUCTS LLC
2105 Technology Dr (12308-1143)
PHONE.................................518 372-5155
EMP: 152
SALES (corp-wide): 10.6B **Privately Held**
SIC: 2834 3295 2087 Vitamin, nutrient & hematinic preparations for human use; vitamin preparations; minerals, ground or treated; flavoring extracts & syrups
HQ: Dsm Nutritional Products, Llc
    45 Waterview Blvd
    Parsippany NJ 07054
    800 526-0189

(G-14262)
ENER-G-ROTORS INC
17 Fern Ave (12306-2708)
PHONE.................................518 372-2608
Michael Newell, *Ch of Bd*
Edward Zampella III, *President*
EMP: 5
SALES (est): 946K **Privately Held**
SIC: 3621 7694 5084 5063 Motors & generators; armature rewinding shops; hydraulic systems equipment & supplies; electrical apparatus & equipment

(G-14263)
ENERGY PANEL STRUCTURES INC
Also Called: Fingerlakes Construction
864 Burdeck St (12306-1218)
PHONE.................................518 355-6708
Kirt Burghdorf, *Vice Pres*
EMP: 7
SALES (corp-wide): 190.3MM **Privately Held**
SIC: 3448 2452 Prefabricated metal buildings; prefabricated wood buildings
HQ: Energy Panel Structures, Inc.
    603 N Van Gordon Ave
    Graettinger IA 51342
    712 859-3219

(G-14264)
ENVIRONMENT-ONE CORPORATION
Also Called: E/One Utility Systems
2773 Balltown Rd (12309-1090)
PHONE.................................518 346-6161
Eric Lacoppola, *President*
Geoffrey Hawks, *Treasurer*
Christopher Nedwick, *Sales Staff*
Dean Pierce, *Manager*
Jessica Flores, *Info Tech Mgr*
▲ EMP: 135
SQ FT: 78,000

▲ = Import ▼=Export
◆ =Import/Export

SALES (est): 46.9MM
SALES (corp-wide): 225.3B **Publicly Held**
WEB: www.eone.com
SIC: 3589 3824 Sewage treatment equipment; mechanical & electromechanical counters & devices
HQ: Precision Castparts Corp.
4650 Sw Mcdam Ave Ste 300
Portland OR 97239
503 946-4800

(G-14265)
EPICOR SOFTWARE CORPORATION
Docstar
2165 Technology Dr (12308-1143)
PHONE..........................805 496-6789
Jeff Frankel, *Vice Pres*
Suren Pai, *Branch Mgr*
Tim Lajeunesse, *Technical Staff*
Mark Sanges, *Technical Staff*
EMP: 45 **Publicly Held**
SIC: 3577 Computer peripheral equipment
HQ: Epicor Software Corporation
804 Las Cimas Pkwy # 200
Austin TX 78746

(G-14266)
GENERAL ELECTRIC COMPANY
1 River Rd Bldg 55 (12305-2551)
PHONE..........................518 385-4022
Greg Bouleris, *Vice Pres*
Dan Abey, *Engineer*
Tyler Beasley, *Engineer*
Brian Fahrenkopf, *Engineer*
David Harper, *Engineer*
EMP: 603
SQ FT: 23,808
SALES (corp-wide): 121.6B **Publicly Held**
SIC: 3511 3612 3641 3632 Steam turbines; gas turbines, mechanical drive; autotransformers, electric (power transformers); electric lamps & parts for generalized applications; electric light bulbs, complete; lamps, incandescent filament, electric; lamps, fluorescent, electric; refrigerators, mechanical & absorption: household; freezers, home & farm; television broadcasting stations; research & development on aircraft engines & parts
PA: General Electric Company
41 Farnsworth St
Boston MA 02210
617 443-3000

(G-14267)
GENERAL ELECTRIC COMPANY
1 River Rd Bldg 33 (12305-2551)
PHONE..........................518 385-2211
Anthony Fiorenza, *Opers Staff*
Paul Kehoe, *Engineer*
Chad Bucholtz, *Finance*
John G Rice, *Branch Mgr*
Richard Zeh, *Manager*
EMP: 500
SALES (corp-wide): 121.6B **Publicly Held**
SIC: 3511 Turbines & turbine generator sets
PA: General Electric Company
41 Farnsworth St
Boston MA 02210
617 443-3000

(G-14268)
GENERAL ELECTRIC COMPANY
1 River Rd Bldg 43 (12345-6000)
PHONE..........................203 373-2756
Steve Bolze, *President*
EMP: 458
SALES (corp-wide): 121.6B **Publicly Held**
SIC: 3511 Turbines & turbine generator sets
PA: General Electric Company
41 Farnsworth St
Boston MA 02210
617 443-3000

(G-14269)
GENERAL ELECTRIC COMPANY
1 River Rd (12345-6000)
PHONE..........................518 385-3716
Damian D Foti, *Principal*

EMP: 491
SALES (corp-wide): 121.6B **Publicly Held**
SIC: 3511 Gas turbine generator set units, complete
PA: General Electric Company
41 Farnsworth St
Boston MA 02210
617 443-3000

(G-14270)
GENERAL ELECTRIC COMPANY
1 River Rd Bldg 37 (12345-6000)
PHONE..........................518 385-2211
John G Rice, *President*
Jeff Shaffer, *Branch Mgr*
Daniel Jordy, *Associate*
EMP: 500
SALES (corp-wide): 121.6B **Publicly Held**
SIC: 3511 3621 Gas turbine generator set units, complete; steam turbine generator set units, complete; motors & generators
PA: General Electric Company
41 Farnsworth St
Boston MA 02210
617 443-3000

(G-14271)
GENERAL ELECTRIC COMPANY
1 Research Cir (12309-1027)
P.O. Box 8 (12301-0008)
PHONE..........................518 387-5000
Jim Bollacker, *Engineer*
Jeremy Van Dam, *Engineer*
Bruce Amm, *Senior Engr*
Bugra Ertas, *Senior Engr*
Jixian Yao, *Senior Engr*
EMP: 500
SALES (corp-wide): 121.6B **Publicly Held**
SIC: 3511 Turbines & turbine generator sets
PA: General Electric Company
41 Farnsworth St
Boston MA 02210
617 443-3000

(G-14272)
GENERAL ELECTRIC COMPANY
705 Corporation Park (12302-1092)
PHONE..........................518 385-3439
Robert Flag, *Branch Mgr*
EMP: 8
SALES (corp-wide): 121.6B **Publicly Held**
SIC: 3511 Turbines & turbine generator sets
PA: General Electric Company
41 Farnsworth St
Boston MA 02210
617 443-3000

(G-14273)
GENERAL ELECTRIC INTL INC
1 River Rd Bldg 53202j (12345-6000)
PHONE..........................518 385-2211
Ernie Frasier, *Manager*
EMP: 9
SALES (corp-wide): 121.6B **Publicly Held**
SIC: 3511 3621 3433 Gas turbine generator set units, complete; steam turbine generator set units, complete; motors & generators; solar heaters & collectors
HQ: General Electric International, Inc.
191 Rosa Parks St
Cincinnati OH 45202
617 443-3000

(G-14274)
GRANDVIEW BLOCK & SUPPLY CO
1705 Hamburg St (12304-4699)
PHONE..........................518 346-7981
Salvatore Salamone, *President*
Samuel Salamone, *Vice Pres*
James Salamone, *Admin Sec*
EMP: 20 **EST:** 1946
SQ FT: 22,500
SALES (est): 3.3MM **Privately Held**
SIC: 3271 5032 Blocks, concrete or cinder: standard; masons' materials

(G-14275)
GRANDVIEW CONCRETE CORP
1705 Hamburg St (12304-4673)
PHONE..........................518 346-7981
George Salamone, *President*
Attilio A Salamone, *Shareholder*
Frank J Salamone, *Shareholder*
EMP: 24
SQ FT: 22,500
SALES (est): 3.1MM **Privately Held**
SIC: 3273 Ready-mixed concrete

(G-14276)
GREEN ENVIRO MACHINE LLC
Also Called: Gem
2366 Algonquin Rd (12309-1425)
PHONE..........................407 461-6412
Janice Lachman,
EMP: 5
SALES: 950K **Privately Held**
SIC: 3581 Automatic vending machines

(G-14277)
GUARDIAN CONCRETE PRODUCTS INC
Also Called: Guardian Concrete Steps
2140 Maxon Rd Ext (12308-1102)
PHONE..........................518 372-0080
Edward F Herba III, *CEO*
Glenda Jablonski, *Office Mgr*
EMP: 12
SQ FT: 13,000
SALES (est): 2.1MM **Privately Held**
SIC: 3272 5211 5039 Concrete products, precast; masonry materials & supplies; septic tanks

(G-14278)
HOHMANN & BARNARD INC
Sandell Moisture
310 Wayto Rd (12303-4538)
PHONE..........................518 357-9757
EMP: 21
SALES (corp-wide): 225.3B **Publicly Held**
SIC: 3496 3462 Clips & fasteners, made from purchased wire; iron & steel forgings
HQ: Hohmann & Barnard, Inc.
30 Rasons Ct
Hauppauge NY 11788
631 234-0600

(G-14279)
HP HOOD LLC
816 Burdeck St (12306-1213)
PHONE..........................518 218-9097
EMP: 299
SALES (corp-wide): 2.2B **Privately Held**
SIC: 2026 Fluid milk
PA: Hp Hood Llc
6 Kimball Ln Ste 400
Lynnfield MA 01940
617 887-8441

(G-14280)
IGT GLOBAL SOLUTIONS CORP
1 Broadway Ctr Fl 2 (12305-2554)
PHONE..........................518 382-2900
Ed Bourghan, *Branch Mgr*
EMP: 70
SALES (corp-wide): 4.8B **Privately Held**
WEB: www.gtech.com
SIC: 3575 Computer terminals
HQ: Igt Global Solutions Corporation
10 Memorial Blvd
Providence RI 02903
401 392-1000

(G-14281)
INTERSOURCE MANAGEMENT GROUP
144 Erie Blvd (12305-2203)
PHONE..........................518 372-6798
EMP: 29
SALES (corp-wide): 1.9MM **Privately Held**
SIC: 3511 Turbines & turbine generator sets & parts
PA: Intersource Management Group
7 Corporate Dr Ste 3
Halfmoon NY 12065
518 372-6798

(G-14282)
JIM QUINN
Also Called: Jim Quinn and Associates
12 Morningside Dr (12303-5610)
PHONE..........................518 356-0398
Jim Quinn, *Owner*
EMP: 10
SALES (est): 634.7K **Privately Held**
SIC: 2426 7641 Carvings, furniture: wood; office furniture repair & maintenance

(G-14283)
JOHN C DOLPH COMPANY
200 Von Roll Dr (12306-2443)
PHONE..........................732 329-2333
Jack Hasson, *President*
▼ **EMP:** 26 **EST:** 1910
SQ FT: 50,000
SALES (est): 7.5MM
SALES (corp-wide): 323.3MM **Privately Held**
WEB: www.johncdolph.com
SIC: 2851 2821 Varnishes; epoxy resins
PA: Von Roll Holding Ag
Passwangstrasse 20
Breitenbach SO
617 855-111

(G-14284)
KERYAKOS INC
1080 Catalyn St Fl 2 (12303-1835)
PHONE..........................518 344-7092
Charles Contompasis, *President*
Marika Contompasis, *Principal*
Laurie Ives, *Vice Pres*
EMP: 15
SALES (est): 1.8MM **Privately Held**
SIC: 2253 5137 Sweaters & sweater coats, knit; sweaters, women's & children's

(G-14285)
KING ROAD MATERIALS INC
145 Cordell Rd (12303-2701)
PHONE..........................518 382-5354
Chris Hensler, *Manager*
EMP: 11
SQ FT: 500
SALES (corp-wide): 30.6B **Privately Held**
SIC: 2951 Asphalt & asphaltic paving mixtures (not from refineries)
HQ: King Road Materials, Inc.
8 Southwoods Blvd
Albany NY 12211
518 381-9995

(G-14286)
LATHAM INTERNATIONAL INC
Also Called: Latham Manufacturing
706 Corporation Park 1 (12302-1047)
PHONE..........................518 346-5292
Tony Pagano, *Branch Mgr*
EMP: 12
SALES (corp-wide): 177.3MM **Privately Held**
WEB: www.pacificpools.com
SIC: 3081 Vinyl film & sheet
PA: Latham International, Inc.
787 Watervliet Shaker Rd
Latham NY 12110
518 783-7776

(G-14287)
LUCIDEON
2210 Technology Dr (12308-1145)
PHONE..........................518 382-0082
Dacia Detiberus, *Business Mgr*
David Hodson, *Sales Engr*
Joe Beagle, *Manager*
Sean Borkowski, *Technical Staff*
EMP: 13
SALES (est): 1.6MM **Privately Held**
SIC: 3297 Nonclay refractories

(G-14288)
METAL COATED FIBERS INC
679 Mariaville Rd (12306-6806)
PHONE..........................518 280-8514
Robert Duval, *President*
EMP: 22 **EST:** 2012
SALES (est): 1.2MM **Privately Held**
SIC: 3624 Fibers, carbon & graphite

(G-14289)
MILLIVAC INSTRUMENTS INC
2818 Curry Rd (12303-3463)
PHONE....................................518 355-8300
Imek Metzger, *President*
Pola Metzger, *Corp Secy*
Jan Metzger, *Vice Pres*
EMP: 7
SQ FT: 12,000
SALES (est): 1.2MM **Privately Held**
WEB: www.millivacinstruments.com
SIC: 3825 Test equipment for electronic &
electric measurement

(G-14290)
MISCELLNOUS IR
FABRICATORS INC
1404 Dunnsville Rd (12306-5509)
PHONE....................................518 355-1822
Helmut Giesselmann, *Ch of Bd*
Gunther Giesselmann, *President*
Daniel Eaton, *Financial Exec*
Thomas Giesselmann, *Manager*
Reinhart Giesselmann, *Admin Sec*
EMP: 22 EST: 1966
SQ FT: 22,000
SALES (est): 5.6MM **Privately Held**
SIC: 3441 1791 7699 Fabricated struc-
tural metal; iron work, structural; metal re-
shaping & replating services

(G-14291)
NEW MOUNT PLEASANT
BAKERY
941 Crane St (12303-1140)
PHONE....................................518 374-7577
Joe Riitano, *President*
Funda Topcuoglu, *Opers Staff*
Raheem Dawodu, *Corp Comm Staff*
Lara Kline, *Marketing Staff*
Kenneth TSE, *Network Enginr*
EMP: 50 EST: 1932
SQ FT: 15,000
SALES (est): 4.8MM **Privately Held**
SIC: 2051 5461 2052 Bread, cake & re-
lated products; bakeries; cookies & crack-
ers

(G-14292)
OLSON SIGN COMPANY INC
Also Called: Olson Signs & Graphics
1750 Valley Rd Ext (12302)
PHONE....................................518 370-2118
Richard Olson, *President*
Kelly Lee Olson, *Vice Pres*
EMP: 8
SQ FT: 6,200
SALES: 580K **Privately Held**
SIC: 3993 Electric signs; displays &
cutouts, window & lobby

(G-14293)
P1 GENERATOR WINDINGS LLC
(PA)
2165 Technology Dr (12308-1143)
PHONE....................................518 930-2879
Ron Pigliavento, *CFO*
David W Dussault, *Mng Member*
EMP: 4
SQ FT: 11,000
SALES (est): 1.1MM **Privately Held**
SIC: 3621 Coils, for electric motors or gen-
erators

(G-14294)
PACKAGE ONE INC
414 Union St (12305-1107)
PHONE....................................518 344-5425
David W Dussault, *President*
John Junge, *Engineer*
Lawrence Pigliavento, *CFO*
▲ EMP: 75
SQ FT: 30,000
SALES (est): 17.9MM **Privately Held**
SIC: 3568 Power transmission equipment

(G-14295)
PIZZA BLENDS LLC
Western Blending
1411 Rottrdm Indstl Park (12306)
PHONE....................................518 356-6650
Bob Morris, *Manager*
Butch Mitchell, *Executive*
EMP: 7

SALES (corp-wide): 626.8MM **Privately Held**
SIC: 2045 2041 Prepared flour mixes &
doughs; pizza dough, prepared
HQ: Pizza Blends Llc
400 112th Ave Ne Ste 350
Bellevue WA 98004
800 826-1200

(G-14296)
PRINTZ AND PATTERNZ LLC
Also Called: Printz Pttrnz Scrn-Prnting EMB
1550 Altamont Ave (12303-2147)
PHONE....................................518 944-6020
Daniel Crowley, *Mng Member*
Mike Crowley,
EMP: 6 EST: 2009
SALES (est): 778.1K **Privately Held**
SIC: 2752 2281 2396 Commercial print-
ing, lithographic; embroidery yarn, spun;
screen printing on fabric articles

(G-14297)
RAND PRODUCTS
MANUFACTURING CO
Also Called: Rand Mfg
1602 Van Vranken Ave (12308-2239)
PHONE....................................518 374-9871
Henry W Frick, *President*
Karen Frick Connlly, *Manager*
Karen Lewis, *Manager*
EMP: 5 EST: 1977
SQ FT: 7,000
SALES (est): 470K **Privately Held**
WEB: www.randmfg.com
SIC: 3444 Radiator shields or enclosures,
sheet metal

(G-14298)
RAY SIGN INC
Also Called: Color Pro Sign
28 Colonial Ave (12304-4122)
PHONE....................................518 377-1371
Russell Hazen, *President*
EMP: 13 EST: 1980
SQ FT: 5,000
SALES (est): 1.6MM **Privately Held**
SIC: 3993 1799 7389 Electric signs; sign
installation & maintenance; sign painting
& lettering shop

(G-14299)
REN TOOL & MANUFACTURING
CO
1801 Chrisler Ave (12303-1517)
PHONE....................................518 377-2123
Renato Belletti, *President*
Ellen Belletti, *Corp Secy*
EMP: 10 EST: 1949
SQ FT: 7,000
SALES (est): 1.5MM **Privately Held**
SIC: 3599 Machine shop, jobbing & repair

(G-14300)
SAMPSONS PRSTHTIC
ORTHOTIC LAB
Also Called: Sampsons Prsthtic Orthotic Lab
1737 State St (12304-1832)
PHONE....................................518 374-6011
William Sampson, *President*
EMP: 24
SQ FT: 3,500
SALES (est): 3MM **Privately Held**
WEB: www.sampsons.com
SIC: 3842 5999 Limbs, artificial; orthope-
dic & prosthesis applications

(G-14301)
SANZDRANZ LLC
388 Broadway (12305-2520)
PHONE....................................518 894-8625
Sandro Gerbini, *Branch Mgr*
EMP: 6
SALES (corp-wide): 231K **Privately Held**
SIC: 2043 Cereal breakfast foods
PA: Sanzdranz Llc
83 Dumbarton Dr
Delmar NY 12054
518 894-8625

(G-14302)
SCHENECTADY STEEL CO INC
18 Mariaville Rd (12306-1398)
PHONE....................................518 355-3220
Claudio Zullo, *President*

Charles Chamulak, *Vice Pres*
Jeffrey Hoffmann, *Treasurer*
Robert Gennett, *Admin Sec*
EMP: 44
SQ FT: 77,700
SALES: 22.1MM **Privately Held**
SIC: 3441 Building components, structural
steel

(G-14303)
SCOTIA BEVERAGES INC
Also Called: Adirondack Beverage Co Inc
701 Corporation Park (12302-1060)
PHONE....................................518 370-3621
Ralph Crowley Jr, *President*
Angelo Mastrangelo, *Chairman*
Michael Mulrain, *Corp Secy*
Christopher Crowley, *Vice Pres*
Douglas Martin, *Vice Pres*
▲ EMP: 1000
SQ FT: 240,000
SALES: 180MM
SALES (corp-wide): 404.9MM **Privately
Held**
WEB: www.adirondackbeverages.com
SIC: 2086 Soft drinks: packaged in cans,
bottles, etc.; pasteurized & mineral wa-
ters, bottled & canned
PA: Polar Corp.
1001 Southbridge St
Worcester MA 01610
508 753-6383

(G-14304)
SI GROUP INC (DH)
2750 Balltown Rd (12309-1006)
P.O. Box 1046 (12301-1046)
PHONE....................................518 347-4200
Frank Bozich, *President*
Rich Preziotti, *President*
Thomas J Masterson, *Vice Pres*
William Conway, *Prdtn Mgr*
Harve Mobley, *Prdtn Mgr*
◆ EMP: 150 EST: 1906
SALES (est): 1B **Privately Held**
WEB: www.schenectadyinternational.com
SIC: 2865 3087 2851 Phenol, alkylated &
cumene; custom compound purchased
resins; enamels
HQ: Si Group Usa Holdings (Usha) Corp.
4 Mountainview Ter
Danbury CT 06810
203 702-6140

(G-14305)
SIERRA PROCESSING LLC
2 Moyer Ave (12306)
PHONE....................................518 433-0020
William Wilczak,
Dave Fusco,
EMP: 15
SALES (est): 1.7MM
SALES (corp-wide): 4.6B **Privately Held**
SIC: 2611 Pulp manufactured from waste
or recycled paper
HQ: Waste Connections Us, Inc.
3 Waterway Square Pl # 110
The Woodlands TX 77380

(G-14306)
SKYTRAVEL (USA) LLC
20 Talon Dr (12309-1839)
PHONE....................................518 888-2610
Hongwei Jin, *Owner*
EMP: 10 EST: 2015
SALES (est): 575.6K **Privately Held**
SIC: 3593 Fluid power cylinders, hydraulic
or pneumatic

(G-14307)
SQP INC
Also Called: Speciality Quality Packaging
602 Potential Pkwy (12302-1041)
PHONE....................................518 831-6800
Barbara Slaming, *President*
▲ EMP: 140
SALES (est): 26.6MM **Publicly Held**
WEB: www.usfoodservice.com
SIC: 2676 2656 Sanitary paper products;
straws, drinking: made from purchased
material
HQ: Us Foods, Inc.
9399 W Higgins Rd # 100
Rosemont IL 60018

(G-14308)
STS STEEL INC
301 Nott St Bldg 304 (12305)
PHONE....................................518 370-2693
James A Stori, *Ch of Bd*
Jim Stori, *President*
Glenn Tabolt, *Vice Pres*
Justin Millington, *Production*
EMP: 65
SQ FT: 85,000
SALES (est): 17.4MM **Privately Held**
WEB: www.stssteel.com
SIC: 3441 Building components, structural
steel; fabricated structural metal for
bridges

(G-14309)
SUPERPOWER INC
450 Duane Ave Ste 1 (12304-2631)
PHONE....................................518 346-1414
Toru Fukushima, *Chairman*
Ross B McClure, *Opers Mgr*
Bob Schmidt, *Mfg Staff*
Erin Corcuera, *Purch Mgr*
Lancelot Hope, *Engineer*
▲ EMP: 29
SALES (est): 8MM **Privately Held**
SIC: 3643 Current-carrying wiring devices
PA: Furukawa Electric Co.,Ltd.
2-2-3, Marunouchi
Chiyoda-Ku TKY 100-0

(G-14310)
TABLECLOTHS FOR GRANTED
LTD
510 Union St (12305-1117)
PHONE....................................518 370-5481
Rudolph R Grant, *President*
David Siders, *Vice Pres*
Richard Walsh, *Admin Sec*
EMP: 11
SALES (est): 1MM **Privately Held**
SIC: 2392 Tablecloths: made from pur-
chased materials; towels, dishcloths &
dust cloths

(G-14311)
TATTERSALL INDUSTRIES LLC
Also Called: Frank Murken Products
2125 Technology Dr (12308-1143)
PHONE....................................518 381-4270
Derek Sutherland, *Plant Mgr*
James Dominelli, *Sales Mgr*
Chuck Polge, *Sales Staff*
John Tattersall, *Mng Member*
▼ EMP: 20 EST: 1963
SQ FT: 35,000
SALES (est): 7.6MM **Privately Held**
WEB: www.fmproducts.com
SIC: 3429 5085 5169 Manufactured hard-
ware (general); rubber goods, mechani-
cal; chemicals & allied products

(G-14312)
TRAC MEDICAL SOLUTIONS INC
2165 Technology Dr (12308-1143)
PHONE....................................518 346-7799
John Botti, *Ch of Bd*
Jeff Frankel, *President*
Brad Pivar, *Vice Pres*
EMP: 7
SALES: 500K
SALES (corp-wide): 12.9MM **Publicly
Held**
WEB: www.tracmed.com
SIC: 7372 Application computer software
PA: Aeon Global Health Corp.
2225 Centennial Dr
Gainesville GA 30504
888 661-0225

(G-14313)
UNICELL BODY COMPANY INC
170 Cordell Rd (12303-2702)
PHONE....................................716 853-8628
Stephen Morris, *Partner*
Carmin Sperduti, *Branch Mgr*
EMP: 14
SALES (corp-wide): 20MM **Privately
Held**
WEB: www.unicell.com
SIC: 3713 5084 Truck bodies (motor vehi-
cles); industrial machinery & equipment

▲ = Import ▼=Export
◆ =Import/Export

PA: Unicell Body Company, Inc
571 Howard St
Buffalo NY 14206
716 853-8628

(G-14314)
VINCYS PRINTING LTD
1832 Curry Rd (12306-4237)
PHONE..................................518 355-4363
Evelyn L Vincinguerra, *President*
EMP: 10 **EST:** 1967
SQ FT: 3,000
SALES (est): 1.4MM **Privately Held**
WEB: www.vincysprinting.com
SIC: 2752 2741 Commercial printing, off-set; miscellaneous publishing

(G-14315)
VON ROLL USA INC
200 Von Roll Dr (12306-2443)
P.O. Box 1404, New Haven CT (06505-1404)
PHONE..................................203 562-2171
EMP: 50
SALES (corp-wide): 336.1MM **Privately Held**
SIC: 2899 3644 Mfg Chemical Preparations Mfg Nonconductive Wiring Devices
HQ: Von Roll Usa, Inc.
200 Von Roll Dr
Schenectady NY 12306
518 344-7100

(G-14316)
VON ROLL USA INC (HQ)
200 Von Roll Dr (12306-2443)
PHONE..................................518 344-7100
Jon Roberts, *CEO*
Eran Rosenzweig, *Ch of Bd*
Andrew T Harrin, *President*
Sanjay Dave, *Area Mgr*
Jurg Brunner, *Vice Pres*
▲ **EMP:** 130
SQ FT: 200,000
SALES (est): 46.1MM
SALES (corp-wide): 323.3MM **Privately Held**
SIC: 3644 Insulators & insulation materials, electrical
PA: Von Roll Holding Ag
Passwangstrasse 20
Breitenbach SO
617 855-111

(G-14317)
VON ROLL USA HOLDING INC
1 W Campbell Rd (12306)
PHONE..................................518 344-7200
Rudolf Zaengerle, *President*
Jurg Brunner, *Treasurer*
Barbara Dickhute, *Manager*
Walter Beebe, *Admin Sec*
EMP: 13
SALES (est): 2MM
SALES (corp-wide): 323.3MM **Privately Held**
SIC: 3644 2891 Insulators & insulation materials, electrical; epoxy adhesives
PA: Von Roll Holding Ag
Passwangstrasse 20
Breitenbach SO
617 855-111

(G-14318)
WHITE EAGLE PACKING CO INC
922 Congress St (12303-1728)
PHONE..................................518 374-4366
Gary Markiewicz, *President*
George Markiewicz, *Vice Pres*
EMP: 12 **EST:** 1951
SQ FT: 15,000
SALES (est): 1.6MM **Privately Held**
SIC: 2013 Frankfurters from purchased meat

Schenevus
Otsego County

(G-14319)
A AND L HOME FUEL LLC
601 Smokey Ave (12155-4012)
PHONE..................................607 638-1994
Frank Competiello, *Principal*
F Competiello, *Principal*

EMP: 9
SALES (est): 1.2MM **Privately Held**
SIC: 2869 Fuels

(G-14320)
SCEHENVUS FIRE DIST
Also Called: Scehenvus Gram Hose Co
40 Main St (12155-2020)
PHONE..................................607 638-9017
Chief Pete Comion, *CEO*
EMP: 65 **EST:** 1900
SALES (est): 3.8MM **Privately Held**
SIC: 3711 Fire department vehicles (motor vehicles), assembly of

Schoharie
Schoharie County

(G-14321)
COBLESKILL STONE PRODUCTS INC
Also Called: Schoharie Quarry/Asphalt
163 Eastern Ave (12157-3209)
P.O. Box 220, Cobleskill (12043-0220)
PHONE..................................518 295-7121
Pete Gray, *Manager*
EMP: 12
SQ FT: 1,104
SALES (corp-wide): 126.7MM **Privately Held**
WEB: www.cobleskillstone.com
SIC: 1422 Crushed & broken limestone
PA: Cobleskill Stone Products, Inc.
112 Rock Rd
Cobleskill NY 12043
518 234-0221

(G-14322)
MASICK SOIL CONSERVATION CO
Also Called: Carver Sand & Gravel
4860 State Route 30 (12157-2906)
PHONE..................................518 827-5354
Carver Laraway, *Owner*
EMP: 11
SQ FT: 800
SALES (est): 500K **Privately Held**
SIC: 3274 0711 Agricultural lime; lime spreading services

Schuylerville
Saratoga County

(G-14323)
EMPIRE BUILDING PRODUCTS INC
12 Spring St (12871-1049)
PHONE..................................518 695-6094
EMP: 5
SQ FT: 1,500
SALES (est): 584.8K **Privately Held**
SIC: 2439 2431 Mfg Structural Wood Members Mfg Millwork
PA: Vermont Timber Frames, Inc
458 Morse Rd
Bennington VT 05201

(G-14324)
GASSHO BODY & MIND INC
76 Broad St (12871-1301)
P.O. Box 910, Saratoga Springs (12866-0836)
PHONE..................................518 695-9991
Louis Hotchkiss, *President*
Junko Kobori, *Vice Pres*
◆ **EMP:** 5
SALES (est): 897.4K **Privately Held**
SIC: 2844 2044 5122 Face creams or lotions; bran, rice; toiletries

Scio
Allegany County

(G-14325)
HYDRAMEC INC
4393 River St (14880-9702)
P.O. Box 69 (14880-0069)
PHONE..................................585 593-5190
Gregg D Shear, *President*
James Vossler, *Vice Pres*
Gregg Shear, *Facilities Mgr*
Ruth Coats, *Treasurer*
Karen Torrence, *Info Tech Dir*
▲ **EMP:** 23 **EST:** 1924
SQ FT: 23,000
SALES (est): 4.6MM **Privately Held**
WEB: www.hydrameconline.com
SIC: 3423 3542 Hand & edge tools; machine tools, metal forming type

Scipio Center
Cayuga County

(G-14326)
CUSTOM CONTROLS
2804 Skillett Rd (13147-3127)
PHONE..................................315 253-4785
EMP: 6
SALES (est): 702.2K **Privately Held**
SIC: 3613 Mfg Switchgear/Switchboards

(G-14327)
VANSRIDGE DAIRY LLC
2831 Black St (13147-3173)
PHONE..................................315 364-8569
Sharon Vannostrand, *Partner*
EMP: 30
SALES (est): 1.5MM **Privately Held**
SIC: 3523 Barn, silo, poultry, dairy & livestock machinery

Scotia
Schenectady County

(G-14328)
ARCHITCTRAL SHETMETAL PDTS INC
1329 Amsterdam Rd (12302-6306)
P.O. Box 2150 (12302-0150)
PHONE..................................518 381-6144
Toll Free:..................................888
Gary Curcio, *President*
William Donnan, *Vice Pres*
Jay Ingersoll, *Vice Pres*
EMP: 6
SQ FT: 8,000
SALES (est): 1.1MM **Privately Held**
SIC: 3444 Sheet metal specialties, not stamped; metal roofing & roof drainage equipment

(G-14329)
DIMENSION FABRICATORS INC
2000 7th St (12302-1051)
PHONE..................................518 374-1936
Scott Stevens, *President*
Joel Patrie, *Principal*
Coleen Stevens, *Corp Secy*
Scott Mushaw, *Vice Pres*
Valerie Borst, *Manager*
▲ **EMP:** 50
SQ FT: 165,000
SALES (est): 19.2MM **Privately Held**
WEB: www.dimensionfab.com
SIC: 3449 Bars, concrete reinforcing; fabricated steel

(G-14330)
GRENO INDUSTRIES INC
2820 Amsterdam Rd (12302-6323)
P.O. Box 542, Schenectady (12301-0542)
PHONE..................................518 393-4195
Robert W Golden, *CEO*
Eileen Guarino, *President*
John Butler, *Production*
Vincent Guarino, *Treasurer*
Pauline Caldarone, *Accounting Mgr*
▲ **EMP:** 6

SQ FT: 70,000
SALES: 8.4MM **Privately Held**
WEB: www.greno.com
SIC: 3599 Machine shop, jobbing & repair

(G-14331)
HADP LLC
602 Potential Pkwy (12302-1041)
PHONE..................................518 831-6824
Paul Epstein,
Adam Epstein,
David Epstein,
EMP: 11
SALES (est): 1.2MM **Privately Held**
SIC: 2656 Plates, paper: made from purchased material

(G-14332)
INTERACTIVE INSTRUMENTS INC
704 Corporation Park # 1 (12302-1078)
PHONE..................................518 347-0955
Robert Skala, *President*
James Hutchison, *Vice Pres*
EMP: 6
SQ FT: 9,000
SALES (est): 920.3K **Privately Held**
WEB: www.interactiveinstruments.com
SIC: 3599 Custom machinery; machine shop, jobbing & repair

(G-14333)
JBS LLC
Also Called: J B S
6 Maple Ave (12302-4612)
PHONE..................................518 346-0001
John Busino, *Mng Member*
EMP: 20
SQ FT: 18,000
SALES (est): 3.7MM **Privately Held**
SIC: 3441 Fabricated structural metal

(G-14334)
NEFAB PACKAGING NORTH EAST LLC
203 Glenville Indus Park (12302-1072)
PHONE..................................518 346-9105
Brad Lawyer, *Manager*
EMP: 37
SALES (corp-wide): 496.7MM **Privately Held**
SIC: 2448 Wood pallets & skids
HQ: Nefab Packaging, Inc.
204 Airline Dr Ste 100
Coppell TX 75019
469 444-5264

(G-14335)
OAK-BARK CORPORATION
Also Called: Silar Laboratories Division
37 Maple Ave (12302-4613)
PHONE..................................518 372-5691
Bob Ruskino, *Manager*
EMP: 8
SQ FT: 256
SALES (corp-wide): 11.2MM **Privately Held**
WEB: www.wrightcorp.com
SIC: 2869 Formaldehyde (formalin)
PA: Oak-Bark Corporation
1224 Old Nc Highway 87
Riegelwood NC 28456
910 655-9225

(G-14336)
SHIPMTES/PRINTMATES HOLDG CORP (PA)
Also Called: Velocity Print Solutions
705 Corporation Park # 2 (12302-1092)
PHONE..................................518 370-1158
James Stiles, *CEO*
David Benny, *General Mgr*
Michael Mello, *CFO*
Lorraine Duchessi, *Accounts Mgr*
EMP: 85
SQ FT: 60,000
SALES (est): 34.3MM **Privately Held**
WEB: www.sm-pm.com
SIC: 2752 5111 7334 7319 Commercial printing, offset; printing & writing paper; photocopying & duplicating services; distribution of advertising material or sample services; direct mail advertising services

(G-14337)
SPECIALTY QUALITY PACKG LLC
Also Called: Sqp
602 Potential Pkwy (12302-1041)
PHONE..................................914 580-3200
Paul Epstein, *Mng Member*
▲ EMP: 81
SQ FT: 267,000
SALES (est): 36.6MM **Privately Held**
SIC: 2679 Papier mache articles, except statuary & art goods

Scottsville
Monroe County

(G-14338)
ADRIA MACHINE & TOOL INC
966 North Rd (14546-9770)
P.O. Box 208 (14546-0208)
PHONE..................................585 889-3360
Janos Poloznik, *President*
John Hehnen, *Opers Mgr*
John Hartman, *Department Mgr*
EMP: 4
SQ FT: 7,000
SALES: 1MM **Privately Held**
WEB: www.adriamachine.com
SIC: 3599 Machine shop, jobbing & repair

(G-14339)
COOPERVISION INC
711 North Rd (14546-1238)
PHONE..................................585 889-3301
Dennis Snyder, *Mfg Staff*
James Gardner, *Purch Mgr*
Scott Reynolds, *Supervisor*
Al Rodriguez, *Program Dir*
EMP: 594
SALES (corp-wide): 2.5B **Publicly Held**
SIC: 3851 Contact lenses
HQ: Coopervision, Inc.
209 High Point Dr Ste 100
Victor NY 14564

(G-14340)
HEANY INDUSTRIES INC
249 Briarwood Ln (14546-1244)
P.O. Box 38 (14546-0038)
PHONE..................................585 889-2700
S Scott Zolnier, *Ch of Bd*
Charles Aldridge, *Vice Pres*
Theresa Dunn, *Purchasing*
Brian Hill, *MIS Dir*
▲ EMP: 58 EST: 1937
SQ FT: 18,000
SALES (est): 10MM **Privately Held**
WEB: www.heany.com
SIC: 3299 3479 2851 2816 Ceramic fiber; coating of metals with plastic or resins; paints & allied products; inorganic pigments

(G-14341)
JACK W MILLER
Also Called: Miller Truck Rental
2339 North Rd (14546-9737)
PHONE..................................585 538-2399
Jack W Miller, *Owner*
EMP: 9
SQ FT: 13,000
SALES (est): 1.5MM **Privately Held**
SIC: 3519 7538 Diesel engine rebuilding; diesel engine repair: automotive

(G-14342)
POWER AND CNSTR GROUP INC
Also Called: Livingston Lighting and Power
86 River Rd (14546-9503)
PHONE..................................585 889-6020
Philip Brooks, *Branch Mgr*
EMP: 26
SALES (corp-wide): 60MM **Privately Held**
WEB: www.valleysandandgravel.com
SIC: 3648 3647 Street lighting fixtures; streetcar lighting fixtures
PA: Power & Construction Group, Inc.
119 River Rd
Scottsville NY 14546
585 889-8500

(G-14343)
SABIN METAL CORPORATION
1647 Wheatland Center Rd (14546-9709)
P.O. Box 905 (14546-0905)
PHONE..................................585 538-2194
John Waldon, *Maint Spvr*
Mike Nichols, *Engineer*
Vicki Strong, *Accounting Dir*
Sherrye Cook, *Human Res Dir*
Rick Dolby, *Human Resources*
EMP: 125
SALES (corp-wide): 39.9MM **Privately Held**
WEB: www.sabinmetal.com
SIC: 3341 3339 Secondary precious metals; primary nonferrous metals
PA: Sabin Metal Corporation
300 Pantigo Pl Ste 102
East Hampton NY 11937
631 329-1695

(G-14344)
SWAIN TECHNOLOGY INC
963 North Rd (14546-1228)
P.O. Box 33 (14546-0033)
PHONE..................................585 889-2786
Daniel Swain, *President*
Linda Swain, *Vice Pres*
EMP: 15
SQ FT: 11,000
SALES (est): 1.7MM **Privately Held**
WEB: www.swaintech.com
SIC: 3479 Coating of metals & formed products

Sea Cliff
Nassau County

(G-14345)
GOTHAM T-SHIRT CORP
211 Glen Cove Ave Unit 5 (11579-1432)
PHONE..................................516 676-0900
Howard Zwang, *Ch of Bd*
EMP: 5
SALES (est): 496.7K **Privately Held**
SIC: 2752 Commercial printing, lithographic

(G-14346)
NORTH AMERICAN MBL SYSTEMS INC
31 Lafayette Ave (11579-1840)
PHONE..................................718 898-8700
Thomas Crowley, *President*
Connor Crowley, *Owner*
EMP: 33
SALES (est): 5.3MM **Privately Held**
SIC: 3663 Radio broadcasting & communications equipment

(G-14347)
ROBS REALLY GOOD LLC
100 Roslyn Ave (11579-1274)
P.O. Box 355 (11579-0355)
PHONE..................................516 671-4411
Carey Johnston, *Sales Staff*
Robert Ehrlich, *Mng Member*
EMP: 10
SALES (est): 1.5MM **Privately Held**
SIC: 2096 Potato chips & similar snacks

Seaford
Nassau County

(G-14348)
A & A GRAPHICS INC II
615 Arlington Dr (11783-1135)
PHONE..................................516 735-0078
Eli P Pandolfi, *President*
EMP: 3 EST: 1999
SQ FT: 5,000
SALES (est): 1.2MM **Privately Held**
SIC: 2759 Commercial printing

(G-14349)
KYRA COMMUNICATIONS CORP
3864 Bayberry Ln (11783-1503)
PHONE..................................516 783-6244
Richard Doherty, *President*
Carol Doherty, *Vice Pres*

EMP: 14
SALES (est): 928.6K **Privately Held**
SIC: 2741 8734 Miscellaneous publishing; testing laboratories

Selden
Suffolk County

(G-14350)
CENTRAL GARDEN & PET COMPANY
1100 Middle Country Rd (11784-2513)
PHONE..................................631 451-8021
Stacey Rossi, *Manager*
EMP: 9
SALES (corp-wide): 2.2B **Publicly Held**
WEB: www.centralgardenandpet.com
SIC: 2048 Prepared feeds
PA: Central Garden & Pet Company
1340 Treat Blvd Ste 600
Walnut Creek CA 94597
925 948-4000

(G-14351)
CREATIVE STONE & CABINETS CORP
448 Middle Country Rd # 1 (11784-2657)
PHONE..................................631 772-6548
Juan Cuzco, *President*
EMP: 6
SALES (est): 890K **Privately Held**
SIC: 2434 Wood kitchen cabinets

(G-14352)
DATORIB INC
Also Called: Minuteman Press
974 Middle Country Rd (11784-2535)
PHONE..................................631 698-6222
William J Passeggio, *President*
EMP: 5
SQ FT: 1,850
SALES (est): 637.8K **Privately Held**
SIC: 2752 Commercial printing, lithographic

(G-14353)
ILAB AMERICA INC
45 Hemlock St (11784-1327)
PHONE..................................631 615-5053
Wayne Boyle, *President*
EMP: 6
SALES: 800K **Privately Held**
WEB: www.ilabamerica.com
SIC: 3651 Amplifiers: radio, public address or musical instrument

(G-14354)
NORTHERN METALWORKS CORP
15 King Ave (11784-2314)
PHONE..................................646 523-1689
Shakir Qureshi, *President*
EMP: 5
SALES (est): 257.3K **Privately Held**
SIC: 3449 Miscellaneous metalwork

(G-14355)
PROGRESSIVE ORTHOTICS LTD (PA)
280 Middle Country Rd G (11784-2532)
PHONE..................................631 732-5556
Bruce Goodman, *President*
EMP: 9
SQ FT: 2,400
SALES (est): 905.9K **Privately Held**
WEB: www.progressiveorthotics.com
SIC: 3842 3841 5999 5047 Limbs, artificial; orthopedic appliances; surgical & medical instruments; orthopedic & prosthesis applications; medical & hospital equipment

Selkirk
Albany County

(G-14356)
CQ TRAFFIC CONTROL DEVICES LLC
Also Called: Cq Traffic Control Products
1521 Us Rte 9w (12158)
P.O. Box 192 (12158-0192)
PHONE..................................518 767-0057
William Quattrochi,
Frank Conrad,
Carol Quattrochi,
Douglas Robbins,
EMP: 5
SALES (est): 881K **Privately Held**
SIC: 3669 Pedestrian traffic control equipment

(G-14357)
GE PLASTICS
1 Noryl Ave (12158-9784)
PHONE..................................518 475-5011
Jeffery Immelt, *Principal*
◆ EMP: 5
SALES (est): 860.2K **Privately Held**
SIC: 2821 Plastics materials & resins

(G-14358)
OLDCASTLE INFRASTRUCTURE INC
Also Called: Oldcastle Precast Bldg Systems
123 County Route 101 (12158-2606)
PHONE..................................518 767-2112
Edward Soler, *Manager*
EMP: 40
SALES (corp-wide): 30.6B **Privately Held**
WEB: www.oldcastle-precast.com
SIC: 3272 Concrete products, precast
HQ: Oldcastle Infrastructure, Inc.
7000 Cntl Prkaway Ste 800
Atlanta GA 30328
470 602-2000

(G-14359)
PALPROSS INCORPORATED
Also Called: L P Transportation
Maple Ave Rr 396 (12158)
P.O. Box 95 (12158-0095)
PHONE..................................845 469-2188
Andrew Palmer, *Manager*
EMP: 10
SQ FT: 2,400
SALES (corp-wide): 3.6MM **Privately Held**
SIC: 3537 Trucks, tractors, loaders, carriers & similar equipment
PA: Palpross Incorporated
Rr Box 17m
Chester NY 10918
845 469-2188

(G-14360)
SABIC INNOVATIVE PLAS US LLC
1 Noryl Ave (12158-9765)
PHONE..................................518 475-5011
Charlie Crew, *Manager*
EMP: 258 **Privately Held**
WEB: www.sabic-ip.com
SIC: 2821 Plastics materials & resins
HQ: Sabic Innovative Plastics Us Llc
2500 Citywest Blvd # 100
Houston TX 77042

Seneca Castle
Ontario County

(G-14361)
CASTLE HARVESTER CO INC
Also Called: Castle Harvstr Met Fabricators
3165 Seneca Castle Rd (14547)
P.O. Box 167 (14547-0167)
PHONE..................................585 526-5884
Michael Kunes, *President*
EMP: 9 EST: 1969
SQ FT: 10,000
SALES (est): 1.3MM **Privately Held**
SIC: 3441 Building components, structural steel

Seneca Falls
Seneca County

(G-14362)
GOULDS PUMPS LLC (HQ)
Also Called: Goulds Pumps Incorporated
240 Fall St (13148-1573)
PHONE..................................315 568-2811
Robert Pagano, *Ch of Bd*
Aris Chicles, *President*
Ken Napolitano, *President*
Christine Bayles, *Purch Agent*
Jaime Valdez, *Purch Agent*
◆ **EMP:** 1100 **EST:** 1984
SALES (est): 75.6MM
SALES (corp-wide): 2.7B **Publicly Held**
WEB: www.gouldspumps.com
SIC: 3561 5084 Pumps & pumping equipment; industrial pumps & parts; pumps, oil well & field; pumps, domestic: water or sump; industrial machinery & equipment
PA: Itt Inc.
1133 Westchester Ave N-100
White Plains NY 10604
914 641-2000

(G-14363)
GOULDS PUMPS LLC
Also Called: ITT Accounts Payable
280 Fall St (13148-1544)
P.O. Box 750 (13148-0750)
PHONE..................................315 568-2811
EMP: 45
SALES (corp-wide): 2.7B **Publicly Held**
WEB: www.gouldspumps.com
SIC: 3561 Pumps & pumping equipment
HQ: Goulds Pumps Llc
240 Fall St
Seneca Falls NY 13148
315 568-2811

(G-14364)
ITT CORPORATION
A-C Pump Division
240 Fall St (13148-1590)
PHONE..................................315 568-2811
Aaron Hagen, *Purch Agent*
Dave Menapace, *Buyer*
Steve Durham, *Engineer*
Daniel Parker, *Engineer*
James Dawley, *Project Engr*
EMP: 58
SALES (corp-wide): 2.7B **Publicly Held**
SIC: 3625 3823 3363 3812 Control equipment, electric; fluidic devices, circuits & systems for process control; aluminum die-castings; radar systems & equipment; infrared object detection equipment; fluid power pumps & motors; pumps & pumping equipment
HQ: Itt Llc
1133 Westchester Ave N-100
White Plains NY 10604
914 641-2000

(G-14365)
ITT ENGINEERED VALVES LLC (DH)
240 Fall St (13148-1590)
Rural Route 750 (13148)
PHONE..................................662 257-6982
Randy Garman, *General Mgr*
▲ **EMP:** 58
SALES (est): 14.8MM
SALES (corp-wide): 2.7B **Publicly Held**
SIC: 3592 Valves
HQ: Itt Llc
1133 Westchester Ave N-100
White Plains NY 10604
914 641-2000

(G-14366)
ITT GOULDS PUMPS INC (HQ)
240 Fall St (13148-1573)
PHONE..................................914 641-2129
Michael J Savinelli, *Principal*
Tim Murney, *Project Mgr*
Christine Bayles, *Buyer*
Luis Rivas, *Manager*
Arleen Bailey, *Administration*
EMP: 4500

SALES (est): 75.6MM
SALES (corp-wide): 2.7B **Publicly Held**
SIC: 3561 5084 Pumps & pumping equipment; industrial machinery & equipment
PA: Itt Inc.
1133 Westchester Ave N-100
White Plains NY 10604
914 641-2000

(G-14367)
ITT LLC
Also Called: ITT Monitoring Control
240 Fall St (13148-1590)
PHONE..................................315 568-4733
Doug Brown, *Manager*
EMP: 5
SALES (corp-wide): 2.7B **Publicly Held**
SIC: 3625 Control equipment, electric
HQ: Itt Llc
1133 Westchester Ave N-100
White Plains NY 10604
914 641-2000

(G-14368)
ITT LLC
2881 E Bayard Street Ext (13148-8745)
PHONE..................................914 641-2000
Kyle Fenter, *Project Mgr*
Don Radford, *Branch Mgr*
EMP: 58
SALES (corp-wide): 2.7B **Publicly Held**
WEB: www.ittind.com
SIC: 3625 3823 3363 3812 Control equipment, electric; fluidic devices, circuits & systems for process control; aluminum die-castings; radar systems & equipment; infrared object detection equipment
HQ: Itt Llc
1133 Westchester Ave N-100
White Plains NY 10604
914 641-2000

(G-14369)
MONTEZUMA WINERY LLC
2981 Us Route 20 (13148-9423)
PHONE..................................315 568-8190
Bill Martin,
▲ **EMP:** 9
SALES (est): 766.9K **Privately Held**
WEB: www.montezumawinery.com
SIC: 2084 Wines

(G-14370)
SENECA FALLS CAPITAL INC (PA)
Also Called: Seneca Falls Machine
314 Fall St (13148-1543)
PHONE..................................315 568-5804
Attila Libertiny, *President*
EMP: 2
SQ FT: 115,000
SALES (est): 5MM **Privately Held**
SIC: 3541 Machine tools, metal cutting type

(G-14371)
SENECA FALLS MACHINE TOOL CO
Also Called: Seneca Falls Technology Group
314 Fall St (13148-1543)
PHONE..................................315 568-5804
Attila Libertiny, *President*
EMP: 60
SQ FT: 115,000
SALES: 3MM **Privately Held**
WEB: www.sftg.com
SIC: 3541 3545 Machine tools, metal cutting type; machine tool accessories
PA: Seneca Falls Capital, Inc.
314 Fall St
Seneca Falls NY 13148

(G-14372)
SENECA FLS SPC & LOGISTICS CO (PA)
50 Johnston St (13148-1279)
PHONE..................................315 568-4139
Stephen M Bregande, *President*
Bruce Hilton, *Vice Pres*
Christopher Woods, *Vice Pres*
Michael Schleahr, *CFO*
▲ **EMP:** 80 **EST:** 1880

SALES (est): 75.6MM
SALES (corp-wide): 2.7B **Publicly Held**
SIC: 3561 5084 Pumps & pumping equipment; industrial machinery & equipment
PA: Itt Inc.
1133 Westchester Ave N-100
White Plains NY 10604
914 641-2000

(G-14373)
TI GROUP AUTO SYSTEMS LLC
240 Fall St (13148-1590)
PHONE..................................315 568-7042
Danielle Roetting, *Manager*
EMP: 5
SALES (corp-wide): 3.9B **Privately Held**
WEB: www.tiautomotive.com
SIC: 3317 3312 3599 3052 Tubes, seamless steel; tubes, steel & iron; hose, flexible metallic; plastic hose; fuel systems & parts, motor vehicle
HQ: Ti Group Automotive Systems, Llc
2020 Taylor Rd
Auburn Hills MI 48326
248 296-8000

(G-14374)
WILSON PRESS LLC
56 Miller St (13148-1585)
PHONE..................................315 568-9693
Don Johnson, *President*
Nancy Bellina, *Sales Staff*
Nora Ricci,
EMP: 20
SQ FT: 5,500
SALES: 2MM **Privately Held**
SIC: 2752 2791 2789 2759 Commercial printing, offset; typesetting; bookbinding & related work; commercial printing

(G-14375)
XYLEM INC
Also Called: Global Financial Shared Svcs
2881 E Bayard Street Ext (13148-8745)
PHONE..................................315 239-2499
Eddie Concepcion, *Analyst*
EMP: 84 **Publicly Held**
SIC: 3561 Pumps & pumping equipment
PA: Xylem Inc.
1 International Dr
Rye Brook NY 10573

Setauket
Suffolk County

(G-14376)
ADVANCED RESEARCH MEDIA INC
60 Route 25a Ste 1 (11733-2872)
P.O. Box 2278, East Setauket (11733-0889)
PHONE..................................631 751-9696
Steve Blechman, *CEO*
Elyse Blechman, *President*
EMP: 17
SALES (est): 4.5MM **Privately Held**
SIC: 2721 Magazines: publishing only, not printed on site

(G-14377)
BC SYSTEMS INC
200 N Belle Mead Rd Ste 2 (11733-3463)
PHONE..................................631 751-9370
Gus Blazek, *President*
Gustav Blazek, *President*
Dennis Carrigan, *Vice Pres*
Art Charych, *Vice Pres*
Pam Lomonaco, *Purch Mgr*
EMP: 50
SQ FT: 16,000
SALES (est): 10.2MM **Privately Held**
WEB: www.bcpowersys.com
SIC: 3679 Power supplies, all types: static

(G-14378)
CARL SAFINA CENTER INC
80 N Country Rd (11733-1345)
PHONE..................................808 888-9440
Mayra Marino, *Principal*
Norman Goodman, *Author*
EMP: 9 **EST:** 2015
SQ FT: 564
SALES: 673.2K **Privately Held**
SIC: 3545 Mandrels

(G-14379)
EATINGEVOLVED LLC
10 Technology Dr Unit 4 (11733-4063)
PHONE..................................631 675-2440
Christine Cusano, *CEO*
Richard Gusmano, *COO*
EMP: 16
SALES (est): 742.4K **Privately Held**
SIC: 2064 Candy bars, including chocolate covered bars

(G-14380)
MAUSNER EQUIPMENT CO INC
8 Heritage Ln (11733-3018)
PHONE..................................631 689-7358
EMP: 137
SQ FT: 17,000
SALES: 27.5MM **Privately Held**
SIC: 3545 5084 3823 Precision measuring tools; measuring & testing equipment, electrical; industrial instrmnts msrmnt display/control process variable

Sharon Springs
Schoharie County

(G-14381)
ADELPHI PAPER HANGINGS
102 Main St (13459-3136)
P.O. Box 135 (13459-0135)
PHONE..................................518 284-9066
Chris Ohrstrom, *President*
Steve Larson, *Manager*
EMP: 5
SALES: 380K **Privately Held**
WEB: www.adelphipaperhangings.com
SIC: 2679 Wallpaper

(G-14382)
AMT INCORPORATED
883 Chestnut St (13459-2131)
P.O. Box 338 (13459-0338)
PHONE..................................518 284-2910
Lanning Brandel, *President*
Beth Brandel, *Corp Secy*
EMP: 33
SQ FT: 22,000
SALES (est): 7.9MM **Privately Held**
WEB: www.amtcastings.com
SIC: 3366 3365 3354 3341 Bushings & bearings, copper (nonmachined); aluminum foundries; aerospace castings, aluminum; machinery castings, aluminum; aluminum extruded products; secondary nonferrous metals; steel foundries; miscellaneous nonferrous products; ferrous metals

(G-14383)
MONOLITHIC COATINGS INC
916 Highway Route 20 (13459-3108)
PHONE..................................914 621-2765
EMP: 5
SALES (est): 566.1K **Privately Held**
SIC: 3674 Read-only memory (ROM)

(G-14384)
TIMOTHY L SIMPSON
5819 State Route 145 (13459-3205)
PHONE..................................518 234-1401
Timothy L Simpson, *Principal*
EMP: 6
SALES (est): 492.5K **Privately Held**
SIC: 2411 Logging

Shelter Island
Suffolk County

(G-14385)
COECLES HBR MARINA & BOAT YARD
68 Cartwright Rd (11964)
PHONE..................................631 749-0856
John Needham, *President*
EMP: 15
SALES (corp-wide): 3.3MM **Privately Held**
SIC: 3732 Boat building & repairing

PA: Coecles Harbor Marina & Boatyard, Inc
18 Hudson Ave
Shelter Island NY 11964
631 749-0700

(G-14386)
GOODING & ASSOCIATES INC
15 Dinah Rock Rd (11964)
P.O. Box 1690 (11964-1690)
PHONE..............................631 749-3313
A Gordon Gooding Jr, *President*
Norie Schuchman, *VP Sales*
Joy Strasser, *Office Mgr*
EMP: 14
SALES (est): 1.3MM **Privately Held**
SIC: 2741 Catalogs: publishing & printing

(G-14387)
SHELTER ISLAND REPORTER INC
Also Called: Shelter Island Cmnty Nwspapers
50 N Ferry Rd (11964)
P.O. Box 756 (11964-0756)
PHONE..............................631 749-1000
Troy Gustavson, *President*
Andrew Olsen, *Vice Pres*
◆ **EMP:** 8
SALES (est): 490K **Privately Held**
SIC: 2711 Newspapers, publishing & printing

Sherburne
Chenango County

(G-14388)
CHENANGO VALLEY TECH INC
328 Route 12b (13460)
P.O. Box 1038 (13460-1038)
PHONE..............................607 674-4115
Lloyd Baker, *CEO*
Lucille Baker, *President*
Norm Wynn, *Warehouse Mgr*
Cole Williams, *QC Mgr*
Patti Mace, *Office Mgr*
EMP: 35 **EST:** 1997
SQ FT: 30,000
SALES (est): 7MM **Privately Held**
WEB: www.chenangovalleytech.com
SIC: 3544 3089 Industrial molds; injection molding of plastics

(G-14389)
COLUMBUS WOODWORKING INC
164 Casey Cheese Fctry Rd (13460-5006)
PHONE..............................607 674-4546
Michael Tomaselli, *President*
Stacy Tomaselli, *Corp Secy*
EMP: 5
SQ FT: 15,000
SALES (est): 653.2K **Privately Held**
SIC: 2431 Millwork

(G-14390)
DEB EL FOOD PRODUCTS LLC
35 W State St (13460-9424)
PHONE..............................607 203-5600
Jennifer Nelson, *Branch Mgr*
EMP: 40 **Privately Held**
SIC: 2015 Egg processing
PA: Deb El Food Products Llc
520 Broad St Fl 6
Newark NJ 07102

(G-14391)
KENYON PRESS INC
1 Kenyon Press Dr (13460-5670)
P.O. Box 710 (13460-0710)
PHONE..............................607 674-9066
Ray Kenyon, *President*
Kevin Crandall, *Sales Staff*
Karisha Gulbin, *Sales Staff*
Kim Ottoson, *Sales Staff*
Amanda Foster, *Office Mgr*
EMP: 50
SQ FT: 75,000
SALES (est): 11.7MM **Privately Held**
SIC: 2752 Commercial printing, offset

(G-14392)
MID-YORK PRESS INC
2808 State Highway 80 (13460-4549)
P.O. Box 733 (13460-0733)
PHONE..............................607 674-4491
Robert W Tenney, *Ch of Bd*
Jane Eaton, *Principal*
Mary Mahoney, *Principal*
Cynthia Tenney, *Principal*
Marie Morgan, *Prdtn Mgr*
EMP: 70 **EST:** 1946
SQ FT: 56,000
SALES (est): 27.8MM
SALES (corp-wide): 3.9MM **Privately Held**
WEB: www.midyorkpress.com
SIC: 2679 2752 2711 Paperboard products, converted; commercial printing, offset; newspapers, publishing & printing
PA: Media Tenney Group
28 Robinson Rd
Clinton NY 13323
315 853-5569

(G-14393)
SHERBURNE METAL SALES INC (PA)
40 S Main St (13460-9804)
PHONE..............................607 674-4441
David Harvey, *President*
Gregory Panagiotakis, *Vice Pres*
EMP: 19
SQ FT: 60,000
SALES (est): 36.6MM **Privately Held**
WEB: www.sherburnemetals.com
SIC: 3331 3351 Primary copper; rolled or drawn shapes: copper & copper alloy

(G-14394)
SOUTHERN TIER PET NTRTN LLC
8 W State St (13460-9752)
PHONE..............................607 674-2121
Joe Mullenax, *Plant Mgr*
Matt Winton, *Manager*
Jeremy Macneill,
▲ **EMP:** 42 **EST:** 2012
SALES (est): 8.2MM **Privately Held**
SIC: 2047 Dog food

(G-14395)
STEEL SALES INC
8085 State Hwy 12 (13460)
P.O. Box 539 (13460-0539)
PHONE..............................607 674-6363
Brenda Westcott, *President*
EMP: 31
SQ FT: 20,000
SALES (est): 6.7MM **Privately Held**
WEB: www.steelsalesinc.com
SIC: 3446 3444 3449 5051 Architectural metalwork; sheet metalwork; bars, concrete reinforcing: fabricated steel; metals service centers & offices; steel

(G-14396)
TECNOFIL CHENANGO SAC
40 S Main St (13460-9804)
PHONE..............................607 674-4441
Jose Babadia, *Principal*
◆ **EMP:** 30
SALES (est): 10.4MM **Privately Held**
SIC: 3331 Primary copper

(G-14397)
WHITE HOUSE CABINET SHOP LLC
11 Knapp St (13460-9791)
P.O. Box 877 (13460-0877)
PHONE..............................607 674-9358
Jeff Webster, *Mng Member*
Bruce Webster,
Mike Webster,
EMP: 8
SQ FT: 5,112
SALES (est): 797.9K **Privately Held**
SIC: 2434 Wood kitchen cabinets

Sheridan
Chautauqua County

(G-14398)
COTTON WELL DRILLING CO INC
Center Rd (14135)
P.O. Box 203 (14135-0203)
PHONE..............................716 672-2788
Donald D Cotton, *President*
Mollie Cotton, *Office Mgr*
EMP: 8 **EST:** 1973
SQ FT: 2,400
SALES (est): 916K **Privately Held**
SIC: 1389 Oil & gas wells: building, repairing & dismantling

Sherman
Chautauqua County

(G-14399)
BISSEL-BABCOCK MILLWORK INC
3866 Kendrick Rd (14781-9628)
PHONE..............................716 761-6976
James Babcock, *President*
Paula Babcock, *Admin Sec*
EMP: 11
SQ FT: 5,000
SALES: 1.1MM **Privately Held**
SIC: 2421 Sawmills & planing mills, general

(G-14400)
FIRE APPARATUS SERVICE TECH
7895 Lyons Rd (14781-9657)
PHONE..............................716 753-3538
Danny Karges, *Executive*
EMP: 7
SALES (est): 894.4K **Privately Held**
SIC: 3669 Fire alarm apparatus, electric

(G-14401)
TRIPLE E MANUFACTURING
117 Osborn St (14781-9790)
P.O. Box 438 (14781-0438)
PHONE..............................716 761-6996
Richard Watrous, *Partner*
Pamela Watrous, *Partner*
▲ **EMP:** 18
SQ FT: 12,000
SALES (est): 2MM **Privately Held**
SIC: 2399 Horse & pet accessories, textile

Sherrill
Oneida County

(G-14402)
BRIGGS & STRATTON CORPORATION
4245 Highbridge Rd (13461)
PHONE..............................315 495-0100
Philip Wenzel, *Manager*
EMP: 15
SALES (corp-wide): 1.8B **Publicly Held**
SIC: 3519 Internal combustion engines
PA: Briggs & Stratton Corporation
12301 W Wirth St
Wauwatosa WI 53222
414 259-5333

(G-14403)
DLR ENTERPRISES LLC
Also Called: Noble Wood Shavings
104 E Seneca St (13461-1008)
PHONE..............................315 813-2911
EMP: 5
SALES (est): 793.5K **Privately Held**
SIC: 2421 Sawmill/Planing Mill

(G-14404)
DUTCHLAND PLASTICS LLC
102 E Seneca St (13461-1008)
PHONE..............................315 280-0247
Daven Claerbout, *Branch Mgr*
EMP: 223
SALES (corp-wide): 118.9MM **Privately Held**
SIC: 3089 Injection molding of plastics
PA: Dutchland Plastics, Llc
54 Enterprise Ct
Oostburg WI 53070
920 564-3633

(G-14405)
PATLA ENTERPRISES INC
Also Called: Joe's Jerky
190 E State St (13461-1232)
PHONE..............................315 367-0237
Jodie-Lynn Patla, *President*
EMP: 14
SALES: 500K **Privately Held**
SIC: 2013 1541 5411 Beef, dried: from purchased meat; food products manufacturing or packing plant construction; convenience stores

(G-14406)
SHERRILL MANUFACTURING INC
102 E Seneca St (13461-1008)
PHONE..............................315 280-0727
Gregory L Owens, *CEO*
Matthew A Roberts, *President*
Jose Alvarez, *Opers Mgr*
Alice Roberts, *Admin Asst*
EMP: 140
SQ FT: 1,000,000
SALES (est): 26.4MM **Privately Held**
WEB: www.sherrillmfg.com
SIC: 3421 3914 3471 Cutlery; silverware, silver plated; gold plating

(G-14407)
SILVER CITY GROUP INC
Also Called: Silver City Metals
27577 W Seneca St (13461)
PHONE..............................315 363-0344
Dennis Tormey, *President*
Cliff Wittman, *Vice Pres*
EMP: 5
SQ FT: 2,500
SALES (est): 400K **Privately Held**
SIC: 3914 Pewter ware

(G-14408)
TIBRO WATER TECHNOLOGIES LTD
106 E Seneca St Unit 25 (13461-1008)
PHONE..............................647 426-3415
Dhiren Chandaria, *President*
EMP: 15
SQ FT: 7,000
SALES: 1.2MM
SALES (corp-wide): 3.6MM **Privately Held**
SIC: 2819 Sodium & potassium compounds, exc. bleaches, alkalies, alum.
PA: Tibro International Ltd
1 Scarsdale Rd Unit 300
North York ON M3B 2
647 426-3415

(G-14409)
WESTMOOR LTD
Also Called: Conde Pumps Div
906 W Hamilton Ave (13461-1366)
P.O. Box 99 (13461-0099)
PHONE..............................315 363-1500
James R Hendry, *Ch of Bd*
EMP: 10 **EST:** 1939
SQ FT: 18,000
SALES (est): 2.7MM **Privately Held**
WEB: www.westmoorltd.com
SIC: 3561 3523 Industrial pumps & parts; milking machines

Shirley
Suffolk County

(G-14410)
AMERICAN REGENT INC (HQ)
Also Called: Osteohealth
5 Ramsey Rd (11967-4701)
P.O. Box 9001 (11967-9001)
PHONE..............................631 924-4000
Joseph Kenneth Keller, *President*
Dante Serricchio, *General Mgr*
Alicia Shepard, *Business Mgr*

Joel Steckler, *Business Mgr*
Jackie Beltrani, *Vice Pres*
▲ EMP: 500
SALES (est): 219.9MM **Privately Held**
WEB: www.osteohealth.com
SIC: 2834 Druggists' preparations (pharmaceuticals)

(G-14411)
AMERICAN REGENT INC
Osteohealth Company
5 Ramsey Rd (11967-4701)
PHONE.............................631 924-4000
Joseph Kenneth Keller, *CEO*
EMP: 20 **Privately Held**
WEB: www.osteohealth.com
SIC: 3843 Dental equipment & supplies
HQ: American Regent, Inc.
5 Ramsey Rd
Shirley NY 11967
631 924-4000

(G-14412)
ANORAD CORPORATION
100 Precision Dr Ste 1 (11967-4716)
PHONE.............................631 344-6600
Marco H Wishart, *Ch of Bd*
Geoffrey Storms, *President*
▲ EMP: 102
SALES (est): 17.9MM **Publicly Held**
WEB: www.anorad.com
SIC: 3577 3827 Computer peripheral equipment; optical instruments & lenses
PA: Rockwell Automation, Inc.
1201 S 2nd St
Milwaukee WI 53204

(G-14413)
ANTHONY GIGI INC
Also Called: Russo's Gluten Free Gourmet
45 Ramsey Rd Unit 28 (11967-4712)
PHONE.............................860 984-1943
Neil Russo, *President*
EMP: 5
SQ FT: 2,000
SALES (est): 300K **Privately Held**
SIC: 2046 Gluten meal

(G-14414)
ATLANTIC COLOR CORP
14 Ramsey Rd (11967-4704)
PHONE.............................631 345-3800
Richard Reina, *Ch of Bd*
EMP: 20
SALES (est): 3.1MM **Privately Held**
WEB: www.atlanticcolor.com
SIC: 2752 Commercial printing, offset

(G-14415)
ATLANTIC INDUSTRIAL TECH INC
90 Precision Dr (11967-4702)
PHONE.............................631 234-3131
Robert Ferrara, *Ch of Bd*
Thomas Ferrara, *Vice Pres*
Jennifer Wines, *Manager*
EMP: 35
SQ FT: 20,000
SALES (est): 12.2MM **Privately Held**
WEB: www.aitzone.com
SIC: 3443 8711 7699 3594 Fabricated plate work (boiler shop); engineering services; industrial machinery & equipment repair; fluid power pumps & motors

(G-14416)
B V M ASSOCIATES
999-32 Montrell 414 (11967)
PHONE.............................631 254-6220
Mike Lucyk, *Owner*
EMP: 8 EST: 1978
SQ FT: 5,000
SALES (est): 510K **Privately Held**
SIC: 3577 Computer peripheral equipment

(G-14417)
BIODEX MEDICAL SYSTEMS INC (PA)
20 Ramsey Rd (11967-4704)
PHONE.............................631 924-9000
James Reiss, *Ch of Bd*
Allyson Scerri, *President*
Kate Dimeglio, *Vice Pres*
Bob Ranieri, *Vice Pres*
John Bennett, *Treasurer*
▲ EMP: 170

SQ FT: 83,000
SALES (est): 28.9MM **Privately Held**
WEB: www.biodex.com
SIC: 3842 3841 Radiation shielding aprons, gloves, sheeting, etc.; muscle exercise apparatus, ophthalmic; X-ray apparatus & tubes

(G-14418)
BIODEX MEDICAL SYSTEMS INC
49 Natcon Dr (11967-4700)
PHONE.............................631 924-3146
John Ryan, *Manager*
EMP: 30
SALES (corp-wide): 28.9MM **Privately Held**
WEB: www.biodex.com
SIC: 3842 3841 Radiation shielding aprons, gloves, sheeting, etc.; muscle exercise apparatus, ophthalmic
PA: Biodex Medical Systems, Inc.
20 Ramsey Rd
Shirley NY 11967
631 924-9000

(G-14419)
EASTLAND ELECTRONICS CO INC
999 Montauk Hwy 402 (11967-2130)
PHONE.............................631 580-3800
William Mercurio, *President*
◆ EMP: 7
SALES (est): 1.4MM **Privately Held**
WEB: www.eastlandny.com
SIC: 3679 Electronic circuits

(G-14420)
FIRE ISLAND FUEL
106 Parkwood Dr (11967-3918)
PHONE.............................631 772-1482
Joseph Intravaia, *Principal*
EMP: 6 EST: 2009
SALES (est): 587.3K **Privately Held**
SIC: 2869 Fuels

(G-14421)
FRANK LOWE RBR & GASKET CO INC
44 Ramsey Rd (11967-4704)
PHONE.............................631 777-2707
Ira M Warren, *Ch of Bd*
Randy Cohen, *Vice Pres*
Azhar Chishti, *Plant Mgr*
Ruth Lyons, *Purch Dir*
Pat Edwards, *Payroll Mgr*
▲ EMP: 35
SQ FT: 60,000
SALES (est): 8.3MM **Privately Held**
WEB: www.franklowe.com
SIC: 3053 Gaskets, all materials

(G-14422)
INNOVATION MGT GROUP INC
999 Montauk Hwy (11967-2130)
PHONE.............................800 889-0987
Jerry Hussong, *Vice Pres*
EMP: 10 **Privately Held**
WEB: www.imgpresents.com
SIC: 7372 Prepackaged software
PA: Innovation Management Group, Inc.
5348 Vegas Dr Ste 285
Las Vegas NV 89108

(G-14423)
L I F PUBLISHING CORP (PA)
Also Called: The Fisherman
14 Ramsey Rd (11967-4704)
PHONE.............................631 345-5200
Richard Reina Sr, *President*
Michael Caruso, *Publisher*
Richard S Reina, *Vice Pres*
John Debona, *Adv Mgr*
EMP: 56 EST: 1964
SQ FT: 14,000
SALES (est): 5.7MM **Privately Held**
SIC: 2721 2752 Magazines: publishing only, not printed on site; commercial printing, offset

(G-14424)
MID ATLANTIC GRAPHICS CORP
14 Ramsey Rd (11967-4704)
PHONE.............................631 345-3800
Madaline Lechner, *CEO*

Richard Reina Sr, *President*
Richard S Reina, *Vice Pres*
EMP: 20 EST: 1979
SQ FT: 14,000
SALES (est): 2.4MM
SALES (corp-wide): 5.7MM **Privately Held**
SIC: 2752 Commercial printing, offset
PA: L I F Publishing Corp
14 Ramsey Rd
Shirley NY 11967
631 345-5200

(G-14425)
MODULAR DEVICES INC
Also Called: M D I
1 Roned Rd (11967-4706)
PHONE.............................631 345-3100
Steven E Summer, *President*
Hank Striegl, *General Mgr*
Greg Mink, *COO*
Henry F Striegl Jr, *Vice Pres*
Barbara Hall, *Purch Mgr*
▲ EMP: 55
SQ FT: 60,000
SALES (est): 12.1MM **Privately Held**
WEB: www.modev.com
SIC: 3621 Motors & generators

(G-14426)
NJF PUBLISHING CORP
Also Called: The Fisherman
14 Ramsey Rd (11967-4704)
PHONE.............................631 345-5200
EMP: 6
SQ FT: 1,800
SALES (est): 680K **Privately Held**
SIC: 2721 8412 Periodicals-Publishing/Printing Museum/Art Gallery

(G-14427)
POWR-UPS CORP
1 Roned Rd (11967-4707)
PHONE.............................631 345-5700
Steven Summer, *President*
Debbie Wheeler, *General Mgr*
EMP: 25 EST: 1981
SQ FT: 20,000
SALES: 2.7MM **Privately Held**
WEB: www.powrupscorp.com
SIC: 3625 5063 Motor controls & accessories; electrical apparatus & equipment

(G-14428)
UNCLE WALLYS LLC
41 Natcon Dr (11967-4700)
PHONE.............................631 205-0455
Lou Avignone, *President*
David Nemer, *VP Opers*
Jim Magorrian, *Plant Supt*
Frank Sivilli, *Opers Staff*
Michael Petrucelli, *CFO*
EMP: 35
SQ FT: 60,000
SALES (est): 1.5MM **Privately Held**
WEB: www.unclewallys.com
SIC: 2051 Bread, cake & related products
HQ: Give And Go Prepared Foods Corp
15 Marmac Dr Unit 200
Etobicoke ON M9W 1
416 675-0114

Shokan
Ulster County

(G-14429)
MACK WOOD WORKING
Also Called: General Specialties
2792 State Route 28 (12481-5002)
PHONE.............................845 657-6625
Ben Mack, *Owner*
EMP: 8
SQ FT: 8,000
SALES (est): 500K **Privately Held**
SIC: 2431 Millwork

Sidney
Delaware County

(G-14430)
AMERICAN BLUESTONE LLC
760 Quarry Rd (13838)
P.O. Box 117 (13838-0117)
PHONE.............................607 369-2235
Robert McDuffey, *Mng Member*
Deborah McDuffey,
EMP: 12
SALES (est): 1.5MM **Privately Held**
SIC: 3281 Granite, cut & shaped

(G-14431)
AMPHENOL CORPORATION
Also Called: Amphenol Aerospace Industrial
40-60 Delaware Ave (13838-1395)
PHONE.............................607 563-5364
Canson Zhao, *Opers Dir*
David Acker, *Opers Staff*
Kevin Mansfield, *Purch Agent*
Arlene McCoon, *Purchasing*
Robert Arcykiewicz, *Engineer*
EMP: 345
SQ FT: 675,000
SALES (corp-wide): 8.2B **Publicly Held**
SIC: 3678 Electronic connectors
PA: Amphenol Corporation
358 Hall Ave
Wallingford CT 06492
203 265-8900

(G-14432)
AMPHENOL CORPORATION
Amphenol Aerospace Operations
40-60 Delaware Ave (13838-1395)
PHONE.............................607 563-5011
Gary Anderson, *Vice Pres*
Brendan Harder, *Opers Mgr*
David Cogswell, *Engineer*
Steve Dombrowski, *Engineer*
Eric Hickey, *Engineer*
EMP: 1500
SALES (corp-wide): 8.2B **Publicly Held**
SIC: 3678 Electronic connectors
PA: Amphenol Corporation
358 Hall Ave
Wallingford CT 06492
203 265-8900

(G-14433)
DECKER FOREST PRODUCTS INC
New York State Rte 8 (13838)
P.O. Box 205 (13838-0205)
PHONE.............................607 563-2345
Floyd Decker, *President*
Mark Decker, *Vice Pres*
Carol Decker, *Admin Sec*
EMP: 5
SQ FT: 15,000
SALES (est): 330K **Privately Held**
SIC: 2411 Logging camps & contractors

(G-14434)
EGLI MACHINE COMPANY INC
240 State Highway 7 (13838-2716)
PHONE.............................607 563-3663
Denis Egli, *President*
Charles Howand, *Engineer*
Ellen Egli, *Treasurer*
EMP: 28
SQ FT: 18,000
SALES: 3.5MM **Privately Held**
WEB: www.eglimachine.com
SIC: 3545 3544 3089 Precision tools, machinists'; special dies, tools, jigs & fixtures; molding primary plastic

(G-14435)
REFILL SERVICES LLC
16 Winkler Rd (13838-1056)
PHONE.............................607 369-5864
Austin Wilson, *Mng Member*
EMP: 5
SALES (est): 487.2K **Privately Held**
SIC: 2621 Stationery, envelope & tablet papers

GEOGRAPHIC

(PA)=Parent Co (HQ)=Headquarters (DH)=Div Headquarters
✪ = New Business established in last 2 years

(G-14436)
TRI-TOWN NEWS INC (PA)
Also Called: Sidney Favorite Printing Div
74 Main St (13838-1134)
P.O. Box 570 (13838-0570)
PHONE....................607 561-3515
Paul Hamilton Sr, *President*
Wiley Vincent, *Vice Pres*
EMP: 25 EST: 1925
SQ FT: 10,080
SALES (est): 1.7MM **Privately Held**
WEB: www.powerofprint.com
SIC: 2752 2711 Commercial printing, off-
set; newspapers, publishing & printing

(G-14437)
UFP NEW YORK LLC
13 Winkler Rd (13838-1057)
PHONE....................607 563-1556
James Brennan, *Manager*
EMP: 45
SQ FT: 14,988
SALES (corp-wide): 4.4B **Publicly Held**
WEB: www.ufpinc.com
SIC: 2439 Structural wood members
HQ: Ufp New York, Llc
11 Allen St
Auburn NY 13021
315 253-2758

(G-14438)
UNADILLA SILO COMPANY INC
Also Called: Unadilla Laminated Products
100 West Rd (13838)
P.O. Box 240 (13838-0240)
PHONE....................607 369-9341
Floyd Spencer, *Manager*
EMP: 62
SALES (corp-wide): 5.7MM **Privately
Held**
SIC: 2431 3444 2439 Silo staves, wood;
sheet metalwork; structural wood mem-
bers
PA: Unadilla Silo Company, Inc.
18 Clifton St
Unadilla NY 13849
607 369-9341

(G-14439)
USA CUSTOM PAD CORP (PA)
16 Winkler Rd (13838-1056)
PHONE....................607 563-9550
Eric T Wilson, *Chairman*
Marcia Wilson, *Admin Sec*
◆ **EMP:** 29
SQ FT: 20,000
SALES (est): 7MM **Privately Held**
WEB: www.memopads.com
SIC: 2678 2759 2741 Tablets & pads,
book & writing; from purchased materials;
commercial printing; miscellaneous pub-
lishing

Silver Creek
Chautauqua County

(G-14440)
**CHAUTAUQUA WINE COMPANY
INC**
Also Called: Willow Creek Winery
2627 Chapin Rd (14136-9760)
PHONE....................716 934-9463
Holly Metzger, *President*
Holly Metzter, *President*
EMP: 5 **EST:** 2000
SALES (est): 459K **Privately Held**
WEB: www.willowcreekwinery.com
SIC: 2084 Wines

(G-14441)
EXCELCO DEVELOPMENTS INC
65 Main St (14136-1467)
P.O. Box 230 (14136-0230)
PHONE....................716 934-2651
Christopher J Lanski, *President*
Douglas A Newman, *Exec VP*
Philip J Azzarella, *CFO*
Paul Rozewicz, *Finance Mgr*
Pj Azzarella, *Human Res Mgr*
EMP: 37
SQ FT: 40,000

SALES (est): 6.3MM **Privately Held**
SIC: 3728 3731 3429 Aircraft assemblies,
subassemblies & parts; shipbuilding & repairing; manufactured hardware (general)

(G-14442)
EXCELCO/NEWBROOK INC
16 Mechanic St (14136-1202)
P.O. Box 231 (14136-0231)
PHONE....................716 934-2644
Christopher J Lanski, *CEO*
Geoff Rondeau, *General Mgr*
Paul Narraway, *Engineer*
P J Azzarella, *CFO*
Dan Uszacki, *Technology*
EMP: 85 **EST:** 1952
SQ FT: 93,000
SALES (est): 14.7MM **Privately Held**
WEB: www.excelco.net
SIC: 3728 3731 7692 Aircraft assemblies,
subassemblies & parts; shipbuilding & re-
pairing; welding repair

Silver Springs
Wyoming County

(G-14443)
MORTON SALT INC
45 Ribaud Ave (14550-9805)
P.O. Box 342 (14550-0342)
PHONE....................585 493-2511
James Bruton, *Production*
Matt Ashley, *Project Engr*
Daniel Border, *Branch Mgr*
Josh Tanski, *Info Tech Mgr*
EMP: 12
SALES (corp-wide): 4.6B **Privately Held**
SIC: 2899 Salt
HQ: Morton Salt, Inc.
444 W Lake St Ste 3000
Chicago IL 60606

Sinclairville
Chautauqua County

(G-14444)
**CARLSON WOOD PRODUCTS
INC**
1705 Bates Rd (14782-9726)
PHONE....................716 287-2923
William Carlson, *President*
Ivetta Carlson, *Vice Pres*
EMP: 19 **EST:** 1973
SQ FT: 4,000
SALES: 1.3MM **Privately Held**
SIC: 2426 2421 Lumber, hardwood dimen-
sion; kiln drying of lumber

(G-14445)
**CONTAINER TSTG SOLUTIONS
LLC (PA)**
17 Lester St (14782)
PHONE....................716 487-3300
Brian Johnson, *Ch of Bd*
EMP: 9
SALES (est): 1.5MM **Privately Held**
SIC: 2834 Solutions, pharmaceutical

Skaneateles
Onondaga County

(G-14446)
ANYELAS VINEYARDS LLC
2433 W Lake Rd (13152-9471)
PHONE....................315 685-3797
James Nocek,
EMP: 13
SQ FT: 5,000
SALES: 200K **Privately Held**
SIC: 2084 Wines

(G-14447)
BURDICK PUBLICATIONS INC
Also Called: EB&I Marketing
2352 E Lake Rd (13152-8924)
P.O. Box 977 (13152-0977)
PHONE....................315 685-9500
Elaina K Burdick, *CEO*

Mary Mahoney, *Vice Pres*
EMP: 6
SQ FT: 1,200
SALES: 1MM **Privately Held**
WEB: www.burdickpubs.com
SIC: 2741 Miscellaneous publishing

(G-14448)
CHOHEHCO LLC
78 State St (13152-1218)
PHONE....................315 420-4624
Vedran Psenicnik,
EMP: 7 **EST:** 2014
SALES (est): 355.4K **Privately Held**
SIC: 2086 Carbonated beverages, nonal-
coholic: bottled & canned

(G-14449)
**DIGITAL ANALYSIS
CORPORATION**
716 Visions Dr (13152-6475)
P.O. Box 95 (13152-0095)
PHONE....................315 685-0760
Richard Pinkowski, *President*
Joseph Pinkowski, *Project Mgr*
Dennis Klotz, *Prdtn Mgr*
Michael Johnson, *Project Engr*
Sherri Springer, *Accounting Mgr*
EMP: 19
SQ FT: 12,000
SALES: 4.4MM **Privately Held**
WEB: www.digital-analysis.com
SIC: 3823 Industrial instrmnts msrmnt dis-
play/control process variable

(G-14450)
DIVINE PHOENIX LLC
Also Called: Divine Phoenix Books
2985 Benson Rd (13152-9638)
P.O. Box 1001 (13152-5001)
PHONE....................585 737-1482
Laura Ponticello, *Principal*
EMP: 585
SQ FT: 850
SALES: 30K **Privately Held**
SIC: 2731 Book publishing

(G-14451)
**G E INSPECTION
TECHNOLOGIES LP**
721 Visions Dr (13152-6475)
PHONE....................315 554-2000
Todd Brugger, *Branch Mgr*
EMP: 175 **Privately Held**
SIC: 3829 8734 7359 3651 Physical
property testing equipment; testing labo-
ratories; equipment rental & leasing;
household audio & video equipment
HQ: G E Inspection Technologies, Lp
721 Visions Dr
Skaneateles NY 13152
315 554-2000

(G-14452)
GENERAL ELECTRIC COMPANY
721 Visions Dr (13152-6475)
PHONE....................315 554-2000
John Barenys, *Buyer*
Sandra Gonzalez, *Buyer*
Lisa Hryckowian, *Buyer*
Ted Chilek, *Engineer*
Jeff Anderson, *Branch Mgr*
EMP: 8
SALES (corp-wide): 121.6B **Publicly
Held**
WEB: www.gecommercialfinance.com
SIC: 3699 3651 3634 Electrical equip-
ment & supplies; household audio & video
equipment; electric housewares & fans
PA: General Electric Company
41 Farnsworth St
Boston MA 02210
617 443-3000

(G-14453)
HABA USA
4407 Jordan Rd (13152-9371)
PHONE....................800 468-6873
Hugh Reed, *Vice Pres*
▲ **EMP:** 7
SALES (est): 72.6K **Privately Held**
SIC: 3944 Games, toys & children's vehi-
cles

(G-14454)
HABERMAASS CORPORATION
Also Called: T C Timber
4407 Jordan Rd (13152-8300)
P.O. Box 42 (13152-0042)
PHONE....................315 729-0070
Klaus Habermaass, *President*
Rolf Sievers, *Vice Pres*
Peter Reynolds, *Natl Sales Mgr*
Ashley Ware, *Sales Staff*
▲ **EMP:** 12
SQ FT: 150,000
SALES (est): 2.1MM
SALES (corp-wide): 425.2MM **Privately
Held**
SIC: 3944 5092 Games, toys & children's
vehicles; toys & hobby goods & supplies
PA: Habermaass Gmbh
August-Grosch-Str. 28-38
Bad Rodach 96476
956 492-9444

(G-14455)
HANSON AGGREGATES PA LLC
Rr 321 (13152)
PHONE....................315 685-3321
Ken Slater, *Plant Mgr*
Phil Wheeler, *Manager*
EMP: 25
SQ FT: 2,160
SALES (corp-wide): 20.6B **Privately Held**
SIC: 1442 1422 Common sand mining;
crushed & broken limestone
HQ: Hanson Aggregates Pennsylvania, Llc
7660 Imperial Way
Allentown PA 18195
610 366-4626

(G-14456)
SCALE-TRONIX INC
4341 State Street Rd (13152-9338)
PHONE....................914 948-8117
Carolyn Lepler, *President*
David C Hale, *Principal*
EMP: 38
SQ FT: 5,000
SALES (est): 7.4MM **Privately Held**
SIC: 3596 Baby scales; bathroom scales;
weighing machines & apparatus

(G-14457)
TESSY PLASTICS CORP (PA)
700 Visions Dr (13152-6475)
PHONE....................315 689-3924
Roland Beck, *President*
Greg Levengood, *COO*
Joe Raffa, *Vice Pres*
Colin Goodale, *Opers Staff*
Nils Hammerich, *Opers Staff*
◆ **EMP:** 260
SQ FT: 240,000
SALES (est): 334.6MM **Privately Held**
WEB: www.tessy.com
SIC: 3089 3549 Injection molding of plas-
tics; assembly machines, including robotic

(G-14458)
U S TECH CORPORATION
6 Hawthorne Woods Ct (13152-1408)
PHONE....................315 437-7207
Alexander E Gelston II, *President*
Janis J Soule, *Vice Pres*
EMP: 12
SALES: 6MM **Privately Held**
SIC: 3812 Search & detection systems &
instruments

Skaneateles Falls
Onondaga County

(G-14459)
WELCH ALLYN INC
Data Collection Division
4341 State Street Rd (13153-5301)
P.O. Box 220 (13153-0220)
PHONE....................315 685-4100
Dewey Shimer, *Branch Mgr*
Beth Rice, *Comp Spec*
EMP: 1000
SALES (corp-wide): 2.8B **Publicly Held**
SIC: 3841 3577 Diagnostic apparatus,
medical; computer peripheral equipment

HQ: Welch Allyn Inc
4341 State Street Rd
Skaneateles Falls NY 13153
315 685-4100

(G-14460)
WELCH ALLYN INC (HQ)
4341 State Street Rd (13153-5301)
P.O. Box 220 (13153-0220)
PHONE..................315 685-4100
John Tierney, *President*
Joseph Hennigan, *COO*
Duane E Wiedor, *Senior VP*
Jim Evans, *Vice Pres*
Nathan Lacomb, *Vice Pres*
◆ EMP: 1400
SALES (est): 783.1MM
SALES (corp-wide): 2.8B **Publicly Held**
SIC: 3841 2835 3827 Diagnostic apparatus, medical; otoscopes, except electromedical; ophthalmic instruments & apparatus; blood pressure apparatus; in vitro & in vivo diagnostic substances; optical instruments & lenses
PA: Hill-Rom Holdings, Inc.
130 E Randolph St # 1000
Chicago IL 60601
312 819-7200

(G-14461)
WELCH ALLYN INC
Also Called: Lighting Products Division
4619 Jordan Rd (13153-5313)
P.O. Box 187 (13153-0187)
PHONE..................315 685-4347
Joshua Grant, *Engineer*
William Bolton, *Branch Mgr*
EMP: 1000
SALES (corp-wide): 2.8B **Publicly Held**
SIC: 3841 3641 Diagnostic apparatus, medical; electric lamps
HQ: Welch Allyn Inc
4341 State Street Rd
Skaneateles Falls NY 13153
315 685-4100

(G-14462)
WELCH ALLYN INC
4341 State Street Rd (13153-5301)
PHONE..................503 530-7500
Steve Meyer, *President*
Gary Hockett, *Sales Staff*
Caroline Webb, *Sales Staff*
Jessica Amidon, *Marketing Staff*
John Prior, *Marketing Staff*
EMP: 5
SALES (est): 840.6K **Privately Held**
SIC: 3841 Surgical & medical instruments

Slate Hill
Orange County

(G-14463)
RICHARD ROTHBARD INC
1866 Route 284 (10973-4208)
P.O. Box 480 (10973-0480)
PHONE..................845 355-2300
Richard Rothbard, *President*
Joanna Rothbard, *Admin Sec*
EMP: 9
SQ FT: 1,500
SALES (est): 675.2K **Privately Held**
SIC: 2499 Decorative wood & woodwork

Sleepy Hollow
Westchester County

(G-14464)
TRADER INTERNTNAL PUBLICATIONS
50 Fremont Rd (10591-1118)
P.O. Box 687, Tarrytown (10591-0687)
PHONE..................914 631-6856
Jean Sudol, *President*
Edward R Sudol, *Corp Secy*
EMP: 6
SALES: 500K **Privately Held**
SIC: 2741 2721 Miscellaneous publishing; periodicals; publishing only; trade journals; publishing only, not printed on site

(G-14465)
VALERIE BOHIGIAN
Also Called: Valian Associates
225 Hunter Ave (10591-1316)
PHONE..................914 631-8866
Valerie Bohigian, *Owner*
EMP: 6
SALES (est): 230K **Privately Held**
WEB: www.valianassociates.com
SIC: 3914 Trophies, pewter

Slingerlands
Albany County

(G-14466)
LONG LUMBER AND SUPPLY CORP
2100 New Scotland Rd (12159-3419)
PHONE..................518 439-1661
Richard L Long Jr, *President*
Robert P Long, *Vice Pres*
EMP: 10 EST: 1945
SQ FT: 10,000
SALES (est): 1MM **Privately Held**
SIC: 2511 2499 5712 5211 Wood lawn & garden furniture; fencing, wood; furniture stores; fencing

(G-14467)
SABRE ENERGY SERVICES LLC
1891 New Scotland Rd (12159-3628)
PHONE..................518 514-1572
Steven D Oesterle, *CEO*
John Y Mason, *Ch of Bd*
Gillian Webster, *Administration*
EMP: 13
SALES: 3.6MM **Privately Held**
SIC: 2819 1389 Sulfur chloride; cementing oil & gas well casings

(G-14468)
TECHNOLOGY PARTNERS INC
Also Called: Provider Ally
1399 New Scotland Rd # 499
(12159-4228)
PHONE..................518 621-2993
EMP: 36
SALES (corp-wide): 40MM **Privately Held**
SIC: 7372 Business oriented computer software
PA: Technology Partners, Llc
8757 Red Oak Blvd Ste 200
Charlotte NC 28217
704 553-1004

Sloansville
Schoharie County

(G-14469)
FLORIDA NORTH INC (PA)
134 Vanderwerken Rd (12160-2211)
PHONE..................518 868-2888
Daniel Nelson, *President*
EMP: 15
SQ FT: 85,000
SALES: 650K **Privately Held**
WEB: www.makarioscondos.com
SIC: 3949 Swimming pools, plastic

Sloatsburg
Rockland County

(G-14470)
CUSTOM EUROPEAN IMPORTS INC
Also Called: Tri State Awnings
100 Sterling Mine Rd (10974-2502)
PHONE..................845 357-5718
Martin Lichtman, *President*
Aron Deutsch, *Sales Staff*
▲ EMP: 20
SALES (est): 1.8MM **Privately Held**
SIC: 2394 Canvas & related products

(G-14471)
HNST MOLD INSPECTIONS LLC (PA)
15 Johnsontown Rd (10974-1101)
PHONE..................845 215-9258
John Skelly, *Mng Member*
EMP: 4 EST: 2010
SALES (est): 1.4MM **Privately Held**
SIC: 3544 Industrial molds

Smithtown
Suffolk County

(G-14472)
A & G HEAT SEALING
1 Albatross Ln (11787-3301)
PHONE..................631 724-7764
George Ciunga, *President*
EMP: 8
SQ FT: 12,000
SALES (est): 790.8K **Privately Held**
WEB: www.agheatsealing.com
SIC: 3089 3565 Plastic processing; packaging machinery

(G-14473)
ANCHOR CANVAS LLC
556 W Jericho Tpke (11787-2601)
PHONE..................631 265-5602
Jon Hansen,
EMP: 6
SQ FT: 8,000
SALES (est): 675.7K **Privately Held**
SIC: 2394 Canvas & related products

(G-14474)
CERTIFIED FLAMEPROOFING CORP
17 N Ingelore Ct (11787-1544)
PHONE..................631 265-4824
Edwards Fallom, *President*
EMP: 6
SALES (est): 436.1K **Privately Held**
SIC: 3251 Fireproofing tile, clay

(G-14475)
DIGITAL ASSOCIATES LLC
50 Karl Ave Ste 303 (11787-2744)
PHONE..................631 983-6075
Vincent RE,
EMP: 8
SALES (est): 247.7K **Privately Held**
SIC: 7372 Publishers' computer software

(G-14476)
DUKE OF IRON INC
1039 W Jericho Tpke (11787-3205)
PHONE..................631 543-3600
Paul Montelbano, *President*
EMP: 6
SQ FT: 8,000
SALES: 1MM **Privately Held**
WEB: www.dukeofiron.com
SIC: 3446 Ornamental metalwork

(G-14477)
EASTEND ENFORCEMENT PRODUCTS
50 Dillmont Dr (11787-1602)
P.O. Box 309, Center Moriches (11934-0309)
PHONE..................631 878-8424
John Koenig, *Owner*
Edityh Koenig, *Manager*
EMP: 5
SALES (est): 339.3K **Privately Held**
SIC: 3559 Ammunition & explosives, loading machinery

(G-14478)
G N R PLASTICS INC
Also Called: G N R Co
11 Wandering Way (11787-1147)
PHONE..................631 724-8758
EMP: 9
SQ FT: 10,000
SALES (est): 760K **Privately Held**
SIC: 3544 3089 Mfg Dies/Tools/Jigs/Fixtures Mfg Plastic Products

(G-14479)
IGAMBIT INC (PA)
1050 W Jericho Tpke Ste A (11787-3242)
PHONE..................631 670-6777
John Salerno, *Ch of Bd*
Elisa Lugman, *CFO*
EMP: 6
SQ FT: 1,000
SALES: 60.2K **Publicly Held**
SIC: 7372 Business oriented computer software

(G-14480)
JERIC KNIT WEAR
61 Hofstra Dr (11787-2053)
PHONE..................631 979-8827
Jerry Lobel, *Owner*
EMP: 5
SALES (est): 452.3K **Privately Held**
SIC: 2253 Sweaters & sweater coats, knit

(G-14481)
KANTIAN SKINCARE LLC
496 Smithtown Byp (11787-5005)
PHONE..................631 780-4711
Jonathan Klein,
Richard Klein,
EMP: 5 EST: 2012
SALES (est): 513.5K **Privately Held**
SIC: 2844 Cosmetic preparations

(G-14482)
LB GRAPH-X & PRINTING INC
227 E Main St (11787-2807)
PHONE..................212 246-2600
J David Garcia, *Co-President*
Bernice Garcia, *Co-President*
EMP: 8
SQ FT: 10,000
SALES (est): 1.3MM **Privately Held**
WEB: www.lbgrx.com
SIC: 2752 Commercial printing, lithographic

(G-14483)
PBL INDUSTRIES CORP
49 Dillmont Dr (11787-1635)
PHONE..................631 979-4266
William Loffman, *President*
EMP: 10
SALES (est): 950K **Privately Held**
SIC: 3499 Fabricated metal products

(G-14484)
PERFECT FORMS AND SYSTEMS INC
35 Riverview Ter (11787-1155)
PHONE..................631 462-1100
Joseph Messana, *President*
EMP: 15
SALES (est): 1.6MM **Privately Held**
SIC: 2752 Business form & card printing, lithographic

(G-14485)
PRECISION DENTAL CABINETS INC (PA)
900 W Jericho Tpke (11787-3206)
PHONE..................631 543-3870
Peter Loscialpo, *President*
Joseph Pisk, *Vice Pres*
EMP: 13
SQ FT: 12,000
SALES (est): 2.3MM **Privately Held**
SIC: 3843 2434 1751 Cabinets, dental; wood kitchen cabinets; cabinet building & installation

(G-14486)
PSI TRANSIT MIX CORP
34 E Main St (11787-2804)
P.O. Box 178 (11787-0178)
PHONE..................631 382-7930
Albino Almeida, *President*
EMP: 5
SALES (est): 478K **Privately Held**
SIC: 2951 Concrete, asphaltic (not from refineries); concrete, bituminous

(G-14487)
SMITHTOWN NEWS INC
Also Called: North Shore News Group
1 Brooksite Dr (11787-3493)
P.O. Box 805 (11787-0805)
PHONE..................631 265-2100

G
E
O
G
R
A
P
H
I
C

Bernard Paley, *President*
EMP: 32
SQ FT: 7,000
SALES (est): 2MM **Privately Held**
WEB: www.thesmithtownnews.com
SIC: 2711 Commercial printing & newspaper publishing combined

(G-14488)
T-COMPANY LLC
16 Monitor Rd (11787-1867)
PHONE..................................646 290-6365
Mark Grottano, *Mng Member*
Lisa Frizol,
Agatha Grottano,
EMP: 5
SQ FT: 2,100
SALES (est): 400K **Privately Held**
SIC: 2599 Factory furniture & fixtures

(G-14489)
VITAKEM NUTRACEUTICAL INC
811 W Jericho Tpke (11787-3232)
PHONE..................................631 956-8343
EMP: 250
SQ FT: 35,000
SALES: 15MM **Privately Held**
SIC: 2023 Mfg Dietary Supplements Products

Smyrna
Chenango County

(G-14490)
JD GRANARY LLC
7 Railroad St (13464)
P.O. Box 12 (13464-0012)
PHONE..................................607 627-6294
Mark Justh,
EMP: 5
SALES (est): 139.9K **Privately Held**
SIC: 2048 Livestock feeds

Sodus
Wayne County

(G-14491)
MIZKAN AMERICAS INC
7673 Sodus Center Rd (14551-9539)
PHONE..................................315 483-6944
Kevin Perry, *Engineer*
Ted Pouley, *Manager*
Masud Khan, *Technology*
EMP: 10 **Privately Held**
SIC: 2099 Vinegar
HQ: Mizkan America, Inc.
    1661 Feehanville Dr # 200
    Mount Prospect IL 60056
    847 590-0059

(G-14492)
NYKON INC
Also Called: Ramco Arts
8175 Stell Rd (14551-9530)
PHONE..................................315 483-0504
Alice Cuvelier, *Principal*
EMP: 9
SQ FT: 5,000
SALES (est): 867.3K **Privately Held**
WEB: www.nykon.net
SIC: 3651 Music distribution apparatus

(G-14493)
TERMATEC MOLDING INC
28 Foley Dr (14551-1044)
P.O. Box 96 (14551-0096)
PHONE..................................315 483-4150
Brad Cuvelier, *President*
Lyle Wilson, *Prdtn Mgr*
EMP: 15 **EST:** 1979
SQ FT: 6,500
SALES (est): 2.4MM **Privately Held**
SIC: 3089 Injection molding of plastics

Solvay
Onondaga County

(G-14494)
BERRY GLOBAL INC
1500 Milton Ave (13209-1622)
PHONE..................................315 484-0397
David Heigel, *Manager*
Peter Miller, *Manager*
EMP: 178 **Publicly Held**
SIC: 3089 3081 Bottle caps, molded plastic; unsupported plastics film & sheet
HQ: Berry Global, Inc.
    101 Oakley St
    Evansville IN 47710
    812 424-2904

(G-14495)
CRUCIBLE INDUSTRIES LLC
575 State Fair Blvd (13209-1560)
PHONE..................................800 365-1180
Scott Maclane, *Engineer*
Erica Aller, *Human Res Mgr*
Jamey Duncan, *Natl Sales Mgr*
William Mastroe, *Manager*
Jim Beckman,
◆ **EMP:** 290
SALES (est): 120.8MM **Privately Held**
SIC: 3312 Bars, iron: made in steel mills

(G-14496)
EASTERN COMPANY
Also Called: Frazer & Jones Division
3000 Milton Ave (13209)
P.O. Box 4955, Syracuse (13221-4955)
PHONE..................................315 468-6251
Leonard F Leganza, *Branch Mgr*
David Huddleson, *Manager*
EMP: 100
SALES (corp-wide): 234.2MM **Publicly Held**
WEB: www.easterncompany.com
SIC: 3322 Malleable iron foundries
PA: The Eastern Company
    112 Bridge St
    Naugatuck CT 06770
    203 729-2255

(G-14497)
EVENT SERVICES CORPORATION
6171 Airport Rd (13209-9754)
P.O. Box 587 (13209-0587)
PHONE..................................315 488-9357
Kevin Jankiewicz, *President*
EMP: 6
SALES (est): 440K **Privately Held**
SIC: 2099 Food preparations

Somers
Westchester County

(G-14498)
GRAYHAWK LEASING LLC (HQ)
1 Pepsi Way (10589-2212)
PHONE..................................914 767-6000
Saad Abdul-Latif, *CEO*
EMP: 7
SALES (est): 2.1MM
SALES (corp-wide): 64.6B **Publicly Held**
SIC: 2086 7359 Bottled & canned soft drinks; rental store, general
PA: Pepsico, Inc.
    700 Anderson Hill Rd
    Purchase NY 10577
    914 253-2000

(G-14499)
PEPSI BTLG GROUP GLOBL FIN LLC (DH)
1 Pepsi Way Ste 1 # 1 (10589-2212)
PHONE..................................914 767-6000
Eric J Ross, *President*
EMP: 7
SALES (est): 2.8MM
SALES (corp-wide): 64.6B **Publicly Held**
SIC: 2086 Carbonated soft drinks, bottled & canned

HQ: Pepsi-Cola Metropolitan Bottling Company, Inc.
    1111 Westchester Ave
    White Plains NY 10604
    914 767-6000

(G-14500)
RICHARD C OWEN PUBLISHERS INC
243 Route 100 (10589-3203)
P.O. Box 585, Katonah (10536-0585)
PHONE..................................914 232-3903
Richard C Owen, *President*
Phyllis Morrison, *Office Mgr*
▲ **EMP:** 11
SQ FT: 5,000
SALES: 1.5MM **Privately Held**
WEB: www.rcowen.com
SIC: 2731 Books: publishing only

(G-14501)
SIMPLE BREWER
346 Route 202 (10589-3278)
PHONE..................................845 490-0182
Gregory Gates, *Principal*
EMP: 20 **EST:** 2012
SALES (est): 2.8MM **Privately Held**
SIC: 2082 Malt beverages

South Bethlehem
Albany County

(G-14502)
OLDCASTLE INFRASTRUCTURE INC
100 S County Rte 101 (12161)
PHONE..................................518 767-2116
Sheila Connor, *Manager*
EMP: 10
SALES (corp-wide): 30.6B **Privately Held**
WEB: www.oldcastle-precast.com
SIC: 3272 3446 3273 Concrete products, precast; pipe, concrete or lined with concrete; open flooring & grating for construction; ready-mixed concrete
HQ: Oldcastle Infrastructure, Inc.
    7000 Cntl Prkaway Ste 800
    Atlanta GA 30328
    470 602-2000

South Colton
St. Lawrence County

(G-14503)
J & S LOGGING INC
3860 State Highway 56 (13687)
P.O. Box 458 (13687-0458)
PHONE..................................315 262-2112
Stephen Poste, *President*
Patricia Poste, *Vice Pres*
Teresa Fisher, *Director*
Jerry Poste, *Director*
EMP: 20
SALES (est): 2.3MM **Privately Held**
SIC: 2411 4212 Logging camps & contractors; local trucking, without storage

(G-14504)
NORTHEASTERN SIGN CORP
102 Cold Brook Dr (13687)
P.O. Box 340 (13687-0340)
PHONE..................................315 265-6657
Anne Clarkson, *President*
EMP: 8 **EST:** 1991
SQ FT: 1,600
SALES (est): 983.3K **Privately Held**
SIC: 3993 Signs & advertising specialties

South Dayton
Cattaraugus County

(G-14505)
BIRDS EYE FOODS INC
Also Called: Comstock Foods Division
Mechanic St (14138)
PHONE..................................716 988-3218
Sam Chiavetta, *Branch Mgr*
EMP: 6

SALES (corp-wide): 9.5B **Publicly Held**
SIC: 2037 Vegetables, quick frozen & cold pack, excl. potato products
HQ: Birds Eye Foods, Inc.
    121 Woodcrest Rd
    Cherry Hill NJ 08003
    585 383-1850

(G-14506)
CHERRY CREEK WOODCRAFT INC (PA)
Also Called: Great Impressions
1 Cherry St (14138-9736)
P.O. Box 267 (14138-0267)
PHONE..................................716 988-3211
Michael Lord, *Ch of Bd*
Martin Goldman, *President*
David Nelson, *Info Tech Mgr*
Charlene Sterlace, *Executive*
EMP: 34
SQ FT: 60,000
SALES (est): 4.4MM **Privately Held**
SIC: 2499 Trophy bases, wood

(G-14507)
COUNTRY SIDE SAND & GRAVEL
8458 Route 62 (14138-9756)
PHONE..................................716 988-3271
Jason Rosier, *Manager*
EMP: 10
SALES (corp-wide): 29.8MM **Privately Held**
SIC: 1442 Construction sand mining; gravel mining
HQ: Country Side Sand & Gravel Inc
    Taylor Hollow Rd
    Collins NY 14034
    716 988-3271

South Fallsburg
Sullivan County

(G-14508)
ALLIED WINE CORP
Also Called: Rosedub
121 Main St (12779)
P.O. Box 88, Ellenville (12428-0088)
PHONE..................................845 796-4160
Moshe Schwartz, *President*
Abe Schwartz, *Vice Pres*
EMP: 10 **EST:** 1992
SQ FT: 18,000
SALES (est): 320.7K **Privately Held**
SIC: 2084 Wines; brandy & brandy spirits

(G-14509)
MB FOOD PROCESSING INC
5190 S Fallsburg Main St (12779)
P.O. Box 13 (12779-0013)
PHONE..................................845 436-5001
Dean Koplik, *President*
EMP: 350 **EST:** 2000
SALES (est): 1.8MM
SALES (corp-wide): 815.7K **Privately Held**
WEB: www.murraychicken.com
SIC: 2015 Poultry slaughtering & processing
PA: M.B. Consulting Group, Ltd.
    5190 S Fallsburg Main
    South Fallsburg NY 12779
    845 434-5050

(G-14510)
MURRAY BRESKY CONSULTANTS LTD (PA)
Also Called: Murray's Chicken
5190 Main St (12779)
P.O. Box P (12779-2015)
PHONE..................................845 436-5001
Murray Bresky, *President*
Ellen Gold, *Corp Secy*
Dean Koplik, *Vice Pres*
Shannon Helmuth, *Manager*
EMP: 299
SQ FT: 40,000
SALES (est): 42.7MM **Privately Held**
SIC: 2015 Poultry slaughtering & processing

South Glens Falls
Saratoga County

(G-14511)
AMES ADVANCED MATERIALS CORP (HQ)
50 Harrison Ave (12803-4912)
PHONE...................................518 792-5808
Frank Barber, *President*
▲ EMP: 58
SALES (est): 24MM
SALES (corp-wide): 32MM **Privately Held**
SIC: 3399 Silver powder; flakes, metal
PA: Ames Goldsmith Corp.
50 Harrison Ave
South Glens Falls NY 12803
518 792-5808

(G-14512)
ARCA INK LLC
30 Bluebird Rd (12803-5707)
PHONE...................................518 798-0100
Robert Chadwick Jr, *Mng Member*
Wendy Lafountain-Chadwick, *Mng Member*
EMP: 6
SQ FT: 9,000
SALES (est): 971.5K **Privately Held**
SIC: 2759 Screen printing

(G-14513)
HEXION INC
64 Fernan Rd (12803-5047)
P.O. Box B (12803)
PHONE...................................518 792-8040
Kathleen Ervine, *Manager*
EMP: 20 **Privately Held**
SIC: 2821 2869 2891 Melamine resins;
melamine-formaldehyde; formaldehyde
(formalin); adhesives & sealants
HQ: Hexion Inc.
180 E Broad St Fl 26
Columbus OH 43215
614 225-4000

(G-14514)
MDI EAST INC
Also Called: Bates Industries
22 Hudson Falls Rd Ste 6 (12803-5069)
PHONE...................................518 747-8730
Tom Pendergrass, *Plant Mgr*
EMP: 50
SALES (corp-wide): 17.3MM **Privately Held**
SIC: 3089 Injection molding of plastics
HQ: Mdi East, Inc.
6918 Ed Perkic St
Riverside CA 92504
951 509-6918

(G-14515)
NORTHEAST PROMOTIONAL GROUP IN
75 Main St (12803-4706)
PHONE...................................518 793-1024
Deana Endieveri, *President*
Jim Chamberlin, *Vice Pres*
Mike Endieveri, *Vice Pres*
Kindra Chamberlin, *Treasurer*
Holly Dekleine, *Accounts Exec*
EMP: 5
SALES (est): 628.4K **Privately Held**
WEB: www.nepromo.com
SIC: 3993 7389 Advertising novelties; embroidering of advertising on shirts, etc.

(G-14516)
NORTHEAST STITCHES & INK INC
Also Called: Sperry Advertising
95 Main St (12803-4706)
PHONE...................................518 798-5549
Deana Endieveri, *President*
Kindra Chamberlin, *Corp Secy*
James Chamberlin, *Vice Pres*
Michael Endieveri, *Vice Pres*
EMP: 34
SQ FT: 20,000
SALES (est): 2.9MM **Privately Held**
WEB: www.nestitchesink.com
SIC: 2395 2396 Embroidery products, except schiffli machine; automotive & apparel trimmings

(G-14517)
O RAMA LIGHT INC
22 Hudson Falls Rd Ste 52 (12803-5067)
PHONE...................................518 539-9000
John N Potochnak, *CEO*
Dan Baldwin, *Co-Owner*
Mary Baldwin, *Office Mgr*
▲ EMP: 20 EST: 2009
SALES (est): 2.6MM **Privately Held**
SIC: 3577 Computer peripheral equipment

(G-14518)
SIGNWORKS
22 Hudson Falls Rd 54 (12803-5050)
PHONE...................................518 745-0700
Robert G Stoya, *CEO*
EMP: 16
SALES (est): 1.9MM **Privately Held**
SIC: 3993 Signs & advertising specialties

South Hempstead
Nassau County

(G-14519)
ACCESSORIES FOR ELECTRONICS
Also Called: Afe
620 Mead Ter (11550-8011)
PHONE...................................631 847-0158
William J Epstein, *President*
Peter Wright, *Treasurer*
EMP: 26
SQ FT: 3,000
SALES (est): 4.9MM **Privately Held**
WEB: www.afeaccess.com
SIC: 3678 3679 Electronic connectors;
electronic circuits

South Otselic
Chenango County

(G-14520)
GLADDING BRAIDED PRODUCTS LLC
110 County Road 13a (13155)
P.O. Box 164 (13155-0164)
PHONE...................................315 653-7211
Sparky Christakos, *President*
Mike Radziwon, *Vice Pres*
Charles Bishop, *VP Prdtn*
▲ EMP: 40
SQ FT: 85,000
SALES: 11MM **Privately Held**
WEB: www.gladdingbraid.com
SIC: 2298 Rope, except asbestos & wire;
cordage: abaca, sisal, henequen, hemp,
jute or other fiber; cord, braided

South Ozone Park
Queens County

(G-14521)
CONTINENTAL LIFT TRUCK INC
12718 Foch Blvd (11420-2824)
PHONE...................................718 738-4738
Giuseppe Donofrio, *CEO*
▲ EMP: 16
SALES (est): 4.4MM **Privately Held**
SIC: 3537 Forklift trucks

South Richmond Hill
Queens County

(G-14522)
BUSINESS NEVER STOPS LLC
13404 97th Ave Ste 2 (11419-1616)
PHONE...................................888 479-3111
Sean Burgess, *Mng Member*
EMP: 8
SALES: 68K **Privately Held**
SIC: 2741 7334 7313 ; photocopying &
duplicating services; electronic media advertising representatives

(G-14523)
MAIZTECA FOODS INC
13005 Liberty Ave (11419-3121)
PHONE...................................718 641-3933
Sixto Reyes, *CEO*
Carlos Reyes, *President*
EMP: 40
SQ FT: 10,000
SALES: 3.5MM **Privately Held**
SIC: 2099 Tortillas, fresh or refrigerated

(G-14524)
SHOP SKY INC
10471 128th St (11419-3011)
PHONE...................................347 686-4616
Andrei Omar, *CEO*
Faiza Nasroor, *Executive Asst*
◆ EMP: 13
SALES: 200K **Privately Held**
SIC: 2844 Depilatories (cosmetic); face
creams or lotions; lipsticks

South Salem
Westchester County

(G-14525)
THE CENTRO COMPANY INC
215 Silver Spring Rd (10590-2525)
PHONE...................................914 533-2200
Alan Greene, *Ch of Bd*
Susan Green, *President*
EMP: 5
SALES (est): 556.7K **Privately Held**
SIC: 3061 Mechanical rubber goods

Southampton
Suffolk County

(G-14526)
AMERICAN COUNTRY QUILTS & LIN
Also Called: Judi Boisson American Country
134 Mariner Dr Unit C (11968-3482)
P.O. Box 5084 (11969-5084)
PHONE...................................631 283-5466
Judi Boisson, *President*
Erin Boisson, *Vice Pres*
EMP: 8
SQ FT: 4,000
SALES (est): 624.7K **Privately Held**
SIC: 2395 2269 3269 5023 Quilted fabrics or cloth; linen fabrics: dyeing, finishing & printing; art & ornamental ware,
pottery; linens & towels; linens, table;
decorative home furnishings & supplies;
mail order house; antiques

(G-14527)
BEST MDLR HMS AFRBE P Q& S IN
495 County Road 39 (11968-5236)
PHONE...................................631 204-0049
John Distefano, *Ch of Bd*
Laureiann Distefano, *Vice Pres*
EMP: 14
SALES (est): 1.6MM **Privately Held**
SIC: 2452 Modular homes, prefabricated,
wood

(G-14528)
CENTRAL KITCHEN CORP
871 County Road 39 (11968-5227)
PHONE...................................631 283-1029
Robert Grigo, *President*
Doreen Grigo, *Corp Secy*
Michelle Thomas, *Admin Asst*
EMP: 10
SQ FT: 4,000
SALES (est): 1.4MM **Privately Held**
WEB: www.centralkitchenscorp.com
SIC: 2434 5712 1751 5031 Wood kitchen
cabinets; cabinet work, custom; cabinets,
except custom made: kitchen; cabinet &
finish carpentry; cabinet building & installation; kitchen cabinets

(G-14529)
DANS PAPER INC
Also Called: South of The Highway
158 County Road 39 (11968-5252)
P.O. Box 630, Bridgehampton (11932-0630)
PHONE...................................631 537-0500
Roy E Brown, *Chairman*
Stacy Dermont, *Senior Editor*
EMP: 68
SQ FT: 2,500
SALES (est): 4.3MM
SALES (corp-wide): 8.9MM **Privately Held**
WEB: www.danspapers.com
SIC: 2711 Newspapers: publishing only,
not printed on site
PA: News Communications Inc
501 Madison Ave Fl 23
New York NY 10022
212 689-2500

(G-14530)
FRONTIERS UNLIMITED INC
Also Called: Homes Land Eastrn Long Island
52 Jagger Ln (11968-4822)
PHONE...................................631 283-4663
EMP: 8
SQ FT: 1,300
SALES: 1.5MM **Privately Held**
SIC: 2721 Periodicals-Publishing/Printing

(G-14531)
GABANI INC
81 Lee Ave (11968-4518)
PHONE...................................631 283-4930
Gabrielle Sampietro, *President*
Miguel Sampietro, *Treasurer*
EMP: 6 EST: 1978
SQ FT: 900
SALES (est): 42.6K **Privately Held**
SIC: 2253 Knit outerwear mills

(G-14532)
HAMPTONS MEDIA LLC
Also Called: Hamptons Magazine
67 Hampton Rd Unit 5 (11968-4962)
PHONE...................................631 283-6900
Nicole Nadboy, *Director*
Jason Binn,
EMP: 5
SALES: 149.3K
SALES (corp-wide): 41MM **Privately Held**
SIC: 2721 Magazines: publishing only, not
printed on site
HQ: Niche Media Holdings, Llc
257 Park Ave S Fl 5
New York NY 10010
702 990-2500

(G-14533)
MORRIS GOLF VENTURES
Sebonac Inlet Rd (11968)
PHONE...................................631 283-0559
James Morris, *Owner*
EMP: 25
SALES (est): 1.7MM **Privately Held**
SIC: 3949 Golf equipment

(G-14534)
PAULPAC LLC
104 Foster Xing (11968-4955)
P.O. Box 2849 (11969-2849)
PHONE...................................631 283-7610
Michela Keszlies,
EMP: 6
SALES: 500K **Privately Held**
WEB: www.paulpac.com
SIC: 2393 Textile bags

(G-14535)
PECONIC IRONWORKS LTD
33 Flying Point Rd # 108 (11968-5280)
PHONE...................................631 204-0323
Patrick Grace, *President*
Thomas Berglin, *Vice Pres*
EMP: 13 EST: 1997
SALES: 2.4MM **Privately Held**
SIC: 3446 Architectural metalwork

(G-14536)
ROCKWELL VIDEO SOLUTIONS LLC
10 Koral Dr (11968-4307)
PHONE..............................631 745-0582
Adam Cusack,
EMP: 15
SALES (est): 950K **Privately Held**
SIC: 3999 Manufacturing industries

(G-14537)
SHADE & SHUTTER SYSTEMS OF NY
260 Hampton Rd (11968-5028)
PHONE..............................631 208-0275
EMP: 6
SALES (est): 630K **Privately Held**
SIC: 3442 Louvers, shutters, jalousies & similar items

(G-14538)
SOUTHAMPTON TOWN NEWSPAPERS (PA)
Also Called: Press of Manorville & Moriches
135 Windmill Ln (11968-4840)
P.O. Box 1207 (11969-1207)
PHONE..............................631 283-4100
Joseph Louchheim, *President*
Nick Thomas, *Business Mgr*
Paul Conroy, *Sales Mgr*
Sara Struble, *Accounts Exec*
Keith Schultz, *Sales Executive*
EMP: 50
SQ FT: 1,500
SALES (est): 3.1MM **Privately Held**
WEB: www.southamptonpress.com
SIC: 2711 2741 Newspapers: publishing only, not printed on site; miscellaneous publishing

(G-14539)
THOMAS MATTHEWS WDWKG LTD
15 Powell Ave (11968-3425)
PHONE..............................631 287-3657
Thomas Matthews, *Branch Mgr*
EMP: 14 **Privately Held**
SIC: 2499 Woodenware, kitchen & household
PA: Thomas Matthews Woodworking Ltd.
225 Ocean View Pkwy
Southampton NY 11968

(G-14540)
THOMAS MATTHEWS WDWKG LTD (PA)
225 Ocean View Pkwy (11968-5523)
P.O. Box 520, Bridgehampton (11932-0520)
PHONE..............................631 287-2023
Thomas Matthew, *President*
EMP: 6
SALES (est): 1.1MM **Privately Held**
SIC: 2499 Woodenware, kitchen & household

Southfields
Orange County

(G-14541)
KARLYN INDUSTRIES INC
16 Spring St (10975)
P.O. Box 310 (10975-0310)
PHONE..............................845 351-2249
Hans Bierdumpfel, *President*
Margaret Bierdumpfel, *Vice Pres*
Joyce Lasalle, *Treasurer*
▲ **EMP:** 15
SQ FT: 10,000
SALES (est): 2.4MM **Privately Held**
WEB: www.karlynsti.com
SIC: 3714 3694 Motor vehicle parts & accessories; spark plugs for internal combustion engines

Southold
Suffolk County

(G-14542)
ACADEMY PRINTING SERVICES INC
Also Called: Peconic B Shopper
42 Hortons Ln (11971)
P.O. Box 848 (11971-0848)
PHONE..............................631 765-3346
Michael Hagerman, *President*
Rita Hagerman, *Vice Pres*
EMP: 6
SQ FT: 4,000
SALES (est): 926.2K **Privately Held**
SIC: 2752 2759 Photo-offset printing; commercial printing

(G-14543)
FUTURE SCREW MACHINE PDTS INC
41155 County Road 48 (11971-5041)
PHONE..............................631 765-1610
Ellen Hufe, *President*
EMP: 10
SQ FT: 2,700
SALES (est): 1.8MM **Privately Held**
SIC: 3599 Machine shop, jobbing & repair

(G-14544)
INTERNODAL INTERNATIONAL INC
54800 Route 25 (11971-4648)
P.O. Box 606 (11971-0606)
PHONE..............................631 765-0037
Rosemary Verrecchio, *President*
Joe Stadler, *Vice Pres*
EMP: 25
SALES (est): 1.4MM **Privately Held**
WEB: www.internodalinternational.com
SIC: 7372 7389 Prepackaged software; design services

(G-14545)
NEW ENGLAND BARNS INC
45805 Route 25 (11971-4670)
P.O. Box 1447, Mattituck (11952-0925)
PHONE..............................631 445-1461
William Gorman, *Owner*
EMP: 22
SALES (est): 1.5MM **Privately Held**
SIC: 2439 Timbers, structural: laminated lumber

(G-14546)
WALLACE HOME DESIGN CTR
44500 County Road 48 (11971-5034)
P.O. Box 181, Peconic (11958-0181)
PHONE..............................631 765-3890
George Wallace, *President*
Rene Lisowy, *Owner*
EMP: 6
SQ FT: 2,400
SALES (est): 839.5K **Privately Held**
SIC: 2211 2511 2512 5713 Draperies & drapery fabrics, cotton; wood household furniture; upholstered household furniture; carpets; window furnishings

Sparrow Bush
Orange County

(G-14547)
ETERNAL LINE
1237 State Route 42 (12780-5042)
PHONE..............................845 856-1999
Marius Winograd, *Owner*
Agnes Winograd, *Co-Owner*
EMP: 2
SALES: 1.2MM **Privately Held**
SIC: 3911 Jewelry, precious metal

Speculator
Hamilton County

(G-14548)
STEPHENSON LUMBER COMPANY INC
Rr 8 (12164)
PHONE..............................518 548-7521
John Shaw, *Manager*
EMP: 5
SALES (corp-wide): 5.9MM **Privately Held**
WEB: www.riversidetruss.com
SIC: 2439 5211 Arches, laminated lumber; millwork & lumber
PA: Stephenson Lumber Company, Inc.
Riverside Station Rd
Riparius NY 12862
518 494-4733

Spencer
Tioga County

(G-14549)
R HADLEY CORPORATION
89 Tompkins St (14883-9759)
PHONE..............................607 589-4415
Jacinto Maratea, *CEO*
Elliot Dutra, *COO*
Mary Jansky, *Purch Agent*
Tracy McCutcheon, *Purch Agent*
Gianna Maratea, *CFO*
▲ **EMP:** 80
SQ FT: 90,000
SALES: 12MM **Privately Held**
WEB: www.raymondhadley.com
SIC: 2099 2041 Almond pastes; flour: blended, prepared or self-rising

(G-14550)
STARFIRE SWORDS LTD INC
74 Railroad Ave (14883-9543)
P.O. Box 74 (14883-0074)
PHONE..............................607 589-7244
Maciej Zakrzewski, *President*
Sandy Russell, *Vice Pres*
Alexandra White, *Vice Pres*
EMP: 20
SALES (est): 2.7MM **Privately Held**
WEB: www.starfireswords.com
SIC: 3421 Swords

Spencerport
Monroe County

(G-14551)
AMERICAN CUSTOM METALS INC
10 Turner Dr (14559-1931)
PHONE..............................585 694-4893
Patrick Revenew, *President*
EMP: 8
SALES (est): 1.1MM **Privately Held**
SIC: 3353 Coils, sheet aluminum

(G-14552)
AZTEC MFG OF ROCHESTER
19 Hickory Ln (14559-2511)
PHONE..............................585 352-8152
James Monsees, *Ch of Bd*
EMP: 7
SQ FT: 5,382
SALES (est): 903.8K **Privately Held**
SIC: 3541 Machine tools, metal cutting type

(G-14553)
BOSS PRECISION LTD
2440 S Union St (14559-2230)
PHONE..............................585 352-7070
Gerd Herrman, *Ch of Bd*
Paul Dugan, *Vice Pres*
Alec Ollies, *Treasurer*
EMP: 60
SQ FT: 45,000
SALES (est): 10.9MM **Privately Held**
SIC: 3444 Sheet metal specialties, not stamped

(G-14554)
BULLET INDUSTRIES INC
Also Called: Coyote Motorsports
7 Turner Dr (14559-1930)
PHONE..............................585 352-0836
Mark Lipari, *CEO*
EMP: 6 **EST:** 2007
SALES (est): 451.8K **Privately Held**
SIC: 3799 7539 Recreational vehicles; machine shop, automotive

(G-14555)
DOLOMITE PRODUCTS COMPANY INC
2540 S Union St (14559-2232)
PHONE..............................585 352-0460
Wally Przybcien, *Principal*
EMP: 16
SALES (corp-wide): 30.6B **Privately Held**
SIC: 2951 Asphalt paving mixtures & blocks
HQ: Dolomite Products Company Inc.
1150 Penfield Rd
Rochester NY 14625
315 524-1998

(G-14556)
IMCO INC
15 Turner Dr (14559-1930)
PHONE..............................585 352-7810
David Demallie, *Principal*
Audrey Mair, *Director*
EMP: 47
SQ FT: 25,000
SALES (est): 9.1MM **Privately Held**
SIC: 3089 Injection molding of plastics

(G-14557)
KLEIN REINFORCING SERVICES INC
11 Turner Dr (14559-1930)
PHONE..............................585 352-9433
Mark Kulzer, *President*
EMP: 15
SQ FT: 15,000
SALES (est): 3.7MM **Privately Held**
SIC: 3449 Bars, concrete reinforcing: fabricated steel

(G-14558)
MANUFACTURERS TOOL & DIE CO
3 Turner Dr (14559-1930)
P.O. Box 139 (14559-0139)
PHONE..............................585 352-1080
Douglas Sullivan, *President*
Dan Sullivan, *Vice Pres*
Gail Sullivan, *Office Mgr*
EMP: 5
SQ FT: 10,000
SALES: 300K **Privately Held**
SIC: 3544 Special dies & tools

(G-14559)
ROTATION DYNAMICS CORPORATION
Rotadyne
3581 Big Ridge Rd (14559-1709)
PHONE..............................585 352-9023
Dan Farrell, *Principal*
Dave Baldwin, *Plant Mgr*
EMP: 36
SALES (corp-wide): 145.7MM **Privately Held**
SIC: 3069 2796 Rolls, solid or covered rubber; platemaking services
PA: Rotation Dynamics Corporation
1101 Windham Pkwy
Romeoville IL 60446
630 769-9255

(G-14560)
WESTSIDE NEWS INC
Also Called: Suburban News
1835 N Union St (14559-1153)
P.O. Box 106 (14559-0106)
PHONE..............................585 352-3411
Keith Ryan, *Ch of Bd*
EMP: 18
SQ FT: 1,000

▲ = Import ▼=Export
◆ =Import/Export

SALES (est): 1.4MM **Privately Held**
SIC: 2711 Newspapers: publishing only, not printed on site

Speonk
Suffolk County

(G-14561)
BUNCEE LLC
170 Montauk Hwy Speonk (11972)
P.O. Box 429 (11972-0429)
PHONE................................631 591-1390
Claire Cucchi, *COO*
Christopher Del Basso, *Marketing Staff*
Arvind Agarwal, *Manager*
Marie Arturi,
Josh Allen, *Education*
EMP: 10
SALES (est): 897K **Privately Held**
SIC: 7372 Prepackaged software

(G-14562)
HENPECKED HUSBAND FARMS CORP
1212 Speonk Riverhead Rd (11972-2532)
P.O. Box 752 (11972-0752)
PHONE................................631 728-2800
Raayah Churgin, *Principal*
Jennifer Roberts, *Administration*
EMP: 6
SQ FT: 12,000
SALES (est): 417.4K **Privately Held**
SIC: 2869 Industrial organic chemicals

(G-14563)
JOHN T MONTECALVO INC
1233 Speonk Riverhead Rd (11972)
P.O. Box 460 (11972-0460)
PHONE................................631 325-1492
Debbie Timpone, *Branch Mgr*
EMP: 7
SALES (corp-wide): 4.6MM **Privately Held**
SIC: 2951 1611 Asphalt paving mixtures & blocks; surfacing & paving
PA: John T. Montecalvo, Inc.
48 Railroad Ave
Center Moriches NY
631 325-1492

Sprakers
Montgomery County

(G-14564)
BILL LAKE HOMES CONSTRUCTION
188 Flanders Rd (12166-4519)
P.O. Box 105 (12166-0105)
PHONE................................518 673-2424
William Lake, *President*
Greg Erhardt, *Office Mgr*
EMP: 56
SALES (est): 8MM **Privately Held**
WEB: www.billlakehomes.com
SIC: 2452 Modular homes, prefabricated, wood

Spring Valley
Rockland County

(G-14565)
CREATIVE KIDS FAR EAST INC
750 Chestnut Ridge Rd # 301 (10977-6444)
PHONE................................844 252-7263
Samuel Lapa, *Chairman*
Daniel Delapa, *Executive*
▲ **EMP:** 120
SALES (est): 14.2MM **Privately Held**
WEB: www.creativekidsltd.com
SIC: 3944 5092 Games, toys & children's vehicles; toys & hobby goods & supplies

(G-14566)
DELUXE CORPORATION
9 Lincoln Ave (10977-8938)
PHONE................................845 362-4054
Yakov Breuer, *Branch Mgr*

EMP: 267
SALES (corp-wide): 2B **Publicly Held**
SIC: 2782 Checkbooks
PA: Deluxe Corporation
3680 Victoria St N
Shoreview MN 55126
651 483-7111

(G-14567)
EAGLE REGALIA CO INC
Also Called: Abbot Flag Co Div
747 Chestnut Ridge Rd # 101 (10977-6224)
PHONE................................845 425-2245
Michael Kartzmer, *President*
▲ **EMP:** 10 **EST:** 1910
SQ FT: 4,000
SALES (est): 730K **Privately Held**
SIC: 2399 3999 2395 3911 Flags, fabric; banners, made from fabric; badges, metal: policemen, firemen, etc.; plaques, picture, laminated; emblems, embroidered; medals, precious or semiprecious metal

(G-14568)
EZ LIFT OPERATOR CORP
Also Called: EZ Lift Garage Door Service
111 S Main St (10977-5617)
PHONE................................845 356-1676
EMP: 10
SALES: 870K **Privately Held**
SIC: 3699 5084 5211 1751 Mfg Elec Mach/Equip/Supp Whol Industrial Equip Ret Lumber/Building Mtrl Carpentry Contractor

(G-14569)
FINAL TOUCH PRINTING INC
29 Decatur Ave Unit 1 (10977-4782)
PHONE................................845 352-2677
Shmiel Elger, *Chairman*
EMP: 13
SALES (est): 1.3MM **Privately Held**
SIC: 2752 Commercial printing, lithographic

(G-14570)
FROZEN PASTRY PRODUCTS CORP
41 Lincoln Ave (10977-1918)
PHONE................................845 364-9833
Dov Sandburg, *President*
EMP: 33
SQ FT: 8,000
SALES (est): 3.1MM **Privately Held**
SIC: 2041 Doughs, frozen or refrigerated

(G-14571)
GOLDEN TASTE INC
318 Roosevelt Ave (10977-5824)
PHONE................................845 356-4133
Rachel Perlmutter, *President*
Rafiel Perlmutter, *Vice Pres*
EMP: 32
SQ FT: 20,000
SALES: 6MM **Privately Held**
SIC: 2099 Salads, fresh or refrigerated

(G-14572)
ION-TOF USA INC
100 Red Schoolhouse Rd A-1 (10977-7049)
PHONE................................845 352-8082
Ewald Niehuis, *President*
Alfred Benninghoven, *Treasurer*
Marianne Leoatta, *Manager*
EMP: 7
SQ FT: 2,200
SALES (est): 1MM
SALES (corp-wide): 9.9MM **Privately Held**
WEB: www.ion-tof.com
SIC: 3826 Analytical instruments
PA: Iontof Technologies Gmbh
Heisenbergstr. 15
Munster 48149
251 162-2100

(G-14573)
JAY BAGS INC
55 Union Rd Ste 104 (10977-3900)
PHONE................................845 459-6500
Gitty Rubin, *Principal*
▲ **EMP:** 3 **EST:** 2010
SQ FT: 20,000

SALES (est): 2MM **Privately Held**
SIC: 2673 5113 Bags: plastic, laminated & coated; bags, paper & disposable plastic

(G-14574)
LECHLER LABORATORIES INC
Also Called: Lechler Labs
100 Red Schoolhse Rd C2 (10977-7049)
PHONE................................845 426-6800
Martin Melik, *Chairman*
Jimmy Varghese, *Research*
EMP: 25 **EST:** 1957
SALES (est): 4.1MM **Privately Held**
WEB: www.lechlerlabs.com
SIC: 2844 5961 Cosmetic preparations; colognes; catalog & mail-order houses

(G-14575)
LECROY CORPORATION (PA)
700 Chestnut Ridge Rd (10977-6435)
PHONE................................845 425-2000
Harkness Adams, *Chairman*
Conrad Fernandes, *Vice Pres*
David Graef, *Vice Pres*
Joe Mendolia, *Vice Pres*
Roberto Petrillo, *Vice Pres*
EMP: 24 **EST:** 1995
SALES (est): 7.5MM **Privately Held**
SIC: 3825 Instruments to measure electricity

(G-14576)
LIPTIS PHARMACEUTICALS USA INC
110 Red Schoolhouse Rd (10977-7032)
PHONE................................845 627-0260
Sherin Awad, *CEO*
Dick Klaus, *President*
Jenny Avalos, *Vice Pres*
Maria Belliard, *Purchasing*
Ndiogou Toure, *Manager*
▲ **EMP:** 1022
SALES (est): 123.1MM
SALES (corp-wide): 1.2MM **Privately Held**
WEB: www.liptis.com
SIC: 2834 Pharmaceutical preparations
PA: Liptis Switzerland Sa
D4 Platz 3
Root Langenbold LU 6039
227 040-505

(G-14577)
LOUIS SCHWARTZ
Also Called: Supreme Leather Products
28 Lawrence St (10977-5038)
PHONE................................845 356-6624
Louis Schwartz, *Owner*
EMP: 6 **EST:** 1949
SQ FT: 7,500
SALES (est): 220K **Privately Held**
SIC: 2386 Garments, leather

(G-14578)
MBH FURNITURE INNOVATIONS INC
28 Lincoln Ave (10977-1915)
PHONE................................845 354-8202
Simcha Greenberg, *CEO*
EMP: 6
SALES (est): 620.1K **Privately Held**
SIC: 2519 Household furniture, except wood or metal: upholstered

(G-14579)
MEASUPRO INC (PA)
Also Called: Smart Weigh
1 Alpine Ct (10977-5647)
PHONE................................845 425-8777
EMP: 14
SALES (est): 3.8MM **Privately Held**
SIC: 3596 Weighing machines & apparatus

(G-14580)
PALISADES PAPER INC
13 Jackson Ave (10977-1910)
PHONE................................845 354-0333
Jochanan Schwaite, *President*
EMP: 6
SALES: 2MM **Privately Held**
SIC: 2621 Parchment paper

(G-14581)
RESERVE CONFECTIONS INC
Also Called: Reserve Confections Chocolate
3 Perlman Dr Ste 105 (10977-5281)
P.O. Box 186, Monsey (10952-0186)
PHONE................................845 371-7744
Juda Fisch, *President*
▲ **EMP:** 11 **EST:** 2014
SALES (est): 1MM **Privately Held**
SIC: 2066 Chocolate

(G-14582)
STRATIVA PHARMACEUTICALS
1 Ram Ridge Rd (10977-6714)
PHONE................................201 802-4000
Paul V Campanelli, *CEO*
Terrance J Coughlin, *COO*
Michael A Tropiano, *Exec VP*
Anthony Guacci, *Vice Pres*
Sal Gencarelli, *Mfg Spvr*
EMP: 12
SALES (est): 1MM **Privately Held**
SIC: 2834 Druggists' preparations (pharmaceuticals)

(G-14583)
TRAFFIC LOGIX CORPORATION
3 Harriet Ln (10977-1302)
PHONE................................866 915-6449
Louis Newman, *CEO*
Mindy N Cohen, *General Mgr*
Ben Cohen, *Treasurer*
John Painter, *Manager*
▼ **EMP:** 7
SQ FT: 100
SALES (est): 1.2MM **Privately Held**
SIC: 3812 3069 5084 Radar systems & equipment; molded rubber products; safety equipment

(G-14584)
ULTRA CLARITY CORP
3101 Parkview Dr (10977-4979)
PHONE................................719 470-1010
Goldie Halpert, *CEO*
Samuel Halpert, *Principal*
EMP: 5 **EST:** 2014
SALES (est): 289.2K **Privately Held**
SIC: 3496 5051 Cable, uninsulated wire: made from purchased wire; cable, wire

(G-14585)
UNEEDA ENTERPRIZES INC
640 Chestnut Ridge Rd (10977-5653)
P.O. Box 209 (10977-0209)
PHONE................................800 431-2494
Bruce Fuchs, *President*
Herman Fuchs, *President*
Richard Caporusso, *Vice Pres*
Phyllis Crystal, *Vice Pres*
Mina Fuchs, *Treasurer*
▲ **EMP:** 110 **EST:** 1967
SQ FT: 58,000
SALES (est): 22MM **Privately Held**
WEB: www.uneeda.com
SIC: 3291 5084 5085 Abrasive products; industrial machinery & equipment; abrasives

(G-14586)
UNIVERSITY TABLE CLOTH COMPANY
10 Centre St (10977)
P.O. Box 82, Nanuet (10954-0082)
PHONE................................845 371-3876
Debra Timco, *President*
▲ **EMP:** 11 **EST:** 1998
SQ FT: 5,000
SALES (est): 901.3K **Privately Held**
SIC: 2392 Tablecloths: made from purchased materials

(G-14587)
US POLYCHEMICAL HOLDING CORP
584 Chestnut Ridge Rd (10977-5648)
PHONE................................845 356-5530
David Cherry, *CEO*
Kelly Simore, *Controller*
Kelly Seymour, *Accounting Mgr*
EMP: 24 **EST:** 2012
SALES (est): 4.8MM **Privately Held**
SIC: 2899 Chemical preparations

GEOGRAPHIC

Springfield Gardens
Queens County

(G-14588)
DUNDY GLASS & MIRROR CORP
12252 Montauk St (11413-1034)
PHONE....................................718 723-5800
Eric Latin, *President*
Florence Latin, *Treasurer*
Ellen Latin, *Admin Sec*
▲ EMP: 25 EST: 1900
SQ FT: 17,000
SALES (est): 4.2MM **Privately Held**
WEB: www.dundyglass.com
SIC: 3231 Mirrored glass; furniture tops,
glass: cut, beveled or polished

Springville
Erie County

(G-14589)
DELOCON WHOLESALE INC
270 W Main St (14141-1175)
P.O. Box 4 (14141-0004)
PHONE....................................716 592-2711
Sherwin Lape, *President*
EMP: 15
SALES (est): 2.2MM **Privately Held**
WEB: www.delocon.com
SIC: 2541 5211 Counter & sink tops; lum-
ber & other building materials

(G-14590)
FLUIDAMPR
180 Zoar Valley Rd (14141-9248)
PHONE....................................716 592-1000
Keith Horschel, *Sales Staff*
EMP: 5
SALES (est): 246.1K **Privately Held**
SIC: 3089 Automotive parts, plastic

(G-14591)
GERNATT ASPHALT PRODUCTS INC
Benz Dr (14141)
PHONE....................................716 496-5111
Mark Smith, *Vice Pres*
EMP: 7
SALES (corp-wide): 29.8MM **Privately Held**
WEB: www.gernatt.com
SIC: 2951 Asphalt paving mixtures &
blocks
PA: Gernatt Asphalt Products, Inc.
13870 Taylor Hollow Rd
Collins NY 14034
716 532-3371

(G-14592)
GRAMCO INC (PA)
299 Waverly St (14141-1055)
P.O. Box 68 (14141-0068)
PHONE....................................716 592-2845
Robert D Mattison, *President*
Nancy J Human, *Vice Pres*
Torrance H Brooks, *Admin Sec*
EMP: 3
SQ FT: 800
SALES (est): 6.7MM **Privately Held**
WEB: www.gramcoonline.com
SIC: 2048 5999 Feed concentrates; feed
& farm supply

(G-14593)
HEARY BROS LGHTNING PROTECTION
11291 Moore Rd (14141-9614)
PHONE....................................716 941-6141
Kenneth Heary, *President*
Edwin Hear, *Officer*
EMP: 40
SQ FT: 22,800
SALES (est): 3MM **Privately Held**
WEB: www.hearybros.com
SIC: 3643 Lightning protection equipment

(G-14594)
PEERLESS-WINSMITH INC
172 Eaton St (14141-1197)
PHONE....................................716 592-9311

Brian Hallstrom, *General Mgr*
Cathy Keller, *Purchasing*
Robert Holdsworth, *Engineer*
Bob Geiser, *Design Engr*
Dennis Wolbert, *Controller*
EMP: 225
SALES (corp-wide): 260.7MM **Privately Held**
WEB: www.peerlesswinsmith.com
SIC: 3566 5063 Gears, power transmis-
sion, except automotive; power transmis-
sion equipment, electric
HQ: Peerless-Winsmith, Inc.
5200 Upper Metro Pl # 110
Dublin OH 43017
614 526-7000

(G-14595)
PERFECTION GEAR INC
172 Eaton St (14141-1165)
PHONE....................................716 592-9310
Kim Neyrett, *Manager*
EMP: 150
SALES (corp-wide): 260.7MM **Privately Held**
SIC: 3566 Reduction gears & gear units for
turbines, except automotive
HQ: Perfection Gear, Inc.
9 N Bear Creek Rd
Asheville NC 28806
828 253-0000

(G-14596)
QUAKER BOY INC (PA)
Also Called: Quaker Boy Turkey Calls
195 W Main St (14141-1017)
PHONE....................................716 662-3979
Richard C Kirby, *President*
▲ EMP: 50
SALES (est): 4.9MM **Privately Held**
WEB: www.quakerboy.com
SIC: 3949 5961 Game calls; hunting
equipment; mail order house

(G-14597)
SPRINGVILLE MFG CO INC
8798 North St (14141-9648)
P.O. Box 367 (14141-0367)
PHONE....................................716 592-4957
Daniel J Schmauss, *President*
Joseph Schmauss, *Shareholder*
Michael Schmauss, *Shareholder*
EMP: 31 EST: 1958
SQ FT: 28,000
SALES (est): 7MM **Privately Held**
WEB: www.springvillemfg.com
SIC: 3593 3599 Fluid power cylinders, hy-
draulic or pneumatic; machine shop, job-
bing & repair

Staatsburg
Dutchess County

(G-14598)
CURRANT COMPANY LLC
Also Called: Currantc
59 Walnut Ln (12580-6346)
PHONE....................................845 266-8999
Greg Quinn,
▲ EMP: 5
SALES (est): 540.1K **Privately Held**
WEB: www.currantc.com
SIC: 2026 Yogurt

(G-14599)
DUTCHESS PLUMBING & HEATING
28 Reservoir Rd (12580-5317)
PHONE....................................845 889-8255
Steven Eckelman, *President*
Maryanne Eckelman, *Vice Pres*
EMP: 5
SALES (est): 420K **Privately Held**
SIC: 2759 Commercial printing

(G-14600)
PROTECTIVE POWER SYSTMS & CNTR
Also Called: AC DC Power Systems & Contrls
2092 Rt 9 G Staatsburg (12580)
P.O. Box 119 (12580-0119)
PHONE....................................845 721-1875
Andrea Patierno, *CEO*

John Patierno, *Vice Pres*
EMP: 11
SALES (est): 2.9MM **Privately Held**
WEB: www.protectivepowersystems.com
SIC: 3621 Motors & generators

(G-14601)
UNIFUSE LLC
2092 Route 9g (12580-5426)
PHONE....................................845 889-4000
Jeff Bookstein, *Managing Dir*
Jeffrey Bookstein, *Managing Dir*
Dan Aiello, *Principal*
EMP: 15
SQ FT: 50,000
SALES (est): 2.9MM **Privately Held**
WEB: www.unifuse.com
SIC: 3089 Injection molding of plastics

Stafford
Genesee County

(G-14602)
CAROLINA EASTERN-CROCKER LLC (PA)
8610 Route 237 (14143-9514)
P.O. Box 68, Le Roy (14482-0068)
PHONE....................................585 345-4141
Carol Thompson, *General Mgr*
Bill Crocker,
EMP: 35 EST: 1998
SALES (est): 10.2MM **Privately Held**
SIC: 2048 Livestock feeds

(G-14603)
GENESEE BUILDING PRODUCTS LLC
7982 Byron Stafford Rd (14143)
P.O. Box 747 (14143-0747)
PHONE....................................585 548-2726
Ronald Wheeler, *Mng Member*
EMP: 11
SQ FT: 20,000
SALES (est): 4.7MM **Privately Held**
SIC: 3444 Gutters, sheet metal

(G-14604)
HANSON AGGREGATES EAST LLC
5870 Main Rd (14143-9519)
PHONE....................................585 343-1787
Jeff Curry, *Manager*
EMP: 22
SALES (corp-wide): 20.6B **Privately Held**
SIC: 2951 Asphalt paving mixtures &
blocks
HQ: Hanson Aggregates East Llc
3131 Rdu Center Dr
Morrisville NC 27560
919 380-2500

(G-14605)
RJ PRECISION LLC
6662 Main Rd (14143-9554)
PHONE....................................585 768-8030
Kathleen Johns, *Partner*
Robert Johns,
EMP: 5
SQ FT: 5,300
SALES: 820K **Privately Held**
SIC: 3441 Fabricated structural metal

Stamford
Delaware County

(G-14606)
AUDIO-SEARS CORP
2 South St (12167-1211)
PHONE....................................607 652-7305
David Hartwell, *President*
Shawn Hartwell, *Vice Pres*
Vincent Pricolo, *Sales Dir*
▲ EMP: 81 EST: 1956
SQ FT: 25,000
SALES (est): 13.1MM **Privately Held**
WEB: www.audiosears.com
SIC: 3661 Telephones & telephone appara-
tus

(G-14607)
CATSKILL CRAFTSMEN INC
15 W End Ave (12167-1296)
PHONE....................................607 652-7321
Duncan Axtell, *Ch of Bd*
Duncan Axtel, *President*
Henry Cioccari, *Purchasing*
Ken Smith, *CFO*
Adam Cornell, *Sales Staff*
▲ EMP: 55
SQ FT: 94,000
SALES (est): 7.7MM **Privately Held**
WEB: www.catskillcraftsmen.com
SIC: 2434 2499 2511 Wood kitchen cabi-
nets; woodenware, kitchen & household;
kitchen & dining room furniture

(G-14608)
MACADOODLES
26 River St (12167-1014)
PHONE....................................607 652-9019
Michelle Caiazza, *Owner*
EMP: 6
SALES (est): 524.6K **Privately Held**
WEB: www.macadoodles.com
SIC: 2024 Ice cream & frozen desserts

(G-14609)
STONE CREST INDUSTRIES INC
Also Called: Generic Compositors
152 Starheim Rd (12167-1757)
PHONE....................................607 652-2665
Gerald Stoner, *President*
Ellen Thorn, *CFO*
EMP: 5
SALES (est): 332.7K **Privately Held**
WEB: www.genericcomp.com
SIC: 2791 Typesetting

Stanfordville
Dutchess County

(G-14610)
GALLANT GRAPHICS LTD
242 Attlebury Hill Rd (12581-5635)
PHONE....................................845 868-1166
Melvin Eiger, *President*
Ralph Brunks, *Vice Pres*
Julian Thorn, *Vice Pres*
▲ EMP: 26
SALES (est): 4.7MM **Privately Held**
WEB: www.gallantgraphics.com
SIC: 2752 2796 2791 2759 Commercial
printing, offset; platemaking services;
typesetting; commercial printing

Stanley
Ontario County

(G-14611)
GIZMO PRODUCTS INC
2257 County Road 4 Bldg 3 (14561-9528)
PHONE....................................585 301-0970
Peter Blokhuis, *President*
Lisa Blokhuis, *Info Tech Mgr*
EMP: 8
SALES: 900K **Privately Held**
SIC: 3823 Level & bulk measuring instru-
ments, industrial process

Staten Island
Richmond County

(G-14612)
828 EXPRESS INC
619 Elbe Ave (10304-3412)
PHONE....................................917 577-9019
Nelson Liu, *President*
EMP: 9
SALES (est): 1.1MM **Privately Held**
SIC: 3443 Containers, shipping (bombs,
etc.): metal plate

(G-14613)
A K A COMPUTER CONSULTING INC
1412 Richmond Rd (10304-2312)
PHONE....................................718 351-5200

▲ = Import ▼ =Export
◆ =Import/Export

Alex Kleyff, *Founder*
Eva Kleyff, *Vice Pres*
EMP: 5
SQ FT: 1,200
SALES (est): 812.6K **Privately Held**
WEB: www.akaconsulting.com
SIC: 7372 Prepackaged software

(G-14614)
A&B MCKEON GLASS INC
69 Roff St (10304-1856)
PHONE................................718 525-2152
Charles Bell, *President*
EMP: 5 **EST:** 1976
SQ FT: 750
SALES (est): 560K **Privately Held**
SIC: 3449 1542 1793 1761 Curtain wall,
metal; store front construction; glass &
glazing work; architectural sheet metal
work

(G-14615)
A/C DESIGN & FABRICATION CORP
638 Sharrotts Rd Ste 1 (10309-1974)
PHONE................................718 227-8100
Jeff Arcello, *President*
▲ **EMP:** 5
SALES (est): 828.6K **Privately Held**
SIC: 3441 Fabricated structural metal

(G-14616)
ALBA HOUSE PUBLISHERS
2187 Victory Blvd (10314-6603)
PHONE................................718 698-2759
Ignatius Staniszewski, *CEO*
▲ **EMP:** 25
SALES (est): 1.1MM **Privately Held**
SIC: 2731 Books: publishing only

(G-14617)
ALL SHORE INDUSTRIES INC
1 Edgewater St Ste 215 (10305-4900)
PHONE................................718 720-0018
Sandor Goldner, *CEO*
Norman Goldner, *President*
▲ **EMP:** 10
SQ FT: 5,000
SALES (est): 1.8MM **Privately Held**
SIC: 3679 3677 3699 Electronic circuits;
electronic coils, transformers & other in-
ductors; appliance cords for household
electrical equipment

(G-14618)
ALL SIGNS
Also Called: Woodside Decorator
63 Bridgetown St (10314-6211)
PHONE................................973 736-2113
Vincent Iannuzzelli, *Owner*
EMP: 7
SALES: 600K **Privately Held**
SIC: 3993 Electric signs

(G-14619)
ARC TEC WLDG & FABRICATION INC
15 Harrison Ave (10302-1328)
PHONE................................718 982-9274
Kim R Genduso, *President*
EMP: 5
SALES (est): 673.3K **Privately Held**
SIC: 7692 Welding repair

(G-14620)
ARIMED ORTHOTICS PROSTHETICS
235 Dongan Hills Ave 2d (10305-1246)
PHONE................................718 979-6155
Steven Mirones, *Branch Mgr*
EMP: 14
SALES (corp-wide): 3.4MM **Privately Held**
SIC: 3842 Orthopedic appliances
PA: Arimed Orthotics, Prosthetics And Pe-
dorthics, Inc.
302 Livingston St
Brooklyn NY 11217
718 875-8754

(G-14621)
ATHLETIC CAP CO INC
123 Fields Ave (10314-5066)
PHONE................................718 398-1300
Arthur Farkas, *Ch of Bd*

Ira Farkas, *Vice Pres*
EMP: 40
SQ FT: 9,000
SALES (est): 1.2MM **Privately Held**
SIC: 2353 2396 2395 Hats & caps; auto-
motive & apparel trimmings; pleating &
stitching

(G-14622)
B & R TOOL INC
955 Rensselaer Ave (10309-2227)
PHONE................................718 948-2729
William Nobile, *President*
EMP: 6
SALES (est): 567K **Privately Held**
SIC: 3469 Metal stampings

(G-14623)
BANDS N BOWS
34 Fieldway Ave (10308-2930)
PHONE................................718 984-4316
Ted Mazola, *Principal*
EMP: 5
SALES (est): 296.7K **Privately Held**
SIC: 2339 Scarves, hoods, headbands,
etc.: women's

(G-14624)
BARBERA TRANSDUSER SYSTEMS
21 Louis St (10304-2111)
PHONE................................718 816-3025
Richard Barbera, *Partner*
Katherine Sanfilippo, *Partner*
EMP: 10
SALES (est): 983K **Privately Held**
SIC: 3931 5736 Guitars & parts, electric &
nonelectric; musical instrument stores

(G-14625)
BEETINS WHOLESALE INC
125 Ravenhurst Ave (10310-2633)
PHONE................................718 524-0899
Gamade Perera, *CEO*
EMP: 13
SALES (est): 1.8MM **Privately Held**
SIC: 2679 Paper products, converted

(G-14626)
BILLING BLOCKS INC
147 North Ave (10314-2653)
PHONE................................718 442-5006
Dan Kuper, *President*
EMP: 10
SALES (est): 338.2K **Privately Held**
WEB: www.billingblocks.com
SIC: 7372 2752 Prepackaged software;
custom computer programming services

(G-14627)
BLINDS TO GO (US) INC
2845 Richmond Ave (10314-5883)
PHONE................................718 477-9523
Bill Forte, *Manager*
EMP: 30
SALES (corp-wide): 266.7MM **Privately Held**
SIC: 2591 5719 Window blinds; window
furnishings
HQ: Blinds To Go (U.S.) Inc.
101 W State Rt 4
Paramus NJ 07652
201 441-9260

(G-14628)
BLOOD MOON PRODUCTIONS LTD
75 Saint Marks Pl (10301-1606)
PHONE................................718 556-9410
Danforth Prince, *CEO*
EMP: 7
SALES (est): 494.9K **Privately Held**
WEB: www.bloodmoonproductions.com
SIC: 2741 Miscellaneous publishing

(G-14629)
BORO PARK CUTTING TOOL CORP
106b Wakefield Ave (10314-3624)
PHONE................................718 720-0610
Vito Rubino, *President*
Steven Bruzese, *General Mgr*
Vincent Bruzese, *Treasurer*
EMP: 21
SQ FT: 10,000

SALES: 1MM **Privately Held**
SIC: 3545 5251 Cutting tools for machine
tools; tools

(G-14630)
BRAZE ALLOY INC
3075 Richmond Ter (10303-1303)
PHONE................................718 815-5757
Princie Sevaratnam, *President*
EMP: 5 **EST:** 2011
SALES (est): 554.8K **Privately Held**
SIC: 3356 Solder: wire, bar, acid core, &
rosin core

(G-14631)
BRITISH SCIENCE CORPORATION (PA)
2550 Victory Blvd Ste 305 (10314-6635)
PHONE................................212 980-8700
David H Kingsley, *President*
Yvonne Kingsley, *Corp Secy*
EMP: 8
SALES (est): 1.1MM **Privately Held**
SIC: 2844 7299 Shampoos, rinses, condi-
tioners: hair; scalp treatment service

(G-14632)
BUD RAVIOLI CENTER INC
Also Called: Pastosa Ravioli
3817 Richmond Ave (10312-3828)
PHONE................................718 356-4600
Benito Di Rosa, *President*
Lucy Di Rosa, *Vice Pres*
EMP: 6
SQ FT: 3,000
SALES (est): 818.8K **Privately Held**
WEB: www.pastosa.com
SIC: 2099 Food preparations

(G-14633)
C & R DE SANTIS INC
Also Called: Royal Press
2645 Forest Ave Ste 2 (10303-1503)
PHONE................................718 447-5076
EMP: 22
SQ FT: 5,000
SALES: 83.9K **Privately Held**
WEB: www.royalpress.com
SIC: 2672 2752 Coated & laminated
paper; commercial printing, offset

(G-14634)
CABINET FACTORY INC
2333 Highland Blvd (10306)
PHONE................................718 351-8922
Michael Dellamonica, *President*
EMP: 12
SALES (est): 1.4MM **Privately Held**
SIC: 2434 Wood kitchen cabinets

(G-14635)
CADDELL DRY DOCK & REPR CO INC
Also Called: Caddell Ship Yards
1515 Richmond Ter (10310-1114)
P.O. Box 100327 (10310-0327)
PHONE................................718 442-2112
John B Caddell, *CEO*
Steven P Kalil, *President*
Cynthia Patelli, *Corp Secy*
Luc Vaval, *Sr Corp Ofcr*
Bill Chapman, *Vice Pres*
EMP: 180 **EST:** 1903
SQ FT: 100,000
SALES (est): 34MM **Privately Held**
WEB: www.caddelldrydock.com
SIC: 3731 Shipbuilding & repairing

(G-14636)
CALIA TECHNICAL INC
Also Called: Calia Consultants
420 Jefferson Blvd (10312-2334)
PHONE................................718 447-3928
Anthony Calia, *President*
Robert Santagata, *Vice Pres*
EMP: 6
SALES: 650K **Privately Held**
SIC: 3625 8742 Control equipment, elec-
tric; training & development consultant

(G-14637)
CARMINE STREET BAGELS INC
Also Called: Bagels On The Square
107 Park Dr N (10314-5702)
PHONE................................212 691-3041

Joseph Turchiano, *Ch of Bd*
Neil Guy, *President*
EMP: 10
SQ FT: 2,000
SALES (est): 870.7K **Privately Held**
SIC: 2051 Bakery: wholesale or whole-
sale/retail combined

(G-14638)
CHUTES AND COMPACTORS OF NY
1011 Westwood Ave (10314-4243)
PHONE................................718 494-2247
EMP: 14
SALES (est): 2.4MM **Privately Held**
SIC: 3444 Sheet metalwork

(G-14639)
COCA-COLA BTLG CO OF NY INC
400 Western Ave (10303-1199)
PHONE................................718 420-6800
Susan Stavan, *Branch Mgr*
EMP: 12
SALES (corp-wide): 31.8B **Publicly Held**
SIC: 2086 Bottled & canned soft drinks
HQ: The Coca-Cola Bottling Company Of
New York Inc
2500 Windy Ridge Pkwy Se
Atlanta GA 30339
770 989-3000

(G-14640)
COFFEE HOLDING CO INC (PA)
3475 Victory Blvd Ste 4 (10314-6785)
PHONE................................718 832-0800
Andrew Gordon, *President*
David Gordon, *Exec VP*
Erik Hansen, *Exec VP*
Dorothy Roche, *Director*
◆ **EMP:** 74
SALES: 90.6MM **Publicly Held**
WEB: www.coffeeholding.com
SIC: 2095 5149 Roasted coffee; coffee,
green or roasted

(G-14641)
COMMERCIAL LUBRICANTS MOOVE
229 Arlington Ave (10303-1605)
PHONE................................718 720-3434
Gary Stetz, *Principal*
EMP: 34
SALES (est): 1.3MM **Privately Held**
SIC: 2992 Lubricating oils & greases

(G-14642)
CONTEMPRA DESIGN INC
20 Grille Ct (10309-1400)
PHONE................................718 984-8586
James Pelligrino, *President*
Dominique Bifiory, *Corp Secy*
EMP: 6
SQ FT: 4,000
SALES: 800K **Privately Held**
SIC: 2541 1799 Table or counter tops,
plastic laminated; showcases, except re-
frigerated: wood; counter top installation

(G-14643)
CORMAN USA INC
1140 Bay St Ste 2c (10305-4910)
PHONE................................718 727-7455
Giorgio Mantovani, *Ch of Bd*
▲ **EMP:** 9
SALES: 1.2MM
SALES (corp-wide): 83.8MM **Privately Held**
SIC: 2676 Feminine hygiene paper prod-
ucts
PA: Corman Spa
Via Liguria 3
Lacchiarella MI 20084
029 008-097

(G-14644)
D MALDARI & SONS INC
287 Natick St (10306-1654)
PHONE................................718 499-3555
Chris Maldari, *President*
▲ **EMP:** 30 **EST:** 1902
SALES (est): 4.5MM **Privately Held**
WEB: www.maldari.com
SIC: 3544 Extrusion dies

(G-14645)
DI DOMENICO PACKAGING CO INC
304 Bertram Ave (10312-5200)
PHONE........................718 727-5454
Vincent A Di Domenico, *President*
Michael A Di Domenico, *President*
Steven M Di Domenico, *Vice Pres*
Michael Di Domenico, *Manager*
EMP: 6
SQ FT: 21,000
SALES: 1MM **Privately Held**
SIC: 2631 3089 Folding boxboard; setup boxboard; blister or bubble formed packaging, plastic

(G-14646)
DIMARZIO INC
1388 Richmond Ter 1 (10310-1118)
P.O. Box 100387 (10310-0387)
PHONE........................718 442-6655
Lawrence Dimarzio, *President*
Steven Blucher II, *Vice Pres*
Louis Butera, *Engineer*
Glenn Simmons, *Director*
▲ EMP: 30
SQ FT: 2,000
SALES (est): 4.3MM **Privately Held**
WEB: www.dimarzio.com
SIC: 3931 Musical instruments

(G-14647)
DOUG LAMBERTSON OD
2555 Richmond Ave Ste 4 (10314-5848)
PHONE........................718 698-9300
Doug Lambertson, *Principal*
EMP: 5
SALES (est): 132.3K **Privately Held**
SIC: 3851 Ophthalmic goods

(G-14648)
E I DU PONT DE NEMOURS & CO
10 Teleport Dr (10311-1001)
PHONE........................718 761-0043
Jennifer Dupont, *Branch Mgr*
EMP: 182
SALES (corp-wide): 30.6B **Publicly Held**
SIC: 2879 Agricultural chemicals
HQ: E. I. Du Pont De Nemours And Company
974 Centre Rd Bldg 735
Wilmington DE 19805
302 485-3000

(G-14649)
EAG ELECTRIC INC
496 Mosel Ave (10304-1621)
PHONE........................201 376-5103
Christopher Todd, *Vice Pres*
EMP: 6
SALES: 500K **Privately Held**
SIC: 3534 Elevators & moving stairways

(G-14650)
EASTERN ENTERPRISE CORP
Also Called: Vinyl Tech Window
465 Bay St Ste 2 (10304-3842)
PHONE........................718 727-8600
Al Gargiulo Jr, *President*
Mary Waller, *Manager*
EMP: 15
SALES (est): 1.6MM **Privately Held**
SIC: 3089 Windows, plastic

(G-14651)
ENVIRO SERVICE & SUPPLY CORP
45b Marble Loop (10309-1326)
PHONE........................347 838-6500
Dom Guercio, *President*
Christopher Lorippo, *Vice Pres*
EMP: 10
SALES (est): 1.2MM **Privately Held**
SIC: 2842 2869 2841 Specialty cleaning preparations; sanitation preparations, disinfectants & deodorants; disinfectants, household or industrial plant; industrial organic chemicals; soap & other detergents

(G-14652)
F & D SERVICES INC
Also Called: F & D Printing
34 E Augusta Ave (10308-1323)
PHONE........................718 984-1635
Frank Sisino, *President*

Donald Marcus, *Vice Pres*
EMP: 14
SQ FT: 2,400
SALES (est): 1.2MM **Privately Held**
SIC: 2752 Letters, circular or form: lithographed; commercial printing, offset

(G-14653)
FEDEX OFFICE & PRINT SVCS INC
2456 Richmond Ave Ste C (10314-6028)
PHONE........................718 982-5223
David Grubb, *Manager*
Melissa Montgomery, *Manager*
Christine Oneil, *Manager*
Mico Perez, *Manager*
EMP: 6
SALES (corp-wide): 69.6B **Publicly Held**
WEB: www.kinkos.com
SIC: 2759 5099 7334 Commercial printing; signs, except electric; photocopying & duplicating services
HQ: Fedex Office And Print Services, Inc.
7900 Legacy Dr
Plano TX 75024
800 463-3339

(G-14654)
GANGI DISTRIBUTORS INC
Also Called: Snapple Distributors
135 Mcclean Ave (10305-4677)
PHONE........................718 442-5745
Santo Spallina, *President*
EMP: 12
SQ FT: 5,000
SALES (est): 890K **Privately Held**
SIC: 2086 Bottled & canned soft drinks

(G-14655)
GENERAL TRADE MARK LA
31 Hylan Blvd Apt 14c (10305-2079)
PHONE........................718 979-7261
EMP: 30 EST: 1924
SQ FT: 20,000
SALES (est): 3.3MM **Privately Held**
SIC: 2759 2671 Commercial Printing Mfg Packaging Paper/Film

(G-14656)
GLENDA INC
Also Called: Victory Sports
1732 Victory Blvd (10314-3510)
PHONE........................718 442-8981
George Siller, *President*
Glenda Siller, *Corp Secy*
EMP: 5
SQ FT: 2,500
SALES: 500K **Privately Held**
SIC: 2395 5941 Emblems, embroidered; sporting goods & bicycle shops

(G-14657)
GOTTLIEB SCHWARTZ FAMILY
724 Collfield Ave (10314-4253)
PHONE........................718 761-2010
EMP: 50 EST: 1973
SALES: 203.3K **Privately Held**
SIC: 3444 Mfg Sheet Metalwork

(G-14658)
GRADO GROUP INC
66 Willow Ave (10305-1829)
PHONE........................718 556-4200
Richard Grado, *President*
EMP: 7 EST: 2000
SQ FT: 2,900
SALES (est): 810.9K **Privately Held**
SIC: 2759 Advertising literature: printing

(G-14659)
GRAPHIC SIGNS & AWNINGS LTD
165 Industrial Loop Ste 1 (10309-1109)
PHONE........................718 227-6000
Mike Demarco, *Vice Pres*
EMP: 5
SALES: 355K **Privately Held**
SIC: 3993 5999 Signs, not made in custom sign painting shops; awnings

(G-14660)
GREAT ATL PR-CAST CON STATUARY
225 Ellis St (10307-1128)
PHONE........................718 948-5677

Frank Fresca, *President*
EMP: 4
SQ FT: 5,000
SALES: 4MM **Privately Held**
SIC: 3272 Concrete products, precast

(G-14661)
HOMESELL INC
4010 Hylan Blvd (10308-3331)
PHONE........................718 514-0346
Frank Lopa, *CEO*
Paul Lopa, *General Mgr*
Tracy Hardyal, *Admin Sec*
EMP: 10
SQ FT: 1,200
SALES (est): 620K **Privately Held**
WEB: www.homesell.com
SIC: 2721 Magazines: publishing & printing

(G-14662)
I D TEL CORP
Also Called: Metro Tel Communications
55 Canal St (10304-3809)
PHONE........................718 876-6000
Anthony Giammanco, *President*
Edward Pavia, *Vice Pres*
Barbara Syracuse, *Sales Staff*
▲ EMP: 12
SQ FT: 4,000
SALES: 1MM **Privately Held**
SIC: 3661 Telephones & telephone apparatus

(G-14663)
IADC INC
845 Father Capodanno Blvd (10305-4039)
PHONE........................718 238-0623
EMP: 10
SALES (est): 690K **Privately Held**
SIC: 3089 Mfg Plastic Products

(G-14664)
IMAGES SI INC
Also Called: Images Scientific Instruments
109 Woods Of Arden Rd (10312-5049)
PHONE........................718 966-3694
John Iovine, *President*
Melissa Serao, *Office Mgr*
◆ EMP: 10
SALES: 1MM **Privately Held**
WEB: www.imagesco.com
SIC: 3829 Measuring & controlling devices

(G-14665)
INFINITE SOFTWARE SOLUTIONS
Also Called: Md-Reports
1110 South Ave Ste 303 (10314-3411)
PHONE........................718 982-1315
Srikanth Gosike, *Principal*
Hari Gandham, *Vice Pres*
Akeel Joseph, *Regl Sales Mgr*
Mahesh Muthyala, *Sales Staff*
Sagarika Ramanan, *Sales Executive*
EMP: 12
SALES (est): 1.5MM **Privately Held**
WEB: www.infinitesoftsol.com
SIC: 3695 5045 Computer software tape & disks: blank, rigid & floppy; computer software

(G-14666)
ISLAND STAIRS CORP
178 Industrial Loop (10309-1145)
PHONE........................347 645-0560
Vassili Lijnev, *President*
EMP: 6
SQ FT: 5,000
SALES (est): 484.5K **Privately Held**
WEB: www.islandstairs.com
SIC: 2431 Staircases & stairs, wood

(G-14667)
ITTS INDUSTRIAL INC
165 Industrial Loop C (10309-1143)
PHONE........................718 605-6934
Sclix Tricoche, *CEO*
Felix Tricoche, *CEO*
▲ EMP: 5
SQ FT: 8,000
SALES (est): 1.3MM **Privately Held**
SIC: 3354 Bars, extruded, aluminum

(G-14668)
J T PRINTING 21
165 Industrial Loop Ste 5 (10309-1109)
PHONE........................718 484-3939
EMP: 6
SALES (est): 169.5K **Privately Held**
SIC: 2759 Screen printing

(G-14669)
J V HARING & SON
Also Called: Haring, J V & Son
1277 Clove Rd Ste 2 (10301-4339)
PHONE........................718 720-1947
Connie Mauro, *President*
EMP: 10
SQ FT: 1,000
SALES (est): 760K **Privately Held**
SIC: 2752 Commercial printing, lithographic

(G-14670)
JMS ICES INC
Also Called: Ralph's Ices
501 Port Richmond Ave (10302-1720)
PHONE........................718 448-0853
Michael Scolaro, *President*
Larry Silvestro, *Corp Secy*
John Scolaro, *Vice Pres*
EMP: 15
SQ FT: 5,000
SALES (est): 3.6MM **Privately Held**
SIC: 2024 Ices, flavored (frozen dessert)

(G-14671)
JOSEPH A FILIPPAZZO SOFTWARE
106 Lovell Ave (10314-4905)
PHONE........................718 987-1626
EMP: 5 EST: 2010
SALES (est): 230K **Privately Held**
SIC: 7372 Prepackaged Software Services

(G-14672)
JOSEPH FEDELE
Also Called: Rainbow Custom Counter Tops
1950b Richmond Ter (10302-1206)
PHONE........................718 448-3658
Joseph Fedele, *Owner*
Rachel Fedele, *Office Mgr*
EMP: 6
SQ FT: 5,000
SALES (est): 580K **Privately Held**
SIC: 2541 5211 5031 1799 Counter & sink tops; cabinets, lockers & shelving; cabinets, kitchen; kitchen cabinets; counter top installation

(G-14673)
KING SHERAZ TRADING CORP
245 Little Clove Rd (10301-4133)
PHONE........................646 944-2800
Sheraz Bhutta, *CEO*
◆ EMP: 10
SQ FT: 7,000
SALES: 250K **Privately Held**
SIC: 2381 Dyeing gloves, woven or knit: for the trade

(G-14674)
KLEEN STIK INDUSTRIES INC
44 Lenzie St (10312-6118)
PHONE........................718 984-5031
Edwin Wallace, *President*
Rosalie Wallace, *Admin Sec*
▲ EMP: 17
SQ FT: 20,000
SALES (est): 1.8MM **Privately Held**
WEB: www.kleenstik.net
SIC: 2672 Tape, pressure sensitive: made from purchased materials

(G-14675)
LAROSA CUPCAKES
314 Lake Ave (10303-2610)
PHONE........................347 866-3920
EMP: 8
SALES (est): 437.2K **Privately Held**
SIC: 2051 Bread, cake & related products

(G-14676)
LASER AND VARICOSE VEIN TRTMNT
500 Seaview Ave Ste 240 (10305-3403)
PHONE........................718 667-1777
Inam Haq, *Principal*

▲ = Import ▼=Export
◆ =Import/Export

EMP: 8
SALES (est): 975K **Privately Held**
SIC: 3845 Laser systems & equipment, medical

(G-14677)
LOOBRICA INTERNATIONAL CORP
41 Darnell Ln (10309-1933)
PHONE..................347 997-0296
Marshall Weinberg, *Principal*
▲ **EMP:** 8 **EST:** 2012
SALES (est): 960K **Privately Held**
SIC: 2992 8733 Lubricating oils & greases; scientific research agency

(G-14678)
M & L STEEL & ORNAMENTAL IRON
27 Housman Ave (10303-2701)
PHONE..................718 816-8660
Lubomir P Svoboda, *President*
▲ **EMP:** 14
SALES (est): 3.1MM **Privately Held**
SIC: 3441 1791 Fabricated structural metal; iron work, structural

(G-14679)
MAXINE DENKER INC (PA)
Also Called: Tokens
212 Manhattan St (10307-1805)
PHONE..................212 689-1440
Maxine Denker, *President*
Carla Elson, *Vice Pres*
EMP: 1
SALES (est): 1.3MM **Privately Held**
SIC: 3911 3965 Jewelry, precious metal; buckles & buckle parts; hair curlers

(G-14680)
MAY SHIP REPAIR CONTG CORP
3075 Richmond Ter Ste 3 (10303-1300)
PHONE..................718 442-9700
Mohamed M Adam, *President*
Kenneth Boothe, *Vice Pres*
Sajira Premabandu, *Accountant*
Yvonne Heredia, *Office Mgr*
Angel Heredia, *Supervisor*
▲ **EMP:** 45
SQ FT: 1,800
SALES (est): 9.9MM **Privately Held**
WEB: www.mayship.com
SIC: 3731 3732 Shipbuilding & repairing; boat building & repairing

(G-14681)
MORAN SHIPYARD CORPORATION (DH)
2015 Richmond Ter (10302-1298)
PHONE..................718 981-5600
Malcolm W McLeod, *President*
Peter Keyes, *Vice Pres*
Brian Burtner, *Purchasing*
Lee Christensen, *Treasurer*
Joseph De'angelo, *Treasurer*
▲ **EMP:** 187
SQ FT: 26,400
SALES (est): 10.5MM **Privately Held**
HQ: Moran Towing Corporation
50 Locust Ave Ste 10
New Canaan CT 06840
203 442-2800

(G-14682)
NEWSPAPER DELIVERY SOLUTIONS
309 Bradley Ave (10314-5154)
PHONE..................718 370-1111
Peter Priolo, *CEO*
EMP: 5 **EST:** 2011
SALES (est): 235.2K **Privately Held**
SIC: 2711 Newspapers

(G-14683)
NORTH AMERICAN DF INC (PA)
4591 Hylan Blvd (10312-6405)
PHONE..................718 698-2500
Chrissy Mazzola, *President*
EMP: 8
SQ FT: 5,000
SALES (est): 2MM **Privately Held**
SIC: 2759 Advertising literature: printing

(G-14684)
NORTH AMERICAN MFG ENTPS INC
Also Called: Mht Lighting
1961 Richmond Ter (10302-1201)
PHONE..................718 524-4370
Thomas Spinelli, *Ch of Bd*
Stephen Mazzaferro, *General Mgr*
▲ **EMP:** 45 **EST:** 2009
SQ FT: 56,000
SALES (est): 9.5MM **Privately Held**
SIC: 3646 Commercial indusl & institutional electric lighting fixtures

(G-14685)
NORTH EAST FUEL GROUP INC
51 Stuyvesant Ave (10312-3721)
PHONE..................718 984-6774
Richard D Auria, *Principal*
EMP: 6
SALES (est): 670.9K **Privately Held**
SIC: 2869 Fuels

(G-14686)
NORTHEASTERN FUEL CORP
51 Stuyvesant Ave (10312-3721)
PHONE..................917 560-6241
Richard Dauria, *Principal*
EMP: 6
SALES (est): 832.9K **Privately Held**
SIC: 2869 Fuels

(G-14687)
OH HOW CUTE INC
38 Androvette St (10309-1302)
PHONE..................347 838-6031
Margaret Delia, *President*
EMP: 6
SQ FT: 800
SALES: 80K **Privately Held**
SIC: 2064 5199 5092 5145 Cake ornaments, confectionery; gifts & novelties; balloons, novelty; candy

(G-14688)
PHOTOGRAVE CORPORATION
Also Called: Www.picturesongold.com
1140 S Railroad Ave (10306-3371)
PHONE..................718 667-4825
Bernard Schifter, *CEO*
Daniel Schifter, *President*
▲ **EMP:** 23
SQ FT: 3,000
SALES (est): 9.4MM **Privately Held**
WEB: www.photograve.com
SIC: 3911 Jewelry, precious metal

(G-14689)
PIAZZAS ICE CREAM ICE HSE INC
41 Housman Ave (10303-2701)
PHONE..................718 818-8811
Salvatore J Piazz, *Ch of Bd*
Sam Conte, *Manager*
EMP: 16 **EST:** 2010
SALES (est): 2.5MM **Privately Held**
SIC: 2024 Ice cream, bulk

(G-14690)
PLAYFITNESS CORP
27 Palisade St (10305-4711)
PHONE..................917 497-5443
Pavel Asanov, *CEO*
EMP: 5
SALES (est): 366.4K **Privately Held**
SIC: 7372 7999 7389 Educational computer software; physical fitness instruction;

(G-14691)
PORT AUTHORITY OF NY & NJ
2777 Goethals Rd N Fl 2 (10303-1107)
PHONE..................718 390-2534
Jerry Deltufo, *Manager*
EMP: 90
SALES (corp-wide): 4.8B **Privately Held**
WEB: www.portnynj.com
SIC: 3441 Bridge sections, prefabricated highway
PA: The Port Authority Of New York & New Jersey
4 World Trade Ctr 150
New York NY 10007
212 435-7000

(G-14692)
POWER METRICS INTL INC
1961 Richmond Ter (10302-1201)
PHONE..................718 524-4370
Thomas Spinelli, *President*
EMP: 15
SALES (est): 1.5MM **Privately Held**
SIC: 3699 Electrical equipment & supplies

(G-14693)
PREMIER GLASS NEW YORK INC
Also Called: Premier Glass Services
22 Brienna Ct (10309-4601)
PHONE..................718 967-7179
Michael Messina, *CEO*
EMP: 5
SALES (est): 203.2K **Privately Held**
SIC: 3172 Cases, glasses

(G-14694)
PREPARATORY MAGAZINE GROUP
1200 South Ave Ste 202 (10314-3424)
PHONE..................718 761-4800
Luciano Rammairone, *President*
Gina Biancardi, *President*
EMP: 55
SQ FT: 9,000
SALES: 2.5MM **Privately Held**
SIC: 2721 Magazines: publishing only, not printed on site

(G-14695)
QPS DIE CUTTERS FINISHERS CORP
140 Alverson Ave (10309-1776)
PHONE..................718 966-1811
Eva Choina, *President*
Semion Goldsman, *Vice Pres*
EMP: 42
SQ FT: 35,000
SALES (est): 3.5MM **Privately Held**
SIC: 3999 Advertising display products

(G-14696)
R & L PRESS INC
896 Forest Ave (10310-2413)
PHONE..................718 447-8557
Ron Patterson, *President*
EMP: 5
SQ FT: 4,000
SALES (est): 854.5K **Privately Held**
SIC: 2752 Promotional printing, lithographic; commercial printing, offset

(G-14697)
R & L PRESS OF SI INC
Also Called: Luke's Copy Shop
2461 Hylan Blvd (10306-3146)
PHONE..................718 667-3258
Luke Callas, *President*
Kim Catanese, *Manager*
EMP: 3
SQ FT: 1,200
SALES: 2.3MM **Privately Held**
SIC: 2752 7334 Commercial printing, offset; photocopying & duplicating services

(G-14698)
RALPHS FAMOUS ITALIAN ICES
4212c Hylan Blvd (10308-3314)
PHONE..................718 605-5052
Ray Longo, *Owner*
EMP: 5
SALES (est): 161.4K **Privately Held**
SIC: 2024 5143 Ice cream & frozen desserts; ice cream & ices

(G-14699)
RAMHOLTZ PUBLISHING INC
Also Called: Collegebound Teen Magazine
1200 South Ave Ste 202 (10314-3424)
PHONE..................718 761-4800
Luciano Rammairone, *CEO*
Gina Biancardi, *Vice Pres*
EMP: 60
SQ FT: 10,000
SALES (est): 5.5MM **Privately Held**
SIC: 2721 Magazines: publishing only, not printed on site

(G-14700)
RD2 CONSTRUCTION & DEM LLC
63 Trossach Rd (10304-2131)
PHONE..................718 980-1650
Peter Dagostino,
EMP: 15
SALES (est): 2.2MM **Privately Held**
SIC: 1442 Construction sand & gravel

(G-14701)
REMSEN FUEL INC
4668 Amboy Rd (10312-4150)
PHONE..................718 984-9551
Natha Singh, *President*
EMP: 6 **EST:** 2012
SALES (est): 595.4K **Privately Held**
SIC: 2869 Fuels

(G-14702)
REYNOLDS SHIPYARD CORPORATION
200 Edgewater St (10305-4996)
P.O. Box 50010 (10305-0010)
PHONE..................718 981-2800
Michael Reynolds, *President*
▲ **EMP:** 10
SQ FT: 30,000
SALES (est): 1.3MM **Privately Held**
SIC: 3731 Cargo vessels, building & repairing; tugboats, building & repairing; barges, building & repairing; scows, building & repairing

(G-14703)
RGM SIGNS INC
Also Called: Blue Boy
1234 Castleton Ave (10310-1717)
PHONE..................718 442-0598
Ron Malanga, *President*
EMP: 6
SQ FT: 684
SALES (est): 646.8K **Privately Held**
WEB: www.rgmsigns.com
SIC: 3993 2752 5999 1799 Signs, not made in custom sign painting shops; offset & photolithographic printing; awnings; sign installation & maintenance

(G-14704)
RICHMOND READY MIX CORP
328 Park St (10306-1859)
PHONE..................917 731-8400
EMP: 9 **EST:** 2015
SALES (est): 896.2K **Privately Held**
SIC: 3273 Ready-mixed concrete

(G-14705)
RICHMOND READY MIX CORP II
291 Chelsea Rd (10314-7112)
PHONE..................917 731-8400
Joe Garry, *President*
Scot D'Arco, *Vice Pres*
EMP: 28 **EST:** 2015
SALES: 15MM **Privately Held**
SIC: 3273 Ready-mixed concrete

(G-14706)
SCARA-MIX INC
2537 Richmond Ter (10303-2390)
P.O. Box 30313 (10303-0313)
PHONE..................718 442-7357
EMP: 45 **EST:** 1981
SQ FT: 17,000
SALES (est): 5.2MM **Privately Held**
SIC: 3273 Mfg Ready-Mixed Concrete

(G-14707)
SEA BREEZE FISH & SEAFOOD OF S (PA)
240 Page Ave (10307-1170)
PHONE..................718 984-0447
Paula Dimino, *Ch of Bd*
EMP: 15
SALES (est): 3.1MM **Privately Held**
SIC: 2092 5421 Seafoods, frozen: prepared; fish markets

(G-14708)
SECOND GENERATION WOOD STAIRS
2581 Richmond Ter Ste 3 (10303-2323)
PHONE..................718 370-0085
EMP: 10

SALES (est): 740K **Privately Held**
SIC: 2431 Staircases, stairs & railings

(G-14709)
SHAMROCK MATERIALS LLC
100 Signal Hill Rd (10301)
PHONE.................................718 273-9223
Thomas Corbett Jr, *Mng Member*
EMP: 100 **EST:** 2000
SQ FT: 5,000
SALES (est): 14.3MM **Privately Held**
SIC: 3273 Ready-mixed concrete

(G-14710)
SIGN MEN
389 Wild Ave Ste G (10314-4758)
PHONE.................................718 227-7446
Ricki D Amato, *Owner*
EMP: 7
SALES (est): 162.8K **Privately Held**
SIC: 3993 Advertising novelties

(G-14711)
SPECIAL TEES
250 Buel Ave (10305-1204)
PHONE.................................718 980-0987
Joanne Homsey, *Prgrmr*
Vicent Bonomi, *Program Dir*
EMP: 24 **EST:** 1995
SALES (est): 1.6MM **Privately Held**
WEB: www.specialtees-si.com
SIC: 2759 Screen printing

(G-14712)
ST JOHN
229 Morrison Ave (10310-2836)
PHONE.................................718 720-8367
Barbara A Logan, *Principal*
Jane Barry, *Associate Dir*
EMP: 5
SALES (est): 241.5K **Privately Held**
SIC: 2339 Sportswear, women's

(G-14713)
**STATEN ISLAND PARENT
MAGAZINE**
16 Shenandoah Ave Ste 2 (10314-3652)
PHONE.................................718 761-4800
Orlando Frank, *Owner*
EMP: 6
SALES (est): 410.5K **Privately Held**
SIC: 2721 Magazines: publishing only, not printed on site

(G-14714)
STATEN ISLAND STAIR INC
439 Sharrotts Rd (10309-1414)
PHONE.................................718 317-9276
Fran Imber, *President*
EMP: 5
SALES: 500K **Privately Held**
SIC: 2431 Staircases & stairs, wood

(G-14715)
**STONEY CROFT CONVERTERS
INC**
Also Called: Alltek Labeling Systems
364 Sharrotts Rd (10309-1990)
PHONE.................................718 608-9800
John Conti, *President*
Ann Holbert, *Vice Pres*
Alan Sherman, *Accounts Mgr*
EMP: 16
SQ FT: 7,000
SALES (est): 4MM **Privately Held**
WEB: www.allteklabeling.com
SIC: 2672 2679 Labels (unprinted), gummed: made from purchased materials; labels, paper: made from purchased material

(G-14716)
STRADA SOFT INC
20 Clifton Ave (10305-4912)
PHONE.................................718 556-6940
Lou Esposito, *Principal*
EMP: 8
SALES: 300K **Privately Held**
WEB: www.stradasoft.com
SIC: 7372 Prepackaged software

(G-14717)
SUPERIOR CONFECTIONS INC
1150 South Ave (10314-3404)
PHONE.................................718 698-3300

George Kaye, *President*
Peter Kaye, *Vice Pres*
▲ **EMP:** 100 **EST:** 1951
SQ FT: 40,000
SALES (est): 10.1MM **Privately Held**
SIC: 2066 Chocolate candy, solid

(G-14718)
SUPREME CHOCOLATIER LLC
1150 South Ave Fl 1 (10314-3404)
PHONE.................................718 761-9600
Michael Kaye, *Marketing Staff*
George Kaye, *Info Tech Dir*
▲ **EMP:** 50 **EST:** 1999
SALES (est): 9.1MM **Privately Held**
WEB: www.supremechocolatier.com
SIC: 2061 Raw cane sugar

(G-14719)
TDS WOODWORKING INC
Also Called: TDS Woodcraft
104 Port Richmond Ave (10302-1334)
PHONE.................................718 442-5298
Salvatore Piscicelli, *President*
EMP: 10
SALES (est): 1.2MM **Privately Held**
SIC: 2431 Millwork

(G-14720)
TEAM BUILDERS INC
Also Called: Team Builders Management
88 New Dorp Plz S Ste 303 (10306-2902)
PHONE.................................718 979-1005
Christine B Fasier, *President*
EMP: 11
SQ FT: 1,100
SALES: 2MM **Privately Held**
SIC: 7372 Business oriented computer software

(G-14721)
TECH PRODUCTS INC
105 Willow Ave (10305-1896)
PHONE.................................718 442-4900
Kenneth Nelson Sr, *President*
Carey Nelson, *Corp Secy*
Resat Karagozler, *Plant Mgr*
Robert Rosenbaum, *CFO*
John Darnell, *Controller*
▼ **EMP:** 43 **EST:** 1948
SQ FT: 1,600
SALES (est): 7.3MM **Privately Held**
WEB: www.techproducts.com
SIC: 3953 3993 Marking devices; signs & advertising specialties

(G-14722)
**TODT HILL AUDIOLOGICAL
SVCS**
78 Todt Hill Rd Ste 202 (10314-4528)
PHONE.................................718 816-1952
Theresa Cannon, *President*
EMP: 5
SALES (est): 587K **Privately Held**
SIC: 3842 8049 Hearing aids; audiologist

(G-14723)
TORTILLERIA OAXACA
121 Port Richmond Ave (10302-1307)
PHONE.................................347 355-7336
EMP: 5
SALES (est): 182.9K **Privately Held**
SIC: 2099 Tortillas, fresh or refrigerated

(G-14724)
TRADE MARK GRAPHICS INC
3982 Amboy Rd (10308-2408)
PHONE.................................718 306-0001
Avery Marder, *President*
EMP: 7
SALES (est): 870K **Privately Held**
SIC: 2752 Commercial printing, offset

(G-14725)
VCP MOBILITY INC
4131 Richmond Ave (10312-5633)
PHONE.................................718 356-7827
EMP: 400
SALES (corp-wide): 402.8MM **Privately
Held**
SIC: 3842 Wheelchairs
HQ: Vcp Mobility, Inc.
    6899 Winchester Cir # 200
    Boulder CO 80301
    303 218-4500

(G-14726)
VEZ INC
Also Called: Fastsigns
3801 Victory Blvd Ste 5 (10314-6759)
PHONE.................................718 273-7002
Rich Vezzuto, *President*
Kurt Kracsun, *Vice Pres*
EMP: 6
SQ FT: 2,500
SALES: 900K **Privately Held**
WEB: www.veztek.com
SIC: 3993 2759 Signs & advertising specialties; business forms: printing

(G-14727)
VF OUTDOOR INC
2655 Richmond Ave # 1570 (10314-5821)
PHONE.................................718 698-6215
EMP: 46
SALES (corp-wide): 13.8MM **Publicly
Held**
SIC: 2329 Men's & boys' leather, wool & down-filled outerwear
HQ: Vf Outdoor, Llc
    2701 Harbor Bay Pkwy
    Alameda CA 94502
    510 618-3500

(G-14728)
VIOLETTES CELLAR LLC
2271 Hylan Blvd (10306-3253)
PHONE.................................718 650-5050
Philip Farinacci, *Owner*
EMP: 13
SALES (est): 1.5MM **Privately Held**
SIC: 2599 5812 Bar, restaurant & cafeteria furniture; caterers

(G-14729)
YPIS OF STATEN ISLAND INC
130 Stuyvesant Pl Ste 5 (10301-1900)
PHONE.................................718 815-4557
Dominick Brancato, *Exec Dir*
EMP: 2
SALES: 5.5MM **Privately Held**
SIC: 7372 Business oriented computer software

Stephentown
Rensselaer County

(G-14730)
**ATLANTIS EQUIPMENT
CORPORATION**
16941 Ny 22 (12168)
P.O. Box 310 (12168-0310)
PHONE.................................518 733-5910
Louis Schroeter, *President*
Richard W Keeler Jr, *Vice Pres*
EMP: 18
SQ FT: 40,000
SALES: 5MM **Privately Held**
SIC: 3599 3441 7692 3444 Machine shop, jobbing & repair; fabricated structural metal; welding repair; sheet metal-work

(G-14731)
FOUR FAT FOWL INC
473 State Route 43 (12168-2937)
PHONE.................................518 733-5230
Willard Bridgham IV, *President*
Josie Madison, *Opers Mgr*
Shaleena Bridgham, *Sales Mgr*
EMP: 5
SALES: 325K **Privately Held**
SIC: 2022 Natural cheese

(G-14732)
ZWACK INCORPORATED
15875 Ny 22 (12168)
P.O. Box 100 (12168-0100)
PHONE.................................518 733-5135
Frank J Zwack, *President*
Maria Zwack, *Admin Sec*
EMP: 50 **EST:** 1971
SQ FT: 30,000
SALES (est): 9.2MM **Privately Held**
WEB: www.zwackinc.com
SIC: 3541 3714 5082 Machine tools, metal cutting type; sanders, motor vehicle safety; general construction machinery & equipment

Stillwater
Saratoga County

(G-14733)
STILLWATER WOOD & IRON
114 N Hudson Ave (12170)
P.O. Box 736 (12170-0736)
PHONE.................................518 664-4501
Charles Robert Hallum, *Owner*
C Robert Hallum, *Owner*
Bob Hallum, *Partner*
EMP: 5
SQ FT: 13,000
SALES: 650K **Privately Held**
WEB: www.stillwaterfdny.com
SIC: 2511 Unassembled or unfinished furniture, household: wood

Stittville
Oneida County

(G-14734)
DYNA-VAC EQUIPMENT INC
8963 State Route 365 (13469-1021)
PHONE.................................315 865-8084
Hal Reigi, *President*
Laurie Reigi, *Vice Pres*
EMP: 11
SQ FT: 6,000
SALES: 1.8MM **Privately Held**
WEB: www.dynavacequipment.com
SIC: 3589 Sewer cleaning equipment, power

Stone Ridge
Ulster County

(G-14735)
FTS SYSTEMS INC (DH)
3538 Main St (12484-5601)
PHONE.................................845 687-5300
Claus Kinder, *Principal*
Patty Dern, *Administration*
EMP: 85 **EST:** 1971
SQ FT: 34,000
SALES (est): 7.6MM
SALES (corp-wide): 1.4B **Privately Held**
WEB: www.ftssystems.com
SIC: 3821 3823 3585 Laboratory equipment: fume hoods, distillation racks, etc.; industrial instrmnts msrmnt display/control process variable; refrigeration & heating equipment
HQ: S P Industries, Inc.
    935 Mearns Rd
    Warminster PA 18974
    215 672-7800

(G-14736)
PK30 SYSTEM LLC
3607 Atwood Rd (12484-5446)
P.O. Box 656 (12484-0656)
PHONE.................................212 473-8050
Philip Kerzner, *Owner*
EMP: 13
SALES (est): 2MM **Privately Held**
SIC: 3442 3446 3429 Store fronts, prefabricated, metal; architectural metalwork; builders' hardware

Stony Brook
Suffolk County

(G-14737)
**COGNITIVEFLOW SENSOR
TECH**
9 Melville Ct (11790-1851)
PHONE.................................631 513-9369
EMP: 9 **EST:** 2011
SALES (est): 775K **Privately Held**
SIC: 3841 Mfg Surgical/Medical Instruments

▲ = Import ▼=Export
◆ =Import/Export

(G-14738)
ELIMA-DRAFT INCORPORATED
20 Hopewell Dr (11790-2324)
PHONE..............................631 375-2830
Robert W Viggers, *Ch of Bd*
EMP: 5
SQ FT: 2,100
SALES: 125K **Privately Held**
SIC: 3585 5075 Air conditioning equipment, complete; air conditioning & ventilation equipment & supplies

(G-14739)
INTELIBS INC
1500 Stony Brook Rd Ste 3 (11794-4600)
PHONE..............................877 213-2640
Seyong Park, *President*
Dorene Weiland, *Executive*
EMP: 5
SALES (est): 929K **Privately Held**
SIC: 3663

(G-14740)
MT FUEL CORP
9 Bayles Ave (11790-2121)
PHONE..............................631 445-2047
Robert Trivigno, *Principal*
EMP: 6
SALES (est): 455.2K **Privately Held**
SIC: 2869 Fuels

(G-14741)
STONY BROOK UNIVERSITY
Also Called: University Advertising Agency
310 Administration Bldg (11794-0001)
PHONE..............................631 632-6434
Jennifer Acosta, *Dean*
Heath Martin, *Dean*
Alan Tucker, *Dean*
Suzanne Shane, *Counsel*
Maryanne Reinhardt, *Finance Dir*
EMP: 40 **Privately Held**
WEB: www.sunysb.edu
SIC: 2752 8221 9411 Commercial printing, lithographic; colleges universities & professional schools; administration of educational programs;
HQ: Stony Brook University
100 Nicolls Rd
Stony Brook NY 11794
631 632-6000

(G-14742)
TRANSISTOR POWER TECH INC
(PA)
Also Called: Tpti
38 Robert Cres (11790-3204)
PHONE..............................631 491-0265
Yehuda Fogel, *President*
EMP: 5
SQ FT: 1,000
SALES (est): 467K **Privately Held**
SIC: 3679 Microwave components

Stony Point
Rockland County

(G-14743)
FANTASY GLASS COMPAN
61 Beach Rd (10980-2035)
PHONE..............................845 786-5818
Greggory Barbutl, *Owner*
EMP: 5
SALES (est): 339.5K **Privately Held**
SIC: 3732 Boats, fiberglass: building & repairing

(G-14744)
GOTHAM INK & COLOR CO INC
19 Holt Dr (10980-1919)
PHONE..............................845 947-4000
William Olson, *General Mgr*
Joseph Simons, *Vice Pres*
EMP: 20 **EST:** 1937
SQ FT: 25,000
SALES (est): 3.7MM **Privately Held**
SIC: 2893 Printing ink

(G-14745)
KEON OPTICS INC
30 John F Kennedy Dr (10980-3207)
PHONE..............................845 429-7103
Kevin McKeon, *President*

EMP: 10
SQ FT: 1,300
SALES (est): 815.2K **Privately Held**
SIC: 3827 Optical instruments & lenses

(G-14746)
LIGHTING SERVICES INC (PA)
2 Holt Dr (10980-1920)
PHONE..............................845 942-2800
Daniel Gelman, *President*
Ken Kane, *Exec VP*
Rose Miller, *Purch Agent*
James Brown, *Controller*
Alexander Gonzales, *Accountant*
▲ **EMP:** 100 **EST:** 1958
SQ FT: 50,000
SALES (est): 16.6MM **Privately Held**
WEB: www.lightingservicesinc.com
SIC: 3646 Commercial indusl & institutional electric lighting fixtures

(G-14747)
PRECISION TECHNIQUES INC
25 Holt Dr (10980-1919)
P.O. Box 1149, Yorktown Heights (10598-8149)
PHONE..............................718 991-1440
Paul Mangione, *President*
Joseph De Savage, *Corp Secy*
▲ **EMP:** 85
SQ FT: 70,000
SALES (est): 11MM **Privately Held**
WEB: www.precisiontechniquesinc.com
SIC: 3089 4783 Injection molding of plastics; packing & crating

(G-14748)
STONY POINT GRAPHICS LTD
Also Called: Shell Ann Printing
79 S Liberty Dr (10980-2321)
PHONE..............................845 786-3322
Phillip Laquidara, *President*
Felix Laquidara, *Vice Pres*
Loraine Laquidara, *Admin Sec*
EMP: 5
SQ FT: 4,000
SALES: 300K **Privately Held**
SIC: 2752 2759 Commercial printing, offset; letterpress printing

(G-14749)
TIMES SQUARE STAGE LTG CO INC
Also Called: Time Square Lighting
5 Holt Dr (10980-1919)
PHONE..............................845 947-3034
Robert Riccadelli, *President*
Robert Hilzen, *Shareholder*
Bernie Reider, *Shareholder*
Felix Sansone,
▲ **EMP:** 50 **EST:** 1938
SQ FT: 32,000
SALES (est): 11MM **Privately Held**
WEB: www.tslight.com
SIC: 3648 Lighting equipment

(G-14750)
US GLOBAL LUBRICANTS INC
22 Hudson Dr (10980-1406)
PHONE..............................845 271-4277
Robert Gonnelli, *Manager*
EMP: 15 **EST:** 2013
SALES: 3.7MM **Privately Held**
SIC: 2992 Lubricating oils & greases

Stormville
Dutchess County

(G-14751)
GALLI SHIRTS AND SPORTS AP
246 Judith Dr (12582-5262)
PHONE..............................845 226-7305
Vincent Gallipani, *President*
Erika Gallipani, *Vice Pres*
EMP: 5
SALES: 300K **Privately Held**
WEB: www.gallishirts.com
SIC: 2396 7311 Screen printing on fabric articles; advertising consultant

(G-14752)
PACKAGE PAVEMENT COMPANY INC (PA)
3530 Route 52 (12582-5651)
P.O. Box 408 (12582-0408)
PHONE..............................845 221-2224
Darren Doherty, *Ch of Bd*
Frank J Doherty, *President*
Paul Doherty, *General Mgr*
Gary Lancour, *General Mgr*
Eileen Doherty, *Vice Pres*
▲ **EMP:** 95 **EST:** 1951
SQ FT: 5,000
SALES (est): 15.4MM **Privately Held**
SIC: 2951 Asphalt & asphaltic paving mixtures (not from refineries)

Stottville
Columbia County

(G-14753)
IRV SCHRODER & SONS INC
2906 Atlantic Ave (12172-7700)
P.O. Box 300 (12172-0300)
PHONE..............................518 828-0194
Jim Schroder, *President*
EMP: 20
SQ FT: 6,000
SALES (est): 3.5MM **Privately Held**
SIC: 3441 1791 Fabricated structural metal; structural steel erection

Stuyvesant
Columbia County

(G-14754)
MAPLE HILL CREAMERY LLC (PA)
285 Allendale Rd W (12173-2611)
P.O. Box 323, Kinderhook (12106-0323)
PHONE..............................518 758-7777
Peter Meck, *Vice Pres*
Anne Trost, *Opers Staff*
Charles Zentay, *CFO*
Peter T Joseph, *Mng Member*
EMP: 19
SQ FT: 6,000
SALES: 8MM **Privately Held**
SIC: 2026 Yogurt

Stuyvesant Falls
Columbia County

(G-14755)
BETHS FARM KITCHEN
504 Rte 46 (12174)
P.O. Box 113 (12174-0113)
PHONE..............................518 799-3414
Beth Linskey, *Owner*
EMP: 8
SALES (est): 591.2K **Privately Held**
WEB: www.bethsfarmkitchen.com
SIC: 2099 Food preparations

Suffern
Rockland County

(G-14756)
ADVANCED MEDICAL MFG CORP
Also Called: Crown Medical Products
7-11 Suffern Pl Ste 2 (10901-5501)
PHONE..............................845 369-7535
Ron Resnick, *Owner*
EMP: 20
SALES (est): 1.4MM **Privately Held**
SIC: 2393 Cushions, except spring & carpet: purchased materials

(G-14757)
AMERICAN BEST CABINETS INC
Also Called: Malibu Cabinets
397 Spook Rock Rd (10901-5319)
PHONE..............................845 369-6666
▲ **EMP:** 39
SQ FT: 26,000
SALES (est): 3.9MM **Privately Held**
SIC: 2514 Mfg Metal Household Furniture

(G-14758)
BEER MARKETERS INSIGHTS INC
49 E Maple Ave (10901-5507)
PHONE..............................845 507-0040
Benj Steinman, *President*
Irene Steinman, *Treasurer*
EMP: 8
SALES (est): 969.1K **Privately Held**
WEB: www.beerinsights.com
SIC: 2721 8742 Trade journals: publishing & printing; management consulting services

(G-14759)
CLASSIC CABINETS
375 Spook Rock Rd (10901-5314)
PHONE..............................845 357-4331
John Cheman, *Owner*
EMP: 10
SALES (est): 767.5K **Privately Held**
WEB: www.classcabs.com
SIC: 2434 Wood kitchen cabinets

(G-14760)
E-FINNERGY GROUP LLC
Also Called: Day One Lighting
355 Spook Rock Rd (10901-5314)
PHONE..............................845 547-2424
Mendel Hecht, *Mng Member*
EMP: 4
SALES (est): 1.3MM **Privately Held**
SIC: 3645 Residential lighting fixtures

(G-14761)
EMPIRE COACHWORKS INTL LLC
475 Haverstraw Rd (10901-3135)
PHONE..............................732 257-7981
Edward Vergopia, *Mng Member*
Micheal Misseri,
EMP: 70
SQ FT: 88,000
SALES (est): 5.3MM **Privately Held**
SIC: 3711 Automobile bodies, passenger car, not including engine, etc.

(G-14762)
LE CHOCOLATE OF ROCKLAND LLC
1 Ramapo Ave (10901-5805)
PHONE..............................845 533-4125
Simon Rottenburg,
▲ **EMP:** 25
SALES (est): 4.6MM **Privately Held**
SIC: 2066 Chocolate

(G-14763)
NY CUTTING INC
Also Called: Uppercut
3 Chestnut St Ste 1 (10901-5476)
PHONE..............................646 434-1355
Solomon Katz, *CEO*
▲ **EMP:** 6
SALES: 1MM **Privately Held**
SIC: 2392 2621 Placemats, plastic or textile; towels, tissues & napkins: paper & stock

(G-14764)
QUALITEA IMPORTS INC
74 Lafayette Ave (10901-5557)
PHONE..............................917 624-6750
Pinchas Nussenzweig, *President*
EMP: 5
SALES (est): 139.9K **Privately Held**
SIC: 2099 Food preparations

(G-14765)
RADIATION SHIELDING SYSTEMS
415 Spook Rock Rd (10901-5308)
PHONE..............................888 631-2278

Ed Delia, *CEO*
Seth Warnock, *Vice Pres*
Gary Novick, *Executive*
EMP: 11
SALES (est): 1.7MM **Privately Held**
WEB: www.radiationshieldingsystems.com
SIC: 3444 3271 Radiator shields or enclosures, sheet metal; blocks, concrete: radiation-proof

(G-14766)
ROYAL TEES INC
29 Lafayette Ave (10901-5405)
PHONE..................845 357-9448
Al Rosenblatt, *President*
EMP: 5
SQ FT: 8,000
SALES: 750K **Privately Held**
WEB: www.royaltees.com
SIC: 2759 2395 2752 5611 Screen printing; embroidery & art needlework; transfers, decalcomania or dry: lithographed; clothing, sportswear, men's & boys'; women's sportswear

(G-14767)
SUPER CONDUCTOR MATERIALS INC
Also Called: SCM
391 Spook Rock Rd (10901-5319)
P.O. Box 701, Tallman (10982-0701)
PHONE..................845 368-0240
Aftab Dar, *President*
Neelam Dar, *Corp Secy*
▼ **EMP:** 14
SQ FT: 10,000
SALES (est): 2.3MM **Privately Held**
WEB: www.scm-inc.com
SIC: 3674 Semiconductors & related devices

(G-14768)
UNITED ROCKLAND HOLDING CO INC
9 N Airmont Rd (10901-5153)
P.O. Box 68, Tallman (10982-0068)
PHONE..................845 357-1900
Paul Wishnoff, *President*
Stanley Wishnoff, *Chairman*
Mitchell Kolata, *Treasurer*
Linda Olivo, *Manager*
EMP: 20 EST: 1961
SQ FT: 20,000
SALES (est): 1.6MM **Privately Held**
WEB: www.unitedrocklandstairs.com
SIC: 2431 Staircases & stairs, wood; stair railings, wood

Sugar Loaf
Orange County

(G-14769)
IRINIRI DESIGNS LTD
1358 Kings Hwy (10981)
P.O. Box 378 (10981-0378)
PHONE..................845 469-7934
Rit Goldman, *Ch of Bd*
Nirit Rechtman, *President*
EMP: 12
SQ FT: 1,653
SALES (est): 1.4MM **Privately Held**
SIC: 3911 5944 Jewelry, precious metal; jewelry stores

Sunnyside
Queens County

(G-14770)
ANOTHER 99 CENT PARADISE
4206 Greenpoint Ave (11104-3004)
PHONE..................718 786-4578
Ali Gohar, *Principal*
EMP: 5
SALES (est): 452.5K **Privately Held**
SIC: 3643 Outlets, electric: convenience

(G-14771)
DEANCO DIGITAL PRINTING LLC
Also Called: NY Print Partners
4545 39th St (11104-4401)
PHONE..................212 371-2025
Joe Aziz, *Mng Member*
Pete Lamba,
EMP: 10
SQ FT: 2,500
SALES (est): 1.2MM **Privately Held**
SIC: 2752 Commercial printing, offset

(G-14772)
EASTERN CONCEPTS LTD
Also Called: Green Mountain Graphics
4125 39th St (11104-4201)
P.O. Box 1417, Long Island City (11101-0417)
PHONE..................718 472-3377
Eric Greenberg, *President*
Rhonda Greenberg, *Admin Sec*
EMP: 11
SQ FT: 6,000
SALES (est): 1.5MM **Privately Held**
WEB: www.gm-graphics.com
SIC: 3993 Signs, not made in custom sign painting shops

(G-14773)
NODUS NOODLE CORPORATION
4504 Queens Blvd (11104-2304)
PHONE..................718 309-3725
Thomas SAE Tang, *CEO*
EMP: 8
SALES (est): 335.2K **Privately Held**
SIC: 2098 Noodles (e.g. egg, plain & water), dry

(G-14774)
S DONADIC INC
Also Called: Sdi
4525 39th St (11104-4401)
PHONE..................718 361-9888
Steven Donadic, *President*
EMP: 60
SQ FT: 7,000
SALES: 2MM **Privately Held**
SIC: 2434 2431 2426 2421 Wood kitchen cabinets; millwork; hardwood dimension & flooring mills; sawmills & planing mills, general

(G-14775)
T S B A GROUP INC (PA)
3830 Woodside Ave (11104-1004)
PHONE..................718 565-6000
Samuel Brown, *Chairman*
Anthony Difiglia, *Marketing Mgr*
Susan Mannarino, *Sr Software Eng*
EMP: 30
SQ FT: 70,000
SALES (est): 19.4MM **Privately Held**
SIC: 3822 1731 Temperature controls, automatic; energy management controls

Surprise
Greene County

(G-14776)
ROYAL METAL PRODUCTS INC
463 West Rd (12176-1709)
PHONE..................518 966-4442
David M Johannesen, *President*
Steven Johannesen, *Vice Pres*
Robert Johannesen, *Treasurer*
EMP: 40 EST: 1956
SQ FT: 49,600
SALES (est): 4.8MM **Privately Held**
WEB: www.royalmetalproducts.com
SIC: 2514 3446 2522 3444 Metal household furniture; architectural metalwork; office furniture, except wood; sheet metalwork; products of purchased glass

Syosset
Nassau County

(G-14777)
ANDOR DESIGN CORP
20 Pond View Dr (11791-4409)
PHONE..................516 364-1619
Ralph Silvera, *President*
EMP: 7
SALES (est): 880K **Privately Held**
WEB: www.andordesign.com
SIC: 3829 Tensile strength testing equipment; testing equipment: abrasion, shearing strength, etc.

(G-14778)
BEKTROM FOODS INC (PA)
Also Called: Lots O' Luv
6800 Jericho Tpke 207w (11791-4445)
PHONE..................516 802-3800
Thomas Barbella, *President*
▲ **EMP:** 7
SALES (est): 12.5MM **Privately Held**
SIC: 2045 2099 Prepared flour mixes & doughs; packaged combination products: pasta, rice & potato

(G-14779)
BOILEROOM FABRICATION LLC
62 Oak Dr (11791-4605)
PHONE..................516 488-4848
Richard Constantino, *Mng Member*
EMP: 9
SALES (est): 343.9K **Privately Held**
SIC: 3443 Boilers: industrial, power, or marine

(G-14780)
BUFFALO DENTAL MFG CO INC
Also Called: Bdm
159 Lafayette Dr (11791-3933)
P.O. Box 678 (11791-0678)
PHONE..................516 496-7200
Donald Nevin, *President*
Marshall Nevin, *Chairman*
Doris Nevin, *Admin Sec*
▲ **EMP:** 50 EST: 1869
SQ FT: 25,000
SALES (est): 7.9MM **Privately Held**
SIC: 3843 Dental equipment

(G-14781)
CONTI AUTO BODY CORP
44 Jericho Tpke (11791)
PHONE..................516 921-6435
Liam Martin, *Principal*
EMP: 7
SALES (est): 775.7K **Privately Held**
SIC: 3711 3713 7532 Automobile bodies, passenger car, not including engine, etc.; truck & bus bodies; top & body repair & paint shops

(G-14782)
COSENSE INC
125 Coachman Pl W (11791-3059)
PHONE..................516 364-9161
Naim Dam, *President*
Sal Stiperi, *Vice Pres*
EMP: 35
SQ FT: 10,000
SALES (est): 7.2MM
SALES (corp-wide): 13.9B **Privately Held**
WEB: www.cosense.com
SIC: 3829 Measuring & controlling devices
HQ: Measurement Specialties, Inc.
1000 Lucas Way
Hampton VA 23666
757 766-1500

(G-14783)
DANDREA INC
115 Eileen Way Ste 106 (11791-5302)
P.O. Box 391, Port Washington (11050-0392)
PHONE..................516 496-2200
Anthony J D'Andrea, *President*
Rosemary D'Andrea, *Corp Secy*
◆ **EMP:** 40 EST: 1922
SQ FT: 12,000
SALES (est): 4.5MM **Privately Held**
SIC: 3931 5736 Musical instruments; musical instrument stores

(G-14784)
DEAL TO WIN INC
Also Called: Monogram Online
575 Unerhill Blvd Ste 325 (11791)
PHONE..................718 609-1165
Shlomi Matalon, *President*
EMP: 30
SALES (est): 2.2MM **Privately Held**
SIC: 3999 Barber & beauty shop equipment

(G-14785)
DELANEY BOOKS INC
212 Michael Dr (11791-5379)
PHONE..................516 921-8888
Michael Rudman, *President*
Frances Rudman, *Vice Pres*
EMP: 15
SQ FT: 5,000
SALES (est): 1.5MM **Privately Held**
WEB: www.passbooks.com
SIC: 2731 Books: publishing only
PA: National Learning Corp
212 Michael Dr
Syosset NY 11791
516 921-8888

(G-14786)
ETERNAL LOVE PARFUMS CORP
Also Called: Eternal Love Perfumes
485 Underhill Blvd # 207 (11791-3434)
PHONE..................516 921-6100
Mahender Sabhnani, *President*
◆ **EMP:** 4
SALES (est): 4.2MM **Privately Held**
WEB: www.eternalloveparfums.com
SIC: 2844 5122 Toilet preparations; perfumes

(G-14787)
FLUID METERING INC (HQ)
5 Aerial Way Ste 500 (11791-5593)
PHONE..................516 922-6050
Harry E Pinkerton III, *President*
Robert A Warren Jr, *Vice Pres*
EMP: 50 EST: 1959
SALES (est): 14.9MM
SALES (corp-wide): 5.1B **Publicly Held**
WEB: www.fmipump.com
SIC: 3561 Pumps & pumping equipment
PA: Roper Technologies, Inc.
6901 Prof Pkwy E Ste 200
Sarasota FL 34240
941 556-2601

(G-14788)
FRANK MERRIWELL INC
212 Michael Dr (11791-5305)
PHONE..................516 921-8888
Jack Rudman, *President*
Frances Rudman, *Vice Pres*
EMP: 15
SQ FT: 5,000
SALES (est): 1.5MM **Privately Held**
WEB: www.frankmerriwell.com
SIC: 2731 Books: publishing only
PA: National Learning Corp
212 Michael Dr
Syosset NY 11791
516 921-8888

(G-14789)
GENERAL MICROWAVE CORPORATION (HQ)
227a Michael Dr (11791-5306)
PHONE..................516 802-0900
Deanna Lund, *CEO*
Eric Demarco, *President*
Michael Fink, *Vice Pres*
Data Links, *Corp Comm Staff*
Marie Mendoza, *Admin Sec*
EMP: 11 EST: 1960
SQ FT: 3,000
SALES: 10MM **Publicly Held**
SIC: 3674 5065 3825 6794 Hybrid integrated circuits; electronic parts & equipment; electronic parts; test equipment for electronic & electrical circuits; patent owners & lessors; microwave components; analytical instruments

(G-14790)
KK INTERNATIONAL TRADING CORP
219 Lafayette Dr (11791-3939)
PHONE.....................516 801-4741
Mihail Kriheli, *President*
Edward Kriheli, *Vice Pres*
EMP: 37 EST: 1991
SALES (est): 214.1K **Privately Held**
WEB: www.slimlinelighter.com
SIC: 2111 5194 Cigarettes; tobacco & to-
bacco products

(G-14791)
KNOLL PRINTING & PACKAGING INC
Also Called: Knoll Worldwide
149 Eileen Way (11791-5302)
PHONE.....................516 621-0100
Jeremy Cohen, *Ch of Bd*
Linda Drew, *Vice Pres*
Lou Scarinci, *Vice Pres*
Coleen Corporal, *Prdtn Mgr*
▲ EMP: 24
SALES (est): 5MM **Privately Held**
WEB: www.knollpack.com
SIC: 2657 3081 3086 Folding paperboard
boxes; packing materials, plastic sheet;
packaging & shipping materials, foamed
plastic

(G-14792)
KUSH OASIS ENTERPRISES LLC
228 Martin Dr (11791-5406)
PHONE.....................516 513-1316
Sanjeev Malhotra, *Vice Pres*
Jyoti Jaiswal,
▲ EMP: 5
SALES (est): 210K **Privately Held**
SIC: 2393 Textile bags

(G-14793)
MEDICAL INFORMATION SYSTEMS
28 Patricia Ln (11791-5824)
PHONE.....................516 621-7200
Irving Silverberg, *President*
Roy Silverberg, *Exec VP*
Hazel Silverberg, *Admin Sec*
EMP: 5
SALES: 2.3MM **Privately Held**
WEB: www.medinfosystems.com
SIC: 2741 Miscellaneous publishing

(G-14794)
MESTEL BROTHERS STAIRS & RAILS
11 Gary Rd Ste 102 (11791-6211)
PHONE.....................516 496-4127
Barry Mestel, *President*
EMP: 236
SALES (est): 13.1MM **Privately Held**
WEB: www.mestelbrothersstairs.com
SIC: 2431 3446 1751 Staircases & stairs,
wood; architectural metalwork; carpentry
work

(G-14795)
NASCO ENTERPRISES INC
95 Woodcrest Dr (11791-3037)
PHONE.....................516 921-9696
Naimish P Shah, *President*
▲ EMP: 1
SALES: 1MM **Privately Held**
SIC: 3841 Catheters

(G-14796)
NATIONAL LEARNING CORP (PA)
212 Michael Dr (11791-5379)
PHONE.....................516 921-8888
Michael Rudman, *President*
Frances Rudman, *Vice Pres*
EMP: 15
SQ FT: 15,000
SALES: 1.5MM **Privately Held**
WEB: www.delaneybooks.com
SIC: 2731 Book clubs: publishing & print-
ing

(G-14797)
NATIONAL RDING STYLES INST INC
Also Called: N R S I
179 Lafayette Dr (11791-3933)
P.O. Box 737 (11791-0737)
PHONE.....................516 921-5500
Marie Carbo, *President*
Juliet Ditroia, *Corp Secy*
EMP: 12
SQ FT: 6,400
SALES: 1.5MM **Privately Held**
WEB: www.nrsi.com
SIC: 2741 8748 Miscellaneous publishing;
educational consultant

(G-14798)
NEW JERSEY PULVERIZING CO INC (PA)
4 Rita St (11791-5918)
PHONE.....................516 921-9595
Martin Tanzer, *President*
Barbara Tanzer, *Vice Pres*
Barbara Deegan, *Treasurer*
EMP: 3 EST: 1915
SQ FT: 2,500
SALES (est): 2.8MM **Privately Held**
SIC: 1446 Industrial sand

(G-14799)
PRINCE BLACK DISTILLERY INC
Also Called: Black Prince
425 Underhill Blvd Unit 4 (11791-3433)
PHONE.....................212 695-6187
Robert Guttag, *President*
◆ EMP: 29 EST: 1934
SALES (est): 5.1MM **Privately Held**
WEB: www.blackprincedistillery.com
SIC: 2085 Distilled & blended liquors

(G-14800)
QUALBUYS LLC
6800 Jericho Tpke 120w (11791-4436)
PHONE.....................855 884-3274
Amy Kajiya, *COO*
EMP: 5 EST: 2011
SALES (est): 177.7K **Privately Held**
SIC: 3999 Barber & beauty shop equip-
ment

(G-14801)
REAL EST BOOK OF LONG ISLAND
575 Underhill Blvd # 110 (11791-3426)
PHONE.....................516 364-5000
Bryan Flynn, *President*
EMP: 10
SQ FT: 1,600
SALES: 2MM **Privately Held**
SIC: 2721 7319 Periodicals: publishing
only; magazines: publishing only, not
printed on site; distribution of advertising
material or sample services

(G-14802)
ROTA FILE CORPORATION
Also Called: Rota Tool
159 Lafayette Dr (11791-3933)
P.O. Box 678 (11791-0678)
PHONE.....................516 496-7200
Don Nevin, *President*
Richard Byalick, *General Mgr*
EMP: 20
SALES (est): 2.2MM **Privately Held**
WEB: www.rotafile.com
SIC: 3545 Cutting tools for machine tools

(G-14803)
TRACCO LLC
6800 Jericho Tpke 101w (11791-4436)
PHONE.....................516 938-4588
David Horowitz,
EMP: 5
SALES (est): 139.9K **Privately Held**
SIC: 2099 Food preparations

(G-14804)
VIDEO TECHNOLOGY SERVICES INC
5 Aerial Way Ste 300 (11791-5594)
PHONE.....................516 937-9700
Andres Sierra, *President*
EMP: 12
SQ FT: 7,200
SALES (est): 2.1MM **Privately Held**
WEB: www.videotechnologyservices.com
SIC: 3651 7622 5099 Household video
equipment; video repair; video & audio
equipment

(G-14805)
VIVONA BUSINESS PRINTERS INC
Also Called: PIP Printing
343 Jackson Ave (11791-4123)
PHONE.....................516 496-3453
Joseph Vivona, *CEO*
Joe Vivona, *President*
Anne Marie Bono, *Vice Pres*
EMP: 8
SALES (est): 1.3MM **Privately Held**
SIC: 2752 Commercial printing, offset

(G-14806)
ZASTECH INC
15 Ryan St (11791-2129)
PHONE.....................516 496-4777
Raymond Zhou, *CEO*
▲ EMP: 20
SALES (est): 1.5MM **Privately Held**
SIC: 3674 Semiconductors & related de-
vices

Syracuse
Onondaga County

(G-14807)
219 SOUTH WEST
219 S West St (13202-1874)
PHONE.....................315 474-2065
EMP: 8
SALES (est): 560K **Privately Held**
SIC: 2448 Mfg Wood Pallets/Skids

(G-14808)
A ZIMMER LTD
Also Called: Syracuse New Times
W Tenesee St (13204)
PHONE.....................315 422-7011
Arthur Zimmer, *President*
Gregg Gambell, *General Mgr*
Shirley Zimmer, *CFO*
Bill De Lapp, *Manager*
EMP: 84
SQ FT: 24,000
SALES (est): 5.5MM **Privately Held**
WEB: www.syracusenewtimes.com
SIC: 2711 5521 Newspapers, publishing &
printing; used car dealers

(G-14809)
ALL TIMES PUBLISHING LLC
Also Called: Syracuse New Times
1415 W Genesee St (13204-2119)
PHONE.....................315 422-7011
William Brod, *CEO*
James Coleman, *Vice Pres*
Bill Brod, *Officer*
EMP: 24
SALES (est): 2MM **Privately Held**
SIC: 2711 Newspapers

(G-14810)
ALL-STATE DIVERSIFIED PDTS INC
8 Dwight Park Dr (13209-1034)
PHONE.....................315 472-4728
EMP: 50
SALES (est): 5.3MM **Privately Held**
SIC: 3443 Mfg Fabricated Plate Work

(G-14811)
ALLIED DECORATIONS CO INC
Also Called: Allied Sign Co
720 Erie Blvd W (13204-2226)
PHONE.....................315 637-0273
Michael E Pfohl, *President*
Kim Charette, *Office Mgr*
EMP: 15
SQ FT: 45,000
SALES (est): 2MM **Privately Held**
WEB: www.alliedsigncompany.com
SIC: 3993 7389 Electric signs; decoration
service for special events; trade show
arrangement

(G-14812)
ALPHA PRINTING CORP
131 Falso Dr (13211-2106)
P.O. Box 26 (13211-0026)
PHONE.....................315 454-5507
Stephen Larose, *President*
EMP: 12
SQ FT: 5,000
SALES (est): 1.5MM **Privately Held**
SIC: 2752 Commercial printing, offset

(G-14813)
ALTIUS AVIATION LLC
113 Tuskegee Rd Ste 2 (13211-1332)
PHONE.....................315 455-7555
Vaughn J Crawford, *Mng Member*
EMP: 6 EST: 2008
SALES (est): 860.2K **Privately Held**
SIC: 3721 6722 8742 Aircraft; manage-
ment investment, open-end; management
consulting services

(G-14814)
ANSUN GRAPHICS INC
6392 Deere Rd Ste 4 (13206-1317)
PHONE.....................315 437-6869
Jeff Schoenfeld, *President*
Pat Burke, *IT/INT Sup*
Joe Marrinan, *Shareholder*
Todd Thomas, *Admin Sec*
EMP: 12
SALES (est): 1.8MM **Privately Held**
WEB: www.ansun.biz
SIC: 2752 Commercial printing, litho-
graphic

(G-14815)
ARCOM AUTOMATICS LLC
185 Ainsley Dr (13210-4202)
P.O. Box 6729 (13217-6729)
PHONE.....................315 422-1230
Gregory A Tresness, *President*
EMP: 8
SALES (est): 1.5MM **Privately Held**
WEB: www.arcomlabs.com
SIC: 3663 Cable television equipment

(G-14816)
ARMOURED ONE LLC
386 N Midler Ave Ste 26 (13206-2276)
PHONE.....................315 720-4186
Thomas Czyz, *CEO*
Joe Guarrera Jr, *Vice Pres*
Scott Hare, *Vice Pres*
Theresa Morgan, *CFO*
Tino Amodei, *CTO*
EMP: 200
SQ FT: 180,000
SALES (est): 11.4MM **Privately Held**
SIC: 3231 Safety glass: made from pur-
chased glass

(G-14817)
ARO-GRAPH CORPORATION
Also Called: Aro-Graph Displays
847 North Ave (13206-1630)
PHONE.....................315 463-8693
Neal Burrei, *President*
Carol Burrei, *Vice Pres*
EMP: 5 EST: 1946
SQ FT: 7,000
SALES (est): 828.5K **Privately Held**
WEB: www.arograph.com
SIC: 2752 2396 Decals, lithographed;
screen printing on fabric articles

(G-14818)
ARROW-COMMUNICATION LABS INC
Also Called: Arcom Labs
185 Ainsley Dr (13210-4202)
P.O. Box 6729 (13217-6729)
PHONE.....................315 422-1230
Andrew Tresness, *President*
Tim Schwab, *CIO*
▲ EMP: 300
SQ FT: 30,000
SALES (est): 50.2MM
SALES (corp-wide): 52.8MM **Privately
Held**
SIC: 3663 Cable television equipment
PA: Northern Catv Sales Inc
185 Ainsley Dr
Syracuse NY
315 422-1230

G E O G R A P H I C

(G-14819)
ARTISTRY IN WOOD OF SYRACUSE
230 Ainsley Dr (13210-4203)
PHONE..............................315 431-4022
Gregory W McCartney, *President*
EMP: 17
SALES (est): 3.3MM Privately Held
SIC: 2599 2531 5046 Factory furniture & fixtures; public building & related furniture; library furniture; store fixtures

(G-14820)
ATLAS BITUMINOUS CO INC
173 Farrell Rd (13209-1823)
P.O. Box 219, Liverpool (13088-0219)
PHONE..............................315 457-2394
Charmaine Jones, *President*
Robert Shattel, *Treasurer*
James Shattel, *Admin Sec*
EMP: 11 EST: 1963
SQ FT: 2,500
SALES (est): 2.1MM Privately Held
SIC: 2951 6513 Asphalt & asphaltic paving mixtures (not from refineries); apartment hotel operation

(G-14821)
AUTOMATION CORRECT LLC
Also Called: Automationcorrect.com
405 Parrish Ln (13205-3323)
PHONE..............................315 299-3589
Neil Waelder, *Manager*
EMP: 5
SALES (est): 696.1K Privately Held
WEB: www.automationcorrect.com
SIC: 3825 Test equipment for electronic & electrical circuits

(G-14822)
AUTOMATION PAPERS INC
Also Called: National Pad & Paper
6361 Thompson Rd Stop 1 (13206-1412)
P.O. Box 572, Fayetteville (13066-0572)
PHONE..............................315 432-0565
David T Carroll, *President*
Donald T Carroll, *Vice Pres*
Jean Carroll, *Admin Sec*
▼ EMP: 7
SQ FT: 17,000
SALES (est): 1.1MM Privately Held
SIC: 2621 Writing paper

(G-14823)
AVALON COPY CENTERS AMER INC (PA)
Also Called: Avalon Document Services
901 N State St (13208-2515)
PHONE..............................315 471-3333
John P Midgley, *CEO*
Shawn Thrall, *President*
Patrick Beckett, *Managing Prtnr*
Jon Willette, *COO*
Chris Haag, *Exec VP*
EMP: 65
SQ FT: 13,000
SALES (est): 19MM Privately Held
SIC: 2741 7375 7336 7334 Art copy: publishing & printing; information retrieval services; commercial art & graphic design; photocopying & duplicating services

(G-14824)
BABBITT BEARINGS INC (PA)
Also Called: Babbit Bearings
734 Burnet Ave (13203-2999)
PHONE..............................315 479-6603
Tracy S Stevenson, *CEO*
H Thomas Wart, *Vice Pres*
Christopher Curfman, *Production*
John Cerrone, *Treasurer*
Marian Wart, *Admin Sec*
EMP: 90
SQ FT: 34,000
SALES (est): 14.3MM Privately Held
SIC: 3599 Machine shop, jobbing & repair

(G-14825)
BABBITT BEARINGS INCORPORATED
734 Burnet Ave (13203-2999)
PHONE..............................315 479-6603
Charles R Wart Jr, *President*
John Cerrone, *Treasurer*
Marian Wart, *Admin Sec*

EMP: 75 EST: 1970
SQ FT: 60,000
SALES (est): 5.2MM
SALES (corp-wide): 14.3MM Privately Held
WEB: www.babbitt-inc.com
SIC: 3599 3568 Machine shop, jobbing & repair; power transmission equipment
PA: Babbitt Bearings, Inc.
734 Burnet Ave
Syracuse NY 13203
315 479-6603

(G-14826)
BARNES GROUP INC
Associated Spring
1225 State Fair Blvd (13209-1011)
PHONE..............................315 457-9200
Fax: 315 457-9228
EMP: 8
SQ FT: 22,448
SALES (corp-wide): 1.4B Publicly Held
SIC: 3495 3469 Mfg Wire Springs And Metal Stampings
PA: Barnes Group Inc.
123 Main St
Bristol CT 06010
860 583-7070

(G-14827)
BELLA FIGURA LETTERPRESS
509 W Fayette St (13204-2986)
PHONE..............................866 699-6040
Virginia Hart, *Principal*
EMP: 5
SALES (est): 257.3K Privately Held
SIC: 2759 Letterpress printing

(G-14828)
BENCHMARK MEDIA SYSTEMS INC
203 E Hampton Pl Ste 2 (13206-1676)
PHONE..............................315 437-6300
Ruth S Burdick, *CEO*
Allen H Burdick, *President*
John Siau, *Vice Pres*
David Siau, *Prdtn Mgr*
Rory Rall, *Sales Mgr*
EMP: 14
SQ FT: 5,500
SALES (est): 2.6MM Privately Held
WEB: www.benchmarkmedia.com
SIC: 3663 Radio & TV communications equipment

(G-14829)
BILLY BEEZ USA LLC
9090 Destiy Usa Dr L301 (13204)
PHONE..............................315 741-5099
EMP: 14
SALES (corp-wide): 16.7MM Privately Held
SIC: 3949 5137 7999 Playground equipment; women's & children's dresses, suits, skirts & blouses; amusement ride
PA: Billy Beez Usa, Llc
3 W 35th St Fl 3 # 3
New York NY 10001
646 606-2249

(G-14830)
BITZER SCROLL INC
6055 Court Street Rd (13206-1749)
PHONE..............................315 463-2101
Peter P Narreau, *CEO*
Richard Kobor, *President*
Tom O'Donnell, *Engineer*
Frank Wilson, *Engineer*
James Shea, *Controller*
▲ EMP: 90
SALES (est): 46.1MM
SALES (corp-wide): 847.8MM Privately Held
SIC: 3822 Air conditioning & refrigeration controls
PA: Bitzer Sc
Peter-Schaufler-Platz 1
Sindelfingen 71065
703 193-20

(G-14831)
BLACKBURN TRUCK BODIES LLC
6216 Thompson Rd Ste 3 (13206-1418)
PHONE..............................315 448-3236
Jeff Blackburn, *Mng Member*

Ryan Blackburn, *Mng Member*
EMP: 5
SALES (est): 241.6K Privately Held
SIC: 3713 5531 Truck & bus bodies; automotive accessories

(G-14832)
BOMAC INC
6477 Ridings Rd (13206-1110)
PHONE..............................315 433-9181
Kevin T Knecht, *President*
Mark Pauls, *Vice Pres*
Michael Rudd, *VP Engrg*
Rocky Yemma, *Cust Mgr*
EMP: 18 EST: 1959
SQ FT: 22,000
SALES (est): 4.7MM Privately Held
WEB: www.bomacinc.com
SIC: 3625 Electric controls & control accessories, industrial

(G-14833)
BOXCAR PRESS INCORPORATED
509 W Fayette St Ste 135 (13204-2987)
PHONE..............................315 473-0930
Harold Kyle, *Ch of Bd*
Debbi Urbanski, *Vice Pres*
Alison Cotsonas, *Project Mgr*
Adriana Sosnowski, *Opers Mgr*
Brian Pribis, *Prgrmr*
EMP: 30
SALES (est): 5.5MM Privately Held
WEB: www.boxcarpress.com
SIC: 2752 5084 Commercial printing, offset; printing trades machinery, equipment & supplies

(G-14834)
BROADNET TECHNOLOGIES INC
2-212 Center For Science (13244-0001)
PHONE..............................315 443-3694
Michael Sun, *CEO*
EMP: 15 EST: 2000
SQ FT: 2,000
SALES (est): 1.3MM Privately Held
SIC: 3577 Optical scanning devices

(G-14835)
BUFFALO STRUCTURAL STEEL INC
213 Teall Ave (13210-1218)
PHONE..............................814 827-1350
Tim Powell, *Branch Mgr*
EMP: 25 Privately Held
WEB: www.buffalostructural.com
SIC: 3441 Fabricated structural metal
PA: Buffalo Structural Steel, Inc.
60 Bryant Woods S
Amherst NY 14228

(G-14836)
BURR & SON INC
Also Called: Dover Enterprises
119 Seeley Rd (13224-1113)
PHONE..............................315 446-1550
J Peter Burr, *President*
EMP: 5 EST: 1973
SQ FT: 3,000
SALES (est): 360K Privately Held
WEB: www.doverent.com
SIC: 2759 Imprinting; engraving

(G-14837)
BUSCH PRODUCTS INC
110 Baker St (13206-1701)
PHONE..............................315 474-8422
Robert Brown Sr, *President*
Darlene Brown, *Vice Pres*
Paul Conley, *Engineer*
Lisa Verrillo, *Cust Mgr*
EMP: 50
SALES (est): 6.4MM Privately Held
WEB: www.buschproducts.com
SIC: 3281 Cut stone & stone products

(G-14838)
C & M PRODUCTS INC
1209 N Salina St Ste 1 (13208-1581)
PHONE..............................315 471-3303
Charles Mott, *President*
EMP: 6 EST: 1965
SQ FT: 5,600

SALES (est): 579.5K Privately Held
SIC: 3479 3499 3089 Name plates: engraved, etched, etc.; trophies, metal, except silver; laminating of plastic

(G-14839)
C M E CORP
Also Called: Central Marking Equipment
1005 W Fayette St Ste 3c (13204-2840)
PHONE..............................315 451-7101
Leedom Kettell, *President*
EMP: 11
SQ FT: 12,000
SALES: 1MM Privately Held
SIC: 3555 3953 Printing plates; marking devices

(G-14840)
CALTEX INTERNATIONAL LTD
60 Presidential Plz # 1405 (13202-2444)
PHONE..............................315 425-1040
Kapil Kevin Sodhi, *President*
Jennifer Hetherington, *Vice Pres*
EMP: 39
SQ FT: 26,000
SALES: 6.4MM Privately Held
WEB: www.iscbiostrat.com
SIC: 2869 2842 3826 Industrial organic chemicals; specialty cleaning preparations; environmental testing equipment

(G-14841)
CAMFIL USA INC
Also Called: Edco Sales
6060 Tarbell Rd (13206-1301)
PHONE..............................315 468-3849
EMP: 12
SALES (corp-wide): 921.6MM Privately Held
SIC: 3564 Blowers & fans
HQ: Camfil Usa, Inc.
1 N Corporate Dr
Riverdale NJ 07457
973 616-7300

(G-14842)
CAROLS POLAR PARLOR
3800 W Genesee St (13219-1928)
PHONE..............................315 468-3404
Carol Franceschetti, *Owner*
EMP: 5
SALES (est): 358.5K Privately Held
SIC: 2024 Ice cream & frozen desserts

(G-14843)
CARPENTER INDUSTRIES INC
1 General Motors Dr # 10 (13206-1129)
P.O. Box 888 (13206-0888)
PHONE..............................315 463-4284
Tenley Tibbits, *President*
EMP: 11
SQ FT: 25,000
SALES (est): 1.6MM Privately Held
WEB: www.carpenterindustries.com
SIC: 3471 3441 Sand blasting of metal parts; fabricated structural metal

(G-14844)
CARRIER CORPORATION
Carrier Pkwy Tr 20 (13221)
P.O. Box 4808 (13221-4808)
PHONE..............................315 432-6000
Randall J Hogan, *President*
EMP: 400
SALES (corp-wide): 66.5B Publicly Held
WEB: www.carrier.com
SIC: 3822 3585 3433 Refrigeration/air-conditioning defrost controls; refrigeration & heating equipment; heating equipment, except electric
HQ: Carrier Corporation
13995 Pasteur Blvd
Palm Beach Gardens FL 33418
800 379-6484

(G-14845)
CARRIER CORPORATION
Carrier Global Account (13221)
P.O. Box 4808 (13221-4808)
PHONE..............................315 432-6000
Geraud Damis, *Branch Mgr*
EMP: 1200
SALES (corp-wide): 66.5B Publicly Held
WEB: www.carrier.com
SIC: 3585 Refrigeration & heating equipment

▲ = Import ▼=Export
◆ =Import/Export

HQ: Carrier Corporation
13995 Pasteur Blvd
Palm Beach Gardens FL 33418
800 379-6484

(G-14846)
CATHEDRAL CANDLE CO
510 Kirkpatrick St (13208-2100)
PHONE..................................315 422-9119
Louis J Steigerwald III, *Ch of Bd*
Mark Steigerwald, *Vice Pres*
John Hogan, *Treasurer*
Robert Alexander, *Sales Staff*
Linda D Rohde, *Admin Sec*
▲ EMP: 52 EST: 1897
SQ FT: 17,000
SALES (est): 7.2MM **Privately Held**
WEB: www.cathedralcandle.com
SIC: 3999 5049 Candles; religious sup-
plies

(G-14847)
CHAMPION MILLWORK INC
140 Hiawatha Pl (13208-1268)
PHONE..................................315 463-0711
Micheal Duffy, *President*
EMP: 25
SALES: 4.6MM **Privately Held**
SIC: 2431 Millwork

(G-14848)
CHEMTRADE CHEMICALS US LLC
Also Called: General Chemical
1421 Willis Ave (13204-1051)
P.O. Box 16 (13209-0016)
PHONE..................................315 430-7650
Biagio Vavala, *Plant Mgr*
Biagio Bavala, *Opers-Prdtn-Mfg*
Kathleen Nese, *Technology*
EMP: 40
SALES (corp-wide): 1.2B **Privately Held**
SIC: 2819 Industrial inorganic chemicals
HQ: Chemtrade Chemicals Us Llc
90 E Halsey Rd
Parsippany NJ 07054

(G-14849)
CHEMTRADE CHEMICALS US LLC
Also Called: Syracuse Technical Center
344 W Genesee St Ste 100 (13202-1010)
PHONE..................................315 478-2323
Joseph Hurd, *Manager*
EMP: 5
SALES (corp-wide): 1.2B **Privately Held**
SIC: 2819 Sodium compounds or salts,
inorg., ex. refined sod. chloride
HQ: Chemtrade Chemicals Us Llc
90 E Halsey Rd
Parsippany NJ 07054

(G-14850)
CITY PATTERN SHOP INC
4052 New Court Ave (13206-1639)
P.O. Box 6 (13206-0006)
PHONE..................................315 463-5239
Paul M Clisson, *President*
Robert Leonard, *Vice Pres*
EMP: 10 EST: 1961
SQ FT: 7,500
SALES (est): 1.2MM **Privately Held**
WEB: www.citypatternshop.com
SIC: 3543 Industrial patterns

(G-14851)
CLARK CONCRETE CO INC (PA)
Also Called: Clark Trucking Co Div
434 E Brighton Ave (13210-4144)
PHONE..................................315 478-4101
Donald W Clark, *President*
Lyndon S Clark, *Vice Pres*
Stephen Clark, *Vice Pres*
EMP: 6 EST: 1920
SQ FT: 8,000
SALES (est): 1.8MM **Privately Held**
SIC: 3273 4212 Ready-mixed concrete;
local trucking, without storage

(G-14852)
CLEAN ALL OF SYRACUSE LLC
838 Erie Blvd W (13204-2228)
PHONE..................................315 472-9189
Severino Gonnella, *President*
Angela Gonnella, *Vice Pres*
EMP: 9

SQ FT: 40,000
SALES (est): 980K **Privately Held**
SIC: 2842 5999 Cleaning or polishing
preparations; swimming pool chemicals,
equipment & supplies

(G-14853)
CNY BUSINESS REVIEW INC
Also Called: Business Journal
211 W Jefferson St Ste 1 (13202-2561)
PHONE..................................315 472-3104
Norman Poltenson, *President*
Kurt Bramer, *Business Mgr*
Dony Bardenett, *Marketing Staff*
EMP: 14
SALES (est): 1MM **Privately Held**
WEB: www.cnybj.com
SIC: 2711 2721 Newspapers: publishing
only, not printed on site; periodicals

(G-14854)
CNYSHIRTS
6392 Deere Rd Ste 1 (13206-1323)
PHONE..................................315 432-1789
Jeremy Hibbert, *Mng Member*
EMP: 7 EST: 2012
SALES: 350K **Privately Held**
SIC: 2759 Screen printing

(G-14855)
COASTEL CABLE TOOLS INC
Also Called: Coastel Cable Tools Intl
344 E Brighton Ave (13210-4142)
PHONE..................................315 471-5361
Edward Dale, *President*
Mary Shaver, *Vice Pres*
John Lumia, *Manager*
EMP: 21
SQ FT: 42,000
SALES (est): 2MM **Privately Held**
WEB: www.coasteltools.com
SIC: 3541 3423 Machine tools, metal cut-
ting type; hand & edge tools

(G-14856)
COCA-COLA BTLG CO OF NY INC
298 Farrell Rd (13209-1876)
PHONE..................................315 457-9221
Lucky Wyrick, *Sales/Mktg Mgr*
Heaven Donner, *Manager*
EMP: 10
SQ FT: 117,740
SALES (corp-wide): 31.8B **Publicly Held**
SIC: 2086 Bottled & canned soft drinks
HQ: The Coca-Cola Bottling Company Of
New York Inc
2500 Windy Ridge Pkwy Se
Atlanta GA 30339
770 989-3000

(G-14857)
COLD SPRINGS R & D INC
1207 Van Vleck Rd Ste A (13209-1017)
PHONE..................................315 413-1237
Scott Grimshaw, *President*
Valerie Grimshaw, *Vice Pres*
EMP: 10
SQ FT: 10,000
SALES (est): 1.3MM **Privately Held**
WEB: www.csrdinc.com
SIC: 3674 Semiconductors & related de-
vices

(G-14858)
CONCEPTS IN WOOD OF CNY
4021 New Court Ave (13206-1640)
PHONE..................................315 463-8084
David Fuleihan, *President*
EMP: 25
SQ FT: 16,000
SALES (est): 3.4MM **Privately Held**
SIC: 2521 2511 2431 Cabinets, office:
wood; filing cabinets (boxes), office:
wood; wood household furniture; millwork

(G-14859)
CONSTAS PRINTING CORPORATION
Also Called: Taylor Copy Services
1120 Burnet Ave (13203-3210)
PHONE..................................315 474-2176
Diane M Brindak, *Ch of Bd*
Diane Constas, *President*
Claudia Constas, *Vice Pres*
EMP: 7

SQ FT: 2,400
SALES (est): 798.5K **Privately Held**
SIC: 2752 7334 Commercial printing, off-
set; photocopying & duplicating services

(G-14860)
COOKIE CONNECTION INC
705 Park Ave (13204-2223)
PHONE..................................315 422-2253
Kathleen Sniezak, *President*
Elizabeth Johnson, *Vice Pres*
EMP: 5
SQ FT: 1,500
SALES (est): 295.5K **Privately Held**
SIC: 2051 Bakery: wholesale or whole-
sale/retail combined

(G-14861)
COOPER & CLEMENT INC
1840 Lemoyne Ave (13208-1367)
PHONE..................................315 454-8135
John Clement, *President*
Inga Clement, *Vice Pres*
Ole Westergaard, *Vice Pres*
EMP: 29
SQ FT: 35,000
SALES (est): 4.4MM **Privately Held**
SIC: 2759 2396 Promotional printing; au-
tomotive & apparel trimmings

(G-14862)
COOPER CROUSE-HINDS LLC (HQ)
Also Called: Cooper Crouse Hinds Elec Pdts
1201 Wolf St (13208-1376)
P.O. Box 4999 (13221-4999)
PHONE..................................315 477-7000
Alexander M Cutler, *CEO*
Grant L Gawronski, *President*
Kurt Schulz, *Sales Staff*
Mark Toby, *Info Tech Dir*
Bill Saylor, *Officer*
◆ EMP: 500
SQ FT: 1,000,000
SALES (est): 370.3MM **Privately Held**
WEB: www.coopercrouse-hinds.com
SIC: 3699 Fire control or bombing equip-
ment, electronic

(G-14863)
COOPER CROUSE-HINDS MTL INC
Also Called: Eaton Crouse-Hinds
1201 Wolf St (13208-1376)
P.O. Box 4999 (13221-4999)
PHONE..................................315 477-7000
Scott Hearn, *President*
Walter Fedor, *Production*
Asiri Jayawardena, *Engineer*
Don Gilbert, *Sales Staff*
Mario Romero, *Marketing Staff*
EMP: 200
SALES (est): 20.1MM **Privately Held**
SIC: 3648 Airport lighting fixtures: runway
approach, taxi or ramp
PA: Eaton Corporation Public Limited Com-
pany
Eaton House
Dublin

(G-14864)
COOPER INDUSTRIES LLC
Also Called: Cooper Molded Products
Wolf & 7th North St (13208)
PHONE..................................315 477-7000
Everett Miles, *Maint Spvr*
Curt J Andersson, *Branch Mgr*
Kathy Kursar, *Technology*
Thomas J Bonk, *Director*
Dave Sensinger, *Director*
EMP: 19 **Privately Held**
SIC: 3646 3648 3613 5063 Commercial
indusl & institutional electric lighting fix-
tures; lighting equipment; switchgear &
switchgear accessories; electrical sup-
plies; electrical equipment & supplies;
construction machinery
HQ: Cooper Industries, Llc
600 Travis St Ste 5400
Houston TX 77002
713 209-8400

(G-14865)
COUNTERTOPS & CABINETS INC
4073 New Court Ave (13206-1646)
PHONE..................................315 433-1038
Emil Henry, *President*
Nick Henry, *Admin Sec*
EMP: 5
SQ FT: 3,200
SALES (est): 752K **Privately Held**
WEB: www.cnytops.com
SIC: 2541 1799 Counter & sink tops;
counter top installation

(G-14866)
CREATIVE LAMINATES INC
4003 Eastbourne Dr (13206-1631)
PHONE..................................315 463-7580
Dennis N Brackly, *President*
EMP: 19
SQ FT: 12,000
SALES (est): 146.4K **Privately Held**
WEB: www.creativelaminates.com
SIC: 2431 Doors & door parts & trim, wood

(G-14867)
CRITICAL LINK LLC
6712 Brooklawn Pkwy # 203 (13211-2110)
PHONE..................................315 425-4045
Neha Chopra, *Project Mgr*
Julie Romagnoli, *Purchasing*
Alex Block, *Engineer*
Tom Catalino, *Engineer*
Bill Halpin, *Engineer*
EMP: 20 EST: 1997
SQ FT: 8,000
SALES (est): 6MM **Privately Held**
SIC: 3571 8711 Electronic computers; en-
gineering services

(G-14868)
CRYOMECH INC
113 Falso Dr (13211-2106)
PHONE..................................315 455-2555
Peter Gifford, *President*
Rich Dausman, *COO*
Mitch Collins, *Purch Agent*
Tabitha Sebastino, *Sales Mgr*
Richard Irvine, *Manager*
▲ EMP: 100
SQ FT: 24,000
SALES (est): 29.5MM **Privately Held**
WEB: www.cryomech.com
SIC: 3559 Cryogenic machinery, industrial

(G-14869)
CUMMINS NORTHEAST LLC
6193 Eastern Ave (13211-2208)
PHONE..................................315 437-2296
Robin Riewaldt, *Opers-Prdtn-Mfg*
EMP: 36
SQ FT: 13,760
SALES (corp-wide): 23.7B **Publicly Held**
SIC: 3519 5063 Internal combustion en-
gines; electrical apparatus & equipment
HQ: Cummins Northeast, Llc
30 Braintree Hill Park # 101
Braintree MA 02184

(G-14870)
CUSTOM SHEET METAL CORP
1 General Motors Dr Ste 5 (13206-1122)
PHONE..................................315 463-9105
Wilson C Brown, *President*
EMP: 8
SQ FT: 5,000
SALES (est): 1.1MM **Privately Held**
SIC: 3444 Sheet metal specialties, not
stamped

(G-14871)
D & D MOTOR SYSTEMS INC
215 Park Ave (13204-2459)
PHONE..................................315 701-0861
Mike Dearoff, *President*
Eric Dearoff, *Vice Pres*
Vic Dejohn, *Engineer*
◆ EMP: 20
SALES (est): 4.8MM **Privately Held**
WEB: www.ddmotorsystems.com
SIC: 3621 Motors & generators

(G-14872)
D N GANNON FABRICATING INC
404 Wavel St (13206-1728)
P.O. Box 6572 (13217-6572)
PHONE..............................315 463-7466
Frank Deuel, *President*
John Noel, *Vice Pres*
EMP: 5 **EST:** 1981
SQ FT: 15,000
SALES (est): 550K **Privately Held**
SIC: 3441 Building components, structural steel

(G-14873)
DAILY ORANGE CORPORATION
744 Ostrom Ave (13244-2977)
PHONE..............................315 443-2314
Julie Mdooling, *General Mgr*
Dave Seal, *Editor*
Nancy Peck, *Adv Dir*
EMP: 50
SALES: 251.4K **Privately Held**
WEB: www.dailyorange.com
SIC: 2711 Newspapers: publishing only, not printed on site

(G-14874)
DARCO MANUFACTURING INC
6756 Thompson Rd (13211-2122)
P.O. Box 6304 (13217-6304)
PHONE..............................315 432-8905
David A Redding, *President*
Laura Miller, *General Mgr*
EMP: 42
SQ FT: 22,000
SALES (est): 10.5MM **Privately Held**
SIC: 3599 Machine shop, jobbing & repair

(G-14875)
DAVID FEHLMAN
Also Called: Rollers Unlimited
6729 Pickard Dr (13211-2123)
P.O. Box 5059 (13220-5059)
PHONE..............................315 455-8888
David Fehlman, *Owner*
EMP: 5
SQ FT: 3,200
SALES (est): 341.9K **Privately Held**
SIC: 3599 3562 3366 3312 Machine & other job shop work; ball & roller bearings; copper foundries; blast furnaces & steel mills; synthetic rubber; platemaking services

(G-14876)
DEPENDABLE TOOL & DIE CO INC
129 Dwight Park Cir # 2 (13209-1010)
PHONE..............................315 453-5696
Anthony D Dantuono, *President*
Andrea Tarolli, *Admin Sec*
EMP: 8
SQ FT: 20,000
SALES (est): 1.2MM **Privately Held**
SIC: 3544 Special dies & tools

(G-14877)
DUPLI GRAPHICS CORPORATION (HQ)
Also Called: Dupli Envelope & Graphics
6761 Thompson Rd (13211-2119)
P.O. Box 11500 (13218-1500)
PHONE..............................315 234-7286
J Kemper Matt, *Ch of Bd*
J Kemper Matt Jr, *President*
Susan Davirro, *Purch Agent*
Todd Luchsinger, *CFO*
Paul Gehring, *Manager*
EMP: 117
SQ FT: 150,000
SALES (est): 29.6MM
SALES (corp-wide): 49.5MM **Privately Held**
WEB: www.duplionline.com
SIC: 2752 2759 Commercial printing, lithographic; envelopes: printing
PA: Matt Industries Inc
6761 Thompson Rd
Syracuse NY 13211
315 472-1316

(G-14878)
DUPLI GRAPHICS CORPORATION
Grafek Direct
Dupli Park Dr (13218)
P.O. Box 11500 (13218-1500)
PHONE..............................315 422-4732
Kemper J Matt, *President*
Robert Cuthill, *Sales Executive*
EMP: 8
SALES (corp-wide): 49.5MM **Privately Held**
WEB: www.duplionline.com
SIC: 2759 2752 Envelopes: printing; commercial printing, offset
HQ: Dupli Graphics Corporation
6761 Thompson Rd
Syracuse NY 13211
315 234-7286

(G-14879)
DYNAMIC HYBIRDS INC
1201 E Fayette St Ste 11 (13210-1933)
PHONE..............................315 426-8110
Don Hazelmyer, *President*
EMP: 7
SQ FT: 2,500
SALES (est): 1MM **Privately Held**
WEB: www.hybridcircuit.com
SIC: 3679 Electronic circuits

(G-14880)
EAGLE MEDIA PARTNERS LP (PA)
Also Called: Eagle Newspapers
2501 James St Ste 100 (13206-2996)
PHONE..............................315 434-8889
H Douglas Barclay, *Partner*
Edward S Green, *Partner*
Stewart Hancock, *Partner*
David Northrup, *Partner*
EMP: 33
SQ FT: 7,000
SALES (est): 3.6MM **Privately Held**
WEB: www.cnylink.com
SIC: 2711 Commercial printing & newspaper publishing combined; newspapers, publishing & printing

(G-14881)
EASTWOOD LITHO IMPRESSIONS LLC
4020 New Court Ave (13206-1663)
P.O. Box 131 (13206-0131)
PHONE..............................315 437-2626
Patrick Mohr, *Treasurer*
Chris Cox, *Controller*
Cathy Tracey, *Sales Staff*
Christina Huebner, *Marketing Mgr*
EMP: 14
SALES (est): 2.8MM **Privately Held**
SIC: 2759 2752 2791 2789 Letterpress printing; commercial printing, lithographic; typesetting; bookbinding & related work

(G-14882)
EATON CORPORATION
Also Called: Ephesus Lighting
125 E Jefferson St (13202-2020)
PHONE..............................315 579-2872
Anthony Saraceni, *Business Mgr*
Terry Tuper, *Engineer*
Michael Quijano, *Director*
EMP: 30 **Privately Held**
SIC: 3645 Fluorescent lighting fixtures, residential
HQ: Eaton Corporation
1000 Eaton Blvd
Cleveland OH 44122
440 523-5000

(G-14883)
EATONS CROUSE HINDS BUSINESS
1201 Wolf St (13208-1375)
PHONE..............................315 477-7000
EMP: 17
SALES (est): 2.9MM **Privately Held**
SIC: 3625 Mfg Relays/Industrial Controls

(G-14884)
ELEVATOR INTERIORS INC
1116 S Salina St (13202-3517)
PHONE..............................315 218-7186
Joe Piepho, *President*

Christopher J Duke, *President*
James E Cosbey, *Vice Pres*
EMP: 20
SQ FT: 5,000
SALES: 6MM **Privately Held**
SIC: 3534 Elevators & equipment

(G-14885)
ELIZABETH WOOD
Also Called: Endoscopic Procedure Center
4900 Broad Rd (13215-2265)
PHONE..............................315 492-5470
Elizabeth Wood, *Principal*
EMP: 5
SALES (est): 905.2K **Privately Held**
SIC: 3845 Endoscopic equipment, electromedical

(G-14886)
ELTON EL MANTLE INC
6072 Court Street Rd (13206-1711)
P.O. Box 3166 (13220-3166)
PHONE..............................315 432-9067
Elton Mantle, *President*
EMP: 5 **EST:** 2000
SALES (est): 356.3K **Privately Held**
SIC: 3621 Motors, electric

(G-14887)
EMPIRE BREWING COMPANY INC
120 Walton St (13202-1571)
PHONE..............................315 925-8308
David Katleski, *President*
Kregg Schuster, *Manager*
Karen Katleski, *Supervisor*
EMP: 64
SALES: 3MM **Privately Held**
SIC: 2082 5812 Ale (alcoholic beverage); American restaurant

(G-14888)
EMPIRE DIVISION INC
201 Kirkpatrick St # 207 (13208-2075)
PHONE..............................315 476-6273
Vincent Williams, *President*
EMP: 72
SQ FT: 9,000
SALES (est): 5MM **Privately Held**
SIC: 3589 3621 5063 5064 Vacuum cleaners & sweepers, electric: industrial; water purification equipment, household type; motors, electric; motors, electric; vacuum cleaners, household; water purification equipment; cleaning equipment & supplies; motors, electric; water purification equipment

(G-14889)
ERHARD & GILCHER INC
235 Cortland Ave (13202-3825)
P.O. Box 84 (13209-0084)
PHONE..............................315 474-1072
Peter Coyne, *President*
Rosemary Coyne, *Corp Secy*
Lance McGee, *Vice Pres*
EMP: 35 **EST:** 1913
SQ FT: 25,000
SALES (est): 3.6MM **Privately Held**
SIC: 2789 Bookbinding & related work

(G-14890)
EVERGREEN CORP CENTRAL NY
Also Called: Evergreen Manufacturing
235 Cortland Ave (13202-3825)
PHONE..............................315 454-4175
Rene Musso, *President*
EMP: 18
SQ FT: 4,500
SALES (est): 2.9MM **Privately Held**
SIC: 3544 2759 Paper cutting dies; commercial printing

(G-14891)
EXCEL ALUMINUM PRODUCTS INC
563 N Salina St (13208-2530)
PHONE..............................315 471-0925
Frank Tafel Jr, *President*
Raymond Tafel, *Admin Sec*
EMP: 5
SQ FT: 2,000

SALES: 250K **Privately Held**
SIC: 3442 5031 Storm doors or windows, metal; windows; doors

(G-14892)
FALSO INDUSTRIES INC
Also Called: Falso Metal Fabricating
4100 New Court Ave (13206-1698)
P.O. Box 6129 (13217-6129)
PHONE..............................315 463-0266
Raymond Falso, *President*
Dean Sharron, *General Mgr*
Richard Iorio, *Corp Secy*
Norb Kieffer, *Plant Mgr*
Steve Sleight, *QC Mgr*
EMP: 20
SQ FT: 19,000
SALES (est): 3.8MM **Privately Held**
WEB: www.falsoindustries.com
SIC: 3444 Sheet metalwork

(G-14893)
FELDMEIER EQUIPMENT INC (PA)
6800 Townline Rd (13211-1325)
P.O. Box 474 (13211-0474)
PHONE..............................315 823-2000
Robert E Feldmeier, *CEO*
Robert Feldmeier, *Vice Pres*
Jean Jackson, *Vice Pres*
David Pollock, *Vice Pres*
Ken Osborne, *Plant Mgr*
EMP: 100 **EST:** 1953
SQ FT: 60,000
SALES (est): 94.1MM **Privately Held**
WEB: www.feldmeier.com
SIC: 3443 Tanks, standard or custom fabricated: metal plate

(G-14894)
FORTECH INC
Also Called: Fortech Div
223 4th North St (13208-1299)
PHONE..............................315 478-2048
Adrian E Ferraris, *President*
Betty Ferraris, *Vice Pres*
EMP: 8
SQ FT: 26,000
SALES (est): 715K **Privately Held**
WEB: www.fortechfab.com
SIC: 3599 Machine & other job shop work

(G-14895)
FRAZER & JONES CO
Also Called: Frasier and Jones
3000 Milton Ave (13209)
P.O. Box 4955 (13221-4955)
PHONE..............................315 468-6251
Mark Novakowski, *Principal*
Stan Newsome, *Plant Supt*
Deborah Kinville, *Human Res Mgr*
Muhamed Ramic, *Manager*
Ronke Onalaja, *Consultant*
EMP: 90
SQ FT: 182,784
SALES (est): 9.7MM **Privately Held**
WEB: www.frazerandjones.com
SIC: 3325 Steel foundries

(G-14896)
FUTON CITY DISCOUNTERS INC
Also Called: Sleep Master
6361 Thompson Rd (13206-1448)
PHONE..............................315 437-1328
Charles Vanpatten, *President*
EMP: 18
SALES (est): 3.4MM **Privately Held**
SIC: 2599 5712 Factory furniture & fixtures; furniture stores

(G-14897)
G A BRAUN INC
461 E Brighton Ave (13210-4143)
P.O. Box 3029 (13220-3029)
PHONE..............................315 475-3123
Steve Bregande, *Principal*
Jim Corrigan, *Vice Pres*
Gary Ostrum, *VP Sales*
CJ Spencer, *Regl Sales Mgr*
Matt Gallagher, *Sales Staff*
EMP: 25
SALES (corp-wide): 45.7MM **Privately Held**
SIC: 3582 Commercial laundry equipment

PA: G. A. Braun, Inc.
79 General Irwin Blvd
North Syracuse NY 13212
315 475-3123

(G-14898)
G C HANFORD
MANUFACTURING CO (PA)
Also Called: Hanford Pharmaceuticals
304 Oneida St (13202-3433)
P.O. Box 1017 (13201-1017)
PHONE....................................315 476-7418
George R Hanford, *Principal*
George W Hanford, *Principal*
Joseph J Heath, *Principal*
Peter Ward, *Principal*
Ronald Lauback, *Vice Pres*
EMP: 186 **EST:** 1846
SQ FT: 80,000
SALES (est): 48.4MM **Privately Held**
WEB: www.hanford.com
SIC: 2834 2833 5122 Penicillin preparations; antibiotics; pharmaceuticals

(G-14899)
GARDALL SAFE CORPORATION
219 Lamson St Ste 1 (13206-2879)
P.O. Box 240 (13206-0240)
PHONE....................................315 432-9115
Edward Baroody, *Ch of Bd*
David A Patton, *Treasurer*
Jim Riccardi, *Director*
Cathy Necsi,
◆ **EMP:** 25 **EST:** 1950
SQ FT: 85,000
SALES (est): 4.9MM **Privately Held**
WEB: www.gardall.com
SIC: 3499 Safes & vaults, metal

(G-14900)
GARDNER DNVER
OBERDORFER PUMPS
5900 Firestone Dr (13206-1103)
PHONE....................................315 437-0361
Robin Watkins, *Principal*
Rick Cadotte, *Director*
▲ **EMP:** 30
SQ FT: 50,000
SALES (est): 5.2MM
SALES (corp-wide): 2.6B **Publicly Held**
SIC: 3561 Industrial pumps & parts
HQ: Gardner Denver, Inc.
222 E Erie St Ste 500
Milwaukee WI 53202

(G-14901)
GEAR MOTIONS
INCORPORATED (PA)
Also Called: Nixon Gear
1750 Milton Ave (13209-1626)
PHONE....................................315 488-0100
Samuel R Haines, *President*
Dean Burroes, *President*
EMP: 50 **EST:** 1973
SQ FT: 45,000
SALES (est): 18MM **Privately Held**
WEB: www.gearmotions.com
SIC: 3462 Gears, forged steel

(G-14902)
GENERAL ELECTRIC COMPANY
5990 E Molloy Rd (13211)
PHONE....................................315 456-3304
Matthew J Battle, *Branch Mgr*
EMP: 20
SQ FT: 8,000
SALES (corp-wide): 121.6B **Publicly Held**
SIC: 7694 Electric motor repair
PA: General Electric Company
41 Farnsworth St
Boston MA 02210
617 443-3000

(G-14903)
GENERATION POWER LLC
238 W Division St (13204-1412)
PHONE....................................315 234-2451
Steve Starrantino, *Vice Pres*
Bob Zywicki,
Jay Bernhardt,
EMP: 9
SALES (est): 1.8MM **Privately Held**
SIC: 3621 Motors & generators

(G-14904)
GEORGE RETZOS
Also Called: Columbus Baking Co
502 Pearl St (13203-1702)
PHONE....................................315 422-2913
James Retzos, *Owner*
EMP: 5 **EST:** 1934
SALES (est): 485.6K **Privately Held**
SIC: 2051 Bread, all types (white, wheat, rye, etc): fresh or frozen

(G-14905)
GREENLEAF CABINET MAKERS
LLC
6691 Pickard Dr (13211-2114)
PHONE....................................315 432-4600
Gerard Davis, *Mng Member*
EMP: 10 **EST:** 2001
SQ FT: 3,000
SALES (est): 1.5MM **Privately Held**
SIC: 2541 Wood partitions & fixtures

(G-14906)
H C YOUNG TOOL & MACHINE
CO
3700 New Court Ave (13206-1674)
PHONE....................................315 463-0663
Gordon K Young, *President*
EMP: 5 **EST:** 1935
SQ FT: 1,000
SALES (est): 553K **Privately Held**
WEB: www.hcyoung.com
SIC: 3599 Machine shop, jobbing & repair

(G-14907)
HANGER PROSTHETICS &
Also Called: Hanger Clinic
522 Liberty St 1 (13204-1249)
PHONE....................................315 492-6608
Vinit Asar, *Branch Mgr*
EMP: 5
SALES (corp-wide): 1B **Publicly Held**
SIC: 3842 Surgical appliances & supplies
HQ: Hanger Prosthetics & Orthotics East, Inc.
33 North Ave Ste 101
Tallmadge OH 44278

(G-14908)
HANGER PRSTHETCS & ORTHO
INC
910 Erie Blvd E Ste 3 (13210-1060)
PHONE....................................315 472-5200
Roy Ostrander, *Manager*
EMP: 5
SALES (corp-wide): 1B **Publicly Held**
SIC: 3842 Limbs, artificial
HQ: Hanger Prosthetics & Orthotics, Inc.
10910 Domain Dr Ste 300
Austin TX 78758
512 777-3800

(G-14909)
HARRISON BAKERY WEST
1306 W Genesee St (13204-2184)
PHONE....................................315 422-1468
James Rothfeld, *President*
EMP: 30
SQ FT: 15,000
SALES (est): 5.2MM **Privately Held**
SIC: 2051 5461 Bread, all types (white, wheat, rye, etc): fresh or frozen; cakes; bakery: except frozen; doughnuts, except frozen; bread; cakes; doughnuts

(G-14910)
HART RIFLE BARREL INC
1680 Jamesville Ave (13210-4236)
P.O. Box 182, La Fayette (13084-0182)
PHONE....................................315 677-9841
Jack Sutton, *Partner*
James Hart, *Partner*
EMP: 7 **EST:** 1955
SQ FT: 2,000
SALES: 750K **Privately Held**
WEB: www.hartbarrels.com
SIC: 3484 Rifles or rifle parts, 30 mm. & below

(G-14911)
HERALD NEWSPAPERS
COMPANY INC (HQ)
Also Called: Post Standard, The
220 S Warren St (13202-1676)
PHONE....................................315 470-0011
Tim Kennedy, *President*
Rachael Raney, *Publisher*
Logan Martinez, *Editor*
Stephen A Rogers, *Chairman*
Donald E Newhouse, *Treasurer*
EMP: 612
SQ FT: 50,000
SALES (est): 342.5MM
SALES (corp-wide): 5.5B **Privately Held**
WEB: www.post-standard.com
SIC: 2711 Commercial printing & newspaper publishing combined
PA: Advance Publications, Inc.
1 World Trade Ctr Fl 43
New York NY 10007
718 981-1234

(G-14912)
HY-GRADE METAL PRODUCTS
CORP
906 Burnet Ave (13203-3206)
PHONE....................................315 475-4221
Michael Donegan, *President*
EMP: 7
SQ FT: 10,000
SALES (est): 544.5K **Privately Held**
WEB: www.hy-grademetal.com
SIC: 3469 Spinning metal for the trade

(G-14913)
INDEPENDENT FIELD SVC LLC
(PA)
6744 Pickard Dr (13211-2115)
PHONE....................................315 559-9243
Aaron Barbaro, *Owner*
EMP: 7
SQ FT: 8,000
SALES (est): 1.3MM **Privately Held**
SIC: 3621 Power generators

(G-14914)
J & J PRINTING INC (PA)
500 Cambridge Ave (13208-1415)
PHONE....................................315 458-7411
Matthew Joseph Farr, *President*
Betty Farr, *Vice Pres*
EMP: 10 **EST:** 1969
SQ FT: 3,000
SALES (est): 1.6MM **Privately Held**
SIC: 2752 Commercial printing, offset

(G-14915)
JACOBS WOODWORKING LLC
801 W Fayette St (13204-2805)
PHONE....................................315 427-8999
Jacob Gerros, *Mng Member*
EMP: 7
SALES (est): 632.5K **Privately Held**
SIC: 2431 Millwork

(G-14916)
JAQUITH INDUSTRIES INC
600 E Brighton Ave (13210-4248)
PHONE....................................315 478-5700
D Scott Jaquith, *President*
Adam Antczak, *Buyer*
Mark Peck, *CFO*
Jeff Waful,
Giovanna Whalen, *Assistant*
◆ **EMP:** 50
SQ FT: 120,000
SALES: 10.1MM **Privately Held**
WEB: www.jaquith.com
SIC: 3312 3648 3728 3444 Blast furnaces & steel mills; lighting equipment; aircraft parts & equipment; sheet metalwork; fabricated plate work (boiler shop); manufactured hardware (general)

(G-14917)
JOHN A EBERLY INC
136 Beattie St (13224-1102)
P.O. Box 149, Pompey (13138-0149)
PHONE....................................315 449-3034
John Lee, *President*
EMP: 7 **EST:** 1912
SQ FT: 6,000
SALES (est): 1.3MM **Privately Held**
WEB: www.jaeberly.com
SIC: 3421 5084 Scissors, shears, clippers, snips & similar tools; textile machinery & equipment

(G-14918)
JOHN F KRELL JR
Also Called: Syracuse Hvac
4046 W Seneca Trpk (13215)
PHONE....................................315 492-3201
John F Krell, *Partner*
Andrew Krell, *Partner*
EMP: 5
SALES (est): 609.8K **Privately Held**
SIC: 3585 Heating & air conditioning combination units

(G-14919)
JOHNSTON DANDY COMPANY
Cook, E F Co
100 Dippold Ave (13208-1320)
PHONE....................................315 455-5773
Michael Myers, *General Mgr*
Kimberly Pinkham, *Controller*
EMP: 7
SQ FT: 12,540
SALES (est): 1.1MM
SALES (corp-wide): 10.4MM **Privately Held**
WEB: www.johnstondandy.com
SIC: 3547 3554 Rolling mill machinery; paper industries machinery
PA: Johnston Dandy Company
148 Main St
Lincoln ME 04457
207 794-6571

(G-14920)
JORDON BOX COMPANY INC
Also Called: Jordan Box Co
140 Dickerson St (13202-2309)
P.O. Box 1054 (13201-1054)
PHONE....................................315 422-3419
Rick Casper, *President*
EMP: 20
SQ FT: 30,000
SALES: 700K **Privately Held**
WEB: www.jordanboxco.com
SIC: 2652 Setup paperboard boxes

(G-14921)
JOY EDWARD COMPANY
Also Called: Joy Process Mechanical
105 Enderberry Cir (13224-2003)
PHONE....................................315 474-3360
Leonard P Markert III, *CEO*
Cindy Ryan, *Controller*
Lyn Markert Hathaway, *Admin Sec*
EMP: 40 **EST:** 1875
SQ FT: 40,000
SALES (est): 15.8MM **Privately Held**
SIC: 3441 1711 Fabricated structural metal; mechanical contractor

(G-14922)
JPW STRUCTURAL
CONTRACTING INC
Also Called: Jpw Riggers & Erectors
6376 Thompson Rd (13206-1406)
PHONE....................................315 432-1111
John P Wozniczka III, *Ch of Bd*
Patricia Wozniczka, *Corp Secy*
Don Feola, *Exec VP*
Jody Wozniczka, *Vice Pres*
Drew Given, *Engineer*
EMP: 25
SQ FT: 70,000
SALES (est): 8.1MM **Privately Held**
SIC: 3441 Fabricated structural metal

(G-14923)
K&G OF SYRACUSE INC
2500 Erie Blvd E (13224-1110)
PHONE....................................315 446-1921
Karamjit Grewal, *Principal*
EMP: 5
SALES (est): 526.1K **Privately Held**
SIC: 3578 Automatic teller machines (ATM)

(G-14924)
KASSIS SUPERIOR SIGN CO
INC
6699 Old Thompson Rd (13211-2118)
PHONE....................................315 463-7446
Joseph Kassis, *CEO*
Anthony Sklaney, *CFO*
Edda Kassis, *Admin Sec*
Cristina Caceres, *Admin Asst*
EMP: 19

SALES (est): 4.5MM **Privately Held**
WEB: www.kassissigns.com
SIC: **3444** 5039 Sheet metalwork; awnings

(G-14925)
KILIAN MANUFACTURING CORP (HQ)
1728 Burnet Ave (13206-3340)
P.O. Box 6974 (13217-6974)
PHONE..................................315 432-0700
Don Wierbinski, *President*
David Bourdeau, *Engineer*
Richard Mitchell, *Engineer*
David Sheridan, *Controller*
Keith Flynn, *Human Res Mgr*
▲ EMP: 73 EST: 1921
SQ FT: 100,000
SALES (est): 70.2MM
SALES (corp-wide): 1.1B **Publicly Held**
SIC: **3562** 3429 Ball bearings & parts; manufactured hardware (general)
PA: Altra Industrial Motion Corp.
    300 Granite St Ste 201
    Braintree MA 02184
    781 917-0600

(G-14926)
KINANECO INC (PA)
Also Called: Kinaneco Printing Systems
2925 Milton Ave (13209-2519)
PHONE..................................315 468-6201
Greg Kinane, *Chairman*
Peter T Kinane, *Chairman*
Gail Foster, *Accounting Mgr*
Gregory Kinane, *Human Res Dir*
Paul Manganiello, *Manager*
EMP: 20 EST: 1973
SQ FT: 6,000
SALES (est): 3.6MM **Privately Held**
WEB: www.kinaneco.com
SIC: **2759** 2752 7311 2754 Business forms; printing; commercial printing, offset; advertising agencies; color printing, gravure

(G-14927)
KNISE & KRICK INC
324 Pearl St (13203-1998)
P.O. Box 6508 (13217-6508)
PHONE..................................315 422-3516
John P Extrom, *President*
Beth Moore, *Admin Sec*
EMP: 20 EST: 1926
SQ FT: 30,000
SALES (est): 3.3MM **Privately Held**
WEB: www.knisekrick.com
SIC: **3544** 7389 3599 Jigs & fixtures; metal cutting services; machine & other job shop work

(G-14928)
KODIAK CUTTING TOOLS LLC
2700 Bellevue Ave (13219-3238)
PHONE..................................800 892-1006
Edward Nolan, *Mng Member*
EMP: 5
SQ FT: 2,000
SALES (est): 244.3K **Privately Held**
SIC: **3541** Machine tools, metal cutting type

(G-14929)
LEADING ELEMENT LLC
247 W Fayette St Ste 302 (13202-2251)
PHONE..................................315 479-8790
EMP: 5
SALES (est): 482.4K **Privately Held**
SIC: **2819** Elements

(G-14930)
LEMOYNE MACHINE PRODUCTS CORP
106 Evelyn Ter (13208-1321)
PHONE..................................315 454-0708
Marvin Kisselstein, *President*
Robert Grandinetti, *Vice Pres*
EMP: 5
SQ FT: 5,000
SALES (est): 643.1K **Privately Held**
SIC: **3562** Ball & roller bearings

(G-14931)
LIBERTY FOOD AND FUEL
1131 N Salina St (13208-2027)
PHONE..................................315 299-4039

Anwa Nagnaji, *Manager*
EMP: 6
SALES (est): 766.4K **Privately Held**
SIC: **2869** Fuels

(G-14932)
LIFT SAFE - FUEL SAFE INC
515 E Brighton Ave (13210-4210)
PHONE..................................315 423-7702
Daniel Sorber, *CEO*
EMP: 5
SALES (est): 1.1MM **Privately Held**
SIC: **2869** Fuels

(G-14933)
LINDE GAS NORTH AMERICA LLC
Also Called: Lifegas
147 Midler Park Dr (13206-1817)
PHONE..................................315 431-4081
Richard Kelley, *Branch Mgr*
EMP: 19 **Privately Held**
SIC: **2813** Nitrogen; oxygen, compressed or liquefied
HQ: Linde Gas North America Llc
    200 Somerset Corp Blvd # 7000
    Bridgewater NJ 08807

(G-14934)
LOCKHEED MARTIN CORPORATION
6060 Tarbell Rd (13206-1301)
PHONE..................................315 456-6604
Mark Schmidt, *Branch Mgr*
EMP: 45 **Publicly Held**
WEB: www.lockheedmartin.com
SIC: **3812** Sonar systems & equipment; radar systems & equipment
PA: Lockheed Martin Corporation
    6801 Rockledge Dr
    Bethesda MD 20817

(G-14935)
LOCKHEED MARTIN INTEGRTD SYSTM
497 Electronics Pkwy (13221)
P.O. Box 4840 (13221-4840)
PHONE..................................315 456-3333
EMP: 26 **Publicly Held**
SIC: **3812** Search & navigation equipment
HQ: Lockheed Martin Integrated Systems, Llc
    6801 Rockledge Dr
    Bethesda MD 20817

(G-14936)
LOUIS IANNETTONI
1841 Lemoyne Ave (13208-1328)
PHONE..................................315 454-3231
Louis Iannettoni, *Owner*
EMP: 65
SALES (est): 4.5MM **Privately Held**
SIC: **3363** Aluminum die-castings

(G-14937)
M & W ALUMINUM PRODUCTS INC
321 Wavel St (13206-1726)
PHONE..................................315 414-0005
Uriah P Montclair, *President*
EMP: 16
SQ FT: 12,330
SALES (est): 2.7MM **Privately Held**
WEB: www.mwalum.com
SIC: **3465** Body parts, automobile: stamped metal

(G-14938)
MATT INDUSTRIES INC (PA)
Also Called: Grphics Grafek
6761 Thompson Rd (13211-2119)
P.O. Box 11500 (13218-1500)
PHONE..................................315 472-1316
J Kemper Matt, *President*
David Martin, *Division Mgr*
Thomas Booth, *Vice Pres*
Tom Booth, *Vice Pres*
John Mather, *Vice Pres*
EMP: 120
SQ FT: 150,000
SALES (est): 49.5MM **Privately Held**
SIC: **2759** 5112 Envelopes: printing; envelopes

(G-14939)
MELOON FOUNDRIES LLC
1841 Lemoyne Ave (13208-1389)
PHONE..................................315 454-3231
Robert Evans, *President*
Cecelia Bleich, *Office Mgr*
EMP: 42
SQ FT: 90,000
SALES (est): 9.6MM
SALES (corp-wide): 43.7MM **Privately Held**
SIC: **3365** 3366 3291 Aluminum foundries; copper foundries; brass foundry; bronze foundry; abrasive products
HQ: Evans Industries, Inc.
    200 Renaissance Ctr # 3150
    Detroit MI 48243
    313 259-2266

(G-14940)
METALICO ALUMINUM RECOVERY INC
Also Called: Metalico Syracuse
6223 Thompson Rd (13206-1405)
P.O. Box 88, East Syracuse (13057-0088)
PHONE..................................315 463-9500
Carlos E Aguero, *President*
Michael J Drury, *COO*
Arnold S Graber, *Exec VP*
David Delbianco, *Vice Pres*
Mike Drury, *Vice Pres*
▲ EMP: 40
SALES (est): 9.7MM
SALES (corp-wide): 110.2MM **Privately Held**
SIC: **3341** 5093 Aluminum smelting & refining (secondary); scrap & waste materials
PA: Metalico, Inc.
    135 Dermody St
    Cranford NJ 07016
    908 497-9610

(G-14941)
MIDDLE AGES BREWING COMPANY
120 Wilkinson St Ste 1 (13204-2490)
PHONE..................................315 476-4250
Mary Rubenstein, *President*
Isaac Rubenstein, *Vice Pres*
Marc Rubenstein, *Treasurer*
Jason Allen, *Sales Mgr*
Matt Vogelsang, *Manager*
▲ EMP: 6
SQ FT: 10,000
SALES (est): 658K **Privately Held**
SIC: **2082** Beer (alcoholic beverage)

(G-14942)
MIDGLEY PRINTING CORP
433 W Onondaga St (13202-3277)
PHONE..................................315 475-1864
Lena Midgley, *President*
David Midgley, *Vice Pres*
Bruce Midgley, *Admin Sec*
EMP: 9 EST: 1955
SQ FT: 10,000
SALES (est): 1.1MM **Privately Held**
SIC: **2752** 2759 2791 2789 Commercial printing, offset; letterpress printing; typesetting; bookbinding & related work

(G-14943)
MIDSTATE SPRING INC
Also Called: Syracuse Midstate Spring
4054 New Court Ave (13206-1639)
P.O. Box 850 (13206-0850)
PHONE..................................315 437-2623
Walter Melnikow, *President*
John Kirby, *General Mgr*
Mike Komurek, *COO*
Paul S Bernet, *Vice Pres*
Keith Miller, *Production*
▲ EMP: 41
SQ FT: 13,000
SALES (est): 10.2MM **Privately Held**
WEB: www.midstatespring.com
SIC: **3493** 3495 Steel springs, except wire; wire springs

(G-14944)
MINIMILL TECHNOLOGIES INC
5792 Widewaters Pkwy # 1 (13214-1847)
PHONE..................................315 692-4557

Kamala G Rajan, *President*
Joseph Gasperetti, *Senior VP*
Srinivasan Balaji, *Vice Pres*
Donnie Parks, *Vice Pres*
George Rice, *Vice Pres*
EMP: 14
SALES: 6MM **Privately Held**
SIC: **2621** Paper mills

(G-14945)
MITTEN MANUFACTURING INC (PA)
5960 Court Street Rd (13206-1706)
PHONE..................................315 437-7564
John P Mitten Jr, *CEO*
Jack Mitten, *Principal*
Michele McBride-Liu, *Vice Pres*
EMP: 18
SALES (est): 3.4MM **Privately Held**
SIC: **3999** Atomizers, toiletry

(G-14946)
MONAGHAN MEDICAL CORPORATION
Also Called: Sales & Marketing Office
327 W Fayette St Ste 214 (13202-1516)
PHONE..................................315 472-2136
Michael Amato, *Vice Pres*
EMP: 8
SALES (corp-wide): 9.9MM **Privately Held**
WEB: www.monaghanmed.com
SIC: **3842** Respiratory protection equipment, personal
PA: Monaghan Medical Corporation
    5 Latour Ave Ste 1600
    Plattsburgh NY 12901
    518 561-7330

(G-14947)
MUENCH-KREUZER CANDLE COMPANY (PA)
Also Called: Emkay Candle Company
617 Hiawatha Blvd E (13208-1228)
PHONE..................................315 471-4515
John P Brogan, *Ch of Bd*
▲ EMP: 80
SQ FT: 100,000
SALES (est): 9.9MM **Privately Held**
WEB: www.emkaycandle.com
SIC: **3999** Candles

(G-14948)
MUZET INC
104 S Main St (13212-3104)
PHONE..................................315 452-0050
Frank Crawford, *Manager*
EMP: 10
SALES (corp-wide): 2.2MM **Privately Held**
SIC: **3931** Musical instruments
PA: Muzet Inc
    219 W Commercial St
    East Rochester NY 14445
    585 586-5320

(G-14949)
N E CONTROLS LLC
7048 Interstate Island Rd (13209-9712)
PHONE..................................315 626-2480
Mike Daniluk, *Production*
Mary Longman, *Engineer*
Anthony Taro, *Engineer*
Brad Stone, *Sales Mgr*
Al Weaver,
EMP: 12
SQ FT: 6,000
SALES: 950K **Privately Held**
WEB: www.necontrols.com
SIC: **3625** 5084 Control equipment, electric; industrial machinery & equipment

(G-14950)
NEPTUNE SOFT WATER INC
1201 E Fayette St Ste 6 (13210-1896)
PHONE..................................315 446-5151
William Olivieri, *President*
EMP: 15 EST: 1963
SQ FT: 4,500
SALES (est): 2.4MM **Privately Held**
SIC: **3589** 5999 5074 Water treatment equipment, industrial; water purification equipment, household type; water purification equipment; water purification equipment

▲ = Import ▼=Export
◆ =Import/Export

(G-14951)
NEW YORK MARKING DEVICES CORP (PA)
Also Called: Jessel Marking Equipment
2207 Teall Ave (13206-1544)
P.O. Box 234 (13206-0234)
PHONE..............................315 463-8641
Joseph L Stummer Jr, *President*
Amy Stummer, *Vice Pres*
Ellen Stummer, *Vice Pres*
Peter J Stummer, *Vice Pres*
Kathy Stummer, *Office Mgr*
EMP: 14
SQ FT: 7,800
SALES: 1.7MM **Privately Held**
WEB: www.nymarking.com
SIC: 3953 Embossing seals & hand stamps

(G-14952)
OBERDORFER PUMPS INC
5900 Firestone Dr (13206-1103)
PHONE..............................315 437-0361
Kevin Digney, *CEO*
Timothy C Brown, *President*
Phillip J Stuecker, *Vice Pres*
EMP: 43
SQ FT: 46,000
SALES (est): 10.4MM
SALES (corp-wide): 2.6B **Publicly Held**
WEB: www.oberdorfer-pumps.com
SIC: 3561 Industrial pumps & parts
HQ: Gardner Denver, Inc.
222 E Erie St Ste 500
Milwaukee WI 53202

(G-14953)
OESTREICH METAL WORKS INC
6131 Court Street Rd (13206-1302)
PHONE..............................315 463-4268
Steve Tallman, *President*
EMP: 5
SQ FT: 4,000
SALES (est): 588.2K **Privately Held**
SIC: 3564 Blowing fans: industrial or commercial; ventilating fans: industrial or commercial; exhaust fans: industrial or commercial

(G-14954)
OMEGA FURNITURE MANUFACTURING
102 Wavel St (13206-1303)
PHONE..............................315 463-7428
George Sakellariou, *President*
EMP: 12
SQ FT: 10,000
SALES (est): 600K **Privately Held**
WEB: www.omegafmi.com
SIC: 2521 5712 Wood office furniture; furniture stores

(G-14955)
ONE TREE DIST
200 Midler Park Dr (13206-1819)
P.O. Box 373 (13206-0373)
PHONE..............................315 701-2924
EMP: 6
SALES (est): 690.9K **Privately Held**
SIC: 2421 Building & structural materials, wood

(G-14956)
ONEIDA AIR SYSTEMS INC
1001 W Fayette St Ste 2a (13204-2873)
PHONE..............................315 476-5151
Robert Witter, *President*
Jen McManus, *Controller*
◆ **EMP:** 50
SQ FT: 60,000
SALES (est): 13.5MM **Privately Held**
WEB: www.oneida-air.com
SIC: 3553 3564 Woodworking machinery; purification & dust collection equipment

(G-14957)
OPTOGENICS OF SYRACUSE INC
2840 Erie Blvd E (13224-1304)
P.O. Box 4894 (13221-4894)
PHONE..............................315 446-3000
Kurt Schrantz, *President*
Yani Alvarez, *Marketing Mgr*
Marybeth Busch, *Manager*
Jarrid Pearson, *Manager*
EMP: 100
SQ FT: 7,000
SALES (est): 13.2MM
SALES (corp-wide): 1.4MM **Privately Held**
WEB: www.optogenics.com
SIC: 3851 Eyeglasses, lenses & frames
HQ: Essilor Laboratories Of America, Inc.
13515 N Stemmons Fwy
Dallas TX 75234
972 241-4141

(G-14958)
P C I PAPER CONVERSIONS INC (HQ)
3584 Walters Rd (13209-9700)
PHONE..............................315 437-1641
Lloyd M Withers, *President*
Matthew Withers, *Vice Pres*
Raymond Ryan, *Treasurer*
Jill Ladd, *Manager*
Richard Bedford, *Maintence Staff*
◆ **EMP:** 120 **EST:** 1973
SQ FT: 121,300
SALES (est): 19.8MM
SALES (corp-wide): 49.5MM **Privately Held**
WEB: www.riverleaf.com
SIC: 2679 2678 2672 Paper products, converted; stationery products; coated & laminated paper
PA: Matt Industries Inc.
6761 Thompson Rd
Syracuse NY 13211
315 472-1316

(G-14959)
P C I PAPER CONVERSIONS INC
Stik-Withit Printworks
6761 Thompson Rd (13211-2119)
PHONE..............................315 703-8300
Howard Kaye, *Managing Dir*
EMP: 100
SALES (corp-wide): 49.5MM **Privately Held**
SIC: 2891 Adhesives & sealants
HQ: P. C. I. Paper Conversions, Inc.
3584 Walters Rd
Syracuse NY 13209
315 437-1641

(G-14960)
P C I PAPER CONVERSIONS INC
Coated Products Division
6761 Thompson Rd (13211-2119)
PHONE..............................315 634-3317
Howard Kaye, *Managing Dir*
Theresa Brown, *Mfg Mgr*
EMP: 25
SALES (corp-wide): 49.5MM **Privately Held**
SIC: 2891 Adhesives & sealants
HQ: P. C. I. Paper Conversions, Inc.
3584 Walters Rd
Syracuse NY 13209
315 437-1641

(G-14961)
P C I PAPER CONVERSIONS INC
Notes
6761 Thompson Rd (13211-2119)
PHONE..............................315 437-1641
Peter McDermott, *Manager*
EMP: 10
SALES (corp-wide): 49.5MM **Privately Held**
SIC: 2679 Novelties, paper: made from purchased material
HQ: P. C. I. Paper Conversions, Inc.
3584 Walters Rd
Syracuse NY 13209
315 437-1641

(G-14962)
PARATORE SIGNS INC
1551 Brewerton Rd (13208-1403)
PHONE..............................315 455-5551
John Paratore, *CEO*
Ian Vincent, *Prdtn Mgr*
Valoree Paratore, *VP Sls/Mktg*
Paige J Paratore, *Treasurer*
EMP: 6 **EST:** 1950
SQ FT: 13,000

SALES (est): 783.9K **Privately Held**
WEB: www.paratoresigns.com
SIC: 2759 7389 Screen printing; sign painting & lettering shop

(G-14963)
PASS & SEYMOUR INC (DH)
50 Boyd Ave (13209-2313)
P.O. Box 4822 (13221-4822)
PHONE..............................315 468-6211
Halsey Cook, *CEO*
Greg Janes, *President*
Steve Schoffstall, *Principal*
Thomas Garrett, *District Mgr*
Mark Sapyta, *District Mgr*
▼ **EMP:** 353
SQ FT: 300,000
SALES (est): 379.2MM
SALES (corp-wide): 21.2MM **Privately Held**
WEB: www.passandseymour.com
SIC: 3643 5731 Current-carrying wiring devices; consumer electronic equipment
HQ: Legrand Holding, Inc.
60 Woodlawn St
West Hartford CT 06110
860 233-6251

(G-14964)
PILKINGTON NORTH AMERICA INC
6412 Deere Rd Ste 1 (13206-1133)
PHONE..............................315 438-3341
EMP: 225 **Privately Held**
SIC: 3211 Flat glass
HQ: Pilkington North America, Inc.
811 Madison Ave Fl 3
Toledo OH 43604
419 247-3731

(G-14965)
PINOS PRESS INC
201 E Jefferson St (13202-2644)
PHONE..............................315 935-0110
Maria Marzocchi, *President*
Michael Marzocchi, *Vice Pres*
EMP: 6
SQ FT: 15,000
SALES: 467K **Privately Held**
SIC: 2079 Olive oil

(G-14966)
POST-STANDARD CNY DEPARTMENT
101 N Salina St (13202-1036)
PHONE..............................315 470-2188
Dylan Carpenter, *Accounts Exec*
Madilen Sim, *Sales Staff*
Gerard Carroll, *Adv Mgr*
EMP: 6
SALES (est): 343.6K **Privately Held**
SIC: 2711 Newspapers, publishing & printing

(G-14967)
PRINTING PRMTNAL SOLUTIONS LLC
Also Called: Printing Promotional Solutions
2320 Milton Ave Ste 5 (13209-2197)
PHONE..............................315 474-1110
Todd Ruetsch,
EMP: 17
SALES (est): 2.8MM **Privately Held**
SIC: 2752 Commercial printing, lithographic

(G-14968)
PRINTWORKS PRINTING & DESIGN
5982 E Molloy Rd (13211-2130)
PHONE..............................315 433-8587
Michael Kinsella, *President*
EMP: 5
SALES (est): 475K **Privately Held**
SIC: 2759 Commercial printing

(G-14969)
QUADRANT BIOSCIENCES INC
505 Irving Ave Ste 3100ab (13210-1718)
PHONE..............................315 614-2325
Richard Uhlig, *CEO*
Bryan Greene, *VP Opers*
EMP: 18
SQ FT: 2,600

SALES (est): 749.3K **Privately Held**
SIC: 3845 Patient monitoring apparatus

(G-14970)
R K B OPTO-ELECTRONICS INC (PA)
6677 Moore Rd (13211-2112)
PHONE..............................315 455-6636
Bruce Dobbie, *President*
William Dobbie, *Chairman*
Fay Colvin, *Plant Mgr*
Alex Fern Ndez, *Sales Dir*
Son Hui Yo, *Admin Sec*
EMP: 10
SQ FT: 12,500
SALES (est): 1.6MM **Privately Held**
WEB: www.rkbopto.com
SIC: 3823 3825 Industrial instrmnts msrmnt display/control process variable; instruments to measure electricity

(G-14971)
RAM FABRICATING LLC
412 Wavel St (13206-1728)
PHONE..............................315 437-6654
Charlie Meakin, *Vice Pres*
Mike Skowron, *Engineer*
Drew Lopitz, *Accounts Mgr*
Don Riggs, *Manager*
Cindy Wilcox, *Technology*
EMP: 30
SQ FT: 15,000
SALES (est): 7.2MM **Privately Held**
SIC: 3498 Tube fabricating (contract bending & shaping)

(G-14972)
RAULLI AND SONS INC (PA)
213 Teall Ave (13210-1291)
PHONE..............................315 479-6693
Richie Raulli, *President*
Thomas Raulli, *Vice Pres*
Paul Raulli, *Treasurer*
EMP: 60
SQ FT: 40,000
SALES (est): 17.9MM **Privately Held**
WEB: www.raulliandsons.com
SIC: 3441 3446 Fabricated structural metal; architectural metalwork; gates, ornamental metal; railings, prefabricated metal; stairs, staircases, stair treads: prefabricated metal

(G-14973)
RAULLI AND SONS INC
660 Burnet Ave (13203-2404)
PHONE..............................315 474-1370
Dennis Raulli, *Manager*
Robert Raulli, *Manager*
EMP: 15
SQ FT: 9,276
SALES (corp-wide): 17.9MM **Privately Held**
WEB: www.raulliandsons.com
SIC: 3446 Stairs, staircases, stair treads: prefabricated metal
PA: Raulli And Sons, Inc.
213 Teall Ave
Syracuse NY 13210
315 479-6693

(G-14974)
RAULLI AND SONS INC
920 Canal St (13210-1204)
PHONE..............................315 479-2515
Joseph Ruscitto, *Branch Mgr*
EMP: 7
SALES: 670.6K
SALES (corp-wide): 17.9MM **Privately Held**
SIC: 3291 Abrasive metal & steel products
PA: Raulli And Sons, Inc.
213 Teall Ave
Syracuse NY 13210
315 479-6693

(G-14975)
RB WOODCRAFT INC
1860 Erie Blvd E Ste 1 (13210-1255)
PHONE..............................315 474-2429
Raymond A Brooks, *President*
Bill Arkerson, *Project Dir*
Jeremiah McCadam, *Prdtn Mgr*
Eric Reissig, *Purch Mgr*
Edward Vancott, *Purch Mgr*
EMP: 50

SQ FT: 40,000
SALES (est): 9.3MM Privately Held
WEB: www.rbwoodcraft.com
SIC: 2431 Interior & ornamental woodwork & trim

(G-14976)
REHABLITATION TECH OF SYRACUSE
Also Called: Rehab Tech
1101 Erie Blvd E Ste 209 (13210-1144)
PHONE....................................315 426-9920
Michael T Hall, *President*
Theresa Hall, *Vice Pres*
EMP: 5
SQ FT: 3,000
SALES (est): 747.1K Privately Held
SIC: 3842 Orthopedic appliances; prosthetic appliances

(G-14977)
ROBOSHOP INC
226 Midler Park Dr (13206-1819)
PHONE....................................315 437-6454
Frank Giovinazzo, *President*
Matthew Eddy, *Vice Pres*
Mike Carno, *Sales Engr*
EMP: 7 EST: 1997
SQ FT: 4,500
SALES (est): 500K Privately Held
SIC: 3599 Custom machinery

(G-14978)
ROBS CYCLE SUPPLY
613 Wolf St (13208-1141)
PHONE....................................315 292-6878
Robert Woodward, *President*
EMP: 9
SALES (est): 1MM Privately Held
SIC: 3751 Motorcycles & related parts

(G-14979)
ROTH GLOBAL PLASTICS INC
Also Called: Fralo
1 General Motors Dr (13206-1117)
P.O. Box 245 (13211-0245)
PHONE....................................315 475-0100
Jochen Drewniok, *Ch of Bd*
Joseph Brown, *Senior VP*
Theresa Lauer, *Senior VP*
John Pezzi, *Vice Pres*
▲ EMP: 20 EST: 2007
SQ FT: 100,000
SALES (est): 5.5MM Privately Held
WEB: www.fralo.net
SIC: 3089 Septic tanks, plastic

(G-14980)
ROYAL ADHESIVES & SEALANTS LLC
Also Called: Advanced Polymers Intl
3584 Walters Rd Rsd (13209-9700)
PHONE....................................315 451-1755
Ted Clark, *CEO*
Theresa Brown, *Director*
EMP: 15
SALES (corp-wide): 3B Publicly Held
SIC: 2891 Adhesives & sealants
HQ: Royal Adhesives And Sealants Llc
　　2001 W Washington St
　　South Bend IN 46628
　　574 246-5000

(G-14981)
RVC INC
Also Called: River Valley Paper Co
2801 Court St (13208-3238)
P.O. Box 1911, Akron OH (44309-1911)
PHONE....................................330 631-8320
EMP: 5
SALES (corp-wide): 708.7MM Privately Held
SIC: 2711 Newspapers
HQ: Rvc Inc.
　　120 E Mill St Ste 337
　　Akron OH 44308
　　330 535-1001

(G-14982)
SAAKSHI INC
Also Called: North Salina Cigar Store
851 N Salina St (13208-2512)
PHONE....................................315 475-3988
Jay Vave, *Principal*
EMP: 6

SALES (est): 903K Privately Held
SIC: 3999 Cigarette & cigar products & accessories

(G-14983)
SABRE ENTERPRISES INC
6799 Townline Rd (13211-1904)
P.O. Box 68 (13211-0068)
PHONE....................................315 430-3127
Bob Dumas, *President*
Gerald Vecchiarelli, *Vice Pres*
Scott Wilkinson, *Treasurer*
John White, *Admin Sec*
EMP: 7 EST: 2009
SQ FT: 10,000
SALES (est): 648.2K Privately Held
SIC: 3711 Snow plows (motor vehicles), assembly of

(G-14984)
SAGELIFE PARENTING LLC
Also Called: Sagemylife
235 Harrison St Ste 2 (13202-3119)
PHONE....................................315 299-5713
EMP: 5 EST: 2014
SQ FT: 34,000
SALES (est): 188.5K Privately Held
SIC: 2741 Internet Publishing And Broadcasting

(G-14985)
SANDYS BUMPER MART INC
120 Wall St (13204-2182)
PHONE....................................315 472-8149
Sandor Bozo, *President*
Romana Bozo, *Vice Pres*
Alex Bozo, *Sales Executive*
EMP: 7 EST: 1970
SQ FT: 10,500
SALES (est): 870.4K Privately Held
SIC: 3471 Electroplating of metals or formed products

(G-14986)
SCANCORP INC
1840 Lemoyne Ave (13208-1329)
PHONE....................................315 454-5596
John Clement, *President*
Ole Westergaard, *Vice Pres*
EMP: 16
SQ FT: 35,000
SALES (est): 1.2MM Privately Held
WEB: www.scancorp.com
SIC: 2759 Promotional printing; screen printing

(G-14987)
SCHILLING FORGE INC
606 Factory Ave (13208-1437)
PHONE....................................315 454-4421
Brent A Driscoll, *CEO*
James E Stitt, *Ch of Bd*
Douglas S Pelsue, *President*
John W Whelpley, *Corp Secy*
▲ EMP: 26 EST: 1975
SQ FT: 30,000
SALES (est): 3.2MM
SALES (corp-wide): 148.8MM Privately Held
WEB: www.schillingforge.com
SIC: 3841 3843 3462 3423 Surgical instruments & apparatus; dental equipment & supplies; iron & steel forgings; hand & edge tools; cutlery
PA: Cutco Corporation
　　1116 E State St
　　Olean NY 14760
　　716 372-3111

(G-14988)
SCHNEIDER BROTHERS CORPORATION
7371 Eastman Rd (13212-2504)
PHONE....................................315 458-8369
William D Schneider, *President*
Chris C Schneider, *Corp Secy*
Robert Schneider, *Vice Pres*
EMP: 35
SQ FT: 11,000
SALES (est): 6.6MM Privately Held
SIC: 3441 Fabricated structural metal

(G-14989)
SCIENTIFIC TOOL CO INC
101 Arterial Rd (13206-1585)
PHONE....................................315 431-4243

Duane Krull, *President*
Chuck Gorman, *President*
Dave Spies, *Vice Pres*
▲ EMP: 36
SQ FT: 16,000
SALES (est): 4.8MM Privately Held
SIC: 3599 Machine shop, jobbing & repair

(G-14990)
SEAL & DESIGN INC
Higbee Division
6741 Thompson Rd (13211-2119)
PHONE....................................315 432-8021
Larry Higbee, *President*
EMP: 40
SALES (corp-wide): 49.8MM Privately Held
SIC: 3053 Gaskets, all materials
PA: Seal & Design Inc.
　　4015 Casillio Pkwy
　　Clarence NY 14031
　　716 759-2222

(G-14991)
SECUREIT TACTICAL INC (PA)
6691 Commerce Blvd (13211-2211)
PHONE....................................800 651-8835
Thomas Kubiniec, *President*
EMP: 15
SALES (est): 1.6MM Privately Held
SIC: 3499 Locks, safe & vault: metal

(G-14992)
SELFLOCK SCREW PRODUCTS CO INC
Also Called: SSP
461 E Brighton Ave (13210-4143)
PHONE....................................315 541-4464
David M Freund, *President*
Daniel H Kuhns, *Vice Pres*
EMP: 30 EST: 1920
SQ FT: 50,000
SALES: 4.5MM Privately Held
WEB: www.selflockscrew.com
SIC: 3451 3541 Screw machine products; machine tools, metal cutting type

(G-14993)
SENECA SIGNS LLC
Also Called: Sign-A-Rama
102 Headson Dr (13214-1102)
PHONE....................................315 446-9420
Steve Werner,
EMP: 5
SALES (est): 815K Privately Held
SIC: 3993 Signs & advertising specialties

(G-14994)
SHENFIELD STUDIO LLC
Also Called: Shenfeld Studio Tile
6361 Thompson Rd Stop 12 (13206-1412)
PHONE....................................315 436-8869
Robert C Shenfeld, *Mng Member*
EMP: 10
SALES: 930K Privately Held
SIC: 3292 Floor tile, asphalt

(G-14995)
SMOOTHIES STRAWBERRY NYSF
581 State Fair Blvd (13209-1551)
PHONE....................................315 406-4250
EMP: 5
SALES (est): 183.9K Privately Held
SIC: 2037 Frozen fruits & vegetables

(G-14996)
SPARKCHARGE INC
304 S Franklin St Ste 200 (13202-1529)
PHONE....................................315 480-3645
Joshua Aviv, *CEO*
Richard Whitney, *Engineer*
Christopher Ellis, *CTO*
EMP: 5
SALES (est): 696.8K Privately Held
SIC: 3629 3691 3699 Electronic generation equipment; storage batteries; alkaline cell storage batteries; pulse amplifiers

(G-14997)
SPAULDING LAW PRINTING INC
231 Walton St Ste 103 (13202-1230)
PHONE....................................315 422-4805
Alexander Douglas, *President*
EMP: 3

SQ FT: 1,000
SALES: 1MM Privately Held
SIC: 2759 Commercial printing

(G-14998)
SPECIALTY WLDG & FABG NY INC (PA)
1025 Hiawatha Blvd E (13208-1359)
P.O. Box 145 (13211-0145)
PHONE....................................315 426-1807
Michael P Murphy, *Ch of Bd*
Randal Stier, *President*
Jack Griffiths, *Vice Pres*
Joseph Karaszewski, *QC Mgr*
Jackie Stier, *Admin Sec*
EMP: 61
SQ FT: 135,000
SALES (est): 27.8MM Privately Held
WEB: www.specweld.com
SIC: 3441 Fabricated structural metal

(G-14999)
SRCTEC LLC
5801 E Taft Rd Ste 6 (13212-3275)
PHONE....................................315 452-8700
Drew James, *President*
Mary Hartnett, *Vice Pres*
Robert Bernhardt, *Engineer*
Greg Boehler, *Engineer*
Tom Chappini, *Engineer*
EMP: 150
SALES (est): 34.7MM
SALES (corp-wide): 141.4MM Privately Held
WEB: www.srctecinc.com
SIC: 3812 Antennas, radar or communications
PA: Src, Inc.
　　7502 Round Pond Rd
　　North Syracuse NY 13212
　　315 452-8000

(G-15000)
STEPS PLUS INC
6375 Thompson Rd (13206-1495)
PHONE....................................315 432-0885
Richard R Kopp, *Ch of Bd*
Judy Taylor, *Vice Pres*
Robert H Kopp, *Treasurer*
Bert Kopp, *Admin Sec*
EMP: 100 EST: 1967
SQ FT: 18,000
SALES (est): 14.7MM Privately Held
WEB: www.steps-plus.com
SIC: 3446 Architectural metalwork

(G-15001)
STERI-PHARMA LLC
429 S West St (13202-2326)
PHONE....................................315 473-7180
Lisa Bukowski, *Office Mgr*
Nick Walip, *Branch Mgr*
John Connelly, *Maintence Staff*
EMP: 34
SQ FT: 775
SALES (est): 7.9MM Privately Held
WEB: www.hanford.com
SIC: 2834 Pharmaceutical preparations
PA: Steri-Pharma, Llc
　　120 N State Rt 17
　　Paramus NJ 07652

(G-15002)
SYRACO PRODUCTS INC
Also Called: Syracuse Stamping Company
1054 S Clinton St (13202-3409)
PHONE....................................315 476-5306
Fred V Honnold, *Ch of Bd*
Elizabeth Hartnett, *Treasurer*
EMP: 14 EST: 1993
SQ FT: 103,000
SALES (est): 7.7MM Privately Held
WEB: www.syraco.com
SIC: 3429 3491 2655 Manufactured hardware (general); industrial valves; spools, fiber: made from purchased material

(G-15003)
SYRACUSE CASING CO INC
528 Erie Blvd W (13204-2423)
PHONE....................................315 475-0309
Peter Frey Jr, *President*
Christine Frey, *Corp Secy*
▲ EMP: 16
SQ FT: 150,000

(G-15004)
SYRACUSE CATHOLIC PRESS ASSN
Also Called: Catholic Sun, The
421 S Warren St Fl 2 (13202-2640)
P.O. Box 511 (13201-0511)
PHONE..................................315 422-8153
Mark Klenz, *Advt Staff*
Rev Donald Bourgeois, *Manager*
L D Costanza, *Associate*
EMP: 6
SALES: 850K **Privately Held**
SIC: 2711 Newspapers

(G-15005)
SYRACUSE COMPUTER FORMS INC
Also Called: Hansen & Hansen Qulty Prtg Div
216 Burnet Ave (13203-2335)
P.O. Box 6761 (13217-6761)
PHONE..................................315 478-0108
Ted Hansen, *CEO*
Michael Hansen, *President*
Toni Hansen, *CFO*
Mary Hansen, *Admin Sec*
Sue Letterman,
EMP: 20
SQ FT: 38,172
SALES (est): 3.3MM **Privately Held**
WEB: www.hansenqp.com
SIC: 2761 2752 2796 2791 Computer forms, manifold or continuous; commercial printing, lithographic; commercial printing, offset; platemaking services; typesetting

(G-15006)
SYRACUSE CULTURAL WORKERS PRJ
400 Lodi St (13203-2069)
P.O. Box 6367 (13217-6367)
PHONE..................................315 474-1132
Teresa Florack, *Principal*
John Faley, *Business Mgr*
Andy Mager, *Sales Mgr*
Marie Summerwood, *Mktg Coord*
Dick Cool, *Co-Director*
▲ EMP: 10
SQ FT: 1,800
SALES (est): 1.4MM **Privately Held**
WEB: www.syracuseculturalworkers.com
SIC: 2732 5961 Books: printing & binding; pamphlets: printing & binding, not published on site; books, mail order (except book clubs); mail order house

(G-15007)
SYRACUSE INDUSTRIAL SLS CO LTD
1850 Lemoyne Ave (13208-1282)
PHONE..................................315 478-5751
Fax: 315 472-0855
EMP: 11
SQ FT: 4,500
SALES (est): 1.8MM **Privately Held**
SIC: 2431 5251 Mfg Millwork Ret Hardware

(G-15008)
SYRACUSE LABEL CO INC
Also Called: Syracuse Label & Surround Prtg
200 Stewart Dr (13212-3426)
PHONE..................................315 422-1037
Peter Rhodes, *Ch of Bd*
Kathy Alaimo, *President*
Mark Howard, *Vice Pres*
Kevin Ekbom, *VP Mfg*
Kevin Gagnon, *VP Prdtn*
EMP: 86 EST: 1974
SQ FT: 35,000
SALES (est): 23.7MM **Privately Held**
WEB: www.syrlabel.com
SIC: 2672 2759 Labels (unprinted), gummed: made from purchased materials; commercial printing

(G-15009)
SYRACUSE PROSTHETIC CENTER INC
1124 E Fayette St (13210-1922)
PHONE..................................315 476-9697

John Tyo, *President*
Sheila Harrington, *Vice Pres*
EMP: 5
SQ FT: 2,000
SALES (est): 682.8K **Privately Held**
WEB: www.cnyprocenter.com
SIC: 3842 Prosthetic appliances

(G-15010)
SYRACUSE UNIVERSITY PRESS INC
621 Skytop Rd Ste 110 (13244-4416)
PHONE..................................315 443-5534
Enid Darby, *Manager*
Yatish Hegde, *Technology*
Alice Pfeiffer, *Director*
Pamela Socker, *Director*
Elizabeth August, *Professor*
▲ EMP: 21
SALES (est): 2.6MM
SALES (corp-wide): 1B **Privately Held**
SIC: 2731 Books: publishing only
PA: Syracuse University
900 S Crouse Ave Ste 620
Syracuse NY 13244
315 443-1870

(G-15011)
TERRELLS POTATO CHIP CO INC
218 Midler Park Dr (13206-1819)
PHONE..................................315 437-2786
Jack Terrell, *President*
Brenda Terrell, *Admin Sec*
EMP: 70 EST: 1946
SQ FT: 30,000
SALES (est): 11.6MM **Privately Held**
SIC: 2096 5145 Potato chips & other potato-based snacks; popcorn & supplies; pretzels; potato chips

(G-15012)
THERMOPATCH CORPORATION (PA)
2204 Erie Blvd E (13224-1100)
P.O. Box 8007 (13217-8007)
PHONE..................................315 446-8110
Tom Depuit, *Ch of Bd*
Mark Matteson, *Production*
Greg Garcia, *Engineer*
Richard Hawley, *VP Finance*
Elizabeth Bessey, *Human Res Mgr*
EMP: 100
SQ FT: 52,000
SALES (est): 37.9MM **Privately Held**
WEB: www.thermopatch.com
SIC: 3953 3582 7359 Figures (marking devices), metal; labeling machines, industrial

(G-15013)
TOMPKINS SRM LLC
Also Called: Tomkins USA
623 Oneida St (13202-3414)
PHONE..................................315 422-8763
Mike Mosher, *General Mgr*
James Pittman, *Sales Staff*
William Savage,
EMP: 6
SQ FT: 31,705
SALES (est): 1.1MM **Privately Held**
SIC: 3559 Sewing machines & attachments, industrial

(G-15014)
TONY BAIRD ELECTRONICS INC
461 E Brighton Ave (13210-4143)
PHONE..................................315 422-4430
Tony Jeffrey Baird, *CEO*
EMP: 4
SQ FT: 1,060
SALES (est): 1.5MM **Privately Held**
WEB: tonybairdelectronics.com
SIC: 3679 5999 Harness assemblies for electronic use: wire or cable; liquid crystal displays (LCD); audio-visual equipment & supplies

(G-15015)
TRI KOLOR PRINTING & STY
1035 Montgomery St (13202-3507)
P.O. Box 669 (13201-0669)
PHONE..................................315 474-6753
Charles De Wolf, *Owner*

EMP: 10
SQ FT: 12,000
SALES: 580K **Privately Held**
SIC: 2752 2759 2791 7336 Commercial printing, offset; letterpress printing; typesetting; graphic arts & related design

(G-15016)
TV GUILFOIL & ASSOCIATES INC (PA)
121 Dwight Park Cir (13209-1005)
P.O. Box 187, Solvay (13209-0187)
PHONE..................................315 453-0920
Phillip H Allen III, *President*
Tim Allen, *Admin Sec*
▲ EMP: 7
SQ FT: 10,000
SALES (est): 816.6K **Privately Held**
WEB: www.tvguilfoil.com
SIC: 3999 Candles

(G-15017)
UNIMAR INC
3195 Vickery Rd (13212-4574)
PHONE..................................315 699-4400
Michael Marley, *President*
Beth Andrews, *General Mgr*
Greg Thomas, *Project Engr*
Gary Saturno, *Sales Staff*
Terry Zarnowski, *Business Dir*
◆ EMP: 14
SQ FT: 21,000
SALES (est): 4.8MM **Privately Held**
SIC: 3625 5084 5063 Relays & industrial controls; controlling instruments & accessories; lighting fixtures, commercial & industrial

(G-15018)
UPSTATE PRINTING INC
433 W Onondaga St (13202-3209)
PHONE..................................315 475-6140
Jack Rotondo, *President*
Cindy Pascarella, *Vice Pres*
Debi Rotondo, *Treasurer*
Patti Vinciguerra, *Marketing Staff*
EMP: 14
SALES (est): 2.1MM **Privately Held**
SIC: 2752 Commercial printing, offset

(G-15019)
US BEVERAGE NET INC
225 W Jefferson St (13202-2401)
PHONE..................................315 579-2025
Mark Young, *President*
EMP: 12
SALES (est): 1.2MM **Privately Held**
SIC: 3556 7371 Beverage machinery; custom computer programming services

(G-15020)
VEHICLE SAFETY DEPT
5801 E Taft Rd Ste 4 (13212-3273)
PHONE..................................315 458-6683
James Donnery, *Manager*
EMP: 18
SALES (est): 1.2MM **Privately Held**
SIC: 3714 Sanders, motor vehicle safety

(G-15021)
VERTEX INNOVATIVE SOLUTIONS
6671 Commerce Blvd (13211-2211)
PHONE..................................315 437-6711
Paul Snow, *Chairman*
Bill Snow, *Vice Pres*
EMP: 18
SALES (est): 3.1MM **Privately Held**
SIC: 3648 Lighting equipment

(G-15022)
VETERAN AIR LLC
Also Called: Veteran Air Filtration
7174 State Fair Blvd (13209-1835)
PHONE..................................315 720-1101
Christopher Clark, *Vice Pres*
David Clark, *Vice Pres*
Lawrence Clark, *Vice Pres*
Steven Clark, *Vice Pres*
Alexandra Johnsin,
EMP: 5 **Privately Held**
SIC: 3564 Air cleaning systems

(G-15023)
WARD SALES CO INC
1117 W Fayette St Ste 1 (13204-2733)
PHONE..................................315 476-5276
Richard Hayko, *President*
Joseph Hayko, *Vice Pres*
EMP: 6
SQ FT: 30,000
SALES (est): 648.6K **Privately Held**
WEB: www.wardsalescompany.com
SIC: 2261 3953 3942 5199 Screen printing of cotton broadwoven fabrics; screens, textile printing; stuffed toys, including animals; advertising specialties

(G-15024)
WEATHER PRODUCTS CORPORATION
Also Called: Dynamic Pak
102 W Division St Fl 1 (13204-1470)
PHONE..................................315 474-8593
W Davies Birchenough Jr, *Ch of Bd*
Herman Garcia, *Vice Pres*
EMP: 8
SQ FT: 30,000
SALES (est): 1.4MM **Privately Held**
SIC: 3089 7389 Thermoformed finished plastic products; packaging & labeling services; labeling bottles, cans, cartons, etc.

(G-15025)
WESTROCK - SOLVAY LLC (DH)
53 Indl Dr (13204)
PHONE..................................315 484-9050
Peter Tantalo, *General Mgr*
Peter Buck,
David H Chrismer,
▲ EMP: 150
SQ FT: 300,000
SALES (est): 76.8MM
SALES (corp-wide): 16.2B **Publicly Held**
WEB: www.solvaypaperboard.com
SIC: 2631 Container board
HQ: Westrock Rkt, Llc
1000 Abernathy Rd Ste 125
Atlanta GA 30328
770 448-2193

(G-15026)
WESTROCK CP LLC
53 Industrial Dr (13204-1035)
PHONE..................................315 484-9050
EMP: 86
SALES (corp-wide): 16.2B **Publicly Held**
SIC: 2631 Container board
HQ: Westrock Cp, Llc
1000 Abernathy Rd
Atlanta GA 30328

(G-15027)
WESTROCK RKT COMPANY
53 Indl Dr (13204)
PHONE..................................770 448-2193
EMP: 162
SALES (corp-wide): 16.2B **Publicly Held**
WEB: www.rocktenn.com
SIC: 2631 Folding boxboard
HQ: Westrock Rkt, Llc
1000 Abernathy Rd Ste 125
Atlanta GA 30328
770 448-2193

(G-15028)
WIZARD EQUIPMENT INC
Also Called: Bob's Signs
10 Dwight Park Dr Ste 3 (13209-1098)
PHONE..................................315 414-9999
Bob Reilly, *President*
Robert Barnes, *Vice Pres*
EMP: 5
SALES: 200K **Privately Held**
SIC: 3993 Signs, not made in custom sign painting shops

(G-15029)
WOLFF & DUNGEY INC
325 Temple St (13202-3417)
P.O. Box 3673 (13220-3673)
PHONE..................................315 475-2105
Maurice Birchmeyer, *CEO*
Charles M Reschke, *Vice Pres*
John Birchmeyer, *Admin Sec*
EMP: 30
SQ FT: 20,000

SALES (est): 4.5MM **Privately Held**
SIC: **3365** 3543 Aluminum foundries; industrial patterns

(G-15030)
WOOD ETC INC
1175 State Fair Blvd # 2 (13209-1082)
PHONE................................315 484-9663
Kathleen Schmidt, *President*
Arnold Schmidt, *Vice Pres*
Jesse Schmidt, *Vice Pres*
EMP: 18
SQ FT: 30,000
SALES (est): 2.6MM **Privately Held**
SIC: **2521** 2599 2434 Cabinets, office: wood; cabinets, factory; wood kitchen cabinets

---

Tallman
Rockland County

(G-15031)
KRAMARTRON PRECISION INC
2 Spook Rock Rd Unit 107 (10982)
P.O. Box 355 (10982-0355)
PHONE................................845 368-3668
Brian Kramer, *President*
EMP: 5 EST: 1974
SQ FT: 3,000
SALES: 500K **Privately Held**
SIC: **3599** Machine shop, jobbing & repair

(G-15032)
LUCIDA USA LLC
Also Called: Lucida Surfaces USA
321 Route 59 Unit 327 (10982-7518)
PHONE................................845 877-7008
Yanky Bennish,
EMP: 5 EST: 2015
SALES: 5MM **Privately Held**
SIC: **3253** Ceramic wall & floor tile

Tappan
Rockland County

(G-15033)
AG TECH WELDING CORP
238 Oak Tree Rd (10983-2812)
PHONE................................845 398-0005
Martin De Joia, *President*
Agnes De Joia, *Corp Secy*
EMP: 6
SQ FT: 5,000
SALES (est): 69.3K **Privately Held**
SIC: **3599** 1799 Machine shop, jobbing & repair; welding on site

(G-15034)
CARIBBEAN FOODS DELIGHT INC
117 Route 303 Ste B (10983-2136)
PHONE................................845 398-3000
Vincent Hosang, *President*
Jeanette Hosang, *Vice Pres*
◆ EMP: 80
SQ FT: 100,000
SALES (est): 17.5MM **Privately Held**
WEB: www.caribbeanfooddelights.com
SIC: **2013** 2011 Frozen meats from purchased meat; meat packing plants

(G-15035)
EN TECH CORP
375 Western Hwy (10983-1317)
PHONE................................845 398-0776
EMP: 15
SALES (corp-wide): 7.8MM **Privately Held**
SIC: **3321** Gray & ductile iron foundries
PA: En Tech Corp
　91 Ruckman Rd
　Closter NJ 07624
　718 389-2058

(G-15036)
NATIONWIDE CUSTOM SERVICES
Also Called: Custom Studio Division
77 Main St (10983-2400)
PHONE................................845 365-0414

Norman Shaifer, *President*
Helen Newman, *Vice Pres*
EMP: 8
SQ FT: 2,000
SALES (est): 590K **Privately Held**
SIC: **2731** 8661 Books: publishing & printing; religious organizations

(G-15037)
PULMUONE FOODS USA INC
30 Rockland Park Ave (10983-2629)
PHONE................................845 365-3300
Chang Hwang, *Branch Mgr*
EMP: 25 **Privately Held**
SIC: **2024** Tofu desserts, frozen
HQ: Pulmuone Foods Usa, Inc.
　2315 Moore Ave
　Fullerton CA 92833

(G-15038)
RJ HARVEY INSTRUMENT CORP
Also Called: Romark Diagnostics
11 Jane St (10983-2503)
PHONE................................845 359-3943
Robert Maines, *President*
Angelo D'Imperio, *Vice Pres*
EMP: 10
SQ FT: 3,600
SALES (est): 1.1MM **Privately Held**
WEB: www.rjharveyinst.com
SIC: **3841** 3829 Diagnostic apparatus, medical; measuring & controlling devices

---

Tarrytown
Westchester County

(G-15039)
AEROLASE CORPORATION
777 Old Saw Mill River Rd # 2 (10591-6717)
PHONE................................914 345-8300
Pavel Efremkin, *CEO*
Tina Tucker, *District Mgr*
Joseph Hurley, *COO*
Wanda Rodriguez, *Research*
Ryan McFadden, *Project Engr*
EMP: 100
SQ FT: 3,000
SALES (est): 14.5MM **Privately Held**
WEB: www.friendlylight.com
SIC: **3841** Surgical lasers

(G-15040)
AMPACET CORPORATION (PA)
660 White Plains Rd # 360 (10591-5171)
PHONE................................914 631-6600
Robert A Defalco, *Ch of Bd*
George Love, *Partner*
Jack Singer, *Exec VP*
Robert Felding, *Senior VP*
Sam Bhoumik, *Vice Pres*
◆ EMP: 948
SQ FT: 36,000
SALES (est): 567.4MM **Privately Held**
WEB: www.ampacet.com
SIC: **2821** Plastics materials & resins

(G-15041)
BASF CORPORATION
500 White Plains Rd (10591-5102)
PHONE................................914 785-2000
Michael Heinz, *CEO*
Joseph Gasperino, *Chief Engr*
EMP: 15
SALES (corp-wide): 71.7B **Privately Held**
SIC: **2869** Industrial organic chemicals
HQ: Basf Corporation
　100 Park Ave
　Florham Park NJ 07932
　973 245-6000

(G-15042)
CROSS BORDER TRANSACTIONS LLC (PA)
580 White Plains Rd # 660 (10591-5198)
PHONE................................646 767-7342
David Bukovac, *CEO*
Donald Scherer, *Ch of Bd*
Mimi Song, *Vice Pres*
Lisa Zimbalist, *Vice Pres*
Alyssa Dorfman, *CFO*
EMP: 14 EST: 2015

SALES (est): 7.9MM **Privately Held**
SIC: **7372** Business oriented computer software

(G-15043)
DENTEK ORAL CARE INC (HQ)
660 White Plains Rd # 250 (10591-5171)
PHONE................................865 983-1300
John M Jansheski, *CEO*
David Fox, *President*
▲ EMP: 63
SQ FT: 64,000
SALES (est): 9.6MM
SALES (corp-wide): 975.7MM **Publicly Held**
WEB: www.usdentek.com
SIC: **3843** Dental equipment & supplies
PA: Prestige Consumer Healthcare Inc.
　660 White Plains Rd
　Tarrytown NY 10591
　914 524-6800

(G-15044)
FOSECO INC
777 Old Saw Mill River Rd (10591-6717)
PHONE................................914 345-4760
EMP: 10
SALES (corp-wide): 2.3B **Privately Held**
SIC: **2899** 3569 Mfg Exorterneic Compunds Fluxes And Ceramic Filters
HQ: Foseco, Inc.
　20200 Sheldon Rd
　Cleveland OH 44142
　440 826-4548

(G-15045)
H ARNOLD WOOD TURNING INC
220 White Plins Rd Ste 24 (10591)
P.O. Box 278, Mamaroneck (10543-0278)
PHONE................................914 381-0801
Bruce Arnold, *President*
Jonathan Arnold, *Vice Pres*
Ann Arnold, *CFO*
Sonia D McSweeney, *Manager*
▲ EMP: 31 EST: 1930
SQ FT: 920
SALES (est): 5.3MM **Privately Held**
WEB: www.arnoldwood.com
SIC: **2431** Millwork

(G-15046)
INTERNATIONAL SOCIETY FOR MEDL
520 White Plains Rd (10591-5102)
PHONE................................520 820-8594
Terry Pena, *Ch of Bd*
EMP: 1
SALES: 1.6MM **Privately Held**
SIC: **2741** Miscellaneous publishing

(G-15047)
MEDTECH PRODUCTS INC (HQ)
Also Called: New Skin
660 White Plains Rd (10591-5139)
PHONE................................914 524-6810
Matthew Mannelly, *President*
Timothy J Connors, *Exec VP*
Jean A Boyko PHD, *Senior VP*
John Parkinson, *Senior VP*
Samuel C Cowley, *Vice Pres*
◆ EMP: 16
SQ FT: 7,000
SALES (est): 14.9MM
SALES (corp-wide): 975.7MM **Publicly Held**
SIC: **2841** 2834 Soap & other detergents; pharmaceutical preparations
PA: Prestige Consumer Healthcare Inc.
　660 White Plains Rd
　Tarrytown NY 10591
　914 524-6800

(G-15048)
MICRO POWDERS INC (PA)
Also Called: M P I
580 White Plains Rd # 400 (10591-5198)
PHONE................................914 332-6400
James Strauss, *President*
Tom Laakso, *Sales Dir*
Bob Stearns, *Regl Sales Mgr*
Phyllis Strauss, *Admin Sec*
◆ EMP: 26
SQ FT: 2,500

SALES (est): 11.1MM **Privately Held**
WEB: www.micropowders.com
SIC: **3952** 3555 2899 2893 Wax, artists'; printing trades machinery; chemical preparations; printing ink; cyclic crudes & intermediates; specialty cleaning, polishes & sanitation goods

(G-15049)
MOMENTIVE PERFORMANCE MTLS INC
Also Called: OSI Specialties
769 Old Saw Mill River Rd (10591-6732)
PHONE................................914 784-4807
Michael Pigeon, *Manager*
EMP: 80
SALES (corp-wide): 2.7B **Publicly Held**
WEB: www.gewaterford.com
SIC: **2843** 2099 2821 8731 Surface active agents; emulsifiers, food; plastics materials & resins; commercial physical research; chemical preparations
HQ: Momentive Performance Materials Inc.
　260 Hudson River Rd
　Waterford NY 12188

(G-15050)
MSM DESIGNZ INC
505 White Plains Rd # 204 (10591-5101)
PHONE................................914 909-5900
Mario S Mirabella, *President*
Anthony Terlizzi, *Manager*
Caroline Martin, *Account Dir*
EMP: 2
SALES (est): 1MM **Privately Held**
SIC: **2759** 7389 7311 8742 Commercial printing; design services; advertising agencies; marketing consulting services; advertising specialties; graphic arts & related design

(G-15051)
OPTIMUM SEMICONDUCTOR TECH
120 White Plains Rd Fl 4 (10591-5526)
PHONE................................914 287-8500
Daniel R Watkins, *Principal*
Brian Jackson, *Senior Engr*
Susan Calabro, *Human Resources*
Joseph Hoane, *Fellow*
EMP: 9 EST: 2010
SALES (est): 1.2MM **Privately Held**
SIC: **3674** Semiconductors & related devices

(G-15052)
POLICY ADM SOLUTIONS INC
505 White Plains Rd (10591-5101)
PHONE................................914 332-4320
Peter Pantelides, *President*
EMP: 45
SALES: 7.5MM **Privately Held**
SIC: **3571** Mainframe computers

(G-15053)
PRESTIGE BRANDS INTL LLC
660 White Plains Rd (10591-5139)
PHONE................................914 524-6800
Timothy J Connors, *Exec VP*
Jean A Boyko PHD, *Senior VP*
Samuel C Cowley, *Vice Pres*
Ronald M Lombardi, *CFO*
Matthew M Mannelly,
◆ EMP: 12
SALES (est): 186.4K
SALES (corp-wide): 975.7MM **Publicly Held**
SIC: **2834** Pharmaceutical preparations
PA: Prestige Consumer Healthcare Inc.
　660 White Plains Rd
　Tarrytown NY 10591
　914 524-6800

(G-15054)
PRESTIGE CONSMR HEALTHCARE INC (PA)
Also Called: PRESTIGE BRANDS
660 White Plains Rd (10591-5139)
PHONE................................914 524-6800
Ronald M Lombardi, *Ch of Bd*
Timothy J Connors, *Exec VP*
Christopher Heye, *Senior VP*
William C P'Pool, *Senior VP*
Jean Boyko, *Vice Pres*
EMP: 63

SALES: 975.7MM **Publicly Held**
SIC: 2834 5122 5169 Pharmaceutical preparations; pharmaceuticals; specialty cleaning & sanitation preparations

(G-15055)
RAUCH INDUSTRIES INC
828 S Broadway (10591-6600)
PHONE..................................704 867-5333
Bruce Charbeck, *Branch Mgr*
EMP: 20
SALES (corp-wide): 200.2MM **Privately Held**
SIC: 3231 Christmas tree ornaments: made from purchased glass
PA: Rauch Industries, Inc.
3800a Little Mountain Rd
Gastonia NC 28056
704 867-5333

(G-15056)
REGENERON PHARMACEUTICALS INC (PA)
777 Old Saw Mill River Rd # 10 (10591-6707)
PHONE..................................914 847-7000
Leonard S Schleifer, *President*
Nanci Babb, *District Mgr*
Neil Stahl, *Exec VP*
Daniel P Van Plew, *Exec VP*
Marion McCourt, *Senior VP*
▲ **EMP:** 277
SQ FT: 1,467,000
SALES: 6.7B **Publicly Held**
WEB: www.regeneron.com
SIC: 2834 Pharmaceutical preparations

(G-15057)
REGENRON HLTHCARE SLUTIONS INC
745 Old Saw Mill River Rd (10591-6701)
PHONE..................................914 847-7000
Robert Terifay, *General Mgr*
David Robinson, *Vice Pres*
Joseph Larosa, *Admin Sec*
EMP: 603
SALES (est): 17.5MM
SALES (corp-wide): 6.7B **Publicly Held**
SIC: 2834 Pharmaceutical preparations
PA: Regeneron Pharmaceuticals Inc
777 Old Saw Mill River Rd # 10
Tarrytown NY 10591
914 847-7000

(G-15058)
RHINO SPORTS & LEISURE LLC
Also Called: Rhino Rugby
303 S Broadway Ste 450 (10591-5484)
PHONE..................................844 877-4466
John Prusmack, *Mng Member*
EMP: 30
SALES (est): 2.4MM **Privately Held**
SIC: 2389 5131 5699 Apparel for handicapped; trimmings, apparel; caps & gowns (academic vestments)

(G-15059)
SIEMENS HLTHCARE DGNOSTICS INC
511 Benedict Ave (10591-5005)
PHONE..................................914 631-0475
EMP: 39
SALES (corp-wide): 89.6B **Privately Held**
SIC: 2835 8734 Mfg Diagnostic Substances Testing Laboratory
HQ: Siemens Healthcare Diagnostics Inc.
511 Benedict Ave
Tarrytown NY 10591
914 631-8000

(G-15060)
SNEAKY CHEF FOODS LLC
520 White Plains Rd (10591-5102)
PHONE..................................914 301-3277
Missy Chase Lapine, *CEO*
Helen Spanjer, *COO*
Laurence Chase, *Vice Pres*
▲ **EMP:** 10 **EST:** 2012
SALES (est): 1.1MM **Privately Held**
SIC: 2033 2099 Spaghetti & other pasta sauce: packaged in cans, jars, etc.; peanut butter

(G-15061)
SPIC AND SPAN COMPANY
660 White Plains Rd # 250 (10591-5171)
PHONE..................................914 524-6823
Matthew M Mannelly, *CEO*
Mark Pettie, *Ch of Bd*
Peter Anderson, *CFO*
EMP: 12 **EST:** 2000
SQ FT: 6,000
SALES (est): 2MM
SALES (corp-wide): 975.7MM **Publicly Held**
SIC: 2842 Cleaning or polishing preparations
PA: Prestige Consumer Healthcare Inc.
660 White Plains Rd
Tarrytown NY 10591
914 524-6800

(G-15062)
SPX CORPORATION
220 White Plains Rd (10591-5837)
PHONE..................................914 366-7402
EMP: 5
SALES (corp-wide): 1.5B **Publicly Held**
SIC: 3443 Heat exchangers, condensers & components
PA: Spx Corporation
13320a Balntyn Corp Pl
Charlotte NC 28277
980 474-3700

(G-15063)
TARRYTOWN BAKERY INC
150 Wildey St (10591-2910)
PHONE..................................914 631-0209
Michael J Birrittella, *President*
EMP: 10 **EST:** 1940
SQ FT: 5,000
SALES (est): 1MM **Privately Held**
WEB: www.plazaview.com
SIC: 2051 5461 Bread, all types (white, wheat, rye, etc): fresh or frozen; bakeries

(G-15064)
ZIP-JACK INDUSTRIES LTD
Also Called: Zip Jack Custom Umbrellas
73 Carrollwood Dr (10591-5210)
PHONE..................................914 592-2000
Emanuel Dubinsky, *President*
Charlotte L Dubinsky, *Treasurer*
▲ **EMP:** 25
SQ FT: 20,000
SALES (est): 2.3MM **Privately Held**
WEB: www.zipjack.com
SIC: 3999 5699 Garden umbrellas; umbrellas

Thiells
Rockland County

(G-15065)
STEEL TECH SA LLC
7 Hillside Dr (10984-1431)
P.O. Box 361 (10984-0361)
PHONE..................................845 786-3691
Allen Klein,
EMP: 5
SALES: 430K **Privately Held**
SIC: 3441 Fabricated structural metal

Thompsonville
Sullivan County

(G-15066)
MONTICELLO BLACK TOP CORP
80 Patio Dr (12784)
P.O. Box 95 (12784-0095)
PHONE..................................845 434-7280
Joseph Gottlieb, *President*
EMP: 5
SQ FT: 4,000
SALES (est): 729.9K **Privately Held**
SIC: 2951 5032 Concrete, asphaltic (not from refineries); sand, construction; gravel

Thornwood
Westchester County

(G-15067)
AUTOMATED CONTROL LOGIC INC
Also Called: Acl
578 Commerce St (10594-1327)
PHONE..................................914 769-8880
Preston Bruenn, *President*
Joe Escaravage, *Info Tech Mgr*
EMP: 12
SALES (est): 3.4MM **Privately Held**
WEB: www.automatedcontrollogic.com
SIC: 3674 3825 1711 Solid state electronic devices; test equipment for electronic & electrical circuits; heating & air conditioning contractors

(G-15068)
COMMERCE OFFSET LTD
657 Commerce St (10594-1399)
PHONE..................................914 769-6671
Fax: 914 769-7845
EMP: 5
SQ FT: 8,400
SALES (est): 540K **Privately Held**
SIC: 2752 Lithographic Commercial Printing

(G-15069)
FENBAR PRCISION MACHINISTS INC
633 Commerce St (10594-1302)
PHONE..................................914 769-5506
Leonard Vallender, *President*
Gloria Vallender, *Corp Secy*
EMP: 10
SQ FT: 6,500
SALES (est): 2.9MM **Privately Held**
WEB: www.fenbar.com
SIC: 3599 Machine shop, jobbing & repair

(G-15070)
HOUGHTON MIFFLIN HARCOURT PUBG
28 Claremont Ave (10594-1042)
PHONE..................................914 747-2709
Glenn Polin, *Owner*
EMP: 124
SALES (corp-wide): 1.3B **Publicly Held**
WEB: www.hmco.com
SIC: 2731 Textbooks: publishing only, not printed on site
HQ: Houghton Mifflin Harcourt Publishing Company
125 High St Ste 900
Boston MA 02110
617 351-5000

(G-15071)
THORNWOOD PRODUCTS LTD
Also Called: All Star Fabricators
401 Claremont Ave Ste 7 (10594-1038)
PHONE..................................914 769-9161
Peter Cuneo, *President*
EMP: 30
SALES (est): 3.7MM **Privately Held**
SIC: 2599 1799 Cabinets, factory; counter top installation

Three Mile Bay
Jefferson County

(G-15072)
ST LAWRENCE LUMBER INC
27140 County Route 57 (13693-7205)
PHONE..................................315 649-2990
Gregory L Hoppel, *President*
Julie Hoppel, *Vice Pres*
EMP: 7
SALES: 1MM **Privately Held**
WEB: www.stlawrencelumber.com
SIC: 2421 Sawmills & planing mills, general

Ticonderoga
Essex County

(G-15073)
ADIRONDACK WASTE MGT INC
Also Called: Adirondack Sanitary Service
963 New York State 9n (12883)
PHONE..................................518 585-2224
R D Seargent Condit, *President*
Cindy Condit, *Vice Pres*
Doran Rockhill, *Treasurer*
EMP: 7
SQ FT: 1,000
SALES: 300K **Privately Held**
SIC: 2842 Sanitation preparations

(G-15074)
INTERNATIONAL PAPER COMPANY
568 Shore Airport Rd (12883-2890)
PHONE..................................518 585-6761
Andrew Ozdoba, *Purch Mgr*
Bob Ballard, *Buyer*
Stephen Treat, *Controller*
Chris Mallon, *Branch Mgr*
Matthew Bush, *Supervisor*
EMP: 650
SQ FT: 1,920
SALES (corp-wide): 23.3B **Publicly Held**
WEB: www.internationalpaper.com
SIC: 2621 Paper mills
PA: International Paper Company
6400 Poplar Ave
Memphis TN 38197
901 419-9000

(G-15075)
LIBBYS BAKERY CAFE LLC
92 Montcalm St (12883-1352)
P.O. Box 61 (12883-0061)
PHONE..................................603 918-8825
Andrew Rasmus, *Principal*
Claire Brown, *Principal*
Katherine Lewis, *Principal*
EMP: 5
SALES (est): 407.8K **Privately Held**
SIC: 2051 Cakes, pies & pastries

(G-15076)
SPECIALTY MINERALS INC
35 Highland St (12883-1520)
P.O. Box 352 (12883-0352)
PHONE..................................518 585-7982
Elaine Bertrand, *General Mgr*
EMP: 6 **Publicly Held**
WEB: www.specialtyminerals.com
SIC: 2819 Industrial inorganic chemicals
HQ: Specialty Minerals Inc.
622 3rd Ave Fl 38
New York NY 10017
212 878-1800

(G-15077)
TICONDEROGA MCH & WLDG CORP
55 Race Track Rd (12883-4003)
PHONE..................................518 585-7444
EMP: 5 **EST:** 1954
SQ FT: 980
SALES (est): 36.3K **Privately Held**
SIC: 3599 Machine Shop

Tillson
Ulster County

(G-15078)
WINERACKSCOM INC
819 Route 32 (12486-1724)
P.O. Box 67, High Falls (12440-0067)
PHONE..................................845 658-7181
Michael Babcock, *President*
Howard Babcock, *Vice Pres*
Jennifer Cristaldi, *Administration*
EMP: 26 **EST:** 1990
SQ FT: 20,000
SALES (est): 4.7MM **Privately Held**
SIC: 2541 Wood partitions & fixtures

Tomkins Cove
Rockland County

(G-15079)
TILCON NEW YORK INC
Fort Of Elm (10986)
P.O. Box 217 (10986-0217)
PHONE..............................845 942-0602
Rich Moon, *Superintendent*
Nathalie Boboshko, *Credit Mgr*
EMP: 22
SQ FT: 2,184
SALES (corp-wide): 30.6B **Privately Held**
WEB: www.tilconny.com
SIC: 1442 Sand mining; gravel & pebble
　　mining
HQ: Tilcon New York Inc.
　　9 Entin Rd
　　Parsippany NJ 07054
　　973 366-7741

Tonawanda
Erie County

(G-15080)
3M COMPANY
305 Sawyer Ave (14150-7718)
PHONE..............................716 876-1596
Mike Mazur, *Manager*
EMP: 400
SALES (corp-wide): 32.7B **Publicly Held**
WEB: www.mmm.com
SIC: 3089 2823 Sponges, plastic; cellu-
　　losic manmade fibers
PA: 3m Company
　　3m Center
　　Saint Paul MN 55144
　　651 733-1110

(G-15081)
ACE SPECIALTY CO INC
695 Ensminger Rd (14150-6698)
PHONE..............................716 874-3670
Patrick J Allen, *President*
EMP: 9
SQ FT: 25,000
SALES (est): 1.1MM **Privately Held**
WEB: www.acespecialtycompany.com
SIC: 3544 Special dies & tools

(G-15082)
ADAMS SFC INC (HQ)
225 E Park Dr (14150-7813)
P.O. Box 963, Buffalo (14240-0963)
PHONE..............................716 877-2608
Jack H Berg, *President*
Carole L Berg, *Admin Sec*
▲ **EMP:** 40
SQ FT: 65,000
SALES (est): 6.9MM
SALES (corp-wide): 62.5MM **Privately
Held**
WEB: www.pacerpumps.com
SIC: 3569 3563 Filters, general line: in-
　　dustrial; vacuum (air extraction) systems,
　　industrial
PA: Service Filtration Corp.
　　2900 Macarthur Blvd
　　Northbrook IL 60062
　　847 509-2900

(G-15083)
ALFA LAVAL KATHABAR INC
91 Sawyer Ave (14150-7716)
PHONE..............................716 875-2000
EMP: 520
SALES (est): 155.8K
SALES (corp-wide): 4.5B **Privately Held**
SIC: 3585 Humidifiers & dehumidifiers
HQ: Alfa Laval U.S. Holding Inc.
　　5400 Intl Trade Dr
　　Richmond VA 23231

(G-15084)
ALFA LAVAL NIAGARA INC (DH)
Also Called: Niagara Blower Company
91 Sawyer Ave (14150-7716)
PHONE..............................800 426-5169
John C Atanasio, *Ch of Bd*
Peter G Demakos, *President*
Craig D Boyce, *Vice Pres*

Brad Wildey, *QC Mgr*
Mark Vogel, *Sales Mgr*
▼ **EMP:** 80 **EST:** 1904
SQ FT: 60,000
SALES (est): 30MM
SALES (corp-wide): 4.5B **Privately Held**
WEB: www.niagarablower.com
SIC: 3585 Air conditioning units, complete:
　　domestic or industrial

(G-15085)
ALRY TOOL AND DIE CO INC
386 Fillmore Ave (14150-2417)
P.O. Box 43 (14151-0043)
PHONE..............................716 693-2419
Michael J Allen, *President*
Daniel T Allen, *Corp Secy*
Francis D Allen Jr, *Vice Pres*
Thomas Allen, *Vice Pres*
EMP: 20 **EST:** 1944
SQ FT: 23,500
SALES (est): 2.8MM **Privately Held**
WEB: www.alry.com
SIC: 3462 3544 Machinery forgings, fer-
　　rous; dies & die holders for metal cutting,
　　forming, die casting

(G-15086)
ARROW GRINDING INC
525 Vicke St Tonaw Ctr (14150)
PHONE..............................716 693-3333
John C Goller, *President*
Kathy Goller, *Corp Secy*
Doug Deschamps, *Mfg Staff*
EMP: 25
SQ FT: 25,000
SALES (est): 4.1MM **Privately Held**
SIC: 3599 Machine shop, jobbing & repair

(G-15087)
AVANTI U S A LTD
412 Young St (14150-4037)
P.O. Box 113, North Tonawanda (14120-
0113)
PHONE..............................716 695-5800
G J Caruso, *President*
Gregory J Van Norman, *Vice Pres*
EMP: 15
SQ FT: 4,863
SALES (est): 2MM **Privately Held**
SIC: 3842 4225 3089 Surgical appliances
　　& supplies; general warehousing; injec-
　　tion molding of plastics

(G-15088)
**B & W HEAT TREATING
COMPANY**
2780 Kenmore Ave (14150-7775)
PHONE..............................716 876-8184
Clifford Calvello, *Owner*
EMP: 8 **EST:** 1948
SQ FT: 14,000
SALES (est): 1.2MM **Privately Held**
SIC: 3398 3471 Metal heat treating; clean-
　　ing, polishing & finishing

(G-15089)
**BCO INDUSTRIES WESTERN NY
INC**
77 Oriskany Dr (14150-6722)
P.O. Box 100 (14151-0100)
PHONE..............................716 877-2800
Janet Soltzman, *President*
Douglas Saltzman, *President*
EMP: 31
SALES (est): 4.5MM **Privately Held**
WEB: www.bcoworld.com
SIC: 2759 2791 Thermography; visiting
　　cards (including business): printing; fac-
　　simile letters: printing; stationery: printing;
　　typesetting

(G-15090)
BIMBO BAKERIES USA INC
Also Called: Best Foods Baking Group
1960 Niagara Falls Blvd (14150-5542)
PHONE..............................716 692-9140
Catherine E Irish, *Branch Mgr*
EMP: 5 **Privately Held**
WEB: www.gwbakeries.com
SIC: 2051 Bakery: wholesale or whole-
　　sale/retail combined
HQ: Bimbo Bakeries Usa, Inc
　　255 Business Center Dr # 200
　　Horsham PA 19044
　　215 347-5500

(G-15091)
BONCRAFT INC
777 E Park Dr (14150-6708)
PHONE..............................716 662-9720
Timothy Bubar, *CEO*
James Bubar Jr, *President*
Mike Ruda, *Maint Spvr*
Jason Braungart, *Manager*
EMP: 75 **EST:** 1952
SQ FT: 20,400
SALES (est): 10.5MM **Privately Held**
WEB: www.boncraft.com
SIC: 2752 2791 2789 Commercial print-
　　ing, offset; typesetting; bookbinding & re-
　　lated work

(G-15092)
BOULEVARD PRINTING
1330 Niagara Falls Blvd # 2 (14150-8900)
PHONE..............................716 837-3800
John Battistella, *Owner*
EMP: 6
SALES (est): 644.9K **Privately Held**
SIC: 2752 Commercial printing, offset

(G-15093)
**BRIGHTON TOOL & DIE
DESIGNERS (PA)**
Also Called: Brighton Design
463 Brighton Rd (14150-6966)
PHONE..............................716 876-0879
Chris Banas, *President*
Chris Eanas, *President*
EMP: 15
SQ FT: 2,000
SALES (est): 1.7MM **Privately Held**
SIC: 3544 Special dies & tools

(G-15094)
**BROTHERS-IN-LAWN
PROPERTY**
176 Vulcan (14150)
PHONE..............................716 279-6191
Rodney Koeppen, *President*
EMP: 9
SALES (est): 783.8K **Privately Held**
SIC: 3711 0781 Snow plows (motor vehi-
　　cles), assembly of; landscape services

(G-15095)
CENTRAL REDE SIGN CO INC
317 Wheeler St (14150-3828)
PHONE..............................716 213-0797
Neal Wilcox, *Principal*
John Wilcox, *VP Sales*
EMP: 5
SALES (est): 698.5K **Privately Held**
SIC: 3993 Signs & advertising specialties

(G-15096)
CENTRISOURCE INC
777 E Park Dr (14150-6708)
PHONE..............................716 871-1105
David Zenger, *President*
Joseph Zenger, *Treasurer*
EMP: 5
SALES (est): 440K **Privately Held**
SIC: 2732 Book printing

(G-15097)
CLIFFORD H JONES INC
608 Young St (14150-4195)
PHONE..............................716 693-2444
Phillip Jones, *President*
EMP: 15
SQ FT: 18,000
SALES (est): 4MM **Privately Held**
WEB: www.chjones.com
SIC: 3544 3089 Forms (molds), for
　　foundry & plastics working machinery; in-
　　jection molding of plastics

(G-15098)
**COCA-COLA BTLG CO BUFFALO
INC**
200 Milens Rd (14150-6795)
PHONE..............................716 874-4610
John F Bitzer III, *President*
Rick Horn Jr, *General Mgr*
Todd Evans, *Human Res Mgr*
▲ **EMP:** 170
SQ FT: 75,000

SALES (est): 999.7K
SALES (corp-wide): 361.4MM **Privately
Held**
SIC: 2086 Bottled & canned soft drinks
PA: Abarta, Inc.
　　200 Alpha Dr
　　Pittsburgh PA 15238
　　412 963-6226

(G-15099)
DIGITAL INSTRUMENTS INC
580 Ensminger Rd (14150-6668)
PHONE..............................716 874-5848
John Swanson, *President*
▲ **EMP:** 10
SQ FT: 6,000
SALES (est): 2.1MM **Privately Held**
WEB: www.digitalinstruments.com
SIC: 3625 Industrial controls: push button,
　　selector switches, pilot

(G-15100)
DISC-LOCK LLC
400 Rrverwalk Pkwy Ste 600 (14150)
PHONE..............................310 560-9940
Adam Pratt, *President*
Greg White, *Manager*
▲ **EMP:** 6
SQ FT: 35,000
SALES (est): 542.8K **Privately Held**
SIC: 3452 Bolts, nuts, rivets & washers;
　　lock washers; bolts, metal

(G-15101)
E-ZOIL PRODUCTS INC
234 Fillmore Ave (14150-2340)
PHONE..............................716 213-0106
Glenn Miller, *President*
Chris Miller, *Vice Pres*
Christopher Miller, *Vice Pres*
Bill Morgan, *Natl Sales Mgr*
Stacey Czerwinski, *Marketing Mgr*
▲ **EMP:** 25
SQ FT: 10,000
SALES (est): 5.8MM **Privately Held**
WEB: www.ezoil.com
SIC: 2911 Fuel additives

(G-15102)
EMULSO CORP
2750 Kenmore Ave (14150-7707)
PHONE..............................716 854-2889
William Breeser, *President*
Susan Spencer, *Executive Asst*
EMP: 6
SQ FT: 30,000
SALES (est): 550K **Privately Held**
WEB: www.emulso.com
SIC: 2842 2841 5087 Soap: granulated,
　　liquid, cake, flaked or chip; waxes for
　　wood, leather & other materials; furniture
　　polish or wax; janitors' supplies

(G-15103)
FCMP INC
230 Fire Tower Dr (14150-5832)
PHONE..............................716 692-4623
David Callendrier, *President*
▲ **EMP:** 17 **EST:** 2000
SQ FT: 20,000
SALES (est): 3.7MM **Privately Held**
WEB: www.fcmp.com
SIC: 3714 3592 Bearings, motor vehicle;
　　pistons & piston rings

(G-15104)
FIBER LAMINATIONS LIMITED
Also Called: C/O M&M Fowarding
600 Main St (14150-3723)
PHONE..............................716 692-1825
William Neal, *Branch Mgr*
EMP: 13
SALES (corp-wide): 11.6MM **Privately
Held**
SIC: 3089 Automotive parts, plastic
PA: Fibre Laminations Ltd
　　651 Burlington St E
　　Hamilton ON L8L 4
　　905 312-9152

(G-15105)
FMC CORPORATION
Also Called: F M C Peroxygen Chemicals Div
78 Sawyer Ave Ste 1 (14150-7751)
PHONE..............................716 879-0400
Robert Service, *Manager*

▲ = Import ▼=Export
◆ =Import/Export

Dina Richman, *Manager*
Brian Verrelli, *Technology*
EMP: 200
SALES (corp-wide): 4.7B **Publicly Held**
WEB: www.fmc.com
SIC: 2812 Alkalies & chlorine
PA: Fmc Corporation
2929 Walnut St
Philadelphia PA 19104
215 299-6000

(G-15106)
GREAT LAKES GEAR CO INC
126 E Niagara St Ste 2 (14150-1215)
PHONE..................716 694-0715
Donald Eggleston, *President*
Robert Rees, *President*
Timothy Rees, *Vice Pres*
Karen Carey, *Manager*
EMP: 8
SQ FT: 4,500
SALES: 900K **Privately Held**
SIC: 3462 Gears, forged steel

(G-15107)
GREAT LAKES METAL TREATING
300 E Niagara St (14150-1218)
P.O. Box 118 (14151-0118)
PHONE..................716 694-1240
Thomas Snyder, *President*
EMP: 10
SQ FT: 18,000
SALES (est): 966.9K **Privately Held**
SIC: 3398 Metal heat treating

(G-15108)
GREEN BUFFALO FUEL LLC
Also Called: Gbf
720 Riverview Blvd (14150-7824)
PHONE..................716 768-0600
Peter Coleman, *CEO*
EMP: 10 EST: 2012
SALES (est): 1.2MM **Privately Held**
SIC: 1311 1321 Natural gas production; butane (natural) production

(G-15109)
GREIF INC
2122 Colvin Blvd (14150-6908)
PHONE..................716 836-4200
Clinton Gathins, *Opers-Prdtn-Mfg*
Brian Ellis, *Purch Mgr*
Karen Muranyi, *Executive*
Hershel Reich, *Admin Sec*
EMP: 70
SALES (corp-wide): 3.8B **Publicly Held**
WEB: www.greif.com
SIC: 2655 Drums, fiber: made from purchased material
PA: Greif, Inc.
425 Winter Rd
Delaware OH 43015
740 549-6000

(G-15110)
HDM HYDRAULICS LLC
125 Fire Tower Dr (14150-5880)
PHONE..................716 694-8004
William Anderson, *President*
▲ **EMP:** 100
SQ FT: 46,560
SALES (est): 24.9MM
SALES (corp-wide): 501.5MM **Privately Held**
WEB: www.ligonindustries.com
SIC: 3511 Hydraulic turbine generator set units, complete
PA: Ligon Industries, Llc
1927 1st Ave N Ste 500
Birmingham AL 35203
205 322-3302

(G-15111)
HEBELER LLC (PA)
2000 Military Rd (14150-6704)
PHONE..................716 873-9300
Kenneth Snyder, *President*
Ahmed Lahrache, *COO*
Jonathan Nelson, *Project Mgr*
Christophe Quaranta, *Facilities Mgr*
Christopher Toth, *Purch Agent*
▲ **EMP:** 140 EST: 1929
SQ FT: 100,000

SALES (est): 31.8MM **Privately Held**
WEB: www.hebeler.com
SIC: 3441 Fabricated structural metal

(G-15112)
HEBELER PROCESS SOLUTIONS LLC
2000 Military Rd (14150-6704)
PHONE..................716 873-9300
Kenneth Snyder, *President*
Kenneth Snyder, *President*
EMP: 20 EST: 2016
SALES (est): 1.7MM **Privately Held**
SIC: 3599 Custom machinery

(G-15113)
HERR MANUFACTURING CO INC
17 Pearce Ave (14150-6711)
PHONE..................716 754-4341
Bruce Mc Lean, *President*
EMP: 25 EST: 1913
SALES (est): 3.1MM **Privately Held**
SIC: 3552 Textile machinery

(G-15114)
IMA LIFE NORTH AMERICA INC
2175 Military Rd (14150-6001)
PHONE..................716 695-6354
Giovanni Pecchioli, *President*
Sergio Marzo, *Corp Secy*
Ernesto Renzi, *Vice Pres*
Cheri Hahn, *Purchasing*
Fran Nesbit, *Engineer*
◆ **EMP:** 150
SQ FT: 43,000
SALES: 70MM **Privately Held**
SIC: 2834 Druggists' preparations (pharmaceuticals)
HQ: I.M.A. Industria Macchine Automatiche Spa
Via Bruno Tosarelli 182/184
Castenaso BO 40055
051 651-4111

(G-15115)
INPRO CORPORATION
Fireline 520
250 Cooper Ave Ste 102 (14150-6633)
PHONE..................716 332-4699
Aj Shaw, *Manager*
EMP: 8
SALES (corp-wide): 144.9MM **Privately Held**
SIC: 3499 Barricades, metal
PA: Inpro Corporation
S80w18766 Apollo Dr
Muskego WI 53150
262 679-9010

(G-15116)
INTEGUMENT TECHNOLOGIES INC
72 Pearce Ave (14150-6711)
PHONE..................716 873-1199
Terrence G Vargo, *President*
EMP: 16
SALES (est): 2.4MM **Privately Held**
WEB: www.integument.com
SIC: 3081 Plastic film & sheet

(G-15117)
KELLER TECHNOLOGY CORPORATION (PA)
2320 Military Rd (14150-6005)
P.O. Box 103, Buffalo (14217-0103)
PHONE..................716 693-3840
Michael A Keller, *Ch of Bd*
Arthur Keller Jr, *Ch of Bd*
Barnaby Keller, *President*
Peter Keller, *Vice Pres*
Joe Fournier, *Mfg Mgr*
▲ **EMP:** 250 EST: 1947
SQ FT: 200,000
SALES (est): 63.1MM **Privately Held**
WEB: www.kellertechnology.com
SIC: 3599 Custom machinery

(G-15118)
LAFARGE NORTH AMERICA INC
4001 River Rd (14150-6513)
PHONE..................716 876-8788
Mark Joslin, *Branch Mgr*
EMP: 13
SALES (corp-wide): 27.6B **Privately Held**
SIC: 3241 Cement, hydraulic

HQ: Lafarge North America Inc.
8700 W Bryn Mawr Ave
Chicago IL 60631
773 372-1000

(G-15119)
LORNAMEAD INC
175 Cooper Ave (14150-6656)
PHONE..................646 745-3643
James A Nass, *Branch Mgr*
EMP: 76 **Privately Held**
SIC: 2844 Cosmetic preparations
HQ: Lornamead, Inc
1359 Broadway Fl 17
New York NY 10018
716 874-7190

(G-15120)
MANTH MFG INC
131 Fillmore Ave (14150-2337)
P.O. Box 866 (14151-0866)
PHONE..................716 693-6525
Duane Manth, *President*
EMP: 35
SQ FT: 14,000
SALES: 1.9MM **Privately Held**
SIC: 3599 Machine shop, jobbing & repair

(G-15121)
MAY TOOL & DIE INC
9 Hackett Dr (14150-3797)
PHONE..................716 695-1033
Martin J May, *President*
Frederick J May, *Vice Pres*
Joseph O May, *Vice Pres*
Mary Kreher, *Admin Sec*
EMP: 5 EST: 1970
SQ FT: 8,000
SALES: 500K **Privately Held**
SIC: 3599 Machine shop, jobbing & repair

(G-15122)
MIDLAND MACHINERY CO INC
101 Cranbrook Road Ext Exd (14150-4110)
PHONE..................716 692-1200
Barre W Banks, *President*
Dave Rinard, *Design Engr*
Darrell Banks, *Sls & Mktg Exec*
Barre Banks, *Manager*
Carol Massimi,
▲ **EMP:** 59 EST: 1969
SQ FT: 15,000
SALES (est): 14.8MM **Privately Held**
WEB: www.midlandmachinery.com
SIC: 3531 Asphalt plant, including gravel-mix type; mixers, concrete; pavers

(G-15123)
MODU-CRAFT INC (PA)
276 Creekside Dr (14150-1435)
PHONE..................716 694-0709
Kenneth Babka, *President*
EMP: 5 EST: 1972
SQ FT: 30,000
SALES: 1MM **Privately Held**
SIC: 3821 2599 2542 Laboratory furniture; factory furniture & fixtures; partitions & fixtures, except wood

(G-15124)
MORNINGSTAR CONCRETE PRODUCTS
528 Young St (14150-4107)
PHONE..................716 693-4020
Juanita Morningstar, *President*
Ray D Morningstar, *Vice Pres*
EMP: 14 EST: 1913
SQ FT: 120,000
SALES (est): 1.7MM **Privately Held**
WEB: www.morningsturf.com
SIC: 3273 Ready-mixed concrete

(G-15125)
NEW YORK IMAGING SERVICE INC
255 Cooper Ave (14150-6641)
PHONE..................716 834-8022
Rob Muzzio, *Branch Mgr*
EMP: 11
SALES (corp-wide): 15.2MM **Privately Held**
SIC: 3844 X-ray apparatus & tubes
PA: New York Imaging Service Inc.
1 Dalfonso Rd
Newburgh NY 12550
845 561-6947

(G-15126)
NIABRAZE LLC
675 Ensminger Rd (14150-6609)
PHONE..................716 447-1082
Albert Bluemle Sr, *President*
David Gardner, *Opers Mgr*
Thomas Bluemle, *Treasurer*
EMP: 14
SALES (est): 2.3MM **Privately Held**
SIC: 3291 3425 Abrasive products; saw blades for hand or power saws

(G-15127)
NIGHTINGALE CORP
750 Ensminger Rd Ste 108 (14150-6640)
PHONE..................905 896-3434
Wiliam Breen, *CEO*
Edward Breen, *President*
EMP: 5 EST: 2018
SQ FT: 2,696
SALES: 1MM
SALES (corp-wide): 1.9MM **Privately Held**
SIC: 2522 Office chairs, benches & stools, except wood
PA: Nightingale Corp
2301 Dixie Rd
Mississauga ON L4Y 1
905 896-3434

(G-15128)
NORTH DELAWARE PRINTING INC
645 Delaware St Ste 1 (14150-5390)
PHONE..................716 692-0576
Michael J Brown, *President*
Steven Brown, *Vice Pres*
EMP: 9
SQ FT: 3,200
SALES (est): 1.5MM **Privately Held**
WEB: www.northdelawareprinting.com
SIC: 2752 7334 Commercial printing, offset; photocopying & duplicating services

(G-15129)
ODEN MACHINERY INC (PA)
600 Ensminger Rd (14150-6637)
PHONE..................716 874-3000
Ronald Sarto, *CEO*
Tony Fwedersky, *President*
Gregory E Simsa, *CFO*
Dave Carroll, *Sales Mgr*
Dj Reynolds, *Sales Mgr*
EMP: 20
SQ FT: 25,000
SALES: 4.5MM **Privately Held**
SIC: 3823 Thermometers, filled system: industrial process type

(G-15130)
PADDOCK CHEVROLET GOLF DOME
175 Brompton Rd (14150-4534)
PHONE..................716 504-4059
Jeff Rainey, *Director*
EMP: 25
SALES (est): 1.2MM **Privately Held**
WEB: www.tonawanda.ny.us
SIC: 3949 7999 Driving ranges, golf, electronic; tennis services & professionals

(G-15131)
PDM STUDIOS INC
510 Main St (14150-3853)
PHONE..................716 694-8337
Paul Michalski, *President*
EMP: 6
SALES (est): 533.4K **Privately Held**
SIC: 2759 Screen printing

(G-15132)
PEROXYCHEM LLC
35 Sawyer Ave (14150-7751)
PHONE..................716 873-0812
Thomas Ball, *Exec VP*
Walter Kramer, *Vice Pres*
Kathy Garris, *Production*
Lei Wang, *Engineer*
Mike Donnelly, *Treasurer*
EMP: 100 **Privately Held**
SIC: 2812 Alkalies & chlorine
HQ: Peroxychem Llc
1 Commerce Sq 2005 Mark
Philadelphia PA 19103
267 422-2400

(G-15133)
PRAXAIR INC
175 E Park Dr (14150-7891)
P.O. Box 44 (14151-0044)
PHONE..............................716 879-2000
Joel Emmet, *Principal*
Christopher Nelson, *Opers Mgr*
Lawrence Bool, *Research*
James J White, *Research*
Richard Cyganovich, *Engineer*
EMP: 15 **Privately Held**
SIC: 2813 Industrial gases
HQ: Praxair, Inc.
　　10 Riverview Dr
　　Danbury CT 06810
　　203 837-2000

(G-15134)
PRAXAIR INC
135 E Park Dr (14150)
PHONE..............................716 879-4000
John Lewendowski, *Principal*
EMP: 50 **Privately Held**
SIC: 2813 Industrial gases
HQ: Praxair, Inc.
　　10 Riverview Dr
　　Danbury CT 06810
　　203 837-2000

(G-15135)
R J REYNOLDS TOBACCO COMPANY
275 Cooper Ave Ste 116 (14150-6643)
PHONE..............................716 871-1553
Tracy Wozniak, *Principal*
EMP: 226
SALES (corp-wide): 31.4B **Privately Held**
SIC: 2111 Cigarettes
HQ: R. J. Reynolds Tobacco Company
　　401 N Main St
　　Winston Salem NC 27101
　　336 741-5000

(G-15136)
S R INSTRUMENTS INC (PA)
600 Young St (14150-4188)
PHONE..............................716 693-5977
John Siegel, *President*
Vern Siegel, *Engineer*
Chris McAlpin, *Info Tech Mgr*
Will Smith, *Director*
Vernon Siegel, *Admin Sec*
EMP: 48
SQ FT: 25,000
SALES (est): 6.2MM **Privately Held**
WEB: www.srinstruments.com
SIC: 3825 3596 Measuring instruments & meters, electric; weighing machines & apparatus

(G-15137)
SAFESPAN PLATFORM SYSTEMS INC
237 Fillmore Ave (14150-2339)
PHONE..............................716 694-1100
Lambros Apostolopoulos, *President*
EMP: 40 **Privately Held**
SIC: 3312 Slabs, steel; structural shapes & pilings, steel
PA: Safespan Platform Systems, Inc.
　　252 Fillmore Ave
　　Tonawanda NY 14150

(G-15138)
SCHWABEL FABRICATING CO INC (PA)
349 Sawyer Ave (14150-7796)
PHONE..............................716 876-2086
Gerald Schwabel, *President*
Paul Schwabel, *Vice Pres*
Janice Malburg, *Office Mgr*
William Schwabel, *Admin Sec*
EMP: 23
SQ FT: 30,000
SALES (est): 3.1MM **Privately Held**
WEB: www.schwabelfab.com
SIC: 3443 3599 3552 Heat exchangers, plate type; vessels, process or storage (from boiler shops): metal plate; tanks, standard or custom fabricated: metal plate; machine shop, jobbing & repair; textile machinery

(G-15139)
SCIENTIFICS DIRECT INC
532 Main St (14150-3853)
PHONE..............................716 773-7500
Paul Gerspach, *Ch of Bd*
▲ **EMP:** 17 **EST:** 2012
SALES (est): 2.3MM **Privately Held**
SIC: 3229 5049 5961 Scientific glassware; scientific & engineering equipment & supplies;

(G-15140)
SERVICE FILTRATION CORP
225 E Park Dr (14150-7813)
P.O. Box 963, Buffalo (14240-0963)
PHONE..............................716 877-2608
EMP: 30
SALES (corp-wide): 62.5MM **Privately Held**
WEB: www.pacerpumps.com
SIC: 3569 3677 Filters, general line: industrial; filtration devices, electronic
PA: Service Filtration Corp.
　　2900 Macarthur Blvd
　　Northbrook IL 60062
　　847 509-2900

(G-15141)
SNYDER INDUSTRIES INC (PA)
340 Wales Ave (14150-2513)
PHONE..............................716 694-1240
Thomas W Snyder, *Ch of Bd*
Thomas Dunch, *Vice Pres*
Charlie Rudolph, *Vice Pres*
Marie Snyder, *Vice Pres*
Keith Snyder, *Treasurer*
EMP: 101 **EST:** 1971
SQ FT: 24,000
SALES (est): 23.7MM **Privately Held**
WEB: www.snyderindustriesinc.com
SIC: 3599 Machine shop, jobbing & repair

(G-15142)
SUPERIOR PRINTING INK CO INC
777 E Park Dr (14150-6708)
PHONE..............................716 877-0250
EMP: 5
SALES (corp-wide): 151.6MM **Privately Held**
SIC: 2893 Printing ink
PA: Superior Printing Ink Co Inc
　　100 North St
　　Teterboro NJ 07608
　　201 478-5600

(G-15143)
SURE FLOW EQUIPMENT INC
250 Cooper Ave Ste 102 (14150-6633)
P.O. Box 321 (14151-0321)
PHONE..............................800 263-8251
John Wordsworth, *President*
Greg Brownstein, *Sales Staff*
Danny Miles, *Sales Staff*
EMP: 50
SALES (est): 12.6MM **Privately Held**
SIC: 3494 5072 Valves & pipe fittings; hardware

(G-15144)
SWIFT RIVER ASSOCIATES INC
4051 River Rd (14150-6513)
PHONE..............................716 875-0902
Kenneth Rawe Sr, *President*
Tony Pariso, *Corp Secy*
Carmen Pariso, *Vice Pres*
Kenneth Rawe Jr, *Vice Pres*
EMP: 7
SALES (est): 1.1MM **Privately Held**
SIC: 2951 Concrete, asphaltic (not from refineries)

(G-15145)
TONAWANDA COKE CORPORATION
3875 River Rd (14150-6591)
P.O. Box 5007 (14151-5007)
PHONE..............................716 876-6222
J D Crane, *CEO*
Michael K Durkin, *President*
Ken Thrun, *Project Engr*
Michael Durkin, *CFO*
Robert Kolvek, *Corp Comm Staff*
▲ **EMP:** 130
SQ FT: 150,000

SALES (est): 46.3MM **Privately Held**
WEB: www.tonawandacoke.com
SIC: 3312 Coke produced in chemical recovery coke ovens

(G-15146)
TONAWANDA LIMB & BRACE INC
545 Delaware St Ste 2 (14150-5336)
PHONE..............................716 695-1131
Robert Catipovic, *President*
Richard C Catipovic, *Vice Pres*
Nancy Sardina, *Manager*
EMP: 5
SQ FT: 14,000
SALES (est): 728.4K **Privately Held**
SIC: 3842 Limbs, artificial; prosthetic appliances

(G-15147)
TREEHOUSE PRIVATE BRANDS INC
570 Fillmore Ave (14150-2509)
PHONE..............................716 693-4715
Christopher Lemay, *Finance*
Karen Reed, *Manager*
EMP: 175
SALES (corp-wide): 5.8B **Publicly Held**
SIC: 2052 Cookies
HQ: Treehouse Private Brands, Inc.
　　2021 Spring Rd Ste 600
　　Oak Brook IL 60523

(G-15148)
TREYCO PRODUCTS CORP
131 Fillmore Ave (14150-2396)
P.O. Box 866 (14151-0866)
PHONE..............................716 693-6525
Duane Manth, *President*
▲ **EMP:** 5 **EST:** 1961
SQ FT: 10,000
SALES (est): 520.8K **Privately Held**
WEB: www.treyco.com
SIC: 3421 Scissors, shears, clippers, snips & similar tools; shears, hand; clippers, fingernail & toenail; snips, tinners'

(G-15149)
UNIFRAX I LLC
Fiberfrax Manufacturing
360 Fire Tower Dr (14150-5893)
PHONE..............................716 696-3000
Scott Penman, *Production*
John Di Matteo, *Engineer*
Ralph Paddock, *Engineer*
Salvatore Riniolo, *Project Engr*
Mark Travers, *Data Proc Staff*
EMP: 165 **Privately Held**
WEB: www.insulfrax.com
SIC: 3297 3299 3296 Nonclay refractories; ceramic fiber; mineral wool
PA: Unifrax I Llc
　　600 Rverwalk Pkwy Ste 120
　　Tonawanda NY 14150

(G-15150)
UNIFRAX I LLC (PA)
600 Rverwalk Pkwy Ste 120 (14150)
PHONE..............................716 768-6500
David E Brooks, *President*
Eugene Turczynski, *Maint Spvr*
Ashley Howard, *Purch Mgr*
Joan Fetty, *Engineer*
Duane Hartsell, *Engineer*
◆ **EMP:** 110
SALES (est): 379.9MM **Privately Held**
WEB: www.insulfrax.com
SIC: 3299 Ceramic fiber

(G-15151)
UOP LLC
175 E Park Dr (14150-7844)
P.O. Box 986 (14151-0986)
PHONE..............................716 879-7600
Charles J Schorr, *General Mgr*
EMP: 21
SALES (corp-wide): 41.8B **Publicly Held**
WEB: www.uop.com
SIC: 2819 Catalysts, chemical
HQ: Uop Llc
　　25 E Algonquin Rd
　　Des Plaines IL 60016
　　847 391-2000

(G-15152)
VIATRAN CORPORATION (DH)
199 Fire Tower Dr (14150-5813)
PHONE..............................716 564-7813
George A Fraas, *CEO*
Kenneth H Brown, *Ch of Bd*
Dennis Scully, *Vice Pres*
Debbie Bunce, *Production*
Todd Avery, *QC Mgr*
EMP: 50 **EST:** 1965
SQ FT: 18,000
SALES (est): 7MM
SALES (corp-wide): 5.1B **Publicly Held**
WEB: www.viatran.com
SIC: 3823 3825 5084 Pressure measurement instruments, industrial; instruments to measure electricity; industrial machinery & equipment

(G-15153)
WASHINGTON MILLS TONAWANDA INC (HQ)
1000 E Niagara St (14150-1306)
PHONE..............................716 693-4550
Ronald Campbell, *Chairman*
Kersi Dordi, *Vice Pres*
Armand Ladage, *Vice Pres*
John Redshaw, *VP Sales*
Nancy Gates, *Admin Sec*
▲ **EMP:** 30 **EST:** 1914
SQ FT: 273,000
SALES (est): 51MM
SALES (corp-wide): 175.7MM **Privately Held**
WEB: www.exolon.com
SIC: 3291 Aluminum oxide (fused) abrasives
PA: Washington Mills Group, Inc.
　　20 N Main St
　　North Grafton MA 01536
　　508 839-6511

(G-15154)
WOODWARD INDUSTRIES INC
233 Fillmore Ave Ste 23 (14150-2316)
PHONE..............................716 692-2242
Daniel Woodward, *President*
Deke Lemieux, *Project Mgr*
Jeanette Woodward, *Office Mgr*
EMP: 16 **EST:** 1953
SQ FT: 18,845
SALES (est): 1.5MM **Privately Held**
WEB: www.woodwardind.com
SIC: 3543 Industrial patterns

(G-15155)
WSF INDUSTRIES INC
7 Hackett Dr (14150-3798)
P.O. Box 400, Buffalo (14217-0400)
PHONE..............................716 692-4930
John Hettrick Jr, *CEO*
Gary Fornasiero, *President*
Nancy Warner, *Buyer*
Curtis Smith, *QC Mgr*
Chuck Becker, *Design Engr*
▼ **EMP:** 25 **EST:** 1941
SQ FT: 66,000
SALES: 2.1MM **Privately Held**
WEB: www.wsf-inc.com
SIC: 3443 Autoclaves, industrial

(G-15156)
ZENGER GROUP INC
777 E Park Dr (14150-6708)
PHONE..............................716 871-1058
Stephen Zenger, *Ch of Bd*
Gloria Caroll, *Info Tech Mgr*
EMP: 44
SALES (est): 4.5MM
SALES (corp-wide): 16.7MM **Privately Held**
SIC: 2752 Commercial printing, lithographic
PA: Zenger Group Inc.
　　777 E Park Dr
　　Tonawanda NY 14150
　　716 871-1058

▲ = Import ▼ = Export
◆ = Import/Export

Troy
Albany County

(G-15157)
ALBANY NIPPLE AND PIPE MFG
60 Cohoes Ave Ste 100a (12183-1518)
PHONE..............................518 270-2162
Robert Moss, *President*
EMP: 20
SALES (est): 2.4MM **Privately Held**
SIC: 3498 Tube fabricating (contract bending & shaping)

(G-15158)
HONEYWELL INTERNATIONAL INC
3 Tibbits Ave (12183-1433)
PHONE..............................518 270-0200
Michael Bennett, *Vice Pres*
Tom White, *Vice Pres*
Tom Sherwood, *Finance*
Jennifer Nguyen, *Marketing Staff*
Steve Kratz, *Branch Mgr*
EMP: 80
SALES (corp-wide): 41.8B **Publicly Held**
WEB: www.honeywell.com
SIC: 3724 Aircraft engines & engine parts
PA: Honeywell International Inc.
300 S Tryon St
Charlotte NC 28202
973 455-2000

(G-15159)
KAYS CAPS INC (PA)
65 Arch St (12183-1599)
PHONE..............................518 273-6079
Roberta Fine, *Ch of Bd*
EMP: 8
SQ FT: 1,000
SALES (est): 637.3K **Privately Held**
WEB: www.kayscaps.com
SIC: 2353 Uniform hats & caps

(G-15160)
LONG ISLAND PIPE SUPPLY INC
75 Cohoes Ave (12183-1506)
PHONE..............................518 270-2159
Bob Moss, *President*
Kathy Fields, *CFO*
EMP: 6
SALES (corp-wide): 2.6B **Privately Held**
SIC: 3498 Fabricated pipe & fittings
HQ: Miles Moss Of Albany, Inc.
586 Commercial Ave
Garden City NY 11530
516 222-8008

(G-15161)
SEALY MATTRESS CO ALBANY INC
30 Veterans Memorial Dr (12183-1517)
PHONE..............................518 880-1600
David J McIlquham, *President*
EMP: 300
SQ FT: 265,000
SALES (est): 37.3MM
SALES (corp-wide): 2.7B **Publicly Held**
SIC: 2515 Mattresses, innerspring or box spring
HQ: Sealy Mattress Company
1 Office Parkway Rd
Trinity NC 27370
336 861-3500

Troy
Rensselaer County

(G-15162)
A I T COMPUTERS INC
157 Hoosick St (12180-2375)
PHONE..............................518 266-9010
Ahmed Ali, *President*
EMP: 3
SQ FT: 2,000
SALES: 1MM **Privately Held**
WEB: www.aitcomputers.com
SIC: 3577 5734 Computer peripheral equipment; computer & software stores

(G-15163)
APPRENDA INC
433 River St Ste 4001 (12180-2357)
PHONE..............................518 383-2130
EMP: 73 **EST:** 2007
SALES (est): 9.2MM **Privately Held**
SIC: 7372 Prepackaged Software Services

(G-15164)
ARDEX COSMETICS OF AMERICA
744 Pawling Ave (12180-6212)
PHONE..............................518 283-6700
Nubar Sukljian, *President*
▲ **EMP:** 20
SQ FT: 250,000
SALES (est): 2.1MM **Privately Held**
SIC: 2844 Cosmetic preparations

(G-15165)
DEAKON HOMES AND INTERIORS
Also Called: Troy Cabinet Manufacturing Div
16 Industrial Park Rd (12180-6197)
PHONE..............................518 271-0342
Diane F Decurtis, *President*
John De Curtis, *General Mgr*
EMP: 15
SQ FT: 7,000
SALES (est): 1.4MM **Privately Held**
WEB: www.troycabinet.com
SIC: 2434 1521 2541 2522 Wood kitchen cabinets; general remodeling, single-family houses; wood partitions & fixtures; office furniture, except wood; wood office furniture; wood household furniture

(G-15166)
DOWD - WITBECK PRINTING CORP
Also Called: Alchar Printing
599 Pawling Ave (12180-5823)
PHONE..............................518 274-2421
Toll Free:...........................877
Denise Padula, *President*
John E Hupe, *Vice Pres*
Laura Erano, *Train & Dev Mgr*
Chip Kress, *Sales Staff*
Debbie Goode, *Manager*
EMP: 18
SQ FT: 10,200
SALES (est): 2.3MM **Privately Held**
WEB: www.alchar.com
SIC: 2752 2796 2791 2789 Commercial printing, offset; platemaking services; typesetting; bookbinding & related work; commercial art & graphic design

(G-15167)
DYNAMIC APPLICATIONS INC
120 Defreest Dr Ste 255 (12180-7633)
PHONE..............................518 283-4654
John P Reilly, *President*
Jonathan Radin, *Vice Pres*
EMP: 9
SQ FT: 1,000
SALES (est): 631.4K **Privately Held**
WEB: www.dynamicapps.com
SIC: 7372 Prepackaged software

(G-15168)
FLOAT TECH INC
216 River St Ste 1 (12180-3848)
PHONE..............................518 266-0964
Cecilia Domingos, *President*
EMP: 6
SALES (est): 480K **Privately Held**
SIC: 2385 Waterproof outerwear

(G-15169)
GEORGE M DUJACK
Also Called: Du Serv Development Co
80 Town Office Rd (12180-8817)
PHONE..............................518 279-1303
George M Dujack, *Owner*
EMP: 5 **EST:** 1973
SALES: 400K **Privately Held**
SIC: 2821 Silicone resins

(G-15170)
GURLEY PRECISION INSTRS INC
514 Fulton St (12180-3315)
PHONE..............................518 272-6300
O Patrick Brady, *Ch of Bd*
Yuiry Benderskiy, *Mfg Staff*
Evan Defilippo, *Engineer*
Boris Mintseris, *Engineer*
Ronald H Laberge, *CFO*
EMP: 105
SQ FT: 78,000
SALES (est): 24.3MM **Privately Held**
WEB: www.gurley.com
SIC: 3827 3824 3829 3823 Optical instruments & lenses; water meters; physical property testing equipment; industrial instrmnts msrmnt display/control process variable; semiconductors & related devices; radio & TV communications equipment

(G-15171)
HAMILTON PRINTING COMPANY INC
22 Hamilton Ave (12180)
PHONE..............................518 732-2161
John Paeglow, *CEO*
William Greenawalt, *Vice Pres*
Brian F Payne, *Vice Pres*
▲ **EMP:** 140 **EST:** 1912
SQ FT: 100,000
SALES (est): 15.2MM **Privately Held**
WEB: www.hamprint.com
SIC: 2732 2789 Books: printing & binding; binding only: books, pamphlets, magazines, etc.

(G-15172)
INDUSTRIAL TOOL & DIE CO INC
14 Industrial Park Rd (12180-6197)
PHONE..............................518 273-7383
Paul V Cacciotti, *President*
▲ **EMP:** 14
SQ FT: 17,000
SALES (est): 2.4MM **Privately Held**
SIC: 3599 Machine shop, jobbing & repair

(G-15173)
INTERNTNAL ELCTRONIC MCHS CORP
Also Called: I E M
850 River St (12180-1239)
PHONE..............................518 268-1636
Zack Mian, *President*
Robert Foss, *Research*
Peter Hayes, *Engineer*
Keith Morgado, *Engineer*
Bill Peabody, *Design Engr*
◆ **EMP:** 29
SQ FT: 35,000
SALES: 5MM **Privately Held**
WEB: www.iem.net
SIC: 3825 8711 Instruments to measure electricity; engineering services

(G-15174)
NEXT ADVANCE INC (PA)
2113 Ny 7 Ste 1 (12180-9188)
PHONE..............................518 674-3510
Ian Glasgow, *President*
EMP: 15
SALES (est): 212.3K **Privately Held**
WEB: www.nextadvance.com
SIC: 3821 Clinical laboratory instruments, except medical & dental

(G-15175)
NIBBLE INC BAKING CO
451 Broadway Apt 5 (12180-3355)
PHONE..............................518 334-3950
EMP: 8
SALES (est): 475K **Privately Held**
SIC: 2051 Bread, cake & related products

(G-15176)
NORTHEAST PALLET & CONT CO INC
1 Mann Ave Bldg 300 (12180)
PHONE..............................518 271-0535
James F Price, *President*
EMP: 16
SQ FT: 18,000
SALES (est): 1.4MM **Privately Held**
SIC: 2449 2448 Rectangular boxes & crates, wood; pallets, wood

(G-15177)
PB MAPINFO CORPORATION
1 Global Vw (12180-8371)
PHONE..............................518 285-6000
Murray Martin, *CEO*
John E O'Hara, *Ch of Bd*
David Woroboff, *President*
Barret Johnson, *Vice Pres*
Andrew Naden, *Vice Pres*
EMP: 903
SQ FT: 150,000
SALES (est): 668.1K
SALES (corp-wide): 3.5B **Publicly Held**
WEB: www.mapinfo.com
SIC: 7372 Business oriented computer software
PA: Pitney Bowes Inc.
3001 Summer St Ste 3
Stamford CT 06905
203 356-5000

(G-15178)
PERROTTAS BAKERY INC
766 Pawling Ave (12180-6294)
PHONE..............................518 283-4711
Charles A Perrotta, *President*
Louis Perrotta, *Corp Secy*
EMP: 9 **EST:** 1962
SQ FT: 5,000
SALES (est): 925.9K **Privately Held**
SIC: 2051 5461 Bakery: wholesale or wholesale/retail combined; bakeries

(G-15179)
PITNEY BOWES SOFTWARE INC
Also Called: Thompson Group
350 Jordan Rd Ste 1 (12180-8358)
PHONE..............................518 285-6000
John Hobson, *General Mgr*
Christopher Allbritton, *Sales Staff*
Jim Karpen, *Business Anlyst*
EMP: 14
SALES (corp-wide): 3.5B **Publicly Held**
WEB: www.mapinfo.com
SIC: 7372 7371 Business oriented computer software; computer software development & applications
HQ: Pitney Bowes Software Inc.
27 Waterview Dr
Shelton CT 06484
855 839-5119

(G-15180)
PLACID BAKER
250 Broadway (12180-3235)
PHONE..............................518 326-2657
Margaret Obert, *Principal*
EMP: 8 **EST:** 2009
SALES (est): 637.9K **Privately Held**
SIC: 2051 Cakes, bakery: except frozen

(G-15181)
R J VALENTE GRAVEL INC (PA)
1 Madison St (12180-5145)
PHONE..............................518 432-4470
Roderick J Valente, *Ch of Bd*
Joseph Panza, *Controller*
EMP: 60
SQ FT: 5,000
SALES (est): 19.4MM **Privately Held**
SIC: 1442 Construction sand & gravel

(G-15182)
RAITH AMERICA INC
Also Called: Vistec Lithography
300 Jordan Rd (12180-8346)
PHONE..............................518 874-3000
Rainer Schmid, *Branch Mgr*
EMP: 33
SALES (corp-wide): 25MM **Privately Held**
SIC: 2752 Color lithography
PA: Raith America, Inc.
1377 Long IIsland Motor P
Islandia NY
518 874-3020

(G-15183)
RARE FORM BREWING COMPANY
90 Congress St (12180-4123)
PHONE..............................518 313-9256
Jennifer Kemp, *President*
EMP: 7 **EST:** 2015
SALES (est): 268.2K **Privately Held**
SIC: 2082 Beer (alcoholic beverage)

(G-15184)
ROSS VALVE MFG
75 102nd St (12180-1125)
PHONE................................518 274-0961
EMP: 8
SALES (est): 740.2K Privately Held
SIC: 3494 Valves & pipe fittings

(G-15185)
RW GATE COMPANY (PA)
79 102nd St (12180-1125)
PHONE................................518 874-4750
Andy Ross, *Principal*
Bill Ross, *Principal*
Evan Whipps, *Principal*
EMP: 10
SALES: 6.3MM Privately Held
SIC: 3441 Dam gates, metal plate

(G-15186)
RW GATE COMPANY
75 102nd St (12180-1125)
PHONE................................518 874-4750
EMP: 60
SALES (corp-wide): 6.3MM Privately Held
SIC: 3441 Dam gates, metal plate
PA: Rw Gate Company
79 102nd St
Troy NY 12180
518 874-4750

(G-15187)
SCRIVEN DUPLICATING SERVICE
Also Called: Scriven Press
100 Eastover Rd (12182-1108)
PHONE................................518 233-8180
Kevin Rafferty, *President*
Brian Rafferty, *Vice Pres*
EMP: 6
SQ FT: 4,800
SALES (est): 750K Privately Held
SIC: 2752 Photo-offset printing

(G-15188)
SHAMRON MILLS LTD
484 River St (12180-2215)
PHONE................................212 354-0430
Ronnye Shamron, *President*
▲ EMP: 3
SQ FT: 3,000
SALES: 3MM Privately Held
WEB: www.shamron.com
SIC: 2389 Hospital gowns

(G-15189)
SILVER GRIFFIN INC
691 Hoosick Rd (12180-8818)
PHONE................................518 272-7771
Paul Noonan, *President*
EMP: 15
SALES (est): 1.2MM Privately Held
SIC: 2759 7299 7334 Commercial printing; wedding chapel, privately operated; ; photocopying & duplicating services

(G-15190)
STANDARD MANUFACTURING CO INC (PA)
Also Called: Sportsmaster Apparel
750 2nd Ave (12182-2290)
P.O. Box 380 (12182-0380)
PHONE................................518 235-2200
George Arakelian, *CEO*
Dorothy King, *Corp Secy*
Christian Arakelian, *Vice Pres*
Daren Arakelian, *Vice Pres*
▲ EMP: 65
SQ FT: 250,000
SALES (est): 8.9MM Privately Held
SIC: 2337 2339 2329 Jackets & vests, except fur & leather: women's; women's & misses' outerwear; jackets (suede, leatherette, etc.), sport: men's & boys'; men's & boys' leather, wool & down-filled outerwear

(G-15191)
SUNWARD ELECTRONICS INC
Also Called: Dog Guard
258 Broadway Ste 2a (12180)
PHONE................................518 687-0030
Rose Watkins, *President*
Richard Dawson, *Marketing Staff*

EMP: 11
SQ FT: 5,000
SALES (est): 1.8MM Privately Held
WEB: www.teacherspetproducts.com
SIC: 3496 3612 Fencing, made from purchased wire; transformers, except electric

(G-15192)
TROY BOILER WORKS INC
2800 7th Ave (12180-1587)
PHONE................................518 274-2650
Louis E Okonski, *President*
John E Okonski Sr, *President*
Richard Okonski, *Treasurer*
Jack Okonski, *Manager*
Joe Thierry, *Manager*
EMP: 50
SQ FT: 25,000
SALES (est): 14.6MM Privately Held
WEB: www.troyboilerworks.com
SIC: 3443 7699 Vessels, process or storage (from boiler shops): metal plate; tanks, standard or custom fabricated: metal plate; boiler & boiler shop work; boiler repair shop

(G-15193)
UNITED AIRCRAFT TECH INC
Also Called: Uat
30 3rd St (12180-3906)
PHONE................................518 286-8867
Daryian Rhysing, *Principal*
Rakshit Amba, *Principal*
Donald Devito, *Principal*
Evaguel Rhysing, *Principal*
Louis Russell, *Principal*
EMP: 5
SALES (est): 359K Privately Held
SIC: 3429 Aircraft & marine hardware, inc. pulleys & similar items

(G-15194)
VITAL VIO INC
185 Jordan Rd Ste 1 (12180-7611)
PHONE................................914 245-6048
Colleen Costello, *CEO*
Meghan Olson, *Business Mgr*
Meredith Palmer, *Director*
Robert Barron, *Associate*
EMP: 10
SALES (est): 245.6K Privately Held
SIC: 3646 7342 Commercial indusl & institutional electric lighting fixtures; disinfecting services

(G-15195)
VM CHOPPY & SONS LLC
4 Van Buren St (12180-5596)
PHONE................................518 266-1444
Vincent J Choppy, *Purchasing*
Whitney Adams, *Office Mgr*
Anne F Choppy, *Mng Member*
Vincent M Choppy,
EMP: 30
SQ FT: 35,000
SALES (est): 5.7MM Privately Held
WEB: www.vmchoppyandsons.com
SIC: 3444 Sheet metal specialties, not stamped

(G-15196)
WANT-AD DIGEST INC
Also Called: Classified Advertising
870 Hoosick Rd Ste 1 (12180-6622)
PHONE................................518 279-1181
William Engelke, *President*
Rose Engelke, *Vice Pres*
Rose Hastings, *Director*
EMP: 18
SQ FT: 2,000
SALES (est): 192.9K Privately Held
WEB: www.wantaddigest.com
SIC: 2741 5521 Directories: publishing & printing; used car dealers

(G-15197)
WEIGHING & SYSTEMS TECH INC
274 2nd St (12180-4616)
PHONE................................518 274-2797
EMP: 7
SALES (corp-wide): 695K Privately Held
SIC: 3596 Mfg Scales/Balances-Nonlaboratory

PA: Weighing & Systems Technology, Inc.
4558 Morgan Pl
Liverpool NY 12180
315 451-7940

(G-15198)
WELDCOMPUTER CORPORATION
105 Jordan Rd Ste 1 (12180-7612)
PHONE................................518 283-2897
Robert Cohen, *President*
Dr Keith Strain, *Vice Pres*
EMP: 13
SQ FT: 4,000
SALES: 1.5MM Privately Held
WEB: www.weldcomputer.com
SIC: 3625 Control equipment, electric

Trumansburg
Tompkins County

(G-15199)
EAGLE ENVELOPE COMPANY (DH)
8091 Trumansburg Rd (14886)
P.O. Box 236, Ithaca (14851-0236)
PHONE................................607 387-3195
J Kemper Matt Sr, *CEO*
Richard Spingarn, *President*
EMP: 9
SQ FT: 3,000
SALES (est): 1MM
SALES (corp-wide): 49.5MM Privately Held
WEB: www.eagleprint.com
SIC: 2759 Envelopes: printing
HQ: Dupli Graphics Corporation
6761 Thompson Rd
Syracuse NY 13211
315 234-7286

(G-15200)
FLO-TECH ORTHOTIC & PROSTHETIC
7325 Halseyville Rd (14886-9135)
P.O. Box 462 (14886-0462)
PHONE................................607 387-3070
Robert N Brown Sr, *CEO*
Kathleen Brown, *President*
Mike Assunto, *Vice Pres*
Bruce Chamberlin, *Manager*
EMP: 8
SALES: 900K Privately Held
WEB: www.1800flo-tech.com
SIC: 3842 Prosthetic appliances

(G-15201)
FORCE DYNAMICS INC
4995 Voorheis Rd (14886-9435)
PHONE................................607 546-5023
Micheal D Wiernicki, *Principal*
EMP: 19
SALES (est): 2.4MM Privately Held
WEB: www.force-dynamics.com
SIC: 3559 Special industry machinery

(G-15202)
WASHBURN MANUFACTURING TECH
9828 State Route 96 (14886-9327)
PHONE................................607 387-3991
Thomas Washburn, *President*
EMP: 8
SQ FT: 2,000
SALES: 1MM Privately Held
SIC: 3599 Custom machinery

Tuckahoe
Westchester County

(G-15203)
AUTOMTIVE UPHL CNVERTIBLE TOPS
170 Marbledale Rd (10707-3118)
PHONE................................914 961-4242
Frank Ackermann, *President*
Ron Ackermann, *Vice Pres*
EMP: 5
SQ FT: 5,000

SALES (est): 370K Privately Held
SIC: 2394 2399 Convertible tops, canvas or boat: from purchased materials; automotive covers, except seat & tire covers

(G-15204)
GLOBAL FOOD SOURCE & CO INC
114 Carpenter Ave (10707-2104)
PHONE................................914 320-9615
Albert J Savarese, *President*
▲ EMP: 4
SALES (est): 5MM Privately Held
SIC: 2032 Canned specialties

(G-15205)
MEDI-RAY INC
150 Marbledale Rd (10707-3197)
PHONE................................877 898-3003
Ralph F Farella, *President*
Barry N Dansky, *Treasurer*
Joyce Adkins, *Data Proc Staff*
Barry Dansky, *Executive*
▲ EMP: 63
SQ FT: 23,000
SALES (est): 11.5MM Privately Held
WEB: www.mediray.com
SIC: 3412 3842 5063 7623 Metal barrels, drums & pails; orthopedic appliances; electrical apparatus & equipment; refrigeration service & repair; nonferrous foundries; nonferrous rolling & drawing

(G-15206)
STOFFEL POLYGON SYSTEMS INC
199 Marbledale Rd (10707-3117)
PHONE................................914 961-2000
John F Stoffel, *President*
Arlene M Gruber, *Admin Sec*
EMP: 10
SQ FT: 22,180
SALES (est): 1.2MM Privately Held
WEB: www.stoffelpolygon.com
SIC: 3462 Iron & steel forgings

Tully
Onondaga County

(G-15207)
APPLIED CONCEPTS INC
397 State Route 281 (13159-2486)
PHONE................................315 696-6676
Kurt Shaffer, *CEO*
Stephen C Soos, *President*
John Dickson, *Design Engr*
EMP: 28 EST: 1998
SQ FT: 16,000
SALES: 4MM Privately Held
WEB: www.acipower.com
SIC: 3679 Power supplies, all types: static

(G-15208)
BARBER & DELINE ENRGY SVCS LLC
10 Community Dr (13159)
PHONE................................315 696-8961
Eva Deline, *Mng Member*
EMP: 10
SALES (est): 643.7K Privately Held
SIC: 1389 1381 Construction, repair & dismantling services; drilling water intake wells

(G-15209)
BARBER & DELINE LLC
995 State Route 11a (13159-2426)
PHONE................................607 749-2619
Eva Deline,
EMP: 10
SQ FT: 3,000
SALES (est): 2.7MM Privately Held
WEB: www.barber-deline.com
SIC: 1381 1781 Service well drilling; water well drilling

▲ = Import ▼=Export
◆ =Import/Export

Tupper Lake
Franklin County

(G-15210)
LIZOTTE LOGGING INC
5 White Pine Ln (12986-1054)
PHONE...................................518 359-2200
Jeannel Lizotte, *President*
Cynthia Lizotte, *Admin Sec*
EMP: 15
SALES (est): 1.8MM **Privately Held**
SIC: 2411 Logging camps & contractors

(G-15211)
MITCHELL STONE PRODUCTS LLC
161 Main St (12986-1023)
PHONE...................................518 359-7029
Paul Mitchell, *Principal*
EMP: 6 **EST:** 2016
SALES (est): 184.7K **Privately Held**
SIC: 1442 Construction sand & gravel

(G-15212)
PAUL J MITCHELL LOGGING INC
15 Mitchell Ln (12986-1056)
PHONE...................................518 359-7029
Paul J Mitchell, *President*
Mary Michell, *Admin Sec*
EMP: 26
SQ FT: 7,000
SALES (est): 3.6MM **Privately Held**
SIC: 2411 Logging camps & contractors

(G-15213)
RICHARDS LOGGING LLC
201 State Route 3 (12986-7705)
PHONE...................................518 359-2775
Bruce Richards, *Mng Member*
Lawrence Richards,
EMP: 15
SALES (est): 2.6MM **Privately Held**
SIC: 2411 Logging camps & contractors

(G-15214)
TRILAKE THREE PRESS CORP
136 Park St (12986-1818)
PHONE...................................518 359-2462
Dan McClelland, *President*
Judy McClelland, *Vice Pres*
John Morris, *Director*
EMP: 6
SQ FT: 3,500
SALES (est): 340K **Privately Held**
SIC: 2711 Newspapers, publishing & printing

(G-15215)
TUPPER LAKE HARDWOODS INC
167 Pitchfork Pond Rd (12986-1047)
P.O. Box 748 (12986-0748)
PHONE...................................518 359-8248
Greg Paneaudeau, *President*
Robert Gibeault, *General Mgr*
EMP: 32 **EST:** 1994
SQ FT: 21,356
SALES (est): 3.6MM **Privately Held**
SIC: 2421 2426 Sawmills & planing mills, general; hardwood dimension & flooring mills

Tuxedo Park
Orange County

(G-15216)
I & I SYSTEMS
66 Table Rock Rd (10987-4720)
PHONE...................................845 753-9126
Shan Custello, *President*
EMP: 6
SALES (est): 634.5K **Privately Held**
SIC: 3953 Letters (marking devices), metal

(G-15217)
INTERNATIONAL PAPER COMPANY
1422 Long Meadow Rd (10987-3500)
PHONE...................................845 986-6409
Virginia Rizzo, *Manager*
EMP: 140
SALES (corp-wide): 23.3B **Publicly Held**
WEB: www.internationalpaper.com
SIC: 2621 8731 Paper mills; commercial physical research
PA: International Paper Company
6400 Poplar Ave
Memphis TN 38197
901 419-9000

Ulster Park
Ulster County

(G-15218)
DYNO NOBEL INC
161 Ulster Ave (12487-5019)
PHONE...................................845 338-2144
Margaret Seeger, *Opers-Prdtn-Mfg*
EMP: 55 **Privately Held**
SIC: 2892 3489 Explosives; ordnance & accessories
HQ: Dyno Nobel Inc.
2795 E Cottonwood Pkwy # 500
Salt Lake City UT 84121
801 364-4800

(G-15219)
MORESCA CLOTHING AND COSTUME
361 Union Center Rd (12487-5232)
PHONE...................................845 331-6012
Lena Dun, *President*
EMP: 10
SQ FT: 11,000
SALES (est): 1.4MM **Privately Held**
WEB: www.moresca.com
SIC: 2389 5699 5136 5137 Costumes; costumes, masquerade or theatrical; men's & boys' clothing; women's & children's clothing

Unadilla
Otsego County

(G-15220)
AMES COMPANIES INC
196 Clifton St (13849-2418)
P.O. Box 644 (13849-0644)
PHONE...................................607 369-9595
Alexander Miller, *Branch Mgr*
EMP: 61
SQ FT: 25,000
SALES (corp-wide): 1.5B **Publicly Held**
WEB: www.ames.com
SIC: 3423 Garden & farm tools, including shovels
HQ: The Ames Companies Inc
465 Railroad Ave
Camp Hill PA 17011
717 737-1500

(G-15221)
ATOMIC INFORMATION SYSTEMS
Also Called: Atomicdbonline.com
1580 State Highway 357 (13849-2399)
PHONE...................................716 713-5402
Jean Le Tennier, *President*
EMP: 50
SALES (corp-wide): 10MM **Privately Held**
SIC: 7372 7371 Prepackaged software; custom computer programming services
PA: Atomic Information Systems Corp
5500 N Bailey Ave Unit 36
Amherst NY
716 713-5402

Union Springs
Cayuga County

(G-15222)
HEART & HANDS WINE COMPANY INC
4162 State Route 90 (13160-3171)
PHONE...................................315 889-8500
Tom Higgins, *Ch of Bd*
EMP: 5 **EST:** 2009
SALES (est): 498.9K **Privately Held**
SIC: 2084 Wines

Uniondale
Nassau County

(G-15223)
AITHACA CHEMICAL CORP
50 Charles Lindbergh Blvd # 400 (11553-3626)
PHONE...................................516 229-2330
Eric Kastens, *President*
EMP: 10
SQ FT: 300
SALES (est): 1.3MM **Privately Held**
WEB: www.aithaca.com
SIC: 2819 5169 Chemicals, high purity: refined from technical grade; chemicals & allied products

(G-15224)
CAMBRIDGE WHOS WHO PUBG INC (PA)
498 Rxr Plz Fl 4 (11556-0400)
PHONE...................................516 833-8440
Mitchel Robbins, *CEO*
Randy Narod, *President*
Eric Lee, *COO*
EMP: 45
SALES (est): 20.3MM **Privately Held**
SIC: 2741 8748 Miscellaneous publishing; business consulting

(G-15225)
COTY US LLC
726 Eab Plz (11556-0726)
PHONE...................................212 389-7000
Rich Garzon, *Branch Mgr*
EMP: 284 **Publicly Held**
SIC: 2844 Perfumes & colognes; cosmetic preparations
HQ: Coty Us Llc
350 5th Ave
New York NY 10118

(G-15226)
ELIZABETH WILSON
Also Called: Elizabeth's
579 Edgemere Ave (11553-2517)
PHONE...................................516 486-2157
Elizabeth Wilson, *Owner*
EMP: 4
SQ FT: 1,200
SALES (est): 2.2MM **Privately Held**
WEB: www.elizabethwilson.com
SIC: 2339 Aprons, except rubber or plastic: women's, misses', juniors'

(G-15227)
FEI COMMUNICATIONS INC
55 Charles Lindbergh Blvd (11553-3689)
PHONE...................................516 794-4500
Harry Newman, *VP Finance*
EMP: 180
SALES (est): 29.7MM
SALES (corp-wide): 49.5MM **Publicly Held**
WEB: www.freqelec.com
SIC: 3679 Electronic circuits
PA: Frequency Electronics, Inc.
55 Charles Lindbergh Blvd # 2
Uniondale NY 11553
516 794-4500

(G-15228)
FEI-ZYFER INC
55 Charles Lindbergh Blvd (11553-3689)
PHONE...................................714 933-4045
EMP: 9

SALES (corp-wide): 49.5MM **Publicly Held**
SIC: 3663 Antennas, transmitting & communications
HQ: Fei-Zyfer, Inc.
7321 Lincoln Way
Garden Grove CA 92841

(G-15229)
FREQUENCY ELECTRONICS INC (PA)
55 Charles Lindbergh Blvd # 2 (11553-3699)
PHONE...................................516 794-4500
Martin B Bloch, *Ch of Bd*
Stanton D Sloane, *President*
James Davis, *President*
Steven Strang, *President*
Oleandro Mancini, *Senior VP*
EMP: 202 **EST:** 1961
SALES: 49.5MM **Publicly Held**
WEB: www.freqelec.com
SIC: 3825 3812 3669 3679 Elapsed time meters, electronic; frequency meters: electrical, mechanical & electronic; search & detection systems & instruments; detection apparatus: electronic/magnetic field, light/heat; intercommunication systems, electric; microwave components

(G-15230)
HEARST BUSINESS MEDIA (HQ)
Also Called: F C W Division
50 Charles Lindbergh Blvd # 103 (11553-3654)
PHONE...................................516 227-1300
Rich Malloch, *CEO*
EMP: 57
SALES (est): 9.8MM
SALES (corp-wide): 8.3B **Privately Held**
SIC: 2721 2741 Magazines: publishing only, not printed on site; directories: publishing only, not printed on site
PA: The Hearst Corporation
300 W 57th St Fl 42
New York NY 10019
212 649-2000

(G-15231)
LOCKHEED MARTIN CORPORATION
55 Charles Lindbergh Blvd # 1 (11553-3682)
PHONE...................................516 228-2000
Marie Bruzzi, *Senior Engr*
Frank Pare, *Senior Engr*
Earl Matchett, *Branch Mgr*
Paul Monaghen, *Technology*
Charles Reibeling, *Technology*
EMP: 225 **Publicly Held**
WEB: www.lockheedmartin.com
SIC: 3812 Search & navigation equipment
PA: Lockheed Martin Corporation
6801 Rockledge Dr
Bethesda MD 20817

(G-15232)
MERCHANT SERVICE PYMNT ACCESS
626 Rxr Plz (11556-0626)
PHONE...................................212 561-5516
Sean Ellis, *President*
EMP: 5 **EST:** 2017
SALES: 10MM **Privately Held**
SIC: 3578 Calculating & accounting equipment

(G-15233)
TDK USA CORPORATION (HQ)
455 Rxr Plz (11556-3811)
PHONE...................................516 535-2600
Francis J Sweeney Jr, *Ch of Bd*
◆ **EMP:** 68
SQ FT: 60,000
SALES (est): 213.2MM **Privately Held**
SIC: 3679 8741 Recording & playback apparatus, including phonograph; administrative management; financial management for business

Unionville
Orange County

(G-15234)
ROYAL FIREWORKS PRTG CO INC
First Ave (10988)
PHONE...........................845 726-3333
Thomas Kemnitz, *President*
EMP: 13
SQ FT: 66,000
SALES (est): 1.6MM **Privately Held**
SIC: 2732 Book printing

Upper Jay
Essex County

(G-15235)
AMSTUTZE WOODWORKING (PA)
246 Springfield Rd (12987-3200)
PHONE...........................518 946-8206
Steve Amstutz, *Principal*
EMP: 5
SALES (est): 456.5K **Privately Held**
SIC: 2431 Millwork

Utica
Oneida County

(G-15236)
ADIRONDACK DISTILLING COMPANY
601 Varick St (13502-4025)
PHONE...........................315 316-0387
Jordan Karp, *Principal*
Anita Elwell, *Business Mgr*
EMP: 8 EST: 2014
SALES (est): 901.9K **Privately Held**
SIC: 2085 Distilled & blended liquors

(G-15237)
ADVANCE ENERGY SYSTEMS NY LLC
17 Tilton Rd (13501-6411)
PHONE...........................315 735-5125
EMP: 5
SALES (est): 649.2K **Privately Held**
SIC: 3699 Mfg Electrical Equipment/Supplies

(G-15238)
AEROMED INC
1821 Broad St Ste 1 (13501-1115)
P.O. Box 768, Amsterdam (12010-0768)
PHONE...........................518 843-9144
William E Palmer, *President*
EMP: 5
SALES (est): 721.5K **Privately Held**
WEB: www.aeromed.com
SIC: 3564 Air purification equipment

(G-15239)
AUSTIN MOHAWK AND COMPANY LLC
2175 Beechgrove Pl (13501-1705)
PHONE...........................315 793-3000
John B Millet, *Plant Mgr*
Richard Davies, *Controller*
▲ EMP: 29
SQ FT: 20,000
SALES (est): 5.5MM **Privately Held**
WEB: www.austinmohawk.com
SIC: 3444 3448 Canopies, sheet metal; prefabricated metal buildings

(G-15240)
BAGEL GROVE INC
7 Burrstone Rd (13502)
PHONE...........................315 724-8015
Anne Wadsworth, *President*
EMP: 25
SQ FT: 2,600

SALES: 450K **Privately Held**
WEB: www.bagelgrove.com
SIC: 2051 5149 5461 Bagels, fresh or frozen; crackers, cookies & bakery products; bagels

(G-15241)
BICK & HEINTZ INC
1101 Stark St (13502-4417)
P.O. Box 395 (13503-0395)
PHONE...........................315 733-7577
Thomas Bick, *President*
Robert J Bick, *Treasurer*
EMP: 18
SQ FT: 8,500
SALES (est): 2.7MM **Privately Held**
SIC: 3599 5531 7538 Machine shop, jobbing & repair; truck equipment & parts; general truck repair

(G-15242)
BRODOCK PRESS INC (PA)
502 Court St Ste G (13502-4233)
PHONE...........................315 735-9577
Lawrence Lelievre, *President*
Craig S Brodock, *Chairman*
Bryan Brodock, *VP Opers*
Paul Besig, *Traffic Mgr*
EMP: 74 EST: 1960
SQ FT: 80,000
SALES (est): 12MM **Privately Held**
WEB: www.brodock.com
SIC: 2759 2752 2791 2789 Letterpress printing; commercial printing, lithographic; typesetting; bookbinding & related work

(G-15243)
CLARA PAPA
Also Called: Kennel Klub
1323 Blandina St 1 (13501-1915)
PHONE...........................315 733-2660
Clara Papa, *Owner*
EMP: 5
SQ FT: 15,000
SALES (est): 227.6K **Privately Held**
SIC: 3999 5199 Pet supplies; pet supplies

(G-15244)
CNY BUSINESS SOLUTIONS
502 Court St Ste 206 (13502-0001)
PHONE...........................315 733-5031
Jennifer Racquet, *President*
Wendy Aiello, *Principal*
EMP: 5 EST: 2010
SALES (est): 472.6K **Privately Held**
SIC: 3577 Printers & plotters

(G-15245)
COLLINITE CORPORATION
Also Called: Collinite Wax
1520 Lincoln Ave (13502-5200)
PHONE...........................315 732-2282
Patrick Taylor, *President*
Mark Taylor, *President*
Michael Taylor, *President*
Christine Taylor, *Admin Sec*
EMP: 8 EST: 1912
SQ FT: 6,000
SALES (est): 914.7K **Privately Held**
WEB: www.collinite.com
SIC: 2842 5169 5999 5961 Cleaning or polishing preparations; polishing preparations & related products; waxes, except petroleum; cleaning equipment & supplies; mail order house

(G-15246)
CONMED ANDOVER MEDICAL INC (HQ)
525 French Rd Ste 3 (13502-5994)
PHONE...........................315 797-8375
Joseph J Corasanti, *CEO*
EMP: 14
SALES (est): 8.4MM
SALES (corp-wide): 859.6MM **Publicly Held**
SIC: 3845 Electromedical apparatus
PA: Conmed Corporation
525 French Rd
Utica NY 13502
315 797-8375

(G-15247)
CONMED CORPORATION
Endoscopic Technologies Div
525 French Rd (13502-5994)
PHONE...........................315 797-8375
Dennis Werger, *Manager*
EMP: 8
SALES (corp-wide): 859.6MM **Publicly Held**
SIC: 3845 8731 3841 Electromedical equipment; commercial physical research; surgical & medical instruments
PA: Conmed Corporation
525 French Rd
Utica NY 13502
315 797-8375

(G-15248)
CONMED CORPORATION (PA)
525 French Rd (13502-5994)
PHONE...........................315 797-8375
Mark E Tryniski, *Ch of Bd*
Curt R Hartman, *President*
Heather L Cohen, *Exec VP*
Daniel S Jonas, *Exec VP*
Peter K Shagory, *Exec VP*
◆ EMP: 277
SQ FT: 500,000
SALES: 859.6MM **Publicly Held**
SIC: 3845 3841 Electromedical apparatus; electrocardiographs; patient monitoring apparatus; surgical instruments & apparatus; trocars; suction therapy apparatus; probes, surgical

(G-15249)
CRANESVILLE BLOCK CO INC
Also Called: Cranesville Concrete Co
895 Catherine St (13501-1409)
PHONE...........................315 732-2135
Mark Smith, *Branch Mgr*
EMP: 25
SQ FT: 3,462
SALES (corp-wide): 45MM **Privately Held**
SIC: 3273 Ready-mixed concrete
PA: Cranesville Block Co., Inc.
1250 Riverfront Ctr
Amsterdam NY 12010
518 684-6154

(G-15250)
CYBERSPORTS INC (PA)
11 Avery Pl (13502-5401)
PHONE...........................315 737-7150
Todd Hobin, *President*
Candice Hobin, *Vice Pres*
EMP: 7
SALES (est): 698.3K **Privately Held**
WEB: www.cybersportsinc.com
SIC: 7372 Prepackaged software

(G-15251)
DACOBE ENTERPRISES LLC
901 Broad St Ste 10 (13501-1500)
PHONE...........................315 368-0093
Geoff Thorp, *President*
EMP: 10
SALES: 5MM **Privately Held**
SIC: 3089 Plastic processing

(G-15252)
DANFOSS SILICON POWER LLC
330 Technology Dr (13502-1306)
PHONE...........................515 239-6376
Kim Fausing, *President*
EMP: 15
SALES (est): 2.6MM
SALES (corp-wide): 250.7K **Privately Held**
SIC: 3599 Custom machinery
HQ: Danfoss A/S
Nordborgvej 81
Nordborg 6430
748 822-22

(G-15253)
DARMAN MANUFACTURING COINC
1410 Lincoln Ave (13502-5019)
PHONE...........................315 724-9632
Pamela Darman, *CEO*
Cynthia J Lane, *Controller*
▼ EMP: 16 EST: 1936
SQ FT: 20,800

SALES: 2MM **Privately Held**
WEB: www.darmanco.com
SIC: 3429 Cabinet hardware

(G-15254)
DEIORIO FOODS INC (PA)
Also Called: De Iorio's Bakery
2200 Bleecker St (13501-1739)
PHONE...........................315 732-7612
George Lampros, *CEO*
John Lafever, *Maint Spvr*
John Carrigg, *CFO*
Karla Ortiz, *Asst Controller*
Tom Foster, *Sales Staff*
EMP: 200 EST: 1924
SALES (est): 55.5MM **Privately Held**
WEB: www.deiorios.com
SIC: 2053 Frozen bakery products, except bread

(G-15255)
DICO PRODUCTS CORPORATION
200 Seward Ave (13502-5750)
PHONE...........................315 797-0470
Bradford Lees Divine, *President*
▲ EMP: 15
SALES (est): 1.2MM **Privately Held**
WEB: www.dicoproducts.com
SIC: 3496 3429 3291 2392 Hardware cloth, woven wire; manufactured hardware (general); abrasive products; household furnishings

(G-15256)
DIMANCO INC (PA)
Also Called: Divine Bros
200 Seward Ave (13502-5750)
PHONE...........................315 797-0470
B Lees Divine, *President*
Eric Smith, *Regional Mgr*
Brad Divine, *Vice Pres*
George Weaver, *Vice Pres*
Brian Carpenter, *Plant Mgr*
◆ EMP: 3
SQ FT: 170,000
SALES (est): 28.4MM **Privately Held**
WEB: www.dimanco.com
SIC: 3291 3562 Buffing or polishing wheels, abrasive or nonabrasive; casters

(G-15257)
DINOS SAUSAGE & MEAT CO INC
722 Catherine St (13501-1304)
PHONE...........................315 732-2661
Anthony Ferrucci, *President*
EMP: 11
SQ FT: 6,300
SALES (est): 1.7MM **Privately Held**
SIC: 2013 Sausages & related products, from purchased meat

(G-15258)
DIVA FARMS LTD
1301 Broad St (13501-1605)
PHONE...........................315 735-4397
Margherita Schuller, *President*
EMP: 7
SQ FT: 2,000
SALES (est): 550K **Privately Held**
SIC: 2099 Seasonings & spices

(G-15259)
DIVINE BROTHERS COMPANY
Also Called: Dico Products
200 Seward Ave (13502-5750)
PHONE...........................315 797-0470
Bradford W Divine, *President*
Charles H Divine, *Vice Pres*
Thomas Banks, *CFO*
◆ EMP: 112 EST: 1892
SQ FT: 112,000
SALES (est): 9.8MM
SALES (corp-wide): 28.4MM **Privately Held**
WEB: www.divinebrothers.com
SIC: 3291 Buffing or polishing wheels, abrasive or nonabrasive
PA: Dimanco Inc.
200 Seward Ave
Utica NY 13502
315 797-0470

(G-15260)
ECR INTERNATIONAL INC (PA)
Also Called: Utica Boilers
2201 Dwyer Ave (13501-1101)
P.O. Box 4729 (13504-4729)
PHONE..............................315 797-1310
Ronald J Passafaro, *President*
Timothy R Reed, *President*
Bob Shea, *Regional Mgr*
Eric Dorozynski, *Plant Mgr*
Michael Cariseo, *Purch Mgr*
◆ **EMP:** 100 **EST:** 1928
SQ FT: 190,000
SALES (est): 107.2MM **Privately Held**
WEB: www.ecrinternational.com
SIC: 3433 3443 Boilers, low-pressure
heating: steam or hot water; fabricated
plate work (boiler shop)

(G-15261)
FALVO MANUFACTURING CO INC
20 Harbor Point Rd (13502-2502)
P.O. Box 215 (13503-0215)
PHONE..............................315 724-7925
Eugene T Falvo, *President*
EMP: 15
SQ FT: 26,000
SALES (est): 2.5MM **Privately Held**
SIC: 2441 2512 2522 2541 Packing
cases, wood: nailed or lock corner; uphol-
stered household furniture; office cabinets
& filing drawers: except wood; store fix-
tures, wood

(G-15262)
FARRINGTON PACKAGING CORP
2007 Beechgrove Pl (13501-1703)
P.O. Box 6538 (13504-6538)
PHONE..............................315 733-4600
Raymond Mele, *President*
Gerard Morrissey, *Controller*
Bill Richardson, *Manager*
EMP: 40
SALES (est): 4.6MM **Privately Held**
SIC: 2631 2541 Packaging board; wood
partitions & fixtures

(G-15263)
FEDERAL SHEET METAL WORKS INC
1416 Dudley Ave (13501-4611)
P.O. Box 273 (13503-0273)
PHONE..............................315 735-4730
Leonard A Capuana, *President*
Michael Capuana, *Treasurer*
EMP: 12
SQ FT: 7,500
SALES: 1.5MM **Privately Held**
SIC: 3444 Sheet metalwork

(G-15264)
FOURTEEN ARNOLD AVE CORP
Also Called: PROGRESS INDUSTRIES
SALES
14 Arnold Ave (13502-5602)
PHONE..............................315 272-1700
Angela Van Derhoof, *President*
EMP: 13
SALES: 312.3K **Privately Held**
SIC: 3565 Packing & wrapping machinery

(G-15265)
G W CANFIELD & SON INC
600 Plant St (13502-4712)
PHONE..............................315 735-5522
Mark W Canfield, *President*
Anne C Kuhn, *Vice Pres*
EMP: 6
SQ FT: 5,000
SALES (est): 868.7K **Privately Held**
WEB: www.gwcanfield.com
SIC: 2752 Commercial printing, offset

(G-15266)
GAMETIME SPORTSWEAR PLUS LLC
1206 Belle Ave (13501-2614)
PHONE..............................315 724-5893
Michael Macchione,
EMP: 6
SQ FT: 3,200

SALES (est): 468.8K **Privately Held**
SIC: 2329 5699 Athletic (warmup, sweat &
jogging) suits: men's & boys'; sports apparel

(G-15267)
GATEHOUSE MEDIA LLC
Also Called: Observer Dispatch
350 Willowbrook Office Pa (13501)
PHONE..............................315 792-5000
Donna Donnovan, *Principal*
Maria Birnell, *Editor*
Rob Booth, *Editor*
Barbara Laible, *Editor*
Gary Casey, *Opers Staff*
EMP: 31
SALES (corp-wide): 1.5B **Privately Held**
WEB: www.gatehousemedia.com
SIC: 2711 Newspapers, publishing & print-
ing
HQ: Gatehouse Media, Llc
175 Sullys Trl Fl 3
Pittsford NY 14534
585 598-0030

(G-15268)
GATEHOUSE MEDIA LLC
Also Called: Evening Telegram
221 Oriskany St E (13501-1201)
P.O. Box 551, Herkimer (13350-0551)
PHONE..............................315 866-2220
Beth Brewer, *Adv Dir*
EMP: 10
SALES (corp-wide): 1.5B **Privately Held**
WEB: www.gatehousemedia.com
SIC: 2711 Newspapers, publishing & print-
ing
HQ: Gatehouse Media, Llc
175 Sullys Trl Fl 3
Pittsford NY 14534
585 598-0030

(G-15269)
H F BROWN MACHINE CO INC
708 State St (13502-3458)
PHONE..............................315 732-6129
James F Chubbuck, *President*
Joseph Chubbuck, *Vice Pres*
George Chubbuck, *Treasurer*
EMP: 10 **EST:** 1946
SQ FT: 26,000
SALES (est): 1.3MM **Privately Held**
SIC: 3599 Machine shop, jobbing & repair

(G-15270)
HARBOR POINT MINERAL PDTS INC
71 Wurz Ave (13502-2533)
PHONE..............................315 797-1300
Raymond P Villeneuve, *Ch of Bd*
Kevin Crane, *President*
Jeff Matuszczak, *Opers Mgr*
▲ **EMP:** 10
SQ FT: 14,800
SALES (est): 1.7MM **Privately Held**
SIC: 2048 Prepared feeds

(G-15271)
HPK INDUSTRIES LLC
1208 Broad St (13501-1604)
P.O. Box 4682 (13504-4682)
PHONE..............................315 724-0196
Michael A Liberatore,
▲ **EMP:** 15
SQ FT: 11,000
SALES (est): 1.6MM **Privately Held**
WEB: www.hpkindustries.com
SIC: 2389 5131 Disposable garments &
accessories; piece goods & notions

(G-15272)
HUMAN ELECTRONICS INC
155 Genesee St (13501)
PHONE..............................315 724-9850
Philip Szeliga, *President*
EMP: 5 **EST:** 1999
SQ FT: 16,000
SALES (est): 568K **Privately Held**
WEB: www.humanelectronics.com
SIC: 3571 4813 Electronic computers;
telephone communication, except radio

(G-15273)
HUMAN TECHNOLOGIES CORPORATION
Also Called: Graphtex A Div of Htc
2260 Dwyer Ave (13501-1193)
PHONE..............................315 735-3532
Tom Keller, *Manager*
EMP: 10
SQ FT: 7,600
SALES (corp-wide): 16.4MM **Privately
Held**
WEB: www.htcorp.net
SIC: 2396 2759 2395 Screen printing on
fabric articles; screen printing; embroidery
products, except schiffli machine
PA: Human Technologies Corporation
2260 Dwyer Ave
Utica NY 13501
315 724-9891

(G-15274)
IDG LLC
Also Called: Microfoam
31 Faass Ave (13502-3350)
PHONE..............................315 797-1000
Kevin Sharrow, *Manager*
EMP: 49
SALES (corp-wide): 259.3MM **Privately
Held**
SIC: 3069 Rolls, solid or covered rubber
HQ: Idg, Llc
1480 Gould Dr
Cookeville TN 38506
931 432-4000

(G-15275)
INDIUM CORPORATION OF AMERICA
1676 Lincoln Ave (13502-5398)
PHONE..............................315 793-8200
Ning Lee, *Vice Pres*
John Sovinsky, *Opers Staff*
Ivan Castellanos, *Technical Mgr*
Graham Wilson, *Engineer*
Brad Anderson, *Controller*
EMP: 30
SQ FT: 31,210
SALES (corp-wide): 245.7MM **Privately
Held**
WEB: www.indium.com
SIC: 3356 2899 Solder: wire, bar, acid
core, & rosin core; chemical preparations
PA: Indium Corporation Of America
34 Robinson Rd
Clinton NY 13323
800 446-3486

(G-15276)
INDIUM CORPORATION OF AMERICA
111 Business Park Dr (13502-6303)
PHONE..............................315 381-2330
Jeffrey Vanslyke, *Technical Staff*
EMP: 38
SALES (corp-wide): 245.7MM **Privately
Held**
SIC: 3356 Solder: wire, bar, acid core, &
rosin core
PA: Indium Corporation Of America
34 Robinson Rd
Clinton NY 13323
800 446-3486

(G-15277)
INFRARED COMPONENTS CORP
2306 Bleecker St (13501-1746)
PHONE..............................315 732-1544
Thomas Clynne, *President*
EMP: 20
SQ FT: 17,000
SALES (est): 3.1MM **Privately Held**
SIC: 3812 Infrared object detection equip-
ment; detection apparatus:
electronic/magnetic field, light/heat

(G-15278)
INTERNATIONAL PAPER COMPANY
50 Harbor Point Rd (13502-2502)
PHONE..............................315 797-5120
EMP: 160
SALES (corp-wide): 23.3B **Publicly Held**
SIC: 2621 Paper mills

PA: International Paper Company
6400 Poplar Ave
Memphis TN 38197
901 419-9000

(G-15279)
KELLY FOUNDRY & MACHINE CO
300 Hubbell St Ste 308 (13501-1404)
PHONE..............................315 732-8313
Geogia M Kelley, *President*
Marsha J Kelly, *Corp Secy*
James S Kelly III, *Vice Pres*
Mark James Kelly, *Vice Pres*
Mark Kelly, *Vice Pres*
EMP: 48 **EST:** 1892
SQ FT: 14,632
SALES (est): 7.5MM **Privately Held**
WEB: www.kellyfoundry.com
SIC: 3369 3999 3953 Nonferrous
foundries; plaques, picture, laminated;
marking devices

(G-15280)
MANNYS CHEESECAKE INC
1221 Pleasant St (13501-4893)
PHONE..............................315 732-0639
Richard Alpert, *President*
EMP: 5
SQ FT: 3,500
SALES: 200K **Privately Held**
SIC: 2052 2051 5461 Cookies; cakes,
pies & pastries; cookies; cakes

(G-15281)
METAL SOLUTIONS INC
1821 Broad St Ste 5 (13501-1115)
PHONE..............................315 732-6271
Joseph Cattadoris Jr, *President*
Cathy Cattadoris-Thiaville, *Vice Pres*
John Kulis, *Shareholder*
EMP: 110 **EST:** 1954
SQ FT: 110,000
SALES (est): 15.1MM **Privately Held**
WEB: www.nhsmetal.com
SIC: 3444 Sheet metalwork

(G-15282)
METALLOGIX DESIGN FABRICATION
1305 Conkling Ave (13501-4618)
PHONE..............................315 738-4554
Joel Grimaldi, *Owner*
EMP: 20
SALES (est): 2.9MM **Privately Held**
SIC: 3444 Sheet metalwork

(G-15283)
MID YORK WEEKLY & PENNYSAVER
221 Oriskany St E (13501-1201)
PHONE..............................315 792-4990
Donna Donnovan, *Principal*
EMP: 5
SALES (est): 155.2K **Privately Held**
WEB: www.utica.gannett.com
SIC: 2711 Commercial printing & newspa-
per publishing combined; newspapers,
publishing & printing

(G-15284)
MILLENNIUM ANTENNA CORP
1001 Broad St Ste 401 (13501-1545)
PHONE..............................315 798-9374
David Schroeter, *President*
EMP: 10
SQ FT: 2,000
SALES (est): 950K **Privately Held**
WEB: www.millenniumantenna.com
SIC: 3663 8711 8731 Antennas, transmit-
ting & communications; engineering serv-
ices; electronic research

(G-15285)
MOBILE MINI INC
2222 Oriskany St W Ste 3 (13502-2925)
PHONE..............................315 732-4555
Marc Allen, *Branch Mgr*
EMP: 10

SALES (corp-wide): 593.2MM **Publicly Held**
WEB: www.mobilemini.com
SIC: **3448** 3441 3412 7359 Buildings, portable: prefabricated metal; fabricated structural metal; metal barrels, drums & pails; equipment rental & leasing
PA: Mobile Mini, Inc.
4646 E Van Buren St # 400
Phoenix AZ 85008
480 894-6311

(G-15286)
MUNSON MACHINERY COMPANY INC
210 Seward Ave (13502-5750)
PHONE....................................315 797-0090
Charles H Divine, *CEO*
Jackie Miller, *Purch Agent*
Robert Batson, *Engineer*
Dier Vinnie, *Engineer*
Dan Simmons, *Design Engr*
▲ EMP: 40 EST: 1828
SQ FT: 45,000
SALES (est): 11.3MM
SALES (corp-wide): 28.4MM **Privately Held**
WEB: www.munsonmachinery.com
SIC: **3532** 3531 3559 3541 Crushing, pulverizing & screening equipment; mixers: ore, plaster, slag, sand, mortar, etc.; refinery, chemical processing & similar machinery; machine tools, metal cutting type; buffing & polishing machines; grinding machines, metalworking; metalworking machinery
PA: Dimanco Inc.
200 Seward Ave
Utica NY 13502
315 797-0470

(G-15287)
NATHAN STEEL CORP
36 Wurz Ave (13502-2534)
P.O. Box 299 (13503-0299)
PHONE....................................315 797-1335
Edward Kowalsky, *President*
EMP: 15
SQ FT: 12,000
SALES (est): 4.1MM **Privately Held**
SIC: **3441** 5051 Fabricated structural metal; steel

(G-15288)
NORTH COUNTRY BOOKS INC
220 Lafayette St (13502-4312)
PHONE....................................315 735-4877
Robert Igoe, *President*
▲ EMP: 5
SQ FT: 5,000
SALES: 1.1MM **Privately Held**
WEB: www.northcountrybooks.com
SIC: **2732** 5192 Books: printing only; books

(G-15289)
OHIO BAKING COMPANY INC
Also Called: Spano's Bread
10585 Cosby Manor Rd (13502-1207)
PHONE....................................315 724-2033
Joseph A Spano, *President*
EMP: 20 EST: 1930
SQ FT: 4,000
SALES (est): 3.5MM **Privately Held**
SIC: **2041** 2051 5149 5461 Pizza dough, prepared; pizza mixes; bread, all types (white, wheat, rye, etc): fresh or frozen; bakery products; bakeries

(G-15290)
ORBCOMM INC
125 Business Park Dr (13502-6305)
PHONE....................................703 433-6396
EMP: 11
SALES (corp-wide): 276.1MM **Publicly Held**
SIC: **3663** Satellites, communications
PA: Orbcomm Inc.
395 W Passaic St Ste 325
Rochelle Park NJ 07662
703 433-6300

(G-15291)
PRINT SHOPPE
311 Turner St Ste 310 (13501-1766)
PHONE....................................315 792-9585
Steven Finch, *Partner*
Thomas Stewart, *Partner*
EMP: 7
SALES (est): 763.9K **Privately Held**
SIC: **2759** Screen printing

(G-15292)
ROBERT BOSCH LLC
2118 Beechgrove Pl (13501-1706)
PHONE....................................315 733-3312
EMP: 25
SALES (corp-wide): 268.9MM **Privately Held**
SIC: **3841** Mfg Surgical/Medical Instruments
HQ: Robert Bosch Llc
2800 S 25th Ave
Broadview IL 60155
708 865-5200

(G-15293)
SCOOBY RENDERING & INC
Also Called: Scooby Dog Food
1930 Oriskany St W (13502-2920)
PHONE....................................315 793-1014
Michael P Dote, *President*
EMP: 5
SQ FT: 3,000
SALES (est): 719.8K **Privately Held**
SIC: **2047** Dog food

(G-15294)
SHIPRITE SERVICES INC
Also Called: Shiprite Software
1312 Genesee St (13502-4700)
PHONE....................................315 427-2422
J Mark Ford, *President*
EMP: 16
SQ FT: 8,400
SALES (est): 1.2MM **Privately Held**
SIC: **7372** 7359 7334 Prepackaged software; shipping container leasing; photocopying & duplicating services

(G-15295)
STURGES MANUFACTURING CO INC
2030 Sunset Ave (13502-5500)
P.O. Box 59 (13503-0059)
PHONE....................................315 732-6159
Richard R Griffith, *Principal*
Tyler Griffith, *Vice Pres*
Norma Jean Rice, *Vice Pres*
Sharon Bubb, *Manager*
Marty Fredsell, *Manager*
▲ EMP: 75 EST: 1909
SQ FT: 58,000
SALES (est): 15.7MM **Privately Held**
WEB: www.sturgesmfg.com
SIC: **2241** Strapping webs; webbing, woven

(G-15296)
T C PETERS PRINTING CO INC
2336 W Whitesboro St (13502-3235)
PHONE....................................315 724-4149
Richard Peters, *CEO*
Douglas Peters, *President*
EMP: 9
SQ FT: 13,200
SALES (est): 1.4MM **Privately Held**
SIC: **2752** Commercial printing, offset

(G-15297)
USA SEWING INC
901 Broad St Ste 2 (13501-1500)
PHONE....................................315 792-8017
John D Inserra, *President*
Linda Taglimonte, *Manager*
EMP: 49
SALES (est): 4MM **Privately Held**
SIC: **3151** Leather gloves & mittens

(G-15298)
UTICA CUTLERY COMPANY
Also Called: Walco Stainless
820 Noyes St (13502-5053)
P.O. Box 10527 (13503-1527)
PHONE....................................315 733-4663
A Edward Allen Jr, *Ch of Bd*
David S Allen, *Ch of Bd*
Bonnette Iocovozzi, *President*
David Allen, *COO*
Phil Benbenek, *Exec VP*
▲ EMP: 60 EST: 1910
SQ FT: 100,000

SALES (est): 12.2MM **Privately Held**
WEB: www.kutmaster.com
SIC: **3914** 3421 5023 5072 Flatware, stainless steel; cutlery, stainless steel; knives: butchers', hunting, pocket, etc.; stainless steel flatware; cutlery

(G-15299)
UTICA METAL PRODUCTS INC
1526 Lincoln Ave (13502-5298)
PHONE....................................315 732-6163
Charles J Fields, *Ch of Bd*
Monte L Craig, *Vice Ch Bd*
Robert Moore, *COO*
Archie Omeragic, *Marketing Staff*
Hilary Walton, *Office Mgr*
EMP: 73
SQ FT: 30,000
SALES (est): 13.8MM **Privately Held**
WEB: www.uticametals.com
SIC: **3465** 3471 Body parts, automobile: stamped metal; hub caps, automobile: stamped metal; anodizing (plating) of metals or formed products

(G-15300)
WHERE IS UTICA COF RASTING INC
92 Genesee St (13502-3519)
PHONE....................................315 269-8898
Frank Ilias, *President*
EMP: 15
SQ FT: 1,000
SALES (est): 300K **Privately Held**
SIC: **2095** 0161 Coffee roasting (except by wholesale grocers); green lima bean farm

---

Valatie
Columbia County

(G-15301)
WEISS INDUSTRIES INC
Also Called: Precision Machine Parts
27 Blossom Ln (12184-9201)
PHONE....................................518 784-9643
Michael Weiss, *President*
EMP: 7
SALES (est): 778.3K **Privately Held**
SIC: **3599** Machine shop, jobbing & repair

Valhalla
Westchester County

(G-15302)
AXIOM SOFTWARE LTD
115 E Stevens Ave Ste 320 (10595-1263)
PHONE....................................914 769-8800
Jeffrey Yagoda, *President*
Rocco Troiano, *Vice Pres*
EMP: 10
SQ FT: 4,800
SALES (est): 1.3MM **Privately Held**
SIC: **7372** Prepackaged software

(G-15303)
EPOCH MICROELECTRONICS INC
420 Columbus Ave Ste 204 (10595-1382)
PHONE....................................914 332-8570
Ken Suyama, *President*
Aleksander Dec, *Vice Pres*
EMP: 9
SALES (est): 1.1MM **Privately Held**
WEB: www.epochmicro.com
SIC: **3825** Integrated circuit testers

(G-15304)
LEGACY VALVE LLC
14 Railroad Ave (10595-1609)
P.O. Box 107 (10595-0107)
PHONE....................................914 403-5075
Charles Cassidy, *President*
EMP: 14
SALES (est): 2.9MM **Privately Held**
SIC: **3494** Pipe fittings

(G-15305)
PEPSICO
100 Summit Lake Dr # 103 (10595-2318)
PHONE....................................914 801-1500

▲ EMP: 34
SALES (est): 4.3MM **Privately Held**
SIC: **2086** Carb Sft Drnkbtlcn

(G-15306)
PEPSICO INC
100 E Stevens Ave (10595-1299)
PHONE....................................914 742-4500
Noel E Anderson, *Vice Pres*
Raymond McGarvey, *Research*
Kyle Shandix, *Research*
Jennifer Pauley, *Human Res Mgr*
Christopher Quintana, *Security Mgr*
EMP: 380
SALES (corp-wide): 64.6B **Publicly Held**
WEB: www.pepsico.com
SIC: **2086** Carbonated soft drinks, bottled & canned
PA: Pepsico, Inc.
700 Anderson Hill Rd
Purchase NY 10577
914 253-2000

(G-15307)
PRESBREY-LELAND INC
Also Called: Presbrey- Leland Memorials
250 Lakeview Ave (10595-1618)
PHONE....................................914 949-2264
Nancy Dylan, *President*
EMP: 5 EST: 1982
SALES (est): 634.2K **Privately Held**
SIC: **3272** 5999 Monuments, concrete; monuments, finished to custom order; monuments & tombstones

(G-15308)
RETIA MEDICAL LLC (PA)
7 Dana Rd Ste 121 (10595-1554)
PHONE....................................914 594-1986
Marc Zemel,
EMP: 5
SALES (est): 679.8K **Privately Held**
SIC: **3841** Surgical & medical instruments

(G-15309)
RUHLE COMPANIES INC
Also Called: Farrand Controls Division
99 Wall St (10595-1462)
PHONE....................................914 287-4000
Frank S Ruhle, *Ch of Bd*
Robert E Ruhle, *Exec VP*
Michael Frenz, *Mfg Spvr*
Richard Babcock, *Production*
EMP: 50
SQ FT: 33,000
SALES (est): 8.3MM **Privately Held**
WEB: www.ruhle.com
SIC: **3679** 3625 3577 3674 Transducers, electrical; control equipment, electric; computer peripheral equipment; semiconductors & related devices; radio & TV communications equipment; motors & generators

(G-15310)
SPELLMAN HIGH VLTAGE ELEC CORP
1 Commerce Park (10595-1455)
PHONE....................................914 686-3600
Graham Chick, *Prdtn Mgr*
Joanne Rizzuto, *Accounting Mgr*
Loren Skeist, *Branch Mgr*
EMP: 86
SALES (corp-wide): 297.2MM **Privately Held**
SIC: **3674** Semiconductors & related devices
PA: Spellman High-Voltage Electronics Corporation
475 Wireless Blvd
Hauppauge NY 11788
631 630-3000

(G-15311)
VTB HOLDINGS INC (HQ)
100 Summit Lake Dr (10595-1339)
PHONE....................................914 345-2255
Juergen Stark, *CEO*
John Hanson, *CFO*
EMP: 6 EST: 2010
SALES: 207.1MM **Publicly Held**
SIC: **3651** Sound reproducing equipment

▲ = Import ▼=Export
◆ =Import/Export

Valley Cottage
Rockland County

(G-15312)
AERO HEALTHCARE (US) LLC
616 Corporate Way Ste 6 (10989-2047)
PHONE...........................855 225-2376
Brian Parker, *General Mgr*
Daryl Parker, *Project Mgr*
▲ EMP: 5 EST: 2012
SALES (est): 912.5K **Privately Held**
SIC: 3842 5099 Bandages & dressings;
tape, adhesive: medicated or non-med-
icated; lifesaving & survival equipment
(non-medical)
PA: Aero Healthcare Partnership
63 Seaton St
Armidale NSW 2350

(G-15313)
AREMCO PRODUCTS INC
707 Executive Blvd (10989-2020)
P.O. Box 517 (10989-0517)
PHONE...........................845 268-0039
Peter Schwartz, *President*
Esther Schwartz, *Admin Sec*
▲ EMP: 15
SQ FT: 15,500
SALES (est): 4.3MM **Privately Held**
WEB: www.aremco.com
SIC: 3559 2891 2952 3253 Refinery,
chemical processing & similar machinery;
adhesives; cement, except linoleum & tile;
coating compounds, tar; ceramic wall &
floor tile

(G-15314)
CEROVENE INC (PA)
612 Corporate Way Ste 10 (10989-2027)
PHONE...........................845 267-2055
Manish Shah, *President*
Ray Difalco, *Vice Pres*
Nikhil Patel, *Research*
Carol Masker, *Manager*
EMP: 10
SQ FT: 40,000
SALES: 8MM **Privately Held**
WEB: www.cerovene.com
SIC: 2834 Pharmaceutical preparations

(G-15315)
FIRST SBF HOLDING INC (PA)
Also Called: Gevril
9 Pinecrest Rd Ste 101 (10989-1443)
PHONE...........................845 425-9882
Samuel Friedmann, *CEO*
Keith Burns, *COO*
David Yurowitz, *Vice Pres*
Rachel Itzkowitz, *Bookkeeper*
Pierre Petit, *Officer*
▼ EMP: 49
SALES (est): 16.1MM **Privately Held**
WEB: www.gevril.com
SIC: 3873 Watches & parts, except crys-
tals & jewels.

(G-15316)
INNOTECH GRAPHIC EQP CORP
614 Corporate Way Ste 5 (10989-2026)
PHONE...........................845 268-6900
EMP: 8
SQ FT: 7,500
SALES (est): 800K **Privately Held**
SIC: 3555 5084 Mfg Printing Trades Ma-
chinery Whol Industrial Equipment

(G-15317)
LANDMARK GROUP INC
Also Called: National Ramp
709 Executive Blvd Ste A (10989-2024)
PHONE...........................845 358-0350
Garth Walker, *Ch of Bd*
Diobhann Chapman, *Manager*
Scott Coulter, *Technical Staff*
EMP: 40
SALES (est): 9.2MM **Privately Held**
SIC: 3448 Ramps: prefabricated metal

(G-15318)
LEXAR GLOBAL LLC
711 Executive Blvd Ste K (10989-2006)
PHONE...........................845 352-9700
Guy Jacobs, *President*

▲ EMP: 9
SQ FT: 18,000
SALES: 4.9MM **Privately Held**
SIC: 3555 Printing trade parts & attach-
ments

(G-15319)
MP DISPLAYS LLC
704 Executive Blvd Ste 1 (10989-2010)
PHONE...........................845 268-4113
Michael Parkes, *Mng Member*
▲ EMP: 9
SQ FT: 5,300
SALES (est): 1.7MM **Privately Held**
WEB: www.mpdisplays.com
SIC: 2653 3577 Display items, corrugated:
made from purchased materials; display
items, solid fiber: made from purchased
materials; graphic displays, except
graphic terminals

(G-15320)
NORTH SUNSHINE LLC
616 Corporate Way Ste 2-3 (10989-2044)
PHONE...........................307 027-1634
EMP: 15 EST: 2016
SALES: 800K **Privately Held**
SIC: 2273 5713 Mfg Carpets/Rugs Ret
Floor Covering

(G-15321)
REAL CO INC
616 Corporate Way (10989-2044)
PHONE...........................347 433-8549
Raphaele Chartrand, *Principal*
Muhammad Elkateb, *COO*
▲ EMP: 8 EST: 2014
SALES (est): 258.8K **Privately Held**
SIC: 2044 2099 2899 Rice milling; sugar;
salt

(G-15322)
ROSSI TOOL & DIES INC
161 Route 303 (10989-1922)
PHONE...........................845 267-8246
James Veltidi, *President*
EMP: 6 EST: 1952
SQ FT: 4,000
SALES (est): 699.7K **Privately Held**
SIC: 3544 3599 Dies & die holders for
metal cutting, forming, die casting; ma-
chine shop, jobbing & repair

(G-15323)
**SCIENTA PHARMACEUTICALS
LLC**
612 Corporate Way Ste 9 (10989-2027)
PHONE...........................845 589-0774
EMP: 5
SQ FT: 2,000
SALES (est): 320K **Privately Held**
SIC: 2834 Mfg Pharmaceutical Prepara-
tions

(G-15324)
ST KILLIANS AMERICA INC
614 Corporate Way Ste 3 (10989-2026)
PHONE...........................917 648-4351
EMP: 8
SALES (est): 831.9K **Privately Held**
SIC: 3999 Candles

(G-15325)
STAR PRESS PEARL RIVER INC
614 Corporate Way Ste 8 (10989-2026)
PHONE...........................845 268-2294
Marino Nicolich, *President*
EMP: 6 EST: 1969
SALES (est): 1.1MM **Privately Held**
SIC: 2752 2759 Commercial printing, off-
set; letterpress printing

(G-15326)
**STATEWIDE FIREPROOF DOOR
CO**
178 Charles Blvd (10989-2437)
PHONE...........................845 268-6043
Joseph Caneiro, *President*
EMP: 11 EST: 1965
SQ FT: 11,000
SALES (est): 1.7MM **Privately Held**
SIC: 3442 Fire doors, metal

(G-15327)
**STROMBERG BRAND
CORPORATION**
Also Called: Stormberg Brand
12 Ford Products Rd (10989-1238)
PHONE...........................914 739-7410
Richard Stromberg, *CEO*
Helen Stromberg, *President*
Michael Pastore, *Accounting Mgr*
EMP: 10
SQ FT: 9,000
SALES (est): 600K **Privately Held**
WEB: www.strombergbrand.com
SIC: 2759 Screen printing

(G-15328)
SUPPLYNET INC (PA)
706 Executive Blvd Ste B (10989-2039)
PHONE...........................800 826-0279
Robert Berkey, *President*
Beverly Lewis, *CFO*
Margie Valle, *Technology*
EMP: 6
SQ FT: 7,500
SALES: 7.3MM **Privately Held**
WEB: www.thesupplynet.com
SIC: 3678 Electronic connectors

(G-15329)
WEROK LLC
18 Ford Products Rd (10989-1238)
PHONE...........................845 675-7710
Brian Kaplan, *Managing Prtnr*
EMP: 6
SALES (est): 3.3MM **Privately Held**
SIC: 3441 Fabricated structural metal

(G-15330)
ZEO HEALTH LTD
159 Route 303 (10989-1922)
P.O. Box 870, Waxhaw NC (28173-1006)
PHONE...........................845 353-5185
Micah Portney, *President*
EMP: 16
SQ FT: 5,000
SALES: 500K **Privately Held**
SIC: 2834 Vitamin, nutrient & hematinic
preparations for human use

Valley Falls
Rensselaer County

(G-15331)
**STEPHEN BADER COMPANY
INC**
10 Charles St (12185-3437)
P.O. Box 297 (12185-0297)
PHONE...........................518 753-4456
Daniel W Johnson, *President*
Rosemarie Johnson, *Vice Pres*
Carrie Johnson, *Admin Sec*
▼ EMP: 10 EST: 1951
SQ FT: 14,000
SALES (est): 1.5MM **Privately Held**
WEB: www.stephenbader.com
SIC: 3541 Grinding machines, metalwork-
ing

Valley Stream
Nassau County

(G-15332)
ADC INDUSTRIES INC (PA)
181a E Jamaica Ave (11580-6069)
PHONE...........................516 596-1304
Joseph Mannino, *President*
EMP: 25
SQ FT: 2,000
SALES: 4.5MM **Privately Held**
WEB: www.airlockdoor.com
SIC: 3491 Valves, automatic control

(G-15333)
ANSA SYSTEMS OF USA INC
145 Hook Creek Blvd B6a1 (11581-2293)
PHONE...........................718 835-3743
John Olusoga, *President*
EMP: 5
SALES: 500K **Privately Held**
SIC: 7372 Application computer software

(G-15334)
**AUTOMATED OFFICE SYSTEMS
INC**
Also Called: Aos
71 S Central Ave (11580-5495)
PHONE...........................516 396-5555
Larry Sachs, *President*
EMP: 10
SQ FT: 5,000
SALES (est): 483.5K **Privately Held**
WEB: www.aosdata.com
SIC: 7372 Business oriented computer
software

(G-15335)
BLACK BEAR COMPANY INC
90 E Hawthorne Ave (11580-6302)
PHONE...........................718 784-7330
Barret T Schleicher, *President*
Jennifer Trubia, *Treasurer*
▲ EMP: 20
SQ FT: 25,000
SALES (est): 3.8MM **Privately Held**
WEB: www.blackbearoil.com
SIC: 2992 Lubricating oils

(G-15336)
BRAUN BROS BRUSHES INC
35 4th St (11581-1231)
P.O. Box 2822, Babylon (11703-0822)
PHONE...........................631 667-2179
James Braun, *President*
Pamela Sue Gagas, *Purch Mgr*
EMP: 5 EST: 1946
SQ FT: 1,400
SALES (est): 554.8K **Privately Held**
WEB: www.braunbrosbrushes.com
SIC: 3991 5085 Brushes, household or in-
dustrial; brushes, industrial

(G-15337)
CITY REAL ESTATE BOOK INC
9831 S Franklin Ave (11580)
PHONE...........................516 593-2949
Charles Danas, *President*
EMP: 8
SALES: 500K **Privately Held**
SIC: 2721 Magazines: publishing & printing

(G-15338)
CNI MEAT & PRODUCE INC
Also Called: Key Foods
500 W Merrick Rd (11580-5233)
PHONE...........................516 599-5929
▲ EMP: 5
SALES (est): 225K **Privately Held**
SIC: 2011 2013 Meat by-products from
meat slaughtered on site; sausages &
other prepared meats

(G-15339)
ELLIS PRODUCTS CORP (PA)
Also Called: Style Plus Hosiery Mills
628 Golf Dr (11581-3550)
PHONE...........................516 791-3732
Seymour Ellis, *President*
EMP: 4 EST: 1954
SALES (est): 6.2MM **Privately Held**
SIC: 3944 2251 Electronic game ma-
chines, except coin-operated; panty hose

(G-15340)
**FACILAMATIC INSTRUMENT
CORP**
39 Clinton Ave (11580-6024)
PHONE...........................516 825-6300
Dennis West, *President*
John E Bergquist, *Vice Pres*
EMP: 15
SQ FT: 15,000
SALES: 1.8MM **Privately Held**
SIC: 3812 Aircraft/aerospace flight instru-
ments & guidance systems; gyro gimbals;
gyrocompasses; gyropilots

(G-15341)
**FREQUENCY SELECTIVE
NETWORKS**
12 N Cottage St (11580-4647)
PHONE...........................718 424-7500
Julius Tischkewitsch, *President*
Michael Izzolo, *Vice Pres*
EMP: 10
SQ FT: 10,000

SALES (est): 1.5MM Privately Held
SIC: 3677 Filtration devices, electronic

(G-15342)
GLOBAL PAYMENT TECH INC
20 E Sunrise Hwy (11581-1260)
PHONE..............................516 887-0700
Stephen Katz, *Branch Mgr*
EMP: 10
SALES (corp-wide): 12.2MM Publicly
Held
WEB: www.gptx.com
SIC: 3581 Mechanisms & parts for auto-
matic vending machines
PA: Global Payment Technologies, Inc.
170 Wilbur Pl Ste 600
Bohemia NY 11716
631 563-2500

(G-15343)
**HIGH PERFORMANCE SFTWR
USA INC**
Also Called: Zuant
145 Hook Creek Blvd (11581-2299)
PHONE..............................866 616-4958
Lauren Byrge, *Business Mgr*
Pete Gillett, *Director*
EMP: 30
SALES (est): 159.2K Privately Held
SIC: 7372 Application computer software

(G-15344)
JERRYS BAGELS
Also Called: Jerry's Bagels & Bakery
951 Rosedale Rd (11581-2318)
PHONE..............................516 791-0063
Jerry Jacobs, *Owner*
EMP: 8
SALES (est): 586.6K Privately Held
SIC: 2051 Bakery: wholesale or whole-
sale/retail combined

(G-15345)
L M N PRINTING COMPANY INC
23 W Merrick Rd Ste A (11580-5757)
P.O. Box 696 (11582-0696)
PHONE..............................516 285-8526
Nora Aly, *President*
Noreen Carro, *Vice Pres*
EMP: 25
SQ FT: 5,200
SALES (est): 3.8MM Privately Held
WEB: www.lmnprinting.com
SIC: 2752 2791 Commercial printing, off-
set; typesetting

(G-15346)
**LELAB DENTAL LABORATORY
INC**
Also Called: Le Lab
550 W Merrick Rd Ste 8 (11580-5101)
PHONE..............................516 561-5050
Edmond Mardirossia, *President*
Maronlyn Mardirossian, *Vice Pres*
EMP: 5
SQ FT: 1,000
SALES (est): 669.1K Privately Held
SIC: 3843 Dental equipment & supplies

(G-15347)
MEZZOPRINT LLC (PA)
201 E Merrick Rd Ste 3 (11580-5952)
PHONE..............................347 480-9199
Robert Rickheeram, *Administration*
Andre Pertab,
EMP: 3
SQ FT: 1,000
SALES (est): 29.9MM Privately Held
SIC: 2261 2396 Screen printing of cotton
broadwoven fabrics; screen printing on
fabric articles

(G-15348)
MICHAEL FIORE LTD
126 E Fairview Ave (11580-5930)
PHONE..............................516 561-8238
Michael Fiore, *President*
EMP: 6
SQ FT: 6,000
SALES: 2MM Privately Held
SIC: 3545 Machine tool accessories

(G-15349)
**NEW YORK RHBILITATIVE SVCS
LLC**
214 E Sunrise Hwy (11581-1315)
PHONE..............................516 239-0990
Michael Nadata,
EMP: 14
SALES (est): 1.9MM Privately Held
SIC: 3842 Prosthetic appliances

(G-15350)
ONE IN A MILLION INC
51 Franklin Ave (11580-2847)
P.O. Box 234111, Great Neck (11023-4111)
PHONE..............................516 829-1111
Sasan Shavanson, *President*
EMP: 6
SQ FT: 2,000
SALES (est): 800K Privately Held
SIC: 2759 5112 2284 Screen printing; sta-
tionery; embroidery thread

(G-15351)
PARNASA INTERNATIONAL INC
Also Called: C-Air International
181 S Franklin Ave # 400 (11581-1138)
PHONE..............................516 394-0400
Glenn Schacher, *President*
Lucille Schacher, *Admin Sec*
▲ EMP: 8
SALES (est): 520K Privately Held
SIC: 2099 Food preparations

(G-15352)
PRECISELED INC
52 Railroad Ave (11580-6031)
PHONE..............................516 418-5337
Daniel Machlis, *President*
David Schachner, *Project Mgr*
▲ EMP: 10 EST: 2015
SQ FT: 13,000
SALES (est): 608.1K Privately Held
SIC: 3646 3645 Commercial indusl & insti-
tutional electric lighting fixtures; residen-
tial lighting fixtures

(G-15353)
PRO METAL OF NY CORP
814 W Merrick Rd (11580-4829)
PHONE..............................516 285-0440
Michael Marin, *President*
EMP: 5
SALES (est): 701.3K Privately Held
SIC: 3585 1761 Heating & air conditioning
combination units; sheet metalwork

(G-15354)
PSG INNOVATIONS INC
924 Kilmer Ln (11581-3130)
PHONE..............................917 299-8986
Philip Green, *CEO*
EMP: 15 EST: 2010
SQ FT: 2,500
SALES: 16MM Privately Held
SIC: 3648 Flashlights

(G-15355)
RAYS ITALIAN BAKERY INC
Also Called: Roma Ray Bakery
45 Railroad Ave (11580-6030)
PHONE..............................516 825-9170
Robert Degiovanni, *President*
Vincent Giovanni, *Vice Pres*
Dario Degiovanni, *Admin Sec*
EMP: 12
SQ FT: 10,000
SALES (est): 1.2MM Privately Held
SIC: 2051 Bread, cake & related products

(G-15356)
**READY TO ASSEMBLE
COMPANY INC**
Also Called: Debra Fisher
115 S Corona Ave (11580-6217)
PHONE..............................516 825-4397
Bruce Wulwick, *CEO*
Phyllis Wulwick, *Treasurer*
EMP: 20
SALES (est): 2.1MM Privately Held
SIC: 2519 7389 Household furniture, ex-
cept wood or metal: upholstered;

(G-15357)
ROMA BAKERY INC
45 Railroad Ave (11580-6030)
PHONE..............................516 825-9170
Jacoui Digiovanni, *President*
EMP: 17
SQ FT: 10,000
SALES (est): 1.8MM Privately Held
SIC: 2051 Bread, cake & related products

(G-15358)
SENERA CO INC
834 Glenridge Ave (11581-3019)
PHONE..............................516 639-3774
Seema Gupta, *President*
EMP: 10
SALES: 100K Privately Held
SIC: 3674 Switches, silicon control

(G-15359)
SHEPHERDS PI LLC
31 Keller St (11580-2641)
PHONE..............................516 647-8151
Imani Shepherd,
EMP: 5
SALES: 250K Privately Held
SIC: 2741

(G-15360)
SOUTH SHORE READY MIX INC
116 E Hawthorne Ave (11580-6331)
PHONE..............................516 872-3049
Joseph Dilemme, *President*
EMP: 5
SQ FT: 10,000
SALES (est): 712.7K Privately Held
SIC: 3273 Ready-mixed concrete

(G-15361)
**TOTAL DNTL IMPLANT SLTIONS
LLC**
Also Called: Tag Dental Implant Solutions
260 W Sunrise Hwy (11581-1011)
PHONE..............................212 877-3777
Ariel Goldschlag,
EMP: 5
SALES: 750K Privately Held
SIC: 3843 Dental equipment & supplies

(G-15362)
**UNIVERSAL 3D INNOVATION
INC**
1085 Rockaway Ave (11581-2137)
PHONE..............................516 837-9423
Tomer Yariz, *President*
EMP: 10
SQ FT: 5,000
SALES: 2.5MM Privately Held
SIC: 3993 Signs, not made in custom sign
painting shops

Van Hornesville
Herkimer County

(G-15363)
OGD V-HVAC INC
174 Pumkinhook Rd (13475)
PHONE..............................315 858-1002
Ormonde G Drham III, *President*
Linda Bowers, *Administration*
EMP: 20
SALES: 400K Privately Held
SIC: 3999 Manufacturing industries

Vernon
Oneida County

(G-15364)
CHEPAUME INDUSTRIES LLC
6201 Cooper St (13476-4022)
PHONE..............................315 829-6400
Chester Poplaski,
Melissa Foppes,
EMP: 6
SQ FT: 17,114
SALES (est): 569.1K Privately Held
WEB: www.chepaume.com
SIC: 3479 Coating electrodes

(G-15365)
FOUR DIRECTIONS INC
4677 State Route 5 (13476-3525)
PHONE..............................315 829-8388
Peter Wiezalis, *Director*
Kelli Bradley, *Administration*
EMP: 20
SALES (est): 760.1K Privately Held
WEB: www.fourdirectionsmedia.com
SIC: 2711 Newspapers: publishing only,
not printed on site
HQ: Oneida Nation Enterprises
5218 Patrick Rd
Verona NY 13478

(G-15366)
HP HOOD LLC
19 Ward St (13476-4415)
P.O. Box 930 (13476-0930)
PHONE..............................315 829-3339
Phil Campbell, *Plant Mgr*
EMP: 100
SQ FT: 800
SALES (corp-wide): 2.2B Privately Held
WEB: www.hphood.com
SIC: 2024 2022 2026 Ice cream & frozen
desserts; processed cheese; cream,
sweet
PA: Hp Hood Llc
6 Kimball Ln Ste 400
Lynnfield MA 01940
617 887-8441

(G-15367)
J H RHODES COMPANY INC
10 Ward St (13476-4416)
PHONE..............................315 829-3600
J Rhodes, *Principal*
EMP: 12
SALES (corp-wide): 51.6MM Privately
Held
SIC: 3674 Semiconductors & related de-
vices
HQ: J H Rhodes Company Inc.
2800 N 44th St Ste 675
Phoenix AZ 85008
602 449-8689

Vernon Center
Oneida County

(G-15368)
**MCDONOUGH HARDWOODS
LTD**
6426 Skinner Rd (13477-3840)
PHONE..............................315 829-3449
Daniel McDonough, *CEO*
James McDonough, *Treasurer*
EMP: 25
SALES (est): 1.1MM Privately Held
SIC: 2421 Sawmills & planing mills, gen-
eral

Vestal
Broome County

(G-15369)
**ADVANCED MTL ANALYTICS
LLC**
85 Murray Hl Rd Ste 2115 (13850)
PHONE..............................321 684-0528
Swastisharan Dey,
EMP: 5
SQ FT: 500
SALES (est): 350K Privately Held
SIC: 3826 Analytical instruments

(G-15370)
**BARNEY & DICKENSON INC
(PA)**
520 Prentice Rd (13850-2197)
PHONE..............................607 729-1536
Mary Murphy Harrison, *President*
Robert S Murphy Jr, *Vice Pres*
EMP: 51
SQ FT: 100,000
SALES (est): 8.1MM Privately Held
SIC: 3273 5032 1771 Ready-mixed con-
crete; concrete mixtures; sand, construc-
tion; gravel; concrete pumping

▲ = Import ▼=Export
◆ =Import/Export

(G-15371)
BHV SHEET MTAL FABRICATORS INC (PA)
505 Prentice Rd 507 (13850-2105)
PHONE....................................607 797-1196
Robert Reid, *President*
Chris Reid, *Vice Pres*
Diane M Reid, *Vice Pres*
▼ **EMP:** 42
SQ FT: 18,000
SALES (est): 7.4MM **Privately Held**
WEB: www.bhvfab.com
SIC: 3444 Sheet metalwork

(G-15372)
BIMBO BAKERIES USA INC
Also Called: Stroehmann Bakeries 90
1624 Castle Gardens Rd (13850-1102)
PHONE....................................800 856-8544
Bruce Gross, *Manager*
EMP: 20 **Privately Held**
SIC: 2051 5149 Breads, rolls & buns; groceries & related products
HQ: Bimbo Bakeries Usa, Inc
255 Business Center Dr # 200
Horsham PA 19044
215 347-5500

(G-15373)
BOB MURPHY INC (PA)
3127 Vestal Rd (13850)
PHONE....................................607 729-3553
Mary Murphy Harrison, *President*
Robert S Murphy Jr, *Vice Pres*
EMP: 19 **EST:** 1952
SQ FT: 130,000
SALES (est): 2MM **Privately Held**
SIC: 3441 5031 Fabricated structural metal; building materials, exterior; building materials, interior

(G-15374)
C & C READY-MIX CORPORATION (PA)
3112 Vestal Rd (13850-2110)
P.O. Box 157 (13851-0157)
PHONE....................................607 797-5108
Nicholas D Cerretani Jr, *President*
Nichols Cerretani Jr, *President*
Anthony Cerretani, *Vice Pres*
EMP: 25
SQ FT: 1,500
SALES: 5.3MM **Privately Held**
WEB: www.ccreadymix.com
SIC: 3273 2951 Ready-mixed concrete; asphalt & asphaltic paving mixtures (not from refineries)

(G-15375)
CARR COMMUNICATIONS GROUP LLC
Also Called: Carr Printing
513 Prentice Rd (13850-2105)
PHONE....................................607 748-0481
Chris Osborn, *Purchasing*
James Petritz,
Anthony Defilio,
David Gannon,
Donald Kahen,
EMP: 18
SQ FT: 11,000
SALES: 1.5MM **Privately Held**
SIC: 2752 Commercial printing, offset

(G-15376)
DETEKION SECURITY SYSTEMS INC
200 Plaza Dr Ste 1 (13850-3680)
PHONE....................................607 729-7179
James Walsh, *President*
Alexander Haker, *Vice Pres*
Karen Walter, *Accountant*
Bill Walsh, *Accounts Mgr*
William Walsh, *Shareholder*
EMP: 18
SQ FT: 7,200
SALES (est): 3.7MM **Privately Held**
SIC: 3699 5063 1731 Security control equipment & systems; burglar alarm systems; fire detection & burglar alarm systems specialization

(G-15377)
GANNETT CO INC
Also Called: Binghamton Press
4421 Vestal Pkwy E (13850-3556)
P.O. Box 1270, Binghamton (13902-1270)
PHONE....................................607 798-1234
Sherman Bodner, *President*
Marge Nelson, *Credit Staff*
Cindy Jarvis, *Director*
EMP: 77
SQ FT: 100,498
SALES (corp-wide): 2.9B **Publicly Held**
WEB: www.gannett.com
SIC: 2711 Newspapers
PA: Gannett Co., Inc.
7950 Jones Branch Dr
Mc Lean VA 22102
703 854-6000

(G-15378)
GEOWEB3D INC
4104 Vestal Rd Ste 202 (13850-3554)
P.O. Box 2019, Binghamton (13902-2019)
PHONE....................................607 323-1114
Robert Holicky, *CEO*
Vincent Autieri, *COO*
Christian Maire, *Vice Pres*
EMP: 15
SQ FT: 3,300
SALES (est): 458.7K **Privately Held**
WEB: www.geoweb3d.com
SIC: 7372 7371 Application computer software; computer software development

(G-15379)
GREAT AMERICAN INDUSTRIES INC (DH)
300 Plaza Dr (13850-3647)
PHONE....................................607 729-9331
Burton I Koffman, *Ch of Bd*
Richard E Koffman, *Senior VP*
◆ **EMP:** 1 **EST:** 1928
SQ FT: 2,000
SALES (est): 68.4MM
SALES (corp-wide): 4MM **Privately Held**
SIC: 3086 5031 5074 3442 Plastics foam products; building materials, interior; plumbing fittings & supplies; metal doors, sash & trim; metal doors; wet suits, rubber; watersports equipment & supplies; diving equipment & supplies
HQ: Public Loan Company Inc
300 Plaza Dr
Vestal NY 13850
607 584-5274

(G-15380)
K HEIN MACHINES INC
341 Vestal Pkwy E (13850-1631)
PHONE....................................607 748-1546
Walter C Hein Sr, *CEO*
W Charles Hein Jr, *President*
Steven W Hein, *Vice Pres*
EMP: 9
SQ FT: 15,000
SALES (est): 650.2K **Privately Held**
WEB: www.kheinmachines.com
SIC: 3599 Machine shop, jobbing & repair

(G-15381)
NATIONAL PIPE & PLASTICS INC (PA)
Also Called: Nppi
3421 Vestal Rd (13850-2188)
PHONE....................................607 729-9381
David J Culbertson, *CEO*
Farouk Aziz, *General Mgr*
Charles E Miller, *Vice Pres*
Charles Miller, *Vice Pres*
Victoria Schoelier, *Purch Mgr*
◆ **EMP:** 170
SQ FT: 157,000
SALES (est): 92.9MM **Privately Held**
WEB: www.nationalpipe.com
SIC: 3084 Plastics pipe

(G-15382)
SCORPION SECURITY PRODUCTS INC
330 N Jensen Rd (13850-2132)
PHONE....................................607 724-9999
Pete Gulick, *President*
Anuj Thakral, *COO*
Brandon Schuldt, *Accounts Mgr*
▲ **EMP:** 18 **EST:** 2008

SQ FT: 4,700
SALES (est): 242K **Privately Held**
SIC: 3699 Security devices

(G-15383)
SPST INC
Also Called: Embroidery Screen Prtg Netwrk
119b Rano Blvd (13850-2729)
PHONE....................................607 798-6952
James Porter, *President*
EMP: 5
SALES (est): 450K **Privately Held**
SIC: 2759 Screen printing

(G-15384)
SUPERIOR PRINT ON DEMAND
165 Charles St (13850-2431)
PHONE....................................607 240-5231
Jeff Valent, *Principal*
EMP: 8 **EST:** 2011
SALES (est): 596.1K **Privately Held**
SIC: 2752 2759 7389 Offset & photolithographic printing; financial note & certificate printing & engraving; personal service agents, brokers & bureaus

(G-15385)
SWITCHED SOURCE LLC
85 Murray Hl Rd Ste 2225 (13850)
PHONE....................................708 207-1479
Charles Murray,
EMP: 5
SALES (est): 177.1K **Privately Held**
SIC: 3621 Rotary converters (electrical equipment)

(G-15386)
TRUEBITE INC
Also Called: Fotofiles
2590 Glenwood Rd (13850-6115)
PHONE....................................607 785-7664
Edward J Calafut, *President*
◆ **EMP:** 23
SQ FT: 6,000
SALES (est): 4.5MM **Privately Held**
WEB: www.truebite.com
SIC: 3499 3674 Magnets, permanent: metallic; photoelectric magnetic devices

(G-15387)
VESTAL ASPHALT INC
201 Stage Rd (13850-1608)
PHONE....................................607 785-3393
Neil I Guiles, *President*
Garrett Guiles, *VP Opers*
Kim Hickok, *Controller*
Timothy Howell, *Manager*
Patricia Schaffer, *Manager*
EMP: 19
SQ FT: 3,000
SALES (est): 8.8MM **Privately Held**
WEB: www.vestalasphalt.com
SIC: 2951 Asphalt & asphaltic paving mixtures (not from refineries)

(G-15388)
XEKU CORPORATION
2520 Vestal Pkwy E222 (13850-2078)
PHONE....................................607 761-1447
Charles S Jakaitis, *Principal*
EMP: 12
SALES (est): 830K **Privately Held**
SIC: 3829 Measuring & controlling devices

Victor
Ontario County

(G-15389)
331 HOLDING INC
Also Called: U S TEC
100 Rawson Rd Ste 205 (14564-1100)
PHONE....................................585 924-1740
EMP: 32
SALES (est): 4MM **Privately Held**
SIC: 3699 7373 1731 Mfg Electrical Equipment/Supplies Computer Systems Design Electrical Contractor

(G-15390)
ADVANCED INTERCONNECT MFG INC (HQ)
Also Called: A I M
780 Canning Pkwy (14564-8983)
PHONE....................................585 742-2220
John Durst, *President*
Shawn Hodgeman, *Controller*
▲ **EMP:** 62
SQ FT: 50,000
SALES (est): 14.9MM
SALES (corp-wide): 61MM **Privately Held**
SIC: 3679 Harness assemblies for electronic use: wire or cable
PA: Floturn, Inc.
4236 Thunderbird Ln
West Chester OH 45014
513 860-8040

(G-15391)
AMERICAN SPORTS MEDIA
106 Cobblestone Court Dr # 323 (14564-1045)
PHONE....................................585 924-4250
David Aultman, *Principal*
EMP: 6
SALES (est): 403K **Privately Held**
SIC: 2711 Newspapers, publishing & printing

(G-15392)
AVCOM OF VIRGINIA INC
Also Called: Ramsey Electronics
590 Fishers Station Dr (14564-9744)
PHONE....................................585 924-4560
Jay Evans, *Ch of Bd*
John G Ramsey, *President*
Richard Oddo, *CFO*
Patrick Tkaczow, *Technical Staff*
EMP: 53
SQ FT: 10,000
SALES (est): 7.8MM
SALES (corp-wide): 30MM **Privately Held**
WEB: www.brynavon.com
SIC: 3825 5961 8331 3651 Test equipment for electronic & electrical circuits; catalog & mail-order houses; job training & vocational rehabilitation services; household audio & video equipment
PA: Brynavon Group, Inc
2000 Montgomery Ave
Villanova PA 19085
610 525-2102

(G-15393)
BIOREM ENVIRONMENTAL INC
100 Rawson Rd Ste 230 (14564-1177)
PHONE....................................585 924-2220
Peter Bruijns, *CEO*
▲ **EMP:** 40
SALES (est): 7.9MM
SALES (corp-wide): 18.4MM **Privately Held**
SIC: 3822 Electric air cleaner controls, automatic
HQ: Biorem Technologies Inc
7496 Wellington Road 34
Puslinch ON N0B 2
519 767-9100

(G-15394)
BIOWORKS INC (PA)
100 Rawson Rd Ste 205 (14564-1100)
PHONE....................................585 924-4362
Bill Foster, *President*
Peter Eppeira, *Opers Staff*
Joe Gionta, *Finance Dir*
Julie Caulfield, *Cust Mgr*
Jeffrey Luke, *Marketing Mgr*
▲ **EMP:** 3
SQ FT: 1,380
SALES (est): 5MM **Privately Held**
WEB: www.bioworksinc.com
SIC: 2879 Fungicides, herbicides

(G-15395)
BRISTOL INSTRUMENTS INC
770 Canning Pkwy (14564-8983)
P.O. Box I, Fishers (14453-0759)
PHONE....................................585 924-2620
Brian Samoriski, *President*
Michael Houk, *Vice Pres*
Steve Person, *Vice Pres*
Steven Person, *Vice Pres*

John Theodorsen, *Vice Pres*
EMP: 6
SQ FT: 2,000
SALES (est): 1.5MM **Privately Held**
WEB: www.bristol-inst.com
SIC: 3826 Analytical instruments

(G-15396)
BUCKEYE CORRUGATED INC
Koch Container Div
797 Old Dutch Rd (14564-8972)
PHONE....................................585 924-1600
Robert Harris, *President*
Karen Schafer, *Safety Dir*
Robert Bailey, *Engineer*
Michael Fay, *Design Engr*
Norbert Wolf, *Controller*
EMP: 80
SALES (corp-wide): 82MM **Privately Held**
WEB: www.buckeyecorrugated.com
SIC: 2653 3993 Boxes, corrugated: made from purchased materials; signs & advertising specialties
PA: Buckeye Corrugated, Inc
  822 Kumho Dr Ste 400
  Fairlawn OH 44333
  330 576-0590

(G-15397)
CHARLES A ROGERS ENTPS INC
Also Called: Car Engineering and Mfg
51 Victor Heights Pkwy (14564-8926)
P.O. Box 627 (14564-0627)
PHONE....................................585 924-6400
Charles A Rogers, *CEO*
Yvette Rogers Pagano, *President*
Brian Rumsey, *Vice Pres*
Cheryl Hixon, *Office Mgr*
EMP: 45
SQ FT: 40,000
SALES (est): 16.3MM **Privately Held**
WEB: www.car-eng.com
SIC: 3469 3549 3544 Stamping metal for the trade; metalworking machinery; special dies & tools

(G-15398)
CLEARCOVE SYSTEMS INC
7910 Rae Blvd (14564-8820)
PHONE....................................585 734-3012
Gregory Westbrook, *CEO*
Gary Miller, *President*
Terry Wright, *Chief Engr*
EMP: 10 EST: 2014
SQ FT: 750
SALES (est): 2.3MM **Privately Held**
SIC: 3589 Water treatment equipment, industrial

(G-15399)
CONSTELLATION BRANDS INC (PA)
207 High Point Dr # 100 (14564-1061)
PHONE....................................585 678-7100
Robert Sands, *CEO*
Richard Sands, *Ch of Bd*
F Paul Hetterich, *President*
William A Newlands, *President*
Christopher Stenzel, *President*
EMP: 95
SALES: 8.1B **Publicly Held**
WEB: www.cbrands.com
SIC: 2084 5182 5181 2082 Wines, brandy & brandy spirits; wine & distilled beverages; wine; neutral spirits; beer & other fermented malt liquors; beer (alcoholic beverage); distilled & blended liquors; concentrates, drink

(G-15400)
CONSTRUCTION ROBOTICS LLC
795 Canning Pkwy (14564-8924)
PHONE....................................585 742-2004
Rafael Astacio, *Surgery Dir*
Nathan Podkaminer,
EMP: 22
SALES (est): 274K **Privately Held**
SIC: 3531 Construction machinery

(G-15401)
COOPERVISION INC
209 High Point Dr (14564-1061)
PHONE....................................585 385-6810
▲ EMP: 250
SQ FT: 35,000
SALES (est): 31.2MM
SALES (corp-wide): 1.8B **Publicly Held**
SIC: 3851 Mfg Ophthalmic Goods
HQ: Coopervision, Inc.
  209 High Point Dr
  Victor NY 14564
  585 385-6810

(G-15402)
COOPERVISION INC (HQ)
209 High Point Dr Ste 100 (14564-1061)
PHONE....................................585 385-6810
Thomas Bender, *Ch of Bd*
Adam Kronstat, *Vice Pres*
Mary Rothermel, *Vice Pres*
Charles Derringer, *Research*
Ashley Kimbrew, *Sales Staff*
◆ EMP: 65
SQ FT: 20,000
SALES: 329.5MM
SALES (corp-wide): 2.5B **Publicly Held**
SIC: 3851 Contact lenses
PA: The Cooper Companies Inc
  6140 Stoneridge Mall Rd # 590
  Pleasanton CA 94588
  925 460-3600

(G-15403)
DAKOTA SOFTWARE CORPORATION
1082 Chapelhill Dr (14564-1532)
PHONE....................................216 765-7100
Reginald C Shiverick, *President*
EMP: 9
SALES (corp-wide): 7.7MM **Privately Held**
WEB: www.dakotasoft.com
SIC: 7372 Prepackaged software
PA: Dakota Software Corporation
  1375 Euclid Ave Ste 500
  Cleveland OH 44115
  216 765-7100

(G-15404)
DAY AUTOMATION SYSTEMS INC (PA)
7931 Rae Blvd (14564-9017)
PHONE....................................585 924-4630
Eric J Orban, *CEO*
Robert Ormsby, *Vice Pres*
Richard Hitchcock, *Project Mgr*
Kenneth Reukauf, *Project Mgr*
Jeremy Ryan, *Opers Mgr*
EMP: 74
SALES (est): 29.6MM **Privately Held**
WEB: www.dayasi.com
SIC: 3822 Temperature controls, automatic

(G-15405)
DICE AMERICA INC
7676 Netlink Dr (14564-9419)
P.O. Box 360 (14564-0360)
PHONE....................................585 869-6200
Jeff Shufelt, *President*
EMP: 8
SALES: 650K **Privately Held**
WEB: www.diceamerica.com
SIC: 2821 Plastics materials & resins

(G-15406)
ELECTRICAL CONTROLS LINK
100 Rawson Rd Ste 220 (14564-1100)
PHONE....................................585 924-7010
Eric Mehserle, *Project Mgr*
Jim Flynn, *Controller*
EMP: 42
SALES (est): 3.2MM **Privately Held**
WEB: www.han-tek.com
SIC: 3829 Measuring & controlling devices

(G-15407)
ENETICS INC
830 Canning Pkwy (14564-8940)
PHONE....................................585 924-5010
William C Bush, *President*
Thomas Jacobson, *Software Engr*
EMP: 6
SQ FT: 6,000
SALES (est): 1MM **Privately Held**
WEB: www.enetics.com
SIC: 3625 Relays & industrial controls

(G-15408)
EXHIBITS & MORE
7615 Omnitech Pl Ste 4a (14564-9767)
PHONE....................................585 924-4040
Brian Pitre, *Principal*
EMP: 5
SALES (est): 207.4K **Privately Held**
SIC: 2711 5999 7319 Newspapers, publishing & printing; miscellaneous retail stores; display advertising service

(G-15409)
FLEX ENTERPRISES INC
820 Canning Pkwy (14564-8940)
PHONE....................................585 742-1000
Linda Murphy, *CEO*
Guy Murphy, *President*
▲ EMP: 30
SQ FT: 15,000
SALES (est): 5.2MM **Privately Held**
WEB: www.flexenterprises.com
SIC: 3052 5085 Rubber & plastics hose & beltings; industrial supplies; hose, belting & packing; gaskets

(G-15410)
FLIGHTLINE ELECTRONICS INC (DH)
Also Called: Ultra Elec Flightline Systems
7625 Omnitech Pl (14564-9816)
PHONE....................................585 924-4000
Paul Fardellone, *President*
Carlos Santiago, *Principal*
Anthony Diduro, *Vice Pres*
Kelly Selner, *Purch Mgr*
Sue Henning, *Buyer*
EMP: 100
SQ FT: 33,000
SALES (est): 38.7MM
SALES (corp-wide): 984.8MM **Privately Held**
WEB: www.ultra-fei.com
SIC: 3812 Search & navigation equipment
HQ: Ultra Electronics Defense Inc.
  4101 Smith School Rd
  Austin TX 78744
  512 327-6795

(G-15411)
GOOD HEALTH HEALTHCARE NEWSPPR
106 Cobblestone Court Dr (14564-1045)
PHONE....................................585 421-8109
Wagner Dotto, *Owner*
EMP: 10
SALES (est): 264.3K **Privately Held**
WEB: www.cnyhealth.com
SIC: 2711 Newspapers: publishing only, not printed on site

(G-15412)
HUNTER MACHINE INC
6551 Anthony Dr (14564-1400)
P.O. Box 50 (14564-0050)
PHONE....................................585 924-7480
John D Vouros, *President*
Shane Wing, *Opers Mgr*
EMP: 20
SQ FT: 11,600
SALES: 5MM **Privately Held**
WEB: www.hmicncmachining.com
SIC: 3599 Machine shop, jobbing & repair

(G-15413)
INDUSTRIAL INDXING SYSTEMS INC
626 Fishers Run (14564-9732)
PHONE....................................585 924-9181
William Schnaufer, *President*
Jon Cassano, *Vice Pres*
Chris Draper, *Purch Agent*
Kevin Sackett, *Engineer*
Andrew Wakefield, *Engineer*
EMP: 22 EST: 1977
SQ FT: 13,000
SALES (est): 5.2MM **Privately Held**
WEB: www.iis-servo.com
SIC: 3625 Relays & industrial controls

(G-15414)
JOHN RAMSEY ELEC SVCS LLC
Also Called: Jre Test
7940 Rae Blvd (14564-8933)
PHONE....................................585 298-9596
Donna Dedes, *General Mgr*
John G Ramsey,
Bruce Sidari,
EMP: 8
SALES (est): 2.8MM **Privately Held**
SIC: 3825 Test equipment for electronic & electric measurement

(G-15415)
KIRTAS INC
749 Phillips Rd Ste 300 (14564-9434)
PHONE....................................585 924-5999
EMP: 6
SALES (corp-wide): 1.2MM **Privately Held**
SIC: 3678 Electronic connectors
PA: Ristech Information Systems Inc
  5115 Harvester Rd Unit 8
  Burlington ON L7L 0
  905 631-7451

(G-15416)
KIRTAS INC
7620 Omnitech Pl (14564-9428)
P.O. Box 729, Bolton MA (01740-0729)
PHONE....................................585 924-2420
Robb Richardson, *CEO*
▼ EMP: 27
SQ FT: 12,000
SALES (est): 3.9MM
SALES (corp-wide): 1.2MM **Privately Held**
WEB: www.kirtastech.com
SIC: 3678 Electronic connectors
PA: Ristech Information Systems Inc
  5115 Harvester Rd Unit 8
  Burlington ON L7L 0
  905 631-7451

(G-15417)
LIFETIME STAINLESS STEEL CORP
7387 Ny 96 850 (14564)
PHONE....................................585 924-9393
Stephen Foti, *Branch Mgr*
EMP: 6
SALES (corp-wide): 2.9MM **Privately Held**
SIC: 3263 Cookware, fine earthenware
PA: Lifetime Stainless Steel Corp
  28 Willow Pond Way Ste 1
  Penfield NY

(G-15418)
LOGICAL CONTROL SOLUTIONS INC
829 Phillips Rd Ste 100 (14564-9431)
PHONE....................................585 424-5340
James Urbanczyk, *President*
Susan Lampi, *General Mgr*
Neil Comstra, *Vice Pres*
EMP: 18
SQ FT: 45,000
SALES (est): 3.9MM **Privately Held**
SIC: 3822 Temperature controls, automatic

(G-15419)
MAGNET-NDCTIVE SYSTEMS LTD USA
Also Called: Ultra Electronics Inc
7625 Omnitech Pl (14564-9816)
PHONE....................................585 924-4000
Russell Greenway, *President*
Bill Gill, *Treasurer*
Robert Thomas, *Program Mgr*
▲ EMP: 22
SQ FT: 10,000
SALES (est): 4.6MM
SALES (corp-wide): 984.8MM **Privately Held**
SIC: 3663 Receiver-transmitter units (transceiver)
HQ: Ultra Electronics Inc
  107 Church Hill Rd
  Sandy Hook CT 06482
  203 270-3695

(G-15420)
NEW SCALE TECHNOLOGIES INC
121 Victor Heights Pkwy (14564-8938)
PHONE..............................585 924-4450
David Henderson, *CEO*
Allison Leet, *Vice Pres*
Heidi Quinlivan, *VP Sls/Mktg*
EMP: 25
SQ FT: 10,000
SALES: 4MM **Privately Held**
WEB: www.newscaletech.com
SIC: 3823 Controllers for process variables, all types

(G-15421)
NEWTEX INDUSTRIES INC (PA)
Also Called: Trident Partners III
8050 Victor Mendon Rd (14564-9109)
PHONE..............................585 924-9135
Jerome Joliet, *CEO*
Douglas Bailey, *President*
Matthew Krempl, *VP Opers*
Kathie Laduca, *Accounting Mgr*
Lindsey Marvin, *Accounts Mgr*
▲ EMP: 45
SQ FT: 103,000
SALES (est): 9MM **Privately Held**
WEB: www.newtex.com
SIC: 2221 2295 2241 Fiberglass fabrics; coated fabrics, not rubberized; narrow fabric mills

(G-15422)
NEXT STEP PUBLISHING INC
Also Called: Next Step Magazine, The
2 W Main St Ste 200 (14564-1153)
PHONE..............................585 742-1260
David Mammano, *President*
Lisa Mietelski, *Cust Mgr*
EMP: 15
SQ FT: 1,500
SALES (est): 2.1MM **Privately Held**
SIC: 2721 8748 Magazines: publishing only, not printed on site; business consulting

(G-15423)
PACE WINDOW AND DOOR CORP (PA)
Also Called: Pace Window & Door
7224 State Route 96 (14564-9754)
PHONE..............................585 924-8350
Robert Mehalso, *Ch of Bd*
Steven Abramson, *President*
Kelly Beer, *Purchasing*
Christina Shea, *Office Mgr*
EMP: 50
SQ FT: 21,000
SALES (est): 8.7MM **Privately Held**
WEB: www.pacewindows.com
SIC: 3089 1751 Plastic hardware & building products; window & door (prefabricated) installation

(G-15424)
PREMIER PACKAGING CORPORATION
6 Framark Dr (14564-1136)
P.O. Box 352 (14564-0352)
PHONE..............................585 924-8460
Robert B Bzdick, *Principal*
Joan T Bzdick, *Treasurer*
EMP: 32
SQ FT: 40,000
SALES (est): 6MM
SALES (corp-wide): 18.5MM **Publicly Held**
WEB: www.premiercustompkg.com
SIC: 2657 2675 2677 Folding paperboard boxes; die-cut paper & board; envelopes
PA: Document Security Systems Inc
200 Canal View Blvd # 300
Rochester NY 14623
585 325-3610

(G-15425)
PROGRESSIVE MCH & DESIGN LLC (PA)
Also Called: Pmd
727 Rowley Rd (14564-9728)
PHONE..............................585 924-5250
Hannah Fox, *General Mgr*
Steve Cairns, *Project Mgr*
Ron Richards, *Project Mgr*

Bruce Allison, *Safety Mgr*
Ilya Beylkin, *Engineer*
EMP: 225
SQ FT: 26,000
SALES: 46.6MM **Privately Held**
WEB: www.pmdautomation.com
SIC: 3599 Machine shop, jobbing & repair; custom machinery

(G-15426)
RAMSEY ELECTRONICS LLC
590 Fishers Station Dr (14564-9744)
PHONE..............................585 924-4560
Richard Oddo, *CFO*
EMP: 20
SALES (est): 5.5MM **Privately Held**
SIC: 3825 5065 Test equipment for electronic & electric measurement; electronic parts & equipment

(G-15427)
RAPID PRINT AND MARKETING INC
8 High St (14564-1105)
PHONE..............................585 924-1520
David Gaudieri, *Owner*
EMP: 5
SQ FT: 3,000
SALES (est): 987K **Privately Held**
SIC: 2752 7334 Commercial printing, offset; photocopying & duplicating services

(G-15428)
REDCOM LABORATORIES INC (PA)
1 Redcom Ctr (14564-9785)
PHONE..............................585 924-6567
Dinah Weisberg, *CEO*
Klaus Gueldenpfennig, *President*
Chris Hasenauer, *COO*
Charles Breidensien, *Vice Pres*
Dinah Gueldenpfennig, *Vice Pres*
▲ EMP: 147 EST: 1978
SQ FT: 140,000
SALES (est): 22.9MM **Privately Held**
WEB: www.redcom.com
SIC: 3661 8748 Switching equipment, telephone; communications consulting

(G-15429)
SENSODX II LLC
600 Fishers Station Dr # 124 (14564-9784)
PHONE..............................585 202-4552
Steve Dietl, *Vice Pres*
Mike Murry, *Vice Pres*
John Thomas McDevitt,
Robert Mehalso,
EMP: 9
SALES: 1.5MM **Privately Held**
SIC: 3841 Surgical & medical instruments

(G-15430)
SENSOR FILMS INCORPORATED
687 Rowley Rd (14564-9728)
PHONE..............................585 738-3500
Peter Hessney, *Principal*
Richard Hecht, *Engineer*
EMP: 25 EST: 2013
SALES: 1.6MM **Privately Held**
SIC: 3699 Sound signaling devices, electrical

(G-15431)
SERVICE EDUCATION INCORPORATED
790 Canning Pkwy Ste 1 (14564-9019)
PHONE..............................585 264-9240
Terence Wolfe, *President*
EMP: 6
SQ FT: 2,100
SALES (est): 300K **Privately Held**
WEB: www.serviceed.com
SIC: 2741 Technical manuals: publishing & printing

(G-15432)
STUDIO GLASS BATCH LLC
7491 Modock Rd (14564-8702)
PHONE..............................585 924-9579
William Glasner,
EMP: 6
SALES: 250K **Privately Held**
SIC: 3231 Products of purchased glass

(G-15433)
SURMOTECH LLC
7676 Netlink Dr (14564-9419)
PHONE..............................585 742-1220
Jerry F Valentine, *CEO*
Arthur Kaempffe, *Vice Pres*
Joseph Oca, *Opers Mgr*
John Kinnear, *Production*
Patty Doud, *Senior Buyer*
▲ EMP: 100
SQ FT: 20,000
SALES (est): 33.7MM **Privately Held**
WEB: www.surmotech.com
SIC: 3679 Electronic circuits

(G-15434)
SYCAMORE HILL DESIGNS INC
7585 Modock Rd (14564-9104)
PHONE..............................585 820-7322
Frank Vallone, *President*
EMP: 5
SALES (est): 300K **Privately Held**
SIC: 3484 Small arms

(G-15435)
SYRACUSA SAND AND GRAVEL INC
1389 Malone Rd (14564-9147)
P.O. Box 2 (14564-0002)
PHONE..............................585 924-7146
Scott Syracusa, *President*
Mark Syracusa, *Vice Pres*
EMP: 10
SQ FT: 1,000
SALES (est): 1.8MM **Privately Held**
SIC: 1442 Construction sand mining; gravel mining

(G-15436)
TEKNIC INC
115 Victor Heights Pkwy (14564-8938)
PHONE..............................585 784-7454
Thomas Bucella, *Ch of Bd*
Abe Amirana, *Buyer*
David Fuchs, *Design Engr*
Erik Morrell, *Business Dir*
▲ EMP: 35
SQ FT: 10,000
SALES (est): 7.7MM **Privately Held**
WEB: www.teknic.com
SIC: 3625 Motor controls & accessories

(G-15437)
TELOG INSTRUMENTS INC
830 Canning Pkwy (14564-8940)
PHONE..............................585 742-3000
Barry L Ceci, *President*
Charlene Donofrio, *Buyer*
Everett Lago, *Engineer*
George Mayoue, *Sales Mgr*
Kerry Hoffman, *Sales Staff*
EMP: 30
SQ FT: 20,000
SALES: 5.7MM
SALES (corp-wide): 3.1B **Publicly Held**
WEB: www.telog.com
SIC: 3829 3823 Measuring & controlling devices; industrial instrmnts msrmnt display/control process variable
PA: Trimble Inc.
935 Stewart Dr
Sunnyvale CA 94085
408 481-8000

(G-15438)
THE CALDWELL MANUFACTURING CO
Advantage Mfg
Holland Industrial Park (14564)
PHONE..............................585 352-2803
Michelle McCorry, *Manager*
EMP: 42
SALES (corp-wide): 66.5MM **Privately Held**
SIC: 3495 Wire springs
PA: The Caldwell Manufacturing Company
2605 Manitou Rd Ste 100
Rochester NY 14624
585 352-3790

(G-15439)
TRIAD NETWORK TECHNOLOGIES
75b Victor Heights Pkwy (14564-8926)
PHONE..............................585 924-8505

Pete Sweltz, *President*
Paul Rheude, *General Mgr*
Frank Carusone, *Vice Pres*
Don Munn, *Accounts Exec*
Jeff Pulli, *Accounts Exec*
EMP: 20
SQ FT: 3,500
SALES (est): 3.3MM **Privately Held**
WEB: www.triadnt.com
SIC: 2298 Cable, fiber

(G-15440)
VICTOR INSULATORS INC
280 Maple Ave (14564-1385)
PHONE..............................585 924-2127
Ira Knickerbocker, *Ch of Bd*
Andrew E Schwalm, *President*
Chris Rishel, *Safety Mgr*
Nelson McKee, *Sales Mgr*
Robert Dowdle, *Manager*
▲ EMP: 105
SQ FT: 327,000
SALES (est): 17MM **Privately Held**
WEB: www.victorinsulatorsinc.com
SIC: 3264 Insulators, electrical: porcelain

(G-15441)
W STUART SMITH INC
Also Called: Heritage Packaging
625 Fishers Run (14564-8905)
PHONE..............................585 742-3310
William S Smith, *Ch of Bd*
Kristin J Smith, *Vice Pres*
Randy Demkowicz, *Engineer*
Evan Smith, *Controller*
Scott Floyd, *Sales Engr*
◆ EMP: 40
SQ FT: 50,000
SALES (est): 8.7MM **Privately Held**
WEB: www.heritagepackaging.com
SIC: 3086 Packaging & shipping materials, foamed plastic

(G-15442)
WASHER SOLUTIONS INC
760 Canning Pkwy Ste A (14564-9018)
PHONE..............................585 742-6388
Mickie T Pitts, *CEO*
Christina Fields, *Opers Staff*
Rachel Pitts, *Technology*
Kim Rosenwinge, *Technician*
EMP: 10 EST: 2001
SQ FT: 1,200
SALES (est): 2.2MM **Privately Held**
WEB: www.washersolutions.com
SIC: 3519 Gas engine rebuilding

(G-15443)
WILLIAMSON LAW BOOK CO
790 Canning Pkwy Ste 2 (14564-9019)
PHONE..............................585 924-3400
Greg Chwiecko, *President*
Thomas Osborne, *Treasurer*
EMP: 12 EST: 1870
SQ FT: 10,800
SALES (est): 1.2MM **Privately Held**
WEB: www.wlbonline.com
SIC: 2761 7371 Manifold business forms; computer software development

---

Voorheesville
Albany County

(G-15444)
ATLAS COPCO COMPTEC LLC (DH)
46 School Rd (12186-9696)
PHONE..............................518 765-3344
Peter Wagner, *President*
Holly Simboli, *Principal*
Peter Carey, *Engineer*
◆ EMP: 330 EST: 1970
SQ FT: 100,000
SALES (est): 131.1MM
SALES (corp-wide): 10.5B **Privately Held**
WEB: www.atlascopco-act.com
SIC: 3563 Air & gas compressors including vacuum pumps
HQ: Atlas Copco North America Llc
6 Century Dr Ste 310
Parsippany NJ 07054
973 397-3400

(G-15445)
SPAULDING & ROGERS MFG INC
3252 New Scotland Rd (12186)
PHONE..............................518 768-2070
Huck Spaulding, *Ch of Bd*
Josephine Spaulding, *President*
Bill Lawyer, *Principal*
▲ EMP: 70
SALES (est): 8.3MM **Privately Held**
WEB: www.spaulding-rogers.com
SIC: 3952 Artists' equipment

Waccabuc
Westchester County

(G-15446)
MANN CONSULTANTS LLC
67 Chapel Rd (10597-1001)
PHONE..............................914 763-0512
Stuart Mann,
Jeffrey Mandelbaum,
EMP: 22
SALES (est): 1MM **Privately Held**
SIC: 2253 2329 T-shirts & tops, knit; men's & boys' sportswear & athletic clothing

Waddington
St. Lawrence County

(G-15447)
STRUCTURAL WOOD CORPORATION
Also Called: Roll Lock Truss
243 Lincoln Ave (13694-3203)
P.O. Box 339 (13694-0339)
PHONE..............................315 388-4442
Michael McGee, *CEO*
Peter Rieter, *President*
Bob Rochefort, *Production*
Jim Lyon, *Finance Mgr*
EMP: 32
SQ FT: 20,000
SALES (est): 4.4MM **Privately Held**
WEB: www.rolllocktruss.com
SIC: 2439 5031 5211 Trusses, wooden roof; doors & windows; lumber & other building materials

Wading River
Suffolk County

(G-15448)
A I P PRINTING & STATIONERS
Also Called: Airport Printing & Stationers
6198 N Country Rd (11792-1625)
PHONE..............................631 929-5529
George A Waldemar, *President*
EMP: 8 EST: 1973
SALES (est): 760K **Privately Held**
SIC: 2752 Lithographing on metal

(G-15449)
FREDERICK COWAN & COMPANY INC
144 Beach Rd (11792-1305)
PHONE..............................631 369-0360
Thomas L Cowan, *President*
Mildred Cowan, *Corp Secy*
EMP: 14 EST: 1957
SQ FT: 20,000
SALES (est): 2.2MM **Privately Held**
WEB: www.fcowan.com
SIC: 3612 3433 Ignition transformers, for use on domestic fuel burners; gas burners, industrial

(G-15450)
LO-CO FUEL CORP
10 Stephen Dr (11792-2126)
PHONE..............................631 929-5086
Michael Lopez, *Principal*
EMP: 6
SALES (est): 486.5K **Privately Held**
SIC: 2869 Fuels

(G-15451)
SAFEGUARD INC
578 Sound Ave (11792)
P.O. Box 922 (11792-0922)
PHONE..............................631 929-3273
Charlie Zimmerman, *President*
EMP: 15
SALES (est): 2.5MM **Privately Held**
SIC: 2899 Fire retardant chemicals

(G-15452)
SPLIT ROCK TRADING CO INC
22 Creek Rd (11792-2501)
P.O. Box 841, Shoreham (11786-0841)
PHONE..............................631 929-3261
Jim Loscalzo, *President*
Peggy Vonbernewitz, *Corp Secy*
EMP: 7
SQ FT: 13,000
SALES: 480K **Privately Held**
WEB: www.splitrockvideo.com
SIC: 3499 5012 5013 5531 Novelties & specialties, metal; automobiles; motorcycles; automotive supplies & parts; automotive accessories; automobiles, new & used; motorcycles

(G-15453)
SWISS SPECIALTIES INC
15 Crescent Ct (11792-3004)
PHONE..............................631 567-8800
Daniel J George, *President*
EMP: 14
SQ FT: 5,000
SALES: 1.9MM **Privately Held**
SIC: 3541 Screw machines, automatic

Wainscott
Suffolk County

(G-15454)
ANTIQUE LUMBER MODRN MLLWK LLC
328 Montauk Hwy (11975-2000)
PHONE..............................631 726-7026
Quana White,
EMP: 5
SALES (est): 443.6K **Privately Held**
SIC: 2431 Millwork

(G-15455)
MAPEASY INC
54 Industrial Rd (11975-2001)
P.O. Box 80 (11975-0080)
PHONE..............................631 537-6213
Gary Bradhering, *President*
Chris Harris, *Vice Pres*
▲ EMP: 12
SQ FT: 11,000
SALES (est): 980.4K **Privately Held**
WEB: www.mapeasy.com
SIC: 2741 4724 Maps: publishing & printing; travel agencies

Walden
Orange County

(G-15456)
AMPAC PAPER LLC (DH)
30 Coldenham Rd (12586-2036)
P.O. Box 271 (12586-0271)
PHONE..............................845 713-6600
John Q Baumann, *CEO*
Robert Tillis, *President*
Jon Dill, *CFO*
Michael Conaton, *Admin Sec*
▲ EMP: 5
SQ FT: 200,000
SALES (est): 82.2MM
SALES (corp-wide): 1.1B **Privately Held**
WEB: www.ampaconline.com
SIC: 2674 2621 5162 Shopping bags: made from purchased materials; paper mills; plastics materials
HQ: Ampac Packaging, Llc
12025 Tricon Rd
Cincinnati OH 45246
513 671-1777

(G-15457)
C & C ATHLETIC INC
Also Called: Viking Jackets & Athletic Wear
11 Myrtle Ave (12586-2340)
PHONE..............................845 713-4670
Andrea Conklin, *President*
EMP: 5
SQ FT: 4,000
SALES (est): 318.7K **Privately Held**
WEB: www.vikingathletic.com
SIC: 2759 2339 Screen printing; athletic clothing: women's, misses' & juniors'

(G-15458)
CALFONEX COMPANY
121 Orchard St (12586-1707)
PHONE..............................845 778-2212
Terrance Donovan, *Owner*
EMP: 15
SALES (est): 836.8K **Privately Held**
SIC: 2899 Chemical preparations

(G-15459)
DWYER FARM LLC
40 Bowman Ln (12586-2100)
PHONE..............................914 456-2742
Brian Dwyer, *Principal*
Christopher Dwyer, *Principal*
Jeannie Dwyer, *Principal*
Joseph Dwyer, *Principal*
Mel Dwyer, *Principal*
EMP: 6
SALES (est): 185.1K **Privately Held**
SIC: 2026 Farmers' cheese

(G-15460)
PACIFIC DIE CAST INC
Also Called: Qssi
827 Route 52 Ste 2 (12586-2747)
PHONE..............................845 778-6374
Melissa Durant, *Principal*
EMP: 15
SALES (corp-wide): 11.6MM **Privately Held**
SIC: 3544 Special dies & tools
PA: Pacific Die Cast, Inc.
12802 Commodity Pl
Tampa FL 33626
813 316-2221

(G-15461)
ROMAR CONTRACTING INC
630 State Route 52 (12586-2709)
P.O. Box 658 (12586-0658)
PHONE..............................845 778-2737
Rod Winchell, *President*
Kyle Winchell, *Technology*
EMP: 5
SALES: 500K **Privately Held**
SIC: 3441 Fabricated structural metal

(G-15462)
SPENCE ENGINEERING COMPANY INC
Also Called: Nicholson Steam Trap
150 Coldenham Rd (12586-2909)
PHONE..............................845 778-5566
A William Higgins, *Ch of Bd*
David A Bloss Sr, *President*
Alan R Carlsen, *Vice Pres*
Dan Cole, *Engineer*
Jay Deman, *Marketing Mgr*
▲ EMP: 150 EST: 1926
SQ FT: 79,000
SALES (est): 26.5MM
SALES (corp-wide): 1.1B **Publicly Held**
WEB: www.spenceengineering.com
SIC: 3491 3444 3612 3494 Pressure valves & regulators, industrial; metal ventilating equipment; transformers, except electric; valves & pipe fittings
PA: Circor International, Inc.
30 Corporate Dr Ste 200
Burlington MA 01803
781 270-1200

(G-15463)
TILCON NEW YORK INC
272 Berea Rd (12586-2906)
PHONE..............................845 778-5591
Reinis Siplls, *Branch Mgr*
EMP: 27

SALES (corp-wide): 30.6B **Privately Held**
WEB: www.tilconny.com
SIC: 1429 Trap rock, crushed & broken-quarrying; dolomitic marble, crushed & broken-quarrying
HQ: Tilcon New York Inc.
9 Entin Rd
Parsippany NJ 07054
973 366-7741

(G-15464)
WALLKILL LODGE NO 627 F&AM
61 Main St (12586-1824)
P.O. Box 311 (12586-0311)
PHONE..............................845 778-7148
Mark Balck, *President*
EMP: 14 EST: 2001
SQ FT: 7,326
SALES (est): 514.7K **Privately Held**
SIC: 2711 Newspapers

Wales Center
Erie County

(G-15465)
AM BICKFORD INC
12318 Big Tree Rd (14169)
PHONE..............................716 652-1590
John Bickford, *President*
EMP: 12
SQ FT: 5,000
SALES (est): 1.8MM **Privately Held**
WEB: www.ambickford.com
SIC: 3841 Surgical & medical instruments

(G-15466)
HALE ELECTRICAL DIST SVCS INC
12088 Big Tree Rd (14169)
P.O. Box 221 (14169-0221)
PHONE..............................716 818-7595
David Neveaux, *President*
EMP: 6
SALES: 1.5MM **Privately Held**
SIC: 3612 Distribution transformers, electric

Wallkill
Ulster County

(G-15467)
ARTCRAFT BUILDING SERVICES
85 Old Hoagerburgh Rd (12589-3419)
PHONE..............................845 895-3893
Pasqual J Petrucci, *President*
Janice A Petrucci, *Vice Pres*
EMP: 5
SQ FT: 3,000
SALES (est): 660.6K **Privately Held**
SIC: 3537 Platforms, stands, tables, pallets & similar equipment; dollies (hand or power trucks), industrial except mining

(G-15468)
CATSMO LLC
Also Called: Solex Catsmo Fine Foods
25 Myers Rd (12589-3516)
PHONE..............................845 895-2296
Markus Draxler, *CEO*
Frederic Pothier, *CFO*
◆ EMP: 12 EST: 1995
SQ FT: 15,000
SALES (est): 2.6MM **Privately Held**
WEB: www.catsmo.com
SIC: 2091 Salmon, smoked

(G-15469)
FAIR-RITE PRODUCTS CORP (PA)
1 Commercial Row (12589-4438)
P.O. Box 288 (12589-0288)
PHONE..............................845 895-2055
Richard Parker, *Ch of Bd*
Carole U Parker, *President*
Larry Surrells, *Division Mgr*
Benjamin Friedman, *General Mgr*
Richard Eckmann, *Site Mgr*
▲ EMP: 125 EST: 1952
SQ FT: 80,000

▲ = Import ▼ =Export
◆ =Import/Export

SALES (est): 18.9MM **Privately Held**
WEB: www.fair-rite.com
SIC: 3679 Cores, magnetic

(G-15470)
JAMES B CROWELL & SONS INC
242 Lippincott Rd (12589-3643)
PHONE.................................845 895-3464
James Crowell III, *President*
Wendy Sutherland, *Vice Pres*
EMP: 9 EST: 1872
SQ FT: 4,800
SALES (est): 1MM **Privately Held**
SIC: 3544 Industrial molds

(G-15471)
RICHTER CHARLES METAL STMP&SP
80 Cottage St (12589-3128)
P.O. Box 297 (12589-0297)
PHONE.................................845 895-2025
David Richter, *President*
EMP: 40
SQ FT: 50,000
SALES (est): 3.3MM **Privately Held**
SIC: 3469 Metal stampings

(G-15472)
RICHTER METALCRAFT CORPORATION
Also Called: Charles Richter
80 Cottage St (12589-3128)
P.O. Box 297 (12589-0297)
PHONE.................................845 895-2025
David Richter, *President*
Carol Morgan, *Vice Pres*
Carl Ulrich, *Engineer*
Louise Tancriedi, *Admin Sec*
EMP: 35 EST: 1934
SQ FT: 50,000
SALES (est): 4.4MM **Privately Held**
WEB: www.charlesrichter.com
SIC: 3469 Stamping metal for the trade

(G-15473)
SELECT-TECH INC
3050 State Route 208 (12589-4431)
P.O. Box 259 (12589-0259)
PHONE.................................845 895-8111
William Diener, *President*
Thomas Diener, *Treasurer*
▲ EMP: 5
SQ FT: 25,000
SALES (est): 600K **Privately Held**
WEB: www.select-tech.com
SIC: 3291 Abrasive products

Walton
Delaware County

(G-15474)
BEYOND DESIGN INC
807 Pines Brook Rd (13856-2381)
PHONE.................................607 865-7487
Barbara A Salvatore, *President*
EMP: 7
SALES (est): 638.4K **Privately Held**
SIC: 3299 Architectural sculptures: gypsum, clay, papier mache, etc.

(G-15475)
KRAFT HEINZ FOODS COMPANY
Also Called: Kraft Foods
261 Delaware St (13856-1099)
PHONE.................................607 865-7131
Cynthia Waggoner, *Opers-Prdtn-Mfg*
EMP: 200
SALES (corp-wide): 26.2B **Publicly Held**
WEB: www.kraftfoods.com
SIC: 2026 2022 Fermented & cultured milk products; cheese, natural & processed
HQ: Kraft Heinz Foods Company
1 Ppg Pl Fl 34
Pittsburgh PA 15222
412 456-5700

(G-15476)
NORTHEAST FABRICATORS LLC
30-35 William St (13856-1497)
P.O. Box 65 (13856-0065)
PHONE.................................607 865-4031
Steve Schick, *Purch Mgr*
George Sonner, *Engineer*
Judy Beardslee, *Human Res Mgr*
Kathy Cole, *Office Mgr*
Peter Phraner, *Manager*
EMP: 70 EST: 1997
SQ FT: 80,000
SALES (est): 18.5MM **Privately Held**
SIC: 3444 3441 Sheet metalwork; fabricated structural metal

Walworth
Wayne County

(G-15477)
MEDCO MACHINE LLC
2320 Walworth Marion Rd (14568-9501)
P.O. Box 454 (14568-0454)
PHONE.................................315 986-2109
Mark Medyn,
EMP: 6
SQ FT: 4,800
SALES (est): 801.2K **Privately Held**
SIC: 3599 Machine shop, jobbing & repair

(G-15478)
ROCHESTER ASPHALT MATERIALS
Also Called: Dolomite Group
1200 Atlantic Ave (14568-9792)
PHONE.................................315 524-4619
Harvey Smeatin, *Manager*
EMP: 7
SALES (corp-wide): 30.6B **Privately Held**
SIC: 3531 Asphalt plant, including gravel-mix type
HQ: Rochester Asphalt Materials Inc
1150 Penfield Rd
Rochester NY 14625
585 381-7010

(G-15479)
SOFTWARE & GENERAL SERVICES CO
Also Called: S and G Imaging
1365 Fairway 5 Cir (14568-9444)
PHONE.................................315 986-4184
EMP: 6
SALES (est): 480K **Privately Held**
SIC: 7372 Data Management/Pim Consulting Services

Wampsville
Madison County

(G-15480)
DIEMOLDING CORPORATION
100 Donald Hicks Dew Dr (13163)
P.O. Box 26 (13163-0026)
PHONE.................................315 363-4710
Donald H Dew, *CEO*
Mark Vanderveen, *Ch of Bd*
Dennis O'Brien, *President*
Donald Lukas, *Vice Pres*
Carl Cook, *Plant Mgr*
◆ EMP: 125 EST: 1920
SQ FT: 50,000
SALES (est): 33MM **Privately Held**
WEB: www.diemolding.com
SIC: 2655 Containers, laminated phenolic & vulcanized fiber

(G-15481)
DIEMOLDING CORPORATION
Also Called: Dietooling
N Court St (13163)
PHONE.................................315 363-4710
EMP: 17
SALES (corp-wide): 17.2MM **Privately Held**
SIC: 3544 Mfg Dies/Tools/Jigs/Fixtures

PA: Diemolding Corporation
100 Donald Hicks Dew Dr
Wampsville NY 13163
315 363-4710

Wantagh
Nassau County

(G-15482)
1/2 OFF CARDS WANTAGH INC
1162 Wantagh Ave (11793-2110)
PHONE.................................516 809-9832
Steven Bodenstein, *CEO*
EMP: 5
SALES (est): 489.6K **Privately Held**
SIC: 2771 Greeting cards

(G-15483)
CHRISTOPHER ANTHONY PUBG CO
Also Called: Christiny
2151 Spruce St (11793-4119)
PHONE.................................516 826-9205
Anthony Fannin, *President*
Jo Ann Fannin, *Admin Sec*
▼ EMP: 19 EST: 1978
SALES: 2.5MM **Privately Held**
WEB: www.christony.com
SIC: 2741 Catalogs: publishing only, not printed on site

(G-15484)
GREENVALE BAGEL INC
3060 Merrick Rd (11793-4395)
PHONE.................................516 221-8221
Cesidia Facchini, *President*
Ralph Facchini, *Vice Pres*
Claudio Facchini, *Treasurer*
EMP: 30
SQ FT: 1,200
SALES (est): 3.1MM **Privately Held**
SIC: 2051 Bagels, fresh or frozen; bakery: wholesale or wholesale/retail combined

(G-15485)
LIFESCAN INC
15 Tardy Ln N (11793-1928)
PHONE.................................516 557-2693
EMP: 258
SALES (corp-wide): 552.7MM **Privately Held**
SIC: 2835 Blood derivative diagnostic agents
HQ: Lifescan, Inc.
20 Valley Stream Pkwy # 100
Malvern PA 19355
800 227-8862

(G-15486)
MORTGAGE PRESS LTD
1220 Wantagh Ave (11793-2202)
PHONE.................................516 409-1400
Russell Sickmen, *CEO*
Joel M Berman, *President*
Andrew Berman, *Exec VP*
EMP: 22
SQ FT: 4,000
SALES (est): 1.7MM **Privately Held**
WEB: www.mortgagepress.com
SIC: 2711 2741 Newspapers; miscellaneous publishing

(G-15487)
NBETS CORPORATION
Also Called: Wantagh 5 & 10
1901 Wantagh Ave (11793-3930)
PHONE.................................516 785-1259
John Norris, *Ch of Bd*
EMP: 8
SALES (est): 855.8K **Privately Held**
SIC: 2392 Household furnishings

(G-15488)
R M F HEALTH MANAGEMENT L L C
Also Called: Professional Health Imaging
3361 Park Ave (11793-3735)
PHONE.................................718 854-5400
Syndney Bernstein, *Executive*
Robyn Feldstein,
EMP: 21
SQ FT: 9,600

SALES (est): 2.9MM **Privately Held**
SIC: 3844 Nuclear irradiation equipment

(G-15489)
WANTAGH COMPUTER CENTER
10 Stanford Ct (11793-1863)
PHONE.................................516 826-2189
Sidney B Nudelman, *CEO*
EMP: 14
SQ FT: 4,000
SALES (est): 1.1MM **Privately Held**
SIC: 3577 3571 Computer peripheral equipment; electronic computers
PA: S B Nudelman Inc
10 Stanford Ct
Wantagh NY 11793

Wappingers Falls
Dutchess County

(G-15490)
CONTEMPORARY VISIONS LLC (PA)
Also Called: Sonneman-A Way of Light
151 Airport Dr (12590-6161)
PHONE.................................845 926-5469
Sonny Park, *Principal*
▲ EMP: 5
SALES (est): 1.2MM **Privately Held**
SIC: 3646 Commercial indusl & institutional electric lighting fixtures

(G-15491)
DRA IMAGING PC
169 Myers Corners Rd # 250 (12590-3868)
PHONE.................................845 296-1057
Richard Friedland, *CEO*
EMP: 27
SALES (est): 5.1MM **Privately Held**
SIC: 3844 X-ray apparatus & tubes

(G-15492)
FLAVORMATIC INDUSTRIES LLC
90 Brentwood Dr (12590-3344)
PHONE.................................845 297-9100
Jeffrey Harris, *CEO*
Ronald Back, *Exec VP*
Frank Wells, *VP Mktg*
◆ EMP: 20 EST: 1887
SQ FT: 21,000
SALES (est): 4.3MM
SALES (corp-wide): 10.2MM **Privately Held**
WEB: www.flavormatic.com
SIC: 2087 5169 Beverage bases, concentrates, syrups, powders & mixes; beverage bases; extracts, flavoring; essential oils
PA: Flavor Producers, Llc
8521 Fllbrook Ave Ste 380
West Hills CA 91304
818 307-4062

(G-15493)
G BOPP USA INC
4 Bill Horton Way (12590-2018)
P.O. Box 393, Hopewell Junction (12533-0393)
PHONE.................................845 296-1065
George Baker, *COO*
Kathy Piciocchi, *Opers Mgr*
▲ EMP: 7
SALES (est): 1.2MM
SALES (corp-wide): 69MM **Privately Held**
SIC: 3496 Wire cloth & woven wire products
PA: G. Bopp & Co Ag
Bachmannweg 21
ZUrich ZH 8046
443 776-666

(G-15494)
GEM REPRODUCTION SERVICES CORP
Also Called: Signal Graphics Printing
1299 Route 9 Ste 105 (12590-4918)
PHONE.................................845 298-0172
Gary Mensching, *President*
Elizabeth Mensching, *Admin Sec*
EMP: 5
SQ FT: 3,300

G
E
O
G
R
A
P
H
I
C

SALES (est): 956.9K **Privately Held**
SIC: 2752 2759 Commercial printing, off-set; commercial printing

(G-15495)
GLAXOSMITHKLINE LLC
6 Alpert Dr (12590-4602)
PHONE..................................845 797-3259
EMP: 26
SALES (corp-wide): 39.5B **Privately Held**
SIC: 2834 Pharmaceutical preparations
HQ: Glaxosmithkline Llc
5 Crescent Dr
Philadelphia PA 19112
215 751-4000

(G-15496)
HIGHLAND VALLEY SUPPLY INC
30 Airport Dr (12590-6164)
P.O. Box 292 (12590-0292)
PHONE..................................845 849-2863
Raymond Marsella, *President*
EMP: 15
SQ FT: 11,000
SALES (est): 3.2MM **Privately Held**
WEB: www.highlandvalleysupply.com
SIC: 3644 Electric conduits & fittings

(G-15497)
HUDSON VALLEY LIGHTING INC
151 Airport Dr (12590-6161)
P.O. Box 393 (12590-0393)
PHONE..................................845 561-0300
David Littman, *President*
Brent Fields, *Vice Pres*
Holly Bilchak, *Opers Mgr*
Andrew Grimm, *Controller*
Dottie Byrnes, *Technology*
◆ **EMP:** 75 **EST:** 1960
SQ FT: 65,000
SALES (est): 17.9MM **Privately Held**
WEB: www.hudsonvalleylighting.com
SIC: 3646 3645 Commercial indusl & institutional electric lighting fixtures; residential lighting fixtures

(G-15498)
MONEAST INC
Also Called: Sir Speedy
1708 Route 9 Ste 3 (12590-1367)
P.O. Box 1, Ford VA (23850-0001)
PHONE..................................845 298-8898
David Monto, *President*
Randall J Easter, *Treasurer*
Mary Alice Monto, *Admin Sec*
Mary Monto, *Admin Sec*
EMP: 6
SQ FT: 2,800
SALES (est): 907.5K **Privately Held**
SIC: 2752 2791 2789 Commercial printing, lithographic; typesetting; bookbinding & related work

(G-15499)
THINK GREEN JUNK REMOVAL INC
29 Meadow Wood Ln (12590-5937)
PHONE..................................845 297-7771
George Makris, *Owner*
EMP: 7
SALES (est): 842.5K **Privately Held**
SIC: 3089 Garbage containers, plastic

(G-15500)
UNBROKEN RTR USA INC
110 Airport Dr (12590-6185)
PHONE..................................541 640-9457
Steinar Kristijansson, *President*
EMP: 6
SALES (est): 185.1K **Privately Held**
SIC: 2023 Dietary supplements, dairy & non-dairy based

(G-15501)
WAPPINGERS FALLS SHOPPER INC
Also Called: Beacon Press News
84 E Main St (12590-2504)
PHONE..................................845 297-3723
Albert M Osten, *President*
EMP: 50 **EST:** 1959
SQ FT: 12,000

SALES (est): 3.6MM **Privately Held**
SIC: 2711 2752 Newspapers: publishing only, not printed on site; commercial printing, lithographic

Warnerville
Schoharie County

(G-15502)
ZMZ MFG INC
300 Mickle Hollow Rd (12187-2507)
PHONE..................................518 234-4336
Lisa Zaba Miller, *Principal*
EMP: 8
SALES (est): 697.5K **Privately Held**
SIC: 3999 Manufacturing industries

Warrensburg
Warren County

(G-15503)
LUMAZU LLC
141 Garnet Lake Rd (12885-5907)
PHONE..................................518 623-3372
Sheila Flanagan,
EMP: 5 **Privately Held**
SIC: 2022 2024 Cheese spreads, dips, pastes & other cheese products; sherbets, dairy based
PA: Lumazu, Llc
484 S Johnsburg Rd
Warrensburg NY 12885

(G-15504)
LUMAZU LLC (PA)
Also Called: Nettle Meadow Farm
484 S Johnsburg Rd (12885-5944)
PHONE..................................518 623-3372
Sheila Flanagan,
Lorraine Lambiase,
EMP: 15
SQ FT: 7,500
SALES: 1.4MM **Privately Held**
SIC: 2022 2024 Cheese spreads, dips, pastes & other cheese products; sherbets, dairy based

(G-15505)
NORTHEASTERN PRODUCTS CORP (PA)
Also Called: Nepco
115 Sweet Rd (12885-4754)
P.O. Box 98 (12885-0098)
PHONE..................................518 623-3161
Paul Schiavi, *CEO*
Gary Schiavi, *President*
Richard Morgan, *Sales Mgr*
EMP: 23
SQ FT: 2,400
SALES (est): 11MM **Privately Held**
WEB: www.nep-co.com
SIC: 2493 Reconstituted wood products

(G-15506)
TUMBLEHOME BOATSHOP
684 State Route 28 (12885-5301)
PHONE..................................518 623-5050
Reuben Smith, *Owner*
Cynde Smith, *Managing Prtnr*
EMP: 6
SALES (est): 580.2K **Privately Held**
SIC: 3732 Boats, fiberglass: building & repairing

Warsaw
Wyoming County

(G-15507)
FAIRVIEW PAPER BOX CORP
200 Allen St (14569-1562)
PHONE..................................585 786-5230
Donald Zaas, *Ch of Bd*
Joel Zaas, *President*
Mark Cassese, *COO*
John L Asimakopoulos, *CFO*
EMP: 26
SQ FT: 55,000

SALES (est): 5.5MM
SALES (corp-wide): 59.4MM **Privately Held**
WEB: www.boxit.com
SIC: 2657 Folding paperboard boxes
PA: The Apex Paper Box Company
5555 Walworth Ave
Cleveland OH 44102
216 631-4000

(G-15508)
MORTON BUILDINGS INC
5616 Route 20a E (14569-9302)
PHONE..................................585 786-8191
John Edmunds, *Opers-Prdtn-Mfg*
Ed Neudeck, *Sales Mgr*
EMP: 40
SQ FT: 5,122
SALES (corp-wide): 463.7MM **Privately Held**
WEB: www.mortonbuildings.com
SIC: 3448 5039 Buildings, portable: prefabricated metal; prefabricated structures
PA: Morton Buildings, Inc.
252 W Adams St
Morton IL 61550
800 447-7436

(G-15509)
UPSTATE DOOR INC (PA)
26 Industrial St (14569-1550)
PHONE..................................585 786-3880
Robert J Fontaine, *CEO*
Brock Beckstrand, *Safety Mgr*
Guy Riendeau, *Sales Staff*
Mark Volage, *Sales Staff*
Jennifer Gniazdowski, *Mktg Coord*
▲ **EMP:** 40
SQ FT: 55,000
SALES (est): 7.6MM **Privately Held**
WEB: www.upstatedoor.com
SIC: 2431 Door frames, wood

Warwick
Orange County

(G-15510)
AMERICAN TOWMAN NETWORK INC
Also Called: American Towman Expeditions
2 Overlook Dr Ste 5 (10990-1810)
PHONE..................................845 986-4546
Steven L Calitri, *President*
Neila Smith, *President*
Dennie Ortiz, *Publisher*
Jimmy Santos, *General Mgr*
Annmarie Nitti, *Art Dir*
EMP: 12
SALES (est): 1.6MM **Privately Held**
WEB: www.towman.com
SIC: 2721 7549 Magazines: publishing only, not printed on site; towing services; towing service, automotive

(G-15511)
DANGELO HOME COLLECTIONS INC
Also Called: Victoria Dngelo Intr Cllctions
39 Warwick Tpke (10990-3632)
P.O. Box 271 (10990-0271)
PHONE..................................917 267-8920
Victoria D'Angelo, *President*
Stuart Morrison, *Vice Pres*
▲ **EMP:** 7
SQ FT: 16,000
SALES: 750K **Privately Held**
WEB: www.dangelohome.com
SIC: 2431 Woodwork, interior & ornamental

(G-15512)
DIGITAL UNITED COLOR PRTG INC
Also Called: Warwick Press
33 South St (10990-1624)
P.O. Box 708 (10990-0708)
PHONE..................................845 986-9846
Scott J Lieberman, *Ch of Bd*
EMP: 8
SALES (est): 1.2MM **Privately Held**
SIC: 2752 Commercial printing, offset

(G-15513)
DREAM GREEN PRODUCTIONS
Also Called: Dream Fabric Printing
39 Warwick Tpke (10990-3632)
P.O. Box 271 (10990-0271)
PHONE..................................917 267-8920
Victoria D'Angelo, *Principal*
EMP: 5
SALES (est): 220K **Privately Held**
SIC: 2399 Fabricated textile products

(G-15514)
GARDEN STATE SHAVINGS INC
16 Almond Tree Ln (10990-2442)
PHONE..................................845 544-2835
Kimberlee Martin, *CEO*
Barry Luyster, *Vice Pres*
▼ **EMP:** 15
SQ FT: 60,000
SALES (est): 1.4MM **Privately Held**
SIC: 2421 Sawdust, shavings & wood chips

(G-15515)
KECK GROUP INC (PA)
314 State Route 94 S (10990-3379)
PHONE..................................845 988-5757
Robert Koeck, *CEO*
EMP: 12
SQ FT: 20,000
SALES (est): 814.2K **Privately Held**
WEB: www.keckgroup.com
SIC: 2531 Pews, church

(G-15516)
KINGS QUARTET CORP
270 Kings Hwy (10990-3417)
PHONE..................................845 986-9090
Gary Bernstein, *President*
David Bernstein, *Treasurer*
Bernard Bernstein, *Admin Sec*
Kenneth Bernstein, *Admin Sec*
EMP: 5 **EST:** 1992
SALES (est): 309.8K **Privately Held**
SIC: 2435 Plywood, hardwood or hardwood faced

(G-15517)
KNG CONSTRUCTION CO INC
19 Silo Ln (10990-2872)
PHONE..................................212 595-1451
Mark V Azzopardi, *President*
EMP: 10
SALES (est): 1.2MM **Privately Held**
SIC: 2431 1542 1521 Woodwork, interior & ornamental; commercial & office buildings, renovation & repair; general remodeling, single-family houses

(G-15518)
LABARBA-Q LLC
32 Highland Ave (10990-1819)
PHONE..................................845 806-6227
Joseph Labarbera,
EMP: 12 **EST:** 2015
SALES (est): 782.1K **Privately Held**
SIC: 2033 Barbecue sauce: packaged in cans, jars, etc.

(G-15519)
MECHANICAL RUBBER PDTS CO INC
Also Called: Minisink Rubber
77 Forester Ave Ste 1 (10990-1107)
P.O. Box 593 (10990-0593)
PHONE..................................845 986-2271
Cedric Glasper, *President*
Bill Thomas, *General Mgr*
Walter Kielb, *Sales Mgr*
Barry Moellman, *Sales Staff*
Lisa Rice, *Sales Staff*
EMP: 15
SQ FT: 53,000
SALES (est): 2.8MM **Privately Held**
SIC: 3061 3089 Mechanical rubber goods; molding primary plastic

(G-15520)
MEECO SULLIVAN LLC
3 Chancellor Ln (10990-3411)
PHONE..................................800 232-3625
EMP: 225
SQ FT: 50,000

▲ = Import ▼=Export
◆ =Import/Export

SALES: 22MM **Privately Held**
SIC: **2499** 4493 Mfg Wood Products Marina Operation

(G-15521)
TRACK 7 INC
3 Forester Ave (10990-1129)
PHONE..............................845 544-1810
Betsy Mitchell, *Principal*
EMP: 6
SALES (est): 990.8K **Privately Held**
SIC: **2653** Corrugated & solid fiber boxes

(G-15522)
TRANSPRTTION COLLABORATIVE INC
Also Called: Trans Tech Bus
7 Lake Station Rd (10990-3426)
PHONE..............................845 988-2333
John Phraner, *Ch of Bd*
EMP: 39
SALES (est): 9.4MM **Privately Held**
SIC: **3711** Motor vehicles & car bodies

Washingtonville
Orange County

(G-15523)
BRISTOL GIFT CO INC
8 North St (10992-1113)
PHONE..............................845 496-2821
EMP: 15
SQ FT: 7,000
SALES (est): 2.3MM **Privately Held**
SIC: **3499** Mfg Misc Fabricated Metal Products

(G-15524)
BROTHERHOOD AMERICAS
Also Called: Vinevrest Co
100 Brotherhood Plaza Dr (10992-2262)
P.O. Box 190 (10992-0190)
PHONE..............................845 496-3661
Hernan Donoso, *President*
Cesar Baeza, *Corp Secy*
▲ EMP: 35
SALES (est): 7.1MM **Privately Held**
WEB: www.brotherhoodwinery.net
SIC: **2084** Wines

Wassaic
Dutchess County

(G-15525)
PAWLING CORPORATION (PA)
32 Nelson Hill Rd (12592-2121)
PHONE..............................845 373-9300
Jason W Smith, *Ch of Bd*
Greg Holen, *General Mgr*
Ron Peck, *Purch Mgr*
Warren Rozelle, *Purch Mgr*
Debbie Silvernail, *Research*
▼ EMP: 105
SALES (est): 40.2MM **Privately Held**
WEB: www.pawling.com
SIC: **3061** 3069 3089 2821 Mechanical rubber goods; custom compounding of rubber materials; rubber floor coverings, mats & wallcoverings; mats or matting, rubber; molding primary plastic; extruded finished plastic products; silicone resins

(G-15526)
PRESRAY CORPORATION
Also Called: Door Dam
32 Nelson Hill Rd (12592-2121)
P.O. Box 200 (12592-0200)
PHONE..............................845 373-9300
Theodore C Hollander, *Ch of Bd*
Jason Smith, *President*
Kevin Harris, *General Mgr*
Todd Smith, *General Mgr*
Jered Tuberville, *Opers Mgr*
▲ EMP: 25 EST: 1955
SQ FT: 50,000
SALES (est): 6.1MM
SALES (corp-wide): 40.2MM **Privately Held**
WEB: www.presray.com
SIC: **3442** Metal doors

PA: Pawling Corporation
32 Nelson Hill Rd
Wassaic NY 12592
845 373-9300

(G-15527)
WALL PROTECTION PRODUCTS LLC
Also Called: Wallguard.com
32 Nelson Hill Rd (12592-2121)
P.O. Box 1109, Dover Plains (12522-1109)
PHONE..............................877 943-6826
Ralph Skokan, *CFO*
Rose Davis, *Sales Mgr*
Rose Benson, *Manager*
EMP: 30
SALES (est): 3.1MM **Privately Held**
SIC: **3069** Rubber floor coverings, mats & wallcoverings

Water Mill
Suffolk County

(G-15528)
CAR DOCTOR MOTOR SPORTS LLC
Also Called: Car Doctor, The
610 Scuttle Hole Rd (11976-2520)
P.O. Box 1384, Amagansett (11930-1384)
PHONE..............................631 537-1548
Ryan Pilla, *Owner*
EMP: 6
SALES (est): 450K **Privately Held**
SIC: **3949** Cartridge belts, sporting type

(G-15529)
DEERFIELD MILLWORK INC
58 Deerfield Rd Unit 2 (11976-2151)
PHONE..............................631 726-9663
Keith Dutcher, *President*
EMP: 11
SQ FT: 5,000
SALES (est): 1.8MM **Privately Held**
WEB: www.deerfieldmillwork.com
SIC: **2431** 8712 Moldings, wood: unfinished & prefinished; architectural services

(G-15530)
DUCK WALK VINYARDS
231 Montauk Hwy (11976-2639)
P.O. Box 962 (11976-0962)
PHONE..............................631 726-7555
Herodotus Damianos, *President*
Alexander Damianos, *Vice Pres*
EMP: 20
SQ FT: 22,470
SALES (est): 1.9MM **Privately Held**
WEB: www.duckwalk.com
SIC: **2084** Wines

(G-15531)
WALPOLE WOODWORKERS INC
779 Montauk Hwy (11976-2607)
P.O. Box 1281 (11976-1281)
PHONE..............................631 726-2859
Lou Maglio, *President*
EMP: 8
SALES (corp-wide): 83.9MM **Privately Held**
WEB: www.walpolewoodworkers.com
SIC: **2499** 5211 5712 2452 Fencing, wood; fencing; outdoor & garden furniture; prefabricated wood buildings; prefabricated metal buildings; wood household furniture
PA: Walpole Outdoors Llc
100 Rver Ridge Dr Ste 302
Norwood MA 02062
508 668-2800

(G-15532)
WONDER NATURAL FOODS CORP (PA)
670 Montauk Hwy Unit 2 (11976-3700)
P.O. Box 2568, Southampton (11969-2568)
PHONE..............................631 726-4433
Lloyd Lasdon, *CEO*
Stuart Lasdon, *COO*
▲ EMP: 8

SALES (est): 1MM **Privately Held**
WEB: www.peanutwonder.com
SIC: **2099** Peanut butter

Waterford
Saratoga County

(G-15533)
CASCADES TSSUE GROUP-SALES INC
148 Hudson River Rd (12188-1908)
PHONE..............................518 238-1900
Andre Lair, *Manager*
EMP: 100
SALES (corp-wide): 3.5B **Privately Held**
SIC: **2621** Paper mills
HQ: Cascades Tissue Group-Sales Inc.
148 Hudson River Rd
Waterford NY 12188
819 363-5100

(G-15534)
CASCADES TSSUE GROUP-SALES INC (HQ)
148 Hudson River Rd (12188-1908)
P.O. Box 369 (12188-0369)
PHONE..............................819 363-5100
Daniel Morneau, *President*
Gary A Hayden, *Chairman*
Maryse Fernet, *Vice Pres*
David Pierro, *Vice Pres*
Mark Sormanti, *Vice Pres*
▲ EMP: 40
SALES (est): 30.8MM
SALES (corp-wide): 3.5B **Privately Held**
SIC: **2621** Absorbent paper
PA: Cascades Inc
404 Boul Marie-Victorin
Kingsey Falls QC J0A 1
819 363-5100

(G-15535)
CASCADES USA INC
148 Hudson River Rd (12188-1908)
PHONE..............................518 880-3600
Sal Sciarrino, *President*
David L Pierro, *Corp Secy*
Allan Hogg, *Asst Treas*
Tad Allen, *Sales Staff*
Stacy Eaker, *Taxation*
EMP: 5
SALES (est): 1.4MM
SALES (corp-wide): 3.5B **Privately Held**
SIC: **2621** Paper mills
HQ: Cascades Canada Ulc
404 Boul Marie-Victorin
Kingsey Falls QC J0A 1
819 363-5100

(G-15536)
EVONIK CORPORATION
7 Schoolhouse Ln (12188-1931)
P.O. Box 188 (12188-0188)
PHONE..............................518 233-7090
Gina Pettinelli, *Counsel*
Alexander Weber, *Vice Pres*
Jonathan Shan, *Opers Mgr*
Chuck Wilpers, *Warehouse Mgr*
Cabrini Grob, *Buyer*
EMP: 32
SALES (corp-wide): 2.6B **Privately Held**
SIC: **2869** Industrial organic chemicals
HQ: Evonik Corporation
299 Jefferson Rd
Parsippany NJ 07054
973 929-8000

(G-15537)
HALFMOON TOWN WATER DEPARTMENT
8 Brookwood Rd (12188-1206)
PHONE..............................518 233-7489
Frank Tironi, *Director*
EMP: 9
SALES (est): 603.6K **Privately Held**
SIC: **2899** Water treating compounds

(G-15538)
MAXIMUM SECURITY PRODUCTS CORP
Also Called: Hillside Iron Works
3 Schoolhouse Ln (12188-1931)
PHONE..............................518 233-1800
Joseph Burch, *President*
Harold Hatfield, *Corp Secy*
Robert Magee, *Vice Pres*
▲ EMP: 50
SQ FT: 100,000
SALES (est): 10.7MM **Privately Held**
WEB: www.maximumsecuritycorp.com
SIC: **3499** 2542 2531 3446 Fire- or burglary-resistive products; partitions & fixtures, except wood; public building & related furniture; stairs, fire escapes, balconies, railings & ladders

(G-15539)
MILLWOOD INC
430 Hudson River Rd (12188-1916)
P.O. Box 275 (12188-0275)
PHONE..............................518 233-1475
Mike Cusack, *Branch Mgr*
EMP: 17 **Privately Held**
SIC: **3565** 5084 Packaging machinery; packaging machinery & equipment
PA: Millwood, Inc.
3708 International Blvd
Vienna OH 44473

(G-15540)
MOM HOLDING COMPANY (PA)
260 Hudson River Rd (12188-1910)
PHONE..............................518 233-3330
Stephen Sukjung Lim, *Ch of Bd*
EMP: 2
SALES (est): 2.7B **Publicly Held**
SIC: **2869** 2821 3479 3679 Silicones; silicone resins; coating of metals with silicon; electronic crystals

(G-15541)
MOMENTIVE PERFORMANCE LLC (DH)
260 Hudson River Rd (12188-1910)
PHONE..............................281 325-3536
Douglas A Johns, *Vice Pres*
EMP: 1
SALES (est): 1.5MM
SALES (corp-wide): 2.7B **Publicly Held**
SIC: **2899** Chemical preparations

(G-15542)
MOMENTIVE PERFORMANCE MTLS INC (DH)
Also Called: Mpm
260 Hudson River Rd (12188-1910)
PHONE..............................518 233-3330
John G Boss, *President*
Erick Asmussen, *Senior VP*
John D Moran, *Senior VP*
Erick R Asmussen, *CFO*
Marvin O Schlanger, *Bd of Directors*
◆ EMP: 20
SALES: 2.7B **Publicly Held**
WEB: www.gewaterford.com
SIC: **2869** 2821 3479 3679 Silicones; silicone resins; coating of metals with silicon; electronic crystals; quartz crystals, for electronic application
HQ: Mpm Intermediate Holdings Inc.
260 Hudson River Rd
Waterford NY 12188
518 237-3330

(G-15543)
MPM HOLDINGS INC (HQ)
Also Called: Momentive
260 Hudson River Rd (12188-1910)
PHONE..............................518 233-3330
John G Boss, *President*
John D Moran, *Senior VP*
Erick R Asmussen, *CFO*
Theodore Butz, *Bd of Directors*
John Dionne, *Bd of Directors*
EMP: 5
SALES: 2.7B **Publicly Held**
SIC: **2869** 2821 3479 3679 Silicones; silicone resins; coating of metals with silicon; electronic crystals; quartz crystals, for electronic application

G E O G R A P H I C

PA: Mom Holding Company
260 Hudson River Rd
Waterford NY 12188
518 233-3330

(G-15544)
MPM INTERMEDIATE HOLDINGS INC (DH)
260 Hudson River Rd (12188-1910)
PHONE..............................518 237-3330
John G Boss, *President*
Brian D Berger, *CFO*
EMP: 2 **EST:** 2006
SALES (est): 2.7B **Publicly Held**
SIC: 2869 3479 3679 Silicones; coating of metals with silicon; electronic crystals; quartz crystals, for electronic application
HQ: Mpm Holdings Inc.
260 Hudson River Rd
Waterford NY 12188
518 233-3330

(G-15545)
MPM SILICONES LLC
Also Called: Momentive
260 Hudson River Rd (12188-1910)
PHONE..............................518 233-3330
Jack Boss, *CEO*
Erick Asnussen, *CFO*
Brian Berger, *Treasurer*
Jeffrey Stelling, *Finance*
EMP: 4600
SALES (est): 228.8MM
SALES (corp-wide): 2.7B **Publicly Held**
SIC: 2869 Silicones
HQ: Momentive Performance Materials Inc.
260 Hudson River Rd
Waterford NY 12188

(G-15546)
SOFT-TEX INTERNATIONAL INC (PA)
Also Called: Soft-Tex Manufacturing Co
428 Hudson River Rd (12188-1916)
P.O. Box 278 (12188-0278)
PHONE..............................800 366-2324
Jeff Chilton, *CEO*
Michael Wilker, *Senior VP*
Keith Bolton, *Vice Pres*
Erik Sanchez, *Vice Pres*
John Timmerman, *Vice Pres*
◆ **EMP:** 90
SQ FT: 120,000
SALES (est): 19.4MM **Privately Held**
WEB: www.bedpillows.com
SIC: 2392 Cushions & pillows

(G-15547)
STEPPING STONES ONE DAY SIGNS
105 Broad St (12188-2313)
P.O. Box 128 (12188-0128)
PHONE..............................518 237-5774
John Matson, *President*
Paul Matson, *Vice Pres*
EMP: 5
SQ FT: 3,000
SALES (est): 517.4K **Privately Held**
SIC: 3993 Signs & advertising specialties

(G-15548)
UPSTATE PIPING PRODUCTS INC
95 Hudson River Rd (12188-1937)
P.O. Box 321 (12188-0321)
PHONE..............................518 238-3457
Bob Lafountain, *President*
EMP: 3 **EST:** 2017
SQ FT: 7,500
SALES: 2MM **Privately Held**
SIC: 3462 Flange, valve & pipe fitting forgings, ferrous

(G-15549)
URSULA OF SWITZERLAND INC (PA)
Also Called: Ursula Company Store
31 Mohawk Ave (12188-2290)
PHONE..............................518 237-2580
Ursula G Rickenbacher, *President*
Meinrad Rickenbacher, *Treasurer*
EMP: 22 **EST:** 1965
SQ FT: 35,000

SALES (est): 2.5MM **Privately Held**
WEB: www.ursula.com
SIC: 2335 2337 2331 Gowns, formal; women's & misses' suits & coats; women's & misses' blouses & shirts

---

Waterloo
Seneca County

(G-15550)
EVANS CHEMETICS LP
228 E Main St (13165-1534)
PHONE..............................315 539-9221
David Schamberger, *Engineer*
Pat Wrobel, *Engineer*
Bernie Souza, *Sales Mgr*
Frank Dipasquale, *Branch Mgr*
Samantha Gotthardt, *Manager*
EMP: 55
SALES (corp-wide): 91MM **Privately Held**
WEB: www.evanschemetics.com
SIC: 2899 Acids
HQ: Evans Chemetics Lp
Glenpointe Center West 4
Teaneck NJ 07666
201 992-3100

(G-15551)
FINGER LAKES CONVEYORS INC
2359 State Route 414 E (13165-9633)
PHONE..............................315 539-9246
Michael J Gelder, *Ch of Bd*
Karen Owens, *Officer*
EMP: 9
SQ FT: 37,000
SALES: 806.5K **Privately Held**
WEB: www.flconveyors.com
SIC: 3499 Fire- or burglary-resistive products; machinery installation

(G-15552)
FRAZIER INDUSTRIAL COMPANY
1291 Waterloo Geneva Rd (13165-1201)
PHONE..............................315 539-9256
Staci Predicho, *Human Resources*
EMP: 55
SQ FT: 62,116
SALES (corp-wide): 281.2MM **Privately Held**
WEB: www.ecologic.com
SIC: 2542 3441 Pallet racks: except wood; fabricated structural metal
PA: Frazier Industrial Company
91 Fairview Ave
Long Valley NJ 07853
908 876-3001

(G-15553)
GHARANA INDUSTRIES LLC
Also Called: Ganesh Foods
61 Swift St (13165-1124)
PHONE..............................315 651-4004
◆ **EMP:** 6
SQ FT: 122,000
SALES (est): 420K **Privately Held**
SIC: 2022 Mfg Cheese

(G-15554)
HAMPSHIRE CHEMICAL CORP
228 E Main St (13165-1529)
P.O. Box 700 (13165-0700)
PHONE..............................315 539-9221
Richard Babiarz, *Partner*
EMP: 100
SALES (corp-wide): 61B **Publicly Held**
SIC: 2869 2899 2819 Industrial organic chemicals; chemical preparations; industrial inorganic chemicals
HQ: Hampshire Chemical Corp
2 E Spit Brook Rd
Nashua NH 03060

(G-15555)
MARROS EQUIPMENT & TRUCKS
2354 State Route 414 (13165-8473)
PHONE..............................315 539-8702
John Marro Jr, *President*
EMP: 14 **EST:** 1946
SQ FT: 14,400

SALES (est): 1.4MM **Privately Held**
SIC: 3713 3536 Truck bodies (motor vehicles); hoists

(G-15556)
PETER PRODUCTIONS DEVIVI INC
2494 Kingdom Rd (13165-9400)
PHONE..............................315 568-8484
Peter Devivi, *President*
EMP: 10
SQ FT: 9,000
SALES (est): 1.5MM **Privately Held**
WEB: www.tapertite.com
SIC: 2431 Millwork

(G-15557)
ZYP PRECISION LLC
1098 Birdsey Rd (13165-9404)
PHONE..............................315 539-3667
Edward Huff,
EMP: 5
SALES (est): 365.2K **Privately Held**
SIC: 3541 Lathes, metal cutting & polishing

Watertown
Jefferson County

(G-15558)
ALLIED MOTION TECHNOLOGIES INC
Also Called: Stature Electric
22543 Fisher Rd (13601-1090)
P.O. Box 6660 (13601-6660)
PHONE..............................315 782-5910
Ron Wenzen, *Branch Mgr*
EMP: 200
SALES (corp-wide): 310.6MM **Publicly Held**
WEB: www.alliedmotion.com
SIC: 3621 3546 Electric motor & generator parts; motors, electric; power-driven handtools
PA: Allied Motion Technologies Inc.
495 Commerce Dr Ste 3
Amherst NY 14228
716 242-8634

(G-15559)
BARRETT PAVING MATERIALS INC
26572 State Route 37 (13601-5789)
PHONE..............................315 788-2037
Sylvain Gross, *General Mgr*
Scott Zellar, *Safety Mgr*
Frank Simmons, *Branch Mgr*
EMP: 12
SQ FT: 820
SALES (corp-wide): 83.5MM **Privately Held**
WEB: www.barrettpaving.com
SIC: 3273 2951 1611 Ready-mixed concrete; asphalt paving mixtures & blocks; highway & street construction
HQ: Barrett Paving Materials Inc.
3 Becker Farm Rd Ste 307
Roseland NJ 07068
973 533-1001

(G-15560)
BIMBO BAKERIES USA INC
1100 Water St (13601-2146)
PHONE..............................315 782-4189
Rick Kimbell, *Manager*
EMP: 165 **Privately Held**
SIC: 2051 Bakery: wholesale or wholesale/retail combined
HQ: Bimbo Bakeries Usa, Inc
255 Business Center Dr # 200
Horsham PA 19044
215 347-5500

(G-15561)
BOTTLING GROUP LLC
Also Called: Pepsi Beverages Company
1035 Bradley St (13601-1248)
PHONE..............................315 788-6751
Eric Foss, *CEO*
Dan Wiseman, *General Mgr*
Darel Jones, *Info Tech Dir*
Lewis Hatch, *Info Tech Mgr*
Winnie Parker, *Administration*
EMP: 39 **EST:** 1999

SALES (est): 4.3MM **Privately Held**
SIC: 2086 Carbonated soft drinks, bottled & canned

(G-15562)
CAR-FRESHNER CORPORATION (HQ)
Also Called: Little Trees
21205 Little Tree Dr (13601-5861)
P.O. Box 719 (13601-0719)
PHONE..............................315 788-6250
Richard O Flechtner, *Chairman*
Amber Geidel, *Safety Mgr*
Tamara West, *Engineer*
Nichole Phillips, *Human Res Mgr*
Travis Washburn, *Sales Mgr*
◆ **EMP:** 250 **EST:** 1952
SQ FT: 30,000
SALES (est): 75.5MM **Privately Held**
WEB: www.little-trees.com
SIC: 2842 Deodorants, nonpersonal

(G-15563)
CAR-FRESHNER CORPORATION
22569 Fisher Cir (13601-1058)
P.O. Box 719 (13601-0719)
PHONE..............................315 788-6250
Robert Swank, *Principal*
EMP: 59 **Privately Held**
WEB: www.little-trees.com
SIC: 2842 Cleaning or polishing preparations
HQ: Car-Freshner Corporation
21205 Little Tree Dr
Watertown NY 13601
315 788-6250

(G-15564)
CHRISTIAN BUS ENDEAVORS INC (PA)
Also Called: Coughlin Printing Group
210 Court St Ste 10 (13601-4546)
PHONE..............................315 788-8560
Michael A Biolsi, *President*
Brian Peck, *Principal*
Laura Biolsi, *Accounts Mgr*
EMP: 10
SQ FT: 5,000
SALES (est): 1.6MM **Privately Held**
WEB: www.amfcoughlin.com
SIC: 2759 7374 Commercial printing; computer graphics service

(G-15565)
CLEMENTS BURRVILLE SAWMILL
18181 Van Allen Rd N (13601-5711)
PHONE..............................315 782-4549
Philip Clement, *President*
Betty Clement, *Vice Pres*
EMP: 9
SQ FT: 8,820
SALES: 700K **Privately Held**
SIC: 2448 2426 2421 Pallets, wood; hardwood dimension & flooring mills; sawmills & planing mills, general

(G-15566)
COCA-COLA REFRESHMENTS USA INC
22614 County Route 51 (13601-5064)
PHONE..............................315 785-8907
Jess Duck, *Manager*
EMP: 33
SALES (corp-wide): 31.8B **Publicly Held**
WEB: www.cokecce.com
SIC: 2086 Bottled & canned soft drinks
HQ: Coca-Cola Refreshments Usa, Inc.
2500 Windy Ridge Pkwy Se
Atlanta GA 30339
770 989-3000

(G-15567)
CURRENT APPLICATIONS INC
275 Bellew Ave S (13601-2381)
P.O. Box 321 (13601-0321)
PHONE..............................315 788-4689
George M Anderson, *President*
Christopher Gilbert, *Vice Pres*
Robert Olin, *Vice Pres*
Roger Snyder, *Treasurer*
▲ **EMP:** 49
SQ FT: 20,000

▲ = Import ▼=Export
◆ =Import/Export

SALES (est): 10.6MM **Privately Held**
WEB: www.currentapps.com
SIC: 3621 Motors, electric

(G-15568)
CYCLOTHERM OF WATERTOWN INC
787 Pearl St (13601-9111)
PHONE..........................315 782-1100
Charles E Stafford, *President*
EMP: 25
SQ FT: 20,000
SALES (est): 885.7K **Privately Held**
SIC: 3443 3554 Boiler shop products: boilers, smokestacks, steel tanks; paper industries machinery

(G-15569)
DOCO QUICK PRINT INC
808 Huntington St (13601-2864)
P.O. Box 6370 (13601-6370)
PHONE..........................315 782-6623
Carolyn Osborne, *President*
Daniel Osborne, *Treasurer*
EMP: 6
SQ FT: 3,000
SALES (est): 770.2K **Privately Held**
SIC: 2752 Commercial printing, offset

(G-15570)
GERTRUDE HAWK CHOCOLATES INC
21182 Salmon Run Mall Loo (13601-2248)
EMP: 20
SALES (corp-wide): 240.6MM **Privately Held**
SIC: 2064 Mfg Candy/Confectionery
PA: Gertrude Hawk Chocolates, Inc.
9 Keystone Industrial Par
Dunmore PA 18512
570 342-7556

(G-15571)
HANSON AGGREGATES PA LLC
25133 Nys Rt 3 (13601-1718)
P.O. Box 130 (13601-0130)
PHONE..........................315 782-2300
Dan O'Connor, *Manager*
Daniel Oconnor, *Manager*
EMP: 10
SALES (corp-wide): 20.6B **Privately Held**
SIC: 1442 5032 Gravel mining; stone, crushed or broken
HQ: Hanson Aggregates Pennsylvania, Llc
7660 Imperial Way
Allentown PA 18195
610 366-4626

(G-15572)
HENDERSON PRODUCTS INC
Also Called: Henderson Truck Equipment
22686 Fisher Rd Ste A (13601-1088)
PHONE..........................315 785-0994
Dave O'Brien, *Manager*
EMP: 22 **Publicly Held**
WEB: www.henderson-mfg.com
SIC: 3822 Ice maker controls
HQ: Henderson Products, Inc.
1085 S 3rd St
Manchester IA 52057
563 927-2828

(G-15573)
JAIN IRRIGATION INC
740 Water St (13601-2114)
PHONE..........................315 755-4400
Aric Olson, *President*
EMP: 70
SALES (corp-wide): 65.4MM **Privately Held**
SIC: 3052 3523 Plastic hose; fertilizing, spraying, dusting & irrigation machinery
PA: Jain Irrigation Holdings Corporation
6975 S Union Park Ctr # 600
Midvale UT 84047
909 395-5200

(G-15574)
JEFFERSON CONCRETE CORP
22850 County Route 51 (13601-5081)
PHONE..........................315 788-4171
Mark Thompson, *CEO*
EMP: 55
SQ FT: 37,000

SALES (est): 8.9MM **Privately Held**
WEB: www.jeffconcrete.com
SIC: 3272 Manhole covers or frames, concrete; septic tanks, concrete; tanks, concrete; burial vaults, concrete or precast terrazzo

(G-15575)
JOHN VESPA INC (PA)
Also Called: Vespa Sand & Stone
19626 Overlook Dr (13601-5443)
PHONE..........................315 788-6330
John Vespa Jr, *President*
Dorothy Vespa, *Admin Sec*
EMP: 13 **EST:** 1941
SQ FT: 2,400
SALES: 1.5MM **Privately Held**
SIC: 1422 1442 Crushed & broken limestone; construction sand mining; gravel mining

(G-15576)
KENAL SERVICES CORP
Also Called: Metal Man Services
1109 Water St (13601-2147)
PHONE..........................315 788-9226
Kenneth Moseley, *President*
Michael Vecchio, *CFO*
EMP: 7
SQ FT: 15,272
SALES (est): 600K **Privately Held**
WEB: www.metalmanservices.com
SIC: 3446 Architectural metalwork

(G-15577)
KENT NUTRITION GROUP INC
810 Waterman Dr (13601-2371)
PHONE..........................315 788-0032
Brad Coolidge, *Opers-Prdtn-Mfg*
EMP: 10
SQ FT: 13,608
SALES (corp-wide): 449.1MM **Privately Held**
WEB: www.blueseal.com
SIC: 2048 Livestock feeds
HQ: Kent Nutrition Group, Inc.
1600 Oregon St
Muscatine IA 52761
866 647-1212

(G-15578)
KNORR BRAKE HOLDING CORP (DH)
748 Starbuck Ave (13601-1620)
PHONE..........................315 786-5356
Heinz Hermann Thiele, *President*
David Kilcran, *Engineer*
Dawn Wetzel, *Admin Asst*
▲ **EMP:** 1
SALES (est): 1.2B
SALES (corp-wide): 711.6K **Privately Held**
SIC: 3743 5013 Railroad equipment; motor vehicle supplies & new parts
HQ: Knorr-Bremse Ag
Moosacher Str. 80
Munchen 80809
893 547-0

(G-15579)
KNORR BRAKE TRUCK SYSTEMS CO (DH)
Also Called: New York Air Brake
748 Starbuck Ave (13601-1620)
P.O. Box 6760 (13601-6760)
PHONE..........................315 786-5200
Peter Riedlinger, *Vice Ch Bd*
Heinz Hermann Thiele, *President*
Jason Connell, *Vice Pres*
John Chatterton, *VP Opers*
Tim Sheridan, *Opers Staff*
▲ **EMP:** 445
SQ FT: 250,000
SALES (est): 1.1B
SALES (corp-wide): 711.6K **Privately Held**
SIC: 3743 Brakes, air & vacuum: railway

(G-15580)
KNOWLTON TECHNOLOGIES LLC
213 Factory St (13601-2748)
PHONE..........................315 782-0600
Frederick G Rudmann, *CEO*
Anthony Closs, *Asst Supt*

James Ganter, *Exec VP*
James Lee, *Vice Pres*
Marty Crossman, *Safety Mgr*
◆ **EMP:** 130
SQ FT: 287,000
SALES (est): 61.8MM **Publicly Held**
SIC: 2621 Filter paper; specialty papers
PA: Eastman Chemical Company
200 S Wilcox Dr
Kingsport TN 37660

(G-15581)
LCO DESTINY LLC
Also Called: Timeless Frames
1 Fisher Cir (13601)
P.O. Box 28 (13601-0028)
PHONE..........................315 782-3302
John Pope, *Vice Pres*
Kevin Davis, *Production*
Greg Gaston, *CFO*
Kathy Watson, *Human Res Dir*
Debra Shambo, *Business Anlyst*
◆ **EMP:** 300
SQ FT: 90,000
SALES (est): 66.3MM **Privately Held**
WEB: www.timelessframes.com
SIC: 2499 Picture frame molding, finished; picture & mirror frames, wood

(G-15582)
MARTINS DENTAL STUDIO
Also Called: Martin Dental Studio
162 Sterling St (13601-3311)
P.O. Box 228 (13601-0228)
PHONE..........................315 788-0800
Richard Martin Jr, *President*
EMP: 7
SQ FT: 1,400
SALES (est): 951.7K **Privately Held**
SIC: 3843 8072 Teeth, artificial (not made in dental laboratories); dental laboratories

(G-15583)
NEW YORK AIR BRAKE LLC
781 Pearl St (13601)
PHONE..........................315 786-5576
Michael Hawthorne, *President*
EMP: 35
SALES (corp-wide): 711.6K **Privately Held**
SIC: 3743 4783 Brakes, air & vacuum: railway; railway motor cars; containerization of goods for shipping; crating goods for shipping; packing goods for shipping
HQ: New York Air Brake Llc
748 Starbuck Ave
Watertown NY 13601

(G-15584)
NEW YORK AIR BRAKE LLC (DH)
748 Starbuck Ave (13601-1620)
P.O. Box 6760 (13601-6760)
PHONE..........................315 786-5219
Heinz Thiele, *Ch of Bd*
J Paul Morgan, *President*
Marshall G Beck, *Senior VP*
Zach Chatterton, *Buyer*
Mitchell Sanchez, *Engineer*
▲ **EMP:** 226
SALES: 22.5MM
SALES (corp-wide): 711.6K **Privately Held**
SIC: 3743 Brakes, air & vacuum: railway

(G-15585)
NORTHERN AWNING & SIGN COMPANY
Also Called: N A S C O
22891 County Route 51 (13601-5005)
PHONE..........................315 782-8515
Michael Fitzgerald, *President*
EMP: 5
SQ FT: 4,000
SALES (est): 581.4K **Privately Held**
WEB: www.nascosigns.com
SIC: 3993 3444 2394 Signs & advertising specialties; sheet metalwork; awnings, fabric: made from purchased materials

(G-15586)
NORTHERN NY NEWSPAPERS CORP
Also Called: Watertown Daily Times
260 Washington St (13601-4669)
PHONE..........................315 782-1000
John B Johnson Jr, *CEO*
Joseph M Butler, *Mayor*
Patrick Nelson, *Mayor*
Richard R Babbitt, *CFO*
Robert Elias, *Natl Sales Mgr*
EMP: 210
SQ FT: 30,000
SALES (est): 13.2MM
SALES (corp-wide): 32MM **Privately Held**
WEB: www.lowville.com
SIC: 2711 2752 Newspapers: publishing only, not printed on site; commercial printing, lithographic
PA: Johnson Newspaper Corporation
260 Washington St
Watertown NY
315 782-1000

(G-15587)
PETRE ALII PETROLEUM
Also Called: Express Mart
1268 Arsenal St (13601-2214)
PHONE..........................315 785-1037
EMP: 6
SALES: 200K **Privately Held**
SIC: 2911 Petroleum Refiner

(G-15588)
SEMCO CERAMICS INC
363 Eastern Blvd (13601-3140)
PHONE..........................315 782-3000
Alfred E Calligaris, *President*
Tony Marra, *Vice Pres*
Douglas E Miller, *Asst Controller*
EMP: 3
SQ FT: 30,000
SALES (est): 4MM
SALES (corp-wide): 178.3MM **Privately Held**
SIC: 3253 3251 Ceramic wall & floor tile; structural brick & blocks
PA: The Stebbins Engineering And Manufacturing Company
363 Eastern Blvd
Watertown NY 13601
315 782-3000

(G-15589)
TAYLOR CONCRETE PRODUCTS INC
20475 Old Rome Rd (13601-5509)
PHONE..........................315 788-2191
Thomas O'Connor, *President*
Scott Kitto, *Vice Pres*
Ellen O'Connor, *Vice Pres*
Richard O'Connor, *Vice Pres*
Richard Oconnor, *Vice Pres*
EMP: 21 **EST:** 1932
SQ FT: 2,500
SALES: 4.1MM **Privately Held**
WEB: www.taylorconcrete.com
SIC: 3271 5032 3272 Blocks, concrete or cinder: standard; concrete & cinder block; concrete & cinder block; concrete products

(G-15590)
TIMELESS DECOR LLC
22419 Fisher Rd (13601-1090)
P.O. Box 28 (13601-0028)
PHONE..........................315 782-5759
Kathy Watson, *Human Res Dir*
Lisa Weber,
EMP: 118
SALES (est): 13MM **Privately Held**
SIC: 2599 3231 3952 7699 Hotel furniture; framed mirrors; frames for artists' canvases; picture framing, custom; art, picture frames & decorations

(G-15591)
WATERTOWN 1785 LLC
Also Called: Thousand Island Diamond Center
21875 Towne Center Dr (13601-5898)
PHONE..........................315 785-0062
Scott Brown, *Managing Prtnr*
EMP: 6

SALES (est): 196.1K
SALES (corp-wide): 69.2MM **Privately Held**
SIC: 3911 Jewelry apparel
PA: The Sporn Company Inc
227 Main St
Burlington VT 05401
802 865-2624

(G-15592)
WATERTOWN CONCRETE INC
24471 State Route 12 (13601-5784)
PHONE..............................315 788-1040
Joseph Belcher, *President*
Jason Belcher, *Vice Pres*
Chris Gregory, *Finance Mgr*
EMP: 16
SQ FT: 10,000
SALES (est): 2MM **Privately Held**
SIC: 3273 Ready-mixed concrete

(G-15593)
ZIEGLER TRUCK & DIESL REPR INC
22249 Fabco Rd (13601-1775)
PHONE..............................315 782-7278
Charles E Ziegler, *President*
Helen Ziegler, *Admin Sec*
EMP: 5
SALES: 425K **Privately Held**
SIC: 3531 Construction machinery

Waterville
Oneida County

(G-15594)
CENTER STATE PROPANE LLC (PA)
1130 Mason Rd Ste 2 (13480-2140)
PHONE..............................315 841-4044
James Wratten,
Mike Buell,
EMP: 4
SALES (est): 1.1MM **Privately Held**
SIC: 1321 Butane (natural) production

(G-15595)
F & R ENTERPRISES INC (PA)
Also Called: Pumilia's Pizza Shell
1594 State Route 315 (13480-1516)
P.O. Box 345 (13480-0345)
PHONE..............................315 841-8189
John Pumilia, *President*
EMP: 7
SALES (est): 1.1MM **Privately Held**
SIC: 2038 Pizza, frozen

Watervliet
Albany County

(G-15596)
ACTASYS INC (PA)
805 25th St (12189)
PHONE..............................914 432-2336
Miles Flamenbaum, *CEO*
Michael Amitay, *President*
Daniele Gallardo, *President*
David Menicovich, *President*
◆ EMP: 6
SQ FT: 230,000
SALES: 360K **Privately Held**
SIC: 3714 Motor vehicle parts & accessories

(G-15597)
BIGBEE STEEL AND TANK COMPANY
Also Called: New York Tank Co
958 19th St (12189-1752)
PHONE..............................518 273-0801
Kristina Engleka, *Controller*
Dwight McCombs, *Credit Mgr*
Chris Myers, *Credit Mgr*
Joseph Werner, *Regl Sales Mgr*
Adam Hemminger, *Sales Staff*
EMP: 25

SALES (corp-wide): 42.1MM **Privately Held**
WEB: www.highlandtank.com
SIC: 3443 3714 Farm storage tanks, metal plate; motor vehicle parts & accessories
PA: Bigbee Steel And Tank Company Inc
4535 Elizabethtown Rd
Manheim PA 17545
814 893-5701

(G-15598)
BONDED CONCRETE INC (PA)
303 Watervliet Shaker Rd (12189-3424)
P.O. Box 189 (12189-0189)
PHONE..............................518 273-5800
Salvatore O Clemente, *Ch of Bd*
Thomas A Clemente, *President*
Philip Clemente, *Vice Pres*
Scott Face, *Safety Dir*
Jude Clemente, *Treasurer*
EMP: 25 EST: 1964
SQ FT: 10,000
SALES: 10.8MM **Privately Held**
WEB: www.bondedconcrete.com
SIC: 3273 Ready-mixed concrete

(G-15599)
CARDISH MACHINE WORKS INC
7 Elm St (12189-1826)
PHONE..............................518 273-2329
Eugene J Cardish Jr, *President*
Charles Cardish, *Vice Pres*
EMP: 33 EST: 1933
SALES: 6.3MM **Privately Held**
WEB: www.cardishmachineworks.com
SIC: 3599 Machine shop, jobbing & repair

(G-15600)
COMFORTEX CORPORATION (DH)
Also Called: Comfortex Window Fashions
21 Elm St (12189-1770)
PHONE..............................518 273-3333
Thomas Marusak, *President*
Suk-Joung Kahng, *Principal*
Jim Barss, *VP Opers*
Jack Dooley, *Facilities Mgr*
Pat Harris, *Warehouse Mgr*
◆ EMP: 132
SQ FT: 100,000
SALES (est): 56.9MM **Privately Held**
WEB: www.comfortex.com
SIC: 2591 Window blinds; window shades
HQ: Hunter Douglas Inc.
1 Blue Hill Plz Ste 1569
Pearl River NY 10965
845 664-7000

(G-15601)
EXTREME MOLDING LLC
25 Gibson St Ste 2 (12189-3375)
PHONE..............................518 326-9319
Lynn Momrow,
Joanne Moon,
▲ EMP: 50
SQ FT: 13,500
SALES (est): 4MM **Privately Held**
WEB: www.extrememolding.com
SIC: 3089 Injection molding of plastics

(G-15602)
GENERAL BUSINESS SUPPLY INC
Also Called: Tech Valley Printing
2550 9th Ave (12189-1962)
PHONE..............................518 720-3939
EMP: 55
SALES (est): 5.3MM **Privately Held**
SIC: 2759 2752 Business forms: printing; commercial printing, offset

(G-15603)
HARTCHROM INC
25 Gibson St Ste 1 (12189-3342)
PHONE..............................518 880-0411
Edgar Oehler, *CEO*
▲ EMP: 18 EST: 2001
SQ FT: 33,000

SALES: 4.9MM
SALES (corp-wide): 1.3B **Privately Held**
WEB: www.hartchrom.com
SIC: 3471 3541 Plating of metals or formed products; anodizing (plating) of metals or formed products; grinding, polishing, buffing, lapping & honing machines
PA: Arbonia Ag
Amriswilerstrasse 50
Arbon TG
714 474-141

(G-15604)
LWA WORKS INC
2622 7th Ave Ste 50s (12189-1963)
PHONE..............................518 271-8360
Lance Weinheimer, *President*
▲ EMP: 5
SALES (est): 500K **Privately Held**
WEB: www.lanartworks.com
SIC: 3599 Machine shop, jobbing & repair

(G-15605)
SAINT-GOBAIN ABRASIVES INC
Also Called: Coated Abrasive Division
2600 10th Ave (12189-1766)
PHONE..............................518 266-2200
Judy Alison, *Manager*
EMP: 400
SQ FT: 1,880
SALES (corp-wide): 215.9MM **Privately Held**
WEB: www.sgabrasives.com
SIC: 3291 Abrasive products
HQ: Saint-Gobain Abrasives, Inc.
1 New Bond St
Worcester MA 01606
508 795-5000

(G-15606)
SOLID SEALING TECHNOLOGY INC
44 Dalliba Ave Ste 240 (12189-4017)
PHONE..............................518 874-3600
Gary L Balfour, *Ch of Bd*
Alan Fuierer, *President*
Gary Balfour, *Principal*
EMP: 25
SQ FT: 10,000
SALES (est): 5.4MM **Publicly Held**
WEB: www.solidsealing.com
SIC: 3629 Rectifiers (electrical apparatus)
HQ: Heico Electronic Technologies Corp.
3000 Taft St
Hollywood FL 33021
954 987-6101

(G-15607)
STRECKS INC
Also Called: Streck's Machinery
800 1st St (12189-3501)
PHONE..............................518 273-4410
Lloyd Demaranville, *President*
Christine Demaranville, *Vice Pres*
▲ EMP: 20 EST: 1952
SQ FT: 50,000
SALES (est): 3.3MM **Privately Held**
SIC: 3599 7692 7629 Machine shop, jobbing & repair; welding repair; electrical repair shops

(G-15608)
TIS ANSONIA LLC
70 Cohoes Rd (12189-1829)
PHONE..............................518 272-4920
Mary Matwa, *Principal*
▲ EMP: 11
SALES (est): 1MM **Privately Held**
SIC: 7694 Electric motor repair

(G-15609)
TROY BELTING AND SUPPLY CO (PA)
70 Cohoes Rd (12189-1895)
PHONE..............................518 272-4920
Jason W Smith, *Ch of Bd*
Dennis Pierce, *Business Mgr*
Lapoint Matt, *Project Mgr*
Mike Moran, *Opers Mgr*
Doug Gerrity, *Sales Mgr*
EMP: 67
SQ FT: 55,000

SALES (est): 16.5MM **Privately Held**
WEB: www.troybelting.com
SIC: 7694 3052 5084 5085 Electric motor repair; rubber & plastics hose & beltings; industrial machinery & equipment; industrial supplies; conveyors & conveying equipment; motors & generators

(G-15610)
TROY INDUSTRIAL SOLUTIONS
70 Cohoes Rd (12189-1829)
PHONE..............................518 272-4920
Jason Smith, *Vice Pres*
EMP: 12
SALES (est): 1.2MM **Privately Held**
SIC: 7694 Electric motor repair

(G-15611)
UTILITY SYSTEMS TECH INC
70 Cohoes Rd (12189-1829)
P.O. Box 110, Latham (12110-0110)
PHONE..............................518 326-4142
Robert Degeneff, *President*
Doug Marble, *President*
Mark Degeneffe, *General Mgr*
David Wightman, *General Mgr*
Jeff Foran, *Engineer*
EMP: 13
SALES (est): 2.8MM **Privately Held**
WEB: www.ustpower.com
SIC: 3643 Current-carrying wiring devices

(G-15612)
WICKED SMART LLC
700 5th Ave (12189-3610)
PHONE..............................518 459-2855
Nicole Martyn, *Sales Staff*
Sarah Brewer, *Marketing Mgr*
Todd Van Epps, *Mng Member*
Marcie Van Epps,
EMP: 15
SALES: 1.1MM **Privately Held**
SIC: 2396 2395 Screen printing on fabric articles; embroidery & art needlework

---

Watkins Glen
Schuyler County

(G-15613)
BMS MANUFACTURING CO INC
2857 County Line Rd (14891-9615)
PHONE..............................607 535-2426
William C Meehan Jr, *CEO*
EMP: 45
SQ FT: 50,000
SALES (est): 7.2MM **Privately Held**
WEB: www.bmsmanufacturing.com
SIC: 7692 3599 3441 Welding repair; machine & other job shop work; fabricated structural metal

(G-15614)
LAKEWOOD VINEYARDS INC
4024 State Route 14 (14891-9630)
PHONE..............................607 535-9252
Christopher Lamont Stamp, *President*
David A Stamp, *Vice Pres*
Beverly Stamp, *Treasurer*
Teresa Knapp, *Shareholder*
Michael E Stamp, *Shareholder*
▲ EMP: 12
SQ FT: 7,500
SALES (est): 930K **Privately Held**
WEB: www.lakewoodvineyards.com
SIC: 2084 Wines

(G-15615)
SKYLARK PUBLICATIONS LTD
Also Called: Hi-Lites
217 N Franklin St (14891-1201)
PHONE..............................607 535-9866
Damir Lazaric, *Managing Prtnr*
Flyod Vlajic, *Partner*
EMP: 5
SQ FT: 3,184
SALES (est): 423.5K **Privately Held**
SIC: 2741 Shopping news: publishing only, not printed on site

(G-15616)
SUIT-KOTE CORPORATION
Also Called: Central Asphalt
20 Fairgrounds Ln (14891-1632)
PHONE..................................607 535-2743
Kevin Suits, *Branch Mgr*
EMP: 30
SQ FT: 11,524
SALES (corp-wide): 272.8MM **Privately Held**
WEB: www.suit-kote.com
SIC: 2951 1611 2952 Asphalt paving mixtures & blocks; highway & street construction; asphalt felts & coatings
PA: Suit-Kote Corporation
1911 Lorings Crossing Rd
Cortland NY 13045
607 753-1100

(G-15617)
US SALT LLC
3580 Salt Point Rd (14891)
P.O. Box 110 (14891-0110)
PHONE..................................607 535-2721
EMP: 100
SALES (corp-wide): 5MM **Privately Held**
SIC: 2899 Salt
HQ: Us Salt, Llc
3580 Salt Point Rd
Watkins Glen NY 14891

(G-15618)
US SALT LLC (DH)
3580 Salt Point Rd (14891)
P.O. Box 110 (14891-0110)
PHONE..................................888 872-7258
Elizabeth Rowe, *Vice Pres*
Barb Adesso, *Office Mgr*
Mitchell Dascher,
▼ EMP: 13
SALES (est): 28.1MM
SALES (corp-wide): 5MM **Privately Held**
SIC: 2899 Salt
HQ: B.S.C. Holding, Inc.
10955 Lowell Ave Ste 500
Overland Park KS 66210
913 262-7263

Waverly
Tioga County

(G-15619)
CHARM MFG CO INC
Also Called: Charm Pools
251 State Route 17c (14892-9507)
P.O. Box 294 (14892-0294)
PHONE..................................607 565-8161
Jane Spicer, *President*
Linda Spicer, *Corp Secy*
Kay Onofre, *Vice Pres*
Richard Spicer, *Vice Pres*
EMP: 50
SQ FT: 50,000
SALES: 2.1MM **Privately Held**
WEB: www.charmpools.com
SIC: 3949 5091 5999 Swimming pools, except plastic; hot tubs; spa equipment & supplies; hot tub & spa chemicals, equipment & supplies; sauna equipment & supplies

(G-15620)
DORY ENTERPRISES INC
184 Sr 17c (14892)
P.O. Box 389 (14892-0389)
PHONE..................................607 565-7079
Robert Rynone, *President*
EMP: 10
SQ FT: 3,000
SALES (est): 1.4MM **Privately Held**
SIC: 2653 5113 Corrugated boxes, partitions, display items, sheets & pad; bags, paper & disposable plastic

(G-15621)
GRANITE WORKS LLC
133 William Donnelly (14892-1547)
PHONE..................................607 565-7012
Rai Leigh, *Sales Staff*
Jason Vandyk,
▲ EMP: 20
SALES (est): 3.3MM **Privately Held**
SIC: 3281 Curbing, granite or stone

(G-15622)
HANCOR INC
1 Wm Donnelly Ind Pkwy (14892-1599)
PHONE..................................607 565-3033
Dave Markie, *Manager*
EMP: 80
SALES (corp-wide): 1.3B **Publicly Held**
SIC: 3082 3084 Tubes, unsupported plastic; plastics pipe
HQ: Hancor, Inc.
4640 Trueman Blvd
Hilliard OH 43026
614 658-0050

(G-15623)
LEPRINO FOODS COMPANY
400 Leprino Ave (14892-1351)
PHONE..................................570 888-9658
Kate Blanchard, *Human Res Mgr*
Neil Brown, *Manager*
Charles Cannavino, *Supervisor*
EMP: 230
SALES (corp-wide): 1.7B **Privately Held**
WEB: www.leprinofoods.com
SIC: 2022 Natural cheese
PA: Leprino Foods Company
1830 W 38th Ave
Denver CO 80211
303 480-2600

(G-15624)
NEWS NOW WAVERLY
446 Broad St Apt 2 (14892-1471)
PHONE..................................607 296-6769
Michael Palmer, *President*
EMP: 15
SALES (est): 273.6K **Privately Held**
SIC: 2711 2741 Newspapers, publishing & printing;

Wayland
Steuben County

(G-15625)
BELANGERS GRAVEL & STONE INC
10184 State Route 21 (14572-9544)
PHONE..................................585 728-3906
Norb Belanger, *Ch of Bd*
EMP: 7
SALES (est): 665.9K **Privately Held**
SIC: 1442 Construction sand & gravel

(G-15626)
GUNLOCKE COMPANY LLC (HQ)
1 Gunlocke Dr (14572-9515)
PHONE..................................585 728-5111
Don Wharton,
▲ EMP: 148
SQ FT: 720,000
SALES (est): 179.7MM
SALES (corp-wide): 2.2B **Publicly Held**
WEB: www.gunlocke.com
SIC: 2521 Wood office furniture
PA: Hni Corporation
600 E 2nd St
Muscatine IA 52761
563 272-7400

(G-15627)
SPECIALTY SERVICES
Also Called: Accent Printing &GRaphics
2631e Naples St (14572)
P.O. Box 397 (14572-0397)
PHONE..................................585 728-5650
Randall Bergvall, *Owner*
EMP: 5
SQ FT: 12,000
SALES (est): 432.4K **Privately Held**
SIC: 2541 2431 Display fixtures, wood; millwork

Wayne
Schuyler County

(G-15628)
NEW MARKET PRODUCTS LLC
9671 Back St (14893)
P.O. Box 135 (14893-0135)
PHONE..................................607 292-6226

Aaron Hoover,
Samuel Hoover,
EMP: 9
SQ FT: 7,500
SALES: 500K **Privately Held**
SIC: 3545 Tool holders

Webster
Monroe County

(G-15629)
APPLIED ENERGY SOLUTIONS LLC
251 Gallant Fox Ln (14580-9034)
PHONE..................................585 538-3270
Vern P Fleming,
Vern Fleming,
EMP: 44
SALES (est): 10.2MM **Privately Held**
WEB: www.appliedenergysol.com
SIC: 3629 Battery chargers, rectifying or nonrotating

(G-15630)
ASHLY AUDIO INC
847 Holt Rd Ste 1 (14580-9193)
PHONE..................................585 872-0010
David Parse, *CEO*
William Thompson, *Chairman*
John Sexton, *Vice Pres*
Mike Bow, *Engineer*
Jim Schwenzer, *Cust Mgr*
▲ EMP: 42
SQ FT: 25,000
SALES (est): 10.8MM **Privately Held**
WEB: www.ashly.com
SIC: 3651 3663 Household audio equipment; radio & TV communications equipment

(G-15631)
AUTOMATION EVOLUTION LLC
800 Salt Rd (14580-9666)
PHONE..................................585 241-6010
Fritz P Ruebeck, *Mng Member*
Travis Schurman,
EMP: 7
SQ FT: 41,000
SALES: 400K **Privately Held**
SIC: 3823 Industrial process control instruments

(G-15632)
CALVARY DESIGN TEAM INC (PA)
Also Called: Calvary Robotics
855 Publishers Pkwy (14580-2587)
PHONE..................................585 347-6127
Mark Chaney, *President*
Ross Gansz, *General Mgr*
Ken Strittmatter, *Managing Dir*
Jim Diederich, *Business Mgr*
Mark Hoyland, *Vice Pres*
◆ EMP: 200
SQ FT: 375,000
SALES: 65.4MM **Privately Held**
WEB: www.calvauto.com
SIC: 3599 8711 Custom machinery; mechanical engineering; industrial engineers

(G-15633)
CDA MACHINE INC
514 Vosburg Rd (14580-1043)
PHONE..................................585 671-5959
William Crosby, *President*
EMP: 9
SQ FT: 13,400
SALES (est): 1MM **Privately Held**
WEB: www.cdamachine.com
SIC: 3599 Machine shop, jobbing & repair

(G-15634)
CGS FABRICATION LLC
855 Publishers Pkwy (14580-2587)
PHONE..................................585 347-6127
Mark Chaney, *Owner*
EMP: 15 EST: 2012
SALES: 21.6MM **Privately Held**
SIC: 3469 Machine parts, stamped or pressed metal

(G-15635)
CLASSIC AUTOMATION LLC (PA)
800 Salt Rd (14580-9666)
PHONE..................................585 241-6010
Margaret Nichols, *Vice Pres*
Fritz Ruebeck, *Mng Member*
▲ EMP: 40
SQ FT: 17,000
SALES: 10MM **Privately Held**
SIC: 3823 Controllers for process variables, all types; boiler controls: industrial, power & marine type

(G-15636)
CLINTON SIGNS INC
1407 Empire Blvd (14580-2101)
PHONE..................................585 482-1620
Michael S Mammano III, *President*
EMP: 6 EST: 1938
SALES: 400K **Privately Held**
WEB: www.clintonsigns.com
SIC: 3993 7389 1799 7336 Electric signs; sign painting & lettering shop; sign installation & maintenance; commercial art & graphic design

(G-15637)
DATA-PAC MAILING SYSTEMS CORP
1217 Bay Rd Ste 12 (14580-1958)
PHONE..................................585 671-0210
Richard A Yankloski, *President*
Ken Yankloski, *Exec VP*
Ana Yankloski, *Vice Pres*
Richard Yankloski, *Treasurer*
EMP: 10
SQ FT: 3,000
SALES (est): 2.4MM **Privately Held**
WEB: www.data-pac.com
SIC: 3571 Electronic computers

(G-15638)
DIGITAL HOME CREATIONS INC
350 Shadowbrook Dr (14580-9108)
PHONE..................................585 576-7070
Ryan J Hills, *CEO*
EMP: 5
SALES: 1.4MM **Privately Held**
SIC: 3491 3651 Automatic regulating & control valves; household audio & video equipment

(G-15639)
EAST SIDE MACHINE INC
625 Phillips Rd (14580-9786)
PHONE..................................585 265-4560
Paul Derleth, *President*
Lou Rossetti, *Vice Pres*
EMP: 26
SQ FT: 16,000
SALES (est): 5.4MM **Privately Held**
WEB: www.esm1.com
SIC: 3599 Machine shop, jobbing & repair

(G-15640)
EMPIRE STATE WEEKLIES INC
Also Called: Wayne County Mail
46 North Ave (14580-3308)
PHONE..................................585 671-1533
David Young, *President*
EMP: 20 EST: 1945
SQ FT: 5,100
SALES (est): 1.5MM **Privately Held**
WEB: www.empirestateweeklies.com
SIC: 2711 Job printing & newspaper publishing combined

(G-15641)
GRIFFIN MANUFACTURING COMPANY
1656 Ridge Rd (14580-3697)
P.O. Box 308 (14580-0308)
PHONE..................................585 265-1991
Angelo Papia, *President*
Kristin P Papia, *Managing Dir*
Darryl Papia, *Vice Pres*
Gary Papia, *Vice Pres*
Terry Papia, *Vice Pres*
▲ EMP: 20 EST: 1946
SQ FT: 6,000
SALES (est): 3.7MM **Privately Held**
WEB: www.grifhold.com
SIC: 3545 Cutting tools for machine tools

(G-15642)
INGENIOUS INGENUITY INC
Also Called: Vertigo Drones
1804 Tebor Rd Ste 2 (14580-9746)
PHONE...................................800 834-5279
Andrew Lake, *CEO*
EMP: 14
SQ FT: 4,200
SALES (est): 2.9MM **Privately Held**
SIC: 3721 5043 5092 Aircraft; motorized aircraft; cameras & photographic equipment; educational toys; vehicles, children's

(G-15643)
JOHNSON CONTROLS INC
237 Birch Ln (14580-1301)
PHONE...................................585 671-1930
Peter Baranello, *Manager*
EMP: 25 **Privately Held**
SIC: 2531 Seats, automobile
HQ: Johnson Controls, Inc.
5757 N Green Bay Ave
Milwaukee WI 53209
414 524-1200

(G-15644)
KAL MANUFACTURING CORPORATION
657 Basket Rd (14580-9764)
PHONE...................................585 265-4310
Alan Liwush, *CEO*
Richard Liwush, *Ch of Bd*
Brian Hooker, *Safety Mgr*
Mike Bates, *Electrical Engi*
Tim Lindsay, *Sales Mgr*
EMP: 37 **EST:** 1943
SQ FT: 50,000
SALES (est): 10.1MM **Privately Held**
WEB: www.kal-mfg.com
SIC: 3444 3845 3599 3441 Sheet metalwork; electromedical equipment; machine & other job shop work; fabricated structural metal; miscellaneous metalwork

(G-15645)
MIRROR SHOW MANAGEMENT INC
855 Hard Rd (14580-8949)
PHONE...................................585 232-4020
Donna Shultz, *President*
Laurie Kamal, *Vice Pres*
Thomas Macallister, *Vice Pres*
Thomas G McAllister, *Vice Pres*
Tammy Wilkes, *Vice Pres*
▲ **EMP:** 57
SQ FT: 65,000
SALES (est): 9.7MM **Privately Held**
WEB: www.mirrorshow.com
SIC: 2541 Display fixtures, wood

(G-15646)
OPTICOOL SOLUTIONS LLC
Also Called: Opticool Technologies
855 Publishers Pkwy (14580-2587)
PHONE...................................585 347-6127
Nicole Cannon, *Purch Mgr*
EMP: 17
SALES (est): 4.6MM **Privately Held**
SIC: 3585 Parts for heating, cooling & refrigerating equipment

(G-15647)
PLANAR OPTICS INC
858 Hard Rd (14580-8950)
PHONE...................................585 671-0100
Horst Koch, *President*
EMP: 7 **EST:** 1965
SQ FT: 5,400
SALES (est): 1MM **Privately Held**
SIC: 3827 Optical instruments & lenses

(G-15648)
PRINT TECH INC
11 Stablegate Dr (14580-9382)
PHONE...................................585 202-3888
Rick Rosso, *President*
David Vella, *CFO*
EMP: 5
SQ FT: 1,700
SALES (est): 770.3K **Privately Held**
WEB: www.printtech.com
SIC: 2752 7389 Commercial printing, lithographic; printing broker

(G-15649)
R D SPECIALTIES INC
560 Salt Rd (14580-9718)
PHONE...................................585 265-0220
Douglas R Krasucki, *President*
Grace Krasucki, *Treasurer*
EMP: 15 **EST:** 1936
SQ FT: 8,000
SALES (est): 1.1MM **Privately Held**
WEB: www.rdspecialties.com
SIC: 3312 Bar, rod & wire products

(G-15650)
RADAX INDUSTRIES INC
700 Basket Rd Ste A (14580-9757)
PHONE...................................585 265-2055
Rocco Sacco, *Ch of Bd*
Richard Sacco, *President*
Barbara Sacco, *Treasurer*
Amy Years Formicola, *Admin Sec*
EMP: 27 **EST:** 1967
SQ FT: 55,000
SALES (est): 6.5MM **Privately Held**
WEB: www.radax.com
SIC: 3452 Screws, metal

(G-15651)
RESPONSE CARE INC
38 Commercial St (14580-3106)
PHONE...................................585 671-4144
Myron Kowal, *President*
Richard Moore, *Co-Owner*
EMP: 7
SQ FT: 6,500
SALES (est): 1MM **Privately Held**
SIC: 3669 Intercommunication systems, electric

(G-15652)
SCHUTT CIDER MILL
1063 Plank Rd (14580-9399)
PHONE...................................585 872-2924
Martin Schutt, *Owner*
EMP: 10
SQ FT: 3,308
SALES (est): 765.8K **Privately Held**
WEB: www.schuttsapplemill.com
SIC: 2099 5499 5149 Cider, nonalcoholic; juices, fruit or vegetable; juices

(G-15653)
SICK INC
Lazerdata Division
855 Publishers Pkwy (14580-2587)
P.O. Box 448 (14580-0448)
PHONE...................................585 347-2000
EMP: 50 **Privately Held**
SIC: 3599 Mfg General Industrial Machinery
HQ: Sick, Inc
6900 W 110th St
Minneapolis MN 55438
952 941-6780

(G-15654)
SKANDACOR DIRECT INC
545 Basket Rd (14580-9610)
PHONE...................................585 265-9020
Johnathan Congdon, *President*
Brad Drever, *Managing Dir*
▲ **EMP:** 7
SQ FT: 6,000
SALES (est): 2.5MM **Privately Held**
SIC: 3555 Printing trades machinery

(G-15655)
STUDCO BUILDING SYSTEMS US LLC
Also Called: Ezconcept
1700 Boulter Indus Pkwy (14580-9763)
PHONE...................................585 545-3000
Ben Stevens, *Managing Dir*
Allan Parr, *Mng Member*
▲ **EMP:** 73
SQ FT: 65,000
SALES (est): 16.5MM **Privately Held**
WEB: www.studcosystems.com
SIC: 3444 Studs & joists, sheet metal

(G-15656)
TG POLYMERS INC
667 Hills Pond Rd (14580-4034)
PHONE...................................585 670-9427
Thomas G Seidewand, *President*
EMP: 1

SALES: 7MM **Privately Held**
SIC: 2673 7389 Bags: plastic, laminated & coated;

(G-15657)
TRICON MACHINE LLC
820 Coventry Dr (14580-8422)
PHONE...................................585 671-0679
Gary German, *
EMP: 7 **EST:** 1979
SQ FT: 10,000
SALES: 1MM **Privately Held**
WEB: www.triconmachine.com
SIC: 3599 Custom machinery

(G-15658)
TRIDENT PRECISION MFG INC
734 Salt Rd (14580-9718)
PHONE...................................585 265-2010
Nicholas Juskiw, *President*
Andrew Juskiw, *VP Opers*
Dan Nuijens, *Plant Mgr*
Kelly Brayer, *Purch Agent*
Diane Cialini, *Buyer*
▲ **EMP:** 95 **EST:** 1979
SQ FT: 60,000
SALES (est): 31.6MM **Privately Held**
WEB: www.tridentprecision.com
SIC: 3469 3545 3569 7373 Stamping metal for the trade; machine tool accessories; assembly machines, non-metalworking; computer-aided design (CAD) systems service; computer-aided manufacturing (CAM) systems service; laser welding, drilling & cutting equipment; sheet metalwork

(G-15659)
UNISEND LLC
249 Gallant Fox Ln (14580-9034)
PHONE...................................585 414-9575
Sheikh Wasim Khaled, *Principal*
Steve Muratore, *Principal*
EMP: 5 **EST:** 2012
SALES (est): 375.6K **Privately Held**
SIC: 3822 Building services monitoring controls, automatic

(G-15660)
UNISTEL LLC
860 Hard Rd (14580-8825)
PHONE...................................585 341-4600
Sankar Sewnauth, *
Mark Curletta, *
▲ **EMP:** 99
SALES: 8.2MM **Privately Held**
SIC: 3999 2099 Manufacturing industries; seasonings & spices

(G-15661)
WEBSTER ONTRIO WLWRTH PNNYSVER
164 E Main St (14580-3230)
P.O. Box 1135 (14580-7835)
PHONE...................................585 265-3620
Geoffrey Mohr, *Partner*
Mary Jill Mohr, *Partner*
EMP: 12
SQ FT: 1,000
SALES (est): 770.7K **Privately Held**
WEB: www.websterpennysaver.com
SIC: 2711 Newspapers

(G-15662)
WEBSTER PRINTING CORPORATION
46 North Ave (14580-3008)
PHONE...................................585 671-1533
W David Young, *President*
Leslie Young, *Admin Sec*
EMP: 18
SQ FT: 2,500
SALES (est): 1.5MM **Privately Held**
SIC: 2759 2791 2789 2752 Newspapers: printing; typesetting; bookbinding & related work; commercial printing, lithographic

(G-15663)
XEROX CORPORATION
800 Phillips Rd Ste 20599 (14580-9791)
PHONE...................................585 422-4564
Fax: 585 422-8576
EMP: 700

SALES (corp-wide): 10.2B **Publicly Held**
SIC: 3861 Mfg Photographic Equipment/Supplies
PA: Xerox Corporation
201 Merritt 7
Norwalk CT 06851
203 968-3000

(G-15664)
ZOMEGA TERAHERTZ CORPORATION
806 Admiralty Way (14580-3912)
PHONE...................................585 347-4337
Thomas Tongue, *CEO*
Wendy Zhang, *CFO*
EMP: 15
SALES (est): 3MM **Privately Held**
SIC: 3829 Measuring & controlling devices

Weedsport
Cayuga County

(G-15665)
BARBER WELDING INC
Also Called: Alpha Boats Unlimited
2517 Rte 31 W (13166)
P.O. Box 690 (13166-0690)
PHONE...................................315 834-6645
Stephen L Walczyk, *President*
Dave Dunham, *Plant Mgr*
▲ **EMP:** 20
SQ FT: 18,000
SALES (est): 2.5MM **Privately Held**
WEB: www.barberweldinginc.com
SIC: 7692 3441 Welding repair; fabricated structural metal

Wellsville
Allegany County

(G-15666)
ANNIES ICE
35 Herman Ave (14895-9513)
PHONE...................................585 593-5605
Laurie Hennessey, *Partner*
Joseph Hennessy, *Partner*
EMP: 5 **EST:** 1993
SALES (est): 210.9K **Privately Held**
SIC: 2097 Manufactured ice

(G-15667)
ARVOS INC (DH)
Also Called: Air Preheater
3020 Truax Rd (14895-9531)
P.O. Box 372 (14895-0372)
PHONE...................................585 593-2700
David Breckinridge, *President*
Brent Beachy, *President*
Karsten Stckrath, *President*
Ludger Heuberg, *CFO*
Guillaume Boutillot, *Marketing Staff*
EMP: 2
SALES (est): 163.9MM
SALES (corp-wide): 104.5MM **Privately Held**
SIC: 3443 Air preheaters, nonrotating: plate type
HQ: Triton Beratungsgesellschaft Gmbh
Schillerstr. 20
Frankfurt Am Main 60313
699 210-20

(G-15668)
CURRENT CONTROLS INC
353 S Brooklyn Ave (14895-1446)
PHONE...................................585 593-1544
Robert Landon, *President*
Carl Baxter, *Engineer*
Jeremy McNaughton, *Engineer*
Jason Hamer, *Sales Mgr*
Bruce McNaughton, *Manager*
EMP: 150 **EST:** 1982
SQ FT: 25,000
SALES (est): 30.6MM **Privately Held**
WEB: www.currentcontrols.com
SIC: 3612 Control transformers

(G-15669)
CURTISS-WRIGHT ELECTRO-
37 Coats St Ste 200 (14895-1003)
PHONE...................................585 596-3482

▲ = Import ▼=Export
◆ =Import/Export

David Schurra, *General Mgr*
EMP: 47
SALES (corp-wide): 2.4B **Publicly Held**
SIC: 3491 Automatic regulating & control valves; process control regulator valves; valves, automatic control
HQ: Curtiss-Wright Electro-Mechanical Corporation
1000 Wright Way
Cheswick PA 15024
724 275-5000

(G-15670)
DRESSER-RAND COMPANY
37 Coats St (14895-1003)
P.O. Box 592 (14895-0592)
PHONE..................................585 596-3100
Eric Seelye, *Engineer*
Rod Blunk, *Program Mgr*
Doug Martin, *Manager*
Dawn Jordan, *IT/INT Sup*
Toni Austin, *Administration*
EMP: 650
SALES (corp-wide): 95B **Privately Held**
WEB: www.dresser-rand.com
SIC: 3491 3511 Industrial valves; turbines & turbine generator sets; turbines & turbine generator sets & parts
HQ: Dresser-Rand Company
500 Paul Clark Dr
Olean NY 14760
716 375-3000

(G-15671)
GENESEE METAL PRODUCTS INC
106 Railroad Ave (14895-1143)
PHONE..................................585 968-6000
Michael P Oleksiak, *President*
EMP: 20
SQ FT: 28,000
SALES (est): 2.9MM **Privately Held**
SIC: 3441 Fabricated structural metal

(G-15672)
MATTESON LOGGING INC
2808 Beech Hill Rd (14895-9779)
PHONE..................................585 593-3037
Brian Matteson, *President*
Pammy Matteson, *Vice Pres*
EMP: 5
SALES (est): 411.3K **Privately Held**
SIC: 2411 Logging camps & contractors

(G-15673)
NORTHERN LIGHTS ENTPS INC
Also Called: Northern Lights Candles
3474 Andover Rd (14895-9525)
PHONE..................................800 836-8797
Andrew Glanzman, *President*
Jeannie Skiffington, *Principal*
Bernard T Wieszczyk, *Principal*
Christina Glanzman, *Vice Pres*
Brittany Zwiefka, *Production*
◆ **EMP:** 120 **EST:** 1977
SQ FT: 20,000
SALES (est): 15MM **Privately Held**
WEB: www.northernlightscandles.com
SIC: 3999 5999 Candles; candle shops

(G-15674)
RELEASE COATINGS NEW YORK INC
125 S Brooklyn Ave (14895-1453)
P.O. Box 622 (14895-0622)
PHONE..................................585 593-2335
Ralph Naples, *President*
Ralph A Naples, *President*
EMP: 5
SQ FT: 7,200
SALES (est): 1.1MM **Privately Held**
SIC: 2822 Synthetic rubber

(G-15675)
SANDLE CUSTOM BEARING CORP
1110 State Route 19 (14895-9120)
PHONE..................................585 593-7000
Eric Sandle, *President*
Diana Sandle, *Admin Sec*
▼ **EMP:** 9
SQ FT: 4,000
SALES (est): 1.6MM **Privately Held**
SIC: 3562 Ball & roller bearings

(G-15676)
SIEMENS GOVERNMENT TECH INC
Also Called: Sgt Dresser-Rand
37 Coats St (14895-1003)
P.O. Box 592 (14895-0592)
PHONE..................................585 593-1234
EMP: 405
SALES (corp-wide): 95B **Privately Held**
WEB: www.dresser-rand.com
SIC: 3511 Turbines & turbine generator sets & parts
HQ: Siemens Government Technologies, Inc.
2231 Crystal Dr Ste 700
Arlington VA 22202
703 480-8901

West Babylon
Suffolk County

(G-15677)
110 SAND COMPANY
170 Cabot St (11704-1102)
PHONE..................................631 694-2822
Tom Murphy, *Manager*
EMP: 17
SALES (corp-wide): 5.8MM **Privately Held**
SIC: 1442 Construction sand & gravel
PA: 110 Sand Company
136 Spagnoli Rd
Melville NY 11747
631 694-2822

(G-15678)
A-MARK MACHINERY CORP
101 Lamar St (11704-1301)
PHONE..................................631 643-6300
Marcel Edelstein, *President*
Shelly Edelstein, *Corp Secy*
Paul Schwartz, *Vice Pres*
▲ **EMP:** 15
SQ FT: 24,000
SALES (est): 5.3MM **Privately Held**
SIC: 3555 Printing trades machinery

(G-15679)
A-QUICK BINDERY LLC
30 Gleam St Unit C (11704-1207)
PHONE..................................631 491-1110
Nick Koutsoliontos, *Owner*
John Liontos,
EMP: 5
SALES (est): 778.1K **Privately Held**
SIC: 2789 Bookbinding & related work

(G-15680)
ABERDEEN BLOWER & SHTMTL WORKS
401 Columbus Ave (11704-5541)
P.O. Box 1134 (11704-0134)
PHONE..................................631 661-6100
Peter Levine, *President*
John Rolleri, *Partner*
EMP: 7 **EST:** 1950
SALES (est): 1.5MM **Privately Held**
SIC: 3444 Sheet metal specialties, not stamped

(G-15681)
ADCOMM GRAPHICS INC
21 Lamar St (11704-1301)
PHONE..................................212 645-1298
EMP: 25
SQ FT: 5,000
SALES (est): 2.1MM **Privately Held**
SIC: 2741 7336 Misc Publishing Commercial Art/Graphic Design

(G-15682)
ADVANCE PRECISION INDUSTRIES
9 Mahan St Unit A (11704-1319)
PHONE..................................631 491-0910
Anton Korconkiewicz, *President*
EMP: 6 **EST:** 1963
SQ FT: 4,000
SALES (est): 479.1K **Privately Held**
SIC: 3599 Machine shop, jobbing & repair

(G-15683)
ADVANCED COATING TECHNIQUES
Also Called: A C T
311 Wyandanch Ave (11704-1501)
PHONE..................................631 643-4555
Anthony Gaitan, *President*
Maria Gaitan, *Corp Secy*
EMP: 20 **EST:** 1974
SQ FT: 50,000
SALES (est): 2.6MM **Privately Held**
WEB: www.advancedcoatingtech.com
SIC: 3479 Galvanizing of iron, steel or endformed products; coating of metals & formed products

(G-15684)
AIRCRAFT FINISHING CORP (PA)
100 Field St Unit A (11704-5550)
PHONE..................................631 422-5000
Sam Serigano, *President*
John Serigano, *Vice Pres*
Kathleen Serigano, *Treasurer*
Ann Serigano, *Admin Sec*
EMP: 16
SQ FT: 18,000
SALES (est): 2MM **Privately Held**
SIC: 3471 3479 Plating of metals or formed products; painting of metal products

(G-15685)
ALLMETAL CHOCOLATE MOLD CO INC
135 Dale St (11704-1103)
PHONE..................................631 752-2888
Joseph Micelli, *President*
John Micelli, *Admin Sec*
EMP: 10
SQ FT: 10,000
SALES (est): 1.3MM **Privately Held**
WEB: www.micelli.com
SIC: 3544 Industrial molds

(G-15686)
AMACON CORPORATION
49 Alder St Unit A (11704-1093)
PHONE..................................631 293-1888
Costas Antoniou, *President*
Ted Antoniou, *Vice Pres*
Henry Mancura, *Vice Pres*
Donald O'Day, *Vice Pres*
EMP: 11 **EST:** 1969
SALES (est): 1.2MM **Privately Held**
WEB: www.amacon.com
SIC: 3599 Machine shop, jobbing & repair

(G-15687)
AMERICAN ACRYLIC CORPORATION
400 Sheffield Ave (11704-5333)
PHONE..................................631 422-2200
Mandell Ziegler, *CEO*
Thomas C Ziegler, *President*
Marjorie Klyne, *Admin Sec*
◆ **EMP:** 20
SQ FT: 20,000
SALES (est): 1.8MM **Privately Held**
WEB: www.americanacrylic.com
SIC: 3083 3081 2821 Laminated plastics plate & sheet; unsupported plastics film & sheet; plastics materials & resins

(G-15688)
AMERICAN METAL SPINNING PDTS
21 Eads St (11704-1125)
PHONE..................................631 454-6276
Clark Morse, *President*
EMP: 9
SQ FT: 8,000
SALES (est): 726K **Privately Held**
WEB: www.amermetalspinning.com
SIC: 3469 Spinning metal for the trade

(G-15689)
AMSCOR INC
119 Lamar St (11704-1301)
PHONE..................................800 825-9800
Scott Silberglied, *President*
Michael Silberglied, *Vice Pres*
EMP: 15
SQ FT: 10,000
SALES: 2.5MM **Privately Held**
WEB: www.amscorinc.com
SIC: 2542 Shelving, office & store: except wood

(G-15690)
AQUA SHIELD INC
114 Bell St (11704-1004)
PHONE..................................631 420-4490
Igor Korsunski, *President*
EMP: 9
SALES: 1.3MM **Privately Held**
WEB: www.aquashieldonline.com
SIC: 3089 1799 Awnings, fiberglass & plastic combination; awning installation

(G-15691)
AUTOMATION SOURCE TECHNOLOGIES (PA)
21 Otis St Unit B (11704-1440)
PHONE..................................631 643-1678
Peter Dougherty,
▲ **EMP:** 12 **EST:** 2012
SALES (est): 2MM **Privately Held**
SIC: 3621 Phase or rotary converters (electrical equipment)

(G-15692)
BABYLON IRON WORKS INC
205 Edison Ave (11704-1030)
PHONE..................................631 643-3311
Raymond Zahralban, *President*
EMP: 16
SQ FT: 14,000
SALES (est): 3.4MM **Privately Held**
SIC: 3446 Architectural metalwork

(G-15693)
BARTOLOMEO PUBLISHING INC
Also Called: Northport Printing
100 Cabot St Unit A (11704-1133)
PHONE..................................631 420-4949
Dan Bartolomeo, *President*
Patricia Bartolomeo, *Vice Pres*
EMP: 5
SQ FT: 17,200
SALES (est): 1.3MM **Privately Held**
SIC: 2759 2752 Screen printing; letterpress printing; flexographic printing; commercial printing, offset

(G-15694)
BEAM MANUFACTURING CORP
Also Called: Sigro Precision
107 Otis St Unit A (11704-1444)
PHONE..................................631 253-2724
Ernie Lampeter, *President*
EMP: 6 **EST:** 1966
SQ FT: 4,000
SALES (est): 856K **Privately Held**
SIC: 3599 Machine shop, jobbing & repair

(G-15695)
BROOKVALE RECORDS INC
Also Called: Looney Tunes CD Store
31 Brookvale Ave (11704-7901)
PHONE..................................631 587-7722
Kral Groger, *President*
EMP: 11
SALES (est): 950K **Privately Held**
SIC: 2782 Record albums

(G-15696)
BSD TOP DIRECT INC
68 Route 109 (11704-6208)
PHONE..................................646 468-0156
Elisha Mishael, *CEO*
EMP: 5
SALES (est): 330K **Privately Held**
SIC: 2096 Potato chips & similar snacks

(G-15697)
BURTON INDUSTRIES INC
243 Wyandanch Ave Ste A (11704-1593)
PHONE..................................631 643-6660
Charles Seelinger, *CEO*
Richard Santos, *President*
Warren Hartman, *Vice Pres*
Thomas Seelinger, *Vice Pres*
EMP: 35 **EST:** 1971
SQ FT: 38,000
SALES (est): 7.8MM **Privately Held**
WEB: www.burtonheat.com
SIC: 3398 Metal heat treating

GEOGRAPHIC

(G-15698)
BUSINESS CARD EXPRESS INC
300 Farmingdale Rd (11704)
PHONE....................631 669-3400
William Richards, *President*
Jerry Peirano, *Treasurer*
EMP: 40
SQ FT: 11,000
SALES (est): 5.4MM **Privately Held**
SIC: 2759 2752 Thermography; commercial printing, lithographic

(G-15699)
C J & C SHEET METAL CORP
433 Falmouth Rd (11704-5654)
PHONE....................631 376-9425
James Thurau, *President*
EMP: 12
SALES (est): 970K **Privately Held**
SIC: 3444 Sheet metalwork

(G-15700)
CENTURY READY MIX INC
615 Cord Ave (11704)
P.O. Box 1065 (11704-0065)
PHONE....................631 888-2200
Nicolina Nicolia, *President*
EMP: 6
SALES (est): 426K **Privately Held**
SIC: 3273 5039 Ready-mixed concrete; mobile homes

(G-15701)
CHECK-MATE INDUSTRIES INC
370 Wyandanch Ave (11704-1524)
PHONE....................631 491-1777
Regina M Vieweg, *CEO*
Michael Zambardi, *Engineer*
Lucille Scavone, *Admin Asst*
Jacquilene Santaro, *Legal Staff*
Jacquelyn Santoro, *Legal Staff*
EMP: 45
SQ FT: 23,000
SALES (est): 13MM **Privately Held**
SIC: 3469 Metal stampings

(G-15702)
CHEM-TAINER INDUSTRIES INC (PA)
Also Called: Todd Enterprises
361 Neptune Ave (11704-5800)
PHONE....................631 422-8300
Stuart Pivar, *Ch of Bd*
James Glen, *President*
Anthony Lamb, *Vice Pres*
Frank Tamburello, *Natl Sales Mgr*
Joe Maiello, *Sales Executive*
◆ EMP: 50
SQ FT: 20,000
SALES (est): 46.5MM **Privately Held**
WEB: www.chemtainer.com
SIC: 3089 Plastic containers, except foam

(G-15703)
CHURCH BULLETIN INC
200 Dale St (11704-1124)
P.O. Box 1659, Massapequa (11758-0911)
PHONE....................631 249-4994
George Keenan Jr, *President*
EMP: 15
SALES (est): 1.6MM **Privately Held**
WEB: www.thechurchbulletininc.com
SIC: 2741 Business service newsletters: publishing & printing

(G-15704)
COMPUTERIZED METAL BENDING SER
91 Cabot St Unit A (11704-1132)
PHONE....................631 249-1177
Kenneth Rosner, *President*
EMP: 16 EST: 2010
SALES (est): 980.2K **Privately Held**
SIC: 3441 Fabricated structural metal

(G-15705)
CUSTOM FRAME & MOLDING CO
97 Lamar St 101 (11704-1308)
PHONE....................631 491-9091
Nick Maminakis, *President*
Dr Steven Lewen, *Vice Pres*
Michelle Lewen, *Admin Sec*
EMP: 12
SQ FT: 15,000
SALES (est): 1.5MM **Privately Held**
SIC: 3499 Picture frames, metal

(G-15706)
DBS INTERIORS CORP
Also Called: Island Interiors
81 Otis St (11704-1405)
P.O. Box 1780 (11704-0780)
PHONE....................631 491-3013
EMP: 12
SQ FT: 7,000
SALES (est): 2MM **Privately Held**
SIC: 2519 2541 2517 2511 Mfg Household Furniture Mfg Wood Partitions/Fixt Mfg Wd Tv/Radio Cabinets Mfg Wood Household Furn Mfg Wood Kitchen Cabinet

(G-15707)
DISPLAY COMPONENTS MFG INC
Also Called: D C M
267 Edison Ave (11704-1020)
PHONE....................631 420-0600
James P Devine III, *President*
Julie Braga, *Controller*
Donna Devine, *Admin Sec*
EMP: 30
SQ FT: 25,000
SALES (est): 5.1MM **Privately Held**
WEB: www.displaycomponents.com
SIC: 2542 Fixtures: display, office or store: except wood

(G-15708)
EAST CAST CLOR COMPOUNDING INC
Also Called: Linli Color
15 Kean St (11704-1208)
PHONE....................631 491-9000
George Benz, *CEO*
Tony Arra, *President*
Jon Shuman, *Vice Pres*
EMP: 9
SQ FT: 10,000
SALES (est): 1.6MM **Privately Held**
WEB: www.linlicolor.com
SIC: 2865 3089 Dyes & pigments; extruded finished plastic products

(G-15709)
EMPIRE AIR SYSTEMS LLC
Also Called: Empire Air Hvac
80 Kean St Ste 1 (11704-1221)
PHONE....................718 377-1549
Lior Binyamin,
Shmuel Cohen Zada,
EMP: 15
SALES (est): 1.6MM **Privately Held**
SIC: 3585 Air conditioning equipment, complete

(G-15710)
EQUUS POWER I LP
380 Patton Ave (11704-1413)
PHONE....................847 908-2878
EMP: 7
SALES (corp-wide): 733K **Privately Held**
SIC: 3612 Transformers, except electric
PA: Equus Power I, L.P.
1900 E Golf Rd Ste 1030
Schaumburg IL 60173
847 908-2878

(G-15711)
FAMOUS BOX SCOOTER CO
75 Rogers Ct (11704-6540)
PHONE....................631 943-2013
Charles Rubino, *Owner*
EMP: 5
SALES (est): 217.8K **Privately Held**
SIC: 3944 Scooters, children's

(G-15712)
G FUEL LLC (PA)
Also Called: Gamma Lab
113 Alder St (11704-1001)
PHONE....................877 426-6262
Clifford Morgan, *CEO*
Matthew Alvarez, *Controller*
Nick Lacagnina, *Marketing Staff*
▼ EMP: 38
SQ FT: 19,000
SALES (est): 7.8MM **Privately Held**
SIC: 2834 Vitamin, nutrient & hematinic preparations for human use

(G-15713)
GREAT EASTERN PASTA WORKS LLC
Also Called: Pasta People
385 Sheffield Ave (11704-5326)
PHONE....................631 956-0889
Kambiz Morakkabi,
EMP: 20
SQ FT: 1,500
SALES (est): 2.1MM **Privately Held**
SIC: 2099 5149 Pasta, uncooked: packaged with other ingredients; pasta & rice

(G-15714)
ISOLATION TECHNOLOGY INC
73 Nancy St Unit A (11704-1428)
P.O. Box 460, Massapequa (11758-0460)
PHONE....................631 253-3314
Bob Grefe, *President*
Robert Joyner, *Treasurer*
▲ EMP: 6
SQ FT: 4,000
SALES (est): 1.1MM **Privately Held**
WEB: www.isolationtech.com
SIC: 3699 Electric sound equipment

(G-15715)
J & T METAL PRODUCTS CO INC
89 Eads St (11704-1105)
PHONE....................631 226-7400
Thomas Lander, *President*
EMP: 20
SQ FT: 18,000
SALES (est): 1.9MM **Privately Held**
SIC: 3443 Industrial vessels, tanks & containers; tanks, standard or custom fabricated: metal plate

(G-15716)
J C INDUSTRIES INC
89 Eads St (11704-1186)
PHONE....................631 420-1920
Joseph V Celano, *Ch of Bd*
James Celano, *Vice Pres*
EMP: 30
SQ FT: 14,000
SALES (est): 5.4MM **Privately Held**
WEB: www.jcindustries.com
SIC: 3411 Metal cans

(G-15717)
J T D STAMPING CO INC
403 Wyandanch Ave (11704-1599)
PHONE....................631 643-4144
Giovanni Bianco, *President*
Aldo D'Adamo, *Vice Pres*
Claudia Mina, *Technology*
EMP: 39
SQ FT: 20,000
SALES (est): 3.5MM **Privately Held**
WEB: www.jtdstamping.com
SIC: 3599 Machine shop, jobbing & repair

(G-15718)
JALEX INDUSTRIES LTD
86 Nancy St (11704-1404)
PHONE....................631 491-5072
Alexander Jedynski, *President*
EMP: 15
SQ FT: 7,000
SALES (est): 1.9MM **Privately Held**
SIC: 3541 Machine tools, metal cutting type

(G-15719)
JAVIN MACHINE CORP
31 Otis St (11704-1405)
PHONE....................631 643-3322
Geri Spiezio, *CEO*
Sal Spiezio, *President*
Vincent Spiezio, *President*
John Zielinski, *QC Mgr*
Regina Heinz, *Office Mgr*
EMP: 15
SQ FT: 16,000
SALES (est): 3MM **Privately Held**
WEB: www.javinmachine.net
SIC: 3599 Machine shop, jobbing & repair

(G-15720)
JF MACHINE SHOP INC
89 Otis St Unit A (11704-1442)
PHONE....................631 491-7273
Anthony Schiavone, *President*
Robert Botticelli, *Business Mgr*
EMP: 7
SQ FT: 9,000
SALES (est): 1.5MM **Privately Held**
WEB: www.jfmachine.com
SIC: 3599 Machine shop, jobbing & repair

(G-15721)
JOHNNYS MACHINE SHOP
81 Mahan St (11704-1303)
PHONE....................631 338-9733
Juan Campos, *Owner*
EMP: 5
SALES (est): 200K **Privately Held**
SIC: 3599 Machine shop, jobbing & repair

(G-15722)
KESSLER THERMOMETER CORP
40 Gleam St (11704-1205)
PHONE....................631 841-5500
Robert Peyser, *President*
▲ EMP: 9
SALES (est): 1.1MM **Privately Held**
SIC: 3823 Thermometers, filled system: industrial process type

(G-15723)
KING ALBUM INC
20 Kean St (11704-1209)
PHONE....................631 253-9500
Warren King, *President*
EMP: 20
SQ FT: 7,700
SALES (est): 2.2MM **Privately Held**
SIC: 2782 Albums

(G-15724)
L K MANUFACTURING CORP
56 Eads St (11704-1106)
P.O. Box 167, Huntington Station (11746-0137)
PHONE....................631 243-6910
Robert Lutzker, *President*
Kay Kelly, *Vice Pres*
Samuel Martin, *Vice Pres*
EMP: 22
SQ FT: 15,000
SALES (est): 1.9MM **Privately Held**
WEB: www.lkmfg.com
SIC: 3089 5065 Kitchenware, plastic; electronic parts & equipment

(G-15725)
LETTERAMA INC (PA)
111 Cabot St (11704-1100)
PHONE....................516 349-0800
Mark Costa, *President*
▼ EMP: 6 EST: 1959
SQ FT: 30,000
SALES: 3MM **Privately Held**
SIC: 3993 Signs & advertising specialties

(G-15726)
LINZER PRODUCTS CORP (DH)
248 Wyandanch Ave (11704-1506)
PHONE....................631 253-3333
Brent Swenson, *President*
Tony Hazantonis, *General Mgr*
Robinson Ted, *Vice Pres*
Mark Saji, *Treasurer*
Rosemary Mailinger, *Asst Controller*
▲ EMP: 200 EST: 1892
SQ FT: 166,000
SALES: 120MM **Privately Held**
SIC: 3991 5198 Paint & varnish brushes; paint brushes, rollers, sprayers

(G-15727)
M T D CORPORATION
41 Otis St (11704-1405)
PHONE....................631 491-3905
Matthew Turnbull, *President*
Michael Deletto, *Vice Pres*
EMP: 10
SQ FT: 6,500
SALES (est): 1.2MM **Privately Held**
WEB: www.makeupart.net
SIC: 2521 2511 Wood office furniture; wood household furniture

(G-15728)
MAGELLAN AEROSPACE PROCESSING
Also Called: Ripak Aerospace Processing
165 Field St (11704-1210)
PHONE......................631 694-1818
Phillip Underwood, *President*
Karen Yoshiki-Gravelsins, *Vice Pres*
John Dekker, *CFO*
EMP: 8
SQ FT: 72,000
SALES (est): 217.6K
SALES (corp-wide): 732.9MM **Privately Held**
SIC: 3724 3429 Aircraft engines & engine parts; aircraft hardware
PA: Magellan Aerospace Corporation
3160 Derry Rd E
Mississauga ON L4T 1
905 677-1889

(G-15729)
MATRIX MACHINING CORP
69 B Nancy St Unitb (11704)
PHONE......................631 643-6690
Joseph Abdale, *President*
Ray Abdale, *Corp Secy*
EMP: 6
SQ FT: 4,700
SALES (est): 997.1K **Privately Held**
SIC: 3599 Machine shop, jobbing & repair

(G-15730)
MATRIX RAILWAY CORP
69 Nancy St Unit A (11704-1425)
PHONE......................631 643-1483
Nelson Rivas, *Ch of Bd*
▲ EMP: 9
SQ FT: 4,000
SALES (est): 1.9MM **Privately Held**
WEB: www.matrixrailway.com
SIC: 3743 Railroad equipment

(G-15731)
METRO DYNAMICS SCIE
20 Nancy St Unit A (11704-1448)
PHONE......................631 842-4300
Steve Plaener, *President*
EMP: 15
SQ FT: 6,000
SALES (est): 1.6MM **Privately Held**
SIC: 3812 Search & navigation equipment

(G-15732)
MILLWRIGHT WDWRK INSTALLETION
991 Peconic Ave (11704-5629)
PHONE......................631 587-2635
Martin Sherlock, *President*
EMP: 20
SQ FT: 16,000
SALES (est): 2.1MM **Privately Held**
SIC: 2431 1751 Millwork; finish & trim carpentry

(G-15733)
MPI CONSULTING INCORPORATED
Also Called: Wal Machine
87 Jersey St (11704-1206)
PHONE......................631 253-2377
William A Toscano, *CEO*
Jennifer Luizzi, *Vice Pres*
Gary Sporing, *Engineer*
EMP: 13 EST: 1966
SQ FT: 18,000
SALES (est): 5.5MM **Privately Held**
SIC: 3728 Aircraft body & wing assemblies & parts

(G-15734)
NEWMAT NORTHEAST CORP
81b Mahan St (11704-1303)
PHONE......................631 253-9277
Timothy T Greco, *President*
EMP: 11
SQ FT: 8,000
SALES (est): 2.7MM **Privately Held**
SIC: 2821 1742 Polyvinyl chloride resins (PVC); acoustical & ceiling work

(G-15735)
OUR TERMS FABRICATORS INC
48 Cabot St (11704-1109)
PHONE......................631 752-1517
John Friese, *President*
Greg D'Arrigo, *Vice Pres*
EMP: 32
SQ FT: 18,000
SALES (est): 4.5MM **Privately Held**
WEB: www.ourtermsfabricators.com
SIC: 3231 Furniture tops, glass: cut, beveled or polished

(G-15736)
PEYSER INSTRUMENT CORPORATION
Also Called: Chase Instrument Co
40 Gleam St (11704-1205)
PHONE......................631 841-3600
Robert Peyser, *President*
Leonard Peyser, *Vice Pres*
▲ EMP: 20
SQ FT: 1,500
SALES (est): 2.8MM **Privately Held**
SIC: 3829 5049 Hydrometers, except industrial process type; analytical instruments

(G-15737)
PMB PRECISION PRODUCTS INC
Also Called: Spartan Instruments
725 Mount Ave (11704-1700)
PHONE......................631 491-6753
Michael Belesis, *President*
Jan Craw, *Principal*
Richard Jackson, *Sales Mgr*
EMP: 16
SALES (est): 3MM **Privately Held**
SIC: 3399 Metal fasteners

(G-15738)
PREMIUM WOODWORKING LLC
108 Lamar St (11704-1312)
PHONE......................631 485-3133
Bhevendra Persaud,
EMP: 5
SQ FT: 5,000
SALES (est): 2MM **Privately Held**
SIC: 2434 Wood kitchen cabinets

(G-15739)
QUALITY SAW & KNIFE INC
115 Otis St (11704-1429)
PHONE......................631 491-4747
Fredrick Luberto, *President*
Paul Siegfried, *Vice Pres*
EMP: 10
SQ FT: 3,000
SALES (est): 800K **Privately Held**
SIC: 3425 7699 Saw blades, chain type; saw blades for hand or power saws; knife, saw & tool sharpening & repair

(G-15740)
R & J DISPLAYS INC
96 Otis St (11704-1430)
PHONE......................631 491-3500
Lance Landau, *President*
EMP: 30
SQ FT: 20,000
SALES (est): 3.2MM **Privately Held**
SIC: 3993 Displays & cutouts, window & lobby

(G-15741)
RGH ASSOCIATES INC
Also Called: Richards Screw Machine
86 Nancy St (11704-1404)
PHONE......................631 643-1111
Richard Honan, *President*
Richard Goldsmith, *Corp Secy*
EMP: 19
SQ FT: 7,200
SALES (est): 6.5MM **Privately Held**
SIC: 3599 Machine shop, jobbing & repair

(G-15742)
RICHARD MANNO & COMPANY INC
42 Lamar St (11704-1302)
PHONE......................631 643-2200
Vincent Manno, *President*
Ilian Dimitrov, *General Mgr*
Vincent Chiappone, *Exec VP*
Jason Wagner, *Exec VP*
Christine Burns, *Vice Pres*
▲ EMP: 54
SQ FT: 18,000
SALES (est): 10.4MM **Privately Held**
WEB: www.richardmanno.com
SIC: 3599 Machine shop, jobbing & repair

(G-15743)
ROSE GRAPHICS LLC
109 Kean St (11704-1208)
PHONE......................516 547-6142
Anthony F Severino,
EMP: 10
SQ FT: 8,000
SALES: 2MM **Privately Held**
SIC: 2759 Commercial printing

(G-15744)
S & D WELDING CORP
Also Called: S&D Welding
229 Edison Ave Ste A (11704-1042)
PHONE......................631 454-0383
Mark Dubicki, *President*
Lucia Dubicki, *Treasurer*
EMP: 5
SALES: 275K **Privately Held**
SIC: 7692 1799 5046 Welding repair; welding on site; commercial cooking & food service equipment

(G-15745)
SAGE KNITWEAR INC
103 Jersey St Unit D (11704-1219)
P.O. Box 748231, Rego Park (11374-8231)
PHONE......................718 628-7902
Payam Ebrani, *President*
EMP: 5
SQ FT: 3,500
SALES (est): 604.1K **Privately Held**
SIC: 2253 Sweaters & sweater coats, knit; dresses, knit; skirts, knit

(G-15746)
SAV THERMO INC
133 Cabot St (11704-1101)
PHONE......................631 249-9444
Vincent Caputi, *President*
Anthony Bangaroo, *Vice Pres*
EMP: 10
SQ FT: 10,000
SALES (est): 1.6MM **Privately Held**
SIC: 3089 Trays, plastic

(G-15747)
SONAER INC
68 Lamar St Unit D (11704-1316)
PHONE......................631 756-4780
Donald Cierco, *Ch of Bd*
Donald Ciervo, *Ch of Bd*
EMP: 8
SQ FT: 3,000
SALES (est): 1.1MM **Privately Held**
WEB: www.sonozap.com
SIC: 3679 Electronic circuits

(G-15748)
SONICOR INC
82 Otis St (11704-1406)
PHONE......................631 920-6555
Michael J Parker, *President*
Augusto D' Agostino, *Manager*
Augusto Dagostino, *Info Tech Mgr*
▲ EMP: 12 EST: 1966
SQ FT: 3,500
SALES (est): 2.7MM **Privately Held**
WEB: www.sonicor.com
SIC: 3569 3559 3554 3699 Separators for steam, gas, vapor or air (machinery); electroplating machinery & equipment; paper mill machinery: plating, slitting, waxing, etc.; welding machines & equipment, ultrasonic; cleaning equipment, ultrasonic, except medical & dental; medical cleaning equipment, ultrasonic

(G-15749)
STERLING TOGGLE INC
99 Mahan St (11704-1303)
PHONE......................631 491-0500
William Horne Jr, *President*
Susan Horne, *Vice Pres*
Debra Irving, *Vice Pres*
Debbie Irving, *Manager*
EMP: 12
SALES (est): 2.3MM **Privately Held**
WEB: www.sterlingtoggle.com
SIC: 3555 Printing trades machinery

(G-15750)
STRAHL & PITSCH INC
230 Great East Neck Rd (11704-7602)
P.O. Box 1098 (11704-0098)
PHONE......................631 669-0175
William France, *Ch of Bd*
William Deluca, *President*
Hans Kestler, *Vice Pres*
Roger McKenna, *Vice Pres*
Thitiporn Pollock, *Vice Pres*
◆ EMP: 40 EST: 1904
SALES (est): 16.5MM **Privately Held**
WEB: www.spwax.com
SIC: 2842 Waxes for wood, leather & other materials

(G-15751)
SUPER WEB INC
97 Lamar St (11704-1308)
PHONE......................631 643-9100
Marcel Edelstein, *Ch of Bd*
Paul Schwartz, *Vice Pres*
Shelly Edelstein, *Admin Sec*
▲ EMP: 30
SQ FT: 27,000
SALES (est): 7.6MM **Privately Held**
WEB: www.superwebusa.com
SIC: 3555 5084 Printing trades machinery; printing trades machinery, equipment & supplies

(G-15752)
SWEET TOOTH ENTERPRISES LLC
Also Called: Micelli Chocolate Mold Co
135 Dale St (11704-1103)
PHONE......................631 752-2888
Tim Goddeau, *Opers Mgr*
Paul Hamilton,
EMP: 20
SALES (est): 3.7MM **Privately Held**
SIC: 3544 Industrial molds

(G-15753)
TRIANGLE GRINDING MACHINE CORP
66 Nancy St Unit A (11704-1436)
PHONE......................631 643-3636
Santo Turano, *President*
Domingo Turano, *Vice Pres*
George Turano, *Vice Pres*
EMP: 5
SQ FT: 800
SALES (est): 636.6K **Privately Held**
SIC: 3599 Machine shop, jobbing & repair

(G-15754)
US ELECTROPLATING CORP
100 Field St Unit A (11704-1294)
PHONE......................631 293-1998
Robert Birmbaum, *President*
EMP: 6 EST: 1971
SQ FT: 3,000
SALES (est): 526K **Privately Held**
SIC: 3471 Plating of metals or formed products; polishing, metals or formed products

(G-15755)
VANDILAY INDUSTRIES INC
Also Called: Dualtron Manufacturing
60 Bell St Unit A (11704-1038)
PHONE......................631 226-3064
Don Ehrlich, *President*
Chris Schleimer, *Vice Pres*
EMP: 22 EST: 1997
SQ FT: 22,000
SALES (est): 4.1MM **Privately Held**
WEB: www.dualtron.com
SIC: 3545 Machine tool accessories

(G-15756)
VILLAGE VIDEO PRODUCTIONS INC
Also Called: Village Video News
107 Alder St (11704-1001)
PHONE......................631 752-9311
Robert Wolf, *President*
Christopher Pendy, *Editor*
Annette Perretta, *Editor*
Shari Rabinowitz, *Editor*
Maryellen Hauslaib, *Opers Dir*
EMP: 6
SQ FT: 2,000

SALES (est): 876.3K **Privately Held**
WEB: www.vvn.com
SIC: 3663 Satellites, communications

(G-15757)
YANKEE FUEL INC
780 Sunrise Hwy (11704-6105)
PHONE.................................631 880-8810
Ibrahim Sergi, *Principal*
EMP: 5
SALES (est): 387.2K **Privately Held**
SIC: 2869 Fuels

West Burlington
Otsego County

(G-15758)
CONTROL LOGIC CORPORATION
2533 State Highway 80 (13482-9717)
PHONE.................................607 965-6423
Randy Holdredge, *President*
Joanne Holdredge, *Admin Sec*
EMP: 6
SALES (est): 460K **Privately Held**
WEB: www.controllogic.com
SIC: 3577 Printers, computer

West Coxsackie
Greene County

(G-15759)
GOOD NOODLES INC
Also Called: Sfoglini Pasta
25 Vermilyea Ln (12192-1700)
PHONE.................................518 731-7278
Julie Wurfel, *CEO*
Scott Ketchum, *President*
EMP: 14
SQ FT: 37,000
SALES: 1.2MM **Privately Held**
SIC: 2099 Pasta, uncooked: packaged with other ingredients

West Edmeston
Madison County

(G-15760)
SCULLY SANITATION
11146 Skaneateles Tpke (13485-3060)
PHONE.................................315 899-8996
Timothy Scully, *Partner*
Kevin Scully, *Partner*
EMP: 8
SALES: 300K **Privately Held**
SIC: 2842 Sanitation preparations, disinfectants & deodorants

West Falls
Erie County

(G-15761)
BUTTERWOOD DESSERTS INC
Also Called: Swamp Island Dessert Co
1863 Davis Rd (14170-9701)
PHONE.................................716 652-0131
Fax: 585 652-1759
EMP: 40
SQ FT: 15,000
SALES (est): 3.4MM **Privately Held**
SIC: 2099 2053 2052 Mfg Food Preparations Mfg Frozen Bakery Prdts Mfg Cookies/Crackers

(G-15762)
TEAM FABRICATION INC
1055 Davis Rd (14170-9734)
P.O. Box 32 (14170-0032)
PHONE.................................716 655-4038
Robert Hopkins, *President*
EMP: 8
SQ FT: 2,376
SALES (est): 1.5MM **Privately Held**
WEB: www.teamfabrication.com
SIC: 3441 Fabricated structural metal

West Harrison
Westchester County

(G-15763)
WESTFAIR COMMUNICATIONS INC
Also Called: Westchester County Bus Jurnl
701 Westchester Ave 100w (10604-3420)
PHONE.................................914 694-3600
Dolores Delbello, *CEO*
John Mack Carter, *Shareholder*
EMP: 35
SALES (est): 2.5MM **Privately Held**
SIC: 2711 2721 Newspapers: publishing only, not printed on site; periodicals

West Haverstraw
Rockland County

(G-15764)
VIN-CLAIR INC
Also Called: Vin-Clair Bindery
132 E Railroad Ave (10993-1418)
PHONE.................................845 429-4998
Lou Maiello, *President*
Florence Maiello, *Vice Pres*
EMP: 10
SQ FT: 17,000
SALES (est): 77.3K **Privately Held**
SIC: 2789 Bookbinding & related work

(G-15765)
YOUR FURNITURE DESIGNERS INC
Also Called: Yfd Cabinetry
118 E Railroad Ave (10993-1416)
PHONE.................................845 947-3046
Jose A Mata, *President*
EMP: 5
SALES (est): 654.4K **Privately Held**
SIC: 2521 2434 2542 2511 Wood office furniture; wood kitchen cabinets; vanities, bathroom: wood; shelving, office & store: except wood; wood bedroom furniture

West Hempstead
Nassau County

(G-15766)
ARTISAN WOODWORKING LTD
Also Called: Artisan Custom Interiors
163 Hempstead Tpke (11552-1622)
PHONE.................................516 486-0818
Michael Aiello, *President*
Janet Aiello, *Corp Secy*
EMP: 6
SQ FT: 6,500
SALES (est): 834.8K **Privately Held**
WEB: www.artisancustominteriors.com
SIC: 2511 Wood household furniture

(G-15767)
AUTOMOTION PARKING SYSTEMS LLC
411 Hempstead Tpke # 200 (11552-1350)
PHONE.................................516 565-5600
Perry Finkelman, *Managing Dir*
Jordan Rinzler, *Vice Pres*
Daniel McCrossin, *Opers Mgr*
ARI Milstein, *Exec Dir*
Jeffrey Hyde, *Director*
▲ **EMP:** 2
SQ FT: 1,000
SALES (est): 2.1MM **Privately Held**
SIC: 3559 Parking facility equipment & supplies

(G-15768)
CENTAR FUEL CO INC
700 Nassau Blvd (11552-3531)
PHONE.................................516 538-2424
John Skei, *Principal*
EMP: 5 **EST:** 2007
SALES (est): 563.8K **Privately Held**
SIC: 2869 Fuels

(G-15769)
D-BEST EQUIPMENT CORP
77 Hempstead Gardens Dr (11552-2635)
PHONE.................................516 358-0965
Marc Cali, *CEO*
EMP: 24 **EST:** 1999
SALES (est): 5MM **Privately Held**
SIC: 2869 Enzymes

(G-15770)
INDEPENDENT HOME PRODUCTS LLC
59 Hempstead Gardens Dr (11552-2641)
PHONE.................................718 541-1256
Abbie Spetner, *Principal*
Yale Lipschik, *CFO*
▲ **EMP:** 20
SALES (est): 3.1MM **Privately Held**
SIC: 3088 3431 Hot tubs, plastic or fiberglass; bathtubs: enameled iron, cast iron or pressed metal

(G-15771)
INTERNTONAL CONSMR CONNECTIONS
Also Called: Wilson Picture Frames
5 Terminal Rd Unit A (11552-1151)
PHONE.................................516 481-3438
Mark Sternberg, *President*
Alan Kohn, *Shareholder*
EMP: 12
SQ FT: 5,000
SALES (est): 750K **Privately Held**
SIC: 2499 7699 Picture & mirror frames, wood; picture framing, custom

(G-15772)
J GIMBEL INC
275 Hempstead Tpke Ste A (11552-1540)
PHONE.................................718 296-5200
Jackie Sherman, *President*
Leonard Gimbel, *Vice Pres*
Lorie Gimbel, *Treasurer*
EMP: 20
SQ FT: 17,000
SALES (est): 2.5MM **Privately Held**
WEB: www.rollershades.com
SIC: 2591 Blinds vertical

(G-15773)
KONRAD PROSTHETICS & ORTHOTICS (PA)
596 Jennings Ave (11552-3706)
PHONE.................................516 485-9164
Kurt Konrad, *President*
Elsbeth Konrad, *Corp Secy*
EMP: 10
SQ FT: 200
SALES (est): 1.2MM **Privately Held**
SIC: 3842 7352 5999 Surgical appliances & supplies; invalid supplies rental; artificial limbs

(G-15774)
LANCO MANUFACTURING CO
384 Hempstead Tpke (11552-1304)
PHONE.................................516 292-8953
Joseph Lancer, *Partner*
Irwin Lamcer, *Partner*
Irwin Lancer, *Partner*
EMP: 5
SQ FT: 10,000
SALES (est): 39.3K **Privately Held**
SIC: 3561 Pumps & pumping equipment

(G-15775)
MAGIC TECH CO LTD
401 Hempstead Tpke (11552-1311)
PHONE.................................516 539-7944
EMP: 5
SALES (est): 440K **Privately Held**
SIC: 3699 5065 Mfg And Dist Karoke Machines

(G-15776)
MULTITONE FINISHING CO INC
56 Hempstead Gardens Dr (11552-2642)
PHONE.................................516 485-1043
Edward Mc Carthy, *President*
Harvey Pollack, *Vice Pres*
EMP: 8 **EST:** 1963
SQ FT: 4,700
SALES (est): 726K **Privately Held**
SIC: 3471 Finishing, metals or formed products

(G-15777)
MUTUAL ENGRAVING COMPANY INC
497 Hempstead Ave (11552-2738)
P.O. Box 129 (11552-0129)
PHONE.................................516 489-0534
Salvatore Forelli, *President*
Robert Forelli, *Vice Pres*
Lou Ewanitsko, *Treasurer*
EMP: 65 **EST:** 1939
SQ FT: 15,000
SALES (est): 8.7MM **Privately Held**
WEB: www.mutualengraving.com
SIC: 2754 2796 2791 2752 Stationery: gravure printing; platemaking services; typesetting; commercial printing, lithographic

(G-15778)
PROFESSIONAL REMODELERS INC
340 Hempstead Ave Unit A (11552-2061)
PHONE.................................516 565-9300
Thomas Stallone, *President*
EMP: 5
SALES (est): 486.2K **Privately Held**
SIC: 1389 Construction, repair & dismantling services

(G-15779)
SIGN GUYS NEW YORK CITY INC (PA)
Also Called: Sign Guys Nyc
237 Oak St (11552-2135)
PHONE.................................718 414-2310
Emma Michael, *President*
EMP: 5
SQ FT: 1,200
SALES (est): 495.1K **Privately Held**
SIC: 3993 Signs & advertising specialties

(G-15780)
STONE EXPO & CABINETRY LLC
7 Terminal Rd (11552-1105)
PHONE.................................516 292-2988
Annie Liu, *Manager*
▲ **EMP:** 14
SALES (est): 1.8MM **Privately Held**
SIC: 2434 2542 Wood kitchen cabinets; counters or counter display cases: except wood

(G-15781)
US PUMP CORP
707 Woodfield Rd (11552-3826)
P.O. Box 357 (11552-0357)
PHONE.................................516 303-7799
Nissim Isaacson, *Ch of Bd*
Kevan Woodworth, *Officer*
Lauren Cahill, *Admin Asst*
▲ **EMP:** 6
SALES (est): 799.9K **Privately Held**
SIC: 1381 1241 Drilling water intake wells; redrilling oil & gas wells; mining services: lignite

West Henrietta
Monroe County

(G-15782)
ALSTOM SIGNALING INC (DH)
Also Called: Alstrom Trnspt Info Solutions
1025 John St (14586-9781)
PHONE.................................585 783-2000
Ulisses Camillo, *CEO*
Thierry Best, *Managing Dir*
Gian-Luca Erbacci, *Vice Pres*
Ellen O'Neill, *Vice Pres*
Craig Daniels, *Project Dir*
▲ **EMP:** 277
SALES (est): 89.7MM
SALES (corp-wide): 63.2MM **Privately Held**
WEB: www.alstomsignalsolutions.com
SIC: 3669 Railroad signaling devices, electric; signaling apparatus, electric
HQ: Alstom Transportation Inc.
641 Lexington Ave Fl 28
New York NY 10022
212 692-5353

(G-15783)
AMERICAN FILTRATION TECH INC
100 Thruway Park Dr (14586-9798)
PHONE...................................585 359-4130
Richard Felber, *President*
EMP: 13
SQ FT: 36,000
SALES (est): 2.9MM **Privately Held**
SIC: 3569 3564 Filters, general line: industrial; blowers & fans

(G-15784)
APOLLO OPTICAL SYSTEMS INC
925 John St (14586-9780)
PHONE...................................585 272-6170
G Michael Morris, *CEO*
Daniel McGarry, *President*
Claude Tribastone, *President*
Gwen Murphy, *QC Mgr*
Kirk McMinn, *Engineer*
EMP: 38
SALES (est): 7.7MM **Privately Held**
WEB: www.apollooptical.com
SIC: 3827 Optical instruments & lenses

(G-15785)
APPAIRENT TECHNOLOGIES INC (PA)
150 Lucius Gordon Dr (14586-9687)
PHONE...................................585 214-2460
Chris O'Donnell, *CEO*
Jim Allen, *President*
Preston Keller, *President*
EMP: 5
SQ FT: 2,500
SALES (est): 1.2MM **Privately Held**
WEB: www.appairent.com
SIC: 3663 Radio broadcasting & communications equipment

(G-15786)
B C MANUFACTURING INC
100 Thruway Park Dr (14586-9798)
PHONE...................................585 482-1080
Bob Collins, *President*
Steve Hakes, *Mfg Dir*
Lyle Yonovich, *Technology*
EMP: 5
SQ FT: 5,500
SALES (est): 800.5K **Privately Held**
SIC: 3599 Machine shop, jobbing & repair

(G-15787)
BRANDYS MOLD AND TOOL CTR LTD (PA)
10 Riverton Way (14586-9754)
PHONE...................................585 334-8333
Michaela Perkins, *President*
Dan Morse, *General Mgr*
Franz Brandstetter, *Vice Pres*
EMP: 15
SALES (est): 1.4MM **Privately Held**
SIC: 3089 Injection molding of plastics

(G-15788)
BRINKMAN PRECISION INC
Also Called: B P I
100 Park Centre Dr (14586-9688)
PHONE...................................585 429-5001
Andrew J Laniak, *CEO*
Robert J Brinkman, *Ch of Bd*
James Gardner, *General Mgr*
Stan Forte, *Plant Mgr*
Bob Coffey, *Engineer*
EMP: 85
SALES (est): 18.3MM
SALES (corp-wide): 99.2MM **Privately Held**
WEB: www.brinkmanprecision.com
SIC: 3324 5047 Aerospace investment castings, ferrous; medical equipment & supplies
PA: Brinkman International Group, Inc.
167 Ames St
Rochester NY 14611
585 429-5000

(G-15789)
COHBER PRESS INC (PA)
Also Called: Kodak Gallery - Cohber
1000 John St (14586-9757)
P.O. Box 93100, Rochester (14692-7300)
PHONE...................................585 475-9100
Eric C Webber, *Ch of Bd*
Rick Moll, *President*
Howard Buzz, *Chairman*
Daniel Mahany, *COO*
Chris Bowen, *Vice Pres*
EMP: 95 **EST:** 1925
SQ FT: 49,000
SALES (est): 20.8MM **Privately Held**
WEB: www.cohber.com
SIC: 2752 2791 2789 Commercial printing, offset; photo-offset printing; typesetting; bookbinding & related work

(G-15790)
COOPERVISION INC
180 Thruway Park Dr (14586-9798)
PHONE...................................585 385-6810
Michelle McDonagh, *Director*
EMP: 594
SALES (corp-wide): 2.5B **Publicly Held**
SIC: 3851 Contact lenses
HQ: Coopervision, Inc.
209 High Point Dr Ste 100
Victor NY 14564

(G-15791)
DELPHI POWERTRAIN SYSTEMS LLC
5500 W Henrietta Rd (14586-9701)
PHONE...................................585 359-6000
Bruce Gardephe, *Engineer*
Jim Zizzleman, *Manager*
Mike Miller, *Manager*
EMP: 209
SALES (corp-wide): 1.5MM **Privately Held**
WEB: www.delphiauto.com
SIC: 3714 Motor vehicle parts & accessories
HQ: Delphi Powertrain Systems, Llc
5825 Innovation Dr
Troy MI 48098
248 813-2000

(G-15792)
DELPHI POWERTRAIN SYSTEMS LLC
5500 W Henrietta Rd (14586-9701)
PHONE...................................585 359-6000
Jim Zizleman, *Manager*
EMP: 486
SALES (corp-wide): 1.5MM **Privately Held**
WEB: www.delphiauto.com
SIC: 3714 8731 3694 3564 Motor vehicle parts & accessories; commercial physical research; engine electrical equipment; blowers & fans
HQ: Delphi Powertrain Systems, Llc
5825 Innovation Dr
Troy MI 48098
248 813-2000

(G-15793)
DELPHI POWERTRAIN SYSTEMS LLC
5500 W Henrietta Rd (14586-9701)
PHONE...................................585 359-6000
Walter Piock, *Branch Mgr*
EMP: 31
SALES (corp-wide): 1.5MM **Privately Held**
SIC: 3714 Motor vehicle parts & accessories
HQ: Delphi Powertrain Systems, Llc
5825 Innovation Dr
Troy MI 48098
248 813-2000

(G-15794)
FORTEQ NORTH AMERICA INC
150 Park Centre Dr (14586-9688)
PHONE...................................585 427-9410
Martin Van Manen, *CEO*
Rune Bakke, *Principal*
Joseph Buonocure, *Principal*
Luc Widmer, *CFO*
James Carboni, *Controller*
▲ **EMP:** 70
SQ FT: 29,000
SALES (est): 25.2MM
SALES (corp-wide): 142.3MM **Privately Held**
SIC: 3089 Plastic containers, except foam

PA: Transmission Technology Holding Ag
C/O Bar & Karrer
Zug ZG 6301
582 615-900

(G-15795)
GENESEE METAL STAMPINGS INC
975 John St (14586-9780)
PHONE...................................585 475-0450
Gerard Caschette, *Principal*
Bruce Ball, *COO*
EMP: 5
SALES (est): 574.8K **Privately Held**
SIC: 3469 Stamping metal for the trade

(G-15796)
GEOSPATIAL SYSTEMS INC (HQ)
150 Lucius Gordon Dr # 211 (14586-9687)
PHONE...................................585 427-8310
Maxime Elbaz, *President*
Steven Randy Olson, *Vice Pres*
Robert Delach, *CFO*
EMP: 11
SQ FT: 3,000
SALES (est): 1.3MM
SALES (corp-wide): 2.9B **Publicly Held**
SIC: 3861 Aerial cameras
PA: Teledyne Technologies Inc
1049 Camino Dos Rios
Thousand Oaks CA 91360
805 373-4545

(G-15797)
HAMMER PACKAGING CORP (PA)
200 Lucius Gordon Dr (14586-9685)
P.O. Box 22678, Rochester (14692-2678)
PHONE...................................585 424-3880
James E Hammer, *President*
Jason Hammer, *Vice Pres*
Marty Karpie, *Vice Pres*
Louis Lovoli, *Vice Pres*
Tom Mason, *Vice Pres*
▲ **EMP:** 350 **EST:** 1912
SQ FT: 92,000
SALES (est): 119.2MM **Privately Held**
WEB: www.hammerpackaging.com
SIC: 2759 Labels & seals: printing

(G-15798)
KATIKATI INC
150 Lucius Gordon Dr (14586-9687)
PHONE...................................585 678-1764
Prathap James Ambaichelvan, *CEO*
Sanjay Hiranandani, *COO*
Allyson Hiranandani, *Vice Pres*
EMP: 5
SALES (est): 276.1K **Privately Held**
SIC: 3714 5013 8733 Motor vehicle electrical equipment; testing equipment, electrical: automotive; research institute

(G-15799)
OUTDOOR GROUP LLC
1325 John St (14586-9121)
PHONE...................................877 503-5483
Corey Risden, *Production*
Joshua Sidebottom, *Engineer*
Chuck Hathaway, *VP Mktg*
Greg Steil,
Lauren Laperle, *Analyst*
EMP: 150 **EST:** 2012
SALES (est): 18.7MM **Privately Held**
SIC: 3949 Archery equipment, general

(G-15800)
PERFECT FORM MANUFACTURING LLC
1325 John St (14586-9121)
PHONE...................................585 500-5923
Joshua Sidebottom, *Engineer*
Greg Steil,
Dylan Bates,
Peter Crawford,
Matthew Kruger,
EMP: 5
SQ FT: 3,200
SALES (est): 76.9K **Privately Held**
SIC: 3949 Bows, archery

(G-15801)
POLYSHOT CORPORATION
75 Lucius Gordon Dr (14586-9682)
PHONE...................................585 292-5010
Douglas C Hepler, *CEO*
Lou Borrelli, *President*
▲ **EMP:** 40
SQ FT: 13,000
SALES (est): 5.3MM **Privately Held**
WEB: www.polyshot.com
SIC: 3544 Industrial molds

(G-15802)
ROCHESTER PRECISION OPTICS LLC
Also Called: R P O
850 John St (14586-9748)
PHONE...................................585 292-5450
Randall Shaw, *President*
Mike Davenport, *Production*
Helen Bilak, *Purch Mgr*
Stacey Faugh, *Senior Buyer*
Jennifer Smith, *Buyer*
◆ **EMP:** 300
SQ FT: 104,500
SALES (est): 56.3MM **Privately Held**
WEB: www.rpoptics.com
SIC: 3827 Lenses, optical: all types except ophthalmic; lens mounts; lens grinding equipment, except ophthalmic; optical elements & assemblies, except ophthalmic

(G-15803)
SEMANS ENTERPRISES INC
Also Called: New Cov Manufacturing
25 Hendrix Rd Ste E (14586-9205)
PHONE...................................585 444-0097
William A Semans II, *Ch of Bd*
Carol Maue- Semans, *Vice Pres*
EMP: 19
SQ FT: 10,000
SALES: 1.8MM **Privately Held**
SIC: 3449 Miscellaneous metalwork

(G-15804)
SIMPORE INC
150 Lucius Gordon Dr # 110 (14586-9687)
PHONE...................................585 748-5980
Richard D Richmond, *Ch of Bd*
Thomas Gaborski, *President*
Jared Carter, *Research*
EMP: 7
SQ FT: 400
SALES (est): 852K **Privately Held**
WEB: www.simpore.com
SIC: 3821 Laboratory equipment: fume hoods, distillation racks, etc.

(G-15805)
SWAGELOK WESTERN NY
10 Thruway Park Dr (14586-9702)
PHONE...................................585 359-8470
EMP: 5
SALES (est): 569.2K **Privately Held**
SIC: 3823 Mfg Process Control Instruments

(G-15806)
VUZIX CORPORATION (PA)
25 Hendrix Rd Ste A (14586-9205)
PHONE...................................585 359-5900
Paul J Travers, *President*
Lance Anderson, *Vice Pres*
Robert Schultz, *Research*
Grant Russell, *CFO*
Richard Falcone, *Sales Mgr*
EMP: 24 **EST:** 1997
SQ FT: 29,000
SALES: 8MM **Publicly Held**
WEB: www.icuiti.com
SIC: 3577 Computer peripheral equipment

(G-15807)
WAVODYNE THERAPEUTICS INC
150 Lucius Gordon Dr (14586-9687)
PHONE...................................954 632-6630
James New, *CEO*
EMP: 2 **EST:** 2015
SQ FT: 200
SALES: 500MM **Privately Held**
SIC: 2834 Druggists' preparations (pharmaceuticals)

West Hurley
Ulster County

(G-15808)
ANATOLI INC
43 Basin Rd Ste 11 (12491-5201)
PHONE....................845 334-9000
Kostas Michalopoulos, *President*
EMP: 16
SQ FT: 4,300
SALES (est): 2.1MM **Privately Held**
SIC: 3911 3961 5094 Jewelry, precious metal; costume jewelry; jewelry

West Islip
Suffolk County

(G-15809)
ACT COMMUNICATIONS GROUP INC
170 Higbie Ln (11795-3238)
PHONE....................631 669-2403
Richard Carpenter, *President*
Robert Carpenter, *Vice Pres*
EMP: 18
SQ FT: 1,000
SALES (est): 1.5MM **Privately Held**
WEB: www.actcommgroup.com
SIC: 2791 2752 7311 Typesetting; commercial printing, offset; advertising agencies

(G-15810)
ACTION BULLET RESISTANT
263 Union Blvd (11795-3007)
PHONE....................631 422-0888
Leonard J Simonetti, *President*
Trish Simonetti, *Manager*
Laura Muench, *Office Admin*
John H Schindler, *Admin Sec*
EMP: 12
SQ FT: 14,000
SALES (est): 2.3MM **Privately Held**
WEB: www.actionbullet.com
SIC: 3442 Window & door frames

(G-15811)
JEM TOOL & DIE CORP
81 Paris Ct (11795-2815)
PHONE....................631 539-8734
Roy Stevens, *President*
Bill Jimenez, *Vice Pres*
EMP: 10 EST: 1961
SQ FT: 8,000
SALES (est): 1.1MM **Privately Held**
SIC: 3545 Machine tool attachments & accessories

(G-15812)
PROFESSIONAL SOLUTIONS PRINT
543 Hunter Ave 3 (11795-1638)
PHONE....................631 231-9300
Karl Snyder, *President*
EMP: 6
SALES: 750K **Privately Held**
SIC: 2752 Commercial printing, lithographic

(G-15813)
V A P TOOL & DYE
436 W 4th St (11795-2414)
PHONE....................631 587-5262
Victor Pons, *Owner*
EMP: 7
SQ FT: 4,700
SALES (est): 400K **Privately Held**
SIC: 3599 Machine shop, jobbing & repair

West Monroe
Oswego County

(G-15814)
ROBINSON CONCRETE INC
Also Called: Cemento,
2735 State Route 49 (13167-3249)
PHONE....................315 676-4333

Vinnie Vitale, *Branch Mgr*
EMP: 128
SALES (corp-wide): 26.1MM **Privately Held**
SIC: 3273 Ready-mixed concrete
PA: Robinson Concrete, Inc.
3486 Franklin Street Rd
Auburn NY 13021
315 253-6666

West Nyack
Rockland County

(G-15815)
AMP-LINE CORP
3 Amethyst Ct (10994-1142)
PHONE....................845 623-3288
Guosen Luo, *President*
EMP: 10
SALES: 1MM **Privately Held**
SIC: 3699 3679 Pulse amplifiers; electronic loads & power supplies

(G-15816)
ANGEL MEDIA AND PUBLISHING
Also Called: Rockland Review Publishing
26 Snake Hill Rd (10994-1625)
PHONE....................845 727-4949
Joseph Miele, *President*
EMP: 6
SALES (est): 407.4K **Privately Held**
WEB: www.rocklandreviewnews.com
SIC: 2711 Newspapers: publishing only, not printed on site

(G-15817)
BEL-BEE PRODUCTS INCORPORATED
100 Snake Hill Rd Ste 1 (10994-1627)
PHONE....................845 353-0300
Vincent Belmont, *Ch of Bd*
Patricia Musumeci, *Purch Mgr*
EMP: 15
SQ FT: 25,000
SALES (est): 3MM **Privately Held**
WEB: www.bel-bee.com
SIC: 3544 Special dies & tools

(G-15818)
BILLY BEEZ USA LLC
1282 Palisades Center Dr (10994-6202)
PHONE....................845 915-4709
EMP: 20
SALES (corp-wide): 16.7MM **Privately Held**
SIC: 3949 5137 7999 Playground equipment; women's & children's dresses, suits, skirts & blouses; amusement ride
PA: Billy Beez Usa, Llc
3 W 35th St Fl 3 # 3
New York NY 10001
646 606-2249

(G-15819)
BYLADA FOODS LLC
250 W Nyack Rd Ste 110 (10994-1745)
PHONE....................845 623-1300
Meade Bradshaw, *Branch Mgr*
EMP: 42
SALES (corp-wide): 9.4MM **Privately Held**
SIC: 2099 Food preparations
PA: Bylada Foods Llc
140 W Commercial Ave
Moonachie NJ 07074
201 933-7474

(G-15820)
CROTON WATCH CO INC
250 W Nyack Rd Ste 114 (10994-1745)
PHONE....................800 443-7639
David Mermelstein, *Ch of Bd*
▲ EMP: 26
SQ FT: 18,000
SALES (est): 4.8MM **Privately Held**
WEB: www.crotonwatch.com
SIC: 3873 Watches & parts, except crystals & jewels

(G-15821)
GANNETT STLLITE INFO NTWRK LLC
1 Crosfield Ave (10994-2222)
PHONE....................845 578-2300
Tony Davenport, *Branch Mgr*
EMP: 30
SALES (corp-wide): 2.9B **Publicly Held**
WEB: www.usatoday.com
SIC: 2711 2752 Newspapers: publishing only, not printed on site; commercial printing, lithographic
HQ: Gannett Satellite Information Network, Llc
7950 Jones Branch Dr
Mc Lean VA 22102
703 854-6000

(G-15822)
GENERAL BEARING CORPORATION (DH)
44 High St (10994-2702)
PHONE....................845 358-6000
David L Gussack, *CEO*
Thomas J Uhlig, *President*
Don Morris, *Regional Mgr*
Joseph Hoo, *Vice Pres*
Ed Lynch, *Vice Pres*
▲ EMP: 120 EST: 1958
SQ FT: 190,000
SALES (est): 125.9MM
SALES (corp-wide): 9.5B **Privately Held**
WEB: www.generalbearing.com
SIC: 3562 Ball bearings & parts
HQ: Skf Usa Inc.
890 Forty Foot Rd
Lansdale PA 19446
267 436-6000

(G-15823)
INTERCOS AMERICA INC
11 Centerock Rd (10994-2214)
PHONE....................845 732-3900
EMP: 5
SALES (corp-wide): 49.7MM **Privately Held**
SIC: 2844 Cosmetic preparations
HQ: Intercos America, Inc.
200 N Route 303
Congers NY 10920

(G-15824)
INTERCOS AMERICA INC
120 Brookhill Dr (10994-2127)
PHONE....................845 732-3910
EMP: 7 EST: 2016
SALES (est): 131.8K **Privately Held**
SIC: 2844 Toilet preparations

(G-15825)
JOURNAL NEWS
200 N Route 303 (10994-1619)
PHONE....................845 578-2324
EMP: 5
SALES (est): 216.8K **Privately Held**
SIC: 2711 Newspapers, publishing & printing

(G-15826)
MACABEE FOODS LLC
250 W Nyack Rd Ste 110 (10994-1745)
PHONE....................845 623-1300
Laurence Silverman, *CFO*
Robert Silverman,
EMP: 5
SALES (est): 553K **Privately Held**
SIC: 2038 Frozen specialties

(G-15827)
MAINLY MONOGRAMS INC
Also Called: Mercury Apparel
260 W Nyack Rd Ste 1 (10994-1750)
PHONE....................845 624-4923
Dan Alexander Sr, *CEO*
Dan Alexander Jr, *CFO*
Zaharo Ula Alexander, *Treasurer*
EMP: 45
SQ FT: 19,000
SALES (est): 5.1MM **Privately Held**
SIC: 2395 7336 5611 5621 Embroidery products, except schiffli machine; silk screen design; clothing, sportswear, men's & boys'; women's sportswear; gifts & novelties

(G-15828)
NICE-PAK PRODUCTS INC
100 Brookhill Dr (10994)
PHONE....................845 353-6090
Jennifer Thriston, *Manager*
EMP: 25
SALES (corp-wide): 378.5MM **Privately Held**
SIC: 2621 Towels, tissues & napkins: paper & stock; sanitary tissue paper
PA: Nice-Pak Products, Inc.
2 Nice Pak Park
Orangeburg NY 10962
845 365-1700

(G-15829)
PEARSON EDUCATION INC
59 Brookhill Dr (10994-2122)
PHONE....................201 236-7000
Michael Schuering, *Exec VP*
Cheryl Gayser, *Human Res Mgr*
EMP: 14
SALES (corp-wide): 5.3B **Privately Held**
WEB: www.phgenit.com
SIC: 2721 2731 Periodicals; book publishing
HQ: Pearson Education, Inc.
221 River St
Hoboken NJ 07030
201 236-7000

(G-15830)
PICCINI MNM INC
35 Highland Ave (10994-1719)
PHONE....................845 741-6770
Richard Piccininni, *President*
EMP: 7
SALES: 700K **Privately Held**
SIC: 2499 Decorative wood & woodwork

(G-15831)
PLASTIC-CRAFT PRODUCTS CORP
744 W Nyack Rd (10994-1998)
P.O. Box K (10994-0713)
PHONE....................845 358-3010
Mark Brecher, *President*
Yung Nguyen, *Vice Pres*
Marge Garrieson, *Treasurer*
Krista Goldstein, *Sales Staff*
Stan Danser, *Sales Associate*
EMP: 33
SQ FT: 30,000
SALES: 4.5MM **Privately Held**
SIC: 3089 5162 Injection molding of plastics; plastics materials & basic shapes

(G-15832)
ROCKLAND MANUFACTURING CO
44 High St (10994-2702)
PHONE....................845 358-6000
Seymour Gussack, *CEO*
Bruce Pope, *Manager*
EMP: 5
SALES (est): 297.2K **Privately Held**
SIC: 3531 Construction machinery

(G-15833)
TILCON NEW YORK INC
1 Crusher Rd (10994-1601)
PHONE....................845 358-3100
Dave Buccafusca, *Foreman/Supr*
Rudolph Knight, *Accountant*
Nathalie Ippolito, *Credit Staff*
Tom Rorrer, *Sales Staff*
Bob Pecorella, *Marketing Mgr*
EMP: 65
SALES (corp-wide): 30.6B **Privately Held**
WEB: www.tilconny.com
SIC: 1429 1442 1423 Trap rock, crushed & broken-quarrying; dolomitic marble, crushed & broken-quarrying; construction sand & gravel; crushed & broken granite
HQ: Tilcon New York Inc.
9 Entin Rd
Parsippany NJ 07054
973 366-7741

▲ = Import ▼=Export
◆ =Import/Export

West Point
Orange County

(G-15834)
PENN ENTERPRISES INC
845 Washington Rd (10996-1111)
PHONE..................................845 446-0765
Joseph Fotovich, *Principal*
EMP: 13 **Privately Held**
WEB: www.pennenterprises.com
SIC: 3633 Household laundry equipment
PA: Penn Enterprises, Inc
5260 S Stonehaven Dr
Springfield MO 65809

West Sand Lake
Rensselaer County

(G-15835)
BONDED CONCRETE INC
Rr 43 (12196)
PHONE..................................518 674-2854
Tom Coemente, *President*
EMP: 10
SALES (corp-wide): 10.8MM **Privately Held**
WEB: www.bondedconcrete.com
SIC: 3273 Ready-mixed concrete
PA: Bonded Concrete, Inc.
303 Watervliet Shaker Rd
Watervliet NY 12189
518 273-5800

(G-15836)
TROY SAND & GRAVEL CO INC (PA)
34 Grange Rd (12196-2051)
P.O. Box 171, Watervliet (12189-0171)
PHONE..................................518 203-5115
Jude Clemente, *President*
Thomas Clemente, *Vice Pres*
Philip Clemente, *Treasurer*
Salvatore Clemente, *Admin Sec*
EMP: 6 **EST:** 1958
SQ FT: 1,000
SALES (est): 16.2MM **Privately Held**
WEB: www.troysg.com
SIC: 1442 Sand mining

(G-15837)
TROY SAND & GRAVEL CO INC
Rr 43 (12196)
P.O. Box 489 (12196-0489)
PHONE..................................518 674-2854
Jude Clemente, *President*
EMP: 15
SALES (corp-wide): 16.2MM **Privately Held**
SIC: 1442 5032 Construction sand & gravel; stone, crushed or broken
PA: Troy Sand & Gravel Co., Inc.
34 Grange Rd
West Sand Lake NY 12196
518 203-5115

West Sayville
Suffolk County

(G-15838)
ACCUCUT INC
120 Easy St (11796-1238)
PHONE..................................631 567-2868
Dan Carbone, *CEO*
Joanne Caruso, *Administration*
EMP: 5
SALES: 370K **Privately Held**
SIC: 3441 Fabricated structural metal

(G-15839)
DOR-A-MAR CANVAS PRODUCTS CO
182 Cherry Ave (11796-1200)
PHONE..................................631 750-9202
Thomas Degirolamo, *President*
EMP: 18 **EST:** 1959
SQ FT: 6,000
SALES: 1.5MM **Privately Held**
WEB: www.doramar.com
SIC: 2394 Awnings, fabric: made from purchased materials

(G-15840)
FIRE ISLAND SEA CLAM CO INC
132 Atlantic Ave (11796-1904)
P.O. Box 2124, Montauk (11954-0905)
PHONE..................................631 589-2199
John Kingston, *President*
Jean Kingston, *Admin Sec*
EMP: 3
SQ FT: 3,500
SALES: 10MM **Privately Held**
WEB: www.fireislandassn.org
SIC: 2431 5812 Moldings, wood: unfinished & prefinished; seafood restaurants

(G-15841)
KUSSMAUL ELECTRONICS CO INC
170 Cherry Ave (11796-1200)
PHONE..................................631 218-0298
Thomas H Nugent, *Ch of Bd*
Marilyn Kussmaul, *Vice Pres*
Phil Sgroi, *Engineer*
Brian Cassell, *Regl Sales Mgr*
Colin Chambless, *Regl Sales Mgr*
◆ **EMP:** 50 **EST:** 1970
SQ FT: 30,000
SALES (est): 11.3MM
SALES (corp-wide): 13.7MM **Privately Held**
WEB: www.maul.com
SIC: 3629 3625 Battery chargers, rectifying or nonrotating; control equipment, electric
HQ: Mission Critical Electronics, Llc
2200 Ross Ave Ste 4050
Dallas TX 75201

(G-15842)
PECK & HALE LLC
180 Division Ave (11796-1303)
PHONE..................................631 589-2510
John Szeglin, *President*
Jose Diaz Bujan, *Opers Staff*
Richard Belkin, *Engineer*
Christos Efstathiou, *Engineer*
Joseph Royt, *Engineer*
▲ **EMP:** 40 **EST:** 1946
SQ FT: 27,000
SALES (est): 8.8MM **Privately Held**
WEB: www.peckhale.com
SIC: 3743 3462 3496 Railroad equipment; iron & steel forgings; miscellaneous fabricated wire products

West Seneca
Erie County

(G-15843)
ABI PACKAGING INC
1703 Union Rd (14224-2060)
PHONE..................................716 677-2900
Roger Severson, *CEO*
EMP: 20
SALES (est): 1.5MM **Privately Held**
SIC: 3086 Packaging & shipping materials, foamed plastic

(G-15844)
BIG DATA BIZVIZ LLC
1075 East And West Rd (14224-3669)
PHONE..................................716 803-2367
Avin Jain, *CEO*
Rajesh Thanki, *CEO*
EMP: 2
SALES (est): 1.5MM **Privately Held**
SIC: 7372 Business oriented computer software

(G-15845)
BUFFALO HEARG & SPEECH
1026 Union Rd (14224-3445)
PHONE..................................716 558-1105
Joe Cozzo, *CEO*
EMP: 45
SALES (corp-wide): 443.2K **Privately Held**
SIC: 3842 Hearing aids

PA: Buffalo Hearing And Speech Center Foundation, Inc.
50 E North St
Buffalo NY 14203
716 885-8318

(G-15846)
EBENEZER RAILCAR SERVICES INC
1005 Indian Church Rd (14224-1305)
P.O. Box 363, Buffalo (14224-0363)
PHONE..................................716 674-5650
Jeffrey F Schmarje, *President*
Robert Wingels, *Vice Pres*
EMP: 80 **EST:** 1981
SQ FT: 30,000
SALES: 20.1MM
SALES (corp-wide): 24.9MM **Privately Held**
WEB: www.ersindustries.com
SIC: 3743 4789 Railroad equipment; railroad car repair
PA: Ers Industries, Inc.
1005 Indian Church Rd
West Seneca NY 14224
716 675-2040

(G-15847)
FIVE STAR INDUSTRIES INC
114 Willowdale Dr (14224-3571)
PHONE..................................716 674-2589
Greg Vastola, *President*
Joel Long, *Vice Pres*
EMP: 27
SQ FT: 10,000
SALES (est): 4.4MM **Privately Held**
SIC: 3444 3599 Sheet metalwork; machine shop, jobbing & repair

(G-15848)
GEMCOR AUTOMATION LLC
100 Gemcor Dr (14224-2055)
PHONE..................................716 674-9300
Michael Mahfet, *President*
Gary Szymkowiak, *Opers Staff*
David Dietrich, *Engineer*
Robert Flaig, *Engineer*
Art Deabold, *Manager*
EMP: 87
SQ FT: 90,000
SALES (est): 16.9MM
SALES (corp-wide): 386.8MM **Privately Held**
SIC: 3542 Spinning, spline rolling & winding machines
HQ: Ascent Aerospace, Llc
16445 23 Mile Rd
Macomb MI 48042
586 726-0500

(G-15849)
GORDEN AUTOMOTIVE EQUIPMENT
60 N America Dr (14224-2225)
PHONE..................................716 674-2700
Richard Deney, *President*
Thomas Gormley, *Exec VP*
Herman Deney, *Vice Pres*
Michael Russo, *Treasurer*
EMP: 10 **EST:** 1963
SALES (est): 978K **Privately Held**
SIC: 3599 Machine shop, jobbing & repair

(G-15850)
KATHERINE BLIZNIAK (PA)
525 Bullis Rd (14224-2511)
PHONE..................................716 674-8545
Katherine Blizniak, *President*
EMP: 6
SALES (est): 619.1K **Privately Held**
SIC: 3732 5091 Boat building & repairing; boat accessories & parts

(G-15851)
KEMPER SYSTEM AMERICA INC (DH)
1200 N America Dr (14224-5303)
PHONE..................................716 558-2971
Andreas H Wiggenhagen, *President*
Christian Schaefer, *CFO*
James Arnold, *Director*
▲ **EMP:** 54

SALES (est): 12.9MM
SALES (corp-wide): 322.5MM **Privately Held**
WEB: www.kempersystem.net
SIC: 2899 7389 Chemical preparations;
HQ: Kemper System Gmbh & Co. Kg
Hollandische Str. 32-36
Vellmar 34246
561 829-50

(G-15852)
MAYER BROS APPLE PRODUCTS INC (PA)
3300 Transit Rd (14224-2525)
PHONE..................................716 668-1787
John A Mayer, *Ch of Bd*
▲ **EMP:** 95 **EST:** 1852
SQ FT: 2,800
SALES (est): 31.7MM **Privately Held**
WEB: www.mayerbros.com
SIC: 2033 2086 5499 5963 Fruit juices: fresh; pasteurized & mineral waters, bottled & canned; juices, fruit or vegetable; bottled water delivery

(G-15853)
SE-MAR ELECTRIC CO INC
101 South Ave (14224-2090)
PHONE..................................716 674-7404
Robert Haungs, *President*
John Simson, *Principal*
Nancy J Haungs, *Treasurer*
▲ **EMP:** 20
SQ FT: 30,000
SALES: 5.1MM **Privately Held**
SIC: 3613 5571 Control panels, electric; motorcycles

(G-15854)
SENECA WEST PRINTING INC
860 Center Rd (14224-2207)
PHONE..................................716 675-8010
Charles Pohlman, *President*
Charles Pohlman Jr, *Vice Pres*
EMP: 6 **EST:** 1965
SQ FT: 4,000
SALES (est): 703.3K **Privately Held**
SIC: 2752 2759 Lithographing on metal; letterpress printing

(G-15855)
THYSSENKRUPP MATERIALS NA INC
Copper & Brass Sales
19 Ransier Dr (14224-2259)
PHONE..................................585 279-0000
Dick Blake, *Branch Mgr*
EMP: 5
SALES (corp-wide): 39.8B **Privately Held**
SIC: 3317 3465 Tubes, wrought: welded or lock joint; automotive stampings
HQ: Thyssenkrupp Materials Na, Inc.
22355 W 11 Mile Rd
Southfield MI 48033
248 233-5600

(G-15856)
YOST NEON DISPLAYS INC
20 Ransier Dr (14224-2230)
PHONE..................................716 674-6780
Michael Yost, *President*
Deborah Yost, *Vice Pres*
EMP: 5
SALES (est): 475.4K **Privately Held**
WEB: www.yostneon.com
SIC: 3993 1751 Neon signs; cabinet building & installation

West Winfield
Herkimer County

(G-15857)
CHRISTIAN FABRICATION LLC
122 South St (13491-2827)
PHONE..................................315 822-0135
Jamie Christian, *Sales Staff*
EMP: 3
SQ FT: 1,296
SALES: 1.5MM **Privately Held**
SIC: 3441 7353 Fabricated structural metal; heavy construction equipment rental

(G-15858)
PRECISIONMATICS CO INC
Also Called: Helmer Avenue
1 Helmer Ave (13491)
P.O. Box 250 (13491-0250)
PHONE..................................315 822-6324
Laslo Pustay, *Ch of Bd*
John Macintosh, *Engineer*
Peter McClave, *Engineer*
John Pustay, *Treasurer*
Amanda Gehrke, *Sales Staff*
EMP: 50
SQ FT: 22,000
SALES (est): 9.1MM **Privately Held**
WEB: www.precisionmatics.com
SIC: 3599 Machine shop, jobbing & repair;
custom machinery

Westbrookville
Sullivan County

(G-15859)
GLASS MENAGERIE INC
1756 Rte 209 (12785)
P.O. Box 478 (12785-0478)
PHONE..................................845 754-8344
Dumitru Costea, *President*
Barbara REA, *Vice Pres*
EMP: 5 **EST:** 1977
SQ FT: 6,000
SALES (est): 40.7K **Privately Held**
SIC: 3229 Novelty glassware

Westbury
Nassau County

(G-15860)
ACCURATE WELDING SERVICE INC
Also Called: Accurate Welding Svce
615 Main St (11590-4903)
PHONE..................................516 333-1730
Joseph Titone, *President*
Charles Titone Jr, *Vice Pres*
EMP: 5
SQ FT: 5,800
SALES (est): 300K **Privately Held**
SIC: 3599 7692 3446 Machine shop, jobbing & repair; welding repair; architectural metalwork

(G-15861)
ADVANCED FROZEN FOODS INC
28 Urban Ave (11590-4822)
P.O. Box 887 (11590-0887)
PHONE..................................516 333-6344
Roy Tuccillo, *President*
Desiree Cano, *Manager*
▲ **EMP:** 50
SALES (est): 8.4MM **Privately Held**
SIC: 2015 Poultry slaughtering & processing

(G-15862)
ADVANCED SURFACE FINISHING
111 Magnolia Ave (11590-4719)
PHONE..................................516 876-9710
Peter Tobias, *President*
EMP: 25
SQ FT: 15,000
SALES: 1.8MM **Privately Held**
WEB: www.advancedsurfacefinishing.com
SIC: 3479 Coating of metals & formed products; painting, coating & hot dipping

(G-15863)
AERO STRCTURES LONG ISLAND INC (PA)
717 Main St (11590-5021)
PHONE..................................516 997-5757
William Gross, *CEO*
Leonard Gross, *President*
Alex Voda, *Controller*
EMP: 79
SQ FT: 91,000
SALES: 30MM **Privately Held**
SIC: 3728 Aircraft body & wing assemblies & parts

(G-15864)
AIRNET COMMUNICATIONS CORP
Also Called: Airnet North Division
609 Cantiague Rock Rd # 5 (11590-1721)
PHONE..................................516 338-0008
Louis Pryce, *Manager*
EMP: 15 **Privately Held**
WEB: www.airnetcom.com
SIC: 3663 Radio & TV communications equipment
HQ: Airnet Communications Corporation
295 North Dr Ste G
Melbourne FL 32934

(G-15865)
ALASKA SPRING PHRMCUTICALS INC
609 Cantiague Rock Rd # 1 (11590-1721)
PHONE..................................516 205-6020
Ahmad Sher, *President*
Upasana Sharma, *QC Mgr*
Geo Jossy, *Sales Staff*
EMP: 27 **EST:** 2010
SQ FT: 20,000
SALES (est): 5.9MM **Privately Held**
SIC: 2834 Pharmaceutical preparations

(G-15866)
ALL TYPE SCREW MACHINE PDTS
Also Called: Skelton Screw Products Co
100 New York Ave (11590-4909)
PHONE..................................516 334-5100
Eileen Sinn, *President*
EMP: 6
SQ FT: 5,000
SALES: 300K **Privately Held**
SIC: 3451 Screw machine products

(G-15867)
AMERICAN LINEAR MANUFACTURERS (PA)
629 Main St (11590-4923)
PHONE..................................516 333-1351
Frank Tabone, *President*
EMP: 10
SQ FT: 2,000
SALES: 4.3MM **Privately Held**
SIC: 3545 3599 Machine tool accessories; custom machinery

(G-15868)
AMERICAN OFFICE SUPPLY INC
400 Post Ave Ste 105 (11590-2226)
PHONE..................................516 294-9444
Joseph Caldwell, *President*
Jospeh Caldwell, *President*
EMP: 11
SALES (est): 1.6MM **Privately Held**
WEB: www.aoslink.com
SIC: 2759 5943 Commercial printing; stationery stores

(G-15869)
AN EXCELSIOR ELEVATOR CORP
640 Main St Unit 2 (11590-4937)
PHONE..................................516 408-3070
Eric Petzold, *CEO*
Nancy Snyder, *Manager*
EMP: 16
SALES (est): 3.4MM **Privately Held**
SIC: 3534 5084 7699 Elevators & equipment; elevators; elevators: inspection, service & repair

(G-15870)
ARKWIN INDUSTRIES INC (HQ)
686 Main St (11590-5093)
PHONE..................................516 333-2640
William Maglio, *Ch of Bd*
Daniel Berlin, *President*
Richard Vonsalzen, *General Mgr*
Frank Robilotto, *Chairman*
Robert Hultmark, *Vice Pres*
EMP: 242 **EST:** 1951
SQ FT: 110,000
SALES: 71.2MM
SALES (corp-wide): 3.8B **Publicly Held**
WEB: www.arkwin.com
SIC: 3728 Aircraft assemblies, subassemblies & parts

PA: Transdigm Group Incorporated
1301 E 9th St Ste 3000
Cleveland OH 44114
216 706-2960

(G-15871)
AVANEL INDUSTRIES INC
121 Hopper St (11590-4803)
PHONE..................................516 333-0990
Ingo Kurth, *President*
Chris Kurth, *Vice Pres*
EMP: 12
SQ FT: 8,500
SALES (est): 1.5MM **Privately Held**
WEB: www.avanelindustries.com
SIC: 3825 Test equipment for electronic & electric measurement; scientific & engineering equipment & supplies

(G-15872)
BIOIVT LLC (PA)
123 Frost St Ste 115 (11590-5034)
PHONE..................................516 483-1196
Jeff Gatz, *CEO*
EMP: 73
SALES (est): 29.3MM **Privately Held**
SIC: 2836 Veterinary biological products

(G-15873)
CAB-NETWORK INC
Also Called: Four Quarter
1500 Shames Dr Unit B (11590-1772)
PHONE..................................516 334-8666
Martin Chin, *President*
Patrick Chin, *Treasurer*
EMP: 6
SQ FT: 11,000
SALES: 975K **Privately Held**
SIC: 2511 Kitchen & dining room furniture

(G-15874)
COMPUTER INSTRUMENTS CORP
963a Brush Hollow Rd (11590-1710)
PHONE..................................516 876-8400
Elsa Markovits Wilen, *President*
Don Wilen, *Vice Pres*
Mark Molder, *Director*
EMP: 40 **EST:** 1950
SQ FT: 20,000
SALES (est): 5.6MM **Privately Held**
WEB: www.computerinstruments.com
SIC: 3812 3823 3824 3829 Search & navigation equipment; industrial flow & liquid measuring instruments; fluid meters & counting devices; integrating & totalizing meters for gas & liquids; measuring & controlling devices; aircraft & motor vehicle measurement equipment

(G-15875)
DEPENDABLE ACME THREADED PDTS
167 School St (11590-3371)
PHONE..................................516 338-4700
Annette Farragher, *President*
Magdalene Vogric, *Corp Secy*
EMP: 6 **EST:** 1958
SQ FT: 3,000
SALES: 500K **Privately Held**
WEB: www.dependableacme.com
SIC: 3452 Nuts, metal

(G-15876)
DIONICS-USA INC
96b Urban Ave (11590-4823)
PHONE..................................516 997-7474
Bernard Kravitz, *President*
Kenneth Davis, *Director*
EMP: 7
SALES (est): 877.1K **Privately Held**
SIC: 3674 Integrated circuits, semiconductor networks, etc.

(G-15877)
E B B GRAPHICS INC
Also Called: Sir Speedy
75 State St (11590-5004)
PHONE..................................516 750-5510
Jack Bloom, *President*
Brandon Bloom, *Principal*
Adrienne Bloom, *Vice Pres*
EMP: 10
SQ FT: 1,000

SALES (est): 1.4MM **Privately Held**
WEB: www.sirspeedyny.net
SIC: 2791 2789 2752 Typesetting; bookbinding & related work; commercial printing, lithographic; commercial printing, offset

(G-15878)
EAGLE METALS CORP
134 Linden Ave (11590-3228)
P.O. Box 45, East Setauket (11733-0045)
PHONE..................................516 338-5100
Joseph Russo, *President*
EMP: 10
SQ FT: 5,000
SALES (est): 1.4MM **Privately Held**
SIC: 3446 Gratings, tread: fabricated metal

(G-15879)
EAST HILLS INSTRUMENT INC
60 Shames Dr (11590-1767)
PHONE..................................516 621-8686
Cary Ratner, *CEO*
EMP: 19
SQ FT: 10,000
SALES (est): 4.2MM **Privately Held**
SIC: 3821 3823 3824 3825 Laboratory measuring apparatus; industrial instrmnts msrmnt display/control process variable; fluid meters & counting devices; instruments to measure electricity; analytical instruments; measuring & controlling devices

(G-15880)
EI ELECTRONICS INC
Also Called: Electro Industries
1800 Shames Dr (11590-1730)
PHONE..................................516 334-0870
Erran Kagan, *Ch of Bd*
Tom David, *Sales Mgr*
Joanne San Roque, *Sales Engr*
Luke Singh, *Sales Engr*
Daniel Odihi, *Sales Staff*
EMP: 11
SALES (est): 1.4MM **Privately Held**
SIC: 3825 Meters: electric, pocket, portable, panelboard, etc.

(G-15881)
ELM TRANSIT MIX CORPORATION
Also Called: Elm Ready Mix
482 Grand Blvd (11590-4602)
PHONE..................................516 333-6144
Sandy Nicolia, *President*
Antonio Nicolia, *Vice Pres*
Liliana Legarreta, *Accountant*
EMP: 12
SALES (est): 2.5MM **Privately Held**
SIC: 3273 Ready-mixed concrete

(G-15882)
EMITLED INC
Also Called: Led Next
2300 Shames Dr (11590-1748)
PHONE..................................516 531-3533
Asi Levy, *President*
EMP: 5
SALES (est): 649.3K **Privately Held**
SIC: 3641 Electric light bulbs, complete

(G-15883)
EXECUTIVE BUSINESS MEDIA INC
Also Called: EBM
825 Old Country Rd (11590-5589)
P.O. Box 1500 (11590-0812)
PHONE..................................516 334-3030
Helen Scheller, *Chairman*
Fred Schane, *Vice Pres*
EMP: 50 **EST:** 1962
SQ FT: 4,100
SALES (est): 26MM **Privately Held**
WEB: www.ebmpubs.com
SIC: 2721 Magazines: publishing only, not printed on site

(G-15884)
FABRIC QUILTERS UNLIMITED INC
1400 Shames Dr (11590-1780)
PHONE..................................516 333-2866
John Brunning, *President*
EMP: 25

SQ FT: 7,500
SALES: 1.7MM **Privately Held**
SIC: 2392 2391 2591 Bedspreads & bed
sets: made from purchased materials;
comforters & quilts: made from purchased
materials; draperies, plastic & textile: from
purchased materials; window blinds; window shades

(G-15885)
FEINSTEIN IRON WORKS INC
990 Brush Hollow Rd (11590-1783)
PHONE..............................516 997-8300
Daniel Feinstein, *CEO*
Howard Feinstein, *President*
Murray Gold, *Vice Pres*
Howard Morris,
EMP: 32 **EST:** 1931
SQ FT: 45,000
SALES (est): 8.4MM **Privately Held**
WEB: www.feinsteinironworks.com
SIC: 3441 Fabricated structural metal

(G-15886)
FOUR K MACHINE SHOP INC
54 Brooklyn Ave (11590-4902)
PHONE..............................516 997-0752
Aaron Feder, *President*
Steven Braverman, *Corp Secy*
Joe Roysman, *Vice Pres*
EMP: 6
SQ FT: 5,000
SALES: 700K **Privately Held**
SIC: 3599 Machine shop, jobbing & repair

(G-15887)
**G & G C MACHINE & TOOL CO
INC**
18 Sylvester St (11590-4911)
PHONE..............................516 873-0999
George Christoforou, *President*
Georgia Christoforou, *Vice Pres*
EMP: 7
SQ FT: 8,200
SALES (est): 887.6K **Privately Held**
SIC: 3599 Machine shop, jobbing & repair

(G-15888)
G A RICHARDS & CO INC
717 Main St (11590-5021)
PHONE..............................516 334-5412
Benjamin Jankowski, *President*
Edward Kaider, *Vice Pres*
EMP: 12
SQ FT: 5,500
SALES (est): 2.1MM **Privately Held**
SIC: 3469 Machine parts, stamped or
pressed metal

(G-15889)
GARY ROTH & ASSOCIATES LTD
1400 Old Country Rd # 305 (11590-5119)
PHONE..............................516 333-1000
Gary Roth, *Partner*
EMP: 30
SALES (est): 4MM **Privately Held**
SIC: 3578 8742 Billing machines; man-
agement consulting services

(G-15890)
**GENERAL CRYOGENIC TECH
LLC**
400 Shames Dr (11590-1753)
PHONE..............................516 334-8200
Ralph Cohan, *General Mgr*
Sunita Assi, *CFO*
J Hanny Ruddy,
Peter Dahal,
EMP: 10
SALES: 1.8MM **Privately Held**
SIC: 3559 Cryogenic machinery, industrial

(G-15891)
**H FREUND WOODWORKING CO
INC**
589 Main St (11590-4900)
PHONE..............................516 334-3774
Frank Freund, *President*
Hubert Freund Jr, *Vice Pres*
EMP: 15
SQ FT: 13,000
SALES: 1.2MM **Privately Held**
SIC: 2521 Wood office furniture

(G-15892)
**HALCYON BUSINESS
PUBLICATIONS**
Also Called: Area Development Magazine
400 Post Ave Ste 304 (11590-2226)
PHONE..............................800 735-2732
Dennis Shea, *President*
Dennis J Shea, *President*
Richard Bodo, *Vice Pres*
EMP: 16
SQ FT: 3,700
SALES (est): 2.4MM **Privately Held**
WEB: www.locationusa.com
SIC: 2721 Magazines: publishing only, not
printed on site

(G-15893)
**HANGER PRSTHETCS & ORTHO
INC**
5502 Brush Hollow Rd (11590-1719)
PHONE..............................516 338-4466
Bradford Deudne, *Principal*
EMP: 5
SALES (corp-wide): 1B **Publicly Held**
SIC: 3842 Surgical appliances & supplies
HQ: Hanger Prosthetics & Orthotics, Inc.
10910 Domain Dr Ste 300
Austin TX 78758
512 777-3800

(G-15894)
HARPER PRODUCTS LTD
Also Called: Pencoa
117 State St (11590-5022)
PHONE..............................516 997-2330
Robert Perlmutter, *CEO*
Rick Perlmutter, *President*
Karen Miller, *Vice Pres*
Helen Perlmutter, *Vice Pres*
Larry Sitten, *Vice Pres*
▲ **EMP:** 106
SQ FT: 30,000
SALES (est): 13.4MM **Privately Held**
SIC: 3951 Pens & mechanical pencils

(G-15895)
IMPERIAL INSTRUMENT CORP
Also Called: Imperial Instrmnt & Mach
18 Sylvester St (11590-4911)
P.O. Box 650326, Fresh Meadows (11365-
0326)
PHONE..............................516 739-6644
Andre Cassata, *President*
EMP: 7 **EST:** 1956
SQ FT: 5,000
SALES (est): 725.8K **Privately Held**
SIC: 3599 Machine shop, jobbing & repair

(G-15896)
**IMPRESS GRAPHIC
TECHNOLOGIES**
141 Linden Ave (11590-3227)
P.O. Box 13187, Hauppauge (11788-0577)
PHONE..............................516 781-0845
Darlene Bifone, *President*
John P Bifone, *Vice Pres*
▲ **EMP:** 12
SQ FT: 7,500
SALES (est): 1.4MM **Privately Held**
SIC: 2759 Commercial printing

(G-15897)
J B TOOL & DIE CO INC
629 Main St (11590-4923)
PHONE..............................516 333-1480
Frank Tabone, *President*
Joseph Tabone, *Vice Pres*
EMP: 28 **EST:** 1946
SQ FT: 14,000
SALES: 2MM **Privately Held**
WEB: www.jbtool-die.com
SIC: 3599 3544 Machine shop, jobbing &
repair; special dies, tools, jigs & fixtures

(G-15898)
JOHN HASSALL LLC (HQ)
609 Cantiague Rock Rd # 1 (11590-1721)
PHONE..............................516 334-6200
Monty Gillespie, *President*
▲ **EMP:** 63
SQ FT: 65,000

SALES (est): 13.9MM
SALES (corp-wide): 165.3MM **Privately
Held**
SIC: 3452 3399 Rivets, metal; metal fas-
teners
PA: Novaria Group, L.L.C.
6300 Ridglea Pl Ste 800
Fort Worth TX 76116
817 381-3810

(G-15899)
JOHN HASSALL LLC
Also Called: Sky Aerospace Products
609 Cantiague Rock Rd # 1 (11590-1721)
PHONE..............................323 869-0150
Monty Gillespie, *President*
▼ **EMP:** 75
SQ FT: 17,000
SALES (est): 6.9MM
SALES (corp-wide): 165.3MM **Privately
Held**
WEB: www.skymfg.net
SIC: 3452 Bolts, nuts, rivets & washers
HQ: John Hassall, Llc
609 Cantiague Rock Rd # 1
Westbury NY 11590
516 334-6200

(G-15900)
JUDITH LEWIS PRINTER INC
1915 Ladenburg Dr (11590-5917)
P.O. Box 778 (11590-0106)
PHONE..............................516 997-7777
Judith Lewis, *President*
EMP: 6
SQ FT: 2,000
SALES (est): 600.9K **Privately Held**
SIC: 2752 2759 Commercial printing, off-
set; letterpress printing

(G-15901)
KAS DIRECT LLC
Also Called: Babyganics
1600 Stewart Ave Ste 411 (11590-6654)
PHONE..............................516 934-0541
Kevin Schwartz, *CEO*
Larry Jewett, *Vice Pres*
Mark Ellis, *CFO*
Kellee Kinnier, *Manager*
EMP: 50 **EST:** 2008
SQ FT: 15,000
SALES (est): 16.1MM
SALES (corp-wide): 3.6B **Privately Held**
SIC: 2676 Infant & baby paper products
PA: S. C. Johnson & Son, Inc.
1525 Howe St
Racine WI 53403
262 260-2000

(G-15902)
KEMP METAL PRODUCTS INC
2300 Shames Dr (11590-1748)
PHONE..............................516 997-8860
Mark Raskin, *President*
Richard Raskin, *Corp Secy*
EMP: 30 **EST:** 1946
SQ FT: 10,000
SALES (est): 8.9MM **Privately Held**
WEB: www.kempmetalproducts.com
SIC: 3915 Jewelry parts, unassembled

(G-15903)
LENNY & BILL LLC
717 Main St (11590-5021)
PHONE..............................516 997-5757
William Gross, *CEO*
Leonard Gross, *President*
EMP: 99
SALES (est): 21MM
SALES (corp-wide): 30MM **Privately
Held**
SIC: 3728 Aircraft parts & equipment
PA: Aero Structures Long Island, Inc.
717 Main St
Westbury NY 11590
516 997-5757

(G-15904)
**LIBERTY BRASS TURNING CO
INC**
1200 Shames Dr Unit C (11590-1766)
PHONE..............................718 784-2911
David Zuckerwise, *CEO*
Peter Zuckerwise, *President*
Marshall Johnson, *Safety Mgr*
Barry Bogel, *CFO*

Joyce Sarich, *Sales Staff*
▲ **EMP:** 45
SQ FT: 20,000
SALES (est): 12.9MM **Privately Held**
WEB: www.libertybrass.com
SIC: 3451 3429 3432 Screw machine
products; manufactured hardware (gen-
eral); plumbing fixture fittings & trim

(G-15905)
LONG ISLAND COMPOST CORP
100 Urban Ave (11590-4823)
PHONE..............................516 334-6600
Charles Vigliotti, *CEO*
Dominic Vigliotti, *Shareholder*
EMP: 120
SALES (est): 29.3MM **Privately Held**
WEB: www.licompost.com
SIC: 2875 Compost

(G-15906)
LOTUS APPAREL DESIGNS INC
Also Called: Courbee
661 Oakwood Ct (11590-5926)
PHONE..............................646 236-9363
Fang Mercedes, *President*
Rey Mercedes, *Vice Pres*
▲ **EMP:** 2
SALES (est): 1.3MM **Privately Held**
SIC: 2339 Service apparel, washable:
women's

(G-15907)
LOVE UNLIMITED NY INC
762 Summa Ave (11590-5011)
PHONE..............................718 359-8500
Tom Terrino, *CEO*
EMP: 45 **EST:** 1953
SQ FT: 25,000
SALES (est): 7.1MM **Privately Held**
WEB: www.mbslove.com
SIC: 2759 2752 Decals: printing; commer-
cial printing, lithographic

(G-15908)
MATCH EYEWEAR LLC
1600 Shames Dr (11590-1761)
PHONE..............................516 877-0170
Helen Junda, *VP Finance*
Shawn Chesanek, *Regl Sales Mgr*
Bob Rosenthal, *Sales Staff*
Liz Tontodonati, *Marketing Staff*
Joanne Conti, *Manager*
▲ **EMP:** 35
SQ FT: 17,000
SALES: 4MM **Privately Held**
WEB: www.floateyewear.com
SIC: 3229 3827 5995 Optical glass; opti-
cal instruments & lenses; optical goods
stores

(G-15909)
**MATERIAL MEASURING
CORPORATION**
121 Hopper St (11590-4803)
PHONE..............................516 334-6167
Ingo O Kurth, *President*
EMP: 5
SALES: 340K **Privately Held**
SIC: 3821 Laboratory equipment: fume
hoods, distillation racks, etc.

(G-15910)
METPAR CORP
95 State St (11590-5006)
PHONE..............................516 333-2600
Ronald S Mondolino, *President*
Vincent Salierno, *Site Mgr*
Jimmy Fallarino, *Mfg Staff*
Howard Young, *Purch Mgr*
Jim Storey, *VP Sales*
◆ **EMP:** 80 **EST:** 1952
SQ FT: 65,000
SALES (est): 21.8MM **Privately Held**
WEB: www.metpar.com
SIC: 3431 3088 Metal sanitary ware; toilet
fixtures, plastic

(G-15911)
MONTERO INTERNATIONAL INC
Also Called: Pardazzio Uomo
155 Sullivan Ln 1 (11590-3221)
PHONE..............................212 695-1787
Raymond Hagigi, *President*
▲ **EMP:** 6

SALES (est): 772.8K **Privately Held**
SIC: 2329 2325 Shirt & slack suits: men's, youths' & boys'; men's & boys' dress slacks & shorts

(G-15912)
NEW YORK READY MIX INC
Also Called: Commercial Concrete
120 Rushmore St (11590-4816)
PHONE............................516 338-6969
Rick Cerrone, *President*
Ron Notaroantonio, *Vice Pres*
EMP: 5
SQ FT: 4,000
SALES (est): 615.7K **Privately Held**
SIC: 3271 Blocks, concrete or cinder: standard

(G-15913)
P & L DEVELOPMENT LLC
200 Hicks St (11590-3323)
PHONE............................516 986-1700
Mitchell Singer, *Branch Mgr*
EMP: 88 **Privately Held**
SIC: 2834 Pharmaceutical preparations
PA: P & L Development, Llc
609 Cantiague Rock Rd 2a
Westbury NY 11590

(G-15914)
P & L DEVELOPMENT LLC
Also Called: Pl Developments New York
275 Grand Blvd Unit 1 (11590-3570)
PHONE............................516 986-1700
EMP: 88 **Privately Held**
SIC: 2834 Pharmaceutical preparations
PA: P & L Development, Llc
609 Cantiague Rock Rd 2a
Westbury NY 11590

(G-15915)
P & L DEVELOPMENT LLC (PA)
Also Called: Pl Developments
609 Cantiague Rock Rd 2a (11590-1721)
PHONE............................516 986-1700
Mitchell Singer, *Ch of Bd*
Evan Singer, *President*
John Francis, *Senior VP*
Dana S Toops, *Senior VP*
Linda Singer, *Vice Pres*
◆ **EMP:** 58
SALES (est): 262MM **Privately Held**
WEB: www.pldevelopments.com
SIC: 2834 Pharmaceutical preparations

(G-15916)
PARFUSE CORP
65 Kinkel St (11590-4914)
PHONE............................516 997-8888
Angelina J Paris, *President*
Amy Kuna, *Corp Secy*
Donald A Paris, *Vice Pres*
EMP: 35
SQ FT: 10,000
SALES (est): 4.1MM **Privately Held**
SIC: 7692 3398 3341 Brazing; metal heat treating; secondary nonferrous metals

(G-15917)
PNI CAPITAL PARTNERS
1400 Old Country Rd # 103 (11590-5119)
PHONE............................516 466-7120
Michael Packman, *Ch of Bd*
EMP: 7
SALES (est): 698.6K **Privately Held**
SIC: 3452 Pins

(G-15918)
POWER SCRUB IT INC
Also Called: Alltec Products
75 Urban Ave (11590-4829)
PHONE............................516 997-2500
Louis Mangione, *President*
EMP: 13 **EST:** 1995
SALES (est): 1.9MM **Privately Held**
SIC: 3589 High pressure cleaning equipment

(G-15919)
PRECISION MECHANISMS CORP
50 Bond St (11590-5002)
PHONE............................516 333-5955
Daniel Z Petrasek, *President*
Emilia Petrasek, *Vice Pres*
EMP: 30 **EST:** 1957
SQ FT: 5,000

SALES (est): 5.9MM **Privately Held**
WEB: www.precisionmechanisms.com
SIC: 3566 3625 3593 3545 Gears, power transmission, except automotive; relays & industrial controls; fluid power cylinders & actuators; machine tool accessories

(G-15920)
PRINT EARLY LLC
821 Prospect Ave Apt 1a (11590-3779)
PHONE............................718 915-7368
Autumn Zawadzki,
▲ **EMP:** 20 **EST:** 2010
SALES (est): 235.7K **Privately Held**
SIC: 2752 Commercial printing, offset

(G-15921)
PROCOMPONENTS INC (PA)
Also Called: P C I Manufacturing Div
900 Merchants Concourse (11590-5142)
PHONE............................516 683-0909
Barry Reed Lubman, *President*
Alan Lubman, *Corp Secy*
Mitchel Lubman, *Vice Pres*
EMP: 25 **EST:** 1984
SALES (est): 3.4MM **Privately Held**
SIC: 3672 3674 8711 Printed circuit boards; semiconductors & related devices; consulting engineer

(G-15922)
R C HENDERSON STAIR BUILDERS
100 Summa Ave (11590-5000)
PHONE............................516 876-9898
Richard Henderson, *President*
Jason Henderson, *Vice Pres*
Julie Henderson, *Treasurer*
EMP: 10
SQ FT: 8,000
SALES: 1MM **Privately Held**
SIC: 2431 Staircases & stairs, wood; stair railings, wood

(G-15923)
RUBIES COSTUME COMPANY INC
601 Cantiague Rock Rd (11590-1708)
PHONE............................516 333-3473
Marck Bege, *Branch Mgr*
EMP: 40
SALES (corp-wide): 366.5MM **Privately Held**
SIC: 2389 Costumes
PA: Rubie's Costume Company, Inc.
12008 Jamaica Ave
Richmond Hill NY 11418
718 846-1008

(G-15924)
S & B MACHINE WORKS INC
111 New York Ave (11590-4924)
PHONE............................516 997-2666
Eileen Sinn, *CEO*
Frederick Sinn Jr, *President*
EMP: 23
SQ FT: 10,000
SALES (est): 4.7MM **Privately Held**
WEB: www.sbmachineworks.com
SIC: 3444 3599 Sheet metal specialties, not stamped; machine shop, jobbing & repair

(G-15925)
SENTINE PRINTING INC
Also Called: Sir Speedy
75 State St (11590-5004)
PHONE............................516 334-7400
Brandon Bloom, *President*
Steve Ross, *President*
EMP: 5
SQ FT: 2,200
SALES (est): 560.4K **Privately Held**
SIC: 2752 2791 2789 2499 Commercial printing, lithographic; typesetting; bookbinding & related work; signboards, wood

(G-15926)
SPECTRONICS CORPORATION
956 Brush Hollow Rd (11590-1714)
PHONE............................516 333-4840
William B Cooper, *Ch of Bd*
Jonathan D Cooper, *President*
Daniel Cooper, *General Mgr*
Richard Cooper, *Vice Pres*
John Duerr, *Vice Pres*

▲ **EMP:** 190 **EST:** 1950
SQ FT: 98,000
SALES (est): 58.8MM **Privately Held**
WEB: www.spectroline.com
SIC: 3646 3544 Fluorescent lighting fixtures, commercial; special dies, tools, jigs & fixtures

(G-15927)
TAYLOR COMMUNICATIONS INC
1600 Stewart Ave Ste 301 (11590-6611)
PHONE............................718 352-0220
Chris Petro, *Branch Mgr*
EMP: 10
SALES (corp-wide): 2.8B **Privately Held**
WEB: www.stdreg.com
SIC: 2761 Manifold business forms
HQ: Taylor Communications, Inc.
1725 Roe Crest Dr
North Mankato MN 56003
507 625-2828

(G-15928)
TEE PEE AUTO SALES CORP
Also Called: Tri-State Towing Equipment NY
52 Swan St (11590)
PHONE............................516 338-9333
Tom Decillis, *President*
Peter Pizzo, *Vice Pres*
EMP: 10
SALES (est): 1.5MM **Privately Held**
SIC: 3711 Truck & tractor truck assembly

(G-15929)
TEMPO INDUSTRIES INC
90 Hopper St (11590-4802)
PHONE............................516 334-6900
Stuart Braunstein, *President*
Jade Beetle, *Principal*
◆ **EMP:** 1
SALES: 1MM **Privately Held**
SIC: 3993 7389 Advertising novelties; telephone services

(G-15930)
TISHCON CORP (PA)
30 New York Ave (11590-4907)
P.O. Box 331 (11590-0300)
PHONE............................516 333-3056
Raj K Chopra, *Ch of Bd*
Vipin Patel, *President*
Arun K Chopra, *Senior VP*
Abdul Siddiqui, *Manager*
▲ **EMP:** 125 **EST:** 1977
SALES (est): 58.9MM **Privately Held**
WEB: www.qgel.com
SIC: 2834 Vitamin preparations; pills, pharmaceutical

(G-15931)
TISHCON CORP
Also Called: Geotec
37 Brooklyn Ave (11590-4901)
P.O. Box 331 (11590-0300)
PHONE............................516 333-3056
Raj Chopra, *Manager*
EMP: 150
SALES (corp-wide): 58.9MM **Privately Held**
WEB: www.qgel.com
SIC: 2834 Vitamin preparations
PA: Tishcon Corp.
30 New York Ave
Westbury NY 11590
516 333-3056

(G-15932)
TISHCON CORP
41 New York Ave (11590-4908)
PHONE............................516 333-3050
Raj Chopra, *Branch Mgr*
EMP: 150
SALES (corp-wide): 58.9MM **Privately Held**
SIC: 2834 Vitamin preparations
PA: Tishcon Corp.
30 New York Ave
Westbury NY 11590
516 333-3056

(G-15933)
TISHCON CORP
36 New York Ave (11590-4907)
PHONE............................516 333-3050
Hemant Pandit, *Branch Mgr*
EMP: 150

SALES (corp-wide): 58.9MM **Privately Held**
WEB: www.qgel.com
SIC: 2834 Vitamin preparations; pills, pharmaceutical
PA: Tishcon Corp.
30 New York Ave
Westbury NY 11590
516 333-3056

(G-15934)
TRIUMPH GROUP INC
Also Called: Triumph Structures-Long Island
717 Main St (11590-5021)
PHONE............................516 997-5757
EMP: 62
SALES (corp-wide): 3.8B **Publicly Held**
SIC: 3724 Mfg Aircraft Engines/Parts
PA: Triumph Group, Inc.
899 Cassatt Rd Ste 210
Berwyn PA 19312
610 251-1000

(G-15935)
TWIN COUNTY RECYCLING CORP (PA)
113 Magnolia Ave (11590-4719)
PHONE............................516 827-6900
Carlos Lizza, *President*
EMP: 13
SQ FT: 2,000
SALES (est): 1.2MM **Privately Held**
WEB: www.twincountyunitedway.com
SIC: 2951 4953 5032 Asphalt paving mixtures & blocks; recycling, waste materials; aggregate

(G-15936)
UTILITY MANUFACTURING CO INC
700 Main St (11590-5020)
PHONE............................516 997-6300
Wilbur Kranz, *CEO*
Audie Kranz, *President*
EMP: 30
SQ FT: 44,000
SALES (est): 7MM **Privately Held**
WEB: www.utilitychemicals.com
SIC: 2899 2891 Chemical preparations; adhesives & sealants

(G-15937)
VALPLAST INTERNATIONAL CORP
200 Shames Dr (11590-1784)
PHONE............................516 442-3923
Peter S Nagy, *President*
Peter Nagy, *Vice Pres*
▲ **EMP:** 11 **EST:** 1958
SQ FT: 10,500
SALES: 2.5MM **Privately Held**
WEB: www.valplast.com
SIC: 3559 3843 Plastics working machinery; dental equipment & supplies

(G-15938)
VESCOM STRUCTURAL SYSTEMS INC
Also Called: Tms Development
1327 Roosevelt Way (11590-6688)
PHONE............................516 876-8100
Joel Person, *President*
EMP: 10
SALES (est): 58.6K **Privately Held**
WEB: www.vescomstructures.com
SIC: 3299 Floor composition, magnesite

(G-15939)
WD CERTIFIED CONTRACTING LLC
112 Magnolia Ave 101-A (11590-4720)
PHONE............................516 493-9319
Pierre Desrosiers, *Vice Pres*
Walter Desrosiers,
EMP: 10
SALES (est): 896.4K **Privately Held**
SIC: 2521 1522 Wood office furniture; residential construction

(G-15940)
WORLD BEST SPORTING GOODS INC
225 Post Ave (11590-3021)
PHONE............................800 489-0908

▲ = Import ▼ =Export
◆ =Import/Export

Jay Lee, *CEO*
Jerry Choe, *Director*
EMP: 13
SQ FT: 5,000
SALES: 2.7MM **Privately Held**
SIC: 3949 Sporting & athletic goods

Westerlo
Albany County

(G-15941)
HANNAY REELS INC
553 State Route 143 (12193-7700)
PHONE..............................518 797-3791
Eric A Hannay, *CEO*
Roger A Hannay, *Ch of Bd*
Marcia Casullo, *General Mgr*
Elaine Hannay Gruener, *Vice Pres*
David G Hannay, *Vice Pres*
◆ **EMP:** 147 **EST:** 1933
SQ FT: 205,000
SALES: 55.9MM **Privately Held**
WEB: www.hannay.com
SIC: 3569 3499 Firehose equipment: driers, rack & reels; reels, cable: metal

Westernville
Oneida County

(G-15942)
G J OLNEY INC
9057 Dopp Hill Rd (13486)
P.O. Box 280 (13486-0280)
PHONE..............................315 827-4208
G Joseph Olney, *President*
David Olney, *Vice Pres*
Jackie Wolanin, *Office Mgr*
EMP: 20 **EST:** 1917
SQ FT: 4,000
SALES (est): 3.7MM **Privately Held**
SIC: 3556 Food products machinery

Westfield
Chautauqua County

(G-15943)
20 BLISS ST INC
61 E Main St (14787-1305)
PHONE..............................716 326-2790
Ralph Wilson, *President*
Janice Wilson, *Vice Pres*
EMP: 5
SALES: 200K **Privately Held**
SIC: 1321 Natural gasoline production

(G-15944)
A TRUSTED NAME INC
Also Called: Proforma
35 Franklin St (14787-1039)
PHONE..............................716 326-7400
Jeff Gerdy, *President*
EMP: 12
SQ FT: 4,000
SALES (est): 894.9K **Privately Held**
WEB: www.atrustedname.com
SIC: 2395 5199 5941 Decorative & novelty stitching, for the trade; advertising specialties; sporting goods & bicycle shops

(G-15945)
BETTER BAKED FOODS LLC
25 Jefferson St (14787-1010)
P.O. Box D (14787)
PHONE..............................716 326-4651
Gregory Leone, *Manager*
EMP: 100
SQ FT: 66,400
SALES (corp-wide): 5.3B **Privately Held**
WEB: www.betterbaked.com
SIC: 2051 Bread, cake & related products
HQ: Better Baked Foods, Llc
  56 Smedley St
  North East PA 16428
  814 725-8778

(G-15946)
MAZZA CHAUTAUQUA CELLARS LLC
8398 W Route 20 (14787-9748)
PHONE..............................716 793-9463
EMP: 10
SALES (corp-wide): 2.4MM **Privately Held**
SIC: 2084 Wines
PA: Mazza Chautauqua Cellars, Llc
  11580 Lake Rd
  North East PA 16428
  814 725-8695

(G-15947)
NATIONAL GRAPE COOP ASSN INC (PA)
80 State St (14787)
PHONE..............................716 326-5200
Randolph Graham, *President*
Brent Roggie, *General Mgr*
Joseph C Falcone, *Vice Pres*
Harold Smith, *Vice Pres*
Jerry A Czebotar, *Director*
◆ **EMP:** 20
SQ FT: 50,000
SALES: 608.4MM **Privately Held**
SIC: 2033 2037 Fruit juices: packaged in cans, jars, etc.; fruit juices: concentrated, hot pack; tomato juice: packaged in cans, jars, etc.; jams, jellies & preserves: packaged in cans, jars, etc.; frozen fruits & vegetables; fruit juices, frozen; fruit juice concentrates, frozen

(G-15948)
QUALITY GUIDES
Also Called: Westfield Publication
39 E Main St (14787-1303)
P.O. Box 38 (14787-0038)
PHONE..............................716 326-3163
Ogden Newspapers, *Owner*
EMP: 7
SALES (est): 311.4K **Privately Held**
SIC: 2711 Newspapers: publishing only, not printed on site

(G-15949)
RENOLD INC
100 Bourne St (14787-9706)
PHONE..............................716 326-3121
Mike Conley, *Ch of Bd*
Richard Kain, *Purch Mgr*
Cathy Meleen, *Purch Mgr*
Ben Dill, *Engineer*
Cathy Ware, *Controller*
▲ **EMP:** 100 **EST:** 1920
SQ FT: 100,000
SALES (est): 24.7MM
SALES (corp-wide): 260.3MM **Privately Held**
WEB: www.renoldajax.com
SIC: 3535 3566 3568 Conveyors & conveying equipment; belt conveyor systems, general industrial use; speed changers, drives & gears; couplings, shaft: rigid, flexible, universal joint, etc.
HQ: Renold Holdings Inc.
  100 Bourne St
  Westfield NY 14787
  716 326-3121

(G-15950)
WAFFENBAUCH USA
165 Academy St (14787-1308)
PHONE..............................716 326-4508
Sam Villafrank, *CEO*
EMP: 48
SALES: 250K **Privately Held**
SIC: 1382 Oil & gas exploration services

(G-15951)
WELCH FOODS INC A COOPERATIVE
2 S Portage St (14787-1492)
PHONE..............................716 326-5252
Robert W McMillin, *Principal*
Thomas M Curtin, *Manager*
EMP: 175
SALES (corp-wide): 608.4MM **Privately Held**
WEB: www.welchs.com
SIC: 2033 Fruit juices: packaged in cans, jars, etc.

HQ: Welch Foods Inc., A Cooperative
  575 Virginia Rd
  Concord MA 01742
  978 371-1000

(G-15952)
WELCH FOODS INC A COOPERATIVE
100 N Portage St (14787-1092)
PHONE..............................716 326-3131
Andrew Mullen, *Buyer*
Wilson Haller, *Branch Mgr*
EMP: 26
SALES (corp-wide): 608.4MM **Privately Held**
WEB: www.welchs.com
SIC: 2033 Canned fruits & specialties
HQ: Welch Foods Inc., A Cooperative
  575 Virginia Rd
  Concord MA 01742
  978 371-1000

(G-15953)
WINE GROUP INC
Also Called: Mogen David Winegroup
85 Bourne St (14787-9706)
P.O. Box 128 (14787-0128)
PHONE..............................716 326-3151
Jean Schwartz, *Manager*
EMP: 60
SQ FT: 83,120
SALES (corp-wide): 148.2MM **Privately Held**
SIC: 2084 Wines
HQ: The Wine Group Inc
  17000 E State Highway 120
  Ripon CA 95366
  209 599-4111

Westhampton
Suffolk County

(G-15954)
DAVE SANDEL CRANES INC
56 S Country Rd (11977-1314)
PHONE..............................631 325-5588
David Sandel, *President*
EMP: 7
SALES: 1MM **Privately Held**
SIC: 3531 Cranes

(G-15955)
HAMPTON SAND CORP
1 High St (11977)
P.O. Box 601, Speonk (11972-0601)
PHONE..............................631 325-5533
Barbara Dawson, *President*
EMP: 8
SQ FT: 1,000
SALES (est): 1.2MM **Privately Held**
SIC: 1442 5261 5032 4953 Sand mining; gravel mining; top soil; brick, stone & related material; recycling, waste materials

Westhampton Beach
Suffolk County

(G-15956)
FRAME WORKS AMERICA INC
Also Called: Spectaculars
146 Mill Rd (11978-2345)
PHONE..............................631 288-1300
William Vetri, *President*
EMP: 40
SQ FT: 1,500
SALES: 3MM **Privately Held**
SIC: 3851 Eyeglasses, lenses & frames

(G-15957)
MICHAEL K LENNON INC
Also Called: Pine Barrens Printing
851 Riverhead Rd (11978-1210)
P.O. Box 704, Westhampton (11977-0704)
PHONE..............................631 288-5200
Michael K Lennon, *President*
EMP: 30
SQ FT: 11,000
SALES (est): 4.6MM **Privately Held**
WEB: www.pinebarrensprinting.com
SIC: 2752 Commercial printing, offset

(G-15958)
SHUGAR PUBLISHING
Also Called: Qsr Medical Communications
99b Main St (11978-2607)
PHONE..............................631 288-4404
Vivian Mahl, *President*
C S Pithumoni, *Editor*
Dorine Kitay, *Manager*
EMP: 8
SQ FT: 250
SALES: 1.5MM **Privately Held**
WEB: www.practicalgastro.com
SIC: 2721 Periodicals: publishing only

(G-15959)
SOUTHAMPTON TOWN NEWSPAPERS
Also Called: Western Edition
12 Mitchell Rd (11978-2609)
P.O. Box 1071 (11978-7071)
PHONE..............................631 288-1100
Cailin Brophy, *Editor*
Frank Costanca, *Manager*
EMP: 10
SALES (corp-wide): 3.1MM **Privately Held**
WEB: www.southamptonpress.com
SIC: 2711 Newspapers: publishing only, not printed on site
PA: Southampton Town Newspapers Inc
  135 Windmill Ln
  Southampton NY 11968
  631 283-4100

Westmoreland
Oneida County

(G-15960)
MOHAWK METAL MFG & SLS
4901 State Route 233 (13490-1309)
PHONE..............................315 853-7663
William F Schrock, *President*
EMP: 5
SQ FT: 20,000
SALES (est): 2.2MM **Privately Held**
SIC: 2421 Building & structural materials, wood

(G-15961)
PERSONAL GRAPHICS CORPORATION
5123 State Route 233 (13490-1311)
PHONE..............................315 853-3421
Paul Hillman, *President*
EMP: 7
SQ FT: 7,000
SALES: 380K **Privately Held**
SIC: 2759 Screen printing

(G-15962)
RISING STARS SOCCER CLUB CNY
4980 State Route 233 (13490-1308)
P.O. Box 423, Rome (13442-0423)
PHONE..............................315 381-3096
Frank Conestabile, *Owner*
EMP: 10
SALES: 423.4K **Privately Held**
SIC: 3949 Sporting & athletic goods

(G-15963)
SHAFER & SONS
Also Called: Storage Sheds
4932 State Route 233 (13490-1308)
PHONE..............................315 853-5285
John H Shafer, *Partner*
Jason Shafer, *Partner*
Joe Shafer, *Partner*
Kathleen Shafer, *Partner*
EMP: 5
SQ FT: 8,000
SALES (est): 709.8K **Privately Held**
WEB: www.ssheds.com
SIC: 2452 5039 Prefabricated buildings, wood; prefabricated buildings

(G-15964)
SIERSON CRANE INC
4822 State Route 233 (13490-1306)
P.O. Box 358 (13490-0358)
PHONE..............................315 723-6914
Mitchell R Sierson, *President*

EMP: 13
SALES (est): 1.6MM **Privately Held**
SIC: 7692 Welding repair

Westtown
Orange County

(G-15965)
FROST PUBLICATIONS INC
55 Laurel Hill Dr (10998-3921)
PHONE..................845 726-3232
Don Frost, *Owner*
EMP: 5
SALES (est): 396.3K **Privately Held**
SIC: 2721 1521 Periodicals: publishing & printing; single-family housing construction

(G-15966)
GRANT-NOREN
83 Ridge Rd (10998-2602)
PHONE..................845 726-4281
Daniel Grant, *Partner*
Ingela Noren, *Partner*
EMP: 5
SALES: 180K **Privately Held**
SIC: 2499 Picture & mirror frames, wood

White Plains
Westchester County

(G-15967)
1KTGOLD INC
Also Called: 3 Barker Ave Ste 290
3 Barker Ave Ste 290 (10601-1545)
PHONE..................212 302-8200
Enrique Verdeguer, *CEO*
EMP: 16
SALES (est): 546.6K **Privately Held**
SIC: 3911 Jewelry, precious metal

(G-15968)
A & C/FURIA ELECTRIC MOTORS
75 Lafayette Ave (10603-1613)
PHONE..................914 949-0585
Andrew Cerone, *President*
EMP: 11
SQ FT: 5,000
SALES (est): 2.1MM **Privately Held**
SIC: 7694 7699 5999 5251 Electric motor repair; pumps & pumping equipment; compressor repair; motors, electric; pumps & pumping equipment; fans, electric

(G-15969)
ALAMAR PRINTING INC
Also Called: PIP Printing
190 E Post Rd Frnt 1 (10601-4918)
PHONE..................914 993-9007
Mary Jane Goldman, *President*
EMP: 10
SQ FT: 6,500
SALES (est): 1.5MM **Privately Held**
SIC: 2752 2754 Commercial printing, offset; business form & card printing, gravure; promotional printing, gravure; stationery & invitation printing, gravure

(G-15970)
ALCONOX INC
30 Glenn St Ste 309 (10603-3252)
PHONE..................914 948-4040
Rhoda Schemin, *President*
Elliot Lebowitz, *COO*
Jill Zisnan, *Vice Pres*
Reggie Balines, *Accounts Mgr*
Michelle Modica, *Mktg Coord*
EMP: 6 **EST:** 1946
SQ FT: 4,000
SALES (est): 1.3MM **Privately Held**
WEB: www.alconox.com
SIC: 3841 Surgical & medical instruments

(G-15971)
ALTA METAL FINISHING CORP
126 Oakley Ave (10601-3904)
PHONE..................914 946-1916
Andres Enriquez, *Vice Pres*

EMP: 5
SQ FT: 7,500
SALES (est): 175K **Privately Held**
SIC: 3471 Finishing, metals or formed products

(G-15972)
AMENDOLA MBL & STONE CTR INC
560 Tarrytown Rd (10607-1316)
PHONE..................914 997-7968
Sergio Amendola, *President*
Joseph Amendola, *Vice Pres*
Shauna Dibuono, *Sales Staff*
Maria Amendola, *Admin Sec*
▲ **EMP:** 62
SQ FT: 3,500
SALES (est): 7.7MM **Privately Held**
SIC: 3281 2493 5999 5211 Granite, cut & shaped; marbleboard (stone face hard board); stones, crystalline: rough; tile, ceramic

(G-15973)
AMERICAN INTL MEDIA LLC
Also Called: Rugby Magazine
11 Martine Ave Ste 870 (10606-4025)
PHONE..................845 359-4225
EMP: 10
SQ FT: 3,000
SALES (est): 890K **Privately Held**
SIC: 2721 Periodicals-Publishing/Printing

(G-15974)
AMERICAN METAL WORKS INC
164 Ferris Ave (10603-3445)
PHONE..................914 682-2979
EMP: 5 **EST:** 2015
SALES (est): 373.7K **Privately Held**
SIC: 7692 Welding repair

(G-15975)
APPLE PRESS
23 Harrison Blvd Ste 2 (10604-1935)
PHONE..................914 723-6660
Jody Majthenyi, *Owner*
EMP: 7
SQ FT: 4,800
SALES (est): 559.3K **Privately Held**
SIC: 2752 7334 Commercial printing, offset; photocopying & duplicating services

(G-15976)
ARLON VISCOR LTD
1133 Westchester Ave (10604-3516)
PHONE..................914 461-1300
Arlon, *Principal*
EMP: 858
SALES (est): 26.3MM
SALES (corp-wide): 1.5B **Publicly Held**
SIC: 3356 Nonferrous rolling & drawing
HQ: Bairnco Corporation
1133 Westchester Ave N-222
White Plains NY 10604
914 461-1300

(G-15977)
BAIRNCO CORPORATION (DH)
1133 Westchester Ave N-222 (10604-3516)
PHONE..................914 461-1300
Glen M Kassan, *Ch of Bd*
John J Quicke, *President*
Lawrence C Maingot, *CFO*
◆ **EMP:** 20
SQ FT: 11,000
SALES (est): 89.4MM
SALES (corp-wide): 1.5B **Publicly Held**
WEB: www.bairnco.com
SIC: 2821 3556 Plastics materials & resins; meat, poultry & seafood processing machinery; slicers, commercial, food

(G-15978)
BAKER PRODUCTS INC
5 Oakley Rd (10606-3701)
PHONE..................212 459-2323
Jeff Brown, *President*
▲ **EMP:** 6
SQ FT: 1,500
SALES: 1.2MM **Privately Held**
SIC: 3111 3172 Case leather; cosmetic bags

(G-15979)
BALLANTRAE LITHOGRAPHERS INC
96 Wayside Dr (10607-2726)
PHONE..................914 592-3275
Steve Quagliano, *President*
Ralph Bocchimuzzo, *Vice Pres*
Rocco Quagliano, *Treasurer*
EMP: 6
SQ FT: 5,000
SALES (est): 380K **Privately Held**
SIC: 2752 Commercial printing, offset

(G-15980)
BEACON PRESS INC
32 Cushman Rd (10606-3706)
PHONE..................212 691-5050
Kenneth B Weiner, *President*
EMP: 4 **EST:** 1913
SQ FT: 3,000
SALES: 2MM **Privately Held**
WEB: www.beaconpress.com
SIC: 2752 Commercial printing, offset

(G-15981)
BENFIELD CONTROL SYSTEMS INC
55 Lafayette Ave (10603)
PHONE..................914 948-3231
Daniel J McLaughlin, *President*
Roy C Kohli, *Chairman*
William Roloff, *CFO*
Maria Bradley, *Human Res Mgr*
EMP: 10
SALES (est): 4.8MM
SALES (corp-wide): 196.7MM **Privately Held**
WEB: www.benfieldcontrolsystems.com
SIC: 3613 8711 Control panels, electric; engineering services
PA: H.H. Benfield Electric Supply Company, Inc.
25 Lafayette Ave
White Plains NY 10603
914 948-6660

(G-15982)
BOTTLING GROUP LLC
Also Called: Pepsi Beverages Company
1111 Westchester Ave (10604-3525)
PHONE..................800 789-2626
James B Lindsey Jr, *President*
Marjorie Lindsey, *Corp Secy*
Dick Graeber, *Vice Pres*
Gean Anne Asturp, *Admin Sec*
EMP: 400 **EST:** 1932
SQ FT: 1,000,000
SALES (est): 92.6MM
SALES (corp-wide): 64.6B **Publicly Held**
SIC: 2086 Carbonated soft drinks, bottled & canned; soft drinks: packaged in cans, bottles, etc.
HQ: Pepsi-Cola Bottling Group
1111 Westchester Ave
White Plains NY 10604
914 767-6000

(G-15983)
BOTTLING GROUP LLC (HQ)
Also Called: Pepsi Beverages Company
1111 Westchester Ave (10604-3525)
PHONE..................914 253-2000
Albert P Carey, *CEO*
Zein Abdalla, *President*
David Delot, *Managing Dir*
Megan Hurley, *Managing Dir*
Robert Housley, *VP Finance*
◆ **EMP:** 14
SALES (est): 11.5B
SALES (corp-wide): 64.6B **Publicly Held**
WEB: www.bottlinggroup.com
SIC: 2086 Bottled & canned soft drinks; carbonated soft drinks, bottled & canned; carbonated beverages, nonalcoholic: bottled & canned
PA: Pepsico, Inc.
700 Anderson Hill Rd
Purchase NY 10577
914 253-2000

(G-15984)
BRISTOL/WHITE PLAINS
305 North St (10605-2208)
PHONE..................914 681-1800
Diane Mandracchia, *Principal*

EMP: 8
SALES (est): 985.7K **Privately Held**
SIC: 2621 Bristols

(G-15985)
BUNGE LIMITED FINANCE CORP
50 Main St (10606-1901)
PHONE..................914 684-2800
Brian Zachman, *Principal*
Premchand Kanne Ganti, *Treasurer*
Ji Yan, *Manager*
Gloria Gutierrez, *Executive Asst*
Angel Gilkey, *Personnel Assit*
EMP: 53
SALES (est): 36MM **Privately Held**
SIC: 2079 Edible fats & oils
PA: Bunge Limited
C/O Conyers, Dill & Pearman
Hamilton HM11

(G-15986)
BYRAM CONCRETE & SUPPLY LLC
145 Virginia Rd (10603-2232)
PHONE..................914 682-4477
Paul Schmieder, *COO*
John R Percham, *Mng Member*
Charlie Smallen, *Manager*
EMP: 11
SALES (est): 1.3MM
SALES (corp-wide): 171.1MM **Privately Held**
SIC: 3273 Ready-mixed concrete
PA: Peckham Industries, Inc.
20 Haarlem Ave Ste 200
White Plains NY 10603
914 949-2000

(G-15987)
C P CHEMICAL CO INC
25 Home St (10606-2306)
PHONE..................914 428-2517
Walter Hasselman Jr, *President*
EMP: 5
SQ FT: 20,000
SALES: 900K **Privately Held**
WEB: www.tripolymer.com
SIC: 3086 2899 2873 Insulation or cushioning material, foamed plastic; foam charge mixtures; fertilizers: natural (organic), except compost

(G-15988)
CAMEO PROCESS CORP
15 Stewart Pl Apt 7g (10603-3808)
PHONE..................914 948-0082
Edwin Goldstein, *President*
S G Goldstein, *Treasurer*
EMP: 2
SALES: 6MM **Privately Held**
SIC: 2671 Resinous impregnated paper for packaging

(G-15989)
CARBONFREE CHEMICALS SPE I LLC
1 N Lexington Ave (10601-1712)
PHONE..................914 421-4900
Nadeem S Nisar, *President*
Nadeem Nisar, *Managing Dir*
Heather Taormina, *Admin Asst*
EMP: 40
SALES (est): 1.6MM **Privately Held**
SIC: 3624 Carbon & graphite products

(G-15990)
CARL ZEISS INC (DH)
1 N Broadway Ste 401 (10601-2317)
P.O. Box 5943, New York (10087-5943)
PHONE..................914 747-1800
Cheryl Sarli, *President*
Dr Michael Kaschke, *Principal*
James Olivo, *Exec VP*
Meg Donohue, *Vice Pres*
Sean Kelly, *Vice Pres*
◆ **EMP:** 120 **EST:** 1925
SALES (est): 163.7MM
SALES (corp-wide): 449.3K **Privately Held**
SIC: 3827 5049 3829 5084 Optical instruments & apparatus; optical goods; measuring & controlling devices; instruments & control equipment; analytical instruments

HQ: Carl Zeiss Ag
    Carl-Zeiss-Str. 22
    Oberkochen 73447
    736 420-0

(G-15991)
CARL ZEISS MICROSCOPY LLC
1 N Broadway Ste 15 (10601-2335)
P.O. Box 5943, New York (10087-5943)
PHONE..................914 681-7840
James Sharp, *President*
Kenneth Patterson, *President*
Steve Cognato, *Controller*
EMP: 300 EST: 2001
SQ FT: 18,000
SALES (est): 69MM
SALES (corp-wide): 449.3K **Privately Held**
WEB: www.zeiss.com/micro
SIC: 3827 Optical instruments & lenses
HQ: Carl Zeiss, Inc.
    1 N Broadway Ste 401
    White Plains NY 10601
    914 747-1800

(G-15992)
CARL ZEISS SBE LLC
1 N Broadway Ste 401 (10601-2317)
PHONE..................914 747-1132
Robert Pignataro, *General Mgr*
Manfred Hanke, *Vice Pres*
Robert Quinn, *Credit Staff*
Scott A Margolin, *Admin Sec*
▲ EMP: 24
SALES (est): 6.8MM
SALES (corp-wide): 449.3K **Privately Held**
SIC: 3827 Optical instruments & lenses
HQ: Carl Zeiss, Inc.
    1 N Broadway Ste 401
    White Plains NY 10601
    914 747-1800

(G-15993)
CLASSIC COLLECTIONS FINE ART
20 Haarlem Ave Ste 408 (10603-2233)
PHONE..................914 591-4500
Larry Tolchin, *President*
EMP: 6
SQ FT: 5,000
SALES (est): 596K **Privately Held**
SIC: 2741 Art copy: publishing only, not printed on site

(G-15994)
CN GROUP INCORPORATED
76 Mamaroneck Ave (10601-4217)
PHONE..................914 358-5690
EMP: 910
SALES (est): 43.7MM **Privately Held**
SIC: 3089 3841 2821 Mfg Plastic Products Mfg Surgical/Medical Instruments Mfg Plastic Materials/Resins

(G-15995)
COMBE INCORPORATED (PA)
1101 Westchester Ave (10604-3503)
PHONE..................914 694-5454
Christopher B Combe, *President*
Jason Friedlander, *General Mgr*
Joanne Shkreli, *Principal*
Jessica Eichel, *Counsel*
Richard G Powers, *Exec VP*
◆ EMP: 240 EST: 1949
SQ FT: 68,000
SALES (est): 174.7MM **Privately Held**
WEB: www.combe.com
SIC: 2834 2841 Pharmaceutical preparations; soap: granulated, liquid, cake, flaked or chip

(G-15996)
COPY STOP INC
Also Called: L K Printing
50 Main St Ste 32 (10606-1920)
PHONE..................914 428-5188
Richard Koh, *President*
EMP: 5
SQ FT: 800
SALES (est): 744.3K **Privately Held**
SIC: 2752 Commercial printing, offset

(G-15997)
DANONE NUTRICIA EARLY
100 Hillside Ave (10603-2861)
PHONE..................914 872-8556
Luciana Nunez, *General Mgr*
EMP: 20 EST: 2014
SQ FT: 30,000
SALES (est): 1.5MM **Privately Held**
SIC: 2023 Canned baby formula

(G-15998)
DANONE US LLC (HQ)
1 Maple Ave (10605-1476)
PHONE..................914 872-8400
Thibaut Helleputte, *General Mgr*
Vanessa Vlahakis, *General Mgr*
Sergio Fuster, *Vice Pres*
Thomas Rondot, *Vice Pres*
Claudia Sargent, *Vice Pres*
▲ EMP: 100
SQ FT: 35,000
SALES (est): 1.1B
SALES (corp-wide): 762.4MM **Privately Held**
WEB: www.dannon.com
SIC: 2026 Yogurt
PA: Danone
    17 Boulevard Haussmann
    Paris 9e Arrondissement 75009
    149 485-000

(G-15999)
DAVID YURMAN ENTERPRISES LLC
125 Westchester Ave # 1060 (10601-4546)
PHONE..................914 539-4444
David Yurman, *CEO*
Liz Candela, *Sales Staff*
Brenda Santiago, *Analyst*
EMP: 9
SALES (corp-wide): 215.1MM **Privately Held**
SIC: 3911 Jewelry, precious metal
PA: David Yurman Enterprises Llc
    24 Vestry St
    New York NY 10013
    212 896-1550

(G-16000)
EFFICIENCY PRINTING CO INC
126 S Lexington Ave (10606-2510)
P.O. Box 157, Valhalla (10595-0157)
PHONE..................914 949-8611
Fax: 914 949-8516
EMP: 13 EST: 1944
SQ FT: 5,000
SALES (est): 1.4MM **Privately Held**
SIC: 2752 2759 Commercial Printer

(G-16001)
ELECTRO PLATING SERVICE INC
127 Oakley Ave (10601-3937)
PHONE..................914 948-3777
Julian Galperin, *President*
EMP: 12 EST: 1930
SQ FT: 27,000
SALES (est): 353.8K **Privately Held**
WEB: www.smithwarren.com
SIC: 3471 Electroplating of metals or formed products

(G-16002)
ESCHOLAR LLC
222 Bloomingdale Rd # 107 (10605-1517)
PHONE..................914 989-2900
Shawn Bay, *CEO*
Wolf Boehme, *President*
EMP: 11
SQ FT: 2,500
SALES (est): 2.5MM **Privately Held**
WEB: www.escholar.com
SIC: 3695 5045 Computer software tape & disks: blank, rigid & floppy; computer software

(G-16003)
ETHIS COMMUNICATIONS INC
44 Church St Ste 200 (10601-1919)
PHONE..................212 791-1440
David Kellner, *Owner*
Ying Guo, *Editor*
Lindsay Hermanson, *Prdtn Mgr*
Mike Smolinsky, *Manager*
Jennifer Zweibel, *Manager*

EMP: 7
SALES (est): 737.4K **Privately Held**
SIC: 2741 Miscellaneous publishing

(G-16004)
EXCELL PRINT & PROMOTIONS INC
50 Main St Ste 100 (10606-1901)
PHONE..................914 437-8668
David Quas, *President*
EMP: 8
SALES (est): 586.6K **Privately Held**
SIC: 2759 7389 Promotional printing;

(G-16005)
F-O-R SOFTWARE LLC (PA)
Also Called: Two-Four Software
10 Bank St Ste 880 (10606-1946)
PHONE..................914 220-8800
David Accolla, *Director*
Kevin Ouderkirk,
John Flowers,
EMP: 21
SQ FT: 2,100
SALES (est): 3.1MM **Privately Held**
WEB: www.twofour.com
SIC: 7372 Business oriented computer software

(G-16006)
FARMERS HUB LLC (HQ)
Also Called: House of Serengeti
8 Francine Ct (10607-1201)
PHONE..................914 380-2945
Oseovbie Imoukhuede, *Mng Member*
EMP: 6
SALES (est): 227.3K **Privately Held**
SIC: 2099 Tea blending
PA: Heureka Llc
    8 Francine Ct
    White Plains NY 10607
    914 380-2945

(G-16007)
FORDHAM MARBLE COMPANY INC
45 Crane Ave (10603-3702)
PHONE..................914 682-6699
Mario Serdo, *Branch Mgr*
EMP: 15
SALES (corp-wide): 4.2MM **Privately Held**
SIC: 3272 3281 Art marble, concrete; cut stone & stone products
PA: Fordham Marble Company, Inc.
    1931 W Farms Rd
    Bronx NY 10460
    718 893-3380

(G-16008)
GARRETT J CRONIN
Also Called: Minute Man Printing Company
1 Stuart Way (10607-1805)
PHONE..................914 761-9299
Garrett J Cronin, *Principal*
EMP: 5
SALES (est): 171.7K **Privately Held**
SIC: 2759 7389 Commercial printing;

(G-16009)
GAS RECOVERY SYSTEMS LLC (HQ)
Also Called: Gas Recovery Systems Illinois
1 N Lexington Ave Ste 620 (10601-1721)
PHONE..................914 421-4903
Thomas Gesicki, *President*
Anthony Albao, *Vice Pres*
EMP: 12
SQ FT: 2,500
SALES (est): 37.8MM
SALES (corp-wide): 198.8MM **Privately Held**
SIC: 1389 Removal of condensate gasoline from field (gathering) lines
PA: Fortistar Llc
    1 N Lexington Ave Ste 620
    White Plains NY 10601
    914 421-4900

(G-16010)
GREAT BRANDS OF EUROPE INC
Also Called: Lu Biscuits
100 Hillside Ave Fl 3 (10603-2862)
PHONE..................914 872-8804

Elio Pacheco, *Vice Pres*
▲ EMP: 6
SALES (est): 508.4K **Privately Held**
WEB: www.danone.com
SIC: 2052 Cookies

(G-16011)
GREENKISSNY INC
75 S Broadway (10601-4413)
PHONE..................914 304-4323
Ann Anderson, *CEO*
EMP: 6
SALES (est): 150.9K **Privately Held**
SIC: 2834 Pharmaceutical preparations

(G-16012)
HANDCRAFT CABINETRY INC
230 Ferris Ave Ste 1 (10603-3461)
PHONE..................914 681-9437
Michael Ford, *President*
EMP: 9
SQ FT: 4,000
SALES (est): 1.3MM **Privately Held**
WEB: www.handcraftcabinetry.com
SIC: 2517 Home entertainment unit cabinets, wood

(G-16013)
HANDY & HARMAN HOLDING CORP
1133 Westchester Ave N-222 (10604-3571)
PHONE..................914 461-1300
EMP: 77 EST: 2015
SALES (est): 115.9K
SALES (corp-wide): 1.5B **Publicly Held**
SIC: 3356 Nonferrous rolling & drawing
PA: Steel Partners Holdings L.P.
    590 Madison Ave Rm 3202
    New York NY 10022
    212 520-2300

(G-16014)
HOGIL PHARMACEUTICAL CORP
237 Mmaroneck Ave Ste 207 (10605)
PHONE..................914 681-1800
David Trager, *President*
Howard Wendy, *Chairman*
▲ EMP: 10
SQ FT: 3,500
SALES (est): 2.1MM **Privately Held**
WEB: www.hogil.com
SIC: 2834 3841 5047 5122 Pharmaceutical preparations; surgical & medical instruments; medical & hospital equipment; drugs, proprietaries & sundries

(G-16015)
INFORMA BUSINESS MEDIA INC
Fleet Owner Magazine
707 Westchester Ave # 101 (10604-3102)
PHONE..................914 949-8500
Paul Kisseberth, *Branch Mgr*
EMP: 14
SALES (corp-wide): 3B **Privately Held**
SIC: 2731 Book publishing
HQ: Informa Business Media, Inc.
    605 3rd Ave
    New York NY 10158
    212 204-4200

(G-16016)
ITT AEROSPACE CONTROLS LLC
4 W Red Oak Ln (10604-3603)
PHONE..................914 641-2000
Allen Briere, *Sales Staff*
Menotti Lombardi, *Mng Member*
Matthew Oliver, *Manager*
Joe Cockman, *Director*
Kathleen Tolar, *Admin Sec*
EMP: 7
SALES (est): 1.1MM
SALES (corp-wide): 2.7B **Publicly Held**
SIC: 3625 Motor controls & accessories
HQ: Itt Llc
    1133 Westchester Ave N-100
    White Plains NY 10604
    914 641-2000

(G-16017)
ITT INC (PA)
1133 Westchester Ave N-100 (10604-3543)
PHONE..................914 641-2000
Frank T Macinnis, *Ch of Bd*

G E O G R A P H I C

Denise L Ramos, *President*
Farrokh Batliwala, *President*
Aris C Chicles, *President*
Carlo Ghirardo, *President*
EMP: 131 **EST:** 1920
SALES: 2.7B **Publicly Held**
SIC: 3594 3625 3823 3812 Fluid power pumps & motors; control equipment, electric; fluidic devices, circuits & systems for process control; radar systems & equipment

(G-16018)
ITT INDUSTRIES HOLDINGS INC (DH)
1133 Westchester Ave N-100 (10604-3543)
PHONE.................................914 641-2000
Mary Beth Gustafsson, *President*
Steve Giuliano, *Senior VP*
Daryl Bowker, *Vice Pres*
Michael Savinelli, *Vice Pres*
Thomas Scalera, *CFO*
EMP: 8 **EST:** 2004
SALES (est): 2.1MM
SALES (corp-wide): 2.7B **Publicly Held**
SIC: 2611 4731 Pulp mills; freight consolidation
HQ: International Standard Electric Corporation
1105 N Market St Ste 1217
Wilmington DE 19801
302 427-3769

(G-16019)
ITT INTERNATIONAL HOLDINGS INC (DH)
1133 Westchester Ave (10604-3516)
PHONE.................................914 641-2000
Dale Roberts, *Engineer*
Michael Savinelli, *Asst Treas*
Richard Irwin, *Technical Staff*
EMP: 6
SALES (est): 30.6MM
SALES (corp-wide): 2.7B **Publicly Held**
SIC: 3625 Control equipment, electric
HQ: Itt Llc
1133 Westchester Ave N-100
White Plains NY 10604
914 641-2000

(G-16020)
ITT LLC (HQ)
1133 Westchester Ave N-100 (10604-3543)
PHONE.................................914 641-2000
Denise L Ramos, *President*
Farrokh Batliwala, *President*
Aris C Chicles, *President*
Neil W Yeargin, *President*
Steven C Giuliano, *Vice Pres*
◆ **EMP:** 450 **EST:** 1920
SALES: 2.5B
SALES (corp-wide): 2.7B **Publicly Held**
WEB: www.ittind.com
SIC: 3594 3625 3823 3812 Fluid power pumps & motors; control equipment, electric; fluidic devices, circuits & systems for process control; radar systems & equipment
PA: Itt Inc.
1133 Westchester Ave N-100
White Plains NY 10604
914 641-2000

(G-16021)
JOURNAL NEWS
1133 Westchester Ave N-110 (10604-3511)
PHONE.................................914 694-5000
EMP: 6
SALES (est): 180.7K **Privately Held**
SIC: 2711 Newspapers-Publishing/Printing

(G-16022)
KINRO MANUFACTURING INC (DH)
200 Mmaroneck Ave Ste 301 (10601)
PHONE.................................817 483-7791
Jason Lippert, *President*
Scott Mereness, *Vice Pres*
Gary McPhail, *CFO*
▲ **EMP:** 1
SALES (est): 138.6MM
SALES (corp-wide): 2.4B **Publicly Held**
SIC: 3442 Metal doors, sash & trim

HQ: Kinro Manufacturing, Inc.
3501 County Road 6 E
Elkhart IN 46514
574 535-1125

(G-16023)
L K PRINTING CORP
Also Called: Royal Press
50 Main St Ste 32 (10606-1920)
PHONE.................................914 761-1944
Richard Koh, *President*
Joshua Greene, *Vice Pres*
EMP: 6
SQ FT: 1,200
SALES: 700K **Privately Held**
SIC: 2752 Commercial printing, offset

(G-16024)
L S Z INC
Also Called: Alconox
30 Glenn St Ste 309 (10603-3252)
PHONE.................................914 948-4040
Elliot Lebowitz, *CEO*
EMP: 8
SALES (est): 680.9K **Privately Held**
WEB: www.ledizolv.com
SIC: 2841 Detergents, synthetic organic or inorganic alkaline

(G-16025)
LIFE PILL LABORATORIES LLC
50 Main St Ste 100 (10606-1901)
PHONE.................................914 682-2146
Alfred Sparman,
Lena Wills, *Admin Sec*
EMP: 6
SALES (est): 267.4K **Privately Held**
SIC: 2834 Pharmaceutical preparations

(G-16026)
LSIL & CO INC
Also Called: Lori Silverman Shoes
2 Greene Ln (10605-5111)
PHONE.................................914 761-0998
Lori Silverman, *President*
EMP: 6
SALES (est): 510.3K **Privately Held**
SIC: 3144 5661 Boots, canvas or leather: women's; women's shoes

(G-16027)
MAIO FUEL COMPANY LP
46 Fairview Ave (10603-3403)
PHONE.................................914 683-1154
Mario Cafagno, *Principal*
EMP: 5
SALES (est): 252.2K **Privately Held**
SIC: 2869 Fuels

(G-16028)
MEASUREMENT INCORPORATED
34 S Broadway Ste 601 (10601-4428)
PHONE.................................914 682-1969
Nina Gottlieb, *Research*
EMP: 18
SALES (corp-wide): 83MM **Privately Held**
SIC: 2759 Commercial printing
PA: Measurement Incorporated
423 Morris St
Durham NC 27701
919 683-2413

(G-16029)
META-THERM CORP
Also Called: Bio-Nutritional Products
70 W Red Oak Ln (10604-3602)
PHONE.................................914 697-4840
Murray Flashner, *President*
▲ **EMP:** 15
SQ FT: 15,000
SALES: 4MM **Privately Held**
SIC: 2099 Food preparations

(G-16030)
MICROSOFT CORPORATION
125 Westchester Ave (10601-4522)
PHONE.................................914 323-2150
EMP: 599
SALES (corp-wide): 125.8B **Publicly Held**
SIC: 7372 Application computer software

PA: Microsoft Corporation
1 Microsoft Way
Redmond WA 98052
425 882-8080

(G-16031)
MITSUI PLASTICS INC (DH)
10 Bank St Ste 1010 (10606-1952)
PHONE.................................914 287-6800
Teruya Mogi, *President*
David Matsushita, *Exec VP*
Fumiyoshi Shingai, *Vice Pres*
Kevi Siladi, *CFO*
Harold Siegriest, *Controller*
◆ **EMP:** 34
SQ FT: 11,000
SALES: 97.4MM **Privately Held**
SIC: 2821 Plastics materials & resins
HQ: Mitsui & Co. (U.S.A.), Inc.
200 Park Ave Fl 36
New York NY 10166
212 878-4000

(G-16032)
NATIONAL HEALTH PROM ASSOC
711 Westchester Ave # 301 (10604-3539)
PHONE.................................914 421-2525
Gilbert J Botvin, *President*
Monica Mitchell, *Accounting Mgr*
EMP: 22
SQ FT: 120,000
SALES (est): 1.9MM **Privately Held**
SIC: 2741 Miscellaneous publishing

(G-16033)
NESTLE USA INC
1311 Mmroneck Ave Ste 350 (10605)
PHONE.................................914 272-4021
David Rosenbluth, *Principal*
EMP: 139
SALES (corp-wide): 92B **Privately Held**
SIC: 2023 Evaporated milk
HQ: Nestle Usa, Inc.
1812 N Moore St Ste 118
Rosslyn VA 22209
818 549-6000

(G-16034)
NEW ENGLAND RECLAMATION INC
20 Haarlem Ave (10603-2223)
PHONE.................................914 949-2000
Janet Peckham, *Ch of Bd*
John Peckhan, *President*
James V De Forest, *Exec VP*
Thomas Vitti, *Treasurer*
EMP: 15
SALES (est): 1.4MM
SALES (corp-wide): 171.1MM **Privately Held**
WEB: www.peckham.com
SIC: 3399 Metal powders, pastes & flakes
PA: Peckham Industries, Inc.
20 Haarlem Ave Ste 200
White Plains NY 10603
914 949-2000

(G-16035)
NU2 SYSTEMS LLC
155 Lafayette Ave (10603-1602)
PHONE.................................914 719-7272
EMP: 10
SQ FT: 15,000
SALES (est): 419K **Privately Held**
SIC: 3669 Communications Equipment, Nec, Nsk

(G-16036)
ORENOVA GROUP LLC
10 New King St Ste 106 (10604-1208)
PHONE.................................914 517-3000
Barrie Levitt MD, *Mng Member*
EMP: 5
SALES: 206.2K **Privately Held**
SIC: 2834 Pharmaceutical preparations

(G-16037)
OSAKA GAS ENERGY AMERICA CORP
1 N Lexington Ave Ste 504 (10601-1724)
PHONE.................................914 253-5500
Shojiro Oka, *Principal*
▲ **EMP:** 15

SALES (est): 771.5K **Privately Held**
SIC: 2911 Gases & liquefied petroleum gases
PA: Osaka Gas Co., Ltd.
4-1-2, Hiranomachi, Chuo-Ku
Osaka OSK 541-0

(G-16038)
PAC PLASTICS LLC
455 Tarrytown Rd Ste 1266 (10607-1313)
PHONE.................................631 545-0382
Ron Pac,
EMP: 3
SQ FT: 2,000
SALES: 4MM **Privately Held**
SIC: 2821 Plastics materials & resins

(G-16039)
PARAMOUNT CORD & BRACKETS
6 Tournament Dr (10605-5121)
PHONE.................................212 325-9100
Gary Rosenkranz, *President*
EMP: 8
SQ FT: 8,000
SALES (est): 640K **Privately Held**
WEB: www.pccords.com
SIC: 2211 Corduroys, cotton; basket weave fabrics, cotton

(G-16040)
PATTERSON BLACKTOP CORP (HQ)
20 Haarlem Ave (10603-2223)
PHONE.................................914 949-2000
John Peckham, *President*
Janet G Peckham, *President*
John R Peckham, *President*
James V De Forest, *Exec VP*
Thomas Vitti, *Treasurer*
EMP: 30
SALES (est): 2.7MM
SALES (corp-wide): 171.1MM **Privately Held**
SIC: 2951 Asphalt paving mixtures & blocks
PA: Peckham Industries, Inc.
20 Haarlem Ave Ste 200
White Plains NY 10603
914 949-2000

(G-16041)
PATTERSON MATERIALS CORP (HQ)
20 Haarlem Ave (10603-2223)
PHONE.................................914 949-2000
Janet G Peckham, *Co-President*
John R Peckham, *Co-President*
James V De Forest, *Exec VP*
EMP: 17
SQ FT: 15,000
SALES (est): 2.8MM
SALES (corp-wide): 171.1MM **Privately Held**
SIC: 2951 Asphalt paving mixtures & blocks
PA: Peckham Industries, Inc.
20 Haarlem Ave Ste 200
White Plains NY 10603
914 949-2000

(G-16042)
PEARSON LONGMAN LLC (DH)
10 Bank St Ste 1030 (10606-1952)
PHONE.................................212 641-2400
Jeff Taylor, *President*
Roger A Brown, *Vice Pres*
John Stallon, *Vice Pres*
Herbert Yeates, *Treasurer*
Cliff Dsouza, *Info Tech Mgr*
EMP: 40
SALES (est): 102.5MM
SALES (corp-wide): 5.3B **Privately Held**
SIC: 2731 2711 Books: publishing & printing; newspapers, publishing & printing
HQ: Pearson Inc.
1330 Hudson St
New York NY 10013
212 641-2400

(G-16043)
PECKHAM ASPHALT RESALE CORP (HQ)
20 Haarlem Ave Ste 200 (10603-2223)
PHONE.................................914 949-2000

▲ = Import ▼=Export
◆ =Import/Export

John R Peckham, *President*
John Peckham, *President*
James V De Forest, *Exec VP*
Gary Mac Meteals, *Vice Pres*
Thomas Vitti, *Treasurer*
EMP: 13
SQ FT: 15,000
SALES (est): 2.4MM
SALES (corp-wide): 171.1MM **Privately Held**
SIC: 2951 Asphalt paving mixtures & blocks
PA: Peckham Industries, Inc.
20 Haarlem Ave Ste 200
White Plains NY 10603
914 949-2000

(G-16044)
PECKHAM INDUSTRIES INC (PA)
20 Haarlem Ave Ste 200 (10603-2223)
PHONE..................914 949-2000
John R Peckham, *President*
Mark Petramale, *General Mgr*
Jack Reynaud, *Assistant VP*
Gary W Metcalf, *Vice Pres*
Joseph Wildermuth, *Vice Pres*
▲ **EMP:** 30 **EST:** 1924
SQ FT: 15,000
SALES (est): 171.1MM **Privately Held**
WEB: www.peckham.com
SIC: 2951 Concrete, asphaltic (not from refineries)

(G-16045)
PECKHAM MATERIALS CORP (HQ)
20 Haarlem Ave Ste 200 (10603-2223)
PHONE..................914 686-2045
John R Peckham, *President*
Gary Metcalf, *Vice Pres*
Peter Simoneau, *Vice Pres*
Joe Wildermuth, *Vice Pres*
John Giorgianne, *Plant Mgr*
EMP: 100 **EST:** 1961
SQ FT: 5,000
SALES (est): 24.5MM
SALES (corp-wide): 171.1MM **Privately Held**
SIC: 2951 1611 5032 Asphalt & asphaltic paving mixtures (not from refineries); concrete, asphaltic (not from refineries); highway & street paving contractor; paving mixtures
PA: Peckham Industries, Inc.
20 Haarlem Ave Ste 200
White Plains NY 10603
914 949-2000

(G-16046)
PEPSI-COLA BOTTLING GROUP (DH)
Also Called: Pepsico
1111 Westchester Ave (10604-4000)
PHONE..................914 767-6000
Sean Bishop, *President*
Micheal Matney, *Vice Pres*
◆ **EMP:** 2
SALES (est): 185.3MM
SALES (corp-wide): 64.6B **Publicly Held**
SIC: 2086 Carbonated soft drinks, bottled & canned
HQ: Pepsi-Cola Metropolitan Bottling Company, Inc.
1111 Westchester Ave
White Plains NY 10604
914 767-6000

(G-16047)
PEPSI-COLA METRO BTLG CO INC (HQ)
Also Called: Pepsico
1111 Westchester Ave (10604-4000)
PHONE..................914 767-6000
Philip A Marineau, *President*
Iryna Kozlova, *General Mgr*
Robert Carl Biggart, *Chairman*
Dick W Boyce, *Senior VP*
George Kovoor, *Senior VP*
◆ **EMP:** 5
SQ FT: 100,000

SALES (est): 19.5B
SALES (corp-wide): 64.6B **Publicly Held**
WEB: www.joy-of-cola.com
SIC: 2086 2087 Carbonated soft drinks, bottled & canned; syrups, drink
PA: Pepsico, Inc.
700 Anderson Hill Rd
Purchase NY 10577
914 253-2000

(G-16048)
PEPSI-COLA OPERATING COMPANY (HQ)
1111 Westchester Ave (10604-4000)
PHONE..................914 767-6000
John Kayhill, *President*
Alex Baxter, *Vice Pres*
Jeff Johnson, *Vice Pres*
Mark Smith, *Vice Pres*
C Campo, *Project Mgr*
EMP: 43
SALES (est): 23.7MM
SALES (corp-wide): 64.6B **Publicly Held**
SIC: 2086 Bottled & canned soft drinks
PA: Pepsico, Inc.
700 Anderson Hill Rd
Purchase NY 10577
914 253-2000

(G-16049)
PEPSICO INC
1111 Westchester Ave (10604-4000)
PHONE..................914 253-2000
Henry Feng, *Manager*
Joana Pinto, *Manager*
Susan Woods, *Director*
EMP: 309
SALES (corp-wide): 64.6B **Publicly Held**
SIC: 2086 Carbonated soft drinks, bottled & canned
PA: Pepsico, Inc.
700 Anderson Hill Rd
Purchase NY 10577
914 253-2000

(G-16050)
PEPSICO INC
150 Airport Rd Hngr V (10604-1219)
PHONE..................914 253-3474
Archie Walker, *Branch Mgr*
Robert A Baldwin, *Manager*
EMP: 28
SALES (corp-wide): 64.6B **Publicly Held**
WEB: www.pepsico.com
SIC: 2086 Carbonated soft drinks, bottled & canned
PA: Pepsico, Inc.
700 Anderson Hill Rd
Purchase NY 10577
914 253-2000

(G-16051)
PETER PAUPER PRESS INC
202 Mmaroneck Ave Ste 400 (10601)
PHONE..................914 681-0144
Laurence Beilenson, *President*
Evelyn Beilenson, *Principal*
Nick Beilenson, *Principal*
Vicki Fischer, *Editor*
Talia Levy, *Editor*
▲ **EMP:** 25 **EST:** 1982
SQ FT: 4,004
SALES (est): 3.2MM **Privately Held**
WEB: www.peterpauper.com
SIC: 2731 Books: publishing only

(G-16052)
PFIZER INC
4 Martine Ave (10606-4016)
PHONE..................914 437-5868
EMP: 146
SALES (corp-wide): 49.6B **Publicly Held**
SIC: 2834 Mfg Pharmaceutical Medicinal Preparations
PA: Pfizer Inc.
235 E 42nd St
New York NY 10017
212 733-2323

(G-16053)
PLASTICYCLE CORPORATION (PA)
245 Main St Ste 430 (10601-2425)
PHONE..................914 997-6882
Anthony R Corso, *Ch of Bd*
Joseph Cirillo, *Principal*

Bobby Jackson, *Plant Mgr*
Mike Tolkov, *Manager*
EMP: 40 **EST:** 1998
SQ FT: 40,000
SALES (est): 9.7MM **Privately Held**
SIC: 2821 Plastics materials & resins

(G-16054)
PREMIER BRANDS AMERICA INC (PA)
170 Hamilton Ave Ste 201 (10601-1717)
PHONE..................914 667-6200
Steven D Corsun, *Ch of Bd*
Alexander Corsun, *President*
Glenn Livi, *Vice Pres*
Alex Corsun, *Project Mgr*
Osvaldo Cruz, *Prdtn Mgr*
▲ **EMP:** 148
SQ FT: 75,000
SALES (est): 35.9MM **Privately Held**
WEB: www.premier-brands.com
SIC: 3842 3131 2842 Surgical appliances & supplies; orthopedic appliances; footwear cut stock; shoe polish or cleaner

(G-16055)
PREMIER WOODCRAFT LTD
277 Martine Ave 214 (10601-3401)
PHONE..................610 383-6624
EMP: 40
SQ FT: 30,000
SALES (est): 3.7MM **Privately Held**
SIC: 2511 2522 2521 2434 Mfg Wood Household Furn Mfg Nonwood Office Furn Mfg Wood Office Furn Mfg Wood Kitchen Cabinet

(G-16056)
RITANI LLC
30 Dr Martin Luther (10601-1400)
PHONE..................888 974-8264
Jacob Genud, *Controller*
Peter Wish, *Sales Staff*
Josh Marion, *Director*
Cantor Fitzgerald,
EMP: 25
SALES (est): 3.9MM **Privately Held**
SIC: 3911 Jewelry, precious metal

(G-16057)
S & H UNIFORM CORP
1 Aqueduct Rd (10606-1003)
PHONE..................914 937-6800
Rhoda Ross, *CEO*
Glen Ross, *President*
Rosa Greco, *Cust Mgr*
Carol Schiffman, *Accounts Exec*
Bettie Green, *Marketing Mgr*
▼ **EMP:** 65
SQ FT: 50,000
SALES (est): 11.4MM **Privately Held**
WEB: www.sandhuniforms.com
SIC: 2326 7389 Men's & boys' work clothing; telemarketing services

(G-16058)
SABRA DIPPING COMPANY LLC (PA)
777 Westchester Ave Fl 3 (10604-3520)
PHONE..................914 372-3900
Tomer Harpaz, *CEO*
Jeff Connelly, *Plant Mgr*
Andrew Howell, *Mfg Mgr*
Matthew Stowell, *Opers Spvr*
Eddie Gunn, *Opers Staff*
▲ **EMP:** 75
SALES (est): 252.3MM **Privately Held**
SIC: 2099 Food preparations

(G-16059)
SAFE FLIGHT INSTRUMENT CORP
20 New King St (10604-1204)
PHONE..................914 946-9500
Randall Greene, *President*
Joe Wilson, *Vice Pres*
Greg Tassio, *Prdtn Mgr*
Pete Barna, *Facilities Mgr*
Victor Falcaro, *Purch Mgr*
▲ **EMP:** 150 **EST:** 1946
SQ FT: 42,600

SALES (est): 27.4MM **Privately Held**
WEB: www.safeflight.com
SIC: 3812 7699 Aircraft flight instruments; aircraft control systems, electronic; aircraft flight instrument repair

(G-16060)
SAPPI NORTH AMERICA INC
925 Westchester Ave # 115 (10604-3562)
PHONE..................914 696-5544
Bradley McLain, *Marketing Staff*
Brent Demichael, *Branch Mgr*
Deborah Hackett, *Director*
EMP: 60
SALES (corp-wide): 5.3B **Privately Held**
SIC: 2679 Paper products, converted
HQ: Sappi North America, Inc.
255 State St Fl 4
Boston MA 02109
617 423-7300

(G-16061)
SOFTLINK INTERNATIONAL
297 Knollwood Rd Ste 301 (10607-1849)
PHONE..................914 574-8197
Prakash S Kamat, *CEO*
Sunil Nikhar, *President*
EMP: 45
SQ FT: 1,200
SALES: 2.1MM **Privately Held**
WEB: www.softlinkinternational.com
SIC: 7372 Prepackaged software

(G-16062)
STARFUELS INC (HQ)
50 Main St (10606-1901)
PHONE..................914 289-4800
Robert Ryneveld, *Managing Dir*
John Surless, *Broker*
EMP: 3 **EST:** 2012
SALES: 21.5MM
SALES (corp-wide): 1MM **Privately Held**
SIC: 3339 2911 1241 Precious metals; oils, fuel; coal mining services
PA: Starcommodities, Inc.
285 Grand Ave Bldg 3
Englewood NJ 07631
201 685-0400

(G-16063)
STEEL EXCEL INC (HQ)
1133 Westchester Ave (10604-3516)
PHONE..................914 461-1300
Jack L Howard, *CEO*
Douglas Woodworth, *CFO*
▲ **EMP:** 6
SALES (est): 119.3MM
SALES (corp-wide): 1.5B **Publicly Held**
WEB: www.adaptec.com
SIC: 1389 7032 Oil & gas wells: building, repairing & dismantling; sporting & recreational camps
PA: Steel Partners Holdings L.P.
590 Madison Ave Rm 3202
New York NY 10022
212 520-2300

(G-16064)
STUDIO FUN INTERNATIONAL INC
44 S Broadway Fl 7 (10601-4417)
PHONE..................914 238-1000
Harold Clark, *President*
William Magill, *Vice Pres*
Clifford Dupree, *Admin Sec*
▲ **EMP:** 30
SALES (est): 8.2MM **Privately Held**
WEB: www.rd.com
SIC: 2731 Book publishing
HQ: Trusted Media Brands, Inc.
750 3rd Ave Fl 3
New York NY 10017
914 238-1000

(G-16065)
SYMBIO TECHNOLOGIES LLC
333 Mamaroneck Ave (10605-1440)
PHONE..................914 576-1205
Boyoung Kwon, *Opers Mgr*
Diane Romm, *Marketing Staff*
Gideon Romm, *CTO*
Roger Del Russo,
Roger D Russo,
EMP: 7

SALES (est): 1MM **Privately Held**
WEB: www.symbio-technologies.com
SIC: 3575 Computer terminals

(G-16066)
TELEMERGENCY LTD
3 Quincy Ln (10605-5431)
PHONE.................................914 629-4222
Elliot I Baum, *President*
▲ EMP: 5
SQ FT: 1,400
SALES (est): 530K **Privately Held**
WEB: www.telemergency300.com
SIC: 3669 Emergency alarms

(G-16067)
TRUSTED MEDIA BRANDS INC
44 S Broadway Fl 7 (10601-4417)
PHONE.................................914 244-5244
Michael Garzone, *Vice Pres*
Bill Jankowski, *Info Tech Dir*
EMP: 12 **Privately Held**
SIC: 2721 2731 5961 2741 Magazines:
publishing only, not printed on site; books:
publishing only; books, mail order (except
book clubs); record &/or tape (music or
video) club, mail order; miscellaneous
publishing
HQ: Trusted Media Brands, Inc.
750 3rd Ave Fl 3
New York NY 10017
914 238-1000

(G-16068)
VERONA PHARMA INC
50 Main St Ste 1000 (10606-1900)
PHONE.................................914 797-5007
Jan-Anders Karlsson, *CEO*
Kenneth Newman, *Vice Pres*
EMP: 11 EST: 2017
SALES (est): 584.1K **Privately Held**
SIC: 2834 Pharmaceutical preparations

(G-16069)
VIBRA TECH INDUSTRIES INC
126 Oakley Ave (10601-3904)
PHONE.................................914 946-1916
Kenneth Strati, *President*
EMP: 11 EST: 1962
SQ FT: 12,000
SALES: 730K **Privately Held**
SIC: 3471 Finishing, metals or formed
products

(G-16070)
WATKINS WELDING AND MCH SP INC
87 Westmoreland Ave (10606-2316)
PHONE.................................914 949-6168
Charles G Watkins, *President*
Inge Watkins, *Treasurer*
EMP: 7
SQ FT: 1,850
SALES: 300K **Privately Held**
SIC: 7692 3599 Welding repair; machine
shop, jobbing & repair

(G-16071)
WAYNE PRINTING INC
Also Called: Wayne Printing & Lithographic
70 W Red Oak Ln Fl 4 (10604-3602)
PHONE.................................914 761-2400
Jeffrey Wayne, *President*
EMP: 10 EST: 1946
SQ FT: 1,000
SALES (est): 1.5MM **Privately Held**
WEB: www.wayneprinting.com
SIC: 2752 Commercial printing, offset

(G-16072)
WESTCHESTER LAW JOURNAL INC
Also Called: Wlj Printers
199 Main St Ste 301 (10601-3206)
PHONE.................................914 948-0715
Lyle Salmon, *President*
Richard L Salmon, *Vice Pres*
Marjorie Salmon, *Director*
▲ EMP: 5
SQ FT: 1,350
SALES (est): 457.9K **Privately Held**
WEB: www.westchesterlawjournal.com
SIC: 2721 7389 Trade journals: publishing
only, not printed on site; legal & tax serv-
ices

(G-16073)
WESTCHESTER MAILING SERVICE
Also Called: Westmail Press
39 Westmoreland Ave Fl 2 (10606-1937)
PHONE.................................914 948-1116
George Lusk, *President*
EMP: 30
SQ FT: 15,000
SALES (est): 3.2MM **Privately Held**
SIC: 2752 7331 2791 2789 Commercial
printing, offset; mailing service; typeset-
ting; bookbinding & related work

(G-16074)
WESTCHESTER WINE WAREHOUSE LLC
53 Tarrytown Rd Ste 1 (10607-1655)
PHONE.................................914 824-1400
Rudi Pali, *Store Mgr*
Rajesh Khurana, *Marketing Staff*
Ben Khurana,
EMP: 15
SALES (est): 2.4MM **Privately Held**
WEB: www.westchesterwine.com
SIC: 2084 2389 Wines; cummerbunds

(G-16075)
WRKBOOK LLC
19 Brookdale Ave (10603-3201)
PHONE.................................914 355-1293
William De Andrade, *CEO*
Eric Wiener, *CTO*
EMP: 10 EST: 2017
SALES: 50K **Privately Held**
SIC: 7372 7389 Prepackaged software;

Whitehall
Washington County

(G-16076)
MAPLEWOOD ICE CO INC
9785 State Route 4 (12887-2317)
P.O. Box 62 (12887-0062)
PHONE.................................518 499-2345
David O Wood, *President*
Donna Wood, *Corp Secy*
Douglas Wood, *Vice Pres*
EMP: 30
SQ FT: 6,000
SALES (est): 5.9MM **Privately Held**
SIC: 2097 5078 Manufactured ice; refrig-
eration equipment & supplies

(G-16077)
STEWARTS SHOPS CORP
60 Poultney St (12887-1516)
PHONE.................................518 499-9376
James Kelley, *Branch Mgr*
EMP: 12
SALES (corp-wide): 1.5B **Privately Held**
WEB: www.stewartsshops.com
SIC: 2024 5411 Ice cream & ice milk; con-
venience stores
PA: Stewart's Shops Corp.
2907 State Route 9
Ballston Spa NY 12020
518 581-1201

(G-16078)
VERMONT STRUCTURAL SLATE CO
Buckley Rd (12887)
PHONE.................................518 499-1912
Robert Tucker, *Manager*
EMP: 12
SALES (corp-wide): 10.3MM **Privately Held**
WEB: www.vermontstructuralslate.com
SIC: 3281 Cut stone & stone products
PA: Vermont Structural Slate Co Inc
3 Prospect St
Fair Haven VT 05743
802 265-4933

Whitesboro
Oneida County

(G-16079)
COLLEGE CALENDAR COMPANY
148 Clinton St (13492-2501)
P.O. Box 148 (13492-0148)
PHONE.................................315 768-8242
Carter Reul, *Owner*
Steve Tibits, *Manager*
EMP: 10
SALES: 850K **Privately Held**
SIC: 2721 Magazines: publishing only, not
printed on site

(G-16080)
EVERSAN INC
34 Main St Ste 3 (13492-1041)
PHONE.................................315 736-3967
Mustafa Evke, *CEO*
Allan R Roberts, *Vice Pres*
John Liberty, *Sales Staff*
Nick Wilson, *Sales Staff*
▲ EMP: 14 EST: 1996
SALES (est): 2.6MM **Privately Held**
WEB: www.eversan.com
SIC: 3625 3674 3993 Timing devices,
electronic; microprocessors; scoreboards,
electric

(G-16081)
QUALITY COMPONENTS FRAMING SYS
44 Mohawk St Bldg 10 (13492-1232)
PHONE.................................315 768-1167
Daniel R Webb, *President*
EMP: 13
SQ FT: 30,000
SALES (est): 1.5MM **Privately Held**
WEB: www.qcwallpanels.com
SIC: 3253 Clay wall & floor tile

(G-16082)
S R SLOAN INC (PA)
8111 Halsey Rd (13492-3707)
P.O. Box 560, New Hartford (13413-0560)
PHONE.................................315 736-7730
Sheldon R Sloan, *CEO*
Stephen R Sloan, *President*
Melissa Cummings, *CFO*
Steve Spudie, *Sales Associate*
EMP: 77 EST: 1960
SQ FT: 60,000
SALES (est): 16.9MM **Privately Held**
WEB: www.srsloan.com
SIC: 2431 2439 Staircases & stairs, wood;
trusses, wooden roof

(G-16083)
TELECOMMUNICATION CONCEPTS
Also Called: T C I
329 Oriskany Blvd (13492-1424)
PHONE.................................315 736-8523
Don Ryan, *President*
EMP: 5
SALES (est): 760.5K **Privately Held**
WEB:
www.telecommunicationconcepts.com
SIC: 3661 1731 Telephones & telephone
apparatus; telephone & telephone equip-
ment installation

(G-16084)
TURBINE ENGINE COMP UTICA
8273 Halsey Rd (13492-3803)
PHONE.................................315 768-8070
Rob Cohen, *President*
Travis Brisack, *Engineer*
Robert Cartmell, *Engineer*
Anthony Hand, *Engineer*
Michael Potsko, *Engineer*
EMP: 1300
SQ FT: 250,000
SALES (est): 191.5MM **Privately Held**
SIC: 3724 3511 3429 3842 Aircraft en-
gines & engine parts; turbines & turbine
generator sets & parts; clamps, couplings,
nozzles & other metal hose fittings; surgi-
cal appliances & supplies; guided missile
& space vehicle parts & auxiliary equip-
ment

PA: U C A Holdings, Inc.
1 W Pack Sq Ste 305
Asheville NC 28801

(G-16085)
WHITESBORO SPRING & ALIGNMENT (PA)
Also Called: Whitesboro Spring Svce
247 Oriskany Blvd (13492-1596)
PHONE.................................315 736-4441
Stewart Wattenbe Jr, *President*
Melanie Wattenbe, *CFO*
EMP: 11
SQ FT: 2,500
SALES (est): 1.1MM **Privately Held**
SIC: 3493 7539 7538 Leaf springs: auto-
mobile, locomotive, etc.; brake repair, au-
tomotive; general automotive repair shops

Whitestone
Queens County

(G-16086)
ANTICO CASALE USA LLC
1244 Clintonville St 2c (11357-1469)
PHONE.................................718 357-2000
Gaetano De Luca, *Prdtn Mgr*
Antonio Scognamiglio, *Sales Staff*
Gerard Ambrosio, *Mng Member*
Fiori Franzese,
▲ EMP: 4
SQ FT: 800
SALES: 2.6MM **Privately Held**
SIC: 2032 Italian foods: packaged in cans,
jars, etc.

(G-16087)
APHRODITIES
2007 Francis Lewis Blvd (11357-3930)
PHONE.................................718 224-1774
John Milonas, *Owner*
EMP: 8
SALES (est): 784.5K **Privately Held**
SIC: 2051 5812 Bread, cake & related
products; coffee shop; cafe

(G-16088)
ATLAS FENCE & RAILING CO INC
Also Called: Atlas Fence Co
15149 7th Ave (11357-1236)
PHONE.................................718 767-2200
Toll Free:.................................866 -
Tom Pappas, *President*
EMP: 20
SQ FT: 12,000
SALES (est): 3.7MM **Privately Held**
SIC: 3446 2499 3089 Fences, gates,
posts & flagpoles; fences or posts, orna-
mental iron or steel; fencing, docks &
other outdoor wood structural products;
fences, gates & accessories: plastic

(G-16089)
BA SPORTS NUTRITION LLC
Also Called: Bodyarmor
1720 Whitestone Expy # 101 (11357-3000)
PHONE.................................718 357-7402
Thomas Hadley, *CFO*
Kevin Talbot, *Controller*
Maylynda Monte, *HR Admin*
Blaise Ffrench, *Marketing Staff*
Mike Repole, *Mng Member*
EMP: 106
SALES (est): 125MM **Privately Held**
SIC: 2086 Fruit drinks (less than 100%
juice): packaged in cans, etc.

(G-16090)
CARAVELLA FOOD CORP
16611 Cryders Ln (11357-2832)
PHONE.................................646 552-0455
Tatiana Odato, *President*
Danny Odato, *Vice Pres*
◆ EMP: 12
SQ FT: 3,500
SALES (est): 590.1K **Privately Held**
SIC: 3556 Oilseed crushing & extracting
machinery

(G-16091)
CROWN AIRCRAFT LIGHTING INC
1021 Clintonville St # 4 (11357-1845)
P.O. Box 570432 (11357-0432)
PHONE.......................718 767-3410
Michelle Virgilio, *President*
Linda Virgilio, *Vice Pres*
EMP: 9
SQ FT: 4,000
SALES (est): 990.8K **Privately Held**
SIC: 3728 Aircraft parts & equipment

(G-16092)
CT PUBLICATIONS CO
Also Called: Queens Times
1120 154th St (11357-1955)
PHONE.......................718 592-2196
James Lisa, *President*
EMP: 7
SALES: 240K **Privately Held**
WEB: www.queenstimes.com
SIC: 2741 Miscellaneous publishing

(G-16093)
FINANCIAL TECHNOLOGIES 360 INC
Also Called: Fin-Tech360
15436 24th Ave (11357-3727)
PHONE.......................646 588-8853
Remo Bidnali, *CEO*
John Marshall, *COO*
Murali Saravu, *CIO*
EMP: 7
SALES: 500K **Privately Held**
SIC: 7372 Application computer software

(G-16094)
HUDSON EASTERN INDUSTRIES INC
1118 143rd Pl (11357-2355)
P.O. Box 570085 (11357-0085)
PHONE.......................917 295-5818
Theresa Marino, *Principal*
EMP: 5
SALES (est): 202.7K **Privately Held**
SIC: 3999 Manufacturing industries

(G-16095)
JENMAR DOOR & GLASS INC
15038 12th Ave (11357-1808)
PHONE.......................718 767-7900
Millie Risi, *CEO*
Alan Risi, *Principal*
EMP: 5
SQ FT: 12,000
SALES (est): 294.3K **Privately Held**
SIC: 3442 Metal doors

(G-16096)
L3HARRIS TECHNOLOGIES INC
1902 Whitestone Expy # 204 (11357-3059)
PHONE.......................718 767-1100
Dominic Catinella, *Manager*
EMP: 18
SALES (corp-wide): 6.8B **Publicly Held**
SIC: 3663 5065 Radio & TV communications equipment; telephone equipment
PA: L3harris Technologies, Inc.
1025 W Nasa Blvd
Melbourne FL 32919
321 727-9100

(G-16097)
LIF INDUSTRIES INC
Also Called: LI Fireproof Door
1105 Clintonville St (11357-1813)
P.O. Box 570171 (11357-0171)
PHONE.......................718 767-8800
Nick Parise, *Branch Mgr*
EMP: 50
SQ FT: 23,136
SALES (corp-wide): 22.9MM **Privately Held**
SIC: 3442 3429 7699 5211 Fire doors, metal; manufactured hardware (general); door & window repair; door & window products; door frames, all materials
PA: Lif Industries, Inc.
5 Harbor Park Dr Ste 1
Port Washington NY 11050
516 390-6800

(G-16098)
NEW YORK DIGITAL PRINT CTR INC
15050 14th Rd Ste 1 (11357-2607)
PHONE.......................718 767-1953
Joann Derasmo, *President*
EMP: 6
SALES (est): 914.1K **Privately Held**
SIC: 2752 Commercial printing, offset

(G-16099)
PEPPERMINTS SALON INC
15722 Powells Cove Blvd (11357-1332)
PHONE.......................718 357-6304
Evangelia Parlionas, *President*
Margarita Parlionas, *Admin Sec*
EMP: 10
SALES (est): 1.1MM **Privately Held**
SIC: 2844 Cosmetic preparations

(G-16100)
SECURITY DEFENSE SYSTEM
15038 12th Ave (11357-1808)
PHONE.......................718 769-7900
Millie Risi, *President*
EMP: 8
SQ FT: 8,000
SALES: 11.5MM **Privately Held**
SIC: 3699 7382 Security devices; protective devices, security

(G-16101)
TOCARE LLC
Also Called: Whitestone Pharmacy
15043b 14th Ave Fl 1 (11357-1864)
PHONE.......................718 767-0618
Roberto Viola,
Nella Viola,
EMP: 10
SALES (est): 1.1MM **Privately Held**
SIC: 2834 5122 Pharmaceutical preparations; pharmaceuticals

(G-16102)
TRIBCO LLC
Also Called: Queens Tribune
15050 14th Rd Ste 2 (11357-2607)
PHONE.......................718 357-7400
Michael Schenkler,
Gary Ackerman,
EMP: 44
SQ FT: 2,000
SALES (est): 3.2MM **Privately Held**
WEB: www.queenstribune.com
SIC: 2711 Newspapers: publishing only, not printed on site

(G-16103)
WHITESTONE PANETTERIA LLC
15045 12th Rd (11357-1809)
PHONE.......................516 543-9788
EMP: 8
SALES (est): 583.5K **Privately Held**
SIC: 2051 Bread, cake & related products

(G-16104)
WORLD JOURNAL LLC (HQ)
14107 20th Ave Fl 2 (11357-6093)
PHONE.......................718 746-8889
Howard Lee, *Vice Chairman*
Abby Mui, *Accounting Mgr*
Jerry Cao, *Accounts Mgr*
Susan Chung, *Accounts Exec*
Sandra Lee, *Accounts Exec*
▲ EMP: 150
SQ FT: 50,000
SALES (est): 49.7MM **Privately Held**
WEB: www.wjnews.net
SIC: 2711 Newspapers, publishing & printing
PA: Cooper Investors Inc.
14107 20th Ave Ste 602
Flushing NY 11357
718 767-8895

Whitney Point
Broome County

(G-16105)
ADVANCED GRAPHICS COMPANY INC
2607 Main St (13862-2223)
P.O. Box 311 (13862-0311)
PHONE.......................607 692-7875
Rosemarie Fralick, *President*
▼ EMP: 10 EST: 1957
SQ FT: 5,000
SALES (est): 591.8K **Privately Held**
SIC: 3479 2759 Name plates: engraved, etched, etc.; screen printing

(G-16106)
GREEN CONVEYOR & MCH GROUP LLC
8300 State Route 79 (13862-2504)
PHONE.......................607 692-7050
Thomas Taylor,
EMP: 8 EST: 2006
SALES (est): 1.1MM **Privately Held**
SIC: 3535 Conveyors & conveying equipment

(G-16107)
POINT CANVAS COMPANY INC
5952 State Route 26 (13862-1211)
PHONE.......................607 692-4381
Lori Warfield, *President*
Sharon Dahulich, *Vice Pres*
Wayne Dahulich, *Treasurer*
Danny Warfield, *Admin Sec*
EMP: 5
SALES (est): 75K **Privately Held**
SIC: 2394 2395 5199 Canvas & related products; embroidery & art needlework; canvas products

---

Wht Sphr Spgs
Sullivan County

(G-16108)
KLEIN & SONS LOGGING INC
3114 State Route 52 (12787-5802)
PHONE.......................845 292-6682
Ronald Klein, *President*
Dale Klein, *Admin Sec*
EMP: 18
SQ FT: 3,900
SALES (est): 2.3MM **Privately Held**
SIC: 2411 Logging camps & contractors

Williamson
Wayne County

(G-16109)
ALARD EQUIPMENT CORPORATION
6483 Lake Ave (14589-9504)
P.O. Box 57 (14589-0057)
PHONE.......................315 589-4511
Alvin E Shults, *President*
Edward Shults, *Vice Pres*
Diane Jenkins, *Sales Mgr*
Susan Laird, *Admin Sec*
▼ EMP: 20
SQ FT: 12,000
SALES (est): 4.5MM **Privately Held**
WEB: www.alard.com
SIC: 3556 Food products machinery

(G-16110)
KEURIG DR PEPPER INC
Also Called: Mott's
4363 State Route 104 (14589-9332)
PHONE.......................315 589-4911
John Adam, *Facilities Dir*
Heather Kinmond, *Opers Mgr*
Stephen Taylor, *Opers Mgr*
Stephen Brisson, *Engineer*
Daniel Henderson, *Engineer*
EMP: 250 **Publicly Held**
WEB: www.maunalai.com

SIC: 2086 2087 2084 Soft drinks: packaged in cans, bottles, etc.; flavoring extracts & syrups; wines, brandy & brandy spirits
PA: Keurig Dr Pepper Inc.
53 South Ave
Burlington MA 01803

(G-16111)
LAGONER FARMS INC
6895 Lake Ave (14589-9570)
PHONE.......................315 904-4109
Mark Lagoner, *President*
Dianna Lagoner, *Admin Sec*
EMP: 52
SQ FT: 8,000
SALES (est): 1.6MM **Privately Held**
SIC: 2033 0191 5431 Fruits: packaged in cans, jars, etc.; general farms, primarily crop; fruit & vegetable markets

(G-16112)
SALMON CREK CABINETRY INC
6687 Salmon Creek Rd (14589-9557)
PHONE.......................315 589-5419
Charles Ciurca, *President*
EMP: 21
SALES (est): 1.5MM **Privately Held**
SIC: 2434 Wood kitchen cabinets

(G-16113)
THATCHER COMPANY NEW YORK INC
4135 Rte 104 (14589)
P.O. Box 118 (14589-0118)
PHONE.......................315 589-9330
Craig N Thatcher, *President*
J Christopher Pavlick, *Vice Pres*
Diane T Barlow, *Admin Sec*
▲ EMP: 45
SALES: 15.7MM
SALES (corp-wide): 177.6MM **Privately Held**
SIC: 2819 5169 Industrial inorganic chemicals; chemicals & allied products
PA: Thatcher Group, Inc
1905 W Fortune Rd
Salt Lake City UT 84104
801 972-4587

(G-16114)
TRIHEX MANUFACTURING INC
6708 Pound Rd (14589-9751)
PHONE.......................315 589-9331
Roger Lester, *President*
Dina Lester, *Manager*
EMP: 6 EST: 1979
SQ FT: 12,000
SALES: 600K **Privately Held**
SIC: 3451 3452 Screw machine products; bolts, nuts, rivets & washers

---

Williamstown
Oswego County

(G-16115)
C G & SON MACHINING INC
87 Nichols Rd (13493-2415)
PHONE.......................315 964-2430
Brian Gardner, *CEO*
EMP: 5
SALES: 703.6K **Privately Held**
SIC: 7692 Welding repair

Williamsville
Erie County

(G-16116)
17 BAKERS LLC
8 Los Robles St (14221-6719)
PHONE.......................844 687-6836
Anthony Habib, *CEO*
Anthony Habibm, *CEO*
Ashley Battaglia, *Principal*
EMP: 10 EST: 2015
SALES (est): 342.9K **Privately Held**
SIC: 2052 Bakery products, dry

(G-16117)
ABBOTT LABORATORIES
Also Called: Abbott Diagnostics Division
6255 Sheridan Dr Ste 406 (14221-4825)
PHONE.................................716 633-1904
Richard Stark, *Manager*
EMP: 11
SALES (corp-wide): 30.5B **Publicly Held**
WEB: www.abbott.com
SIC: 2834 Pharmaceutical preparations
PA: Abbott Laboratories
100 Abbott Park Rd
Abbott Park IL 60064
224 667-6100

(G-16118)
ALDRICH SOLUTIONS INCORPORATED
80 Earhart Dr Ste 14 (14221-7804)
PHONE.................................716 634-1790
Jason Aldrich, *Owner*
Anthony Porpora, *Sales Staff*
EMP: 5
SALES (est): 351.5K **Privately Held**
SIC: 3599 Machine shop, jobbing & repair

(G-16119)
ALEXANDRIA PROFESSIONAL LLC
5500 Main St Ste 103 (14221-6737)
PHONE.................................716 242-8514
Lina Kennedy, *Branch Mgr*
EMP: 10
SALES (corp-wide): 1.6MM **Privately Held**
SIC: 2844 Toilet preparations
PA: 938023 Ontario Inc
85 Lakeshore Rd Unit A
St Catharines ON L2N 2
800 957-8427

(G-16120)
ASHTON-POTTER USA LTD
Also Called: Hig Capital
10 Curtwright Dr (14221-7072)
PHONE.................................716 633-2000
Miles S Nadal, *Ch of Bd*
Barry Switzer, *President*
Joe Sheeran, *Senior VP*
Kelly Smith, *Senior VP*
Bob Morreale, *Vice Pres*
▲ EMP: 170
SQ FT: 104,000
SALES (est): 27.8MM **Privately Held**
WEB: www.ashtonpotter.com
SIC: 2754 2759 Trading stamps: gravure
printing; trading stamps: printing
HQ: H.I.G. Capital, L.L.C.
1450 Brickell Ave Fl 31
Miami FL 33131
305 379-2322

(G-16121)
BEE PUBLICATIONS INC
Also Called: Amherst Bee
5564 Main St (14221-5410)
PHONE.................................716 632-4700
Trey Measer, *President*
Bryan Jackson, *Editor*
Brenda Denk, *Advt Staff*
Teresa Eastman, *Advt Staff*
Cynthia Guszik, *Advt Staff*
EMP: 55
SQ FT: 3,000
SALES (est): 3.1MM **Privately Held**
WEB: www.beenews.com
SIC: 2711 Newspapers: publishing only,
not printed on site

(G-16122)
BELTONE CORPORATION
7474 Transit Rd (14221-6173)
PHONE.................................716 565-1015
EMP: 5
SALES (corp-wide): 1.6B **Privately Held**
SIC: 3842 Hearing aids
HQ: Beltone Corporation
2601 Patriot Blvd
Glenview IL 60026
847 832-3300

(G-16123)
BLUEBIRD TRANSPORTATION LLC
Also Called: Bluebird Mobility
5477 Main St (14221-6701)
PHONE.................................716 395-0000
Andrew J Shaevel, *CEO*
EMP: 10
SALES: 250K **Privately Held**
SIC: 7372 Prepackaged software

(G-16124)
BROETJE AUTOMATION-USA INC
165 Lawrence Bell Dr # 116 (14221-7900)
PHONE.................................716 204-8640
Ken Benczkowski, *President*
Jeremy Harris, *General Mgr*
Jim Lazarus, *Sales Staff*
EMP: 120
SQ FT: 200,000
SALES (est): 22MM
SALES (corp-wide): 14.1B **Privately Held**
SIC: 3365 Aerospace castings, aluminum
HQ: Broetje-Automation Gmbh
Am Autobahnkreuz 14
Rastede 26180
440 296-60

(G-16125)
CABOODLE PRINTING INC
1975 Wehrle Dr Ste 120 (14221-7022)
PHONE.................................716 693-6000
John Doyle, *President*
Scott Lepir, *Partner*
Gary Wodarczak, *Vice Pres*
EMP: 6
SALES (est): 887.3K **Privately Held**
WEB: www.caboodleprinting.com
SIC: 2752 Commercial printing, offset

(G-16126)
CANADA GOOSE US INC (DH)
300 International Dr (14221-5781)
PHONE.................................888 276-6297
Dani Reiss, *President*
EMP: 8
SALES (est): 1.6MM
SALES (corp-wide): 15.3B **Privately Held**
SIC: 2339 2337 Women's & misses' outer-
wear; women's & misses' suits & coats
HQ: Canada Goose Holdings Inc
250 Bowie Ave
Toronto ON M6E 4
416 780-9850

(G-16127)
CLOUD TORONTO INC
1967 Wehrle Dr Ste 1 (14221-8452)
PHONE.................................408 569-4542
Adam Noop, *Owner*
EMP: 10
SALES: 2.5MM **Privately Held**
SIC: 3679 Electronic circuits

(G-16128)
DAWN FOOD PRODUCTS INC
160 Lawrence Bell Dr # 120 (14221-7897)
PHONE.................................716 830-8214
EMP: 107
SALES (corp-wide): 1.6B **Privately Held**
SIC: 2045 Doughnut mixes, prepared: from
purchased flour
HQ: Dawn Food Products, Inc.
3333 Sargent Rd
Jackson MI 49201

(G-16129)
ELASTOMERS INC
2095 Wehrle Dr (14221-7097)
PHONE.................................716 633-4883
Robert J Kunkel Sr, *President*
Robert J Kunkel Jr, *Vice Pres*
EMP: 8
SQ FT: 12,250
SALES: 700K **Privately Held**
SIC: 2821 Elastomers, nonvulcanizable
(plastics)

(G-16130)
ENGINEERED PLASTICS INC
300 International Dr # 100 (14221-5783)
PHONE.................................800 682-2525
Ken Szekely, *President*
▲ EMP: 20

SQ FT: 2,000
SALES (est): 3.8MM **Privately Held**
SIC: 3996 Tile, floor: supported plastic

(G-16131)
FELENE INC
5522 Main St Apt 3 (14221-6758)
PHONE.................................716 276-3583
Tim Kelly, *Principal*
Stephen Point, *Principal*
EMP: 6
SALES (est): 185.1K **Privately Held**
SIC: 2085 Vodka (alcoholic beverage)

(G-16132)
HOWDEN NORTH AMERICA INC
Also Called: Howden Fan Company
1775 Wehrle Dr (14221-7093)
PHONE.................................716 817-6900
Darryl Halter, *Principal*
EMP: 100
SALES (corp-wide): 224.5MM **Privately
Held**
WEB: www.howdenbuffalo.com
SIC: 3564 8711 Ventilating fans: industrial
or commercial; engineering services
PA: Howden North America Inc.
2475 George Urban Blvd # 120
Depew NY 14043
330 867-8540

(G-16133)
LEGAL SERVICING LLC
2801 Wehrle Dr Ste 5 (14221-7381)
PHONE.................................716 565-9300
EMP: 6
SALES (est): 584.3K **Privately Held**
SIC: 1389 Roustabout service

(G-16134)
MOTOROLA SOLUTIONS SLS & SVCS
4990 Meadowbrook Rd (14221-4216)
PHONE.................................716 633-5022
John Clark, *Manager*
EMP: 35
SALES (corp-wide): 7.3B **Publicly Held**
WEB: www.motorola-labs.com
SIC: 3663 Radio & TV communications
equipment
HQ: Motorola Solutions Sales And Services
2000 Progress Pkwy
Schaumburg IL 60196
847 576-5000

(G-16135)
ORTHO-CLINICAL DIAGNOSTICS INC
15 Limestone Dr (14221-7051)
PHONE.................................716 631-1281
Sue Riester, *Branch Mgr*
EMP: 37
SQ FT: 5,600
SALES (corp-wide): 594.4MM **Privately
Held**
WEB: www.orthoclinical.com
SIC: 2835 Blood derivative diagnostic
agents
PA: Ortho-Clinical Diagnostics, Inc.
1001 Route 202
Raritan NJ 08869
908 218-8000

(G-16136)
PATUGA LLC
7954 Transit Rd 316 (14221-4117)
PHONE.................................716 204-7220
Joseph Pandolfino,
EMP: 5 EST: 2015
SALES (est): 270.4K **Privately Held**
SIC: 3911 7389 Jewelry, precious metal;

(G-16137)
SCHMITT SALES INC
Also Called: Robo Self Serve
5095 Main St (14221-5203)
PHONE.................................716 632-8595
Joe Betts, *Manager*
EMP: 8
SQ FT: 2,347
SALES (est): 480.8K
SALES (corp-wide): 49.4MM **Privately
Held**
WEB: www.schmittsales.com
SIC: 1389 Gas field services

PA: Schmitt Sales, Inc.
2101 Saint Ritas Ln
Buffalo NY 14221
716 639-1500

(G-16138)
SENECA RESOURCES COMPANY LLC
165 Lawrence Bell Dr (14221-7900)
PHONE.................................716 630-6750
Scott Brown, *Principal*
EMP: 18
SALES (corp-wide): 1.5B **Publicly Held**
WEB: www.srcx.com
SIC: 1382 Oil & gas exploration services
HQ: Seneca Resources Company, Llc
1201 La St Ste 2600
Houston TX 77002
713 654-2600

(G-16139)
SKINCARE PRODUCTS INC
5933 Main St Apt 208 (14221-8700)
PHONE.................................917 837-5255
Allan Vanhoven, *CEO*
EMP: 9 EST: 2013
SALES: 900K **Privately Held**
SIC: 2834 7991 7389 Dermatologicals;
spas; design services

(G-16140)
SOLMAC INC
1975 Wehrle Dr Ste 130 (14221-7022)
PHONE.................................716 630-7061
Borris Soldo, *President*
John Barrett, *General Mgr*
EMP: 9
SALES (est): 1.7MM **Privately Held**
SIC: 3599 Machine shop, jobbing & repair

(G-16141)
SRC LIQUIDATION COMPANY
435 Lawrence Bell Dr # 4 (14221-8440)
PHONE.................................716 631-3900
EMP: 5 **Publicly Held**
SIC: 2754 Printing
PA: Src Liquidation Company
600 Albany St
Dayton OH 45402
937 221-1000

(G-16142)
SUCCESSWARE INC
8860 Main St 102 (14221-7640)
PHONE.................................716 565-2338
Phil Di RE, *President*
Roy Powell, *Treasurer*
Gerri Di RE, *Admin Asst*
EMP: 15
SQ FT: 1,600
SALES (est): 906.2K
SALES (corp-wide): 30.9MM **Privately
Held**
WEB: www.successware21.com
SIC: 7372 Prepackaged software
HQ: Clockwork, Inc.
12 Greenway Plz Ste 250
Houston TX 77046
941 366-9692

(G-16143)
TEALEAFS
5416 Main St (14221-5362)
PHONE.................................716 688-8022
Sydney Hoffman, *Owner*
EMP: 5
SALES (est): 397.4K **Privately Held**
SIC: 2087 Beverage bases

(G-16144)
TOWN OF AMHERST
Also Called: Park's Department
450 Maple Rd (14221-3162)
PHONE.................................716 631-7113
Dan Raily, *Manager*
EMP: 40
SQ FT: 15,600 **Privately Held**
WEB: www.apdny.org
SIC: 2531 9111 Picnic tables or benches,
park; mayors' offices
PA: Town Of Amherst
5583 Main St Ste 1
Williamsville NY 14221
716 631-7082

(G-16145)
TRICOR DIRECT INC (HQ)
Also Called: Seton Identification Products
2491 Wehrle Dr (14221-7141)
PHONE.....................716 626-1616
Tim Smith, *President*
▼ EMP: 4 EST: 1981
SQ FT: 150,000
SALES (est): 120.5MM
SALES (corp-wide): 1.1B **Publicly Held**
WEB: www.seton.com
SIC: 3479 Name plates: engraved, etched, etc.
PA: Brady Corporation
6555 W Good Hope Rd
Milwaukee WI 53223
414 358-6600

(G-16146)
WEST SENECA BEE INC
5564 Main St (14221-5410)
PHONE.....................716 632-4700
EMP: 60
SQ FT: 4,500
SALES (est): 1.5MM **Privately Held**
SIC: 2711 Newspapers-Publishing/Printing

Williston Park
Nassau County

(G-16147)
GREENWAY CABINETRY INC
485 Willis Ave (11596-1725)
PHONE.....................516 877-0009
Frank Tommasini, *President*
EMP: 10
SALES (est): 630K **Privately Held**
SIC: 2434 Wood kitchen cabinets

(G-16148)
SCHARF AND BREIT INC
2 Hillside Ave Ste F (11596-2335)
PHONE.....................516 282-0287
Christopher Aives, *President*
EMP: 50 EST: 1939
SQ FT: 22,000
SALES (est): 3.5MM **Privately Held**
SIC: 2329 Sweaters & sweater jackets: men's & boys'

(G-16149)
T RS GREAT AMERICAN REST
17 Hillside Ave (11596-2303)
PHONE.....................516 294-1680
Patrick Miele, *President*
EMP: 10
SALES (est): 918.8K **Privately Held**
SIC: 2035 Seasonings & sauces, except tomato & dry

Willsboro
Essex County

(G-16150)
COMMONWEALTH HOME FASHION INC
31 Station Rd (12996)
P.O. Box 339 (12996-0339)
PHONE.....................514 384-8290
Harvey Levenson, *President*
Barry Goodman, *VP Sales*
Barb Wilson, *Manager*
Sebastian Beleca, *Info Tech Dir*
▲ EMP: 90
SQ FT: 151,000
SALES (est): 8.2MM
SALES (corp-wide): 39.8MM **Privately Held**
WEB: www.comhomfash.com
SIC: 2391 Curtains & draperies
PA: Decors De Maison Commonwealth Inc
8800 Boul Pie-Ix
Montreal QC H1Z 3
514 384-8290

(G-16151)
GENERAL COMPOSITES INC
39 Myers Way (12996-4539)
PHONE.....................518 963-7333
Joseph M Callahan Jr, *CEO*

Jeffrey G Allott, *Ch of Bd*
Ed Marvin, *Engineer*
Allison Whalen, *Office Mgr*
▲ EMP: 41
SQ FT: 40,000
SALES (est): 7.7MM **Privately Held**
WEB: www.generalcomposites.com
SIC: 3089 8711 Synthetic resin finished products; consulting engineer

Wilmington
Essex County

(G-16152)
ADIRONDACK CHOCOLATE CO LTD (PA)
Also Called: Candy Man
5680 Ny State Rte 86 (12997)
PHONE.....................518 946-7270
Joe Dougherty, *President*
EMP: 10 EST: 1962
SQ FT: 800
SALES (est): 1MM **Privately Held**
WEB: www.candymanonline.com
SIC: 2066 5441 Chocolate candy, solid; candy

Wilson
Niagara County

(G-16153)
LYNX PRODUCT GROUP LLC
Also Called: Chalmers Medical Group
650 Lake St (14172-9600)
PHONE.....................716 751-3100
Bob Urtel, *Production*
Dawn Coe, *Purchasing*
James Scime, *Engineer*
Donald Basil,
David T Beckinghausen,
EMP: 38
SQ FT: 28,000
SALES (est): 9.6MM
SALES (corp-wide): 73.1MM **Privately Held**
WEB: www.lynxpg.com
SIC: 3582 Washing machines, laundry: commercial, incl. coin-operated
PA: K S T Industries Inc
6400 Northam Dr
Mississauga ON L4V 1
905 362-6400

(G-16154)
VALAIR INC
87 Harbor St (14172-9749)
P.O. Box 27 (14172-0027)
PHONE.....................716 751-9480
Donald E Sinclair Jr, *Ch of Bd*
John Sinclair, *President*
Linda J Sinclair, *Corp Secy*
EMP: 12 EST: 1971
SQ FT: 4,000
SALES (est): 1.9MM **Privately Held**
SIC: 3599 Machine shop, jobbing & repair

(G-16155)
WOODCOCK BROTHERS BREWING COMP
638 Lake St (14172-9600)
P.O. Box 66 (14172-0066)
PHONE.....................716 333-4000
Tim Woodcock, *President*
EMP: 11
SALES (est): 1MM **Privately Held**
SIC: 2082 Beer (alcoholic beverage)

Wilton
Saratoga County

(G-16156)
JOINTA LIME COMPANY
269 Ballard Rd (12831-1597)
PHONE.....................518 580-0300
Thomas Longe, *President*
EMP: 600
SALES (est): 156.5K **Privately Held**
SIC: 1422 Crushed & broken limestone

Windsor
Broome County

(G-16157)
DEVONIAN STONE NEW YORK INC
463 Atwell Hill Rd (13865-3623)
PHONE.....................607 655-2600
Robert Bellospirito, *President*
▲ EMP: 28
SQ FT: 7,000
SALES (est): 2.1MM **Privately Held**
WEB: www.devonianstone.com
SIC: 3281 1459 Cut stone & stone products; stoneware clay mining

(G-16158)
WINDSOR UNITED INDUSTRIES LLC
10 Park St (13865)
PHONE.....................607 655-3300
Dennis Garges,
EMP: 40
SALES (est): 3.4MM **Privately Held**
SIC: 2499 Decorative wood & woodwork

Wingdale
Dutchess County

(G-16159)
HUNT COUNTRY FURNITURE INC (PA)
19 Dog Tail Corners Rd (12594-1218)
P.O. Box 396, Dover Plains (12522-0396)
PHONE.....................845 832-6601
Todd Gazzoli, *General Mgr*
Randy Williams, *Chairman*
▲ EMP: 80
SQ FT: 60,000
SALES (est): 9.6MM **Privately Held**
WEB: www.huntcountryfurniture.com
SIC: 2511 2599 Chairs, household, except upholstered: wood; restaurant furniture, wood or metal

(G-16160)
WESTCHESTER MODULAR HOMES INC
30 Reagans Mill Rd (12594-1101)
PHONE.....................845 832-9400
Charles W Hatcher, *President*
Steve Sokol, *Opers Mgr*
Zachary Revella, *Purch Agent*
Dave Wrocklage, *Regl Sales Mgr*
Lisa Napolitano, *Sales Staff*
EMP: 125
SQ FT: 104,000
SALES (est): 20.9MM **Privately Held**
WEB: www.westchestermodular.com
SIC: 2452 Modular homes, prefabricated, wood

Wolcott
Wayne County

(G-16161)
CAHOON FARMS INC
10951 Lummisville Rd (14590-9549)
P.O. Box 190 (14590-0190)
PHONE.....................315 594-8081
Donald D Cahoon Jr, *President*
William Cahoon, *Vice Pres*
Sheila Rigerman, *QC Mgr*
Jolene Green, *Comptroller*
Carol Wray, *Human Res Mgr*
EMP: 35 EST: 1942
SQ FT: 44,000
SALES (est): 9.2MM **Privately Held**
SIC: 2033 0723 2037 0175 Fruit juices: fresh; fruit (fresh) packing services; frozen fruits & vegetables; deciduous tree fruits

(G-16162)
CARBALLO CONTRACT MACHINING
Also Called: C C M
6205 Lake Ave (14590-1040)
PHONE.....................315 594-2511
Jeannie Brockmyer, *Owner*
Bryan Brockmyre, *Production*
EMP: 5
SQ FT: 3,000
SALES (est): 344.5K **Privately Held**
WEB: www.ccmprecision.biz
SIC: 3599 Machine shop, jobbing & repair

(G-16163)
EAGLE WELDING MACHINE
13458 Ridge Rd (14590-9602)
PHONE.....................315 594-1845
Gary Buckalew, *Principal*
EMP: 9
SALES (est): 1MM **Privately Held**
SIC: 7692 Welding repair

(G-16164)
MARSHALL INGREDIENTS LLC
5786 Limekiln Rd (14590-9354)
PHONE.....................800 796-9353
EMP: 6
SALES (corp-wide): 866.5K **Privately Held**
SIC: 2034 Fruits, dried or dehydrated, except freeze-dried
PA: Marshall Ingredients Llc
5740 Limekiln Rd
Wolcott NY

(G-16165)
WAYUGA COMMUNITY NEWSPAPERS
Also Called: Waguya News
12039 E Main St (14590-1021)
PHONE.....................315 594-2506
Chuck Palermo, *Manager*
EMP: 6
SQ FT: 5,004
SALES (est): 278.3K
SALES (corp-wide): 2MM **Privately Held**
WEB: www.wayuga.com
SIC: 2711 4225 Newspapers, publishing & printing; general warehousing
PA: Wayuga Community Newspapers Inc
6784 Main St
Red Creek NY 13143
315 754-6229

Woodbury
Nassau County

(G-16166)
ARIZONA BEVERAGE COMPANY LLC (HQ)
Also Called: Arizona Beverages USA
60 Crossways Park Dr W # 400 (11797-2018)
PHONE.....................516 812-0300
Jim Dar, *Vice Pres*
Jay Petragnani, *Vice Pres*
Rick Vaccaro, *Vice Pres*
Maureen Guest, *Sales Staff*
Francie Patton, *Chief Mktg Ofcr*
▼ EMP: 3
SALES (est): 2.7MM
SALES (corp-wide): 90.2MM **Privately Held**
SIC: 2086 Iced tea & fruit drinks, bottled & canned
PA: Hornell Brewing Co., Inc.
60 Crossways Park Dr W # 400
Woodbury NY 11797
516 812-0300

(G-16167)
CLEVER DEVICES LTD (PA)
300 Crossways Park Dr (11797-2035)
PHONE.....................516 433-6100
Frank Ingrassia, *President*
Dean Soucy, *Senior VP*
John Locascio, *Manager*
EMP: 43
SQ FT: 10,000

GEOGRAPHIC

SALES (est): 20.2MM **Privately Held**
WEB: www.cleverdevices.net
SIC: 3679 3663 Recording & playback apparatus, including phonograph; radio & TV communications equipment

(G-16168)
COMPOSITECH LTD
4 Fairbanks Blvd (11797-2604)
PHONE.................................516 835-1458
Jonas Medney, *Ch of Bd*
Christopher F Johnson, *President*
Richard Depoto, *Vice Pres*
Ralph W Segalowitz, *Vice Pres*
Samuel S Gross, *Treasurer*
EMP: 110
SQ FT: 33,000
SALES (est): 11.5MM **Privately Held**
WEB: www.compositech.com
SIC: 3674 6794 Semiconductors & related devices; patent owners & lessors

(G-16169)
CRAZY COWBOY BREWING CO LLC
60 Crossways Park Dr W # 400 (11797-2018)
PHONE.................................516 812-0576
David Menashi, *CEO*
EMP: 25
SALES (est): 948.7K **Privately Held**
SIC: 2082 Malt beverage products

(G-16170)
E & W MANUFACTURING CO INC
15 Pine Dr (11797-1509)
PHONE.................................516 367-8571
Elliot Wald, *President*
EMP: 21
SQ FT: 15,000
SALES (est): 1.7MM **Privately Held**
SIC: 3991 Paint brushes

(G-16171)
F & V DISTRIBUTION COMPANY LLC
1 Arizona Plz (11797-1125)
PHONE.................................516 812-0393
Don Vultaggio, *Principal*
EMP: 9 **Privately Held**
SIC: 2086 Iced tea & fruit drinks, bottled & canned
PA: F & V Distribution Company, Llc
60 Crossways Park Dr W # 400
Woodbury NY 11797

(G-16172)
GLOBAL VIDEO LLC (HQ)
Also Called: Guidance Channel
1000 Woodbury Rd Ste 1 (11797-2530)
P.O. Box 760, Plainview (11803-0760)
PHONE.................................516 222-2600
David Rust, *President*
EMP: 60
SALES (est): 22.8MM
SALES (corp-wide): 673.4MM **Publicly Held**
WEB: www.sunburstvm.com
SIC: 2741 5961 5092 6719 Catalogs: publishing & printing; book club, mail order; educational toys; investment holding companies, except banks
PA: School Specialty, Inc.
W6316 Design Dr
Greenville WI 54942
920 734-5712

(G-16173)
HOWARD CHARLES INC
180 Froehlich Farm Blvd (11797-2923)
P.O. Box 854, Nanuet (10954-0854)
PHONE.................................917 902-6934
Charles Breslin, *Principal*
EMP: 7
SALES (est): 685.4K **Privately Held**
SIC: 3089 Plastic kitchenware, tableware & houseware

(G-16174)
INLAND PRINTING COMPANY INC
36 Orchard Dr (11797-2830)
P.O. Box 414, Syosset (11791-0414)
PHONE.................................516 367-4700
Steven E Spaeth, *President*

Susan Spaeth, *Vice Pres*
EMP: 3
SALES: 7.5MM **Privately Held**
SIC: 2752 Commercial printing, offset

(G-16175)
LENCORE ACOUSTICS CORP (PA)
1 Crossways Park Dr W (11797-2014)
PHONE.................................516 682-9292
Jack D Leonard, *Ch of Bd*
Jonathan Leonard, *Vice Pres*
Alison Friedson, *Purch Mgr*
Cheryl McLaughlin, *Bookkeeper*
David Smith, *Business Dir*
EMP: 10
SQ FT: 2,200
SALES (est): 6.1MM **Privately Held**
WEB: www.lencore.com
SIC: 3446 Partitions & supports/studs, including accoustical systems; acoustical suspension systems, metal

(G-16176)
LI SCRIPT LLC
333 Crossways Park Dr (11797-2066)
PHONE.................................631 321-3850
Michael Shamalov, *Owner*
EMP: 30
SALES (est): 6.7MM **Privately Held**
SIC: 2752 Commercial printing, lithographic

(G-16177)
MANHATTAN MILLING & DRYING CO
78 Pond Rd (11797-1616)
PHONE.................................516 496-1041
EMP: 20
SQ FT: 37,500
SALES (est): 1.2MM **Privately Held**
SIC: 2099 Spice Reconditioning

(G-16178)
NEW YORK COMPUTER CONSULTING
14 Pheasant Ln (11797-1900)
PHONE.................................516 921-1932
Sandra M Biondi, *President*
Bruce Biondi, *Vice Pres*
EMP: 6
SQ FT: 1,500
SALES (est): 664.4K **Privately Held**
WEB: www.nycomputer.net
SIC: 7372 7371 Prepackaged software; computer software systems analysis & design, custom

(G-16179)
PHOTO INDUSTRY INC
Also Called: Pemystifying Diital
7600 Jericho Tpke Ste 301 (11797-1705)
PHONE.................................516 364-0016
Allan Lavine, *President*
Jerry Grossman, *Vice Pres*
EMP: 10
SQ FT: 1,200
SALES (est): 980K **Privately Held**
SIC: 2721 Magazines: publishing only, not printed on site

(G-16180)
PROVIDENT FUEL INC
4 Stillwell Ln (11797-1104)
PHONE.................................516 224-4427
Douglas Robalino, *Principal*
EMP: 8
SALES (est): 1.1MM **Privately Held**
SIC: 2869 Fuels

(G-16181)
RESEARCH FRONTIERS INC (PA)
240 Crossways Park Dr (11797-2033)
PHONE.................................516 364-1902
Joseph M Harary, *President*
Michael R Lapointe, *Vice Pres*
Steven M Slovak, *Vice Pres*
Seth L Van Voorhees, *CFO*
Gregory Grimes, *Bd of Directors*
EMP: 7
SQ FT: 9,500
SALES: 1.4MM **Publicly Held**
WEB: www.refr-spd.com
SIC: 3829 Measuring & controlling devices

(G-16182)
ROYAL PAINT ROLLER CORP
Also Called: Royal Paint Roller Mfg
1 Harvard Dr (11797-3302)
PHONE.................................516 367-4370
Randy Boritz, *President*
Gloria Boritz, *Admin Sec*
EMP: 25 EST: 1968
SQ FT: 23,000
SALES (est): 2MM **Privately Held**
SIC: 3991 Paint rollers

(G-16183)
SORFIN YOSHIMURA LTD
100 Crossways Park Dr W # 215 (11797-2012)
PHONE.................................516 802-4600
Scott Fink, *President*
◆ EMP: 9
SALES (est): 203.2K **Privately Held**
SIC: 3825 Battery testers, electrical

(G-16184)
VEECO INSTRUMENTS INC
100 Sunnyside Blvd Ste B (11797-2925)
PHONE.................................516 677-0200
Edward Braun, *President*
Keith Johnson, *President*
Alan Kass, *Business Mgr*
Ellen Lasala, *Production*
Tracy McDermott, *Buyer*
EMP: 230
SALES (corp-wide): 542MM **Publicly Held**
WEB: www.veeco.com
SIC: 3826 3823 Analytical instruments; industrial instrmnts msrmnt display/control process variable
PA: Veeco Instruments Inc.
1 Terminal Dr
Plainview NY 11803
516 677-0200

(G-16185)
WIN-HOLT EQUIPMENT CORP (PA)
Also Called: Win-Holt Equipment Group
20 Crossways Park Dr N # 205 (11797-2007)
PHONE.................................516 222-0335
Jonathan J Holtz, *CEO*
Dominick Scarfogliero, *President*
Jason Womack, *President*
Jose Ponce, *COO*
Jim Madden, *Vice Pres*
▲ EMP: 45 EST: 1946
SQ FT: 10,000
SALES (est): 83.1MM **Privately Held**
WEB: www.winholt.com
SIC: 2099 Food preparations

(G-16186)
WOODBURY SYSTEMS GROUP INC
30 Glenn Dr (11797-2104)
P.O. Box 346, Plainview (11803-0346)
PHONE.................................516 364-2653
William L Fitzgerald, *President*
Deirdre Volpe, *Vice Pres*
EMP: 6
SALES: 792.5K **Privately Held**
WEB: www.woodsysgrp.com
SIC: 7372 Prepackaged software

Woodhaven
Queens County

(G-16187)
JO-VIN DECORATORS INC
9423 Jamaica Ave (11421-2287)
PHONE.................................718 441-9350
Vincent Pappalando, *Ch of Bd*
Leo Pappalardo, *Admin Sec*
EMP: 40 EST: 1956
SQ FT: 20,000
SALES (est): 4.8MM **Privately Held**
WEB: www.jo-vin.com
SIC: 2391 2299 2392 2394 Curtains & draperies; tops & top processing, man-made or other fiber; bedspreads & bed sets: made from purchased materials; shades, canvas: made from purchased materials

(G-16188)
STEINDL CAST STONE CO INC
9107 76th St (11421-2817)
PHONE.................................718 296-8530
John Steindl Jr, *President*
James Steindl, *Vice Pres*
EMP: 6 EST: 1928
SQ FT: 2,800
SALES: 500K **Privately Held**
WEB: www.steindlcaststone.com
SIC: 3272 Cast stone, concrete

Woodhull
Steuben County

(G-16189)
OWLETTS SAW MILLS
4214 Cook Rd (14898-9630)
PHONE.................................607 525-6340
Walt Owlett, *Owner*
EMP: 5
SALES (est): 324.4K **Privately Held**
SIC: 2421 Sawmills & planing mills, general

Woodmere
Nassau County

(G-16190)
BENISHTY BROTHERS CORP
233 Mosher Ave (11598-1655)
PHONE.................................646 339-9991
EMP: 5
SALES (est): 342.5K **Privately Held**
SIC: 3524 Lawn & garden mowers & accessories

(G-16191)
GLASGOW PRODUCTS INC
886 Lakeside Dr (11598-1916)
PHONE.................................516 374-5937
Paul J Glasgow, *President*
Dorothy Glasgow, *Treasurer*
EMP: 25 EST: 1969
SQ FT: 3,000
SALES (est): 3.1MM **Privately Held**
WEB: www.glasgowproducts.com
SIC: 3535 8711 Conveyors & conveying equipment; consulting engineer

(G-16192)
LAVISH LAYETTE INC (PA)
876 Woodmere Pl (11598-2052)
PHONE.................................347 962-9955
EMP: 5 EST: 2013
SALES (est): 337K **Privately Held**
SIC: 2339 2335 Women's & misses' athletic clothing & sportswear; women's, juniors' & misses' dresses

(G-16193)
SHANE TEX INC
Also Called: Henry Segal Co
717 Longacre Ave (11598-2338)
PHONE.................................516 486-7522
Martin Segal, *Ch of Bd*
Robert Segal, *President*
▲ EMP: 18 EST: 1926
SQ FT: 30,000
SALES: 4MM **Privately Held**
WEB: www.henrysegal.com
SIC: 2311 2337 2335 Tailored suits & formal jackets; men's & boys' uniforms; uniforms, except athletic: women's, misses' & juniors'; women's & misses' suits & skirts; bridal & formal gowns

Woodridge
Sullivan County

(G-16194)
PROFESSIONAL CAB DETAILING CO
Also Called: Procab
Navograrsky Rd (12789)
P.O. Box 727 (12789-0727)
PHONE.................................845 436-7282
Keith Bahr-Tioson, *Owner*

EMP: 10
SQ FT: 15,000
SALES (est): 600K **Privately Held**
WEB: www.procab.com
SIC: 2511 2431 Kitchen & dining room furniture; millwork

Woodside
Queens County

(G-16195)
A SUNSHINE GLASS & ALUMINUM
2610 Brooklyn Queens Expy (11377-7822)
PHONE..............................718 932-8080
Scong Lee, *Principal*
Justin Lee, *Manager*
▲ **EMP:** 20
SALES (est): 1.6MM **Privately Held**
SIC: 3211 5023 Flat glass; glassware

(G-16196)
BALDWIN RIBBON & STAMPING CORP
3956 63rd St (11377-3649)
PHONE..............................718 335-6700
Ronald Steinberg, *President*
EMP: 15
SQ FT: 5,000
SALES (est): 2MM **Privately Held**
SIC: 2399 3999 Emblems, badges & insignia; military insignia

(G-16197)
BIELECKY BROS INC (PA)
5022 72nd St (11377-6084)
PHONE..............................718 424-4764
Edwood Bielecky, *President*
EMP: 22
SQ FT: 24,000
SALES (est): 3.3MM **Privately Held**
WEB: www.bieleckybrothers.com
SIC: 2519 Rattan furniture: padded or plain; wicker & rattan furniture

(G-16198)
BLACK & DECKER CORPORATION
5615 Queens Blvd (11377-4741)
PHONE..............................718 335-1042
Michael Domdrowski, *Manager*
EMP: 9
SQ FT: 6,525
SALES (corp-wide): 13.9B **Publicly Held**
WEB: www.blackanddecker.com
SIC: 3546 Power-driven handtools
HQ: The Black & Decker Corporation
701 E Joppa Rd
Towson MD 21286
410 716-3900

(G-16199)
C & T TOOL & INSTRUMENT CO
Also Called: C&T Tool & Instrmnt
4125 58th St (11377-4748)
PHONE..............................718 429-1253
EMP: 24
SQ FT: 1,690
SALES (est): 2.2MM **Privately Held**
SIC: 3599 3542 3444 3441 Mfg Industrial Machinery Mfg Machine Tool-Forming Mfg Sheet Metalwork Structural Metal Fabrctn

(G-16200)
C L PRECISION MACHINE & TL CO
5015 70th St (11377-6020)
PHONE..............................718 651-8475
George Lolis, *President*
EMP: 5 **EST:** 1967
SQ FT: 1,200
SALES: 250K **Privately Held**
SIC: 3599 Machine shop, jobbing & repair

(G-16201)
CAR-GO INDUSTRIES INC (PA)
5007 49th St (11377-7335)
PHONE..............................718 472-1443
Drori Benman, *President*
EMP: 8
SQ FT: 5,000

SALES (est): 9.3MM **Privately Held**
SIC: 3714 Motor vehicle parts & accessories

(G-16202)
CODY PRINTING CORP
3728 56th St (11377-2438)
PHONE..............................718 651-8854
Kyu Hwang, *CEO*
Kyung Shin, *President*
EMP: 9
SQ FT: 3,000
SALES (est): 1.5MM **Privately Held**
WEB: www.codyprinting.com
SIC: 2752 Commercial printing, offset

(G-16203)
DAMIANOU SPORTSWEAR INC
6001 31st Ave Ste 2 (11377-1205)
P.O. Box 463, Roslyn Heights (11577-0463)
PHONE..............................718 204-5600
Paul Damianou, *President*
Pat Damianou, *Corp Secy*
Elenitsa Damianou, *Vice Pres*
EMP: 62
SQ FT: 24,000
SALES (est): 5.5MM **Privately Held**
SIC: 2335 Women's, juniors' & misses' dresses

(G-16204)
DOMOTECK INTERIORS INC
2430 Brooklyn Queens Expy # 1 (11377-7825)
PHONE..............................718 433-4300
Raja Mustafa, *President*
Konstantinos Mabrikos, *Vice Pres*
EMP: 5
SQ FT: 5,000
SALES: 500K **Privately Held**
SIC: 1411 Limestone & marble dimension stone; argillite, dimension-quarrying

(G-16205)
ECUADOR NEWS INC
6403 Roosevelt Ave Fl 2 (11377-3643)
PHONE..............................718 205-7014
Edgar Arboleda, *President*
EMP: 15
SALES (est): 875.1K **Privately Held**
WEB: www.ecuadornews.net
SIC: 2711 Newspapers: publishing only, not printed on site

(G-16206)
FIRECOM INC (PA)
Also Called: Bio Service
3927 59th St (11377-3435)
PHONE..............................718 899-6100
Paul Mendez, *Ch of Bd*
Antoine Sayour, *President*
Howard L Kogen, *COO*
Howard Kogen, *COO*
Antoine J Sayour, *Senior VP*
EMP: 130 **EST:** 1978
SQ FT: 16,000
SALES (est): 51.6MM **Privately Held**
SIC: 3669 1799 Fire detection systems, electric; fire escape installation

(G-16207)
FIRST LINE PRINTING INC
3728 56th St (11377-2438)
PHONE..............................718 606-0860
Sergio Torres, *President*
EMP: 10
SQ FT: 10,000
SALES (est): 2.2MM **Privately Held**
SIC: 2752 Commercial printing, offset

(G-16208)
GENESIS ELECTRICAL MOTORS
Also Called: Genesis Electl Motor
6010 32nd Ave (11377-2019)
PHONE..............................718 274-7030
Hercules Minnelli, *President*
Beatrice Minnelli, *Corp Secy*
EMP: 5
SQ FT: 4,000
SALES (est): 864.9K **Privately Held**
SIC: 7694 Electric motor repair

(G-16209)
GLOBE ELECTRONIC HARDWARE INC
3424 56th St (11377-2122)
P.O. Box 770727 (11377-0727)
PHONE..............................718 457-0303
Caroline Dennehy, *President*
Paul Murphy, *COO*
Patrick M Dennehy, *Vice Pres*
EMP: 14 **EST:** 1976
SQ FT: 8,800
SALES (est): 2.5MM **Privately Held**
WEB: www.globelectronics.com
SIC: 3451 5072 Screw machine products; hardware

(G-16210)
KETCHAM PUMP CO INC
3420 64th St (11377-2398)
PHONE..............................718 457-0800
Stuart Hruska, *President*
EMP: 15 **EST:** 1903
SQ FT: 10,000
SALES (est): 3.7MM **Privately Held**
SIC: 3561 Pumps & pumping equipment

(G-16211)
KOKOROKO CORPORATION
Also Called: Kokoroko Bakery
4755 47th St (11377-6546)
PHONE..............................718 433-4321
Ivonne D Penaherrera, *President*
EMP: 7
SALES (est): 611.8K **Privately Held**
SIC: 2051 Bakery: wholesale or wholesale/retail combined

(G-16212)
MC COY TOPS AND INTERIORS INC
Also Called: Mc Coy Tops and Covers
6914 49th Ave (11377-6002)
PHONE..............................718 458-5800
John Proimos, *President*
EMP: 8
SQ FT: 6,000
SALES (est): 740K **Privately Held**
SIC: 2399 2394 Seat covers, automobile; convertible tops, canvas or boat: from purchased materials

(G-16213)
METALOCKE INDUSTRIES INC
3202 57th St (11377-1919)
PHONE..............................718 267-9200
Susanna Hollnsteiner, *President*
Tom Sadi, *President*
Tanveer Sadiq, *Vice Pres*
EMP: 6 **EST:** 1936
SQ FT: 10,000
SALES: 1MM **Privately Held**
SIC: 3429 5031 2431 5211 Manufactured hardware (general); millwork; millwork; millwork & lumber

(G-16214)
METRO MACHINING & FABRICATING
3234 61st St (11377-2030)
PHONE..............................718 545-0104
Nicholas Dorazio, *President*
EMP: 7
SALES (est): 570K **Privately Held**
SIC: 3599 Machine shop, jobbing & repair

(G-16215)
NATIONAL ELEV CAB & DOOR CORP
Also Called: Necd
5315 37th Ave (11377-2474)
PHONE..............................718 478-5900
Harold Friedman, *CEO*
John Ferella, *President*
Jeffrey Friedman, *Exec VP*
Jimmy Betancourt, *Accounting Mgr*
Michele Sargent, *Agent*
▲ **EMP:** 50 **EST:** 1930
SQ FT: 30,000
SALES (est): 16.8MM **Privately Held**
WEB: www.necd.com
SIC: 3534 Elevators & equipment

(G-16216)
NYC TRADE PRINTERS CORP
3245 62nd St (11377-2031)
PHONE..............................718 606-0610
Ely Toledo, *President*
EMP: 12
SQ FT: 5,000
SALES (est): 1.6MM **Privately Held**
SIC: 2711 Commercial printing & newspaper publishing combined

(G-16217)
ORTHOPEDIC TREATMENT FACILITY
4906 Queens Blvd (11377-4462)
PHONE..............................718 898-7326
Gary Marano, *President*
Anthony Marano, *Vice Pres*
EMP: 8
SQ FT: 2,800
SALES: 700K **Privately Held**
SIC: 3842 Limbs, artificial; braces, orthopedic

(G-16218)
PACEMAKER PACKAGING CORP
7200 51st Rd (11377-7631)
PHONE..............................718 458-1188
Emil Romotzki, *President*
Helga Romotzki, *Admin Sec*
EMP: 10 **EST:** 1964
SQ FT: 7,000
SALES (est): 1.8MM **Privately Held**
SIC: 3565 Packaging machinery

(G-16219)
PFEIL & HOLING INC
5815 Northern Blvd (11377-2297)
PHONE..............................718 545-4600
Sy Stricker, *President*
David Gordils, *General Mgr*
Margo Stricker, *Corp Secy*
David Stricker, *Vice Pres*
Erica Romanoff, *Purchasing*
◆ **EMP:** 75 **EST:** 1923
SQ FT: 50,000
SALES (est): 14.6MM **Privately Held**
WEB: www.cakedeco.com
SIC: 2064 5046 5999 Cake ornaments, confectionery; bakery equipment & supplies; cake decorating supplies

(G-16220)
PIEMONTE HOME MADE RAVIOLI CO (PA)
Also Called: Piemonte Company
3436 65th St (11377-2329)
PHONE..............................718 429-1972
Mario Bertorelli, *President*
Flavio Bertorelli, *Vice Pres*
▲ **EMP:** 16 **EST:** 1945
SQ FT: 14,000
SALES (est): 1.7MM **Privately Held**
WEB: www.piemonteravioli.com
SIC: 2098 5812 Macaroni products (e.g. alphabets, rings & shells), dry; noodles (e.g. egg, plain & water), dry; spaghetti, dry; eating places

(G-16221)
PLAYBILL INCORPORATED
3715 61st St (11377-2593)
PHONE..............................718 335-4033
Jenna Perrino, *Prdtn Dir*
Lewis Cole, *Finance Other*
Adrienne Scott, *Marketing Staff*
EMP: 20
SALES (corp-wide): 20.3MM **Privately Held**
SIC: 2789 Bookbinding & repairing: trade, edition, library, etc.
PA: Playbill Incorporated
729 7th Ave Fl 4
New York NY 10019
212 557-5757

(G-16222)
RE 99 CENTS INC
4905 Roosevelt Ave (11377-4457)
PHONE..............................718 639-2325
EMP: 6 **EST:** 2009
SALES (est): 492.6K **Privately Held**
SIC: 3643 Mfg Conductive Wiring Devices

(G-16223)
RED WHITE & BLUE ENTPS CORP
3443 56th St (11377-2121)
PHONE..............................718 565-8080
Vasilios Katranis, *President*
EMP: 5
SALES (est): 634.2K **Privately Held**
SIC: 2521 5712 2541 2434 Wood office filing cabinets & bookcases; customized furniture & cabinets; table or counter tops, plastic laminated; wood kitchen cabinets

(G-16224)
ROBERT-MASTERS CORP
3217 61st St (11377-2029)
PHONE..............................718 545-1030
Roberto C Orellana, *President*
▲ EMP: 7
SQ FT: 10,000
SALES (est): 1MM **Privately Held**
SIC: 3442 Rolling doors for industrial buildings or warehouses, metal

(G-16225)
SPAETH DESIGN INC
6006 37th Ave (11377-2541)
PHONE..............................718 606-9685
Sandra L Spaeth, *President*
David Spaeth, *Chairman*
Dorothy Spaeth, *Corp Secy*
▲ EMP: 35 EST: 1945
SQ FT: 27,000
SALES (est): 7.6MM **Privately Held**
WEB: www.spaethdesign.com
SIC: 2653 Display items, corrugated: made from purchased materials

(G-16226)
SPECTRUM ON BROADWAY
6106 34th Ave (11377-2228)
PHONE..............................718 932-5388
Harvey Brooks, *President*
Michael Gyscek, *Vice Pres*
Joseph Morra, *Vice Pres*
EMP: 12
SALES (est): 1.8MM **Privately Held**
WEB: www.spectrumsignsinc.com
SIC: 3993 Electric signs

(G-16227)
SPECTRUM SIGNS INC
6106 34th Ave (11377-2228)
PHONE..............................631 756-1010
Harvey Brooks, *President*
Michael Gyscek, *Vice Pres*
Joseph Morra, *Vice Pres*
EMP: 45
SQ FT: 20,000
SALES (est): 5.5MM **Privately Held**
SIC: 3993 Electric signs; signs, not made in custom sign painting shops

(G-16228)
STAINLESS METALS INC
6001 31st Ave Ste 1 (11377-1205)
PHONE..............................718 784-1454
Fred Meier, *President*
Dan Meier, *Vice Pres*
EMP: 11 EST: 1927
SQ FT: 14,000
SALES (est): 2.3MM **Privately Held**
WEB: www.stainlessmetals.com
SIC: 3443 3431 Tanks, standard or custom fabricated: metal plate; sinks: enameled iron, cast iron or pressed metal

(G-16229)
STONE BOSS INDUSTRIES INC
2604 Borough Pl (11377-7816)
PHONE..............................718 278-2677
Kathy Carlini, *Principal*
EMP: 14
SALES (corp-wide): 5.6MM **Privately Held**
SIC: 2436 Softwood veneer & plywood
PA: Stone Boss Industries Inc.
　　15-01 Pollitt Dr Ste 2
　　Fair Lawn NJ 07410
　　201 254-2450

(G-16230)
SYNERGX SYSTEMS INC (HQ)
3927 59th St (11377-3435)
PHONE..............................516 433-4700

Paul Mendez, *President*
John A Poserina, *CFO*
EMP: 89
SQ FT: 16,400
SALES (est): 18.8MM
SALES (corp-wide): 53.7MM **Privately Held**
WEB: www.synergxsystems.com
SIC: 3669 7382 Emergency alarms; fire alarm apparatus, electric; fire detection systems, electric; transportation signaling devices; security systems services; burglar alarm maintenance & monitoring
PA: Firecom, Inc.
　　3927 59th St
　　Woodside NY 11377
　　718 899-6100

(G-16231)
UNITED PRINT GROUP INC
Also Called: United Business Forms
4523 47th St (11377-5225)
P.O. Box 1430, Long Island City (11101-0430)
PHONE..............................718 392-4242
Robert Sanchez, *Ch of Bd*
Henry Morales, *Vice Pres*
Norma Sanchez, *Treasurer*
EMP: 16
SALES (est): 2.9MM **Privately Held**
WEB: www.unitedpg.com
SIC: 2759 3993 Business forms: printing; advertising artwork

(G-16232)
UTLEYS INCORPORATED
3123 61st St (11377-1222)
PHONE..............................718 956-1661
George Utley III, *President*
John Utley, *Vice Pres*
EMP: 45 EST: 1945
SQ FT: 6,500
SALES (est): 7MM **Privately Held**
WEB: www.utleys.com
SIC: 3565 Packaging machinery

(G-16233)
VERNON PLATING WORKS INC
3318 57th St (11377-2298)
PHONE..............................718 639-1124
Kenneth Abrahami, *CEO*
Alan Hyman, *President*
EMP: 15
SQ FT: 20,000
SALES (est): 1.6MM **Privately Held**
SIC: 3471 Plating of metals or formed products

Woodstock
Ulster County

(G-16234)
BIG INDIE - BEAUTIFUL BOY LLC (PA)
41 Plochmann Ln (12498-1615)
PHONE..............................917 464-5599
Declan Baldwin,
EMP: 5 EST: 2017
SQ FT: 300
SALES (est): 733K **Privately Held**
SIC: 3861 Motion picture film

(G-16235)
CUSTOM PATCHES INC
1760 Glasco Tpke (12498-2120)
P.O. Box 22, Mount Marion (12456-0022)
PHONE..............................845 679-6320
Sophia Preza, *President*
Kari Gilbert, *Manager*
EMP: 35
SALES (est): 500K **Privately Held**
SIC: 2395 Embroidery & art needlework

(G-16236)
MARSHA FLEISHER
Also Called: Loominus Handwoven
18 Tinker St (12498-1233)
PHONE..............................845 679-6500
Marsha Fleisher, *Owner*
Andrea Rose, *General Mgr*
EMP: 10

SALES (est): 786.4K **Privately Held**
SIC: 2282 5632 2211 Weaving yarn: throwing & twisting; women's accessory & specialty stores; broadwoven fabric mills, cotton

(G-16237)
ROTRON INCORPORATED (HQ)
Also Called: Ametek Rotron
55 Hasbrouck Ln (12498-1894)
PHONE..............................845 679-2401
Robert J Vogel, *President*
Michael Ryan, *General Mgr*
Michael Denicola, *Vice Pres*
Mariana Alonso, *Accountant*
Donna Comeau, *Accountant*
▲ EMP: 300
SQ FT: 110,000
SALES (est): 215.8MM
SALES (corp-wide): 4.8B **Publicly Held**
WEB: www.rotronmilaero.com
SIC: 3564 Blowers & fans
PA: Ametek, Inc.
　　1100 Cassatt Rd
　　Berwyn PA 19312
　　610 647-2121

(G-16238)
ROTRON INCORPORATED
Also Called: Ametek Rotron
9 Hasbrouck Ln (12498)
PHONE..............................845 679-2401
Charles Lohwasser, *Principal*
EMP: 44
SALES (corp-wide): 4.8B **Publicly Held**
SIC: 3564 Blowers & fans
HQ: Rotron Incorporated
　　55 Hasbrouck Ln
　　Woodstock NY 12498
　　845 679-2401

Woodville
Jefferson County

(G-16239)
RURAL HILL SAND AND GRAV CORP
10262 County Route 79 (13650-2028)
P.O. Box 128, Belleville (13611-0128)
PHONE..............................315 846-5212
David Staie, *President*
EMP: 12 EST: 1956
SQ FT: 1,000
SALES (est): 1.8MM **Privately Held**
SIC: 1442 3273 Construction sand mining; gravel mining; ready-mixed concrete

Wyandanch
Suffolk County

(G-16240)
A & D ENTRANCES LLC
105 Wyandanch Ave (11798-4441)
PHONE..............................718 989-2441
David L Viteri, *President*
Kimberly Viteri, *Vice Pres*
Raisa Colon, *Project Mgr*
Bradley Myers, *Purch Mgr*
◆ EMP: 15
SALES (est): 4.3MM **Privately Held**
SIC: 3534 Elevators & equipment

(G-16241)
ACCRA SHEETMETAL LLC
1359 Straight Path (11798-4336)
P.O. Box 1219 (11798-0219)
PHONE..............................631 643-2100
Orlando Stokes,
EMP: 7
SQ FT: 4,000
SALES (est): 500K **Privately Held**
SIC: 3444 Sheet metalwork

(G-16242)
ADVANCE GRAFIX EQUIPMENT INC
150 Wyandanch Ave (11798-4436)
PHONE..............................917 202-4593
Bally Mohan, *President*
EMP: 4

SALES (est): 1.2MM **Privately Held**
SIC: 3555 Printing presses

(G-16243)
CANNOLI FACTORY INC
75 Wyandanch Ave (11798-4441)
PHONE..............................631 643-2700
Michael Zucaro, *President*
▲ EMP: 50
SQ FT: 30,000
SALES (est): 9.5MM **Privately Held**
SIC: 2051 5149 Pastries, e.g. danish: except frozen; bakery products

(G-16244)
CORINTHIAN CAST STONE INC
115 Wyandanch Ave (11798-4441)
PHONE..............................631 920-2340
Jason Hirschhorn, *Ch of Bd*
Jason Duran, *Controller*
▲ EMP: 47 EST: 1998
SQ FT: 20,000
SALES (est): 15.4MM **Privately Held**
WEB: www.corinthiancaststone.com
SIC: 3272 Stone, cast concrete

(G-16245)
EHRLICH ENTERPRISES INC
Also Called: Floymar Manufacturing
82 Wyandanch Ave Unit C (11798-4457)
PHONE..............................631 956-0690
Don Ehrlich, *President*
Al Schneider, *General Mgr*
EMP: 16
SQ FT: 18,000
SALES (est): 1.6MM **Privately Held**
SIC: 3599 Machine shop, jobbing & repair

(G-16246)
OIL AND LUBRICANT DEPOT LLC
Also Called: Oil Depot, The
44 Island Container Plz (11798-2200)
PHONE..............................631 841-5000
Steven Krausman, *Mng Member*
EMP: 10 EST: 2011
SALES (est): 2MM **Privately Held**
SIC: 2992 Lubricating oils & greases

(G-16247)
T G M PRODUCTS INC
90 Wyandanch Ave Unit E (11798-4458)
PHONE..............................631 491-0515
Thomas G Miller, *President*
EMP: 6
SALES (est): 679.6K **Privately Held**
SIC: 3841 Surgical instruments & apparatus

(G-16248)
WELD-BUILT BODY CO INC
276 Long Island Ave (11798-3199)
PHONE..............................631 643-9700
Joseph Milan, *President*
Diana Nelson, *Vice Pres*
EMP: 30 EST: 1949
SQ FT: 55,000
SALES (est): 2.1MM **Privately Held**
WEB: www.weldbuilt.com
SIC: 3713 Truck bodies (motor vehicles); car carrier bodies

Wyoming
Wyoming County

(G-16249)
AKA ENTERPRISES
164 Main St (14591-9703)
P.O. Box 58 (14591-0058)
PHONE..............................716 474-4579
Andy Kreutter, *Owner*
EMP: 20
SALES: 4MM **Privately Held**
SIC: 2434 Wood kitchen cabinets

(G-16250)
MARKIN TUBING LP (PA)
1 Markin Ln (14591)
P.O. Box 242 (14591-0242)
PHONE..............................585 495-6211
Maurice J Cunniffe, *Partner*
Allen I Skott, *Partner*
William Carter, *Partner*

John W Dyke, *Partner*
Dan Cunniffe, *COO*
▲ **EMP:** 107
SQ FT: 250,000
SALES (est): 30.1MM **Privately Held**
SIC: 3317 Tubes, wrought: welded or lock joint

(G-16251)
MARKIN TUBING INC
Pearl Creek Rd (14591)
PHONE.................................585 495-6211
Barton P Dambra, *President*
Maurice Cunnife, *Chairman*
Arthur A Smith, *Vice Pres*
Diane Fowler, *Sales Mgr*
EMP: 150
SALES (est): 20.7MM **Privately Held**
WEB: www.markintubing.com
SIC: 3317 3312 Tubes, wrought: welded or lock joint; structural shapes & pilings, steel

(G-16252)
TEXAS BRINE COMPANY LLC
Also Called: Plant Office
1346 Saltvale Rd (14591-9511)
PHONE.................................585 495-6228
Ted Grabowski, *President*
Brian Stacy, *Plant Mgr*
Scott Borne, *Opers Spvr*
Sandra Wilkinson, *Office Mgr*
Bill Wood, *Manager*
EMP: 8
SALES (corp-wide): 274.6MM **Privately Held**
SIC: 2819 Brine
HQ: Texas Brine Company, Llc
4800 San Felipe St
Houston TX 77056
713 877-2700

(G-16253)
TMP TECHNOLOGIES INC
Also Called: Advanced Rubber Products
6110 Lamb Rd (14591-9754)
PHONE.................................585 495-6231
Holly Mitchell, *General Mgr*
Eric Snyder, *Prdtn Mgr*
Robert Flowers, *Manager*
EMP: 60
SALES (corp-wide): 21.3MM **Privately Held**
WEB: www.tmptech.com
SIC: 3069 Medical & laboratory rubber sundries & related products
PA: Tmp Technologies, Inc.
1200 Northland Ave
Buffalo NY 14215
716 895-6100

Yaphank
Suffolk County

(G-16254)
AARCO PRODUCTS INC
21 Old Dock Rd (11980-9734)
PHONE.................................631 924-5461
George M Demartino, *Ch of Bd*
Joel Goldberg, *Engineer*
Scott Schillinger, *Administration*
▲ **EMP:** 15 **EST:** 1975
SQ FT: 10,000
SALES (est): 3.8MM **Privately Held**
WEB: www.aarcoproducts.com
SIC: 2493 2542 Bulletin boards, wood; office & store showcases & display fixtures

(G-16255)
AMERICAN ELECTRONIC PRODUCTS
Also Called: A E P
86 Horseblock Rd Unit F (11980-9743)
PHONE.................................631 924-1299
Robert Gazza, *President*
Warren Azzinaro, *Vice Pres*
EMP: 15
SQ FT: 6,000
SALES (est): 2.2MM **Privately Held**
SIC: 2899 Ink or writing fluids

(G-16256)
CABLES UNLIMITED INC
3 Old Dock Rd (11980-9702)
PHONE.................................631 563-6363
Darren Clark, *President*
EMP: 40
SQ FT: 12,000
SALES: 7.5MM
SALES (corp-wide): 50.2MM **Publicly Held**
WEB: www.cables-unlimited.com
SIC: 3679 5063 Harness assemblies for electronic use: wire or cable; electronic wire & cable
PA: Rf Industries, Ltd.
7610 Miramar Rd Ste 6000
San Diego CA 92126
858 549-6340

(G-16257)
CHIPLOGIC INC
14a Old Dock Rd (11980-9701)
PHONE.................................631 617-6317
Harry Perry, *President*
Carmen Ramos, *QC Mgr*
EMP: 10 **EST:** 2010
SQ FT: 3,500
SALES (est): 1.5MM **Privately Held**
SIC: 3679 Electronic circuits

(G-16258)
COSA XENTAUR CORPORATION
Also Called: Alpha Omega Intruments
84 Horseblock Rd Unit G (11980-9742)
PHONE.................................631 345-3434
Joe Burton, *Opers Mgr*
Chad Boudreaux, *Regl Sales Mgr*
John Dooley, *Sales Staff*
Lawerence Chasen, *Manager*
Christopher Rodriguez, *Manager*
EMP: 10
SALES (corp-wide): 20MM **Privately Held**
WEB: www.cosa-instrument.com
SIC: 3823 Analyzers, industrial process type; coulometric analyzers, industrial process type; combustion control instruments; moisture meters, industrial process type
PA: Cosa Xentaur Corporation
4140 World Houston Pkwy # 180
Houston TX 77032
713 947-9591

(G-16259)
EMS DEVELOPMENT CORPORATION (DH)
Also Called: Ultra Electronics, Ems
95 Horseblock Rd Unit 2 (11980-2301)
PHONE.................................631 924-4736
Peter A Crawford, *President*
Ellen Kren, *Buyer*
Carol Haunstein, *QC Mgr*
Neal Fergenson, *Engineer*
Magill James, *Engineer*
▲ **EMP:** 60 **EST:** 1972
SQ FT: 60,000
SALES (est): 22.1MM
SALES (corp-wide): 984.8MM **Privately Held**
WEB: www.ultra-ems.com
SIC: 3825 3613 3677 3621 Instruments to measure electricity; time switches, electrical switchgear apparatus; switchgear & switchgear accessories; electronic coils, transformers & other inductors; electric motor & generator parts; rectifiers (electrical apparatus)
HQ: Ultra Electronics Defense Inc.
4101 Smith School Rd
Austin TX 78744
512 327-6795

(G-16260)
EMS DEVELOPMENT CORPORATION
95 Horseblock Rd Unit 2a (11980-2301)
PHONE.................................631 345-6200
Peter Crawford, *President*
EMP: 90

SALES (corp-wide): 984.8MM **Privately Held**
SIC: 3675 3677 3577 3612 Electronic capacitors; electronic coils, transformers & other inductors; computer peripheral equipment; power & distribution transformers
HQ: Ems Development Corporation
95 Horseblock Rd Unit 2
Yaphank NY 11980
631 924-4736

(G-16261)
EMTRON HYBRIDS INC
86 Horseblock Rd Unit G (11980-9743)
PHONE.................................631 924-9668
Damian Emery, *President*
EMP: 15
SQ FT: 6,000
SALES (est): 2.5MM **Privately Held**
WEB: www.emtronhybrids.com
SIC: 3674 2396 Hybrid integrated circuits; automotive & apparel trimmings

(G-16262)
GEORGIA-PACIFIC LLC
319 Yaphank Ave (11980-9644)
PHONE.................................631 924-7401
Craig Bigliotta, *General Mgr*
EMP: 20
SALES (corp-wide): 40.6B **Privately Held**
WEB: www.gp.com
SIC: 2611 5211 5031 Pulp mills; lumber products; lumber: rough, dressed & finished
HQ: Georgia-Pacific Llc
133 Peachtree St Nw
Atlanta GA 30303
404 652-4000

(G-16263)
H B MILLWORK INC
9 Old Dock Rd (11980-9702)
PHONE.................................631 924-4195
Timothy Hollowell, *Principal*
EMP: 6
SALES (corp-wide): 2.8MM **Privately Held**
WEB: www.hbmillwork.com
SIC: 2431 Millwork
PA: H B Millwork Inc
500 Long Island Ave
Medford NY 11763
631 289-8086

(G-16264)
L D FLECKEN INC
11 Old Dock Rd Unit 11 # 11 (11980-9622)
PHONE.................................631 777-4881
Leo D Flecken, *President*
EMP: 13
SQ FT: 8,000
SALES (est): 1.5MM **Privately Held**
WEB: www.ldflecken.com
SIC: 3499 Metal household articles

(G-16265)
LYNTRONICS INC
7 Old Dock Rd Unit 1 (11980-9637)
PHONE.................................631 205-1061
Anthony Vigliotti, *President*
EMP: 20
SQ FT: 12,000
SALES (est): 3.1MM **Privately Held**
SIC: 3679 5063 Harness assemblies for electronic use: wire or cable; batteries, dry cell

(G-16266)
MASTER-HALCO INC
19 Zorn Blvd (11980-2102)
PHONE.................................631 585-8150
Bob Locurto, *Manager*
EMP: 14 **Privately Held**
WEB: www.fenceonline.com
SIC: 3315 5039 5031 1799 Chain link fencing; wire fence, gates & accessories; fencing, wood; fence construction
HQ: Master-Halco, Inc.
3010 Lbj Fwy Ste 800
Dallas TX 75234
972 714-7300

(G-16267)
NANOPROBES INC
95 Horseblock Rd Unit 1 (11980-2301)
PHONE.................................631 205-9490
James Hainfeld, *President*
Fred Furuya, *Vice Pres*
Frederic R Furuya, *Vice Pres*
Cat Hainfeld, *Marketing Staff*
Claudia Cifuentes, *Manager*
EMP: 14
SALES (est): 250K **Privately Held**
WEB: www.nanoprobes.com
SIC: 2836 Biological products, except diagnostic

(G-16268)
RUGA GRINDING & MFG CORP
84 Horseblock Rd Unit A (11980-9742)
PHONE.................................631 924-5067
Harry Gaenzle, *President*
Ronnie Ganzle, *Treasurer*
Joie Cascillo, *Admin Sec*
EMP: 8
SQ FT: 5,000
SALES (est): 881.1K **Privately Held**
SIC: 3599 Machine shop, jobbing & repair

(G-16269)
SCOTTS COMPANY LLC
Also Called: Vigliotti's Great Garden
445 Horseblock Rd (11980-9629)
PHONE.................................631 816-2831
Charles Vigliotti, *President*
Richard Schwerer, *Manager*
EMP: 20
SALES (corp-wide): 2.6B **Publicly Held**
WEB: www.licompost.com
SIC: 2875 5261 5083 2421 Compost; fertilizer; landscaping equipment; sawmills & planing mills, general
HQ: The Scotts Company Llc
14111 Scottslawn Rd
Marysville OH 43040
937 644-0011

(G-16270)
SEARLES GRAPHICS INC (PA)
56 Old Dock Rd (11980-9701)
PHONE.................................631 345-2202
Kenneth Searles, *President*
Richard Searles, *Vice Pres*
Gary Lorandini, *Prdtn Mgr*
Leigh Searles, *CFO*
Ted Demaio, *Manager*
EMP: 35
SALES (est): 4.5MM **Privately Held**
WEB: www.searlesgraphics.com
SIC: 2752 Commercial printing, offset

(G-16271)
SHAD INDUSTRIES INC
7 Old Dock Rd Unit 1 (11980-9637)
PHONE.................................631 504-6028
Lenore A Veltry, *President*
EMP: 5
SALES (est): 457.1K **Privately Held**
SIC: 3692 Primary batteries, dry & wet

(G-16272)
SOKOLIN LLC (PA)
Also Called: Sokolin Wine
445 Sills Rd Unit K (11980)
P.O. Box 1206, Bridgehampton (11932-1206)
PHONE.................................631 537-4434
Benjamin Calloway, *Vice Pres*
David Smydo, *Mng Member*
Daron Watson, *Consultant*
Dave Sokolin,
EMP: 27 **EST:** 1934
SQ FT: 15,000
SALES (est): 4.3MM **Privately Held**
SIC: 2084 Wines

(G-16273)
SWITCHES AND SENSORS INC
86 Horseblock Rd Unit J (11980-9743)
PHONE.................................631 924-2167
Joe Calvitto, *President*
Rudolph Baldeo, *Engineer*
EMP: 10
SQ FT: 6,200
SALES (est): 1.6MM **Privately Held**
SIC: 3625 Switches, electronic applications

(G-16274)
TIMTRONICS LLC
35 Old Dock Rd (11980-9702)
PHONE....................................631 345-6509
Prakash Khatri, *President*
William Krause, *Mng Member*
EMP: 4
SALES: 5MM **Privately Held**
SIC: 3826 Differential thermal analysis instruments

(G-16275)
TRIBOLOGY INC
Also Called: Tech Lube
35 Old Dock Rd (11980-9702)
PHONE....................................631 345-3000
William Krause, *President*
Bruce Stebbins, *President*
Paul Anderson, *Mktg Dir*
▲ EMP: 25
SQ FT: 21,000
SALES (est): 6MM **Privately Held**
WEB: www.techlube.com
SIC: 2992 2842 Oils & greases, blending & compounding; specialty cleaning, polishes & sanitation goods

(G-16276)
TWIN PANE INSULATED GL CO INC
86 Horseblock Rd Unit D (11980-9743)
P.O. Box 279 (11980-0279)
PHONE....................................631 924-1060
William F Willett, *President*
Rachel Willett, *Treasurer*
EMP: 15
SQ FT: 11,000
SALES (est): 2.8MM **Privately Held**
SIC: 3211 5039 Construction glass; glass construction materials

(G-16277)
US EPOXY INC
11 Old Dock Rd Unit 7 (11980-9622)
PHONE....................................800 332-3883
Edward Beller, *President*
EMP: 5
SQ FT: 3,000
SALES (est): 371.1K **Privately Held**
SIC: 2891 Epoxy adhesives

(G-16278)
W J ALBRO MACHINE WORKS INC
Also Called: Albro Gear & Instrument
86 Horseblock Rd Unit L (11980-9743)
PHONE....................................631 345-0657
Kevin Albro, *President*
William Albro, *Vice Pres*
William Ambro Jr, *Treasurer*
EMP: 6
SQ FT: 2,000
SALES (est): 775K **Privately Held**
SIC: 3599 3728 3621 3566 Custom machinery; gears, aircraft power transmission; aircraft propellers & associated equipment; motors & generators; speed changers, drives & gears; iron & steel forgings

(G-16279)
XENTAUR CORPORATION
84 Horseblock Rd Unit G (11980-9742)
PHONE....................................631 345-3434
Christopher Mueller, *CEO*
Craig Allshouse, *President*
Brian Flanagan, *Engineer*
Betty Kenyon, *Controller*
David Hailey, *Manager*
EMP: 23
SALES (est): 5.4MM **Privately Held**
WEB: www.xentaur.com
SIC: 3823 Industrial instrmnts msrmnt display/control process variable

Yonkers
Westchester County

(G-16280)
AD IMAGE INC
646 Saw Mill River Rd (10710-4013)
P.O. Box 2038, River Vale NJ (07675-9001)
PHONE....................................914 476-0000
Jeff Klein, *President*
Brett Radmin, *Vice Pres*
EMP: 25
SQ FT: 3,500
SALES: 2.5MM **Privately Held**
WEB: www.greek101.com
SIC: 2759 Screen printing

(G-16281)
ALETEIA USA INC
86 Main St Ste 303 (10701-8805)
PHONE....................................914 502-1855
Axel D'Epinay, *CFO*
EMP: 5
SQ FT: 900
SALES (est): 157.9K **Privately Held**
SIC: 2741

(G-16282)
ALPHA-EN CORPORATION (PA)
28 Wells Ave Ste 2 (10701-7045)
PHONE....................................914 418-2000
Sam Pitroda, *CEO*
Jerome I Feldman, *Ch of Bd*
Jim Kilman, *Vice Ch Bd*
Michael Feldman, *Managing Dir*
George McKeegan, *Vice Pres*
EMP: 8
SQ FT: 8,000
SALES (est): 1.3MM **Publicly Held**
SIC: 2819 6794 Lithium compounds, inorganic; patent buying, licensing, leasing

(G-16283)
ALTMAN STAGE LIGHTING CO INC
Also Called: Altman Lighting
57 Alexander St (10701-2714)
PHONE....................................914 476-7987
Robert Altman, *Ch of Bd*
Russell Altman, *Business Mgr*
Dwarak Parvatum, *COO*
Chris Fennell, *Warehouse Mgr*
Eva Garcia, *Purchasing*
▲ EMP: 125 EST: 1953
SQ FT: 75,000
SALES (est): 42.9MM **Privately Held**
WEB: www.altmanlighting.com
SIC: 3648 3646 Stage lighting equipment; commercial indusl & institutional electric lighting fixtures

(G-16284)
AMERICAN CANVAS BINDERS CORP
430 Nepperhan Ave (10701-6601)
PHONE....................................914 969-0300
Richard Maslowski, *President*
EMP: 6
SQ FT: 10,000
SALES (est): 412K **Privately Held**
SIC: 2241 Narrow fabric mills

(G-16285)
AMERICAN SUGAR REFINING INC
1 Federal St (10705-1079)
PHONE....................................914 376-3386
Stacey Shaefer, *Project Engr*
Becky Serafini, *Marketing Staff*
Michael Mahoney, *Manager*
Kenneth Blanch, *Director*
Phil Nizza, *Director*
EMP: 26
SALES (est): 4MM **Privately Held**
SIC: 2062 Cane sugar refining

(G-16286)
APF MANAGEMENT COMPANY LLC
60 Fullerton Ave (10704-1097)
PHONE....................................914 665-5400
Max Munn, *CEO*

EMP: 110
SALES (est): 8.7MM **Privately Held**
SIC: 3231 Framed mirrors

(G-16287)
APF MANUFACTURING COMPANY LLC (PA)
Also Called: Apf Munn Master Frame Makers
60 Fullerton Ave (10704-1097)
PHONE....................................914 963-6300
Oudit Harbhajan,
EMP: 33 EST: 2014
SQ FT: 52,000
SALES (est): 4.2MM **Privately Held**
SIC: 2499 3231 Picture & mirror frames, wood; framed mirrors

(G-16288)
API INTERNATIONAL GROUP LLC
1767 Ctr Park Ave Ste 277 (10710)
PHONE....................................877 215-0017
▲ EMP: 5
SALES (est): 312.7K **Privately Held**
SIC: 2822 3561 Synthetic rubber; pumps & pumping equipment

(G-16289)
BARRON METAL PRODUCTS INC
286 Nepperhan Ave (10701-3403)
PHONE....................................914 965-1232
Richard Cleary, *President*
Robert Cleary, *Vice Pres*
EMP: 20
SQ FT: 15,000
SALES (est): 1.9MM **Privately Held**
SIC: 3544 3469 Special dies & tools; metal stampings

(G-16290)
BARTIZAN DATA SYSTEMS LLC
217 Riverdale Ave (10705-1131)
PHONE....................................914 965-7977
Lewis C Hoff,
Elizabeth Mazei,
EMP: 25
SQ FT: 43,000
SALES (est): 1.9MM **Privately Held**
WEB: www.bartizan.com
SIC: 3555 Engraving machinery & equipment, except plates

(G-16291)
BELMAY HOLDING CORPORATION
Also Called: Scent 2 Market
1 Odell Plz Ste 123 (10701-6800)
PHONE....................................914 376-1515
Theodore Kesten, *CEO*
Greg Banwer, *Vice Pres*
Alan Kesten, *Treasurer*
▲ EMP: 25 EST: 1967
SQ FT: 26,000
SALES (est): 9.5MM **Privately Held**
WEB: www.belmay.com
SIC: 2844 Hair preparations, including shampoos

(G-16292)
BRUCCI LTD
861 Nepperhan Ave (10703-2013)
PHONE....................................914 965-0707
Murray Bober, *Ch of Bd*
Howard Marcus, *Vice Pres*
Allan Shapiro, *Treasurer*
EMP: 25
SQ FT: 10,800
SALES (est): 3.8MM **Privately Held**
SIC: 2844 5399 Cosmetic preparations; warehouse club stores

(G-16293)
CAROLINAS DESSERTS INC
1562 Central Park Ave (10710-6001)
PHONE....................................914 779-4000
EMP: 8
SALES (est): 577.5K **Privately Held**
SIC: 2051 Bakery: wholesale or wholesale/retail combined

(G-16294)
CAROLYN RAY INC
578 Nepperhan Ave Ste C10 (10701-6670)
PHONE....................................914 476-0619

Carolyn Ray, *President*
EMP: 6
SALES (est): 695.4K **Privately Held**
WEB: www.carolynray.com
SIC: 2261 Finishing plants, cotton

(G-16295)
CEP TECHNOLOGIES CORPORATION (PA)
763 Saw Mill River Rd (10710-4001)
PHONE....................................914 968-4100
Kenneth W Kaufman, *President*
Francine Kaufman, *Vice Pres*
▲ EMP: 48 EST: 1960
SQ FT: 22,000
SALES (est): 10.4MM **Privately Held**
SIC: 3469 Stamping metal for the trade

(G-16296)
CLOVER WIRE FORMING CO INC
1021 Saw Mill River Rd (10710-3292)
PHONE....................................914 375-0400
George Margareten, *President*
▲ EMP: 30 EST: 1957
SQ FT: 35,000
SALES (est): 5.8MM **Privately Held**
WEB: www.cloverwire.com
SIC: 3496 3316 Miscellaneous fabricated wire products; cold finishing of steel shapes

(G-16297)
CONSUMER REPORTS INC (PA)
Also Called: CONSUMERS UNION
101 Truman Ave (10703-1044)
PHONE....................................914 378-2000
Walter D Bristol, *Ch of Bd*
James Guest, *President*
Marta Tellado, *President*
Jeff Bartlett, *Editor*
Marvin Lipman, *Editor*
EMP: 400 EST: 1936
SQ FT: 180,000
SALES (est): 241.7MM **Privately Held**
SIC: 2741 2721 7389 Miscellaneous publishing; magazines: publishing only, not printed on site; fund raising organizations

(G-16298)
COSTELLO BROS PETROLEUM CORP (PA)
990 Mclean Ave Ste 3 (10704-4101)
PHONE....................................914 237-3189
Frank Costello, *President*
Kristopher Costello, *Vice Pres*
EMP: 6
SQ FT: 1,200
SALES (est): 737.7K **Privately Held**
SIC: 2999 5983 Fuel briquettes & waxes; fuel oil dealers

(G-16299)
CREATIVE SOLUTIONS GROUP INC (PA)
Also Called: Diam International
555 Tuckahoe Rd (10710-5709)
PHONE....................................914 771-4200
Edward Winder, *CEO*
Williaml Ecker, *Ch of Bd*
▲ EMP: 500
SALES (est): 84.5MM **Privately Held**
WEB: www.diam-int.com
SIC: 3993 Displays & cutouts, window & lobby

(G-16300)
DAYLEEN INTIMATES INC
Also Called: Dominique Intimate Apparel
540 Nepperhan Ave (10701-6630)
PHONE....................................914 969-5900
Mike Chernoff, *President*
▲ EMP: 24
SQ FT: 20,000
SALES (est): 6MM **Privately Held**
SIC: 2341 4225 Women's & children's undergarments; general warehousing & storage

(G-16301)
DIMAIO MILLWORK CORPORATION
12 Bright Pl (10705-1342)
PHONE....................................914 476-1937
Ralph Dimaio Jr, *President*
Oren McDermid, *Project Mgr*

2020 Harris
New York Manufacturers Directory
▲ = Import ▼=Export
◆ =Import/Export

EMP: 35
SQ FT: 20,000
SALES (est): 5.5MM **Privately Held**
WEB: www.dimaiomillwork.com
SIC: 2431 Millwork

(G-16302)
DOLLAR POPULAR INC
473 S Broadway (10705-3249)
P.O. Box 312150, Jamaica (11431-2150)
PHONE..............................914 375-0361
Muhammad Irfan, *Ch of Bd*
EMP: 9 **EST:** 2008
SALES (est): 713.4K **Privately Held**
SIC: 3643 Outlets, electric: convenience

(G-16303)
DOMINO FOODS INC
Also Called: Domino Sugar
1 Federal St (10705-1079)
PHONE..............................800 729-4840
Laura Harkins, *Vice Pres*
Maria Machita, *Vice Pres*
Armando Tabernilla, *Vice Pres*
Robert Fuller, *Engineer*
Gaston Cantenes, *Manager*
EMP: 13
SALES (corp-wide): 2B **Privately Held**
SIC: 2062 Granulated cane sugar from
purchased raw sugar or syrup
HQ: Domino Foods Inc.
99 Wood Ave S Ste 901
Iselin NJ 08830
732 590-1173

(G-16304)
ECKER WINDOW CORP
1 Odell Plz (10701-1402)
PHONE..............................914 776-0000
Robert Ecker, *CEO*
Jim De Koch, *Vice Pres*
David Ecker, *Vice Pres*
Howard Ecker, *Vice Pres*
Harold Morales, *Technology*
EMP: 100
SQ FT: 5,000
SALES (est): 22.3MM **Privately Held**
SIC: 2431 1751 Windows & window parts
& trim, wood; window & door installation &
erection

(G-16305)
ECONOCRAFT WORLDWIDE
MFG INC
56 Worth St Frnt Unit (10701-5508)
PHONE..............................914 966-2280
Shlomo Malki, *President*
Eran Malki, *Vice Pres*
Amir Malki, *Admin Sec*
▼ **EMP:** 5
SQ FT: 27,000
SALES (est): 907.3K **Privately Held**
WEB: www.econocraft.com
SIC: 3589 Car washing machinery

(G-16306)
ELECTRONIC DEVICES INC
(HQ)
Also Called: E D I
21 Gray Oaks Ave (10710-3205)
PHONE..............................914 965-4400
Jimmy Huang, *President*
Nancy Alcantara, *General Mgr*
Steven Huang, *Vice Pres*
Henry Kolokowsky, *Vice Pres*
Mary Natrella, *Accounting Mgr*
▲ **EMP:** 30
SQ FT: 45,000
SALES (est): 1.2MM **Privately Held**
WEB: www.edidiodes.com
SIC: 3674 5065 Rectifiers, solid state;
diodes, solid state (germanium, silicon,
etc.); solid state electronic devices; elec-
tronic parts & equipment
PA: North Technology Inc
161 Tices Ln
East Brunswick NJ 08816
732 390-2828

(G-16307)
EMPIRE OPEN MRI
1915 Central Park Ave # 25 (10710-2949)
PHONE..............................914 961-1777
Michael Singer, *Owner*
EMP: 6

SALES (est): 541.9K **Privately Held**
SIC: 3845 Ultrasonic scanning devices,
medical

(G-16308)
FABRIC CONCEPTS FOR
INDUSTRY
Also Called: Awning Man, The
354 Ashburton Ave (10701-6014)
PHONE..............................914 375-2565
Daniel Burke, *President*
EMP: 17
SALES (est): 1.5MM **Privately Held**
SIC: 2394 Awnings, fabric: made from pur-
chased materials

(G-16309)
FITZGERALD PUBLISHING CO
INC
Also Called: Golden Legacy Ilstrd Histry
1853 Central Park Ave # 8 (10710-2948)
PHONE..............................914 793-5016
Bertram Fitzgerald, *President*
Jeanette Fitzgerald, *Vice Pres*
EMP: 5
SALES (est): 300K **Privately Held**
SIC: 2741 Miscellaneous publishing

(G-16310)
FLEETCOM INC
1081 Yonkers Ave (10704-3123)
PHONE..............................914 776-5582
Mike Rosenzweig, *President*
Melissa Duffy, *Representative*
EMP: 15 **EST:** 1984
SALES (est): 1MM **Privately Held**
SIC: 3663 Radio broadcasting & communi-
cations equipment

(G-16311)
FOWLER ROUTE CO INC
25 Sunnyside Dr (10705-1763)
PHONE..............................917 653-4640
EMP: 56
SALES (corp-wide): 14MM **Privately
Held**
SIC: 3582 Commercial laundry equipment
PA: Fowler Route Co., Inc.
565 Rahway Ave
Union NJ 07083
908 686-3400

(G-16312)
GANNETT STLLITE INFO NTWRK
INC
Also Called: Herald Statesman
1 Odell Plz (10701-1402)
PHONE..............................914 965-5000
John Gambrill, *Branch Mgr*
EMP: 50
SALES (corp-wide): 2.9B **Publicly Held**
WEB: www.usatoday.com
SIC: 2711 Newspapers: publishing only,
not printed on site
HQ: Gannett Satellite Information Network,
Llc
7950 Jones Branch Dr
Mc Lean VA 22102
703 854-6000

(G-16313)
GLOBAL LIGHTING INC
201 Saw Mill River Rd 3 (10701-5711)
PHONE..............................914 591-4095
Nadeem Razi, *CEO*
EMP: 8
SALES (est): 227.5K **Privately Held**
SIC: 3646 5063 Chandeliers, commercial;
lighting fixtures

(G-16314)
GOLDEN RENEWABLE ENERGY
LLC
430 Nepperhan Ave (10701-6601)
PHONE..............................914 920-9800
Michael Moreno, *COO*
George Allen, *Engineer*
Nicholas Canosa,
Franklin Canosa,
Jason Provost,
EMP: 5
SALES (est): 950K **Privately Held**
SIC: 2869 Fuels

(G-16315)
GRAPHITE METALLIZING CORP
(PA)
Also Called: Graphalloy
1050 Nepperhan Ave (10703-1432)
PHONE..............................914 968-8400
Eben T Walker, *Ch of Bd*
Viridiana Bermejo, *Business Mgr*
Giovanni Loconte, *Plant Mgr*
Audrey Tostanoski, *Purchasing*
James Cox, *Engineer*
◆ **EMP:** 190 **EST:** 1913
SQ FT: 95,000
SALES (est): 36MM **Privately Held**
WEB: www.graphalloy.com
SIC: 3624 Brushes & brush stock contacts,
electric

(G-16316)
GREYSTON BAKERY INC
104 Alexander St (10701-2535)
PHONE..............................914 375-1510
Michael Brady, *Ch of Bd*
Koren Pitts, *Clerk*
◆ **EMP:** 130
SQ FT: 10,000
SALES (est): 22.5MM
SALES (corp-wide): 2.1MM **Privately
Held**
WEB: www.greystonbakery.com
SIC: 2051 Cakes, pies & pastries
PA: Greyston Foundation Inc.
21 Park Ave
Yonkers NY 10703
914 376-3900

(G-16317)
HANA SHEET METAL INC
9 Celli Pl 11 (10701-4805)
PHONE..............................914 377-0773
Awni A Hana, *Ch of Bd*
EMP: 8
SALES (est): 1.5MM **Privately Held**
SIC: 3444 Sheet metalwork

(G-16318)
HEMISPHERE NOVELTIES INC
167 Saw Mill River Rd 3c (10701-6621)
P.O. Box 1240 (10703-8240)
PHONE..............................914 378-4100
Max Wolfeld, *President*
Jeffrey Wolfeld, *Corp Secy*
◆ **EMP:** 25
SQ FT: 12,000
SALES (est): 3.6MM **Privately Held**
WEB: www.hemispherenovelties.com
SIC: 3172 3965 5091 5131 Personal
leather goods; fasteners, buttons, nee-
dles & pins; fishing tackle; buttons; belt &
buckle assembly kits

(G-16319)
HIGHER POWER INDUSTRIES
INC
11 Sunny Slope Ter (10703-1714)
PHONE..............................914 709-9800
Warren J Azzara, *President*
Anna Dibello Battista, *Vice Pres*
EMP: 9
SQ FT: 5,500
SALES (est): 8MM **Privately Held**
SIC: 3743 Locomotives & parts

(G-16320)
HORNE ORGANIZATION INC (PA)
15 Arthur Pl (10701-1702)
PHONE..............................914 572-1330
Leon H Horne Jr, *President*
Jackie Arce, *Office Mgr*
EMP: 10 **EST:** 1974
SQ FT: 1,500
SALES (est): 2.6MM **Privately Held**
SIC: 2752 7336 Commercial printing, litho-
graphic; graphic arts & related design

(G-16321)
ITR INDUSTRIES INC (PA)
441 Saw Mill River Rd (10701-4913)
PHONE..............................914 964-7063
Mario F Rolla, *Ch of Bd*
Adrienne Rola, *President*
Peter M Rolla, *President*
Brian Fialkowski, *General Mgr*
Gary Drossman, *CFO*
▲ **EMP:** 21

SALES (est): 201.7MM **Privately Held**
SIC: 3431 3429 3446 3088 Shower
stalls, metal; manufactured hardware
(general); architectural metalwork; shower
stalls, fiberglass & plastic

(G-16322)
J KENDALL LLC
Also Called: J K Fertility
71 Belvedere Dr (10705-2813)
PHONE..............................646 739-4956
Julius K Smalls, *CEO*
EMP: 5
SALES (est): 370K **Privately Held**
SIC: 2759 Screen printing

(G-16323)
KAWASAKI RAIL CAR INC (DH)
29 Wells Ave Bldg 4 (10701-8815)
PHONE..............................914 376-4700
Hiroji Iwasaki, *CEO*
Yuichi Yamamoto, *President*
Steven Vangellow, *General Mgr*
Yoshinori Kanehana, *Exec VP*
Quinn Bond, *Project Mgr*
▲ **EMP:** 197
SQ FT: 150,000
SALES (est): 79.2MM **Privately Held**
SIC: 3743 Railroad equipment, except lo-
comotives; railway motor cars; train cars
& equipment, freight or passenger
HQ: Kawasaki Motors Manufacturing Corp.,
U.S.A.
6600 Nw 27th St
Lincoln NE 68524
402 476-6600

(G-16324)
KIMBER MFG INC (PA)
1120 Saw Mill River Rd (10710-3224)
PHONE..............................888 243-4522
Leslie Edelmen, *Ch of Bd*
Kieran Kelly, *Mfg Mgr*
Bill Southward, *Mfg Mgr*
Chris Dennis, *Production*
Donald Little, *Engineer*
◆ **EMP:** 220
SQ FT: 50,000
SALES (est): 79.1MM **Privately Held**
WEB: www.kimbermfg.com
SIC: 3599 Machine shop, jobbing & repair

(G-16325)
KIMBER MFG INC
1 Lawton St (10705-2617)
PHONE..............................406 758-2222
Greg Grogan, *Vice Pres*
Denis Morland, *Production*
Barry Volaski, *Purchasing*
Mikhail Borin, *Engineer*
Lucio Di Trolio, *Engineer*
EMP: 24
SALES (corp-wide): 79.1MM **Privately
Held**
WEB: www.kimbermfg.com
SIC: 3599 Machine shop, jobbing & repair
PA: Kimber Mfg., Inc.
1120 Saw Mill River Rd
Yonkers NY 10710
888 243-4522

(G-16326)
LEGGIADRO INTERNATIONAL
INC (PA)
65 Main St 2 (10701-2739)
PHONE..............................212 997-8766
Brooks Ross, *President*
Ann Ross, *Corp Secy*
◆ **EMP:** 50
SALES (est): 9.2MM **Privately Held**
SIC: 2339 Sportswear, women's

(G-16327)
LESER ENTERPRISES LTD
Also Called: Color Story
1767 Central Park Ave # 514 (10710-2828)
PHONE..............................212 832-8013
Robert Leser, *President*
EMP: 1
SALES (est): 1.3MM **Privately Held**
WEB: www.colorstory.com
SIC: 3911 Jewelry, precious metal

(G-16328)
LIGHTING BY DOM YONKERS INC
Also Called: Sparkle Light Manufacturing
253 S Broadway (10705-1351)
PHONE....................914 968-8700
Dominick Di Gennaro Jr, *President*
EMP: 5 EST: 1979
SQ FT: 5,000
SALES (est): 640K **Privately Held**
SIC: 3646 Commercial indusl & institutional electric lighting fixtures

(G-16329)
M SANTOLIQUIDO CORP
Also Called: San Signs & Awnings
925 Saw Mill River Rd (10710-3238)
PHONE....................914 375-6674
Michael Santoliquido, *President*
Lucille Santoliquido, *Vice Pres*
EMP: 11
SQ FT: 10,000
SALES (est): 1.3MM **Privately Held**
WEB: www.sansigns.com
SIC: 3993 Electric signs

(G-16330)
MAGNIFICAT INC
86 Main St Ste 303 (10701-8805)
P.O. Box 822 (10702-0822)
PHONE....................914 502-1820
Fleurus Mame, *CEO*
Romain Lize, *Exec VP*
Axel D'Epinay, *CFO*
Francois Piebo, *Accountant*
◆ EMP: 18 EST: 1998
SALES (est): 2.8MM
SALES (corp-wide): 51.4K **Privately Held**
SIC: 2721 Periodicals
PA: Magnificat Films
     10 Rue De Penthievre
     Paris
     954 464-343

(G-16331)
MARBLE WORKS INC
681 Saw Mill River Rd (10710-4004)
PHONE....................914 376-3653
Sabo Barmaksiz, *President*
Sezen Barmaksiz, *Opers Dir*
▲ EMP: 30
SALES (est): 3.5MM **Privately Held**
SIC: 3281 Granite, cut & shaped; marble, building: cut & shaped

(G-16332)
MARPLEX FURNITURE CORPORATION
167 Saw Mill Rver Rd Fl 1 Flr 1 (10701)
PHONE....................914 969-7755
Peter Bizzarro, *President*
EMP: 5
SQ FT: 13,000
SALES (est): 527.4K **Privately Held**
SIC: 2541 Display fixtures, wood

(G-16333)
MICROMOLD PRODUCTS INC
7 Odell Plz 133 (10701-1407)
PHONE....................914 969-2850
Arthur Lukach, *Ch of Bd*
Justin Lukach, *President*
Yuri Zhuravel, *Production*
Frank Pino, *Human Resources*
Tricia Lombardo, *Sales Staff*
EMP: 25 EST: 1954
SQ FT: 13,000
SALES (est): 5.3MM **Privately Held**
WEB: www.micromold.com
SIC: 3089 3494 3053 3084 Plastic containers, except foam; valves & pipe fittings; gaskets, packing & sealing devices; plastics pipe; steel pipe & tubes; fabricated pipe & fittings

(G-16334)
MIRROR-TECH MANUFACTURING CO
286 Nepperhan Ave (10701-3403)
PHONE....................914 965-1232
Richard Cleary, *President*
EMP: 16 EST: 1961
SQ FT: 7,000

SALES: 750K **Privately Held**
SIC: 3231 Mirrored glass; mirrors, truck & automobile: made from purchased glass

(G-16335)
OCTOPUS ADVANCED SYSTEMS INC
27 Covington Rd (10710-3515)
PHONE....................914 771-6110
Nikolai Prokhorenkov, *Ch of Bd*
EMP: 1
SALES (est): 2MM **Privately Held**
SIC: 3669 Emergency alarms

(G-16336)
ON LINE POWER TECHNOLOGIES
113 Sunnyside Dr (10705-2830)
PHONE....................914 968-4440
Linda Hack, *President*
Bruce Hack, *Vice Pres*
EMP: 2
SALES (est): 10MM **Privately Held**
SIC: 3568 5063 7389 Power transmission equipment; electrical apparatus & equipment;

(G-16337)
OUREM IRON WORKS INC
498 Nepperhan Ave Ste 5 (10701-6604)
PHONE....................914 476-4856
Arthur Viera, *President*
EMP: 12 EST: 1977
SQ FT: 25,000
SALES (est): 2.9MM **Privately Held**
SIC: 3446 1799 Fences or posts, ornamental iron or steel; fence construction

(G-16338)
P PASCAL INC
Also Called: P Pascal Coffee Roasters
960 Nepperhan Ave (10703-1726)
P.O. Box 347 (10703-0347)
PHONE....................914 969-7933
Dean Pialtos, *President*
James Ranni, *Corp Secy*
Barbara Pialtos, *Vice Pres*
Charles Pialtos, *Vice Pres*
EMP: 27
SQ FT: 15,000
SALES (est): 4.4MM **Privately Held**
SIC: 2095 Roasted coffee

(G-16339)
PANE DORO
166 Ludlow St (10705-1036)
PHONE....................914 964-0043
Roger Nehme, *Owner*
EMP: 15
SALES (est): 986.1K **Privately Held**
SIC: 2051 Bread, cake & related products

(G-16340)
PENNYSAVER GROUP INC
80 Alexander St (10701-2715)
PHONE....................914 966-1400
Ed Levitt, *Manager*
EMP: 10
SALES (corp-wide): 7.6MM **Privately Held**
WEB: www.nysaver.com
SIC: 2711 Newspapers, publishing & printing
PA: Pennysaver Group Inc.
     510 Fifth Ave
     Pelham NY
     914 592-5222

(G-16341)
PETER RACING
Also Called: Jaguars
73 Market St (10710-7616)
PHONE....................914 968-4150
Michael Demartino, *Vice Pres*
Scott Massey, *Vice Pres*
Steven Ziff, *Vice Pres*
Chris Sutton, *Accounts Exec*
Jeff Miranda, *Sales Staff*
EMP: 48
SALES (est): 971K **Privately Held**
SIC: 2273 Carpets & rugs

(G-16342)
PIETRO DEMARCO IMPORTERS INC
1185 Saw Mill River Rd (10710-3240)
PHONE....................914 969-3201
Pietro Demarco, *President*
Anthony Demarco, *Vice Pres*
▲ EMP: 10
SALES (est): 1.2MM **Privately Held**
SIC: 2079 Olive oil

(G-16343)
POMPIAN MANUFACTURING CO INC
280 Nepperhan Ave (10701-3403)
PHONE....................914 476-7076
Fax: 914 476-7095
EMP: 8
SQ FT: 10,000
SALES: 900K **Privately Held**
SIC: 3645 5063 Mfg & Whol Electrical Equipment & Electronic Ballast

(G-16344)
PREPAC DESIGNS INC
25 Abner Pl (10704-3015)
PHONE....................914 524-7800
Manuel Mendez, *President*
Noemi Pabon, *Relations*
▲ EMP: 5
SQ FT: 1,500
SALES: 2.5MM **Privately Held**
WEB: www.designerschoiceline.com
SIC: 3161 Luggage

(G-16345)
REFINED SUGARS INC
1 Federal St (10705-1079)
PHONE....................914 963-2400
Jack Lay, *Principal*
EMP: 6 EST: 2009
SALES (est): 630.9K **Privately Held**
SIC: 2062 Cane sugar refining

(G-16346)
ROBERT VIGGIANI
Also Called: Irv & Vic Sportswear Co
37 Vredenburgh Ave Ste B (10704-2150)
PHONE....................914 423-4046
Robert Viggiani, *Owner*
EMP: 5
SQ FT: 975
SALES (est): 510.6K **Privately Held**
SIC: 2329 5699 Riding clothes:, men's, youths' & boys'; riding apparel

(G-16347)
RUMSEY CORP
Also Called: B2b Cleaning Services
15 Rumsey Rd (10705-1623)
PHONE....................914 751-3640
Anna Negron, *President*
EMP: 6
SALES (est): 300K **Privately Held**
SIC: 3672 7349 Printed circuit boards; building & office cleaning services; office cleaning or charring; cleaning service, industrial or commercial; window cleaning

(G-16348)
SKIL-CARE CORPORATION
29 Wells Ave Bldg 4 (10701-8815)
PHONE....................914 963-2040
Martin Prenskean, *Ch of Bd*
Arnold Silverman, *President*
Stephen Warhaftig, *Vice Pres*
Jeffrey Steckler, *Mktg Coord*
▲ EMP: 135
SQ FT: 55,000
SALES (est): 17.7MM **Privately Held**
WEB: www.skilcare.com
SIC: 3842 2392 2241 Wheelchairs; household furnishings; narrow fabric mills

(G-16349)
STANSON AUTOMATED LLC
145 Saw Mill River Rd # 2 (10701-6615)
PHONE....................866 505-7826
Stewart Iskowitz, *Mng Member*
Joel Iskowitz, *Mng Member*
EMP: 10
SALES (est): 910K **Privately Held**
SIC: 3578 Automatic teller machines (ATM)

(G-16350)
STAR DESK PAD CO INC
60 Mclean Ave (10705-2317)
PHONE....................914 963-9400
Sidney Newman, *President*
▲ EMP: 45
SQ FT: 60,000
SALES: 2.4MM **Privately Held**
WEB: www.stardesk.com
SIC: 3199 3999 Desk sets, leather; desk pads, except paper

(G-16351)
T C DUNHAM PAINT COMPANY INC
761 Nepperhan Ave (10703-2313)
PHONE....................914 969-4202
Isaac Schwartz, *Ch of Bd*
Ely Fisch, *Vice Pres*
Eoy Fisch, *Vice Pres*
EMP: 25
SQ FT: 5,000
SALES (est): 11MM **Privately Held**
WEB: www.dunhampaint.com
SIC: 2851 Paints & paint additives

(G-16352)
TODD SYSTEMS INC
50 Ash St (10701-3900)
PHONE....................914 963-3400
Kenneth Todd, *President*
K H Todd, *Chairman*
Ruthann Todd, *Vice Pres*
◆ EMP: 60 EST: 1964
SQ FT: 25,000
SALES (est): 9.4MM **Privately Held**
WEB: www.toddsystems.com
SIC: 3677 Electronic transformers

(G-16353)
TOPPS-ALL PRODUCTS OF YONKERS
148 Ludlow St Ste 2 (10705-7014)
PHONE....................914 968-4226
Edward J Bolwell Jr, *President*
Keith Cherry, *Education*
Christopher Seitz, *Advisor*
EMP: 15 EST: 1939
SALES (est): 2.5MM **Privately Held**
SIC: 2842 Cleaning or polishing preparations; automobile polish

(G-16354)
VALENTI NECKWEAR CO INC
540 Nepperhan Ave Ste 564 (10701-6611)
PHONE....................914 969-0700
Albert Valentine, *President*
EMP: 8
SALES: 250K **Privately Held**
WEB: www.valentineckwear.com
SIC: 2323 2339 Men's & boys' neckwear; neckwear & ties: women's, misses' & juniors'

(G-16355)
VINYLINE WINDOW AND DOOR INC
636 Saw Mill River Rd (10710-4019)
PHONE....................914 476-3500
Carmen Cangialosi, *President*
Henry Nagani, *Owner*
Robert Gramagila, *Vice Pres*
EMP: 10
SQ FT: 10,000
SALES: 600K **Privately Held**
SIC: 3089 Windows, plastic

(G-16356)
WINESOFT INTERNATIONAL CORP
503 S Broadway Ste 220 (10705-6202)
PHONE....................914 400-6247
Marco Vicens, *Manager*
EMP: 6
SALES (est): 253.2K **Privately Held**
WEB: www.winesoftusa.com
SIC: 7372 Application computer software

(G-16357)
WINGS FOR WHEELS INC
Also Called: Mr Sign
590 Tuckahoe Rd (10710-5736)
PHONE....................914 961-0276
David Lenkowsky, *President*
EMP: 5

SQ FT: 3,000
SALES (est): 160K **Privately Held**
SIC: 3993 Signs & advertising specialties

(G-16358)
YEWTREE MILLWORKS CORP
372 Ashburton Ave (10701-6015)
PHONE..................................914 320-5851
Keith Murphy, *President*
EMP: 5
SALES (est): 266.2K **Privately Held**
SIC: 2851 Paints & allied products

(G-16359)
YONKERS CABINET INC
1179 Yonkers Ave (10704-3210)
PHONE..................................914 668-2133
Wai Hing Yip, *Ch of Bd*
EMP: 7
SALES (est): 755.1K **Privately Held**
SIC: 2434 Wood kitchen cabinets

(G-16360)
YONKERS TIME PUBLISHING CO
Also Called: Martinelli Publications
40 Larkin Plz (10701-2748)
PHONE..................................914 965-4000
Franchesca Martinelli, *Owner*
EMP: 15
SQ FT: 6,000
SALES (est): 520K **Privately Held**
WEB: www.martinellipublications.com
SIC: 2711 Newspapers: publishing only,
  not printed on site

(G-16361)
YONKERS WHL BEER DISTRS INC
424 Riverdale Ave (10705-2908)
PHONE..................................914 963-8600
Richard McDine, *Owner*
EMP: 5
SALES (est): 347.5K **Privately Held**
SIC: 2082 Beer (alcoholic beverage)

York
Livingston County

(G-16362)
DAVIS TRAILER WORLD LLC
Also Called: Davis Trlr World & Cntry Mall
1640 Main St (14592)
P.O. Box 260 (14592-0260)
PHONE..................................585 538-6640
Mike Osterman, *Sales Staff*
Dean Davis,
Susan Davis,
EMP: 10 EST: 1987
SALES (est): 3MM **Privately Held**
WEB: www.davistrailerworld.com
SIC: 3715 Truck trailers

Yorktown Heights
Westchester County

(G-16363)
CROWN DELTA CORPORATION
1550 Front St (10598-4638)
PHONE..................................914 245-8910
Anthony Konopka, *CEO*
Anthony J Konopka, *CFO*
Maureen Barone, *Human Resources*
▲ EMP: 35
SQ FT: 30,000
SALES (est): 9.6MM **Privately Held**
WEB: www.crowndelta.com
SIC: 2869 Silicones

(G-16364)
FOLEYS GRAPHIC CENTER INC
Also Called: Foley Graphics
1661 Front St Ste 3 (10598-4650)
PHONE..................................914 245-3625
Joseph Foley III, *President*
Brenda Piekutowski, *Production*
Katy Foley, *Manager*
EMP: 25
SQ FT: 7,000

SALES (est): 2.7MM **Privately Held**
WEB: www.foleygraphics.com
SIC: 2754 2791 2789 2752 Commercial
  printing, gravure; typesetting; bookbinding
  & related work; commercial printing, lithographic; blueprinting service

(G-16365)
GAME SPORTSWEAR LTD
1401 Front St (10598-4663)
PHONE..................................914 962-1701
Enrico Genovese, *President*
Leslie Tandler, *Vice Pres*
Gina M Furano, *Treasurer*
Virginia Genovese, *Admin Sec*
Jennifer Lopez, *Administration*
▲ EMP: 110
SQ FT: 76,000
SALES (est): 20.3MM **Privately Held**
SIC: 2253 Knit outerwear mills;
  women's & misses' outerwear

(G-16366)
INTERNATIONAL BUS MCHS CORP
IBM
1101 Kitchawan Rd (10598)
P.O. Box 218 (10598-0218)
PHONE..................................914 945-3000
Val Rahmani, *General Mgr*
Sesh Murthy, *Vice Pres*
Margaret Serafin, *Project Mgr*
Chris Suda, *Project Mgr*
Mary Yost, *Project Mgr*
EMP: 3000
SALES (corp-wide): 79.5B **Publicly Held**
WEB: www.ibm.com
SIC: 3571 Electronic computers
PA: International Business Machines Cor-
  poration
  1 New Orchard Rd Ste 1 # 1
  Armonk NY 10504
  914 499-1900

(G-16367)
MAKARENKO STUDIOS INC
2984 Saddle Ridge Dr (10598-2327)
PHONE..................................914 968-7673
Boris Makarenko, *President*
Sviatoslaw Makarenko, *Treasurer*
EMP: 5
SALES (est): 290K **Privately Held**
SIC: 3231 1542 Stained glass: made from
  purchased glass; religious building con-
  struction

(G-16368)
MEGA GRAPHICS INC
1725 Front St Ste 1 (10598-4651)
PHONE..................................914 962-1402
Robert Pierro, *Principal*
EMP: 5
SALES (est): 418.2K **Privately Held**
SIC: 2759 Commercial printing

(G-16369)
NORTHERN TIER PUBLISHING CORP
Also Called: North County News
1520 Front St (10598-4638)
PHONE..................................914 962-4748
EMP: 11
SQ FT: 2,000
SALES (est): 710.7K **Privately Held**
SIC: 2711 Newspapers-Publishing/Printing

(G-16370)
Q OMNI INC
1994 Commerce St (10598-4412)
PHONE..................................914 962-2726
Kwan Lee, *Owner*
EMP: 6
SALES (est): 542.4K **Privately Held**
SIC: 3582 Drycleaning equipment & ma-
  chinery, commercial

(G-16371)
RICHARD ANTHONY CORP
Also Called: Richard Anthony Custom Mllwk
1500 Front St Ste 12 (10598-4648)
P.O. Box 240 (10598-0240)
PHONE..................................914 922-7141
Richard Scavelli, *CEO*
Angela Desiena, *Vice Pres*
EMP: 28

SALES (est): 2.8MM **Privately Held**
SIC: 2431 Millwork

(G-16372)
SIGNS INK LTD
3255 Crompond Rd (10598-3605)
PHONE..................................914 739-9059
Dick Hederson, *President*
Matthew Beachak, *Vice Pres*
Steve Chester, *Sales Mgr*
Timothy Beachak, *Sales Staff*
Esteban Baquero, *Department Mgr*
EMP: 10
SQ FT: 1,000
SALES (est): 1.6MM **Privately Held**
SIC: 3993 Electric signs

(G-16373)
SPITALE CNSTR RESOURCES INC
2025 Crompond Rd (10598-4236)
PHONE..................................914 352-6366
Eric Spitale, *President*
EMP: 6
SALES (est): 780.1K **Privately Held**
SIC: 3479 Painting, coating & hot dipping

(G-16374)
WOODTRONICS INC
1661 Front St Ste 3 (10598-4650)
PHONE..................................914 962-5205
Jan Efraimsen, *President*
EMP: 5
SQ FT: 4,500
SALES (est): 510K **Privately Held**
SIC: 2499 Decorative wood & woodwork

Yorkville
Oneida County

(G-16375)
HUBBELL GALVANIZING INC
5124 Commercial Dr (13495-1109)
P.O. Box 37, New York Mills (13417-0037)
PHONE..................................315 736-8311
Daniel Merritt Hubbell, *President*
EMP: 7
SALES (est): 112.7K **Privately Held**
SIC: 3479 Coating, rust preventive; coating
  electrodes

(G-16376)
O W HUBBELL & SONS INC
Also Called: Hubbell Galvanising
5124 Commercial Dr (13495-1109)
P.O. Box 37, New York Mills (13417-0037)
PHONE..................................315 736-8311
Allen W Hubbell, *Ch of Bd*
Jock Hubbell, *President*
Pete Hubbell, *VP Mktg*
▲ EMP: 35 EST: 1925
SQ FT: 8,000
SALES (est): 5.1MM
SALES (corp-wide): 3.7MM **Privately Held**
WEB: www.hubbellgalvanizing.com
SIC: 3479 Galvanizing of iron, steel or end-
  formed products
PA: W Hubbell & Sons Inc
  5124 Commercial Dr
  Yorkville NY 13495
  315 736-8311

(G-16377)
ORISKANY MANUFACTURING LLC
2 Wurz Ave (13495-1118)
PHONE..................................315 732-4962
Michael Fitzgerald, *CEO*
Don Darling, *Controller*
EMP: 15 EST: 2009
SALES (est): 2.1MM **Privately Held**
SIC: 3999 Manufacturing industries

(G-16378)
ORISKANY MFG TECH LLC
Also Called: Omt
2 Wurz Ave (13495-1118)
PHONE..................................315 732-4962
Dave Pelligrini, *Vice Pres*
Clayton McKeon, *Opers Mgr*
Stephen Palmieri, *Production*
Mike Reile, *Production*

Thomas Dutcher, *Purch Mgr*
▲ EMP: 30
SQ FT: 30,000
SALES (est): 7.4MM **Privately Held**
WEB: www.oriskanymfg.com
SIC: 3441 3317 Fabricated structural
  metal; welded pipe & tubes

(G-16379)
OTIS ELEVATOR COMPANY
5172 Commercial Dr (13495-1110)
PHONE..................................315 736-0167
Nikki Josey, *General Mgr*
Larry Blank, *Superintendent*
Christopher Heatherly, *Superintendent*
Kim Boyle, *Project Mgr*
Derek Mento, *Project Mgr*
EMP: 12
SALES (corp-wide): 66.5B **Publicly Held**
WEB: www.otis.com
SIC: 3534 7699 Elevators & equipment;
  elevators: inspection, service & repair
HQ: Otis Elevator Company
  1 Carrier Pl
  Farmington CT 06032
  860 674-3000

(G-16380)
VICKS LITHOGRAPH & PRTG CORP (PA)
5166 Commercial Dr (13495-1173)
P.O. Box 270 (13495-0270)
PHONE..................................315 272-2401
Dwight E Vicks III, *Ch of Bd*
Dwight E Vicks III, *Ch of Bd*
Dwight E Vicks Jr, *Chairman*
Tom Luker, *Accounts Mgr*
Mike O'Donnell, *Manager*
EMP: 110
SQ FT: 130,000
SALES (est): 22MM **Privately Held**
SIC: 2732 2789 2752 Books: printing
  only; bookbinding & related work; com-
  mercial printing, lithographic

(G-16381)
VICKS LITHOGRAPH & PRTG CORP
5210 Commercial Dr (13495-1111)
P.O. Box 270 (13495-0270)
PHONE..................................315 736-9344
Frank Driscoll, *Manager*
EMP: 130
SALES (est): 3.2MM
SALES (corp-wide): 22MM **Privately Held**
SIC: 2732 2752 Book printing; commercial
  printing, lithographic
PA: Vicks Lithograph & Printing Corp.
  5166 Commercial Dr
  Yorkville NY 13495
  315 272-2401

(G-16382)
W HUBBELL & SONS INC (PA)
5124 Commercial Dr (13495-1109)
P.O. Box 37, New York Mills (13417-0037)
PHONE..................................315 736-8311
Allen W Hubbell, *President*
Allen W Hubbel, *Principal*
Steve Mulvihill, *Principal*
Emmite White, *HR Admin*
Nate Mastro, *Supervisor*
EMP: 40
SQ FT: 8,000
SALES (est): 3.7MM **Privately Held**
SIC: 3479 Galvanizing of iron, steel or end-
  formed products

(G-16383)
WAYNES WELDING INC
66 Calder Ave (13495-1601)
PHONE..................................315 768-6146
Wayne A Ramsey, *President*
EMP: 20
SQ FT: 9,000
SALES (est): 2.7MM **Privately Held**
SIC: 7692 3599 Automotive welding; ma-
  chine shop, jobbing & repair

GEOGRAPHIC

Youngstown
Niagara County

(G-16384)
**KINETIC FUEL TECHNOLOGY
INC**
Also Called: Kinetic Laboratories
1205 Balmer Rd (14174-9797)
PHONE.................................716 745-1461
Timothy M Booth, *Ch of Bd*
Eric Fragale, *President*
EMP: 5
SQ FT: 4,500
SALES (est): 1.2MM **Privately Held**
SIC: 2911 Fuel additives

SIC NO	PRODUCT

A

3291 Abrasive Prdts
2891 Adhesives & Sealants
3563 Air & Gas Compressors
3585 Air Conditioning & Heating Eqpt
3721 Aircraft
3724 Aircraft Engines & Engine Parts
3728 Aircraft Parts & Eqpt, NEC
2812 Alkalies & Chlorine
3363 Aluminum Die Castings
3354 Aluminum Extruded Prdts
3365 Aluminum Foundries
3355 Aluminum Rolling & Drawing, NEC
3353 Aluminum Sheet, Plate & Foil
3483 Ammunition, Large
3826 Analytical Instruments
2077 Animal, Marine Fats & Oils
1231 Anthracite Mining
2389 Apparel & Accessories, NEC
2387 Apparel Belts
3446 Architectural & Ornamental Metal Work
7694 Armature Rewinding Shops
3292 Asbestos products
2952 Asphalt Felts & Coatings
3822 Automatic Temperature Controls
3581 Automatic Vending Machines
3465 Automotive Stampings
2396 Automotive Trimmings, Apparel Findings, Related Prdts

B

2673 Bags: Plastics, Laminated & Coated
2674 Bags: Uncoated Paper & Multiwall
3562 Ball & Roller Bearings
2836 Biological Prdts, Exc Diagnostic Substances
2782 Blankbooks & Looseleaf Binders
3312 Blast Furnaces, Coke Ovens, Steel & Rolling Mills
3564 Blowers & Fans
3732 Boat Building & Repairing
3452 Bolts, Nuts, Screws, Rivets & Washers
2732 Book Printing, Not Publishing
2789 Bookbinding
2731 Books: Publishing & Printing
3131 Boot & Shoe Cut Stock & Findings
2342 Brassieres, Girdles & Garments
2051 Bread, Bakery Prdts Exc Cookies & Crackers
3251 Brick & Structural Clay Tile
3991 Brooms & Brushes
3995 Burial Caskets
2021 Butter

C

3578 Calculating & Accounting Eqpt
2064 Candy & Confectionery Prdts
2033 Canned Fruits, Vegetables & Preserves
2032 Canned Specialties
2394 Canvas Prdts
3624 Carbon & Graphite Prdts
3955 Carbon Paper & Inked Ribbons
3592 Carburetors, Pistons, Rings & Valves
2273 Carpets & Rugs
2823 Cellulosic Man-Made Fibers
3241 Cement, Hydraulic
3253 Ceramic Tile
2043 Cereal Breakfast Foods
2022 Cheese
1479 Chemical & Fertilizer Mining
2899 Chemical Preparations, NEC
2067 Chewing Gum
2361 Children's & Infants' Dresses & Blouses
3261 China Plumbing Fixtures & Fittings
3262 China, Table & Kitchen Articles
2066 Chocolate & Cocoa Prdts
2111 Cigarettes
2121 Cigars
2257 Circular Knit Fabric Mills
3255 Clay Refractories
1459 Clay, Ceramic & Refractory Minerals, NEC
1241 Coal Mining Svcs
3479 Coating & Engraving, NEC
2095 Coffee
3316 Cold Rolled Steel Sheet, Strip & Bars
3582 Commercial Laundry, Dry Clean & Pressing Mchs
2759 Commercial Printing
2754 Commercial Printing: Gravure
2752 Commercial Printing: Lithographic
3646 Commercial, Indl & Institutional Lighting Fixtures

3669 Communications Eqpt, NEC
3577 Computer Peripheral Eqpt, NEC
3572 Computer Storage Devices
3575 Computer Terminals
3271 Concrete Block & Brick
3272 Concrete Prdts
3531 Construction Machinery & Eqpt
1442 Construction Sand & Gravel
2679 Converted Paper Prdts, NEC
3535 Conveyors & Eqpt
2052 Cookies & Crackers
3366 Copper Foundries
1021 Copper Ores
2298 Cordage & Twine
2653 Corrugated & Solid Fiber Boxes
3961 Costume Jewelry & Novelties
2261 Cotton Fabric Finishers
2211 Cotton, Woven Fabric
2074 Cottonseed Oil Mills
3466 Crowns & Closures
1311 Crude Petroleum & Natural Gas
1423 Crushed & Broken Granite
1422 Crushed & Broken Limestone
1429 Crushed & Broken Stone, NEC
3643 Current-Carrying Wiring Devices
2391 Curtains & Draperies
3087 Custom Compounding Of Purchased Plastic Resins
3281 Cut Stone Prdts
3421 Cutlery
2865 Cyclic-Crudes, Intermediates, Dyes & Org Pigments

D

3843 Dental Eqpt & Splys
2835 Diagnostic Substances
2675 Die-Cut Paper & Board
3544 Dies, Tools, Jigs, Fixtures & Indl Molds
1411 Dimension Stone
2047 Dog & Cat Food
3942 Dolls & Stuffed Toys
2591 Drapery Hardware, Window Blinds & Shades
2381 Dress & Work Gloves
2034 Dried Fruits, Vegetables & Soup
1381 Drilling Oil & Gas Wells

E

3263 Earthenware, Whiteware, Table & Kitchen Articles
3634 Electric Household Appliances
3641 Electric Lamps
3694 Electrical Eqpt For Internal Combustion Engines
3629 Electrical Indl Apparatus, NEC
3699 Electrical Machinery, Eqpt & Splys, NEC
3845 Electromedical & Electrotherapeutic Apparatus
3313 Electrometallurgical Prdts
3675 Electronic Capacitors
3677 Electronic Coils & Transformers
3679 Electronic Components, NEC
3571 Electronic Computers
3678 Electronic Connectors
3676 Electronic Resistors
3471 Electroplating, Plating, Polishing, Anodizing & Coloring
3534 Elevators & Moving Stairways
3431 Enameled Iron & Metal Sanitary Ware
2677 Envelopes
2892 Explosives

F

2241 Fabric Mills, Cotton, Wool, Silk & Man-Made
3499 Fabricated Metal Prdts, NEC
3498 Fabricated Pipe & Pipe Fittings
3443 Fabricated Plate Work
3069 Fabricated Rubber Prdts, NEC
3441 Fabricated Structural Steel
2399 Fabricated Textile Prdts, NEC
2295 Fabrics Coated Not Rubberized
2297 Fabrics, Nonwoven
3523 Farm Machinery & Eqpt
3965 Fasteners, Buttons, Needles & Pins
2875 Fertilizers, Mixing Only
2655 Fiber Cans, Tubes & Drums
2091 Fish & Seafoods, Canned & Cured
2092 Fish & Seafoods, Fresh & Frozen
3211 Flat Glass
2087 Flavoring Extracts & Syrups
2045 Flour, Blended & Prepared
2041 Flour, Grain Milling
3824 Fluid Meters & Counters

3593 Fluid Power Cylinders & Actuators
3594 Fluid Power Pumps & Motors
3492 Fluid Power Valves & Hose Fittings
2657 Folding Paperboard Boxes
3556 Food Prdts Machinery
2099 Food Preparations, NEC
3149 Footwear, NEC
2053 Frozen Bakery Prdts
2037 Frozen Fruits, Juices & Vegetables
2038 Frozen Specialties
2371 Fur Goods
2599 Furniture & Fixtures, NEC

G

3944 Games, Toys & Children's Vehicles
3524 Garden, Lawn Tractors & Eqpt
3053 Gaskets, Packing & Sealing Devices
2369 Girls' & Infants' Outerwear, NEC
3221 Glass Containers
3231 Glass Prdts Made Of Purchased Glass
1041 Gold Ores
3321 Gray Iron Foundries
2771 Greeting Card Publishing
3769 Guided Missile/Space Vehicle Parts & Eqpt, NEC
3761 Guided Missiles & Space Vehicles
2861 Gum & Wood Chemicals
3275 Gypsum Prdts

H

3423 Hand & Edge Tools
3425 Hand Saws & Saw Blades
3171 Handbags & Purses
3429 Hardware, NEC
2426 Hardwood Dimension & Flooring Mills
2435 Hardwood Veneer & Plywood
2353 Hats, Caps & Millinery
3433 Heating Eqpt
3536 Hoists, Cranes & Monorails
2252 Hosiery, Except Women's
2251 Hosiery, Women's Full & Knee Length
2392 House furnishings: Textile
3142 House Slippers
3639 Household Appliances, NEC
3651 Household Audio & Video Eqpt
3631 Household Cooking Eqpt
2519 Household Furniture, NEC
3633 Household Laundry Eqpt
3632 Household Refrigerators & Freezers
3635 Household Vacuum Cleaners

I

2097 Ice
2024 Ice Cream
2819 Indl Inorganic Chemicals, NEC
3823 Indl Instruments For Meas, Display & Control
3569 Indl Machinery & Eqpt, NEC
3567 Indl.Process Furnaces & Ovens
3537 Indl Trucks, Tractors, Trailers & Stackers
2813 Industrial Gases
2869 Industrial Organic Chemicals, NEC
3543 Industrial Patterns
1446 Industrial Sand
3491 Industrial Valves
2816 Inorganic Pigments
3825 Instrs For Measuring & Testing Electricity
3519 Internal Combustion Engines, NEC
3462 Iron & Steel Forgings
1011 Iron Ores

J

3915 Jewelers Findings & Lapidary Work
3911 Jewelry: Precious Metal

K

2253 Knit Outerwear Mills
2254 Knit Underwear Mills
2259 Knitting Mills, NEC

L

3821 Laboratory Apparatus & Furniture
2258 Lace & Warp Knit Fabric Mills
3952 Lead Pencils, Crayons & Artist's Mtrls
2386 Leather & Sheep Lined Clothing
3151 Leather Gloves & Mittens
3199 Leather Goods, NEC
3111 Leather Tanning & Finishing
3648 Lighting Eqpt, NEC

S I C

SIC NO	PRODUCT
3274	Lime
3996	Linoleum & Hard Surface Floor Coverings, NEC
2085	Liquors, Distilled, Rectified & Blended
2411	Logging
2992	Lubricating Oils & Greases
3161	Luggage

M

SIC NO	PRODUCT
2098	Macaroni, Spaghetti & Noodles
3545	Machine Tool Access
3541	Machine Tools: Cutting
3542	Machine Tools: Forming
3599	Machinery & Eqpt, Indl & Commercial, NEC
3322	Malleable Iron Foundries
2083	Malt
2082	Malt Beverages
2761	Manifold Business Forms
3999	Manufacturing Industries, NEC
3953	Marking Devices
2515	Mattresses & Bedsprings
3829	Measuring & Controlling Devices, NEC
3586	Measuring & Dispensing Pumps
2011	Meat Packing Plants
3568	Mechanical Power Transmission Eqpt, NEC
2833	Medicinal Chemicals & Botanical Prdts
2329	Men's & Boys' Clothing, NEC
2323	Men's & Boys' Neckwear
2325	Men's & Boys' Separate Trousers & Casual Slacks
2321	Men's & Boys' Shirts
2311	Men's & Boys' Suits, Coats & Overcoats
2322	Men's & Boys' Underwear & Nightwear
2326	Men's & Boys' Work Clothing
3143	Men's Footwear, Exc Athletic
3412	Metal Barrels, Drums, Kegs & Pails
3411	Metal Cans
3442	Metal Doors, Sash, Frames, Molding & Trim
3497	Metal Foil & Leaf
3398	Metal Heat Treating
2514	Metal Household Furniture
1081	Metal Mining Svcs
1099	Metal Ores, NEC
3469	Metal Stampings, NEC
3549	Metalworking Machinery, NEC
2026	Milk
2023	Milk, Condensed & Evaporated
2431	Millwork
3296	Mineral Wool
3295	Minerals & Earths: Ground Or Treated
3532	Mining Machinery & Eqpt
3496	Misc Fabricated Wire Prdts
2741	Misc Publishing
3449	Misc Structural Metal Work
1499	Miscellaneous Nonmetallic Mining
2451	Mobile Homes
3061	Molded, Extruded & Lathe-Cut Rubber Mechanical Goods
3716	Motor Homes
3714	Motor Vehicle Parts & Access
3711	Motor Vehicles & Car Bodies
3751	Motorcycles, Bicycles & Parts
3621	Motors & Generators
3931	Musical Instruments

N

SIC NO	PRODUCT
1321	Natural Gas Liquids
2711	Newspapers: Publishing & Printing
2873	Nitrogenous Fertilizers
3297	Nonclay Refractories
3644	Noncurrent-Carrying Wiring Devices
3364	Nonferrous Die Castings, Exc Aluminum
3463	Nonferrous Forgings
3369	Nonferrous Foundries: Castings, NEC
3357	Nonferrous Wire Drawing
3299	Nonmetallic Mineral Prdts, NEC
1481	Nonmetallic Minerals Svcs, Except Fuels

O

SIC NO	PRODUCT
2522	Office Furniture, Except Wood
3579	Office Machines, NEC
1382	Oil & Gas Field Exploration Svcs
1389	Oil & Gas Field Svcs, NEC
3533	Oil Field Machinery & Eqpt
3851	Ophthalmic Goods
3827	Optical Instruments
3489	Ordnance & Access, NEC
3842	Orthopedic, Prosthetic & Surgical Appliances/Splys

P

SIC NO	PRODUCT
3565	Packaging Machinery
2851	Paints, Varnishes, Lacquers, Enamels
2671	Paper Coating & Laminating for Packaging

SIC NO	PRODUCT
2672	Paper Coating & Laminating, Exc for Packaging
3554	Paper Inds Machinery
2621	Paper Mills
2631	Paperboard Mills
2542	Partitions & Fixtures, Except Wood
2951	Paving Mixtures & Blocks
3951	Pens & Mechanical Pencils
2844	Perfumes, Cosmetics & Toilet Preparations
2721	Periodicals: Publishing & Printing
3172	Personal Leather Goods
2879	Pesticides & Agricultural Chemicals, NEC
2911	Petroleum Refining
2834	Pharmaceuticals
3652	Phonograph Records & Magnetic Tape
2874	Phosphatic Fertilizers
3861	Photographic Eqpt & Splys
2035	Pickled Fruits, Vegetables, Sauces & Dressings
3085	Plastic Bottles
3086	Plastic Foam Prdts
3083	Plastic Laminated Plate & Sheet
3084	Plastic Pipe
3088	Plastic Plumbing Fixtures
3089	Plastic Prdts
3082	Plastic Unsupported Profile Shapes
3081	Plastic Unsupported Sheet & Film
2821	Plastics, Mtrls & Nonvulcanizable Elastomers
2796	Platemaking & Related Svcs
2395	Pleating & Stitching For The Trade
3432	Plumbing Fixture Fittings & Trim, Brass
3264	Porcelain Electrical Splys
2096	Potato Chips & Similar Prdts
3269	Pottery Prdts, NEC
2015	Poultry Slaughtering, Dressing & Processing
3546	Power Hand Tools
3612	Power, Distribution & Specialty Transformers
3448	Prefabricated Metal Buildings & Cmpnts
2452	Prefabricated Wood Buildings & Cmpnts
7372	Prepackaged Software
2048	Prepared Feeds For Animals & Fowls
3229	Pressed & Blown Glassware, NEC
3692	Primary Batteries: Dry & Wet
3399	Primary Metal Prdts, NEC
3339	Primary Nonferrous Metals, NEC
3334	Primary Production Of Aluminum
3331	Primary Smelting & Refining Of Copper
3672	Printed Circuit Boards
2893	Printing Ink
3555	Printing Trades Machinery & Eqpt
2999	Products Of Petroleum & Coal, NEC
2531	Public Building & Related Furniture
2611	Pulp Mills
3561	Pumps & Pumping Eqpt

R

SIC NO	PRODUCT
3663	Radio & T V Communications, Systs & Eqpt, Broadcast/Studio
3671	Radio & T V Receiving Electron Tubes
3743	Railroad Eqpt
3273	Ready-Mixed Concrete
2493	Reconstituted Wood Prdts
3695	Recording Media
3625	Relays & Indl Controls
3645	Residential Lighting Fixtures
2044	Rice Milling
2384	Robes & Dressing Gowns
3547	Rolling Mill Machinery & Eqpt
3351	Rolling, Drawing & Extruding Of Copper
3356	Rolling, Drawing-Extruding Of Nonferrous Metals
3021	Rubber & Plastic Footwear
3052	Rubber & Plastic Hose & Belting

S

SIC NO	PRODUCT
2068	Salted & Roasted Nuts & Seeds
2656	Sanitary Food Containers
2676	Sanitary Paper Prdts
2013	Sausages & Meat Prdts
2421	Saw & Planing Mills
3596	Scales & Balances, Exc Laboratory
2397	Schiffli Machine Embroideries
3451	Screw Machine Prdts
3812	Search, Detection, Navigation & Guidance Systs & Instrs
3341	Secondary Smelting & Refining Of Nonferrous Metals
3674	Semiconductors
3589	Service Ind Machines, NEC
2652	Set-Up Paperboard Boxes
3444	Sheet Metal Work
3731	Shipbuilding & Repairing
2079	Shortening, Oils & Margarine
3993	Signs & Advertising Displays
2262	Silk & Man-Made Fabric Finishers
2221	Silk & Man-Made Fiber

SIC NO	PRODUCT
1044	Silver Ores
3914	Silverware, Plated & Stainless Steel Ware
3484	Small Arms
3482	Small Arms Ammunition
2841	Soap & Detergents
2086	Soft Drinks
2436	Softwood Veneer & Plywood
2842	Spec Cleaning, Polishing & Sanitation Preparations
3559	Special Ind Machinery, NEC
2429	Special Prdt Sawmills, NEC
3566	Speed Changers, Drives & Gears
3949	Sporting & Athletic Goods, NEC
2678	Stationery Prdts
3511	Steam, Gas & Hydraulic Turbines & Engines
3325	Steel Foundries, NEC
3324	Steel Investment Foundries
3317	Steel Pipe & Tubes
3493	Steel Springs, Except Wire
3315	Steel Wire Drawing & Nails & Spikes
3691	Storage Batteries
3259	Structural Clay Prdts, NEC
2439	Structural Wood Members, NEC
2063	Sugar, Beet
2061	Sugar, Cane
2062	Sugar, Cane Refining
2843	Surface Active & Finishing Agents, Sulfonated Oils
3841	Surgical & Medical Instrs & Apparatus
3613	Switchgear & Switchboard Apparatus
2824	Synthetic Organic Fibers, Exc Cellulosic
2822	Synthetic Rubber (Vulcanizable Elastomers)

T

SIC NO	PRODUCT
3795	Tanks & Tank Components
3661	Telephone & Telegraph Apparatus
2393	Textile Bags
2269	Textile Finishers, NEC
2299	Textile Goods, NEC
3552	Textile Machinery
2284	Thread Mills
2296	Tire Cord & Fabric
3011	Tires & Inner Tubes
2141	Tobacco Stemming & Redrying
2131	Tobacco, Chewing & Snuff
3799	Transportation Eqpt, NEC
3792	Travel Trailers & Campers
3713	Truck & Bus Bodies
3715	Truck Trailers
2791	Typesetting

U

SIC NO	PRODUCT
1094	Uranium, Radium & Vanadium Ores

V

SIC NO	PRODUCT
3494	Valves & Pipe Fittings, NEC
2076	Vegetable Oil Mills
3647	Vehicular Lighting Eqpt

W

SIC NO	PRODUCT
3873	Watch & Clock Devices & Parts
2385	Waterproof Outerwear
3548	Welding Apparatus
7692	Welding Repair
2046	Wet Corn Milling
2084	Wine & Brandy
3495	Wire Springs
2331	Women's & Misses' Blouses
2335	Women's & Misses' Dresses
2339	Women's & Misses' Outerwear, NEC
2337	Women's & Misses' Suits, Coats & Skirts
3144	Women's Footwear, Exc Athletic
2341	Women's, Misses' & Children's Underwear & Nightwear
2441	Wood Boxes
2449	Wood Containers, NEC
2511	Wood Household Furniture
2512	Wood Household Furniture, Upholstered
2434	Wood Kitchen Cabinets
2521	Wood Office Furniture
2448	Wood Pallets & Skids
2499	Wood Prdts, NEC
2491	Wood Preserving
2517	Wood T V, Radio, Phono & Sewing Cabinets
2541	Wood, Office & Store Fixtures
3553	Woodworking Machinery
2231	Wool, Woven Fabric

X

SIC NO	PRODUCT
3844	X-ray Apparatus & Tubes

Y

SIC NO	PRODUCT
2281	Yarn Spinning Mills
2282	Yarn Texturizing, Throwing, Twisting & Winding Mills

SIC INDEX

Standard Industrial Classification Numerical Index

SIC NO	PRODUCT

10 metal mining

1011 Iron Ores
1021 Copper Ores
1041 Gold Ores
1044 Silver Ores
1081 Metal Mining Svcs
1094 Uranium, Radium & Vanadium Ores
1099 Metal Ores, NEC

12 coal mining

1231 Anthracite Mining
1241 Coal Mining Svcs

13 oil and gas extraction

1311 Crude Petroleum & Natural Gas
1321 Natural Gas Liquids
1381 Drilling Oil & Gas Wells
1382 Oil & Gas Field Exploration Svcs
1389 Oil & Gas Field Svcs, NEC

14 mining and quarrying of nonmetallic minerals, except fuels

1411 Dimension Stone
1422 Crushed & Broken Limestone
1423 Crushed & Broken Granite
1429 Crushed & Broken Stone, NEC
1442 Construction Sand & Gravel
1446 Industrial Sand
1459 Clay, Ceramic & Refractory Minerals, NEC
1479 Chemical & Fertilizer Mining
1481 Nonmetallic Minerals Svcs, Except Fuels
1499 Miscellaneous Nonmetallic Mining

20 food and kindred products

2011 Meat Packing Plants
2013 Sausages & Meat Prdts
2015 Poultry Slaughtering, Dressing & Processing
2021 Butter
2022 Cheese
2023 Milk, Condensed & Evaporated
2024 Ice Cream
2026 Milk
2032 Canned Specialties
2033 Canned Fruits, Vegetables & Preserves
2034 Dried Fruits, Vegetables & Soup
2035 Pickled Fruits, Vegetables, Sauces & Dressings
2037 Frozen Fruits, Juices & Vegetables
2038 Frozen Specialties
2041 Flour, Grain Milling
2043 Cereal Breakfast Foods
2044 Rice Milling
2045 Flour, Blended & Prepared
2046 Wet Corn Milling
2047 Dog & Cat Food
2048 Prepared Feeds For Animals & Fowls
2051 Bread, Bakery Prdts Exc Cookies & Crackers
2052 Cookies & Crackers
2053 Frozen Bakery Prdts
2061 Sugar, Cane
2062 Sugar, Cane Refining
2063 Sugar, Beet
2064 Candy & Confectionery Prdts
2066 Chocolate & Cocoa Prdts
2067 Chewing Gum
2068 Salted & Roasted Nuts & Seeds
2074 Cottonseed Oil Mills
2076 Vegetable Oil Mills
2077 Animal, Marine Fats & Oils
2079 Shortening, Oils & Margarine
2082 Malt Beverages
2083 Malt
2084 Wine & Brandy
2085 Liquors, Distilled, Rectified & Blended
2086 Soft Drinks
2087 Flavoring Extracts & Syrups
2091 Fish & Seafoods, Canned & Cured
2092 Fish & Seafoods, Fresh & Frozen
2095 Coffee
2096 Potato Chips & Similar Prdts
2097 Ice
2098 Macaroni, Spaghetti & Noodles
2099 Food Preparations, NEC

21 tobacco products

2111 Cigarettes
2121 Cigars
2131 Tobacco, Chewing & Snuff
2141 Tobacco Stemming & Redrying

22 textile mill products

2211 Cotton, Woven Fabric
2221 Silk & Man-Made Fiber
2231 Wool, Woven Fabric
2241 Fabric Mills, Cotton, Wool, Silk & Man-Made
2251 Hosiery, Women's Full & Knee Length
2252 Hosiery, Except Women's
2253 Knit Outerwear Mills
2254 Knit Underwear Mills
2257 Circular Knit Fabric Mills
2258 Lace & Warp Knit Fabric Mills
2259 Knitting Mills, NEC
2261 Cotton Fabric Finishers
2262 Silk & Man-Made Fabric Finishers
2269 Textile Finishers, NEC
2273 Carpets & Rugs
2281 Yarn Spinning Mills
2282 Yarn Texturizing, Throwing, Twisting & Winding Mills
2284 Thread Mills
2295 Fabrics Coated Not Rubberized
2296 Tire Cord & Fabric
2297 Fabrics, Nonwoven
2298 Cordage & Twine
2299 Textile Goods, NEC

23 apparel and other finished products made from fabrics and similar material

2311 Men's & Boys' Suits, Coats & Overcoats
2321 Men's & Boys' Shirts
2322 Men's & Boys' Underwear & Nightwear
2323 Men's & Boys' Neckwear
2325 Men's & Boys' Separate Trousers & Casual Slacks
2326 Men's & Boys' Work Clothing
2329 Men's & Boys' Clothing, NEC
2331 Women's & Misses' Blouses
2335 Women's & Misses' Dresses
2337 Women's & Misses' Suits, Coats & Skirts
2339 Women's & Misses' Outerwear, NEC
2341 Women's, Misses' & Children's Underwear & Nightwear
2342 Brassieres, Girdles & Garments
2353 Hats, Caps & Millinery
2361 Children's & Infants' Dresses & Blouses
2369 Girls' & Infants' Outerwear, NEC
2371 Fur Goods
2381 Dress & Work Gloves
2384 Robes & Dressing Gowns
2385 Waterproof Outerwear
2386 Leather & Sheep Lined Clothing
2387 Apparel Belts
2389 Apparel & Accessories, NEC
2391 Curtains & Draperies
2392 House furnishings: Textile
2393 Textile Bags
2394 Canvas Prdts
2395 Pleating & Stitching For The Trade
2396 Automotive Trimmings, Apparel Findings, Related Prdts
2397 Schiffli Machine Embroideries
2399 Fabricated Textile Prdts, NEC

24 lumber and wood products, except furniture

2411 Logging
2421 Saw & Planing Mills
2426 Hardwood Dimension & Flooring Mills
2429 Special Prdt Sawmills, NEC
2431 Millwork
2434 Wood Kitchen Cabinets
2435 Hardwood Veneer & Plywood
2436 Softwood Veneer & Plywood
2439 Structural Wood Members, NEC
2441 Wood Boxes
2448 Wood Pallets & Skids
2449 Wood Containers, NEC
2451 Mobile Homes
2452 Prefabricated Wood Buildings & Cmpnts
2491 Wood Preserving
2493 Reconstituted Wood Prdts
2499 Wood Prdts, NEC

25 furniture and fixtures

2511 Wood Household Furniture
2512 Wood Household Furniture, Upholstered
2514 Metal Household Furniture
2515 Mattresses & Bedsprings
2517 Wood T V, Radio, Phono & Sewing Cabinets
2519 Household Furniture, NEC
2521 Wood Office Furniture
2522 Office Furniture, Except Wood
2531 Public Building & Related Furniture

2541 Wood, Office & Store Fixtures
2542 Partitions & Fixtures, Except Wood
2591 Drapery Hardware, Window Blinds & Shades
2599 Furniture & Fixtures, NEC

26 paper and allied products

2611 Pulp Mills
2621 Paper Mills
2631 Paperboard Mills
2652 Set-Up Paperboard Boxes
2653 Corrugated & Solid Fiber Boxes
2655 Fiber Cans, Tubes & Drums
2656 Sanitary Food Containers
2657 Folding Paperboard Boxes
2671 Paper Coating & Laminating for Packaging
2672 Paper Coating & Laminating, Exc for Packaging
2673 Bags: Plastics, Laminated & Coated
2674 Bags: Uncoated Paper & Multiwall
2675 Die-Cut Paper & Board
2676 Sanitary Paper Prdts
2677 Envelopes
2678 Stationery Prdts
2679 Converted Paper Prdts, NEC

27 printing, publishing, and allied industries

2711 Newspapers: Publishing & Printing
2721 Periodicals: Publishing & Printing
2731 Books: Publishing & Printing
2732 Book Printing, Not Publishing
2741 Misc Publishing
2752 Commercial Printing: Lithographic
2754 Commercial Printing: Gravure
2759 Commercial Printing, NEC
2761 Manifold Business Forms
2771 Greeting Card Publishing
2782 Blankbooks & Looseleaf Binders
2789 Bookbinding
2791 Typesetting
2796 Platemaking & Related Svcs

28 chemicals and allied products

2812 Alkalies & Chlorine
2813 Industrial Gases
2816 Inorganic Pigments
2819 Indl Inorganic Chemicals, NEC
2821 Plastics, Mtrls & Nonvulcanizable Elastomers
2822 Synthetic Rubber (Vulcanizable Elastomers)
2823 Cellulosic Man-Made Fibers
2824 Synthetic Organic Fibers, Exc Cellulosic
2833 Medicinal Chemicals & Botanical Prdts
2834 Pharmaceuticals
2835 Diagnostic Substances
2836 Biological Prdts, Exc Diagnostic Substances
2841 Soap & Detergents
2842 Spec Cleaning, Polishing & Sanitation Preparations
2843 Surface Active & Finishing Agents, Sulfonated Oils
2844 Perfumes, Cosmetics & Toilet Preparations
2851 Paints, Varnishes, Lacquers, Enamels
2861 Gum & Wood Chemicals
2865 Cyclic-Crudes, Intermediates, Dyes & Org Pigments
2869 Industrial Organic Chemicals, NEC
2873 Nitrogenous Fertilizers
2874 Phosphatic Fertilizers
2875 Fertilizers, Mixing Only
2879 Pesticides & Agricultural Chemicals, NEC
2891 Adhesives & Sealants
2892 Explosives
2893 Printing Ink
2899 Chemical Preparations, NEC

29 petroleum refining and related industries

2911 Petroleum Refining
2951 Paving Mixtures & Blocks
2952 Asphalt Felts & Coatings
2992 Lubricating Oils & Greases
2999 Products Of Petroleum & Coal, NEC

30 rubber and miscellaneous plastics products

3011 Tires & Inner Tubes
3021 Rubber & Plastic Footwear
3052 Rubber & Plastic Hose & Belting
3053 Gaskets, Packing & Sealing Devices
3061 Molded, Extruded & Lathe-Cut Rubber Mechanical Goods
3069 Fabricated Rubber Prdts, NEC
3081 Plastic Unsupported Sheet & Film
3082 Plastic Unsupported Profile Shapes
3083 Plastic Laminated Plate & Sheet
3084 Plastic Pipe

SIC NO	PRODUCT

3085 Plastic Bottles
3086 Plastic Foam Prdts
3087 Custom Compounding Of Purchased Plastic Resins
3088 Plastic Plumbing Fixtures
3089 Plastic Prdts

31 leather and leather products

3111 Leather Tanning & Finishing
3131 Boot & Shoe Cut Stock & Findings
3142 House Slippers
3143 Men's Footwear, Exc Athletic
3144 Women's Footwear, Exc Athletic
3149 Footwear, NEC
3151 Leather Gloves & Mittens
3161 Luggage
3171 Handbags & Purses
3172 Personal Leather Goods
3199 Leather Goods, NEC

32 stone, clay, glass, and concrete products

3211 Flat Glass
3221 Glass Containers
3229 Pressed & Blown Glassware, NEC
3231 Glass Prdts Made Of Purchased Glass
3241 Cement, Hydraulic
3251 Brick & Structural Clay Tile
3253 Ceramic Tile
3255 Clay Refractories
3259 Structural Clay Prdts, NEC
3261 China Plumbing Fixtures & Fittings
3262 China, Table & Kitchen Articles
3263 Earthenware, Whiteware, Table & Kitchen Articles
3264 Porcelain Electrical Splys
3269 Pottery Prdts, NEC
3271 Concrete Block & Brick
3272 Concrete Prdts
3273 Ready-Mixed Concrete
3274 Lime
3275 Gypsum Prdts
3281 Cut Stone Prdts
3291 Abrasive Prdts
3292 Asbestos products
3295 Minerals & Earths: Ground Or Treated
3296 Mineral Wool
3297 Nonclay Refractories
3299 Nonmetallic Mineral Prdts, NEC

33 primary metal industries

3312 Blast Furnaces, Coke Ovens, Steel & Rolling Mills
3313 Electrometallurgical Prdts
3315 Steel Wire Drawing & Nails & Spikes
3316 Cold Rolled Steel Sheet, Strip & Bars
3317 Steel Pipe & Tubes
3321 Gray Iron Foundries
3322 Malleable Iron Foundries
3324 Steel Investment Foundries
3325 Steel Foundries, NEC
3331 Primary Smelting & Refining Of Copper
3334 Primary Production Of Aluminum
3339 Primary Nonferrous Metals, NEC
3341 Secondary Smelting & Refining Of Nonferrous Metals
3351 Rolling, Drawing & Extruding Of Copper
3353 Aluminum Sheet, Plate & Foil
3354 Aluminum Extruded Prdts
3355 Aluminum Rolling & Drawing, NEC
3356 Rolling, Drawing-Extruding Of Nonferrous Metals
3357 Nonferrous Wire Drawing
3363 Aluminum Die Castings
3364 Nonferrous Die Castings, Exc Aluminum
3365 Aluminum Foundries
3366 Copper Foundries
3369 Nonferrous Foundries: Castings, NEC
3398 Metal Heat Treating
3399 Primary Metal Prdts, NEC

34 fabricated metal products, except machinery and transportation equipment

3411 Metal Cans
3412 Metal Barrels, Drums, Kegs & Pails
3421 Cutlery
3423 Hand & Edge Tools
3425 Hand Saws & Saw Blades
3429 Hardware, NEC
3431 Enameled Iron & Metal Sanitary Ware
3432 Plumbing Fixture Fittings & Trim, Brass
3433 Heating Eqpt
3441 Fabricated Structural Steel
3442 Metal Doors, Sash, Frames, Molding & Trim
3443 Fabricated Plate Work
3444 Sheet Metal Work
3446 Architectural & Ornamental Metal Work
3448 Prefabricated Metal Buildings & Cmpnts

3449 Misc Structural Metal Work
3451 Screw Machine Prdts
3452 Bolts, Nuts, Screws, Rivets & Washers
3462 Iron & Steel Forgings
3463 Nonferrous Forgings
3465 Automotive Stampings
3466 Crowns & Closures
3469 Metal Stampings, NEC
3471 Electroplating, Plating, Polishing, Anodizing & Coloring
3479 Coating & Engraving, NEC
3482 Small Arms Ammunition
3483 Ammunition, Large
3484 Small Arms
3489 Ordnance & Access, NEC
3491 Industrial Valves
3492 Fluid Power Valves & Hose Fittings
3493 Steel Springs, Except Wire
3494 Valves & Pipe Fittings, NEC
3495 Wire Springs
3496 Misc Fabricated Wire Prdts
3497 Metal Foil & Leaf
3498 Fabricated Pipe & Pipe Fittings
3499 Fabricated Metal Prdts, NEC

35 industrial and commercial machinery and computer equipment

3511 Steam, Gas & Hydraulic Turbines & Engines
3519 Internal Combustion Engines, NEC
3523 Farm Machinery & Eqpt
3524 Garden, Lawn Tractors & Eqpt
3531 Construction Machinery & Eqpt
3532 Mining Machinery & Eqpt
3533 Oil Field Machinery & Eqpt
3534 Elevators & Moving Stairways
3535 Conveyors & Eqpt
3536 Hoists, Cranes & Monorails
3537 Indl Trucks, Tractors, Trailers & Stackers
3541 Machine Tools: Cutting
3542 Machine Tools: Forming
3543 Industrial Patterns
3544 Dies, Tools, Jigs, Fixtures & Indl Molds
3545 Machine Tool Access
3546 Power Hand Tools
3547 Rolling Mill Machinery & Eqpt
3548 Welding Apparatus
3549 Metalworking Machinery, NEC
3552 Textile Machinery
3553 Woodworking Machinery
3554 Paper Inds Machinery
3555 Printing Trades Machinery & Eqpt
3556 Food Prdts Machinery
3559 Special Ind Machinery, NEC
3561 Pumps & Pumping Eqpt
3562 Ball & Roller Bearings
3563 Air & Gas Compressors
3564 Blowers & Fans
3565 Packaging Machinery
3566 Speed Changers, Drives & Gears
3567 Indl Process Furnaces & Ovens
3568 Mechanical Power Transmission Eqpt, NEC
3569 Indl Machinery & Eqpt, NEC
3571 Electronic Computers
3572 Computer Storage Devices
3575 Computer Terminals
3577 Computer Peripheral Eqpt, NEC
3578 Calculating & Accounting Eqpt
3579 Office Machines, NEC
3581 Automatic Vending Machines
3582 Commercial Laundry, Dry Clean & Pressing Mchs
3585 Air Conditioning & Heating Eqpt
3586 Measuring & Dispensing Pumps
3589 Service Ind Machines, NEC
3592 Carburetors, Pistons, Rings & Valves
3593 Fluid Power Cylinders & Actuators
3594 Fluid Power Pumps & Motors
3596 Scales & Balances, Exc Laboratory
3599 Machinery & Eqpt, Indl & Commercial, NEC

36 electronic and other electrical equipment and components, except computer

3612 Power, Distribution & Specialty Transformers
3613 Switchgear & Switchboard Apparatus
3621 Motors & Generators
3624 Carbon & Graphite Prdts
3625 Relays & Indl Controls
3629 Electrical Indl Apparatus, NEC
3631 Household Cooking Eqpt
3632 Household Refrigerators & Freezers
3633 Household Laundry Eqpt
3634 Electric Household Appliances
3635 Household Vacuum Cleaners
3639 Household Appliances, NEC

3641 Electric Lamps
3643 Current-Carrying Wiring Devices
3644 Noncurrent-Carrying Wiring Devices
3645 Residential Lighting Fixtures
3646 Commercial, Indl & Institutional Lighting Fixtures
3647 Vehicular Lighting Eqpt
3648 Lighting Eqpt, NEC
3651 Household Audio & Video Eqpt
3652 Phonograph Records & Magnetic Tape
3661 Telephone & Telegraph Apparatus
3663 Radio & T V Communications, Systs & Eqpt, Broadcast/Studio
3669 Communications Eqpt, NEC
3671 Radio & T V Receiving Electron Tubes
3672 Printed Circuit Boards
3674 Semiconductors
3675 Electronic Capacitors
3676 Electronic Resistors
3677 Electronic Coils & Transformers
3678 Electronic Connectors
3679 Electronic Components, NEC
3691 Storage Batteries
3692 Primary Batteries: Dry & Wet
3694 Electrical Eqpt For Internal Combustion Engines
3695 Recording Media
3699 Electrical Machinery, Eqpt & Splys, NEC

37 transportation equipment

3711 Motor Vehicles & Car Bodies
3713 Truck & Bus Bodies
3714 Motor Vehicle Parts & Access
3715 Truck Trailers
3716 Motor Homes
3721 Aircraft
3724 Aircraft Engines & Engine Parts
3728 Aircraft Parts & Eqpt, NEC
3731 Shipbuilding & Repairing
3732 Boat Building & Repairing
3743 Railroad Eqpt
3751 Motorcycles, Bicycles & Parts
3761 Guided Missiles & Space Vehicles
3769 Guided Missile/Space Vehicle Parts & Eqpt, NEC
3792 Travel Trailers & Campers
3795 Tanks & Tank Components
3799 Transportation Eqpt, NEC

38 measuring, analyzing and controlling instruments; photographic, medical an

3812 Search, Detection, Navigation & Guidance Systs & Instrs
3821 Laboratory Apparatus & Furniture
3822 Automatic Temperature Controls
3823 Indl Instruments For Meas, Display & Control
3824 Fluid Meters & Counters
3825 Instrs For Measuring & Testing Electricity
3826 Analytical Instruments
3827 Optical Instruments
3829 Measuring & Controlling Devices, NEC
3841 Surgical & Medical Instrs & Apparatus
3842 Orthopedic, Prosthetic & Surgical Appliances/Splys
3843 Dental Eqpt & Splys
3844 X-ray Apparatus & Tubes
3845 Electromedical & Electrotherapeutic Apparatus
3851 Ophthalmic Goods
3861 Photographic Eqpt & Splys
3873 Watch & Clock Devices & Parts

39 miscellaneous manufacturing industries

3911 Jewelry: Precious Metal
3914 Silverware, Plated & Stainless Steel Ware
3915 Jewelers Findings & Lapidary Work
3931 Musical Instruments
3942 Dolls & Stuffed Toys
3944 Games, Toys & Children's Vehicles
3949 Sporting & Athletic Goods, NEC
3951 Pens & Mechanical Pencils
3952 Lead Pencils, Crayons & Artist's Mtrls
3953 Marking Devices
3955 Carbon Paper & Inked Ribbons
3961 Costume Jewelry & Novelties
3965 Fasteners, Buttons, Needles & Pins
3991 Brooms & Brushes
3993 Signs & Advertising Displays
3995 Burial Caskets
3996 Linoleum & Hard Surface Floor Coverings, NEC
3999 Manufacturing Industries, NEC

73 business services

7372 Prepackaged Software

76 miscellaneous repair services

7692 Welding Repair
7694 Armature Rewinding Shops

SIC SECTION

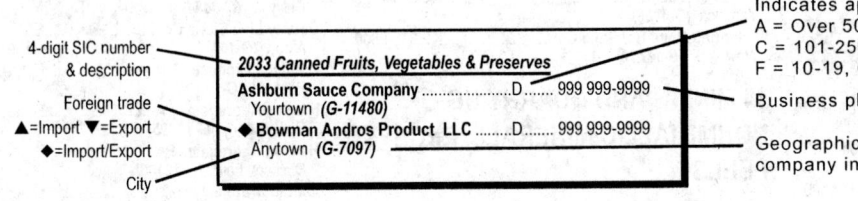

2033 Canned Fruits, Vegetables & Preserves

4-digit SIC number & description →

Ashburn Sauce Company ....D...... 999 999-9999
Yourtown *(G-11480)*

Foreign trade
▲=Import ▼=Export
◆=Import/Export
City

◆ Bowman Andros Product LLC ....D...... 999 999-9999
Anytown *(G-7097)*

Indicates approximate employment figure
A = Over 500 employees, B = 251-500
C = 101-250, D = 51-100, E = 20-50
F = 10-19, G = 5-9

Business phone

Geographic Section entry number where full company information appears.

See footnotes for symbols and codes identification.

- The SIC codes in this section are from the latest Standard Industrial Classification manual published by the U.S. Government's Office of Management and Budget. For more information regarding SICs, see the Explanatory Notes.
- Companies may be listed under multiple classifications.

10 METAL MINING

1011 Iron Ores

▲ Essar Steel Minnesota LLC ....F....... 212 292-2600
New York *(G-9399)*

1021 Copper Ores

Global Gold Corporation ....F...... 914 925-0020
Rye *(G-14079)*

1041 Gold Ores

Andes Gold Corporation ....D.... 212 541-2495
New York *(G-8576)*

▲ Capital Gold Corporation ....G...... 212 668-0842
New York *(G-8912)*

Fuda Group (usa) Corporation ....G.... 646 751-7488
New York *(G-9549)*

Global Gold Corporation ....F.... 914 925-0020
Rye *(G-14079)*

Gncc Capital Inc ....G...... 702 951-9793
New York *(G-9635)*

Surtic Mining Company LLC ....F...... 718 434-0477
Brooklyn *(G-2481)*

1044 Silver Ores

Global Gold Corporation ....F....... 914 925-0020
Rye *(G-14079)*

◆ Rochester Silver Works LLC ....E....... 585 477-9501
Rochester *(G-13696)*

1081 Metal Mining Svcs

Advanced Biomedical Tech Inc ....G....... 718 766-7898
New York *(G-8476)*

Bedrock Industries ....G...... 202 400-0839
New York *(G-8749)*

◆ Coremet Trading Inc ....G...... 212 964-3600
New York *(G-9103)*

1094 Uranium, Radium & Vanadium Ores

Global Gold Corporation ....F....... 914 925-0020
Rye *(G-14079)*

1099 Metal Ores, NEC

American Douglas Metals Inc ....F....... 716 856-3170
Buffalo *(G-2630)*

12 COAL MINING

1231 Anthracite Mining

Puglisi & Co ....E....... 212 300-2285
New York *(G-10925)*

1241 Coal Mining Svcs

Dowa International Corp ....F....... 212 697-3217
New York *(G-9261)*

Lessoilcom ....G....... 516 319-5052
Franklin Square *(G-4961)*

Starfuels Inc ....G....... 914 289-4800
White Plains *(G-16062)*

Trimet Coal LLC ....E....... 718 951-3654
Brooklyn *(G-2521)*

▲ US Pump Corp ....G....... 516 303-7799
West Hempstead *(G-15781)*

13 OIL AND GAS EXTRACTION

1311 Crude Petroleum & Natural Gas

Chanse Petroleum Corporation ....G.... 212 682-3789
New York *(G-8970)*

China N E Petro Holdings Ltd ....A.... 212 307-3568
New York *(G-8991)*

County Energy Corp ....G.... 718 626-7000
Brooklyn *(G-1692)*

Flownet LLC ....G.... 716 685-4036
Lancaster *(G-6807)*

Green Buffalo Fuel LLC ....F..... 716 768-0600
Tonawanda *(G-15108)*

▲ Hess Corporation ....B...... 212 997-8500
New York *(G-9771)*

Hess Energy Exploration Ltd ....G.... 732 750-6500
New York *(G-9772)*

Hess Explrtion Prod Hldngs Ltd ....G.... 732 750-6000
New York *(G-9773)*

Hess Pipeline Corporation ....C..... 212 997-8500
New York *(G-9775)*

Hess Tioga Gas Plant LLC ....C..... 212 997-8500
New York *(G-9776)*

Lukoil Americas Corporation ....C..... 212 421-4141
New York *(G-10282)*

MRC Global (us) Inc ....F...... 607 739-8575
Horseheads *(G-6129)*

Petro River Oil Corp ....G.... 469 828-3900
New York *(G-10818)*

Repsol Oil & Gas Usa LLC ....G.... 607 562-4000
Horseheads *(G-6133)*

Reserve Gas Company Inc ....G.... 716 937-9484
Alden *(G-173)*

Resource PTRlm&ptrochmcl Intl ....E.... 212 537-3856
New York *(G-11020)*

Rocket Tech Fuel Corp ....F...... 516 810-8947
Bay Shore *(G-708)*

Speedway LLC ....F...... 631 738-2536
Lake Grove *(G-6760)*

Stedman Energy Inc ....G.... 716 789-3018
Mayville *(G-7685)*

Zenith Energy US Logistics ....G.... 212 993-1280
New York *(G-11820)*

1321 Natural Gas Liquids

20 Bliss St Inc ....G.... 716 326-2790
Westfield *(G-15943)*

Center State Propane LLC ....G.... 315 841-4044
Waterville *(G-15594)*

Green Buffalo Fuel LLC ....F...... 716 768-0600
Tonawanda *(G-15108)*

Nfe Management LLC ....F...... 212 798-6100
New York *(G-10620)*

Okra Energy LLC ....G.... 206 495-7574
New York *(G-10683)*

Western Oil and Gas JV Inc ....G.... 914 967-4758
Rye *(G-14086)*

1381 Drilling Oil & Gas Wells

Alden Aurora Gas Company Inc ....G.... 716 937-9484
Alden *(G-165)*

Barber & Deline Enrgy Svcs LLC ....F....... 315 696-8961
Tully *(G-15208)*

Barber & Deline LLC ....F...... 607 749-2619
Tully *(G-15209)*

Copper Ridge Oil Inc ....G.... 716 372-4021
Jamestown *(G-6505)*

Geotechnical Drilling Inc ....D.... 516 616-6055
Mineola *(G-7977)*

Lenape Energy Inc ....G.... 585 344-1200
Alexander *(G-177)*

Schneider Amalco Inc ....F...... 917 470-9674
New York *(G-11154)*

Steel Partners Holdings LP ....D.... 212 520-2300
New York *(G-11352)*

Turner Undgrd Instllations Inc ....E.... 585 359-2531
Henrietta *(G-5862)*

U S Energy Development Corp ....D.... 716 636-0401
Getzville *(G-5183)*

▲ US Pump Corp ....G.... 516 303-7799
West Hempstead *(G-15781)*

Western Oil and Gas JV Inc ....G.... 914 967-4758
Rye *(G-14086)*

1382 Oil & Gas Field Exploration Svcs

Able Environmental Services ....G.... 631 567-6585
Bohemia *(G-961)*

Aegis Oil Limited Ventures LLC ....F...... 646 233-4900
New York *(G-8487)*

America Capital Energy Corp ....G.... 212 983-8316
New York *(G-8540)*

▲ Aquifer Drilling & Testing Inc ....D.... 516 616-6026
Mineola *(G-7958)*

▲ Aterra Exploration LLC ....E.... 212 315-0030
New York *(G-8663)*

Bistate Oil Management Corp ....F...... 212 935-4110
New York *(G-8803)*

Hess Energy Exploration Ltd ....G.... 732 750-6500
New York *(G-9772)*

Hess Explrtion Prod Hldngs Ltd ....G.... 732 750-6000
New York *(G-9773)*

KKR Ntral Rsources Fund I-A LP ....G.... 212 750-8300
New York *(G-10113)*

Lenape Energy Inc ....G.... 585 344-1200
Alexander *(G-177)*

Lenape Resources Inc ....F...... 585 344-1200
Alexander *(G-178)*

Mac Fadden Holdings Inc ....E.... 212 979-4805
New York *(G-10303)*

Madoff Energy III LLC ....G.... 212 744-1918
New York *(G-10316)*

Native Amercn Enrgy Group Inc ....G.... 718 408-2323
Forest Hills *(G-4923)*

Norse Energy Corp USA ....G.... 716 568-2048
Buffalo *(G-2891)*

Occidental Energy Mktg Inc ....G.... 212 632-4950
New York *(G-10675)*

Range Rsurces - Appalachia LLC ....E.... 716 753-3385
Mayville *(G-7684)*

Sanguine Gas Exploration LLC ....E.... 212 582-8555
New York *(G-11132)*

Schlumberger Technology Corp ....C.... 607 378-0105
Horseheads *(G-6136)*

Seneca Resources Company LLC ....F...... 716 630-6750
Williamsville *(G-16138)*

Somerset Production Co LLC ....G.... 716 932-6480
Buffalo *(G-2985)*

▲ Springfield Oil Services Inc ....E.... 914 315-6812
Harrison *(G-5559)*

U S Energy Development Corp ....D.... 716 636-0401
Getzville *(G-5183)*

Waffenbauch USA ....E.... 716 326-4508
Westfield *(G-15950)*

Warren Energy Services LLC ....F...... 212 697-9660
New York *(G-11725)*

Wellspring Omni Holdings Corp ....A.... 212 318-9800
New York *(G-11742)*

SIC

1389 Oil & Gas Field Svcs, NEC

A & Mt Realty Group LLC ....F 718 974-5871
Brooklyn *(G-1429)*

Ah Elctronic Test Eqp Repr Ctr ....F 631 234-8979
Central Islip *(G-3260)*

Alba Fuel Corp ....G 718 931-1700
Bronx *(G-1199)*

Alice Perkins ....G 716 378-5100
Salamanca *(G-14121)*

Archrock Inc ....G 716 763-1553
Lakewood *(G-6777)*

Arm Construction Company Inc ....G 646 235-6520
East Elmhurst *(G-4103)*

Babula Construction Inc ....G 716 681-0886
Lancaster *(G-6797)*

Barber & Deline Enrgy Svcs LLC ......F 315 696-8961
Tully *(G-15208)*

Bass Oil & Chemical Llc ....F 718 628-4444
Brooklyn *(G-1564)*

Bluebar Oil Co Inc ....G 315 245-4328
Blossvale *(G-955)*

Case Brothers Inc ....G 716 925-7172
Limestone *(G-6937)*

Cotton Well Drilling Co Inc ....G 716 672-2788
Sheridan *(G-14398)*

Darrell Mitchell ....G 646 659-7075
Arverne *(G-407)*

Dimension Development Corp ....G 718 361-8825
Long Island City *(G-7202)*

Dlh Energy Service LLC ....G 716 410-0028
Lakewood *(G-6782)*

DTI Financial Inc ....E 212 661-7673
New York *(G-9274)*

Essar Americas ....G 212 292-2600
New York *(G-9398)*

Fame Construction Inc ....E 718 626-1000
Astoria *(G-423)*

Fuel Energy Services USA Ltd ....E 607 846-2650
Horseheads *(G-6124)*

Gas Field Specialists Inc ....D 716 378-6422
Horseheads *(G-6125)*

Gas Recovery Systems LLC ....F 914 421-4903
White Plains *(G-16009)*

Gotham Energy 360 LLC ....G 917 338-1023
New York *(G-9647)*

Grit Energy Services Inc ....G 212 701-4500
New York *(G-9680)*

I & S of NY Inc ....F 716 373-7001
Allegany *(G-189)*

Jay Little Oil Well Servi ....G 716 925-8905
Limestone *(G-6938)*

Jemcap Servicing LLC ....G 212 213-9353
New York *(G-9993)*

Legal Servicing LLC ....G 716 565-9300
Williamsville *(G-16133)*

Lenape Energy Inc ....G 585 344-1200
Alexander *(G-177)*

Marcellus Energy Services LLC ....E 607 236-0038
Candor *(G-3162)*

Metro Group Inc ....D 718 729-7200
Long Island City *(G-7295)*

Northeastern Air Quality Inc ....F 518 857-3641
Albany *(G-108)*

P & C Gas Measurements Service ......F 716 257-3412
Cattaraugus *(G-3221)*

Petro Inc ....G 516 686-1900
Hicksville *(G-5944)*

Professional Remodelers Inc ....G 516 565-9300
West Hempstead *(G-15778)*

Sabre Energy Services LLC ....F 518 514-1572
Slingerlands *(G-14467)*

Schlumberger Technology Corp ....C 607 378-0105
Horseheads *(G-6136)*

Schmitt Sales Inc ....G 716 632-8595
Williamsville *(G-16137)*

Schneider Amalco Inc ....F 917 470-9674
New York *(G-11154)*

Sovereign Servicing System LLC ......F 914 779-1400
Bronxville *(G-1403)*

▲ **Steel Excel Inc** ....G 914 461-1300
White Plains *(G-16063)*

Superior Energy Services Inc ....G 716 483-0100
Jamestown *(G-6547)*

T A S Sales Service LLC ....G 518 234-4919
Cobleskill *(G-3500)*

Terra Energy Resource Tech Inc ....F 212 286-9197
New York *(G-11453)*

U S Energy Development Corp ....D 716 636-0401
Getzville *(G-5183)*

Uniformed Fire Officer Assoiat ....F 212 293-9300
New York *(G-11586)*

Vick Construction Inc ....G 718 313-7625
Jamaica *(G-6486)*

Wellspring Omni Holdings Corp ....A 212 318-9800
New York *(G-11742)*

14 MINING AND QUARRYING OF NONMETALLIC MINERALS, EXCEPT FUELS

1411 Dimension Stone

Alice Perkins ....G 716 378-5100
Salamanca *(G-14121)*

Dominic De Nigris Inc ....E 718 597-4460
Bronx *(G-1241)*

Domoteck Interiors Inc ....G 718 433-4300
Woodside *(G-16204)*

Imerys Usa Inc ....F 315 287-0780
Gouverneur *(G-5321)*

▲ **Minerals Technologies Inc** ....E 212 878-1800
New York *(G-10476)*

▲ **New York Quarries Inc** ....E 518 756-3138
Alcove *(G-163)*

Suffolk Granite Manufacturing ....E 631 226-4774
Lindenhurst *(G-6977)*

Vermont Multicolor Slate ....G 518 642-2400
Middle Granville *(G-7871)*

1422 Crushed & Broken Limestone

Barrett Paving Materials Inc ....F 315 737-9471
Clayville *(G-3454)*

Buffalo Crushed Stone Inc ....E 716 826-7310
Buffalo *(G-2672)*

Buffalo Crushed Stone Inc ....E 716 632-6963
Clarence *(G-3427)*

Cayuga Crushed Stone Inc ....E 607 533-4273
Lansing *(G-6840)*

Cobleskill Stone Products Inc ....F 518 295-7121
Schoharie *(G-14321)*

Cobleskill Stone Products Inc ....E 518 234-0221
Cobleskill *(G-3498)*

Cobleskill Stone Products Inc ....F 607 637-4271
Hancock *(G-5535)*

Dolomite Products Company Inc ....E 315 524-1998
Rochester *(G-13354)*

Hanson Aggregates PA Inc ....E 315 858-1100
Jordanville *(G-6632)*

Hanson Aggregates PA Inc ....F 518 568-2444
Saint Johnsville *(G-14117)*

Hanson Aggregates PA LLC ....E 315 469-5501
Jamesville *(G-6560)*

Hanson Aggregates PA LLC ....E 315 685-3321
Skaneateles *(G-14455)*

Hanson Aggregates PA LLC ....F 315 393-3743
Ogdensburg *(G-12205)*

Hanson Aggregates PA LLC ....E 585 624-1220
Honeoye Falls *(G-6074)*

Hanson Aggregates PA LLC ....F 315 821-7222
Oriskany Falls *(G-12400)*

Hanson Aggregates PA LLC ....E 315 789-6202
Oaks Corners *(G-12162)*

Jml Quarries Inc ....E 845 932-8206
Cochecton *(G-3502)*

John Vespa Inc ....F 315 788-6330
Watertown *(G-15575)*

Jointa Lime Company ....A 518 580-0300
Wilton *(G-16156)*

Lilac Quarries LLC ....G 607 867-4016
Mount Upton *(G-8118)*

Patterson Materials Corp ....E 845 832-6000
New Windsor *(G-8377)*

Schaefer Entps Deposit Inc ....E 607 467-4990
Deposit *(G-4002)*

Shelby Crushed Stone Inc ....E 585 798-4501
Medina *(G-7746)*

Upstone Materials Inc ....E 518 891-0236
Saranac Lake *(G-14160)*

1423 Crushed & Broken Granite

MCM Natural Stone Inc ....F 585 586-6510
Rochester *(G-13540)*

Suffolk Granite Manufacturing ....E 631 226-4774
Lindenhurst *(G-6977)*

Tilcon New York Inc ....D 845 358-3100
West Nyack *(G-15833)*

1429 Crushed & Broken Stone, NEC

Barrett Paving Materials Inc ....F 315 737-9471
Clayville *(G-3454)*

County Line Stone Co Inc ....E 716 542-5435
Akron *(G-16)*

Dolomite Products Company Inc ....E 585 586-2568
Penfield *(G-12570)*

Hanson Aggregates PA LLC ....F 315 393-3743
Ogdensburg *(G-12205)*

Hanson Aggregates PA LLC ....F 315 821-7222
Oriskany Falls *(G-12400)*

Labrador Stone Inc ....G 570 465-2120
Binghamton *(G-893)*

Masten Enterprises LLC ....C 845 932-8206
Cochecton *(G-3503)*

Peckham Materials Corp ....E 518 747-3353
Hudson Falls *(G-6192)*

Rock Iroquois Products Inc ....E 585 637-6834
Brockport *(G-1179)*

Shelby Crushed Stone Inc ....E 585 798-4501
Medina *(G-7746)*

Sparclean MBL Refinishing Inc ....G 718 445-2351
Ridgewood *(G-13160)*

Tilcon New York Inc ....E 845 778-5591
Walden *(G-15463)*

Tilcon New York Inc ....D 845 480-3249
Flushing *(G-4899)*

Tilcon New York Inc ....G 845 615-0216
Goshen *(G-5314)*

Tilcon New York Inc ....D 845 457-3158
Montgomery *(G-8067)*

Tilcon New York Inc ....D 845 358-3100
West Nyack *(G-15833)*

Upstone Materials Inc ....D 518 561-5321
Plattsburgh *(G-12787)*

Western Slate Inc ....E 802 287-2210
Granville *(G-5356)*

1442 Construction Sand & Gravel

110 Sand Company ....E 631 694-2822
Melville *(G-7751)*

110 Sand Company ....F 631 694-2822
West Babylon *(G-15677)*

A Colarusso and Son Inc ....E 518 828-3218
Hudson *(G-6146)*

Barrett Paving Materials Inc ....G 607 723-5367
Binghamton *(G-856)*

Belangers Gravel & Stone Inc ....E 585 728-3906
Wayland *(G-15625)*

Buffalo Crushed Stone Inc ....F 716 566-9636
Franklinville *(G-4965)*

Buffalo Crushed Stone Inc ....G 607 587-8102
Alfred Station *(G-184)*

Callanan Industries Inc ....E 845 331-6868
Kingston *(G-6683)*

Carver Sand & Gravel LLC ....E 518 355-6034
Altamont *(G-193)*

Central Dover Development ....G 917 709-3266
Dover Plains *(G-4031)*

Country Side Sand & Gravel ....G 716 988-3271
Collins *(G-3569)*

Country Side Sand & Gravel ....F 716 988-3271
South Dayton *(G-14507)*

D & A Sand & Gravel Inc ....E 516 248-9444
Mineola *(G-7967)*

Dalrymple Grav & Contg Co Inc ....F 607 739-0391
Pine City *(G-12627)*

Dalrymple Holding Corp ....G 607 737-6200
Pine City *(G-12628)*

Dicks Concrete Co Inc ....E 845 374-5966
New Hampton *(G-8234)*

Diehl Development Inc ....G 585 494-2920
Bergen *(G-813)*

E F Lippert Co Inc ....F 716 373-1100
Allegany *(G-187)*

E Tetz & Sons Inc ....D 845 692-4486
Middletown *(G-7905)*

East Coast Mines Ltd ....E 631 653-5445
East Quogue *(G-4156)*

Genoa Sand & Gravel Lnsg ....G 607 533-4551
Freeville *(G-5034)*

Gernatt Asphalt Products Inc ....E 716 532-3371
Collins *(G-3571)*

Greenebuild LLC ....G 917 562-0556
Brooklyn *(G-1910)*

H L Robinson Sand & Gravel ....F 607 659-5153
Candor *(G-3161)*

Hampton Sand Corp ....G 631 325-5533
Westhampton *(G-15955)*

Hanson Aggregates East LLC ....G...... 315 536-9391
Penn Yan *(G-12585)*
Hanson Aggregates East LLC ....E...... 315 548-4913
Phelps *(G-12604)*
Hanson Aggregates PA Inc ....G...... 315 858-1100
Jordanville *(G-6632)*
Hanson Aggregates PA Inc ....F...... 518 568-2444
Saint Johnsville *(G-14117)*
Hanson Aggregates PA LLC ....E...... 585 624-1220
Honeoye Falls *(G-6074)*
Hanson Aggregates PA LLC ....E...... 315 469-5501
Jamesville *(G-6560)*
Hanson Aggregates PA LLC ....E...... 315 685-3321
Skaneateles *(G-14455)*
Hanson Aggregates PA LLC ....F...... 315 782-2300
Watertown *(G-15571)*
Hanson Aggregates PA LLC ....F...... 315 821-7222
Oriskany Falls *(G-12400)*
Hanson Aggregates PA LLC ....G...... 315 789-6202
Oaks Corners *(G-12162)*
Hanson Aggregates PA LLC ....E...... 585 624-3800
Honeoye Falls *(G-6073)*
Hanson Aggregates PA LLC ....F...... 585 436-3250
Rochester *(G-13458)*
IA Construction Corporation ....G...... 716 933-8787
Portville *(G-12935)*
John Vespa Inc ....F...... 315 788-6330
Watertown *(G-15575)*
Johnson S Sand Gravel Inc ....G...... 315 771-1450
La Fargeville *(G-6734)*
Lafarge North America Inc ....E...... 716 651-9235
Lancaster *(G-6813)*
Lafarge North America Inc ....E...... 518 756-5000
Ravena *(G-13069)*
Lazarek Inc ....G...... 315 343-1242
Oswego *(G-12413)*
Little Valley Sand & Gravel ....G...... 716 938-6676
Little Valley *(G-6999)*
McEwan Trucking & Grav Produc ....G...... 716 609-1828
East Concord *(G-4100)*
Milestone Construction Corp ....G...... 718 459-8500
Flushing *(G-4875)*
Mitchell Stone Products LLC ....G...... 518 359-7029
Tupper Lake *(G-15211)*
Northeast Solite Corporation ....E...... 845 246-2177
Mount Marion *(G-8112)*
Northern Crushing LLC ....G...... 518 365-8452
Averill Park *(G-509)*
R G King General Construction ....G...... 315 583-3560
Adams Center *(G-3)*
R J Valente Gravel Inc ....D...... 518 432-4470
Troy *(G-15181)*
R J Valente Gravel Inc ....E...... 518 279-1001
Cropseyville *(G-3803)*
R J Valente Gravel Inc ....F...... 518 432-4470
Rensselaer *(G-13090)*
Rd2 Construction & Dem LLC ....F...... 718 980-1650
Staten Island *(G-14700)*
Republic Construction Co Inc ....G...... 914 235-3654
New Rochelle *(G-8353)*
Robinson Concrete Inc ....E...... 315 253-6666
Auburn *(G-493)*
Rock Mountain Farms Inc ....G...... 845 647-9084
Ellenville *(G-4311)*
Rural Hill Sand and Grav Corp ....F...... 315 846-5212
Woodville *(G-16239)*
Rush Gravel Corp ....G...... 585 533-1740
Honeoye Falls *(G-6079)*
Sagaponack Sand & Gravel Corp ....E...... 631 537-2424
Bridgehampton *(G-1167)*
Seneca Stone Corporation ....G...... 607 737-6200
Pine City *(G-12629)*
Seven Springs Gravel Pdts LLC ....G...... 585 343-4336
Batavia *(G-624)*
Shelby Crushed Stone Inc ....E...... 585 798-4501
Medina *(G-7746)*
Smith Sand & Gravel Inc ....G...... 315 673-4124
Marcellus *(G-7563)*
Sparrow Mining Co ....G...... 718 519-6600
Bronx *(G-1367)*
Speyside Holdings LLC ....E...... 845 928-2221
Highland Mills *(G-5969)*
Syracusa Sand and Gravel Inc ....F...... 585 924-7146
Victor *(G-15435)*
Tilcon New York Inc ....E...... 845 942-0602
Tomkins Cove *(G-15079)*
Tilcon New York Inc ....D...... 845 358-3100
West Nyack *(G-15833)*
Titus Mountain Sand & Grav LLC ....G...... 518 483-3740
Malone *(G-7492)*

Tri City Highway Products Inc ....E...... 607 722-2967
Binghamton *(G-914)*
Tri-City Highway Products Inc ....E...... 518 294-9964
Richmondville *(G-13130)*
Troy Sand & Gravel Co Inc ....G...... 518 203-5115
West Sand Lake *(G-15836)*
Troy Sand & Gravel Co Inc ....F...... 518 674-2854
West Sand Lake *(G-15837)*
United Materials LLC ....E...... 716 662-0564
Orchard Park *(G-12381)*
US Allegro Inc ....E...... 347 408-6601
Maspeth *(G-7640)*

1446 Industrial Sand

◆ American Minerals Inc ....F...... 646 747-4222
New York *(G-8556)*
New Jersey Pulverizing Co Inc ....G...... 516 921-9595
Syosset *(G-14798)*
Precision Elctro Mnrl Pmco Inc ....E...... 716 284-2484
Niagara Falls *(G-11968)*
St Silicones Inc ....G...... 518 664-0745
Mechanicville *(G-7695)*

1459 Clay, Ceramic & Refractory Minerals, NEC

Applied Minerals Inc ....F...... 212 226-4265
Brooklyn *(G-1520)*
Callahan & Nannini Quarry Inc ....G...... 845 496-4323
Salisbury Mills *(G-14134)*
▲ Devonian Stone New York Inc ....E...... 607 655-2600
Windsor *(G-16157)*
Grosso Materials Inc ....F...... 845 361-5211
Montgomery *(G-8061)*

1479 Chemical & Fertilizer Mining

▲ American Rock Salt Company LLC ..E...... 585 991-6878
Retsof *(G-13094)*
Steel City Salt LLC ....G...... 716 532-0000
Collins *(G-3572)*

1481 Nonmetallic Minerals Svcs, Except Fuels

CB Minerals LLC ....F...... 914 777-3330
Mamaroneck *(G-7502)*
▲ Crystal Ceres Industries Inc ....D...... 716 283-0445
Niagara Falls *(G-11918)*
Resource Capital Funds LP ....G...... 631 692-9111
Jericho *(G-6592)*

1499 Miscellaneous Nonmetallic Mining

Avs Gem Stone Corp ....G...... 212 944-6380
New York *(G-8695)*
◆ Barton Mines Company LLC ....C...... 518 798-5462
Glens Falls *(G-5242)*
▲ Capital Gold Corporation ....G...... 212 668-0842
New York *(G-8912)*
Didco Inc ....F...... 212 997-5022
Rego Park *(G-13076)*
Hargrave Development ....F...... 716 877-7880
Kenmore *(G-6650)*
Herkimer Diamond Mines Inc ....E...... 315 891-7355
Herkimer *(G-5864)*
Kotel Importers Inc ....E...... 212 245-6200
New York *(G-10130)*
Ray Griffiths Inc ....G...... 212 689-7209
New York *(G-10985)*
Romance & Co Inc ....G...... 212 382-0337
New York *(G-11079)*
Signature Diamond Entps LLC ....E...... 212 869-5115
New York *(G-11235)*

20 FOOD AND KINDRED PRODUCTS

2011 Meat Packing Plants

A To Z Kosher Meat Products Co ....E...... 718 384-7400
Brooklyn *(G-1436)*
Bliss-Poston The Second Wind ....G...... 212 481-1055
New York *(G-8813)*
◆ Caribbean Foods Delight Inc ....D...... 845 398-3000
Tappan *(G-15034)*
Chefs Delight Packing Co ....F...... 718 388-8581
Brooklyn *(G-1662)*
▲ Cni Meat & Produce Inc ....G...... 516 599-5929
Valley Stream *(G-15338)*
▼ Crescent Duck Farm Inc ....E...... 631 722-8700
Aquebogue *(G-365)*
Dinewise Inc ....G...... 631 694-1111
Farmingdale *(G-4617)*

▲ Domestic Casing Co ....G...... 718 522-1902
Brooklyn *(G-1756)*
◆ DRG New York Holdings Corp ....D...... 914 668-9000
Mount Vernon *(G-8138)*
Frank Wardynski & Sons Inc ....E...... 716 854-6083
Buffalo *(G-2759)*
Gold Medal Packing Inc ....D...... 315 337-1911
Oriskany *(G-12391)*
Hilltown Pork Inc ....F...... 518 781-4050
Canaan *(G-3119)*
Ives Farm Market ....G...... 315 592-4880
Fulton *(G-5065)*
Kamerys Wholesale Meats Inc ....G...... 716 372-6756
Olean *(G-12237)*
Orleans Custom Packing Inc ....G...... 585 314-8227
Holley *(G-6036)*
▼ Robert & William Inc ....G...... 631 727-5780
Riverhead *(G-13187)*
▲ Sahlen Packing Company Inc ....D...... 716 852-8677
Buffalo *(G-2973)*
Sam A Lupo & Sons Inc ....E...... 800 388-5352
Endicott *(G-4472)*
Side Hill Farmers Coop Inc ....E...... 315 697-9862
Canastota *(G-3157)*
The Smoke House of Catskills ....G...... 845 246-8767
Saugerties *(G-14215)*
Tri-Town Packing Corp ....G...... 315 389-5101
Brasher Falls *(G-1113)*
Tyson Deli Inc ....B...... 716 566-3189
Buffalo *(G-3024)*
We Work ....G...... 877 673-6628
New York *(G-11733)*

2013 Sausages & Meat Prdts

▲ Alle Processing Corp ....C...... 718 894-2000
Maspeth *(G-7587)*
Alps Provision Co Inc ....E...... 718 721-4477
Astoria *(G-414)*
Arnolds Meat Food Products ....E...... 718 384-8071
Brooklyn *(G-1532)*
Bianca Burgers LLC ....F...... 516 764-9591
Rockville Centre *(G-13826)*
Big Johns Adirondack Inc ....G...... 518 587-3680
Saratoga Springs *(G-14166)*
Brooklyn Bangers LLC ....F...... 718 875-3535
Brooklyn *(G-1611)*
Brooklyn Casing Co Inc ....G...... 718 522-0866
Brooklyn *(G-1613)*
Buffalo Provisions Co Inc ....F...... 718 292-4300
Elmhurst *(G-4332)*
Camellia General Provision Co ....E...... 716 893-5352
Buffalo *(G-2691)*
◆ Caribbean Foods Delight Inc ....D...... 845 398-3000
Tappan *(G-15034)*
▲ Cni Meat & Produce Inc ....G...... 516 599-5929
Valley Stream *(G-15338)*
De Ans Pork Products Inc ....E...... 718 788-2464
Brooklyn *(G-1731)*
Dinos Sausage & Meat Co Inc ....F...... 315 732-2661
Utica *(G-15257)*
▲ Domestic Casing Co ....G...... 718 522-1902
Brooklyn *(G-1756)*
Elmgang Enterprises I Inc ....F...... 212 868-4142
New York *(G-9350)*
Frank Wardynski & Sons Inc ....E...... 716 854-6083
Buffalo *(G-2759)*
Grossglockner Inc ....G...... 585 266-4960
Canandaigua *(G-3134)*
Hanzlian Sausage Incorporated ....G...... 716 891-5247
Cheektowaga *(G-3353)*
Hilltown Pork Inc ....F...... 518 781-4050
Canaan *(G-3119)*
Jacks Gourmet LLC ....F...... 718 954-4681
Brooklyn *(G-1983)*
Julian Freirich Company Inc ....E...... 718 361-9111
Long Island City *(G-7256)*
Lancaster Quality Pork Inc ....F...... 718 439-8822
Brooklyn *(G-2046)*
Life Earth Company ....G...... 310 751-0627
New York *(G-10211)*
Marathon Enterprises Inc ....D...... 718 665-2560
Bronx *(G-1306)*
Milan Provision Co Inc ....E...... 718 899-7678
Corona *(G-3745)*
Mineo & Sapio Meats Inc ....G...... 716 884-2398
Buffalo *(G-2866)*
Mr Pierogi LLC ....F...... 718 499-7821
Brooklyn *(G-2177)*
Muddy Trail Jerky Co ....G...... 518 642-2194
Granville *(G-5353)*

▲ Niagara Tying Service Inc ....E 716 825-0066
Buffalo (G-2888)

Orchard Sausages Inc ....F 718 381-9388
Brooklyn (G-2233)

Original Crunch Roll Fctry LLC ......G 716 402-5030
Amherst (G-240)

Patla Enterprises Inc ....F 315 367-0237
Sherrill (G-14405)

Picone Meat Specialties Ltd ....G 914 381-3002
Mamaroneck (G-7519)

Pork King Sausage Inc ....E 718 542-2810
Bronx (G-1341)

◆ Prime Food Processing Corp ......D 718 963-2323
Brooklyn (G-2284)

Provisionaire & Co LLC ....G 646 681-8600
Brooklyn (G-2304)

▲ Rapa Independent North America ..G 518 561-0513
Plattsburgh (G-12774)

Reliable Brothers Inc ....E 518 273-6732
Green Island (G-5441)

Rosina Food Products Inc ....C 716 668-0123
Buffalo (G-2962)

Rosina Holding Inc ....G 716 668-0123
Buffalo (G-2963)

Salarinos Italian Foods Inc ....F 315 697-9766
Canastota (G-3156)

Schaller Manufacturing Corp ....D 718 721-5480
New York (G-11149)

Schaller Manufacturing Corp ....F 212 879-3047
New York (G-11150)

Schonwetter Enterprises Inc ....E 518 237-0171
Cohoes (G-3515)

Schrader Meat Market ....F 607 869-6328
Romulus (G-13879)

▲ Sun Ming Jan Inc ....F 718 418-8221
Brooklyn (G-2469)

▲ Syracuse Casing Co Inc ....F 315 475-0309
Syracuse (G-15003)

Tower Isles Frozen Foods Ltd ....D 718 495-2626
Brooklyn (G-2515)

White Eagle Packing Co Inc ....F 518 374-4366
Schenectady (G-14318)

Wilson Beef Farms LLC ....F 607 545-8308
Canaseraga (G-3148)

Zweigles Inc ....D 585 546-1740
Rochester (G-13816)

2015 Poultry Slaughtering, Dressing & Processing

▲ Advanced Frozen Foods Inc ....E 516 333-6344
Westbury (G-15861)

▲ Alle Processing Corp ....C 718 894-2000
Maspeth (G-7587)

Campanellis Poultry Farm Inc ....G 845 482-2222
Bethel (G-828)

▼ Crescent Duck Farm Inc ....E 631 722-8700
Aquebogue (G-365)

Deb El Food Products LLC ....F 845 295-8050
Rock Hill (G-13818)

Deb El Food Products LLC ....E 607 203-5600
Sherburne (G-14390)

Fruit Fresh Up Inc ....E 716 683-3200
Depew (G-3983)

Goya Foods Inc ....D 716 549-0076
Angola (G-359)

Hlw Acres LLC ....G 585 591-0795
Attica (G-457)

◆ Hoskie Co Inc ....D 718 628-8672
Brooklyn (G-1944)

Hudson Valley Foie Gras LLC ....F 845 292-2500
Ferndale (G-4790)

JW Consulting Inc ....G 845 325-7070
Monroe (G-8024)

▲ K&Ns Foods Usa LLC ....C 315 598-8080
Fulton (G-5067)

MB Food Processing Inc ....B 845 436-5001
South Fallsburg (G-14509)

Murray Bresky Consultants Ltd ......G 845 436-5001
South Fallsburg (G-14510)

Sing Ah Poultry ....G 718 625-7253
Brooklyn (G-2421)

Vineland Kosher Poultry Inc ....F 718 921-1347
Brooklyn (G-2560)

Wendels Poultry Farm ....G 716 592-2299
East Concord (G-4101)

2021 Butter

◆ O-At-Ka Milk Products Coop Inc ...B 585 343-0536
Batavia (G-622)

Pure Ghee Inc ....G 917 214-5431
Glen Head (G-5213)

2022 Cheese

Agri-Mark Inc ....D 518 497-6644
Chateaugay (G-3329)

Artisanal Brands Inc ....E 914 441-3591
Bronxville (G-1399)

Castelli America LLC ....D 716 782-2101
Ashville (G-408)

Cemac Foods Corp ....F 914 835-0526
Harrison (G-5549)

Crosswinds Farm & Creamery ....G 607 327-0363
Ovid (G-12423)

East Hill Creamery LLC ....G 585 237-3622
Perry (G-12597)

Emkay Trading Corp ....G 914 592-9000
Elmsford (G-4407)

Emkay Trading Corp ....E 585 492-3800
Arcade (G-373)

▲ Empire Cheese Inc ....C 585 968-1552
Cuba (G-3813)

▲ Euphrates Inc ....D 518 762-3488
Johnstown (G-6616)

Fly Creek Cder Mill Orchrd Inc ......G 607 547-9692
Fly Creek (G-4909)

Four Fat Fowl Inc ....G 518 733-5230
Stephentown (G-14731)

Friendship Dairies LLC ....C 585 973-3031
Friendship (G-5052)

◆ Galaxy Nutritional Foods Inc ....E 401 667-5000
Albany (G-79)

◆ Gharana Industries LLC ....G 315 651-4004
Waterloo (G-15553)

Great Lakes Cheese NY Inc ....D 315 232-4511
Adams (G-2)

▲ Habco Corp ....E 631 789-1400
Amityville (G-266)

HP Hood LLC ....D 315 829-3339
Vernon (G-15366)

HP Hood LLC ....E 607 295-8134
Arkport (G-393)

▲ Hudson Valley Creamery LLC ....F 518 851-2570
Hudson (G-6163)

Instantwhip of Buffalo Inc ....E 716 892-7031
Buffalo (G-2811)

Kraft Heinz Foods Company ....B 315 376-6575
Lowville (G-7416)

Kraft Heinz Foods Company ....B 607 527-4584
Campbell (G-3116)

Kraft Heinz Foods Company ....C 607 865-7131
Walton (G-15475)

Lactalis American Group Inc ....D 716 827-2622
Buffalo (G-2843)

◆ Lactalis American Group Inc ....B 716 823-6262
Buffalo (G-2844)

Leprino Foods Company ....C 570 888-9658
Waverly (G-15623)

Losurdo Foods Inc ....C 315 344-2444
Heuvelton (G-5867)

Lumazu LLC ....G 518 623-3372
Warrensburg (G-15503)

Lumazu LLC ....F 518 623-3372
Warrensburg (G-15504)

Mondelez Global LLC ....D 845 567-4701
Newburgh (G-11875)

▼ Mongiello Sales Inc ....E 845 436-4200
Hurleyville (G-6268)

Mongiellos Itln Cheese Spc LLC .....C 845 436-4200
Hurleyville (G-6269)

▲ Noga Dairies Inc ....F 516 293-5448
Farmingdale (G-4695)

Original Hrkmer Cnty Chese Inc .....D 315 895-7428
Ilion (G-6280)

Pecoraro Dairy Products Inc ....G 718 388-2379
Brooklyn (G-2251)

Rainbeau Ridge Farm ....G 914 234-2197
Bedford Hills (G-772)

Sandvoss Farms LLC ....G 585 297-7044
East Bethany (G-4099)

Sargento Foods Inc ....C 920 893-8484
New York (G-11138)

Sorrento Lactalis Inc ....F 716 823-6262
Buffalo (G-2989)

▲ Taam Tov Foods Inc ....G 718 788-8880
Brooklyn (G-2488)

Upstate Farms Cheese LLC ....E 607 527-4584
Campbell (G-3117)

Wny Cheese Enterprise LLC ....E 585 243-6516
Pavilion (G-12524)

◆ World Cheese Co Inc ....F 718 965-1700
Brooklyn (G-2595)

2023 Milk, Condensed & Evaporated

America Health Corp ....G 800 860-1868
New York (G-8541)

B&B Sports Nutrition LLC ....G 520 869-5434
New York (G-8707)

Baby Central LLC ....G 718 372-2229
Brooklyn (G-1558)

Century Tom Inc ....G 347 654-3179
Jamaica (G-6431)

Danone Nutricia Early ....E 914 872-8556
White Plains (G-15997)

Dynatabs LLC ....F 718 376-6084
Brooklyn (G-1769)

El-Gen LLC ....G 631 218-3400
Bohemia (G-1010)

Eli Consumer Healthcare LLC ....F 914 943-3107
Irvington (G-6307)

Friendship Dairies LLC ....C 585 973-3031
Friendship (G-5052)

FriesIndcmpina Ingrdnts N Amer .....E 607 746-0196
Delhi (G-3965)

◆ Hain Celestial Group Inc ....C 516 587-5000
New Hyde Park (G-8272)

Infant Formula Laboratory Svc ....F 718 257-3000
Brooklyn (G-1957)

J Rettenmaier USA LP ....D 716 693-4009
North Tonawanda (G-12075)

◆ Kerry Bfnctnal Ingredients Inc .....G 608 363-1200
Norwich (G-12123)

Makers Nutrition LLC ....E 631 456-5397
Hauppauge (G-5706)

Makers Nutrition LLC ....G 844 625-3771
Commack (G-3594)

◆ Nationwide Dairy Inc ....G 347 689-8148
Brooklyn (G-2191)

Nestle Usa Inc ....C 914 272-4021
White Plains (G-16033)

Nestle Usa Inc ....C 212 688-2490
New York (G-10568)

Nyb Distributors Inc ....G 516 937-0666
Jericho (G-6587)

◆ O-At-Ka Milk Products Coop Inc ...B 585 343-0536
Batavia (G-622)

◆ Rich Products Corporation ....A 716 878-8000
Buffalo (G-2954)

◆ Sugar Foods Corporation ....E 212 753-6900
New York (G-11385)

Unbroken Rtr Usa Inc ....G 541 640-9457
Wappingers Falls (G-15500)

Upstate Niagara Coop Inc ....C 716 892-2121
Buffalo (G-3033)

Vitakem Nutraceutical Inc ....C 631 956-8343
Smithtown (G-14489)

2024 Ice Cream

Ample Hills Creamery Inc ....E 347 725-4061
Brooklyn (G-1506)

Ample Hills Creamery Inc ....E 718 809-1678
Brooklyn (G-1507)

Ample Hills Holdings Inc ....G 347 725-4061
Brooklyn (G-1508)

Beyond Better Foods LLC ....G 212 888-1120
Bronx (G-1213)

Bleecker Pastry Tartufo Inc ....G 718 937-9830
Long Island City (G-7180)

Blue Marble Ice Cream LLC ....G 718 858-5551
Brooklyn (G-1593)

Blue Pig Ice Cream Factory ....G 914 271-3850
Croton On Hudson (G-3806)

Byrne Dairy Inc ....B 315 475-2121
La Fayette (G-6737)

Carols Polar Parlor ....G 315 468-3404
Syracuse (G-14842)

Chobani Idaho LLC ....G 208 432-2248
Norwich (G-12119)

▼ Crowley Foods Inc ....E 800 637-0019
Binghamton (G-869)

Delicioso Coco Helado Inc ....F 718 292-1930
Bronx (G-1240)

Df Mavens Inc ....E 347 813-4705
Astoria (G-417)

Elegant Desserts By Metro Inc ....F 718 388-1323
Brooklyn (G-1792)

Ffc Holding Corp Subsidiaries ....B 716 366-5400
Dunkirk (G-4057)

◆ Fieldbrook Foods Corporation ......C 716 366-5400
Dunkirk (G-4058)

Four Brothers Italian Bakery..............G......914 741-5434
  Hawthorne (G-5812)
Fresh Ice Cream Company LLC..........F......347 603-6021
  Brooklyn (G-1868)
Fresh Ice Cream Company LLC..........E......347 603-6021
  Brooklyn (G-1869)
G Pesso & Sons Inc.............................G......718 224-9130
  Bayside (G-738)
▲ Grom Columbus LLC.........................G......212 974-3444
  New York (G-9683)
HP Hood LLC..D......315 829-3339
  Vernon (G-15366)
HP Hood LLC..A......607 772-6580
  Binghamton (G-882)
Indulge Desserts Holdings LLC..........G......212 231-8600
  New York (G-9883)
JMS Ices Inc..F......718 448-0853
  Staten Island (G-14670)
Jones Humdinger.................................F......607 771-6501
  Binghamton (G-892)
Kan Pak LLC.......................................G......620 440-2319
  Penn Yan (G-12589)
Kozy Shack Enterprises LLC...............C......516 870-3000
  Hicksville (G-5920)
La Cremeria..G......212 226-6758
  New York (G-10156)
La Newyorkina LLC..............................G......917 669-4591
  Brooklyn (G-2041)
▲ LArte Del Gelato Gruppo Inc............F......718 383-6600
  Long Island City (G-7269)
Lickity Splits.......................................G......585 345-6091
  Batavia (G-619)
Lumazu LLC...G......518 623-3372
  Warrensburg (G-15503)
Lumazu LLC...F......518 623-3372
  Warrensburg (G-15504)
Macadoodles.......................................G......607 652-9019
  Stamford (G-14608)
▲ Macedonia Ltd..................................F......718 462-3596
  Brooklyn (G-2100)
Marvel Dairy Whip Inc..........................G......516 889-4232
  Lido Beach (G-6928)
MSQ Corporation.................................G......718 465-0900
  Queens Village (G-13025)
My Most Favorite Food.........................G......212 580-5130
  New York (G-10524)
Ninas Custard.....................................E......716 636-0345
  Getzville (G-5179)
Nutrifast LLC..F......347 671-3181
  New York (G-10658)
NY Froyo LLC......................................G......516 312-4588
  Deer Park (G-3915)
▼ Olympic Ice Cream Co Inc...............E......718 849-6200
  Richmond Hill (G-13118)
Paleteria Fernandez Inc.......................F......914 315-1598
  Mamaroneck (G-7518)
Paleteria Fernandez Inc.......................G......914 939-3694
  Port Chester (G-12826)
▲ Perrys Ice Cream Company Inc.........B......716 542-5492
  Akron (G-20)
Phyljohn Distributors Inc.....................F......518 459-2775
  Albany (G-115)
Piazzas Ice Cream Ice Hse Inc............F......718 818-8811
  Staten Island (G-14689)
Primo Frozen Desserts Inc...................G......718 252-2312
  Brooklyn (G-2285)
Pulmuone Foods Usa Inc.....................E......845 365-3300
  Tappan (G-15037)
Purity Ice Cream Co Inc.......................F......607 272-1545
  Ithaca (G-6408)
Quaker Bonnet Inc...............................G......716 885-7208
  Buffalo (G-2941)
▼ Quality Dairy Farms Inc....................E......315 942-2611
  Boonville (G-1109)
Ralphs Famous Italian Ices.................G......718 605-5052
  Staten Island (G-14698)
Scoops R US Incorporated...................G......212 730-7959
  New York (G-11168)
Smartys Corner....................................G......607 239-5276
  Endicott (G-4473)
Stewarts Processing Corp....................D......518 581-1200
  Ballston Spa (G-588)
Stewarts Shops Corp............................F......518 499-9376
  Whitehall (G-16077)
▲ Sweet Melodys LLC...........................G......716 580-3227
  East Amherst (G-4080)
Swirl Bliss LLC....................................G......516 867-9475
  North Baldwin (G-12009)
Textured Fd Innvations Tfi LLC............G......515 731-3663
  Carle Place (G-3182)

Tia Lattrell...G......845 373-9494
  Amenia (G-203)
▲ TLC-Lc Inc......................................E......212 756-8900
  New York (G-11501)
Unilever United States Inc...................F......212 546-0200
  New York (G-11588)
Unilever United States Inc...................C......212 546-0200
  New York (G-11589)
▲ Van Leeuwen Artisan Ice Cream......G......718 701-1630
  Brooklyn (G-2552)
Vanilla Sky LLC...................................G......347 738-4195
  Long Island City (G-7392)
Victory Garden....................................G......212 206-7273
  New York (G-11678)
Washburns Dairy Inc...........................G......518 725-0629
  Gloversville (G-5299)
Wicked Spoon Inc................................F......646 335-2890
  New York (G-11753)
Zings Company LLC.............................G......631 454-0339
  Farmingdale (G-4767)

2026 Milk

Aethera LLC...E......215 324-9222
  New York (G-8489)
Bliss Foods Inc....................................G......212 732-8888
  New York (G-8811)
Bliss Foods Inc....................................F......212 732-8888
  New York (G-8812)
Byrne Dairy Inc....................................B......315 475-2121
  La Fayette (G-6737)
Chobani LLC..F......646 998-3800
  New York (G-8994)
◆ Chobani LLC....................................C......607 337-1246
  Norwich (G-12118)
Chobani LLC..G......607 847-6181
  New Berlin (G-8221)
▼ Crowley Foods Inc............................E......800 637-0019
  Binghamton (G-869)
▲ Currant Company LLC........................G......845 266-8999
  Staatsburg (G-14598)
Cville Yoghurt Inc................................G......315 430-4966
  Cortland (G-3765)
Dairy Farmers America Inc...................E......816 801-6440
  East Syracuse (G-4205)
▲ Danone Us LLC.................................D......914 872-8400
  White Plains (G-15998)
Dean Foods Company..........................D......315 452-5001
  East Syracuse (G-4207)
Dwyer Farm LLC..................................G......914 456-2742
  Walden (G-15459)
Emkay Trading Corp............................E......585 492-3800
  Arcade (G-373)
◆ Fage USA Holdings...........................G......518 762-5912
  Johnstown (G-6617)
Finger Lakes Cheese Trail....................F......607 857-5726
  Odessa (G-12200)
Garelick Farms LLC.............................C......518 283-0820
  East Greenbush (G-4114)
▼ Hanan Products Company Inc...........E......516 938-1000
  Hicksville (G-5915)
HP Hood LLC..D......607 295-8134
  Arkport (G-393)
HP Hood LLC..G......315 363-3870
  Oneida (G-12246)
HP Hood LLC..B......315 658-2132
  La Fargeville (G-6733)
HP Hood LLC..B......518 218-9097
  Schenectady (G-14279)
HP Hood LLC..A......607 772-6580
  Binghamton (G-882)
HP Hood LLC..D......315 829-3339
  Vernon (G-15366)
Instantwhip of Buffalo Inc....................E......716 892-7031
  Buffalo (G-2811)
Kesso Foods Inc..................................G......718 777-5303
  East Elmhurst (G-4108)
▲ Kong Kee Food Corp.........................E......718 937-2746
  Long Island City (G-7264)
Kraft Heinz Foods Company.................C......607 865-7131
  Walton (G-15475)
Kraft Heinz Foods Company.................B......607 527-4584
  Campbell (G-3116)
Maple Hill Creamery LLC......................F......518 758-7777
  Stuyvesant (G-14754)
Midland Farms Inc...............................D......518 436-7038
  Menands (G-7846)
Mountain Side Farms Inc......................E......718 526-3442
  Jamaica (G-6462)
▲ Noga Dairies Inc...............................F......516 293-5448
  Farmingdale (G-4695)

◆ O-At-Ka Milk Products Coop Inc.......B......585 343-0536
  Batavia (G-622)
Oatly Inc..E......646 625-4633
  New York (G-10673)
P & F Bakers Inc..................................F......516 931-6821
  Hicksville (G-5938)
Purity Ice Cream Co Inc.......................F......607 272-1545
  Ithaca (G-6408)
Saputo Dairy Foods Usa LLC...............D......607 746-2141
  Delhi (G-3966)
Steuben Foods Incorporated................C......716 655-4000
  Elma (G-4329)
Steuben Foods Incorporated................F......718 291-3333
  Elma (G-4328)
Stewarts Processing Corp....................D......518 581-1200
  Ballston Spa (G-588)
Swirls Twirls Incorporated....................G......516 541-9400
  Massapequa (G-7652)
Upstate Farms Dairy LLC.....................G......716 892-3156
  Buffalo (G-3031)
Upstate Niagara Coop Inc....................D......716 892-3156
  Buffalo (G-3032)
Upstate Niagara Coop Inc....................E......585 458-1880
  Rochester (G-13789)
Upstate Niagara Coop Inc....................E......716 484-7178
  Jamestown (G-6551)
Upstate Niagara Coop Inc....................D......315 389-5111
  North Lawrence (G-12033)
Upstate Niagara Coop Inc....................C......716 892-2121
  Buffalo (G-3033)
Whitney Foods Inc................................F......718 291-3333
  Jamaica (G-6488)
Wny Enterprise LLC.............................E......585 243-6514
  Pavilion (G-12525)
Yiamas Dairy Farms LLC......................G......347 766-7177
  Bayside (G-745)
Yogolicious Inc....................................G......914 236-3455
  Briarcliff Manor (G-1163)

2032 Canned Specialties

▲ A & G Food Distributors LLC.............G......917 939-3457
  Franklin Square (G-4958)
▲ Antico Casale Usa LLC.....................G......718 357-2000
  Whitestone (G-16086)
◆ Beech-Nut Nutrition Company...........B......518 839-0300
  Amsterdam (G-319)
Borgattis Ravioli Egg Noodles.............G......718 367-3799
  Bronx (G-1216)
Delicious Foods Inc.............................F......718 446-9352
  Corona (G-3738)
Dinewise Inc..G......631 694-1111
  Farmingdale (G-4617)
Eataly Net Usa LLC.............................G......212 897-2895
  New York (G-9308)
Edesia World Wide LLC........................G......646 705-3505
  New York (G-9320)
◆ Eve Sales Corp.................................F......718 589-6800
  Bronx (G-1255)
Fireside Holdings LLC..........................G......718 564-4335
  Monsey (G-8038)
▲ Global Food Source & Co Inc............G......914 320-9615
  Tuckahoe (G-15204)
Goya Foods Inc....................................G......716 549-0076
  Angola (G-359)
Grandma Browns Beans Inc.................F......315 963-7221
  Mexico (G-7866)
Indira Foods Inc...................................F......718 343-1500
  Floral Park (G-4819)
Kawasho Foods USA Inc.......................F......212 841-7400
  New York (G-10080)
Marketplace Slutions Group LLC..........E......631 868-0111
  Holbrook (G-6009)
◆ Sahadi Fine Foods Inc......................E......718 369-0100
  Brooklyn (G-2381)
Sangster Foods Inc..............................F......212 993-9129
  Brooklyn (G-2383)
Steuben Foods Incorporated................F......718 291-3333
  Elma (G-4328)

2033 Canned Fruits, Vegetables & Preserves

Amiram Dror Inc..................................F......212 979-9505
  Brooklyn (G-1504)
Andros Bowman Products LLC.............G......540 217-4100
  Lyndonville (G-7444)
◆ Apple & Eve LLC...............................D......516 621-1122
  Port Washington (G-12863)
▲ Brads Organic LLC............................G......845 429-9080
  Haverstraw (G-5804)
Brooklyns Best Pasta Co Inc................G......917 881-3007
  Brooklyn (G-1624)

S
I
C

Cahoon Farms Inc....E.... 315 594-8081
Wolcott *(G-16161)*
Cheribundi Inc....E.... 800 699-0460
Geneva *(G-5150)*
◆ **Cliffstar LLC**....A.... 716 366-6100
Dunkirk *(G-4052)*
Dells Cherries LLC....E.... 718 624-4380
Brooklyn *(G-1734)*
Dells Cherries LLC....E.... 718 624-4380
Brooklyn *(G-1735)*
Fly Creek Cder Mill Orchrd Inc....G.... 607 547-9692
Fly Creek *(G-4909)*
Fresh Fanatic Inc....G.... 516 521-6574
Brooklyn *(G-1867)*
◆ **Giovanni Food Co Inc**....D.... 315 457-2373
Baldwinsville *(G-548)*
Goya Foods Inc....D.... 716 549-0076
Angola *(G-359)*
Green Valley Foods LLC....G.... 315 926-4280
Marion *(G-7569)*
Hc Brill Co Inc....G.... 716 685-4000
Lancaster *(G-6810)*
Jets Lefrois Corp....G.... 585 637-5003
Brockport *(G-1178)*
Jus By Julie LLC....G.... 718 266-3906
Brooklyn *(G-2014)*
Kaltech Food Packaging Inc....E.... 845 856-1210
Port Jervis *(G-12852)*
Kensington & Sons LLC....E.... 646 430-8298
New York *(G-10091)*
▲ **L and S Packing Co**....D.... 631 845-1717
Amityville *(G-287)*
Labarba-Q LLC....F.... 845 806-6227
Warwick *(G-15518)*
Lagoner Farms Inc....D.... 315 904-4109
Williamson *(G-16111)*
◆ **Lidestri Foods Inc**....B.... 585 377-7700
Fairport *(G-4504)*
Life Juice Brands LLC....G.... 585 944-7982
Pittsford *(G-12646)*
▲ **Mayer Bros Apple Products Inc**....D.... 716 668-1787
West Seneca *(G-15852)*
Mizkan America Inc....D.... 585 765-9171
Lyndonville *(G-7445)*
◆ **Motts LLP**....C.... 972 673-8088
Elmsford *(G-4418)*
◆ **National Grape Coop Assn Inc**....E.... 716 326-5200
Westfield *(G-15947)*
New York Pasta Authority Inc....F.... 347 787-2130
Brooklyn *(G-2209)*
◆ **Old Dutch Mustard Co Inc**....G.... 516 466-0522
Great Neck *(G-5408)*
Olive Branch Foods LLC....G.... 631 343-7070
Islandia *(G-6342)*
Organic Nectars Inc....G.... 845 246-0506
Saugerties *(G-14206)*
Pressed Juice LLC....G.... 646 573-9157
Brooklyn *(G-2281)*
Sarabeths Kitchen LLC....G.... 718 589-2900
Bronx *(G-1360)*
▲ **Sbk Preserves Inc**....E.... 800 773-7378
Bronx *(G-1361)*
◆ **Seneca Foods Corporation**....E.... 315 926-8100
Marion *(G-7574)*
Seneca Foods Corporation....C.... 315 781-8733
Geneva *(G-5162)*
Seneca Foods Corporation....E.... 585 658-2211
Leicester *(G-6911)*
▲ **Sneaky Chef Foods LLC**....F.... 914 301-3277
Tarrytown *(G-15060)*
Spf Holdings II LLC....G.... 212 750-8300
New York *(G-11320)*
Super Sauces Inc....G.... 347 497-2537
Brooklyn *(G-2472)*
US Juice Partners LLC....G.... 516 621-1122
Port Washington *(G-12930)*
◆ **Victoria Fine Foods LLC**....D.... 718 649-1635
Brooklyn *(G-2556)*
Victoria Fine Foods Holding Co....G.... 718 649-1635
Brooklyn *(G-2557)*
Vincents Food Corp....F.... 516 481-3544
Carle Place *(G-3183)*
Wax Jams LLC....F.... 914 834-7886
Larchmont *(G-6844)*
Welch Foods Inc A Cooperative....C.... 716 326-5252
Westfield *(G-15951)*
Welch Foods Inc A Cooperative....E.... 716 326-3131
Westfield *(G-15952)*
Wolfgang B Gourmet Foods Inc....F.... 518 719-1727
Catskill *(G-3218)*

2034 Dried Fruits, Vegetables & Soup

▲ **Allied Food Products Inc**....F.... 718 230-4227
Brooklyn *(G-1488)*
◆ **Associated Brands Inc**....B.... 585 798-3475
Medina *(G-7727)*
Goya Foods Inc....D.... 716 549-0076
Angola *(G-359)*
◆ **Hain Celestial Group Inc**....C.... 516 587-5000
New Hyde Park *(G-8272)*
Marshall Ingredients LLC....G.... 800 796-9353
Wolcott *(G-16164)*
◆ **Settons Intl Foods Inc**....D.... 631 543-8090
Commack *(G-3598)*
Shoreline Fruit LLC....D.... 585 765-2639
Lyndonville *(G-7446)*
▲ **Wm E Martin and Sons Co Inc**....E.... 516 605-2444
Roslyn *(G-14047)*

2035 Pickled Fruits, Vegetables, Sauces & Dressings

Allen Pickle Works Inc....F.... 516 676-0640
Glen Cove *(G-5187)*
American Specialty Mfg Co....F.... 585 544-5600
Rochester *(G-13231)*
Baldwin Richardson Foods Co....B.... 315 986-2727
Macedon *(G-7461)*
Batampte Pickle Products Inc....D.... 718 251-2100
Brooklyn *(G-1566)*
Bushwick Kitchen LLC....G.... 917 297-1045
Brooklyn *(G-1631)*
Conway Import Co Inc....G.... 914 592-1312
Elmsford *(G-4402)*
Culture Clash Corporation....G.... 631 933-8179
Amityville *(G-261)*
Elwood International Inc....F.... 631 842-6600
Copiague *(G-3651)*
French Associates Inc....F.... 718 387-9880
Fresh Meadows *(G-5041)*
Goya Foods Inc....D.... 716 549-0076
Angola *(G-359)*
Gravymaster Inc....E.... 203 453-1893
Canajoharie *(G-3120)*
Heintz & Weber Co Inc....G.... 716 852-7171
Buffalo *(G-2797)*
Instantwhip of Buffalo Inc....E.... 716 892-7031
Buffalo *(G-2811)*
Jets Lefrois Corp....G.... 585 637-5003
Brockport *(G-1178)*
Kensington & Sons LLC....E.... 646 430-8298
New York *(G-10091)*
▲ **L and S Packing Co**....D.... 631 845-1717
Amityville *(G-287)*
Lucinas Gourmet Food Inc....G.... 646 835-9784
Long Island City *(G-7280)*
▲ **Mandarin Soy Sauce Inc**....E.... 845 343-1505
Middletown *(G-7918)*
◆ **Materne North America Corp**....B.... 212 675-7881
New York *(G-10383)*
Mizkan America Inc....F.... 585 798-5720
Medina *(G-7742)*
Mizkan America Inc....D.... 585 765-9171
Lyndonville *(G-7445)*
▲ **Moldova Pickles & Salads Inc**....G.... 718 284-2220
Brooklyn *(G-2168)*
◆ **Old Dutch Mustard Co Inc**....G.... 516 466-0522
Great Neck *(G-5408)*
◆ **Pure Golds Family Corp**....D.... 516 483-5600
Hempstead *(G-5848)*
▲ **Rob Salamida Company Inc**....F.... 607 729-4868
Johnson City *(G-6608)*
T RS Great American Rest....F.... 516 294-1680
Williston Park *(G-16149)*
▲ **Twin Marquis Inc**....D.... 718 386-6868
Brooklyn *(G-2532)*
Unilever United States Inc....F.... 212 546-0200
New York *(G-11588)*
Unilever United States Inc....C.... 212 546-0200
New York *(G-11589)*
United Farm Processing Corp....C.... 718 933-6060
Bronx *(G-1387)*
United Pickle Products Corp....E.... 718 933-6060
Bronx *(G-1388)*
◆ **Victoria Fine Foods LLC**....D.... 718 649-1635
Brooklyn *(G-2556)*
Victoria Fine Foods Holding Co....G.... 718 649-1635
Brooklyn *(G-2557)*
◆ **Wanjashan International LLC**....F.... 845 343-1505
Middletown *(G-7937)*
Whalens Horseradish Products....G.... 518 587-6404
Galway *(G-5082)*

2037 Frozen Fruits, Juices & Vegetables

Atlantic Farm & Food Inc....F.... 718 441-3152
Richmond Hill *(G-13108)*
Berryfield Bottling LLC....E.... 315 781-2749
Geneva *(G-5146)*
Birds Eye Foods Inc....G.... 716 988-3218
South Dayton *(G-14505)*
Blend Smoothie Bar....G.... 845 568-7366
New Windsor *(G-8361)*
C O P R A Inc....G.... 917 224-1727
New York *(G-8881)*
Cahoon Farms Inc....E.... 315 594-8081
Wolcott *(G-16161)*
Cheribundi Inc....E.... 800 699-0460
Geneva *(G-5150)*
▲ **Dynamic Health Labs Inc**....E.... 718 858-0100
Brooklyn *(G-1767)*
Farmtobottle LLC....G.... 631 944-8422
Locust Valley *(G-7122)*
Fly Creek Cder Mill Orchrd Inc....G.... 607 547-9692
Fly Creek *(G-4909)*
Grace Love Inc....F.... 646 402-4325
Garden City Park *(G-5121)*
Grass Roots Juicery....E.... 718 486-2838
Brooklyn *(G-1908)*
Hain Blueprint Inc....F.... 212 414-5741
New Hyde Park *(G-8271)*
Kj Astoria Gourmet Inc....G.... 718 545-6900
Astoria *(G-426)*
◆ **National Grape Coop Assn Inc**....E.... 716 326-5200
Westfield *(G-15947)*
◆ **Pepsico Inc**....A.... 914 253-2000
Purchase *(G-13010)*
◆ **Prime Food Processing Corp**....D.... 718 963-2323
Brooklyn *(G-2284)*
Pura Fruta LLC....F.... 415 279-5727
Long Island City *(G-7332)*
Pure Green Holdings Inc....F.... 917 209-8811
New York *(G-10927)*
◆ **Seneca Foods Corporation**....E.... 315 926-8100
Marion *(G-7574)*
Smoothies Strawberry Nysf....G.... 315 406-4250
Syracuse *(G-14995)*
T & Smoothie Inc....G.... 631 804-6653
Patchogue *(G-12513)*
Tami Great Food Corp....G.... 845 352-7901
Monsey *(G-8052)*
Textured Fd Innvations Tfi LLC....G.... 515 731-3663
Carle Place *(G-3182)*

2038 Frozen Specialties

▲ **3021743 Holdings Inc**....E.... 585 589-6399
Albion *(G-152)*
▲ **Alle Processing Corp**....C.... 718 894-2000
Maspeth *(G-7587)*
▲ **America NY RI Wang Fd Group Co**....E.... 631 231-8999
Bay Shore *(G-647)*
America NY RI Wang Fd Group Co....F.... 631 231-8999
Maspeth *(G-7589)*
Beetnpath LLC....G.... 607 319-5585
Ithaca *(G-6364)*
Codinos Limited Inc....E.... 518 372-3308
Schenectady *(G-14258)*
D R M Management Inc....E.... 716 668-0333
Depew *(G-3978)*
Delicious Foods Inc....F.... 718 446-9352
Corona *(G-3738)*
Dufour Pastry Kitchens Inc....E.... 718 402-8800
Bronx *(G-1243)*
▲ **Dvash Foods Inc**....F.... 845 578-1959
Monsey *(G-8037)*
F & R Enterprises Inc....G.... 315 841-8189
Waterville *(G-15595)*
Finger Food Products Inc....E.... 716 297-4888
Sanborn *(G-14141)*
Food Basket USA Company Ltd....E.... 631 231-8999
Bay Shore *(G-680)*
▲ **Julians Recipe LLC**....G.... 888 640-8880
Brooklyn *(G-2011)*
Juno Chefs....D.... 845 294-5400
Goshen *(G-5310)*
Kraft Heinz Foods Company....B.... 585 226-4400
Avon *(G-513)*
Les Chateaux De France Inc....E.... 516 239-6795
Inwood *(G-6297)*
Macabee Foods LLC....G.... 845 623-1300
West Nyack *(G-15826)*
▲ **Milmar Food Group II LLC**....C.... 845 294-5400
Goshen *(G-5311)*

Moretta Cilento Ltd Lblty Co..............G..... 631 386-8654
  Huntington (G-6214)
Rhosey LLC..G..... 718 382-1226
  Brooklyn (G-2343)
Salarinos Italian Foods Inc................F..... 315 697-9766
  Canastota (G-3156)
▲ Seviroli Foods Inc...........................C..... 516 222-6220
  Garden City (G-5115)
Tami Great Food Corp.......................G..... 845 352-7901
  Monsey (G-8052)
Textured Fd Innvations Tfi LLC........G..... 515 731-3663
  Carle Place (G-3182)
Tio Foods LLC.....................................F..... 917 946-1160
  New York (G-11498)
▲ Tuv Taam Corp.................................E..... 718 855-2207
  Brooklyn (G-2530)
Unilever United States Inc................F..... 212 546-0200
  New York (G-11588)
Unilever United States Inc................C..... 212 546-0200
  New York (G-11589)
Van Rip Inc..E..... 415 529-5403
  Brooklyn (G-2553)
◆ Wlf Founders Corporation...............D..... 718 777-8899
  Astoria (G-446)

2041 Flour, Grain Milling

ADM Milling Co.....................................D..... 716 849-7333
  Buffalo (G-2621)
Archer-Daniels-Midland Company.....D..... 716 849-7333
  Buffalo (G-2643)
Archer-Daniels-Midland Company.....E..... 518 828-4691
  Hudson (G-6147)
Archer-Daniels-Midland Company.....D..... 518 828-4691
  Hudson (G-6148)
Archer-Daniels-Midland Company.....G..... 585 346-2311
  Lakeville (G-6773)
Ardent Mills LLC.................................D..... 518 447-1700
  Albany (G-43)
Aryzta LLC..F..... 585 235-8160
  Rochester (G-13250)
◆ Birkett Mills.....................................G..... 315 536-3311
  Penn Yan (G-12578)
Birkett Mills...E..... 315 536-4112
  Penn Yan (G-12579)
Cochecton Mills Inc............................E..... 845 932-8282
  Cochecton (G-3501)
Frozen Pastry Products Corp..............E..... 845 364-9833
  Spring Valley (G-14570)
General Mills Inc.................................E..... 716 856-6060
  Buffalo (G-2771)
Ohio Baking Company Inc...................E..... 315 724-2033
  Utica (G-15289)
Pizza Blends LLC.................................G..... 518 356-6650
  Schenectady (G-14295)
▲ R Hadley Corporation......................D..... 607 589-4415
  Spencer (G-14549)
◆ Sheppard Grain Enterprises LLC.....E..... 315 548-9271
  Phelps (G-12608)

2043 Cereal Breakfast Foods

◆ Associated Brands Inc.....................B..... 585 798-3475
  Medina (G-7727)
Chia Usa LLC......................................G..... 212 226-7512
  New York (G-8985)
Gabila Food Products Inc...................E..... 631 789-2220
  Copiague (G-3654)
General Mills Inc.................................D..... 716 856-6060
  Buffalo (G-2772)
Group International LLC.......................G..... 718 475-8805
  Flushing (G-4855)
◆ Pepsico Inc.......................................A..... 914 253-2000
  Purchase (G-13010)
Sangster Foods Inc.............................F..... 212 993-9129
  Brooklyn (G-2383)
Sanzdranz LLC....................................G..... 518 894-8625
  Delmar (G-3969)
Sanzdranz LLC....................................G..... 518 894-8625
  Schenectady (G-14301)

2044 Rice Milling

◆ Gassho Body & Mind Inc..................G..... 518 695-9991
  Schuylerville (G-14324)
▲ Real Co Inc.......................................G..... 347 433-8549
  Valley Cottage (G-15321)

2045 Flour, Blended & Prepared

▲ Allied Food Products Inc..................F..... 718 230-4227
  Brooklyn (G-1488)

Bektrom Foods Inc..............................G..... 516 802-3800
  Syosset (G-14778)
Cohens Bakery Inc..............................E..... 716 892-8149
  Buffalo (G-2702)
Dawn Food Products Inc.....................C..... 716 830-8214
  Williamsville (G-16128)
Elis Bread (eli Zabar) Inc....................F..... 212 772-2011
  New York (G-9342)
New Hope Mills Inc.............................F..... 315 252-2676
  Auburn (G-486)
Pizza Blends LLC.................................G..... 518 356-6650
  Schenectady (G-14295)
Rhosey LLC..G..... 718 382-1226
  Brooklyn (G-2343)

2046 Wet Corn Milling

Anthony Gigi Inc..................................G..... 860 984-1943
  Shirley (G-14413)
Attis Ethanol Fulton LLC....................D..... 315 593-0500
  Fulton (G-5054)
▲ Sweetwater Energy Inc....................G..... 585 647-5760
  Rochester (G-13751)

2047 Dog & Cat Food

American Cat Club LLC.......................G..... 212 779-1140
  New York (G-8546)
◆ Colgate-Palmolive Company............A..... 212 310-2000
  New York (G-9051)
Farmers Dog Inc..................................G..... 646 780-7957
  New York (G-9473)
Hills Pet Products Inc.........................G..... 212 310-2000
  New York (G-9786)
Hound & Gatos Pet Foods Corp........G..... 212 618-1917
  New York (G-9822)
Nestle Purina Petcare Company.........B..... 716 366-8080
  Dunkirk (G-4061)
◆ Pet Proteins LLC..............................G..... 888 293-1029
  New York (G-10812)
Robert Abady Dog Food Co Ltd.........F..... 845 473-1900
  Poughkeepsie (G-12979)
Scooby Rendering & Inc......................G..... 315 793-1014
  Utica (G-15293)
▲ Southern Tier Pet Ntrtn LLC...........E..... 607 674-2121
  Sherburne (G-14394)

2048 Prepared Feeds For Animals & Fowls

Bailey Boonville Mills Inc...................G..... 315 942-2131
  Boonville (G-1103)
Baker Commodities Inc.......................E..... 585 482-1880
  Rochester (G-13259)
Cargill Incorporated............................D..... 585 345-1160
  Batavia (G-607)
Cargill Incorporated............................G..... 716 665-6570
  Kennedy (G-6657)
Cargill Incorporated............................E..... 315 287-0241
  Gouverneur (G-5317)
Cargill Incorporated............................E..... 315 622-3533
  Liverpool (G-7005)
Carolina Eastern-Crocker LLC...........E..... 585 345-4141
  Stafford (G-14602)
Central Garden & Pet Company.........G..... 631 451-8021
  Selden (G-14350)
Cochecton Mills Inc............................G..... 845 932-8282
  Cochecton (G-3501)
Commodity Resource Corporation.....F..... 585 538-9500
  Caledonia (G-3069)
Eastport Feeds Inc..............................G..... 631 325-0077
  Eastport (G-4251)
Gramco Inc...G..... 716 592-2845
  Springville (G-14592)
Grand Maes Cntry Naturals LLC.......G..... 212 348-8171
  New York (G-9659)
▲ Harbor Point Mineral Pdts Inc........F..... 315 797-1300
  Utica (G-15270)
Heath Manufacturing Company..........G..... 800 444-3140
  Batavia (G-617)
JD Granary LLC...................................G..... 607 627-6294
  Smyrna (G-14490)
Kent Nutrition Group Inc....................F..... 315 788-0032
  Watertown (G-15577)
Lowville Farmers Coop Inc.................E..... 315 376-6587
  Lowville (G-7417)
Lutz Feed Co Inc.................................E..... 607 432-7984
  Oneonta (G-12273)
Narrowsburg Feed & Grain Co..........F..... 845 252-3936
  Narrowsburg (G-8210)
Nutra-Vet Research Corp....................F..... 845 473-1900
  Poughkeepsie (G-12976)
Pine Tree Farms Inc............................E..... 607 532-4312
  Interlaken (G-6286)

Scotts Feed Inc...................................E..... 518 483-3110
  Malone (G-7489)
Veterinary Biochemical Ltd................G..... 845 473-1900
  Poughkeepsie (G-12989)
Wagners LLC..G..... 516 933-6580
  Jericho (G-6598)

2051 Bread, Bakery Prdts Exc Cookies & Crackers

3rd Avenue Doughnut Inc...................F..... 718 748-3294
  Brooklyn (G-1416)
40 Street Baking Inc...........................G..... 212 683-4700
  Brooklyn (G-1418)
527 Franco Bakery Corporation.........G..... 718 993-4200
  Bronx (G-1182)
999 Bagels Inc.....................................G..... 718 915-0742
  Brooklyn (G-1426)
A & M Appel Distributing Inc.............G..... 516 735-1172
  Massapequa (G-7642)
A Angonoa Inc.....................................C..... 718 762-4466
  College Point (G-3531)
A T A Bagel Shoppe Inc......................G..... 718 352-4948
  Bayside (G-733)
Above The Rest Baking Corp..............D..... 718 313-9222
  Bronx (G-1189)
Addeo Bakers Inc................................F..... 718 367-8316
  Bronx (G-1197)
Aladdin Bakers Inc..............................D..... 718 499-1818
  Brooklyn (G-1475)
Alicias Bakery Inc...............................G..... 914 235-4689
  New Rochelle (G-8318)
Always Baked Fresh Inc.....................G..... 631 648-0811
  Holbrook (G-5985)
Amiram Dror Inc..................................F..... 212 979-9505
  Brooklyn (G-1504)
Andreas Protein Cakery Inc................G..... 646 801-9826
  New York (G-8579)
Aphrodities...G..... 718 224-1774
  Whitestone (G-16087)
Aryzta LLC..C..... 585 235-8160
  Rochester (G-13251)
Aryzta LLC..F..... 585 235-8160
  Rochester (G-13250)
B & D Enterprises Utica Inc...............D..... 315 735-3311
  New Hartford (G-8236)
Bagel Club Inc.....................................F..... 718 423-6106
  Bayside (G-735)
Bagel Grove Inc...................................E..... 315 724-8015
  Utica (G-15240)
Bagel Land...E..... 585 442-3080
  Rochester (G-13257)
Bagelovers Inc.....................................F..... 607 844-3683
  Dryden (G-4037)
Bakery & Coffee Shop.........................G..... 315 287-1829
  Gouverneur (G-5316)
Better Baked Foods LLC......................D..... 716 326-4651
  Westfield (G-15945)
Bien Cuit LLC.......................................F..... 718 852-0200
  Brooklyn (G-1583)
Bimbo Bakeries....................................G..... 631 274-4906
  Deer Park (G-3846)
Bimbo Bakeries....................................F..... 518 463-2221
  Albany (G-50)
Bimbo Bakeries Usa Inc......................G..... 716 692-9140
  Tonawanda (G-15090)
Bimbo Bakeries Usa Inc......................G..... 718 601-1561
  Bronx (G-1214)
Bimbo Bakeries Usa Inc......................G..... 718 545-0291
  Long Island City (G-7177)
Bimbo Bakeries Usa Inc......................F..... 845 255-4345
  New Paltz (G-8305)
Bimbo Bakeries Usa Inc......................E..... 516 877-2850
  Mineola (G-7961)
Bimbo Bakeries Usa Inc......................C..... 716 372-8444
  Olean (G-12225)
Bimbo Bakeries Usa Inc......................G..... 631 951-5183
  Bay Shore (G-657)
Bimbo Bakeries Usa Inc......................F..... 516 887-1024
  Lynbrook (G-7427)
Bimbo Bakeries Usa Inc......................G..... 315 379-9069
  Canton (G-3163)
Bimbo Bakeries Usa Inc......................F..... 518 563-1320
  Plattsburgh (G-12735)
Bimbo Bakeries Usa Inc......................G..... 718 463-6300
  Maspeth (G-7597)
Bimbo Bakeries Usa Inc......................F..... 518 489-4053
  Albany (G-51)
Bimbo Bakeries Usa Inc......................E..... 203 531-2311
  Bay Shore (G-658)

Bimbo Bakeries Usa Inc ....D 315 253-9782
Auburn (G-467)

Bimbo Bakeries Usa Inc ....F 716 706-0450
Lancaster (G-6798)

Bimbo Bakeries Usa Inc ....D 845 568-0943
Newburgh (G-11860)

Bimbo Bakeries Usa Inc ....E 800 856-8544
Vestal (G-15372)

Bimbo Bakeries Usa Inc ....C 315 782-4189
Watertown (G-15560)

Bimbo Bakeries Usa Inc ....F 845 294-5282
Goshen (G-5305)

Blackbirds Brooklyn LLC ....E 917 362-4080
Brooklyn (G-1592)

Blondie S Bakeshop Inc ....G 631 424-4545
Centerport (G-3254)

Bread Factory LLC ....E 914 637-8150
New Rochelle (G-8321)

Brooklyn Sweet Spot Inc ....G 718 522-2577
Brooklyn (G-1622)

▲ Cannoli Factory Inc ....E 631 643-2700
Wyandanch (G-16243)

Caputo Bakery Inc ....G 718 875-6871
Brooklyn (G-1645)

Carmine Street Bagels Inc ....F 212 691-3041
Staten Island (G-14637)

Carolinas Desserts Inc ....G 914 779-4000
Yonkers (G-16293)

Carter Street Bakery Inc ....G 585 749-7104
Rochester (G-13298)

Chambord LLC ....E 718 859-1110
Brooklyn (G-1659)

Charlotte Neuville Design LLC ....G 646 530-4570
Brooklyn (G-1661)

Chocnyc LLC ....G 917 804-4848
New York (G-8995)

Circle 5 Deli Corp ....G 718 525-5687
Jamaica (G-6433)

Coccadotts Inc ....F 518 438-4937
Albany (G-67)

Cohens Bakery Inc ....E 716 892-8149
Buffalo (G-2702)

Commitment 2000 Inc ....G 716 439-1206
Buffalo (G-2706)

Cookie Connection Inc ....G 315 422-2253
Syracuse (G-14860)

Cupcake Contessas Corporation ....G 516 307-1222
North Bellmore (G-12017)

Cuzins Duzin Corp ....G 347 724-6200
Kew Gardens (G-6663)

D-Lite Donuts ....G 718 626-5953
Astoria (G-416)

Daly Meghan ....F 347 699-3259
Brooklyn (G-1720)

Damascus Bakery Inc ....D 718 855-1456
Brooklyn (G-1721)

Dancing Deer Baking Co LLC ......E 617 442-7300
Castleton On Hudson (G-3202)

Delicias Andinas Food Corp ....G 718 416-2922
Flushing (G-4847)

Dipaolo Baking Co Inc ....D 585 303-5013
Rochester (G-13348)

Eileens Special Cheesecake ....E 212 966-5585
New York (G-9330)

Enterprise Bagels Inc ....F 845 896-3823
Fishkill (G-4799)

Famous Doughnuts Inc ....G 716 834-6356
Buffalo (G-2751)

Fayda Manufacturing Corp ....F 718 456-9331
Brooklyn (G-1835)

FB Sale LLC ....G 315 986-9999
Macedon (G-7465)

Felix Roma & Sons Inc ....D 607 748-3336
Endicott (G-4456)

▲ Ferrara Bakery & Cafe Inc ....C 212 226-6150
New York (G-9484)

Flour Power Bakery Cafe ....G 917 747-6895
Livingston Manor (G-7053)

Food Gems Ltd ....E 718 296-7788
Ozone Park (G-12462)

Fotis Oneonta Italian Bakery ....G 607 432-3871
Oneonta (G-12271)

Fratellis LLC ....G 607 722-5663
Binghamton (G-878)

Fritters & Buns Inc ....G 845 227-6609
Hopewell Junction (G-6093)

Fung Wong Bakery Inc ....E 212 267-4037
New York (G-9553)

Gabila & Sons Mfg Inc ....E 631 789-2220
Copiague (G-3653)

Geddes Bakery Co Inc ....E 315 437-8084
North Syracuse (G-12043)

Gennaris Itln French Bky Inc ....G 516 997-8968
Carle Place (G-3174)

George Retzos ....G 315 422-2913
Syracuse (G-14904)

Giovanni Bakery Corp ....F 212 695-4296
New York (G-9614)

Glenn Wayne Wholesale Bky Inc ....D 631 289-9200
Bohemia (G-1018)

▼ Gluten Free Bake Shop Inc ....E 845 782-5307
Mountainville (G-8193)

Golden Glow Cookie Co Inc ....E 718 379-6223
Bronx (G-1267)

Good Bread Bakery ....E 914 939-3900
Port Chester (G-12822)

Gourmet Toast Corp ....G 718 852-4536
Brooklyn (G-1903)

Great American Dessert Co LLC ....D 718 894-3494
Maspeth (G-7620)

Greenvale Bagel Inc ....E 516 221-8221
Wantagh (G-15484)

◆ Greyston Bakery Inc ....E 914 375-1510
Yonkers (G-16316)

H & S Edible Products Corp ....E 914 413-3489
Mount Vernon (G-8146)

H H B Bakery of Little Neck ....G 718 631-7004
Flushing (G-4856)

Hagadah Passover Bakery ....G 718 638-1589
Brooklyn (G-1918)

Hahns Old Fashioned Cake Co .....F 631 249-3456
Farmingdale (G-4643)

Hana Pastries Inc ....G 718 369-7593
Brooklyn (G-1923)

Harrison Bakery West ....E 315 422-1468
Syracuse (G-14909)

Have Your Cake Kitchen LLC ......G 646 820-8074
Brooklyn (G-1927)

▲ Heidelberg Group Inc ....E 315 866-0999
Herkimer (G-5863)

Herris Gourmet Inc ....G 917 578-2308
Brooklyn (G-1934)

Hum Limited Liability Corp ....G 631 525-2174
Nesconset (G-8218)

Indulge Desserts Holdings LLC ....G 212 231-8600
New York (G-9883)

J & S Licata Bros Inc ....F 718 805-6924
Richmond Hill (G-13117)

Jane Bakes Inc ....G 845 920-1100
Pearl River (G-12535)

Jarets Stuffed Cupcakes ....G 607 658-9096
Endicott (G-4460)

Jerrys Bagels ....G 516 791-0063
Valley Stream (G-15344)

JGM Wholesale Bakery Inc ....G 631 396-0131
Amityville (G-282)

Jim Romas Bakery Inc ....E 607 748-7425
Endicott (G-4463)

▲ JJ Cassone Bakery Inc ....B 914 939-1568
Port Chester (G-12823)

Jonathan Lord Corp ....F 631 563-4445
Bohemia (G-1030)

Juniors Cheesecake Inc ....G 718 852-5257
Brooklyn (G-2013)

King Cracker Corp ....E 516 539-9251
Hempstead (G-5842)

Kokoroko Corporation ....G 718 433-4321
Woodside (G-16211)

Kossars On Grand LLC ....E 212 473-4810
New York (G-10129)

L American Ltd ....F 716 372-9480
Olean (G-12238)

La Prima Bakery Inc ....F 718 584-4442
Bronx (G-1297)

Ladybird Bakery Inc ....G 718 499-8108
Brooklyn (G-2042)

Larosa Cupcakes ....G 347 866-3920
Staten Island (G-14675)

Libbys Bakery Cafe LLC ....G 603 918-8825
Ticonderoga (G-15075)

Lillys Homestyle Bakeshop Inc ....D 718 491-2904
Brooklyn (G-2074)

Ljmm Inc ....G 845 454-5876
Poughkeepsie (G-12967)

M & M Bagel Corp ....F 516 295-1222
Cedarhurst (G-3240)

Mac Crete Corporation ....E 718 932-1803
Long Island City (G-7284)

Made Close LLC ....G 917 837-1357
Brooklyn (G-2102)

Mannys Cheesecake Inc ....G 315 732-0639
Utica (G-15280)

Maplehurst Bakeries LLC ....B 315 735-5000
Frankfort (G-4953)

Maxwell Bakery Inc ....E 718 498-2200
Brooklyn (G-2127)

McKee Foods Corporation ....A 631 979-9364
Hauppauge (G-5710)

Mds Hot Bagels Deli Inc ....G 718 438-5650
Brooklyn (G-2129)

Melita Corp ....C 718 392-7280
Astoria (G-429)

Millers Bulk Food and Bakery ......G 585 798-9700
Medina (G-7741)

Miss Grimble Associates Inc ....F 718 665-2253
Bronx (G-1316)

Modern Itln Bky of W Babylon ......C 631 589-7300
Oakdale (G-12153)

Mrs Baking Distribution Corp ....G 718 460-6700
College Point (G-3555)

New Hope Mills Mfg Inc ....E 315 252-2676
Auburn (G-487)

New Mount Pleasant Bakery ....E 518 374-7577
Schenectady (G-14291)

New Star Bakery ....E 718 961-8868
Flushing (G-4877)

Nibble Inc Baking Co ....E 518 334-3950
Troy (G-15175)

Niebylski Bakery Inc ....E 718 721-5152
Astoria (G-431)

▼ Nightingale Food Entps Inc ....G 347 577-1630
New York (G-10626)

Nildas Desserts Limited ....F 845 454-5876
Poughkeepsie (G-12975)

Ohio Baking Company Inc ....E 315 724-2033
Utica (G-15289)

Operative Cake Corp ....E 718 278-5600
Bronx (G-1329)

Ossining Bakery Lmp Inc ....G 914 941-2654
Ossining (G-12405)

OWayne Enterprises Inc ....E 718 326-2200
Maspeth (G-7632)

Oz Baking Company Ltd ....G 516 466-5114
Great Neck (G-5410)

▲ Palagonia Bakery Co Inc ....D 718 272-5400
Brooklyn (G-2242)

Pane DOro ....F 914 964-0043
Yonkers (G-16339)

▼ Peking Food LLC ....E 718 628-8080
Brooklyn (G-2252)

Perrottas Bakery Inc ....E 518 283-4711
Troy (G-15178)

Pesces Bakery Inc ....G 845 246-4730
Saugerties (G-14208)

Placid Baker ....E 518 326-2657
Troy (G-15180)

Presser Kosher Baking Corp ....E 718 375-5088
Brooklyn (G-2282)

Quaker Bonnet Inc ....G 716 885-7208
Buffalo (G-2941)

R & H Baking Co Inc ....E 718 852-1768
Brooklyn (G-2318)

Rays Italian Bakery Inc ....F 516 825-9170
Valley Stream (G-15355)

▲ Rays Restaurant & Bakery Inc ....G 718 441-7707
Jamaica (G-6469)

Reisman Bros Bakery Inc ....F 718 331-1975
Brooklyn (G-2337)

Richard Engdal Baking Corp ....F 914 777-9600
Mamaroneck (G-7521)

Rm Bakery LLC ....E 718 472-3036
Bronx (G-1351)

Rnd Food Service Inc ....F 917 291-0061
New York (G-11057)

Rock Hill Bakehouse Ltd ....E 518 743-1627
Gansevoort (G-5086)

Roma Bakery Inc ....F 516 825-9170
Valley Stream (G-15357)

Roslyn Bread Company Inc ....E 516 625-1470
Roslyn Heights (G-14056)

◆ Royal Sweet Bakery Inc ....F 718 567-7770
Brooklyn (G-2362)

Saint Honore Pastry Shop Inc ......G 516 767-2555
Port Washington (G-12921)

▼ Saj of Freeport Corp ....C 516 623-8800
Freeport (G-5021)

Sapienza Pastry Inc ....E 516 352-5232
Elmont (G-4389)

▲ Satispie LLC ....E 716 982-4600
Rochester (G-13715)

Scaife Enterprises Inc ....F 585 454-5231
  Fairport (G-4519)
◆ Secure International ....G 716 206-2500
  Lancaster (G-6833)
Settepani Inc ....E 718 349-6524
  Brooklyn (G-2397)
Silver Bell Baking Co ....G 718 335-9539
  Middle Village (G-7884)
Slims Bagels Unlimited Inc ....E 718 229-1140
  Oakland Gardens (G-12160)
Smith Street Bread Co LLC ....F 718 797-9712
  Brooklyn (G-2431)
Soutine Inc ....G 212 496-1450
  New York (G-11306)
Stebe Shcjhjff ....F 839 383-9833
  Poughkeepsie (G-12985)
Sugarbear Cupcakes ....G 917 698-9005
  Jamaica (G-6476)
▲ Sullivan St Bky - Hlls Kit Inc .....E 212 265-5580
  New York (G-11386)
T&B Bakery Corp ....G 646 642-4300
  Maspeth (G-7638)
Tarrytown Bakery Inc ....F 914 631-0209
  Tarrytown (G-15063)
Tates Wholesale LLC ....C 631 780-6511
  East Moriches (G-4140)
Triboro Bagel Co Inc ....E 718 359-9245
  Flushing (G-4901)
Uncle Wallys LLC ....E 631 205-0455
  Shirley (G-14428)
Village Lantern Baking Corp ....G 631 225-1690
  Lindenhurst (G-6984)
Vito & Sons Bakery ....F 201 617-8501
  Brooklyn (G-2566)
Waldorf Bakers Inc ....F 718 665-2253
  Bronx (G-1394)
▲ Wenner Bread Products Inc ......B 800 869-6262
  Ronkonkoma (G-14026)
Wenner Bread Products Inc ....E 800 869-6262
  Ronkonkoma (G-14027)
Wenner Bread Products Inc ....F 800 869-6262
  Bayport (G-732)
Whitestone Panetteria LLC ....G 516 543-9788
  Whitestone (G-16103)
Worlds Best Cookie Dough Inc ......G 347 592-3422
  New York (G-11783)

2052 Cookies & Crackers

17 Bakers LLC ....F 844 687-6836
  Williamsville (G-16116)
212kiddish Inc ....G 718 705-7227
  Brooklyn (G-1411)
▲ Aron Streit Inc ....G 212 475-7000
  Orangeburg (G-12307)
Aryzta LLC ....C 585 235-8160
  Rochester (G-13251)
Butterwood Desserts Inc ....E 716 652-0131
  West Falls (G-15761)
Chipita America Inc ....E 845 292-2540
  Ferndale (G-4787)
Cone Buddy System Inc ....F 585 427-9940
  Rochester (G-13322)
▲ Cookies United LLC ....C 631 581-4000
  Islip (G-6351)
Cooking With Chef Michelle LLC ....G 516 662-2324
  Calverton (G-3079)
◆ Creative Food Ingredients Inc ...C 585 237-2213
  Perry (G-12596)
D F Stauffer Biscuit Co Inc ....E 585 968-2700
  Cuba (G-3811)
Dancing Deer Baking Co LLC ....E 617 442-7300
  Castleton On Hudson (G-3202)
Danny Macaroons Inc....................G 260 622-8463
  New York (G-9168)
▲ Elenis Nyc Inc ....E 718 361-8136
  Long Island City (G-7213)
Falcones Cookie Land Ltd ....F 718 236-4200
  Brooklyn (G-1830)
Golden Glow Cookie Co Inc ....E 718 379-6223
  Bronx (G-1267)
▲ Great Brands of Europe Inc ....G 914 872-8804
  White Plains (G-16010)
Jonathan Lord Corp ....F 631 563-4445
  Bohemia (G-1030)
▲ Kaltec Food Packaging Inc ....G 845 856-9888
  Port Jervis (G-12851)
Keebler Company ....F 585 948-8010
  Oakfield (G-12157)
Ladybird Bakery Inc......................G 718 499-8108
  Brooklyn (G-2042)

▲ Larte Del Gelato Inc ....G 212 366-0570
  New York (G-10174)
Linden Cookies Inc ....E 845 268-5050
  Congers (G-3617)
Lloyd Price Icon Food Brands ....F 914 764-8624
  Pound Ridge (G-12993)
Mannys Cheesecake Inc ....G 315 732-0639
  Utica (G-15280)
Mindful Foods Inc ....G 646 708-0454
  New York (G-10475)
My Most Favorite Food ....G 212 580-5130
  New York (G-10524)
New Mount Pleasant Bakery ....E 518 374-7577
  Schenectady (G-14291)
Pdi Cone Co Inc ....D 716 825-8750
  Buffalo (G-2909)
◆ Pepsico Inc ....A 914 253-2000
  Purchase (G-13010)
Quaker Bonnet Inc ....G 716 885-7208
  Buffalo (G-2941)
Sapienza Pastry Inc ....E 516 352-5232
  Elmont (G-4389)
Top Seedz LLC ....G 716 380-2612
  Buffalo (G-3015)
Treehouse Private Brands Inc ....C 716 693-4715
  Tonawanda (G-15147)
U Serve Brands Inc ....F 877 632-6654
  New York (G-11572)
United Baking Co Inc ....F 631 413-5116
  Central Islip (G-3291)
Wonton Food Inc ....E 718 784-8178
  Long Island City (G-7406)
▲ Wonton Food Inc ....C 718 628-6868
  Brooklyn (G-2593)

2053 Frozen Bakery Prdts

Bello LLC ....C 516 623-8800
  Freeport (G-4987)
Butterwood Desserts Inc................E 716 652-0131
  West Falls (G-15761)
▲ Circle Peak Capital MGT LLC.......E 646 230-8812
  New York (G-9010)
Culinary Arts Specialties Inc ....D 716 656-8943
  Cheektowaga (G-3343)
Deiorio Foods Inc ....C 315 732-7612
  Utica (G-15254)
Dufour Pastry Kitchens Inc ....E 718 402-8800
  Bronx (G-1243)
Fratellis LLC ....E 607 722-5663
  Binghamton (G-878)
▲ LArte Del Gelato Gruppo Inc.......F 718 383-6600
  Long Island City (G-7269)
Liddabit Sweets ....G 917 912-1370
  Brooklyn (G-2068)
Maplehurst Bakeries LLC ....B 315 735-5000
  Frankfort (G-4953)
Micosta Enterprises Inc ....G 518 822-9708
  Hudson (G-6171)
◆ Rich Holdings Inc ....D 716 878-8000
  Buffalo (G-2953)
◆ Rich Products Corporation ....A 716 878-8000
  Buffalo (G-2954)
▲ Wenner Bread Products Inc.........B 800 869-6262
  Ronkonkoma (G-14026)
Wenner Bread Products Inc ....E 800 869-6262
  Ronkonkoma (G-14027)

2061 Sugar, Cane

▲ Supreme Chocolatier LLC ....E 718 761-9600
  Staten Island (G-14718)
US Sweeteners Corp ....E 718 854-8714
  Brooklyn (G-2549)

2062 Sugar, Cane Refining

American Sugar Refining Inc ....E 914 376-3386
  Yonkers (G-16285)
Cane Sugar LLC ....G 212 329-2695
  New York (G-8904)
Domino Foods Inc ....F 800 729-4840
  Yonkers (G-16303)
Refined Sugars Inc ....G 914 963-2400
  Yonkers (G-16345)
▲ Sweeteners Plus LLC ....D 585 728-3770
  Lakeville (G-6776)

2063 Sugar, Beet

Beets Love Production LLC ....E 585 270-2471
  Rochester (G-13265)

New York Sugars LLC.....................F 585 500-0155
  Rochester (G-13573)

2064 Candy & Confectionery Prdts

▲ 5th Avenue Chocolatiere Ltd...........G 212 935-5454
  Freeport (G-4977)
Aigner Chocolates ....G 718 544-1850
  Forest Hills (G-4915)
Amiram Dror Inc ....G 212 979-9505
  Brooklyn (G-1504)
Anyas Licorice Inc ....G 917 935-1916
  Brooklyn (G-1515)
Bader Enterprise Inc ....G 718 965-9434
  Brooklyn (G-1560)
C Howard Company Inc...................G 631 286-7940
  Bellport (G-795)
▼ Calico Cottage Inc ....E 631 841-2100
  Amityville (G-257)
▲ Chocolat Moderne LLC ....G 212 229-4797
  New York (G-8996)
▲ Chocolate Delivery Systems Inc.......E 716 877-3146
  Buffalo (G-2696)
Chocolate Pizza Company Inc ....G 315 673-4098
  Marcellus (G-7561)
Chocolations LLC ....G 914 777-3600
  Mamaroneck (G-7503)
Dilese International Inc..................F 716 855-3500
  Buffalo (G-2729)
Eatingevolved LLC ....F 631 675-2440
  Setauket (G-14379)
▲ Fairbanks Mfg LLC ....E 845 341-0002
  Middletown (G-7908)
Fine and Raw Chocolate ....G 718 366-3633
  Brooklyn (G-1844)
Fruit Fresh Up Inc ....E 716 683-3200
  Depew (G-3983)
Gertrude Hawk Chocolates Inc..........E
  Watertown (G-15570)
▲ Godiva Chocolatier Inc ....E 212 984-5900
  New York (G-9636)
Golden Chocolate Inc ....G 718 330-1000
  Brooklyn (G-1897)
Gravymaster Inc ....E 203 453-1893
  Canajoharie (G-3120)
Handsome Dans LLC ....G 917 965-2499
  New York (G-9719)
Hercules Candy Co ....G 315 463-4339
  East Syracuse (G-4216)
Hudson Valley Chocolatier Inc ....F 845 831-8240
  Beacon (G-753)
▼ In Room Plus Inc ....E 716 838-9433
  Buffalo (G-2808)
Jo-Mart Candies Corp....................F 718 375-1277
  Brooklyn (G-1996)
Joseph Shalhoub & Son Inc ....F 718 871-6300
  Brooklyn (G-2002)
◆ Joyva Corp ....D 718 497-0170
  Brooklyn (G-2006)
Keep Healthy Inc ....F 631 651-9090
  Northport (G-12106)
Koppers Choclat Specialty Inc ....G 917 834-2290
  New York (G-10126)
L A Burdick Chocolates ....F 212 796-0143
  New York (G-10149)
Lady-N-Th-wndow Chocolates Inc ....F 631 549-1059
  Huntington (G-6210)
▲ Lanco Corporation ....C 631 231-2300
  Ronkonkoma (G-13964)
▲ Landies Candies Co Inc ....F 716 834-8212
  Buffalo (G-2847)
Little Bird Chocolates Inc...............E 646 620-6395
  Plainview (G-12697)
Momn Pops Inc ....E 845 567-0640
  Cornwall (G-3729)
▲ Mrchocolatecom LLC ....F 718 875-9772
  Brooklyn (G-2179)
▲ N Make Mold Inc ....E 716 877-3146
  Buffalo (G-2878)
▼ Naples Vly Mrgers Acqstons LLC.....G 585 490-1339
  Naples (G-8209)
◆ Nassau Candy Distributors Inc ....C 516 433-7100
  Hicksville (G-5933)
Noras Candy Shop ....F 315 337-4530
  Rome (G-13860)
OH How Cute Inc ....G 347 838-6031
  Staten Island (G-14687)
Pachanga Inc ....F 212 832-0022
  New York (G-10737)
Papa Bubble ....G 212 966-2599
  New York (G-10747)

S
I
C

◆ Pfeil & Holing Inc ....D 718 545-4600
  Woodside (G-16219)
Premium Sweets USA Inc ....G 718 739-6000
  Jamaica (G-6466)
▲ Richardson Brands Company .....C 800 839-8938
  Canajoharie (G-3121)
Robert Pikcilingis ....F 518 355-1860
  Altamont (G-198)
Roger L Urban Inc ....E 716 693-5391
  North Tonawanda (G-12089)
Salty Road Inc ....G 347 673-3925
  Brooklyn (G-2382)
◆ Satin Fine Foods Inc ....D 845 469-1034
  Chester (G-3386)
▲ Scaccianoce Inc ....F 718 991-4462
  Bronx (G-1362)
Seaward Candies ....G 585 638-6761
  Holley (G-6038)
◆ Settons Intl Foods Inc ....E 631 543-8090
  Commack (G-3598)
▲ Simply Natural Foods LLC ....C 631 543-9600
  Commack (G-3599)
Stones Homemade Candies Inc .....G 315 343-8401
  Oswego (G-12422)
◆ Sweetworks Inc ....C 716 634-4545
  Buffalo (G-2998)
◆ Tomric Systems Inc ....F 716 854-6050
  Buffalo (G-3013)
Valenti Distributing ....G 716 824-2304
  Blasdell (G-924)
◆ Vidal Candies USA Inc ....G 609 781-8169
  New York (G-11679)
◆ Vigneri Chocolate Inc ....G 585 254-6160
  Rochester (G-13797)
Wellspring Corp ....G 212 529-5454
  New York (G-11741)

2066 Chocolate & Cocoa Prdts

▲ 5th Avenue Chocolatiere LLC ....E 516 868-8070
  Freeport (G-4976)
▲ 5th Avenue Chocolatiere Ltd .....G 212 935-5454
  Freeport (G-4977)
Adirondack Chocolate Co Ltd .....F 518 946-7270
  Wilmington (G-16152)
Aethera LLC ....E 215 324-9222
  New York (G-8489)
Aigner Chocolates ....G 718 544-1850
  Forest Hills (G-4915)
Amiram Dror Inc ....F 212 979-9505
  Brooklyn (G-1504)
◆ Associated Brands Inc ....B 585 798-3475
  Medina (G-7727)
Big Heart Pet Brands ....E 716 891-6566
  Buffalo (G-2664)
▲ Cemoi Inc ....G 212 583-4920
  New York (G-8946)
Chocolate Lady LLC ....G 516 532-0551
  Port Jervis (G-12845)
Chocolate Pizza Company Inc .....F 315 673-4098
  Marcellus (G-7561)
Commodore Chocolatier USA Inc ...F 845 561-3960
  Newburgh (G-11861)
Ctac Holdings LLC ....F 212 924-2280
  Brooklyn (G-1707)
Dilese International Inc ....F 716 855-3500
  Buffalo (G-2729)
Dolce Vite International LLC .....G 713 962-5767
  Brooklyn (G-1754)
Doma Marketing Inc ....G 516 684-1111
  Port Washington (G-12874)
Eating Evolved Inc ....G 516 510-2601
  Hauppauge (G-5643)
Emvi Inc ....G 518 883-5111
  Broadalbin (G-1173)
Fox 416 Corp ....E 718 385-4600
  Brooklyn (G-1864)
▲ Godiva Chocolatier Inc ....E 212 984-5900
  New York (G-9636)
Greenwood Winery LLC ....G 315 432-8132
  East Syracuse (G-4213)
Jo-Mart Candies Corp ....F 718 375-1277
  Brooklyn (G-1996)
◆ Joyva Corp ....D 718 497-0170
  Brooklyn (G-2006)
Lady-N-Th-wndow Chocolates Inc ..F 631 549-1059
  Huntington (G-6210)
◆ Lanco Corporation ....C 631 231-2300
  Ronkonkoma (G-13964)
▲ Le Chocolate of Rockland LLC ...E 845 533-4125
  Suffern (G-14762)

LMC 49th Inc ....E 718 361-9161
  Long Island City (G-7277)
LMC 49th Inc ....F 212 744-7117
  New York (G-10237)
▲ Max Brenner Union Square LLC ...G 646 467-8803
  New York (G-10390)
Mbny LLC ....F 646 467-8810
  New York (G-10394)
Menrose USA LLC ....G 718 221-5540
  Brooklyn (G-2137)
Micosta Enterprises Inc ....G 518 822-9708
  Hudson (G-6171)
Momn Pops Inc ....E 845 567-0640
  Cornwall (G-3729)
Nibmor Project LLC ....F 718 374-5091
  Great Neck (G-5405)
Noras Candy Shop ....F 315 337-4530
  Rome (G-13860)
Parkside Candy Co Inc ....F 716 833-7540
  Buffalo (G-2907)
▲ Reserve Confections Inc ....F 845 371-7744
  Spring Valley (G-14581)
Robert Pikcilingis ....F 518 355-1860
  Altamont (G-198)
Roger L Urban Inc ....E 716 693-5391
  North Tonawanda (G-12089)
◆ Settons Intl Foods Inc ....D 631 543-8090
  Commack (G-3598)
▲ Simply Natural Foods LLC ....C 631 543-9600
  Commack (G-3599)
▲ Superior Confections Inc ....G 718 698-3300
  Staten Island (G-14717)
◆ Sweetworks Inc ....C 716 634-4545
  Buffalo (G-2998)
The Chocolate Shop ....G 716 882-5055
  Buffalo (G-3008)
Van Rip Inc ....E 415 529-5403
  Brooklyn (G-2553)
Yes Were Nuts Ltd ....G 516 374-1940
  Hewlett (G-5877)

2067 Chewing Gum

▲ Ford Gum & Machine Company Inc .D 716 542-4561
  Akron (G-17)
◆ Sweetworks Inc ....C 716 634-4545
  Buffalo (G-2998)

2068 Salted & Roasted Nuts & Seeds

Our Daily Eats LLC ....F 518 810-8412
  Albany (G-110)
◆ Sahadi Fine Foods Inc ....E 718 369-0100
  Brooklyn (G-2381)
▲ Scaccianoce Inc ....F 718 991-4462
  Bronx (G-1362)
◆ Settons Intl Foods Inc ....D 631 543-8090
  Commack (G-3598)
◆ Sugar Foods Corporation ....E 212 753-6900
  New York (G-11385)
Whitsons Food Svc Bronx Corp ....B 631 424-2700
  Islandia (G-6346)

2074 Cottonseed Oil Mills

▲ Perimondo LLC ....G 212 749-0721
  New York (G-10804)

2076 Vegetable Oil Mills

▲ Jax Coco USA LLC ....G 347 688-8198
  New York (G-9979)

2077 Animal, Marine Fats & Oils

Baker Commodities Inc ....E 585 482-1880
  Rochester (G-13259)
Darling Ingredients Inc ....F 716 895-0655
  Buffalo (G-2721)
Textured Fd Innvations Tfi LLC ...G 515 731-3663
  Carle Place (G-3182)

2079 Shortening, Oils & Margarine

▲ Bonelli Foods LLC ....G 212 346-0942
  New York (G-8834)
Bunge Limited Finance Corp ......D 914 684-2800
  White Plains (G-15985)
C B S Food Products Corp ....F 718 452-2500
  Brooklyn (G-1635)
Consumer Flavoring Extract Co ....F 718 435-0201
  Brooklyn (G-1682)
Gourmet Factory Inc ....G 631 231-4548
  Hauppauge (G-5662)

Healthy Brand Oil Corp ....E 718 937-0806
  Long Island City (G-7239)
◆ Kerry Bfnctnal Ingredients Inc ..D 608 363-1200
  Norwich (G-12123)
L LLC ....E 716 885-3918
  Buffalo (G-2841)
Lesieur Cristal Inc ....G 646 604-4314
  Long Island City (G-7270)
▲ Pietro Demarco Importers Inc ...F 914 969-3201
  Yonkers (G-16342)
Pinos Press Inc ....G 315 935-0110
  Syracuse (G-14965)

2082 Malt Beverages

Anheuser-Busch LLC ....G 315 638-0365
  Baldwinsville (G-541)
Anheuser-Busch LLC ....C 315 638-0365
  Baldwinsville (G-542)
Anheuser-Busch LLC ....C 212 573-8800
  New York (G-8585)
Anheuser-Busch Companies LLC ....G 718 589-2610
  Bronx (G-1206)
Anheuser-Busch Inbev Fin Inc ....F 212 573-8800
  New York (G-8586)
Anheuser-Busch Inbev Svcs LLC ...G 314 765-4729
  New York (G-8587)
Barrier Brewing Company LLC .....G 516 316-4429
  Long Beach (G-7135)
Brazen Street LLC ....E 516 305-7951
  Brooklyn (G-1606)
▲ Brewery Ommegang Ltd ....E 607 286-4144
  Cooperstown (G-3638)
▲ Castle Brands Inc ....E 646 356-0200
  New York (G-8930)
Constellation Brands Inc ....D 585 678-7100
  Victor (G-15399)
Coopers Cave Ale Co S-Corp .....F 518 792-0007
  Glens Falls (G-5246)
Cooperstown Brewing Co LLC ......G 607 286-9330
  Oneonta (G-12268)
Crazy Cowboy Brewing Co LLC .....E 516 812-0576
  Woodbury (G-16169)
Duvel Mortgage USA Inc ....G 607 267-6121
  Cooperstown (G-3640)
Empire Brewing Company Inc ......D 315 925-8308
  Syracuse (G-14887)
Equilibrium Brewery LLC ....G 201 245-0292
  Middletown (G-7907)
Gilded Otter Brewing Co ....D 845 256-1700
  New Paltz (G-8306)
◆ High Falls Brewing Company LLC ..C 585 263-9318
  Rochester (G-13466)
High Falls Operating Co LLC .....A 585 546-1030
  Rochester (G-13467)
Hoptron Brewtique ....G 631 438-0296
  Patchogue (G-12502)
Horns & Halos Cft Brewing LLC ...E 585 507-7248
  Caledonia (G-3071)
Hyde Park Brewing Co Inc ....E 845 229-8277
  Hyde Park (G-6272)
Indian Ladder Farmstead Brewer ..G 518 577-1484
  Altamont (G-194)
Keegan Ales LLC ....F 845 331-2739
  Kingston (G-6695)
Keuka Brewing Co LLC ....G 607 868-4648
  Hammondsport (G-5531)
Kings Cnty Brwers Cllective LLC ..F 917 207-2739
  Brooklyn (G-2031)
▲ Labatt USA LLC ....D 716 604-1050
  Buffalo (G-2842)
Lic Brewery LLC ....G 917 832-6840
  Long Island City (G-7271)
Liquid State Brewing Co Inc .....G 607 319-6209
  Ithaca (G-6392)
Lock 1 Distilling Company LLC ....G 315 934-4376
  Phoenix (G-12616)
Long Ireland Brewing LLC ....G 631 403-4303
  Riverhead (G-13179)
▲ Mad Scntsts Brwing Prtners LLC ..E 347 766-2739
  Brooklyn (G-2101)
▲ Middle Ages Brewing Company ....G 315 476-4250
  Syracuse (G-14941)
Mikkeller Nyc ....G 917 572-0357
  Flushing (G-4874)
Millercoors LLC ....E 585 385-0670
  Pittsford (G-12652)
Montauk Brewing Company Inc .....F 631 668-8471
  Montauk (G-8055)
Murphs Famous Inc ....G 516 398-0417
  Rockville Centre (G-13831)

Newburgh Brewing Company LLC......F 845 569-2337
Newburgh *(G-11876)*

▼ North American Breweries Inc.....F 585 546-1030
Rochester *(G-13581)*

North Amrcn Brwries Hldngs LLC.....E 585 546-1030
Rochester *(G-13582)*

Oyster Bay Brewing Company ....F 516 802-5546
Oyster Bay *(G-12452)*

Rare Form Brewing Company ....G 518 313-9256
Troy *(G-15183)*

Remarkable Liquids LLC...............D 518 861-5351
Altamont *(G-197)*

Rohrbach Brewing Company Inc .....D 585 594-9800
Rochester *(G-13704)*

▲ Shmaltz Brewing Company...........E 518 406-5430
Clifton Park *(G-3474)*

Simple Brewer ....E 845 490-0182
Somers *(G-14501)*

Spectacle Brewing LLC ....E 845 942-8776
Garnerville *(G-5135)*

Valcour Brewing Company LLC ....E 518 324-2337
Plattsburgh *(G-12789)*

▲ Vanberg & Dewulf Co Inc ....G 607 547-8184
Cooperstown *(G-3641)*

Vernon Wine & Liquor Inc ....G 718 784-5096
Long Island City *(G-7394)*

Wagner Vineyards & Brewing Co ....G 607 582-6574
Lodi *(G-7133)*

Woodcock Brothers Brewing Comp .....F 716 333-4000
Wilson *(G-16155)*

Yonkers Whl Beer Distrs Inc ....G 914 963-8600
Yonkers *(G-16361)*

2083 Malt

▲ Great Western Malting Co ....G 800 496-7732
Champlain *(G-3312)*

Queen City Malting LLC ....G 716 481-1313
Buffalo *(G-2943)*

2084 Wine & Brandy

Adirondack Winery LLC ....G 518 668-9463
Lake George *(G-6756)*

Allied Wine Corp ....F 845 796-4160
South Fallsburg *(G-14508)*

Americana Vineyards & Winery ....F 607 387-6801
Interlaken *(G-6283)*

Anthony Road Wine Co Inc ....F 315 536-2182
Penn Yan *(G-12577)*

Anyelas Vineyards LLC ....F 315 685-3797
Skaneateles *(G-14446)*

Arrowhead Spring Vineyards LLC.......G 716 434-8030
Lockport *(G-7060)*

Atwater Estate Vineyards LLC ....E 607 546-8463
Burdett *(G-3055)*

Bad Seed Cider Co LLC..................G 914 474-4422
Highland *(G-5957)*

Bibo International LLC ....F 617 304-2242
New York *(G-8780)*

Billsboro Winery ....G 315 789-9538
Geneva *(G-5147)*

Brooklyn Winery LLC ....F 347 763-1506
Brooklyn *(G-1623)*

▲ Brotherhood Americas ....E 845 496-3661
Washingtonville *(G-15524)*

Casa Larga Vineyards ....E 585 223-4210
Fairport *(G-4492)*

Casa Larga Vineyards ....G 585 223-4210
Fairport *(G-4493)*

Cascade Mountain Winery & Rest......F 845 373-9021
Amenia *(G-201)*

▲ Cava Spiliadis USA ....E 212 247-8214
New York *(G-8939)*

Chautauqua Wine Company Inc ....G 716 934-9463
Silver Creek *(G-14440)*

Clinton Vineyards Inc ....G 845 266-5372
Clinton Corners *(G-3487)*

Cobblestone Frm Winery Vinyrd ....F 315 549-1004
Romulus *(G-13878)*

Constellation Brands Inc.................D 585 678-7100
Victor *(G-15399)*

Constellation Brands Inc.................E 585 393-4880
Canandaigua *(G-3129)*

Constellation Brands Smo LLC ....G 585 396-7161
New York *(G-9088)*

Coyote Moon LLC ....F 315 686-5600
Clayton *(G-3453)*

▼ Cruzin Management Inc................E 212 641-8700
New York *(G-9126)*

Damiani Wine Cellars LLC..............G 607 546-5557
Burdett *(G-3056)*

David F De Marco...........................G 315 536-0882
Penn Yan *(G-12581)*

◆ Davos Brands LLC ....F 212 779-1911
New York *(G-9189)*

Deer Run Enterprises Inc ....G 585 346-0850
Geneseo *(G-5143)*

Di Borghese Castello LLC.................F 631 734-5111
Cutchogue *(G-3815)*

▲ Dorset Farms ....F 631 734-6010
Peconic *(G-12545)*

▲ Dreyfus Ashby Inc......................E 212 818-0770
New York *(G-9271)*

Duck Walk Vinyards ....E 631 726-7555
Water Mill *(G-15530)*

▲ Dutch Spirits LLC.......................F 518 398-1022
Pine Plains *(G-12633)*

Dutchess Wines LLC......................G 845 876-1319
Rhinebeck *(G-13099)*

▲ Eagle Crest Vineyard LLC ....G 585 346-5760
Conesus *(G-3605)*

East Branch Winery Inc ....G 607 292-3999
Dundee *(G-4045)*

▲ East End Vineyards LLC..............G 718 468-0500
Queens Village *(G-13019)*

Edrington Group Usa LLC................E 212 352-6000
New York *(G-9322)*

Fly Creek Cder Mill Orchrd Inc ....G 607 547-9692
Fly Creek *(G-4909)*

Fox Run Vineyards Inc ....F 315 536-4616
Penn Yan *(G-12584)*

Freedom Run Winery Inc ....G 716 433-4136
Lockport *(G-7076)*

Greenwood Winery LLC ....E 315 432-8132
East Syracuse *(G-4213)*

Hazlitts 1852 Vineyards Inc ....E 607 546-9463
Hector *(G-5825)*

Heart & Hands Wine Company Inc ......G 315 889-8500
Union Springs *(G-15222)*

▲ Hermann J Wiemer Vineyard ....G 607 243-7971
Dundee *(G-4047)*

Heron Hill Vineyards Inc..................E 607 868-4241
Hammondsport *(G-5530)*

Hickory Road Land Co LLC...............G 607 243-9114
Dundee *(G-4048)*

Hoffman & Hoffman ....G 315 536-4773
Penn Yan *(G-12586)*

Hosmer Inc ....F 888 467-9463
Ovid *(G-12424)*

Hunt Country Vineyards ....E 315 595-2812
Branchport *(G-1111)*

▲ J Petrocelli Wine Cellars LLC ....E 631 765-1100
Peconic *(G-12546)*

J R Dill Winery LLC........................G 607 546-5757
Burdett *(G-3058)*

Joseph Zakon Winery Ltd ....G 718 604-1430
Brooklyn *(G-2003)*

Keurig Dr Pepper Inc ....C 315 589-4911
Williamson *(G-16110)*

▲ Konstantin D FRAnk& Sons Vini ....E 607 868-4884
Hammondsport *(G-5532)*

L & D Acquisition LLC....................F 585 531-9000
Naples *(G-8207)*

Lafayette Chateau ....E 607 546-2062
Hector *(G-5826)*

▲ Lakewood Vineyards Inc ....F 607 535-9252
Watkins Glen *(G-15614)*

Lamoreaux Landing WI ....D 607 582-6162
Lodi *(G-7131)*

Leonard Oakes Estate Winery ....G 585 318-4418
Medina *(G-7739)*

Lieb Cellars LLC...........................E 631 298-1942
Mattituck *(G-7677)*

Lucas Vineyards Inc ....F 607 532-4825
Interlaken *(G-6285)*

Malina Management Company Inc ......E 607 535-9614
Montour Falls *(G-8075)*

Mazza Chautauqua Cellars LLC..........F 716 793-9463
Westfield *(G-15946)*

Merritt Estate Winery Inc.................F 716 965-4800
Forestville *(G-4931)*

▲ Millbrook Winery Inc...................F 845 677-8383
Millbrook *(G-7944)*

▲ Montezuma Winery LLC...............G 315 568-8190
Seneca Falls *(G-14369)*

Negys New Land Vinyrd Winery ....G 315 585-4432
Geneva *(G-5160)*

▲ North House Vineyards Inc ....G 631 779-2817
Jamesport *(G-6490)*

Olde Chtqua Vneyards Ltd Lblty ....F 716 792-2749
Portland *(G-12933)*

▲ Paumanok Vineyards Ltd ....E 631 722-8800
Aquebogue *(G-366)*

Pellegrini Vineyards LLC ....G 631 734-4111
Cutchogue *(G-3816)*

Pindar Vineyards LLC ....E 631 734-6200
Peconic *(G-12547)*

PM Spirits LLC ....F 347 689-4414
Brooklyn *(G-2267)*

Prejean Winery Inc ....G 315 536-7524
Penn Yan *(G-12590)*

▲ Premium Wine Group LLC ....E 631 298-1900
Mattituck *(G-7678)*

Pugliese Vineyards Inc ....G 631 734-4057
Cutchogue *(G-3817)*

Quinn and Co of NY Ltd ....D 212 868-1900
New York *(G-10958)*

Railex Wine Services LLC ....E 631 369-7000
Riverhead *(G-13186)*

Red Newt Cellars Inc ....F 607 546-4100
Hector *(G-5827)*

Red Tail Ridge Inc ....F 315 536-4580
Penn Yan *(G-12591)*

Rock Stream Vineyards...................G 607 243-8322
Rock Stream *(G-13819)*

Royal Wine Corporation ....F 845 236-4000
Marlboro *(G-7582)*

Schulze Vineyards & Winery LLC........F 716 778-8090
Burt *(G-3061)*

Sheldrake Point Vineyard LLC ....F 607 532-8967
Ovid *(G-12426)*

▲ Shinn Winery LLC ....G 631 804-0367
Mattituck *(G-7679)*

Sokolin LLC ....E 631 537-4434
Yaphank *(G-16272)*

◆ Solstars Inc ....G 212 605-0430
New York *(G-11290)*

Spanish Artisan Wine Group LLC ....G 914 414-6982
Patterson *(G-12520)*

Spring Lake Winery LLC ....G 716 439-5253
Lockport *(G-7107)*

Standing Stone Vineyards ....E 607 582-6051
Hector *(G-5828)*

Swedish Hill Vineyard Inc ....D 607 403-0029
Romulus *(G-13881)*

Thirsty Owl Wine Company Inc ....G 607 869-5805
Ovid *(G-12427)*

Thousand Islands Winery LLC ....E 315 482-9306
Alexandria Bay *(G-181)*

Tickle Hill Winery ....G 607 546-7740
Hector *(G-5829)*

Tug Hill Vineyards ....G 315 376-4336
Lowville *(G-7422)*

Ventosa Vineyards LLC ....G 315 719-0000
Geneva *(G-5166)*

Wagner Vineyards LLC ....G 607 582-6976
Lodi *(G-7132)*

Wagner Vineyards & Brewing Co ....E 607 582-6574
Lodi *(G-7133)*

Westchester Wine Warehouse LLC......F 914 824-1400
White Plains *(G-16074)*

Wine Group Inc ....D 716 326-3151
Westfield *(G-15953)*

Wine Services Inc ....G 631 722-3800
Riverhead *(G-13193)*

▲ Wolffer Estate Vineyard Inc ....E 631 537-5106
Sagaponack *(G-14103)*

Woodbury Vineyards Inc ....G 716 679-9463
Fredonia *(G-4973)*

2085 Liquors, Distilled, Rectified & Blended

21st Century Spirits Corp................G 718 499-0606
Brooklyn *(G-1412)*

Adirondack Distilling Company..........G 315 316-0387
Utica *(G-15236)*

Anheusr-Bsch Coml Strategy LLC ......F 347 429-1082
New York *(G-8588)*

Braided Oak Spirits LLC..................F 845 381-1525
Middletown *(G-7896)*

▲ Castle Brands Inc......................E 646 356-0200
New York *(G-8930)*

Cocktail Crate LLC ....G 718 316-2033
Long Island City *(G-7188)*

Constellation Brands Inc.................D 585 678-7100
Victor *(G-15399)*

▼ Cruzin Management Inc................E 212 641-8700
New York *(G-9126)*

▲ Dutch Spirits LLC.......................F 518 398-1022
Pine Plains *(G-12633)*

Ellicottville Distillery LLC.................G 716 597-6121
Ellicottville *(G-4313)*

Evolution Spirits Inc ....G...... 917 543-7880
New York (G-9432)

Felene Inc ....G...... 716 276-3583
Williamsville (G-16131)

Finger Lakes Distilling.............................F...... 607 546-5510
Burdett (G-3057)

George Lake Distilling Company..........G...... 518 639-1025
Queensbury (G-13040)

Honeoye Falls Distillery LLC ....F...... 201 780-4618
Honeoye Falls (G-6075)

Infirmary Nyc ....G...... 504 606-6280
New York (G-9885)

Iron Smoke Whiskey LLC ....G...... 585 388-7584
Fairport (G-4499)

▲ Leblon Holdings LLC ....E...... 212 741-2675
New York (G-10187)

▲ Leblon LLC ....E...... 786 281-5672
New York (G-10188)

Lockhouse Distillery ....G...... 716 768-4898
Buffalo (G-2852)

Madison County Distillery LLC ....G...... 315 391-6070
Cazenovia (G-3229)

▲ New York Distilling Co LLC ....B...... 718 473-2955
Brooklyn (G-2206)

New York Distilling Co LLC ....G...... 917 893-7519
Brooklyn (G-2207)

◆ Prince Black Distillery Inc ....E...... 212 695-6187
Syosset (G-14799)

Prohibition Distillery LLC ....G...... 917 685-8989
Roscoe (G-14035)

◆ Russian Standard Vodka USA Inc ....G...... 212 679-1894
New York (G-11100)

◆ Sovereign Brands LLC ....G...... 212 343-8366
New York (G-11307)

Stilltheone Distillery LLC ....G...... 914 217-0347
Harrison (G-5561)

▲ Tuthilltown Spirits LLC ....F...... 845 255-1527
Gardiner (G-5131)

Watermans Distillery LLC ....G...... 607 258-0274
Apalachin (G-363)

2086 Soft Drinks

3v Company Inc ....E...... 718 858-7333
Brooklyn (G-1417)

4 Star Brands Inc ....G...... 516 944-0472
Elmhurst (G-4331)

A Health Obsession LLC ....E...... 347 850-4587
Brooklyn (G-1435)

Alpha Wolf LLC ....G...... 516 778-5812
Carle Place (G-3169)

Alpine Water USA LLC ....G...... 203 912-9723
Dayton (G-3822)

American Bottling Company...................F...... 516 714-0002
Ronkonkoma (G-13902)

▼ Arizona Beverage Company LLC ......G...... 516 812-0300
Woodbury (G-16166)

Ba Sports Nutrition LLC ....C...... 718 357-7402
Whitestone (G-16089)

Beverage Works Incorporated ....G...... 718 834-0500
Brooklyn (G-1581)

Beverage Works Nj Inc ....E...... 631 293-3501
Farmingdale (G-4593)

Beverage Works Ny Inc ....E...... 718 812-2034
Brooklyn (G-1582)

Beverages Foods & Service Inds ....D...... 914 253-2000
Purchase (G-13002)

▲ Big Geyser Inc ....C...... 718 821-2200
Maspeth (G-7596)

▲ Blue Star Beverages Corp ....G...... 718 381-3535
Brooklyn (G-1596)

Borabora Fruit Juices Inc ....G...... 914 438-8744
Highland (G-5958)

Bottling Group LLC................................E...... 315 788-6751
Watertown (G-15561)

Bottling Group LLC................................B...... 800 789-2626
White Plains (G-15982)

◆ Bottling Group LLC...........................G...... 914 253-2000
White Plains (G-15983)

▲ Boylan Bottling Co Inc ....E...... 800 289-7978
New York (G-8842)

▲ Brands Within Reach LLC ....G...... 847 720-9090
Mamaroneck (G-7499)

▲ Canada Dry Bottling Co NY LP ....D...... 718 358-2000
College Point (G-3538)

Canada Dry Bottling Co NY LP ....D...... 718 786-8550
Maspeth (G-7598)

Canada Dry Bottling Co NY LP ....E...... 631 694-7575
Melville (G-7764)

◆ Cell-Nique Corporation ....G...... 203 856-8550
Castleton On Hudson (G-3200)

▲ Central Coca-Cola Btlg Co Inc..........B...... 914 789-1100
Elmsford (G-4399)

Cham Cold Brew LLC............................G...... 646 926-0206
New York (G-8968)

Chateau Imports Ltd ....G...... 516 841-6343
Port Washington (G-12867)

Cheribundi Inc ....E...... 800 699-0460
Geneva (G-5150)

Chohehco LLC ....G...... 315 420-4624
Skaneateles (G-14448)

◆ Cliffstar LLC ....A...... 716 366-6100
Dunkirk (G-4052)

Clintons Ditch Coop Co Inc ....C...... 315 699-2695
Cicero (G-3417)

Coca-Cola Bottling Company ....E...... 518 483-0422
Malone (G-7484)

▲ Coca-Cola Btlg Co Buffalo Inc..........C...... 716 874-4610
Tonawanda (G-15098)

Coca-Cola Btlg Co of NY Inc ....F...... 845 562-3037
New Windsor (G-8364)

Coca-Cola Btlg Co of NY Inc ....F...... 914 789-1572
Elmsford (G-4400)

Coca-Cola Btlg Co of NY Inc ....F...... 518 459-2010
Albany (G-66)

Coca-Cola Btlg Co of NY Inc ....F...... 718 416-7575
Maspeth (G-7599)

Coca-Cola Btlg Co of NY Inc ....G...... 315 457-9221
Syracuse (G-14856)

Coca-Cola Btlg Co of NY Inc ....F...... 631 434-3535
Hauppauge (G-5620)

Coca-Cola Btlg Co of NY Inc ....F...... 718 420-6800
Staten Island (G-14639)

Coca-Cola Btlg Co of NY Inc ....F...... 914 789-1580
Elmsford (G-4401)

Coca-Cola Refreshments USA Inc ....E...... 718 401-5200
Bronx (G-1227)

Coca-Cola Refreshments USA Inc ....G...... 315 785-8907
Watertown (G-15566)

Coca-Cola Refreshments USA Inc ....F...... 914 592-0806
Hawthorne (G-5811)

Cornell Beverages Inc ....F...... 718 381-3000
Brooklyn (G-1688)

Crystal Rock LLC ....G...... 716 626-7460
Buffalo (G-2714)

Dirty Lemon Beverages LLC ....G...... 877 897-7784
New York (G-9233)

Doheny Nice and Easy ....G...... 518 793-1733
Glens Falls (G-5247)

East Coast Cultures LLC ....F...... 917 261-3010
Kingston (G-6690)

▼ Energy Brands Inc ....E...... 212 545-6000
New York (G-9374)

F & V Distribution Company LLC ....G...... 516 812-0393
Woodbury (G-16171)

Fancy Flamingo LLC ....G...... 516 209-7306
New York (G-9468)

Farmtobottle LLC ....G...... 631 944-8422
Locust Valley (G-7122)

Fevertree USA Inc ....F...... 718 852-5577
New York (G-9486)

Gangi Distributors Inc ....F...... 718 442-5745
Staten Island (G-14654)

Global Brands Inc ....G...... 845 358-1212
Nyack (G-12144)

◆ Good-O-Beverage Inc ....F...... 718 328-6400
Bronx (G-1268)

Grayhawk Leasing LLC ....G...... 914 767-6000
Somers (G-14498)

Green Zone Food Service Inc ....G...... 917 709-1728
Corona (G-3739)

◆ Hain Celestial Group Inc ....C...... 516 587-5000
New Hyde Park (G-8272)

Heart of Tea ....F...... 917 725-3164
New York (G-9757)

Hmo Beverage Corporation ....G...... 917 371-6100
Brooklyn (G-1936)

Hydrive Energy ....G...... 914 925-9100
Rye (G-14081)

Johnnie Ryan Co Inc ....F...... 716 282-1606
Niagara Falls (G-11943)

Juices Enterprises Inc ....G...... 718 953-1860
Brooklyn (G-2010)

Just Beverages LLC ....F...... 480 388-1133
Glens Falls (G-5252)

Just Goods Inc ....F...... 855 282-5878
New York (G-10046)

Keurig Dr Pepper Inc ....C...... 315 589-4911
Williamson (G-16110)

Keurig Dr Pepper Inc ....D...... 914 846-2300
Elmsford (G-4414)

Keurig Dr Pepper Inc ....G...... 718 246-6200
Brooklyn (G-2025)

La Cola 1 Inc ....G...... 917 509-6669
New York (G-10155)

Life Earth Company ....G...... 310 751-0627
New York (G-10211)

▲ Liquid Management Partners LLC....F...... 516 775-5050
New Hyde Park (G-8280)

Load/N/Go Beverage Corp ....F...... 585 218-4019
Rochester (G-13521)

Long Blockchain Corp............................C...... 855 542-2832
Farmingdale (G-4672)

Long Island Brand Bevs LLC ....D...... 855 542-2832
Long Island City (G-7279)

Manhattan Special Bottling ....F...... 718 388-4144
Brooklyn (G-2109)

▲ Mayer Bros Apple Products Inc........D...... 716 668-1787
West Seneca (G-15852)

Monfefo LLC ....G...... 347 779-2600
Brooklyn (G-2169)

N Y Winstons Inc ....G...... 212 665-3166
New York (G-10529)

New York Bottling Co Inc ....F...... 718 963-3232
Bronx (G-1323)

▲ New York Spring Water Inc ....E...... 212 777-4649
New York (G-10602)

Nexbev Industries LLC ....F...... 646 648-1255
Blauvelt (G-931)

▲ Nirvana Inc ....C...... 315 942-4900
Forestport (G-4928)

Owens Table Mixers LLC ....G...... 650 303-7342
New York (G-10722)

Pepsi Beverages Co ....G...... 518 782-2150
Latham (G-6871)

Pepsi Bottling Ventures LLC...................E...... 631 226-9000
Amityville (G-303)

Pepsi Btlg Group Globl Fin LLC..............G...... 914 767-6000
Somers (G-14499)

Pepsi-Cola Bottling Co NY Inc ....F...... 914 699-2600
Mount Vernon (G-8169)

Pepsi-Cola Bottling Co NY Inc ....A...... 718 392-1000
College Point (G-3559)

Pepsi-Cola Bottling Co NY Inc ....D...... 718 892-1570
Bronx (G-1335)

◆ Pepsi-Cola Bottling Group ....G...... 914 767-6000
White Plains (G-16046)

◆ Pepsi-Cola Metro Btlg Co Inc ....G...... 914 767-6000
White Plains (G-16047)

Pepsi-Cola Metro Btlg Co Inc ....G...... 914 253-2000
Purchase (G-13008)

Pepsi-Cola Metro Btlg Co Inc ....D...... 607 795-2122
Horseheads (G-6131)

Pepsi-Cola Metro Btlg Co Inc ....C...... 585 454-5220
Rochester (G-13614)

Pepsi-Cola Metro Btlg Co Inc ....B...... 518 834-7811
Keeseville (G-6645)

Pepsi-Cola Newburgh Btlg Inc................C...... 845 562-5400
Newburgh (G-11882)

Pepsi-Cola Operating Company ....E...... 914 767-6000
White Plains (G-16048)

Pepsi-Cola Sales and Dist Inc................G...... 914 253-2000
Purchase (G-13009)

Pepsico ....F...... 419 252-0247
Hawthorne (G-5821)

▲ Pepsico ....E...... 914 801-1500
Valhalla (G-15305)

Pepsico Inc ....G...... 914 253-2000
New York (G-10798)

Pepsico Inc ....G...... 914 253-2000
White Plains (G-16049)

Pepsico Inc ....B...... 914 742-4500
Valhalla (G-15306)

Pepsico Inc ....A...... 914 253-2000
Purchase (G-13011)

Pepsico Inc ....E...... 914 253-3474
White Plains (G-16050)

Pepsico Inc ....F...... 914 253-2713
Purchase (G-13012)

◆ Pepsico Inc ....A...... 914 253-2000
Purchase (G-13010)

Pepsico Capital Resources Inc...............G...... 914 253-2000
Purchase (G-13013)

Pepsico Design & Innovation ....G...... 917 405-9307
New York (G-10799)

Pepsico Sales Inc ....G...... 914 253-2000
Purchase (G-13014)

Purely Maple LLC ....F...... 203 997-9309
New York (G-10930)

Rochester Coca Cola Bottling ....E...... 607 739-5678
Horseheads (G-6135)

Rochester Coca Cola Bottling ....D....... 585 546-3900
  Rochester *(G-13685)*
Royal Crown Financial ....G....... 718 234-7237
  Brooklyn *(G-2359)*
Saratoga Spring Water Company ....E....... 518 584-6363
  Saratoga Springs *(G-14193)*
Save More Beverage Corp ....G....... 518 371-2520
  Halfmoon *(G-5499)*
▲ Scotia Beverages Inc ....A....... 518 370-3621
  Schenectady *(G-14303)*
Shopping Center Wine & Liquor ....G....... 914 528-1600
  Mohegan Lake *(G-8011)*
Snapp Too Enterprise ....G....... 718 224-5252
  Flushing *(G-4893)*
Snapple Beverage Corp ....D....... 914 612-4000
  Rye Brook *(G-14094)*
Soto Sake Corporation ....G....... 305 781-3906
  Brooklyn *(G-2442)*
Stewarts Processing Corp ....D....... 518 581-1200
  Ballston Spa *(G-588)*
Switch Beverage Company LLC ....F....... 203 202-7383
  Port Washington *(G-12928)*
Treo Brands LLC ....F....... 914 341-1850
  Harrison *(G-5562)*
Unilever United States Inc ....F....... 212 546-0200
  New York *(G-11588)*
Unilever United States Inc ....F....... 212 546-0200
  New York *(G-11589)*

2087 Flavoring Extracts & Syrups

3v Company Inc ....E....... 718 858-7333
  Brooklyn *(G-1417)*
Agua Enerviva LLC ....F....... 516 597-5440
  Bethpage *(G-832)*
American Juice Company LLC ....G....... 347 620-0252
  New York *(G-8555)*
Baldwin Richardson Foods Co ....B....... 315 986-2727
  Macedon *(G-7461)*
Bi Nutraceuticals Inc ....G....... 631 533-4934
  Islandia *(G-6325)*
▲ Boylan Bottling Co Inc ....E....... 800 289-7978
  New York *(G-8842)*
▲ Buffalo Blends Inc ....E....... 716 825-4422
  Buffalo *(G-2671)*
◆ Citrus and Allied Essences Ltd ....E....... 516 354-1200
  Floral Park *(G-4812)*
Cocktail Crate LLC ....G....... 718 316-2033
  Long Island City *(G-7188)*
◆ Comax Manufacturing Corp ....D....... 631 249-0505
  Melville *(G-7769)*
Constellation Brands Inc ....D....... 585 678-7100
  Victor *(G-15399)*
Consumer Flavoring Extract Co ....F....... 718 435-0201
  Brooklyn *(G-1682)*
Craftmaster Flavor Technology ....F....... 631 789-8607
  Amityville *(G-260)*
Danisco US Inc ....D....... 585 277-4300
  Rochester *(G-13338)*
▲ Delbia Do Company Inc ....G....... 718 585-2226
  Bronx *(G-1238)*
Delbia Do Company Inc ....F....... 718 585-2226
  Bronx *(G-1239)*
DSM Nutritional Products LLC ....C....... 518 372-5155
  Schenectady *(G-14261)*
DSM Nutritional Products LLC ....C....... 518 372-5155
  Glenville *(G-5271)*
▲ Esense LLC ....F....... 718 887-9779
  Long Island City *(G-7215)*
◆ Flavormatic Industries LLC ....E....... 845 297-9100
  Wappingers Falls *(G-15492)*
Fox 416 Corp ....E....... 718 385-4600
  Brooklyn *(G-1864)*
Interntnal Flvors Frgrnces Inc ....C....... 212 765-5500
  New York *(G-9924)*
Keurig Dr Pepper Inc ....C....... 315 589-4911
  Williamson *(G-16110)*
Life On Earth Inc ....F....... 646 844-9897
  New York *(G-10212)*
Mapleland Farms LLC ....G....... 518 854-7669
  Salem *(G-14133)*
◆ Motts LLP ....C....... 972 673-8088
  Elmsford *(G-4418)*
Mr Smoothie ....G....... 845 296-1686
  Poughkeepsie *(G-12973)*
▼ Myx Beverage LLC ....F....... 585 978-3542
  Oyster Bay *(G-12451)*
Natural Organics Labs Inc ....B....... 631 957-5600
  Melville *(G-7807)*
◆ Pepsi-Cola Metro Btlg Co Inc ....G....... 914 767-6000
  White Plains *(G-16047)*

◆ Pepsico Inc ....A....... 914 253-2000
  Purchase *(G-13010)*
▼ Roar Beverages LLC ....E....... 631 683-5565
  Port Washington *(G-12918)*
▲ Sabila Corp ....G....... 845 981-7128
  Pine Island *(G-12631)*
◆ Star Kay White Inc ....D....... 845 268-2600
  Congers *(G-3618)*
Synergy Flavors NY Company LLC ....G....... 585 232-6647
  Rochester *(G-13753)*
Tealeafs ....G....... 716 688-8022
  Williamsville *(G-16143)*
Torre Products Co Inc ....G....... 212 925-8989
  Mount Vernon *(G-8184)*
◆ Virginia Dare Extract Co Inc ....C....... 718 788-6320
  Brooklyn *(G-2561)*

2091 Fish & Seafoods, Canned & Cured

◆ Acme Smoked Fish Corp ....D....... 954 942-5598
  Brooklyn *(G-1458)*
▲ Banner Smoked Fish Inc ....D....... 718 449-1992
  Brooklyn *(G-1561)*
Blue Ocean Food Trading LLC ....G....... 718 689-4291
  Brooklyn *(G-1594)*
◆ Catsmo LLC ....F....... 845 895-2296
  Wallkill *(G-15468)*
▲ Diamond Seafoods Inc ....G....... 503 351-3240
  New York *(G-9222)*
Incro Marketing USA Corp ....G....... 917 365-5552
  New York *(G-9876)*
▲ Premium Ocean LLC ....C....... 917 231-1061
  Bronx *(G-1344)*
Samaki Inc ....G....... 845 858-1012
  Port Jervis *(G-12856)*
Sangster Foods Inc ....F....... 212 993-9129
  Brooklyn *(G-2383)*

2092 Fish & Seafoods, Fresh & Frozen

6th Ave Gourmet Inc ....G....... 845 782-9067
  Monroe *(G-8013)*
AB Seafood Trading Inc ....G....... 718 353-8848
  Flushing *(G-4832)*
Entrepreneur Ventures Inc ....G....... 631 261-1111
  Northport *(G-12103)*
◆ Foo Yuan Food Products Co Inc ....C....... 212 925-2840
  Long Island City *(G-7226)*
Montauk Inlet Seafood Inc ....G....... 631 668-3419
  Montauk *(G-8056)*
◆ Rich Products Corporation ....A....... 716 878-8000
  Buffalo *(G-2954)*
Sea Breeze Fish & Seafood of S ....F....... 718 984-0447
  Staten Island *(G-14707)*

2095 Coffee

Anandsar Inc ....E....... 551 556-5555
  Oakland Gardens *(G-12159)*
Arista Coffee Inc ....F....... 347 531-0813
  Maspeth *(G-7592)*
▲ Bh Coffee Company LLC ....D....... 914 377-2500
  Elmsford *(G-4396)*
Birch Guys LLC ....G....... 917 763-0751
  Long Island City *(G-7178)*
BK Associates Intl Inc ....F....... 607 432-1499
  Oneonta *(G-12259)*
▲ Brads Organic LLC ....G....... 845 429-9080
  Haverstraw *(G-5804)*
Brooklyn Roasting Works LLC ....G....... 718 855-1000
  Brooklyn *(G-1621)*
CCS North America LLC ....G....... 312 834-2165
  Mohegan Lake *(G-8009)*
◆ Coffee Holding Co Inc ....D....... 718 832-0800
  Staten Island *(G-14640)*
▼ Coffee Holding Company Inc ....G....... 718 832-0800
  Brooklyn *(G-1674)*
Death Wish Coffee Company LLC ....E....... 518 400-1050
  Ballston Spa *(G-571)*
▲ Eldorado Coffee Roasters Ltd ....D....... 718 418-4100
  Maspeth *(G-7612)*
Elite Roasters Inc ....E....... 716 626-0307
  East Amherst *(G-4077)*
▲ Empire Coffee Company Inc ....E....... 914 934-1100
  Port Chester *(G-12820)*
Gillies Coffee Company ....F....... 718 499-7766
  Brooklyn *(G-1886)*
John A Vassilaros & Son Inc ....E....... 718 886-4140
  Flushing *(G-4865)*
Jonathan Brose ....G....... 716 417-8978
  Lockport *(G-7086)*
List & Beisler GMBH ....E....... 646 866-6960
  New York *(G-10225)*

▲ Orens Daily Roast Inc ....G....... 212 348-5400
  New York *(G-10710)*
P Pascal Inc ....E....... 914 969-7933
  Yonkers *(G-16338)*
▲ Paul De Lima Company Inc ....D....... 315 457-3725
  Liverpool *(G-7031)*
Paul De Lima Company Inc ....E....... 315 457-3725
  Cicero *(G-3422)*
Peaks Coffee Company ....G....... 315 565-1900
  Cazenovia *(G-3233)*
Pintail Coffee Inc ....G....... 631 396-0808
  Farmingdale *(G-4708)*
▲ Regal Trading Inc ....E....... 914 694-6100
  Purchase *(G-13015)*
▲ S J McCullagh Inc ....C....... 716 856-3473
  Buffalo *(G-2970)*
Sangster Foods Inc ....F....... 212 993-9129
  Brooklyn *(G-2383)*
Star Mountain JFK Inc ....G....... 718 553-6787
  Jamaica *(G-6475)*
Vega Coffee Inc ....G....... 415 881-7969
  New York *(G-11653)*
Where Is Utica Cof Rasting Inc ....F....... 315 269-8898
  Utica *(G-15300)*
▲ White Coffee Corp ....D....... 718 204-7900
  Astoria *(G-445)*

2096 Potato Chips & Similar Prdts

▲ Brads Organic LLC ....G....... 845 429-9080
  Haverstraw *(G-5804)*
BSD Top Direct Inc ....G....... 646 468-0156
  West Babylon *(G-15696)*
▲ Emmi USA Inc ....F....... 845 268-9990
  Orangeburg *(G-12313)*
Frito-Lay North America Inc ....D....... 607 775-7000
  Binghamton *(G-879)*
◆ Hain Celestial Group Inc ....C....... 516 587-5000
  New Hyde Park *(G-8272)*
◆ Ideal Snacks Corporation ....C....... 845 292-7000
  Liberty *(G-6924)*
◆ Pepsico Inc ....A....... 914 253-2000
  Purchase *(G-13010)*
Proformance Foods Inc ....G....... 703 869-3413
  Brooklyn *(G-2299)*
Robs Really Good LLC ....F....... 516 671-4411
  Sea Cliff *(G-14347)*
Saratoga Chips LLC ....G....... 877 901-6950
  Saratoga Springs *(G-14192)*
Switch Beverage Company LLC ....F....... 203 202-7383
  Port Washington *(G-12928)*
Terrells Potato Chip Co Inc ....D....... 315 437-2786
  Syracuse *(G-15011)*
▲ TLC-Lc Inc ....E....... 212 756-8900
  New York *(G-11501)*

2097 Ice

Adirondack Ice & Air Inc ....F....... 518 483-4340
  Malone *(G-7481)*
Annies Ice ....G....... 585 593-5605
  Wellsville *(G-15666)*
Arctic Glacier Newburgh Inc ....G....... 718 456-2013
  Brooklyn *(G-1525)*
Arctic Glacier Newburgh Inc ....F....... 845 561-0549
  Newburgh *(G-11858)*
Clayville Ice Co Inc ....G....... 315 839-5405
  Clayville *(G-3455)*
Henry Newman LLC ....F....... 607 273-8512
  Dryden *(G-4038)*
Huntington Ice & Cube Corp ....F....... 718 456-2013
  Brooklyn *(G-1947)*
Ice Cube Inc ....G....... 613 254-0071
  Deer Park *(G-3882)*
Maplewood Ice Co Inc ....E....... 518 499-2345
  Whitehall *(G-16076)*
South Shore Ice Co Inc ....F....... 516 379-2056
  Roosevelt *(G-14033)*

2098 Macaroni, Spaghetti & Noodles

Bedessee Imports Ltd ....E....... 718 272-1300
  Brooklyn *(G-1569)*
Borgattis Ravioli Egg Noodles ....G....... 718 367-3799
  Bronx *(G-1216)*
Canton Noodle Corporation ....G....... 212 226-3276
  New York *(G-8907)*
Cassinelli Food Products Inc ....F....... 718 274-4881
  Long Island City *(G-7184)*
Deer Park Macaroni Co Inc ....F....... 631 667-4600
  Deer Park *(G-3861)*
Deer Park Macaroni Co Inc ....F....... 631 667-4600
  Deer Park *(G-3862)*

S
I
C

Momofuku 171 First Avenue LLC ....D....... 212 777-7773
New York *(G-10496)*

Nodus Noodle Corporation ....G....... 718 309-3725
Sunnyside *(G-14773)*

▲ Piemonte Home Made Ravioli Co .....F....... 718 429-1972
Woodside *(G-16220)*

Piemonte Home Made Ravioli Co ....G....... 212 226-0475
New York *(G-10838)*

Queen Ann Macaroni Mfg Co Inc ....G....... 718 256-1061
Brooklyn *(G-2314)*

Ramen & Yakitori Okidoki Inc ....G....... 718 806-1677
Astoria *(G-437)*

Ravioli Store Inc ....G....... 718 729-9300
Long Island City *(G-7340)*

▲ Twin Marquis Inc ....D....... 718 386-6868
Brooklyn *(G-2532)*

Wing Heung Noodle Inc ....F....... 212 966-7496
New York *(G-11765)*

Wing Kei Noodle Inc ....F....... 212 226-1644
New York *(G-11766)*

Wonton Food Inc ....F....... 212 677-8865
New York *(G-11776)*

2099 Food Preparations, NEC

3v Company Inc ....E....... 718 858-7333
Brooklyn *(G-1417)*

ABC Peanut Butter LLC ....B....... 212 661-6886
New York *(G-8427)*

Ahhmigo LLC ....F....... 212 315-1818
New York *(G-8497)*

▲ Allied Food Products Inc ....F....... 718 230-4227
Brooklyn *(G-1488)*

Anandsar Inc ....E....... 551 556-5555
Oakland Gardens *(G-12159)*

Andros Bowman Products LLC ....G....... 540 217-4100
Lyndonville *(G-7444)*

Armour Bearer Group Inc ....G....... 646 812-4487
Arverne *(G-406)*

Aromasong Usa Inc ....F....... 718 838-9669
Brooklyn *(G-1533)*

◆ Associated Brands Inc ....B....... 585 798-3475
Medina *(G-7727)*

Bainbridge & Knight LLC ....E....... 212 986-5100
New York *(G-8720)*

Baldwin Richardson Foods Co ....B....... 315 986-2727
Macedon *(G-7461)*

▲ Barilla America Ny Inc ....C....... 585 226-5600
Avon *(G-512)*

▲ Bektrom Foods Inc ....G....... 516 802-3800
Syosset *(G-14778)*

Beths Farm Kitchen ....E....... 518 799-3414
Stuyvesant Falls *(G-14755)*

Blue Ridge Tea & Herb Co Ltd ....G....... 718 625-3100
Brooklyn *(G-1595)*

▲ Bombay Kitchen Foods Inc ....F....... 516 767-7401
Port Washington *(G-12865)*

▲ Brads Organic LLC ....G....... 845 429-9080
Haverstraw *(G-5804)*

Brooklyns Best Pasta Co Inc ....G....... 917 881-3007
Brooklyn *(G-1624)*

Brooklynwrap Inc ....G....... 718 258-8088
Brooklyn *(G-1625)*

Bud Ravioli Center Inc ....G....... 718 356-4600
Staten Island *(G-14632)*

Buna Besta Tortillas ....G....... 347 987-3995
Brooklyn *(G-1628)*

Butterwood Desserts Inc ....E....... 716 652-0131
West Falls *(G-15761)*

Bylada Foods LLC ....E....... 845 623-1300
West Nyack *(G-15819)*

Cafe Spice Gct Inc ....C....... 845 863-0910
New Windsor *(G-8362)*

Capitol City Specialties Co ....G....... 518 486-8935
Albany *(G-57)*

Castella Imports Inc ....E....... 631 231-5500
Hauppauge *(G-5611)*

◆ Castella Imports Inc ....C....... 631 231-5500
Edgewood *(G-4264)*

Chan Kee Dried Bean Curd Inc ....G....... 718 622-0820
Brooklyn *(G-1660)*

▲ Chemicolloid Laboratories Inc ....F....... 516 747-2666
New Hyde Park *(G-8256)*

Child Nutrition Prog Dept Ed ....D....... 212 371-1000
New York *(G-8986)*

▲ China Huaren Organic Pdts Inc ......G....... 212 232-0120
New York *(G-8988)*

Cookiebaker LLC ....G....... 716 878-8000
Buffalo *(G-2710)*

D R M Management Inc ....E....... 716 668-0333
Depew *(G-3978)*

De Matteis Food Corp ....G....... 646 629-8554
New York *(G-9191)*

Diva Farms Ltd ....G....... 315 735-4397
Utica *(G-15258)*

Event Services Corporation ....G....... 315 488-9357
Solvay *(G-14497)*

▲ Extreme Spices Inc ....G....... 917 496-4081
Maspeth *(G-7613)*

Fanshawe Foods LLC ....F....... 212 757-3130
New York *(G-9469)*

▲ Far Eastern Coconut Company ....F....... 631 851-8800
Central Islip *(G-3274)*

Farm To Table Community Inc ....E....... 845 383-1761
Kingston *(G-6692)*

Farmers Hub LLC ....E....... 914 380-2945
White Plains *(G-16006)*

Fleischmanns Vinegar Co Inc ....G....... 315 587-4414
North Rose *(G-12034)*

Flik International/Compass ....F....... 212 450-4750
New York *(G-9510)*

Freshly Inc ....E....... 844 373-7459
New York *(G-9540)*

▼ Fruitcrown Products Corp ....G....... 631 694-5800
Farmingdale *(G-4633)*

Gillies Coffee Company ....F....... 718 499-7766
Brooklyn *(G-1886)*

▼ Glenn Foods Inc ....F....... 516 377-1400
Freeport *(G-4999)*

Golden Taste Inc ....G....... 845 356-4133
Spring Valley *(G-14571)*

Good Noodles Inc ....F....... 518 731-7278
West Coxsackie *(G-15759)*

▲ Gourmet Boutique LLC ....C....... 718 977-1200
Jamaica *(G-6445)*

Gourmet Crafts Inc ....F....... 718 372-0505
Brooklyn *(G-1902)*

Gourmet Toast Corp ....G....... 718 852-4536
Brooklyn *(G-1903)*

Gravymaster Inc ....E....... 203 453-1893
Canajoharie *(G-3120)*

Great Eastern Pasta Works LLC ....G....... 631 956-0889
West Babylon *(G-15713)*

H & S Edible Products Corp ....E....... 914 413-3489
Mount Vernon *(G-8146)*

H&F Products Inc ....G....... 845 651-6100
Florida *(G-4824)*

◆ Harney & Sons Tea Corp ....C....... 518 789-2100
Millerton *(G-7947)*

HP Hood LLC ....D....... 607 295-8134
Arkport *(G-393)*

Instantwhip of Buffalo Inc ....E....... 716 892-7031
Buffalo *(G-2811)*

▲ Johns Ravioli Company Inc ....F....... 914 576-7030
New Rochelle *(G-8345)*

◆ Joyva Corp ....D....... 718 497-0170
Brooklyn *(G-2006)*

Kale Factory Inc ....G....... 917 363-6361
Brooklyn *(G-2020)*

Kaneka America LLC ....D....... 212 705-4340
New York *(G-10066)*

◆ Kerry Bfnctnal Ingredients Inc ....D....... 608 363-1200
Norwich *(G-12123)*

Koppert Cress USA LLC ....E....... 631 779-3640
Riverhead *(G-13176)*

◆ Kozy Shack Enterprises LLC ....C....... 516 870-3000
Hicksville *(G-5919)*

Kozy Shack Enterprises LLC ....C....... 516 870-3000
Hicksville *(G-5920)*

Kraft Heinz Foods Company ....B....... 585 226-4400
Avon *(G-513)*

La Escondida Inc ....G....... 845 562-1387
Newburgh *(G-11872)*

▲ La Flor Products Company Inc ....E....... 631 851-9601
Hauppauge *(G-5690)*

Labella Pasta Inc ....G....... 845 331-9130
Kingston *(G-6698)*

Lakeside Cider Mill Farm Inc ....G....... 518 399-8359
Ballston Lake *(G-560)*

▲ Lams Foods Inc ....F....... 718 217-0476
Queens Village *(G-13024)*

Land OLakes Inc ....G....... 516 681-2980
Hicksville *(G-5922)*

▲ Larte Del Gelato Inc ....E....... 212 366-0570
New York *(G-10174)*

▲ Lidestri Beverages LLC ....F....... 585 377-7700
Fairport *(G-4503)*

Losurdo Foods Inc ....E....... 518 842-1500
Amsterdam *(G-333)*

Lucky Lous Inc ....G....... 631 672-1932
Lake Grove *(G-6759)*

Lugo Nutrition Inc ....G....... 302 573-2503
Nyack *(G-12145)*

M & M Food Products Inc ....F....... 718 821-1970
Brooklyn *(G-2093)*

Maizteca Foods Inc ....E....... 718 641-3933
South Richmond Hill *(G-14523)*

Manhattan Milling & Drying Co ....E....... 516 496-1041
Woodbury *(G-16177)*

▲ Maramont Corporation ....B....... 718 439-8900
Brooklyn *(G-2112)*

▲ Martens Country Kit Pdts LLC ....F....... 315 776-8821
Port Byron *(G-12809)*

▲ Mediterrean Dyro Company ....E....... 718 786-4888
Long Island City *(G-7293)*

Merb LLC ....F....... 631 393-3621
Brooklyn *(G-2139)*

▲ Meta-Therm Corp ....F....... 914 697-4840
White Plains *(G-16029)*

Milnot Holding Corporation ....G....... 518 839-0300
Amsterdam *(G-337)*

Mizkan America Inc ....F....... 585 798-5720
Medina *(G-7742)*

Mizkan America Inc ....D....... 585 765-9171
Lyndonville *(G-7445)*

Mizkan Americas Inc ....F....... 315 483-6944
Sodus *(G-14491)*

Moira New Hope Food Pantry ....G....... 518 529-6524
Moira *(G-8012)*

Momentive Performance Mtls Inc ....D....... 914 784-4807
Tarrytown *(G-15049)*

Mondelez Global LLC ....G....... 585 345-3300
Batavia *(G-620)*

More Good ....G....... 845 765-0115
Beacon *(G-754)*

Mullers Cider House LLC ....G....... 585 287-5875
Rochester *(G-13562)*

▲ Natural Lab Inc ....E....... 718 321-8848
Flushing *(G-4876)*

Natural Matters Inc ....G....... 212 337-3077
New York *(G-10552)*

New York Ravioli Pasta Co Inc ....E....... 516 270-2852
New Hyde Park *(G-8285)*

New York Sugars LLC ....F....... 585 500-0155
Rochester *(G-13573)*

Nine Pin Ciderworks LLC ....E....... 518 449-9999
Albany *(G-106)*

North Shore Farms Two Ltd ....G....... 516 280-6880
Mineola *(G-7991)*

◆ Old Dutch Mustard Co Inc ....G....... 516 466-0522
Great Neck *(G-5408)*

Omg Desserts Inc ....F....... 585 698-1561
Rochester *(G-13590)*

▲ Once Again Nut Butter Collectv ......B....... 585 468-2535
Nunda *(G-12133)*

Original Hrkmer Cnty Chese Inc ....D....... 315 895-7428
Ilion *(G-6280)*

Panda Plates Inc ....G....... 888 997-6623
New York *(G-10745)*

▲ Parnasa International Inc ....E....... 516 394-0400
Valley Stream *(G-15351)*

Peaceful Valley Maple Farm ....G....... 518 762-0491
Johnstown *(G-6623)*

▲ Peanut Butter & Co Inc ....E....... 212 757-3130
New York *(G-10776)*

Pelican Bay Ltd ....F....... 718 729-9300
Long Island City *(G-7323)*

Pellicano Specialty Foods Inc ....F....... 716 822-2366
Buffalo *(G-2910)*

Pennant Ingredients Inc ....D....... 585 235-8160
Rochester *(G-13613)*

Ponti Rossi Inc ....G....... 347 506-9616
Brooklyn *(G-2269)*

Pride Pak Inc ....D....... 905 828-2149
Medina *(G-7743)*

Private Lbel Fods Rchester Inc ....E....... 585 254-9205
Rochester *(G-13646)*

Pure Functional Foods Inc ....E....... 315 294-0733
Savannah *(G-14221)*

◆ Pure Golds Family Corp ....G....... 516 483-5600
Hempstead *(G-5848)*

Qualitea Imports Inc ....G....... 917 624-6750
Suffern *(G-14764)*

▲ R Hadley Corporation ....D....... 607 589-4415
Spencer *(G-14549)*

Radicle Farm LLC ....G....... 315 226-3294
New York *(G-10970)*

▲ Raw Indulgence Ltd ....F....... 866 498-4671
Elmsford *(G-4425)*

Rawpothecary Inc ....G 917 783-7770
Brooklyn *(G-2328)*

▲ Real Co Inc ....G 347 433-8549
Valley Cottage *(G-15321)*

▲ Redland Foods Corp ....F 716 288-9061
Cheektowaga *(G-3360)*

◆ Rich Products Corporation ....A 716 878-8000
Buffalo *(G-2954)*

▲ Rob Salamida Company Inc ....F 607 729-4868
Johnson City *(G-6608)*

Royal Kosher Foods LLC ....G 347 221-1867
Brooklyn *(G-2360)*

▲ Sabra Dipping Company LLC ....D 914 372-9400
White Plains *(G-16058)*

Salvador Colletti Blank ....G 718 217-6725
Douglaston *(G-4028)*

Sapienza Pastry Inc ....E 516 352-5232
Elmont *(G-4389)*

Schutt Cider Mill ....F 585 872-2924
Webster *(G-15652)*

▲ Seasons Soyfood Inc ....G 718 797-9896
Brooklyn *(G-2393)*

Seneca Foods Corporation ....F 315 926-4277
Marion *(G-7575)*

◆ Settons Intl Foods Inc ....D 631 543-8090
Commack *(G-3598)*

▲ Sneaky Chef Foods LLC ....F 914 301-3277
Tarrytown *(G-15060)*

▲ SOS Chefs New York Inc ....G 212 505-5813
New York *(G-11301)*

Spf Holdings II LLC ....G 212 750-8300
New York *(G-11320)*

Spread-Mmms LLC ....G 917 727-8116
Brooklyn *(G-2447)*

▲ Steinway Pasta & Gelati Inc ....F 718 246-5414
Lindenhurst *(G-6974)*

◆ Sugar Foods Corporation ....E 212 753-6900
New York *(G-11385)*

Sugar Shack Desert Company Inc ....G 518 523-7540
Lake Placid *(G-6768)*

Sunrise Snacks Rockland Inc ....F 845 352-2676
Monsey *(G-8049)*

Tea Life LLC ....G 516 365-7711
Manhasset *(G-7542)*

Tortilla Heaven Inc ....E 845 339-1550
Kingston *(G-6715)*

Tortilleria Oaxaca ....G 347 355-7336
Staten Island *(G-14723)*

Tracco LLC ....G 516 938-4588
Syosset *(G-14803)*

▲ Tuv Taam Corp ....E 718 855-2207
Brooklyn *(G-2530)*

▲ Twin Marquis Inc ....D 718 386-6868
Brooklyn *(G-2532)*

◆ U S Sugar Co Inc ....E 716 828-1170
Buffalo *(G-3025)*

UFS Industries Inc ....D 914 664-6262
Mount Vernon *(G-8190)*

Ultra Thin Ready To Bake Pizza ....E 516 679-6655
Deer Park *(G-3943)*

▲ Unistel LLC ....D 585 341-4600
Webster *(G-15660)*

◆ Victoria Fine Foods LLC ....D 718 649-1635
Brooklyn *(G-2556)*

Victoria Fine Foods Holding Co ....D 718 649-1635
Brooklyn *(G-2557)*

Vinegar Hill Asset LLC ....G 718 469-0342
Brooklyn *(G-2559)*

▲ VIP Foods Inc ....E 718 821-5330
Ridgewood *(G-13166)*

Whitsons Food Svc Bronx Corp ....B 631 424-2700
Islandia *(G-6346)*

▲ Win-Holt Equipment Corp ....E 516 222-0335
Woodbury *(G-16185)*

▲ Wm E Martin and Sons Co Inc ....E 516 605-2444
Roslyn *(G-14047)*

▲ Wonder Natural Foods Corp ....G 631 726-4433
Water Mill *(G-15532)*

Wonton Food Inc ....E 718 784-8178
Long Island City *(G-7406)*

▲ Wonton Food Inc ....C 718 628-6868
Brooklyn *(G-2593)*

Wonton Food Inc ....F 212 677-8865
New York *(G-11776)*

21 TOBACCO PRODUCTS

2111 Cigarettes

East End ....F 716 532-2622
Collins *(G-3570)*

Jacobs Tobacco Company ....E 518 358-4948
Hogansburg *(G-5980)*

Kk International Trading Corp ....E 516 801-4741
Syosset *(G-14790)*

Onondaga Nation ....G 315 469-3230
Nedrow *(G-8216)*

Philip Morris Globl Brands Inc ....G 917 663-2000
New York *(G-10827)*

Philip Morris Intl Inc ....D 917 663-2000
New York *(G-10828)*

PMI Global Services Inc ....E 917 663-2000
New York *(G-10858)*

R J Reynolds Tobacco Company ....C 716 871-1553
Tonawanda *(G-15135)*

Schweitzer-Mauduit Intl Inc ....C 518 329-4222
Ancram *(G-355)*

▲ Seneca Manufacturing Company ......G 716 945-4400
Salamanca *(G-14128)*

Seneca Nation Enterprise ....F 716 934-7430
Irving *(G-6304)*

Vector Group Ltd ....C 212 409-2800
New York *(G-11651)*

2121 Cigars

American Cigar ....G 718 969-0008
Fresh Meadows *(G-5037)*

Mafco Consolidated Group Inc ....F 212 572-8600
New York *(G-10318)*

2131 Tobacco, Chewing & Snuff

Elab Smokers Boutique ....G 585 865-4513
Rochester *(G-13381)*

Mafco Consolidated Group Inc ....F 212 572-8600
New York *(G-10318)*

National Tobacco Company LP ....F 212 253-8185
New York *(G-10548)*

Standard Diversified Inc ....E 302 248-1100
Mineola *(G-8001)*

2141 Tobacco Stemming & Redrying

Schweitzer-Mauduit Intl Inc ....C 518 329-4222
Ancram *(G-355)*

22 TEXTILE MILL PRODUCTS

2211 Cotton, Woven Fabric

1510 Associates LLC ....G 212 828-8720
New York *(G-8389)*

A and J Apparel Corp ....G 212 398-8899
New York *(G-8413)*

A3 Apparel LLC ....G 888 403-9669
New York *(G-8422)*

Accolade USA Inc ....F 302 257-5688
Cheektowaga *(G-3336)*

Advanced Fashions Technology ....G 212 221-0606
New York *(G-8480)*

▲ Apollo Apparel Group LLC ....F 212 398-6585
New York *(G-8604)*

Avitto Leather Goods Inc ....G 212 219-7501
New York *(G-8693)*

▲ Axis Na LLC ....F 212 302-1959
New York *(G-8698)*

◆ Basileus Company LLC ....F 315 963-3516
Manlius *(G-7543)*

▲ Benartex LLC ....G 212 840-3250
New York *(G-8755)*

▲ Beyond Loom Inc ....G 212 575-3100
New York *(G-8773)*

▲ Blu Sand LLC ....G 212 564-1147
New York *(G-8816)*

Brooklyn Denim Co. ....F 718 782-2600
Brooklyn *(G-1616)*

▲ Brunschwig & Fils LLC ....F 800 538-1880
Bethpage *(G-833)*

◆ Cai Inc ....G 212 819-0008
New York *(G-8886)*

Charming Fashion Inc ....G 212 730-2872
New York *(G-8976)*

Creation Baumann USA Inc ....E 516 764-7431
Rockville Centre *(G-13827)*

Cy Fashion Corp ....G 212 730-8600
New York *(G-9139)*

Designway Ltd ....G 212 254-2220
New York *(G-9209)*

Do Over LLC ....G 212 302-2336
New York *(G-9243)*

▲ Equipment Apparel LLC ....D 212 502-1890
New York *(G-9390)*

Fab Industries Corp ....B 516 498-3200
Great Neck *(G-5385)*

▲ French Accnt Rugs & Tapestries ......G 212 686-6097
New York *(G-9535)*

Geordie Magee Uphl & Canvas ....G 315 676-7679
Brewerton *(G-1135)*

◆ Gerli & Co Inc ....B 212 213-1919
New York *(G-9603)*

H Group LLC ....F 212 719-5500
New York *(G-9703)*

Haleys Comet Seafood Corp ....E 212 571-1828
New York *(G-9711)*

Hanesbrands Inc ....E 212 576-9300
New York *(G-9721)*

High Alchemy LLC ....F 212 224-9600
New York *(G-9780)*

▲ Horizon Apparel Mfg Inc ....G 516 361-4878
Atlantic Beach *(G-453)*

In2green LLC ....G 914 693-5054
Hastings On Hudson *(G-5573)*

Internationl Studios Inc ....G 212 819-1616
New York *(G-9923)*

Joy of Learning ....G 718 443-6463
Brooklyn *(G-2004)*

▲ Jrg Apparel Group Company Ltd ......E 212 997-0900
New York *(G-10034)*

Knightly Endeavors ....G 845 340-0949
Kingston *(G-6697)*

▲ La Lame Inc ....G 212 921-9770
New York *(G-10158)*

◆ Lydall Thermal/Acoustical Inc ....C 518 273-6320
Green Island *(G-5440)*

▲ Magic Brands International LLC ....F 212 563-4999
New York *(G-10324)*

Marsha Fleisher ....F 845 679-6500
Woodstock *(G-16236)*

▼ Mason Contract Products LLC ....D 516 328-6900
New Hyde Park *(G-8282)*

Meder Textile Co Inc ....G 516 883-0409
Port Washington *(G-12904)*

Medline Industries Inc ....B 845 344-3301
Middletown *(G-7919)*

Melwood Partners Inc ....F 631 923-0134
Melville *(G-7803)*

Mgk Group Inc ....E 212 989-2732
New York *(G-10448)*

Michael Stuart Inc ....F 718 821-0704
Brooklyn *(G-2151)*

Navas Designs Inc ....E 818 988-9050
New York *(G-10556)*

▲ Neilson International Inc ....G 631 454-0400
Farmingdale *(G-4693)*

Nochairs Inc ....G 917 748-8731
New York *(G-10635)*

◆ Northpoint Trading Inc ....F 212 481-8001
New York *(G-10645)*

◆ Northwest Company LLC ....C 516 484-6996
Roslyn *(G-14045)*

▲ Ortex Home Textile Inc ....G 718 241-7298
Brooklyn *(G-2234)*

Paramount Cord & Brackets ....G 212 325-9100
White Plains *(G-16039)*

▲ Phoenix Usa LLC ....G 646 351-6598
New York *(G-10830)*

Premium 5 Kids LLC ....F 212 563-4999
New York *(G-10880)*

▲ Renaissnce Crpt Tapestries Inc ....F 212 696-0080
New York *(G-11011)*

▲ Scalamandre Wallpaper Inc ....B 631 467-8800
Hauppauge *(G-5760)*

Schneider Mills Inc ....C 828 632-0801
New York *(G-11158)*

SD Eagle Global Inc ....G 516 822-1778
Jericho *(G-6594)*

Shahin Designs Ltd ....G 212 737-7225
New York *(G-11203)*

Shindo Usa Inc ....G 212 868-9311
New York *(G-11215)*

▲ Sita Finishing Inc ....F 718 417-5295
Brooklyn *(G-2424)*

Sky Laundromat Inc ....E 718 639-7070
Jamaica *(G-6473)*

Ssjjj Manufacturing LLC ....B 516 498-3200
Great Neck *(G-5423)*

Success Apparel LLC ....D 212 502-1890
New York *(G-11384)*

▲ US Design Group Ltd ....F 212 354-4070
New York *(G-11623)*

Versailles Drapery Upholstery ....F 212 533-2059
Long Island City *(G-7395)*

Vf Services LLC............................G....... 212 575-7820
New York *(G-11671)*

Wallace Home Design Ctr ....G....... 631 765-3890
Southold *(G-14546)*

◆ Westpoint Home LLC ....A....... 212 930-2000
New York *(G-11746)*

Westpoint International Inc ....A....... 212 930-2000
New York *(G-11747)*

▲ Xing Lin USA Intl Corp ....G....... 212 947-4846
New York *(G-11798)*

2221 Silk & Man-Made Fiber

ABC Elastic Corp ....G....... 718 388-2953
Brooklyn *(G-1447)*

Albany International Corp ....C....... 518 445-2200
Rensselaer *(G-13084)*

Apex Texicon Inc ....E....... 516 239-4400
New York *(G-8602)*

Art People Inc ....G....... 212 431-4865
New York *(G-8629)*

▲ Beyond Loom Inc ....G....... 212 575-3100
New York *(G-8773)*

◆ Chf Industries Inc ....E....... 212 951-7800
New York *(G-8984)*

▲ Concepts Nyc Inc ....E....... 212 244-1033
New York *(G-9076)*

Creation Baumann USA Inc ....E....... 516 764-7431
Rockville Centre *(G-13827)*

Eastern Silk Mills Inc ....G....... 212 730-1300
New York *(G-9305)*

Ess Bee Industries Inc................E....... 718 894-5202
Brooklyn *(G-1814)*

◆ Fabric Resources Intl Ltd ....F....... 516 829-4550
Great Neck *(G-5386)*

◆ Fiber Glass Industries Inc ....D....... 518 842-4000
Amsterdam *(G-327)*

Fibrix LLC ....G....... 716 683-4100
Depew *(G-3981)*

▲ Frp Apparel Group LLC ....G....... 212 695-8000
New York *(G-9544)*

◆ Gerli & Co Inc ....B....... 212 213-1919
New York *(G-9603)*

Himatsingka America Inc ....E....... 212 252-0802
New York *(G-9788)*

▲ Himatsingka Holdings NA Inc ....G....... 212 824-2949
New York *(G-9789)*

Intertex USA Inc ....F....... 212 279-3601
New York *(G-9925)*

◆ Ivi Services Inc ....D....... 607 729-5111
Binghamton *(G-889)*

▲ Jag Manufacturing Inc ....E....... 518 762-9558
Johnstown *(G-6620)*

Jakob Schlaepfer Inc ....G....... 212 221-2323
New York *(G-9970)*

JM Manufacturer Inc ....G....... 212 869-0626
New York *(G-10010)*

Kragel Co Inc ....G....... 716 648-1344
Hamburg *(G-5512)*

▲ La Lame Inc ....G....... 212 921-9770
New York *(G-10158)*

▼ Laregence Inc ....E....... 212 736-2548
New York *(G-10173)*

Marly Home Industries USA Inc ....F....... 718 388-3030
Brooklyn *(G-2118)*

Mgk Group Inc ....E....... 212 989-2732
New York *(G-10448)*

National Contract Industries ....G....... 212 249-0045
New York *(G-10541)*

▲ New York Poplin LLC ....G....... 718 768-3296
Brooklyn *(G-2210)*

▲ Newtex Industries Inc ....E....... 585 924-9135
Victor *(G-15421)*

Pierce Arrow Drapery Mfg ....G....... 716 876-3023
Buffalo *(G-2918)*

▲ Polytex Inc ....D....... 716 549-5100
Angola *(G-360)*

▲ Scalamandre Silks Inc ....D....... 212 980-3888
New York *(G-11147)*

▲ Scalamandre Wallpaper Inc ......B....... 631 467-8800
Hauppauge *(G-5760)*

Schneider Mills Inc ....C....... 828 632-0801
New York *(G-11158)*

Shengkun North America Inc ....F....... 212 217-2460
New York *(G-11211)*

Stern & Stern Industries Inc ....D....... 607 324-4485
Hornell *(G-6111)*

Superior Fiber Mills Inc ....E....... 718 782-7500
New York *(G-2475)*

Tli Import Inc ....G....... 917 578-4568
Brooklyn *(G-2508)*

Toltec Fabrics Inc ....C....... 212 706-9310
New York *(G-11506)*

Toray Industries Inc ....G....... 212 697-8150
New York *(G-11517)*

▲ US Home Textiles Group LLC .....G....... 212 768-3030
New York *(G-11625)*

V Technical Textiles Inc ....G....... 315 597-1674
Palmyra *(G-12494)*

◆ Westpoint Home LLC ....A....... 212 930-2000
New York *(G-11746)*

▲ Zorlu USA Inc ....D....... 212 689-4622
New York *(G-11830)*

2231 Wool, Woven Fabric

▲ Acker & LI Mills Corporation ......G....... 212 307-7247
New York *(G-8448)*

▲ Alicia Adams Alpaca Inc ....G....... 845 868-3366
Millbrook *(G-7941)*

▲ Beyond Loom Inc ....G....... 212 575-3100
New York *(G-8773)*

◆ Citisource Industries Inc ....E....... 212 683-1033
New York *(G-9015)*

Eldeen Clothing Inc ....G....... 212 719-9190
New York *(G-9333)*

◆ Fabric Resources Intl Ltd ....F....... 516 829-4550
Great Neck *(G-5386)*

▲ Hawkins Fabrics Inc ....E....... 518 773-9550
Johnstown *(G-6618)*

▲ Light House Hill Marketing ....F....... 212 354-1338
New York *(G-10216)*

▲ Loomstate LLC ....E....... 212 219-2300
New York *(G-10254)*

Nazim Izzak Inc ....G....... 212 920-5546
Long Island City *(G-7304)*

▲ Oakhurst Partners LLC ....G....... 212 502-3220
New York *(G-10672)*

▲ Pinder International Inc ....G....... 631 273-0324
Hauppauge *(G-5741)*

▲ Scalamandre Wallpaper Inc ......B....... 631 467-8800
Hauppauge *(G-5760)*

◆ Warren Corporation ....C....... 917 379-3434
New York *(G-11724)*

Woolmark Americas Inc ....G....... 347 767-3160
New York *(G-11777)*

▲ Yarnz International Inc ....G....... 212 868-5883
New York *(G-11807)*

2241 Fabric Mills, Cotton, Wool, Silk & Man-Made

Albany International Corp ....C....... 518 445-2200
Rensselaer *(G-13084)*

Ambind Corp ....G....... 716 836-4365
Buffalo *(G-2628)*

American Canvas Binders Corp ....G....... 914 969-0300
Yonkers *(G-16284)*

▲ American Trim Mfg Inc ....E....... 518 239-8151
Durham *(G-4070)*

▲ Bardwil Industries Inc ....C....... 212 944-1870
New York *(G-8727)*

Breton Industries Inc ....C....... 518 842-3030
Amsterdam *(G-320)*

Champion Zipper Corp ....G....... 212 239-0414
New York *(G-8969)*

▲ Colonial Tag & Label Co Inc ......F....... 516 482-0508
Great Neck *(G-5377)*

▲ Danray Textiles Corp ....F....... 212 354-5213
New York *(G-9169)*

Depot Label Company Inc ....G....... 631 467-2952
Patchogue *(G-12499)*

Eiseman-Ludmar Co Inc ....F....... 516 932-6990
Hicksville *(G-5904)*

◆ Essential Ribbons Inc ....G....... 212 967-4173
New York *(G-9402)*

▲ Fashion Ribbon Co Inc ....E....... 718 482-0100
Long Island City *(G-7221)*

Imperial-Harvard Label Co ....F....... 212 736-8420
New York *(G-9869)*

Itc Mfg Group Inc ....F....... 212 684-3696
New York *(G-9947)*

▲ J & M Textile Co Inc ....F....... 212 268-8000
New York *(G-9953)*

Jakob Schlaepfer Inc ....G....... 212 221-2323
New York *(G-9970)*

▲ La Lame Inc ....G....... 212 921-9770
New York *(G-10158)*

Label Source Inc ....G....... 212 244-1403
New York *(G-10159)*

▲ Labels Inter-Global Inc ....F....... 212 398-0006
New York *(G-10160)*

Labeltex Mills Inc ....G....... 212 279-6165
New York *(G-10161)*

Marketing Action Xecutives Inc ......G....... 212 971-9155
New York *(G-10370)*

▲ Mergence Studios Ltd ....F....... 212 288-5616
Hauppauge *(G-5714)*

New York Binding Co Inc ....E....... 718 729-2454
Long Island City *(G-7309)*

▲ Newtex Industries Inc ....E....... 585 924-9135
Victor *(G-15421)*

◆ R-Pac International Corp ....E....... 212 465-1818
New York *(G-10968)*

▲ Scalamandre Silks Inc ....D....... 212 980-3888
New York *(G-11147)*

▲ Schoen Trimming & Cord Co Inc ...F....... 212 255-3949
New York *(G-11159)*

▲ Skil-Care Corporation ....C....... 914 963-2040
Yonkers *(G-16348)*

Solstiss Inc ....G....... 212 719-9194
New York *(G-11291)*

▲ Sturges Manufacturing Co Inc ....D....... 315 732-6159
Utica *(G-15295)*

Valley Industrial Products Inc ....E....... 631 385-9300
Huntington *(G-6231)*

2251 Hosiery, Women's Full & Knee Length

Brach Knitting Mills Inc ....F....... 845 651-4450
Florida *(G-4821)*

▲ Classic Hosiery Inc ....E....... 845 342-6661
Middletown *(G-7899)*

Ellis Products Corp ....G....... 516 791-3732
Valley Stream *(G-15339)*

▲ Fine Sheer Industries Inc ....F....... 212 594-4224
New York *(G-9495)*

◆ Gina Group LLC ....E....... 212 947-2445
New York *(G-9612)*

◆ Hot Sox Company Incorporated ...D....... 212 957-2000
New York *(G-9818)*

Silky Tones Inc ....G....... 718 218-5598
Brooklyn *(G-2412)*

▲ Trimfit Inc ....E....... 215 245-1122
New York *(G-11546)*

2252 Hosiery, Except Women's

▲ Ace Drop Cloth Canvas Pdts Inc ...E....... 718 731-1550
Bronx *(G-1193)*

▲ Ashko Group LLC ....F....... 212 594-6050
New York *(G-8645)*

Bombas LLC ....G....... 800 314-0980
New York *(G-8832)*

Centric Socks LLC ....E....... 646 839-7000
New York *(G-8957)*

Customize Elite Socks LLC ....G....... 212 533-8551
New York *(G-9136)*

▲ Fine Sheer Industries Inc ....F....... 212 594-4224
New York *(G-9495)*

◆ Gina Group LLC ....E....... 212 947-2445
New York *(G-9612)*

▲ Haddad Hosiery LLC ....G....... 212 251-0022
New York *(G-9707)*

▲ High Point Design LLC ....F....... 212 354-2400
New York *(G-9781)*

◆ Hot Sox Company Incorporated ...D....... 212 957-2000
New York *(G-9818)*

La Strada Dance Footwear Inc ....G....... 631 242-1401
Deer Park *(G-3895)*

▲ Leadertex Intl Inc ....E....... 212 563-2242
New York *(G-10183)*

▲ Look By M Inc ....G....... 212 213-4019
New York *(G-10251)*

Lr Acquisition LLC ....F....... 212 301-8765
New York *(G-10274)*

▲ Majesty Brands LLC ....G....... 212 283-3400
New York *(G-10335)*

▲ Ness Legwear LLC ....G....... 212 335-0777
New York *(G-10567)*

New Hampton Creations Inc ....G....... 212 244-7474
New York *(G-10584)*

◆ Palmbay Ltd ....G....... 718 424-3388
Flushing *(G-4884)*

Sockbin ....G....... 917 519-1119
Brooklyn *(G-2433)*

Socks and More of NY Inc ....G....... 718 769-1785
Brooklyn *(G-2434)*

Sticky Socks LLC ....G....... 212 541-5927
New York *(G-11363)*

Strassburg Medical LLC ....G....... 800 452-0631
North Tonawanda *(G-12092)*

▲ Trimfit Inc ....E....... 215 245-1122
New York *(G-11546)*

United Retail II ....G...... 212 966-9692
New York *(G-11599)*

▲ You and ME Legwear LLC ....F 212 279-9292
New York *(G-11812)*

2253 Knit Outerwear Mills

▲ 180s LLC ....E 410 534-6320
New York *(G-8390)*

79 Metro Ltd ....G...... 212 944-4030
New York *(G-8408)*

A & B Finishing Inc ....E 718 522-4702
Brooklyn *(G-1427)*

Accurate Knitting Corp ....G...... 646 552-2216
Brooklyn *(G-1451)*

Alpha Knitting Mills Inc ....F 718 628-6300
Brooklyn *(G-1491)*

Andrea Strongwater ....G...... 212 873-0905
New York *(G-8578)*

▲ Asian Global Trading Corp ....G...... 718 786-0998
New York *(G-8647)*

▲ B & B Sweater Mills Inc ....F 718 456-8693
Brooklyn *(G-1555)*

▲ Betsy & Adam Ltd ....E 212 302-3750
New York *(G-8770)*

▲ Binghamton Knitting Co Inc ....E 607 722-6941
Binghamton *(G-858)*

Blueberry Knitting Inc ....E 718 599-6520
Brooklyn *(G-1597)*

Central Mills Inc ....C 212 764-9011
New York *(G-8952)*

▲ Charter Ventures LLC ....F 212 868-0222
New York *(G-8977)*

◆ Domani Fashions Corp ....G...... 718 797-0505
Brooklyn *(G-1755)*

▲ Dressy Tessy Inc ....G...... 212 869-0750
New York *(G-9269)*

E I Du Pont De Nemours & Co ....E 716 876-4420
Buffalo *(G-2734)*

Elegant Headwear Co Inc ....G...... 212 695-8520
New York *(G-9336)*

▲ Emerald Holdings Inc ....G...... 718 797-4404
Brooklyn *(G-1798)*

Fashion Avenue Knits Inc ....F 718 456-9000
New York *(G-9476)*

▲ Freedom Rains Inc ....G...... 646 710-4512
New York *(G-9534)*

Gabani Inc...G...... 631 283-4930
Southampton *(G-14531)*

▲ GAME Sportswear Ltd ....C 914 962-1701
Yorktown Heights *(G-16365)*

▲ Gce International Inc ....D 212 704-4800
New York *(G-9580)*

▲ Gildan Apparel USA Inc ....D 212 476-0341
New York *(G-9609)*

▲ Golden Leaves Knitwear Inc ....E 718 875-8235
Brooklyn *(G-1898)*

Great Adirondack Yarn Company ....F 518 843-3381
Amsterdam *(G-329)*

▲ Hamil America Inc ....F 212 244-2645
New York *(G-9714)*

Hania By Anya Cole LLC ....G...... 212 302-3550
New York *(G-9722)*

▲ Hertling Trousers Inc ....E 718 784-6100
Brooklyn *(G-1935)*

IaMmaliamills LLC.............................G...... 805 845-2137
Brooklyn *(G-1950)*

▲ J & D Walter Distributors Inc ....F 518 449-1606
Glenmont *(G-5238)*

J & E Talit Inc...................................G...... 718 850-1333
Richmond Hill *(G-13116)*

Jeric Knit Wear ....G...... 631 979-8827
Smithtown *(G-14480)*

Jfs Inc..E 646 264-1200
New York *(G-10001)*

▲ Jj Basics LLC ....E 212 768-4779
New York *(G-10008)*

▲ Julia Knit Inc ....G...... 718 848-1900
Ozone Park *(G-12464)*

K & S Childrens Wear Inc ....E 718 624-0006
Brooklyn *(G-2016)*

KD Dids Inc ....E 718 402-2012
Bronx *(G-1289)*

Keryakos Inc.....................................F 518 344-7092
Schenectady *(G-14284)*

▲ Knit Illustrated Inc ....E 212 268-9054
New York *(G-10116)*

Lids Corporation ....G...... 518 459-7060
Albany *(G-97)*

▲ Lloyds Fashions Inc ....D 631 435-3353
Brentwood *(G-1125)*

Lynch Knitting Mills Inc ....E 718 821-3436
Brooklyn *(G-2090)*

▲ M B M Manufacturing Inc ....F 718 769-4148
Brooklyn *(G-2096)*

Machinit Inc......................................G...... 631 454-9297
Farmingdale *(G-4675)*

Mann Consultants LLC ....E 914 763-0512
Waccabuc *(G-15446)*

Manrico Usa Inc ....G...... 212 794-4200
New York *(G-10350)*

Matchables Inc ....F 718 389-9318
Brooklyn *(G-2123)*

Mdj Sales Associates Inc ....G...... 914 420-5897
Mamaroneck *(G-7515)*

Mongru Neckwear Inc ....E 718 706-0406
Long Island City *(G-7299)*

Native Textiles Inc ....G...... 212 951-5100
New York *(G-10549)*

New York Sweater Company Inc ....E 845 629-9533
New York *(G-10603)*

North Star Knitting Mills Inc..............G...... 718 894-4848
Glendale *(G-5230)*

NY Denim Inc....................................G...... 212 764-6668
New York *(G-10659)*

Phillips-Van Heusen Europe ....F 212 381-3500
New York *(G-10829)*

Precision Apparel Mfg LLC ....G...... 201 805-2664
New York *(G-10874)*

Premier Knits Ltd ....F 718 323-8264
Ozone Park *(G-12466)*

◆ Pvh Corp ....D 212 381-3500
New York *(G-10933)*

Pvh Corp ....G...... 212 549-6000
New York *(G-10934)*

Rags Knitwear Ltd ....F 718 782-8417
Brooklyn *(G-2322)*

◆ Ralph Lauren Corporation ....B 212 318-7000
New York *(G-10975)*

Riviera Sun Inc ....G...... 212 546-9220
New York *(G-11050)*

S & T Knitting Co Inc ....E 607 722-7558
Conklin *(G-3628)*

S & V Knits Inc ....E 631 752-1595
Farmingdale *(G-4730)*

Sage Knitwear Inc ....G...... 718 628-7902
West Babylon *(G-15745)*

Sarug Inc..D 718 339-2791
Brooklyn *(G-2384)*

▲ Summit Apparel Inc ....E 631 213-8299
Hauppauge *(G-5777)*

Sweater Brand Inc ....G...... 718 797-0505
Brooklyn *(G-2482)*

▲ T & R Knitting Mills Inc ....E 718 497-4017
Glendale *(G-5233)*

T & R Knitting Mills Inc ....F 212 840-8665
New York *(G-11415)*

Tomas Maier ....G...... 212 988-8686
New York *(G-11510)*

▲ United Knitwear International ....G...... 212 354-2920
New York *(G-11598)*

Warm ....F 212 925-1200
New York *(G-11719)*

Warnaco Inc......................................F 718 722-3000
Brooklyn *(G-2575)*

Winter Water Factory ....G...... 646 387-3247
Brooklyn *(G-2592)*

WR Design Corp................................E 212 354-9000
New York *(G-11791)*

2254 Knit Underwear Mills

▲ Balanced Tech Corp ....E 212 768-8330
New York *(G-8722)*

In Toon Amkor Fashions Inc ....E 718 937-4546
Long Island City *(G-7247)*

Maidenform LLC................................F 201 436-9200
New York *(G-10331)*

Native Textiles Inc ....G...... 212 951-5100
New York *(G-10549)*

2257 Circular Knit Fabric Mills

A-One Moving & Storage Inc ....E 718 266-6002
Brooklyn *(G-1443)*

Apex Aridyne Corp ....G...... 516 239-4400
Inwood *(G-6287)*

Apex Texicon Inc ....E 516 239-4400
New York *(G-8602)*

Cap USA Jerseyman Harlem Inc ....G...... 212 222-7942
New York *(G-8909)*

Gehring Tricot Corporation ....C 315 429-8551
Dolgeville *(G-4023)*

Hill Knitting Mills Inc........................E 718 846-5000
Richmond Hill *(G-13115)*

▲ Lifestyle Design Usa Ltd ....G...... 212 279-9400
New York *(G-10214)*

2258 Lace & Warp Knit Fabric Mills

Apex Aridyne Corp ....G...... 516 239-4400
Inwood *(G-6287)*

Apex Texicon Inc ....E 516 239-4400
New York *(G-8602)*

Eagle Lace Dyeing Corp ....F 212 947-2712
New York *(G-9297)*

Fab Industries Corp ....B 516 498-3200
Great Neck *(G-5385)*

▲ Gehring Tricot Corporation ....D 315 429-8551
Dolgeville *(G-4022)*

Gehring Tricot Corporation ....C 315 429-8551
Dolgeville *(G-4023)*

George Knitting Mills Corp ....G...... 212 242-3300
New York *(G-9600)*

Helmont Mills Inc ....G...... 518 568-7913
Saint Johnsville *(G-14118)*

Hosel & Ackerson Inc ....G...... 212 575-1490
New York *(G-9814)*

Hudson Fabrics LLC ....F 518 671-6100
Hudson *(G-6162)*

▲ Klauber Brothers Inc ....E 212 686-2531
New York *(G-10114)*

Litchfield Fabrics of NC ....G...... 518 773-9500
Gloversville *(G-5288)*

Mary Bright Inc ....G...... 212 677-1970
New York *(G-10377)*

Mohawk Fabric Company Inc ....F 518 842-3090
Amsterdam *(G-338)*

Orbit Industries LLC ....F 914 244-1500
Mount Kisco *(G-8101)*

Solstiss Inc ....G...... 212 719-9194
New York *(G-11291)*

Somerset Dyeing & Finishing ....E 518 773-7383
Gloversville *(G-5291)*

▲ Somerset Industries Inc ....E 518 773-7383
Gloversville *(G-5292)*

Ssjjj Manufacturing LLC ....B 516 498-3200
Great Neck *(G-5423)*

Sunwin Global Industry Inc................G...... 646 370-6196
New York *(G-11395)*

Super-Trim Inc ....E 212 255-2370
New York *(G-11396)*

▲ Veratex Inc ....F 212 683-9300
New York *(G-11659)*

2259 Knitting Mills, NEC

▲ Bank-Miller Co Inc ....E 914 227-9357
Pelham *(G-12565)*

▲ Hawkins Fabrics Inc ....E 518 773-9500
Johnstown *(G-6618)*

Maidenform LLC................................F 201 436-9200
New York *(G-10331)*

Nochairs Inc ....G...... 917 748-8731
New York *(G-10635)*

▲ Sextet Fabrics Inc ....F 516 593-0608
Roosevelt *(G-14032)*

2261 Cotton Fabric Finishers

All About Art Inc ....F 718 321-0755
Flushing *(G-4837)*

B & K Dye Cutting Inc ....G...... 718 497-5216
Brooklyn *(G-1556)*

Basiloff LLC......................................G...... 646 671-0353
New York *(G-8737)*

Carolyn Ray Inc ....G...... 914 476-0619
Yonkers *(G-16294)*

Central Textiles Inc ....F 212 213-8740
New York *(G-8953)*

Dyenamix Inc.....................................G...... 212 941-6642
New York *(G-9287)*

Dynamic Screenprinting......................G...... 518 487-4256
Albany *(G-72)*

Lee Dyeing Company NC Inc ....F 518 736-5232
Johnstown *(G-6622)*

Loremanss Embroidery Engrav ....F 518 834-9205
Keeseville *(G-6643)*

Marcel Finishing Corp ....E 718 381-2889
Plainview *(G-12699)*

Mezzoprint LLC ....G...... 347 480-9199
Valley Stream *(G-15347)*

Mountain T-Shirts Inc ....G...... 518 943-4533
Catskill *(G-3215)*

Printery ....G...... 315 253-7403
Auburn *(G-491)*

Prismatic Dyeing & Finshg Inc ....D 845 561-1800
Newburgh *(G-11883)*

Reynolds Drapery Service Inc ....F 315 845-8632
Newport *(G-11899)*

▲ Santee Print Works ....B 212 997-1570
New York *(G-11134)*

Sciane Enterprises Inc ....G 845 452-2400
Poughkeepsie *(G-12982)*

Steve Poli Sales ....G 315 487-0394
Camillus *(G-3110)*

Tramwell Inc ....G 315 789-2762
Geneva *(G-5164)*

Ward Sales Co Inc ....G 315 476-5276
Syracuse *(G-15023)*

2262 Silk & Man-Made Fabric Finishers

American Spray-On Corp ....E 212 929-2100
New York *(G-8559)*

▲ Beckmann Converting Inc ....E 518 842-0073
Amsterdam *(G-318)*

Central Textiles Inc ....F 212 213-8740
New York *(G-8953)*

Dyenamix Inc ....E 212 941-6642
New York *(G-9287)*

Eastern Silk Mills Inc ....E 212 730-1300
New York *(G-9305)*

Efs Designs LLC ....G 718 852-9511
Brooklyn *(G-1785)*

◆ Fabric Resources Intl Ltd ....F 516 829-4550
Great Neck *(G-5386)*

▲ Gehring Tricot Corporation ....D 315 429-8551
Dolgeville *(G-4022)*

Intertex USA Inc ....F 212 279-3601
New York *(G-9925)*

Knucklehead Embroidery Inc ....G 607 797-2725
Johnson City *(G-6605)*

Marcel Finishing Corp ....E 718 381-2889
Plainview *(G-12699)*

▲ Mv Corp Inc ....C 631 273-8020
Bay Shore *(G-695)*

Prismatic Dyeing & Finshg Inc ....D 845 561-1800
Newburgh *(G-11883)*

▲ Raxon Fabrics Corp ....F 212 532-6816
New York *(G-10984)*

Rescuestuff Inc ....G 718 318-7570
Peekskill *(G-12555)*

Screen Gems Inc ....G 845 561-0036
New Windsor *(G-8382)*

Toltec Fabrics Inc ....E 212 706-9310
New York *(G-11506)*

Valley Stream Sporting Gds Inc ....E 516 593-7800
Lynbrook *(G-7442)*

2269 Textile Finishers, NEC

American Country Quilts & Lin ....G 631 283-5466
Southampton *(G-14526)*

▲ China Ting Fshion Group USA LL ....G 212 716-1600
New York *(G-8993)*

◆ Duck River Textiles Inc ....F 212 679-2980
New York *(G-9277)*

Hosel & Ackerson Inc ....E 212 575-1490
New York *(G-9814)*

▲ Majestic Rayon Corporation ....E 212 929-6443
New York *(G-10334)*

Marcel Finishing Corp ....E 718 381-2889
Plainview *(G-12699)*

National Spinning Co Inc ....E 212 382-6400
New York *(G-10546)*

Newcastle Fabrics Corp ....E 718 388-6600
Brooklyn *(G-2212)*

Prismatic Dyeing & Finshg Inc ....D 845 561-1800
Newburgh *(G-11883)*

Skin Prints Inc ....G 845 920-8756
Pearl River *(G-12541)*

2273 Carpets & Rugs

Aladdin Manufacturing Corp ....C 212 561-8715
New York *(G-8504)*

Auto-Mat Company Inc ....E 516 938-7373
Hicksville *(G-5886)*

Bloomsburg Carpet Inds Inc ....G 212 688-7447
New York *(G-8814)*

▲ Carpet Fabrications Intl ....E 914 381-6060
Mamaroneck *(G-7500)*

Daniels Bath & Beyond ....G 718 765-1915
Brooklyn *(G-1724)*

Eskayel Inc ....G 347 703-8084
Brooklyn *(G-1812)*

▲ Excellent Art Mfg Corp ....F 718 388-7075
Inwood *(G-6292)*

Interfaceflor LLC ....E 212 686-8284
New York *(G-9915)*

Kalati Company Inc ....G 516 423-9132
Great Neck *(G-5397)*

▲ Loom Concepts LLC ....G 212 813-9586
New York *(G-10253)*

▲ Lorena Canals USA Inc ....G 844 567-3622
Hastings On Hudson *(G-5575)*

▲ Mark Nelson Designs LLC ....F 646 422-7020
New York *(G-10365)*

Mgk Group Inc ....G 212 989-2732
New York *(G-10448)*

Michaelian & Kohlberg Inc ....G 212 431-9009
New York *(G-10454)*

North Sunshine LLC ....F 307 027-1634
Valley Cottage *(G-15320)*

◆ Northpoint Trading Inc ....F 212 481-8001
New York *(G-10645)*

Odegard Inc ....F 212 545-0069
Long Island City *(G-7313)*

Peter Racing ....F 914 968-4150
Yonkers *(G-16341)*

▲ Renaissnce Crpt Tapestries Inc ....F 212 696-0080
New York *(G-11011)*

Rosecore Division ....F 516 504-4530
Great Neck *(G-5418)*

Safavieh Inc ....A 516 945-1900
Port Washington *(G-12920)*

▲ Scalamandre Silks Inc ....D 212 980-3888
New York *(G-11147)*

Shyam Ahuja Limited ....G 212 644-5910
New York *(G-11221)*

▲ Sunrise Tile Inc ....G 718 939-0538
Flushing *(G-4896)*

Tdg Operations LLC ....G 212 779-4300
New York *(G-11440)*

Tiger 21 LLC ....G 212 360-1700
New York *(G-11485)*

▲ Tsar USA LLC ....F 646 415-7968
New York *(G-11555)*

Wells Rugs Inc ....G 516 676-2056
Glen Cove *(G-5204)*

2281 Yarn Spinning Mills

Advanced Yarn Technologies Inc ....E 518 239-6600
Durham *(G-4069)*

▲ Colortex Inc ....G 212 564-2000
New York *(G-9057)*

Great Adirondack Yarn Company ....F 518 843-3381
Amsterdam *(G-329)*

▲ Missiontex Inc ....G 718 532-9053
Brooklyn *(G-2161)*

National Spinning Co Inc ....E 212 382-6400
New York *(G-10546)*

Printz and Patternz LLC ....G 518 944-6020
Schenectady *(G-14296)*

▼ United Thread Mills Corp ....G 516 536-3900
Oceanside *(G-12195)*

2282 Yarn Texturizing, Throwing, Twisting & Winding Mills

Janes Designer Yrn Pttrns Inc ....G 347 260-3071
New York *(G-9974)*

▲ La Lame Inc ....G 212 921-9770
New York *(G-10158)*

▲ Majestic Rayon Corporation ....E 212 929-6443
New York *(G-10334)*

Marsha Fleisher ....F 845 679-6500
Woodstock *(G-16236)*

2284 Thread Mills

Albany International Corp ....C 607 749-7226
Homer *(G-6060)*

American Quality Embroidery ....G 631 467-3200
Ronkonkoma *(G-13903)*

One In A Million Inc ....G 516 829-1111
Valley Stream *(G-15350)*

▼ United Thread Mills Corp ....G 516 536-3900
Oceanside *(G-12195)*

V Technical Textiles Inc ....G 315 597-1674
Palmyra *(G-12494)*

2295 Fabrics Coated Not Rubberized

▲ A-One Laminating Corp ....G 718 266-6002
Brooklyn *(G-1442)*

A-One Moving & Storage Inc ....G 718 266-6002
Brooklyn *(G-1443)*

Architectural Fiberglass Corp ....E 631 842-4772
Copiague *(G-3645)*

▲ Beckmann Converting Inc ....E 518 842-0073
Amsterdam *(G-318)*

Breton Industries Inc ....C 518 842-3030
Amsterdam *(G-320)*

▲ Chemprene Inc ....C 845 831-2800
Beacon *(G-749)*

▲ Chemprene Holding Inc ....C 845 831-2800
Beacon *(G-750)*

▲ Comfort Care Textiles Inc ....E 631 543-0531
Commack *(G-3584)*

▲ Eurotex Inc ....F 716 205-8861
Niagara Falls *(G-11925)*

◆ Fabric Resources Intl Ltd ....F 516 829-4550
Great Neck *(G-5386)*

◆ GE Polymershapes ....F 516 433-4092
Hicksville *(G-5910)*

GM Insulation Corp ....F 516 354-6000
Elmont *(G-4385)*

Kaneka America LLC ....D 212 705-4340
New York *(G-10066)*

Kiltronx Enviro Systems Corp ....E 917 971-7177
Hauppauge *(G-5682)*

New York Cutting & Gumming Co ....E 212 563-4146
Middletown *(G-7924)*

▲ Newtex Industries Inc ....E 585 924-9135
Victor *(G-15421)*

▼ Perry Plastics Inc ....F 718 747-5600
Flushing *(G-4887)*

▲ Tonoga Inc ....C 518 658-3202
Petersburg *(G-12600)*

▲ Tpi Industries LLC ....E 845 692-2820
Middletown *(G-7935)*

V Technical Textiles Inc ....G 315 597-1674
Palmyra *(G-12494)*

2296 Tire Cord & Fabric

Albany International Corp ....C 518 445-2230
Menands *(G-7838)*

Designatronics Incorporated ....B 516 328-3300
New Hyde Park *(G-8261)*

Haines Equipment Inc ....E 607 566-8531
Avoca *(G-510)*

York Industries Inc ....E 516 746-3736
Garden City Park *(G-5126)*

2297 Fabrics, Nonwoven

Albany International Corp ....C 518 445-2200
Rensselaer *(G-13084)*

◆ Fabrication Enterprises Inc ....E 914 591-9300
Elmsford *(G-4409)*

▲ Legendary Auto Interiors Ltd ....E 315 331-1212
Newark *(G-11843)*

Mgk Group Inc ....E 212 989-2732
New York *(G-10448)*

◆ Saint-Gobain Adfors Amer Inc ....D 716 775-3900
Grand Island *(G-5343)*

Saint-Gobain Adfors Amer Inc ....D 585 589-4401
Albion *(G-161)*

2298 Cordage & Twine

Albany International Corp ....C 607 749-7226
Homer *(G-6060)*

All-Lifts Incorporated ....E 518 465-3461
Albany *(G-37)*

▲ Continental Cordage Corp ....D 315 655-9800
Cazenovia *(G-3225)*

Cortland Company Inc ....D 607 753-8276
Cortland *(G-3759)*

Cortland Line Mfg LLC ....E 607 756-2851
Cortland *(G-3760)*

◆ Fiber Instrument Sales Inc ....C 315 736-2206
Oriskany *(G-12390)*

Fiberone LLC ....F 315 434-8877
East Syracuse *(G-4211)*

▲ Gladding Braided Products LLC ....E 315 653-7211
South Otselic *(G-14520)*

Laseoptics Corp ....F 716 462-5078
Buffalo *(G-2848)*

Sphere Cables & Chips Inc ....E 212 619-3132
New York *(G-11322)*

T M International LLC ....G 718 842-0949
Bronx *(G-1377)*

Triad Network Technologies ....E 585 924-8505
Victor *(G-15439)*

2299 Textile Goods, NEC

A Thousand Cranes Inc ....F 212 724-9596
New York *(G-8419)*

▲ Ace Drop Cloth Canvas Pdts Inc ......E 718 731-1550
   Bronx (G-1193)
◆ American Home Mfg LLC ....G 212 643-0680
   New York (G-8551)
▲ Arabella Textiles LLC ....G 212 679-0611
   New York (G-8616)
Architectural Textiles USA Inc ....E 212 213-6972
   New York (G-8619)
◆ Benson Mills Inc ....E 718 236-6743
   Brooklyn (G-1576)
Blc Textiles Inc ....E 844 500-7900
   Mineola (G-7962)
Buperiod PBC ....G 917 406-9804
   Brooklyn (G-1629)
◆ Copen United LLC ....G 212 819-0008
   New York (G-9097)
▲ David King Linen Inc ....F 718 241-7298
   New York (G-9180)
Dean Trading Corp ....F 718 485-0600
   Brooklyn (G-1732)
Eskayel Inc ....G 347 703-8084
   Brooklyn (G-1812)
▲ Feldman Company Inc ....F 212 966-1303
   New York (G-9482)
Fibrix LLC ....E 716 683-4100
   Depew (G-3981)
Fil Doux Inc ....F 212 202-1459
   Brooklyn (G-1842)
▲ Gappa Textiles Inc ....G 212 481-7100
   New York (G-9572)
▲ Ghani Textiles Inc ....G 718 859-4561
   Brooklyn (G-1884)
▲ Global Resources Sg Inc ....F 212 686-1411
   New York (G-9632)
Ino-Tex LLC ....G 212 400-2205
   New York (G-9899)
◆ Ivi Services Inc ....D 607 729-5111
   Binghamton (G-889)
J Rettenmaier USA LP ....D 716 693-4040
   North Tonawanda (G-12074)
J Rettenmaier USA LP ....D 716 693-4009
   North Tonawanda (G-12075)
▲ James Thompson & Company Inc ..E 212 686-4242
   New York (G-9972)
Jo-Vin Decorators Inc ....E 718 441-9350
   Woodhaven (G-16187)
Jonice Industires ....G 516 640-4283
   Hempstead (G-5841)
▲ K F I Inc ....G 516 546-2904
   Roosevelt (G-14031)
▲ La Lame Inc ....G 212 921-9770
   New York (G-10158)
◆ Lintex Linens Inc ....B 212 679-8046
   New York (G-10222)
▲ Lr Paris LLC ....F 845 709-8013
   New York (G-10275)
▲ Manrico Usa Inc ....G 212 794-4200
   New York (G-10351)
▲ Navy Plum LLC ....G 845 641-7441
   Monsey (G-8041)
Novita Fabrics Furnishing Corp ....F 516 299-4500
   Mineola (G-7994)
Rli Schlgel Specialty Pdts LLC ....G 585 627-5919
   Rochester (G-13675)
Rovel Manufacturing Co Inc ....G 516 365-2752
   Roslyn (G-14046)
S Hellerman Inc ....G 718 622-2995
   Brooklyn (G-2377)
◆ Sabbsons International Inc ....F 718 360-1947
   Brooklyn (G-2379)
◆ Sam Salem & Son LLC ....F 212 695-6020
   New York (G-11124)
▼ Shannon Global Enrgy Solutions ..D 716 693-7954
   North Tonawanda (G-12090)
▲ Simple Elegance New York Inc ....F 718 360-1947
   Brooklyn (G-2419)
Sk Capital Partners II LP ....F 212 826-2700
   New York (G-11254)
Sk Titan Holdings LLC ....G 212 826-2700
   New York (G-11255)
◆ Soundcoat Company Inc ....D 631 242-2200
   Deer Park (G-3938)
Southern Adrndck Fbr Prdcrs CP ......G 518 692-2700
   Greenwich (G-5476)
Superior Fiber Mills Inc ....E 718 782-7500
   Brooklyn (G-2475)
Thistle Hill Weavers ....G 518 284-2729
   Cherry Valley (G-3368)
▼ TRM Linen Inc ....G 718 686-6075
   Brooklyn (G-2524)

Vincent Manufacturing Co Inc ....F 315 823-0280
   Little Falls (G-6995)
▲ Yankee Corp ....F 718 589-1377
   Bronx (G-1397)

23 APPAREL AND OTHER FINISHED PRODUCTS MADE FROM FABRICS AND SIMILAR MATERIAL

2311 Men's & Boys' Suits, Coats & Overcoats

▲ Adrian Jules Ltd ....D 585 342-5886
   Rochester (G-13207)
▲ Advance Apparel Intl Inc ....G 212 944-0984
   New York (G-8467)
Allytex LLC ....G 518 376-7539
   Ballston Spa (G-568)
Bindle and Keep ....G 917 740-5002
   Brooklyn (G-1588)
▲ Blue Duck Trading Ltd ....G 212 268-3122
   New York (G-8818)
▲ Canali USA Inc ....E 212 767-0205
   New York (G-8901)
Centric Brands Inc ....D 646 582-6000
   New York (G-8955)
▲ Check Group LLC ....D 212 221-4700
   New York (G-8978)
▲ Christian Casey LLC ....E 212 500-2200
   New York (G-8998)
Christian Casey LLC ....E 212 500-2200
   New York (G-8998)
▲ Concorde Apparel Company LLC ..G 212 307-7848
   New York (G-9078)
Crisada Inc ....G 718 729-9730
   Long Island City (G-7194)
▲ Crye Precision LLC ....C 718 246-3838
   Brooklyn (G-1705)
▲ Excelled Sheepskin & Lea Coat ....F 212 594-5843
   New York (G-9443)
▲ G-III Apparel Group Ltd ....B 212 403-0500
   New York (G-9560)
G-III Apparel Group Ltd ....F 212 840-7272
   New York (G-9562)
Giliberto Designs Inc ....E 212 695-0216
   New York (G-9610)
▲ Great 4 Image Inc ....E 518 424-2058
   Rensselaer (G-13088)
◆ Hugo Boss Usa Inc ....D 212 940-0600
   New York (G-9835)
J & X Production Inc ....F 718 200-1228
   New York (G-9249)
John Kochis Custom Designs ....G 212 244-6046
   New York (G-10016)
▲ Kozinn+sons Merchant Tailors ....E 212 643-1916
   New York (G-10132)
▲ L F Fashion Orient Intl Co Ltd ....G 917 667-3398
   New York (G-10151)
Lvl Xiii Brands Inc ....F 646 530-2795
   New York (G-10287)
◆ M Hidary & Co Inc ....D 212 736-6540
   New York (G-10296)
▲ Manchu New York Inc ....G 212 921-5050
   New York (G-10340)
▲ Martin Greenfield Clothiers ....C 718 497-5480
   Brooklyn (G-2120)
Med-Eng LLC ....E 315 713-0130
   Ogdensburg (G-12209)
▲ Michael Andrews LLC ....F 212 677-1755
   New York (G-10451)
▲ Mv Corp Inc ....C 631 273-8020
   Bay Shore (G-695)
▲ Occunomix International LLC ....E 631 741-1940
   Port Jeff STA (G-12837)
Opposuits USA Inc ....E 917 438-8878
   New York (G-10700)
Otex Protective Inc ....G 585 232-7160
   Rochester (G-13600)
Pat & Rose Dress Inc ....D 212 279-1357
   New York (G-10768)
Primo Coat Corp ....E 718 349-2070
   Long Island City (G-7329)
Proper Cloth LLC ....G 646 964-4221
   New York (G-10914)
Ps38 LLC ....G 212 302-1108
   New York (G-10918)
◆ Ralph Lauren Corporation ....B 212 318-7000
   New York (G-10975)
▲ Roth Clothing Co Inc ....G 718 384-4927
   Brooklyn (G-2356)

Royal Clothing Corp ....G 718 436-5841
   Brooklyn (G-2358)
▲ Salsa Professional Apparel LLC ....G 212 575-6565
   New York (G-11122)
▲ Shane Tex Inc ....F 516 486-7522
   Woodmere (G-16193)
Strong Group Inc ....G 516 766-6300
   Oceanside (G-12192)
Tom James Company ....F 212 593-0204
   New York (G-11509)
Uniforms By Park Coats Inc ....E 718 499-1182
   Brooklyn (G-2536)
▲ Urban Textiles Inc ....F 212 777-1900
   New York (G-11617)
Vf Imagewear Inc ....G 718 352-2363
   Bayside (G-744)
▲ Wp Lavori USA Inc ....G 212 244-6074
   New York (G-11790)
Yong Ji Productions Inc ....G 917 559-4616
   Corona (G-3752)

2321 Men's & Boys' Shirts

Americo Group Inc ....E 212 563-2700
   New York (G-8560)
◆ Americo Group Inc ....E 212 563-2700
   New York (G-8561)
◆ Andy & Evan Industries Inc ....G 212 967-7908
   New York (G-8581)
Arthur Gluck Shirtmakers Inc ....F 212 755-8165
   Brooklyn (G-1537)
▲ August Silk Inc ....E 212 643-2400
   New York (G-8678)
August Silk Inc ....G 212 643-2400
   New York (G-8679)
▲ Ben Wachter Associates Inc ....G 212 736-4064
   New York (G-8754)
◆ Bowe Industries Inc ....D 718 441-6464
   Glendale (G-5219)
Bowe Industries Inc ....D 718 441-6464
   Glendale (G-5220)
▲ Check Group LLC ....D 212 221-4700
   New York (G-8978)
▲ Christian Casey LLC ....E 212 500-2200
   New York (G-8997)
Christian Casey LLC ....E 212 500-2200
   New York (G-8998)
Colony Holdings Intl LLC ....F 212 868-2800
   New York (G-9054)
Cyberlimit Inc ....F 212 840-9597
   New York (G-9140)
◆ Donna Karan International Inc ......F 212 789-1500
   New York (G-9250)
Donna Karan International Inc ....G 212 768-5800
   New York (G-9250)
◆ Garan Incorporated ....C 212 563-1292
   New York (G-9573)
▼ Garan Manufacturing Corp ....G 212 563-2000
   New York (G-9574)
Gbg National Brands Group LLC ......G 646 839-7000
   New York (G-9577)
Gce International Inc ....D 773 263-1210
   New York (G-9582)
Grayers America Inc ....F 310 953-2742
   New York (G-9668)
◆ Great Universal Corp ....E 917 302-0065
   New York (G-9670)
Groupe 16sur20 LLC ....F 212 625-1620
   New York (G-9685)
▲ Grunt Apparel Inc ....G 646 878-6171
   New York (G-9689)
◆ Haddad Bros Inc ....F 212 563-2117
   New York (G-9706)
Ibrands International LLC ....F 212 354-1330
   New York (G-9853)
Interbrand LLC ....G 212 840-9595
   New York (G-9913)
Jacks and Jokers 52 LLC ....G 917 740-2595
   New York (G-9961)
Jordache Enterprises Inc ....D 212 944-1330
   New York (G-10024)
◆ Jordache Enterprises Inc ....C 212 643-8400
   New York (G-10025)
Just Brass Inc ....G 212 724-5447
   New York (G-10045)
▲ Kt Group Inc ....G 212 760-2500
   New York (G-10144)
Lt2 LLC ....E 212 684-1510
   New York (G-10277)
▲ M S B International Ltd ....F 212 302-5551
   New York (G-10299)

S I C

▲ Mega Sourcing Inc ....G..... 646 682-0304
  Merrick (G-7861)

Miltons of New York Inc ....G..... 212 997-3359
  New York (G-10471)

▲ Mulitex Usa Inc ....G..... 212 398-0440
  New York (G-10518)

▲ Nat Nast Company Inc ....E..... 212 575-1186
  New York (G-10536)

Oved Mens LLC ....E..... 212 563-4999
  New York (G-10719)

Oxford Industries Inc ....F..... 212 840-2288
  New York (G-10726)

Perry Ellis International Inc ....F..... 212 536-5400
  New York (G-10807)

Perry Ellis International Inc ....G..... 212 536-5499
  New York (G-10808)

◆ Perry Ellis Menswear LLC ....C..... 212 221-7500
  New York (G-10809)

Phillips-Van Heusen Europe ....F..... 212 381-3500
  New York (G-10829)

◆ Pvh Corp ....D..... 212 381-3500
  New York (G-10933)

Pvh Corp ....G..... 845 561-0233
  New Windsor (G-8379)

Pvh Corp ....G..... 631 254-8200
  Deer Park (G-3924)

Pvh Corp ....G..... 212 549-6000
  New York (G-10934)

Pvh Corp ....G..... 212 719-2600
  New York (G-10937)

◆ Ralph Lauren Corporation ....B..... 212 318-7000
  New York (G-10975)

▲ Roffe Accessories Inc ....E..... 212 213-1440
  New York (G-11071)

Saad Collection Inc ....G..... 212 937-0341
  New York (G-11111)

▲ Schwartz Textile LLC ....E..... 718 499-8243
  Brooklyn (G-2389)

Sifonya Inc ....G..... 212 620-4512
  New York (G-11229)

◆ Warnaco Inc ....B..... 212 287-8000
  New York (G-11721)

Warnaco Inc ....F..... 718 722-3000
  Brooklyn (G-2575)

Whittall & Shon ....G..... 212 594-2626
  New York (G-11752)

Yale Trouser Corporation ....F..... 516 255-0700
  Oceanside (G-12199)

2322 Men's & Boys' Underwear & Nightwear

Becks Classic Mfg Inc ....D..... 631 435-3800
  Brentwood (G-1116)

▲ Candlesticks Inc ....F..... 212 947-8900
  New York (G-8903)

▲ Check Group LLC ....D..... 212 221-4700
  New York (G-8978)

▲ Christian Casey LLC ....E..... 212 500-2200
  New York (G-8997)

Christian Casey LLC ....E..... 212 500-2200
  New York (G-8998)

▲ Comme-Ci Comme-CA AP Group ..E..... 631 300-1035
  Hauppauge (G-5623)

▲ Revolutionwear Inc ....G..... 617 669-9191
  New York (G-11030)

▲ Sleepwear Holdings Inc ....C..... 516 466-4738
  New York (G-11268)

▲ Tommy John Inc ....E..... 800 708-3490
  New York (G-11512)

◆ Twist Intimate Group LLC ....G..... 212 695-5990
  New York (G-11564)

◆ Warnaco Group Inc ....E..... 212 287-8000
  New York (G-11720)

◆ Warnaco Inc ....B..... 212 287-8000
  New York (G-11721)

Warnaco Inc ....F..... 718 722-3000
  Brooklyn (G-2575)

▲ Waterbury Garment LLC ....E..... 212 725-1500
  New York (G-11730)

▲ Wickers Sportswear Inc ....G..... 631 543-1640
  Commack (G-3604)

2323 Men's & Boys' Neckwear

Countess Mara Inc ....G..... 212 768-7300
  New York (G-9111)

Emunas Sales Inc ....F..... 718 621-3138
  Brooklyn (G-1803)

JS Blank & Co Inc ....E..... 212 689-4835
  New York (G-10035)

Mallory & Church LLC ....G..... 212 868-7888
  New York (G-10337)

MANE Enterprises Inc ....D..... 718 472-4955
  Long Island City (G-7287)

Mongru Neckwear Inc ....E..... 718 706-0406
  Long Island City (G-7299)

◆ Perry Ellis Menswear LLC ....C..... 212 221-7500
  New York (G-10809)

◆ Ralph Lauren Corporation ....B..... 212 318-7000
  New York (G-10975)

Randa Accessories Lea Gds LLC ..D..... 212 354-5100
  New York (G-10979)

▲ Roffe Accessories Inc ....E..... 212 213-1440
  New York (G-11071)

▲ S Broome and Co Inc ....D..... 718 663-6800
  Long Island City (G-7350)

▲ Tie King Inc ....E..... 718 768-8484
  Brooklyn (G-2504)

Tie King Inc ....G..... 212 714-9611
  New York (G-11484)

Valenti Neckwear Co Inc ....G..... 914 969-0700
  Yonkers (G-16354)

W B Bow Tie Corp ....F..... 212 683-6130
  New York (G-11712)

◆ Warnaco Inc ....B..... 212 287-8000
  New York (G-11721)

Wetherall Contracting NY Inc ......G..... 718 894-7011
  Middle Village (G-7885)

2325 Men's & Boys' Separate Trousers & Casual Slacks

▲ Adrian Jules Ltd ....D..... 585 342-5886
  Rochester (G-13207)

Bruno & Canio Ltd ....E..... 845 624-3060
  Nanuet (G-8197)

Centric Brands Inc ....D..... 646 582-6000
  New York (G-8955)

Centric Denim Usa LLC ....G..... 646 839-7000
  New York (G-8956)

▲ Check Group LLC ....D..... 212 221-4700
  New York (G-8978)

▲ Christian Casey LLC ....E..... 212 500-2200
  New York (G-8997)

Christian Casey LLC ....E..... 212 500-2200
  New York (G-8998)

Denim King Depot LLC ....E..... 917 477-0550
  New York (G-9201)

◆ Donna Karan International Inc ...F..... 212 789-1500
  New York (G-9249)

Donna Karan International Inc .....G..... 212 768-5800
  New York (G-9250)

Groupe 16sur20 LLC ....E..... 212 625-1620
  New York (G-9685)

Guess Inc ....E..... 716 298-3561
  Niagara Falls (G-11934)

Halabieh Group Inc ....E..... 347 987-8263
  New York (G-9710)

▲ Hertling Trousers Inc ....E..... 718 784-6100
  Brooklyn (G-1935)

◆ Hugo Boss Usa Inc ....D..... 212 940-0600
  New York (G-9835)

▲ Int Trading USA LLC ....C..... 212 760-2338
  New York (G-9906)

Jordache Enterprises Inc ....D..... 212 944-1330
  New York (G-10024)

◆ Jordache Enterprises Inc ....C..... 212 643-8400
  New York (G-10025)

Kalikow Brothers LP ....E..... 212 643-0315
  New York (G-10060)

Kaltex America Inc ....F..... 212 971-0575
  New York (G-10062)

Leng Universal Inc ....F..... 212 398-6800
  New York (G-10196)

Levi Strauss & Co ....F..... 917 213-6263
  Flushing (G-4870)

◆ M Hidary & Co Inc ....D..... 212 736-6540
  New York (G-10296)

▲ M S B International Ltd ....F..... 212 302-5551
  New York (G-10299)

▲ Martin Greenfield Clothiers ....C..... 718 497-5480
  Brooklyn (G-2120)

Messex Group Inc ....G..... 646 229-2582
  New York (G-10442)

Miltons of New York Inc ....G..... 212 997-3359
  New York (G-10471)

▲ Montero International Inc ....E..... 212 695-1787
  Westbury (G-15911)

▲ Mulitex Usa Inc ....G..... 212 398-0440
  New York (G-10518)

▲ One Jeanswear Group LLC ....B..... 212 575-2571
  New York (G-10690)

◆ Passport Brands Inc ....E..... 646 459-2625
  New York (G-10767)

Pat & Rose Dress Inc ....D..... 212 279-1357
  New York (G-10768)

Perry Ellis International Inc ....F..... 212 536-5400
  New York (G-10807)

◆ Perry Ellis Menswear LLC ....C..... 212 221-7500
  New York (G-10809)

Primo Coat Corp ....E..... 718 349-2070
  Long Island City (G-7329)

◆ Ralph Lauren Corporation ....B..... 212 318-7000
  New York (G-10975)

◆ Ryba General Merchandise Inc ..E..... 718 522-2028
  Brooklyn (G-2368)

Sean John Clothing Inc ....G..... 212 500-2200
  New York (G-11173)

Sean John Clothing Inc ....G..... 212 500-2200
  New York (G-11174)

Yale Trouser Corporation ....F..... 516 255-0700
  Oceanside (G-12199)

2326 Men's & Boys' Work Clothing

5 Star Apparel LLC ....G..... 212 563-1233
  New York (G-8404)

▲ Ace Drop Cloth Canvas Pdts Inc ..E..... 718 731-1550
  Bronx (G-1193)

American Apparel Ltd ....G..... 516 504-4559
  Great Neck (G-5364)

Badgley Mischka Licensing LLC ..E..... 212 921-1585
  New York (G-8713)

Beardslee Realty ....G..... 516 747-5557
  Mineola (G-7960)

▲ Best Medical Wear Ltd ....G..... 718 858-5544
  Brooklyn (G-1579)

▲ Billion Tower Intl LLC ....F..... 212 220-0608
  New York (G-8791)

Broadway Knitting Mills Inc ....G..... 716 692-4421
  North Tonawanda (G-12059)

Classic Designer Workshop Inc ..G..... 212 730-8480
  New York (G-9024)

Dalcom USA Ltd ....F..... 516 466-7733
  Great Neck (G-5380)

Doral Apparel Group Inc ....G..... 917 208-5652
  New York (G-9254)

▲ Du Monde Trading Inc ....E..... 212 944-1306
  New York (G-9275)

▲ E J Manufacturing Inc ....G..... 516 313-9380
  Bellmore (G-782)

Enzo Manzoni LLC ....E..... 212 464-7000
  Brooklyn (G-1807)

Far East Industries Inc ....G..... 718 687-2482
  New Hyde Park (G-8268)

Ferris USA LLC ....G..... 617 895-8102
  New York (G-9485)

◆ HC Contracting Inc ....D..... 212 643-9292
  New York (G-9740)

Hillary Merchant Inc ....G..... 646 575-9242
  New York (G-9785)

▲ Itochu Prominent USA LLC ....C..... 212 827-5715
  New York (G-9948)

Kse Sportsman Media Inc ....D..... 212 852-6600
  New York (G-10142)

Lady Brass Co Inc ....G..... 516 887-8040
  Hewlett (G-5870)

LLC Major Major ....E..... 212 354-8550
  New York (G-10236)

Lynn Brands LLC ....E..... 626 376-8948
  New York (G-10289)

Medline Industries Inc ....B..... 845 344-3301
  Middletown (G-7919)

▲ Mesh LLC ....E..... 646 839-7000
  New York (G-10440)

New York Hospital Disposable .....E..... 718 384-1620
  Brooklyn (G-2208)

Norcorp Inc ....E..... 914 666-1310
  Mount Kisco (G-8100)

▲ Occunomix International LLC .....E..... 631 741-1940
  Port Jeff STA (G-12837)

▲ Penfli Industries Inc ....F..... 212 947-6080
  Great Neck (G-5413)

▲ Rag & Bone Industries LLC ....D..... 212 278-8214
  New York (G-10971)

Richard Manufacturing Co Inc .....G..... 718 254-0958
  Brooklyn (G-2344)

▼ S & H Uniform Corp ....D..... 914 937-6800
  White Plains (G-16057)

▲ Salsa Professional Apparel LLC ..G..... 212 575-6565
  New York (G-11122)

Shanghai Harmony AP Intl LLC ....E..... 646 569-5680
  New Rochelle (G-8354)

Stealth Inc...F 718 252-7900
 Brooklyn *(G-2455)*
▲ Untuckit LLC.....................................D 347 524-9111
 New York *(G-11612)*
Untuckit LLC..C 646 724-1857
 New York *(G-11613)*
▲ Ventura Enterprise Co Inc..............E 212 391-0170
 New York *(G-11656)*
Vf Imagewear Inc.................................F 718 352-2363
 Bayside *(G-744)*

2329 Men's & Boys' Clothing, NEC

▲ A Bogen Enterprises Inc...............G 718 951-9533
 Brooklyn *(G-1432)*
Adpro Sports LLC..............................D 716 854-5116
 Buffalo *(G-2622)*
▲ Alexander Wang Incorporated.........D 212 532-3103
 New York *(G-8514)*
Alleson of Rochester Inc...................E 315 548-3635
 Geneva *(G-5145)*
▲ Alpha 6 Distributions LLC.............F 516 801-8290
 Locust Valley *(G-7121)*
▲ American Challenge Enterprises....G 631 595-7171
 Bay Shore *(G-648)*
American Clssic Outfitters Inc.........D 585 237-6111
 Perry *(G-12595)*
Apogee Retail NY................................G 516 731-1727
 Levittown *(G-6912)*
Bandit International Ltd.....................F 718 402-2100
 Bronx *(G-1210)*
▲ Beluga Inc..E 212 594-5511
 New York *(G-8753)*
◆ Benetton Trading Usa Inc.............G 212 593-0290
 New York *(G-8757)*
Bernette Apparel LLC.........................F 212 279-5526
 New York *(G-8762)*
▲ Big Idea Brands LLC.....................F 212 938-0270
 New York *(G-8787)*
Bilco Industries Inc...........................F 917 783-5008
 New York *(G-8790)*
Billion Tower USA LLC.......................G 212 220-0608
 New York *(G-8792)*
Brigantine Inc....................................G 212 354-8550
 New York *(G-8851)*
Broadway Knitting Mills Inc...............G 716 692-4421
 North Tonawanda *(G-12059)*
▲ Broken Threads Inc.......................G 212 730-4351
 New York *(G-8860)*
▲ Brunschwig & Fils LLC.................F 800 538-1880
 Bethpage *(G-833)*
By Robert James................................G 212 253-2121
 New York *(G-8876)*
Caps Teamwear Inc............................G 585 663-1750
 Rochester *(G-13295)*
▲ Caribbean Fashion Group Inc........G 212 706-8851
 New York *(G-8916)*
Caroda Inc..E 212 630-9986
 New York *(G-8919)*
Central Mills Inc.................................C 212 764-9011
 New York *(G-8952)*
City Jeans Inc.....................................G 718 239-5353
 Bronx *(G-1226)*
▲ Comme-Ci Comme-CA AP Group....E 631 300-1035
 Hauppauge *(G-5623)*
Continental Knitting Mills...................G 631 242-5330
 Deer Park *(G-3853)*
▲ Cotton Emporium Inc.....................G 718 894-3365
 Glendale *(G-5223)*
Craftatlantic LLC................................F 646 726-4205
 New York *(G-9117)*
▲ David Peyser Sportswear Inc........C 631 231-7788
 Bay Shore *(G-670)*
David Peyser Sportswear Inc............E 212 695-7716
 New York *(G-9181)*
▲ Eb Couture Ltd...............................E 212 912-0190
 New York *(G-9310)*
▲ Endurance LLC...............................E 212 719-2500
 New York *(G-9372)*
◆ Eternal Fortune Fashion LLC........G 212 965-5322
 New York *(G-9412)*
Ferris USA LLC...................................G 617 895-8102
 New York *(G-9485)*
Feyem USA Inc...................................G 845 363-6253
 Brewster *(G-1149)*
▲ G-III Apparel Group Ltd................B 212 403-0500
 New York *(G-9560)*
Gametime Sportswear Plus LLC.........G 315 724-5893
 Utica *(G-15266)*
◆ General Sportwear Company Inc......C 212 764-5820
 New York *(G-9591)*

Groupe 16sur20 LLC...........................F 212 625-1620
 New York *(G-9685)*
Haculla Nyc Inc..................................F 718 886-3163
 Fresh Meadows *(G-5042)*
Halabieh Group Inc............................F 347 987-8263
 New York *(G-9710)*
Hansae Co Ltd....................................F 212 354-6690
 New York *(G-9724)*
▼ Herman Kay Company Ltd.............C 212 239-2025
 New York *(G-9768)*
◆ Hf Mfg Corp....................................D 212 594-9142
 New York *(G-9777)*
Hockey Facility..................................G 518 452-7396
 Albany *(G-86)*
House Pearl Fashions (us) Ltd.........F 212 840-3183
 New York *(G-9826)*
Hpe Clothing Corporation..................F 946 356-0474
 New York *(G-9829)*
▲ I Spiewak & Sons Inc...................E 212 695-1620
 New York *(G-9849)*
Icer Sports LLC..................................F 212 221-4700
 New York *(G-9855)*
Ifg Corp...C 212 629-9600
 New York *(G-9860)*
Ifg Corp...G 212 239-8615
 New York *(G-9861)*
Jacob Hidary Foundation Inc............F 212 736-6540
 New York *(G-9965)*
Joseph (uk) Inc..................................G 212 570-0077
 New York *(G-10026)*
Just Bottoms & Tops Inc...................F 212 564-3202
 New York *(G-10044)*
Kicks Closet Sportswear Inc.............G 347 577-0857
 Bronx *(G-1292)*
▲ Kidz World Inc................................F 212 563-4949
 New York *(G-10098)*
▲ King Sales Inc................................F 718 301-9862
 Brooklyn *(G-2029)*
▲ Komar Luxury Brands....................G 646 472-0060
 New York *(G-10125)*
Linder New York LLC..........................G 646 678-5819
 New York *(G-10221)*
▲ London Paris Ltd...........................G 718 564-4793
 Brooklyn *(G-2083)*
Longevity Brands LLC.........................G 212 231-7877
 New York *(G-10248)*
Luxe Imagine Consulting LLC............G 212 273-9770
 New York *(G-10286)*
◆ M Hidary & Co Inc.........................D 212 736-6540
 New York *(G-10296)*
Maiyet Inc...G 212 343-9999
 New York *(G-10333)*
Mann Consultants LLC........................E 914 763-0512
 Waccabuc *(G-15446)*
Mayberry Shoe Company Inc..............G 315 692-4086
 Manlius *(G-7549)*
▲ Mee Accessories LLC....................B 917 262-1000
 New York *(G-10421)*
▲ Miss Group.....................................G 212 391-2535
 New York *(G-10481)*
▲ Montero International Inc...............G 212 695-1787
 Westbury *(G-15911)*
▲ North American Mills Inc...............F 212 695-6146
 New York *(G-10642)*
▲ Nyc Idol Apparel Inc......................G 212 997-9797
 New York *(G-10661)*
On The Double Inc.............................G 518 431-3571
 Germantown *(G-5169)*
◆ One Step Up Ltd............................D 212 398-1110
 New York *(G-10691)*
Oxford Industries Inc.........................E 212 247-7712
 New York *(G-10725)*
P & I Sportswear Inc..........................G 718 934-4587
 New York *(G-10731)*
Predator Mountainwear Inc................G 315 727-3241
 Auburn *(G-490)*
Premier Brnds Group Hldngs LLC.....G 212 575-2571
 New York *(G-10878)*
Prestige Global NY Sls Corp.............G 212 776-4322
 New York *(G-10885)*
Pride & Joys Inc................................F 212 594-9820
 New York *(G-10888)*
▲ Pti-Pacific Inc...............................G 212 414-8495
 New York *(G-10920)*
Pvh Corp..G 212 381-3800
 New York *(G-10935)*
▲ Rainforest Inc................................F 212 575-7620
 New York *(G-10973)*
◆ Ralph Lauren Corporation............B 212 318-7000
 New York *(G-10975)*

▲ Ramsbury Property Us Inc.............F 212 223-6250
 New York *(G-10976)*
Robert Viggiani..................................G 914 423-4046
 Yonkers *(G-16346)*
Rp55 Inc..G 212 840-4035
 New York *(G-11093)*
▲ S & S Fashions Inc.......................G 718 328-0001
 Bronx *(G-1354)*
◆ Sanctuary Brands LLC..................F 212 704-4014
 New York *(G-11129)*
▼ Sb Corporation...............................G 212 822-3166
 New York *(G-11143)*
Scharf and Breit Inc...........................E 516 282-0287
 Williston Park *(G-16148)*
▲ Schwartz Textile LLC.....................F 718 499-8243
 Brooklyn *(G-2389)*
Siskind Group Inc..............................F 212 840-0880
 New York *(G-11251)*
▲ Sister Sister Inc.............................G 212 629-9600
 New York *(G-11252)*
▲ Standard Manufacturing Co Inc....D 518 235-2200
 Troy *(G-15190)*
Swimwear Anywhere Inc.....................E 845 858-4141
 Port Jervis *(G-12858)*
Tamka Sport LLC................................G 718 224-7820
 Douglaston *(G-4030)*
Tbhl International LLC.........................F 212 799-2007
 New York *(G-11438)*
◆ Tibana Finishing Inc......................F 718 417-5375
 Glendale *(G-5234)*
▲ Tillsonburg Company USA Inc........E 267 994-8096
 New York *(G-11488)*
▲ Uniqlo USA LLC.............................C 877 486-4756
 New York *(G-11593)*
Valley Stream Sporting Gds Inc.........E 516 593-7800
 Lynbrook *(G-7442)*
▲ Versailles Industries LLC..............G 212 792-9615
 New York *(G-11664)*
Vf Outdoor Inc....................................E 718 698-6215
 Staten Island *(G-14727)*
Vf Outdoor LLC...................................E 845 928-4900
 Central Valley *(G-3301)*
◆ Warnaco Group Inc.......................E 212 287-8000
 New York *(G-11720)*
◆ Warnaco Inc...................................B 212 287-8000
 New York *(G-11721)*
Warnaco Inc..F 718 722-3000
 Brooklyn *(G-2575)*
Worth Imports LLC..............................G 212 398-5410
 New York *(G-11786)*

2331 Women's & Misses' Blouses

79 Metro Ltd.......................................G 212 944-4030
 New York *(G-8408)*
▲ Accessries Direct Intl USA Inc......E 646 448-8200
 New York *(G-8443)*
Agi Brooks Production Co Inc............F 212 268-1533
 New York *(G-8493)*
▲ Alexander Wang Incorporated.........D 212 532-3103
 New York *(G-8514)*
▲ Alfred Dunner Inc..........................B 212 478-4300
 New York *(G-8515)*
Amerex Corporation............................G 212 221-3151
 New York *(G-8539)*
▲ Anna Sui Corp...............................E 212 941-8406
 New York *(G-8593)*
Apparel Group Ltd..............................E 212 328-1200
 New York *(G-8607)*
▲ August Silk Inc..............................G 212 643-2400
 New York *(G-8678)*
August Silk Inc...................................G 212 643-2400
 New York *(G-8679)*
▲ Ben Wachter Associates Inc..........G 212 736-4064
 New York *(G-8754)*
▲ Bernard Chaus Inc........................D 212 354-1280
 New York *(G-8760)*
Bernard Chaus Inc.............................G 646 562-4700
 New York *(G-8761)*
◆ Bowe Industries Inc.......................D 718 441-6464
 Glendale *(G-5219)*
Brach Knitting Mills Inc.....................F 845 651-4450
 Florida *(G-4821)*
Cyberlimit Inc....................................F 212 840-9597
 New York *(G-9140)*
▲ Cynthia Rowley Inc........................F 212 242-3803
 New York *(G-9142)*
◆ Donna Karan International Inc........F 212 789-1500
 New York *(G-9249)*
Donna Karan International Inc............G 212 768-5800
 New York *(G-9250)*

Elie Tahari Ltd ..... G 212 763-2000
New York *(G-9339)*

Elie Tahari Ltd ..... D 212 763-2000
New York *(G-9340)*

Embassy Apparel Inc ..... F 212 768-8330
New York *(G-9356)*

Feyem USA Inc ..... G 845 363-6253
Brewster *(G-1149)*

Fourtys Ny Inc ..... F 212 382-0301
New York *(G-9524)*

Fuller Sportswear Co Inc ..... G 516 773-3353
Great Neck *(G-5391)*

Gabrielle Andra ..... G 212 366-9624
New York *(G-9565)*

◆ Garan Incorporated ..... C 212 563-1292
New York *(G-9573)*

▼ Garan Manufacturing Corp ..... G 212 563-2000
New York *(G-9574)*

▲ Gce International Inc ..... D 212 704-4800
New York *(G-9580)*

Geoffrey Beene Inc ..... E 212 371-5570
New York *(G-9597)*

▲ Gildan Apparel USA Inc ..... D 212 476-0341
New York *(G-9609)*

Grey State Apparel LLC ..... E 212 255-4216
New York *(G-9675)*

Hansae Co Ltd ..... F 212 354-6690
New York *(G-9724)*

Icer Sports LLC ..... F 212 221-4700
New York *(G-9855)*

◆ International Direct Group Inc ..... E 212 921-9036
New York *(G-9919)*

▲ Jeanjer LLC ..... A 212 944-1330
New York *(G-9991)*

Jl Parc LLC ..... G 718 271-0703
Rego Park *(G-13078)*

Jordache Enterprises Inc ..... D 212 944-1330
New York *(G-10024)*

◆ Jordache Enterprises Inc ..... C 212 643-8400
New York *(G-10025)*

◆ Kate Spade Holdings LLC ..... B 212 354-4900
New York *(G-10076)*

▼ Krasner Group Inc ..... G 212 268-4100
New York *(G-10136)*

Ksk International Inc ..... E 212 354-7770
New York *(G-10143)*

◆ Land n Sea Inc ..... D 212 444-6000
New York *(G-10168)*

Lea & Viola Inc ..... G 646 918-6866
New York *(G-10181)*

▲ Liberty Apparel Company Inc ..... E 718 625-4000
New York *(G-10209)*

Lt2 LLC ..... E 212 684-1510
New York *(G-10277)*

Lynn Brands LLC ..... E 212 921-5495
New York *(G-10288)*

▲ M S B International Ltd ..... F 212 302-5551
New York *(G-10299)*

◆ Maggy London International Ltd ..... D 212 944-7199
New York *(G-10323)*

▲ Mega Sourcing Inc ..... G 646 682-0304
Merrick *(G-7861)*

▲ Mulitex Usa Inc ..... G 212 398-0440
New York *(G-10518)*

▲ Necessary Objects Ltd ..... E 212 334-9888
Long Island City *(G-7305)*

▲ Nyc Knitwear Inc ..... E 212 840-1313
New York *(G-10662)*

Orchard Apparel Group Ltd ..... G 212 268-8701
New York *(G-10706)*

Orchid Manufacturing Co Inc ..... F 212 840-5700
New York *(G-10708)*

Paddy Lee Fashions Inc ..... F 718 786-6020
Long Island City *(G-7318)*

Pat & Rose Dress Inc ..... D 212 279-1357
New York *(G-10768)*

▲ Permit Fashion Group Inc ..... G 212 912-0988
Melville *(G-7815)*

Phillips-Van Heusen Europe ..... F 212 381-3500
New York *(G-10829)*

Plugg LLC ..... F 212 840-6655
New York *(G-10857)*

◆ Pvh Corp ..... D 212 381-3500
New York *(G-10933)*

Pvh Corp ..... G 212 549-6000
New York *(G-10934)*

Pvh Corp ..... G 212 719-2600
New York *(G-10937)*

▲ Ramy Brook LLC ..... E 212 744-2789
New York *(G-10978)*

▲ Raven New York LLC ..... G 212 584-9690
New York *(G-10983)*

▲ Rhoda Lee Inc ..... D 212 840-5700
New York *(G-11035)*

Robert Danes Danes Inc ..... G 212 226-1351
New York *(G-11060)*

▲ S & S Manufacturing Co Inc ..... D 212 444-6000
New York *(G-11106)*

Saad Collection Inc ..... G 212 937-0341
New York *(G-11111)*

Soho Apparel Ltd ..... G 212 840-1109
New York *(G-11285)*

Spencer AB Inc ..... G 646 831-3728
New York *(G-11318)*

Stitch & Couture Inc ..... E 212 947-9204
New York *(G-11364)*

T Rj Shirts Inc ..... G 347 642-3071
East Elmhurst *(G-4111)*

Tahari ASL LLC ..... B 212 763-2800
New York *(G-11424)*

◆ Tibana Finishing Inc ..... E 718 417-5375
Glendale *(G-5234)*

◆ Triumph Apparel Corporation ..... E 212 302-2606
New York *(G-11548)*

Turn On Products Inc ..... F 212 764-4545
New York *(G-11560)*

▲ Turn On Products Inc ..... D 212 764-2121
New York *(G-11559)*

Ursula of Switzerland Inc ..... E 518 237-2580
Waterford *(G-15549)*

Vanity Room Inc ..... F 212 921-7154
New York *(G-11642)*

▲ Ventura Enterprise Co Inc ..... E 212 391-0170
New York *(G-11656)*

Yeohlee Inc ..... F 212 631-8099
New York *(G-11808)*

2335 Women's & Misses' Dresses

◆ A & M Rosenthal Entps Inc ..... E 646 638-9600
New York *(G-8411)*

Ace & Jig LLC ..... G 347 227-0318
Brooklyn *(G-1454)*

Agi Brooks Production Co Inc ..... F 212 268-1533
New York *(G-8493)*

Allison Che Fashion Inc ..... F 212 391-1433
New York *(G-8519)*

Alvina Vlenta Couture Collectn ..... F 212 921-7058
New York *(G-8533)*

Alvina Vlenta Couture Collectn ..... F 212 921-7058
New York *(G-8534)*

AM Retail Group Inc ..... C 716 297-0752
Niagara Falls *(G-11902)*

▲ Amj DOT LLC ..... G 718 775-3288
Brooklyn *(G-1505)*

Anna B Inc ..... G 516 680-6609
New York *(G-8592)*

▲ Anna Sui Corp ..... E 212 941-8406
New York *(G-8593)*

▲ Arteast LLC ..... E 646 859-6020
New York *(G-8633)*

▲ August Silk Inc ..... E 212 643-2400
New York *(G-8678)*

August Silk Inc ..... G 212 643-2400
New York *(G-8679)*

Bari-Jay Fashions Inc ..... E 212 921-1551
New York *(G-8730)*

Birnbaum & Bullock Ltd ..... G 212 242-2914
New York *(G-8801)*

▲ Cachet Industries Inc ..... E 212 944-2188
New York *(G-8885)*

Carol Peretz ..... F 516 248-6300
Mineola *(G-7964)*

▲ China Ting Fshion Group USA LL ..... G 212 716-1600
New York *(G-8993)*

Christian Siriano Holdings LLC ..... G 212 695-5494
New York *(G-9000)*

▲ Christos Inc ..... E 212 921-0025
New York *(G-9003)*

▲ Couture Inc ..... G 212 921-1166
New York *(G-9112)*

Crisada Inc ..... G 718 729-9730
Long Island City *(G-7194)*

▲ Csco LLC ..... E 212 375-6180
New York *(G-9127)*

CTS LLC ..... G 212 278-0058
New York *(G-9128)*

▲ Cynthia Rowley Inc ..... F 212 242-3803
New York *(G-9142)*

Dalma Dress Mfg Co Inc ..... E 212 391-8296
Greenvale *(G-5461)*

Damianou Sportswear Inc ..... D 718 204-5600
Woodside *(G-16203)*

◆ Donna Karan International Inc ..... F 212 789-1500
New York *(G-9249)*

Donna Karan International Inc ..... G 212 768-5800
New York *(G-9250)*

Elana Laderos Ltd ..... F 212 764-0840
New York *(G-9332)*

Elizabeth Fillmore LLC ..... G 212 647-0863
New York *(G-9347)*

▲ Faviana International Inc ..... E 212 594-4422
New York *(G-9479)*

G-III Apparel Group Ltd ..... E 212 403-0500
New York *(G-9561)*

Geoffrey Beene Inc ..... E 212 371-5570
New York *(G-9597)*

▲ Halmode Apparel Inc ..... A 212 819-9114
New York *(G-9712)*

Haute By Blair Stanley LLC ..... G 212 557-7868
New York *(G-9736)*

▲ I S C A Corp ..... F 212 719-5123
New York *(G-9847)*

J R Nites ..... G 212 354-9670
New York *(G-9958)*

JBS Limited ..... E 212 764-4600
New York *(G-9984)*

◆ JBS Limited ..... E 212 221-8403
New York *(G-9985)*

▲ Jiranimo Industries Ltd ..... F 212 921-5106
New York *(G-10007)*

▲ Jon Teri Sports Inc ..... E 212 398-0657
New York *(G-10021)*

▲ Jovani Fashion Ltd ..... E 212 279-0222
New York *(G-10031)*

▲ Judys Group Inc ..... E 212 921-0515
New York *(G-10037)*

▲ Jump Design Group Inc ..... C 212 869-3300
New York *(G-10040)*

◆ Kasper Group LLC ..... C 212 354-4311
New York *(G-10075)*

▲ Kelly Grace Corp ..... C 212 704-9603
New York *(G-10088)*

▼ Krasner Group Inc ..... G 212 268-4100
New York *(G-10136)*

▲ L F Fashion Orient Intl Co Ltd ..... G 917 667-3398
New York *(G-10151)*

Lavish Layette Inc ..... G 347 962-9955
Woodmere *(G-16192)*

Leanne Marshall Designs Inc ..... F 646 918-6349
New York *(G-10184)*

▲ Lily & Taylor Inc ..... F 212 564-5459
New York *(G-10220)*

Lmr Group Inc ..... G 212 730-9221
New York *(G-10238)*

▲ Lou Sally Fashions Corp ..... E 212 354-9670
New York *(G-10269)*

Lou Sally Fashions Corp ..... E 212 354-1283
New York *(G-10270)*

▲ McCall Pattern Company ..... C 212 465-6800
New York *(G-10396)*

▲ Millennium Productions Inc ..... F 212 944-6203
New York *(G-10467)*

Mmj Apparel LLC ..... E 212 354-8550
New York *(G-10486)*

▲ Nasserati Inc ..... G 212 947-8100
New York *(G-10535)*

▲ Necessary Objects Ltd ..... E 212 334-9888
Long Island City *(G-7305)*

Nine West Holdings Inc ..... G 212 391-5000
New York *(G-10630)*

▲ Paris Wedding Center Corp ..... F 347 368-4085
Flushing *(G-4885)*

Paris Wedding Center Corp ..... E 212 267-8088
New York *(G-10761)*

Parsley Apparel Corp ..... E 631 981-7181
Ronkonkoma *(G-13992)*

Pat & Rose Dress Inc ..... D 212 279-1357
New York *(G-10768)*

Paula Varsalona Ltd ..... F 212 570-9100
New York *(G-10772)*

Plugg LLC ..... F 212 840-6655
New York *(G-10857)*

▲ Product Development Intl LLC ..... G 212 279-6170
New York *(G-10903)*

▲ Pronovias USA Inc ..... E 212 897-6393
New York *(G-10911)*

Quality Patterns Inc ..... D 212 704-0355
New York *(G-10950)*

▲ R & M Richards Inc ..... C 212 921-8820
New York *(G-10965)*

▲ Raven New York LLC ....G...... 212 584-9690
New York (G-10983)

Rogan LLC ....G...... 212 680-1407
New York (G-11072)

▲ Rogan LLC ....E...... 646 496-9339
New York (G-11073)

◆ Ronni Nicole Group LLC ....E...... 212 764-1000
New York (G-11080)

Sg Nyc LLC ....E...... 310 210-1837
New York (G-11197)

▲ Shane Tex Inc ....F...... 516 486-7522
Woodmere (G-16193)

Spencer AB Inc ....G...... 646 831-3728
New York (G-11318)

▲ SSG Fashions Ltd ....G...... 212 221-0933
New York (G-11343)

Stitch & Couture Inc ....E...... 212 947-9204
New York (G-11364)

Tabrisse Collections Inc ....F...... 212 921-1014
New York (G-11422)

Tahari ASL LLC ....B...... 212 763-2800
New York (G-11424)

▲ Texport Fabrics Corp ....F...... 212 226-6066
New York (G-11456)

▲ Thread LLC ....G...... 212 414-8844
New York (G-11477)

Tom & Linda Platt Inc ....F...... 212 221-7208
New York (G-11507)

Turn On Products Inc ....F...... 212 764-4545
New York (G-11560)

Ursula of Switzerland Inc ....E...... 518 237-2580
Waterford (G-15549)

V Technical Textiles Inc ....G...... 315 597-1674
Palmyra (G-12494)

Vanity Room Inc ....F...... 212 921-7154
New York (G-11642)

▲ Vera Wang Group LLC ....C...... 212 575-6400
New York (G-11657)

▲ Worth Collection Ltd ....E...... 212 268-0312
New York (G-11785)

Yeohlee Inc ....F...... 212 631-8099
New York (G-11808)

2337 Women's & Misses' Suits, Coats & Skirts

2h International Corp ....G...... 347 623-9380
Forest Hills (G-4914)

79 Metro Ltd ....G...... 212 944-4030
New York (G-8408)

Adrienne Landau Designs Inc ....F...... 212 695-8362
New York (G-8464)

▲ Age Manufacturers Inc ....D...... 718 927-0048
Brooklyn (G-1471)

Agi Brooks Production Co Inc ....F...... 212 268-1533
New York (G-8493)

▲ Alfred Dunner Inc ....B...... 212 478-4300
New York (G-8515)

▲ Alicia Adams Alpaca Inc ....G...... 845 868-3366
Millbrook (G-7941)

▲ Anna Sui Corp ....E...... 212 941-8406
New York (G-8593)

Bindle and Keep ....G...... 917 740-5002
Brooklyn (G-1588)

▲ Blatt Searle & Company Ltd ....E...... 212 730-7717
Long Island City (G-7179)

Bruno & Canio Ltd ....E...... 845 624-3060
Nanuet (G-8197)

Canada Goose Us Inc ....G...... 888 276-6297
Williamsville (G-16126)

▼ Carolina Herrera Ltd ....E...... 212 944-5757
New York (G-8923)

Centric Brands Inc ....G...... 212 925-5727
New York (G-8954)

Centric Brands Inc ....D...... 646 582-6000
New York (G-8955)

▲ Countess Corporation ....G...... 212 869-7070
New York (G-9110)

◆ Donna Karan International Inc ....F...... 212 789-1500
New York (G-9249)

Donna Karan International Inc ....G...... 212 768-5800
New York (G-9250)

Elie Tahari Ltd ....D...... 631 329-8883
East Hampton (G-4122)

Elie Tahari Ltd ....D...... 973 671-6300
New York (G-9341)

Elie Tahari Ltd ....D...... 212 763-2000
New York (G-9340)

Elie Tahari Ltd ....G...... 212 763-2000
New York (G-9339)

▲ Excelled Sheepskin & Lea Coat ....F...... 212 594-5843
New York (G-9443)

▲ G-III Apparel Group Ltd ....B...... 212 403-0500
New York (G-9560)

G-III Leather Fashions Inc ....B...... 212 403-0500
New York (G-9563)

G18 Corporation ....G...... 212 869-0010
New York (G-9564)

Geoffrey Beene Inc ....E...... 212 371-5570
New York (G-9597)

▲ Global Gold Inc ....F...... 212 239-4657
New York (G-9629)

◆ Hampshire Sub II Inc ....D...... 631 321-0923
New York (G-9716)

▲ Harrison Sportswear Inc ....F...... 212 391-1051
New York (G-9730)

▼ Herman Kay Company Ltd ....C...... 212 239-2025
New York (G-9768)

◆ Hugo Boss Usa Inc ....D...... 212 940-0600
New York (G-9835)

▲ Itochu Prominent USA LLC ....C...... 212 827-5715
New York (G-9948)

◆ J Percy For Mrvin Rchards Ltd ....E...... 212 944-5300
New York (G-9956)

▲ Jeanjer LLC ....A...... 212 944-1330
New York (G-9991)

▲ Jon Teri Sports Inc ....E...... 212 398-0657
New York (G-10021)

▲ Judys Group Inc ....E...... 212 921-0515
New York (G-10037)

Kayo of California ....G...... 212 354-6336
New York (G-10083)

▲ Kozinn+sons Merchant Tailors ....E...... 212 643-1916
New York (G-10132)

Lady Brass Co Inc ....G...... 516 887-8040
Hewlett (G-5870)

▲ Levy Group Inc ....C...... 212 398-0707
New York (G-10206)

▲ Lf Outerwear LLC ....D...... 212 239-2025
New York (G-10207)

▲ Lily & Taylor Inc ....F...... 212 564-5459
New York (G-10220)

▲ Marlou Garments Inc ....F...... 516 739-7100
New Hyde Park (G-8281)

Miny Group Inc ....D...... 212 925-6722
New York (G-10479)

Mp Studio Inc ....G...... 212 302-5666
New York (G-10510)

▲ Nyc Idol Apparel Inc ....G...... 212 997-9797
New York (G-10661)

Opposuits USA Inc ....E...... 917 438-8878
New York (G-10700)

Pat & Rose Dress Inc ....D...... 212 279-1357
New York (G-10768)

▲ Permit Fashion Group Inc ....G...... 212 912-0988
Melville (G-7815)

◆ Premier Brnds Group Hldngs LLC ....B...... 215 785-4000
New York (G-10876)

Primo Coat Corp ....E...... 718 349-2070
Long Island City (G-7329)

Ps38 LLC ....G...... 212 302-1108
New York (G-10918)

▲ R & M Richards Inc ....C...... 212 921-8820
New York (G-10965)

Rhoda Lee Inc ....D...... 212 840-5700
New York (G-11035)

▲ Shane Tex Inc ....F...... 516 486-7522
Woodmere (G-16193)

▲ Standard Manufacturing Co Inc ....D...... 518 235-2200
Troy (G-15190)

Terrapin Station Ltd ....G...... 716 874-6677
Buffalo (G-3007)

Theory LLC ....D...... 212 762-2300
New York (G-11462)

Theory LLC ....G...... 212 879-0265
New York (G-11463)

▲ Tiger J LLC ....E...... 212 465-9300
New York (G-11486)

Turn On Products Inc ....F...... 212 764-4545
New York (G-11560)

Uniforms By Park Coats Inc ....E...... 718 499-1182
Brooklyn (G-2536)

▲ Uniqlo USA LLC ....F...... 877 486-4756
New York (G-11593)

Ursula of Switzerland Inc ....E...... 518 237-2580
Waterford (G-15549)

View Collections Inc ....F...... 212 944-4030
New York (G-11680)

Yeohlee Inc ....F...... 212 631-8099
New York (G-11808)

2339 Women's & Misses' Outerwear, NEC

1 Atelier LLC ....G...... 917 916-2968
New York (G-8388)

18 Rocks LLC ....E...... 631 465-9990
Melville (G-7752)

▲ 31 Phillip Lim LLC ....E...... 212 354-6540
New York (G-8401)

525 America LLC ....G...... 212 921-5688
New York (G-8405)

◆ 5th & Ocean Clothing Inc ....C...... 716 604-9000
Buffalo (G-2613)

▲ 6th Avenue Showcase Inc ....G...... 212 382-0400
New York (G-8407)

A & B Finishing Inc ....E...... 718 522-4702
Brooklyn (G-1427)

▲ Accessory Street LLC ....F...... 212 686-8990
New York (G-8442)

▲ Accessries Direct Intl USA Inc ....E...... 646 448-8200
New York (G-8443)

Adpro Sports LLC ....D...... 716 854-5116
Buffalo (G-2622)

Aerobic Wear Inc ....G...... 631 673-1830
Huntington Station (G-6235)

▲ Age Manufacturers Inc ....D...... 718 927-0048
Brooklyn (G-1471)

▲ Alfred Dunner Inc ....B...... 212 478-4300
New York (G-8515)

Alleson of Rochester Inc ....E...... 315 548-3635
Geneva (G-5145)

Ally Nyc Corp ....G...... 212 447-7277
New York (G-8523)

▲ Alpha 6 Distributions LLC ....G...... 516 801-8290
Locust Valley (G-7121)

▲ Amber Bever Inc ....G...... 212 391-4911
Brooklyn (G-1495)

American Apparel Trading Corp ....G...... 212 764-5990
New York (G-8544)

▲ American Challenge Enterprises ....G...... 631 595-7171
Bay Shore (G-648)

▲ Angel-Made In Heaven Inc ....F...... 212 869-5678
New York (G-8583)

Angel-Made In Heaven Inc ....G...... 718 832-4778
Brooklyn (G-1510)

▲ Anna Sui Corp ....E...... 212 941-8406
New York (G-8593)

▲ Argee America Inc ....G...... 212 768-9840
New York (G-8621)

Authentic Brands Group LLC ....C...... 212 760-2410
New York (G-8680)

▲ Avalin LLC ....F...... 212 842-2286
New York (G-8686)

AZ Yashir Bapaz Inc ....G...... 212 947-7357
New York (G-8700)

▲ B Tween LLC ....F...... 212 819-9040
New York (G-8706)

Bag Bazaar Ltd ....E...... 212 689-3508
New York (G-8717)

▲ Bagznyc Corp ....F...... 212 643-8202
New York (G-8718)

Bam Sales LLC ....G...... 212 781-3000
New York (G-8724)

Bandit International Ltd ....F...... 718 402-2100
Bronx (G-1210)

Bands N Bows ....G...... 718 984-4316
Staten Island (G-14623)

▲ Bank-Miller Co Inc ....E...... 914 227-9357
Pelham (G-12565)

▲ Bernard Chaus Inc ....D...... 212 354-1280
New York (G-8760)

Bernard Chaus Inc ....C...... 646 562-4700
New York (G-8761)

Bilco Industries Inc ....F...... 917 783-5008
New York (G-8790)

▲ Blue Duck Trading Ltd ....G...... 212 268-3122
New York (G-8818)

Botkier Ny LLC ....G...... 212 343-2782
New York (G-8838)

Brigantine Inc ....G...... 212 354-8550
New York (G-8851)

C & C Athletic Inc ....G...... 845 713-4670
Walden (G-15457)

▲ Cai Design Inc ....F...... 212 401-9973
New York (G-8887)

Canada Goose Inc ....G...... 888 276-6297
New York (G-8900)

Canada Goose Us Inc ....G...... 888 276-6297
Williamsville (G-16126)

▲ Candlesticks Inc ....F...... 212 947-8900
New York (G-8903)

S
I
C

▲ Caribbean Fashion Group Inc..........G...... 212 706-8851
New York (G-8916)

▲ Carolina Amato Inc ....G...... 212 768-9095
New York (G-8922)

▼ Carolina Herrera Ltd ....E...... 212 944-5757
New York (G-8923)

Casuals Etc Inc ....D...... 212 838-1319
New York (G-8932)

◆ Cathy Daniels Ltd ....E...... 212 354-8000
Old Westbury (G-12222)

◆ Central Apparel Group Ltd ....F...... 212 868-6505
New York (G-8950)

Central Mills Inc ....C...... 212 764-9011
New York (G-8952)

Centric Brands Inc ....D...... 646 582-6000
New York (G-8955)

Centric Denim Usa LLC ....G...... 646 839-7000
New York (G-8956)

Centric West LLC ....C...... 646 839-7000
New York (G-8958)

▲ China Ting Fshion Group USA LL ....G...... 212 716-1600
New York (G-8993)

▲ Christina Sales Inc ....F...... 212 391-0710
New York (G-9001)

▲ City Sites Sportswear Inc ....E...... 718 375-2990
Brooklyn (G-1668)

▲ Collection Xiix Ltd ....F...... 212 686-8990
New York (G-9053)

▲ Comint Apparel Group LLC ....E...... 212 947-7474
New York (G-9065)

▲ Comme-Ci Comme-CA AP Group .....E...... 631 300-1035
Hauppauge (G-5623)

Continental Knitting Mills ....G...... 631 242-5330
Deer Park (G-3853)

▲ Cynthia Rowley Inc ....F...... 212 242-3803
New York (G-9142)

▲ Daily Wear Sportswear Corp ....G...... 718 972-0533
Brooklyn (G-1719)

Dalma Dress Mfg Co Inc ....E...... 212 391-8296
Greenvale (G-5461)

Dana Michele LLC ....G...... 917 757-7777
New York (G-9161)

▲ Dani II Inc ....F...... 212 869-5999
New York (G-9165)

Danice Stores Inc ....F...... 212 665-0389
New York (G-9166)

Denim King Depot LLC ....E...... 917 477-0550
New York (G-9201)

▲ DFA New York LLC ....E...... 212 523-0021
New York (G-9215)

Dianos Kathryn Designs ....G...... 212 267-1584
New York (G-9223)

◆ Donna Karan International Inc ....F...... 212 789-1500
New York (G-9249)

Donna Karan International Inc ....E...... 212 768-5800
New York (G-9250)

Doral Apparel Group Inc ....G...... 917 208-5652
New York (G-9254)

Double Take Fashions Inc ....F...... 718 832-9000
New York (G-9256)

▼ Dr Jayscom ....G...... 888 437-5297
New York (G-9264)

▲ Drew Philips Corp ....F...... 212 354-0095
New York (G-9270)

▲ Du Monde Trading Inc ....E...... 212 944-1306
New York (G-9275)

El-La Design Inc ....G...... 212 382-1080
New York (G-9331)

Elie Tahari Ltd ....E...... 212 763-2000
New York (G-9339)

◆ Elizabeth Gillett Ltd ....G...... 212 629-7993
New York (G-9348)

Elizabeth Wilson ....G...... 516 486-2157
Uniondale (G-15226)

Elliot Mann Nyc Inc ....G...... 212 260-0658
New York (G-9349)

▲ Emerald Holdings Inc ....G...... 718 797-4404
Brooklyn (G-1798)

Emerson & Oliver LLC ....G...... 585 775-9929
Rochester (G-13385)

▲ F & J Designs Inc ....G...... 212 302-8755
New York (G-9454)

▲ Fad Inc ....E...... 631 385-2460
Huntington (G-6205)

Falls Manufacturing Inc ....G...... 518 672-7189
Philmont (G-12613)

Fashion Ave Sweater Knits LLC ....C...... 212 302-8282
New York (G-9475)

▲ Feldman Manufacturing Corp ....D...... 718 433-1700
Long Island City (G-7222)

First Love Fashions LLC ....F...... 212 256-1089
New York (G-9501)

▲ French Atmosphere Inc ....F...... 516 371-9100
New York (G-9536)

Fusion Pro Performance Ltd ....F...... 917 833-0761
New York (G-9554)

▲ G-III Apparel Group Ltd ....B...... 212 403-0500
New York (G-9560)

G-III Leather Fashions Inc ....E...... 212 403-0500
New York (G-9563)

▲ GAME Sportswear Ltd ....C...... 914 962-1701
Yorktown Heights (G-16365)

◆ Garan Incorporated ....C...... 212 563-1292
New York (G-9573)

▼ Garan Manufacturing Corp ....C...... 212 563-2000
New York (G-9574)

Geoffrey Beene Inc ....E...... 212 371-5570
New York (G-9597)

▲ Gfb Fashions Ltd ....G...... 212 239-9230
New York (G-9605)

Giulietta LLC ....G...... 212 334-1859
Brooklyn (G-1887)

◆ Gloria Apparel Inc ....F...... 212 947-0869
New York (G-9633)

▲ Gogo Jeans Inc ....E...... 212 944-2391
New York (G-9637)

▲ Golden Leaves Knitwear Inc ....E...... 718 875-8235
Brooklyn (G-1898)

▲ Great Wall Corp ....C...... 212 704-4372
Long Island City (G-7235)

▲ H2gear Fashions LLC ....G...... 347 787-7508
Brooklyn (G-1917)

▲ Halmode Apparel Inc ....A...... 212 819-9114
New York (G-9712)

◆ Hampshire Sub II Inc ....D...... 631 321-0923
New York (G-9716)

▲ HB Athletic Inc ....F...... 914 560-8422
New Rochelle (G-8340)

◆ HC Contracting Inc ....D...... 212 643-9292
New York (G-9740)

Hearts of Palm LLC ....E...... 212 944-6660
New York (G-9758)

Hearts of Palm LLC ....D...... 212 944-6660
New York (G-9759)

▲ Hedaya Home Fashions Inc ....C...... 212 889-1111
New York (G-9761)

▼ Herman Kay Company Ltd ....C...... 212 239-2025
New York (G-9768)

Hoehn Inc ....F...... 518 463-8900
Albany (G-87)

◆ Hot Line Industries Inc ....F...... 516 764-0400
Bellmore (G-783)

House Pearl Fashions (us) Ltd ....F...... 212 840-3183
New York (G-9826)

I Shalom & Co Inc ....C...... 212 532-7911
New York (G-9848)

Ifg Corp ....C...... 212 629-9600
New York (G-9860)

◆ Ikeddi Enterprises Inc ....F...... 212 302-7644
New York (G-9863)

Ikeddi Enterprises Inc ....G...... 212 302-7644
New York (G-9864)

▲ Int Trading USA LLC ....C...... 212 760-2338
New York (G-9906)

J & E Talit Inc ....G...... 718 850-1333
Richmond Hill (G-13116)

◆ J Percy For Mrvin Rchards Ltd ....E...... 212 944-5300
New York (G-9956)

Jaxis Inc ....G...... 212 302-7611
Brooklyn (G-1989)

Jaya Apparel Group LLC ....E...... 212 764-4980
New York (G-9981)

▲ Jeanjer LLC ....A...... 212 944-1330
New York (G-9991)

Jesse Joeckel ....G...... 631 668-2772
Montauk (G-8054)

JI Parc LLC ....G...... 718 271-0703
Rego Park (G-13078)

◆ Joe Benbasset Inc ....E...... 212 594-8440
New York (G-10014)

Jomat New York Inc ....F...... 718 369-7641
Brooklyn (G-1998)

▲ Jonathan Michael Coat Corp ....D...... 212 239-9230
New York (G-10023)

Jordache Enterprises Inc ....D...... 212 944-1330
New York (G-10024)

◆ Jordache Enterprises Inc ....E...... 212 643-8400
New York (G-10025)

▲ Judys Group Inc..............................E...... 212 921-0515
New York (G-10037)

Just Bottoms & Tops Inc ....F...... 212 564-3202
New York (G-10044)

▼ K T P Design Co Inc ....F...... 212 481-6613
New York (G-10052)

Kaltex America Inc ....F...... 212 971-0575
New York (G-10062)

Kasper Group LLC ....G...... 212 354-4311
New York (G-10074)

Kayo of California ....G...... 212 354-6336
New York (G-10083)

Kicks Closet Sportswear Inc ....G...... 347 577-0857
Bronx (G-1292)

▼ Krasner Group Inc ....G...... 212 268-4100
New York (G-10136)

Ksk International Inc ....E...... 212 354-7770
New York (G-10143)

▲ L D Weiss Inc ....G...... 212 697-3023
New York (G-10150)

▲ Lahoya Enterprise Inc ....E...... 718 886-8799
College Point (G-3550)

▲ Lai Apparel Design Inc ....E...... 212 382-1075
New York (G-10165)

◆ Land n Sea Inc ....D...... 212 444-6000
New York (G-10168)

Lavish Layette Inc ....G...... 347 962-9955
Woodmere (G-16192)

Leesa Designs Ltd ....G...... 631 261-3991
Centerport (G-3256)

◆ Leggiadro International Inc ....E...... 212 997-8766
Yonkers (G-16326)

Leng Universal Inc ....F...... 212 398-6800
New York (G-10196)

▲ Leslie Stuart Co Inc ....G...... 212 629-4551
New York (G-10204)

▲ Liberty Apparel Company Inc ....E...... 718 625-4000
New York (G-10209)

Life Style Design Group ....E...... 212 391-8666
New York (G-10213)

▲ Light Inc ....G...... 212 629-3255
New York (G-10217)

▲ Lily & Taylor Inc ....F...... 212 564-5459
New York (G-10220)

▲ Liquid Knits Inc ....F...... 718 706-6600
Long Island City (G-7275)

▲ Lotus Apparel Designs Inc ....G...... 646 236-9363
Westbury (G-15906)

Luxe Imagine Consulting LLC ....G...... 212 273-9770
New York (G-10286)

▲ Mag Brands LLC ....D...... 212 629-9600
New York (G-10319)

Maiyet Inc ....G...... 212 343-9999
New York (G-10333)

Malia Mills Inc ....F...... 212 354-4200
Brooklyn (G-2105)

▲ Manchu New York Inc ....G...... 212 921-5050
New York (G-10340)

▲ Manchu Times Fashion Inc ....G...... 212 921-5050
New York (G-10341)

▲ Mango Usa Inc ....E...... 718 998-6050
Brooklyn (G-2106)

Marcasiano Inc ....G...... 212 614-9412
New York (G-10354)

▲ Marconi Intl USA Co Ltd ....E...... 212 391-2626
New York (G-10357)

Marina Holding Corp ....F...... 718 646-9283
Brooklyn (G-2115)

Mayberry Shoe Company Inc...............G...... 315 692-4086
Manlius (G-7549)

▲ Medi-Tech International Corp...........G...... 800 333-0109
Brooklyn (G-2132)

▲ Meryl Diamond Ltd ....D...... 212 730-0333
New York (G-10439)

Michael Feldman Inc ....D...... 718 433-1700
Long Island City (G-7296)

◆ Mikael Aghal LLC ....F...... 212 596-4010
New York (G-10463)

▲ Millennium Productions Inc ....F...... 212 944-6203
New York (G-10467)

Miltons of New York Inc......................G...... 212 997-3359
New York (G-10471)

MISS Sportswear Inc ....F...... 212 391-2535
Brooklyn (G-2159)

▲ MISS Sportswear Inc ....G...... 212 391-2535
New York (G-10482)

MISS Sportswear Inc ....F...... 718 369-6012
Brooklyn (G-2160)

▲ Moes Wear Apparel Inc ....F...... 718 940-1597
Brooklyn (G-2167)

Morelle Products Ltd ....F...... 212 391-8070
New York (G-10502)

▲ Mv Corp Inc ....C 631 273-8020
Bay Shore *(G-695)*

▲ Mystic Inc ....C 212 239-2025
New York *(G-10528)*

Naito International Corp ....F 718 309-2425
Rockville Centre *(G-13832)*

▲ Necessary Objects Ltd ....E 212 334-9888
Long Island City *(G-7305)*

▲ New Concepts of New York LLC ....E 212 695-4999
Brooklyn *(G-2201)*

▲ New York Accessory Group Inc ....E 212 532-7911
New York *(G-10592)*

Nlhe LLC ....E 212 594-0012
Brooklyn *(G-2217)*

▲ Noah Enterprises Ltd ....E 212 736-2888
New York *(G-10634)*

▲ Ocean Waves Swim LLC ....G 212 967-4481
New York *(G-10676)*

▲ ODY Accessories Inc ....E 212 239-0580
New York *(G-10680)*

On The Double Inc ....G 518 431-3571
Germantown *(G-5169)*

▲ One Jeanswear Group LLC ....B 212 575-2571
New York *(G-10690)*

◆ One Step Up Ltd ....D 212 398-1110
New York *(G-10691)*

Only Hearts Ltd ....E 212 268-0886
New York *(G-10694)*

P & I Sportswear Inc ....G 718 934-4587
New York *(G-10731)*

Pacific Alliance Usa Inc ....G 336 500-8184
New York *(G-10738)*

▲ Pacific Alliance Usa Inc ....D 646 839-7000
New York *(G-10739)*

Paddy Lee Fashions Inc ....F 718 786-6020
Long Island City *(G-7318)*

Park Avenue Sportswear Ltd ....F 718 369-0520
Brooklyn *(G-2248)*

◆ Passport Brands Inc ....E 646 459-2625
New York *(G-10767)*

Pat & Rose Dress Inc ....D 212 279-1357
New York *(G-10768)*

▲ Penfli Industries Inc ....F 212 947-6080
Great Neck *(G-5413)*

▲ Permit Fashion Group Inc ....G 212 912-0988
Melville *(G-7815)*

Petrunia LLC ....G 607 277-1930
Ithaca *(G-6405)*

▲ Planet Gold Clothing Co Inc ......C 646 432-5100
New York *(G-10851)*

Plugg LLC ....F 212 840-6655
New York *(G-10857)*

▲ Popnyc 1 LLC ....G 646 684-4600
New York *(G-10865)*

Premier Brnds Group Hldngs LLC ....G 212 642-3860
New York *(G-10877)*

Premier Brnds Group Hldngs LLC ....E 212 642-3860
New York *(G-10879)*

Premier Brnds Group Hldngs LLC ....G 212 575-2571
New York *(G-10878)*

Pride & Joys Inc ....F 212 594-9820
New York *(G-10888)*

Primo Coat Corp ....E 718 349-2070
Long Island City *(G-7329)*

▲ Pti-Pacific Inc ....G 212 414-8495
New York *(G-10920)*

Pvh Corp ....D 212 502-6300
New York *(G-10936)*

Pvh Corp ....G 212 381-3800
New York *(G-10935)*

RAK Finishing Corp ....E 718 416-4242
Howard Beach *(G-6141)*

▲ Ramsbury Property Us Inc ....F 212 223-6250
New York *(G-10976)*

Rene Portier Inc ....G 718 853-7896
Brooklyn *(G-2341)*

▲ Republic Clothing Corporation ....E 212 719-3000
New York *(G-11016)*

Republic Clothing Group Inc ....C 212 719-3000
New York *(G-11017)*

▲ Rhoda Lee Inc ....D 212 840-5700
New York *(G-11035)*

Richard Manufacturing Co Inc .....G 718 254-0958
Brooklyn *(G-2344)*

▲ Ritchie Corp ....F 212 768-0083
New York *(G-11049)*

Robespierre Inc ....G 212 764-8810
New York *(G-11063)*

Rogers Group Inc ....E 212 643-9292
New York *(G-11075)*

▲ Rvc Enterprises LLC ....E 212 391-4600
New York *(G-11101)*

▲ S & S Manufacturing Co Inc ....D 212 444-6000
New York *(G-11106)*

S & V Knits Inc ....E 631 752-1595
Farmingdale *(G-4730)*

▲ S Broome and Co Inc ....D 718 663-6800
Long Island City *(G-7350)*

▲ S2 Sportswear Inc ....F 347 335-0713
Brooklyn *(G-2378)*

Salisbury Sportswear Inc ....E 516 221-9519
Bellmore *(G-789)*

▲ Salsa Professional Apparel LLC ....G 212 575-6565
New York *(G-11122)*

▲ Sarina Accessories LLC ....F 212 239-8106
New York *(G-11139)*

▲ Sea Waves Inc ....G 516 766-4201
Oceanside *(G-12189)*

▲ Sensational Collection Inc ....G 212 840-7388
New York *(G-11191)*

Shanghai Harmony AP Intl LLC .....E 646 569-5680
New Rochelle *(G-8354)*

Shirl-Lynn of New York ....F 315 363-5898
Oneida *(G-12254)*

Siskind Group Inc ....F 212 840-0880
New York *(G-11251)*

▲ Smooth Industries Incorporated ....E 212 869-1080
New York *(G-11276)*

Snowman ....G 212 239-8818
New York *(G-11280)*

Spectrum Apparel Inc ....D 212 239-2025
New York *(G-11315)*

▲ SRP Apparel Group Inc ....G 212 764-4810
New York *(G-11341)*

Ssa Trading Ltd ....F 646 465-9500
New York *(G-11342)*

▲ SSG Fashions Ltd ....G 212 221-0933
New York *(G-11343)*

St John ....G 718 720-8367
Staten Island *(G-14712)*

St John ....G 718 771-4541
Brooklyn *(G-2448)*

▲ Standard Manufacturing Co Inc ....D 518 235-2200
Troy *(G-15190)*

Stony Apparel Corp ....G 212 391-0022
New York *(G-11367)*

▲ Street Beat Sportswear Inc ....F 718 302-1500
Brooklyn *(G-2463)*

▲ Sunynams Fashions Ltd ....G 212 268-5200
Roslyn Heights *(G-14058)*

▲ Survival Inc ....G 631 385-5060
Centerport *(G-3258)*

Swatfame Inc ....G 212 944-8022
New York *(G-11406)*

◆ Swimwear Anywhere Inc ....D 631 420-1400
Farmingdale *(G-4746)*

Swimwear Anywhere Inc ....E 845 858-4141
Port Jervis *(G-12858)*

Tahari ASL LLC ....B 212 763-2800
New York *(G-11424)*

▲ Tailored Sportsman LLC ....F 646 366-8733
New York *(G-11425)*

Tamka Sport LLC ....G 718 224-7820
Douglaston *(G-4030)*

Tbhi International LLC ....F 212 799-2007
New York *(G-11438)*

▲ THE Design Group Inc ....F 212 681-1548
New York *(G-11459)*

▲ Tiger J LLC ....E 212 465-9300
New York *(G-11486)*

▲ Tillsonburg Company USA Inc ......E 267 994-8096
New York *(G-11488)*

Toni Industries Inc ....F 212 921-0700
Great Neck *(G-5428)*

▲ TR Designs Inc ....E 212 398-9300
New York *(G-11527)*

▲ Turn On Products Inc ....D 212 764-2121
New York *(G-11559)*

Turn On Products Inc ....F 212 764-4545
New York *(G-11560)*

▲ Untuckit LLC ....D 347 524-9111
New York *(G-11612)*

Untuckit LLC ....C 646 724-1857
New York *(G-11613)*

◆ Urban Apparel Group Inc ....E 212 947-7009
New York *(G-11615)*

▲ Uspa Accessories LLC ....C 212 868-2590
New York *(G-11631)*

Valenti Neckwear Co Inc ....G 914 969-0700
Yonkers *(G-16354)*

▲ Venus Manufacturing Co Inc ....D 315 639-3100
Dexter *(G-4007)*

Vf Imagewear Inc ....E 718 352-2363
Bayside *(G-744)*

Vf Outdoor LLC ....E 845 928-4900
Central Valley *(G-3301)*

◆ Warnaco Group Inc ....E 212 287-8000
New York *(G-11720)*

X Vision Inc ....G 917 412-3570
New York *(G-11796)*

Yigal-Azrouel Inc ....E 212 302-1194
New York *(G-11809)*

▲ Z-Ply Corp ....E 212 398-7011
New York *(G-11814)*

▼ Zar Group LLC ....F 212 944-2510
New York *(G-11816)*

◆ Zg Apparel Group LLC ....E 212 944-2510
New York *(G-11822)*

Zia Power Inc ....E 845 661-8388
New York *(G-11823)*

▲ Zoomers Inc ....E 718 369-2656
Brooklyn *(G-2606)*

2341 Women's, Misses' & Children's Underwear & Nightwear

Allure Fashions Inc ....G 516 829-2470
Great Neck *(G-5363)*

▲ Ariela and Associates Intl LLC .....C 212 683-4131
New York *(G-8623)*

Becks Classic Mfg Inc ....D 631 435-3800
Brentwood *(G-1116)*

▲ Candlesticks Inc ....F 212 947-8900
New York *(G-8903)*

Classic Designer Workshop Inc ....G 212 730-8480
New York *(G-9024)*

▲ Comme-Ci Comme-CA AP Group ....E 631 300-1035
Hauppauge *(G-5623)*

▲ Dayleen Intimates Inc ....E 914 969-5900
Yonkers *(G-16300)*

Delta Galil USA Inc ....G 212 710-6440
New York *(G-9199)*

Faye Bernard Loungewear ....G 718 951-7245
Brooklyn *(G-1836)*

▲ Halo Innovations Inc ....E 952 259-1500
Brooklyn *(G-1920)*

▲ Handcraft Manufacturing Corp ....D 212 251-0022
New York *(G-9718)*

◆ Intimateco LLC ....G 212 239-4411
New York *(G-9928)*

▲ Kokin Inc ....E 212 643-8225
New York *(G-10123)*

▲ Komar Layering LLC ....E 212 725-1500
New York *(G-10124)*

▲ Komar Luxury Brands ....G 646 472-0060
New York *(G-10125)*

Lady Ester Lingerie Corp ....E 212 689-1729
New York *(G-10162)*

Loungehouse LLC ....E 646 524-2965
New York *(G-10272)*

Luxerdame Co Inc ....E 718 752-9800
Long Island City *(G-7282)*

Mrt Textile Inc ....G 800 674-1073
New York *(G-10515)*

Natori Company Incorporated ....E 212 532-7796
New York *(G-10551)*

▲ Natori Company Incorporated ......D 212 532-7796
New York *(G-10550)*

Only Hearts Ltd ....E 212 268-0886
New York *(G-10694)*

▲ Pearl River Textiles Inc ....G 212 629-5490
New York *(G-10778)*

▲ Sleepwear Holdings Inc ....C 516 466-4738
New York *(G-11268)*

Vanity Fair Brands LP ....C 212 548-1548
New York *(G-11641)*

◆ Warnaco Group Inc ....E 212 287-8000
New York *(G-11720)*

◆ Warnaco Inc ....B 212 287-8000
New York *(G-11721)*

Warnaco Inc ....F 718 722-3000
Brooklyn *(G-2575)*

▲ Waterbury Garment LLC ....E 212 725-1500
New York *(G-11730)*

▲ Wickers Sportswear Inc ....G 631 543-1640
Commack *(G-3604)*

2342 Brassieres, Girdles & Garments

Burlen Corp ....F 212 684-0052
New York *(G-8869)*

S I C

E P Sewing Pleating Inc E 212 967-2575
New York *(G-9290)*
East Coast Molders Inc C 516 240-6000
Oceanside *(G-12170)*
Higgins Supply Company Inc D 607 836-6474
Mc Graw *(G-7688)*
Luxerdame Co Inc E 718 752-9800
Long Island City *(G-7282)*
Naked Brand Group Inc G 212 851-8050
New York *(G-10531)*
▲ New York Elegance Entps Inc F 212 685-3088
New York *(G-10595)*
▲ Prime Garments Inc F 212 354-7294
Rockville Centre *(G-13833)*
▼ Rago Foundations LLC E 718 728-8436
Astoria *(G-436)*
Sensual Inc E 212 869-1450
New York *(G-11192)*
▲ Valmont Inc F 212 685-1653
New York *(G-11636)*
Wacoal America Inc E 212 743-9600
New York *(G-11715)*
◆ Warnaco Group Inc E 212 287-8000
New York *(G-11720)*
◆ Warnaco Inc B 212 287-8000
New York *(G-11721)*
Warnaco Inc F 718 722-3000
Brooklyn *(G-2575)*

2353 Hats, Caps & Millinery

▲ A-1 Skull Cap Corp E 718 633-9333
Brooklyn *(G-1441)*
Albrizio Inc G 212 719-5290
Brooklyn *(G-1479)*
Athletic Cap Co Inc E 718 398-1300
Staten Island *(G-14621)*
Bollman Hat Company G 212 981-9836
New York *(G-8831)*
Bonk Sam Unforms Civilian Cap E 718 585-0665
Bronx *(G-1215)*
▲ Cookies Inc A 917 261-4981
New York *(G-9095)*
Dorel Hat Co E 845 831-5231
Beacon *(G-751)*
▲ Flexfit Llc D 516 932-8800
Hicksville *(G-5907)*
Gce International Inc F 212 868-0500
New York *(G-9581)*
Gramercy Designs Inc G 201 919-8570
New York *(G-9656)*
Hankin Brothers Cap Co F 716 892-8840
Buffalo *(G-2792)*
◆ Hat Attack Inc E 718 994-1000
Bronx *(G-1273)*
Hepa-Hat Incorporated F 914 271-9747
Croton On Hudson *(G-3809)*
Kays Caps Inc G 518 273-6079
Troy *(G-15159)*
▲ Kim Eugenia Inc G 212 674-1345
New York *(G-10100)*
▲ Kingform Cap Company Inc D 516 822-2501
Hicksville *(G-5918)*
▲ Kokin Inc E 212 643-8225
New York *(G-10123)*
▲ Kraft Hat Manufacturers Inc D 845 735-6200
Pearl River *(G-12536)*
▲ Lenore Marshall Inc G 212 947-5945
New York *(G-10197)*
▲ Lloyds Fashions Inc D 631 435-3353
Brentwood *(G-1125)*
Matthews Hats G 718 859-4683
Brooklyn *(G-2126)*
Mega Power Sports Corporation G 212 627-3380
New York *(G-10423)*
New ERA Cap Co Inc B 716 604-9000
Buffalo *(G-2882)*
◆ New ERA Cap Co Inc B 716 604-9000
Buffalo *(G-2883)*
New ERA Cap Co Inc F 716 549-0445
Derby *(G-4006)*
Paletot Ltd F 212 268-3774
New York *(G-10741)*
▲ Weinfeld Skull Cap Mfg Co Inc G 718 854-3864
Brooklyn *(G-2579)*
Whittall & Shon G 212 594-2626
New York *(G-11752)*

2361 Children's & Infants' Dresses & Blouses

◆ Andy & Evan Industries Inc G 212 967-7908
New York *(G-8581)*
◆ Bowe Industries Inc D 718 441-6464
Glendale *(G-5219)*
◆ Brooke Maya Inc E 212 268-2626
New York *(G-8861)*
▲ Cheri Mon Baby LLC G 212 354-5511
New York *(G-8981)*
▲ Consolidated Childrens AP Inc G 212 239-8615
New York *(G-9085)*
Cream Bebe F 917 578-2088
Brooklyn *(G-1695)*
E-Play Brands LLC G 212 563-2646
New York *(G-9294)*
◆ Garan Incorporated C 212 563-1292
New York *(G-9573)*
▼ Garan Manufacturing Corp G 212 563-2000
New York *(G-9574)*
Gce International Inc F 212 868-0500
New York *(G-9581)*
◆ General Sportwear Company Inc C 212 764-5820
New York *(G-9591)*
◆ Gerson & Gerson Inc C 212 244-6775
New York *(G-9604)*
▲ Grand Knitting Mills Inc E 631 226-5000
Amityville *(G-265)*
◆ Great Universal Corp E 917 302-0065
New York *(G-9670)*
▲ Gw Acquisition LLC E 212 736-4848
New York *(G-9700)*
◆ Haddad Bros Inc F 212 563-2117
New York *(G-9706)*
Hard Ten Clothing Inc G 212 302-1321
New York *(G-9725)*
◆ JM Originals Inc C 845 647-3003
Ellenville *(G-4307)*
Jordache Enterprises Inc D 212 944-1330
New York *(G-10024)*
◆ Jordache Enterprises Inc C 212 643-8400
New York *(G-10025)*
◆ Land n Sea Inc D 212 444-6000
New York *(G-10168)*
▲ Manchu New York Inc G 212 921-5050
New York *(G-10340)*
Michael Stuart Inc E 718 821-0704
Brooklyn *(G-2151)*
▲ S & C Bridal LLC F 212 789-7000
New York *(G-11104)*
S & C Bridals LLC G 213 624-4477
New York *(G-11105)*
▲ Silly Phillie Creations Inc E 718 492-6300
Brooklyn *(G-2413)*
◆ Skip Hop Inc E 646 902-9874
New York *(G-11259)*
Skip Hop Holdings Inc G 212 868-9850
New York *(G-11260)*
Sports Products America LLC E 212 594-5511
New York *(G-11328)*
◆ Star Childrens Dress Co Inc D 212 279-1524
New York *(G-11348)*
Thats My Girl Inc F 212 695-0020
Brooklyn *(G-2500)*
▲ Zinnias Inc F 718 746-8551
Bellerose *(G-777)*

2369 Girls' & Infants' Outerwear, NEC

6 Shore Road LLC G 212 274-9666
New York *(G-8406)*
Aerobic Wear Inc G 631 673-1830
Huntington Station *(G-6235)*
◆ Babyfair Inc E 212 736-7989
New York *(G-8711)*
▲ Best Brands Consumer Pdts Inc G 212 684-7456
New York *(G-8766)*
▲ Candlesticks Inc F 212 947-8900
New York *(G-8903)*
Detour Apparel Inc E 212 221-3265
New York *(G-9211)*
▲ Devil Dog Manufacturing Co Inc G 845 647-4411
Ellenville *(G-4306)*
◆ Domani Fashions Corp G 718 797-0505
Brooklyn *(G-1755)*
E-Play Brands LLC G 212 563-2646
New York *(G-9294)*
▲ Fine Sheer Industries Inc F 212 594-4224
New York *(G-9495)*
First Brands LLC E 646 432-4366
Merrick *(G-7855)*
▲ Franco Apparel Group Inc D 212 967-7272
New York *(G-9530)*
◆ Garan Incorporated C 212 563-1292
New York *(G-9573)*
▼ Garan Manufacturing Corp G 212 563-2000
New York *(G-9574)*
◆ General Sportwear Company Inc C 212 764-5820
New York *(G-9591)*
◆ Gerson & Gerson Inc C 212 244-6775
New York *(G-9604)*
▲ Gw Acquisition LLC E 212 736-4848
New York *(G-9700)*
▲ Ideal Creations Inc E 212 563-5928
New York *(G-9857)*
◆ In Mocean Group LLC D 212 944-0317
New York *(G-9873)*
◆ Isfel Co Inc G 212 736-6216
New York *(G-9945)*
▲ Jeanjer LLC A 212 944-1330
New York *(G-9991)*
Jgx LLC G 212 575-1244
New York *(G-10002)*
◆ JM Originals Inc C 845 647-3003
Ellenville *(G-4307)*
Jomat New York Inc E 718 369-7641
Brooklyn *(G-1998)*
Jordache Enterprises Inc D 212 944-1330
New York *(G-10024)*
◆ Jordache Enterprises Inc C 212 643-8400
New York *(G-10025)*
K & S Childrens Wear Inc E 718 624-0006
Brooklyn *(G-2016)*
Kahn-Lucas-Lancaster Inc D 212 239-2407
New York *(G-10057)*
◆ Land n Sea Inc D 212 444-6000
New York *(G-10168)*
Leng Universal Inc F 212 398-6800
New York *(G-10196)*
▲ Lf Sourcing (millwork) LLC G 212 827-3352
New York *(G-10208)*
▲ Liberty Apparel Company Inc E 718 625-4000
New York *(G-10209)*
◆ Lollytogs Ltd D 212 502-6000
New York *(G-10246)*
Longevity Brands LLC G 212 231-7877
New York *(G-10248)*
◆ M Hidary & Co Inc D 212 736-6540
New York *(G-10296)*
Michael Stuart Inc E 718 821-0704
Brooklyn *(G-2151)*
Miltons of New York Inc G 212 997-3359
New York *(G-10471)*
Nyc Bronx Inc G 917 417-0509
Bronx *(G-1327)*
◆ Oxygen Inc G 516 433-1144
Hicksville *(G-5936)*
Pink Crush LLC G 718 788-6978
New York *(G-10844)*
▲ Pti-Pacific Inc G 212 414-8495
New York *(G-10920)*
Rogers Group Inc E 212 643-9292
New York *(G-11075)*
◆ S Rothschild & Co Inc C 212 354-8550
New York *(G-11110)*
Sch Dpx Corporation G 917 405-5377
New York *(G-11148)*
▲ Silly Phillie Creations Inc E 718 492-6300
Brooklyn *(G-2413)*
▲ Sister Sister Inc G 212 629-9600
New York *(G-11252)*
Sleepy Head Inc F 718 237-9655
Brooklyn *(G-2427)*
Swatfame Inc G 212 944-8022
New York *(G-11406)*
◆ Warnaco Group Inc E 212 287-8000
New York *(G-11720)*
▲ Waterbury Garment LLC E 212 725-1500
New York *(G-11730)*
Yigal-Azrouel Inc E 212 302-1194
New York *(G-11809)*
▲ Z-Ply Corp E 212 398-7011
New York *(G-11814)*
▲ Zinnias Inc F 718 746-8551
Bellerose *(G-777)*

2371 Fur Goods

▲ Anage Inc F 212 944-6533
New York *(G-8571)*
Anastasia Furs International F 212 868-9241
New York *(G-8574)*
▲ Avante G 516 782-4888
Great Neck *(G-5369)*
B Smith Furs Inc F 212 967-5290
New York *(G-8705)*

▲ Best Brands Consumer Pdts Inc ......G...... 212 684-7456
New York *(G-8766)*

▲ Blum & Fink Inc ....F...... 212 695-2606
New York *(G-8823)*

▲ CPT Usa LLC ....E...... 212 575-1616
New York *(G-9114)*

▲ Dennis Basso Couture Inc ....F...... 212 794-4500
New York *(G-9203)*

First Brands LLC ....E...... 646 432-4366
Merrick *(G-7855)*

Fox Unlimited Inc ....G...... 212 736-3071
New York *(G-9526)*

Georgy Creative Fashions Inc ....G...... 212 279-4885
New York *(G-9602)*

◆ J Percy For Mrvin Rchards Ltd .....E...... 212 944-5300
New York *(G-9956)*

Jerry Sorbara Furs Inc ....F...... 212 594-3897
New York *(G-9995)*

◆ Kaitery Furs Ltd ....G...... 718 204-1396
Long Island City *(G-7260)*

Miller & Berkowitz Ltd ....F...... 212 244-5459
New York *(G-10468)*

Mink Mart Inc ....G...... 212 868-2785
New York *(G-10478)*

Mksf Inc ....G...... 212 563-3877
New York *(G-10485)*

Moschos Furs Inc ....G...... 212 244-0255
New York *(G-10506)*

Samuel Schulman Furs Inc ....G...... 212 736-5550
New York *(G-11127)*

Sekas International Ltd ....F...... 212 629-6095
New York *(G-11184)*

▲ Stallion Inc ....E...... 718 706-0111
Long Island City *(G-7362)*

Stefan Furs Inc ....G...... 212 594-2788
New York *(G-11354)*

Steves Original Furs Inc ....E...... 212 967-8007
New York *(G-11362)*

Superior Furs Inc ....F...... 516 365-4123
Manhasset *(G-7541)*

USA Furs By George Inc ....G...... 212 643-1415
New York *(G-11629)*

Xanadu ....G...... 212 465-0580
New York *(G-11797)*

2381 Dress & Work Gloves

Falls Manufacturing Inc ....G...... 518 672-7189
Philmont *(G-12613)*

◆ Fownes Brothers & Co Inc ....E...... 800 345-6837
New York *(G-9525)*

Fownes Brothers & Co Inc ....E...... 518 752-4411
Gloversville *(G-5283)*

Gce International Inc ....F...... 212 868-0500
New York *(G-9581)*

◆ King Sheraz Trading Corp ....F...... 646 944-2800
Staten Island *(G-14673)*

▲ Manzella Knitting ....G...... 716 825-0808
Orchard Park *(G-12363)*

▲ Worldwide Protective Pdts LLC ....C...... 877 678-4568
Hamburg *(G-5525)*

2384 Robes & Dressing Gowns

Authentic Brands Group LLC ....C...... 212 760-2410
New York *(G-8680)*

▲ Komar Luxury Brands ....G...... 646 472-0060
New York *(G-10125)*

Lady Ester Lingerie Corp ....E...... 212 689-1729
New York *(G-10162)*

Mata Fashions LLC ....G...... 917 716-7894
New York *(G-10380)*

▲ Natori Company Incorporated ......D...... 212 532-7796
New York *(G-10550)*

◆ Palmbay Ltd ....G...... 718 424-3388
Flushing *(G-4884)*

Sketch Studio Trading Inc ....G...... 212 244-2875
New York *(G-11257)*

2385 Waterproof Outerwear

A W R Group Inc ....F...... 718 729-0412
Long Island City *(G-7141)*

◆ Essex Manufacturing Inc ....D...... 212 239-0080
New York *(G-9404)*

Float Tech Inc ....G...... 518 266-0964
Troy *(G-15168)*

▲ Hercules Group Inc ....E...... 212 813-8000
Port Washington *(G-12883)*

▲ Levy Group Inc ....C...... 212 398-0707
New York *(G-10206)*

▲ Mpdw Inc ....G...... 925 631-6878
New York *(G-10512)*

▲ Top Fortune Usa Ltd ....G...... 516 608-2694
Lynbrook *(G-7441)*

2386 Leather & Sheep Lined Clothing

▲ Andrew M Schwartz LLC ....G...... 212 391-7070
New York *(G-8580)*

Cockpit Usa Inc ....F...... 212 575-1616
New York *(G-9046)*

▲ Excelled Sheepskin & Lea Coat ...F...... 212 594-5843
New York *(G-9443)*

▲ G-III Apparel Group Ltd ....B...... 212 403-0500
New York *(G-9560)*

G-III Leather Fashions Inc ....G...... 212 403-0500
New York *(G-9563)*

Georgy Creative Fashions Inc ....G...... 212 279-4885
New York *(G-9602)*

▲ J Lowy Co ....G...... 718 338-7324
Brooklyn *(G-1979)*

◆ J Percy For Mrvin Rchards Ltd .....E...... 212 944-5300
New York *(G-9956)*

Lost Worlds Inc ....G...... 212 923-3423
New York *(G-10267)*

Louis Schwartz ....G...... 845 356-6624
Spring Valley *(G-14577)*

Studio One Leather Design Inc ......F...... 212 760-1701
New York *(G-11379)*

▲ US Authentic LLC ....G...... 914 767-0295
Katonah *(G-6639)*

Zwuits Inc ....F...... 929 387-2323
Larchmont *(G-6845)*

2387 Apparel Belts

Barrera Jose & Maria Co Ltd ....E...... 212 239-1994
New York *(G-8733)*

Centric Brands Inc ....D...... 646 582-6000
New York *(G-8955)*

▲ Courtlandt Boot Jack Co Inc ....E...... 718 445-6200
Flushing *(G-4846)*

▲ Daniel M Friedman & Assoc Inc ....E...... 212 695-5545
New York *(G-9167)*

Gbg USA Inc ....D...... 646 839-7083
New York *(G-9578)*

Gbg USA Inc ....E...... 212 615-3400
New York *(G-9579)*

Nassau Suffolk Brd of Womens ......G...... 631 666-8835
Bay Shore *(G-696)*

▲ New Classic Inc ....F...... 718 609-1100
Long Island City *(G-7306)*

P M Belts Usa Inc ....E...... 800 762-3580
Brooklyn *(G-2240)*

◆ Perry Ellis Menswear LLC ....C...... 212 221-7500
New York *(G-10809)*

Randa Accessories Lea Gds LLC ...D...... 212 354-5100
New York *(G-10979)*

Sandy Duftler Designs Ltd ....F...... 516 379-3084
North Baldwin *(G-12007)*

Sh Leather Novelty Company ....G...... 718 387-7742
Brooklyn *(G-2400)*

◆ Tapestry Inc ....B...... 212 594-1850
New York *(G-11434)*

▲ Trafalgar Company LLC ....G...... 212 768-8800
New York *(G-11531)*

Universal Elliot Corp ....G...... 212 736-8877
New York *(G-11606)*

Xinya International Trading Co ....G...... 212 216-9681
New York *(G-11799)*

2389 Apparel & Accessories, NEC

▲ A Lunt Design Inc ....F...... 716 662-0781
Orchard Park *(G-12334)*

▲ Accessries Direct Intl USA Inc ......E...... 646 448-8200
New York *(G-8443)*

▲ Adf Accessories Inc ....G...... 516 450-5755
Oceanside *(G-12164)*

▲ Apollo Apparel Group LLC ....F...... 212 398-6585
New York *(G-8604)*

Astor Accessories LLC ....G...... 212 695-6146
New York *(G-8657)*

Barbara Matera Ltd ....D...... 212 475-5006
New York *(G-8725)*

Brooklyn Denim Co ....F...... 718 782-2600
Brooklyn *(G-1616)*

▲ Carter Enterprises LLC ....E...... 718 853-5052
Brooklyn *(G-1650)*

Costume Armour Inc ....F...... 845 534-9120
Cornwall *(G-3728)*

Craft Clerical Clothes Inc ....G...... 212 764-6122
New York *(G-9184)*

Creative Costume Co ....G...... 212 564-5552
Liverpool *(G-7008)*

Cygnet Studio Inc ....F...... 646 450-4550
New York *(G-9141)*

D-C Theatricks ....G...... 716 847-0180
Buffalo *(G-2719)*

David & Young Co Inc ....G...... 212 594-6034
New York *(G-9177)*

Davis ....G...... 716 833-4678
Buffalo *(G-2722)*

▲ Dreamwave LLC ....E...... 212 594-4250
New York *(G-9267)*

▲ Dvf Studio LLC ....D...... 212 741-6607
New York *(G-9283)*

Dvf Studio LLC ....G...... 646 576-8009
New York *(G-9284)*

▲ Eb Couture Ltd ....J...... 212 912-0190
New York *(G-9310)*

Eric Winterling Inc ....E...... 212 629-7686
New York *(G-9393)*

▼ Euroco Costumes Inc ....G...... 212 629-9665
New York *(G-9420)*

Foot Locker Retail Inc ....F...... 516 827-5306
Hicksville *(G-5908)*

▲ Gce International Inc ....D...... 212 704-4800
New York *(G-9580)*

▲ HB Athletic Inc ....F...... 914 560-8422
New Rochelle *(G-8340)*

Hoehn Inc ....F...... 518 463-8900
Albany *(G-87)*

▲ Hpk Industries LLC ....F...... 315 724-0196
Utica *(G-15271)*

Hudson Dying & Finishing LLC ....E...... 518 752-4389
Gloversville *(G-5286)*

I Shalom & Co Inc ....C...... 212 532-7911
New York *(G-9848)*

Izquierdo Studios Ltd ....F...... 212 807-9757
New York *(G-9950)*

J & C Finishing ....E...... 718 456-1087
Ridgewood *(G-13147)*

JC California Inc ....G...... 212 334-4380
New York *(G-9986)*

Jersey Express Inc ....F...... 716 834-6151
Buffalo *(G-2821)*

▲ Jimeale Incorporated ....G...... 917 686-5383
New York *(G-10005)*

▲ JM Studio Inc ....F...... 646 546-5514
New York *(G-10011)*

John Kristiansen New York Inc ....F...... 212 388-1097
New York *(G-10017)*

Jolibe Atelier LLC ....G...... 917 319-5908
New York *(G-10020)*

Jonathan Meizler LLC ....G...... 212 213-2977
New York *(G-10022)*

▲ Joseph Industries Inc ....E...... 212 764-0010
New York *(G-10027)*

◆ Kidz Concepts LLC ....D...... 212 398-1110
New York *(G-10097)*

Kiton Building Corp ....E...... 212 486-3224
New York *(G-10111)*

Koon Enterprises LLC ....G...... 718 886-3163
Fresh Meadows *(G-5043)*

▲ L D Weiss Inc ....E...... 212 697-3023
New York *(G-10150)*

▼ Lakeland Industries Inc ....C...... 631 981-9700
Ronkonkoma *(G-13963)*

Linder New York LLC ....F...... 646 678-5819
New York *(G-10221)*

▲ Lr Paris LLC ....F...... 845 709-8013
New York *(G-10275)*

M2 Fashion Group Holdings Inc ......G...... 917 208-2948
New York *(G-10302)*

Masquerade LLC ....F...... 212 673-4546
New York *(G-10379)*

▲ Meryl Diamond Ltd ....D...... 212 730-0333
New York *(G-10439)*

Moresca Clothing and Costume ......F...... 845 331-6012
Ulster Park *(G-15219)*

Mountain and Isles LLC ....F...... 212 354-1890
New York *(G-10509)*

My Hanky Inc ....G...... 646 321-0869
Brooklyn *(G-2182)*

▲ New York Accessory Group Inc .....F...... 212 532-7911
New York *(G-10592)*

New York Hospital Disposable ....E...... 718 384-1620
Brooklyn *(G-2208)*

▲ NY Orthopedic Usa Inc ....D...... 718 852-5330
Brooklyn *(G-2225)*

◆ Onia LLC ....E...... 646 701-0008
New York *(G-10693)*

Parsons-Meares Ltd ....D...... 212 242-3378
Long Island City *(G-7320)*

S I C

Patient-Wear LLC ....G.... 914 740-7770
 Bronx *(G-1333)*

◆ Perry Ellis Menswear LLC ....C.... 212 221-7500
 New York *(G-10809)*

▲ Ppr Direct Marketing LLC ....G.... 718 965-8600
 Brooklyn *(G-2275)*

▲ Prolink Industries Inc ....F.... 212 354-5690
 New York *(G-10907)*

RA Newhouse Inc...............................D.... 516 248-6670
 Mineola *(G-7995)*

Randa Accessories Lea Gds LLC ....D.... 212 354-5100
 New York *(G-10979)*

Rhino Sports & Leisure LLC ....E.... 844 877-4466
 Tarrytown *(G-15058)*

Ribz LLC ....G.... 212 764-9595
 New York *(G-11036)*

▲ Rjm2 Ltd ....G.... 212 944-1660
 New York *(G-11054)*

Robert Miller Associates LLC ....F.... 718 392-1640
 Long Island City *(G-7343)*

▲ Rose Solomon Co ....E.... 718 855-1788
 Brooklyn *(G-2355)*

▲ Rosetti Handbags and ACC ....E.... 646 839-7945
 New York *(G-11085)*

▲ Roth Clothing Co Inc ....G.... 718 384-4927
 Brooklyn *(G-2356)*

◆ Rubies Costume Company Inc ....B.... 718 846-1008
 Richmond Hill *(G-13122)*

Rubies Costume Company Inc ....D.... 631 777-3300
 Bay Shore *(G-711)*

Rubies Costume Company Inc ....C.... 718 441-0834
 Richmond Hill *(G-13123)*

Rubies Costume Company Inc ....G.... 631 951-3688
 Bay Shore *(G-712)*

Rubies Costume Company Inc ....E.... 516 333-3473
 Westbury *(G-15923)*

Rubies Costume Company Inc ....F.... 631 435-7912
 Bay Shore *(G-713)*

Rubies Costume Company Inc ....C.... 718 846-1008
 Richmond Hill *(G-13124)*

Rubies Masquerade Company LLC .....G.... 718 846-1008
 Richmond Hill *(G-13125)*

▲ S & B Fashion Inc ....G.... 718 482-1386
 Long Island City *(G-7349)*

Schneeman Studio Limited ....G.... 212 244-3330
 New York *(G-11153)*

▲ Setton Brothers Inc ....G.... 646 902-6011
 Brooklyn *(G-2398)*

▲ Shamron Mills Ltd ....G.... 212 354-0430
 Troy *(G-15188)*

◆ Skiva International Inc ....E.... 212 736-9520
 New York *(G-11261)*

South Central Boyz............................G.... 718 496-7270
 Brooklyn *(G-2444)*

▲ Swank Inc ....B.... 212 867-2600
 New York *(G-11403)*

▲ Timeless Fashions LLC ....G.... 212 730-9328
 New York *(G-11495)*

Tr Apparel LLC ....G.... 646 358-3888
 New York *(G-11526)*

▲ Trafalgar Company LLC ....G.... 212 768-8800
 New York *(G-11531)*

Trash and Vaudeville Inc ....G.... 212 777-1727
 New York *(G-11534)*

Twcc Product and Sales......................E.... 212 614-9364
 New York *(G-11563)*

▲ Ufo Contemporary Inc ....F.... 212 226-5400
 New York *(G-11576)*

Unified Inc led ....F.... 646 370-4650
 New York *(G-11583)*

Westchester Wine Warehouse LLC......F.... 914 824-1400
 White Plains *(G-16074)*

White Plains Coat Apron Co Inc ....G.... 914 736-2610
 Peekskill *(G-12563)*

2391 Curtains & Draperies

Abalene Decorating Services ....E.... 718 782-2000
 New York *(G-8425)*

Anthony Lawrence of New York ....E.... 212 206-8820
 Long Island City *(G-7159)*

Associated Drapery & Equipment ....F.... 516 671-5245
 Monroe *(G-8014)*

◆ Baby Signature Inc ....G.... 212 686-1700
 New York *(G-8710)*

◆ Belle Maison USA Ltd ....E.... 718 805-0200
 Richmond Hill *(G-13110)*

Bettertex Inc ....F.... 212 431-3373
 New York *(G-8771)*

◆ Bramson House Inc ....C.... 516 764-5006
 Freeport *(G-4988)*

C & G of Kingston Inc ....D.... 845 331-0148
 Kingston *(G-6681)*

Cabriole Designs Inc ....G.... 212 593-4528
 New York *(G-8884)*

▲ Commonwealth Home Fashion Inc ..D.... 514 384-8290
 Willsboro *(G-16150)*

◆ County Draperies Inc ....E.... 845 342-9009
 Middletown *(G-7901)*

Daniels Bath & Beyond ....G.... 718 765-1915
 Brooklyn *(G-1724)*

Deangelis Ltd ....E.... 212 348-8225
 Glen Head *(G-5205)*

Drapery Industries Inc ....F.... 585 232-2992
 Rochester *(G-13356)*

Fabric Quilters Unlimited Inc ....E.... 516 333-2866
 Westbury *(G-15884)*

▲ J Edlin Interiors Ltd ....F.... 212 243-2111
 New York *(G-9955)*

Jo-Vin Decorators Inc ....E.... 718 441-9350
 Woodhaven *(G-16187)*

Laminated Window Products Inc ....F.... 631 242-6883
 Bay Shore *(G-687)*

▼ Laregence Inc ....E.... 212 736-2548
 New York *(G-10173)*

Majestic Curtains LLC ....G.... 718 898-0774
 Elmhurst *(G-4336)*

▼ Mason Contract Products LLC ....D.... 516 328-6900
 New Hyde Park *(G-8282)*

▲ Mistdoda Inc ....E.... 919 735-7111
 New York *(G-10483)*

▲ Mutual Sales Corp ....E.... 718 361-8373
 Long Island City *(G-7300)*

Northast Coml Win Trtments Inc ....D.... 845 331-0148
 Kingston *(G-6704)*

Puregrab LLC ....G.... 718 935-1959
 Brooklyn *(G-2307)*

◆ Revman International Inc ....E.... 212 894-3100
 New York *(G-11028)*

Reynolds Drapery Service Inc ....F.... 315 845-8632
 Newport *(G-11899)*

◆ Richloom Fabrics Corp ....F.... 212 685-5400
 New York *(G-11042)*

▲ Richloom Fabrics Group Inc ....E.... 212 685-5400
 New York *(G-11043)*

Seaway Mats Inc ....G.... 518 483-2560
 Malone *(G-7490)*

Showeray Co ....D.... 718 965-3633
 Brooklyn *(G-2406)*

Shyam Ahuja Limited ....G.... 212 644-5910
 New York *(G-11221)*

Terbo Ltd ....G.... 718 847-2860
 Richmond Hill *(G-13127)*

Wayne Decorators Inc ....G.... 718 529-4200
 Jamaica *(G-6487)*

Wcd Window Coverings Inc ....E.... 845 336-4511
 Lake Katrine *(G-6764)*

2392 House furnishings: Textile

388 Associates Inc ....G.... 267 367-0990
 Brooklyn *(G-1414)*

AEP Environmental LLC......................F.... 716 446-0739
 Buffalo *(G-2625)*

▲ Alen Sands York Associates Ltd ......F.... 212 563-6305
 New York *(G-8511)*

Alexandra Ferguson LLC.....................G.... 718 788-7768
 New Rochelle *(G-8317)*

▲ Anhui Skyworth LLC ....D.... 917 940-6903
 Hempstead *(G-5831)*

Apex Real Holdings Inc ....G.... 877 725-2150
 Brooklyn *(G-1517)*

▲ Area Inc ....G.... 212 924-7084
 New York *(G-8620)*

▲ Arlee Home Fashions Inc ....D.... 212 689-0020
 New York *(G-8624)*

▲ August Silk Inc ....E.... 212 643-2400
 New York *(G-8678)*

August Silk Inc ....G.... 212 643-2400
 New York *(G-8679)*

◆ Baby Signature Inc ....G.... 212 686-1700
 New York *(G-8710)*

▲ Bardwil Industries Inc ....C.... 212 944-1870
 New York *(G-8727)*

◆ Belle Maison USA Ltd ....E.... 718 805-0200
 Richmond Hill *(G-13110)*

◆ Bramson House Inc ....C.... 516 764-5006
 Freeport *(G-4988)*

▲ Broder Mfg Inc ....G.... 718 366-1667
 Brooklyn *(G-1610)*

C & G of Kingston Inc ....D.... 845 331-0148
 Kingston *(G-6681)*

▲ Caddy Concepts Inc ....F.... 516 570-6279
 Great Neck *(G-5372)*

▲ Catalina Products Corp ....E.... 718 336-8288
 Brooklyn *(G-1655)*

◆ Cathay Home Inc ....E.... 212 213-0988
 New York *(G-8937)*

▲ Continental Quilting Co Inc ....E.... 718 499-9100
 New Hyde Park *(G-8259)*

◆ County Draperies Inc ....E.... 845 342-9009
 Middletown *(G-7901)*

◆ Cpac Inc ....E.... 585 382-3223
 Leicester *(G-6908)*

◆ Creative Home Furnishings ....G.... 631 582-8000
 Central Islip *(G-3270)*

Creative Scents USA Inc ....E.... 718 522-5901
 Brooklyn *(G-1698)*

Daniels Bath & Beyond ....G.... 718 765-1915
 Brooklyn *(G-1724)*

◆ Dico Products Corporation ....F.... 315 797-0470
 Utica *(G-15255)*

▲ E & F Home Fashions Inc ....G.... 718 968-9719
 Brooklyn *(G-1770)*

▲ Elegant Linen Inc ....E.... 718 492-0297
 Brooklyn *(G-1793)*

Ess Bee Industries Inc.......................E.... 718 894-5202
 Brooklyn *(G-1814)*

◆ Ex-Cell Home Fashions Inc ....C.... 919 735-7111
 New York *(G-9435)*

▲ Excellent Art Mfg Corp ....F.... 718 388-7075
 Inwood *(G-6292)*

EY Industries Inc ....F.... 718 624-9122
 Brooklyn *(G-1824)*

Fabric Quilters Unlimited Inc ....E.... 516 333-2866
 Westbury *(G-15884)*

▲ Franks Cushions Inc......................F.... 718 848-1216
 Maspeth *(G-7617)*

▲ Handy Laundry Products Corp ....G.... 845 701-1111
 Airmont *(G-11)*

▲ Hedaya Home Fashions Inc ....C.... 212 889-1111
 New York *(G-9761)*

◆ Himatsingka America Inc ....E.... 212 824-2949
 New York *(G-9787)*

Hollander HM Fshons Hldngs LLC.......E.... 212 575-0400
 New York *(G-9804)*

Hollander Sleep Products LLC ....D.... 212 575-0400
 New York *(G-9805)*

▲ Home Fashions Intl LLC ....E.... 212 689-3579
 New York *(G-9807)*

Home Fashions Intl LLC ....F.... 212 684-0091
 New York *(G-9808)*

◆ Indigo Home Inc ....G.... 212 684-4146
 New York *(G-9881)*

◆ Ingenious Designs LLC ....C.... 631 254-3376
 Ronkonkoma *(G-13948)*

Jo-Vin Decorators Inc ....E.... 718 441-9350
 Woodhaven *(G-16187)*

◆ Josie Accessories Inc ....D.... 212 889-6376
 New York *(G-10029)*

▲ Kaltex North America Inc ....E.... 212 894-3200
 New York *(G-10063)*

◆ Kartell Us Inc ....E.... 212 966-6665
 New York *(G-10070)*

◆ Kim Seybert Inc ....F.... 212 564-7850
 New York *(G-10101)*

Medline Industries Inc ....B.... 845 344-3301
 Middletown *(G-7919)*

Mgk Group Inc ....E.... 212 989-2732
 New York *(G-10448)*

Michael Stuart Inc ....E.... 718 821-0704
 Brooklyn *(G-2151)*

Moga Trading Company Inc.................G.... 718 760-2966
 Corona *(G-3746)*

▲ National Wire & Metal Tech Inc ......E.... 716 661-9180
 Jamestown *(G-6534)*

▲ Nationwide Tarps Incorporated ....D.... 518 843-1545
 Amsterdam *(G-341)*

Nbets Corporation ....E.... 516 785-1259
 Wantagh *(G-15487)*

◆ Northpoint Trading Inc ....F.... 212 481-8001
 New York *(G-10645)*

▲ NY Cutting Inc ....G.... 646 434-1355
 Suffern *(G-14763)*

Paramount Textiles Inc.......................F.... 212 966-1040
 New York *(G-10756)*

Performance Sourcing Group Inc ....E.... 914 636-2100
 Scarsdale *(G-14240)*

◆ Place Vendome Holding Co Inc ....E.... 212 696-0765
 New York *(G-10850)*

Premier Skirting Products Inc ....F.... 516 239-6581
 Lawrence *(G-6890)*

▲ Q Squared Design LLC ....E 212 686-8860
New York *(G-10942)*

▲ R & M Industries Inc ....F 212 366-6414
New York *(G-10964)*

Repellem Consumer Pdts Corp ....F 631 273-3992
Bohemia *(G-1070)*

◆ Revman International Inc ....E 212 894-3100
New York *(G-11028)*

◆ Richloom Fabrics Corp ....F 212 685-5400
New York *(G-11042)*

▲ Richloom Fabrics Group Inc ....G 212 685-5400
New York *(G-11043)*

▲ Royal Copenhagen Inc ....F 845 454-4442
Poughkeepsie *(G-12980)*

Showeray Co ....D 718 965-3633
Brooklyn *(G-2406)*

▲ Silly Phillie Creations Inc ....E 718 492-6300
Brooklyn *(G-2413)*

▲ Skil-Care Corporation ....C 914 963-2040
Yonkers *(G-16348)*

Sleepable Sofas Ltd ....D 973 546-4502
New York *(G-11267)*

▲ Sleeping Partners Intl Inc ....F 212 254-1515
Brooklyn *(G-2426)*

◆ Soft-Tex International Inc ....D 800 366-2324
Waterford *(G-15546)*

Sterling Shelf Liners Inc ....G 631 676-5175
Holbrook *(G-6022)*

◆ Sunham Home Fashions LLC ....D 212 695-1218
New York *(G-11393)*

Sure Fit Inc ....E 212 395-9340
New York *(G-11398)*

Tablecloths For Granted Ltd ....D 518 370-5481
Schenectady *(G-14310)*

Terbo Ltd ....G 718 847-2860
Richmond Hill *(G-13127)*

▲ University Table Cloth Company ......F 845 371-3876
Spring Valley *(G-14586)*

Vr Bags Inc ....G 212 714-1494
Bronx *(G-1393)*

Wayne Decorators Inc ....G 718 529-4200
Jamaica *(G-6487)*

William Harvey Studio Inc ....G 718 599-4343
Brooklyn *(G-2586)*

2393 Textile Bags

◆ Ace Bag & Burlap Company Inc ......F 718 319-9300
Bronx *(G-1192)*

▲ Ace Drop Cloth Canvas Pdts Inc .....E 718 731-1550
Bronx *(G-1193)*

Advanced Medical Mfg Corp ....E 845 369-7535
Suffern *(G-14756)*

Carry Hot Inc ....E 212 279-7535
New York *(G-8925)*

GPM Associates LLC ....G 585 359-1770
Rush *(G-14071)*

GPM Associates LLC ....E 585 335-3940
Dansville *(G-3819)*

▲ H G Maybeck Co Inc ....E 718 297-4410
Jamaica *(G-6447)*

▲ Health Matters America Inc ....F 716 235-8772
Buffalo *(G-2796)*

◆ Ivi Services Inc ....D 607 729-5111
Binghamton *(G-889)*

▲ Jag Manufacturing Inc ....E 518 762-9558
Johnstown *(G-6620)*

Jakes Sneakers Inc ....G 718 233-1132
Brooklyn *(G-1988)*

Johnson Outdoors Inc ....C 607 779-2200
Binghamton *(G-891)*

Kragel Co Inc ....G 716 648-1344
Hamburg *(G-5512)*

▲ Kush Oasis Enterprises LLC ....G 516 513-1316
Syosset *(G-14792)*

Mgk Group Inc ....E 212 989-2732
New York *(G-10448)*

Paulpac LLC ....G 631 283-7610
Southampton *(G-14534)*

Prima Satchel Inc ....G 929 367-7770
Monroe *(G-8029)*

▼ Select Fabricators Inc ....F 585 393-0650
Canandaigua *(G-3142)*

▲ Spray Moret LLC ....G 917 213-9592
New York *(G-11331)*

Wayne Decorators Inc ....G 718 529-4200
Jamaica *(G-6487)*

2394 Canvas Prdts

125-127 Main Street Corp ....F 631 477-1500
Greenport *(G-5456)*

Abble Awning Co Inc ....G 516 822-1200
Bethpage *(G-830)*

▲ Ace Canvas & Tent Corp ....F 631 981-9705
Ronkonkoma *(G-13886)*

▲ Ace Drop Cloth Canvas Pdts Inc .....E 718 731-1550
Bronx *(G-1193)*

Acme Awning Co Inc ....F 718 409-1881
Bronx *(G-1195)*

▼ Air Structures Amercn Tech Inc ......E 914 937-4500
Port Chester *(G-12812)*

Allen Boat Co Inc ....G 716 842-0800
Buffalo *(G-2626)*

AMS Star Structures Inc ....G 914 584-0898
Nyack *(G-12135)*

Anchor Canvas LLC ....G 631 265-5602
Smithtown *(G-14473)*

Automtve Uphl Cnvertible Tops ....G 914 961-4242
Tuckahoe *(G-15203)*

Awning Mart Inc ....G 315 699-5928
Cicero *(G-3416)*

Breton Industries Inc ....C 518 842-3030
Amsterdam *(G-320)*

Broadway Neon Sign Corp ....F 908 241-4177
Ronkonkoma *(G-13918)*

Brock Awnings Ltd ....F 631 765-5200
Hampton Bays *(G-5533)*

C E King & Sons Inc ....G 631 324-4944
East Hampton *(G-4118)*

Canvas Products Company Inc ....F 516 742-1058
Mineola *(G-7963)*

Capitol Awning Co Inc ....F 212 505-1717
Jamaica *(G-6430)*

Classic Awnings Inc ....F 716 649-0390
Hamburg *(G-5503)*

Coverall Manufacturing ....G 315 622-2852
Baldwinsville *(G-546)*

▲ Covergrip Corporation ....G 855 268-3747
Manorville *(G-7552)*

▲ Custom Canvas Manufacturing Co ..E 716 852-6372
Buffalo *(G-2717)*

▲ Custom European Imports Inc ....G 845 357-5718
Sloatsburg *(G-14470)*

▲ Dhs Systems LLC ....F 845 359-6066
Orangeburg *(G-12312)*

Di Sanos Creative Canvas Inc ....G 315 894-3137
Frankfort *(G-4949)*

Dor-A-Mar Canvas Products Co ....F 631 750-9202
West Sayville *(G-15839)*

◆ Durasol Systems Inc ....D 845 610-1100
Chester *(G-3375)*

Fabric Concepts For Industry ....F 914 375-2565
Yonkers *(G-16308)*

▲ Jag Manufacturing Inc ....E 518 762-9558
Johnstown *(G-6620)*

Jamestown Awning Inc ....G 716 483-1435
Jamestown *(G-6520)*

Jo-Vin Decorators Inc ....E 718 441-9350
Woodhaven *(G-16187)*

Johnson Outdoors Inc ....C 607 779-2200
Binghamton *(G-891)*

Ke Durasol Awnings Inc ....F 845 610-1100
Chester *(G-3380)*

Kingston Building Products LLC ....G 914 665-0707
Mount Vernon *(G-8156)*

Kohler Awning Inc ....E 716 685-3333
Buffalo *(G-2839)*

Kragel Co Inc ....G 716 648-1344
Hamburg *(G-5512)*

Kraus & Sons Inc ....F 212 620-0408
New York *(G-10137)*

Laminated Window Products Inc ....F 631 242-6883
Bay Shore *(G-687)*

Lanza Corp ....G 914 937-6360
Port Chester *(G-12824)*

▲ Leiter Sukkahs Inc ....G 718 436-0303
Brooklyn *(G-2061)*

Mauceri Sign Inc ....F 718 656-7700
Jamaica *(G-6458)*

Mc Coy Tops and Interiors Inc ....G 718 458-5800
Woodside *(G-16212)*

▼ Melbourne C Fisher Yacht Sails ......G 631 673-5055
Huntington Station *(G-6253)*

▼ Meyco Products Inc ....E 631 421-9800
Melville *(G-7804)*

▲ Nationwide Tarps Incorporated ....D 518 843-1545
Amsterdam *(G-341)*

Northern Awning & Sign Company ......G 315 782-8515
Watertown *(G-15585)*

Perma Tech Inc ....E 716 854-0707
Buffalo *(G-2915)*

Point Canvas Company Inc ....G 607 692-4381
Whitney Point *(G-16107)*

Quantum Sails Rochester LLC ....G 585 342-5200
Rochester *(G-13664)*

Sausbiers Awning Shop Inc ....G 518 828-3748
Hudson *(G-6178)*

▼ Select Fabricators Inc ....F 585 393-0650
Canandaigua *(G-3142)*

Service Canvas Co Inc ....F 716 853-0558
Buffalo *(G-2979)*

Steinway Awning II LLC ....G 718 729-2965
Astoria *(G-442)*

TG Peppe Inc ....G 516 239-7852
Lawrence *(G-6893)*

Toptec Products LLC ....F 631 421-9800
Melville *(G-7831)*

Ulmer Sales LLC ....F 718 885-1700
Port Chester *(G-12830)*

Utility Canvas Inc ....G 845 255-9290
Gardiner *(G-5132)*

Vinyl Works Inc ....E 518 786-1200
Latham *(G-6880)*

▲ Y & A Trading Inc ....F 718 436-6333
Brooklyn *(G-2598)*

2395 Pleating & Stitching For The Trade

A Trusted Name Inc ....F 716 326-7400
Westfield *(G-15944)*

▲ Active World Solutions Inc ....G 718 922-9404
Brooklyn *(G-1459)*

Aditiany Inc ....G 212 997-8440
New York *(G-8460)*

All About Art Inc ....F 718 321-0755
Flushing *(G-4837)*

All American Awards Inc ....F 631 567-2025
Bohemia *(G-968)*

American Country Quilts & Lin ....G 631 283-5466
Southampton *(G-14526)*

American Quality Embroidery ....G 631 467-3200
Ronkonkoma *(G-13903)*

Arena Graphics Inc ....G 516 767-5108
Port Washington *(G-12864)*

Athletic Cap Co Inc ....E 718 398-1300
Staten Island *(G-14621)*

Casual Friday Inc ....G 585 544-9470
Rochester *(G-13300)*

Control Research Inc ....G 631 225-1111
Amityville *(G-259)*

Corporate Loss Preven ....G 516 409-0002
Massapequa *(G-7646)*

Custom Patches Inc ....E 845 679-6320
Woodstock *(G-16235)*

Design Archives Inc ....G 212 768-0617
New York *(G-9205)*

Dirt T Shirts Inc ....E 845 336-4230
Kingston *(G-6689)*

▲ Eagle Regalia Co Inc ....F 845 425-2245
Spring Valley *(G-14567)*

East Coast Embroidery Ltd ....G 631 254-3878
Deer Park *(G-3866)*

Eiseman-Ludmar Co Inc ....F 516 932-6990
Hicksville *(G-5904)*

Expressions Punching & Digitiz ....G 718 291-1177
Jamaica *(G-6441)*

F X Graphix Inc ....G 716 871-1511
Buffalo *(G-2750)*

Glenda Inc ....G 718 442-8981
Staten Island *(G-14656)*

▲ Holland & Sherry Inc ....E 212 542-8410
New York *(G-9803)*

Hosel & Ackerson Inc ....G 212 575-1490
New York *(G-9814)*

Human Technologies Corporation ......F 315 735-3532
Utica *(G-15273)*

Instant Monogramming Inc ....G 585 654-5550
Rochester *(G-13480)*

▲ Jomari Industries Inc ....E 845 357-5773
Airmont *(G-13)*

Kabrics ....G 607 962-6344
Corning *(G-3717)*

Karishma Fashions Inc ....G 718 565-5404
Jackson Heights *(G-6420)*

Kevin J Kassman ....G 585 529-4245
Rochester *(G-13502)*

Knucklehead Embroidery Inc ....G 607 797-2725
Johnson City *(G-6605)*

Loremanss Embroidery Engrav ....F 518 834-9205
Keeseville *(G-6643)*

Mainly Monograms Inc ....E 845 624-4923
West Nyack *(G-15827)*

Milaaya Inc ....G....... 212 764-6386
New York (G-10465)

Mrinalini Inc ....G....... 646 510-2747
New York (G-10513)

Northeast Stitches & Ink Inc ....E....... 518 798-5549
South Glens Falls (G-14516)

▲ NY Embroidery Inc ....E....... 516 822-6456
Hicksville (G-5934)

On The Job Embroidery & AP ....G....... 914 381-3556
Mamaroneck (G-7516)

Pass Em-Entries Inc ....F....... 718 392-0100
Long Island City (G-7321)

Penn & Fletcher Inc ....F....... 212 239-6868
Long Island City (G-7324)

Pink Inc ....G....... 212 352-8282
New York (G-10843)

Planet Embroidery ....F....... 718 381-4827
Ridgewood (G-13155)

Point Canvas Company Inc ....G....... 607 692-4381
Whitney Point (G-16107)

Quist Industries Ltd ....F....... 718 243-2800
Brooklyn (G-2316)

Rescuestuff Inc ....G....... 718 318-7570
Peekskill (G-12555)

Round Top Knit & Screening ....G....... 518 622-3600
Round Top (G-14064)

Royal Tees Inc ....G....... 845 357-9448
Suffern (G-14766)

Sand Hill Industries Inc ....G....... 518 885-7991
Ballston Spa (G-586)

Sciane Enterprises Inc ....G....... 845 452-2400
Poughkeepsie (G-12982)

Screen Gems Inc ....G....... 845 561-0036
New Windsor (G-8382)

Screen The World Inc ....F....... 631 475-0023
Holtsville (G-6052)

Sports Depot Inc ....G....... 516 965-4668
Baldwin (G-536)

Stephen M Kiernan ....E....... 716 836-6300
Buffalo (G-2992)

Stucki Embroidery Works Inc ....F....... 845 657-2308
Boiceville (G-1100)

Stylist Pleating Corp ....F....... 718 384-8181
Brooklyn (G-2468)

Todd Walbridge ....G....... 585 254-3018
Rochester (G-13768)

Trimworld Inc ....F....... 212 354-8973
New York (G-11547)

U All Inc ....E....... 518 438-2558
Albany (G-138)

Uniform Namemakers Inc......................F....... 716 626-5474
Buffalo (G-3028)

Verdonette Inc ....G....... 212 719-2003
New York (G-11660)

Vogue Too Plting Stitching EMB ....F....... 212 354-1022
New York (G-11703)

Voyager Emblems Inc ....C....... 416 255-3421
Buffalo (G-3039)

Wicked Smart LLC ....F....... 518 459-2855
Watervliet (G-15612)

2396 Automotive Trimmings, Apparel Findings, Related Prdts

Acorn Products Corp.............................F....... 315 894-4868
Ilion (G-6276)

Albert Siy ....G....... 718 359-0389
Flushing (G-4836)

American Spray-On Corp ....E....... 212 929-2100
New York (G-8559)

▲ Amoseastern Apparel Inc ....F....... 212 730-6350
New York (G-8565)

Angel Textiles Inc ....G....... 212 532-0900
New York (G-8582)

▲ Apple Imprints Apparel Inc ....E....... 716 893-1130
Buffalo (G-2641)

▲ Apsco Sports Enterprises Inc ....D....... 718 965-9500
Brooklyn (G-1522)

Aro-Graph Corporation ....G....... 315 463-8693
Syracuse (G-14817)

▲ Artistic Ribbon Novelty Co Inc ....E....... 212 255-4224
New York (G-8637)

Athletic Cap Co Inc ....E....... 718 398-1300
Staten Island (G-14621)

Barnaby Prints Inc ....F....... 845 477-2501
Greenwood Lake (G-5479)

Bondy Printing Corp.............................G....... 631 242-1510
Bay Shore (G-659)

Bpe Studio Inc.....................................G....... 212 868-9896
New York (G-8843)

C H Thompson Company Inc ....D....... 607 724-1094
Binghamton (G-866)

◆ Cai Inc ....G....... 212 819-0008
New York (G-8886)

Casual Friday Inc ....F....... 585 544-9470
Rochester (G-13300)

Coe Displays Inc ....G....... 718 937-5658
Long Island City (G-7189)

Cooper & Clement Inc ....E....... 315 454-8135
Syracuse (G-14861)

Creative Images & Applique ....D....... 718 821-8700
Maspeth (G-7602)

Decal Makers Inc ....E....... 516 221-7200
Bellmore (G-781)

Dirt T Shirts Inc ....E....... 845 336-4230
Kingston (G-6689)

Eagle Lace Dyeing Corp ....F....... 212 947-2712
New York (G-9297)

Emtron Hybrids Inc ....E....... 631 924-9668
Yaphank (G-16261)

Flp Group LLC ....F....... 315 252-7583
Auburn (G-476)

Folder Factory Inc ....F....... 540 477-3852
Melville (G-7783)

▲ Freeport Screen & Stamping ....E....... 516 379-0330
Freeport (G-4998)

Galli Shirts and Sports AP ....G....... 845 226-7305
Stormville (G-14751)

Human Technologies Corporation ....F....... 315 735-3532
Utica (G-15273)

Ihd Motorsports LLC.............................F....... 979 690-1669
Binghamton (G-886)

Irene Cerone ....G....... 315 668-2899
Brewerton (G-1136)

J M L Productions Inc ....D....... 718 643-1674
Brooklyn (G-1980)

Jack J Florio Jr ....G....... 716 434-9123
Lockport (G-7085)

Kenmar Shirts Inc ....E....... 718 824-3880
Bronx (G-1291)

Kevin J Kassman ....G....... 585 529-4245
Rochester (G-13502)

L I C Screen Printing Inc ....E....... 516 546-7289
Merrick (G-7858)

▲ Legendary Auto Interiors Ltd...........G....... 315 331-1212
Newark (G-11843)

Lending Trimming Co Inc ....D....... 212 242-7502
New York (G-10195)

Loremanss Embroidery Engrav ....F....... 518 834-9205
Keeseville (G-6643)

Mas Cutting Inc ....G....... 212 869-0826
New York (G-10378)

Master Craft Finishers Inc ....E....... 631 586-0540
Deer Park (G-3904)

Master Image Printing Inc ....G....... 914 347-4400
Elmsford (G-4416)

Mezzoprint LLC....................................G....... 347 480-9199
Valley Stream (G-15347)

Mountain T-Shirts Inc ....G....... 518 943-4533
Catskill (G-3215)

New York Binding Co Inc ....E....... 718 729-2454
Long Island City (G-7309)

Northeast Stitches & Ink Inc ....E....... 518 798-5549
South Glens Falls (G-14516)

Original Tube Tshirt ....G....... 845 291-7031
Goshen (G-5312)

▲ Pangea Brands LLC ....G....... 617 638-0001
New York (G-10746)

Patrick Rohan ....F....... 718 781-2573
Monticello (G-8072)

Paula Varsalona Ltd ....F....... 212 570-9100
New York (G-10772)

▲ Perfect Shoulder Company Inc ....E....... 914 699-8100
Mount Vernon (G-8170)

Polkadot Usa Inc ....G....... 914 835-3697
Mamaroneck (G-7520)

Printz and Patternz LLC ....G....... 518 944-6020
Schenectady (G-14296)

Rainbow Lettering ....G....... 607 732-5751
Elmira (G-4366)

Randy Sixberry ....G....... 315 265-6211
Potsdam (G-12940)

Rli Schlgel Specialty Pdts LLC ....F....... 585 627-5919
Rochester (G-13675)

Round Top Knit & Screening ....G....... 518 622-3600
Round Top (G-14064)

Sellco Industries Inc ....E....... 607 756-7594
Cortland (G-3788)

Solidus Industries Inc ....D....... 607 749-4540
Homer (G-6067)

Starline Usa Inc ....C....... 716 773-0100
Grand Island (G-5344)

Todd Walbridge ....G....... 585 254-3018
Rochester (G-13768)

U All Inc ....E....... 518 438-2558
Albany (G-138)

Viewsport International Inc ....F....... 585 259-1562
Penfield (G-12576)

Wicked Smart LLC ....F....... 518 459-2855
Watervliet (G-15612)

2397 Schiffli Machine Embroideries

American Images Inc ....F....... 716 825-8888
Buffalo (G-2631)

Rmb Embroidery Service ....G....... 585 271-5560
Rochester (G-13676)

2399 Fabricated Textile Prdts, NEC

AAa Amercn Flag Dctg Co Inc ....G....... 212 279-3524
New York (G-8423)

Accel Printing & Graphics ....G....... 914 241-3369
Mount Kisco (G-8086)

Ace Banner & Flag Company ....F....... 212 620-9111
New York (G-8445)

Arista Flag Corporation ....F....... 845 246-7700
Saugerties (G-14197)

Automtve Uphl Cnvertible Tops ....G....... 914 961-4242
Tuckahoe (G-15203)

Baldwin Ribbon & Stamping Corp ....F....... 718 335-6700
Woodside (G-16196)

Becks Classic Mfg Inc ....D....... 631 435-3800
Brentwood (G-1116)

▲ Big Apple Sign Corp ....D....... 212 629-3650
New York (G-8785)

Big Apple Sign Corp ....E....... 631 342-0303
Islandia (G-6326)

Breton Industries Inc ....C....... 518 842-3030
Amsterdam (G-320)

City Signs Inc ....G....... 718 375-5933
Brooklyn (G-1667)

Dkm Sales LLC.....................................E....... 716 893-7777
Buffalo (G-2730)

Dream Green Productions ....G....... 917 267-8920
Warwick (G-15513)

▲ Eagle Regalia Co Inc ....F....... 845 425-2245
Spring Valley (G-14567)

Hampton Transport Inc ....E....... 631 716-4445
Coram (G-3693)

Jim Henson Company Inc ....E....... 212 794-2400
Long Island City (G-7253)

▲ Kamali Group Inc ....F....... 516 627-4000
Great Neck (G-5399)

Koring Bros Inc ....G....... 888 233-1292
New Rochelle (G-8346)

Kraus & Sons Inc ....F....... 212 620-0408
New York (G-10137)

Mc Coy Tops and Interiors Inc ....G....... 718 458-5800
Woodside (G-16212)

▲ National Flag & Display Co Inc ....E....... 212 228-6600
New York (G-10542)

National Parachute Industries ....E....... 908 782-1646
Palenville (G-12479)

Osprey Boat ....G....... 631 331-4153
Mount Sinai (G-8116)

▲ Penthouse Manufacturing Co Inc .....B....... 516 379-1300
Freeport (G-5014)

Regal Emblem Co Inc ....F....... 212 925-8833
New York (G-11001)

Saratoga Horseworks Ltd ....E....... 518 843-6756
Amsterdam (G-347)

Sellco Industries Inc ....E....... 607 756-7594
Cortland (G-3788)

▲ Sherwood Group Inc ....G....... 240 731-8573
New York (G-11212)

▲ Skd Tactical Inc ....E....... 845 897-2889
Highland Falls (G-5966)

Stonegate Stabless ....E....... 518 746-7133
Fort Edward (G-4944)

▲ Triple E Manufacturing ....F....... 716 761-6996
Sherman (G-14401)

Tulmar Manufacturing Inc ....G....... 315 393-7191
Ogdensburg (G-12212)

24 LUMBER AND WOOD PRODUCTS, EXCEPT FURNITURE

2411 Logging

3b Timber Company Inc ....F....... 315 942-6580
Boonville (G-1102)

Attica Package Company Inc ....F 585 591-0510
 Attica (G-456)
▼ B & B Forest Products Ltd ....F 518 622-0811
 Cairo (G-3063)
Baker Logging & Firewood ....G 585 374-5733
 Naples (G-8206)
Bart Ostrander Trckg Log Corp ....G 518 661-6535
 Mayfield (G-7681)
▲ C J Logging Equipment Inc ....E 315 942-5431
 Boonville (G-1106)
Central Timber Co Inc ....G 518 638-6338
 Granville (G-5348)
Chad Pierson ....G 518 251-0186
 Bakers Mills (G-529)
Chip It All Ltd ....G 631 473-2040
 Port Jefferson (G-12840)
Couture Timber Harvesting ....G 607 836-4719
 Mc Graw (G-7687)
Daniel & Lois Lyndaker Logging ....G 315 346-6527
 Castorland (G-3207)
Davis Logging & Lumber ....G 315 245-1040
 Camden (G-3100)
Decker Forest Products Inc ....G 607 563-2345
 Sidney (G-14433)
Donald Snyder Jr ....F 315 265-4485
 Potsdam (G-12936)
Ed Beach Forest Management ....G 607 538-1745
 Bloomville (G-952)
Finger Lakes Timber Co Inc ....G 585 346-2990
 Livonia (G-7054)
George Chilson Logging ....G 607 732-1558
 Elmira (G-4353)
GL & RL Logging Inc ....F 518 883-3936
 Broadalbin (G-1174)
Got Wood ....G 315 405-3384
 Constableville (G-3634)
Guldenschuh Logging & Lbr LLC ....G 585 538-4750
 Caledonia (G-3070)
Harris Logging Inc ....E 518 792-1083
 Queensbury (G-13042)
Homer Logging Contractor ....G 607 753-8553
 Homer (G-6065)
J & S Logging Inc ....E 315 262-2112
 South Colton (G-14503)
Kevin Regan Logging Ltd ....G 315 245-3890
 Camden (G-3103)
Klein & Sons Logging Inc ....F 845 292-6682
 Wht Sphr Spgs (G-16108)
Lizotte Logging Inc ....F 518 359-2200
 Tupper Lake (G-15210)
Lyndaker Timber Harvesting LLC ....F 315 346-1328
 Castorland (G-3208)
Matteson Logging Inc ....G 585 593-3037
 Wellsville (G-15672)
Mountain Forest Products Inc ....G 518 597-3674
 Crown Point (G-3810)
Murray Logging LLC ....G 518 834-7372
 Keeseville (G-6644)
Northern Timber Harvesting LLC ....F 585 233-7330
 Alfred Station (G-185)
Oak Valley Logging Inc ....G 518 622-8249
 Cairo (G-3067)
Paul J Mitchell Logging Inc ....E 518 359-7029
 Tupper Lake (G-15212)
Peters LLC ....G 607 637-5470
 Hancock (G-5538)
Richard Bauer Logging ....G 585 343-4149
 Alexander (G-179)
Richards Logging LLC ....F 518 359-2775
 Tupper Lake (G-15213)
Russell Bass ....F 607 637-5253
 Hancock (G-5539)
Schaefer Logging Inc ....F 607 467-4990
 Deposit (G-4003)
Seaway Timber Harvesting Inc ....D 315 769-5970
 Massena (G-7671)
Smoothbore International Inc ....G 315 754-8124
 Red Creek (G-13070)
Snyder Logging ....F 315 265-1462
 Potsdam (G-12941)
Tim Cretin Logging & Sawmill ....F 315 946-4476
 Lyons (G-7453)
Timothy L Simpson ....G 518 234-1401
 Sharon Springs (G-14384)
Tonche Timber LLC ....G 845 389-3489
 Amsterdam (G-348)
Van Cpeters Logging Inc ....G 607 637-3574
 Hancock (G-5540)
Wadsworth Logging Inc ....F 518 863-6870
 Gloversville (G-5298)

Westrock Container LLC ....D 518 842-2450
 Amsterdam (G-353)

2421 Saw & Planing Mills

A D Bowman & Son Lumber Co ....E 607 692-2595
 Castle Creek (G-3199)
Adams Lumber Co Inc ....F 716 358-2815
 Cattaraugus (G-3219)
Amish Structure ....F 607 257-1070
 Dryden (G-4036)
Angelica Forest Products Inc ....G 585 466-3205
 Angelica (G-356)
Axtell Bradtke Lumber Co ....F 607 265-3850
 Masonville (G-7583)
B & B Lumber Company Inc ....C 866 282-0582
 Jamesville (G-6555)
B & J Lumber Co Inc ....E 518 677-3845
 Cambridge (G-3091)
Bissel-Babcock Millwork Inc ....F 716 761-6976
 Sherman (G-14399)
Bono Sawdust Supply Co Inc ....G 718 446-1374
 Corona (G-3734)
Brookside Lumber Inc ....G 315 497-0937
 Moravia (G-8081)
Builders Firstsource Inc ....E 860 528-2293
 Middletown (G-7897)
Cannonsville Lumber Inc ....G 607 467-3380
 Deposit (G-3998)
Capital Sawmill Service ....G 518 479-0729
 Nassau (G-8212)
Carlson Wood Products Inc ....F 716 287-2923
 Sinclairville (G-14444)
Casters Custom Sawing ....G 315 387-5104
 Sandy Creek (G-14154)
Clements Burrville Sawmill ....G 315 782-4549
 Watertown (G-15565)
Cote Hardwood Products Inc ....F 607 898-5737
 Locke (G-7057)
▲ Curran Renewable Energy LLC ......E 315 769-2000
 Massena (G-7667)
Dansville Logging & Lumber ....E 585 335-5879
 Dansville (G-3818)
Dlr Enterprises LLC ....G 315 813-2911
 Sherrill (G-14403)
Donver Incorporated ....F 716 945-1910
 Kill Buck (G-6669)
Embassy Millwork Inc ....F 518 839-0965
 Amsterdam (G-326)
Farney Lumber Corporation ....F 315 346-6013
 Lowville (G-7415)
▼ Garden State Shavings Inc ....F 845 544-2835
 Warwick (G-15514)
◆ GM Palmer Inc ....F 585 492-2990
 Arcade (G-374)
Greene Lumber Co LP ....E 607 278-6101
 Davenport (G-3821)
Gutchess Freedom Inc ....D 716 492-2824
 Freedom (G-4974)
Gutchess Hardwoods Inc ....G 607 753-3393
 Cortland (G-3770)
◆ Gutchess Lumber Co Inc ....C 607 753-3393
 Cortland (G-3771)
Gutchess Lumber Co Inc ....E 716 492-2824
 Freedom (G-4975)
Hennig Custom Woodwork Corp ....G 516 536-3460
 Oceanside (G-12174)
◆ J & J Log & Lumber Corp ....D 845 832-6535
 Dover Plains (G-4032)
J A Yansick Lumber Co Inc ....E 585 492-4312
 Arcade (G-376)
L J Valente Inc ....G 518 674-3750
 Averill Park (G-508)
Machina Deus Lex Inc ....G 917 577-0972
 Jamaica (G-6455)
Mallery Lumber LLC ....G 607 637-2236
 Hancock (G-5537)
McDonough Hardwoods Ltd ....E 315 829-3449
 Vernon Center (G-15368)
Meltz Lumber Co of Mellenville ....E 518 672-7021
 Hudson (G-6170)
Mettowee Lumber & Plastics Co ....C 518 642-1100
 Granville (G-5352)
Mohawk Metal Mfg & Sls ....G 315 853-7663
 Westmoreland (G-15960)
One Tree Dist ....G 315 701-2924
 Syracuse (G-14955)
Owletts Saw Mills ....G 607 525-6340
 Woodhull (G-16189)
▼ PA Pellets LLC ....F 814 848-9970
 Pittsford (G-12654)

Pallets Inc ....E 518 747-4177
 Fort Edward (G-4941)
PDJ Inc ....E 315 655-8824
 Cazenovia (G-3232)
Petteys Lumber ....G 518 792-5943
 Fort Ann (G-4934)
Piccini Industries Ltd ....E 845 365-0614
 Orangeburg (G-12325)
Potter Lumber Co Inc ....F 716 373-1260
 Allegany (G-190)
Rudy Stempel & Family Sawmill ....G 518 872-0431
 East Berne (G-4098)
Russell Bass ....F 607 637-5253
 Hancock (G-5539)
S Donadic Inc ....D 718 361-9888
 Sunnyside (G-14774)
▼ Salamanca Lumber Company Inc ......E 716 945-4810
 Salamanca (G-14126)
Scotts Company LLC ....E 631 816-2831
 Yaphank (G-16269)
Sirianni Hardwoods Inc ....E 607 962-4688
 Painted Post (G-12476)
Spiegel Woodworks Inc ....F 845 336-8090
 Kingston (G-6710)
St Lawrence Lumber Inc ....G 315 649-2990
 Three Mile Bay (G-15072)
Swanson Lumber ....G 716 499-1726
 Gerry (G-5171)
Tri State Hardwoods Ltd ....G 845 687-7814
 Kingston (G-6716)
▲ Tri-State Brick & Stone NY Inc .....D 212 366-0300
 New York (G-11540)
Tupper Lake Hardwoods Inc ....E 518 359-8248
 Tupper Lake (G-15215)
Upstate Increte Incorporated ....G 585 254-2010
 Rochester (G-13788)
Wagner Hardwoods LLC ....C 607 594-3321
 Cayuta (G-3223)
Wagner Hardwoods LLC ....G 607 229-8198
 Friendship (G-5053)
▼ Wagner Millwork Inc ....D 607 687-5362
 Owego (G-12439)
Wagner Nineveh Inc ....G 607 693-2689
 Afton (G-8)
Weather Tight Exteriors ....G 631 375-5108
 Ridge (G-13135)
Wolski Wood Works Inc ....G 718 577-9816
 Flushing (G-4906)
Wyde Lumber ....F 845 513-5571
 Monticello (G-8073)

2426 Hardwood Dimension & Flooring Mills

A D Bowman & Son Lumber Co ....E 607 692-2595
 Castle Creek (G-3199)
◆ Artistic Frame Corp ....C 212 289-2100
 New York (G-8636)
B & B Lumber Company Inc ....C 866 282-0582
 Jamesville (G-6555)
Carlson Wood Products Inc ....F 716 287-2923
 Sinclairville (G-14444)
Clements Burrville Sawmill ....G 315 782-4549
 Watertown (G-15565)
Custom Woodwork Ltd ....F 631 727-5260
 Riverhead (G-13173)
Donver Incorporated ....F 716 945-1910
 Kill Buck (G-6669)
Essequattro USA Inc ....G 917 862-0005
 New York (G-9403)
Fibron Products Inc ....E 716 886-2378
 Buffalo (G-2752)
▼ Fitzpatrick and Weller Inc ....D 716 699-2393
 Ellicottville (G-4314)
Fountain Tile Outlet Inc ....E 718 927-4555
 Brooklyn (G-1862)
Guldenschuh Logging & Lbr LLC ....G 585 538-4750
 Caledonia (G-3070)
◆ Gutchess Lumber Co Inc ....C 607 753-3393
 Cortland (G-3771)
H B Millwork Inc ....E 631 289-8086
 Medford (G-7709)
Horizon Floors I LLC ....G 212 509-9686
 New York (G-9812)
◆ J & J Log & Lumber Corp ....D 845 832-6535
 Dover Plains (G-4032)
J A Yansick Lumber Co Inc ....E 585 492-4312
 Arcade (G-376)
Jim Quinn ....F 518 356-0398
 Schenectady (G-14282)
▲ Legno Veneto USA ....G 716 651-9169
 Depew (G-3986)

SIC

Madison & Dunn....G....585 563-7760
Rochester (G-13528)
Mason Carvings Inc....G....716 484-7884
Jamestown (G-6531)
◆ MP Caroll Inc....F....716 683-8520
Cheektowaga (G-3355)
North Hudson Woodcraft Corp....E....315 429-3105
Dolgeville (G-4024)
▼ Norton-Smith Hardwoods Inc....G....716 945-0346
Salamanca (G-14125)
Petteys Lumber....G....518 792-5943
Fort Ann (G-4934)
Potter Lumber Co Inc....E....716 373-1260
Allegany (G-190)
Premier Hardwood Products Inc....E....315 492-1786
Jamesville (G-6561)
Randolph Dimension Corporation....F....716 358-6901
Randolph (G-13064)
Revival Industries Inc....F....315 868-1085
Ilion (G-6282)
S Donadic Inc....D....718 361-9888
Sunnyside (G-14774)
▲ Tectonic Flooring USA LLC....G....212 686-2700
New York (G-11448)
Tupper Lake Hardwoods Inc....E....518 359-8248
Tupper Lake (G-15215)
Vitobob Furniture Inc....G....516 676-1696
Long Island City (G-7396)
▼ Wagner Millwork Inc....D....607 687-5362
Owego (G-12439)

2429 Special Prdt Sawmills, NEC

RWS Manufacturing Inc....G....518 361-1657
Queensbury (G-13054)

2431 Millwork

A Losee & Sons....G....516 676-3060
Glen Cove (G-5186)
A W Hamel Stair Mfg Inc....F....518 346-3031
Schenectady (G-14244)
Ace Fire Door Corp....E....718 901-0001
Bronx (G-1194)
Adams Interior Fabrications....F....631 249-8282
Massapequa (G-7644)
Adirondack Stairs Inc....F....845 246-2525
Saugerties (G-14196)
▲ Adriatic Wood Products Inc....E....718 922-4621
Brooklyn (G-1462)
American Wood Column Corp....G....718 782-3163
Brooklyn (G-1503)
Amstutze Woodworking....G....518 946-8206
Upper Jay (G-15235)
Antique Lumber Modrn Mllwk LLC....G....631 726-7026
Wainscott (G-15454)
Apollo Windows & Doors Inc....F....718 386-3326
Brooklyn (G-1518)
Arbr Studios LLC....F....585 254-7607
Rochester (G-13242)
Architctral Mllwk Installation....E....631 499-0755
East Northport (G-4142)
Architectural Enhancements Inc....F....845 343-9663
Middletown (G-7893)
Armada New York LLC....F....718 852-8105
Brooklyn (G-1531)
Artistic Iron Works Inc....G....631 665-4285
Bay Shore (G-652)
Atlantic Stairs Corp....G....718 417-8818
Brooklyn (G-1548)
▲ Attica Millwork Inc....F....585 591-2333
Attica (G-455)
Auburn Custom Millwork Inc....G....315 253-3843
Auburn (G-460)
Bator Bintor Inc....F....347 546-6503
Brooklyn (G-1567)
▲ Bauerschmidt & Sons Inc....D....718 528-3500
Jamaica (G-6429)
Beaver Creek Industries Inc....G....607 545-6382
Canaseraga (G-3147)
Bennett Stair Company Inc....G....518 384-1554
Ballston Lake (G-558)
Bloch Industries LLC....D....585 334-9600
Rochester (G-13272)
Blooming Grove Stair Co....G....845 783-4245
Monroe (G-8016)
Blooming Grove Stair Co....G....845 791-4016
Monticello (G-8069)
BNC Innovative Woodworking....F....718 277-2800
Brooklyn (G-1598)
Braga Woodworks....G....845 342-4636
Middletown (G-7895)
Brauen Constrution....G....585 492-0042
Arcade (G-371)
Broadway Neon Sign Corp....F....908 241-4177
Ronkonkoma (G-13918)
▲ Burt Millwork Corporation....E....718 257-4601
Albertson (G-146)
Capital District Stairs Inc....G....518 383-2449
Halfmoon (G-5491)
Capital Kit Cab & Door Mfrs....G....718 886-0303
College Point (G-3539)
Carob Industries Inc....F....631 225-0900
Lindenhurst (G-6945)
◆ Case Group LLC....E....518 720-3100
Green Island (G-5433)
Champion Millwork Inc....E....315 463-0711
Syracuse (G-14847)
Chautauqua Woods Corporation....E....716 366-3808
Dunkirk (G-4051)
Christiana Millwork Inc....E....315 492-9099
Jamesville (G-6557)
▲ City Store Gates Mfg Corp....E....718 939-9700
College Point (G-3540)
Clearwood Custom Carpentry and....E....315 432-8422
East Syracuse (G-4204)
Columbus Woodworking Inc....G....607 674-4546
Sherburne (G-14389)
Concepts In Wood of CNY....E....315 463-8084
Syracuse (G-14858)
Cousins Furniture & Hm Imprvs....E....631 254-3752
Deer Park (G-3854)
Craftsmen Woodworkers Ltd....E....718 326-3350
Maspeth (G-7601)
Creative Laminates Inc....F....315 463-7580
Syracuse (G-14866)
Crown Mill Work Corp....G....845 371-2200
Nanuet (G-8199)
Crown Woodworking Corp....G....718 974-6415
Brooklyn (G-1702)
Cuan Corp....G....917 579-3774
Roslyn Heights (G-14049)
Cuccio-Zanetti Inc....G....518 587-1363
Middle Grove (G-7872)
▲ Custom Door & Mirror Inc....E....631 414-7725
Farmingdale (G-4609)
Custom Stair & Millwork Co....G....315 839-5793
Sauquoit (G-14218)
Custom Wood Inc....G....718 927-4700
Brooklyn (G-1713)
D K P Wood Railings & Stairs....F....631 665-8656
Bay Shore (G-669)
D R Cornue Woodworks....G....315 655-9463
Cazenovia (G-3226)
▲ DAngelo Home Collections Inc....G....917 267-8920
Warwick (G-15511)
Dbs Interiors Corp....F....631 491-3013
West Babylon (G-15706)
DC Contracting & Building Corp....F....631 385-1117
Huntington Station (G-6244)
Deer Pk Stair Bldg Mllwk Inc....E....631 363-5000
Blue Point (G-956)
Deerfield Millwork Inc....F....631 726-9663
Water Mill (G-15529)
Dimaio Millwork Corporation....E....914 476-1937
Yonkers (G-16301)
▲ Dorm Company Corporation....G....502 551-6195
Cheektowaga (G-3345)
Duncan & Son Carpentry Inc....E....914 664-4311
Mount Vernon (G-8139)
Ecker Window Corp....D....914 776-0000
Yonkers (G-16304)
Ed Negron Fine Woodworking....G....718 246-1016
Brooklyn (G-1781)
Efj Inc....D....518 234-4799
Cobleskill (G-3499)
EM Pfaff & Son Inc....F....607 739-3691
Horseheads (G-6121)
Empire Building Products Inc....G....518 695-6094
Schuylerville (G-14323)
▲ Fancy Windows & Doors Mfg Corp....G....718 366-7800
Brooklyn (G-1832)
Fire Island Sea Clam Co Inc....G....631 589-2199
West Sayville (G-15840)
Five Star Millwork LLC....F....845 920-0247
Pearl River (G-12530)
Fontrick Door Inc....E....585 345-6032
Batavia (G-614)
Grace Ryan & Magnus Mllwk LLC....D....914 665-0902
Mount Vernon (G-8144)
◆ Griffon Corporation....E....212 957-5000
New York (G-9676)
▲ Gw Manufacturing....E....718 386-8078
Poughkeepsie (G-12960)
▲ H Arnold Wood Turning Inc....E....914 381-0801
Tarrytown (G-15045)
H B Millwork Inc....E....631 289-8086
Medford (G-7709)
H B Millwork Inc....G....631 924-4195
Yaphank (G-16263)
Highland Organization Corp....E....631 991-3240
Deer Park (G-3880)
Hulley Holding Company Inc....F....716 332-3982
Kenmore (G-6653)
Humboldt Woodworking....G....718 707-0022
Long Island City (G-7244)
I Meglio Corp....E....631 617-6900
Hauppauge (G-5674)
▲ Ideal Wood Products Inc....E....315 823-1124
Little Falls (G-6989)
Ignelzi Interiors Inc....E....718 464-0279
Queens Village (G-13021)
Inform Studio Inc....F....718 401-6149
Bronx (G-1282)
Island Stairs Corp....G....347 645-0560
Staten Island (G-14666)
Island Street Lumber Co Inc....G....716 692-4127
North Tonawanda (G-12072)
J Percoco Industries Inc....G....631 312-4572
Bohemia (G-1025)
Jacobs Woodworking LLC....G....315 427-8999
Syracuse (G-14915)
James King Woodworking Inc....G....518 761-6091
Queensbury (G-13044)
Jays Furniture Products Inc....E....716 876-8854
Buffalo (G-2816)
JEm Wdwkg & Cabinets Inc....F....518 828-5361
Hudson (G-6165)
John Langenbacher Co Inc....E....718 328-0141
Bronx (G-1288)
KB Millwork Inc....G....516 280-2183
Levittown (G-6916)
Kelly Window Systems Inc....E....631 420-8500
Farmingdale (G-4664)
Kng Construction Co Inc....F....212 595-1451
Warwick (G-15517)
Living Doors Inc....F....631 924-5393
Medford (G-7717)
Mack Wood Working....G....845 657-6625
Shokan (G-14429)
Marretti USA Inc....G....212 255-5565
New York (G-10373)
Mason Woodworks LLC....G....917 363-7052
Brooklyn (G-2121)
Masonite International Corp....F....607 775-0615
Binghamton (G-895)
Medina Millworks LLC....G....585 798-2969
Medina (G-7740)
Mensch Mill & Lumber Corp....E....718 359-7500
Bronx (G-1309)
Mestel Brothers Stairs & Rails....C....516 496-4127
Syosset (G-14794)
Metalocke Industries Inc....G....718 267-9200
Woodside (G-16213)
Michael Bernstein Design Assoc....E....718 456-9277
Brooklyn (G-2150)
Michbi Doors Inc....D....631 231-9050
Farmingdale (G-4683)
Millco Woodworking LLC....F....585 526-6844
Hall (G-5500)
▲ Miller Blaker Inc....D....718 665-0500
Bronx (G-1315)
Millwright Wdwrk Installetion....E....631 587-2635
West Babylon (G-15732)
Mind Designs Inc....G....631 563-3644
Farmingville (G-4782)
Monroe Stair Products Inc....E....845 783-4245
Monroe (G-8028)
Monroe Stair Products Inc....G....845 791-4016
Monticello (G-8071)
▲ Nordic Interior Inc....C....718 456-7000
Brooklyn (G-2219)
Northern Forest Pdts Co Inc....G....315 942-6955
Boonville (G-1107)
Ohana Metal & Iron Works Inc....F....845 344-7520
Montgomery (G-8063)
Old Souls Inc....G....845 809-5886
Cold Spring (G-3522)
Old World Mouldings Inc....G....631 563-8660
Bohemia (G-1057)
Overhead Door Corporation....D....518 828-7652
Hudson (G-6173)

P & B Woodworking Inc .... F 845 744-2508
Pine Bush *(G-12626)*

P H Custom Woodworking Corp .... E 917 801-1444
Bronx *(G-1330)*

Paul David Enterprises Inc .... G 646 667-5530
New York *(G-10770)*

Pella Corporation .... B 607 223-2023
Johnson City *(G-6607)*

Pella Corporation .... B 516 385-3622
Albertson *(G-150)*

Pella Corporation .... B 516 385-3622
Albertson *(G-151)*

Pella Corporation .... C 631 208-0710
Calverton *(G-3083)*

Peter Productions Devivi Inc .... F 315 568-8484
Waterloo *(G-15556)*

▲ Pgs Millwork Inc .... D 518 828-2608
Hudson *(G-6175)*

Piccini Industries Ltd .... E 845 365-0614
Orangeburg *(G-12325)*

Professional Cab Detailing Co .... F 845 436-7282
Woodridge *(G-16194)*

Props Displays & Interiors .... F 212 620-3840
New York *(G-10915)*

Quaker Millwork & Lumber Inc .... E 716 662-3388
Orchard Park *(G-12375)*

▲ Quality Millwork Corp .... E 718 892-2250
Bronx *(G-1348)*

Quality Stair Builders Inc .... F 631 694-0711
Farmingdale *(G-4719)*

Quality Woodworking Corp .... F 718 875-3437
Brooklyn *(G-2313)*

R C Henderson Stair Builders .... F 516 876-9898
Westbury *(G-15922)*

Ragnatelli Inc .... E 718 765-4050
Brooklyn *(G-2321)*

Randolph Dimension Corporation .... F 716 358-6901
Randolph *(G-13064)*

RB Woodcraft Inc .... E 315 474-2429
Syracuse *(G-14975)*

Red Tail Moulding & Mllwk LLC .... G 516 852-4613
Center Moriches *(G-3247)*

Richard Anthony Corp .... E 914 922-7141
Yorktown Heights *(G-16371)*

Rj Millworkers Inc .... E 607 433-0525
Oneonta *(G-12281)*

Rochester Colonial Mfg Corp .... D 585 254-8191
Rochester *(G-13686)*

Rochester Lumber Company .... E 585 924-7171
Farmington *(G-4778)*

Rockaway Stairs Ltd .... G 718 945-0047
Far Rockaway *(G-4567)*

Roode Hoek & Co Inc .... F 718 522-5921
Brooklyn *(G-2354)*

Royal Windows Mfg Corp .... E 631 435-8888
Bay Shore *(G-710)*

Royalton Millwork & Design .... G 716 439-4092
Lockport *(G-7104)*

S Donadic Inc .... D 718 361-9888
Sunnyside *(G-14774)*

S R Sloan Inc .... D 315 736-7730
Whitesboro *(G-16082)*

▲ Scanga Woodworking Corp .... E 845 265-9115
Cold Spring *(G-3525)*

Second Generation Wood Stairs .... F 718 370-0085
Staten Island *(G-14708)*

Select Interior Door Ltd .... E 585 535-9900
North Java *(G-12032)*

Shawmut Woodworking & Sup Inc .... C 212 920-8900
New York *(G-11209)*

Specialty Services .... G 585 728-5650
Wayland *(G-15627)*

Spiegel Woodworks Inc .... F 845 336-8090
Kingston *(G-6710)*

Stairworld Inc .... G 718 441-9722
Fresh Meadows *(G-5046)*

Staten Island Stair Inc .... G 718 317-9276
Staten Island *(G-14714)*

Stealth Archtctral Windows Inc .... F 718 821-6666
Brooklyn *(G-2454)*

Super Millwork Inc .... G 631 293-5025
Melville *(G-7825)*

Syracuse Industrial Sls Co Ltd .... F 315 478-5751
Syracuse *(G-15007)*

TDS Woodworking Inc .... F 718 442-5298
Staten Island *(G-14719)*

Tiedemann Waldemar Inc .... F 716 875-5665
Buffalo *(G-3010)*

Truth Hardware Corporation .... G 585 627-5964
Rochester *(G-13777)*

Unadilla Silo Company Inc .... D 607 369-9341
Sidney *(G-14438)*

Unicenter Millwork Inc .... G 716 741-8201
Clarence Center *(G-3450)*

United Rockland Holding Co Inc .... E 845 357-1900
Suffern *(G-14768)*

Universal Custom Millwork Inc .... D 518 330-6622
Amsterdam *(G-351)*

Upbeat Upholstery & Design LLC .... G 347 480-3980
Brooklyn *(G-2547)*

▲ Upstate Door Inc .... E 585 786-3880
Warsaw *(G-15509)*

Vander Heyden Woodworking .... G 212 242-0525
New York *(G-11639)*

▼ Wagner Millwork Inc .... D 607 687-5362
Owego *(G-12439)*

Wolfe Lumber Mill Inc .... G 716 772-7750
Gasport *(G-5140)*

Wood Innovations of Suffolk .... G 631 698-2345
Oceanside *(G-12198)*

Wood Talk .... G 631 940-3085
Bay Shore *(G-725)*

▲ Woodworks .... F 845 677-3960
Salt Point *(G-14135)*

Xylon Industries Inc .... G 631 293-4717
Farmingdale *(G-4766)*

Yesteryears Vintage Doors LLC .... G 315 324-5250
Hammond *(G-5528)*

Zanzano Woodworking Inc .... F 914 725-6025
Scarsdale *(G-14243)*

2434 Wood Kitchen Cabinets

Able Kitchen .... F 877 268-1264
Cedarhurst *(G-3238)*

Affordble Gran Cbntry Outl Inc .... F 845 564-0500
Newburgh *(G-11857)*

Aka Enterprises .... E 716 474-4579
Wyoming *(G-16249)*

▲ Aki Cabinets Inc .... E 718 721-2541
Astoria *(G-413)*

American Classic Kitchens Inc .... G 212 838-9308
New York *(G-8547)*

Andike Millwork Inc .... G 718 894-1796
Maspeth *(G-7590)*

▲ Artone LLC .... D 716 664-2232
Jamestown *(G-6495)*

Auburn-Watson Corp .... F 716 876-8000
Depew *(G-3970)*

Aucapina Cabinets Inc .... G 718 609-9054
Maspeth *(G-7594)*

▲ Bauerschmidt & Sons Inc .... D 718 528-3500
Jamaica *(G-6429)*

Bloch Industries LLC .... D 585 334-9600
Rochester *(G-13272)*

Cabinet Factory Inc .... F 718 351-8922
Staten Island *(G-14634)*

Cabinet Shapes Corp .... F 718 784-6255
Long Island City *(G-7182)*

Cabinetry By Tbr Inc .... G 516 365-8500
Manhasset *(G-7531)*

Cabinets By Stanley Inc .... G 718 222-5861
Brooklyn *(G-1639)*

Cambridge Kitchens Mfg Inc .... F 516 935-5100
Hicksville *(G-5891)*

Candlelight Cabinetry Inc .... C 716 434-2114
Lockport *(G-7063)*

Capital Kit Cab & Door Mfrs .... G 718 886-0303
College Point *(G-3539)*

Carefree Kitchens Inc .... G 631 567-2120
Holbrook *(G-5988)*

Carlos & Alex Atelier Inc .... E 718 441-8911
Richmond Hill *(G-13111)*

Casa Collection Inc .... G 718 694-0272
Brooklyn *(G-1653)*

▲ Catskill Craftsmen Inc .... D 607 652-7321
Stamford *(G-14607)*

Central Kitchen Corp .... F 631 283-1029
Southampton *(G-14528)*

Chicone Builders LLC .... G 607 535-6540
Montour Falls *(G-8074)*

Classic Cabinets .... F 845 357-4331
Suffern *(G-14759)*

Clearwood Custom Carpentry and .... E 315 432-8422
East Syracuse *(G-4204)*

Cleary Custom Cabinets Inc .... F 516 939-2475
Hicksville *(G-5895)*

Columbia Cabinets LLC .... G 212 972-7550
Armonk *(G-396)*

Columbia Cabinets LLC .... F 518 283-1700
Saratoga Springs *(G-14170)*

▼ Craft Custom Woodwork Co Inc .... F 718 821-2162
Maspeth *(G-7600)*

Creative Stone & Cabinets Corp .... G 631 772-6548
Selden *(G-14351)*

Custom CAS Inc .... E 718 726-3575
Long Island City *(G-7195)*

Custom Woodcraft LLC .... F 315 843-4234
Munnsville *(G-8195)*

D & M Custom Cabinets Inc .... F 516 678-2818
Oceanside *(G-12168)*

Dak Mica and Wood Products .... G 631 467-0749
Ronkonkoma *(G-13929)*

Dbs Interiors Corp .... F 631 491-3013
West Babylon *(G-15706)*

Deakon Homes and Interiors .... F 518 271-0342
Troy *(G-15165)*

Di Fiore and Sons Custom Wdwkg .... G 718 278-1663
Long Island City *(G-7201)*

East End Country Kitchens Inc .... F 631 727-2258
Calverton *(G-3080)*

EC Wood & Company Inc .... F 718 388-2287
Deer Park *(G-3868)*

EM Pfaff & Son Inc .... F 607 739-3691
Horseheads *(G-6121)*

Enterprise Wood Products Inc .... F 718 853-9243
Brooklyn *(G-1806)*

Euro Woodworking Inc .... G 718 246-9172
Brooklyn *(G-1817)*

Fina Cabinet Corp .... G 718 409-2900
Mount Vernon *(G-8141)*

Finger Lkes Stirs Cabinets LLC .... G 315 638-3150
Baldwinsville *(G-547)*

Fra-Rik Formica Fabg Co Inc .... G 718 597-3335
Bronx *(G-1262)*

▲ Glissade New York LLC .... E 631 756-4800
Farmingdale *(G-4638)*

Greenway Cabinetry Inc .... F 516 877-0009
Williston Park *(G-16147)*

Hearth Cabinets and More Ltd .... G 315 641-1197
Liverpool *(G-7011)*

Home Ideal Inc .... G 718 762-8998
Flushing *(G-4860)*

Huntington Woodworking Inc .... G 631 271-7897
Northport *(G-12105)*

Ignelzi Interiors Inc .... E 718 464-0279
Queens Village *(G-13021)*

J Percoco Industries Inc .... G 631 312-4572
Bohemia *(G-1025)*

Jordache Woodworking Corp .... F 718 349-3373
Brooklyn *(G-1999)*

K-Binet Inc .... G 845 348-1149
Blauvelt *(G-929)*

▲ Kw Distributors Group Inc .... F 718 843-3500
Ozone Park *(G-12465)*

Longo Commercial Cabinets Inc .... E 631 225-4290
Lindenhurst *(G-6956)*

Lyn Jo Kitchens Inc .... G 718 336-6060
Brooklyn *(G-2089)*

Maple Tree Kitchen & Bath Inc .... F 845 236-3660
Marlboro *(G-7581)*

▲ Material Process Systems Inc .... F 718 302-3081
Brooklyn *(G-2124)*

Matteo & Antonio Bartolotta .... F 315 252-2220
Auburn *(G-485)*

McGraw Wood Products LLC .... E 607 836-6465
Mc Graw *(G-7689)*

Methods Tooling & Mfg Inc .... E 845 246-7100
Mount Marion *(G-8111)*

▲ Metro Kitchens Corp .... F 718 434-1166
Brooklyn *(G-2147)*

Michael Bernstein Design Assoc .... E 718 456-9277
Brooklyn *(G-2150)*

Michael P Mmarr .... G 315 623-9380
Constantia *(G-3636)*

Millco Woodworking LLC .... F 585 526-6844
Hall *(G-5500)*

Modern Cabinet Company Inc .... E 845 473-4900
Poughkeepsie *(G-12971)*

Mostly Mica Inc .... G 631 586-4200
Bay Shore *(G-694)*

▲ N Y Elli Design Corp .... F 718 228-0014
Ridgewood *(G-13152)*

Nagad Cabinets Inc .... G 718 382-7200
Brooklyn *(G-2185)*

Neo Cabinetry LLC .... F 718 403-0456
Brooklyn *(G-2196)*

▲ New York Vanity and Mfg Co .... E 718 417-1010
Freeport *(G-5010)*

Nexis 3 LLC .... E 585 285-4120
Rochester *(G-13576)*

S
I
C

NY Cabinet Factory Inc .... F 718 256-6541
  Brooklyn *(G-2224)*
Old Souls Inc .... G 845 809-5886
  Cold Spring *(G-3522)*
▲ Pgs Millwork Inc .... D 518 828-2608
  Hudson *(G-6175)*
Piccini Industries Ltd .... E 845 365-0614
  Orangeburg *(G-12325)*
Precision Built Tops LLC .... G 607 336-5417
  Norwich *(G-12126)*
Precision Dental Cabinets Inc ...... F 631 543-3870
  Smithtown *(G-14485)*
Premier Woodcraft Ltd .... E 610 383-6624
  White Plains *(G-16055)*
Premium Woodworking LLC .... G 631 485-3133
  West Babylon *(G-15738)*
R & M Thermofoil Doors Inc .... G 718 206-4991
  Jamaica *(G-6468)*
Red White & Blue Entps Corp ...... G 718 565-8080
  Woodside *(G-16223)*
Ribble Lumber Inc .... G 315 536-6221
  Penn Yan *(G-12592)*
Royal Custom Cabinets .... G 315 376-6042
  Lowville *(G-7421)*
S & V Custom Furniture Mfg .... F 516 746-8299
  Mineola *(G-7999)*
S Donadic Inc .... D 718 361-9888
  Sunnyside *(G-14774)*
▲ Salko Kitchens Inc .... F 845 565-4420
  New Windsor *(G-8381)*
Salmon Crek Cabinetry Inc .... E 315 589-5419
  Williamson *(G-16112)*
Serway Bros Inc .... G 315 337-0601
  Rome *(G-13872)*
Silva Cabinetry Inc .... E 914 737-7697
  Buchanan *(G-2610)*
Skyline Custom Cabinetry Inc ...... G 631 393-2983
  Farmingdale *(G-4733)*
▲ Stone Expo & Cabinetry LLC ..... F 516 292-2988
  West Hempstead *(G-15780)*
Tristate Contract Sales LLC .... G 845 782-2614
  Chester *(G-3392)*
Upbeat Upholstery & Design LLC ... G 347 480-3980
  Brooklyn *(G-2547)*
Upstate Cabinet Company Inc ...... F 585 429-5090
  Rochester *(G-13787)*
Viola Cabinet Corporation .... G 716 284-6327
  Niagara Falls *(G-11989)*
▲ W Designe Inc .... E 914 736-1058
  Peekskill *(G-12559)*
White House Cabinet Shop LLC ..... G 607 674-9358
  Sherburne *(G-14397)*
William Brooks Woodworking .... F 718 495-9767
  Brooklyn *(G-2585)*
▲ Win Wood Cabinetry Inc .... G 516 304-2216
  Greenvale *(G-5466)*
Wood Etc Inc .... F 315 484-9663
  Syracuse *(G-15030)*
Yonkers Cabinet Inc .... G 914 668-2133
  Yonkers *(G-16359)*
Your Furniture Designers Inc .... G 845 947-3046
  West Haverstraw *(G-15765)*
Your Way Custom Cabinets Inc ..... G 914 371-1870
  Mount Vernon *(G-8192)*

2435 Hardwood Veneer & Plywood

Geonex International Corp .... G 212 473-4555
  New York *(G-9599)*
Kings Quartet Corp .... G 845 986-9090
  Warwick *(G-15516)*
▲ Veneer One Inc .... E 516 536-6480
  Oceanside *(G-12196)*

2436 Softwood Veneer & Plywood

H B Millwork Inc .... E 631 289-8086
  Medford *(G-7709)*
Stone Boss Industries Inc .... F 718 278-2677
  Woodside *(G-16229)*

2439 Structural Wood Members, NEC

Architctral Mllwk Installation ...... E 631 499-0755
  East Northport *(G-4142)*
Empire Building Products Inc .... G 518 695-6094
  Schuylerville *(G-14323)*
Faulkner Truss Company Inc .... G 315 536-8894
  Dresden *(G-4035)*
Harvest Homes Inc .... E 518 895-2341
  Delanson *(G-3960)*
New England Barns Inc .... E 631 445-1461
  Southold *(G-14545)*

Pdj Components Inc .... E 845 469-9191
  Chester *(G-3382)*
Proof Industries Inc .... G 631 694-7663
  Farmingdale *(G-4717)*
Rochester Lumber Company .... E 585 924-7171
  Farmington *(G-4778)*
S R Sloan Inc .... D 315 736-7730
  Whitesboro *(G-16082)*
Steele Truss Company Inc .... E 518 562-4663
  Plattsburgh *(G-12780)*
Stephenson Lumber Company Inc ... E 518 548-7521
  Speculator *(G-14548)*
Structural Wood Corporation .... E 315 388-4442
  Waddington *(G-15447)*
Timber Frames Inc .... E 585 374-6405
  Canandaigua *(G-3144)*
Ufp New York LLC .... E 716 496-5484
  Chaffee *(G-3308)*
Ufp New York LLC .... E 518 828-2888
  Hudson *(G-6182)*
Ufp New York LLC .... E 315 253-2758
  Auburn *(G-501)*
Ufp New York LLC .... E 607 563-1556
  Sidney *(G-14437)*
Unadilla Silo Company Inc .... D 607 369-9341
  Sidney *(G-14438)*

2441 Wood Boxes

Abbot & Abbot Box Corp .... F 888 930-5972
  Long Island City *(G-7143)*
Bragley Mfg Co Inc .... E 718 622-7469
  Brooklyn *(G-1605)*
Bristol Boarding Inc .... G 585 271-7860
  Rochester *(G-13283)*
Falvo Manufacturing Co Inc .... F 315 724-7925
  Utica *(G-15261)*
Great Lakes Specialites .... E 716 672-4622
  Fredonia *(G-4970)*
M &L Industry of NY Inc .... G 845 827-6255
  Highland Mills *(G-5968)*
McGraw Wood Products LLC .... E 607 836-6465
  Mc Graw *(G-7689)*
McIntosh Box & Pallet Co Inc ...... F 315 789-8750
  Geneva *(G-5159)*
McIntosh Box & Pallet Co Inc ...... D 315 675-8511
  Bernhards Bay *(G-826)*
McIntosh Box & Pallet Co Inc ...... E 315 446-9350
  Rome *(G-13855)*
McNeilly Wood Products Inc .... E 845 457-9651
  Campbell Hall *(G-3118)*
Philpac Corporation .... E 716 875-8005
  Buffalo *(G-2917)*
Reuter Pallet Pkg Sys Inc .... G 845 457-9937
  Montgomery *(G-8066)*
Technical Packaging Inc .... F 516 223-2300
  Baldwin *(G-537)*

2448 Wood Pallets & Skids

219 South West .... G 315 474-2065
  Syracuse *(G-14807)*
A D Bowman & Son Lumber Co ..... E 607 692-2595
  Castle Creek *(G-3199)*
Abbot & Abbot Box Corp .... F 888 930-5972
  Long Island City *(G-7143)*
▲ Airline Container Services .... G 516 371-4125
  Lido Beach *(G-6927)*
B & B Lumber Company Inc .... C 866 282-0582
  Jamesville *(G-6555)*
B&B Albany Pallet Company LLC ... G 315 492-1786
  Jamesville *(G-6556)*
Berry Industrial Group Inc .... G 845 353-8338
  Nyack *(G-12137)*
Best Pallet & Crate LLC .... E 518 438-2945
  Albany *(G-49)*
CDF Indstrial Pckg Sltions Inc ...... F 716 672-2984
  Fredonia *(G-4968)*
Clements Burrville Sawmill .... G 315 782-4549
  Watertown *(G-15565)*
▼ Concord Express Cargo Inc .... G 718 276-7200
  Jamaica *(G-6437)*
Custom Shipping Products Inc ...... F 716 355-4437
  Clymer *(G-3496)*
Dimensional Mills Inc .... G 518 746-1047
  Hudson Falls *(G-6185)*
Dwa Pallet Inc .... G 518 746-1047
  Hudson Falls *(G-6186)*
Essex Box & Pallet Co Inc .... E 518 834-7279
  Keeseville *(G-6641)*
Four-Way Pallet Corp .... E 631 351-3401
  Huntington Station *(G-6247)*

G & H Wood Products LLC .... F 716 372-0341
  Olean *(G-12236)*
Great Lakes Specialites .... E 716 672-4622
  Fredonia *(G-4970)*
Just Wood Pallets Inc .... G 718 644-7013
  New Windsor *(G-8370)*
Lindley Wood Works Inc .... E 607 523-7786
  Lindley *(G-6986)*
McIntosh Box & Pallet Co Inc ...... D 315 675-8511
  Bernhards Bay *(G-826)*
McIntosh Box & Pallet Co Inc ...... E 315 789-8750
  Geneva *(G-5159)*
McIntosh Box & Pallet Co Inc ...... E 315 446-9350
  Rome *(G-13855)*
McNeilly Wood Products Inc .... E 845 457-9651
  Campbell Hall *(G-3118)*
Nefab Packaging North East LLC ... E 518 346-9105
  Scotia *(G-14334)*
Neville Mfg Svc & Dist Inc .... E 716 834-3038
  Cheektowaga *(G-3357)*
North Shore Pallet Inc .... G 631 673-4700
  Huntington Station *(G-6256)*
Northeast Pallet & Cont Co Inc ..... F 518 271-0535
  Troy *(G-15176)*
Ongweoweh Corp .... D 607 266-7070
  Ithaca *(G-6403)*
Orleans Pallet Company Inc .... F 585 589-0781
  Albion *(G-158)*
Pallet Division Inc .... G 585 328-3780
  Rochester *(G-13606)*
Pallet Services Inc .... C 716 873-7700
  Clarence *(G-3438)*
Pallet Services Inc .... E 585 647-4020
  Rochester *(G-13607)*
Pallets Inc .... E 518 747-4177
  Fort Edward *(G-4941)*
Pallets R US Inc .... E 631 758-2360
  Bellport *(G-806)*
Paul Bunyan Products Inc .... E 315 696-6164
  Cortland *(G-3782)*
Peco Pallet Inc .... E 914 376-5444
  Irvington *(G-6313)*
Peter C Herman Inc .... E 315 926-4100
  Marion *(G-7573)*
Pooran Pallet Inc .... G 718 938-7970
  Bronx *(G-1340)*
Reuter Pallet Pkg Sys Inc .... G 845 457-9937
  Montgomery *(G-8066)*
Sanjay Pallets Inc .... G 347 590-2485
  Bronx *(G-1359)*
▼ Sg Blocks Inc .... F 646 240-4235
  Brooklyn *(G-2399)*
Steven Coffey Pallet S Inc .... G 585 261-6783
  Rochester *(G-13747)*
Taylor Brothers Inc .... F 607 625-2828
  Apalachin *(G-362)*
Vansantis Development Inc .... E 315 461-0113
  Liverpool *(G-7046)*
Wolfe Lumber Mill Inc .... G 716 772-7750
  Gasport *(G-5140)*

2449 Wood Containers, NEC

Abbot & Abbot Box Corp .... F 888 930-5972
  Long Island City *(G-7143)*
David Isseks & Sons Inc .... E 212 966-8694
  New York *(G-9179)*
Essex Box & Pallet Co Inc .... E 518 834-7279
  Keeseville *(G-6641)*
Great Lakes Specialites .... E 716 672-4622
  Fredonia *(G-4970)*
Hood Industries Inc .... F 716 836-0301
  Buffalo *(G-2800)*
J & M Packaging Inc .... F 631 608-3069
  Hauppauge *(G-5679)*
Northeast Pallet & Cont Co Inc ..... F 518 271-0535
  Troy *(G-15176)*
Pluribus Products Inc .... E 718 852-1614
  Bayville *(G-747)*
R D A Container Corporation .... E 585 247-2323
  Gates *(G-5142)*
Rosenwach Tank Co Inc .... E 212 972-4411
  Astoria *(G-439)*
Wolfe Lumber Mill Inc .... G 716 772-7750
  Gasport *(G-5140)*

2451 Mobile Homes

All Star Carts & Vehicles Inc .... D 631 666-5581
  Bay Shore *(G-646)*
Champion Home Builders Inc .... C 315 841-4122
  Sangerfield *(G-14155)*

Leatherstocking Mobile Home PA.........G....... 315 839-5691
Sauquoit *(G-14219)*

2452 Prefabricated Wood Buildings & Cmpnts

Alta Industries Ltd ....F....... 845 586-3336
Halcottsville *(G-5487)*
Bandec LLC ....G....... 516 627-1971
Jericho *(G-6572)*
Beaver Mountain Log Homes Inc..........G....... 607 467-2700
Hancock *(G-5534)*
Best Mdlr HMS Afrbe P Q& S In...........F....... 631 204-0049
Southampton *(G-14527)*
Bill Lake Homes Construction..............D....... 518 673-2424
Sprakers *(G-14564)*
Cort Contracting ....F....... 845 758-1190
Red Hook *(G-13073)*
Duro-Shed Inc ....E....... 585 344-0800
Buffalo *(G-2732)*
Eastern Exterior Wall................E....... 631 589-3880
Bohemia *(G-1009)*
Energy Panel Structures Inc................G....... 315 923-7777
Clyde *(G-3489)*
Energy Panel Structures Inc................G....... 585 343-1777
Clyde *(G-3490)*
Energy Panel Structures Inc................G....... 518 355-6708
Schenectady *(G-14263)*
Fishers Storage Sheds................G....... 585 382-9580
Leicester *(G-6910)*
Harvest Homes Inc................E....... 518 895-2341
Delanson *(G-3960)*
House Ur Home Inc................G....... 347 585-3308
Monroe *(G-8023)*
Jabo Agricultural Inc ....G....... 631 475-1800
Patchogue *(G-12503)*
Lapp Management Corp................G....... 607 243-5141
Himrod *(G-5976)*
Northern Design & Bldg Assoc ....E....... 518 747-2200
Queensbury *(G-13050)*
Roscoe Brothers Inc................F....... 607 844-3750
Dryden *(G-4040)*
Shafer & Sons ....G....... 315 853-5285
Westmoreland *(G-15963)*
▲ Shelter Enterprises Inc................D....... 518 237-4100
Cohoes *(G-3516)*
Timberbuilt Inc ....F....... 716 337-0012
North Collins *(G-12029)*
Walpole Woodworkers Inc ....G....... 631 726-2859
Water Mill *(G-15531)*
Westchester Modular Homes Inc ....C....... 845 832-9400
Wingdale *(G-16160)*
Whitley East LLC................D....... 718 403-0050
Brooklyn *(G-2582)*
Wood Tex Products LLC ....D....... 607 243-5141
Himrod *(G-5977)*

2491 Wood Preserving

▲ Colorspec Coatings Intl Inc ....F....... 631 472-8251
Holbrook *(G-5992)*
Donver Incorporated................F....... 716 945-1910
Kill Buck *(G-6669)*
Genesee Reserve Buffalo LLC..............E....... 716 824-3116
Buffalo *(G-2774)*
Northeast Treaters Inc ....E....... 518 945-2660
Athens *(G-447)*
Northeast Treaters NY LLC ....E....... 518 945-2660
Athens *(G-448)*
◆ Osmose Holdings Inc................A....... 716 882-5905
Depew *(G-3991)*
Wego International Floors LLC.............F....... 516 487-3510
Great Neck *(G-5431)*

2493 Reconstituted Wood Prdts

▲ Aarco Products Inc ....F....... 631 924-5461
Yaphank *(G-16254)*
▲ Amendola MBL & Stone Ctr Inc........D....... 914 997-7968
White Plains *(G-15972)*
Bedford Wdwrk Instllations Inc ....G....... 914 764-9434
Bedford *(G-762)*
▲ Continental Buchanan LLC..............D....... 703 480-3800
Buchanan *(G-2608)*
Hi-Temp Fabrication Inc ....F....... 716 852-5655
Buffalo *(G-2798)*
Niagara Fiberboard Inc................E....... 716 434-8881
Lockport *(G-7097)*
Northeastern Products Corp................E....... 518 623-3161
Warrensburg *(G-15505)*
Superior Interiors NY Corp ....F....... 845 274-7600
Monsey *(G-8050)*

Zircar Refr Composites Inc ....F....... 845 651-2200
Florida *(G-4828)*

2499 Wood Prdts, NEC

A Van Hoek Woodworking Limited........G....... 718 599-4388
Brooklyn *(G-1437)*
◆ Aakron Rule Corp................C....... 716 542-5483
Akron *(G-15)*
▲ Abbott Industries Inc ....B....... 718 291-0800
Jamaica *(G-6423)*
AC Moore Incorporated................G....... 516 796-5831
Bethpage *(G-831)*
Adams Interior Fabrications ....F....... 631 249-8282
Massapequa *(G-7644)*
▲ Amci Ltd................D....... 718 937-5858
Long Island City *(G-7155)*
American Woods & Veneers Works ......E....... 718 937-2195
Long Island City *(G-7157)*
Andike Millwork Inc ....G....... 718 894-1796
Maspeth *(G-7590)*
Apf Manufacturing Company LLC........E....... 914 963-6300
Yonkers *(G-16287)*
Art Essentials of New York ....G....... 845 368-1100
Airmont *(G-10)*
Atelier Viollet Corp................G....... 718 782-1727
Brooklyn *(G-1545)*
Atlas Fence & Railing Co Inc ....E....... 718 767-2200
Whitestone *(G-16088)*
Babcock Co Inc................E....... 607 776-3341
Bath *(G-630)*
◆ Betterbee Inc................F....... 518 314-0575
Greenwich *(G-5469)*
▲ Brooks Woodworking Inc................F....... 914 666-2029
Mount Kisco *(G-8088)*
Budd Woodwork Inc ....F....... 718 389-1110
Brooklyn *(G-1627)*
Cabinet Shapes Corp................F....... 718 784-6255
Long Island City *(G-7182)*
▲ Catskill Craftsmen Inc ....D....... 607 652-7321
Stamford *(G-14607)*
▲ Cffco USA Inc ....G....... 718 747-1118
Jericho *(G-6573)*
▲ Channel Manufacturing Inc...............E....... 516 944-6271
Port Washington *(G-12866)*
Charles Freihofer Baking Co ....G....... 518 463-2221
Albany *(G-60)*
Cherry Creek Woodcraft Inc ....E....... 716 988-3211
South Dayton *(G-14506)*
▲ Cowee Forest Products Inc..............E....... 518 658-2233
Berlin *(G-823)*
Craz Woodworking Assoc Inc................F....... 631 205-1890
Bellport *(G-796)*
Daniel Demarco and Assoc Inc ....E....... 631 598-7000
Amityville *(G-262)*
Designs By Robert Scott Inc................E....... 718 609-2535
Brooklyn *(G-1738)*
Di Fiore and Sons Custom Wdwkg ....G....... 718 278-1663
Long Island City *(G-7201)*
Digital Fabrication Wkshp Inc................G....... 518 249-6500
Hudson *(G-6153)*
Drummond Framing Inc ....F....... 212 647-1701
New York *(G-9273)*
Ed Negron Fine Woodworking..............G....... 718 246-1016
Brooklyn *(G-1781)*
Elephants Custom Furniture Inc ....D....... 917 509-3581
Brooklyn *(G-1796)*
Encore Retail Systems Inc................F....... 718 385-3443
Mamaroneck *(G-7509)*
Essex Box & Pallet Co Inc................E....... 518 834-7279
Keeseville *(G-6641)*
▲ FG Galassi Moulding Co Inc ....G....... 845 258-2100
Goshen *(G-5308)*
Fibron Products Inc ....E....... 716 886-2378
Buffalo *(G-2752)*
Frame Shoppe & Art Gallery ....G....... 516 365-6014
Manhasset *(G-7534)*
▲ Fred M Lawrence Co Inc................E....... 631 617-6853
Bay Shore *(G-681)*
Fruit Fresh Up Inc ....E....... 716 683-3200
Depew *(G-3983)*
Galas Framing Services ....F....... 718 706-0007
Long Island City *(G-7228)*
General Art Company Inc................F....... 212 255-1298
New York *(G-9588)*
▲ Globus Cork Inc ....F....... 347 963-4059
Brooklyn *(G-1892)*
Grant-Noren................G....... 845 726-4281
Westtown *(G-15966)*
Graphics Slution Providers Inc ....F....... 845 677-5088
Lagrangeville *(G-6748)*

Green Renewable Inc................E....... 518 658-2233
Berlin *(G-824)*
Grohe America Inc ....G....... 212 206-8820
New York *(G-9681)*
Hennig Custom Woodwork Corp..........G....... 516 536-3460
Oceanside *(G-12174)*
Hubray Inc ....F....... 800 645-2855
North Baldwin *(G-12006)*
▲ Imperial Frames & Albums LLC.......G....... 718 832-9793
Brooklyn *(G-1953)*
Innova Interiors Inc................E....... 718 401-2122
Bronx *(G-1283)*
Interntonal Consmr Connections ....F....... 516 481-3438
West Hempstead *(G-15771)*
Interstate Wood Products Inc...............E....... 631 842-4488
Amityville *(G-277)*
Ivan Horning................G....... 315 536-3028
Penn Yan *(G-12587)*
Jeffrey John................G....... 631 842-2850
Amityville *(G-281)*
Jordache Woodworking Corp...............F....... 718 349-3373
Brooklyn *(G-1999)*
Julius Lowy Frame Restoring Co..........E....... 212 861-8585
New York *(G-10039)*
K & B Woodworking Inc ....G....... 518 634-7253
Cairo *(G-3066)*
Lanwood Industries Inc................E....... 718 786-3000
Bay Shore *(G-688)*
Lanza Corp ....G....... 914 937-6360
Port Chester *(G-12824)*
◆ Lco Destiny LLC ....B....... 315 782-3302
Watertown *(G-15581)*
Long Lumber and Supply Corp ....F....... 518 439-1661
Slingerlands *(G-14466)*
M & R Woodworking & Finishing ....G....... 718 486-5480
Brooklyn *(G-2094)*
▲ M A Moslow & Bros Inc ....E....... 716 896-2950
Buffalo *(G-2854)*
McGraw Wood Products LLC ....E....... 607 836-6465
Mc Graw *(G-7689)*
McIntosh Box & Pallet Co Inc...............E....... 315 446-9350
Rome *(G-13855)*
Meeco Sullivan LLC................C....... 800 232-3625
Warwick *(G-15520)*
◆ N Sketch Build Inc................G....... 800 975-0597
Fishkill *(G-4802)*
New Heydenryk LLC................F....... 212 206-9611
Long Island City *(G-7307)*
◆ Northast Ctr For Bekeeping LLC.......F....... 800 632-3379
Greenwich *(G-5474)*
Northern Forest Pdts Co Inc................G....... 315 942-6955
Boonville *(G-1107)*
P B & H Moulding Corporation ....E....... 315 455-1756
Fayetteville *(G-4785)*
Paramount Graphix................G....... 845 367-5003
Port Jervis *(G-12854)*
Pdj Components Inc ....E....... 845 469-9191
Chester *(G-3382)*
Pella Corporation................C....... 631 208-0710
Calverton *(G-3083)*
▲ Pgs Millwork Inc................D....... 518 828-2608
Hudson *(G-6175)*
Piccini Mnm Inc................G....... 845 741-6770
West Nyack *(G-15830)*
Picture Perfect Framing ....G....... 718 851-1884
Brooklyn *(G-2257)*
Premium Mulch & Materials Inc............F....... 631 320-3666
Coram *(G-3698)*
Prime Wood Products ....G....... 518 792-1407
Queensbury *(G-13053)*
▲ Putnam Rolling Ladder Co Inc.........F....... 212 226-5147
New York *(G-10932)*
Putnam Rolling Ladder Co Inc..............F....... 718 381-8219
Brooklyn *(G-2308)*
Quattro Frameworks Inc................F....... 718 361-2620
Astoria *(G-435)*
▲ R P M Industries Inc................E....... 315 255-1105
Auburn *(G-492)*
Revival Industries Inc................F....... 315 868-1085
Ilion *(G-6282)*
Richard Rothbard Inc ....G....... 845 355-2300
Slate Hill *(G-14463)*
Rose Fence Inc................F....... 516 223-0777
Baldwin *(G-533)*
Ryers Creek Corp................E....... 607 523-6617
Corning *(G-3720)*
Sentine Printing Inc ....G....... 516 334-7400
Westbury *(G-15925)*
Sky Frame & Art Inc................E....... 212 925-7856
New York *(G-11263)*

S I C

▲ Structural Industries Inc ....C 631 471-5200
  Bohemia **(G-1082)**
Superior Wood Turnings ....F 716 483-1254
  Jamestown **(G-6549)**
Thomas Matthews Wdwkg Ltd ....F ... 631 287-3657
  Southampton **(G-14539)**
Thomas Matthews Wdwkg Ltd ....G ... 631 287-2023
  Southampton **(G-14540)**
Ultimate Styles of America ....F ... 631 254-0219
  Bay Shore **(G-724)**
Walpole Woodworkers Inc ....G ... 631 726-2859
  Water Mill **(G-15531)**
Wholesale Mulch & Sawdust Inc ....G ... 607 687-2637
  Owego **(G-12440)**
Windsor United Industries LLC ....G ... 607 655-3300
  Windsor **(G-16158)**
Wood Innovations of Suffolk ....G ... 631 698-2345
  Oceanside **(G-12198)**
Woodmotif Inc ....F ... 516 564-8325
  Hempstead **(G-5852)**
Woodtronics Inc ....G ... 914 962-5205
  Yorktown Heights **(G-16374)**
▲ York Ladder Inc ....F ... 718 784-6666
  Long Island City **(G-7411)**

25 FURNITURE AND FIXTURES

2511 Wood Household Furniture

A & S Woodworking Inc ....G 518 821-0832
  Hudson **(G-6145)**
Acem Corp ....G 631 242-2440
  Deer Park **(G-3828)**
American Epoxy and Metal Inc ....G ... 718 828-7828
  Scarsdale **(G-14233)**
Anthony Lawrence of New York ....E ... 212 206-8820
  Long Island City **(G-7159)**
Arthur Brown W Mfg Co ....F ... 631 243-5594
  Deer Park **(G-3842)**
Artisan Woodworking Ltd ....G ... 516 486-0818
  West Hempstead **(G-15766)**
Atelier Viollet Corp ....G ... 718 782-1727
  Brooklyn **(G-1545)**
▲ Benchmark Furniture Mfg ....D ... 718 257-4707
  Brooklyn **(G-1574)**
Bento Box LLC ....G ... 718 260-8200
  Brooklyn **(G-1577)**
Black River Woodworking LLC ....G ... 315 376-8405
  Castorland **(G-3206)**
◆ Bush Industries Inc ....C ... 716 665-2000
  Jamestown **(G-6500)**
Cab-Network Inc ....G ... 516 334-8666
  Westbury **(G-15873)**
Carlos & Alex Atelier Inc ....E ... 718 441-8911
  Richmond Hill **(G-13111)**
Carver Creek Enterprises Inc ....G ... 585 657-7511
  Bloomfield **(G-942)**
▲ Catskill Craftsmen Inc ....D ... 607 652-7321
  Stamford **(G-14607)**
▲ Charles H Beckley Inc ....F ... 718 665-2218
  Bronx **(G-1224)**
Comerford Hennessy At Home Inc ......G ... 631 537-6200
  Bridgehampton **(G-1165)**
▲ Community Products LLC ....C ... 845 658-8799
  Rifton **(G-13167)**
Concepts In Wood of CNY ....E ... 315 463-8084
  Syracuse **(G-14858)**
Conesus Lake Association Inc ....E ... 585 346-6864
  Lakeville **(G-6774)**
Cousins Furniture & Hm Imprvs ....E ... 631 254-3752
  Deer Park **(G-3854)**
Custom Display Manufacture ....G ... 516 783-6491
  North Bellmore **(G-12018)**
Custom Woodcraft LLC ....F ... 315 843-4234
  Munnsville **(G-8195)**
▲ D & W Design Inc ....E ... 845 343-3366
  Middletown **(G-7903)**
David Sutherland Showrooms - N ....G ... 212 871-9717
  New York **(G-9183)**
Dbs Interiors Corp ....F ... 631 491-3013
  West Babylon **(G-15706)**
Dcl Furniture Manufacturing ....E ... 516 248-2683
  Mineola **(G-7968)**
Deakon Homes and Interiors ....E ... 518 271-0342
  Troy **(G-15165)**
Designs By Robert Scott Inc ....E ... 718 609-2535
  Brooklyn **(G-1738)**
▲ Dinette Depot Ltd ....D ... 516 515-9623
  Brooklyn **(G-1748)**
Ducduc LLC ....F ... 212 226-1868
  New York **(G-9276)**

▲ Dune Inc ....G ... 212 925-6171
  New York **(G-9279)**
▲ Eclectic Cntract Furn Inds Inc ....F ... 212 967-5504
  New York **(G-9316)**
El Greco Woodworking Inc ....E ... 716 483-0315
  Jamestown **(G-6508)**
Emilia Interiors Inc ....F ... 718 629-4202
  Brooklyn **(G-1800)**
▲ Ercole Nyc Inc ....F ... 212 675-2218
  Brooklyn **(G-1810)**
Eugenia Selective Living Inc ....E ... 631 277-1461
  Islip **(G-6352)**
Falcon Chair and Table Inc ....E ... 716 664-7136
  Falconer **(G-4540)**
▲ Feinkind Inc ....G ... 800 289-6136
  Irvington **(G-6308)**
▲ Fiber-Seal of New York Inc ....G ... 212 888-5580
  New York **(G-9487)**
Final Dimension Inc ....G ... 718 786-0100
  Maspeth **(G-7615)**
▲ Forecast Consoles Inc ....E ... 631 253-9000
  Hauppauge **(G-5653)**
French & Itln Furn Craftsmen ....G ... 718 599-5001
  Brooklyn **(G-1866)**
Furniture Doctor Inc ....G ... 585 657-6941
  Bloomfield **(G-947)**
Glendale Architectural WD Pdts ....E ... 718 326-2700
  Glendale **(G-5226)**
▲ Harden Furniture LLC ....C ... 315 675-3600
  Mc Connellsville **(G-7686)**
▲ Hunt Country Furniture Inc ....D ... 845 832-6601
  Wingdale **(G-16159)**
Icon Design LLC ....E ... 585 768-6040
  Le Roy **(G-6901)**
▲ Inova LLC ....E ... 866 528-2804
  Guilderland Center **(G-5486)**
Inter Craft Custom Furniture ....G ... 718 278-2573
  Astoria **(G-425)**
J Percoco Industries Inc ....G ... 631 312-4572
  Bohemia **(G-1025)**
K & B Woodworking Inc ....G ... 518 634-7253
  Cairo **(G-3066)**
Kazac Inc ....G ... 631 249-7299
  Farmingdale **(G-4662)**
Kittinger Company Inc ....E ... 716 876-1000
  Buffalo **(G-2835)**
Knoll Inc ....D ... 212 343-4124
  New York **(G-10118)**
▲ L& JG Stickley Incorporated ....A ... 315 682-5500
  Manlius **(G-7548)**
Lanoves Inc ....G ... 718 384-1880
  Brooklyn **(G-2047)**
Lemode Concepts Inc ....G ... 631 841-0796
  Amityville **(G-291)**
Little Wolf Cabinet Shop Inc ....E ... 212 734-1116
  New York **(G-10230)**
Long Lumber and Supply Corp ....F ... 518 439-1661
  Slingerlands **(G-14466)**
Ltdm Incorporated ....G ... 718 965-1339
  Brooklyn **(G-2088)**
▲ M & C Furniture ....G ... 718 422-2136
  Brooklyn **(G-2091)**
M T D Corporation ....F ... 631 491-3905
  West Babylon **(G-15727)**
Machias Furniture Factory Inc ....G ... 716 353-8687
  Machias **(G-7472)**
◆ Mackenzie-Childs LLC ....C ... 315 364-6118
  Aurora **(G-504)**
Manchester Wood Inc ....G ... 518 642-9518
  Granville **(G-5351)**
McGraw Wood Products LLC ....E ... 607 836-6465
  Mc Graw **(G-7689)**
Mica International Ltd ....G ... 516 378-3400
  Freeport **(G-5008)**
New Day Woodwork Inc ....E ... 718 275-1721
  Glendale **(G-5229)**
▲ Patrick Mackin Custom Furn ....G ... 718 237-2592
  Brooklyn **(G-2250)**
Peter S Curtis ....G ... 315 782-7363
  Evans Mills **(G-4487)**
Piccini Industries Ltd ....E ... 845 365-0614
  Orangeburg **(G-12325)**
▼ Pillow Perfections Ltd Inc ....G ... 718 383-2259
  Brooklyn **(G-2259)**
Plexi Craft Quality Products ....E ... 212 924-3244
  New York **(G-10856)**
Premier Woodcraft Ltd ....G ... 610 383-6624
  White Plains **(G-16055)**
◆ Premiere Living Products LLC ....F ... 631 873-4337
  Dix Hills **(G-4013)**

Professional Cab Detailing Co ....F ... 845 436-7282
  Woodridge **(G-16194)**
Raff Enterprises ....G ... 518 218-7883
  Albany **(G-123)**
Recycled Brooklyn Group LLC ....F ... 917 902-0662
  Brooklyn **(G-2334)**
▼ Reis D Furniture Mfg ....E ... 516 248-5676
  Mineola **(G-7997)**
◆ Renco Group Inc ....G ... 212 541-6000
  New York **(G-11012)**
Ridge Cabinet & Showcase Inc ....E ... 585 663-0560
  Rochester **(G-13673)**
Sitecraft Inc ....G ... 718 729-4900
  Astoria **(G-441)**
Stillwater Wood & Iron ....G ... 518 664-4501
  Stillwater **(G-14733)**
▲ Sundown Ski & Sport Shop Inc ....D ... 631 737-8600
  Lake Grove **(G-6761)**
▲ Triple J Bedding LLC ....G ... 718 643-8005
  Brooklyn **(G-2523)**
Universal Designs Inc ....G ... 718 721-1111
  Long Island City **(G-7389)**
Wallace Home Design Ctr ....G ... 631 765-3890
  Southold **(G-14546)**
Walpole Woodworkers Inc ....G ... 631 726-2859
  Water Mill **(G-15531)**
Walter P Sauer LLC ....E ... 718 937-0600
  Brooklyn **(G-2574)**
William Somerville Maintenance ....G ... 212 534-4600
  New York **(G-11759)**
Woodmotif Inc ....F ... 516 564-8325
  Hempstead **(G-5852)**
◆ World Trading Center Inc ....G ... 631 273-3330
  Hauppauge **(G-5803)**
Your Furniture Designers Inc ....G ... 845 947-3046
  West Haverstraw **(G-15765)**

2512 Wood Household Furniture, Upholstered

▲ Artone LLC ....D ... 716 664-2232
  Jamestown **(G-6495)**
August Studios ....G ... 718 706-6487
  Long Island City **(G-7172)**
▲ Avanti Furniture Corp ....F ... 516 293-8220
  Farmingdale **(G-4590)**
▲ Classic Sofa Ltd ....D ... 212 620-0485
  New York **(G-9026)**
Deangelis Ltd ....E ... 212 348-8225
  Glen Head **(G-5205)**
Elan Upholstery Inc ....F ... 631 563-0650
  Bohemia **(G-1011)**
Falvo Manufacturing Co Inc ....F ... 315 724-7925
  Utica **(G-15261)**
▲ Fiber-Seal of New York Inc ....G ... 212 888-5580
  New York **(G-9487)**
Furniture By Craftmaster Ltd ....G ... 631 750-0658
  Bohemia **(G-1014)**
H & H Furniture Co ....G ... 718 850-5252
  Jamaica **(G-6446)**
Hallagan Manufacturing Co Inc ....G ... 315 331-4640
  Newark **(G-11840)**
▲ Harden Furniture LLC ....C ... 315 675-3600
  Mc Connellsville **(G-7686)**
▲ Jackson Dakota Inc ....G ... 212 838-9444
  New York **(G-9962)**
Jays Furniture Products Inc ....E ... 716 876-8854
  Buffalo **(G-2816)**
Kittinger Company Inc ....E ... 716 876-1000
  Buffalo **(G-2835)**
◆ Mackenzie-Childs LLC ....C ... 315 364-6118
  Aurora **(G-504)**
Matteo & Antonio Bartolotta ....F ... 315 252-2220
  Auburn **(G-485)**
Mazza Classics Incorporated ....G ... 631 390-9060
  Farmingdale **(G-4679)**
Pheonix Custom Furniture Ltd ....E ... 212 727-2648
  Long Island City **(G-7325)**
◆ Princeton Upholstery Co Inc ....D ... 845 343-2196
  Middletown **(G-7928)**
Rob Herschenfeld Design Inc ....F ... 718 456-6801
  Brooklyn **(G-2350)**
Simon S Decorating Inc ....G ... 718 339-2931
  Brooklyn **(G-2418)**
▲ Slava Industries Incorporated ....G ... 718 499-4850
  Brooklyn **(G-2425)**
Sleepable Sofas Ltd ....D ... 973 546-4502
  New York **(G-11267)**
▲ Smith & Watson ....E ... 212 686-6444
  New York **(G-11274)**

Two Worlds Arts Ltd ... G ... 212 929-2210 — Brooklyn *(G-2533)*
Versailles Drapery Upholstery ... F ... 212 533-2059 — Long Island City *(G-7395)*
Wallace Home Design Ctr ... G ... 631 765-3890 — Southold *(G-14546)*
Yepes Fine Furniture ... E ... 718 383-0221 — Brooklyn *(G-2600)*

2514 Metal Household Furniture

Acem Corp ... G ... 631 242-2440 — Deer Park *(G-3828)*
▲ American Best Cabinets Inc ... E ... 845 369-6666 — Suffern *(G-14757)*
◆ Charles P Rogers Brass Beds ... F ... 212 675-4400 — New York *(G-8975)*
▲ CIDC Corp ... F ... 718 342-5820 — Glendale *(G-5222)*
▲ D & W Design Inc ... E ... 845 343-3366 — Middletown *(G-7903)*
◆ Embassy Dinettes Inc ... G ... 631 253-2292 — Deer Park *(G-3871)*
▲ F&M Ornamental Designs LLC ... E ... 908 241-7776 — New York *(G-9456)*
Furniture Doctor Inc ... G ... 585 657-6941 — Bloomfield *(G-947)*
▲ Glissade New York LLC ... E ... 631 756-4800 — Farmingdale *(G-4638)*
▲ Hellas Stone Inc ... G ... 718 545-4716 — Astoria *(G-424)*
La Forge Francaise Ltd Inc ... G ... 631 591-0572 — Riverhead *(G-13177)*
▲ Majestic Home Imprvs Distr ... G ... 718 853-5079 — Brooklyn *(G-2103)*
Manhattan Cabinets Inc ... G ... 212 548-2436 — New York *(G-10342)*
Meeker Sales Corp ... G ... 718 384-5400 — Brooklyn *(G-2133)*
Methods Tooling & Mfg Inc ... E ... 845 246-7100 — Mount Marion *(G-8111)*
▲ NK Medical Products Inc ... G ... 716 759-7200 — Amherst *(G-235)*
▲ Novum Medical Products Ny LLC ... F ... 716 759-7200 — Amherst *(G-236)*
Precision Orna Ir Works Inc ... G ... 718 379-5200 — Bronx *(G-1342)*
◆ Renco Group Inc ... G ... 212 541-6000 — New York *(G-11012)*
Royal Metal Products Inc ... E ... 518 966-4442 — Surprise *(G-14776)*
▲ Slava Industries Incorporated ... G ... 718 499-4850 — Brooklyn *(G-2425)*
Steelcraft Manufacturing Co ... F ... 718 277-2404 — Brooklyn *(G-2456)*

2515 Mattresses & Bedsprings

Acworth Foundation ... G ... 631 784-7802 — Huntington *(G-6197)*
▲ Brook North Farms Inc ... F ... 315 834-9390 — Auburn *(G-469)*
▲ Charles H Beckley Inc ... F ... 718 665-2218 — Bronx *(G-1224)*
Dixie Foam Ltd ... G ... 212 645-8999 — Brooklyn *(G-1750)*
Duxiana Dux Bed ... G ... 212 755-2600 — New York *(G-9282)*
▼ Ideal Manufacturing Inc ... E ... 585 872-7190 — East Rochester *(G-4165)*
KKR Millennium GP LLC ... A ... 212 750-8300 — New York *(G-10112)*
◆ M R C Industries Inc ... C ... 516 328-6900 — Port Washington *(G-12903)*
Metro Mattress Corp ... E ... 716 205-2300 — Niagara Falls *(G-11951)*
Natural Dreams LLC ... G ... 718 760-4202 — Corona *(G-3747)*
▲ Otis Bedding Mfg Co Inc ... E ... 716 825-2599 — Buffalo *(G-2900)*
◆ Quality Foam Inc ... F ... 718 381-3644 — Brooklyn *(G-2309)*
Rollers Inc ... G ... 716 837-0700 — Buffalo *(G-2961)*
▲ Royal Bedding Co Buffalo Inc ... E ... 716 895-1414 — Buffalo *(G-2966)*
Sealy Mattress Co Albany Inc ... B ... 518 880-1600 — Troy *(G-15161)*
Sleep Improvement Center Inc ... F ... 516 536-5799 — Rockville Centre *(G-13836)*
Sleepable Sofas Ltd ... D ... 973 546-4502 — New York *(G-11267)*
▲ Steinbock-Braff Inc ... E ... 718 972-6500 — Brooklyn *(G-2460)*
◆ VSM Investors LLC ... G ... 212 351-1600 — New York *(G-11708)*

2517 Wood T V, Radio, Phono & Sewing Cabinets

Dbs Interiors Corp ... F ... 631 491-3013 — West Babylon *(G-15706)*
Handcraft Cabinetry Inc ... G ... 914 681-9437 — White Plains *(G-16012)*
Time Base Corporation ... E ... 631 293-4068 — Edgewood *(G-4288)*
▲ W Designe Inc ... E ... 914 736-1058 — Peekskill *(G-12559)*

2519 Household Furniture, NEC

3phase Industries LLC ... G ... 347 763-2942 — Brooklyn *(G-1415)*
Albert Menin Interiors Ltd ... F ... 212 876-3041 — Bronx *(G-1200)*
Anandamali Inc ... F ... 212 343-8964 — New York *(G-8573)*
Bielecky Bros Inc ... E ... 718 424-4764 — Woodside *(G-16197)*
▲ Comely International Trdg Inc ... G ... 212 683-1240 — New York *(G-9064)*
Culin/Colella Inc ... G ... 914 698-7727 — Mamaroneck *(G-7507)*
Dbs Interiors Corp ... F ... 631 491-3013 — West Babylon *(G-15706)*
Eugenia Selective Living Inc ... F ... 631 277-1461 — Islip *(G-6352)*
Harome Designs LLC ... E ... 631 864-1900 — Commack *(G-3591)*
▲ Holland & Sherry Inc ... E ... 212 542-8410 — New York *(G-9803)*
▲ L& JG Stickley Incorporated ... A ... 315 682-5500 — Manlius *(G-7548)*
Matthew Shively LLC ... G ... 914 937-3531 — Port Chester *(G-12825)*
◆ Max Header ... E ... 680 888-9786 — New York *(G-10389)*
Mbh Furniture Innovations Inc ... G ... 845 354-8202 — Spring Valley *(G-14578)*
▲ Olollo Inc ... G ... 877 701-0110 — Brooklyn *(G-2230)*
Ready To Assemble Company Inc ... E ... 516 825-4397 — Valley Stream *(G-15356)*
Safcore LLC ... F ... 917 627-5263 — Brooklyn *(G-2380)*
Two Worlds Arts Ltd ... G ... 212 929-2210 — New York *(G-11566)*
Universal Interiors LLC ... F ... 518 298-4400 — Champlain *(G-3320)*
▲ Vondom LLC ... G ... 212 207-3252 — New York *(G-11706)*
Yogibo LLC ... F ... 518 456-1762 — Albany *(G-143)*

2521 Wood Office Furniture

▲ Artone LLC ... D ... 716 664-2232 — Jamestown *(G-6495)*
B D B Typewriter Supply Works ... E ... 718 232-4800 — Brooklyn *(G-1557)*
▲ Bauerschmidt & Sons Inc ... D ... 718 528-3500 — Jamaica *(G-6429)*
Bloch Industries LLC ... D ... 585 334-9600 — Rochester *(G-13272)*
Breather Products US Inc ... E ... 800 471-8704 — New York *(G-8850)*
◆ Bush Industries Inc ... C ... 716 665-2000 — Jamestown *(G-6500)*
▼ Ccn International Inc ... D ... 315 789-4400 — Geneva *(G-5149)*
Centre Interiors Wdwkg Co Inc ... E ... 718 323-1343 — Ozone Park *(G-12458)*
Chicone Builders LLC ... G ... 607 535-6540 — Montour Falls *(G-8074)*
Commercial Display Design LLC ... F ... 607 336-7353 — Oneonta *(G-12266)*
Concepts In Wood of CNY ... E ... 315 463-8084 — Syracuse *(G-14858)*
▼ Craft Custom Woodwork Co Inc ... F ... 718 821-2162 — Maspeth *(G-7600)*
Culin/Colella Inc ... G ... 914 698-7727 — Mamaroneck *(G-7507)*
DAF Office Networks Inc ... G ... 315 699-7070 — Cicero *(G-3418)*
Davinci Designs Inc ... F ... 631 595-1095 — Deer Park *(G-3859)*
Dcl Furniture Manufacturing ... E ... 516 248-2683 — Mineola *(G-7968)*
Deakon Homes and Interiors ... F ... 518 271-0342 — Troy *(G-15165)*
Designs By Robert Scott Inc ... E ... 718 609-2535 — Brooklyn *(G-1738)*
▲ E-Systems Group LLC ... E ... 607 775-1100 — Conklin *(G-3624)*
Eugenia Selective Living Inc ... F ... 631 277-1461 — Islip *(G-6352)*
Exhibit Corporation America ... E ... 718 937-2600 — Long Island City *(G-7217)*
F E Hale Mfg Co ... D ... 315 894-5490 — Frankfort *(G-4950)*
Fina Cabinet Corp ... G ... 718 409-2900 — Mount Vernon *(G-8141)*
▲ Forecast Consoles Inc ... E ... 631 253-9000 — Hauppauge *(G-5653)*
Furniture By Craftmaster Ltd ... G ... 631 750-0658 — Bohemia *(G-1014)*
Glendale Architectural WD Pdts ... E ... 718 326-2700 — Glendale *(G-5226)*
Gothic Cabinet Craft Inc ... D ... 347 881-1420 — Maspeth *(G-7618)*
▲ Gunlocke Company LLC ... C ... 585 728-5111 — Wayland *(G-15626)*
H Freund Woodworking Co Inc ... F ... 516 334-3774 — Westbury *(G-15891)*
▲ Harden Furniture LLC ... C ... 315 675-3600 — Mc Connellsville *(G-7686)*
Heartwood Specialties Inc ... G ... 607 654-0102 — Hammondsport *(G-5529)*
Hni Corporation ... C ... 212 683-2232 — New York *(G-9798)*
House Ur Home Inc ... G ... 347 585-3308 — Monroe *(G-8023)*
◆ Humanscale Corporation ... E ... 212 725-4749 — New York *(G-9839)*
▲ Innovant Inc ... G ... 212 929-4883 — Islandia *(G-6336)*
Interior Solutions of Wny LLC ... G ... 716 332-0372 — Buffalo *(G-2813)*
Kazac Inc ... G ... 631 249-7299 — Farmingdale *(G-4662)*
Kimball Office Inc ... E ... 212 753-6161 — New York *(G-10102)*
Kittinger Company Inc ... E ... 716 876-1000 — Buffalo *(G-2835)*
Knoll Inc ... D ... 716 891-1700 — Buffalo *(G-2836)*
Knoll Inc ... D ... 212 343-4124 — New York *(G-10118)*
▲ Lake Country Woodworkers Ltd ... E ... 585 374-6353 — Naples *(G-8208)*
Longo Commercial Cabinets Inc ... E ... 631 225-4290 — Lindenhurst *(G-6956)*
M T D Corporation ... F ... 631 491-3905 — West Babylon *(G-15727)*
▲ Manhattan Comfort Inc ... G ... 908 888-0818 — Brooklyn *(G-2107)*
Materials Design Workshop ... F ... 718 893-1954 — Bronx *(G-1308)*
Matteo & Antonio Bartolotta ... F ... 315 252-2220 — Auburn *(G-485)*
▲ Miller Blaker Inc ... D ... 718 665-0500 — Bronx *(G-1315)*
Millers Millworks Inc ... E ... 585 494-1420 — Bergen *(G-818)*
▲ N Y Elli Design Corp ... F ... 718 228-0014 — Ridgewood *(G-13152)*
New Dimensions Office Group ... D ... 718 387-0995 — Brooklyn *(G-2203)*
Omega Furniture Manufacturing ... F ... 315 463-7428 — Syracuse *(G-14954)*
Pheonix Custom Furniture Ltd ... E ... 212 727-2648 — Long Island City *(G-7325)*
Piccini Industries Ltd ... E ... 845 365-0614 — Orangeburg *(G-12325)*
▲ Poppin Inc ... D ... 212 391-7200 — New York *(G-10866)*
Premier Woodcraft Ltd ... E ... 610 383-6624 — White Plains *(G-16055)*
▲ Prince Seating Corp ... E ... 718 363-2300 — Brooklyn *(G-2287)*
◆ Princeton Upholstery Co Inc ... D ... 845 343-2196 — Middletown *(G-7928)*
Red White & Blue Entps Corp ... G ... 718 565-8080 — Woodside *(G-16223)*

Riverfront Costume Design ....G 716 693-2501
North Tonawanda (G-12087)

Stylecraft Interiors Inc ....F 516 487-2133
Great Neck (G-5427)

▲ Technology Desking Inc ....E 212 257-6998
New York (G-11446)

Universal Designs Inc ....G 718 721-1111
Long Island City (G-7389)

▲ Upstate Office Liquidators Inc ....F 607 722-9234
Johnson City (G-6609)

WD Certified Contracting LLC ....F 516 493-9319
Westbury (G-15939)

Wood Etc Inc ....F 315 484-9663
Syracuse (G-15030)

Woodmotif Inc ....F 516 564-8325
Hempstead (G-5852)

Your Furniture Designers Inc ....G 845 947-3046
West Haverstraw (G-15765)

Zographos Designs Ltd ....G 212 545-0227
New York (G-11828)

2522 Office Furniture, Except Wood

3phase Industries LLC ....G 347 763-2942
Brooklyn (G-1415)

Able Steel Equipment Co Inc ....F 718 361-9240
Long Island City (G-7144)

Allcraft Fabricators Inc ....G 631 951-4100
Hauppauge (G-5583)

Aronowitz Metal Works ....G 845 356-1660
Monsey (G-8035)

▲ Artistic Products LLC ....E 631 435-0200
Hauppauge (G-5595)

▲ Artone LLC ....D 716 664-2232
Jamestown (G-6495)

Aztec Industries Inc ....G 631 585-1331
Ronkonkoma (G-13910)

▲ Bisley Inc ....G 212 675-3055
New York (G-8802)

▲ Davies Office Refurbishing Inc ....C 518 449-2040
Albany (G-69)

Davinci Designs Inc ....F 631 595-1095
Deer Park (G-3859)

Dcl Furniture Manufacturing ....E 516 248-2683
Mineola (G-7968)

Deakon Homes and Interiors ....F 518 271-0342
Troy (G-15165)

▲ E-Systems Group LLC ....F 607 775-1100
Conklin (G-3624)

Eugenia Selective Living Inc ....F 631 277-1461
Islip (G-6352)

Exhibit Corporation America ....F 718 937-2600
Long Island City (G-7217)

Falvo Manufacturing Co Inc ....F 315 724-7925
Utica (G-15261)

▲ Forecast Consoles Inc ....E 631 253-9000
Hauppauge (G-5653)

FX INC ....F 212 244-2240
New York (G-9556)

Gothic Cabinet Craft Inc ....D 347 881-1420
Maspeth (G-7618)

◆ Hergo Ergonomic Support Syst ....E 888 222-7270
Oceanside (G-12175)

Herman Miller Inc ....E 212 753-3022
New York (G-9769)

Hudson Valley Office Furn Inc ....G 845 565-6673
Newburgh (G-11869)

Inscape Inc ....E 716 665-6210
Falconer (G-4545)

Integrated Tech Support Svcs ....G 718 454-2497
Saint Albans (G-14106)

▲ International Office ....G 212 334-4617
New York (G-9922)

Knoll Inc ....D 212 343-4124
New York (G-10118)

Larson Metal Manufacturing Co ....G 716 665-6807
Jamestown (G-6529)

▲ Lucia Group Inc ....G 631 392-4900
Deer Park (G-3900)

Modern Metal Fabricators Inc ....G 518 966-4142
Hannacroix (G-5541)

▲ Natural Stone & Cabinet Inc ....G 718 388-2988
Brooklyn (G-2192)

New Dimensions Office Group ....D 718 387-0995
Brooklyn (G-2203)

Nightingale Corp ....G 905 896-3434
Tonawanda (G-15127)

Piccini Industries Inc ....E 845 365-0614
Orangeburg (G-12325)

▲ Poppin Inc ....D 212 391-7200
New York (G-10866)

Premier Woodcraft Ltd ....E 610 383-6624
White Plains (G-16055)

Riverfront Costume Design ....G 716 693-2501
North Tonawanda (G-12087)

Roberts Office Furn Cncpts Inc ....E 315 451-9185
Liverpool (G-7038)

Royal Metal Products Inc ....E 518 966-4442
Surprise (G-14776)

Seating Inc ....E 800 468-2475
Nunda (G-12134)

▼ Ulrich Planfiling Eqp Corp ....E 716 763-1815
Lakewood (G-6786)

◆ Vitra Inc ....F 212 463-5700
New York (G-11698)

Workplace Interiors LLC ....E 585 425-7420
Fairport (G-4530)

Zographos Designs Ltd ....G 212 545-0227
New York (G-11828)

2531 Public Building & Related Furniture

Able Steel Equipment Co Inc ....F 718 361-9240
Long Island City (G-7144)

American Bptst Chrches Mtro NY ....G 212 870-3195
New York (G-8545)

Artistry In Wood of Syracuse ....F 315 431-4022
Syracuse (G-14819)

▲ Artone LLC ....D 716 664-2232
Jamestown (G-6495)

B/E Aerospace Inc ....E 631 563-6400
Bohemia (G-978)

E & D Specialty Stands Inc ....E 716 337-0161
North Collins (G-12025)

East/West Industries Inc ....E 631 981-5900
Ronkonkoma (G-13932)

▲ Forecast Consoles Inc ....E 631 253-9000
Hauppauge (G-5653)

▲ Inova LLC ....E 866 528-2804
Guilderland Center (G-5486)

Jays Furniture Products Inc ....E 716 876-8854
Buffalo (G-2816)

Jcdecaux Mallscape LLC ....F 646 834-1200
New York (G-9988)

Johnson Controls Inc ....D 518 884-8313
Ballston Spa (G-578)

Johnson Controls Inc ....G 518 694-4822
Albany (G-92)

Johnson Controls Inc ....E 585 671-1930
Webster (G-15643)

Johnson Controls Inc ....C 585 724-2232
Rochester (G-13495)

Keck Group Inc ....F 845 988-5757
Warwick (G-15515)

▲ Maximum Security Products Corp ....E 518 233-1800
Waterford (G-15538)

Maxsecure Systems Inc ....G 800 657-4336
Buffalo (G-2863)

▲ N Y Elli Design Corp ....F 718 228-0014
Ridgewood (G-13152)

Pluribus Products Inc ....E 718 852-1614
Bayville (G-747)

Rosenwach Tank Co Inc ....E 212 972-4411
Astoria (G-439)

Seating Inc ....E 800 468-2475
Nunda (G-12134)

▲ Steeldeck Ny Inc ....E 718 599-3700
Brooklyn (G-2457)

▼ Stidd Systems Inc ....E 631 477-2400
Greenport (G-5458)

▲ Studio 21 LA Inc ....E 718 965-6579
Brooklyn (G-2464)

◆ Testori Interiors Inc ....E 518 298-4400
Champlain (G-3317)

Town of Amherst ....E 716 631-7113
Williamsville (G-16144)

Town of Hartford ....G 315 724-0654
New Hartford (G-8247)

Tymor Park ....G 845 724-5691
Lagrangeville (G-6755)

▲ Unifor Inc ....F 212 673-3434
New York (G-11585)

Universal Interiors LLC ....F 518 298-4400
Champlain (G-3320)

2541 Wood, Office & Store Fixtures

Abaco Steel Products Inc ....G 631 589-1800
Bohemia (G-960)

▲ Abbott Industries Inc ....B 718 291-0800
Jamaica (G-6423)

All Merchandise Display Corp ....G 718 257-2221
Highland Mills (G-5967)

Allegany Laminating and Supply ....G 716 372-2424
Allegany (G-186)

Alrod Associates Inc ....F 631 981-2193
Ronkonkoma (G-13900)

Arcy Plastic Laminates Inc ....E 518 235-0753
Albany (G-42)

▲ Array Marketing Group Inc ....E 212 750-3367
New York (G-8625)

▲ Artone LLC ....D 716 664-2232
Jamestown (G-6495)

Auburn Custom Millwork Inc ....G 315 253-3843
Auburn (G-460)

Bator Bintor Inc ....F 347 546-6503
Brooklyn (G-1567)

▲ Bauerschmidt & Sons Inc ....D 718 528-3500
Jamaica (G-6429)

Bloch Industries LLC ....D 585 334-9600
Rochester (G-13272)

Contempra Design Inc ....G 718 984-8586
Staten Island (G-14642)

Countertops & Cabinets Inc ....G 315 433-1038
Syracuse (G-14865)

Creative Counter Tops Inc ....G 845 471-6480
Poughkeepsie (G-12950)

Custom Countertops Inc ....G 716 685-2871
Depew (G-3977)

Custom Design Kitchens Inc ....F 518 355-4446
Duanesburg (G-4044)

Custom Wood Inc ....G 718 927-4700
Brooklyn (G-1713)

▲ David Flatt Furniture Ltd ....D 718 937-7944
Long Island City (G-7198)

Dbs Interiors Corp ....G 631 491-3013
West Babylon (G-15706)

Deakon Homes and Interiors ....F 518 271-0342
Troy (G-15165)

Delocon Wholesale Inc ....G 716 592-2711
Springville (G-14589)

E F Thresh Inc ....G 315 437-7301
East Syracuse (G-4208)

Empire Archtctural Systems Inc ....E 518 773-5109
Johnstown (G-6615)

Empire Fabricators Inc ....G 585 235-3050
Rochester (G-13387)

Encore Retail Systems Inc ....E 718 385-3443
Mamaroneck (G-7509)

Falvo Manufacturing Co Inc ....F 315 724-7925
Utica (G-15261)

Farrington Packaging Corp ....G 315 733-4600
Utica (G-15262)

▲ Fifty Door Partners LLC ....E 845 562-3332
New Windsor (G-8367)

Fina Cabinet Corp ....G 718 409-2900
Mount Vernon (G-8141)

Fleetwood Cabinet Co Inc ....G 516 379-2139
Brooklyn (G-1853)

▲ Forecast Consoles Inc ....E 631 253-9000
Hauppauge (G-5653)

Frank J Martello ....G 585 235-2780
Rochester (G-13423)

Gaughan Construction Corp ....G 718 850-9577
Richmond Hill (G-13114)

▲ Gotham City Industries Inc ....G 914 713-3449
Scarsdale (G-14236)

Greenleaf Cabinet Makers LLC ....F 315 432-4600
Syracuse (G-14905)

▲ Hamlet Products Inc ....F 914 665-0307
Mount Vernon (G-8147)

Heartwood Specialties Inc ....G 607 654-0102
Hammondsport (G-5529)

Home Ideal Inc ....G 718 762-8998
Flushing (G-4860)

▲ Home4u Inc ....G 347 262-7214
Brooklyn (G-1941)

Hunter Metal Industries Inc ....D 631 475-5900
East Patchogue (G-4154)

▲ Icestone LLC ....E 718 624-4900
Brooklyn (G-1951)

▲ Industrial Support Inc ....D 716 662-2954
Buffalo (G-2809)

Integrated Wood Components Inc ....E 607 467-1739
Deposit (G-4000)

Inter State Laminates Inc ....E 518 283-8355
Poestenkill (G-12803)

J M P Display Fixture Co Inc ....G 718 649-0333
Brooklyn (G-1981)

Johnny Mica Inc ....G 631 225-5213
Lindenhurst (G-6953)

Joseph Fedele ....G 718 448-3658
Staten Island (G-14672)

▲ Karp Associates Inc ....D...... 631 768-8300
  Melville (G-7798)
Kitchen Specialty Craftsmen ....G...... 607 739-0833
  Elmira (G-4361)
L & J Interiors Inc ....G...... 631 218-0838
  Bohemia (G-1031)
▲ Leo D Bernstein & Sons Inc ....E...... 212 337-9578
  New York (G-10198)
▲ Lifestyle-Trimco ....E...... 718 257-9101
  Brooklyn (G-2069)
Longo Commercial Cabinets Inc ....E... 631 225-4290
  Lindenhurst (G-6956)
Ludwig and Larsen ....G...... 718 369-0999
  Ridgewood (G-13151)
▲ Madjek Inc ....D...... 631 842-4475
  Amityville (G-293)
◆ Marietta Corporation ....B...... 607 753-6746
  Cortland (G-3775)
Marplex Furniture Corporation ....G... 914 969-7755
  Yonkers (G-16332)
Metropolitan Granite & MBL Inc ....G... 585 342-7020
  Rochester (G-13543)
Michael P Mmarr ....G...... 315 623-9380
  Constantia (G-3636)
▲ Mirror Show Management Inc ....D...... 585 232-4020
  Webster (G-15645)
▲ Mrp Supports LLC ....F...... 716 332-7673
  Orchard Park (G-12367)
▲ New Business Solutions Inc .....E...... 631 789-1500
  Amityville (G-298)
New Dimensions Office Group ....D...... 718 387-0995
  Brooklyn (G-2203)
Nlr Counter Tops LLC ....G...... 347 295-0410
  New York (G-10632)
Old Souls Inc ....G...... 845 809-5886
  Cold Spring (G-3522)
▲ Premier Woodworking Inc ......E...... 631 236-4100
  Hauppauge (G-5749)
R H Guest Inc ....G...... 718 675-7600
  Brooklyn (G-2319)
Red White & Blue Entps Corp ....G...... 718 565-8080
  Woodside (G-16223)
Rochester Countertop Inc ....F...... 585 338-2260
  Rochester (G-13687)
Serway Bros Inc ....G...... 315 337-0601
  Rome (G-13872)
Sharonana Enterprises Inc ....E...... 631 875-5619
  Coram (G-3699)
Solid Surfaces Inc ....D...... 585 292-5340
  Rochester (G-13736)
▲ Space-Craft Worldwide Inc .....E...... 631 603-3000
  Hauppauge (G-5768)
Specialty Services ....G...... 585 728-5650
  Wayland (G-15627)
Steelcraft Manufacturing Co .....F...... 718 277-2404
  Brooklyn (G-2456)
▲ Steeldeck Ny Inc ....F...... 718 599-3700
  Brooklyn (G-2457)
Stein Industries Inc ....E...... 631 789-2222
  Amityville (G-307)
Stereo Advantage Inc ....F...... 716 656-7161
  Cheektowaga (G-3362)
Telesca-Heyman Inc ....F...... 212 534-3442
  New York (G-11450)
Triad Counter Corp ....E...... 631 750-0615
  Bohemia (G-1088)
Universal Designs Inc ....G...... 718 721-1111
  Long Island City (G-7389)
Vitarose Corp of America ....G...... 718 951-9700
  Brooklyn (G-2565)
Wilbedone Inc ....E...... 607 756-8813
  Cortland (G-3791)
Wilsonart Intl Holdings LLC ......E...... 516 935-6980
  Bethpage (G-846)
Winerackscom Inc ....E...... 845 658-7181
  Tillson (G-15078)
Wolak Inc ....G...... 315 839-5366
  Clayville (G-3459)

2542 Partitions & Fixtures, Except Wood

260 Oak Street Inc ....G...... 877 852-4676
  Buffalo (G-2612)
▲ Aarco Products Inc ....F...... 631 924-5461
  Yaphank (G-16254)
Abaco Steel Products Inc ....G...... 631 589-1800
  Bohemia (G-960)
▲ Abbott Industries Inc ....B...... 718 291-0800
  Jamaica (G-6423)
Able Steel Equipment Co Inc .....F...... 718 361-9240
  Long Island City (G-7144)

Air Crafters Inc ....C...... 631 471-7788
  Ronkonkoma (G-13893)
▲ All American Metal Corporation ....G... 516 223-1760
  Freeport (G-4982)
All American Metal Corporation ....E... 516 623-0222
  Freeport (G-4983)
Alrod Associates Inc ....F...... 631 981-2193
  Ronkonkoma (G-13900)
American Standard Mfg Inc ......E...... 518 868-2512
  Central Bridge (G-3259)
Amscor Inc ....F...... 800 825-9800
  West Babylon (G-15689)
ASAP Rack Rental Inc ....G...... 718 499-4495
  Brooklyn (G-1539)
Avf Group Inc ....F...... 951 360-7111
  Cheektowaga (G-3339)
Bobrick Washroom Equipment Inc ....D... 518 877-7444
  Clifton Park (G-3463)
▲ Bridge Metal Industries LLC .....C...... 914 663-9200
  Mount Vernon (G-8125)
Clark Specialty Co Inc ....E...... 607 776-3193
  Bath (G-632)
◆ Core Group Displays Inc ....E...... 845 876-5109
  Rhinebeck (G-13098)
Custom Fixtures Inc ....G...... 718 965-1141
  Brooklyn (G-1710)
Dakota Systems Mfg Corp ....E...... 631 249-5811
  Farmingdale (G-4613)
Data Control Inc ....G...... 585 265-2980
  Ontario (G-12287)
Display Components Mfg Inc .....E...... 631 420-0600
  West Babylon (G-15707)
Display Shop Inc ....F...... 646 202-9494
  New York (G-9237)
▲ Display Technologies LLC ....D...... 718 321-3100
  New Hyde Park (G-8262)
▲ E-Systems Group LLC ....E...... 607 775-1100
  Conklin (G-3624)
Evans & Paul LLC ....E...... 516 576-0800
  Plainview (G-12684)
▲ Fifty Door Partners LLC ....E...... 845 562-3332
  New Windsor (G-8367)
◆ Fixtures 2000 Inc ....B...... 631 236-4100
  Hauppauge (G-5651)
Four S Showcase Manufacturing ....G... 718 649-4900
  Brooklyn (G-1863)
Frazier Industrial Company ....D...... 315 539-9256
  Waterloo (G-15552)
▼ Gaylord Bros Inc ....G...... 315 457-5070
  North Syracuse (G-12042)
▲ GF Packaging LLC ....E...... 716 692-2705
  Cheektowaga (G-3351)
▲ Glaro Inc ....D...... 631 234-1717
  Hauppauge (G-5661)
▲ Glasbau Hahn America LLC ......G...... 845 566-3331
  Newburgh (G-11867)
◆ Global Steel Products Corp ......C...... 631 586-3455
  Deer Park (G-3878)
Green Beacon Solutions LLC .....G...... 617 485-5000
  New York (G-9671)
▲ Hamlet Products Inc ....F...... 914 665-0307
  Mount Vernon (G-8147)
Hawver Display Inc ....E...... 585 544-2290
  Rochester (G-13461)
◆ Hergo Ergonomic Support Syst ....E... 888 222-7270
  Oceanside (G-12175)
Hunter Metal Industries Inc ......D...... 631 475-5900
  East Patchogue (G-4154)
◆ Inscape (new York) Inc ....D...... 716 665-6210
  Falconer (G-4544)
Inscape Inc ....E...... 716 665-6210
  Falconer (G-4545)
Jack Luckner Steel Shelving Co ....D... 718 363-0500
  Maspeth (G-7623)
Joldeson One Aerospace Inds .....D...... 718 848-7396
  Ozone Park (G-12463)
▲ Knickerbocker Partition Corp .....C...... 516 546-0550
  Melville (G-7799)
Ledan Inc ....E...... 631 239-1226
  Northport (G-12107)
▲ Lifestyle-Trimco ....E...... 718 257-9101
  Brooklyn (G-2069)
Locker Masters Inc ....F...... 518 288-3203
  Granville (G-5349)
▲ Lucia Group Inc ....G...... 631 392-4900
  Deer Park (G-3900)
Ludwig and Larsen ....G...... 718 369-0999
  Ridgewood (G-13151)
Manhattan Display Inc ....G...... 718 392-1365
  Long Island City (G-7289)

▲ Mass Mdsg Self Selection Eqp ....E... 631 234-3300
  Bohemia (G-1044)
▲ Maximum Security Products Corp ....E... 518 233-1800
  Waterford (G-15538)
▲ Millennium Stl Rack Rntals Inc ....G... 718 965-4736
  Brooklyn (G-2155)
▲ Milton Merl & Associates Inc .....G... 212 634-9292
  New York (G-10470)
▲ Mobile Media Inc ....E...... 845 744-8080
  Pine Bush (G-12625)
Modern Craft Bar Rest Equip .....G...... 631 226-5647
  Lindenhurst (G-6961)
Modu-Craft Inc ....G...... 716 694-0709
  Tonawanda (G-15123)
Nationwide Exhibitor Svcs Inc ....E...... 631 467-2034
  Central Islip (G-3285)
▲ New Business Solutions Inc .....E...... 631 789-1500
  Amityville (G-298)
▲ Parabit Systems Inc ....E...... 516 378-4800
  Bellmore (G-786)
R H Guest Inc ....G...... 718 675-7600
  Brooklyn (G-2319)
Sterling Shelf Liners Inc ....G...... 631 676-5175
  Holbrook (G-6022)
Steven Kraus Associates Inc .....G...... 631 923-2033
  Huntington (G-6225)
▲ Stone Expo & Cabinetry LLC .....F...... 516 292-2988
  West Hempstead (G-15780)
▲ Sturdy Store Displays Inc ....E...... 718 389-9919
  Brooklyn (G-2467)
Traco Manufacturing Inc ....G...... 585 343-2434
  Batavia (G-628)
Tri-Boro Shelving Inc ....G...... 718 782-8527
  Ridgewood (G-13165)
Trylon Wire & Metal Works Inc ....E... 718 542-4472
  Bronx (G-1384)
▲ Visual Millwork & Fix Mfg Inc ....D... 718 267-7800
  Deer Park (G-3952)
Yaloz Mould & Die Co Inc ....E...... 718 389-1131
  Brooklyn (G-2599)
Your Furniture Designers Inc .....G...... 845 947-3046
  West Haverstraw (G-15765)

2591 Drapery Hardware, Window Blinds & Shades

Abalene Decorating Services .....E...... 718 782-2000
  New York (G-8425)
Blinds To Go (us) Inc ....E...... 718 477-9523
  Staten Island (G-14627)
▲ Blindtek Designer Systems Inc ....F... 914 347-7100
  Ardsley (G-387)
◆ Comfortex Corporation ....C...... 518 273-3333
  Watervliet (G-15600)
D & D Window Tech Inc ....G...... 212 308-2822
  New York (G-9145)
Drapery Industries Inc ....F...... 585 232-2992
  Rochester (G-13356)
Fabric Quilters Unlimited Inc .....E...... 516 333-2866
  Westbury (G-15884)
◆ Hunter Douglas Inc ....D...... 845 664-7000
  Pearl River (G-12533)
Instant Verticals Inc ....F...... 631 501-0001
  Farmingdale (G-4650)
J Gimbel Inc ....E...... 718 296-5200
  West Hempstead (G-15772)
KPP Ltd ....G...... 516 338-5201
  Jericho (G-6585)
▲ Levolor Inc ....B...... 845 664-7000
  Pearl River (G-12537)
▼ Manhattan Shade & Glass Co Inc ....E... 212 288-5616
  Great Neck (G-5402)
Manhattan Shade & Glass Co Inc ....E... 212 288-5616
  Hauppauge (G-5707)
◆ Mechoshade Systems Inc ....C...... 718 729-2020
  Long Island City (G-7292)
Nu Ways Inc ....G...... 585 254-7510
  Rochester (G-13587)
◆ P E Guerin ....D...... 212 243-5270
  New York (G-10733)
Pj Decorators Inc ....E...... 516 735-9693
  East Meadow (G-4139)
Solar Screen Co Inc ....G...... 718 592-8222
  Corona (G-3750)
Tentina Window Fashions Inc .....C...... 631 957-9585
  Lindenhurst (G-6980)
TLC Vision (usa) Corporation .....G...... 914 395-3949
  Hartsdale (G-5570)
Vertical Research Partners LLC ....F... 212 257-6499
  New York (G-11667)

SIC

Wcd Window Coverings Inc...............E.......845 336-4511
  Lake Katrine (G-6764)
▲ Windowcraft Inc.............................F.......516 294-3580
  Garden City Park (G-5125)
Windowtex Inc...................................F.......877 294-3580
  New Hyde Park (G-8303)

2599 Furniture & Fixtures, NEC

▼ A-Plus Restaurant Equipment......G.......718 522-2656
  Brooklyn (G-1444)
▲ Adirondack Scenic Inc..................D.......518 638-8000
  Argyle (G-392)
▲ AFC Industries Inc.......................D.......718 747-0237
  College Point (G-3535)
All Star Carts & Vehicles Inc..........D.......631 666-5581
  Bay Shore (G-646)
Armada New York LLC......................F.......718 852-8105
  Brooklyn (G-1531)
Artistry In Wood of Syracuse..........F.......315 431-4022
  Syracuse (G-14819)
Brandt Equipment LLC.....................G.......718 994-0800
  Bronx (G-1217)
Bullock Boys LLC.............................F.......518 783-6161
  Latham (G-6850)
Carts Mobile Food Eqp Corp............E.......718 788-5540
  Brooklyn (G-1652)
Dellet Industries Inc........................F.......718 965-0101
  Brooklyn (G-1733)
Dine Rite Seating Products Inc........G.......631 226-8899
  Lindenhurst (G-6950)
Durall Dolly LLC................................F.......802 728-7122
  Brooklyn (G-1764)
Evans & Paul LLC.............................G.......516 576-0800
  Plainview (G-12684)
Futon City Discounters Inc...............F.......315 437-1328
  Syracuse (G-14896)
G Z G Rest & Kit Met Works.............G.......718 788-8621
  Brooklyn (G-1875)
Halfway House LLC...........................G.......518 873-2198
  Elizabethtown (G-4301)
▲ Hunt Country Furniture Inc...........F.......845 832-6601
  Wingdale (G-16159)
Ideoli Group Inc...............................F.......212 705-8769
  Port Washington (G-12887)
Inova LLC..F.......518 861-3400
  Altamont (G-195)
▲ Inova LLC....................................G.......866 528-2804
  Guilderland Center (G-5486)
Interiors-Pft Inc...............................E.......212 244-9600
  Long Island City (G-7249)
J P Installations Warehouse............F.......914 576-3188
  New Rochelle (G-8344)
Kedco Inc...F.......516 454-7800
  Farmingdale (G-4663)
Kinfolk Studios Inc...........................F.......770 617-5592
  Brooklyn (G-2026)
Kinfolk Studios Inc...........................F.......347 799-2946
  Brooklyn (G-2027)
Kinplex Corp....................................G.......631 242-4800
  Edgewood (G-4274)
L & D Manufacturing Corp................G.......718 665-5226
  Bronx (G-1295)
Lafayette Pub Inc.............................E.......212 925-4242
  New York (G-10163)
▲ Lb Furniture Industries LLC..........C.......518 828-1501
  Hudson (G-6169)
▲ Maxsun Corporation....................F.......718 418-6800
  Maspeth (G-7628)
Modern Craft Bar Rest Equip............G.......631 226-5647
  Lindenhurst (G-6961)
Modu-Craft Inc.................................F.......716 694-0709
  North Tonawanda (G-12078)
Modu-Craft Inc.................................F.......716 694-0709
  Tonawanda (G-15123)
Monroe Table Company Inc..............F.......716 945-7700
  Salamanca (G-14124)
▲ N3a Corporation.........................D.......516 284-6799
  Inwood (G-6299)
▲ NK Medical Products Inc.............G.......716 759-7200
  Amherst (G-235)
▲ Novum Medical Products Ny LLC...F.......716 759-7200
  Amherst (G-236)
R V H Estates Inc.............................G.......914 664-9888
  Mount Vernon (G-8176)
▲ Ramler International Ltd...............E.......516 353-3106
  Jericho (G-6591)
Restaurant 570 8th Avenue LLC.......F.......646 722-8191
  New York (G-11021)
Rollhaus Seating Products Inc.........F.......718 729-9111
  Long Island City (G-7344)

S & V Restaurants Corp...................E.......718 220-1140
  Bronx (G-1357)
Sandys Deli Inc...............................G.......518 297-6951
  Rouses Point (G-14068)
Smart Space Products LLC...............G.......877 777-2441
  New York (G-11272)
▼ Starliner Shipping & Travel..........G.......718 385-1515
  Brooklyn (G-2453)
T O Gronlund Company Inc...............F.......212 679-3535
  New York (G-11419)
T-Company LLC................................G.......646 290-6365
  Smithtown (G-14488)
Tao Group LLC.................................G.......646 625-4818
  New York (G-11431)
Thornwood Products Ltd..................E.......914 769-9161
  Thornwood (G-15071)
Timeless Decor LLC.........................C.......315 782-5759
  Watertown (G-15590)
Violettes Cellar LLC.........................F.......718 650-5050
  Staten Island (G-14728)
◆ VSM Investors LLC......................E.......212 351-1600
  New York (G-11708)
Wood Etc Inc....................................F.......315 484-9663
  Syracuse (G-15030)

26 PAPER AND ALLIED PRODUCTS

2611 Pulp Mills

Advanced Recovery & Recycl LLC.....F.......315 450-3301
  Baldwinsville (G-540)
Andritz Inc.......................................E.......518 745-2988
  Glens Falls (G-5240)
APC Paper Company Inc...................D.......315 384-4225
  Norfolk (G-11997)
▲ Cenibra Inc.................................G.......212 818-8242
  New York (G-8947)
Central Nat Pulp & Ppr Sls Inc.........A.......914 696-9000
  Purchase (G-13003)
Easm Machine Works LLC.................E.......518 747-5326
  Fort Edward (G-4939)
Fcr LLC..G.......845 926-1071
  Beacon (G-752)
Georgia-Pacific Corrugared LLC.......D.......585 343-3800
  Batavia (G-615)
Georgia-Pacific LLC..........................G.......631 924-7401
  Yaphank (G-16262)
Hamlin Bottle & Can Return Inc........G.......585 259-1301
  Brockport (G-1177)
Harvest Technologies Inc.................G.......518 899-7124
  Ballston Spa (G-576)
International Paper Company.............C.......607 775-1550
  Conklin (G-3625)
ITT Industries Holdings Inc..............G.......914 641-2000
  White Plains (G-16018)
Norton Pulpstones Incorporated.......G.......716 433-9400
  Lockport (G-7099)
Parsons & Whittemore Inc................B.......914 937-9009
  Port Chester (G-12827)
Parsons Whittemore Entps Corp.......E.......914 937-9009
  Port Chester (G-12828)
R D S Mountain View Trucking..........G.......315 823-4265
  Little Falls (G-6987)
◆ Repapers Corporation.................F.......305 691-1635
  Hicksville (G-5945)
Sierra Processing LLC......................F.......518 433-0020
  Schenectady (G-14305)
Suffolk Indus Recovery Corp............D.......631 732-6403
  Coram (G-3700)

2621 Paper Mills

▲ A-One Laminating Corp................G.......718 266-6002
  Brooklyn (G-1442)
Albany International Corp..................C.......518 445-2230
  Menands (G-7838)
▲ Ampac Paper LLC........................G.......845 713-6600
  Walden (G-15456)
Andex Corp.......................................E.......585 328-3790
  Rochester (G-13236)
APC Paper Company Inc...................D.......315 384-4225
  Norfolk (G-11997)
Atlas Recycling LLC..........................G.......212 925-3280
  New York (G-8672)
▼ Automation Papers Inc................G.......315 432-0565
  Syracuse (G-14822)
▲ Bigrow Paper Mfg Corp................F.......718 624-4439
  Brooklyn (G-1584)
Bristol Core Inc...............................F.......585 919-0302
  Canandaigua (G-3126)
Bristol/White Plains.........................G.......914 681-1800
  White Plains (G-15984)

BSD Aluminum Foil LLC....................E.......347 689-3875
  Brooklyn (G-1626)
Burrows Paper Corporation..............D.......315 823-2300
  Little Falls (G-6987)
Burrows Paper Corporation..............D.......315 823-2300
  Little Falls (G-6988)
▲ Carta Usa LLC.............................E.......585 436-3012
  Rochester (G-13297)
Cascades New York Inc....................C.......716 285-3681
  Niagara Falls (G-11912)
Cascades New York Inc....................E.......585 527-8110
  Rochester (G-13299)
Cascades New York Inc....................C.......518 346-6151
  Schenectady (G-14254)
Cascades New York Inc....................E.......716 681-1560
  Depew (G-3976)
Cascades New York Inc....................E.......518 689-1020
  Albany (G-58)
Cascades Tssue Group-Sales Inc.....D.......518 238-1900
  Waterford (G-15533)
▲ Cascades Tssue Group-Sales Inc...E.......819 363-5100
  Waterford (G-15534)
Cascades USA Inc............................E.......518 880-3600
  Waterford (G-15535)
Citigroup Inc....................................E.......212 816-6000
  New York (G-9014)
Clearwater Paper Corporation..........D.......315 287-1200
  Gouverneur (G-5319)
▲ Cottrell Paper Company Inc.........E.......518 885-1702
  Rock City Falls (G-13817)
◆ Crosstex International Inc............D.......631 582-6777
  Hauppauge (G-5631)
▲ Daniel O Reich Incorporated........F.......718 748-6000
  Brooklyn (G-1723)
Datagraphic Business Systems.........F.......516 485-9069
  Brentwood (G-1118)
Donne Dieu Paper Mill Inc................E.......212 226-0573
  Brooklyn (G-1757)
Dunmore Corporation.......................D.......845 279-5061
  Brewster (G-1147)
Dunn Paper - Natural Dam Inc..........D.......315 287-1200
  Gouverneur (G-5320)
Easm Machine Works LLC.................E.......518 747-5326
  Fort Edward (G-4939)
Elgreco Gt Inc..................................G.......718 777-7922
  Astoria (G-420)
Essity Prof Hygiene N Amer LLC.......E.......518 692-8434
  Greenwich (G-5470)
Essity Prof Hygiene N Amer LLC.......C.......518 583-2785
  Saratoga Springs (G-14173)
Euro Fine Paper Inc..........................G.......516 238-5253
  Garden City (G-5098)
Fibercel Packaging LLC....................E.......716 933-8703
  Portville (G-12934)
▲ Flower Cy Tissue Mills Co Inc.......D.......585 458-9200
  Rochester (G-13417)
◆ Freeport Paper Industries Inc......D.......631 851-1555
  Central Islip (G-3276)
Georgia-Pacific LLC..........................A.......518 561-3500
  Plattsburgh (G-12748)
▼ Gooding Co Inc............................E.......716 266-6252
  Lockport (G-7082)
Gratitude & Company Inc..................G.......607 277-3188
  Ithaca (G-6383)
Hollingsworth & Vose Company........C.......518 695-8000
  Greenwich (G-5473)
Huhtamaki Inc..................................A.......315 593-5311
  Fulton (G-5064)
International Paper Company.............A.......518 585-6761
  Ticonderoga (G-15074)
International Paper Company.............C.......845 986-6409
  Tuxedo Park (G-15217)
International Paper Company.............C.......315 797-5120
  Utica (G-15278)
International Paper Company.............C.......607 775-1550
  Conklin (G-3625)
▲ Irving Consumer Products Inc.......B.......518 747-4151
  Fort Edward (G-4940)
Kimberly-Clark Corporation..............D.......212 554-4252
  New York (G-10103)
◆ Knowlton Technologies LLC.........C.......315 782-0600
  Watertown (G-15580)
◆ Lenaro Paper Co Inc....................F.......631 439-8800
  Central Islip (G-3282)
Lion Die-Cutting Co Inc....................E.......718 383-8841
  Brooklyn (G-2077)
Minimill Technologies Inc.................F.......315 692-4557
  Syracuse (G-14944)
▲ Mohawk Fine Papers Inc.............B.......518 237-1740
  Cohoes (G-3510)

Morcon Inc ....D 518 677-8511
  Eagle Bridge *(G-4072)*
National Paper Converting Inc ....G 607 687-6049
  Owego *(G-12434)*
◆ Nice-Pak Products Inc ....B 845 365-1700
  Orangeburg *(G-12324)*
Nice-Pak Products Inc ....E 845 353-6090
  West Nyack *(G-15828)*
North End Paper Co Inc ....G 315 593-8100
  Fulton *(G-5073)*
▲ NY Cutting Inc ....G 646 434-1355
  Suffern *(G-14763)*
◆ Omniafiltra LLC ....G 315 346-7300
  Beaver Falls *(G-761)*
Palisades Paper Inc ....G 845 354-0333
  Spring Valley *(G-14580)*
▲ Paper Solutions Inc ....G 718 499-4666
  Brooklyn *(G-2244)*
◆ Plastirun Corporation ....D 631 273-2626
  Brentwood *(G-1126)*
Post Heritage Inc ....G 646 286-7579
  Brooklyn *(G-2271)*
◆ Potsdam Specialty Paper Inc ....D 315 265-4000
  Potsdam *(G-12939)*
▲ Precare Corp ....G 631 667-1055
  Hauppauge *(G-5746)*
▲ Precision Charts Inc ....E 631 244-8295
  Bohemia *(G-1064)*
◆ Professnal Dsposables Intl Inc .....E 800 999-6423
  Orangeburg *(G-12329)*
Refill Services LLC ....G 607 369-5864
  Sidney *(G-14435)*
Sabin Robbins Paper Company ....E 513 874-5270
  New York *(G-11112)*
▲ Scalamandre Wallpaper Inc ....B 631 467-8800
  Hauppauge *(G-5760)*
Schweitzer-Mauduit Intl Inc ....C 518 329-4222
  Ancram *(G-355)*
Stephen Singer Pattern Co Inc ....F 212 947-2902
  New York *(G-11359)*
Summit Fincl Disclosure LLC ....E 212 913-0510
  New York *(G-11390)*
▲ T & L Trading Co ....G 718 782-5550
  Brooklyn *(G-2484)*
Tag Envelope Co Inc ....E 718 389-6844
  College Point *(G-3567)*
Twin Rivers Paper Company LLC ....C 315 348-8491
  Lyons Falls *(G-7456)*
Twin Rivers Paper Company LLC ....B 315 823-2300
  Little Falls *(G-6994)*
▲ US Alliance Paper Inc ....C 631 254-3030
  Edgewood *(G-4290)*
Verso Corporation ....B 212 599-2700
  New York *(G-11665)*
Westrock Container LLC ....D 518 842-2450
  Amsterdam *(G-353)*

2631 Paperboard Mills

Alpine Paper Box Co Inc ....E 718 345-4040
  Brooklyn *(G-1492)*
▲ American Wire Tie Inc ....E 716 337-2412
  North Collins *(G-12023)*
▲ Burt Rigid Box Inc ....F 607 433-2510
  Oneonta *(G-12262)*
▼ Continental Kraft Corp ....G 516 681-9090
  Jericho *(G-6575)*
Di Domenico Packaging Co Inc ....G 718 727-5454
  Staten Island *(G-14645)*
Enterprise Folding Box Co Inc ....E 716 876-6421
  Buffalo *(G-2747)*
Farrington Packaging Corp ....E 315 733-4600
  Utica *(G-15262)*
▲ Greenpac Mill LLC ....C 716 299-0560
  Niagara Falls *(G-11933)*
International Paper Company ....D 607 775-1550
  Conklin *(G-3625)*
Lydall Performance Mtls US Inc ....D 518 686-3400
  Hoosick Falls *(G-6085)*
M&F Stringing LLC ....E 914 664-1600
  Mount Vernon *(G-8160)*
Ms Paper Products Co Inc ....G 718 624-0248
  Brooklyn *(G-2180)*
Niagara Fiberboard Inc ....E 716 434-8881
  Lockport *(G-7097)*
Pactiv LLC ....E 585 248-1213
  Pittsford *(G-12655)*
Paper Box Corp ....D 212 226-7490
  New York *(G-10748)*
Pdf Seal Incorporated ....E 631 595-7035
  Hauppauge *(G-5737)*

Pkg Group ....G 212 965-0112
  New York *(G-10849)*
Prestige Box Corporation ....E 516 773-3115
  Great Neck *(G-5415)*
Professional Packg Svcs Inc ....E 518 677-5100
  Eagle Bridge *(G-4073)*
▲ Tin Box Company of America Inc ...E 631 845-1600
  Farmingdale *(G-4757)*
▲ Westrock - Solvay Llc ....C 315 484-9050
  Syracuse *(G-15025)*
Westrock Container LLC ....D 518 842-2450
  Amsterdam *(G-353)*
Westrock Cp LLC ....D 315 484-9050
  Syracuse *(G-15026)*
Westrock Mwv LLC ....C 212 688-5000
  New York *(G-11748)*
Westrock Rkt LLC ....F 315 487-6111
  Camillus *(G-3114)*
Westrock Rkt Company ....C 770 448-2193
  Syracuse *(G-15027)*

2652 Set-Up Paperboard Boxes

A Fleisig Paper Box Corp ....F 212 226-7490
  New York *(G-8415)*
American Package Company Inc ....E 718 389-4444
  Brooklyn *(G-1500)*
▲ Brick & Ballerstein Inc ....D 718 497-1400
  Ridgewood *(G-13142)*
Burt Rigid Box Inc ....D 607 433-2510
  Oneonta *(G-12261)*
Drescher Paper Box Inc ....F 716 854-0288
  Clarence *(G-3429)*
Earlville Paper Box Co Inc ....E 315 691-2131
  Earlville *(G-4076)*
▲ F M Howell & Company ....E 607 734-6291
  Elmira *(G-4351)*
Jordon Box Company Inc ....E 315 422-3419
  Syracuse *(G-14920)*
Lionel Habas Associates Inc ....F 212 860-8454
  New York *(G-10223)*
Parlor City Paper Box Co Inc ....D 607 772-0600
  Binghamton *(G-903)*
▲ Paul T Freund Corporation ....D 315 597-4873
  Palmyra *(G-12493)*
Prestige Box Corporation ....E 516 773-3115
  Great Neck *(G-5415)*
Propak Inc ....G 518 677-5100
  Eagle Bridge *(G-4074)*
▲ Pure Trade Us Inc ....E 212 256-1600
  New York *(G-10928)*
▲ Seneca FLS Spc & Logistics Co .....D 315 568-4139
  Seneca Falls *(G-14372)*

2653 Corrugated & Solid Fiber Boxes

Action Paper Co Inc ....G 718 665-1652
  Bronx *(G-1196)*
Ares Printing and Packg Corp ....C 718 858-8760
  Brooklyn *(G-1527)*
▼ Arma Container Corp ....E 631 254-1200
  Deer Park *(G-3841)*
Brand Box USA LLC ....G 607 584-7682
  Binghamton *(G-863)*
Buckeye Corrugated Inc ....D 585 924-1600
  Victor *(G-15396)*
Burt Rigid Box Inc ....D 607 433-2510
  Oneonta *(G-12261)*
Cattaraugus Containers Inc ....E 716 676-2000
  Franklinville *(G-4966)*
▲ Color Carton Corp ....D 718 665-0840
  Bronx *(G-1228)*
Dory Enterprises Inc ....F 607 565-7079
  Waverly *(G-15620)*
Fennell Industries LLC ....E 607 733-6693
  Elmira *(G-4352)*
Fiber USA Corp ....E 718 888-1512
  Flushing *(G-4852)*
Gavin Mfg Corp ....E 631 467-0040
  Farmingdale *(G-4636)*
▲ General Die and Die Cutng Inc .....D 516 665-3584
  Massapequa Park *(G-7655)*
◆ General Fibre Products Corp ....D 516 358-7500
  New Hyde Park *(G-8270)*
International Paper Company ....C 585 663-1000
  Rochester *(G-13482)*
International Paper Company ....D 607 775-1550
  Conklin *(G-3625)*
International Paper Company ....F 716 852-2144
  Buffalo *(G-2814)*
International Paper Company ....D 518 372-6461
  Glenville *(G-5272)*

J & M Packaging Inc ....F 631 608-3069
  Hauppauge *(G-5679)*
Jamestown Cont of Rochester ....D 585 254-9190
  Rochester *(G-13489)*
▼ Jamestown Container Corp ....C 716 665-4623
  Falconer *(G-4547)*
Key Container Corp ....G 631 582-3847
  East Islip *(G-4129)*
Lakeside Container Corp ....F 518 561-6150
  Plattsburgh *(G-12757)*
Land Packaging Corp ....F 914 472-5976
  Scarsdale *(G-14238)*
M C Packaging Corporation ....E 631 643-3763
  Babylon *(G-522)*
▲ Mkt329 Inc ....E 631 249-5500
  Farmingdale *(G-4688)*
▲ Mp Displays LLC ....G 845 268-4113
  Valley Cottage *(G-15319)*
▲ Niagara Sheets LLC ....G 716 692-1129
  North Tonawanda *(G-12079)*
Norampac New York City Inc ....C 718 340-2100
  Maspeth *(G-7630)*
▲ Orange Die Cutting Corp ....G 845 562-0900
  Newburgh *(G-11879)*
▲ Orcon Industries Corp ....D 585 768-7000
  Le Roy *(G-6905)*
Packaging Corporation America ....C 315 457-6780
  Liverpool *(G-7029)*
Pactiv LLC ....G 315 457-6780
  Liverpool *(G-7030)*
Pactiv LLC ....E 585 248-1213
  Pittsford *(G-12655)*
Paperworks Industries Inc ....C 315 638-4355
  Baldwinsville *(G-552)*
Parlor City Paper Box Co Inc ....D 607 772-0600
  Binghamton *(G-903)*
Philpac Corporation ....E 716 875-8005
  Buffalo *(G-2917)*
President Cont Group II LLC ....E 845 516-1600
  Middletown *(G-7927)*
Prestige Box Corporation ....E 516 773-3115
  Great Neck *(G-5415)*
Professional Packg Svcs Inc ....E 518 677-5100
  Eagle Bridge *(G-4073)*
R D A Container Corporation ....E 585 247-2323
  Gates *(G-5142)*
▲ Seneca FLS Spc & Logistics Co .....D 315 568-4139
  Seneca Falls *(G-14372)*
▲ Spaeth Design Inc ....E 718 606-9685
  Woodside *(G-16225)*
▲ Specialized Packg Group Inc ....C 315 638-4355
  Baldwinsville *(G-553)*
Specialized Packg Radisson LLC ....C 315 638-4355
  Baldwinsville *(G-554)*
Syracuse Corrugated Box Corp ....F 315 437-9901
  East Syracuse *(G-4241)*
▲ Technical Library Service Inc ....F 212 219-0771
  Brooklyn *(G-2495)*
Technical Packaging Inc ....F 516 223-2300
  Baldwin *(G-537)*
Tin Inc ....D 607 775-1550
  Conklin *(G-3629)*
Track 7 Inc ....G 845 544-1810
  Warwick *(G-15521)*
Valentine Packaging Corp ....F 718 418-6000
  Maspeth *(G-7641)*
Westrock - Southern Cont LLC ....C 315 487-6111
  Camillus *(G-3113)*
Westrock Container LLC ....C 518 842-2450
  Amsterdam *(G-353)*
Westrock Cp LLC ....C 716 694-1000
  North Tonawanda *(G-12098)*
Westrock Cp LLC ....C 770 448-2193
  New Hartford *(G-8248)*
Westrock Rkt LLC ....C 631 586-6000
  Deer Park *(G-3953)*
Westrock Rkt LLC ....C 770 448-2193
  Camillus *(G-3115)*

2655 Fiber Cans, Tubes & Drums

Acran Spill Containment Inc ....F 631 841-2300
  Massapequa *(G-7643)*
American Intrmdal Cont Mfg LLC ....G 631 774-6790
  Hauppauge *(G-5591)*
Caraustar Industries Inc ....G 716 874-0393
  Buffalo *(G-2692)*
Carthage Fibre Drum Inc ....F 315 493-2730
  Carthage *(G-3194)*
Consolidated Container Co LLC ....C 585 262-6470
  Rochester *(G-13325)*

S I C

◆ Diemolding Corporation ....C 315 363-4710
Wampsville *(G-15480)*
Greif Inc ....D 716 836-4200
Tonawanda *(G-15109)*
Industrial Paper Tube Inc ....F 718 893-5000
Bronx *(G-1281)*
Philpac Corporation ....E 716 875-8005
Buffalo *(G-2917)*
▲ Skydyne Company ....D 845 858-6400
Port Jervis *(G-12857)*
Syraco Products Inc ....F 315 476-5306
Syracuse *(G-15002)*

2656 Sanitary Food Containers

Amscan Inc ....F 845 469-9116
Chester *(G-3370)*
Apexx Omni-Graphics Inc ....D 718 326-3330
Maspeth *(G-7591)*
Consolidated Container Co LLC ....C 585 262-6470
Rochester *(G-13325)*
Ecoquality Inc ....G 718 887-7876
Brooklyn *(G-1780)*
Elgreco Gt Inc ....G 718 777-7922
Astoria *(G-420)*
Hadp LLC ....F 518 831-6824
Scotia *(G-14331)*
International Paper Company ....C 607 775-1550
Conklin *(G-3625)*
Pactiv LLC ....E 518 562-6101
Plattsburgh *(G-12766)*
◆ Plastirun Corporation ....D 631 273-2626
Brentwood *(G-1126)*
▲ Sqp Inc ....C 518 831-6800
Schenectady *(G-14307)*

2657 Folding Paperboard Boxes

Abbot & Abbot Box Corp ....F 888 930-5972
Long Island City *(G-7143)*
Alpha Packaging Industries Inc ....E 718 267-4115
Long Island City *(G-7152)*
▲ Arkay Packaging Corporation ....E 631 273-2000
Hauppauge *(G-5593)*
Burt Rigid Box Inc ....D 607 433-2510
Oneonta *(G-12261)*
Cattaraugus Containers Inc ....E 716 676-2000
Franklinville *(G-4966)*
Climax Packaging Inc ....C 315 376-8000
Lowville *(G-7414)*
▲ Color Carton Corp ....D 718 665-0840
Bronx *(G-1228)*
Designers Folding Box Corp ....E 716 853-5141
Buffalo *(G-2728)*
Diamond Packaging Holdings LLC ......G 585 334-8030
Rochester *(G-13343)*
◆ Diamond Paper Box Company ....B 585 334-8030
Rochester *(G-13344)*
Disc Graphics Inc ....C 631 300-1129
Hauppauge *(G-5637)*
▲ Disc Graphics Inc ....D 631 234-1400
Hauppauge *(G-5638)*
▲ F M Howell & Company ....D 607 734-6291
Elmira *(G-4351)*
Fairview Paper Box Corp ....E 585 786-5230
Warsaw *(G-15507)*
Flower City Printing Inc ....C 585 663-9000
Rochester *(G-13415)*
Gavin Mfg Corp ....E 631 467-0040
Farmingdale *(G-4636)*
▼ Gaylord Bros Inc ....D 315 457-5070
North Syracuse *(G-12042)*
Genpak Industries Inc ....E 518 798-9511
Middletown *(G-7910)*
▲ HSM Packaging Corporation ....D 315 476-7996
Liverpool *(G-7012)*
▲ Knoll Printing & Packaging Inc .....E 516 621-0100
Syosset *(G-14791)*
M C Packaging Corporation ....E 631 643-3763
Babylon *(G-522)*
◆ Mod-Pac Corp ....C 716 898-8480
Buffalo *(G-2869)*
Multi Packg Solutions Intl Ltd ....E 646 885-0005
New York *(G-10520)*
◆ Novel Box Company Ltd ....E 718 965-2222
Brooklyn *(G-2221)*
Pactiv LLC ....C 518 562-6101
Plattsburgh *(G-12766)*
Paper Box Corp ....D 212 226-7490
New York *(G-10748)*
Premier Packaging Corporation ....E 585 924-8460
Victor *(G-15424)*

Prestige Box Corporation ....E 516 773-3115
Great Neck *(G-5415)*
▲ Specialized Packg Group Inc ....G 315 638-4355
Baldwinsville *(G-553)*
Specialized Packg Radisson LLC ......C 315 638-4355
Baldwinsville *(G-554)*
▲ Standard Group ....E 718 335-5500
Great Neck *(G-5424)*
▲ Standard Group LLC ....C 718 507-6430
Great Neck *(G-5425)*
Viking Industries Inc ....D 845 883-6325
New Paltz *(G-8314)*
Visitainer Corp ....E 718 636-0300
Brooklyn *(G-2564)*

2671 Paper Coating & Laminating for Packaging

▲ Allied Converters Inc ....E 914 235-1585
New Rochelle *(G-8319)*
American Packaging Corporation ......C 585 537-4650
Churchville *(G-3408)*
American Packaging Corporation ......G 585 254-2002
Rochester *(G-13229)*
American Packaging Corporation ......G 585 254-9500
Rochester *(G-13230)*
Anasia Inc ....G 718 588-1407
Bronx *(G-1205)*
Apexx Omni-Graphics Inc ....D 718 326-3330
Maspeth *(G-7591)*
Ares Box LLC ....D 718 858-8760
Brooklyn *(G-1526)*
Berry Plastics Corporation ....B 315 986-6270
Macedon *(G-7463)*
Brook & Whittle Limited ....F 716 691-4348
Amherst *(G-214)*
Brook & Whittle Limited ....F 716 853-1688
Buffalo *(G-2666)*
Cameo Process Corp ....G 914 948-0082
White Plains *(G-15988)*
CCL Label Inc ....F 716 852-2155
Buffalo *(G-2693)*
Classic Labels Inc ....E 631 467-2300
Patchogue *(G-12498)*
Colad Group LLC ....D 716 961-1776
Buffalo *(G-2703)*
Cove Point Holdings LLC ....E 212 599-3388
New York *(G-9113)*
Craft Packaging Inc ....G 718 633-4045
Brooklyn *(G-1694)*
De Luxe Packaging Corp ....E 416 754-4633
Saugerties *(G-14200)*
Depot Label Company Inc ....G 631 467-2952
Patchogue *(G-12499)*
▲ Dolco LLC ....E 585 657-7777
Bloomfield *(G-946)*
▲ F M Howell & Company ....D 607 734-6291
Elmira *(G-4351)*
▲ Folene Packaging LLC ....G 917 626-6740
Brooklyn *(G-1857)*
◆ General Fibre Products Corp ....D 516 358-7500
New Hyde Park *(G-8270)*
General Trade Mark La ....G 718 979-7261
Staten Island *(G-14655)*
International Paper Company ....C 585 663-1000
Rochester *(G-13482)*
▲ K Sidrane Inc ....E 631 393-6974
Farmingdale *(G-4659)*
Mason Transparent Package Inc ....G 718 792-6000
Bronx *(G-1307)*
Multi Packaging Solutions Inc ....E 516 488-2000
Hicksville *(G-5932)*
◆ Multi Packaging Solutions Inc ......E 646 885-0005
New York *(G-10519)*
Nameplate Mfrs of Amer ....G 631 752-0055
Farmingdale *(G-4690)*
Nova Packaging Ltd Inc ....G 914 232-8406
Katonah *(G-6637)*
Pactiv LLC ....E 518 562-6101
Plattsburgh *(G-12766)*
Patco Tapes Inc ....G 718 497-1527
Maspeth *(G-7634)*
Penta-Tech Coated Products LLC ......F 315 986-4098
Macedon *(G-7468)*
Pliant LLC ....B 315 986-6286
Macedon *(G-7469)*
▲ Printex Packaging Corporation .....D 631 234-4300
Islandia *(G-6343)*
▲ Quality Circle Products Inc ....D 914 736-6600
Montrose *(G-8078)*

▲ RMS Packaging Inc ....F 914 205-2070
Peekskill *(G-12556)*
Saint-Gobain Prfmce Plas Corp ....C 518 642-2200
Granville *(G-5355)*
◆ Shaant Industries Inc ....C 716 366-3654
Dunkirk *(G-4066)*
Smart USA Inc ....F 631 969-1111
Bay Shore *(G-715)*
▲ Time Release Sciences Inc ....C 716 823-4580
Buffalo *(G-3011)*
◆ Transcntinental Ultra Flex Inc ......B 718 272-9100
Brooklyn *(G-2516)*
▲ Tri-Plex Packaging Corporation ....E 212 481-6070
New York *(G-11539)*
◆ Universal Packg Systems Inc ....A 631 543-2277
Hauppauge *(G-5792)*
Valley Industrial Products Inc ....E 631 385-9300
Huntington *(G-6231)*
W E W Container Corporation ....E 718 827-8150
Brooklyn *(G-2572)*
Westrock Mwv LLC ....C 212 688-5000
New York *(G-11748)*

2672 Paper Coating & Laminating, Exc for Packaging

▲ A-One Laminating Corp ....G 718 266-6002
Brooklyn *(G-1442)*
Albany International Corp ....D 518 447-6400
Menands *(G-7839)*
Avery Dennison Corporation ....C 626 304-2000
New York *(G-8690)*
Berry Specialty Tapes LLC ....E 631 727-6000
Riverhead *(G-13172)*
C & R De Santis Inc ....E 718 447-5076
Staten Island *(G-14633)*
CCL Label Inc ....F 716 852-2155
Buffalo *(G-2693)*
Classic Labels Inc ....E 631 467-2300
Patchogue *(G-12498)*
Clp Holdings LLC ....G 917 846-5094
New York *(G-9038)*
Cove Point Holdings LLC ....E 212 599-3388
New York *(G-9113)*
Cytec Industries Inc ....D 716 372-9650
Olean *(G-12231)*
Dunmore Corporation ....D 845 279-5061
Brewster *(G-1147)*
Eis Legacy LLC ....E 585 426-5330
Rochester *(G-13380)*
◆ Felix Schoeller North Amer Inc .....D 315 298-8425
Pulaski *(G-12994)*
Greenbush Tape & Label Inc ....E 518 465-2389
Albany *(G-82)*
Itac Label & Tag Corp ....G 718 625-2148
Brooklyn *(G-1973)*
Janice Moses Represents ....G 212 898-4898
New York *(G-9975)*
▲ K Sidrane Inc ....E 631 393-6974
Farmingdale *(G-4659)*
▲ Kleen Stik Industries Inc ....F 718 984-5031
Staten Island *(G-14674)*
Label Gallery Inc ....E 607 334-3244
Norwich *(G-12124)*
Liberty Label Mfg Inc ....F 631 737-2365
Holbrook *(G-6006)*
◆ Merco Hackensack Inc ....G 845 357-3699
Hillburn *(G-5970)*
Micro Essential Laboratory ....E 718 338-3618
Brooklyn *(G-2152)*
▲ Mohawk Fine Papers Inc ....B 518 237-1740
Cohoes *(G-3510)*
Neenah Northeast LLC ....G 315 376-3571
Lowville *(G-7419)*
New York Cutting & Gumming Co ......E 212 563-0145
Middletown *(G-7924)*
Oaklee International Inc ....D 631 436-7900
Ronkonkoma *(G-13985)*
◆ P C I Paper Conversions Inc ....C 315 437-1641
Syracuse *(G-14958)*
Patco Tapes Inc ....G 718 497-1527
Maspeth *(G-7634)*
Princeton Label & Packaging ....E 609 490-0800
Patchogue *(G-12510)*
▲ Rochester 100 Inc ....C 585 475-0200
Rochester *(G-13679)*
▲ S & S Prtg Die-Cutting Co Inc ......E 718 388-8990
Brooklyn *(G-2372)*
Stoney Croft Converters Inc ....F 718 608-9800
Staten Island *(G-14715)*

Syracuse Label Co Inc ....D 315 422-1037
Syracuse *(G-15008)*

T L F Graphics Inc ....D 585 272-5500
Rochester *(G-13757)*

◆ Tape-It Inc ....E 631 243-4100
Bay Shore *(G-721)*

▲ Tri-Flex Label Corp ....E 631 293-0411
Farmingdale *(G-4758)*

▲ Uniflex Holdings LLC ....F 516 932-2000
Hauppauge *(G-5790)*

Valley Industrial Products Inc ....E 631 385-9300
Huntington *(G-6231)*

2673 Bags: Plastics, Laminated & Coated

◆ Ace Bag & Burlap Company Inc ......F 718 319-9300
Bronx *(G-1192)*

▲ Aladdin Packaging LLC ....D 631 273-4747
Hauppauge *(G-5582)*

Alco Plastics Inc ....E 716 683-3020
Lancaster *(G-6793)*

▲ Allied Converters Inc ....E 914 235-1585
New Rochelle *(G-8319)*

▲ Amby International Inc ....G 718 645-0964
Brooklyn *(G-1496)*

American Packaging Corporation ......G 585 254-2002
Rochester *(G-13229)*

American Packaging Corporation ......C 585 254-9500
Rochester *(G-13230)*

◆ API Industries Inc ....B 845 365-2200
Orangeburg *(G-12305)*

API Industries Inc ....C 845 365-2200
Orangeburg *(G-12306)*

▲ Bag Arts The Art Packaging LLC ......G 212 684-7020
New York *(G-8716)*

▲ Bags Unlimited Inc ....E 585 436-6282
Rochester *(G-13258)*

Berry Global Inc ....C 315 986-2161
Macedon *(G-7462)*

Centre De Conformite ICC Inc ......C 716 283-0002
Niagara Falls *(G-11914)*

Clear View Bag Company Inc ......C 518 458-7153
Albany *(G-61)*

Colden Closet LLC ....G 716 713-6125
East Aurora *(G-4084)*

D Bag Lady Inc ....G 585 425-8095
Fairport *(G-4495)*

Edco Supply Corporation ....D 718 788-8108
Brooklyn *(G-1782)*

Elgreco Gt Inc ....G 718 777-7922
Astoria *(G-420)*

Excellent Poly Inc ....F 718 768-6555
Brooklyn *(G-1820)*

Filmpak Extrusion LLC ....D 631 293-6767
Melville *(G-7782)*

▲ Fortune Poly Products Inc ......F 718 361-0767
Jamaica *(G-6442)*

▼ Franklin Poly Film Inc ....E 718 492-3523
Brooklyn *(G-1865)*

Garb-O-Liner Inc ....G 914 235-1585
New Rochelle *(G-8334)*

Golden Group International Ltd ......G 845 440-1025
Patterson *(G-12517)*

▲ H G Maybeck Co Inc ....E 718 297-4410
Jamaica *(G-6447)*

◆ Ivi Services Inc ....D 607 729-5111
Binghamton *(G-889)*

Jad Corp of America ....E 718 762-8900
College Point *(G-3548)*

▲ Jay Bags Inc ....G 845 459-6500
Spring Valley *(G-14573)*

▲ JM Murray Center Inc ....C 607 756-9913
Cortland *(G-3774)*

▲ Josh Packaging Inc ....E 631 822-1660
Hauppauge *(G-5681)*

▲ Maco Bag Corporation ....C 315 226-1000
Newark *(G-11844)*

◆ Magcrest Packaging Inc ....G 845 425-0451
Monsey *(G-8039)*

Manhattan Poly Bag Corporation ......E 917 689-7549
Brooklyn *(G-2108)*

Mason Transparent Package Inc ......E 718 792-6000
Bronx *(G-1307)*

▲ Metropolitan Packg Mfg Corp ......E 718 383-2700
Brooklyn *(G-2149)*

Mint-X Products Corporation ....F 877 646-8224
College Point *(G-3554)*

Modern Plastic Bags Mfg Inc ......G 718 237-2985
Brooklyn *(G-2166)*

▲ New York Packaging Corp ....D 516 746-0600
New Hyde Park *(G-8284)*

▲ New York Packaging II LLC ....E 516 746-0600
Garden City Park *(G-5122)*

◆ Noteworthy Industries Inc ....C 518 842-2662
Amsterdam *(G-344)*

Nova Packaging Ltd Inc ....E 914 232-8406
Katonah *(G-6637)*

▲ Pacific Poly Product Corp ....F 718 786-7129
Long Island City *(G-7317)*

▲ Pack America Corp ....G 212 508-6666
New York *(G-10740)*

Pactiv LLC ....C 585 394-5125
Canandaigua *(G-3138)*

Pactiv LLC ....C 518 793-2524
Glens Falls *(G-5264)*

Paradise Plastics LLC ....E 718 788-3733
Brooklyn *(G-2246)*

▲ Paramount Equipment Inc ....E 631 981-4422
Ronkonkoma *(G-13991)*

▲ Poly Craft Industries Corp ....E 631 630-6731
Hauppauge *(G-5744)*

◆ Poly-Pak Industries Inc ....B 800 969-1933
Melville *(G-7816)*

▲ Primo Plastics Inc ....E 718 349-1000
Brooklyn *(G-2286)*

▲ Protective Lining Corp ....D 718 854-3838
Brooklyn *(G-2302)*

Rainbow Poly Bag Co Inc ....E 718 386-3500
Brooklyn *(G-2326)*

▲ Rege Inc ....E 845 565-7772
New Windsor *(G-8380)*

Repellem Consumer Pdts Corp ......F 631 273-3992
Bohemia *(G-1070)*

▲ Rtr Bag & Co Ltd ....G 212 620-0011
New York *(G-11095)*

Salerno Packaging Inc ....F 518 563-3636
Plattsburgh *(G-12775)*

▼ Select Fabricators Inc ....F 585 393-0650
Canandaigua *(G-3142)*

Supreme Poly Plastics Inc ....E 718 456-9300
Brooklyn *(G-2478)*

▲ T M I Plastics Industries Inc ......F 718 383-0363
Brooklyn *(G-2485)*

▲ Tai Seng ....G 718 399-6311
Brooklyn *(G-2491)*

Technipoly Manufacturing Inc ......E 718 383-0363
Brooklyn *(G-2496)*

Tg Polymers Inc ....G 585 670-9427
Webster *(G-15656)*

▲ Trinity Packaging Corporation ......F 914 273-4111
Armonk *(G-404)*

Trinity Packaging Corporation ....E 716 668-3111
Buffalo *(G-3020)*

▲ Uniflex Holdings LLC ....F 516 932-2000
Hauppauge *(G-5790)*

United Plastics Inc ....G 718 389-2255
Brooklyn *(G-2539)*

W E W Container Corporation ....E 718 827-8150
Brooklyn *(G-2572)*

2674 Bags: Uncoated Paper & Multiwall

333 J & M Food Corp ....F 718 381-1493
Ridgewood *(G-13136)*

American Packaging Corporation ......C 585 254-9500
Rochester *(G-13230)*

▲ Ampac Paper LLC ....G 845 713-6600
Walden *(G-15456)*

APC Paper Company Inc ....D 315 384 4225
Norfolk *(G-11997)*

▲ Bag Arts The Art Packaging LLC ......G 212 684-7020
New York *(G-8716)*

▲ Custom Eco Friendly LLC ....F 347 227-0229
Roslyn *(G-14041)*

Elgreco Gt Inc ....G 718 777-7922
Astoria *(G-420)*

▲ R P Fedder Corp ....E 585 288-1600
Rochester *(G-13666)*

▲ Rtr Bag & Co Ltd ....G 212 620-0011
New York *(G-11095)*

Seoul Shopping Bag Inc ....G 718 439-9226
Brooklyn *(G-2394)*

◆ Shalam Imports Inc ....F 718 686-6271
Brooklyn *(G-2402)*

▲ Uniflex Holdings LLC ....F 516 932-2000
Hauppauge *(G-5790)*

Westrock Container LLC ....D 518 842-2450
Amsterdam *(G-353)*

2675 Die-Cut Paper & Board

Able National Corp ....E 718 386-8801
Brooklyn *(G-1450)*

All Out Die Cutting Inc ....E 718 346-6666
Brooklyn *(G-1486)*

Allied Sample Card Co Inc ....E 718 238-0523
Brooklyn *(G-1489)*

American Dsplay Die Ctters Inc ......E 212 645-1274
New York *(G-8549)*

Art Industries of New York ....E 212 633-9200
New York *(G-8628)*

▲ Borden & Riley Paper Co Inc ......E 718 454-9494
Hollis *(G-6040)*

Dia ....G 212 675-4097
New York *(G-9216)*

▲ General Die and Die Cutng Inc ......D 516 665-3584
Massapequa Park *(G-7655)*

◆ General Fibre Products Corp ....D 516 358-7500
New Hyde Park *(G-8270)*

Hubray Inc ....F 800 645-2855
North Baldwin *(G-12006)*

◆ Kleer-Fax Inc ....D 631 225-1100
Amityville *(G-286)*

Leather Indexes Corp ....D 516 827-1900
Hicksville *(G-5923)*

Lion Die-Cutting Co Inc ....E 718 383-8841
Brooklyn *(G-2077)*

Manufacturers Indexing Pdts ....G 631 271-0956
Halesite *(G-5488)*

New Horizon Graphics Inc ....E 631 231-8055
Hauppauge *(G-5727)*

New York Cutting & Gumming Co ......E 212 563-4146
Middletown *(G-7924)*

Norampac New York City Inc ....C 718 340-2100
Maspeth *(G-7630)*

▲ Paperworld Inc ....E 516 221-2702
Bellmore *(G-785)*

Precision Diecutting Inc ....G 315 776-8465
Port Byron *(G-12811)*

Premier Packaging Corporation ......E 585 924-8460
Victor *(G-15424)*

▲ S & S Prtg Die-Cutting Co Inc ......F 718 388-8990
Brooklyn *(G-2372)*

Spectrum Prtg Lithography Inc ......E 212 255-3131
New York *(G-11316)*

Ums Manufacturing LLC ....F 518 562-2410
Plattsburgh *(G-12786)*

2676 Sanitary Paper Prdts

▲ Alyk Inc ....E 866 232-0970
New York *(G-8535)*

Attends Healthcare Inc ....A 212 338-5100
New York *(G-8675)*

Becks Classic Mfg Inc ....D 631 435-3800
Brentwood *(G-1116)*

◆ Bentley Manufacturing Inc ....G 212 714-1800
New York *(G-8759)*

▲ Cellu Tissue - Long Island LLC ......C 631 232-2626
Central Islip *(G-3267)*

▲ Corman USA Inc ....G 718 727-7455
Staten Island *(G-14643)*

◆ Crosstex International Inc ....D 631 582-6777
Hauppauge *(G-5631)*

Deluxe Packaging Corp ....F 845 246-6090
Saugerties *(G-14201)*

◆ First Quality Products Inc ....G 516 829-4949
Great Neck *(G-5388)*

▲ Florelle Tissue Corporation ....F 647 997-7405
Brownville *(G-2607)*

Georgia-Pacific LLC ....G 518 561-3500
Plattsburgh *(G-12748)*

HFC Prestige Intl US LLC ....A 212 389-7800
New York *(G-9778)*

Kas Direct LLC ....E 516 934-0541
Westbury *(G-15901)*

Kimberly-Clark Corporation ....D 212 554-4252
New York *(G-10103)*

L VII Resilient LLC ....F 631 987-5819
Medford *(G-7716)*

▲ Maxim Hygiene Products Inc ......F 516 621-3323
Mineola *(G-7988)*

Monthly Gift Inc ....G 888 444-9661
New York *(G-10501)*

▲ Mr Disposable Inc ....F 718 388-8574
Brooklyn *(G-2175)*

▲ N3a Corporation ....D 516 284-6799
Inwood *(G-6299)*

◆ Nice-Pak Products Inc ....B 845 365-1700
Orangeburg *(G-12324)*

Nutek Disposables Inc ....G 516 829-3030
Great Neck *(G-5406)*

▲ Precare Corp ....G 631 667-1055
Hauppauge *(G-5746)*

◆ **Professnl Dsposables Intl Inc** ....E 800 999-6423
Orangeburg *(G-12329)*

◆ **Rochester Midland Corporation** ....C 585 336-2200
Rochester *(G-13690)*

▲ **Select Products Holdings LLC** ....E 631 421-6000
Huntington *(G-6224)*

◆ **Skip Hop Inc** ....E 646 902-9874
New York *(G-11259)*

Skip Hop Holdings Inc ....G 212 868-9850
New York *(G-11260)*

▲ **Sqp Inc** ....C 518 831-6800
Schenectady *(G-14307)*

◆ **US Nonwovens Corp** ....D 631 952-0100
Brentwood *(G-1132)*

Waymor1 Inc ....E 518 677-8511
Cambridge *(G-3097)*

2677 Envelopes

3dflam Inc ....F 631 647-2694
Bay Shore *(G-641)*

Apec Paper Industries Ltd ....G 212 730-0088
New York *(G-8601)*

Buffalo Envelope Inc ....G 716 686-0100
Depew *(G-3973)*

▲ **Cambridge-Pacific Inc** ....E 518 677-5988
Cambridge *(G-3092)*

Conformer Products Inc ....F 516 504-6300
Great Neck *(G-5378)*

East Cast Envlope Graphics LLC ....E 718 326-2424
Maspeth *(G-7609)*

Jacmax Industries LLC ....G 718 439-3743
Brooklyn *(G-1984)*

◆ **Kleer-Fax Inc** ....D 631 225-1100
Amityville *(G-286)*

Mercury Envelope Co Inc ....D 516 678-6744
Rockville Centre *(G-13830)*

◆ **Poly-Pak Industries Inc** ....B 800 969-1933
Melville *(G-7816)*

Premier Packaging Corporation ....E 585 924-8460
Victor *(G-15424)*

▲ **Rochester 100 Inc** ....C 585 475-0200
Rochester *(G-13679)*

Westrock Mwv LLC ....C 212 688-5000
New York *(G-11748)*

X-L Envelope and Printing Inc ....F 716 852-2135
Buffalo *(G-3051)*

2678 Stationery Prdts

Allen William & Company Inc ....C 212 675-6461
Glendale *(G-5218)*

▲ **Anne Taintor Inc** ....G 718 483-9312
Brooklyn *(G-1512)*

Drimark ....F 516 484-6200
Bethpage *(G-834)*

Duck Flats Pharma ....G 315 689-3407
Elbridge *(G-4297)*

▲ **General Diaries Corporation** ....F 516 371-2244
Inwood *(G-6294)*

▲ **Innovative Designs LLC** ....E 212 695-0892
New York *(G-9897)*

◆ **Kleer-Fax Inc** ....D 631 225-1100
Amityville *(G-286)*

Leather Indexes Corp ....D 516 827-1900
Hicksville *(G-5923)*

◆ **P C I Paper Conversions Inc** ....C 315 437-1641
Syracuse *(G-14958)*

Paper Magic Group Inc ....G 631 521-3682
New York *(G-10749)*

▲ **Princton Archtctural Press LLC** ....F 518 671-6100
Hudson *(G-6176)*

◆ **USA Custom Pad Corp** ....E 607 563-9550
Sidney *(G-14439)*

Westrock Mwv LLC ....C 212 688-5000
New York *(G-11748)*

2679 Converted Paper Prdts, NEC

Accent Label & Tag Co Inc ....G 631 244-7066
Ronkonkoma *(G-13885)*

Adelphi Paper Hangings ....G 518 284-9066
Sharon Springs *(G-14381)*

▲ **Aigner Label Holder Corp** ....F 845 562-4510
New Windsor *(G-8358)*

▲ **Allied Converters Inc** ....E 914 235-1585
New Rochelle *(G-8319)*

Aniiwe Inc ....G 347 683-1891
Brooklyn *(G-1511)*

Apexx Omni-Graphics Inc ....D 718 326-3330
Maspeth *(G-7591)*

▼ **Auto Data Systems Inc** ....E 631 667-2382
Deer Park *(G-3843)*

Avco Industries Inc ....F 631 851-1555
Central Islip *(G-3264)*

Beetins Wholesale Inc ....F 718 524-0899
Staten Island *(G-14625)*

◆ **CCT (us) Inc** ....F 716 297-7509
Niagara Falls *(G-11913)*

Depot Label Company Inc ....G 631 467-2952
Patchogue *(G-12499)*

Eagles Nest Holdings LLC ....E 513 874-5270
New York *(G-9298)*

Emergent Power Inc ....G 201 441-3590
Latham *(G-6856)*

Eskayel Inc ....G 347 703-8084
Brooklyn *(G-1812)*

Flavor Paper Ltd ....F 718 422-0230
Brooklyn *(G-1851)*

Folia Water Inc ....G 412 802-5083
New York *(G-9514)*

▲ **Gardei Industries LLC** ....F 716 693-7100
North Tonawanda *(G-12069)*

Gavin Mfg Corp ....E 631 467-0040
Farmingdale *(G-4636)*

▼ **Gaylord Bros Inc** ....D 315 457-5070
North Syracuse *(G-12042)*

◆ **General Fibre Products Corp** ....D 516 358-7500
New Hyde Park *(G-8270)*

Gerald McGlone ....G 518 482-2613
Colonie *(G-3574)*

◆ **Global Tissue Group Inc** ....E 631 924-3019
Medford *(G-7708)*

▼ **Gooding Co Inc** ....E 716 266-6252
Lockport *(G-7082)*

◆ **Graphic Cntrls Acqisition Corp** ....F 716 853-7500
Buffalo *(G-2780)*

Graphic Controls Holdings Inc ....F 716 853-7500
Buffalo *(G-2781)*

▲ **Howard J Moore Company Inc** ....E 631 351-8467
Plainview *(G-12688)*

▲ **Interntnal Bus Cmmncations Inc** ....E 516 352-4505
New Hyde Park *(G-8275)*

Jerry Tomaselli ....F 718 965-1400
Brooklyn *(G-1991)*

▲ **K Sidrane Inc** ....E 631 393-6974
Farmingdale *(G-4659)*

▲ **Katz Group Americas Inc** ....E 716 995-3059
Sanborn *(G-14144)*

Larkin Anya Ltd ....G 718 361-1827
Long Island City *(G-7268)*

Lydall Performance Mtls US Inc ....F 315 346-3100
Beaver Falls *(G-760)*

▲ **M C Packaging Corporation** ....C 631 694-3012
Farmingdale *(G-4674)*

M C Packaging Corporation ....E 631 643-3763
Babylon *(G-522)*

▲ **Marketing Group International** ....G 631 754-8095
Northport *(G-12109)*

Master Image Printing Inc ....G 914 347-4400
Elmsford *(G-4416)*

Mid-York Press Inc ....D 607 674-4491
Sherburne *(G-14392)*

National Advertising & Prtg ....G 212 629-7650
New York *(G-10540)*

◆ **Noteworthy Industries Inc** ....C 518 842-2662
Amsterdam *(G-344)*

◆ **P C I Paper Conversions Inc** ....C 315 437-1641
Syracuse *(G-14958)*

P C I Paper Conversions Inc ....F 315 437-1641
Syracuse *(G-14961)*

▲ **Pack America Corp** ....G 212 508-6666
New York *(G-10740)*

▲ **Paperworld Inc** ....E 516 221-2702
Bellmore *(G-785)*

Precision Label Corporation ....F 631 270-4490
Hauppauge *(G-5747)*

Quadra Flex Corp ....G 607 758-7066
Cortland *(G-3785)*

▲ **Quality Circle Products Inc** ....D 914 736-6600
Montrose *(G-8078)*

RB Converting Inc ....G 607 777-1325
Binghamton *(G-905)*

Sappi North America Inc ....D 914 696-5544
White Plains *(G-16060)*

▼ **Setterstix Inc** ....E 716 257-3451
Cattaraugus *(G-3222)*

▲ **Shell Containers Inc** ....E 516 352-4505
New Hyde Park *(G-8292)*

▲ **Specialty Quality Packg LLC** ....D 914 580-3200
Scotia *(G-14337)*

Stanley Paper Co Inc ....F 518 489-1131
Albany *(G-131)*

Stickershopcom Inc ....G 631 563-4323
Bayport *(G-731)*

Stoney Croft Converters Inc ....F 718 608-9800
Staten Island *(G-14715)*

Sunnyside Decorative Prints Co ....G 516 671-1935
Glen Cove *(G-5203)*

Tag Envelope Co Inc ....E 718 389-6844
College Point *(G-3567)*

▲ **Tri-Flex Label Corp** ....E 631 293-0411
Farmingdale *(G-4758)*

▲ **Tri-Seal International Inc** ....A 845 353-3300
Blauvelt *(G-937)*

▲ **Trinity Packaging Corporation** ....F 914 273-4111
Armonk *(G-404)*

Waymor1 Inc ....E 518 677-8511
Cambridge *(G-3097)*

Web-Tech Packaging Inc ....F 716 684-4520
Lancaster *(G-6839)*

27 PRINTING, PUBLISHING, AND ALLIED INDUSTRIES

2711 Newspapers: Publishing & Printing

21st Century Fox America Inc ....G 212 782-8000
New York *(G-8395)*

50+ Lifestyle ....G 631 286-0058
Bellport *(G-791)*

◆ **A C J Communications Inc** ....F 631 587-5612
Babylon *(G-517)*

A Zimmer Ltd ....D 315 422-7011
Syracuse *(G-14808)*

Adirondack Publishing Co Inc ....E 518 891-2600
Saranac Lake *(G-14156)*

Advance Magazine Publs Inc ....C 212 450-7000
New York *(G-8473)*

▲ **Advance Publications Inc** ....D 718 981-1234
New York *(G-8475)*

Advertiser Perceptions Inc ....G 212 626-6683
New York *(G-8486)*

Advertiser Publications Inc ....F 845 783-1111
Chester *(G-3369)*

▲ **Afro Times Newspaper** ....F 718 636-9500
Brooklyn *(G-1470)*

After 50 Inc ....G 716 832-9300
Lancaster *(G-6791)*

Albany Catholic Press Assoc ....G 518 453-6688
Albany *(G-31)*

Albany Student Press Inc ....E 518 442-5665
Albany *(G-36)*

Albion-Holley Pennysaver Inc ....E 585 589-5641
Albion *(G-153)*

Algemeiner Journal Inc ....E 718 771-0400
Brooklyn *(G-1483)*

All Island Media Inc ....E 631 698-8400
Edgewood *(G-4261)*

All Island Media Inc ....E 516 942-8400
Hicksville *(G-5880)*

All Times Publishing LLC ....E 315 422-7011
Syracuse *(G-14809)*

Alm Media LLC ....B 212 457-9400
New York *(G-8524)*

Alm Media Holdings Inc ....B 212 457-9400
New York *(G-8525)*

American City Bus Journals Inc ....E 716 541-1654
Buffalo *(G-2629)*

American Sports Media ....G 585 924-4250
Victor *(G-15391)*

American Sports Media LLC ....G 585 377-9636
Rochester *(G-13232)*

Amnews Corporation ....E 212 932-7400
New York *(G-8564)*

Angel Media and Publishing ....G 845 727-4949
West Nyack *(G-15816)*

Angola Penny Saver Inc ....F 716 549-1164
Angola *(G-358)*

AR Publishing Company Inc ....F 212 482-0303
New York *(G-8615)*

Architects Newspaper LLC ....F 212 966-0630
New York *(G-8618)*

Asahi Shimbun America Inc ....F 212 398-0257
New York *(G-8643)*

Aspect Printing Inc ....E 347 789-4284
Brooklyn *(G-1542)*

Auburn Publishing Co ....D 315 253-5311
Auburn *(G-462)*

Bangla Patrika Inc ....G 718 482-9923
Long Island City *(G-7174)*

Bee Publications Inc ....D 716 632-4700
Williamsville *(G-16121)*

Belsito Communications Inc..............F......845 534-9700
New Windsor *(G-8360)*

Beth Kobliner Company LLC..........G....212 501-8407
New York *(G-8768)*

Bleezarde Publishing Inc.................G....518 756-2030
Ravena *(G-13067)*

Blue and White Publishing Inc..........F....215 431-3339
New York *(G-8817)*

BNH Lead Examiner Corp..............718 807-1365
Brooklyn *(G-1600)*

Boonville Herald Inc.....................G....315 942-4449
Boonville *(G-1104)*

Bradford Publications Inc.............C....716 373-2500
Olean *(G-12226)*

Brasilans Press Pblcations Inc..........E....212 764-6161
New York *(G-8848)*

Brooklyn Journal Publications..........E....718 422-7400
Brooklyn *(G-1618)*

Brooklyn Rail Inc........................F....718 349-8427
Brooklyn *(G-1620)*

Brown Publishing LLC...................G....585 484-0432
Rochester *(G-13284)*

Buffalo Law Journal.....................F....716 541-1600
Buffalo *(G-2675)*

▲ Buffalo News Inc......................A....716 849-4401
Buffalo *(G-2680)*

Buffalo Standard Printing Corp..........F....716 835-9454
Buffalo *(G-2684)*

Bureau of National Affairs Inc...........E....212 687-4530
New York *(G-8868)*

Business First of New York..............E....716 854-5822
Buffalo *(G-2686)*

Business First of New York..............E....518 640-6800
Albany *(G-54)*

Business Journals.........................F....212 790-5100
New York *(G-8873)*

Camden News Inc........................G....315 245-1849
Camden *(G-3098)*

Canandaigua Msgnr Incorporated........C....585 394-0770
Canandaigua *(G-3127)*

Canarsie Courier Inc.....................F....718 257-0600
Brooklyn *(G-1642)*

Capital Region Wkly Newspapers........E....518 877-7160
Albany *(G-56)*

Catskill Delaware Publications..........F....845 887-5200
Callicoon *(G-3075)*

Catskill Mountain Publishing............F....845 586-2601
Arkville *(G-394)*

Chester West County Press...............G....914 684-0006
Mount Vernon *(G-8129)*

China Daily Distribution Corp............E....212 537-8888
New York *(G-8987)*

China Newsweek Corporation............F....212 481-2510
New York *(G-8992)*

▲ Chinese Medical Report Inc..........G....718 359-5676
Flushing *(G-4842)*

Christian Press Inc......................G....718 886-4400
Flushing *(G-4843)*

Chronicle Express.......................F....315 536-4422
Penn Yan *(G-12580)*

Citizen Publishing Corp.................F....845 627-1414
Nanuet *(G-8198)*

City Newspaper.........................G....585 244-3329
Rochester *(G-13315)*

Citywire LLC.............................F....646 503-2216
New York *(G-9021)*

Cnhi LLC.................................E....585 798-1400
Medina *(G-7732)*

Cnhi LLC.................................D....716 693-1000
Niagara Falls *(G-11915)*

Cnhi LLC.................................D....716 282-2311
Niagara Falls *(G-11916)*

Cnhi LLC.................................E....716 439-9222
Lockport *(G-7065)*

CNY Business Review Inc................F....315 472-3104
Syracuse *(G-14853)*

Columbia Daily Spectator................E....212 854-9550
New York *(G-9058)*

Community Media Group Inc..............D....315 789-3333
Geneva *(G-5151)*

Community Media Group LLC............G....518 439-4949
Delmar *(G-3968)*

Community Media LLC....................E....212 229-1890
New York *(G-9070)*

Community News Group LLC.............C....718 260-2500
Brooklyn *(G-1680)*

Community Newspaper Group LLC.....E....607 432-1000
Oneonta *(G-12267)*

Community Newspaper Group LLC.....E....518 565-4114
Plattsburgh *(G-12743)*

Copia Interactive LLC....................F....212 481-0520
New York *(G-9098)*

Cortland Standard Printing Co............D....607 756-5665
Cortland *(G-3764)*

Country Folks...........................G....585 343-9721
Batavia *(G-612)*

Courier-Life Inc.........................C....718 260-2500
Brooklyn *(G-1693)*

Daily Cornell Sun.......................E....607 273-0746
Ithaca *(G-6378)*

Daily Freeman...........................F....845 331-5000
Kingston *(G-6688)*

Daily Gazette Company..................B....518 374-4141
Schenectady *(G-14260)*

Daily Mail & Greene Cnty News..........F....518 943-2100
Hudson *(G-6152)*

Daily Muse Inc..........................E....646 357-3201
New York *(G-9153)*

▲ Daily News LP.........................A....212 210-2100
New York *(G-9154)*

Daily Orange Corporation................E....315 443-2314
Syracuse *(G-14873)*

▼ Daily Racing Form Inc.................C....212 366-7600
New York *(G-9155)*

Daily Racing Form LLC...................F....212 514-2180
New York *(G-9156)*

Daily Record............................F....585 232-2035
Rochester *(G-13336)*

Daily World Press Inc....................E....212 922-9201
New York *(G-9157)*

Dale Press Inc..........................E....718 543-6200
Bronx *(G-1236)*

Danet Inc...............................F....718 266-4444
Brooklyn *(G-1722)*

Dans Paper Inc..........................D....631 537-0500
Southampton *(G-14529)*

Das Yidishe Licht Inc....................G....718 387-3166
Brooklyn *(G-1726)*

Dbg Media...............................G....718 599-6828
Brooklyn *(G-1730)*

Delaware County Times Inc...............G....607 746-2176
Delhi *(G-3963)*

Denton Publications Inc.................D....518 873-6368
Elizabethtown *(G-4299)*

Denton Publications Inc.................E....518 561-9680
Plattsburgh *(G-12744)*

Der Blatt Inc............................F....845 783-1148
Monroe *(G-8019)*

Digital One USA Inc.....................F....718 396-4890
Flushing *(G-4848)*

▲ Document Journal Inc.................G....646 586-3099
New York *(G-9244)*

DOT Publishing.........................F....315 593-2510
Fulton *(G-5058)*

▲ Dow Jones & Company Inc..........B....609 627-2999
New York *(G-9258)*

Dow Jones & Company Inc..............E....212 597-5983
New York *(G-9259)*

Dray Enterprises Inc....................F....585 768-2201
Le Roy *(G-6899)*

E W Smith Publishing Co Inc.............F....845 562-1218
New Windsor *(G-8366)*

Eagle Media Partners LP.................E....315 434-8889
Syracuse *(G-14880)*

East Hampton Ind News Inc..............E....631 324-2500
East Hampton *(G-4120)*

East Hampton Star Inc...................E....631 324-0002
East Hampton *(G-4121)*

Ecclesiastical Communications..........F....212 688-2399
New York *(G-9314)*

Economist Newspaper NA Inc...........E....212 554-0676
New York *(G-9319)*

Ecuador News Inc.......................F....718 205-7014
Woodside *(G-16205)*

El Diario LLC............................C....212 807-4600
Brooklyn *(G-1788)*

Empire Publishing Inc...................F....516 829-4000
Far Rockaway *(G-4564)*

Empire State Weeklies Inc...............E....585 671-1533
Webster *(G-15640)*

Event Journal Inc.......................F....516 470-1811
Jericho *(G-6578)*

Evercore Partners Svcs E LLC............A....212 857-3100
New York *(G-9425)*

Exhibits & More.........................G....585 924-4040
Victor *(G-15408)*

Expositor Newspapers Inc...............G....585 427-2468
Rochester *(G-13407)*

▲ Fairchild Publications Inc.............A....212 630-4000
New York *(G-9463)*

Finger Lakes Media Inc..................F....607 243-7600
Dundee *(G-4046)*

Firefighters Journal.....................E....718 391-0283
Long Island City *(G-7223)*

First Choice News Inc....................G....212 477-2044
New York *(G-9498)*

Five Islands Publishing Inc..............F....631 583-5345
Bronx *(G-1258)*

Four Directions Inc......................E....315 829-8388
Vernon *(G-15365)*

▲ Francepress LLC.......................F....646 202-9828
New York *(G-9528)*

Fredonia Pennysaver Inc.................G....716 679-1509
Fredonia *(G-4969)*

French Morning LLC.....................G....646 290-7463
New York *(G-9537)*

▲ FT Publications Inc....................D....212 641-6500
New York *(G-9547)*

FT Publications Inc......................E....212 641-2420
New York *(G-9548)*

Fulton Newspapers Inc...................E....315 598-6397
Fulton *(G-5059)*

Gallagher Printing Inc....................E....716 873-2434
Buffalo *(G-2764)*

Gannett Co Inc..........................D....585 232-7100
Rochester *(G-13428)*

Gannett Co Inc..........................E....914 278-9315
New Rochelle *(G-8333)*

Gannett Co Inc..........................D....607 798-1234
Vestal *(G-15377)*

Gannett Stllite Info Ntwrk Inc............E....914 965-5000
Yonkers *(G-16312)*

Gannett Stllite Info Ntwrk Inc............E....585 798-1400
Medina *(G-7735)*

Gannett Stllite Info Ntwrk LLC............E....845 578-2300
West Nyack *(G-15821)*

Gannett Stllite Info Ntwrk LLC............E....845 454-2000
Poughkeepsie *(G-12956)*

Gannett Stllite Info Ntwrk LLC............F....914 381-3400
Mamaroneck *(G-7511)*

▲ Gatehouse Media LLC................B....585 598-0030
Pittsford *(G-12641)*

Gatehouse Media LLC...................E....315 792-5000
Utica *(G-15267)*

Gatehouse Media LLC...................G....607 776-2121
Bath *(G-633)*

Gatehouse Media LLC...................E....315 866-2220
Utica *(G-15268)*

Gatehouse Media LLC...................D....607 936-4651
Corning *(G-3715)*

Gatehouse Media LLC...................D....585 394-0770
Canandaigua *(G-3133)*

Gatehouse Media LLC...................C....607 324-1425
Hornell *(G-6107)*

Gatehuse Media PA Holdings Inc........E....585 598-0030
Pittsford *(G-12642)*

General Media Strategies Inc............G....212 586-4141
New York *(G-9590)*

Gleaner Company Ltd....................G....718 657-0788
Jamaica *(G-6444)*

Glens Falls Newspapers Inc..............G....518 792-3131
Glens Falls *(G-5250)*

Good Health Healthcare Newsppr........F....585 421-8109
Victor *(G-15411)*

Guardian News & Media LLC............E....917 900-4663
New York *(G-9691)*

Guest of A Guest Inc.....................G....212 206-0397
New York *(G-9694)*

Guidance Group Inc.....................F....631 756-4618
Melville *(G-7788)*

▲ Hagedorn Communications Inc........D....914 636-7400
New Rochelle *(G-8336)*

Hagedorn Communications Inc...........G....914 636-7400
New York *(G-9708)*

Haitian Times Inc........................G....718 230-8700
New Rochelle *(G-8337)*

Hamodia Corp...........................G....718 338-5637
Brooklyn *(G-1921)*

Hamodia Corp...........................F....718 853-9094
Brooklyn *(G-1922)*

▲ Hearst Communications Inc...........A....212 649-2000
New York *(G-9743)*

Hearst Communications Inc..............G....212 247-1014
New York *(G-9744)*

Hearst Corporation.......................A....518 454-5694
Albany *(G-85)*

Hearst Corporation.......................E....212 649-2275
New York *(G-9754)*

Herald Newspapers Company Inc........A....315 470-0011
Syracuse *(G-14911)*

Herald Publishing Company LLC..........G..... 315 470-2022
New York (G-9767)

High Ridge News LLC.............................G..... 718 548-7412
Bronx (G-1276)

Highline Media LLC.................................C..... 859 692-2100
New York (G-9784)

Home Reporter Inc.................................E..... 718 238-6600
Brooklyn (G-1940)

Hudson Group (hg) Inc.........................G..... 212 971-6800
New York (G-9832)

Hudson Valley Black Press...................G..... 845 562-1313
Newburgh (G-11868)

Huersch Marketing Group LLC............F..... 518 874-1045
Green Island (G-5437)

IMG The Daily...G..... 212 541-5640
New York (G-9868)

▲ Impremedia LLC................................D..... 212 807-4600
Brooklyn (G-1954)

India Abroad Publications Inc ....D..... 212 929-1727
New York (G-9880)

Informa Uk Ltd.......................................G..... 646 957-8966
New York (G-9892)

Investmentnews LLC..............................E..... 212 210-0100
New York (G-9935)

Investors Business Daily Inc ....F..... 212 626-7676
New York (G-9936)

Irish Echo Newspaper Corp ....F..... 212 482-4818
New York (G-9942)

Irish Tribune Inc ....F..... 212 684-3366
New York (G-9943)

Irwin Futures LLC ....G..... 518 884-9008
Ballston Spa (G-577)

Ithaca Journal News Co Inc ....E..... 607 272-2321
Ithaca (G-6389)

Jewish Journal.......................................G..... 718 630-9350
Brooklyn (G-1994)

Jewish Press Inc ....C..... 718 330-1100
Brooklyn (G-1995)

Jewish Week Inc ....E..... 212 921-7822
New York (G-9998)

Jobs Weekly Inc ....F..... 716 648-5627
Hamburg (G-5510)

John Lor Publishing Ltd.........................E..... 631 475-1000
Patchogue (G-12504)

Johnson Acquisition Corp ....F..... 518 828-1616
Hudson (G-6167)

Johnson Newspaper Corporation ....G..... 518 483-4700
Malone (G-7486)

Journal News..G..... 914 694-5000
White Plains (G-16021)

Journal News..G..... 845 578-2324
West Nyack (G-15825)

Journal Register Company ....D..... 518 584-4242
Saratoga Springs (G-14184)

▲ Korea Central Daily News Inc ....D..... 718 361-7700
Long Island City (G-7265)

▲ Korea Times New York Inc ....D..... 718 784-4526
Long Island City (G-7266)

Korea Times New York Inc ....G..... 718 961-7979
Flushing (G-4868)

L & M Publications Inc...........................E..... 516 378-3133
Garden City (G-5103)

Lee Enterprises Incorporated................C..... 518 792-3131
Glens Falls (G-5255)

Lee Newspapers Inc ....F..... 518 673-3237
Palatine Bridge (G-12477)

Lee Publications Inc ....D..... 518 673-3237
Palatine Bridge (G-12478)

LI Community Newspapers Inc..............G..... 516 747-8282
Mineola (G-7985)

Litmor Publishing Corp ....F..... 516 931-0012
Garden City (G-5105)

Livingston County News ....G..... 585 243-1234
Geneseo (G-5144)

Lmg National Publishing Inc ....E..... 585 598-6874
Fairport (G-4505)

Local Media Group Inc ....B..... 845 341-1100
Middletown (G-7915)

Local Media Group Inc ....E..... 845 341-1100
Middletown (G-7916)

Local Media Group Inc ....D..... 845 341-1100
Middletown (G-7917)

Local Media Group Inc ....F..... 845 794-3712
Monticello (G-8070)

Local Media Group Inc ....F..... 845 340-4910
Kingston (G-6700)

Local Media Group Holdings LLC ....G..... 585 598-0030
Pittsford (G-12647)

Long Island Business News ....E..... 631 737-1700
Ronkonkoma (G-13967)

Long Island Cmnty Nwsppers Inc ....D..... 516 482-4490
Mineola (G-7987)

Long Island Cmnty Nwsppers Inc ....F..... 631 427-7000
Huntington (G-6212)

Long Islander Newspapers LLC ....G..... 631 427-7000
Huntington (G-6213)

Los Angles Tmes Cmmnctions LLC .....F..... 212 692-7170
New York (G-10265)

Los Angles Tmes Cmmnctions LLC .....E..... 212 418-9600
New York (G-10266)

Louis Vuitton North Amer Inc ....G..... 212 644-2574
New York (G-10271)

Lowville Newspaper Corporation ....G..... 315 376-3525
Lowville (G-7418)

◆ Macandrews & Forbes Inc ....E..... 212 572-8600
New York (G-10305)

Made Fresh Daily ....G..... 212 285-2253
New York (G-10313)

Main Street Connect LLC ....G..... 203 803-4110
Armonk (G-400)

Manchester Newspaper Inc...................E..... 518 642-1234
Granville (G-5350)

Manhattan Media LLC ....F..... 212 268-8600
New York (G-10344)

Manhattan Times Inc ....F..... 212 569-5800
New York (G-10346)

Mark I Publications Inc ....E..... 718 205-8000
Glendale (G-5228)

Market Place Publications ....E..... 516 997-7909
Carle Place (G-3178)

Massapequa Post ....E..... 516 798-5100
Massapequa Park (G-7659)

McClary Media Inc ....G..... 800 453-6397
Amsterdam (G-334)

Melmont Fine Pringng/Graphics............G..... 516 939-2253
Bethpage (G-839)

Merchandiser Inc ....G..... 315 462-6411
Clifton Springs (G-3479)

Miami Media LLC...................................F..... 212 268-8600
New York (G-10450)

Mid York Weekly & Pennysaver ....G..... 315 792-4990
Utica (G-15283)

Mid-York Press Inc ....D..... 607 674-4491
Sherburne (G-14392)

Ming Pao (new York) Inc ....F..... 212 334-2220
New York (G-10477)

Minority Reporter Inc............................G..... 585 225-3628
Rochester (G-13550)

Minority Reporter Inc............................E..... 585 301-4199
Rochester (G-13551)

Moneypaper Inc ....F..... 914 925-0022
Rye (G-14083)

Mortgage Press Ltd ....E..... 516 409-1400
Wantagh (G-15486)

Nassau County Publications ....G..... 516 481-5400
Hempstead (G-5846)

▲ National Herald Inc ....E..... 718 784-5255
Long Island City (G-7303)

NC Audience Exchange LLC.................F..... 212 416-3400
New York (G-10559)

Neighbor Newspapers ....G..... 631 226-2636
Farmingdale (G-4692)

Neighbor To Neighbor News Inc ....G..... 585 492-2525
Arcade (G-378)

New Living Inc ....G..... 631 751-8819
Patchogue (G-12507)

New Media Investment Group Inc ....B..... 212 479-3160
New York (G-10586)

New Republic ....G..... 212 989-8200
New York (G-10589)

New Ski Inc ....E..... 607 277-7000
Ithaca (G-6401)

New York Cvl Srvc Emplys Pblsh ....F..... 212 962-2690
New York (G-10593)

New York Daily Challenge Inc ....E..... 718 636-9500
Brooklyn (G-2205)

New York Daily News ....G..... 212 248-2100
New York (G-10594)

▲ New York IL Bo Inc ....F..... 718 961-1538
Flushing (G-4878)

New York Press Inc ....E..... 212 268-8600
New York (G-10601)

New York Times Company ....B..... 212 556-1234
New York (G-10604)

New York Times Company ....F..... 718 281-7000
Flushing (G-4879)

New York Times Company ....C..... 212 556-4300
New York (G-10606)

New York University ....E..... 212 998-4300
New York (G-10607)

New York1 News Operations ....F..... 212 379-3311
New York (G-10608)

News Communications Inc ....F..... 212 689-2500
New York (G-10611)

News Corporation ....C..... 212 416-3400
New York (G-10612)

News India Usa LLC ....G..... 212 675-7515
New York (G-10613)

News India USA Inc ....F..... 212 675-7515
New York (G-10614)

News Now Waverly ....F..... 607 296-6769
Waverly (G-15624)

News of The Highlands Inc ....F..... 845 534-7771
Cornwall (G-3731)

News Report Inc ....G..... 718 851-6607
Brooklyn (G-2213)

Newsday LLC ....B..... 631 843-4050
Melville (G-7808)

Newsday LLC ....C..... 631 843-3135
Melville (G-7809)

Newspaper Delivery Solutions ....G..... 718 370-1111
Staten Island (G-14682)

Newspaper Publisher LLC ....F..... 607 775-0472
Conklin (G-3626)

Newspaper Times Union ....F..... 518 454-5676
Albany (G-105)

Newsweek LLC ....G..... 646 867-7100
New York (G-10616)

Newsweek Media Group Inc ....D..... 646 867-7100
New York (G-10617)

Nick Lugo Inc ....F..... 212 348-2100
New York (G-10623)

Nikkei America Inc ....E..... 212 261-6200
New York (G-10627)

Nikkei America Holdings Inc ....D..... 212 261-6200
New York (G-10628)

Nordic Press Inc....................................G..... 212 686-3356
New York (G-10639)

North Country This Week Inc................E..... 315 265-1000
Potsdam (G-12938)

Northern NY Newspapers Corp ....C..... 315 782-1000
Watertown (G-15586)

Northern Tier Publishing Corp ....F..... 914 962-4748
Yorktown Heights (G-16369)

▲ Noticia Hispanoamericana Inc ....E..... 516 223-5678
Bayside (G-741)

Novoye Rsskoye Slovo Pubg Corp ....D..... 646 460-4566
Brooklyn (G-2222)

Nyc Community Media LLC ....F..... 212 229-1890
Brooklyn (G-2226)

Nyc Trade Printers Corp........................F..... 718 606-0610
Woodside (G-16216)

Nyp Holdings Inc..................................D..... 718 260-2500
Brooklyn (G-2227)

▲ Nyp Holdings Inc.............................B..... 212 997-9272
New York (G-10666)

Nyt Capital LLC ....F..... 212 556-1234
New York (G-10669)

Nytimes Corporate................................G..... 212 556-1234
New York (G-10670)

Oak Lone Publishing Co Inc ....E..... 518 792-1126
Glens Falls (G-5262)

Observer Daily Sunday Newsppr ....G..... 716 366-3000
Dunkirk (G-4062)

Observer Media LLC ....E..... 716 755-2400
New York (G-10674)

Ogden Newspapers Inc ....C..... 716 487-1111
Jamestown (G-6535)

Oneida Publications Inc ....E..... 315 363-5100
Oneida (G-12251)

Ottaway Newspapers Inc.......................G..... 845 343-2181
Middletown (G-7925)

Owego Pennysaver Press Inc................F..... 607 687-2434
Owego (G-12436)

Page Front Group Inc ....G..... 716 823-8222
Lackawanna (G-6742)

Panagraphics Inc ....G..... 716 312-8088
Orchard Park (G-12370)

Panzarella Prtg & Packg Inc.................G..... 716 853-4480
Amherst (G-241)

Patchogue Advance Inc ....E..... 631 475-1000
Patchogue (G-12509)

▲ Peace Times Weekly Inc...................G..... 718 762-6500
Flushing (G-4886)

◆ Pearson Inc ....D..... 212 641-2400
New York (G-10782)

Pearson Longman LLC...........................E..... 212 641-2400
White Plains (G-16042)

Pennysaver Group Inc...........................F..... 914 966-1400
Yonkers (G-16340)

Pennysaver Group Inc F 845 627-3600
New City *(G-8228)*
Permanent Observer Mission G 212 883-0140
New York *(G-10806)*
Post Journal F 716 487-1111
Jamestown *(G-6536)*
Post-Standard CNY Department G 315 470-2188
Syracuse *(G-14966)*
Prometheus International Inc F 718 472-0700
Jackson Heights *(G-6421)*
Prospect News Inc F 212 374-2800
New York *(G-10916)*
Publishing Group America Inc F 646 658-0550
New York *(G-10923)*
Putnam Cnty News Recorder LLC F 845 265-2468
Cold Spring *(G-3523)*
Quality Guides G 716 326-3163
Westfield *(G-15948)*
Queens Ldgr/Grenpoint Star Inc F 718 639-7000
Maspeth *(G-7636)*
R W Publications Div of Wtrhs E 716 714-5620
Elma *(G-4325)*
R W Publications Div of Wtrhs E 716 714-5620
Elma *(G-4326)*
Realtimetraderscom E 716 632-6600
Buffalo *(G-2950)*
Record G 518 270-1200
Saratoga Springs *(G-14190)*
Record Advertiser E 716 693-1000
North Tonawanda *(G-12085)*
Record Review LLC F 914 244-0533
Katonah *(G-6638)*
Republican Registrar Inc G 315 497-1551
Moravia *(G-8083)*
Richner Communications Inc C 516 569-4000
Garden City *(G-5113)*
Richner Communications Inc G 516 569-4000
Lawrence *(G-6891)*
Ridgewood Times Prtg & Pubg E 718 821-7500
Ridgewood *(G-13158)*
Rochester Area Mdia Prtners LL F 585 244-3329
Rochester *(G-13680)*
Rochester Business Journal E 585 546-8303
Rochester *(G-13683)*
Rochester Catholic Press F 585 529-9530
Rochester *(G-13684)*
Rochester Democrat & Chronicle E 585 232-7100
Rochester *(G-13688)*
Rocket Communications Inc F 716 873-2594
Buffalo *(G-2959)*
Rome Main Street Alliance Inc G 315 271-8356
Rome *(G-13868)*
Royal News Corp F 212 564-8972
New York *(G-11090)*
Ruby Newco LLC G 212 852-7000
New York *(G-11096)*
Russkaya Reklama Inc E 718 769-3000
Brooklyn *(G-2367)*
Rvc Inc G 330 631-8320
Syracuse *(G-14981)*
S G New York LLC F 631 698-8400
Edgewood *(G-4281)*
S G New York LLC E 631 665-4000
Bohemia *(G-1072)*
S I Communications Inc F 914 725-2500
Scarsdale *(G-14241)*
Sag Harbor Express G 631 725-1700
Sag Harbor *(G-14100)*
Salamanca Press Penny Saver E 716 945-1500
Salamanca *(G-14127)*
Sample News Group LLC D 315 343-3800
Oswego *(G-12420)*
Saugerties Delicioso Inc G 845 217-5072
Saugerties *(G-14211)*
Sb New York Inc D 212 457-7790
New York *(G-11144)*
Schneps Media LLC G 718 224-5863
Brooklyn *(G-2387)*
Schneps Publications Inc E 718 260-2500
Bayside *(G-742)*
School News Nationwide Inc G 718 753-9920
Brooklyn *(G-2388)*
Seabay Media Holdings LLC G 212 457-7790
New York *(G-11172)*
Second Amendment Foundation G 716 885-6408
Buffalo *(G-2978)*
Seneca County Area Shopper G 607 532-4333
Ovid *(G-12425)*
Seneca Media Inc D 607 324-1425
Hornell *(G-6110)*
Service Advertising Group Inc F 718 361-6161
Long Island City *(G-7355)*
◆ **Shelter Island Reporter Inc** G 631 749-1000
Shelter Island *(G-14387)*
Sing Tao Newspapers NY Ltd F 212 431-9030
Brooklyn *(G-2422)*
Sing Tao Newspapers NY Ltd E 718 821-0123
Brooklyn *(G-2423)*
▲ **Sing Tao Newspapers NY Ltd** E 212 699-3800
New York *(G-11248)*
SM News Plus Incorporated G 212 888-0153
New York *(G-11270)*
Smithtown News Inc E 631 265-2100
Smithtown *(G-14487)*
South Shore Tribune Inc G 516 431-5628
Island Park *(G-6322)*
Southampton Town Newspapers E 631 283-4100
Southampton *(G-14538)*
Southampton Town Newspapers F 631 288-1100
Westhampton Beach *(G-15959)*
Spartacist Publishing Co E 212 732-7860
New York *(G-11310)*
Spartan Publishing Inc F 716 664-7373
Jamestown *(G-6541)*
Sports Pblications Prod NY LLC D 212 366-7700
New York *(G-11327)*
Sports Reporter Inc G 212 737-2750
New York *(G-11329)*
Ssrja LLC F 718 725-7020
Jamaica *(G-6474)*
▲ **St Lawrence County Newspapers** D 315 393-1003
Canton *(G-3167)*
Star Community Publishing C 631 843-4050
Melville *(G-7824)*
Star Sports Corp E 516 773-4075
Great Neck *(G-5426)*
Star-Gazette Fund Inc C 607 734-5151
Elmira *(G-4368)*
Steffen Publishing Inc D 315 865-4100
Holland Patent *(G-6034)*
Stratconglobal Inc G 212 989-2355
New York *(G-11369)*
Straus Communications F 845 782-4000
Chester *(G-3388)*
Straus Newspapers Inc E 845 782-4000
Chester *(G-3389)*
Stuart Communications Inc F 845 252-7414
Narrowsburg *(G-8211)*
Sun-Times Media Group Inc E 716 945-1644
Salamanca *(G-14131)*
Syracuse Catholic Press Assn G 315 422-8153
Syracuse *(G-15004)*
Tablet Publishing Company Inc E 718 965-7333
Brooklyn *(G-2490)*
Tech Times LLC G 646 599-7201
New York *(G-11444)*
Tegna Inc C 716 849-2222
Buffalo *(G-3005)*
Tenney Media Group D 315 853-5569
Clinton *(G-3486)*
Terrance Brown G 716 648-6171
Hamburg *(G-5523)*
The Earth Times Foundation G 718 297-0488
Brooklyn *(G-2501)*
The Sandhar Corp G 718 523-0819
Jamaica *(G-6480)*
Thestreet Inc D 212 321-5000
New York *(G-11465)*
Thousand Islands Printing Co G 315 482-2581
Alexandria Bay *(G-180)*
Times Beacon Record Newspapers F 631 331-1154
East Setauket *(G-4188)*
Times Review Newspaper Corp E 631 354-8031
Mattituck *(G-7680)*
Tioga County Courier G 607 687-0108
Owego *(G-12438)*
Tompkins Weekly Inc G 607 539-7100
Ithaca *(G-6413)*
Tri-Town News Inc E 607 561-3515
Sidney *(G-14436)*
Tri-Village Publishers Inc D 518 843-1100
Amsterdam *(G-349)*
Tribco LLC E 718 357-7400
Whitestone *(G-16102)*
Tribune Entertainment Co Del E 203 866-2204
New York *(G-11543)*
Tricycle Foundation Inc G 800 873-9871
New York *(G-11544)*
Trilake Three Press Corp G 518 359-2462
Tupper Lake *(G-15214)*
Tryp Times Square G 212 246-8800
New York *(G-11554)*
Ubm Inc A 212 600-3000
New York *(G-11574)*
Ubm LLC F 516 562-5000
New York *(G-11575)*
Ubm LLC D 516 562-7800
New Hyde Park *(G-8298)*
Ulster County Press Office G 845 687-4480
High Falls *(G-5956)*
Ulster Publishing Co Inc E 845 334-8205
Kingston *(G-6718)*
Ulster Publishing Co Inc F 845 255-7005
New Paltz *(G-8313)*
Unified Media Inc F 917 595-2710
New York *(G-11584)*
Urdu Times G 718 297-8700
Jamaica *(G-6485)*
USA Today International Corp G 703 854-3400
New York *(G-11630)*
Village Herald G 516 569-4403
Lawrence *(G-6894)*
Vnovom Svete G 212 302-9480
New York *(G-11701)*
Vpj Publication Inc E 718 845-3221
Howard Beach *(G-6143)*
W H White Publications Inc G 914 725-2500
Dobbs Ferry *(G-4021)*
W M T Publications Inc F 585 244-3329
Rochester *(G-13798)*
Wallkill Lodge No 627 F&Am F 845 778-7148
Walden *(G-15464)*
Wallkill Valley Publications E 845 561-0170
Newburgh *(G-11893)*
Wappingers Falls Shopper Inc E 845 297-3723
Wappingers Falls *(G-15501)*
Wave Publishing Co Inc F 718 634-4000
Rockaway Beach *(G-13823)*
Wayuga Community Newspapers E 315 754-6229
Red Creek *(G-13071)*
Wayuga Community Newspapers G 315 594-2506
Wolcott *(G-16165)*
Webster Ontrio Wlwrth Pnnysver F 585 265-3620
Webster *(G-15661)*
Weekly Ajkal F 718 565-2100
Jackson Heights *(G-6422)*
Weekly Business News Corp G 212 689-5888
New York *(G-11735)*
Weisbeck Publishing Printing G 716 937-9226
Alden *(G-176)*
West Seneca Bee Inc D 716 632-4700
Williamsville *(G-16146)*
Westbury Times D 516 747-8282
Mineola *(G-8003)*
Westfair Communications Inc E 914 694-3600
West Harrison *(G-15763)*
Westside News Inc F 585 352-3411
Spencerport *(G-14560)*
William B Collins Company D 518 773-8272
Gloversville *(G-5300)*
William Boyd Printing Co Inc C 518 339-5832
Latham *(G-6881)*
William J Kline & Son Inc D 518 843-1100
Amsterdam *(G-354)*
Williamsburg Bulletin G 718 387-0123
Brooklyn *(G-2588)*
Wolfe Publications Inc C 585 394-0770
Canandaigua *(G-3145)*
▲ **World Journal LLC** C 718 746-8889
Whitestone *(G-16104)*
World Journal LLC F 718 871-5000
Brooklyn *(G-2596)*
Worldwide Media Svcs Group Inc B 212 545-4800
New York *(G-11784)*
Wp Company LLC G 212 445-5050
New York *(G-11789)*
Yonkers Time Publishing Co F 914 965-4000
Yonkers *(G-16360)*
Zenith Color Comm Group Inc E 212 989-4400
Long Island City *(G-7413)*

2721 Periodicals: Publishing & Printing

21st Century Fox America Inc D 212 447-4600
New York *(G-8397)*
21st Century Fox America Inc D 212 852-7000
New York *(G-8396)*
▲ **2600 Enterprises Inc** F 631 474-2677
Saint James *(G-14107)*
A Guideposts Church Corp C 212 251-8100
New York *(G-8417)*

SIC

Abp International Inc ....E 212 490-3999
New York *(G-8433)*

Academy of Political Science ....G 212 870-2500
New York *(G-8437)*

Access Intelligence LLC ....A 212 204-4269
New York *(G-8440)*

Adirondack Life Inc ....F 518 946-2191
Jay *(G-6565)*

Adirondack Life Inc ....G 518 946-2191
Jay *(G-6566)*

Advance Magazine Publs Inc ....G 212 286-8582
New York *(G-8469)*

▲ Advance Magazine Publs Inc ....A 212 286-2860
New York *(G-8470)*

Advance Magazine Publs Inc ....D 212 790-4422
New York *(G-8471)*

Advance Magazine Publs Inc ....D 212 286-2860
New York *(G-8472)*

Advance Magazine Publs Inc ....C 212 450-7000
New York *(G-8473)*

Advance Magazine Publs Inc ....D 212 697-0126
New York *(G-8474)*

▲ Advance Publications Inc ....F 718 981-1234
New York *(G-8475)*

Advanced Research Media Inc ....F 631 751-9696
Setauket *(G-14376)*

Adventure Publishing Group ....E 212 575-4510
New York *(G-8485)*

Aeon America Inc ....G 914 584-0275
Brooklyn *(G-1468)*

▲ Alcoholics Anonymous Grapevine ....F 212 870-3400
New York *(G-8509)*

Alm Media LLC ....F 212 457-9400
New York *(G-8524)*

Alm Media Holdings Inc ....B 212 457-9400
New York *(G-8525)*

▲ Alpha Media Group Inc ....B 212 302-2626
New York *(G-8526)*

American Agora Foundation Inc ....E 212 590-6870
New York *(G-8543)*

American Graphic Design Awards ....G 212 696-4380
New York *(G-8550)*

▲ American Inst Chem Engners Inc ....D 646 495-1355
New York *(G-8552)*

American Institute Physics Inc ....C 516 576-2410
Melville *(G-7760)*

American Intl Media LLC ....F 845 359-4225
White Plains *(G-15973)*

American Jewish Committee ....G 212 891-1400
New York *(G-8553)*

American Jewish Congress ....E 212 879-4500
New York *(G-8554)*

American Physical Society ....D 631 591-4025
Ridge *(G-13132)*

American Towman Network Inc ....F 845 986-4546
Warwick *(G-15510)*

Analysts In Media (aim) Inc ....E 212 488-1777
New York *(G-8572)*

Animal Fair Media Inc ....F 212 629-0392
New York *(G-8590)*

Annointed Buty Ministries LLC ....G 646 867-3796
Brooklyn *(G-1513)*

Archaelogy Magazine ....E 718 472-3050
Long Island City *(G-7163)*

Archie Comic Publications Inc ....D 914 381-5155
Pelham *(G-12564)*

Artifex Press LLC ....F 212 414-1482
New York *(G-8635)*

▲ Artnews Ltd ....F 212 398-1690
New York *(G-8639)*

Aspire One Communications LLC ....F 201 281-2998
Cornwall *(G-3725)*

Aspire One Communications Inc ....G 845 534-6110
Cornwall *(G-3726)*

Association For Cmpt McHy Inc ....D 212 869-7440
New York *(G-8654)*

Athlon Spt Communications Inc ....F 212 478-1910
New York *(G-8665)*

Atlantic Monthly Group Inc ....E 202 266-7000
New York *(G-8666)*

Backstage LLC ....E 212 493-4243
Brooklyn *(G-1559)*

▲ Bazaar ....G 212 903-5497
New York *(G-8742)*

Bedford Freeman & Worth ....C 212 576-9400
New York *(G-8745)*

Bedford Communications Inc ....E 212 807-8220
New York *(G-8747)*

Beer Marketers Insights Inc ....G 845 507-0040
Suffern *(G-14758)*

Bellerophon Publications Inc ....E 212 627-9977
New York *(G-8752)*

Bernhard Arnold & Company Inc ....G 212 907-1500
New York *(G-8763)*

▲ Bertelsmann Inc ....E 212 782-1000
New York *(G-8764)*

Bertelsmann Pubg Group Inc ....A 212 782-1000
New York *(G-8765)*

▲ Beverage Media Group Inc ....F 212 571-3232
New York *(G-8772)*

Binah Magazines Corp ....E 718 305-5200
Brooklyn *(G-1587)*

Bizbash Media Inc ....D 646 638-3602
New York *(G-8804)*

BJ Magazines Inc ....G 212 367-9705
New York *(G-8805)*

Blackbook Media Corp ....E 212 334-1800
New York *(G-8807)*

Blue Horizon Media Inc ....F 212 661-7878
New York *(G-8819)*

Bnei Aram Soba Inc ....F 718 645-4460
Brooklyn *(G-1599)*

BNP Media Inc ....G 646 849-7100
New York *(G-8826)*

Boardman Simons Publishing ....E 212 620-7200
New York *(G-8863)*

Brownstone Publishers Inc ....E 212 473-8200
New York *(G-8863)*

Buffalo Spree Publishing Inc ....E 716 783-9119
Buffalo *(G-2683)*

Bust Inc ....G 212 675-1707
Brooklyn *(G-1634)*

Bz Publishing Inc ....F 631 421-4158
Melville *(G-7763)*

C Q Communications Inc ....E 516 681-2922
Hicksville *(G-5890)*

Cambridge University Press ....E 212 337-5000
New York *(G-8897)*

Canopy Canopy Canopy Inc ....F 347 529-5182
New York *(G-8905)*

Capco Marketing ....F 315 699-1687
Baldwinsville *(G-544)*

Capital Partners LLC ....D 212 935-4990
New York *(G-8913)*

Capital Reg Wkly Newsppr Group ....F 518 674-2841
Averill Park *(G-506)*

Carol Group Ltd ....G 212 505-2030
New York *(G-8921)*

▼ Centennial Media LLC ....F 646 527-7320
New York *(G-8948)*

Center For Inquiry Inc ....F 716 636-4869
Amherst *(G-217)*

Cfo Publishing LLC ....E 212 459-3004
New York *(G-8964)*

Choice Magazine Listening Inc ....G 516 883-8280
Port Washington *(G-12868)*

City and State Ny LLC ....E 212 268-0442
New York *(G-9016)*

City Real Estate Book Inc ....G 516 593-2949
Valley Stream *(G-15337)*

Civil Svc Rtred Employees Assn ....F 718 937-0290
Long Island City *(G-7185)*

◆ Clp Pb LLC ....E 212 340-8100
New York *(G-9039)*

▲ CMX Media LLC ....G 917 793-5831
New York *(G-9042)*

CNY Business Review Inc ....G 315 472-3104
Syracuse *(G-14853)*

Coda Media Inc ....G 917 478-2565
New York *(G-9047)*

College Calendar Company ....F 315 768-8242
Whitesboro *(G-16079)*

Commentary Inc ....F 212 891-1400
New York *(G-9066)*

Commonweal Foundation Inc ....F 212 662-4200
New York *(G-9068)*

Complex Media Inc ....E 917 793-5831
New York *(G-9074)*

Conde Nast Entertainment LLC ....A 212 286-2860
New York *(G-9079)*

Conference Board Inc ....C 212 759-0900
New York *(G-9081)*

Congress For Jewish Culture ....E 212 505-8040
New York *(G-9083)*

Consumer Reports Inc ....B 914 378-2000
Yonkers *(G-16297)*

Continuity Publishing Inc ....F 212 869-4170
New York *(G-9090)*

Convenience Store News ....G 214 217-7800
New York *(G-9093)*

Cornell University ....E 607 254-2473
Ithaca *(G-6377)*

Cosmopolitan Magazine ....G 212 649-2000
New York *(G-9106)*

Crain Communications Inc ....C 212 210-0100
New York *(G-9118)*

Creative Magazine Inc ....G 516 378-0800
Merrick *(G-7853)*

Credit Union Journal Inc ....G 212 803-8200
New York *(G-9122)*

▲ Daily Beast Company LLC ....E 212 445-4600
New York *(G-9152)*

Data Key Communication LLC ....F 315 445-2347
Fayetteville *(G-4783)*

Davler Media Group LLC ....E 212 315-0800
New York *(G-9188)*

Delaware County Times Inc ....G 607 746-2176
Delhi *(G-3963)*

Demos Medical Publishing LLC ....F 516 889-1791
New York *(G-9200)*

Dennis Publishing Inc ....D 646 717-9500
New York *(G-9204)*

Denton Publications Inc ....G 518 561-9680
Plattsburgh *(G-12744)*

Direct Mktg Edctl Fndation Inc ....G 212 790-1512
New York *(G-9231)*

Discover Media LLC ....E 212 624-4800
New York *(G-9235)*

Dissent Magazine ....E 212 316-3120
New York *(G-9238)*

Distinction Magazine Inc ....E 631 843-3522
Melville *(G-7775)*

Dj Publishing Inc ....F 516 767-2500
Port Washington *(G-12873)*

Doctorow Communications Inc ....F 845 708-5166
New City *(G-8225)*

Dotto Wagner ....G 315 342-8020
Oswego *(G-12409)*

▲ Dow Jones & Company Inc ....B 609 627-2999
New York *(G-9258)*

Dow Jones & Company Inc ....E 212 597-5983
New York *(G-9259)*

Dow Jones Aer Company Inc ....A 212 416-2000
New York *(G-9259)*

Downtown Media Group LLC ....F 646 723-4510
New York *(G-9263)*

E C Publications Inc ....E 212 728-1844
New York *(G-9289)*

E W Williams Publications ....G 212 661-1516
New York *(G-9292)*

Earl G Graves Pubg Co Inc ....D 212 242-8000
New York *(G-9299)*

Ebner Publishing International ....G 646 742-0740
New York *(G-9311)*

Economist Intelligence Unit NA ....D 212 554-0600
New York *(G-9318)*

Eidosmedia Inc ....E 646 795-2100
New York *(G-9329)*

Elite Traveler LLC ....F 646 430-7900
New York *(G-9346)*

Elmont North Little League ....G 516 775-8210
Elmont *(G-4384)*

Entrepreneur Media Inc ....F 646 502-5463
New York *(G-9383)*

Envy Publishing Group Inc ....G 212 253-9874
New York *(G-9385)*

Equal Opprtnity Pblcations Inc ....F 631 421-9421
Melville *(G-7778)*

▲ Essence Communications Inc ....G 212 522-1212
Brooklyn *(G-1815)*

Essence Ventures LLC ....C 212 522-1212
New York *(G-9400)*

Essential Publications US LLC ....G 646 707-0898
New York *(G-9401)*

Excelsior Publications ....G 607 746-7600
Delhi *(G-3964)*

Executive Business Media Inc ....E 516 334-3030
Westbury *(G-15883)*

▲ Faces Magazine Inc ....F 201 843-4004
Poughkeepsie *(G-12954)*

Fader Inc ....F 212 741-7100
New York *(G-9461)*

Fahy-Williams Publishing Inc ....F 315 781-6820
Geneva *(G-5153)*

▲ Fairchild Publications Inc ....A 212 630-4000
New York *(G-9463)*

Fairchild Publishing LLC ....G 212 286-3897
New York *(G-9464)*

Family Publishing Group Inc ....E 914 381-7474
Mamaroneck *(G-7510)*

Fashion Calendar International ....G....... 212 289-0420
New York (G-9477)
Foleon Inc ....F....... 347 727-6809
New York (G-9513)
Formula 4 Media LLC ....F....... 516 305-4709
Great Neck (G-5390)
Fortune Media USA Corporation ....C....... 212 522-1212
New York (G-9518)
Forum Publishing Co ....G....... 631 754-5000
Centerport (G-3255)
Foundtion For A Mndful Soc Inc ....G....... 902 431-8062
New York (G-9520)
Four M Studios ....C....... 212 557-6600
New York (G-9521)
Four M Studios ....F....... 212 499-2000
New York (G-9522)
Four M Studios ....D....... 515 284-2157
New York (G-9523)
Francis Emory Fitch Inc ....E....... 212 619-3800
New York (G-9529)
Fridge Magazine Inc ....G....... 212 997-7673
New York (G-9541)
Frontiers Unlimited Inc ....G....... 631 283-4663
Southampton (G-14530)
Frost Publications Inc ....G....... 845 726-3232
Westtown (G-15965)
▲ Frozen Food Digest Inc ....G....... 212 557-8600
New York (G-9543)
Fun Media Inc ....E....... 646 472-0135
New York (G-9552)
Future Media Group Inc ....D....... 646 854-1375
New York (G-9555)
Getting The Word Out Inc ....G....... 518 891-9352
Saranac Lake (G-14158)
Glamour Magazine ....G....... 212 286-2860
New York (G-9618)
Global Entity Media Inc ....G....... 631 580-7772
Ronkonkoma (G-13943)
Global Finance Magazine ....G....... 212 524-3223
New York (G-9625)
Global Finance Media Inc ....F....... 212 447-7900
New York (G-9626)
▲ Golfing Magazine ....G....... 516 822-5446
Hicksville (G-5914)
Government Data Publication ....E....... 347 789-8719
Brooklyn (G-1904)
▲ Graphis Inc ....F....... 212 532-9387
New York (G-9666)
Green Apple Courage Inc ....G....... 716 614-4673
Buffalo (G-2785)
Gruner + Jahr Prtg & Pubg Co ....C....... 212 463-1000
New York (G-9687)
◆ Gruner + Jahr USA Group Inc ....B....... 866 323-9336
New York (G-9688)
Guernica Inc ....F....... 646 327-7138
New York (G-9692)
Guilford Publications Inc ....D....... 212 431-9800
New York (G-9696)
H F W Communications Inc ....F....... 315 703-7979
East Syracuse (G-4214)
H W Wilson Company Inc ....B....... 718 588-8635
Bronx (G-1271)
Halcyon Business Publications ....F....... 800 735-2732
Westbury (G-15892)
Hamptons Media LLC ....G....... 631 283-6900
Southampton (G-14532)
Harpers Magazine Foundation ....E....... 212 420-5720
New York (G-9729)
Hart Energy Publishing Lllp ....G....... 212 621-4621
New York (G-9734)
Hatherleigh Company Ltd ....G....... 607 538-1092
Hobart (G-5978)
Haymarket Group Ltd ....F....... 212 239-0855
New York (G-9737)
▲ Haymarket Media Inc ....C....... 646 638-6000
New York (G-9738)
Healthy Way of Life Magazine ....G....... 718 616-1681
Brooklyn (G-1929)
Hearst Business Media ....D....... 516 227-1300
Uniondale (G-15230)
Hearst Business Publishing Inc ....F....... 212 969-7500
New York (G-9742)
Hearst Communications Inc ....C....... 212 649-2000
New York (G-9745)
Hearst Corporation ....E....... 212 649-3100
New York (G-9746)
Hearst Corporation ....E....... 212 903-5366
New York (G-9747)
Hearst Corporation ....B....... 212 767-5800
New York (G-9748)
Hearst Corporation ....D....... 516 382-4580
New York (G-9749)
Hearst Corporation ....A....... 518 454-5694
Albany (G-85)
Hearst Corporation ....D....... 212 649-4271
New York (G-9750)
Hearst Corporation ....D....... 212 204-4300
New York (G-9751)
Hearst Corporation ....D....... 212 903-5000
New York (G-9752)
Hearst Corporation ....D....... 212 649-3204
New York (G-9753)
Hearst Corporation ....E....... 212 649-2275
New York (G-9754)
▲ Hearst Holdings Inc ....F....... 212 649-2000
New York (G-9756)
Her Money Media Inc ....G....... 917 882-3284
Briarcliff Manor (G-1161)
Herman Hall Communications ....F....... 718 941-1879
Brooklyn (G-1933)
Highline Media LLC ....C....... 859 692-2100
New York (G-9784)
▲ Historic TW Inc ....E....... 212 484-8000
New York (G-9794)
Homesell Inc ....F....... 718 514-0346
Staten Island (G-14661)
Human Life Foundation Inc ....G....... 212 685-5210
New York (G-9837)
▲ Humana Press Inc ....E....... 212 460-1500
New York (G-9838)
I On Youth ....G....... 716 832-6509
Buffalo (G-2804)
Icarus Enterprises Inc ....G....... 917 969-4461
New York (G-9854)
Icd Publications Inc ....E....... 631 246-9300
Islandia (G-6335)
Imek Media LLC ....E....... 212 422-9000
New York (G-9866)
Impact Journals LLC ....G....... 800 922-0957
Orchard Park (G-12354)
Impressions Inc ....G....... 212 594-5954
New York (G-9871)
Index Magazine ....G....... 212 243-1428
New York (G-9879)
Informa Business Media Inc ....C....... 212 204-4200
New York (G-9888)
▲ Informa Media Inc ....B....... 212 204-4200
New York (G-9889)
Informa Media Inc ....G....... 212 204-4200
New York (G-9890)
Ink Publishing Corporation ....G....... 347 294-1220
Brooklyn (G-1958)
Institute of Electrical and El ....E....... 212 705-8900
New York (G-9905)
Intellignc The Ftr Cmptng Nwsl ....F....... 212 222-1123
New York (G-9909)
Intellitravel Media Inc ....G....... 646 695-6700
New York (G-9910)
Intercultural Alliance Artists ....G....... 917 406-1202
Flushing (G-4862)
Interhellenic Publishing Inc ....G....... 212 967-5016
New York (G-9916)
International Center For Postg ....G....... 607 257-5860
Ithaca (G-6387)
International Data Group Inc ....E....... 212 331-7883
New York (G-9918)
Interview New York ....G....... 857 928-4120
New York (G-9926)
Irish America Inc ....E....... 212 725-2993
New York (G-9941)
Japan America Learning Ctr Inc ....F....... 914 723-7600
Scarsdale (G-14237)
Jerome Levy Forecasting Center ....G....... 914 244-8617
Mount Kisco (G-8094)
▲ Jobson Medical Information LLC ....C....... 212 274-7000
New York (G-10013)
JSD Communications Inc ....F....... 914 588-1841
Bedford (G-763)
Kbs Communications LLC ....F....... 212 765-7124
New York (G-10085)
Kids Discover LLC ....G....... 212 677-4457
New York (G-10096)
L I F Publishing Corp ....D....... 631 345-5200
Shirley (G-14423)
Lagardere North America Inc ....E....... 212 477-7373
New York (G-10164)
▲ Latina Media Ventures LLC ....E....... 212 642-0200
New York (G-10177)
Laurtom Inc ....E....... 914 273-2233
Mount Kisco (G-8098)
Leadership Connect Inc ....D....... 212 627-4140
New York (G-10182)
Livid Magazine ....F....... 929 340-7123
Brooklyn (G-2080)
Locations Magazine ....G....... 212 288-4745
New York (G-10240)
▲ Lockwood Trade Journal Co Inc ....E....... 212 391-2060
Long Island City (G-7278)
Ltb Media (usa) Inc ....D....... 212 447-9555
New York (G-10278)
Lucky Magazine ....F....... 212 286-6220
New York (G-10279)
Luminary Publishing Inc ....F....... 845 334-8600
Kingston (G-6701)
Luria Communications Inc ....G....... 631 329-4922
East Hampton (G-4125)
M Shanken Communications Inc ....C....... 212 684-4224
New York (G-10301)
Mac Fadden Holdings Inc ....E....... 212 979-4805
New York (G-10303)
▲ Macfadden Cmmnctions Group LLC ....C....... 212 979-4800
New York (G-10306)
Macmillan Holdings LLC ....F....... 212 576-9428
New York (G-10308)
Mag Inc ....E....... 607 257-6970
Ithaca (G-6395)
Magazine I Spectrum E ....E....... 212 419-7555
New York (G-10320)
◆ Magnificat Inc ....F....... 914 502-1820
Yonkers (G-16330)
Manhattan Media LLC ....F....... 212 268-8600
New York (G-10344)
Mann Publications Inc ....E....... 212 840-6266
New York (G-10347)
Mansueto Ventures LLC ....C....... 212 389-5300
New York (G-10353)
▲ Marie Claire USA ....D....... 212 841-8493
New York (G-10360)
Maritime Activity Reports ....E....... 212 477-6700
New York (G-10362)
▲ Mark Levine ....F....... 212 677-4457
New York (G-10364)
▲ Martha Stewart Living ....C....... 212 827-8000
New York (G-10374)
▲ Martha Stewart Living Omni LLC ....B....... 212 827-8000
New York (G-10375)
Martinelli Holdings LLC ....E....... 302 504-1361
Harrison (G-5555)
Mary Ann Liebert Inc ....D....... 914 740-2100
New Rochelle (G-8347)
Mass Appeal Magazine ....G....... 718 858-0979
Brooklyn (G-2122)
Mathisen Ventures Inc ....G....... 212 986-1025
New York (G-10384)
McMahon Group LLC ....D....... 212 957-5300
New York (G-10402)
Med Reviews LLC ....E....... 212 239-5860
New York (G-10407)
Media Press Corp ....E....... 212 791-6347
New York (G-10410)
Medikidz Usa Inc ....G....... 646 895-9319
New York (G-10418)
Mergent Inc ....B....... 212 413-7700
New York (G-10433)
Metrosource Publishing Inc ....F....... 212 691-5127
New York (G-10446)
Miami Media LLC ....F....... 212 268-8600
New York (G-10450)
Mishpacha Magazine Inc ....G....... 718 686-9339
Brooklyn (G-2158)
Modern Farmer Media Inc ....F....... 518 828-7447
Hudson (G-6172)
Music & Sound Retailer Inc ....E....... 516 767-2500
Port Washington (G-12908)
Nation Company LLC ....E....... 212 209-5400
New York (G-10538)
Nation Magazine ....E....... 212 209-5400
New York (G-10539)
National Ggraphic Partners LLC ....G....... 212 656-0726
New York (G-10543)
National Review Inc ....E....... 212 679-7330
New York (G-10545)
Nautilusthink Inc ....G....... 646 239-6858
New York (G-10555)
NCM Publishers Inc ....G....... 212 691-9100
New York (G-10560)
New Art Publications Inc ....F....... 718 636-9100
Brooklyn (G-2200)
New Hope Media LLC ....G....... 646 366-0830
New York (G-10585)

SIC

New York Fshion Week Guide LLC ....F 646 757-9119
New York (G-10598)

New York Media LLC ....C 212 508-0700
New York (G-10599)

New York Moves Magazine LLC ....F 212 396-2394
New York (G-10600)

Next Step Publishing Inc ....F 585 742-1260
Victor (G-15422)

Niche Media Holdings LLC ....E 702 990-2500
New York (G-10621)

Nickelodeon Magazines Inc ....G 212 541-1949
New York (G-10624)

Njf Publishing Corp ....G 631 345-5200
Shirley (G-14426)

▲ Northeast Group ....D 518 563-8214
Plattsburgh (G-12763)

Northeast Prtg & Dist Co Inc ....G 514 577-3545
Plattsburgh (G-12764)

Northside Media Group LLC ....F 917 318-6513
Brooklyn (G-2220)

Nova Science Publishers Inc ....F 631 231-7269
Hauppauge (G-5728)

Nsgv Inc ....E 212 367-3100
New York (G-10652)

Nyemac Inc ....G 631 668-1303
Montauk (G-8057)

Nylon LLc ....E 212 226-6454
New York (G-10663)

Nylon Media LLC ....F 212 226-6454
New York (G-10664)

Nyrev Inc ....E 212 757-8070
New York (G-10667)

Odyssey Mag Pubg Group Inc ....C 212 545-4800
New York (G-10681)

Optionline LLC ....E 516 218-3225
Garden City (G-5111)

Outdoor Sportsman Group ....G 323 791-7190
New York (G-10718)

Paper Publishing Company Inc ....E 212 226-4405
New York (G-10750)

Parade Publications Inc ....E 212 450-7000
New York (G-10754)

Parents Guide Network Corp ....E 212 213-8840
New York (G-10757)

Paris Review Foundation Inc ....G 212 343-1333
New York (G-10760)

Pati Inc ....F 718 244-6788
Jamaica (G-6464)

Pearson Education Inc ....F 201 236-7000
West Nyack (G-15829)

▲ Penhouse Media Group Inc ....C 212 702-6000
New York (G-10795)

Pensions & Investments ....E 212 210-0763
New York (G-10796)

Periodical Services Co Inc ....F 518 822-9300
Hudson (G-6174)

Photo Industry Inc ....F 516 364-0016
Woodbury (G-16179)

Playbill Incorporated ....E 212 557-5757
New York (G-10853)

Pointwise Information Service ....F 315 457-4111
Liverpool (G-7033)

Preparatory Magazine Group ....D 718 761-4800
Staten Island (G-14694)

Prescribing Reference Inc ....D 646 638-6000
New York (G-10881)

Professnal Spt Pblications Inc ....D 212 697-1460
New York (G-10904)

Professnal Spt Pblications Inc ....D 516 327-9500
Elmont (G-4388)

Promenade Magazines Inc ....F 212 888-3500
New York (G-10908)

Psychonomic Society Inc ....E 512 381-1494
New York (G-10919)

Public Relations Soc Amer Inc ....E 212 460-1400
New York (G-10922)

Q Communications Inc ....G 212 594-6520
New York (G-10940)

Quartz Media LLC ....E 646 539-6604
New York (G-10954)

Quest Media Llc ....F 646 840-3404
New York (G-10956)

Ragozin Data ....E 212 674-3123
Long Island City (G-7338)

Raharney Capital LLC ....G 212 220-9084
Brooklyn (G-2323)

Ralph Martinelli ....E 914 345-3055
Elmsford (G-4424)

Ramholtz Publishing Inc ....D 718 761-4800
Staten Island (G-14699)

Rda Holding Co ....E 914 238-1000
New York (G-10990)

Readers Digest Assn Incthe ....F 414 423-0100
New York (G-10993)

Readers Digest Sls & Svcs Inc ....C 914 238-1000
Pleasantville (G-12799)

Real Est Book of Long Island ....F 516 364-5000
Syosset (G-14801)

Real Estate Media Inc ....E 212 929-6976
New York (G-10994)

Redbook Magazine ....F 212 649-3331
New York (G-10997)

◆ Relx Inc ....E 212 309-8100
New York (G-11005)

Relx Inc ....E 212 463-6644
New York (G-11006)

Relx Inc ....B 212 633-3900
New York (G-11007)

Rfp LLC ....E 212 838-7733
New York (G-11032)

Risk Society Management Pubg ....E 212 286-9364
New York (G-11048)

Rnd Enterprises Inc ....E 212 627-0165
New York (G-11056)

Rolling Stone Magazine ....E 212 484-1616
New York (G-11077)

Romantic Times Inc ....F 718 237-1097
Brooklyn (G-2353)

Ross Communications Associates ....F 631 393-5089
Melville (G-7820)

Rough Draft Publishing LLC ....F 212 741-4773
New York (G-11087)

Rsl Media LLC ....E 212 307-6760
New York (G-11094)

Ruby Newco LLC ....G 212 852-7000
New York (G-11096)

Rye Record ....F 914 713-3213
Rye (G-14085)

▲ S C Magazine ....G 646 638-6018
New York (G-11107)

Sandow Media LLC ....F 646 805-0200
New York (G-11131)

Saveur Magazine ....E 212 219-7400
New York (G-11141)

▲ Scholastic Corporation ....A 212 343-6100
New York (G-11160)

◆ Scholastic Inc ....A 212 343-6100
New York (G-11161)

Scoutnews LLC ....F 203 855-1400
Melville (G-7821)

Security Letter ....E 212 348-1553
New York (G-11177)

Shoreline Publishing Inc ....G 914 738-7869
Pelham (G-12568)

Shugar Publishing ....G 631 288-4404
Westhampton Beach (G-15958)

Simmons-Boardman Pubg Corp ....G 212 620-7200
New York (G-11243)

Sky Art Media Inc ....G 917 355-9022
New York (G-11262)

Small Business Advisors Inc ....F 516 374-1387
Atlantic Beach (G-454)

Smart & Strong LLC ....E 212 938-2051
New York (G-11271)

Smooth Magazine ....E 212 925-1150
New York (G-11277)

Society For The Study ....G 212 822-8806
New York (G-11283)

Sound Communications Inc ....E 516 767-2500
Port Washington (G-12927)

▲ Source Media LLC ....C 212 803-8200
New York (G-11304)

Spin Magazine Media ....E 212 231-7400
New York (G-11323)

▲ Sports Illustrated For Kids ....E 212 522-1212
New York (G-11326)

Spotlight Publications LLC ....G 914 345-9473
Elmsford (G-4435)

Springer Adis Us LLC ....E 212 460-1500
New York (G-11333)

Springer Healthcare LLC ....E 212 460-1500
New York (G-11334)

Springer Publishing Co LLC ....E 212 431-4370
New York (G-11338)

◆ Springer Scnce + Bus Media LLC .....D 212 460-1500
New York (G-11339)

Standard Analytics Io Inc ....G 917 882-5422
New York (G-11344)

Staten Island Parent Magazine ....G 718 761-4800
Staten Island (G-14713)

Steffen Publishing Inc ....D 315 865-4100
Holland Patent (G-6034)

Stuff Magazine ....G 212 302-2626
New York (G-11380)

Suburban Publishing Inc ....F 845 463-0542
Fishkill (G-4804)

Suffolk Community Council Inc ....G 631 434-9277
Deer Park (G-3940)

Summit Professional Networks ....D 212 557-7480
New York (G-11391)

Surface Magazine ....G 646 805-0200
New York (G-11400)

Surface Media LLC ....G 212 229-1500
New York (G-11401)

Sussex Publishers LLC ....E 212 260-7210
New York (G-11402)

Swaps Monitor Publications Inc ....F 212 742-8550
New York (G-11404)

Swift Fulfillment Services ....G 516 593-1198
Lynbrook (G-7440)

T V Trade Media Inc ....F 212 288-3933
New York (G-11420)

Testa Communications Inc ....E 516 767-2500
Port Washington (G-12929)

The PRS Group Inc ....F 315 431-0511
East Syracuse (G-4242)

Thestreet Inc ....D 212 321-5000
New York (G-11465)

Thomas Publishing Company LLC ....G 212 695-0500
New York (G-11470)

Thomas Publishing Company LLC ....G 212 695-0500
New York (G-11471)

Thomas Publishing Company LLC ....B 212 695-0500
New York (G-11468)

TI Gotham Inc ....E 212 522-1212
New York (G-11479)

TI Gotham Inc ....E 212 522-1633
New York (G-11480)

◆ TI Gotham Inc ....A 212 522-1212
New York (G-11481)

TI Gotham Inc ....E 212 522-0361
New York (G-11482)

Time Inc Affluent Media Group ....G 212 382-5600
New York (G-11490)

Time Out America LLC ....C 646 432-3000
New York (G-11491)

▲ Time Out New York Partners LP ....D 646 432-3000
New York (G-11494)

Time Warner Companies Inc ....D 212 484-8000
New York (G-11494)

Towse Publishing Co ....F 914 235-3095
New Rochelle (G-8355)

Trader Interntnal Publications ....G 914 631-6856
Sleepy Hollow (G-14464)

Trans-High Corporation ....E 212 387-0500
New York (G-11532)

▲ Trend Pot Inc ....E 212 431-9970
New York (G-11536)

◆ Trusted Media Brands Inc ....A 914 238-1000
New York (G-11553)

Trusted Media Brands Inc ....E 914 244-5454
White Plains (G-16067)

TV Guide Magazine LLC ....G 800 866-1400
New York (G-11561)

▲ TV Guide Magazine Group Inc ....D 212 852-7500
New York (G-11562)

▲ U S Japan Publication NY Inc ....G 212 252-8833
New York (G-11571)

Ubm Inc ....A 212 600-3000
New York (G-11574)

Ubm LLC ....D 516 562-7800
New Hyde Park (G-8298)

Ubm LLC ....F 516 562-5000
New York (G-11575)

Ulster Publishing Co Inc ....E 845 334-8205
Kingston (G-6718)

Universal Cmmncations of Miami ....C 212 986-5100
New York (G-11604)

Untitled Media ....E 212 780-0960
New York (G-11611)

Uptown Media Group LLC ....E 212 360-5073
New York (G-11614)

Urbandaddy Inc ....F 212 929-7905
New York (G-11618)

US China Magazine ....E 212 663-4333
New York (G-11622)

▲ US News & World Report Inc ....C 212 716-6800
New York (G-11626)

US Weekly LLC ....D 212 484-1616
New York (G-11628)

Valassis Communications Inc ....G 585 627-4138
Rochester (G-13793)
Valiant Entertainment LLC ....E 212 972-0361
New York (G-11635)
Value Line Inc ....D 212 907-1500
New York (G-11637)
Value Line Publishing LLC ....C 201 842-8054
New York (G-11638)
◆ Vanity Fair ....F 212 286-7919
New York (G-11640)
Vending Times Inc ....F 516 442-1850
Rockville Centre (G-13840)
Veranda Publications Inc ....G 212 903-5206
New York (G-11658)
Vibe Media Group LLC ....D 212 448-7300
New York (G-11675)
Vickers Stock Research Corp ....E 212 425-7500
New York (G-11676)
▲ Visionaire Publishing LLC ....E 646 434-6091
New York (G-11693)
Wall Street Reporter Magazine ....D 212 363-2600
New York (G-11717)
Wallkill Valley Publications ....E 845 561-0170
Newburgh (G-11893)
Watch Journal LLC ....G 212 229-1500
New York (G-11727)
Weider Publications LLC ....C 212 545-4800
New York (G-11736)
Welcome Magazine Inc ....F 716 839-3121
Amherst (G-254)
▲ Wenner Media LLC ....C 212 484-1616
New York (G-11743)
▲ Westchester Law Journal Inc ....G 914 948-0715
White Plains (G-16072)
Western New York Family Mag ....G 716 836-3486
Buffalo (G-3046)
Westfair Communications Inc ....E 914 694-3600
West Harrison (G-15763)
Wine & Spirits Magazine Inc ....G 212 695-4660
New York (G-11764)
Winsight LLC ....G 646 708-7309
New York (G-11769)
Womens E News Inc ....G 212 244-1720
New York (G-11775)
Working Mother Media Inc ....D 212 351-6400
New York (G-11778)
World Business Media LLC ....F 212 344-0759
Massapequa Park (G-7662)
World Guide Publishing ....E 800 331-7840
New York (G-11781)
Wsn Inc ....G 212 924-7620
New York (G-11792)
Yale Robbins Inc ....D 212 683-5700
New York (G-11805)
▲ Ziff Davis Publishing LLC ....D 212 503-3500
New York (G-11824)

2731 Books: Publishing & Printing

450 Ridge St Inc ....G 716 754-2789
Lewiston (G-6919)
A Lesley Dummett............................G 646 541-1168
Saint Albans (G-14104)
▲ Abbeville Press Inc ....E 212 366-5585
New York (G-8426)
Adir Publishing Co...........................F 718 633-9437
Brooklyn (G-1461)
▲ Advance Publications Inc ....D 718 981-1234
New York (G-8475)
Ai Entertainment Holdings LLC ....F 212 247-6400
New York (G-8499)
Aip Publishing LLC ....C 516 576-2200
Melville (G-7757)
▲ Alba House Publishers ....E 718 698-2759
Staten Island (G-14616)
▲ Allworth Communications Inc ....F 212 777-8395
New York (G-8522)
Alm Media LLC ....B 212 457-9400
New York (G-8524)
Alm Media Holdings Inc ....B 212 457-9400
New York (G-8525)
Amereon Ltd 631 298-5100
Mattituck (G-7676)
▲ American Inst Chem Engners Inc....D 646 495-1355
New York (G-8552)
American Institute Physics Inc...........C 516 576-2410
Melville (G-7760)
Amherst Media Inc ....G 716 874-4450
Buffalo (G-2633)
◆ Amplify Education Inc ....B 212 213-8177
Brooklyn (G-1509)

▼ Amsco School Publications Inc....D 212 886-6500
New York (G-8568)
Annuals Publishing Co Inc ....G 212 505-0950
New York (G-8594)
▲ Anthroposophic Press Inc ....G 518 851-2054
Clifton Park (G-3461)
Apollo Investment Fund VII LP ....G 212 515-3200
New York (G-8605)
◆ Assouline Publishing Inc ....F 212 989-6769
New York (G-8655)
▲ Ateres Publishing & Bk Bindery .....F 718 935-9355
Brooklyn (G-1546)
Atlas & Company LLC ....G 212 234-3100
New York (G-8669)
◆ Barrons Educational Series Inc ......C 631 434-3311
Hauppauge (G-5602)
Bedford Freeman & Worth ....D 212 375-7000
New York (G-8746)
Bedford Freeman & Worth ....D 212 576-9400
New York (G-8745)
Bedrock Communications ....G 212 532-4150
New York (G-8748)
▲ Benchmark Education Co LLC ....D 914 637-7200
New Rochelle (G-8320)
▲ Bertelsmann Inc ....E 212 782-1000
New York (G-8764)
Bertelsmann Pubg Group Inc ....A 212 782-1000
New York (G-8765)
▲ Bicker Inc ....F 212 688-0085
New York (G-8781)
◆ Bloomsbury Publishing Inc ....D 212 419-5300
New York (G-8815)
Bmg Rights Management (us) LLC .....E 212 561-3000
New York (G-8824)
Boardman Simons Publishing ....E 212 620-7200
New York (G-8827)
▲ Bobley-Harmann Corporation ....G 516 433-3800
Ronkonkoma (G-13917)
Booklinks Publishing Svcs LLC ....G 718 852-2116
Brooklyn (G-1602)
Booklyn Artists Alliance Inc..............G 718 383-9621
Brooklyn (G-1603)
Boydell & Brewer Inc ....F 585 275-0419
Rochester (G-13279)
▲ Bright Kids Nyc Inc ....E 917 539-4575
New York (G-8852)
British American Publishing ....D 518 786-6000
Latham (G-6849)
Brown Publishing Network Inc...........G 212 682-3330
New York (G-8862)
▼ Burns Archive Phtgraphic Distr.......G 212 889-1938
New York (G-8870)
Byliner Inc......................................E 415 680-3608
New York (G-8879)
Callaway Arts & Entrmt Inc ....F 646 465-4667
New York (G-8892)
Cambridge University Press ....D 212 337-5000
New York (G-8897)
Campus Course Paks Inc ....G 516 877-3967
Garden City (G-5094)
Canopy Books LLC ....G 516 354-4888
Massapequa (G-7645)
Castle Connolly Medical Ltd ....E 212 367-8400
New York (G-8931)
CB Publishing LLC ....G 516 354-4888
Floral Park (G-4811)
CCC Publications Inc ....F 718 306-1008
Brooklyn (G-1656)
▲ Central Cnfrnce of Amrcn Rbbis .....F 212 972-3636
New York (G-8951)
Chain Store Age Magazine ....G 212 756-5000
New York (G-8966)
Changdu Technology (usa) Co ....F 917 340-1976
North Bellmore (G-12015)
▼ Church Publishing Incorporated .....G 212 592-1800
New York (G-9004)
Cinderella Press Ltd ....G 212 431-3130
New York (G-9006)
Codesters Inc ....G 646 232-1025
New York (G-9048)
▲ Columbia University Press ....E 212 459-0600
New York (G-9060)
Columbia University Press ....E 212 459-0600
New York (G-9061)
Columbia University Press ....E 212 459-0600
New York (G-9062)
Confrtrnity of Precious Blood............G 718 436-1120
Brooklyn (G-1681)
Congress For Jewish Culture ....G 212 505-8040
New York (G-9083)

Continuum Intl Pubg Group Inc..........F 646 649-4215
New York (G-9092)
Cornell University ....D 607 277-2338
Ithaca (G-6376)
Crabtree Publishing Inc ....E 212 496-5040
New York (G-9115)
Curriculum Associates LLC ....F 978 313-1355
Brooklyn (G-1709)
D C I Technical Inc ....F 516 355-0464
Franklin Square (G-4960)
Daheshist Publishing Co Ltd ....F 212 581-8360
New York (G-9151)
Definition Press Inc ....F 212 777-4490
New York (G-9195)
Delaney Books Inc ....F 516 921-8888
Syosset (G-14785)
Demos Medical Publishing LLC ....F 516 889-1791
New York (G-9200)
Der Yid Inc ....E 718 797-3900
Brooklyn (G-1737)
Divine Phoenix LLC ....A 585 737-1482
Skaneateles (G-14450)
Dreams To Print ....G 718 483-8020
Brooklyn (G-1761)
E W Williams Publications ....G 212 661-1516
New York (G-9292)
Eagle Art Publishing Inc...................G 212 685-7411
New York (G-9296)
Edwin Mellen Press Inc ....E 716 754-2796
Lewiston (G-6921)
▲ Egmont US Inc ....G 212 685-0102
New York (G-9328)
F P H Communications ....G 212 528-1728
New York (G-9455)
Faces Magazine Inc ....D 845 454-7420
Poughkeepsie (G-12955)
▲ Fairchild Publications Inc ....A 212 630-4000
New York (G-9463)
Family Publishing Group Inc ....E 914 381-7474
Mamaroneck (G-7510)
Feminist Press Inc ....G 212 817-7915
New York (G-9483)
Four M Studios ....D 515 284-2157
New York (G-9523)
◆ Foxhill Press Inc ....E 212 995-9620
New York (G-9527)
Frank Merriwell Inc ....F 516 921-8888
Syosset (G-14788)
Franklin Report LLC ....G 212 639-9100
New York (G-9533)
French Publishers Agency Inc ....F 212 254-4540
New York (G-9538)
Ggp Publishing Inc ....F 914 834-8896
Harrison (G-5553)
Government Data Publication ....E 347 789-8719
Brooklyn (G-1904)
Gq Magazine ....G 212 286-2860
New York (G-9653)
Grand Central Publishing ....E 212 364-1200
New York (G-9658)
▲ Graphis Inc ....F 212 532-9387
New York (G-9666)
Grey House Publishing Inc ....E 518 789-8700
Amenia (G-202)
Grolier International Inc ....E 212 343-6100
New York (G-9682)
Guilford Publications Inc ....D 212 431-9800
New York (G-9696)
Guilford Publications Inc ....G 800 365-7006
New York (G-9697)
H W Wilson Company Inc..................B 718 588-8635
Bronx (G-1271)
◆ Hachette Book Group Inc ....B 800 759-0190
New York (G-9704)
Hachette Book Group USA ....E 212 364-1200
New York (G-9705)
Harpercollins ....F 212 207-7000
New York (G-9726)
▲ Harpercollins Publishers LLC.........A 212 207-7000
New York (G-9727)
Harpercollins Publishers LLC.............E 212 553-4200
New York (G-9728)
▲ Harry N Abrams Incorporated.........D 212 206-7715
New York (G-9731)
Hearst Corporation ....E 212 649-2275
New York (G-9754)
◆ Henry Holt and Company LLC.........D 646 307-5095
New York (G-9766)
Highline Media LLC...........................C 859 692-2100
New York (G-9784)

SIC

▲ Hippocrene Books Inc .... G 212 685-4371
New York *(G-9792)*

Houghton Mifflin Harcourt Co .... G 212 420-5800
New York *(G-9819)*

Houghton Mifflin Harcourt Pubg .... E 212 420-5800
New York *(G-9820)*

Houghton Mifflin Harcourt Pubg .... C 914 747-2709
Thornwood *(G-15070)*

▲ Hudson Park Press Inc .... G 212 929-8898
New York *(G-9833)*

▲ Humana Press Inc .... E 212 460-1500
New York *(G-9838)*

Iat Interactive LLC .... E 914 273-2233
Mount Kisco *(G-8093)*

▲ Infobase Holdings Inc .... D 212 967-8800
New York *(G-9886)*

Infobase Publishing Company .... G 212 967-8800
New York *(G-9887)*

Informa Business Media Inc .... F 914 949-8500
White Plains *(G-16015)*

Ir Media Group (usa) Inc .... E 212 425-9649
New York *(G-9939)*

James Morgan Publishing .... G 212 655-5470
New York *(G-9971)*

▲ Jonathan David Publishers Inc .... F 718 456-8611
Middle Village *(G-7880)*

▲ Judaica Press Inc .... G 718 972-6202
Brooklyn *(G-2008)*

▲ Juris Publishing Inc .... F 631 351-5430
Huntington *(G-6209)*

▲ K T A V Publishing House Inc .... F 201 963-9524
Brooklyn *(G-2019)*

Kaplan Inc .... E 212 752-1840
New York *(G-10067)*

Kensington Publishing Corp .... D 212 407-1500
New York *(G-10092)*

▲ Klutz .... E 650 687-2600
New York *(G-10115)*

Kobalt Music Pubg Amer Inc .... D 212 247-6204
New York *(G-10119)*

▲ Kodansha USA Inc .... G 917 322-6200
New York *(G-10122)*

Kwesi Legesse LLC .... G 347 581-9872
Brooklyn *(G-2037)*

▲ Le Book Publishing Inc .... G 212 334-5252
New York *(G-10180)*

Learningexpress LLC .... E 646 274-6454
New York *(G-10185)*

▲ Lee & Low Books Incorporated ...... F 212 779-4400
New York *(G-10189)*

Legal Strategies Inc .... G 516 377-3940
Merrick *(G-7860)*

Lippincott Massie McQuilkin L .... F 212 352-2055
New York *(G-10224)*

▲ Literary Classics of US .... F 212 308-3360
New York *(G-10226)*

▲ Little Bee Books Inc .... E 212 321-0237
New York *(G-10228)*

Liveright Publishing Corp .... G 212 354-5500
New York *(G-10234)*

Living Well Innovations Inc .... G 646 517-3200
Hauppauge *(G-5693)*

Looseleaf Law Publications Inc .... F 718 359-5559
Flushing *(G-4873)*

Macmillan College Pubg Co Inc .... F 212 702-2000
New York *(G-10307)*

▲ Macmillan Publishers Inc .... A 646 307-5151
New York *(G-10309)*

◆ Macmillan Publishing Group LLC .... B 212 674-5145
New York *(G-10310)*

▲ Malhame Publs & Importers Inc ..... E 631 694-8600
Bohemia *(G-1043)*

▲ Marshall Cavendish Corp .... E 914 332-8888
Rye Brook *(G-14091)*

▲ Martha Stewart Living .... C 212 827-8000
New York *(G-10374)*

Mary Ann Liebert Inc .... D 914 740-2100
New Rochelle *(G-8347)*

Mathisen Ventures Inc .... G 212 986-1025
New York *(G-10384)*

McGraw-Hill Education Inc .... D 646 766-2000
New York *(G-10397)*

McGraw-Hill Globl Edcatn Hldng .... D 800 338-3987
New York *(G-10398)*

McGraw-Hill School Education H .... B 646 766-2000
New York *(G-10399)*

McGraw-Hill School Educatn LLC .... A 646 766-2060
New York *(G-10400)*

Mediaplanet Publishing Hse Inc .... E 646 922-1400
New York *(G-10414)*

Medikidz Usa Inc .... G 646 895-9319
New York *(G-10418)*

Meegenius Inc .... G 212 283-7285
New York *(G-10422)*

▲ Melcher Media Inc .... F 212 727-2322
New York *(G-10428)*

Merkos Llnyonei Chinuch Inc .... E 718 778-0226
Brooklyn *(G-2143)*

▲ Mesorah Publications Ltd .... E 718 921-9000
Brooklyn. *(G-2145)*

Metro Creative Graphics Inc .... E 212 947-5100
New York *(G-10444)*

Michel Design Works Ltd .... F 914 763-2244
Katonah *(G-6635)*

Micro Publishing Inc .... G 212 533-9180
New York *(G-10456)*

Modern Language Assn Amer Inc .... C 646 576-5000
New York *(G-10488)*

▲ Monacelli Press LLC .... G 212 229-9925
New York *(G-10497)*

◆ Mondo Publishing Inc .... G 212 268-3560
New York *(G-10498)*

▲ Moznaim Publishing Co Inc .... G 718 853-0525
Brooklyn *(G-2173)*

▲ Mud Puddle Books Inc .... G 212 647-9168
New York *(G-10517)*

◆ Multi Packaging Solutions Inc .... E 646 885-0005
New York *(G-10519)*

N A R Associates Inc .... G 845 557-8713
Barryville *(G-598)*

National Learning Corp .... F 516 921-8888
Syosset *(G-14796)*

Nationwide Custom Services .... G 845 365-0414
Tappan *(G-15036)*

Natural E Creative LLC .... F 516 488-1143
New Hyde Park *(G-8283)*

▲ NBM Publishing Inc .... G 646 559-4681
New York *(G-10558)*

NC Audience Exchange LLC .... F 212 416-3400
New York *(G-10559)*

New City Press Inc .... G 845 229-0335
Hyde Park *(G-6273)*

New Directions Publishing .... E 212 255-0230
New York *(G-10579)*

New Press .... E 212 629-8802
New York *(G-10588)*

New York Legal Publishing .... G 518 459-1100
Menands *(G-7847)*

New York Qrtrly Foundation Inc .... F 917 843-8825
Brooklyn *(G-2211)*

News Corporation .... C 212 416-3400
New York *(G-10612)*

News India USA Inc .... F 212 675-7515
New York *(G-10614)*

North Shore Home Improver .... F 631 474-2824
Port Jeff STA *(G-12835)*

Nova Science Publishers Inc .... F 631 231-7269
Hauppauge *(G-5728)*

▲ Osprey Publishing Inc .... G 212 419-5300
New York *(G-10715)*

Other Press LLC .... G 212 414-0054
New York *(G-10716)*

Oxford Book Company Inc .... G 212 227-2120
New York *(G-10723)*

◆ Oxford University Press LLC .... B 212 726-6000
New York *(G-10727)*

Oxford University Press LLC .... G 212 726-6000
New York *(G-10728)*

Ozmodyl Ltd .... G 212 226-0622
New York *(G-10730)*

P J D Publications Ltd .... G 516 626-0650
New Hyde Park *(G-8288)*

Pace Walkers of America Inc .... F 631 444-2147
Port Jefferson *(G-12843)*

▲ Palgrave Macmillan Ltd .... G 646 307-5028
New York *(G-10742)*

◆ Papercutz Inc .... G 646 559-4681
New York *(G-10751)*

▲ Parachute Publishing LLC .... E 212 337-6743
New York *(G-10753)*

Pearson Education Inc .... E 845 340-8700
Kingston *(G-6706)*

Pearson Education Inc .... F 212 782-3337
New York *(G-10779)*

Pearson Education Inc .... E 212 366-2000
New York *(G-10780)*

Pearson Education Inc .... F 201 236-7000
West Nyack *(G-15829)*

▲ Pearson Education Holdings Inc ...... A 201 236-6716
New York *(G-10781)*

◆ Pearson Inc .... D 212 641-2400
New York *(G-10782)*

Pearson Longman LLC .... C 917 981-2200
New York *(G-10783)*

Pearson Longman LLC .... E 212 641-2400
White Plains *(G-16042)*

Pegasus Books NY Ltd .... G 646 343-9502
New York *(G-10789)*

▲ Penguin Putnam Inc .... G 212 366-2000
New York *(G-10791)*

Penguin Random House LLC .... E 212 782-1000
New York *(G-10792)*

▲ Penguin Random House LLC .... B 212 782-9000
New York *(G-10793)*

Penguin Random House LLC .... A 212 572-6162
New York *(G-10794)*

Penguin Random House LLC .... C 212 366-2377
Albany *(G-114)*

Peri-Facts Academy .... G 585 275-6037
Rochester *(G-13616)*

Peter Lang Publishing Inc .... F 212 647-7700
New York *(G-10814)*

▲ Peter Mayer Publishers Inc .... F 212 673-2210
New York *(G-10815)*

▲ Peter Pauper Press Inc .... E 914 681-0144
White Plains *(G-16051)*

▲ Phaidon Press Inc .... E 212 652-5400
New York *(G-10825)*

▲ Philipp Feldheim Inc .... G 845 356-2282
Nanuet *(G-8203)*

Picador USA .... F 646 307-5629
New York *(G-10835)*

Poetry Mailing List Marsh Hawk .... G 516 766-1891
Oceanside *(G-12185)*

Poets House Inc .... F 212 431-7920
New York *(G-10860)*

▲ Powerhouse Cultural Entrmt Inc ..... F 212 604-9074
Brooklyn *(G-2273)*

Preserving Chrstn Publications .... G 315 942-6617
Boonville *(G-1108)*

▲ Prestel Publishing LLC .... E 212 995-2720
New York *(G-10884)*

▲ Princton Archtctural Press LLC ...... F 518 671-6100
Hudson *(G-6176)*

Project Energy Savers LLC .... F 718 596-6448
Brooklyn *(G-2300)*

▲ Prometheus Books Inc .... G 716 691-0133
Buffalo *(G-2935)*

PSR Press Ltd .... F 716 754-2266
Lewiston *(G-6923)*

▲ Quarto Group Inc .... E 212 779-0700
New York *(G-10953)*

Rapid Intellect Group Inc .... F 518 929-3210
Chatham *(G-3332)*

Rda Holding Co .... E 914 238-1000
New York *(G-10990)*

Readers Dgest Yung Fmilies Inc .... E 914 238-1000
Pleasantville *(G-12798)*

◆ Relx Inc .... E 212 309-8100
New York *(G-11005)*

Repertoire International De Ll .... E 212 817-1990
New York *(G-11015)*

Research Centre of Kabbalah .... G 718 805-0380
Richmond Hill *(G-13121)*

▲ Richard C Owen Publishers Inc ...... F 914 232-3903
Somers *(G-14500)*

▲ Rizzoli Intl Publications Inc .... E 212 387-3400
New York *(G-11051)*

Rizzoli Intl Publications Inc .... E 212 387-3572
New York *(G-11052)*

▲ Rosen Publishing Group Inc .... C 212 777-3017
New York *(G-11084)*

▲ Ryland Peters & Small Inc .... G 646 791-5410
New York *(G-11103)*

S P Books Inc .... G 212 431-5011
New York *(G-11109)*

Samuel French Inc .... E 212 206-8990
New York *(G-11126)*

▲ Scholastic Corporation .... G 212 343-6100
New York *(G-11160)*

◆ Scholastic Inc .... A 212 343-6100
New York *(G-11161)*

Scholastic Inc .... E 212 343-6100
New York *(G-11162)*

Scholium International Inc .... G 516 883-8032
Port Washington *(G-12923)*

Second Chance Press Inc .... G 631 725-1101
Sag Harbor *(G-14102)*

▲ Seven Stories Press Inc .... G 212 226-8760
New York *(G-11196)*

▲ Sheridan House Inc ....G...... 914 725-5431
   Scarsdale *(G-14242)*
Simmons-Boardman Pubg Corp ......G...... 212 620-7200
   New York *(G-11243)*
Simon & Schuster Inc ....D...... 212 698-7000
   New York *(G-11244)*
Simon Schuster Digital Sls Inc ....D...... 212 698-4391
   New York *(G-11246)*
▲ Skyhorse Publishing Inc ....E...... 212 643-6816
   New York *(G-11264)*
Social Register Association ....F...... 646 612-7314
   New York *(G-11281)*
Soho Press Inc ....G...... 212 260-1900
   New York *(G-11286)*
Spartacist Publishing Co ....E...... 212 732-7860
   New York *(G-11310)*
Springer Adis Us LLC ....F...... 212 460-1500
   New York *(G-11333)*
▲ Springer Nature ....D...... 212 460-1500
   New York *(G-11335)*
Springer Nature Cust Serv Cent ......B...... 212 460-1500
   New York *(G-11337)*
Springer Publishing Co LLC ....E...... 212 431-4370
   New York *(G-11338)*
◆ Springer Scnce + Bus Media LLC ....D...... 212 460-1500
   New York *(G-11339)*
▲ Square One Publishers Inc ....F...... 516 535-2010
   Garden City Park *(G-5124)*
Station Hill of Barrytown ....G...... 845 758-5293
   Barrytown *(G-597)*
Steffen Publishing Inc ....D...... 315 865-4100
   Holland Patent *(G-6034)*
STf Services Inc ....E...... 315 463-8506
   East Syracuse *(G-4239)*
Stonesong Press LLC ....G...... 212 929-4600
   New York *(G-11366)*
Storybooks Forever ....F...... 716 822-7845
   Buffalo *(G-2994)*
▲ Studio Fun International Inc ....E...... 914 238-1000
   White Plains *(G-16064)*
Suny At Binghamton ....D...... 607 777-2316
   Binghamton *(G-910)*
Sweet Mouth Inc ....E...... 800 433-7758
   New York *(G-11407)*
▲ Syracuse University Press Inc........E...... 315 443-5534
   Syracuse *(G-15010)*
T G S Inc ....G...... 516 629-6905
   Locust Valley *(G-7130)*
Targum Press USA Inc ....G...... 248 355-2266
   Brooklyn *(G-2493)*
Thornwillow Press Ltd ....G...... 212 980-0738
   New York *(G-11476)*
TI Gotham Inc ....E...... 212 522-1212
   New York *(G-11479)*
Time Home Entertainment Inc ....E...... 212 522-1212
   New York *(G-11489)*
Tom Doherty Associates Inc ....E...... 212 388-0100
   New York *(G-11508)*
◆ Trusted Media Brands Inc ....A...... 914 238-1000
   New York *(G-11553)*
Trusted Media Brands Inc ....F...... 914 244-5244
   White Plains *(G-16067)*
▲ Unisystems Inc ....E...... 212 826-0850
   New York *(G-11596)*
▲ United Synggue Cnsrvtive Jdism ...E...... 212 533-7800
   New York *(G-11602)*
▲ Vaad LHafotzas Sichoes................F...... 718 778-5436
   Brooklyn *(G-2550)*
▲ Vandam Inc ....F...... 212 929-0416
   Long Island City *(G-7391)*
Vaultcom Inc ....E...... 212 366-4212
   New York *(G-11650)*
Verso Inc ....G...... 718 246-8160
   Brooklyn *(G-2554)*
◆ W W Norton & Company Inc ....C...... 212 354-5500
   New York *(G-11713)*
W W Norton & Company Inc ....G...... 212 354-5500
   New York *(G-11714)*
▲ Waldman Publishing Corporation ...F...... 212 730-9590
   New York *(G-11716)*
Warodean Corporation ....G...... 718 359-5559
   Flushing *(G-4905)*
◆ William H Sadlier Inc ....C...... 212 233-3646
   New York *(G-11757)*
William S Hein & Co Inc ....C...... 716 882-2600
   Getzville *(G-5184)*
William S Hein & Co Inc ....D...... 716 882-2600
   Buffalo *(G-3049)*
Windows Media Publishing LLC ....E...... 917 732-7892
   Brooklyn *(G-2591)*

Wolters Kluwer US Inc ....F...... 212 894-8920
   New York *(G-11774)*
Woodward/White Inc ....F...... 718 509-6082
   Brooklyn *(G-2594)*
◆ Workman Publishing Co Inc ....C...... 212 254-5900
   New York *(G-11779)*
Workman Publishing Co Inc ....C...... 212 254-5900
   New York *(G-11780)*
Worth Publishers Inc ....C...... 212 475-6000
   New York *(G-11787)*
▲ YS Publishing Co Inc ....G...... 212 682-9360
   New York *(G-11813)*
▲ Ziff Davis Publishing LLC ....D...... 212 503-3500
   New York *(G-11824)*
Zinepak LLC ....F...... 212 706-8621
   New York *(G-11825)*

2732 Book Printing, Not Publishing

450 Ridge St Inc ....G...... 716 754-2789
   Lewiston *(G-6919)*
Bedford Freeman & Worth ....C...... 212 576-9400
   New York *(G-8745)*
Bmg Printing and Promotion LLC ......C...... 631 231-9200
   Bohemia *(G-982)*
Book1one LLC ....G...... 585 458-2101
   Rochester *(G-13278)*
Bridge Enterprises Inc ....G...... 718 625-6622
   Brooklyn *(G-1607)*
Cct Inc ....G...... 212 532-3355
   New York *(G-8940)*
Centrisource Inc ....G...... 716 871-1105
   Tonawanda *(G-15096)*
E Graphics Corporation ....G...... 718 486-9767
   Brooklyn *(G-1772)*
▲ Experiment LLC ....E...... 212 889-1659
   New York *(G-9447)*
Flare Multicopy Corp ....E...... 718 258-8860
   Brooklyn *(G-1849)*
▲ Hamilton Printing Company Inc ......C...... 518 732-2161
   Troy *(G-15171)*
▲ Hudson Valley Paper Works Inc ......F...... 845 569-8883
   Newburgh *(G-11870)*
In-House Inc ....F...... 718 445-9007
   College Point *(G-3544)*
▲ Kravitz Design Inc ....G...... 212 625-1644
   New York *(G-10139)*
▲ Literary Classics of US ....F...... 212 308-3360
   New York *(G-10226)*
▲ Logical Operations Inc ....E...... 585 350-7000
   Rochester *(G-13522)*
▲ North Country Books Inc ....G...... 315 735-4877
   Utica *(G-15288)*
Panzarella Prtg & Packg Inc ....G...... 716 853-4480
   Amherst *(G-241)*
Printing Factory LLC ....F...... 718 451-0500
   Brooklyn *(G-2291)*
Promotional Sales Books LLC............G...... 212 675-0364
   New York *(G-10909)*
Royal Fireworks Prtg Co Inc ....F...... 845 726-3333
   Unionville *(G-15234)*
Steffen Publishing Inc ....D...... 315 865-4100
   Holland Patent *(G-6034)*
▼ Sterling Pierce Company Inc ....E...... 516 593-1170
   East Rockaway *(G-4174)*
Stop Entertainment Inc....................F...... 212 242-7867
   Monroe *(G-8031)*
▲ Syracuse Cultural Workers Prj ....F...... 315 474-1132
   Syracuse *(G-15006)*
Tobay Printing Co Inc ....E...... 631 842-3300
   Copiague *(G-3684)*
◆ Twp America Inc ....G...... 212 274-8090
   New York *(G-11567)*
Vicks Lithograph & Prtg Corp ....C...... 315 272-2401
   Yorkville *(G-16380)*
Vicks Lithograph & Prtg Corp............C...... 315 736-9344
   Yorkville *(G-16381)*
Willis Mc Donald Co Inc ....F...... 212 366-1526
   New York *(G-11761)*
Worzalla Publishing Company ....C...... 212 967-7909
   New York *(G-11788)*

2741 Misc Publishing

▲ 212 Media LLC ....E...... 212 710-3092
   New York *(G-8394)*
Abkco Music & Records Inc..............E...... 212 399-0300
   New York *(G-8430)*
Abkco Music Inc ....F...... 212 399-0300
   New York *(G-8431)*
ABRA Media Inc ....G...... 518 398-1010
   Pine Plains *(G-12632)*

Absolute Color Corporation..............G...... 212 868-0404
   New York *(G-8436)*
Adcomm Graphics Inc ....E...... 212 645-1298
   West Babylon *(G-15681)*
Adirondack Pennysaver Inc..............E...... 518 563-0100
   Plattsburgh *(G-12731)*
Ahae Press Inc ....G...... 914 471-8671
   Mount Kisco *(G-8087)*
Ai Media Group Inc ....F...... 212 660-2400
   New York *(G-8500)*
Albany Student Press Inc ....E...... 518 442-5665
   Albany *(G-36)*
Albion-Holley Pennysaver Inc ....E...... 585 589-5641
   Albion *(G-153)*
Aleteia Usa Inc ....G...... 914 502-1855
   Yonkers *(G-16281)*
▼ Alfred Mainzer Inc ....E...... 718 392-4200
   Long Island City *(G-7148)*
Alm Media LLC ....G...... 212 457-9400
   New York *(G-8524)*
Alm Media Holdings Inc ....B...... 212 457-9400
   New York *(G-8525)*
Alphonse Lduc - Rbert King Inc ....G...... 508 238-8118
   New York *(G-8527)*
America Press Inc ....E...... 212 581-4640
   New York *(G-8542)*
American Hsptals Patient Guide ......F...... 518 346-1099
   Schenectady *(G-14245)*
American Society of Composers........B...... 212 621-6000
   New York *(G-8558)*
Amy Pak Publishing Inc ....G...... 585 964-8188
   Holley *(G-6035)*
An Group Inc ....G...... 631 549-4090
   Melville *(G-7761)*
Answer Printing Inc ....F...... 212 922-2922
   New York *(G-8595)*
Art Asiapacific Publishing LLC ....G...... 212 255-6003
   New York *(G-8627)*
Associated Publishing Company ....E...... 325 676-4032
   Buffalo *(G-2644)*
Atlas Music Publishing LLC ....G...... 646 502-5170
   New York *(G-8670)*
Auto Market Publications Inc............G...... 631 667-0500
   Deer Park *(G-3844)*
Avalon Copy Centers Amer Inc ....D...... 315 471-3333
   Syracuse *(G-14823)*
Avalon Copy Centers Amer Inc ....G...... 716 995-7777
   Buffalo *(G-2651)*
Award Publishing Limited ....G...... 212 246-0405
   New York *(G-8696)*
Bdg Media Inc ....G...... 917 551-6510
   New York *(G-8743)*
▲ Black Book Photography Inc ....F...... 212 979-6700
   New York *(G-8806)*
Blood Moon Productions Ltd ....G...... 718 556-9410
   Staten Island *(G-14628)*
▲ Boosey and Hawkes Inc ....E...... 212 358-5300
   New York *(G-8836)*
Bourne Music Publishers ....F...... 212 391-4300
   New York *(G-8841)*
Bright Line Eting Slutions LLC............E...... 585 245-2956
   Pittsford *(G-12637)*
Brownstone Publishers Inc................E...... 212 473-8200
   New York *(G-8863)*
Bulkley Dunton ....E...... 212 863-1800
   New York *(G-8866)*
Burdick Publications Inc ....G...... 315 685-9500
   Skaneateles *(G-14447)*
Business Directory Inc ....F...... 718 486-8099
   Brooklyn *(G-1632)*
Business Expert Press LLC ....F...... 212 661-8810
   New York *(G-8871)*
Business Never Stops LLC ....G...... 888 479-3111
   South Richmond Hill *(G-14522)*
Buzzoole Inc ....G...... 347 964-0120
   New York *(G-8875)*
Byliner Inc ....E...... 415 680-3608
   New York *(G-8879)*
◆ Bys Publishing LLC ....G...... 315 655-9431
   Cazenovia *(G-3224)*
▲ C F Peters Corp ....E...... 718 416-7800
   Glendale *(G-5221)*
Cambridge Info Group Inc ....F...... 301 961-6700
   New York *(G-8896)*
Cambridge Whos Who Pubg Inc ....E...... 516 833-8440
   Uniondale *(G-15224)*
Carl Fischer LLC ....E...... 212 777-0900
   New York *(G-8917)*
Catapult LLC ....G...... 303 717-0334
   New York *(G-8935)*

Catholic News Publishing Co ....F 914 632-7771
Mamaroneck *(G-7501)*

Cayuga Press Cortland Inc ....E 888 229-8421
Liverpool *(G-7007)*

Ceo Cast Inc ....F 212 732-4300
New York *(G-8961)*

Charing Cross Music Inc ....G 212 541-7571
New York *(G-8971)*

Cherry Lane Magazine LLC ....D 212 561-3000
New York *(G-8982)*

▼ Christopher Anthony Pubg Co ....F 516 826-9205
Wantagh *(G-15483)*

Church Bulletin Inc ....F 631 249-4994
West Babylon *(G-15703)*

City of New York ....E 718 965-8787
Brooklyn *(G-1665)*

▲ City Post Express Inc ....G 718 995-8690
Jamaica *(G-6435)*

Classic Collections Fine Art ....G 914 591-4500
White Plains *(G-15993)*

Classpass Inc ....E 888 493-5953
New York *(G-9027)*

Clearstep Technologies LLC ....G 315 952-3628
Camillus *(G-3108)*

Cnhi Co ....D 716 282-2311
Niagara Falls *(G-11916)*

Coastal Publications Inc ....F 631 725-1700
Sag Harbor *(G-14097)*

Color Unlimited Inc ....G 212 802-7547
New York *(G-9055)*

Community Cpons Frnchising Inc .....E 516 277-1968
Glen Cove *(G-5190)*

Complete Publishing Solutions ....G 212 242-7321
New York *(G-9073)*

Comps Inc ....F 516 676-0400
Glen Cove *(G-5191)*

Consumer Reports Inc ....B 914 378-2000
Yonkers *(G-16297)*

CT Publications Co ....G 718 592-2196
Whitestone *(G-16092)*

D C I Technical Inc ....F 516 355-0464
Franklin Square *(G-4960)*

Dailycandy Inc ....E 646 230-8719
New York *(G-9158)*

Dapper Dads Inc ....G 917 903-8045
Brooklyn *(G-1725)*

Dayton T Brown Inc ....B 631 589-6300
Bohemia *(G-1001)*

Dezawy LLC ....G 917 436-8820
New York *(G-9214)*

Directory Major Malls Inc ....G 845 348-7000
Nyack *(G-12141)*

▲ DK Publishing ....F 212 366-2000
New York *(G-9241)*

Dlc Comprehensive Medical PC ....F 718 857-1200
Brooklyn *(G-1752)*

Dohnsco Inc ....G 516 773-4800
Manhasset *(G-7533)*

Draper Associates Incorporated ....F 212 255-2727
New York *(G-9266)*

Dryve LLC ....G 646 279-3648
Bronx *(G-1242)*

Dwell Life Inc ....E 212 382-2010
New York *(G-9285)*

East Meet East Inc ....G 646 481-0033
New York *(G-9303)*

Easy Book Publishing Inc ....G 518 459-6281
Albany *(G-73)*

Elite Daily Inc ....F 212 402-9097
New York *(G-9343)*

◆ Elsevier Inc ....B 212 989-5800
New York *(G-9352)*

Energy Intelligence Group Inc ....E 212 532-1112
New York *(G-9375)*

Enhance A Colour Corp ....E 212 490-3620
New York *(G-9379)*

Enjoy City North Inc ....D 607 584-5061
Binghamton *(G-876)*

Epost International Inc ....G 212 352-9390
New York *(G-9388)*

Ethis Communications Inc ....G 212 791-1440
White Plains *(G-16003)*

Euphorbia Productions Ltd ....E 212 533-1700
New York *(G-9418)*

▲ Experiment Publishing LLC ....G 212 889-1273
New York *(G-9448)*

Family Publications Ltd ....F 212 947-2177
New York *(G-9467)*

Fantasy Sports Media Group Inc ....E 416 917-6002
New York *(G-9472)*

Fashionex Inc ....G 914 271-6121
New York *(G-9478)*

First Games Publr Netwrk Inc ....D 212 983-0501
New York *(G-9499)*

Fischler Hockey Service ....F 212 749-4152
New York *(G-9505)*

Fitzgerald Publishing Co Inc ....G 914 793-5016
Yonkers *(G-16309)*

▲ Foundation Center Inc ....C 212 620-4230
New York *(G-9519)*

Franklin-Douglas Inc ....F 516 883-0121
Port Washington *(G-12880)*

Fredonia Pennysaver Inc ....G 716 679-1509
Fredonia *(G-4969)*

Freeville Publishing Co Inc ....G 607 844-9119
Freeville *(G-5033)*

Froebe Group LLC ....G 646 649-2150
New York *(G-9542)*

▲ G Schirmer Inc ....E 212 254-2100
New York *(G-9559)*

G Schirmer Inc ....E 845 469-4699
Chester *(G-3378)*

▲ Galison Publishing LLC ....E 212 354-8840
New York *(G-9566)*

Gannett Co Inc ....G 607 352-2702
Johnson City *(G-6600)*

Gds Publishing Inc ....F 212 796-2000
New York *(G-9583)*

Gen Publishing Inc ....D 914 834-3880
New Rochelle *(G-8335)*

Genius Media Group Inc ....F 509 670-7502
Brooklyn *(G-1883)*

Glassview LLC ....E 646 844-4922
New York *(G-9619)*

Global Grind Digital ....E 212 840-9399
New York *(G-9630)*

Global Video LLC ....G 516 222-2600
Woodbury *(G-16172)*

Golden Eagle Marketing LLC ....G 212 726-1242
New York *(G-9641)*

Golf Directories USA Inc ....G 516 365-5351
Manhasset *(G-7535)*

Gooding & Associates Inc ....F 631 749-3313
Shelter Island *(G-14386)*

Government Data Publication ....G 347 789-8719
Brooklyn *(G-1904)*

Grant Hamilton ....G 716 652-0320
East Aurora *(G-4089)*

Grants Financial Publishing ....F 212 809-7994
New York *(G-9663)*

Grey House Publishing Inc ....E 518 789-8700
Amenia *(G-202)*

Guest Informat LLC ....F 212 557-3010
New York *(G-9693)*

Guilford Publications Inc ....D 212 431-9800
New York *(G-9696)*

Guilford Publications Inc ....G 800 365-7006
New York *(G-9697)*

Hagedorn Communications Inc ....G 914 636-7400
New York *(G-9708)*

Hampton Press Incorporated ....G 646 638-3800
New York *(G-9717)*

Harborside Press ....G 631 470-4967
Huntington *(G-6206)*

Hart Energy Publishing Lllp ....G 212 621-4621
New York *(G-9734)*

Hearst Business Media ....D 516 227-1300
Uniondale *(G-15230)*

Hearst Digital Studios Inc ....E 212 969-7552
New York *(G-9755)*

Heed LLC ....E 646 708-7111
New York *(G-9762)*

Helium Media Inc ....G 917 596-4081
New York *(G-9763)*

▲ Helvetica Press Incorporated ....G 212 737-1857
New York *(G-9764)*

Her Money Media Inc ....G 917 882-3284
Briarcliff Manor *(G-1161)*

Herff Jones LLC ....E 607 936-2366
Corning *(G-3716)*

Hibert Publishing LLC ....G 914 381-7474
Rye *(G-14080)*

◆ Hibu Inc ....C 516 730-1900
East Meadow *(G-4137)*

Highline Media LLC ....C 859 692-2100
New York *(G-9784)*

▲ Historic TW Inc ....F 212 484-8000
New York *(G-9794)*

History Publishing Company LLC ....G 845 398-8161
Palisades *(G-12481)*

Hola Publishing Co ....G 718 424-3129
Long Island City *(G-7243)*

Holmes Group The Inc ....G 212 333-2300
New York *(G-9806)*

▲ Humana Press Inc ....E 212 460-1500
New York *(G-9838)*

Humor Rainbow Inc ....E 646 402-9113
New York *(G-9840)*

Integrated Copyright Group ....E 615 329-3999
New York *(G-9907)*

International Society For Medl ....G 520 820-8594
Tarrytown *(G-15046)*

Intuition Publishing Limited ....G 212 838-7115
New York *(G-9933)*

Israeli Yellow Pages ....G 718 520-1000
Kew Gardens *(G-6665)*

Jewish Heritage For Blind ....G 718 338-4999
Brooklyn *(G-1993)*

▲ Jobson Medical Information LLC .....C 212 274-7000
New York *(G-10013)*

▲ John Szoke Graphics Inc ....G 212 219-8300
New York *(G-10019)*

Kalel Partners LLC ....F 347 561-7804
Flushing *(G-4866)*

Kendor Music Inc ....F 716 492-1254
Delevan *(G-3962)*

Kitcheco Inc ....G 917 388-7479
New York *(G-10110)*

Kjckd Inc ....G 518 435-9696
Latham *(G-6862)*

Korangy Publishing Inc ....C 212 260-1332
New York *(G-10127)*

▲ Korean Yellow Pages ....F 718 461-0073
Flushing *(G-4869)*

Kraus Organization Limited ....D 212 686-5411
New York *(G-10138)*

Kyra Communications Corp ....F 516 783-6244
Seaford *(G-14349)*

Lagunatic Music & Filmworks ....F 212 353-9600
Brooklyn *(G-2044)*

Language and Graphics Inc ....G 212 315-5266
New York *(G-10172)*

Leadership Connect Inc ....D 212 627-4140
New York *(G-10182)*

Lefrak Entertainment Co Ltd ....G 212 586-3600
New York *(G-10192)*

Lightbulb Press Inc ....E 212 485-8800
New York *(G-10218)*

Lino Press Inc ....E 718 665-2625
Bronx *(G-1304)*

Llcs Publishing Corp ....G 718 569-2703
Brooklyn *(G-2081)*

London Theater News Ltd ....F 212 517-8608
New York *(G-10247)*

Long Islands Best Inc ....G 855 542-3785
Bohemia *(G-1036)*

Lucky Peach LLC ....G 212 228-0031
New York *(G-10280)*

Ludlow Music Inc ....F 212 594-9795
New York *(G-10281)*

Luminary Publishing Inc ....F 845 334-8600
Kingston *(G-6701)*

Mailers-Pblsher Wlfare Tr Fund ....G 212 869-5986
New York *(G-10332)*

▲ Mapeasy Inc ....F 631 537-6213
Wainscott *(G-15455)*

Market Partners International ....G 212 447-0855
New York *(G-10369)*

Marketresearchcom Inc ....F 212 807-2600
New York *(G-10371)*

Mary Ann Liebert Inc ....D 914 740-2100
New Rochelle *(G-8347)*

Mathisen Ventures Inc ....G 212 986-1025
New York *(G-10384)*

▲ Media Transcripts Inc ....E 212 362-1481
New York *(G-10411)*

Media Trust LLC ....G 212 802-1162
New York *(G-10412)*

Medical Daily Inc ....E 646 867-7100
New York *(G-10416)*

Medical Information Systems ....G 516 621-7200
Syosset *(G-14793)*

Mens Journal LLC ....A 212 484-1616
New York *(G-10431)*

▲ Menucha Publishers Inc ....F 718 232-0856
Brooklyn *(G-2138)*

Merrill Corporation ....D 212 620-5600
New York *(G-10437)*

Metro Group Inc ....G 716 434-4055
Lockport *(G-7092)*

Michael Karp Music Inc ....G...... 212 840-3285
New York *(G-10453)*

Millennium Medical Publishing ....F...... 212 995-2211
New York *(G-10466)*

Mindbodygreen LLC ....E...... 347 529-6952
Brooklyn *(G-2156)*

Minyanville Media Inc ....E...... 212 991-6200
New York *(G-10480)*

Mom Dad Publishing Inc ....E...... 646 476-9170
New York *(G-10495)*

Morey Publishing ....E...... 516 284-3300
Farmingdale *(G-4689)*

Mortgage Press Ltd ....E...... 516 409-1400
Wantagh *(G-15486)*

Mosby Holdings Corp ....G...... 212 309-8100
New York *(G-10505)*

Mt Morris Shopper Inc ....G...... 585 658-3520
Mount Morris *(G-8114)*

Mtm Publishing Inc ....G...... 212 242-6930
New York *(G-10516)*

Multi-Health Systems Inc ....D...... 800 456-3003
Cheektowaga *(G-3356)*

▲ Music Sales Corporation ....G...... 212 254-2100
New York *(G-10521)*

Napean LLC ....G...... 917 968-6757
New York *(G-10533)*

Narratively Inc ....E...... 203 536-0332
Brooklyn *(G-2188)*

National Health Prom Assoc ....E...... 914 421-2525
White Plains *(G-16032)*

National Rding Styles Inst Inc ....F...... 516 921-5500
Syosset *(G-14797)*

National RES Mktg Council Inc ....G...... 914 591-4297
Irvington *(G-6311)*

Nature Publishing Co ....G...... 212 726-9200
New York *(G-10553)*

Neu Group Inc ....F...... 914 232-4068
Katonah *(G-6636)*

New York Legal Publishing ....G...... 518 459-1100
Menands *(G-7847)*

New York Times Company ....G...... 212 556-1200
New York *(G-10605)*

Newbay Media LLC ....D...... 212 378-0400
New York *(G-10609)*

News Now Waverly ....F...... 607 296-6769
Waverly *(G-15624)*

Nigun Music ....F...... 718 977-5700
Brooklyn *(G-2216)*

Nimbletv Inc ....F...... 646 502-7010
New York *(G-10629)*

O Val Nick Music Co Inc ....G...... 212 873-2179
New York *(G-10671)*

Oakwood Publishing Co ....G...... 516 482-7720
Great Neck *(G-5407)*

One Story Inc ....G...... 917 816-3659
Brooklyn *(G-2232)*

Openroad Integrated Media Inc ....E...... 212 691-0900
New York *(G-10698)*

Outreach Publishing Corp ....G...... 718 773-0525
Brooklyn *(G-2239)*

Oyster Bay Publications LLC ....G...... 516 922-1300
Oyster Bay *(G-12453)*

Pace Editions Inc ....G...... 212 421-3237
New York *(G-10735)*

Pace Editions Inc ....G...... 212 643-6353
New York *(G-10736)*

Panzarella Prtg & Packg Inc ....G...... 716 853-4480
Amherst *(G-241)*

▲ Peer International Corp ....E...... 212 265-3910
New York *(G-10785)*

Peermusic III Ltd ....F...... 212 265-3910
New York *(G-10787)*

Peermusic Ltd ....F...... 212 265-3910
New York *(G-10788)*

▲ Per Annum Inc ....E...... 212 647-8700
New York *(G-10800)*

Pictoure Inc ....G...... 212 641-0098
New York *(G-10836)*

Portfolio Media Inc ....C...... 646 783-7100
New York *(G-10868)*

Press Express ....G...... 914 592-3790
Elmsford *(G-4422)*

Primary Wave Publishing LLC ....E...... 212 661-6990
New York *(G-10889)*

Princess Music Publishing Co ....E...... 212 586-0240
New York *(G-10892)*

Pro Publica Inc ....D...... 212 514-5250
New York *(G-10901)*

Professnal Spt Pblications Inc ....E...... 516 327-9500
Elmont *(G-4387)*

Publicis Health LLC ....E...... 212 771-5500
Long Island City *(G-7330)*

Publishers Clearing House LLC ....E...... 516 249-4063
Melville *(G-7818)*

Pwxyz LLC ....E...... 212 377-5500
New York *(G-10939)*

Qtalk Publishing LLC ....G...... 877 549-1841
New York *(G-10946)*

Quality Patterns Inc ....D...... 212 704-0355
New York *(G-10950)*

Qworldstar Inc ....G...... 212 768-4500
New York *(G-10962)*

R W Publications Div of Wtrhs ....E...... 716 714-5620
Elma *(G-4325)*

Rda Holding Co ....E...... 914 238-1000
New York *(G-10990)*

Redspring Communications Inc.........E...... 518 587-0547
Saratoga Springs *(G-14191)*

Refinery 29 Inc ....D...... 212 966-3112
New York *(G-11000)*

▲ Reliable Press II Inc ....F...... 718 840-5812
Hempstead *(G-5849)*

Renegade Nation Online LLC ....G...... 212 868-9000
New York *(G-11014)*

Repertoire International De LI ....E...... 212 817-1990
New York *(G-11015)*

Reservoir Media Management Inc ......F...... 212 675-0541
New York *(G-11018)*

Riot New Media Group Inc ....G...... 604 700-4896
Brooklyn *(G-2346)*

Rizzoli Intl Publications Inc..............E...... 212 308-2000
New York *(G-11053)*

Rolling Stone Magazine ....G...... 212 484-1616
New York *(G-11077)*

Rosemont Press Incorporated ....G...... 212 239-4770
Deer Park *(G-3929)*

▲ Rough Guides US Ltd ....D...... 212 414-3635
New York *(G-11088)*

Royalty Network Inc ....G...... 212 967-4300
New York *(G-11092)*

Rsl Media LLC ....G...... 212 307-6760
New York *(G-11094)*

S G New York LLC ....E...... 631 665-4000
Bohemia *(G-1072)*

Sacks and Company New York...........G...... 212 741-1000
New York *(G-11113)*

Sag Harbor Express............................G...... 631 725-1700
Sag Harbor *(G-14100)*

Sagelife Parenting LLC ....G...... 315 299-5713
Syracuse *(G-14984)*

Salamanca Press Penny Saver...........E...... 716 945-1500
Salamanca *(G-14127)*

Scholastic Inc ....D...... 212 343-7100
New York *(G-11163)*

Screen Gems-EMI Music Inc ....D...... 212 786-8000
New York *(G-11170)*

Seabay Media Holdings LLC ....G...... 212 457-7790
New York *(G-11172)*

Selby Marketing Associates Inc ....F...... 585 377-0750
Rochester *(G-13722)*

Select Information Exchange...............F...... 212 496-6435
New York *(G-11186)*

Sephardic Yellow Pages ....E...... 718 998-0299
Brooklyn *(G-2395)*

Service Advertising Group Inc ....F...... 718 361-6161
Long Island City *(G-7355)*

Service Education Incorporated..........G...... 585 264-9240
Victor *(G-15431)*

▲ Shapiro Bernstein & Co Inc ....F...... 212 588-0878
New York *(G-11207)*

Sharedbook Inc ....E...... 646 442-8840
New York *(G-11208)*

Shepherds PI LLC ....G...... 516 647-8151
Valley Stream *(G-15359)*

▲ Sing Tao Newspapers NY Ltd ....E...... 212 699-3800
New York *(G-11248)*

Skylark Publications Ltd ....G...... 607 535-9866
Watkins Glen *(G-15615)*

Slosson Eductl Publications...............F...... 716 652-0930
East Aurora *(G-4096)*

Sneaker News Inc ....G...... 347 687-1588
New York *(G-11278)*

Social Science Electronic Pubg ....F...... 585 442-8170
Rochester *(G-13734)*

◆ Sony Music Holdings Inc ....A...... 212 833-8000
New York *(G-11299)*

▲ Sony/Atv Music Publishing LLC ......E...... 212 833-7730
New York *(G-11300)*

Southampton Town Newspapers ....E...... 631 283-4100
Southampton *(G-14538)*

Space 150 ....C...... 612 332-6458
Brooklyn *(G-2445)*

Spirit Music Group Inc ....E...... 212 533-7672
New York *(G-11324)*

Sportsgrid Inc ....F...... 646 849-4085
New York *(G-11330)*

▼ Springer Nature America Inc............B...... 212 726-9200
New York *(G-11336)*

Standard Analytics Io Inc ....G...... 917 882-5422
New York *(G-11344)*

Statebook LLC ....G...... 845 383-1991
Kingston *(G-6711)*

Stephen Singer Pattern Co Inc ....F...... 212 947-2902
New York *(G-11359)*

STf Services Inc ....E...... 315 463-8506
East Syracuse *(G-4239)*

Straight Arrow Publishing Co ....C...... 212 484-1616
New York *(G-11368)*

Student Lifeline Inc ....E...... 516 327-0800
Franklin Square *(G-4964)*

Summit Communications......................G...... 914 273-5504
Armonk *(G-402)*

Super Express USA Pubg Corp ....F...... 212 227-5800
Richmond Hill *(G-13126)*

Supermedia LLC ....D...... 212 513-9700
New York *(G-11397)*

Tablet Publishing Company Inc..........E...... 718 965-7333
Brooklyn *(G-2490)*

Tango Publishing Corporation ....E...... 646 773-3060
New York *(G-11430)*

Taylor & Francis Group LLC ....C...... 212 216-7800
New York *(G-11437)*

◆ Te Neues Publishing Co LP ....E...... 212 627-9090
New York *(G-11441)*

Thehuffingtonpostcom Inc ....E...... 212 245-7844
New York *(G-11460)*

Theskimm Inc ....F...... 646 213-4754
New York *(G-11464)*

Thomas Publishing Company LLC ......B...... 212 695-0500
New York *(G-11468)*

Thomas Publishing Company LLC ......D...... 212 695-0500
New York *(G-11469)*

Thomson Reuters Corporation ....F...... 212 393-9461
New York *(G-11474)*

▲ Thomson Reuters Corporation ....A...... 646 223-4000
New York *(G-11475)*

Time Warner Companies Inc...............D...... 212 484-8000
New York *(G-11494)*

Total Webcasting Inc ....G...... 845 883-0909
New Paltz *(G-8311)*

Trader Interntnal Publications ....G...... 914 631-6856
Sleepy Hollow *(G-14464)*

Tradewins Publishing Corp................G...... 631 361-6916
Saint James *(G-14115)*

Trading Edge Ltd ....G...... 347 699-7079
Ridgewood *(G-13164)*

Treiman Publications Corp ....G...... 607 657-8473
Berkshire *(G-822)*

Tribune Entertainment Co Del ....E...... 203 866-2204
New York *(G-11543)*

Tribune Media Services Inc ....B...... 518 792-9914
Queensbury *(G-13059)*

▲ Triumph Learning LLC ....E...... 212 652-0200
New York *(G-11549)*

◆ Trusted Media Brands Inc................A...... 914 238-1000
New York *(G-11553)*

Trusted Media Brands Inc ....F...... 914 244-5244
White Plains *(G-16067)*

Tunecore Inc ....F...... 646 651-1060
Brooklyn *(G-2528)*

Turbo Express Inc ....G...... 718 723-3686
Jamaica *(G-6483)*

Two Palms Press Inc ....E...... 212 965-8598
New York *(G-11565)*

Ubm Inc ....A...... 212 600-3000
New York *(G-11574)*

Ucc Guide Inc ....F...... 518 434-0909
Albany *(G-139)*

Underline Communications LLC ....F...... 212 994-4340
New York *(G-11581)*

▲ Universal Edition Inc ....D...... 917 213-2177
New York *(G-11605)*

Urban Mapping Inc ....F...... 415 946-8170
New York *(G-11616)*

◆ USA Custom Pad Corp ....E...... 607 563-9550
Sidney *(G-14439)*

Value Line Inc ....D...... 212 907-1500
New York *(G-11637)*

▲ Vandam Inc ....F...... 212 929-0416
Long Island City *(G-7391)*

Vending Times Inc ....F 516 442-1850
Rockville Centre (G-13840)

Vendome Group LLC ....D 646 795-3899
New York (G-11654)

Viamedia Corporation ....G 718 485-7792
Brooklyn (G-2555)

Viewfinder Inc ....G 212 831-0939
New York (G-11681)

Vincys Printing Ltd ....F 518 355-4363
Schenectady (G-14314)

Vinous Group LLC ....G 917 275-5184
New York (G-11685)

Visant Secondary Holdings Corp ....E 914 595-8200
Armonk (G-405)

Want-Ad Digest Inc ....F 518 279-1181
Troy (G-15196)

▼ Warner Music Inc ....D 212 275-2000
New York (G-11723)

Watchanish LLC ....F 917 558-0404
New York (G-11728)

Wayuga Community Newspapers ....E 315 754-6229
Red Creek (G-13071)

Welcome Rain Publishers LLC ....E 212 686-1909
New York (G-11738)

Wmg Acquisition Corp ....F 212 275-2000
New York (G-11771)

▲ Won & Lee Inc ....E 516 222-0712
Garden City (G-5119)

Worldwide Media Svcs Group Inc ....B 212 545-4800
New York (G-11784)

Yam TV LLC ....G 917 932-5418
New York (G-11806)

Yellow Pages Inc ....G 845 639-6060
New City (G-8231)

Zazoom LLC ....F 212 321-2100
New York (G-11817)

2752 Commercial Printing: Lithographic

1 800 Postcards Inc ....D 212 741-1070
New York (G-8387)

12pt Printing LLC ....G 718 376-2120
Brooklyn (G-1410)

2 1 2 Postcards Inc ....E 212 767-8227
New York (G-8391)

2 X 4 Inc ....E 212 647-1170
New York (G-8392)

21st Century Fox America Inc ....D 212 852-7000
New York (G-8396)

450 Ridge St Inc ....G 716 754-2789
Lewiston (G-6919)

514 Adams Corporation ....G 516 352-6948
Deer Park (G-3825)

518 Prints LLC ....G 518 674-5346
Averill Park (G-505)

6727 11th Ave Corp ....F 718 837-8787
Brooklyn (G-1421)

A & M Litho Inc ....E 516 342-9727
Bethpage (G-829)

▲ A Esteban & Company Inc ....E 212 989-7000
New York (G-8414)

A I P Printing & Stationers ....G 631 929-5529
Wading River (G-15448)

A M & J Digital ....G 518 434-2579
Menands (G-7836)

A National Printing Co Inc ....G 631 243-3395
Bohemia (G-958)

A Q P Inc ....G 585 256-1690
Rochester (G-13194)

AC Envelope Inc ....G 516 420-0646
Farmingdale (G-4572)

Academy Printing Services Inc ....G 631 765-3346
Southold (G-14542)

Accuprint ....G 518 456-2431
Albany (G-27)

Ace Printing & Publishing Inc ....F 718 939-0040
Flushing (G-4834)

Act Communications Group Inc ....F 631 669-2403
West Islip (G-15809)

Ad-Vantage Printing Inc ....F 718 820-0688
Kew Gardens (G-6661)

Add Associates Inc ....G 315 449-3474
Cicero (G-3415)

Adirondack Publishing Co Inc ....E 518 891-2600
Saranac Lake (G-14156)

Ads-N-Color Inc ....E 718 797-0900
Brooklyn (G-1463)

▲ Advance Publications Inc ....D 718 981-1234
New York (G-8475)

Advanced Business Group Inc ....F 212 398-1010
New York (G-8477)

Advanced Copy Center Inc ....G 212 388-1001
New York (G-8478)

Advanced Digital Printing LLC ....E 718 649-1500
New York (G-8479)

Advanced Printing New York Inc ....G 212 840-8108
New York (G-8481)

▲ Advantage Quick Print Inc ....E 212 989-5644
New York (G-8483)

Advertising Lithographers ....F 212 966-7771
Long Island City (G-7146)

Agrecolor Inc ....G 516 741-8700
Mineola (G-7957)

Ahw Printing Corp ....F 516 536-3600
Oceanside (G-12165)

Alamar Printing Inc ....F 914 993-9007
White Plains (G-15969)

Albany Letter Shop Inc ....G 518 434-1172
Albany (G-32)

Albert Siy ....G 718 359-0389
Flushing (G-4836)

All Color Business Spc Ltd ....G 516 420-0649
Deer Park (G-3833)

All Time Products Inc ....G 718 464-1400
Queens Village (G-13016)

All-Color Offset Printers Inc ....G 516 420-0649
Deer Park (G-3834)

Allen William & Company Inc ....C 212 675-6461
Glendale (G-5218)

Allied Reproductions Inc ....E 212 255-2472
New York (G-8518)

Allstatebannerscom Corporation ......G 718 300-1256
Long Island City (G-7150)

Alpha Printing Corp ....F 315 454-5507
Syracuse (G-14812)

Alpina Color Graphics Inc ....G 212 285-2700
New York (G-8528)

Alpina Copyworld Inc ....F 212 683-3511
New York (G-8529)

Alpine Business Group Inc ....F 212 989-4198
New York (G-8530)

Always Printing ....G 914 481-5209
Port Chester (G-12814)

Amax Printing Inc ....F 718 384-8600
Maspeth (G-7588)

American Business Forms Inc ....G 716 836-5111
Amherst (G-209)

American Print Solutions Inc ....G 718 246-7800
Brooklyn (G-1501)

Amsterdam Printing & Litho Inc ....F 518 792-6501
Queensbury (G-13030)

Amsterdam Printing & Litho Inc ....G 518 842-6000
Amsterdam (G-316)

Amsterdam Printing & Litho Inc ....E 518 842-6000
Amsterdam (G-317)

Andrew J George ....G 518 462-4662
Albany (G-40)

▲ Anne Taintor Inc ....G 718 483-9312
Brooklyn (G-1512)

Ansun Graphics Inc ....F 315 437-6869
Syracuse (G-14814)

Answer Printing Inc ....F 212 922-2922
New York (G-8595)

Apple Press ....G 914 723-6660
White Plains (G-15975)

April Printing Co Inc ....G 212 685-7455
New York (G-8612)

Ares Printing and Packg Corp ....C 718 858-8760
Brooklyn (G-1527)

Argo Printing Inc ....D 718 729-2700
Long Island City (G-7164)

Argo Lithographers Inc ....E 718 729-2700
Long Island City (G-7166)

Arista Innovations Inc ....E 516 746-2262
Mineola (G-7959)

Arnold Printing Corp ....F 607 272-7800
Ithaca (G-6363)

Arnold Taylor Printing Inc ....F 516 781-0564
Bellmore (G-779)

Aro-Graph Corporation ....G 315 463-8693
Syracuse (G-14817)

Art Digital Technologies LLC ....F 646 649-4820
Brooklyn (G-1535)

Art Scroll Printing Corp ....F 212 929-2413
New York (G-8631)

Artina Group Inc ....G 914 592-1850
Elmsford (G-4394)

Artscroll Printing Corp ....E 212 929-2413
New York (G-8640)

Asn Inc ....E 718 894-0800
Maspeth (G-7593)

At Copy Inc ....G 718 624-6136
Brooklyn (G-1543)

Atlantic Color Corp ....E 631 345-3800
Shirley (G-14414)

Atlas Print Solutions Inc ....E 212 949-8775
New York (G-8671)

Avm Printing Inc ....F 631 351-1331
Hauppauge (G-5599)

B & P Jays Inc ....G 716 668-8408
Buffalo (G-2654)

B D B Typewriter Supply Works ....E 718 232-4800
Brooklyn (G-1557)

B Q P Inc ....G 518 793-4999
Queensbury (G-13034)

Ballantrae Lithographers Inc ....G 914 592-3275
White Plains (G-15979)

Barone Offset Printing Corp ....E 212 989-5500
Mohegan Lake (G-8008)

Bartolomeo Publishing Inc ....G 631 420-4949
West Babylon (G-15693)

Batavia Press LLC ....E 585 343-4429
Batavia (G-603)

Bates Jackson Engraving Co Inc ....G 716 854-3000
Buffalo (G-2657)

Baum Christine and John Corp ....G 585 621-8910
Rochester (G-13261)

Beacon Press Inc ....G 212 691-5050
White Plains (G-15980)

Beastons Budget Printing Inc ....G 585 244-2721
Rochester (G-13264)

Beehive Press Inc ....G 718 654-1200
Bronx (G-1211)

Bel Aire Offset Corp ....G 718 539-8333
College Point (G-3537)

▲ Benchemark Printing Inc ....D 518 393-1361
Schenectady (G-14249)

Benchmark Graphics Ltd ....F 212 683-1711
New York (G-8756)

Bennett Multimedia Inc ....F 718 629-1454
Brooklyn (G-1575)

Bernard Hall ....G 585 425-3340
Fairport (G-4489)

▲ Beyer Graphics Inc ....D 631 543-3900
Commack (G-3579)

Billing Coding and Prtg Inc ....G 718 827-9409
Brooklyn (G-1586)

Bishop Print Shop Inc ....G 607 965-8155
Edmeston (G-4294)

Bittner Company LLC ....F 585 214-1790
Rochester (G-13270)

Bk Printing Inc ....G 315 565-5396
East Syracuse (G-4200)

Bklynfavors Party Print ....G 718 277-0233
Brooklyn (G-1590)

Bluesoho ....F 646 805-2583
New York (G-8822)

Bmg Printing and Promotion LLC ......G 631 231-9200
Bohemia (G-982)

Boka Printing Inc ....G 607 725-3235
Binghamton (G-862)

Boncraft Inc ....D 716 662-9720
Tonawanda (G-15091)

Bondy Printing Corp ....G 631 242-1510
Bay Shore (G-659)

Boulevard Printing ....G 716 837-3800
Tonawanda (G-15092)

Boxcar Press Incorporated ....E 315 473-0930
Syracuse (G-14833)

BP Beyond Printing Inc ....G 516 328-2700
Hempstead (G-5834)

▼ BP Digital Imaging LLC ....G 607 753-0022
Cortland (G-3757)

Brennans Quick Print Inc ....E 518 793-4999
Glens Falls (G-5243)

Bridge Printing Inc ....G 212 243-5390
Long Island City (G-7181)

Brigar X-Press Solutions Inc ....D 518 438-7817
Albany (G-52)

Brodock Press Inc ....D 315 735-9577
Utica (G-15242)

Brooklyn Circus Inc ....F 718 858-0919
Brooklyn (G-1614)

Brooklyn Printers Inc ....G 718 511-7994
Brooklyn (G-1619)

Brooks Litho Digital Group Inc ....G 631 789-4500
Deer Park (G-3850)

Business Card Express Inc ....▲ 631 669-3400
West Babylon (G-15698)

C & R De Santis Inc ....E 718 447-5076
Staten Island (G-14633)

C To C Design & Print Inc...............F...... 631 885-4020
Ronkonkoma *(G-13919)*

Cabba Printing Incorporated ....G...... 212 319-4747
New York *(G-8883)*

Caboodle Printing Inc ....G...... 716 693-6000
Williamsville *(G-16125)*

Canaan Printing Inc ....F...... 718 729-3100
Bayside *(G-736)*

Canandaigua Msgnr Incorported ......C...... 585 394-0770
Canandaigua *(G-3127)*

Canastota Publishing Co Inc ....G...... 315 697-9010
Canastota *(G-3151)*

Candid Litho Printing Ltd ....D...... 212 431-3800
Farmingdale *(G-4596)*

Canfield & Tack Inc ....D...... 585 235-7710
Rochester *(G-13293)*

Canyon Publishing Inc ....F...... 212 334-0227
New York *(G-8908)*

Capital Dst Print & Imaging ....G...... 518 456-6773
Schenectady *(G-14251)*

Carges Entps of Canandaigua ....G...... 585 394-2600
Canandaigua *(G-3128)*

Carlara Group Ltd ....G...... 914 769-2020
Pleasantville *(G-12795)*

Carnels Printing Inc ....G...... 516 883-3355
Great Neck *(G-5374)*

Carr Communications Group LLC......F...... 607 748-0481
Vestal *(G-15375)*

Castlereagh Printcraft Inc ....D...... 516 623-1728
Freeport *(G-4989)*

Cathedral Corporation ....C...... 315 338-0021
Rome *(G-13846)*

Catskill Delaware Publications ....F...... 845 887-5200
Callicoon *(G-3075)*

Cayuga Press Cortland Inc ....E...... 888 229-8421
Liverpool *(G-7007)*

▲ Cazar Printing & Advertising ....G...... 718 446-4606
Corona *(G-3735)*

Cedar Graphics Inc ....D...... 631 467-1444
Ronkonkoma *(G-13923)*

Cedar West Inc ....D...... 631 467-1444
Ronkonkoma *(G-13924)*

Chakra Communications Inc ....E...... 607 748-7491
Endicott *(G-4446)*

Challenge Graphics Svcs Inc ....E...... 631 586-0171
Deer Park *(G-3851)*

Chenango Union Printing Inc ....G...... 607 334-2112
Norwich *(G-12116)*

Cherry Lane Lithographing Corp ....E...... 516 293-9294
Plainview *(G-12668)*

▲ China Imprint LLC........................G...... 585 563-3391
Rochester *(G-13313)*

Chromagraphics Press Inc ....G...... 631 367-6160
Melville *(G-7766)*

CHv Printed Company ....F...... 516 997-1101
East Meadow *(G-4132)*

Cilyox Inc ....F...... 716 853-3809
Buffalo *(G-2697)*

Circle Press Inc ....D...... 212 924-4277
New York *(G-9011)*

CK Printing Corp ....G...... 718 965-0388
Brooklyn *(G-1669)*

Clarsons Corp ....F...... 585 235-8775
Rochester *(G-13317)*

▲ Classic Business Solutions ....G...... 212 563-9100
New York *(G-9023)*

Classic Color Graphics Inc ....G...... 516 822-9090
Hicksville *(G-5893)*

Classic Color Graphics Inc ....G...... 516 822-9090
Hicksville *(G-5894)*

Cloud Printing ....G...... 212 775-0888
New York *(G-9036)*

Cobico Productions Inc.....................G...... 347 417-5883
New York *(G-9045)*

Cody Printing Corp ....G...... 718 651-8854
Woodside *(G-16202)*

Coe Displays Inc ....G...... 718 937-5658
Long Island City *(G-7189)*

Cohber Press Inc ....D...... 585 475-9100
West Henrietta *(G-15789)*

Colad Group LLC ....D...... 716 961-1776
Buffalo *(G-2703)*

Color Card LLC ....F...... 631 232-1300
Central Islip *(G-3269)*

▲ Color Carton Corp........................D...... 718 665-0840
Bronx *(G-1228)*

Color-Aid Corporation ....G...... 212 673-5500
Hudson Falls *(G-6184)*

Colorfast..F...... 212 929-2440
New York *(G-9056)*

Colorfully Yours Inc ....F...... 631 242-8600
Bay Shore *(G-666)*

Combine Graphics Corp ....G...... 212 695-4044
Forest Hills *(G-4918)*

Commerce Offset Ltd ....G...... 914 769-6671
Thornwood *(G-15068)*

Commercial Press Inc ....G...... 315 274-0028
Canton *(G-3164)*

Commercial Print & Imaging.............E...... 716 597-0100
Buffalo *(G-2705)*

Community Media LLC ....E...... 212 229-1890
New York *(G-9070)*

Community Newspaper Group LLC ....E...... 607 432-1000
Oneonta *(G-12267)*

Compass Printing Plus ....G...... 518 523-3308
Saranac Lake *(G-14157)*

Complemar Print LLC ....F...... 716 875-7238
Buffalo *(G-2707)*

Composite Forms Inc ....E...... 914 937-1808
Port Chester *(G-12815)*

▲ Compucolor Associates Inc............E...... 516 358-0000
New Hyde Park *(G-8258)*

▲ Concept Printing Inc......................G...... 845 353-4040
Nyack *(G-12139)*

Consolidated Color Press Inc............F...... 212 929-8197
New York *(G-9086)*

Constas Printing Corporation ....G...... 315 474-2176
Syracuse *(G-14859)*

Copy Stop Inc ....G...... 914 428-5188
White Plains *(G-15996)*

Coral Color Process Ltd ....G...... 631 543-5200
Commack *(G-3585)*

▲ Coral Graphic Services Inc ....G...... 516 576-2100
Hicksville *(G-5897)*

Cosmos Communications Inc ....C...... 718 482-1800
Long Island City *(G-7193)*

Courier Printing Corp ....E...... 607 467-2191
Deposit *(G-3999)*

Craig Envelope Corp ....E...... 718 786-4277
Hicksville *(G-5898)*

Crater Service Group Inc ....G...... 585 482-7770
Rochester *(G-13328)*

Crawford Print Shop Inc ....G...... 607 359-4970
Addison *(G-4)*

Create-A-Card Inc ....G...... 631 584-2273
Saint James *(G-14108)*

Creative Forms Inc ....G...... 212 431-7540
New York *(G-9119)*

Creative Juices Prtg Graphics ....F...... 631 249-2211
Deer Park *(G-3855)*

Creative Printing Corp......................G...... 212 226-3870
New York *(G-9120)*

Cronin Enterprises Inc ....G...... 914 345-9600
Elmsford *(G-4405)*

Custom Prtrs Guilderland Inc ....F...... 518 456-2811
Guilderland *(G-5485)*

D G M Graphics Inc ....F...... 516 223-2220
Merrick *(G-7854)*

D W S Associates Inc ....E...... 631 667-6666
Deer Park *(G-3858)*

Daily Record ....F...... 585 232-2035
Rochester *(G-13336)*

Dan Trent Company Inc ....G...... 716 822-1422
Buffalo *(G-2720)*

Dark Star Lithograph Corp ....G...... 845 634-3780
New City *(G-8224)*

Datorib Inc ....G...... 631 698-6222
Selden *(G-14352)*

David Helsing ....G...... 607 796-2681
Horseheads *(G-6120)*

Dawn Paper Co Inc ....F...... 516 596-9110
East Rockaway *(G-4172)*

Deanco Digital Printing LLC ....F...... 212 371-2025
Sunnyside *(G-14771)*

Decal Makers Inc ....E...... 516 221-7200
Bellmore *(G-781)*

Decal Techniques Inc ....G...... 631 491-1800
Bay Shore *(G-671)*

Dell Communications Inc ....G...... 212 989-3434
New York *(G-9198)*

Delta Press Inc ....E...... 212 989-3445
High Falls *(G-5955)*

Denton Printing Corporation ....F...... 631 586-4333
Bohemia *(G-1003)*

Denton Publications Inc ....D...... 518 873-6368
Elizabethtown *(G-4299)*

Dependable Lithographers Inc ....F...... 718 472-4200
Long Island City *(G-7199)*

▲ Design Distributors Inc..................D...... 631 242-2000
Deer Park *(G-3863)*

Design Lithographers Inc ....F...... 212 645-8900
New York *(G-9206)*

Designlogocom Inc..........................G...... 212 564-0200
New York *(G-9208)*

Dick Bailey Service Inc ....F...... 718 522-4363
Brooklyn *(G-1742)*

Digital Color Concepts Inc ....E...... 212 989-4888
New York *(G-9226)*

Digital United Color Prtg Inc ....G...... 845 986-9846
Warwick *(G-15512)*

Direct Print Inc ....G...... 212 987-6003
New York *(G-9232)*

Discover Casting Inc ....G...... 212 398-5050
New York *(G-9234)*

Dispatch Graphics Inc ....G...... 212 307-5943
New York *(G-9236)*

Distinctive Printing Inc ....G...... 212 727-3000
New York *(G-9239)*

Diversified Envelope Ltd ....F...... 585 615-4697
Rochester *(G-13350)*

Doco Quick Print Inc ....G...... 315 782-6623
Watertown *(G-15569)*

Donmar Printing Co ....F...... 516 280-2239
Mineola *(G-7969)*

Donnelley Financial LLC ....D...... 212 351-9000
New York *(G-9252)*

Dowd - Witbeck Printing Corp ....F...... 518 274-2421
Troy *(G-15166)*

Downright Printing Corp ....G...... 516 619-7200
Bellerose *(G-774)*

DP Murphy Co Inc ....D...... 631 673-9400
Deer Park *(G-3865)*

DPM of Western New York LLC ....D...... 716 775-8001
Grand Island *(G-5327)*

DPM of Western New York LLC ....D...... 716 684-3825
Cheektowaga *(G-3346)*

Dupli Graphics Corporation ....G...... 315 234-7286
Syracuse *(G-14877)*

Dupli Graphics Corporation ....G...... 315 422-4732
Syracuse *(G-14878)*

Dyenamix Inc ....G...... 212 941-6642
New York *(G-9287)*

E B B Graphics Inc...........................F...... 516 750-5510
Westbury *(G-15877)*

E W Smith Publishing Co Inc.............F...... 845 562-1218
New Windsor *(G-8366)*

Eagle Graphics Inc ....G...... 585 244-5006
Rochester *(G-13361)*

Earth Enterprises Inc ....E...... 212 741-3999
New York *(G-9301)*

East Coast Business Forms Inc ....G...... 631 231-9300
Saint James *(G-14110)*

East Coast Thermographers Inc.........E...... 718 321-3211
College Point *(G-3541)*

East Ridge Quick Print ....F...... 585 266-4911
Rochester *(G-13364)*

Eastern Hills Printing ....G...... 716 741-3300
Clarence *(G-3431)*

Eastwood Litho Impressions LLC.......F...... 315 437-2626
Syracuse *(G-14881)*

Echo Appellate Press Inc ....G...... 516 432-3601
Long Beach *(G-7136)*

Edwards Graphic Co Inc ....G...... 718 548-6858
Bronx *(G-1252)*

Efficiency Printing Co Inc ....F...... 914 949-8611
White Plains *(G-16000)*

Electronic Printing Inc......................G...... 631 218-2200
Hauppauge *(G-5646)*

Empire Press Co ....G...... 718 756-9500
Brooklyn *(G-1801)*

Endeavor Printing LLC ....G...... 718 570-2720
Long Island City *(G-7214)*

Engrav-O-Type Press Inc ....F...... 585 262-7590
Rochester *(G-13393)*

Entermarket ....G...... 914 437-7268
Mount Kisco *(G-8092)*

Enterprise Press Inc ....C...... 212 741-2111
New York *(G-9382)*

Evenhouse Printing ....G...... 716 649-2666
Hamburg *(G-5508)*

Excel Graphics Services Inc ....F...... 212 929-2183
New York *(G-9441)*

Excellent Photo Copies ....G...... 718 384-7272
Brooklyn *(G-1819)*

Excellent Printing Inc ....G...... 718 384-7272
Brooklyn *(G-1821)*

Excelsior Graphics Inc ....G...... 212 730-6200
New York *(G-9444)*

Excelsus Solutions LLC ....E...... 585 533-0003
Rochester *(G-13405)*

S
I
C

F & B Photo Offset Co Inc ....G...... 516 431-5433
Island Park *(G-6317)*

F & D Services Inc ....F...... 718 984-1635
Staten Island *(G-14652)*

F J Remey Co Inc ....E...... 516 741-5112
Mineola *(G-7974)*

F5 Networks Inc ....G...... 888 882-7535
New York *(G-9458)*

Fambus Inc ....G...... 607 785-3700
Endicott *(G-4455)*

Fasprint ....G...... 518 483-4631
Malone *(G-7485)*

Federal Envelope Inc ....F...... 212 243-8380
New York *(G-9480)*

Figueroa Claribell ....G...... 718 772-8521
Bronx *(G-1256)*

Final Touch Printing Inc ....F...... 845 352-2677
Spring Valley *(G-14569)*

Finer Touch Printing Corp ....E...... 516 944-8000
Port Washington *(G-12879)*

▲ First Displays Inc ....F...... 347 642-5972
Long Island City *(G-7224)*

First Line Printing Inc ....E...... 718 606-0860
Woodside *(G-16207)*

▲ Five Star Prtg & Mailing Svcs ....F...... 212 929-0300
New York *(G-9508)*

Flare Multicopy Corp ....E...... 718 258-8860
Brooklyn *(G-1849)*

Flower City Printing Inc ....G...... 585 512-1235
Rochester *(G-13416)*

Flower City Printing Inc ....C...... 585 663-9000
Rochester *(G-13415)*

Flp Group LLC ....F...... 315 252-7583
Auburn *(G-476)*

▲ Flynns Inc ....E...... 212 339-8700
New York *(G-9512)*

Folder Factory Inc ....F...... 540 477-3852
Melville *(G-7783)*

Foleys Graphic Center Inc ....E...... 914 245-3625
Yorktown Heights *(G-16364)*

Fort Orange Press Inc ....E...... 518 489-3233
Albany *(G-78)*

Forward Enterprises Inc ....F...... 585 235-7670
Rochester *(G-13421)*

Francis Emory Fitch Inc ....E...... 212 619-3800
New York *(G-9529)*

Frederick Coon Inc ....E...... 716 683-6812
Elma *(G-4318)*

Freeville Publishing Co Inc ....F...... 607 844-9119
Freeville *(G-5033)*

Fulton Newspapers Inc ....E...... 315 598-6397
Fulton *(G-5059)*

G & P Printing Inc ....G...... 212 274-8092
New York *(G-9557)*

G F Labels LLC ....F...... 518 798-6643
Queensbury *(G-13039)*

G W Canfield & Son Inc ....G...... 315 735-5522
Utica *(G-15265)*

Gallagher Printing Inc ....F...... 716 873-2434
Buffalo *(G-2764)*

▲ Gallant Graphics Ltd ....E...... 845 868-1166
Stanfordville *(G-14610)*

Gannett Stllite Info Ntwrk LLC ....E...... 845 578-2300
West Nyack *(G-15821)*

Gatehouse Media LLC ....D...... 585 394-0770
Canandaigua *(G-3133)*

Gateway Prtg & Graphics Inc ....E...... 716 823-3873
Hamburg *(G-5509)*

Gazette Press Inc ....E...... 914 963-8300
Rye *(G-14077)*

Gem Reproduction Services Corp ....G...... 845 298-0172
Wappingers Falls *(G-15494)*

General Business Supply Inc ....D...... 518 720-3939
Watervliet *(G-15602)*

Geneva Printing Company Inc ....G...... 315 789-8191
Geneva *(G-5156)*

Genie Instant Printing Co Inc ....E...... 212 575-8258
New York *(G-9595)*

Glens Falls Printing LLC ....F...... 518 793-0555
Glens Falls *(G-5251)*

Global Graphics Inc ....F...... 718 939-4967
Flushing *(G-4854)*

Gmp LLC ....D...... 914 939-0571
Port Chester *(G-12821)*

Gn Printing ....E...... 718 784-1713
Long Island City *(G-7231)*

Golos Printing Inc ....G...... 607 732-1896
Elmira Heights *(G-4377)*

▼ Gooding Co Inc ....E...... 716 266-6252
Lockport *(G-7082)*

Gotham T-Shirt Corp ....G...... 516 676-0900
Sea Cliff *(G-14345)*

Government Data Publication ....E...... 347 789-8719
Brooklyn *(G-1904)*

GPM Associates LLC ....E...... 585 335-3940
Dansville *(G-3819)*

Grafconect Corp ....G...... 212 714-1795
New York *(G-9655)*

Grand Meridian Printing Inc ....E...... 718 937-3888
Maspeth *(G-7619)*

Grand Prix Litho Inc ....E...... 631 242-4182
Hauppauge *(G-5663)*

◆ Graphic Cntrls Acqisition Corp ....B...... 716 853-7500
Buffalo *(G-2780)*

Graphic Controls Holdings Inc ....F...... 716 853-7500
Buffalo *(G-2781)*

Graphic Fabrications Inc ....G...... 516 763-3222
Rockville Centre *(G-13828)*

Graphic Lab Inc ....E...... 212 682-1815
New York *(G-9664)*

Graphicomm Inc ....G...... 716 283-0830
Niagara Falls *(G-11932)*

Graphics Plus Printing Inc ....E...... 607 299-0500
Cortland *(G-3769)*

Great Eastern Color Lith ....C...... 845 454-7420
Poughkeepsie *(G-12959)*

Green Girl Prtg & Msgnr Inc ....G...... 212 575-0357
New York *(G-9672)*

Grover Cleveland Press Inc ....F...... 716 564-2222
Amherst *(G-226)*

Guaranteed Printing Svc Co Inc ....E...... 212 929-2410
Long Island City *(G-7236)*

H T L & S Ltd ....F...... 718 435-4474
Brooklyn *(G-1916)*

H&E Service Corp ....D...... 646 472-1936
Garden City *(G-5101)*

Haig Press Inc ....E...... 631 582-5800
Hauppauge *(G-5665)*

Harmon and Castella Printing ....F...... 845 471-9163
Hyde Park *(G-6271)*

Hearst Corporation ....A...... 518 454-5694
Albany *(G-85)*

Hempstead Sentinel Inc ....F...... 516 486-5000
Hempstead *(G-5838)*

Heritage Printing Center ....G...... 518 563-8240
Plattsburgh *(G-12751)*

HI Speed Envelope Co Inc ....F...... 718 617-1600
Mount Vernon *(G-8148)*

High End Print Solutions Inc ....F...... 585 325-5320
Rochester *(G-13465)*

Hillside Printing Inc ....F...... 718 658-6719
Jamaica *(G-6448)*

Hks Printing Company Inc ....F...... 212 675-2529
New York *(G-9797)*

Holdens Screen Supply Corp ....G...... 212 627-2727
New York *(G-9802)*

▲ Hooek Produktion Inc ....G...... 212 367-9111
New York *(G-9809)*

Horne Organization Inc ....F...... 914 572-1330
Yonkers *(G-16320)*

Hospitality Graphics Inc ....G...... 212 643-6700
New York *(G-9816)*

Huckleberry Inc ....G...... 631 630-5450
Hauppauge *(G-5673)*

▲ Hudson Envelope Corporation ....F...... 212 473-6666
New York *(G-9831)*

▲ Hudson Park Press Inc ....G...... 212 929-8898
New York *(G-9833)*

Hudson Printing Co Inc ....G...... 718 937-8600
New York *(G-9834)*

Hugh F McPherson Inc ....G...... 716 668-6107
Cheektowaga *(G-3354)*

I 2 Print Inc ....F...... 718 937-8800
Long Island City *(G-7245)*

Image Sales & Marketing Inc ....G...... 516 238-7023
Massapequa Park *(G-7656)*

Impala Press Ltd ....G...... 631 588-4262
Ronkonkoma *(G-13947)*

In-House Inc ....F...... 718 445-9007
College Point *(G-3544)*

In-Step Marketing Inc ....F...... 212 797-3450
New York *(G-9874)*

Ink Well ....G...... 718 253-9736
Brooklyn *(G-1959)*

Ink-It Printing Inc ....G...... 718 229-5590
College Point *(G-3545)*

Inland Printing Company Inc ....G...... 516 367-4700
Woodbury *(G-16174)*

Instant Again LLC ....E...... 585 436-8003
Rochester *(G-13479)*

Instant Stream Inc ....E...... 917 438-7182
New York *(G-9904)*

Insty-Prints of Buffalo Inc ....G...... 716 853-6483
Buffalo *(G-2812)*

International Newsppr Prtg Co ....E...... 516 626-6095
Glen Head *(G-5208)*

Iron Horse Graphics Ltd ....G...... 631 537-3400
Bridgehampton *(G-1166)*

Iver Printing Inc ....G...... 718 275-2070
New Hyde Park *(G-8276)*

J & J Printing Inc ....F...... 315 458-7411
Syracuse *(G-14914)*

J A T Printing Inc ....G...... 631 427-1155
Huntington *(G-6208)*

J F B & Sons Lithographers ....D...... 631 467-1444
Lake Ronkonkoma *(G-6771)*

J P Printing Inc ....G...... 516 293-6110
Farmingdale *(G-4655)*

J V Haring & Son ....F...... 718 720-1947
Staten Island *(G-14669)*

J3 Printing Inc ....G...... 516 304-6103
Queens Village *(G-13022)*

Jack J Florio Jr ....G...... 716 434-9123
Lockport *(G-7085)*

Jacobs Press Inc ....F...... 315 252-4861
Auburn *(G-481)*

Jam Printing Publishing Inc ....G...... 914 345-8400
Elmsford *(G-4413)*

James Conolly Printing Co ....E...... 585 426-4150
Rochester *(G-13488)*

Jane Lewis ....G...... 607 722-0584
Binghamton *(G-890)*

Japan Printing & Graphics Inc ....E...... 212 406-2905
New York *(G-9976)*

JDS Graphics Inc ....F...... 973 330-3300
New York *(G-9989)*

Johnnys Ideal Printing Co ....G...... 518 828-6666
Hudson *(G-6166)*

Jon Lyn Ink Inc ....G...... 516 546-2312
Merrick *(G-7857)*

◆ Joseph Paul ....G...... 718 693-4269
Brooklyn *(G-2001)*

Judith Lewis Printer Inc ....G...... 516 997-7777
Westbury *(G-15900)*

Jurist Company Inc ....G...... 212 243-8008
Long Island City *(G-7257)*

Just Press Print LLC ....E...... 585 783-1300
Rochester *(G-13500)*

Kaleidoscope Imaging Inc ....E...... 212 631-9947
New York *(G-10058)*

Karr Graphics Corp ....E...... 212 645-6000
Long Island City *(G-7261)*

Kas-Ray Industries Inc ....E...... 212 620-3144
New York *(G-10071)*

Kaufman Brothers Printing ....G...... 212 563-1854
New York *(G-10079)*

Kaymil Printing Company Inc ....G...... 212 594-3718
New York *(G-10082)*

Keeners East End Litho Inc ....G...... 631 324-8565
East Hampton *(G-4124)*

Keller Bros & Miller Inc ....G...... 716 854-2374
Buffalo *(G-2831)*

Kent Associates Inc ....G...... 212 675-0722
New York *(G-10093)*

Kenyon Press Inc ....E...... 607 674-9066
Sherburne *(G-14391)*

Key Brand Entertainment Inc ....C...... 212 966-5400
New York *(G-10095)*

Kim Jae Printing Co Inc ....G...... 212 691-6289
Roslyn Heights *(G-14053)*

Kinaneco Inc ....E...... 315 468-6201
Syracuse *(G-14926)*

Kingsbury Printing Co Inc ....E...... 518 747-6606
Queensbury *(G-13046)*

Kjckd Inc ....G...... 518 435-9696
Latham *(G-6862)*

▲ Kling Magnetics Inc ....E...... 518 392-4000
Chatham *(G-3331)*

Kurtskraft Inc ....G...... 516 944-4449
Port Washington *(G-12898)*

◆ Kwik Ticket Inc ....F...... 718 421-3800
Brooklyn *(G-2038)*

L & K Graphics Inc ....G...... 631 667-2269
Deer Park *(G-3893)*

L I F Publishing Corp ....D...... 631 345-5200
Shirley *(G-14423)*

L K Printing Corp ....G...... 914 761-1944
White Plains *(G-16023)*

L M N Printing Company Inc ....E...... 516 285-8526
Valley Stream *(G-15345)*

Label Gallery Inc ....E ... 607 334-3244
Norwich *(G-12124)*

Lake Placid Advertisers Wkshp ....E ... 518 523-3359
Lake Placid *(G-6767)*

Lake View Graphics Inc ....G ... 607 687-7033
Owego *(G-12432)*

▼ Laser Printer Checks Corp ....G ... 845 782-5837
Monroe *(G-8025)*

Lb Graph-X & Printing Inc ....G ... 212 246-2600
Smithtown *(G-14482)*

Leader Printing Inc ....F ... 516 546-1544
Merrick *(G-7859)*

Lee Printing Inc ....G ... 718 237-1651
Brooklyn *(G-2057)*

Lehmann Printing Company Inc ....G ... 212 929-2395
New York *(G-10193)*

Leigh Scott Enterprises Inc ....G ... 718 343-5440
Bellerose *(G-775)*

Lennons Litho Inc ....F ... 315 866-3156
Herkimer *(G-5866)*

Leonardo Printing Corp ....G ... 914 664-7890
Mount Vernon *(G-8157)*

Levon Graphics Corp ....D ... 631 753-2022
Deer Park *(G-3897)*

LI Script LLC ....E ... 631 321-3850
Woodbury *(G-16176)*

Liberty Label Mfg Inc ....F ... 631 737-2365
Holbrook *(G-6006)*

Litho Dynamics Inc ....G ... 914 769-1759
Hawthorne *(G-5817)*

Lithomatic Business Forms Inc ....G ... 212 255-6700
New York *(G-10227)*

Litmor Publishing Corp ....F ... 516 931-0012
Garden City *(G-5105)*

Lmg National Publishing Inc ....E ... 585 598-6874
Fairport *(G-4505)*

Logo Print Company ....G ... 607 324-5403
Hornell *(G-6109)*

Loudon Ltd ....G ... 631 757-4447
East Northport *(G-4149)*

Louis Heindl & Son Inc ....G ... 585 454-5080
Rochester *(G-13523)*

Love Unlimited NY Inc ....E ... 718 359-8500
Westbury *(G-15907)*

Loy L Press Inc ....G ... 716 634-5966
Buffalo *(G-2853)*

Lynmar Printing Corp ....G ... 631 957-8500
Amityville *(G-292)*

▲ M L Design Inc ....G ... 212 233-0213
New York *(G-10298)*

M T M Printing Co Inc ....F ... 718 353-3297
College Point *(G-3552)*

M&M Printing Inc ....F ... 516 796-3020
Carle Place *(G-3177)*

Madison Printing Corp ....G ... 607 273-3535
Ithaca *(G-6394)*

Magazines & Brochures Inc ....G ... 716 875-9699
Buffalo *(G-2857)*

Mahin Impressions Inc ....G ... 212 871-9777
Riverhead *(G-13182)*

Malone Industrial Press Inc ....G ... 518 483-5880
Malone *(G-7488)*

Manifestation-Glow Press Inc ....G ... 718 380-5259
Jamaica *(G-6457)*

Mansfield Press Inc ....F ... 212 265-5411
New York *(G-10352)*

Marcal Printing Inc ....G ... 516 942-9500
Hicksville *(G-5925)*

Marcy Printing Inc ....G ... 718 935-9100
Brooklyn *(G-2114)*

Mark T Westinghouse ....G ... 518 678-3262
Catskill *(G-3214)*

Marlow Printing Co Inc ....E ... 718 625-4948
Brooklyn *(G-2117)*

▼ Marsid Group Ltd ....G ... 516 334-1603
Carle Place *(G-3179)*

Master Image Printing Inc ....G ... 914 347-4400
Elmsford *(G-4416)*

Master Printing USA Inc ....F ... 718 456-0962
Island Park *(G-6319)*

Mc Squared Nyc Inc ....F ... 212 947-2260
New York *(G-10395)*

McG Graphics Inc ....G ... 631 499-0730
Dix Hills *(G-4012)*

McPc Inc ....D ... 212 583-6000
New York *(G-10403)*

Mdi Holdings LLC ....A ... 212 559-1127
New York *(G-10404)*

Mdr Printing Corp ....G ... 516 627-3221
Manhasset *(G-7538)*

▲ Medallion Associates Inc ....E ... 212 929-9130
New York *(G-10408)*

▲ Mercury Print Productions Inc ....C ... 585 458-7900
Rochester *(G-13542)*

Merrill New York Company Inc ....C ... 212 229-6500
New York *(G-10438)*

Messenger Press ....G ... 518 885-9231
Ballston Spa *(G-582)*

Michael K Lennon Inc ....E ... 631 288-5200
Westhampton Beach *(G-15957)*

Mickelberry Communications Inc ....G ... 212 832-0303
New York *(G-10455)*

Microera Printers Inc ....E ... 585 783-1300
Rochester *(G-13547)*

Mid Atlantic Graphics Corp ....E ... 631 345-3800
Shirley *(G-14424)*

Mid-York Press Inc ....D ... 607 674-4491
Sherburne *(G-14392)*

Middletown Press ....G ... 845 343-1895
Middletown *(G-7920)*

Midgley Printing Corp ....G ... 315 475-1864
Syracuse *(G-14942)*

Midstate Printing Corp ....E ... 315 475-4101
Liverpool *(G-7026)*

Mikam Graphics LLC ....D ... 212 684-9393
New York *(G-10464)*

Miller Place Printing Inc ....G ... 631 473-1158
Miller Place *(G-7945)*

Miller Printing & Litho Inc ....G ... 518 842-0001
Amsterdam *(G-336)*

▲ Mines Press Inc ....G ... 888 559-2634
Cortland Manor *(G-3797)*

Minuteman Press Inc ....G ... 845 623-2277
Nanuet *(G-8202)*

◆ Minuteman Press Intl Inc ....E ... 631 249-1370
Farmingdale *(G-4685)*

Minuteman Press Intl Inc ....G ... 718 343-5440
Jamaica *(G-6461)*

Mitchell Prtg & Mailing Inc ....F ... 315 343-3531
Oswego *(G-12414)*

MJB Printing Corp ....G ... 631 581-0177
Islip *(G-6355)*

Mod-Pac Corp ....D ... 716 447-9013
Buffalo *(G-2870)*

Monarch Graphics Inc ....F ... 631 232-1300
Central Islip *(G-3284)*

Moneast Inc ....G ... 845 298-8898
Wappingers Falls *(G-15498)*

Monte Press Inc ....G ... 718 325-4999
Bronx *(G-1319)*

Mooney-Keehley Inc ....G ... 585 271-1573
Rochester *(G-13559)*

Moore Printing Company Inc ....G ... 585 394-1533
Canandaigua *(G-3136)*

Multimedia Services Inc ....E ... 607 936-3186
Corning *(G-3718)*

Multiple Imprssons of Rchester ....G ... 585 546-1160
Rochester *(G-13563)*

Mutual Engraving Company Inc ....D ... 516 489-0534
West Hempstead *(G-15777)*

Nameplate Mfrs of Amer ....E ... 631 752-0055
Farmingdale *(G-4690)*

Nasco Printing Corporation ....G ... 212 229-2462
New York *(G-10534)*

Nash Printing Inc ....F ... 516 935-4567
Plainview *(G-12704)*

National Reproductions Inc ....E ... 212 619-3800
New York *(G-10544)*

NCR Corporation ....C ... 607 273-5310
Ithaca *(G-6400)*

Nesher Printing Inc ....E ... 212 760-2521
New York *(G-10566)*

New Goldstar 1 Printing Corp ....G ... 212 343-3909
New York *(G-10583)*

New Horizon Graphics Inc ....E ... 631 231-8055
Hauppauge *(G-5727)*

New York Digital Print Ctr Inc ....G ... 718 767-1953
Whitestone *(G-16098)*

New York Typing & Printing Co ....G ... 718 268-7900
Forest Hills *(G-4925)*

Newburgh Envelope Corp ....G ... 845 566-4211
Newburgh *(G-11877)*

Newport Graphics Inc ....E ... 212 924-2600
New York *(G-10610)*

North Delaware Printing Inc ....G ... 716 692-0576
Tonawanda *(G-15128)*

Northeast Commercial Prtg Inc ....G ... 518 459-5047
Albany *(G-107)*

▲ Northeast Prtg & Dist Co Inc ....E ... 518 563-8214
Plattsburgh *(G-12765)*

Northern NY Newspapers Corp ....C ... 315 782-1000
Watertown *(G-15586)*

▲ Nova Inc ....G ... 212 967-1139
New York *(G-10648)*

Observer Daily Sunday Newsppr ....D ... 716 366-3000
Dunkirk *(G-4062)*

Office Grabs NY Inc ....G ... 212 444-1331
Brooklyn *(G-2229)*

▼ Official Offset Corporation ....E ... 631 957-8500
Amityville *(G-299)*

Orbis Brynmore Lithographics ....G ... 212 987-2100
New York *(G-10703)*

Orffeo Printing & Imaging Inc ....G ... 716 681-5757
Lancaster *(G-6819)*

▲ Orlandi Inc ....D ... 631 756-0110
Farmingdale *(G-4698)*

Orlandi Inc ....E ... 631 756-0110
Farmingdale *(G-4699)*

Ozipko Enterprises Inc ....G ... 585 424-6740
Rochester *(G-13602)*

P & W Press Inc ....E ... 646 486-3417
New York *(G-10732)*

P D R Inc ....E ... 516 829-5300
Plainview *(G-12706)*

Pace Editions Inc ....G ... 212 643-6353
New York *(G-10736)*

Paladino Prtg & Graphics Inc ....G ... 718 279-6000
Flushing *(G-4883)*

Pama Enterprises Inc ....G ... 516 504-6300
Great Neck *(G-5411)*

▲ Panther Graphics Inc ....E ... 585 546-7163
Rochester *(G-13608)*

▲ Paper House Productions Inc ....E ... 845 246-7261
Saugerties *(G-14207)*

Park Slope Copy Center ....F ... 718 783-0268
Brooklyn *(G-2249)*

Parkside Printing Co Inc ....F ... 516 933-5423
Jericho *(G-6588)*

Parrinello Printing Inc ....F ... 716 633-7780
Buffalo *(G-2908)*

Patrick Ryans Modern Press ....F ... 518 434-2921
Albany *(G-112)*

▲ Paul Michael Group Inc ....G ... 631 585-5700
Ronkonkoma *(G-13993)*

Paya Printing of NY Inc ....G ... 516 625-8346
Albertson *(G-149)*

PBR Graphics Inc ....G ... 518 458-2909
Albany *(G-113)*

Peachtree Enterprises Inc ....E ... 212 989-3445
Long Island City *(G-7322)*

Perfect Forms and Systems Inc ....E ... 631 462-1100
Smithtown *(G-14484)*

Persch Service Print Inc ....G ... 716 366-2677
Dunkirk *(G-4063)*

Petit Printing Corp ....G ... 716 871-9490
Getzville *(G-5181)*

Phillip Tissicher ....F ... 718 282-3310
Brooklyn *(G-2255)*

Phoenix Graphics Inc ....E ... 585 232-4040
Rochester *(G-13621)*

Photo Agents Ltd ....G ... 631 421-0258
Huntington *(G-6217)*

Pic A Poc Enterprises Inc ....G ... 631 981-2094
Ronkonkoma *(G-13995)*

Pine Bush Printing Co Inc ....G ... 518 456-2431
Albany *(G-116)*

Pioneer Printers Inc ....F ... 716 693-7100
North Tonawanda *(G-12082)*

PIP Inc ....G ... 518 861-0133
Latham *(G-6873)*

Pixos Print ....G ... 585 500-4600
Rochester *(G-13625)*

Platinum Printing & Graphics ....G ... 631 249-3325
Farmingdale *(G-4711)*

Pollack Graphics Inc ....G ... 212 727-8400
New York *(G-10861)*

Pop Printing Incorporated ....F ... 212 808-7800
Brooklyn *(G-2270)*

Positive Print Litho Offset ....G ... 212 431-4850
New York *(G-10870)*

◆ Positive Promotions Inc ....C ... 631 648-1200
Hauppauge *(G-5745)*

Post Road ....F ... 203 545-2122
New York *(G-10871)*

Pre Cycled Inc ....G ... 845 278-7611
Brewster *(G-1158)*

Precision Envelope Co Inc ....G ... 631 694-3990
Farmingdale *(G-4715)*

Preebro Printing ....G ... 718 633-7300
Brooklyn *(G-2279)*

S I C

Presstek Printing	G	585 266-2770	
Rochester (G-13641)			
Presstek Printing LLC	F	585 467-8140	
Rochester (G-13642)			
Presstek Printing LLC	F	585 266-2770	
Rochester (G-13643)			
Prestige Envelope & Lithograph	F	631 521-7043	
Merrick (G-7863)			
Pricet Printing	G	315 655-0369	
Cazenovia (G-3234)			
Print & Graphics Group	G	518 371-4649	
Clifton Park (G-3470)			
▲ Print Better Inc	G	347 348-1841	
Ridgewood (G-13156)			
Print Center Inc	G	718 643-9559	
Cold Spring Harbor (G-3529)			
Print Cottage LLC	F	516 369-1749	
Massapequa Park (G-7660)			
▲ Print Early LLC	E	718 915-7368	
Westbury (G-15920)			
▲ Print House Inc	D	718 443-7500	
Brooklyn (G-2288)			
Print It Here	G	516 308-7785	
Massapequa (G-7648)			
Print It Inc	G	845 371-2227	
Monsey (G-8044)			
Print Management Group Inc	G	212 213-1555	
New York (G-10895)			
Print Market Inc	G	631 940-8181	
Deer Park (G-3922)			
▲ Print Media Inc	D	212 563-4040	
New York (G-10896)			
Print On Demand Initiative Inc	F	585 239-6044	
Rochester (G-13644)			
Print Seforim Bzul Inc	G	718 679-1011	
Brooklyn (G-2290)			
Print Solutions Plus Inc	G	315 234-3801	
Liverpool (G-7036)			
Print Tech Inc	G	585 202-3888	
Webster (G-15648)			
Printcorp Inc	E	631 696-0641	
Ronkonkoma (G-13996)			
Printech Business Systems Inc	F	212 290-2542	
New York (G-10897)			
Printed Image	G	716 821-1880	
Buffalo (G-2932)			
Printers 3 Inc	F	631 351-1331	
Hauppauge (G-5750)			
Printing Prep Inc	E	716 852-5011	
Buffalo (G-2933)			
Printing Prmtnal Solutions LLC	F	315 474-1110	
Syracuse (G-14967)			
Printing Resources Inc	E	518 482-2470	
Albany (G-119)			
Printing Sales Group Limited	E	718 258-8860	
Brooklyn (G-2293)			
Printing Spectrum Inc	F	631 689-1010	
East Setauket (G-4185)			
Printing X Press Ions	G	631 242-1992	
Dix Hills (G-4014)			
Printinghouse Press Ltd	G	212 719-0990	
New York (G-10899)			
Printout Copy Corp	E	718 855-4040	
Brooklyn (G-2294)			
Printroc Inc	G	585 461-2556	
Rochester (G-13645)			
Printutopia	F	718 788-1545	
Brooklyn (G-2295)			
Printz and Patternz LLC	G	518 944-6020	
Schenectady (G-14296)			
Pro Printing	G	516 561-9700	
Lynbrook (G-7435)			
Professional Solutions Print	G	631 231-9300	
West Islip (G-15812)			
Profile Printing & Graphics	G	631 273-2727	
Hauppauge (G-5751)			
Progressive Color Graphics	G	212 292-8787	
Great Neck (G-5416)			
Progressive Graphics & Prtg	G	315 331-3635	
Newark (G-11850)			
Prompt Printing Inc	G	631 454-6524	
Farmingdale (G-4716)			
Pronto Printer	G	914 737-0800	
Cortlandt Manor (G-3798)			
Psychonomic Society Inc	E	512 381-1494	
New York (G-10919)			
▲ Publimax Printing Corp	G	718 366-7133	
Ridgewood (G-13157)			
Quad/Graphics Inc	A	518 581-4000	
Saratoga Springs (G-14189)			

Quad/Graphics Inc	C	212 672-1300	
New York (G-10947)			
Quad/Graphics Inc	A	212 206-5535	
New York (G-10948)			
Quad/Graphics Inc	A	212 741-1001	
New York (G-10949)			
Quality Graphics Tri State	G	845 735-2523	
Pearl River (G-12539)			
Quicker Printer Inc	G	607 734-8622	
Elmira (G-4365)			
Quickprint	G	585 394-2600	
Canandaigua (G-3141)			
R & J Graphics Inc	F	631 293-6611	
Farmingdale (G-4721)			
R & L Press Inc	G	718 447-8557	
Staten Island (G-14696)			
R & L Press of SI Inc	G	718 667-3258	
Staten Island (G-14697)			
R D Printing Associates Inc	G	631 390-5964	
Farmingdale (G-4722)			
▲ R Hochman Papers Incorporated	F	516 466-6414	
Brooklyn (G-2320)			
Raith America Inc	E	518 874-3000	
Troy (G-15182)			
Rapid Print and Marketing Inc	G	585 924-1520	
Victor (G-15427)			
Rapid Rays Printing & Copying	G	716 852-0550	
Buffalo (G-2947)			
Rapid Reproductions LLC	G	607 843-2221	
Oxford (G-12442)			
Rapid Service Engraving Co	G	716 896-4555	
Buffalo (G-2948)			
Rasco Graphics Inc	G	212 206-0447	
New York (G-10981)			
Ready Check Glo Inc	G	516 547-1849	
East Northport (G-4151)			
Redi Records Payroll	F	718 854-6990	
Brooklyn (G-2335)			
Reflex Offset Inc	G	516 746-4142	
Deer Park (G-3927)			
Register Graphics Inc	G	716 358-2921	
Randolph (G-13065)			
REM Printing Inc	G	518 438-7338	
Albany (G-126)			
Remsen Graphics Corp	G	718 643-7500	
Brooklyn (G-2340)			
Resonant Legal Media LLC	G	800 781-3591	
New York (G-11019)			
Rgm Signs Inc	G	718 442-0598	
Staten Island (G-14703)			
Richard Ruffner	F	631 234-4600	
Central Islip (G-3287)			
Richmar Printing Inc	G	631 617-6915	
Bay Shore (G-706)			
RIT Printing Corp	F	631 586-6220	
Bay Shore (G-707)			
Rmd Holding Inc	G	845 628-0030	
Mahopac (G-7478)			
Rmf Print Management Group	F	716 683-4351	
Depew (G-3997)			
▲ Rmf Printing Technologies Inc	E	716 683-7500	
Lancaster (G-6830)			
Robert Tabatznik Assoc Inc	F	845 336-4555	
Kingston (G-6708)			
▲ Rosemont Press Incorporated	E	212 239-4770	
New York (G-11082)			
Rosen Mandell & Immerman Inc	E	212 691-2277	
New York (G-11083)			
Royal Tees Inc	G	845 357-9448	
Suffern (G-14766)			
Rv Printing	G	631 567-8658	
Holbrook (G-6019)			
Ryan Printing Inc	E	845 535-3235	
Blauvelt (G-933)			
Sample News Group LLC	D	315 343-3800	
Oswego (G-12420)			
Sand Hill Industries Inc	G	518 885-7991	
Ballston Spa (G-586)			
▲ Sanford Printing Inc	G	718 461-1202	
Flushing (G-4891)			
Scotti Graphics Inc	E	212 367-9602	
Long Island City (G-7352)			
Scriven Duplicating Service	G	518 233-8180	
Troy (G-15187)			
Seaboard Graphic Services LLC	E	315 652-4200	
East Syracuse (G-4237)			
Searles Graphics Inc	E	631 345-2202	
Yaphank (G-16270)			
Select-A-Form Inc	D	631 981-3076	
Holbrook (G-6020)			

Seneca West Printing Inc	G	716 675-8010	
West Seneca (G-15854)			
Sentine Printing Inc	G	516 334-7400	
Westbury (G-15925)			
Sharp Printing Inc	G	716 731-3994	
Sanborn (G-14149)			
Shield Press Inc	G	212 431-7489	
New York (G-11213)			
Shipman Printing Inds Inc	E	716 504-7700	
Niagara Falls (G-11980)			
Shipman Printing Inds Inc	F	716 504-7700	
Sanborn (G-14150)			
Shipmtes/Printmates Holdg Corp	D	518 370-1158	
Scotia (G-14336)			
Shoreline Publishing Inc	G	914 738-7869	
Pelham (G-12568)			
Sign Shop Inc	G	631 226-4145	
Copiague (G-3678)			
Sign World Inc	E	212 619-9000	
Brooklyn (G-2410)			
Sizzal LLC	E	212 354-6123	
Long Island City (G-7359)			
Sloane Design Inc	G	212 539-0184	
Brooklyn (G-2429)			
Solarz Bros Printing Corp	G	718 383-1330	
Brooklyn (G-2439)			
Source Envelope Inc	G	866 284-0707	
Farmingdale (G-4735)			
South Bridge Press Inc	E	212 233-4047	
New York (G-11305)			
Spectrum Prtg Lithography Inc	E	212 255-3131	
New York (G-11316)			
Speedway Press Inc	G	315 343-3531	
Oswego (G-12421)			
Speedy Enterprise USA Corp	G	718 463-3000	
Flushing (G-4894)			
Sputnick 84 LLC	G	844 667-7468	
New York (G-11340)			
St James Printing Inc	G	631 981-2095	
Ronkonkoma (G-14014)			
▲ St Lawrence County Newspapers	D	315 393-1003	
Canton (G-3167)			
▲ Standwill Packaging Inc	E	631 752-1236	
Farmingdale (G-4739)			
Star Press Pearl River Inc	G	845 268-2294	
Valley Cottage (G-15325)			
▲ Star Quality Printing Inc	F	631 273-1900	
Hauppauge (G-5775)			
Steffen Publishing Inc	D	315 865-4100	
Holland Patent (G-6034)			
Sterling North America Inc	E	631 243-6933	
Hauppauge (G-5776)			
▼ Sterling Pierce Company Inc	E	516 593-1170	
East Rockaway (G-4174)			
Steval Graphics Concepts Inc	F	516 576-0220	
Plainview (G-12716)			
Stevens Bandes Graphics Corp	F	212 675-1128	
New York (G-11361)			
Stevenson Printing Co Inc	G	516 676-1233	
Glen Cove (G-5202)			
Stony Brook University	E	631 632-6434	
Stony Brook (G-14741)			
Stony Point Graphics Ltd	G	845 786-3322	
Stony Point (G-14748)			
Stubbs Printing Inc	G	315 769-8641	
Massena (G-7672)			
Studio 22 Print	G	212 679-2656	
New York (G-11377)			
Studley Prtg Publications Inc	F	518 563-1414	
Plattsburgh (G-12782)			
Stylistic Press Inc	F	212 675-0797	
New York (G-11382)			
Suffolk Copy Center Inc	G	631 665-0570	
Bay Shore (G-718)			
Summit MSP LLC	G	716 433-1014	
Lockport (G-7108)			
Summit MSP LLC	G	716 433-1014	
Lockport (G-7109)			
Sun Printing Incorporated	E	607 337-3034	
Norwich (G-12128)			
Superior Print On Demand	G	607 240-5231	
Vestal (G-15384)			
Syracuse Computer Forms Inc	E	315 478-0108	
Syracuse (G-15005)			
T C Peters Printing Co Inc	G	315 724-4149	
Utica (G-15296)			
Taylor Communications Inc	E	718 361-1000	
Long Island City (G-7378)			
Technipoly Manufacturing Inc	E	718 383-0363	
Brooklyn (G-2496)			

◆ Tele-Pak Inc ....E 845 426-2300
Monsey *(G-8053)*

Teller Printing Corp ....G 718 486-3662
Brooklyn *(G-2499)*

The Kingsbury Printing Co Inc ....G 518 747-6606
Queensbury *(G-13058)*

Thomas Group Inc ....F 212 947-6400
New York *(G-11467)*

Thomson Press (india) Limited ....G 646 318-0369
Long Island City *(G-7382)*

Three Star Offset Printing ....F 516 867-8223
Freeport *(G-5029)*

Tobay Printing Co Inc ....G 631 842-3300
Copiague *(G-3684)*

Tom & Jerry Printcraft Forms ....E 914 777-7468
Mamaroneck *(G-7525)*

Torsaf Printers Inc ....G 516 569-5577
Hewlett *(G-5873)*

Total Concept Graphic Inc ....G 212 229-2626
New York *(G-11520)*

Tovie Asarese Royal Prtg Co ......G 716 885-7692
Buffalo *(G-3016)*

Trade Mark Graphics Inc ....G 718 306-0001
Staten Island *(G-14724)*

Transaction Printer Group ....G 607 274-2500
Ithaca *(G-6415)*

◆ Transcntinental Ultra Flex Inc ....B 718 272-9100
Brooklyn *(G-2516)*

Transcontinental Printing GP ......G 716 626-3078
Amherst *(G-249)*

Tremont Offset Inc ....G 718 892-7333
Bronx *(G-1380)*

Tri Kolor Printing & Sty ....F 315 474-6753
Syracuse *(G-15015)*

Tri-Star Offset Corp ....E 718 894-5555
Maspeth *(G-7639)*

Tri-Town News Inc ....E 607 561-3515
Sidney *(G-14436)*

Triad Printing Inc ....G 845 343-2722
Middletown *(G-7936)*

Tripi Engraving Co Inc ....E 718 383-6500
Brooklyn *(G-2522)*

Troy Sign & Printing ....G 718 994-4482
Bronx *(G-1382)*

True Type Printing Co Inc ....G 718 706-6900
Amityville *(G-315)*

Tucker Printers Inc ....D 585 359-3030
Henrietta *(G-5861)*

▲ Twenty-First Century Press Inc ....F 716 837-0800
Buffalo *(G-3023)*

Twin Counties Pro Printers Inc ....F 518 828-3278
Hudson *(G-6181)*

U Invite Limited ....G 212 739-0620
New York *(G-11570)*

Upstate Printing Inc ....F 315 475-6140
Syracuse *(G-15018)*

V & J Graphics Inc ....G 315 363-1933
Oneida *(G-12255)*

V C N Group Ltd Inc ....G 516 223-4812
North Baldwin *(G-12010)*

▲ Variable Graphics LLC ....G 212 691-2323
New York *(G-11643)*

Veterans Offset Printing Inc ....G 585 288-2900
Rochester *(G-13796)*

Vicks Lithograph & Prtg Corp ....C 315 736-9344
Yorkville *(G-16381)*

Vicks Lithograph & Prtg Corp ....C 315 272-2401
Yorkville *(G-16380)*

Vincys Printing Ltd ....F 518 355-4363
Schenectady *(G-14314)*

VIP Printing ....G 718 641-9361
Howard Beach *(G-6142)*

▲ Virgil Mountain Inc ....G 212 378-0007
New York *(G-11686)*

Vivona Business Printers Inc ......G 516 496-3453
Syosset *(G-14805)*

Wallkill Valley Publications ....E 845 561-0170
Newburgh *(G-11893)*

Walnut Printing Inc ....G 718 707-0100
Long Island City *(G-7397)*

Wappingers Falls Shopper Inc ....E 845 297-3723
Wappingers Falls *(G-15501)*

Warren Printing Inc ....F 212 627-5000
Long Island City *(G-7398)*

Waterhouse Publications Inc ......E 716 662-4200
Orchard Park *(G-12383)*

Wayne Printing Inc ....F 914 761-2400
White Plains *(G-16071)*

Webb-Mason Inc ....E 716 276-8792
Buffalo *(G-3043)*

Webster Printing Corporation .....F 585 671-1533
Webster *(G-15662)*

Weeks & Reichel Printing Inc .....G 631 589-1443
Sayville *(G-14232)*

Weicro Graphics Inc ....E 631 253-3360
Brooklyn *(G-2578)*

Westchester Mailing Service ......E 914 948-1116
White Plains *(G-16073)*

Westmore Litho Corp ....G 718 361-9403
Long Island City *(G-7400)*

Westypo Printers Inc ....G 914 737-7394
Peekskill *(G-12562)*

Whitestone Dev Group LLC ......G 585 482-7770
Rochester *(G-13804)*

William Boyd Printing Co Inc .....C 518 339-5832
Latham *(G-6881)*

William Charles Prtg Co Inc ......E 516 349-0900
Plainview *(G-12728)*

William J Kline & Son Inc ....D 518 843-1100
Amsterdam *(G-354)*

William J Ryan ....G 585 392-6200
Hilton *(G-5975)*

Wilson Press LLC ....E 315 568-9693
Seneca Falls *(G-14374)*

Winner Press Inc ....E 718 937-7715
Long Island City *(G-7404)*

Winson Surnamer Inc ....G 718 729-8787
Long Island City *(G-7405)*

▲ Won & Lee Inc ....E 516 222-0712
Garden City *(G-5119)*

Woodbury Printing Plus + Inc ....G 845 928-6610
Central Valley *(G-3302)*

Worldwide Ticket Craft ....D 516 538-6200
Merrick *(G-7865)*

Wynco Press One Inc ....G 516 354-6145
Glen Oaks *(G-5215)*

X Myles Mar Inc ....E 212 683-2015
New York *(G-11795)*

X-L Envelope and Printing Inc ....F 716 852-2135
Buffalo *(G-3051)*

Zacmel Graphics LLC ....G 631 944-6031
Deer Park *(G-3957)*

Zenger Group Inc ....E 716 871-1058
Tonawanda *(G-15156)*

Zenger Partners LLC ....E 716 876-2284
Kenmore *(G-6656)*

2754 Commercial Printing: Gravure

Alamar Printing Inc ....F 914 993-9007
White Plains *(G-15969)*

Alfa Card Inc ....G 718 326-7107
Glendale *(G-5217)*

American Packaging Corporation ....C 585 254-9500
Rochester *(G-13230)*

American Print Solutions Inc ......G 718 208-2309
Brooklyn *(G-1502)*

▲ Ashton-Potter USA Ltd ....C 716 633-2000
Williamsville *(G-16120)*

C C Industries Inc ....F 518 581-7633
Saratoga Springs *(G-14167)*

▲ Clintrak Clinical Labeling S ....D 888 479-3900
Bohemia *(G-988)*

Color Industries LLC ....G 718 392-8301
Long Island City *(G-7190)*

Copy Corner Inc ....G 718 388-4545
Brooklyn *(G-1687)*

Dijifi LLC ....F 646 519-2447
Brooklyn *(G-1746)*

Foleys Graphic Center Inc ....E 914 245-3625
Yorktown Heights *(G-16364)*

◆ Gruner + Jahr USA Group Inc ....B 866 323-9336
New York *(G-9688)*

Jack J Florio Jr ....G 716 434-9123
Lockport *(G-7085)*

Janco Press Inc ....F 631 563-3003
Bohemia *(G-1027)*

Karr Graphics Corp ....E 212 645-6000
Long Island City *(G-7261)*

Kinaneco Inc ....G 315 468-6201
Syracuse *(G-14926)*

Liberty Label Mfg Inc ....F 631 737-2365
Holbrook *(G-6006)*

Macadame Inc ....G 212 477-1930
Brooklyn *(G-2099)*

Mastro Graphic Arts Inc ....E 585 436-7570
Rochester *(G-13537)*

McG Graphics Inc ....G 631 499-0730
Dix Hills *(G-4012)*

Mod-Pac Corp ....D 716 447-9013
Buffalo *(G-2870)*

Mrs John L Strong & Co LLC ....F 212 838-3775
New York *(G-10514)*

Mutual Engraving Company Inc ....D 516 489-0534
West Hempstead *(G-15777)*

▲ Niagara Label Company Inc ......F 716 542-3000
Akron *(G-18)*

Paya Printing of NY Inc ....G 516 625-8346
Albertson *(G-149)*

Sommer and Sons Printing Inc ....F 716 822-4311
Buffalo *(G-2986)*

SRC Liquidation Company ....G 716 631-3900
Williamsville *(G-16141)*

◆ Tele-Pak Inc ....E 845 426-2300
Monsey *(G-8053)*

Trust of Colum Unive In The Ci ....F 212 854-2793
New York *(G-11552)*

2759 Commercial Printing

2 1 2 Postcards Inc ....E 212 767-8227
New York *(G-8391)*

4 Over 4com Inc ....G 718 932-2700
Astoria *(G-412)*

461 New Lots Avenue LLC ....G 347 303-9305
Brooklyn *(G-1419)*

5 Stars Printing Corp ....F 718 461-4612
Flushing *(G-4831)*

6727 11th Ave Corp ....F 718 837-8787
Brooklyn *(G-1421)*

A & A Graphics Inc II ....G 516 735-0078
Seaford *(G-14348)*

▲ A Graphic Printing Inc ....G 212 233-9696
New York *(G-8416)*

A Promos USA Inc ....F 516 377-0186
Freeport *(G-4978)*

A Tradition of Excellence Inc ......G 845 638-4595
New City *(G-8223)*

◆ Abigal Press Inc ....D 718 641-5350
Ozone Park *(G-12457)*

AC Envelope Inc ....G 516 420-0646
Farmingdale *(G-4572)*

Academy Printing Services Inc ....G 631 765-3346
Southold *(G-14542)*

Accel Printing & Graphics ....G 914 241-3369
Mount Kisco *(G-8086)*

Acme Screenprinting LLC ....G 716 565-1052
Buffalo *(G-2619)*

Action Envelope & Prtg Co Inc ....F 631 225-3900
Melville *(G-7754)*

Actioncraft Products Inc ....G 516 883-6423
Port Washington *(G-12859)*

▲ Active World Solutions Inc ....G 718 922-9404
Brooklyn *(G-1459)*

Ad Image Inc ....E 914 476-0000
Yonkers *(G-16280)*

Ad Publications Inc ....F 585 248-2888
Pittsford *(G-12635)*

Adirondack Pennysaver Inc ....E 518 563-0100
Plattsburgh *(G-12731)*

Advance Finance Group LLC ......D 212 630-5900
New York *(G-8468)*

▼ Advanced Graphics Company Inc ....F 607 692-7875
Whitney Point *(G-16105)*

Albert Siy ....G 718 359-0389
Flushing *(G-4836)*

Alicia F Herdlein ....G 585 344-4411
Batavia *(G-599)*

▲ Allsafe Technologies Inc ....D 716 691-0400
Amherst *(G-208)*

Alpina Copyworld Inc ....F 212 683-3511
New York *(G-8529)*

Alpine Business Group Inc ....F 212 989-4198
New York *(G-8530)*

AMA Precision Screening Inc ......F 585 293-0820
Churchville *(G-3407)*

Amax Printing Inc ....F 718 384-8600
Maspeth *(G-7588)*

◆ American Casting and Mfg Corp ....D 800 342-0333
Plainview *(G-12662)*

American Office Supply Inc ....F 516 294-9444
Westbury *(G-15868)*

Amerikom Group Inc ....D 212 675-1329
New York *(G-8562)*

Amstead Press Corp ....G 347 416-2373
New York *(G-8569)*

Apple Enterprises Inc ....E 718 361-2200
Long Island City *(G-7160)*

Arca Ink LLC ....G 518 798-0100
South Glens Falls *(G-14512)*

Arena Graphics Inc	G	516 767-5108	Port Washington *(G-12864)*
Argo Envelope Corp	D	718 729-2700	Long Island City *(G-7164)*
Argo Lithographers Inc	E	718 729-2700	Long Island City *(G-7166)*
Arista Innovations Inc	E	516 746-2262	Mineola *(G-7959)*
▲ Artistic Typography Corp	F	212 463-8880	New York *(G-8638)*
Artscroll Printing Corp	E	212 929-2413	New York *(G-8640)*
Artwill Group LLC	E	845 826-3692	Blauvelt *(G-926)*
▲ Ashton-Potter USA Ltd	C	716 633-2000	Williamsville *(G-16120)*
Asn Inc	E	718 894-0800	Maspeth *(G-7593)*
Aspect Printing Inc	E	347 789-4284	Brooklyn *(G-1542)*
Baffler Foundation Inc	G	203 362-8147	New York *(G-8714)*
▲ Bags Unlimited Inc	E	585 436-6282	Rochester *(G-13258)*
Balajee Enterprises Inc	G	212 629-6150	New York *(G-8721)*
Barnaby Prints Inc	F	845 477-2501	Greenwood Lake *(G-5479)*
Bartolomeo Publishing Inc	G	631 420-4949	West Babylon *(G-15693)*
Batavia Legal Printing Inc	G	585 768-2100	Le Roy *(G-6896)*
Batavia Press LLC	E	585 343-4429	Batavia *(G-603)*
Bates Jackson Engraving Co Inc	E	716 854-3000	Buffalo *(G-2657)*
Bco Industries Western NY Inc	E	716 877-2800	Tonawanda *(G-15089)*
BDR Creative Concepts Inc	F	516 942-7768	Farmingdale *(G-4591)*
Bedford Freeman & Worth	C	212 576-9400	New York *(G-8745)*
Beebie Printing & Art Agcy Inc	G	518 725-4528	Gloversville *(G-5279)*
Beis Moshiach Inc	E	718 778-8000	Brooklyn *(G-1571)*
Bella Figura Letterpress	G	866 699-6040	Syracuse *(G-14827)*
▲ Benchemark Printing Inc	D	518 393-1361	Schenectady *(G-14249)*
Berkshire Business Forms Inc	F	518 828-2600	Hudson *(G-6150)*
Bestmade Printing LLC	F	718 384-0719	Brooklyn *(G-1580)*
Bestype Digital Imaging LLC	F	212 966-6886	New York *(G-8767)*
Bidpress LLC	G	267 973-8876	New York *(G-8782)*
▲ Big Apple Sign Corp	D	212 629-3650	New York *(G-8785)*
Bizbash Media Inc	D	646 638-3602	New York *(G-8804)*
Bkny Printing Corp	E	718 875-4219	Brooklyn *(G-1591)*
▲ Bobley-Harmann Corporation	G	516 433-3800	Ronkonkoma *(G-13917)*
Body Builders Inc	G	718 492-7997	Brooklyn *(G-1601)*
Bondy Printing Corp	G	631 242-1510	Bay Shore *(G-659)*
BP Beyond Printing Inc	G	516 328-2700	Hempstead *(G-5834)*
Bradley Marketing Group Inc	G	212 967-6100	New York *(G-8844)*
Bridge Fulfillment Inc	G	718 625-6622	Brooklyn *(G-1608)*
Brodock Press Inc	D	315 735-9577	Utica *(G-15242)*
Brooks Litho Digital Group Inc	G	631 789-4500	Deer Park *(G-3850)*
Buffalo Newspress Inc	C	716 852-1600	Buffalo *(G-2681)*
Burr & Son Inc	G	315 446-1550	Syracuse *(G-14836)*
Business Card Express Inc	E	631 669-3400	West Babylon *(G-15698)*
C & C Athletic Inc	G	845 713-4670	Walden *(G-15457)*
Cama Graphics Inc	F	718 707-9747	Long Island City *(G-7183)*
Candid Worldwide LLC	G	212 799-5300	Farmingdale *(G-4597)*
▲ Century Direct LLC	C	212 763-0600	Islandia *(G-6328)*
Chakra Communications Inc	E	607 748-7491	Endicott *(G-4446)*
Check-O-Matic Inc	G	845 781-7675	Monroe *(G-8018)*
Chenango Union Printing Inc	G	607 334-2112	Norwich *(G-12116)*
Christian Bus Endeavors Inc	F	315 788-8560	Watertown *(G-15564)*
Chroma Communications Inc	G	631 289-8871	Medford *(G-7703)*
Citation Healthcare Labels LLC	G	631 293-4646	Hauppauge *(G-5616)*
Classic Album	E	718 388-2818	Brooklyn *(G-1670)*
Classic Labels Inc	E	631 467-2300	Patchogue *(G-12498)*
Cnyshirts	G	315 432-1789	Syracuse *(G-14854)*
Colad Group LLC	D	716 961-1776	Buffalo *(G-2703)*
Colonial Label Systems Inc	E	631 254-0111	Bay Shore *(G-664)*
▲ Colonial Tag & Label Co Inc	F	516 482-0508	Great Neck *(G-5377)*
Color Card LLC	F	631 232-1300	Central Islip *(G-3269)*
Comgraph Sales Service	G	716 601-7243	Elma *(G-4317)*
Commercial Press Inc	G	315 274-0028	Canton *(G-3164)*
Con-Tees Custom Printing Ltd	G	914 664-0251	Mount Vernon *(G-8133)*
Control Research Inc	G	631 225-1111	Amityville *(G-259)*
Cooper & Clement Inc	E	315 454-8135	Syracuse *(G-14861)*
Copy Room Inc	F	212 371-8600	New York *(G-9099)*
Copy X/Press Ltd	D	631 585-2200	Ronkonkoma *(G-13925)*
Craig Envelope Corp	E	718 786-4277	Hicksville *(G-5898)*
Create-A-Card Inc	G	631 584-2273	Saint James *(G-14108)*
Crisray Printing Corp	E	631 293-3770	Farmingdale *(G-4605)*
Curtis Prtg Co The Del Press	G	518 477-4820	Castleton On Hudson *(G-3201)*
Custom 101 Prints Inc	F	718 708-4425	Bronx *(G-1234)*
Custom Sportswear Corp	G	914 666-9200	Bedford Hills *(G-766)*
D B F Associates	G	718 328-0005	Bronx *(G-1235)*
D G M Graphics Inc	F	516 223-2220	Merrick *(G-7854)*
D3 Repro Group Inc	G	347 507-1075	Long Island City *(G-7197)*
Dash Printing Inc	G	212 643-8534	New York *(G-9171)*
Data Flow Inc	G	631 436-9200	Medford *(G-7705)*
▲ Data Palette Info Svcs LLC	D	718 433-1060	Port Washington *(G-12871)*
Delft Printing Inc	G	716 683-1100	Lancaster *(G-6802)*
Dental Tribune America LLC	F	212 244-7181	Forest Hills *(G-4919)*
▲ Design Distributors Inc	D	631 242-2000	Deer Park *(G-3863)*
DEW Graphics Inc	E	212 727-8820	New York *(G-9213)*
Diamond Inscription Tech	F	646 366-7944	New York *(G-9221)*
Digital Evolution Inc	E	212 732-2722	New York *(G-9227)*
Dit Prints Incorporated	G	518 885-4400	Ballston Spa *(G-572)*
Diversified Envelope Ltd	F	585 615-4697	Rochester *(G-13350)*
Division Den-Bar Enterprises	G	914 381-2220	Mamaroneck *(G-7508)*
Dkm Sales LLC	E	716 893-7777	Buffalo *(G-2730)*
Doctor Print Inc	E	631 873-4560	Hauppauge *(G-5640)*
Donald Bruhnke	F	212 600-1260	New York *(G-9247)*
Doremus FP LLC	E	212 366-3800	New York *(G-9255)*
▲ Drns Corp	E	718 369-4530	Brooklyn *(G-1763)*
Dupli Graphics Corporation	G	315 422-4732	Syracuse *(G-14878)*
Dupli Graphics Corporation	C	315 234-7286	Syracuse *(G-14877)*
Dutchess Plumbing & Heating	G	845 889-8255	Staatsburg *(G-14599)*
Dynamic Packaging Inc	F	718 388-0800	Brooklyn *(G-1768)*
E&I Printing	F	212 206-0506	New York *(G-9293)*
Eagle Envelope Company	G	607 387-3195	Trumansburg *(G-15199)*
East Coast Thermographers Inc	E	718 321-3211	College Point *(G-3541)*
Eastwood Litho Impressions LLC	F	315 437-2626	Syracuse *(G-14881)*
Effective Slling Solutions LLC	G	716 771-8503	Lake View *(G-6772)*
Efficiency Printing Co Inc	F	914 949-8611	White Plains *(G-16000)*
Efs Designs LLC	G	718 852-9511	Brooklyn *(G-1785)*
Ehs Group LLC	G	914 937-6162	Port Chester *(G-12819)*
Elm Graphics Inc	G	315 737-5984	New Hartford *(G-8239)*
Empire Business Forms Inc	F	845 562-7780	Newburgh *(G-11864)*
Enterprise Press Inc	C	212 741-2111	New York *(G-9382)*
Evergreen Corp Central NY	F	315 454-4175	Syracuse *(G-14890)*
Excell Print & Promotions Inc	G	914 437-8668	White Plains *(G-16004)*
Exotic Print and Paper Inc	F	212 807-0465	New York *(G-9446)*
▲ Expedi-Printing Inc	C	516 513-0919	Great Neck *(G-5383)*
F & B Photo Offset Co Inc	G	516 431-5433	Island Park *(G-6317)*
Fairmount Press	G	212 255-2300	New York *(G-9465)*
Federal Envelope Inc	F	212 243-8380	New York *(G-9480)*
Fedex Office & Print Svcs Inc	G	718 982-5223	Staten Island *(G-14653)*
Fineline Thermographers Inc	G	718 643-1100	Brooklyn *(G-1845)*
First2print Inc	G	212 868-6886	New York *(G-9502)*
Fleaheart Inc	F	718 521-4958	Brooklyn *(G-1852)*
Flp Group LLC	F	315 252-7583	Auburn *(G-476)*
Folder Factory Inc	F	540 477-3852	Melville *(G-7783)*
Force Digital Media Inc	G	631 243-0243	Deer Park *(G-3874)*
Forward Enterprises Inc	F	585 235-7670	Rochester *(G-13421)*
Franklin Packaging Inc	G	631 582-8900	Northport *(G-12104)*
Frederick Coon Inc	E	716 683-6812	Elma *(G-4318)*
▲ Freeport Screen & Stamping	E	516 379-0330	Freeport *(G-4998)*
Freeville Publishing Co Inc	F	607 844-9119	Freeville *(G-5033)*
Fresh Prints LLC	E	917 826-2752	New York *(G-9539)*
Fulcrum Promotions & Prtg LLC	G	203 909-6362	New York *(G-9550)*
Fulton Screen Printing	G	315 593-2220	Fulton *(G-5060)*
Gailer Stamping Diecutting LLC	F	212 243-5662	Long Island City *(G-7227)*
▲ Gallant Graphics Ltd	E	845 868-1166	Stanfordville *(G-14610)*
Garrett J Cronin	G	914 761-9299	White Plains *(G-16008)*
Gary Stock Corporation	G	914 276-2700	Croton Falls *(G-3805)*
▲ Gatehouse Media LLC	B	585 598-0030	Pittsford *(G-12641)*

Gazette Press Inc .... E 914 963-8300
Rye **(G-14077)**

GE Healthcare Fincl Svcs Inc .... G 212 713-2000
New York **(G-9584)**

Gem Reproduction Services Corp ..... G 845 298-0172
Wappingers Falls **(G-15494)**

General Business Supply Inc .... D 518 720-3939
Watervliet **(G-15602)**

General Trade Mark La .... E 718 979-7261
Staten Island **(G-14655)**

Genie Instant Printing Co Inc .... F 212 575-8258
New York **(G-9595)**

Glenn Horowitz Bookseller Inc .... G 212 691-9100
New York **(G-9620)**

Golos Printing Inc .... G 607 732-1896
Elmira Heights **(G-4377)**

Grado Group Inc .... G 718 556-4200
Staten Island **(G-14658)**

Grand Meridian Printing Inc .... E 718 937-3888
Maspeth **(G-7619)**

Graph-Tex Inc .... F 607 756-7791
Cortland **(G-3767)**

Graph-Tex Inc .... G 607 756-1875
Cortland **(G-3768)**

Graphic Printing .... G 718 701-4433
Bronx **(G-1269)**

Graphics 247 Corp .... G 718 729-2470
Long Island City **(G-7233)**

Graphics For Industry Inc .... F 212 889-6202
New York **(G-9665)**

Graphics Plus Printing Inc .... E 607 299-0500
Cortland **(G-3769)**

Graphics Service Bureau Inc .... F 212 684-3600
Long Island City **(G-7234)**

Greenbush Tape & Label Inc .... E 518 465-2389
Albany **(G-82)**

Grover Cleveland Press Inc .... F 716 564-2222
Amherst **(G-226)**

Gruber Display Co Inc .... F 718 882-8220
Bronx **(G-1270)**

GTM Alap Inc .... G 833 345-2748
Brooklyn **(G-1913)**

H T L & S Ltd .... F 718 435-4474
Brooklyn **(G-1916)**

Haig Press Inc .... E 631 582-5800
Hauppauge **(G-5665)**

▲ Hammer Packaging Corp .... B 585 424-3880
West Henrietta **(G-15797)**

Handone Studios Inc .... G 585 421-8175
Fairport **(G-4498)**

Harmon and Castella Printing .... F 845 471-9163
Hyde Park **(G-6271)**

Herrmann Group LLC .... G 716 876-9798
Kenmore **(G-6651)**

HI Speed Envelope Co Inc .... F 718 617-1600
Mount Vernon **(G-8148)**

Hi-Tech Packg World-Wide LLC ...... G 845 947-1912
New Windsor **(G-8369)**

Horace J Metz .... G 716 873-9103
Kenmore **(G-6652)**

Hospitality Inc .... E 212 268-1930
New York **(G-9817)**

▲ Hudson Envelope Corporation .... E 212 473-6666
New York **(G-9831)**

Human Technologies Corporation .... F 315 735-3532
Utica **(G-15273)**

▲ I N K T Inc .... F 212 957-2700
New York **(G-9846)**

Image Typography Inc .... G 631 218-6932
Holbrook **(G-6000)**

▲ Impress Graphic Technologies .... F 516 781-0845
Westbury **(G-15896)**

Imprint Branded Content LLC .... G 212 888-8073
New York **(G-9872)**

Incodema3d LLC .... E 607 269-4390
Freeville **(G-5035)**

Industrial Test Eqp Co Inc .... E 516 883-6423
Port Washington **(G-12888)**

Info Label Inc .... F 518 664-0791
Halfmoon **(G-5493)**

Integrated Graphics Inc .... G 212 592-5600
New York **(G-9908)**

Iron Horse Graphics Ltd .... G 631 537-3400
Bridgehampton **(G-1166)**

Island Silkscreen Inc .... G 631 757-4567
East Northport **(G-4147)**

Issacs Yisroel .... G 718 851-7430
Brooklyn **(G-1971)**

Itc Mfg Group Inc .... F 212 684-3696
New York **(G-9947)**

J Kendall LLC .... G 646 739-4956
Yonkers **(G-16322)**

J M L Productions Inc .... D 718 643-1674
Brooklyn **(G-1980)**

J N White Associates Inc .... D 585 237-5191
Perry **(G-12598)**

J T Printing 21 .... G 718 484-3939
Staten Island **(G-14668)**

Jack J Florio Jr .... G 716 434-9123
Lockport **(G-7085)**

Janco Press Inc .... F 631 563-3003
Bohemia **(G-1027)**

Japan Printing & Graphics Inc ...... G 212 406-2905
New York **(G-9976)**

Joed Press .... G 212 243-3620
New York **(G-10015)**

John Auguliaro Printing Co .... G 718 382-5283
Brooklyn **(G-1997)**

Johnnys Ideal Printing Co .... G 518 828-6666
Hudson **(G-6166)**

▲ Jomar Industries Inc .... E 845 357-5773
Airmont **(G-13)**

Jomart Associates Inc .... E 212 627-2153
Islandia **(G-6339)**

Jon Lyn Ink Inc .... G 516 546-2312
Merrick **(G-7857)**

Judith Lewis Printer Inc .... G 516 997-7777
Westbury **(G-15900)**

K & B Stamping Co Inc .... G 914 664-8555
Mount Vernon **(G-8154)**

Kallen Corp .... G 212 242-1470
New York **(G-10061)**

Karr Graphics Corp .... E 212 645-6000
Long Island City **(G-7261)**

▲ Kates Paperie Ltd .... G 212 966-3904
New York **(G-10077)**

Kaufman Brothers Printing .... G 212 563-1854
New York **(G-10079)**

Kaymill Printing Company Inc .... G 212 594-3718
New York **(G-10082)**

▲ Kenan International Trading ...... G 718 672-4922
Corona **(G-3742)**

Kenmar Shirts Inc .... E 718 824-3880
Bronx **(G-1291)**

Kim Jae Printing Co Inc .... G 212 691-6289
Roslyn Heights **(G-14053)**

Kinaneco Inc .... E 315 468-6201
Syracuse **(G-14926)**

Knucklehead Embroidery Inc .... G 607 797-2725
Johnson City **(G-6605)**

Kurtskraft Inc .... G 516 944-4449
Port Washington **(G-12898)**

L & M Uniserv Corp .... G 718 854-3700
Brooklyn **(G-2040)**

L I C Screen Printing Inc .... E 516 546-7289
Merrick **(G-7858)**

▲ Labels Inter-Global Inc .... F 212 398-0006
New York **(G-10160)**

Lake Placid Advertisers Wkshp ..... E 518 523-3359
Lake Placid **(G-6767)**

Landlord Guard Inc .... F 212 695-6505
New York **(G-10169)**

Lennons Litho Inc .... F 315 866-3156
Herkimer **(G-5866)**

Leo Paper Inc .... G 917 305-0708
New York **(G-10200)**

Levon Graphics Corp .... D 631 753-2022
Deer Park **(G-3897)**

Linco Printing Inc .... E 718 937-5141
Long Island City **(G-7273)**

Linda Campbell .... G 718 994-4026
Bronx **(G-1303)**

Linden Forms & Systems Inc .... E 212 219-1100
Brooklyn **(G-2076)**

Lion In The Sun Park Slope Ltd ..... G 718 369-4006
Brooklyn **(G-2078)**

Logomax Inc .... G 631 420-0484
Farmingdale **(G-4671)**

Loremanss Embroidery Engrav ...... F 518 834-9205
Keeseville **(G-6643)**

Louis Heindl & Son Inc .... G 585 454-5080
Rochester **(G-13523)**

Love Unlimited NY Inc .... E 718 359-8500
Westbury **(G-15907)**

Loy L Press Inc .... G 716 634-5966
Buffalo **(G-2853)**

M C Packaging Corporation .... E 631 643-3763
Babylon **(G-522)**

M T M Printing Co Inc .... F 718 353-3297
College Point **(G-3552)**

Magazines & Brochures Inc .... G 716 875-9699
Buffalo **(G-2857)**

Malone Industrial Press Inc .... G 518 483-5880
Malone **(G-7488)**

Mark T Westinghouse .... G 518 678-3262
Catskill **(G-3214)**

Marlow Printing Co Inc .... E 718 625-4948
Brooklyn **(G-2117)**

Mart-Tex Athletics Inc .... E 631 454-9583
Farmingdale **(G-4678)**

Mason Transparent Package Inc ..... E 718 792-6000
Bronx **(G-1307)**

Maspeth Press Inc .... G 718 429-2363
Maspeth **(G-7626)**

Master Image Printing Inc .... G 914 347-4400
Elmsford **(G-4416)**

▲ Mastercraft Decorators Inc .... E 585 223-5150
Fairport **(G-4506)**

Mastro Graphic Arts Inc .... E 585 436-7570
Rochester **(G-13537)**

Matt Industries Inc .... C 315 472-1316
Syracuse **(G-14938)**

Matthew-Lee Corporation .... F 631 226-0100
Lindenhurst **(G-6959)**

McAuliffe Paper Inc .... E 315 453-2222
Liverpool **(G-7024)**

Measurement Incorporated .... F 914 682-1969
White Plains **(G-16028)**

▲ Medallion Associates Inc .... E 212 929-9130
New York **(G-10408)**

Mega Graphics Inc .... G 914 962-1402
Yorktown Heights **(G-16368)**

Merchandiser Inc .... G 315 462-6411
Clifton Springs **(G-3479)**

Merrill Communications LLC .... G 212 620-5600
New York **(G-10435)**

Merrill Corporation .... G 917 934-7300
New York **(G-10436)**

Merrill New York Company Inc ...... C 212 229-6500
New York **(G-10438)**

Metro Creative Graphics Inc .... E 212 947-5100
New York **(G-10444)**

Middletown Press .... G 845 343-1895
Middletown **(G-7920)**

Midgley Printing Corp .... G 315 475-1864
Syracuse **(G-14942)**

Miller Place Printing Inc .... G 631 473-1158
Miller Place **(G-7945)**

Mimeocom Inc .... B 212 847-3000
New York **(G-10472)**

▲ Mines Press Inc .... G 888 559-2634
Cortlandt Manor **(G-3797)**

Mini Graphics Inc .... D 516 223-6464
Hauppauge **(G-5720)**

Mixture Screen Printing .... G 845 561-2857
Newburgh **(G-11873)**

Modern Decal Co .... G 315 622-2778
Liverpool **(G-7027)**

Moore Printing Company Inc .... E 585 394-1533
Canandaigua **(G-3136)**

Mpe Graphics Inc .... F 631 582-8900
Bohemia **(G-1048)**

Msm Designz Inc .... G 914 909-5900
Tarrytown **(G-15050)**

◆ Multi Packaging Solutions Inc .... E 646 885-0005
New York **(G-10519)**

▲ Mv Corp Inc .... C 631 273-8020
Bay Shore **(G-695)**

Nathan Printing Express Inc .... G 914 472-0914
Scarsdale **(G-14239)**

New Art Signs Co Inc .... G 718 443-0900
Glen Head **(G-5210)**

New Buffalo Shirt Factory Inc ...... G 716 436-5839
Buffalo **(G-2881)**

▲ New Deal Printing Corp .... E 718 729-5800
New York **(G-10578)**

New York Christian Times Inc .... G 718 638-6397
Brooklyn **(G-2204)**

New York Legal Publishing .... G 518 459-1100
Menands **(G-7847)**

▲ Niagara Label Company Inc .... G 716 542-3000
Akron **(G-18)**

Niagara Sample Book Co Inc .... F 716 284-6151
Niagara Falls **(G-11954)**

Noble Checks Inc .... G 212 537-6241
Brooklyn **(G-2218)**

Nomad Editions LLC .... E 212 918-0992
Bronxville **(G-1402)**

North American DF Inc .... G 718 698-2500
Staten Island **(G-14683)**

North American Graphics Inc ... F ... 212 725-2200
New York ***(G-10641)***

North Six Inc ... F ... 212 463-7227
New York ***(G-10643)***

Northwind Graphics ... G ... 518 899-9651
Ballston Spa ***(G-584)***

▼ Nyc Vinyl Screen Printing Inc ... G ... 718 784-1360
Cold Spring Harbor ***(G-3528)***

Nyc Vinyl Screen Printing Inc ... E ... 718 784-1360
Long Island City ***(G-7312)***

Nys Nyu-Cntr Intl Cooperation ... E ... 212 998-3680
New York ***(G-10668)***

Okey Enterprises Inc ... G ... 212 213-2640
New York ***(G-10682)***

One In A Million Inc ... G ... 516 829-1111
Valley Stream ***(G-15350)***

Ontario Label Graphics Inc ... F ... 716 434-8505
Lockport ***(G-7100)***

P & W Press Inc ... E ... 646 486-3417
New York ***(G-10732)***

Pace Editions Inc ... G ... 212 643-6353
New York ***(G-10736)***

Paratore Signs Inc ... G ... 315 455-5551
Syracuse ***(G-14962)***

▲ Paris Art Label Co Inc ... D ... 631 467-2300
Patchogue ***(G-12508)***

Park Avenue Imprints LLC ... G ... 716 822-5737
Buffalo ***(G-2906)***

Patrick Rohan ... G ... 718 781-2573
Monticello ***(G-8072)***

Patrick Kraft ... G ... 315 343-9376
Oswego ***(G-12419)***

Patrick Ryans Modern Press ... F ... 518 434-2921
Albany ***(G-112)***

Paulin Investment Company ... E ... 631 957-8500
Amityville ***(G-302)***

PDM Studios Inc ... G ... 716 694-8337
Tonawanda ***(G-15131)***

PDQ Shipping Services ... G ... 845 255-5500
New Paltz ***(G-8310)***

Penny Lane Printing Inc ... D ... 585 226-8111
Avon ***(G-515)***

Personal Graphics Corporation ... G ... 315 853-3421
Westmoreland ***(G-15961)***

Peter Papastrat ... G ... 607 723-8112
Binghamton ***(G-904)***

Photo Agents Ltd ... G ... 631 421-0258
Huntington ***(G-6217)***

▲ Poly-Flex Corp ... F ... 631 586-9500
Edgewood ***(G-4277)***

Pony Farm Press & Graphics ... G ... 607 432-9020
Oneonta ***(G-12280)***

Precision Envelope Co Inc ... G ... 631 694-3990
Farmingdale ***(G-4715)***

Precision Label Corporation ... F ... 631 270-4490
Hauppauge ***(G-5747)***

Premier Ink Systems Inc ... E ... 845 782-5802
Harriman ***(G-5546)***

Presstek Printing LLC ... F ... 585 266-2770
Rochester ***(G-13643)***

Print City Corp ... F ... 212 487-9778
New York ***(G-10894)***

Print Mall ... G ... 718 437-7700
Brooklyn ***(G-2289)***

Print Shoppe ... G ... 315 792-9585
Utica ***(G-15291)***

Printech Business Systems Inc ... F ... 212 290-2542
New York ***(G-10897)***

Printery ... G ... 516 922-3250
Oyster Bay ***(G-12454)***

Printfacility Inc ... G ... 212 349-4009
New York ***(G-10898)***

Printing Max New York Inc ... G ... 718 692-1400
Brooklyn ***(G-2292)***

Printing Resources Inc ... E ... 518 482-2470
Albany ***(G-119)***

Printworks Printing & Design ... G ... 315 433-8587
Syracuse ***(G-14968)***

Proof 7 Ltd ... F ... 212 680-1843
New York ***(G-10913)***

Quadra Flex Corp ... G ... 607 758-7066
Cortland ***(G-3785)***

Quality Impressions Inc ... G ... 646 613-0002
Long Island City ***(G-7336)***

Quality Offset LLC ... G ... 347 342-4660
Long Island City ***(G-7337)***

Quist Industries Ltd ... F ... 718 243-2800
Brooklyn ***(G-2316)***

R & M Graphics of New York ... F ... 212 929-0294
New York ***(G-10963)***

R R Donnelley & Sons Company ... F ... 716 763-2613
Lakewood ***(G-6784)***

R R Donnelley & Sons Company ... D ... 716 773-0647
Grand Island ***(G-5341)***

R R Donnelley & Sons Company ... D ... 518 438-9722
Albany ***(G-121)***

R R Donnelley & Sons Company ... G ... 646 755-8125
New York ***(G-10967)***

Rainbow Lettering ... G ... 607 732-5751
Elmira ***(G-4366)***

Regal Screen Printing Intl ... G ... 845 356-8181
New City ***(G-8229)***

Rfn Inc ... F ... 516 764-5100
Bay Shore ***(G-705)***

Richard Ruffner ... F ... 631 234-4600
Central Islip ***(G-3287)***

Richs Sttches EMB Screenprint ... G ... 845 621-2175
Mahopac ***(G-7477)***

▲ Rike Enterprises Inc ... F ... 631 277-8338
Islip ***(G-6356)***

RIT Printing Corp ... F ... 631 586-6220
Bay Shore ***(G-707)***

Rose Graphics LLC ... F ... 516 547-6142
West Babylon ***(G-15743)***

Ross L Sports Screening Inc ... F ... 716 824-5350
Buffalo ***(G-2964)***

Round Top Knit & Screening ... G ... 518 622-3600
Round Top ***(G-14064)***

Royal Tees Inc ... G ... 845 357-9448
Suffern ***(G-14766)***

▲ S & S Prtg Die-Cutting Co Inc ... F ... 718 388-8990
Brooklyn ***(G-2372)***

S L C Industries Incorporated ... F ... 607 775-2299
Binghamton ***(G-907)***

Salamanca Press Penny Saver ... E ... 716 945-1500
Salamanca ***(G-14127)***

Sand Hill Industries Inc ... G ... 518 885-7991
Ballston Spa ***(G-586)***

Scan-A-Chrome Color Inc ... G ... 631 532-6146
Copiague ***(G-3675)***

Scancorp Inc ... F ... 315 454-5596
Syracuse ***(G-14986)***

Scotti Graphics Inc ... E ... 212 367-9602
Long Island City ***(G-7352)***

Screen The World Inc ... F ... 631 475-0023
Holtsville ***(G-6052)***

Select-A-Form Inc ... D ... 631 981-3076
Holbrook ***(G-6020)***

Seneca West Printing Inc ... G ... 716 675-8010
West Seneca ***(G-15854)***

Sephardic Yellow Pages ... E ... 718 998-0299
Brooklyn ***(G-2395)***

Seri Systems Inc ... E ... 585 272-5515
Rochester ***(G-13724)***

Shade Tree Greetings Inc ... F ... 585 442-4580
Rochester ***(G-13725)***

Shapeways Inc ... C ... 914 356-5816
New York ***(G-11206)***

Shapeways Inc ... G ... 646 470-3576
Long Island City ***(G-7356)***

▲ Sherwood Group Inc ... G ... 240 731-8573
New York ***(G-11212)***

Shipman Printing Inds Inc ... E ... 716 504-7700
Niagara Falls ***(G-11980)***

Shore Line Monogramming Inc ... F ... 914 698-8000
Mamaroneck ***(G-7523)***

Short Run Forms Inc ... D ... 631 567-7171
Bohemia ***(G-1078)***

Sign Shop Inc ... G ... 631 226-4145
Copiague ***(G-3678)***

Silk Screen Art Inc ... F ... 518 762-8423
Johnstown ***(G-6627)***

Silver Griffin Inc ... F ... 518 272-7771
Troy ***(G-15189)***

◆ Sino Printing Inc ... F ... 212 334-6896
New York ***(G-11250)***

Soho Letterpress Inc ... F ... 718 788-2518
Brooklyn ***(G-2435)***

Source Envelope Inc ... G ... 866 284-0707
Farmingdale ***(G-4735)***

Spaulding Law Printing Inc ... G ... 315 422-4805
Syracuse ***(G-14997)***

Special Tees ... E ... 718 980-0987
Staten Island ***(G-14711)***

Spectrum Prtg Lithography Inc ... E ... 212 255-3131
New York ***(G-11316)***

Spst Inc ... G ... 607 798-6952
Vestal ***(G-15383)***

St James Printing Inc ... G ... 631 981-2095
Ronkonkoma ***(G-14014)***

▲ Standwill Packaging Inc ... E ... 631 752-1236
Farmingdale ***(G-4739)***

Star Press Pearl River Inc ... G ... 845 268-2294
Valley Cottage ***(G-15325)***

Starcraft Press Inc ... G ... 718 383-6700
Long Island City ***(G-7366)***

Starfire Printing Inc ... G ... 631 736-1495
Holtsville ***(G-6053)***

Stellar Printing Inc ... D ... 718 361-1600
Long Island City ***(G-7369)***

Stickershopcom Inc ... G ... 631 563-4323
Bayport ***(G-731)***

Stony Point Graphics Ltd ... G ... 845 786-3322
Stony Point ***(G-14748)***

Stromberg Brand Corporation ... F ... 914 739-7410
Valley Cottage ***(G-15327)***

Structured 3d Inc ... G ... 346 704-2614
Amityville ***(G-308)***

Superior Print On Demand ... G ... 607 240-5231
Vestal ***(G-15384)***

Swift Multigraphics LLC ... G ... 585 442-8000
Rochester ***(G-13752)***

Syracuse Label Co Inc ... D ... 315 422-1037
Syracuse ***(G-15008)***

▲ Syracuse Letter Company Inc ... F ... 315 476-8328
Bridgeport ***(G-1169)***

T L F Graphics Inc ... D ... 585 272-5500
Rochester ***(G-13757)***

T S O General Corp ... E ... 631 952-5320
Brentwood ***(G-1127)***

T&K Printing Inc ... F ... 718 439-9454
Brooklyn ***(G-2487)***

T-Base Communications USA Inc ... E ... 315 713-0013
Ogdensburg ***(G-12211)***

T-Shirt Factory Inc ... F ... 845 454-2255
Poughkeepsie ***(G-12987)***

Table Tops Paper Corp ... G ... 718 831-6440
Brooklyn ***(G-2489)***

Takeout Printing LLC ... G ... 845 564-2609
Newburgh ***(G-11888)***

Tannens ... G ... 718 292-4646
Bronx ***(G-1378)***

▲ Tape Printers Inc ... F ... 631 249-5585
Farmingdale ***(G-4750)***

Tapemaker Supply Company LLC ... G ... 914 693-3407
Hartsdale ***(G-5569)***

Tara Rific Screen Printing Inc ... G ... 718 583-6864
Bronx ***(G-1379)***

Tc Transcontinental USA Inc ... G ... 818 993-4767
New York ***(G-11439)***

Tcmf Inc ... D ... 607 724-1094
Binghamton ***(G-912)***

◆ Tele-Pak Inc ... E ... 845 426-2300
Monsey ***(G-8053)***

The Gramecy Group ... G ... 518 348-1325
Clifton Park ***(G-3476)***

Todd Walbridge ... G ... 585 254-3018
Rochester ***(G-13768)***

Toppan Merrill USA Inc ... C ... 212 596-7747
New York ***(G-11515)***

Toprint Ltd ... G ... 718 439-0469
Brooklyn ***(G-2512)***

Total Solution Graphics Inc ... G ... 718 706-1540
Long Island City ***(G-7383)***

Tovie Asarese Royal Prtg Co ... G ... 716 885-7692
Buffalo ***(G-3016)***

◆ Transcntinental Ultra Flex Inc ... B ... 718 272-9100
Brooklyn ***(G-2516)***

Tri Kolor Printing & Sty ... F ... 315 474-6753
Syracuse ***(G-15015)***

▲ Tri Star Label Inc ... G ... 914 237-4800
Mount Vernon ***(G-8186)***

Tri-State Envelope Corporation ... F ... 212 736-3110
New York ***(G-11541)***

Tripi Engraving Co Inc ... E ... 718 383-6500
Brooklyn ***(G-2522)***

U All Inc ... E ... 518 438-2558
Albany ***(G-138)***

United Print Group Inc ... F ... 718 392-4242
Woodside ***(G-16231)***

▲ Universal Screening Associates ... F ... 718 232-2744
Brooklyn ***(G-2545)***

Unlimited Ink Inc ... E ... 631 582-0696
Hauppauge ***(G-5793)***

◆ USA Custom Pad Corp ... E ... 607 563-9550
Sidney ***(G-14439)***

Varick Street Litho Inc ... G ... 646 843-0800
New York ***(G-11644)***

Venus Printing Company ... F ... 212 967-8900
Hewlett ***(G-5875)***

Veterans Offset Printing Inc .... G 585 288-2900
Rochester (G-13796)

Vez Inc .... G 718 273-7002
Staten Island (G-14726)

▲ Viking Athletics Ltd .... E 631 957-8000
Lindenhurst (G-6982)

Voss Signs LLC .... E 315 682-6418
Manlius (G-7550)

W N Vanalstine & Sons Inc .... D 518 237-1436
Cohoes (G-3520)

Waterhouse Publications Inc .... E 716 662-4200
Orchard Park (G-12383)

Webster Printing Corporation .... F 585 671-1533
Webster (G-15662)

Weeks & Reichel Printing Inc .... G 631 589-1443
Sayville (G-14232)

Weicro Graphics Inc .... E 631 253-3360
Brooklyn (G-2578)

Were Forms Inc .... G 585 482-4400
Rochester (G-13802)

Westypo Printers Inc .... G 914 737-7394
Peekskill (G-12562)

Willco Fine Art Ltd .... F 718 935-9567
New York (G-11755)

William Charles Prtg Co Inc .... E 516 349-0900
Plainview (G-12728)

William J Ryan .... G 585 392-6200
Hilton (G-5975)

Willis Mc Donald Co Inc .... F 212 366-1526
New York (G-11761)

Wilson Press LLC .... G 315 568-9693
Seneca Falls (G-14374)

▲ Won & Lee Inc .... E 516 222-0712
Garden City (G-5119)

Worldwide Ticket Craft .... D 516 538-6200
Merrick (G-7865)

X Myles Mar Inc .... E 212 683-2015
New York (G-11795)

X Press Screen Printing .... G 716 679-7788
Dunkirk (G-4068)

Xl Graphics Inc .... G 212 929-8700
New York (G-11800)

Xpress Printing Inc .... G 516 605-1000
Plainview (G-12729)

Yoman Madeo Fano .... G 631 438-0246
Patchogue (G-12514)

▲ Zacks Enterprises Inc .... E 800 366-4924
Orangeburg (G-12333)

2761 Manifold Business Forms

▲ Abra-Ka-Data Systems Ltd .... E 631 667-5550
Deer Park (G-3827)

Amsterdam Printing & Litho Inc .... F 518 842-6000
Amsterdam (G-316)

Amsterdam Printing & Litho Inc .... E 518 842-6000
Amsterdam (G-317)

Bmg Printing and Promotion LLC .... G 631 231-9200
Bohemia (G-982)

Boces Business Office .... F 607 763-3300
Binghamton (G-861)

Five Boro Holding LLC .... F 718 431-9500
Brooklyn (G-1848)

Gateway Prtg & Graphics Inc .... E 716 823-3873
Hamburg (G-5509)

Linden Forms & Systems Inc .... E 212 219-1100
Brooklyn (G-2076)

Maggio Data Forms .... C 631 348-0343
Hauppauge (G-5704)

Marcy Business Forms Inc .... G 718 935-9100
Brooklyn (G-2113)

◆ Multi Packaging Solutions Inc .... E 646 885-0005
New York (G-10519)

P P I Business Forms Inc .... G 716 825-1241
Buffalo (G-2903)

R R Donnelley & Sons Company .... D 716 773-0300
Grand Island (G-5342)

Resonant Legal Media LLC .... D 800 781-3591
New York (G-11019)

Richard Ruffner .... F 631 234-4600
Central Islip (G-3287)

Select-A-Form Inc .... D 631 981-3076
Holbrook (G-6020)

▲ Specialized Printed Forms Inc .... E 585 538-2381
Caledonia (G-3073)

Syracuse Computer Forms Inc .... E 315 478-0108
Syracuse (G-15005)

Taylor Communications Inc .... F 937 221-1303
Melville (G-7828)

Taylor Communications Inc .... F 718 352-0220
Westbury (G-15927)

Williamson Law Book Co .... F 585 924-3400
Victor (G-15443)

2771 Greeting Card Publishing

1/2 Off Cards Wantagh Inc .... G 516 809-9832
Wantagh (G-15482)

▲ Anne Taintor Inc .... G 718 483-9312
Brooklyn (G-1512)

Avanti Press Inc .... E 212 414-1025
New York (G-8687)

Massimo Friedman Inc .... E 716 836-0408
Buffalo (G-2862)

▲ Paper House Productions Inc .... E 845 246-7261
Saugerties (G-14207)

Paper Magic Group Inc .... B 631 521-3682
New York (G-10749)

▲ Quotable Cards Inc .... G 212 420-7552
New York (G-10960)

Shade Tree Greetings Inc .... F 585 442-4580
Rochester (G-13725)

2782 Blankbooks & Looseleaf Binders

▲ Albumx Corp .... D 914 939-6878
Port Chester (G-12813)

Brookvale Records Inc .... F 631 587-7722
West Babylon (G-15695)

Classic Album .... E 718 388-2818
Brooklyn (G-1670)

▲ Classic Album LLC .... D 718 388-2818
Brooklyn (G-1671)

Colad Group LLC .... D 716 961-1776
Buffalo (G-2703)

Consolidated Loose Leaf Inc .... E 212 924-5800
New York (G-9087)

Dalee Bookbinding Co Inc .... F 914 965-1660
Croton On Hudson (G-3807)

▲ Datamax International Inc .... E 212 693-0933
New York (G-9175)

Deluxe Corporation .... B 845 362-4054
Spring Valley (G-14566)

Dorose Novelty Co Inc .... E 718 451-3088
East Elmhurst (G-4106)

Federal Sample Card Corp .... D 718 458-1344
Elmhurst (G-4334)

Folder Factory Inc .... F 540 477-3852
Melville (G-7783)

Foster - Gordon Manufacturing .... G 631 589-6776
Bohemia (G-1013)

▲ General Diaries Corporation .... F 516 371-2244
Inwood (G-6294)

GPM Associates LLC .... E 585 335-3940
Dansville (G-3819)

King Album Inc .... E 631 253-9500
West Babylon (G-15723)

Lanwood Industries Inc .... E 718 786-3000
Bay Shore (G-688)

Leather Craftsmen Inc .... D 631 752-9000
Farmingdale (G-4670)

Leather Indexes Corp .... D 516 827-1900
Hicksville (G-5923)

Motema Music LLC .... G 212 860-6969
New York (G-10508)

Niagara Sample Book Co Inc .... F 716 284-6151
Niagara Falls (G-11954)

▲ Quotable Cards Inc .... G 212 420-7552
New York (G-10960)

Renegade Nation Ltd .... F 212 868-9000
New York (G-11013)

▲ Roger Michael Press Inc .... D 732 752-0800
New York (G-2352)

Sellco Industries Inc .... E 607 756-7594
Cortland (G-3788)

Simon & Simon LLC .... G 202 419-0490
New York (G-11245)

Tm Music Inc .... F 212 471-4000
New York (G-11502)

Tommy Boy Entertainment LLC .... F 212 388-8300
New York (G-11511)

Wmg Acquisition Corp .... F 212 275-2000
New York (G-11771)

2789 Bookbinding

514 Adams Corporation .... G 516 352-6948
Deer Park (G-3825)

A-1 Products Inc .... G 718 789-1818
Brooklyn (G-1440)

A-Quick Bindery LLC .... G 631 491-1110
West Babylon (G-15679)

Agrecolor Inc .... F 516 741-8700
Mineola (G-7957)

Argo Lithographers Inc .... E 718 729-2700
Long Island City (G-7166)

Arista Innovations Inc .... E 516 746-2262
Mineola (G-7959)

▲ Ateres Publishing & Bk Bindery ..... F 718 935-9355
Brooklyn (G-1546)

Baum Christine and John Corp .... G 585 621-8910
Rochester (G-13261)

Beastons Budget Printing Inc .... G 585 244-2721
Rochester (G-13264)

▲ Benchemark Printing Inc .... D 518 393-1361
Schenectady (G-14249)

Bernard Hall .... G 585 425-3340
Fairport (G-4489)

▲ Beyer Graphics Inc .... D 631 543-3900
Commack (G-3579)

Bg Bindery Inc .... G 631 767-4242
Maspeth (G-7595)

Boncraft Inc .... D 716 662-9720
Tonawanda (G-15091)

Bondy Printing Corp .... G 631 242-1510
Bay Shore (G-659)

Brodock Press Inc .... G 315 735-9577
Utica (G-15242)

Brooks Litho Digital Group Inc .... G 631 789-4500
Deer Park (G-3850)

C & C Bindery Co Inc .... E 631 752-7078
Farmingdale (G-4595)

Carlara Group Ltd .... G 914 769-2020
Pleasantville (G-12795)

Carnels Printing Inc .... G 516 883-3355
Great Neck (G-5374)

Castlereagh Printcraft Inc .... D 516 623-1728
Freeport (G-4989)

Chakra Communications Inc .... E 607 748-7491
Endicott (G-4446)

Challenge Graphics Svcs Inc .... F 631 586-0171
Deer Park (G-3851)

Classic Album .... E 718 388-2818
Brooklyn (G-1670)

Cohber Press Inc .... D 585 475-9100
West Henrietta (G-15789)

Copy Corner Inc .... G 718 388-4545
Brooklyn (G-1687)

Copy Room Inc .... F 212 371-8600
New York (G-9099)

Cosmos Communications Inc .... C 718 482-1800
Long Island City (G-7193)

D G M Graphics Inc .... F 516 223-2220
Merrick (G-7854)

Dalee Bookbinding Co Inc .... F 914 965-1660
Croton On Hudson (G-3807)

David Helsing .... G 607 796-2681
Horseheads (G-6120)

Dependable Lithographers Inc .... F 718 472-4200
Long Island City (G-7199)

▲ Dime Trading Inc .... G 718 797-0303
Brooklyn (G-1747)

Dispatch Graphics Inc .... F 212 307-5943
New York (G-9236)

Division Den-Bar Enterprises .... G 914 381-2220
Mamaroneck (G-7508)

Dowd - Witbeck Printing Corp .... F 518 274-2421
Troy (G-15166)

DP Murphy Co Inc .... D 631 673-9400
Deer Park (G-3865)

E B B Graphics Inc .... F 516 750-5510
Westbury (G-15877)

Eastwood Litho Impressions LLC .... F 315 437-2626
Syracuse (G-14881)

Erhard & Gilcher Inc .... E 315 474-1072
Syracuse (G-14889)

Flare Multicopy Corp .... E 718 258-8860
Brooklyn (G-1849)

Flp Group LLC .... F 315 252-7583
Auburn (G-476)

Foleys Graphic Center Inc .... E 914 245-3625
Yorktown Heights (G-16364)

Foster - Gordon Manufacturing .... G 631 589-6776
Bohemia (G-1013)

Fulton Newspapers Inc .... E 315 598-6397
Fulton (G-5059)

Gateway Prtg & Graphics Inc .... E 716 823-3873
Hamburg (G-5509)

Gazette Press Inc .... E 914 963-8300
Rye (G-14077)

Gild-Rite Inc .... G 631 752-9000
Farmingdale (G-4637)

Gold Pride Press Inc .... E 585 224-8800
Rochester (G-13448)

Graphicomm Inc ....G 716 283-0830
Niagara Falls *(G-11932)*

Haig Press Inc ....E 631 582-5800
Hauppauge *(G-5665)*

▲ Hamilton Printing Company Inc ......C 518 732-2161
Troy *(G-15171)*

Hudson Printing Co Inc ....E 718 937-8600
New York *(G-9834)*

In-House Inc ....F 718 445-9007
College Point *(G-3544)*

▲ J Mackenzie Ltd ....E 585 321-1770
Rochester *(G-13485)*

Jack J Florio Jr ....G 716 434-9123
Lockport *(G-7085)*

James Conolly Printing Co ....E 585 426-4150
Rochester *(G-13488)*

Jane Lewis ....G 607 722-0584
Binghamton *(G-890)*

Johnnys Ideal Printing Co ....G 518 828-6666
Hudson *(G-6166)*

Jon Lyn Ink Inc ....G 516 546-2312
Merrick *(G-7857)*

Kaufman Brothers Printing ....G 212 563-1854
New York *(G-10079)*

Louis Heindl & Son Inc ....E 585 454-5080
Rochester *(G-13523)*

Loy L Press Inc ....G 716 634-5966
Buffalo *(G-2853)*

▲ Melcher Media Inc ....F 212 727-2322
New York *(G-10428)*

▲ Mercury Print Productions Inc ......C 585 458-7900
Rochester *(G-13542)*

Midgley Printing Corp ....G 315 475-1864
Syracuse *(G-14942)*

▲ Mines Press Inc ....C 888 559-2634
Cortlandt Manor *(G-3797)*

Moneast Inc ....G 845 298-8898
Wappingers Falls *(G-15498)*

Multiple Imprssons of Rchester ......G 585 546-1160
Rochester *(G-13563)*

Mutual Library Bindery Inc ....E 315 455-6638
East Syracuse *(G-4227)*

Newport Graphics Inc ....E 212 924-2600
New York *(G-10610)*

On The Spot Binding Inc ....E 718 497-2200
Ridgewood *(G-13154)*

Piroke Trade Inc ....G 646 515-1537
Brooklyn *(G-2263)*

Playbill Incorporated ....E 718 335-4033
Woodside *(G-16221)*

Prestige Envelope & Lithograph ......F 631 521-7043
Merrick *(G-7863)*

Printech Business Systems Inc ......F 212 290-2542
New York *(G-10897)*

Printing Resources Inc ....E 518 482-2470
Albany *(G-119)*

Pro Printing ....G 516 561-9700
Lynbrook *(G-7435)*

Progressive Graphics & Prtg ....G 315 331-3635
Newark *(G-11850)*

Prompt Bindery Co Inc ....F 212 675-5181
New York *(G-10910)*

Psychonomic Society Inc ....E 512 381-1494
New York *(G-10919)*

Quad/Graphics Inc ....A 518 581-4000
Saratoga Springs *(G-14189)*

Quality Bindery Service Inc ....E 716 883-5185
Buffalo *(G-2942)*

Reynolds Book Bindery LLC ....F 607 772-8937
Binghamton *(G-906)*

Richard Ruffner ....F 631 234-4600
Central Islip *(G-3287)*

Rip-It Rip-It Shred-It Corp ....E 516 818-5825
Holbrook *(G-6017)*

Rmd Holding Inc ....G 845 628-0030
Mahopac *(G-7478)*

▲ Roger Michael Press Inc ....D 732 752-0800
Brooklyn *(G-2352)*

▲ Rosemont Press Incorporated ......E 212 239-4770
New York *(G-11082)*

Rosen Mandell & Immerman Inc .....E 212 691-2277
New York *(G-11083)*

S L C Industries Incorporated ......F 607 775-2299
Binghamton *(G-907)*

Sentine Printing Inc ....G 516 334-7400
Westbury *(G-15925)*

Shipman Printing Inds Inc ....E 716 504-7700
Niagara Falls *(G-11980)*

Spectrum Prtg Lithography Inc ....E 212 255-3131
New York *(G-11316)*

▼ Sterling Pierce Company Inc ....E 516 593-1170
East Rockaway *(G-4174)*

Thomas Group Inc ....F 212 947-6400
New York *(G-11467)*

Tobay Printing Co Inc ....E 631 842-3300
Copiague *(G-3684)*

Tom & Jerry Printcraft Forms ....E 914 777-7468
Mamaroneck *(G-7525)*

▲ Twenty-First Century Press Inc ......F 716 837-0800
Buffalo *(G-3023)*

Vicks Lithograph & Prtg Corp ....C 315 272-2401
Yorkville *(G-16380)*

Vin-Clair Inc ....F 845 429-4998
West Haverstraw *(G-15764)*

Webster Printing Corporation ....F 585 671-1533
Webster *(G-15662)*

Westchester Mailing Service ....E 914 948-1116
White Plains *(G-16073)*

Whitford Development Inc ....F 631 471-7711
Port Jefferson *(G-12844)*

William Charles Prtg Co Inc ....E 516 349-0900
Plainview *(G-12728)*

Wilson Press LLC ....E 315 568-9693
Seneca Falls *(G-14374)*

▲ Won & Lee Inc ....E 516 222-0712
Garden City *(G-5119)*

Wynco Press One Inc ....G 516 354-6145
Glen Oaks *(G-5215)*

X Myles Mar Inc ....E 212 683-2015
New York *(G-11795)*

Zenger Partners LLC ....E 716 876-2284
Kenmore *(G-6656)*

2791 Typesetting

514 Adams Corporation ....G 516 352-6948
Deer Park *(G-3825)*

Act Communications Group Inc ......F 631 669-2403
West Islip *(G-15809)*

▲ Advance Publications Inc ....D 718 981-1234
New York *(G-8475)*

Agrecolor Inc ....F 516 741-8700
Mineola *(G-7957)*

Alabaster Group Inc ....G 516 867-8223
Freeport *(G-4981)*

Albion-Holley Pennysaver Inc ....E 585 589-5641
Albion *(G-153)*

Arista Innovations Inc ....E 516 746-2262
Mineola *(G-7959)*

▲ Art Resources Transfer Inc ....G 212 255-2919
New York *(G-8630)*

▲ Artistic Typography Corp ....E 212 463-8880
New York *(G-8638)*

Artscroll Printing Corp ....E 212 929-2413
New York *(G-8640)*

Bates Jackson Engraving Co Inc .....E 716 854-3000
Buffalo *(G-2657)*

Baum Christine and John Corp ....G 585 621-8910
Rochester *(G-13261)*

Bco Industries Western NY Inc ....E 716 877-2800
Tonawanda *(G-15089)*

Beastons Budget Printing Inc ....G 585 244-2721
Rochester *(G-13264)*

Beehive Press Inc ....E 718 654-1200
Bronx *(G-1211)*

▲ Benchemark Printing Inc ....D 518 393-1361
Schenectady *(G-14249)*

Bernard Hall ....G 585 425-3340
Fairport *(G-4489)*

▲ Beyer Graphics Inc ....F 631 543-3900
Commack *(G-3579)*

Boncraft Inc ....D 716 662-9720
Tonawanda *(G-15091)*

Bondy Printing Corp ....G 631 242-1510
Bay Shore *(G-659)*

Brodock Press Inc ....D 315 735-9577
Utica *(G-15242)*

Brooks Litho Digital Group Inc ......E 631 789-4500
Deer Park *(G-3850)*

Bytheway Publishing Services ....F 607 334-8365
Norwich *(G-12114)*

Carlara Group Ltd ....G 914 769-2020
Pleasantville *(G-12795)*

Carnels Printing Inc ....G 516 883-3355
Great Neck *(G-5374)*

Castlereagh Printcraft Inc ....D 516 623-1728
Freeport *(G-4989)*

Chakra Communications Inc ....E 607 748-7491
Endicott *(G-4446)*

Challenge Graphics Svcs Inc ....E 631 586-0171
Deer Park *(G-3851)*

Clarsons Corp ....F 585 235-8775
Rochester *(G-13317)*

Cohber Press Inc ....D 585 475-9100
West Henrietta *(G-15789)*

Consolidated Color Press Inc ....E 212 929-8197
New York *(G-9086)*

Cortland Standard Printing Co ....D 607 756-5665
Cortland *(G-3764)*

Cosmos Communications Inc ....C 718 482-1800
Long Island City *(G-7193)*

Csw Inc ....F 585 247-4010
Rochester *(G-13331)*

D G M Graphics Inc ....F 516 223-2220
Merrick *(G-7854)*

Desktop Publishing Concepts ....F 631 752-1934
Farmingdale *(G-4614)*

Digital Color Concepts Inc ....E 212 989-4888
New York *(G-9226)*

Digital Page LLC ....F 518 446-9129
Albany *(G-70)*

Dispatch Graphics Inc ....E 212 307-5943
New York *(G-9236)*

Dowd - Witbeck Printing Corp ....F 518 274-2421
Troy *(G-15166)*

DP Murphy Co Inc ....G 631 673-9400
Deer Park *(G-3865)*

Draper Associates Incorporated ......F 212 255-2727
New York *(G-9266)*

E B B Graphics Inc ....F 516 750-5510
Westbury *(G-15877)*

Eastwood Litho Impressions LLC .....F 315 437-2626
Syracuse *(G-14881)*

Empire Press Co ....G 718 756-9500
Brooklyn *(G-1801)*

Flare Multicopy Corp ....E 718 258-8860
Brooklyn *(G-1849)*

Flp Group LLC ....F 315 252-7583
Auburn *(G-476)*

Foleys Graphic Center Inc ....E 914 245-3625
Yorktown Heights *(G-16364)*

Fort Orange Press Inc ....E 518 489-3233
Albany *(G-78)*

Fulton Newspapers Inc ....G 315 598-6397
Fulton *(G-5059)*

▲ Gallant Graphics Ltd ....E 845 868-1166
Stanfordville *(G-14610)*

Gateway Prtg & Graphics Inc ....E 716 823-3873
Hamburg *(G-5509)*

Gazette Press Inc ....E 914 963-8300
Rye *(G-14077)*

▲ Gg Design and Printing ....E 718 321-3220
New York *(G-9606)*

Graphic Fabrications Inc ....E 516 763-3222
Rockville Centre *(G-13828)*

Graphicomm Inc ....G 716 283-0830
Niagara Falls *(G-11932)*

Hks Printing Company Inc ....F 212 675-2529
New York *(G-9797)*

Hugh F McPherson Inc ....G 716 668-6107
Cheektowaga *(G-3354)*

In-House Inc ....F 718 445-9007
College Point *(G-3544)*

Jack J Florio Jr ....G 716 434-9123
Lockport *(G-7085)*

James Conolly Printing Co ....E 585 426-4150
Rochester *(G-13488)*

Jane Lewis ....G 607 722-0584
Binghamton *(G-890)*

Johnnys Ideal Printing Co ....G 518 828-6666
Hudson *(G-6166)*

Jon Lyn Ink Inc ....G 516 546-2312
Merrick *(G-7857)*

L M N Printing Company Inc ....E 516 285-8526
Valley Stream *(G-15345)*

Lake Placid Advertisers Wkshp ....E 518 523-3359
Lake Placid *(G-6767)*

Leigh Scott Enterprises Inc ....G 718 343-5440
Bellerose *(G-775)*

Litmor Publishing Corp ....F 516 931-0012
Garden City *(G-5105)*

Loudon Ltd ....G 631 757-4447
East Northport *(G-4149)*

Louis Heindl & Son Inc ....E 585 454-5080
Rochester *(G-13523)*

Loy L Press Inc ....G 716 634-5966
Buffalo *(G-2853)*

Mechon Beiss Uvas ....G 718 436-1489
Brooklyn *(G-2131)*

▲ Medallion Associates Inc ....E 212 929-9130
New York *(G-10408)*

▲ Mercury Print Productions Inc..........C....... 585 458-7900
Rochester (G-13542)
Midgley Printing Corp..........G....... 315 475-1864
Syracuse (G-14942)
▲ Mines Press Inc..........C....... 888 559-2634
Cortlandt Manor (G-3797)
Moneast Inc..........G....... 845 298-8898
Wappingers Falls (G-15498)
Multiple Imprssons of Rchester..........G....... 585 546-1160
Rochester (G-13563)
Mutual Engraving Company Inc..........D....... 516 489-0534
West Hempstead (G-15777)
News India USA Inc..........F....... 212 675-7515
New York (G-10614)
Newspaper Publisher LLC..........F....... 607 775-0472
Conklin (G-3626)
▼ Official Offset Corporation..........E....... 631 957-8500
Amityville (G-299)
P D R Inc..........G....... 516 829-5300
Plainview (G-12706)
Panagraphics Inc..........G....... 716 312-8088
Orchard Park (G-12370)
Patrick Ryans Modern Press..........F....... 518 434-2921
Albany (G-112)
Presstek Printing LLC..........F....... 585 467-8140
Rochester (G-13642)
Prestige Envelope & Lithograph..........F....... 631 521-7043
Merrick (G-7863)
Printery..........G....... 516 922-3250
Oyster Bay (G-12454)
Printing Resources Inc..........E....... 518 482-2470
Albany (G-119)
Pro Printing..........G....... 516 561-9700
Lynbrook (G-7435)
Progressive Graphics & Prtg..........G....... 315 331-3635
Newark (G-11850)
Publishing Synthesis Ltd..........G....... 212 219-0135
New York (G-10924)
Quad/Graphics Inc..........A....... 518 581-4000
Saratoga Springs (G-14189)
Quicker Printer Inc..........G....... 607 734-8622
Elmira (G-4365)
Rmd Holding Inc..........G....... 845 628-0030
Mahopac (G-7478)
Rubber Stamps Inc..........E....... 212 675-1180
Mineola (G-7998)
Scotti Graphics Inc..........E....... 212 367-9602
Long Island City (G-7352)
Sentine Printing Inc..........G....... 516 334-7400
Westbury (G-15925)
▲ Star Composition Services Inc..........G....... 212 684-4001
Brooklyn (G-2452)
Stone Crest Industries Inc..........G....... 607 652-2665
Stamford (G-14609)
Syracuse Computer Forms Inc..........E....... 315 478-0108
Syracuse (G-15005)
Thomas Group Inc..........F....... 212 947-6400
New York (G-11467)
Times Review Newspaper Corp..........E....... 631 354-8031
Mattituck (G-7680)
Tobay Printing Co Inc..........E....... 631 842-3300
Copiague (G-3684)
Tom & Jerry Printcraft Forms..........E....... 914 777-7468
Mamaroneck (G-7525)
Torsaf Printers Inc..........G....... 516 569-5577
Hewlett (G-5873)
Tri Kolor Printing & Sty..........F....... 315 474-6753
Syracuse (G-15015)
Tripi Engraving Co Inc..........E....... 718 383-6500
Brooklyn (G-2522)
Voss Signs LLC..........E....... 315 682-6418
Manlius (G-7550)
Wallkill Valley Publications..........E....... 845 561-0170
Newburgh (G-11893)
Waterhouse Publications Inc..........E....... 716 662-4200
Orchard Park (G-12383)
Webster Printing Corporation..........F....... 585 671-1533
Webster (G-15662)
Westchester Mailing Service..........E....... 914 948-1116
White Plains (G-16073)
Wilson Press LLC..........E....... 315 568-9693
Seneca Falls (G-14374)
Woodbury Printing Plus + Inc..........G....... 845 928-6610
Central Valley (G-3302)
Worldwide Ticket Craft..........D....... 516 538-6200
Merrick (G-7865)
Wynco Press One Inc..........G....... 516 354-6145
Glen Oaks (G-5215)
X Myles Mar Inc..........E....... 212 683-2015
New York (G-11795)
Zenger Partners LLC..........E....... 716 876-2284
Kenmore (G-6656)

2796 Platemaking & Related Svcs

Absolute Color Corporation..........G....... 212 868-0404
New York (G-8436)
Allstate Sign & Plaque Corp..........F....... 631 242-2828
Deer Park (G-3836)
Charles Henricks Inc..........F....... 212 243-5800
New York (G-8973)
Circle Press Inc..........D....... 212 924-4277
New York (G-9011)
Csw Inc..........F....... 585 247-4010
Rochester (G-13331)
▲ Custom House Engravers Inc..........G....... 631 567-3004
Bohemia (G-995)
D & A Offset Services Inc..........F....... 212 924-0612
New York (G-9144)
David Fehlman..........G....... 315 455-8888
Syracuse (G-14875)
Dowd - Witbeck Printing Corp..........F....... 518 274-2421
Troy (G-15166)
Eastern Color Stripping Inc..........F....... 631 563-3700
Bohemia (G-1008)
▲ Gallant Graphics Ltd..........E....... 845 868-1166
Stanfordville (G-14610)
Gazette Press Inc..........E....... 914 963-8300
Rye (G-14077)
Karr Graphics Corp..........E....... 212 645-6000
Long Island City (G-7261)
Koehlr-Gibson Mkg Graphics Inc..........E....... 716 838-5960
Buffalo (G-2838)
Lazer Incorporated..........E....... 336 744-8047
Rochester (G-13514)
Leo P Callahan Inc..........F....... 607 797-7314
Binghamton (G-894)
Lgn Materials & Solutions..........F....... 888 414-0005
Mount Vernon (G-8158)
Micro Publishing Inc..........G....... 212 533-9180
New York (G-10456)
Miroddi Imaging Inc..........G....... 516 624-6898
Oyster Bay (G-12450)
Mutual Engraving Company Inc..........D....... 516 489-0534
West Hempstead (G-15777)
New Dimension Awards Inc..........G....... 718 236-8200
Brooklyn (G-2202)
P & H Thermotech Inc..........G....... 585 624-1310
Lima (G-6934)
Rapid Service Engraving Co..........G....... 716 896-4555
Buffalo (G-2948)
▲ Rigidized Metals Corporation..........E....... 716 849-4703
Buffalo (G-2955)
Rotation Dynamics Corporation..........E....... 585 352-9023
Spencerport (G-14559)
Syracuse Computer Forms Inc..........E....... 315 478-0108
Syracuse (G-15005)
Tobay Printing Co Inc..........E....... 631 842-3300
Copiague (G-3684)
Tripi Engraving Co Inc..........E....... 718 383-6500
Brooklyn (G-2522)
Wilcro Inc..........G....... 716 632-4204
Buffalo (G-3047)

28 CHEMICALS AND ALLIED PRODUCTS

2812 Alkalies & Chlorine

Church & Dwight Co Inc..........F....... 518 887-5109
Schenectady (G-14255)
FMC Corporation..........C....... 716 879-0400
Tonawanda (G-15105)
Indian Springs Mfg Co Inc..........F....... 315 635-6101
Baldwinsville (G-549)
Occidental Chemical Corp..........E....... 716 278-7795
Niagara Falls (G-11959)
Occidental Chemical Corp..........E....... 716 773-8100
Grand Island (G-5340)
Occidental Chemical Corp..........G....... 716 694-3827
North Tonawanda (G-12080)
Occidental Chemical Corp..........C....... 716 278-7794
Niagara Falls (G-11960)
Olin Chlor Alkali Logistics..........C....... 716 278-6411
Niagara Falls (G-11961)
Peroxychem LLC..........D....... 716 873-0812
Tonawanda (G-15132)

2813 Industrial Gases

Air Products and Chemicals Inc..........D....... 518 463-4273
Glenmont (G-5235)
Airgas Inc..........F....... 518 690-0068
Albany (G-30)
Fountainhead Group Inc..........C....... 708 598-7100
New York Mills (G-11833)
Linde Gas North America LLC..........E....... 518 713-2015
Cohoes (G-3508)
Linde Gas North America LLC..........F....... 315 431-4081
Syracuse (G-14933)
Matheson Tri-Gas Inc..........G....... 518 203-5003
Cohoes (G-3509)
Messer LLC..........E....... 716 847-0748
Buffalo (G-2865)
Messer LLC..........D....... 518 439-8187
Feura Bush (G-4791)
Messer Merchant Production LLC..........G....... 315 593-1360
Fulton (G-5071)
Neon..........F....... 212 727-5628
New York (G-10563)
◆ Oxair Ltd..........G....... 716 298-8288
Niagara Falls (G-11962)
Praxair Inc..........F....... 716 879-2000
Tonawanda (G-15133)
Praxair Inc..........E....... 716 649-1600
Hamburg (G-5516)
Praxair Inc..........E....... 518 482-4360
Albany (G-117)
Praxair Inc..........E....... 716 286-4600
Niagara Falls (G-11966)
Praxair Inc..........C....... 845 359-4200
Orangeburg (G-12326)
Praxair Inc..........E....... 716 879-4000
Tonawanda (G-15134)
Praxair Distribution Inc..........G....... 315 457-5821
Liverpool (G-7034)
Praxair Distribution Inc..........G....... 716 879-2185
Buffalo (G-2927)
Praxair Distribution Inc..........F....... 315 735-6153
Marcy (G-7565)

2816 Inorganic Pigments

Applied Minerals Inc..........F....... 212 226-4265
Brooklyn (G-1520)
▲ Heany Industries Inc..........D....... 585 889-2700
Scottsville (G-14340)

2819 Indl Inorganic Chemicals, NEC

Aithaca Chemical Corp..........F....... 516 229-2330
Uniondale (G-15223)
Alpha-En Corporation..........G....... 914 418-2000
Yonkers (G-16282)
Ames Goldsmith Corp..........F....... 518 792-7435
Glens Falls (G-5239)
Amtek Research LLC..........E....... 416 400-2906
Niagara Falls (G-11905)
Anchor Commerce Trading Corp..........G....... 516 881-3485
Atlantic Beach (G-452)
Arch Chemicals Inc..........C....... 585 436-3030
Rochester (G-13243)
Arkema Inc..........C....... 585 243-6359
Piffard (G-12623)
Auterra Inc..........G....... 518 382-9600
Schenectady (G-14246)
Benzsay & Harrison Inc..........G....... 518 895-2311
Delanson (G-3958)
◆ Buffalo Tungsten Inc..........D....... 716 683-9170
Depew (G-3975)
Byk USA Inc..........E....... 845 469-5800
Chester (G-3372)
Calgon Carbon Corporation..........G....... 716 531-9113
North Tonawanda (G-12061)
Carbide-Usa LLC..........G....... 607 331-9353
Elmira (G-4342)
Carbon Activated Corporation..........G....... 716 662-2005
Orchard Park (G-12344)
Carbon Activated Corporation..........E....... 716 677-6661
Blasdell (G-918)
CB Minerals LLC..........F....... 914 777-3330
Mamaroneck (G-7502)
▼ Cerion Energy Inc..........E....... 585 271-5630
Rochester (G-13308)
Cerion LLC..........F....... 585 271-5630
Rochester (G-13309)
Chemtrade Chemicals US LLC..........E....... 315 430-7650
Syracuse (G-14848)
Chemtrade Chemicals US LLC..........G....... 315 478-2323
Syracuse (G-14849)
Danisco US Inc..........D....... 585 277-4300
Rochester (G-13338)
▲ Dynasty Chemical Corp..........E....... 518 463-1146
Menands (G-7842)

S I C

Element St Johns Corp ....G 917 349-2139
Brooklyn (G-1794)

◆ Elementis Srl Inc ....C 845 692-3914
Huguenot (G-6193)

◆ Esm Group Inc ....F 716 446-8914
Amherst (G-222)

Esm Group Inc ....G 724 265-1766
Buffalo (G-2749)

Esm Special Metals & Tech Inc ....E 716 446-8914
Amherst (G-224)

Ferro Corporation ....E 585 586-8770
East Rochester (G-4162)

Ferro Corporation ....C 315 536-3357
Penn Yan (G-12582)

Ferro Electronics Materials ....C 716 278-9400
Niagara Falls (G-11928)

FMC Corporation ....E 716 735-3761
Middleport (G-7888)

▲ Germanium Corp America Inc ......F 315 853-4900
Clinton (G-3482)

Hampshire Chemical Corp ....D 315 539-9221
Waterloo (G-15554)

▲ Innovative Municipal Pdts US ......E 800 387-5777
Glenmont (G-5237)

Isonics Corporation ....G 212 356-7400
New York (G-9946)

◆ Kowa American Corporation ....E 212 303-7800
New York (G-10131)

Lakeshore Carbide Inc ....G 716 462-4349
Buffalo (G-2846)

Lawn Elements Inc ....F 631 656-9711
Holbrook (G-6005)

Leading Element LLC ....G 315 479-8790
Syracuse (G-14929)

▼ Meliorum Technologies Inc ....G 585 313-0616
Rochester (G-13541)

▲ Minerals Technologies Inc ....E 212 878-1800
New York (G-10476)

Moog Inc ....D 716 731-6300
Niagara Falls (G-11952)

Multisorb Tech Intl LLC ....G 716 824-8900
Buffalo (G-2875)

Multisorb Technologies Inc ....E 716 656-1402
Buffalo (G-2876)

New Mountain Capital LLC ....D 212 720-0300
New York (G-10587)

Next Potential LLC ....G 401 742-5190
New York (G-10619)

▲ Niagara Refining LLC ....E 716 706-1400
Depew (G-3989)

◆ Norfalco LLC ....F 416 775-1431
New York (G-10640)

◆ North American Hoganas Inc ......E 716 285-3451
Niagara Falls (G-11956)

Nouryon Surface Chemistry ....C 914 674-5008
Dobbs Ferry (G-4018)

Poly Scientific R&D Corp ....E 631 586-0400
Bay Shore (G-698)

▲ Polyset Company Inc ....E 518 664-6000
Mechanicville (G-7693)

Precision Elctro Mnrl Pmco Inc ......E 716 284-2484
Niagara Falls (G-11968)

PVS Chemical Solutions Inc ......D 716 825-5762
Buffalo (G-2938)

S E A Supplies Ltd ....F 516 694-6677
Plainview (G-12712)

Sabre Energy Services LLC ....F 518 514-1572
Slingerlands (G-14467)

Scientific Polymer Products ....G 585 265-0413
Ontario (G-12302)

Signa Chemistry Inc ....F 212 933-4101
New York (G-11234)

Somerville Acquisitions Co Inc ......F 845 856-5261
Huguenot (G-6194)

Somerville Tech Group Inc ....D 908 782-9500
Huguenot (G-6195)

Specialty Minerals Inc ....G 518 585-7982
Ticonderoga (G-15076)

Srlh Holdings Inc ....C 929 529-7951
Huguenot (G-6196)

▼ Tangram Company LLC ....E 631 758-0460
Holtsville (G-6055)

Texas Brine Company LLC ....G 585 495-6228
Wyoming (G-16252)

▲ Thatcher Company New York Inc ......E 315 589-9330
Williamson (G-16113)

Tibro Water Technologies Ltd ....F 647 426-3415
Sherrill (G-14408)

Transport National Dev Inc ....E 716 662-0270
Orchard Park (G-12380)

UOP LLC ....E 716 879-7600
Tonawanda (G-15151)

US Peroxide ....G 716 775-5585
Grand Island (G-5347)

◆ Vanchlor Company Inc ....F 716 434-2624
Lockport (G-7117)

Vanchlor Company Inc ....F 716 434-2624
Lockport (G-7118)

◆ Washingtom Mills Elec Mnrls ......D 716 278-6600
Niagara Falls (G-11991)

2821 Plastics, Mtrls & Nonvulcanizable Elastomers

◆ Adam Scott Designs Inc ....E 212 420-8866
New York (G-8453)

◆ American Acrylic Corporation ......E 631 422-2200
West Babylon (G-15687)

American Epoxy and Metal Inc ......G 718 828-7828
Scarsdale (G-14233)

◆ Ampacet Corporation ....A 914 631-6600
Tarrytown (G-15040)

◆ APS American Polymers Svcs Inc ......G 212 362-7711
New York (G-8613)

◆ Ashley Resin Corp ....F 718 851-8111
Brooklyn (G-1541)

Atc Plastics LLC ....E 212 375-2515
New York (G-8660)

◆ Bairnco Corporation ....E 914 461-1300
White Plains (G-15977)

◆ Bamberger Polymers Inc ....E 516 622-3600
Jericho (G-6571)

Bso Energy Corp ....F 212 520-1827
New York (G-8865)

Ccmi Inc ....G 315 781-3270
Geneva (G-5148)

Clarence Resins and Chemicals ......G 716 406-9804
Clarence Center (G-3444)

CN Group Incorporated ....A 914 358-5690
White Plains (G-15994)

Craftech ....D 518 828-5011
Chatham (G-3330)

Creations In Lucite Inc ....E 718 871-2000
Brooklyn (G-1696)

Cytec Industries Inc ....D 716 372-9650
Olean (G-12231)

◆ Dewitt Plastics Inc ....F 315 255-1209
Auburn (G-473)

Dice America Inc ....G 585 869-6200
Victor (G-15405)

Durez Corporation ....F 716 286-0100
Niagara Falls (G-11921)

E I Du Pont De Nemours & Co ......E 716 876-4420
Buffalo (G-2734)

Eastman Chemical Company ....D 585 722-2905
Rochester (G-13365)

Elastomers Inc ....G 716 633-4883
Williamsville (G-16129)

Empire Plastics Inc ....G 607 754-9132
Endwell (G-4479)

Endurart Inc ....E 212 473-7000
New York (G-9373)

Everfab Inc ....D 716 655-1550
East Aurora (G-4086)

▲ Fougera Pharmaceuticals Inc ......G 631 454-7677
Melville (G-7785)

◆ GE Plastics ....E 518 475-5011
Selkirk (G-14357)

▲ General Vy-Coat LLC ....E 718 266-6002
Brooklyn (G-1882)

George M Dujack ....G 518 279-1303
Troy (G-15169)

Global Plastics LLC ....E 800 417-4605
New York (G-9631)

Hanet Plastics Usa Inc ....G 518 324-5850
Plattsburgh (G-12750)

Hazen Holdings LLC ....G 607 542-9365
Jericho (G-6581)

Hexion Inc ....E 518 792-8040
South Glens Falls (G-14513)

Imbibitive Tech Amer Corp ....G 888 843-2323
Niagara Falls (G-11936)

Imbibitive Technologies Corp ....G 888 843-2323
Niagara Falls (G-11937)

International Casein Corp Cal ....G 516 466-4363
Great Neck (G-5394)

▼ John C Dolph Company ....E 732 329-2333
Schenectady (G-14283)

▲ Jrlon Inc ....D 315 597-4067
Palmyra (G-12489)

◆ Kent Chemical Corporation ....E 212 521-1700
New York (G-10094)

Macneil Polymers Inc ....F 716 681-7755
Buffalo (G-2856)

Majestic Mold & Tool Inc ....F 315 695-2079
Phoenix (G-12617)

Manufacturers Indexing Pdts ....G 631 271-0956
Halesite (G-5488)

Maviano Corp ....G 845 494-2598
Monsey (G-8040)

▲ MB Plastics Inc ....E 718 523-1180
Greenlawn (G-5454)

▲ Mega Plastic Group Inc ....G 347 737-8444
Brooklyn (G-2134)

▼ Meliorum Technologies Inc ....G 585 313-0616
Rochester (G-13541)

◆ Mitsui Chemicals America Inc ......E 914 253-0777
Rye Brook (G-14092)

◆ Mitsui Plastics Inc ....E 914 287-6800
White Plains (G-16031)

Mom Holding Company ....G 518 233-3330
Waterford (G-15540)

◆ Momentive Performance Mtls Inc ......E 518 233-3330
Waterford (G-15542)

Momentive Performance Mtls Inc ......D 914 784-4807
Tarrytown (G-15049)

Mpm Holdings Inc ....G 518 233-3330
Waterford (G-15543)

▲ Nationwide Tarps Incorporated ......D 518 843-1545
Amsterdam (G-341)

Newmat Northeast Corp ....F 631 253-9277
West Babylon (G-15734)

Pac Plastics LLC ....G 631 545-0382
White Plains (G-16038)

Parker-Hannifin Corporation ....E 315 926-4211
Marion (G-7572)

▼ Pawling Corporation ....C 845 373-9300
Wassaic (G-15525)

Perfect Poly Inc ....E 631 265-0539
Nesconset (G-8220)

Plaslok Corp ....E 716 681-7755
Buffalo (G-2921)

Plasticycle Corporation ....C 914 997-6882
White Plains (G-16053)

Polycast Industries Inc ....E 631 595-2530
Bay Shore (G-699)

▼ Polymers Merona Inc ....F 631 862-8010
Saint James (G-14112)

▲ Queen City Manufacturing Inc ......G 716 877-1102
Buffalo (G-2944)

Rodgard Corporation ....E 716 852-1435
Buffalo (G-2960)

Sabic Innovative Plas US LLC ......B 518 475-5011
Selkirk (G-14360)

Sabic Innovative Plastics ....E 713 448-7474
East Greenbush (G-4116)

Saint-Gobain Prfmce Plas Corp ......C 518 686-7301
Hoosick Falls (G-6088)

Saint-Gobain Prfmce Plas Corp ......C 518 686-7301
Hoosick Falls (G-6089)

Saint-Gobain Prfmce Plas Corp ......C 518 642-2200
Granville (G-5355)

Sk Capital Partners II LP ....F 212 826-2700
New York (G-11254)

Sk Titan Holdings LLC ....F 212 826-2700
New York (G-11255)

◆ Solepoxy Inc ....D 716 372-6300
Olean (G-12241)

Solid Surfaces Inc ....G 585 292-5340
Rochester (G-13736)

Spectra Polymers & Color Spc ......F 631 694-6943
Farmingdale (G-4738)

Telechemische Inc ....G 845 561-3237
Newburgh (G-11889)

▼ Terphane Holdings LLC ....G 585 657-5800
Bloomfield (G-948)

◆ Terphane LLC ....D 585 657-5800
Bloomfield (G-949)

▼ Tmp Technologies Inc ....D 716 895-6100
Buffalo (G-3012)

◆ Toray Holding (usa) Inc ....E 212 697-8150
New York (G-11516)

Toray Industries Inc ....G 212 697-8150
New York (G-11517)

▲ Transpo Industries Inc ....E 914 636-1000
New Rochelle (G-8356)

Tri-Seal Holdings Inc ....D 845 353-3300
Blauvelt (G-936)

▼ Urethane Technology Co Inc ....F 845 561-5500
Newburgh (G-11892)

Wilsonart Intl Holdings LLC ....E 516 935-6980
  Bethpage *(G-846)*
WR Smith & Sons Inc ....G 845 620-9400
  Nanuet *(G-8205)*

2822 Synthetic Rubber (Vulcanizable Elastomers)

▲ API International Group LLC ....G 877 215-0017
  Yonkers *(G-16288)*
Canton Bio-Medical Inc ....E 518 283-5963
  Poestenkill *(G-12801)*
David Fehlman ....G 315 455-8888
  Syracuse *(G-14875)*
▲ Depco Inc ....F 631 582-1995
  Hauppauge *(G-5635)*
▲ Dynax Corporation ....G 914 764-0202
  Pound Ridge *(G-12992)*
▲ Formosa Polymer Corporation ....G 718 326-1769
  Maspeth *(G-7616)*
Geon Performance Solutions LLC ....E 888 910-0536
  New York *(G-9598)*
▲ Hilord Chemical Corporation ....G 631 234-7373
  Hauppauge *(G-5671)*
▲ Integrated Liner Tech Inc ....E 518 621-7422
  Rensselaer *(G-13089)*
Release Coatings New York Inc ....G 585 593-2335
  Wellsville *(G-15674)*
Silicone Products & Technology ....C 716 684-1155
  Lancaster *(G-6835)*
Snow Craft 216 Inc ....F 718 757-6121
  Freeport *(G-5026)*
▲ Specialty Silicone Pdts Inc ....D 518 885-8826
  Ballston Spa *(G-587)*
Vasquez Tito ....F 212 944-0441
  New York *(G-11648)*

2823 Cellulosic Man-Made Fibers

3M Company ....B 716 876-1596
  Tonawanda *(G-15080)*
◆ Cortland Cable Company Inc ....E 607 753-8276
  Cortland *(G-3758)*
Cytec Industries Inc ....D 716 372-9650
  Olean *(G-12231)*
E I Du Pont De Nemours & Co ....D 716 876-4420
  Buffalo *(G-2734)*
J Rettenmaier USA LP ....D 716 693-4040
  North Tonawanda *(G-12074)*
J Rettenmaier USA LP ....D 716 693-4009
  North Tonawanda *(G-12075)*

2824 Synthetic Organic Fibers, Exc Cellulosic

Dal-Tile Corporation ....G 718 894-9574
  Maspeth *(G-7604)*
▲ Dynax Corporation ....G 914 764-0202
  Pound Ridge *(G-12992)*
Fibrix LLC ....E 716 683-4100
  Depew *(G-3981)*
▲ Jaclyn LLC ....D 201 909-6000
  New York *(G-9963)*
Marly Home Industries USA Inc ....F 718 388-3030
  Brooklyn *(G-2118)*
Solid Surface Acrylics LLC ....F 716 743-1870
  North Tonawanda *(G-12091)*
Solutia Business Entps Inc ....F 314 674-1000
  New York *(G-11293)*
◆ Stein Fibers Ltd ....E 518 489-5700
  Albany *(G-132)*

2833 Medicinal Chemicals & Botanical Prdts

Abh Natures Products Inc ....E 631 249-5783
  Edgewood *(G-4258)*
Accredo Health Incorporated ....G 718 353-3012
  Flushing *(G-4833)*
▼ Ajes Pharmaceuticals LLC ....E 631 608-1728
  Copiague *(G-3644)*
Albany Molecular Research Inc ....F 518 433-7700
  Rensselaer *(G-13085)*
Albany Molecular Research Inc ....F 518 512-2000
  Rensselaer *(G-13086)*
Alo Acquisition LLC ....G 518 464-0279
  Albany *(G-38)*
Asept Pak Inc ....E 518 651-2026
  Malone *(G-7483)*
Bi Nutraceuticals Inc ....G 631 533-4934
  Islandia *(G-6325)*
◆ Bio-Botanica Inc ....D 631 231-0987
  Hauppauge *(G-5604)*

Biobat Inc ....G 718 270-1011
  Brooklyn *(G-1589)*
Biotemper ....G 516 302-7985
  Carle Place *(G-3172)*
Conversion Labs Inc ....F 866 351-5907
  New York *(G-9094)*
Cosmic Enterprise ....G 718 342-6257
  Brooklyn *(G-1691)*
Custom Nutraceuticals LLC ....G 631 755-1388
  Bohemia *(G-996)*
G C Hanford Manufacturing Co ....C 315 476-7418
  Syracuse *(G-14898)*
▲ Gemini Pharmaceuticals Inc ....B 631 543-3334
  Commack *(G-3590)*
Good Earth Inc ....G 716 684-8111
  Lancaster *(G-6808)*
Great Life Elixirs LLC ....D 332 204-1953
  New York *(G-9669)*
Healthee Endeavors Inc ....G 718 653-5499
  Bronx *(G-1274)*
Healthy N Fit Intl Inc ....F 800 338-5200
  Brewster *(G-1150)*
Kamwo Meridian Herbs LLC ....E 212 966-6370
  New York *(G-10064)*
Kannalife Sciences Inc ....G 516 669-3219
  Lloyd Harbor *(G-7056)*
Lee Yuen Fung Trading Co Inc ....F 212 594-9595
  New York *(G-10191)*
Lyteline LLC ....G 657 333-5983
  New York *(G-10290)*
Matys Healthy Products LLC ....G 585 218-0507
  Pittsford *(G-12651)*
▲ Mercer Milling Co ....E 315 701-1334
  Liverpool *(G-7025)*
Natures Bounty Co ....F 631 472-2817
  Bayport *(G-729)*
Natures Bounty Co ....D 631 244-2021
  Ronkonkoma *(G-13980)*
Nbty Inc ....G 631 200-2062
  Holbrook *(G-6014)*
◆ Nbty Manufacturing LLC ....E 631 567-9500
  Ronkonkoma *(G-13982)*
Nutra Solutions USA Inc ....E 631 392-1900
  Deer Park *(G-3914)*
Nutraqueen LLC ....F 347 368-6568
  New York *(G-10657)*
Nutrascience Labs Inc ....E 631 247-0660
  Farmingdale *(G-4696)*
◆ Only Natural Inc ....F 516 897-7001
  Oceanside *(G-12183)*
Pfizer Inc ....A 212 733-2323
  New York *(G-10821)*
Pfizer Overseas LLC ....G 212 733-2323
  New York *(G-10824)*
Plant Science Laboratories LLC ....G 716 228-4553
  Buffalo *(G-2920)*
Proper Chemical Ltd ....G 631 420-8000
  Farmingdale *(G-4718)*
Setauket Manufacturing Co ....G 631 231-7272
  Ronkonkoma *(G-14008)*
Supplement Mfg Partner Inc ....F 516 368-2656
  Edgewood *(G-4283)*
Vitalize Labs LLC ....G 212 966-6130
  New York *(G-11696)*
Wacf Enterprise Inc ....E 631 745-5841
  Northport *(G-12111)*
▲ Wellquest International Inc ....G 212 689-9094
  New York *(G-11740)*

2834 Pharmaceuticals

3v Company Inc ....E 718 858-7333
  Brooklyn *(G-1417)*
5th Avenue Pharmacy Inc ....G 718 439-8585
  Brooklyn *(G-1420)*
872 Hunts Point Pharmacy Inc ....G 718 991-3519
  Bronx *(G-1183)*
888 Pharmacy Inc ....F 718 871-8833
  Brooklyn *(G-1425)*
A & Z Pharmaceutical Inc ....D 631 952-3802
  Hauppauge *(G-5576)*
◆ A & Z Pharmaceutical Inc ....B 631 952-3802
  Hauppauge *(G-5577)*
Abbott Laboratories ....F 716 633-1904
  Williamsville *(G-16117)*
Abeona Therapeutics Inc ....E 646 813-4712
  New York *(G-8429)*
Abh Pharma Inc ....D 866 922-4669
  Edgewood *(G-4259)*
Abraxis Bioscience LLC ....G 716 773-0800
  Grand Island *(G-5324)*

▲ Acorda Therapeutics Inc ....C 914 347-4300
  Ardsley *(G-383)*
Actinium Pharmaceuticals Inc ....E 646 677-3870
  New York *(G-8451)*
Advance Pharmaceutical Inc ....D 631 981-4600
  Holtsville *(G-6044)*
▲ Affymax Inc ....G 650 812-8700
  New York *(G-8491)*
Aiping Pharmaceutical Inc ....G 631 952-3802
  Hauppauge *(G-5581)*
Alaska Spring Phrmcuticals Inc ....E 516 205-6020
  Westbury *(G-15865)*
▲ Alfred Khalily Inc ....F 516 504-0059
  Great Neck *(G-5362)*
Allied Pharmacy Products Inc ....G 516 374-8862
  Hicksville *(G-5882)*
▲ Altaire Pharmaceuticals Inc ....C 631 722-5988
  Aquebogue *(G-364)*
Amarantus Bscence Holdings Inc ....F 917 686-5317
  New York *(G-8536)*
American Bio Medica Corp ....D 518 758-8158
  Kinderhook *(G-6670)*
American Hlth Formulations Inc ....G 631 392-1756
  Hauppauge *(G-5590)*
American Hormones Inc ....F 845 471-7272
  Poughkeepsie *(G-12943)*
▲ American Regent Inc ....B 631 924-4000
  Shirley *(G-14410)*
Amneal Pharmaceuticals LLC ....E 908 231-1911
  Brookhaven *(G-1405)*
Amneal Pharmaceuticals LLC ....E 631 952-0214
  Brookhaven *(G-1406)*
Amneal Pharmaceuticals NY LLC ....E 631 952-0214
  Commack *(G-3576)*
▲ Amneal Pharmaceuticals NY LLC .....E 908 947-3120
  Brookhaven *(G-1407)*
AMP Nutraceuticals Inc ....G 631 676-5537
  Ronkonkoma *(G-13906)*
Anacor Pharmaceuticals Inc ....E 212 733-2323
  New York *(G-8570)*
Anavex Life Sciences Corp ....F 844 689-3939
  New York *(G-8575)*
Angiogenex Inc ....G 347 468-6799
  New York *(G-8584)*
Anima Mundi Herbals LLC ....G 415 279-5727
  Long Island City *(G-7158)*
Anterios Inc ....G 212 303-1683
  New York *(G-8596)*
Apothecus Pharmaceutical Corp ....F 516 624-8200
  Oyster Bay *(G-12444)*
Aratana Therapeutics Inc ....G 212 827-0020
  New York *(G-8617)*
Ark Sciences Inc ....G 646 943-1520
  Islandia *(G-6324)*
▲ Ascent Pharmaceuticals Inc ....D 631 851-0550
  Central Islip *(G-3262)*
Asence Inc ....E 347 335-2606
  New York *(G-8644)*
Athenex Inc ....D 716 427-2950
  Buffalo *(G-2646)*
Athenex Pharma Solutions LLC ....G 877 463-7823
  Clarence *(G-3426)*
Athenex Pharmaceutical Div LLC ....F 877 463-7823
  Buffalo *(G-2647)*
Atlantic Essential Pdts Inc ....D 631 434-8333
  Hauppauge *(G-5596)*
Auri Nutrascience Inc ....G 631 454-0020
  Farmingdale *(G-4587)*
Auven Therapeutics MGT LP ....F 212 616-4000
  New York *(G-8683)*
Avenue Therapeutics Inc ....G 781 652-4500
  New York *(G-8689)*
Axim Biotechnologies Inc ....F 212 751-0001
  New York *(G-8697)*
Azurrx Biopharma Inc ....F 646 699-7855
  Brooklyn *(G-1554)*
▲ Bactolac Pharmaceutical Inc ....C 631 951-4908
  Hauppauge *(G-5600)*
Bactolac Pharmaceutical Inc ....E 631 951-4908
  Hauppauge *(G-5601)*
▲ Barc Usa Inc ....E 516 719-1052
  New Hyde Park *(G-8253)*
Bausch & Lomb Holdings Inc ....G 585 338-6000
  New York *(G-8741)*
Baxter Healthcare Corporation ....B 800 356-3454
  Medina *(G-7729)*
Beyondspring Inc ....D 646 305-6387
  New York *(G-8775)*
Beyondspring Phrmceuticals Inc ....F 646 305-6387
  New York *(G-8776)*

SIC

Bi Nutraceuticals Inc ....D 631 232-1105
Central Islip (G-3266)

◆ Bio-Botanica Inc ....D 631 231-0987
Hauppauge (G-5604)

Biomed Pharmaceuticals Inc ....G 914 592-0525
Hawthorne (G-5810)

▲ Biospecifics Technologies Corp....G 516 593-7000
Lynbrook (G-7428)

Biotie Therapies Inc ....F 650 244-4850
Ardsley (G-386)

Bli International Inc ....C 631 940-9000
Deer Park (G-3847)

Bristol-Myers Squibb Company ....A 212 546-4000
New York (G-8856)

Bristol-Myers Squibb Company ....E 315 432-2000
East Syracuse (G-4201)

Bristol-Myers Squibb Company ....C 516 832-2191
Garden City (G-5093)

Bristol-Myers Squibb Intl Corp ....E 212 546-4000
New York (G-8857)

Caligor Rx Inc ....E 212 988-0590
New York (G-8891)

Campbell Alliance Group Inc ....E 212 377-2740
New York (G-8899)

Canbiola Inc ....G 954 253-4443
Hicksville (G-5892)

Cas Biosciences LLC ....C 844 227-2467
New York (G-8928)

Cellectis Inc ....F 347 809-5980
New York (G-8942)

Central Islip Pharmacy Inc ....G 631 234-6039
Central Islip (G-3268)

Century Grand Inc ....F 212 925-3838
New York (G-8960)

Cerovene Inc ....F 845 359-1101
Orangeburg (G-12308)

Cerovene Inc ....F 845 267-2055
Valley Cottage (G-15314)

Chartwell Pharma Nda B2 Holdin ....G 845 268-5000
Congers (G-3612)

Chartwell Pharmaceuticals LLC ....D 845 268-5000
Congers (G-3613)

Checkpoint Therapeutics Inc ....F 781 652-4500
New York (G-8979)

▲ Chembio Diagnostics Inc ....D 631 924-1135
Medford (G-7702)

Citypharma Inc ....G 917 832-6035
Jackson Heights (G-6419)

Cleveland Biolabs Inc ....F 716 849-6810
Buffalo (G-2699)

Cognigen Corporation ....D 716 633-3463
Buffalo (G-2701)

◆ Combe Incorporated ....C 914 694-5454
White Plains (G-15995)

Container Tstg Solutions LLC ....F 716 487-3300
Jamestown (G-6504)

Container Tstg Solutions LLC ....G 716 487-3300
Sinclairville (G-14445)

Contract Pharmacal Corp ....E 631 231-4610
Hauppauge (G-5625)

Contract Pharmacal Corp ....C 631 231-4610
Hauppauge (G-5626)

Contract Pharmacal Corp ....E 631 231-4610
Hauppauge (G-5627)

Contract Pharmacal Corp ....D 631 231-4610
Hauppauge (G-5628)

Contract Pharmacal Corp ....C 631 231-4610
Hauppauge (G-5629)

Contract Pharmacal Corp ....G 631 231-4610
Hauppauge (G-5630)

Coopersurgical Inc ....F 716 693-6230
North Tonawanda (G-12064)

▲ CRS Nuclear Services LLC ....F 716 810-0688
Cheektowaga (G-3342)

Delcath Systems Inc ....E 212 489-2100
New York (G-9197)

▲ Devos Ltd ....C 800 473-2138
Holbrook (G-5996)

Dr Reddys Laboratories NY Inc ....E 518 827-7702
Middleburgh (G-7886)

DSM Nutritional Products LLC ....C 518 372-5155
Schenectady (G-14261)

DSM Nutritional Products LLC ....C 518 372-5155
Glenville (G-5271)

Durata Therapeutics Inc ....G 646 871-6400
New York (G-9281)

Easton Pharmaceuticals Inc ....G 347 284-0192
Lewiston (G-6920)

▼ Edlaw Pharmaceuticals Inc ....E 631 454-6888
Farmingdale (G-4623)

Eli Lilly and Company ....F 516 622-2244
New Hyde Park (G-8265)

Emilior Phrm Compounding Inc ....E 646 350-0033
Bronx (G-1254)

Emphascience ....G 585 348-9415
Pittsford (G-12639)

▲ Encysive Pharmaceuticals Inc........E 212 733-2323
New York (G-9368)

Enumeral Biomedical Corp ....G 347 227-4787
New York (G-9384)

Enzo Life Sciences Inc ....E 631 694-7070
Farmingdale (G-4625)

◆ Enzo Life Sciences Intl Inc ....E 610 941-0430
Farmingdale (G-4626)

Eon Labs Inc ....F 516 478-9700
New Hyde Park (G-8267)

▲ Epic Pharma LLC ....C 718 276-8600
Laurelton (G-6882)

Erika T Schwartz MD PC ....E 212 873-3420
New York (G-9395)

Eyenovia Inc ....E 917 289-1117
New York (G-9453)

▲ FB Laboratories Inc ....E 631 963-6450
Hauppauge (G-5649)

Fera Pharmaceuticals LLC ....E 516 277-1449
Locust Valley (G-7123)

Flushing Pharmacy Inc ....C 718 260-8999
Brooklyn (G-1856)

Forest Laboratories LLC ....E 212 421-7850
Hauppauge (G-5654)

Forest Labs ....G 631 755-1185
Farmingdale (G-4632)

Forest Research Institute Inc ....F 631 858-5200
Commack (G-3588)

Fortress Biotech Inc ....F 781 652-4500
New York (G-9517)

▲ Fougera Pharmaceuticals Inc ....C 631 454-7677
Melville (G-7785)

Fougera Pharmaceuticals Inc ....C 631 454-7677
Hicksville (G-5909)

Fresenius Kabi Usa LLC ....B 716 773-0053
Grand Island (G-5330)

Fresenius Kabi USA LLC ....B 716 773-0800
Grand Island (G-5331)

◆ Futurebiotics LLC ....E 631 273-6300
Hauppauge (G-5656)

G C Hanford Manufacturing Co ....C 315 476-7418
Syracuse (G-14898)

▼ G Fuel LLC ....E 877 426-6262
West Babylon (G-15712)

▲ Gemini Pharmaceuticals Inc ....B 631 543-3334
Commack (G-3590)

▲ Generic Pharmaceutical Svcs ....E 631 348-6900
Hauppauge (G-5658)

Genzyme Corporation ....D 212 698-0300
New York (G-9596)

▲ Geritrex LLC ....E 914 668-4003
Middletown (G-7912)

Geritrex Holdings Inc ....E 914 668-4003
Mount Vernon (G-8142)

Ges Ges ....G 631 291-9624
Hauppauge (G-5660)

Glaxosmithkline LLC ....E 845 341-7590
Montgomery (G-8060)

Glaxosmithkline LLC ....E 845 797-3259
Wappingers Falls (G-15495)

Glaxosmithkline LLC ....E 585 738-9025
Rochester (G-13443)

Glaxosmithkline LLC ....E 716 913-5679
Buffalo (G-2776)

Glaxosmithkline LLC ....E 518 852-9637
Mechanicville (G-7692)

Glaxosmithkline LLC ....D 518 239-6901
East Durham (G-4102)

Global Alliance For Tb ....E 212 227-7540
New York (G-9622)

Glycobia Inc ....G 607 339-0051
Ithaca (G-6382)

Greenkissny Inc ....G 914 304-4323
White Plains (G-16011)

Greentree Pharmacy Inc ....F 718 768-2700
Brooklyn (G-1911)

Guosa Life Sciences Inc ....F 718 813-7806
New York (G-9699)

▲ H W Naylor Co Inc ....F 607 263-5145
Morris (G-8084)

Health Care Products ....G 631 789-8228
Amityville (G-268)

Healthone Pharmacy Inc ....F 718 495-9015
Brooklyn (G-1928)

▲ Hi-Tech Pharmacal Co Inc ....C 631 789-8228
Amityville (G-270)

Hi-Tech Pharmacal Co Inc ....E 631 789-8228
Amityville (G-271)

Hi-Tech Pharmacal Co Inc ....F 631 789-8228
Amityville (G-272)

Hi-Tech Pharmacal Co Inc ....F 631 789-8228
Amityville (G-273)

Hitech Pharm ....G 631 789-8228
Amityville (G-274)

Hoffmann-La Roche Inc ....G 973 890-2291
New York (G-9799)

▲ Hogil Pharmaceutical Corp ....F 914 681-1800
White Plains (G-16014)

Hookipa Pharma Inc ....D 431 890-6360
New York (G-9810)

Hospira Inc ....C 716 684-9400
Buffalo (G-2801)

Ibio Inc ....E 302 355-0650
New York (G-9852)

Ichor Therapeutics Inc ....G 315 677-8400
La Fayette (G-6738)

◆ Ima Life North America Inc ....C 716 695-6354
Tonawanda (G-15114)

Innogenix Inc ....F 631 450-4704
Amityville (G-276)

Innovative Labs LLC ....D 631 231-5522
Hauppauge (G-5676)

Intercept Pharmaceuticals Inc ....D 646 747-1000
New York (G-9914)

▲ Intra-Cellular Therapies Inc ....E 646 440-9333
New York (G-9929)

Intstrux LLC ....G 646 688-2782
New York (G-9932)

Invagen Pharmaceuticals Inc ....C 631 949-6367
Central Islip (G-3278)

▲ Invagen Pharmaceuticals Inc ....B 631 231-3233
Hauppauge (G-5678)

Ip Med Inc ....G 516 766-3800
Oceanside (G-12176)

Irx Therapeutics Inc ....G 347 442-0640
Brooklyn (G-1970)

Iveric Bio Inc ....E 212 845-8200
New York (G-9949)

Izun Pharmaceuticals Corp ....F 212 618-6357
New York (G-9951)

Jerome Stvens Phrmcuticals Inc ....C 631 567-1113
Bohemia (G-1028)

◆ JRS Pharma LP ....G 845 878-8300
Patterson (G-12518)

▲ Kabco Pharmaceuticals Inc ....C 631 842-3600
Amityville (G-283)

Kadmon Corporation LLC ....F 212 308-6000
New York (G-10055)

Kadmon Holdings Inc ....D 212 308-6000
New York (G-10056)

Kaneka America LLC ....D 212 705-4340
New York (G-10066)

Kannalife Sciences Inc ....G 516 669-3219
Lloyd Harbor (G-7056)

Kbl Healthcare LP ....G 212 319-5555
New York (G-10084)

◆ Kent Chemical Corporation ....E 212 521-1700
New York (G-10094)

Kingston Pharma LLC ....D 315 705-4019
Massena (G-7668)

▲ Klg Usa LLC ....A 845 856-5311
Port Jervis (G-12853)

Life Pill Laboratories LLC ....G 914 682-2146
White Plains (G-16025)

▲ Liptis Pharmaceuticals USA Inc ......A 845 627-0260
Spring Valley (G-14576)

LNK International Inc ....D 631 435-3500
Hauppauge (G-5694)

LNK International Inc ....C 631 435-3500
Hauppauge (G-5695)

LNK International Inc ....G 631 435-3500
Hauppauge (G-5696)

LNK International Inc ....B 631 543-3787
Hauppauge (G-5697)

LNK International Inc ....C 631 435-3500
Hauppauge (G-5698)

LNK International Inc ....C 631 231-4020
Hauppauge (G-5699)

▲ Lotta Luv Beauty LLC ....F 646 786-2847
New York (G-10268)

Maks Pharma & Diagnostics Inc ....G 631 270-1528
Baldwin (G-532)

▲ Marco Hi-Tech JV LLC ....G 212 798-8100
New York (G-10355)

◆ Marietta Corporation ....B 607 753-6746
   Cortland (G-3775)
Medek Laboratories Inc ....E 845 943-4988
   Monroe (G-8027)
◆ Medtech Products Inc ....F 914 524-6810
   Tarrytown (G-15047)
◆ Mentholatum Company ....E 716 677-2500
   Orchard Park (G-12366)
◆ Mercer Milling Co ....E 315 701-1334
   Liverpool (G-7025)
Mesoblast Inc ....G 212 880-2060
   New York (G-10441)
◆ Mtc Industries Inc ....F 631 274-4818
   Hauppauge (G-5724)
Mustang Bio Inc ....E 781 652-4500
   New York (G-10522)
Mylan Health Management LLC ....G 917 262-2950
   New York (G-10526)
Nanorx Inc ....G 914 671-0224
   Chappaqua (G-3326)
Natural Organics Labs Inc ....B 631 957-5600
   Melville (G-7807)
Natures Bounty Inc ....G 631 567-9500
   Bohemia (G-1050)
▲ Natures Bounty Inc ....A 631 200-2000
   Ronkonkoma (G-13981)
▲ Natures Value Inc ....B 631 846-2500
   Coram (G-3695)
ND Labs Inc ....F 516 612-4900
   Lynbrook (G-7434)
Neurotrope Inc ....G 973 242-0005
   New York (G-10574)
▲ Norwich Pharmaceuticals Inc ....B 607 335-3000
   Norwich (G-12125)
Novartis Corporation ....D 718 276-8600
   Laurelton (G-6883)
Novartis Pharmaceuticals Corp ......G 888 669-6682
   New York (G-10649)
Novartis Pharmaceuticals Corp ......G 718 276-8600
   Laurelton (G-6884)
Noven Pharmaceuticals Inc ....E 212 682-4420
   New York (G-10650)
Nutraceutical Wellness Inc ....G 888 454-3320
   New York (G-10656)
Nutrascience Labs Inc ....E 631 247-0660
   Farmingdale (G-4696)
Nutratech Labs Inc ....G 315 695-2256
   Phoenix (G-12618)
NY Phrmacy Compounding Ctr Inc ..G 201 403-5151
   Astoria (G-432)
Ony Biotech Inc ....E 716 636-9096
   Amherst (G-239)
Ony Inc Baird Researchpark ....E 716 636-9096
   Buffalo (G-2898)
Oova Inc ....G 215 880-3125
   New York (G-10696)
Orenova Group LLC ....G 914 517-3000
   White Plains (G-16036)
Ortho-Clinical Diagnostics Inc ....F 585 453-3000
   Rochester (G-13594)
OSI Pharmaceuticals LLC ....D 631 847-0175
   Farmingdale (G-4700)
◆ OSI Pharmaceuticals LLC ....G 631 962-2000
   Farmingdale (G-4701)
Ovid Therapeutics Inc ....E 646 661-7661
   New York (G-10721)
P & L Development LLC ....D 516 986-1700
   Westbury (G-15913)
P & L Development LLC ....D 631 693-8000
   Copiague (G-3667)
P & L Development LLC ....D 516 986-1700
   Westbury (G-15914)
◆ P & L Development LLC ....D 516 986-1700
   Westbury (G-15915)
Pace Up Pharmaceuticals LLC ....G 631 450-4495
   Lindenhurst (G-6969)
▲ Pall Corporation ....A 516 484-5400
   Port Washington (G-12913)
▲ Par Pharmaceutical Inc ....B 845 573-5500
   Chestnut Ridge (G-3396)
Par Phrmceutical Companies Inc ....E 845 573-5500
   Chestnut Ridge (G-3397)
Par Sterile Products LLC ....E 845 573-5500
   Chestnut Ridge (G-3398)
▲ Parmed Pharmaceuticals LLC ....D 716 773-1113
   Niagara Falls (G-11963)
Pedinol Pharmacal Inc ....G 800 733-4665
   Farmingdale (G-4703)
Perrigo Company ....E 718 960-9900
   Bronx (G-1336)

Perrigo New York Inc ....F 718 901-2800
   Bronx (G-1337)
▲ Perrigo New York Inc ....B 718 960-9900
   Bronx (G-1338)
▲ Pfizer HCP Corporation ....F 212 733-2323
   New York (G-10820)
Pfizer Inc ....B 518 297-6611
   Rouses Point (G-14066)
Pfizer Inc ....C 914 437-5868
   White Plains (G-16052)
Pfizer Inc ....C 937 746-3603
   New York (G-10822)
Pfizer Inc ....D 212 733-6276
   New York (G-10823)
Pfizer Inc ....A 212 733-2323
   New York (G-10821)
Pfizer Overseas LLC ....G 212 733-2323
   New York (G-10824)
PH David J Rossi ....G 585 455-1160
   Rochester (G-13619)
▲ Pharbest Pharmaceuticals Inc ....E 631 249-5130
   Farmingdale (G-4705)
Pharmalife Inc ....G 631 249-4040
   Farmingdale (G-4706)
▲ Pharmavantage LLC ....G 631 321-8171
   Babylon (G-523)
Phoenix Laboratories Inc ....C 516 822-1230
   Farmingdale (G-4707)
Polygen Pharmaceuticals Inc ....E 631 392-4044
   Edgewood (G-4278)
Precision Pharma Services Inc ....C 631 752-7314
   Melville (G-7817)
Premium Processing Corp ....D 631 232-1105
   Babylon (G-525)
◆ Prestige Brands Intl LLC ....F 914 524-6800
   Tarrytown (G-15053)
Prestige Consmr Healthcare Inc .....D 914 524-6800
   Tarrytown (G-15054)
▲ Prime Pack LLC ....F 732 253-7734
   New York (G-10890)
Progenics Pharmaceuticals Inc ....D 646 975-2500
   New York (G-10905)
Protein Sciences Corporation ....F 203 686-0800
   Pearl River (G-12538)
Puracap Laboratories LLC ....G 270 586-6386
   Laurelton (G-6885)
▲ Purity Products Inc ....D 516 767-1967
   Plainview (G-12709)
Quality Nature Inc ....G 718 484-4666
   Brooklyn (G-2310)
Quogue Capital LLC ....G 212 554-4475
   New York (G-10959)
Randob Labs Ltd ....G 845 534-2197
   Cornwall (G-3732)
Rasna Therapeutics Inc ....G 646 396-4087
   New York (G-10982)
▲ Regeneron Pharmaceuticals Inc ....B 914 847-7000
   Tarrytown (G-15056)
Regeneron Pharmaceuticals Inc ......E 518 488-6000
   Rensselaer (G-13091)
Regenron Hlthcare Slutions Inc ....A 914 847-7000
   Tarrytown (G-15057)
Relmada Therapeutics Inc ....E 646 677-3853
   New York (G-11004)
Retrophin LLC ....G 646 564-3680
   New York (G-11024)
Rij Pharmaceutical Corporation ......E 845 692-5799
   Middletown (G-7929)
Rk Pharma Inc ....G 646 884-3765
   Pearl River (G-12540)
Rls Holdings Inc ....G 716 418-7274
   Clarence (G-3441)
Roche Tcrc Inc ....G 800 626-3553
   New York (G-11067)
Rocket Pharmaceuticals Inc ....E 646 440-9100
   New York (G-11068)
Ropack USA Inc ....F 631 482-7777
   Commack (G-3596)
▲ Safetec of America Inc ....D 716 895-1822
   Buffalo (G-2971)
Salutem Group LLC ....G 347 620-2640
   New York (G-11123)
Saptalil Pharmacueticals Inc ....G 631 231-2751
   Hauppauge (G-5758)
Saptalis Pharmaceuticals LLC ....E 631 231-2751
   Hauppauge (G-5759)
Scarguard Labs LLC ....F 516 482-8050
   Great Neck (G-5422)
Sciarra Laboratories Inc ....G 516 933-7853
   Hicksville (G-5947)

▲ Sciegen Pharmaceuticals Inc ....D 631 951-4908
   Hauppauge (G-5762)
Scienta Pharmaceuticals LLC ....G 845 589-0774
   Valley Cottage (G-15323)
Seelos Corporation ....G 646 998-6475
   New York (G-11179)
Seelos Therapeutics Inc ....F 646 998-6475
   New York (G-11180)
Seidlin Consulting ....G 212 496-2043
   New York (G-11183)
Sellas Life Sciences Group Inc ....G 917 438-4353
   New York (G-11188)
Shrineeta Pharmacy ....G 212 234-7959
   New York (G-11219)
Shrineeta Pharmacy Inc ....E 212 234-7959
   New York (G-11220)
Siga Technologies Inc ....E 212 672-9100
   New York (G-11230)
Silver Oak Pharmacy Inc ....G 718 922-3400
   Brooklyn (G-2414)
Sincerus LLC ....G 800 419-2804
   Brooklyn (G-2420)
Skills Alliance Inc ....G 646 492-5300
   New York (G-11258)
Skincare Products Inc ....G 917 837-5255
   Williamsville (G-16139)
Specgx LLC ....A 607 538-9124
   Hobart (G-5979)
Stemline Therapeutics Inc ....E 646 502-2311
   New York (G-11356)
Steri-Pharma LLC ....E 315 473-7180
   Syracuse (G-15001)
Sterrx LLC ....E 518 324-7879
   Plattsburgh (G-12781)
Strativa Pharmaceuticals ....F 201 802-4000
   Spring Valley (G-14582)
Sunquest Pharmaceuticals Inc ....F 855 478-6779
   Hicksville (G-5950)
Syntho Pharmaceuticals Inc ....G 631 755-9898
   Farmingdale (G-4747)
Tg Therapeutics Inc ....D 212 554-4484
   New York (G-11457)
▲ Time-Cap Laboratories Inc ....C 631 753-9090
   Farmingdale (G-4756)
▲ Tishcon Corp ....C 516 333-3056
   Westbury (G-15930)
Tishcon Corp ....C 516 333-3056
   Westbury (G-15931)
Tishcon Corp ....C 516 333-3050
   Westbury (G-15932)
Tishcon Corp ....C 516 333-3050
   Westbury (G-15933)
▼ Tmp Technologies Inc ....D 716 895-6100
   Buffalo (G-3012)
Tocare LLC ....F 718 767-0618
   Whitestone (G-16101)
Tongli Pharmaceuticals USA Inc ......F 212 842-8837
   Flushing (G-4900)
Tonix Pharmaceuticals Inc ....G 917 288-8908
   New York (G-11513)
Tonix Phrmceuticals Holdg Corp ......G 212 980-9155
   New York (G-11514)
▲ Topiderm Inc ....C 631 226-7979
   Amityville (G-312)
▲ Topix Pharmaceuticals Inc ....C 631 226-7979
   Amityville (G-313)
Tyme Technologies Inc ....F 212 461-2315
   New York (G-11569)
Ultra-Tab Laboratories Inc ....G 845 691-8361
   Highland (G-5964)
▼ Unipharm Inc ....D 212 594-3260
   New York (G-11592)
United-Guardian Inc ....E 631 273-0900
   Hauppauge (G-5791)
▲ Unither Manufacturing LLC ....C 585 475-9000
   Rochester (G-13783)
Unither Manufacturing LLC ....F 585 274-5430
   Rochester (G-13784)
Urogen Ltd ....G 646 768-9780
   New York (G-11619)
Urogen Pharma Inc ....F 646 506-4663
   New York (G-11620)
Vaccinex Inc ....E 585 271-2700
   Rochester (G-13792)
▲ Velocity Pharma LLC ....G 631 393-2905
   Farmingdale (G-4761)
Ventrus Biosciences Inc ....G 646 706-5208
   New York (G-11655)
Verona Pharma Inc ....F 914 797-5007
   White Plains (G-16068)

S
I
C

Vida-Blend LLC ....E 518 627-4138
Amsterdam *(G-352)*

Viropro Inc ....E 650 300-5190
New York *(G-11688)*

Vita-Gen Laboratories LLC ....G 631 450-4357
Commack *(G-3602)*

▲ Vita-Nat Inc ....G 631 293-6000
Farmingdale *(G-4762)*

Vitalis LLC ....G 646 831-7338
New York *(G-11695)*

◆ Vitane Pharmaceuticals Inc ....E 845 267-6700
Congers *(G-3620)*

Viwit Pharmaceuticals Inc ....G 201 701-9787
Castleton On Hudson *(G-3205)*

Vvs International Inc ....G 212 302-5410
New York *(G-11710)*

Wavodyne Therapeutics Inc ....G 954 632-6630
West Henrietta *(G-15807)*

Wellmill LLC ....E 631 465-9245
Commack *(G-3603)*

Wyeth Holdings LLC ....D 845 602-5000
Pearl River *(G-12543)*

◆ Wyeth LLC ....A 212 733-2323
New York *(G-11793)*

▲ X-Gen Pharmaceuticals Inc ....G 607 562-2700
Big Flats *(G-849)*

X-Gen Pharmaceuticals Inc ....E 631 261-8188
Northport *(G-12112)*

Xstelos Holdings Inc ....G 212 729-4962
New York *(G-11802)*

Y-Mabs Therapeutics Inc ....F 917 817-2992
New York *(G-11803)*

Ys Marketing Inc ....E 718 778-6080
Brooklyn *(G-2603)*

Zenith Solutions ....G 718 575-8570
Saugerties *(G-14217)*

Zeo Health Ltd ....F 845 353-5185
Valley Cottage *(G-15330)*

▲ Zitomer LLC ....G 212 737-5560
New York *(G-11827)*

2835 Diagnostic Substances

Bella International Inc ....G 716 484-0102
Jamestown *(G-6496)*

Biochemical Diagnostics Inc ....E 631 595-9200
Edgewood *(G-4263)*

▲ Biopool Us Inc ....G 716 483-3851
Jamestown *(G-6497)*

▲ Chembio Diagnostic Systems Inc ..C 631 924-1135
Medford *(G-7701)*

Danisco US Inc ....D 585 256-5200
Rochester *(G-13337)*

◆ E-Z-Em Inc ....G 609 524-2864
Melville *(G-7777)*

Enzo Life Sciences Inc ....E 631 694-7070
Farmingdale *(G-4625)*

Gotham Veterinary Center PC ....E 212 222-1900
New York *(G-9648)*

Immco Diagnostics Inc ....G 716 691-0091
Buffalo *(G-2807)*

Ithaca Pregancy Center ....G 607 753-3909
Cortland *(G-3772)*

Kannalife Sciences Inc ....G 516 669-3219
Lloyd Harbor *(G-7056)*

Ken-Ton Open Mri PC ....G 716 876-7000
Kenmore *(G-6654)*

Lesanne Life Sciences LLC ....G 914 234-0860
Bedford *(G-764)*

Lifelink Monitoring Corp ....E 845 336-2098
Bearsville *(G-758)*

Lifescan Inc ....B 516 557-2693
Wantagh *(G-15485)*

Northeast Doulas ....G 845 621-0654
Mahopac *(G-7476)*

Ortho-Clinical Diagnostics Inc ......E 716 631-1281
Williamsville *(G-16135)*

Ortho-Clinical Diagnostics Inc ......E 585 453-3000
Rochester *(G-13597)*

Petnet Solutions Inc ....G 865 218-2000
New York *(G-10817)*

Siemens Hlthcare Dgnostics Inc ....E 914 631-0475
Tarrytown *(G-15059)*

Tiziana Therapeutics Inc ....G 646 396-4970
New York *(G-11500)*

Ufc Biotechnology Inc ....F 716 603-3652
Amherst *(G-251)*

▲ US Diagnostics Inc ....E 866 216-5308
New York *(G-11624)*

◆ Welch Allyn Inc ....A 315 685-4100
Skaneateles Falls *(G-14460)*

Working Family Solutions Inc ....G 845 802-6182
Saugerties *(G-14216)*

2836 Biological Prdts, Exc Diagnostic Substances

▲ Acorda Therapeutics Inc ....C 914 347-4300
Ardsley *(G-383)*

Advance Biofactures Corp ....E 516 593-7000
Lynbrook *(G-7423)*

▲ Akshar Extracts Inc ....G 631 588-9727
Ronkonkoma *(G-13895)*

Albany Molecular Research Inc ......G 518 512-2234
Albany *(G-33)*

◆ Albany Molecular Research Inc ....B 518 512-2000
Albany *(G-34)*

Angus Chemical Company ....F 716 283-1434
Niagara Falls *(G-11906)*

AV Therapeutics Inc ....E 917 497-5523
New York *(G-8684)*

Bioivt LLC ....D 516 483-1196
Westbury *(G-15872)*

Biomup Usa Inc ....G 800 436-6266
New York *(G-8799)*

Coral Blood Service ....F 800 483-4888
Elmsford *(G-4403)*

Cypress Bioscience Inc ....F 858 452-2323
New York *(G-9143)*

D C I Plasma Center Inc ....G 914 241-1646
Mount Kisco *(G-8090)*

Debmar-Mercury ....G 212 669-5025
New York *(G-9193)*

▲ Ecological Laboratories Inc ....D 516 823-3441
Island Park *(G-6316)*

Instrumentation Laboratory Co ....C 845 680-0028
Orangeburg *(G-12321)*

International Aids Vaccine Ini ....D 646 381-8066
Brooklyn *(G-1964)*

International Aids Vccné Inttv ....D 212 847-1111
New York *(G-9917)*

Invitrogen Corp ....G 716 774-6700
Grand Island *(G-5333)*

Ip Med Inc ....G 516 766-3800
Oceanside *(G-12176)*

Kadmon Holdings Inc ....D 212 308-6000
New York *(G-10056)*

Lake Immunogenics Inc ....F 585 265-1973
Ontario *(G-12293)*

Man of World ....G 212 915-0017
New York *(G-10339)*

Meiragtx Holdings PLC ....E 646 490-2965
New York *(G-10424)*

Nanoprobes Inc ....G 631 205-9490
Yaphank *(G-16267)*

Nelco Laboratories Inc ....E 631 242-0082
Deer Park *(G-3910)*

Omrix Biopharmaceuticals Inc ....C 908 218-0707
New York *(G-10687)*

Prevail Therapeutics Inc ....E 917 336-9310
New York *(G-10886)*

Renmatix Inc ....C 315 356-4780
Rome *(G-13867)*

Rentschler Biotechnologie GMBH ...G 631 656-7137
Hauppauge *(G-5754)*

Roar Biomedical Inc ....G 631 591-2749
Calverton *(G-3085)*

Siga Technologies Inc ....E 212 672-9100
New York *(G-11230)*

Stemcultures LLC ....G 518 621-0848
Rensselaer *(G-13092)*

Synergy Pharmaceuticals Inc ....E 212 227-8611
New York *(G-11413)*

Vyera Pharmaceuticals LLC ....E 646 356-5577
New York *(G-11711)*

Wyeth Holdings LLC ....D 845 602-5000
Pearl River *(G-12543)*

◆ Wyeth LLC ....A 212 733-2323
New York *(G-11793)*

2841 Soap & Detergents

Aura Detergent LLC ....G 718 824-2162
Bronx *(G-1208)*

▼ Baums Castorine Company Inc .....G 315 336-8154
Rome *(G-13844)*

Bfma Holding Corporation ....G 607 753-6746
Cortland *(G-3755)*

Bocks Inc ....F 833 437-3363
New York *(G-8828)*

Cleanse TEC ....E 718 346-9111
Hauppauge *(G-5617)*

◆ Colgate-Palmolive Company ....A 212 310-2000
New York *(G-9051)*

Colgate-Palmolive Nj Inc ....E 212 310-2000
New York *(G-9052)*

◆ Combe Incorporated ....C 914 694-5454
White Plains *(G-15995)*

Cosco Enterprises Inc ....G 718 383-4488
Ridgewood *(G-13143)*

Cosco Interprises Inc ....E 718 417-8995
Ridgewood *(G-13144)*

◆ Cpac Inc ....E 585 382-3223
Leicester *(G-6908)*

◆ Crosstex International Inc ....D 631 582-6777
Hauppauge *(G-5631)*

Dr Jacobs Naturals LLC ....E 718 265-1522
Brooklyn *(G-1759)*

Ecolab Inc ....F 716 683-6298
Cheektowaga *(G-3347)*

Emulso Corp ....G 716 854-2889
Tonawanda *(G-15102)*

Enviro Service & Supply Corp ....F 347 838-6500
Staten Island *(G-14651)*

Glissen Chemical Co Inc ....D 718 436-4200
Brooklyn *(G-1890)*

▲ H & H Laboratories Inc ....F 718 624-8041
Brooklyn *(G-1914)*

H & H Laboratories Inc ....G 718 624-8041
Brooklyn *(G-1915)*

HFC Prestige Intl US LLC ....A 212 389-7800
New York *(G-9778)*

◆ King Research Inc ....E 718 788-0122
Brooklyn *(G-2028)*

L S Z Inc ....G 914 948-4040
White Plains *(G-16024)*

Marietta Corporation ....B 607 753-0982
Cortland *(G-3776)*

Marietta Corporation ....A 323 589-8181
Cortland *(G-3777)*

Maybelline Inc ....A 212 885-1310
New York *(G-10392)*

◆ Medtech Products Inc ....F 914 524-6810
Tarrytown *(G-15047)*

▲ Monroe Fluid Technology Inc ......E 585 392-3434
Hilton *(G-5973)*

Mooseberry Soap Co LLC ....G 315 332-8913
Newark *(G-11847)*

Natures Warehouse ....F 800 215-4372
Philadelphia *(G-12612)*

Pro-Line Solutions Inc ....G 914 664-0002
Mount Vernon *(G-8173)*

RAD Soap Co LLC ....F 518 461-9667
Albany *(G-122)*

▲ Robert Racine ....E 518 677-0224
Cambridge *(G-3096)*

Ronbar Laboratories Inc ....F 718 937-6755
Long Island City *(G-7345)*

S & S Soap Co Inc ....E 718 585-2900
Bronx *(G-1355)*

Schneider M Soap & Chemical Co ...G 718 389-1000
Ridgewood *(G-13159)*

Sunfeather Natural Soap Co Inc ......G 315 265-1776
Potsdam *(G-12942)*

▲ T S Pink Corp ....F 607 432-1100
Oneonta *(G-12282)*

Unilever United States Inc ....F 212 546-0200
New York *(G-11588)*

Unilever United States Inc ....C 212 546-0200
New York *(G-11589)*

2842 Spec Cleaning, Polishing & Sanitation Preparations

Adirondack Waste MGT Inc ....G 518 585-2224
Ticonderoga *(G-15073)*

American Wax Company Inc ....E 718 392-8080
Long Island City *(G-7156)*

▲ Bennett Manufacturing Co Inc .....C 716 937-9161
Alden *(G-166)*

Bono Sawdust Supply Co Inc ....G 718 446-1374
Corona *(G-3734)*

Caltex International Ltd ....G 315 425-1040
Syracuse *(G-14840)*

◆ Car-Freshner Corporation ....C 315 788-6250
Watertown *(G-15562)*

Car-Freshner Corporation ....D 315 788-6250
Watertown *(G-15563)*

Castoleum Corporation ....F 914 664-5877
Mount Vernon *(G-8128)*

▲ Chemclean Corporation ....E 718 525-4500
Jamaica *(G-6432)*

City of New York............................C.... 718 236-2693
Brooklyn (G-1666)

Clean All of Syracuse LLC ....G.... 315 472-9189
Syracuse (G-14852)

Cleanse TEC ....E.... 718 346-9111
Hauppauge (G-5617)

◆ Colgate-Palmolive Company ....A .. 212 310-2000
New York (G-9051)

Collinite Corporation ....G.... 315 732-2282
Utica (G-15245)

Connie French Cleaners Inc ....G.... 516 487-1343
Great Neck (G-5379)

Connies Laundry ....G.... 716 822-2800
Buffalo (G-2709)

Conrad Blasius Equipment Co ....G.... 516 753-1200
Plainview (G-12672)

◆ Cpac Inc ....E.... 585 382-3223
Leicester (G-6908)

▲ Crescent Marketing Inc ....C.... 716 337-0145
North Collins (G-12024)

◆ Crosstex International Inc ....D.... 631 582-6777
Hauppauge (G-5631)

Emulso Corp ....G.... 716 854-2889
Tonawanda (G-15102)

Enviro Service & Supply Corp ....F.... 347 838-6500
Staten Island (G-14651)

FBC Chemical Corporation ....G.... 716 681-1581
Lancaster (G-6806)

Finger Lakes Chemicals Inc............E.... 585 454-4760
Rochester (G-13410)

Four Sasons Multi-Services Inc ....G.... 347 843-6262
Bronx (G-1261)

George Basch Co Inc ....F.... 516 378-8100
North Bellmore (G-12019)

▲ Gliptone Manufacturing Inc ....F.... 631 285-7250
Ronkonkoma (G-13942)

Griffin Chemical Company LLC ....G.... 716 693-2465
North Tonawanda (G-12071)

Grillbot LLC ....G.... 646 258-5639
New York (G-9677)

HFC Prestige Intl US LLC ....A 212 389-7800
New York (G-9778)

James Richard Specialty Chem........G.... 914 478-7500
Hastings On Hudson (G-5574)

▲ Jescar Enterprises Inc................G.... 845 352-5850
Nanuet (G-8201)

◆ King Research Inc ....E.... 718 788-0122
Brooklyn (G-2028)

Mdi Holdings LLC ....A 212 559-1127
New York (G-10404)

◆ Micro Powders Inc ....E.... 914 332-6400
Tarrytown (G-15048)

Noble Pine Products Co Inc............F.... 914 664-5877
Mount Vernon (G-8165)

Nuvite Chemical Compounds Corp....F 718 383-8351
Brooklyn (G-2223)

Olin Chlor Alkali Logistics ....C.... 716 278-6411
Niagara Falls (G-11961)

Omg Cleaners Inc ....G.... 718 282-2011
Brooklyn (G-2231)

P S M Group Inc ....E.... 716 532-6686
Forestville (G-4932)

Premier Brands America Inc ....E.... 718 325-3000
Mount Vernon (G-8172)

Premier Brands America Inc ....F.... 718 325-3000
Bronx (G-1343)

▲ Premier Brands America Inc ....C.... 914 667-6200
White Plains (G-16054)

▲ Progressive Products LLC............G.... 914 417-6022
Rye Brook (G-14093)

Pure Green LLC ....G.... 800 306-9122
Oyster Bay (G-12455)

◆ Rochester Midland Corporation......C.... 585 336-2200
Rochester (G-13690)

Royce Associates A Ltd Partnr ....G.... 516 367-6298
Jericho (G-6593)

Safe Seat USA Inc ....F.... 516 586-8240
Plainview (G-12713)

▲ Safetec of America Inc................D.... 716 895-1822
Buffalo (G-2971)

Scully Sanitation ....G.... 315 899-8996
West Edmeston (G-15760)

Sensor & Decontamination Inc..........F.... 301 526-8389
Binghamton (G-908)

Simply Amazing Enterprises Inc ......G.... 631 503-6452
Melville (G-7823)

Solvents Company Inc ....F.... 631 595-9300
Kingston (G-6709)

Spic and Span Company ....F.... 914 524-6823
Tarrytown (G-15061)

Spray Nine Corporation ....D.... 800 477-7299
Johnstown (G-6629)

◆ Strahl & Pitsch Inc......................E.... 631 669-0175
West Babylon (G-15750)

Tjb Sunshine Enterprises ....F.... 518 384-6483
Ballston Lake (G-565)

Topps-All Products of Yonkers..........F.... 914 968-4226
Yonkers (G-16353)

▲ Tribology Inc ....E.... 631 345-3000
Yaphank (G-16275)

TWI-Laq Industries Inc ....E.... 718 638-5860
Bronx (G-1385)

U S Plychmical Overseas Corp..........E.... 845 356-5530
Chestnut Ridge (G-3400)

▲ US Nonwovens Corp ....C.... 631 236-4491
Brentwood (G-1130)

US Nonwovens Corp ....C.... 631 232-0001
Hauppauge (G-5794)

US Nonwovens Corp ....B.... 631 952-0100
Commack (G-3600)

US Nonwovens Corp ....C.... 631 952-0100
Brentwood (G-1131)

◆ US Nonwovens Corp ....D.... 631 952-0100
Brentwood (G-1132)

▲ Walter G Legge Company Inc ....G.... 914 737-5040
Peekskill (G-12560)

Wedding Gown Preservation Co ....D.... 607 748-7999
Endicott (G-4478)

2843 Surface Active & Finishing Agents, Sulfonated Oils

▲ Androme Leather Inc ....F.... 518 773-7945
Gloversville (G-5277)

Bigsky Technologies LLC ....G.... 585 270-5282
Rochester (G-13269)

Comander Terminals LLC ....F.... 516 922-7600
Oyster Bay (G-12446)

Halmark Architectural Finshg............E.... 718 272-1831
Brooklyn (G-1919)

Momentive Performance Mtls Inc........D.... 914 784-4807
Tarrytown (G-15049)

Suit-Kote Corporation ....F.... 716 683-8850
Buffalo (G-2995)

2844 Perfumes, Cosmetics & Toilet Preparations

Abbe Laboratories Inc ....F.... 631 756-2223
Farmingdale (G-4571)

AEP Environmental LLC ....F.... 716 446-0739
Buffalo (G-2625)

Alabu Inc ....G.... 518 665-0411
Mechanicville (G-7690)

Alan F Bourguet ....F.... 516 883-4315
Port Washington (G-12861)

Alexandria Professional LLC............F.... 716 242-8514
Williamsville (G-16119)

◆ All Cultures Inc ....E.... 631 293-3143
Greenlawn (G-5451)

▲ Allan John Company ....F.... 212 940-2210
New York (G-8516)

Angel Tips Nail Salon ....G.... 718 225-8300
Little Neck (G-6996)

Antimony New York LLC ....G.... 917 232-1836
New York (G-8598)

▲ Ardex Cosmetics of America ....E.... 518 283-6700
Troy (G-15164)

Aromasong Usa Inc ....F.... 718 838-9669
Brooklyn (G-1533)

Bastide Inc ....D.... 646 356-0460
New York (G-8739)

▲ Becca Inc ....D.... 646 568-6250
New York (G-8744)

▲ Belmay Holding Corporation ....E.... 914 376-1515
Yonkers (G-16291)

◆ Bio-Botanica Inc ....D.... 631 231-0987
Hauppauge (G-5604)

◆ Borghese Inc ....E.... 212 659-5318
New York (G-8837)

British Science Corporation ....G.... 212 980-8700
Staten Island (G-14631)

Brucci Ltd ....E.... 914 965-0707
Yonkers (G-16292)

◆ Bycmac Corp ....E.... 845 255-0884
Gardiner (G-5127)

◆ California Fragrance Company ....E.... 631 424-4023
Huntington Station (G-6241)

Cassini Parfums Ltd ....G.... 212 753-7540
New York (G-8929)

▲ China Huaren Organic Pdts Inc ......G.... 212 232-0120
New York (G-8988)

◆ Christian Dior Perfumes LLC ....E.... 212 931-2200
New York (G-8999)

Clark Botanicals Inc ....F.... 914 826-4319
Bronxville (G-1400)

Classique Perfumes Inc ....G.... 718 657-8200
Jamaica (G-6436)

Clean Beauty Collective Inc ....E.... 212 269-1387
New York (G-9030)

▲ Clinique Laboratories LLC ....G.... 212 572-4200
New York (G-9032)

Clinique Services Inc ....G.... 212 572-4200
New York (G-9033)

Colgat-Plmolive Centl Amer Inc ....F.... 212 310-2000
New York (G-9050)

◆ Colgate-Palmolive Company ....A .. 212 310-2000
New York (G-9051)

Colgate-Palmolive Company ....B.... 718 506-3961
Queens Village (G-13018)

Common Good LLC ....G.... 646 246-1441
Brooklyn (G-1679)

Common Sense Natural Soap............E.... 518 677-0224
Cambridge (G-3093)

Conopco Inc ....E.... 585 647-8322
Rochester (G-13324)

◆ Coty Inc ....D.... 212 389-7300
New York (G-9107)

◆ Coty US LLC ....C.... 212 389-7000
New York (G-9108)

Coty US LLC ....B.... 212 389-7000
Uniondale (G-15225)

◆ Cpac Inc ....E.... 585 382-3223
Leicester (G-6908)

▲ D & H Amazing Deals Inc..............G.... 347 318-3805
Brooklyn (G-1714)

Delbia Do Company Inc ....E.... 718 585-2226
Bronx (G-1239)

▲ Delbia Do Company Inc ....E.... 718 585-2226
Bronx (G-1238)

▲ Dermatech Labs Inc ....F.... 631 225-1700
Lindenhurst (G-6949)

Distribio USA LLC ....G.... 212 989-6077
New York (G-9240)

Editions De Prfums Madison LLC......G.... 646 666-0527
New York (G-9321)

◆ EL Erman International Ltd............G.... 212 444-9440
Brooklyn (G-1789)

▲ Elias Fragrances Inc....................F.... 718 693-6400
Rye Brook (G-14088)

▲ Elite Parfums Ltd ....G.... 212 983-2640
New York (G-9345)

Elizabeth Arden Inc ....C.... 845 810-2175
Central Valley (G-3299)

▼ Eos Products LLC ....D.... 212 929-6367
New York (G-9386)

Epic Beauty Co LLC ....G.... 212 327-3059
New York (G-9387)

◆ Essie Cosmetics Ltd ....D.... 212 818-1500
New York (G-9405)

Estee Lauder Companies Inc............A 917 606-3240
New York (G-9406)

Estee Lauder Companies Inc............A 212 572-4200
New York (G-9407)

Estee Lauder Companies Inc............G.... 212 756-4800
New York (G-9408)

Estee Lauder Companies Inc............F.... 646 762-7718
New York (G-9409)

Estee Lauder Companies Inc............D.... 631 694-2601
Melville (G-7779)

◆ Estee Lauder Companies Inc ....A 212 572-4200
New York (G-9410)

Estee Lauder Companies Inc............A 212 572-4200
Melville (G-7780)

Estee Lauder Companies Inc............A 646 602-7590
New York (G-9411)

Estee Lauder Inc ....D.... 631 531-1000
Melville (G-7781)

◆ Eternal Love Parfums Corp ....G.... 516 921-6100
Syosset (G-14786)

Ex-It Medical Devices Inc ....G.... 212 653-0637
New York (G-9436)

▲ F L Demeter Inc ....E.... 516 487-5187
Great Neck (G-5384)

◆ Forsythe Cosmetic Group Ltd..........E.... 516 239-4200
Freeport (G-4997)

▲ Four Paws Products Ltd................D.... 631 436-7421
Ronkonkoma (G-13940)

▲ Fragrance Acquisitions LLC............D.... 845 534-9172
Newburgh (G-11865)

▲ Fsr Beauty Ltd ....G 212 447-0036
New York (G-9546)

◆ Gassho Body & Mind Inc ....G 518 695-9991
Schuylerville (G-14324)

Glacee Skincare LLC ....G 212 690-7632
New York (G-9617)

Good Home Co Inc ....G 212 352-1509
New York (G-9644)

▲ H & H Laboratories Inc ....F 718 624-8041
Brooklyn (G-1914)

H & H Laboratories Inc ....F 718 624-8041
Brooklyn (G-1915)

◆ Hain Celestial Group Inc ....C 516 587-5000
New Hyde Park (G-8272)

Hair Ventures LLC ....F 718 664-7689
Irvington (G-6310)

HFC Prestige Intl US LLC ....A 212 389-7800
New York (G-9778)

Hnc Enterprises LLC ....G 904 448-9387
Brooklyn (G-1937)

Hogan Flavors & Fragrances ....E 212 598-4310
New York (G-9800)

Iles Formula Inc ....G 315 834-2478
New York (G-9865)

▲ Inter Parfums Inc ....D 212 983-2640
New York (G-9911)

Inter Parfums Usa LLC ....G 212 983-2640
New York (G-9912)

Intercos America Inc ....G 845 732-3900
West Nyack (G-15823)

Intercos America Inc ....G 845 732-3910
West Nyack (G-15824)

Interntnal Flvors Frgrnces Inc ....C 212 765-5500
New York (G-9924)

◆ Jean Philippe Fragrances LLC ....D 212 983-2640
New York (G-9990)

▲ JP Filling Inc ....D 845 534-4793
Mountainville (G-8194)

Judith N Graham Inc ....G 914 921-5446
Rye (G-14082)

June Jacobs Labs LLC ....D 212 471-4830
New York (G-10042)

Kantian Skincare LLC ....G 631 780-4711
Smithtown (G-14481)

Kind Group LLC ....G 212 645-0800
New York (G-10104)

◆ King Research Inc ....E 718 788-0122
Brooklyn (G-2028)

▲ Klg Usa LLC ....A 845 856-5311
Port Jervis (G-12853)

▲ Lady Burd Exclusive Cosmt Inc .....C 631 454-0444
Farmingdale (G-4669)

▲ Le Labo Holding LLC ....E 646 490-6200
Brooklyn (G-2053)

Le Labo Holding LLC ....E 646 719-1740
Brooklyn (G-2054)

Lechler Laboratories Inc ....E 845 426-6800
Spring Valley (G-14574)

Liddell Corporation ....F 716 297-8557
Niagara Falls (G-11946)

LOreal Usa Inc ....B 212 818-1500
New York (G-10258)

LOreal Usa Inc ....B 917 606-9554
New York (G-10259)

LOreal Usa Inc ....B 212 389-4201
New York (G-10260)

LOreal Usa Inc ....B 646 658-5477
New York (G-10261)

▲ LOreal USA Products Inc ....G 212 818-1500
New York (G-10262)

Lornamead Inc ....D 646 745-3643
Tonawanda (G-15119)

◆ Lornamead Inc ....D 716 874-7190
New York (G-10264)

◆ Maesa LLC ....E 212 674-5555
New York (G-10317)

Malin + Goetz Inc ....F 212 244-7771
New York (G-10336)

▲ Mana Products Inc ....B 718 361-2550
Long Island City (G-7285)

Mana Products Inc ....B 718 361-5204
Long Island City (G-7286)

◆ Marietta Corporation ....B 607 753-6746
Cortland (G-3775)

Marvellissima Intl Ltd ....G 212 682-7306
New York (G-10376)

Maybelline Inc ....A 212 885-1310
New York (G-10392)

Medisonic Inc ....F 516 653-2345
Great Neck (G-5403)

Mehron Inc ....E 845 426-1700
Chestnut Ridge (G-3395)

◆ Meiyume USA Inc ....E 646 927-2370
New York (G-10425)

Memo America Inc ....G 646 356-0460
New York (G-10429)

◆ Mentholatum Company ....E 716 677-2500
Orchard Park (G-12366)

Michel Design Works Ltd ....F 914 763-2244
Katonah (G-6635)

▲ MZB Accessories LLC ....D 718 472-7500
Long Island City (G-7301)

Nature Only Inc ....G 917 922-6539
Forest Hills (G-4924)

▲ Naturpathica Holistic Hlth Inc ....D 631 329-8792
East Hampton (G-4126)

Nava Global Partners Inc ....G 516 737-7127
Great Neck (G-5404)

Nea Naturals Inc ....G 845 522-8042
New Windsor (G-8373)

New Avon LLC ....F 716 572-4842
Buffalo (G-2880)

New Avon LLC ....B 212 282-6000
New York (G-10577)

▲ Newburgh Distribution Corp ....G 845 561-6330
New Windsor (G-8375)

Nr Fragrances & Cosmetics Inc ....G 212 686-4006
New York (G-10651)

Oasis Cosmetic Labs Inc ....G 631 758-0038
Holtsville (G-6051)

Olan Laboratories Inc ....G 631 582-2082
Hauppauge (G-5730)

Old Williamsburgh Corp ....D 631 952-0100
Hauppauge (G-5731)

◆ P S Pibbs Inc ....D 718 445-8046
Flushing (G-4882)

▲ Paula Dorf Cosmetics Inc ....G 212 582-0073
New York (G-10771)

Peppermints Salon Inc ....F 718 357-6304
Whitestone (G-16099)

▲ Perfumers Workshop Intl Ltd ....G 212 644-8950
New York (G-10803)

▲ Peter Thomas Roth Labs LLC ....E 212 581-5800
New York (G-10816)

Plastic & Reconstructive Svcs ....G 914 584-5605
Mount Kisco (G-8102)

Precision Cosmetics Mfg Co ....G 914 667-1200
Mount Vernon (G-8171)

Prescriptives Inc ....G 212 572-4400
New York (G-10882)

Procter & Gamble Company ....C 646 885-4201
New York (G-10902)

▲ Puig Usa Inc ....F 917 208-3219
New York (G-10931)

Pureology Research LLC ....F 212 984-4360
New York (G-10931)

Quality King Distributors Inc ....C 631 439-2027
Ronkonkoma (G-13998)

Quip Nyc Inc ....G 917 331-3993
Brooklyn (G-2315)

REB Lybss Inc ....G 845 238-5633
Monroe (G-8030)

▼ Redken 5th Avenue NYC LLC ....C 212 818-1500
New York (G-10998)

Restorsea LLC ....G 212 828-8878
New York (G-11022)

▲ Revlon Inc ....B 212 527-4000
New York (G-11026)

▲ Revlon Consumer Products Corp .....B 212 527-4000
New York (G-11027)

▲ Robell Research Inc ....G 212 755-6577
New York (G-11059)

▲ Robert Racine ....E 518 677-0224
Cambridge (G-3096)

Salonclick LLC ....F 718 643-6793
New York (G-11121)

Scent-A-Vision Inc ....E 631 424-4905
Huntington Station (G-6259)

Scientific Solutions Globl LLC ....F 516 543-3376
Carle Place (G-3181)

▲ Selective Beauty Corporation ....F 585 336-7600
New York (G-11187)

◆ Shiseido Americas Corporation ....G 212 805-2300
New York (G-11218)

◆ Shop Sky Inc ....G 347 686-4616
South Richmond Hill (G-14524)

Simply Active Cosmetics Inc ....G 646 554-6421
New York (G-11247)

Sixthscents Paper Products Ltd ....G 212 627-5066
Long Island City (G-7358)

▼ Skin Atelier Inc ....F 845 294-1202
Goshen (G-5313)

Sml Acquisition LLC ....C 914 592-3130
Elmsford (G-4434)

◆ Soft Sheen Products Inc ....G 212 818-1500
New York (G-11284)

▲ Solabia USA Inc ....G 212 847-2397
New York (G-11288)

Sundial Brands ....G 631 842-8800
Farmingdale (G-4743)

▲ Sundial Brands LLC ....C 631 842-8800
Amityville (G-309)

Sundial Group LLC ....E 631 842-8800
Amityville (G-311)

Takasago Intl Corp USA ....D 845 751-0622
Harriman (G-5547)

Temptu Inc ....G 718 937-9503
Long Island City (G-7379)

▲ Thompson Ferrier LLC ....G 212 244-2212
New York (G-11473)

▲ Topiderm Inc ....C 631 226-7979
Amityville (G-312)

▼ Unike Products Inc ....G 347 686-4616
Jamaica (G-6484)

Unilever United States Inc ....F 212 546-0200
New York (G-11588)

Unilever United States Inc ....C 212 546-0200
New York (G-11589)

United-Guardian Inc ....G 631 273-0900
Hauppauge (G-5791)

◆ Universal Packg Systems Inc ....A 631 543-2277
Hauppauge (G-5792)

▲ Verla International Ltd ....B 845 561-2440
New Windsor (G-8386)

▲ Victoria Albi International ....F 212 689-2600
New York (G-11677)

Vitiprints LLC ....G 646 591-4343
New York (G-11697)

Westman Atelier LLC ....G 917 297-0842
New York (G-11745)

Xania Labs Inc ....G 718 361-2550
Long Island City (G-7409)

▲ Zela International Co ....E 518 436-1833
Albany (G-144)

Zotos International Inc ....B 315 781-3207
Geneva (G-5167)

2851 Paints, Varnishes, Lacquers, Enamels

A & B Color Corp ....G 718 441-5482
Kew Gardens (G-6660)

Absolute Coatings Inc ....E 914 636-0700
New Rochelle (G-8316)

Akzo Nobel Coatings Inc ....G 631 242-6020
Deer Park (G-3832)

▲ Angiotech Biocoatings Corp ....E 585 321-1130
Henrietta (G-5854)

Atc Plastics LLC ....E 212 375-2515
New York (G-8660)

Atlas Coatings Group Corp ....D 718 469-8787
Brooklyn (G-1549)

B & F Architectural Support Gr ....E 212 279-6488
New York (G-8702)

Barson Composites Corporation ....E 516 752-7882
Old Bethpage (G-12215)

Benjamin Moore & Co ....E 518 736-1723
Johnstown (G-6611)

Cytec Industries Inc ....D 716 372-9650
Olean (G-12231)

Delta Polymers Inc ....G 631 254-6240
Bay Shore (G-673)

Designer Epoxy Finishes Inc ....G 646 943-6044
Melville (G-7774)

Dlz Holdings South Inc ....F 607 723-1727
Binghamton (G-872)

Elantas Pdg Inc ....G 716 372-9650
Olean (G-12235)

▲ Emco Finishing Products Inc ....G 716 483-1176
Jamestown (G-6510)

◆ Enecon Corporation ....D 516 349-0022
Medford (G-7706)

Eric S Turner & Company Inc ....F 914 235-7114
New Rochelle (G-8329)

Fayette Street Coatings Inc ....F 315 488-5401
Liverpool (G-7010)

▲ Fougera Pharmaceuticals Inc ....C 631 454-7677
Melville (G-7785)

G & M Dege Inc ....F 631 475-1450
Patchogue (G-12501)

Garco Manufacturing Corp Inc ....G 718 287-3330
Brooklyn (G-1877)

General Coatings Tech Inc ....E..... 718 821-1232
  Ridgewood (G-13146)
▲ General Vy-Coat LLC ....E..... 718 266-6002
  Brooklyn (G-1882)
▲ Heany Industries Inc ....D..... 585 889-2700
  Scottsville (G-14340)
▼ John C Dolph Company ....E..... 732 329-2333
  Schenectady (G-14283)
▲ Jrlon Inc ....D..... 315 597-4067
  Palmyra (G-12489)
Liberty Panel Center Inc ....F..... 718 647-2763
  Brooklyn (G-2067)
Masterdisk Corporation ....F..... 212 541-5022
  Elmsford (G-4417)
▲ Mercury Paint Corporation ....D..... 718 469-8787
  Brooklyn (G-2141)
Nautical Marine Paint Corp ....E..... 718 462-7000
  Brooklyn (G-2193)
◆ Nortek Powder Coating LLC ....F..... 315 337-2339
  Rome (G-13861)
◆ Paint Over Rust Products Inc ....E..... 914 636-0700
  New Rochelle (G-8348)
▲ Peter Kwasny Inc ....G..... 727 641-1462
  Hauppauge (G-5740)
Philadelphia Coatings LLC ....F..... 917 929-4738
  New York (G-10826)
Rapid Removal LLC ....F..... 716 665-4663
  Falconer (G-4553)
Reddi Car Corp ....G..... 631 589-3141
  Sayville (G-14231)
Robert Greenburg ....G..... 845 586-2226
  Margaretville (G-7567)
Royce Associates A Ltd Partnr ....G..... 516 367-6298
  Jericho (G-6593)
Si Group Inc ....C..... 518 347-4200
  Rotterdam Junction (G-14061)
◆ Si Group Inc ....C..... 518 347-4200
  Schenectady (G-14304)
▲ Sml Brothers Holding Corp ....D..... 718 402-2000
  Bronx (G-1366)
Starlite Pnt & Varnish Co Inc ....G..... 718 292-6420
  Bronx (G-1371)
T C Dunham Paint Company Inc ....E..... 914 969-4202
  Yonkers (G-16351)
▼ T J Ronan Paint Corp ....E..... 718 292-1100
  Bronx (G-1376)
▼ Uc Coatings LLC ....E..... 716 833-9366
  Buffalo (G-3026)
Yewtree Millworks Corp ....G..... 914 320-5851
  Yonkers (G-16358)

2861 Gum & Wood Chemicals

▲ Metro Products & Services LLC ......G..... 866 846-8486
  Brooklyn (G-2148)
▲ Oci USA Inc ....G..... 646 589-6180
  New York (G-10677)
Ocip Holding LLC ....G..... 646 589-6180
  New York (G-10678)
Prismatic Dyeing & Finshg Inc ....D..... 845 561-1800
  Newburgh (G-11883)
◆ Tioga Hardwoods Inc ....G..... 607 657-8686
  Berkshire (G-821)
Westrock Mwv LLC ....C..... 212 688-5000
  New York (G-11748)

2865 Cyclic-Crudes, Intermediates, Dyes & Org Pigments

▲ Crowley Tar Products Co Inc ....G..... 212 682-1200
  New York (G-9123)
Durez Corporation ....F..... 716 286-0100
  Niagara Falls (G-11921)
East Cast Clor Compounding Inc ....G..... 631 491-9000
  West Babylon (G-15708)
F M Group Inc ....F..... 845 589-0102
  Congers (G-3614)
◆ Jos H Lowenstein and Sons Inc ....D..... 718 388-5410
  Brooklyn (G-2000)
▲ LTS Inc ....F..... 845 494-2940
  Orangeburg (G-12322)
Magic Tank LLC ....G..... 877 646-2442
  New York (G-10328)
◆ Micro Powders Inc ....E..... 914 332-6400
  Tarrytown (G-15048)
◆ Mitsui Chemicals America Inc ....E..... 914 253-0777
  Rye Brook (G-14092)
Premier Brands America Inc ....E..... 718 325-3000
  Mount Vernon (G-8172)
◆ Si Group Inc ....C..... 518 347-4200
  Schenectady (G-14304)

Si Group Inc ....C..... 518 347-4200
  Rotterdam Junction (G-14060)
▲ Sml Brothers Holding Corp ....D..... 718 402-2000
  Bronx (G-1366)

2869 Industrial Organic Chemicals, NEC

A and L Home Fuel LLC ....G..... 607 638-1994
  Schenevus (G-14319)
Akzo Nobel Chemicals LLC ....G..... 845 276-8200
  Brewster (G-1139)
American Hlth Formulations Inc ....G..... 631 392-1756
  Hauppauge (G-5590)
Ames Goldsmith Corp ....F..... 518 792-7435
  Glens Falls (G-5239)
Arcadia Chem Preservative LLC ....G..... 516 466-5258
  Great Neck (G-5366)
Arkema Inc ....C..... 585 243-6359
  Piffard (G-12623)
Attis Ethanol Fulton LLC ....D..... 315 593-0500
  Fulton (G-5054)
Avstar Fuel Systems Inc ....G..... 315 255-1955
  Auburn (G-465)
◆ Balchem Corporation ....B..... 845 326-5600
  New Hampton (G-8232)
Baoma Industrial Inc ....G..... 631 218-6515
  Bohemia (G-979)
BASF Corporation ....B..... 914 737-2554
  Peekskill (G-12548)
BASF Corporation ....F..... 914 785-2000
  Tarrytown (G-15041)
BASF Corporation ....B..... 518 465-6534
  Rensselaer (G-13087)
BASF Corporation ....C..... 631 689-0200
  East Setauket (G-4177)
Caltex International Ltd ....E..... 315 425-1040
  Syracuse (G-14840)
Castle Fuels Corporation ....E..... 914 381-6600
  Harrison (G-5548)
Centar Fuel Co Inc ....G..... 516 538-2424
  West Hempstead (G-15768)
China Ruitai Intl Holdings Ltd ....G..... 718 740-2278
  Hollis (G-6041)
Classic Flavors Fragrances Inc ....G..... 212 777-0004
  New York (G-9025)
Comax Aromatics Corporation ....E..... 631 249-0505
  Melville (G-7768)
Comboland Packing Corp ....D..... 718 858-4200
  Brooklyn (G-1677)
Consolidated Edison Co NY Inc ....F..... 914 933-2936
  Rye (G-14076)
Craftmaster Flavor Technology ....F..... 631 789-8607
  Amityville (G-260)
▲ Crown Delta Corporation ....E..... 914 245-8910
  Yorktown Heights (G-16363)
◆ Cumberland Packing Corp ....B..... 718 858-4200
  Brooklyn (G-1708)
D-Best Equipment Corp ....E..... 516 358-0965
  West Hempstead (G-15769)
Danisco US Inc ....D..... 585 256-5200
  Rochester (G-13337)
Degennaro Fuel Service LLC ....F..... 518 239-6350
  Medusa (G-7750)
Dib Managmnt Inc ....F..... 718 439-8190
  Brooklyn (G-1741)
Dulcette Technologies LLC ....G..... 631 752-8700
  Lindenhurst (G-6951)
Enviro Service & Supply Corp ....F..... 347 838-6500
  Staten Island (G-14651)
Evonik Corporation ....E..... 518 233-7090
  Waterford (G-15536)
Family Fuel Co Inc ....G..... 718 232-2009
  Brooklyn (G-1831)
Fire Island Fuel ....G..... 631 772-1482
  Shirley (G-14420)
Flavors Holdings Inc ....F..... 212 572-8677
  New York (G-9509)
Friendly Fuel Incorporated ....G..... 518 581-7036
  Saratoga Springs (G-14176)
Friendly Star Fuel Inc ....G..... 718 369-8801
  Brooklyn (G-1870)
Fuel Energy Services USA Ltd ....G..... 607 846-2650
  Horseheads (G-6124)
Fuel Soul ....G..... 516 379-0810
  Merrick (G-7856)
Full Motion Beverage Inc ....G..... 631 585-1100
  Plainview (G-12686)
Genencor International Inc ....G..... 585 256-5200
  Rochester (G-13432)
Givaudan Fragrances Corp ....C..... 212 649-8800
  New York (G-9615)

Golden Renewable Energy LLC ....G..... 914 920-9800
  Yonkers (G-16314)
Hampshire Chemical Corp ....D..... 315 539-9221
  Waterloo (G-15554)
Henpecked Husband Farms Corp ....G..... 631 728-2800
  Speonk (G-14562)
Hexion Inc ....E..... 518 792-8040
  South Glens Falls (G-14513)
Highrange Fuels Inc ....G..... 914 930-8300
  Cortlandt Manor (G-3796)
Hudson Technologies Company ....E..... 845 735-6000
  Pearl River (G-12532)
Hunts Point Clean Energy LLC ....G..... 203 451-5143
  Pearl River (G-12534)
▼ International Mtls & Sups Inc ....G..... 518 834-9899
  Keeseville (G-6642)
Interntnal Flvors Frgrnces Inc ....C..... 212 765-5500
  New York (G-9924)
▲ Islechem LLC ....E..... 716 773-8401
  Grand Island (G-5334)
J&R Fuel of LI Inc ....G..... 631 234-1959
  Central Islip (G-3281)
Jmg Fuel Inc ....G..... 631 579-4319
  Ronkonkoma (G-13955)
◆ Jos H Lowenstein and Sons Inc ....D..... 718 388-5410
  Brooklyn (G-2000)
JRs Fuels Inc ....G..... 518 622-9939
  Cairo (G-3065)
◆ Kent Chemical Corporation ....E..... 212 521-1700
  New York (G-10094)
Kore Infrastructure LLC ....G..... 646 532-9060
  Glen Cove (G-5196)
Leroux Fuels ....F..... 518 563-3653
  Plattsburgh (G-12758)
Liberty Food and Fuel ....G..... 315 299-4039
  Syracuse (G-14931)
Lift Safe - Fuel Safe Inc ....G..... 315 423-7702
  Syracuse (G-14932)
Lo-Co Fuel Corp ....G..... 631 929-5086
  Wading River (G-15450)
Logo ....G..... 212 846-2568
  New York (G-10243)
Mafco Consolidated Group Inc ....F..... 212 572-8600
  New York (G-10318)
Maio Fuel Company LP ....G..... 914 683-1154
  White Plains (G-16027)
▲ Marval Industries Inc ....D..... 914 381-2400
  Mamaroneck (G-7514)
Metro Fuel LLC ....C..... 212 836-9608
  New York (G-10445)
MNS Fuel LLC ....F..... 516 735-3835
  Ronkonkoma (G-13976)
Molecular Glasses Inc ....G..... 585 210-2861
  Rochester (G-13556)
Mom Holding Company ....G..... 518 233-3330
  Waterford (G-15540)
◆ Momentive Performance Mtls Inc .....E..... 518 233-3330
  Waterford (G-15542)
Mpm AR LLC ....G..... 518 233-3397
  Albany (G-102)
Mpm Holdings Inc ....G..... 518 233-3330
  Waterford (G-15543)
Mpm Intermediate Holdings Inc ....G..... 518 237-3330
  Waterford (G-15544)
Mpm Silicones LLC ....A..... 518 233-3330
  Waterford (G-15545)
Mt Fuel Corp ....G..... 631 445-2047
  Stony Brook (G-14740)
N & L Fuel Corp ....G..... 718 863-3538
  Bronx (G-1320)
Nagle Fuel Corporation ....G..... 212 304-4618
  New York (G-10530)
North East Fuel Group Inc ....G..... 718 984-6774
  Staten Island (G-14685)
Northeastern Fuel Corp ....G..... 917 560-6241
  Staten Island (G-14686)
Nouryon Functional Chem LLC ....D..... 845 276-8200
  Brewster (G-1156)
Nouryon Surface Chemistry ....G..... 716 778-8554
  Burt (G-3060)
Oak-Bark Corporation ....G..... 518 372-5691
  Scotia (G-14335)
Patdan Fuel Corporation ....G..... 718 326-3668
  Middle Village (G-7883)
Poly Scientific R&D Corp ....E..... 631 586-0400
  Bay Shore (G-698)
Polymer Slutions Group Fin LLC ....G..... 212 771-1717
  New York (G-10863)
Pretty Fuel Inc ....G..... 315 823-4063
  Little Falls (G-6991)

S I C

Provident Fuel Inc ....G ... 516 224-4427
 Woodbury (G-16180)
Quality Fuel 1 Corporation ....G ... 631 392-4090
 North Babylon (G-12002)
Remsen Fuel Inc ....G ... 718 984-9551
 Staten Island (G-14701)
Rising Tide Fuel LLC ....G ... 631 374-7361
 Amityville (G-305)
▲ Rose Solomon Co ....E ... 718 855-1788
 Brooklyn (G-2355)
Royce Associates A Ltd Partnr ....G ... 516 367-6298
 Jericho (G-6593)
San Esters Corporation ....F ... 212 223-0020
 New York (G-11128)
Solvents Company Inc ....F ... 631 595-9300
 Kingston (G-6709)
Southbay Fuel Injectors ....G ... 516 442-4707
 Rockville Centre (G-13838)
▲ Specialty Silicone Pdts Inc ....D ... 518 885-8826
 Ballston Spa (G-587)
◆ Sugar Foods Corporation ....E ... 212 753-6900
 New York (G-11385)
Sundial Fragrances & Flavors ....E ... 631 842-8800
 Amityville (G-310)
Symrise Inc ....E ... 646 459-5000
 New York (G-11410)
Telechemische Inc ....G ... 845 561-3237
 Newburgh (G-11889)
▲ Twin Lake Chemical Inc ....F ... 716 433-3824
 Lockport (G-7115)
Unified Solutions For Clg Inc ....E ... 718 782-8800
 Brooklyn (G-2535)
▲ United Biochemicals LLC ....E ... 716 731-5161
 Sanborn (G-14151)
Value Fragrances & Flavors ....F ... 845 294-5726
 Goshen (G-5315)
◆ Vandemark Chemical Inc ....D ... 716 433-6764
 Lockport (G-7119)
Wecare Organics LLC ....E ... 315 689-1937
 Jordan (G-6631)
Western New York Energy LLC ....E ... 585 798-9693
 Medina (G-7749)
Yankee Fuel Inc ....G ... 631 880-8810
 West Babylon (G-15757)
York Fuel Incorporated ....E ... 718 951-0202
 Brooklyn (G-2602)
Zymtrnix Catalytic Systems Inc ....G ... 607 351-2639
 Ithaca (G-6418)

2873 Nitrogenous Fertilizers

C P Chemical Co Inc ....G ... 914 428-2517
 White Plains (G-15987)
◆ Oci USA Inc ....G ... 646 589-6180
 New York (G-10677)
Ocip Holding LLC ....G ... 646 589-6180
 New York (G-10678)
Rt Solutions LLC ....G ... 585 245-3456
 Rochester (G-13709)
Scotts Company LLC ....G ... 631 478-6843
 Hauppauge (G-5763)

2874 Phosphatic Fertilizers

◆ International Ord Tech Inc ....D ... 716 664-1100
 Jamestown (G-6518)
Mdi Holdings LLC ....A ... 212 559-1127
 New York (G-10404)
Occidental Chemical Corp ....C ... 716 278-7794
 Niagara Falls (G-11960)

2875 Fertilizers, Mixing Only

Biosoil Farm Inc ....G ... 518 344-4920
 Glenville (G-5270)
Carolina Eastern-Vail Inc ....E ... 518 854-9785
 Salem (G-14132)
Commodity Resource Corporation ....F ... 585 538-9500
 Caledonia (G-3069)
Long Island Compost Corp ....C ... 516 334-6600
 Westbury (G-15905)
Scotts Company LLC ....E ... 631 816-2831
 Yaphank (G-16269)

2879 Pesticides & Agricultural Chemicals, NEC

Agrochem Inc ....E ... 518 226-4850
 Saratoga Springs (G-14164)
▲ Bioworks Inc ....G ... 585 924-4362
 Victor (G-15394)
E I Du Pont De Nemours & Co ....C ... 718 761-0043
 Staten Island (G-14648)

FMC Corporation ....E ... 716 735-3761
 Middleport (G-7888)
Green Amazon LLC ....G ... 585 300-1319
 Rochester (G-13451)
Island Marketing Corp ....G ... 516 739-0500
 Mineola (G-7981)
Noble Pine Products Co Inc ....F ... 914 664-5877
 Mount Vernon (G-8165)

2891 Adhesives & Sealants

Able National Corp ....E ... 718 386-8801
 Brooklyn (G-1450)
Adirondack Spclty Adhsives Inc ....F ... 518 869-5736
 Albany (G-28)
Advanced Polymer Solutions LLC ....G ... 516 621-5800
 Port Washington (G-12860)
All Out Die Cutting Inc ....E ... 718 346-6666
 Brooklyn (G-1486)
▲ Angiotech Biocoatings Corp ....E ... 585 321-1130
 Henrietta (G-5854)
▲ Aremco Products Inc ....F ... 845 268-0039
 Valley Cottage (G-15313)
▲ Astro Chemical Company Inc ....E ... 518 399-5338
 Ballston Lake (G-557)
◆ Beacon Adhesives Inc ....E ... 914 699-3400
 Mount Vernon (G-8124)
Best Adhesives Co Inc ....G ... 718 417-3800
 Ridgewood (G-13141)
Classic Labels Inc ....E ... 631 467-2300
 Patchogue (G-12498)
▲ Continental Buchanan LLC ....D ... 703 480-3800
 Buchanan (G-2608)
▲ Deal International Inc ....E ... 585 288-4444
 Rochester (G-13341)
Hexion Inc ....E ... 518 792-8040
 South Glens Falls (G-14513)
Hudson Industries Corporation ....E ... 518 762-4638
 Johnstown (G-6619)
J M Canty Inc ....E ... 716 625-4227
 Lockport (G-7084)
Legacy USA LLC ....F ... 718 292-5333
 Bronx (G-1299)
Meridian Adhesives Group LLC ....G ... 212 771-1717
 New York (G-10434)
P C I Paper Conversions Inc ....G ... 315 703-8300
 Syracuse (G-14959)
P C I Paper Conversions Inc ....G ... 315 634-3317
 Syracuse (G-14960)
Polycast Industries Inc ....E ... 631 595-2530
 Bay Shore (G-699)
▲ Polyset Company Inc ....E ... 518 664-6000
 Mechanicville (G-7693)
R-Co Products Corporation ....F-G ... 800 854-7657
 Lakewood (G-6785)
Ran Mar Enterprises Ltd ....F ... 631 666-4754
 Bay Shore (G-704)
Royal Adhesives & Sealants LLC ....E ... 315 451-1755
 Syracuse (G-14980)
▲ Saint Gobain Grains & Powders ....A ... 716 731-8200
 Niagara Falls (G-11976)
Saint-Gobain Prfmce Plas Corp ....C ... 518 642-2200
 Granville (G-5355)
US Epoxy Inc ....G ... 800 332-3883
 Yaphank (G-16277)
Utility Manufacturing Co Inc ....E ... 516 997-6300
 Westbury (G-15936)
Von Roll USA Holding Inc ....F ... 518 344-7200
 Schenectady (G-14317)
Walsh & Hughes Inc ....G ... 631 427-5904
 Huntington Station (G-6266)
Wild Works Incorporated ....G ... 716 891-4197
 Albany (G-142)

2892 Explosives

Dyno Nobel Inc ....D ... 845 338-2144
 Ulster Park (G-15218)
Maxam North America Inc ....G ... 315 322-8651
 Ogdensburg (G-12208)

2893 Printing Ink

Atlas Coatings Corp ....D ... 718 402-2000
 Bronx (G-1207)
Bishop Print Shop Inc ....G ... 607 965-8155
 Edmeston (G-4294)
▲ Calchem Corporation ....E ... 631 423-5696
 Ronkonkoma (G-13920)
Flint Group US LLC ....E ... 585 458-1223
 Rochester (G-13413)
Gotham Ink & Color Co Inc ....E ... 845 947-4000
 Stony Point (G-14744)

Intrinsiq Materials Inc ....G ... 585 301-4432
 Rochester (G-13483)
INX International Ink Co ....E ... 716 366-6010
 Dunkirk (G-4059)
◆ Micro Powders Inc ....E ... 914 332-6400
 Tarrytown (G-15048)
Millennium Rmnfctred Toner Inc ....F ... 718 585-9887
 Bronx (G-1314)
◆ Mitsubishi Chemical Amer Inc ....E ... 212 223-3043
 New York (G-10484)
▲ Specialty Ink Co Inc ....F ... 631 586-3666
 Blue Point (G-957)
◆ Standard Screen Supply Corp ....E ... 212 627-2727
 New York (G-11346)
Superior Printing Ink Co Inc ....E ... 716 877-0250
 Tonawanda (G-15142)
Wikoff Color Corporation ....F ... 585 458-0653
 Rochester (G-13805)

2899 Chemical Preparations, NEC

Aiping Pharmaceutical Inc ....G ... 631 952-3802
 Hauppauge (G-5581)
▲ Alonzo Fire Works Display Inc ....G ... 518 664-9994
 Mechanicville (G-7691)
American Electronic Products ....F ... 631 924-1299
 Yaphank (G-16255)
Amtek Research LLC ....G ... 416 400-2906
 Niagara Falls (G-11905)
Anabec Inc ....G ... 716 759-1674
 Clarence (G-3425)
▲ Ask Chemicals Hi-Tech LLC ....C ... 607 587-9146
 Alfred Station (G-183)
▲ Aufhauser Corporation ....F ... 516 694-8696
 Plainview (G-12665)
◆ Balchem Corporation ....B ... 845 326-5600
 New Hampton (G-8232)
Barson Composites Corporation ....E ... 516 752-7882
 Old Bethpage (G-12215)
Bass Oil Company Inc ....E ... 718 628-4444
 Brooklyn (G-1565)
▼ Bcp Ingredients Inc ....D ... 845 326-5600
 New Hampton (G-8233)
Beyond Beauty Basics LLC ....F ... 516 731-7100
 Levittown (G-6913)
▲ Bonide Products LLC ....G ... 315 736-8231
 Oriskany (G-12384)
◆ C & A Service Inc ....E ... 516 354-1200
 Floral Park (G-4810)
C P Chemical Co Inc ....G ... 914 428-2517
 White Plains (G-15987)
Calfonex Company ....F ... 845 778-2212
 Walden (G-15458)
◆ Citrus and Allied Essences Ltd ....E ... 516 354-1200
 Floral Park (G-4812)
Classic Flavors Fragrances Inc ....G ... 212 777-0004
 New York (G-9025)
Concrete Designs Inc ....G ... 607 738-0309
 Elmira (G-4345)
◆ Coventya Inc ....D ... 216 351-1500
 Oriskany (G-12386)
Coventya Inc ....F ... 315 768-6635
 Oriskany (G-12387)
Crystal Fusion Tech Inc ....E ... 631 253-9800
 Lindenhurst (G-6946)
Cytec Industries Inc ....D ... 716 372-9650
 Olean (G-12231)
Danisco US Inc ....D ... 585 256-5200
 Rochester (G-13337)
▲ Ecological Laboratories Inc ....D ... 516 823-3441
 Island Park (G-6316)
Engineering Maint Pdts Inc ....F ... 516 624-9774
 Oyster Bay (G-12447)
Evans Chemetics LP ....G ... 315 539-9221
 Waterloo (G-15550)
F M Group Inc ....F ... 845 589-0102
 Congers (G-3614)
◆ Fireworks By Grucci Inc ....E ... 631 286-0088
 Bellport (G-799)
▼ Fitzsimmons Systems Inc ....F ... 315 214-7010
 Cazenovia (G-3227)
▼ Flame Control Coatings LLC ....E ... 716 282-1399
 Niagara Falls (G-11929)
Foseco Inc ....F ... 914 345-4760
 Tarrytown (G-15044)
Fppf Chemical Co Inc ....G ... 716 856-9607
 Buffalo (G-2758)
◆ Geliko LLC ....E ... 212 876-5620
 New York (G-9585)
Gordon Fire Equipment LLC ....G ... 845 691-5700
 Highland (G-5959)

▲ Greenfield Manufacturing Inc ....F 518 581-2368
   Saratoga Springs *(G-14180)*

Halfmoon Town Water Department ....G...... 518 233-7489
   Waterford *(G-15537)*

Hampshire Chemical Corp ....D...... 315 539-9221
   Waterloo *(G-15554)*

Hanson Aggregates PA LLC ....F 585 436-3250
   Rochester *(G-13458)*

▼ I A S National Inc ....E 631 423-6900
   Huntington Station *(G-6249)*

Icynene US Acquisition Corp ....G...... 800 758-7325
   Buffalo *(G-2805)*

Indium Corporation of America ....F 315 793-8200
   Utica *(G-15275)*

Instrumentation Laboratory Co ....C...... 845 680-0028
   Orangeburg *(G-12321)*

International Fire-Shield Inc ....F 315 255-1006
   Auburn *(G-479)*

◆ Island Pyrochemical Inds Corp ......C...... 516 746-2100
   Mineola *(G-7983)*

Johnson Manufacturing Company ....F 716 881-3030
   Buffalo *(G-2824)*

Kaneka America LLC ....D...... 212 705-4340
   New York *(G-10066)*

▲ Kemper System America Inc ....D...... 716 558-2971
   West Seneca *(G-15851)*

◆ Kent Chemical Corporation ....E 212 521-1700
   New York *(G-10094)*

Luxfer Magtech Inc ....D...... 631 727-8600
   Riverhead *(G-13181)*

Mdi Holdings LLC ....A...... 212 559-1127
   New York *(G-10404)*

◆ Micro Powders Inc ....E 914 332-6400
   Tarrytown *(G-15048)*

Momentive Performance LLC ....G...... 281 325-3536
   Waterford *(G-15541)*

Momentive Performance Mtls Inc ....D...... 914 784-4807
   Tarrytown *(G-15049)*

▲ Monroe Fluid Technology Inc ....E 585 392-3434
   Hilton *(G-5973)*

Morton Salt Inc ....F 585 493-2511
   Silver Springs *(G-14443)*

Nalco Company LLC ....E 518 796-1985
   Saratoga Springs *(G-14185)*

Natures Warehouse ....F 800 215-4372
   Philadelphia *(G-12612)*

New Fine Chemicals Inc ....G...... 631 321-8151
   Lindenhurst *(G-6963)*

Nouryon Surface Chemistry ....G...... 716 778-8554
   Burt *(G-3060)*

Nouryon Surface Chemistry ....C...... 914 674-5008
   Dobbs Ferry *(G-4018)*

▲ Penetron International Ltd ....F 631 941-9700
   East Setauket *(G-4183)*

Pure Kemika LLC ....G...... 718 745-2200
   Bellmore *(G-787)*

PVS Chemical Solutions Inc ....D...... 716 825-5762
   Buffalo *(G-2938)*

Pwf Enterprise LLC ....F 315 695-2223
   Phoenix *(G-12620)*

▲ Real Co Inc ....G...... 347 433-8549
   Valley Cottage *(G-15321)*

Reddi Car Corp ....G...... 631 589-3141
   Sayville *(G-14231)*

Reliance Fluid Tech LLC ....E 716 332-0988
   Niagara Falls *(G-11972)*

◆ Rochester Midland Corporation ......C...... 585 336-2200
   Rochester *(G-13690)*

Roto Salt Company Inc ....E 315 536-3742
   Penn Yan *(G-12593)*

Royce Associates A Ltd Partnr ....G...... 516 367-6298
   Jericho *(G-6593)*

Safeguard Inc ....F 631 929-3273
   Wading River *(G-15451)*

Solenis LLC ....G...... 718 383-1717
   Brooklyn *(G-2440)*

Solenis LLC ....G...... 315 461-4730
   Liverpool *(G-7040)*

Solvents Company Inc ....F 631 595-9300
   Kingston *(G-6709)*

▲ Specialty Ink Co Inc ....F 631 586-3666
   Blue Point *(G-957)*

▼ Supresta US LLC ....E 914 674-9434
   Ardsley *(G-390)*

▲ Tam Ceramics LLC ....D...... 716 278-9480
   Niagara Falls *(G-11985)*

▼ Tangram Company LLC ....E 631 758-0460
   Holtsville *(G-6055)*

Technic Inc ....F 516 349-0700
   Plainview *(G-12718)*

▲ Topaz Industries Inc ....F 631 207-0700
   Holtsville *(G-6057)*

Torre Products Co Inc ....G...... 212 925-8989
   Mount Vernon *(G-8184)*

US Polychemical Holding Corp ....E 845 356-5530
   Spring Valley *(G-14587)*

US Salt LLC ....D...... 607 535-2721
   Watkins Glen *(G-15617)*

▼ US Salt LLC ....F 888 872-7258
   Watkins Glen *(G-15618)*

Utility Manufacturing Co Inc ....E 516 997-6300
   Westbury *(G-15936)*

Venue Graphics Supply Inc ....F 718 361-1690
   Long Island City *(G-7393)*

Von Roll Usa Inc ....E 203 562-2171
   Schenectady *(G-14315)*

Water Wise of America Inc ....F 585 232-1210
   Rochester *(G-13799)*

◆ Watson Bowman Acme Corp ....C...... 716 691-8162
   Amherst *(G-253)*

Wyeth Holdings LLC ....D...... 845 602-5000
   Pearl River *(G-12543)*

Yiwen Usa Inc ....F 212 370-0828
   New York *(G-11810)*

▲ Young Explosives Corp ....D...... 585 394-1783
   Canandaigua *(G-3146)*

Yr Blanc & Co LLC ....G...... 716 800-3999
   Buffalo *(G-3053)*

29 PETROLEUM REFINING AND RELATED INDUSTRIES

2911 Petroleum Refining

209 Discount Oil ....E 845 386-2090
   Middletown *(G-7891)*

Algafuel America ....G...... 516 295-2257
   Hewlett *(G-5869)*

◆ C & A Service Inc ....G...... 516 354-1200
   Floral Park *(G-4810)*

California Petro Trnspt Corp ....G...... 212 302-5151
   New York *(G-8889)*

◆ Citrus and Allied Essences Ltd ......E 516 354-1200
   Floral Park *(G-4812)*

▲ E-Zoil Products Inc ....G...... 716 213-0106
   Tonawanda *(G-15101)*

Ergun Inc ....G...... 631 721-0049
   Roslyn Heights *(G-14050)*

Fppf Chemical Co Inc ....G...... 716 856-9607
   Buffalo *(G-2758)*

Fuel Energy Services USA Ltd ....E 607 846-2650
   Horseheads *(G-6124)*

Heat USA II LLC ....E 212 564-4328
   New York *(G-9760)*

▲ Hess Corporation ....B 212 997-8500
   New York *(G-9771)*

Hess Oil Virgin Island Corp ....A...... 212 997-8500
   New York *(G-9774)*

Hess Pipeline Corporation ....C...... 212 997-8500
   New York *(G-9775)*

Hygrade Fuel Inc ....G...... 516 741-0723
   Mineola *(G-7980)*

Iep Energy Holding LLC ....A...... 212 702-4300
   New York *(G-9859)*

▲ Industrial Raw Materials LLC ....F 212 688-8080
   Plainview *(G-12689)*

◆ Kent Chemical Corporation ....E 212 521-1700
   New York *(G-10094)*

Kinetic Fuel Technology Inc ....G...... 716 745-1461
   Youngstown *(G-13384)*

Koch Supply & Trading LP ....G...... 212 319-4895
   New York *(G-10121)*

▲ Koster Keunen Waxes Ltd ....F 631 589-0400
   Sayville *(G-14229)*

Motiva Enterprises LLC ....G...... 516 371-4780
   Lawrence *(G-6889)*

Northern Biodiesel Inc ....G...... 585 545-4534
   Ontario *(G-12294)*

Oil Solutions Intl Inc ....G...... 631 608-8889
   Amityville *(G-300)*

▲ Osaka Gas Energy America Corp ......F 914 253-5500
   White Plains *(G-16037)*

Performance Diesel Service LLC ....F 315 854-5269
   Plattsburgh *(G-12767)*

Petre Alii Petroleum ....G...... 315 785-1037
   Watertown *(G-15587)*

R H Crown Co Inc ....E 518 762-4589
   Johnstown *(G-6626)*

Solvents Company Inc ....F 631 595-9300
   Kingston *(G-6709)*

Starfuels Inc ....G...... 914 289-4800
   White Plains *(G-16062)*

Suit-Kote Corporation ....F 585 268-7127
   Belmont *(G-811)*

2951 Paving Mixtures & Blocks

A Colarusso and Son Inc ....E 518 828-3218
   Hudson *(G-6146)*

Advanced Pavement Group Corp ....G...... 631 277-8400
   Islip *(G-6349)*

Alliance Paving Materials Inc ....G...... 315 337-0795
   Rome *(G-13841)*

Atlas Bituminous Co Inc ....F 315 457-2394
   Syracuse *(G-14820)*

Barrett Paving Materials Inc ....E 315 353-6611
   Norwood *(G-12131)*

Barrett Paving Materials Inc ....E 315 652-4585
   Liverpool *(G-7000)*

Barrett Paving Materials Inc ....F 315 737-9471
   Clayville *(G-3454)*

Barrett Paving Materials Inc ....G...... 607 723-5367
   Binghamton *(G-856)*

Barrett Paving Materials Inc ....F 315 788-2037
   Watertown *(G-15559)*

Bross Quality Paving ....G...... 845 532-7116
   Ellenville *(G-4305)*

C & C Ready-Mix Corporation ....E 607 797-5108
   Vestal *(G-15374)*

C & C Ready-Mix Corporation ....F 607 687-1690
   Owego *(G-12429)*

Callanan Industries Inc ....E 845 457-3158
   Montgomery *(G-8058)*

▲ Callanan Industries Inc ....C...... 518 374-2222
   Albany *(G-55)*

Callanan Industries Inc ....G...... 845 331-6868
   Kingston *(G-6683)*

Canal Asphalt Inc ....G...... 914 667-8500
   Mount Vernon *(G-8127)*

Cobleskill Stone Products Inc ....F 607 432-8321
   Oneonta *(G-12265)*

Cobleskill Stone Products Inc ....F 607 637-4271
   Hancock *(G-5535)*

Cofire Paving Corporation ....E 718 463-1403
   Flushing *(G-4845)*

Cold Mix Manufacturing Corp ....F 718 463-1444
   Mount Vernon *(G-8132)*

Deans Paving Inc ....G...... 315 736-7601
   Marcy *(G-7564)*

Doctor Pavers ....E 516 342-6016
   Commack *(G-3586)*

Dolomite Products Company Inc ....E 315 524-1998
   Rochester *(G-13354)*

Dolomite Products Company Inc ....F 607 324-3636
   Hornell *(G-6103)*

Dolomite Products Company Inc ....F 585 768-7295
   Le Roy *(G-6898)*

Dolomite Products Company Inc ....F 585 352-0460
   Spencerport *(G-14555)*

Gernatt Asphalt Products Inc ....E 716 496-5111
   Springville *(G-14591)*

Grace Associates Inc ....G...... 718 767-9000
   Harrison *(G-5554)*

Graymont Materials Inc ....E 518 561-5200
   Plattsburgh *(G-12749)*

Hanson Aggregates East LLC ....E 585 343-1787
   Stafford *(G-14604)*

Hanson Aggregates PA LLC ....F 585 624-3800
   Honeoye Falls *(G-6073)*

Iroquois Rock Products Inc ....F 585 381-7010
   Rochester *(G-13484)*

J Pahura Contractors ....G...... 585 589-5793
   Albion *(G-156)*

Jet-Black Sealers Inc ....F 716 891-4197
   Buffalo *(G-2822)*

John T Montecalvo Inc ....G...... 631 325-1492
   Speonk *(G-14563)*

Kal-Harbour Inc ....F 518 266-0690
   Albany *(G-93)*

King Road Materials Inc ....E 518 381-9995
   Albany *(G-94)*

King Road Materials Inc ....F 518 382-5354
   Schenectady *(G-14285)*

Kings Park Asphalt Corporation ....G...... 631 269-9774
   Hauppauge *(G-5683)*

Lafarge North America Inc ....E 518 756-5000
   Ravena *(G-13069)*

▲ McConnaughay Technologies ....G...... 607 753-1100
   Cortland *(G-3778)*

Monticello Black Top Corp ....G...... 845 434-7280
   Thompsonville *(G-15066)*

SIC

▲ Nicolia Concrete Products Inc ....D 631 669-0700
   Lindenhurst (G-6965)

Northeastern Sealcoat Inc ....F 585 544-4372
   Rochester (G-13583)

Northern Bituminous Mix Inc ....G 315 598-2141
   Fulton (G-5074)

▲ Package Pavement Company Inc ....D 845 221-2224
   Stormville (G-14752)

Pallette Stone Corporation ....E 518 584-2421
   Gansevoort (G-5084)

Patterson Blacktop Corp ....E 845 628-3425
   Carmel (G-3189)

Patterson Blacktop Corp ....E 914 949-2000
   White Plains (G-16040)

Patterson Materials Corp ....F 914 949-2000
   White Plains (G-16041)

Peckham Asphalt Resale Corp ....F 914 949-2000
   White Plains (G-6193)

Peckham Asphalt Resale Corp ....E 518 945-1120
   Athens (G-449)

▲ Peckham Industries Inc ....E 914 949-2000
   White Plains (G-16044)

Peckham Industries Inc ....E 518 943-0155
   Catskill (G-3216)

Peckham Industries Inc ....F 518 893-2176
   Greenfield Center (G-5450)

Peckham Industries Inc ....G 518 945-1120
   Athens (G-450)

Peckham Materials Corp ....G 845 562-5370
   Newburgh (G-11881)

Peckham Materials Corp ....D 914 686-2045
   White Plains (G-16045)

Peckham Materials Corp ....E 518 945-1120
   Athens (G-451)

Peckham Materials Corp ....F 518 494-2313
   Chestertown (G-3394)

Peckham Materials Corp ....E 518 747-3353
   Hudson Falls (G-6192)

Peckham Road Corp ....E 518 792-3157
   Queensbury (G-13051)

Posillico Materials LLC ....F 631 249-1872
   Farmingdale (G-4713)

PSI Transit Mix Corp ....G 631 382-7930
   Smithtown (G-14486)

R Schleider Contracting Corp ....G 631 269-4249
   Kings Park (G-6676)

Rochester Asphalt Materials ....E 585 381-7010
   Rochester (G-13681)

Rochester Seal Pro LLC ....G 585 594-3818
   Rochester (G-13695)

Sheldon Slate Products Co Inc ....E 518 642-1280
   Middle Granville (G-7870)

◆ Suit-Kote Corporation ....C 607 753-1100
   Cortland (G-3789)

Suit-Kote Corporation ....F 315 735-8501
   Oriskany (G-12396)

Suit-Kote Corporation ....E 607 535-2743
   Watkins Glen (G-15616)

Suit-Kote Corporation ....E 716 664-3750
   Jamestown (G-6545)

Swift River Associates Inc ....G 716 875-0902
   Tonawanda (G-15144)

Thalle Industries Inc ....E 914 762-3415
   Briarcliff Manor (G-1162)

Tilcon New York Inc ....D 845 638-3594
   Haverstraw (G-5808)

Tilcon New York Inc ....G 845 562-3240
   New Windsor (G-8384)

Tri City Highway Products Inc ....E 607 722-2967
   Binghamton (G-914)

Tri-City Highway Products Inc ....E 518 294-9964
   Richmondville (G-13130)

Twin County Recycling Corp ....F 516 827-6900
   Westbury (G-15935)

▲ Unilock New York Inc ....F 845 278-6700
   Brewster (G-1159)

Universal Ready Mix Inc ....G 516 746-4535
   New Hyde Park (G-8301)

Upstone Materials Inc ....G 518 873-2275
   Lewis (G-6918)

Upstone Materials Inc ....D 518 561-5321
   Plattsburgh (G-12787)

Vestal Asphalt Inc ....F 607 785-3393
   Vestal (G-15387)

Zielinskis Asphalt Inc ....F 315 306-4057
   Oriskany Falls (G-12401)

2952 Asphalt Felts & Coatings

▲ Aremco Products Inc ....F 845 268-0039
   Valley Cottage (G-15313)

Barrett Paving Materials Inc ....E 315 353-6611
   Norwood (G-12131)

Callanan Industries Inc ....E 845 457-3158
   Montgomery (G-8058)

Countryside Truss LLC ....G 315 985-0643
   Saint Johnsville (G-14116)

Empire Emulsions LLC ....E 845 610-5350
   Chester (G-3376)

Johns Manville Corporation ....E 518 565-3000
   Plattsburgh (G-12755)

K-D Stone Inc ....E 518 642-2082
   Middle Granville (G-7869)

◆ Marathon Roofing Products Inc ....F 716 685-3340
   Orchard Park (G-12364)

Northeastern Sealcoat Inc ....F 585 544-4372
   Rochester (G-13583)

Peckham Materials Corp ....E 518 747-3353
   Hudson Falls (G-6192)

▲ Polyset Company Inc ....E 518 664-6000
   Mechanicville (G-7693)

Savage & Son Installations LLC ....E 585 342-7533
   Rochester (G-13716)

Sheldon Slate Products Co Inc ....E 518 642-1280
   Middle Granville (G-7870)

Spray-Tech Finishing Inc ....F 716 664-6317
   Jamestown (G-6542)

Suit-Kote Corporation ....E 607 535-2743
   Watkins Glen (G-15616)

Tntpaving ....G 607 372-4911
   Endicott (G-4475)

2992 Lubricating Oils & Greases

▲ Battenfeld Grease Oil Corp NY ....E 716 695-2100
   North Tonawanda (G-12058)

▼ Battenfeld-American Inc ....E 716 822-8410
   Buffalo (G-2658)

▼ Baums Castorine Company Inc ....G 315 336-8154
   Rome (G-13844)

Beka World LP ....G 716 685-3717
   Buffalo (G-2660)

▲ Black Bear Company Inc ....E 718 784-7330
   Valley Stream (G-15335)

▲ Blaser Production Inc ....E 845 294-3200
   Goshen (G-5306)

◆ Blaser Swisslube Holding Corp ....F 845 294-3200
   Goshen (G-5307)

Castoleum Corporation ....E 914 664-5877
   Mount Vernon (G-8128)

◆ Chemlube International LLC ....F 914 381-5800
   Harrison (G-5550)

◆ Chemlube Marketing Inc ....F 914 381-5800
   Harrison (G-5551)

Commercial Lubricants Moove ....E 718 720-3434
   Staten Island (G-14641)

◆ Finish Line Technologies Inc ....E 631 666-7300
   Hauppauge (G-5650)

Industrial Oil Tank Service ....G 315 736-6080
   Oriskany (G-12392)

▲ Inland Vacuum Industries Inc ....F 585 293-3330
   Churchville (G-3412)

▲ Loobrica International Corp ....G 347 997-0296
   Staten Island (G-14677)

Mdi Holdings LLC ....A 212 559-1127
   New York (G-10404)

▲ Monroe Fluid Technology Inc ....E 585 392-3434
   Hilton (G-5973)

Oil and Lubricant Depot LLC ....F 631 841-5000
   Wyandanch (G-16246)

Polycast Industries Inc ....E 631 595-2530
   Bay Shore (G-699)

Remcoda LLC ....G 212 354-1330
   New York (G-11009)

Safety-Kleen Systems Inc ....F 716 855-2212
   Buffalo (G-2972)

▲ Specialty Silicone Pdts Inc ....D 518 885-8826
   Ballston Spa (G-587)

▲ Summit Lubricants Inc ....E 585 815-0798
   Batavia (G-626)

▲ Tribology Inc ....E 631 345-3000
   Yaphank (G-16275)

US Global Lubricants Inc ....F 845 271-4277
   Stony Point (G-14750)

2999 Products Of Petroleum & Coal, NEC

◆ Cooks Intl Ltd Lblty Co ....G 212 741-4407
   New York (G-9096)

Costello Bros Petroleum Corp ....G 914 237-3189
   Yonkers (G-16298)

Hh Liquidating Corp ....A 646 282-2500
   New York (G-9779)

▲ Premier Ingridients Inc ....G 516 641-6763
   Great Neck (G-5414)

30 RUBBER AND MISCELLANEOUS PLASTICS PRODUCTS

3011 Tires & Inner Tubes

East Coast Intl Tire Group Inc ....G 718 386-9088
   Maspeth (G-7610)

East Coast Intl Tire Inc ....F 718 386-9088
   Maspeth (G-7611)

▼ Handy & Harman Ltd ....A 212 520-2300
   New York (G-9720)

McCarthy Tire Svc Co NY Inc ....F 518 449-5185
   Menands (G-7845)

Roli Retreads Inc ....E 631 694-7670
   Farmingdale (G-4726)

Sph Group Holdings LLC ....F 212 520-2300
   New York (G-11321)

3021 Rubber & Plastic Footwear

◆ Anthony L & S LLC ....E 212 386-7245
   New York (G-8597)

▲ Detny Footwear Inc ....G 212 423-1040
   New York (G-9210)

Great Shoes Inc ....F 718 813-1945
   Islandia (G-6333)

Homegrown For Good LLC ....F 857 540-6361
   New Rochelle (G-8342)

Inkkas LLC ....G 646 845-9803
   New York (G-9895)

Little Eric Shoes On Madison ....G 212 717-1513
   New York (G-10229)

▲ Mango Usa Inc ....E 718 998-6050
   Brooklyn (G-2106)

Nike Inc ....E 631 960-0184
   Islip Terrace (G-6359)

Nike Inc ....E 716 298-5615
   Niagara Falls (G-11955)

▲ Soludos LLC ....F 212 219-1101
   New York (G-11292)

▲ Timing Group LLC ....G 646 878-2600
   New York (G-11497)

Vans Inc ....F 631 724-1011
   Lake Grove (G-6762)

3052 Rubber & Plastic Hose & Belting

▲ Anchor Tech Products Corp ....E 914 592-0240
   Elmsford (G-4393)

Cataract Hose Co ....C 914 941-9019
   Ossining (G-12402)

Deer Park Driveshaft & Hose ....G 631 667-4091
   Deer Park (G-3860)

▲ Flex Enterprises Inc ....E 585 742-1000
   Victor (G-15409)

Habasit America Inc ....D 716 824-8484
   Buffalo (G-2787)

▲ Hitachi Cable America Inc ....F 914 694-9200
   Purchase (G-13004)

Index Incorporated ....F 440 632-5400
   Bronx (G-1280)

Jain Irrigation Inc ....D 315 755-4400
   Watertown (G-15573)

Jed Lights Inc ....F 516 812-5001
   Deer Park (G-3888)

◆ Mason Industries Inc ....C 631 348-0282
   Hauppauge (G-5708)

▲ Mercer Rubber Co ....E 631 348-0282
   Hauppauge (G-5713)

Moreland Hose & Belting Corp ....G 631 563-7071
   Oakdale (G-12154)

▲ Peraflex Hose Inc ....F 716 876-8806
   Buffalo (G-2913)

◆ Standard Motor Products Inc ....B 718 392-0200
   Long Island City (G-7364)

TI Group Auto Systems LLC ....G 315 568-7042
   Seneca Falls (G-14373)

Troy Belting and Supply Co ....D 518 272-4920
   Watervliet (G-15609)

Van Slyke Belting LLC ....G 518 283-5479
   Poestenkill (G-12805)

▲ WF Lake Corp ....E 518 798-9934
   Queensbury (G-13060)

3053 Gaskets, Packing & Sealing Devices

A L Sealing ....G 315 699-6900
   Chittenango (G-3402)

▲ Allstate Gasket & Packing Inc...........F 631 254-4050
Deer Park *(G-3835)*

American Sealing Technology..........F 631 254-0019
Deer Park *(G-3838)*

Apple Rubber Products Inc................C 716 684-7649
Lancaster *(G-6796)*

◆ Bag Arts Ltd.................................G 212 684-7020
New York *(G-8715)*

Boonville Manufacturing Corp..........G 315 942-4368
Boonville *(G-1105)*

Commercial Gaskets New York ....F 212 244-8130
New York *(G-9067)*

▲ Frank Lowe Rbr & Gasket Co Inc ....E 631 777-2707
Shirley *(G-14421)*

Gaddis Industrial Equipment..............F 516 759-3100
Glen Cove *(G-5194)*

Garlock Sealing Tech LLC.................A 315 597-4811
Palmyra *(G-12487)*

GM Components Holdings LLC...........D 716 439-2402
Lockport *(G-7081)*

Hollingsworth & Vose Company.........C 518 695-8000
Greenwich *(G-5473)*

Jed Lights Inc....................................F 516 812-5001
Deer Park *(G-3888)*

John Crane Inc...................................D 315 593-6237
Fulton *(G-5066)*

▲ Loomis Root Inc..........................F 716 564-7668
Amherst *(G-230)*

Lydall Performance Mtls US Inc ....C 315 592-8100
Fulton *(G-5070)*

Lydall Performance Mtls US Inc ....D 518 686-3400
Hoosick Falls *(G-6085)*

▲ Make-Waves Instrument Corp........E 716 681-7524
Buffalo *(G-2860)*

Micromold Products Inc....................E 914 969-2850
Yonkers *(G-16333)*

◆ Noroc Enterprises Inc..................C 718 585-3230
Bronx *(G-1325)*

▲ Prince Rubber & Plas Co Inc ....E 225 272-1653
Buffalo *(G-2931)*

▲ SAS Industries Inc.......................F 631 727-1441
Manorville *(G-7553)*

Schlegel Electronic Mtls Inc ....F 585 295-2030
Rochester *(G-13717)*

▲ Schlegel Systems Inc...................C 585 427-7200
Rochester *(G-13718)*

Seal & Design Inc..............................E 315 432-8021
Syracuse *(G-14990)*

SKF USA Inc......................................D 716 661-2600
Falconer *(G-4556)*

Technical Packaging Inc....................F 516 223-2300
Baldwin *(G-537)*

Temper Corporation...........................E 518 853-3467
Fonda *(G-4912)*

Unique Packaging Corporation ....G 514 341-5872
Champlain *(G-3319)*

Web Seal Inc.....................................E 585 546-1320
Rochester *(G-13800)*

▲ Xto Incorporated ....D 315 451-7807
Liverpool *(G-7050)*

3061 Molded, Extruded & Lathe-Cut Rubber Mechanical Goods

Apple Rubber Products Inc................C 716 684-7649
Lancaster *(G-6796)*

Bridgestone APM Company................D 419 423-9552
Sanborn *(G-14137)*

◆ Camso Manufacturing Usa Ltd........D 518 561-7528
Plattsburgh *(G-12740)*

Delford Industries Inc.......................D 845 342-3901
Middletown *(G-7904)*

Finzer Holding LLC............................E 315 597-1147
Palmyra *(G-12486)*

Mechanical Rubber Pdts Co Inc ....F 845 986-2271
Warwick *(G-15519)*

▲ Moldtech Inc................................E 716 685-3344
Lancaster *(G-6818)*

Ms Spares LLC..................................G 607 223-3024
Clay *(G-3451)*

▼ Pawling Corporation.....................C 845 373-9300
Wassaic *(G-15525)*

Pawling Engineered Pdts Inc.............C 845 855-1000
Pawling *(G-12527)*

Pilot Products Inc.............................F 718 728-2141
Long Island City *(G-7326)*

R & A Industrial Products..................G 716 823-4300
Buffalo *(G-2945)*

The Centro Company Inc ....G 914 533-2200
South Salem *(G-14525)*

▲ Triangle Rubber Co Inc.................E 631 589-9400
Bohemia *(G-1089)*

3069 Fabricated Rubber Prdts, NEC

◆ Adam Scott Designs Inc ....E 212 420-8866
New York *(G-8453)*

▲ Apple Rubber Products Inc............C 716 684-6560
Lancaster *(G-6795)*

Apple Rubber Products Inc................C 716 684-7649
Lancaster *(G-6796)*

Buffalo Lining & Fabricating...............G 716 883-6500
Buffalo *(G-2676)*

▼ Cementex Latex Corp....................F 212 741-1770
New York *(G-8944)*

Certified Health Products Inc.............E 718 339-7498
Brooklyn *(G-1658)*

▲ Chemprene Inc.............................C 845 831-2800
Beacon *(G-749)*

▲ Chemprene Holding Inc.................C 845 831-2800
Beacon *(G-750)*

Continental Latex Corp.....................F 718 783-7883
Brooklyn *(G-1683)*

Enbi Indiana Inc................................G 585 647-1627
Rochester *(G-13389)*

Enviroform Recycled Pdts Inc............G 315 789-1810
Geneva *(G-5152)*

Finzer Holding LLC............................E 315 597-1147
Palmyra *(G-12486)*

Foam Products Inc............................E 718 292-4830
Bronx *(G-1260)*

◆ Great American Industries Inc........G 607 729-9331
Vestal *(G-15379)*

▲ Hampton Art LLC..........................E 631 924-1335
Medford *(G-7710)*

Hti Recycling LLC..............................E 716 433-9294
Lockport *(G-7083)*

Hutchinson Industries Inc..................E 716 852-1435
Buffalo *(G-2802)*

Idg LLC...E 315 797-1000
Utica *(G-15274)*

Impladent Ltd...................................E 718 465-1810
Jamaica *(G-6449)*

Inflation Systems Inc........................E 914 381-8070
Mamaroneck *(G-7512)*

Jamestown Scientific Inds LLC ....F 716 665-3224
Jamestown *(G-6525)*

Kelson Products Inc..........................G 716 825-2585
Orchard Park *(G-12359)*

Life Medical Technologies LLC ....F 845 894-2121
Hopewell Junction *(G-6099)*

◆ Magic Touch Icewares Intl ....G 212 794-2852
New York *(G-10329)*

▲ Mam USA Corporation...................F 914 269-2500
Purchase *(G-13007)*

◆ Mason Industries Inc.....................C 631 348-0282
Hauppauge *(G-5708)*

▲ Mercer Rubber Co.........................C 631 348-0282
Hauppauge *(G-5713)*

Mhxco Foam Company LLC................F 518 843-8400
Amsterdam *(G-335)*

▲ Moldtech Inc................................E 716 685-3344
Lancaster *(G-6818)*

Newyork Pedorthic Associates ....G 718 236-7700
Brooklyn *(G-2214)*

▲ Package Print Technologies ....F 716 871-9905
Buffalo *(G-2904)*

Par-Foam Products Inc......................C 716 855-2066
Buffalo *(G-2905)*

▼ Pawling Corporation.....................C 845 373-9300
Wassaic *(G-15525)*

◆ Power Up Manufacturing Inc ....E 716 876-4890
Buffalo *(G-2925)*

▲ Prince Rubber & Plas Co Inc ....E 225 272-1653
Buffalo *(G-2931)*

Remedies Surgical Supplies...............G 718 599-5301
Brooklyn *(G-2339)*

Rli Schlgel Specialty Pdts LLC ....G 585 627-5919
Rochester *(G-13675)*

Rotation Dynamics Corporation..........E 585 352-9023
Spencerport *(G-14559)*

Rubber Stamps Inc............................E 212 675-1180
Mineola *(G-7998)*

▼ Rubberform Recycled Pdts LLC.......F 716 478-0404
Lockport *(G-7105)*

▲ Schlegel Systems Inc...................C 585 427-7200
Rochester *(G-13718)*

SD Christie Associates Inc ....G 914 734-1800
Peekskill *(G-12557)*

Seaway Mats Inc...............................G 518 483-2560
Malone *(G-7490)*

Short Jj Associates Inc ....F 315 986-3511
Macedon *(G-7470)*

▲ Tire Conversion Tech Inc ....E 518 372-1600
Latham *(G-6876)*

▼ Tmp Technologies Inc...................D 716 895-6100
Buffalo *(G-3012)*

Tmp Technologies Inc........................D 585 495-6231
Wyoming *(G-16253)*

▼ Traffic Logix Corporation...............G 866 915-6449
Spring Valley *(G-14583)*

▲ Triangle Rubber Co Inc.................E 631 589-9400
Bohemia *(G-1089)*

▲ Turner Bellows Inc.......................E 585 235-4456
Rochester *(G-13778)*

United Rubber Supply Co Inc ....G 212 233-6650
New York *(G-11600)*

Vehicle Manufacturers Inc.................E 631 851-1700
Hauppauge *(G-5795)*

Wall Protection Products LLC.............G 877 943-6826
Wassaic *(G-15527)*

3081 Plastic Unsupported Sheet & Film

▲ Ace Canvas & Tent Corp...............F 631 981-9705
Ronkonkoma *(G-13886)*

Albert F Stager Inc............................G 315 434-7240
East Syracuse *(G-4193)*

◆ American Acrylic Corporation.........E 631 422-2200
West Babylon *(G-15687)*

◆ API Industries Inc.........................B 845 365-2200
Orangeburg *(G-12305)*

API Industries Inc.............................C 845 365-2200
Orangeburg *(G-12306)*

▲ Astra Products Inc........................E 631 464-4747
Copiague *(G-3648)*

Berry Global Inc................................C 315 986-2161
Macedon *(G-7462)*

Berry Global Inc................................C 315 484-0397
Solvay *(G-14494)*

Berry Plastics Corporation ....B 315 986-6270
Macedon *(G-7463)*

Bfgg Investors Group LLC..................G 585 424-3456
Rochester *(G-13268)*

Clear View Bag Company Inc ....C 518 458-7153
Albany *(G-61)*

▲ Comco Plastics Inc.......................E 718 849-9000
Huntington Station *(G-6242)*

Dunmore Corporation........................D 845 279-5061
Brewster *(G-1147)*

Edco Supply Corporation...................D 718 788-8108
Brooklyn *(G-1782)*

Excellent Poly Inc.............................F 718 768-6555
Brooklyn *(G-1834)*

Farber Trucking Corp.........................E 516 378-4860
Freeport *(G-4995)*

▲ Favorite Plastic Corp....................C 718 253-7000
Brooklyn *(G-1834)*

▼ Franklin Poly Film Inc....................E 718 492-3523
Brooklyn *(G-1865)*

Great Lakes Plastics Co Inc ....E 716 896-3100
Buffalo *(G-2783)*

Integument Technologies Inc ....F 716 873-1199
Tonawanda *(G-15116)*

◆ Island Pyrochemical Inds Corp ....E 516 746-2100
Mineola *(G-7983)*

◆ Kent Chemical Corporation ....E 212 521-1700
New York *(G-10094)*

Kings Film & Sheet Inc......................E 718 624-7510
Brooklyn *(G-2032)*

Knf Clean Room Products Corp ....E 631 588-7000
Ronkonkoma *(G-13958)*

▲ Knoll Printing & Packaging Inc........E 516 621-0100
Syosset *(G-14791)*

Latham International Inc....................F 518 346-5292
Schenectady *(G-14286)*

◆ Latham International Inc................G 518 783-7776
Latham *(G-6865)*

▲ Maco Bag Corporation...................C 315 226-1000
Newark *(G-11844)*

Msi Inc...F 845 639-6683
New City *(G-8227)*

▲ Nap Industries Inc........................D 718 625-4948
Brooklyn *(G-2187)*

▲ Nationwide Tarps Incorporated ......D 518 843-1545
Amsterdam *(G-341)*

Nova Packaging Ltd Inc.....................E 914 232-8406
Katonah *(G-6637)*

Oaklee International Inc.....................D 631 436-7900
Ronkonkoma *(G-13985)*

Orafol Americas Inc..........................E 585 272-0309
Henrietta *(G-5859)*

Pace Polyethylene Mfg Co Inc............E 914 381-3000
　Harrison *(G-5557)*

Pacific Designs Intl Inc.....................G....... 718 364-2867
　Bronx *(G-1331)*

▲ Plascal Corp ....G....... 516 249-2200
　Farmingdale *(G-4710)*

Pliant LLC ....B....... 315 986-6286
　Macedon *(G-7469)*

▲ Potential Poly Bag Inc ....G....... 718 258-0800
　Brooklyn *(G-2272)*

R & F Boards & Dividers Inc ....G....... 718 331-1529
　Brooklyn *(G-2317)*

Rainbow Poly Bag Co Inc ....E....... 718 386-3500
　Brooklyn *(G-2326)*

Robeco/Ascot Products Inc ....G....... 516 248-1521
　Garden City *(G-5114)*

Sand Hill Industries Inc ....G....... 518 885-7991
　Ballston Spa *(G-586)*

▲ Scapa North America ....E....... 315 413-1111
　Liverpool *(G-7039)*

◆ Shaant Industries Inc ....E....... 716 366-3654
　Dunkirk *(G-4066)*

◆ Swimline Corp ....C....... 631 254-2155
　Edgewood *(G-4284)*

Toray Industries Inc ....G....... 212 697-8150
　New York *(G-11517)*

Tri-Seal Holdings Inc ....D....... 845 353-3300
　Blauvelt *(G-936)*

Trinity Packaging Corporation............E....... 716 668-3111
　Buffalo *(G-3020)*

▲ Turner Bellows Inc ....E....... 585 235-4456
　Rochester *(G-13778)*

Vinyl Materials Inc ....E....... 631 586-9444
　Deer Park *(G-3951)*

3082 Plastic Unsupported Profile Shapes

Chelsea Plastics Inc ....F....... 212 924-4530
　New York *(G-8980)*

▲ Comco Plastics Inc ....E....... 718 849-9000
　Huntington Station *(G-6242)*

▲ Finger Lakes Extrusion Corp ....E....... 585 905-0632
　Canandaigua *(G-3132)*

▼ Franklin Poly Film Inc ....E....... 718 492-3523
　Brooklyn *(G-1865)*

Great Lakes Plastics Co Inc ....E....... 716 896-3100
　Buffalo *(G-2783)*

Hancor Inc ....D....... 607 565-3033
　Waverly *(G-15622)*

Howard J Moore Company Inc ....E....... 631 351-8467
　Plainview *(G-12688)*

◆ Mitsui Chemicals America Inc.......E....... 914 253-0777
　Rye Brook *(G-14092)*

▲ Ontario Plastics Inc ....E....... 585 663-2644
　Rochester *(G-13591)*

3083 Plastic Laminated Plate & Sheet

▼ ADC Acquisition Company..............E....... 518 377-6471
　Niskayuna *(G-11994)*

Advanced Structures Corp ....F....... 631 667-5000
　Deer Park *(G-3830)*

Allred & Associates Inc ....E....... 315 252-2559
　Elbridge *(G-4296)*

◆ American Acrylic Corporation........E....... 631 422-2200
　West Babylon *(G-15687)*

Architctral Dsign Elements LLC..........G....... 718 218-7800
　Brooklyn *(G-1523)*

▲ Clear Cast Technologies Inc ....E....... 914 945-0848
　Ossining *(G-12403)*

Displays By Rioux Inc ....G....... 315 458-3639
　North Syracuse *(G-12039)*

▲ Favorite Plastic Corp ....C....... 718 253-7000
　Brooklyn *(G-1834)*

◆ Griffon Corporation ....E....... 212 957-5000
　New York *(G-9676)*

▲ Inland Paper Products Corp ....E....... 718 827-8150
　Brooklyn *(G-1960)*

Inter State Laminates Inc ....E....... 518 283-8355
　Poestenkill *(G-12803)*

Iridium Industries Inc..........................E....... 516 504-9700
　Great Neck *(G-5395)*

Jaguar Industries Inc ....F....... 845 947-1800
　Haverstraw *(G-5805)*

Jay Moulding Corporation ....F....... 518 237-4200
　Cohoes *(G-3507)*

◆ Nalge Nunc International Corp.......A....... 585 498-2661
　Rochester *(G-13565)*

On Time Plastics Inc ....G....... 516 442-4280
　Freeport *(G-5011)*

Strux Corp ....E....... 516 768-3969
　Lindenhurst *(G-6976)*

Synthetic Textiles Inc ....F....... 716 842-2598
　Buffalo *(G-2999)*

▲ Unico Special Products Inc............E....... 845 562-9255
　Newburgh *(G-11890)*

3084 Plastic Pipe

▲ BMC LLC.......................................E....... 716 681-7755
　Buffalo *(G-2665)*

Hancor Inc ....D....... 607 565-3033
　Waverly *(G-15622)*

Micromold Products Inc ....E....... 914 969-2850
　Yonkers *(G-16333)*

◆ National Pipe & Plastics Inc..........C....... 607 729-9381
　Vestal *(G-15381)*

North American Pipe Corp ....F....... 516 338-2863
　East Williston *(G-4249)*

▲ Prince Rubber & Plas Co Inc ....E....... 225 272-1653
　Buffalo *(G-2931)*

3085 Plastic Bottles

▲ Alphamed Bottles Inc ....E....... 631 524-5577
　Central Islip *(G-3261)*

Alpla Inc ....G....... 607 250-8101
　Cortland *(G-3754)*

▼ Capitol Plastic Products Inc ....E....... 518 627-0051
　Amsterdam *(G-322)*

◆ Chapin International Inc................C....... 585 343-3140
　Batavia *(G-608)*

◆ Chapin Manufacturing Inc ....C....... 585 343-3140
　Batavia *(G-609)*

Cortland Plastics Intl LLC ....E....... 607 662-0120
　Cortland *(G-3762)*

David Johnson ....F....... 315 493-4735
　Carthage *(G-3197)*

Intrapac International Corp ....E....... 518 561-2030
　Plattsburgh *(G-12753)*

Kybod Group LLC ....G....... 408 306-1657
　New York *(G-10146)*

Monroe Cnty Chapter Nysarc Inc ....G....... 585 698-1320
　Rochester *(G-13557)*

◆ Nalge Nunc International Corp.......A....... 585 498-2661
　Rochester *(G-13565)*

Pvc Container Corporation ....C....... 518 672-7721
　Philmont *(G-12614)*

◆ Samco Scientific LLC ....C....... 800 625-4327
　Rochester *(G-13712)*

▲ Schless Bottles Inc ....E....... 718 236-2790
　Brooklyn *(G-2386)*

3086 Plastic Foam Prdts

ABI Packaging Inc...............................E....... 716 677-2900
　West Seneca *(G-15843)*

Arm Rochester Inc..............................F....... 585 354-5077
　Rochester *(G-13245)*

Barclay Brown Corp ....F....... 718 376-7166
　Brooklyn *(G-1563)*

Berry Plastics Corporation ....E....... 315 986-6270
　Macedon *(G-7463)*

▲ Burnett Process Inc ....G....... 585 254-8080
　Rochester *(G-13288)*

C P Chemical Co Inc ....G....... 914 428-2517
　White Plains *(G-15987)*

Carlisle Construction Mtls LLC ....D....... 386 753-0786
　Montgomery *(G-8059)*

Chesu Inc ....F....... 239 564-2803
　East Hampton *(G-4119)*

Dura Foam Inc ....E....... 718 894-2488
　Maspeth *(G-7608)*

Fedex Ground Package Sys Inc ....G....... 800 463-3339
　Plattsburgh *(G-12747)*

First Qlty Packg Solutions LLC ....F....... 516 829-3030
　Great Neck *(G-5387)*

Foam Products Inc ....E....... 718 292-4830
　Bronx *(G-1260)*

▲ General Vy-Coat LLC ....E....... 718 266-6002
　Brooklyn *(G-1882)*

◆ Great American Industries Inc.......E....... 607 729-9331
　Vestal *(G-15379)*

▲ Interntnal Bus Cmmncations Inc....E....... 516 352-4505
　New Hyde Park *(G-8275)*

J & M Packaging Inc ....F....... 631 608-3069
　Hauppauge *(G-5679)*

▼ Jamestown Container Corp............C....... 716 665-4623
　Falconer *(G-4547)*

Jem Container Corp............................F....... 800 521-0145
　Plainview *(G-12692)*

▲ Knoll Printing & Packaging Inc.......E....... 516 621-0100
　Syosset *(G-14791)*

▲ Lamar Plastics Packaging Ltd.........D....... 516 378-2500
　Freeport *(G-5004)*

◆ Latham International Inc................G....... 518 783-7776
　Latham *(G-6865)*

Latham Pool Products Inc...................E....... 260 432-8731
　Latham *(G-6868)*

New York State Foam Enrgy LLC ....G....... 845 534-4656
　Cornwall *(G-3730)*

▲ Orcon Industries Corp ....D....... 585 768-7000
　Le Roy *(G-6905)*

Par-Foam Products Inc ....C....... 716 855-2066
　Buffalo *(G-2905)*

Philpac Corporation ....E....... 716 875-8005
　Buffalo *(G-2917)*

Plastpac Inc ....E....... 908 272-7200
　Brooklyn *(G-2265)*

Pliant LLC ....B....... 315 986-6286
　Macedon *(G-7469)*

▲ Printex Packaging Corporation.......D....... 631 234-4300
　Islandia *(G-6343)*

Professional Packg Svcs Inc...............E....... 518 677-5100
　Eagle Bridge *(G-4073)*

R D A Container Corporation ....E....... 585 247-2323
　Gates *(G-5142)*

Rimco Plastics Corp ....E....... 607 739-3864
　Horseheads *(G-6134)*

Saint-Gobain Prfmce Plas Corp..........C....... 518 642-2200
　Granville *(G-5355)*

▲ Shell Containers Inc ....E....... 516 352-4505
　New Hyde Park *(G-8292)*

▲ Shelter Enterprises Inc ....D....... 518 237-4100
　Cohoes *(G-3516)*

▲ Skd Distribution Corp ....E....... 718 525-6000
　Jericho *(G-6596)*

Snow Craft Co Inc ....E....... 516 739-1399
　New Hyde Park *(G-8293)*

◆ Soundcoat Company Inc ....D....... 631 242-2200
　Deer Park *(G-3938)*

Strux Corp ....E....... 516 768-3969
　Lindenhurst *(G-6976)*

Technical Packaging Inc ....F....... 516 223-2300
　Baldwin *(G-537)*

▲ Thermal Foams/Syracuse Inc ....G....... 716 874-6474
　Buffalo *(G-3009)*

Thermal Foams/Syracuse Inc ....E....... 315 699-8734
　Cicero *(G-3424)*

▼ Tmp Technologies Inc ....D....... 716 895-6100
　Buffalo *(G-3012)*

TSS Foam Industries Corp ....F....... 585 538-2321
　Caledonia *(G-3074)*

◆ W Stuart Smith Inc ....E....... 585 742-3310
　Victor *(G-15441)*

Walnut Packaging Inc ....E....... 631 293-3836
　Farmingdale *(G-4764)*

3087 Custom Compounding Of Purchased Plastic Resins

Advance Chemicals Usa Inc ....G....... 718 633-1030
　Brooklyn *(G-1464)*

Atc Plastics LLC..................................E....... 212 375-2515
　New York *(G-8660)*

Cryovac Inc ....C....... 585 436-3211
　Rochester *(G-13329)*

Lahr Recycling & Resins Inc................F....... 585 425-8608
　Fairport *(G-4502)*

▲ Marval Industries Inc ....D....... 914 381-2400
　Mamaroneck *(G-7514)*

▲ Polyset Company Inc ....E....... 518 664-6000
　Mechanicville *(G-7693)*

◆ Si Group Inc ....C....... 518 347-4200
　Schenectady *(G-14304)*

3088 Plastic Plumbing Fixtures

Allegany Laminating and Supply ....G....... 716 372-2424
　Allegany *(G-186)*

An-Cor Industrial Plastics Inc.............D....... 716 695-3141
　North Tonawanda *(G-12052)*

▼ Bow Industrial Corporation............D....... 518 561-0190
　Champlain *(G-3309)*

D & M Enterprises Incorporated..........G....... 914 937-6430
　Port Chester *(G-12816)*

Gms Hicks Street Corporation ....E....... 718 858-1010
　Brooklyn *(G-1894)*

H Rindustries......................................G....... 516 487-3825
　Mineola *(G-7979)*

▲ Independent Home Products LLC....E....... 718 541-1256
　West Hempstead *(G-15770)*

▲ ITR Industries Inc ....E....... 914 964-7063
　Yonkers *(G-16321)*

◆ Metpar Corp ....D....... 516 333-2600
　Westbury *(G-15910)*

▲ Quality Enclosures Inc ....E 631 234-0115
   Central Islip (G-3286)

3089 Plastic Prdts

▲ 311 Industries Corp.......................G 607 846-4520
   Endicott (G-4442)

3M Company ....B 716 876-1596
   Tonawanda (G-15080)

A & G Heat Sealing ....G 631 724-7764
   Smithtown (G-14472)

▲ A R Arena Products Inc ....E 585 277-1680
   Rochester (G-13195)

A R V Precision Mfg Inc ....G 631 293-9643
   Farmingdale (G-4569)

A-1 Products Inc ....G 718 789-1818
   Brooklyn (G-1440)

Aaron Tool & Mold Inc ....G 585 426-5100
   Rochester (G-13197)

▲ Abbott Industries Inc ....B 718 291-0800
   Jamaica (G-6423)

▲ Abr Molding Andy LLC ....F 212 576-1821
   Ridgewood (G-13138)

Ace Molding & Tool Inc ....G 631 567-2355
   Bohemia (G-965)

Acme Awning Co Inc ....F 718 409-1881
   Bronx (G-1195)

◆ Adirondack Plas & Recycl Inc ....E 518 746-9212
   Argyle (G-391)

▲ Adore Floors Inc..............................G 631 843-0900
   Farmingdale (G-4573)

▲ Advent Tool & Mold Inc ....C 585 254-2000
   Rochester (G-13214)

Albany International Corp ....C 607 749-7226
   Homer (G-6060)

◆ Albea Cosmetics America Inc ....E 212 371-5100
   New York (G-8507)

◆ Albest Metal Stamping Corp............E 718 388-6000
   Brooklyn (G-1477)

▲ Allen Field Co Inc ....F 631 665-2782
   Brightwaters (G-1170)

▲ Alliance Precision Plas Corp ....C 585 426-5310
   Rochester (G-13219)

Alliance Precision Plas Corp ....D 585 426-5310
   Rochester (G-13220)

Alliance-Mcalpin Ny LLC ....F 585 426-5310
   Rochester (G-13221)

▲ Allsafe Technologies Inc ....D 716 691-0400
   Amherst (G-208)

Alpha Incorporated ....G 718 765-1614
   Brooklyn (G-1490)

Aluminum Injection Mold Co LLC ....G 585 502-6087
   Le Roy (G-6895)

Amcor Rigid Packaging Usa LLC .....E 716 366-2440
   Dunkirk (G-4049)

◆ American Casting and Mfg Corp ......D 800 342-0333
   Plainview (G-12662)

American Casting and Mfg Corp ......G 516 349-7010
   Plainview (G-12663)

American Package Company Inc ......E 718 389-4444
   Brooklyn (G-1500)

American Visuals Inc........................G 631 694-6104
   Farmingdale (G-4584)

An-Cor Industrial Plastics Inc ....D 716 695-3141
   North Tonawanda (G-12052)

▲ Anka Tool & Die Inc ....E 845 268-4116
   Congers (G-3607)

▲ Anna Young Assoc Ltd ....C 516 546-4400
   Freeport (G-4985)

Apexx Omni-Graphics Inc ....D 718 326-3330
   Maspeth (G-7591)

Aqua Shield Inc ....G 631 420-4490
   West Babylon (G-15690)

Aquarium Pump & Piping Systems ...F 631 567-5555
   Sayville (G-14222)

▼ Armstrong Mold Corporation ....E 315 437-1517
   East Syracuse (G-4196)

Armstrong Mold Corporation ....D 315 437-1517
   East Syracuse (G-4197)

Atlas Fence & Railing Co Inc ....E 718 767-2200
   Whitestone (G-16088)

Auburn Vacuum Forming Co Inc ....G 315 253-2440
   Auburn (G-464)

▲ Autronic Plastics Inc.......................C 516 333-7577
   Central Islip (G-3263)

▲ Avanti Advanced Mfg Corp ....F 716 791-9001
   Buffalo (G-2652)

Avanti U S A Ltd ....F 716 695-5800
   Tonawanda (G-15087)

Aztec Tool Co Inc ....E 631 243-1144
   Edgewood (G-4262)

▲ Baird Mold Making Inc ....G 631 667-0322
   Bay Shore (G-655)

◆ Baralan Usa Inc ....E 718 849-5768
   Richmond Hill (G-13109)

Barton Tool Inc ....G 716 665-2801
   Falconer (G-4535)

Berry Global Inc ....C 315 986-2161
   Macedon (G-7462)

Berry Global Inc ....C 315 484-0397
   Solvay (G-14494)

▲ Billie-Ann Plastics Pkg Corp ....E 718 497-3409
   Brooklyn (G-1585)

Bin Optics ....G 604 257-3200
   Ithaca (G-6367)

▼ Bo-Mer Plastics LLC ....E 315 252-7216
   Auburn (G-468)

Bragley Mfg Co Inc ....E 718 622-7469
   Brooklyn (G-1605)

Brandys Mold and Tool Ctr Ltd ....F 585 334-8333
   West Henrietta (G-15787)

Bst United Corp ....F 631 777-2110
   Farmingdale (G-4594)

Buffalo Polymer Processors Inc.......E 716 537-3153
   Holland (G-6028)

Burnham Polymeric Inc.....................G 518 792-3040
   Fort Edward (G-4937)

Buttons & Trimcom Inc ....F 212 868-1971
   New York (G-8874)

C & M Products Inc ....G 315 471-3303
   Syracuse (G-14838)

◆ Cambridge Security Seals LLC ....E 845 520-4111
   Pomona (G-12806)

Capco Wai Shing LLC ....G 212 268-1976
   New York (G-8910)

Capitol Cups Inc...............................E 518 627-0051
   Amsterdam (G-321)

Carolina Precision Plas LLC ....D 631 981-0743
   Ronkonkoma (G-13922)

Cast-All Corporation ....E 516 741-4025
   Mineola (G-7965)

Castino Corporation..........................G 845 229-0341
   Hyde Park (G-6270)

Cdj Stamping Inc ....G 585 224-8120
   Rochester (G-13301)

▼ Cementex Latex Corp ....F 212 741-1770
   New York (G-8944)

Centro Inc ....B 212 791-9450
   New York (G-8959)

▲ Century Mold Company Inc ....E 585 352-8600
   Rochester (G-13306)

▲ Century Mold Mexico LLC ....G 585 352-8600
   Rochester (G-13307)

Certainteed Corporation ....B 716 827-7560
   Buffalo (G-2695)

▲ Champlain Plastics Inc.....................D 518 297-3700
   Rouses Point (G-14065)

◆ Chem-Tainer Industries Inc ....E 631 422-8300
   West Babylon (G-15702)

Chem-Tek Systems Inc ....F 631 253-3010
   Bay Shore (G-662)

Chenango Valley Tech Inc ....E 607 674-4115
   Sherburne (G-14388)

Christi Plastics Inc ....G 585 436-8510
   Rochester (G-13314)

Cjk Manufacturing LLC ....F 585 663-6370
   Rochester (G-13316)

Clifford H Jones Inc ....F 716 693-2444
   Tonawanda (G-15097)

CN Group Incorporated ....A 914 358-5690
   White Plains (G-15994)

▲ Colonie Plastics Corp ....C 631 434-6969
   Bay Shore (G-665)

▲ Commodore Machine Co Inc ....E 585 657-6916
   Bloomfield (G-943)

◆ Confer Plastics Inc ....C 800 635-3213
   North Tonawanda (G-12063)

Consolidated Container Co LLC.........F 585 343-9351
   Batavia (G-611)

Continental Latex Corp ....F 718 783-7883
   Brooklyn (G-1683)

CPI of Falconer Inc ....E 716 664-4444
   Falconer (G-4537)

Craftech ....D 518 828-5011
   Chatham (G-3330)

Craftech Industries Inc ....D 518 828-5001
   Hudson (G-6151)

▲ CSP Technologies Inc......................E 518 627-0051
   Amsterdam (G-324)

CT Industrial Supply Co Inc ....F 718 417-3226
   Brooklyn (G-1706)

▲ Currier Plastics Inc ....D 315 255-1779
   Auburn (G-471)

▲ Custom Door & Mirror Inc ....E 631 414-7725
   Farmingdale (G-4609)

▲ Custom House Engravers Inc ....E 631 567-3004
   Bohemia (G-995)

Custom Lucite Creations Inc ....F 718 871-2000
   Brooklyn (G-1712)

Custom Molding Solutions Inc ....E 585 293-1702
   Churchville (G-3410)

▲ Cy Plastics Works Inc ....D 585 229-2555
   Honeoye (G-6068)

Dacobe Enterprises LLC ....G 315 368-0093
   Utica (G-15251)

Dawnex Industries Inc ....F 718 384-0199
   Brooklyn (G-1729)

Di Domenico Packaging Co Inc ....G 718 727-5454
   Staten Island (G-14645)

Diamond Packaging Holdings LLC .....E 585 334-8030
   Rochester (G-13343)

▲ Digitac Inc ....F 732 215-4020
   Brooklyn (G-1744)

Displays By Rioux Inc ....G 315 458-3639
   North Syracuse (G-12039)

▲ Dolco LLC ....E 585 657-7777
   Bloomfield (G-946)

Dortronics Systems Inc.....................E 631 725-0505
   Sag Harbor (G-14098)

Dutchland Plastics LLC ....C 315 280-0247
   Sherrill (G-14404)

◆ E & T Plastic Mfg Co Inc ....E 718 729-6226
   Long Island City (G-7208)

East Cast Clor Compounding Inc.......G 631 491-9000
   West Babylon (G-15708)

East Pattern & Model Corp.................F 585 461-3240
   Rochester (G-13363)

East Pattern & Model Corp.................F 585 461-3240
   Rochester (G-13362)

Eastern Enterprise Corp....................F 718 727-8600
   Staten Island (G-14650)

Eastern Industrial Steel Corp ....F 845 639-9749
   New City (G-8226)

▲ Eck Plastic Arts Inc ....E 607 722-3227
   Binghamton (G-873)

Egli Machine Company Inc ....E 607 563-3663
   Sidney (G-14434)

▲ Elara Fdsrvice Disposables LLC ......G 877 893-3244
   Jericho (G-6577)

Em-Kay Molds Inc ....G 716 895-6180
   Buffalo (G-2742)

▲ Engineered Composites Inc.............E 716 362-0295
   Buffalo (G-2745)

▲ Epp Team Inc ....D 585 454-4995
   Rochester (G-13396)

Erie Engineered Products Inc ....E 716 206-0204
   Lancaster (G-6805)

Ernie Green Industries Inc ....D 585 295-8951
   Rochester (G-13398)

Ernie Green Industries Inc ....C 585 647-2300
   Rochester (G-13399)

Ernie Green Industries Inc ....E 585 647-2300
   Rochester (G-13400)

▲ Etna Products Co Inc ....F 212 989-7591
   New York (G-9413)

▲ Eugene G Danner Mfg Inc ....E 631 234-5261
   Central Islip (G-3273)

Everblock Systems LLC ....G 844 422-5625
   New York (G-9424)

▲ Extreme Molding LLC ....E 518 326-9319
   Watervliet (G-15601)

Farber Plastics Inc ....E 516 378-4860
   Freeport (G-4994)

Faro Industries Inc ....F 585 647-6000
   Rochester (G-13408)

Fbm Galaxy Inc ....F 315 463-5144
   East Syracuse (G-4210)

Fei Products LLC ....E 716 693-6230
   North Tonawanda (G-12067)

▲ Felchar Manufacturing Corp ....A 607 723-4076
   Binghamton (G-877)

Fiber Laminations Limited ....F 716 692-1825
   Tonawanda (G-15104)

▲ Fibre Materials Corp ....E 516 349-1660
   Plainview (G-12685)

▲ Finger Lakes Extrusion Corp............E 585 905-0632
   Canandaigua (G-3132)

Fluidampr ....G 716 592-1000
   Springville (G-14590)

Form A Rockland Plastics Inc............G 315 848-3300
   Cranberry Lake (G-3801)

Form-Tec Inc	E	516 867-0200	
Freeport (G-4996)			
Formatix Corp	E	631 467-3399	
Ronkonkoma (G-13939)			
Formed Plastics Inc	D	516 334-2300	
Carle Place (G-3173)			
▲ Forteq North America Inc	D	585 427-9410	
West Henrietta (G-15794)			
G and G Service	G	518 785-9247	
Latham (G-6857)			
G N R Plastics Inc	G	631 724-8758	
Smithtown (G-14478)			
▲ Gagne Associates Inc	E	800 800-5954	
Johnson City (G-6599)			
▲ Galt Industries Inc	G	212 758-0770	
New York (G-9568)			
Gen-West Associates LLC	G	315 255-1779	
Auburn (G-477)			
▲ General Composites Inc	E	518 963-7333	
Willsboro (G-16151)			
Genpak LLC	C	845 343-7971	
Middletown (G-7911)			
◆ Germanow-Simon Corporation	E	585 232-1440	
Rochester (G-13438)			
▲ Global Hanger & Display Inc	G	631 475-5900	
East Patchogue (G-4153)			
Global Marine Power Inc	E	631 208-2933	
Calverton (G-3081)			
Global Security Tech LLC	F	917 838-4507	
Cedarhurst (G-3239)			
GPM Associates LLC	E	585 335-3940	
Dansville (G-3819)			
GSE Composites Inc	F	631 389-1300	
Hauppauge (G-5664)			
H & H Hulls Inc	G	518 828-1339	
Hudson (G-6159)			
H Risch Inc	D	585 442-0110	
Rochester (G-13454)			
▲ Hamlet Products Inc	F	914 665-0307	
Mount Vernon (G-8147)			
▲ Hansa Plastics Inc	F	631 269-9050	
Kings Park (G-6673)			
Harbec Inc	D	585 265-0010	
Ontario (G-12290)			
Hart To Hart Industries Inc	G	716 492-2709	
Chaffee (G-3307)			
Hornet Group Inc	D	845 858-6400	
Port Jervis (G-12850)			
Howard Charles Inc	G	917 902-6934	
Woodbury (G-16173)			
Iadc Inc	F	718 238-0623	
Staten Island (G-14663)			
Ilion Plastics Inc	F	315 894-4868	
Ilion (G-6278)			
Illinois Tool Works Inc	D	860 435-2574	
Millerton (G-7948)			
Imco Inc	E	585 352-7810	
Spencerport (G-14556)			
Industrial Paper Tube Inc	F	718 893-5000	
Bronx (G-1281)			
◆ Ingenious Designs LLC	C	631 254-3376	
Ronkonkoma (G-13948)			
▼ Innovative Plastics Corp	C	845 359-7500	
Orangeburg (G-12320)			
Inteva Products LLC	B	248 655-8886	
New York (G-9927)			
Iridium Industries Inc	E	516 504-9700	
Great Neck (G-5395)			
▲ ISO Plastics Corp	D	914 663-8300	
Mount Vernon (G-8152)			
ITW Deltar	G	860 435-2574	
Millerton (G-7949)			
J M R Plastics Corporation	G	718 898-9825	
Middle Village (G-7879)			
J T Systematic	G	607 754-0929	
Endwell (G-4480)			
Jamestown Plastics Inc	D	716 792-4144	
Brocton (G-1181)			
Joe Pietryka Incorporated	E	845 855-1201	
Pawling (G-12526)			
JSM Vinyl Products Inc	F	516 775-4520	
New Hyde Park (G-8278)			
▲ K & H Industries Inc	E	716 312-0088	
Hamburg (G-5511)			
K & H Precision Products Inc	E	585 624-4894	
Honeoye Falls (G-6076)			
K2 Plastics Inc	G	585 494-2727	
Bergen (G-816)			
Kaneka America LLC	D	212 705-4340	
New York (G-10066)			
Kasson & Keller Inc	A	518 853-3421	
Fonda (G-4910)			
Kc Tag Co	G	518 842-6666	
Amsterdam (G-332)			
◆ Kelta Inc	G	631 789-5000	
Edgewood (G-4273)			
Kenney Manufacturing Displays	F	631 231-5563	
Bay Shore (G-686)			
Kernow North America	F	585 586-3590	
Pittsford (G-12645)			
◆ Kleer-Fax Inc	F	631 225-1100	
Amityville (G-286)			
▲ Kling Magnetics Inc	E	518 392-4000	
Chatham (G-3331)			
◆ Kobe Steel USA Holdings Inc	G	212 751-9400	
New York (G-10120)			
▲ Koonichi Inc	G	718 886-8338	
Fresh Meadows (G-5044)			
L I C Screen Printing Inc	E	516 546-7289	
Merrick (G-7858)			
L K Manufacturing Corp	E	631 243-6910	
West Babylon (G-15724)			
Leidel Corporation	E	631 244-0900	
Bohemia (G-1034)			
▲ M & M Molding Corp	C	631 582-1900	
Central Islip (G-3283)			
M I T Poly-Cart Corp	E	212 724-7290	
New York (G-10297)			
◆ Macauto Usa Inc	E	585 342-2060	
Rochester (G-13525)			
Madison Lifestyle Ny LLC	G	212 725-4002	
New York (G-10315)			
▲ Major-IPC Inc	G	845 292-2200	
Liberty (G-6925)			
Mam Molding Inc	G	607 433-2121	
Oneonta (G-12274)			
Markwik Corp	F	516 470-1990	
Hicksville (G-5928)			
▲ Marval Industries Inc	D	914 381-2400	
Mamaroneck (G-7514)			
Mdi East Inc	E	518 747-8730	
South Glens Falls (G-14514)			
Mechanical Rubber Pdts Co Inc	F	845 986-2271	
Warwick (G-15519)			
Mehr Foil Corp	G	631 648-9742	
Ronkonkoma (G-13972)			
Memory Protection Devices Inc	F	631 249-0001	
Farmingdale (G-4680)			
▲ Mercury Plastics Corp	E	718 498-5400	
Brooklyn (G-2142)			
▲ Metal Cladding Inc	D	716 434-5513	
Lockport (G-7091)			
Metropltan Data Sltons MGT Inc	F	516 586-5520	
Farmingdale (G-4682)			
Mettowee Lumber & Plastics Co	C	518 642-1100	
Granville (G-5352)			
Micromold Products Inc	E	914 969-2850	
Yonkers (G-16333)			
Midbury Industries Inc	F	516 868-0600	
Freeport (G-5009)			
Miller Technology Inc	G	631 694-2224	
Farmingdale (G-4684)			
Milne Mfg Inc	F	716 772-2536	
Gasport (G-5139)			
Minico Industries Inc	F	631 595-1455	
Bay Shore (G-693)			
▲ Mirage Moulding Mfg Inc	F	631 843-6168	
Farmingdale (G-4686)			
▲ Mold-A-Matic Corporation	E	607 433-2121	
Oneonta (G-12276)			
Mold-Rite Plastics LLC	G	518 561-1812	
Plattsburgh (G-12759)			
▲ Monarch Plastics Inc	E	716 569-2175	
Frewsburg (G-5051)			
▲ Msi-Molding Solutions Inc	E	315 736-2412	
Rome (G-13857)			
◆ Multi Packaging Solutions Inc	E	646 885-0005	
New York (G-10519)			
◆ Nalge Nunc International Corp	A	585 498-2661	
Rochester (G-13565)			
Natech Plastics Inc	E	631 580-3506	
Ronkonkoma (G-13979)			
Neo Plastics LLC	E	646 542-1499	
Brooklyn (G-2197)			
New York Cutting & Gumming Co	E	212 563-4146	
Middletown (G-7924)			
New York Manufactured Products	F	585 254-9353	
Rochester (G-13570)			
Niagara Fiberglass Inc	E	716 822-3921	
Buffalo (G-2884)			
◆ Nordon Inc	D	585 546-6200	
Rochester (G-13578)			
Nordon Inc	E	585 546-6200	
Rochester (G-13579)			
Nordon Inc	E	585 546-6200	
Rochester (G-13580)			
▲ Northeast Windows Usa Inc	E	516 378-6577	
Merrick (G-7862)			
Norwesco Inc	F	607 687-8081	
Owego (G-12435)			
◆ Novel Box Company Ltd	E	718 965-2222	
Brooklyn (G-2221)			
▲ Novelty Crystal Corp	D	718 458-6700	
Long Island City (G-7310)			
◆ Ocala Group LLC	F	516 233-2750	
New Hyde Park (G-8286)			
▲ Oneida Molded Plastics LLC	C	315 363-7980	
Oneida (G-12250)			
Oneonta Fence	G	607 433-6707	
Oneonta (G-12278)			
▲ Ontario Plastics Inc	E	585 663-2644	
Rochester (G-13591)			
P M Plastics Inc	E	716 662-1255	
Orchard Park (G-12369)			
P V C Molding Technologies	F	315 331-1212	
Newark (G-11849)			
Pace Window and Door Corp	E	585 924-8350	
Victor (G-15423)			
Pactiv Corporation	E	518 743-3100	
Glens Falls (G-5263)			
Pactiv LLC	A	585 393-3149	
Canandaigua (G-3139)			
Pactiv LLC	C	585 394-5125	
Canandaigua (G-3138)			
Pactiv LLC	C	518 793-2524	
Glens Falls (G-5264)			
Patmian LLC	B	212 758-0770	
New York (G-10769)			
▼ Pawling Corporation	C	845 373-9300	
Wassaic (G-15525)			
Pawling Engineered Pdts Inc	C	845 855-1000	
Pawling (G-12527)			
Peconic Plastics Inc	F	631 653-3676	
Quogue (G-13061)			
▲ Peek A Boo USA Inc	G	201 533-8700	
New York (G-10784)			
▲ Pelican Products Co Inc	E	718 860-3220	
Bronx (G-1334)			
Peninsula Plastics Ltd	D	716 854-3050	
Buffalo (G-2911)			
Performance Advantage Co Inc	F	716 683-7413	
Lancaster (G-6824)			
Perma Tech Inc	E	716 854-0707	
Buffalo (G-2915)			
Philcom Ltd	G	716 875-8005	
Buffalo (G-2916)			
Pietryka Plastics LLC	E	845 855-1201	
Pawling (G-12528)			
Pii Holdings Inc	G	716 876-9951	
Buffalo (G-2919)			
Piper Plastics Corp	E	631 842-6889	
Copiague (G-3668)			
Piper Plastics Corp	G	631 842-6889	
Copiague (G-3669)			
Plascoline Inc	F	917 410-5754	
New York (G-10852)			
Plastic Solutions Inc	E	631 234-9013	
Bayport (G-730)			
Plastic Sys/Gr Bflo Inc	G	716 835-7555	
Buffalo (G-2922)			
Plastic Works	G	914 576-2050	
New Rochelle (G-8349)			
Plastic-Craft Products Corp	E	845 358-3010	
West Nyack (G-15831)			
Plasticware LLC	F	845 267-0790	
Monsey (G-8043)			
Plastitel Usa Inc	G	800 667-2313	
Chazy (G-3335)			
Pleasure Chest Sales Ltd	F	212 242-2158	
New York (G-10854)			
◆ PMI Industries LLC	E	585 464-8050	
Rochester (G-13627)			
Polymer Conversions Inc	D	716 662-8550	
Orchard Park (G-12372)			
Polymer Engineered Pdts Inc	D	585 426-1811	
Rochester (G-13629)			
▲ Powertex Inc	E	518 297-4000	
Rouses Point (G-14067)			
Precision Extrusion Inc	E	518 792-1199	
Glens Falls (G-5265)			

▲ Precision Packaging Pdts Inc ....C 585 638-8200
Holley *(G-6037)*

▲ Precision Techniques Inc ....D 718 991-1440
Stony Point *(G-14747)*

Prestige Hangers Str Fixs Corp ....G 718 522-6777
Brooklyn *(G-2283)*

Primoplast Inc ....F 631 750-0680
Bohemia *(G-1066)*

▲ Prince Rubber & Plas Co Inc ....E 225 272-1653
Buffalo *(G-2931)*

▲ Printex Packaging Corporation ....D 631 234-4300
Islandia *(G-6343)*

◆ Protective Industries Inc ....B 716 876-9951
Buffalo *(G-2936)*

Pulse Plastics Products Inc ....E 718 328-5224
Bronx *(G-1346)*

Pvc Container Corporation ....C 518 672-7721
Philmont *(G-12614)*

Pvc Industries Inc ....E 518 877-8670
Clifton Park *(G-3471)*

Pylantis New York LLC ....G 310 429-5911
Groton *(G-5484)*

▲ Q Squared Design LLC ....E 212 686-8860
New York *(G-10942)*

Quality Lineals Usa Inc ....D 516 378-6577
Merrick *(G-7864)*

Quoin LLC ....A 914 967-9400
Rye *(G-14084)*

▲ R P M Industries Inc ....E 315 255-1105
Auburn *(G-492)*

▲ Rainbow Plastics Inc ....F 718 218-7288
Brooklyn *(G-2325)*

Richardson Molding LLC ....D 716 282-1261
Niagara Falls *(G-11973)*

Richlar Industries Inc ....F 315 463-5144
East Syracuse *(G-4234)*

Rimco Plastics Corp ....E 607 739-3864
Horseheads *(G-6134)*

Robinson Knife ....F 716 685-6300
Buffalo *(G-2958)*

Roechling Medical Rochester LP ....D 585 254-2000
Rochester *(G-13702)*

▲ Romold Inc ....F 585 529-4440
Rochester *(G-13705)*

▲ Roth Global Plastics Inc ....E 315 475-0100
Syracuse *(G-14979)*

Royce Associates A Ltd Partnr ....G 516 367-6298
Jericho *(G-6593)*

RSC Molding Inc ....E 516 351-9871
Freeport *(G-5020)*

Rus Auto Parts Inc ....G 800 410-2669
Brooklyn *(G-2365)*

Russell Plastics Tech Co Inc ....C 631 963-8602
Lindenhurst *(G-6971)*

Saint-Gobain Prfmce Plas Corp ....E 518 283-5963
Poestenkill *(G-12804)*

SAV Thermo Inc ....F 631 249-9444
West Babylon *(G-15746)*

▲ Schlegel Systems Inc ....C 585 427-7200
Rochester *(G-13718)*

Seal Reinforced Fiberglass Inc ....E 631 842-2230
Copiague *(G-3676)*

Seal Reinforced Fiberglass Inc ....G 631 842-2230
Copiague *(G-3677)*

Seaway Mats Inc ....G 518 483-2560
Malone *(G-7490)*

Senior Brands LLC ....G 212 213-5100
New York *(G-11190)*

Shamrock Plastic Corporation ....G 585 328-6040
Rochester *(G-13726)*

Shamrock Plastics & Tool Inc ....G 585 328-6040
Rochester *(G-13727)*

Sigma Worldwide LLC ....G 646 217-0629
New York *(G-11231)*

Silgan Plastics LLC ....C 315 536-5690
Penn Yan *(G-12594)*

Silvatrim Corp ....C 212 675-0933
New York *(G-11239)*

▲ Skd Distribution Corp ....E 718 525-6000
Jericho *(G-6596)*

Somar North America Corp ....G 716 458-0742
Olean *(G-12242)*

▲ Sonoco-Crellin Intl Inc ....B 518 392-2000
Chatham *(G-3333)*

▲ Southern Tier Plastics Inc ....F 607 723-2601
Binghamton *(G-909)*

Space Age Plstic Fbrcators Inc ....F 718 324-4062
Queens Village *(G-13026)*

Space Sign ....F 718 961-1112
College Point *(G-3565)*

Specialty Model & Mold Inc ....G 631 475-0840
Ronkonkoma *(G-14012)*

Specialty Products Inc ....E 866 869-4335
Center Moriches *(G-3248)*

Staroba Plastics Inc ....C 716 537-3153
Holland *(G-6031)*

▲ Sterling Molded Products Inc ....E 845 344-4546
Middletown *(G-7933)*

▲ Structural Industries Inc ....C 631 471-5200
Bohemia *(G-1082)*

Stuart Mold & Manufacturing ....F 716 488-9765
Falconer *(G-4558)*

◆ Summit Manufacturing LLC ....G 631 952-1570
Bay Shore *(G-719)*

▲ Surprise Plastics Inc ....C 718 492-6355
Brooklyn *(G-2480)*

◆ Swimways Corp ....C 757 460-1156
Long Island City *(G-7377)*

Syntec Technologies Inc ....D 585 768-2513
Rochester *(G-13754)*

▲ Syracuse Plastics LLC ....C 315 637-9881
Liverpool *(G-7043)*

T A Tool & Molding Inc ....F 631 293-0172
Farmingdale *(G-4748)*

Termatec Molding Inc ....F 315 483-4150
Sodus *(G-14493)*

◆ Tessy Plastics Corp ....B 315 689-3924
Skaneateles *(G-14457)*

Tessy Plastics Corp ....A 315 689-3924
Elbridge *(G-4298)*

▲ Thermold Corporation ....C 315 697-3924
Canastota *(G-3158)*

Think Green Junk Removal Inc ....G 845 297-7771
Wappingers Falls *(G-15499)*

▲ Tii Technologies Inc ....E 516 364-9300
Edgewood *(G-4287)*

Tint World ....G 631 458-1999
Medford *(G-7725)*

Titherington Design & Mfg ....F 518 324-2205
Plattsburgh *(G-12785)*

▲ Toolroom Express Inc ....D 607 723-5373
Conklin *(G-3630)*

Toray Industries Inc ....G 212 697-8150
New York *(G-11517)*

▲ Transpo Industries Inc ....E 914 636-1000
New Rochelle *(G-8356)*

Tri-State Window Factory Corp ....D 631 667-8600
Deer Park *(G-3942)*

Trico Holding Corporation ....A 716 852-5700
Buffalo *(G-3019)*

Trimac Molding Services ....G 607 967-2900
Bainbridge *(G-527)*

Tully Products Inc ....G 716 773-3166
Grand Island *(G-5346)*

▲ TVI Imports LLC ....G 631 793-3077
Massapequa Park *(G-7661)*

Unifab Inc ....G 585 235-1760
Rochester *(G-13782)*

Unifuse LLC ....F 845 889-4000
Staatsburg *(G-14601)*

United Plastics Inc ....G 718 389-2255
Brooklyn *(G-2539)*

Usheco Inc ....G 845 658-9200
Kingston *(G-6721)*

▲ Van Blarcom Closures Inc ....C 718 855-3810
Brooklyn *(G-2551)*

◆ Viele Manufacturing Corp ....B 718 893-2200
Bronx *(G-1392)*

Villeroy & Boch Usa Inc ....F 212 213-8149
New York *(G-11684)*

Vinyl Materials Inc ....E 631 586-9444
Deer Park *(G-3951)*

Vinyline Window and Door Inc ....F 914 476-3500
Yonkers *(G-16355)*

Visitainer Corp ....E 718 636-0300
Brooklyn *(G-2564)*

Vitarose Corp of America ....G 718 951-9700
Brooklyn *(G-2565)*

Vpulse Inc ....G 646 729-5675
Brooklyn *(G-2570)*

▲ W Kintz Plastics Inc ....F 518 296-8513
Howes Cave *(G-6144)*

Waddington North America Inc ....C 585 638-8200
Holley *(G-6039)*

Weather Products Corporation ....G 315 474-8593
Syracuse *(G-15024)*

Weber Intl Packg Co LLC ....D 518 561-8282
Plattsburgh *(G-12790)*

Window Tech Systems Inc ....E 518 899-9000
Ballston Spa *(G-589)*

Zone Fabricators Inc ....F 718 272-0200
Ozone Park *(G-12470)*

31 LEATHER AND LEATHER PRODUCTS

3111 Leather Tanning & Finishing

A-1 Products Inc ....G 718 789-1818
Brooklyn *(G-1440)*

◆ Adam Scott Designs Inc ....E 212 420-8866
New York *(G-8453)*

▲ Androme Leather Inc ....F 518 773-7945
Gloversville *(G-5277)*

Ariel Tian LLC ....G 212 457-1266
Forest Hills *(G-4917)*

▲ Arrow Leather Finishing Inc ....E 518 762-3121
Johnstown *(G-6610)*

▲ Aston Leather Inc ....G 212 481-2760
New York *(G-8656)*

Automotive Leather Group LLC ....F 516 627-4000
Great Neck *(G-5368)*

▲ Baker Products Inc ....E 212 459-2323
White Plains *(G-15978)*

▲ Carville National Leather Corp ....F 518 762-1634
Johnstown *(G-6613)*

Centric Brands Inc ....E 646 582-6000
New York *(G-8955)*

▲ Colonial Tanning Corporation ....C 518 725-7171
Gloversville *(G-5281)*

◆ Corium Corporation ....F 914 381-0100
Mamaroneck *(G-7505)*

▲ Cromwell Leather Company Inc ....F 914 381-0100
Mamaroneck *(G-7506)*

▲ Edsim Leather Co Inc ....E 212 695-8500
New York *(G-9323)*

Givi Inc ....F 212 586-5029
New York *(G-9616)*

Graphic Image Associates LLC ....D 631 249-9600
Melville *(G-7787)*

Hastings Hide Inc ....E 516 295-2400
Inwood *(G-6295)*

◆ Hat Attack Inc ....E 718 994-1000
Bronx *(G-1273)*

Hohenforst Splitting Co Inc ....E 518 725-0012
Gloversville *(G-5285)*

▲ Jaclyn LLC ....D 201 909-6000
New York *(G-9963)*

John Gailer Inc ....E 212 243-5662
Long Island City *(G-7254)*

Justin Gregory Inc ....G 631 249-5187
Deer Park *(G-3890)*

Kamali Automotive Group Inc ....F 516 627-4000
Great Neck *(G-5398)*

▲ Kamali Group Inc ....F 516 627-4000
Great Neck *(G-5399)*

Leather Hub Worldwide LLC ....C 310 386-2247
New York *(G-10186)*

▲ Legendary Auto Interiors Ltd ....E 315 331-1212
Newark *(G-11843)*

Mohawk River Leather Works ....F 518 853-3900
Fultonville *(G-5080)*

◆ Myers Group LLC ....G 973 761-6414
New York *(G-10525)*

▲ Pan American Leathers Inc ....E 978 741-4150
New York *(G-10744)*

▲ Pearl Leather Finishers Inc ....F 518 762-4543
Johnstown *(G-6624)*

▲ Pearl Leather Group LLC ....E 516 627-4047
Great Neck *(G-5412)*

▲ Rainbow Leather Inc ....F 718 939-8762
College Point *(G-3562)*

Shadal LLC ....E 212 319-5946
New York *(G-11200)*

▲ Simco Leather Corporation ....E 518 762-7100
Johnstown *(G-6628)*

▲ Street Smart Designs Inc ....E 646 865-0056
New York *(G-11370)*

Studio One Leather Design Inc ....F 212 760-1701
New York *(G-11379)*

System of AME Binding ....E 631 390-8560
Central Islip *(G-3290)*

Tandy Leather Factory Inc ....G 845 480-3588
Nyack *(G-12146)*

Tradition Leather Inc ....E 518 725-2555
Gloversville *(G-5297)*

Vic Demayos Inc ....G 845 626-4343
Accord *(G-1)*

◆ Wood & Hyde Leather Co Inc ....E 518 725-7105
Gloversville *(G-5301)*

S I C

3131 Boot & Shoe Cut Stock & Findings

▲ Age Manufacturers Inc ....D 718 927-0048
Brooklyn *(G-1471)*
Counter Evolution ....G 212 647-7505
New York *(G-9109)*
Custom Countertops Inc ....G 716 685-2871
Depew *(G-3977)*
Custom Design Kitchens Inc ....F 518 355-4446
Duanesburg *(G-4044)*
MBA Orthotics Inc ....G 631 392-4755
Bay Shore *(G-691)*
Premier Brands America Inc ....F 718 325-3000
Bronx *(G-1343)*
▲ Premier Brands America Inc ....C 914 667-6200
White Plains *(G-16054)*
Priscilla Quart Co Firts ....G 516 365-2755
Manhasset *(G-7540)*
▲ Randall Loeffler Inc ....E 212 226-8787
New York *(G-10980)*

3142 House Slippers

RG Barry Corporation ....F 212 244-3145
New York *(G-11033)*

3143 Men's Footwear, Exc Athletic

Air Skate & Air Jump Corp ....G 212 967-1201
New York *(G-8503)*
▲ Air Skate & Air Jump Corp ....F 212 967-1201
Brooklyn *(G-1473)*
Artisan Boot & Shoe Co LLC ....F 585 813-2825
Batavia *(G-602)*
▲ Bh Brand Inc ....E 212 239-1635
New York *(G-8777)*
▲ Detny Footwear Inc ....G 212 423-1040
New York *(G-9210)*
▲ GH Bass & Co ....E 646 768-4600
New York *(G-9607)*
◆ Jerry Miller Molded Shoes Inc ....F 716 881-3920
Buffalo *(G-2820)*
Kcp Holdco Inc ....F 212 265-1500
New York *(G-10086)*
▲ Kenneth Cole Productions Inc ....B 212 265-1500
New York *(G-10089)*
Lake View Manufacturing LLC ....F 315 364-7892
King Ferry *(G-6671)*
▲ Neumann Jutta New York Inc ....F 212 982-7048
New York *(G-10572)*
Nicholas Kirkwood LLC ....F 646 559-5239
New York *(G-10622)*
▲ Pedifix Inc ....E 845 277-2850
Brewster *(G-1157)*
Phillips-Van Heusen Europe ....F 212 381-3500
New York *(G-10829)*
◆ Pvh Corp ....D 212 381-3500
New York *(G-10933)*
Pvh Corp ....G 212 549-6000
New York *(G-10934)*
▲ Steven Madden Ltd ....B 718 446-1800
Long Island City *(G-7370)*
T O Dey Service Corp ....F 212 683-6300
New York *(G-11418)*
◆ Tapestry Inc ....B 212 594-1850
New York *(G-11434)*
▲ Tic TAC Toes Mfg Corp ....D 518 773-8187
Gloversville *(G-5296)*
Tru Mold Shoes Inc ....F 716 881-4484
Buffalo *(G-3022)*

3144 Women's Footwear, Exc Athletic

▲ Adl Design Inc ....G 516 949-6658
Huntington *(G-6198)*
Attitudes Footwear Inc ....G 212 754-9113
New York *(G-8676)*
▲ Bh Brand Inc ....E 212 239-1635
New York *(G-8777)*
▲ Detny Footwear Inc ....G 212 423-1040
New York *(G-9210)*
▲ Everlast Worldwide Inc ....E 212 239-0990
New York *(G-9428)*
▲ GH Bass & Co ....E 646 768-4600
New York *(G-9607)*
Jag Footwear ACC & Ret Corp ....A 800 999-1877
New York *(G-9967)*
◆ Jerry Miller Molded Shoes Inc ....F 716 881-3920
Buffalo *(G-2820)*
▲ Kenneth Cole Productions Inc ....B 212 265-1500
New York *(G-10089)*
Lake View Manufacturing LLC ....F 315 364-7892
King Ferry *(G-6671)*
Lsil & Co Inc ....G 914 761-0998
White Plains *(G-16026)*
▲ Mango Usa Inc ....E 718 998-6050
Brooklyn *(G-2106)*
▲ Neumann Jutta New York Inc ....F 212 982-7048
New York *(G-10572)*
Nicholas Kirkwood LLC ....F 646 559-5239
New York *(G-10622)*
▲ Pedifix Inc ....E 845 277-2850
Brewster *(G-1157)*
S & W Ladies Wear ....G 718 431-2800
Brooklyn *(G-2374)*
Scott Silverstein Llc ....G 212 781-1818
New York *(G-11169)*
▲ Steven Madden Ltd ....B 718 446-1800
Long Island City *(G-7370)*
T O Dey Service Corp ....F 212 683-6300
New York *(G-11418)*
◆ Tapestry Inc ....B 212 594-1850
New York *(G-11434)*
▲ Tic TAC Toes Mfg Corp ....D 518 773-8187
Gloversville *(G-5296)*
Tru Mold Shoes Inc ....F 716 881-4484
Buffalo *(G-3022)*

3149 Footwear, NEC

Custom Sports Lab Inc ....G 212 832-1648
New York *(G-9135)*
▲ Everlast Worldwide Inc ....E 212 239-0990
New York *(G-9428)*
▲ GH Bass & Co ....E 646 768-4600
New York *(G-9607)*
Kicks Closet Sportswear Inc ....G 347 577-0857
Bronx *(G-1292)*
La Strada Dance Footwear Inc ....G 631 242-1401
Deer Park *(G-3895)*
▲ Mango Usa Inc ....E 718 998-6050
Brooklyn *(G-2106)*
Mayberry Shoe Company Inc ....G 315 692-4086
Manlius *(G-7549)*
McM Products USA Inc ....E 646 756-4090
New York *(G-10401)*
▲ Steven Madden Ltd ....B 718 446-1800
Long Island City *(G-7370)*
▲ Vsg International LLC ....G 718 300-8171
Brooklyn *(G-2571)*

3151 Leather Gloves & Mittens

American Target Marketing Inc ....E 518 725-4369
Gloversville *(G-5276)*
▲ Fieldtex Products Inc ....C 585 427-2940
Rochester *(G-13409)*
◆ Fownes Brothers & Co Inc ....E 800 345-6837
New York *(G-9525)*
Fownes Brothers & Co Inc ....E 518 752-4411
Gloversville *(G-5283)*
▲ J & D Walter Distributors Inc ....F 518 449-1606
Glenmont *(G-5238)*
Protech (llc) ....E 518 725-7785
Gloversville *(G-5289)*
Samco LLC ....E 518 725-4705
Gloversville *(G-5290)*
USA Sewing Inc ....E 315 792-8017
Utica *(G-15297)*

3161 Luggage

▲ 212 Biz LLC ....G 212 391-4444
New York *(G-8393)*
◆ Adam Scott Designs Inc ....E 212 420-8866
New York *(G-8453)*
Atlantic Specialty Co Inc ....E 845 356-2502
Monsey *(G-8036)*
Barclay Brown Corp ....F 718 376-7166
Brooklyn *(G-1563)*
Bragley Mfg Co Inc ....E 718 622-7469
Brooklyn *(G-1605)*
Calvin Klein Inc ....E 212 292-9000
New York *(G-8894)*
▲ Carry-All Canvas Bag Co Inc ....G 718 375-4230
Brooklyn *(G-1649)*
Deluxe Travel Store Inc ....G 718 435-8111
Brooklyn *(G-1736)*
▲ Dlx Industries Inc ....D 718 272-9420
Brooklyn *(G-1753)*
Donna Morgan LLC ....E 212 575-2550
New York *(G-9251)*
Ead Cases ....F 845 343-2111
Middletown *(G-7906)*
Fibre Case & Novelty Co Inc ....G 212 254-6060
New York *(G-9488)*
▲ Fieldtex Products Inc ....C 585 427-2940
Rochester *(G-13409)*
◆ Fish & Crown Ltd ....D 212 707-9603
New York *(G-9506)*
Goyard Inc ....G 212 813-0005
New York *(G-9650)*
Goyard Miami LLC ....G 212 813-0005
New York *(G-9651)*
▲ Goyard NM Beverly Hills LLC ....G 212 355-3872
New York *(G-9652)*
Hornet Group Inc ....D 845 858-6400
Port Jervis *(G-12850)*
Junk In My Trunk Inc ....G 631 420-5865
Farmingdale *(G-4658)*
▲ Lo & Sons Inc ....F 917 775-4025
Brooklyn *(G-2082)*
▲ Merzon Leather Co Inc ....C 718 782-6260
Brooklyn *(G-2144)*
▲ Prepac Designs Inc ....G 914 524-7800
Yonkers *(G-16344)*
Progressive Fibre Products Co ....E 212 566-2720
New York *(G-10906)*
Randa Accessories Lea Gds LLC ....D 212 354-5100
New York *(G-10979)*
Rhino Trunk & Case Inc ....F 585 244-4553
Rochester *(G-13671)*
▲ Rimowa Inc ....F 214 360-4268
New York *(G-11044)*
▲ Roadie Products Inc ....E 631 567-8588
Holbrook *(G-6018)*
◆ Rose Trunk Mfg Co Inc ....F 516 766-6686
Oceanside *(G-12187)*
Sigma Worldwide LLC ....G 646 217-0629
New York *(G-11231)*
▲ Three Point Ventures LLC ....F 585 697-3444
Rochester *(G-13767)*
▲ Trafalgar Company LLC ....G 212 768-8800
New York *(G-11531)*
▲ Trunk & Trolley LLC ....G 212 947-9001
New York *(G-11551)*

3171 Handbags & Purses

▲ Affordable Luxury Group Inc ....G 631 523-9266
New York *(G-8490)*
▲ Ahq LLC ....E 212 328-1560
New York *(G-8498)*
Atalla Handbags Inc ....G 718 965-5500
Brooklyn *(G-1544)*
▲ Bagznyc Corp ....F 212 643-8202
New York *(G-8718)*
▲ Baikal Inc ....D 212 239-4650
New York *(G-8719)*
Coach Inc ....F 718 760-0624
Elmhurst *(G-4333)*
◆ Coach Services Inc ....E 212 594-1850
New York *(G-9043)*
Dani Accessories Inc ....E 631 692-4505
Cold Spring Harbor *(G-3527)*
◆ Essex Manufacturing Inc ....D 212 239-0080
New York *(G-9404)*
Formart Corp ....F 212 819-1819
New York *(G-9516)*
Jag Footwear ACC & Ret Corp ....A 800 999-1877
New York *(G-9967)*
Kcp Holdco Inc ....F 212 265-1500
New York *(G-10086)*
▲ Kenneth Cole Productions Inc ....B 212 265-1500
New York *(G-10089)*
McM Products USA Inc ....E 646 756-4090
New York *(G-10401)*
Paradiso Cnsld Entps LLC ....G 585 924-3937
Rochester *(G-13609)*
▲ Pure Trade Us Inc ....E 212 256-1600
New York *(G-10928)*
Quilted Koala Ltd ....F 800 223-5678
New York *(G-10957)*
◆ Renco Group Inc ....G 212 541-6000
New York *(G-11012)*
▲ Roadie Products Inc ....E 631 567-8588
Holbrook *(G-6018)*
▲ Rodem Incorporated ....F 212 779-7122
New York *(G-11070)*
Tapestry Inc ....G 212 615-2082
New York *(G-11433)*
◆ Tapestry Inc ....B 212 594-1850
New York *(G-11434)*

3172 Personal Leather Goods

▲ Ada Gems Corp ....G 212 719-0100
New York *(G-8452)*

Astucci US Ltd ....F 718 752-9700
  Long Island City (G-7169)
▲ Astucci US Ltd ....G 212 725-3171
  New York (G-8658)
Atlantic Specialty Co Inc ....E 845 356-2502
  Monsey (G-8036)
▲ Baker Products Inc ....G 212 459-2323
  White Plains (G-15978)
▲ Bauble Bar Inc ....E 646 846-2044
  New York (G-8740)
▲ Datamax International Inc ....E 212 693-0933
  New York (G-9175)
Elco Manufacturing Co Inc ....F 516 767-3577
  Port Washington (G-12877)
▲ Excelled Sheepskin & Lea Coat ...F 212 594-5843
  New York (G-9443)
Fahrenheit NY Inc ....G 212 354-6554
  New York (G-9462)
▲ First Manufacturing Co Inc ....E 516 763-0400
  Oceanside (G-12172)
Form A Rockland Plastics Inc ....G 315 848-3300
  Cranberry Lake (G-3801)
Grownbeans Inc ....G 212 989-3486
  New York (G-9686)
▲ Helgen Industries Inc ....C 631 841-6300
  Amityville (G-269)
◆ Hemisphere Novelties Inc ....E 914 378-4100
  Yonkers (G-16318)
House of Portfolios Co Inc ....E 212 206-7323
  New York (G-9824)
House of Portfolios Co Inc ....F 212 206-7323
  New York (G-9825)
International Time Products ....G 516 931-0005
  Jericho (G-6584)
▲ Jaclyn LLC...............................D 201 909-6000
  New York (G-9963)
Just Brass Inc ....G 212 724-5447
  New York (G-10045)
K Displays...................................F 718 854-6045
  Brooklyn (G-2017)
Leather Artisan ....G 518 359-3102
  Childwold (G-3401)
▲ M G New York Inc ....F 212 371-5566
  New York (G-10293)
▲ Merzon Leather Co Inc ....C 718 782-6260
  Brooklyn (G-2144)
Mhg Studio Inc ....G 212 674-7610
  New York (G-10449)
▲ Neumann Jutta New York Inc .....F 212 982-7048
  New York (G-10572)
▲ Penthouse Manufacturing Co Inc ...B 516 379-1300
  Freeport (G-5014)
Premier Glass New York Inc ....G 718 967-7179
  Staten Island (G-14693)
Randa Accessories Lea Gds LLC ...D 212 354-5100
  New York (G-10979)
Roma Industries LLC....................G 212 268-0723
  New York (G-11078)
Slim Line Case Co Inc ....F 585 546-3639
  Rochester (G-13733)
◆ Tapestry Inc ....B 212 594-1850
  New York (G-11434)
▲ Trafalgar Company LLC ....G 212 768-8800
  New York (G-11531)
Unique Packaging Corporation .....G 514 341-5872
  Champlain (G-3319)

3199 Leather Goods, NEC

Adirondack Leather Pdts Inc ....F 607 547-5798
  Fly Creek (G-4908)
Billykirk.......................................G 212 217-0679
  New York (G-8794)
▲ Courtlandt Boot Jack Co Inc ....E 718 445-6200
  Flushing (G-4846)
Deluxe Travel Store Inc ....G 718 435-8111
  Brooklyn (G-1736)
▲ Dvf Studio LLC ....D 212 741-6607
  New York (G-9283)
Dvf Studio LLC.............................G 646 576-8009
  New York (G-9284)
East West Global Sourcing Inc .....G 917 887-2286
  Brooklyn (G-1775)
Equicenter Inc ....E 585 742-2522
  Honeoye Falls (G-6071)
Fahrenheit NY Inc ....G 212 354-6554
  New York (G-9462)
▼ Finger Lakes Lea Crafters LLC ...F 315 252-4107
  Auburn (G-475)
▲ First Manufacturing Co Inc ....E 516 763-0400
  Oceanside (G-12172)

▲ Helgen Industries Inc ....C 631 841-6300
  Amityville (G-269)
▲ Import-Export Corporation ....F 718 707-0880
  Long Island City (G-7246)
▲ Jaclyn LLC...............................D 201 909-6000
  New York (G-9963)
Kamali Leather LLC ....G 518 762-2522
  Johnstown (G-6621)
Leather Outlet ....G 518 668-0328
  Lake George (G-6757)
Max 200 Performance Dog Eqp ...E 315 776-9588
  Port Byron (G-12810)
McM Products USA Inc ....E 646 756-4090
  New York (G-10401)
▲ Star Desk Pad Co Inc ....E 914 963-9400
  Yonkers (G-16350)
◆ Tucano Usa Inc ....G 212 966-9211
  New York (G-11557)
◆ Unique Overseas Inc ....G 516 466-9792
  Great Neck (G-5429)

32 STONE, CLAY, GLASS, AND CONCRETE PRODUCTS

3211 Flat Glass

▲ A Sunshine Glass & Aluminum ...E 718 932-8080
  Woodside (G-16195)
Corning Incorporated ....D 315 379-3200
  Canton (G-3165)
Corning Incorporated ....A 607 974-9000
  Painted Post (G-12473)
Elite Glass Fabrication LLC ....B 201 333-8100
  New York (G-9344)
Europrojects Intl Inc ....F 917 262-0795
  New York (G-9421)
Express Building Supply Inc ....E 516 608-0379
  Oceanside (G-12171)
▲ Global Glass Corp ....G 516 681-2309
  Hicksville (G-5912)
Guardian Industries LLC ....B 315 787-7000
  Geneva (G-5157)
▲ Hecht & Sohn Glass Co Inc........G 718 782-8295
  Brooklyn (G-1930)
▲ Lafayette Mirror & Glass Co........G 718 768-0660
  New Hyde Park (G-8279)
▲ Lazer Marble & Granite Corp ......G 718 859-9644
  Brooklyn (G-2049)
▼ Manhattan Shade & Glass Co Inc ...E 212 288-5616
  Great Neck (G-5402)
Manhattan Shade & Glass Co Inc ...E 212 288-5616
  Hauppauge (G-5707)
Mr Glass Tempering LLC...............F 718 576-3826
  Brooklyn (G-2176)
◆ Munn Works LLC ....E 914 665-6100
  Mount Vernon (G-8164)
Pilkington North America Inc ....C 315 438-3341
  Syracuse (G-14964)
RG Glass Creations Inc ....E 212 675-0030
  New York (G-11034)
Saxon Glass Technologies Inc .....F 607 587-9630
  Alfred (G-182)
◆ Schott Corporation ....D 914 831-2200
  Elmsford (G-4428)
Schott Gemtron Corporation ....C 423 337-3522
  Elmsford (G-4429)
▲ Schott Solar Pv LLC ....G 888 457-6527
  Elmsford (G-4432)
South Seneca Vinyl LLC...............G 315 585-6050
  Romulus (G-13880)
▼ Stefan Sydor Optics Inc ....E 585 271-7300
  Rochester (G-13745)
▲ Tempco Glass Fabrication LLC ...D 718 461-6888
  Flushing (G-4898)
Twin Pane Insulated GL Co Inc......F 631 924-1060
  Yaphank (G-16276)
Window-Fix Inc............................E 718 854-3475
  Brooklyn (G-2589)
▲ Zered Inc ....F 718 353-7464
  College Point (G-3568)

3221 Glass Containers

Anchor Glass Container Corp ....B 607 737-1933
  Elmira Heights (G-4374)
◆ Baralan Usa Inc ....E 718 849-5768
  Richmond Hill (G-13109)
Certainteed Corporation ....C 716 823-3684
  Lackawanna (G-6740)
▲ Glopak USA Corp ....E 844 445-6725
  Hicksville (G-5913)

Intrapac International Corp ....C 518 561-2030
  Plattsburgh (G-12753)
◆ Lidestri Foods Inc ....B 585 377-7700
  Fairport (G-4504)
Owens-Brockway Glass Cont Inc ...C 315 258-3211
  Auburn (G-489)
Pennsauken Packing Company LLC ...G 585 377-7700
  Fairport (G-4514)
▲ Rocco Bormioli Glass Co Inc ......E 212 719-0606
  New York (G-11066)
▲ Saint Gobain Grains & Powders ...A 716 731-8200
  Niagara Falls (G-11976)
◆ Schott Corporation ....D 914 831-2200
  Elmsford (G-4428)
▲ SGD North America ....E 212 753-4200
  New York (G-11198)
SGD Pharma Packaging Inc ....F 212 223-7100
  New York (G-11199)
Velvet Healing By Alma Corp ....G 347 271-4220
  Bronx (G-1390)

3229 Pressed & Blown Glassware, NEC

Architectural Glass Inc.................F 845 831-3116
  Beacon (G-748)
▼ Bedford Downing Glass ....G 718 418-6409
  Brooklyn (G-1570)
Biolitec Inc ....E 413 525-0600
  New York (G-8798)
▲ Bronx Wstchester Tempering Inc ...E 914 663-9400
  Mount Vernon (G-8126)
Co-Optics America Lab Inc ....E 607 432-0557
  Oneonta (G-12264)
Complete Fiber Solutions Inc ....G 718 828-8900
  Bronx (G-1230)
◆ Corning Incorporated ....A 607 974-9000
  Corning (G-3705)
Corning Incorporated ....G 607 974-9000
  Corning (G-3706)
Corning Incorporated ....E 607 974-1274
  Painted Post (G-12472)
Corning Incorporated ....G 607 974-9000
  Corning (G-3707)
Corning Incorporated ....D 315 379-3200
  Canton (G-3165)
Corning Incorporated ....E 607 433-3100
  Oneonta (G-12269)
Corning Incorporated ....E 607 248-1200
  Corning (G-3708)
Corning Incorporated ....G 646 521-9600
  New York (G-9105)
Corning Incorporated ....E 607 974-4488
  Corning (G-3709)
Corning Incorporated ....E 607 974-8496
  Corning (G-3710)
Corning Incorporated ....A 607 974-9000
  Painted Post (G-12473)
▼ Corning International Corp ....G 607 974-9000
  Corning (G-3711)
Corning Specialty Mtls Inc ....G 607 974-9000
  Corning (G-3713)
Corning Tropel Corporation ....C 585 377-3200
  Fairport (G-4494)
◆ Corning Vitro Corporation ....A 607 974-8605
  Corning (G-3714)
▲ Daylight Technology USA Inc ......G 973 255-8100
  Maspeth (G-7605)
▲ Depp Glass Inc ....F 718 784-8500
  Long Island City (G-7200)
Formcraft Display Products ....G 914 632-1410
  New Rochelle (G-8330)
▲ Gillinder Brothers Inc ....D 845 856-5375
  Port Jervis (G-12849)
Glass Menagerie Inc ....G 845 754-8344
  Westbrookville (G-15859)
Glasteel Parts & Services Inc ....E 585 235-1010
  Rochester (G-13442)
▲ Gray Glass Inc ....E 718 217-2943
  Queens Village (G-13020)
Ion Optics Inc ....F 518 339-6853
  Albany (G-89)
▲ Jay Strongwater Holdings LLC.....A 646 657-0558
  New York (G-9980)
▲ Jinglebell Inc ....G 914 219-5395
  Armonk (G-399)
◆ King Research Inc ....E 718 788-0122
  Brooklyn (G-2028)
▲ Led Lumina USA LLC ....G 631 750-4433
  Bohemia (G-1032)
◆ Lighting Holdings Intl LLC...........A 845 306-1850
  Purchase (G-13006)

S I C

▲ Match Eyewear LLC ....E 516 877-0170
Westbury *(G-15908)*

▼ Navitar Inc ....D 585 359-4000
Rochester *(G-13568)*

New York Enrgy Synthetics Inc ....G 212 634-4787
New York *(G-10596)*

Niche Design Inc ....F 212 777-2101
Beacon *(G-755)*

Owens Corning Sales LLC ....B 518 475-3600
Feura Bush *(G-4792)*

▲ Pasabahce USA ....G 212 683-1600
New York *(G-10766)*

Photonic Controls LLC ....F 607 562-4585
Horseheads *(G-6132)*

Schott Corporation ....D 315 255-2791
Auburn *(G-494)*

◆ Schott Corporation ....D 914 831-2200
Elmsford *(G-4428)*

▲ Schott North America Inc ....D 914 831-2200
Elmsford *(G-4431)*

▲ Scientifics Direct Inc ....F 716 773-7500
Tonawanda *(G-15139)*

Semrok Inc ....D 585 594-7050
Rochester *(G-13723)*

Somers Stain Glass Inc ....F 631 586-7772
Deer Park *(G-3937)*

▼ Stefan Sydor Optics Inc ....E 585 271-7300
Rochester *(G-13745)*

◆ Volpi Manufacturing USA Co Inc ......E 315 255-1737
Auburn *(G-502)*

3231 Glass Prdts Made Of Purchased Glass

Adirondack Stained Glass Works ....G 518 725-0387
Gloversville *(G-5275)*

Apf Management Company LLC ....C 914 665-5400
Yonkers *(G-16286)*

Apf Manufacturing Company LLC ......E 914 963-6300
Yonkers *(G-16287)*

Armoured One LLC ....C 315 720-4186
Syracuse *(G-14816)*

Batavia Precision Glass LLC ....G 585 343-6050
Buffalo *(G-2656)*

Benson Industries Inc ....F 212 779-3230
New York *(G-8758)*

C B Management Services Inc..........F 845 735-2300
Pearl River *(G-12529)*

Carvart Glass Inc ....E 212 675-0030
New York *(G-8926)*

Community Glass Inc ....G 607 737-8860
Elmira *(G-4344)*

▲ Depp Glass Inc ....F 718 784-8500
Long Island City *(G-7200)*

Dillmeier Enterprises Inc ....F 800 325-0596
Garden City *(G-5095)*

▲ Dundy Glass & Mirror Corp..........E 718 723-5800
Springfield Gardens *(G-14588)*

Dunlea Whl GL & Mirror Inc ....G 914 664-5277
Mount Vernon *(G-8140)*

Executive Mirror Doors Inc ....G 631 234-1090
Ronkonkoma *(G-13937)*

Exquisite Glass & Stone Inc ....G 718 937-9266
Astoria *(G-422)*

Flickinger Glassworks Inc ....G 718 875-1531
Brooklyn *(G-1854)*

Flour City Growlers Inc ....F 585 360-8709
Rochester *(G-13414)*

G & M Clearview Inc..............G 845 781-4877
Monroe *(G-8021)*

▲ Glassfab Inc ....E 585 262-4000
Rochester *(G-13441)*

▲ Global Glass Corp ....G 516 681-2309
Hicksville *(G-5912)*

▲ Gmd Industries Inc ....G 718 445-8779
College Point *(G-3543)*

Granville Glass & Granite ....G 518 812-0492
Hudson Falls *(G-6189)*

▲ Gray Glass Inc ....E 718 217-2943
Queens Village *(G-13020)*

▲ Hecht & Sohn Glass Co Inc ....G 718 782-8295
Brooklyn *(G-1930)*

Immco Diagnostics Inc ....G 716 691-0091
Buffalo *(G-2807)*

▲ Jimmy Crystal New York Co Ltd ......E 212 594-0858
New York *(G-10006)*

▲ Jinglebell Inc ....G 914 219-5395
Armonk *(G-399)*

▲ Kasson & Keller Inc ....A 518 853-3421
Fonda *(G-4910)*

▲ Lafayette Mirror & Glass Co..........G 718 768-0660
New Hyde Park *(G-8279)*

Lalique North America Inc ....E 212 355-6550
New York *(G-10167)*

Makarenko Studios Inc..............G 914 968-7673
Yorktown Heights *(G-16367)*

Manhattan Shade & Glass Co Inc ......E 212 288-5616
Hauppauge *(G-5707)*

Michbi Doors Inc ....D 631 231-9050
Farmingdale *(G-4683)*

Mirror-Tech Manufacturing Co ....F 914 965-1232
Yonkers *(G-16334)*

Mri Northtowns Group PC ....F 716 836-4646
Buffalo *(G-2873)*

◆ Munn Works LLC ....E 914 665-6100
Mount Vernon *(G-8164)*

Oldcastle Building Envelope ....F 212 957-5400
New York *(G-10685)*

Oldcastle Buildingenvelope Inc..........C 631 234-2200
Hauppauge *(G-5732)*

Oneida International Inc ....G 315 361-3000
Oneida *(G-12249)*

Oneida Silversmiths Inc ....G 315 361-3000
Oneida *(G-12252)*

Our Terms Fabricators Inc ....E 631 752-1517
West Babylon *(G-15735)*

Pal Manufacturing Corp ....E 516 937-1990
Hicksville *(G-5940)*

Potters Industries LLC ....E 315 265-4920
Norwood *(G-12132)*

Press Glass Na Inc..............G 212 631-3044
New York *(G-10883)*

▲ Quality Enclosures Inc ....E 631 234-0115
Central Islip *(G-3286)*

Rauch Industries Inc..............F 704 867-5333
Tarrytown *(G-15055)*

RB Wyatt Mfg Co Inc ....F 718 209-9682
Brooklyn *(G-2330)*

Rochester Colonial Mfg Corp ....D 585 254-8191
Rochester *(G-13686)*

◆ Rochester Insulated Glass Inc ....D 585 289-3611
Manchester *(G-7528)*

Rohlfs Stined Leaded GL Studio ....E 914 699-4848
Mount Vernon *(G-8178)*

◆ Rosco Inc ....C 718 526-2601
Jamaica *(G-6471)*

Royal Metal Products Inc ....E 518 966-4442
Surprise *(G-14776)*

Select Interior Door Ltd ....E 585 535-9900
North Java *(G-12032)*

Somers Stain Glass Inc ....F 631 586-7772
Deer Park *(G-3937)*

▲ Stark Aquarium Products Co Inc ......E 718 445-5357
Flushing *(G-4895)*

Studio Glass Batch LLC ....G 585 924-9579
Victor *(G-15432)*

Sunburst Studios Inc ....G 718 768-6360
Brooklyn *(G-2470)*

▲ Swift Glass Co Inc ....D 607 733-7166
Elmira Heights *(G-4381)*

▲ Taylor Made Group LLC ....E 518 725-0681
Gloversville *(G-5294)*

▲ Taylor Products Inc ....G 518 773-9312
Gloversville *(G-5295)*

TEC Glass & Inst LLC ....G 315 926-7639
Marion *(G-7576)*

Timeless Decor LLC ....G 315 782-5759
Watertown *(G-15590)*

Upstate Insulated Glass Inc ....G 315 475-4960
Central Square *(G-3297)*

Vitarose Corp of America ....G 718 951-9700
Brooklyn *(G-2565)*

Vitrix Inc ....G 607 936-8707
Corning *(G-3723)*

3241 Cement, Hydraulic

Ciment St-Laurent Inc..............C 518 943-4040
Catskill *(G-3210)*

Euro Gear (usa) Inc ....E 518 578-1775
Plattsburgh *(G-12746)*

Holcim (us) Inc ....G 518 828-8478
Hudson *(G-6160)*

Lafarge Building Materials Inc ....F 518 756-5000
Ravena *(G-13068)*

Lafarge North America Inc ....G 716 651-9235
Lancaster *(G-6813)*

Lafarge North America Inc ....G 716 772-2621
Lockport *(G-7087)*

Lafarge North America Inc ....D 914 930-3027
Buchanan *(G-2609)*

Lafarge North America Inc ....F 716 876-8788
Tonawanda *(G-15118)*

Lafarge North America Inc ....E 518 756-5000
Ravena *(G-13069)*

▲ Lehigh Cement Company ....C 518 792-1137
Glens Falls *(G-5256)*

Lehigh Cement Company LLC ....E 518 792-1137
Glens Falls *(G-5257)*

Pallette Stone Corporation ....E 518 584-2421
Gansevoort *(G-5084)*

Upstone Materials Inc ....G 518 873-2275
Lewis *(G-6918)*

3251 Brick & Structural Clay Tile

Certified Flameproofing Corp ....G 631 265-4824
Smithtown *(G-14474)*

Everblock Systems LLC ....G 844 422-5625
New York *(G-9424)*

◆ Noroc Enterprises Inc ....C 718 585-3230
Bronx *(G-1325)*

Semco Ceramics Inc ....G 315 782-3000
Watertown *(G-15588)*

▲ Stone and Bath Gallery ....G 718 438-4500
Brooklyn *(G-2462)*

3253 Ceramic Tile

▲ Aremco Products Inc ....F 845 268-0039
Valley Cottage *(G-15313)*

Dal-Tile Corporation ....G 914 835-1801
Harrison *(G-5552)*

▲ Ercole Nyc Inc ....F 212 675-2218
Brooklyn *(G-1810)*

▲ Hastings Tile & Bath Inc ....E 631 285-3330
Ronkonkoma *(G-13946)*

▲ Lazer Marble & Granite Corp ....G 718 859-9644
Brooklyn *(G-2049)*

Lucida Usa LLC ....G 845 877-7008
Tallman *(G-15032)*

Quality Components Framing Sys ......F 315 768-1167
Whitesboro *(G-16081)*

Semco Ceramics Inc ....G 315 782-3000
Watertown *(G-15588)*

3255 Clay Refractories

Filtros Ltd ....E 585 586-8770
East Rochester *(G-4163)*

◆ Saint-Gobain Strl Ceramics ....A 716 278-6233
Niagara Falls *(G-11979)*

Upstate Refractory Svcs Inc ....E 315 331-2955
Newark *(G-11855)*

3259 Structural Clay Prdts, NEC

▲ American Chimney Supplies Inc ......G 631 434-2020
Hauppauge *(G-5588)*

Bistrian Cement Corporation ....F 631 324-1123
East Hampton *(G-4117)*

▲ Boston Valley Pottery Inc ....C 716 649-7490
Orchard Park *(G-12340)*

Chimney Doctors Americas Corp..........G 631 868-3586
Bayport *(G-728)*

Jq Woodworking Inc ....G 516 766-3424
Oceanside *(G-12177)*

Lenon Models Inc ....G 212 229-1581
Bronx *(G-1301)*

3261 China Plumbing Fixtures & Fittings

◆ AMG JV LLC ....G 212 602-1818
New York *(G-8563)*

▲ Gamma Products Inc ....D 845 562-3332
New Windsor *(G-8368)*

▲ Kraus USA Inc ....F 800 775-0703
Port Washington *(G-12897)*

▲ Larcent Enterprises Inc ....E 845 562-3332
New Windsor *(G-8371)*

▲ Stone and Bath Gallery ....G 718 438-4500
Brooklyn *(G-2462)*

3262 China, Table & Kitchen Articles

Jill Fagin Enterprises Inc ....G 212 674-9383
New York *(G-10003)*

◆ Korin Inc ....E 212 587-7021
New York *(G-10128)*

Oneida International Inc ....G 315 361-3000
Oneida *(G-12249)*

Oneida Silversmiths Inc ....G 315 361-3000
Oneida *(G-12252)*

Prime Cook (wttc) Inc ....G 646 881-0068
Flushing *(G-4888)*

Swissmar Inc ....G 905 764-1121
Niagara Falls *(G-11983)*

3263 Earthenware, Whiteware, Table & Kitchen Articles

Ceramica Varm ....G.... 914 381-6215
New Rochelle (G-8324)
▲ Green Wave International Inc..........G.... 718 499-3371
Brooklyn (G-1909)
◆ Korin Inc ....E.... 212 587-7021
New York (G-10128)
Lifetime Stainless Steel Corp ....G.... 585 924-9393
Victor (G-15417)
◆ Mackenzie-Childs LLC ....C.... 315 364-6118
Aurora (G-504)
Williams-Sonoma Stores Inc ....F.... 212 633-2203
New York (G-11760)

3264 Porcelain Electrical Splys

▲ Arnold Magnetic Tech Corp ....C.... 585 385-9010
Rochester (G-13246)
▲ Cetek Inc ....E.... 845 452-3510
Poughkeepsie (G-12948)
Corning Incorporated ....E.... 607 974-1274
Painted Post (G-12472)
▲ Eneflux Armtek Magnetics Inc ....G.... 516 576-3434
Medford (G-7707)
Ferro Electronics Materials ....C.... 716 278-9400
Niagara Falls (G-11928)
◆ Ferro Electronics Materials ....G.... 315 536-3357
Penn Yan (G-12583)
Filtros Ltd ....E.... 585 586-8770
East Rochester (G-4163)
▲ Hitachi Metals America Ltd ....E.... 914 694-9200
Purchase (G-13005)
◆ Hoosier Magnetics Inc ....E.... 315 323-5832
Ogdensburg (G-12206)
Lapp Insulator Company LLC..............G.... 585 768-6221
Le Roy (G-6902)
◆ Pfisterer Lapp LLC ....G.... 585 768-6221
Le Roy (G-6906)
▲ Victor Insulators Inc ....C.... 585 924-2127
Victor (G-15440)

3269 Pottery Prdts, NEC

American Country Quilts & Lin............G.... 631 283-5466
Southampton (G-14526)
▲ Saint Gobain Grains & Powders.....A.... 716 731-8200
Niagara Falls (G-11976)
▲ Saint-Gbain Advnced Crmics LLC...C.... 716 278-6066
Niagara Falls (G-11977)
Schiller Stores Inc ....G.... 845 928-4316
Central Valley (G-3300)

3271 Concrete Block & Brick

Ace Cntracting Consulting Corp ....G.... 631 567-4752
Bohemia (G-964)
All American Concrete Corp ....G.... 718 497-3301
Brooklyn (G-1484)
Arnan Development Corp......................D.... 607 432-8391
Oneonta (G-12257)
Barrasso & Sons Trucking Inc............E.... 631 581-0360
Islip Terrace (G-6358)
Brickit..E.... 631 727-8977
Hauppauge (G-5608)
Chenango Concrete Corp ....F.... 607 334-2545
Norwich (G-12115)
Chimney Doctors Americas Corp.........G.... 631 868-3586
Bayport (G-728)
Colonie Block and Supply Co...............G.... 518 869-8411
Colonie (G-3573)
Cossitt Concrete Products Inc ....F.... 315 824-2700
Hamilton (G-5526)
▲ Cranesville Block Co Inc ....E.... 518 684-6154
Amsterdam (G-323)
Cranesville Block Co Inc ....E.... 315 773-2296
Felts Mills (G-4786)
Creative Yard Designs Inc ....G.... 315 706-6143
Manlius (G-7545)
Crest Haven Precast Inc......................G.... 518 483-4750
Burke (G-3059)
Dicks Concrete Co Inc ....E.... 845 374-5966
New Hampton (G-8234)
Dkn Ready Mix LLC ....G.... 718 218-6418
Brooklyn (G-1751)
Duke Concrete Products Inc ....E.... 518 793-7743
Queensbury (G-13037)
Edgewood Industries Inc ....G.... 516 227-2447
Garden City (G-5097)
Everblock Systems LLC ....G.... 844 422-5625
New York (G-9424)

Felicetti Concrete Products ....G.... 716 284-5740
Niagara Falls (G-11926)
▼ Fort Miller Service Corp ....F.... 518 695-5000
Greenwich (G-5472)
▼ Get Real Surfaces Inc ....E.... 845 337-4483
Poughkeepsie (G-12957)
Gone South Concrete Block Inc ....E.... 315 598-2141
Fulton (G-5062)
Grace Associates Inc ....E.... 718 767-9000
Harrison (G-5554)
Grandview Block & Supply Co ....E.... 518 346-7981
Schenectady (G-14274)
Great American Awning & Patio ....F.... 518 899-2300
Ballston Spa (G-575)
▲ Imperia Masonry Supply Corp ....E.... 914 738-0900
Pelham (G-12566)
Jenna Concrete Corporation ....E.... 718 842-5250
Bronx (G-1286)
Jenna Harlem River Inc ....G.... 718 842-5997
Bronx (G-1287)
Lafarge North America Inc ....E.... 518 756-5000
Ravena (G-13069)
Modern Block LLC ....G.... 315 923-7443
Clyde (G-3493)
Montfort Brothers Inc ....E.... 845 896-6694
Fishkill (G-4801)
New York Ready Mix Inc ....G.... 516 338-6969
Westbury (G-15912)
▲ Nicolia Concrete Products Inc.........D.... 631 669-0700
Lindenhurst (G-6965)
Northeast Mesa LLC ....F.... 845 878-9344
Carmel (G-3188)
Palumbo Block Co Inc ....E.... 845 832-6100
Dover Plains (G-4033)
Phelps Cement Products Inc ....E.... 315 548-9415
Phelps (G-12606)
Radiation Shielding Systems ....F.... 888 631-2278
Suffern (G-14765)
Smithtown Concrete Products ....F.... 631 265-1815
Saint James (G-14114)
Suffolk Cement Products Inc ....E.... 631 727-2317
Calverton (G-3088)
Superior Block Corp ....F.... 718 421-0900
Brooklyn (G-2473)
Taylor Concrete Products Inc ....E.... 315 788-2191
Watertown (G-15589)
Troys Landscape Supply Co Inc..........F.... 518 785-1526
Cohoes (G-3518)
Unilock Ltd ....E.... 716 822-6074
Buffalo (G-3029)
▲ Unilock New York Inc ....E.... 845 278-6700
Brewster (G-1159)

3272 Concrete Prdts

A & R Concrete Products LLC ....E.... 845 562-0640
New Windsor (G-8357)
Access Products Inc............................G.... 800 679-4022
Buffalo (G-2617)
Accurate Precast ....F.... 718 345-2910
Brooklyn (G-1452)
▲ Afco Precast Sales Corp ....D.... 631 924-7114
Middle Island (G-7873)
▲ Alp Stone Inc ....F.... 718 706-6166
Long Island City (G-7151)
Alpine Building Supply Inc ....G.... 718 456-2522
Ridgewood (G-13139)
▲ American Chimney Supplies Inc .....G.... 631 434-2020
Hauppauge (G-5588)
Apollo Management V LP ....E.... 914 467-6510
Purchase (G-13001)
Arnan Development Corp......................D.... 607 432-8391
Oneonta (G-12257)
Baliva Concrete Products Inc ....G.... 585 328-8442
Rochester (G-13260)
Barrett Paving Materials Inc................F.... 315 737-9471
Clayville (G-3454)
Beck Vault Company ....G.... 315 337-7590
Rome (G-13845)
Binghamton Burial Vault Co Inc ....F.... 607 722-4931
Binghamton (G-857)
Binghamton Precast & Sup Corp ....E.... 607 722-0334
Binghamton (G-859)
Bistrian Cement Corporation...............F.... 631 324-1123
East Hampton (G-4117)
Blackstone International Inc ....G.... 631 289-5490
Holtsville (G-6045)
Bonsal American Inc ....F.... 585 343-4741
Batavia (G-605)
Bonsal American Inc ....G.... 631 208-8073
Calverton (G-3077)

Callanan Industries Inc........................E.... 315 697-9569
Canastota (G-3150)
▲ Callanan Industries Inc ....C.... 518 374-2222
Albany (G-55)
Callanan Industries Inc........................E.... 845 331-6868
Kingston (G-6683)
Callanan Industries Inc........................E.... 518 785-5666
Latham (G-6851)
▲ Castek Inc ....G.... 914 636-1000
New Rochelle (G-8323)
▲ Chim-Cap Corp................................E.... 800 262-9622
Farmingdale (G-4598)
Chimney Doctors Americas Corp.........G.... 631 868-3586
Bayport (G-728)
City Mason Corp ....F.... 718 658-3796
Jamaica (G-6434)
▲ Coastal Pipeline Products Corp ......E.... 631 369-4000
Calverton (G-3078)
▲ Copeland Coating Company Inc......F.... 518 766-2932
Nassau (G-8213)
Coral Cast LLC ....E.... 516 349-1300
Plainview (G-12674)
▲ Corinthian Cast Stone Inc ....E.... 631 920-2340
Wyandanch (G-16244)
Cossitt Concrete Products Inc ....F.... 315 824-2700
Hamilton (G-5526)
Creative Stone Mfg Inc ....G.... 718 386-7425
Brooklyn (G-1699)
David Kucera Inc ....E.... 845 255-1044
Gardiner (G-5128)
Diamond Precast Products Inc............F.... 631 874-3777
Center Moriches (G-3245)
Dillner Precast Inc...............................G.... 631 421-9130
Lloyd Harbor (G-7055)
Dillner Precast Inc...............................G.... 631 421-9130
Huntington Station (G-6245)
Duke Company ....G.... 607 347-4455
Ithaca (G-6379)
Duranm Inc ....G.... 914 774-3367
Cortlandt Manor (G-3793)
East Main Associates ....D.... 585 624-1990
Lima (G-6931)
▲ Eaton Brothers Corp ....G.... 716 649-8250
Hamburg (G-5505)
Elderlee Incorporated ....C.... 315 789-6670
Oaks Corners (G-12161)
Express Concrete Inc ....G.... 631 273-4224
Brentwood (G-1121)
Fordham Marble Company Inc ....F.... 914 682-6699
White Plains (G-16007)
Foro Marble Co Inc ....E.... 718 852-2322
Brooklyn (G-1859)
▲ Fort Miller Group Inc ....B.... 518 695-5000
Greenwich (G-5471)
▼ Fort Miller Service Corp ....F.... 518 695-5000
Greenwich (G-5472)
Galle & Zinter Inc ....G.... 716 833-4212
Buffalo (G-2765)
Gamble & Gamble Inc ....G.... 716 731-3239
Sanborn (G-14142)
Geotech Associates Ltd ....G.... 631 286-0251
Brookhaven (G-1408)
▼ Get Real Surfaces Inc ....E.... 845 337-4483
Poughkeepsie (G-12957)
Glens Falls Ready Mix Inc ....F.... 518 793-1695
Queensbury (G-13041)
Grace Associates Inc ....G.... 718 767-9000
Harrison (G-5554)
Great ATL Pr-Cast Con Statuary.........G.... 718 948-5677
Staten Island (G-14660)
Guardian Concrete Products Inc..........F.... 518 372-0080
Schenectady (G-14277)
H F Cary & Sons...................................G.... 607 598-2563
Lockwood (G-7120)
Hanson Aggregates East LLC ....G.... 716 372-1574
Allegany (G-188)
Ideal Burial Vault Company ....G.... 585 599-2242
Corfu (G-3703)
Island Ready Mix Inc ....E.... 631 874-3777
Center Moriches (G-3246)
Jefferson Concrete Corp ....D.... 315 788-4171
Watertown (G-15574)
Jenna Concrete Corporation ....E.... 718 842-5250
Bronx (G-1286)
Jenna Harlem River Inc ....G.... 718 842-5997
Bronx (G-1287)
John E Potente & Sons Inc ....G.... 516 935-8585
Hicksville (G-5917)
▲ Key Cast Stone Company Inc ....E.... 631 789-2145
Amityville (G-285)

S
I
C

Lafarge North America Inc ....E 518 756-5000
Ravena (G-13069)

Lakelands Concrete Pdts Inc ....E 585 624-1990
Lima (G-6932)

Lhv Precast Inc ....E 845 336-8880
Kingston (G-6699)

Long Island Geotech ....G 631 473-1044
Port Jefferson (G-12841)

Long Island Green Guys ....G 631 664-4306
Riverhead (G-13180)

Long Island Precast Inc ....E 631 286-0240
Brookhaven (G-1409)

M K Ulrich Construction Inc ....F 716 893-5777
Buffalo (G-2855)

Meditub Incorporated ....F 866 633-4882
Lawrence (G-6888)

Mid-Hudson Concrete Pdts Inc ....F 845 265-3141
Cold Spring (G-3521)

Murcadom Corporation ....F 585 412-2176
Canandaigua (G-3137)

▲ Nicolia Concrete Products Inc ....D 631 669-0700
Lindenhurst (G-6965)

▲ Nicolock Paving Stones LLC ....D 631 669-0700
Lindenhurst (G-6968)

Northeast Concrete Pdts Inc ....F 518 563-0700
Plattsburgh (G-12762)

▲ NY Tempering LLC ....G 718 326-8989
Maspeth (G-7631)

Oldcastle Infrastructure Inc ....F 518 767-2116
South Bethlehem (G-14502)

Oldcastle Infrastructure Inc ....E 518 767-2112
Selkirk (G-14358)

P J R Industries Inc ....F 716 825-9300
Buffalo (G-2902)

Pelkowski Precast Corp ....F 631 269-5727
Kings Park (G-6675)

Preload Concrete Structures ....E 631 231-8100
Hauppauge (G-5748)

Presbrey-Leland Inc ....G 914 949-2264
Valhalla (G-15307)

Quikrete Companies LLC ....E 716 213-2027
Lackawanna (G-6743)

Quikrete Companies LLC ....G 315 673-2020
Marcellus (G-7562)

Rain Catchers Seamless Gutters ....G 516 520-1956
Bethpage (G-844)

Robinson Concrete Inc ....E 315 253-6666
Auburn (G-493)

Roman Stone Construction Co ....E 631 667-0566
Bay Shore (G-709)

▲ Royal Marble & Granite Inc ....G 516 536-5900
Oceanside (G-12188)

St Raymond Monument Co ....G 718 824-3600
Bronx (G-1369)

Stag Brothers Cast Stone Co ....G 718 629-0975
Brooklyn (G-2449)

Standard Industries Inc ....F 212 821-1600
New York (G-11345)

Steindl Cast Stone Co Inc ....G 718 296-8530
Woodhaven (G-16188)

▲ Suhor Industries Inc ....F 585 377-5100
Fairport (G-4526)

Suhor Industries Inc ....G 716 483-6818
Jamestown (G-6544)

Sunnycrest Inc ....E 315 252-7214
Auburn (G-496)

Superior Aggregates Supply LLC ....E 516 333-2923
Lindenhurst (G-6979)

Superior Walls Upstate NY Inc ....E 585 624-9390
Lima (G-6936)

Superior Wlls of Hdson Vly Inc ....E 845 485-4033
Poughkeepsie (G-12986)

Taylor Concrete Products Inc ....G 315 788-2191
Watertown (G-15589)

Towne House Restorations Inc ....G 718 497-9200
Long Island City (G-7385)

▲ Transpo Industries Inc ....E 914 636-1000
New Rochelle (G-8356)

Trinic LLC ....F 607 775-1948
Kirkwood (G-6732)

▲ Unilock New York Inc ....G 845 278-6700
Brewster (G-1159)

Universal Step Inc ....G 315 437-7611
East Syracuse (G-4247)

Upstone Materials Inc ....G 518 873-2275
Lewis (G-6918)

Urban Precast LLC ....E 845 331-6299
Kingston (G-6720)

▲ Walter G Legge Company Inc ....G 914 737-5040
Peekskill (G-12560)

Wel Made Enterprises Inc ....F 631 752-1238
Farmingdale (G-4765)

Woodards Concrete Products Inc ....E 845 361-3471
Bullville (G-3054)

▲ Woodside Granite Industries ....G 585 589-6500
Albion (G-162)

3273 Ready-Mixed Concrete

Advanced Ready Mix Corp ....F 718 497-5020
Brooklyn (G-1465)

Advanced Transit Mix Corp ....G 718 497-5020
Brooklyn (G-1466)

All American Transit Mix Corp ....G 718 417-3654
Brooklyn (G-1485)

Anbriella Sand & Gravel Corp ....E 631 586-2111
Bay Shore (G-650)

Atlas Concrete Batching Corp ....D 718 523-3000
Jamaica (G-6426)

Atlas Transit Mix Corp ....C 718 523-3000
Jamaica (G-6427)

Barney & Dickenson Inc ....D 607 729-1536
Vestal (G-15370)

Barrett Paving Materials Inc ....F 315 788-2037
Watertown (G-15559)

Best Concrete Mix Corp ....E 718 463-5500
Flushing (G-4841)

Bonded Concrete Inc ....E 518 273-5800
Watervliet (G-15598)

Bonded Concrete Inc ....E 518 674-2854
West Sand Lake (G-15835)

▲ Brewster Transit Mix Corp ....D 845 279-3738
Brewster (G-1144)

Brewster Transit Mix Corp ....E 845 279-3738
Brewster (G-1145)

Byram Concrete & Supply LLC ....F 914 682-4477
White Plains (G-15986)

C & C Ready-Mix Corporation ....E 607 797-5108
Vestal (G-15374)

C & C Ready-Mix Corporation ....F 607 687-1690
Owego (G-12429)

Capital Concrete Inc ....G 716 648-8001
Hamburg (G-5502)

Casa Redimix Concrete Corp ....F 718 589-1555
Bronx (G-1220)

Ccz Ready Mix Concrete Corp ....F 516 579-7352
Levittown (G-6914)

Cemex Cement Inc ....D 212 317-6000
New York (G-8945)

Century Ready Mix Inc ....G 631 888-2200
West Babylon (G-15700)

Champion Materials Inc ....G 315 493-2654
Carthage (G-3196)

Chenango Concrete Corp ....F 518 294-9964
Richmondville (G-13129)

Clark Concrete Co Inc ....G 315 478-4101
Syracuse (G-14851)

Clemente Latham Concrete Corp ....D 518 374-2222
Schenectady (G-14257)

Corona Ready Mix Inc ....F 718 271-5940
Corona (G-3737)

Cortland Ready Mix Inc ....F 607 753-3063
Cortland (G-3763)

Cossitt Concrete Products Inc ....G 315 824-2700
Hamilton (G-5526)

Costanza Ready Mix Inc ....G 516 783-4444
North Bellmore (G-12016)

Cranesville Block Co Inc ....E 315 732-2135
Utica (G-15249)

Cranesville Block Co Inc ....E 845 896-5687
Fishkill (G-4798)

Cranesville Block Co Inc ....E 845 331-1775
Kingston (G-6687)

Cranesville Block Co Inc ....E 315 384-4000
Norfolk (G-11998)

▲ Cranesville Block Co Inc ....E 518 684-6154
Amsterdam (G-323)

Cranesville Block Co Inc ....E 315 773-2296
Felts Mills (G-4786)

Custom Mix Inc ....G 516 797-7090
Massapequa Park (G-7654)

Dalrymple Grav & Contg Co Inc ....F 607 739-0391
Pine City (G-12627)

Dalrymple Holding Corp ....E 607 737-6200
Pine City (G-12628)

Deer Park Sand & Gravel Corp ....E 631 586-2323
Bay Shore (G-672)

Dicks Concrete Co Inc ....E 845 374-5966
New Hampton (G-8234)

Dunkirk Construction Products ....G 716 366-5220
Dunkirk (G-4053)

E Tetz & Sons Inc ....D 845 692-4486
Middletown (G-7905)

East Coast Spring Mix Inc ....G 845 355-1215
New Hampton (G-8235)

Elam Materials Inc ....F 585 658-2248
Mount Morris (G-8113)

Electric City Concrete Co Inc ....E 518 887-5560
Amsterdam (G-325)

Elm Transit Mix Corporation ....F 516 333-6144
Westbury (G-15881)

Empire Transit Mix Inc ....E 718 384-3000
Brooklyn (G-1802)

F H Stickles & Son Inc ....F 518 851-9048
Livingston (G-7052)

Ferrara Bros Inc ....E 718 939-3030
Flushing (G-4851)

Frey Concrete Inc ....G 716 213-5832
North Tonawanda (G-12068)

Fulmont Ready-Mix Company Inc ....F 518 887-5560
Amsterdam (G-328)

G & J Rdymx & Msnry Sup Inc ....F 718 454-0800
Hollis (G-6043)

Glens Falls Ready Mix Inc ....F 518 793-1695
Queensbury (G-13041)

Grandview Concrete Corp ....E 518 346-7981
Schenectady (G-14275)

Haley Concrete Inc ....F 716 492-0849
Delevan (G-3961)

Hanson Aggregates East LLC ....F 585 798-0762
Medina (G-7737)

Hanson Aggregates East LLC ....F 716 372-1574
Falconer (G-4542)

Hanson Aggregates East LLC ....E 315 548-4913
Phelps (G-12604)

Hanson Aggregates New York LLC ....F 716 665-4620
Jamesville (G-6558)

Hanson Aggregates New York LLC ....F 716 665-4620
Jamestown (G-6515)

Hanson Aggregates New York LLC ....F 585 638-5841
Pavilion (G-12523)

Hanson Aggregates New York LLC ....C 315 469-5501
Jamesville (G-6559)

Hanson Aggregates New York LLC ....F 607 776-7945
Bath (G-635)

Hanson Aggregates New York LLC ....G 607 276-5881
Almond (G-191)

Inwood Material ....F 516 371-1842
Inwood (G-6296)

Iroquois Rock Products Inc ....F 585 381-7010
Rochester (G-13484)

Island Ready Mix Inc ....E 631 874-3777
Center Moriches (G-3246)

James Town Macadam Inc ....D 716 665-4504
Falconer (G-4546)

Jenna Concrete Corporation ....E 718 842-5250
Bronx (G-1286)

Jenna Harlem River Inc ....G 718 842-5997
Bronx (G-1287)

Jet Redi Mix Concrete Inc ....F 631 580-3640
Ronkonkoma (G-13954)

King Road Materials Inc ....E 518 382-5354
Albany (G-95)

Kings Park Ready Mix Corp ....F 631 269-4330
Kings Park (G-6674)

Kings Ready Mix Inc ....E 718 853-4644
Roslyn Heights (G-14054)

Knight Sttlement Sand Grav LLC ....E 607 776-2048
Bath (G-637)

Lafarge North America Inc ....G 716 854-5791
Buffalo (G-2845)

Lafarge North America Inc ....E 518 756-5000
Ravena (G-13069)

Lage Industries Corporation ....F 718 342-3400
Brooklyn (G-2043)

Lazarek Inc ....G 315 343-1242
Oswego (G-12413)

Lehigh Cement Company ....E 518 943-5940
Catskill (G-3212)

Lehigh Cement Company LLC ....E 718 522-0800
Brooklyn (G-2060)

Lehigh Northeast Cement Co ....E 518 792-1137
Catskill (G-3213)

Liberty Ready Mix Inc ....F 718 526-1700
Jamaica (G-6453)

Long Island Ready Mix ....G 516 485-5260
Hempstead (G-5843)

Manitou Concrete ....D 585 424-6040
Rochester (G-13531)

Manzione Ready Mix Corp ....G 718 628-3837
Brooklyn (G-2111)

Mastro Concrete Inc ....G...... 718 528-6788
  Rosedale (G-14037)

Mix N Mac LLC ....G...... 845 381-5536
  Middletown (G-7921)

Morningstar Concrete Products ....F...... 716 693-4020
  Tonawanda (G-15124)

N Y Western Concrete Corp ....G...... 585 343-6850
  Batavia (G-621)

Nex-Gen Ready Mix Corp ....G...... 347 231-0073
  Bronx (G-1324)

Nicolia Ready Mix Inc ....D...... 631 669-7000
  Lindenhurst (G-6966)

Nicolia Ready Mix Inc ....E...... 631 669-7000
  Lindenhurst (G-6967)

Northern Ready Mix LLC ....F...... 315 336-7900
  North Syracuse (G-12048)

Oldcastle Infrastructure Inc ....F...... 518 767-2116
  South Bethlehem (G-14502)

Oldcastle Materials Inc ....G...... 585 424-6410
  Rochester (G-13588)

Otsego Ready Mix Inc ....F...... 607 432-3400
  Oneonta (G-12279)

Precision Ready Mix Inc ....G...... 718 658-5600
  Jamaica (G-6465)

Presti Ready Mix Concrete Inc ....G...... 516 378-6006
  Freeport (G-5016)

Quality Ready Mix Inc ....F...... 516 437-0100
  New Hyde Park (G-8289)

Queens Ready Mix Inc ....G...... 718 526-4919
  Jamaica (G-6467)

Residential Fences Corp ....E...... 631 205-9758
  Ridge (G-13134)

Richmond Ready Mix Corp ....G...... 917 731-8400
  Staten Island (G-14704)

Richmond Ready Mix Corp II ....E...... 917 731-8400
  Staten Island (G-14705)

Robinson Concrete Inc ....E...... 315 253-6666
  Auburn (G-493)

Robinson Concrete Inc ....C...... 315 676-4333
  West Monroe (G-15814)

Robinson Concrete Inc ....F...... 315 492-6200
  Jamesville (G-6562)

Robinson Concrete Inc ....F...... 315 676-4662
  Brewerton (G-1137)

Rochester Asphalt Materials ....D...... 585 924-7360
  Farmington (G-4777)

Rochester Asphalt Materials ....G...... 585 381-7010
  Rochester (G-13681)

Rural Hill Sand and Grav Corp ....F...... 315 846-5212
  Woodville (G-16239)

Russian Mix Inc ....G...... 347 385-7198
  Brooklyn (G-2366)

Saunders Concrete Co Inc ....F...... 607 756-7905
  Cortland (G-3787)

Scara-Mix Inc ....E...... 718 442-7357
  Staten Island (G-14706)

Seville Central Mix Corp ....G...... 516 868-3000
  Freeport (G-5024)

Seville Central Mix Corp ....D...... 516 293-6190
  Old Bethpage (G-12219)

Seville Central Mix Corp ....E...... 516 239-8333
  Lawrence (G-6892)

Shamrock Materials LLC ....D...... 718 273-9223
  Staten Island (G-14709)

South Shore Ready Mix Inc ....G...... 516 872-3049
  Valley Stream (G-15360)

Star Ready Mix East Inc ....F...... 631 289-8787
  East Hampton (G-4128)

Star Ready-Mix Inc ....F...... 631 289-8787
  Medford (G-7724)

Stephen Miller Gen Contrs Inc ....E...... 518 661-5601
  Gloversville (G-5293)

Suffolk Cement Precast Inc ....G...... 631 727-4432
  Calverton (G-3087)

Suffolk Cement Products Inc ....E...... 631 727-2317
  Calverton (G-3088)

Sullivan Concrete Inc ....F...... 845 888-2235
  Cochecton (G-3504)

T Mix Inc ....G...... 646 379-6814
  Brooklyn (G-2486)

TEC - Crete Transit Mix Corp ....E...... 718 657-6880
  Ridgewood (G-13163)

Thousand Island Ready Mix Con ....G...... 315 686-3203
  La Fargeville (G-6735)

Torrington Industries Inc ....G...... 315 676-4662
  Central Square (G-3296)

United Materials LLC ....D...... 716 683-1432
  North Tonawanda (G-12097)

United Materials LLC ....E...... 716 731-2332
  Sanborn (G-14152)

United Materials LLC ....G...... 716 662-0564
  Orchard Park (G-12381)

United Transit Mix Inc ....F...... 718 416-3400
  Brooklyn (G-2540)

Upstate Materials Inc ....G...... 518 483-2671
  Malone (G-7493)

Upstone Materials Inc ....F...... 315 265-8036
  Plattsburgh (G-12788)

Upstone Materials Inc ....G...... 315 764-0251
  Massena (G-7673)

Upstone Materials Inc ....G...... 518 873-2275
  Lewis (G-6918)

Upstone Materials Inc ....D...... 518 561-5321
  Plattsburgh (G-12787)

US Concrete Inc ....E...... 718 433-0111
  Long Island City (G-7390)

US Concrete Inc ....E...... 718 853-4644
  Roslyn Heights (G-14059)

US Concrete Inc ....E...... 718 438-6800
  Brooklyn (G-2548)

W F Saunders & Sons Inc ....F...... 315 469-3217
  Nedrow (G-8217)

W F Saunders & Sons Inc ....F...... 607 257-6930
  Etna (G-4486)

Watertown Concrete Inc ....F...... 315 788-1040
  Watertown (G-15592)

3274 Lime

Lime Energy Co ....G...... 704 892-4442
  Buffalo (G-2849)

Masick Soil Conservation Co ....F...... 518 827-5354
  Schoharie (G-14322)

▲ Minerals Technologies Inc ....E...... 212 878-1800
  New York (G-10476)

3275 Gypsum Prdts

▲ Continental Buchanan LLC ....D...... 703 480-3800
  Buchanan (G-2608)

East Pattern & Model Corp ....E...... 585 461-3240
  Rochester (G-13362)

Lafarge North America Inc ....D...... 914 930-3027
  Buchanan (G-2609)

United States Gypsum Company ....C...... 585 948-5221
  Oakfield (G-12158)

3281 Cut Stone Prdts

6478 Ridge Road LLC ....E...... 716 625-8400
  Lockport (G-7058)

Adirondack Precision Cut Stone ....F...... 518 681-3060
  Queensbury (G-13029)

Alart Inc ....G...... 212 840-1508
  New York (G-8505)

▲ Amendola MBL & Stone Ctr Inc ....D...... 914 997-7968
  White Plains (G-15972)

American Bluestone LLC ....F...... 607 369-2235
  Sidney (G-14430)

Aurora Stone Group LLC ....F...... 315 471-6869
  East Syracuse (G-4199)

▲ Barra & Trumbore Inc ....G...... 845 626-5442
  Kerhonkson (G-6658)

Busch Products Inc ....E...... 315 474-8422
  Syracuse (G-14837)

Callanan Industries Inc ....E...... 845 331-6868
  Kingston (G-6683)

Capital Stone LLC ....G...... 518 382-7588
  Schenectady (G-14252)

Capital Stone Saratoga LLC ....G...... 518 226-8677
  Saratoga Springs (G-14168)

Dalrymple Holding Corp ....E...... 607 737-6200
  Pine City (G-12588)

Denton Stoneworks Inc ....F...... 516 746-1500
  Garden City Park (G-5120)

▲ Devonian Stone New York Inc ....E...... 607 655-2600
  Windsor (G-16157)

Dicamillo Marble and Granite ....E...... 845 878-0078
  Patterson (G-12515)

Dominic De Nigris Inc ....E...... 718 597-4460
  Bronx (G-1241)

Douglas Patterson & Sons Inc ....G...... 716 433-8100
  Lockport (G-7070)

▲ European Marble Works Co Inc ....F...... 718 387-9778
  Garden City (G-5099)

◆ Evergreen Slate Company Inc ....D...... 518 642-2530
  Middle Granville (G-7867)

Fordham Marble Company Inc ....F...... 914 682-6699
  White Plains (G-16007)

▲ GDi Custom Marble & Gran Inc ....F...... 718 996-9100
  Brooklyn (G-1881)

Geneva Granite Co Inc ....F...... 315 789-8142
  Geneva (G-5155)

▲ Glen Plaza Marble & Gran Inc ....G...... 516 671-1100
  Glen Cove (G-5195)

Granite Tops Inc ....E...... 914 699-2909
  Mount Vernon (G-8145)

▲ Granite Works LLC ....E...... 607 565-7012
  Waverly (G-15621)

Graymont Materials Inc ....E...... 518 561-5200
  Plattsburgh (G-12749)

Hanson Aggregates East LLC ....F...... 315 493-3721
  Great Bend (G-5358)

Hanson Aggregates PA LLC ....E...... 315 789-6202
  Oaks Corners (G-12162)

▲ Hilltop Slate Inc ....E...... 518 642-1453
  Middle Granville (G-7868)

House of Stone Inc ....G...... 845 782-7271
  Monroe (G-8022)

▲ Icestone LLC ....E...... 718 624-4900
  Brooklyn (G-1951)

▲ International Stone Accessrs ....G...... 718 522-5399
  Brooklyn (G-1966)

Iroquois Rock Products Inc ....F...... 585 381-7010
  Rochester (G-13484)

Jamestown Kitchen & Bath Inc ....G...... 716 665-2299
  Jamestown (G-6523)

▲ Marble Works Inc ....E...... 914 376-3653
  Yonkers (G-16331)

Masonville Stone Incorporated ....G...... 607 265-3597
  Masonville (G-7584)

MCM Natural Stone Inc ....F...... 585 586-6510
  Rochester (G-13540)

▲ Minerals Technologies Inc ....E...... 212 878-1800
  New York (G-10476)

Monroe Industries Inc ....G...... 585 226-8230
  Avon (G-514)

▲ New York Quarries Inc ....F...... 518 756-3138
  Alcove (G-163)

North American Slate Inc ....E...... 518 642-1702
  Granville (G-5354)

North Shore Monuments Inc ....G...... 516 759-2156
  Glen Head (G-5212)

Northeast Solite Corporation ....E...... 845 246-2177
  Mount Marion (G-8112)

Pallette Stone Corporation ....E...... 518 584-2421
  Gansevoort (G-5084)

PR & Stone & Tile Inc ....G...... 718 383-1115
  Brooklyn (G-2276)

Puccio Design International ....F...... 516 248-6426
  Garden City (G-5112)

Roto Salt Company Inc ....E...... 315 536-3742
  Penn Yan (G-12593)

▲ Royal Marble & Granite Inc ....G...... 516 536-5900
  Oceanside (G-12188)

Sanford Stone LLC ....E...... 607 467-1313
  Deposit (G-4001)

Seneca Stone Corporation ....G...... 607 737-6200
  Pine City (G-12629)

Sheldon Slate Products Co Inc ....E...... 518 642-1280
  Middle Granville (G-7870)

Stone & Terrazzo World Inc ....G...... 718 361-6899
  Long Island City (G-7371)

Suffolk Granite Manufacturing ....G...... 631 226-4774
  Lindenhurst (G-6977)

Thalle Industries Inc ....E...... 914 762-3415
  Briarcliff Manor (G-1162)

▲ Unilock New York Inc ....E...... 845 278-6700
  Brewster (G-1159)

▲ Unique MBL Gran Orgnztion Corp ...G...... 718 482-0440
  Long Island City (G-7387)

Vermont Structural Slate Co ....F...... 518 499-1912
  Whitehall (G-16078)

W F Saunders & Sons Inc ....F...... 315 469-3217
  Nedrow (G-8217)

White Plains Marble Inc ....G...... 914 347-6000
  Elmsford (G-4441)

3291 Abrasive Prdts

09 Flshy Bll/Dsert Sunrise LLC ....G...... 518 583-6638
  Saratoga Springs (G-14161)

American Douglas Metals Inc ....F...... 716 856-3170
  Buffalo (G-2630)

▲ Barker Brothers Incorporated ....D...... 718 456-6400
  Ridgewood (G-13140)

◆ Barton Mines Company LLC ....C...... 518 798-5462
  Glens Falls (G-5242)

Bedrock Landscaping Mtls Corp ....G...... 631 587-4950
  Babylon (G-518)

▼ Brick-It Inc ....G...... 631 244-3993
  Hauppauge (G-5607)

▲ Buffalo Abrasives Inc ....E...... 716 693-3856
  North Tonawanda (G-12060)

Conrad Blasius Equipment Co ....G 516 753-1200
Plainview *(G-12672)*

◆ Datum Alloys Inc ....G 607 239-6274
Endicott *(G-4448)*

▲ Dedeco International Sales Inc ....D 845 887-4840
Long Eddy *(G-7139)*

▲ Dico Products Corporation ....F 315 797-0470
Utica *(G-15255)*

◆ Dimanco Inc ....G 315 797-0470
Utica *(G-15256)*

◆ Divine Brothers Company ....C 315 797-0470
Utica *(G-15259)*

▼ EAC Holdings of NY Corp ....E 716 822-2500
Buffalo *(G-2735)*

◆ Electro Abrasives LLC ....E 716 822-2500
Buffalo *(G-2740)*

Global Abrasive Products Inc ....E 716 438-0047
Lockport *(G-7077)*

Imerys Fsed Mnrl Ngara FLS Inc ....G 716 286-1234
Niagara Falls *(G-11938)*

Imerys Fsed Mnrl Ngara FLS Inc ....G 716 286-1250
Niagara Falls *(G-11939)*

◆ Imerys Fsed Mnrl Ngara FLS Inc ....E 716 286-1250
Niagara Falls *(G-11940)*

Jta USA Inc ....G 718 722-0902
Brooklyn *(G-2007)*

Lunzer Inc ....G 201 794-2800
New York *(G-10284)*

Malyn Industrial Ceramics Inc ....G 716 741-1510
Clarence Center *(G-3448)*

Meloon Foundries LLC ....E 315 454-3231
Syracuse *(G-14939)*

Niabraze LLC ....F 716 447-1082
Tonawanda *(G-15126)*

▲ Pellets LLC ....G 716 693-1750
North Tonawanda *(G-12081)*

▲ Precision Abrasives Corp ....E 716 826-5833
Orchard Park *(G-12373)*

Precision Elctro Mnrl Pmco Inc ....E 716 284-2484
Niagara Falls *(G-11968)*

Raulli and Sons Inc. ....G 315 479-2515
Syracuse *(G-14974)*

Saint-Gbain Advnced Crmics LLC ......E 716 691-2000
Amherst *(G-242)*

Saint-Gobain Abrasives Inc ....B 518 266-2200
Watervliet *(G-15605)*

▲ Select-Tech Inc ....G 845 895-8111
Wallkill *(G-15473)*

Smm - North America Trade Corp ......G 212 604-0710
New York *(G-11275)*

Sunbelt Industries Inc ....F 315 823-2947
Little Falls *(G-6993)*

▲ Uneeda Enterprizes Inc ....C 800 431-2494
Spring Valley *(G-14585)*

Warren Cutlery Corp ....F 845 876-3444
Rhinebeck *(G-13103)*

◆ Washington Mills Elec Mnrls ....D 716 278-6600
Niagara Falls *(G-11991)*

▲ Washington Mills Tonawanda Inc ....E 716 693-4550
Tonawanda *(G-15153)*

3292 Asbestos products

▲ Adore Floors Inc ....G 631 843-0900
Farmingdale *(G-4573)*

Andujar Asbestos and Lead ....F 716 228-6757
Buffalo *(G-2634)*

Regional MGT & Consulting Inc ....F 718 599-3718
Brooklyn *(G-2336)*

Shenfield Studio LLC ....F 315 436-8869
Syracuse *(G-14994)*

3295 Minerals & Earths: Ground Or Treated

A&B Conservation LLC ....G 845 282-7272
Monsey *(G-8033)*

Allied Aero Services Inc ....G 631 277-9368
Brentwood *(G-1114)*

DSM Nutritional Products LLC ....C 518 372-5155
Schenectady *(G-14261)*

DSM Nutritional Products LLC ....C 518 372-5155
Glenville *(G-5271)*

Magnesium Technologies Corp ....F 905 689-7361
Buffalo *(G-2858)*

▲ Minerals Technologies Inc ....E 212 878-1800
New York *(G-10476)*

Norlite LLC ....B 518 235-0030
Cohoes *(G-3511)*

Northeast Solite Corporation ....E 845 246-2646
Saugerties *(G-14205)*

Northeast Solite Corporation ....E 845 246-2177
Mount Marion *(G-8112)*

Nutech Biosciences Inc ....F 315 505-6500
Oneida *(G-12248)*

Oro Avanti Inc ....G 516 487-5185
Great Neck *(G-5409)*

Skyline LLC ....E 631 403-4131
East Setauket *(G-4187)*

3296 Mineral Wool

▲ Burnett Process Inc ....G 585 254-8080
Rochester *(G-13288)*

Elliot Industries Inc ....G 716 287-3100
Ellington *(G-4316)*

Fbm Galaxy Inc ....F 315 463-5144
East Syracuse *(G-4210)*

Lencore Acoustics Corp ....G 315 384-9114
Norfolk *(G-11999)*

Owens Corning Sales LLC ....G 518 475-3600
Feura Bush *(G-4792)*

Richlar Industries Inc ....F 315 463-5144
East Syracuse *(G-4234)*

◆ Soundcoat Company Inc ....D 631 242-2200
Deer Park *(G-3938)*

▲ Ssf Production LLC ....F 518 324-3407
Plattsburgh *(G-12778)*

Unifrax Corporation ....E 716 278-3800
Niagara Falls *(G-11987)*

Unifrax I LLC ....C 716 696-3000
Tonawanda *(G-15149)*

3297 Nonclay Refractories

▲ Blasch Precision Ceramics Inc ....D 518 436-1263
Menands *(G-7841)*

Capitol Restoration Corp ....G 516 783-1425
North Bellmore *(G-12014)*

Filtros Ltd ....E 585 586-8770
East Rochester *(G-4163)*

Global Alumina Services Co ....B 212 309-8060
New York *(G-9623)*

Lucideon ....F 518 382-0082
Schenectady *(G-14287)*

◆ Monofrax LLC ....C 716 483-7200
Falconer *(G-4550)*

▼ Rembar Company LLC ....E 914 693-2620
Dobbs Ferry *(G-4019)*

Roccera LLC ....G 585 426-0887
Rochester *(G-13678)*

Saint-Gobain Dynamics Inc ....F 716 278-6007
Niagara Falls *(G-11978)*

▲ Silicon Carbide Products Inc ....G 607 562-8599
Horseheads *(G-6137)*

Surmet Ceramics Corporation ....F 716 875-4091
Buffalo *(G-2997)*

Unifrax I LLC ....C 716 696-3000
Tonawanda *(G-15149)*

▲ Zircar Ceramics Inc ....E 845 651-6600
Florida *(G-4827)*

▲ Zircar Refr Composites Inc ....G 845 651-4481
Florida *(G-4829)*

▲ Zircar Zirconia Inc ....E 845 651-3040
Florida *(G-4830)*

3299 Nonmetallic Mineral Prdts, NEC

American Crmic Process RES LLC ....G 315 828-6268
Phelps *(G-12601)*

American Wood Column Corp ....G 718 782-3163
Brooklyn *(G-1503)*

Argosy Composite Advanced Mate ......F 212 268-0003
New York *(G-8622)*

B & F Architectural Support Gr ....E 212 279-6488
New York *(G-8702)*

B & R Promotional Products ....G 212 563-0040
New York *(G-8703)*

Beyond Design Inc ....G 607 865-7487
Walton *(G-15474)*

▲ Cetek Inc ....E 845 452-3510
Poughkeepsie *(G-12948)*

Dream Statuary Inc ....G 718 647-2024
Brooklyn *(G-1760)*

Enrg Inc ....F 716 873-2939
Buffalo *(G-2746)*

Essex Works Ltd ....F 718 495-4575
Brooklyn *(G-1816)*

Everblock Systems LLC ....G 844 422-5625
Brooklyn *(G-9424)*

▲ Foster Reeve & Associates Inc ....G 718 609-0090
Brooklyn *(G-1861)*

Fra-Rik Formica Fabg Co Inc ....G 718 597-3335
Bronx *(G-1262)*

Glasson Sculpture Works ....G 845 255-2969
Gardiner *(G-5129)*

Halo Associates ....G 212 691-9549
New York *(G-9713)*

▲ Heany Industries Inc ....D 585 889-2700
Scottsville *(G-14340)*

Jonas Louis Paul Studios Inc ....G 518 851-2211
Hudson *(G-6168)*

Kodiak Studios Inc ....G 718 769-5399
Brooklyn *(G-2034)*

▲ Reliance Mica Co Inc ....G 718 788-0282
Rockaway Park *(G-13825)*

▲ S & J Trading Inc ....G 718 347-1323
Floral Park *(G-4820)*

▲ Starfire Systems Inc ....F 518 899-9336
Glenville *(G-5273)*

Studio Associates of New York ....G 212 268-1163
New York *(G-11378)*

▲ Ufx Holding I Corporation ....G 212 644-5900
New York *(G-11577)*

Ufx Holding II Corporation ....G 212 644-5900
New York *(G-11578)*

Unifrax Holding Co ....G 212 644-5900
New York *(G-11587)*

◆ Unifrax I LLC ....C 716 768-6500
Tonawanda *(G-15150)*

Unifrax I LLC ....C 716 696-3000
Tonawanda *(G-15149)*

Vescom Structural Systems Inc ....F 516 876-8100
Westbury *(G-15938)*

33 PRIMARY METAL INDUSTRIES

3312 Blast Furnaces, Coke Ovens, Steel & Rolling Mills

A-1 Iron Works Inc ....G 718 927-4766
Brooklyn *(G-1439)*

Albaluz Films LLC ....G 347 613-2321
New York *(G-8506)*

▲ Allvac ....F 716 433-4411
Lockport *(G-7059)*

▲ American Chimney Supplies Inc ......G 631 434-2020
Hauppauge *(G-5588)*

Artistic Iron Works Inc. ....G 631 665-4285
Bay Shore *(G-652)*

B H M Metal Products Co ....G 845 292-5297
Kauneonga Lake *(G-6640)*

Baker Tool & Die ....G 716 694-2025
North Tonawanda *(G-12056)*

Baker Tool & Die & Die ....G 716 694-2025
North Tonawanda *(G-12057)*

◆ Bebitz USA Inc ....G 516 280-8378
Hicksville *(G-5889)*

Belmet Products Inc ....E 718 542-8220
Bronx *(G-1212)*

Bonura and Sons Iron Works ....F 718 381-4100
Franklin Square *(G-4959)*

CFS Enterprises Inc. ....E 718 585-0500
Bronx *(G-1223)*

China Industrial Steel Inc ....G 646 328-1502
New York *(G-8989)*

Coventry Manufacturing Co Inc ....E 914 668-2212
Mount Vernon *(G-8134)*

◆ Crucible Industries LLC ....B 800 365-1180
Solvay *(G-14495)*

Dakota Systems Mfg Corp ....G 631 249-5811
Farmingdale *(G-4613)*

David Fehlman ....G 315 455-8888
Syracuse *(G-14875)*

◆ Dunkirk Specialty Steel LLC ....C 716 366-1000
Dunkirk *(G-4055)*

Elderlee Incorporated ....C 315 789-6670
Oaks Corners *(G-12161)*

Empire Steel Works Inc ....F 516 561-3500
Hicksville *(G-5905)*

Fuller Tool Incorporated ....F 315 891-3183
Newport *(G-11898)*

▼ Handy & Harman Ltd ....A 212 520-2300
New York *(G-9720)*

Hmi Metal Powders ....C 315 839-5421
Clayville *(G-3456)*

▲ Homogeneous Metals Inc ....D 315 839-5421
Clayville *(G-3457)*

Hudson Valley Steel Products ....G 845 565-2270
Newburgh *(G-11871)*

Image Iron Works Inc. ....G 718 592-8276
Corona *(G-3740)*

◆ Jaquith Industries Inc ....E 315 478-5700
Syracuse *(G-14916)*

Jfe Engineering Corporation ....F 212 310-9320
New York *(G-9999)*

Jfe Steel America Inc..............G.....212 310-9320
New York (G-10000)

▲ Juniper Elbow Co Inc.............C.....718 326-2546
Middle Village (G-7881)

Kenbenco Inc..............F.....845 246-3066
Saugerties (G-14203)

L&B Fabricators LLC............F.....585 265-2731
Ontario (G-12292)

Lino International Inc..............G.....516 482-7100
Great Neck (G-5401)

▲ Mardek LLC..............G.....585 735-9333
Pittsford (G-12649)

Markin Tubing LP..............F.....585 495-6211
Buffalo (G-2861)

Markin Tubing Inc..............C.....585 495-6211
Wyoming (G-16251)

Matrix Steel Company Inc..............G.....718 381-6800
Brooklyn (G-2125)

N C Iron Works Inc..............G.....718 633-4660
Brooklyn (G-2184)

◆ Niagara Specialty Metals Inc.............E.....716 542-5552
Akron (G-19)

Nitro Wheels Inc..............F.....716 337-0709
North Collins (G-12027)

▲ Nucor Steel Auburn Inc.............B.....315 253-4561
Auburn (G-488)

Quality Stainless Steel NY Inc.............F.....718 748-1785
Brooklyn (G-2311)

Quest Manufacturing Inc..............E.....716 312-8000
Hamburg (G-5518)

R D Specialties Inc..............F.....585 265-0220
Webster (G-15649)

◆ Renco Group Inc..............G.....212 541-6000
New York (G-11012)

Republic Steel Inc..............B.....716 827-2800
Blasdell (G-920)

Rochester Structural LLC...........E.....585 436-1250
Rochester (G-13700)

Safespan Platform Systems Inc...........E.....716 694-1100
Tonawanda (G-15137)

Samuel Son & Co (usa) Inc...........G.....716 856-6500
Blasdell (G-921)

Sims Group USA Holdings Corp...........D.....718 786-6031
Long Island City (G-7357)

Sph Group Holdings LLC..............F.....212 520-2300
New York (G-11321)

Spin-Rite Corporation..............F.....585 266-5200
Rochester (G-13739)

Tdy Industries LLC..............E.....716 433-4411
Lockport (G-7110)

TI Group Auto Systems LLC..............G.....315 568-7042
Seneca Falls (G-14373)

Tms International LLC..............G.....315 253-8925
Auburn (G-499)

▲ Tonawanda Coke Corporation...........C.....716 876-6222
Tonawanda (G-15145)

Tri Valley Iron Inc..............F.....845 365-1013
Palisades (G-12483)

Vell Company Inc..............G.....845 365-1013
Palisades (G-12484)

◆ Viraj - USA Inc..............G.....516 280-8380
Hicksville (G-5953)

3313 Electrometallurgical Prdts

◆ CCA Holding Inc..............C.....716 446-8800
Amherst (G-216)

Globe Metallurgical Inc..............D.....716 804-0862
Niagara Falls (G-11931)

▲ Golden Egret LLC..............G.....516 922-2839
East Norwich (G-4152)

▲ Medima LLC..............C.....716 741-0400
Clarence (G-3436)

3315 Steel Wire Drawing & Nails & Spikes

A&B Iron Works Inc..............G.....347 466-3193
Brooklyn (G-1438)

▲ Able Industries Inc..............F.....914 739-5685
Cortlandt Manor (G-3792)

▲ Aerospace Wire & Cable Inc...........E.....718 358-2345
College Point (G-3534)

▲ American Wire Tie Inc.............E.....716 337-2412
North Collins (G-12023)

▲ Aruvil International Inc..............G.....212 447-5020
New York (G-8642)

Bekaert Corporation..............E.....716 830-1321
Amherst (G-212)

▲ Braun Horticulture Inc..............G.....716 282-6101
Niagara Falls (G-11909)

▲ Cobra Manufacturing Corp.............G.....845 514-2505
Lake Katrine (G-6763)

▲ Continental Cordage Corp.............D.....315 655-9800
Cazenovia (G-3225)

◆ Dragon Trading Inc..............G.....212 717-1496
New York (G-9265)

▲ Dsr International Corp..............G.....631 427-2600
Great Neck (G-5382)

EB Acquisitions LLC............D.....212 355-3310
New York (G-9309)

Forsyth Industries Inc..............E.....716 652-1070
Buffalo (G-2757)

▲ Hohmann & Barnard Inc..............E.....631 234-0600
Hauppauge (G-5672)

▲ Island Industries Corp..............G.....631 451-8825
Coram (G-3694)

▲ Lee Spring Company LLC..............C.....888 777-4647
Brooklyn (G-2058)

Liberty Fabrication Inc..............G.....718 495-5735
Brooklyn (G-2066)

Master-Halco Inc..............F.....631 585-8150
Yaphank (G-16266)

▲ Nyi Building Products Inc..............F.....518 458-7500
Clifton Park (G-3469)

Omega Wire Inc..............D.....315 689-7115
Jordan (G-6630)

Oneonta Fence..............G.....607 433-6707
Oneonta (G-12278)

▲ Rolling Gate Supply Corp..............G.....718 366-5258
Glendale (G-5232)

Rose Fence Inc..............F.....516 223-0777
Baldwin (G-533)

▲ Sigmund Cohn Corp..............D.....914 664-5300
Mount Vernon (G-8180)

Spectrum Cable Corporation..............G.....585 235-7714
Rochester (G-13738)

▲ Styles Manufacturing Corp..............E.....516 763-5303
Oceanside (G-12193)

▲ Tappan Wire & Cable Inc..............G.....845 353-9000
Blauvelt (G-935)

Technical Wldg Fabricators LLC...........F.....518 463-2229
Albany (G-134)

Web Associates Inc..............G.....716 883-3377
Buffalo (G-3042)

3316 Cold Rolled Steel Sheet, Strip & Bars

▼ Aero-Data Metal Crafters Inc.............E.....631 471-7733
Ronkonkoma (G-13892)

▲ Clover Wire Forming Co Inc.............E.....914 375-0400
Yonkers (G-16296)

◆ Gibraltar Industries Inc..............D.....716 826-6500
Buffalo (G-2775)

Northeast Cnstr Inds Inc..............F.....845 565-1000
Montgomery (G-8062)

◆ Renco Group Inc..............G.....212 541-6000
New York (G-11012)

Rough Brothers Holding Co..............G.....716 826-6500
Buffalo (G-2965)

Worthington Industries Inc..............D.....315 336-5500
Rome (G-13877)

3317 Steel Pipe & Tubes

Coventry Manufacturing Co Inc.............E.....914 668-2212
Mount Vernon (G-8134)

Liberty Pipe Incorporated..............G.....516 747-2472
Mineola (G-7986)

▲ Markin Tubing LP..............C.....585 495-6211
Wyoming (G-16250)

Markin Tubing LP..............F.....585 495-6211
Buffalo (G-2861)

Markin Tubing Inc..............C.....585 495-6211
Wyoming (G-16251)

McHone Industries Inc..............D.....716 945-3380
Salamanca (G-14122)

Micromold Products Inc..............E.....914 969-2850
Yonkers (G-16333)

▲ Oriskany Mfg Tech LLC..............E.....315 732-4962
Yorkville (G-16378)

Stony Brook Mfg Co Inc..............E.....631 369-9530
Calverton (G-3086)

Thyssenkrupp Materials NA Inc...........G.....585 279-0000
West Seneca (G-15855)

TI Group Auto Systems LLC..............G.....315 568-7042
Seneca Falls (G-14373)

▼ Tricon Piping Systems Inc..............F.....315 697-8787
Canastota (G-3159)

▲ Welded Tube Usa Inc..............D.....716 828-1111
Lackawanna (G-6746)

3321 Gray Iron Foundries

Acme Nipple Mfg Co Inc..............G.....716 873-7491
Buffalo (G-2618)

Auburn Foundry Inc..............F.....315 253-4441
Auburn (G-461)

◆ Dragon Trading Inc..............G.....212 717-1496
New York (G-9265)

En Tech Corp..............F.....845 398-0776
Tappan (G-15035)

Field Wares LLC..............G.....508 380-6545
Brooklyn (G-1841)

▲ Hitachi Metals America Ltd...........E.....914 694-9200
Purchase (G-13005)

Jamestown Iron Works Inc..............F.....716 665-2818
Falconer (G-4548)

Matrix Steel Company Inc..............G.....718 381-6800
Brooklyn (G-2125)

McWane Inc..............B.....607 734-2211
Elmira (G-4362)

▲ Noresco Industrial Group Inc...........E.....516 759-3355
Glen Cove (G-5197)

Penner Elbow Company Inc..............F.....718 526-9000
Elmhurst (G-4337)

S M S C Inc..............G.....315 942-4394
Boonville (G-1110)

Speyside Foundry Holdings LLC..............G.....212 994-0308
New York (G-11319)

3322 Malleable Iron Foundries

Eastern Company..............D.....315 468-6251
Solvay (G-14496)

Emcom Industries Inc..............G.....716 852-3711
Buffalo (G-2743)

▲ Noresco Industrial Group Inc...........E.....516 759-3355
Glen Cove (G-5197)

◆ Plattco Corporation..............E.....518 563-4640
Plattsburgh (G-12768)

3324 Steel Investment Foundries

Brinkman Precision Inc..............D.....585 429-5001
West Henrietta (G-15788)

Consoldted Precision Pdts Corp.............B.....315 687-0014
Chittenango (G-3404)

▲ Cpp-Syracuse..............E.....315 687-0014
Chittenango (G-3406)

Jbf Stainless LLC..............E.....315 569-2800
Frankfort (G-4952)

Quality Castings Inc..............E.....732 409-3203
Long Island City (G-7335)

Worldwide Resources Inc..............F.....718 760-5000
Brooklyn (G-2597)

3325 Steel Foundries, NEC

A & V Castings Inc..............G.....212 997-0042
New York (G-8412)

Amt Incorporated..............E.....518 284-2910
Sharon Springs (G-14382)

Brinkman Intl Group Inc..............G.....585 429-5000
Rochester (G-13281)

C J Winter Machine Tech..............E.....585 429-5000
Rochester (G-13290)

Eastern Industrial Steel Corp.............F.....845 639-9749
New City (G-8226)

Frazer & Jones Co..............D.....315 468-6251
Syracuse (G-14895)

Speyside Foundry Holdings LLC..............G.....212 994-0308
New York (G-11319)

Steel Craft Rolling Door..............F.....631 608-8662
Copiague (G-3679)

3331 Primary Smelting & Refining Of Copper

Sherburne Metal Sales Inc..............F.....607 674-4441
Sherburne (G-14393)

◆ Tecnofil Chenango SAC..............E.....607 674-4441
Sherburne (G-14396)

3334 Primary Production Of Aluminum

Alcoa USA Corp..............G.....315 764-4011
Massena (G-7664)

Alcoa USA Corp..............E.....315 764-4106
Massena (G-7665)

American Std Shtmtl Sup Corp.............F.....718 888-9350
Flushing (G-4839)

Greene Brass & Alum Fndry LLC...........G.....607 656-4204
Bloomville (G-954)

3339 Primary Nonferrous Metals, NEC

▲ AAA Catalytic Recycling Inc...........F.....631 920-7944
Farmingdale (G-4570)

All American Funding & Ref LLC...........G.....516 978-7531
Farmingdale (G-4578)

Ames Goldsmith Corp ....F 518 792-7435
  Glens Falls *(G-5239)*
Billanti Casting Co Inc ....E 516 775-4800
  New Hyde Park *(G-8254)*
Dennis Metals Inc ....G 516 487-5747
  Great Neck *(G-5381)*
Doral Refining Corp ....E 516 223-3684
  Freeport *(G-4992)*
Electro Alloy Recovery Inc ....G 631 879-7530
  Bohemia *(G-1012)*
General Refining & Semlt Corp .....G 516 538-4747
  Hempstead *(G-5836)*
General Refining Corporation ....G 516 538-4747
  Hempstead *(G-5837)*
Globe Metallurgical Inc ....D 716 804-0862
  Niagara Falls *(G-11931)*
Goldmark Products Inc ....E 631 777-3343
  Farmingdale *(G-4639)*
▼ Handy & Harman Ltd ....A 212 520-2300
  New York *(G-9720)*
Hh Liquidating Corp ....A 646 282-2500
  New York *(G-9779)*
Marco Industries Ltd ....G 212 798-8100
  New York *(G-10356)*
Marina Jewelry Co Inc ....G 212 354-5027
  New York *(G-10361)*
Materion Advanced Materials ......G 800 327-1355
  Brewster *(G-1154)*
▲ Medima LLC ....C 716 741-0400
  Clarence *(G-3436)*
▲ Rochester Silver Works LLC ......G 585 743-1610
  Rochester *(G-13697)*
S & W Metal Trading Corp ....G 212 719-5070
  Brooklyn *(G-2375)*
Sabin Metal Corporation ....C 585 538-2194
  Scottsville *(G-14343)*
▲ Saes Smart Materials Inc ....E 315 266-2026
  New Hartford *(G-8245)*
▲ Sigmund Cohn Corp ....D 914 664-5300
  Mount Vernon *(G-8180)*
Sph Group Holdings LLC ....F 212 520-2300
  New York *(G-11321)*
Starfuels Inc ....G 914 289-4800
  White Plains *(G-16062)*
Tdy Industries LLC ....E 716 433-4411
  Lockport *(G-7110)*
▲ Umicore Elec Mtls USA Inc ....C 518 792-7700
  Glens Falls *(G-5267)*
Umicore USA Inc ....E 919 874-7171
  Glens Falls *(G-5268)*
Wallace Refiners Inc ....G 212 391-2649
  New York *(G-11718)*
Zerovalent Nanometals Inc ....G 585 298-8592
  Rochester *(G-13814)*

3341 Secondary Smelting & Refining Of Non-ferrous Metals

Advanced Precision Technology ....F 845 279-3540
  Brewster *(G-1138)*
Amt Incorporated ....E 518 284-2910
  Sharon Springs *(G-14382)*
Ben Weitsman of Albany LLC ....E 518 462-4444
  Albany *(G-46)*
Cora Materials Corp ....F 516 488-6300
  New Hyde Park *(G-8260)*
Encore Refining and Recycleing .....G 631 319-1910
  Holbrook *(G-5999)*
General Refining & Semlt Corp .....G 516 538-4747
  Hempstead *(G-5836)*
▲ Germanium Corp America Inc ......F 315 853-4900
  Clinton *(G-3482)*
Island Recycling Corp ....G 631 234-6688
  Central Islip *(G-3279)*
Karbra Company ....C 212 736-9300
  New York *(G-10069)*
▲ Metalico Aluminum Recovery Inc ....E 315 463-9500
  Syracuse *(G-14940)*
Parfuse Corp ....E 516 997-8888
  Westbury *(G-15916)*
Pluribus Products Inc ....E 718 852-1614
  Bayville *(G-747)*
S & W Metal Trading Corp ....G 212 719-5070
  Brooklyn *(G-2375)*
▲ Sabin Metal Corporation ....F 631 329-1695
  East Hampton *(G-4127)*
Sabin Metal Corporation ....C 585 538-2194
  Scottsville *(G-14343)*
Sims Group USA Holdings Corp ....D 718 786-6031
  Long Island City *(G-7357)*

Special Metals Corporation ....D 716 366-5663
  Dunkirk *(G-4067)*

3351 Rolling, Drawing & Extruding Of Copper

Aurubis Buffalo Inc ....F 716 879-6700
  Buffalo *(G-2648)*
▲ Aurubis Buffalo Inc ....B 716 879-6700
  Buffalo *(G-2649)*
Camden Wire Co Inc ....A 315 245-3800
  Camden *(G-3099)*
▲ Continental Cordage Corp ....D 315 655-9800
  Cazenovia *(G-3225)*
International Wire Group ....F 315 245-3800
  Camden *(G-3101)*
Jaguar Industries Inc ....F 845 947-1800
  Haverstraw *(G-5805)*
◆ Milward Alloys Inc ....E 716 434-5536
  Lockport *(G-7093)*
Omega Wire Inc ....D 315 689-7115
  Jordan *(G-6630)*
▲ Omega Wire Inc ....B 315 245-3800
  Camden *(G-3104)*
▲ Owi Corporation ....G 315 245-4305
  Camden *(G-3105)*
Sherburne Metal Sales Inc ....F 607 674-4441
  Sherburne *(G-14393)*

3353 Aluminum Sheet, Plate & Foil

Alcoa Fastening Systems ....G 585 368-5049
  Rochester *(G-13216)*
◆ Alufoil Products Co Inc ....F 631 231-4141
  Hauppauge *(G-5585)*
American Custom Metals Inc ....G 585 694-4893
  Spencerport *(G-14551)*
American Douglas Metals Inc ......F 716 856-3170
  Buffalo *(G-2630)*
Arconic Fstening Systems Rings ....G 800 278-4825
  Kingston *(G-6678)*
Arconic Inc ....G 315 764-4011
  Massena *(G-7666)*
BSD Aluminum Foil LLC ....E 347 689-3875
  Brooklyn *(G-1626)*
En Foil LLC ....G 516 466-9500
  New Hyde Park *(G-8266)*
Golden Argosy LLC ....G 212 268-0003
  New York *(G-9640)*
Novelis Corporation ....B 315 342-1036
  Oswego *(G-12416)*
Novelis Corporation ....B 315 349-0121
  Oswego *(G-12417)*

3354 Aluminum Extruded Prdts

◆ A-Fab Initiatives Inc ....F 716 877-5257
  Buffalo *(G-2616)*
Amt Incorporated ....E 518 284-2910
  Sharon Springs *(G-14382)*
Apollo Management V LP ....E 914 467-6510
  Purchase *(G-13001)*
Arconic Inc ....G 315 764-4011
  Massena *(G-7666)*
▼ Flagpoles Incorporated ....D 631 751-5500
  East Setauket *(G-4178)*
▲ Itts Industrial Inc ....G 718 605-6934
  Staten Island *(G-14667)*
▼ J Sussman Inc ....E 718 297-0228
  Jamaica *(G-6450)*
Jem Threading Specialties Inc ....G 718 665-3341
  Bronx *(G-1285)*
▲ Keymark Corporation ....A 518 853-3421
  Fonda *(G-4911)*
▲ Minitec Framing Systems LLC .....E 585 924-4690
  Farmington *(G-4775)*
North American Pipe Corp ....F 516 338-2863
  East Williston *(G-4249)*
▼ North Coast Outfitters Ltd ....E 631 727-5580
  Riverhead *(G-13183)*
▲ Nyahb Inc ....G 845 352-5300
  Monsey *(G-8042)*
Pioneer Window Holdings Inc ....E 518 762-5526
  Johnstown *(G-6625)*
Super Sweep Inc ....F 631 223-8205
  Huntington Station *(G-6261)*
Swiss Tool Corporation ....E 631 842-7766
  Copiague *(G-3681)*

3355 Aluminum Rolling & Drawing, NEC

Alcoa Corporation ....B 412 315-2900
  Massena *(G-7663)*

Arconic Inc ....G 315 764-4011
  Massena *(G-7666)*
Irtronics Instruments Inc ....F 914 693-6291
  Ardsley *(G-389)*
◆ Mitsubishi Chemical Amer Inc ......E 212 223-3043
  New York *(G-10484)*
▲ N A Alumil Corporation ....G 718 355-9393
  Long Island City *(G-7302)*
▲ Novelis Inc ....E 315 349-0121
  Oswego *(G-12418)*
▲ SI Partners Inc ....G 516 433-1415
  Hicksville *(G-5948)*

3356 Rolling, Drawing-Extruding Of Nonferrous Metals

Arlon Viscor Ltd ....A 914 461-1300
  White Plains *(G-15976)*
▲ Aufhauser Corporation ....F 516 694-8696
  Plainview *(G-12665)*
Aufhauser Manufacturing Corp ....E 516 694-8696
  Plainview *(G-12666)*
Braze Alloy Inc ....G 718 815-5757
  Staten Island *(G-14630)*
▲ Continental Cordage Corp ....D 315 655-9800
  Cazenovia *(G-3225)*
▲ Cpp-Syracuse Inc ....E 315 687-0014
  Chittenango *(G-3406)*
Handy & Harman Holding Corp ......D 914 461-1300
  White Plains *(G-16013)*
Hh Liquidating Corp ....A 646 282-2500
  New York *(G-9779)*
▲ Indium Corporation of America ......E 800 446-3486
  Clinton *(G-3483)*
Indium Corporation of America ......E 315 793-8200
  Utica *(G-15275)*
Indium Corporation of America ......E 315 381-2330
  Utica *(G-15276)*
Jewelers Solder Supply Inc ....E 718 637-1256
  Brooklyn *(G-1992)*
▲ Medi-Ray Inc ....D 877 898-3003
  Tuckahoe *(G-15205)*
Mustard Tin ....G 315 769-8409
  Massena *(G-7669)*
▲ Nationwide Precision Pdts Corp .....B 585 272-7100
  Rochester *(G-13567)*
Nickel City Studios Photo Jour ....G 716 200-0956
  Buffalo *(G-2889)*
RB Diamond Inc ....G 212 398-4560
  New York *(G-10989)*
◆ Selectrode Industries Inc ....D 631 547-5470
  Huntington Station *(G-6260)*
▲ Sigmund Cohn Corp ....D 914 664-5300
  Mount Vernon *(G-8180)*
Special Metals Corporation ....B 315 798-2900
  New Hartford *(G-8246)*
T L Diamond & Company Inc ....G 212 249-6660
  New York *(G-11416)*
Tin Rage Productions Inc ....G 718 398-0787
  Brooklyn *(G-2506)*
Titanium Dem Remediation Group ....F 716 433-4100
  Lockport *(G-7112)*
▲ Vestal Electronic Devices LLC ......F 607 773-8461
  Endicott *(G-4477)*

3357 Nonferrous Wire Drawing

▲ C S Business Systems Inc ....E 716 886-6521
  Buffalo *(G-2688)*
Caldwell Bennett Inc ....E 315 337-8540
  Oriskany *(G-12385)*
Camden Wire Co Inc ....A 315 245-3800
  Camden *(G-3099)*
Colonial Wire & Cable Co Inc ....D 631 234-8500
  Hauppauge *(G-5621)*
Colonial Wire Cable Co NJ ....G 631 234-8500
  Hauppauge *(G-5622)*
Complete Fiber Solutions Inc ....G 718 828-8900
  Bronx *(G-1230)*
▲ Continental Cordage Corp ....D 315 655-9800
  Cazenovia *(G-3225)*
▲ Convergent Cnnctivity Tech Inc ....G 845 651-5250
  Florida *(G-4822)*
Corning Incorporated ....A 607 974-9000
  Painted Post *(G-12473)*
◆ Corning Incorporated ....A 607 974-9000
  Corning *(G-3705)*
Corning Incorporated ....E 607 248-1200
  Corning *(G-3708)*
Corning Optcal Cmmncations LLC ....F 607 974-7543
  Corning *(G-3712)*

Corning Specialty Mtls Inc ....G..... 607 974-9000
Corning (G-3713)

◆ Cortland Cable Company Inc ....E..... 607 753-8276
Cortland (G-3758)

Crhmdu Isulations LLC ....G..... 516 353-7749
Port Washington (G-12870)

▲ Fiberall Corp ....E..... 516 371-5200
Inwood (G-6293)

▲ Fiberdyne Labs Inc ....D..... 315 895-8470
Frankfort (G-4951)

▲ International Wire Group Inc...........B..... 315 245-2000
Camden (G-3102)

Jaguar Industries Inc......................F..... 845 947-1800
Haverstraw (G-5805)

▲ Kris-Tech Wire Company Inc ....E..... 315 339-5268
Rome (G-13853)

▲ Leviton Manufacturing Co Inc ....B..... 631 812-6000
Melville (G-7800)

▲ Monroe Cable Company Inc ....C..... 845 692-2800
Middletown (G-7922)

Performance Wire & Cable Inc ....F..... 315 245-2594
Camden (G-3106)

▲ Rdi Inc ....F..... 914 773-1000
Mount Kisco (G-8104)

◆ Remee Products Corp ....D..... 845 651-4431
Florida (G-4826)

Rockland Insulated Wire Cable ....G..... 845 429-3103
Haverstraw (G-5806)

Siemens Corporation.......................F..... 202 434-7800
New York (G-11226)

Siemens USA Holdings Inc ....B..... 212 258-4000
New York (G-11228)

Sinclair Technologies Inc ....E..... 716 874-3682
Hamburg (G-5521)

Steelflex Electro Corp......................D..... 516 226-4466
Lindenhurst (G-6973)

▲ Tappan Wire & Cable Inc ....C..... 845 353-9000
Blauvelt (G-935)

Tdg Acquistion Co LLC ....E..... 585 500-4625
Henrietta (G-5860)

TLC-The Light Connection Inc ....D..... 315 736-7384
Oriskany (G-12399)

▲ United Wire Technologies Inc ....F..... 315 623-7203
Constantia (G-3637)

Universal Builders Supply Inc ....F..... 845 758-8801
Red Hook (G-13074)

▲ Whirlwind Music Distrs Inc ....D..... 800 733-9473
Rochester (G-13803)

3363 Aluminum Die Castings

◆ Albest Metal Stamping Corp.............E....... 718 388-6000
Brooklyn (G-1477)

Crown Die Casting Corp.....................E....... 914 667-5400
Mount Vernon (G-8135)

Greene Brass & Alum Fndry LLC ....G....... 607 656-4204
Bloomville (G-954)

▲ Greenfield Industries Inc..................D....... 516 623-9230
Freeport (G-5001)

ITT Corporation ....D....... 315 568-2811
Seneca Falls (G-14364)

ITT LLC..D....... 914 641-2000
Seneca Falls (G-14368)

Louis Iannettoni ....D....... 315 454-3231
Syracuse (G-14936)

▲ Pinnacle Manufacturing Co Inc ....E....... 585 343-5664
Batavia (G-623)

Tpi Arcade Inc ....D....... 585 492-0122
Arcade (G-382)

3364 Nonferrous Die Castings, Exc Aluminum

◆ Albest Metal Stamping Corp.............E....... 718 388-6000
Brooklyn (G-1477)

▲ AM Cast Inc ....F....... 631 750-1644
Bohemia (G-970)

◆ American Casting and Mfg Corp.........D....... 800 342-0333
Plainview (G-12662)

American Casting and Mfg Corp.........G....... 516 349-7010
Plainview (G-12663)

Cast-All Corporation ....E....... 516 741-4025
Mineola (G-7965)

Crown Die Casting Corp.....................E....... 914 667-5400
Mount Vernon (G-8135)

Crown Novelty Works Inc...................G....... 631 253-0949
Melville (G-7772)

Greenfield Die Casting Corp ....E....... 516 623-9230
Freeport (G-5000)

Mar-A-Thon Filters Inc ....G....... 631 957-4774
Lindenhurst (G-6957)

▲ Pinnacle Manufacturing Co Inc ....E..... 585 343-5664
Batavia (G-623)

3365 Aluminum Foundries

Airflex Industrial Inc ....E..... 631 752-1234
Farmingdale (G-4575)

American Blade Mfg LLC ....F..... 607 432-4518
Oneonta (G-12256)

American Blade Mfg LLC ....G..... 607 656-4204
Greene (G-5443)

Amt Incorporated ....E..... 518 284-2910
Sharon Springs (G-14382)

▼ Armstrong Mold Corporation............E..... 315 437-1517
East Syracuse (G-4196)

Armstrong Mold Corporation..............D..... 315 437-1517
East Syracuse (G-4197)

◆ August Thomsen Corp ....E..... 516 676-7100
Glen Cove (G-5189)

▼ Auto-Mate Technologies LLC...........F..... 631 727-8886
Riverhead (G-13171)

Broetje Automation-Usa Inc...............C..... 716 204-8640
Williamsville (G-16124)

Consoldted Precision Pdts Corp..........B..... 315 687-0014
Chittenango (G-3404)

Corbett Stves Pttern Works Inc ....E..... 585 546-7109
Rochester (G-13326)

Crown Die Casting Corp.....................E..... 914 667-5400
Mount Vernon (G-8135)

East Pattern & Model Corp..................E..... 585 461-3240
Rochester (G-13362)

East Pattern & Model Corp..................F..... 585 461-3240
Rochester (G-13363)

Eastern Castings Co ....F..... 518 677-5610
Cambridge (G-3094)

Eastern Strategic Materials................E..... 212 332-1619
New York (G-9306)

◆ Hitachi Metals America Ltd ....E..... 914 694-9200
Purchase (G-13005)

J & J Bronze & Aluminum Cast ....E..... 718 383-2111
Brooklyn (G-1976)

Mehr Foil Corp.................................G..... 631 648-9742
Ronkonkoma (G-13972)

Meloon Foundries LLC ....E..... 315 454-3231
Syracuse (G-14939)

Micro Instrument Corp ....D..... 585 458-3150
Rochester (G-13545)

◆ Milward Alloys Inc ....E..... 716 434-5536
Lockport (G-7093)

▲ Ppi Corp ....D..... 585 243-0300
Rochester (G-13633)

Pyrotek Incorporated ....D..... 607 756-3050
Cortland (G-3784)

Smart USA Inc ....F..... 631 969-1111
Bay Shore (G-715)

Taylor Metalworks Inc.......................C..... 716 662-3113
Orchard Park (G-12378)

Wolff & Dungey Inc ....E..... 315 475-2105
Syracuse (G-15029)

3366 Copper Foundries

American Blade Mfg LLC ....G..... 607 656-4204
Greene (G-5443)

American Blade Mfg LLC ....F..... 607 432-4518
Oneonta (G-12256)

Amt Incorporated ....E..... 518 284-2910
Sharon Springs (G-14382)

Art Bedi-Makky Foundry Corp ....G..... 718 383-4191
Brooklyn (G-1534)

David Fehlman ....G..... 315 455-8888
Syracuse (G-14875)

▲ Eastern Finding Corp ....F..... 516 747-6640
New Hyde Park (G-8263)

J & J Bronze & Aluminum Cast ....E..... 718 383-2111
Brooklyn (G-1976)

Meloon Foundries LLC ....E..... 315 454-3231
Syracuse (G-14939)

▲ Modern Art Foundry Inc ....E..... 718 728-2030
Astoria (G-430)

Omega Wire Inc ....E..... 315 337-4300
Rome (G-13862)

Omega Wire Inc ....D..... 315 689-7115
Jordan (G-6630)

Ross Precision Mfg Inc ....F..... 518 273-3912
Green Island (G-5442)

3369 Nonferrous Foundries: Castings, NEC

Allstar Casting Corporation ....E..... 212 563-0909
New York (G-8520)

Buffalo Metal Casting Co Inc ....E..... 716 874-6211
Buffalo (G-2677)

▲ Cardona Industries USA Ltd ....G..... 516 466-5200
Great Neck (G-5373)

Carrera Casting Corp.........................C..... 212 382-3296
New York (G-8924)

Cast-All Corporation ....E..... 516 741-4025
Mineola (G-7965)

City Casting Corp.............................G..... 212 938-0511
New York (G-9017)

Controlled Castings Corp ....E..... 516 349-1718
Plainview (G-12673)

▲ Cpp-Syracuse Inc ....E..... 315 687-0014
Chittenango (G-3406)

Crown Die Casting Corp.....................E..... 914 667-5400
Mount Vernon (G-8135)

Globalfoundries US Inc ....D..... 518 305-9013
Malta (G-7495)

Globalfoundries US Inc ....F..... 408 462-3900
Ballston Spa (G-574)

Greenfield Die Casting Corp ....E..... 516 623-9230
Freeport (G-5000)

J & J Bronze & Aluminum Cast ....E..... 718 383-2111
Brooklyn (G-1976)

▼ Jamestown Bronze Works Inc ....G..... 716 665-2302
Jamestown (G-6521)

K & H Precision Products Inc ....E..... 585 624-4894
Honeoye Falls (G-6076)

Karbra Company ....C..... 212 736-9300
New York (G-10069)

Kelly Foundry & Machine Co ....E..... 315 732-8313
Utica (G-15279)

Lamothermic Corp ....D..... 845 278-6161
Brewster (G-1153)

▲ Medi-Ray Inc ....D..... 877 898-3003
Tuckahoe (G-15205)

Miller Technology Inc ....G..... 631 694-2224
Farmingdale (G-4684)

◆ Plattco Corporation ....E..... 518 563-4640
Plattsburgh (G-12768)

Plattco Corporation ....F..... 518 563-4640
Plattsburgh (G-12769)

▲ Polich Tallix Inc ....D..... 845 567-9464
Rock Tavern (G-13821)

Quality Castings Inc ....E..... 732 409-3203
Long Island City (G-7335)

Speyside Foundry Holdings LLC ....G..... 212 994-0308
New York (G-11319)

Summit Aerospace Inc ....G..... 718 433-1326
Long Island City (G-7374)

Wemco Casting LLC ....D..... 631 563-8050
Bohemia (G-1098)

▲ Zierick Manufacturing Corp ....D..... 800 882-8020
Mount Kisco (G-8108)

3398 Metal Heat Treating

A1 International Heat Treating ....G..... 718 863-5552
Bronx (G-1188)

B & W Heat Treating Company ....G..... 716 876-8184
Tonawanda (G-15088)

Bodycote Syracuse Heat Treatin ....E..... 315 451-0000
Liverpool (G-7001)

Bodycote Thermal Proc Inc ....E..... 585 436-7876
Rochester (G-13276)

BSV Metal Finishers Inc ....E..... 585 747-7070
Rochester (G-13285)

Buffalo Armory LLC ....G..... 716 935-6346
Buffalo (G-2670)

Burke Frging Heat Treating Inc...........E..... 585 235-6060
Rochester (G-13287)

Burton Industries Inc ....E..... 631 643-6660
West Babylon (G-15697)

Cpp - Steel Treaters ....E..... 315 736-3081
Oriskany (G-12388)

Elmira Heat Treating Inc ....E..... 607 734-1577
Elmira (G-4350)

Expedient Heat Treating Corp..............G..... 716 433-1177
North Tonawanda (G-12066)

◆ Gibraltar Industries Inc ....D..... 716 826-6500
Buffalo (G-2775)

▲ Graywood Companies Inc ....A..... 585 738-8889
Rochester (G-13450)

Great Lakes Metal Treating ....F..... 716 694-1240
Tonawanda (G-15107)

Hercules Heat Treating Corp...............E..... 718 625-1266
Brooklyn (G-1932)

Hi-Temp Brazing Inc ....E..... 631 491-4917
Deer Park (G-3879)

◆ International Ord Tech Inc ....D..... 716 664-1100
Jamestown (G-6518)

Jasco Heat Treating Inc ....E..... 585 388-0071
Fairport (G-4501)

Metal Improvement Company LLC.......D....... 607 533-7000
Lansing (G-6841)
Milgo Industrial Inc ....D....... 718 388-6476
Brooklyn (G-2153)
Milgo Industrial Inc ....G....... 718 387-0406
Brooklyn (G-2154)
Parfuse Corp ....E....... 516 997-8888
Westbury (G-15916)
Rochester Steel Treating Works..........F....... 585 546-3348
Rochester (G-13699)
Rough Brothers Holding Co ....G....... 716 826-6500
Buffalo (G-2965)

3399 Primary Metal Prdts, NEC

Advantech Industries Inc ....C....... 585 247-0701
Rochester (G-13213)
Aip Mc Holdings LLC........................G....... 212 627-2360
New York (G-8502)
▲ Ames Advanced Materials Corp......D....... 518 792-5808
South Glens Falls (G-14511)
Ames Goldsmith Corp ....F....... 518 792-7435
Glens Falls (G-5239)
Bridge Components Inc ....G....... 716 731-1184
Sanborn (G-14136)
◆ Buffalo Tungsten Inc ....D....... 716 683-9170
Depew (G-3975)
Cintube Ltd ....F....... 518 324-3333
Plattsburgh (G-12742)
Custom Design Metals Inc ....G....... 631 563-2444
Bohemia (G-994)
▲ Cws Powder Coatings Company LP G....... 845 398-2911
Blauvelt (G-927)
Hje Company Inc ....G....... 518 792-8733
Queensbury (G-13043)
▼ HK Metal Trading Ltd ....G....... 212 868-3333
New York (G-9796)
▲ John Hassall LLC.........................D....... 516 334-6200
Westbury (G-15898)
New England Reclamation Inc ....F....... 914 949-2000
White Plains (G-16034)
Oerlikon Metco (us) Inc ....G....... 716 270-2228
Amherst (G-238)
Pmb Precision Products Inc ....F....... 631 491-6753
West Babylon (G-15737)
Reed Systems Ltd ....F....... 845 647-3660
Ellenville (G-4310)
▼ Rembar Company LLC ....G....... 914 693-2620
Dobbs Ferry (G-4019)
Robert J Deluca Associates...............G....... 845 357-3212
New York (G-11061)
Specialty Fabricators......................F....... 631 433-0258
Oakdale (G-12155)
Tam Ceramics Group of Ny LLC..........D....... 716 278-9400
Niagara Falls (G-11984)
Trico Holding Corporation ....A....... 716 852-5700
Buffalo (G-3019)
◆ Universal Metals Inc.....................G....... 516 829-0896
Great Neck (G-5430)

34 FABRICATED METAL PRODUCTS, EXCEPT MACHINERY AND TRANSPORTATION EQUIPMENT

3411 Metal Cans

Anheuser-Busch Companies LLC.......G....... 718 589-2610
Bronx (G-1206)
Arconic Fastening Systems................F....... 585 368-5049
Rochester (G-13244)
Ardagh Metal Packaging USA Inc ....C....... 607 584-3300
Conklin (G-3621)
Ball Metal Beverage Cont Corp ....C....... 845 692-3800
Middletown (G-7894)
Ball Metal Beverage Cont Corp ....C....... 518 587-6030
Saratoga Springs (G-14165)
Brakewell Stl Fabricators Inc...............E....... 845 469-9131
Chester (G-3371)
Cmc-Kuhnke Inc..............................F....... 518 694-3310
Albany (G-62)
Crown Cork & Seal Usa Inc ....C....... 845 343-9586
Middletown (G-7902)
Erie Engineered Products Inc ....E....... 716 206-0204
Lancaster (G-6805)
Hornet Group Inc ....D....... 845 858-6400
Port Jervis (G-12850)
J C Industries Inc ....E....... 631 420-1920
West Babylon (G-15716)
Marley Spoon Inc ....C....... 866 228-4513
New York (G-10372)

Metal Container Corporation ....C....... 845 567-1500
New Windsor (G-8372)
◆ Reynolds Metals Company LLC........G....... 212 518-5400
New York (G-11031)
Silgan Containers Mfg Corp ....C....... 315 946-4826
Lyons (G-7452)

3412 Metal Barrels, Drums, Kegs & Pails

Abbot & Abbot Box Corp ....F....... 888 930-5972
Long Island City (G-7143)
Erie Engineered Products Inc ....E....... 716 206-0204
Lancaster (G-6805)
Hornet Group Inc ....D....... 845 858-6400
Port Jervis (G-12850)
J R Cooperage Co Inc.......................G....... 718 387-1664
Brooklyn (G-1982)
▲ Medi-Ray Inc ....D....... 877 898-3003
Tuckahoe (G-15205)
Mobile Mini Inc ....D....... 315 732-4555
Utica (G-15285)
Westrock - Southern Cont LLC............C....... 315 487-6111
Camillus (G-3113)
Westrock Cp LLC ....C....... 716 694-1000
North Tonawanda (G-12098)

3421 Cutlery

Advanced Machine Design Co Inc ....E....... 716 826-2000
Buffalo (G-2624)
BSD Aluminum Foil LLC ....E....... 347 689-3875
Brooklyn (G-1626)
Gibar Inc ....C....... 315 452-5656
Cicero (G-3420)
HFC Prestige Intl US LLC ....A....... 212 389-7800
New York (G-9778)
Inquiring Minds Inc ....F....... 845 246-5775
Saugerties (G-14202)
John A Eberly Inc............................G....... 315 449-3034
Syracuse (G-14917)
▲ Klein Cutlery LLC.........................D....... 585 928-2500
Bolivar (G-1101)
◆ Korin Inc ....E....... 212 587-7021
New York (G-10128)
◆ Lifetime Brands Inc ....B....... 516 683-6000
Garden City (G-5104)
Mpdraw LLC ....E....... 212 228-8383
New York (G-10511)
▲ Novelty Crystal Corp ....D....... 718 458-6700
Long Island City (G-7310)
Oneida International Inc ....E....... 315 361-3000
Oneida (G-12249)
Oneida Silversmiths Inc ....E....... 315 361-3000
Oneida (G-12252)
◆ Ontario Knife Company ....D....... 716 676-5527
Franklinville (G-4967)
Palladia Inc ....E....... 212 206-3669
New York (G-10743)
Ratan Ronkonkoma ....G....... 631 588-6800
Ronkonkoma (G-14001)
▲ Revlon Consumer Products Corp .....B....... 212 527-4000
New York (G-11027)
▲ Schilling Forge Inc ....E....... 315 454-4421
Syracuse (G-14987)
Schrader Meat Market.......................F....... 607 869-6328
Romulus (G-13879)
Servotronics Inc.............................C....... 716 655-5990
Elma (G-4327)
Sherrill Manufacturing Inc ....C....... 315 280-0727
Sherrill (G-14406)
Starfire Swords Ltd Inc ....E....... 607 589-7244
Spencer (G-14550)
▲ Treyco Products Corp ....G....... 716 693-6525
Tonawanda (G-15148)
▲ Utica Cutlery Company ....D....... 315 733-4663
Utica (G-15298)
Warren Cutlery Corp ....F....... 845 876-3444
Rhinebeck (G-13103)
Woods Knife Corporation ....E....... 516 798-4972
Massapequa (G-7653)

3423 Hand & Edge Tools

Allway Tools Inc ....D....... 718 792-3636
Bronx (G-1202)
Ames Companies Inc........................E....... 607 739-4544
Pine Valley (G-12634)
Ames Companies Inc........................D....... 607 369-9595
Unadilla (G-15220)
Best Way Tools By Anderson Inc ....G....... 631 586-4702
Deer Park (G-3845)
Boucheron Joaillerie USA Inc..............E....... 212 715-7330
New York (G-8839)

Classic Tool Design Inc.....................E....... 845 562-8700
New Windsor (G-8363)
Clopay Ames True Temper..................F....... 212 957-5096
New York (G-9035)
Coastel Cable Tools Inc ....E....... 315 471-5361
Syracuse (G-14855)
▲ Dead Ringer LLC ....G....... 585 355-4685
Rochester (G-13340)
▲ Design Source By Lg Inc ....E....... 212 274-0022
New York (G-9207)
▲ Dresser-Argus Inc ....G....... 718 643-1540
Brooklyn (G-1762)
Edward C Lyons Company Inc ....G....... 718 515-5361
Bronx (G-1250)
Edward C Muller Corp ....E....... 718 881-7270
Bronx (G-1251)
Empire Devleopment ....G....... 716 789-2097
Mayville (G-7682)
Gei International Inc ....E....... 315 463-9261
East Syracuse (G-4212)
Huron TI Cutter Grinding Inc ....E....... 631 420-7000
Farmingdale (G-4646)
▲ Hydramec Inc ....F....... 585 593-5190
Scio (G-14325)
◆ Ivy Classic Industries Inc ....E....... 914 632-8200
New Rochelle (G-8343)
▲ Lancaster Knives Inc ....E....... 716 683-5050
Lancaster (G-6814)
Metro City Group Inc ....E....... 516 781-2500
Bellmore (G-784)
Nyc District Council Ubcja ....G....... 212 366-7500
New York (G-10660)
Robinson Tools LLC ....E....... 585 586-5432
Penfield (G-12573)
Royal Molds Inc...............................F....... 718 382-7686
Brooklyn (G-2361)
▲ Schilling Forge Inc ....E....... 315 454-4421
Syracuse (G-14987)
▲ Snyder Manufacturing Inc ....E....... 716 945-0354
Salamanca (G-14129)
◆ Swimline International Corp.............C....... 631 254-2155
Edgewood (G-4285)
▲ U S Air Tool Co Inc ....G....... 631 471-3300
Ronkonkoma (G-14019)
Wall Tool & Tape Corp ....E....... 718 641-6813
Ozone Park (G-12468)
Winters Railroad Service Inc ....G....... 716 337-2668
North Collins (G-12030)
Woods Knife Corporation ....E....... 516 798-4972
Massapequa (G-7653)
York Industries Inc ....E....... 516 746-3736
Garden City Park (G-5126)

3425 Hand Saws & Saw Blades

Allway Tools Inc ....D....... 718 792-3636
Bronx (G-1202)
◆ Amana Tool Corp ....D....... 631 752-1300
Farmingdale (G-4582)
▲ Diamond Saw Works Inc ....E....... 716 496-7417
Chaffee (G-3305)
Dinosaw Inc ....E....... 518 828-9942
Hudson (G-6154)
Niabraze LLC.................................F....... 716 447-1082
Tonawanda (G-15126)
Quality Saw & Knife Inc ....F....... 631 491-4747
West Babylon (G-15739)
▼ Suffolk McHy & Pwr TI Corp ....G....... 631 289-7153
Patchogue (G-12512)

3429 Hardware, NEC

A & L Doors & Hardware LLC ....F....... 718 585-8400
Bronx (G-1184)
Advantage Wholesale Supply LLC.......D....... 718 284-5346
Brooklyn (G-1467)
American Casting and Mfg Corp ....G....... 516 349-7010
Plainview (G-12663)
Amertac Holdings Inc ....G....... 610 336-1330
Monsey (G-8034)
Barry Industries Inc ....F....... 212 242-5200
New York (G-8734)
Bfg Marine Inc ....F....... 631 586-5500
Bay Shore (G-656)
Boa Security Technologies Corp..........G....... 516 480-6822
Huntington (G-6202)
Boehm Surgical Instrument Corp.........F....... 585 436-6584
Rochester (G-13277)
▲ Cant Live Without It LLC ....D....... 844 517-9355
New York (G-8906)
Cast-All Corporation ....E....... 516 741-4025
Mineola (G-7965)

▲ City Store Gates Mfg Corp ....E 718 939-9700
College Point *(G-3540)*

▲ Classic Brass Inc ....D 716 763-1400
Lakewood *(G-6780)*

▲ Crest Lock Co Inc ....F 718 345-9898
Brooklyn *(G-1700)*

D Best Service Co Inc ....G 718 972-6133
Brooklyn *(G-1715)*

Daniel Demarco and Assoc Inc ....E 631 598-7000
Amityville *(G-262)*

▼ Darman Manufacturing Coinc ....F 315 724-9632
Utica *(G-15253)*

▲ Decorative Hardware ....F 914 238-5251
Chappaqua *(G-3324)*

▲ Delta Lock Company LLC ....F 631 238-7035
Bohemia *(G-1002)*

Designatronics Incorporated ....B 516 328-3300
New Hyde Park *(G-8261)*

▲ Dico Products Corporation ....F 315 797-0470
Utica *(G-15255)*

Dortronics Systems Inc ....E 631 725-0505
Sag Harbor *(G-14098)*

Dover Marine Mfg & Sup Co Inc ....G 631 667-4300
Deer Park *(G-3864)*

Eazy Locks LLC ....G 718 327-7770
Far Rockaway *(G-4563)*

▲ ER Butler & Co Inc ....E 212 925-3565
New York *(G-9392)*

Excelco Developments Inc ....E 716 934-2651
Silver Creek *(G-14441)*

Fastener Dimensions Inc ....E 718 847-6321
Ozone Park *(G-12461)*

G Marks Hdwr Liquidating Corp ....D 631 225-5400
Amityville *(G-263)*

Grow Computer Inc ....G 646 535-2037
Brooklyn *(G-1912)*

▲ H A Guden Company Inc ....E 631 737-2900
Ronkonkoma *(G-13945)*

Industrial Electronic Hardware ....D 718 492-4440
Brooklyn *(G-1956)*

Ingham Industries Inc ....E 631 242-2493
Holbrook *(G-6001)*

International Key Supply LLC ....F 631 983-6096
Farmingdale *(G-4652)*

▲ ITR Industries Inc ....E 914 964-7063
Yonkers *(G-16321)*

◆ Jaquith Industries Inc ....E 315 478-5700
Syracuse *(G-14916)*

▲ Kenstan Lock & Hardware Co Inc ...E 631 423-1977
Plainview *(G-12694)*

▲ Key High Vacuum Products Inc ......E 631 584-5959
Nesconset *(G-8219)*

▲ Kilian Manufacturing Corp ....D 315 432-0700
Syracuse *(G-14925)*

Kyntec Corporation ....G 716 810-6956
Buffalo *(G-2840)*

▲ Legendary Auto Interiors Ltd ....E 315 331-1212
Newark *(G-11843)*

Lewis Avenue LLC ....F 718 669-0579
Brooklyn *(G-2064)*

▲ Liberty Brass Turning Co Inc ....E 718 784-2911
Westbury *(G-15904)*

Lif Industries Inc ....E 718 767-8800
Whitestone *(G-16097)*

Magellan Aerospace Processing ....G 631 694-1818
West Babylon *(G-15728)*

Metalocke Industries Inc ....G 718 267-9200
Woodside *(G-16213)*

Morgik Metal Designs ....F 212 463-0304
New York *(G-10503)*

◆ Nanz Custom Hardware Inc ....E 212 367-7000
New York *(G-10532)*

Nanz Custom Hardware Inc ....C 212 367-7000
Deer Park *(G-3908)*

◆ Napco Security Tech Inc ....C 631 842-9400
Amityville *(G-297)*

◆ Nielsen Hardware Corporation ....E 607 821-1475
Binghamton *(G-902)*

◆ Northknight Logistics Inc ....F 716 283-3090
Niagara Falls *(G-11957)*

▲ Orbital Holdings Inc ....E 951 360-7100
Buffalo *(G-2899)*

◆ P & F Industries Inc ....E 631 694-9800
Melville *(G-7813)*

◆ P E Guerin ....D 212 243-5270
New York *(G-10733)*

Pk30 System LLC ....F 212 473-8050
Stone Ridge *(G-14736)*

Real Design Inc ....F 315 429-3071
Dolgeville *(G-4026)*

Rollson Inc ....E 631 423-9578
Huntington *(G-6221)*

◆ Rosco Inc ....C 718 526-2601
Jamaica *(G-6471)*

▲ Safe Skies LLC ....G 888 632-5027
New York *(G-11114)*

Southco Inc ....B 585 624-2545
Honeoye Falls *(G-6080)*

Syraco Products Inc ....F 315 476-5306
Syracuse *(G-15002)*

▼ Tattersall Industries LLC ....E 518 381-4270
Schenectady *(G-14311)*

▲ Taylor Made Group LLC ....E 518 725-0681
Gloversville *(G-5294)*

Tools & Stamping Corp ....G 718 392-4040
Brooklyn *(G-2510)*

Trico Manufacturing Corp ....G 718 349-6565
Brooklyn *(G-2520)*

Truth Hardware Corporation ....G 585 627-5964
Rochester *(G-13777)*

Turbine Engine Comp Utica ....A 315 768-8070
Whitesboro *(G-16084)*

United Aircraft Tech Inc ....G 518 286-8867
Troy *(G-15193)*

▲ United Metal Industries Inc ....G 516 354-6800
New Hyde Park *(G-8299)*

▲ Water Street Brass Corporation ....E 716 763-0059
Lakewood *(G-6787)*

▲ Weber-Knapp Company ....C 716 484-9135
Jamestown *(G-6553)*

William H Jackson Company ....G 718 784-4482
Long Island City *(G-7403)*

◆ Wolo Mfg Corp ....E 631 242-0333
Deer Park *(G-3955)*

Yaloz Mould & Die Co Inc ....E 718 389-1131
Brooklyn *(G-2599)*

York Industries Inc ....E 516 746-3736
Garden City Park *(G-5126)*

Zip Products Inc ....F 585 482-0044
Rochester *(G-13815)*

3431 Enameled Iron & Metal Sanitary Ware

◆ Advance Tabco Inc ....D 631 242-8270
Hauppauge *(G-5578)*

▲ Independent Home Products LLC .....E 718 541-1256
West Hempstead *(G-15770)*

▲ ITR Industries Inc ....E 914 964-7063
Yonkers *(G-16321)*

Kenbenco Inc ....F 845 246-3066
Saugerties *(G-14203)*

Ketcham Medicine Cabinets ....E 631 615-6151
Ronkonkoma *(G-13957)*

▲ Kraus USA Inc ....F 800 775-0703
Port Washington *(G-12897)*

◆ Metpar Corp ....D 516 333-2600
Westbury *(G-15910)*

▲ Sola Home Expo Inc ....G 718 646-3383
Brooklyn *(G-2436)*

Stainless Metals Inc ....F 718 784-1454
Woodside *(G-16228)*

Vanity Fair Bathmart Inc ....F 718 584-6700
Bronx *(G-1389)*

◆ Vigo Industries LLC ....G 866 591-7792
New York *(G-11682)*

▲ Watermark Designs Holdings Ltd .....D 718 257-2800
Brooklyn *(G-2576)*

3432 Plumbing Fixture Fittings & Trim, Brass

A B S Brass Products Inc ....F 718 497-2115
Brooklyn *(G-1431)*

Acme Parts Inc ....E 718 649-1750
Brooklyn *(G-1457)*

Artys Sprnklr Svc Instllation ....F 516 538-4371
East Meadow *(G-4131)*

Corona Plumbing & Htg Sup Inc ....G 718 424-4133
Corona *(G-3736)*

Coronet Parts Mfg Co Inc ....E 718 649-1750
Brooklyn *(G-1689)*

Coronet Parts Mfg Co Inc ....E 718 649-1750
Brooklyn *(G-1690)*

▲ ER Butler & Co Inc ....E 212 925-3565
New York *(G-9392)*

Faucets and More Incorporated ....G 734 328-2387
Brooklyn *(G-1833)*

G Sicuranza Ltd ....G 516 759-0259
Glen Cove *(G-5193)*

Giagni Enterprises LLC ....G 914 699-6500
Mount Vernon *(G-8143)*

Hanco Metal Products Inc ....F 212 787-5992
Brooklyn *(G-1924)*

L A S Replacement Parts Inc ....F 718 583-4700
Bronx *(G-1296)*

▲ Liberty Brass Turning Co Inc ....E 718 784-2911
Westbury *(G-15904)*

Malyn Industrial Ceramics Inc ....G 716 741-1510
Clarence Center *(G-3448)*

◆ P E Guerin ....D 212 243-5270
New York *(G-10733)*

Roccera LLC ....F 585 426-0887
Rochester *(G-13678)*

Toto USA Inc ....G 917 237-0665
New York *(G-11521)*

▲ Watermark Designs Holdings Ltd ....D 718 257-2800
Brooklyn *(G-2576)*

3433 Heating Eqpt

A Nuclimate Qulty Systems Inc ....F 315 431-0226
East Syracuse *(G-4192)*

American Comfort Direct LLC ....E 201 364-8309
New York *(G-8548)*

Atlantis Energy Systems Inc ....G 916 438-2930
Poughkeepsie *(G-12946)*

Best Boilers Inc ....F 718 372-4210
Brooklyn *(G-1578)*

Biotech Energy Inc ....G 800 340-1387
Plattsburgh *(G-12736)*

Carrier Corporation ....B 315 432-6000
Syracuse *(G-14844)*

▲ Chentronics LLC ....E 607 334-5531
Norwich *(G-12117)*

▲ Chicken Hawk Racing Inc ....G 845 758-0700
Red Hook *(G-13072)*

▲ CIDC Corp ....F 718 342-5820
Glendale *(G-5222)*

Dandelion Energy Inc ....F 603 781-2663
New York *(G-9163)*

◆ Dyson-Kissner-Moran Corp ....E 212 661-4600
Poughkeepsie *(G-12952)*

Economy Pump & Motor Repr Inc ....G 718 433-2600
Astoria *(G-418)*

◆ ECR International Inc ....D 315 797-1310
Utica *(G-15260)*

ECR International Inc ....C 716 366-5500
Dunkirk *(G-4056)*

◆ Embassy Industries Inc ....C 631 435-0209
Hauppauge *(G-5647)*

Empire Industrial Burner Svc ....F 631 242-4619
Deer Park *(G-3872)*

Fisonic Corp ....G 212 732-3777
Long Island City *(G-7225)*

▲ Fisonic Corp ....F 716 763-0295
New York *(G-9507)*

Frederick Cowan & Company Inc ....F 631 369-0360
Wading River *(G-15449)*

▲ Fulton Heating Solutions Inc ....D 315 298-5121
Pulaski *(G-12998)*

▼ Fulton Volcanic Inc ....D 315 298-5121
Pulaski *(G-12999)*

General Electric Intl Inc ....G 518 385-2211
Schenectady *(G-14273)*

Great Rock Automation Inc ....F 631 270-1508
Farmingdale *(G-4640)*

▲ Integrated Solar Tech LLC ....G 914 249-9364
Binghamton *(G-888)*

▲ Juniper Elbow Co Inc ....C 718 326-2546
Middle Village *(G-7881)*

◆ Mx Solar USA LLC ....C 732 356-7300
New York *(G-10523)*

Nanopv Corporation ....C 609 851-3666
Liverpool *(G-7028)*

New Energy Systems Group ....C 917 573-0302
New York *(G-10580)*

▲ Omega Heater Company Inc ....D 631 588-8820
Ronkonkoma *(G-13986)*

▲ Prism Solar Technologies Inc ....E 845 883-4200
Highland *(G-5962)*

◆ RE Hansen Industries Inc ....C 631 471-2900
Saint James *(G-14113)*

▲ Roberts-Gordon LLC ....D 716 852-4400
Buffalo *(G-2957)*

Rockmills Steel Products Corp ....F 718 366-8300
Great Neck *(G-5417)*

▲ Slant/Fin Corporation ....B 516 484-2600
Greenvale *(G-5464)*

Solar Energy Systems LLC ....F 718 389-1545
Brooklyn *(G-2437)*

Vincent Genovese ....G 631 281-8170
Mastic Beach *(G-7675)*

3441 Fabricated Structural Steel

760 NI Holdings ....E 716 821-1391
Buffalo *(G-2614)*

▲ A & T Iron Works Inc ....E 914 632-8992
New Rochelle *(G-8315)*

◆ A-Fab Initiatives Inc ....F 716 877-5257
Buffalo *(G-2616)*

▲ A/C Design & Fabrication Corp........G 718 227-8100
Staten Island *(G-14615)*

AAA Welding and Fabrication of ....G 585 254-2830
Rochester *(G-13196)*

Abalon Precision Mfg Corp ....E 914 665-7700
Mount Vernon *(G-8120)*

▲ Acadia Stairs ....G 845 765-8600
Fishkill *(G-4797)*

Accucut Inc ....G 631 567-2868
West Sayville *(G-15838)*

Ackroyd Metal Fabricators Inc.........F 518 434-1281
Menands *(G-7837)*

Adsco Manufacturing Corp ....D 716 827-5450
Buffalo *(G-2623)*

Advanced Thermal Systems Inc........E 716 681-1800
Lancaster *(G-6790)*

▼ Aero-Data Metal Crafters Inc..........C 631 471-7733
Ronkonkoma *(G-13892)*

Aldo Frustacci Iron Works Inc ....F 718 768-0707
Brooklyn *(G-1480)*

Alken Industries Inc ....E 631 467-2000
Ronkonkoma *(G-13896)*

All-City Metal Inc ....E 718 937-3975
Maspeth *(G-7586)*

Alloy Metal Works Inc ....G 631 694-8163
Farmingdale *(G-4580)*

Alpha Iron Works LLC ....F 585 424-7260
Rochester *(G-13224)*

American Aerogel Corporation ....E 585 328-2140
Rochester *(G-13228)*

Apollo Steel Corporation ....F 716 283-8758
Niagara Falls *(G-11907)*

Asp Industries Inc ....E 585 254-9130
Rochester *(G-13253)*

Atlantis Equipment Corporation..........F 518 733-5910
Stephentown *(G-14730)*

B H M Metal Products Co ....G 845 292-5297
Kauneonga Lake *(G-6640)*

▲ Barber Welding Inc ....E 315 834-6645
Weedsport *(G-15665)*

Barker Steel LLC ....E 518 465-6221
Albany *(G-44)*

Barry Steel Fabrication Inc ....E 716 433-2144
Lockport *(G-7061)*

Bear Metal Works Inc ....F 716 824-4350
Buffalo *(G-2659)*

Bellmore Steel Products Corp ....F 516 785-9667
Bellmore *(G-780)*

▲ Bennett Manufacturing Co Inc........C 716 937-9161
Alden *(G-166)*

Bereza Iron Works Inc ....E 585 254-6311
Rochester *(G-13266)*

Blackstone Advanced Tech LLC..........C 716 665-5410
Jamestown *(G-6498)*

Bms Manufacturing Co Inc ....E 607 535-2426
Watkins Glen *(G-15613)*

Bob Murphy Inc ....F 607 729-3553
Vestal *(G-15373)*

Bombardier Transportation ....D 607 324-0216
Hornell *(G-6102)*

Bombardier Trnsp Holdings USA ....D 607 776-4791
Bath *(G-631)*

Bristol Metals Inc ....F 585 657-7665
Bloomfield *(G-941)*

Buffalo Metal Fabricating Corp ....F 716 892-7800
Buffalo *(G-2678)*

Buffalo Structural Steel Inc ....E 814 827-1350
Syracuse *(G-14835)*

Burnt Hills Fabricators Inc ....E 518 885-1115
Ballston Spa *(G-570)*

C & C Custom Metal Fabricators ....G 631 235-9646
Hauppauge *(G-5610)*

C & C Metal Fabrications Inc ....E 315 598-7607
Fulton *(G-5055)*

C & T Tool & Instrument Co ....E 718 429-1253
Woodside *(G-16199)*

Cameron Bridge Works LLC ....E 607 734-9456
Horseheads *(G-6116)*

▲ Cameron Mfg & Design Inc............C 607 739-3606
Horseheads *(G-6117)*

Carpenter Industries Inc ....F 315 463-4284
Syracuse *(G-14843)*

Castle Harvester Co Inc..................G 585 526-5884
Seneca Castle *(G-14361)*

CBM Fabrications Inc ....E 518 399-8023
Ballston Lake *(G-559)*

Chautauqua Machine Spc LLC ....F 716 782-3276
Ashville *(G-409)*

Christian Fabrication LLC ....G 315 822-0135
West Winfield *(G-15857)*

Cives Corporation ....C 315 287-2200
Gouverneur *(G-5318)*

Cobbe Industries Inc ....G 716 287-2661
Gerry *(G-5170)*

Cobra Operating Industries LLC ....G 607 639-1700
Afton *(G-7)*

Coco Architectureal Grilles...............G 631 482-9449
Farmingdale *(G-4600)*

Computerized Metal Bending Ser........F 631 249-1177
West Babylon *(G-15704)*

Cottonwood Metals Inc ....G 646 807-8674
Bohemia *(G-991)*

County Fabricators ....F 914 741-0219
Pleasantville *(G-12796)*

Cyncal Steel Fabricators Inc ....F 631 254-5600
Bay Shore *(G-668)*

D N Gannon Fabricating Inc ....G 315 463-7466
Syracuse *(G-14872)*

Dennies Manufacturing Inc ....E 585 393-4646
Canandaigua *(G-3130)*

Diversified Manufacturing Inc............F 716 681-7670
Lancaster *(G-6803)*

Donald Stefan ....G 716 492-1110
Chaffee *(G-3306)*

Duquettes Steel & Structural F ....F 518 563-3161
Plattsburgh *(G-12745)*

E B Atlas Steel Corp ....F 716 876-0900
Buffalo *(G-2733)*

Eastern Manufacturing Inc ....F 716 741-4572
Clarence *(G-3432)*

Eastern Trading Partners Corp..........G 212 202-1451
Brooklyn *(G-1778)*

Eastern Welding Inc......................G 631 727-0306
Riverhead *(G-13174)*

Elevator Accessories Mfg ....F 914 739-7004
Peekskill *(G-12550)*

Elite Steel Fabricators Inc ....G 631 285-1008
Ronkonkoma *(G-13935)*

Empire Industrial Systems Corp ....F 631 242-4619
Bay Shore *(G-678)*

Empire Metal Fabricators Inc ....G 585 288-2140
Rochester *(G-13388)*

Empro Niagara Inc ....G 716 433-2769
Lockport *(G-7073)*

Eps Iron Works Inc ....G 516 294-5840
Mineola *(G-7972)*

Erie Engineered Products Inc ....E 716 206-0204
Lancaster *(G-6805)*

Everfab Inc.................................D 716 655-1550
East Aurora *(G-4086)*

Excel Industries Inc ....E 716 542-5468
Clarence *(G-3434)*

Farmingdale Iron Works Inc.............G 631 249-5995
Farmingdale *(G-4629)*

Feinstein Iron Works Inc ....F 516 997-8300
Westbury *(G-15885)*

Fence Plaza Corp ....G 718 469-2200
Brooklyn *(G-1838)*

Five Corners Repair Inc ....F 585 322-7369
Bliss *(G-939)*

▼ Flagpoles Incorporated ....D 631 751-5500
East Setauket *(G-4178)*

▲ Fort Miller Group Inc ....B 518 695-5000
Greenwich *(G-5471)*

FPL Fbrctors Erctors Group LLC ....G 917 334-6968
Howard Beach *(G-6139)*

▲ Framing Technology Inc...............E 585 464-8470
Rochester *(G-13422)*

Frazier Industrial Company ....D 315 539-9256
Waterloo *(G-15552)*

Fred A Nudd Corporation ....E 315 524-2531
Ontario *(G-12289)*

Fred Santucci Inc ....F 716 483-1411
Jamestown *(G-6511)*

Gasport Welding & Fabg Inc ....F 716 772-7205
Gasport *(G-5137)*

Genesee Metal Products Inc ....E 585 968-6000
Wellsville *(G-15671)*

George Industries LLC ....D 607 748-3371
Endicott *(G-4458)*

◆ Gibraltar Industries Inc................D 716 826-6500
Buffalo *(G-2775)*

Glenridge Fabricators Inc ....F 718 456-2297
Glendale *(G-5227)*

Hansen Steel ....E 585 398-2020
Farmington *(G-4772)*

▲ Hebeler LLC ....C 716 873-9300
Tonawanda *(G-15111)*

Homer Iron Works LLC ....G 607 749-3963
Homer *(G-6064)*

Industrial Fabricating Corp ....E 315 437-3353
East Syracuse *(G-4218)*

▲ Industrial Support Inc ....D 716 662-2954
Buffalo *(G-2809)*

◆ Inscape (new York) Inc ....D 716 665-6210
Falconer *(G-4544)*

Inter Metal Fabricators Inc ....F 718 852-4000
Brooklyn *(G-1962)*

International Metals Trdg LLC ....G 866 923-0182
Melville *(G-7796)*

Irony Limited Inc ....G 631 329-4065
East Hampton *(G-4123)*

Irv Schroder & Sons Inc ....E 518 828-0194
Stottville *(G-14753)*

J F M Sheet Metal Inc ....G 631 737-8494
Ronkonkoma *(G-13950)*

J M Haley Corp ....C 631 845-5200
Farmingdale *(G-4654)*

Jaab Precision Inc ....G 631 218-3725
Ronkonkoma *(G-13953)*

James Woerner Inc ....G 631 454-9330
Farmingdale *(G-4656)*

Jaxson LLC ....G 631 842-7775
Amityville *(G-279)*

Jbs LLC ....G 518 346-0001
Scotia *(G-14333)*

Jentsch & Co Inc ....G 716 852-4111
Buffalo *(G-2819)*

Joy Edward Company ....E 315 474-3360
Syracuse *(G-14921)*

Jpw Structural Contracting Inc...........E 315 432-1111
Syracuse *(G-14922)*

K & E Fabricating Company Inc ....F 716 829-1829
Buffalo *(G-2827)*

Kal Manufacturing Corporation ....E 585 265-4310
Webster *(G-15644)*

KDO Industries Inc ....G 631 608-4612
Amityville *(G-284)*

King Steel Iron Work Corp ....F 718 384-7500
Brooklyn *(G-2030)*

Kleinfelder John ....G 716 753-3163
Mayville *(G-7683)*

Knj Fabricators LLC ....F 347 234-6985
Bronx *(G-1294)*

Koenig Iron Works Inc....................E 718 433-0900
Long Island City *(G-7263)*

Kryten Iron Works Inc....................E 914 345-0990
Hawthorne *(G-5816)*

Kuno Steel Products Corp ....F 516 938-8500
Hicksville *(G-5921)*

L&B Fabricators LLC ....E 585 265-2731
Ontario *(G-12292)*

Lindenhurst Fabricators Inc ....G 631 226-3737
Lindenhurst *(G-6954)*

Linita Design & Mfg Corp ....E 716 566-7753
Lackawanna *(G-6741)*

M & E Mfg Co Inc ....D 845 331-7890
Kingston *(G-6702)*

▲ M & L Steel & Ornamental Iron ....F 718 816-8660
Staten Island *(G-14678)*

▲ Mageba USA LLC ....E 212 317-1991
New York *(G-10321)*

▲ Major-IPC Inc ....G 845 292-2200
Liberty *(G-6925)*

▲ Marex Aquisition Corp ....E 585 458-3940
Rochester *(G-13536)*

▲ Marovato Industries Inc................F 718 389-0800
Brooklyn *(G-2119)*

◆ Mason Industries Inc...................C 631 348-0282
Hauppauge *(G-5708)*

Maspeth Welding Inc ....E 718 497-5430
Maspeth *(G-7627)*

Metal Crafts Inc ....G 718 443-3333
Brooklyn *(G-2146)*

Metal Fab LLC ....G 607 775-3200
Binghamton *(G-898)*

Metal Works of NY Inc ....G 718 525-9440
Jamaica *(G-6459)*

Metro Iron Corp ....G 631 842-5929
Amityville *(G-296)*

Miller Metal Fabricating Inc..............G 585 359-3400
Rochester *(G-13549)*

Miscellnous Ir Fabricators Inc ....E 518 355-1822
  Schenectady *(G-14290)*

Mobile Mini Inc ....F 315 732-4555
  Utica *(G-15285)*

▲ Modern Mechanical Fab Inc ....G 518 298-5177
  Champlain *(G-3315)*

Mount Vernon Iron Works Inc ....G 914 668-7064
  Mount Vernon *(G-8163)*

Nathan Steel Corp ....F 315 797-1335
  Utica *(G-15287)*

Nb Elctrcal Enclsures Mfrs Inc ....G 718 272-8792
  Brooklyn *(G-2194)*

Nci Group Inc ....D 315 339-1245
  Rome *(G-13859)*

Neversink Steel Corp ....G 845 292-4611
  Liberty *(G-6926)*

New Age Ironworks Inc ....F 718 277-1895
  Brooklyn *(G-2199)*

New Vision Industries Inc ....F 607 687-7700
  Endicott *(G-4466)*

New York Manufactured Products ......F 585 254-9353
  Rochester *(G-13570)*

Nextgen Building Components ....E 585 924-7171
  Farmington *(G-4776)*

North E Rggers Erectors NY Inc ....E 518 842-6377
  Amsterdam *(G-342)*

Northeast Fabricators LLC.................D 607 865-4031
  Walton *(G-15476)*

Oehlers Wldg & Fabrication Inc..........F 716 821-1800
  Buffalo *(G-2894)*

Orange County Ironworks LLC ....G 845 769-3000
  Montgomery *(G-8064)*

▲ Oriskany Mfg Tech LLC ....E 315 732-4962
  Yorkville *(G-16378)*

P K G Equipment Incorporated ....E 585 436-4650
  Rochester *(G-13605)*

Patsy Strocchia & Sons Iron Wo ....F 516 625-8800
  Albertson *(G-148)*

Pcx Aerostructures LLC ....E 631 467-2632
  Farmingdale *(G-4702)*

Penasack Machine Company Inc ....E 585 589-7044
  Albion *(G-159)*

Peralta Metal Works Inc ....G 718 649-8661
  Brooklyn *(G-2254)*

Perma Tech Inc ....E 716 854-0707
  Buffalo *(G-2915)*

▲ Pierce Industries LLC ....E 585 458-0888
  Rochester *(G-13623)*

Pierce Steel Fabricators ....F 716 372-7652
  Olean *(G-12240)*

Pirod Inc ....E 631 231-7660
  Hauppauge *(G-5742)*

Port Authority of NY & NJ ....D 718 390-2534
  Staten Island *(G-14691)*

Precision Metals Corp ....E 631 586-5032
  Bay Shore *(G-700)*

Precision Polish LLC ....E 315 894-3792
  Frankfort *(G-4955)*

Precision Spclty Fbrctions LLC............F 716 824-2108
  Buffalo *(G-2929)*

Prime Materials Recovery Inc ....G 315 697-5251
  Canastota *(G-3154)*

▲ Productand Design Inc ....F 718 858-2440
  Brooklyn *(G-2297)*

Pwf Enterprise LLC...........................F 315 695-2223
  Phoenix *(G-12620)*

R&S Steel LLC ....E 315 281-0123
  Rome *(G-13865)*

Raulli and Sons Inc ....D 315 479-6693
  Syracuse *(G-14972)*

REO Welding Inc ....F 518 238-1022
  Cohoes *(G-3514)*

▲ Risa Management Corp ....E 718 361-2606
  Maspeth *(G-7637)*

Riverside Iron LLC ....F 315 535-4864
  Gouverneur *(G-5322)*

RJ Precision LLC ....G 585 768-8030
  Stafford *(G-14605)*

▲ Robert E Derecktor Inc ....D 914 698-0962
  Mamaroneck *(G-7522)*

Roman Iron Works Inc ....F 516 621-1103
  Greenvale *(G-5463)*

Romar Contracting Inc ....G 845 778-2737
  Walden *(G-15461)*

Roth Design & Consulting Inc ....E 718 209-0193
  Brooklyn *(G-2357)*

Rothe Welding Inc............................G 845 246-3051
  Saugerties *(G-14210)*

Rough Brothers Holding Co ....E 716 826-6500
  Buffalo *(G-2965)*

Rs Automation ....F 585 589-0199
  Albion *(G-160)*

▲ Rus Industries Inc ....E 716 284-7828
  Niagara Falls *(G-11975)*

Rw Gate Company ....F 518 874-4750
  Troy *(G-15185)*

Rw Gate Company ....D 518 874-4750
  Troy *(G-15186)*

▼ Salit Specialty Rebar Inc ....E 716 299-1990
  Buffalo *(G-2974)*

Schenectady Steel Co Inc ....E 518 355-3220
  Schenectady *(G-14302)*

Schneider Brothers Corporation ....E 315 458-8369
  Syracuse *(G-14988)*

Schuler-Subra Inc ....G 716 893-3100
  Buffalo *(G-2975)*

▲ Seibel Modern Mfg & Wldg Corp ....D 716 683-1536
  Lancaster *(G-6834)*

Sentry Metal Blast Inc ....E 716 285-5241
  Lockport *(G-7106)*

Silverstone Shtmtl Fbrications ....G 718 422-0380
  Brooklyn *(G-2416)*

Specialty Steel Fabg Corp ....F 718 893-6326
  Bronx *(G-1368)*

Specialty Wldg & Fabg NY Inc ....D 315 426-1807
  Syracuse *(G-14998)*

Steel Tech SA LLC ....G 845 786-3691
  Thiells *(G-15065)*

▲ Stone Bridge Iron and Stl Inc.........D 518 695-3752
  Gansevoort *(G-5087)*

▼ Stone Well Bodies & Mch Inc.........E 315 497-3512
  Genoa *(G-5168)*

STS Steel Inc ....D 518 370-2693
  Schenectady *(G-14308)*

Team Fabrication Inc ....G 716 655-4038
  West Falls *(G-15762)*

Titan Steel Corp ....F 315 656-7046
  Kirkville *(G-6727)*

Tms Structures Inc ....C 646 740-7646
  New York *(G-11503)*

Torino Indus Fabrication Inc ....G 631 509-1640
  Bellport *(G-809)*

Triton Builders Inc ....E 631 841-2534
  Amityville *(G-314)*

Tropical Driftwood Originals ....G 516 623-0980
  Roosevelt *(G-14034)*

Tymetal Corp ....E 518 692-9930
  Fort Edward *(G-4945)*

Tymetal Corp ....E 518 692-9930
  Greenwich *(G-5477)*

Ulster Precision Inc ....E 845 338-0995
  Kingston *(G-6717)*

United Iron Inc ....E 914 667-5700
  Mount Vernon *(G-8191)*

United Structure Solution Inc ....F 347 227-7526
  New York *(G-11601)*

Universal Metal Works LLC................F 315 598-7607
  Fulton *(G-5076)*

▲ Vance Metal Fabricators Inc...........D 315 789-5626
  Geneva *(G-5165)*

Vulcan Iron Works Inc ....G 631 395-6846
  Manorville *(G-7555)*

Vulcraft of New York Inc ....C 607 529-9000
  Chemung *(G-3366)*

Ward Steel Company Inc ....E 315 451-4566
  Liverpool *(G-7047)*

◆ Watson Bowman Acme Corp ....C 716 691-8162
  Amherst *(G-253)*

Welding Metallurgy Inc ....D 631 586-5200
  Edgewood *(G-4293)*

Werok LLC ....F 845 675-7710
  Valley Cottage *(G-15329)*

Whitacre Engineering Company..........G 315 622-1075
  Liverpool *(G-6554)*

Wilston Enterprises Inc ....F 716 483-1411
  Jamestown *(G-6554)*

Winters Railroad Service Inc ....G 716 337-2668
  North Collins *(G-12030)*

Xli Manufacturing LLC ....E 585 436-2250
  Rochester *(G-13812)*

3442 Metal Doors, Sash, Frames, Molding & Trim

A & L Doors & Hardware LLC ....F 718 585-8400
  Bronx *(G-1184)*

▲ A & S Window Associates Inc..........E 718 275-7900
  Glendale *(G-5216)*

A G M Deco Inc.................................F 718 624-6200
  Brooklyn *(G-1433)*

▲ A G M Deco Inc ....D 718 624-6200
  Brooklyn *(G-1434)*

Accurate Metal Weather Strip ....G 914 668-6042
  Mount Vernon *(G-8121)*

Ace Fire Door Corp ....E 718 901-0001
  Bronx *(G-1194)*

▲ Acme Architectural Pdts Inc ....D 718 384-7800
  Brooklyn *(G-1456)*

Action Bullet Resistant......................F 631 422-0888
  West Islip *(G-15810)*

Advanced Door Solutions Inc ....C 631 773-6100
  Holbrook *(G-5984)*

Air Tite Manufacturing Inc.................C 516 897-0295
  Long Beach *(G-7134)*

All United Window Corp ....E 718 624-0490
  Brooklyn *(G-1487)*

Altype Fire Door Corporation ....G 718 292-3500
  Bronx *(G-1203)*

▲ Alumil Fabrication Inc....................F 845 469-2874
  Long Island City *(G-7153)*

Alvio-US Corp ....E 631 664-0618
  Hauppauge *(G-5586)*

Amarr Company ....F 585 426-8290
  Rochester *(G-13226)*

Assa Abloy Entrance Systems US ....E 315 492-6600
  East Syracuse *(G-4198)*

Corkhill Manufacturing Co Inc............G 718 528-7413
  Jamaica *(G-6438)*

D D & L Inc ....F 607 729-9131
  Binghamton *(G-870)*

Dawson Metal Company Inc ....C 716 664-3811
  Jamestown *(G-6506)*

▲ Dayton Industries Inc ....E 718 542-8144
  Bronx *(G-1237)*

Dural Door Company Inc ....F 718 729-1333
  Long Island City *(G-7206)*

East Pattern & Model Corp.................F 585 461-3240
  Rochester *(G-13363)*

Eastern Storefronts & Mtls Inc ....F 631 471-7065
  Ronkonkoma *(G-13933)*

◆ Ellison Bronze Inc ....D 716 665-6522
  Falconer *(G-4538)*

Empire Archtctural Systems Inc..........E 518 773-5109
  Johnstown *(G-6615)*

Excel Aluminum Products Inc ....G 315 471-0925
  Syracuse *(G-14891)*

▲ F A Alpine Windows Mfg ....F 845 469-5700
  Chester *(G-3377)*

Fha Firedoor Corp ....G 718 366-1700
  Central Islip *(G-3275)*

Five Boro Doors Mouldings Inc...........G 718 865-9371
  Oceanside *(G-12173)*

Gamma North Corporation ....E 716 902-5100
  Alden *(G-169)*

General Fire-Proof Door Corp.............E 718 893-5500
  Bronx *(G-1265)*

◆ Global Steel Products Corp ....C 631 586-3455
  Deer Park *(G-3878)*

◆ Great American Industries Inc ....G 607 729-9331
  Vestal *(G-15379)*

◆ Griffon Corporation ....E 212 957-5000
  New York *(G-9676)*

Gscp Emax Acquisition LLC ....G 212 902-1000
  New York *(G-9690)*

▲ Hopes Windows Inc ....C 716 665-5124
  Jamestown *(G-6516)*

I Fix Screen ....G 631 421-1938
  Centereach *(G-3251)*

◆ Inscape (new York) Inc ....D 716 665-6210
  Falconer *(G-4544)*

Inter-Fence Co Inc ....E 718 939-9700
  College Point *(G-3546)*

Interntional Fireprof Door Inc ....F 718 783-1310
  Brooklyn *(G-1967)*

▲ Interstate Window Corporation ....D 631 231-0800
  Brentwood *(G-1123)*

It Windows & Doors Inc ....G 646 220-8398
  Rye Brook *(G-14090)*

▼ J Sussman Inc ....E 718 297-0228
  Jamaica *(G-6450)*

▲ Jaidan Industries Inc ....F 516 944-3650
  Port Washington *(G-12891)*

Jenmar Door & Glass Inc ....G 718 767-7900
  Whitestone *(G-16095)*

▲ Karey Kassl Corp ....E 516 349-8484
  Plainview *(G-12693)*

▲ Karp Associates Inc ....D 631 768-8300
  Melville *(G-7798)*

▲ Kasson & Keller Inc ....A 518 853-3421
  Fonda *(G-4910)*

S
I
C

Kelly Window Systems Inc ....E 631 420-8500
Farmingdale *(G-4664)*

▲ Kinro Manufacturing Inc ....G 817 483-7791
White Plains *(G-16022)*

L & L Overhead Garage Doors ....G 718 721-2518
Long Island City *(G-7267)*

Lif Industries Inc ....D 516 390-6800
Port Washington *(G-12899)*

Lif Industries Inc ....E 718 767-8800
Whitestone *(G-16097)*

▼ M & D Installers Inc ....G 718 782-6978
Brooklyn *(G-2092)*

Markar Architectural Products ....G 716 685-4104
Lancaster *(G-6817)*

▲ McKeon Rolling Stl Door Co Inc .....E 631 803-3000
Bellport *(G-803)*

Mercury Lock and Door Service ....E 718 542-7048
Bronx *(G-1310)*

Metalline Fire Door Co Inc ....E 718 583-2320
Bronx *(G-1311)*

Michbi Doors Inc ....D 631 231-9050
Farmingdale *(G-4683)*

Milanese Commercial Door LLC ....F 518 658-0398
Berlin *(G-825)*

Milgo Industrial Inc ....D 718 388-6476
Brooklyn *(G-2153)*

Milgo Industrial Inc ....E 718 387-0406
Brooklyn *(G-2154)*

Munschauer Inc ....F 716 895-8888
Buffalo *(G-2877)*

New Bgnnngs Win Door Dstrs LLC ...F 845 214-0698
Poughkeepsie *(G-12974)*

◆ Optimum Window Mfg Corp ....E 845 647-1900
Ellenville *(G-4309)*

Overhead Door Corporation ....D 518 828-7652
Hudson *(G-6173)*

Pal Manufacturing Corp ....E 516 937-1990
Hicksville *(G-5940)*

Pioneer Window Holdings Inc ....F 516 822-7000
Roslyn Heights *(G-14055)*

Pioneer Window Holdings Inc ....E 518 762-5526
Johnstown *(G-6625)*

Pk30 System LLC ....F 212 473-8050
Stone Ridge *(G-14736)*

▲ Presray Corporation ....E 845 373-9300
Wassaic *(G-15526)*

Raydoor Inc ....G 212 421-0641
New York *(G-10988)*

Revival Sash & Door LLC ....G 973 500-4242
New York *(G-11025)*

▲ Robert-Masters Corp ....G 718 545-1030
Woodside *(G-16224)*

Rochester Colonial Mfg Corp ....D 585 254-8191
Rochester *(G-13686)*

Rochester Lumber Company ....G 585 924-7171
Farmington *(G-4778)*

Rohlfs Stined Leaded GL Studio ....E 914 699-4848
Mount Vernon *(G-8178)*

Roly Door Sales Inc ....G 716 877-1515
Hamburg *(G-5520)*

Shade & Shutter Systems of NY ....G 631 208-0275
Southampton *(G-14537)*

Slanto Manufacturing Inc ....E 516 759-5721
Glen Cove *(G-5201)*

Statewide Fireproof Door Co ....F 845 268-6043
Valley Cottage *(G-15326)*

Steelmasters Inc ....E 718 498-2854
Brooklyn *(G-2458)*

Sunrise Door Solutions ....G 631 464-4139
Copiague *(G-3680)*

Superior Stl Door Trim Co Inc ....F 716 665-3256
Jamestown *(G-6548)*

Supreme Fire Proof Door Co ....F 718 665-4224
Bronx *(G-1374)*

Texas Home Security Inc ....E 516 747-2100
New Hyde Park *(G-8296)*

Thermal Tech Doors Inc ....E 516 745-0100
Garden City *(G-5118)*

Thompson Overhead Door Co Inc ......F 718 788-2470
Brooklyn *(G-2503)*

Truth Hardware Corporation ....G 585 627-5964
Rochester *(G-13777)*

United Steel Products Inc ....D 914 968-7782
Flushing *(G-4904)*

▲ United Steel Products Inc ....D 718 478-5330
Corona *(G-3751)*

Universal Fire Proof Door ....E 718 455-8442
Brooklyn *(G-2543)*

Vr Containment LLC ....G 917 972-3441
Fresh Meadows *(G-5048)*

Window Tech Systems Inc ....E 518 899-9000
Ballston Spa *(G-589)*

Windowman Inc (usa) ....G 718 246-2626
Brooklyn *(G-2590)*

3443 Fabricated Plate Work

828 Express Inc ....G 917 577-9019
Staten Island *(G-14612)*

▲ A K Allen Co Inc ....C 516 747-5450
Melville *(G-7753)*

A L Eastmond & Sons Inc ....D 718 378-3000
Bronx *(G-1186)*

▲ Aavid Niagara LLC ....E 716 297-0652
Niagara Falls *(G-11900)*

▲ Acro Industries Inc ....C 585 254-3661
Rochester *(G-13204)*

▲ Aerco International Inc ....C 845 580-8000
Blauvelt *(G-925)*

▲ Aero-Data Metal Crafters Inc ....C 631 471-7733
Ronkonkoma *(G-13892)*

All-State Diversified Pdts Inc ....E 315 472-4728
Syracuse *(G-14810)*

▲ Allstate Gasket & Packing Inc ....C 631 254-4050
Deer Park *(G-3835)*

American Boiler Tank Wldg Inc ....E 518 463-5012
Albany *(G-39)*

◆ American Precision Inds Inc ....C 716 691-9100
Amherst *(G-210)*

▼ Amherst Stnless Fbrication LLC .....E 716 691-7012
Amherst *(G-211)*

◆ API Heat Transf Thermasys Corp ....E 716 684-6700
Buffalo *(G-2638)*

API Heat Transfer Company ....F 716 684-6700
Buffalo *(G-2639)*

API Heat Transfer Inc ....C 585 496-5755
Arcade *(G-368)*

◆ API Heat Transfer Inc ....B 716 684-6700
Buffalo *(G-2640)*

Arvos Inc ....G 585 593-2700
Wellsville *(G-15667)*

Atlantic Industrial Tech Inc ....E 631 234-3131
Shirley *(G-14415)*

Aurora Indus Machining Inc ....E 716 826-7911
Orchard Park *(G-12338)*

Bigbee Steel and Tank Company ....E 518 273-0801
Watervliet *(G-15597)*

Blackstone Advanced Tech LLC ....C 716 665-5410
Jamestown *(G-6498)*

Boileroom Fabrication LLC ....E 516 488-4848
Syosset *(G-14779)*

Bos-Hatten Inc ....E 716 662-7030
Orchard Park *(G-12339)*

Breton Industries Inc ....C 518 842-3030
Amsterdam *(G-320)*

Bridgehampton Steel & Wldg Inc ....F 631 537-2486
Bridgehampton *(G-1164)*

Bruce Pierce ....G 716 731-9310
Sanborn *(G-14138)*

◆ Buflovak LLC ....E 716 895-2100
Buffalo *(G-2685)*

Byelocorp Scientific Inc ....E 212 785-2580
New York *(G-8877)*

Cardinal Tank Corp ....E 718 625-4350
Brooklyn *(G-1647)*

▲ Charles Ross & Son Company ....D 631 234-0500
Hauppauge *(G-5614)*

Chart Industries Inc ....E 716 691-0202
Amherst *(G-218)*

▲ Cigar Box Studios Inc ....F 845 236-9283
Marlboro *(G-7579)*

CMS Heat Transfer Division Inc ....E 631 968-0084
Bohemia *(G-990)*

Contech Engnered Solutions LLC ......F 716 870-9091
Orchard Park *(G-12348)*

▼ Costanzos Welding Inc ....E 716 282-0845
Niagara Falls *(G-11917)*

Crown Tank Company LLC ....F 855 276-9682
Horseheads *(G-6119)*

Cyclotherm of Watertown Inc ....E 315 782-1100
Watertown *(G-15568)*

David Isseks & Sons Inc ....E 212 966-8694
New York *(G-9179)*

Direkt Force LLC ....E 716 652-3022
East Aurora *(G-4085)*

◆ ECR International Inc ....D 315 797-1310
Utica *(G-15260)*

ECR International Inc ....C 716 366-5500
Dunkirk *(G-4056)*

Empire Industrial Systems Corp ....F 631 242-4619
Bay Shore *(G-678)*

Endicott Precision Inc ....C 607 754-7076
Endicott *(G-4451)*

Energy Nuclear Operations ....E 315 342-0055
Oswego *(G-12410)*

Erie Engineered Products Inc ....E 716 206-0204
Lancaster *(G-6805)*

Exergy LLC ....E 516 832-9300
Garden City *(G-5100)*

Expert Industries Inc ....E 718 434-6060
Brooklyn *(G-1823)*

Feldmeier Equipment Inc ....D 315 823-2000
Syracuse *(G-14893)*

Fluid Handling LLC ....C 716 897-2800
Cheektowaga *(G-3348)*

Fross Industries Inc ....E 716 297-0652
Niagara Falls *(G-11930)*

Fuel Efficiency Inc ....E 315 923-2511
Clyde *(G-3491)*

◆ Fulton Boiler Works Inc ....D 315 298-5121
Pulaski *(G-12995)*

Fulton Boiler Works Inc ....C 315 298-5121
Pulaski *(G-12996)*

Fulton China LLC ....G 315 298-0112
Pulaski *(G-12997)*

Gasport Welding & Fabg Inc ....F 716 772-7205
Gasport *(G-5137)*

General Oil Equipment Co Inc ....E 716 691-7012
Amherst *(G-225)*

Glenridge Fabricators Inc ....F 718 456-2297
Glendale *(G-5227)*

◆ Global Steel Products Corp ....C 631 586-3455
Deer Park *(G-3878)*

◆ Graham Corporation ....B 585 343-2216
Batavia *(G-616)*

Hyperbaric Technologies Inc ....G 518 842-3030
Amsterdam *(G-330)*

Industrial Fabricating Corp ....E 315 437-8234
East Syracuse *(G-4219)*

Inex Inc ....E 716 537-2270
Holland *(G-6029)*

J & T Metal Products Co Inc ....E 631 226-7400
West Babylon *(G-15715)*

J D Cousins Inc ....E 716 824-1098
Buffalo *(G-2815)*

J M Canty Inc ....E 716 625-4227
Lockport *(G-7084)*

J W Stevens Co Inc ....G 315 472-6311
East Syracuse *(G-4223)*

◆ Jaquith Industries Inc ....E 315 478-5700
Syracuse *(G-14916)*

Jbren Corp ....F 716 332-5928
Buffalo *(G-2817)*

John R Robinson Inc ....E 718 786-6088
Long Island City *(G-7255)*

K Industries Inc ....G 631 897-2125
Bellport *(G-801)*

Kintex Inc ....D 716 297-0652
Niagara Falls *(G-11944)*

Lane Enterprises Inc ....F 607 776-3366
Bath *(G-638)*

▲ Lifetime Chimney Supply LLC ....G 516 576-8144
Plainview *(G-12696)*

Manhattan Cooling Towers Inc ....F 212 279-1045
Long Island City *(G-7288)*

Manning Lewis Div Rubicon Inds ....E 908 687-2400
Brooklyn *(G-2110)*

▲ Marex Aquisition Corp ....C 585 458-3940
Rochester *(G-13536)*

Methods Tooling & Mfg Inc ....E 845 246-7100
Mount Marion *(G-8111)*

Metrofab Pipe Incorporated ....F 516 349-7373
Plainview *(G-12701)*

Miller Metal Fabricating Inc ....G 585 359-3400
Rochester *(G-13549)*

◆ Mitsubishi Chemical Amer Inc ....E 212 223-3043
New York *(G-10484)*

Modutank Inc ....F 718 392-1112
Long Island City *(G-7298)*

Mono-Systems Inc ....E 716 821-1344
Buffalo *(G-2871)*

▲ Motivair Corporation ....E 716 691-9222
Amherst *(G-233)*

Niagara Cooler Inc ....G 716 434-1235
Lockport *(G-7096)*

Nitram Energy Inc ....E 716 662-6540
Orchard Park *(G-12368)*

North American Svcs Group LLC ....F 518 885-1820
Ballston Spa *(G-583)*

Perforated Screen Surfaces E 866 866-8690
Conklin *(G-3627)*
Pfaudler US Inc C 585 235-1000
Rochester *(G-13618)*
Roemac Industrial Sales Inc G 716 692-7332
North Tonawanda *(G-12088)*
Rosenwach Tank Co Inc E 212 972-4411
Astoria *(G-439)*
Ross Metal Fabricators Inc E 631 586-7000
Deer Park *(G-3930)*
RPI of Indiana Inc E 330 279-2421
Brooklyn *(G-2363)*
Saraga Industries Corp G 631 842-4049
Amityville *(G-306)*
Sargent Manufacturing Inc G 212 722-7000
New York *(G-11137)*
Schwabel Fabricating Co Inc E 716 876-2086
Tonawanda *(G-15138)*
▲ Seibel Modern Mfg & Wldg Corp D 716 683-1536
Lancaster *(G-6834)*
▲ Slant/Fin Corporation B 516 484-2600
Greenvale *(G-5464)*
Slantco Manufacturing Inc G 516 484-2600
Greenvale *(G-5465)*
SPX Cooling Technologies Inc G 914 697-5030
Irvington *(G-6314)*
SPX Corporation G 914 366-7402
Tarrytown *(G-15062)*
SPX Corporation E 631 467-2632
Ronkonkoma *(G-14013)*
SPX Corporation B 585 436-5550
Rochester *(G-13741)*
Stainless Metals Inc F 718 784-1454
Woodside *(G-16228)*
▲ Stavo Industries Inc F 845 331-4552
Kingston *(G-6712)*
Steele Truss and Panel LLC G 518 562-4663
Plattsburgh *(G-12779)*
Steelways Inc E 845 562-0860
Newburgh *(G-11887)*
Stutzman Management Corp F 800 735-2013
Lancaster *(G-6836)*
Supreme Boilers Inc G 718 342-2220
Brooklyn *(G-2476)*
Taylor Tank Company Inc E 718 434-1300
Brooklyn *(G-2494)*
Themis Chimney Inc F 718 937-4716
Brooklyn *(G-2502)*
Troy Boiler Works Inc E 518 274-2650
Troy *(G-15192)*
United Wind Inc E 888 313-3353
Brooklyn *(G-2541)*
Vertarib Inc G 561 683-0888
Jericho *(G-6597)*
◆ Vship Co F 718 706-8566
Astoria *(G-443)*
Wastequip Manufacturing Co LLC E 800 235-0734
New Lebanon *(G-8304)*
Water Cooling Corp G 718 723-6500
Rosedale *(G-14038)*
Wayne Integrated Tech Corp E 631 242-0213
Edgewood *(G-4291)*
Weslor Industries Inc E 315 871-4405
Lyons *(G-7454)*
West Metal Works Inc E 716 895-4900
Buffalo *(G-3045)*
▼ Wsf Industries Inc E 716 692-4930
Tonawanda *(G-15155)*
▲ Yula Corporation E 718 991-0900
Bronx *(G-1398)*
Zone Fabricators Inc F 718 272-0200
Ozone Park *(G-12470)*

3444 Sheet Metal Work

A & L Shtmtl Fabrications Corp E 718 842-1600
Bronx *(G-1185)*
Aabco Sheet Metal Co Inc D 718 821-1166
Ridgewood *(G-13137)*
Aberdeen Blower & Shtmtl Works G 631 661-6100
West Babylon *(G-15680)*
Accra Sheetmetal LLC G 631 643-2100
Wyandanch *(G-16241)*
Accurate Specialty Metal Fabri E 718 418-6895
Middle Village *(G-7876)*
▲ Acme Architectural Pdts Inc D 718 384-7800
Brooklyn *(G-1456)*
▲ Acro Industries Inc C 585 254-3661
Rochester *(G-13204)*
Acro-Fab Ltd E 315 564-6688
Hannibal *(G-5542)*
Advanced Precision Technology F 845 279-3540
Brewster *(G-1138)*
Advantage Metalwork Finshg LLC D 585 454-0160
Rochester *(G-13212)*
Advantech Industries Inc C 585 247-0701
Rochester *(G-13213)*
Aero Trades Mfg Corp E 516 746-3360
Mineola *(G-7955)*
▼ Aero-Data Metal Crafters Inc C 631 471-7733
Ronkonkoma *(G-13892)*
Aeroduct Inc E 516 248-9550
Mineola *(G-7956)*
▲ AFP Enterprises Inc C 585 254-1128
Rochester *(G-13215)*
Air Louver & Damper Inc F 718 392-3232
Long Island City *(G-7147)*
Aj Genco Mch Sp McHy Rdout Svc F 716 664-4925
Falconer *(G-4532)*
Albany Mtal Fbrcation Holdings G 518 463-5161
Albany *(G-35)*
Aldo Frustacci Iron Works Inc F 718 768-0707
Brooklyn *(G-1480)*
Aleta Industries Inc F 718 349-0040
Brooklyn *(G-1482)*
Alkemy Machine LLC G 585 436-8730
Rochester *(G-13217)*
All Island Blower & Shtmtl F 631 567-7070
Bohemia *(G-969)*
All Metal Specialties Inc E 716 664-6009
Jamestown *(G-6492)*
All Star Carts & Vehicles Inc D 631 666-5581
Bay Shore *(G-646)*
All Star Sheet Metal Inc F 718 456-1567
Farmingdale *(G-4579)*
▲ Allen Machine Products Inc E 631 630-8800
Hauppauge *(G-5584)*
Alliance Welding & Steel Fabg F 516 775-7600
Floral Park *(G-4806)*
Allure Metal Works Inc F 631 588-0220
Ronkonkoma *(G-13899)*
Alpine Machine Inc F 607 272-1344
Ithaca *(G-6362)*
▲ Alternative Service Inc F 631 345-9500
Bellport *(G-793)*
American Std Shtmtl Sup Corp F 718 888-9350
Flushing *(G-4839)*
Apparatus Mfg Inc G 845 471-5116
Poughkeepsie *(G-12944)*
▲ Arcadia Mfg Group Inc E 518 434-6213
Green Island *(G-5432)*
Arcadia Mfg Group Inc G 518 434-6213
Menands *(G-7840)*
Architctral Shetmetal Pdts Inc G 518 381-6144
Scotia *(G-14328)*
Arlan Damper Corporation E 631 589-7431
Bohemia *(G-976)*
Art Precision Metal Products F 631 842-8889
Copiague *(G-3647)*
▲ Ascension Industries Inc C 716 693-9381
North Tonawanda *(G-12054)*
Asm USA Inc F 212 925-2906
New York *(G-8649)*
Asp Industries Inc E 585 254-9130
Rochester *(G-13253)*
Atech-Seh Metal Fabricator E 716 895-8888
Buffalo *(G-2645)*
Atlantis Equipment Corporation F 518 733-5910
Stephentown *(G-14730)*
Auburn Tank & Manufacturing Co F 315 255-2788
Auburn *(G-463)*
▲ Austin Mohawk and Company LLC E 315 793-3000
Utica *(G-15239)*
Auto Body Services LLC F 631 431-4640
Lindenhurst *(G-6941)*
Avalanche Fabrication Inc F 585 545-4000
Ontario *(G-12285)*
◆ B & B Sheet Metal Inc E 718 433-2501
Long Island City *(G-7173)*
B & H Precision Fabricators F 631 563-9620
Bohemia *(G-977)*
B & R Sheet G 718 558-5544
Jamaica *(G-6428)*
Banner Metalcraft Inc D 631 563-7303
Ronkonkoma *(G-13913)*
Bargold Storage Systems LLC E 718 247-7000
Long Island City *(G-7175)*
Batavia Enclosures Inc G 585 344-1797
Arcade *(G-369)*
Berjen Metal Industries Ltd G 631 673-7979
Huntington *(G-6201)*
Best Tinsmith Supply Inc G 518 863-2541
Northville *(G-12113)*
▼ Bhv Sheet Mtal Fabricators Inc E 607 797-1196
Vestal *(G-15371)*
Billings Sheet Metal Inc G 716 372-6165
Olean *(G-12224)*
Blackstone Advanced Tech LLC C 716 665-5410
Jamestown *(G-6498)*
Bmg Systems F 716 432-5160
Depew *(G-3972)*
Boss Precision Ltd D 585 352-7070
Spencerport *(G-14553)*
Broadway Neon Sign Corp F 908 241-4177
Ronkonkoma *(G-13918)*
Brothers Roofing Supplies Co E 718 779-0280
East Elmhurst *(G-4104)*
Brzozka Industries Inc F 631 588-8164
Holbrook *(G-5987)*
Building New Bridges LLC F 315 960-1242
Remsen *(G-13083)*
C & T Tool & Instrument Co E 718 429-1253
Woodside *(G-16199)*
C J & C Sheet Metal Corp F 631 376-9425
West Babylon *(G-15699)*
▲ Cannon Industries Inc D 585 254-8080
Rochester *(G-13294)*
CBM Fabrications Inc E 518 399-8023
Ballston Lake *(G-559)*
Celtic Sheet Metal Inc E 845 267-3400
Congers *(G-3611)*
Center Sheet Metal Inc C 718 378-4476
Bronx *(G-1222)*
▲ Cetek Inc E 845 452-3510
Poughkeepsie *(G-12948)*
Chamtek Mfg Inc F 585 328-4900
Rochester *(G-13311)*
Chutes and Compactors of NY F 718 494-2247
Staten Island *(G-14638)*
Citros Building Materials Co E 718 779-0727
East Elmhurst *(G-4105)*
City Cooling Enterprises Inc G 718 331-7400
Brooklyn *(G-1664)*
Clark Specialty Co Inc E 607 776-3193
Bath *(G-632)*
Contractors Sheet Metal LLC C 718 786-2505
Long Island City *(G-7191)*
Craft-Tech Mfg Corp G 631 563-4949
Bohemia *(G-992)*
Crown Die Casting Corp E 914 667-5400
Mount Vernon *(G-8135)*
Custom Sheet Metal Corp G 315 463-9105
Syracuse *(G-14870)*
Cutting Edge Metal Works E 631 981-8333
Holtsville *(G-6048)*
Cw Metals Inc E 917 416-7906
Long Island City *(G-7196)*
D & G Sheet Metal Co Inc F 718 326-9111
Maspeth *(G-7603)*
D and D Sheet Metal Corp F 718 465-7585
Jamaica *(G-6440)*
Dart Awning Inc G 516 544-2082
Freeport *(G-4991)*
Dawson Metal Company Inc C 716 664-3811
Jamestown *(G-6506)*
Dayton T Brown Inc B 631 589-6300
Bohemia *(G-1001)*
Delta Sheet Metal Corp C 718 429-5805
Hicksville *(G-5901)*
Dimar Manufacturing Corp C 716 759-0351
Clarence *(G-3428)*
▲ Dj Acquisition Management Corp D 585 265-3000
Ontario *(G-12288)*
Doortec Archtctural Met GL LLC E 718 567-2730
Brooklyn *(G-1758)*
Dundas-Jafine Inc E 716 681-9690
Alden *(G-168)*
Duravent Inc E 518 463-7284
Albany *(G-71)*
E G M Restaurant Equipment Mfg G 718 782-9800
Brooklyn *(G-1771)*
Elderlee Incorporated C 315 789-6670
Oaks Corners *(G-12161)*
Elevator Accessories Mfg F 914 739-7004
Peekskill *(G-12550)*
Elmsford Sheet Metal Works Inc D 914 739-6300
Cortlandt Manor *(G-3794)*
Empire Air Specialties Inc E 518 689-4440
Albany *(G-75)*
Empire Ventilation Eqp Co Inc F 718 728-2143
Florida *(G-4823)*

Endicott Precision Inc ....C 607 754-7076
Endicott *(G-4451)*
Engineering Mfg Tech LLC ....D 607 754-7111
Endicott *(G-4453)*
Expert Industries Inc ....E 718 434-6060
Brooklyn *(G-1823)*
F M L Industries Inc ....G 607 749-7273
Homer *(G-6062)*
Falso Industries Inc ....E 315 463-0266
Syracuse *(G-14892)*
Federal Sheet Metal Works Inc ....F 315 735-4730
Utica *(G-15263)*
Fenton Mobility Products Inc ....G 716 484-7014
Randolph *(G-13062)*
Five Star Industries Inc ....E 716 674-2589
West Seneca *(G-15847)*
Franchet Metal Craft Inc ....G 718 658-6400
Jamaica *(G-6443)*
Fred A Nudd Corporation ....E 315 524-2531
Ontario *(G-12289)*
Genesee Building Products LLC ....F 585 548-2726
Stafford *(G-14603)*
Goergen-Mackwirth Co Inc ....E 716 874-4800
Buffalo *(G-2778)*
Golden Group International Ltd ....G 845 440-1025
Patterson *(G-12517)*
Gottlieb Schwartz Family ....E 718 761-2010
Staten Island *(G-14657)*
Greene Technologies Inc ....D 607 656-4166
Greene *(G-5446)*
Gt Innovations LLC ....G 585 739-7659
Bergen *(G-814)*
H & M Leasing Corp ....G 631 225-5246
Copiague *(G-3656)*
H Klein & Sons Inc ....E 516 746-0163
Mineola *(G-7978)*
Hana Sheet Metal Inc ....G 914 377-0773
Yonkers *(G-16317)*
Hansen Steel ....E 585 398-2020
Farmington *(G-4772)*
Harbor Elc Fabrication Tls Inc ....E 914 636-4400
New Rochelle *(G-8339)*
Hart To Hart Industries Inc ....G 716 492-2709
Chaffee *(G-3307)*
Hatfield Metal Fab Inc ....E 845 454-9078
Poughkeepsie *(G-12961)*
◆ **Hergo Ergonomic Support Syst** ....E 888 222-7270
Oceanside *(G-12175)*
Hermann Gerdens Inc ....G 631 841-3132
Copiague *(G-3658)*
Hi-Tech Industries NY Inc ....E 607 217-7361
Johnson City *(G-6601)*
Hrd Metal Products Inc ....G 631 243-6700
Deer Park *(G-3881)*
Hri Metals LLC ....G 518 822-1013
Hudson *(G-6161)*
◆ **Hunter Douglas Inc** ....D 845 664-7000
Pearl River *(G-12533)*
I Rauchs Sons Inc ....E 718 507-8844
East Elmhurst *(G-4107)*
IEC Electronics Corp ....D 585 647-1760
Rochester *(G-13474)*
Illinois Tool Works Inc ....E 607 770-4945
Binghamton *(G-887)*
Imperial Damper & Louver Co ....E 718 731-3800
Bronx *(G-1279)*
▼ **Incodema Inc** ....E 607 277-7070
Ithaca *(G-6385)*
Industrial Fabricating Corp ....E 315 437-3353
East Syracuse *(G-4218)*
Intellimetal Inc ....D 585 424-3260
Rochester *(G-13481)*
Interior Metals ....E 718 439-7324
Brooklyn *(G-1963)*
J&T Metal Inc ....G 631 471-5335
Ronkonkoma *(G-13952)*
Jamestown Advanced Pdts Corp ....E 716 483-3406
Jamestown *(G-6519)*
◆ **Jaquith Industries Inc** ....E 315 478-5700
Syracuse *(G-14916)*
Jar Metals Inc ....F 845 425-8901
Nanuet *(G-8200)*
▲ **Juniper Elbow Co Inc** ....C 718 326-2546
Middle Village *(G-7881)*
K Barthelmes Mfg Co Inc ....F 585 328-8140
Rochester *(G-13501)*
Kal Manufacturing Corporation ....E 585 265-4310
Webster *(G-15644)*
Karo Sheet Metal Inc ....E 718 542-8420
Brooklyn *(G-2021)*
Kassis Superior Sign Co Inc ....F 315 463-7446
Syracuse *(G-14924)*
Kellys Sheet Metal Inc ....F 718 774-4750
Brooklyn *(G-2023)*
▲ **Kenan International Trading** ....G 718 672-4922
Corona *(G-3742)*
Ksm Group Ltd ....G 716 751-6006
Newfane *(G-11894)*
L&B Fabricators LLC ....F 585 265-2731
Ontario *(G-12292)*
▲ **Lambro Industries Inc** ....D 631 842-8088
Amityville *(G-290)*
Lane Enterprises Inc ....E 518 885-4385
Ballston Spa *(G-579)*
Leader Sheet Metal Inc ....F 347 271-4961
Bronx *(G-1298)*
Liffey Sheet Metal Corp ....F 347 381-1134
Long Island City *(G-7272)*
Lotus Awnings Enterprises Inc ....G 718 965-4824
Brooklyn *(G-2086)*
Maloya Laser Inc ....E 631 543-2327
Commack *(G-3595)*
Manufacturing Resources Inc ....E 631 481-0041
Rochester *(G-13532)*
▲ **Marex Aquisition Corp** ....C 585 458-3940
Rochester *(G-13536)*
Mariah Metal Products Inc ....G 516 938-9783
Hicksville *(G-5926)*
▲ **McAlpin Industries Inc** ....C 585 266-3060
Rochester *(G-13538)*
McHone Industries Inc ....D 716 945-3380
Salamanca *(G-14122)*
MD International Industries ....E 631 254-3100
Deer Park *(G-3906)*
▲ **Melto Metal Products Co Inc** ....E 516 546-8866
Freeport *(G-5007)*
Met Weld International LLC ....D 518 765-2318
Altamont *(G-196)*
Metal Solutions Inc ....C 315 732-6271
Utica *(G-15281)*
Metal Tek Products ....G 516 586-4514
Plainview *(G-12700)*
Metallogix Design Fabrication ....E 315 738-4554
Utica *(G-15282)*
Metalsmith Inc ....G 631 467-1500
Holbrook *(G-6011)*
Methods Tooling & Mfg Inc ....E 845 246-7100
Mount Marion *(G-8111)*
Metro Duct Systems Inc ....F 718 278-4294
Long Island City *(G-7294)*
Middleby Corporation ....E 631 226-6688
Lindenhurst *(G-6960)*
◆ **Mitsubishi Chemical Amer Inc** ....E 212 223-3043
New York *(G-10484)*
▼ **Monarch Metal Fabrication Inc** ....G 631 563-8967
Bohemia *(G-1047)*
Monroe Piping & Shtmtl LLC ....D 585 482-0200
Rochester *(G-13558)*
Ms Spares LLC ....G 607 223-3024
Clay *(G-3451)*
N & L Instruments Inc ....F 631 471-4000
Ronkonkoma *(G-13978)*
Nci Group Inc ....D 315 339-1245
Rome *(G-13859)*
Nelson Air Device Corporation ....C 718 729-3801
Maspeth *(G-7629)*
▼ **North Coast Outfitters Ltd** ....E 631 727-5580
Riverhead *(G-13183)*
Northeast Fabricators LLC ....D 607 865-4031
Walton *(G-15476)*
Northern Awning & Sign Company ....G 315 782-8515
Watertown *(G-15585)*
Olympic Manufacturing Inc ....E 631 231-8900
Hauppauge *(G-5733)*
Omc Inc ....C 718 731-5001
Bronx *(G-1328)*
P R B Metal Products Inc ....F 631 467-1800
Ronkonkoma *(G-13989)*
Pal Aluminum Inc ....G 516 937-1990
Hicksville *(G-5939)*
Pathfinder Industries Inc ....E 315 593-2483
Fulton *(G-5075)*
PDQ Manufacturing Co Inc ....E 845 889-3123
Rhinebeck *(G-13100)*
Penner Elbow Company Inc ....F 718 526-9000
Elmhurst *(G-4337)*
Phoenix Envmtl Svcs Corp ....F 718 381-8100
Glendale *(G-5231)*
Pirnat Precise Metals Inc ....G 631 293-9169
Farmingdale *(G-4709)*
Plattsburgh Sheet Metal Inc ....G 518 561-4930
Plattsburgh *(G-12770)*
Precision Fabrication LLC ....G 585 591-3449
Attica *(G-458)*
Precision Metals Corp ....E 631 586-5032
Bay Shore *(G-700)*
Precision Mtal Fabricators Inc ....F 718 832-9805
Brooklyn *(G-2277)*
Precision Systems Mfg Inc ....E 315 451-3480
Liverpool *(G-7035)*
Product Integration & Mfg Inc ....E 585 436-6260
Rochester *(G-13649)*
Prokosch and Sonn Sheet Metal ....E 845 562-4211
Newburgh *(G-11884)*
Protofast Holding Corp ....G 631 753-2549
Copiague *(G-3671)*
R & J Sheet Metal Distributors ....G 518 433-1525
Albany *(G-120)*
R D R Industries Inc ....F 315 866-5020
Mohawk *(G-8007)*
Radiation Shielding Systems ....F 888 631-2278
Suffern *(G-14765)*
Rainbow Awning Co Inc ....G 716 297-3939
Niagara Falls *(G-11970)*
Rand Products Manufacturing Co ....G 518 374-9871
Schenectady *(G-14297)*
Read Manufacturing Company Inc ....E 631 567-4487
Holbrook *(G-6016)*
Reynolds Manufacturing Inc ....F 607 562-8936
Big Flats *(G-848)*
▲ **Rigidized Metals Corporation** ....E 716 849-4703
Buffalo *(G-2955)*
▲ **Robert E Derecktor Inc** ....D 914 698-0962
Mamaroneck *(G-7522)*
Rochester Colonial Mfg Corp ....D 585 254-8191
Rochester *(G-13686)*
Rollson Inc ....E 631 423-9578
Huntington *(G-6221)*
Royal Metal Products Inc ....E 518 966-4442
Surprise *(G-14776)*
S & B Machine Works Inc ....E 516 997-2666
Westbury *(G-15924)*
S & J Sheet Metal Supply ....G 718 384-0800
Brooklyn *(G-2369)*
S & T Machine Inc ....F 718 272-2484
Brooklyn *(G-2373)*
Savaco Inc ....G 716 751-9455
Newfane *(G-11895)*
Service Mfg Group Inc ....E 716 893-1482
Buffalo *(G-2981)*
Service Mfg Group Inc ....F 716 893-1482
Buffalo *(G-2980)*
Shanghai Stove Inc ....F 718 599-4583
Brooklyn *(G-2403)*
Simmons Fabricating Svc Inc ....G 845 635-3755
Pleasant Valley *(G-12794)*
Smg Metal Products LLC ....G 716 633-6439
Cheektowaga *(G-3361)*
Solidus Industries Inc ....D 607 749-4540
Homer *(G-6067)*
Space Sign ....F 718 961-1112
College Point *(G-3565)*
▲ **Spence Engineering Company Inc** ....C 845 778-5566
Walden *(G-15462)*
Standard Industrial Works Inc ....F 631 888-0130
Bay Shore *(G-717)*
Steel Sales Inc ....E 607 674-6363
Sherburne *(G-14395)*
Steel Work Inc ....G 585 232-1555
Rochester *(G-13744)*
Steelcraft Manufacturing Co ....F 718 277-2404
Brooklyn *(G-2456)*
Sterling Industries Inc ....E 631 753-3070
Farmingdale *(G-4742)*
▲ **Studco Building Systems US LLC** ....D 585 545-3000
Webster *(G-15655)*
Superior Elec Enclosure Inc ....G 718 797-9090
Brooklyn *(G-2474)*
Superior Exteriors of Buffalo ....F 716 873-1000
East Amherst *(G-4079)*
T Lemme Mechanical Inc ....E 518 436-4136
Menands *(G-7849)*
Tatra Mfg Corporation ....F 631 691-1184
Copiague *(G-3682)*
▲ **TCS Industries Inc** ....D 585 426-1160
Rochester *(G-13759)*
Technimetal Precision Inds ....E 631 231-8900
Hauppauge *(G-5782)*
Themis Chimney Inc ....F 718 937-4716
Brooklyn *(G-2502)*

Tri-Metal Industries Inc............E......716 691-3323
Amherst (G-250)

Tri-State Metals LLC.............F......914 347-8157
Elmsford (G-4437)

▲ Tri-Technologies Inc............E......914 699-2001
Mount Vernon (G-8187)

▲ Trident Precision Mfg Inc............D......585 265-2010
Webster (G-15658)

Tripar Manufacturing Co Inc............G......631 563-0855
Bohemia (G-1090)

Truform Manufacturing Corp............D......585 458-1090
Rochester (G-13776)

Trylon Wire & Metal Works Inc............E......718 542-4472
Bronx (G-1384)

Ucr Steel Group LLC............F......718 764-3414
Ronkonkoma (G-14020)

Ulster Precision Inc............E......845 338-0995
Kingston (G-6717)

Unadilla Silo Company Inc............D......607 369-9341
Sidney (G-14438)

United Sheet Metal Corp............E......718 482-1197
Long Island City (G-7388)

Universal Precision Corp............E......585 321-9760
Rochester (G-13785)

Universal Shielding Corp............E......631 667-7900
Deer Park (G-3945)

▲ Vance Metal Fabricators Inc............D......315 789-5626
Geneva (G-5165)

Vin Mar Precision Metals Inc............F......631 563-6608
Copiague (G-3688)

Vitarose Corp of America............G......718 951-9700
Brooklyn (G-2565)

VM Choppy & Sons LLC............E......518 266-1444
Troy (G-15195)

◆ Voss Manufacturing Inc............D......716 731-5062
Sanborn (G-14153)

▲ Wainland Inc............E......718 626-2233
Astoria (G-444)

Wayne Integrated Tech Corp............E......631 242-0213
Edgewood (G-4291)

Wenig Corporation............E......718 542-3600
Bronx (G-1396)

Weslor Industries Inc............E......315 871-4405
Lyons (G-7454)

Wg Sheet Metal Corp............E......718 235-3093
Brooklyn (G-2581)

William Kanes Mfg Corp............G......718 346-1515
Brooklyn (G-2587)

Xli Manufacturing LLC............E......585 436-2250
Rochester (G-13812)

▲ Zahk Sales Inc............G......631 851-0851
Islandia (G-6347)

3446 Architectural & Ornamental Metal Work

786 Iron Works Corp............G......718 418-4808
Brooklyn (G-1424)

▲ A & T Iron Works Inc............E......914 632-8992
New Rochelle (G-8315)

A1 Ornamental Iron Works Inc............G......718 265-3055
Brooklyn (G-1445)

Aca Quality Building Pdts LLC............E......718 991-2423
Bronx (G-1191)

Accurate Welding Service Inc............G......516 333-1730
Westbury (G-15860)

▲ Acme Architectural Pdts Inc............D......718 384-7800
Brooklyn (G-1456)

▼ Aero-Data Metal Crafters Inc............C......631 471-7733
Ronkonkoma (G-13892)

Airflex Corp............D......631 752-1219
Farmingdale (G-4574)

Airflex Industrial Inc............E......631 752-1234
Farmingdale (G-4575)

Airflex Industrial Inc............D......631 752-1234
Farmingdale (G-4576)

Aldo Frustacci Iron Works Inc............F......718 768-0707
Brooklyn (G-1480)

Aldos Iron Works Inc............G......718 834-0408
Brooklyn (G-1481)

All American Metal Corporation............E......516 623-0222
Freeport (G-4983)

All American Stairs & Railing............F......718 441-8400
Richmond Hill (G-13107)

▲ Allied Bronze Corp (del Corp)............E......646 421-6400
New York (G-8517)

▲ Arcadia Mfg Group Inc............E......518 434-6213
Green Island (G-5432)

Arcadia Mfg Group Inc............G......518 434-6213
Menands (G-7840)

Armento Incorporated............E......716 875-2423
Kenmore (G-6648)

Artistic Iron Works Inc............G......631 665-4285
Bay Shore (G-652)

Atlas Fence & Railing Co Inc............E......718 767-2200
Whitestone (G-16088)

Babylon Iron Works Inc............F......631 643-3311
West Babylon (G-15692)

Bobrick Washroom Equipment Inc............D......518 877-7444
Clifton Park (G-3463)

Bracci Ironworks Inc............F......718 629-2374
Brooklyn (G-1604)

C & F Iron Works Inc............F......914 592-2450
Elmsford (G-4397)

C & F Steel Design............F......914 592-3928
Elmsford (G-4398)

Cabezon Design Group Inc............G......718 488-9868
Brooklyn (G-1638)

Caliper Studio Inc............E......718 302-2427
Brooklyn (G-1640)

Cianfarani Armando............G......518 393-7755
Schenectady (G-14256)

▲ City Store Gates Mfg Corp............E......718 939-9700
College Point (G-3540)

Creative Metal Fabricators............G......631 567-2266
Bohemia (G-993)

D V S Iron & Aluminum Works............G......718 768-7961
Brooklyn (G-1716)

Duke of Iron Inc............G......631 543-3600
Smithtown (G-14476)

E & J Iron Works Inc............E......718 665-6040
Bronx (G-1247)

E F Iron Works & Construction............G......631 242-4766
Bay Shore (G-677)

▲ E S P Metal Crafts Inc............G......718 381-2443
Brooklyn (G-1773)

Eagle Metals Corp............F......516 338-5100
Westbury (G-15878)

Ej Group Inc............G......315 699-2601
Cicero (G-3419)

Elevator Accessories Mfg............F......914 739-7004
Peekskill (G-12550)

Empire Steel Works Inc............F......516 561-3500
Hicksville (G-5905)

Fence Plaza Corp............G......718 469-2200
Brooklyn (G-1838)

▼ Flagpoles Incorporated............D......631 751-5500
East Setauket (G-4178)

Flushing Iron Weld Inc............E......718 359-2208
Flushing (G-4853)

Forest Iron Works Inc............F......516 671-4229
Locust Valley (G-7125)

▼ Giumenta Corp............E......718 832-1200
Brooklyn (G-1888)

Giumenta Corp............E......718 832-1200
Brooklyn (G-1889)

◆ Global Steel Products Corp............C......631 586-3455
Deer Park (G-3878)

Grillmaster Inc............E......718 272-9191
Howard Beach (G-6140)

Hi-Tech Metals Inc............E......718 894-1212
Maspeth (G-7622)

Imperial Damper & Louver Co............E......718 731-3800
Bronx (G-1279)

Inter-Fence Co Inc............E......718 939-9700
College Point (G-3546)

Iron Art Inc............G......914 592-7977
Elmsford (G-4412)

Irony Limited Inc............G......631 329-4065
East Hampton (G-4123)

▲ ITR Industries Inc............E......914 964-7063
Yonkers (G-16321)

Jamaica Iron Works Inc............F......718 657-4849
Jamaica (G-6451)

Jamestown Fab Stl & Sup Inc............G......716 665-2227
Jamestown (G-6522)

▲ Jaxson Rollforming Inc............E......631 842-7775
Amityville (G-280)

Jerry Cardullo Iron Works Inc............F......631 242-8881
Bay Shore (G-685)

▲ Jonathan Metal & Glass Ltd............C......718 846-8000
Jamaica (G-6452)

Kenal Services Corp............G......315 788-9226
Watertown (G-15576)

Kendi Iron Works Inc............G......718 821-2722
Brooklyn (G-2024)

▼ Keuka Studios Inc............E......585 624-5960
Rush (G-14073)

Kleinfelder John............G......716 753-3163
Mayville (G-7683)

Kms Contracting Inc............F......718 495-6500
Brooklyn (G-2033)

Koenig Iron Works Inc............E......718 433-0900
Long Island City (G-7263)

Kryten Iron Works Inc............G......914 345-0990
Hawthorne (G-5816)

Lencore Acoustics Corp............E......516 682-9292
Woodbury (G-16175)

Lopopolo Iron Works Inc............G......718 339-0572
Brooklyn (G-2085)

Ludwig and Larsen............G......718 369-0999
Ridgewood (G-13151)

M B C Metal Inc............G......718 384-6713
Brooklyn (G-2095)

Martin Orna Ir Works II Inc............G......516 354-3923
Elmont (G-4386)

▲ Material Process Systems Inc............F......718 302-3081
Brooklyn (G-2124)

▲ Maximum Security Products Corp............E......518 233-1800
Waterford (G-15538)

McAllisters Precision Wldg Inc............F......518 221-3455
Menands (G-7844)

Mestel Brothers Stairs & Rails............C......516 496-4127
Syosset (G-14794)

Metalworks Inc............E......718 319-0011
Bronx (G-1312)

▼ Metro Door Inc............D......800 669-3667
Islandia (G-6340)

Milgo Industrial Inc............G......718 388-6476
Brooklyn (G-2153)

Milgo Industrial Inc............G......718 387-0406
Brooklyn (G-2154)

▲ Mison Concepts Inc............E......516 933-8000
Hicksville (G-5930)

▲ Modern Art Foundry Inc............E......718 728-2030
Astoria (G-430)

Moon Gates Company............G......718 426-0023
East Elmhurst (G-4110)

Morgik Metal Designs............F......212 463-0304
New York (G-10503)

Moro Corporation............E......607 724-4241
Binghamton (G-899)

New Dimensions Office Group............D......718 387-0995
Brooklyn (G-2203)

▲ Old Dutchmans Wrough Iron Inc............G......716 688-2034
Getzville (G-5180)

Oldcastle Infrastructure Inc............F......518 767-2116
South Bethlehem (G-14502)

Ornametal Inc............G......845 562-5151
Newburgh (G-11880)

Ourem Iron Works Inc............F......914 476-4856
Yonkers (G-16337)

▲ Paragon Aquatics............E......845 452-5500
Lagrangeville (G-6752)

Peconic Ironworks Ltd............F......631 204-0323
Southampton (G-14535)

Phoenix Metal Designs Inc............E......516 597-4100
Brooklyn (G-2256)

Pk30 System LLC............F......212 473-8050
Stone Ridge (G-14736)

◆ Pole-Tech Co Inc............F......631 689-5525
East Setauket (G-4184)

Railings By New Star Brass............E......516 358-1153
Brooklyn (G-2324)

Raulli and Sons Inc............G......315 474-1370
Syracuse (G-14973)

Raulli and Sons Inc............D......315 479-6693
Syracuse (G-14972)

Raulli Iron Works Inc............F......315 337-8070
Rome (G-13866)

Riverside Iron LLC............F......315 535-4864
Gouverneur (G-5322)

Rollson Inc............E......631 423-9578
Huntington (G-6221)

Roman Iron Works Inc............F......516 621-1103
Greenvale (G-5463)

Royal Metal Products Inc............E......518 966-4442
Surprise (G-14776)

▲ S A Baxter LLC............G......845 469-7995
Chester (G-3385)

Steel Sales Inc............E......607 674-6363
Sherburne (G-14395)

Steel Work Inc............G......585 232-1555
Rochester (G-13744)

Steps Plus Inc............D......315 432-0885
Syracuse (G-15000)

Studio 40 Inc............G......212 420-8631
Brooklyn (G-2465)

Superior Metal & Woodwork Inc............E......631 465-9004
Farmingdale (G-4744)

Tee Pee Fence and Railing............F......718 658-8323
Jamaica (G-6479)

SIC

◆ Tensator Inc .... D 631 666-0300
　Bay Shore (G-722)

Tonys Ornamental Ir Works Inc .... E 315 337-3730
　Rome (G-13874)

Tri State Shearing Bending Inc .... F 718 485-2200
　Brooklyn (G-2518)

Triple H Construction Inc .... E 516 280-8252
　Jamaica (G-6481)

Tropical Driftwood Originals .... G 516 623-0980
　Roosevelt (G-14034)

Tymetal Corp .... E 518 692-9930
　Fort Edward (G-4945)

Tymetal Corp .... E 518 692-9930
　Greenwich (G-5477)

United Iron Inc .... E 914 667-5700
　Mount Vernon (G-8191)

United Steel Products Inc .... D 914 968-7782
　Flushing (G-4904)

Universal Steel Fabricators .... F 718 342-0782
　Brooklyn (G-2546)

Village Wrought Iron Inc .... F 315 683-5589
　Fabius (G-4488)

Vr Containment LLC .... G 917 972-3441
　Fresh Meadows (G-5048)

Waverly Iron Corp .... E 631 732-2800
　Medford (G-7726)

West End Iron Works Inc .... G 518 456-1105
　Albany (G-141)

Z-Studios Dsign Fbrication LLC .... G 347 512-4210
　Brooklyn (G-2604)

3448 Prefabricated Metal Buildings & Cmp-nts

All American Building .... G 607 797-7123
　Binghamton (G-851)

▲ Austin Mohawk and Company LLC . E 315 793-3000
　Utica (G-15239)

◆ Birdair Inc .... D 716 633-9500
　Amherst (G-213)

Countryside Truss LLC .... G 315 985-0643
　Saint Johnsville (G-14116)

Deraffele Mfg Co Inc .... E 914 636-6850
　New Rochelle (G-8326)

Energy Panel Structures Inc .... G 315 923-7777
　Clyde (G-3489)

Energy Panel Structures Inc .... G 585 343-1777
　Clyde (G-3490)

Energy Panel Structures Inc .... G 518 355-6708
　Schenectady (G-14263)

▲ Fillmore Greenhouses Inc .... E 585 567-2678
　Portageville (G-12932)

▲ Guardian Booth LLC .... F 844 992-6684
　Orangeburg (G-12317)

Guardian Booth LLC .... F 844 992-6684
　Orangeburg (G-12318)

Landmark Group Inc .... E 845 358-0350
　Valley Cottage (G-15317)

Latium USA Trading LLC .... D 631 563-4000
　Holbrook (G-6004)

Man Products Inc .... E 631 789-6500
　Farmingdale (G-4676)

▼ Metallic Ladder Mfg Corp .... F 716 358-6201
　Randolph (G-13063)

Metals Building Products .... F 844 638-2527
　Holbrook (G-6010)

Mobile Mini Inc .... F 315 732-4555
　Utica (G-15285)

Morton Buildings Inc .... E 585 786-8191
　Warsaw (G-15508)

Nci Group Inc .... D 315 339-1245
　Rome (G-13859)

Overhead Door Corporation .... D 518 828-7652
　Hudson (G-6173)

Precision Fabrication LLC .... G 585 591-3449
　Attica (G-458)

Sunbilt Solar Pdts By Sussman .... D 718 297-0228
　Jamaica (G-6477)

T Shore Products Ltd .... G 315 252-9174
　Auburn (G-497)

Universal Shielding Corp .... E 631 667-7900
　Deer Park (G-3945)

Walpole Woodworkers Inc .... G 631 726-2859
　Water Mill (G-15531)

3449 Misc Structural Metal Work

A&B McKeon Glass Inc .... G 718 525-2152
　Staten Island (G-14614)

▲ Abasco Inc .... E 716 649-4790
　Hamburg (G-5501)

Accurate Metal Weather Strip .... G 914 668-6042
　Mount Vernon (G-8121)

Agl Industries Inc .... E 718 326-7597
　Maspeth (G-7585)

Arista Steel Designs Corp .... G 718 965-7077
　Brooklyn (G-1529)

▲ Baco Enterprises Inc .... D 718 589-6225
　Bronx (G-1209)

Barker Steel LLC .... E 518 465-6221
　Albany (G-44)

City Evolutionary .... G 718 861-7585
　Bronx (G-1225)

Coral Management Corp .... G 718 893-9286
　Bronx (G-1231)

DAgostino Iron Works Inc .... G 585 235-8850
　Rochester (G-13335)

▲ Designs By Novello Inc .... G 914 934-7711
　Port Chester (G-12817)

▲ Dimension Fabricators Inc .... E 518 374-1936
　Scotia (G-14429)

Empire Metal Finishing Inc .... E 718 545-6700
　Astoria (G-421)

Ferro Fabricators Inc .... F 718 703-0007
　Brooklyn (G-1839)

GCM Metal Industries Inc .... F 718 386-4059
　Brooklyn (G-1879)

Halmark Architectural Finshg .... F 718 272-1831
　Brooklyn (G-1919)

Harbor Wldg & Fabrication Corp .... F 631 667-1880
　Copiague (G-3657)

Hornet Group Inc .... D 845 858-6400
　Port Jervis (G-12850)

◆ Inscape (new York) Inc .... D 716 665-6210
　Falconer (G-4544)

Janed Enterprises .... F 631 694-4494
　Farmingdale (G-4657)

Jpl Designs Ltd .... G 212 689-7096
　New York (G-10032)

Kal Manufacturing Corporation .... E 585 265-4310
　Webster (G-15644)

Klein Reinforcing Services Inc .... F 585 352-9433
　Spencerport (G-14557)

Kraman Iron Works Inc .... F 212 460-8400
　New York (G-10135)

▲ Lakeside Capital Corporation .... F 716 664-2555
　Jamestown (G-6528)

Lane Enterprises Inc .... E 518 885-4385
　Ballston Spa (G-579)

▲ Longstem Organizers Inc .... G 914 777-2174
　Jefferson Valley (G-6568)

▲ Metal Products Intl LLC .... E 716 215-1930
　Niagara Falls (G-11950)

Metalsigma Usa Inc .... E 212 731-4346
　New York (G-10443)

New York Steel Services Co .... G 718 291-7770
　Jamaica (G-6463)

Northern Metalworks Corp .... G 646 523-1689
　Selden (G-14354)

Orange County Ironworks LLC .... E 845 769-3000
　Montgomery (G-8064)

▲ Orbital Holdings Inc .... E 951 360-7100
　Buffalo (G-2899)

▲ Paragon Aquatics .... G 845 452-5500
　Lagrangeville (G-6752)

Ppi Corp .... E 585 880-7277
　Rochester (G-13632)

▲ Risa Management Corp .... E 718 361-2606
　Maspeth (G-7637)

Riverside Iron LLC .... F 315 535-4864
　Gouverneur (G-5322)

▲ Rolite Mfg Inc .... E 716 683-0259
　Lancaster (G-6831)

▲ Rollform of Jamestown Inc .... F 716 665-5310
　Jamestown (G-6539)

Semans Enterprises Inc .... F 585 444-0097
　West Henrietta (G-15803)

Signature Metal MBL Maint LLC .... D 718 292-8280
　Bronx (G-1365)

Sims Steel Corporation .... E 631 587-8670
　Lindenhurst (G-6972)

▲ Siw Inc .... F 631 888-0130
　Bay Shore (G-714)

Steel Sales Inc .... E 607 674-6363
　Sherburne (G-14395)

Tebbens Steel LLC .... F 631 208-8330
　Calverton (G-3089)

Tonys Ornamental Ir Works Inc .... E 315 337-3730
　Rome (G-13874)

Torino Industrial Inc .... F 631 509-1640
　Bellport (G-810)

United Iron Inc .... E 914 667-5700
　Mount Vernon (G-8191)

Weslor Industries Inc .... E 315 871-4405
　Lyons (G-7454)

West Metal Works Inc .... E 716 895-4900
　Buffalo (G-3045)

Wide Flange Inc .... F 718 492-8705
　Brooklyn (G-2583)

3451 Screw Machine Prdts

Acme Precision Screw Pdts Inc .... F 585 328-2028
　Rochester (G-13203)

Action Machined Products Inc .... F 631 842-2333
　Copiague (G-3643)

Albert Gates Inc .... D 585 594-9401
　North Chili (G-12021)

All Type Screw Machine Pdts .... G 516 334-5100
　Westbury (G-15866)

▲ Alpha Fasteners Corp .... G 516 867-6188
　Freeport (G-4984)

American-Swiss Products Co Inc .... G 585 292-1720
　Pittsford (G-12636)

▲ Anderson Precision Inc .... D 716 484-1148
　Jamestown (G-6494)

Andros Manufacturing Corp .... G 585 663-5700
　Rochester (G-13237)

Brinkman Intl Group Inc .... G 585 429-5000
　Rochester (G-13281)

C R C Manufacturing Inc .... F 585 254-8820
　Rochester (G-13291)

C&C Automatics Inc .... E 315 331-1436
　Newark (G-11838)

CAM-Tech Industries Inc .... E 585 425-2090
　Fairport (G-4491)

Century Metal Parts Corp .... E 631 667-0800
　Bay Shore (G-661)

Craftech Industries Inc .... D 518 828-5001
　Hudson (G-6151)

Curtis Screw Co Inc .... E 716 898-7800
　Buffalo (G-2716)

Emory Machine & Tool Co Inc .... E 585 436-9610
　Farmington (G-4771)

Five Star Tool Co Inc .... E 585 328-9580
　Rochester (G-13412)

Gem Manufacturing Inc .... G 585 235-1670
　Rochester (G-13431)

Globe Electronic Hardware Inc .... F 718 457-0303
　Woodside (G-16209)

Gsp Components Inc .... D 585 436-3377
　Rochester (G-13452)

Hanco Metal Products Inc .... F 212 787-5992
　Brooklyn (G-1924)

J & J Swiss Precision Inc .... E 631 243-5584
　Deer Park (G-3884)

Kaddis Manufacturing Corp .... G 585 624-3070
　Honeoye Falls (G-6077)

Lexington Machining LLC .... D 585 235-0880
　Rochester (G-13516)

Lexington Machining LLC .... E 585 235-0880
　Rochester (G-13517)

▲ Liberty Brass Turning Co Inc .... E 718 784-2911
　Westbury (G-15904)

M Manastrip-M Corporation .... E 518 664-2089
　Clifton Park (G-3467)

Manacraft Precision Inc .... F 914 654-0967
　Pelham (G-12567)

Manth-Brownell Inc .... C 315 687-7263
　Kirkville (G-6724)

Marmach Machine Inc .... G 585 768-8800
　Le Roy (G-6904)

Micro Threaded Products Inc .... G 585 288-0080
　Rochester (G-13546)

Muller Tool Inc .... E 716 895-3658
　Buffalo (G-2874)

Multimatic Products Inc .... D 800 767-7633
　Ronkonkoma (G-13977)

▲ Murphy Manufacturing Co Inc .... G 585 223-0100
　Fairport (G-4509)

Norwood Screw Machine Parts .... F 516 481-6644
　Mineola (G-7993)

▲ Park-Ohio Inds Trsry Co Inc .... F 212 966-3310
　Albany (G-111)

▲ Ppi Corp .... D 585 243-0300
　Rochester (G-13633)

Ranney Precision .... F 716 731-6418
　Niagara Falls (G-11971)

Selflock Screw Products Co Inc .... E 315 541-4464
　Syracuse (G-14992)

Supreme Screw Products Inc .... D 718 293-6600
　Plainview (G-12717)

T & L Automatics Inc .... C 585 647-3717
Rochester *(G-13756)*
TAC Screw Products Inc .... F 585 663-5840
Rochester *(G-13758)*
Taylor Metalworks Inc .... C 716 662-3113
Orchard Park *(G-12378)*
Teale Machine Company Inc .... D 585 244-6700
Rochester *(G-13761)*
▲ Thuro Metal Products Inc .... E 631 435-0444
Brentwood *(G-1128)*
▲ Tri-Technologies Inc .... E 914 699-2001
Mount Vernon *(G-8187)*
Trihex Manufacturing Inc .... G 315 589-9331
Williamson *(G-16114)*
Triple Point Manufacturing .... G 631 218-4988
Bohemia *(G-1091)*
Umbro Machine & Tool Co Inc .... F 845 876-4669
Rhinebeck *(G-13102)*
Vanguard Metals Inc .... F 631 234-6500
Central Islip *(G-3292)*
Verns Machine Co Inc .... E 315 926-4223
Marion *(G-7577)*
Xli Manufacturing LLC .... E 585 436-2250
Rochester *(G-13812)*

3452 Bolts, Nuts, Screws, Rivets & Washers

▲ Alcoa Fastening Systems .... C 845 334-7203
Kingston *(G-6677)*
Allied Bolt Products LLC .... E 516 512-7600
New Hyde Park *(G-8249)*
▲ American Pride Fasteners LLC .... E 631 940-8292
Bay Shore *(G-649)*
Anthony Manno & Co Inc .... G 631 445-1834
Deer Park *(G-3840)*
▲ Baco Enterprises Inc .... D 718 589-6225
Bronx *(G-1209)*
Buckley Qc Fasteners Inc .... E 716 662-1490
Orchard Park *(G-12341)*
Craftech Industries Inc .... D 518 828-5001
Hudson *(G-6151)*
Dependable Acme Threaded Pdts .... G 516 338-4700
Westbury *(G-15875)*
▲ Disc-Lock LLC .... G 310 560-9940
Tonawanda *(G-15100)*
Fastener Dimensions Inc .... E 718 847-6321
Ozone Park *(G-12461)*
Huck International Inc .... C 845 331-7300
Kingston *(G-6694)*
Jem Threading Specialties Inc .... G 718 665-3341
Bronx *(G-1285)*
John F Rafter Inc .... G 716 992-3425
Eden *(G-4256)*
▲ John Hassall LLC .... D 516 334-6200
Westbury *(G-15898)*
▼ John Hassall LLC .... D 323 869-0150
Westbury *(G-15899)*
Kinemotive Corporation .... E 631 249-6440
Farmingdale *(G-4666)*
LD McCauley LLC .... C 716 662-6744
Orchard Park *(G-12362)*
◆ Marksmen Manufacturing Corp .... E 800 305-6942
Deer Park *(G-3903)*
▲ Park-Ohio Inds Trsry Co Inc .... F 212 966-3310
Albany *(G-111)*
Pin Pharma Inc .... G 212 543-2583
New York *(G-10841)*
Pins N Needles .... F 212 535-6222
New York *(G-10845)*
Pni Capital Partners .... G 516 466-7120
Westbury *(G-15917)*
Radax Industries Inc .... E 585 265-2055
Webster *(G-15650)*
Rochester Stampings Inc .... F 585 467-5241
Rochester *(G-13698)*
Schaefer Machine Co Inc .... E 516 248-6880
Mineola *(G-8000)*
Simon Defense Inc .... G 516 217-6000
Ronkonkoma *(G-14009)*
Socket Products Mfg Corp .... G 631 232-9870
Islandia *(G-6344)*
Southco Inc .... B 585 624-2545
Honeoye Falls *(G-6080)*
Superior Washer & Gasket Corp .... D 631 273-8282
Hauppauge *(G-5778)*
Ta Chen International Inc .... F 845 352-5300
Monsey *(G-8051)*
▲ Tamperproof Screw Company Inc .... F 516 931-1616
Hicksville *(G-5951)*
Teka Precision Inc .... G 845 753-1900
Nyack *(G-12147)*

Treo Industries Inc .... G 631 737-4022
Bohemia *(G-1087)*
Trihex Manufacturing Inc .... G 315 589-9331
Williamson *(G-16114)*
▲ Zierick Manufacturing Corp .... D 800 882-8020
Mount Kisco *(G-8108)*
Zip Products Inc .... F 585 482-0044
Rochester *(G-13815)*

3462 Iron & Steel Forgings

Alry Tool and Die Co Inc .... E 716 693-2419
Tonawanda *(G-15085)*
▲ Ball Chain Mfg Co Inc .... D 914 664-7500
Mount Vernon *(G-8123)*
▲ Biltron Automotive Products .... E 631 928-8613
Port Jeff STA *(G-12833)*
Burke Frging Heat Treating Inc .... E 585 235-6060
Rochester *(G-13287)*
Delaware Valley Forge Co Inc .... G 716 447-9140
Buffalo *(G-2724)*
Delaware Valley Forge Inc .... E 716 447-9140
Buffalo *(G-2725)*
◆ Designatronics Incorporated .... G 516 328-3300
Hicksville *(G-5902)*
◆ Dragon Trading Inc .... G 212 717-1496
New York *(G-9265)*
▲ Firth Rixson Inc .... D 585 328-1383
Rochester *(G-13411)*
Gear Motions Incorporated .... E 716 885-1080
Buffalo *(G-2769)*
Gear Motions Incorporated .... E 315 488-0100
Syracuse *(G-14901)*
Great Lakes Gear Co Inc .... G 716 694-0715
Tonawanda *(G-15106)*
▲ Hammond & Irving Inc .... D 315 253-6265
Auburn *(G-478)*
▲ Hohmann & Barnard Inc .... E 631 234-0600
Hauppauge *(G-5672)*
Hohmann & Barnard Inc .... E 518 357-9757
Schenectady *(G-14278)*
Industrial Mch Gear Works LLC .... G 516 695-4442
Rockville Centre *(G-13829)*
▲ Jrlon Inc .... D 315 597-4067
Palmyra *(G-12489)*
Kurz and Zobel Inc .... G 585 254-9060
Rochester *(G-13506)*
Mattessich Iron LLC .... G 315 409-8496
Memphis *(G-7835)*
Metrofab Pipe Incorporated .... F 516 349-7373
Plainview *(G-12701)*
▲ Peck & Hale LLC .... E 631 589-2510
West Sayville *(G-15842)*
Perfect Gear & Instrument .... F 516 328-3330
Hicksville *(G-5943)*
Perfect Gear & Instrument .... E 516 873-6122
Garden City Park *(G-5123)*
Pro-Gear Co Inc .... G 716 684-3811
Buffalo *(G-2934)*
Riley Gear Corporation .... E 716 694-0900
North Tonawanda *(G-12086)*
S R & R Industries Inc .... G 845 692-8329
Middletown *(G-7931)*
▲ Schilling Forge Inc .... E 315 454-4421
Syracuse *(G-14987)*
▲ Secs Inc .... E 914 667-5600
Mount Vernon *(G-8179)*
Special Metals Corporation .... D 716 366-5663
Dunkirk *(G-4067)*
Stoffel Polygon Systems Inc .... F 914 961-2000
Tuckahoe *(G-15206)*
Superior Motion Controls Inc .... E 516 420-2921
Farmingdale *(G-4745)*
Superite Gear Instr of Hppauge .... G 631 234-0100
Hauppauge *(G-5779)*
Upstate Piping Products Inc .... G 518 238-3457
Waterford *(G-15548)*
Viking Iron Works Inc .... F 845 471-5010
Poughkeepsie *(G-12990)*
▲ Vulcan Steam Forging Co .... E 716 875-3680
Buffalo *(G-3040)*
W J Albro Machine Works Inc .... G 631 345-0657
Yaphank *(G-16278)*
York Industries Inc .... E 516 746-3736
Garden City Park *(G-5126)*

3463 Nonferrous Forgings

Arconic Inc .... G 315 764-4011
Massena *(G-7666)*
▲ Nak International Corp .... D 516 334-6245
Locust Valley *(G-7128)*

Penn State Mtal Fbrctors No 2 .... G 718 786-8814
Brooklyn *(G-2253)*
Special Metals Corporation .... D 716 366-5663
Dunkirk *(G-4067)*

3465 Automotive Stampings

Albert Kemperle Inc .... E 718 629-1084
Brooklyn *(G-1476)*
Autokiniton US Holdings Inc .... G 212 338-5100
New York *(G-8681)*
Kustom Korner .... F 716 646-0173
Hamburg *(G-5513)*
M & W Aluminum Products Inc .... F 315 414-0005
Syracuse *(G-14937)*
P R B Metal Products Inc .... F 631 467-1800
Ronkonkoma *(G-13989)*
Qpbc Inc .... E 718 685-1900
Long Island City *(G-7333)*
▲ Racing Industries Inc .... E 631 905-0100
Calverton *(G-3084)*
Thyssenkrupp Materials NA Inc .... G 585 279-0000
West Seneca *(G-15855)*
Utica Metal Products Inc .... D 315 732-6163
Utica *(G-15299)*

3466 Crowns & Closures

Protocase Incorporated .... C 866 849-3911
Lewiston *(G-6922)*
Reynolds Packaging McHy Inc .... D 716 358-6451
Falconer *(G-4554)*
▲ Van Blarcom Closures Inc .... C 718 855-3810
Brooklyn *(G-2551)*

3469 Metal Stampings, NEC

4m Precision Industries Inc .... E 315 252-8415
Auburn *(G-459)*
Able National Corp .... E 718 386-8801
Brooklyn *(G-1450)*
Acme Architectural Products .... B 718 360-0700
Brooklyn *(G-1455)*
▲ Acro Industries Inc .... C 585 254-3661
Rochester *(G-13204)*
Advanced Structures Corp .... F 631 667-5000
Deer Park *(G-3830)*
◆ Albest Metal Stamping Corp .... E 718 388-6000
Brooklyn *(G-1477)*
Albest Metal Stamping Corp .... E 718 388-6000
Brooklyn *(G-1478)*
All Out Die Cutting Inc .... E 718 346-6666
Brooklyn *(G-1486)*
▲ Allen Machine Products Inc .... E 631 630-8800
Hauppauge *(G-5584)*
◆ Allied Metal Spinning Corp .... D 718 893-3300
Bronx *(G-1201)*
Alton Manufacturing Inc .... D 585 458-2600
Rochester *(G-13225)*
American Metal Spinning Pdts .... G 631 454-6276
West Babylon *(G-15688)*
American Mtal Stmping Spinning .... F 718 384-1500
Brooklyn *(G-1499)*
Arnell Inc .... G 516 486-7098
Hempstead *(G-5833)*
Arro Manufacturing LLC .... F 716 763-6203
Lakewood *(G-6778)*
▼ Arro Tool & Die Inc .... F 716 763-6203
Lakewood *(G-6779)*
Art Precision Metal Products .... F 631 842-8889
Copiague *(G-3647)*
B & R Tool Inc .... G 718 948-2729
Staten Island *(G-14622)*
B H M Metal Products Co .... G 845 292-5297
Kauneonga Lake *(G-6640)*
Bailey Manufacturing Co LLC .... E 716 965-2731
Forestville *(G-4930)*
Barnes Group Inc .... G 315 457-9200
Syracuse *(G-14826)*
Barron Metal Products Inc .... E 914 965-1232
Yonkers *(G-16289)*
Bcs Access Systems Us LLC .... B 315 258-3469
Auburn *(G-466)*
Belmet Products Inc .... E 718 542-8220
Bronx *(G-1212)*
Belrix Industries Inc .... G 716 821-5964
Buffalo *(G-2661)*
Bowen Products Corporation .... G 315 498-4481
Nedrow *(G-8214)*
Bridgeport Metalcraft Inc .... G 315 623-9597
Constantia *(G-3635)*
C & H Precision Tools Inc .... E 631 758-3806
Holtsville *(G-6047)*

▲ Cameo Metal Products Inc ....E 718 788-1106
Brooklyn *(G-1641)*

▲ Cannon Industries Inc ....D 585 254-8080
Rochester *(G-13294)*

▲ Cep Technologies Corporation ....E 914 968-4100
Yonkers *(G-16295)*

Cgs Fabrication LLC ....F 585 347-6127
Webster *(G-15634)*

Charles A Rogers Entps Inc ....E 585 924-6400
Victor *(G-15397)*

Check-Mate Industries Inc ....E 631 491-1777
West Babylon *(G-15701)*

Cobbe Industries Inc ....E 716 287-2661
Gerry *(G-5170)*

Coil Stamping Inc ....F 631 588-3040
Holbrook *(G-5991)*

Colonial Precision Machinery ....G 631 249-0738
Farmingdale *(G-4601)*

Compac Development Corporation ......D 631 881-4903
Edgewood *(G-4265)*

Compar Manufacturing Corp ....E 212 304-2777
New York *(G-9071)*

Corbett Stves Pttern Works Inc ....E 585 546-7109
Rochester *(G-13326)*

◆ Corning Vitro Corporation ....A 607 974-8605
Corning *(G-3714)*

◆ Creative Design and Mch Inc ....E 845 778-9001
Rock Tavern *(G-13820)*

Crosby Company ....E 716 852-3522
Buffalo *(G-2713)*

Custom Metal Incorporated ....F 631 643-4075
Farmingdale *(G-4610)*

D-K Manufacturing Corp ....E 315 592-4327
Fulton *(G-5057)*

▲ Dayton Industries Inc ....E 718 542-8144
Bronx *(G-1237)*

Dayton Rogers New York LLC ....D 585 349-4040
Rochester *(G-13339)*

Die-Matic Products LLC ....E 516 433-7900
Plainview *(G-12679)*

▼ Dunkirk Metal Products Wny LLC .....E 716 366-2555
Dunkirk *(G-4054)*

Electric Motors and Pumps Inc ....G 718 935-9118
Brooklyn *(G-1790)*

Endicott Precision Inc ....E 607 754-7076
Endicott *(G-4451)*

Engineering Mfg Tech LLC ....D 607 754-7111
Endicott *(G-4453)*

Erdle Perforating Holdings Inc ....D 585 247-4700
Rochester *(G-13397)*

Forkey Construction & Fabg Inc ....E 607 849-4879
Cortland *(G-3766)*

Forsyth Industries Inc ....E 716 652-1070
Buffalo *(G-2757)*

▲ Freeport Screen & Stamping ....E 516 379-0330
Freeport *(G-4998)*

G A Richards & Co Inc ....F 516 334-5412
Westbury *(G-15888)*

▲ Gasser & Sons Inc ....D 631 543-6600
Commack *(G-3589)*

Gay Sheet Metal Dies Inc ....G 716 877-0208
Buffalo *(G-2768)*

Gem Metal Spinning & Stamping ....E 718 729-7014
Long Island City *(G-7230)*

Genesee Metal Stampings Inc ....G 585 475-0450
West Henrietta *(G-15795)*

German Machine & Assembly Inc ....E 585 546-4200
Rochester *(G-13437)*

◆ Gleason Works ....A 585 473-1000
Rochester *(G-13445)*

Great Lakes Pressed Steel Corp ....E 716 885-4037
Buffalo *(G-2784)*

Greene Technologies Inc ....D 607 656-4166
Greene *(G-5446)*

Hy-Grade Metal Products Corp ....G 315 475-4221
Syracuse *(G-14912)*

▲ Hyman Podrusnick Co Inc ....G 718 853-4502
Brooklyn *(G-1949)*

◆ International Ord Tech Inc ....D 716 664-1100
Jamestown *(G-6518)*

Johnson & Hoffman LLC ....G 516 742-3333
Carle Place *(G-3175)*

▲ Kerns Manufacturing Corp ....C 718 784-4044
Long Island City *(G-7262)*

▼ Koch Metal Spinning Co Inc ....D 716 835-3631
Buffalo *(G-2837)*

▲ Lancaster Knives Inc ....E 716 683-5050
Lancaster *(G-6814)*

▲ Lb Furniture Industries LLC ....C 518 828-1501
Hudson *(G-6169)*

Long Island Metalform Inc ....F 631 242-9088
Deer Park *(G-3899)*

M F Manufacturing Enterprises ....G 516 822-5135
Hicksville *(G-5924)*

Maehr Industries Inc ....F 631 924-1661
Bellport *(G-802)*

▲ Magic Novelty Co Inc ....E 212 304-2777
New York *(G-10325)*

Mantel & Mantel Stamping Corp ....E 631 467-1916
Ronkonkoma *(G-13969)*

▲ Marex Aquisition Corp ....C 585 458-3940
Rochester *(G-13536)*

Matov Industries Inc ....E 718 392-5060
Long Island City *(G-7291)*

McHone Industries Inc ....E 716 945-3380
Salamanca *(G-14122)*

Mega Tool & Mfg Corp ....E 607 734-8398
Elmira *(G-4363)*

Nash Metalware Co Inc ....F 315 339-5794
Rome *(G-13858)*

National Computer & Electronic ....G 631 242-7222
Deer Park *(G-3909)*

National Die & Button Mould Co ....E 201 939-7800
Brooklyn *(G-2189)*

▲ National Wire & Metal Tech Inc ....E 716 661-9180
Jamestown *(G-6534)*

◆ Novel Box Company Ltd ....E 718 965-2222
Brooklyn *(G-2221)*

▲ OEM Solutions Inc ....G 716 864-9324
Clarence *(G-3437)*

◆ Oxo International Inc ....C 212 242-3333
New York *(G-10729)*

▲ P & G Steel Products Co Inc ....E 716 896-7900
Buffalo *(G-2901)*

P R B Metal Products Inc ....E 631 467-1800
Ronkonkoma *(G-13989)*

Pall Corporation ....A 607 753-6041
Cortland *(G-3779)*

Pervi Precision Company Inc ....G 631 589-5557
Bohemia *(G-2928)*

◆ Phoenix Metal Products Inc ....F 516 546-4200
Freeport *(G-5015)*

Precision Photo-Fab Inc ....D 716 821-9393
Buffalo *(G-2928)*

▲ Progressus Company Inc ....F 516 255-0245
Rockville Centre *(G-13834)*

Pronto Tool & Die Co Inc ....E 631 981-8920
Ronkonkoma *(G-13997)*

Quality Metal Stamping LLC ....G 516 255-9000
Rockville Centre *(G-13835)*

▲ R G Flair Co Inc ....G 631 586-7311
Bay Shore *(G-703)*

▲ Revol Usa LLC ....F 678 456-8671
New York *(G-11029)*

Reynolds Manufacturing Inc ....C 607 562-8936
Big Flats *(G-848)*

Richter Charles Metal STMp&sp ....E 845 895-2025
Wallkill *(G-15471)*

Richter Metalcraft Corporation ....E 845 895-2025
Wallkill *(G-15472)*

▲ Rigidized Metals Corporation ....E 716 849-4703
Buffalo *(G-2955)*

Rochester Stampings Inc ....E 585 467-5241
Rochester *(G-13698)*

▲ Rolite Mfg Inc ....E 716 683-0259
Lancaster *(G-6831)*

Russco Metal Spinning Co Inc ....F 516 872-6055
Baldwin *(G-534)*

▲ S & S Prtg Die-Cutting Co Inc ....F 718 388-8990
Brooklyn *(G-2372)*

S D Z Metal Spinning Stamping ....F 718 778-3600
Brooklyn *(G-2376)*

Schiller Stores Inc ....G 631 208-9400
Riverhead *(G-13188)*

Seneca Ceramics Corp ....G 315 781-0100
Phelps *(G-12607)*

Sharon Manufacturing Co Inc ....G 631 242-8870
Deer Park *(G-3936)*

Simplex Manufacturing Co Inc ....F 315 252-7524
Auburn *(G-495)*

Smithers Tools & Mch Pdts Inc ....D 845 876-3063
Rhinebeck *(G-13101)*

Solidus Industries Inc ....D 607 749-4540
Homer *(G-6067)*

Square Stamping Mfg Corp ....G 315 896-2641
Barneveld *(G-596)*

▼ Stampcrete International Ltd ....E 315 451-2837
Liverpool *(G-7042)*

▲ Stamped Fittings Inc ....E 607 733-9988
Elmira Heights *(G-4380)*

▲ Stever-Locke Industries Inc ....G 585 624-3450
Honeoye Falls *(G-6081)*

Surving Studios ....F 845 355-1430
Middletown *(G-7934)*

Tooling Enterprises Inc ....F 716 842-0445
Buffalo *(G-3014)*

Tools & Stamping Corp ....G 718 392-4040
Brooklyn *(G-2510)*

▲ Tri-Technologies Inc ....E 914 699-2001
Mount Vernon *(G-8187)*

Trico Holding Corporation ....A 716 852-5700
Buffalo *(G-3019)*

▲ Trident Precision Mfg Inc ....D 585 265-2010
Webster *(G-15658)*

▲ Twinco Mfg Co Inc ....E 631 231-0022
Hauppauge *(G-5789)*

▲ Unicel Corporation ....E 760 741-3912
Deer Park *(G-3944)*

Universal Shielding Corp ....E 631 667-7900
Deer Park *(G-3945)*

Van Reenen Tool & Die Inc ....F 585 288-6000
Rochester *(G-13794)*

Vanity Fair Bathmart Inc ....F 718 584-6700
Bronx *(G-1389)*

◆ Vigo Industries LLC ....C 866 591-7792
New York *(G-11682)*

Volkert Precision Tech Inc ....F 718 464-9500
Queens Village *(G-13027)*

Vosky Precision Machining Corp ....F 631 737-3200
Ronkonkoma *(G-14025)*

W & H Stampings Inc ....E 631 234-6161
Hauppauge *(G-5798)*

Web Associates Inc ....G 716 883-3377
Buffalo *(G-3042)*

Wessie Machine Inc ....G 315 926-4060
Marion *(G-7578)*

Wilmax Usa LLC ....F 917 388-2790
New York *(G-11762)*

WR Smith & Sons Inc ....G 845 620-9400
Nanuet *(G-8205)*

Zeta Machine Corp ....G 631 471-8832
Ronkonkoma *(G-14029)*

3471 Electroplating, Plating, Polishing, Anodizing & Coloring

21st Century Finishes Inc ....F 516 221-7000
North Bellmore *(G-12013)*

Abetter Processing Corp ....F 718 252-2223
Brooklyn *(G-1448)*

Able Anodizing Corp ....F 718 252-0660
Brooklyn *(G-1449)*

ABS Metal Corp ....G 646 302-9018
Hewlett *(G-5868)*

Aircraft Finishing Corp ....F 631 422-5000
West Babylon *(G-15684)*

Airmarine Electroplating Corp ....G 516 623-4406
Freeport *(G-4980)*

Alta Metal Finishing Corp ....G 914 946-1916
White Plains *(G-15971)*

▲ Apti Pro Systems 2000 Inc ....D 585 265-0160
Ontario *(G-12283)*

Astro Electroplating Inc ....E 631 968-0656
Bay Shore *(G-653)*

B & W Heat Treating Company ....G 716 876-8184
Tonawanda *(G-15088)*

Barnes Metal Finishing Inc ....F 585 798-4817
Medina *(G-7728)*

Bfg Manufacturing Services Inc ....E 716 362-0888
Buffalo *(G-2663)*

Buffalo Metal Finishing Co ....F 716 883-2751
Buffalo *(G-2679)*

C H Thompson Company Inc ....D 607 724-1094
Binghamton *(G-866)*

Carpenter Industries Inc ....F 315 463-4284
Syracuse *(G-14843)*

Coating Technology Inc ....E 585 546-7170
Rochester *(G-13320)*

Control Electropolishing Corp ....F 718 858-6634
Brooklyn *(G-1684)*

D & I Finishing Inc ....G 631 471-3034
Bohemia *(G-998)*

D & W Enterprises LLC ....F 585 590-6727
Medina *(G-7733)*

Deming Electro-Plating Corp ....G 585 968-2355
Cuba *(G-3812)*

Dura Spec Inc ....F 718 526-3053
North Baldwin *(G-12004)*

Eastside Oxide Co ....E 607 734-1253
Elmira *(G-4349)*

Electro Plating Service Inc ....F 914 948-3777
White Plains (G-16001)

Empire Metal Finishing Inc ....E ... 718 545-6700
Astoria (G-421)

▼ Epner Technology Incorporated .....E ... 718 782-5948
Brooklyn (G-1808)

Epner Technology Incorporated ....E ... 718 782-8722
Brooklyn (G-1809)

Eric S Turner & Company Inc ....F 914 235-7114
New Rochelle (G-8329)

▲ Ever-Nu-Metal Products Inc ....F 646 423-5833
Brooklyn (G-1818)

F & H Metal Finishing Co Inc ....F 585 798-2151
Medina (G-7734)

Fallon Inc ....E ... 718 326-7226
Maspeth (G-7614)

Finest Cc Corp ....G 917 574-4525
Bronx (G-1257)

First Impressions Finishing ....G 631 467-2244
Ronkonkoma (G-13938)

Forge Metal Finishing Inc ....G 585 730-7340
Rochester (G-13420)

Galmer Ltd ....G 718 392-4609
Long Island City (G-7229)

General Galvanizing Sup Co Inc .....D ... 718 589-4300
Bronx (G-1266)

General Plating LLC ....E ... 585 423-0830
Rochester (G-13433)

Greene Technologies Inc ....D ... 607 656-4166
Greene (G-5446)

Halmark Architectural Finshg ....E ... 718 272-1831
Brooklyn (G-1919)

Hamburg Finishing Works Inc ....G 716 362-0888
Buffalo (G-2791)

▲ Hartchrom Inc ....F 518 880-0411
Watervliet (G-15603)

▲ Jay Strongwater Holdings LLC ......A 646 657-0558
New York (G-9980)

John Larocca & Son Inc ....G 631 423-5256
Huntington Station (G-6251)

Key Tech Finishing ....E ... 716 832-1232
Buffalo (G-2832)

▲ Keymark Corporation ....A 518 853-3421
Fonda (G-4911)

Keystone Corporation ....E ... 800 880-9747
Buffalo (G-2834)

L W S Inc ....F 631 580-0472
Ronkonkoma (G-13960)

Maracle Industrial Finshg Co ....E ... 585 387-9077
Rochester (G-13534)

Master Craft Finishers Inc ....E ... 631 586-0540
Deer Park (G-3904)

McAlpin Industries Inc ....E ... 585 544-5335
Rochester (G-13539)

Metal Man Restoration ....F 914 662-4218
Mount Vernon (G-8161)

Multitone Finishing Co Inc ....G 516 485-1043
West Hempstead (G-15776)

▲ Nas CP Corp ....E ... 718 961-6757
College Point (G-3556)

Nassau Chromium Plating Co Inc .....F 516 746-6666
Mineola (G-7990)

North East Finishing Co Inc ....F 631 789-8000
Copiague (G-3666)

Oerlikon Blzers Cating USA Inc ....E ... 716 564-8557
Buffalo (G-2895)

Praxair Surface Tech Inc ....C 845 398-8322
Orangeburg (G-12327)

▲ Precious Plate Inc ....D ... 716 283-0690
Niagara Falls (G-11967)

Premier Finishing Inc ....F 716 484-6271
Jamestown (G-6537)

Psb Ltd ....F 585 654-7078
Rochester (G-13651)

Qos Enterprises LLC ....G 585 454-0550
Rochester (G-13657)

Rainbow Powder Coating Corp ....G 631 586-4019
Deer Park (G-3926)

Rayco of Schenectady Inc ....F 518 212-5113
Amsterdam (G-346)

Reynolds Tech Fabricators Inc ....E ... 315 437-0532
East Syracuse (G-4233)

Rochester Overnight Pltg LLC ....D ... 585 328-4590
Rochester (G-13692)

Saccomize Inc ....G 818 287-3000
Bronx (G-1358)

Sandys Bumper Mart Inc ....G 315 472-8149
Syracuse (G-14985)

Sas Maintenance Services Inc ....F 718 837-2124
Brooklyn (G-2385)

Sherrill Manufacturing Inc ....C 315 280-0727
Sherrill (G-14406)

Silverman & Gorf Inc ....G 718 625-1309
Brooklyn (G-2415)

Square One Coating Systems LLC ....G 315 790-5921
Oriskany (G-12395)

Surface Finish Technology ....E ... 607 732-2909
Elmira (G-4369)

T & M Plating Inc ....E ... 212 967-1110
New York (G-11414)

Tcmf Inc ....D ... 607 724-1094
Binghamton (G-912)

Tompkins Metal Finishing Inc ....D ... 585 344-2600
Batavia (G-627)

Tripp Plating Works Inc ....G 716 894-2424
Buffalo (G-3021)

Tronic Plating Co Inc ....F 516 293-7883
Farmingdale (G-4760)

Tropical Driftwood Originals ....G 516 623-0980
Roosevelt (G-14034)

Tru-Tone Metal Products Inc ....E ... 718 386-5960
Brooklyn (G-2526)

US Electroplating Corp ....G 631 293-1998
West Babylon (G-15754)

Utica Metal Products Inc ....D ... 315 732-6163
Utica (G-15299)

Vernon Plating Works Inc ....F 718 639-1124
Woodside (G-16233)

Vibra Tech Industries Inc ....F 914 946-1916
White Plains (G-16069)

▲ Victoria Plating Co Inc ....D ... 718 589-1550
Bronx (G-1391)

West Falls Machine Co Inc ....F 716 655-0440
East Aurora (G-4097)

Witt Preparations LLC ....G 716 948-4002
Cheektowaga (G-3365)

3479 Coating & Engraving, NEC

72 Steel and Aluminium Work ....G 917 667-3033
Brooklyn (G-1422)

Accurate Pnt Powdr Coating Inc ......F 585 235-1650
Rochester (G-13201)

Advanced Coating Service LLC ....G 585 247-3970
Rochester (G-13209)

Advanced Coating Techniques ....E ... 631 643-4555
West Babylon (G-15683)

▼ Advanced Graphics Company Inc ...F 607 692-7875
Whitney Point (G-16105)

Advanced Surface Finishing ....E ... 516 876-9710
Westbury (G-15862)

Aircraft Finishing Corp ....F 631 422-5000
West Babylon (G-15684)

All Spec Finishing Inc ....E ... 607 770-9174
Binghamton (G-852)

▲ Angiotech Biocoatings Corp ....E ... 585 321-1130
Henrietta (G-5854)

Applause Coating LLC ....F 631 231-5223
Brentwood (G-1115)

Ascribe Inc ....E ... 585 413-0298
Rochester (G-13252)

Barson Composites Corporation ......E ... 516 752-7882
Old Bethpage (G-12215)

Buffalo Finishing Works Inc ....G 716 893-5266
Buffalo (G-2673)

Buffalo Metal Finishing Co ....F 716 883-2751
Buffalo (G-2679)

C & M Products Inc ....G 315 471-3303
Syracuse (G-14838)

C H Thompson Company Inc ....D ... 607 724-1094
Binghamton (G-866)

Chepaume Industries LLC ....G 315 829-6400
Vernon (G-15364)

Chromalloy Gas Turbine LLC ....E ... 845 692-8912
Middletown (G-7898)

Clad Metal Specialties Inc ....F 631 666-7750
Bay Shore (G-663)

Cnv Architectural Coatings Inc ....G 718 418-9584
Brooklyn (G-1672)

▲ Custom House Engravers Inc ....G 631 567-3004
Bohemia (G-995)

Custom Laser Inc ....E ... 716 434-8600
Lockport (G-7066)

D & I Finishing Inc ....G 631 471-3034
Bohemia (G-998)

Deloka LLC ....G 315 946-6910
Lyons (G-7449)

Duzmor Painting Inc ....G 585 768-4760
Le Roy (G-6900)

Dynocoat Inc ....F 631 244-9344
Holbrook (G-5997)

Eastern Silver of Boro Park ....G 718 854-5600
Brooklyn (G-1777)

▲ Electronic Coating Tech Inc ....F 518 688-2048
Cohoes (G-3506)

Elegance Coating Ltd ....D ... 518 298-2888
Champlain (G-3311)

F & H Metal Finishing Co Inc ....F 585 798-2151
Medina (G-7734)

▲ Fougera Pharmaceuticals Inc ....C 631 454-7677
Melville (G-7785)

▲ Frontier Ht-Dip Glvanizing Inc ......F 716 875-2091
Buffalo (G-2761)

Future Spray Finishing Co ....G 631 242-6252
Deer Park (G-3877)

Greene Technologies Inc ....D ... 607 656-4166
Greene (G-5446)

Harold Wood Co Inc ....G 716 873-1535
Buffalo (G-2794)

Hatfield Metal Fab Inc ....E ... 845 454-9078
Poughkeepsie (G-12961)

▲ Heany Industries Inc ....D ... 585 889-2700
Scottsville (G-14340)

▲ Hilord Chemical Corporation ....E ... 631 234-7373
Hauppauge (G-5671)

Hitemco Med Applications Inc ....C 516 752-7882
Old Bethpage (G-12217)

Hubbell Galvanizing Inc ....G 315 736-8311
Yorkville (G-16375)

Hudson Valley Coatings LLC ....G 845 398-1778
Congers (G-3615)

Industrial Paint Services Corp ....F 607 687-0107
Owego (G-12430)

▼ Jamestown Bronze Works Inc ....G 716 665-2302
Jamestown (G-6521)

▲ Jrlon Inc ....D ... 315 597-4067
Palmyra (G-12489)

Js Coating Solutions Inc ....G 585 471-8354
Rochester (G-13497)

▲ Keymark Corporation ....A 518 853-3421
Fonda (G-4911)

Kwong CHI Metal Fabrication ....G 718 369-6429
Brooklyn (G-2039)

▲ Lodolce Machine Co Inc ....E ... 845 246-7017
Saugerties (G-14204)

Mac Artspray Finishing Corp ....F 718 649-3800
Brooklyn (G-2098)

Master Craft Finishers Inc ....E ... 631 586-0540
Deer Park (G-3904)

▲ Metal Cladding Inc ....D ... 716 434-5513
Lockport (G-7091)

Micromatter Tech Inc USA ....G 631 580-2522
Holbrook (G-6012)

Modern Coating and Research ....F 315 597-3517
Palmyra (G-12491)

Modern Coating and Research ....F 315 597-3517
Palmyra (G-12492)

Mom Holding Company ....G 518 233-3330
Waterford (G-15540)

◆ Momentive Performance Mtls Inc ...E ... 518 233-3330
Waterford (G-15542)

Mpm Holdings Inc ....G 518 233-3330
Waterford (G-15543)

Mpm Intermediate Holdings Inc ....G 518 237-3330
Waterford (G-15544)

Nameplate Mfrs of Amer ....E ... 631 752-0055
Farmingdale (G-4690)

Newchem Inc ....G 315 331-7680
Ithaca (G-6402)

▲ O W Hubbell & Sons Inc ....E ... 315 736-8311
Yorkville (G-16376)

Oerlikon Blzers Cating USA Inc ....E ... 716 270-2228
Amherst (G-237)

Oerlikon Blzers Cating USA Inc ....E ... 716 564-8557
Buffalo (G-2895)

Piper Plastics Corp ....E ... 631 842-6889
Copiague (G-3668)

Precision Design Systems Inc ....E ... 585 426-4500
Rochester (G-13635)

Pro-Tech Catings Solutions Inc ....G 631 707-9400
Edgewood (G-4279)

Pro-Teck Coating Inc ....F 716 537-2619
Holland (G-6030)

▲ Qualicoat Inc ....D ... 585 293-2650
Churchville (G-3414)

R S T Cable and Tape Inc ....G 631 981-0096
Ronkonkoma (G-14000)

Rayana Designs Inc ....E ... 718 786-2040
Carle Place (G-3180)

Read Manufacturing Company Inc ....E ... 631 567-4487
Holbrook (G-6016)

Rims Like New Inc ....F 845 537-0396
  Middletown (G-7930)

Sentry Metal Blast Inc.........................E 716 285-5241
  Lockport (G-7106)

Sequa Corporation ....E 201 343-1122
  Orangeburg (G-12332)

Solidus Industries Inc.........................D 607 749-4540
  Homer (G-6067)

Spitale Cnstr Resources Inc ....G 914 352-6366
  Yorktown Heights (G-16373)

Static Coatings Inc.............................G 516 764-0040
  Oceanside (G-12191)

Static Coatings Inc.............................G 646 296-0754
  Lynbrook (G-7439)

Steel Partners Holdings LP ....D 212 520-2300
  New York (G-11352)

Stuart-Dean Co Inc ....F 718 472-1326
  Long Island City (G-7372)

▲ Superior Metals & Processing ....G 718 545-7500
  Long Island City (G-7375)

Swain Technology Inc ....F 585 889-2786
  Scottsville (G-14344)

Tailored Coatings Inc..........................E 716 893-4869
  Buffalo (G-3002)

The Gramecy Group ....G 518 348-1325
  Clifton Park (G-3476)

Tobeyco Manufacturing Co Inc ....F 607 962-2446
  Corning (G-3722)

▼ Tricor Direct Inc...............................G 716 626-1616
  Williamsville (G-16145)

Trojan Metal Fabrication Inc ....E 631 968-5040
  Bay Shore (G-723)

W Hubbell & Sons Inc ....E 315 736-8311
  Yorkville (G-16382)

▲ W W Custom Clad Inc ....G 518 673-3322
  Canajoharie (G-3122)

W W Custom Clad Inc ....D 518 673-3322
  Canajoharie (G-3123)

With You Designs LLC ....G 800 413-0670
  Red Hook (G-13075)

3482 Small Arms Ammunition

Benjamin Sheridan Corporation...........G 585 657-6161
  Bloomfield (G-940)

CIC International Ltd............................D 212 213-0089
  Brooklyn (G-1663)

▲ Crosman Corporation ....E 585 657-6161
  Bloomfield (G-945)

Crosman Corporation ....E 585 398-3920
  Farmington (G-4769)

3483 Ammunition, Large

CIC International Ltd............................D 212 213-0089
  Brooklyn (G-1663)

Circor Aerospace Inc ....D 631 737-1900
  Hauppauge (G-5615)

3484 Small Arms

Benjamin Sheridan Corporation...........G 585 657-6161
  Bloomfield (G-940)

▲ Crosman Corporation ....E 585 657-6161
  Bloomfield (G-945)

Crosman Corporation ....E 585 398-3920
  Farmington (G-4769)

Dan Wesson Corp ....F 607 336-1174
  Norwich (G-12120)

Dark Storm Industries LLC ....G 631 967-3170
  Oakdale (G-12150)

Hart Rifle Barrel Inc ....G 315 677-9841
  Syracuse (G-14910)

Kyntec Corporation ....G 716 810-6956
  Buffalo (G-2840)

Oriskany Arms Inc ....F 315 737-2196
  Oriskany (G-12393)

▼ Redding-Hunter Inc..........................E 607 753-3331
  Cortland (G-3786)

Remington Arms Company LLC............A 315 895-3482
  Ilion (G-6281)

Sycamore Hill Designs Inc ....G 585 820-7322
  Victor (G-15434)

▲ Tri-Technologies Inc ....E 914 699-2001
  Mount Vernon (G-8187)

3489 Ordnance & Access, NEC

CIC International Ltd............................D 212 213-0089
  Brooklyn (G-1663)

Dyno Nobel Inc....................................D 845 338-2144
  Ulster Park (G-15218)

▼ Island Ordnance Systems LLC ....F 516 746-2100
  Mineola (G-7982)

▲ Magellan Aerospace NY Inc ....C 718 699-4000
  Corona (G-3744)

3491 Industrial Valves

ADC Industries Inc..............................E 516 596-1304
  Valley Stream (G-15332)

▲ Air System Products Inc ....F 716 683-0435
  Lancaster (G-6792)

Byelocorp Scientific Inc ....E 212 785-2580
  New York (G-8877)

Caithness Equities Corporation ....E 212 599-2112
  New York (G-8888)

Curtiss-Wright Electro-.......................E 585 596-3482
  Wellsville (G-15669)

◆ Curtiss-Wright Flow Control ....C 631 293-3800
  Farmingdale (G-4607)

Curtiss-Wright Flow Ctrl Corp ....C 631 293-3800
  Farmingdale (G-4608)

Digital Home Creations Inc ....G 585 576-7070
  Webster (G-15638)

Dresser-Rand Company ....A 585 596-3100
  Wellsville (G-15670)

◆ Flomatic Corporation ....E 518 761-9797
  Glens Falls (G-5249)

▲ Flow-Safe Inc ....E 716 662-2585
  Orchard Park (G-12352)

Hy Cert Services Inc ....G 631 231-7005
  Brentwood (G-1122)

J H Buscher Inc...................................E 716 667-2003
  Orchard Park (G-12357)

▲ Jeg Online Ventures LLC ....F 800 983-8230
  Islandia (G-6337)

▲ John N Fehlinger Co Inc ....F 212 233-5656
  New York (G-10018)

McWane Inc ....B 607 734-2211
  Elmira (G-4362)

▲ Murphy Manufacturing Co Inc ....E 585 223-0100
  Fairport (G-4509)

◆ Plattco Corporation ....E 518 563-4640
  Plattsburgh (G-12768)

▲ Precision Valve & Automtn Inc ....C 518 371-2684
  Cohoes (G-3513)

▲ Spence Engineering Company Inc ...C 845 778-5566
  Walden (G-15462)

Syraco Products Inc ....F 315 476-5306
  Syracuse (G-15002)

▲ Total Energy Fabrication Corp ....G 580 363-1500
  North Salem (G-12037)

Trac Regulators Inc.............................E 914 699-9352
  Mount Vernon (G-8185)

Tyco Simplexgrinnell ....E 315 437-9664
  East Syracuse (G-4245)

◆ William E Williams Valve Corp ....E 718 392-1660
  Long Island City (G-7402)

3492 Fluid Power Valves & Hose Fittings

▲ A K Allen Co Inc ....C 516 747-5450
  Melville (G-7753)

Aalborg Instrs & Contrls Inc ....D 845 398-3160
  Orangeburg (G-12304)

▲ Aerco International Inc ....C 845 580-8000
  Blauvelt (G-925)

▲ BW Elliott Mfg Co LLC ....B 607 772-0404
  Binghamton (G-865)

Direkt Force LLC ....E 716 652-3022
  East Aurora (G-4085)

Dmic Inc ....C 716 743-4360
  North Tonawanda (G-12065)

Dynamic Sealing Tech Inc ....E 716 376-0708
  Olean (G-12233)

▲ Key High Vacuum Products Inc ....E 631 584-5959
  Nesconset (G-8219)

Kinemotive Corporation ....E 631 249-6440
  Farmingdale (G-4666)

▲ KSA Manufacturing LLC ....F 315 488-0809
  Camillus (G-3109)

Lourdes Industries Inc ....D 631 234-6600
  Hauppauge (G-5700)

Moog Inc ....B 716 687-4954
  East Aurora (G-4093)

◆ Moog Inc ....A 716 805-2604
  Elma (G-4321)

Own Instrument Inc ....F 914 668-6546
  Mount Vernon (G-8167)

Servotronics Inc ....C 716 655-5990
  Elma (G-4323)

▲ Steel & Obrien Mfg Inc ....D 585 492-5800
  Arcade (G-381)

Tactair Fluid Controls Inc ....C 315 451-3928
  Liverpool (G-7044)

Upstate Tube Inc ....G 315 488-5636
  Camillus (G-3112)

Young & Franklin Inc ....D 315 457-3110
  Liverpool (G-7051)

3493 Steel Springs, Except Wire

Angelica Spring Company Inc ....F 585 466-7892
  Angelica (G-357)

Isolation Dynamics Corp ....E 631 491-5670
  Farmingdale (G-4653)

▲ Lee Spring Company LLC ....C 888 777-4647
  Brooklyn (G-2058)

▲ Midstate Spring Inc ....E 315 437-2623
  Syracuse (G-14943)

▲ Red Onyx Industrial Pdts LLC ....G 516 459-6035
  Huntington (G-6219)

Temper Corporation ....E 518 853-3467
  Fonda (G-4912)

Whitesboro Spring & Alignment...........F 315 736-4441
  Whitesboro (G-16085)

Whiting Door Mfg Corp ....D 716 542-3070
  Akron (G-24)

3494 Valves & Pipe Fittings, NEC

▲ A K Allen Co Inc ....C 516 747-5450
  Melville (G-7753)

Aalborg Instrs & Contrls Inc ....D 845 398-3160
  Orangeburg (G-12304)

Advanced Thermal Systems Inc ....E 716 681-1800
  Lancaster (G-6790)

▲ Anderson Precision Inc ....D 716 484-1148
  Jamestown (G-6494)

◆ Curtiss-Wright Flow Control ....C 631 293-3800
  Farmingdale (G-4607)

▼ Devin Mfg Inc ....F 585 496-5770
  Arcade (G-372)

Dynamic Products Inc ....G 631 270-4833
  Farmingdale (G-4619)

◆ Flomatic Corporation ....E 518 761-9797
  Glens Falls (G-5249)

Ford Regulator Valve Corp ....G 718 497-3255
  Brooklyn (G-1858)

Goodman Main Stopper Mfg Co ....F 718 875-5140
  Brooklyn (G-1900)

Holyoke Fittings Inc ....F 718 649-0710
  Brooklyn (G-1939)

J H Robotics Inc..................................E 607 729-3758
  Johnson City (G-6603)

▲ Key High Vacuum Products Inc ....E 631 584-5959
  Nesconset (G-8219)

Kingston Hoops Summer ....G 845 401-6830
  Kingston (G-6696)

Lance Valves ....G 716 681-5825
  Lancaster (G-6815)

Legacy Valve LLC ....F 914 403-5075
  Valhalla (G-15304)

Lemode Plumbing & Heating ....E 718 545-3336
  Astoria (G-427)

M Manastrip-M Corporation ....G 518 664-2089
  Clifton Park (G-3467)

▲ Make-Waves Instrument Corp ....E 716 681-7524
  Buffalo (G-2860)

Micromold Products Inc ....E 914 969-2850
  Yonkers (G-16333)

Rand Machine Products, Inc.................C 716 665-5217
  Falconer (G-4552)

Ross Valve Mfg ....G 518 274-0961
  Troy (G-15184)

Sigmamotor Inc ....E 716 735-3115
  Middleport (G-7890)

▲ Spence Engineering Company Inc ...C 845 778-5566
  Walden (G-15462)

▲ Steel & Obrien Mfg Inc ....D 585 492-5800
  Arcade (G-381)

Sure Flow Equipment Inc ....E 800 263-8251
  Tonawanda (G-15143)

▲ United Pipe Nipple Co Inc ....F 516 295-2468
  Hewlett (G-5874)

Venco Sales Inc...................................E 631 754-0782
  Huntington (G-6233)

Westchester Valve & Fitting Co ....G 914 762-6600
  Clifton Park (G-3477)

William E William Valve Corp................E 718 392-1660
  Long Island City (G-7401)

◆ William E Williams Valve Corp ....E 718 392-1660
  Long Island City (G-7402)

3495 Wire Springs

Ajax Wire Specialty Co Inc ....F 516 935-2333
Hicksville (G-5879)
Barnes Group Inc ....G..... 315 457-9200
Syracuse (G-14826)
Commerce Spring Corp ....F 631 293-4844
Farmingdale (G-4602)
Commercial Communications LLC ......G..... 845 343-9078
Middletown (G-7900)
Fennell Spring Company LLC ....D...... 607 739-3541
Horseheads (G-6123)
Kinemotive Corporation ....E 631 249-6440
Farmingdale (G-4666)
▲ Lee Spring Company LLC ....C...... 888 777-4647
Brooklyn (G-2058)
▲ Midstate Spring Inc ....E 315 437-2623
Syracuse (G-14943)
▼ Pullman Mfg Corporation ....G..... 585 334-1350
Rochester (G-13652)
Teka Precision Inc.............................G..... 845 753-1900
Nyack (G-12147)
◆ The Caldwell Manufacturing Co ....D...... 585 352-3790
Rochester (G-13764)
The Caldwell Manufacturing Co ....E 585 352-2803
Victor (G-15438)
Unimex Corporation ....D...... 800 886-0390
New York (G-11591)
Unimex Corporation ....C...... 718 236-2222
Brooklyn (G-2537)

3496 Misc Fabricated Wire Prdts

369 River Road Inc ....E 716 694-5001
North Tonawanda (G-12050)
▲ Abbott Industries Inc ....B...... 718 291-0800
Jamaica (G-6423)
▲ Aeroflex Incorporated ....B...... 516 694-6700
Plainview (G-12660)
◆ Albest Metal Stamping Corp ....E 718 388-6000
Brooklyn (G-1477)
All-Lifts Incorporated ....E 518 465-3461
Albany (G-37)
▲ American Wire Tie Inc ....E 716 337-2412
North Collins (G-12023)
Angelica Spring Company Inc ....F 585 466-7892
Angelica (G-357)
Bayshore Wire Products Corp ....F 631 451-8825
Coram (G-3692)
▲ Better Wire Products Inc ....E 716 883-3377
Buffalo (G-2662)
▲ Bison Steel Incorporated ....G..... 716 683-0900
Depew (G-3971)
▲ Brook North Farms Inc ....F 315 834-9390
Auburn (G-469)
▲ Cable Management Solutions Inc......E 631 674-0004
Bay Shore (G-660)
▲ Chemprene Inc ....C...... 845 831-2800
Beacon (G-749)
▲ Chemprene Holding Inc ....C...... 845 831-2800
Beacon (G-750)
▲ Clover Wire Forming Co Inc ....E 914 375-0400
Yonkers (G-16296)
▼ Cobra Systems Inc ....F 845 338-6675
Bloomington (G-951)
◆ Columbus McKinnon Corporation ......C....... 716 689-5400
Getzville (G-5174)
Columbus McKinnon Corporation ....C....... 716 689-5400
Getzville (G-5175)
Columbus McKinnon Corporation ....C....... 716 689-5400
Getzville (G-5176)
Compar Manufacturing Corp ....E 212 304-2777
New York (G-9071)
▲ Continental Cordage Corp ....D...... 315 655-9800
Cazenovia (G-3225)
◆ Cortland Cable Company Inc ....E 607 753-8276
Cortland (G-3758)
▲ Cuba Specialty Mfg Co Inc ....F 585 567-4176
Fillmore (G-4793)
Cuddeback Machining Inc ....G..... 585 392-5889
Hilton (G-5972)
▲ Dico Products Corporation ....F 315 797-0470
Utica (G-15255)
Engineering Mfg Tech LLC ....D....... 607 754-7111
Endicott (G-4453)
Flanagans Creative Disp Inc ....E 845 858-2542
Port Jervis (G-12848)
Flatcut LLC ....G...... 212 542-5732
Brooklyn (G-1850)
▲ G Bopp USA Inc ....G..... 845 296-1065
Wappingers Falls (G-15493)

Habasit America Inc..........................D...... 716 824-8484
Buffalo (G-2787)
Hanes Supply Inc ....F 518 438-0139
Albany (G-83)
▲ Hohmann & Barnard Inc ....E 631 234-0600
Hauppauge (G-5672)
Hohmann & Barnard Inc ....E 518 357-9757
Schenectady (G-14278)
Interstate Wood Products Inc ....E 631 842-4488
Amityville (G-277)
J Davis Manufacturing Co Inc ....E 315 337-7574
Rome (G-13852)
Joldeson One Aerospace Inds ....D...... 718 848-7396
Ozone Park (G-12463)
Kehr-Buffalo Wire Frame Co Inc...........E 716 897-2288
Buffalo (G-2830)
Lyn Jo Enterprises Ltd ....G..... 716 753-2776
Jamestown (G-6530)
▲ Magic Novelty Co Inc ....E 212 304-2777
New York (G-10325)
◆ Nexans Energy USA Inc ....C....... 845 469-2141
Chester (G-3381)
Oneida Sales & Service Inc................E 716 822-8205
Buffalo (G-2897)
▲ Owl Wire & Cable LLC ....C...... 315 697-2011
Canastota (G-3153)
▲ Peck & Hale LLC ....E 631 589-2510
West Sayville (G-15842)
Quality Industrial Services.................F 716 667-7703
Orchard Park (G-12376)
Reelcology Inc...................................F 845 258-1880
Pine Island (G-12630)
◆ Renco Group Inc ....G..... 212 541-6000
New York (G-11012)
Rose Fence Inc..................................D...... 516 790-2308
Halesite (G-5489)
Rose Fence Inc ....F 516 223-0777
Baldwin (G-533)
◆ Sampla Belting North Amer LLC ......E 716 667-7450
Lackawanna (G-6745)
▲ Samzong Inc ....G..... 718 475-1843
Monsey (G-8047)
SCI Bore Inc......................................G..... 212 674-7128
New York (G-11165)
◆ Selectrode Industries Inc................D...... 631 547-5470
Huntington Station (G-6260)
▲ Sigmund Cohn Corp ....D...... 914 664-5300
Mount Vernon (G-8180)
Sinclair International Company ....D...... 518 798-2361
Queensbury (G-13057)
Star Wire Mesh Fabricators ....G..... 212 831-4133
New York (G-11349)
Sunward Electronics Inc ....F 518 687-0030
Troy (G-15191)
Teka Precision Inc..............................G..... 845 753-1900
Nyack (G-12147)
Trylon Wire & Metal Works Inc ....E 718 542-4472
Bronx (G-1384)
Ultra Clarity Corp ....G..... 719 470-1010
Spring Valley (G-14584)
Utility Engineering Co ....F 845 735-8900
Pearl River (G-12542)
▲ Weico Wire & Cable Inc ....E 631 254-2970
Edgewood (G-4292)

3497 Metal Foil & Leaf

◆ Alufoil Products Co Inc ....F 631 231-4141
Hauppauge (G-5585)
American Packaging Corporation ....G....... 585 254-2002
Rochester (G-13229)
American Packaging Corporation ....C....... 585 254-9500
Rochester (G-13230)
De Luxe Packaging Corp ....E 416 754-4633
Saugerties (G-14200)
Oak-Mitsui Inc ....D...... 518 686-8060
Hoosick Falls (G-6086)
▲ Oak-Mitsui Technologies LLC..........E 518 686-4961
Hoosick Falls (G-6087)
Pactiv LLC ....C...... 518 793-2524
Glens Falls (G-5264)
Quick Roll Leaf Mfg Co Inc ....E 845 457-1500
Montgomery (G-8065)
Steel Partners Holdings LP ....D...... 212 520-2300
New York (G-11352)
Thermal Process Cnstr Co ....E 631 293-6400
Farmingdale (G-4754)
Tri-State Food Jobbers Inc ....G..... 718 921-1211
Brooklyn (G-2519)

3498 Fabricated Pipe & Pipe Fittings

Accord Pipe Fabricators Inc ....E 718 657-3900
Jamaica (G-6424)
Advanced Thermal Systems Inc..........E 716 681-1800
Lancaster (G-6790)
Albany Nipple and Pipe Mfg ....E 518 270-2162
Troy (G-15157)
▲ Arcadia Mfg Group Inc ....E 518 434-6213
Green Island (G-5432)
Arcadia Mfg Group Inc ....G..... 518 434-6213
Menands (G-7840)
▲ Cobey Inc ....C...... 716 362-9550
Buffalo (G-2700)
Coventry Manufacturing Co Inc...........E 914 668-2212
Mount Vernon (G-8134)
D & G Welding Inc ....G..... 716 873-3088
Buffalo (G-2718)
Daikin Applied Americas Inc ....D...... 315 253-2771
Auburn (G-472)
Falcon Perspectives Inc ....G..... 718 706-9168
Long Island City (G-7220)
Flatcut LLC ....G..... 212 542-5732
Brooklyn (G-1850)
J D Steward Inc ....G..... 718 358-0169
Flushing (G-4864)
James Woerner Inc ....G..... 631 454-9330
Farmingdale (G-4656)
▲ Juniper Elbow Co Inc ....E 718 326-2546
Middle Village (G-7881)
▲ Juniper Industries Florida Inc...........G..... 718 326-2546
Middle Village (G-7882)
▲ Leo International Inc ....E 718 290-8005
Brooklyn (G-2063)
◆ Leroy Plastics Inc ....D...... 585 768-8158
Le Roy (G-6903)
Long Island Pipe Supply Inc ....G..... 718 456-7877
Flushing (G-4872)
Long Island Pipe Supply Inc ....G..... 518 270-2159
Troy (G-15160)
M Manastrip-M Corporation ....G..... 518 664-2089
Clifton Park (G-3467)
Micromold Products Inc ....E 914 969-2850
Yonkers (G-16333)
Miles Moss of Albany Inc ....E 516 222-8008
Garden City (G-5108)
Miles Moss of New York Inc ....E 516 222-8008
Garden City (G-5109)
Piping Solutions Inc ....G..... 646 258-5381
Brooklyn (G-2262)
Ram Fabricating LLC ....E 315 437-6654
Syracuse (G-14971)
▲ Spinco Metal Products Inc ....D...... 315 331-6285
Newark (G-11852)
Star Tubing Corp ....G..... 716 483-1703
Jamestown (G-6543)
Tag Flange & Machining Inc................G..... 516 536-1300
Oceanside (G-12194)
▲ Total Piping Solutions Inc ....F 716 372-0160
Olean (G-12243)
Truly Tubular Fitting Corp ....F 914 664-8686
Mount Vernon (G-8188)
Tube Fabrication Company Inc.............F 716 673-1871
Fredonia (G-4971)

3499 Fabricated Metal Prdts, NEC

▲ Access Display Group Inc ....E 516 678-7772
Freeport (G-4979)
Alpine Paper Box Co Inc ....E 718 345-4040
Brooklyn (G-1492)
American Standard Mfg Inc ....E 518 868-2512
Central Bridge (G-3259)
Aquarium Pump & Piping Systems.......F 631 567-5555
Sayville (G-14222)
▲ Arnold Magnetic Tech Corp ....C...... 585 385-9010
Rochester (G-13246)
Brakewell Stl Fabricators Inc..............E 845 469-9131
Chester (G-3371)
Bristol Gift Co Inc ....F 845 496-2821
Washingtonville (G-15523)
Brooklyn Cstm Met Fbrction Inc...........G..... 718 499-1573
Brooklyn (G-1615)
Buttons & Trimcom Inc ....F 212 868-1971
New York (G-8874)
C & M Products Inc ....G..... 315 471-3303
Syracuse (G-14838)
▲ Carpentier Industries LLC ....F 585 385-5550
East Rochester (G-4160)
◆ Chapin International Inc ....E 585 343-3140
Batavia (G-608)

◆ Chapin Manufacturing Inc ....C 585 343-3140
  Batavia (G-609)
Clad Industries LLC ....G 585 413-4359
  Macedon (G-7464)
▲ Classic Medallics Inc ....E 718 392-5410
  Mount Vernon (G-8131)
Consolidated Barricades Inc ....G 518 922-7944
  Fultonville (G-5078)
Criterion Bell & Specialty ....E 718 788-2600
  Brooklyn (G-1701)
Crystalizations Systems Inc ....F 631 467-0090
  Holbrook (G-5993)
Custom Frame & Molding Co ....F 631 491-9091
  West Babylon (G-15705)
Di Highway Sign Structure Corp ....E 315 736-8312
  New York Mills (G-11831)
Dimar Manufacturing Corp ....C 716 759-0351
  Clarence (G-3428)
Dobrin Industries Inc ....G 800 353-2229
  Lockport (G-7069)
Dz9 Power LLC ....G 877 533-5530
  Olean (G-12234)
Elias Artmetal Inc ....F 516 873-7501
  Mineola (G-7970)
Empire Metal Finishing Inc ....E 718 545-6700
  Astoria (G-421)
Finger Lakes Conveyors Inc ....G 315 539-9246
  Waterloo (G-15551)
Frame Shoppe & Art Gallery ....G 516 365-6014
  Manhasset (G-7534)
Galmer Ltd ....G 718 392-4609
  Long Island City (G-7229)
◆ Gardall Safe Corporation ....E 315 432-9115
  Syracuse (G-14899)
▲ Garment Care Systems LLC ....G 518 674-1826
  Averill Park (G-507)
◆ Gibraltar Industries Inc ....D 716 826-6500
  Buffalo (G-2775)
◆ Hannay Reels Inc ....C 518 797-3791
  Westerlo (G-15941)
Hatfield Metal Fab Inc ....E 845 454-9078
  Poughkeepsie (G-12961)
▲ Icestone LLC ....E 718 624-4900
  Brooklyn (G-1951)
Inpro Corporation ....G 716 332-4699
  Tonawanda (G-15115)
▲ Inter Pacific Consulting Corp ....G 718 460-2787
  Flushing (G-4861)
James D Rubino Inc ....E 631 244-8730
  Bohemia (G-1026)
▲ Jay Strongwater Holdings LLC ......A 646 657-0558
  New York (G-9980)
JE Monahan Fabrications LLC ....F 518 761-0414
  Queensbury (G-13045)
▼ Jordan Panel Systems Corp ....E 631 754-4900
  East Northport (G-4148)
▲ Kefa Industries Group Inc ....G 718 568-9297
  Rego Park (G-13079)
Kwong CHI Metal Fabrication ....G 718 369-6429
  Brooklyn (G-2039)
L D Flecken Inc ....F 631 777-4881
  Yaphank (G-16264)
▲ Lr Paris LLC ....F 845 709-8013
  New York (G-10275)
Machinery Mountings Inc ....F 631 851-0480
  Hauppauge (G-5703)
Magnaworks Technology Inc ....G 631 218-3431
  Bohemia (G-1042)
▲ Magnetic Aids Inc ....G 845 863-1400
  Marlboro (G-7580)
▲ Materion Brewster LLC ....D 845 279-0900
  Brewster (G-1155)
▲ Maximum Security Products Corp ...E 518 233-1800
  Waterford (G-15538)
McD Metals LLC ....F 518 456-9694
  Albany (G-98)
▼ Metallic Ladder Mfg Corp ....F 716 358-6201
  Randolph (G-13063)
Mpl Metal Inc ....G 718 338-4952
  Brooklyn (G-2174)
National Maint Contg Corp ....D 716 285-1583
  Niagara Falls (G-11953)
New Dimension Awards Inc ....G 718 236-8200
  Brooklyn (G-2202)
New York Manufactured Products .....F 585 254-9353
  Rochester (G-13570)
▲ Nrd LLC ....E 716 773-7634
  Grand Island (G-5339)
PBL Industries Corp ....F 631 979-4266
  Smithtown (G-14483)

Peak Motion Inc ....G 716 534-4925
  Clarence (G-3439)
▲ Peelle Company ....G 631 231-6000
  Hauppauge (G-5738)
Picture Perfect Framing ....E 718 851-1884
  Brooklyn (G-2257)
▲ Polich Tallix Inc ....D 845 567-9464
  Rock Tavern (G-13821)
▲ Polymag Inc ....E 631 286-4111
  Bellport (G-807)
▲ Precision Magnetics LLC ....E 585 385-9010
  Rochester (G-13639)
Protocase Incorporated ....C 866 849-3911
  Lewiston (G-6922)
Range Repair Warehouse ....G 585 235-0980
  Penfield (G-12572)
Raytech Corp Asbestos Personal .....A 516 747-0300
  Mineola (G-7996)
Reelcology Inc ....F 845 258-1880
  Pine Island (G-12630)
Romac Electronics Inc ....E 516 349-7900
  Plainview (G-12711)
Rough Brothers Holding Co ....G 716 826-6500
  Buffalo (G-2965)
▲ Rush Gold Manufacturing Ltd ....D 516 781-3155
  Bellmore (G-788)
Secureit Tactical Inc ....F 800 651-8835
  Syracuse (G-14991)
▲ Sono-Tek Corporation ....D 845 795-2020
  Milton (G-7952)
Split Rock Trading Co Inc ....G 631 929-3261
  Wading River (G-15452)
▲ Structural Industries Inc ....C 631 471-5200
  Bohemia (G-1082)
▲ Stylebuilt Accessories Inc ....F 917 439-0578
  East Rockaway (G-4175)
Total Metal Resource ....F 718 384-7818
  Brooklyn (G-2513)
◆ Truebite Inc ....E 607 785-7664
  Vestal (G-15386)
Ulster County Iron Works LLC ....G 845 255-0003
  New Paltz (G-8312)

35 INDUSTRIAL AND COMMERCIAL MACHINERY AND COMPUTER EQUIPMENT

3511 Steam, Gas & Hydraulic Turbines & Engines

Atlantic Projects Company Inc ....F 518 878-2065
  Clifton Park (G-3462)
Awr Energy Inc ....F 585 469-7750
  Plattsburgh (G-12733)
▲ Cooper Turbocompressor Inc ....B 716 896-6600
  Buffalo (G-2711)
Dresser-Rand Company ....B 585 596-3100
  Wellsville (G-15670)
Dresser-Rand Group Inc ....B 716 375-3000
  Olean (G-12232)
Frontier Hydraulics Corp ....F 716 694-2070
  Buffalo (G-2762)
GE Global Research ....A 518 387-5000
  Niskayuna (G-11995)
General Electric Company ....A 518 385-4022
  Schenectady (G-14266)
General Electric Company ....B 518 385-2211
  Schenectady (G-14267)
General Electric Company ....B 203 373-2756
  Schenectady (G-14268)
General Electric Company ....B 518 385-3716
  Schenectady (G-14269)
General Electric Company ....B 518 385-2211
  Schenectady (G-14270)
General Electric Company ....B 518 387-5000
  Schenectady (G-14271)
General Electric Company ....B 518 385-7620
  Niskayuna (G-11996)
General Electric Company ....B 518 385-3439
  Schenectady (G-14272)
General Electric Intl Inc ....G 518 385-2211
  Schenectady (G-14273)
▲ Hdm Hydraulics LLC ....D 716 694-8004
  Tonawanda (G-15110)
Intersource Management Group ....G 518 372-6798
  Halfmoon (G-5494)
Intersource Management Group ....E 518 372-6798
  Schenectady (G-14281)

▲ Mannesmann Corporation ....D 212 258-4000
  New York (G-10348)
Mission Critical Energy Inc ....G 716 276-8465
  Getzville (G-5178)
◆ Prime Turbine Parts LLC ....G 518 306-7306
  Saratoga Springs (G-14188)
Siemens Government Tech Inc ....B 585 593-1234
  Wellsville (G-15676)
Signa Chemistry Inc ....F 212 933-4101
  New York (G-11234)
▲ Stork H & E Turbo Blading Inc ....C 607 277-4968
  Ithaca (G-6411)
Tgp Flying Cloud Holdings LLC ....E 646 829-3900
  New York (G-11458)
Turbine Engine Comp Utica ....A 315 768-8070
  Whitesboro (G-16084)
Turbo Machined Products LLC ....E 315 895-3010
  Frankfort (G-4957)
Tuthill Corporation ....B 631 727-1097
  Riverhead (G-13191)
Weaver Wind Energy LLC ....G 607 379-9463
  Freeville (G-5036)
Worldwide Gas Turbine Pdts Inc ......G 518 877-7200
  Clifton Park (G-3478)

3519 Internal Combustion Engines, NEC

AB Engine ....G 518 557-3510
  Latham (G-6846)
Briggs & Stratton Corporation ....F 315 495-0100
  Sherrill (G-14402)
Cummins - Allison Corp ....D 718 263-2482
  Kew Gardens (G-6662)
Cummins Inc ....A 716 456-2111
  Lakewood (G-6781)
Cummins Northeast LLC ....E 315 437-2296
  Syracuse (G-14869)
Cummins-Wagner-Siewert LLC ....E 585 482-9640
  Rochester (G-13332)
D & W Diesel Inc ....F 518 437-1300
  Latham (G-6853)
Jack W Miller ....G 585 538-2399
  Scottsville (G-14341)
▲ Mannesmann Corporation ....D 212 258-4000
  New York (G-10348)
Perkins International Inc ....G 309 675-1000
  Buffalo (G-2914)
Washer Solutions Inc ....F 585 742-6388
  Victor (G-15442)

3523 Farm Machinery & Eqpt

Asp Blade Intrmdate Hldngs Inc ....A 212 476-8000
  New York (G-8650)
Bdp Industries Inc ....E 518 695-6851
  Greenwich (G-5468)
▲ Bean King International LLC ....F 845 268-3135
  Congers (G-3609)
◆ Chapin Manufacturing Inc ....G 585 343-3140
  Batavia (G-609)
Don Beck Inc ....G 585 493-3040
  Castile (G-3198)
Eastern Welding Inc ....G 631 727-0306
  Riverhead (G-13174)
◆ Fountainhead Group Inc ....C 315 736-0037
  New York Mills (G-11832)
▲ Good Earth Organics Corp ....E 716 684-8111
  Lancaster (G-6809)
▼ Growtech Industries LLC ....G 315 335-9692
  Buffalo (G-2786)
Haines Equipment Inc ....E 607 566-8531
  Avoca (G-510)
House of The Foaming Case Inc ....G 718 454-0101
  Saint Albans (G-14105)
Jain Irrigation Inc ....D 315 755-4400
  Watertown (G-15573)
L&M Specialty Fabrication ....G 585 283-4847
  Albion (G-157)
Landpro Equipment LLC ....E 716 665-3110
  Falconer (G-4549)
▲ Oxbo International Corporation ....D 585 548-2665
  Byron (G-3062)
Plant-Tech2o Inc ....G 516 483-7845
  Hempstead (G-5847)
Renaldos Sales & Service Ctr ....G 716 337-3760
  North Collins (G-12028)
Richard Stewart ....G 518 632-5363
  Hartford (G-5566)
Road Cases USA Inc ....E 631 563-0633
  Bohemia (G-1071)
Vansridge Dairy LLC ....E 315 364-8569
  Scipio Center (G-14327)

Westmoor Ltd ....F 315 363-1500
Sherrill (G-14409)
Zappala Farms AG Systems Inc ....E 315 626-6293
Cato (G-3209)

3524 Garden, Lawn Tractors & Eqpt

Benishty Brothers Corp ....G...... 646 339-9991
Woodmere (G-16190)
Capital E Financial Group ....F 212 319-6550
New York (G-8911)
◆ Chapin International Inc ....C 585 343-3140
Batavia (G-608)
◆ Chapin Manufacturing Inc ....C 585 343-3140
Batavia (G-609)
Clopay Ames True Temper ....F 212 957-5096
New York (G-9035)
▲ Eaton Brothers Corp ....G...... 716 649-8250
Hamburg (G-5505)
Fradan Manufacturing Corp ....F 914 632-3653
New Rochelle (G-8332)
Rhett M Clark Inc............................G...... 585 538-9570
Caledonia (G-3072)
Saxby Implement Corp ....F 585 624-2938
Mendon (G-7852)

3531 Construction Machinery & Eqpt

▲ AAAA York Inc ....F 718 784-6666
Long Island City (G-7142)
Air-Flo Mfg Co Inc............................D 607 733-8284
Elmira (G-4340)
Applied Technology Mfg Corp ....E 607 687-2200
Owego (G-12428)
Asp Blade Intrmdate Hldngs Inc...........A 212 476-8000
New York (G-8650)
▲ BW Elliott Mfg Co LLC ....B 607 772-0404
Binghamton (G-865)
Ceno Technologies Inc ....G...... 716 885-5050
Buffalo (G-2694)
City of Jamestown...........................D 716 483-7545
Jamestown (G-6501)
Cives Corporation...........................D 315 543-2321
Harrisville (G-5565)
Construction Robotics LLC ....E 585 742-2004
Victor (G-15400)
Cooper Industries LLC ....F 315 477-7000
Syracuse (G-14864)
Crane Equipment & Service Inc...........G...... 716 689-5400
Amherst (G-219)
Dave Sandel Cranes Inc ....G...... 631 325-5588
Westhampton (G-15954)
Diamond Coring & Cutting Inc.............G...... 718 381-4545
Maspeth (G-7606)
◆ Dover Global Holdings Inc ....F 212 922-1640
New York (G-9257)
Drillco National Group Inc ....E 718 726-9801
Long Island City (G-7204)
ET Oakes Corporation ....E 631 232-0002
Hauppauge (G-5648)
Gei International Inc ....E 315 463-9261
East Syracuse (G-4212)
Highway Garage...............................G...... 518 568-2837
Saint Johnsville (G-14119)
Kinedyne Inc..................................F 716 667-6833
Orchard Park (G-12360)
◆ Kinshofer Usa Inc ....E 716 731-4333
Sanborn (G-14145)
Kyntec Corporation ....G...... 716 810-6956
Buffalo (G-2840)
Line Ward Corporation ....G...... 716 675-7373
Buffalo (G-2850)
Lomin Construction Company ....G...... 516 759-5734
Glen Head (G-5209)
▲ Midland Machinery Co Inc................D 716 692-1200
Tonawanda (G-15122)
▲ Munson Machinery Company Inc....E 315 797-0090
Utica (G-15286)
New Eagle Silo Corp ....G...... 585 492-1300
Arcade (G-379)
North American Supply LLC ....G...... 607 432-1480
Oneonta (G-12277)
▲ Northrock Industries Inc ....E 631 924-6130
Bohemia (G-1055)
Oneida Sales & Service Inc................E 716 822-8205
Buffalo (G-2897)
▲ Oswald Manufacturing Co Inc ....E 516 883-8850
Port Washington (G-12910)
◆ Ozteck Industries Inc ....E 516 883-8857
Port Washington (G-12911)
Park Ave Bldg & Roofg Sups LLC ....E 718 403-0100
Brooklyn (G-2247)

Pauls Rods & Restos Inc ....G...... 631 665-7637
Deer Park (G-3917)
Peckham Materials Corp ....E 518 747-3353
Hudson Falls (G-6192)
Penn Can Equipment Corporation ....G...... 315 378-0337
Lyons (G-7451)
Penn State Mtal Fbrctors No 2 ....G...... 718 786-8814
Brooklyn (G-2253)
Pier-Tech Inc..................................E 516 442-5420
Oceanside (G-12184)
▲ Precision Product Inc ....G...... 718 852-7127
Brooklyn (G-2278)
Presti Ready Mix Concrete Inc ....G...... 516 378-6006
Freeport (G-5016)
Primoplast Inc................................F 631 750-0680
Bohemia (G-1066)
Pro-Tech Wldg Fabrication Inc ....E 585 436-9855
Rochester (G-13647)
▲ Professional Pavers Corp ....E 718 784-7853
Rego Park (G-13081)
Railworks Transit Systems Inc ....F 212 502-7900
New York (G-10972)
Rapistak Corporation ....G...... 716 822-2804
Buffalo (G-2949)
Rochester Asphalt Materials ....G...... 315 524-4619
Walworth (G-15478)
Rockland Manufacturing Co ....G...... 845 358-6000
West Nyack (G-15832)
RTD Manufacturing Inc......................G...... 315 337-3151
Rome (G-13871)
S R & R Industries Inc ....G...... 845 692-8329
Middletown (G-7931)
▲ Schutte-Buffalo Hammermill LLC.......E 716 855-1202
Buffalo (G-2976)
Seville Central Mix Corp....................D 516 293-6190
Old Bethpage (G-12219)
T S P Corp.....................................F 585 768-6769
Le Roy (G-6907)
Technopaving New York Inc................G...... 631 351-6472
Huntington Station (G-6263)
TLC Industries Inc...........................F 718 596-2842
Brooklyn (G-2507)
Town of Ohio ....E 315 392-2055
Forestport (G-4929)
Vanhouten Motorsports ....G...... 315 387-6312
Lacona (G-6747)
X-Treme Ready Mix Inc......................G...... 718 739-3384
Jamaica (G-6489)
Ziegler Truck & Diesl Repr Inc ....G...... 315 782-7278
Watertown (G-15593)

3532 Mining Machinery & Eqpt

American Material Processing...............F 315 318-0017
Phoenix (G-12615)
▲ Drillco Equipment Co Inc ....E 718 777-5986
Long Island City (G-7203)
Flatcut LLC ....G...... 212 542-5732
Brooklyn (G-1850)
Lawson M Whiting Inc ....G...... 315 986-3064
Macedon (G-7467)
▲ Munson Machinery Company Inc....E 315 797-0090
Utica (G-15286)
Universal Metal Fabricators ....F 845 331-8248
Kingston (G-6719)

3533 Oil Field Machinery & Eqpt

Anchor Commerce Trading Corp ....G...... 516 881-3485
Atlantic Beach (G-452)
Basin Holdings LLC ....E 212 695-7376
New York (G-8738)
◆ Blue Tee Corp ....G...... 212 598-0880
New York (G-8820)
◆ Derrick Corporation ....C 716 683-9010
Buffalo (G-2727)
Derrick Corporation ....B 716 685-4892
Cheektowaga (G-3344)
▼ Desmi-Afti Inc ....E 716 662-0632
Orchard Park (G-12351)
Schlumberger Technology Corp ....C 607 378-0105
Horseheads (G-6136)
Smith International Inc ....F 585 265-2330
Ontario (G-12303)

3534 Elevators & Moving Stairways

◆ A & D Entrances LLC.......................F 718 989-2441
Wyandanch (G-16240)
Access Elevator & Lift Inc...................G...... 716 483-3696
Jamestown (G-6491)
◆ Allround Logistics Inc ....G...... 718 544-8945
Forest Hills (G-4916)

An Excelsior Elevator Corp..................F 516 408-3070
Westbury (G-15869)
Ankom Development LLC ....G...... 315 986-1937
Macedon (G-7458)
Automated Elevator Systems ....E 845 595-1063
Greenwood Lake (G-5478)
Bhi Elevator Cabs Inc ....F 516 431-5665
Island Park (G-6315)
Big Apple Elevtr Srv & Consult ....G...... 212 279-0700
New York (G-8784)
CEC Elevator Cab Corp......................D 718 328-3632
Bronx (G-1221)
◆ Dover Global Holdings Inc ....F 212 922-1640
New York (G-9257)
Dural Door Company Inc....................F 718 729-1333
Long Island City (G-7206)
E Z Entry Doors Inc..........................F 716 434-3440
Lockport (G-7072)
Eag Electric Inc ....F 201 376-5103
Staten Island (G-14649)
▲ Eazylift Albany LLC.........................G...... 518 452-6929
Latham (G-6855)
Elevator Accessories Mfg ....F 914 739-7004
Peekskill (G-12550)
Elevator Interiors Inc ....E 315 218-7186
Syracuse (G-14884)
Elevator Ventures Corporation ....D 212 375-1900
Ozone Park (G-12460)
GAI Manufacturing Co LLC ....D 718 292-9000
Bronx (G-1264)
Herbert Wolf Corp ....G...... 718 392-2424
Long Island City (G-7241)
Interface Products Co Inc ....G...... 631 242-4605
Bay Shore (G-683)
Island Custom Stairs Inc ....G...... 631 205-5335
Medford (G-7713)
▲ Monitor Elevator Products LLC..........D 631 543-4334
Hauppauge (G-5723)
▲ National Elev Cab & Door Corp ....E 718 478-5900
Woodside (G-16215)
Otis Elevator Company ....F 315 736-0167
Yorkville (G-16379)
Otis Elevator Company ....E 917 339-9600
New York (G-10717)
Palmer Industries Inc.......................G...... 607 754-8741
Endicott (G-4468)
Rokon Tech LLC...............................G...... 718 429-0729
Elmhurst (G-4338)
S & H Enterprises Inc ....G...... 888 323-8755
Queensbury (G-13055)
Schindler Elevator Corporation ....C 212 708-1000
New York (G-11151)
Schindler Elevator Corporation ....E 800 225-3123
New York (G-11152)
Velis Associates Inc ....G...... 631 225-4220
Lindenhurst (G-6981)

3535 Conveyors & Eqpt

American Material Processing...............F 315 318-0017
Phoenix (G-12615)
Automated Biomass Systems LLC ....F 607 849-7800
Marathon (G-7556)
▲ Chemprene Inc ....C 845 831-2800
Beacon (G-749)
▲ Chemprene Holding Inc...................C 845 831-2800
Beacon (G-750)
◆ Columbus McKinnon Corporation......C 716 689-5400
Getzville (G-5174)
Columbus McKinnon Corporation ....C 716 689-5400
Getzville (G-5175)
Columbus McKinnon Corporation ....C 716 689-5400
Getzville (G-5176)
▲ Crownbrook ACC LLC ....C 718 626-0760
Brooklyn (G-1703)
◆ Dairy Conveyor Corp ....D 845 278-7878
Brewster (G-1146)
▼ Desmi-Afti Inc ....E 716 662-0632
Orchard Park (G-12351)
Excel Conveyor LLC ....F 718 474-0001
Rockaway Beach (G-13822)
General Splice Corporation ....G...... 914 271-5131
Croton On Hudson (G-3808)
Glasgow Products Inc ....E 516 374-5937
Woodmere (G-16191)
Green Conveyor & Mch Group LLC ......G...... 607 692-7050
Whitney Point (G-16106)
Haines Equipment Inc ....E 607 566-8531
Avoca (G-510)
Hohl Machine & Conveyor Co Inc ....E 716 882-7210
Buffalo (G-2799)

▼ I J White Corporation ....D 631 293-3788
　Farmingdale *(G-4647)*

▲ J D Handling Systems Inc ....F 518 828-9676
　Ghent *(G-5185)*

Joldeson One Aerospace Inds ....D 718 848-7396
　Ozone Park *(G-12463)*

▲ Nerak Systems Inc ....F 914 763-8259
　Fishkill *(G-4803)*

Northeast Conveyors Inc ....F 585 768-8912
　Lima *(G-6933)*

Noto Industrial Corp ....G 631 736-7600
　Coram *(G-3697)*

◆ Raymond Corporation ....A 607 656-2311
　Greene *(G-5448)*

Raymond Corporation ....E 315 643-5000
　East Syracuse *(G-4232)*

Re-Al Industrial Corp ....G 716 542-4556
　Akron *(G-21)*

▲ Renold Inc ....D 716 326-3121
　Westfield *(G-15949)*

▲ Rlp Holdings Inc ....G 716 852-0832
　Buffalo *(G-2956)*

Rota Pack Inc ....F 631 274-1037
　Farmingdale *(G-4727)*

Shako Inc ....G 315 437-1294
　East Syracuse *(G-4238)*

Specialty Conveyor Corp ....G 347 707-0490
　Farmingdale *(G-4737)*

Troy Belting and Supply Co ....D 518 272-4920
　Watervliet *(G-15609)*

▲ Ward Industrial Equipment Inc ....G 716 856-6966
　Buffalo *(G-3041)*

3536 Hoists, Cranes & Monorails

▼ Acme Marine Hoist Inc................631 472-3030
　Calverton *(G-3076)*

C M Insurance Company Inc ....G 716 689-5409
　Getzville *(G-5173)*

◆ Columbus McKinnon Corporation ...C 716 689-5400
　Getzville *(G-5174)*

Columbus McKinnon Corporation ...C 716 689-5400
　Getzville *(G-5175)*

Columbus McKinnon Corporation ...C 716 689-5400
　Getzville *(G-5176)*

Debrucque Cleveland Tramrail S .....G 315 697-5160
　Canastota *(G-3152)*

Dun-Rite Spclized Carriers LLC........F 718 991-1100
　Bronx *(G-1244)*

▲ Gorbel Inc ....C 585 924-6262
　Fishers *(G-4796)*

Kleinfelder John...........................G 716 753-3163
　Mayville *(G-7683)*

Konecranes Inc ....F 585 359-4450
　Henrietta *(G-5857)*

▲ Mannesmann Corporation ....D 212 258-4000
　New York *(G-10348)*

Marros Equipment & Trucks ....F 315 539-8702
　Waterloo *(G-15555)*

▲ Mohawk Resources Ltd ....D 518 842-1431
　Amsterdam *(G-339)*

▲ Reimann & Georger Corporation......E 716 895-1156
　Buffalo *(G-2951)*

T Shore Products Ltd ....G 315 252-9174
　Auburn *(G-497)*

Thego Corporation........................G 631 776-2472
　Bellport *(G-808)*

◆ US Hoists Corp ....G 631 472-3030
　Calverton *(G-3090)*

3537 Indl Trucks, Tractors, Trailers & Stackers

Artcraft Building Services ....G 845 895-3893
　Wallkill *(G-15467)*

ASAP Rack Rental Inc ....G 718 499-4495
　Brooklyn *(G-1539)*

▲ Channel Manufacturing Inc ....E 516 944-6271
　Port Washington *(G-12866)*

◆ Columbus McKinnon Corporation ...C 716 689-5400
　Getzville *(G-5174)*

Columbus McKinnon Corporation ...C 716 689-5400
　Getzville *(G-5175)*

Columbus McKinnon Corporation ...C 716 689-5400
　Getzville *(G-5176)*

▲ Continental Lift Truck Inc ....F 718 738-4738
　South Ozone Park *(G-14521)*

Crown Equipment Corporation........D 516 822-5100
　Hicksville *(G-5900)*

▼ Devin Mfg Inc............................F 585 496-5770
　Arcade *(G-372)*

DI Manufacturing Inc ....E 315 432-8977
　North Syracuse *(G-12040)*

◆ Ducon Technologies Inc ....B 631 694-1700
　New York *(G-9278)*

Ducon Technologies Inc ....E 631 420-4900
　Farmingdale *(G-4618)*

E-One Inc ....D 716 646-6790
　Hamburg *(G-5504)*

Elramida Holdings Inc ....E 646 280-0503
　Brooklyn *(G-1797)*

Jasper Transport LLC....................G 315 729-5760
　Penn Yan *(G-12588)*

◆ Koke Inc ....E 800 535-5303
　Queensbury *(G-13047)*

Meteor Express Inc ....F 718 551-9177
　Jamaica *(G-6460)*

Mil & Mir Steel Pdts Co Inc ....G 718 328-7596
　Bronx *(G-1313)*

Palpross Incorporated ....F 845 469-2188
　Selkirk *(G-14359)*

Pb08 Inc ....G 347 866-7353
　Hicksville *(G-5941)*

Raymond Corporation ....E 315 643-5000
　East Syracuse *(G-4232)*

◆ Raymond Corporation ....A 607 656-2311
　Greene *(G-5448)*

Raymond Sales Corporation ....E 607 656-2311
　Greene *(G-5449)*

Sherco Services LLC ....E 516 676-3028
　Glen Cove *(G-5200)*

Stanley Industrial Eqp LLC ....G 315 656-8733
　Kirkville *(G-6726)*

W W Trading Co Inc ....G 718 935-1085
　Brooklyn *(G-2573)*

Ward Lafrance Truck Corp ....F 518 893-1865
　Saratoga Springs *(G-14195)*

3541 Machine Tools: Cutting

Abtex Corporation ....E 315 536-7403
　Dresden *(G-4034)*

Advanced Machine Design Co Inc ...E 716 826-2000
　Buffalo *(G-2624)*

Alpine Machine Inc ....F 607 272-1344
　Ithaca *(G-6362)*

▲ Alternative Service Inc ....E 631 345-9500
　Bellport *(G-793)*

Alton Manufacturing Inc ....D 585 458-2600
　Rochester *(G-13225)*

▲ Ascension Industries Inc..............C 716 693-9381
　North Tonawanda *(G-12054)*

Aztec Mfg of Rochester ....G 585 352-8152
　Spencerport *(G-14552)*

▲ Baldwin Machine Works Inc ....G 631 842-9110
　Copiague *(G-3649)*

▲ Brinkman Products Inc ....B 585 235-4545
　Rochester *(G-13282)*

Bystronic Inc ....G 631 231-1212
　Hauppauge *(G-5609)*

Coastel Cable Tools Inc ....E 315 471-5361
　Syracuse *(G-14855)*

Connex Grinding & Machining ....G 315 946-4340
　Lyons *(G-7448)*

Dinosaw Inc ....E 518 828-9942
　Hudson *(G-6154)*

Dunlap Machine LLC ....F 315 926-1013
　Marion *(G-7568)*

Five Star Tool Co Inc ....E 585 328-9580
　Rochester *(G-13412)*

Folam Tool Co Inc ....G 716 688-1347
　Buffalo *(G-2756)*

Gallery of Machines LLC ....E 607 849-6028
　Marathon *(G-7557)*

Gb Aero Engine LLC ....E 914 925-9600
　Rye *(G-14078)*

Genco John ....G 716 483-5446
　Jamestown *(G-6512)*

◆ Gleason Corporation ....A 585 473-1000
　Rochester *(G-13444)*

◆ Gleason Works ....A 585 473-1000
　Rochester *(G-13445)*

▲ Graywood Companies Inc ....A 585 738-8889
　Rochester *(G-13450)*

H S Assembly Inc ....G 585 266-4287
　Rochester *(G-13455)*

Halpern Tool Corp ....G 914 633-0038
　New Rochelle *(G-8338)*

◆ Hardinge Inc ....B 607 734-2281
　Elmira *(G-4355)*

▲ Hartchrom Inc ....F 518 880-0411
　Watervliet *(G-15603)*

High Speed Hammer Company Inc ....F 585 266-4287
　Rochester *(G-13468)*

IPC/Razor LLC ....D 212 551-4500
　New York *(G-9938)*

J Vogler Enterprise LLC ....F 585 247-1625
　Rochester *(G-13486)*

Jalex Industries Ltd ....F 631 491-5072
　West Babylon *(G-15718)*

Johnson Mch & Fibr Pdts Co Inc ....F 716 665-2003
　Jamestown *(G-6527)*

Kodiak Cutting Tools LLC ....G 800 892-1006
　Syracuse *(G-14928)*

◆ Kps Capital Partners LP ....E 212 338-5100
　New York *(G-10133)*

Kyocera Precision Tools Inc ....F 607 687-0012
　Owego *(G-12431)*

▲ Lancaster Knives Inc ....F 716 683-5050
　Lancaster *(G-6814)*

Lk Industries Inc ....G 716 941-9202
　Glenwood *(G-5274)*

▲ Montrose Equipment Sales Inc.......F 718 388-7446
　Brooklyn *(G-2170)*

Mortech Industries Inc ....G 845 628-6138
　Mahopac *(G-7475)*

Multimatic Products Inc ....D 800 767-7633
　Ronkonkoma *(G-13977)*

▲ Munson Machinery Company Inc.....E 315 797-0090
　Utica *(G-15286)*

Myles Tool Company Inc ....E 716 731-1300
　Sanborn *(G-14146)*

Nifty Bar Grinding & Cutting ....G 585 381-0450
　Penfield *(G-12571)*

Omc2 LLC ....G 415 580-0262
　Peekskill *(G-12554)*

▼ Omega Consolidated Corporation .....E 585 392-9262
　Hilton *(G-5974)*

▲ Omega Tool Measuring Mchs Inc ....E 585 598-7800
　Fairport *(G-4510)*

P & R Industries Inc ....E 585 266-6725
　Rochester *(G-13604)*

Ppi Corp ....E 585 880-7277
　Rochester *(G-13632)*

▲ Ppi Corp ....D 585 243-0300
　Rochester *(G-13633)*

▲ Precise Tool & Mfg Inc................E 585 247-0700
　Rochester *(G-13634)*

Producto Corporation ....C 716 484-7131
　Jamestown *(G-6538)*

R Steiner Technologies Inc ....E 585 425-5912
　Fairport *(G-4518)*

Rapid Precision Machining Inc ....G 585 467-0780
　Rochester *(G-13669)*

RTD Manufacturing Inc..................G 315 337-3151
　Rome *(G-13871)*

▲ Rush Machinery Inc ....E 585 554-3070
　Rushville *(G-14075)*

▲ S & S Machinery Corp ....D 718 492-7400
　Brooklyn *(G-2370)*

S & S Machinery Corp ....E 718 492-7400
　Brooklyn *(G-2371)*

Selflock Screw Products Co Inc ....G 315 541-4464
　Syracuse *(G-14992)*

Seneca Falls Capital Inc ....G 315 568-5804
　Seneca Falls *(G-14370)*

Seneca Falls Machine Tool Co.........D 315 568-5804
　Seneca Falls *(G-14371)*

▲ Simmons Machine Tool Corp ....C 518 462-5431
　Menands *(G-7848)*

▼ Stephen Bader Company Inc ....F 518 753-4456
　Valley Falls *(G-15331)*

Swiss Specialties Inc ....F 631 567-8800
　Wading River *(G-15453)*

Teka Precision Inc ....E 845 753-1900
　Nyack *(G-12147)*

Transport National Dev Inc ....E 716 662-0270
　Orchard Park *(G-12379)*

Truemade Products Inc ....G 631 981-4755
　Ronkonkoma *(G-14018)*

Verns Machine Co Inc ....G 315 926-4223
　Marion *(G-7577)*

Wazer Inc ....E 201 580-6486
　Brooklyn *(G-2577)*

Welch Machine Inc ....G 585 647-3578
　Rochester *(G-13801)*

▼ World LLC ....F 631 940-9121
　Deer Park *(G-3956)*

Zwack Incorporated ....E 518 733-5135
　Stephentown *(G-14732)*

Zyp Precision LLC ....G 315 539-3667
　Waterloo *(G-15557)*

3542 Machine Tools: Forming

Adaptive Mfg Tech Inc .... E 631 580-5400
Ronkonkoma *(G-13888)*

Advanced Machine Design Co Inc .... E 716 826-2000
Buffalo *(G-2624)*

American Racing Headers Inc .... E 631 608-1427
Deer Park *(G-3837)*

Arconic Inc .... G 716 358-6451
Falconer *(G-4534)*

Austin Industries Inc .... F 585 589-1353
Albion *(G-154)*

Bdp Industries Inc .... E 518 695-6851
Greenwich *(G-5468)*

Brinkman Intl Group Inc .... G 585 429-5000
Rochester *(G-13281)*

Buffalo Machine Tls of Niagara .... F 716 201-1310
Lockport *(G-7062)*

C & T Tool & Instrument Co .... E 718 429-1253
Woodside *(G-16199)*

C J Winter Machine Tech .... E 585 429-5000
Rochester *(G-13290)*

Commodore Manufacutring Corp ...... E 718 788-2600
Brooklyn *(G-1678)*

◆ Dover Global Holdings Inc .... F 212 922-1640
New York *(G-9257)*

Dunlap Machine LLC .... F 315 926-1013
Marion *(G-7568)*

▼ Ecko Fin & Tooling Inc .... F 716 487-0200
Jamestown *(G-6507)*

Factory East .... E 718 280-1558
Brooklyn *(G-1828)*

Gemcor Automation LLC .... D 716 674-9300
West Seneca *(G-15848)*

▲ Gh Induction Atmospheres LLC ..... E 585 368-2120
Rochester *(G-13440)*

Hawthorne Garden Company .... F 516 883-6550
Port Washington *(G-12882)*

High Speed Hammer Company Inc .... F 585 266-4287
Rochester *(G-13468)*

▲ Hydramec Inc .... E 585 593-5190
Scio *(G-14325)*

◆ Kobe Steel USA Holdings Inc .... G 212 751-9400
New York *(G-10120)*

Lourdes Systems Inc .... E 631 234-7077
Hauppauge *(G-5701)*

Manhasset Tool & Die Co Inc .... F 716 684-6066
Lancaster *(G-6816)*

Miller Mechanical Services Inc .... E 518 792-0430
Glens Falls *(G-5259)*

▼ Mpi Incorporated .... C 845 471-7630
Poughkeepsie *(G-12972)*

Precision Eforming LLC .... F 607 753-7730
Cortland *(G-3783)*

Prim Hall Enterprises Inc .... F 518 561-7408
Plattsburgh *(G-12772)*

Producto Corporation .... C 716 484-7131
Jamestown *(G-6538)*

Raloid Tool Co Inc .... F 518 664-4261
Mechanicville *(G-7694)*

Schaefer Machine Co Inc .... E 516 248-6880
Mineola *(G-8000)*

Servotec Usa LLC .... G 518 671-6120
Hudson *(G-6179)*

▼ Smart High Voltage Solutions .... F 631 563-6724
Bohemia *(G-1080)*

Special Metals Corporation .... D 716 366-5663
Dunkirk *(G-4067)*

▲ Standard Paper Box Machine Co ... E 718 328-3300
Bronx *(G-1370)*

◆ Strippit Inc .... C 716 542-4511
Akron *(G-22)*

Taumel Metalforming Corp .... E 845 878-3100
Patterson *(G-12521)*

◆ Trueforge Global McHy Corp .... G 516 825-7040
Rockville Centre *(G-13839)*

▲ U S Air Tool Co Inc .... E 631 471-3300
Ronkonkoma *(G-14019)*

Uhmac Inc .... F 716 537-2343
Holland *(G-6032)*

▼ Win Set Technologies LLC .... F 631 234-7077
Centereach *(G-3253)*

3543 Industrial Patterns

A & T Tooling LLC .... G 716 601-7299
Lancaster *(G-6788)*

▼ Armstrong Mold Corporation .... E 315 437-1517
East Syracuse *(G-4196)*

Armstrong Mold Corporation .... D 315 437-1517
East Syracuse *(G-4197)*

Bianca Group Ltd .... G 212 768-3011
New York *(G-8779)*

City Pattern Shop Inc .... F 315 463-5239
Syracuse *(G-14850)*

G Haynes Holdings Inc .... G 607 538-1160
Bloomville *(G-953)*

K & H Precision Products Inc .... E 585 624-4894
Honeoye Falls *(G-6076)*

Speyside Foundry Holdings LLC ..... G 212 994-0308
New York *(G-11319)*

Studio One Leather Design Inc .... F 212 760-1701
New York *(G-11379)*

W N R Pattern & Tool Inc .... G 716 681-9334
Lancaster *(G-6838)*

Wolff & Dungey Inc .... E 315 475-2105
Syracuse *(G-15029)*

Woodward Industries Inc .... F 716 692-2242
Tonawanda *(G-15154)*

3544 Dies, Tools, Jigs, Fixtures & Indl Molds

A & D Tool Inc .... G 631 243-4339
Dix Hills *(G-4008)*

▲ Accede Mold & Tool Co Inc .... D 585 254-6490
Rochester *(G-13199)*

Ace Specialty Co Inc .... G 716 874-3670
Tonawanda *(G-15081)*

▲ Advent Tool & Mold Inc .... C 585 254-2000
Rochester *(G-13214)*

All Out Die Cutting Inc .... E 718 346-6666
Brooklyn *(G-1486)*

▲ Alliance Precision Plas Corp .... C 585 426-5310
Rochester *(G-13219)*

Alliance Precision Plas Corp .... G 585 426-5310
Rochester *(G-13220)*

Allmetal Chocolate Mold Co Inc .... F 631 752-2888
West Babylon *(G-15685)*

▲ Allstate Tool and Die Inc .... D 585 426-0400
Rochester *(G-13222)*

Alry Tool and Die Co Inc .... E 716 693-2419
Tonawanda *(G-15085)*

Alton Manufacturing Inc .... D 585 458-2600
Rochester *(G-13225)*

▲ Amada Tool America Inc .... E 585 344-3900
Batavia *(G-601)*

American Dsplay Die Ctters Inc .... E 212 645-1274
New York *(G-8549)*

American Orthotic Lab Co Inc .... G 718 961-6487
College Point *(G-3536)*

▲ Anka Tool & Die Inc .... E 845 268-4116
Congers *(G-3607)*

Arnell Inc .... G 516 486-7098
Hempstead *(G-5833)*

Arro Manufacturing LLC .... F 716 763-6203
Lakewood *(G-6778)*

▼ Arro Tool & Die Inc .... F 716 763-6203
Lakewood *(G-6779)*

Art Precision Metal Products .... F 631 842-8889
Copiague *(G-3647)*

Artisan Management Group Inc .... G 716 569-4094
Frewsburg *(G-5049)*

▲ Ascension Industries Inc .... C 716 693-9381
North Tonawanda *(G-12054)*

Barron Metal Products Inc .... E 914 965-1232
Yonkers *(G-16289)*

Bel-Bee Products Incorporated .... F 845 353-0300
West Nyack *(G-15817)*

Bennett Die & Tool Inc .... E 607 739-5629
Horseheads *(G-6115)*

Bennett Die & Tool Inc .... F 607 273-2836
Ithaca *(G-6365)*

Blue Chip Mold Inc .... F 585 647-1790
Rochester *(G-13273)*

Brayley Tool & Machine Inc .... G 585 342-7190
Rochester *(G-13280)*

Brighton Tool & Die Designers .... F 716 876-0879
Tonawanda *(G-15093)*

Carbaugh Tool Company Inc .... E 607 739-3293
Elmira *(G-4341)*

▲ Century Mold Company Inc .... D 585 352-8600
Rochester *(G-13306)*

Chamtek Mfg Inc .... E 585 328-4900
Rochester *(G-13311)*

Charles A Rogers Entps Inc .... E 585 924-6400
Victor *(G-15397)*

Chenango Valley Tech Inc .... F 607 674-4115
Sherburne *(G-14388)*

Clifford H Jones Inc .... F 716 693-2444
Tonawanda *(G-15097)*

Cosmo Electronic Machine Corp ...... E 631 249-2535
Farmingdale *(G-4603)*

Cuddeback Machining Inc .... G 585 392-5889
Hilton *(G-5972)*

▲ Cy Plastics Works Inc .... D 585 229-2555
Honeoye *(G-6068)*

▲ D Maldari & Sons Inc .... E 718 499-3555
Staten Island *(G-14644)*

Dependable Tool & Die Co Inc .... G 315 453-5696
Syracuse *(G-14876)*

▲ Diemax of Rochester Inc .... G 585 288-3912
Rochester *(G-13345)*

Diemolding Corporation .... F 315 363-4710
Wampsville *(G-15481)*

Dixon Tool and Manufacturing .... F 585 235-1352
Rochester *(G-13351)*

Dynamic Dies Inc .... F 585 247-4010
Rochester *(G-13360)*

East Pattern & Model Corp .... E 585 461-3240
Rochester *(G-13362)*

East Pattern & Model Corp .... E 585 461-3240
Rochester *(G-13363)*

▲ Eberhardt Enterprises Inc .... E 585 458-7681
Rochester *(G-13379)*

▼ Eden Tool & Die Inc .... G 716 992-4240
Eden *(G-4255)*

Egli Machine Company Inc .... E 607 563-3663
Sidney *(G-14434)*

Electronic Die Corp .... F 718 455-3200
Brooklyn *(G-1791)*

Enhanced Tool Inc .... E 716 691-5200
Amherst *(G-221)*

Etna Tool & Die Corporation .... F 212 475-4350
New York *(G-9414)*

Everfab Inc .... D 716 655-1550
East Aurora *(G-4086)*

Evergreen Corp Central NY .... F 315 454-4175
Syracuse *(G-14890)*

▲ F M EDM Inc .... G 716 655-1784
East Aurora *(G-4088)*

Fuller Tool Incorporated .... F 315 891-3183
Newport *(G-11898)*

G N R Plastics Inc .... G 631 724-8758
Smithtown *(G-14478)*

Gatti Tool & Mold Inc .... F 585 328-1350
Rochester *(G-13429)*

Gay Sheet Metal Dies Inc .... G 716 877-0208
Buffalo *(G-2768)*

▲ General Die and Die Cutng Inc ...... D 516 665-3584
Massapequa Park *(G-7655)*

◆ Globmarble LLC .... G 347 717-4088
Brooklyn *(G-1891)*

▲ Graywood Companies Inc .... A 585 738-8889
Rochester *(G-13450)*

Great Lakes Pressed Steel Corp ...... E 716 885-4037
Buffalo *(G-2784)*

Handy Tool & Mfg Co Inc .... E 718 478-9203
Brooklyn *(G-1926)*

HNST Mold Inspections LLC .... G 845 215-9258
Sloatsburg *(G-14471)*

Hy-Tech Mold Inc .... F 585 247-2450
Rochester *(G-13472)*

▲ Hytech Tool & Die Inc .... G 716 488-2796
Jamestown *(G-6517)*

Intek Precision .... E 585 293-0853
Churchville *(G-3413)*

Inter Molds Inc .... G 631 667-8580
Bay Shore *(G-682)*

J B Tool & Die Co Inc .... G 516 333-1480
Westbury *(G-15897)*

J T Systematic .... G 607 754-0929
Endwell *(G-4480)*

James B Crowell & Sons Inc .... G 845 895-3464
Wallkill *(G-15470)*

James Wire Die Co .... G 315 894-3233
Ilion *(G-6279)*

K & H Precision Products Inc .... E 585 624-4894
Honeoye Falls *(G-6076)*

K D M Die Company Inc .... F 716 828-9000
Buffalo *(G-2828)*

Keyes Machine Works Inc .... E 585 426-5059
Gates *(G-5141)*

Knise & Krick Inc .... E 315 422-3516
Syracuse *(G-14927)*

▲ Light Waves Concept Inc .... F 212 677-6400
Brooklyn *(G-2072)*

Long Island Tool & Die Inc .... E 631 225-0600
Copiague *(G-3662)*

M J M Tooling Corp .... G 718 292-3590
Bronx *(G-1305)*

Machinecraft Inc .... E 585 436-1070
Rochester *(G-13526)*

S
I
C

Magnus Precision Mfg Inc..................D.....315 548-8032
Phelps (G-12605)
Manhasset Tool & Die Co Inc..............F.....716 684-6066
Lancaster (G-6816)
▲ Mannesmann Corporation...............D.....212 258-4000
New York (G-10348)
Mantel & Mantel Stamping Corp.........G.....631 467-1916
Ronkonkoma (G-13969)
Manufacturers Tool & Die Co..............G.....585 352-1080
Spencerport (G-14558)
Mega Tool & Mfg Corp.......................E.....607 734-8398
Elmira (G-4363)
Micro Instrument Corp........................G.....585 458-3150
Rochester (G-13545)
Micron Inds Rochester Inc..................G.....585 247-6130
Rochester (G-13548)
Moldcraft Inc.....................................E.....716 684-1126
Depew (G-3988)
Ms Machining Inc...............................E.....607 723-1105
Binghamton (G-900)
Multifold Die Ctng Finshg Corp...........G.....631 232-1235
Islandia (G-6341)
Mustang-Major Tool & Die Co.............G.....716 992-9200
Eden (G-4257)
▲ Nas CP Corp..................................E.....718 961-6757
College Point (G-3556)
National Steel Rule Die Inc.................F.....718 402-1396
Bronx (G-1322)
Niagara Fiberglass Inc........................E.....716 822-3921
Buffalo (G-2884)
Niagara Punch & Die Corp..................G.....716 896-7619
Buffalo (G-2886)
▼ Nicoform Inc.................................E.....585 454-5530
Rochester (G-13577)
Nijon Tool Co Inc...............................F.....631 242-3434
Deer Park (G-3912)
◆ Nordon Inc...................................D.....585 546-6200
Rochester (G-13578)
Nordon Inc..E.....585 546-6200
Rochester (G-13579)
Nordon Inc..E.....585 546-6200
Rochester (G-13580)
Northern Design Inc...........................G.....716 652-7071
East Aurora (G-4095)
▲ P & G Steel Products Co Inc...........D.....716 896-7900
Buffalo (G-2901)
P & H Machine Shop Inc.....................G.....585 247-5500
Rochester (G-13603)
P & R Industries Inc...........................E.....585 266-6725
Rochester (G-13604)
P Tool & Die Co Inc...........................E.....585 889-1340
North Chili (G-12022)
Pacific Die Cast Inc...........................F.....845 778-6374
Walden (G-15460)
Palma Tool & Die Company Inc..........E.....716 681-4464
Lancaster (G-6820)
Paragon Steel Rule Dies Inc..............F.....585 254-3395
Rochester (G-13610)
Patmian LLC.....................................B.....212 758-0770
New York (G-10769)
Peak Motion Inc.................................G.....716 534-4925
Clarence (G-3439)
Phelinger Tool & Die Corp..................G.....716 685-1780
Alden (G-172)
Pivot Punch Corporation.....................D.....716 625-8000
Lockport (G-7101)
Plastic Solutions Inc..........................E.....631 234-9013
Bayport (G-730)
◆ PMI Industries LLC........................E.....585 464-8050
Rochester (G-13627)
▲ Polyshot Corporation.....................E.....585 292-5010
West Henrietta (G-15801)
Ppi Corp...E.....585 880-7277
Rochester (G-13632)
Precise Punch Corporation.................F.....716 625-8000
Lockport (G-7102)
▲ Precision Grinding & Mfg Corp.......C.....585 458-4300
Rochester (G-13636)
Precision Systems Mfg Inc.................E.....315 451-3480
Liverpool (G-7035)
Prime Tool & Die LLC.........................G.....607 334-5435
Norwich (G-12127)
Producto Corporation.........................C.....716 484-7131
Jamestown (G-6538)
Pronto Tool & Die Co Inc....................E.....631 981-8920
Ronkonkoma (G-13997)
Quality Lineals Usa Inc......................G.....516 378-6577
Freeport (G-5018)
Raloid Tool Co Inc.............................F.....518 664-4261
Mechanicville (G-7694)

Rand Machine Products, Inc...............C.....716 665-5217
Falconer (G-4552)
Rid Lom Precision Mfg........................E.....585 594-8600
Rochester (G-13672)
Rochester Stampings Inc....................F.....585 467-5241
Rochester (G-13698)
Rochester Tool and Mold Inc..............F.....585 464-9336
Rochester (G-13701)
Roechling Medical Rochester LP.........D.....585 254-2000
Rochester (G-13702)
Rossi & Dies Inc...............................G.....845 267-8246
Valley Cottage (G-15322)
Royal Molds Inc.................................F.....718 382-7686
Brooklyn (G-2361)
S B Whistler & Sons Inc.....................E.....585 798-3000
Medina (G-7745)
Saturn Industries Inc.........................E.....518 828-9956
Hudson (G-6177)
Sb Molds LLC....................................D.....845 352-3700
Monsey (G-8048)
Silicone Products & Technology..........C.....716 684-1155
Lancaster (G-6835)
Specialty Model & Mold Inc................G.....631 475-0840
Ronkonkoma (G-14012)
▲ Spectronics Corporation................E.....516 333-4840
Westbury (G-15926)
Stamp Rite Tool & Die Inc..................F.....718 752-0334
Long Island City (G-7363)
Star Mold Co Inc...............................G.....631 694-2283
Farmingdale (G-4740)
◆ Strippit Inc...................................C.....716 542-4511
Akron (G-22)
Stuart Tool & Die Inc.........................E.....716 488-1975
Falconer (G-4559)
Sweet Tooth Enterprises LLC.............E.....631 752-2888
West Babylon (G-15752)
Synergy Tooling Systems Inc..............E.....716 834-4457
Amherst (G-246)
T A Tool & Molding Inc.......................F.....631 293-0172
Farmingdale (G-4748)
Thayer Tool & Die Inc........................G.....716 782-4841
Ashville (G-411)
Tips & Dies Inc.................................F.....315 337-4161
Rome (G-13873)
Tooling Enterprises Inc.......................E.....716 842-0445
Buffalo (G-3014)
Tools & Stamping Corp.......................E.....718 392-4040
Brooklyn (G-2510)
Trimaster/Htech Holding LLC..............G.....212 257-6772
New York (G-11545)
Trinity Tools Inc.................................E.....716 694-1111
North Tonawanda (G-12096)
Universal Tooling Corporation.............F.....716 985-4691
Gerry (G-5172)
Van Reenen Tool & Die Inc.................E.....585 288-6000
Rochester (G-13794)
▲ Van Thomas Inc.............................E.....585 426-1414
Rochester (G-13795)
W N R Pattern & Tool Inc....................G.....716 681-9334
Lancaster (G-6838)
Z Works Inc.......................................G.....631 750-0612
Bohemia (G-1099)

3545 Machine Tool Access

Advance D Tech Inc...........................F.....845 534-8248
Cornwall (G-3724)
▲ Advent Tool & Mold Inc..................C.....585 254-2000
Rochester (G-13214)
Ale-Techniques Inc............................F.....845 687-7200
High Falls (G-5954)
Ameri-Cut Tool Grinding Inc................G.....716 692-3900
North Tonawanda (G-12051)
American Linear Manufacturers...........F.....516 333-1351
Westbury (G-15867)
▲ Baldwin Machine Works Inc............G.....631 842-9110
Copiague (G-3649)
Bdp Industries Inc.............................E.....518 695-6851
Greenwich (G-5468)
Bnm Product Service...........................G.....631 750-1586
Holbrook (G-5986)
Boro Park Cutting Tool Corp...............E.....718 720-0610
Staten Island (G-14629)
Brinkman Intl Group Inc......................E.....585 429-5000
Rochester (G-13281)
C J Winter Machine Tech.....................E.....585 429-5000
Rochester (G-13290)
Carl Safina Center Inc........................G.....808 888-9440
Setauket (G-14378)
Circo File Corp..................................G.....516 922-1848
Oyster Bay (G-12445)

▲ Curran Manufacturing Corp............E.....631 273-1010
Hauppauge (G-5633)
Curran Manufacturing Corp................E.....631 273-1010
Hauppauge (G-5634)
Custom Service Solutions Inc.............G.....585 637-3760
Brockport (G-1175)
◆ Designatronics Incorporated..........G.....516 328-3300
Hicksville (G-5902)
Dinosaw Inc......................................E.....518 828-9942
Hudson (G-6154)
Dock Hardware Incorporated..............F.....585 266-7920
Rochester (G-13352)
Dorsey Metrology Intl Inc....................E.....845 229-2929
Poughkeepsie (G-12951)
Drt Aerospace LLC............................E.....585 247-5940
Rochester (G-13357)
Dura-Mill Inc.....................................E.....518 899-2255
Ballston Spa (G-573)
Egli Machine Company Inc.................E.....607 563-3663
Sidney (G-14434)
Everfab Inc.......................................D.....716 655-1550
East Aurora (G-4086)
▲ Flexbar Machine Corporation..........E.....631 582-8440
Islandia (G-6332)
Fred M Velepec Co Inc.......................E.....718 821-6636
Glendale (G-5225)
▲ Gardei Industries LLC....................F.....716 693-7100
North Tonawanda (G-12069)
Genesee Manufacturing Co Inc..........G.....585 266-3201
Rochester (G-13435)
▲ Graywood Companies Inc..............A.....585 738-8889
Rochester (G-13450)
▲ Griffin Manufacturing Company.......E.....585 265-1991
Webster (G-15641)
◆ Hardinge Inc.................................B.....607 734-2281
Elmira (G-4355)
Hubbard Tool and Die Corp................E.....315 337-7840
Rome (G-13851)
Huron TI Cutter Grinding Inc...............E.....631 420-7000
Farmingdale (G-4646)
Innovative Automation Inc...................F.....631 439-3300
Farmingdale (G-4649)
J H Robotics Inc...............................E.....607 729-3758
Johnson City (G-6603)
Jasco Tools LLC................................D.....585 254-7000
Rochester (G-13490)
JD Tool Inc.......................................G.....607 786-3129
Endicott (G-4462)
Jem Tool & Die Corp..........................F.....631 539-8734
West Islip (G-15811)
◆ Kps Capital Partners LP.................E.....212 338-5100
New York (G-10133)
▲ Lancaster Knives Inc.....................E.....716 683-5050
Lancaster (G-6814)
▲ M & S Precision Machine Co LLC....F.....518 747-1193
Queensbury (G-13048)
Macinnes Tool Corporation.................E.....585 467-1920
Rochester (G-13527)
▲ Make-Waves Instrument Corp.........E.....716 681-7524
Buffalo (G-2860)
Mausner Equipment Co Inc.................C.....631 689-7358
Setauket (G-14380)
Melland Gear Instr of Huppauge.........E.....631 234-0100
Hauppauge (G-5712)
Messer LLC.......................................D.....716 773-7552
Grand Island (G-5337)
Methods Tooling & Mfg Inc.................E.....845 246-7100
Mount Marion (G-8111)
Michael Fiore Ltd..............................G.....516 561-8238
Valley Stream (G-15348)
Miller Metal Fabricating Inc................G.....585 359-3400
Rochester (G-13549)
Morgood Tools Inc.............................D.....585 436-8828
Rochester (G-13560)
Myles Tool Company Inc....................E.....716 731-1300
Sanborn (G-14146)
New Market Products LLC..................E.....607 292-6226
Wayne (G-15628)
Northfeld Precision Instr Corp.............E.....516 431-1112
Island Park (G-6321)
Novatech Inc.....................................E.....716 892-6682
Cheektowaga (G-3358)
▲ Omega Tool Measuring Mchs Inc....E.....585 598-7800
Fairport (G-4510)
◆ Park Enterprises Rochester Inc.......C.....585 546-4200
Rochester (G-13611)
Parlec LLC..D.....585 425-4400
Fairport (G-4513)
▲ Ppi Corp......................................D.....585 243-0300
Rochester (G-13633)

▲ Precision Grinding & Mfg Corp ....C...... 585 458-4300
  Rochester (G-13636)
Precision Mechanisms Corp ....E...... 516 333-5955
  Westbury (G-15919)
▲ Production Metal Cutting Inc ....F...... 585 458-7136
  Rochester (G-13650)
Prz Technologies Inc ....F...... 716 683-1300
  Lancaster (G-6827)
Ptc Precision LLC ....E...... 607 748-8294
  Endwell (G-4483)
Robert J Faraone ....G...... 585 232-7160
  Rochester (G-13677)
Roechling Medical Rochester LP ....D...... 585 254-2000
  Rochester (G-13702)
Ross JC Inc ....G...... 716 439-1161
  Lockport (G-7103)
Rota File Corporation ....E...... 516 496-7200
  Syosset (G-14802)
▲ S & S Machinery Corp ....D...... 718 492-7400
  Brooklyn (G-2370)
S S Precision Gear & Instr ....E...... 718 457-7474
  Corona (G-3749)
◆ Schenck Corporation ....D...... 631 242-4010
  Deer Park (G-3932)
▲ Schenck USA Corp ....D...... 631 242-4010
  Deer Park (G-3933)
Scomac Inc ....F...... 585 494-2200
  Bergen (G-820)
Seneca Falls Machine Tool Co ....D...... 315 568-5804
  Seneca Falls (G-14371)
Sinn- Tech Industries Inc ....F...... 631 643-1171
  Bohemia (G-1079)
Socket Products Mfg Corp ....G...... 631 232-9870
  Islandia (G-6344)
Steiner Technologies Inc ....F...... 585 425-5910
  Fairport (G-4523)
Streamline Precision Inc ....G...... 585 421-9050
  Fairport (G-4524)
Streamline Precision Inc ....G...... 585 421-9050
  Fairport (G-4525)
◆ Strippit Inc ....C...... 716 542-4511
  Akron (G-22)
▲ Thuro Metal Products Inc ....E...... 631 435-0444
  Brentwood (G-1128)
Townline Machine Co Inc ....E...... 315 462-3413
  Clifton Springs (G-3481)
Transport National Dev Inc ....E...... 716 662-0270
  Orchard Park (G-12380)
▲ Trident Precision Mfg Inc ....D...... 585 265-2010
  Webster (G-15658)
Trimaster/Htech Holding LLC ....G...... 212 257-6772
  New York (G-11545)
Trinity Tools Inc ....E...... 716 694-1111
  North Tonawanda (G-12096)
▲ Truebite Inc ....F...... 607 786-3184
  Endicott (G-4476)
Universal Tooling Corporation ....F...... 716 985-4691
  Gerry (G-5172)
Vandilay Industries Inc ....E...... 631 226-3064
  West Babylon (G-15755)
Velmex Inc ....E...... 585 657-6151
  Bloomfield (G-950)
Xactra Technologies Inc ....D...... 585 426-2030
  Rochester (G-13810)

3546 Power Hand Tools

Allied Motion Technologies Inc ....C...... 315 782-5910
  Watertown (G-15558)
▲ Awt Supply Corp ....G...... 516 437-9105
  Elmont (G-4383)
Black & Decker (us) Inc ....B...... 914 235-6300
  Brewster (G-1143)
Black & Decker (us) Inc ....G...... 631 952-2008
  Hauppauge (G-5605)
Black & Decker Corporation ....G...... 718 335-1042
  Woodside (G-16198)
▲ Dynabrade Inc ....C...... 716 631-0100
  Clarence (G-3430)
Huck International Inc ....C...... 845 331-7300
  Kingston (G-6694)
◆ Ivy Classic Industries Inc ....E...... 914 632-8200
  New Rochelle (G-8343)
▲ Meritool LLC ....E...... 716 699-6005
  Salamanca (G-14123)
◆ P & F Industries Inc ....E...... 631 694-9800
  Melville (G-7813)
◆ Rbhammers Corp ....F...... 845 353-5042
  Blauvelt (G-932)
▲ Reimann & Georger Corporation .....E...... 716 895-1156
  Buffalo (G-2951)

Stature Electric Inc ....F...... 716 242-7535
  Amherst (G-244)
▼ Thomas C Wilson LLC ....E...... 718 729-3360
  Long Island City (G-7381)

3547 Rolling Mill Machinery & Eqpt

Anthony Manufacturing Inc ....G...... 631 957-9424
  Lindenhurst (G-6940)
◆ Ivy Classic Industries Inc ....E...... 914 632-8200
  New Rochelle (G-8343)
Johnston Dandy Company ....G...... 315 455-5773
  Syracuse (G-14919)
▲ Mannesmann Corporation ....D...... 212 258-4000
  New York (G-10348)
Polymag Tek Inc ....F...... 585 235-8390
  Rochester (G-13628)

3548 Welding Apparatus

Lynne B Enterprises Inc ....E...... 631 254-6975
  Deer Park (G-3901)
McAllisters Precision Wldg Inc ....F...... 518 221-3455
  Menands (G-7844)
Riverview Industries Inc ....G...... 845 265-5284
  Cold Spring (G-3524)
▲ Vante Inc ....F...... 716 778-7691
  Newfane (G-11896)

3549 Metalworking Machinery, NEC

Advanced Machine Design Co Inc .....E...... 716 826-2000
  Buffalo (G-2624)
▲ Alliance Automation Systems ....C...... 585 426-2700
  Rochester (G-13218)
▲ Autostat Corporation ....F...... 516 379-9447
  Roosevelt (G-14030)
◆ Bartell Machinery Systems LLC ......C...... 315 336-7600
  Rome (G-13843)
Carpenter Manufacturing Co ....G...... 315 682-9176
  Manlius (G-7544)
Charles A Rogers Entps Inc ....E...... 585 924-6400
  Victor (G-15397)
Duall Finishing Inc ....G...... 716 827-1707
  Buffalo (G-2731)
▲ Esm II Inc ....E...... 716 446-8888
  Amherst (G-223)
▲ Expert Metal Slitters Corp ....G...... 718 361-2735
  Long Island City (G-7219)
◆ Hardinge Inc ....B...... 607 734-2281
  Elmira (G-4355)
Hje Company Inc ....G...... 518 792-8733
  Queensbury (G-13043)
▲ Hover-Davis Inc ....C...... 585 352-9590
  Rochester (G-13471)
Manufacturing Resources Inc ....E...... 631 481-0041
  Rochester (G-13532)
▲ MGS Manufacturing Inc ....E...... 315 337-3350
  Rome (G-13856)
▲ Mold-A-Matic Corporation ....E...... 607 433-2121
  Oneonta (G-12276)
Mono-Systems Inc ....E...... 716 821-1344
  Buffalo (G-2871)
Mtwli Precision Corp ....G...... 631 244-3767
  Bohemia (G-1049)
▲ Munson Machinery Company Inc ....E...... 315 797-0090
  Utica (G-15286)
Pems Tool & Machine Inc ....E...... 315 823-3595
  Little Falls (G-6990)
Precision Systems Mfg Inc ....G...... 315 451-3480
  Liverpool (G-7035)
▲ Reelex Packaging Solutions Inc ......E...... 845 878-7878
  Patterson (G-12519)
Riverside Machinery Company ....G...... 718 492-7400
  Brooklyn (G-2349)
▲ S & S Machinery Corp ....D...... 718 492-7400
  Brooklyn (G-2370)
S & S Machinery Corp ....G...... 718 492-7400
  Brooklyn (G-2371)
Serge Duct Designs Inc ....E...... 718 783-7799
  Brooklyn (G-2396)
▲ Standard Bots Company ....G...... 646 876-2687
  Locust Valley (G-7129)
◆ Strippit Inc ....C...... 716 542-4511
  Akron (G-22)
◆ Tessy Plastics Corp ....B...... 315 689-3924
  Skaneateles (G-14457)
◆ Van Blarcom Closures Inc ....E...... 718 855-3810
  Brooklyn (G-2551)
▲ Voss Manufacturing Inc ....D...... 716 731-5062
  Sanborn (G-14153)
▲ Xto Incorporated ....D...... 315 451-7807
  Liverpool (G-7050)

3552 Textile Machinery

Aglika Trade LLC ....F...... 727 424-1944
  Middle Village (G-7877)
Angel Textiles Inc ....G...... 212 532-0900
  New York (G-8582)
Big Apple Sign Corp ....E...... 631 342-0303
  Islandia (G-6326)
Chroma Logic ....G...... 716 736-2458
  Ripley (G-13169)
Corbertex LLC ....G...... 212 971-0008
  New York (G-9101)
◆ Eastman Machine Company ....C...... 716 856-2200
  Buffalo (G-2738)
EMC Tech Inc ....E...... 716 488-9071
  Falconer (G-4539)
Herr Manufacturing Co Inc ....E...... 716 754-4341
  Tonawanda (G-15113)
Herrmann Group LLC ....G...... 716 876-9798
  Kenmore (G-6651)
Mjk Cutting Inc ....E...... 718 384-7613
  Brooklyn (G-2162)
Mohawk Valley Knt McHy Co Inc ....F...... 315 736-3038
  New York Mills (G-11835)
Rfb Associates Inc ....E...... 518 271-0551
  Fort Edward (G-4943)
Schwabel Fabricating Co Inc ....E...... 716 876-2086
  Tonawanda (G-15138)
Screen Team Inc ....G...... 718 786-2424
  Long Island City (G-7353)
Simtec Industries Corporation ....G...... 631 293-0080
  Farmingdale (G-4732)
Thread Check Inc ....G...... 631 231-1515
  Hauppauge (G-5784)

3553 Woodworking Machinery

901 D LLC ....E...... 845 369-1111
  Airmont (G-9)
Corbett Stves Pttern Works Inc ....E...... 585 546-7109
  Rochester (G-13326)
Downtown Interiors Inc ....F...... 212 337-0230
  New York (G-9262)
◆ Hardinge Inc ....B...... 607 734-2281
  Elmira (G-4355)
Hat Factory Furniture Co ....E...... 914 788-6288
  Peekskill (G-12552)
◆ James L Taylor Mfg Co ....E...... 845 452-3780
  Poughkeepsie (G-12964)
James L Taylor Mfg Co ....G...... 845 452-3780
  Poughkeepsie (G-12965)
◆ Merritt Machinery LLC ....G...... 716 434-5558
  Lockport (G-7090)
◆ Oneida Air Systems Inc ....E...... 315 476-5151
  Syracuse (G-14956)
Phoenix Wood Wrights Ltd ....F...... 631 727-9691
  Riverhead (G-13184)
US Sander LLC ....G...... 518 875-9157
  Esperance (G-4485)
Wood-Mizer Holdings Inc ....G...... 315 564-5722
  Hannibal (G-5543)

3554 Paper Inds Machinery

Automecha International Ltd ....E...... 607 843-2235
  Oxford (G-12441)
Cyclotherm of Watertown Inc ....E...... 315 782-1100
  Watertown (G-15568)
Fbm Galaxy Inc ....F...... 315 463-5144
  East Syracuse (G-4210)
Gailer Stamping Diecutting LLC ....F...... 212 243-5662
  Long Island City (G-7227)
GL&v USA Inc ....E...... 518 747-2444
  Hudson Falls (G-6188)
Haanen Packard Machinery Inc ....E...... 518 747-2330
  Hudson Falls (G-6190)
Jacob Inc ....E...... 646 450-3067
  Brooklyn (G-1985)
Johnston Dandy Company ....G...... 315 455-5773
  Syracuse (G-14919)
Kadant Inc ....F...... 518 793-8801
  Glens Falls (G-5253)
Lake Image Systems Inc ....F...... 585 321-3630
  Henrietta (G-5858)
Richlar Industries Inc ....F...... 315 463-5144
  East Syracuse (G-4234)
Rsb Associates Inc ....F...... 518 281-5067
  Altamont (G-199)
Sinclair International Company ....D...... 518 798-2361
  Queensbury (G-13057)
▲ Sonicor Inc ....F...... 631 920-6555
  West Babylon (G-15748)

SIC

▲ Standard Paper Box Machine Co .....E 718 328-3300
Bronx (G-1370)

Verso Corporation ....B 212 599-2700
New York (G-11665)

3555 Printing Trades Machinery & Eqpt

▲ A-Mark Machinery Corp ....F 631 643-6300
West Babylon (G-15678)

AC Envelope Inc ....G 516 420-0646
Farmingdale (G-4572)

Advance Grafix Equipment Inc ....G 917 202-4593
Wyandanch (G-16242)

Anand Printing Machinery Inc ....E 631 667-3079
Deer Park (G-3839)

Apexx Omni-Graphics Inc ....D 718 326-3330
Maspeth (G-7591)

▲ Awt Supply Corp ....G 516 437-9105
Elmont (G-4383)

Bartizan Data Systems LLC ....E 914 965-7977
Yonkers (G-16290)

▲ Bmp America Inc ....C 585 798-0950
Medina (G-7730)

C M E Corp ....F 315 451-7101
Syracuse (G-14839)

Castlereagh Printcraft Inc ....D 516 623-1728
Freeport (G-4989)

Copy4les Inc ....F 212 487-9778
New York (G-9100)

Csw Inc ....F 585 247-4010
Rochester (G-13331)

Daige Products Inc ....F 516 621-2100
Albertson (G-147)

Davis International Inc ....F 585 421-8175
Fairport (G-4496)

Exacta LLC ....G 716 406-2303
Clarence Center (G-3445)

Halm Instrument Co Inc ....D 516 676-6700
Glen Head (G-5207)

◆ Hodgins Engraving Co Inc ....D 585 343-4444
Batavia (G-618)

▲ Impressions International Inc ....G 585 442-5240
Rochester (G-13477)

Innotech Graphic Eqp Corp ....G 845 268-6900
Valley Cottage (G-15316)

◆ International Imaging Mtls Inc ....B 716 691-6333
Amherst (G-227)

▲ Lexar Global LLC ....G 845 352-9700
Valley Cottage (G-15318)

▲ Mekatronics Incorporated ....E 516 883-6805
Port Washington (G-12907)

◆ Micro Powders Inc ....G 914 332-6400
Tarrytown (G-15048)

▲ Package Print Technologies ....F 716 871-9905
Buffalo (G-2904)

▲ Perretta Graphics Corp ....E 845 473-0550
Poughkeepsie (G-12978)

Prim Hall Enterprises Inc ....F 518 561-7408
Plattsburgh (G-12772)

Rollers Inc ....G 716 837-0700
Buffalo (G-2961)

Rubber Stamps Inc ....E 212 675-1180
Mineola (G-7998)

▲ Skandacor Direct Inc ....G 585 265-9020
Webster (G-15654)

Southern Graphic Systems LLC ....E 315 695-7079
Phoenix (G-12621)

Specilty Bus Mchs Holdings LLC ....E 212 587-9600
New York (G-11314)

Sterling Toggle Inc ....F 631 491-0500
West Babylon (G-15749)

▲ Super Web Inc ....E 631 643-9100
West Babylon (G-15751)

Universal Metal Fabricators ....F 845 331-8248
Kingston (G-6719)

◆ Vits International Inc ....E 845 353-5000
Blauvelt (G-938)

Voodoo Manufacturing Inc ....E 646 893-8366
Brooklyn (G-2569)

Woerner Industries Inc ....E 585 436-1934
Rochester (G-13807)

3556 Food Prdts Machinery

Acai of America Inc ....G 862 205-9334
New York (G-8438)

◆ Ag-Pak Inc ....F 716 772-2651
Gasport (G-5136)

▼ Alard Equipment Corporation ....E 315 589-4511
Williamson (G-16109)

◆ Bairnco Corporation ....E 914 461-1300
White Plains (G-15977)

Bake-Rite International Inc ....G 518 395-3340
Schenectady (G-14248)

Bari Engineering Corp ....E 212 966-2080
New York (G-8729)

Blue Toad Hard Cider ....E 585 424-5508
Rochester (G-13274)

▲ Brooklyn Brew Shop LLC ....F 718 874-0119
Brooklyn (G-1612)

◆ Buflovak LLC ....E 716 895-2100
Buffalo (G-2685)

C-Flex Bearing Co Inc ....F 315 895-7454
Frankfort (G-4948)

◆ Caravella Food Corp ....F 646 552-0455
Whitestone (G-16090)

Carts Mobile Food Eqp Corp ....E 718 788-5540
Brooklyn (G-1652)

▲ Chemicolloid Laboratories Inc ....F 516 747-2666
New Hyde Park (G-8256)

Chester-Jensen Company ....F 610 876-6276
Cattaraugus (G-3220)

Delaval Inc ....F 585 599-4696
Corfu (G-3702)

Delsur Parts ....G 631 630-1606
Brentwood (G-1119)

Desu Machinery Corporation ....D 716 681-5798
Depew (G-3979)

Esquire Mechanical Corp ....E 718 625-4006
Brooklyn (G-1813)

ET Oakes Corporation ....D 631 232-0002
Hauppauge (G-5648)

Expert Industries Inc ....E 718 434-6060
Brooklyn (G-1823)

G J Olney Inc ....E 315 827-4208
Westernville (G-15942)

Goodnature Products Inc ....E 800 875-3381
Buffalo (G-2779)

Haines Equipment Inc ....F 607 566-8531
Avoca (G-510)

Home Maide Incorporated ....F 845 837-1700
Harriman (G-5544)

Janel Corporation ....G 516 256-8143
Lynbrook (G-7432)

Kedco Inc ....E 516 454-7800
Farmingdale (G-4663)

Kings Cnty Brwers Cllctive LLC ....F 917 207-2739
Brooklyn (G-2031)

Kinplex Corp ....E 631 242-4800
Edgewood (G-4274)

Los Olivos Ltd ....C 631 773-6439
Farmingdale (G-4673)

Lyophilization Systems Inc ....G 845 338-0456
New Paltz (G-8309)

Mary F Morse ....G 315 866-2741
Mohawk (G-8006)

Mohawk Valley Manufacturing ....G 315 797-0851
Frankfort (G-4954)

◆ National Equipment Corporation ......F 718 585-0200
Harrison (G-5556)

National Equipment Corporation ....F 718 585-0200
Bronx (G-1321)

▲ Olmstead Products Corp ....F 516 681-3700
Hicksville (G-5935)

P & M LLC ....E 631 842-2200
Amityville (G-301)

Pic Nic LLC ....F 914 245-6500
Amawalk (G-200)

▲ Precision N Amer Fd McHy LLC ....F 518 462-3387
Albany (G-118)

◆ Purvi Enterprises Incorporated ....G 347 808-9448
Maspeth (G-7635)

Sidco Food Distribution Corp ....F 718 733-3939
Bronx (G-1363)

▲ Simply Natural Foods LLC ....E 631 543-9600
Commack (G-3599)

Singlecut Beersmiths LLC ....F 718 606-0788
Astoria (G-440)

SPX Flow Us LLC ....A 716 692-3000
Getzville (G-5182)

US Beverage Net Inc ....E 315 579-2025
Syracuse (G-15019)

▲ Vr Food Equipment Inc ....F 315 531-8133
Farmington (G-4780)

Wired Coffee and Bagel Inc ....F 518 506-3194
Malta (G-7498)

3559 Special Ind Machinery, NEC

▲ Addex Inc ....G 781 344-5800
Newark (G-11837)

◆ Adirondack Plas & Recycl Inc ....E 518 746-9212
Argyle (G-391)

▲ Andela Tool & Machine Inc ....G 315 858-0055
Richfield Springs (G-13105)

◆ Arbe Machinery Inc ....F 631 756-2477
Farmingdale (G-4586)

▲ Aremco Products Inc ....F 845 268-0039
Valley Cottage (G-15313)

▲ Automotion Parking Systems LLC ....G 516 565-5600
West Hempstead (G-15767)

B&K Precision Corporation ....G 631 369-2665
Manorville (G-7551)

Ben Weitsman of Albany LLC ....E 518 462-4444
Albany (G-46)

Blue Star Products Inc ....F 631 952-3204
Hauppauge (G-5606)

▲ Cameo Metal Products Inc ....E 718 788-1106
Brooklyn (G-1641)

◆ Caswell Inc ....F 315 946-1213
Lyons (G-7447)

CBA Group LLC ....A 607 779-7522
Conklin (G-3622)

▲ Charles Ross & Son Company ....D 631 234-0500
Hauppauge (G-5614)

Cleaning Tech Group LLC ....E 716 665-2340
Jamestown (G-6502)

Cpp - Guaymas ....C 315 687-0014
Chittenango (G-3405)

Crumbrubber Technology Inc ....F 718 468-3988
Hollis (G-6042)

▲ Cryomech Inc ....D 315 455-2555
Syracuse (G-14868)

Curtin-Hebert Co Inc ....F 518 725-7157
Gloversville (G-5282)

Cvd Equipment Corporation ....E 845 246-3631
Saugerties (G-14199)

Cvd Equipment Corporation ....F 631 582-4365
Central Islip (G-3272)

◆ Designatronics Incorporated ....G 516 328-3300
Hicksville (G-5902)

Digital Matrix Corp ....E 516 481-7990
Farmingdale (G-4616)

Eastend Enforcement Products ....G 631 878-8424
Smithtown (G-14477)

Eltee Tool & Die Co ....F 607 748-4301
Endicott (G-4449)

Emhart Glass Manufacturing Inc ....C 607 734-3671
Horseheads (G-6122)

Force Dynamics Inc ....F 607 546-5023
Trumansburg (G-15201)

General Cryogenic Tech LLC ....F 516 334-8200
Westbury (G-15890)

George Ponte Inc ....E 914 243-4202
Jefferson Valley (G-6567)

Globalfoundries US Inc ....E 512 457-3900
Hopewell Junction (G-6095)

Gordon S Anderson Mfg Co ....E 845 677-3304
Millbrook (G-7942)

Haanen Packard Machinery Inc ....G 518 747-2330
Hudson Falls (G-6190)

Herbert Jaffe Inc ....G 718 392-1956
Long Island City (G-7240)

▲ Hitachi Metals America Ltd ....E 914 694-9200
Purchase (G-13005)

Illinois Tool Works Inc ....E 716 681-8222
Lancaster (G-6811)

▲ Innovation Associates Inc ....C 607 798-9376
Johnson City (G-6602)

▼ Innovation In Motion Inc ....E 407 878-7561
Long Beach (G-7137)

Innovative Cleaning Solutions ....G 716 731-4408
Sanborn (G-14143)

James Morris ....E 315 824-8519
Hamilton (G-5527)

Kabar Manufacturing Corp ....E 631 694-1036
Farmingdale (G-4661)

▲ Kabar Manufacturing Corp ....E 631 694-6857
Farmingdale (G-4660)

▲ Maharlika Holdings LLC ....F 631 319-6203
Ronkonkoma (G-13968)

Michael Benalt Inc ....E 845 628-1008
Mahopac (G-7474)

▲ Munson Machinery Company Inc ......E 315 797-0090
Utica (G-15286)

◆ National Equipment Corporation ......F 718 585-0200
Harrison (G-5556)

National Equipment Corporation ....F 718 585-0200
Bronx (G-1321)

Northeast Data ....G 845 331-5554
Kingston (G-6705)

Nycon Diamond & Tools Corp ....E 855 937-6922
Bohemia (G-1056)

◆ **Optipro Systems LLC** ....D 585 265-0160
Ontario *(G-12296)*

P K G Equipment Incorporated ....E 585 436-4650
Rochester *(G-13605)*

▲ **Park Assist LLC** ....D 646 666-7525
New York *(G-10762)*

Parkmatic Car Prkg Systems LLC ....G 516 224-7700
Long Island City *(G-7319)*

Parkmatic Car Prkg Systems LLC ....G 800 422-5438
College Point *(G-3558)*

Pearl Technologies Inc ....E 315 365-3742
Savannah *(G-14220)*

◆ **Pfaudler Inc** ....B 585 235-1000
Rochester *(G-13617)*

▲ **Precision Process Inc** ....D 716 731-1587
Niagara Falls *(G-11969)*

◆ **Qes Solutions Inc** ....D 585 783-1455
Rochester *(G-13656)*

▲ **Quality Strapping Inc** ....D 718 418-1111
Brooklyn *(G-2312)*

▼ **Queenaire Technologies Inc** ....G 315 393-5454
Ogdensburg *(G-12210)*

R & B Machinery Corp ....G 716 894-3332
Buffalo *(G-2946)*

Reefer Tek Llc ....F 347 590-1067
Bronx *(G-1350)*

Reynolds Tech Fabricators Inc ....E 315 437-0532
East Syracuse *(G-4233)*

Rfb Associates Inc ....F 518 271-0551
Fort Edward *(G-4943)*

Riverview Associates Inc ....F 585 235-5980
Rochester *(G-13674)*

Shred Center ....G 716 664-3052
Jamestown *(G-6540)*

Sj Associates Inc ....E 516 942-3232
Jericho *(G-6595)*

▲ **Sonicor Inc** ....F 631 920-6555
West Babylon *(G-15748)*

Spectrum Catalysts Inc ....G 631 560-3683
Central Islip *(G-3288)*

SPX Corporation ....E 585 436-5550
Rochester *(G-13740)*

Stainless Design Concepts Ltd ....E 845 246-3631
Saugerties *(G-14213)*

Surepure Inc ....G 917 368-8480
New York *(G-11399)*

T-Rex Supply Corporation ....G 516 308-0505
Hempstead *(G-5850)*

Technic Inc ....F 516 349-0700
Plainview *(G-12718)*

Tompkins Srm LLC ....G 315 422-8763
Syracuse *(G-15013)*

Ui Acquisition Holding Co ....G 607 779-7522
Conklin *(G-3631)*

Ui Holding Company ....G 607 779-7522
Conklin *(G-3632)*

▲ **Ultrepet LLC** ....D 781 275-6400
Albany *(G-140)*

◆ **Universal Instruments Corp** ....C 800 842-9732
Conklin *(G-3633)*

Universal Thin Film Lab Corp ....G 845 562-0601
Newburgh *(G-11891)*

▲ **Valplast International Corp** ....F 516 442-3923
Westbury *(G-15937)*

▲ **Veeco Instruments Inc** ....B 516 677-0200
Plainview *(G-12725)*

West Metal Works Inc ....E 716 895-4900
Buffalo *(G-3045)*

Wilt Industries Inc ....G 518 548-4961
Lake Pleasant *(G-6769)*

Witt Preparations LLC ....G 716 948-4002
Cheektowaga *(G-3365)*

3561 Pumps & Pumping Eqpt

Air Flow Pump Corp ....G 718 241-2800
Brooklyn *(G-1472)*

▲ **Air Techniques Inc** ....B 516 433-7676
Melville *(G-7758)*

▲ **API International Group LLC** ....G 877 215-0017
Yonkers *(G-16288)*

◆ **Armstrong Pumps Inc** ....D 716 693-8813
North Tonawanda *(G-12053)*

Century-Tech Inc ....F 718 326-9400
Hempstead *(G-5835)*

Curaegis Technologies Inc ....E 585 254-1100
Rochester *(G-13333)*

Daikin Applied Americas Inc ....D 315 253-2771
Auburn *(G-472)*

▲ **Federal Pump Corporation** ....E 718 451-2000
New York *(G-9481)*

Fisonic Corp ....G 212 732-3777
Long Island City *(G-7225)*

▲ **Fisonic Corp** ....F 716 763-0295
New York *(G-9507)*

Flow Control LLC ....C 914 323-5700
Rye Brook *(G-14089)*

◆ **Fluid Handling LLC** ....G 716 897-2800
Cheektowaga *(G-3349)*

Fluid Metering Inc ....E 516 922-6050
Syosset *(G-14787)*

▲ **Gardner Dnver Oberdorfer Pumps** ....E 315 437-0361
Syracuse *(G-14900)*

Geopump Inc ....G 585 798-6666
Medina *(G-7736)*

◆ **Goulds Pumps LLC** ....A 315 568-2811
Seneca Falls *(G-14362)*

Goulds Pumps LLC ....E 315 568-2811
Seneca Falls *(G-14363)*

ITT Corporation ....D 315 568-2811
Seneca Falls *(G-14364)*

ITT Goulds Pumps Inc ....A 914 641-2129
Seneca Falls *(G-14366)*

▲ **John N Fehlinger Co Inc** ....F 212 233-5656
New York *(G-10018)*

Ketcham Pump Co Inc ....F 718 457-0800
Woodside *(G-16210)*

Lanco Manufacturing Co ....G 516 292-8953
West Hempstead *(G-15774)*

◆ **Liberty Pumps Inc** ....C 800 543-2550
Bergen *(G-817)*

▲ **Mannesmann Corporation** ....D 212 258-4000
New York *(G-10348)*

McWane Inc ....B 607 734-2211
Elmira *(G-4362)*

Messer LLC ....D 716 773-7552
Grand Island *(G-5337)*

Oberdorfer Pumps Inc ....E 315 437-0361
Syracuse *(G-14952)*

▲ **Oyster Bay Pump Works Inc** ....F 516 933-4500
Hicksville *(G-5937)*

Pentair Water Pool and Spa Inc ......E 845 452-5500
Lagrangeville *(G-6753)*

◆ **Pulsafeeder Inc** ....C 585 292-8000
Rochester *(G-13653)*

Pumpcrete Corporation ....G 716 667-7867
Orchard Park *(G-12374)*

▲ **Stavo Industries Inc** ....F 845 331-4552
Kingston *(G-6712)*

Trench & Marine Pump Co Inc ....E 212 423-9098
Bronx *(G-1381)*

◆ **Voss Usa Inc** ....C 212 995-2255
New York *(G-11707)*

◆ **Wastecorp Pumps LLC** ....F 888 829-2783
New York *(G-11726)*

Water Cooling Corp ....G 718 723-6500
Rosedale *(G-14038)*

Westmoor Ltd ....F 315 363-1500
Sherrill *(G-14409)*

Xylem Inc ....D 315 239-2499
Seneca Falls *(G-14375)*

Xylem Inc ....B 914 323-5700
Rye Brook *(G-14095)*

3562 Ball & Roller Bearings

A Hyatt Ball Co Ltd ....G 518 747-0272
Fort Edward *(G-4936)*

American Refuse Supply Inc ....G 718 893-8157
Bronx *(G-1204)*

Auburn Bearing & Mfg Inc ....G 315 986-7600
Macedon *(G-7460)*

David Fehlman ....G 315 455-8888
Syracuse *(G-14875)*

◆ **Dimanco Inc** ....G 315 797-0470
Utica *(G-15256)*

Enbi Rochester Inc ....E 585 647-1651
Rochester *(G-13390)*

▲ **General Bearing Corporation** ....C 845 358-6000
West Nyack *(G-15822)*

▲ **Kilian Manufacturing Corp** ....D 315 432-0700
Syracuse *(G-14925)*

Lemoyne Machine Products Corp ....G 315 454-0708
Syracuse *(G-14930)*

▲ **Mageba USA LLC** ....E 212 317-1991
New York *(G-10321)*

▲ **Nes Bearing Company Inc** ....E 716 372-6532
Olean *(G-12239)*

Raydon Precision Bearing Co ....G 516 887-2582
Lynbrook *(G-7436)*

▼ **Sandle Custom Bearing Corp** ....G 585 593-7000
Wellsville *(G-15675)*

▲ **Schatz Bearing Corporation** ....D 845 452-6000
Poughkeepsie *(G-12981)*

SKF USA Inc ....D 716 661-2869
Falconer *(G-4555)*

SKF USA Inc ....D 716 661-2600
Falconer *(G-4557)*

SKF USA Inc ....D 716 661-2600
Falconer *(G-4556)*

Workshop Art Fabrication ....F 845 331-0385
Kingston *(G-6723)*

3563 Air & Gas Compressors

▲ **Adams Sfc Inc** ....E 716 877-2608
Tonawanda *(G-15082)*

▲ **Air Techniques Inc** ....B 516 433-7676
Melville *(G-7758)*

◆ **Atlas Copco Comptec LLC** ....B 518 765-3344
Voorheesville *(G-15444)*

Auto Body Services LLC ....F 631 431-4640
Lindenhurst *(G-6941)*

Bedford Precision Parts Corp ....E 914 241-2211
Bedford Hills *(G-765)*

Buffalo Compressed Air Inc ....G 716 783-8673
Cheektowaga *(G-3340)*

◆ **Chapin International Inc** ....C 585 343-3140
Batavia *(G-608)*

◆ **Chapin Manufacturing Inc** ....C 585 343-3140
Batavia *(G-609)*

Comairco Equipment Inc ....G 716 656-0211
Cheektowaga *(G-3341)*

▲ **Cooper Turbocompressor Inc** ....B 716 896-6600
Buffalo *(G-2711)*

▲ **Crosman Corporation** ....E 585 657-6161
Bloomfield *(G-945)*

Crosman Corporation ....E 585 398-3920
Farmington *(G-4769)*

Dresser-Rand (delaware) LLC ....C 607 937-2011
Painted Post *(G-12474)*

Dresser-Rand Group Inc ....D 716 375-3000
Olean *(G-12232)*

▲ **Eastern Air Products LLC** ....F 716 391-1866
Lancaster *(G-6804)*

▲ **Edwards Vacuum LLC** ....D 800 848-9800
Sanborn *(G-14140)*

◆ **Fountainhead Group Inc** ....C 315 736-0037
New York Mills *(G-11832)*

Fountainhead Group Inc ....C 708 598-7100
New York Mills *(G-11833)*

GM Components Holdings LLC ....B 716 439-2463
Lockport *(G-7079)*

GM Components Holdings LLC ....B 716 439-2011
Lockport *(G-7080)*

◆ **Graham Corporation** ....B 585 343-2216
Batavia *(G-616)*

Ingersoll-Rand Company ....E 716 896-6600
Buffalo *(G-2810)*

▲ **Precision Plus Vacuum Parts** ....D 716 297-2039
Sanborn *(G-14147)*

Screw Compressor Tech Inc ....F 716 827-6600
Buffalo *(G-2977)*

Spfm Corp ....G 718 788-6800
Brooklyn *(G-2446)*

Turbopro Inc ....G 716 681-8651
Alden *(G-175)*

Vac Air Service Inc ....F 716 665-2206
Jamestown *(G-6552)*

3564 Blowers & Fans

Acme Engineering Products Inc ....E 518 236-5659
Mooers *(G-8079)*

Aeromed Inc ....G 518 843-9144
Utica *(G-15238)*

Air Crafters Inc ....C 631 471-7788
Ronkonkoma *(G-13893)*

Air Engineering Filters Inc ....G 914 238-5945
Chappaqua *(G-3322)*

Air Export Mechanical ....G 917 709-5310
Flushing *(G-4835)*

▲ **Airgle Corporation** ....G 866 501-7750
Ronkonkoma *(G-13894)*

American Filtration Tech Inc ....F 585 359-4130
West Henrietta *(G-15783)*

Apgn Inc ....E 518 324-4150
Plattsburgh *(G-12732)*

Applied Safety LLC ....G 718 608-6292
Long Island City *(G-7161)*

◆ **Austin Air Systems Limited** ....D 716 856-3700
Buffalo *(G-2650)*

Beecher Emssn Sltn Tchnlgs LLC ......F 607 796-0149
Horseheads *(G-6113)*

S I C

Beltran Associates Inc ....E 718 252-2996
Brooklyn *(G-1572)*
▲ **Beltran Technologies Inc** ....E 718 338-3311
Brooklyn *(G-1573)*
▲ **Buffalo Filter LLC** ....D 716 835-7000
Lancaster *(G-6799)*
Camfil Usa Inc ....F 315 468-3849
Syracuse *(G-14841)*
▲ **Canarm Ltd** ....G 800 267-4427
Ogdensburg *(G-12203)*
Clean Gas Systems Inc ....E 631 467-1600
Commack *(G-3583)*
Daikin Applied Americas Inc ....D 315 253-2771
Auburn *(G-472)*
Delphi Powertrain Systems LLC ....B 585 359-6000
West Henrietta *(G-15792)*
Ducon Technologies Inc ....E 631 420-4900
Farmingdale *(G-4618)*
◆ **Ducon Technologies Inc** ....B 631 694-1700
New York *(G-9278)*
Dundas-Jafine Inc ....E 716 681-9690
Alden *(G-168)*
Filta Clean Co Inc ....E 718 495-3800
Brooklyn *(G-1843)*
Filtros Ltd ....E 585 586-8770
East Rochester *(G-4163)*
Flanders Precisionaire NY ....G 518 751-5640
Hudson *(G-6156)*
▲ **Healthway Home Products Inc** ....E 315 298-2904
Pulaski *(G-13000)*
Healthway Products Company ....E 315 207-1410
Oswego *(G-12411)*
◆ **Hilliard Corporation** ....B 607 733-7121
Elmira *(G-4357)*
Hilliard Corporation ....G 607 733-7121
Elmira *(G-4358)*
◆ **Howden North America Inc** ....D 330 867-8540
Depew *(G-3985)*
Howden North America Inc ....D 716 817-6900
Williamsville *(G-16132)*
Isolation Systems Inc ....F 716 694-6390
North Tonawanda *(G-12073)*
Jr Engineering Enterprise LLC ....G 716 909-2693
Grand Island *(G-5335)*
JT Systems Inc ....F 315 622-1980
Liverpool *(G-7019)*
▲ **Low-Cost Mfg Co Inc** ....G 516 627-3282
Carle Place *(G-3176)*
Nexstar Holding Corp ....G 716 929-9000
Amherst *(G-234)*
▼ **North American Filter Corp** ....D 800 265-8943
Newark *(G-11848)*
◆ **Northland Filter Intl LLC** ....E 315 207-1410
Oswego *(G-12415)*
Oestreich Metal Works Inc ....G 315 463-4268
Syracuse *(G-14953)*
◆ **Oneida Air Systems Inc** ....E 315 476-5151
Syracuse *(G-14956)*
Parker-Hannifin Corporation ....D 716 685-4040
Lancaster *(G-6822)*
Phytofilter Technologies Inc ....G 518 507-6399
Saratoga Springs *(G-14187)*
Pliotron Company America LLC ....G 716 298-4457
Niagara Falls *(G-11965)*
▲ **R P Fedder Corp** ....E 585 288-1600
Rochester *(G-13666)*
Rapid Fan & Blower Inc ....F 718 786-2060
Long Island City *(G-7339)*
Roome Technologies Inc ....G 585 229-4437
Honeoye *(G-6069)*
▲ **Rotron Incorporated** ....B 845 679-2401
Woodstock *(G-16237)*
Rotron Incorporated ....E 845 679-2401
Woodstock *(G-16238)*
Sbb Inc ....G 315 422-2376
East Syracuse *(G-4236)*
◆ **Standard Motor Products Inc** ....B 718 392-0200
Long Island City *(G-7364)*
Sullivan Bazinet Bongio Inc ....E 315 437-6500
East Syracuse *(G-4240)*
Vent-A-Kiln Corporation ....G 716 876-2023
Buffalo *(G-3035)*
Veteran Air LLC ....G 315 720-1101
Syracuse *(G-15022)*

3565 Packaging Machinery

A & G Heat Sealing ....G 631 724-7764
Smithtown *(G-14472)*
All Packaging McHy & Sups Corp ....F 631 588-7310
Ronkonkoma *(G-13897)*
Automecha International Ltd ....E 607 843-2235
Oxford *(G-12441)*
Brooks Bottling Co LLC ....F 607 432-1782
Oneonta *(G-12260)*
Crandall Filling Machinery Inc ....G 716 897-3486
Buffalo *(G-2712)*
Desu Machinery Corporation ....D 716 681-5798
Depew *(G-3979)*
◆ **Dover Global Holdings Inc** ....F 212 922-1640
New York *(G-9257)*
▲ **Elmar Industries Inc** ....D 716 681-5650
Depew *(G-3980)*
Filling Equipment Co Inc ....F 718 445-2111
College Point *(G-3542)*
Fourteen Arnold Ave Corp ....F 315 272-1700
Utica *(G-15264)*
Global Packaging Services LLC ....G 646 648-0355
Glen Head *(G-5206)*
Haines Equipment Inc ....E 607 566-8531
Avoca *(G-510)*
▲ **Kabar Manufacturing Corp** ....E 631 694-6857
Farmingdale *(G-4660)*
◆ **Kaps-All Packaging Systems** ....D 631 574-8778
Riverhead *(G-13175)*
Millwood Inc ....F 518 233-1475
Waterford *(G-15539)*
▲ **Modern Packaging Inc** ....D 631 595-2437
Deer Park *(G-3907)*
National Equipment Corporation ....E 718 585-0200
Bronx *(G-1321)*
Niagara Scientific Inc ....E 315 437-0821
East Syracuse *(G-4228)*
▲ **Orics Industries Inc** ....E 718 461-8613
Farmingdale *(G-4697)*
Overhead Door Corporation ....D 518 828-7652
Hudson *(G-6173)*
Pacemaker Packaging Corp ....F 718 458-1188
Woodside *(G-16218)*
◆ **Packaging Dynamics Ltd** ....F 631 563-4499
Bohemia *(G-1058)*
Reynolds Packaging McHy Inc ....D 716 358-6451
Falconer *(G-4554)*
Rfb Associates Inc ....F 518 271-0551
Fort Edward *(G-4943)*
Rota Pack Inc ....F 631 274-1037
Farmingdale *(G-4727)*
Save O Seal Corporation Inc ....G 914 592-3031
Elmsford *(G-4427)*
Sharon Manufacturing Co Inc ....G 631 242-8870
Deer Park *(G-3936)*
▲ **Turbofil Packaging Mchs LLC** ....F 914 239-3878
Mount Vernon *(G-8189)*
◆ **Universal Packg Systems Inc** ....A 631 543-2277
Hauppauge *(G-5792)*
Utleys Incorporated ....E 718 956-1661
Woodside *(G-16232)*
▲ **Vetroelite Inc** ....G 925 724-7900
New York *(G-11668)*
Volckening Inc ....E 718 748-0294
Brooklyn *(G-2568)*

3566 Speed Changers, Drives & Gears

American Torque Inc ....F 718 526-2433
Jamaica *(G-6425)*
▲ **Biltron Automotive Products** ....E 631 928-8613
Port Jeff STA *(G-12833)*
▲ **Buffalo Gear Inc** ....E 716 731-2100
Sanborn *(G-14139)*
Designatronics Incorporated ....B 516 328-3300
New Hyde Park *(G-8261)*
◆ **Gleason Works** ....A 585 473-1000
Rochester *(G-13445)*
Harmonic Drive LLC ....G 631 231-6630
Hauppauge *(G-5667)*
▲ **Interparts International Inc** ....E 516 576-2000
Plainview *(G-12691)*
▲ **John G Rubino Inc** ....E 315 253-7396
Auburn *(G-482)*
▲ **Jrlon Inc** ....D 315 597-4067
Palmyra *(G-12489)*
Khk Usa Inc ....G 516 248-3850
Mineola *(G-7984)*
Magna Products Corp ....E 585 647-2280
Rochester *(G-13529)*
McGuigan Inc ....E 631 750-6222
Bohemia *(G-1045)*
Niagara Gear Corporation ....E 716 874-3131
Buffalo *(G-2885)*
Nidec Indus Automtn USA LLC ....E 716 774-1193
Grand Island *(G-5338)*
▲ **Nuttall Gear L L C** ....E 716 298-4100
Niagara Falls *(G-11958)*
Oliver Gear Inc ....E 716 885-1080
Buffalo *(G-2896)*
◆ **Ondrivesus Corp** ....E 516 771-6777
Freeport *(G-5012)*
Peerless-Winsmith Inc ....C 716 592-9311
Springville *(G-14594)*
Perfection Gear Inc ....C 716 592-9310
Springville *(G-14595)*
Precipart Corporation ....C 631 694-3100
Farmingdale *(G-4714)*
Precision Mechanisms Corp ....E 516 333-5955
Westbury *(G-15919)*
▲ **Renold Inc** ....D 716 326-3121
Westfield *(G-15949)*
Rochester Gear Inc ....E 585 254-5442
Rochester *(G-13689)*
W J Albro Machine Works Inc ....G 631 345-0657
Yaphank *(G-16278)*

3567 Indl Process Furnaces & Ovens

▲ **Ambrell Corporation** ....F 585 889-0236
Rochester *(G-13227)*
◆ **Buflovak LLC** ....E 716 895-2100
Buffalo *(G-2685)*
Concealed Baseboard Htg Co LLC ....F 212 378-6710
New York *(G-9075)*
◆ **Cooks Intl Ltd Lblty Co** ....G 212 741-4407
New York *(G-9096)*
Cosmos Electronic Machine Corp ....E 631 249-2535
Farmingdale *(G-4604)*
Cvd Equipment Corporation ....F 631 582-4365
Central Islip *(G-3272)*
◆ **Embassy Industries Inc** ....C 631 435-0209
Hauppauge *(G-5647)*
▼ **Fulton Volcanic Inc** ....D 315 298-5121
Pulaski *(G-12999)*
◆ **Harper International Corp** ....D 716 276-9900
Buffalo *(G-2795)*
Harper International Corp ....G 716 276-9900
Depew *(G-3984)*
▲ **Hpi Co Inc** ....G 718 851-2753
Brooklyn *(G-1945)*
J H Buhrmaster Company Inc ....G 518 843-1700
Amsterdam *(G-331)*
Messer LLC ....D 716 773-7552
Grand Island *(G-5337)*
Parker-Hannifin Corporation ....D 716 685-4040
Lancaster *(G-6823)*
Radiant Pro Ltd ....G 516 763-5678
Oceanside *(G-12186)*
Specified Air Solutions LLC ....E 716 852-4400
Buffalo *(G-2991)*
Thermal Process Cnstr Co ....E 631 293-6400
Farmingdale *(G-4754)*
Ultraflex Power Technologies ....G 631 467-6814
Ronkonkoma *(G-14021)*
Vincent Genovese ....G 631 281-8170
Mastic Beach *(G-7675)*

3568 Mechanical Power Transmission Eqpt, NEC

Advanced Thermal Systems Inc ....E 716 681-1800
Lancaster *(G-6790)*
Babbitt Bearings Incorporated ....D 315 479-6603
Syracuse *(G-14825)*
▲ **BW Elliott Mfg Co LLC** ....B 607 772-0404
Binghamton *(G-865)*
C-Flex Bearing Co Inc ....F 315 895-7454
Frankfort *(G-4948)*
Champlain Hudson Power Ex Inc ....G 518 465-0710
Albany *(G-59)*
Designatronics Incorporated ....B 516 328-3300
New Hyde Park *(G-8261)*
Eaw Electronic Systems Inc ....G 845 471-5290
Poughkeepsie *(G-12953)*
◆ **Howden North America Inc** ....D 330 867-8540
Depew *(G-3985)*
Hudson Power Transmission Co ....G 718 622-3869
Brooklyn *(G-1946)*
Huron Tl Cutter Grinding Inc ....E 631 420-7000
Farmingdale *(G-4646)*
Kaddis Manufacturing Corp ....G 585 624-3070
Honeoye Falls *(G-6077)*
Kinemotive Corporation ....E 631 249-6440
Farmingdale *(G-4666)*
Liston Manufacturing Inc ....E 716 695-2111
North Tonawanda *(G-12077)*

Ls Power Equity Partners LP ....G 212 615-3456
New York (G-10276)
Machine Components Corp ....E 516 694-7222
Plainview (G-12698)
◆ Magtrol Inc ....E 716 668-5555
Buffalo (G-2859)
Metallized Carbon Corporation...............C 914 941-3738
Ossining (G-12404)
On Line Power Technologies ....G 914 968-4440
Yonkers (G-16336)
▲ Package One Inc ....D 518 344-5425
Schenectady (G-14294)
▲ Renold Inc ....D 716 326-3121
Westfield (G-15949)
▲ Sepac Inc ....E 607 732-2030
Elmira (G-4367)
◆ Watson Bowman Acme Corp...............C 716 691-8162
Amherst (G-253)
York Industries Inc ....E 516 746-3736
Garden City Park (G-5126)

3569 Indl Machinery & Eqpt, NEC

Acme Engineering Products Inc...............E 518 236-5659
Mooers (G-8079)
▲ Adams Sfc Inc ....E 716 877-2608
Tonawanda (G-15082)
▲ Advanced Tchncal Solutions Inc ....F 914 214-8230
Mahopac (G-7473)
Airsep Corporation ....D 716 691-0202
Amherst (G-204)
▲ Alliance Automation Systems ....C 585 426-2700
Rochester (G-13218)
Allied Inspection Services LLC ....F 716 489-3199
Falconer (G-4533)
▲ American Felt & Filter Co Inc ....D 845 561-3560
New Windsor (G-8359)
American Filtration Tech Inc ....F 585 359-4130
West Henrietta (G-15783)
American Material Processing...............F 315 318-0017
Phoenix (G-12615)
◆ Audubon Machinery Corporation...............D 716 564-5165
North Tonawanda (G-12055)
Automated Cells & Eqp Inc ....F 607 936-1341
Painted Post (G-12471)
Better Power Inc ....G 585 475-1321
Rochester (G-13267)
Bowen Products Corporation ....G 315 498-4481
Nedrow (G-8214)
▲ Bullex Inc ....F 518 689-2023
Albany (G-53)
Burnett Process Inc ....E 585 277-1623
Rochester (G-13289)
Cleaning Tech Group LLC ....E 716 665-2340
Jamestown (G-6502)
◆ Cross Filtration Ltd Lblty Co ....F 315 412-1539
Moravia (G-8082)
▲ Distech Systems Inc ....G 585 254-7020
Rochester (G-13349)
Dynamasters Inc ....G 585 458-9970
Rochester (G-13359)
Eastern Precision Mfg ....G 845 358-1951
Nyack (G-12142)
▲ Filter Tech Inc ....D 315 682-8815
Manlius (G-7546)
▲ Finesse Creations Inc ....F 718 692-2100
Brooklyn (G-1846)
First Due Fire Equipment Inc ....F 845 222-1329
Garnerville (G-5134)
Foseco Inc ....F 914 345-4760
Tarrytown (G-15044)
◆ Fountainhead Group Inc ....C 315 736-0037
New York Mills (G-11832)
Graver Technologies LLC ....E 585 624-1330
Honeoye Falls (G-6072)
◆ Hannay Reels Inc ....C 518 797-3791
Westerlo (G-15941)
◆ Hilliard Corporation ....B 607 733-7121
Elmira (G-4357)
Hilliard Corporation ....G 607 733-7121
Elmira (G-4358)
Honeybee Robotics Ltd ....E 212 966-0661
Brooklyn (G-1942)
▲ Hubco Inc ....G 716 683-5940
Alden (G-170)
Island Automated Gate Co LLC ....G 631 425-0196
Huntington Station (G-6250)
J H Robotics Inc ....E 607 729-3758
Johnson City (G-6603)
Javlyn Process Systems LLC ....E 585 424-5580
Rochester (G-13491)

Kyntec Corporation ....G 716 810-6956
Buffalo (G-2840)
Lifc Corp ....G 516 426-5737
Port Washington (G-12900)
Lydall Performance Mtls Inc ....F 518 273-6320
Green Island (G-5439)
Markpericom ....G 516 208-6824
Oceanside (G-12182)
McHone Industries Inc ....D 716 945-3380
Salamanca (G-14122)
New Vision Industries Inc ....F 607 687-7700
Endicott (G-4466)
▼ North American Filter Corp ....D 800 265-8943
Newark (G-11848)
▲ Pall Corporation ....A 516 484-5400
Port Washington (G-12913)
Pall Corporation ....A 607 753-6041
Cortland (G-3779)
Parker-Hannifin Corporation ....D 716 685-4040
Lancaster (G-6822)
Peregrine Industries Inc ....G 631 838-2870
New York (G-10801)
Pyrotek Incorporated ....F 716 731-3221
Sanborn (G-14148)
Quality Manufacturing Sys LLC...............G 716 763-0988
Lakewood (G-6783)
◆ Reliable Autmtc Sprnklr Co Inc ....B 800 431-1588
Elmsford (G-4426)
Rfb Associates Inc ....F 518 271-0551
Fort Edward (G-4943)
▲ SC Supply Chain Management LLC .G 212 344-3322
New York (G-11146)
Sentry Automatic Sprinkler ....F 631 723-3095
Riverhead (G-13189)
Service Filtration Corp ....E 716 877-2608
Tonawanda (G-15140)
Sidco Filter Corporation ....F 585 289-3100
Manchester (G-7529)
Sigelock Systems LLC ....G 888 744-3562
Oceanside (G-12190)
Sinclair International Company ....D 518 798-2361
Queensbury (G-13057)
▲ Sonicor Inc ....F 631 920-6555
West Babylon (G-15748)
▲ Stavo Industries Inc ....F 845 331-4552
Kingston (G-6712)
Stavo Industries Inc ....E 845 331-5389
Kingston (G-6713)
▲ Sussman-Automatic Corporation...............D 718 937-4500
Long Island City (G-7376)
▲ Taylor Devices Inc ....C 716 694-0800
North Tonawanda (G-12095)
▲ Trident Precision Mfg Inc ....D 585 265-2010
Webster (G-15658)
Tyco Simplexgrinnell ....E 315 437-9664
East Syracuse (G-4245)
Universal Metal Fabricators ....F 845 331-8248
Kingston (G-6719)
▲ Veeco Process Equipment Inc ....C 516 677-0200
Plainview (G-12726)
William R Shoemaker Inc ....G 716 649-0511
Hamburg (G-5524)

3571 Electronic Computers

Apple Commuter Inc ....G 917 299-0066
New Hyde Park (G-8250)
▲ Argon Corp ....F 516 487-5314
Great Neck (G-5367)
Arnouse Digital Devices Corp ....D 516 673-4444
New Hyde Park (G-8251)
B-Reel Films Inc ....E 917 388-3836
New York (G-8708)
▲ Binghamton Simulator Co Inc ....E 607 321-2980
Binghamton (G-860)
Computer Conversions Corp ....E 631 261-3300
East Northport (G-4143)
Critical Link LLC ....E 315 425-4045
Syracuse (G-14867)
Data-Pac Mailing Systems Corp ....F 585 671-0210
Webster (G-15637)
Datacom Systems Inc ....E 315 463-9541
East Syracuse (G-4206)
Dees Audio & Vision ....G 585 719-9256
Rochester (G-13342)
▲ Digicom International Inc ....F 631 249-8999
Farmingdale (G-4615)
Digitac LLC ....G 732 669-7637
Brooklyn (G-1745)
Doar Inc ....G 516 872-8140
Lynbrook (G-7430)

▲ Dynamic Decisions Inc ....E 908 755-5000
Fresh Meadows (G-5039)
▲ E-Systems Group LLC ....E 607 775-1100
Conklin (G-3624)
Ebc Technologies LLC ....D 631 729-8182
Hauppauge (G-5644)
Electronic Systems Inc ....G 631 589-4389
Holbrook (G-5998)
▲ Elo Touch Solutions Inc ....E 585 427-2802
Rochester (G-13384)
Facsimile Cmmncations Inds Inc ....D 212 741-6400
New York (G-9460)
G S Communications USA Inc ....E 718 389-7371
Brooklyn (G-1874)
Go Go Apple Inc ....G 646 264-8909
Elmhurst (G-4335)
H&L Computers Inc ....E 516 873-8088
Flushing (G-4857)
Hi-Tech Advanced Solutions Inc ....F 718 926-3488
Forest Hills (G-4921)
HP Inc ....E 650 857-1501
Albany (G-88)
HP Inc ....G 650 857-1501
New York (G-9828)
Human Electronics Inc ....G 315 724-9850
Utica (G-15272)
IBM World Trade Corporation ....G 914 765-1900
Armonk (G-397)
International Bus Mchs Corp ....A 914 945-3000
Yorktown Heights (G-16366)
International Bus Mchs Corp ....A 845 433-1234
Poughkeepsie (G-12963)
J & N Computer Services Inc ....F 585 388-8780
Fairport (G-4500)
M&C Associates LLC ....E 631 467-8760
Hauppauge (G-5702)
Medsim-Eagle Simulation Inc ....F 607 658-9354
Endicott (G-4464)
N & G of America Inc ....F 516 428-3414
Plainview (G-12703)
N & L Instruments Inc ....F 631 471-4000
Ronkonkoma (G-13978)
NCR Corporation ....C 516 876-7200
Jericho (G-6586)
North Atlantic Industries Inc ....C 631 567-1100
Bohemia (G-1053)
Northpoint Digital LLC ....G 212 819-1700
New York (G-10644)
▲ Partech Inc ....C 315 738-0600
New Hartford (G-8243)
Photon Vision Systems Inc ....F 607 749-2689
Homer (G-6066)
Policy ADM Solutions Inc ....E 914 332-4320
Tarrytown (G-15052)
Revivn Public Benefit Corp ....F 347 762-8193
Brooklyn (G-2342)
Stargate Computer Corp ....G 516 474-4799
Port Jeff STA (G-12838)
▲ Telxon Corporation ....E 631 738-2400
Holtsville (G-6056)
◆ Toshiba Amer Info Systems Inc ....B 949 583-3000
New York (G-11518)
◆ Toshiba America Inc ....E 212 596-0600
New York (G-11519)
Transland Sourcing LLC ....G 718 596-5704
Brooklyn (G-2517)
Wantagh Computer Center ....F 516 826-2189
Wantagh (G-15489)
Wilcro Inc ....G 716 632-4204
Buffalo (G-3047)
Yellow E House Inc ....G 718 888-2000
Flushing (G-4907)

3572 Computer Storage Devices

Datalink Computer Products ....F 914 666-2358
Mount Kisco (G-8091)
EMC Corporation ....C 212 564-6866
New York (G-9359)
Emcs LLC ....G 716 523-2002
Hamburg (G-5507)
Formats Unlimited Inc ....F 631 249-9200
Deer Park (G-3875)
Garland Technology LLC ....E 716 242-8500
Buffalo (G-2767)
Gim Electronics Corp ....F 516 942-3382
Hicksville (G-5911)
Globalfoundries US Inc ....D 518 305-9013
Malta (G-7495)
Quantum Knowledge LLC ....G 631 727-6111
Riverhead (G-13185)

S
I
C

Quantum Logic Corp ....G..... 516 746-1380
New Hyde Park *(G-8290)*

Quantum Mechanics Ny LLC ....G..... 917 519-7077
Huntington *(G-6218)*

Sale 121 Corp ....D..... 240 855-8988
New York *(G-11117)*

◆ Sony Corporation of America...........C..... 212 833-8000
New York *(G-11295)*

▲ Technologies Application LLC ....F..... 607 275-0345
Cortland *(G-3790)*

◆ Toshiba Amer Info Systems Inc ....B..... 949 583-3000
New York *(G-11518)*

William S Hein & Co Inc ....C..... 716 882-2600
Getzville *(G-5184)*

3575 Computer Terminals

AG Neovo Professional Inc...............F..... 212 647-9080
New York *(G-8492)*

Cine Design Group LLC ....G..... 646 747-0734
New York *(G-9007)*

▲ Clayton Dubilier & Rice Fun.............E..... 212 407-5200
New York *(G-9029)*

Doar Inc................G..... 516 872-8140
Lynbrook *(G-7430)*

Igt Global Solutions Corp ....D..... 518 382-2900
Schenectady *(G-14280)*

Integra Microsystem 1988 Inc ....G..... 718 609-6099
Brooklyn *(G-1961)*

Orbit International Corp ....D..... 631 435-8300
Hauppauge *(G-5734)*

PC Solutions & Consulting ....G..... 607 735-0466
Elmira *(G-4364)*

Shadowtv Inc ....G..... 212 445-2540
New York *(G-11201)*

Symbio Technologies LLC ....G..... 914 576-1205
White Plains *(G-16065)*

▲ Touchstone Technology Inc............F..... 585 458-2690
Rochester *(G-13770)*

Ultra-Scan Corporation ....F..... 716 832-6269
Amherst *(G-252)*

3577 Computer Peripheral Eqpt, NEC

A I T Computers Inc ....G..... 518 266-9010
Troy *(G-15162)*

Aalborg Instrs & Contrls Inc ....D..... 845 398-3160
Orangeburg *(G-12304)*

Advanced Barcode Tech Inc ....F..... 516 570-8100
Great Neck *(G-5359)*

Aero-Vision Technologies Inc.............G..... 631 643-8349
Melville *(G-7756)*

◆ Andrea Electronics Corporation ....G..... 631 719-1800
Bohemia *(G-973)*

Annese & Associates Inc ....G..... 716 972-0076
Buffalo *(G-2635)*

▲ Anorad Corporation ....C..... 631 344-6600
Shirley *(G-14412)*

Aruba Networks Inc ....G..... 732 343-1305
New York *(G-8641)*

Atlaz International Ltd ....F..... 516 239-1854
Freeport *(G-4986)*

◆ Aventura Technologies Inc ....E..... 631 300-4000
Commack *(G-3577)*

B V M Associates ....G..... 631 254-6220
Shirley *(G-14416)*

▲ Binghamton Simulator Co Inc ....E..... 607 321-2980
Binghamton *(G-860)*

Blue Skies ....G..... 631 392-1140
Deer Park *(G-3848)*

Broadnet Technologies Inc ....F..... 315 443-3694
Syracuse *(G-14834)*

Cisco Systems Inc ....C..... 212 714-4000
New York *(G-9012)*

▲ Clayton Dubilier & Rice Fun.............E..... 212 407-5200
New York *(G-9029)*

CNy Business Solutions ....G..... 315 733-5031
Utica *(G-15244)*

Cobham Long Island Inc ....G..... 631 231-9100
Hauppauge *(G-5619)*

Control Logic Corporation ....G..... 607 965-6423
West Burlington *(G-15758)*

▲ Data Device Corporation ....B..... 631 567-5600
Bohemia *(G-999)*

Datatran Labs Inc ....G..... 845 856-4313
Port Jervis *(G-12847)*

▲ Digiorange Inc ....G..... 718 801-8244
Brooklyn *(G-1743)*

Dolphin Data Capture LLC ....G..... 516 429-5663
New York *(G-9246)*

▲ Dynamic Decisions Inc ....E..... 908 755-5000
Fresh Meadows *(G-5039)*

◆ Eastman Kodak Company ....B..... 585 724-4000
Rochester *(G-13367)*

Ems Development Corporation ....D..... 631 345-6200
Yaphank *(G-16260)*

Epicor Software Corporation ....E..... 805 496-6789
Schenectady *(G-14265)*

Future Star Digatech ....F..... 718 666-0350
Brooklyn *(G-1872)*

◆ Gasoft Equipment Inc ....F..... 845 863-1010
Newburgh *(G-11866)*

Glowa Manufacturing Inc ....E..... 607 770-0811
Binghamton *(G-880)*

▲ Hauppauge Computer Works Inc ....E..... 631 434-1600
Hauppauge *(G-5668)*

▲ Hauppauge Digital Inc ....E..... 631 434-1600
Hauppauge *(G-5669)*

◆ Hergo Ergonomic Support Syst ....E..... 888 222-7270
Oceanside *(G-12175)*

▲ Hitachi Metals America Ltd ....E..... 914 694-9200
Purchase *(G-13005)*

◆ Humanscale Corporation ....E..... 212 725-4749
New York *(G-9839)*

IBM World Trade Corporation ....G..... 914 765-1900
Armonk *(G-397)*

Innovative Systems of New York ....G..... 516 541-7410
Massapequa Park *(G-7657)*

Iweb Design Inc ....F..... 805 243-8305
Bronx *(G-1284)*

Jadak Technologies Inc ....C..... 315 701-0678
North Syracuse *(G-12047)*

▲ Kantek Inc ....E..... 516 594-4600
Oceanside *(G-12178)*

Lsc Peripherals Incorporated ....G..... 631 244-0707
Bohemia *(G-1038)*

Luminescent Systems Inc...............B..... 716 655-0800
East Aurora *(G-4091)*

Macrolink Inc ....E..... 631 924-8200
Medford *(G-7718)*

Maia Systems LLC ....G..... 718 206-0100
Jamaica *(G-6456)*

Mdi Holdings LLC ....A..... 212 559-1127
New York *(G-10404)*

Medsim-Eagle Simulation Inc ....F..... 607 658-9354
Endicott *(G-4464)*

Mg Imaging ....G..... 212 704-4073
New York *(G-10447)*

Mirion Technologies Ist Corp.............D..... 607 562-4300
Horseheads *(G-6128)*

▲ Mp Displays LLC ....E..... 845 268-4113
Valley Cottage *(G-15319)*

NCR Corporation ....G..... 607 273-5310
Ithaca *(G-6400)*

▲ Norazza Inc ....F..... 716 706-1160
Buffalo *(G-2890)*

▲ O Rama Light Inc ....E..... 518 539-9000
South Glens Falls *(G-14517)*

Office Grabs LLC ....G..... 347 678-3993
Brooklyn *(G-2228)*

Orbit International Corp ....D..... 631 435-8300
Hauppauge *(G-5734)*

P C Rfrs Radiology ....E..... 212 586-5700
Long Island City *(G-7315)*

Pda Panache Corp ....G..... 631 776-0523
Bohemia *(G-1060)*

Peak Performance Design LLC.............G..... 518 302-9198
Cohoes *(G-3512)*

Peoples Choice M R I ....F..... 716 681-7377
Buffalo *(G-2912)*

Performance Technologies Inc.............E..... 585 256-0200
Rochester *(G-13615)*

Phoenix Venture Fund LLC ....E..... 212 759-1909
New York *(G-10831)*

▲ Rdi Inc ....F..... 914 773-1000
Mount Kisco *(G-8104)*

Reliable Elec Mt Vernon Inc ....E..... 914 668-4440
Mount Vernon *(G-8177)*

Ruhle Companies Inc ....G..... 914 287-4000
Valhalla *(G-15309)*

S G I ....G..... 917 386-0385
New York *(G-11108)*

Scroll Media Inc ....E..... 617 395-8904
New York *(G-11171)*

▲ Sima Technologies LLC ....G..... 412 828-9130
Hauppauge *(G-5766)*

◆ Sony Corporation of America...........C..... 212 833-8000
New York *(G-11295)*

▲ Symbol Technologies LLC ....A..... 631 737-6851
Holtsville *(G-6054)*

Symbol Technologies LLC ....F..... 631 738-2400
Bohemia *(G-1083)*

Symbol Technologies LLC ....F..... 631 218-3907
Holbrook *(G-6025)*

T&K Printing Inc...............F..... 718 439-9454
Brooklyn *(G-2487)*

Tokenworks Inc ....G..... 914 704-3100
Bronxville *(G-1404)*

Torrent Ems LLC ....F..... 716 312-4099
Lockport *(G-7113)*

◆ Toshiba Amer Info Systems Inc ....B..... 949 583-3000
New York *(G-11518)*

Transact Technologies Inc ....D..... 607 257-8901
Ithaca *(G-6414)*

▲ Vishay Thin Film LLC ....C..... 716 283-4025
Niagara Falls *(G-11990)*

Vuzix Corporation ....E..... 585 359-5900
West Henrietta *(G-15806)*

Wantagh Computer Center ....F..... 516 826-2189
Wantagh *(G-15489)*

▼ Watson Productions LLC ....E..... 516 334-9766
Hauppauge *(G-5799)*

Welch Allyn Inc...............A..... 315 685-4100
Skaneateles Falls *(G-14459)*

Wilson & Wilson Group ....E..... 212 729-4736
Forest Hills *(G-4927)*

X Brand Editions ....G..... 718 482-7646
Long Island City *(G-7408)*

▲ Z-Axis Inc ....D..... 315 548-5000
Phelps *(G-12611)*

Zebra Technologies Entp Corp ....E..... 800 722-6234
Holtsville *(G-6059)*

3578 Calculating & Accounting Eqpt

Gary Roth & Associates Ltd ....E..... 516 333-1000
Westbury *(G-15889)*

International Merch Svcs Inc ....G..... 914 699-4000
Mount Vernon *(G-8151)*

Jpmorgan Chase Bank Nat Assn ....G..... 718 767-3592
College Point *(G-3549)*

K&G of Syracuse Inc ....G..... 315 446-1921
Syracuse *(G-14923)*

Kenney Manufacturing Displays ....F..... 631 231-5563
Bay Shore *(G-686)*

Merchant Service Pymnt Access ....E..... 212 561-5516
Uniondale *(G-15232)*

Mid Enterprise Inc ....G..... 631 924-3933
Middle Island *(G-7875)*

▲ Parabit Systems Inc ....E..... 516 378-4800
Bellmore *(G-786)*

Powa Technologies Inc ....E..... 347 344-7848
New York *(G-10872)*

Stanson Automated LLC ....E..... 866 505-7826
Yonkers *(G-16349)*

3579 Office Machines, NEC

Action Technologies Inc...............G..... 718 278-1000
Long Island City *(G-7145)*

Automecha International Ltd ....E..... 607 843-2235
Oxford *(G-12441)*

Cummins - Allison Corp ....D..... 718 263-2482
Kew Gardens *(G-6662)*

Gradual LLC ....F..... 347 293-0974
Long Island City *(G-7232)*

National Time Recording Eqp Co ....F..... 212 227-3310
New York *(G-10547)*

Neopost USA Inc ....E..... 631 435-9100
Hauppauge *(G-5726)*

Pitney Bowes Inc ....E..... 212 564-7548
New York *(G-10846)*

Pitney Bowes Inc ....E..... 203 356-5000
New York *(G-10847)*

Pitney Bowes Inc ....F..... 516 822-0900
Jericho *(G-6589)*

▲ Staplex Company Inc ....E..... 718 768-3333
Brooklyn *(G-2451)*

Widmer Time Recorder Company ....F..... 212 227-0405
New York *(G-11754)*

3581 Automatic Vending Machines

American Lckr SEC Systems Inc...........E..... 716 699-2773
Ellicottville *(G-4312)*

Cubic Trnsp Systems Inc ....F..... 212 255-1810
New York *(G-9129)*

Distributors Vending Corp ....F..... 914 472-8981
Ardsley *(G-388)*

Global Payment Tech Inc ....F..... 516 887-0700
Valley Stream *(G-15342)*

▲ Global Payment Tech Inc ....E..... 631 563-2500
Bohemia *(G-1019)*

Green Enviro Machine LLC ....G..... 407 461-6412
Schenectady *(G-14276)*

Vengo Inc ....G...... 866 526-7054
Bethpage *(G-845)*

3582 Commercial Laundry, Dry Clean & Pressing Mchs

Autarkic Holdings Inc ....D...... 516 371-4400
Inwood *(G-6290)*
Fowler Route Co Inc ....D...... 917 653-4640
Yonkers *(G-16311)*
▲ G A Braun Inc ....C...... 315 475-3123
North Syracuse *(G-12041)*
G A Braun Inc ....E...... 315 475-3123
Syracuse *(G-14897)*
Lynx Product Group LLC ....E...... 716 751-3100
Wilson *(G-16153)*
▼ Maxi Companies Inc ....G...... 315 446-1002
De Witt *(G-3824)*
Q Omni Inc ....G...... 914 962-2726
Yorktown Heights *(G-16370)*
Thermopatch Corporation ....D...... 315 446-8110
Syracuse *(G-15012)*
Trio Clean LLC ....F...... 518 627-4055
Amsterdam *(G-350)*

3585 Air Conditioning & Heating Eqpt

A Nuclimate Qulty Systems Inc ....F...... 315 431-0226
East Syracuse *(G-4192)*
A&S Refrigeration Equipment ....G...... 718 993-6030
Bronx *(G-1187)*
AC Air Cooling Co Inc ....F...... 718 933-1011
Bronx *(G-1190)*
Advance Energy Tech Inc ....E...... 518 371-2140
Halfmoon *(G-5490)*
Alfa Laval Kathabar Inc ....A...... 716 875-2000
Tonawanda *(G-15083)*
▼ Alfa Laval Niagara Inc ....D...... 800 426-5169
Tonawanda *(G-15084)*
▲ Atmost Refrigeration Co Inc ......G...... 518 828-2180
Hudson *(G-6149)*
Balticare Inc ....F...... 646 380-9470
New York *(G-8723)*
Besicorp Ltd ....F...... 845 336-7700
Kingston *(G-6680)*
Bombardier Trnsp Holdings USA ...D...... 607 776-4791
Bath *(G-631)*
Carrier Corporation ....A...... 315 432-6000
Syracuse *(G-14845)*
Carrier Corporation ....B...... 315 432-6000
East Syracuse *(G-4202)*
Carrier Corporation ....B...... 315 432-3844
East Syracuse *(G-4203)*
Carrier Corporation ....B...... 315 432-6000
Syracuse *(G-14844)*
Chudnow Manufacturing Co Inc .....E...... 516 593-4222
Oceanside *(G-12167)*
Cleanroom Systems Inc ....E...... 315 452-7400
North Syracuse *(G-12038)*
Coil Craft Inc ....G...... 718 369-1210
Ozone Park *(G-12459)*
Colburns AC Rfrgn ....F...... 716 569-3695
Frewsburg *(G-5050)*
▲ Cold Point Corporation ....E...... 315 339-2331
Rome *(G-13847)*
▲ Columbia Pool Accessories Inc ..G...... 718 993-0389
Bronx *(G-1229)*
Daikin Applied Americas Inc ....D...... 315 253-2771
Auburn *(G-472)*
Dundas-Jafine Inc ....E...... 716 681-9690
Alden *(G-168)*
▲ Duro Dyne Corporation ....C...... 631 249-9000
Bay Shore *(G-674)*
◆ Duro Dyne Machinery Corp ....E...... 631 249-9000
Bay Shore *(G-675)*
◆ Duro Dyne National Corp ....C...... 631 249-9000
Bay Shore *(G-676)*
Economy Pump & Motor Repr Inc ..G...... 718 433-2600
Astoria *(G-418)*
Elima-Draft Incorporated ....G...... 631 375-2830
Stony Brook *(G-14738)*
EMC Tech Inc ....F...... 716 488-9071
Falconer *(G-4539)*
Empire Air Systems LLC ....F...... 718 377-1549
West Babylon *(G-15709)*
▲ Enviromaster International LLC ...D...... 315 336-3716
Rome *(G-13848)*
Environmental Temp Systems LLC ..G...... 516 640-5818
Mineola *(G-7971)*
Foster Refrigerators Entp ....F...... 518 671-6036
Hudson *(G-6157)*

Fts Systems Inc ....D...... 845 687-5300
Stone Ridge *(G-14735)*
GM Components Holdings LLC ....B...... 716 439-2463
Lockport *(G-7079)*
GM Components Holdings LLC ....B...... 716 439-2011
Lockport *(G-7080)*
◆ Graham Corporation ....B...... 585 343-2216
Batavia *(G-616)*
Grillmaster Inc ....E...... 718 272-9191
Howard Beach *(G-6140)*
Healthway Products Company ....E...... 315 207-1410
Oswego *(G-12411)*
▲ Hoshizaki Nrtheastern Dist Ctr ...G...... 516 605-1411
Plainview *(G-12687)*
▲ Hydro-Air Components Inc ....C...... 716 827-6510
Buffalo *(G-2803)*
▲ Ice Air LLC ....E...... 914 668-4700
Mount Vernon *(G-8150)*
JE Miller Inc ....G...... 315 437-6811
East Syracuse *(G-4224)*
John F Krell Jr ....G...... 315 492-3201
Syracuse *(G-14918)*
Kedco Inc ....F...... 516 454-7800
Farmingdale *(G-4663)*
Keeler Services ....G...... 607 776-5757
Bath *(G-636)*
▲ Klearbar Inc ....G...... 516 684-9892
Port Washington *(G-12896)*
Layton Manufacturing Corp ....E...... 718 498-6000
Brooklyn *(G-2048)*
M M Tool and Manufacturing ....E...... 845 691-4140
Highland *(G-5961)*
▼ Mgr Equipment Corp ....E...... 516 239-3030
Inwood *(G-6298)*
◆ Millrock Technology Inc ....E...... 845 339-5700
Kingston *(G-6703)*
Mohawk Group Holdings Inc ....G...... 347 676-1681
New York *(G-10493)*
▲ Motivair Corporation ....E...... 716 691-9222
Amherst *(G-233)*
MSP Technologycom LLC ....B...... 631 424-7542
Centerport *(G-3257)*
▼ Nationwide Coils Inc ....G...... 914 277-7396
Mount Kisco *(G-8099)*
Northern Air Systems Inc ....E...... 585 594-5050
Rochester *(G-13584)*
Northwell Health Inc ....A...... 646 665-6000
New York *(G-10646)*
Opticool Solutions LLC ....F...... 585 347-6127
Webster *(G-15646)*
Parker-Hannifin Corporation ....D...... 716 685-4040
Lancaster *(G-6823)*
◆ Pfannenberg Inc ....D...... 716 685-6866
Lancaster *(G-6825)*
Pfannenberg Manufacturing LLC ...D...... 716 685-6866
Lancaster *(G-6826)*
Pro Metal of NY Corp ....G...... 516 285-0440
Valley Stream *(G-15353)*
◆ RE Hansen Industries Inc ....C...... 631 471-2900
Saint James *(G-14113)*
Roemac Industrial Sales Inc ....G...... 716 692-7332
North Tonawanda *(G-12088)*
▲ Rubicon Industries Corp ....E...... 718 434-4700
Brooklyn *(G-2364)*
S & V Restaurant Eqp Mfrs Inc .....E...... 718 220-1140
Bronx *(G-1356)*
Siemens Industry Inc ....E...... 716 568-0983
Buffalo *(G-2982)*
Specified Air Solutions LLC ....E...... 716 852-4400
Buffalo *(G-2991)*
Split Systems Corp ....E...... 516 223-5511
North Baldwin *(G-12008)*
◆ Standard Motor Products Inc ......B...... 718 392-0200
Long Island City *(G-7364)*
▼ Storflex Holdings Inc ....C...... 607 962-2137
Corning *(G-3721)*
Supermarket Equipment Depo Inc ..G...... 718 665-6200
Bronx *(G-1373)*
Thomson Industries Inc ....E...... 716 691-9100
Amherst *(G-248)*
Trane US Inc ....D...... 718 721-8844
Long Island City *(G-7386)*
Trane US Inc ....G...... 914 593-0303
Elmsford *(G-4436)*
Trane US Inc ....E...... 315 234-1500
East Syracuse *(G-4244)*
Trane US Inc ....E...... 518 785-1315
Latham *(G-6877)*
Trane US Inc ....E...... 585 256-2500
Rochester *(G-13771)*

Trane US Inc ....E...... 716 626-1260
Buffalo *(G-3017)*
Trane US Inc ....E...... 631 952-9477
Plainview *(G-12719)*
▲ Transit Air Inc ....E...... 607 324-0216
Hornell *(G-6112)*
▲ Universal Coolers Inc ....G...... 718 788-8621
Brooklyn *(G-2542)*
Universal Parent and Youth ....F...... 917 754-2426
Brooklyn *(G-2544)*
York International Corporation ....D...... 718 389-4152
Long Island City *(G-7410)*

3586 Measuring & Dispensing Pumps

Aptargroup Inc ....C...... 845 639-3700
Congers *(G-3608)*
▲ Charles Ross & Son Company ....D...... 631 234-0500
Hauppauge *(G-5614)*
Economy Pump & Motor Repr Inc ..G...... 718 433-2600
Astoria *(G-418)*
◆ Pulsafeeder Inc ....C...... 585 292-8000
Rochester *(G-13653)*
Schlumberger Technology Corp .....C...... 607 378-0105
Horseheads *(G-6136)*
▲ Valois of America Inc ....C...... 845 639-3700
Congers *(G-3619)*

3589 Service Ind Machines, NEC

240 Michigan Street Inc ....F...... 716 434-6010
Buffalo *(G-2611)*
Advance Food Service Co Inc ....E...... 631 242-4800
Edgewood *(G-4260)*
◆ Advance Tabco Inc ....D...... 631 242-8270
Hauppauge *(G-5578)*
▲ Airgle Corporation ....E...... 866 501-7750
Ronkonkoma *(G-13894)*
American Comfort Direct LLC ....E...... 201 364-8309
New York *(G-8548)*
Arista Coffee Inc ....F...... 347 531-0813
Maspeth *(G-7592)*
◆ Atlantic Ultraviolet Corp ....E...... 631 234-3275
Hauppauge *(G-5597)*
▲ Attias Oven Corp ....G...... 718 499-0145
Brooklyn *(G-1550)*
◆ Blue Tee Corp ....G...... 212 598-0880
New York *(G-8820)*
Bolton Point Wtr Trtmnt Plant ....G...... 607 277-0660
Ithaca *(G-6370)*
Business Advisory Services ....G...... 718 337-3740
Far Rockaway *(G-4562)*
Carts Mobile Food Eqp Corp ....E...... 718 788-5540
Brooklyn *(G-1652)*
City of Kingston ....F...... 845 331-2490
Kingston *(G-6686)*
City of Olean ....G...... 716 376-5694
Olean *(G-12228)*
City of Oneonta ....G...... 607 433-3470
Oneonta *(G-12263)*
Clearcove Systems Inc ....E...... 585 734-3012
Victor *(G-15398)*
Cresent Services Inc ....G...... 585 657-4104
Bloomfield *(G-944)*
Custom Klean Corp ....F...... 315 865-8101
Holland Patent *(G-6033)*
Dyna-Vac Equipment Inc ....F...... 315 865-8084
Stittville *(G-14734)*
▼ Econocraft Worldwide Mfg Inc ...G...... 914 966-2280
Yonkers *(G-16305)*
Empire Division Inc ....D...... 315 476-6273
Syracuse *(G-14888)*
▲ Environment-One Corporation ....E...... 518 346-6161
Schenectady *(G-14264)*
Fabco Industries Inc ....G...... 631 393-6024
Farmingdale *(G-4628)*
Fantasia International LLC ....G...... 212 869-0432
New York *(G-9470)*
Ferguson Enterprises Inc ....E...... 800 437-1146
New Hyde Park *(G-8269)*
Hobart Corporation ....E...... 585 427-9000
Rochester *(G-13470)*
▲ Hubco Inc ....E...... 716 683-5940
Alden *(G-170)*
▼ I A S National Inc ....E...... 631 423-6900
Huntington Station *(G-6249)*
IMC Teddy Food Service ....E...... 631 789-8881
Amityville *(G-275)*
▲ Integrated Water Management ...G...... 607 844-4276
Dryden *(G-4039)*
▲ Key High Vacuum Products Inc ...E...... 631 584-5959
Nesconset *(G-8219)*

Employee Codes: A=Over 500 employees, B=251-500
C=101-250, D=51-100, E=20-50, F=10-19, G=5-9   2020 Harris
New York Manufacturers Directory   745

S I C

◆ Kinplex Corp ....E 631 242-4800
  Hauppauge (G-5684)

Kinplex Corp ....E 631 242-4800
  Edgewood (G-4274)

Klee Corp ....G 585 272-0320
  Rochester (G-13503)

◆ Korin Inc ....E 212 587-7021
  New York (G-10128)

Liquid Industries Inc ....G 716 628-2999
  Niagara Falls (G-11947)

Menpin Supply Corp ....F 718 415-4168
  Brooklyn (G-2136)

Metro Group Inc ....D 718 729-7200
  Long Island City (G-7295)

Metro Lube ....G 718 947-1167
  Rego Park (G-13080)

National Vac Envmtl Svcs Corp ....E 518 743-0563
  Glens Falls (G-5260)

Neptune Soft Water Inc ....F 315 446-5151
  Syracuse (G-14950)

New Windsor Waste Water Plant ....F 845 561-2550
  New Windsor (G-8374)

Ossining Village of Inc ....G 914 202-9668
  Ossining (G-12406)

Oxford Cleaners ....G 212 734-0006
  New York (G-10724)

▲ Oyster Bay Pump Works Inc ....F 516 933-4500
  Hicksville (G-5937)

Pathfinder 103 Inc ....G 315 363-4260
  Oneida (G-12253)

Pentair Water Pool and Spa Inc ....E 845 452-5500
  Lagrangeville (G-6753)

▲ Pleatco LLC ....G 516 609-0200
  Glen Cove (G-5198)

Power Scrub It Inc ....F 516 997-2500
  Westbury (G-15918)

Pure Planet Waters LLC ....F 718 676-7900
  Brooklyn (G-2306)

R C Kolstad Water Corp ....G 585 216-2230
  Ontario (G-12298)

▲ R-S Restaurant Eqp Mfg Corp ....F 212 925-0335
  New York (G-10969)

Roger & Sons Inc ....G 212 226-4734
  New York (G-11074)

Strategies North America Inc ....G 716 945-6053
  Salamanca (G-14130)

▲ Toga Manufacturing Inc ....G 631 242-4800
  Edgewood (G-4289)

Water Energy Systems LLC ....G 844 822-7665
  New York (G-11729)

▲ Water Technologies Inc ....G 315 986-0000
  Macedon (G-7471)

Wetlook Detailing Inc ....G 212 390-8877
  Brooklyn (G-2580)

Yr Blanc & Co LLC ....G 716 800-3999
  Buffalo (G-3053)

3592 Carburetors, Pistons, Rings & Valves

▲ Fcmp Inc ....F 716 692-4623
  Tonawanda (G-15103)

Helio Precision Products Inc ....G 585 697-5434
  Rochester (G-13464)

▲ ITT Engineered Valves LLC ....D 662 257-6982
  Seneca Falls (G-14365)

Valvetech Inc ....E 315 548-4551
  Phelps (G-12610)

3593 Fluid Power Cylinders & Actuators

▲ A K Allen Co Inc ....C 516 747-5450
  Melville (G-7753)

Actuant Corporation ....E 607 753-8276
  Cortland (G-3753)

▲ Ameritool Mfg Inc ....E 315 668-2172
  Central Square (G-3294)

Direkt Force LLC ....E 716 652-3022
  East Aurora (G-4085)

▲ ITT Enidine Inc ....B 716 662-1900
  Orchard Park (G-12356)

Precision Mechanisms Corp ....E 516 333-5955
  Westbury (G-15919)

Skytravel (usa) LLC ....E 518 888-2610
  Schenectady (G-14306)

Springville Mfg Co Inc ....E 716 592-4957
  Springville (G-14597)

Starcyl USA Corp ....F 877 782-7295
  Champlain (G-3316)

Tactair Fluid Controls Inc ....C 315 451-3928
  Liverpool (G-7044)

Triumph Actuation Systems LLC ....D 516 378-0162
  Freeport (G-5030)

Young & Franklin Inc ....D 315 457-3110
  Liverpool (G-7051)

3594 Fluid Power Pumps & Motors

Atlantic Industrial Tech Inc ....E 631 234-3131
  Shirley (G-14415)

Huck International Inc ....C 845 331-7300
  Kingston (G-6694)

Hydroacoustics Inc ....F 585 359-1000
  Henrietta (G-5856)

ITT Corporation ....D 315 568-2811
  Seneca Falls (G-14364)

ITT Inc ....C 914 641-2000
  White Plains (G-16017)

◆ ITT LLC ....B 914 641-2000
  White Plains (G-16020)

Parker-Hannifin Corporation ....C 716 686-6400
  Lancaster (G-6821)

Parker-Hannifin Corporation ....B 631 231-3737
  Hauppauge (G-5736)

Parker-Hannifin Corporation ....C 585 425-7000
  Fairport (G-4512)

Trench & Marine Pump Co Inc ....F 212 423-9098
  Bronx (G-1381)

Triumph Actuation Systems LLC ....D 516 378-0162
  Freeport (G-5030)

3596 Scales & Balances, Exc Laboratory

Buffalo Scale and Sup Co Inc ....G 716 847-2880
  Buffalo (G-2682)

◆ Circuits & Systems Inc ....E 516 593-4301
  East Rockaway (G-4171)

◆ Itin Scale Co Inc ....E 718 336-5900
  Brooklyn (G-1974)

Measupro Inc ....F 845 425-8777
  Spring Valley (G-14579)

S R Instruments Inc ....E 716 693-5977
  Tonawanda (G-15136)

Scale-Tronix Inc ....E 914 948-8117
  Skaneateles (G-14456)

Weighing & Systems Tech Inc ....G 518 274-2797
  Troy (G-15197)

3599 Machinery & Eqpt, Indl & Commercial, NEC

A & G Precision Corp ....F 631 957-5613
  Amityville (G-255)

A & L Machine Company Inc ....G 631 463-3111
  Islandia (G-6323)

A P Manufacturing ....G 909 228-3049
  Bohemia (G-959)

A R V Precision Mfg Inc ....G 631 293-9643
  Farmingdale (G-4569)

A-Line Technologies Inc ....F 607 772-2439
  Binghamton (G-850)

Absolute Manufacturing Inc ....G 631 563-7466
  Bohemia (G-962)

Acad Design Corp ....G 585 254-6960
  Rochester (G-13198)

▲ Accede Mold & Tool Co Inc ....D 585 254-6490
  Rochester (G-13199)

▲ Accurate Industrial Machining ......G 631 242-0566
  Holbrook (G-5983)

Accurate McHning Incorporation ....F 315 689-1428
  Elbridge (G-4295)

Accurate Tool & Die LLC ....G 585 254-2830
  Rochester (G-13202)

Accurate Welding Service Inc ....G 516 333-1730
  Westbury (G-15860)

Acme Industries of W Babylon ....F 631 737-5231
  Ronkonkoma (G-13887)

▲ Acro Industries Inc ....C 585 254-3661
  Rochester (G-13204)

Acro-Fab Ltd ....G 315 564-6688
  Hannibal (G-5542)

Active Manufacturing Inc ....F 607 775-3162
  Kirkwood (G-6728)

Adaptive Mfg Tech Inc ....F 631 580-5400
  Ronkonkoma (G-13888)

Addison Precision Mfg Corp ....D 585 254-1386
  Rochester (G-13206)

Adria Machine & Tool Inc ....G 585 889-3360
  Scottsville (G-14338)

Advan-Tech Manufacturing Inc ....E 716 667-1500
  Orchard Park (G-12337)

Advance Precision Industries ....G 631 491-0910
  West Babylon (G-15682)

Advanced Machine Inc ....F 585 423-8255
  Rochester (G-13211)

Advanced Mfg Techniques ....G 518 877-8560
  Clifton Park (G-3460)

Advantage Machining Inc ....F 716 731-6418
  Niagara Falls (G-11901)

Aero Specialties Manufacturing ....F 631 242-7200
  Deer Park (G-3831)

AG Tech Welding Corp ....G 845 398-0005
  Tappan (G-15033)

Aj Genco Mch Sp McHy Rdout Svc ....F 716 664-4925
  Falconer (G-4532)

Akraturn Mfg Inc ....D 607 775-2802
  Kirkwood (G-6729)

Aldrich Solutions Incorporated ....G 716 634-1790
  Williamsville (G-16118)

Aljo Precision Products Inc ....E 516 420-4419
  Old Bethpage (G-12213)

Aljo-Gefa Precision Mfg LLC ....E 516 420-4419
  Old Bethpage (G-12214)

Alkemy Machine LLC ....G 585 436-8730
  Rochester (G-13217)

Allen Tool Phoenix Inc ....E 315 463-7533
  East Syracuse (G-4194)

Alliance Innovative Mfg Inc ....E 716 822-1626
  Lackawanna (G-6739)

Allied Industrial Products Co ....G 716 664-3893
  Jamestown (G-6493)

▲ Aloi Solutions LLC ....E 585 292-0920
  Rochester (G-13223)

Alpha Manufacturing Corp ....F 631 249-3700
  Farmingdale (G-4581)

Alpine Machine Inc ....F 607 272-1344
  Ithaca (G-6362)

Alro Machine Tool & Die Co Inc ....F 631 226-5020
  Lindenhurst (G-6939)

Altamont Spray Welding Inc ....G 518 861-8870
  Altamont (G-192)

Amacon Corporation ....E 631 293-1888
  West Babylon (G-15686)

American Linear Manufacturers ....F 516 333-1351
  Westbury (G-15867)

▲ American Wire Tie Inc ....F 716 337-2412
  North Collins (G-12023)

Ancon Gear & Instrument Corp ....F 631 694-5255
  Amityville (G-256)

▲ Antab Mch Sprfinishing Lab Inc .....G 585 865-8290
  Rochester (G-13239)

Applied Technology Mfg Corp ....F 607 687-2200
  Owego (G-12428)

◆ Arbe Machinery Inc ....E 631 756-2477
  Farmingdale (G-4586)

Archimedes Products Inc ....E 631 589-1215
  Bohemia (G-975)

Architectural Coatings Inc ....F 718 418-9584
  Brooklyn (G-1524)

Argencord Machine Corp Inc ....F 631 842-8990
  Copiague (G-3646)

Argo General Machine Work Inc ....G 718 392-4605
  Long Island City (G-7165)

Armstrong Mold Corporation ....G 315 437-1517
  East Syracuse (G-4197)

Arrow Grinding Inc ....E 716 693-3333
  Tonawanda (G-15086)

Art Precision Metal Products ....F 631 842-8889
  Copiague (G-3647)

Artisan Machining Inc ....E 631 589-1416
  Ronkonkoma (G-13909)

Artisan Management Group Inc ....G 716 569-4094
  Frewsburg (G-5049)

Astra Tool & Instrument Mfg ....E 914 747-3863
  Hawthorne (G-5809)

Atlantis Equipment Corporation ....F 518 733-5910
  Stephentown (G-14730)

Atwood Tool & Machine Inc ....E 607 648-6543
  Chenango Bridge (G-3367)

Auburn Bearing & Mfg Inc ....G 315 986-7600
  Macedon (G-7460)

AW Mack Manufacturing Co Inc ....E 845 452-4050
  Poughkeepsie (G-12947)

B & B Precision Mfg Inc ....E 585 226-6226
  Avon (G-511)

B & R Industries Inc ....F 631 736-2275
  Medford (G-7698)

B C Manufacturing Inc ....G 585 482-1080
  West Henrietta (G-15786)

Babbitt Bearings Inc ....D 315 479-6603
  Syracuse (G-14824)

Babbitt Bearings Incorporated ....D 315 479-6603
  Syracuse (G-14825)

Badge Machine Products Inc ....E 585 394-0330
  Canandaigua (G-3125)

Barton Tool Inc ... G ... 716 665-2801
Falconer *(G-4535)*
BEAM Manufacturing Corp ... G ... 631 253-2724
West Babylon *(G-15694)*
Belden Manufacturing Inc ... E ... 607 238-0998
Kirkwood *(G-6730)*
Bick & Heintz Inc ... F ... 315 733-7577
Utica *(G-15241)*
Bill Shea Enterprises Inc ... G ... 585 343-2284
Batavia *(G-604)*
Birch Machine & Tool Inc ... G ... 716 735-9802
Middleport *(G-7887)*
Blading Services Unlimited LLC ... F ... 315 875-5313
Canastota *(G-3149)*
Bliss Machine Inc ... F ... 585 492-5128
Arcade *(G-370)*
Blue Manufacturing Co Inc ... G ... 607 796-2463
Millport *(G-7950)*
Bms Manufacturing Co Inc ... E ... 607 535-2426
Watkins Glen *(G-15613)*
▲ **Brach Machine Inc** ... F ... 585 343-9134
Batavia *(G-606)*
Breed Enterprises Inc ... G ... 585 388-0126
Fairport *(G-4490)*
Broadalbin Manufacturing Corp ... E ... 518 883-5313
Broadalbin *(G-1172)*
Broda Machine Co Inc ... F ... 716 297-3221
Niagara Falls *(G-11910)*
Bruce Pierce ... G ... 716 731-9310
Sanborn *(G-14138)*
Bryant Machine & Development ... F ... 716 894-8282
Buffalo *(G-2667)*
Bryant Machine Co Inc ... F ... 716 894-8282
Buffalo *(G-2668)*
Bryant Manufacturing Wny Inc ... G ... 716 894-8282
Buffalo *(G-2669)*
Buxton Machine and Tool Co Inc ... F ... 716 876-2312
Buffalo *(G-2687)*
C & H Machining Inc ... F ... 631 582-6737
Bohemia *(G-984)*
C & T Tool & Instrument Co ... E ... 718 429-1253
Woodside *(G-16199)*
C L Precision Machine & Tl Co ... G ... 718 651-8475
Woodside *(G-16200)*
C R C Manufacturing Inc ... F ... 585 254-8820
Rochester *(G-13291)*
◆ **Calvary Design Team Inc** ... C ... 585 347-6127
Webster *(G-15632)*
Canfield Machine & Tool LLC ... E ... 315 593-8062
Fulton *(G-5056)*
▲ **Capy Machine Shop Inc** ... E ... 631 694-6916
Melville *(G-7765)*
Carballo Contract Machining ... G ... 315 594-2511
Wolcott *(G-16162)*
Carbaugh Tool Company Inc ... E ... 607 739-3293
Elmira *(G-4341)*
Cardish Machine Works Inc ... E ... 518 273-2329
Watervliet *(G-15599)*
Casey Machine Co Inc ... D ... 716 651-0150
Lancaster *(G-6800)*
Catapult ... G ... 323 839-6204
New York *(G-8934)*
Cayuga Tool and Die Inc ... G ... 607 533-7400
Groton *(G-5482)*
CBM Fabrications Inc ... E ... 518 399-8023
Ballston Lake *(G-559)*
Cda Machine Inc ... G ... 585 671-5959
Webster *(G-15633)*
Cdl Manufacturing Inc ... G ... 585 589-2533
Albion *(G-155)*
▲ **Cem Machine Inc** ... E ... 315 493-4258
Carthage *(G-3195)*
Centerless Technology Inc ... F ... 585 436-2240
Rochester *(G-13305)*
Certified Prcsion McHining Inc ... G ... 631 244-3671
Bohemia *(G-986)*
▲ **Cetek Inc** ... E ... 845 452-3510
Poughkeepsie *(G-12948)*
Charl Industries Inc ... E ... 631 234-0100
Hauppauge *(G-5613)*
Chassix Automotive Corp ... F ... 585 815-1700
Batavia *(G-610)*
Chautqua Prcsion Machining Inc ... F ... 716 763-3752
Ashville *(G-410)*
◆ **Chocovision Corporation** ... F ... 845 473-8003
Poughkeepsie *(G-12949)*
▼ **City Gear Inc** ... G ... 914 450-4746
Irvington *(G-6306)*
Cjn Machinery Corp ... G ... 631 244-8030
Holbrook *(G-5989)*

Classic Auto Crafts Inc ... G ... 518 966-8003
Greenville *(G-5467)*
Cnc Manufacturing Corp ... E ... 718 728-6800
Long Island City *(G-7187)*
Conesus Lake Association Inc ... E ... 585 346-6864
Lakeville *(G-6774)*
Conrad Blasius Equipment Co ... G ... 516 753-1200
Plainview *(G-12672)*
Converter Design Inc ... G ... 518 745-7138
Glens Falls *(G-5245)*
Corbett Stves Pttern Works Inc ... E ... 585 546-7109
Rochester *(G-13326)*
Cortland Machine and Tool Co ... F ... 607 756-5852
Cortland *(G-3761)*
Courser Inc ... E ... 607 739-3861
Elmira *(G-4346)*
Craftsman Manufacturing Co In ... G ... 585 426-5780
Rochester *(G-13327)*
Crowley Fabg Machining Co Inc ... E ... 607 484-0299
Endicott *(G-4447)*
▼ **Cubitek Inc** ... F ... 631 665-6900
Brentwood *(G-1117)*
D J Crowell Co Inc ... G ... 716 684-3343
Alden *(G-167)*
D K Machine Inc ... F ... 518 747-0626
Fort Edward *(G-4938)*
D-K Manufacturing Corp ... E ... 315 592-4327
Fulton *(G-5057)*
Danfoss Silicon Power LLC ... F ... 515 239-6376
Utica *(G-15252)*
Darco Manufacturing Inc ... E ... 315 432-8905
Syracuse *(G-14874)*
Daves Precision Machine Shop ... F ... 845 626-7263
Kerhonkson *(G-6659)*
David Fehlman ... G ... 315 455-8888
Syracuse *(G-14875)*
Deck Bros Inc ... E ... 716 852-0262
Buffalo *(G-2723)*
Delaney Machine Products Ltd ... G ... 631 225-1032
Lindenhurst *(G-6948)*
Dennies Manufacturing Inc ... E ... 585 393-4646
Canandaigua *(G-3130)*
Denny Machine Co Inc ... E ... 716 873-6865
Buffalo *(G-2726)*
Dern Moore Machine Company Inc ... G ... 716 433-6243
Lockport *(G-7068)*
Derosa Fabrications Inc ... E ... 631 563-0640
Bohemia *(G-1004)*
▼ **Devin Mfg Inc** ... F ... 585 496-5770
Arcade *(G-372)*
Dewey Machine & Tool Inc ... G ... 607 749-3930
Homer *(G-6061)*
DMD Machining Technology Inc ... G ... 585 659-8180
Kendall *(G-6647)*
Dormitory Authority - State NY ... G ... 631 434-1487
Brentwood *(G-1120)*
Dougs Machine Shop Inc ... G ... 585 905-0004
Canandaigua *(G-3131)*
Dragow Inc ... E ... 585 786-3603
Gainesville *(G-5081)*
Duetto Integrated Systems Inc ... F ... 631 851-0102
Islandia *(G-6331)*
Dunlap Machine LLC ... F ... 315 926-1013
Marion *(G-7568)*
Dyna-Tech Quality Inc ... G ... 585 458-9970
Rochester *(G-13358)*
Dynak Inc ... F ... 585 271-2255
Churchville *(G-3411)*
E & R Machine Inc ... E ... 716 434-6639
Lockport *(G-7071)*
E B Trottnow Machine Spc ... F ... 716 694-0600
Eden *(G-4254)*
E J Willis Company Inc ... F ... 315 891-7602
Middleville *(G-7940)*
▲ **Eagle Bridge Machine & Tl Inc** ... E ... 518 686-4541
Eagle Bridge *(G-4071)*
Eagle Instruments Inc ... G ... 914 939-6843
Port Chester *(G-12818)*
East Side Machine Inc ... E ... 585 265-4560
Webster *(G-15639)*
Eastern Machine and Electric ... G ... 716 284-8271
Niagara Falls *(G-11922)*
Eastern Precision Machining ... G ... 631 286-4758
Bellport *(G-797)*
EDM Mfg ... G ... 631 669-1966
Babylon *(G-520)*
Edr Industries Inc ... F ... 516 868-1928
Freeport *(G-4993)*
▲ **Edsal Machine Products Inc** ... F ... 718 439-9163
Brooklyn *(G-1784)*

▲ **Edwin J McKenica & Sons Inc** ... F ... 716 823-4646
Buffalo *(G-2739)*
Ehrlich Enterprises Inc ... F ... 631 956-0690
Wyandanch *(G-16245)*
Electro Form Corp ... F ... 607 722-6404
Binghamton *(G-874)*
Elite Machine Inc ... G ... 585 289-4733
Manchester *(G-7527)*
Elite Precise Manufacturer LLC ... G ... 518 993-3040
Fort Plain *(G-4946)*
Elite Turning & Machining Corp ... E ... 585 445-8765
Rochester *(G-13383)*
Emcom Industries Inc ... G ... 716 852-3711
Buffalo *(G-2743)*
Emory Machine & Tool Co Inc ... E ... 585 436-9610
Farmington *(G-4771)*
Empire Plastics Inc ... E ... 607 754-9132
Endwell *(G-4479)*
Endicott Precision Inc ... C ... 607 754-7076
Endicott *(G-4451)*
Engineering Mfg Tech LLC ... D ... 607 754-7111
Endicott *(G-4453)*
Estebania Enterprises Inc ... G ... 585 529-9330
Rochester *(G-13401)*
ET Oakes Corporation ... E ... 631 232-0002
Hauppauge *(G-5648)*
ET Precision Optics Inc ... D ... 585 254-2560
Rochester *(G-13402)*
Etna Tool & Die Corporation ... F ... 212 475-4350
New York *(G-9414)*
Euro Gear (usa) Inc ... G ... 518 578-1775
Plattsburgh *(G-12746)*
Everfab Inc ... D ... 716 655-1550
East Aurora *(G-4086)*
Exact Machining & Mfg ... G ... 585 334-7090
Rochester *(G-13403)*
Excel Industries Inc ... E ... 716 542-5468
Clarence *(G-3434)*
Excel Machine Technologies Inc ... F ... 585 426-1911
Rochester *(G-13404)*
Exigo Precision Inc ... G ... 585 254-5818
Rochester *(G-13406)*
Expert Machine Services Inc ... G ... 718 786-1200
Long Island City *(G-7218)*
F M L Industries Inc ... G ... 607 749-7273
Homer *(G-6062)*
Fabtechny LLC ... F ... 845 338-2000
Kingston *(G-6691)*
Falk Precision Inc ... E ... 315 437-4545
East Syracuse *(G-4209)*
Farrant Screw Machine Products ... G ... 585 457-3213
Java Village *(G-6564)*
Felton Machine Co Inc ... E ... 716 215-9001
Niagara Falls *(G-11927)*
Fenbar Prcision Machinists Inc ... F ... 914 769-5506
Thornwood *(G-15069)*
Fermer Precision Inc ... D ... 315 822-6371
Ilion *(G-6277)*
Ferraro Manufacturing Company ... G ... 631 752-1509
Farmingdale *(G-4630)*
Ferro Machine Co Inc ... G ... 845 398-3641
Orangeburg *(G-12316)*
▲ **Finesse Creations Inc** ... F ... 718 692-2100
Brooklyn *(G-1846)*
Five Star Industries Inc ... E ... 716 674-2589
West Seneca *(G-15847)*
Flashflo Manufacturing Inc ... F ... 716 826-9500
Buffalo *(G-2753)*
Forbes Precision Inc ... F ... 585 865-7069
Rochester *(G-13419)*
Fortech Inc ... G ... 315 478-2048
Syracuse *(G-14894)*
Four K Machine Shop Inc ... G ... 516 997-0752
Westbury *(G-15886)*
Frederick Machine Repair Inc ... G ... 716 332-0104
Buffalo *(G-2760)*
Fronhofer Tool Company Inc ... E ... 518 692-2496
Cossayuna *(G-3799)*
Fross Industries Inc ... E ... 716 297-0652
Niagara Falls *(G-11930)*
Fulton Tool Co Inc ... E ... 315 598-2900
Fulton *(G-5061)*
Fultonville Machine & Tool Co ... F ... 518 853-4441
Fultonville *(G-5079)*
Future Screw Machine Pdts Inc ... F ... 631 765-1610
Southold *(G-14543)*
G & G C Machine & Tool Co Inc ... G ... 516 873-0999
Westbury *(G-15887)*
Gamma Instrument Co Inc ... G ... 516 486-5526
Farmingdale *(G-4635)*

S
I
C

Gefa Instrument Corp	F	516 420-4419		
Old Bethpage (G-12216)				
Genco John	G	716 483-5446		
Jamestown (G-6512)				
General Cutting Inc	F	631 580-5011		
Ronkonkoma (G-13941)				
Genesis Machining Corp	F	516 377-1197		
North Baldwin (G-12005)				
Gentner Precision Components	G	315 597-5734		
Palmyra (G-12488)				
Giuliante Machine Tool Inc	E	914 835-0008		
Peekskill (G-12551)				
Gli-Dex Sales Corp	E	716 692-6501		
North Tonawanda (G-12070)				
Global Precision Inds Inc	F	585 254-0010		
Rochester (G-13446)				
Globe Grinding Corp	F	631 694-1970		
Copiague (G-3655)				
Gmr Manufacturing Inc	G	631 582-2600		
Central Islip (G-3277)				
Gorden Automotive Equipment	F	716 674-2700		
West Seneca (G-15849)				
Gpp Post-Closing Inc	E	585 334-4640		
Rush (G-14072)				
▲ Greno Industries Inc	G	518 393-4195		
Scotia (G-14330)				
Grind	G	646 558-3250		
New York (G-9678)				
H C Young Tool & Machine Co	G	315 463-0663		
Syracuse (G-14906)				
H F Brown Machine Co Inc	F	315 732-6129		
Utica (G-15269)				
H T Specialty Inc	F	585 458-4060		
Rochester (G-13456)				
Hagner Industries Inc	G	716 873-5720		
Buffalo (G-2789)				
Hartman Enterprises Inc	G	315 363-7300		
Oneida (G-12245)				
Harwitt Industries Inc	F	516 623-9787		
Freeport (G-5002)				
Haskell Machine & Tool Inc	F	607 749-2421		
Homer (G-6063)				
Hebeler Process Solutions LLC	E	716 873-9300		
Tonawanda (G-15112)				
Herbert Wolf Corp	G	718 392-2424		
Long Island City (G-7241)				
Herkimer Tool & Machining Corp	F	315 866-2110		
Herkimer (G-5865)				
Hes Inc	G	607 359-2974		
Addison (G-5)				
Hi-Tech Cnc Machining Corp	G	914 668-5090		
Mount Vernon (G-8149)				
Hi-Tech Industries NY Inc	E	607 217-7361		
Johnson City (G-6601)				
Hoercher Industries Inc	G	585 398-2982		
East Rochester (G-4164)				
Hohl Machine & Conveyor Co Inc	E	716 882-7210		
Buffalo (G-2799)				
Howe Machine & Tool Corp	F	516 931-5687		
Bethpage (G-836)				
▲ HSM Machine Works Inc	E	631 924-6600		
Medford (G-7712)				
Hubbard Tool and Die Corp	E	315 337-7840		
Rome (G-13851)				
Hunter Machine Inc	E	585 924-7480		
Victor (G-15412)				
Hw Specialties Co Inc	F	631 589-0745		
Bohemia (G-1020)				
I D Machine Inc	D	607 796-2549		
Elmira (G-4359)				
Imperial Instrument Corp	G	516 739-6644		
Westbury (G-15895)				
Indian Springs Mfg Co Inc	F	315 635-6101		
Baldwinsville (G-549)				
Indus Precision Manufacturing	F	845 268-0782		
Congers (G-3616)				
Industrial Precision Pdts Inc	E	315 343-4421		
Oswego (G-12412)				
Industrial Services of Wny	G	716 799-7788		
Niagara Falls (G-11941)				
▲ Industrial Tool & Die Co Inc	E	518 273-7383		
Troy (G-15172)				
Ingleside Machine Co Inc	D	585 924-3046		
Farmington (G-4774)				
▼ Innex Industries Inc	E	585 247-3575		
Rochester (G-13478)				
Integrity Tool Incorporated	F	315 524-4409		
Ontario (G-12291)				
Interactive Instruments Inc	G	518 347-0955		
Scotia (G-14332)				

International Climbing Mchs	G	607 288-4001		
Ithaca (G-6388)				
Ironshore Holdings Inc	F	315 457-1052		
Liverpool (G-7017)				
Island Instrument Corporation	G	631 243-0550		
Deer Park (G-3883)				
Island Machine Inc	G	518 562-1232		
Plattsburgh (G-12754)				
▲ ISO Plastics Corp	D	914 663-8300		
Mount Vernon (G-8152)				
J & G Machine & Tool Co Inc	F	315 310-7130		
Marion (G-7571)				
J & J Swiss Precision Inc	E	631 243-5584		
Deer Park (G-3884)				
J & J TI Die Mfg & Stampg Corp	G	845 228-0242		
Carmel (G-3186)				
J B Tool & Die Co Inc	E	516 333-1480		
Westbury (G-15897)				
J F Machining Company Inc	G	716 791-3910		
Ransomville (G-13066)				
J R S Precision Machining	G	631 737-1330		
Ronkonkoma (G-13951)				
J T D Stamping Co Inc	E	631 643-4144		
West Babylon (G-15717)				
J T Systematic	G	607 754-0929		
Endwell (G-4480)				
Jack Merkel Inc	E	631 234-2600		
Hauppauge (G-5680)				
Jacobi Tool & Die Mfg Inc	E	631 736-5394		
Medford (G-7714)				
▲ Jam Industries Inc	E	585 458-9830		
Rochester (G-13487)				
Jamar Precision Products Co	E	631 254-0234		
Deer Park (G-3885)				
Jamestown Iron Works Inc	F	716 665-2818		
Falconer (G-4548)				
Javcon Machine Inc	G	631 586-1890		
Deer Park (G-3887)				
Javin Machine Corp	F	631 643-3322		
West Babylon (G-15719)				
Jet Sew Corporation	E	315 896-2683		
Barneveld (G-592)				
Jewelers Machinist Co Inc	G	631 661-5020		
Babylon (G-521)				
JF Machine Shop Inc	G	631 491-7273		
West Babylon (G-15720)				
John J Mazur Inc	G	631 242-4554		
Deer Park (G-3889)				
Johnnys Machine Shop	G	631 338-9733		
West Babylon (G-15721)				
Johnson Mch & Fibr Pdts Co Inc	F	716 665-2003		
Jamestown (G-6527)				
Johnston Precision Inc	G	315 253-4181		
Auburn (G-483)				
Jolin Machining Corp	E	631 589-1305		
Bohemia (G-1029)				
Jordan Machine Inc	G	585 647-3585		
Rochester (G-13496)				
▲ Jrb Machine-Tool Inc	E	716 206-0355		
Buffalo (G-2825)				
Jt Precision Inc	E	716 795-3860		
Barker (G-591)				
Just In Time Cnc Machinin	G	585 247-3850		
Rochester (G-13499)				
Just In Time Cnc Machining	F	585 335-2010		
Dansville (G-3820)				
JW Burg Machine & Tool Inc	G	716 434-0015		
Clarence Center (G-3447)				
▲ K & H Industries Inc	E	716 312-0088		
Hamburg (G-5511)				
K & H Precision Products Inc	E	585 624-4894		
Honeoye Falls (G-6076)				
K D M Die Company Inc	G	716 828-9000		
Buffalo (G-2828)				
K Hein Machines Inc	G	607 748-1546		
Vestal (G-15380)				
Kal Manufacturing Corporation	E	585 265-4310		
Webster (G-15644)				
▲ Keller Technology Corporation	C	716 693-3840		
Tonawanda (G-15117)				
Kenwell Corporation	G	315 592-4263		
Fulton (G-5068)				
Keyes Machine Works Inc	G	585 426-5059		
Gates (G-5141)				
◆ Kimber Mfg Inc	G	888 243-4522		
Yonkers (G-16324)				
Kimber Mfg Inc	E	406 758-2222		
Yonkers (G-16325)				
Kinemotive Corporation	E	631 249-6440		
Farmingdale (G-4666)				

▲ KMA Corporation	G	518 743-1330		
Glens Falls (G-5254)				
Knise & Krick Inc	E	315 422-3516		
Syracuse (G-14927)				
Konar Precision Mfg Inc	G	631 242-4466		
Deer Park (G-3892)				
▲ Kondor Technologies Inc	F	631 471-8832		
Ronkonkoma (G-13959)				
Kramartron Precision Inc	G	845 368-3668		
Tallman (G-15031)				
Kronenberger Mfg Corp	G	585 385-2340		
East Rochester (G-4166)				
Krug Precision Inc	G	516 944-9350		
Manhasset (G-7536)				
Kurtz Truck Equipment Inc	F	607 849-3468		
Marathon (G-7558)				
Kurz and Zobel Inc	G	585 254-9060		
Rochester (G-13506)				
Kz Precision Inc	G	716 683-3202		
Lancaster (G-6812)				
L & S Metals Inc	E	716 692-6865		
North Tonawanda (G-12076)				
L P R Precision Parts & Tls Co	F	631 293-7334		
Farmingdale (G-4667)				
Labco of Palmyra Inc	F	315 597-5202		
Palmyra (G-12490)				
▲ Lagasse Works Inc	E	315 946-9202		
Lyons (G-7450)				
Lakeside Industries Inc	G	716 386-3031		
Bemus Point (G-812)				
Lakeside Precision Inc	E	716 366-5030		
Dunkirk (G-4060)				
Laser & Electron Beam Inc	G	603 626-6080		
New York (G-10175)				
Lasticks Aerospace Inc	F	631 242-8484		
Bay Shore (G-689)				
Leetech Manufacturing Inc	G	631 563-1442		
Bohemia (G-1033)				
Lewis Machine Co Inc	G	718 625-0799		
Brooklyn (G-2065)				
Liberty Machine & Tool	G	315 699-3242		
Cicero (G-3421)				
▲ Linda Tool & Die Corporation	E	718 522-2066		
Brooklyn (G-2075)				
▲ Lodolce Machine Co Inc	E	845 246-7017		
Saugerties (G-14204)				
Loughlin Manufacturing Corp	F	631 585-4422		
Bohemia (G-1037)				
Lovejoy Chaplet Corporation	E	518 686-5232		
Hoosick Falls (G-6084)				
▲ Lwa Works Inc	E	518 271-8360		
Watervliet (G-15604)				
▲ M & S Precision Machine Co LLC	F	518 747-1193		
Queensbury (G-13048)				
Macro Tool & Machine Company	G	845 223-3824		
Lagrangeville (G-6750)				
Maehr Industries Inc	F	631 924-1661		
Bellport (G-802)				
▲ Magellan Aerospace Bethel Inc	C	203 798-9373		
Corona (G-3743)				
Magellan Aerospace NY Inc	C	631 589-2440		
Bohemia (G-1041)				
▲ Makamah Enterprises Inc	F	631 231-0200		
Hauppauge (G-5705)				
Malisa Branko Inc	F	631 225-9741		
Copiague (G-3663)				
Manth Mfg Inc	E	716 693-6525		
Tonawanda (G-15120)				
Mar-A-Thon Filters Inc	G	631 957-4774		
Lindenhurst (G-6957)				
Mardon Tool & Die Co Inc	F	585 254-4545		
Rochester (G-13535)				
◆ Marksmen Manufacturing Corp	E	800 305-6942		
Deer Park (G-3903)				
Massapqua Prcsion McHining Ltd	G	631 789-1485		
Amityville (G-295)				
▲ Master Machine Incorporated	G	716 487-2555		
Jamestown (G-6532)				
Matic Industries Inc	G	718 886-5470		
College Point (G-3553)				
Matrix Machining Corp	G	631 643-6690		
West Babylon (G-15729)				
May Tool & Die Inc	G	716 695-1033		
Tonawanda (G-15121)				
Mayfair Machine Company Inc	G	631 981-6644		
Ronkonkoma (G-13971)				
Mc Ivor Manufacturing Inc	G	716 825-1808		
Buffalo (G-2864)				
McGuigan Inc	E	631 750-6222		
Bohemia (G-1045)				

Meade Machine Co Inc ....G...... 315 923-1703
Clyde (G-3492)

Medco Machine LLC ....G...... 315 986-2109
Walworth (G-15477)

Mega Tool & Mfg Corp ....E...... 607 734-8398
Elmira (G-4363)

Meridian Manufacturing Inc ....G...... 518 885-0450
Ballston Spa (G-581)

Metal Parts Manufacturing Inc ....G...... 315 831-2530
Barneveld (G-593)

Metro Machining & Fabricating ....G...... 718 545-0104
Woodside (G-16214)

Micro Instrument Corp ....D...... 585 458-3150
Rochester (G-13545)

Micro-Tech Machine Inc ....E...... 315 331-6671
Newark (G-11846)

Miles Machine Inc ....F...... 716 484-6026
Jamestown (G-6533)

Milex Precision Inc ....F...... 631 595-2393
Bay Shore (G-692)

Miller Technology Inc ....G...... 631 694-2224
Farmingdale (G-4684)

Minutemen Precsn McHning Tool ......E...... 631 467-4900
Ronkonkoma (G-13975)

Mitchell Machine Tool LLC ....G...... 585 254-7520
Rochester (G-13552)

▲ Modern Packaging Inc ....D...... 631 595-2437
Deer Park (G-3907)

Modern-TEC Manufacturing Inc........G...... 716 625-8700
Lockport (G-7094)

Morco Products Corp ....F...... 718 853-4005
Brooklyn (G-2171)

Ms Machining Inc ....G...... 607 723-1105
Binghamton (G-900)

Ms Spares LLC ....G...... 607 223-3024
Clay (G-3451)

Muller Tool Inc ....E...... 716 895-3658
Buffalo (G-2874)

Nassau Tool Works Inc ....E...... 631 328-7031
Bay Shore (G-697)

Neptune Machine Inc ....E...... 718 852-4100
Brooklyn (G-2198)

NET & Die Inc ....E...... 315 592-4311
Fulton (G-5072)

New Age Precision Tech Inc ....E...... 631 471-4000
Ronkonkoma (G-13983)

New York Manufacturing Corp...........G...... 585 254-9353
Rochester (G-13571)

New York State Tool Co Inc ....F...... 315 737-8985
Chadwicks (G-3303)

Niagara Precision Inc ....E...... 716 439-0956
Lockport (G-7098)

▼ Nicoform Inc ....E...... 585 454-5530
Rochester (G-13577)

Nitro Manufacturing LLC ....G...... 716 646-9900
North Collins (G-12026)

North-East Machine Inc ....G...... 518 746-1837
Hudson Falls (G-6191)

Northeast Hardware Specialties ....F...... 516 487-6868
Mineola (G-7992)

Northeastern Water Jet Inc ....F...... 518 843-4988
Amsterdam (G-343)

Northern Machining Inc ....F...... 315 384-3189
Norfolk (G-12000)

Northern Tier Cnc Inc ....G...... 518 236-4702
Mooers Forks (G-8080)

O & S Machine & Tool Co Inc ....E...... 716 941-5542
Colden (G-3530)

Olmstead Machine Inc ....F...... 315 587-9864
North Rose (G-12036)

Omni Turbine Parts LLC ....F...... 607 564-9922
Newfield (G-11897)

Optics Technology Inc ....G...... 585 586-0950
Pittsford (G-12653)

▲ P & F Industries of NY Corp ....G...... 718 894-3501
Maspeth (G-7633)

P T E Inc ....F...... 516 775-3839
Floral Park (G-4816)

▲ Pall Corporation ....A...... 516 484-5400
Port Washington (G-12913)

Pall Corporation ....A...... 607 753-6041
Cortland (G-3779)

▲ Park-Ohio Inds Trsry Co Inc.........F...... 212 966-3310
Albany (G-111)

Parker Machine Company Inc ....F...... 518 747-0675
Fort Edward (G-4942)

Peko Precision Products Inc ....F...... 585 301-1386
Rochester (G-13612)

Pems Tool & Machine Inc ....E...... 315 823-3595
Little Falls (G-6990)

Performance Mfg Inc ....F...... 716 735-3500
Middleport (G-7889)

Pervi Precision Company Inc ....G...... 631 589-5557
Bohemia (G-1061)

Pol-Tek Industries Ltd ....F...... 716 823-1502
Buffalo (G-2924)

Port Everglades Machine Works ....F...... 516 367-2280
Plainview (G-12708)

Port Jervis Machine Corp ....G...... 845 856-6210
Port Jervis (G-12855)

▼ Posimech Inc ....E...... 631 924-5959
Medford (G-7722)

Ppi Corp ....E...... 585 880-7277
Rochester (G-13632)

▲ Ppi Corp ....D...... 585 243-0300
Rochester (G-13633)

Pre-Tech Plastics Inc ....E...... 518 942-5950
Mineville (G-8005)

Precision Arms Inc ....G...... 845 225-1130
Carmel (G-3190)

Precision Index Equipment Inc.........G...... 631 468-8776
Bohemia (G-1065)

▲ Precision Machine Tech LLC ....D...... 585 467-1840
Rochester (G-13638)

Precision Metals Corp ....E...... 631 586-5032
Bay Shore (G-700)

Precision Systems Mfg Inc ....E...... 315 451-3480
Liverpool (G-7035)

Precision Tool and Mfg ....E...... 518 678-3130
Palenville (G-12480)

Precisionmatics Co Inc ....E...... 315 822-6324
West Winfield (G-15858)

Premier Machining Tech Inc ....G...... 716 608-1311
Buffalo (G-2930)

Premier Prcision Machining LLC ....F...... 716 665-5217
Falconer (G-4551)

Production Milling Company ....G...... 914 666-0792
Bedford Hills (G-771)

Progressive Mch & Design LLC.........C...... 585 924-5250
Victor (G-15425)

Progressive Tool Company Inc ....E...... 607 748-8294
Endwell (G-4482)

Pronto Tool & Die Co Inc ....E...... 631 981-8920
Ronkonkoma (G-13997)

Proto Machine Inc ....F...... 631 392-1159
Bay Shore (G-702)

Prototype Manufacturing Corp.........F...... 716 695-1700
North Tonawanda (G-12083)

▲ Qmc Technologies Inc ....F...... 716 681-0810
Depew (G-3995)

Qta Machining Inc ....F...... 716 862-8108
Buffalo (G-2940)

Qualified Manufacturing Corp ....F...... 631 249-4440
East Islip (G-4130)

Quality Grinding Inc ....G...... 716 480-3766
Hamburg (G-5517)

Quality Machining Service Inc ....G...... 315 736-5774
New York Mills (G-11836)

Qualtech Tool & Machine Inc ....F...... 585 223-9227
Fairport (G-4517)

R & S Machine Center Inc ....F...... 518 563-4016
Plattsburgh (G-12773)

R E F Precision Products ....F...... 631 242-4471
Deer Park (G-3925)

Ram Machining LLC ....G...... 585 426-1007
Rochester (G-13668)

Ram Precision Tool Inc ....G...... 716 759-8722
Lancaster (G-6828)

Rand Machine Products, Inc...........C...... 716 665-5217
Falconer (G-4552)

▼ Redding-Hunter Inc ....E...... 607 753-3331
Cortland (G-3786)

Reliance Machining Inc ....E...... 718 784-0314
Long Island City (G-7341)

Ren Tool & Manufacturing Co..........F...... 518 377-2123
Schenectady (G-14299)

RGH Associates Inc ....F...... 631 643-1111
West Babylon (G-15741)

▲ Richard Manno & Company Inc.........D...... 631 643-2200
West Babylon (G-15742)

Richards Machine Tool Co Inc ....E...... 716 683-3380
Lancaster (G-6829)

Rinaldi Precision Machine ....F...... 631 242-4141
Deer Park (G-3928)

Ripi Precision Co Inc ....F...... 631 694-2453
Farmingdale (G-4724)

Ripley Machine & Tool Co Inc..........F...... 716 736-3205
Ripley (G-13170)

Riverside Machinery Company...........G...... 718 492-7400
Brooklyn (G-2348)

Rjs Machine Works Inc ....G...... 716 826-1778
Lackawanna (G-6744)

Rmw Filtration Products Co LLC.........G...... 631 226-9412
Copiague (G-3674)

Roboshop Inc ....G...... 315 437-6454
Syracuse (G-14977)

Roccera LLC ....F...... 585 426-0887
Rochester (G-13678)

Rochester Atomated Systems Inc........E...... 585 594-3222
Rochester (G-13682)

Rochester Tool and Mold Inc ....F...... 585 464-9336
Rochester (G-13701)

Roger Latari ....G...... 631 580-2422
Ronkonkoma (G-14004)

Rona Precision Inc. ....G...... 631 737-4034
Ronkonkoma (G-14005)

Rossi Tool & Dies Inc ....G...... 845 267-8246
Valley Cottage (G-15322)

Rozal Industries Inc ....E...... 631 420-4277
Farmingdale (G-4728)

RS Precision Industries Inc ....E...... 631 420-0424
Farmingdale (G-4729)

Rt Machined Specialties ....G...... 716 731-2055
Niagara Falls (G-11974)

RTD Manufacturing Inc ....G...... 315 337-3151
Rome (G-13871)

Ruga Grinding & Mfg Corp ....G...... 631 924-5067
Yaphank (G-16268)

S & B Machine Works Inc ....E...... 516 997-2666
Westbury (G-15924)

S & H Machine Company Inc ....F...... 716 834-1194
Buffalo (G-2968)

S & R Tool Inc ....G...... 585 346-2029
Lakeville (G-6775)

S R & R Industries Inc ....G...... 845 692-8329
Middletown (G-7931)

Saturn Industries Inc ....E...... 518 828-9956
Hudson (G-6177)

Schwabel Fabricating Co Inc ....E...... 716 876-2086
Tonawanda (G-15138)

▲ Scientific Tool Co Inc ....E...... 315 431-4243
Syracuse (G-14989)

SDJ Machine Shop Inc ....F...... 585 458-1236
Rochester (G-13720)

Seanair Machine Co Inc ....F...... 631 694-2820
Farmingdale (G-4731)

Seeley Machine Inc ....E...... 518 798-9510
Queensbury (G-13056)

Semi-Linear Inc ....G...... 212 243-2108
New York (G-11189)

▲ Service Machine & Tool Company......E...... 607 732-0413
Elmira Heights (G-4379)

Shar-Mar Machine Company ....G...... 631 567-8040
Bohemia (G-1077)

Sick Inc ....E...... 585 347-2000
Webster (G-15653)

Sigma Manufacturing Inds Inc ....F...... 718 842-9180
Bronx (G-1364)

Sigmamotor Inc ....E...... 716 735-3115
Middleport (G-7890)

Smidgens Inc ....G...... 585 624-1486
Lima (G-6935)

Smith Metal Works Newark Inc ....E...... 315 331-1651
Newark (G-11851)

Smithers Tools & Mch Pdts Inc ....D...... 845 876-3063
Rhinebeck (G-13101)

Snyder Industries Inc ....C...... 716 694-1240
Tonawanda (G-15141)

Solmac Inc ....G...... 716 630-7061
Williamsville (G-16140)

▲ Sotek Inc ....D...... 716 821-5961
Blasdell (G-922)

Source Technologies ....E...... 718 708-0305
Brooklyn (G-2443)

Springville Mfg Co Inc ....E...... 716 592-4957
Springville (G-14597)

Stanfordville Mch & Mfg Co Inc ....D...... 845 868-2266
Poughkeepsie (G-12984)

Staub Machine Company Inc ....E...... 716 649-4211
Hamburg (G-5522)

Stony Manufacturing Inc ....E...... 716 652-6730
Elma (G-4330)

▲ Strecks Inc ....E...... 518 273-4410
Watervliet (G-15607)

Strong Forge & Fabrication ....E...... 585 343-5251
Batavia (G-625)

▲ Superior Technology Inc ....E...... 585 352-6556
Rochester (G-13750)

Superior Welding ....G...... 631 676-2751
Holbrook (G-6024)

Swissway Inc ....E 631 351-5350
  Huntington Station *(G-6262)*
▲ Sylhan LLC ....E 631 243-6600
  Edgewood *(G-4286)*
T M Machine Inc ....G 716 822-0817
  Buffalo *(G-3001)*
T R P Machine Inc ....E 631 567-9620
  Bohemia *(G-1084)*
Tangent Machine & Tool Corp ...F 631 249-3088
  Farmingdale *(G-4749)*
Tarsia Technical Industries ......G 631 231-8322
  Hauppauge *(G-5781)*
Taylor Precision Machining ......G 607 535-3101
  Montour Falls *(G-8077)*
Tchnologies N MRC Ameerica LLC ...G 716 822-4300
  Buffalo *(G-3003)*
Technical Precision Corp ....F 845 473-0548
  Pleasantville *(G-12800)*
Ted Westbrook ....G 716 625-4443
  Lockport *(G-7111)*
Temrick Inc ....G 631 567-8860
  Bohemia *(G-1085)*
Tennyson Machine Co Inc ....F 914 668-5468
  Mount Vernon *(G-8182)*
Theodosiou Inc ....G 718 728-6800
  Long Island City *(G-7380)*
TI Group Auto Systems LLC ......G 315 568-7042
  Seneca Falls *(G-14373)*
Ticonderoga Mch & Wldg Corp ....G 518 585-7444
  Ticonderoga *(G-15077)*
Tioga Tool Inc ....F 607 785-6005
  Endicott *(G-4474)*
Tobeyco Manufacturing Co Inc ....F 607 962-2446
  Corning *(G-3722)*
▲ Toolroom Express Inc ....D 607 723-5373
  Conklin *(G-3630)*
Towpath Machine Corp ....G 315 252-0112
  Auburn *(G-500)*
Trebor Instrument Corp ....G 631 423-7026
  Dix Hills *(G-4016)*
Triangle Grinding Machine Corp ...G 631 643-3636
  West Babylon *(G-15753)*
Tricon Machine LLC ....G 585 671-0679
  Webster *(G-15657)*
Tripar Manufacturing Co Inc ......G 631 563-0855
  Bohemia *(G-1090)*
Triple Point Manufacturing ....G 631 218-4988
  Bohemia *(G-1091)*
Triplett Machine Inc ....D 315 548-3198
  Phelps *(G-12609)*
Triplex Industries Inc ....F 585 621-6920
  Rochester *(G-13773)*
Truarc Fabrication ....G 518 691-0430
  Gansevoort *(G-5088)*
Turning Point Tool LLC ....G 585 288-7380
  Rochester *(G-13779)*
▲ Twinco Mfg Co Inc ....E 631 231-0022
  Hauppauge *(G-5789)*
Two Bills Machine & Tool Co .....F 516 437-2585
  Floral Park *(G-4817)*
U-Cut Enterprises Inc ....E 315 492-9316
  Jamesville *(G-6563)*
Ultra Tool and Manufacturing .....F 585 467-3700
  Rochester *(G-13780)*
United Machining Inc ....G 631 589-6751
  Bohemia *(G-1093)*
Universal Metal Fabricators ....F 845 331-8248
  Kingston *(G-6719)*
▲ Upturn Industries Inc ....E 607 967-2923
  Bainbridge *(G-528)*
Ushers Machine and Tool Co Inc ...E 518 877-5501
  Round Lake *(G-14062)*
V A P Tool & Dye ....G 631 587-5262
  West Islip *(G-15813)*
V Lake Industries Inc ....G 716 885-9141
  Buffalo *(G-3034)*
Valair Inc ....F 716 751-9480
  Wilson *(G-16154)*
Van Laeken Richard ....G 315 331-0289
  Newark *(G-11856)*
Van Reenen Tool & Die Inc ......F 585 288-6000
  Rochester *(G-13794)*
▲ Van Thomas Inc ....E 585 426-1414
  Rochester *(G-13795)*
Vanguard Metals Inc ....F 631 234-6500
  Central Islip *(G-3292)*
Verns Machine Co Inc ....E 315 926-4223
  Marion *(G-7577)*
Victoria Precision Inc ....G 845 473-9309
  Hyde Park *(G-6275)*

Village Decoration Ltd ....E 315 437-2522
  East Syracuse *(G-4248)*
Visimetrics Corporation ....G 716 871-7070
  Buffalo *(G-3038)*
Vosky Precision Machining Corp ...F 631 737-3200
  Ronkonkoma *(G-14025)*
◆ Voss Manufacturing Inc ....D 716 731-5062
  Sanborn *(G-14153)*
Vytek Inc ....F 631 750-1770
  Bohemia *(G-1097)*
W H Jones & Son Inc ....F 716 875-8233
  Kenmore *(G-6655)*
W J Albro Machine Works Inc ....G 631 345-0657
  Yaphank *(G-16278)*
Walsh & Sons Machine Inc ......G 845 526-0301
  Mahopac *(G-7480)*
Washburn Manufacturing Tech ....G 607 387-3991
  Trumansburg *(G-15202)*
Watkins Welding and Mch Sp Inc ...G 914 949-6168
  White Plains *(G-16070)*
Wayne Integrated Tech Corp .....E 631 242-0213
  Edgewood *(G-4291)*
Waynes Welding Inc ....E 315 768-6146
  Yorkville *(G-16383)*
Weaver Machine & Tool Co Inc ...F 315 253-4422
  Auburn *(G-503)*
Weiss Industries Inc ....G 518 784-9643
  Valatie *(G-15301)*
◆ Wendt Corporation ....D 716 391-1200
  Buffalo *(G-3044)*
West Falls Machine Co Inc ......F 716 655-0440
  East Aurora *(G-4097)*
▲ Westchstr Crnkshft Grndng ....G 718 651-3900
  East Elmhurst *(G-4112)*
Wiggby Precision Machine Corp ...G 718 439-6900
  Brooklyn *(G-2584)*
Willard Machine ....F 716 885-1630
  Buffalo *(G-3048)*
William Kanes Mfg Corp ....G 718 346-1515
  Brooklyn *(G-2587)*
William Moon Iron Works Inc .....F 518 943-3861
  Catskill *(G-3217)*
Williams Tool Inc ....E 315 737-7226
  Chadwicks *(G-3304)*
Winn Manufacturing Inc ....G 518 642-3515
  Granville *(G-5357)*
Woods Machine and Tool LLC ....F 607 699-3253
  Nichols *(G-11993)*
Wordingham Machine Co Inc .....E 585 924-2294
  Rochester *(G-13808)*
Wrightcut EDM & Machine Inc ...G 607 733-5018
  Elmira *(G-4373)*
Zip Products Inc ....F 585 482-0044
  Rochester *(G-13815)*

36 ELECTRONIC AND OTHER ELECTRICAL EQUIPMENT AND COMPONENTS, EXCEPT COMPUTER

3612 Power, Distribution & Specialty Transformers

Arstan Products International ....F 516 433-1313
  Hicksville *(G-5885)*
Berkshire Transformer ....G 631 467-5328
  Central Islip *(G-3265)*
Beta Transformer Tech Corp ....E 631 244-7393
  Bohemia *(G-980)*
Buffalo Power Electronics Ctr .....F 716 651-1600
  Depew *(G-3974)*
Caddell Burns Manufacturing Co ...G 631 757-1772
  Northport *(G-12100)*
Cooper Power Systems LLC ......B 716 375-7100
  Olean *(G-12230)*
Current Controls Inc ....C 585 593-1544
  Wellsville *(G-15668)*
Dyco Electronics Inc ....D 607 324-2030
  Hornell *(G-6104)*
Electron Coil Inc ....G 607 336-7414
  Norwich *(G-12121)*
Ems Development Corporation .....D 631 345-6200
  Yaphank *(G-16260)*
Equus Power I LP ....G 847 908-2878
  West Babylon *(G-15710)*
Exxelia-Raf Tabtronics LLC ....E 585 243-4331
  Piffard *(G-12624)*
Frederick Cowan & Company Inc ...F 631 369-0360
  Wading River *(G-15449)*

General Electric Company ....A 518 385-4022
  Schenectady *(G-14266)*
General Electric Company ....E 518 385-7620
  Niskayuna *(G-11996)*
Hale Electrical Dist Svcs Inc ......G 716 818-7595
  Wales Center *(G-15466)*
K Road Power Management LLC ...G 212 351-0535
  New York *(G-10051)*
Kepco Inc ....D 718 461-7000
  Flushing *(G-4867)*
Mitchell Electronics Corp ....E 914 699-3800
  Mount Vernon *(G-8162)*
▲ Niagara Transformer Corp .....D 716 896-6500
  Buffalo *(G-2887)*
▲ Piller Power Systems Inc ......E 845 695-6658
  Middletown *(G-7926)*
Precision Electronics Inc ....F 631 842-4900
  Copiague *(G-3670)*
Railworks Corporation ....G 904 296-5055
  Farmingdale *(G-4723)*
Ram Transformer Technologies ....F 914 632-3988
  New Rochelle *(G-8351)*
Sag Harbor Industries Inc ....E 631 725-0440
  Sag Harbor *(G-14101)*
Schneider Electric It Corp ....F 646 335-0216
  New York *(G-11156)*
Schneider Electric Usa Inc ....F 585 377-1313
  Penfield *(G-12574)*
Schneider Electric Usa Inc ....G 631 567-5710
  Bohemia *(G-1073)*
Siemens Corporation ....F 202 434-7800
  New York *(G-11226)*
Siemens USA Holdings Inc ....B 212 258-4000
  New York *(G-11228)*
▲ Spence Engineering Company Inc ...C 845 778-5566
  Walden *(G-15462)*
Sunward Electronics Inc ....F 518 687-0030
  Troy *(G-15191)*
Supreme Lighting Design LLC .....F 718 812-3347
  Brooklyn *(G-2477)*
▲ Switching Power Inc ....D 631 981-7231
  Ronkonkoma *(G-14016)*
Telephone Sales & Service Co .....E 212 233-8505
  New York *(G-11449)*
Transistor Devices Inc ....E 631 471-7492
  Ronkonkoma *(G-14017)*
Veeco Instruments Inc ....C 516 349-8300
  Plainview *(G-12724)*

3613 Switchgear & Switchboard Apparatus

▲ Abasco Inc ....E 716 649-4790
  Hamburg *(G-5501)*
All City Switchboard Corp ....E 718 956-7244
  Long Island City *(G-7149)*
Allied Circuits LLC ....E 716 551-0285
  Buffalo *(G-2627)*
Atlas Switch Co Inc ....E 516 222-6280
  Garden City *(G-5090)*
Avanti Control Systems Inc ....G 518 921-4368
  Gloversville *(G-5278)*
Benfield Control Systems Inc ......F 914 948-3231
  White Plains *(G-15981)*
Boulay Fabrication Inc ....F 315 677-5247
  La Fayette *(G-6736)*
Claddagh Electronics Ltd ....E 718 784-0571
  Long Island City *(G-7186)*
Cooper Industries LLC ....F 315 477-7000
  Syracuse *(G-14864)*
Cooper Power Systems LLC ......B 716 375-7100
  Olean *(G-12230)*
Custom Controls ....G 315 253-4785
  Scipio Center *(G-14326)*
Electric Swtchbard Sltions LLC ....G 718 643-1105
  New Hyde Park *(G-8264)*
Electrotech Service Eqp Corp .....E 718 626-7700
  Astoria *(G-419)*
▲ Ems Development Corporation ...D 631 924-4736
  Yaphank *(G-16259)*
Inertia Switch Inc ....E 845 359-8300
  Orangeburg *(G-12319)*
◆ Leviton Manufacturing Co Inc ...B 631 812-6000
  Melville *(G-7800)*
Link Control Systems Inc ....F 631 471-3950
  Ronkonkoma *(G-13966)*
▲ Marquardt Switches Inc ....C 315 655-8050
  Cazenovia *(G-3231)*
Micro Instrument Corp ....D 585 458-3150
  Rochester *(G-13545)*
Odyssey Controls Inc ....G 585 548-9800
  Bergen *(G-819)*

Product Station Inc ....F...... 516 942-4220
  Jericho *(G-6590)*
Schneider Electric Usa Inc ......C... 646 335-0220
  New York *(G-11157)*
Schneider Electric Usa Inc ......G... 631 567-5710
  Bohemia *(G-1073)*
▲ Se-Mar Electric Co Inc ....E...... 716 674-7404
  West Seneca *(G-15853)*
Select Controls Inc ....E... 631 567-9010
  Bohemia *(G-1076)*
Sinclair Technologies Inc ....E... 716 874-3682
  Hamburg *(G-5521)*
Smith Control Systems Inc ......F... 518 828-7646
  Hudson *(G-6180)*
Soc America Inc ....F... 631 472-6666
  Ronkonkoma *(G-14010)*
▲ Switching Power Inc ....D... 631 981-7231
  Ronkonkoma *(G-14016)*
Trac Regulators Inc ....E... 914 699-9352
  Mount Vernon *(G-8185)*
▲ Transit Air Inc ....E... 607 324-0216
  Hornell *(G-6112)*

3621 Motors & Generators

▲ Aeroflex Incorporated ....B... 516 694-6700
  Plainview *(G-12660)*
Allied Motion Control Corp ......G... 716 242-7535
  Amherst *(G-205)*
▲ Allied Motion Technologies Inc ....C... 716 242-8634
  Amherst *(G-207)*
Allied Motion Technologies Inc ....C... 315 782-5910
  Watertown *(G-15558)*
◆ American Precision Inds Inc ....C... 716 691-9100
  Amherst *(G-210)*
Ametek Inc ....G... 631 467-8400
  Ronkonkoma *(G-13904)*
Ametek Inc ....D... 607 763-4700
  Binghamton *(G-854)*
Ametek Inc ....D... 585 263-7700
  Rochester *(G-13234)*
Apogee Power Usa Inc ....F... 202 746-2890
  Hartsdale *(G-5567)*
▲ Applied Power Systems Inc ....E... 516 935-2230
  Hicksville *(G-5883)*
▲ ARC Systems Inc ....E... 631 582-8020
  Hauppauge *(G-5592)*
▲ Automation Source Technologies ....F... 631 643-1678
  West Babylon *(G-15691)*
Cellgen Inc ....G... 516 889-9300
  Freeport *(G-4990)*
Cobham Long Island Inc ....B... 516 694-6700
  Plainview *(G-12669)*
Cobham Long Island Inc ....G... 631 231-9100
  Hauppauge *(G-5619)*
Con Rel Auto Electric Inc ....E... 518 356-1646
  Schenectady *(G-14259)*
▲ Current Applications Inc ....E... 315 788-4689
  Watertown *(G-15567)*
◆ D & D Motor Systems Inc ......E... 315 701-0861
  Syracuse *(G-14871)*
Designatronics Incorporated ....B... 516 328-3300
  New Hyde Park *(G-8261)*
EDP Renewables North Amer LLC ....G... 518 426-1650
  Albany *(G-74)*
Electron Coil Inc ....D... 607 336-7414
  Norwich *(G-12121)*
Elton El Mantle Inc ....G... 315 432-9067
  Syracuse *(G-14886)*
Emes Motor Inc ....G... 718 387-2445
  Brooklyn *(G-1799)*
Empire Division Inc ....D... 315 476-6273
  Syracuse *(G-14888)*
▲ Ems Development Corporation ....D... 631 924-4736
  Yaphank *(G-16259)*
Ener-G-Rotors Inc ....G... 518 372-2608
  Schenectady *(G-14262)*
▲ Eni Technology Inc ....B... 585 427-8300
  Rochester *(G-13395)*
▲ Faradyne Motors LLC ....F... 315 331-5985
  Palmyra *(G-12485)*
▲ Felchar Manufacturing Corp ....A... 607 723-4076
  Binghamton *(G-877)*
General Electric Company ....B... 518 385-2211
  Schenectady *(G-14270)*
General Electric Intl Inc ....G... 518 385-2211
  Schenectady *(G-14273)*
Generation Power LLC ....G... 315 234-2451
  Syracuse *(G-14903)*
▲ Getec Inc ....F... 845 292-0800
  Ferndale *(G-4789)*

Got Power Inc ....G... 631 767-9493
  Ronkonkoma *(G-13944)*
Hes Inc ....G... 607 359-2974
  Addison *(G-5)*
▲ IEC Holden Corporation ....F... 518 213-3991
  Plattsburgh *(G-12752)*
Independent Field Svc LLC ....G... 315 559-9243
  Syracuse *(G-14913)*
Industrial Test Eqp Co Inc ....E... 516 883-6423
  Port Washington *(G-12888)*
Intelligen Power Systems LLC ....G... 212 750-0373
  Old Bethpage *(G-12218)*
Island Components Group Inc ....F... 631 563-4224
  Holbrook *(G-6003)*
▲ John G Rubino Inc ....E... 315 253-7396
  Auburn *(G-482)*
Kaddis Manufacturing Corp ......G... 585 624-3070
  Honeoye Falls *(G-6077)*
Lcdrives Corp ....E... 860 712-8926
  Potsdam *(G-12937)*
Magna Products Corp ....E... 585 647-2280
  Rochester *(G-13529)*
▲ Makerbot Industries LLC ....C... 347 334-6800
  Brooklyn *(G-2104)*
Mks Medical Electronics ....C... 585 292-7400
  Rochester *(G-13555)*
▲ Modular Devices Inc ....D... 631 345-3100
  Shirley *(G-14425)*
▲ Moley Magnetics Inc ....F... 716 434-4023
  Lockport *(G-7095)*
Nidec Motor Corporation ....F... 315 434-9303
  East Syracuse *(G-4229)*
P1 Generator Windings LLC ....G... 518 930-2879
  Schenectady *(G-14293)*
▲ Power and Composite Tech LLC ....D... 518 843-6825
  Amsterdam *(G-345)*
Power Gneration Indus Engs Inc ....E... 315 633-9389
  Bridgeport *(G-1168)*
Premco Inc ....F... 914 636-7095
  New Rochelle *(G-8350)*
Princetel Inc ....F... 914 579-2410
  Hawthorne *(G-5822)*
Protective Power Systms & Cntr ....F... 845 721-1875
  Staatsburg *(G-14600)*
Ruhle Companies Inc ....E... 914 287-4000
  Valhalla *(G-15309)*
Sag Harbor Industries Inc ....E... 631 725-0440
  Sag Harbor *(G-14101)*
▲ Sima Technologies LLC ....G... 412 828-9130
  Hauppauge *(G-5766)*
▲ Sopark Corp ....D... 716 822-0434
  Buffalo *(G-2987)*
Stature Electric Inc ....F... 716 242-7535
  Amherst *(G-244)*
Supergen Products LLC ....G... 315 573-7887
  Newark *(G-11853)*
Switched Source LLC ....G... 708 207-1479
  Vestal *(G-15385)*
▲ Taro Manufacturing Company Inc ....F... 315 252-9430
  Auburn *(G-498)*
Troy Belting and Supply Co ....D... 518 272-4920
  Watervliet *(G-15609)*
▲ Vdc Electronics Inc ....F... 631 423-8220
  Huntington *(G-6232)*
W J Albro Machine Works Inc .....G... 631 345-0657
  Yaphank *(G-16278)*
Worldwide Electric Corp LLC .....E... 800 808-2131
  Rochester *(G-13809)*

3624 Carbon & Graphite Prdts

▲ Americarb Inc ....D... 419 281-5800
  Niagara Falls *(G-11903)*
Americarb International Corp ......G... 419 281-5800
  Niagara Falls *(G-11904)*
▲ Carbon Graphite Materials Inc ....E... 716 792-7979
  Brocton *(G-1180)*
Carbonfree Chemicals Spe I LLC ....E... 914 421-4900
  White Plains *(G-15989)*
Go Blue Technologies Ltd ....G... 631 404-6285
  North Babylon *(G-12001)*
◆ Graphite Metallizing Corp ......C... 914 968-8400
  Yonkers *(G-16315)*
Hh Liquidating Corp ....A... 646 282-2500
  New York *(G-9779)*
J V Precision Inc ....G... 518 851-3200
  Hudson *(G-6164)*
Metal Coated Fibers Inc ....E... 518 280-8514
  Schenectady *(G-14288)*
Metallized Carbon Corporation ....C... 914 941-3738
  Ossining *(G-12404)*

▲ Mwi Inc ....D... 585 424-4200
  Rochester *(G-13564)*
Pyrotek Incorporated ....E... 716 731-3221
  Sanborn *(G-14148)*
Saturn Industries Inc ....E... 518 828-9956
  Hudson *(G-6177)*
Xactiv Inc ....F... 585 288-7220
  Fairport *(G-4531)*

3625 Relays & Indl Controls

Adeptronics Incorporated ....G... 631 667-0659
  Bay Shore *(G-643)*
Afi Cybernetics Corporation ....E... 607 732-3244
  Elmira *(G-4339)*
Air Crafters Inc ....C... 631 471-7788
  Ronkonkoma *(G-13893)*
◆ Altronix Corp ....D... 718 567-8181
  Brooklyn *(G-1494)*
◆ American Precision Inds Inc ....C... 716 691-9100
  Amherst *(G-210)*
▲ Anderson Instrument Co Inc ....E... 518 922-5315
  Fultonville *(G-5077)*
Baco Controls Inc ....F... 315 635-2500
  Baldwinsville *(G-543)*
Bakery Innovative Tech Corp ......F... 631 758-3081
  Patchogue *(G-12496)*
Bomac Inc ....F... 315 433-9181
  Syracuse *(G-14832)*
▲ Burgess-Manning Inc ....D... 716 662-6540
  Orchard Park *(G-12343)*
Calia Technical Inc ....G... 718 447-3928
  Staten Island *(G-14636)*
Con Rel Auto Electric Inc ....E... 518 356-1646
  Schenectady *(G-14259)*
◆ Conic Systems Inc ....F... 845 856-4053
  Port Jervis *(G-12846)*
Continental Instruments LLC ......E... 631 842-9400
  Amityville *(G-258)*
▲ Cox & Company Inc ....C... 212 366-0200
  Plainview *(G-12676)*
Crestron Electronics Inc ....D... 201 894-0670
  Orangeburg *(G-12311)*
Datatran Labs Inc ....G... 845 856-4313
  Port Jervis *(G-12847)*
Designatronics Incorporated ......B... 516 328-3300
  New Hyde Park *(G-8261)*
◆ Designatronics Incorporated ....G... 516 328-3300
  Hicksville *(G-5902)*
Deutsch Relays ....F... 631 342-1700
  Hauppauge *(G-5636)*
▲ Digital Instruments Inc ....F... 716 874-5848
  Tonawanda *(G-15099)*
Dortronics Systems Inc ....E... 631 725-0505
  Sag Harbor *(G-14098)*
▲ Dri Relays Inc ....D... 631 342-1700
  Hauppauge *(G-5641)*
◆ Dyson-Kissner-Moran Corp ....E... 212 661-4600
  Poughkeepsie *(G-12952)*
Eaton Corporation ....C... 516 353-3017
  East Meadow *(G-4135)*
Eatons Crouse Hinds Business ....F... 315 477-7000
  Syracuse *(G-14883)*
Electronic Machine Parts LLC ....F... 631 434-3700
  Hauppauge *(G-5645)*
Enetics Inc ....G... 585 924-5010
  Victor *(G-15407)*
Entertron Industries Inc ....E... 716 772-7216
  Lockport *(G-7074)*
▲ Eversan Inc ....F... 315 736-3967
  Whitesboro *(G-16080)*
▲ Fortitude Industries Inc ....D... 607 324-1500
  Hornell *(G-6106)*
G C Controls Inc ....E... 607 656-4117
  Greene *(G-5445)*
▲ Gas Turbine Controls Corp ......E... 914 693-0830
  Hawthorne *(G-5813)*
Gemtrol Inc ....G... 716 894-0716
  Buffalo *(G-2770)*
General Control Systems Inc ......E... 518 270-8045
  Green Island *(G-5435)*
General Oil Equipment Co Inc ....E... 716 691-7012
  Amherst *(G-225)*
Goddard Design Co ....G... 718 599-0170
  Brooklyn *(G-1895)*
▲ Hasco Componets ....E... 516 328-9292
  New Hyde Park *(G-8273)*
▲ I D E Processes Corporation ....F... 718 544-1177
  Kew Gardens *(G-6664)*
I E D Corp ....F... 631 348-0424
  Islandia *(G-6334)*

SIC

▲ ICM Controls Corp ....F 315 233-5266
North Syracuse *(G-12045)*

Industrial Indxing Systems Inc ....E 585 924-9181
Victor *(G-15413)*

Inertia Switch Inc ....E 845 359-8300
Orangeburg *(G-12319)*

◆ Infitec Inc ....D 315 433-1150
East Syracuse *(G-4222)*

▲ Interntnal Cntrls Msrmnts Corp ....C 315 233-5266
North Syracuse *(G-12046)*

ITT Aerospace Controls LLC ....G 914 641-2000
White Plains *(G-16016)*

ITT Corp ....E 716 662-1900
Orchard Park *(G-12355)*

ITT Corporation ....E 585 269-7109
Hemlock *(G-5830)*

ITT Corporation ....D 315 568-2811
Seneca Falls *(G-14364)*

ITT Inc ....C 914 641-2000
White Plains *(G-16017)*

ITT International Holdings Inc ....G 914 641-2000
White Plains *(G-16019)*

ITT LLC ....G 315 568-4733
Seneca Falls *(G-14367)*

ITT LLC ....D 315 258-4904
Auburn *(G-480)*

ITT LLC ....D 914 641-2000
Seneca Falls *(G-14368)*

◆ ITT LLC ....B 914 641-2000
White Plains *(G-16020)*

JE Miller Inc ....F 315 437-6811
East Syracuse *(G-4224)*

Jit International Inc ....G 631 761-5551
Islandia *(G-6338)*

◆ Kearney-National Inc ....F 212 661-4600
New York *(G-10087)*

◆ Kussmaul Electronics Co Inc ....E 631 218-0298
West Sayville *(G-15841)*

L-3 Cmmnctons Ntronix Holdings ....D 212 697-1111
New York *(G-10152)*

L3harris Technologies Inc ....C 631 630-4000
Amityville *(G-289)*

Logitek Inc ....D 631 567-1100
Bohemia *(G-1035)*

Machine Components Corp ....E 516 694-7222
Plainview *(G-12698)*

Magnus Precision Mfg Inc ....D 315 548-8032
Phelps *(G-12605)*

◆ Magtrol Inc ....E 716 668-5555
Buffalo *(G-2859)*

▲ Makerbot Industries LLC ....C 347 334-6800
Brooklyn *(G-2104)*

▲ Marine & Indus Hydraulics Inc ....F 914 698-2036
Mamaroneck *(G-7513)*

▲ Marquardt Switches Inc ....C 315 655-8050
Cazenovia *(G-3231)*

◆ Mason Industries Inc ....C 631 348-0282
Hauppauge *(G-5708)*

Mason Industries Inc ....D 631 348-0282
Hauppauge *(G-5709)*

Messer LLC ....D 716 773-7552
Grand Island *(G-5337)*

▼ Micropen Technologies Corp ....D 585 624-2610
Honeoye Falls *(G-6078)*

Moog Inc ....E 716 687-4778
Elma *(G-4322)*

◆ Moog Inc ....A 716 805-2604
Elma *(G-4321)*

▲ Morris Products Inc ....F 518 743-0523
Queensbury *(G-13049)*

N E Controls LLC ....F 315 626-2480
Syracuse *(G-14949)*

▲ Nas-Tra Automotive Inds Inc ....C 631 225-1225
Lindenhurst *(G-6962)*

National Time Recording Eqp Co ....F 212 227-3310
New York *(G-10547)*

Nitram Energy Inc ....E 716 662-6540
Orchard Park *(G-12368)*

North Point Technologies ....E 607 238-1114
Johnson City *(G-6606)*

North Point Technology LLC ....F 866 885-3377
Endicott *(G-4467)*

Nsi Industries LLC ....C 800 841-2505
Mount Vernon *(G-8166)*

▲ Omntec Mfg Inc ....E 631 981-2001
Ronkonkoma *(G-13987)*

Panelogic Inc ....E 607 962-6319
Corning *(G-3719)*

Peerless Instrument Co Inc ....C 631 396-6500
Farmingdale *(G-4704)*

Peraton Inc ....E 315 838-7000
Rome *(G-13863)*

Powr-UPS Corp ....E 631 345-5700
Shirley *(G-14427)*

Precision Electronics Inc ....F 631 842-4900
Copiague *(G-3670)*

Precision Mechanisms Corp ....E 516 333-5955
Westbury *(G-15919)*

◆ Pulsafeeder Inc ....C 585 292-8000
Rochester *(G-13653)*

Rasp Incorporated ....E 518 747-8020
Gansevoort *(G-5085)*

▲ Rochester Industrial Ctrl Inc ....D 315 524-4555
Ontario *(G-12300)*

Rockwell Automation Inc ....E 585 487-2700
Pittsford *(G-12656)*

Rotork Controls Inc ....F 585 328-1550
Rochester *(G-13707)*

Ruby Automation LLC ....D 585 254-8840
Rochester *(G-13710)*

Ruhle Companies Inc ....E 914 287-4000
Valhalla *(G-15309)*

◆ Schmersal Inc ....E 914 347-4775
Hawthorne *(G-5823)*

Schneider Electric Usa Inc ....G 631 567-5710
Bohemia *(G-1073)*

Select Controls Inc ....E 631 567-9010
Bohemia *(G-1076)*

Service Mfg Group Inc ....F 716 893-1482
Buffalo *(G-2980)*

▲ Soft-Noze Usa Inc ....E 315 732-2726
Frankfort *(G-4956)*

◆ Soundcoat Company Inc ....D 631 242-2200
Deer Park *(G-3938)*

Ssac Inc ....E 800 843-8848
Baldwinsville *(G-555)*

▲ Stetron International Inc ....F 716 854-3443
Buffalo *(G-2993)*

Switches and Sensors Inc ....F 631 924-2167
Yaphank *(G-16273)*

Teale Machine Company Inc ....D 585 244-6700
Rochester *(G-13761)*

Techniflo Corporation ....G 716 741-3500
Clarence Center *(G-3449)*

▲ Teknic Inc ....E 585 784-7454
Victor *(G-15436)*

▲ Tork Inc ....D 914 664-3542
Mount Vernon *(G-8183)*

Transistor Devices Inc ....E 631 471-7492
Ronkonkoma *(G-14017)*

Trident Valve Actuator Co ....F 914 698-2650
Mamaroneck *(G-7526)*

◆ Unimar Inc ....F 315 699-4400
Syracuse *(G-15017)*

US Drives Inc ....D 716 731-1606
Niagara Falls *(G-11988)*

Vibration & Noise Engrg Corp ....G 716 827-4959
Orchard Park *(G-12382)*

▲ Vibration Eliminator Co Inc ....E 631 841-4000
Copiague *(G-3687)*

Vps Control Systems Inc ....F 518 686-0019
Hoosick *(G-6082)*

Weldcomputer Corporation ....F 518 283-2897
Troy *(G-15198)*

Young & Franklin Inc ....D 315 457-3110
Liverpool *(G-7051)*

Zeppelin Electric Company Inc ....G 631 928-9467
East Setauket *(G-4191)*

3629 Electrical Indl Apparatus, NEC

▲ Alliance Control Systems Inc ....G 845 279-4430
Brewster *(G-1140)*

Applied Energy Solutions LLC ....E 585 538-3270
Webster *(G-15629)*

▲ Applied Power Systems Inc ....E 516 935-2230
Hicksville *(G-5883)*

Beltron Products Inc ....E 888 423-5876
Albany *(G-45)*

C & M Circuits Inc ....E 631 589-0208
Bohemia *(G-985)*

Calibration Technologies Inc ....G 631 676-6133
Centereach *(G-3250)*

China Lithium Technologies ....G 212 391-2688
New York *(G-8990)*

▲ Curtis Instruments Inc ....G 914 666-2971
Mount Kisco *(G-8089)*

Curtis/Palmer Hydroelectric LP ....F 518 654-6297
Corinth *(G-3704)*

Cygnus Automation Inc ....E 631 981-0909
Bohemia *(G-997)*

Eluminocity US Inc ....G 651 528-1165
New York *(G-9353)*

▲ Ems Development Corporation ....D 631 924-4736
Yaphank *(G-16259)*

Endicott Research Group Inc ....D 607 754-9187
Endicott *(G-4452)*

Energy Harvesters LLC ....G 617 325-9852
Rochester *(G-13391)*

Exide Technologies ....G 585 344-0656
Batavia *(G-613)*

◆ G B International Trdg Co Ltd ....C 607 785-0938
Endicott *(G-4457)*

General Electric Company ....E 518 459-4110
Albany *(G-80)*

General Electric Company ....B 518 746-5750
Hudson Falls *(G-6187)*

GM Components Holdings LLC ....B 716 439-2463
Lockport *(G-7079)*

GM Components Holdings LLC ....B 716 439-2011
Lockport *(G-7080)*

◆ Kussmaul Electronics Co Inc ....E 631 218-0298
West Sayville *(G-15841)*

▲ Nrd LLC ....E 716 773-7634
Grand Island *(G-5339)*

Plug Power Inc ....G 585 474-3993
Rochester *(G-13626)*

▲ Plug Power Inc ....B 518 782-7700
Latham *(G-6874)*

Solid Sealing Technology Inc ....E 518 874-3600
Watervliet *(G-15606)*

Sparkcharge Inc ....G 315 480-3645
Syracuse *(G-14996)*

▲ Tonoga Inc ....C 518 658-3202
Petersburg *(G-12600)*

Viking Technologies Ltd ....E 631 957-8000
Lindenhurst *(G-6983)*

▲ Walter R Tucker Entps Ltd ....E 607 467-2866
Deposit *(G-4004)*

3631 Household Cooking Eqpt

Applince Installation Svc Corp ....E 716 884-7425
Buffalo *(G-2642)*

◆ Korin Inc ....E 212 587-7021
New York *(G-10128)*

◆ Oxo International Inc ....C 212 242-3333
New York *(G-10729)*

▲ Podravka International USA ....F 212 661-0125
New York *(G-10859)*

Steelstone Group LLC ....G 888 552-0033
Brooklyn *(G-2459)*

◆ Toshiba America Inc ....E 212 596-0600
New York *(G-11519)*

3632 Household Refrigerators & Freezers

Ae Fund Inc ....E 315 698-7650
Brewerton *(G-1134)*

General Electric Company ....A 518 385-4022
Schenectady *(G-14266)*

Robin Industries Ltd ....F 718 218-9616
Brooklyn *(G-2351)*

Sure-Kol Refrigerator Co Inc ....F 718 625-0601
Brooklyn *(G-2479)*

3633 Household Laundry Eqpt

AES Electronics Inc ....G 212 371-8120
New York *(G-8488)*

Autarkic Holdings Inc ....D 516 371-4400
Inwood *(G-6290)*

Coinmach Service Corp ....A 516 349-8555
Plainview *(G-12670)*

CSC SW Holdco Inc ....D 516 349-8555
Plainview *(G-12677)*

Penn Enterprises Inc ....F 845 446-0765
West Point *(G-15834)*

Pluslux LLC ....G 516 371-4400
Inwood *(G-6302)*

Spin Holdco Inc ....G 516 349-8555
Plainview *(G-12715)*

3634 Electric Household Appliances

A & M LLC ....G 212 354-1341
New York *(G-8410)*

▲ Abbott Industries Inc ....B 718 291-0800
Jamaica *(G-6423)*

▲ Advanced Response Corporation ....G 212 459-0887
New York *(G-8482)*

Algonquin Power ....G 315 393-5595
Ogdensburg *(G-12201)*

American Comfort Direct LLC ....E 201 364-8309
New York *(G-8548)*

Bino Products LLC ....E 212 886-6899
New York *(G-8795)*

▲ **Brumis Imports Inc** ....D 646 845-6000
New York *(G-8864)*

Dampits International Inc ....G 212 581-3047
New York *(G-9160)*

▼ **Fulton Volcanic Inc** ....D 315 298-5121
Pulaski *(G-12999)*

General Electric Company ....G 315 554-2000
Skaneateles *(G-14452)*

Goodnature Products Inc ....E 800 875-3381
Buffalo *(G-2779)*

▲ **Harrys Inc** ....D 888 212-6855
New York *(G-9733)*

▲ **Peek A Boo USA Inc** ....E 201 533-8700
New York *(G-10784)*

▲ **Quality Life Inc** ....F 718 939-5787
College Point *(G-3561)*

Quip Nyc Inc ....G 917 331-3993
Brooklyn *(G-2315)*

Remedies Surgical Supplies ....G 718 599-5301
Brooklyn *(G-2339)*

Sundance Industries Inc ....G 845 795-5809
Milton *(G-7953)*

▲ **Tactica International Inc** ....E 212 575-0500
New York *(G-11423)*

▲ **Uniware Houseware Corp** ....E 631 242-7400
Brentwood *(G-1129)*

Valad Electric Heating Corp ....F 888 509-4927
Montgomery *(G-8068)*

Vincent Genovese ....G 631 281-8170
Mastic Beach *(G-7675)*

◆ **World Trading Center Inc** ....G 631 273-3330
Hauppauge *(G-5803)*

3635 Household Vacuum Cleaners

American Comfort Direct LLC ....E 201 364-8309
New York *(G-8548)*

D & C Cleaning Inc ....F 631 789-5659
Copiague *(G-3650)*

▲ **Global Resources Sg Inc** ....F 212 686-1411
New York *(G-9632)*

▲ **Nationwide Sales and Service** ...F 631 491-6625
Farmingdale *(G-4691)*

Tri County Custom Vacuum ....G 845 774-7595
Monroe *(G-8032)*

3639 Household Appliances, NEC

A Gatty Products Inc ....G 914 592-3903
Elmsford *(G-4391)*

▼ **Ajmadison Corp** ....D 718 532-1800
Brooklyn *(G-1474)*

Barrage ....E 212 586-9390
New York *(G-8732)*

Design Solutions LI Inc ....G 631 656-8700
Saint James *(G-14109)*

Hobart Corporation ....E 631 864-3440
Commack *(G-3592)*

Jado Sewing Machines Inc ....E 718 784-2314
Long Island City *(G-7252)*

Mohawk Group Holdings Inc ....G 347 676-1681
New York *(G-10493)*

Talmu NY LLC ....G 347 434-6700
Brooklyn *(G-2492)*

3641 Electric Lamps

◆ **Atlantic Ultraviolet Corp** ....E 631 234-3275
Hauppauge *(G-5597)*

Boehm Surgical Instrument Corp ...F 585 436-6584
Rochester *(G-13277)*

Emitled Inc ....G 516 531-3533
Westbury *(G-15882)*

General Electric Company ....A 518 385-4022
Schenectady *(G-14266)*

Goldstar Lighting LLC ....F 646 543-6811
New York *(G-9643)*

▲ **K & H Industries Inc** ....E 716 312-0088
Hamburg *(G-5511)*

▲ **Kreon Inc** ....G 516 470-9522
Bethpage *(G-837)*

▲ **La Mar Lighting Co Inc** ....E 631 777-7700
Farmingdale *(G-4668)*

▲ **Led Waves Inc** ....F 347 416-6182
Brooklyn *(G-2056)*

◆ **Lighting Holdings Intl LLC** ....A 845 306-1850
Purchase *(G-13006)*

▲ **Lowel-Light Manufacturing Inc** ...E 718 921-0600
New York *(G-2087)*

▲ **Make-Waves Instrument Corp** ......E 716 681-7524
Buffalo *(G-2860)*

Oledworks LLC ....E 585 287-6802
Rochester *(G-13589)*

Philips Elec N Amer Corp ....C 607 776-3692
Bath *(G-639)*

Preston Glass Industries Inc ....E 718 997-8888
Forest Hills *(G-4926)*

▲ **Ric-Lo Productions Ltd** ....G 845 469-2285
Chester *(G-3384)*

▲ **Saratoga Lighting Holdings LLC** ...G 212 906-7800
New York *(G-11136)*

◆ **Satco Products Inc** ....G 631 243-2022
Edgewood *(G-4282)*

Siemens Corporation ....F 202 434-7800
New York *(G-11226)*

Siemens USA Holdings Inc ....B 212 258-4000
New York *(G-11228)*

Welch Allyn Inc ....A 315 685-4347
Skaneateles Falls *(G-14461)*

3643 Current-Carrying Wiring Devices

99cent World and Variety Corp ....G 212 740-0010
New York *(G-8409)*

Andros Manufacturing Corp ....G 585 663-5700
Rochester *(G-13237)*

Another 99 Cent Paradise ....G 718 786-4578
Sunnyside *(G-14770)*

Associated Lightning Rod Co ....F 845 373-8309
Millerton *(G-7946)*

Atc Plastics LLC ....E 212 375-2515
New York *(G-8660)*

Automatic Connector Inc ....F 631 543-5000
Hauppauge *(G-5598)*

Belden Inc ....B 607 796-5600
Horseheads *(G-6114)*

Bronx New Way Corp ....G 347 431-1385
Bronx *(G-1218)*

Charlton Precision Products ....G 845 338-2351
Kingston *(G-6685)*

Command Components Corporation ...G 631 666-4411
Bay Shore *(G-667)*

Cooper Power Systems LLC ....B 716 375-7100
Olean *(G-12230)*

▲ **Cox & Company Inc** ....C 212 366-0200
Plainview *(G-12676)*

Crown Die Casting Corp ....E 914 667-5400
Mount Vernon *(G-8135)*

▲ **Delfingen Us-New York Inc** ....E 716 215-0300
Niagara Falls *(G-11920)*

Dollar Popular Inc ....G 914 375-0361
Yonkers *(G-16302)*

EB Acquisitions LLC ....D 212 355-3310
New York *(G-9309)*

Exxelia-Raf Tabtronics LLC ....E 585 243-4331
Piffard *(G-12624)*

◆ **Fiber Instrument Sales Inc** ....C 315 736-2206
Oriskany *(G-12390)*

Heary Bros Lghtning Protection ....E 716 941-6141
Springville *(G-14593)*

Hubbell Inc ....E 845 586-2707
Margaretville *(G-7566)*

Inertia Switch Inc ....E 845 359-8300
Orangeburg *(G-12319)*

International Key Supply LLC ....F 631 983-6096
Farmingdale *(G-4652)*

Jaguar Industries Inc ....F 845 947-1800
Haverstraw *(G-5805)*

Joldeson One Aerospace Inds ....D 718 848-7396
Ozone Park *(G-12463)*

▲ **K & H Industries Inc** ....E 716 312-0088
Hamburg *(G-5511)*

▲ **Kelta Inc** ....E 631 789-5000
Edgewood *(G-4273)*

L3 Technologies Inc ....A 631 436-7400
Hauppauge *(G-5687)*

◆ **Leviton Manufacturing Co Inc** ......B 631 812-6000
Melville *(G-7800)*

◆ **Lighting Holdings Intl LLC** ....A 845 306-1850
Purchase *(G-13006)*

Lite Brite Manufacturing Inc ....F 718 855-9797
Brooklyn *(G-2079)*

Lourdes Industries Inc ....D 631 234-6600
Hauppauge *(G-5700)*

Ludwig and Larsen ....E 718 369-0999
Ridgewood *(G-13151)*

▲ **Micro Contacts Inc** ....E 516 433-4830
Hicksville *(G-5929)*

Mini-Circuits Fort Wayne LLC ....B 718 934-4500
Brooklyn *(G-2157)*

▲ **Monarch Electric Products Inc** ......G 718 583-7996
Bronx *(G-1318)*

Mono-Systems Inc ....E 716 821-1344
Buffalo *(G-2871)*

▲ **NEa Manufacturing Corp** ....E 516 371-4200
Inwood *(G-6300)*

Orbit International Corp ....D 631 435-8300
Hauppauge *(G-5734)*

▼ **Pass & Seymour Inc** ....B 315 468-6211
Syracuse *(G-14963)*

RE 99 Cents Inc ....G 718 639-2325
Woodside *(G-6222)*

Reynolds Packaging McHy Inc ....D 716 358-6451
Falconer *(G-4554)*

Saturn Industries Inc ....E 518 828-9956
Hudson *(G-6177)*

Schneider Electric Usa Inc ....G 631 567-5710
Bohemia *(G-1073)*

▼ **Sector Microwave Inds Inc** ....E 631 242-2245
Deer Park *(G-3935)*

Sinclair Technologies Inc ....E 716 874-3682
Hamburg *(G-5521)*

Skyko International LLC ....E 518 562-9696
Plattsburgh *(G-12777)*

▲ **Stever-Locke Industries Inc** ....G 585 624-3450
Honeoye Falls *(G-6081)*

▲ **Superpower Inc** ....E 518 346-1414
Schenectady *(G-14309)*

▲ **Switching Power Inc** ....D 631 981-7231
Ronkonkoma *(G-14016)*

Swivelier Company Inc ....D 845 353-1455
Blauvelt *(G-934)*

▲ **Tappan Wire & Cable Inc** ....C 845 353-9000
Blauvelt *(G-935)*

▲ **Tii Technologies Inc** ....E 516 364-9300
Edgewood *(G-4287)*

Utility Systems Tech Inc ....F 518 326-4142
Watervliet *(G-15611)*

▲ **Whirlwind Music Distrs Inc** ....D 800 733-9473
Rochester *(G-13803)*

▲ **Zierick Manufacturing Corp** ....D 800 882-8020
Mount Kisco *(G-8108)*

3644 Noncurrent-Carrying Wiring Devices

Chase Corporation ....F 631 827-0476
Northport *(G-12101)*

Complete SEC & Contrls Inc ....F 631 421-7200
Huntington Station *(G-6243)*

▲ **Gerome Technologies Inc** ....D 518 463-1324
Menands *(G-7843)*

Highland Valley Supply Inc ....F 845 849-2863
Wappingers Falls *(G-15496)*

▲ **J H C Fabrications Inc** ....E 718 649-0065
Brooklyn *(G-1977)*

Lapp Insulator Company LLC ....B 585 768-6221
Le Roy *(G-6902)*

◆ **Pfisterer Lapp LLC** ....B 585 768-6221
Le Roy *(G-6906)*

◆ **Producto Electric Corp** ....E 845 359-4900
Orangeburg *(G-12328)*

▲ **Quadristi LLC** ....F 585 279-3318
Rochester *(G-13658)*

Sphere Cables & Chips Inc ....E 212 619-3132
New York *(G-11322)*

▲ **Varflex Corporation** ....C 315 336-4400
Rome *(G-13876)*

▲ **Veja Electronics Inc** ....D 631 321-6086
Deer Park *(G-3949)*

▲ **Volt Tek Inc** ....F 585 377-2050
Fairport *(G-4529)*

▲ **Von Roll Usa Inc** ....C 518 344-7100
Schenectady *(G-14316)*

Von Roll Usa Inc ....E 203 562-2171
Schenectady *(G-14315)*

Von Roll USA Holding Inc ....F 518 344-7200
Schenectady *(G-14317)*

▲ **Zierick Manufacturing Corp** ....D 800 882-8020
Mount Kisco *(G-8108)*

3645 Residential Lighting Fixtures

◆ **Adesso Inc** ....E 212 736-4440
New York *(G-8456)*

▲ **Aesthonics Inc** ....D 646 723-2463
Brooklyn *(G-1469)*

Artemis Studios Inc ....E 718 788-6022
Brooklyn *(G-1536)*

▲ **Canarm Ltd** ....G 800 267-4427
Ogdensburg *(G-12203)*

▲ **Cooper Lighting LLC** ....C 516 470-1000
Hicksville *(G-5896)*

SIC

Custom Lampshades Inc ....F 718 254-0500
Brooklyn *(G-1711)*

▲ David Weeks Studio ....F 212 966-3433
New York *(G-9184)*

▲ Dreyfus Ashby Inc......................E 212 818-0770
New York *(G-9271)*

E-Finnergy Group LLC ....G 845 547-2424
Suffern *(G-14760)*

Eaton Corporation ....E 315 579-2872
Syracuse *(G-14882)*

▲ ER Butler & Co Inc ....E 212 925-3565
New York *(G-9392)*

◆ Hudson Valley Lighting Inc ....D 845 561-0300
Wappingers Falls *(G-15497)*

▲ Jamaica Lamp Corp ....E 718 776-5039
Queens Village *(G-13023)*

Jimco Lamp & Manufacturing Co ....G 631 218-2152
Islip *(G-6353)*

Judis Lampshades Inc ....G 917 561-3921
Brooklyn *(G-2009)*

▲ Litelab Corp ....C 716 856-4300
Buffalo *(G-2851)*

Matov Industries Inc ....E 718 392-5060
Long Island City *(G-7291)*

▲ Modulighter Inc ....F 212 371-0336
New York *(G-10491)*

New Generation Lighting Inc ....F 212 966-0328
New York *(G-10582)*

Nulux Inc ....E 718 383-1112
Ridgewood *(G-13153)*

Philips Elec N Amer Corp ....C 607 776-3692
Bath *(G-639)*

Pompian Manufacturing Co Inc ....G 914 476-7076
Yonkers *(G-16343)*

▲ Preciseled Inc ....F 516 418-5337
Valley Stream *(G-15352)*

▲ Prestigeline Inc ....D 631 273-3636
Bay Shore *(G-701)*

▲ Quality HM Brands Holdings LLC ......G 718 292-2024
Bronx *(G-1347)*

Quoizel Inc ....E 631 436-4402
Hauppauge *(G-5752)*

Rapid-Lite Fixture Corporation ....F 347 599-2600
Brooklyn *(G-2327)*

Remains Lighting ....E 212 675-8051
New York *(G-11008)*

▲ Sandy Littman Inc ....G 845 562-1112
Newburgh *(G-11886)*

▲ Saratoga Lighting Holdings LLC ......G 212 906-7800
New York *(G-11136)*

Savwatt Usa Inc ....G 646 478-2676
New York *(G-11142)*

▲ Solarwaterway Inc ....E 888 998-5337
Brooklyn *(G-2438)*

◆ Swarovski Lighting Ltd ....C 518 563-7500
Plattsburgh *(G-12783)*

Swarovski Lighting Ltd ....B 518 324-6378
Plattsburgh *(G-12784)*

Swivelier Company Inc ....D 845 353-1455
Blauvelt *(G-934)*

Tarsier Ltd ....C 646 880-8680
New York *(G-11436)*

Tudor Electrical Supply Co Inc ....G 212 867-7550
New York *(G-11558)*

Two Worlds Arts Ltd ....G 212 929-2210
New York *(G-11566)*

Ulster Precision Inc ....E 845 338-0995
Kingston *(G-6717)*

▲ Vaughan Designs Inc ....F 212 319-7070
New York *(G-11649)*

▲ Vision Quest Lighting Inc ....E 631 737-4800
East Setauket *(G-4190)*

▲ Wainland Inc ....E 718 626-2233
Astoria *(G-444)*

3646 Commercial, Indl & Institutional Lighting Fixtures

AEP Environmental LLC ....F 716 446-0739
Buffalo *(G-2625)*

▲ Aesthonics Inc ....D 646 723-2463
Brooklyn *(G-1469)*

▲ Altman Stage Lighting Co Inc ....C 914 476-7987
Yonkers *(G-16283)*

▲ Apparatus Studio ....E 646 527-9732
New York *(G-8606)*

Aquarii Inc ....G 315 672-8807
Camillus *(G-3107)*

Aristocrat Lighting Inc....................F 718 522-0003
Brooklyn *(G-1530)*

Arlee Lighting Corp.......................G 516 595-8558
Inwood *(G-6288)*

Big Shine Worldwide Inc ....G 845 444-5255
Newburgh *(G-11859)*

▲ Canarm Ltd ....G 800 267-4427
Ogdensburg *(G-12203)*

▲ Coldstream Group Inc ....G 914 698-5959
Mamaroneck *(G-7504)*

▲ Contemporary Visions LLC ....G 845 926-5469
Wappingers Falls *(G-15490)*

Cooper Industries LLC ....C 315 477-7000
Syracuse *(G-14864)*

▲ Cooper Lighting LLC ....C 516 470-1000
Hicksville *(G-5896)*

▲ Dreyfus Ashby Inc......................E 212 818-0770
New York *(G-9271)*

▲ Edison Price Lighting Inc ....C 718 685-0700
Long Island City *(G-7209)*

Edison Price Lighting Inc ....D 718 685-0700
Long Island City *(G-7210)*

Electric Lighting Agencies ....E 212 645-4580
New York *(G-9334)*

Energy Conservation & Sup Inc ....F 718 855-5888
Brooklyn *(G-1805)*

G&G Led LLC ....E 800 285-6780
Clifton Park *(G-3464)*

Global Lighting Inc ....G 914 591-4095
Yonkers *(G-16313)*

▲ Green Energy Concepts Inc ....G 845 238-2574
Chester *(G-3379)*

◆ Hudson Valley Lighting Inc ....D 845 561-0300
Wappingers Falls *(G-15497)*

Ideoli Group Inc ....F 212 705-8769
Port Washington *(G-12887)*

▲ Jesco Lighting Inc ....E 718 366-3211
Port Washington *(G-12892)*

▲ Jesco Lighting Group LLC ....E 718 366-3211
Port Washington *(G-12893)*

▲ La Mar Lighting Co Inc ....E 631 777-7700
Farmingdale *(G-4668)*

LDI Lighting Inc ....E 718 384-4490
Brooklyn *(G-2050)*

LDI Lighting Inc ....G 718 384-4490
Brooklyn *(G-2051)*

▲ Legion Lighting Co Inc ....E 718 498-1770
Brooklyn *(G-2059)*

▲ Light Waves Concept Inc ....F 212 677-6400
Brooklyn *(G-2072)*

Lighting By Dom Yonkers Inc ....G 914 968-8700
Yonkers *(G-16328)*

▲ Lighting Services Inc ....D 845 942-2800
Stony Point *(G-14746)*

▲ Linear Lighting Corporation ....C 718 361-7552
Long Island City *(G-7274)*

Lite Brite Manufacturing Inc ....F 718 855-9797
Brooklyn *(G-2079)*

▲ Lite-Makers Inc ....E 718 739-9300
Jamaica *(G-6454)*

Litelab Corp ....E 718 361-6829
Long Island City *(G-7276)*

▲ Litelab Corp ....C 716 856-4300
Buffalo *(G-2851)*

▲ Lukas Lighting Inc ....E 800 841-4011
Long Island City *(G-7281)*

Luminatta Inc ....G 914 664-3600
Mount Vernon *(G-8159)*

Luminescent Systems Inc ....B 716 655-0800
East Aurora *(G-4091)*

Lynne B Enterprises Inc ....E 631 254-6975
Deer Park *(G-3901)*

▲ Magniflood Inc ....E 631 226-1000
Amityville *(G-294)*

Matov Industries Inc ....E 718 392-5060
Long Island City *(G-7291)*

▲ Modulighter Inc ....F 212 371-0336
New York *(G-10491)*

Mtz Enterprises Inc ....G 347 834-2716
Brooklyn *(G-2181)*

▲ North American Mfg Entps Inc.........E 718 524-4370
Staten Island *(G-14684)*

Nulux Inc ....E 718 383-1112
Ridgewood *(G-13153)*

Oledworks LLC ....E 585 287-6802
Rochester *(G-13589)*

▲ Preciseled Inc ....F 516 418-5337
Valley Stream *(G-15352)*

Primelite Manufacturing Corp............G 516 868-4411
Freeport *(G-5017)*

Rapid-Lite Fixture Corporation ....F 347 599-2600
Brooklyn *(G-2327)*

Remains Lighting ....E 212 675-8051
New York *(G-11008)*

◆ Rle Industries LLC ....E 973 276-1444
New York *(G-11055)*

S E A Supplies Ltd ....F 516 694-6677
Plainview *(G-12712)*

▲ Sandy Littman Inc ....G 845 562-1112
Newburgh *(G-11886)*

Santucci Custom Lighting ....F 866 853-1929
Clinton *(G-3485)*

▲ Saratoga Lighting Holdings LLC ......E 212 906-7800
New York *(G-11136)*

Savwatt Usa Inc ....G 646 478-2676
New York *(G-11142)*

◆ Selux Corporation ....C 845 691-7723
Highland *(G-5963)*

Signify North America Corp ....E 646 265-7170
New York *(G-11237)*

Solarpath Inc ....E 201 490-4499
New York *(G-11289)*

▲ Solarwaterway Inc ....E 888 998-5337
Brooklyn *(G-2438)*

▲ Spectronics Corporation ....E 516 333-4840
Westbury *(G-15926)*

Swivelier Company Inc ....E 845 353-1455
Blauvelt *(G-934)*

Twinkle Lighting Inc......................E 718 225-0939
Flushing *(G-4902)*

Versaponents Inc ....F 631 242-3387
Deer Park *(G-3950)*

▲ Vision Quest Lighting Inc ....E 631 737-4800
East Setauket *(G-4190)*

Vital Vio Inc ....G 914 245-6048
Troy *(G-15194)*

Xeleum Lighting LLC ....F 954 617-8170
Mount Kisco *(G-8107)*

▲ Zumtobel Lighting Inc ....C 845 691-6262
Highland *(G-5965)*

3647 Vehicular Lighting Eqpt

Aerospace Lighting Corporation..........D 631 563-6400
Bohemia *(G-967)*

▲ Astronics Corporation ....C 716 805-1599
East Aurora *(G-4082)*

B/E Aerospace Inc ....E 631 563-6400
Bohemia *(G-978)*

Copy Cat ....G 718 934-2192
Brooklyn *(G-1686)*

Licenders ....G 212 759-5200
New York *(G-10210)*

Luminescent Systems Inc ....B 716 655-0800
East Aurora *(G-4091)*

▼ Mobile Fleet Inc ....E 631 206-2920
Hauppauge *(G-5722)*

Power and Cnstr Group Inc ....E 585 889-6020
Scottsville *(G-14342)*

◆ Wolo Mfg Corp ....E 631 242-0333
Deer Park *(G-3955)*

3648 Lighting Eqpt, NEC

▲ Altman Stage Lighting Co Inc ....C 914 476-7987
Yonkers *(G-16283)*

▲ CEIT Corp ....F 518 825-0649
Plattsburgh *(G-12741)*

Cooper Crouse-Hinds Mtl Inc ....C 315 477-7000
Syracuse *(G-14863)*

Cooper Industries LLC ....F 315 477-7000
Syracuse *(G-14864)*

◆ Creative Stage Lighting Co Inc ....E 518 251-3302
North Creek *(G-12031)*

Edison Power & Light Co Inc ....F 718 522-0002
Brooklyn *(G-1783)*

Eluminocity US Inc ....G 651 528-1165
New York *(G-9353)*

▲ Enchante Lites LLC ....G 212 602-1818
New York *(G-9367)*

Exc Holdings I Corp.......................A 212 644-5900
New York *(G-9438)*

Exc Holdings II Corp......................A 212 644-5900
New York *(G-9439)*

Exc Holdings LP ....A 212 644-5900
New York *(G-9440)*

▲ Expo Furniture Designs Inc ....F 516 674-1420
Glen Cove *(G-5192)*

▲ Fabbian USA Corp ....G 973 882-3824
New York *(G-9459)*

General Led Corp..........................F 516 280-2854
Mineola *(G-7976)*

Goddard Design Co ....G 718 599-0170
Brooklyn *(G-1895)*

Gordon S Anderson Mfg Co ....G...... 845 677-3304
   Millbrook *(G-7942)*
Illumination Technologies Inc ....F...... 315 463-4673
   Liverpool *(G-7013)*
Island Lite Louvers Inc ....E...... 631 608-4250
   Amityville *(G-278)*
J M Canty Inc ....E...... 716 625-4227
   Lockport *(G-7084)*
Jag Lighting ....G...... 917 226-3575
   Maspeth *(G-7624)*
◆ Jaquith Industries Inc ....E...... 315 478-5700
   Syracuse *(G-14916)*
Jed Lights Inc ....F...... 516 812-5001
   Deer Park *(G-3888)*
Jt Roselle Lighting & Sup Inc ....F...... 914 666-3700
   Mount Kisco *(G-8095)*
▲ Julian A McDermott Corporation .....E...... 718 456-3606
   Ridgewood *(G-13148)*
▲ La Mar Lighting Co Inc ....E...... 631 777-7700
   Farmingdale *(G-4668)*
Light Blue USA LLC ....G...... 718 475-2515
   Brooklyn *(G-2070)*
Lighting N Beyond LLC ....G...... 718 669-9142
   Blauvelt *(G-930)*
Lighting Sculptures Inc ....F...... 631 242-3387
   Deer Park *(G-3898)*
Lilibrand LLC ....G...... 212 239-8230
   Brooklyn *(G-2073)*
Luminescent Systems Inc ....B...... 716 655-0800
   East Aurora *(G-4091)*
Medtek Skin Care Inc ....E...... 518 745-7264
   Glens Falls *(G-5258)*
Methods Tooling & Mfg Inc ....E...... 845 246-7100
   Mount Marion *(G-8111)*
Mjk Enterprises LLC ....G...... 917 653-9042
   Brooklyn *(G-2163)*
Northern Air Technology Inc ....G...... 585 594-5050
   Rochester *(G-13585)*
◆ Olive Led Lighting Inc ....G...... 718 746-0830
   College Point *(G-3557)*
Power and Cnstr Prod Inc ....E...... 585 889-6020
   Scottsville *(G-14342)*
Psg Innovations Inc ....F...... 917 299-8986
   Valley Stream *(G-15354)*
Revolution Lighting LLC ....E...... 518 779-3655
   Glens Falls *(G-5266)*
▲ Ric-Lo Productions Ltd ....E...... 845 469-2285
   Chester *(G-3384)*
Rodac USA Corp ....E...... 716 741-3931
   Clarence *(G-3442)*
▲ Saratoga Lighting Holdings LLC ......G...... 212 906-7800
   New York *(G-11136)*
Secret Celebrity Licensing LLC ....G...... 212 812-9277
   New York *(G-11175)*
Sensio America ....F...... 877 501-5337
   Clifton Park *(G-3472)*
▲ Sensio America LLC ....F...... 877 501-5337
   Clifton Park *(G-3473)*
Serway Bros Inc ....G...... 315 337-0601
   Rome *(G-13872)*
Shakuff LLC ....G...... 212 675-0383
   Brooklyn *(G-2401)*
▲ Sir Industries Inc ....E...... 631 234-2444
   Hauppauge *(G-5767)*
◆ Star Headlight Lantern Co Inc ....C...... 585 226-9500
   Avon *(G-516)*
Strider Global LLC ....G...... 212 726-1302
   New York *(G-11374)*
Tarsier Ltd ....C...... 646 880-8680
   New York *(G-11436)*
▲ Tecnolux Incorporated ....G...... 718 369-3900
   Brooklyn *(G-2497)*
▲ Times Square Stage Ltg Co Inc ....E...... 845 947-3034
   Stony Point *(G-14749)*
◆ Truck-Lite Co LLC ....B...... 716 665-6214
   Falconer *(G-4560)*
▲ USA Illumination Inc ....E...... 845 565-8500
   New Windsor *(G-8385)*
Vertex Innovative Solutions ....F...... 315 437-6711
   Syracuse *(G-15021)*
Vincent Conigliaro ....F...... 845 340-0489
   Kingston *(G-6722)*
Vivid Rgb Lighting LLC ....G...... 718 635-0817
   Peekskill *(G-12558)*

3651 Household Audio & Video Eqpt

▲ Accent Speaker Technology Ltd ....G...... 631 738-2540
   Holbrook *(G-5982)*
▲ Aguilar Amplification LLC ....F...... 212 431-9109
   New York *(G-8496)*

Amplitech Group Inc ....G...... 631 521-7831
   Bohemia *(G-972)*
◆ Andrea Electronics Corporation ....G...... 631 719-1800
   Bohemia *(G-973)*
▲ Ashly Audio Inc ....E...... 585 872-0010
   Webster *(G-15630)*
▲ Audio Technology New York Inc ....F...... 718 369-7528
   Brooklyn *(G-1552)*
Audio Video Invasion Inc ....F...... 516 345-2636
   Plainview *(G-12664)*
▼ Audiosavings Inc ....F...... 888 445-1555
   Inwood *(G-6289)*
Avcom of Virginia Inc ....D...... 585 924-4560
   Victor *(G-15392)*
AVI-Spl Employee ....B...... 212 840-4801
   Brooklyn *(G-8691)*
B & H Electronics Corp ....E...... 845 782-5000
   Monroe *(G-8015)*
▲ B & K Components Ltd ....D...... 323 776-4277
   Buffalo *(G-2653)*
▲ Bayit Home Automation Corp ....E...... 973 988-2638
   Brooklyn *(G-1568)*
Broadcast Manager Inc ....G...... 212 509-1200
   New York *(G-8858)*
▲ Communication Power Corp ....E...... 631 434-7306
   Hauppauge *(G-5624)*
Convergent Audio Tech Inc ....G...... 585 359-2700
   Rush *(G-14069)*
Covington Sound ....G...... 646 256-7486
   Bronx *(G-1232)*
▲ Digitac Inc ....F...... 732 215-4020
   Brooklyn *(G-1744)*
Digitac LLC ....G...... 732 669-7637
   Brooklyn *(G-1745)*
Digital Home Creations Inc ....G...... 585 576-7070
   Webster *(G-15638)*
Fulcrum Acoustic LLC ....G...... 866 234-0678
   Whitesboro *(G-13426)*
G E Inspection Technologies LP ....C...... 315 554-2000
   Skaneateles *(G-14451)*
General Electric Company ....G...... 315 554-2000
   Skaneateles *(G-14452)*
Gilmores Sound Advice Inc ....F...... 212 265-4445
   New York *(G-9611)*
▲ Global Market Development Inc ....E...... 631 667-1000
   Edgewood *(G-4269)*
Granada Electronics Inc ....G...... 718 387-1157
   Brooklyn *(G-1906)*
Hope International Productions ....F...... 212 247-3188
   New York *(G-9811)*
Ilab America Inc ....G...... 631 615-5053
   Selden *(G-14353)*
◆ Jwin Electronics Corp ....C...... 516 626-7188
   Port Washington *(G-12894)*
Keemotion LLC ....G...... 914 458-3900
   Brooklyn *(G-2022)*
▲ Key Digital Systems Inc ....E...... 914 667-9700
   Mount Vernon *(G-8155)*
L A R Electronics Corp ....G...... 716 285-0555
   Niagara Falls *(G-11945)*
L3 Technologies Inc ....A...... 631 436-7400
   Hauppauge *(G-5687)*
Laird Telemedia ....C...... 845 339-9555
   Mount Marion *(G-8110)*
Lamm Industries Inc ....G...... 718 368-0181
   Brooklyn *(G-2045)*
Masterdisk Corporation ....F...... 212 541-5022
   Elmsford *(G-4417)*
▼ Navitar Inc ....D...... 585 359-4000
   Rochester *(G-13568)*
▲ NEa Manufacturing Corp ....E...... 516 371-4200
   Inwood *(G-6300)*
▲ New Audio LLC ....E...... 212 213-6060
   New York *(G-10576)*
New Wop Records ....G...... 631 617-9732
   Deer Park *(G-3911)*
Nykon Inc ....G...... 315 483-0504
   Sodus *(G-14492)*
Octave Music Group Inc ....G...... 212 991-6540
   New York *(G-10679)*
Professional Technology Inc ....G...... 315 337-4156
   Rome *(G-13864)*
Pure Acoustics Inc ....G...... 718 788-4411
   Brooklyn *(G-2305)*
Request Inc ....E...... 518 899-1254
   Halfmoon *(G-5497)*
Request Serious Play LLC ....G...... 518 899-1254
   Halfmoon *(G-5498)*
Sage Audio Video Tech LLC ....E...... 212 213-1523
   New York *(G-11115)*

Samson Technologies Corp ....D...... 631 784-2200
   Hicksville *(G-5946)*
◆ Scy Manufacturing Inc ....G...... 516 986-3083
   Inwood *(G-6303)*
Shyk International Corp ....G...... 212 663-3302
   New York *(G-11222)*
▲ Sima Technologies LLC ....G...... 412 828-9130
   Hauppauge *(G-5766)*
Sing Trix ....F...... 212 352-1500
   New York *(G-11249)*
◆ Sony Corporation of America ....C...... 212 833-8000
   New York *(G-11295)*
▲ Sound Video Systems Wny LLC ....F...... 716 684-8200
   Buffalo *(G-2990)*
Speaqua Corp ....G...... 858 334-9042
   Deer Park *(G-3939)*
Theodore A Rapp Associates ....G...... 845 469-2100
   Chester *(G-3391)*
Tkm Technologies Inc ....E...... 631 474-4700
   Port Jeff STA *(G-12839)*
◆ Toshiba America Inc ....E...... 212 596-0600
   New York *(G-11519)*
Touchtunes Music Corporation ....D...... 847 419-3300
   New York *(G-11523)*
Tunecore Inc ....E...... 646 651-1060
   Brooklyn *(G-2527)*
Video Technology Services Inc ....F...... 516 937-9700
   Syosset *(G-14804)*
Vincent Conigliaro ....F...... 845 340-0489
   Kingston *(G-6722)*
Vtb Holdings Inc ....G...... 914 345-2255
   Valhalla *(G-15311)*
▲ Whirlwind Music Distrs Inc ....D...... 800 733-9473
   Rochester *(G-13803)*
Widgetworks Unlimited LLC ....G...... 914 666-6395
   Chappaqua *(G-3327)*
▲ Woo Audio Inc ....F...... 917 324-5284
   Long Island City *(G-7407)*
▲ Wyrestorm Technologies LLC ....F...... 518 289-1293
   Round Lake *(G-14063)*
▲ Yorkville Sound Inc ....G...... 716 297-2920
   Niagara Falls *(G-11992)*

3652 Phonograph Records & Magnetic Tape

▲ A To Z Media Inc ....E...... 212 260-0237
   New York *(G-8420)*
Abkco Music & Records Inc ....E...... 212 399-0300
   New York *(G-8430)*
Atlantic Recording Corp ....B...... 212 707-2000
   New York *(G-8667)*
▲ Bertelsmann Inc ....E...... 212 782-1000
   New York *(G-8764)*
Bridge Records Inc ....G...... 914 654-9270
   New Rochelle *(G-8322)*
Chesky Records Inc ....F...... 212 586-7799
   New York *(G-8983)*
Columbia Records Inc ....F...... 212 833-8000
   New York *(G-9059)*
Cult Records LLC ....G...... 718 395-2077
   Brooklyn *(G-9131)*
Eks Manufacturing Inc ....F...... 917 217-0784
   Brooklyn *(G-1787)*
Emusiccom Inc ....D...... 212 201-9240
   New York *(G-9365)*
Europadisk LLC ....E...... 718 407-7300
   Long Island City *(G-7216)*
▲ Extreme Group Holdings LLC ....F...... 212 833-8000
   New York *(G-9450)*
High Quality Video Inc ....F...... 212 686-9534
   New York *(G-9782)*
His Productions USA Inc ....G...... 212 594-3737
   New York *(G-9793)*
▲ Historic TW Inc ....G...... 212 484-8000
   New York *(G-9794)*
Hope International Productions ....F...... 212 247-3188
   New York *(G-9811)*
Lefrak Entertainment Co Ltd ....G...... 212 586-3600
   New York *(G-10192)*
Masterdisk Corporation ....F...... 212 541-5022
   Elmsford *(G-4417)*
Media Technologies Ltd ....G...... 631 467-7900
   Eastport *(G-4252)*
Peer-Southern Productions Inc ....E...... 212 265-3910
   New York *(G-10786)*
Pete Levin Music Inc ....G...... 845 247-9211
   Saugerties *(G-14209)*
Pivot Records LLC ....F...... 718 417-1213
   Brooklyn *(G-2264)*
▲ Recorded Anthology of Amrcn Mus ..F...... 212 290-1695
   Brooklyn *(G-2333)*

S
I
C

Roadrunner Records Inc ....E 212 274-7500
New York (G-11058)

Side Hustle Music Group LLC ....F 800 219-4003
New York (G-11223)

▲ Sony Broadband Entertainment ....F 212 833-6800
New York (G-11294)

◆ Sony Corporation of America ....C 212 833-8000
New York (G-11295)

Sony Music Entertainment ....A 212 833-8000
New York (G-11297)

▲ Sony Music Entertainment Inc ......A 212 833-8000
New York (G-11298)

◆ Sony Music Holdings Inc ....A 212 833-8000
New York (G-11299)

Sterling Sound Inc ....E 212 604-9433
New York (G-11360)

Time Warner Companies Inc ....D 212 484-8000
New York (G-11494)

▲ Universal Mus Group Hldngs Inc .....E 212 333-8000
New York (G-11608)

Universal Music Group Inc ....F 212 333-8237
New York (G-11609)

Vaire LLC ....G 631 271-4933
Huntington Station (G-6265)

Warner Music Group Corp ....C 212 275-2000
New York (G-11722)

▼ Warner Music Inc ....D 212 275-2000
New York (G-11723)

Wea International Inc ....D 212 275-1300
New York (G-11734)

3661 Telephone & Telegraph Apparatus

ABS Talkx Inc ....G 631 254-9100
Bay Shore (G-642)

▼ Aines Manufacturing Corp ....E 631 471-3900
Islip (G-6350)

Alcatel-Lucent USA Inc ....D 516 349-4900
Plainview (G-12661)

Alternative Technology Corp ....G 914 478-5900
Hastings On Hudson (G-5571)

▲ Astrocom Electronics Inc ....D 607 432-1930
Oneonta (G-12258)

▲ Audio-Sears Corp ....D 607 652-7305
Stamford (G-14606)

Avaya Services Inc ....G 866 462-8292
New York (G-8688)

Call Forwarding Technologies ....G 516 621-3600
Greenvale (G-5460)

▲ Clayton Dubilier & Rice Fun ....E 212 407-5200
New York (G-9029)

Corning Incorporated ....E 607 248-1200
Corning (G-3708)

Corning Incorporated ....A 607 974-9000
Painted Post (G-12473)

◆ Corning Incorporated ....A 607 974-9000
Corning (G-3705)

Eagle Telephonics Inc ....F 631 471-3600
Bohemia (G-1007)

▲ ESi Cases & Accessories Inc ....E 212 883-8838
New York (G-9397)

◆ Fiber Instrument Sales Inc ....C 315 736-2206
Oriskany (G-12390)

▲ Fiberwave Corporation ....C 718 802-9011
Brooklyn (G-1840)

▲ Forerunner Technologies Inc ....E 631 337-2100
Edgewood (G-4268)

Fujitsu Ntwrk Cmmnications Inc ....F 845 731-2000
Pearl River (G-12531)

Gac Express Inc ....G 718 438-2227
Brooklyn (G-1876)

▲ I D Tel Corp ....F 718 876-6000
Staten Island (G-14662)

Interdgital Communications LLC ....C 631 622-4000
Melville (G-7795)

▲ Kelta Inc ....E 631 789-5000
Edgewood (G-4273)

L3 Technologies Inc ....A 631 436-7400
Hauppauge (G-5687)

L3harris Technologies Inc ....E 585 244-5830
Rochester (G-13511)

Luxcore Networks Inc ....F 212 618-1724
New York (G-10285)

Maia Systems LLC ....G 718 206-0100
Jamaica (G-6456)

Mitel Networks Inc ....G 877 654-3573
Rochester (G-13553)

▲ Parabit Systems Inc ....E 516 378-4800
Bellmore (G-786)

Performance Technologies Inc ....E 585 256-0200
Rochester (G-13615)

Photonstring Inc ....G 917 966-5717
Godeffroy (G-5302)

Polycom Inc ....E 212 372-6960
New York (G-10862)

▲ Powermate Cellular ....G 718 833-9400
Brooklyn (G-2274)

Quality One Wireless LLC ....C 631 233-3337
Ronkonkoma (G-13999)

R I R Communications Systems ....E 718 706-9957
Mount Vernon (G-8175)

▲ Redcom Laboratories Inc ....C 585 924-6567
Victor (G-15428)

▲ Rus Industries Inc ....E 716 284-7828
Niagara Falls (G-11975)

◆ Sandstone Technologies Corp ....E 585 785-5537
Rochester (G-13713)

Sandstone Technologies Corp ....E 585 785-5537
Rochester (G-13714)

Siemens AG ....G 212 946-2440
New York (G-11225)

Siemens Corporation ....F 202 434-7800
New York (G-11226)

Siemens USA Holdings Inc ....B 212 258-4000
New York (G-11228)

▼ Simrex Corporation ....G 716 206-0174
Buffalo (G-2983)

▲ Snake Tray International LLC ....E 631 674-0004
Bay Shore (G-716)

▼ Splice Technologies Inc ....G 631 924-8108
Manorville (G-7554)

Telecommunication Concepts ....G 315 736-8523
Whitesboro (G-16083)

Telephonics Corporation ....B 631 755-7659
Farmingdale (G-4751)

▲ Telephonics Corporation ....A 631 755-7600
Farmingdale (G-4752)

Terahertz Technologies Inc ....G 315 736-3642
Oriskany (G-12398)

▲ Tii Technologies Inc ....E 516 364-9300
Edgewood (G-4287)

◆ Toshiba Amer Info Systems Inc ......B 949 583-3000
New York (G-11518)

◆ Toshiba America Inc ....E 212 596-0600
New York (G-11519)

U2o Usa LLC ....G 516 813-9500
Plainview (G-12720)

3663 Radio & T V Communications, Systs & Eqpt, Broadcast/Studio

2p Agency Usa Inc ....E 212 203-5586
Brooklyn (G-1413)

Advanced Comm Solutions ....G 914 693-5076
Ardsley (G-384)

Airnet Communications Corp ....F 516 338-0008
Westbury (G-15864)

Ametek CTS Us Inc ....E 631 467-8400
Ronkonkoma (G-13905)

Amplitech Inc ....G 631 521-7738
Bohemia (G-971)

Amplitech Group Inc ....G 631 521-7831
Bohemia (G-972)

◆ Andrea Electronics Corporation .....G 631 719-1800
Bohemia (G-973)

▲ Apex Airtronics Inc ....E 718 485-8560
Brooklyn (G-1516)

Appairent Technologies Inc ....G 585 214-2460
West Henrietta (G-15785)

Arcom Automatics LLC ....G 315 422-1230
Syracuse (G-14815)

▲ Armstrong Transmitter Corp ....F 315 673-1269
Marcellus (G-7560)

▲ Arrow-Communication Labs Inc ....B 315 422-1230
Syracuse (G-14818)

▲ Ashly Audio Inc ....E 585 872-0010
Webster (G-15630)

AVI-Spl Employee ....B 212 840-4801
New York (G-8691)

B & H Electronics Corp ....E 845 782-5000
Monroe (G-8015)

Basil S Kadhim ....G 888 520-5192
New York (G-8736)

Bayside Beepers & Cellular ....G 718 343-3888
Glen Oaks (G-5214)

Belden Inc ....B 607 796-5600
Horseheads (G-6114)

Benchmark Media Systems Inc ....F 315 437-6300
Syracuse (G-14828)

Big Fish Entertainment LLC ....C 646 797-4955
New York (G-8786)

Bullitt Mobile LLC ....D 631 424-1749
Bohemia (G-983)

Century Metal Parts Corp ....E 631 667-0800
Bay Shore (G-661)

Chyronhego Corporation ....D 631 845-2000
Melville (G-7767)

▼ CJ Component Products LLC ....G 631 567-3733
Oakdale (G-12149)

Clever Devices Ltd ....E 516 433-6100
Woodbury (G-16167)

Click It Inc ....D 631 686-2900
Hauppauge (G-5618)

▲ Cmb Wireless Group LLC ....B 631 750-4700
Bohemia (G-989)

Cntry Cross Communications LLC ....F 386 758-9696
Jamestown (G-6503)

▲ Communication Power Corp ....E 631 434-7306
Hauppauge (G-5624)

▲ Comtech PST Corp ....E 631 777-8900
Melville (G-7770)

◆ Comtech Telecom Corp ....C 631 962-7000
Melville (G-7771)

Digifab Systems Inc ....G 212 944-9882
New York (G-9225)

▲ Eagle Comtronics Inc ....C 315 451-3313
Liverpool (G-7009)

Eeg Enterprises Inc ....F 516 293-7472
Farmingdale (G-4624)

▼ Electro-Metrics Corporation ....E 518 762-2600
Johnstown (G-6614)

Elite Cellular Accessories Inc ....E 877 390-2502
Deer Park (G-3869)

▲ Eni Technology Inc ....B 585 427-8300
Rochester (G-13395)

Evado Filip ....G 917 774-8666
New York (G-9423)

Fei-Zyfer Inc ....G 714 933-4045
Uniondale (G-15228)

Fleetcom Inc ....F 914 776-5582
Yonkers (G-16310)

Flycell Inc ....D 212 400-1212
New York (G-9511)

Fujitsu Ntwrk Cmmnications Inc ....F 845 731-2000
Pearl River (G-12531)

◆ GE Mds LLC ....C 585 242-9600
Rochester (G-13430)

Geosync Microwave Inc ....G 631 760-5567
Hauppauge (G-5659)

Ghostek LLC ....F 855 310-3439
Brooklyn (G-1885)

◆ Griffon Corporation ....E 212 957-5000
New York (G-9676)

Gurley Precision Instrs Inc ....C 518 272-6300
Troy (G-15170)

Hamtronics Inc ....G 585 392-9430
Rochester (G-13457)

▼ Harris Globl Cmmunications Inc .....A 585 244-5830
Rochester (G-13460)

Home Tech Inc ....G 914 301-5408
Katonah (G-6633)

Hopewell Precision Inc ....E 845 221-2737
Hopewell Junction (G-6096)

Icell Incorporated ....C 516 590-0007
Hempstead (G-5839)

▲ Icon Enterprises Intl Inc ....E 718 752-9764
Mohegan Lake (G-8010)

Iheartcommunications Inc ....C 585 454-4884
Rochester (G-13475)

▼ Innovation In Motion Inc ....G 407 878-7561
Long Beach (G-7137)

Intelibs Inc ....G 877 213-2640
Stony Brook (G-14739)

It Commodity Sourcing Inc ....G 718 677-1577
Brooklyn (G-1972)

▲ John Mezzalingua Assoc LLC ....C 315 431-7100
Liverpool (G-7018)

▲ L3 Foreign Holdings Inc ....C 212 697-1111
New York (G-10153)

L3 Technologies Inc ....B 631 231-1700
Hauppauge (G-5686)

L3 Technologies Inc ....A 631 436-7400
Hauppauge (G-5687)

L3 Technologies Inc ....D 631 231-1700
Hauppauge (G-5688)

L3 Technologies Inc ....D 631 436-7400
Hauppauge (G-5689)

L3 Technologies Inc ....B 212 697-1111
New York (G-10154)

L3harris Technologies Inc ....A 585 244-5830
Rochester (G-13507)

L3harris Technologies Inc.................B......585 244-5830
Rochester *(G-13512)*

L3harris Technologies Inc.................F......718 767-1100
Whitestone *(G-16096)*

L3harris Technologies Inc.................B......585 244-5830
Rochester *(G-13513)*

L3harris Technologies Inc.................A......631 630-4200
Amityville *(G-288)*

Listec Video Corp...............................G......631 273-3029
Hauppauge *(G-5692)*

Loral Space & Commnctns Holdng.......E......212 697-1105
New York *(G-10255)*

Loral Space Communications Inc........E......212 697-1105
New York *(G-10256)*

Loral Spacecom Corporation...............E......212 697-1105
New York *(G-10257)*

▲ Magnet-Ndctive Systems Ltd USA....E......585 924-4000
Victor *(G-15419)*

Mark Peri International.......................F......516 208-6824
Oceanside *(G-12181)*

Millennium Antenna Corp.....................F......315 798-9374
Utica *(G-15284)*

Mini-Circuits Fort Wayne LLC.............B......718 934-4500
Brooklyn *(G-2157)*

Mirion Tech Imaging LLC......................E......607 562-4300
Horseheads *(G-6127)*

Mitel Networks Inc..............................G......877 654-3573
Rochester *(G-13553)*

Mks Medical Electronics......................C......585 292-7400
Rochester *(G-13555)*

Motorola Solutions Inc........................C......518 348-0833
Halfmoon *(G-5495)*

Motorola Solutions Inc........................C......518 869-9517
Albany *(G-101)*

Motorola Solutions Sls & Svcs............E......716 633-5022
Williamsville *(G-16134)*

Movin On Sounds and SEC Inc............E......516 489-2350
Franklin Square *(G-4962)*

▼ Navitar Inc.......................................D......585 359-4000
Rochester *(G-13568)*

North American MBL Systems Inc.......E......718 898-8700
Sea Cliff *(G-14346)*

Nycom Business Solutions Inc............G......516 345-6000
Franklin Square *(G-4963)*

Orbcomm Inc.......................................F......703 433-6396
Utica *(G-15290)*

▲ Prime View USA Inc.........................G......212 730-4905
New York *(G-10891)*

Quanta Electronics Inc.........................F......631 961-9953
Centereach *(G-3252)*

▲ Quintel Usa Inc................................E......585 420-8364
Rochester *(G-13665)*

Rehabilitation International...................G......212 420-1500
Jamaica *(G-6470)*

Ruhle Companies Inc...........................E......914 287-4000
Valhalla *(G-15309)*

Sartek Industries Inc...........................G......631 473-3555
East Setauket *(G-4186)*

Sdr Technology Inc..............................G......716 583-1249
Alden *(G-174)*

▲ Sentry Technology Corporation.......E......800 645-4224
Ronkonkoma *(G-14007)*

Silverlight Digital LLC..........................G......646 650-5330
New York *(G-11240)*

Sinclair Technologies Inc.....................E......716 874-3682
Hamburg *(G-5521)*

Specialty Microwave Corp....................F......631 737-1919
Ronkonkoma *(G-14014)*

Srtech Industry Corp...........................E......718 496-7001
College Point *(G-3566)*

STI-Co Industries Inc..........................E......716 662-2680
Orchard Park *(G-12377)*

▲ Telephonics Corporation.................A......631 755-7000
Farmingdale *(G-4752)*

▲ Telxon Corporation..........................E......631 738-2400
Holtsville *(G-6056)*

Times Square Studios Ltd....................C......212 930-7720
New York *(G-11496)*

Toura LLC..F......646 652-8668
Brooklyn *(G-2514)*

United Satcom Inc...............................G......718 359-4100
Flushing *(G-4903)*

US Space LLC......................................G......646 278-0371
New York *(G-11627)*

Village Video Productions Inc.............G......631 752-9311
West Babylon *(G-15756)*

▲ Whirlwind Music Distrs Inc.............D......800 733-9473
Rochester *(G-13803)*

Wireless Communications Inc.............G......845 353-5921
Nyack *(G-12148)*

Zetek Corporation...............................F......212 668-1485
New York *(G-11821)*

3669 Communications Eqpt, NEC

Ademco Inc..G......716 631-2197
Cheektowaga *(G-3337)*

All Metro Emrgncy Response Sys........G......516 750-9100
Lynbrook *(G-7424)*

▲ Alstom Signaling Inc........................B......585 783-2000
West Henrietta *(G-15782)*

Andrea Systems LLC...........................E......631 390-3140
Farmingdale *(G-4585)*

Apex Signal Corporation......................D......631 567-1100
Bohemia *(G-974)*

Apple Core Electronics Inc..................F......718 628-4068
Brooklyn *(G-1519)*

AVI-Spl Employee................................B......212 840-4801
New York *(G-8691)*

BNo Intl Trdg Co Inc............................G......716 487-1900
Jamestown *(G-6499)*

Capstream Technologies LLC.............G......716 945-7100
Olean *(G-12227)*

Comet Flasher Inc...............................G......716 821-9595
Buffalo *(G-2704)*

Cq Traffic Control Devices LLC.............G......518 767-0057
Selkirk *(G-14356)*

Curbell Medical Products Inc...............F......716 667-2520
Orchard Park *(G-12349)*

▲ Curbell Medical Products Inc............F......716 667-2520
Orchard Park *(G-12350)*

Datasonic Inc......................................G......516 248-7330
East Meadow *(G-4134)*

Finger Lakes Traffic Ctrl LLC..............E......607 795-7458
Elmira Heights *(G-4376)*

Fire Apparatus Service Tech................G......716 753-3538
Sherman *(G-14400)*

Firecom Inc...C......718 899-6100
Woodside *(G-16206)*

Firemaxx Systems Corp......................E......212 645-7414
New York *(G-9497)*

Firetronics Inc....................................G......516 997-5151
Jericho *(G-6580)*

Frequency Electronics Inc...................E......516 794-4500
Uniondale *(G-15229)*

Fuel Watchman Sales & Service..........F......718 665-6100
Bronx *(G-1263)*

Goddard Design Co.............................G......718 599-0170
Brooklyn *(G-1895)*

Harris Corporation..............................A......413 263-6200
Rochester *(G-13459)*

Intelligent Traffic Systems ....G......631 567-5994
Bohemia *(G-1024)*

Johnson Controls................................D......585 288-6200
Rochester *(G-13493)*

Johnson Controls................................E......518 952-6040
Clifton Park *(G-3465)*

Johnson Controls................................G......845 774-4120
Harriman *(G-5545)*

▲ L3 Foreign Holdings Inc..................C......212 697-1111
New York *(G-10153)*

L3 Technologies Inc............................B......212 697-1111
New York *(G-10154)*

Lifewatch Inc.......................................F......800 716-1433
Hewlett *(G-5871)*

Light Phone Inc..................................G......415 595-0044
Brooklyn *(G-2071)*

Lik LLC...F......516 848-5135
Northport *(G-12108)*

▲ McDowell Research Co Inc..............D......315 332-7100
Newark *(G-11845)*

Mkj Communications Inc.....................E......212 206-0072
Brooklyn *(G-2164)*

◆ Napco Security Tech Inc.................C......631 842-9400
Amityville *(G-297)*

▲ Nrd LLC...E......716 773-7634
Grand Island *(G-5339)*

Nu2 Systems LLC................................F......914 719-7272
White Plains *(G-16035)*

Octopus Advanced Systems Inc.........G......914 771-6110
Yonkers *(G-16335)*

Power Line Constructors Inc...............E......315 853-6183
Clinton *(G-3484)*

Response Care Inc..............................G......585 671-4144
Webster *(G-15651)*

▼ Roanwell Corporation......................E......718 401-0288
Bronx *(G-1352)*

Sentry Devices Corp...........................G......631 491-3191
Dix Hills *(G-4015)*

▼ Simrex Corporation.........................G......716 206-0174
Buffalo *(G-2983)*

◆ Star Headlight Lantern Co Inc.........C......585 226-9500
Avon *(G-516)*

Synergx Systems Inc..........................D......516 433-4700
Woodside *(G-16230)*

Telebyte Inc...E......631 423-3232
Hauppauge *(G-5783)*

▲ Telemergency Ltd............................G......914 629-4222
White Plains *(G-16066)*

▲ Telephonics Corporation.................A......631 755-7000
Farmingdale *(G-4752)*

Tokenize Inc..F......585 981-9919
Rochester *(G-13769)*

Toweriq Inc...F......844 626-7638
Long Island City *(G-7384)*

Traffic Lane Closures LLC...................F......845 228-6100
Carmel *(G-3192)*

▲ Twinco Mfg Co Inc...........................E......631 231-0022
Hauppauge *(G-5789)*

▲ TX Rx Systems Inc...........................C......716 549-4700
Angola *(G-361)*

Unitone Communication Systems........G......212 777-9090
New York *(G-11603)*

◆ Visiontron Corp...............................E......631 582-8600
Hauppauge *(G-5797)*

Zetek Corporation...............................F......212 668-1485
New York *(G-11821)*

3671 Radio & T V Receiving Electron Tubes

Cuebid Technologies Inc.....................G......302 380-3910
New York *(G-9130)*

▲ E-Beam Services Inc........................G......516 622-1422
Hicksville *(G-5903)*

L3harris Technologies Inc...................E......585 244-5830
Rochester *(G-13511)*

◆ New Sensor Corporation..................D......718 937-8300
Long Island City *(G-7308)*

Passur Aerospace Inc.........................G......631 589-6800
Bohemia *(G-1059)*

▲ Thomas Electronics Inc...................C......315 923-2051
Clyde *(G-3495)*

Y & Z Precision Inc.............................F......516 349-8243
Plainview *(G-12730)*

3672 Printed Circuit Boards

◆ A A Technology Inc...........................D......631 913-0400
Ronkonkoma *(G-13882)*

Adco Circuits Inc................................G......716 668-6600
Buffalo *(G-2620)*

▲ Advance Circuit Technology Inc.......E......585 328-2000
Rochester *(G-13208)*

▲ Advance Micro Power Corp..............F......631 471-6157
Ronkonkoma *(G-13889)*

Advanced Digital Info Corp.................E......607 266-4000
Ithaca *(G-6360)*

Advanced Manufacturing Svc Inc........E......631 676-5210
Ronkonkoma *(G-13890)*

American Quality Technology...............F......607 777-9488
Binghamton *(G-853)*

◆ American Tchncal Ceramics Corp....B......631 622-4700
Huntington Station *(G-6237)*

▲ Ansen Corporation...........................G......315 393-3573
Ogdensburg *(G-12202)*

▲ Badger Technologies Inc..................E......585 869-7101
Farmington *(G-4768)*

BCM Electronics Manuf Services........G......631 580-9516
Ronkonkoma *(G-13914)*

Bsu Inc...E......607 272-8100
Ithaca *(G-6373)*

Buffalo Circuits Inc............................G......716 662-2113
Orchard Park *(G-12342)*

▲ C & D Assembly Inc...........................E......607 898-4275
Groton *(G-5481)*

Chautauqua Circuits Inc.....................G......716 366-5771
Dunkirk *(G-4050)*

Coast To Coast Circuits Inc...............E......585 254-2980
Rochester *(G-13319)*

Cygnus Automation Inc.......................E......631 981-0909
Bohemia *(G-997)*

Della Systems Inc..............................F......631 580-0010
Ronkonkoma *(G-13930)*

Duro Business Solutions Inc..............G......646 577-9537
Bronx *(G-1245)*

▲ Electronic Coating Tech Inc.............F......518 688-2048
Cohoes *(G-3506)*

Ems Technologies Inc........................E......607 723-3676
Binghamton *(G-875)*

Ensil Technical Services Inc................E......716 282-1020
Niagara Falls *(G-11924)*

Entertron Industries Inc......................E......716 772-7216
Lockport *(G-7074)*

Falconer Electronics Inc .... D 716 665-4176
  Falconer (G-4541)

Geometric Circuits Inc .... D 631 249-0230
  East Setauket (G-4179)

Hazlow Electronics Inc .... E 585 325-5323
  Rochester (G-13462)

I 3 Manufacturing Services Inc ...... G 607 238-7077
  Binghamton (G-883)

I3 Assembly LLC .... C 607 238-7077
  Binghamton (G-884)

◆ I3 Electronics Inc .... C 607 238-7077
  Binghamton (G-885)

I3 Electronics Inc .... D 607 238-7077
  Endicott (G-4459)

▲ IEC Electronics Corp .... B 315 331-7742
  Newark (G-11841)

Irtronics Instruments Inc .... F 914 693-6291
  Ardsley (G-389)

▲ Isine Inc .... E 631 913-4400
  Melville (G-7797)

Kendall Circuits Inc .... E 631 473-3636
  Mount Sinai (G-8115)

Kingboard Holdings Limited .... A 705 844-1993
  New York (G-10108)

Marco Manufacturing Inc .... E 845 485-1571
  Poughkeepsie (G-12969)

Mpl Inc .... D 607 266-0480
  Ithaca (G-6398)

Nationwide Circuits Inc .... E 585 328-0791
  Rochester (G-13566)

▲ NEa Manufacturing Corp .... E 516 371-4200
  Inwood (G-6300)

▼ Oakdale Industrial Elec Corp ...... F 631 737-4092
  Ronkonkoma (G-13984)

Ormec Systems Corp .... E 585 385-3520
  Rochester (G-13592)

▲ Park Aerospace Corp .... D 631 465-3600
  Melville (G-7814)

Performance Technologies Inc .... E 585 256-0200
  Rochester (G-13615)

Photonamics Inc .... F 585 247-8990
  Rochester (G-13622)

Procomponents Inc .... E 516 683-0909
  Westbury (G-15921)

Rce Manufacturing LLC .... E 631 856-9005
  Hauppauge (G-5753)

▲ Rochester Industrial Ctrl Inc ...... D 315 524-4555
  Ontario (G-12300)

Rumsey Corp .... G 914 751-3640
  Yonkers (G-16347)

S K Circuits Inc .... F 703 376-8718
  Canastota (G-3155)

Sag Harbor Industries Inc .... E 631 725-0440
  Sag Harbor (G-14101)

Sanmina Corporation .... B 607 689-5000
  Owego (G-12437)

▲ Sopark Corp .... D 716 822-0434
  Buffalo (G-2987)

▲ Stetron International Inc .... F 716 854-3443
  Buffalo (G-2993)

▲ Stever-Locke Industries Inc .... G 585 624-3450
  Honeoye Falls (G-6081)

Surf-Tech Manufacturing Corp .... F 631 589-1194
  Ronkonkoma (G-14015)

TCS Electronics Inc .... E 585 337-4301
  Farmington (G-4779)

Transistor Devices Inc .... E 631 471-7492
  Ronkonkoma (G-14017)

Vexos Inc .... F 855 711-3227
  New York (G-11670)

Windsor Technology LLC .... F 585 461-2500
  Rochester (G-13806)

3674 Semiconductors

Able Electronics Inc .... F 631 924-5386
  Bellport (G-792)

Accumetrics Associates Inc .... F 518 393-2200
  Latham (G-6847)

▲ Acolyte Technologies Corp .... F 212 629-3239
  New York (G-8449)

Adco Circuits Inc .... G 716 668-6600
  Buffalo (G-2620)

Advis Inc .... G 585 568-0100
  Caledonia (G-3068)

▼ Aeroflex Holding Corp .... A 516 694-6700
  Plainview (G-12659)

▲ Aeroflex Incorporated .... B 516 694-6700
  Plainview (G-12660)

▲ Air Liquide Electronics .... G 518 605-4936
  Malta (G-7494)

Akoustis Inc .... E 585 919-3073
  Canandaigua (G-3124)

Applied Materials Inc .... G 518 245-1400
  Ballston Spa (G-569)

Applied Materials Inc .... E 845 227-5000
  Hopewell Junction (G-6090)

▲ Artemis Inc .... G 631 232-2424
  Hauppauge (G-5594)

▲ Atlantis Energy Systems Inc ...... F 845 486-4052
  Poughkeepsie (G-12945)

Atlantis Energy Systems Inc .... G 916 438-2930
  Poughkeepsie (G-12946)

Autodyne Manufacturing Co Inc ...... F 631 957-5858
  Lindenhurst (G-6942)

Automated Control Logic Inc .... F 914 769-8880
  Thornwood (G-15067)

Beech Grove Technology Inc .... G 845 223-6844
  Hopewell Junction (G-6091)

Besicorp Ltd .... F 845 336-7700
  Kingston (G-6680)

Bga Technology LLC .... E 631 750-4600
  Bohemia (G-981)

Bharat Electronics Limited .... E 516 248-4021
  Garden City (G-5092)

CAM Touchview Products Inc .... F 631 842-3400
  Sag Harbor (G-14096)

▲ Central Semiconductor Corp ...... D 631 435-1110
  Hauppauge (G-5612)

Ceres Technologies Inc .... D 845 247-4701
  Saugerties (G-14198)

Cobham Long Island Inc .... B 516 694-6700
  Plainview (G-12669)

Cobham Long Island Inc .... G 631 231-9100
  Hauppauge (G-5619)

Cold Springs R & D Inc .... F 315 413-1237
  Syracuse (G-14857)

Compositech Ltd .... C 516 835-1458
  Woodbury (G-16168)

Convergent Med MGT Svcs LLC ...... G 718 921-6159
  Brooklyn (G-1685)

Cooper Power Systems LLC .... B 716 375-7100
  Olean (G-12230)

Corning Incorporated .... E 607 248-1200
  Corning (G-3708)

◆ Corning Incorporated .... A 607 974-9000
  Corning (G-3705)

Corning Incorporated .... A 607 974-9000
  Painted Post (G-12473)

Corning Specialty Mtls Inc .... G 607 974-9000
  Corning (G-3713)

Crystalonics Inc .... F 631 981-6140
  Ronkonkoma (G-13927)

Crystalonics of New York Inc .... F 631 981-6140
  Ronkonkoma (G-13928)

Curtiss-Wright Controls .... F 631 756-4740
  Farmingdale (G-4606)

▲ Cvd Equipment Corporation .... C 631 981-7081
  Central Islip (G-3271)

Cypress Semiconductor Corp .... F 631 261-1358
  Northport (G-12102)

▲ Data Device Corporation .... B 631 567-5600
  Bohemia (G-999)

Dionics-Usa Inc .... G 516 997-7474
  Westbury (G-15876)

DJS Nyc Inc .... G 845 445-8618
  Pomona (G-12807)

Dynamic Photography Inc .... G 516 381-2951
  Roslyn (G-14042)

▲ Electronic Devices Inc .... E 914 965-4400
  Yonkers (G-16306)

Elite Semi Conductor Products .... G 631 884-8400
  Lindenhurst (G-6952)

Ely Beach Solar LLC .... G 718 796-9400
  New York (G-9354)

Emagin Corporation .... C 845 838-7900
  Hopewell Junction (G-6092)

Emtron Hybrids Inc .... F 631 924-9668
  Yaphank (G-16261)

▲ Endicott Interconnect Tech Inc ..... A 866 820-4820
  Endicott (G-4450)

Energy Materials Corporation .... G 315 247-0880
  Rochester (G-13392)

Enrg Inc .... F 716 873-2939
  Buffalo (G-2746)

▲ Eversan Inc .... F 315 736-3967
  Whitesboro (G-16080)

Exc Holdings I Corp .... A 212 644-5900
  New York (G-9438)

Exc Holdings II Corp .... A 212 644-5900
  New York (G-9439)

Exc Holdings LP .... G 212 644-5900
  New York (G-9440)

Excel Technology Inc .... G 718 423-7262
  Fresh Meadows (G-5040)

General Led Holdings LLC .... F 212 629-6830
  New York (G-9589)

General Microwave Corporation ...... F 516 802-0900
  Syosset (G-14789)

General Semiconductor Inc .... G 631 300-3818
  Hauppauge (G-5657)

Globalfoundries US 2 LLC .... C 512 457-3900
  Hopewell Junction (G-6094)

Globalfoundries US Inc .... E 512 457-3900
  Hopewell Junction (G-6095)

Globalfoundries US Inc .... F 408 462-3900
  Ballston Spa (G-574)

Green Logic Led Elec Sup Inc .... E 516 280-2854
  Farmingdale (G-4641)

Gurley Precision Instrs Inc .... C 518 272-6300
  Troy (G-15170)

H K Technologies Inc .... G 718 255-1898
  Long Island City (G-7237)

Hi-Tron Semiconductor Corp .... E 631 231-1500
  Hauppauge (G-5670)

◆ Hipotronics Inc .... C 845 279-8091
  Brewster (G-1151)

Hippo International LLC .... F 617 230-0599
  New York (G-9791)

▲ Hisun Optoelectronics Co Ltd ...... F 718 886-6966
  Flushing (G-4859)

I E D Corp .... F 631 348-0424
  Islandia (G-6334)

Idalia Solar Technologies LLC .... G 212 792-3913
  New York (G-9856)

Ilc Holdings Inc .... G 631 567-5600
  Bohemia (G-1021)

▲ Ilc Industries LLC .... G 631 567-5600
  Bohemia (G-1023)

Imperium Partners Group LLC .... C 212 433-1360
  New York (G-9870)

▲ Intech 21 Inc .... F 516 626-7221
  Port Washington (G-12889)

INTEL Corporation .... D 408 765-8080
  Getzville (G-5177)

International Bus Mchs Corp .... C 800 426-4968
  Hopewell Junction (G-6097)

Intex Company Inc .... D 516 223-0200
  Freeport (G-5003)

▲ Isine Inc .... E 631 913-4400
  Melville (G-7797)

Isonics Corporation .... E 212 356-7400
  New York (G-9946)

J H Rhodes Company Inc .... F 315 829-3600
  Vernon (G-15367)

▲ Kionix Inc .... C 607 257-1080
  Ithaca (G-6391)

KLA Corporation .... F 845 897-1723
  Hopewell Junction (G-6098)

◆ Leviton Manufacturing Co Inc ...... B 631 812-6000
  Melville (G-7800)

Light Blue USA LLC .... G 718 475-2515
  Brooklyn (G-2070)

Lightspin Technologies Inc .... G 301 656-7600
  Endwell (G-4481)

LMD Power of Light Corp .... D 585 272-5420
  Rochester (G-13519)

Logitek Inc .... G 631 567-1100
  Bohemia (G-1035)

▲ LSI Computer Systems .... E 631 271-0400
  Melville (G-7801)

M C Products .... E 631 471-4070
  Holbrook (G-6008)

Marcon Services .... G 516 223-8019
  Freeport (G-5006)

▲ Marktech International Corp .... E 518 956-2980
  Latham (G-6870)

▲ Materion Brewster LLC .... D 845 279-0900
  Brewster (G-1155)

▼ McG Electronics Inc .... E 631 586-5125
  Deer Park (G-3905)

Micro Contract Manufacturing .... D 631 738-7874
  Medford (G-7719)

▲ Micro Semicdtr Researches LLC ..... G 646 863-6070
  New York (G-10457)

Microchip Technology Inc .... G 631 233-3280
  Hauppauge (G-5717)

Microchip Technology Inc .... C 607 785-5992
  Endicott (G-5717)

Micromem Technologies .... F 212 672-1806
  New York (G-10458)

Mini-Circuits Fort Wayne LLC...............B...... 718 934-4500
Brooklyn *(G-2157)*

Monolithic Coatings Inc ....G...... 914 621-2765
Sharon Springs *(G-14383)*

Mosaic Microsystems LLC ....G...... 585 314-7441
Rochester *(G-13561)*

Moser Baer Technologies Inc ....F...... 585 749-0480
Fairport *(G-4508)*

▲ Nationwide Tarps Incorporated ....D...... 518 843-1545
Amsterdam *(G-341)*

▼ Navitar Inc ....D...... 585 359-4000
Rochester *(G-13568)*

Nsi Industries LLC ....C...... 800 841-2505
Mount Vernon *(G-8166)*

Oledworks LLC ....E...... 585 287-6802
Rochester *(G-13589)*

▲ Onyx Solar Group LLC ....G...... 917 951-9732
New York *(G-10695)*

Optimum Semiconductor Tech...........G...... 914 287-8500
Tarrytown *(G-15051)*

Orbit International Corp ....D...... 631 435-8300
Hauppauge *(G-5734)*

▲ Park Aerospace Corp ....D...... 631 465-3600
Melville *(G-7814)*

▲ Passive-Plus Inc ....F...... 631 425-0938
Huntington *(G-6216)*

◆ Philips Medical Systems Mr ....B...... 518 782-1122
Latham *(G-6872)*

Plug Power Inc ....G...... 585 474-3993
Rochester *(G-13626)*

▲ Plug Power Inc ....B...... 518 782-7700
Latham *(G-6874)*

Plures Technologies Inc ....G...... 585 905-0554
Canandaigua *(G-3140)*

Procomponents Inc ....E...... 516 683-0909
Westbury *(G-15921)*

Pvi Solar Inc ....G...... 212 280-2100
New York *(G-10938)*

Renewable Energy Inc ....G...... 718 690-2691
Little Neck *(G-6998)*

Riverhawk Company LP ....E...... 315 624-7171
New Hartford *(G-8244)*

▲ RSM Electron Power Inc ....C...... 631 586-7600
Deer Park *(G-3931)*

RSM Electron Power Inc ....C...... 631 586-7600
Hauppauge *(G-5756)*

Ruhle Companies Inc ....E...... 914 287-4000
Valhalla *(G-15309)*

S3j Electronics LLC ....E...... 716 206-1309
Lancaster *(G-6832)*

▲ Sanrex Corporation ....F...... 516 625-1313
Port Washington *(G-12922)*

Schott Corporation ....D...... 315 255-2791
Auburn *(G-494)*

Schott Lithotec USA Corp ....D...... 845 463-5300
Elmsford *(G-4430)*

▲ Schott Solar Pv LLC ....G...... 888 457-6527
Elmsford *(G-4432)*

Semitronics Corp ....E...... 516 223-0200
Freeport *(G-5023)*

Senera Co Inc ....F...... 516 639-3774
Valley Stream *(G-15358)*

Sinclair Technologies Inc ....E...... 716 874-3682
Hamburg *(G-5521)*

SMC Diode Solutions LLC ....G...... 631 965-0869
Plainview *(G-12714)*

▲ Solar Thin Films Inc ....E...... 212 629-8260
Cedarhurst *(G-3244)*

Solid Cell Inc ....F...... 585 426-5000
Rochester *(G-13735)*

Sonotec US Inc ....C...... 631 415-4758
Islandia *(G-6345)*

▲ Spectron Glass & Electronics...........F...... 631 582-5600
Hauppauge *(G-5769)*

Spectron Systems Technology ....F...... 631 582-5600
Hauppauge *(G-5770)*

Spellman High Vltage Elec Corp ....D...... 914 686-3600
Valhalla *(G-15310)*

▲ Standard Microsystems Corp ....D...... 631 435-6000
Hauppauge *(G-5774)*

▲ Stetron International Inc ....F...... 716 854-3443
Buffalo *(G-2993)*

▲ Sumitomo Elc USA Holdings Inc ......G...... 212 490-6610
New York *(G-11389)*

▼ Super Conductor Materials Inc........F...... 845 368-0240
Suffern *(G-14767)*

Swissbit Na Inc ....G...... 914 935-1400
Port Chester *(G-12829)*

Symwave Inc ....G...... 949 542-4400
Hauppauge *(G-5780)*

Tarsier Ltd...C...... 646 880-8680
New York *(G-11436)*

▲ Tel Technology Center Amer LLC....E...... 512 424-4200
Albany *(G-135)*

Telephonics Corporation......................E...... 631 549-6000
Huntington *(G-6226)*

Telephonics Tlsi Corp..........................C...... 631 470-8854
Huntington *(G-6228)*

Thales Laser SA..................................D...... 585 223-2370
Fairport *(G-4527)*

Thermo Cidtec Inc...............................E...... 315 451-9410
Liverpool *(G-7045)*

Thermoaura Inc...................................F...... 518 813-4997
Albany *(G-136)*

Tlsi Incorporated.................................D...... 631 470-8880
Huntington *(G-6229)*

Tokyo Electron America Inc.................G...... 518 289-3100
Malta *(G-7497)*

Tokyo Electron America Inc.................G...... 518 292-4200
Albany *(G-137)*

▲ Tork Inc ....D...... 914 664-3542
Mount Vernon *(G-8183)*

◆ Truebite Inc ....E...... 607 785-7664
Vestal *(G-15386)*

◆ Veriled Inc ....G...... 877 521-5520
New York *(G-11661)*

Vgg Holding LLC.................................G...... 212 415-6700
New York *(G-11672)*

Viking Technologies Ltd.......................E...... 631 957-8000
Lindenhurst *(G-6983)*

Warner Energy LLC.............................G...... 315 457-3828
Liverpool *(G-7048)*

Washington Foundries Inc....................G...... 516 374-8447
Hewlett *(G-5876)*

▲ Zastech Inc ....E...... 516 496-4777
Syosset *(G-14806)*

3675 Electronic Capacitors

American Tchncal Ceramics Corp........B...... 631 622-4700
Huntington Station *(G-6238)*

◆ American Tchncal Ceramics Corp ....B...... 631 622-4700
Huntington Station *(G-6237)*

AVX Corporation ....D...... 716 372-6611
Olean *(G-12223)*

Electron Coil Inc.................................E...... 607 336-7414
Norwich *(G-12121)*

Ems Development Corporation ....D...... 631 345-6200
Yaphank *(G-16260)*

◆ Hipotronics Inc ....C...... 845 279-8091
Brewster *(G-1151)*

Kemet Properties LLC ....G...... 718 654-8079
Bronx *(G-1290)*

▲ Knowles Cazenovia Inc ....C...... 315 655-8710
Cazenovia *(G-3228)*

▲ MTK Electronics Inc.........................E...... 631 924-7666
Medford *(G-7720)*

▲ Passive-Plus Inc ....F...... 631 425-0938
Huntington *(G-6216)*

▲ Roberts-Gordon LLC ....D...... 716 852-4400
Buffalo *(G-2957)*

▲ Russell Industries Inc ....G...... 516 536-5000
Lynbrook *(G-7437)*

▲ Stk Electronics Inc ....E...... 315 655-8476
Cazenovia *(G-3235)*

Strux Corp ....E...... 516 768-3969
Lindenhurst *(G-6976)*

▲ Tronser Inc.......................................G...... 315 655-9528
Cazenovia *(G-3236)*

Viking Technologies Ltd.......................E...... 631 957-8000
Lindenhurst *(G-6983)*

Voltronics LLC....................................E...... 410 749-2424
Cazenovia *(G-3237)*

3676 Electronic Resistors

Betapast Holdings LLC.........................D...... 631 582-6740
Hauppauge *(G-5603)*

Microgen Systems Inc ....G...... 585 214-2426
Fairport *(G-4507)*

▼ Micropen Technologies Corp.............D...... 585 624-2610
Honeoye Falls *(G-6078)*

▲ Passive-Plus Inc ....F...... 631 425-0938
Huntington *(G-6216)*

▲ Stetron International Inc...................F...... 716 854-3443
Buffalo *(G-2993)*

▲ Vishay Thin Film LLC.......................C...... 716 283-4025
Niagara Falls *(G-11990)*

3677 Electronic Coils & Transformers

▲ Aeroflex Incorporated......................B...... 516 694-6700
Plainview *(G-12660)*

▲ All Shore Industries Inc ....F...... 718 720-0018
Staten Island *(G-14617)*

◆ American Precision Inds Inc ....C...... 716 691-9100
Amherst *(G-210)*

American Precision Inds Inc ....D...... 716 652-3600
East Aurora *(G-4081)*

American Precision Inds Inc ....D...... 585 496-5755
Arcade *(G-367)*

American Trans-Coil Corp....................F...... 516 922-9640
Oyster Bay *(G-12443)*

▲ Applied Power Systems Inc ....E...... 516 935-2230
Hicksville *(G-5883)*

Atlantic Transformer Inc......................F...... 716 795-3258
Barker *(G-590)*

▲ Bel Transformer Inc ....D...... 516 239-5777
Lynbrook *(G-7426)*

▲ Bright Way Supply Inc ....F...... 718 833-2882
Brooklyn *(G-1609)*

Caddell Burns Manufacturing Co ....E...... 631 757-1772
Northport *(G-12100)*

▲ Data Device Corporation ....B...... 631 567-5600
Bohemia *(G-999)*

Electron Coil Inc.................................D...... 607 336-7414
Norwich *(G-12121)*

Ems Development Corporation ....D...... 631 345-6200
Yaphank *(G-16260)*

▲ Ems Development Corporation ....D...... 631 924-4736
Yaphank *(G-16259)*

▲ Eni Technology Inc ....B...... 585 427-8300
Rochester *(G-13395)*

Es Beta Inc ....E...... 631 582-6740
Ronkonkoma *(G-13936)*

▲ Esc Control Electronics LLC ....E...... 631 467-5328
Sayville *(G-14225)*

Exxelia-Raf Tabtronics LLC ....E...... 585 243-4331
Piffard *(G-12624)*

▲ Fil-Coil (fc) Corp ....E...... 631 467-5328
Sayville *(G-14226)*

Fil-Coil International LLC ....F...... 631 467-5328
Sayville *(G-14227)*

Frequency Selective Networks ....F...... 718 424-7500
Valley Stream *(G-15341)*

Fuse Electronics Inc ....G...... 607 352-3222
Kirkwood *(G-6731)*

Gowanda - Bti LLC ....D...... 716 492-4081
Arcade *(G-375)*

▲ Hammond Manufacturing Co Inc......F...... 716 630-7030
Cheektowaga *(G-3352)*

◆ Hipotronics Inc ....C...... 845 279-8091
Brewster *(G-1151)*

Island Audio Engineering ....G...... 631 543-2372
Commack *(G-3593)*

M F L B Inc ....F...... 631 254-8300
Massapequa Park *(G-7658)*

▲ Magnetic Technologies Corp ....D...... 585 385-9010
Rochester *(G-13530)*

Microwave Filter Company Inc ....E...... 315 438-4700
East Syracuse *(G-4226)*

Mini-Circuits Fort Wayne LLC ....B...... 718 934-4500
Brooklyn *(G-2157)*

▲ Misonix Opco Inc ....D...... 631 694-9555
Farmingdale *(G-4687)*

Mitchell Electronics Corp ....E...... 914 699-3800
Mount Vernon *(G-8162)*

Mohawk Electro Techniques Inc...........D...... 315 896-2661
Barneveld *(G-594)*

▲ MTK Electronics Inc.........................E...... 631 924-7666
Medford *(G-7720)*

National Energy Audits LLC ....G...... 631 883-3407
Holbrook *(G-6013)*

▲ NEa Manufacturing Corp ....E...... 516 371-4200
Inwood *(G-6300)*

New York Fan Coil LLC........................G...... 646 580-1344
Coram *(G-3696)*

Precision Electronics Inc ....F...... 631 842-4900
Copiague *(G-3670)*

▲ Rdi Inc ....F...... 914 773-1000
Mount Kisco *(G-8104)*

Sag Harbor Industries Inc ....E...... 631 725-0440
Sag Harbor *(G-14101)*

Service Filtration Corp ....E...... 716 877-2608
Tonawanda *(G-15140)*

◆ Todd Systems Inc ....D...... 914 963-3400
Yonkers *(G-16352)*

Tte Filters LLC....................................G...... 716 532-2234
Gowanda *(G-5323)*

Urban Technologies Inc ....G...... 716 672-2709
Fredonia *(G-4972)*

3678 Electronic Connectors

Accessories For Electronics................E...... 631 847-0158
  South Hempstead *(G-14519)*

▲ Amphenol Cables On Demand Corp F....... 607 321-2115
  Endicott *(G-4443)*

Amphenol Corporation.....................B...... 607 563-5364
  Sidney *(G-14431)*

Amphenol Corporation.....................A...... 607 563-5011
  Sidney *(G-14432)*

▲ Automatic Connector Inc ....F...... 631 543-5000
  Hauppauge *(G-5598)*

Belden Inc..................................B...... 607 796-5600
  Horseheads *(G-6114)*

▲ C S Business Systems Inc ....E...... 716 886-6521
  Buffalo *(G-2688)*

▲ Casa Innovations Inc ....G...... 718 965-6600
  Brooklyn *(G-1654)*

▲ EBY Electro Inc ....E...... 516 576-7777
  Plainview *(G-12681)*

▲ Executive Machines Inc ....E...... 718 965-6600
  Brooklyn *(G-1822)*

▲ Felchar Manufacturing Corp ....A...... 607 723-4076
  Binghamton *(G-877)*

I Trade Technology Ltd ....E...... 615 348-7233
  Airmont *(G-12)*

Ieh Corporation ....C...... 718 492-4440
  Brooklyn *(G-1952)*

Kirtas Inc..................................G...... 585 924-5999
  Victor *(G-15415)*

▼ Kirtas Inc ....E...... 585 924-2420
  Victor *(G-15416)*

◆ Leviton Manufacturing Co Inc ....B...... 631 812-6000
  Melville *(G-7800)*

◆ Mason Industries Inc ....C...... 631 348-0282
  Hauppauge *(G-5708)*

▲ Mill-Max Mfg Corp ....C...... 516 922-6000
  Oyster Bay *(G-12449)*

Mini-Circuits Fort Wayne LLC.............B...... 718 934-4500
  Brooklyn *(G-2157)*

▲ NEa Manufacturing Corp ....E...... 516 371-4200
  Inwood *(G-6300)*

▲ Power Connector Inc ....E...... 631 563-7878
  Bohemia *(G-1062)*

◆ Ppc Broadband Inc ....B...... 315 431-7200
  East Syracuse *(G-4231)*

Princetel Inc..............................F...... 914 579-2410
  Hawthorne *(G-5822)*

▲ Rdi Inc ....F...... 914 773-1000
  Mount Kisco *(G-8104)*

Resonance Technologies Inc...............E...... 631 237-4901
  Ronkonkoma *(G-14002)*

Sitewatch Technology LLC ....G...... 207 778-3246
  East Quogue *(G-4158)*

Supplynet Inc..............................G...... 800 826-0279
  Valley Cottage *(G-15328)*

▲ Taro Manufacturing Company Inc ......F....... 315 252-9430
  Auburn *(G-498)*

◆ Universal Remote Control Inc ....D...... 914 835-4484
  Harrison *(G-5563)*

▲ Whirlwind Music Distrs Inc ....D...... 800 733-9473
  Rochester *(G-13803)*

3679 Electronic Components, NEC

3835 Lebron Rest Eqp & Sup Inc...........E...... 212 942-8258
  New York *(G-8402)*

▲ A K Allen Co Inc ....C...... 516 747-5450
  Melville *(G-7753)*

A R V Precision Mfg Inc...................G...... 631 293-9643
  Farmingdale *(G-4569)*

Accessories For Electronics..............E...... 631 847-0158
  South Hempstead *(G-14519)*

Adco Circuits Inc ....G...... 716 668-6600
  Buffalo *(G-2620)*

▲ Advance Circuit Technology Inc.......E...... 585 328-2000
  Rochester *(G-13208)*

▲ Advanced Interconnect Mfg Inc........D...... 585 742-2220
  Victor *(G-15390)*

▲ Albatros North America Inc ....E...... 518 381-7100
  Ballston Spa *(G-567)*

▲ All Shore Industries Inc ....F...... 718 720-0018
  Staten Island *(G-14617)*

Alloy Machine & Tool Co Inc...............G...... 516 593-3445
  Lynbrook *(G-7425)*

American Quality Technology ....F...... 607 777-9488
  Binghamton *(G-853)*

AMP-Line Corp ....F...... 845 623-3288
  West Nyack *(G-15815)*

▲ Amphenol Intrconnect Pdts Corp.....G...... 607 754-4444
  Endicott *(G-4444)*

Ampro International Inc...................G...... 845 278-4910
  Brewster *(G-1141)*

Amron Electronics Inc ....E...... 631 737-1234
  Ronkonkoma *(G-13907)*

▲ Anaren Inc ....B...... 315 432-8909
  East Syracuse *(G-4195)*

Antenna & Radome Res Assoc ....E...... 631 231-8400
  Bay Shore *(G-651)*

◆ Apollo Display Tech Corp ....E...... 631 580-4360
  Ronkonkoma *(G-13908)*

Applied Concepts Inc ....E...... 315 696-6676
  Tully *(G-15207)*

▲ Applied Power Systems Inc ....E...... 516 935-2230
  Hicksville *(G-5883)*

▲ Apx Technologies Inc ....E...... 516 433-1313
  Hicksville *(G-5884)*

▲ Arnold-Davis LLC ....C...... 607 772-1201
  Binghamton *(G-855)*

Arstan Products International ....E...... 516 433-1313
  Hicksville *(G-5885)*

B H M Metal Products Co ....G...... 845 292-5297
  Kauneonga Lake *(G-6640)*

B3cg Interconnect Usa Inc ....B...... 518 324-4800
  Plattsburgh *(G-12734)*

BC Systems Inc.............................E...... 631 751-9370
  Setauket *(G-14377)*

Becker Electronics Inc ....D...... 631 619-9100
  Ronkonkoma *(G-13915)*

Berkshire Transformer ....G...... 631 467-5328
  Central Islip *(G-3265)*

Bud Barger Assoc Inc ....G...... 631 696-6703
  Farmingville *(G-4781)*

Cables Unlimited Inc......................E...... 631 563-6363
  Yaphank *(G-16256)*

▼ Canfield Electronics Inc ....E...... 631 585-4100
  Lindenhurst *(G-6944)*

Celmet Co ....G...... 585 647-1760
  Newark *(G-11839)*

Centroid Inc...............................E...... 516 349-0070
  Plainview *(G-12667)*

Chiplogic Inc ....F...... 631 617-6317
  Yaphank *(G-16257)*

Clever Devices Ltd ....E...... 516 433-6100
  Woodbury *(G-16167)*

Cloud Toronto Inc ....F...... 408 569-4542
  Williamsville *(G-16127)*

Cobham Holdings Inc ....F...... 716 662-0006
  Orchard Park *(G-12345)*

Cobham Long Island Inc ....B...... 516 694-6700
  Plainview *(G-12669)*

Cobham Long Island Inc ....C...... 631 231-9100
  Hauppauge *(G-5619)*

▲ Condor Electronics Corp ....E...... 585 235-1500
  Rochester *(G-13321)*

Crystal Is Inc ....E...... 518 271-7375
  Green Island *(G-5434)*

D & S Supplies Inc ....F...... 718 721-5256
  Astoria *(G-415)*

Dimension Technologies Inc ....G...... 585 436-3530
  Rochester *(G-13347)*

Dortronics Systems Inc ....E...... 631 725-0505
  Sag Harbor *(G-14098)*

Dynamic Hybirds Inc ....G...... 315 426 8110
  Syracuse *(G-14879)*

◆ Eastland Electronics Co Inc ....G...... 631 580-3800
  Shirley *(G-14419)*

▼ Electronics & Innovation Ltd ....F...... 585 214-0598
  Rochester *(G-13382)*

Engagement Technology LLC ....F...... 914 591-7600
  Elmsford *(G-4408)*

▲ Eni Technology Inc ....B...... 585 427-8300
  Rochester *(G-13395)*

▲ Esc Control Electronics LLC ....E...... 631 467-5328
  Sayville *(G-14225)*

Espey Mfg & Electronics Corp.............E...... 518 584-4100
  Saratoga Springs *(G-14172)*

Exc Holdings I Corp.......................A...... 212 644-5900
  New York *(G-9438)*

Exc Holdings II Corp......................A...... 212 644-5900
  New York *(G-9439)*

Exc Holdings LP ....G...... 212 644-5900
  New York *(G-9440)*

▲ Fair-Rite Products Corp ....C...... 845 895-2055
  Wallkill *(G-15469)*

Fei Communications Inc ....C...... 516 794-4500
  Uniondale *(G-15227)*

Fine Sounds Group Inc ....F...... 212 364-0219
  New York *(G-9996)*

Frequency Electronics Inc ....C...... 516 794-4500
  Uniondale *(G-15229)*

General Microwave Corporation ....F...... 516 802-0900
  Syosset *(G-14789)*

Gotenna Inc ....F...... 718 360-4988
  Brooklyn *(G-1901)*

▲ Grado Laboratories Inc ....F...... 718 435-5340
  Brooklyn *(G-1905)*

▲ Haynes Roberts Inc ....F...... 212 989-1901
  New York *(G-9739)*

Hazlow Electronics Inc ....E...... 585 325-5323
  Rochester *(G-13462)*

◆ Hipotronics Inc ....C...... 845 279-8091
  Brewster *(G-1151)*

▲ Hoff Associates Mfg Reps Inc..........E...... 585 398-2000
  Farmington *(G-4773)*

Hudson Valley Tech Dev Ctr Inc ....E...... 845 391-8214
  Highland *(G-5960)*

Hypres Inc ....E...... 914 592-1190
  Elmsford *(G-4411)*

▲ IEC Electronics Corp ....E...... 315 331-7742
  Newark *(G-11841)*

IEC Electronics Wire Cable Inc ....D...... 585 924-9010
  Newark *(G-11842)*

Imrex LLC ....B...... 516 479-3675
  Oyster Bay *(G-12448)*

Innovative Power Products Inc............E...... 631 563-0088
  Holbrook *(G-6002)*

Island Circuits International ....G...... 516 625-5555
  College Point *(G-3547)*

Island Research and Dev Corp ....D...... 631 471-7100
  Ronkonkoma *(G-13949)*

▲ Jenlor Ltd ....F...... 315 637-9080
  Fayetteville *(G-4784)*

◆ Kearney-National Inc ....F...... 212 661-4600
  New York *(G-10087)*

▲ Keltron Electronics (de Corp) ....F...... 631 567-6300
  Ronkonkoma *(G-13956)*

▲ L3 Foreign Holdings Inc ....C...... 212 697-1111
  New York *(G-10153)*

L3 Technologies Inc.......................E...... 631 289-0363
  Patchogue *(G-12506)*

L3 Technologies Inc.......................B...... 212 697-1111
  New York *(G-10154)*

Lexan Industries Inc ....F...... 631 434-7586
  Bay Shore *(G-690)*

Lighthouse Components ....E...... 917 993-6820
  New York *(G-10219)*

Lion E-Mobility North Amer Inc ....G...... 917 345-6365
  Bronxville *(G-1401)*

Logitek Inc ....D...... 631 567-1100
  Bohemia *(G-1035)*

Lyntronics Inc ....E...... 631 205-1061
  Yaphank *(G-16265)*

M W Microwave Corp ....F...... 516 295-1814
  Lawrence *(G-6887)*

Marcon Electronic Systems LLC ....G...... 516 633-6396
  Freeport *(G-5005)*

Mechanical Pwr Conversion LLC............F...... 607 766-9620
  Binghamton *(G-896)*

▲ Mekatronics Incorporated ....E...... 516 883-6805
  Port Washington *(G-12907)*

▲ Merit Electronic Design Co Inc ....C...... 631 667-9699
  Edgewood *(G-4275)*

Mezmeriz Inc ....G...... 607 216-8140
  Ithaca *(G-6396)*

Microwave Filter Company Inc ....E...... 315 438-4700
  East Syracuse *(G-4226)*

▲ Mid Hdson Wkshp For The Dsbled...E...... 845 471-3820
  Poughkeepsie *(G-12970)*

Mini-Circuits Fort Wayne LLC.............B...... 718 934-4500
  Brooklyn *(G-2157)*

Mirion Technologies Ist Corp.............D...... 607 562-4300
  Horseheads *(G-6128)*

MLS Sales ....G...... 516 681-2736
  Bethpage *(G-840)*

Mom Holding Company ....G...... 518 233-3330
  Waterford *(G-15540)*

◆ Momentive Performance Mtls Inc ......E...... 518 233-3330
  Waterford *(G-15542)*

Mpm Holdings Inc ....G...... 518 233-3330
  Waterford *(G-15543)*

Mpm Intermediate Holdings Inc............G...... 518 237-3330
  Waterford *(G-15544)*

▲ NEa Manufacturing Corp ....E...... 516 371-4200
  Inwood *(G-6300)*

Nelson Holdings Ltd ....G...... 607 772-1794
  Binghamton *(G-901)*

New York Digital Corporation ....F...... 631 630-9798
  Huntington Station *(G-6255)*

▲ North Hills Signal Proc Corp..........E...... 631 244-7393
  Bohemia *(G-1054)*

▼ **Oakdale Industrial Elec Corp**............F 631 737-4092
Ronkonkoma *(G-13984)*
Opus Technology Corporation ....F 631 271-1883
Melville *(G-7812)*
Orbit International Corp ....D....... 631 435-8300
Hauppauge *(G-5734)*
Orbit International Corp ....D....... 631 435-8300
Hauppauge *(G-5735)*
Orthogonal...G....... 585 254-2775
Rochester *(G-13598)*
Paal Technologies Inc ....G....... 631 319-6262
Ronkonkoma *(G-13990)*
▲ **Passive-Plus Inc**...............................F 631 425-0938
Huntington *(G-6216)*
Pcb Group Inc ....E 716 684-0001
Depew *(G-3992)*
Pcb Piezotronics Inc...............................B 716 684-0003
Depew *(G-3994)*
◆ **Philips Medical Systems Mr** ....B 518 782-1122
Latham *(G-6872)*
Plura Broadcast Inc ....G....... 516 997-5675
Massapequa *(G-7647)*
Polycast Industries Inc..........................G....... 631 595-2530
Bay Shore *(G-699)*
▲ **Precision Assembly Tech Inc**............E 631 699-9400
Bohemia *(G-1063)*
Premier Systems LLC............................G....... 631 587-9700
Babylon *(G-524)*
Pvi Solar Inc ....G....... 212 280-2100
New York *(G-10938)*
◆ **Pyragon Inc**...G....... 585 697-0444
Rochester *(G-13654)*
▲ **Quality Contract Assemblies** ....F 585 663-9030
Rochester *(G-13659)*
R L C Electronics Inc.............................D....... 914 241-1334
Mount Kisco *(G-8103)*
▲ **Rdi Inc** ....F 914 773-1000
Mount Kisco *(G-8104)*
Rem-Tronics Inc......................................D....... 716 934-2697
Dunkirk *(G-4064)*
Rochester Industrial Ctrl Inc..................D....... 315 524-4555
Ontario *(G-12301)*
▲ **Rochester Industrial Ctrl Inc**.............D....... 315 524-4555
Ontario *(G-12300)*
Ruhle Companies Inc ....E 914 287-4000
Valhalla *(G-15309)*
▲ **Russell Industries Inc**........................G....... 516 536-5000
Lynbrook *(G-7437)*
SC Textiles Inc..G....... 631 944-6262
Huntington *(G-6223)*
▲ **Scientific Components Corp**.............B 718 934-4500
Brooklyn *(G-2390)*
Scientific Components Corp..................B 718 368-2060
Brooklyn *(G-2391)*
Sendec Corp..E 585 425-5965
Fairport *(G-4520)*
Sln Group Inc..G....... 718 677-5969
Brooklyn *(G-2428)*
Sonaer Inc...G....... 631 756-4780
West Babylon *(G-15747)*
▲ **Sopark Corp** ....D....... 716 822-0434
Buffalo *(G-2987)*
Space Coast Semiconductor Inc...........F 631 414-7131
Farmingdale *(G-4736)*
▲ **Spectron Glass & Electronics**...........F 631 582-5600
Hauppauge *(G-5769)*
Spellman Hgh-Voltage Elec Corp ....B 631 630-3000
Hauppauge *(G-5773)*
▲ **Stetron International Inc**...................F 716 854-3443
Buffalo *(G-2993)*
Sturges Elec Pdts Co Inc ....E 607 844-8604
Dryden *(G-4041)*
Sturges Electronics LLC ....F 607 844-8604
Dryden *(G-4042)*
Superior Motion Controls Inc ....E 516 420-2921
Farmingdale *(G-4745)*
▲ **Surmotech LLC** ....D....... 585 742-1220
Victor *(G-15433)*
T-S-K Electronics Inc...............................G....... 716 693-3916
North Tonawanda *(G-12093)*
TCS Electronics Inc ....E 585 337-4301
Farmington *(G-4779)*
◆ **Tdk USA Corporation** ....D....... 516 535-2600
Uniondale *(G-15233)*
Te Connectivity Corporation....................E 585 785-2500
Rochester *(G-13760)*
Telephonics Corporation...........................E 631 549-6000
Huntington *(G-6226)*
▲ **Telephonics Corporation**......................A....... 631 755-7000
Farmingdale *(G-4752)*

Three Five III-V Materials Inc..................F 212 213-8290
New York *(G-11478)*
Tlsi Incorporated......................................D....... 631 470-8880
Huntington *(G-6229)*
Tony Baird Electronics Inc.......................G....... 315 422-4430
Syracuse *(G-15014)*
Torotron Corporation................................G....... 718 428-6992
Fresh Meadows *(G-5047)*
▲ **Trading Services International**..........F 212 501-0142
New York *(G-11530)*
Traffic Lane Closures LLC ....F 845 228-6100
Carmel *(G-3192)*
Transistor Power Tech Inc ....G....... 631 491-0265
Stony Brook *(G-14742)*
▲ **Ultralife Corporation**..............................B 315 332-7100
Newark *(G-11854)*
Ultravolt Inc ....D....... 631 471-4444
Ronkonkoma *(G-14022)*
Unison Industries LLC..............................B 607 335-5000
Norwich *(G-12130)*
▲ **Vestal Electronic Devices LLC**.........F 607 773-8461
Endicott *(G-4477)*
Voices For All LLC ....G....... 518 261-1664
Mechanicville *(G-7696)*
W D Technology Inc...................................G....... 914 779-8738
Eastchester *(G-4250)*
▲ **Walter G Legge Company Inc** ....G....... 914 737-5040
Peekskill *(G-12560)*
Werlatone Inc...E 845 278-2220
Patterson *(G-12522)*
Xedit Corp..G....... 718 380-1592
Queens Village *(G-13028)*

3691 Storage Batteries

Amco Intl Mfg & Design Inc ....E 718 388-8668
Brooklyn *(G-1497)*
Battery Research and Tstg Inc ....F 315 342-2373
Oswego *(G-12408)*
▲ **Battsco LLC**...G....... 516 586-6544
Hicksville *(G-5888)*
Bren-Trnics Batteries Intl Inc...................G....... 631 499-5155
Commack *(G-3580)*
Bren-Trnics Batteries Intl LLC ....E 631 499-5155
Commack *(G-3581)*
◆ **Bren-Tronics Inc** ....C....... 631 499-5155
Commack *(G-3582)*
Cellec Technologies Inc............................G....... 585 454-9166
Rochester *(G-13304)*
China Lithium Technologies.....................G....... 212 391-2688
New York *(G-8990)*
El-Don Battery Post Inc............................G....... 716 627-3697
Hamburg *(G-5506)*
Exide Technologies....................................G....... 585 344-0656
Batavia *(G-613)*
Johnson Controls Inc ....C....... 585 724-2232
Rochester *(G-13495)*
New Energy Systems Group....................C....... 917 573-0302
New York *(G-10580)*
Sparkcharge Inc...G....... 315 480-3645
Syracuse *(G-14996)*
Synergy Digital...F 718 643-2742
Brooklyn *(G-2483)*
▲ **Ultralife Corporation**..............................B 315 332-7100
Newark *(G-11854)*

3692 Primary Batteries: Dry & Wet

◆ **Bren-Tronics Inc**......................................C....... 631 499-5155
Commack *(G-3582)*
◆ **Electrochem Solutions Inc** ....D....... 716 759-5800
Clarence *(G-3433)*
Shad Industries Inc.....................................G....... 631 504-6028
Yaphank *(G-16271)*

3694 Electrical Eqpt For Internal Combustion Engines

▲ **ARC Systems Inc** ....E 631 582-8020
Hauppauge *(G-5592)*
▲ **Autel US Inc**..G....... 631 923-2620
Farmingdale *(G-4589)*
Con Rel Auto Electric Inc...........................E 518 356-1646
Schenectady *(G-14259)*
Delphi Powertrain Systems LLC...............B 585 359-6000
West Henrietta *(G-15792)*
Eastern Unit Exch Rmnfacturing..............F 718 739-7113
Floral Park *(G-4815)*
Eluminocity US Inc ....G....... 651 528-1165
New York *(G-9353)*
Ev-Box North America Inc.........................G....... 646 930-6305
New York *(G-9422)*

International Key Supply LLC...................F 631 983-6096
Farmingdale *(G-4652)*
▲ **Karlyn Industries Inc** ....F 845 351-2249
Southfields *(G-14541)*
◆ **Kearney-National Inc**...............................F 212 661-4600
New York *(G-10087)*
◆ **Leviton Manufacturing Co Inc**...............B 631 812-6000
Melville *(G-7800)*
▲ **Magnum Shielding Corporation** ....E 585 381-9957
Pittsford *(G-12648)*
Martinez Specialties Inc ....G....... 607 898-3053
Groton *(G-5483)*
▲ **Nas-Tra Automotive Inds Inc**................C....... 631 225-1225
Lindenhurst *(G-6962)*
Prestolite Electric Inc ....C....... 585 492-2278
Arcade *(G-380)*
▲ **Sopark Corp** ....D....... 716 822-0434
Buffalo *(G-2987)*
◆ **Standard Motor Products Inc** ....B 718 392-0200
Long Island City *(G-7364)*
▲ **Taro Manufacturing Company Inc** ....F 315 252-9430
Auburn *(G-498)*
▲ **Zenith Autoparts Corp**............................E 845 344-1382
Middletown *(G-7939)*
▲ **Zierick Manufacturing Corp** ....D....... 800 882-8020
Mount Kisco *(G-8108)*

3695 Recording Media

Aarfid LLC..G....... 716 992-3999
Eden *(G-4253)*
BMA Media Services Inc.............................E 585 385-2060
Rochester *(G-13275)*
Connectiva Systems Inc.............................F 646 722-8741
New York *(G-9084)*
Digiday Media LLC.......................................E 646 419-4357
New York *(G-9224)*
Ember Media Corporation..........................F 212 695-1919
New York *(G-9357)*
Escholar LLC...F 914 989-2900
White Plains *(G-16002)*
Infinite Software Solutions........................F 718 982-1315
Staten Island *(G-14665)*
John J Richardson..F 516 538-6339
Lawrence *(G-6886)*
▲ **L & M Optical Disc LLC** ....D....... 718 649-3500
New York *(G-10148)*
Longtail Studios Inc.....................................E 646 443-8146
New York *(G-10250)*
Multi-Health Systems Inc ....D....... 800 456-3003
Cheektowaga *(G-3356)*
Next Big Sound Inc.......................................G....... 646 657-9837
New York *(G-10618)*
Orpheo USA Corp ....G....... 212 464-8255
New York *(G-10711)*
▲ **Professional Tape Corporation**...............G....... 516 656-5519
Glen Cove *(G-5199)*
◆ **Sony Corporation of America**................C....... 212 833-8000
New York *(G-11295)*
Sony Dadc US Inc ....B 212 833-8800
New York *(G-11296)*
▲ **Stamper Technology Inc** ....G....... 585 247-8370
Rochester *(G-13743)*

3699 Electrical Machinery, Eqpt & Splys, NEC

331 Holding Inc ....E 585 924-1740
Victor *(G-15389)*
3krf LLC ....G....... 516 208-6824
Oceanside *(G-12163)*
A & S Electric ....G....... 212 228-2030
Brooklyn *(G-1430)*
Aabacs Group Inc ....F 718 961-3577
College Point *(G-3532)*
Advance Energy Systems NY LLC ....G....... 315 735-5125
Utica *(G-15237)*
Advanced Mfg Techniques.........................G....... 518 877-8560
Clifton Park *(G-3460)*
Advanced Photonics Inc ....F 631 471-3693
Ronkonkoma *(G-13891)*
▲ **Albatros North America Inc**...................E 518 381-7100
Ballston Spa *(G-567)*
Alexy Associates Inc ....E 845 482-3000
Bethel *(G-827)*
▲ **All Shore Industries Inc** ....F 718 720-0018
Staten Island *(G-14617)*
Altan Robotech (usa) Inc............................G....... 866 291-1101
Goshen *(G-5304)*
Altaquip LLC...G....... 631 580-4740
Ronkonkoma *(G-13901)*
◆ **Altronix Corp**...D....... 718 567-8181
Brooklyn *(G-1494)*

Amertac Holdings Inc ....G...... 610 336-1330
 Monsey (G-8034)

Ameta International Co Ltd ....G...... 416 992-8036
 Buffalo (G-2632)

Ametek Inc ....D...... 585 263-7700
 Rochester (G-13234)

AMP-Line Corp ....F...... 845 623-3288
 West Nyack (G-15815)

Analog Digital Technology LLC ....G...... 585 698-1845
 Rochester (G-13235)

Arise At Marshall Farms Inc ....G...... 315 687-6727
 Chittenango (G-3403)

Assa Abloy Entrance Systems US .E...... 315 492-6600
 East Syracuse (G-4198)

▲ Atlantic Electronic Tech LLC ....G...... 800 296-2177
 Brooklyn (G-1547)

Atlas Switch Co Inc ....E...... 516 222-6280
 Garden City (G-5090)

Audible Difference Inc ....E...... 212 662-4848
 Brooklyn (G-1551)

B & H Electronics Corp ....E...... 845 782-5000
 Monroe (G-8015)

Bare Beauty Laser Hair Removal ..G...... 718 278-2273
 New York (G-8728)

▲ Binghamton Simulator Co Inc ...E...... 607 321-2980
 Binghamton (G-860)

Bombardier Trnsp Holdings USA ..D...... 607 776-4791
 Bath (G-631)

Branson Ultrasonics Corp ....E...... 585 624-8000
 Honeoye Falls (G-6070)

◆ Bren-Tronics Inc ....C...... 631 499-5155
 Commack (G-3582)

BSC Associates LLC ....F...... 607 321-2980
 Binghamton (G-864)

▲ Buffalo Filter LLC ....D...... 716 835-7000
 Lancaster (G-6799)

C & G Video Systems Inc ....G...... 315 452-1490
 Liverpool (G-7003)

◆ Castle Power Solutions LLC ....F...... 518 743-1000
 Hudson Falls (G-6183)

Cathay Global Co Inc ....G...... 718 229-0920
 Bayside Hills (G-746)

Ces Industries Inc ....E...... 631 782-7088
 Islandia (G-6329)

Comsec Ventures International ......E...... 518 523-1600
 Lake Placid (G-6766)

◆ Cooper Crouse-Hinds LLC ....B...... 315 477-7000
 Syracuse (G-14862)

Cooper Industries LLC ....F...... 315 477-7000
 Syracuse (G-14864)

Cooper Power Systems LLC ....B...... 716 375-7100
 Olean (G-12230)

Cooperfriedman Elc Sup Co Inc ....G...... 718 269-4906
 Long Island City (G-7192)

Custom Sound and Video ....E...... 585 424-5000
 Rochester (G-13334)

Dahill Distributors Inc ....G...... 347 371-9453
 Brooklyn (G-1718)

Detekion Security Systems Inc .....F...... 607 729-7179
 Vestal (G-15376)

Dorsey Metrology Intl Inc ....E...... 845 229-2929
 Poughkeepsie (G-12951)

◆ Dyson-Kissner-Moran Corp ....D...... 212 661-4600
 Poughkeepsie (G-12952)

Eastco Manufacturing Corp ....F...... 914 738-5667
 Scarsdale (G-14235)

Emco Electric Services LLC ....E...... 212 420-9766
 New York (G-9360)

▲ Emcom Inc ....D...... 315 255-5300
 Auburn (G-474)

Empire Plastics Inc ....E...... 607 754-9132
 Endwell (G-4479)

Eyelock Corporation ....F...... 855 393-5625
 New York (G-9451)

Eyelock LLC ....F...... 855 393-5625
 New York (G-9452)

EZ Lift Operator Corp ....F...... 845 356-1676
 Spring Valley (G-14568)

Fairview Bell and Intercom ....G...... 718 627-8621
 Brooklyn (G-1829)

◆ Fiber Instrument Sales Inc ....C...... 315 736-2206
 Oriskany (G-12390)

Fire Fox Security Corp ....G...... 917 981-9280
 Brooklyn (G-1847)

Forte Network ....E...... 631 390-9050
 East Northport (G-4146)

Full Circle Studios LLC ....G...... 716 875-7740
 Buffalo (G-2763)

Gb Group Inc ....G...... 212 594-3748
 New York (G-9576)

General Electric Company ....G...... 315 554-2000
 Skaneateles (G-14452)

▲ Gerome Technologies Inc ....D...... 518 463-1324
 Menands (G-7843)

Green Island Power Authority ....F...... 518 273-0661
 Green Island (G-5436)

Gsa Upstate NY ....G...... 631 244-5744
 Oakdale (G-12152)

Guardian Systems Tech Inc ....F...... 716 481-5597
 East Aurora (G-4090)

▲ Hampton Technologies LLC ....E...... 631 924-1335
 Medford (G-7711)

◆ Hergo Ergonomic Support Syst ..F...... 888 222-7270
 Oceanside (G-12175)

Highlander Realty Inc ....E...... 914 235-8073
 New Rochelle (G-8341)

Home Tech LLC ....G...... 914 301-5408
 Katonah (G-6633)

▲ Iba Industrial Inc ....E...... 631 254-6800
 Edgewood (G-4270)

Iconix Inc ....E...... 516 513-1420
 Hauppauge (G-5675)

Ingham Industries Inc ....G...... 631 242-2493
 Holbrook (G-6001)

◆ Innovative Video Tech Inc ....F...... 631 388-5700
 Hauppauge (G-5677)

Intellicheck Inc ....E...... 516 992-1900
 Melville (G-7794)

Intelligent Ctrl Systems LLC ....G...... 516 340-1011
 Farmingdale (G-4651)

▲ Isolation Technology Inc ....G...... 631 253-3314
 West Babylon (G-15714)

Issco Corporation ....E...... 212 732-8748
 Garden City (G-5102)

◆ Itin Scale Co Inc ....E...... 718 336-5900
 Brooklyn (G-1974)

J H M Engineering ....E...... 718 871-1810
 Brooklyn (G-1978)

▲ Kinetic Marketing Inc ....G...... 212 620-0600
 New York (G-10106)

Knf Clean Room Products Corp ......E...... 631 588-7000
 Ronkonkoma (G-13958)

▲ Koregon Enterprises Inc ....G...... 450 218-6836
 Champlain (G-3314)

L-3 Cmmnctons Ntronix Holdings ..D...... 212 697-1111
 New York (G-10152)

L3harris Technologies Inc ....A...... 631 630-4200
 Amityville (G-288)

LMD Power of Light Corp ....E...... 585 272-5420
 Rochester (G-13519)

LTS Ny Inc ....G...... 646 558-3888
 Port Washington (G-12901)

Lyn Jo Enterprises Ltd ....G...... 716 753-2776
 Jamestown (G-6530)

Magic Tech Co Ltd ....G...... 516 539-7944
 West Hempstead (G-15775)

Manhattan Scientifics Inc ....F...... 212 541-2405
 New York (G-10345)

Manhole Brrier SEC Systems Inc ...E...... 516 741-1032
 Kew Gardens (G-6668)

Manufacturing Solutions Inc ....E...... 585 235-3320
 Rochester (G-13533)

Mitsubishi Elc Pwr Pdts Inc ....E...... 516 962-2813
 Melville (G-7806)

◆ Napco Security Tech Inc ....C...... 631 842-9400
 Amityville (G-297)

National Security Systems Inc ....E...... 516 627-2222
 Manhasset (G-7539)

▼ Navitar Inc ....D...... 585 359-4000
 Rochester (G-13568)

Nbn Technologies LLC ....E...... 585 355-5556
 Rochester (G-13569)

▲ Ncc Ny LLC ....E...... 718 943-7000
 Brooklyn (G-2195)

News/Sprts Microwave Rentl Inc ...E...... 619 670-0572
 New York (G-10615)

Northrop Grumman Intl Trdg Inc ...E...... 716 626-7233
 Buffalo (G-2892)

▲ OEM Solutions Inc ....G...... 716 864-9324
 Clarence (G-3437)

Optimum Applied Systems Inc ....F...... 845 471-3333
 Poughkeepsie (G-12977)

▲ Parabit Systems Inc ....E...... 516 378-4800
 Bellmore (G-786)

▲ Piller Power Systems Inc ....E...... 845 695-6658
 Middletown (G-7926)

Power Metrics Intl Inc ....F...... 718 524-4370
 Staten Island (G-14692)

▲ Protex International Corp ....D...... 631 563-4250
 Bohemia (G-1068)

Quantify Energy LLC ....G...... 917 268-1234
 New York (G-10951)

Rbw Studio LLC ....E...... 212 388-1621
 Brooklyn (G-2331)

Red Hawk Fire & Security LLC ....G...... 518 877-7616
 Albany (G-125)

Roo Inc ....F...... 212 905-6100
 New York (G-11081)

▲ Ross Electronics Ltd ....E...... 718 569-6643
 Haverstraw (G-5807)

Schneider Electric Usa Inc ....F...... 518 452-2590
 Albany (G-129)

Schuler-Haas Electric Corp ....G...... 607 936-3514
 Painted Post (G-12475)

▲ Scorpion Security Products Inc ..F...... 607 724-9999
 Vestal (G-15382)

Security Defense System ....G...... 718 769-7900
 Whitestone (G-16100)

▲ Security Dynamics Inc ....F...... 631 392-1701
 Bohemia (G-1075)

Sensor Films Incorporated ....E...... 585 738-3500
 Victor (G-15430)

Shield Security Doors Ltd ....G...... 202 468-3308
 Brooklyn (G-2405)

▲ Sima Technologies LLC ....G...... 412 828-9130
 Hauppauge (G-5766)

Simulaids Inc ....D...... 845 679-2475
 Saugerties (G-14212)

Skae Power Solutions LLC ....E...... 845 365-9103
 Palisades (G-12482)

Smithers Tools & Mch Pdts Inc .....D...... 845 876-3063
 Rhinebeck (G-13101)

▲ Sonicor Inc ....G...... 631 920-6555
 West Babylon (G-15748)

Sparkcharge Inc ....G...... 315 480-3645
 Syracuse (G-14996)

Tectran Inc ....G...... 800 776-5549
 Cheektowaga (G-3364)

Telephonics Corporation ....D...... 631 755-7000
 Farmingdale (G-4753)

Telephonics Corporation ....D...... 631 470-8800
 Huntington (G-6227)

▲ Trident Precision Mfg Inc ....D...... 585 265-2010
 Webster (G-15658)

U E Systems Incorporated ....E...... 914 592-1220
 Elmsford (G-4438)

United Technologies Corp ....D...... 866 788-5095
 Pittsford (G-12657)

Uptek Solutions Corp ....F...... 631 256-5565
 Bohemia (G-1094)

▲ V E Power Door Co Inc ....G...... 631 231-4500
 Brentwood (G-1133)

Windowman Inc (usa) ....G...... 718 246-2626
 Brooklyn (G-2590)

◆ World Trading Center Inc ....G...... 631 273-3330
 Hauppauge (G-5803)

▲ Z-Axis Inc ....D...... 315 548-5000
 Phelps (G-12611)

37 TRANSPORTATION EQUIPMENT

3711 Motor Vehicles & Car Bodies

AB Fire Inc ....G...... 917 416-6444
 Brooklyn (G-1446)

Antiques & Collectible Autos ....G...... 716 825-3990
 Buffalo (G-2636)

Antonicelli Vito Race Car ....G...... 716 684-2205
 Buffalo (G-2637)

Armor Dynamics Inc ....F...... 845 658-9200
 Kingston (G-6679)

▲ Auto Sport Designs Inc ....F...... 631 425-1555
 Huntington Station (G-6239)

Brothers-In-Lawn Property ....G...... 716 279-6191
 Tonawanda (G-15094)

Cabot Coach Builders Inc ....G...... 516 625-4000
 Roslyn Heights (G-14048)

CIC International Ltd ....D...... 212 213-0089
 Brooklyn (G-1663)

Conti Auto Body Corp ....G...... 516 921-6435
 Syosset (G-14781)

▲ Daimler Buses North Amer Inc ...A...... 315 768-8101
 Oriskany (G-12389)

Dejana Trck Utility Eqp Co LLC ......C...... 631 544-9000
 Kings Park (G-6672)

Dejana Trck Utility Eqp Co LLC ......E...... 631 549-0944
 Huntington (G-6204)

Empire Coachworks Intl LLC ....D...... 732 257-7981
 Suffern (G-14761)

Empire Emergency Apparatus Inc ..E...... 716 348-3473
 Niagara Falls (G-11923)

◆ Global Fire Corporation ....E 888 320-1799
New York (G-9627)

▲ Jtekt Torsen North America ....F 585 464-5000
Rochester (G-13498)

Kovatch Mobile Equipment Corp ....F 518 785-0900
Latham (G-6863)

Leonard Bus Sales Inc ....G 607 467-3100
Rome (G-13854)

Marcovicci-Wenz Engineering ....G 631 467-9040
Ronkonkoma (G-13970)

◆ Medical Coaches Incorporated ....E 607 432-1333
Oneonta (G-12275)

Prevost Car (us) Inc ....C 518 957-2052
Plattsburgh (G-12771)

▲ Ranger Design Us Inc ....E 800 565-5321
Ontario (G-12299)

Sabre Enterprises Inc ....G 315 430-3127
Syracuse (G-14983)

Schenvus Fire Dist. ....D 607 638-9017
Schenevus (G-14320)

Siemens Mobility Inc ....F 212 672-4000
New York (G-11227)

Smart Systems Inc ....E 607 776-5380
Bath (G-640)

Tee Pee Auto Sales Corp ....F 516 338-9333
Westbury (G-15928)

Tesla Motors Inc ....A 212 206-1204
New York (G-11455)

Transprttion Collaborative Inc ....E 845 988-2333
Warwick (G-15522)

Troyer Inc. ....F 585 352-5590
Rochester (G-13774)

Wendys Auto Express Inc ....G ....: 845 624-6100
Nanuet (G-8204)

3713 Truck & Bus Bodies

Able Weldbuilt Industries Inc ....F 631 643-9700
Deer Park (G-3826)

Bay Horse Innovations Nyinc ....G 607 898-3337
Groton (G-5480)

Blackburn Truck Bodies LLC ....G 315 448-3236
Syracuse (G-14831)

▲ Brunner International Inc ....C 585 798-6000
Medina (G-7731)

◆ Concrete Mixer Supplycom Inc ....G 716 375-5565
Olean (G-12229)

Conti Auto Body Corp ....G 516 921-6435
Syosset (G-14781)

▲ Daimler Buses North Amer Inc ....A 315 768-8101
Oriskany (G-12389)

Demartini Oil Equipment Svc ....G 518 463-5752
Glenmont (G-5236)

Donver Incorporated ....F 716 945-1910
Kill Buck (G-6669)

Eastern Welding Inc ....G 631 727-0306
Riverhead (G-13174)

Ekostinger Inc ....F 585 739-0450
East Rochester (G-4161)

General Welding & Fabg Inc ....F 585 697-7660
Rochester (G-13434)

Jeffersonville Volunteer ....E 845 482-3110
Jeffersonville (G-6570)

Kurtz Truck Equipment Inc ....F 607 849-3468
Marathon (G-7558)

Marros Equipment & Trucks ....G 315 539-8702
Waterloo (G-15555)

Premium Bldg Components Inc ....E 518 885-0194
Ballston Spa (G-585)

Renaldos Sales & Service Ctr ....G 716 337-3760
North Collins (G-12028)

Rexford Services Inc ....G 716 366-6671
Dunkirk (G-4065)

▲ Tectran Mfg Inc ....D 800 776-5549
Buffalo (G-3004)

Unicell Body Company Inc ....E 716 853-8628
Buffalo (G-3027)

Unicell Body Company Inc ....F 716 853-8628
Schenectady (G-14313)

Unicell Body Company Inc ....F 585 424-2660
Rochester (G-13781)

USA Body Inc ....G 315 852-6123
De Ruyter (G-3823)

Weld-Built Body Co Inc ....E 631 643-9700
Wyandanch (G-16248)

3714 Motor Vehicle Parts & Access

4bumpers Llc ....F 212 721-9600
New York (G-8403)

A-Line Technologies Inc ....F 607 772-2439
Binghamton (G-850)

◆ Actasys Inc ....G 914 432-2336
Watervliet (G-15596)

Agri Services Co ....G 716 937-6618
Alden (G-164)

Allomatic Products Company ....G 516 775-0330
Floral Park (G-4807)

▲ Alloy Metal Products LLC ....F 315 676-2405
Central Square (G-3293)

Aludyne New York LLC ....F 248 728-8642
Batavia (G-600)

American Auto ACC Incrporation ....G 718 886-6600
Flushing (G-4838)

American Refuse Supply Inc ....G 718 893-8157
Bronx (G-1204)

Anchor Commerce Trading Corp ....G 516 881-3485
Atlantic Beach (G-452)

◆ API Heat Transf Thermasys Corp ....C 716 684-6700
Buffalo (G-2638)

▲ ARC Remanufacturing Inc ....D 718 728-0701
Long Island City (G-7162)

Automotive Accessories Group ....B 212 736-8100
New York (G-8682)

Axle Express ....E 518 347-2220
Schenectady (G-14247)

Bam Enterprises Inc ....G 716 773-7634
Grand Island (G-5326)

Banner Transmission & Eng Co ....G 516 221-9459
Melville (G-7762)

Bigbee Steel and Tank Company ....G 518 273-0801
Watervliet (G-15597)

▲ Biltron Automotive Products ....E 631 928-8613
Port Jeff STA (G-12833)

Borgwarner Inc. ....G 607 257-1800
Ithaca (G-6371)

Borgwarner Morse TEC Inc ....D 607 266-5111
Ithaca (G-6372)

Borgwarner Morse TEC LLC ....D 607 257-6700
Cortland (G-3756)

Car-Go Industries Inc ....G 718 472-1443
Woodside (G-16201)

Classic & Performance Spc ....E 716 759-1800
Lancaster (G-6801)

Crestron Electronics Inc ....D 201 894-0670
Orangeburg (G-12311)

▲ CRS Remanufacturing Co Inc ....F 718 739-1720
Jamaica (G-6439)

Cubic Trnsp Systems Inc ....E 212 255-1810
New York (G-9129)

Curtis L Maclean L C ....B 716 898-7800
Buffalo (G-2715)

▲ Custom Sitecom LLC ....G 631 420-4238
Farmingdale (G-4611)

Deer Park Driveshaft & Hose ....G 631 667-4091
Deer Park (G-3860)

Delphi Automotive LLP ....G 716 438-4886
Amherst (G-220)

Delphi Powertrain Systems LLC ....C 585 359-6000
West Henrietta (G-15791)

Delphi Powertrain Systems LLC ....B 585 359-6000
West Henrietta (G-15792)

Delphi Powertrain Systems LLC ....E 585 359-6000
West Henrietta (G-15793)

Delphi Thermal Systems ....F 716 439-2454
Lockport (G-7067)

Dennys Drive Shaft Service ....G 716 875-6640
Kenmore (G-6649)

Dmic Inc. ....G 716 743-4360
North Tonawanda (G-12065)

Drive Shaft Shop Inc ....F 631 348-1818
Hauppauge (G-5642)

Electron Top Mfg Co Inc ....E 718 846-7400
Richmond Hill (G-13112)

Electronic Machine Parts LLC ....F 631 434-3700
Hauppauge (G-5645)

Empire Emergency Apparatus Inc ....F 716 348-3473
Niagara Falls (G-11923)

Enplas America Inc ....G 646 892-7811
New York (G-9381)

Exten II LLC ....F 716 895-2214
East Aurora (G-4087)

▲ Extreme Auto Accessories Corp ....F 718 978-6722
Mineola (G-7973)

Factory Wheel Warehouse Inc ....G 516 605-2131
Commack (G-3587)

▲ Fast By Gast Inc ....G 716 773-1536
Grand Island (G-5329)

▲ Fcmp Inc ....F 716 692-4623
Tonawanda (G-15103)

Flagship One Inc ....F 516 766-2223
Lynbrook (G-7431)

General Motors LLC ....A 716 879-5000
Buffalo (G-2773)

◆ Gleason Works ....A 585 473-1000
Rochester (G-13445)

GM Components Holdings LLC ....C 716 439-2237
Lockport (G-7078)

GM Components Holdings LLC ....B 585 647-7000
Rochester (G-13447)

GM Components Holdings LLC ....B 716 439-2463
Lockport (G-7079)

GM Components Holdings LLC ....B 716 439-2011
Lockport (G-7080)

Interntnal Auto Voluntary Untd ....B 718 743-8732
Brooklyn (G-1968)

▲ Interparts International Inc ....E 516 576-2000
Plainview (G-12691)

▲ ITT Enidine Inc ....C 716 662-1900
Orchard Park (G-12356)

Johnson Controls Inc ....C 585 724-2232
Rochester (G-13495)

▲ Jtekt Torsen North America ....B 585 464-5000
Rochester (G-13498)

K M Drive Line Inc ....G 718 599-0628
Brooklyn (G-2018)

▲ Karlyn Industries Inc ....F 845 351-2249
Southfields (G-14541)

Katikati Inc ....G 585 678-1764
West Henrietta (G-15798)

◆ Kearney-National Inc ....F 212 661-4600
New York (G-10087)

▲ Kerns Manufacturing Corp ....C 718 784-4044
Long Island City (G-7262)

Kurtz Truck Equipment Inc ....F 607 849-3468
Marathon (G-7558)

▲ Lee World Industries LLC ....F 212 265-8866
New York (G-10190)

Lemans Corporation ....G 518 885-7500
Ballston Spa (G-580)

M2 Race Systems Inc ....G 607 882-9078
Ithaca (G-6393)

◆ Magtrol Inc ....E 716 668-5555
Buffalo (G-2859)

Mahle Behr Troy Inc ....C 716 439-3039
Lockport (G-7088)

Mahle Behr USA Inc ....B 716 439-2011
Lockport (G-7089)

Mahle Indstrbeteiligungen GMBH ....D 716 319-6700
Amherst (G-231)

▼ Mahle Manufacturing MGT Inc ....D 248 735-3623
Amherst (G-232)

Marcovicci-Wenz Engineering ....G 631 467-9040
Ronkonkoma (G-13970)

Mohawk Innovative Tech Inc ....F 518 862-4290
Albany (G-100)

▲ Motor Components LLC ....D 607 737-8011
Elmira Heights (G-4378)

▲ Nas-Tra Automotive Inds Inc ....C 631 225-1225
Lindenhurst (G-6962)

◆ P & F Industries Inc ....E 631 694-9800
Melville (G-7813)

▲ Pall Corporation ....A 516 484-5400
Port Washington (G-12913)

Pall Corporation ....A 607 753-6041
Cortland (G-3779)

Par-Foam Products Inc ....C 716 855-2066
Buffalo (G-2905)

Parker-Hannifin Corporation ....D 716 685-4040
Lancaster (G-6822)

Performance Designed By Peters ....F 585 223-9062
Fairport (G-4515)

Phillip J Ortiz Manufacturing ....G 845 226-7030
Hopewell Junction (G-6100)

▲ Powerflow Inc ....D 716 892-1014
Buffalo (G-2926)

Pro Torque ....E 631 218-8700
Bohemia (G-1067)

Pro-Value Distribution Inc ....G 585 783-1461
Rochester (G-13648)

◆ Rosco Inc ....C 718 526-2601
Jamaica (G-6471)

▲ Rpb Distributors LLC ....G 914 244-3600
Mount Kisco (G-8105)

Smith Metal Works Newark Inc ....E 315 331-1651
Newark (G-11851)

▲ Specialty Silicone Pdts Inc ....D 518 885-8826
Ballston Spa (G-587)

◆ Standard Motor Products Inc ....B 718 392-0200
Long Island City (G-7364)

Steering Columns Galore Inc ....G 845 278-5762
Mahopac (G-7479)

S
I
C

Temper Corporation............G...... 518 853-3467
Fonda *(G-4913)*

Tesla Motors Inc............A...... 212 206-1204
New York *(G-11455)*

TI Group Auto Systems LLC............G...... 315 568-7042
Seneca Falls *(G-14373)*

▲ **Titanx Engine Cooling Inc**............B...... 716 665-7129
Jamestown *(G-6550)*

Trico Holding Corporation............A...... 716 852-5700
Buffalo *(G-3019)*

Troyer Inc............F...... 585 352-5590
Rochester *(G-13774)*

Vehicle Safety Dept............F...... 315 458-6683
Syracuse *(G-15020)*

▼ **Whiting Door Mfg Corp**............B...... 716 542-5427
Akron *(G-23)*

◆ **Wolo Mfg Corp**............E...... 631 242-0333
Deer Park *(G-3955)*

Yomiuri International Inc............G...... 212 752-2196
New York *(G-11811)*

Zwack Incorporated............E...... 518 733-5135
Stephentown *(G-14732)*

3715 Truck Trailers

◆ **Blue Tee Corp**............G...... 212 598-0880
New York *(G-8820)*

Cross Country Mfg Inc............F...... 607 656-4103
Greene *(G-5444)*

Davis Trailer World LLC............F...... 585 538-6640
York *(G-16362)*

General Welding & Fabg Inc............G...... 716 652-0033
Elma *(G-4319)*

Rolling Star Manufacturing Inc............E...... 315 896-4767
Barneveld *(G-595)*

Seneca Truck & Trailer Inc............G...... 315 781-1100
Geneva *(G-5163)*

▼ **Stone Well Bodies & Mch Inc**............E...... 315 497-3512
Genoa *(G-5168)*

3716 Motor Homes

Authority Transportation Inc............F...... 888 933-1268
Dix Hills *(G-4010)*

3721 Aircraft

Alliant Tchsystems Oprtons LLC............E...... 631 737-6100
Ronkonkoma *(G-13898)*

Altius Aviation LLC............G...... 315 455-7555
Syracuse *(G-14813)*

Barclay Tagg Racing............E...... 631 404-8269
Floral Park *(G-4809)*

Boeing Company............A...... 201 259-9400
New York *(G-8829)*

Bombardier Trnsp Holdings USA............E...... 518 566-5067
Plattsburgh *(G-12738)*

◆ **Calspan Corporation**............C...... 716 631-6955
Buffalo *(G-2689)*

Calspan Corporation............F...... 716 236-1040
Niagara Falls *(G-11911)*

Calspan Holdings LLC............F...... 716 631-6955
Buffalo *(G-2690)*

CIC International Ltd............D...... 212 213-0089
Brooklyn *(G-1663)*

Easy Aerial Inc............G...... 646 639-4410
Brooklyn *(G-1779)*

Grumman Field Support Services............D...... 516 575-0574
Bethpage *(G-835)*

Ingenious Ingenuity Inc............F...... 800 834-5279
Webster *(G-15642)*

Lesly Enterprise & Associates............G...... 631 988-1301
Deer Park *(G-3896)*

Lockheed Martin Corporation............E...... 716 297-1000
Niagara Falls *(G-11948)*

Lockheed Martin Corporation............D...... 315 793-5800
New Hartford *(G-8241)*

Luminati Aerospace LLC............F...... 631 574-2616
Calverton *(G-3082)*

M & H Research and Dev Corp............G...... 607 734-2346
Beaver Dams *(G-759)*

Moog Inc............B...... 716 687-4954
East Aurora *(G-4093)*

Necessity Systems LLC............G...... 907 322-4084
Kirkville *(G-6725)*

Northrop Grumman Systems Corp............A...... 516 575-0574
Bethpage *(G-842)*

Pro Drones Usa LLC............F...... 718 530-3558
New York *(G-10900)*

Sikorsky Aircraft Corporation............D...... 585 424-1990
Rochester *(G-13731)*

Tech Park Food Services LLC............G...... 585 295-1250
Rochester *(G-13762)*

Xactiv Inc............F...... 585 288-7220
Fairport *(G-4531)*

3724 Aircraft Engines & Engine Parts

Ademco Inc............G...... 716 631-2197
Cheektowaga *(G-3337)*

Advanced Atomization Tech LLC............B...... 315 923-2341
Clyde *(G-3488)*

▲ **ARC Systems Inc**............E...... 631 582-8020
Hauppauge *(G-5592)*

B H Aircraft Company Inc............D...... 631 580-9747
Ronkonkoma *(G-13912)*

Chromalloy American LLC............E...... 845 230-7355
Orangeburg *(G-12309)*

Chromalloy Gas Turbine LLC............C...... 845 359-2462
Orangeburg *(G-12310)*

Chromalloy Gas Turbine LLC............E...... 845 692-8912
Middletown *(G-7898)*

Colonial Group LLC............E...... 516 349-8010
Plainview *(G-12671)*

▲ **Davis Aircraft Products Co Inc**............C...... 631 563-1500
Bohemia *(G-1000)*

▲ **Dyna-Empire Inc**............C...... 516 222-2700
Garden City *(G-5096)*

Eur-Pac Corporation............G...... 203 756-0102
Bay Shore *(G-679)*

Fadec Alliance LLC............C...... 607 770-3342
Endicott *(G-4454)*

Gb Aero Engine LLC............B...... 914 925-9600
Rye *(G-14078)*

General Electric Company............E...... 518 385-7620
Niskayuna *(G-11996)*

General Electric Company............A...... 518 385-4022
Schenectady *(G-14266)*

Honeywell International Inc............D...... 518 270-0200
Troy *(G-15158)*

Honeywell International Inc............E...... 516 577-2661
Melville *(G-7790)*

Honeywell International Inc............E...... 516 577-2000
Melville *(G-7791)*

Honeywell International Inc............A...... 845 342-4400
Middletown *(G-7914)*

Honeywell International Inc............G...... 516 302-9401
New Hyde Park *(G-8274)*

Honeywell International Inc............A...... 212 964-5111
Melville *(G-7792)*

Honeywell International Inc............B...... 516 577-2000
Melville *(G-7793)*

Honeywell International Inc............F...... 315 463-7208
East Syracuse *(G-4217)*

Honeywell International Inc............G...... 631 471-2202
Lake Ronkonkoma *(G-6770)*

▲ **ITT Enidine Inc**............B...... 716 662-1900
Orchard Park *(G-12356)*

▲ **Kerns Manufacturing Corp**............C...... 718 784-4044
Long Island City *(G-7262)*

Lourdes Industries Inc............D...... 631 234-6600
Hauppauge *(G-5700)*

▲ **Magellan Aerospace Bethel Inc**............C...... 203 798-9373
Corona *(G-3743)*

Magellan Aerospace Processing............G...... 631 694-1818
West Babylon *(G-15728)*

McGuigan Inc............E...... 631 750-6222
Bohemia *(G-1045)*

Nell-Joy Industries Inc............E...... 631 842-8989
Copiague *(G-3665)*

SOS International LLC............B...... 212 742-2410
New York *(G-11302)*

▲ **Therm Incorporated**............C...... 607 272-8500
Ithaca *(G-6412)*

Triumph Actuation Systems LLC............D...... 516 378-0162
Freeport *(G-5030)*

Triumph Group Inc............D...... 516 997-5757
Westbury *(G-15934)*

Turbine Engine Comp Utica............A...... 315 768-8070
Whitesboro *(G-16084)*

United Technologies Corp............G...... 315 432-7849
East Syracuse *(G-4246)*

3728 Aircraft Parts & Eqpt, NEC

AAR Allen Services Inc............E...... 516 222-9000
Garden City *(G-5089)*

Aero Strctures Long Island Inc............D...... 516 997-5757
Westbury *(G-15863)*

Aero Trades Mfg Corp............E...... 516 746-3360
Mineola *(G-7955)*

Air Industries Group............D...... 631 881-4920
Bay Shore *(G-644)*

▲ **Air Industries Machining Corp**............C...... 631 328-7000
Bay Shore *(G-645)*

Alken Industries Inc............E...... 631 467-2000
Ronkonkoma *(G-13896)*

Arkwin Industries Inc............C...... 516 333-2640
Westbury *(G-15870)*

▲ **Astronics Corporation**............C...... 716 805-1599
East Aurora *(G-4082)*

Ausco Inc............D...... 516 944-9882
Farmingdale *(G-4588)*

B & B Precision Components Inc............G...... 631 273-3321
Ronkonkoma *(G-13911)*

B/E Aerospace Inc............E...... 631 563-6400
Bohemia *(G-978)*

▲ **Blair Industries Inc**............E...... 631 924-6600
Medford *(G-7699)*

Canfield Aerospace & Mar Inc............E...... 631 648-1050
Ronkonkoma *(G-13921)*

Caravan International Corp............E...... 212 223-7190
New York *(G-8915)*

Circor Aerospace Inc............D...... 631 737-1900
Hauppauge *(G-5615)*

▲ **Cox & Company Inc**............E...... 212 366-0200
Plainview *(G-12676)*

CPI Aerostructures Inc............E...... 631 586-5200
Edgewood *(G-4266)*

Crown Aircraft Lighting Inc............G...... 718 767-3410
Whitestone *(G-16091)*

▲ **Davis Aircraft Products Co Inc**............C...... 631 563-1500
Bohemia *(G-1000)*

Design/OI Inc............F...... 631 474-2134
Port Jeff STA *(G-12834)*

▲ **Dresser-Argus Inc**............E...... 718 643-1540
Brooklyn *(G-1762)*

Drt Aerospace LLC............G...... 585 247-5940
Rochester *(G-13357)*

Ducommun Aerostructures NY Inc............B...... 518 731-2791
Coxsackie *(G-3800)*

▲ **Dyna-Empire Inc**............C...... 516 222-2700
Garden City *(G-5096)*

East/West Industries Inc............E...... 631 981-5900
Ronkonkoma *(G-13932)*

Eastern Precision Machining............G...... 631 286-4758
Bellport *(G-797)*

Engineered Metal Products Inc............G...... 631 842-3780
Copiague *(G-3652)*

Enlighten Air Inc............G...... 917 656-1248
New York *(G-9380)*

Excelco Developments Inc............E...... 716 934-2651
Silver Creek *(G-14441)*

Excelco/Newbrook Inc............G...... 716 934-2644
Silver Creek *(G-14442)*

Fluid Mechanisms Hauppauge Inc............E...... 631 234-0100
Hauppauge *(G-5652)*

GE Aviation Systems LLC............C...... 631 467-5500
Bohemia *(G-1015)*

▲ **GKN Aerospace Monitor Inc**............B...... 562 619-8558
Amityville *(G-264)*

◆ **Gleason Works**............A...... 585 473-1000
Rochester *(G-13445)*

Goodrich Corporation............C...... 315 838-1200
Rome *(G-13849)*

Handy Tool & Mfg Co Inc............E...... 718 478-9203
Brooklyn *(G-1926)*

Hicksville Machine Works Corp............F...... 516 931-1524
Hicksville *(G-5916)*

▲ **HSM Machine Works Inc**............E...... 631 924-6600
Medford *(G-7712)*

Jac Usa Inc............G...... 212 841-7430
New York *(G-9960)*

Jamco Aerospace Inc............E...... 631 586-7900
Deer Park *(G-3886)*

◆ **Jaquith Industries Inc**............E...... 315 478-5700
Syracuse *(G-14916)*

Joldeson One Aerospace Inds............D...... 718 848-7396
Ozone Park *(G-12463)*

Jrsmm LLC............G...... 607 331-1549
Elmira *(G-4360)*

Lai International Inc............E...... 763 780-0060
Green Island *(G-5438)*

Lenny & Bill LLC............D...... 516 997-5757
Westbury *(G-15903)*

Loar Group Inc............C...... 212 210-9348
New York *(G-10239)*

▲ **Magellan Aerospace Bethel Inc**............C...... 203 798-9373
Corona *(G-3743)*

Magellan Aerospace NY Inc............C...... 631 589-2440
Bohemia *(G-1041)*

▲ **Magellan Aerospace NY Inc**............C...... 718 699-4000
Corona *(G-3744)*

MD International Industries............E...... 631 254-3100
Deer Park *(G-3906)*

Metadure Parts & Sales Inc .... F 631 249-2141
Farmingdale (G-4681)

◆ Metal Dynamics Intl Corp .... G 631 231-1153
Hauppauge (G-5715)

Milex Precision Inc .... F 631 595-2393
Bay Shore (G-692)

Military Parts Exchange LLC .... F 631 243-1700
Melville (G-7805)

Min-Max Machine Ltd .... F 631 585-4378
Ronkonkoma (G-13974)

Minutemen Precsn McHning Tool ..... E 631 467-4900
Ronkonkoma (G-13975)

Moelis Capital Partners LLC .... B 212 883-3800
New York (G-10492)

◆ Moog Inc .... A 716 805-2604
Elma (G-4321)

Mpi Consulting Incorporated .... F 631 253-2377
West Babylon (G-15733)

Nassau Tool Works Inc .... E 631 328-7031
Bay Shore (G-697)

Norsk Titanium US Inc .... E 518 324-4010
Plattsburgh (G-12761)

Parker-Hannifin Corporation .... C 631 231-3737
Clyde (G-3494)

▼ Posimech Inc .... E 631 924-5959
Medford (G-7722)

Precision Cnc .... G 631 847-3999
Deer Park (G-3921)

▲ Precision Gear Incorporated .... C 718 321-7200
College Point (G-3560)

Reese Manufacturing Inc .... G 631 842-3780
Copiague (G-3673)

S&L Aerospace Metals LLC .... D 718 326-1821
Flushing (G-4890)

Santa Fe Manufacturing Corp .... G 631 234-0100
Hauppauge (G-5757)

Servotronics Inc .... C 716 655-5990
Elma (G-4327)

▲ Styles Aviation Inc .... G 845 677-8185
Lagrangeville (G-6754)

▼ Sumner Industries Inc .... F 631 666-7290
Bay Shore (G-720)

Superior Motion Controls Inc .... E 516 420-2921
Farmingdale (G-4745)

Tangent Machine & Tool Corp .... F 631 249-3088
Farmingdale (G-4749)

Tek Precision Co Ltd .... E 631 242-0330
Deer Park (G-3941)

Tens Machine Company Inc .... E 631 981-3321
Holbrook (G-6026)

TPC Inc .... G 315 438-8605
East Syracuse (G-4243)

Triumph Actuation Systems LLC ..... D 516 378-0162
Freeport (G-5030)

Universal Armor Systems Corp .... E 631 838-1836
Levittown (G-6917)

Usairports Services Inc .... E 585 527-6835
Rochester (G-13790)

UTC Aerospace Systems .... E 315 838-1200
Rome (G-13875)

Vosky Precision Machining Corp ..... F 631 737-3200
Ronkonkoma (G-14025)

W J Albro Machine Works Inc .... G 631 345-0657
Yaphank (G-16278)

Wilco Industries Inc .... G 631 676-2593
Ronkonkoma (G-14028)

Young & Franklin Inc .... D 315 457-3110
Liverpool (G-7051)

3731 Shipbuilding & Repairing

Caddell Dry Dock & Repr Co Inc ..... C 718 442-2112
Staten Island (G-14635)

◆ Dragon Trading Inc .... G 212 717-1496
New York (G-9265)

Excelco Developments Inc .... E 716 934-2651
Silver Creek (G-14441)

Excelco/Newbrook Inc .... D 716 934-2644
Silver Creek (G-14442)

Gmd Shipyard Corp .... E 718 260-9202
Brooklyn (G-1893)

Huntington Ingalls Inc .... E 518 884-3834
Saratoga Springs (G-14182)

▲ May Ship Repair Contg Corp .... E 718 442-9700
Staten Island (G-14680)

McQuilling Partners Inc .... E 516 227-5718
Garden City (G-5107)

▼ Metalcraft Marine Us Inc .... F 315 501-4015
Cape Vincent (G-3168)

▲ Moran Shipyard Corporation .... C 718 981-5600
Staten Island (G-14681)

Port Everglades Machine Works ...... F 516 367-2280
Plainview (G-12708)

▲ Reynolds Shipyard Corporation ..... F 718 981-2800
Staten Island (G-14702)

▲ Robert E Derecktor Inc .... D 914 698-0962
Mamaroneck (G-7522)

Steelways Inc .... E 845 562-0860
Newburgh (G-11887)

Viking Mar Wldg Ship Repr LLC ..... F 718 758-4116
Brooklyn (G-2558)

World Maritime News .... G 212 477-6700
New York (G-11782)

3732 Boat Building & Repairing

Allen Boat Co Inc .... G 716 842-0800
Buffalo (G-2626)

▼ American Metalcraft Marine .... G 315 686-9891
Clayton (G-3452)

Ashco Management Inc .... F 212 960-8428
Brooklyn (G-1540)

▲ AVS Laminates Inc .... E 631 286-2136
Bellport (G-794)

Cayuga Wooden Boatworks Inc .... E 315 253-7447
Ithaca (G-6374)

Coecles Hbr Marina & Boat Yard ..... F 631 749-0856
Shelter Island (G-14385)

Eastern Welding Inc .... G 631 727-0306
Riverhead (G-13174)

Fantasy Glass Compan .... E 845 786-5818
Stony Point (G-14743)

Gar Wood Custom Boats .... G 518 494-2966
Brant Lake (G-1112)

Global Marine Power Inc .... E 631 208-2933
Calverton (G-3081)

Hampton Shipyards Inc .... F 631 653-6777
East Quogue (G-4157)

▲ Jag Manufacturing Inc .... E 518 762-9558
Johnstown (G-6620)

Katherine Blizniak .... G 716 674-8545
West Seneca (G-15850)

▼ Marathon Boat Group Inc .... F 607 849-3211
Marathon (G-7559)

▲ May Ship Repair Contg Corp .... E 718 442-9700
Staten Island (G-14680)

▼ Metalcraft Marine Us Inc .... F 315 501-4015
Cape Vincent (G-3168)

Mokai Manufacturing Inc .... G 845 566-8287
Newburgh (G-11874)

▲ Robert E Derecktor Inc .... D 914 698-0962
Mamaroneck (G-7522)

Rocking The Boat Inc .... F 718 466-5799
Bronx (G-1353)

Scarano Boat Building Inc .... E 518 463-3401
Albany (G-127)

Scarano Boatbuilding Inc .... E 518 463-3401
Albany (G-128)

Superboats Inc .... G 631 226-1761
Lindenhurst (G-6978)

Tumblehome Boatshop .... E 518 623-5050
Warrensburg (G-15506)

Wooden Boatworks .... G 631 477-6507
Greenport (G-5459)

3743 Railroad Eqpt

Acf Industries Holding LLC .... G 212 702-4363
New York (G-8447)

▲ Bombardier Mass Transit Corp ..... B 518 566-0150
Plattsburgh (G-12737)

Bombardier Transportation .... D 607 324-0216
Hornell (G-6102)

CAF Usa Inc .... D 607 737-3004
Elmira Heights (G-4375)

▲ Cox & Company Inc .... C 212 366-0200
Plainview (G-12676)

▲ Eagle Bridge Machine & TI Inc ..... E 518 686-4541
Eagle Bridge (G-4071)

Ebenezer Railcar Services Inc .... D 716 674-5650
West Seneca (G-15846)

▲ Gray Manufacturing Inds LLC ..... F 607 281-1325
Hornell (G-6108)

Highcrest Investors LLC .... D 212 702-4323
New York (G-8466)

Higher Power Industries Inc .... G 914 709-9800
Yonkers (G-16319)

Horne Products Inc .... G 631 293-0773
Farmingdale (G-4645)

Hudson Machine Works Inc .... C 845 279-1413
Brewster (G-1152)

▲ Kawasaki Rail Car Inc .... C 914 376-4700
Yonkers (G-16323)

Knorr Brake Company LLC .... G 518 561-1387
Plattsburgh (G-12756)

▲ Knorr Brake Holding Corp .... G 315 786-5356
Watertown (G-15578)

▲ Knorr Brake Truck Systems Co ..... B 315 786-5200
Watertown (G-15579)

▲ Koshii Maxelum America Inc .... E 845 471-0500
Poughkeepsie (G-12966)

▲ Matrix Railway Corp .... G 631 643-1483
West Babylon (G-15730)

New York Air Brake LLC .... G 315 786-5576
Watertown (G-15583)

▲ New York Air Brake LLC .... C 315 786-5219
Watertown (G-15584)

▲ Peck & Hale LLC .... E 631 589-2510
West Sayville (G-15842)

Rand Machine Products, Inc. .... C 716 665-5217
Falconer (G-4552)

Seisenbacher Inc .... F 585 730-4960
Rochester (G-13721)

▲ Semec Corp .... E 518 825-0160
Plattsburgh (G-12776)

Siemens Mobility Inc .... F 212 672-4000
New York (G-11227)

Starfire Holding Corporation .... G 914 614-7000
New York (G-11350)

▲ Strato Transit Components LLC ..... G 518 686-4541
Eagle Bridge (G-4075)

Transco Railway Products Inc .... E 716 825-1663
Buffalo (G-3018)

Transco Railway Products Inc .... C 716 824-1219
Blasdell (G-923)

▲ Twinco Mfg Co Inc .... G 631 231-0022
Hauppauge (G-5789)

Westcode Incorporated .... F 607 766-9881
Binghamton (G-916)

Westinghouse A Brake Tech Corp .... D 518 561-0044
Plattsburgh (G-12791)

Westinghouse A Brake Tech Corp .... F 914 347-8650
Elmsford (G-4440)

3751 Motorcycles, Bicycles & Parts

Bignay Inc .... G 786 346-1673
New York (G-8789)

Bike Shopcom LLC .... G 716 236-7500
Niagara Falls (G-11908)

▲ Chicken Hawk Racing Inc .... G 845 758-0700
Red Hook (G-13072)

▲ Evelo Inc .... G 917 251-8743
Rockaway Park (G-13824)

Golub Corporation .... E 518 943-3903
Catskill (G-3211)

Golub Corporation .... G 518 899-6063
Malta (G-7496)

Golub Corporation .... G 315 363-0679
Oneida (G-12244)

Golub Corporation .... G 607 336-2588
Norwich (G-12122)

Golub Corporation .... G 518 583-3697
Saratoga Springs (G-14177)

Golub Corporation .... G 518 822-0076
Hudson (G-6158)

Golub Corporation .... E 845 344-0327
Middletown (G-7913)

Great American Bicycle LLC .... G 518 584-8100
Saratoga Springs (G-14179)

Ihd Motorsports LLC .... F 979 690-1669
Binghamton (G-886)

Indian Larry Legacy .... G 718 609-9184
Brooklyn (G-1955)

▲ KG Motors Inc .... E 607 562-2877
Big Flats (G-847)

Orange County Choppers Inc .... G 845 522-5200
Newburgh (G-11878)

◆ Piaggio Group Americas Inc .... E 212 380-4400
New York (G-10833)

▲ Prestacycle Llc .... G 518 588-5546
Rexford (G-13097)

Robs Cycle Supply .... G 315 292-6878
Syracuse (G-14978)

▲ Social Bicycles LLC .... E 917 746-7624
Brooklyn (G-2432)

Sumax Cycle Products Inc .... F 315 768-1058
Oriskany (G-12397)

Super Price Chopper Inc .... F 716 893-3323
Buffalo (G-2996)

◆ Worksman Trading Corp .... G 718 322-2000
Ozone Park (G-12469)

Ying Ke Youth Age Group Inc .... F 929 402-8458
Dix Hills (G-4017)

S
I
C

3761 Guided Missiles & Space Vehicles

Drt Aerospace LLC ....G...... 585 247-5940
Rochester *(G-13357)*

L3harris Technologies Inc ....A...... 631 630-4200
Amityville *(G-288)*

Lockheed Martin Corporation ....A...... 315 456-0123
Liverpool *(G-7021)*

Lockheed Martin Corporation ....A...... 607 751-2000
Owego *(G-12433)*

3769 Guided Missile/Space Vehicle Parts & Eqpt, NEC

Gb Aero Engine LLC ....B...... 914 925-9600
Rye *(G-14078)*

▲ GKN Aerospace Monitor Inc ....B...... 562 619-8558
Amityville *(G-264)*

▲ L3 Foreign Holdings Inc ....C...... 212 697-1111
New York *(G-10153)*

L3 Technologies Inc ....A...... 631 436-7400
Hauppauge *(G-5687)*

L3 Technologies Inc ....B...... 212 697-1111
New York *(G-10154)*

Lockheed Martin Corporation ....E...... 716 297-1000
Niagara Falls *(G-11948)*

▲ Magellan Aerospace NY Inc ....C...... 718 699-4000
Corona *(G-3744)*

◆ Moog Inc ....A...... 716 805-2604
Elma *(G-4321)*

Saturn Industries Inc ....E...... 518 828-9956
Hudson *(G-6177)*

Servotronics Inc ....C...... 716 655-5990
Elma *(G-4327)*

SKF USA Inc ....D...... 716 661-2869
Falconer *(G-4555)*

SKF USA Inc ....D...... 716 661-2600
Falconer *(G-4557)*

Turbine Engine Comp Utica ....A...... 315 768-8070
Whitesboro *(G-16084)*

Unison Industries LLC ....B...... 607 335-5000
Norwich *(G-12130)*

3792 Travel Trailers & Campers

All Star Carts & Vehicles Inc ....D...... 631 666-5581
Bay Shore *(G-646)*

3795 Tanks & Tank Components

Lourdes Industries Inc ....D...... 631 234-6600
Hauppauge *(G-5700)*

◆ Tecmotiv (usa) Inc ....E...... 716 282-1211
Niagara Falls *(G-11986)*

3799 Transportation Eqpt, NEC

Adirondack Power Sports ....G...... 518 481-6269
Malone *(G-7482)*

Bombardier Trnsp Holdings USA ....D...... 607 776-4791
Bath *(G-631)*

Bullet Industries Inc ....G...... 585 352-0836
Spencerport *(G-14554)*

Clopay Ames True Temper ....F...... 212 957-5096
New York *(G-9035)*

Kens Service & Sales Inc ....F...... 716 683-1155
Elma *(G-4320)*

Performance Custom Trailer ....G...... 518 504-4021
Lake George *(G-6758)*

Tectran Inc ....G...... 800 776-5549
Cheektowaga *(G-3364)*

Truck-Lite Sub Inc ....G...... 800 888-7095
Falconer *(G-4561)*

Truxton Corp ....G...... 718 842-6000
Bronx *(G-1383)*

38 MEASURING, ANALYZING AND CONTROLLING INSTRUMENTS; PHOTOGRAPHIC, MEDICAL AN

3812 Search, Detection, Navigation & Guidance Systs & Instrs

Accipiter Radar Corporation ....G...... 716 508-4432
Orchard Park *(G-12336)*

Accutrak Inc ....F...... 212 925-5330
New York *(G-8444)*

▲ Aeroflex Incorporated ....B...... 516 694-6700
Hauppauge *(G-12660)*

American Aerospace Contrls Inc ....E...... 631 694-5100
Farmingdale *(G-4583)*

Ametek Inc ....D...... 585 263-7700
Rochester *(G-13234)*

Arsenal Holdings LLC ....G...... 212 398-9139
New York *(G-8626)*

▲ Artemis Inc ....G...... 631 232-2424
Hauppauge *(G-5594)*

◆ Aventura Technologies Inc ....E...... 631 300-4000
Commack *(G-3577)*

B & Z Technologies LLC ....G...... 631 675-9666
East Setauket *(G-4176)*

▲ Bae Systems Controls Inc ....A...... 607 770-2000
Endicott *(G-4445)*

Bae Systems Info & Elec Sys ....E...... 603 885-4321
Rome *(G-13842)*

Bae Systems Info & Elec Sys ....F...... 631 912-1525
Greenlawn *(G-5452)*

Bae Systems PLC ....E...... 631 261-7000
Greenlawn *(G-5453)*

Boeing Distribution Svcs Inc ....F...... 845 534-0401
Cornwall *(G-3727)*

C Speed LLC ....E...... 315 453-1043
Liverpool *(G-7004)*

C-Flex Bearing Co Inc ....F...... 315 895-7454
Frankfort *(G-4948)*

CIC International Ltd ....D...... 212 213-0089
Brooklyn *(G-1663)*

CIT Aerospace LLC ....G...... 212 461-5200
New York *(G-9013)*

▲ Clayton Dubilier & Rice Fun ....E...... 212 407-5200
New York *(G-9029)*

Cobham Holdings Inc ....F...... 716 662-0006
Orchard Park *(G-12345)*

◆ Cobham Management Services Inc ..A...... 716 662-0006
Orchard Park *(G-12346)*

Cobham Mission Systems ....B...... 716 662-0006
Orchard Park *(G-12347)*

Computer Instruments Corp ....E...... 516 876-8400
Westbury *(G-15874)*

▲ Cox & Company Inc ....G...... 212 366-0200
Plainview *(G-12676)*

◆ Dyna-Empire Inc ....E...... 516 222-2700
Garden City *(G-5096)*

Eastern Strategic Materials ....E...... 212 332-1619
New York *(G-9306)*

Emergency Beacon Corp ....F...... 914 576-2700
Bronx *(G-1253)*

Excelsior Mlt-Cltural Inst Inc ....F...... 706 627-4285
Flushing *(G-4850)*

Facilamatic Instrument Corp ....F...... 516 825-6300
Valley Stream *(G-15340)*

Flightline Electronics Inc ....D...... 585 924-4000
Victor *(G-15410)*

Frequency Electronics Inc ....C...... 516 794-4500
Uniondale *(G-15229)*

GE Aviation Systems LLC ....D...... 513 243-9104
Bohemia *(G-1016)*

Gryphon Sensors LLC ....F...... 315 452-8882
North Syracuse *(G-12044)*

◆ Ihi Inc ....E...... 212 599-8100
New York *(G-9862)*

Inertia Switch Inc ....E...... 845 359-8300
Orangeburg *(G-12319)*

▲ Inficon Inc ....C...... 315 434-1100
East Syracuse *(G-4220)*

Infrared Components Corp ....E...... 315 732-1544
Utica *(G-15277)*

ITT Corporation ....D...... 315 568-2811
Seneca Falls *(G-14364)*

ITT Inc ....C...... 914 641-2000
White Plains *(G-16017)*

◆ ITT LLC ....B...... 914 641-2000
White Plains *(G-16020)*

ITT LLC ....G...... 914 641-2000
Seneca Falls *(G-14368)*

Joldeson One Aerospace Inds ....D...... 718 848-7396
Ozone Park *(G-12463)*

▲ Kerns Manufacturing Corp ....C...... 718 784-4044
Long Island City *(G-7262)*

Kimdu Corporation ....E...... 516 723-1339
Plainview *(G-12695)*

Krieger Defense Group LLC ....F...... 716 485-1970
Blasdell *(G-919)*

▲ Kwadair LLC ....G...... 646 824-2511
Brooklyn *(G-2036)*

▲ L3 Foreign Holdings Inc ....C...... 212 697-1111
New York *(G-10153)*

L3 Technologies Inc ....B...... 212 697-1111
New York *(G-10154)*

L3harris Technologies Inc ....A...... 585 269-6600
Rochester *(G-13508)*

L3harris Technologies Inc ....B...... 585 269-5001
Rochester *(G-13509)*

L3harris Technologies Inc ....C...... 585 269-5000
Rochester *(G-13510)*

L3harris Technologies Inc ....A...... 631 630-4200
Amityville *(G-288)*

Laufer Wind Group LLC ....F...... 212 792-3912
New York *(G-10178)*

Lockheed Martin Corporation ....G...... 212 953-1510
New York *(G-10241)*

Lockheed Martin Corporation ....A...... 315 456-3386
Liverpool *(G-7020)*

Lockheed Martin Corporation ....B...... 516 228-2000
Uniondale *(G-15231)*

Lockheed Martin Corporation ....A...... 607 751-2000
Owego *(G-12433)*

Lockheed Martin Corporation ....G...... 315 456-6604
Syracuse *(G-14934)*

Lockheed Martin Corporation ....D...... 212 697-1105
New York *(G-10242)*

Lockheed Martin Corporation ....E...... 716 297-1000
Niagara Falls *(G-11948)*

Lockheed Martin Corporation ....A...... 315 456-0123
Liverpool *(G-7021)*

Lockheed Martin Global Inc ....E...... 315 456-2982
Liverpool *(G-7022)*

Lockheed Martin Integrtd Systm ....E...... 315 456-3333
Syracuse *(G-14935)*

Lockheed Martin Overseas ....F...... 315 456-0123
Liverpool *(G-7023)*

Logitek Inc ....D...... 631 567-1100
Bohemia *(G-1035)*

▲ Magellan Aerospace NY Inc ....C...... 718 699-4000
Corona *(G-3744)*

Metro Dynamics Scie ....F...... 631 842-4300
West Babylon *(G-15731)*

Mirion Technologies Ist Corp ....D...... 607 562-4300
Horseheads *(G-6128)*

Mod-A-Can Inc ....D...... 516 931-8545
Hicksville *(G-5931)*

◆ Moog Inc ....A...... 716 805-2604
Elma *(G-4321)*

Moog Inc ....C...... 716 805-8100
East Aurora *(G-4094)*

Moog Inc ....F...... 716 687-7825
Elma *(G-4323)*

Moog Inc ....B...... 716 687-5486
Elma *(G-4323)*

No Longer Empty Inc ....G...... 202 413-4262
New York *(G-10633)*

Northrop Grumman Corporation ....A...... 703 280-2900
Bethpage *(G-841)*

Northrop Grumman Systems Corp ......D...... 716 626-4600
Buffalo *(G-2893)*

Northrop Grumman Systems Corp ......G...... 631 423-1014
Huntington *(G-6215)*

Northrop Grumman Systems Corp ......C...... 516 346-7100
Bethpage *(G-843)*

Orthstar Enterprises Inc ....D...... 607 562-2100
Horseheads *(G-6130)*

Penetradar Corporation ....F...... 716 731-2629
Niagara Falls *(G-11964)*

Premier Prcision Machining LLC ....E...... 716 665-5217
Falconer *(G-4551)*

Rochester Personal Defense LLC ....G...... 585 406-6758
Rochester *(G-13693)*

◆ Rockwell Industries Intl Corp ....E...... 516 927-8300
Plainview *(G-12710)*

Saab Defense and SEC USA LLC ....F...... 315 445-5009
East Syracuse *(G-4235)*

▲ Safe Flight Instrument Corp ....C...... 914 946-9500
White Plains *(G-16059)*

▼ Select Fabricators Inc ....F...... 585 393-0650
Canandaigua *(G-3142)*

Sensormatic Electronics LLC ....F...... 845 365-3125
Orangeburg *(G-12331)*

▲ Sentry Technology Corporation ......E...... 631 739-2000
Ronkonkoma *(G-14006)*

▲ Sentry Technology Corporation ......F...... 800 645-4224
Ronkonkoma *(G-14007)*

SRC Ventures Inc ....C...... 315 452-8000
North Syracuse *(G-12049)*

Srctec LLC ....C...... 315 452-8700
Syracuse *(G-14999)*

Systems Drs C3 Inc ....B...... 716 631-6200
Buffalo *(G-3000)*

▲ Telephonics Corporation ....A...... 631 755-7000
Farmingdale *(G-4752)*

▼ Traffic Logix Corporation ....G...... 866 915-6449
Spring Valley *(G-14583)*

Transistor Devices Inc ....E 631 471-7492
  Ronkonkoma *(G-14017)*
Tusk Manufacturing Inc ....F 631 567-3349
  Bohemia *(G-1092)*
U E Systems Incorporated ....E 914 592-1220
  Elmsford *(G-4438)*
U S Tech Corporation ....F 315 437-7207
  Skaneateles *(G-14458)*
UNI Source Technology ....F 514 748-8888
  Champlain *(G-3318)*
Vacuum Instrument Corporation ....D ... 631 737-0900
  Ronkonkoma *(G-14023)*
Virtualapt Corp ....F 917 293-3173
  Brooklyn *(G-2562)*
◆ VJ Technologies Inc ....E 631 589-8800
  Bohemia *(G-1096)*
Woodbine Products Inc ....E 631 586-3770
  Hauppauge *(G-5802)*
▼ Worldwide Arntcal Cmpnents Inc ....E ... 631 842-3780
  Copiague *(G-3690)*
Worldwide Arntcal Cmpnents Inc ....G ... 631 842-3780
  Copiague *(G-3691)*

3821 Laboratory Apparatus & Furniture

▲ Air Techniques Inc ....B 516 433-7676
  Melville *(G-7758)*
Ankom Technology Corp ....E 315 986-8090
  Macedon *(G-7459)*
Avro Inc ....G 585 445-7588
  Rochester *(G-13254)*
Biodesign Inc of New York ....F 845 454-6610
  Carmel *(G-3184)*
Biospherix Ltd ....E 315 387-3414
  Parish *(G-12495)*
Crystal Linton Technologies ....F 585 444-8784
  Rochester *(G-13330)*
▲ Dynamica Inc ....F 212 818-1900
  New York *(G-9288)*
East Hills Instrument Inc ....F 516 621-8686
  Westbury *(G-15879)*
Fts Systems Inc ....D 845 687-5300
  Stone Ridge *(G-14735)*
◆ Fungilab Inc ....G 631 750-6361
  Hauppauge *(G-5655)*
Healthalliance Hospital ....G 845 338-2500
  Kingston *(G-6693)*
▲ Hyman Podrusnick Co Inc ....G 718 853-4502
  Brooklyn *(G-1949)*
Instrumentation Laboratory Co ....C ... 845 680-0028
  Orangeburg *(G-12321)*
▲ Integrated Liner Tech Inc ....E 518 621-7422
  Rensselaer *(G-13089)*
Integrted Work Envronments LLC ....G ... 716 725-5088
  East Amherst *(G-4078)*
◆ Itin Scale Co Inc ....E 718 336-5900
  Brooklyn *(G-1974)*
▲ J H C Fabrications Inc ....E 718 649-0065
  Brooklyn *(G-1977)*
▲ Jamestown Metal Products LLC ....C ... 716 665-5313
  Jamestown *(G-6524)*
Lab Crafters Inc ....E 631 471-7755
  Ronkonkoma *(G-13961)*
Lomir Inc ....F 518 483-7697
  Malone *(G-7487)*
Maripharm Laboratories ....F 716 984-6520
  Niagara Falls *(G-11949)*
Material Measuring Corporation ....G ... 516 334-6167
  Westbury *(G-15909)*
Modu-Craft Inc ....G 716 694-0709
  Tonawanda *(G-15123)*
Modu-Craft Inc ....G 716 694-0709
  North Tonawanda *(G-12078)*
◆ Nalge Nunc International Corp ....A ... 585 498-2661
  Rochester *(G-13565)*
Newport Corporation ....E 585 248-4246
  Rochester *(G-13574)*
Next Advance Inc ....F 518 674-3510
  Troy *(G-15174)*
Radon Testing Corp of America ....F ... 914 345-3380
  Elmsford *(G-4423)*
S P Industries Inc ....D 845 255-5000
  Gardiner *(G-5130)*
Scientific Industries Inc ....E 631 567-4700
  Bohemia *(G-1074)*
Simpore Inc ....G 585 748-5980
  West Henrietta *(G-15804)*
SPS Medical Supply Corp ....F 585 968-2377
  Cuba *(G-3814)*
▲ Staplex Company Inc ....G 718 768-3333
  Brooklyn *(G-2451)*

Steriliz LLC ....G 585 415-5411
  Rochester *(G-13746)*
▲ Vistalab Technologies Inc ....E 914 244-6226
  Brewster *(G-1160)*
Vivus Technologies LLC ....G 585 798-6658
  Medina *(G-7748)*

3822 Automatic Temperature Controls

▲ A K Allen Co Inc ....C 516 747-5450
  Melville *(G-7753)*
Ademco Inc ....G 716 631-2197
  Cheektowaga *(G-3337)*
Advantex Solutions Inc ....G 718 278-2290
  Bellerose *(G-773)*
Air Louver & Damper Inc ....F 718 392-3232
  Long Island City *(G-7147)*
Airflex Industrial Inc ....E 631 752-1234
  Farmingdale *(G-4575)*
▲ Anderson Instrument Co Inc ....D ... 518 922-5315
  Fultonville *(G-5077)*
Automated Bldg MGT Systems Inc ....E ... 516 216-5603
  Floral Park *(G-4808)*
Bilbee Controls Inc ....F 518 622-3033
  Cairo *(G-3064)*
▲ Biorem Environmental Inc ....E 585 924-2220
  Victor *(G-15393)*
▲ Bitzer Scroll Inc ....D 315 463-2101
  Syracuse *(G-14830)*
Black River Generations LLC ....E 315 773-2314
  Fort Drum *(G-4935)*
Building Management Assoc Inc ....E ... 718 542-4779
  Bronx *(G-1219)*
Care Enterprises Inc ....G 631 472-8155
  Bayport *(G-726)*
Carrier Corporation ....B 315 432-6000
  Syracuse *(G-14844)*
Cascade Technical Services LLC ....F ... 516 596-6300
  Lynbrook *(G-7429)*
Cascade Technical Services LLC ....G ... 518 355-2201
  Schenectady *(G-14253)*
Clean Room Depot Inc ....F 631 589-3033
  Holbrook *(G-5990)*
◆ Cox & Company Inc ....C 212 366-0200
  Plainview *(G-12676)*
Daikin Applied Americas Inc ....D ... 315 253-2771
  Auburn *(G-472)*
Darkpulse Inc ....G 800 436-1436
  New York *(G-9170)*
Day Automation Systems Inc ....D ... 585 924-4630
  Victor *(G-15404)*
E Global Solutions Inc ....G 516 767-5138
  Port Washington *(G-12876)*
East Hudson Watershed Corp ....G ... 845 319-6349
  Patterson *(G-12516)*
Eastern Strategic Materials ....E 212 332-1619
  New York *(G-9306)*
Fuel Watchman Sales & Service ....F ... 718 665-6100
  Bronx *(G-1263)*
Grillmaster Inc ....E 718 272-9191
  Howard Beach *(G-6140)*
Heating & Burner Supply Inc ....G 718 665-0006
  Bronx *(G-1275)*
Henderson Products Inc ....E 315 785-0994
  Watertown *(G-15572)*
◆ Infitec Inc ....D 315 433-1150
  East Syracuse *(G-4222)*
Intellidyne LLC ....F 516 676-0777
  Plainview *(G-12690)*
Intrepid Control Service Inc ....G 718 886-8771
  Flushing *(G-4863)*
Irtronics Instruments Inc ....F 914 693-6291
  Ardsley *(G-389)*
Johnson Controls Inc ....E 585 924-9346
  Rochester *(G-13494)*
Johnson Controls Inc ....E 914 593-5200
  Hawthorne *(G-5815)*
Johnson Controls Inc ....E 716 688-7340
  Buffalo *(G-2823)*
Johnson Controls Inc ....C 585 724-2232
  Rochester *(G-13495)*
Logical Control Solutions Inc ....F 585 424-5340
  Victor *(G-15418)*
Long Island Analytical Labs ....F 631 472-3400
  Holbrook *(G-6007)*
Microb Phase Services ....F 518 877-8948
  Clifton Park *(G-3468)*
Pii Holdings Inc ....G 716 876-9951
  Buffalo *(G-2919)*
Protective Industries Inc ....E 716 876-9951
  Buffalo *(G-2937)*

◆ Protective Industries Inc ....B 716 876-9951
  Buffalo *(G-2936)*
◆ Pulsafeeder Inc ....C 585 292-8000
  Rochester *(G-13653)*
◆ RE Hansen Industries Inc ....C 631 471-2900
  Saint James *(G-14113)*
Reuse Action Incorporated ....G 716 949-0900
  Buffalo *(G-2952)*
Ruskin Company ....G 845 767-4100
  Orangeburg *(G-12330)*
Siemens Industry Inc ....D 716 568-0983
  Amherst *(G-243)*
Siemens Industry Inc ....G 585 797-2300
  Rochester *(G-13728)*
▲ Svyz Trading Corp ....G 718 220-1140
  Bronx *(G-1375)*
T S B A Group Inc ....E 718 565-6000
  Sunnyside *(G-14775)*
▲ Transit Air Inc ....E 607 324-0216
  Hornell *(G-6112)*
Unisend LLC ....G 585 414-9575
  Webster *(G-15659)*
Use Acquisition LLC ....F 516 812-6800
  New Hyde Park *(G-8302)*
Virtual Super LLC ....G 212 685-6400
  New York *(G-11691)*
Zebra Environmental Corp ....F 516 596-6300
  Lynbrook *(G-7443)*

3823 Indl Instruments For Meas, Display & Control

Aalborg Instrs & Contrls Inc ....D ... 845 398-3160
  Orangeburg *(G-12304)*
Ametek Inc ....D 585 263-7700
  Rochester *(G-13234)*
Anchor Commerce Trading Corp ....G ... 516 881-3485
  Atlantic Beach *(G-452)*
▲ Anderson Instrument Co Inc ....D ... 518 922-5315
  Fultonville *(G-5077)*
▲ Applied Power Systems Inc ......E 516 935-2230
  Hicksville *(G-5883)*
Aspex Incorporated ....E 212 966-0410
  New York *(G-8652)*
Aureonic ....G 518 791-9331
  Gansevoort *(G-5083)*
Automation Evolution LLC ....G 585 241-6010
  Webster *(G-15631)*
Beauty America LLC ....E 917 744-1430
  Great Neck *(G-5370)*
Betapast Holdings LLC ....D 631 582-6740
  Hauppauge *(G-5603)*
▼ Betatronix Inc ....E 631 582-6740
  Ronkonkoma *(G-13916)*
◆ Blue Tee Corp ....G 212 598-0880
  New York *(G-8820)*
▲ Calibrated Instruments Inc ......F 914 741-5700
  Manhasset *(G-7532)*
Ceres Technologies Inc ....D 845 247-4701
  Saugerties *(G-14198)*
▲ Classic Automation LLC ....E 585 241-6010
  Webster *(G-15635)*
Computer Instruments Corp ....E 516 876-8400
  Westbury *(G-15874)*
Conax Technologies LLC ....C 716 684-4500
  Buffalo *(G-2708)*
Cosa Xentaur Corporation ....F 631 345-3434
  Yaphank *(G-16258)*
Danaher Corporation ....C 516 443-9432
  New York *(G-9162)*
◆ Defelsko Corporation ....D 315 393-4450
  Ogdensburg *(G-12204)*
Digital Analysis Corporation ....F 315 685-0760
  Skaneateles *(G-14449)*
Digitronik Labs Inc ....F 585 360-0043
  Rochester *(G-13346)*
Display Logic USA Inc ....G 631 406-1922
  Hauppauge *(G-5639)*
▲ Dyna-Empire Inc ....C 516 222-2700
  Garden City *(G-5096)*
East Hills Instrument Inc ....F 516 621-8686
  Westbury *(G-15879)*
Electrcal Instrumentation Ctrl ....F 518 861-5789
  Delanson *(G-3959)*
Electronic Machine Parts LLC ......F 631 434-3700
  Hauppauge *(G-5645)*
Emerson Electric Co ....E 212 244-2490
  New York *(G-9361)*
Emerson Process MGT Lllp ....F 585 214-8340
  Rochester *(G-13386)*

▲ **Eni Mks Products Group** ... F ... 585 427-8300
Rochester *(G-13394)*

Esensors Inc ... F ... 716 837-8719
Buffalo *(G-2748)*

Flexim Americas Corporation ... F ... 631 492-2300
Edgewood *(G-4267)*

Fts Systems Inc ... D ... 845 687-5300
Stone Ridge *(G-14735)*

Gizmo Products Inc ... G ... 585 301-0970
Stanley *(G-14611)*

Gurley Precision Instrs Inc ... C ... 518 272-6300
Troy *(G-15170)*

◆ **Hilliard Corporation** ... B ... 607 733-7121
Elmira *(G-4357)*

Hilliard Corporation ... G ... 607 733-7121
Elmira *(G-4358)*

Industrial Machine Repair ... G ... 607 272-0717
Ithaca *(G-6386)*

▲ **Inficon Inc** ... C ... 315 434-1100
East Syracuse *(G-4220)*

Inficon Holding AG ... G ... 315 434-1100
East Syracuse *(G-4221)*

▲ **Integrated Control Corp** ... E ... 631 673-5100
Huntington *(G-6207)*

ITT Corporation ... D ... 315 568-2811
Seneca Falls *(G-14364)*

ITT Inc ... C ... 914 641-2000
White Plains *(G-16017)*

ITT LLC ... D ... 914 641-2000
Seneca Falls *(G-14368)*

◆ **ITT LLC** ... B ... 914 641-2000
White Plains *(G-16020)*

▲ **Kessler Thermometer Corp** ... G ... 631 841-5500
West Babylon *(G-15722)*

▲ **Koehler Instrument Company Inc** ... D ... 631 589-3800
Holtsville *(G-6050)*

◆ **Ktk Thermal Technologies Inc** ... E ... 585 678-9025
Macedon *(G-7466)*

Macrolink Inc ... E ... 631 924-8200
Medford *(G-7718)*

◆ **Magtrol Inc** ... E ... 716 668-5555
Buffalo *(G-2859)*

Malcon Inc ... F ... 914 666-7146
Bedford Hills *(G-770)*

Mark - 10 Corporation ... E ... 631 842-9200
Copiague *(G-3664)*

Mausner Equipment Co Inc ... C ... 631 689-7358
Setauket *(G-14380)*

Medsafe Systems Inc ... G ... 516 883-8222
Port Washington *(G-12906)*

Mks Instruments Inc ... E ... 585 292-7472
Rochester *(G-13554)*

Nautilus Controls Corp ... G ... 917 676-7005
New York *(G-10554)*

New Scale Technologies Inc ... E ... 585 924-4450
Victor *(G-15420)*

Nidec Indus Automtn USA LLC ... E ... 716 774-1193
Grand Island *(G-5338)*

Nutec Components Inc ... F ... 631 242-1224
Deer Park *(G-3913)*

Oden Machinery Inc ... E ... 716 874-3000
Tonawanda *(G-15129)*

Ormec Systems Corp ... E ... 585 385-3520
Rochester *(G-13592)*

Orthstar Enterprises Inc ... D ... 607 562-2100
Horseheads *(G-6130)*

Parrington Instruments ... G ... 518 373-8420
Rexford *(G-13096)*

Pcb Group Inc ... E ... 716 684-0001
Depew *(G-3992)*

▲ **Pneumercator Company Inc** ... E ... 631 293-8450
Hauppauge *(G-5743)*

Poseidon Systems LLC ... F ... 585 239-6025
Rochester *(G-13630)*

◆ **Pulsafeeder Inc** ... C ... 585 292-8000
Rochester *(G-13653)*

R K B Opto-Electronics Inc ... F ... 315 455-6636
Syracuse *(G-14970)*

Riverhawk Company LP ... E ... 315 624-7171
New Hartford *(G-8244)*

Roessel & Co Inc ... G ... 585 458-5560
Rochester *(G-13703)*

Rosemount Inc ... G ... 585 424-2460
Rochester *(G-13706)*

Rotronic Instrument Corp ... G ... 631 427-3898
Huntington *(G-6222)*

▲ **Rotronic Instrument Corp** ... F ... 631 348-6844
Hauppauge *(G-5755)*

Rwb Controls Inc ... G ... 716 897-4341
Buffalo *(G-2967)*

Schneider Elc Systems USA Inc ... F ... 214 527-3099
New York *(G-11155)*

Schneider Electric Usa Inc ... G ... 631 567-5710
Bohemia *(G-1073)*

Select Controls Inc ... E ... 631 567-9010
Bohemia *(G-1076)*

Sixnet LLC ... D ... 518 877-5173
Ballston Lake *(G-563)*

▲ **Sixnet Holdings LLC** ... G ... 518 877-5173
Ballston Lake *(G-564)*

Solar Metrology LLC ... G ... 845 247-4701
Holbrook *(G-6021)*

Springfield Control Systems ... G ... 718 631-0870
Douglaston *(G-4029)*

Swagelok Western NY ... G ... 585 359-8470
West Henrietta *(G-15805)*

Taber Acquisition Corp ... D ... 716 694-4000
North Tonawanda *(G-12094)*

Tel-Tru Inc ... E ... 585 295-0225
Rochester *(G-13763)*

Telog Instruments Inc ... E ... 585 742-3000
Victor *(G-15437)*

Thread Check Inc ... D ... 631 231-1515
Hauppauge *(G-5784)*

▼ **Transtech Systems Inc** ... E ... 518 370-5558
Latham *(G-6878)*

Vacuum Instrument Corporation ... D ... 631 737-0900
Ronkonkoma *(G-14023)*

Veea Inc ... F ... 212 535-6050
New York *(G-11652)*

Veeco Instruments Inc ... C ... 516 677-0200
Woodbury *(G-16184)*

▲ **Vermont Medical Inc** ... C ... 802 463-9976
Buffalo *(G-3036)*

Vertiv Corporation ... G ... 516 349-8500
Plainview *(G-12727)*

Vetra Systems Corporation ... G ... 631 434-3185
Hauppauge *(G-5796)*

Viatran Corporation ... E ... 716 564-7813
Tonawanda *(G-15152)*

Vibro-Laser Instrs Corp LLC ... G ... 518 874-2700
Glens Falls *(G-5269)*

Webinfinity Americas Inc ... F ... 516 331-5180
Huntington *(G-6234)*

▲ **Weiss Instruments Inc** ... D ... 631 207-1200
Holtsville *(G-6058)*

▲ **Winters Instruments Inc** ... E ... 281 880-8607
Buffalo *(G-3050)*

Xentaur Corporation ... E ... 631 345-3434
Yaphank *(G-16279)*

3824 Fluid Meters & Counters

Aalborg Instrs & Contrls Inc ... D ... 845 398-3160
Orangeburg *(G-12304)*

Cmp Advnced Mech Sltons NY LLC ... C ... 607 352-1712
Binghamton *(G-867)*

Computer Instruments Corp ... E ... 516 876-8400
Westbury *(G-15874)*

▲ **Curtis Instruments Inc** ... C ... 914 666-2971
Mount Kisco *(G-8089)*

◆ **Designatronics Incorporated** ... G ... 516 328-3300
Hicksville *(G-5902)*

East Hills Instrument Inc ... F ... 516 621-8686
Westbury *(G-15879)*

Encore Electronics Inc ... E ... 518 584-5354
Saratoga Springs *(G-14171)*

▲ **Environment-One Corporation** ... C ... 518 346-6161
Schenectady *(G-14264)*

Gurley Precision Instrs Inc ... C ... 518 272-6300
Troy *(G-15170)*

K-Technologies Inc ... E ... 716 828-4444
Buffalo *(G-2829)*

Melland Gear Instr of Huppauge ... E ... 631 234-0100
Hauppauge *(G-5712)*

Schlumberger Technology Corp ... C ... 607 378-0105
Horseheads *(G-6136)*

SPX Flow Us LLC ... D ... 585 436-5550
Rochester *(G-13742)*

Turbo Machined Products LLC ... E ... 315 895-3010
Frankfort *(G-4957)*

Vantage Mfg & Assembly LLC ... E ... 845 471-5290
Poughkeepsie *(G-12988)*

Vepo Solutions LLC ... G ... 914 384-2121
Cross River *(G-3804)*

▲ **Walter R Tucker Entps Ltd** ... E ... 607 467-2866
Deposit *(G-4004)*

3825 Instrs For Measuring & Testing Electricity

Advanced Testing Tech Inc ... C ... 631 231-8777
Hauppauge *(G-5580)*

Agilent Technologies Inc ... A ... 877 424-4536
New York *(G-8494)*

Ah Elctronic Test Eqp Repr Ctr ... F ... 631 234-8979
Central Islip *(G-3260)*

Allied Motion Systems Corp ... F ... 716 691-5868
Amherst *(G-206)*

▲ **Allied Motion Technologies Inc** ... C ... 716 242-8634
Amherst *(G-207)*

American Quality Technology ... F ... 607 777-9488
Binghamton *(G-853)*

Ametek Inc ... D ... 585 263-7700
Rochester *(G-13234)*

Anmar Acquisition LLC ... G ... 585 352-7777
Rochester *(G-13238)*

Apogee Power Usa Inc ... F ... 202 746-2890
Hartsdale *(G-5567)*

Aurora Technical Services Ltd ... G ... 716 652-1463
East Aurora *(G-4083)*

Automated Control Logic Inc ... F ... 914 769-8880
Thornwood *(G-15067)*

Automation Correct LLC ... G ... 315 299-3589
Syracuse *(G-14821)*

Avanel Industries Inc ... F ... 516 333-0990
Westbury *(G-15871)*

Avcom of Virginia Inc ... D ... 585 924-4560
Victor *(G-15392)*

C Speed LLC ... E ... 315 453-1043
Liverpool *(G-7004)*

C-Flex Bearing Co Inc ... F ... 315 895-7454
Frankfort *(G-4948)*

▲ **Cetek Inc** ... E ... 845 452-3510
Poughkeepsie *(G-12948)*

Cgw Corp ... G ... 631 472-6600
Bayport *(G-727)*

Clarke Hess Communication RES ... G ... 631 698-3350
Medford *(G-7704)*

▲ **Clayton Dubilier & Rice Fun** ... E ... 212 407-5200
New York *(G-9029)*

▲ **Comtech PST Corp** ... C ... 631 777-8900
Melville *(G-7770)*

▲ **Curtis Instruments Inc** ... C ... 914 666-2971
Mount Kisco *(G-8089)*

East Hills Instrument Inc ... F ... 516 621-8686
Westbury *(G-15879)*

El Electronics Inc ... F ... 516 334-0870
Westbury *(G-15880)*

▲ **Ems Development Corporation** ... D ... 631 924-4736
Yaphank *(G-16259)*

Enertiv Inc ... G ... 646 350-3525
New York *(G-9376)*

Epoch Microelectronics Inc ... G ... 914 332-8570
Valhalla *(G-15303)*

Everest Bbn Inc ... F ... 212 268-7979
New York *(G-9426)*

Frequency Electronics Inc ... C ... 516 794-4500
Uniondale *(G-15229)*

Gcns Technology Group Inc ... G ... 347 713-8160
Brooklyn *(G-1880)*

General Microwave Corporation ... F ... 516 802-0900
Syosset *(G-14789)*

Hamilton Marketing Corporation ... G ... 585 395-0678
Brockport *(G-1176)*

◆ **Hipotronics Inc** ... C ... 845 279-8091
Brewster *(G-1151)*

▲ **Iet Labs Inc** ... F ... 516 334-5959
Roslyn Heights *(G-14052)*

◆ **Interntnal Elctronic Mchs Corp** ... E ... 518 268-1636
Troy *(G-15173)*

John Ramsey Elec Svcs LLC ... G ... 585 298-9596
Victor *(G-15414)*

L3harris Technologies Inc ... A ... 631 630-4200
Amityville *(G-288)*

Larry Kings Corporation ... G ... 718 481-8741
Rosedale *(G-14036)*

Lecroy Corporation ... E ... 845 425-2000
Spring Valley *(G-14575)*

Lexan Industries Inc ... F ... 631 434-7586
Bay Shore *(G-690)*

Logitek Inc ... D ... 631 567-1100
Bohemia *(G-1035)*

▼ **Ludl Electronic Products Ltd** ... E ... 914 769-6111
Hawthorne *(G-5818)*

▲ **Magnetic Analysis Corporation** ... D ... 914 530-2000
Elmsford *(G-4415)*

◆ **Magtrol Inc** ... E ... 716 668-5555
Buffalo *(G-2859)*

▲ **Make-Waves Instrument Corp**........E....... 716 681-7524
Buffalo *(G-2860)*
Messer LLC........D....... 716 773-7552
Grand Island *(G-5337)*
Millivac Instruments Inc........G....... 518 355-8300
Schenectady *(G-14289)*
▲ **Nas CP Corp**........E....... 718 961-6757
College Point *(G-3556)*
New York Enrgy Synthetics Inc........G....... 212 634-4787
New York *(G-10596)*
North Atlantic Industries Inc........E....... 631 567-1100
Bohemia *(G-1052)*
Northeast Metrology Corp........F....... 716 827-3770
Depew *(G-3990)*
Omni-ID Usa Inc........E....... 585 299-5990
East Rochester *(G-4168)*
Optimized Devices Inc........F....... 914 769-6100
Pleasantville *(G-12797)*
Peerless Instrument Co Inc........C....... 631 396-6500
Farmingdale *(G-4704)*
Performance Systems Contg Inc........E....... 607 277-6240
Ithaca *(G-6404)*
Photonix Technologies Inc........F....... 607 786-4600
Endicott *(G-4471)*
Pragmatics Technology Inc........G....... 845 795-5071
Milton *(G-7951)*
Precision Filters Inc........E....... 607 277-3550
Ithaca *(G-6407)*
Primesouth Inc........F....... 585 567-4191
Fillmore *(G-4794)*
◆ **Pulsafeeder Inc**........C....... 585 292-8000
Rochester *(G-13653)*
Pulsar Technology Systems Inc........G....... 718 361-9292
Long Island City *(G-7331)*
▲ **Quadlogic Controls Corporation**........D....... 212 930-9300
Long Island City *(G-7334)*
R K B Opto-Electronics Inc........F....... 315 455-6636
Syracuse *(G-14970)*
Ramsey Electronics LLC........E....... 585 924-4560
Victor *(G-15426)*
S R Instruments Inc........E....... 716 693-5977
Tonawanda *(G-15136)*
Schlumberger Technology Corp........C....... 607 378-0105
Horseheads *(G-6136)*
Scientific Components Corp........E....... 631 243-4901
Deer Park *(G-3934)*
Scj Associates Inc........E....... 585 359-0600
Rochester *(G-13719)*
◆ **Sorfin Yoshimura Ltd**........G....... 516 802-4600
Woodbury *(G-16183)*
T & C Power Conversion Inc........F....... 585 482-5551
Rochester *(G-13755)*
▲ **Teledyne Lecroy Inc**........C....... 845 425-2000
Chestnut Ridge *(G-3399)*
◆ **Transcat Inc**........B....... 585 352-7777
Rochester *(G-13772)*
Trek Inc........F....... 716 438-7555
Lockport *(G-7114)*
Viatran Corporation........E....... 716 564-7813
Tonawanda *(G-15152)*
W D Technology Inc........G....... 914 779-8738
Eastchester *(G-4250)*
▲ **Walter R Tucker Entps Ltd**........E....... 607 467-2866
Deposit *(G-4004)*
Xelic Incorporated........F....... 585 415-2764
Pittsford *(G-12658)*
▲ **Zumbach Electronics Corp**........D....... 914 241-7080
Mount Kisco *(G-8109)*

3826 Analytical Instruments

A S A Precision Co Inc........G....... 845 482-4870
Jeffersonville *(G-6569)*
Advanced Mtl Analytics LLC........G....... 321 684-0528
Vestal *(G-15369)*
Advion Inc........E....... 607 266-9162
Ithaca *(G-6361)*
Applied Image Inc........E....... 585 482-0300
Rochester *(G-13241)*
Awe Technologies LLC........G....... 631 747-8448
Bay Shore *(G-654)*
Bristol Instruments Inc........G....... 585 924-2620
Victor *(G-15395)*
Brookhaven Instruments Corp........E....... 631 758-3200
Holtsville *(G-6046)*
Caltex International Ltd........E....... 315 425-1040
Syracuse *(G-14840)*
Cambridge Manufacturing LLC........G....... 516 326-1350
New Hyde Park *(G-8255)*
◆ **Carl Zeiss Inc**........C....... 914 747-1800
White Plains *(G-15990)*
Ceres Technologies Inc........D....... 845 247-4701
Saugerties *(G-14198)*
Chromosense LLC........G....... 646 541-2302
Rye Brook *(G-14087)*
Corning Incorporated........A....... 607 974-9000
Painted Post *(G-12473)*
CTB Enterprise LLC........F....... 631 563-0088
Holbrook *(G-5994)*
Dantec Dynamics Inc........G....... 631 654-1290
Holtsville *(G-6049)*
East Cast Envmtl Rstration Inc........G....... 631 600-2000
Farmingdale *(G-4622)*
East Hills Instrument Inc........F....... 516 621-8686
Westbury *(G-15879)*
Elementar Americas Inc........G....... 856 787-0022
Ronkonkoma *(G-13934)*
Equine Imaging LLC........F....... 414 326-0665
Port Washington *(G-12878)*
Finger Lakes Radiology LLC........G....... 315 787-5399
Geneva *(G-5154)*
Gemprint Corporation........E....... 212 997-0007
New York *(G-9586)*
General Microwave Corporation........F....... 516 802-0900
Syosset *(G-14789)*
High Voltage Inc........E....... 518 329-3275
Copake *(G-3642)*
Industrial Municipal Equipment........F....... 631 665-6712
Brightwaters *(G-1171)*
Ion-Tof Usa Inc........G....... 845 352-8082
Spring Valley *(G-14572)*
Islandia Mri Associates PC........F....... 631 234-2828
Central Islip *(G-3280)*
Life Technologies Corporation........D....... 716 774-6700
Grand Island *(G-5336)*
Medpod Inc........G....... 631 863-8090
Melville *(G-7802)*
Micro Photo Acoustics Inc........G....... 631 750-6035
Ronkonkoma *(G-13973)*
▲ **MMC Enterprises Corp**........G....... 800 435-1088
Hauppauge *(G-5721)*
▼ **Multiwire Laboratories Ltd**........G....... 607 257-3378
Ithaca *(G-6399)*
Nanotronics Imaging Inc........E....... 212 401-6209
Brooklyn *(G-2186)*
▲ **Nexgen Enviro Systems Inc**........G....... 631 226-2930
Lindenhurst *(G-6964)*
Niagara Scientific Inc........E....... 315 437-0821
East Syracuse *(G-4228)*
◆ **Nikon Instruments Inc**........D....... 631 547-4200
Melville *(G-7810)*
Nikon Instruments Inc........G....... 631 845-7620
Edgewood *(G-4276)*
▲ **Photonics Industries Intl Inc**........D....... 631 218-2240
Ronkonkoma *(G-13994)*
Phymetrix Inc........G....... 631 627-3950
Medford *(G-7721)*
Porous Materials Inc........F....... 607 257-5544
Ithaca *(G-6406)*
Quality Vision Intl Inc........E....... 585 544-0400
Rochester *(G-13661)*
Rheonix Inc........D....... 607 257-1242
Ithaca *(G-6409)*
Smartpill Corporation........E....... 716 882-0701
Buffalo *(G-2984)*
Spectra Vista Corporation........G....... 845 471-7007
Poughkeepsie *(G-12983)*
Thermo Fisher Scientific Inc........E....... 585 899-7780
Penfield *(G-12575)*
Thermo Fisher Scientific Inc........G....... 716 774-6700
Grand Island *(G-5345)*
Thermo Fisher Scientific Inc........B....... 585 458-8008
Rochester *(G-13765)*
Thermo Fisher Scientific Inc........A....... 585 899-7610
Rochester *(G-13766)*
Timtronics LLC........G....... 631 345-6509
Yaphank *(G-16274)*
Uptek Solutions Corp........F....... 631 256-5565
Bohemia *(G-1094)*
Veeco Instruments Inc........C....... 516 677-0200
Woodbury *(G-16184)*
▲ **Velp Scientific Inc**........G....... 631 573-6002
Bohemia *(G-1095)*

3827 Optical Instruments

21st Century Optics Inc........E....... 347 527-1079
Long Island City *(G-7140)*
Accu Coat Inc........G....... 585 288-2330
Rochester *(G-13200)*
▲ **Advanced Glass Industries Inc**........D....... 585 458-8040
Rochester *(G-13210)*
▲ **Aeroflex Incorporated**........B....... 516 694-6700
Plainview *(G-12660)*
▲ **Anorad Corporation**........C....... 631 344-6600
Shirley *(G-14412)*
Apollo Optical Systems Inc........E....... 585 272-6170
West Henrietta *(G-15784)*
◆ **Applied Coatings Holding Corp**........G....... 585 482-0300
Rochester *(G-13240)*
Applied Image Inc........E....... 585 482-0300
Rochester *(G-13241)*
▲ **Apti Pro Systems 2000 Inc**........D....... 585 265-0160
Ontario *(G-12283)*
Ariel Optics Inc........G....... 585 265-4820
Ontario *(G-12284)*
▼ **Binoptics LLC**........E....... 607 257-3200
Ithaca *(G-6368)*
Caliber Imging Diagnostics Inc........E....... 585 239-9800
Rochester *(G-13292)*
◆ **Carl Zeiss Inc**........C....... 914 747-1800
White Plains *(G-15990)*
Carl Zeiss Microscopy LLC........B....... 914 681-7840
White Plains *(G-15991)*
▲ **Carl Zeiss Sbe LLC**........E....... 914 747-1132
White Plains *(G-15992)*
CK Coatings........G....... 585 502-0425
Le Roy *(G-6897)*
Cobham Long Island Inc........B....... 516 694-6700
Plainview *(G-12669)*
Corning Tropel Corporation........C....... 585 377-3200
Fairport *(G-4494)*
Cross Bronx Optical........G....... 917 667-6611
Bronx *(G-1233)*
▲ **Digitac Inc**........F....... 732 215-4020
Brooklyn *(G-1744)*
Dorsey Metrology Intl Inc........E....... 845 229-2929
Poughkeepsie *(G-12951)*
Double Helix Optics Inc........G....... 917 689-6490
Rochester *(G-13355)*
▲ **Dynamic Laboratories Inc**........E....... 631 231-7474
Ronkonkoma *(G-13931)*
Edroy Products Co Inc........G....... 845 358-6600
Nyack *(G-12143)*
Enplas America Inc........G....... 646 892-7811
New York *(G-9381)*
Exc Holdings I Corp........A....... 212 644-5900
New York *(G-9438)*
Exc Holdings II Corp........A....... 212 644-5900
New York *(G-9439)*
Exc Holdings LP........G....... 212 644-5900
New York *(G-9440)*
◆ **Germanow-Simon Corporation**........E....... 585 232-1440
Rochester *(G-13438)*
Gradient Lens Corporation........E....... 585 235-2620
Rochester *(G-13449)*
Gurley Precision Instrs Inc........C....... 518 272-6300
Troy *(G-15170)*
Halo Optical Products Inc........D....... 518 773-4256
Gloversville *(G-5284)*
◆ **Hart Specialties Inc**........D....... 631 226-5600
Amityville *(G-267)*
Hudson Mirror LLC........E....... 914 930-8906
Peekskill *(G-12553)*
▲ **Jml Optical Industries LLC**........D....... 585 248-8900
Rochester *(G-13492)*
Keon Optics Inc........F....... 845 429-7103
Stony Point *(G-14745)*
Kevin Freeman........G....... 631 447-5321
Patchogue *(G-12505)*
Leica Microsystems Inc........G....... 716 686-3000
Depew *(G-3987)*
Lens Triptar Co Inc........G....... 585 473-4470
Rochester *(G-13515)*
Lightforce Technology Inc........G....... 585 292-5610
Rochester *(G-13518)*
▼ **Lumetrics Inc**........F....... 585 214-2455
Rochester *(G-13524)*
Machida Incorporated........G....... 845 365-0600
Orangeburg *(G-12323)*
▲ **Match Eyewear LLC**........E....... 516 877-0170
Westbury *(G-15908)*
Micatu Inc........G....... 888 705-8836
Horseheads *(G-6126)*
▼ **Navitar Inc**........D....... 585 359-4000
Rochester *(G-13568)*
▲ **Newport Rochester Inc**........D....... 585 262-1325
Rochester *(G-13575)*
Optics Technology Inc........G....... 585 586-0950
Pittsford *(G-12653)*
Optimax Systems Inc........C....... 585 265-1020
Ontario *(G-12295)*

S I C

◆ Optipro Systems LLC ....D 585 265-0160
  Ontario *(G-12296)*

Photon Gear Inc ....F 585 265-3360
  Ontario *(G-12297)*

Planar Optics Inc ....G 585 671-0100
  Webster *(G-15647)*

Plx Inc ....E 631 586-4190
  Deer Park *(G-3919)*

▲ QED Technologies Intl Inc ....D 585 256-6540
  Rochester *(G-13655)*

▲ Quality Vision Intl Inc ....B 585 544-0450
  Rochester *(G-13660)*

▲ Quality Vision Services Inc ......D 585 544-0450
  Rochester *(G-13662)*

Rochester Photonics Corp ....D 585 387-0674
  Rochester *(G-13694)*

◆ Rochester Precision Optics LLC ..B 585 292-5450
  West Henrietta *(G-15802)*

RPC Photonics Inc ....F 585 272-2840
  Rochester *(G-13708)*

Santa Fe Manufacturing Corp ......G 631 234-0100
  Hauppauge *(G-5757)*

▲ Schneider Optics Inc ....E 631 761-5000
  Hauppauge *(G-5761)*

Schott Corporation ....D 315 255-2791
  Auburn *(G-494)*

Spectral Systems LLC ....E 845 896-2200
  Hopewell Junction *(G-6101)*

Spectrum Thin Films Inc ....E 631 901-1010
  Hauppauge *(G-5772)*

▼ Stefan Sydor Optics Inc ....E 585 271-7300
  Rochester *(G-13745)*

Steven John Opticians ....G 718 543-3336
  Bronx *(G-1372)*

Surgical Design Corp ....F 914 273-2445
  Armonk *(G-403)*

▲ Tele-Vue Optics Inc ....E 845 469-4551
  Chester *(G-3390)*

Va Inc ....E 585 385-5930
  Rochester *(G-13791)*

Videk Inc ....E 585 377-0377
  Fairport *(G-4528)*

◆ Welch Allyn Inc ....A 315 685-4100
  Skaneateles Falls *(G-14460)*

Westchester Technologies Inc ....E 914 736-1034
  Peekskill *(G-12561)*

3829 Measuring & Controlling Devices, NEC

Accuvein Inc ....D 816 997-9400
  Medford *(G-7697)*

Amarantus Bscence Holdings Inc ..F 917 686-5317
  New York *(G-8536)*

Andor Design Corp ....G 516 364-1619
  Syosset *(G-14777)*

Aspex Incorporated ....E 212 966-0410
  New York *(G-8652)*

Aurora Technical Services Ltd ......G 716 652-1463
  East Aurora *(G-4083)*

Awe Technologies LLC ....G 631 747-8448
  Bay Shore *(G-654)*

Biodesign Inc of New York ....F 845 454-6610
  Carmel *(G-3184)*

◆ Carl Zeiss Inc ....C 914 747-1800
  White Plains *(G-15990)*

Circor Aerospace Inc ....D 631 737-1900
  Hauppauge *(G-5615)*

Climatronics Corp ....F 541 471-7111
  Bohemia *(G-987)*

Computer Instruments Corp ....E 516 876-8400
  Westbury *(G-15874)*

Cosense Inc ....E 516 364-9161
  Syosset *(G-14782)*

Cubic Trnsp Systems Inc ....F 212 255-1810
  New York *(G-9129)*

Darkpulse Inc ....G 800 436-1436
  New York *(G-9170)*

Dayton T Brown Inc ....B 631 589-6300
  Bohemia *(G-1001)*

◆ Defelsko Corporation ....D 315 393-4450
  Ogdensburg *(G-12204)*

Dispersion Technology Inc ....G 914 241-4777
  Bedford Hills *(G-768)*

Dylix Corporation ....E 716 773-2985
  Grand Island *(G-5328)*

▲ Dyna-Empire Inc ....C 516 222-2700
  Garden City *(G-5096)*

▲ Dynamic Systems Inc ....E 518 283-5350
  Poestenkill *(G-12802)*

East Hills Instrument Inc ....F 516 621-8686
  Westbury *(G-15879)*

Eastern Niagra Radiology ....E 716 882-6544
  Buffalo *(G-2737)*

Electrical Controls Link ....E 585 924-7010
  Victor *(G-15406)*

Electro-Optical Products Corp ....G 718 456-6000
  Ridgewood *(G-13145)*

Elsag North America LLC ....G 877 773-5724
  Brewster *(G-1148)*

Erbessd Reliability LLC ....E 518 874-2700
  Glens Falls *(G-5248)*

▲ Fougera Pharmaceuticals Inc ....C 631 454-7677
  Melville *(G-7785)*

Freeman Technology Inc ....E 732 829-8345
  Bayside *(G-737)*

G E Inspection Technologies LP ....C 315 554-2000
  Skaneateles *(G-14451)*

Gei International Inc ....E 315 463-9261
  East Syracuse *(G-4212)*

◆ Gleason Corporation ....A 585 473-1000
  Rochester *(G-13444)*

◆ Gleason Works ....A 585 473-1000
  Rochester *(G-13445)*

Gurley Precision Instrs Inc ....E 518 272-6300
  Troy *(G-15170)*

H D M Labs Inc ....G 516 431-8357
  Island Park *(G-6318)*

Hci Engineering ....G 315 336-3450
  Rome *(G-13850)*

▲ Helmel Engineering Pdts Inc .....G 716 297-8644
  Niagara Falls *(G-11935)*

▲ Highway Toll ADM LLC ....F 516 684-9584
  Roslyn Heights *(G-14051)*

◆ Hipotronics Inc ....C 845 279-8091
  Brewster *(G-1151)*

◆ Images Si Inc ....F 718 966-3694
  Staten Island *(G-14664)*

Imaginant Inc ....E 585 264-0480
  Pittsford *(G-12643)*

Industrial Test Eqp Co Inc ....E 516 883-6423
  Port Washington *(G-12888)*

◆ Itin Scale Co Inc ....G 718 336-5900
  Brooklyn *(G-1974)*

James A Staley Co Inc ....F 845 878-3344
  Carmel *(G-3187)*

Kem Medical Products Corp ....G 631 454-6565
  Farmingdale *(G-4665)*

Kinemotive Corporation ....E 631 249-6440
  Farmingdale *(G-4666)*

Kistler Instrument Corporation .....E 716 691-5100
  Amherst *(G-228)*

Kld Labs Inc ....E 631 549-4222
  Hauppauge *(G-5685)*

L N D Incorporated ....E 516 678-6141
  Oceanside *(G-12179)*

Liberty Controls Inc ....E 718 461-0600
  College Point *(G-3551)*

Machine Technology Inc ....E 845 454-4030
  Poughkeepsie *(G-12968)*

▲ Magnetic Analysis Corporation ..D 914 530-2000
  Elmsford *(G-4415)*

◆ Magtrol Inc ....E 716 668-5555
  Buffalo *(G-2859)*

▲ Make-Waves Instrument Corp .....E 716 681-7524
  Buffalo *(G-2860)*

◆ Mason Industries Inc ....C 631 348-0282
  Hauppauge *(G-5708)*

Mechanical Technology Inc ....E 518 218-2550
  Albany *(G-99)*

Mirion Tech Conax Nuclear Inc .....E 716 681-1973
  Buffalo *(G-2867)*

Mirion Technologies Ist Corp ....D 607 562-4300
  Horseheads *(G-6128)*

Mobius Labs Inc ....E 518 961-2600
  Rexford *(G-13095)*

MTI Instruments Inc ....F 518 218-2550
  Albany *(G-103)*

▲ North Pk Innovations Group Inc ..E 716 699-2031
  Ellicottville *(G-4315)*

Nuclear Diagnostic Pdts NY Inc ....G 516 575-4201
  Plainview *(G-12705)*

Orolia Usa Inc ....D 585 321-5800
  Rochester *(G-13593)*

▲ Oyster Bay Pump Works Inc ......F 516 933-4500
  Hicksville *(G-5937)*

Pcb Piezotronics Inc ....F 716 684-0001
  Depew *(G-3993)*

Peerless Instrument Co Inc ....C 631 396-6500
  Farmingdale *(G-4704)*

▲ Peyser Instrument Corporation ...E 631 841-3600
  West Babylon *(G-15736)*

Poseidon Systems LLC ....F 585 239-6025
  Rochester *(G-13630)*

Precision Design Systems Inc ......E 585 426-4500
  Rochester *(G-13635)*

Pronto Gas Heating Sups Inc ....G 718 292-0707
  Bronx *(G-1345)*

Qhi Group Incorporated ....G 646 512-5727
  New York *(G-10943)*

▲ Qualitrol Company LLC ....C 586 643-3717
  Fairport *(G-4516)*

Quality Vision Intl Inc ....E 585 544-0400
  Rochester *(G-13661)*

Research Frontiers Inc ....E 516 364-1902
  Woodbury *(G-16181)*

Riverhawk Company LP ....E 315 624-7171
  New Hartford *(G-8244)*

RJ Harvey Instrument Corp ....F 845 359-3943
  Tappan *(G-15038)*

◆ Schenck Corporation ....E 631 242-4010
  Deer Park *(G-3932)*

▲ Schenck USA Corp ....D 631 242-4010
  Deer Park *(G-3933)*

◆ Schott Corporation ....D 914 831-2200
  Elmsford *(G-4428)*

SKF USA Inc ....D 716 661-2600
  Falconer *(G-4556)*

▲ Teledyne Lecroy Inc ....C 845 425-2000
  Chestnut Ridge *(G-3399)*

Telog Instruments Inc ....E 585 742-3000
  Victor *(G-15437)*

Titan Controls Inc ....E 516 358-2407
  New York *(G-11499)*

U E Systems Incorporated ....E 914 592-1220
  Elmsford *(G-4438)*

Vacuum Instrument Corporation ...D 631 737-0900
  Ronkonkoma *(G-14023)*

Vector Magnetics LLC ....E 607 273-8351
  Ithaca *(G-6417)*

Videk Inc ....E 585 377-0377
  Fairport *(G-4528)*

◆ VJ Technologies Inc ....G 631 589-8800
  Bohemia *(G-1096)*

▲ Weiss Instruments Inc ....D 631 207-1200
  Holtsville *(G-6058)*

Xeku Corporation ....E 607 761-1447
  Vestal *(G-15388)*

York Industries Inc ....E 516 746-3736
  Garden City Park *(G-5126)*

Zomega Terahertz Corporation .....F 585 347-4337
  Webster *(G-15664)*

3841 Surgical & Medical Instrs & Apparatus

▲ A Titan Instruments Inc ....F 716 667-9211
  Orchard Park *(G-12335)*

Abyrx Inc ....F 914 357-2600
  Irvington *(G-6305)*

Advanced Back Technologies ....G 631 231-0076
  Hauppauge *(G-5579)*

Advantage Plus Diagnostics Inc ...G 631 393-5044
  Melville *(G-7755)*

Aerolase Corporation ....D 914 345-8300
  Tarrytown *(G-15039)*

▼ Aktina Corp ....E 845 268-0101
  Congers *(G-3606)*

Ala Scientific Instruments Inc ....F 631 393-6401
  Farmingdale *(G-4577)*

Alconox Inc ....G 914 948-4040
  White Plains *(G-15970)*

AM Bickford Inc ....F 716 652-1590
  Wales Center *(G-15465)*

Ambulatory Monitoring Inc ....G 914 693-9240
  Ardsley *(G-385)*

American Bio Medica Corp ....D 518 758-8158
  Kinderhook *(G-6670)*

◆ American Diagnostic Corp ....D 631 273-6155
  Hauppauge *(G-5589)*

Angiodynamics Inc ....E 518 798-1215
  Queensbury *(G-13031)*

Angiodynamics Inc ....B 518 975-1400
  Queensbury *(G-13032)*

Angiodynamics Inc ....B 518 792-4112
  Glens Falls *(G-5241)*

Angiodynamics Inc ....B 518 742-4430
  Queensbury *(G-13033)*

Angiodynamics Inc ....B 518 795-1400
  Latham *(G-6848)*

Argon Medical Devices Inc ....G 585 321-1130
  Henrietta *(G-5855)*

Astra Tool & Instrument Mfg ....E 914 747-3863
  Hawthorne *(G-5809)*

Avery Biomedical Devices Inc ....F 631 864-1600
Commack (G-3578)
Beacon Spch Lnge Pthlgy Phys ....F 516 626-1635
Roslyn (G-14039)
Becton Dickinson and Company ....B 845 353-3371
Nyack (G-12136)
Beyond Air Inc ....F 516 665-8200
Garden City (G-5091)
Biochemical Diagnostics Inc ....E 631 595-9200
Edgewood (G-4263)
▲ Biodex Medical Systems Inc ....C 631 924-9000
Shirley (G-14417)
Biodex Medical Systems Inc ....E 631 924-3146
Shirley (G-14418)
Bioresearch Inc ....G 212 734-5315
Pound Ridge (G-12991)
Boehm Surgical Instrument Corp ....F 585 436-6584
Rochester (G-13277)
▲ Buffalo Filter LLC ....D 716 835-7000
Lancaster (G-6799)
▲ Buxton Medical Equipment Corp ....E 631 957-4500
Lindenhurst (G-6943)
C R Bard Inc ....B 518 793-2531
Queensbury (G-13035)
C R Bard Inc ....A 518 793-2531
Glens Falls (G-5244)
C R Bard Inc ....D 518 793-2531
Queensbury (G-13036)
Caire Inc ....E 716 691-0202
Amherst (G-215)
Caliber Imging Diagnostics Inc ....E 585 239-9800
Rochester (G-13292)
Clerio Vision Inc ....F 617 216-7881
Rochester (G-13318)
CN Group Incorporated ....A 914 358-5690
White Plains (G-15994)
Cognitiveflow Sensor Tech ....G 631 513-9369
Stony Brook (G-14737)
◆ Conmed Corporation ....B 315 797-8375
Utica (G-15248)
Conmed Corporation ....D 315 797-8375
Utica (G-15247)
Corning Tropel Corporation ....C 585 377-3200
Fairport (G-4494)
Daxor Corporation ....F 212 330-8500
New York (G-9190)
Delcath Systems Inc ....E 212 489-2100
New York (G-9197)
Derm-Buro Inc ....E 516 694-8300
Plainview (G-12678)
▲ Designs For Vision Inc ....C 631 585-3300
Bohemia (G-1006)
Drive Medical Spv LLC ....G 516 998-4600
Port Washington (G-12875)
◆ E-Z-Em Inc ....E 609 524-2864
Melville (G-7777)
▲ Elliquence LLC ....F 516 277-9000
Baldwin (G-530)
Endovor Inc ....G 214 679-7385
New York (G-9370)
Endovor LLC ....G 214 679-7385
New York (G-9371)
▲ Esc Control Electronics LLC ....E 631 467-5328
Sayville (G-14225)
Extek Inc ....E 585 533-1672
Rush (G-14070)
Eyeglass Service Industries ....G 914 666-3150
Bedford Hills (G-769)
◆ Fabrication Enterprises Inc ....E 914 591-9300
Elmsford (G-4409)
▲ Flexbar Machine Corporation ....E 631 582-8440
Islandia (G-6332)
Flowmedica Inc ....F 800 772-6446
Queensbury (G-13038)
Fluorologic Inc ....G 585 248-2796
Pittsford (G-12640)
Ftt Medical Inc ....G 585 444-0980
Rochester (G-13425)
◆ Future Diagnostics LLC ....E 347 434-6700
Brooklyn (G-1871)
▲ Gaymar Industries Inc ....B 800 828-7341
Orchard Park (G-12353)
Gradian Health Systems Inc ....G 212 537-0340
New York (G-9654)
▲ Harmac Medical Products Inc ....B 716 897-4500
Buffalo (G-2793)
▲ Hogil Pharmaceutical Corp ....F 914 681-1800
White Plains (G-16014)
Huron Tl Cutter Grinding Inc ....E 631 420-7000
Farmingdale (G-4646)
Hurryworks LLC ....D 516 998-4600
Port Washington (G-12885)
Incredible Scents Inc ....G 516 656-3300
Greenvale (G-5462)
Integer Holdings Corporation ....E 716 937-5100
Alden (G-171)
Integer Holdings Corporation ....D 716 759-5200
Clarence (G-3435)
Ip Med Inc ....G 516 766-3800
Oceanside (G-12176)
J H M Engineering ....E 718 871-1810
Brooklyn (G-1978)
J Jamner Surgical Instrs Inc ....E 914 592-9051
Hawthorne (G-5814)
Jaracz Jr Joseph Paul ....G 716 533-1377
Orchard Park (G-12358)
Ken-Ton Open Mri PC ....G 716 876-7000
Kenmore (G-6654)
Lake Region Medical Inc ....C 716 662-5025
Orchard Park (G-12361)
Liberty Install Inc ....F 631 651-5655
Huntington (G-6211)
Manhattan Eastside Dev Corp ....F 212 305-3275
New York (G-10343)
◆ Medical Depot Inc ....C 516 998-4600
Port Washington (G-12905)
Medical Technology Products ....G 631 285-6640
Greenlawn (G-5455)
Medipoint Inc ....F 516 294-8822
Mineola (G-7989)
Medline Industries Inc ....B 845 344-3301
Middletown (G-7919)
Medsource Technologies LLC ....D 716 662-5025
Orchard Park (G-12365)
Memory Md Inc ....G 917 318-0215
New York (G-10430)
▲ Misonix Opco Inc ....D 631 694-9555
Farmingdale (G-4687)
Modular Medical Corp ....E 718 829-2626
Bronx (G-1317)
◆ Moog Inc ....A 716 805-2604
Elma (G-4321)
▲ Moogs Medical Devices Group ....G 716 652-2000
Buffalo (G-2872)
N Y B P Inc ....G 585 624-2541
Mendon (G-7851)
Nano Vibronix Inc ....G 516 374-8330
Cedarhurst (G-3242)
Nanobionovum LLC ....F 518 581-1171
Saratoga Springs (G-14186)
▲ Nasco Enterprises Inc ....G 516 921-9696
Syosset (G-14795)
Nasiff Associates Inc ....G 315 676-2346
Central Square (G-3295)
▲ Navilyst Medical Inc ....A 800 833-9973
Glens Falls (G-5261)
Njr Medical Devices ....E 440 258-8204
Cedarhurst (G-3243)
▲ Novamed-Usa Inc ....E 914 789-2100
Elmsford (G-4420)
◆ Ocala Group LLC ....F 516 233-2750
New Hyde Park (G-8286)
Omnicare Anesthesia PC ....E 718 433-0044
Astoria (G-433)
▲ Orics Industries Inc ....E 718 461-8613
Farmingdale (G-4697)
Ortho Medical Products ....E 212 879-3700
New York (G-10712)
Ortho-Clinical Diagnostics Inc ....B 585 453-4771
Rochester (G-13595)
Ortho-Clinical Diagnostics Inc ....F 585 453-5200
Rochester (G-13596)
Orthocon Inc ....E 914 357-2600
Irvington (G-6312)
Ovitz Corporation ....G 585 967-2114
Rochester (G-13601)
▲ P-Ryton Corp ....F 718 937-7052
Long Island City (G-7316)
Pall Corporation ....A 607 753-6041
Cortland (G-3779)
▲ Pall Corporation ....A 516 484-5400
Port Washington (G-12913)
Parace Bionics LLC ....G 877 727-2231
New York (G-10752)
Parkchester Dps LLC ....C 718 823-4411
Bronx (G-1332)
Pavmed Inc ....G 212 949-4319
New York (G-10775)
Peter Digioia ....G 516 644-5517
Plainview (G-12707)
Praxis Powder Technology Inc ....E 518 812-0112
Queensbury (G-13052)
Precimed Inc ....E 716 759-5600
Clarence (G-3440)
▲ Proactive Medical Products LLC ....G 845 205-6004
Mount Vernon (G-8174)
Professional Medical Devices ....F 914 835-0614
Harrison (G-5558)
Progressive Orthotics Ltd ....G 631 732-5556
Selden (G-14355)
Rdd Pharma Inc ....G 302 319-9970
New York (G-10991)
▲ Reichert Inc ....C 716 686-4500
Depew (G-3996)
▲ Repro Med Systems Inc ....D 845 469-2042
Chester (G-3383)
Responselink Inc ....G 518 424-7776
Latham (G-6875)
Retia Medical LLC ....G 914 594-1986
Valhalla (G-15308)
RJ Harvey Instrument Corp ....F 845 359-3943
Tappan (G-15038)
Robert Bosch LLC ....E 315 733-3312
Utica (G-15292)
▲ Schilling Forge Inc ....E 315 454-4421
Syracuse (G-14987)
Seedlngs Lf Scnce Ventures LLC ....G 917 913-8511
New York (G-11178)
Seneca TEC Inc ....G 585 381-2645
Fairport (G-4521)
Sensodx II LLC ....G 585 202-4552
Victor (G-15429)
▼ Sigma Intl Gen Med Apprtus LLC ....B 585 798-3901
Medina (G-7747)
Simulaids Inc ....D 845 679-2475
Saugerties (G-14212)
Skyler Brand Ventures LLC ....G 646 979-5904
New York (G-11265)
Soniquence LLC ....F 516 267-6400
Baldwin (G-535)
Sonomed Inc ....E 516 354-0900
New Hyde Park (G-8294)
St Silicones Corporation ....F 518 406-3208
Clifton Park (G-3475)
Striker Orthopedics ....E 585 381-1773
Rochester (G-13749)
Surgical Design Corp ....F 914 273-2445
Armonk (G-403)
Symmetry Medical Inc ....G 845 368-4573
Hillburn (G-5971)
T G M Products Inc ....G 631 491-0515
Wyandanch (G-16247)
Tril Inc ....G 631 645-7989
Copiague (G-3685)
▲ Vante Inc ....F 716 778-7691
Newfane (G-11896)
▲ Vaso Corporation ....F 516 997-4600
Plainview (G-12722)
Vasomedical Solutions Inc ....D 516 997-4600
Plainview (G-12723)
Viterion Corporation ....F 914 333-6033
Elmsford (G-4439)
Vizio Medical Devices LLC ....F 646 845-7382
New York (G-11700)
▲ W A Baum Co Inc ....D 631 226-3940
Copiague (G-3689)
Welch Allyn Inc ....A 315 685-4100
Skaneateles Falls (G-14459)
◆ Welch Allyn Inc ....A 315 685-4100
Skaneateles Falls (G-14460)
Welch Allyn Inc ....A 315 685-4347
Skaneateles Falls (G-14461)
Welch Allyn Inc ....G 503 530-7500
Skaneateles Falls (G-14462)
Wyeth Holdings LLC ....D 845 602-5000
Pearl River (G-12543)

3842 Orthopedic, Prosthetic & Surgical Appliances/Splys

ACS Custom USA LLC ....G 646 559-5642
New York (G-8450)
▲ Advanced Enterprises Inc ....F 845 342-1009
Middletown (G-7892)
Advanced Orthotics & Prostheth ....F 518 472-1023
Albany (G-29)
Advanced Prosthetics Orthotics ....F 516 365-7225
Manhasset (G-7530)
Advantage Orthotics Inc ....G 631 368-1754
East Northport (G-4141)

▲ Aero Healthcare (us) LLC ....G...... 855 225-2376
    Valley Cottage *(G-15312)*

Agnovos Healthcare LLC ....F...... 646 502-5860
    New York *(G-8495)*

Apollo Orthotics Corp ....G...... 516 333-3223
    Carle Place *(G-3170)*

Argon Medical Devices Inc ....G...... 585 321-1130
    Henrietta *(G-5855)*

Arimed Orthotics Prosthetics ....F...... 718 875-8754
    Brooklyn *(G-1528)*

Arimed Orthotics Prosthetics ....F...... 718 979-6155
    Staten Island *(G-14620)*

▲ Atlantic Er Inc ....E...... 516 294-3200
    New Hyde Park *(G-8252)*

Avanti U S A Ltd ....F...... 716 695-5800
    Tonawanda *(G-15087)*

Backtech Inc ....G...... 973 279-0838
    New York *(G-8712)*

Beltone Corporation ....G...... 716 565-1015
    Williamsville *(G-16122)*

Benway-Haworth-Lwlr-Iacosta He ....F...... 518 432-4070
    Albany *(G-47)*

Bio-Chem Barrier Systems LLC ......G...... 631 261-2682
    Northport *(G-12099)*

▲ Biodex Medical Systems Inc ....C...... 631 924-9000
    Shirley *(G-14417)*

Biodex Medical Systems Inc ....E...... 631 924-3146
    Shirley *(G-14418)*

Bionic Eye Technologies Inc ....G...... 845 505-5254
    Ithaca *(G-6369)*

Brannock Device Co Inc ....E...... 315 475-9862
    Liverpool *(G-7002)*

Buffalo Hearg & Speech ....E...... 716 558-1105
    West Seneca *(G-15845)*

Byer California ....G...... 212 944-8989
    New York *(G-8878)*

Caire Inc ....E...... 716 691-0202
    Amherst *(G-215)*

Center For Orthotic & Prosthet........G...... 607 215-0847
    Elmira *(G-4343)*

Center For Prosthetic ....G...... 845 336-7762
    Kingston *(G-6684)*

Centinel Spine LLC ....G...... 212 583-9700
    New York *(G-8949)*

Church Communities NY Inc ....E...... 518 589-5103
    Elka Park *(G-4302)*

Church Communities NY Inc ....E...... 518 589-5103
    Elka Park *(G-4303)*

▲ Cirrus Healthcare Products LLC ....E...... 631 692-7600
    Cold Spring Harbor *(G-3526)*

Cityscape Ob/Gyn PLLC................F...... 212 683-3595
    New York *(G-9020)*

▲ Community Products LLC..............C...... 845 658-8799
    Rifton *(G-13167)*

Community Products LLC ....E...... 845 658-7720
    Chester *(G-3373)*

Community Products LLC ....F...... 845 572-3433
    Chester *(G-3374)*

Community Products LLC ....E...... 518 589-5103
    Elka Park *(G-4304)*

Complete Orthopedic Svcs Inc ....E...... 516 357-9113
    East Meadow *(G-4133)*

Cranial Technologies Inc ....G...... 914 472-0975
    Scarsdale *(G-14234)*

Creative Orthotics & Prosthet..........F...... 607 734-7215
    Elmira *(G-4347)*

Creative Orthotics & Prosthet..........F...... 607 431-2526
    Oneonta *(G-12270)*

Creative Orthotics Prosthetics ....G...... 607 771-4672
    Binghamton *(G-868)*

▲ Crye Precision LLC ....C...... 718 246-3838
    Brooklyn *(G-1705)*

Custom Sports Lab Inc..................G...... 212 832-1648
    New York *(G-9135)*

▲ Cy Plastics Works Inc ....D...... 585 229-2555
    Honeoye *(G-6068)*

Derm-Buro Inc ....E...... 516 694-8300
    Plainview *(G-12678)*

East Cast Orthtics Prosthetics ....F...... 716 856-5192
    Buffalo *(G-2736)*

▲ East Coast Orthoic & Pros Cor .....D...... 516 248-5566
    Deer Park *(G-3867)*

East Coast Orthoic & Pros Cor.........F...... 212 923-2161
    New York *(G-9302)*

Eis Legacy LLC ....E...... 585 426-5330
    Rochester *(G-13380)*

Elwood Specialty Products Inc.........F...... 716 877-6622
    Buffalo *(G-2741)*

Eschen Prosthetic & Orthotic L........E...... 212 606-1262
    New York *(G-9396)*

Eschen Prsthetic Orthotic Labs ....F...... 516 871-0029
    Hicksville *(G-5906)*

◆ Euromed Inc ....D...... 845 359-4039
    Orangeburg *(G-12315)*

Family Hearing Center ....G...... 845 897-3059
    Fishkill *(G-4800)*

Far Rockaway Drugs Inc ....F...... 718 471-2500
    Far Rockaway *(G-4565)*

Fiber Foot Appliances Inc ....F...... 631 465-9199
    Farmingdale *(G-4631)*

Fk Safety Gear Inc ....G...... 516 233-9628
    East Rockaway *(G-4173)*

Flexible Lifeline Systems Inc ....G...... 716 896-4949
    Buffalo *(G-2754)*

Flo-Tech Orthotic & Prosthetic ....G...... 607 387-3070
    Trumansburg *(G-15200)*

Gadabout USA Wheelchairs Inc ....F...... 585 338-2110
    Rochester *(G-13427)*

▲ Getinge Group Logistics Ameri ......C...... 585 475-1400
    Rochester *(G-13439)*

Gfh Orthotic & Prosthetic Labs ....G...... 631 467-3725
    Bohemia *(G-1017)*

Go Blue Technologies Ltd ....G...... 631 404-6285
    North Babylon *(G-12001)*

Grand Slam Holdings LLC ....E...... 212 583-5000
    New York *(G-9660)*

Great Lakes Orthpd Labs Inc ....G...... 716 893-4116
    Buffalo *(G-2782)*

Green Prosthetics & Orthotics ....G...... 716 484-1088
    Jamestown *(G-6514)*

Hakson Safety Wears Inc ....G...... 613 667-3015
    Buffalo *(G-2790)*

▲ Hand Care Inc ....E...... 516 747-5649
    Roslyn *(G-14043)*

Hanger Inc ....G...... 518 435-0840
    Albany *(G-84)*

Hanger Inc ....F...... 607 431-2526
    Oneonta *(G-12272)*

Hanger Inc ....E...... 518 438-4546
    East Syracuse *(G-4215)*

Hanger Inc ....G...... 718 575-5504
    Forest Hills *(G-4920)*

Hanger Prosthetics & ....G...... 315 492-6608
    Syracuse *(G-14907)*

Hanger Prsthetics & Ortho Inc ....G...... 516 338-4466
    Westbury *(G-15893)*

Hanger Prsthetcs & Ortho Inc ....G...... 718 892-1103
    Bronx *(G-1272)*

Hanger Prsthetcs & Ortho Inc ....F...... 607 277-6620
    Ithaca *(G-6384)*

Hanger Prsthetcs & Ortho Inc ....G...... 607 776-8013
    Bath *(G-634)*

Hanger Prsthetcs & Ortho Inc ....G...... 607 771-4672
    Binghamton *(G-881)*

Hanger Prsthetcs & Ortho Inc ....G...... 315 472-5200
    Syracuse *(G-14908)*

Hanger Prsthetcs & Ortho Inc ....D...... 607 795-1220
    Elmira *(G-4354)*

Hanger Prsthetcs & Ortho Inc ....G...... 315 789-4810
    Geneva *(G-5158)*

Hearos LLC ....G...... 844 432-7327
    Latham *(G-6858)*

Hersco-Orthotic Labs Corp ....E...... 718 391-0416
    Long Island City *(G-7242)*

Higgins Supply Company Inc ....D...... 607 836-6474
    Mc Graw *(G-7688)*

Howmedica Osteonics Corp ....G...... 518 783-1880
    Latham *(G-6859)*

Howmedica Osteonics Corp ....G...... 516 484-0897
    Port Washington *(G-12884)*

Hygrade ....G...... 718 488-9000
    Brooklyn *(G-1948)*

Instrumentation Laboratory Co ....C...... 845 680-0028
    Orangeburg *(G-12321)*

Integer Holdings Corporation ....D...... 716 759-5200
    Clarence *(G-3435)*

J P R Pharmacy Inc ....F...... 718 327-0600
    Far Rockaway *(G-4566)*

J-K Prosthetics & Orthotics ....E...... 914 699-2077
    Mount Vernon *(G-8153)*

Kem Medical Products Corp ....G...... 631 454-6565
    Farmingdale *(G-4665)*

Klemmt Orthotics & Prosthetics ....G...... 607 770-4400
    Johnson City *(G-6604)*

Konrad Orthotics & Orthotics ....F...... 516 485-9164
    West Hempstead *(G-15773)*

La Torre Orthopedic Laboratory.........F...... 518 786-8655
    Latham *(G-6864)*

▼ Lakeland Industries Inc ....G...... 631 981-9700
    Ronkonkoma *(G-13963)*

Langer Biomechanics Inc ....D...... 800 645-5520
    Ronkonkoma *(G-13965)*

Latorre Orthopedic Laboratory ....F...... 518 786-8655
    Latham *(G-6869)*

Lehneis Orthotics Prosthetic ....F...... 516 790-1897
    Hauppauge *(G-5691)*

Lehneis Orthotics Prosthetic ....G...... 631 369-3115
    Riverhead *(G-13178)*

Lorelei Orthotics Prosthetics ....G...... 212 727-2011
    New York *(G-10263)*

M H Mandelbaum Orthotic ....F...... 631 473-8668
    Port Jefferson *(G-12842)*

Mark Goldberg Prosthetic ....F...... 631 689-6606
    East Setauket *(G-4180)*

Mayflower Splint Co ....E...... 631 549-5131
    Dix Hills *(G-4011)*

▲ Medi-Ray Inc ....D...... 877 898-3003
    Tuckahoe *(G-15205)*

▲ Medi-Tech International Corp ....G...... 800 333-0109
    Brooklyn *(G-2132)*

Medical Action Industries Inc ....C...... 631 231-4600
    Hauppauge *(G-5711)*

Medline Industries Inc ....B...... 845 344-3301
    Middletown *(G-7919)*

▲ Monaghan Medical Corporation ....D...... 518 561-7330
    Plattsburgh *(G-12760)*

Monaghan Medical Corporation ....G...... 315 472-2136
    Syracuse *(G-14946)*

National Prosthetic Orthot ....G...... 718 767-8400
    Bayside *(G-740)*

New Dynamics Corporation ....E...... 845 692-0022
    Middletown *(G-7923)*

New England Orthotic & Prost ....G...... 212 682-9313
    New York *(G-10581)*

New York Rhbilitative Svcs LLC ....F...... 516 239-0990
    Valley Stream *(G-15349)*

North Shore Orthtics Prsthtics ....G...... 631 928-3040
    Port Jeff STA *(G-12836)*

Nucare Pharmacy Inc ....F...... 212 426-9300
    New York *(G-10653)*

Nucare Pharmacy West LLC ....F...... 212 462-2525
    New York *(G-10654)*

▲ NY Orthopedic Usa Inc ....D...... 718 852-5330
    Brooklyn *(G-2225)*

▲ Occunomix International LLC ....E...... 631 741-1940
    Port Jeff STA *(G-12837)*

Orcam Inc ....F...... 800 713-3741
    New York *(G-10704)*

Ortho Medical Products ....E...... 212 879-3700
    New York *(G-10712)*

Ortho Rite Inc ....E...... 914 235-9100
    Mamaroneck *(G-7517)*

Orthocraft Inc ....G...... 718 951-1700
    Brooklyn *(G-2235)*

Orthopedic Arts Laboratory Inc.........G...... 718 858-2400
    Brooklyn *(G-2236)*

Orthopedic Treatment Facility ....G...... 718 898-7326
    Woodside *(G-16217)*

Orthotics & Prosthetics Dept ....F...... 585 341-9299
    Rochester *(G-13599)*

Overhead Door Corporation ....D...... 518 828-7652
    Hudson *(G-6173)*

▲ Pall Biomedical Inc ....C...... 516 484-3600
    Port Washington *(G-12912)*

Pall Corporation ....A...... 607 753-6041
    Cortland *(G-3779)*

Pall Corporation ....A...... 607 753-6041
    Cortland *(G-3780)*

Pall Corporation ....A...... 516 484-2818
    Port Washington *(G-12914)*

Pall Corporation ....A...... 607 753-6041
    Cortland *(G-3781)*

Palmer Industries Inc ....G...... 607 754-8741
    Endicott *(G-4468)*

▲ Palmer Industries Inc ....E...... 607 754-2957
    Endicott *(G-4469)*

Palmer Industries Inc ....G...... 607 754-8741
    Endicott *(G-4470)*

Paradigm Spine LLC ....E...... 888 273-9897
    New York *(G-10755)*

Peak Performance Design LLC.........G...... 518 302-9198
    Cohoes *(G-3512)*

▲ Premier Brands America Inc ....C...... 914 667-6200
    White Plains *(G-16054)*

Premier Brands America Inc ....F...... 718 325-3000
    Bronx *(G-1343)*

▲ Proficient Surgical Eqp Inc ....G...... 516 487-1175
    Port Washington *(G-12916)*

◆ Profoot Inc ....D...... 718 965-8600
    Brooklyn *(G-2298)*

Progressive Orthotics Ltd ....G..... 631 732-5556
   Selden *(G-14355)*

Progressive Orthotics Ltd ....F..... 631 447-3860
   East Patchogue *(G-4155)*

Prosthetic Rehabilitation Ctr ....G..... 845 565-8255
   Newburgh *(G-11885)*

Prosthetics By Nelson Inc ....F..... 716 894-6666
   Cheektowaga *(G-3359)*

Queue Solutions LLC ....F..... 631 750-6440
   Bohemia *(G-1069)*

Rehablitation Tech of Syracuse ....G..... 315 426-9920
   Syracuse *(G-14976)*

Rigicon Inc ....G..... 631 676-3376
   Ronkonkoma *(G-14003)*

Robert Cohen ....G..... 718 789-0996
   Ozone Park *(G-12467)*

Rochester Orthopedic Labs ....G..... 585 272-1060
   Rochester *(G-13691)*

▲ Roner Inc ....G..... 718 392-6020
   Long Island City *(G-7346)*

Roner Inc ....C..... 718 392-6020
   Long Island City *(G-7347)*

▲ Salsa Professional Apparel LLC ......G..... 212 575-6565
   New York *(G-11122)*

Sampsons Prsthtic Orthotic Lab ....E..... 518 374-6011
   Schenectady *(G-14300)*

Schuster & Richard Labortories ....G..... 718 358-8607
   College Point *(G-3563)*

Scientific Plastics Inc ....F..... 212 967-1199
   New York *(G-11166)*

◆ Silipos Holding LLC ....G..... 716 283-0700
   Niagara Falls *(G-11981)*

▲ Skil-Care Corporation ....C..... 914 963-2040
   Yonkers *(G-16348)*

◆ SPS Medical Supply Corp ....D..... 585 359-0130
   Rush *(G-14074)*

SPS Medical Supply Corp ....F..... 585 968-2377
   Cuba *(G-3814)*

Stafford Labs Orthotics/Prosth ....F..... 845 692-5227
   Middletown *(G-7932)*

Steriliz LLC ....G..... 585 415-5411
   Rochester *(G-13746)*

Steris Corporation ....G..... 845 469-4087
   Chester *(G-3387)*

Stj Orthotic Services Inc ....F..... 631 956-0181
   Lindenhurst *(G-6975)*

Superior Glove Works USA Ltd ....E..... 716 626-9500
   Cheektowaga *(G-3363)*

Synthes Usa LLC ....C..... 607 271-2500
   Horseheads *(G-6138)*

Syracuse Prosthetic Center Inc ....G..... 315 476-9697
   Syracuse *(G-15009)*

▲ Tape Systems Inc ....F..... 914 668-3700
   Mount Vernon *(G-8181)*

Thomas F Egan ....E..... 607 669-4822
   Binghamton *(G-913)*

Todt Hill Audiological Svcs ....G..... 718 816-1952
   Staten Island *(G-14722)*

Tonawanda Limb & Brace Inc ....F..... 716 695-1131
   Tonawanda *(G-15146)*

Tumble Forms Inc ....C..... 315 429-3101
   Dolgeville *(G-4027)*

Turbine Engine Comp Utica ....A..... 315 768-8070
   Whitesboro *(G-16084)*

Ultrapedics Ltd ....G..... 718 748-4806
   Brooklyn *(G-2534)*

Vcp Mobility Inc ....B..... 718 356-7827
   Staten Island *(G-14725)*

◆ VSM Investors LLC ....G..... 212 351-1600
   New York *(G-11708)*

▲ Widex Usa Inc ....D..... 718 360-1000
   Hauppauge *(G-5800)*

William H Shapiro ....G..... 212 263-7037
   New York *(G-11758)*

Womens Health Care PC ....G..... 718 850-0009
   Richmond Hill *(G-13128)*

Wyeth Holdings LLC ....D..... 845 602-5000
   Pearl River *(G-12543)*

Xylon Industries Inc ....G..... 631 293-4717
   Farmingdale *(G-4766)*

3843 Dental Eqpt & Splys

Air Techniques Inc ....G..... 516 433-7676
   Hicksville *(G-5878)*

▲ Air Techniques Inc ....B..... 516 433-7676
   Melville *(G-7758)*

American Regent Inc ....E..... 631 924-4000
   Shirley *(G-14411)*

Boehm Surgical Instrument Corp ....F..... 585 436-6584
   Rochester *(G-13277)*

Brandt Equipment LLC ....G..... 718 994-0800
   Bronx *(G-1217)*

▲ Buffalo Dental Mfg Co Inc ....E..... 516 496-7200
   Syosset *(G-14780)*

Cettel Studio of New York Inc ....G..... 518 494-3622
   Chestertown *(G-3393)*

▲ Cmp Export Co Inc ....E..... 518 434-3147
   Albany *(G-63)*

◆ Cmp Industries LLC ....E..... 518 434-3147
   Albany *(G-64)*

Cmp Industries LLC ....G..... 518 434-3147
   Albany *(G-65)*

▲ Corning Rubber Company Inc ....F..... 631 738-0041
   Ronkonkoma *(G-13926)*

Cpac Equipment Inc ....F..... 585 382-3223
   Leicester *(G-6909)*

◆ Crosstex International Inc ....D..... 631 582-6777
   Hauppauge *(G-5631)*

Crosstex International Inc ....F..... 631 582-6777
   Hauppauge *(G-5632)*

Darby Dental Supply ....G..... 516 688-6421
   Jericho *(G-6576)*

◆ Dedeco International Sales Inc ....D..... 845 887-4840
   Long Eddy *(G-7139)*

▲ DenTek Oral Care Inc ....D..... 865 983-1300
   Tarrytown *(G-15043)*

Gallery 57 Dental ....E..... 212 246-8700
   New York *(G-9567)*

Gan Kavod Inc ....E..... 716 633-2820
   Buffalo *(G-2766)*

◆ Glaxosmithkline LLC ....D..... 518 239-6901
   East Durham *(G-4102)*

Henry Schein Fincl Svcs LLC ....G..... 631 843-5500
   Melville *(G-7789)*

Impladent Ltd ....G..... 718 465-1810
   Jamaica *(G-6449)*

J H M Engineering ....E..... 718 871-1810
   Brooklyn *(G-1978)*

Jeffrey D Menoff DDS PC ....G..... 716 665-1468
   Jamestown *(G-6526)*

▲ JM Murray Center Inc ....C..... 607 756-9913
   Cortland *(G-3774)*

Kay See Dental Mfg Co ....F..... 816 842-2817
   New York *(G-10081)*

Lelab Dental Laboratory Inc ....G..... 516 561-5050
   Valley Stream *(G-15346)*

◆ Lornamead Inc ....D..... 716 874-7190
   New York *(G-10264)*

Lucas Dental Equipment Co Inc ....F..... 631 244-2807
   Bohemia *(G-1039)*

Marotta Dental Studio Inc ....E..... 631 249-7520
   Farmingdale *(G-4677)*

Martins Dental Studio ....G..... 315 788-0800
   Watertown *(G-15582)*

Oramaax Dental Products Inc ....F..... 516 771-8514
   Freeport *(G-5013)*

Precision Dental Cabinets Inc ....F..... 631 543-3870
   Smithtown *(G-14485)*

Professional Manufacturers ....F..... 631 586-2440
   Deer Park *(G-3923)*

Safe-Dent Enterprises LLC ....G..... 845 362-0141
   Monsey *(G-8046)*

▲ Schilling Forge Inc ....E..... 315 454-4421
   Syracuse *(G-14987)*

Smile Specialists ....G..... 877 337-6135
   New York *(G-11273)*

Stylecraft Interiors Inc ....F..... 516 487-2133
   Great Neck *(G-5427)*

Temrex Corporation ....E..... 516 868-6221
   Freeport *(G-5028)*

Tiger Supply Inc ....G..... 631 293-2700
   Farmingdale *(G-4755)*

Total Dntl Implant Sltions LLC ....G..... 212 877-3777
   Valley Stream *(G-15361)*

▲ Valplast International Corp ....F..... 516 442-3923
   Westbury *(G-15937)*

Vincent Martino Dental Lab ....F..... 716 674-7800
   Buffalo *(G-3037)*

3844 X-ray Apparatus & Tubes

▲ Air Techniques Inc ....B..... 516 433-7676
   Melville *(G-7758)*

American Access Care LLC ....F..... 631 582-9729
   Hauppauge *(G-5587)*

▲ Biodex Medical Systems Inc ....C..... 631 924-9000
   Shirley *(G-14417)*

▲ Community Products LLC ....C..... 845 658-8799
   Rifton *(G-13167)*

Dra Imaging PC ....E..... 845 296-1057
   Wappingers Falls *(G-15491)*

▲ Flow X Ray Corporation ....D..... 631 242-9729
   Deer Park *(G-3873)*

Genesis Digital Imaging Inc ....G..... 310 305-7358
   Rochester *(G-13436)*

Mitegen LLC ....G..... 607 266-8877
   Ithaca *(G-6397)*

▼ Multiwire Laboratories Ltd ....G..... 607 257-3378
   Ithaca *(G-6399)*

New York Imaging Service Inc ....F..... 716 834-8022
   Tonawanda *(G-15125)*

Phantom Laboratory Inc ....F..... 518 692-1190
   Greenwich *(G-5475)*

Photo Medic Equipment Inc ....D..... 631 242-6600
   Deer Park *(G-3918)*

▲ Quantum Medical Imaging LLC ....D..... 631 567-5800
   Rochester *(G-13663)*

R M F Health Management L L C ....E..... 718 854-5400
   Wantagh *(G-15488)*

Siemens Corporation ....F..... 202 434-7800
   New York *(G-11226)*

Siemens USA Holdings Inc ....B..... 212 258-4000
   New York *(G-11228)*

Surescan Corporation ....G..... 607 321-0042
   Binghamton *(G-911)*

◆ VJ Technologies Inc ....E..... 631 589-8800
   Bohemia *(G-1096)*

◆ Wolf X-Ray Corporation ....D..... 631 242-9729
   Deer Park *(G-3954)*

3845 Electromedical & Electrotherapeutic Apparatus

Advd Heart Phys & Surgs ....F..... 212 434-3000
   New York *(G-8484)*

Argon Medical Devices Inc ....G..... 585 321-1130
   Henrietta *(G-5855)*

▲ Biofeedback Instrument Corp ....G..... 212 222-5665
   New York *(G-8797)*

▲ Buffalo Filter LLC ....D..... 716 835-7000
   Lancaster *(G-6799)*

C R Bard Inc ....A..... 518 793-2531
   Glens Falls *(G-5244)*

Caire Inc ....E..... 716 691-0202
   Amherst *(G-215)*

Caliber Imging Diagnostics Inc ....E..... 585 239-9800
   Rochester *(G-13292)*

City Sports Imaging Inc ....E..... 212 481-3600
   New York *(G-9019)*

Complex Biosystems Inc ....G..... 315 464-8007
   Baldwinsville *(G-545)*

Conmed Andover Medical Inc ....F..... 315 797-8375
   Utica *(G-15246)*

Conmed Corporation ....D..... 315 797-8375
   Utica *(G-15247)*

◆ Conmed Corporation ....B..... 315 797-8375
   Utica *(G-15248)*

Ddc Technologies Inc ....G..... 516 594-1533
   Oceanside *(G-12169)*

Elizabeth Wood ....G..... 315 492-5470
   Syracuse *(G-14885)*

Empire Open Mri ....G..... 914 961-1777
   Yonkers *(G-16307)*

Equivital Inc ....E..... 646 513-4169
   New York *(G-9391)*

Evoke Neuroscience Inc ....F..... 917 261-6096
   New York *(G-9431)*

Excel Technology Inc ....F..... 212 355-3400
   New York *(G-9442)*

Fonar Corporation ....C..... 631 694-2929
   Melville *(G-7784)*

Gary Gelbfish MD ....G..... 718 258-3004
   Brooklyn *(G-1878)*

Geneva Healthcare LLC ....G..... 646 665-2044
   New York *(G-9593)*

Global Instrumentation LLC ....F..... 315 682-0272
   Manlius *(G-7547)*

Gravity East Village Inc ....G..... 212 388-9788
   New York *(G-9667)*

Health Care Originals Inc ....G..... 585 471-8215
   Rochester *(G-13463)*

Imacor Inc ....E..... 516 393-0970
   Jericho *(G-6583)*

▲ Infimed Inc ....D..... 315 453-4545
   Liverpool *(G-7014)*

Infimed Inc ....G..... 585 383-1710
   Pittsford *(G-12644)*

Integrated Medical Devices ....G..... 315 457-4200
   Liverpool *(G-7016)*

Isimulate LLC ....G..... 877 947-2831
   Albany *(G-90)*

S
I
C

J H M Engineering......................E...... 718 871-1810
Brooklyn *(G-1978)*

Jaracz Jr Joseph Paul.................G...... 716 533-1377
Orchard Park *(G-12358)*

Jarvik Heart Inc........................E...... 212 397-3911
New York *(G-9977)*

Juvly Aesthetics Inc...................D...... 614 686-3627
New York *(G-10049)*

Kal Manufacturing Corporation.....E...... 585 265-4310
Webster *(G-15644)*

Laser and Varicose Vein Trtmnt....G...... 718 667-1777
Staten Island *(G-14676)*

Med Services Inc.......................D...... 631 218-6450
Bohemia *(G-1046)*

▲ Misonix Opco Inc....................D...... 631 694-9555
Farmingdale *(G-4687)*

Nanovibronix Inc.......................F...... 914 233-3004
Elmsford *(G-4419)*

Natus Medical Incorporated.........G...... 631 457-4430
Hauppauge *(G-5725)*

Netech Corporation....................F...... 631 531-0100
Farmingdale *(G-4694)*

Neurosteer Inc..........................F...... 401 837-0351
New York *(G-10573)*

New Primecare..........................G...... 516 822-4031
Hewlett *(G-5872)*

New York Laser & Aestheticks.....G...... 516 627-7777
Roslyn *(G-14044)*

Nirx Medical Technologies LLC....F...... 516 676-6479
Glen Head *(G-5211)*

▲ Novamed-Usa Inc....................E...... 914 789-2100
Elmsford *(G-4420)*

Ocean Cardiac Monitoring...........G...... 631 777-3700
Deer Park *(G-3916)*

Pharmadva LLC.........................G...... 585 469-1410
Rochester *(G-13620)*

◆ Philips Medical Systems Mr.......B...... 518 782-1122
Latham *(G-6872)*

Qrs Technologies Inc.................G...... 315 457-5300
Liverpool *(G-7037)*

Quadrant Biosciences Inc............F...... 315 614-2325
Syracuse *(G-14969)*

Ray Medica Inc..........................E...... 952 885-0500
New York *(G-10986)*

▲ Sonicor Inc...........................F...... 631 920-6555
West Babylon *(G-15748)*

Sonomed Inc.............................E...... 516 354-0900
New Hyde Park *(G-8294)*

▲ Soterix Medical Inc................F...... 888 990-8327
New York *(G-11303)*

Sun Scientific Inc......................G...... 914 479-5108
Dobbs Ferry *(G-4020)*

Ultradian Diagnostics LLC...........G...... 518 618-0046
Rensselaer *(G-13093)*

University of Rochester...............B...... 585 275-3483
Rochester *(G-13786)*

▲ Vaso Corporation...................F...... 516 997-4600
Plainview *(G-12722)*

▲ Vermont Medical Inc..............G...... 802 463-9976
Buffalo *(G-3036)*

▲ Z-Axis Inc............................D...... 315 548-5000
Phelps *(G-12611)*

3851 Ophthalmic Goods

21st Century Optics Inc..............E...... 347 527-1079
Long Island City *(G-7140)*

Acuity Polymers Inc..................G...... 585 458-8409
Rochester *(G-13205)*

Alden Optical Laboratory Inc........F...... 716 937-9181
Lancaster *(G-6794)*

Allure Eyewear LLC....................G...... 631 755-2121
Melville *(G-7759)*

Art-Craft Optical Company Inc......E...... 585 546-6640
Rochester *(G-13249)*

Bausch & Lomb Holdings Inc.......G...... 585 338-6000
New York *(G-8741)*

Bausch & Lomb Incorporated.......D...... 585 338-6000
Rochester *(G-13262)*

Bausch & Lomb Incorporated.......B...... 585 338-6000
Rochester *(G-13263)*

Co-Optics America Lab Inc..........E...... 607 432-0557
Oneonta *(G-12264)*

Colors In Optics Ltd..................D...... 718 845-0300
New Hyde Park *(G-8257)*

Coopervision Inc.......................A...... 585 385-6810
West Henrietta *(G-15790)*

Coopervision Inc.......................A...... 585 889-3301
Scottsville *(G-14339)*

▲ Coopervision Inc..................C...... 585 385-6810
Victor *(G-15401)*

◆ Coopervision Inc...................D...... 585 385-6810
Victor *(G-15402)*

▲ Corinne McCormack Inc...........F...... 212 868-7919
New York *(G-9104)*

Corneal Design Corporation.........F...... 301 670-7076
Lima *(G-6930)*

▲ Davis Vision Inc...................G...... 800 328-4728
Latham *(G-6854)*

▲ Designs For Vision Inc...........C...... 631 585-3300
Bohemia *(G-1006)*

Doug Lambertson Od.................G...... 718 698-9300
Staten Island *(G-14647)*

Equicheck LLC..........................G...... 631 987-6356
Patchogue *(G-12500)*

▲ Esc Control Electronics LLC.......G...... 631 467-5328
Sayville *(G-14225)*

Essilor Laboratories Amer Inc.......E...... 845 365-6700
Orangeburg *(G-12314)*

Frame Works America Inc............G...... 631 288-1300
Westhampton Beach *(G-15956)*

Hirsch Optical Corp....................D...... 516 752-2211
Farmingdale *(G-4644)*

▲ His Vision Inc........................G...... 585 254-0022
Rochester *(G-13469)*

Humanware USA Inc..................D...... 800 722-3393
Champlain *(G-3313)*

J I Intrntnal Contact Lens Lab.......G...... 718 997-1212
Rego Park *(G-13077)*

Kathmando Valley Preservation.....F...... 212 727-0074
New York *(G-10078)*

Lens Lab.................................G...... 718 379-2020
Bronx *(G-1302)*

Lens Lab Express......................G...... 718 921-5488
Brooklyn *(G-2062)*

Lens Lab Express Southern Blvd....G...... 718 626-5184
Astoria *(G-428)*

Luxottica of America Inc..............G...... 516 484-3800
Port Washington *(G-12902)*

M Factory USA Inc.....................G...... 917 410-7878
Brooklyn *(G-2097)*

Mager & Gougelman Inc.............G...... 212 661-3939
New York *(G-10322)*

Mager & Gougelman Inc.............G...... 212 661-3939
Hempstead *(G-5844)*

Mark F Rosenhaft N A O.............G...... 516 374-1010
Cedarhurst *(G-3241)*

Modo Retail LLC.......................E...... 212 965-4900
New York *(G-10489)*

▲ Moscot Wholesale Corp............G...... 212 647-1550
New York *(G-10507)*

North Bronx Retinal & Ophthlmi.....G...... 347 535-4932
Bronx *(G-1326)*

Optika Eyes Ltd........................G...... 631 567-8852
Sayville *(G-14230)*

▲ Optisource International Inc.......E...... 631 924-8360
Bellport *(G-805)*

Optogenics of Syracuse Inc.........D...... 315 446-3000
Syracuse *(G-14957)*

▲ Parker Warby Retail Inc............D...... 646 517-5223
New York *(G-10764)*

Provision Supply LLC..................F...... 347 623-0237
Brooklyn *(G-2303)*

SCR Group NY Inc.....................G...... 516 601-3174
Brooklyn *(G-2392)*

Spectacle Optical Inc..................G...... 646 706-1015
Rego Park *(G-13082)*

Strauss Eye Prosthetics Inc..........G...... 585 424-1350
Rochester *(G-13748)*

Surgical Design Corp.................F...... 914 273-2445
Armonk *(G-403)*

▲ Tri-Supreme Optical LLC............D...... 631 249-2020
Farmingdale *(G-4759)*

Winchester Optical Company........E...... 607 734-4251
Elmira *(G-4372)*

Wyeth Holdings LLC...................D...... 845 602-5000
Pearl River *(G-12543)*

Xinya International Trading Co........G...... 212 216-9681
New York *(G-11799)*

▲ Zyloware Corporation...............D...... 914 708-1200
Port Chester *(G-12831)*

3861 Photographic Eqpt & Splys

▲ Air Techniques Inc..................B...... 516 433-7676
Melville *(G-7758)*

Apexx Omni-Graphics Inc............D...... 718 326-3330
Maspeth *(G-7591)*

Astrodyne Inc..........................G...... 516 536-5755
Oceanside *(G-12166)*

AVI-Spl Employee.....................B...... 212 840-4801
New York *(G-8691)*

Avid Technology Inc..................E...... 212 983-2424
New York *(G-8692)*

▲ Bescor Video Accessories Ltd....F...... 631 420-1717
Farmingdale *(G-4592)*

Big Indie - Beautiful Boy LLC........G...... 917 464-5599
Woodstock *(G-16234)*

▲ Cannon Industries Inc.............D...... 585 254-8080
Rochester *(G-13294)*

Carestream Health Inc.................B...... 585 627-1800
Rochester *(G-13296)*

◆ Champion Photochemistry Inc....D...... 585 760-6444
Rochester *(G-13310)*

Cine Magnetics Inc....................E...... 914 667-6707
Mount Vernon *(G-8130)*

Core Swx LLC..........................E...... 516 595-7488
Plainview *(G-12675)*

◆ Cpac Inc..............................E...... 585 382-3223
Leicester *(G-6908)*

Creatron Services Inc.................G...... 516 437-5119
Floral Park *(G-4813)*

▲ Dnp Electronics America LLC.....D...... 212 503-1060
New York *(G-9242)*

Dolby Laboratories Inc.................F...... 212 767-1700
New York *(G-9245)*

Easterncctv (usa) LLC...............F...... 516 870-3779
Plainview *(G-12680)*

Eastman Kodak Company...........D...... 585 722-2187
Rochester *(G-13366)*

◆ Eastman Kodak Company.........B...... 585 724-4000
Rochester *(G-13367)*

Eastman Kodak Company...........D...... 585 724-5600
Rochester *(G-13368)*

Eastman Kodak Company...........D...... 585 722-9695
Pittsford *(G-12638)*

Eastman Kodak Company...........D...... 585 726-6261
Rochester *(G-13369)*

Eastman Kodak Company...........D...... 585 724-4000
Rochester *(G-13370)*

Eastman Kodak Company...........F...... 800 698-3324
Rochester *(G-13371)*

Eastman Kodak Company...........D...... 585 722-4385
Rochester *(G-13372)*

Eastman Kodak Company...........D...... 585 588-5598
Rochester *(G-13373)*

Eastman Kodak Company...........C...... 585 726-7000
Rochester *(G-13374)*

Eastman Kodak Company...........D...... 585 722-4007
Rochester *(G-13375)*

Eastman Kodak Company...........D...... 585 588-3896
Rochester *(G-13376)*

Eastman Kodak Company...........E...... 585 724-4000
Rochester *(G-13377)*

Eastman Park Micrographics Inc....G...... 866 934-4376
Rochester *(G-13378)*

Ebsco Industries Inc..................E...... 585 398-2000
Farmington *(G-4770)*

Efam Enterprises LLC................E...... 718 204-1760
Long Island City *(G-7211)*

Emda Inc.................................F...... 631 243-6363
Plainview *(G-12683)*

Facsimile Cmmncations Inds Inc....D...... 212 741-6400
New York *(G-9460)*

Fluxdata Incorporated.................G...... 800 425-0176
Rochester *(G-13418)*

Garys Loft...............................G...... 212 244-0970
New York *(G-9575)*

Geospatial Systems Inc.............F...... 585 427-8310
West Henrietta *(G-15796)*

Gpc International Inc..................C...... 631 752-9600
Melville *(G-7786)*

Henrys Deals Inc.......................E...... 347 821-4685
Brooklyn *(G-1931)*

▲ Hilord Chemical Corporation......E...... 631 234-7373
Hauppauge *(G-5671)*

Jack L Popkin & Co Inc...............G...... 718 361-6700
Kew Gardens *(G-6666)*

Just Lamps of New York Inc.........F...... 716 626-2240
Buffalo *(G-2826)*

Kelmar Systems Inc..................F...... 631 421-1230
Huntington Station *(G-6252)*

◆ Kodak Alaris Inc....................B...... 888 242-2424
Rochester *(G-13504)*

Kodak Graphic Communications....F...... 585 724-4000
Rochester *(G-13505)*

Kyle Editing LLC.......................G...... 212 675-3464
New York *(G-10147)*

Labgrafix Printing Inc..................E...... 516 280-8300
Lynbrook *(G-7433)*

Lake Image Systems Inc.............F...... 585 321-3630
Henrietta *(G-5858)*

Lasertech Crtridge RE-Builders ....G....... 518 373-1246
Clifton Park *(G-3466)*

▲ Lowel-Light Manufacturing Inc ......E...... 718 921-0600
Brooklyn *(G-2087)*

▲ Mekatronics Incorporated ....E...... 516 883-6805
Port Washington *(G-12907)*

Mirion Technologies Ist Corp ....D...... 607 562-4300
Horseheads *(G-6128)*

▲ Norazza Inc ....F...... 716 706-1160
Buffalo *(G-2890)*

Qls Solutions Group Inc ....E...... 716 852-2203
Buffalo *(G-2939)*

▲ Rear View Safety Inc ....E...... 855 815-3842
Brooklyn *(G-2332)*

Rockland Colloid Corp ....G...... 845 359-5559
Piermont *(G-12622)*

Rosco Collision Avoidance Inc ....G...... 718 526-2601
Jamaica *(G-6472)*

Seneca TEC Inc ....G...... 585 381-2645
Fairport *(G-4521)*

Shelley Promotions Inc ....G...... 212 924-4987
New York *(G-11210)*

▲ Sima Technologies LLC ....G...... 412 828-9130
Hauppauge *(G-5766)*

Stallion Technologies Inc ....G...... 315 622-1176
Liverpool *(G-7041)*

Thermo Cidtec Inc ....E...... 315 451-9410
Liverpool *(G-7045)*

Tiffen Company LLC ....G...... 631 273-2500
Hauppauge *(G-5785)*

▲ Tiffen Company LLC ....C...... 631 273-2500
Hauppauge *(G-5786)*

Toner-N-More Inc ....G...... 718 232-6200
Brooklyn *(G-2509)*

Truesense Imaging Inc ....C...... 585 784-5500
Rochester *(G-13775)*

▲ Turner Bellows Inc ....E...... 585 235-4456
Rochester *(G-13778)*

Va Inc...E...... 585 385-5930
Rochester *(G-13791)*

▲ Vishay Thin Film LLC ....C...... 716 283-4025
Niagara Falls *(G-11990)*

Watec America Corporation ....E...... 702 434-6111
Middletown *(G-7938)*

Xerox Corporation ....A...... 585 422-4564
Webster *(G-15663)*

Xerox Corporation ....C...... 585 264-5584
Rochester *(G-13811)*

3873 Watch & Clock Devices & Parts

▲ American Time Mfg Ltd ....F....... 585 266-5120
Rochester *(G-13233)*

▲ Croton Watch Co Inc.........................E...... 800 443-7639
West Nyack *(G-15820)*

▲ E Gluck Corporation ....C...... 718 784-0700
Little Neck *(G-6997)*

▲ Ewatchfactory Corp ....G...... 212 564-8318
New York *(G-9433)*

▼ First Sbf Holding Inc ....E...... 845 425-9882
Valley Cottage *(G-15315)*

▲ Game Time LLC ....F...... 914 557-9662
New York *(G-9569)*

▲ Geneva Watch Company Inc ....E...... 212 221-1177
New York *(G-9594)*

H Best Ltd ....F...... 212 354-2400
New York *(G-9701)*

Hammerman Bros Inc.........................G...... 212 956-2800
New York *(G-9715)*

I-Tem Brand LLC ....F...... 718 790-6927
Bronx *(G-1277)*

Justa Company ....G...... 718 932-6139
Long Island City *(G-7258)*

Life Watch Technology Inc ....D...... 917 669-2428
Flushing *(G-4871)*

National Time Recording Eqp Co ....F...... 212 227-3310
New York *(G-10547)*

Olympic Jewelry Inc ....G...... 212 768-7004
New York *(G-10686)*

▲ Pavana USA Inc ....G...... 646 833-8811
New York *(G-10774)*

◆ Pedre Corp ....E...... 212 868-2935
Hicksville *(G-5942)*

▲ Precision International Co Inc ....G...... 212 268-9090
New York *(G-10875)*

Richemont North America Inc ....G...... 212 355-7052
New York *(G-11037)*

Richemont North America Inc ....G...... 212 644-9500
New York *(G-11038)*

▲ Sarina Accessories LLC ....F...... 212 239-8106
New York *(G-11139)*

◆ Stuhrling Original LLC ....E...... 718 840-5760
Brooklyn *(G-2466)*

▲ TWI Watches LLC ....E...... 718 663-3969
Brooklyn *(G-2531)*

▲ Watchcraft Inc ....G...... 347 531-0382
Long Island City *(G-7399)*

39 MISCELLANEOUS MANUFACTURING INDUSTRIES

3911 Jewelry: Precious Metal

1ktgold Inc ....F....... 212 302-8200
White Plains *(G-15967)*

A & V Castings Inc ....G...... 212 997-0042
New York *(G-8412)*

A Jaffe Inc ....C...... 212 843-7464
New York *(G-8418)*

Aaron Group LLC ....D...... 718 392-5454
Mount Vernon *(G-8119)*

Abraham Jwly Designers & Mfrs ....F...... 212 944-1149
New York *(G-8434)*

Abrimian Bros Corp ....F...... 212 382-1106
New York *(G-8435)*

Adamor Inc ....G...... 212 688-8885
New York *(G-8454)*

Adg Jewels LLC ....G...... 212 888-1890
New York *(G-8458)*

Alart Inc ....G...... 212 840-1508
New York *(G-8505)*

◆ Albea Cosmetics America Inc ....E...... 212 371-5100
New York *(G-8507)*

Alchemy Simya Inc ....E...... 646 230-1122
New York *(G-8508)*

◆ Ale Viola LLC ....D...... 212 868-3808
New York *(G-8510)*

Alex Sepkus Inc ....F...... 212 391-8466
New York *(G-8512)*

Alexander Primak Jewelry Inc ....D...... 212 398-0287
New York *(G-8513)*

▲ Alfred Butler Inc ....F...... 516 829-7460
Great Neck *(G-5361)*

All The Rage Inc ....G...... 516 605-2001
Hicksville *(G-5881)*

▲ Almond Jewelers Inc ....F...... 516 933-6000
Port Washington *(G-12862)*

▲ Alpine Creations Ltd ....G...... 212 308-9353
New York *(G-8531)*

◆ Altr Inc ....E...... 212 575-0077
New York *(G-8532)*

Ambras Fine Jewelry Inc ....E...... 718 784-5252
Long Island City *(G-7154)*

American Craft Jewelers Inc...............G...... 718 972-0945
Brooklyn *(G-1498)*

American Originals Corporation ....G...... 212 836-4155
New York *(G-8557)*

Anatoli Inc ....F...... 845 334-9000
West Hurley *(G-15808)*

▲ Anima Group LLC ....G...... 917 913-2053
New York *(G-8589)*

Apicella Jewelers Inc ....E...... 212 840-2024
New York *(G-8603)*

▲ AR & AR Jewelry Inc ....E...... 212 764-7916
New York *(G-8614)*

Arringement International Inc ....G...... 347 323-7974
Flushing *(G-4840)*

Art-TEC Jewelry Designs Ltd ....E...... 212 719-2941
New York *(G-8632)*

Ateliers Tamalet Corp ....E...... 929 325-7976
New York *(G-8661)*

Ateret LLC...G...... 212 819-0777
New York *(G-8662)*

Atlantic Precious Metal Cast...............G...... 718 937-7100
Long Island City *(G-7171)*

Atr Jewelry Inc ....F...... 212 819-0075
New York *(G-8673)*

B K Jewelry Contractor Inc ....E...... 212 398-9093
New York *(G-8704)*

Barber Brothers Jewelry Mfg ....F...... 212 819-0666
New York *(G-8726)*

Baroka Creations Inc ....G...... 212 768-0527
New York *(G-8731)*

Bartholomew Mazza Ltd Inc ....E...... 212 935-4530
New York *(G-8735)*

Bellataire Diamonds Inc ....F...... 212 687-8881
New York *(G-8751)*

Benlee Enterprises LLC ....F...... 212 730-7330
Long Island City *(G-7176)*

◆ BH Multi Com Corp ....E...... 212 944-0020
New York *(G-8778)*

Bielka Inc ....G...... 212 980-6841
New York *(G-8783)*

Billanti Casting Co Inc.......................E...... 516 775-4800
New Hyde Park *(G-8254)*

Bourghol Brothers Inc ....G...... 845 268-9752
Congers *(G-3610)*

Bral Nader Fine Jewelry Inc ....G...... 800 493-1222
New York *(G-8846)*

▲ Brannkey Inc ....D...... 212 371-1515
New York *(G-8847)*

Brilliant Jewelers/Mjj Inc ....C...... 212 353-2326
New York *(G-8854)*

Brilliant Stars Collection Inc ....G...... 516 365-9000
Great Neck *(G-5371)*

Bristol Seamless Ring Corp ....F...... 212 874-2645
New York *(G-8855)*

Burke & Bannayan ....G...... 585 723-1010
Rochester *(G-13286)*

Carbon6 LLC ....G...... 607 229-3611
Brooklyn *(G-1646)*

Carlo Monte Designs Inc ....G...... 212 935-5611
New York *(G-8918)*

Carr Manufacturing Jewelers ....G...... 518 783-6093
Latham *(G-6852)*

Carvin French Jewelers Inc ....E...... 212 755-6474
New York *(G-8927)*

Chaindom Enterprises Inc ....G...... 212 719-4778
New York *(G-8967)*

Chameleon Gems Inc ....F...... 516 829-3333
Great Neck *(G-5375)*

Charis & Mae Inc ....G...... 212 641-0816
New York *(G-8972)*

Charles Krypell Inc ....G...... 212 752-3313
New York *(G-8974)*

Charles Perrella Inc ....E...... 845 348-4777
Nyack *(G-12138)*

▲ Christopher Designs Inc ....G...... 212 382-1013
New York *(G-9002)*

▲ Cigar Oasis LLC ....G...... 516 520-5258
Farmingdale *(G-4599)*

▲ CJ Jewelry Inc ....F...... 212 719-2464
New York *(G-9022)*

▲ Clyde Duneier Inc ....D...... 212 398-1122
New York *(G-9040)*

Concord Jewelry Mfg Co LLC..............E...... 212 719-4030
New York *(G-9077)*

▲ Creative Gold LLC ....E...... 718 686-2225
Brooklyn *(G-1697)*

Crown Jewelers Intl Inc ....G...... 212 420-7800
New York *(G-9124)*

▲ Csi International Inc ....A...... 800 441-2895
Niagara Falls *(G-11919)*

D M J Casting Inc ....G...... 212 719-1951
New York *(G-9146)*

▲ D R S Inc ....E...... 212 819-0237
New York *(G-9147)*

David Friedman Chain Co Inc ....F...... 212 684-1760
New York *(G-9178)*

David Howell Product Design ....E...... 914 666-4080
Bedford Hills *(G-767)*

▲ David S Diamonds Inc ....F...... 212 921-8029
New York *(G-9182)*

David Weisz & Sons USA LLC..............G...... 212 840-4747
New York *(G-9185)*

David Yurman Enterprises LLC ....G...... 914 539-4444
White Plains *(G-15999)*

◆ David Yurman Enterprises LLC...........B...... 212 896-1550
New York *(G-9186)*

David Yurman Enterprises LLC ....G...... 845 928-8660
Central Valley *(G-3298)*

David Yurman Retail LLC ....G...... 877 226-1400
New York *(G-9187)*

Diamond Distributors Inc ....G...... 212 921-9188
New York *(G-9220)*

Diana Kane Incorporated ....G...... 718 638-6520
Brooklyn *(G-1739)*

Dimoda Designs Inc..........................E...... 212 355-8166
New York *(G-9230)*

Discover Casting Inc ....G...... 212 398-5050
New York *(G-9234)*

Donna Distefano Ltd ....G...... 212 594-3757
New York *(G-9248)*

Doris Panos Designs Ltd ....G...... 631 245-0580
Melville *(G-7776)*

▲ Duran Jewelry Inc ....G...... 212 431-1959
New York *(G-9280)*

Dweck Industries Inc ....G...... 718 615-1695
Brooklyn *(G-1765)*

▲ Eagle Regalia Co Inc.........................F...... 845 425-2245
Spring Valley *(G-14567)*

S
I
C

Earring King Jewelry Mfg Inc..............G......718 544-7947 New York *(G-9300)*	▲ Hjn Inc..............F......212 398-9564 New York *(G-9795)*	Krainz Creations Inc..............E......212 583-1555 New York *(G-10134)*
Eastern Jewelry Mfg Co Inc..............E......212 840-0001 New York *(G-9304)*	Horo Creations LLC..............G......212 719-4818 New York *(G-9813)*	▼ Krasner Group Inc..............G......212 268-4100 New York *(G-10136)*
Echo Group Inc..............F......917 608-7440 New York *(G-9315)*	Houles USA Inc..............G......212 935-3900 New York *(G-9821)*	Kurt Gaum Inc..............F......212 719-2836 New York *(G-10145)*
Eclipse Collection Jewelers..............G......212 764-6883 New York *(G-9317)*	Hw Holdings Inc..............G......212 399-1000 New York *(G-9841)*	▲ La Fina Design Inc..............G......212 689-6725 New York *(G-10157)*
Ed Levin Inc..............E......518 677-8595 Cambridge *(G-3095)*	Ilico Jewelry Inc..............G......516 482-0201 Great Neck *(G-5393)*	▲ Lali Jewelry Inc..............G......212 944-2277 New York *(G-10166)*
Efron Designs Ltd..............G......718 482-8440 Long Island City *(G-7212)*	Imena Jewelry Manufacturer Inc..............F......212 827-0073 New York *(G-9867)*	▲ Le Hook Rouge LLC..............G......212 947-6272 Brooklyn *(G-2052)*
Elegant Jewelers Mfg Co Inc..............F......212 869-4951 New York *(G-9337)*	Incon Gems Inc..............F......212 221-8560 New York *(G-9875)*	▲ Le Vian Corp..............C......516 466-7200 Great Neck *(G-5400)*
▼ Ema Jewelry Inc..............D......212 575-8989 New York *(G-9355)*	◆ Indonesian Imports Inc..............D......855 725-5656 New York *(G-9882)*	Leo Ingwer Inc..............E......212 719-1342 New York *(G-10199)*
Emsaru USA Corp..............G......212 459-9355 New York *(G-9363)*	Inori Jewels..............F......347 703-5078 New York *(G-9900)*	Leo Schachter & Co Inc..............D......212 688-2000 New York *(G-10201)*
Eternal Line..............G......845 856-1999 Sparrow Bush *(G-14547)*	Intentions Jewelry LLC..............G......845 226-4650 Lagrangeville *(G-6749)*	Leon Mege Inc..............F......212 768-3868 New York *(G-10203)*
Euro Bands Inc..............F......212 719-9777 New York *(G-9419)*	Iridesse Inc..............F......212 230-6000 New York *(G-9940)*	Leser Enterprises Ltd..............G......212 832-8013 Yonkers *(G-16327)*
F M Abdulky Inc..............F......607 272-7373 Ithaca *(G-6380)*	Iriniri Designs Ltd..............F......845 469-7934 Sugar Loaf *(G-14769)*	▲ Lokai Holdings LLC..............F......646 979-3474 New York *(G-10245)*
F M Abdulky Inc..............G......607 272-7373 Ithaca *(G-6381)*	▲ J C Continental Inc..............G......212 643-2051 Long Island City *(G-7250)*	Love Bright Jewelry Inc..............E......516 620-2509 Oceanside *(G-12180)*
Fam Creations..............E......212 869-4833 New York *(G-9466)*	J J Creations Inc..............E......718 392-2828 Long Island City *(G-7251)*	M & S Quality Co Ltd..............G......212 302-8757 New York *(G-10291)*
Fantasia Jewelry Inc..............E......212 921-9590 New York *(G-9471)*	J R Gold Designs Ltd..............F......212 922-9292 New York *(G-9957)*	M A R A Metals Ltd..............G......718 786-7868 Long Island City *(G-7283)*
Feldman Jewelry Creations Inc..............G......718 438-8895 Brooklyn *(G-1837)*	▲ Jacmel Jewelry Inc..............C......718 349-4300 New York *(G-9964)*	M H Manufacturing Incorporated..............G......212 461-6900 New York *(G-10294)*
Fiesta Jewelry Corporation..............G......212 564-6847 New York *(G-9492)*	Jacobs & Cohen Inc..............E......212 714-2702 New York *(G-9966)*	M Heskia Company Inc..............G......212 768-1845 New York *(G-10295)*
First Image Design Corp..............E......212 221-8282 New York *(G-9500)*	▲ Jacoby Enterprises LLC..............G......718 435-0289 Brooklyn *(G-1987)*	M S Riviera Inc..............E......212 391-0206 New York *(G-10300)*
Five Star Creations Inc..............E......845 783-1187 Monroe *(G-8020)*	Jaguar Casting Co Inc..............E......212 869-0197 New York *(G-9968)*	Magnum Creation Inc..............F......212 869-2600 New York *(G-10330)*
Frank Blancato Inc..............F......212 768-1495 New York *(G-9532)*	Jaguar Jewelry Casting NY Inc..............G......212 768-4848 New York *(G-9969)*	Manny Grunberg Inc..............E......212 302-6173 New York *(G-10349)*
Fuzion Creations Intl LLC..............E......718 369-8800 Brooklyn *(G-1873)*	▲ Jane Bohan Inc..............G......212 529-6090 New York *(G-9973)*	Marina Jewelry Co Inc..............G......212 354-5027 New York *(G-10361)*
Gemoro Inc..............G......212 768-8844 Great Neck *(G-5392)*	Jasani Designs Usa Inc..............G......212 257-6465 New York *(G-9978)*	Mark King Jewelry Inc..............E......212 921-0746 New York *(G-10363)*
Gemveto Jewelry Company Inc..............E......212 755-2522 New York *(G-9587)*	▲ Jay Strongwater Holdings LLC..............A......646 657-0558 New York *(G-9980)*	Mark Robinson Inc..............G......212 223-3515 New York *(G-10366)*
George Lederman Inc..............G......212 753-4556 New York *(G-9601)*	Jay-Aimee Designs Inc..............C......718 609-0333 Great Neck *(G-5396)*	Markowitz Jewelry Co Inc..............E......845 774-1175 Monroe *(G-8026)*
Giovane Ltd..............E......212 332-7373 New York *(G-9613)*	Jayden Star LLC..............E......212 686-0400 New York *(G-9982)*	Marlborough Jewels Inc..............G......718 768-2000 Brooklyn *(G-2116)*
Global Gem Corporation..............G......212 350-9936 New York *(G-9628)*	▲ JC Crystal Inc..............E......212 594-0858 New York *(G-9987)*	▲ Martin Flyer Incorporated..............G......212 840-8899 Manhasset *(G-7537)*
Gold & Diamonds Wholesale Outl..............G......718 438-7888 Brooklyn *(G-1896)*	Jcco Enterprises..............F......716 626-0892 Buffalo *(G-2818)*	◆ Max Header..............E......680 888-9786 New York *(G-10389)*
Goldarama Company Inc..............G......212 730-7299 New York *(G-9638)*	Jeff Cooper Inc..............F......516 333-8200 New York *(G-9992)*	Maxine Denker Inc..............G......212 689-1440 Staten Island *(G-14679)*
Golden Integrity Inc..............E......212 764-6753 New York *(G-9642)*	Jewelry By Sarah Belle..............G......518 793-1626 Fort Ann *(G-4933)*	▲ MB Plastics Inc..............E......718 523-1180 Greenlawn *(G-5454)*
Goldmark Products Inc..............E......631 777-3343 Farmingdale *(G-4639)*	Jewels By Star Ltd..............E......212 308-3490 New York *(G-9996)*	ME & Ro Inc..............E......212 431-8744 New York *(G-10405)*
Gorga Fehren Fine Jewelry LLC..............G......646 861-3595 New York *(G-9646)*	Jeweltex Mfg Corp..............F......212 921-8188 New York *(G-9997)*	▲ Mellem Corporation..............F......607 723-0001 Binghamton *(G-897)*
Gottlieb & Sons Inc..............E......212 575-1907 New York *(G-9649)*	▲ Jimmy Crystal New York Co Ltd..............E......212 594-0858 New York *(G-10006)*	◆ Mer Gems Corp..............G......212 714-9129 New York *(G-10432)*
▲ Gramercy Jewelry Mfg Corp..............E......212 268-0461 New York *(G-9657)*	JK Manufacturing Inc..............G......212 683-3535 Locust Valley *(G-7127)*	▲ Mgd Brands Inc..............E......516 545-0150 Plainview *(G-12702)*
Grandeur Creations Inc..............G......212 643-1277 New York *(G-9661)*	Joan Boyce Ltd..............G......212 867-7474 New York *(G-10012)*	Michael Bondanza Inc..............E......212 869-0043 New York *(G-10452)*
Grinnell Designs Ltd..............E......212 391-5277 New York *(G-9679)*	▲ Jotaly Inc..............A......212 886-6000 New York *(G-10030)*	Midura Jewels Inc..............G......213 265-8090 New York *(G-10462)*
▲ Guild Diamond Products Inc..............F......212 871-0007 New York *(G-9695)*	Jr Licensing LLC..............G......212 244-1230 New York *(G-10033)*	Mimi So International LLC..............E......212 300-8600 New York *(G-10473)*
Gumuchian Fils Ltd..............F......212 588-7084 New York *(G-9698)*	JSA Jewelry Inc..............F......212 764-4504 New York *(G-10036)*	Min Ho Designs Inc..............G......212 838-3667 New York *(G-10474)*
H C Kionka & Co Inc..............F......212 227-3155 New York *(G-9702)*	Julius Cohen Jewelers Inc..............G......212 371-3050 Brooklyn *(G-2012)*	Monelle Jewelry..............G......212 977-9535 New York *(G-10499)*
Hammerman Bros Inc..............G......212 956-2800 New York *(G-9715)*	▲ Justin Ashley Designs Inc..............G......718 707-0200 Long Island City *(G-7259)*	Mwsi Inc..............D......914 347-4200 Hawthorne *(G-5819)*
Hanna Altinis Co Inc..............E......718 706-1134 Long Island City *(G-7238)*	▲ Justperfectmsp Ltd..............E......877 201-0005 New York *(G-10047)*	▲ N Y Bijoux Corp..............G......212 244-9585 Port Washington *(G-12909)*
▲ Hansa Usa LLC..............E......646 412-6407 New York *(G-9723)*	▲ Justyna Kaminska NY Inc..............G......917 423-5527 New York *(G-10048)*	Neil Savalia Inc..............F......212 869-0123 New York *(G-10561)*
▲ Harry Winston Inc..............C......212 399-1000 New York *(G-9732)*	▲ Kaprielian Enterprises Inc..............D......212 645-6623 New York *(G-10068)*	▲ Nicolo Raineri..............G......212 925-6128 New York *(G-10625)*
▲ Haskell Jewels Ltd..............E......212 764-3332 New York *(G-9735)*	Karbra Company..............C......212 736-9300 New York *(G-10069)*	Oscar Heyman & Bros Inc..............E......212 593-0400 New York *(G-10714)*
Henry Design Studios Inc..............G......516 801-2760 Locust Valley *(G-7126)*	Keith Lewis Studio Inc..............G......845 339-5629 New Paltz *(G-8307)*	Overnight Mountings Inc..............D......516 865-3000 New Hyde Park *(G-8287)*
Henry Dunay Designs Inc..............E......212 768-9700 New York *(G-9765)*	Kingold Jewelry Inc..............F......212 509-1700 New York *(G-10109)*	Parijat Jewels Inc..............G......212 302-2549 New York *(G-10759)*

Park West Jewelery Inc ....G....... 646 329-6145
New York *(G-10763)*

Patuga LLC ....G....... 716 204-7220
Williamsville *(G-16136)*

Pearl Erwin Inc ....E....... 212 889-7410
New York *(G-10777)*

Pesselnik & Cohen Inc ....G....... 212 925-0287
New York *(G-10811)*

Peter Atman Inc ....F....... 212 644-8882
New York *(G-10813)*

▲ Photograve Corporation ....E....... 718 667-4825
Staten Island *(G-14688)*

▲ Pink Box Accessories LLC .....G....... 718 435-2821
Brooklyn *(G-2260)*

Pronto Jewelry Inc ....E....... 212 719-9455
New York *(G-10912)*

◆ Q Ed Creations ....G....... 212 391-1155
New York *(G-10941)*

R & R Grosbard Inc ....E....... 212 575-0077
New York *(G-10966)*

R Klein Jewelry Co Inc ....D....... 516 482-3260
Massapequa *(G-7649)*

R M Reynolds ....G....... 315 789-7365
Geneva *(G-5161)*

Rand & Paseka Mfg Co Inc .....E....... 516 867-1500
Freeport *(G-5019)*

Reinhold Brothers Inc ....E....... 212 867-8310
New York *(G-11002)*

Renaissance Bijou Ltd ....G....... 212 869-1969
New York *(G-11010)*

Richards & West Inc ....D....... 585 461-4088
East Rochester *(G-4169)*

Richline Group Inc ....E....... 212 643-2908
New York *(G-11039)*

Richline Group Inc ....C....... 212 764-8454
New York *(G-11040)*

Richline Group Inc ....C....... 914 699-0000
New York *(G-11041)*

Ritani LLC ....E....... 888 974-8264
White Plains *(G-16056)*

▲ Riva Jewelry Manufacturing Inc ...C....... 718 361-3100
Brooklyn *(G-2347)*

Robert Bartholomew Ltd ....E....... 516 767-2970
Port Washington *(G-12919)*

▼ Roberto Coin Inc ....F....... 212 486-4545
New York *(G-11062)*

Robin Stanley Inc.....................G....... 212 871-0007
New York *(G-11064)*

Rosy Blue Inc ....E....... 212 687-8838
New York *(G-11086)*

▲ Royal Jewelry Mfg Inc ....E....... 212 302-2500
Great Neck *(G-5419)*

Royal Miracle Corp ....E....... 212 921-5797
New York *(G-11089)*

Rubinstein Jewelry Mfg Co ....F....... 718 784-8650
Long Island City *(G-7348)*

Rudolf Friedman Inc ....F....... 212 869-5070
New York *(G-11097)*

Rumson Acquisition LLC ....F....... 718 349-4300
New York *(G-11098)*

▲ Ryan Gems Inc ....E....... 212 697-0149
New York *(G-11102)*

▲ S Kashi & Sons Inc ....E....... 212 869-9393
Great Neck *(G-5420)*

S Scharf Inc ....F....... 516 541-9552
Massapequa *(G-7650)*

▲ Samuel B Collection Inc ....F....... 516 466-1826
Great Neck *(G-5421)*

Sanoy Inc ....E....... 212 695-6384
New York *(G-11133)*

Satco Castings Service Inc ......E....... 516 354-1500
New Hyde Park *(G-8291)*

Satellite Incorporated ....G....... 212 221-6687
New York *(G-11140)*

▲ Select Jewelry Inc ....D....... 718 784-3626
Long Island City *(G-7354)*

▲ Shah Diamonds Inc ....F....... 212 888-9393
New York *(G-11202)*

Shanu Gems Inc ....F....... 212 921-4470
New York *(G-11205)*

Sharodine Inc ....E....... 516 767-3548
Port Washington *(G-12926)*

Shining Creations Inc ....G....... 845 358-4911
New City *(G-8230)*

▲ Shiro Limited ....G....... 212 780-0007
New York *(G-11217)*

Simka Diamond Corp ....F....... 212 921-4420
New York *(G-11242)*

◆ Sol Savransky Diamonds Inc ...F....... 212 730-4700
New York *(G-11287)*

Somerset Manufacturers Inc .....E....... 516 626-3832
Roslyn Heights *(G-14057)*

▲ Spark Creations Inc ....F....... 212 575-8385
New York *(G-11308)*

Standard Wedding Band Co ......G....... 516 294-0954
Garden City *(G-5117)*

Stanley Creations Inc ....C....... 718 361-6100
Long Island City *(G-7365)*

Stanmark Jewelry Inc ....G....... 212 730-2557
New York *(G-11347)*

Stone House Associates Inc .....G....... 212 221-7447
New York *(G-11365)*

◆ Sube Inc ....E....... 212 243-6930
New York *(G-11383)*

Sumer Gold Ltd ....G....... 212 354-8677
New York *(G-11388)*

Suna Bros Inc ....E....... 212 869-5670
New York *(G-11392)*

Sunrise Jewelers of NY Inc ......G....... 516 541-1302
Massapequa *(G-7651)*

Tambetti Inc ....G....... 212 751-9584
New York *(G-11427)*

Tamsen Z LLC ....E....... 212 292-6412
New York *(G-11428)*

Tanagro Jewelry Corp ....G....... 212 753-2817
New York *(G-11429)*

Technical Service Industries .....E....... 212 719-9800
Jamaica *(G-6478)*

Teena Creations Inc ....G....... 516 867-1500
Freeport *(G-5027)*

▲ Temple St Clair LLC ....E....... 212 219-8664
New York *(G-11452)*

Thomas Sasson Co Inc ....G....... 212 697-4998
New York *(G-11472)*

Tiga Holdings Inc ....E....... 845 838-3000
Beacon *(G-757)*

▲ Trianon Collection Inc ....E....... 212 921-9450
New York *(G-11542)*

▲ Ultra Fine Jewelry Mfg ....E....... 516 349-2848
Plainview *(G-12721)*

▲ UNI Jewelry Inc ....G....... 212 398-1818
New York *(G-11582)*

Unique Designs Inc ....F....... 212 575-7701
New York *(G-11594)*

United Brothers Jewelry Inc .....G....... 212 921-2558
New York *(G-11597)*

Valentin & Kalich Jwly Mfg Ltd ...E....... 212 575-9044
New York *(G-11633)*

Valentine Jewelry Mfg Co Inc ...G....... 212 382-0606
New York *(G-11634)*

▲ Verragio Ltd ....E....... 212 868-8181
New York *(G-11662)*

Viktor Gold Enterprise Corp ......G....... 212 768-8885
New York *(G-11683)*

Von Musulin Patricia ....G....... 212 206-8345
New York *(G-11704)*

W & B Mazza & Sons Inc ....E....... 516 379-4130
North Baldwin *(G-12012)*

Watertown 1785 LLC ....G....... 315 785-0062
Watertown *(G-15591)*

Weisco Inc ....F....... 212 575-8989
New York *(G-11737)*

William Goldberg Diamond Corp ...C....... 212 980-4343
New York *(G-11756)*

Xomox Jewelry Inc ....G....... 212 944-8428
New York *(G-11801)*

▲ Yofah Religious Articles Inc ...F....... 718 435-3288
Brooklyn *(G-2601)*

Zeeba Jewelry Mfg Inc ....G....... 212 997-1009
New York *(G-11819)*

Zelman & Friedman Jwly Mfg Co ...E....... 718 349-3400
Long Island City *(G-7412)*

3914 Silverware, Plated & Stainless Steel Ware

All American Awards Inc ....F....... 631 567-2025
Bohemia *(G-968)*

Atlantic Trophy Co Inc ....G....... 212 684-6020
New York *(G-8668)*

▲ Csi International Inc ....E....... 800 441-2895
Niagara Falls *(G-11919)*

▲ DWH&s Inc ....E....... 718 993-6405
Bronx *(G-1246)*

▲ Dwm International Inc ....F....... 646 290-7448
Long Island City *(G-7207)*

Endurart Inc ....E....... 212 473-7000
New York *(G-9373)*

Oneida International Inc ....G....... 315 361-3000
Oneida *(G-12249)*

Oneida Silversmiths Inc ....G....... 315 361-3000
Oneida *(G-12252)*

▼ Quest Bead & Cast Inc ....E....... 212 354-1737
New York *(G-10955)*

R Goldsmith ....F....... 718 239-1396
Bronx *(G-1349)*

Sherrill Manufacturing Inc ....C....... 315 280-0727
Sherrill *(G-14406)*

Silver City Group Inc ....G....... 315 363-0344
Sherrill *(G-14407)*

▲ Studio Silversmiths Inc ....E....... 718 418-6785
Ridgewood *(G-13162)*

▲ Utica Cutlery Company ....D....... 315 733-4663
Utica *(G-15298)*

Valerie Bohigian ....G....... 914 631-8866
Sleepy Hollow *(G-14465)*

3915 Jewelers Findings & Lapidary Work

A J M Enterprises ....F....... 716 626-7294
Buffalo *(G-2615)*

Ace Diamond Corp ....G....... 212 730-8231
New York *(G-8446)*

Allstar Casting Corporation ......E....... 212 563-0909
New York *(G-8520)*

Ampex Casting Corporation ......F....... 212 719-1318
New York *(G-8566)*

Antwerp Diamond Distributors ...F....... 212 319-3300
New York *(G-8599)*

Antwerp Sales Intl Inc ....F....... 212 354-6515
New York *(G-8600)*

Asa Manufacturing Inc ....E....... 718 853-3033
Brooklyn *(G-1538)*

Asco Castings Inc ....G....... 212 719-9800
Long Island City *(G-7167)*

Asur Jewelry Inc ....G....... 718 472-1687
Long Island City *(G-7170)*

Baroka Creations Inc ....G....... 212 768-0527
New York *(G-8731)*

Boucheron Joaillerie USA Inc ...G....... 212 715-7330
New York *(G-8839)*

Carrera Casting Corp ....C....... 212 382-3296
New York *(G-8924)*

▲ Christopher Designs Inc ....E....... 212 382-1013
New York *(G-9002)*

Classic Creations Inc ....G....... 516 498-1991
Great Neck *(G-5376)*

▲ Creative Tools & Supply Inc ...G....... 212 279-7077
New York *(G-9121)*

D R S Watch Materials ....E....... 212 819-0470
New York *(G-9148)*

Danhier Co LLC ....F....... 212 563-7683
New York *(G-9164)*

Dialase Inc ....G....... 212 575-8833
New York *(G-9217)*

Diamex Inc ....G....... 212 575-8145
New York *(G-9218)*

Diamond Boutique ....G....... 516 444-3373
Port Washington *(G-12872)*

Diamond Constellation Corp ......G....... 212 819-0324
New York *(G-9219)*

Dresdiam Inc ....E....... 212 819-2217
New York *(G-9268)*

Dweck Industries Inc ....E....... 718 615-1695
Brooklyn *(G-1766)*

▲ E Schreiber Inc ....E....... 212 382-0280
New York *(G-9291)*

Engelack Gem Corporation ....G....... 212 719-3094
New York *(G-9377)*

Eugene Biro Corp ....E....... 212 997-0146
New York *(G-9417)*

Fine Cut Diamonds Corporation ...G....... 212 575-8780
New York *(G-9494)*

Fischer Diamonds Inc ....F....... 212 869-1990
New York *(G-9503)*

▲ Fischler Diamonds Inc ....G....... 212 921-8196
New York *(G-9504)*

◆ Forever Grown Diamonds Inc ...G....... 917 261-4511
New York *(G-9515)*

Frank Billanti Casting Co Inc .....F....... 212 221-0440
New York *(G-9531)*

Gemini Manufactures ....F....... 716 633-0306
Cheektowaga *(G-3350)*

Goldmark Inc ....E....... 718 438-0295
Brooklyn *(G-1899)*

▲ Guild Diamond Products Inc ...F....... 212 871-0007
New York *(G-9695)*

Hershel Horowitz Corp ....G....... 212 719-1710
New York *(G-9770)*

Jaguar Casting Co Inc ....E....... 212 869-0197
New York *(G-9968)*

Jim Wachtler Inc ....G...... 212 755-4367
New York *(G-10004)*

▲ Julius Klein Group ....E...... 212 719-1811
New York *(G-10038)*

Kaleko Bros ....G...... 212 819-0100
New York *(G-10059)*

▲ Kaprielian Enterprises Inc ....D...... 212 645-6623
New York *(G-10068)*

Karbra Company ....C...... 212 736-9300
New York *(G-10069)*

Kemp Metal Products Inc ....G...... 516 997-8860
Westbury *(G-15902)*

▲ Lazare Kaplan Intl Inc ....D...... 212 972-9700
New York *(G-10179)*

Leo Schachter Diamonds LLC ....D...... 212 688-2000
New York *(G-10202)*

Levi Shabtai ....G...... 212 302-7393
New York *(G-10205)*

▲ Magic Novelty Co Inc ....E...... 212 304-2777
New York *(G-10325)*

Max Kahan Inc ....F...... 212 575-4646
New York *(G-10391)*

ME & Ro Inc ....G...... 212 431-8744
New York *(G-10405)*

Miller & Veit Inc ....F...... 212 247-2275
New York *(G-10469)*

Nathan Berrie & Sons Inc ....G...... 516 432-8500
Island Park *(G-6320)*

New York Findings Corp ....F...... 212 925-5745
New York *(G-10597)*

Nyman Jewelry Inc...........................G...... 212 944-1976
New York *(G-10665)*

▲ Perma Glow Ltd Inc ....F...... 212 575-9677
New York *(G-10805)*

▲ R G Flair Co Inc ....E...... 631 586-7311
Bay Shore *(G-703)*

Renco Manufacturing Inc ....G...... 718 392-8877
Long Island City *(G-7342)*

Satco Castings Service Inc ....G...... 516 354-1500
New Hyde Park *(G-8291)*

▲ Shah Diamonds Inc ....F...... 212 888-9393
New York *(G-11202)*

Stephen J Lipkins Inc ....G...... 631 249-8866
Farmingdale *(G-4741)*

Sunshine Diamond Cutter Inc ....G...... 212 221-1028
New York *(G-11394)*

T M W Diamonds Mfg Co ....G...... 212 869-8444
New York *(G-11417)*

Times One Inc ....G...... 718 686-8988
Brooklyn *(G-2505)*

▲ Touch Adjust Clip Co Inc ....G...... 631 589-3077
Bohemia *(G-1086)*

▲ Townley Inc ....E...... 212 779-0544
New York *(G-11524)*

United Gemdiam Inc ....E...... 718 851-5083
Brooklyn *(G-2538)*

Via America Fine Jewelry Inc...........G...... 212 302-1218
New York *(G-11674)*

William Goldberg Diamond Corp.......G...... 212 980-4343
New York *(G-11756)*

Windiam Usa Inc ....G...... 212 542-0949
New York *(G-11763)*

◆ Zak Jewelry Tools Inc ....F...... 212 768-8122
New York *(G-11815)*

Zirconia Creations Intl ....G...... 212 239-3730
New York *(G-11826)*

3931 Musical Instruments

Albert Augustine Ltd ....D...... 718 913-9635
Mount Vernon *(G-8122)*

Barbera Transduser Systems ....F...... 718 816-3025
Staten Island *(G-14624)*

DAddario & Company Inc ....D...... 631 439-3300
Melville *(G-7773)*

DAddario & Company Inc ....E...... 718 599-6660
Brooklyn *(G-1717)*

◆ DAddario & Company Inc ....A...... 631 439-3300
Farmingdale *(G-4612)*

◆ DAndrea Inc ....E...... 516 496-2200
Syosset *(G-14783)*

▲ Dimarzio Inc ....E...... 718 442-6655
Staten Island *(G-14646)*

▲ E & O Mari Inc ....D...... 845 562-4400
Newburgh *(G-11863)*

Elsener Organ Works Inc ....G...... 631 254-2744
Deer Park *(G-3870)*

▲ Evans Manufacturing LLC ....G...... 631 439-3300
Farmingdale *(G-4627)*

Gluck Orgelbau Inc ....G...... 212 233-2684
New York *(G-9634)*

Guitar Specialist Inc ....G...... 914 401-9052
Goldens Bridge *(G-5303)*

▲ Hipshot Products Inc ....F...... 607 532-9404
Interlaken *(G-6284)*

J D Calato Manufacturing Co ....G...... 716 285-3546
Niagara Falls *(G-11942)*

Jason Ladanye Guitar Piano & H .....E...... 518 527-3973
Albany *(G-91)*

Kerner and Merchant........................G...... 315 463-8023
East Syracuse *(G-4225)*

▲ Leonard Carlson ....G...... 518 477-4710
East Greenbush *(G-4115)*

Magic Reed ....F...... 914 630-4006
Larchmont *(G-6842)*

▲ Mari Strings Inc ....F...... 212 799-6781
New York *(G-10359)*

Muzet Inc ....F...... 315 452-0050
Syracuse *(G-14948)*

Nathan Love LLC ....F...... 212 925-7111
New York *(G-10537)*

◆ New Sensor Corporation ....D...... 718 937-8300
Long Island City *(G-7308)*

◆ Paulson & Co Inc ....C...... 212 956-2221
New York *(G-10773)*

Roli USA Inc ....F...... 412 600-4840
New York *(G-11076)*

▲ Sadowsky Guitars Ltd ....F...... 718 433-1990
Long Island City *(G-7351)*

▲ Samson Technologies Corp ....D...... 631 784-2200
Hicksville *(G-5946)*

Siegfrieds Call Inc ....G...... 845 765-2275
Beacon *(G-756)*

Sound Source Inc ....G...... 585 271-5370
Rochester *(G-13737)*

▲ Steinway Inc ....A...... 718 721-2600
Long Island City *(G-7367)*

◆ Steinway and Sons ....C...... 718 721-2600
Long Island City *(G-7368)*

◆ Steinway Musical Instrs Inc ....E...... 781 894-9770
New York *(G-11355)*

▲ Stuart Spector Designs Ltd...........G...... 845 246-6124
Saugerties *(G-14214)*

3942 Dolls & Stuffed Toys

◆ ADC Dolls Inc ....C...... 212 244-4500
New York *(G-8455)*

Beila Group Inc ....F...... 212 260-1948
New York *(G-8750)*

◆ Commonwealth Toy Novelty Inc .....D...... 212 242-4070
New York *(G-9069)*

Community Products LLC ....E...... 518 589-5103
Elka Park *(G-4304)*

Dana Michele LLC ....G...... 917 757-7777
New York *(G-9161)*

Fierce Fun Toys LLC ....G...... 646 322-7172
New York *(G-9491)*

First Brands LLC ....E...... 646 432-4366
Merrick *(G-7855)*

▲ Goldberger Company LLC ....F...... 212 924-1194
New York *(G-9639)*

▲ Jupiter Creations Inc ....G...... 917 493-9393
New York *(G-10043)*

▲ Lovee Doll & Toy Co Inc ....G...... 212 242-1545
New York *(G-10273)*

Madame Alexander Doll 2018 LLC ....G...... 917 576-8381
New York *(G-10311)*

Madame Alexander Doll Co LLC........D...... 212 244-4500
New York *(G-10312)*

Minted Green Inc ....G...... 845 458-1845
Airmont *(G-14)*

Naito International Corp ....F...... 718 309-2425
Rockville Centre *(G-13832)*

◆ Skip Hop Inc ....E...... 646 902-9874
New York *(G-11259)*

Skip Hop Holdings Inc ....G...... 212 868-9850
New York *(G-11260)*

Ward Sales Co Inc ....G...... 315 476-5276
Syracuse *(G-15023)*

▲ Well-Made Toy Mfg Corporation .....E...... 718 381-4225
Port Washington *(G-12931)*

3944 Games, Toys & Children's Vehicles

▲ Babysafe Usa LLC ....G...... 877 367-4141
Afton *(G-6)*

◆ Barron Games Intl Co LLC ....F...... 716 630-0054
Buffalo *(G-2655)*

Buffalo Games LLC ....D...... 716 827-8393
Buffalo *(G-2674)*

C T A Digital Inc ....G...... 718 963-9845
Brooklyn *(G-1636)*

▲ C T A Digital Inc...........................E...... 845 513-0433
Monroe *(G-8017)*

Church Communities NY Inc ....E...... 518 589-5103
Elka Park *(G-4302)*

Church Communities NY Inc ....E...... 518 589-5103
Elka Park *(G-4303)*

Code Red Trading LLC ....E...... 347 782-2608
Brooklyn *(G-1673)*

Compoz A Puzzle Inc ....G...... 516 883-2311
Port Washington *(G-12869)*

▲ Creative Kids Far East Inc ....C...... 844 252-7263
Spring Valley *(G-14565)*

▲ Dakott LLC ....G...... 888 805-6795
New York *(G-9159)*

Dana Michele LLC ....G...... 917 757-7777
New York *(G-9161)*

▲ Design Works Craft Inc ....F...... 631 244-5749
Bohemia *(G-1005)*

Drescher Paper Box Inc ....F...... 716 854-0288
Clarence *(G-3429)*

▲ E C C Corp ....G...... 518 873-6494
Elizabethtown *(G-4300)*

▲ Eeboo Corporation ....F...... 212 222-0823
New York *(G-9325)*

Ellis Products Corp ....G...... 516 791-3732
Valley Stream *(G-15339)*

Famous Box Scooter Co ....G...... 631 943-2013
West Babylon *(G-15711)*

First Brands LLC ....E...... 646 432-4366
Merrick *(G-7855)*

Gargraves Trackage Corporation ....G...... 315 483-6577
North Rose *(G-12035)*

Glitter Slimes LLC ....G...... 845 772-1113
Goshen *(G-5309)*

▲ Haba USA ....G...... 800 468-6873
Skaneateles *(G-14453)*

▲ Habermaass Corporation ....F...... 315 729-0070
Skaneateles *(G-14454)*

▲ Innovative Designs LLC ....E...... 212 695-0892
New York *(G-9897)*

▲ Jupiter Creations Inc ....G...... 917 493-9393
New York *(G-10043)*

Kidz Toyz Inc ....G...... 914 261-1453
Mount Kisco *(G-8096)*

▲ Kling Magnetics Inc ....E...... 518 392-4000
Chatham *(G-3331)*

Littlebits Electronics Inc ....G...... 917 464-4577
New York *(G-10231)*

Master Juvenile Products Inc ....F...... 845 647-8400
Ellenville *(G-4308)*

Matel LLC ....G...... 646 825-6760
New York *(G-10382)*

Mattel Inc ....E...... 310 252-2000
East Aurora *(G-4092)*

▲ Mechanical Displays Inc...............G...... 718 258-5588
Brooklyn *(G-2130)*

Pidyon Controls Inc ....F...... 212 683-9523
New York *(G-10837)*

Pride Lines Ltd ....G...... 631 225-0033
Lindenhurst *(G-6970)*

R F Giardina Co................................F...... 516 922-1364
Oyster Bay *(G-12456)*

Sandbox Brands Inc ....G...... 212 647-8877
New York *(G-11130)*

Spectrum Crafts Inc ....G...... 631 244-5749
Bohemia *(G-1081)*

◆ Swimways Corp ....C...... 757 460-1156
Long Island City *(G-7377)*

Toymax Inc ....G...... 212 633-6611
New York *(G-11525)*

Tucker Jones House Inc ....E...... 631 642-9092
East Setauket *(G-4189)*

Vogel Applied Technologies ....G...... 212 677-3136
New York *(G-11702)*

Way Out Toys Inc ....G...... 212 689-9094
New York *(G-11732)*

Wobbleworks Inc ....E...... 718 618-9904
New York *(G-11772)*

3949 Sporting & Athletic Goods, NEC

728 Berriman LLC ....G...... 718 272-5000
Brooklyn *(G-1423)*

A Hyatt Ball Co Ltd ....G...... 518 747-0272
Fort Edward *(G-4936)*

Absolute Fitness US Corp ....D...... 732 979-8582
Bayside *(G-734)*

Adirondack Outdoor Center LLC.......G...... 315 369-2300
Old Forge *(G-12221)*

Adpro Sports LLC ....D...... 716 854-5116
Buffalo *(G-2622)*

Alternatives For Children ....E 631 271-0777
Dix Hills **(G-4009)**

▲ Apparel Production Inc ....E 212 278-8362
New York **(G-8608)**

▲ Athalon Sportgear Inc ....G 212 268-8070
New York **(G-8664)**

Azibi Ltd ....F 212 869-6550
New York **(G-8701)**

Bears Management Group Inc ....F 585 624-5694
Lima **(G-6929)**

Billy Beez Usa LLC ....F 315 741-5099
Syracuse **(G-14829)**

Billy Beez Usa LLC ....F 646 606-2249
New York **(G-8793)**

Billy Beez Usa LLC ....E 845 915-4709
West Nyack **(G-15818)**

Billy Beez Usa LLC ....G 315 235-3121
New Hartford **(G-8237)**

▼ Blades ....F 212 477-1059
New York **(G-8808)**

Bomber LLC ....G 212 980-2442
New York **(G-8833)**

Bungers Surf Shop ....G 631 244-3646
Sayville **(G-14224)**

Burnt Mill Smithing ....G 585 293-2380
Churchville **(G-3409)**

Burton Corporation ....D 802 862-4500
Champlain **(G-3310)**

Callaway Golf Ball Oprtons Inc ....F 518 725-5744
Johnstown **(G-6612)**

Callaway Golf Ball Oprtons Inc ....C 518 773-2255
Gloversville **(G-5280)**

Car Doctor Motor Sports LLC ....G 631 537-1548
Water Mill **(G-15528)**

Cascade Helmets Holdings Inc ....G 315 453-3073
Liverpool **(G-7006)**

▲ Chapman Skateboard Co Inc ....G 631 321-4773
Deer Park **(G-3852)**

Charm Mfg Co Inc ....E 607 565-8161
Waverly **(G-15619)**

City Sports Inc ....G 212 730-2009
New York **(G-9018)**

Cooperstown Bat Company Inc ....F 607 547-2415
Cooperstown **(G-3639)**

▲ Copper John Corporation ....F 315 258-9269
Auburn **(G-470)**

▲ Cy Plastics Works Inc ....D 585 229-2555
Honeoye **(G-6068)**

▼ Devin Mfg Inc ....F 585 496-5770
Arcade **(G-372)**

◆ Eastern Jungle Gym Inc ....E 845 878-9800
Carmel **(G-3185)**

▲ Everlast Sports Mfg Corp ....E 212 239-0990
New York **(G-9427)**

▲ Everlast Worldwide Inc ....E 212 239-0990
New York **(G-9428)**

▲ Excellent Art Mfg Corp ....F 718 388-7075
Inwood **(G-6292)**

Fishing Valley LLC ....G 716 523-6158
Lockport **(G-7075)**

Fitsmo LLC ....G 585 519-1956
Fairport **(G-4497)**

Florida North Inc ....F 518 868-2888
Sloansville **(G-14469)**

Fly-Tyers Carry-All LLC ....G 607 821-1460
Charlotteville **(G-3328)**

◆ Fownes Brothers & Co Inc ....E 800 345-6837
New York **(G-9525)**

Fownes Brothers & Co Inc ....E 518 752-4411
Gloversville **(G-5283)**

Good Show Sportwear Inc ....F 212 334-8751
New York **(G-9645)**

Grace Wheeler ....G 716 483-1254
Jamestown **(G-6513)**

Grand Slam Safety LLC ....G 315 301-4039
Croghan **(G-3802)**

▼ Gym Store Inc ....G 718 366-7804
Maspeth **(G-7621)**

Hart Sports Inc ....G 631 385-1805
Huntington Station **(G-6248)**

Herrmann Group LLC ....G 716 876-9798
Kenmore **(G-6651)**

Hinspergers Poly Industries ....E 585 798-6625
Medina **(G-7738)**

▲ Hypoxico Inc ....G 212 972-1009
New York **(G-9844)**

◆ Imperial Pools Inc ....C 518 786-1200
Latham **(G-6860)**

▲ International Leisure Pdts Inc ....E 631 254-2155
Edgewood **(G-4272)**

▲ J R Products Inc ....G 716 633-7565
Clarence Center **(G-3446)**

▲ Jag Manufacturing Inc ....E 518 762-9558
Johnstown **(G-6620)**

Joe Moro ....G 607 272-0591
Ithaca **(G-6390)**

Johnson Outdoors Inc ....C 607 779-2200
Binghamton **(G-891)**

Kohlberg Sports Group Inc ....G 914 241-7430
Mount Kisco **(G-8097)**

Latham International Mfg Corp ....B 800 833-3800
Latham **(G-6866)**

▼ Latham Pool Products Inc ....B 518 951-1000
Latham **(G-6867)**

▲ Mac Swed Inc ....F 212 684-7730
New York **(G-10304)**

Makiplastic ....G 716 772-2222
Gasport **(G-5138)**

▲ Maverik Lacrosse LLC ....A 516 213-3050
New York **(G-10388)**

Morris Golf Ventures ....E 631 283-0559
Southampton **(G-14533)**

◆ Nalge Nunc International Corp ....A 585 498-2661
Rochester **(G-13565)**

▼ North Coast Outfitters Ltd ....E 631 727-5580
Riverhead **(G-13183)**

Northern King Lures Inc ....G 585 865-3373
Rochester **(G-13586)**

▲ Olympia Sports Company Inc ....F 914 347-4737
Elmsford **(G-4421)**

▲ Otis Products Inc ....C 315 348-4300
Lyons Falls **(G-7455)**

Outdoor Group LLC ....C 877 503-5483
West Henrietta **(G-15799)**

Paddock Chevrolet Golf Dome ....E 716 504-4059
Tonawanda **(G-15130)**

Perfect Form Manufacturing LLC ....G 585 500-5923
West Henrietta **(G-15800)**

▲ Performance Lacrosse Group Inc ....G 315 453-3073
Liverpool **(G-7032)**

▲ Physicalmind Institute ....F 212 343-2150
New York **(G-10832)**

Pilates Designs LLC ....G 718 721-5929
Astoria **(G-434)**

Pilgrim Surf & Supply ....G 718 218-7456
Brooklyn **(G-2258)**

PNC Sports ....G 516 665-2244
Deer Park **(G-3920)**

Polytech Pool Mfg Inc ....F 718 492-8991
Brooklyn **(G-2268)**

PRC Liquidating Company ....E 212 823-9626
New York **(G-10873)**

▲ Quaker Boy Inc ....G 716 662-3979
Springville **(G-14596)**

Qubicaamf Worldwide LLC ....C 315 376-6541
Lowville **(G-8222)**

Rawlings Sporting Goods Co Inc ....D 315 429-8511
Dolgeville **(G-4025)**

Rising Stars Soccer Club CNY ....F 315 381-3096
Westmoreland **(G-15962)**

◆ Rome Specialty Company Inc ....E 315 337-8200
Rome **(G-13870)**

Rottkamp Tennis Inc ....E 631 421-0040
Huntington Station **(G-6257)**

Sea Isle Custom Rod Builders ....G 516 868-8855
Freeport **(G-5022)**

Seaway Mats Inc ....G 518 483-2560
Malone **(G-7490)**

Shehawken Archery Co Inc ....F 607 967-8333
Bainbridge **(G-526)**

Sportsfield Specialties Inc ....E 607 746-8911
Delhi **(G-3967)**

Stephenson Custom Case Company ....E 905 542-8762
Niagara Falls **(G-11982)**

◆ Swimline Corp ....C 631 254-2155
Edgewood **(G-4284)**

◆ Swimways Corp ....G 757 460-1156
Long Island City **(G-7377)**

▲ TDS Fitness Equipment Corp ....F 607 733-6789
Elmira **(G-4370)**

TDS Foundry Corporation ....G 607 733-6789
Elmira **(G-4371)**

Tosch Products Ltd ....G 315 672-3040
Camillus **(G-3111)**

▲ Viking Athletics Ltd ....E 631 957-8000
Lindenhurst **(G-6982)**

Watson Adventures LLC ....G 212 564-8293
New York **(G-11731)**

▲ Wilbar International Inc ....D 631 951-9800
Hauppauge **(G-5801)**

World Best Sporting Goods Inc ....F 800 489-0908
Westbury **(G-15940)**

3951 Pens & Mechanical Pencils

◆ Aakron Rule Corp ....C 716 542-5483
Akron **(G-15)**

▲ Harper Products Ltd ....C 516 997-2330
Westbury **(G-15894)**

▲ Mark Dri Products Inc ....C 516 484-6200
Bethpage **(G-838)**

▲ Mercury Pen Company Inc ....G 518 899-9653
Ballston Lake **(G-561)**

▲ Pelican Products Co Inc ....E 718 860-3220
Bronx **(G-1334)**

Pintrill LLC ....F 718 782-1000
Brooklyn **(G-2261)**

▲ STS Refill America LLC ....C 516 934-8008
Hicksville **(G-5949)**

Universal Luxury Brands Inc ....G 646 248-5700
New York **(G-11607)**

3952 Lead Pencils, Crayons & Artist's Mtrls

◆ Aakron Rule Corp ....C 716 542-5483
Akron **(G-15)**

Clapper Hollow Designs Inc ....E 518 234-9561
Cobleskill **(G-3497)**

◆ Golden Artist Colors Inc ....C 607 847-6154
New Berlin **(G-8222)**

Handmade Frames Inc ....F 718 782-8364
Brooklyn **(G-1925)**

Lopez Restorations Inc ....F 718 383-1555
Brooklyn **(G-2084)**

◆ Micro Powders Inc ....E 914 332-6400
Tarrytown **(G-15048)**

North America Pastel Artists ....G 718 463-4701
Flushing **(G-4880)**

▲ R & F Handmade Paints Inc ....F 845 331-3112
Kingston **(G-6707)**

▲ Simon Liu Inc ....F 718 567-2011
Brooklyn **(G-2417)**

▲ Sml Brothers Holding Corp ....D 718 402-2000
Bronx **(G-1366)**

▲ Spaulding & Rogers Mfg Inc ....D 518 768-2070
Voorheesville **(G-15445)**

Timeless Decor LLC ....C 315 782-5759
Watertown **(G-15590)**

3953 Marking Devices

A & M Steel Stamps Inc ....G 516 741-6223
Mineola **(G-7954)**

Bianca Group Ltd ....G 212 768-3011
New York **(G-8779)**

C M E Corp ....F 315 451-7101
Syracuse **(G-14839)**

▲ Cannizzaro Seal & Engraving Co ....G 718 513-6125
Brooklyn **(G-1644)**

▼ Crafters Workshop Inc ....G 914 345-2838
Elmsford **(G-4404)**

Dab-O-Matic Corp ....D 914 699-7070
Mount Vernon **(G-8137)**

East Coast Thermographers Inc ....E 718 321-3211
College Point **(G-3541)**

▲ Hampton Art LLC ....E 631 924-1335
Medford **(G-7710)**

◆ Hodgins Engraving Co Inc ....D 585 343-4444
Batavia **(G-618)**

I & I Systems ....G 845 753-9126
Tuxedo Park **(G-15216)**

Joseph Treu Successors Inc ....G 212 691-7026
New York **(G-10028)**

Kelly Foundry & Machine Co ....E 315 732-8313
Utica **(G-15279)**

Koehlr-Gibson Mkg Graphics Inc ....E 716 838-5960
Buffalo **(G-2838)**

Krengel Manufacturing Co Inc ....F 212 227-1901
Fulton **(G-5069)**

Long Island Stamp & Seal Co ....F 718 628-8550
Ridgewood **(G-13150)**

Michael Todd Stevens ....G 585 436-9957
Rochester **(G-13544)**

New York Marking Devices Corp ....G 585 454-5188
Rochester **(G-13572)**

New York Marking Devices Corp ....F 315 463-8641
Syracuse **(G-14951)**

Rubber Stamp X Press ....G 631 423-1322
Huntington Station **(G-6258)**

Rubber Stamps Inc ....E 212 675-1180
Mineola **(G-7998)**

Sales Tax Asset Rceivable Corp ....G 212 788-5874
New York **(G-11119)**

S I C

Samoss Group Ltd ....E 212 239-6677
New York (G-11125)
▲ Specialty Ink Co Inc ....F 631 586-3666
Blue Point (G-957)
▼ Tech Products Inc ....E 718 442-4900
Staten Island (G-14721)
Thermopatch Corporation ....D 315 446-8110
Syracuse (G-15012)
Ul Corp ....G 201 203-4453
Bayside (G-743)
◆ United Silicone Inc ....D 716 681-8222
Lancaster (G-6837)
United Sttes Brnze Sign of Fla ....E 516 352-5155
New Hyde Park (G-8300)
Ward Sales Co Inc ....G 315 476-5276
Syracuse (G-15023)

3955 Carbon Paper & Inked Ribbons

Cartridge Evolution Inc ....G 718 788-0678
Brooklyn (G-1651)
Guttz Corporation of America ....F 914 591-9600
Irvington (G-6309)
◆ International Imaging Mtls Inc ....B 716 691-6333
Amherst (G-227)
Northeast Toner Inc ....G 518 899-5545
Ballston Lake (G-562)
Qls Solutions Group Inc ....E 716 852-2203
Buffalo (G-2939)
Smartoners Inc ....G 718 975-0197
Brooklyn (G-2430)
▲ Summit Technologies LLC ....E 631 590-1040
Holbrook (G-6023)

3961 Costume Jewelry & Novelties

Accessory Plays LLC ....E 212 564-7301
New York (G-8441)
◆ Allure Jewelry and ACC LLC ....F 646 226-8057
New York (G-8521)
Anatoli Inc ....F 845 334-9000
West Hurley (G-15808)
Aniiwe Inc ....G 347 683-1891
Brooklyn (G-1511)
Barrera Jose & Maria Co Ltd ....E 212 239-1994
New York (G-8733)
Beth Ward Studios LLC ....F 646 922-7575
New York (G-8769)
Bnns Co Inc ....G 212 302-1844
New York (G-8825)
Carol For Eva Graham Inc ....F 212 889-8686
New York (G-8920)
Carvin French Jewelers Inc ....E 212 755-6474
New York (G-8927)
Catherine Stein Designs Inc ....E 212 840-1188
New York (G-8938)
Ciner Manufacturing Co Inc ....E 212 947-3770
New York (G-9009)
▲ Columbus Trading Corp ....F 212 564-1780
New York (G-9063)
Custom Pins Inc ....G 888 922-9378
Elmsford (G-4406)
Dabby-Reid Ltd ....F 212 356-0040
New York (G-9150)
▼ Ema Jewelry Inc ....D 212 575-8989
New York (G-9355)
Erickson Beamon Ltd ....F 212 643-4810
New York (G-9394)
▲ Eu Design LLC ....G 212 420-7788
New York (G-9416)
Fantasia Jewelry Inc ....E 212 921-9590
New York (G-9471)
Fashion Accents LLC ....F 401 331-6626
New York (G-9474)
Five Star Creations Inc ....E 845 783-1187
Monroe (G-8020)
Formart Corp ....F 212 819-1819
New York (G-9516)
Greenbeads Llc ....G 212 327-2765
New York (G-9673)
Holbrooke Inc ....G 646 397-4674
New York (G-9801)
▲ I Love Accessories Inc ....G 212 239-1875
New York (G-9845)
◆ International Inspirations LLC ....E 212 465-8500
New York (G-9920)
▲ J & H Creations Inc ....E 212 465-0962
New York (G-9952)
J J Creations Inc ....E 718 392-2828
Long Island City (G-7251)
Jay Turoff ....F 718 856-7300
Brooklyn (G-1990)

Jaymar Jewelry Co Inc ....G 212 564-4788
New York (G-9983)
Jill Fagin Enterprises Inc ....G 212 674-9383
New York (G-10003)
Jj Fantasia Inc ....G 212 868-1198
New York (G-10009)
▲ K2 International Corp ....G 212 947-1734
New York (G-10053)
Kenneth J Lane Inc ....F 212 868-1780
New York (G-10090)
▲ Magic Novelty Co Inc ....G 212 304-2777
New York (G-10325)
Marlborough Jewels Inc ....G 718 768-2000
Brooklyn (G-2116)
▲ Mataci Inc ....D 212 502-1899
New York (G-10381)
Maurice Max Inc ....E 212 334-6573
New York (G-10386)
Mel Bernie and Company Inc ....G 212 889-8570
New York (G-10427)
Mercado Global Inc ....G 718 838-9908
Brooklyn (G-2140)
Mwsi Inc ....D 914 347-4200
Hawthorne (G-5819)
▲ Nes Jewelry Inc ....E 212 502-0025
New York (G-10565)
Noir Jewelry LLC ....G 212 465-8500
New York (G-10637)
Pearl Erwin Inc ....G 212 889-7410
New York (G-10777)
Pepe Creations Inc ....F 212 391-1514
New York (G-10797)
Reino Manufacturing Co Inc ....F 914 636-8990
New Rochelle (G-8352)
▲ Rush Gold Manufacturing Ltd ....D 516 781-3155
Bellmore (G-788)
▲ Salmco Jewelry Corp ....F 212 695-8792
New York (G-11120)
Sanoy Inc ....E 212 695-6384
New York (G-11133)
▲ Sarina Accessories LLC ....F 212 239-8106
New York (G-11139)
Shira Accessories Ltd ....F 212 594-4455
New York (G-11216)
Steezys LLC ....G 646 276-5333
New York (G-11353)
▲ Stephan & Company ACC Ltd ....F 212 481-3888
New York (G-11358)
Swarovski North America Ltd ....G 212 695-1502
New York (G-11405)
▲ Toho Shoji (new York) Inc ....F 212 868-7466
New York (G-11505)
▲ Vetta Jewelry Inc ....E 212 564-8250
New York (G-11669)
▲ Vitafede ....F 646 869-4003
New York (G-11694)
Von Musulin Patricia ....G 212 206-8345
New York (G-11704)
Yacoubian Jewelers Inc ....E 212 302-6729
New York (G-11804)

3965 Fasteners, Buttons, Needles & Pins

▲ American Pride Fasteners LLC ....E 631 940-8292
Bay Shore (G-649)
Buttons & Trimcom Inc ....F 212 868-1971
New York (G-8874)
Champion Zipper Corp ....G 212 239-0414
New York (G-8969)
▲ Clo-Shure Intl Inc ....G 212 268-5029
New York (G-9034)
Columbia Button Nailhead Corp ....F 718 386-3414
Brooklyn (G-1676)
Connection Mold Inc ....G 585 458-6463
Rochester (G-13323)
CPI of Falconer Inc ....E 716 664-4444
Falconer (G-4537)
Cw Fasteners & Zippers Corp ....G 212 594-3203
New York (G-9138)
▲ E-Won Industrial Co Inc ....E 212 750-9610
New York (G-9295)
▲ Empire State Metal Pdts Inc ....E 718 847-1617
Richmond Hill (G-13113)
◆ Emsig Manufacturing Corp ....F 718 784-7717
Brooklyn (G-9364)
Emsig Manufacturing Corp ....E 518 828-7301
Hudson (G-6155)
▲ Eu Design LLC ....G 212 420-7788
New York (G-9416)
◆ Hemisphere Novelties Inc ....F 914 378-4100
Yonkers (G-16318)

Ideal Fastener Corporation ....D 212 244-0260
New York (G-9858)
Itc Mfg Group Inc ....F 212 684-3696
New York (G-9947)
Jem Threading Specialties Inc ....G 718 665-3341
Bronx (G-1285)
Kane-M Inc ....G 973 777-2797
New York (G-10065)
Karp Overseas Corporation ....E 718 784-2105
Maspeth (G-7625)
Kenwin Sales Corp ....G 516 933-7553
Deer Park (G-3891)
Kraus & Sons Inc ....F 212 620-0408
New York (G-10137)
M H Stryke Co Inc ....G 631 242-2660
Deer Park (G-3902)
Maxine Denker Inc ....G 212 689-1440
Staten Island (G-14679)
National Die & Button Mould Co ....E 201 939-7800
Brooklyn (G-2189)
Prym Fashion Americas LLC ....D 212 760-9660
New York (G-10917)
Rings Wire Inc ....G 212 741-9779
New York (G-11045)
▲ Riri USA Inc ....E 212 268-3866
New York (G-11046)
Shimada Shoji (hk) Limited ....G 212 268-0465
New York (G-11214)

3991 Brooms & Brushes

Abtex Corporation ....E 315 536-7403
Dresden (G-4034)
Braun Bros Brushes Inc ....G 631 667-2179
Valley Stream (G-15336)
▲ Braun Industries Inc ....F 516 741-6000
Albertson (G-145)
▲ Brushtech (disc) Inc ....F 518 563-8420
Plattsburgh (G-12739)
◆ Colgate-Palmolive Company ....A 212 310-2000
New York (G-9051)
◆ Cpac Inc ....E 585 382-3223
Leicester (G-6908)
E & W Manufacturing Co Inc ....E 516 367-8571
Woodbury (G-16170)
▲ Excel Paint Applicators Inc ....E 347 221-1968
Inwood (G-6291)
▲ FM Brush Co Inc ....C 718 821-5939
Glendale (G-5224)
▲ Full Circle Home LLC ....E 212 432-0001
New York (G-9551)
K & R Allied Inc ....E 718 625-6610
Brooklyn (G-2015)
▲ Kirschner Brush LLC ....F 718 292-1809
Bronx (G-1293)
▲ Linzer Products Corp ....E 631 253-3333
West Babylon (G-15726)
Pan American Roller Inc ....F 914 762-8700
Ossining (G-12407)
◆ Premier Paint Roller Co LLC ....D 718 441-7700
Richmond Hill (G-13119)
Premier Paint Roller Co LLC ....F 718 441-7700
Richmond Hill (G-13120)
Royal Paint Roller Corp ....E 516 367-4370
Woodbury (G-16182)
Teka Fine Line Brushes Inc ....G 718 692-2928
Brooklyn (G-2498)
Volckening Inc ....E 718 748-0294
Brooklyn (G-2568)
▲ Walter R Tucker Entps Ltd ....F 607 467-2866
Deposit (G-4004)
Young & Swartz Inc ....F 716 852-2171
Buffalo (G-3052)

3993 Signs & Advertising Displays

A B C Mc Cleary Sign Co Inc ....F 315 493-3550
Carthage (G-3193)
A M S Sign Designs ....G 631 467-7722
Centereach (G-3249)
◆ Aakron Rule Corp ....C 716 542-5483
Akron (G-15)
ABC Windows and Signs Corp ....F 718 353-6210
College Point (G-3533)
Accurate Signs & Awnings Inc ....F 718 788-0302
Brooklyn (G-1453)
Acme Signs of Baldwinsville ....G 315 638-4865
Baldwinsville (G-539)
Ad Makers Long Island Inc ....F 631 595-9100
Deer Park (G-3829)
Adirondack Sign Company LLC ....F 518 409-7446
Saratoga Springs (G-14162)

Adirondack Sign Perfect Inc ....G..... 518 409-7446
  Saratoga Springs (G-14163)
Adstream America LLC ....E..... 212 804-8498
  New York (G-8465)
All Signs...............G..... 973 736-2113
  Staten Island (G-14618)
Alley Cat Signs Inc ....F..... 631 924-7446
  Middle Island (G-7874)
Allied Decorations Co Inc ....F..... 315 637-0273
  Syracuse (G-14811)
Allied Maker...............F..... 516 200-9145
  Glen Cove (G-5188)
Allstar Graphics Ltd...............E..... 718 740-2240
  Queens Village (G-13017)
Allstate Sign & Plaque Corp ....F..... 631 242-2828
  Deer Park (G-3836)
American Car Signs Inc...............G..... 518 227-1173
  Duanesburg (G-4043)
American Visuals Inc ....G..... 631 694-6104
  Farmingdale (G-4584)
Amsterdam Printing & Litho Inc ....F..... 518 842-6000
  Amsterdam (G-316)
Amsterdam Printing & Litho Inc ....E..... 518 842-6000
  Amsterdam (G-317)
Architectural Sign Group Inc ....G..... 516 326-1800
  Elmont (G-4382)
Aric Signs & Awnings Inc...............G..... 516 350-0409
  Hempstead (G-5832)
Art Parts Signs Inc...............G..... 585 381-2134
  East Rochester (G-4159)
Artscroll Printing Corp...............E..... 212 929-2413
  New York (G-8640)
Asi Sign Systems Inc ....G..... 646 742-1320
  New York (G-8646)
Asi Sign Systems Inc...............G..... 716 775-0104
  Grand Island (G-5325)
Bannerboy Corporation...............G..... 646 691-6524
  Brooklyn (G-1562)
BC Communications Inc ....G..... 631 549-8833
  Huntington Station (G-6240)
Bedford Precision Parts Corp...............E..... 914 241-2211
  Bedford Hills (G-765)
Big Apple Sign Corp...............E..... 631 342-0303
  Islandia (G-6326)
▲ Big Apple Sign Corp ....D..... 212 629-3650
  New York (G-8785)
Bmg Printing and Promotion LLC ....G..... 631 231-9200
  Bohemia (G-982)
Broadway Neon Sign Corp...............F..... 908 241-4177
  Ronkonkoma (G-13918)
Buckeye Corrugated Inc...............D..... 585 924-1600
  Victor (G-15396)
Cab Signs Inc...............E..... 718 479-2424
  Brooklyn (G-1637)
Central Rede Sign Co Inc ....G..... 716 213-0797
  Tonawanda (G-15095)
▲ Chameleon Color Cards Ltd ....D..... 716 625-9452
  Lockport (G-7064)
Chautauqua Sign Co Inc ....G..... 716 665-2222
  Falconer (G-4536)
Checklist Boards Corporation...............G..... 585 586-0152
  Rochester (G-13312)
City Signs Inc...............G..... 718 375-5933
  Brooklyn (G-1667)
Climax Packaging Inc ....C..... 315 376-8000
  Lowville (G-7414)
Clinton Signs Inc...............G..... 585 482-1620
  Webster (G-15636)
Coe Displays Inc ....G..... 718 937-5658
  Long Island City (G-7189)
Colad Group LLC ....D..... 716 961-1776
  Buffalo (G-2703)
Colonial Redi Record Corp ....E..... 718 972-7433
  Brooklyn (G-1675)
Community Products LLC...............G..... 845 658-8351
  Rifton (G-13168)
▲ Creative Solutions Group Inc ....B..... 914 771-4200
  Yonkers (G-16299)
▲ Crown Sign Systems Inc ....F..... 914 375-2118
  Mount Vernon (G-8136)
Custom Display Manufacture ....G..... 516 783-6491
  North Bellmore (G-12018)
▲ Data Display USA Inc ....C..... 631 218-2130
  Holbrook (G-5995)
Decal Makers Inc...............E..... 516 221-7200
  Bellmore (G-781)
Decree Signs & Graphics Inc...............F..... 973 278-3603
  Floral Park (G-4814)
Designplex LLC...............G..... 845 358-6647
  Nyack (G-12140)

Display Marketing Group Inc ....E..... 631 348-4450
  Islandia (G-6330)
Display Presentations Ltd...............D..... 631 951-4050
  Brooklyn (G-1749)
▲ Display Producers Inc ....E..... 718 904-1200
  New Rochelle (G-8327)
Dkm Sales LLC...............E..... 716 893-7777
  Buffalo (G-2730)
▲ DSI Group Inc ....C..... 800 553-2202
  Maspeth (G-7607)
Dura Engraving Corporation ....E..... 718 706-6400
  Long Island City (G-7205)
East End Sign Design Inc...............G..... 631 399-2574
  Mastic (G-7674)
Eastern Concepts Ltd...............F..... 718 472-3377
  Sunnyside (G-14772)
▼ Eastern Metal of Elmira Inc...............D..... 607 734-2295
  Elmira (G-4348)
▼ Edge Display Group Entp Inc ....F..... 631 498-1373
  Bellport (G-798)
Elderlee Incorporated ....C..... 315 789-6670
  Oaks Corners (G-12161)
▲ Eversan Inc ....F..... 315 736-3967
  Whitesboro (G-16080)
Executive Sign Corp ....G..... 212 397-4050
  Cornwall On Hudson (G-3733)
Executive Sign Corporation ....G..... 212 397-4050
  New York (G-9445)
Exhibit Corporation America ....E..... 718 937-2600
  Long Island City (G-7217)
▲ Faster-Form Corp...............D..... 800 327-3676
  New Hartford (G-8240)
Fastsigns ....F..... 518 456-7446
  Albany (G-76)
First Signs Saratoga Springs ....G..... 518 306-4449
  Saratoga Springs (G-14174)
▲ Five Star Prtg & Mailing Svcs ....F..... 212 929-0300
  New York (G-9508)
Flado Enterprises Inc ....G..... 716 668-6400
  Depew (G-3982)
▲ Flair Display Inc ....D..... 718 324-9330
  Bronx (G-1259)
Flexlume Sign Corporation...............G..... 716 884-2020
  Buffalo (G-2755)
Forrest Engraving Co Inc ....F..... 845 228-0200
  New Rochelle (G-8331)
Fortuna Visual Group Inc ....G..... 646 383-8682
  Brooklyn (G-1860)
▼ Fossil Industries Inc ....E..... 631 254-9200
  Deer Park (G-3876)
G I Certified Inc ....G..... 212 397-1945
  New York (G-9558)
Gloede Neon Signs Ltd Inc ....G..... 845 471-4366
  Poughkeepsie (G-12958)
Grant Graphics LLC...............G..... 518 583-2818
  Saratoga Springs (G-14178)
Graphic Signs & Awnings Ltd ....G..... 718 227-6000
  Staten Island (G-14659)
Graphitek Inc...............F..... 518 686-5966
  Hoosick Falls (G-6083)
Greyline Signs Inc...............G..... 716 947-4526
  Derby (G-4005)
Gupp Signs Inc...............G..... 585 244-5070
  Rochester (G-13453)
Hadley Exhibits Inc ....D..... 716 874-3666
  Buffalo (G-2788)
Hanson Sign Screen Prcess Corp ....E..... 716 661-3900
  Falconer (G-4543)
Hermosa Corp ....E..... 315 768-4320
  New York Mills (G-11834)
HI Tech Signs of NY Inc ....G..... 516 794-7880
  East Meadow (G-4136)
Hollywood Advg Banners Inc ....G..... 631 842-3000
  Copiague (G-3659)
Hollywood Banners Inc ....G..... 631 842-3000
  Copiague (G-3660)
Hollywood Signs Inc...............G..... 917 577-7333
  Brooklyn (G-1938)
Hospitality Graphic Systems...............F..... 212 563-9334
  New York (G-9815)
◆ ID Signsystems Inc ....G..... 585 266-5750
  Rochester (G-13473)
Ideal Signs Inc...............G..... 718 292-9196
  Bronx (G-1278)
Image360...............G..... 585 272-1234
  Rochester (G-13476)
Impressive Imprints Inc ....G..... 631 293-6161
  Farmingdale (G-4648)
Innovative Signage Systems Inc ....F..... 315 469-7783
  Nedrow (G-8215)

Island Nameplate Inc ....G..... 845 651-4005
  Florida (G-4825)
▲ Jaf Converters Inc...............E..... 631 842-3131
  Copiague (G-3661)
Jal Signs Inc...............F..... 516 536-7280
  Baldwin (G-531)
Jax Signs and Neon Inc...............G..... 607 727-3420
  Endicott (G-4461)
Jay Turoff...............F..... 718 856-7300
  Brooklyn (G-1990)
Jem Sign Corp...............G..... 516 867-4466
  Hempstead (G-5840)
▲ Jomar Industries Inc...............G..... 845 357-5773
  Airmont (G-13)
Joseph Struhl Co Inc ....G..... 516 741-3660
  New Hyde Park (G-8277)
JP Signs...............G..... 518 569-3907
  Chazy (G-3334)
K & B Stamping Co Inc ....G..... 914 664-8555
  Mount Vernon (G-8154)
▲ Kenan International Trading ....G..... 718 672-4922
  Corona (G-3742)
Kennyetto Graphics Inc ....E..... 518 883-6360
  Gloversville (G-5287)
King Displays Inc ....F..... 212 629-8455
  New York (G-10107)
▲ Kling Magnetics Inc ....E..... 518 392-4000
  Chatham (G-3331)
KP Industries Inc...............F..... 516 679-3161
  North Bellmore (G-12020)
Kraus & Sons Inc ....F..... 212 620-0408
  New York (G-10137)
L I C Screen Printing Inc ....E..... 516 546-7289
  Merrick (G-7858)
L Miller Design Inc...............G..... 631 242-1163
  Deer Park (G-3894)
L S Sign Co Inc...............F..... 718 469-8600
  Ridgewood (G-13149)
▲ Lamar Plastics Packaging Ltd ....D..... 516 378-2500
  Freeport (G-5004)
◆ Lanco Corporation...............E..... 631 231-2300
  Ronkonkoma (G-13964)
Landmark Signs Elec Maint Corp ....F..... 212 262-3699
  New York (G-10170)
Landmark Signs Elec Maint Corp ....E..... 212 354-7551
  New York (G-10171)
Lanza Corp...............G..... 914 937-6360
  Port Chester (G-12824)
▼ Letterama Inc...............G..... 516 349-0800
  West Babylon (G-15725)
Liberty Awnings & Signs Inc...............G..... 347 203-1470
  East Elmhurst (G-4109)
▲ Lifestyle-Trimco ....E..... 718 257-9101
  Brooklyn (G-2069)
Linear Signs Inc ....F..... 631 532-5330
  Lindenhurst (G-6955)
M Santoliquido Corp ....F..... 914 375-6674
  Yonkers (G-16329)
Marigold Signs Inc ....F..... 516 433-7446
  Hicksville (G-5927)
Mastercraft Manufacturing Co ....G..... 718 729-5620
  Long Island City (G-7290)
Mauceri Sign Inc ....F..... 718 656-7700
  Jamaica (G-6458)
Mekanism Inc...............E..... 212 226-2772
  New York (G-10426)
Metropolitan Signs Inc ....F..... 315 638-1448
  Baldwinsville (G-551)
▲ Millennium Signs & Display Inc ....E..... 516 292-8000
  Hempstead (G-5845)
Miller Mohr Display Inc...............G..... 631 941-2769
  East Setauket (G-4181)
Mixture Screen Printing...............G..... 845 561-2857
  Newburgh (G-11873)
Modern Decal Co...............G..... 315 622-2778
  Liverpool (G-7027)
Modulex New York Inc...............G..... 646 742-1320
  New York (G-10490)
Mohawk Sign Systems Inc ....E..... 518 842-5303
  Amsterdam (G-340)
Monasani Signs Inc ....G..... 631 266-2635
  East Northport (G-4150)
Morris Brothers Sign Svc Inc...............G..... 212 675-9130
  New York (G-10504)
Motion Message Inc...............F..... 631 924-9500
  Bellport (G-804)
Movinads & Signs LLC...............G..... 518 378-3000
  Halfmoon (G-5496)
Mr Sign Usa Inc ....F..... 718 218-3321
  Brooklyn (G-2178)

▼ Mystic Display Co Inc ....G....... 718 485-2651
  Brooklyn *(G-2183)*
Nameplate Mfrs of Amer ....E....... 631 752-0055
  Farmingdale *(G-4690)*
Nas Quick Sign Inc ....G....... 716 876-7599
  Buffalo *(G-2879)*
National Advertising & Prtg ....G....... 212 629-7650
  New York *(G-10540)*
National Prfmce Solutions Inc ....D....... 718 833-4767
  Brooklyn *(G-2190)*
Nationwide Exhibitor Svcs Inc ....F....... 631 467-2034
  Central Islip *(G-3285)*
New Art Signs Co Inc ....G....... 718 443-0900
  Glen Head *(G-5210)*
New Kit On The Block ....G....... 631 757-5655
  Bohemia *(G-1051)*
New Style Signs Limited Inc ....F....... 212 242-7848
  New York *(G-10590)*
▲ Newline Products Inc ....C....... 972 881-3318
  New Windsor *(G-8376)*
Noel Assoc ....G....... 516 371-5420
  Inwood *(G-6301)*
Norampac New York City Inc ....C....... 718 340-2100
  Maspeth *(G-7630)*
North Shore Neon Sign Co Inc ....E....... 718 937-4848
  Flushing *(G-4881)*
Northeast Promotional Group In ....G....... 518 793-1024
  South Glens Falls *(G-14515)*
Northeastern Sign Corp ....G....... 315 265-6657
  South Colton *(G-14504)*
Northern Awning & Sign Company ....G....... 315 782-8515
  Watertown *(G-15585)*
▲ Nysco Products LLC ....D....... 718 792-9000
  Hawthorne *(G-5820)*
Olson Sign Company Inc ....G....... 518 370-2118
  Schenectady *(G-14292)*
On The Mark Digital Printing & ....G....... 716 823-3373
  Hamburg *(G-5515)*
▲ Orlandi Inc ....D....... 631 756-0110
  Farmingdale *(G-4698)*
Orlandi Inc ....E....... 631 756-0110
  Farmingdale *(G-4699)*
Outer Image LLC ....G....... 914 420-3097
  Brooklyn *(G-2238)*
Pama Enterprises Inc ....G....... 516 504-6300
  Great Neck *(G-5411)*
Pereira & ODell LLC ....G....... 212 897-1000
  New York *(G-10802)*
Pierrepont Visual Graphics ....G....... 585 305-9672
  Rochester *(G-13624)*
▲ Platinum Sales Promotion Inc ....G....... 718 361-0200
  Long Island City *(G-7327)*
Polyplastic Forms Inc ....E....... 631 249-5011
  Farmingdale *(G-4712)*
Poncio Signs ....G....... 718 543-4851
  Bronx *(G-1339)*
Precision Signscom Inc ....D....... 631 841-7500
  Amityville *(G-304)*
Premier Sign Systems LLC ....G....... 585 235-0390
  Rochester *(G-13640)*
▲ Promotional Development Inc ....D....... 718 485-8550
  Brooklyn *(G-2301)*
Props Displays & Interiors ....F....... 212 620-3840
  New York *(G-10915)*
Quick Sign F X ....F....... 516 249-6531
  Farmingdale *(G-4720)*
Quorum Group LLC ....D....... 585 798-8888
  Medina *(G-7744)*
R & J Displays Inc ....E....... 631 491-3500
  West Babylon *(G-15740)*
Rapp Signs Inc ....F....... 607 656-8167
  Greene *(G-5447)*
Ray Sign Inc ....F....... 518 377-1371
  Schenectady *(G-14298)*
Reflective Image ....G....... 631 477-3368
  Greenport *(G-5457)*
Resonant Legal Media LLC ....D....... 800 781-3591
  New York *(G-11019)*
Rgm Signs Inc ....G....... 718 442-0598
  Staten Island *(G-14703)*
Riverwood Signs By Dandev Desi ....G....... 845 229-0282
  Hyde Park *(G-6274)*
Rome Sign & Display Co ....G....... 315 336-0550
  Rome *(G-13869)*
▲ Royal Promotion Group Inc ....D....... 212 246-3780
  New York *(G-11091)*
Rpf Associates Inc ....G....... 631 462-7446
  Commack *(G-3597)*
▲ Rsquared Ny Inc ....D....... 631 521-8700
  Edgewood *(G-4280)*

Saxton Corporation ....E....... 518 732-7705
  Castleton On Hudson *(G-3204)*
Seifert Graphics Inc ....F....... 315 736-2744
  Oriskany *(G-12394)*
Sellco Industries Inc ....E....... 607 756-7594
  Cortland *(G-3788)*
Seneca Signs LLC ....G....... 315 446-9420
  Syracuse *(G-14993)*
Sign & Signs ....G....... 718 941-6200
  Brooklyn *(G-2407)*
Sign A Rama Inc ....G....... 631 952-3324
  Hauppauge *(G-5764)*
Sign Center Inc ....F....... 212 967-2113
  New York *(G-11232)*
Sign City of New York Inc ....G....... 718 661-1118
  College Point *(G-3564)*
Sign Company ....G....... 212 967-2113
  New York *(G-11233)*
▲ Sign Design Group New York Inc ....F....... 718 392-0779
  Hauppauge *(G-5765)*
Sign Group Inc ....E....... 718 438-7103
  Brooklyn *(G-2408)*
Sign Guys New York City Inc ....G....... 718 414-2310
  West Hempstead *(G-15779)*
Sign Heaven Corp ....G....... 718 499-4423
  Brooklyn *(G-2409)*
Sign Here Enterprises LLC ....G....... 914 328-3111
  Hartsdale *(G-5568)*
Sign Impressions Inc ....G....... 585 723-0420
  Rochester *(G-13729)*
Sign Language Inc ....G....... 585 237-2620
  Perry *(G-12599)*
Sign Men ....G....... 718 227-7446
  Staten Island *(G-14710)*
Sign Studio Inc ....F....... 518 266-0877
  Cohoes *(G-3517)*
Sign Works Incorporated ....G....... 914 592-0700
  Elmsford *(G-4433)*
Sign World Inc ....E....... 212 619-9000
  Brooklyn *(G-2410)*
Signature Industries Inc ....F....... 516 771-8182
  Freeport *(G-5025)*
Signature Name Plate Co Inc ....G....... 585 321-9960
  Rochester *(G-13730)*
Signexpo Enterprises Inc ....F....... 212 925-8585
  New York *(G-11236)*
▲ Signs & Decal Corp ....E....... 718 486-6400
  Brooklyn *(G-2411)*
Signs Inc ....G....... 518 483-4759
  Malone *(G-7491)*
Signs Ink Ltd ....G....... 914 739-9059
  Yorktown Heights *(G-16372)*
Signs of Success Ltd ....F....... 516 295-6000
  Lynbrook *(G-7438)*
Signworks ....G....... 518 745-0700
  South Glens Falls *(G-14518)*
Sizmek Dsp Inc ....F....... 212 594-8888
  New York *(G-11253)*
▲ Smith Graphics Inc ....G....... 631 420-4180
  Farmingdale *(G-4734)*
Snyders Neon Displays Inc ....G....... 518 857-4100
  Colonie *(G-3575)*
Space Sign ....F....... 718 961-1112
  College Point *(G-3565)*
Spanjer Corp ....G....... 347 448-8033
  Long Island City *(G-7361)*
Specialty Signs Co Inc ....F....... 212 243-8521
  New York *(G-11313)*
Spectrum On Broadway ....F....... 718 932-5388
  Woodside *(G-16226)*
Spectrum Signs Inc ....E....... 631 756-1010
  Woodside *(G-16227)*
Speedy Sign A Rama USA Inc ....G....... 516 783-1075
  Bellmore *(G-790)*
Stamps & Signs Online Corp ....G....... 718 218-0050
  Brooklyn *(G-2450)*
Starlite Media LLC ....E....... 212 909-7700
  New York *(G-11351)*
Steel-Brite Ltd ....F....... 631 589-4044
  Oakdale *(G-12156)*
Stepping Stones One Day Signs ....G....... 518 237-5774
  Waterford *(G-15547)*
Stickershopcom Inc ....G....... 631 563-4323
  Bayport *(G-731)*
Strategic Signage Sourcing LLC ....F....... 518 450-1093
  Saratoga Springs *(G-14194)*
Substrate LLC ....E....... 212 913-9600
  Long Island City *(G-7373)*
Suma Industries Inc ....G....... 646 436-5202
  New York *(G-11387)*

Super Neon Light Co Inc ....G....... 718 236-5667
  Brooklyn *(G-2471)*
Swell LLC ....F....... 646 738-8981
  New York *(G-11408)*
T J Signs Unlimited LLC ....E....... 631 273-4800
  Islip *(G-6357)*
▼ Tech Products Inc ....E....... 718 442-4900
  Staten Island *(G-14721)*
◆ Tempo Industries Inc ....G....... 516 334-6900
  Westbury *(G-15929)*
Terrabilt Inc ....G....... 914 341-1500
  Mamaroneck *(G-7524)*
Three Gems Inc ....G....... 516 248-0388
  New Hyde Park *(G-8297)*
Timely Signs Inc ....G....... 516 285-5339
  Elmont *(G-4390)*
Timely Signs of Kingston Inc ....F....... 845 331-8710
  Kingston *(G-6714)*
Tj Signs Unlimited LLC ....G....... 631 273-4800
  Hicksville *(G-5952)*
Todd Walbridge ....G....... 585 254-3018
  Rochester *(G-13768)*
▲ Trans-Lux Corporation ....D....... 800 243-5544
  New York *(G-11533)*
Tru-Art Sign Co Inc ....F....... 718 658-5068
  Jamaica *(G-6482)*
Turoff Tower Graphics Inc ....F....... 718 856-7300
  Brooklyn *(G-2529)*
Ulrich Sign Co Inc ....E....... 716 434-0167
  Lockport *(G-7116)*
Ultimate Signs & Designs Inc ....E....... 516 481-0800
  Hempstead *(G-5851)*
Unilumin North America Inc ....G....... 732 904-2037
  New York *(G-11590)*
Unique Display Mfg Corp ....G....... 516 546-3800
  Freeport *(G-5031)*
United Print Group Inc ....F....... 718 392-4242
  Woodside *(G-16231)*
United Sttes Brnze Sign of Fla ....E....... 516 352-5155
  New Hyde Park *(G-8300)*
Universal 3d Innovation Inc ....F....... 516 837-9423
  Valley Stream *(G-15362)*
Universal Signs and Svc Inc ....E....... 631 446-1121
  Deer Park *(G-3946)*
USA Signs of America Inc ....D....... 631 254-6900
  Deer Park *(G-3948)*
Valle Signs and Awnings ....F....... 516 408-3440
  Copiague *(G-3686)*
Valley Creek Side Inc ....G....... 315 839-5526
  Clayville *(G-3458)*
Vez Inc ....G....... 718 273-7002
  Staten Island *(G-14726)*
Viana Signs Corp ....F....... 516 887-2000
  Oceanside *(G-12197)*
Victory Signs Inc ....G....... 315 762-0220
  Canastota *(G-3160)*
▲ Visual Citi Inc ....C....... 631 482-3030
  Lindenhurst *(G-6985)*
Visual ID Source Inc ....F....... 516 307-9759
  Mineola *(G-8002)*
Visual Impact Graphics Inc ....G....... 585 548-7118
  Batavia *(G-629)*
Vital Signs & Graphics Co Inc ....G....... 518 237-8372
  Cohoes *(G-3519)*
▲ Von Pok & Chang New York Inc ....G....... 212 599-0556
  New York *(G-11705)*
Voss Signs LLC ....E....... 315 682-6418
  Manlius *(G-7550)*
Wedel Sign Company Inc ....G....... 631 727-4577
  Riverhead *(G-13192)*
Westchester Signs Inc ....G....... 914 666-7446
  Mount Kisco *(G-8106)*
Whispr Group Inc ....F....... 212 924-3979
  New York *(G-11750)*
Wings For Wheels Inc ....G....... 914 961-0276
  Yonkers *(G-16357)*
Wizard Equipment Inc ....G....... 315 414-9999
  Syracuse *(G-15028)*
▲ WI Concepts & Production Inc ....E....... 516 565-5151
  Freeport *(G-5032)*
Woodbury Printing Plus + Inc ....G....... 845 928-6610
  Central Valley *(G-3302)*
Yellowpagecitycom ....F....... 585 410-6688
  Rochester *(G-13813)*
Yost Neon Displays Inc ....G....... 716 674-6780
  West Seneca *(G-15856)*
Z-Car-D Corp ....E....... 631 424-2077
  Huntington Station *(G-6267)*

3995 Burial Caskets

Milso Industries Inc ....F......631 234-1133
  Hauppauge *(G-5719)*
North Hudson Woodcraft Corp ....E......315 429-3105
  Dolgeville *(G-4024)*

3996 Linoleum & Hard Surface Floor Coverings, NEC

East To West Architectral Pdts ....G......631 433-9690
  East Northport *(G-4144)*
▲ Engineered Plastics Inc ....E......800 682-2525
  Williamsville *(G-16130)*

3999 Manufacturing Industries, NEC

A & L Asset Management Ltd ....C......718 566-1500
  Brooklyn *(G-1428)*
A & W Metal Works Inc ....F......845 352-2346
  Garnerville *(G-5133)*
A Fire Inc ....G......631 897-9449
  Ronkonkoma *(G-13883)*
A&M Model Makers LLC ....G......626 813-9661
  Macedon *(G-7457)*
Accessible Bath Tech LLC ....F......518 937-1518
  Albany *(G-26)*
Accurate Pnt Powdr Coating Inc ....G......585 235-1650
  Rochester *(G-13201)*
Active Manufacturing Inc ....F......607 775-3162
  Kirkwood *(G-6728)*
Adel Rootstein (usa) Inc ....E......718 499-5650
  Brooklyn *(G-1460)*
Adults and Children With Learn ....E......516 593-8230
  East Rockaway *(G-4170)*
Advanced Assembly Services Inc ....G......716 217-8144
  Lancaster *(G-6789)*
AFP Manufacturing Corp ....E......516 466-6464
  Great Neck *(G-5360)*
▲ Age Manufacturers Inc ....D......718 927-0048
  Brooklyn *(G-1471)*
▲ Aloi Solutions LLC ....E......585 292-0920
  Rochester *(G-13223)*
▲ American Culture Hair Inc ....E......631 242-3142
  Huntington Station *(G-6236)*
Animal Pantry ....G......631 673-3666
  Huntington *(G-6199)*
Anu Industries LLC ....G......201 735-7475
  Brooklyn *(G-1514)*
▲ Arcadia Mfg Group Inc ....E......518 434-6213
  Green Island *(G-5432)*
Arcadia Mfg Group Inc ....G......518 434-6213
  Menands *(G-7840)*
Arnprior Rpid Mfg Slutions Inc ....C......585 617-6301
  Rochester *(G-13247)*
Arnprior Rpid Mfg Slutions Inc ....F......585 617-6301
  Rochester *(G-13248)*
Artemis Studios Inc ....D......718 788-6022
  Brooklyn *(G-1536)*
Ascribe Inc ....E......585 413-0298
  Rochester *(G-13252)*
◆ Astron Candle Manufacturing Co .....G......718 728-3330
  Long Island City *(G-7168)*
Avoomo Power LLC ....F......718 344-0404
  Brooklyn *(G-1553)*
B & R Promotional Products ....G......212 563-0040
  New York *(G-8703)*
B F G Elcpltg and Mfg Co ....F......716 362-0888
  Blasdell *(G-917)*
Balance Enterprises Inc ....G......516 822-3183
  Hicksville *(G-5887)*
Baldwin Ribbon & Stamping Corp ....F......718 335-6700
  Woodside *(G-16196)*
Bee Green Industries Inc ....G......516 334-3525
  Carle Place *(G-3171)*
Best Priced Products Inc ....G......914 345-3800
  Elmsford *(G-4395)*
◆ Betterbee Inc ....F......518 314-0575
  Greenwich *(G-5469)*
Biocontinuum Group Inc ....G......212 406-1060
  New York *(G-8796)*
Blackbox Biometrics Inc ....E......585 329-3399
  Rochester *(G-13271)*
Blanche P Field LLC ....E......212 355-6616
  New York *(G-8809)*
Blinc Group LLC ....F......212 879-2329
  New York *(G-8810)*
◆ Boom LLC ....E......646 218-0752
  New York *(G-8835)*
Brooklyn Industries LLC ....G......718 788-5250
  Brooklyn *(G-1617)*

Bushwick Bottling LLC ....F......929 666-3618
  Brooklyn *(G-1630)*
Callanan Industries Inc ....G......518 382-5354
  Schenectady *(G-14250)*
▲ Candle In The Window Inc ....F......718 852-5743
  Brooklyn *(G-1643)*
Candles By Foster ....G......914 739-9226
  Peekskill *(G-12549)*
▲ Cathedral Candle Co ....D......315 422-9119
  Syracuse *(G-14846)*
▲ Cemecon Inc ....E......607 562-2363
  Horseheads *(G-6118)*
Ceylan & Co LLC ....G......646 858-3022
  New York *(G-8963)*
◆ Christian Dior Perfumes LLC ....E......212 931-2200
  New York *(G-8999)*
Clara Papa ....G......315 733-2660
  Utica *(G-15243)*
Commercial Fabrics Inc ....F......716 694-0641
  North Tonawanda *(G-12062)*
Consolidated Spring LLC ....F......845 391-8855
  Newburgh *(G-11862)*
Copesetic Inc ....E......315 684-7780
  Morrisville *(G-8085)*
Costume Armour Inc ....F......845 534-9120
  Cornwall *(G-3728)*
Creative Models & Prototypes ....G......516 433-6828
  Hicksville *(G-5899)*
Criterion Bell & Specialty ....E......718 788-2600
  Brooklyn *(G-1701)*
◆ Crusader Candle Co Inc ....E......718 625-0005
  Brooklyn *(G-1704)*
Curiously Creative Candles ....F......631 586-1700
  Deer Park *(G-3857)*
D & M Enterprises Incorporated ....G......914 937-6430
  Port Chester *(G-12816)*
D3 Led LLC ....E......917 757-9671
  New York *(G-9149)*
Daves Cbd LLC ....G......917 833-7306
  Brooklyn *(G-1728)*
▲ De Meo Brothers Inc ....G......212 268-1400
  New York *(G-9192)*
Deal To Win Inc ....E......718 609-1165
  Syosset *(G-14784)*
Deva Concepts LLC ....E......212 343-0344
  New York *(G-9212)*
▲ Diane Studios Inc ....D......718 788-6007
  Brooklyn *(G-1740)*
Dolmen ....F......912 596-1537
  Conklin *(G-3623)*
Donorwall Inc ....G......212 766-9670
  New York *(G-9253)*
Dyco Manufacturing LLC ....D......607 324-2030
  Hornell *(G-6105)*
E-Z Global Wholesale Inc ....G......888 769-7888
  Brooklyn *(G-1774)*
▲ Eagle Regalia Co Inc ....F......845 425-2245
  Spring Valley *(G-14567)*
East Penn Manufacturing Co ....G......631 321-7161
  Babylon *(G-519)*
▲ Eastern Feather & Down Corp ....G......718 387-4100
  Brooklyn *(G-1776)*
Egm Mfg Inc ....G......718 782-9800
  Brooklyn *(G-1786)*
Energy Ahead Inc ....G......718 813-7338
  Brooklyn *(G-1804)*
◆ Eser Realty Corp ....E......718 383-0565
  Brooklyn *(G-1811)*
Essex Industries ....G......518 942-6671
  Mineville *(G-8004)*
◆ Essex Manufacturing Inc ....D......212 239-0080
  New York *(G-9404)*
Eton Institute ....F......855 334-3688
  New York *(G-9415)*
Everstone Industries LLC ....E......347 777-8150
  New York *(G-9429)*
▲ Faster-Form Corp ....D......800 327-3676
  New Hartford *(G-8240)*
Federal Sample Card Corp ....D......718 458-1344
  Elmhurst *(G-4334)*
Fingerprint America Inc ....G......518 435-1609
  Albany *(G-77)*
◆ Fish & Crown Ltd ....D......212 707-9603
  New York *(G-9506)*
Five Star Creations Inc ....E......845 783-1187
  Monroe *(G-8020)*
▲ Four Paws Products Ltd ....D......631 436-7421
  Ronkonkoma *(G-13940)*
Freedom Mfg LLC ....F......518 584-0441
  Saratoga Springs *(G-14175)*

Fun Industries of NY ....F......631 845-3805
  Farmingdale *(G-4634)*
▲ Genesis Mannequins USA II Inc .....G......212 505-6600
  New York *(G-9592)*
Givi Inc ....F......212 586-5029
  New York *(G-9616)*
Goldmont Enterprises Inc ....F......212 947-3633
  Middle Village *(G-7878)*
Goodwill Inds of Greater NY ....C......914 621-0781
  Baldwin Place *(G-538)*
Grand Island Animal Hospital ....E......716 773-7645
  Grand Island *(G-5332)*
Grand Visual LLC ....G......912 529-6215
  Brooklyn *(G-1907)*
▲ Gustbuster Ltd ....G......631 391-9000
  Farmingdale *(G-4642)*
Hair Color Research Group Inc ....E......718 445-6026
  Flushing *(G-4858)*
Handmade Frames Inc ....F......718 782-8364
  Brooklyn *(G-1925)*
◆ Hoskie Co Inc ....D......718 628-8672
  Brooklyn *(G-1944)*
Houghton Mifflin Harcourt Co ....G......212 420-5800
  New York *(G-9819)*
Hs Homeworx LLC ....G......646 870-0406
  New York *(G-9830)*
Hudson Eastern Industries Inc ....G......917 295-5818
  Whitestone *(G-16094)*
▼ Identfication Data Imaging LLC ....G......516 484-6500
  Port Washington *(G-12886)*
Ilc Industries Inc ....E......631 567-5600
  Bohemia *(G-1022)*
Image Tech ....F......716 635-0167
  Buffalo *(G-2806)*
Impressart ....F......631 940-9530
  Edgewood *(G-4271)*
Innovative Industries LLC ....E......718 784-7300
  Long Island City *(G-7248)*
Iquit Cig LLC ....G......718 475-1422
  Brooklyn *(G-1969)*
Islip Miniture Golf ....G......631 940-8900
  Bay Shore *(G-684)*
▲ Ivy Enterprises Inc ....B......516 621-9779
  Port Washington *(G-12890)*
◆ J & A Usa Inc ....G......631 243-3336
  Brentwood *(G-1124)*
J T Systematic ....G......607 754-0929
  Endwell *(G-4480)*
Jacobs Juice Corp ....G......646 255-2860
  Brooklyn *(G-1986)*
▲ Jamaica Lamp Corp ....E......718 776-5039
  Queens Village *(G-13023)*
Jason & Jean Products Inc ....F......718 271-8300
  Corona *(G-3741)*
▲ Jenalex Creative Marketing Inc ....G......212 935-2266
  New York *(G-9994)*
JG Innovative Industries Inc ....G......718 784-7300
  Kew Gardens *(G-6667)*
Jimco Lamp & Manufacturing Co ....G......631 218-2152
  Islip *(G-6353)*
John Gailer Inc ....E......212 243-5662
  Long Island City *(G-7254)*
John Prior ....G......516 520-9801
  East Meadow *(G-4138)*
Joya LLC ....F......718 852-6979
  Brooklyn *(G-2005)*
Just Right Carbines LLC ....G......585 261-5331
  Canandaigua *(G-3135)*
K Dymond Industries Inc ....F......631 828-0826
  Medford *(G-7715)*
Kafko (us) Corp ....G......877 721-7665
  Latham *(G-6861)*
Kaylon Industries LLC ....G......315 303-2119
  Baldwinsville *(G-550)*
Kelly Foundry & Machine Co ....E......315 732-8313
  Utica *(G-15279)*
Ketchum Manufacturing Co Inc ....F......518 696-3331
  Lake Luzerne *(G-6765)*
Kevco Industries ....G......845 255-7407
  New Paltz *(G-8308)*
King Displays Inc ....F......212 629-8455
  New York *(G-10107)*
▲ Kittywalk Systems Inc ....G......516 627-8418
  Port Washington *(G-12895)*
▲ Kkw Corp ....E......631 589-5454
  Sayville *(G-14228)*
▲ Lab-Aids Inc ....E......631 737-1133
  Ronkonkoma *(G-13962)*
Lemetric Hair Centers Inc ....F......212 986-5620
  New York *(G-10194)*

Lemon Brothers Foundation Inc ....F 347 920-2749
Bronx (G-1300)
▲ Leo D Bernstein & Sons Inc ....E 212 337-9578
New York (G-10198)
Liberty Displays Inc ....E 716 743-1757
Amherst (G-229)
▲ Lifestyle-Trimco ....E 718 257-9101
Brooklyn (G-2069)
Lois Kitchen LLC ....G 216 308-9335
New York (G-10244)
Lux Mundi Corp ....G 631 244-4596
Bohemia (G-1040)
M & S Schmalberg Inc ....F 212 244-2090
New York (G-10292)
M and J Hair Center Inc ....F 516 872-1010
Garden City (G-5106)
Mack Studios Displays Inc ....E 315 252-7542
Auburn (G-484)
Madison Mfg & Mch Inc ....G 315 922-4476
Erieville (G-4484)
Malouf Colette Inc ....F 212 941-9588
New York (G-10338)
▲ Meisel-Peskin Co Inc ....D 718 497-1840
Brooklyn (G-2135)
▲ Mgd Brands Inc ....E 516 545-0150
Plainview (G-12702)
Mission Crane Service Inc ....D 718 937-3333
Long Island City (G-7297)
▲ Mitco Manufacturing ....G 516 745-9236
Garden City (G-5110)
Mitten Manufacturing Inc ....F 315 437-7564
Syracuse (G-14945)
▲ Moti Inc ....F 718 436-4280
Brooklyn (G-2172)
▲ Muench-Kreuzer Candle Company ..D 315 471-4515
Syracuse (G-14947)
Nationwide Exhibitor Svcs Inc ....F 631 467-2034
Central Islip (G-3285)
Nitro Manufacturing LLC ....F 716 646-9900
Hamburg (G-5514)
◆ Northast Ctr For Bekeeping LLC ....F 800 632-3379
Greenwich (G-5474)
◆ Northern Lights Entps Inc ....C 800 836-8797
Wellsville (G-15673)
Northern New York Rural ....G 518 891-9460
Saranac Lake (G-14159)
Nubian Heritage ....G 631 265-3551
Hauppauge (G-5729)
Ogd V-Hvac Inc ....E 315 858-1002
Van Hornesville (G-15363)
▲ Ohserase Manufacturing LLC ....E 518 358-9309
Akwesasne (G-25)
▲ Ohserase Manufacturing LLC ....G 518 358-9309
Hogansburg (G-5981)
Oledworks LLC ....E 585 287-6802
Rochester (G-13589)
Omicron Technologies Inc ....E 631 434-7697
Holbrook (G-6015)
Oriskany Manufacturing LLC ....F 315 732-4962
Yorkville (G-16377)
▲ Orlandi Inc ....D 631 756-0110
Farmingdale (G-4698)
Orlandi Inc ....E 631 756-0110
Farmingdale (G-4699)
Oso Industries Inc ....G 917 709-2050
Brooklyn (G-2237)
◆ Our Own Candle Company Inc ....F 716 769-5000
Findley Lake (G-4795)
◆ P S Pibbs Inc ....D 718 445-8046
Flushing (G-4882)
Paratus Industries Inc ....E 716 826-2000
Orchard Park (G-12371)
PCI Industries Corp ....E 914 662-2700
Mount Vernon (G-8168)
Performance Precision Mfg LLC ....G 518 993-3033
Fort Plain (G-4947)
Pom Industries LLC ....G 800 695-4791
New York (G-10864)
Premium Assure Inc ....G 605 252-9999
Brooklyn (G-2280)
◆ Production Resource Group LLC ....D 877 774-7088
Armonk (G-401)
Production Resource Group LLC ....E 845 567-5700
New Windsor (G-8378)
▲ Promotional Development Inc ....D 718 485-8550
Brooklyn (G-2301)
Props Displays & Interiors ....F 212 620-3840
New York (G-10915)
Pyrotek Incorporated ....E 716 731-3221
Sanborn (G-14148)
Qps Die Cutters Finishers Corp ....E 718 966-1811
Staten Island (G-14695)
Qualbuys LLC ....G 855 884-3274
Syosset (G-14800)
Quality Candle Mfg Co Inc ....F 631 842-8475
Copiague (G-3672)
Quest Manufacturing Inc ....E 716 312-8000
Hamburg (G-5519)
▲ R V Dow Enterprises Inc ....F 585 454-5862
Rochester (G-13667)
Rave Inc ....D 716 695-1110
North Tonawanda (G-12084)
Ray Gold Shade Inc ....F 718 377-8892
Brooklyn (G-2329)
Rockwell Video Solutions LLC ....F 631 745-0582
Southampton (G-14536)
Rutcarele Inc ....G 347 830-5353
Corona (G-3748)
Ryers Creek Corp ....E 607 523-6617
Corning (G-3720)
S & H Enterprises Inc ....G 888 323-8755
Queensbury (G-13055)
S B Manufacturing LLC ....F 845 352-3700
Monsey (G-8045)
Saakshi Inc ....G 315 475-3988
Syracuse (G-14982)
Sayeda Manufacturing Corp ....F 631 345-2525
Medford (G-7723)
▲ Select Industries New York Inc ....F 800 723-5333
New York (G-11185)
Shake-N-Go Fashion Inc ....E 516 944-7777
Port Washington (G-12924)
◆ Shake-N-Go Fashion Inc ....C 516 944-7777
Port Washington (G-12925)
Shenzhen Xnhdingsheng Tech Ltd ....E 510 506-5753
Flushing (G-4892)
▲ Sherwood Group Inc ....G 240 731-8573
New York (G-11212)
Shyam Ahuja Limited ....G 212 644-5910
New York (G-11221)
▲ Siegel & Stockman Inc ....G 212 633-1508
New York (G-11224)
▲ Simcha Candle Co Inc ....G 845 783-0406
New Windsor (G-8383)
Skaffles Group LLC ....F 212 944-9494
New York (G-11256)
▲ Soggy Doggy Productions LLC ....G 877 504-4811
Larchmont (G-6843)
Sonaal Industries Inc ....G 718 383-3860
Brooklyn (G-2441)
◆ Spartan Brands Inc ....F 212 340-0320
New York (G-11311)
Specialists Ltd ....F 212 941-7696
Ridgewood (G-13161)
Spectrum Brands Inc ....B 631 232-1200
Hauppauge (G-5771)
St Killians America Inc ....G 917 648-4351
Valley Cottage (G-15324)
▲ Star Desk Pad Co Inc ....E 914 963-9400
Yonkers (G-16350)
Stasi Industries Inc ....G 516 334-2742
Old Bethpage (G-12220)
▲ Steeldeck Ny Inc ....F 718 599-3700
Brooklyn (G-2457)
Stiegelbauer Associates Inc ....E 718 624-0835
Brooklyn (G-2461)
Swift Multigraphics LLC ....G 585 442-8000
Rochester (G-13752)
▲ Tactica International Inc ....E 212 575-0500
New York (G-11423)
Talisman Industries LLC ....G 908 433-7116
New York (G-11426)
Techgrass ....F 646 719-2000
New York (G-11445)
▲ Tent and Table Com LLC ....F 716 570-0258
Buffalo (G-3006)
Thomas F Egan ....E 607 669-4822
Binghamton (G-913)
▲ Thompson Ferrier LLC ....G 212 244-2212
New York (G-11473)
Tii Industries Inc ....F 631 789-5000
Copiague (G-3683)
Tiki Industries Inc ....G 516 779-3629
Riverhead (G-13190)
Toho Company Limited ....G 212 391-9058
New York (G-11504)
▲ Topoo Industries Incorporated ....G 718 331-3755
Brooklyn (G-2511)
Trendsformers Ltd Liability Co ....G 888 700-2423
New York (G-11537)
▼ Tri-Force Sales LLC ....E 732 261-5507
New York (G-11538)
▲ Tri-Plex Packaging Corporation ....E 212 481-6070
New York (G-11539)
Trove Inc ....F 212 268-2046
Brooklyn (G-2525)
▲ TV Guilfoil & Associates Inc ....G 315 453-0920
Syracuse (G-15016)
Ubees Inc ....F 916 505-8470
New York (G-11573)
▲ Unique Petz LLC ....E 212 714-1800
New York (G-11595)
▲ Unistel LLC ....D 585 341-4600
Webster (G-15660)
Unlimited Industries Inc ....G 631 665-5800
Deer Park (G-3947)
V Technical Textiles Inc ....G 315 597-1674
Palmyra (G-12494)
▲ Water Splash Inc ....G 800 936-3430
Champlain (G-3321)
Wave Float Rooms LLC ....G 844 356-2876
Clarence (G-3443)
Woodfalls Industries ....F 518 236-7201
Plattsburgh (G-12792)
▲ Zip-Jack Industries Ltd ....E 914 592-2000
Tarrytown (G-15064)
Zmz Mfg Inc ....G 518 234-4336
Warnerville (G-15502)

73 BUSINESS SERVICES

7372 Prepackaged Software

2k Inc ....G 646 536-3007
New York (G-8398)
30dc Inc ....F 212 962-4400
New York (G-8399)
30dc Inc ....F 212 962-4400
New York (G-8400)
A K A Computer Consulting Inc ....G 718 351-5200
Staten Island (G-14613)
A2ia Corp ....G 917 237-0390
New York (G-8421)
Aarfid LLC ....G 716 992-3999
Eden (G-4253)
Abacus Labs Inc ....E 917 426-6642
New York (G-8424)
Abel Noser Solutions LLC ....E 646 432-4000
New York (G-8428)
Ableton Inc ....G 646 723-4586
New York (G-8432)
Accela Inc ....F 631 563-5005
Ronkonkoma (G-13884)
Accelify Solutions LLC ....E 888 922-2354
New York (G-8439)
Adfin Solutions Inc ....F 650 464-0742
New York (G-8457)
Adgorithmics Inc ....G 646 277-8728
New York (G-8459)
Adl Data Systems Inc ....E 914 591-1800
Elmsford (G-4392)
Adobe Inc ....E 212 471-0904
New York (G-8461)
Adobe Systems Inc ....E 212 471-0904
New York (G-8462)
Adobe Systems Incorporated ....C 212 592-1400
New York (G-8463)
Adtech Us Inc ....C 212 402-4840
New York (G-8466)
Advanced Cmpt Sftwr Consulting ....G 718 300-3577
Bronx (G-1198)
▲ Advanced Comfort Systems Inc ....F 518 884-8444
Ballston Spa (G-566)
Advanced Cyber Security Corp ....E 866 417-9155
Bohemia (G-966)
Agrinetix Cmpt Systems LLC ....F 877 978-5477
Henrietta (G-5853)
Ahmazing Boutique Inc ....G 631 828-1474
Port Jeff STA (G-12832)
Aimsun Inc ....G 917 267-8534
New York (G-8501)
Altana Technologies Inc ....G 516 263-0633
Brooklyn (G-1493)
Amcom Software Inc ....G 212 951-7600
New York (G-8537)
Amenity Analytics Inc ....E 646 786-8316
New York (G-8538)
American Ctr For Edmocracy LLC ....G 716 803-1118
Cheektowaga (G-3338)
Amplience Inc ....G 917 410-7189
New York (G-8567)

◆ Amplify Education Inc	B	212 213-8177	Brooklyn (G-1509)
Andigo New Media Inc	G	212 727-8445	New York (G-8577)
Anju Sylogent LLC	F	480 326-2358	New York (G-8591)
Ansa Systems of USA Inc	G	718 835-3743	Valley Stream (G-15333)
Answermgmt LLC	G	914 318-1301	Albany (G-41)
Appfigures Inc	F	212 343-7900	New York (G-8609)
Appguard Inc	F	703 786-8884	New York (G-8610)
Application Resources Inc	G	516 636-6200	Great Neck (G-5365)
Application Security Inc	D	212 912-4100	New York (G-8611)
Apprenda Inc	D	518 383-2130	Troy (G-15163)
Appsbidder Inc	G	917 880-4269	Brooklyn (G-1521)
APS Enterprise Software Inc	E	631 784-7720	Huntington (G-6200)
Articulate Global Inc	C	800 861-4880	New York (G-8634)
Arumai Technologies Inc	F	914 217-0038	Armonk (G-395)
Asite LLC	D	203 545-3089	New York (G-8648)
Aspen Research Group Ltd	G	212 425-9588	New York (G-8651)
Assessment Technologies Inc	G	646 530-8666	New York (G-8653)
AT&T Corp	F	212 317-7048	New York (G-8659)
Atomic Information Systems	E	716 713-5402	Unadilla (G-15221)
Attachmate Corporation	G	646 704-0042	New York (G-8674)
Augury Inc	E	866 432-0976	New York (G-8677)
Automated & MGT Solutions LLC	G	518 833-0315	East Greenbush (G-4113)
Automated Office Systems Inc	F	516 396-5555	Valley Stream (G-15334)
Avalanche Studios New York Inc	D	212 993-6447	New York (G-8685)
AVM Software Inc	F	646 381-2468	New York (G-8694)
Axiom Software Ltd	F	914 769-8800	Valhalla (G-15302)
Aycan Medical Systems LLC	F	585 271-3078	Rochester (G-13255)
Aydata Management LLC	G	585 271-6133	Rochester (G-13256)
Ayehu Inc	G	408 930-5823	New York (G-8699)
B601 V2 Inc	G	646 391-6431	New York (G-8709)
Base Systems Inc	G	845 278-1991	Brewster (G-1142)
Bespoke Software Inc	F	518 618-0746	Albany (G-48)
Beyondly Inc	E	646 658-3665	New York (G-8774)
Big Data Bizviz LLC	G	716 803-2367	West Seneca (G-15844)
Big White Wall Holding Inc	F	917 281-2649	New York (G-8788)
Bigwood Systems Inc	G	607 257-0915	Ithaca (G-6366)
Billing Blocks Inc	F	718 442-5006	Staten Island (G-14626)
Birdsigns Inc	G	201 388-7613	New York (G-8800)
Blue Wolf Group LLC	D	866 455-9653	New York (G-8821)
Bluebird Transportation LLC	F	716 395-0000	Williamsville (G-16123)
Boeing Digital Solutions Inc	G	212 478-1200	New York (G-8830)
Boulevard Arts Inc	G	917 968-8693	New York (G-8840)
Brainpop LLC	E	212 574-6017	New York (G-8845)
Brainworks Software Dev Corp	E	631 563-5000	Sayville (G-14223)
Braze Inc	D	504 327-7269	New York (G-8849)

Brigadoon Software Inc	G	845 624-0909	Nanuet (G-8196)
Brightidea Incorporated	D	212 594-4500	New York (G-8853)
Broadway Technology LLC	E	646 912-6450	New York (G-8859)
Bull Street LLC	G	212 495-9855	New York (G-8867)
Buncee LLC	F	631 591-1390	Speonk (G-14561)
Business Integrity Inc	G	718 238-2008	New York (G-8872)
Business Management Systems	F	914 245-8558	Brooklyn (G-1633)
Byte Consulting Inc	G	646 500-8606	New York (G-8880)
C S I G Inc	G	845 383-3800	Kingston (G-6682)
Ca Inc	A	800 225-5224	New York (G-8882)
Ca Inc	G	800 225-5224	Islandia (G-6327)
California US Holdings Inc	A	212 726-6500	New York (G-8890)
Callaway Digital Arts Inc	E	212 675-3050	New York (G-8893)
Calypso Technology Inc	E	212 905-0735	New York (G-8895)
Caminus Corporation	D	212 515-3600	New York (G-8898)
Candex Solutions Inc	G	215 650-3214	New York (G-8902)
Capital Programs Inc	G	212 842-4640	New York (G-8914)
Careconnector	G	919 360-2987	Brooklyn (G-1648)
Catalyst Group Inc	G	212 243-7777	New York (G-8933)
Catch Ventures Inc	F	347 620-4351	New York (G-8936)
Catholic News Publishing Co	F	914 632-7771	Mamaroneck (G-7501)
Cbord Group Inc	C	607 257-2410	Ithaca (G-6375)
Cdml Computer Services Ltd	G	718 428-9063	Fresh Meadows (G-5038)
Cegid Corporation	F	212 757-9038	New York (G-8941)
Ceipal LLC	G	585 351-2934	Rochester (G-13302)
Ceipal LLC	G	585 584-1316	Rochester (G-13303)
Celonis Inc	G	941 615-9670	Brooklyn (G-1657)
Celonis Inc	G	973 652-8821	New York (G-8943)
Ceros Inc	E	347 744-9250	New York (G-8962)
Cgi Technologies Solutions Inc	F	212 682-7411	New York (G-8965)
Chequedcom Inc	E	888 412-0699	Saratoga Springs (G-14169)
Chronicles Systems Inc	G	516 992-2553	North Baldwin (G-12003)
Cinch Technologies Inc	G	212 266-0022	New York (G-9005)
Cinedigm Software	G	212 206-9001	New York (G-9008)
Citic Intl (usa) Travel Inc	G	718 888-9577	Flushing (G-4844)
Classroom Inc	E	212 545-8400	New York (G-9028)
▲ Clayton Dubilier & Rice Fun	E	212 407-5200	New York (G-9029)
Clearview Social Inc	G	801 414-7675	Buffalo (G-2698)
Clever Goats Media LLC	G	917 512-0340	New York (G-9031)
Cloud Rock Group LLC	G	516 967-6023	Roslyn (G-14040)
Cloudscale365 Inc	G	888 608-6245	Jericho (G-6574)
Cloudsense Inc	G	917 880-6195	New York (G-9037)
Cmnty Corporation	G	646 712-9949	New York (G-9041)
Coalition On Positive Health	F	212 633-2500	New York (G-9044)
Cognotion Inc	G	347 692-0640	New York (G-9049)

Commercehub Inc	F	518 810-0700	Albany (G-68)
Compelld Inc	G	917 494-4462	New York (G-9072)
Comprehensive Dental Tech	G	607 467-4456	Hancock (G-5536)
Condeco Software Inc	E	408 508-7330	New York (G-9080)
Confiant Inc	F	646 397-4198	New York (G-9082)
Construction Technology Inc	E	914 747-8900	Chappaqua (G-3323)
Contactive Inc	E	646 476-9059	New York (G-9089)
Continuity Software Inc	E	646 216-8628	New York (G-9091)
Coocoo SMS Inc	F	646 459-4260	Huntington (G-6203)
Cordis Solutions Inc	F	917 909-2002	New York (G-9102)
Cross Border Transactions LLC	F	646 767-7342	Tarrytown (G-15042)
Crunched Inc	G	415 484-9909	New York (G-9125)
CTI Software Inc	G	631 253-3550	Deer Park (G-3856)
Cuffs Planning & Models Ltd	G	914 632-1883	New Rochelle (G-8325)
Cultureiq Inc	G	212 755-8633	New York (G-9132)
Curaegis Technologies Inc	E	585 254-1100	Rochester (G-13333)
Cureatr Inc	G	212 203-3927	New York (G-9133)
Curemdcom Inc	G	212 509-6200	New York (G-9134)
Customshow Inc	G	800 255-5303	New York (G-9137)
Cybersports Inc	G	315 737-7150	Utica (G-15250)
Dakota Software Corporation	G	216 765-7100	Victor (G-15403)
Dartcom Incorporated	G	315 790-5456	New Hartford (G-8238)
Dashlane Inc	E	212 596-7510	New York (G-9172)
Data Implementation Inc	G	212 979-2015	New York (G-9173)
Datadog Inc	C	866 329-4466	New York (G-9174)
Davel Systems Inc	G	718 382-6024	Brooklyn (G-1727)
Dbase LLC	G	607 729-0234	Binghamton (G-871)
Deephaven Data Labs LLC	G	855 828-8445	New York (G-9194)
Defran Systems Inc	E	212 727-8342	New York (G-9196)
Deniz Information Systems	G	212 750-5199	New York (G-9202)
Digital Associates LLC	G	631 983-6075	Smithtown (G-14475)
Diligent Board Member Svcs LLC	E	212 741-8181	New York (G-9228)
Diligent Corporation	E	212 741-8181	New York (G-9229)
Document Strategies LLC	F	585 506-9000	Rochester (G-13353)
▲ Docuware Corporation	D	845 563-9045	New Windsor (G-8365)
Dow Jones & Company Inc	E	212 597-5983	New York (G-9259)
Dropcar Operating Company Inc	G	646 342-1595	New York (G-9272)
Dwnld Inc	E	484 483-6572	New York (G-9286)
Dynamic Applications Inc	G	518 283-4654	Troy (G-15167)
E H Hurwitz & Associates	G	718 884-3766	Bronx (G-1248)
Eastnets Americas Corp	F	212 631-0666	New York (G-9307)
Easy Analytic Software Inc	G	718 740-7930	Flushing (G-4849)
Ebeling Associates Inc	F	518 688-8700	Halfmoon (G-5492)
Ebrevia Inc	E	203 870-3000	New York (G-9312)
Eccella Corporation	G	718 612-0451	New York (G-9313)

S I C

Econometric Software Inc ....G 516 938-5254
Plainview **(G-12682)**

Educational Networks Inc ....G 866 526-0200
New York **(G-9324)**

Efront Financial Solutions Inc ....E 212 220-0660
New York **(G-9326)**

Eft Analytics Inc ....G 212 290-2300
New York **(G-9327)**

Electronic Arts Inc ....G 212 672-0722
New York **(G-9335)**

Elepath Inc ....G 347 417-4975
Brooklyn **(G-1795)**

Elevondata Labs Inc ....E 470 222-5438
New York **(G-9338)**

Elodina Inc ....G 646 402-5202
New York **(G-9351)**

Emblaze Systems Inc ....C 212 371-1100
New York **(G-9358)**

Empire Innovation Group LLC ....F 716 852-5000
Buffalo **(G-2744)**

Empirical Resolution Inc ....F 510 671-0222
New York **(G-9362)**

Emx Digital LLC ....G 212 792-6810
New York **(G-9366)**

Endava Inc ....F 212 920-7240
New York **(G-9369)**

English Computer Consulting ....G 212 764-1717
New York **(G-9378)**

Enterprise Tech Group Inc ....F 914 588-0327
New Rochelle **(G-8328)**

Equilend Holdings LLC ....E 212 901-2200
New York **(G-9389)**

Ert Software Inc ....G 845 358-5721
Blauvelt **(G-928)**

Evocate Media LLC ....F 646 361-3014
New York **(G-9430)**

Ex El Enterprises Ltd ....F 212 489-4500
New York **(G-9434)**

Exact Solutions Inc ....F 212 707-8627
New York **(G-9437)**

Exchange My Mail Inc ....F 516 605-1835
Jericho **(G-6579)**

Express Checkout LLC ....G 646 512-2068
New York **(G-9449)**

EZ Newsletter LLC ....F 412 943-7777
Brooklyn **(G-1825)**

EZ Systems US Inc ....C 929 295-0699
Brooklyn **(G-1826)**

F R A M Technologies Inc ....G 718 338-6230
Brooklyn **(G-1827)**

F-O-R Software LLC ....F 212 231-9506
New York **(G-9457)**

F-O-R Software LLC ....E 914 220-8800
White Plains **(G-16005)**

Fastnet Software Intl Inc ....F 888 740-7790
East Northport **(G-4145)**

Fatwire Corporation ....E 516 247-4500
Mineola **(G-7975)**

Fidelus Technologies LLC ....D 212 616-7800
New York **(G-9489)**

Fidesa US Corporation ....B 212 269-9000
New York **(G-9490)**

Filestream Inc ....F 516 759-4100
Locust Valley **(G-7124)**

Financial Technologies 360 Inc ....G 646 588-8853
Whitestone **(G-16093)**

Findmine Inc ....F 925 787-6181
New York **(G-9493)**

Flextrade Systems Inc ....C 516 627-8993
Great Neck **(G-5389)**

Flogic Inc ....F 914 478-1352
Hastings On Hudson **(G-5572)**

Formats Unlimited Inc ....F 631 249-9200
Deer Park **(G-3875)**

Frazer Computing Inc ....G 315 379-3500
Canton **(G-3166)**

▼ Freshop Inc ....E 585 738-6035
Rochester **(G-13424)**

Fruit St Hlth Pub Benefit Corp ....G 347 960-6400
New York **(G-9545)**

Fuel Data Systems Inc ....G 800 447-7870
Middletown **(G-7909)**

Galaxy Software LLC ....G 631 244-8405
Oakdale **(G-12151)**

Gameclub Inc ....G 415 359-5742
New York **(G-9570)**

Games For Change Inc ....G 212 242-4922
New York **(G-9571)**

Geoweb3d Inc ....F 607 323-1114
Vestal **(G-15378)**

Gifts Software Inc ....E 904 438-6000
New York **(G-9608)**

◆ Glitch Inc ....G 866 364-2733
New York **(G-9621)**

Glitnir Ticketing Inc ....G 516 390-5168
Levittown **(G-6915)**

Global Applctions Solution LLC ....G 212 741-9595
New York **(G-9624)**

Globalquest Solutions Inc ....F 716 601-3524
Buffalo **(G-2777)**

Grantoo LLC ....G 646 356-0460
New York **(G-9662)**

Great Dane Parent LLC ....G 518 810-0700
Albany **(G-81)**

Gresham Technologies (us) Inc ....F 646 943-5955
New York **(G-9674)**

Group Commerce Inc ....F 646 346-0598
New York **(G-9684)**

Hailo Network Usa Inc ....G 646 561-8552
New York **(G-9709)**

Hallmark Hlth Care Sltions LLC ....F 516 513-0959
Hauppauge **(G-5666)**

Happy Software LLC ....G 518 584-4668
Saratoga Springs **(G-14181)**

Health Care Compliance ....F 516 478-4100
Jericho **(G-6582)**

Healthix Inc ....F 877 695-4749
New York **(G-9741)**

Heineck Associates Inc ....G 631 207-2347
Bellport **(G-800)**

High Performance Sftwr USA Inc ....E 866 616-4958
Valley Stream **(G-15343)**

Hinge Inc ....F 214 576-9352
New York **(G-9790)**

Hopscotch Technologies Inc ....G 313 408-4285
Brooklyn **(G-1943)**

Hourglass Interactive LLC ....F 954 254-2853
New York **(G-9823)**

Hovee Inc ....F 646 249-6200
New York **(G-9827)**

Hudson Software Corporation ....E 914 773-0400
Elmsford **(G-4410)**

Human Condition Safety Inc ....F 646 867-0644
New York **(G-9836)**

Hvr Mso LLC ....G 833 345-6974
Poughkeepsie **(G-12962)**

Hydrogen Technology Corp ....E 800 315-9554
New York **(G-9842)**

Hyperlaw Inc ....F 212 873-6982
New York **(G-9843)**

IAC Search LLC ....E 212 314-7300
New York **(G-9850)**

Iac/Interactivecorp ....A 212 314-7300
New York **(G-9851)**

Igambit Inc ....G 631 670-6777
Smithtown **(G-14479)**

Incentivate Health LLC ....G 518 469-8491
Saratoga Springs **(G-14183)**

Incycle Software Corp ....F 212 626-2608
New York **(G-9877)**

Indegy Inc ....G 866 801-5394
New York **(G-9878)**

Infinity Augmented Reality Inc ....G 917 677-2084
New York **(G-9884)**

Info Quick Solutions ....E 315 463-1400
Liverpool **(G-7015)**

▲ Infobase Holdings Inc ....D 212 967-8800
New York **(G-9886)**

Infobase Publishing Company ....G 212 967-8800
New York **(G-9887)**

Informa Solutions Inc ....E 516 543-3733
New York **(G-9891)**

Informatica LLC ....F 212 845-7650
New York **(G-9893)**

Informerly Inc ....G 646 238-7137
New York **(G-9894)**

Innofun Digital Entrmt LLC ....F 347 708-0078
New York **(G-9896)**

Innovation MGT Group Inc ....F 800 889-0987
Shirley **(G-14422)**

Innroad Inc ....E 631 458-1437
New York **(G-9898)**

Inprotopia Corporation ....F 917 338-7501
New York **(G-9901)**

Insight Unlimited Inc ....G 914 861-2090
Chappaqua **(G-3325)**

Insight Venture Partners IV ....C 212 230-9200
New York **(G-9902)**

Inspired Entertainment Inc ....F 646 565-3861
New York **(G-9903)**

INTEL Corporation ....D 408 765-8080
Getzville **(G-5177)**

International Bus Mchs Corp ....E 914 499-2000
Armonk **(G-398)**

International Identity LLC ....G 787 864-0379
Brooklyn **(G-1965)**

International MGT Netwrk ....F 646 401-0032
New York **(G-9921)**

Internodal International Inc ....E 631 765-0037
Southold **(G-14544)**

Intralinks Holdings Inc ....E 212 543-7700
New York **(G-9930)**

Intraworlds Inc ....G 631 602-5333
New York **(G-9931)**

Inturn ....G 212 639-9675
New York **(G-9934)**

Invision Inc ....G 212 557-5554
New York **(G-9937)**

Ipsidy Inc ....F 516 274-8700
Long Beach **(G-7138)**

Irv Inc ....E 212 334-4507
New York **(G-9944)**

Ivalua Inc ....F 650 930-9710
Brooklyn **(G-1975)**

J9 Technologies Inc ....E 412 586-5038
New York **(G-9959)**

Joseph A Filippazzo Software ....G 718 987-1626
Staten Island **(G-14671)**

Jumprope Inc ....G 347 927-5867
New York **(G-10041)**

Jvl Ventures LLC ....D 212 365-7555
New York **(G-10050)**

Kaazing Corporation ....E 212 572-4859
New York **(G-10054)**

Kaseya US LLC ....F 415 694-5700
New York **(G-10072)**

Kasisto Inc ....E 917 734-4750
New York **(G-10073)**

Kastor Consulting Inc ....G 718 224-9109
Bayside **(G-739)**

Keynote Systems Corporation ....G 716 564-1332
Buffalo **(G-2833)**

Kik Us Inc ....F 519 505-7616
New York **(G-10099)**

Kindling Inc ....F 212 400-6296
New York **(G-10105)**

Kitcheco Inc ....G 917 388-7479
New York **(G-10110)**

▲ Knoa Software Inc ....E 212 807-9608
New York **(G-10117)**

Kronos Incorporated ....E 518 459-5545
Albany **(G-96)**

Krux Digital Inc ....F 646 476-6261
New York **(G-10140)**

Kryon Systems Inc ....C 800 618-4318
New York **(G-10141)**

Latchable Inc ....E 917 338-3915
New York **(G-10176)**

Learningateway LLC ....E 212 920-7969
Brooklyn **(G-2055)**

Liftforward Inc ....E 917 693-4993
New York **(G-10215)**

Lighf Inc ....G 917 803-3323
Katonah **(G-6634)**

Lincdoc LLC ....G 585 563-1669
East Rochester **(G-4167)**

Live Up Top Inc ....F 866 333-1332
New York **(G-10232)**

Live Vote II Inc ....G 646 343-9053
New York **(G-10233)**

Livetiles Corp ....F 917 472-7887
New York **(G-10235)**

Lmt Technology Solutions ....F 585 784-7470
Rochester **(G-13520)**

Lookbooks Media Inc ....F 646 737-3360
New York **(G-10252)**

Loyaltyplant Inc ....F 551 221-2701
Forest Hills **(G-4922)**

Lubbu Inc ....G 917 693-9600
Sag Harbor **(G-14099)**

Luluvise Inc ....E 914 309-7812
New York **(G-10283)**

Madhat Inc ....G 518 947-0732
New York **(G-10314)**

Magic Numbers Inc ....G 646 839-8578
New York **(G-10326)**

Magic Software Inc ....F 646 827-9788
New York **(G-10327)**

Mall Inc ....G 315 751-9490
Cazenovia **(G-3230)**

Marcus Goldman Inc............F 212 431-0707	Noetic Partners Inc.............F 212 836-4351	Pointman LLC............G...... 716 842-1439
New York (G-10358)	New York (G-10636)	Buffalo (G-2923)
Market Factory Inc............F 212 625-9988	Nook Media LLC............G 212 633-3300	Portfolio Decisionware Inc............E 212 947-1326
New York (G-10367)	New York (G-10638)	New York (G-10867)
Market Logic Software Inc............F 646 405-1041	Nortonlifelock Inc............D 646 487-6000	Portware LLC............D 212 425-5233
New York (G-10368)	New York (G-10647)	New York (G-10869)
Masterlibrarycom LLC............F 585 270-6676	Numerix LLC............D 212 302-2220	Powa Technologies Inc............E 347 344-7848
Pittsford (G-12650)	New York (G-10655)	New York (G-10872)
Matrixcare Inc............G 518 583-6400	Olb Group Inc............G 212 278-0900	Premier Heart LLC............G 516 883-3383
New York (G-10385)	New York (G-10684)	Port Washington (G-12915)
Maven Marketing LLC............F 615 510-3248	Olympic Software & Consulting............G 631 351-0655	Pricing Engine Inc............F 917 549-3289
New York (G-10387)	Melville (G-7811)	New York (G-10887)
Maz Systems Inc............F 855 629-3444	Omx (us) Inc............A 646 428-2800	Prime Research Solutions LLC............F 917 836-7941
New York (G-10393)	New York (G-10688)	Flushing (G-4889)
Mdcare911 LLC............G 917 640-4869	On Demand Books LLC............G 212 966-2222	Principia Partners LLC............D 212 480-2270
Brooklyn (G-2128)	New York (G-10689)	New York (G-10893)
Mealplan Corp............G 909 706-8398	One-Blue LLC............G 212 223-4380	Processing Foundation Inc............G 415 748-2679
New York (G-10406)	New York (G-10692)	Brooklyn (G-2296)
Medaptive Health Inc............G 646 541-7389	Oova Inc............G 215 880-3125	Pts Financial Technology LLC............E 844 825-7634
New York (G-10409)	New York (G-10696)	New York (G-10921)
Mediamorph Inc............G 212 643-0762	Openfin Inc............G 917 450-8822	Purebase Networks Inc............G 646 670-8964
New York (G-10413)	New York (G-10697)	New York (G-10929)
Mediapost Communications LLC............E 212 204-2000	Operateit Inc............G 631 259-4777	Qlogix Entertainment LLC............G 215 459-6315
New York (G-10415)	Ronkonkoma (G-13988)	New York (G-10944)
Medidata Solutions Inc............B 212 918-1800	Operative Media Inc............D 212 994-8930	Qmetis Inc............G 212 500-5000
New York (G-10417)	New York (G-10699)	New York (G-10945)
Medius Software Inc............F 877 295-0058	Oracle America Inc............D 518 427-9353	Quality and Asrn Tech Corp............G 646 450-6762
New York (G-10419)	Albany (G-109)	Ridge (G-13133)
Medscale Plus LLC............G 212 218-4070	Oracle America Inc............D 585 317-4648	Quartet Financial Systems Inc............F 845 358-6071
New York (G-10420)	Fairport (G-4511)	New York (G-10952)
Micro Systems Specialists Inc............G 845 677-6150	Oracle Corporation............C 212 508-7700	Quovo Inc............E 212 643-0695
Millbrook (G-7943)	New York (G-10701)	New York (G-10961)
Microcad Trning Consulting Inc............G 617 923-0500	Orangenius Inc............F 631 742-0648	Radnor-Wallace............G 516 767-2131
Lagrangeville (G-6751)	New York (G-10702)	Port Washington (G-12917)
Microcad Trning Consulting Inc............G 631 291-9484	Orchard App Inc............G 888 217-2718	Raleigh & Drake Pbc............G 212 625-8212
Hauppauge (G-5716)	New York (G-10705)	New York (G-10974)
Microsoft Corporation............A 914 323-2150	Orchard Platform Advisors LLC............E 888 217-2718	Ramsey Solutions LLC............F 888 329-1055
White Plains (G-16030)	New York (G-10707)	New York (G-10977)
Microsoft Corporation............G 631 760-2340	Ordergroove Inc............E 866 253-1261	Rational Retention LLC............E 518 489-3000
Huntington Station (G-6254)	New York (G-10709)	Albany (G-124)
Microsoft Corporation............F 212 245-2100	Orthstar Enterprises Inc............D 607 562-2100	Ray Theta Inc............G 646 757-4956
New York (G-10459)	Horseheads (G-6130)	New York (G-10987)
Microsoft Corporation............D 516 380-1531	Os33 Inc............G 708 336-3466	Reactivecore LLC............G 631 944-1618
Hauppauge (G-5718)	New York (G-10713)	New York (G-10992)
Microstrategy Incorporated............F 888 537-8135	Ougra Inc............G 646 342-4575	Real Factors Inc............G 206 963-6661
New York (G-10460)	Long Island City (G-7314)	Astoria (G-438)
Midas Mdici Group Holdings Inc............G 212 792-0920	Overture Media Inc............G 917 446-7455	Reality Analytics Inc............G 347 363-2200
New York (G-10461)	New York (G-10720)	New York (G-10995)
Mitel Networks Inc............G 877 654-3573	P&C Group Inc............F 212 425-9200	Reason Software Company Inc............F 646 664-1038
Rochester (G-13553)	New York (G-10734)	New York (G-10996)
Mml Software Ltd............E 631 941-1313	P8h Inc............E 212 343-1142	Red Oak Software Inc............G 585 454-3170
East Setauket (G-4182)	Brooklyn (G-2241)	Rochester (G-13670)
Mnn Holding Company LLC............F 404 558-5251	Pap Chat Inc............G 516 350-1888	Reentry Games Inc............G 646 421-0080
Brooklyn (G-2165)	Brooklyn (G-2243)	New York (G-10999)
Mobileapp Systems LLC............G 716 667-2780	Paperstreet Technology Inc............G 704 773-5689	Reliant Security............F 917 338-2200
Buffalo (G-2868)	Brooklyn (G-2245)	New York (G-11003)
Mobo Systems Inc............D 212 260-0895	Par Technology Corporation............D 315 738-0600	Remarkety Inc............G 800 570-7564
New York (G-10487)	New Hartford (G-8242)	Brooklyn (G-2338)
Molabs Inc............G 310 721-6828	Pareteum Corporation............E 212 984-1096	Retina Labs (usa) Inc............F 866 344-2692
New York (G-10494)	New York (G-10758)	New York (G-11023)
Mongodb Inc............C 646 727-4092	Parlor Labs Inc............G 866 801-7323	Revivn Public Benefit Corp............F 347 762-8193
New York (G-10500)	New York (G-10765)	Brooklyn (G-2342)
Mymee Inc............F 917 476-4122	Pb Mapinfo Corporation............A 518 285-6000	Ringlead Inc............F 310 906-0545
New York (G-10527)	Troy (G-15177)	Melville (G-7819)
Navatar Group Inc............E 212 863-9655	Peer Software Incorporated............G 631 979-1770	Rision Inc............G 212 987-2628
New York (G-10557)	Hauppauge (G-5739)	New York (G-11047)
Nemaris Inc............E 646 794-8648	Pegasystems Inc............E 212 626-6550	Ritnoa Inc............E 212 660-2148
New York (G-10562)	New York (G-10790)	Bellerose (G-776)
Nervve Technologies Inc............E 716 800-2250	Perry Street Software Inc............G 415 935-1429	Robly Digital Marketing LLC............E 917 238-0730
New York (G-10564)	New York (G-10810)	New York (G-11065)
Netlogic Inc............E 212 269-3796	Pexip Inc............F 703 338-3544	Robocom Us LLC............F 631 861-2045
New York (G-10569)	New York (G-10819)	Farmingdale (G-4725)
Netsuite Inc............G 646 652-5700	Piano Software Inc............E 646 350-1999	Robot Fruit Inc............G 631 423-7250
New York (G-10570)	New York (G-10834)	Huntington (G-6220)
Network Infrastructure Tech Inc............G 212 404-7340	Pilot Inc............G 212 951-1133	Rockport Pa LLC............F 212 482-8580
New York (G-10571)	New York (G-10839)	New York (G-11069)
Neverware Inc............F 516 302-3223	Pilot Inc............G 212 951-1133	RPS Holdings Inc............E 607 257-7778
New York (G-10575)	New York (G-10840)	Ithaca (G-6410)
New Triad For Collaborative............E 212 873-9610	Pingmd Inc............G 212 632-2665	Runs Inc............E 212 618-1201
New York (G-10591)	New York (G-10842)	New York (G-11099)
New York Computer Consulting............G 516 921-1932	Pitney Bowes Software Inc............F 518 285-6000	Ryba Software Inc............G 718 264-9352
Woodbury (G-16178)	Troy (G-15179)	Fresh Meadows (G-5045)
New York State Assoc............F 518 434-2281	Piwik Pro LLC............E 888 444-0049	Safe Passage International Inc............F 585 292-4910
Albany (G-104)	Rochester (G-10848)	Rochester (G-13711)
Nift Group Inc............G 504 505-1144	Platform Experts Inc............G 646 843-7100	Sakonnet Technology LLC............E 212 849-9267
Brooklyn (G-2215)	Brooklyn (G-2266)	New York (G-11116)
Nikish Software Corp............G 631 754-1618	Playfitness Corp............G 917 497-5443	Sales Hacker Inc............G 516 660-2836
Northport (G-12110)	Staten Island (G-14690)	New York (G-11118)
Ninth Wave Inc............E 212 401-6381	Plectica LLC............F 646 941-8822	San Jae Educational Resou............G 845 364-5458
New York (G-10631)	New York (G-10855)	Pomona (G-12808)

S
I
C

Sapphire Systems Inc	F	212 905-0100
New York *(G-11135)*		
SC Building Solutions LLC	D	800 564-1152
New York *(G-11145)*		
▲ Scholastic Corporation	G	212 343-6100
New York *(G-11160)*		
◆ Scholastic Inc	A	212 343-6100
New York *(G-11161)*		
Schoolnet Inc	C	646 496-9000
New York *(G-11164)*		
Sciterra LLC	G	646 883-3724
New York *(G-11167)*		
Secured Services Inc	G	866 419-3900
New York *(G-11176)*		
Sefaira Inc	E	855 733-2472
New York *(G-11181)*		
Segovia Technology Co	F	212 868-4412
New York *(G-11182)*		
Seriesone Inc	G	212 385-1552
New York *(G-11193)*		
Serraview America Inc	D	800 903-3716
New York *(G-11194)*		
Servicenow Inc	F	914 318-1168
New York *(G-11195)*		
Shake Inc	F	650 544-5479
New York *(G-11204)*		
Sharemethods LLC	F	877 742-7366
Brooklyn *(G-2404)*		
Shiprite Services Inc	F	315 427-2422
Utica *(G-15294)*		
Siemens Product Life Mgmt Sftw	E	585 389-8699
Fairport *(G-4522)*		
Siemens Product Life Mgmt Sftw	B	631 549-2300
Melville *(G-7822)*		
Signpost Inc	C	877 334-2837
New York *(G-11238)*		
Similarweb Inc	F	347 685-5422
New York *(G-11241)*		
Skillsoft Corporation	F	585 240-7500
Rochester *(G-13732)*		
Skyop LLC	F	585 598-4737
Canandaigua *(G-3143)*		
Skystem LLC	G	877 778-3320
New York *(G-11266)*		
Slidebean Incorporated	F	866 365-0588
New York *(G-11269)*		
Slyde Inc	F	917 331-2114
Long Island City *(G-7360)*		
Sneakers Software Inc	F	800 877-9221
New York *(G-11279)*		
▲ Social Bicycles LLC	E	917 746-7624
Brooklyn *(G-2432)*		
Socialed Inc	G	516 297-2172
New York *(G-11282)*		
Softlink International	E	914 574-8197
White Plains *(G-16061)*		
Software & General Services Co	G	315 986-4184
Walworth *(G-15479)*		
Software Engineering Amer Inc	D	516 328-7000
Garden City *(G-5116)*		
Solve Advisors Inc	G	646 699-5041
Rockville Centre *(G-13837)*		
Somml Health Inc	G	518 880-2170
Albany *(G-130)*		
Soroc Technology Corp	G	716 849-5913
Buffalo *(G-2988)*		
Sparta Commercial Services Inc	F	212 239-2666
New York *(G-11309)*		
Special Circle Inc	F	516 595-9988
New Hyde Park *(G-8295)*		
Specialneedsware Inc	F	646 278-9959
New York *(G-11312)*		
Spektrix Inc	G	646 741-5110
New York *(G-11317)*		
Splacer Inc	G	646 853-9789
New York *(G-11325)*		
Spring Inc	G	646 732-0323
New York *(G-11332)*		
SS&c Financial Services LLC	C	914 670-3600
Harrison *(G-5560)*		
Stensul Inc	G	212 380-8620
New York *(G-11357)*		
Stop N Shop LLC	G	518 512-9657
Albany *(G-133)*		
Strada Soft Inc	G	718 556-6940
Staten Island *(G-14716)*		
Street Smarts Vr Inc	G	413 438-7787
New York *(G-11371)*		
Streetcred Nyc LLC	G	646 675-0073
New York *(G-11372)*		

Striata Inc	D	212 918-4677
New York *(G-11373)*		
Structured Retail Products	G	212 224-3692
New York *(G-11375)*		
Structuredweb Inc	E	201 325-3110
New York *(G-11376)*		
Styleclick Inc	D	212 329-0300
New York *(G-11381)*		
Successware Inc	F	716 565-2338
Williamsville *(G-16142)*		
Suite Solutions Inc	G	716 929-3050
Amherst *(G-245)*		
Sutton Place Software Inc	G	631 421-1737
Melville *(G-7826)*		
Symphony Talent LLC	D	212 999-9000
New York *(G-11409)*		
Synced Inc	G	917 565-5591
New York *(G-11411)*		
Synco Technologies Inc	G	212 255-2031
New York *(G-11412)*		
Synergy Resources Inc	D	631 665-2050
Central Islip *(G-3289)*		
Syrasoft LLC	F	315 708-0341
Baldwinsville *(G-556)*		
Systems Trading Inc	G	718 261-8900
Melville *(G-7827)*		
Taazu Inc	E	212 618-1201
New York *(G-11421)*		
Tabi Inc	G	347 701-1051
Flushing *(G-4897)*		
Tap2play LLC	G	914 960-6232
New York *(G-11432)*		
Tapinator Inc	G	914 930-6232
New York *(G-11435)*		
Targetprocess Inc	F	877 718-2617
Amherst *(G-247)*		
Teachergaming LLC	F	866 644-9323
New York *(G-11442)*		
Teachley LLC	G	347 552-1272
New York *(G-11443)*		
Team Builders Inc	F	718 979-1005
Staten Island *(G-14720)*		
Tech Software LLC	G	516 986-3050
Melville *(G-7829)*		
Technology Partners Inc	E	518 621-2993
Slingerlands *(G-14468)*		
Tecsys US Inc	G	800 922-8649
New York *(G-11447)*		
Tel Tech International	E	516 393-5174
Melville *(G-7830)*		
Telmar Information Services	E	212 725-3000
New York *(G-11451)*		
Tequipment Inc	D	516 922-3508
Huntington Station *(G-6264)*		
Terranua US Corp	F	212 852-9028
New York *(G-11454)*		
Theirapp LLC	E	212 896-1255
New York *(G-11461)*		
Thing Daemon Inc	E	917 746-9895
New York *(G-11466)*		
▲ Thomson Reuters Corporation	A	646 223-4000
New York *(G-11475)*		
Tibco Software Inc	G	646 495-2600
New York *(G-11483)*		
Tika Mobile Inc	G	646 650-5545
New York *(G-11487)*		
Time To Know Inc	G	212 230-1210
New York *(G-11493)*		
Total Defense Inc	D	631 257-3258
Hauppauge *(G-5787)*		
Touchcare P LLC	F	646 824-5373
New York *(G-11522)*		
Tpa Computer Corp	F	877 866-6044
Carmel *(G-3191)*		
Trac Medical Solutions Inc	G	518 346-7799
Schenectady *(G-14312)*		
Traddle LLC	G	646 330-0436
New York *(G-11528)*		
Tradeblock Inc	A	212 231-8353
New York *(G-11529)*		
Transportgistics Inc	F	631 567-4100
Mount Sinai *(G-8117)*		
Treauu Inc	G	703 731-0196
New York *(G-11535)*		
Trueex LLC	E	646 786-8526
New York *(G-11550)*		
Trustfort LLC	G	781 787-0906
Holbrook *(G-6027)*		
Ttg LLC	G	917 777-0959
New York *(G-11556)*		

Tunaverse Media Inc	G	631 778-8350
Hauppauge *(G-5788)*		
Tyme Global Technologies LLC	E	212 796-1950
New York *(G-11568)*		
U X World Inc	G	914 375-6167
Hawthorne *(G-5824)*		
UI Information & Insights Inc	E	518 640-9200
Latham *(G-6879)*		
Ullink Inc	F	646 565-6675
New York *(G-11579)*		
Unacast Inc	G	917 670-7852
New York *(G-11580)*		
▲ United Data Systems Inc	G	631 549-6900
Huntington *(G-6230)*		
Unqork Inc	E	844 486-7675
New York *(G-11610)*		
Upstate Records Management LLC	G	518 834-1144
Keeseville *(G-6646)*		
Urthworx Inc	G	646 373-7535
New York *(G-11621)*		
Usq Group LLC	G	212 777-7751
New York *(G-11632)*		
Value Spring Technology Inc	F	917 705-4658
Harrison *(G-5564)*		
Varnish Software Inc	G	201 857-2832
New York *(G-11645)*		
Varonis Systems Inc	C	877 292-8787
New York *(G-11646)*		
Varsity Monitor LLC	G	212 691-6292
New York *(G-11647)*		
Vehicle Tracking Solutions LLC	E	631 586-7400
Commack *(G-3601)*		
Verint Americas Inc	F	631 962-9334
Melville *(G-7832)*		
Verint SEC Intelligence Inc	D	631 962-9300
Melville *(G-7833)*		
Verint Systems Inc	C	631 962-9600
Melville *(G-7834)*		
Verris Inc	G	201 565-1648
New York *(G-11663)*		
Vertana Group LLC	G	646 430-8226
New York *(G-11666)*		
Vhx Corporation	F	347 689-1446
New York *(G-11673)*		
Viridis Learning Inc	G	347 420-9181
New York *(G-11687)*		
Virtual Facility Inc	G	646 891-4861
New York *(G-11689)*		
Virtual Frameworks Inc	G	646 690-8207
New York *(G-11690)*		
Virtusphere Inc	F	607 760-2207
Binghamton *(G-915)*		
Virtuvent Inc	G	855 672-8677
Brooklyn *(G-2563)*		
Vision Logic Inc	G	212 729-4606
New York *(G-11692)*		
Vizbee Inc	G	650 787-1424
New York *(G-11699)*		
Vline Inc	G	512 222-5464
Brooklyn *(G-2567)*		
Vormittag Associates Inc	G	800 824-7776
Ronkonkoma *(G-14024)*		
Vortex Ventures Inc	G	516 946-8345
North Baldwin *(G-12011)*		
Vuniverse Inc	G	212 206-1041
New York *(G-11709)*		
Water Oracle	G	845 876-8327
Rhinebeck *(G-13104)*		
West Internet Trading Company	G	415 484-5848
New York *(G-11744)*		
Wetpaintcom Inc	E	206 859-6300
Floral Park *(G-4818)*		
Whentech LLC	F	212 571-0042
New York *(G-11749)*		
Whiteboard Ventures Inc	F	855 972-6346
New York *(G-11751)*		
Winesoft International Corp	G	914 400-6247
Yonkers *(G-16356)*		
Wink Inc	E	212 389-1382
New York *(G-11767)*		
Wink Labs Inc	E	844 946-5277
New York *(G-11768)*		
Wizq Inc	F	586 381-9040
New York *(G-11770)*		
Wochit Inc	G	212 979-8343
New York *(G-11773)*		
Woodbury Systems Group Inc	G	516 364-2653
Woodbury *(G-16186)*		
Wrkbook LLC	F	914 355-1293
White Plains *(G-16075)*		

X Function Inc ....E 212 231-0092
New York *(G-11794)*

Xborder Entertainment LLC ....G 518 726-7036
Plattsburgh *(G-12793)*

Xenial Inc ....E 845 920-0800
Pearl River *(G-12544)*

Ypis of Staten Island Inc ....G 718 815-4557
Staten Island *(G-14729)*

Zedge Inc ....D 330 577-3424
New York *(G-11818)*

Zipari Inc ....E 855 558-7884
Brooklyn *(G-2605)*

Zoomifier Corporation ....D 800 255-5303
New York *(G-11829)*

Zydoc Med Transcription LLC ....F 631 273-1963
Islandia *(G-6348)*

76 MISCELLANEOUS REPAIR SERVICES

7692 *Welding Repair*

A & J Machine & Welding Inc ....F 631 845-7586
Farmingdale *(G-4568)*

AAA Welding and Fabrication of ....G 585 254-2830
Rochester *(G-13196)*

Accurate Welding Service Inc..........G 516 333-1730
Westbury *(G-15860)*

Acro-Fab Ltd ....E 315 564-6688
Hannibal *(G-5542)*

Airweld Inc ....G 631 924-6366
Ridge *(G-13131)*

Aj Genco Mch Sp McHy Rdout Svc ....F 716 664-4925
Falconer *(G-4532)*

Allen Tool Phoenix Inc ....E 315 463-7533
East Syracuse *(G-4194)*

Alliance Services Corp ....F 516 775-7600
Floral Park *(G-4805)*

Alliance Welding & Steel Fabg ....F 516 775-7600
Floral Park *(G-4806)*

Alpine Machine Inc ....F 607 272-1344
Ithaca *(G-6362)*

Alumi-Tech LLC ....G 585 663-7010
Penfield *(G-12569)*

American Metal Works Inc ....G 914 682-2979
White Plains *(G-15974)*

Andersens Spring & Wldg Corp ....G 516 785-7337
Bellmore *(G-778)*

ARC TEC Wldg & Fabrication Inc ....G 718 982-9274
Staten Island *(G-14619)*

Atlantis Equipment Corporation ....F 518 733-5910
Stephentown *(G-14730)*

▲ Barber Welding Inc ....E 315 834-6645
Weedsport *(G-15665)*

Benemy Welding & Fabrication ....G 315 548-8500
Phelps *(G-12602)*

Bms Manufacturing Co Inc ....E 607 535-2426
Watkins Glen *(G-15613)*

Boilermatic Welding Inds Inc ....E 631 654-1341
Medford *(G-7700)*

Bracci Ironworks Inc.........................F 718 629-2374
Brooklyn *(G-1604)*

Brenseke George Wldg Ir Works ....G 631 271-4870
Deer Park *(G-3849)*

Broadalbin Manufacturing Corp ....E 518 883-5313
Broadalbin *(G-1172)*

Bruce Pierce ....G 716 731-9310
Sanborn *(G-14138)*

C G & Son Machining Inc ....G 315 964-2430
Williamstown *(G-16115)*

CBM Fabrications Inc ....E 518 399-8023
Ballston Lake *(G-559)*

Chautauqua Machine Spc LLC ....F 716 782-3276
Ashville *(G-409)*

Competicion Mower Repair ....G 516 280-6584
Mineola *(G-7966)*

Cs Automation Inc ....F 315 524-5123
Ontario *(G-12286)*

Custom Laser Inc ....E 716 434-8600
Lockport *(G-7066)*

D & G Welding Inc ....G 716 873-3088
Buffalo *(G-2718)*

DC Fabrication & Welding Inc.............G 845 295-0215
Ferndale *(G-4788)*

Deck Bros Inc ....E 716 852-0262
Buffalo *(G-2723)*

Dennies Manufacturing Inc ....E 585 393-4646
Canandaigua *(G-3130)*

Donald Stefan ....G 716 492-1110
Chaffee *(G-3306)*

Dorgan Welding Service ....G 315 462-9030
Phelps *(G-12603)*

E B Industries LLC ....E 631 293-8565
Farmingdale *(G-4620)*

E B Industries LLC ....E 631 293-8565
Farmingdale *(G-4621)*

Eagle Welding Machine ....G 315 594-1845
Wolcott *(G-16163)*

Etna Tool & Die Corporation ....F 212 475-4350
New York *(G-9414)*

Excelco/Newbrook Inc........................D 716 934-2644
Silver Creek *(G-14442)*

F M L Industries Inc ....G 607 749-7273
Homer *(G-6062)*

Flushing Boiler & Welding Co ....G 718 463-1266
Brooklyn *(G-1855)*

Formac Welding Inc ....G 631 421-5525
Huntington Station *(G-6246)*

Fred Santucci Inc ....F 716 483-1411
Jamestown *(G-6511)*

G & C Welding Co Inc ....G 516 883-3228
Port Washington *(G-12881)*

Gasport Welding & Fabg Inc ....F 716 772-7205
Gasport *(G-5137)*

Gc Mobile Services Inc.......................G 914 736-9730
Cortlandt Manor *(G-3795)*

Genco John ....G 716 483-5446
Jamestown *(G-6512)*

General Welding & Fabg Inc ....G 716 652-0033
Elma *(G-4319)*

Guthrie Heli-Arc Inc ....G 585 548-5053
Bergen *(G-815)*

Hadfield Inc ....F 631 981-4314
Saint James *(G-14111)*

Hadleys Fab-Weld Inc ....G 315 926-5101
Marion *(G-7570)*

Hansen Steel ....E 585 398-2020
Farmington *(G-4772)*

Hartman Enterprises Inc ....D 315 363-7300
Oneida *(G-12245)*

Haskell Machine & Tool Inc ....F 607 749-2421
Homer *(G-6063)*

Haun Welding Supply Inc ....G 607 846-2289
Elmira *(G-4356)*

Haun Welding Supply Inc ....G 315 592-5012
Fulton *(G-5063)*

Homer Iron Works LLC ....G 607 749-3963
Homer *(G-6064)*

Ingleside Machine Co Inc ....D 585 924-3046
Farmington *(G-4774)*

Jacksons Welding LLC ....G 607 756-2725
Cortland *(G-3773)*

▼ Kon Tat Group Corporation ....G 718 207-5022
Brooklyn *(G-2035)*

L & S Metals Inc ....E 716 692-6865
North Tonawanda *(G-12076)*

▲ Lagasse Works Inc ....G 315 946-9202
Lyons *(G-7450)*

Linita Design & Mfg Corp ....E 716 566-7753
Lackawanna *(G-6741)*

M M Welding ....E 315 363-3980
Oneida *(G-12247)*

Maple Grove Corp ....E 585 492-5286
Arcade *(G-377)*

Maria Dionisio Welding Inc ....G 631 956-0815
Lindenhurst *(G-6958)*

Maspeth Welding Inc ....E 718 497-5430
Maspeth *(G-7627)*

Meades Welding and Fabricating ....G 631 581-1555
Islip *(G-6354)*

Mega Tool & Mfg Corp ....E 607 734-8398
Elmira *(G-4363)*

Miller Metal Fabricating Inc ....G 585 359-3400
Rochester *(G-13549)*

Mooradian Hydraulics & Eqp Co ....F 518 766-3866
Castleton On Hudson *(G-3203)*

Ms Spares LLC ....G 607 223-3024
Clay *(G-3451)*

NY Iron Inc ....F 718 302-9000
Long Island City *(G-7311)*

Parfuse Corp ....E 516 997-8888
Westbury *(G-15916)*

Phillip J Ortiz Manufacturing ....G 845 226-7030
Hopewell Junction *(G-6100)*

Phoenix Welding & Fabg Inc ....G 315 695-2223
Phoenix *(G-12619)*

Precision Laser Technology LLC ....F 585 458-6208
Rochester *(G-13637)*

Pro-Tech Wldg Fabrication Inc ....G 585 436-9855
Rochester *(G-13647)*

Quality Industrial Services..................F 716 667-7703
Orchard Park *(G-12376)*

R & B Fabrication Inc ....F 315 640-9901
Cicero *(G-3423)*

Reliable Welding & Fabrication ....G 631 758-2637
Patchogue *(G-12511)*

REO Welding Inc ....F 518 238-1022
Cohoes *(G-3514)*

Rini Tank & Truck Service ....F 718 384-6606
Brooklyn *(G-2345)*

Rj Welding & Fabricating Inc ....G 315 523-1288
Clifton Springs *(G-3480)*

Robert M Brown ....F 607 426-6250
Montour Falls *(G-8076)*

Rothe Welding Inc ....G 845 246-3051
Saugerties *(G-14210)*

Ryans Mobile Welding Svc LLC ....G 315 769-5699
Massena *(G-7670)*

S & D Welding Corp ....G 631 454-0383
West Babylon *(G-15744)*

S J B Fabrication..................................F 716 895-0281
Buffalo *(G-2969)*

Sierson Crane Inc ....F 315 723-6914
Westmoreland *(G-15964)*

Smithers Tools & Mch Pdts Inc ....D 845 876-3063
Rhinebeck *(G-13101)*

▲ Strecks Inc ....E 518 273-4410
Watervliet *(G-15607)*

Tomahawk Welding Svcs & Insptn ....G 903 249-4451
Norwich *(G-12129)*

Tracey Welding Co Inc........................G 518 756-6309
Coeymans *(G-3505)*

Ub Welding Corp ....G 347 688-5196
Bronx *(G-1386)*

W R P Welding Ltd ....G 631 249-8859
Farmingdale *(G-4763)*

Walters & Walters Inc ....G 347 202-8535
Bronx *(G-1395)*

Watkins Welding and Mch Sp Inc ....G 914 949-6168
White Plains *(G-16070)*

Waynes Welding Inc ....E 315 768-6146
Yorkville *(G-16383)*

Welding and Brazing Svcs Inc ....G 607 397-1009
Richfield Springs *(G-13106)*

Welding Chapter of New York ....G 212 481-1496
New York *(G-11739)*

Welding Guys LLC ....G 518 898-8323
Menands *(G-7850)*

West Metal Works Inc ....E 716 895-4900
Buffalo *(G-3045)*

7694 *Armature Rewinding Shops*

A & C/Furia Electric Motors ....F 914 949-0585
White Plains *(G-15968)*

Accurate Marine Specialties ....G 631 589-5502
Bohemia *(G-963)*

Bailey Elc Mtr & Pump Sup LLC ....G 585 418-5051
Corfu *(G-3701)*

Bayshore Electric Motors ....G 631 475-1397
Patchogue *(G-12497)*

D & D Elc Mtrs & Cmpsr Inc ....F 631 991-3001
Lindenhurst *(G-6947)*

Daves Electric Motors & Pumps ....G 212 982-2930
New York *(G-9176)*

Electric Motor Specialty Inc ....G 716 487-1458
Jamestown *(G-6509)*

Ener-G-Rotors Inc ....G 518 372-2608
Schenectady *(G-14262)*

General Electric Company ....E 315 456-3304
Syracuse *(G-14902)*

General Electric Company ....E 518 459-4110
Albany *(G-80)*

Genesis Electrical Motors ....G 718 274-7030
Woodside *(G-16208)*

Lawtons Electric Motor Service............G 315 393-2728
Ogdensburg *(G-12207)*

Longo New York Inc.............................F 212 929-7128
New York *(G-10249)*

Power-Flo Technologies Inc ....D 315 399-5801
East Syracuse *(G-4230)*

Power-Flo Technologies Inc ....E 585 426-4607
Rochester *(G-13631)*

Premco Inc ....F 914 636-7095
New Rochelle *(G-8350)*

Prime Electric Motors Inc.....................G 718 784-1124
Long Island City *(G-7328)*

RC Entps Bus & Trck Inc......................G 518 568-5753
Saint Johnsville *(G-14120)*

Sunset Ridge Holdings Inc ....G 716 487-1458
Jamestown *(G-6546)*

Employee Codes: A=Over 500 employees, B=251-500
C=101-250, D=51-100, E=20-50, F=10-19, G=5-9   2020 Harris
New York Manufacturers Directory   789

S
I
C

▲ **Tis Ansonia LLC**...............................F 518 272-4920
Watervliet *(G-15608)*

Troy Belting and Supply Co ....D....... 518 272-4920
Watervliet *(G-15609)*

Troy Industrial Solutions ....F 518 272-4920
Watervliet *(G-15610)*

United Richter Electrical Mtrs ....F 716 855-1945
Buffalo *(G-3030)*

ALPHABETIC SECTION

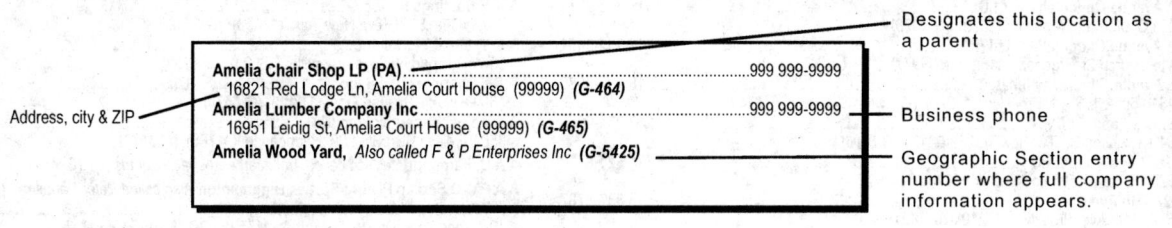

Designates this location as a parent

Amelia Chair Shop LP (PA) 999 999-9999
16821 Red Lodge Ln, Amelia Court House (99999) *(G-464)*

Amelia Lumber Company Inc 999 999-9999
16951 Leidig St, Amelia Court House (99999) *(G-465)*

Amelia Wood Yard, *Also called F & P Enterprises Inc* *(G-5425)*

Address, city & ZIP

Business phone

Geographic Section entry
number where full company
information appears.

See footnotes for symbols and codes identification.

* Companies listed alphabetically.

* Complete physical or mailing address.

---

09 Flshy Bll/Dsert Sunrise LLC 518 583-6638
2 Smith Bridge Rd Saratoga Springs (12866) *(G-14161)*

1 800 Postcards Inc 212 741-1070
149 W 27th St Fl 3 New York (10001) *(G-8387)*

1 Atelier LLC 917 916-2968
347 W 36th St Rm 303 New York (10018) *(G-8388)*

1/2 Off Cards Wantagh Inc 516 809-9832
1162 Wantagh Ave Wantagh (11793) *(G-15482)*

110 Sand Company (PA) 631 694-2822
136 Spagnoli Rd Melville (11747) *(G-7751)*

110 Sand Company 631 694-2822
170 Cabot St West Babylon (11704) *(G-15677)*

116 26 Street, Brooklyn *Also called Angel-Made In Heaven Inc* *(G-1510)*

125-127 Main Street Corp 631 477-1500
125 Main St 127 Greenport (11944) *(G-5456)*

12pt Printing LLC 718 376-2120
2053 E 1st St Brooklyn (11223) *(G-1410)*

1510 Associates LLC 212 828-8720
1500 Lexington Ave New York (10029) *(G-8389)*

17 Bakers LLC 844 687-6836
8 Los Robles St Williamsville (14221) *(G-16116)*

18 Rocks LLC (HQ) 631 465-9990
102 Marcus Dr Melville (11747) *(G-7752)*

180s LLC (HQ) 410 534-6320
1 Liberty Plz Rm 3500 New York (10006) *(G-8390)*

1884 Collection, New York *Also called Anima Group LLC* *(G-8589)*

1928 Jewelry Co, New York *Also called Mel Bernie and Company Inc* *(G-10427)*

1gpn, New York *Also called First Games Publr Netwrk Inc* *(G-9499)*

1ktgold Inc 212 302-8200
3 Barker Ave Ste 290 White Plains (10601) *(G-15967)*

1st Responder Newspaper, New Windsor *Also called Belsito Communications Inc* *(G-8360)*

2 1 2 Postcards Inc 212 767-8227
121 Varick St Frnt B New York (10013) *(G-8391)*

2 X 4 Inc 212 647-1170
180 Varick St Rm 1610 New York (10014) *(G-8392)*

20 Bliss St Inc 716 326-2790
61 E Main St Westfield (14787) *(G-15943)*

209 Discount Oil 845 386-2090
10 Sands Station Rd Middletown (10940) *(G-7891)*

212 Biz LLC (PA) 212 391-4444
1410 Broadway Rm 3203 New York (10018) *(G-8393)*

212 Media LLC 212 710-3092
460 Park Ave S Fl 4 New York (10016) *(G-8394)*

212kiddish Inc 718 705-7227
168 Spencer St Brooklyn (11205) *(G-1411)*

219 South West 315 474-2065
219 S West St Syracuse (13202) *(G-14807)*

21st Century Finishes Inc 516 221-7000
1353 Newbridge Rd Unit A North Bellmore (11710) *(G-12013)*

21st Century Fox America Inc 212 782-8000
1211 Aveof The Am Lowr C3 New York (10036) *(G-8395)*

21st Century Fox America Inc (HQ) 212 852-7000
1211 Ave Of The Americas New York (10036) *(G-8396)*

21st Century Fox America Inc 212 447-4600
200 Madison Ave Fl 8 New York (10016) *(G-8397)*

21st Century Optics Inc (HQ) 347 527-1079
4700 33rd St Ste 1r Long Island City (11101) *(G-7140)*

21st Century Spirits Corp 718 499-0606
137 12th St Brooklyn (11215) *(G-1412)*

240 Michigan Street Inc 716 434-6010
96 Darwin Dr Buffalo (14226) *(G-2611)*

260 Oak Street Inc 877 852-4676
260 Oak St Buffalo (14203) *(G-2612)*

2600 Enterprises Inc 631 474-2677
2 Flowerfield Ste 30 Saint James (11780) *(G-14107)*

2fish 5loaves Comminty Pantry, Arverne *Also called Armour Bearer Group Inc* *(G-406)*

2h International Corp 347 623-9380
6766 108th St Apt D1 Forest Hills (11375) *(G-4914)*

2k Inc 646 536-3007
622 Broadway Fl 6 New York (10012) *(G-8398)*

2nd Skin Armor, Levittown *Also called Universal Armor Systems Corp* *(G-6917)*

2p Agency Usa Inc 212 203-5586
1674 E 22nd St Ste 1 Brooklyn (11229) *(G-1413)*

3 Barker Ave Ste 290, White Plains *Also called 1ktgold Inc* *(G-15967)*

30 Degrees Weatherproof, New York *Also called David Peyser Sportswear Inc* *(G-9181)*

3021743 Holdings Inc 585 589-6399
111 West Ave Ste 2 Albion (14411) *(G-152)*

30dc Inc (PA) 212 962-4400
80 Broad St Fl 5 New York (10004) *(G-8399)*

30dc Inc 212 962-4400
80 Broad St Fl 5 New York (10004) *(G-8400)*

31 Phillip Lim LLC (PA) 212 354-6540
225 Liberty St Fl 33 New York (10281) *(G-8401)*

311 Industries Corp 607 846-4520
434 Airport Rd Endicott (13760) *(G-4442)*

3239603400 La Head Quarters, New York *Also called Peer International Corp* *(G-10785)*

331 Holding Inc 585 924-1740
100 Rawson Rd Ste 205 Victor (14564) *(G-15389)*

333 J & M Food Corp 718 381-1493
333 Seneca Ave Ridgewood (11385) *(G-13136)*

369 River Road Inc 716 694-5001
369 River Rd North Tonawanda (14120) *(G-12050)*

3835 Lebron Rest Eqp & Sup Inc (PA) 212 942-8258
3835 9th Ave New York (10034) *(G-8402)*

388 Associates Inc 267 367-0990
385 Harman St Brooklyn (11237) *(G-1414)*

39th Street Music-Div, New York *Also called Michael Karp Music Inc* *(G-10453)*

3b Timber Company Inc 315 942-6580
8745 Industrial Dr Boonville (13309) *(G-1102)*

3dflam Inc 631 647-2694
1460 N Clinton Ave Ste I9 Bay Shore (11706) *(G-641)*

3doodler, New York *Also called Wobbleworks Inc* *(G-11772)*

3krf LLC 516 208-6824
3516 Hargale Rd Oceanside (11572) *(G-12163)*

3M Company 716 876-1596
305 Sawyer Ave Tonawanda (14150) *(G-15080)*

3phase Industries LLC 347 763-2942
481 Van Buren St Unit 9a Brooklyn (11221) *(G-1415)*

3rd Avenue Doughnut Inc 718 748-3294
7111 3rd Ave Brooklyn (11209) *(G-1416)*

3v Company Inc 718 858-7333
110 Bridge St Ste 3 Brooklyn (11201) *(G-1417)*

4 Over 4com Inc 718 932-2700
1941 46th St Astoria (11105) *(G-412)*

4 Star Brands Inc 516 944-0472
7416 Grand Ave Elmhurst (11373) *(G-4331)*

40 Street Baking Inc 212 683-4700
8617 17th Ave Brooklyn (11214) *(G-1418)*

450 Ridge St Inc 716 754-2789
450 Ridge St Lewiston (14092) *(G-6919)*

461 New Lots Avenue LLC 347 303-9305
461 New Lots Ave Brooklyn (11207) *(G-1419)*

4bumpers Llc 212 721-9600
285 New Wstmnster End Ave New York (10023) *(G-8403)*

4m Precision Industries Inc 315 252-8415
4000 Technology Park Blvd Auburn (13021) *(G-459)*

5 Star Apparel LLC 212 563-1233
31 W 34th St Fl 7 New York (10001) *(G-8404)*

5 Stars Printing Corp 718 461-4612
13330 32nd Ave Flushing (11354) *(G-4831)*

50+ Lifestyle 631 286-0058
146 S Country Rd Ste 4 Bellport (11713) *(G-791)*

514 Adams Corporation 516 352-6948
305 Suburban Ave Deer Park (11729) *(G-3825)*

518 Prints LLC 518 674-5346
1548 Burden Lake Rd Ste 4 Averill Park (12018) *(G-505)*

525 America LLC (PA) 212 921-5688
1411 Broadway Fl 15 New York (10018) *(G-8405)*

527 Franco Bakery Corporation 718 993-4200
527 E 138th St Bronx (10454) *(G-1182)*

A
L
P
H
A
B
E
T
I
C

5th & Ocean Clothing Inc 716 604-9000
160 Delaware Ave Buffalo (14202) ***(G-2613)***
5th Avenue Chocolatiere LLC 516 868-8070
114 Church St Freeport (11520) ***(G-4976)***
5th Avenue Chocolatiere Ltd (PA) 212 935-5454
114 Church St Freeport (11520) ***(G-4977)***
5th Avenue Pharmacy Inc 718 439-8585
4818 5th Ave Ste 1 Brooklyn (11220) ***(G-1420)***
6 Shore Road LLC 212 274-9666
54 Thompson St Fl 5 New York (10012) ***(G-8406)***
6478 Ridge Road LLC 716 625-8400
6251 S Transit Rd Lockport (14094) ***(G-7058)***
6727 11th Ave Corp 718 837-8787
6727 11th Ave Brooklyn (11219) ***(G-1421)***
6th Ave Gourmet Inc 845 782-9067
51 Forest Rd Unit 116 Monroe (10950) ***(G-8013)***
6th Avenue Showcase Inc 212 382-0400
241 W 37th St Frnt 2 New York (10018) ***(G-8407)***
72 Steel and Aluminium Work 917 667-3033
220 42nd St Brooklyn (11232) ***(G-1422)***
728 Berriman LLC 718 272-5000
728 Berriman St Brooklyn (11208) ***(G-1423)***
760 NI Holdings 716 821-1391
760 Northland Ave Buffalo (14211) ***(G-2614)***
786 Iron Works Corp 718 418-4808
50 Morgan Ave Brooklyn (11237) ***(G-1424)***
79 Metro Ltd (PA) 212 944-4030
265 W 37th St Rm 205 New York (10018) ***(G-8408)***
828 Express Inc 917 577-9019
619 Elbe Ave Staten Island (10304) ***(G-14612)***
872 Hunts Point Pharmacy Inc 718 991-3519
872 Hunts Point Ave Bronx (10474) ***(G-1183)***
888 Pharmacy Inc 718 871-8833
4821 8th Ave Brooklyn (11220) ***(G-1425)***
901 D LLC 845 369-1111
360 Route 59 Ste 3 Airmont (10952) ***(G-9)***
999 Bagels Inc 718 915-0742
1410 86th St Brooklyn (11228) ***(G-1426)***
99cent World and Variety Corp 212 740-0010
4242 Broadway New York (10033) ***(G-8409)***
A & A Graphics Inc II 516 735-0078
615 Arlington Dr Seaford (11783) ***(G-14348)***
A & B Color Corp (PA) 718 441-5482
8204 Lefferts Blvd # 356 Kew Gardens (11415) ***(G-6660)***
A & B Finishing Inc 718 522-4702
401 Park Ave Brooklyn (11205) ***(G-1427)***
A & C/Furia Electric Motors 914 949-0585
75 Lafayette Ave White Plains (10603) ***(G-15968)***
A & D Entrances LLC 718 989-2441
105 Wyandanch Ave Wyandanch (11798) ***(G-16240)***
A & D Tool Inc 631 243-4339
30 Pashen Pl Dix Hills (11746) ***(G-4008)***
A & F Trucking & Excavating, Salamanca *Also called Alice Perkins* ***(G-14121)***
A & G Food Distributors LLC 917 939-3457
372 Doris Ave Franklin Square (11010) ***(G-4958)***
A & G Heat Sealing 631 724-7764
1 Albatross Ln Smithtown (11787) ***(G-14472)***
A & G Precision Corp 631 957-5613
680 Albany Ave Amityville (11701) ***(G-255)***
A & J Machine & Welding Inc 631 845-7586
6040 New Hwy Farmingdale (11735) ***(G-4568)***
A & J Washroom Accessories, New Windsor *Also called Gamma Products Inc* ***(G-8368)***
A & L Asset Management Ltd 718 566-1500
143 Alabama Ave Brooklyn (11207) ***(G-1428)***
A & L Doors & Hardware LLC 718 585-8400
375 E 163rd St Frnt 2 Bronx (10451) ***(G-1184)***
A & L Machine Company Inc 631 463-3111
200 Blydenburg Rd Ste 9 Islandia (11749) ***(G-6323)***
A & L Shtmtl Fabrications Corp 718 842-1600
1243 Oakpoint Ave Bronx (10474) ***(G-1185)***
A & M LLC 212 354-1341
29 W 46th St New York (10036) ***(G-8410)***
A & M Appel Distributing Inc 516 735-1172
500 N Atlanta Ave Massapequa (11758) ***(G-7642)***
A & M Home Improvement, Maspeth *Also called Andike Millwork Inc* ***(G-7590)***
A & M Litho Inc 516 342-9727
4 Hunt Pl Bethpage (11714) ***(G-829)***
A & M Rosenthal Entps Inc (PA) 646 638-9600
8 W 38th St Fl 4 New York (10018) ***(G-8411)***
A & M Steel Stamps Inc 516 741-6223
55 Windsor Ave Mineola (11501) ***(G-7954)***
A & Mt Realty Group LLC 718 974-5871
1979 Pacific St Fl 1 Brooklyn (11233) ***(G-1429)***
A & R Concrete Products LLC 845 562-0640
7 Ruscitti Rd New Windsor (12553) ***(G-8357)***
A & S Electric 212 228-2030
952 Flushing Ave Brooklyn (11206) ***(G-1430)***
A & S Window Associates Inc 718 275-7900
8819 76th Ave Glendale (11385) ***(G-5216)***
A & S Woodworking Inc 518 821-0832
9 Partition St Hudson (12534) ***(G-6145)***
A & T Iron Works Inc 914 632-8992
25 Cliff St New Rochelle (10801) ***(G-8315)***
A & T Tooling LLC 716 601-7299
91 Beach Ave Lancaster (14086) ***(G-6788)***
A & V Castings Inc 212 997-0042
257 W 39th St Fl 16w New York (10018) ***(G-8412)***
A & W Metal Works Inc 845 352-2346
55 W Railroad Ave 5 Garnerville (10923) ***(G-5133)***
A & Z Pharmaceutical Inc 631 952-3802
180 Oser Ave Hauppauge (11788) ***(G-5576)***
A & Z Pharmaceutical Inc (PA) 631 952-3802
350 Wireless Blvd Ste 200 Hauppauge (11788) ***(G-5577)***
A A C, Farmingdale *Also called American Aerospace Contrls Inc* ***(G-4583)***
A A P C O Screen Prntng/Sprtwr, Binghamton *Also called Peter Papastrat* ***(G-904)***
A A Technology Inc 631 913-0400
101 Trade Zone Dr Ronkonkoma (11779) ***(G-13882)***
A and J Apparel Corp 212 398-8899
209 W 38th St Rm 1207 New York (10018) ***(G-8413)***
A and L Home Fuel LLC 607 638-1994
601 Smokey Ave Schenevus (12155) ***(G-14319)***
A Angonoa Inc (PA) 718 762-4466
11505 15th Ave College Point (11356) ***(G-3531)***
A B C Mc Cleary Sign Co Inc 315 493-3550
40230 State Route 3 Carthage (13619) ***(G-3193)***
A B S Brass Products Inc 718 497-2115
185 Moore St Brooklyn (11206) ***(G-1431)***
A Bogen Enterprises Inc 718 951-9533
1837 Coney Island Ave Brooklyn (11230) ***(G-1432)***
A C J Communications Inc 631 587-5612
65 Deer Park Ave Ste 2 Babylon (11702) ***(G-517)***
A C M, New York *Also called Association For Cmpt McHy Inc* ***(G-8654)***
A C T, West Babylon *Also called Advanced Coating Techniques* ***(G-15683)***
A Colarusso and Son Inc (PA) 518 828-3218
91 Newman Rd Hudson (12534) ***(G-6146)***
A D Bowman & Son Lumber Co 607 692-2595
1737 Us Highway 11 Castle Creek (13744) ***(G-3199)***
A D C, Hauppauge *Also called American Diagnostic Corp* ***(G-5589)***
A D M, North Tonawanda *Also called Riverfront Costume Design* ***(G-12087)***
A D T, Mineola *Also called Aquifer Drilling & Testing Inc* ***(G-7958)***
A E P, Yaphank *Also called American Electronic Products* ***(G-16255)***
A Esteban & Company Inc (PA) 212 989-7000
132 W 36th St Rm 1000 New York (10018) ***(G-8414)***
A Fire Inc 631 897-9449
23 Parr Dr Ronkonkoma (11779) ***(G-13883)***
A Fleisig Paper Box Corp 212 226-7490
1751 2nd Ave Apt 10a New York (10128) ***(G-8415)***
A G I, Rochester *Also called Advanced Glass Industries Inc* ***(G-13210)***
A G M Deco Inc 718 624-6200
305 Wallabout St 307 Brooklyn (11206) ***(G-1433)***
A G M Deco Inc (PA) 718 624-6200
741 Myrtle Ave Brooklyn (11205) ***(G-1434)***
A Gatty Products Inc 914 592-3903
1 Warehouse Ln Elmsford (10523) ***(G-4391)***
A Gatty Svce, Elmsford *Also called A Gatty Products Inc* ***(G-4391)***
A Graphic Printing Inc 212 233-9696
49 Market St Frnt 2 New York (10002) ***(G-8416)***
A Guideposts Church Corp 212 251-8100
16 E 34th St Fl 21 New York (10016) ***(G-8417)***
A Health Obsession LLC 347 850-4587
2184 Mcdonald Ave Brooklyn (11223) ***(G-1435)***
A Hyatt Ball Co Ltd 518 747-0272
School St Fort Edward (12828) ***(G-4936)***
A I M, Victor *Also called Advanced Interconnect Mfg Inc* ***(G-15390)***
A I P Printing & Stationers 631 929-5529
6198 N Country Rd Wading River (11792) ***(G-15448)***
A I T Computers Inc 518 266-9010
157 Hoosick St Troy (12180) ***(G-15162)***
A J Congress, New York *Also called American Jewish Congress Inc* ***(G-8554)***
A J Gnco Mch Shp/Mchnery Rdout, Falconer *Also called Aj Genco Mch Sp McHy Rdout Svc* ***(G-4532)***
A J Hollander Enterprises, Inwood *Also called Hastings Hide Inc* ***(G-6295)***
A J M Enterprises 716 626-7294
348 Cayuga Rd Buffalo (14225) ***(G-2615)***
A Jaffe Inc 212 843-7464
592 5th Ave Fl 3 New York (10036) ***(G-8418)***
A K A Computer Consulting Inc 718 351-5200
1412 Richmond Rd Staten Island (10304) ***(G-14613)***
A K Allen Co Inc 516 747-5450
1860 Walt Whitman Rd # 900 Melville (11747) ***(G-7753)***
A L Eastmond & Sons Inc (PA) 718 378-3000
1175 Leggett Ave Bronx (10474) ***(G-1186)***
A L Sealing 315 699-6900
2280 Osborne Rd Chittenango (13037) ***(G-3402)***
A Lesley Dummett 646 541-1168
10415 185th St Saint Albans (11412) ***(G-14104)***
A Losee & Sons 516 676-3060
68 Landing Rd Glen Cove (11542) ***(G-5186)***
A Lunt Design Inc 716 662-0781
5755 Big Tree Rd Orchard Park (14127) ***(G-12334)***
A M & J Digital 518 434-2579
800 N Pearl St Ste 5 Menands (12204) ***(G-7836)***
A M I, New York *Also called Weider Publications LLC* ***(G-11736)***

A M S Sign Designs 631 467-7722
2360 Middle Country Rd Centereach (11720) ***(G-3249)***
A National Printing Co Inc 631 243-3395
606 Johnson Ave Ste 31 Bohemia (11716) ***(G-958)***
A Nuclimate Qulty Systems Inc 315 431-0226
6295 E Molloy Rd Ste 3 East Syracuse (13057) ***(G-4192)***
A P Manufacturing 909 228-3049
21 Floyds Run Bohemia (11716) ***(G-959)***
A P S, Hicksville *Also called Applied Power Systems Inc* ***(G-5883)***
A Petteys Lumber, Fort Ann *Also called Petteys Lumber* ***(G-4934)***
A Promos USA Inc 516 377-0186
143 E Merrick Rd Freeport (11520) ***(G-4978)***
A Q P Inc 585 256-1690
2975 Brighton Henrietta T Rochester (14623) ***(G-13194)***
A R Arena Products Inc 585 277-1680
2101 Mount Read Blvd Rochester (14615) ***(G-13195)***
A R V Precision Mfg Inc 631 293-9643
60 Baiting Place Rd Ste B Farmingdale (11735) ***(G-4569)***
A S A Precision Co Inc 845 482-4870
295 Jffersonville N Br Rd Jeffersonville (12748) ***(G-6569)***
A S P, Albany *Also called Albany Student Press Inc* ***(G-36)***
A Strongwater Designs, New York *Also called Andrea Strongwater* ***(G-8578)***
A Sunshine Glass & Aluminum 718 932-8080
2610 Brooklyn Queens Expy Woodside (11377) ***(G-16195)***
A T A Bagel Shoppe Inc 718 352-4948
20814 Cross Island Pkwy Bayside (11360) ***(G-733)***
A T C, Oyster Bay *Also called American Trans-Coil Corp* ***(G-12443)***
A T M, Hornell *Also called Fortitude Industries Inc* ***(G-6106)***
A T T I, Hauppauge *Also called Advanced Testing Tech Inc* ***(G-5580)***
A Thousand Cranes Inc 212 724-9596
208 W 79th St Apt 2 New York (10024) ***(G-8419)***
A Titan Instruments Inc 716 667-9211
10 Centere Dr Orchard Park (14127) ***(G-12335)***
A To Z Kosher Meat Products Co 718 384-7400
123 Borinquen Pl Brooklyn (11211) ***(G-1436)***
A To Z Media Inc (PA) 212 260-0237
243 W 30th St Fl 6 New York (10001) ***(G-8420)***
A Tradition of Excellence Inc 845 638-4595
85b Maple Ave New City (10956) ***(G-8223)***
A Trusted Name Inc 716 326-7400
35 Franklin St Westfield (14787) ***(G-15944)***
A V T, New York *Also called AV Therapeutics Inc* ***(G-8684)***
A Van Hoek Woodworking Limited 718 599-4388
71 Montrose Ave Brooklyn (11206) ***(G-1437)***
A W Hamel Stair Mfg Inc 518 346-3031
3111 Amsterdam Rd Schenectady (12302) ***(G-14244)***
A W R Group Inc 718 729-0412
3715 Hunters Point Ave Long Island City (11101) ***(G-7141)***
A W S, Port Chester *Also called D & M Enterprises Incorporated* ***(G-12816)***
A Weinfeld Skull Cap Mfg, Brooklyn *Also called Weinfeld Skull Cap Mfg Co Inc* ***(G-2579)***
A Yashir Bapa, New York *Also called AZ Yashir Bapaz Inc* ***(G-8700)***
A Zimmer Ltd 315 422-7011
W Tenesee St Syracuse (13204) ***(G-14808)***
A&B Conservation LLC 845 282-7272
12 Maple Leaf Rd Monsey (10952) ***(G-8033)***
A&B Iron Works Inc 347 466-3193
137 Conover St Brooklyn (11231) ***(G-1438)***
A&B McKeon Glass Inc 718 525-2152
69 Roff St Staten Island (10304) ***(G-14614)***
A&M Model Makers LLC 626 813-9661
1675 Wayneport Rd Ste 1 Macedon (14502) ***(G-7457)***
A&S Refrigeration Equipment 718 993-6030
557 Longfellow Ave Bronx (10474) ***(G-1187)***
A-1 Iron Works Inc 718 927-4766
2413 Atlantic Ave Brooklyn (11233) ***(G-1439)***
A-1 Products Inc 718 789-1818
165 Classon Ave Brooklyn (11205) ***(G-1440)***
A-1 Skull Cap Corp 718 633-9333
1212 36th St Brooklyn (11218) ***(G-1441)***
A-Fab Initiatives Inc 716 877-5257
99 Bud Mil Dr Buffalo (14206) ***(G-2616)***
A-Line Technologies Inc 607 772-2439
197 Corporate Dr Binghamton (13904) ***(G-850)***
A-Mark Machinery Corp 631 643-6300
101 Lamar St West Babylon (11704) ***(G-15678)***
A-One Laminating Corp 718 266-6002
1636 Coney Island Ave 2b Brooklyn (11230) ***(G-1442)***
A-One Moving & Storage Inc 718 266-6002
1725 Avenue M Brooklyn (11230) ***(G-1443)***
A-Plus Restaurant Equipment 718 522-2656
623 Sackett St Brooklyn (11217) ***(G-1444)***
A-Quick Bindery LLC 631 491-1110
30 Gleam St Unit C West Babylon (11704) ***(G-15679)***
A.L. Blades, Hornell *Also called Dolomite Products Company Inc* ***(G-6103)***
A.S.I. Fancies Ltd, New York *Also called Antwerp Sales Intl Inc* ***(G-8600)***
A/C Design & Fabrication Corp 718 227-8100
638 Sharrotts Rd Ste 1 Staten Island (10309) ***(G-14615)***
A1 International Heat Treating 718 863-5552
905 Brush Ave Bronx (10465) ***(G-1188)***
A1 Ornamental Iron Works Inc 718 265-3055
61 Jefferson St Brooklyn (11206) ***(G-1445)***
A1 Skullcaps, Brooklyn *Also called A-1 Skull Cap Corp* ***(G-1441)***
A2ia Corp 917 237-0390
24 W 40th St Fl 3 New York (10018) ***(G-8421)***
A3 Apparel LLC 888 403-9669
1407 Broadway Rm 716a New York (10018) ***(G-8422)***
AAa Amercn Flag Dctg Co Inc 212 279-3524
36 W 37th St Rm 409 New York (10018) ***(G-8423)***
AAA Catalytic Recycling Inc 631 920-7944
345 Eastern Pkwy Farmingdale (11735) ***(G-4570)***
AAA Welding and Fabrication of 585 254-2830
1085 Lyell Ave Rochester (14606) ***(G-13196)***
AAAA York Inc 718 784-6666
3720 12th St Long Island City (11101) ***(G-7142)***
Aaaaaa Creative Designs, New York *Also called Paper Box Corp* ***(G-10748)***
Aabacs Group Inc 718 961-3577
1509 132nd St College Point (11356) ***(G-3532)***
Aabco Sheet Metal Co Inc (PA) 718 821-1166
47 40 Metropolitan Ave Ridgewood (11385) ***(G-13137)***
Aakron Rule Corp (PA) 716 542-5483
8 Indianola Ave Akron (14001) ***(G-15)***
Aalborg Instrs & Contrls Inc 845 398-3160
20 Corporate Dr Orangeburg (10962) ***(G-12304)***
Aand D Maintenance, Bridgehampton *Also called Bridgehampton Steel & Wldg Inc* ***(G-1164)***
AAR Allen Services Inc 516 222-9000
747 Zeckendorf Blvd Garden City (11530) ***(G-5089)***
Aarco Products Inc 631 924-5461
21 Old Dock Rd Yaphank (11980) ***(G-16254)***
Aarfid LLC (PA) 716 992-3999
3780 Yochum Rd Eden (14057) ***(G-4253)***
Aaron Group LLC 718 392-5454
115 S Macquesten Pkwy Mount Vernon (10550) ***(G-8119)***
Aaron Tool & Mold Inc 585 426-5100
620 Trolley Blvd Rochester (14606) ***(G-13197)***
Aarrow Promotions, Freeport *Also called A Promos USA Inc* ***(G-4978)***
Aatech, Clyde *Also called Advanced Atomization Tech LLC* ***(G-3488)***
Aavid Niagara LLC (HQ) 716 297-0652
3315 Haseley Dr Niagara Falls (14304) ***(G-11900)***
AB Engine 518 557-3510
4a Northway Ln Latham (12110) ***(G-6846)***
AB Fire Inc 917 416-6444
1554 61st St Brooklyn (11219) ***(G-1446)***
AB Seafood Trading Inc 718 353-8848
3129 Higgins St Flushing (11354) ***(G-4832)***
Abaco Steel Products Inc 631 589-1800
40 Aero Rd Ste 4 Bohemia (11716) ***(G-960)***
Abacus Labs Inc 917 426-6642
14 E 38th St Fl 9 New York (10016) ***(G-8424)***
Abalene Decorating Services 718 782-2000
315 W 39th St Rm 611 New York (10018) ***(G-8425)***
Abalon Precision Mfg Corp 914 665-7700
717 S 3rd Ave Mount Vernon (10550) ***(G-8120)***
Abasco Inc 716 649-4790
5225 Southwestern Blvd Hamburg (14075) ***(G-5501)***
Abbe Laboratories Inc 631 756-2223
1095 Broadhollow Rd Ste E Farmingdale (11735) ***(G-4571)***
Abbeville Press Inc 212 366-5585
116 W 23rd St Fl 5 New York (10011) ***(G-8426)***
Abbeville Publishing Group, New York *Also called Abbeville Press Inc* ***(G-8426)***
Abble Awning Co Inc 516 822-1200
313 Broadway Ste 315 Bethpage (11714) ***(G-830)***
Abbot & Abbot Box Corp 888 930-5972
3711 10th St Long Island City (11101) ***(G-7143)***
Abbot & Abbot Packing Service, Long Island City *Also called Abbot & Abbot Box Corp* ***(G-7143)***
Abbot Flag Co Div, Spring Valley *Also called Eagle Regalia Co Inc* ***(G-14567)***
Abbott Diagnostics Division, Williamsville *Also called Abbott Laboratories* ***(G-16117)***
Abbott Industries Inc (PA) 718 291-0800
9525 149th St Jamaica (11435) ***(G-6423)***
Abbott Laboratories 716 633-1904
6255 Sheridan Dr Ste 406 Williamsville (14221) ***(G-16117)***
ABC Casting, Jamaica *Also called Technical Service Industries* ***(G-6478)***
ABC Elastic Corp (PA) 718 388-2953
889 Metropolitan Ave Brooklyn (11211) ***(G-1447)***
ABC Freight Solutions, Brooklyn *Also called ABC Elastic Corp* ***(G-1447)***
ABC Peanut Butter LLC 212 661-6886
295 Madison Ave Ste 1618 New York (10017) ***(G-8427)***
ABC Television Network, New York *Also called Times Square Studios Ltd* ***(G-11496)***
ABC Windows and Signs Corp 718 353-6210
12606 18th Ave College Point (11356) ***(G-3533)***
Abel Noser Solutions LLC 646 432-4000
1 Battery Park Plz # 601 New York (10004) ***(G-8428)***
Abeona Therapeutics Inc (PA) 646 813-4712
1330 Avenue Of Americas New York (10019) ***(G-8429)***
Abercrombie & Fitch, Brooklyn *Also called Apsco Sports Enterprises Inc* ***(G-1522)***
Aberdeen Blower & Shtmtl Works 631 661-6100
401 Columbus Ave West Babylon (11704) ***(G-15680)***
Abetter Processing Corp 718 252-2223
984 E 35th St Brooklyn (11210) ***(G-1448)***
ABG Accessories, New York *Also called Elegant Headwear Co Inc* ***(G-9336)***
Abgprint, New York *Also called Advanced Business Group Inc* ***(G-8477)***

ALPHABETIC

Abh Natures Products Inc 631 249-5783
131 Heartland Blvd Edgewood (11717) ***(G-4258)***
Abh Pharma Inc 866 922-4669
131 Heartland Blvd Edgewood (11717) ***(G-4259)***
ABI Packaging Inc 716 677-2900
1703 Union Rd West Seneca (14224) ***(G-15843)***
Abigal Press Inc 718 641-5350
9735 133rd Ave Ozone Park (11417) ***(G-12457)***
Abkco Music & Records Inc (PA) 212 399-0300
85 5th Ave Fl 11 New York (10003) ***(G-8430)***
Abkco Music Inc (HQ) 212 399-0300
85 5th Ave Fl 11 New York (10003) ***(G-8431)***
Able Anodizing Corp 718 252-0660
1767 Bay Ridge Ave Brooklyn (11204) ***(G-1449)***
Able Electronics Inc 631 924-5386
18 Sawgrass Dr Bellport (11713) ***(G-792)***
Able Environmental Services 631 567-6585
1599 Ocean Ave Bohemia (11716) ***(G-961)***
Able Industries Inc 914 739-5685
18 Brook Ln Cortlandt Manor (10567) ***(G-3792)***
Able Kitchen 877 268-1264
540 Willow Ave Unit B Cedarhurst (11516) ***(G-3238)***
Able Kitchen Supplies, Cedarhurst *Also called Able Kitchen* ***(G-3238)***
Able National Corp 718 386-8801
49 Wyckoff Ave Brooklyn (11237) ***(G-1450)***
Able Printing, Brooklyn *Also called Weicro Graphics Inc* ***(G-2578)***
Able Steel Equipment Co Inc 718 361-9240
5002 23rd St Long Island City (11101) ***(G-7144)***
Able Weldbuilt Industries Inc 631 643-9700
1050 Grand Blvd Deer Park (11729) ***(G-3826)***
Able Wire Co, Cortlandt Manor *Also called Able Industries Inc* ***(G-3792)***
Ableton Inc 646 723-4586
36 W Colo Blvd Ste 300 New York (10013) ***(G-8432)***
Above The Rest Baking Corp 718 313-9222
531-533 Bryant Ave Bronx (10474) ***(G-1189)***
Abp International Inc 212 490-3999
1466 Broadway Ste 910 New York (10036) ***(G-8433)***
Abr Molding Andy LLC 212 576-1821
1624 Centre St Ridgewood (11385) ***(G-13138)***
ABRA Media Inc 518 398-1010
2773 W Church St Pine Plains (12567) ***(G-12632)***
Abra-Ka-Data Systems Ltd 631 667-5550
39 W Jefryn Blvd Ste 1 Deer Park (11729) ***(G-3827)***
Abraham Jwly Designers & Mfrs 212 944-1149
71 W 47th St Ste 905 New York (10036) ***(G-8434)***
Abraxis Bioscience LLC 716 773-0800
3159 Staley Rd Grand Island (14072) ***(G-5324)***
Abrimian Bros Corp 212 382-1106
48 W 48th St Ste 805 New York (10036) ***(G-8435)***
ABS Metal Corp 646 302-9018
58 Holly Rd Hewlett (11557) ***(G-5868)***
ABS Talkx Inc 631 254-9100
34 Cleveland Ave Bay Shore (11706) ***(G-642)***
Absolute Business Products, Port Washington *Also called Jaidan Industries Inc* ***(G-12891)***
Absolute Coatings Inc 914 636-0700
38 Portman Rd New Rochelle (10801) ***(G-8316)***
Absolute Color Corporation 212 868-0404
109 W 27th St Frnt 2 New York (10001) ***(G-8436)***
Absolute Engineering Company, Bohemia *Also called Absolute Manufacturing Inc* ***(G-962)***
Absolute Fitness US Corp 732 979-8582
21337 39th Ave Ste 322 Bayside (11361) ***(G-734)***
Absolute Manufacturing Inc 631 563-7466
210 Knickerbocker Ave Bohemia (11716) ***(G-962)***
ABT, Great Neck *Also called Advanced Barcode Tech Inc* ***(G-5359)***
Abtex Corporation 315 536-7403
89 Main St Dresden (14441) ***(G-4034)***
Abyrx Inc 914 357-2600
1 Bridge St Ste 121 Irvington (10533) ***(G-6305)***
AC Air Cooling Co Inc 718 933-1011
1637 Stillwell Ave Bronx (10461) ***(G-1190)***
AC DC Power Systems & Contrls, Staatsburg *Also called Protective Power Systms & Cntr* ***(G-14600)***
AC Envelope Inc 516 420-0646
51 Heisser Ln Ste B Farmingdale (11735) ***(G-4572)***
AC Moore Incorporated 516 796-5831
3988 Hempstead Tpke Bethpage (11714) ***(G-831)***
Aca Quality Building Pdts LLC 718 991-2423
1322 Garrison Ave Bronx (10474) ***(G-1191)***
Acad Design Corp 585 254-6960
975 Mount Read Blvd Rochester (14606) ***(G-13198)***
Academy of Political Science 212 870-2500
475 Riverside Dr Ste 1274 New York (10115) ***(G-8437)***
Academy Printing Services Inc 631 765-3346
42 Hortons Ln Southold (11971) ***(G-14542)***
Acadia Stairs 845 765-8600
73 Route 9 Ste 3 Fishkill (12524) ***(G-4797)***
Acai of America Inc 862 205-9334
225 W 34th St Fl 9 New York (10122) ***(G-8438)***
Accede Mold & Tool Co Inc 585 254-6490
1125 Lexington Ave Rochester (14606) ***(G-13199)***
Accel Printing & Graphics 914 241-3369
128 Radio Circle Dr Ste 2 Mount Kisco (10549) ***(G-8086)***
Accela Inc 631 563-5005
100 Comac St Ste 2 Ronkonkoma (11779) ***(G-13884)***
Accelify Solutions LLC 888 922-2354
16 W 36th St Rm 902 New York (10018) ***(G-8439)***
Accent Label & Tag Co Inc (PA) 631 244-7066
348 Woodlawn Ave Ronkonkoma (11779) ***(G-13885)***
Accent Printing &GRaphics, Wayland *Also called Specialty Services* ***(G-15627)***
Accent Speaker Technology Ltd 631 738-2540
1511 Lincoln Ave Holbrook (11741) ***(G-5982)***
Access Display Group Inc 516 678-7772
151 S Main St Freeport (11520) ***(G-4979)***
Access Elevator & Lift Inc (PA) 716 483-3696
1209 E 2nd St Jamestown (14701) ***(G-6491)***
Access Intelligence LLC 212 204-4269
249 W 17th St New York (10011) ***(G-8440)***
Access Products Inc 800 679-4022
241 Main St Ste 100 Buffalo (14203) ***(G-2617)***
Accessible Bath Tech LLC 518 937-1518
6 Albright Ave Albany (12203) ***(G-26)***
Accessories For Electronics 631 847-0158
620 Mead Ter South Hempstead (11550) ***(G-14519)***
Accessory Headquarters, New York *Also called Ahq LLC* ***(G-8498)***
Accessory Plays LLC 212 564-7301
29 W 36th St New York (10018) ***(G-8441)***
Accessory Street LLC 212 686-8990
1370 Broadway New York (10018) ***(G-8442)***
Accessries Direct Intl USA Inc 646 448-8200
1450 Broadway Fl 22 New York (10018) ***(G-8443)***
Accipiter Radar Corporation 716 508-4432
40 Centre Dr Ste 3 Orchard Park (14127) ***(G-12336)***
Accolade USA Inc (PA) 302 257-5688
60 Industrial Pkwy # 397 Cheektowaga (14227) ***(G-3336)***
Accord Pipe Fabricators Inc 718 657-3900
9226 180th St Jamaica (11433) ***(G-6424)***
Accra Sheetmetal LLC 631 643-2100
1359 Straight Path Wyandanch (11798) ***(G-16241)***
Accredo Health Incorporated 718 353-3012
14330 38th Ave Apt 1f Flushing (11354) ***(G-4833)***
Accu Coat Inc 585 288-2330
111 Humboldt St Ste 8 Rochester (14609) ***(G-13200)***
Accucut Inc 631 567-2868
120 Easy St West Sayville (11796) ***(G-15838)***
Accumetrics Associates Inc 518 393-2200
6 British American Blvd # 100 Latham (12110) ***(G-6847)***
Accuprint (PA) 518 456-2431
2005 Western Ave Ste 1 Albany (12203) ***(G-27)***
Accurate Business Systems, Saint James *Also called East Coast Business Forms Inc* ***(G-14110)***
Accurate Industrial Machining 631 242-0566
1711 Church St Holbrook (11741) ***(G-5983)***
Accurate Knitting Corp 646 552-2216
1478 E 26th St Brooklyn (11210) ***(G-1451)***
Accurate Marine Specialties 631 589-5502
2200 Artic Ave Bohemia (11716) ***(G-963)***
Accurate McHning Incorporation 315 689-1428
251 State Route 5 Elbridge (13060) ***(G-4295)***
Accurate Metal Weather Strip 914 668-6042
725 S Fulton Ave Mount Vernon (10550) ***(G-8121)***
Accurate Pnt Powdr Coating Inc 585 235-1650
606 Hague St Rochester (14606) ***(G-13201)***
Accurate Precast 718 345-2910
1957 Pitkin Ave Brooklyn (11207) ***(G-1452)***
Accurate Signs & Awnings Inc 718 788-0302
247 Prospect Ave Ste 2 Brooklyn (11215) ***(G-1453)***
Accurate Specialty Metal Fabri 718 418-6895
6420 Admiral Ave Middle Village (11379) ***(G-7876)***
Accurate Tool & Die LLC 585 254-2830
1085 Lyell Ave Rochester (14606) ***(G-13202)***
Accurate Welding Service Inc 516 333-1730
615 Main St Westbury (11590) ***(G-15860)***
Accurate Welding Svce, Westbury *Also called Accurate Welding Service Inc* ***(G-15860)***
Accusonic Voice Systems, Edgewood *Also called Global Market Development Inc* ***(G-4269)***
Accutrak Inc 212 925-5330
432 Washington St Ste 113 New York (10013) ***(G-8444)***
Accuvein Inc 816 997-9400
3243 Route 112 Ste 2 Medford (11763) ***(G-7697)***
Ace, Brooklyn *Also called Montrose Equipment Sales Inc* ***(G-2170)***
Ace & Jig LLC (PA) 347 227-0318
323 Dean St Ste 2 Brooklyn (11217) ***(G-1454)***
Ace Bag & Burlap Company Inc 718 319-9300
1601 Bronxdale Ave Frnt 4 Bronx (10462) ***(G-1192)***
Ace Banner & Flag Company 212 620-9111
115 W 28th St Apt 3r New York (10001) ***(G-8445)***
Ace Banner Flag & Graphics, New York *Also called Ace Banner & Flag Company* ***(G-8445)***
Ace Canvas & Tent Corp 631 981-9705
155 Raynor Ave Ronkonkoma (11779) ***(G-13886)***
Ace Cntracting Consulting Corp 631 567-4752
1650 Sycamore Ave Ste 18 Bohemia (11716) ***(G-964)***
Ace Diamond Corp 212 730-8231
30 W 47th St Ste 808r New York (10036) ***(G-8446)***
Ace Drop Cloth Canvas Pdts Inc 718 731-1550
4216 Park Ave Bronx (10457) ***(G-1193)***

Ace Drop Cloth Co, Bronx *Also called Ace Drop Cloth Canvas Pdts Inc* **(G-1193)**
Ace Fire Door Corp 718 901-0001
4000 Park Ave Bronx (10457) **(G-1194)**
Ace Manufacturing, Rochester *Also called Jam Industries Inc* **(G-13487)**
Ace Molding & Tool Inc 631 567-2355
51 Floyds Run Bohemia (11716) **(G-965)**
Ace Printing & Publishing Inc 718 939-0040
14951 Roosevelt Ave Flushing (11354) **(G-4834)**
Ace Printing Co, Flushing *Also called Ace Printing & Publishing Inc* **(G-4834)**
Ace Specialty Co Inc 716 874-3670
695 Ensminger Rd Tonawanda (14150) **(G-15081)**
Acec, New York *Also called America Capital Energy Corp* **(G-8540)**
Acem Corp 631 242-2440
45 W Jefryn Blvd Ste 107 Deer Park (11729) **(G-3828)**
Acf Industries Holding LLC (HQ) 212 702-4363
767 5th Ave New York (10153) **(G-8447)**
Acj Communications, Massapequa Park *Also called Massapequa Post* **(G-7659)**
Acker & LI Mills Corporation 212 307-7247
44 W 62nd St Apt 3b New York (10023) **(G-8448)**
Ackroyd Metal Fabricators Inc 518 434-1281
966 Broadway Ste 2 Menands (12204) **(G-7837)**
Acl, Thornwood *Also called Automated Control Logic Inc* **(G-15067)**
Acme Architectural Products 718 360-0700
513 Porter Ave Brooklyn (11222) **(G-1455)**
Acme Architectural Pdts Inc (PA) 718 384-7800
251 Lombardy St Brooklyn (11222) **(G-1456)**
Acme Architectural Walls, Brooklyn *Also called Acme Architectural Pdts Inc* **(G-1456)**
Acme Awning Co Inc 718 409-1881
435 Van Nest Ave Bronx (10460) **(G-1195)**
Acme Engineering Products Inc 518 236-5659
2330 State Route 11 Mooers (12958) **(G-8079)**
Acme Industries of W Babylon 631 737-5231
125 Gary Way Ste 2 Ronkonkoma (11779) **(G-13887)**
Acme Marine, Calverton *Also called US Hoists Corp* **(G-3090)**
Acme Marine Hoist, Bellport *Also called Thego Corporation* **(G-808)**
Acme Marine Hoist Inc 631 472-3030
800 Burman Blvd Calverton (11933) **(G-3076)**
Acme Nipple Mfg Co Inc 716 873-7491
1930 Elmwood Ave Buffalo (14207) **(G-2618)**
Acme Office Group, Brooklyn *Also called New Dimensions Office Group* **(G-2203)**
Acme Parts Inc 718 649-1750
901 Elton St Brooklyn (11208) **(G-1457)**
Acme Precision Screw Pdts Inc 585 328-2028
623 Glide St Rochester (14606) **(G-13203)**
Acme Screenprinting LLC 716 565-1052
247 Cayuga Rd Ste 25e Buffalo (14225) **(G-2619)**
Acme Signs of Baldwinsville 315 638-4865
3 Marble St Baldwinsville (13027) **(G-539)**
Acme Smoked Fish Corp (PA) 954 942-5598
30 Gem St 56 Brooklyn (11222) **(G-1458)**
Acolyte Industries, New York *Also called General Led Holdings LLC* **(G-9589)**
Acolyte Technologies Corp 212 629-3239
44 E 32nd St Rm 901 New York (10016) **(G-8449)**
Acorda Therapeutics Inc (PA) 914 347-4300
420 Saw Mill River Rd Ardsley (10502) **(G-383)**
Acorn, New York *Also called Music Sales Corporation* **(G-10521)**
Acorn Products Corp 315 894-4868
27 Pleasant Ave Ilion (13357) **(G-6276)**
Acran Spill Containment Inc (PA) 631 841-2300
898 N Broadway Ste 1 Massapequa (11758) **(G-7643)**
Acro Industries Inc 585 254-3661
554 Colfax St Rochester (14606) **(G-13204)**
Acro-Fab Ltd 315 564-6688
55 Rochester St Hannibal (13074) **(G-5542)**
Acrolite, Elbridge *Also called Accurate McHning Incorporation* **(G-4295)**
ACS, Ballston Spa *Also called Advanced Comfort Systems Inc* **(G-566)**
ACS Custom USA LLC 646 559-5642
520 W 25th St New York (10001) **(G-8450)**
Act Communications Group Inc 631 669-2403
170 Higbie Ln West Islip (11795) **(G-15809)**
Actasys Inc (PA) 914 432-2336
805 25th St Watervliet (12189) **(G-15596)**
Actinium Pharmaceuticals Inc (PA) 646 677-3870
275 Madison Ave Ste 702 New York (10016) **(G-8451)**
Action Bullet Resistant 631 422-0888
263 Union Blvd West Islip (11795) **(G-15810)**
Action Envelope & Prtg Co Inc 631 225-3900
105 Maxess Rd Ste S215 Melville (11747) **(G-7754)**
Action Envelopes.com, Melville *Also called Action Envelope & Prtg Co Inc* **(G-7754)**
Action Machined Products Inc 631 842-2333
1355 Bangor St Copiague (11726) **(G-3643)**
Action Paper Co Inc 718 665-1652
429 E 164th St Bronx (10456) **(G-1196)**
Action Technologies Inc 718 278-1000
3809 33rd St Apt 1 Long Island City (11101) **(G-7145)**
Actioncraft Products Inc 516 883-6423
2 Manhasset Ave Port Washington (11050) **(G-12859)**
Active Business Systems, Long Island City *Also called Action Technologies Inc* **(G-7145)**
Active Manufacturing Inc 607 775-3162
32 Laughlin Rd Kirkwood (13795) **(G-6728)**

Active Process Supply, New York *Also called Standard Screen Supply Corp* **(G-11346)**
Active World Solutions Inc 718 922-9404
609 Fountain Ave Brooklyn (11208) **(G-1459)**
Actuant Corporation 607 753-8276
44 River St Cortland (13045) **(G-3753)**
Acuity Polymers Inc 585 458-8409
1667 Lake Ave Ste 303 Rochester (14615) **(G-13205)**
Acworth Foundation 631 784-7802
775 Park Ave Ste 255 Huntington (11743) **(G-6197)**
Ad Image Inc 914 476-0000
646 Saw Mill River Rd Yonkers (10710) **(G-16280)**
Ad Makers Long Island Inc 631 595-9100
60 E Jefryn Blvd Ste 3 Deer Park (11729) **(G-3829)**
Ad Publications Inc 585 248-2888
8 Greenwood Park Pittsford (14534) **(G-12635)**
Ad-Vantage Printing Inc 718 820-0688
12034 Queens Blvd Vd Kew Gardens (11415) **(G-6661)**
Ada Gems Corp 212 719-0100
10 W 47th St Ste 707 New York (10036) **(G-8452)**
Adam Scott Designs Inc 212 420-8866
118 E 25th St Fl 11 New York (10010) **(G-8453)**
Adamor Inc 212 688-8885
17 E 48th St Rm 901 New York (10017) **(G-8454)**
Adams Interior Fabrications 631 249-8282
8 Iroquois Pl Massapequa (11758) **(G-7644)**
Adams Lumber Co Inc 716 358-2815
6052 Adams Rd Cattaraugus (14719) **(G-3219)**
Adams Press, Deer Park *Also called 514 Adams Corporation* **(G-3825)**
Adams Ridge, Lancaster *Also called Markar Architectural Products* **(G-6817)**
Adams Sfc Inc (HQ) 716 877-2608
225 E Park Dr Tonawanda (14150) **(G-15082)**
Adaptive Mfg Tech Inc 631 580-5400
181 Remington Blvd Ronkonkoma (11779) **(G-13888)**
ADC Acquisition Company 518 377-6471
2 Commerce Park Rd Niskayuna (12309) **(G-11994)**
ADC Dolls Inc 212 244-4500
112 W 34th St Ste 1207 New York (10120) **(G-8455)**
ADC Industries Inc (PA) 516 596-1304
181a E Jamaica Ave Valley Stream (11580) **(G-15332)**
Adco Circuits Inc 716 668-6600
160 Lawrence Bell Dr # 122 Buffalo (14221) **(G-2620)**
Adcomm Graphics Inc 212 645-1298
21 Lamar St West Babylon (11704) **(G-15681)**
Add Associates Inc (PA) 315 449-3474
6333 Daedalus Rd Cicero (13039) **(G-3415)**
Addeo Bakers Inc 718 367-8316
2372 Hughes Ave Bronx (10458) **(G-1197)**
Addex Inc 781 344-5800
251 Murray St Newark (14513) **(G-11837)**
Addison Precision Mfg Corp 585 254-1386
500 Avis St Rochester (14615) **(G-13206)**
Additude Magazine, New York *Also called New Hope Media LLC* **(G-10585)**
Adel Rootstein (usa) Inc 718 499-5650
145 18th St Brooklyn (11215) **(G-1460)**
Adelphi Paper Hangings 518 284-9066
102 Main St Sharon Springs (13459) **(G-14381)**
Ademco Inc 716 631-2197
307 Cayuga Rd Ste 160 Cheektowaga (14225) **(G-3337)**
Adeptronics Incorporated 631 667-0659
281 Skip Ln Ste C Bay Shore (11706) **(G-643)**
Adesso Inc (PA) 212 736-4440
353 W 39th St Fl 2 New York (10018) **(G-8456)**
Adf Accessories Inc 516 450-5755
3539 Lawson Blvd Oceanside (11572) **(G-12164)**
Adfin Solutions Inc 650 464-0742
25 W 31st St Fl 4 New York (10001) **(G-8457)**
Adg Jewels LLC 212 888-1890
15 W 47th St Ste 600 New York (10036) **(G-8458)**
Adgorithmics Inc (PA) 646 277-8728
260 Madison Ave Fl 8 New York (10016) **(G-8459)**
ADI Global Distribution, Cheektowaga *Also called Ademco Inc* **(G-3337)**
Adir Publishing Co 718 633-9437
1212 36th St Brooklyn (11218) **(G-1461)**
Adirondack Beverage Co Inc, Schenectady *Also called Scotia Beverages Inc* **(G-14303)**
Adirondack Chocolate Co Ltd (PA) 518 946-7270
5680 Ny State Rte 86 Wilmington (12997) **(G-16152)**
Adirondack Daily Enterprise, Saranac Lake *Also called Adirondack Publishing Co Inc* **(G-14156)**
Adirondack Distilling Company 315 316-0387
601 Varick St Utica (13502) **(G-15236)**
ADIRONDACK EXPLORER, Saranac Lake *Also called Getting The Word Out Inc* **(G-14158)**
Adirondack Home News, Holland Patent *Also called Steffen Publishing Inc* **(G-6034)**
Adirondack Ice & Air Inc 518 483-4340
26 Railroad St Malone (12953) **(G-7481)**
Adirondack Leather Pdts Inc 607 547-5798
196 Cemetery Rd Fly Creek (13337) **(G-4908)**
Adirondack Life Inc (PA) 518 946-2191
Rr 9 Box North Jay (12941) **(G-6565)**
Adirondack Life Inc 518 946-2191
12961 Nys Route 9n Jay (12941) **(G-6566)**
Adirondack Life Magazine, Jay *Also called Adirondack Life Inc* **(G-6565)**

A
L
P
H
A
B
E
T
I
C

Adirondack Life Magazine, Jay *Also called Adirondack Life Inc* ***(G-6566)***
Adirondack Outdoor Center LLC (PA)......315 369-2300
2839 State Route 28 Old Forge (13420) ***(G-12221)***
Adirondack Pennysaver Inc......518 563-0100
177 Margaret St Plattsburgh (12901) ***(G-12731)***
Adirondack Plas & Recycl Inc......518 746-9212
453 County Route 45 Argyle (12809) ***(G-391)***
Adirondack Power Sports......518 481-6269
5378 State Route 37 Malone (12953) ***(G-7482)***
Adirondack Precision Cut Stone (PA)......518 681-3060
536 Queensbury Ave Queensbury (12804) ***(G-13029)***
Adirondack Publishing Co Inc (HQ)......518 891-2600
54 Broadway Saranac Lake (12983) ***(G-14156)***
Adirondack Rawlings, Dolgeville *Also called Rawlings Sporting Goods Co Inc* ***(G-4025)***
Adirondack Sanitary Service, Ticonderoga *Also called Adirondack Waste MGT Inc* ***(G-15073)***
Adirondack Scenic Inc......518 638-8000
439 County Route 45 Ste 1 Argyle (12809) ***(G-392)***
Adirondack Sign Company LLC......518 409-7446
72 Ballston Ave Saratoga Springs (12866) ***(G-14162)***
Adirondack Sign Perfect Inc......518 409-7446
72 Ballston Ave Saratoga Springs (12866) ***(G-14163)***
Adirondack Spclty Adhsives Inc......518 869-5736
4258 Albany St Albany (12205) ***(G-28)***
Adirondack Stained Glass Works......518 725-0387
29 W Fulton St Ste 6 Gloversville (12078) ***(G-5275)***
Adirondack Stairs Inc......845 246-2525
990 Kings Hwy Saugerties (12477) ***(G-14196)***
Adirondack Studios, Argyle *Also called Adirondack Scenic Inc* ***(G-392)***
Adirondack Waste MGT Inc......518 585-2224
963 New York State 9n Ticonderoga (12883) ***(G-15073)***
Adirondack Winery LLC......518 668-9463
285 Canada St Lake George (12845) ***(G-6756)***
Adirondack-Aire, Rome *Also called Cold Point Corporation* ***(G-13847)***
Adirondex, Malone *Also called Adirondack Ice & Air Inc* ***(G-7481)***
Aditiany Inc......212 997-8440
37 W 39th St Rm 1100 New York (10018) ***(G-8460)***
Adjmi Apparel Group, New York *Also called Beluga Inc* ***(G-8753)***
Adjustable Shelving, Melville *Also called Karp Associates Inc* ***(G-7798)***
Adl Data Systems Inc......914 591-1800
565 Taxter Rd Ste 100 Elmsford (10523) ***(G-4392)***
Adl Design Inc......516 949-6658
4 W Mall Dr Huntington (11743) ***(G-6198)***
ADM, Buffalo *Also called Archer-Daniels-Midland Company* ***(G-2643)***
ADM, Hudson *Also called Archer-Daniels-Midland Company* ***(G-6147)***
ADM, Hudson *Also called Archer-Daniels-Midland Company* ***(G-6148)***
ADM, Lakeville *Also called Archer-Daniels-Midland Company* ***(G-6773)***
ADM Milling Co......716 849-7333
250 Ganson St Buffalo (14203) ***(G-2621)***
Admor Blinds & Window Fashion, Jericho *Also called KPP Ltd* ***(G-6585)***
Adobe Inc......212 471-0904
8 W 40th St Fl 8 # 8 New York (10018) ***(G-8461)***
Adobe Systems Inc......212 471-0904
1540 Broadway Fl 17 New York (10036) ***(G-8462)***
Adobe Systems Incorporated......212 592-1400
100 5th Ave Fl 5 New York (10011) ***(G-8463)***
Adore Floors Inc......631 843-0900
5 Dubon Ct Farmingdale (11735) ***(G-4573)***
Adotta America, New York *Also called Europrojects Intl Inc* ***(G-9421)***
Adpro Sports LLC......716 854-5116
55 Amherst Villa Rd Buffalo (14225) ***(G-2622)***
Adria Machine & Tool Inc......585 889-3360
966 North Rd Scottsville (14546) ***(G-14338)***
Adrian Jules Ltd......585 342-5886
1392 E Ridge Rd Rochester (14621) ***(G-13207)***
Adrian-Jules Custom Tailor, Rochester *Also called Adrian Jules Ltd* ***(G-13207)***
Adriatic Wood Products Inc......718 922-4621
1994 Industrial Park Rd Brooklyn (11207) ***(G-1462)***
Adrienne Landau Designs Inc......212 695-8362
519 8th Ave Fl 21 New York (10018) ***(G-8464)***
Ads-N-Color Inc......718 797-0900
20 Jay St Ste 530 Brooklyn (11201) ***(G-1463)***
Adsco Manufacturing Corp......716 827-5450
4979 Lake Ave Buffalo (14219) ***(G-2623)***
Adstream America LLC (HQ)......212 804-8498
345 7th Ave Fl 6 New York (10001) ***(G-8465)***
Adtech, Rochester *Also called Analog Digital Technology LLC* ***(G-13235)***
Adtech Us Inc......212 402-4840
770 Broadway Fl 4 New York (10003) ***(G-8466)***
Adults and Children With Learn......516 593-8230
22 Alice Ct East Rockaway (11518) ***(G-4170)***
Advan-Tech Manufacturing Inc......716 667-1500
3645 California Rd Orchard Park (14127) ***(G-12337)***
Advance Apparel Intl Inc......212 944-0984
265 W 37th St Rm 906 New York (10018) ***(G-8467)***
Advance Biofactures Corp......516 593-7000
35 Wilbur St Lynbrook (11563) ***(G-7423)***
Advance Chemicals Usa Inc......718 633-1030
1230 57th St Brooklyn (11219) ***(G-1464)***
Advance Circuit Technology Inc......585 328-2000
19 Jetview Dr Rochester (14624) ***(G-13208)***
Advance Construction Group, New York *Also called B & F Architectural Support Gr* ***(G-8702)***
Advance D Tech Inc......845 534-8248
2 Mill St Stop 19 Cornwall (12518) ***(G-3724)***
Advance Energy Systems NY LLC......315 735-5125
17 Tilton Rd Utica (13501) ***(G-15237)***
Advance Energy Tech Inc......518 371-2140
1 Solar Dr Halfmoon (12065) ***(G-5490)***
Advance Finance Group LLC......212 630-5900
101 Park Ave Frnt New York (10178) ***(G-8468)***
Advance Food Service Co Inc......631 242-4800
200 Heartland Blvd Edgewood (11717) ***(G-4260)***
Advance Grafix Equipment Inc......917 202-4593
150 Wyandanch Ave Wyandanch (11798) ***(G-16242)***
Advance Magazine Publs Inc......212 286-8582
1 World Trade Ctr New York (10007) ***(G-8469)***
Advance Magazine Publs Inc (HQ)......212 286-2860
1 World Trade Ctr Fl 43 New York (10007) ***(G-8470)***
Advance Magazine Publs Inc......212 790-4422
1 World Trade Ctr Fl 20 New York (10007) ***(G-8471)***
Advance Magazine Publs Inc......212 286-2860
1166 Ave Of The Amrcs 1 New York (10036) ***(G-8472)***
Advance Magazine Publs Inc......212 450-7000
711 3rd Ave Rm 700 New York (10017) ***(G-8473)***
Advance Magazine Publs Inc......212 697-0126
750 3rd Ave Frnt G New York (10017) ***(G-8474)***
Advance Micro Power Corp......631 471-6157
2190 Smithtown Ave Ronkonkoma (11779) ***(G-13889)***
Advance Pharmaceutical Inc (PA)......631 981-4600
895 Waverly Ave Holtsville (11742) ***(G-6044)***
Advance Precision Industries......631 491-0910
9 Mahan St Unit A West Babylon (11704) ***(G-15682)***
Advance Pressure Products, Ithaca *Also called Porous Materials Inc* ***(G-6406)***
Advance Publications Inc (PA)......718 981-1234
1 World Trade Ctr Fl 43 New York (10007) ***(G-8475)***
Advance Tabco Inc (HQ)......631 242-8270
325 Wireless Blvd Ste 1 Hauppauge (11788) ***(G-5578)***
Advanced Assembly Services Inc......716 217-8144
44 Knollwood Dr Lancaster (14086) ***(G-6789)***
Advanced Atomization Tech LLC......315 923-2341
124 Columbia St Clyde (14433) ***(G-3488)***
Advanced Back Technologies......631 231-0076
89 Ste F Cabot Ct Hauppauge (11788) ***(G-5579)***
Advanced Barcode Tech Inc......516 570-8100
175 E Shore Rd Ste 228 Great Neck (11023) ***(G-5359)***
Advanced Biomedical Tech Inc......718 766-7898
350 5th Ave Fl 59 New York (10118) ***(G-8476)***
Advanced Business Group Inc......212 398-1010
266 W 37th St Fl 15 New York (10018) ***(G-8477)***
Advanced Cmpt Sftwr Consulting......718 300-3577
2236 Pearsall Ave Bronx (10469) ***(G-1198)***
Advanced Coating Service LLC......585 247-3970
15 Hytec Cir Rochester (14606) ***(G-13209)***
Advanced Coating Techniques......631 643-4555
311 Wyandanch Ave West Babylon (11704) ***(G-15683)***
Advanced Coating Technologies, Amherst *Also called Bekaert Corporation* ***(G-212)***
Advanced Comfort Systems Inc......518 884-8444
12b Commerce Dr Ballston Spa (12020) ***(G-566)***
Advanced Comm Solutions......914 693-5076
38 Ridge Rd Ardsley (10502) ***(G-384)***
Advanced Comm Solutions Ltd, New York *Also called ACS Custom USA LLC* ***(G-8450)***
Advanced Copy Center Inc......212 388-1001
213 W 35th St Ste 501 New York (10001) ***(G-8478)***
Advanced Cyber Security Corp......866 417-9155
3880 Veterans Memorial Hw Bohemia (11716) ***(G-966)***
Advanced Digital Info Corp......607 266-4000
10 Brown Rd Ithaca (14850) ***(G-6360)***
Advanced Digital Printing LLC......718 649-1500
65 W 36th St Fl 11 New York (10018) ***(G-8479)***
Advanced Door Solutions Inc......631 773-6100
1363 Lincoln Ave Ste 7 Holbrook (11741) ***(G-5984)***
Advanced Doors, Holbrook *Also called Advanced Door Solutions Inc* ***(G-5984)***
Advanced Enterprises Inc......845 342-1009
366 Highland Ave Ext Middletown (10940) ***(G-7892)***
Advanced Fashions Technology......212 221-0606
110 W 40th St Rm 1100 New York (10018) ***(G-8480)***
Advanced Foam Products Div, Buffalo *Also called Tmp Technologies Inc* ***(G-3012)***
Advanced Frozen Foods Inc......516 333-6344
28 Urban Ave Westbury (11590) ***(G-15861)***
Advanced Glass Industries Inc......585 458-8040
1335 Emerson St Rochester (14606) ***(G-13210)***
Advanced Graphics Company Inc......607 692-7875
2607 Main St Whitney Point (13862) ***(G-16105)***
Advanced Interconnect Mfg Inc (HQ)......585 742-2220
780 Canning Pkwy Victor (14564) ***(G-15390)***
Advanced Machine Design Co Inc......716 826-2000
45 Roberts Ave Buffalo (14206) ***(G-2624)***
Advanced Machine Inc......585 423-8255
439 Central Ave Ste 108 Rochester (14605) ***(G-13211)***
Advanced Manufacturing Svc Inc......631 676-5210
100 13th Ave Ste 2 Ronkonkoma (11779) ***(G-13890)***
Advanced Medical Mfg Corp......845 369-7535
7-11 Suffern Pl Ste 2 Suffern (10901) ***(G-14756)***

Advanced Mfg Techniques...518 877-8560
  453 Kinns Rd Clifton Park (12065) *(G-3460)*
Advanced Mtl Analytics LLC...321 684-0528
  85 Murray HI Rd Ste 2115 Vestal (13850) *(G-15369)*
Advanced Orthotics & Prostheth.....................................518 472-1023
  350 Northern Blvd Ste 101 Albany (12204) *(G-29)*
Advanced Pavement Group Corp (PA)...............................631 277-8400
  2 W Beech St Islip (11751) *(G-6349)*
Advanced Photonics Inc...631 471-3693
  151 Trade Zone Dr Ronkonkoma (11779) *(G-13891)*
Advanced Polymer Solutions LLC....................................516 621-5800
  99 Seaview Blvd Ste 1a Port Washington (11050) *(G-12860)*
Advanced Polymers Intl, Syracuse *Also called Royal Adhesives & Sealants LLC (G-14980)*
Advanced Precision Technology.....................................845 279-3540
  577 N Main St Ste 7 Brewster (10509) *(G-1138)*
Advanced Printing New York Inc.....................................212 840-8108
  263 W 38th St New York (10018) *(G-8481)*
Advanced Prosthetics Orthotics....................................516 365-7225
  50 Maple Pl Manhasset (11030) *(G-7530)*
Advanced Quickprinting, Rochester *Also called A Q P Inc (G-13194)*
Advanced Ready Mix Corp...718 497-5020
  239 Ingraham St Brooklyn (11237) *(G-1465)*
Advanced Recovery & Recycl LLC..................................315 450-3301
  3475 Linda Ln Baldwinsville (13027) *(G-540)*
Advanced Research Media Inc.......................................631 751-9696
  60 Route 25a Ste 1 Setauket (11733) *(G-14376)*
Advanced Response Corporation...................................212 459-0887
  345 W 58th St Apt 11a New York (10019) *(G-8482)*
Advanced Rubber Products, Wyoming *Also called Tmp Technologies Inc (G-16253)*
Advanced Structures Corp (PA)......................................631 667-5000
  235 W Industry Ct Deer Park (11729) *(G-3830)*
Advanced Surface Finishing...516 876-9710
  111 Magnolia Ave Westbury (11590) *(G-15862)*
Advanced Tchncal Solutions Inc....................................914 214-8230
  8 Lupi Plz Mahopac (10541) *(G-7473)*
Advanced Technology Division, Plainview *Also called Technic Inc (G-12718)*
Advanced Testing Tech Inc (PA).....................................631 231-8777
  110 Ricefield Ln Hauppauge (11788) *(G-5580)*
Advanced Thermal Systems Inc.....................................716 681-1800
  15 Enterprise Dr Lancaster (14086) *(G-6790)*
Advanced Transit Mix Corp...718 497-5020
  610 Johnson Ave Brooklyn (11237) *(G-1466)*
Advanced Yarn Technologies LLC...................................518 239-6600
  4750 State Hwy 145 Durham (12422) *(G-4069)*
Advantage Machining Inc..716 731-6418
  6421 Wendt Dr Niagara Falls (14304) *(G-11901)*
Advantage Metalwork Finshg LLC...................................585 454-0160
  1000 University Ave # 700 Rochester (14607) *(G-13212)*
Advantage Orthotics Inc...631 368-1754
  337 Larkfield Rd East Northport (11731) *(G-4141)*
Advantage Plus Diagnostics Inc....................................631 393-5044
  200 Broadhollow Rd Melville (11747) *(G-7755)*
Advantage Quick Print Inc...212 989-5644
  30 E 33rd St Frnt B New York (10016) *(G-8483)*
Advantage Wholesale Supply LLC..................................718 284-5346
  172 Empire Blvd Brooklyn Brooklyn (11225) *(G-1467)*
Advantage Wood Shop, Cheektowaga *Also called Stereo Advantage Inc (G-3362)*
Advantech Industries Inc...585 247-0701
  3850 Buffalo Rd Rochester (14624) *(G-13213)*
Advantex Solutions Inc...718 278-2290
  24845 Jericho Tpke Bellerose (11426) *(G-773)*
Advd Heart Phys & Surgs..212 434-3000
  130 E 77th St Fl 4 New York (10075) *(G-8484)*
Advent Tool & Mold Inc..585 254-2000
  999 Ridgeway Ave Rochester (14615) *(G-13214)*
Adventure Publishing Group..212 575-4510
  307 7th Ave Rm 1601 New York (10001) *(G-8485)*
Advertiser, Albany *Also called Capital Region Wkly Newspapers (G-56)*
Advertiser Perceptions Inc..212 626-6683
  1120 Ave Of The Americas New York (10036) *(G-8486)*
Advertiser Publications Inc..845 783-1111
  148 State Route 17m Chester (10918) *(G-3369)*
Advertiser, The, Averill Park *Also called Capital Reg Wkly Newsppr Group (G-506)*
Advertising Lithographers...212 966-7771
  2812 41st Ave Long Island City (11101) *(G-7146)*
Advion Inc (PA)...607 266-9162
  61 Brown Rd Ste 100 Ithaca (14850) *(G-6361)*
Advis Inc...585 568-0100
  2218 River Rd Caledonia (14423) *(G-3068)*
Ae Fund Inc...315 698-7650
  5860 Mckinley Rd Brewerton (13029) *(G-1134)*
Aegis Oil Limited Ventures LLC.....................................646 233-4900
  14 Wall St Fl 20 New York (10005) *(G-8487)*
Aeon America Inc...914 584-0275
  68 Jay St Ste 201 Brooklyn (11201) *(G-1468)*
AEP Environmental LLC...716 446-0739
  2495 Main St Ste 230 Buffalo (14214) *(G-2625)*
Aerco International Inc (HQ)..845 580-8000
  100 Oritani Dr Blauvelt (10913) *(G-925)*
Aero Brand Inks, Blue Point *Also called Specialty Ink Co Inc (G-957)*
Aero Healthcare (us) LLC...855 225-2376
  616 Corporate Way Ste 6 Valley Cottage (10989) *(G-15312)*

Aero Specialties Manufacturing......................................631 242-7200
  20 Burt Dr Deer Park (11729) *(G-3831)*
Aero Strctures Long Island Inc (PA)................................516 997-5757
  717 Main St Westbury (11590) *(G-15863)*
Aero Trades Mfg Corp..516 746-3360
  65 Jericho Tpke Mineola (11501) *(G-7955)*
Aero-Data Metal Crafters Inc...631 471-7733
  2085 5th Ave Ronkonkoma (11779) *(G-13892)*
Aero-Vision Technologies Inc (PA)..................................631 643-8349
  7 Round Tree Dr Melville (11747) *(G-7756)*
Aerobic Wear Inc..631 673-1830
  16 Depot Rd Huntington Station (11746) *(G-6235)*
Aeroduct Inc..516 248-9550
  134 Herricks Rd Mineola (11501) *(G-7956)*
Aeroflex Holding Corp...516 694-6700
  35 S Service Rd Plainview (11803) *(G-12659)*
Aeroflex Incorporated (HQ)...516 694-6700
  35 S Service Rd Plainview (11803) *(G-12660)*
Aerolase Corporation..914 345-8300
  777 Old Saw Mill River Rd # 2 Tarrytown (10591) *(G-15039)*
Aeromed Inc..518 843-9144
  1821 Broad St Ste 1 Utica (13501) *(G-15238)*
Aerospace Lighting Corporation (HQ)..............................631 563-6400
  355 Knickerbocker Ave Bohemia (11716) *(G-967)*
Aerospace Wire & Cable Inc..718 358-2345
  12909 18th Ave College Point (11356) *(G-3534)*
AES Electronics Inc...212 371-8120
  135 E 54th St Apt 10j New York (10022) *(G-8488)*
Aesthonics Inc...646 723-2463
  21 Belvidere St Fl 3 Brooklyn (11206) *(G-1469)*
Aethera LLC...215 324-9222
  256 W 12th St New York (10014) *(G-8489)*
Afab Initiative, Buffalo *Also called American Douglas Metals Inc (G-2630)*
AFC Industries Inc...718 747-0237
  1316 133rd Pl Ste 1 College Point (11356) *(G-3535)*
Afco Precast Sales Corp...631 924-7114
  114 Rocky Point Rd Middle Island (11953) *(G-7873)*
Afe, South Hempstead *Also called Accessories For Electronics (G-14519)*
Aferge Mds, Rochester *Also called GE Mds LLC (G-13430)*
Affco, New Windsor *Also called American Felt & Filter Co Inc (G-8359)*
Affiliated Services Group, Huntington *Also called SC Textiles Inc (G-6223)*
Affordable Luxury Group Inc..631 523-9266
  10 W 33rd St Rm 615 New York (10001) *(G-8490)*
Affordble Gran Cbntry Outl Inc.....................................845 564-0500
  179 S Plank Rd Newburgh (12550) *(G-11857)*
Affymax Inc...650 812-8700
  600 5th Ave 2 New York (10020) *(G-8491)*
Afi Cybernetics Corporation...607 732-3244
  713 Batavia St Elmira (14904) *(G-4339)*
AFP Enterprises Inc...585 254-1128
  100 Holleder Pkwy Rochester (14615) *(G-13215)*
AFP Industries, Lancaster *Also called Air System Products Inc (G-6792)*
AFP Manufacturing Corp...516 466-6464
  9 Park Pl Great Neck (11021) *(G-5360)*
African American Observer, New York *Also called General Media Strategies (G-9590)*
Afro Times Newspaper..718 636-9500
  1195 Atlantic Ave Brooklyn (11216) *(G-1470)*
After 50 Inc...716 832-9300
  5 W Main St Ste 2 Lancaster (14086) *(G-6791)*
AG Kids, New York *Also called Premium 5 Kids LLC (G-10880)*
AG Neovo Professional Inc..212 647-9080
  156 5th Ave Ste 434 New York (10010) *(G-8492)*
AG Tech Welding Corp..845 398-0005
  238 Oak Tree Rd Tappan (10983) *(G-15033)*
Ag-Pak Inc...716 772-2651
  8416 Telegraph Rd Gasport (14067) *(G-5136)*
Age Manufacturers Inc...718 927-0048
  10624 Avenue D Brooklyn (11236) *(G-1471)*
Age Timberline Mamba, Farmingdale *Also called Amana Tool Corp (G-4582)*
Agi Brooks Production Co Inc (PA)..................................212 268-1533
  7 E 14th St Apt 615 New York (10003) *(G-8493)*
Agilent Technologies Inc..877 424-4536
  399 Park Ave New York (10022) *(G-8494)*
Agl Industries Inc...718 326-7597
  5912 57th St Maspeth (11378) *(G-7585)*
Aglika Trade LLC..727 424-1944
  5905 74th St Middle Village (11379) *(G-7877)*
Agn Professional, New York *Also called AG Neovo Professional Inc (G-8492)*
Agnovos Healthcare LLC..646 502-5860
  140 Broadway Fl 46 New York (10005) *(G-8495)*
Agrecolor Inc (PA)..516 741-8700
  400 Sagamore Ave Mineola (11501) *(G-7957)*
Agri Services Co..716 937-6618
  13899 North Rd Alden (14004) *(G-164)*
Agri-Mark Inc..518 497-6644
  39 Mccadam Ln Chateaugay (12920) *(G-3329)*
Agrinetix Cmpt Systems LLC..877 978-5477
  370 Summit Point Dr 1a Henrietta (14467) *(G-5853)*
Agrinetix, LLC, Henrietta *Also called Agrinetix Cmpt Systems LLC (G-5853)*
Agrochem Inc...518 226-4850
  26 Freedom Way Saratoga Springs (12866) *(G-14164)*

A
L
P
H
A
B
E
T
I
C

Agua Brands, Bethpage *Also called Agua Enerviva LLC* ***(G-832)***
Agua Enerviva LLC......516 597-5440
15 Grumman Rd W Ste 1300 Bethpage (11714) ***(G-832)***
Aguilar Amplification LLC......212 431-9109
599 Broadway Fl 7 New York (10012) ***(G-8496)***
Ah Elctronic Test Eqp Repr Ctr......631 234-8979
7 Olive St Central Islip (11722) ***(G-3260)***
Ahae Press Inc......914 471-8671
100 S Bedford Rd Ste 340 Mount Kisco (10549) ***(G-8087)***
Ahhmigo LLC......212 315-1818
120 Cent Park S Rm 7c New York (10019) ***(G-8497)***
Ahlstrom Kamyr, Glens Falls *Also called Andritz Inc* ***(G-5240)***
Ahmazing Boutique Inc......631 828-1474
5225 Nesconset Hwy Ste 42 Port Jeff STA (11776) ***(G-12832)***
Ahq LLC......212 328-1560
25 W 39th St Fl 3 New York (10018) ***(G-8498)***
Ahw Printing Corp......516 536-3600
2920 Long Beach Rd Oceanside (11572) ***(G-12165)***
Ai Entertainment Holdings LLC (HQ)......212 247-6400
730 5th Ave Fl 20 New York (10019) ***(G-8499)***
Ai Media Group Inc......212 660-2400
1359 Broadway Fl 5 New York (10018) ***(G-8500)***
Aiche, New York *Also called American Inst Chem Engners Inc* ***(G-8552)***
Aicm, Hauppauge *Also called American Intrmdal Cont Mfg LLC* ***(G-5591)***
Aigner Chocolates (PA)......718 544-1850
10302 Metropolitan Ave Forest Hills (11375) ***(G-4915)***
Aigner Index,, New Windsor *Also called Aigner Label Holder Corp* ***(G-8358)***
Aigner Label Holder Corp......845 562-4510
218 Mac Arthur Ave New Windsor (12553) ***(G-8358)***
Aimee Kestenberg, New York *Also called Affordable Luxury Group Inc* ***(G-8490)***
Aimsun Inc......917 267-8534
20 W 22nd St Ste 612 New York (10010) ***(G-8501)***
Aines Manufacturing Corp......631 471-3900
96 E Bayberry Rd Islip (11751) ***(G-6350)***
Aip Mc Holdings LLC (PA)......212 627-2360
330 Madison Ave Fl 28 New York (10017) ***(G-8502)***
Aip Publishing LLC......516 576-2200
1305 Walt Whitman Rd # 300 Melville (11747) ***(G-7757)***
Aiping Pharmaceutical Inc......631 952-3802
350w Wireless Blvd Hauppauge (11788) ***(G-5581)***
Air Conditioning, Bronx *Also called AC Air Cooling Co Inc* ***(G-1190)***
Air Crafters Inc......631 471-7788
2085 5th Ave Ronkonkoma (11779) ***(G-13893)***
Air Engineering Filters Inc......914 238-5945
17 Memorial Dr Chappaqua (10514) ***(G-3322)***
Air Export Mechanical......917 709-5310
4108 Parsons Blvd Apt 4r Flushing (11355) ***(G-4835)***
Air Flow Pump Corp......718 241-2800
8412 Foster Ave Brooklyn (11236) ***(G-1472)***
Air Flow Pump Supply, Brooklyn *Also called Air Flow Pump Corp* ***(G-1472)***
Air Industries Group (PA)......631 881-4920
1460 5th Ave Bay Shore (11706) ***(G-644)***
Air Industries Machining Corp......631 328-7000
1460 5th Ave Bay Shore (11706) ***(G-645)***
Air Liquide Electronics......518 605-4936
400 Stonebreak Ext Malta (12020) ***(G-7494)***
Air Louver & Damper Inc (PA)......718 392-3232
2121 44th Rd Long Island City (11101) ***(G-7147)***
Air Preheater, Wellsville *Also called Arvos Inc* ***(G-15667)***
Air Products and Chemicals Inc......518 463-4273
461 River Rd Glenmont (12077) ***(G-5235)***
Air Skate & Air Jump Corp......212 967-1201
1385 Broadway New York (10018) ***(G-8503)***
Air Skate & Air Jump Corp (PA)......212 967-1201
2208 E 5th St Brooklyn (11223) ***(G-1473)***
Air Structures Amercn Tech Inc......914 937-4500
211 S Ridge St Ste 3 Port Chester (10573) ***(G-12812)***
Air System Products Inc......716 683-0435
51 Beach Ave Lancaster (14086) ***(G-6792)***
Air Techniques Inc (HQ)......516 433-7676
1295 Walt Whitman Rd Melville (11747) ***(G-7758)***
Air Techniques Inc......516 433-7676
70 Cantiague Rock Rd Hicksville (11801) ***(G-5878)***
Air Tite Manufacturing Inc......516 897-0295
724 Park Pl Ste B Long Beach (11561) ***(G-7134)***
Air-Flo Mfg Co Inc......607 733-8284
365 Upper Oakwood Ave Elmira (14903) ***(G-4340)***
Air-O-Tronics, Cazenovia *Also called Stk Electronics Inc* ***(G-3235)***
Aircraft Finishing Corp (PA)......631 422-5000
100 Field St Unit A West Babylon (11704) ***(G-15684)***
Airflex Corp......631 752-1219
965 Conklin St Farmingdale (11735) ***(G-4574)***
Airflex Industrial Inc (PA)......631 752-1234
965 Conklin St Farmingdale (11735) ***(G-4575)***
Airflex Industrial Inc......631 752-1234
937 Conklin St Farmingdale (11735) ***(G-4576)***
Airgas Inc......518 690-0068
84 Karner Rd Albany (12205) ***(G-30)***
Airgle Corporation......866 501-7750
711 Koehler Ave Ste 3 Ronkonkoma (11779) ***(G-13894)***
Airline Container Services......516 371-4125
354 Harbor Dr Lido Beach (11561) ***(G-6927)***
Airline Container Svces, Lido Beach *Also called Airline Container Services* ***(G-6927)***
Airmarine Electroplating Corp......516 623-4406
388 Woodcleft Ave Freeport (11520) ***(G-4980)***
Airnet Communications Corp......516 338-0008
609 Cantiague Rock Rd # 5 Westbury (11590) ***(G-15864)***
Airnet North Division, Westbury *Also called Airnet Communications Corp* ***(G-15864)***
Airport Press, The, Jamaica *Also called Pati Inc* ***(G-6464)***
Airport Printing & Stationers, Wading River *Also called A I P Printing & Stationers* ***(G-15448)***
Airsep, Amherst *Also called Chart Industries Inc* ***(G-218)***
Airsep Corporation......716 691-0202
260 Creekside Dr Ste 100 Amherst (14228) ***(G-204)***
Airtech Lab, Brooklyn *Also called Dib Managmnt Inc* ***(G-1741)***
Airweld Inc......631 924-6366
1740 Middle Country Rd Ridge (11961) ***(G-13131)***
Aithaca Chemical Corp......516 229-2330
50 Charles Lindbergh Blvd # 400 Uniondale (11553) ***(G-15223)***
Aj Genco Mch Sp McHy Rdout Svc......716 664-4925
235 Carter St Falconer (14733) ***(G-4532)***
Ajax Wire Specialty Co Inc......516 935-2333
119 Bloomingdale Rd Hicksville (11801) ***(G-5879)***
Ajes Pharmaceuticals LLC......631 608-1728
11a Lincoln St Copiague (11726) ***(G-3644)***
Ajmadison Corp......718 532-1800
3605 13th Ave Brooklyn (11218) ***(G-1474)***
AJW Architectural Products, New Windsor *Also called Fifty Door Partners LLC* ***(G-8367)***
Aka Enterprises......716 474-4579
164 Main St Wyoming (14591) ***(G-16249)***
Akhon Samoy Weekly, Flushing *Also called Digital One USA Inc* ***(G-4848)***
Aki Cabinets Inc......718 721-2541
2636 2nd St Astoria (11102) ***(G-413)***
Akoustis Inc......585 919-3073
5450 Campus Dr Ste 100 Canandaigua (14424) ***(G-3124)***
Akraturn Mfg Inc......607 775-2802
1743 Us Route 11 Kirkwood (13795) ***(G-6729)***
Akribos Watches, Brooklyn *Also called TWI Watches LLC* ***(G-2531)***
Akron-Corfu Pennysaver, Elma *Also called R W Publications Div of Wtrhs* ***(G-4325)***
Akshar Extracts Inc......631 588-9727
59 Remington Blvd Ronkonkoma (11779) ***(G-13895)***
Aktina Corp......845 268-0101
360 N Route 9w Congers (10920) ***(G-3606)***
Akzo Nobel Central Research, Dobbs Ferry *Also called Nouryon Surface Chemistry* ***(G-4018)***
Akzo Nobel Chemicals LLC......845 276-8200
281 Fields Ln Brewster (10509) ***(G-1139)***
Akzo Nobel Coatings Inc......631 242-6020
1014 Grand Blvd Ste 6 Deer Park (11729) ***(G-3832)***
Al Cohens Famous Rye Bread Bky, Buffalo *Also called Cohens Bakery Inc* ***(G-2702)***
Ala Scientific Instruments Inc......631 393-6401
60 Marine St Ste 1 Farmingdale (11735) ***(G-4577)***
Alabaster Group Inc......516 867-8223
188 N Main St Freeport (11520) ***(G-4981)***
Alabu Inc......518 665-0411
30 Graves Rd Mechanicville (12118) ***(G-7690)***
Alabu Skin Care, Mechanicville *Also called Alabu Inc* ***(G-7690)***
Aladdin Bakers Inc......718 499-1818
239 26th St Brooklyn (11232) ***(G-1475)***
Aladdin Manufacturing Corp......212 561-8715
295 5th Ave Ste 1412 New York (10016) ***(G-8504)***
Aladdin Packaging LLC......631 273-4747
115 Engineers Rd Ste 100 Hauppauge (11788) ***(G-5582)***
Alamar Printing Inc......914 993-9007
190 E Post Rd Frnt 1 White Plains (10601) ***(G-15969)***
Alan F Bourguet......516 883-4315
63 Essex Ct Port Washington (11050) ***(G-12861)***
Alard Equipment Corporation......315 589-4511
6483 Lake Ave Williamson (14589) ***(G-16109)***
Alart Inc......212 840-1508
578 5th Ave Unit 33 New York (10036) ***(G-8505)***
Alaska Spring Phrmcuticals Inc......516 205-6020
609 Cantiague Rock Rd # 1 Westbury (11590) ***(G-15865)***
Alba Fuel Corp......718 931-1700
2135 Wllmsbrdge Rd Fl 2 Flr 2 Bronx (10461) ***(G-1199)***
Alba House Publishers......718 698-2759
2187 Victory Blvd Staten Island (10314) ***(G-14616)***
Albaluz Films LLC......347 613-2321
954 Lexington Ave New York (10021) ***(G-8506)***
Albany Catholic Press Assoc......518 453-6688
40 N Main Ave Ste 2 Albany (12203) ***(G-31)***
Albany International Corp......518 445-2230
1373 Broadway Menands (12204) ***(G-7838)***
Albany International Corp......607 749-7226
156 S Main St Homer (13077) ***(G-6060)***
Albany International Corp......518 447-6400
1373 Broadway Menands (12204) ***(G-7839)***
Albany International Corp......518 445-2200
253 Troy Rd Rensselaer (12144) ***(G-13084)***
Albany Letter Shop Inc......518 434-1172
16 Van Zandt St Ste 20 Albany (12207) ***(G-32)***
Albany Molecular Research Inc......518 512-2234
21 Corporate Cir Albany (12203) ***(G-33)***
Albany Molecular Research Inc......518 433-7700
81 Columbia Tpke Rensselaer (12144) ***(G-13085)***

Albany Molecular Research Inc (HQ)....................518 512-2000
26 Corporate Cir Albany (12203) *(G-34)*

Albany Molecular Research Inc.........................518 512-2000
33 Riverside Ave Rensselaer (12144) *(G-13086)*

Albany Mtal Fbrcation Holdings........................518 463-5161
67 Henry Johnson Blvd Albany (12210) *(G-35)*

Albany Nipple and Pipe Mfg.............................518 270-2162
60 Cohoes Ave Ste 100a Troy (12183) *(G-15157)*

Albany Student Press Inc...............................518 442-5665
1400 Washington Ave Cc329 Albany (12222) *(G-36)*

Albatros North America Inc............................518 381-7100
6 Mccrea Hill Rd Ballston Spa (12020) *(G-567)*

Albea Cosmetics America Inc (HQ)....................212 371-5100
595 Madison Ave Fl 10 New York (10022) *(G-8507)*

Albert Augustine Ltd....................................718 913-9635
161 S Macquesten Pkwy Mount Vernon (10550) *(G-8122)*

Albert F Stager Inc....................................315 434-7240
6805 Crossbow Dr East Syracuse (13057) *(G-4193)*

Albert Gates Inc.......................................585 594-9401
3434 Union St North Chili (14514) *(G-12021)*

Albert Kemperle Inc....................................718 629-1084
890 E 51st St Brooklyn (11203) *(G-1476)*

Albert Menin Interiors Ltd.............................212 876-3041
2417 3rd Ave Fl 3 Bronx (10451) *(G-1200)*

Albert Siy..718 359-0389
13508 Booth Memorial Ave Flushing (11355) *(G-4836)*

Albest Metal Stamping Corp (PA)......................718 388-6000
1 Kent Ave Brooklyn (11249) *(G-1477)*

Albest Metal Stamping Corp.............................718 388-6000
30 Wythe Ln Brooklyn (11249) *(G-1478)*

Albion-Holley Pennysaver Inc.........................585 589-5641
170 N Main St Albion (14411) *(G-153)*

Albrizio Couture, Brooklyn *Also called Albrizio Inc (G-1479)*

Albrizio Inc...212 719-5290
257 Varet St Ste Mgmt Brooklyn (11206) *(G-1479)*

Albro Gear & Instrument, Yaphank *Also called W J Albro Machine Works Inc (G-16278)*

Albumx Corp...914 939-6878
21 Grace Church St Port Chester (10573) *(G-12813)*

Alcatel-Lucent USA Inc.................................516 349-4900
1 Fairchild Ct Ste 340 Plainview (11803) *(G-12661)*

Alchar Printing, Troy *Also called Dowd - Witbeck Printing Corp (G-15166)*

Alchemy Simya Inc......................................646 230-1122
161 Avnue Of The Americas New York (10013) *(G-8508)*

Alco Plastics Inc.......................................716 683-3020
35 Ward Rd Lancaster (14086) *(G-6793)*

Alco Products Div, Orchard Park *Also called Nitram Energy Inc (G-12368)*

Alcoa, Falconer *Also called Arconic Inc (G-4534)*

Alcoa Corporation......................................412 315-2900
45 County Route 42 Massena (13662) *(G-7663)*

Alcoa Fastening Systems...............................585 368-5049
181 Mckee Rd Rochester (14611) *(G-13216)*

Alcoa Fastening Systems...............................845 334-7203
1 Corporate Dr Kingston (12401) *(G-6677)*

Alcoa USA Corp..315 764-4011
45 County Route 42 Massena (13662) *(G-7664)*

Alcoa USA Corp..315 764-4106
1814 State Highway 131 Massena (13662) *(G-7665)*

Alcoholics Anonymous Grapevine (PA).................212 870-3400
475 Riverside Dr Ste 1264 New York (10115) *(G-8509)*

Alconox, White Plains *Also called L S Z Inc (G-16024)*

Alconox Inc...914 948-4040
30 Glenn St Ste 309 White Plains (10603) *(G-15970)*

Alden Advertiser, Alden *Also called Weisbeck Publishing Printing (G-176)*

Alden Aurora Gas Company Inc..........................716 937-9484
13441 Railroad St Alden (14004) *(G-165)*

Alden Optical Laboratory Inc..........................716 937-9181
6 Lancaster Pkwy Lancaster (14086) *(G-6794)*

Aldo Frustacci Iron Works Inc.........................718 768-0707
165 27th St Brooklyn (11232) *(G-1480)*

Aldos Iron Works Inc...................................718 834-0408
75 Van Brunt St Brooklyn (11231) *(G-1481)*

Aldrich Solutions Incorporated........................716 634-1790
80 Earhart Dr Ste 14 Williamsville (14221) *(G-16118)*

Ale Viola LLC...212 868-3808
259 W 30th St Fl 9-10 New York (10001) *(G-8510)*

Ale-Techniques Inc.....................................845 687-7200
2452 Lucas Tpke Ste B High Falls (12440) *(G-5954)*

Alen Sands York Associates Ltd........................212 563-6305
236 W 26th St Rm 801 New York (10001) *(G-8511)*

Aleta Industries Inc...................................718 349-0040
40 Ash St Brooklyn (11222) *(G-1482)*

Aleteia Usa Inc...914 502-1855
86 Main St Ste 303 Yonkers (10701) *(G-16281)*

Alex Sepkus Inc..212 391-8466
42 W 48th St Ste 501 New York (10036) *(G-8512)*

Alexander Primak Jewelry Inc..........................212 398-0287
529 5th Ave Fl 15 New York (10017) *(G-8513)*

Alexander Wang Incorporated (PA)......................212 532-3103
386 Broadway Fl 3 New York (10013) *(G-8514)*

Alexandra Ferguson LLC.................................718 788-7768
180 Davenport Ave New Rochelle (10805) *(G-8317)*

Alexandre Furs, New York *Also called Samuel Schulman Furs Inc (G-11127)*

Alexandria Professional LLC..........................716 242-8514
5500 Main St Ste 103 Williamsville (14221) *(G-16119)*

Alexandros, New York *Also called Anastasia Furs International (G-8574)*

Alexy Associates Inc...................................845 482-3000
86 Jim Stephenson Rd Bethel (12720) *(G-827)*

Alfa Card Inc...718 326-7107
7915 Cooper Ave Glendale (11385) *(G-5217)*

Alfa Chem, Great Neck *Also called Alfred Khalily Inc (G-5362)*

Alfa Laval Kathabar Inc................................716 875-2000
91 Sawyer Ave Tonawanda (14150) *(G-15083)*

Alfa Laval Niagara Inc (HQ)............................800 426-5169
91 Sawyer Ave Tonawanda (14150) *(G-15084)*

Alfred Butler Inc......................................516 829-7460
107 Grace Ave Great Neck (11021) *(G-5361)*

Alfred Dunner Inc (PA).................................212 478-4300
1333 Broadway Fl 11 New York (10018) *(G-8515)*

Alfred Khalily Inc......................................516 504-0059
2 Harbor Way Great Neck (11024) *(G-5362)*

Alfred Mainzer Inc (PA)................................718 392-4200
2708 40th Ave Long Island City (11101) *(G-7148)*

Algafuel America.......................................516 295-2257
289 Meadowview Ave Hewlett (11557) *(G-5869)*

Algemeiner Journal Inc.................................718 771-0400
508 Montgomery St Brooklyn (11225) *(G-1483)*

Algonquin Books Chapel Hl Div, New York *Also called Workman Publishing Co Inc (G-11779)*

Algonquin Power..315 393-5595
19 Mill St Ogdensburg (13669) *(G-12201)*

Ali Ro, New York *Also called Donna Morgan LLC (G-9251)*

Alice & Trixie, New York *Also called Millennium Productions Inc (G-10467)*

Alice Perkins...716 378-5100
148 Washington St Salamanca (14779) *(G-14121)*

Alicia Adams Alpaca Inc................................845 868-3366
3262 Franklin Ave Millbrook (12545) *(G-7941)*

Alicia F Herdlein......................................585 344-4411
5450 E Main Street Rd Batavia (14020) *(G-599)*

Alicias Bakery Inc.....................................914 235-4689
498 Main St Ste A New Rochelle (10801) *(G-8318)*

Alison Wine & Vineyard, Rhinebeck *Also called Dutchess Wines LLC (G-13099)*

Aljo Precision Products Inc...........................516 420-4419
205 Bethpge Sweet Holw Old Bethpage (11804) *(G-12213)*

Aljo-Gefa Precision Mfg LLC............................516 420-4419
205 Bethpge Sweet Holw Old Bethpage (11804) *(G-12214)*

Alkemy Machine LLC....................................585 436-8730
1600 Lexington Ave 103c Rochester (14606) *(G-13217)*

Alken Industries Inc...................................631 467-2000
2175 5th Ave Ronkonkoma (11779) *(G-13896)*

All About Art Inc.....................................718 321-0755
4128 Murray St Flushing (11355) *(G-4837)*

All American Awards Inc................................631 567-2025
331 Knickerbocker Ave Bohemia (11716) *(G-968)*

All American Building..................................607 797-7123
109 Crestmont Rd Binghamton (13905) *(G-851)*

All American Concrete Corp.............................718 497-3301
239 Ingraham St Brooklyn (11237) *(G-1484)*

All American Funding & Ref LLC........................516 978-7531
345 Eastern Pkwy Farmingdale (11735) *(G-4578)*

All American Metal Corporation........................516 223-1760
200 Buffalo Ave Freeport (11520) *(G-4982)*

All American Metal Corporation........................516 623-0222
200 Buffalo Ave Freeport (11520) *(G-4983)*

All American Stairs & Railing.........................718 441-8400
13023 91st Ave Richmond Hill (11418) *(G-13107)*

All American Transit Mix Corp.........................718 417-3654
46 Knickerbocker Ave Brooklyn (11237) *(G-1485)*

All American Uniform, Bohemia *Also called All American Awards Inc (G-968)*

All Cast Foundry, Brooklyn *Also called J & J Bronze & Aluminum Cast (G-1976)*

All City Switchboard Corp..............................718 956-7244
3541 11th St Long Island City (11106) *(G-7149)*

All Color Business Spc Ltd.............................516 420-0649
305 Suburban Ave Deer Park (11729) *(G-3833)*

All Color Business Specialties, Deer Park *Also called All-Color Offset Printers Inc (G-3834)*

All Craft Jewelry Supply, New York *Also called Creative Tools & Supply Inc (G-9121)*

All Cultures Inc..631 293-3143
12 Gates St Greenlawn (11740) *(G-5451)*

All Island Blower & Shtmtl.............................631 567-7070
1585 Smithtown Ave Unit C Bohemia (11716) *(G-969)*

All Island Media Inc (PA).............................631 698-8400
1 Rodeo Dr Edgewood (11717) *(G-4261)*

All Island Media Inc...................................516 942-8400
325 Duffy Ave Unit 2 Hicksville (11801) *(G-5880)*

All Merchandise Display Corp...........................718 257-2221
4 Pheasant Run Highland Mills (10930) *(G-5967)*

All Metal Specialties Inc..............................716 664-6009
300 Livingston Ave Jamestown (14701) *(G-6492)*

All Metro Emrgncy Response Sys........................516 750-9100
50 Broadway Lynbrook (11563) *(G-7424)*

All Out Die Cutting Inc................................718 346-6666
49 Wyckoff Ave Ste 1 Brooklyn (11237) *(G-1486)*

All Packaging McHy & Sups Corp........................631 588-7310
90 13th Ave Unit 11 Ronkonkoma (11779) *(G-13897)*

All Shore Industries Inc..............................718 720-0018
1 Edgewater St Ste 215 Staten Island (10305) *(G-14617)*

A
L
P
H
A
B
E
T
I
C

All Signs 973 736-2113
63 Bridgetown St Staten Island (10314) *(G-14618)*
All Spec Finishing Inc 607 770-9174
219 Clinton St Binghamton (13905) *(G-852)*
All Star Carts & Vehicles Inc 631 666-5581
1565 5th Industrial Ct B Bay Shore (11706) *(G-646)*
All Star Fabricators, Thornwood *Also called Thornwood Products Ltd (G-15071)*
All Star Sheet Metal Inc 718 456-1567
25 Rome St Farmingdale (11735) *(G-4579)*
All The Rage Inc 516 605-2001
147 W Cherry St Unit 1 Hicksville (11801) *(G-5881)*
All Time Products Inc 718 464-1400
21167 Jamaica Ave Queens Village (11428) *(G-13016)*
All Times Publishing LLC 315 422-7011
1415 W Genesee St Syracuse (13204) *(G-14809)*
All Type Screw Machine Pdts 516 334-5100
100 New York Ave Westbury (11590) *(G-15866)*
All United Window Corp 718 624-0490
97 Classon Ave Brooklyn (11205) *(G-1487)*
All Worth Press, New York *Also called Skyhorse Publishing Inc (G-11264)*
All-City Metal Inc 718 937-3975
5435 46th St Maspeth (11378) *(G-7586)*
All-Color Offset Printers Inc 516 420-0649
305 Suburban Ave Deer Park (11729) *(G-3834)*
All-Lifts Incorporated 518 465-3461
27-39 Thatcher St Albany (12207) *(G-37)*
All-State Diversified Pdts Inc 315 472-4728
8 Dwight Park Dr Syracuse (13209) *(G-14810)*
All-Tech, Brooklyn *Also called Integra Microsystem 1988 Inc (G-1961)*
Allan John Company 212 940-2210
611 5th Ave Fl 7 New York (10022) *(G-8516)*
Allcraft Fabricators Inc 631 951-4100
150 Wireless Blvd Hauppauge (11788) *(G-5583)*
Alle Processing Corp 718 894-2000
5620 59th St Maspeth (11378) *(G-7587)*
Allegany Laminating and Supply 716 372-2424
158 W Main St Ste A Allegany (14706) *(G-186)*
Allegiant Health, Deer Park *Also called Bli International Inc (G-3847)*
Allegra Print & Imaging, Schenectady *Also called Capital Dst Print & Imaging (G-14251)*
Allegra Printing, Buffalo *Also called Loy L Press Inc (G-2853)*
Allen Air, Melville *Also called A K Allen Co Inc (G-7753)*
Allen Boat Co Inc 716 842-0800
370 Babcock St Rear Buffalo (14206) *(G-2626)*
Allen Field Co Inc 631 665-2782
256 Orinoco Dr Ste A Brightwaters (11718) *(G-1170)*
Allen Machine Products Inc 631 630-8800
120 Ricefield Ln Ste 100 Hauppauge (11788) *(G-5584)*
Allen Pickle Works Inc 516 676-0640
36 Garvies Point Rd Glen Cove (11542) *(G-5187)*
Allen Tool Phoenix Inc 315 463-7533
6821 Ellicott Dr East Syracuse (13057) *(G-4194)*
Allen William & Company Inc 212 675-6461
7119 80th St Ste 8315 Glendale (11385) *(G-5218)*
Alleson of Rochester Inc 315 548-3635
833 Canandaigua Rd Ste 40 Geneva (14456) *(G-5145)*
Alley Cat Signs Inc 631 924-7446
506 Middle Country Rd Middle Island (11953) *(G-7874)*
Alliance Automation Systems 585 426-2700
400 Trabold Rd Rochester (14624) *(G-13218)*
Alliance Control Systems Inc 845 279-4430
577 N Main St Ste 9 Brewster (10509) *(G-1140)*
Alliance Innovative Mfg Inc 716 822-1626
1 Alliance Dr Lackawanna (14218) *(G-6739)*
Alliance Paving Materials Inc 315 337-0795
846 Lawrence St Rome (13440) *(G-13841)*
Alliance Precision Plas Corp (PA) 585 426-5310
1220 Lee Rd Rochester (14606) *(G-13219)*
Alliance Precision Plas Corp 585 426-5310
105 Elmore Dr Rochester (14606) *(G-13220)*
Alliance Services Corp 516 775-7600
23 Van Siclen Ave Floral Park (11001) *(G-4805)*
Alliance Welding & Steel Fabg 516 775-7600
15 Van Siclen Ave Floral Park (11001) *(G-4806)*
Alliance-Mcalpin Ny LLC 585 426-5310
1220 Lee Rd Rochester (14606) *(G-13221)*
Alliant Tchsystems Oprtons LLC 631 737-6100
77 Raynor Ave Ronkonkoma (11779) *(G-13898)*
Allied Aero Services Inc 631 277-9368
506 Grand Blvd Brentwood (11717) *(G-1114)*
Allied Bolt Products LLC 516 512-7600
3000 Marcus Ave Ste 3e09 New Hyde Park (11042) *(G-8249)*
Allied Bronze Corp (del Corp) 646 421-6400
32 Avenue Of The Americas New York (10013) *(G-8517)*
Allied Circuits LLC 716 551-0285
22 James E Casey Dr Buffalo (14206) *(G-2627)*
Allied Converters Inc 914 235-1585
64 Drake Ave New Rochelle (10805) *(G-8319)*
Allied Decorations Co Inc 315 637-0273
720 Erie Blvd W Syracuse (13204) *(G-14811)*
Allied Food Products Inc (PA) 718 230-4227
251 Saint Marks Ave Brooklyn (11238) *(G-1488)*
Allied Industrial Products Co 716 664-3893
880 E 2nd St Jamestown (14701) *(G-6493)*
Allied Industries, Jamestown *Also called Allied Industrial Products Co (G-6493)*
Allied Inspection Services LLC 716 489-3199
4 Carter St Falconer (14733) *(G-4533)*
Allied K & R Broom & Brush Co, Brooklyn *Also called K & R Allied Inc (G-2015)*
Allied Maker 516 200-9145
108 Glen Cove Ave Glen Cove (11542) *(G-5188)*
Allied Metal Spinning Corp 718 893-3300
1290 Viele Ave Bronx (10474) *(G-1201)*
Allied Motion Control Corp 716 242-7535
495 Commerce Dr Ste 3 Amherst (14228) *(G-205)*
Allied Motion Systems Corp (HQ) 716 691-5868
495 Commerce Dr Ste 3 Amherst (14228) *(G-206)*
Allied Motion Technologies Inc (PA) 716 242-8634
495 Commerce Dr Ste 3 Amherst (14228) *(G-207)*
Allied Motion Technologies Inc 315 782-5910
22543 Fisher Rd Watertown (13601) *(G-15558)*
Allied Orthopedics, Ozone Park *Also called Robert Cohen (G-12467)*
Allied Pharmacy Products Inc 516 374-8862
100 Tec St Unit F Hicksville (11801) *(G-5882)*
Allied Products, New York *Also called Biofeedback Instrument Corp (G-8797)*
Allied Reproductions Inc 212 255-2472
70 W 36th St Rm 500 New York (10018) *(G-8518)*
Allied Sample Card Co Inc 718 238-0523
140 58th St Ste 7a Brooklyn (11220) *(G-1489)*
Allied Sign Co, Syracuse *Also called Allied Decorations Co Inc (G-14811)*
Allied Wine Corp 845 796-4160
121 Main St South Fallsburg (12779) *(G-14508)*
Allison Che Fashion Inc (PA) 212 391-1433
1400 Broadway Lbby 5 New York (10018) *(G-8519)*
Allmetal Chocolate Mold Co Inc 631 752-2888
135 Dale St West Babylon (11704) *(G-15685)*
Allomatic Products Company 516 775-0330
102 Jericho Tpke Ste 104 Floral Park (11001) *(G-4807)*
Alloy Machine & Tool Co Inc 516 593-3445
169 Vincent Ave Lynbrook (11563) *(G-7425)*
Alloy Metal Products LLC 315 676-2405
193 Us Route 11 Central Square (13036) *(G-3293)*
Alloy Metal Works Inc 631 694-8163
146 Verdi St Farmingdale (11735) *(G-4580)*
Allred & Associates Inc 315 252-2559
321 Rte 5 W Elbridge (13060) *(G-4296)*
Allround Logistics Inc (PA) 718 544-8945
7240 Ingram St Forest Hills (11375) *(G-4916)*
Allround Maritime Services, Forest Hills *Also called Allround Logistics Inc (G-4916)*
Allsafe Technologies Inc 716 691-0400
290 Creekside Dr Amherst (14228) *(G-208)*
Allstar Casting Corporation 212 563-0909
240 W 37th St Frnt 7 New York (10018) *(G-8520)*
Allstar Graphics Ltd 718 740-2240
22034 Jamaica Ave Queens Village (11428) *(G-13017)*
Allstate Banners, Long Island City *Also called Allstatebannerscom Corporation (G-7150)*
Allstate Gasket & Packing Inc 631 254-4050
31 Prospect Pl Deer Park (11729) *(G-3835)*
Allstate Sign & Plaque Corp 631 242-2828
70 Burt Dr Deer Park (11729) *(G-3836)*
Allstate Tool and Die Inc 585 426-0400
15 Coldwater Cres Rochester (14624) *(G-13222)*
Allstatebannerscom Corporation 718 300-1256
3511 9th St Long Island City (11106) *(G-7150)*
Allstateelectronics, Brooklyn *Also called Henrys Deals Inc (G-1931)*
Allsupermarkets, Ridgewood *Also called 333 J & M Food Corp (G-13136)*
Alltec Products, Westbury *Also called Power Scrub It Inc (G-15918)*
Alltek Labeling Systems, Staten Island *Also called Stoney Croft Converters Inc (G-14715)*
Allure Eyewear LLC 631 755-2121
35 Hub Dr Melville (11747) *(G-7759)*
Allure Fashions Inc 516 829-2470
8 Barstow Rd Apt 2e Great Neck (11021) *(G-5363)*
Allure Jewelry and ACC LLC (PA) 646 226-8057
15 W 36th St Fl 12 New York (10018) *(G-8521)*
Allure Metal Works Inc 631 588-0220
71 Hoffman Ln Ronkonkoma (11749) *(G-13899)*
Allvac 716 433-4411
695 Ohio St Lockport (14094) *(G-7059)*
Allway Tools Inc 718 792-3636
1255 Seabury Ave Bronx (10462) *(G-1202)*
Allworth Communications Inc 212 777-8395
10 E 23rd St Ste 510 New York (10010) *(G-8522)*
Allworth Press, New York *Also called Allworth Communications Inc (G-8522)*
Ally Nyc Corp 212 447-7277
230 W 39th St Rm 525 New York (10018) *(G-8523)*
Allytex LLC 518 376-7539
540 Acland Blvd Ballston Spa (12020) *(G-568)*
Alm Media LLC (HQ) 212 457-9400
150 E 42nd St New York (10017) *(G-8524)*
Alm Media Holdings Inc (PA) 212 457-9400
120 Broadway Fl 5 New York (10271) *(G-8525)*
Almond Group, Port Washington *Also called Almond Jewelers Inc (G-12862)*
Almond Jewelers Inc 516 933-6000
16 S Maryland Ave Port Washington (11050) *(G-12862)*

Almost Famous Clothing, New York *Also called Turn On Products Inc* **(G-11559)**
Alo Acquisition LLC (HQ)..............................518 464-0279
26 Corporate Cir Albany (12203) **(G-38)**
Aloi Materials Handling, Rochester *Also called Aloi Solutions LLC* **(G-13223)**
Aloi Solutions LLC (PA)................................585 292-0920
140 Commerce Dr Rochester (14623) **(G-13223)**
Alonzo Fire Works Display Inc (PA).................518 664-9994
12 County Route 75 Mechanicville (12118) **(G-7691)**
Alp Stone Inc..718 706-6166
2520 50th Ave Fl 2 Long Island City (11101) **(G-7151)**
Alpha 6 Distributions LLC..........................516 801-8290
11 Oyster Bay Rd Locust Valley (11560) **(G-7121)**
Alpha Boats Unlimited, Weedsport *Also called Barber Welding Inc* **(G-15665)**
Alpha Fasteners Corp...................................516 867-6188
154 E Merrick Rd Freeport (11520) **(G-4984)**
Alpha Incorporated.......................................718 765-1614
265 80th St Brooklyn (11209) **(G-1490)**
Alpha Iron Works LLC...................................585 424-7260
65 Goodway Dr S Rochester (14623) **(G-13224)**
Alpha Knitting Mills Inc...............................718 628-6300
41 Varick Ave Ste Mgmt Brooklyn (11237) **(G-1491)**
Alpha Manufacturing Corp............................631 249-3700
152 Verdi St Farmingdale (11735) **(G-4581)**
Alpha Media Group Inc (PA)..........................212 302-2626
415 Madison Ave Fl 4 New York (10017) **(G-8526)**
Alpha Omega Intruments, Yaphank *Also called Cosa Xentaur Corporation* **(G-16258)**
Alpha Packaging Industries Inc.....................718 267-4115
2004 33rd St Long Island City (11105) **(G-7152)**
Alpha Printing Corp......................................315 454-5507
131 Falso Dr Syracuse (13211) **(G-14812)**
Alpha Wolf LLC...516 778-5812
241 Rushmore Ave Carle Place (11514) **(G-3169)**
Alpha-En Corporation (PA)............................914 418-2000
28 Wells Ave Ste 2 Yonkers (10701) **(G-16282)**
AlphaGraphics, Rochester *Also called Bittner Company LLC* **(G-13270)**
Alphamed Bottles Inc....................................631 524-5577
300 S Technology Dr Central Islip (11722) **(G-3261)**
Alphonse Lduc - Rbert King Inc.....................508 238-8118
180 Madison Ave 24 New York (10016) **(G-8527)**
Alpina Color Graphics Inc.............................212 285-2700
27 Cliff St Rm 502 New York (10038) **(G-8528)**
Alpina Copyworld Inc (PA).............................212 683-3511
134 E 28th St New York (10016) **(G-8529)**
Alpina Digital, New York *Also called Alpina Copyworld Inc* **(G-8529)**
Alpine Building Supply Inc............................718 456-2522
4626 Metropolitan Ave Ridgewood (11385) **(G-13139)**
Alpine Business Group Inc (PA)......................212 989-4198
30 E 33rd St Frnt A New York (10016) **(G-8530)**
Alpine Creations Ltd....................................212 308-9353
17 E 48th St Fl 6 New York (10017) **(G-8531)**
Alpine Creative Group, New York *Also called Alpine Business Group Inc* **(G-8530)**
Alpine Machine Inc.......................................607 272-1344
1616 Trumansburg Rd Ithaca (14850) **(G-6362)**
Alpine Paper Box Co Inc...............................718 345-4040
2246 Fulton St Brooklyn (11233) **(G-1492)**
Alpine Water USA LLC...................................203 912-9723
70 Park Dr N Dayton (14041) **(G-3822)**
Alpla Inc...607 250-8101
106 Central Ave Cortland (13045) **(G-3754)**
Alps Provision Co Inc...................................718 721-4477
2270 45th St Astoria (11105) **(G-414)**
Alps Sweet Shop, Beacon *Also called Hudson Valley Chocolatier Inc* **(G-753)**
Alro Machine Company, Lindenhurst *Also called Alro Machine Tool & Die Co Inc* **(G-6939)**
Alro Machine Tool & Die Co Inc.....................631 226-5020
585 W Hoffman Ave Lindenhurst (11757) **(G-6939)**
Alrod Associates Inc...................................631 981-2193
710 Union Pkwy Ste 9 Ronkonkoma (11779) **(G-13900)**
Alry Tool and Die Co Inc...............................716 693-2419
386 Fillmore Ave Tonawanda (14150) **(G-15085)**
Alstom Signaling Inc (HQ).............................585 783-2000
1025 John St West Henrietta (14586) **(G-15782)**
Alstrom Trnspt Info Solutions, West Henrietta *Also called Alstom Signaling Inc* **(G-15782)**
Alta Industries Ltd......................................845 586-3336
46966 State Hwy 30 Halcottsville (12438) **(G-5487)**
Alta Log Homes, Halcottsville *Also called Alta Industries Ltd* **(G-5487)**
Alta Metal Finishing Corp.............................914 946-1916
126 Oakley Ave White Plains (10601) **(G-15971)**
Altaire Pharmaceuticals Inc........................631 722-5988
311 West Ln Aquebogue (11931) **(G-364)**
Altamont Spray Welding Inc..........................518 861-8870
133 Lewis Rd Altamont (12009) **(G-192)**
Altan Robotech (usa) Inc..............................866 291-1101
224a Main St Goshen (10924) **(G-5304)**
Altana Technologies Inc..............................516 263-0633
81 Prospect St Brooklyn (11201) **(G-1493)**
Altaquip LLC..631 580-4740
200 13th Ave Unit 6 Ronkonkoma (11779) **(G-13901)**
Alternative Parts, Bellport *Also called Alternative Service Inc* **(G-793)**
Alternative Service Inc.................................631 345-9500
7 Sawgrass Dr Bellport (11713) **(G-793)**

Alternative Technology Corp..........................914 478-5900
1 North St Ste 1 # 1 Hastings On Hudson (10706) **(G-5571)**
Alternatives For Children..............................631 271-0777
600 S Service Rd Dix Hills (11746) **(G-4009)**
Altius Aviation LLC.......................................315 455-7555
113 Tuskegee Rd Ste 2 Syracuse (13211) **(G-14813)**
Altman Lighting, Yonkers *Also called Altman Stage Lighting Co Inc* **(G-16283)**
Altman Stage Lighting Co Inc.........................914 476-7987
57 Alexander St Yonkers (10701) **(G-16283)**
Alton Manufacturing Inc..............................585 458-2600
825 Lee Rd Rochester (14606) **(G-13225)**
Altr Inc...212 575-0077
16 W 46th St Fl 12 New York (10036) **(G-8532)**
Altro Business Forms Div, New York *Also called New Deal Printing Corp* **(G-10578)**
Altronix Corp...718 567-8181
140 58th St Bldg A3w Brooklyn (11220) **(G-1494)**
Altum Press, Long Island City *Also called Cama Graphics Inc* **(G-7183)**
Altype Fire Door Corporation.........................718 292-3500
886 E 149th St Bronx (10455) **(G-1203)**
Aludyne New York LLC..................................248 728-8642
4320 Federal Dr Batavia (14020) **(G-600)**
Aluf Plastics Division, Orangeburg *Also called API Industries Inc* **(G-12305)**
Alufoil Products Co Inc...............................631 231-4141
135 Oser Ave Ste 3 Hauppauge (11788) **(G-5585)**
Alumi-Tech LLC...585 663-7010
1640 Harris Rd Penfield (14526) **(G-12569)**
Alumidock, Randolph *Also called Metallic Ladder Mfg Corp* **(G-13063)**
Alumil Fabrication Inc..................................845 469-2874
4401 21st St Ste 203 Long Island City (11101) **(G-7153)**
Alumil NA Fabrication, Long Island City *Also called N A Alumil Corporation* **(G-7302)**
Aluminum Injection Mold Co LLC....................585 502-6087
8741 Lake Street Rd Ste 4 Le Roy (14482) **(G-6895)**
Alvin J Bart, Glendale *Also called Allen William & Company Inc* **(G-5218)**
Alvina Vlenta Couture Collectn......................212 921-7058
525 Fashion Ave Rm 1703 New York (10018) **(G-8533)**
Alvina Vlenta Couture Collectn......................212 921-7058
225 W 37th St New York (10018) **(G-8534)**
Alvio-US Corp..631 664-0618
89 Cabot Ct Ste M Hauppauge (11788) **(G-5586)**
Always Baked Fresh Inc...............................631 648-0811
331 Dante Ct Ste F Holbrook (11741) **(G-5985)**
Always Printing...914 481-5209
149 Highland St Port Chester (10573) **(G-12814)**
Alyk Inc...866 232-0970
150 W 22nd St Fl 5 New York (10011) **(G-8535)**
AM Bickford Inc..716 652-1590
12318 Big Tree Rd Wales Center (14169) **(G-15465)**
AM Cast Inc (PA)...631 750-1644
34 Aero Rd Bohemia (11716) **(G-970)**
AM Display, Highland Mills *Also called All Merchandise Display Corp* **(G-5967)**
AM Retail Group Inc.....................................716 297-0752
1900 Military Rd Niagara Falls (14304) **(G-11902)**
Am-Best Emblems, Boiceville *Also called Stucki Embroidery Works Inc* **(G-1100)**
Am-Pol Eagle, Buffalo *Also called Buffalo Standard Printing Corp* **(G-2684)**
AMA Precision Screening Inc..........................585 293-0820
456 Sanford Rd N Churchville (14428) **(G-3407)**
Amacon Corporation.....................................631 293-1888
49 Alder St Unit A West Babylon (11704) **(G-15686)**
Amada Tool America Inc................................585 344-3900
4 Treadeasy Ave Ste A Batavia (14020) **(G-601)**
Amana Tool Corp..631 752-1300
120 Carolyn Blvd Farmingdale (11735) **(G-4582)**
Amarantus Bscence Holdings Inc (PA)............917 686-5317
110 Wall St New York (10005) **(G-8536)**
Amarr Company..585 426-8290
550 Mile Crssing Blvd 1 Rochester (14624) **(G-13226)**
Amarr Garage Doors, Rochester *Also called Amarr Company* **(G-13226)**
Amax Printing Inc...718 384-8600
6417 Grand Ave Maspeth (11378) **(G-7588)**
Amazing Meals, Maspeth *Also called Alle Processing Corp* **(G-7587)**
Amber Bever Inc..212 391-4911
8604 Avenue M 1 Brooklyn (11236) **(G-1495)**
Ambind Corp...716 836-4365
Cheektowaga Buffalo (14225) **(G-2628)**
Ambras Fine Jewelry Inc...............................718 784-5252
3100 47th Ave Unit 3 Long Island City (11101) **(G-7154)**
Ambras Fjc, Long Island City *Also called Ambras Fine Jewelry Inc* **(G-7154)**
Ambrell Corporation (HQ)..............................585 889-0236
1655 Lyell Ave Rochester (14606) **(G-13227)**
Ambulatory Monitoring Inc............................914 693-9240
731 Saw Mill River Rd # 3 Ardsley (10502) **(G-385)**
Amby International Inc...................................718 645-0964
1460 E 12th St Brooklyn (11230) **(G-1496)**
Amci Ltd..718 937-5858
3302 48th Ave Long Island City (11101) **(G-7155)**
Amco Intl Mfg & Design Inc...........................718 388-8668
10 Conselyea St Brooklyn (11211) **(G-1497)**
Amcom Software Inc......................................212 951-7600
256 W 38th St Fl 8 New York (10018) **(G-8537)**
Amcor Rigid Packaging Usa LLC....................716 366-2440
1 Cliffstar Ave Dunkirk (14048) **(G-4049)**

A
L
P
H
A
B
E
T
I
C

Amendola MBL & Stone Ctr Inc 914 997-7968
560 Tarrytown Rd White Plains (10607) ***(G-15972)***
Amenity Analytics Inc 646 786-8316
387 Park Ave S Fl 9 New York (10016) ***(G-8538)***
Amereon Ltd 631 298-5100
800 Wickham Ave Mattituck (11952) ***(G-7676)***
Amerex Corporation 212 221-3151
512 7th Ave Fl 9 New York (10018) ***(G-8539)***
Ameri Serv South, Jamestown *Also called Vac Air Service Inc* ***(G-6552)***
Ameri-Cut Tool Grinding Inc 716 692-3900
1020 Oliver St North Tonawanda (14120) ***(G-12051)***
America Capital Energy Corp 212 983-8316
405 Lexington Ave Fl 65 New York (10174) ***(G-8540)***
America Health Corp 800 860-1868
708 3rd Ave Ste 600 New York (10017) ***(G-8541)***
America NY Ri Wang Fd Group Co (PA) 631 231-8999
30 Inez Dr Bay Shore (11706) ***(G-647)***
America NY Ri Wang Fd Group Co 631 231-8999
5885 58th Ave Maspeth (11378) ***(G-7589)***
America Press Inc (PA) 212 581-4640
1212 Ave Of The Americas New York (10036) ***(G-8542)***
American Access Care LLC 631 582-9729
32 Central Ave Hauppauge (11788) ***(G-5587)***
American Acrylic Corporation 631 422-2200
400 Sheffield Ave West Babylon (11704) ***(G-15687)***
American Aerogel Corporation 585 328-2140
460 Buffalo Rd Ste 200a Rochester (14611) ***(G-13228)***
American Aerospace Contrls Inc 631 694-5100
570 Smith St Farmingdale (11735) ***(G-4583)***
American Agora Foundation Inc 212 590-6870
116 E 16th St Fl 8 New York (10003) ***(G-8543)***
American Apparel Ltd 516 504-4559
15 Cuttermill Rd Ste 145 Great Neck (11021) ***(G-5364)***
American Apparel Trading Corp (PA) 212 764-5990
209 W 38th St Rm 1004 New York (10018) ***(G-8544)***
American Auto ACC Incrporation (PA) 718 886-6600
3506 Leavitt St Apt Cfc Flushing (11354) ***(G-4838)***
American Best Cabinets Inc 845 369-6666
397 Spook Rock Rd Suffern (10901) ***(G-14757)***
American Bio Medica Corp (PA) 518 758-8158
122 Smith Rd Kinderhook (12106) ***(G-6670)***
American Blade Mfg LLC (PA) 607 432-4518
138 Roundhouse Rd Oneonta (13820) ***(G-12256)***
American Blade Mfg LLC 607 656-4204
47 Birdsall St Greene (13778) ***(G-5443)***
American Bluestone LLC 607 369-2235
760 Quarry Rd Sidney (13838) ***(G-14430)***
American Boiler Tank Wldg Inc 518 463-5012
53 Pleasant St Albany (12207) ***(G-39)***
American Bottling Company 516 714-0002
2004 Orville Dr N Ronkonkoma (11779) ***(G-13902)***
American Bptst Chrches Mtro NY 212 870-3195
527 W 22nd St New York (10011) ***(G-8545)***
American Business Forms Inc 716 836-5111
3840 E Robinson Rd # 249 Amherst (14228) ***(G-209)***
American Canvas Binders Corp 914 969-0300
430 Nepperhan Ave Yonkers (10701) ***(G-16284)***
American Car Signs Inc 518 227-1173
1483 W Duane Lake Rd Duanesburg (12056) ***(G-4043)***
American Casting and Mfg Corp (PA) 800 342-0333
51 Commercial St Plainview (11803) ***(G-12662)***
American Casting and Mfg Corp 516 349-7010
65 S Terminal Dr Plainview (11803) ***(G-12663)***
American Cat Club LLC 212 779-1140
148 Madison Ave Fl 8 New York (10016) ***(G-8546)***
American Challenge Enterprises 631 595-7171
60 Corbin Ave Ste N Bay Shore (11706) ***(G-648)***
American Chimney Supplies Inc 631 434-2020
129 Oser Ave Ste B Hauppauge (11788) ***(G-5588)***
American Cigar 718 969-0008
6940 Fresh Meadow Ln Fresh Meadows (11365) ***(G-5037)***
American City Bus Journals Inc 716 541-1654
465 Main St Ste 100 Buffalo (14203) ***(G-2629)***
American Classic Kitchens Inc 212 838-9308
150 E 58th St Ste 900 New York (10155) ***(G-8547)***
American Cleaning Solutions, Long Island City *Also called American Wax Company Inc* ***(G-7156)***
American Clssic Outfitters Inc 585 237-6111
200 Main St N Ste 1 Perry (14530) ***(G-12595)***
American Comfort Direct LLC 201 364-8309
708 3rd Ave Fl 6 New York (10017) ***(G-8548)***
American Conveyor, Brooklyn *Also called Crownbrook ACC LLC* ***(G-1703)***
American Country Quilts & Lin 631 283-5466
134 Mariner Dr Unit C Southampton (11968) ***(G-14526)***
American Craft Jewelers Inc (PA) 718 972-0945
3611 14th Ave Ste 522 Brooklyn (11218) ***(G-1498)***
American Crmic Process RES LLC 315 828-6268
835 Mcivor Rd Phelps (14532) ***(G-12601)***
American Ctr For Edmocracy LLC 716 803-1118
435 Cleveland Dr Cheektowaga (14225) ***(G-3338)***
American Culture, Greenlawn *Also called All Cultures Inc* ***(G-5451)***
American Culture Hair Inc 631 242-3142
159 E 2nd St Huntington Station (11746) ***(G-6236)***
American Custom Metals Inc 585 694-4893
10 Turner Dr Spencerport (14559) ***(G-14551)***
American Diagnostic Corp 631 273-6155
55 Commerce Dr Hauppauge (11788) ***(G-5589)***
American Douglas Metals Inc 716 856-3170
99 Bud Mil Dr Buffalo (14206) ***(G-2630)***
American Dsplay Die Ctters Inc 212 645-1274
121 Varick St Rm 301 New York (10013) ***(G-8549)***
American Electronic Products 631 924-1299
86 Horseblock Rd Unit F Yaphank (11980) ***(G-16255)***
American Epoxy and Metal Inc 718 828-7828
83 Cushman Rd Scarsdale (10583) ***(G-14233)***
American Felt & Filter Co Inc 845 561-3560
361 Walsh Ave New Windsor (12553) ***(G-8359)***
American Filtration Tech Inc 585 359-4130
100 Thruway Park Dr West Henrietta (14586) ***(G-15783)***
American Glass Light, Newburgh *Also called Sandy Littman Inc* ***(G-11886)***
American Graphic Design Awards 212 696-4380
89 5th Ave Ste 901 New York (10003) ***(G-8550)***
American Heritage Magazine, New York *Also called Nsgv Inc* ***(G-10652)***
American Hlth Formulations Inc (HQ) 631 392-1756
45 Adams Ave Hauppauge (11788) ***(G-5590)***
American Home Mfg LLC (HQ) 212 643-0680
302 5th Ave Fl 5 New York (10001) ***(G-8551)***
American Hormones Inc 845 471-7272
69 W Cedar St Ste 2 Poughkeepsie (12601) ***(G-12943)***
American Hose & Hydralics, Bronx *Also called American Refuse Supply Inc* ***(G-1204)***
American Hsptals Patient Guide 518 346-1099
1890 Maxon Rd Ext Schenectady (12308) ***(G-14245)***
American Images Inc 716 825-8888
25 Imson St Buffalo (14210) ***(G-2631)***
American Inst Chem Engners Inc (PA) 646 495-1355
120 Wall St Fl 23 New York (10005) ***(G-8552)***
American Institute Physics Inc 516 576-2410
Hntngton Qad Ste 1n1-2 Melville (11747) ***(G-7760)***
American Intl Media LLC 845 359-4225
11 Martine Ave Ste 870 White Plains (10606) ***(G-15973)***
American Intrmdal Cont Mfg LLC 631 774-6790
150 Motor Pkwy Ste 401 Hauppauge (11788) ***(G-5591)***
American Jewish Committee 212 891-1400
561 Fashion Ave Fl 16 New York (10018) ***(G-8553)***
American Jewish Congress Inc (PA) 212 879-4500
825 3rd Ave Fl 181800 New York (10022) ***(G-8554)***
American Juice Company LLC 347 620-0252
224 W 35th St Fl 11 New York (10001) ***(G-8555)***
American Lckr SEC Systems Inc 716 699-2773
12 Martha St Ellicottville (14731) ***(G-4312)***
American Linear Manufacturers (PA) 516 333-1351
629 Main St Westbury (11590) ***(G-15867)***
American Lpg Systems, Huntington *Also called United Data Systems Inc* ***(G-6230)***
American Marking Systems, Fulton *Also called Krengel Manufacturing Co Inc* ***(G-5069)***
American Material Processing 315 318-0017
126 Bankrupt Rd Phoenix (13135) ***(G-12615)***
American Metal, Rome *Also called Nash Metalware Co Inc* ***(G-13858)***
American Metal Spinning Pdts 631 454-6276
21 Eads St West Babylon (11704) ***(G-15688)***
American Metal Works Inc 914 682-2979
164 Ferris Ave White Plains (10603) ***(G-15974)***
American Metalcraft Marine 315 686-9891
690 Riverside Dr Clayton (13624) ***(G-3452)***
American Minerals Inc (HQ) 646 747-4222
21 W 46th St Fl 14 New York (10036) ***(G-8556)***
American Mtal Stmping Spinning 718 384-1500
72 N 15th St Brooklyn (11222) ***(G-1499)***
American Office Supply Inc 516 294-9444
400 Post Ave Ste 105 Westbury (11590) ***(G-15868)***
American Originals Corporation (PA) 212 836-4155
1156 Avenue Of The Americ New York (10036) ***(G-8557)***
American Orthotic Lab Co Inc 718 961-6487
924 118th St College Point (11356) ***(G-3536)***
American Package Company Inc 718 389-4444
226 Franklin St Brooklyn (11222) ***(G-1500)***
American Packaging Corporation 585 254-2002
1555 Lyell Ave Rochester (14606) ***(G-13229)***
American Packaging Corporation 585 537-4650
100 Apc Dr Churchville (14428) ***(G-3408)***
American Packaging Corporation 585 254-9500
777 Driving Park Ave Rochester (14613) ***(G-13230)***
American Physical Society 631 591-4025
1 Research Rd Ridge (11961) ***(G-13132)***
American Precision Inds Inc (HQ) 716 691-9100
45 Hazelwood Dr Amherst (14228) ***(G-210)***
American Precision Inds Inc 716 652-3600
270 Quaker Rd East Aurora (14052) ***(G-4081)***
American Precision Inds Inc 585 496-5755
95 North St Arcade (14009) ***(G-367)***
American Pride Fasteners LLC 631 940-8292
195 S Fehr Way Bay Shore (11706) ***(G-649)***
American Print Solutions Inc 718 246-7800
561 President St Brooklyn (11215) ***(G-1501)***
American Print Solutions Inc (PA) 718 208-2309
2233 Nostrand Ave Ste 7 Brooklyn (11210) ***(G-1502)***

American Printing & Envelope, New York *Also called Apec Paper Industries Ltd* ***(G-8601)***
American Printing and Off Sups, Kingston *Also called Robert Tabatznik Assoc Inc* ***(G-6708)***
American Printing Eqp & Sup, Elmont *Also called Awt Supply Corp* ***(G-4383)***
American Products, Rochester *Also called American Time Mfg Ltd* ***(G-13233)***
American Profile Magazine, New York *Also called Publishing Group America Inc* ***(G-10923)***
American Quality Embroidery (PA)....631 467-3200
740 Koehler Ave Ronkonkoma (11779) ***(G-13903)***
American Quality Technology....607 777-9488
6 Emma St Binghamton (13905) ***(G-853)***
American Racing Headers Inc....631 608-1427
880 Grand Blvd Deer Park (11729) ***(G-3837)***
American Refuse Supply Inc....718 893-8157
521 Longfellow Ave Bronx (10474) ***(G-1204)***
American Regent Inc (HQ)....631 924-4000
5 Ramsey Rd Shirley (11967) ***(G-14410)***
American Regent Inc....631 924-4000
5 Ramsey Rd Shirley (11967) ***(G-14411)***
American Rock Salt Company LLC (PA)....585 991-6878
3846 Retsof Rd Retsof (14539) ***(G-13094)***
American Sealing Technology....631 254-0019
31 Prospect Pl Deer Park (11729) ***(G-3838)***
American Signcrafters, Hicksville *Also called Tj Signs Unlimited LLC* ***(G-5952)***
American Signcrafters, Islip *Also called T J Signs Unlimited LLC* ***(G-6357)***
American Silk Mills, New York *Also called Gerli & Co Inc* ***(G-9603)***
American Society of Composers (PA)....212 621-6000
250 W 57th St Ste 1300 New York (10107) ***(G-8558)***
American Specialty Mfg Co....585 544-5600
272 Hudson Ave Rochester (14605) ***(G-13231)***
American Sports Media....585 924-4250
106 Cobblestone Court Dr # 323 Victor (14564) ***(G-15391)***
American Sports Media LLC (PA)....585 377-9636
2604 Elmwood Ave Ste 343 Rochester (14618) ***(G-13232)***
American Spray-On Corp....212 929-2100
5 Hanover Sq Fl 5 # 5 New York (10004) ***(G-8559)***
American Standard Mfg Inc....518 868-2512
106 Industrial Park Ln Central Bridge (12035) ***(G-3259)***
American Std Shtmtl Sup Corp....718 888-9350
13324 36th Rd Flushing (11354) ***(G-4839)***
American Sugar Refining Inc....914 376-3386
1 Federal St Yonkers (10705) ***(G-16285)***
American Target Marketing Inc....518 725-4369
11 Cayadutta St Gloversville (12078) ***(G-5276)***
American Tchncal Ceramics Corp (HQ)....631 622-4700
1 Norden Ln Huntington Station (11746) ***(G-6237)***
American Tchncal Ceramics Corp....631 622-4700
17 Stepar Pl Huntington Station (11746) ***(G-6238)***
American Time Mfg Ltd....585 266-5120
1600 N Clinton Ave Ste 1 Rochester (14621) ***(G-13233)***
American Torque Inc....718 526-2433
10522 150th St Jamaica (11435) ***(G-6425)***
American Towman Expeditions, Warwick *Also called American Towman Network Inc* ***(G-15510)***
American Towman Network Inc....845 986-4546
2 Overlook Dr Ste 5 Warwick (10990) ***(G-15510)***
American Trans-Coil Corp....516 922-9640
69 Hamilton Ave Ste 3 Oyster Bay (11771) ***(G-12443)***
American Trim Mfg Inc....518 239-8151
4750 State Hwy 145 Durham (12422) ***(G-4070)***
American Turf Monthly, Great Neck *Also called Star Sports Corp* ***(G-5426)***
American Visual Display, Farmingdale *Also called American Visuals Inc* ***(G-4584)***
American Visuals Inc....631 694-6104
90 Gazza Blvd Farmingdale (11735) ***(G-4584)***
American Wax Company Inc....718 392-8080
3930 Review Ave Long Island City (11101) ***(G-7156)***
American Wire Tie Inc (PA)....716 337-2412
2073 Franklin St North Collins (14111) ***(G-12023)***
American Wood Column Corp....718 782-3163
913 Grand St Brooklyn (11211) ***(G-1503)***
American Woods & Veneers Works....718 937-2195
4735 27th St Long Island City (11101) ***(G-7157)***
American-Swiss Products Co Inc....585 292-1720
1987 W Jefferson Rd Pittsford (14534) ***(G-12636)***
Americana Vineyards & Winery....607 387-6801
4367 E Covert Rd Interlaken (14847) ***(G-6283)***
Americarb Inc....419 281-5800
6100 Niagara Falls Blvd Niagara Falls (14304) ***(G-11903)***
Americarb International Corp....419 281-5800
6100 Niagara Falls Blvd Niagara Falls (14304) ***(G-11904)***
Americo Group Inc....212 563-2700
498 7th Ave Fl 8 New York (10018) ***(G-8560)***
Americo Group Inc (PA)....212 563-2700
1411 Broadway Fl 2 New York (10018) ***(G-8561)***
Amerikom Group Inc....212 675-1329
247 W 30th St Rm 6w New York (10001) ***(G-8562)***
Ameritool Mfg Inc....315 668-2172
64 Corporate Park Dr Central Square (13036) ***(G-3294)***
Amertac Holdings Inc (PA)....610 336-1330
25 Robert Pitt Dr Monsey (10952) ***(G-8034)***
Ames Advanced Materials Corp (HQ)....518 792-5808
50 Harrison Ave South Glens Falls (12803) ***(G-14511)***
Ames Companies Inc....607 739-4544
114 Smith Rd Pine Valley (14872) ***(G-12634)***
Ames Companies Inc....607 369-9595
196 Clifton St Unadilla (13849) ***(G-15220)***
Ames Goldsmith Corp....518 792-7435
21 Rogers St Glens Falls (12801) ***(G-5239)***
Amesburytruth, Rochester *Also called Truth Hardware Corporation* ***(G-13777)***
Ameta International Co Ltd....416 992-8036
2221 Kenmore Ave Ste 108 Buffalo (14207) ***(G-2632)***
Ametal International, Brooklyn *Also called Kon Tat Group Corporation* ***(G-2035)***
Ametek Inc....631 467-8400
903 S 2nd St Ronkonkoma (11779) ***(G-13904)***
Ametek Inc....607 763-4700
33 Lewis Rd Ste 6 Binghamton (13905) ***(G-854)***
Ametek CTS Us Inc (PA)....631 467-8400
903 S 2nd St Ronkonkoma (11779) ***(G-13905)***
Ametek Inc....585 263-7700
255 Union St N Rochester (14605) ***(G-13234)***
Ametek Power Instruments, Rochester *Also called Ametek Inc* ***(G-13234)***
Ametek Rotron, Woodstock *Also called Rotron Incorporated* ***(G-16237)***
Ametek Rotron, Woodstock *Also called Rotron Incorporated* ***(G-16238)***
AMG Global, New York *Also called Enchante Lites LLC* ***(G-9367)***
AMG Global NY & Enchante ACC, New York *Also called AMG JV LLC* ***(G-8563)***
AMG JV LLC (HQ)....212 602-1818
15 W 34th St Fl 8 New York (10001) ***(G-8563)***
Amherst Bee, Williamsville *Also called Bee Publications Inc* ***(G-16121)***
Amherst Media Inc....716 874-4450
175 Rano St Ste 200 Buffalo (14207) ***(G-2633)***
Amherst Stnless Fbrication LLC....716 691-7012
60 John Glenn Dr Amherst (14228) ***(G-211)***
AMI, New York *Also called Worldwide Media Svcs Group Inc* ***(G-11784)***
Amica Magazine, New York *Also called Rizzoli Intl Publications Inc* ***(G-11053)***
Amicale Cashmere, New York *Also called Oakhurst Partners LLC* ***(G-10672)***
Amiram Dror Inc (PA)....212 979-9505
226 India St Brooklyn (11222) ***(G-1504)***
Amish Structure....607 257-1070
32 North St Dryden (13053) ***(G-4036)***
Amj DOT LLC....718 775-3288
1726 E 7th St Brooklyn (11223) ***(G-1505)***
Amneal Pharmaceuticals LLC....908 231-1911
50 Horseblock Rd Brookhaven (11719) ***(G-1405)***
Amneal Pharmaceuticals LLC....631 952-0214
50 Horseblock Rd Brookhaven (11719) ***(G-1406)***
Amneal Pharmaceuticals NY LLC....631 952-0214
360 Moreland Rd Ste C Commack (11725) ***(G-3576)***
Amneal Pharmaceuticals NY LLC (HQ)....908 947-3120
50 Horseblock Rd Brookhaven (11719) ***(G-1407)***
Amnews Corporation....212 932-7400
2340 Frdrick Duglass Blvd New York (10027) ***(G-8564)***
Amoseastern Apparel Inc (PA)....212 730-6350
251 W 39th St Fl 12 New York (10018) ***(G-8565)***
AMP Nutraceuticals Inc....631 676-5537
2130 Pond Rd Ste H Ronkonkoma (11779) ***(G-13906)***
AMP-Line Corp....845 623-3288
3 Amethyst Ct West Nyack (10994) ***(G-15815)***
Ampac Paper LLC (HQ)....845 713-6600
30 Coldenham Rd Walden (12586) ***(G-15456)***
Ampacet Corporation (PA)....914 631-6600
660 White Plains Rd # 360 Tarrytown (10591) ***(G-15040)***
Ampaco, Brooklyn *Also called American Package Company Inc* ***(G-1500)***
Ampex Casting Corporation....212 719-1318
23 W 47th St Unit 3 New York (10036) ***(G-8566)***
Amphenol Aerospace Industrial, Sidney *Also called Amphenol Corporation* ***(G-14431)***
Amphenol Cables On Demand Corp....607 321-2115
20 Valley St Endicott (13760) ***(G-4443)***
Amphenol Corporation....607 563-5364
40-60 Delaware Ave Sidney (13838) ***(G-14431)***
Amphenol Corporation....607 563-5011
40-60 Delaware Ave Sidney (13838) ***(G-14432)***
Amphenol Intrconnect Pdts Corp (HQ)....607 754-4444
20 Valley St Endicott (13760) ***(G-4444)***
Ample Hills Creamery Inc (PA)....347 725-4061
305 Nevins St Brooklyn (11215) ***(G-1506)***
Ample Hills Creamery Inc....718 809-1678
623 Vanderbilt Ave Brooklyn (11238) ***(G-1507)***
Ample Hills Holdings Inc....347 725-4061
305 Nevins St Brooklyn (11215) ***(G-1508)***
Amplience Inc....917 410-7189
234 5th Ave Fl 2 New York (10001) ***(G-8567)***
Amplify Education Inc (PA)....212 213-8177
55 Washington St Ste 800 Brooklyn (11201) ***(G-1509)***
Amplitech Inc....631 521-7738
620 Johnson Ave Ste 2 Bohemia (11716) ***(G-971)***
Amplitech Group Inc (PA)....631 521-7831
620 Johnson Ave Ste 2 Bohemia (11716) ***(G-972)***
Ampro International Inc....845 278-4910
30 Coventry Ln Brewster (10509) ***(G-1141)***
Amri, Albany *Also called Albany Molecular Research Inc* ***(G-34)***
Amri, Rensselaer *Also called Albany Molecular Research Inc* ***(G-13086)***
Amri Rensselaer, Rensselaer *Also called Albany Molecular Research Inc* ***(G-13085)***

ALPHABETIC

Amron Electronics Inc 631 737-1234
160 Gary Way Ronkonkoma (11779) *(G-13907)*

AMS Star Structures Inc 914 584-0898
453 S Broadway Nyack (10960) *(G-12135)*

Amscan Everyday Warehouse, Chester Also called Amscan Inc *(G-3370)*

Amscan Inc 845 469-9116
47 Elizabeth Dr Chester (10918) *(G-3370)*

Amsco School Publications Inc 212 886-6500
315 Hudson St Fl 5 New York (10013) *(G-8568)*

Amscor Inc 800 825-9800
119 Lamar St West Babylon (11704) *(G-15689)*

Amstead Press Corp 347 416-2373
225 W 37th St Fl 16 New York (10018) *(G-8569)*

Amsterdam Oil Heat, Amsterdam Also called J H Buhrmaster Company Inc *(G-331)*

Amsterdam Pharmacy, New York Also called Shrineeta Pharmacy Inc *(G-11220)*

Amsterdam Printing & Litho Inc 518 792-6501
428 Corinth Rd Queensbury (12804) *(G-13030)*

Amsterdam Printing & Litho Inc 518 842-6000
166 Wallins Corners Rd Amsterdam (12010) *(G-316)*

Amsterdam Printing & Litho Inc 518 842-6000
166 Wallins Corners Rd Amsterdam (12010) *(G-317)*

Amstutze Woodworking (PA) 518 946-8206
246 Springfield Rd Upper Jay (12987) *(G-15235)*

Amt Incorporated 518 284-2910
883 Chestnut St Sharon Springs (13459) *(G-14382)*

Amtek Research LLC 416 400-2906
1711 Cudaback Ave # 3865 Niagara Falls (14303) *(G-11905)*

Amy Pak Publishing Inc 585 964-8188
3997 Roosevelt Hwy Holley (14470) *(G-6035)*

An Excelsior Elevator Corp 516 408-3070
640 Main St Unit 2 Westbury (11590) *(G-15869)*

An Group Inc 631 549-4090
17 Scott Dr Melville (11747) *(G-7761)*

An-Cor Industrial Plastics Inc 716 695-3141
900 Niagara Falls Blvd North Tonawanda (14120) *(G-12052)*

Anabec Inc 716 759-1674
9393 Main St Clarence (14031) *(G-3425)*

Anacor Pharmaceuticals Inc (HQ) 212 733-2323
235 E 42nd St New York (10017) *(G-8570)*

Anage Inc 212 944-6533
530 Fashion Ave Frnt 5 New York (10018) *(G-8571)*

Analog Digital Technology LLC 585 698-1845
95 Mount Read Blvd # 149 Rochester (14611) *(G-13235)*

Analysis & Design Aplicat Co, Melville Also called Siemens Product Life Mgmt Sftw *(G-7822)*

Analysts In Media (aim) Inc 212 488-1777
55 Broad St Fl 9 New York (10004) *(G-8572)*

Analytics Intell, New York Also called Informa Solutions Inc *(G-9891)*

Anand Printing Machinery Inc 631 667-3079
188 W 16th St Deer Park (11729) *(G-3839)*

Anandamali Inc 212 343-8964
35 N Moore St New York (10013) *(G-8573)*

Anandsar Inc 551 556-5555
5616 201st St Oakland Gardens (11364) *(G-12159)*

Anaren Inc (HQ) 315 432-8909
6635 Kirkville Rd East Syracuse (13057) *(G-4195)*

Anasia Inc 718 588-1407
1175 Jerome Ave Bronx (10452) *(G-1205)*

Anastasia Furs International (PA) 212 868-9241
345 7th Ave Fl 20 New York (10001) *(G-8574)*

Anatoli Inc 845 334-9000
43 Basin Rd Ste 11 West Hurley (12491) *(G-15808)*

Anavex Life Sciences Corp (PA) 844 689-3939
51 W 52nd St Fl 7 New York (10019) *(G-8575)*

Anbriella Sand & Gravel Corp 631 586-2111
145 S 4th St Bay Shore (11706) *(G-650)*

Anchor Canvas LLC 631 265-5602
556 W Jericho Tpke Smithtown (11787) *(G-14473)*

Anchor Commerce Trading Corp 516 881-3485
53 Dutchess Blvd Atlantic Beach (11509) *(G-452)*

Anchor Glass Container Corp 607 737-1933
151 E Mccanns Blvd Elmira Heights (14903) *(G-4374)*

Anchor Tech Products Corp 914 592-0240
4 Vernon Ln Ste 2 Elmsford (10523) *(G-4393)*

Ancon Gear & Instrument Corp (PA) 631 694-5255
29 Seabro Ave Amityville (11701) *(G-256)*

Andela Products, Richfield Springs Also called Andela Tool & Machine Inc *(G-13105)*

Andela Tool & Machine Inc 315 858-0055
493 State Route 28 Richfield Springs (13439) *(G-13105)*

Andersens Spring & Wldg Corp 516 785-7337
2374 Merrick Rd Bellmore (11710) *(G-778)*

Anderson Instrument Co Inc (HQ) 518 922-5315
156 Auriesville Rd Fultonville (12072) *(G-5077)*

Anderson Precision Inc 716 484-1148
20 Livingston Ave Jamestown (14701) *(G-6494)*

Andes Gold Corporation 212 541-2495
405 Lexington Ave New York (10174) *(G-8576)*

Andex Corp 585 328-3790
69 Deep Rock Rd Rochester (14624) *(G-13236)*

Andigo New Media Inc 212 727-8445
150 W 25th St Rm 900 New York (10001) *(G-8577)*

Andike Millwork Inc (PA) 718 894-1796
5818 64th St Fl 2 Maspeth (11378) *(G-7590)*

Andin International Inc., New York Also called Jotaly Inc *(G-10030)*

Andor Design Corp 516 364-1619
20 Pond View Dr Syosset (11791) *(G-14777)*

Andrea Electronics Corporation (PA) 631 719-1800
620 Johnson Ave Ste 1b Bohemia (11716) *(G-973)*

Andrea Strongwater 212 873-0905
465 W End Ave New York (10024) *(G-8578)*

Andrea Systems LLC 631 390-3140
140 Finn Ct Farmingdale (11735) *(G-4585)*

Andreas Protein Cakery Inc 646 801-9826
229 E 85th St Unit 332 New York (10028) *(G-8579)*

Andrew J George 518 462-4662
457 Madison Ave Albany (12210) *(G-40)*

Andrew M Schwartz LLC 212 391-7070
71 Gansevoort St Ste 2a New York (10014) *(G-8580)*

Andritz Inc 518 745-2988
13 Pruyns Island Dr Glens Falls (12801) *(G-5240)*

Androme Leather Inc 518 773-7945
21 Foster St Gloversville (12078) *(G-5277)*

Andros Bowman Products LLC 540 217-4100
151 West Ave Lyndonville (14098) *(G-7444)*

Andros Manufacturing Corp 585 663-5700
30 Hojack Park Rochester (14612) *(G-13237)*

Andujar Asbestos and Lead 716 228-6757
473 4th St Buffalo (14201) *(G-2634)*

Andy & Evan Industries Inc 212 967-7908
1071 Ave Of The Amer # 804 New York (10018) *(G-8581)*

Andy & Evan Shirt Co., The, New York Also called Andy & Evan Industries Inc *(G-8581)*

Angel Media and Publishing 845 727-4949
26 Snake Hill Rd West Nyack (10994) *(G-15816)*

Angel Textiles Inc 212 532-0900
519 8th Ave Fl 21 New York (10018) *(G-8582)*

Angel Tips Nail Salon 718 225-8300
25473 Horace Harding Expy Little Neck (11362) *(G-6996)*

Angel-Made In Heaven Inc (PA) 212 869-5678
525 Fashion Ave Rm 1710 New York (10018) *(G-8583)*

Angel-Made In Heaven Inc 718 832-4778
116 26th St Brooklyn (11232) *(G-1510)*

Angelic Gourmet, Naples Also called Naples Vly Mrgers Acqstons LLC *(G-8209)*

Angelica Forest Products Inc 585 466-3205
54 Closser Ave Angelica (14709) *(G-356)*

Angelica Spring Company Inc 585 466-7892
99 West Ave Angelica (14709) *(G-357)*

Angie Washroom, New Windsor Also called Larcent Enterprises Inc *(G-8371)*

Angiodynamics Inc 518 798-1215
603 Queensbury Ave Queensbury (12804) *(G-13031)*

Angiodynamics Inc 518 975-1400
603 Queensbury Ave Queensbury (12804) *(G-13032)*

Angiodynamics Inc 518 792-4112
10 Glens Fls Technical Pa Glens Falls (12801) *(G-5241)*

Angiodynamics Inc 518 742-4430
543 Queensbury Ave Queensbury (12804) *(G-13033)*

Angiodynamics Inc (PA) 518 795-1400
14 Plaza Dr Latham (12110) *(G-6848)*

Angiogenex Inc (PA) 347 468-6799
425 Madison Ave Ste 902 New York (10017) *(G-8584)*

Angiotech Biocoatings Corp 585 321-1130
336 Summit Point Dr Henrietta (14467) *(G-5854)*

Ango Home, New York Also called Feldman Company Inc *(G-9482)*

Angola Penny Saver Inc 716 549-1164
19 Center St Angola (14006) *(G-358)*

Angus Buffers & Biochemicals, Niagara Falls Also called Angus Chemical
Company *(G-11906)*

Angus Chemical Company 716 283-1434
2236 Liberty Dr Niagara Falls (14304) *(G-11906)*

Anheuser-Busch LLC 315 638-0365
2780 Brundage Rd Baldwinsville (13027) *(G-541)*

Anheuser-Busch LLC 315 638-0365
2885 Belgium Rd Baldwinsville (13027) *(G-542)*

Anheuser-Busch LLC 212 573-8800
250 Park Ave Fl 2 New York (10177) *(G-8585)*

Anheuser-Busch Companies LLC 718 589-2610
510 Food Center Dr Bronx (10474) *(G-1206)*

Anheuser-Busch Inbev Fin Inc 212 573-8800
250 Park Ave New York (10177) *(G-8586)*

Anheuser-Busch Inbev Svcs LLC 314 765-4729
250 Park Ave Fl 2 New York (10177) *(G-8587)*

Anheusr-Bsch Coml Strategy LLC 347 429-1082
125 W 24th St New York (10011) *(G-8588)*

Anhui Skyworth LLC 917 940-6903
44 Kensington Ct Hempstead (11550) *(G-5831)*

Aniiwe Inc 347 683-1891
774 Rockaway Ave Apt 3k Brooklyn (11212) *(G-1511)*

Anima Group LLC 917 913-2053
435 E 79th St Ph H New York (10075) *(G-8589)*

Anima Mundi Herbals LLC 415 279-5727
2323 Borden Ave Long Island City (11101) *(G-7158)*

Animal Fair Media Inc 212 629-0392
545 8th Ave Rm 401 New York (10018) *(G-8590)*

Animal Pantry 631 673-3666
741 W Jericho Tpke Huntington (11743) *(G-6199)*

Anju Sylogent LLC (HQ)..............................480 326-2358
251 W 19th St New York (10011) *(G-8591)*

Anka Tool & Die Inc..................................845 268-4116
150 Wells Ave Congers (10920) *(G-3607)*

Ankom Development LLC..............................315 986-1937
2052 Oneil Rd Macedon (14502) *(G-7458)*

Ankom Technology Corp...............................315 986-8090
2052 Oneil Rd Macedon (14502) *(G-7459)*

Anmar Acquisition LLC (HQ)........................585 352-7777
35 Vantage Point Dr Rochester (14624) *(G-13238)*

Anna B Inc...516 680-6609
55 Great Jones St Apt 6 New York (10012) *(G-8592)*

Anna Sui Corp (PA)....................................212 941-8406
484 Broome St New York (10013) *(G-8593)*

Anna Young Assoc Ltd................................516 546-4400
100 Doxsee Dr Freeport (11520) *(G-4985)*

Anne Taintor Inc......................................718 483-9312
137 Montague St Brooklyn (11201) *(G-1512)*

Annese & Associates Inc.............................716 972-0076
500 Corporate Pkwy # 106 Buffalo (14226) *(G-2635)*

Annies Ice..585 593-5605
35 Herman Ave Wellsville (14895) *(G-15666)*

Annointed Buty Ministries LLC.....................646 867-3796
1697 E 54th St Brooklyn (11234) *(G-1513)*

Annuals Publishing Co Inc..........................212 505-0950
10 E 23rd St Ste 510 New York (10010) *(G-8594)*

Anorad Corporation...................................631 344-6600
100 Precision Dr Ste 1 Shirley (11967) *(G-14412)*

Another 99 Cent Paradise...........................718 786-4578
4206 Greenpoint Ave Sunnyside (11104) *(G-14770)*

Ansa Systems of USA Inc............................718 835-3743
145 Hook Creek Blvd B6a1 Valley Stream (11581) *(G-15333)*

Ansel Printing & Packaging, Amherst *Also called Panzarella Prtg & Packg Inc* *(G-241)*

Ansen Corporation....................................315 393-3573
100 Chimney Point Dr Ogdensburg (13669) *(G-12202)*

Ansun Graphics Inc....................................315 437-6869
6392 Deere Rd Ste 4 Syracuse (13206) *(G-14814)*

Answer Company, The, New York *Also called Answer Printing Inc* *(G-8595)*

Answer Printing Inc...................................212 922-2922
505 8th Ave Rm 1101 New York (10018) *(G-8595)*

Answermgmt LLC.......................................914 318-1301
90 State St Albany (12207) *(G-41)*

Antab Mch Sprfinishing Lab Inc.....................585 865-8290
46 Latta Rd Rochester (14612) *(G-13239)*

Antenna & Radome Res Assoc (PA).................631 231-8400
15 Harold Ct Bay Shore (11706) *(G-651)*

Anterios Inc...212 303-1683
60 E 42nd St Ste 1160 New York (10165) *(G-8596)*

Anthony Gigi Inc......................................860 984-1943
45 Ramsey Rd Unit 28 Shirley (11967) *(G-14413)*

Anthony L & S LLC (PA)..............................212 386-7245
499 Fashion Ave Fl 19s New York (10018) *(G-8597)*

Anthony L&S Footwear Group, New York *Also called Anthony L & S LLC* *(G-8597)*

Anthony Lawrence of New York.....................212 206-8820
3233 47th Ave Long Island City (11101) *(G-7159)*

Anthony Manno & Co Inc.............................631 445-1834
307 Skidmore Rd Ste 2 Deer Park (11729) *(G-3840)*

Anthony Manufacturing Inc..........................631 957-9424
34 Gear Ave Lindenhurst (11757) *(G-6940)*

Anthony Road Wine Co Inc..........................315 536-2182
1020 Anthony Rd Penn Yan (14527) *(G-12577)*

Anthroposophic Press Inc (PA)......................518 851-2054
15 Greenridge Dr Clifton Park (12065) *(G-3461)*

Antico Casale Usa LLC...............................718 357-2000
1244 Clintonville St 2c Whitestone (11357) *(G-16086)*

Antimony New York LLC..............................917 232-1836
120 E 34th St Apt 7g New York (10016) *(G-8598)*

Antique Lumber Modrn Mllwk LLC...................631 726-7026
328 Montauk Hwy Wainscott (11975) *(G-15454)*

Antiques & Collectible Autos........................716 825-3990
35 Dole St Buffalo (14210) *(G-2636)*

Anton Community Newspapers, Mineola *Also called Long Island Cmnty Nwsppers Inc* *(G-7987)*

Antonicelli Vito Race Car............................716 684-2205
3883 Broadway St Buffalo (14227) *(G-2637)*

Antwerp Diamond Distributors.......................212 319-3300
581 5th Ave Fl 5 New York (10017) *(G-8599)*

Antwerp Sales Intl Inc................................212 354-6515
576 5th Ave New York (10036) *(G-8600)*

Anu Industries LLC....................................201 735-7475
1414 Brooklyn Ave Apt 4f Brooklyn (11210) *(G-1514)*

Anvil Knitwear, Inc., New York *Also called Gildan Apparel USA Inc* *(G-9609)*

Anyas Licorice Inc....................................917 935-1916
1027 Grand St Brooklyn (11211) *(G-1515)*

Anyelas Vineyards LLC...............................315 685-3797
2433 W Lake Rd Skaneateles (13152) *(G-14446)*

Aos, Valley Stream *Also called Automated Office Systems Inc* *(G-15334)*

APC Paper Company Inc..............................315 384-4225
100 Remington Ave Norfolk (13667) *(G-11997)*

APC-Mge, New York *Also called Schneider Electric It Corp* *(G-11156)*

Apec Paper Industries Ltd...........................212 730-0088
189 W 89th St Apt 5w New York (10024) *(G-8601)*

Apex Airtronics Inc (PA).............................718 485-8560
2465 Atlantic Ave Brooklyn (11207) *(G-1516)*

Apex Aridyne Corp....................................516 239-4400
168 Doughty Blvd Inwood (11096) *(G-6287)*

Apex Real Holdings Inc..............................877 725-2150
1640 40th St Ste A Brooklyn (11218) *(G-1517)*

Apex Signal Corporation.............................631 567-1100
110 Wilbur Pl Bohemia (11716) *(G-974)*

Apex Texicon Inc (PA)...............................516 239-4400
295 Madison Ave New York (10017) *(G-8602)*

Apexx Omni-Graphics Inc............................718 326-3330
5829 64th St Maspeth (11378) *(G-7591)*

Apf Management Company LLC........................914 665-5400
60 Fullerton Ave Yonkers (10704) *(G-16286)*

Apf Manufacturing Company LLC (PA)...............914 963-6300
60 Fullerton Ave Yonkers (10704) *(G-16287)*

Apf Munn Master Frame Makers, Yonkers *Also called Apf Manufacturing Company LLC* *(G-16287)*

Apg Neuros, Plattsburgh *Also called Apgn Inc* *(G-12732)*

Apgn Inc...518 324-4150
160 Banker Rd Plattsburgh (12901) *(G-12732)*

Aphrodities...718 224-1774
2007 Francis Lewis Blvd Whitestone (11357) *(G-16087)*

API, Central Islip *Also called Autronic Plastics Inc* *(G-3263)*

API Delevan, East Aurora *Also called American Precision Inds Inc* *(G-4081)*

API Heat Transf Thermasys Corp (HQ)..............716 684-6700
2777 Walden Ave Buffalo (14225) *(G-2638)*

API Heat Transfer Company (HQ)....................716 684-6700
2777 Walden Ave Ste 1 Buffalo (14225) *(G-2639)*

API Heat Transfer Inc.................................585 496-5755
91 North St Arcade (14009) *(G-368)*

API Heat Transfer Inc (HQ)..........................716 684-6700
2777 Walden Ave Ste 1 Buffalo (14225) *(G-2640)*

API Industries Inc (PA)..............................845 365-2200
2 Glenshaw St Orangeburg (10962) *(G-12305)*

API Industries Inc....................................845 365-2200
2 Glenshaw St Orangeburg (10962) *(G-12306)*

API International Group LLC..........................877 215-0017
1767 Ctr Park Ave Ste 277 Yonkers (10710) *(G-16288)*

Apicella Jewelers Inc.................................212 840-2024
40 W 39th St Fl 4 New York (10018) *(G-8603)*

Apogee, Deer Park *Also called Lynne B Enterprises Inc* *(G-3901)*

Apogee Power Usa Inc...............................202 746-2890
7 Verne Pl Hartsdale (10530) *(G-5567)*

Apogee Retail NY.....................................516 731-1727
3041 Hempstead Tpke Levittown (11756) *(G-6912)*

Apollo Apparel Group LLC............................212 398-6585
1407 Brdway Ste 2000-200 New York (10018) *(G-8604)*

Apollo Display Tech Corp (PA).......................631 580-4360
87 Raynor Ave Ste 1 Ronkonkoma (11779) *(G-13908)*

Apollo Investment Fund VII LP......................212 515-3200
9 W 57th St Fl 43 New York (10019) *(G-8605)*

Apollo Jeans, New York *Also called Apollo Apparel Group LLC* *(G-8604)*

Apollo Lighting and Hasco Ltg, Mount Vernon *Also called Luminatta Inc* *(G-8159)*

Apollo Management V LP.............................914 467-6510
1 Manhattanville Rd # 201 Purchase (10577) *(G-13001)*

Apollo Optical Systems Inc..........................585 272-6170
925 John St West Henrietta (14586) *(G-15784)*

Apollo Orthotics Corp................................516 333-3223
320 Westbury Ave Carle Place (11514) *(G-3170)*

Apollo Steel Corporation.............................716 283-8758
4800 Tomson Ave Niagara Falls (14304) *(G-11907)*

Apollo Windows & Doors Inc.........................718 386-3326
1003 Metropolitan Ave Brooklyn (11211) *(G-1518)*

Apothecus Pharmaceutical Corp (PA)................516 624-8200
220 Townsend Sq Oyster Bay (11771) *(G-12444)*

Appairent Technologies Inc (PA)....................585 214-2460
150 Lucius Gordon Dr West Henrietta (14586) *(G-15785)*

Apparatus Mfg Inc....................................845 471-5116
13 Commerce St Poughkeepsie (12603) *(G-12944)*

Apparatus Studio (PA)...............................646 527-9732
122 W 30th St Fl 4 New York (10001) *(G-8606)*

Apparel Group Ltd....................................212 328-1200
35 W 36th St Rm 10w New York (10018) *(G-8607)*

Apparel Production Inc...............................212 278-8362
270 W 39th St Rm 1701 New York (10018) *(G-8608)*

Appfigures Inc...212 343-7900
133 Chrystie St Fl 3 New York (10002) *(G-8609)*

Appguard Inc (HQ)....................................703 786-8884
141 W 36th St Rm 17 New York (10018) *(G-8610)*

Applause Coating LLC................................631 231-5223
8b Grand Blvd Brentwood (11717) *(G-1115)*

Apple, Port Washington *Also called US Juice Partners LLC* *(G-12930)*

Apple & Eve LLC (HQ)................................516 621-1122
2 Seaview Blvd Ste 100 Port Washington (11050) *(G-12863)*

Apple Commuter Inc..................................917 299-0066
54 Lake Dr New Hyde Park (11040) *(G-8250)*

Apple Core Electronics Inc...........................718 628-4068
991 Flushing Ave Brooklyn (11206) *(G-1519)*

Apple Digital Printing, Long Island City *Also called Apple Enterprises Inc* *(G-7160)*

Apple Enterprises Inc.................................718 361-2200
1308 43rd Ave Long Island City (11101) *(G-7160)*

A L P H A B E T I C

Apple Imprints Apparel Inc..................................716 893-1130
   2336 Bailey Ave Buffalo (14211) *(G-2641)*
Apple Press...914 723-6660
   23 Harrison Blvd Ste 2 White Plains (10604) *(G-15975)*
Apple Rubber Products Inc (PA)........................716 684-6560
   310 Erie St Lancaster (14086) *(G-6795)*
Apple Rubber Products Inc..................................716 684-7649
   204 Cemetery Rd Lancaster (14086) *(G-6796)*
Application Resources Inc....................................516 636-6200
   15 Cutternill Rd Ste 529 Great Neck (11021) *(G-5365)*
Application Security Inc (HQ).............................212 912-4100
   55 Broad St Rm 10a New York (10004) *(G-8611)*
Applied Coatings Holding Corp (PA)...................585 482-0300
   1653 E Main St Ste 1 Rochester (14609) *(G-13240)*
Applied Concepts Inc..315 696-6676
   397 State Route 281 Tully (13159) *(G-15207)*
Applied Energy Solutions LLC............................585 538-3270
   251 Gallant Fox Ln Webster (14580) *(G-15629)*
Applied Image Inc...585 482-0300
   1653 E Main St Ste 1 Rochester (14609) *(G-13241)*
Applied Materials Inc...518 245-1400
   10 Stonebreak Rd Ste 2 Ballston Spa (12020) *(G-569)*
Applied Materials Inc...845 227-5000
   2531 Route 52 Hopewell Junction (12533) *(G-6090)*
Applied Minerals Inc (PA)..................................212 226-4265
   55 Washington St Ste 301 Brooklyn (11201) *(G-1520)*
Applied Power Systems Inc.................................516 935-2230
   124 Charlotte Ave Hicksville (11801) *(G-5883)*
Applied Safety LLC..718 608-6292
   4349 10th St Ste 311 Long Island City (11101) *(G-7161)*
Applied Technology Mfg Corp...............................607 687-2200
   71 Temple St Owego (13827) *(G-12428)*
Applied Terminal Systems, Auburn *Also called Daikin Applied Americas Inc (G-472)*
Applince Installation Svc Corp (PA)....................716 884-7425
   3190 Genesee St Buffalo (14225) *(G-2642)*
Apprenda Inc...518 383-2130
   433 River St Ste 4001 Troy (12180) *(G-15163)*
Apprise Mobile, New York *Also called Theirapp LLC (G-11461)*
Appsbidder Inc...917 880-4269
   55 Clark St 772 Brooklyn (11201) *(G-1521)*
Apricus, New York *Also called Seelos Therapeutics Inc (G-11180)*
April Printing Co Inc..212 685-7455
   1201 Broadway Ste 710 New York (10001) *(G-8612)*
APS American Polymers Svcs Inc.......................212 362-7711
   104 W 40th St Rm 500 New York (10018) *(G-8613)*
APS Enterprise Software Inc..............................631 784-7720
   775 Park Ave Huntington (11743) *(G-6200)*
Apsco Sports Enterprises Inc.............................718 965-9500
   50th St & 1st Av Bg 57 F5 Brooklyn (11232) *(G-1522)*
Aptar Congers, Congers *Also called Aptargroup Inc (G-3608)*
Aptargroup Inc..845 639-3700
   250 N Route 303 Congers (10920) *(G-3608)*
Apti Pro Systems 2000 Inc.................................585 265-0160
   6368 Dean Pkwy Ontario (14519) *(G-12283)*
Apx Arstan Products, Hicksville *Also called Arstan Products International (G-5885)*
Apx Technologies Inc...516 433-1313
   264 Duffy Ave Hicksville (11801) *(G-5884)*
Aqua Shield Inc..631 420-4490
   114 Bell St West Babylon (11704) *(G-15690)*
Aquarii Inc..315 672-8807
   17 Genesee St Camillus (13031) *(G-3107)*
Aquarium Pump & Piping Systems......................631 567-5555
   528 Chester Rd Sayville (11782) *(G-14222)*
Aquifer Drilling & Testing Inc (HQ)......................516 616-6026
   75 E 2nd St Mineola (11501) *(G-7958)*
AR & AR Jewelry Inc...212 764-7916
   31 W 47th St Fl 15 New York (10036) *(G-8614)*
AR Publishing Company Inc................................212 482-0303
   55 Broad St Rm 20b New York (10004) *(G-8615)*
Arabella Textiles LLC...212 679-0611
   303 5th Ave Rm 1402 New York (10016) *(G-8616)*
Aratana Therapeutics Inc....................................212 827-0020
   35 W 35th St Fl 11 New York (10001) *(G-8617)*
Arbe Machinery Inc..631 756-2477
   54 Allen Blvd Farmingdale (11735) *(G-4586)*
Arbor Valley Flooring, Salamanca *Also called Norton-Smith Hardwoods Inc (G-14125)*
Arborn Printing & Graphics, Mamaroneck *Also called Division Den-Bar Enterprises (G-7508)*
Arbr Studios LLC..585 254-7607
   35 Norman St Rochester (14613) *(G-13242)*
ARC Remanufacturing Inc....................................718 728-0701
   1940 42nd St Long Island City (11105) *(G-7162)*
ARC Systems Inc...631 582-8020
   2090 Joshuas Path Hauppauge (11788) *(G-5592)*
ARC TEC Wldg & Fabrication Inc..........................718 982-9274
   15 Harrison Ave Staten Island (10302) *(G-14619)*
Arca Ink LLC...518 798-0100
   30 Bluebird Rd South Glens Falls (12803) *(G-14512)*
Arcade Glass Works, Chaffee *Also called Hart To Hart Industries Inc (G-3307)*
Arcade Herald, Arcade *Also called Neighbor To Neighbor News Inc (G-378)*
Arcadia Chem Preservative LLC...........................516 466-5258
   100 Great Neck Rd Apt 5b Great Neck (11021) *(G-5366)*

Arcadia Mfg Group Inc (PA).................................518 434-6213
   80 Cohoes Ave Green Island (12183) *(G-5432)*
Arcadia Mfg Group Inc...518 434-6213
   1032 Broadway Menands (12204) *(G-7840)*
Arch Chemicals Inc...585 436-3030
   100 Mckee Rd Rochester (14611) *(G-13243)*
Arch Globl Precision Rochester, Rochester *Also called Jasco Tools LLC (G-13490)*
Archaelogy Magazine..718 472-3050
   3636 33rd St Ste 301 Long Island City (11106) *(G-7163)*
Archer-Daniels-Midland Company........................716 849-7333
   250 Ganson St Buffalo (14203) *(G-2643)*
Archer-Daniels-Midland Company........................518 828-4691
   201 State Route 23b Hudson (12534) *(G-6147)*
Archer-Daniels-Midland Company........................518 828-4691
   Ste B Rr 23 Hudson (12534) *(G-6148)*
Archer-Daniels-Midland Company........................585 346-2311
   3401 Rochester Rd Lakeville (14480) *(G-6773)*
Archie Comic Publications Inc.............................914 381-5155
   629 Fifth Ave Ste 100 Pelham (10803) *(G-12564)*
Archie Comics Publishers, Pelham *Also called Archie Comic Publications Inc (G-12564)*
Archimedes Products Inc....................................631 589-1215
   21 Floyds Run Bohemia (11716) *(G-975)*
Architctral Dsign Elements LLC..........................718 218-7800
   52 Box St Brooklyn (11222) *(G-1523)*
Architctral Mllwk Installation.............................631 499-0755
   590 Elwood Rd East Northport (11731) *(G-4142)*
Architctral Shetmetal Pdts Inc...........................518 381-6144
   1329 Amsterdam Rd Scotia (12302) *(G-14328)*
Architects Newspaper LLC...................................212 966-0630
   21 Murray St Fl 5 New York (10007) *(G-8618)*
Architectural Coatings Inc...................................718 418-9584
   538 Johnson Ave Brooklyn (11237) *(G-1524)*
Architectural Enhancements Inc..........................845 343-9663
   135 Crotty Rd Middletown (10941) *(G-7893)*
Architectural Fiberglass Corp..............................631 842-4772
   1395 Marconi Blvd Copiague (11726) *(G-3645)*
Architectural Glass Inc...845 831-3116
   71 Maple St Apt 2 Beacon (12508) *(G-748)*
Architectural Sign Group Inc................................516 326-1800
   145 Meacham Ave Elmont (11003) *(G-4382)*
Architectural Textiles USA Inc.............................212 213-6972
   36 E 23rd St Ste F New York (10010) *(G-8619)*
Architex International, New York *Also called Architectural Textiles USA Inc (G-8619)*
Archrock Inc..716 763-1553
   305 E Fairmount Ave Ste 4 Lakewood (14750) *(G-6777)*
Arcom Automatics LLC..315 422-1230
   185 Ainsley Dr Syracuse (13210) *(G-14815)*
Arcom Labs, Syracuse *Also called Arrow-Communication Labs Inc (G-14818)*
Arconic Fastening Systems, Kingston *Also called Huck International Inc (G-6694)*
Arconic Fastening Systems...................................585 368-5049
   181 Mckee Rd Rochester (14611) *(G-13244)*
Arconic Fstening Systems Rings..........................800 278-4825
   1 Corporate Dr Kingston (12401) *(G-6678)*
Arconic Inc..716 358-6451
   2632 S Work St Ste 24 Falconer (14733) *(G-4534)*
Arconic Inc..315 764-4011
   45 County Route 42 Massena (13662) *(G-7666)*
Arctic Glacier Newburgh Inc................................718 456-2013
   335 Moffat St Brooklyn (11237) *(G-1525)*
Arctic Glacier Newburgh Inc (HQ)........................845 561-0549
   225 Lake St Newburgh (12550) *(G-11858)*
Arctix, Locust Valley *Also called Alpha 6 Distributions LLC (G-7121)*
Arcworks, Rochester *Also called Monroe Cnty Chapter Nysarc Inc (G-13557)*
Arcy Plastic Laminates Inc (PA)..........................518 235-0753
   555 Patroon Creek Blvd Albany (12206) *(G-42)*
Ardagh Metal Packaging USA Inc........................607 584-3300
   379 Broome Corporate Pkwy Conklin (13748) *(G-3621)*
Ardent Mills LLC...518 447-1700
   101 Normanskill St Albany (12202) *(G-43)*
Ardex Cosmetics of America................................518 283-6700
   744 Pawling Ave Troy (12180) *(G-15164)*
Area Development Magazine, Westbury *Also called Halcyon Business Publications (G-15892)*
Area Inc...212 924-7084
   58 E 11th St Fl 2 New York (10003) *(G-8620)*
Area Warehouse, New York *Also called Area Inc (G-8620)*
Aremco Products Inc...845 268-0039
   707 Executive Blvd Valley Cottage (10989) *(G-15313)*
Arena Graphics Inc...516 767-5108
   52 Main St Frnt Port Washington (11050) *(G-12864)*
Arena Sports Center, Port Washington *Also called Arena Graphics Inc (G-12864)*
Ares Box LLC...718 858-8760
   63 Flushing Ave Unit 224 Brooklyn (11205) *(G-1526)*
Ares Printing and Packg Corp..............................718 858-8760
   Brooklyn Navy Yard Bldg Brooklyn (11205) *(G-1527)*
Argee America Inc...212 768-9840
   1410 Broadway Rm 1204 New York (10018) *(G-8621)*
Argee Sportswear, New York *Also called Argee America Inc (G-8621)*
Argencord Machine Corp Inc................................631 842-8990
   10 Reith St Copiague (11726) *(G-3646)*

Argo Envelope Corp....718 729-2700
4310 21st St Long Island City (11101) *(G-7164)*
Argo General Machine Work Inc....718 392-4605
3816 11th St Long Island City (11101) *(G-7165)*
Argo Lithographers Inc....718 729-2700
4310 21st St Long Island City (11101) *(G-7166)*
Argon Corp (PA)....516 487-5314
160 Great Neck Rd Great Neck (11021) *(G-5367)*
Argon Medical Devices Inc....585 321-1130
336 Summit Point Dr Henrietta (14467) *(G-5855)*
Argosy Composite Advanced Mate....212 268-0003
225 W 34th St Ste 1106 New York (10122) *(G-8622)*
Arh, Deer Park *Also called American Racing Headers Inc (G-3837)*
Aric Signs & Awnings Inc....516 350-0409
153 Baldwin Rd Hempstead (11550) *(G-5832)*
Ariel Optics Inc....585 265-4820
261 David Pkwy Ontario (14519) *(G-12284)*
Ariel Tian LLC....212 457-1266
253 W 35th St Fl 8 Flr 8 Forest Hills (11375) *(G-4917)*
Ariela and Associates Intl LLC (PA)....212 683-4131
1359 Broadway Fl 21 New York (10018) *(G-8623)*
Aries Precision Products, Rochester *Also called Estebania Enterprises Inc (G-13401)*
Arimed Orthotics Prosthetics (PA)....718 875-8754
302 Livingston St Brooklyn (11217) *(G-1528)*
Arimed Orthotics Prosthetics....718 979-6155
235 Dongan Hills Ave 2d Staten Island (10305) *(G-14620)*
Arise At Marshall Farms Inc....315 687-6727
1972 New Boston Rd Chittenango (13037) *(G-3403)*
Arista Coffee Inc....347 531-0813
5901 55th St Maspeth (11378) *(G-7592)*
Arista Flag Corporation....845 246-7700
157 W Saugerties Rd Saugerties (12477) *(G-14197)*
Arista Innovations Inc....516 746-2262
131 Liberty Ave Mineola (11501) *(G-7959)*
Arista Printing, Mineola *Also called Arista Innovations Inc (G-7959)*
Arista Steel Designs Corp....718 965-7077
788 3rd Ave Brooklyn (11232) *(G-1529)*
Aristocrat Lighting Inc....718 522-0003
104 Halleck St Brooklyn (11231) *(G-1530)*
Arizona Beverage Company LLC (HQ)....516 812-0300
60 Crossways Park Dr W # 400 Woodbury (11797) *(G-16166)*
Arizona Beverages USA, Woodbury *Also called Arizona Beverage Company LLC (G-16166)*
Ark Sciences Inc....646 943-1520
1601 Veterans Hwy Ste 315 Islandia (11749) *(G-6324)*
Arkay Packaging Corporation (PA)....631 273-2000
700 Veterans Memorial Hwy # 300 Hauppauge (11788) *(G-5593)*
Arkema Inc....585 243-6359
3289 Genesee St Piffard (14533) *(G-12623)*
Arkwin Industries Inc (HQ)....516 333-2640
686 Main St Westbury (11590) *(G-15870)*
Arlan Damper Corporation....631 589-7431
1598 Lakeland Ave Bohemia (11716) *(G-976)*
Arlee Group, New York *Also called Arlee Home Fashions Inc (G-8624)*
Arlee Home Fashions Inc (PA)....212 689-0020
36 E 31st St Rm 800 New York (10016) *(G-8624)*
Arlee Lighting Corp....516 595-8558
125 Doughty Blvd Inwood (11096) *(G-6288)*
Arlon Viscor Ltd....914 461-1300
1133 Westchester Ave White Plains (10604) *(G-15976)*
Arlyn Scales, East Rockaway *Also called Circuits & Systems Inc (G-4171)*
Arm & Hammer, Schenectady *Also called Church & Dwight Co Inc (G-14255)*
Arm Construction Company Inc....646 235-6520
10001 27th Ave East Elmhurst (11369) *(G-4103)*
Arm Rochester Inc....585 354-5077
740 Driving Park Ave I1 Rochester (14613) *(G-13245)*
Arma Container Corp....631 254-1200
65 N Industry Ct Deer Park (11729) *(G-3841)*
Armada New York LLC....718 852-8105
141 Flushing Ave Unit 404 Brooklyn (11205) *(G-1531)*
Armadillo Bar & Grill, Kingston *Also called Tortilla Heaven Inc (G-6715)*
Armando & Sons General Welding, Schenectady *Also called Cianfarani Armando (G-14256)*
Armento Architectural Arts, Kenmore *Also called Armento Incorporated (G-6648)*
Armento Incorporated....716 875-2423
1011 Military Rd Kenmore (14217) *(G-6648)*
Armitron Watch Div, Little Neck *Also called E Gluck Corporation (G-6997)*
Armor Dynamics Inc....845 658-9200
138 Maple Hill Rd Kingston (12401) *(G-6679)*
Armor Tile, Buffalo *Also called Engineered Composites Inc (G-2745)*
Armour Bearer Group Inc....646 812-4487
424 Beach 65th St Arverne (11692) *(G-406)*
Armoured One LLC....315 720-4186
386 N Midler Ave Ste 26 Syracuse (13206) *(G-14816)*
Armstrong Mold Corporation (PA)....315 437-1517
6910 Manlius Center Rd East Syracuse (13057) *(G-4196)*
Armstrong Mold Corporation....315 437-1517
5860 Fisher Rd East Syracuse (13057) *(G-4197)*
Armstrong Pumps Inc....716 693-8813
93 East Ave North Tonawanda (14120) *(G-12053)*
Armstrong Transmitter Corp....315 673-1269
4835 N Street Rd Marcellus (13108) *(G-7560)*
Arnan Development Corp (PA)....607 432-8391
6459 State Highway 23 Oneonta (13820) *(G-12257)*
Arnell Inc....516 486-7098
73 High St Hempstead (11550) *(G-5833)*
Arnold Magnetic Tech Corp (HQ)....585 385-9010
770 Linden Ave Rochester (14625) *(G-13246)*
Arnold Printing Corp....607 272-7800
604 W Green St Ithaca (14850) *(G-6363)*
Arnold Taylor Printing Inc....516 781-0564
2218 Brody Ln Bellmore (11710) *(G-779)*
Arnold-Davis LLC....607 772-1201
187 Indl Pk Dr Binghamton (13904) *(G-855)*
Arnolds Meat Food Products....718 384-8071
274 Heyward St Brooklyn (11206) *(G-1532)*
Arnouse Digital Devices Corp....516 673-4444
1983 Marcus Ave Ste 104 New Hyde Park (11042) *(G-8251)*
Arnprior Rpid Mfg Slutions Inc (PA)....585 617-6301
2400 Mount Read Blvd # 112 Rochester (14615) *(G-13247)*
Arnprior Rpid Mfg Slutions Inc....585 617-6301
2400 Mount Read Blvd # 1124 Rochester (14615) *(G-13248)*
Aro-Graph Corporation....315 463-8693
847 North Ave Syracuse (13206) *(G-14817)*
Aro-Graph Displays, Syracuse *Also called Aro-Graph Corporation (G-14817)*
Aromafloria, Huntington Station *Also called California Fragrance Company (G-6241)*
Aromasong Usa Inc....718 838-9669
35 Frost St Brooklyn (11211) *(G-1533)*
Aron Streit Inc....212 475-7000
171 Route 303 Orangeburg (10962) *(G-12307)*
Aronowitz Metal Works....845 356-1660
5 Edwin Ln Monsey (10952) *(G-8035)*
Array Marketing Group Inc (HQ)....212 750-3367
200 Madison Ave Ste 2121 New York (10016) *(G-8625)*
Arringement International Inc....347 323-7974
16015 45th Ave Flushing (11358) *(G-4840)*
Arro Manufacturing LLC....716 763-6203
4687 Gleason Rd Lakewood (14750) *(G-6778)*
Arro Tool & Die Inc....716 763-6203
4687 Gleason Rd Lakewood (14750) *(G-6779)*
Arrow Grinding Inc....716 693-3333
525 Vicke St Tonaw Ctr Tonawanda (14150) *(G-15086)*
Arrow Leather Finishing Inc....518 762-3121
228 Pleasant Ave Johnstown (12095) *(G-6610)*
Arrow-Communication Labs Inc....315 422-1230
185 Ainsley Dr Syracuse (13210) *(G-14818)*
Arrowear Athletic Apparel, Lynbrook *Also called Valley Stream Sporting Gds Inc (G-7442)*
Arrowhead Spring Vineyards LLC....716 434-8030
4746 Townline Rd Lockport (14094) *(G-7060)*
Arrowpak, Richmond Hill *Also called Baralan Usa Inc (G-13109)*
Arsenal Holdings LLC (PA)....212 398-9139
885 3rd Ave Rm 2403 New York (10022) *(G-8626)*
Arstan Products International....516 433-1313
264 Duffy Ave Hicksville (11801) *(G-5885)*
Art Asiapacific Publishing LLC....212 255-6003
410 W 24th St Apt 14a New York (10011) *(G-8627)*
Art Bedi-Makky Foundry Corp....718 383-4191
227 India St Ste 31 Brooklyn (11222) *(G-1534)*
Art Boards, Brooklyn *Also called Patrick Mackin Custom Furn (G-2250)*
Art Digital Technologies LLC....646 649-4820
85 Debevoise Ave Brooklyn (11222) *(G-1535)*
Art Essentials of New York (PA)....845 368-1100
25 Church Rd Airmont (10952) *(G-10)*
Art Foam, Lindenhurst *Also called Strux Corp (G-6976)*
Art Industries of New York....212 633-9200
601 W 26th St Rm 1425 New York (10001) *(G-8628)*
Art of Platinum, The, New York *Also called Leon Mege Inc (G-10203)*
Art Parts Signs Inc....585 381-2134
100 Lincoln Pkwy East Rochester (14445) *(G-4159)*
Art People Inc....212 431-4865
594 Broadway Rm 1102 New York (10012) *(G-8629)*
Art Precision Metal Products....631 842-8889
1465 S Strong Ave Copiague (11726) *(G-3647)*
Art Resources Transfer Inc....212 255-2919
526 W 26th St Rm 614 New York (10001) *(G-8630)*
Art Scroll Printing Corp....212 929-2413
230 W 41st St Bsmt 1 New York (10036) *(G-8631)*
Art-Craft Optical Company Inc....585 546-6640
57 Goodway Dr S Rochester (14623) *(G-13249)*
Art-TEC Jewelry Designs Ltd (PA)....212 719-2941
48 W 48th St Ste 401 New York (10036) *(G-8632)*
Artcraft Building Services....845 895-3893
85 Old Hoagerburgh Rd Wallkill (12589) *(G-15467)*
Arteast LLC....646 859-6020
453 Broome St New York (10013) *(G-8633)*
Artemis Inc....631 232-2424
36 Central Ave Hauppauge (11788) *(G-5594)*
Artemis Studios Inc....718 788-6022
34 35th St Ste 2b Brooklyn (11232) *(G-1536)*
Arthur Brown W Mfg Co....631 243-5594
49 E Industry Ct Ste I Deer Park (11729) *(G-3842)*
Arthur Gluck Shirtmakers Inc....212 755-8165
871 E 24th St Brooklyn (11210) *(G-1537)*
Arthur Invitation, New York *Also called Exotic Print and Paper Inc (G-9446)*

(PA)=Parent Co (HQ)=Headquarters (DH)=Div Headquarters

A L P H A B E T I C

Articulate Global Inc...800 861-4880
244 5th Ave Ste 2960 New York (10001) ***(G-8634)***
Artifex Press LLC...212 414-1482
260 W 35th St Ph New York (10001) ***(G-8635)***
Artina Group Inc...914 592-1850
250 Clearbrook Rd Ste 245 Elmsford (10523) ***(G-4394)***
Artisan Bags, Childwold *Also called Leather Artisan* ***(G-3401)***
Artisan Boot & Shoe Co LLC...585 813-2825
3 Treadeasy Ave Batavia (14020) ***(G-602)***
Artisan Custom Interiors, West Hempstead *Also called Artisan Woodworking Ltd* ***(G-15766)***
Artisan Machining Inc...631 589-1416
49 Remington Blvd Ronkonkoma (11779) ***(G-13909)***
Artisan Management Group Inc...716 569-4094
39 Venman St Frewsburg (14738) ***(G-5049)***
Artisan Meats, Canandaigua *Also called Grossglockner Inc* ***(G-3134)***
Artisan Woodworking Ltd...516 486-0818
163 Hempstead Tpke West Hempstead (11552) ***(G-15766)***
Artisanal Brands Inc (PA)...914 441-3591
42 Forest Ln Bronxville (10708) ***(G-1399)***
Artistic Frame Corp (PA)...212 289-2100
979 3rd Ave Ste 1705 New York (10022) ***(G-8636)***
Artistic Group, The, New York *Also called Artistic Typography Corp* ***(G-8638)***
Artistic Iron Works Inc...631 665-4285
94 Saxon Ave Ste A Bay Shore (11706) ***(G-652)***
Artistic Products LLC...631 435-0200
345 Oser Ave Hauppauge (11788) ***(G-5595)***
Artistic Ribbon Novelty Co Inc...212 255-4224
22 W 21st St Fl 3 New York (10010) ***(G-8637)***
Artistic Typography Corp (PA)...212 463-8880
151 W 30th St Fl 8 New York (10001) ***(G-8638)***
Artistry In Wood of Syracuse...315 431-4022
230 Ainsley Dr Syracuse (13210) ***(G-14819)***
Artists, Doo Wop, Deer Park *Also called New Wop Records* ***(G-3911)***
Artnews Ltd (PA)...212 398-1690
475 5th Ave Fl 24 New York (10017) ***(G-8639)***
Artnewsletter, New York *Also called Artnews Ltd* ***(G-8639)***
Artone Furniture By Design, Jamestown *Also called Artone LLC* ***(G-6495)***
Artone LLC (PA)...716 664-2232
1089 Allen St Jamestown (14701) ***(G-6495)***
Artscroll Printing Corp (PA)...212 929-2413
53 W 23rd St Fl 4 New York (10010) ***(G-8640)***
Artube, Great Neck *Also called Iridium Industries Inc* ***(G-5395)***
Artwill Group LLC...845 826-3692
344 Greenbush Rd Blauvelt (10913) ***(G-926)***
Artys Sprnklr Svc Instllation...516 538-4371
234 E Meadow Ave Unit B East Meadow (11554) ***(G-4131)***
Aruba Networks Inc...732 343-1305
556 W 22nd St New York (10011) ***(G-8641)***
Arumai Technologies Inc (PA)...914 217-0038
175 King St Armonk (10504) ***(G-395)***
Arusha Tanzanite, Great Neck *Also called Le Vian Corp* ***(G-5400)***
Aruvil International Inc (PA)...212 447-5020
185 Madison Ave Rm 1701 New York (10016) ***(G-8642)***
Arvos Inc (HQ)...585 593-2700
3020 Truax Rd Wellsville (14895) ***(G-15667)***
Aryzta LLC...585 235-8160
64 Chester St Rochester (14611) ***(G-13250)***
Aryzta LLC...585 235-8160
235 Buffalo Rd Rochester (14611) ***(G-13251)***
Asa Manufacturing Inc...718 853-3033
3611 14th Ave Brooklyn (11218) ***(G-1538)***
Asahi Shimbun America Inc...212 398-0257
620 8th Ave New York (10018) ***(G-8643)***
ASAP Rack Rental Inc...718 499-4495
33 35th St St5 Brooklyn (11232) ***(G-1539)***
Ascap, New York *Also called American Society of Composers* ***(G-8558)***
Ascension Industries Inc (PA)...716 693-9381
1254 Erie Ave North Tonawanda (14120) ***(G-12054)***
Ascent Pharmaceuticals Inc (HQ)...631 851-0550
400 S Technology Dr Central Islip (11722) ***(G-3262)***
Asco Castings Inc (PA)...212 719-9800
3100 47th Ave Ste G Long Island City (11101) ***(G-7167)***
Ascribe Inc...585 413-0298
383 Buell Rd Rochester (14624) ***(G-13252)***
Asence Inc...347 335-2606
65 Broadway Fl 7 New York (10006) ***(G-8644)***
Asept Pak Inc...518 651-2026
64 West St Malone (12953) ***(G-7483)***
Ashco Management Inc...212 960-8428
1937 Mcdonald Ave Brooklyn (11223) ***(G-1540)***
Ashko Group LLC...212 594-6050
10 W 33rd St Rm 1019 New York (10001) ***(G-8645)***
Ashland Water Technologies, Brooklyn *Also called Solenis LLC* ***(G-2440)***
Ashland Water Technologies, Liverpool *Also called Solenis LLC* ***(G-7040)***
Ashley Resin Corp...718 851-8111
1171 59th St Brooklyn (11219) ***(G-1541)***
Ashly Audio Inc...585 872-0010
847 Holt Rd Ste 1 Webster (14580) ***(G-15630)***
Ashton-Potter USA Ltd...716 633-2000
10 Curtwright Dr Williamsville (14221) ***(G-16120)***
Asi Sign Systems, New York *Also called Modulex New York Inc* ***(G-10490)***
Asi Sign Systems Inc...646 742-1320
192 Lexington Ave Rm 1002 New York (10016) ***(G-8646)***
Asi Sign Systems Inc...716 775-0104
2957 Alt Blvd Grand Island (14072) ***(G-5325)***
Asian Global Trading Corp...718 786-0998
1407 Broadway Rm 2310 New York (10018) ***(G-8647)***
Asite LLC...203 545-3089
245 W 29th St Rm 1601 New York (10001) ***(G-8648)***
Ask Chemicals Hi-Tech LLC...607 587-9146
6329 Rte 21 Alfred Station (14803) ***(G-183)***
Asm, Central Bridge *Also called American Standard Mfg Inc* ***(G-3259)***
Asm Mechanical Systems, Ridgewood *Also called Aabco Sheet Metal Co Inc* ***(G-13137)***
Asm USA Inc...212 925-2906
73 Spring St Rm 309 New York (10012) ***(G-8649)***
Asn Inc...718 894-0800
6020 59th Pl Ste 2 Maspeth (11378) ***(G-7593)***
Asp Blade Intrmdate Hldngs Inc...212 476-8000
299 Park Ave Fl 34 New York (10171) ***(G-8650)***
Asp Industries Inc...585 254-9130
9 Evelyn St Rochester (14606) ***(G-13253)***
Aspect Printing Inc...347 789-4284
904 E 51st St Brooklyn (11203) ***(G-1542)***
Aspen Research Group Ltd...212 425-9588
17 State St Fl 15 New York (10004) ***(G-8651)***
Aspex Incorporated...212 966-0410
161 Hudson St Apt 1a New York (10013) ***(G-8652)***
Aspire One Communications LLC...201 281-2998
245 Main St Ste 8 Cornwall (12518) ***(G-3725)***
Aspire One Communications Inc...845 534-6110
246 Main St Cornwall (12518) ***(G-3726)***
Assa Abloy Entrance Systems US...315 492-6600
28 Corporate Cir Ste 1 East Syracuse (13057) ***(G-4198)***
Assembly Equipment Division, Rochester *Also called High Speed Hammer Company Inc* ***(G-13468)***
Assessment Technologies Inc...646 530-8666
1350 Ave Of The Americas New York (10019) ***(G-8653)***
Associated Brands Inc...585 798-3475
4001 Salt Works Rd Medina (14103) ***(G-7727)***
Associated Drapery & Equipment...516 671-5245
3 Kosnitz Dr Unit 111 Monroe (10950) ***(G-8014)***
Associated Lightning Rod Co...845 373-8309
6020 Route 22 Millerton (12546) ***(G-7946)***
Associated Publishing Company (HQ)...325 676-4032
61 John Muir Dr Buffalo (14228) ***(G-2644)***
Association For Cmpt McHy Inc (PA)...212 869-7440
1601 Broadway Fl 10 New York (10019) ***(G-8654)***
Assouline Publishing Inc (PA)...212 989-6769
3 Park Ave Ste 2702 New York (10016) ***(G-8655)***
Aston Leather Inc...212 481-2760
153 W 27th St Ste 406 New York (10001) ***(G-8656)***
Astor Accessories LLC...212 695-6146
1370 Broadway Rm 650 New York (10018) ***(G-8657)***
Astra Products Inc...631 464-4747
6 Bethpage Rd Copiague (11726) ***(G-3648)***
Astra Tool & Instrument Mfg...914 747-3863
369 Bradhurst Ave Hawthorne (10532) ***(G-5809)***
Astro Chemical Company Inc...518 399-5338
3 Mill Rd Ballston Lake (12019) ***(G-557)***
Astro Electroplating Inc...631 968-0656
171 4th Ave Bay Shore (11706) ***(G-653)***
Astrocom Electronics Inc...607 432-1930
115 Dk Lifgren Dr Oneonta (13820) ***(G-12258)***
Astrodyne Inc...516 536-5755
18 Neil Ct Oceanside (11572) ***(G-12166)***
Astron Candle Manufacturing Co...718 728-3330
1125 30th Ave Long Island City (11102) ***(G-7168)***
Astronics Corporation (PA)...716 805-1599
130 Commerce Way East Aurora (14052) ***(G-4082)***
Astucci US Ltd...718 752-9700
4369 9th St Long Island City (11101) ***(G-7169)***
Astucci US Ltd (PA)...212 725-3171
385 5th Ave Rm 1100 New York (10016) ***(G-8658)***
Asur Jewelry Inc...718 472-1687
4709 30th St Ste 403 Long Island City (11101) ***(G-7170)***
At Copy Inc...718 624-6136
25 Flatbush Ave Brooklyn (11217) ***(G-1543)***
AT&T Corp...212 317-7048
767 5th Ave Fl 12a New York (10153) ***(G-8659)***
Atalla Handbags Inc...718 965-5500
559 79th St Brooklyn (11209) ***(G-1544)***
Atc, Huntington Station *Also called American Tchncal Ceramics Corp* ***(G-6237)***
Atc Plastics LLC...212 375-2515
555 Madison Ave Fl 5 New York (10022) ***(G-8660)***
Atco EZ Dock, Auburn *Also called Auburn Tank & Manufacturing Co* ***(G-463)***
Atd Precision Machining, Rochester *Also called Allstate Tool and Die Inc* ***(G-13222)***
Ateaz Organic Coffe & Tea, Oakland Gardens *Also called Anandsar Inc* ***(G-12159)***
Atech-Seh Metal Fabricator...716 895-8888
330 Greene St Buffalo (14206) ***(G-2645)***
Ateco Products, Bay Shore *Also called Sumner Industries Inc* ***(G-720)***
Atelier Viollet Corp...718 782-1727
505 Driggs Ave Brooklyn (11211) ***(G-1545)***

Ateliers Tamalet Corp...929 325-7976
  349 5th Ave New York (10016) *(G-8661)*

Ateres Book Binding, Brooklyn *Also called Ateres Publishing & Bk Bindery (G-1546)*

Ateres Publishing & Bk Bindery.................................718 935-9355
  845 Bedford Ave Brooklyn (11205) *(G-1546)*

Ateret LLC...212 819-0777
  22 W 48th St New York (10036) *(G-8662)*

Aterra Exploration LLC..212 315-0030
  230 W 56th St Apt 53d New York (10019) *(G-8663)*

Athalon Sportgear Inc..212 268-8070
  10 W 33rd St Rm 1012 New York (10001) *(G-8664)*

Athenex Inc (PA)..716 427-2950
  1001 Main St Ste 600 Buffalo (14203) *(G-2646)*

Athenex Pharma Solutions LLC................................877 463-7823
  11342 Main St Clarence (14031) *(G-3426)*

Athenex Pharmaceutical Div LLC (PA).......................877 463-7823
  1001 Main St Ste 600 Buffalo (14203) *(G-2647)*

Athletic Cap Co Inc...718 398-1300
  123 Fields Ave Staten Island (10314) *(G-14621)*

Athlon Spt Communications Inc.................................212 478-1910
  60 E 42nd St Ste 820 New York (10165) *(G-8665)*

ATI, Brooklyn *Also called Anne Taintor Inc (G-1512)*

ATI Specialty Materials, Lockport *Also called Tdy Industries LLC (G-7110)*

Atis Colojet, Ronkonkoma *Also called Maharlika Holdings LLC (G-13968)*

Atlantic Business Products, New York *Also called Facsimile Cmmncations Inds Inc (G-9460)*

Atlantic Color Corp..631 345-3800
  14 Ramsey Rd Shirley (11967) *(G-14414)*

Atlantic Electronic Tech LLC....................................800 296-2177
  285 5th Ave Apt 2b Brooklyn (11215) *(G-1547)*

Atlantic Electronic Technology, Brooklyn *Also called Atlantic Electronic Tech LLC (G-1547)*

Atlantic Er Inc...516 294-3200
  180 Atlantic Ave New Hyde Park (11040) *(G-8252)*

Atlantic Essential Pdts Inc.......................................631 434-8333
  7 Oser Ave Ste 1 Hauppauge (11788) *(G-5596)*

Atlantic Farm & Food Inc..718 441-3152
  11415 Atlantic Ave Richmond Hill (11418) *(G-13108)*

Atlantic Industrial Tech Inc.......................................631 234-3131
  90 Precision Dr Shirley (11967) *(G-14415)*

Atlantic Monthly Group Inc.......................................202 266-7000
  60 Madison Ave New York (10010) *(G-8666)*

Atlantic Precious Metal Cast.....................................718 937-7100
  4132 27th St Long Island City (11101) *(G-7171)*

Atlantic Projects Company Inc...................................518 878-2065
  5 Southside Dr Ste 11s Clifton Park (12065) *(G-3462)*

Atlantic Recording Corp (HQ)....................................212 707-2000
  1633 Broadway Lowr 2c1 New York (10019) *(G-8667)*

Atlantic Records, New York *Also called Atlantic Recording Corp (G-8667)*

Atlantic Specialty Co Inc...845 356-2502
  20 Jeffrey Pl Monsey (10952) *(G-8036)*

Atlantic Stairs Corp..718 417-8818
  284a Meserole St Brooklyn (11206) *(G-1548)*

Atlantic Transformer Inc...716 795-3258
  1674 Quaker Rd Barker (14012) *(G-590)*

Atlantic Trophy Co Inc..212 684-6020
  866 Avenue Of The America New York (10001) *(G-8668)*

Atlantic Ultraviolet Corp...631 234-3275
  375 Marcus Blvd Hauppauge (11788) *(G-5597)*

Atlantic, The, New York *Also called Atlantic Monthly Group Inc (G-8666)*

Atlantis Energy Systems Inc (PA)..............................845 486-4052
  7 Industry St Poughkeepsie (12603) *(G-12945)*

Atlantis Energy Systems Inc......................................916 438-2930
  7 Industry St Poughkeepsie (12603) *(G-12946)*

Atlantis Equipment Corporation.................................518 733-5910
  16941 Ny 22 Stephentown (12168) *(G-14730)*

Atlas & Company LLC...212 234-3100
  355 Lexington Ave Fl 6 New York (10017) *(G-8669)*

Atlas Bituminous Co Inc...315 457-2394
  173 Farrell Rd Syracuse (13209) *(G-14820)*

Atlas Coatings Corp...718 402-2000
  820 E 140th St Bronx (10454) *(G-1207)*

Atlas Coatings Group Corp (PA)................................718 469-8787
  4808 Farragut Rd Brooklyn (11203) *(G-1549)*

Atlas Concrete Batching Corp...................................718 523-3000
  9511 147th Pl Jamaica (11435) *(G-6426)*

Atlas Copco Comptec LLC (HQ).................................518 765-3344
  46 School Rd Voorheesville (12186) *(G-15444)*

Atlas Fence & Railing Co Inc.....................................718 767-2200
  15149 7th Ave Whitestone (11357) *(G-16088)*

Atlas Fence Co, Whitestone *Also called Atlas Fence & Railing Co Inc (G-16088)*

Atlas Industries, Newburgh *Also called Consolidated Spring LLC (G-11862)*

Atlas Music Publishing LLC (PA)................................646 502-5170
  6 E 39th St Ste 1104 New York (10016) *(G-8670)*

Atlas Print Solutions Inc...212 949-8775
  589 8th Ave Fl 4 New York (10018) *(G-8671)*

Atlas Recycling LLC...212 925-3280
  25 Howard St Fl 2 New York (10013) *(G-8672)*

Atlas Switch Co Inc..516 222-6280
  969 Stewart Ave Garden City (11530) *(G-5090)*

Atlas Transit Mix Corp..718 523-3000
  9511 147th Pl Jamaica (11435) *(G-6427)*

Atlaz International Ltd...516 239-1854
  244 E Merrick Rd Freeport (11520) *(G-4986)*

Atmost Refrigeration Co Inc (PA)...............................518 828-2180
  793 Route 66 Hudson (12534) *(G-6149)*

Atomic Information Systems.......................................716 713-5402
  1580 State Highway 357 Unadilla (13849) *(G-15221)*

Atomicdbonline.com, Unadilla *Also called Atomic Information Systems (G-15221)*

Atr Jewelry Inc..212 819-0075
  71 W 47th St Ste 402 New York (10036) *(G-8673)*

Ats, Mahopac *Also called Advanced Tchncal Solutions Inc (G-7473)*

Attachmate Corporation...646 704-0042
  1 Penn Plz Fl 36 New York (10119) *(G-8674)*

Attends Healthcare Inc...212 338-5100
  200 Park Ave New York (10166) *(G-8675)*

Attias Oven Corp...718 499-0145
  926 3rd Ave Brooklyn (11232) *(G-1550)*

Attica Millwork Inc...585 591-2333
  71 Market St Attica (14011) *(G-455)*

Attica Package Company Inc......................................585 591-0510
  45 Windsor St Attica (14011) *(G-456)*

Attis Ethanol Fulton LLC...315 593-0500
  376 Owens Rd Fulton (13069) *(G-5054)*

Attitudes Footwear Inc...212 754-9113
  1040 1st Ave Ste 232 New York (10022) *(G-8676)*

ATW Group, New York *Also called Great Universal Corp (G-9670)*

Atwater Estate Vineyards LLC....................................607 546-8463
  5055 State Route 414 Burdett (14818) *(G-3055)*

Atwater Foods, Lyndonville *Also called Shoreline Fruit LLC (G-7446)*

Atwood Tool & Machine Inc.......................................607 648-6543
  39 Kattelville Rd Chenango Bridge (13745) *(G-3367)*

Auburn Armature, East Syracuse *Also called Power-Flo Technologies Inc (G-4230)*

Auburn Armature, Rochester *Also called Power-Flo Technologies Inc (G-13631)*

Auburn Bearing & Mfg Inc...315 986-7600
  4 State Route 350 Macedon (14502) *(G-7460)*

Auburn Custom Millwork Inc......................................315 253-3843
  315 Genesee St Ste 8 Auburn (13021) *(G-460)*

Auburn Foundry Inc..315 253-4441
  15 Wadsworth St Auburn (13021) *(G-461)*

Auburn Leathercrafters, Auburn *Also called Finger Lakes Lea Crafters LLC (G-475)*

Auburn Publishing Co...315 253-5311
  25 Dill St Auburn (13021) *(G-462)*

Auburn Tank & Manufacturing Co...............................315 255-2788
  24 Mcmaster St Auburn (13021) *(G-463)*

Auburn Vacuum Forming Co Inc.................................315 253-2440
  40 York St Auburn (13021) *(G-464)*

Auburn-Watson Corp (PA)...716 876-8000
  3295 Walden Ave Depew (14043) *(G-3970)*

Aucapina Cabinets Inc..718 609-9054
  5737 57th Dr Maspeth (11378) *(G-7594)*

Audible Difference Inc..212 662-4848
  110 8th St Brooklyn (11215) *(G-1551)*

Audible Difference Lnc, Brooklyn *Also called Audible Difference Inc (G-1551)*

Audio Technology New York Inc..................................718 369-7528
  129 31st St Brooklyn (11232) *(G-1552)*

Audio Video Invasion Inc...516 345-2636
  53 Werman Ct Plainview (11803) *(G-12664)*

Audio-Sears Corp..607 652-7305
  2 South St Stamford (12167) *(G-14606)*

Audiology, Brooklyn *Also called Audio Technology New York Inc (G-1552)*

Audiosavings Inc...888 445-1555
  600 Bayview Ave Ste 200 Inwood (11096) *(G-6289)*

Audubon Machinery Corporation (PA)..........................716 564-5165
  814 Wurlitzer Dr North Tonawanda (14120) *(G-12055)*

Aufhauser Corp Canada, Plainview *Also called Aufhauser Manufacturing Corp (G-12666)*

Aufhauser Corporation (PA).......................................516 694-8696
  39 West Mall Plainview (11803) *(G-12665)*

Aufhauser Manufacturing Corp...................................516 694-8696
  39 West Mall Plainview (11803) *(G-12666)*

Augury Inc..866 432-0976
  263 W 38th St Fl 16 New York (10018) *(G-8677)*

August Graphics, Bronx *Also called D B F Associates (G-1235)*

August Silk Inc (PA)..212 643-2400
  499 7th Ave Fl 5s New York (10018) *(G-8678)*

August Silk Inc..212 643-2400
  499 7th Ave Fl 5s New York (10018) *(G-8679)*

August Studios..718 706-6487
  4008 22nd St Fl 3 Long Island City (11101) *(G-7172)*

August Thomsen Corp...516 676-7100
  36 Sea Cliff Ave Glen Cove (11542) *(G-5189)*

Augusta Studios, Long Island City *Also called August Studios (G-7172)*

Aura, New York *Also called Roo Inc (G-11081)*

Aura Detergent LLC (PA)...718 824-2162
  1746 Crosby Ave Bronx (10461) *(G-1208)*

Aura Essence, Brooklyn *Also called Candle In The Window Inc (G-1643)*

Aurafin Oroamerica, New York *Also called Richline Group Inc (G-11041)*

Aureonic...518 791-9331
  13 Whispering Pines Rd Gansevoort (12831) *(G-5083)*

Auri Nutrascience Inc..631 454-0020
  155 Rome St Farmingdale (11735) *(G-4587)*

Aurora Indus Machining Inc.......................................716 826-7911
  3380 N Benzing Rd Orchard Park (14127) *(G-12338)*

Aurora Machine, Rochester *Also called Alkemy Machine LLC (G-13217)*

A L P H A B E T I C

Aurora Sef, Peekskill *Also called RMS Packaging Inc* ***(G-12556)***
Aurora Shoe Company, King Ferry *Also called Lake View Manufacturing LLC* ***(G-6671)***
Aurora Stone Group LLC 315 471-6869
114 Marcy St East Syracuse (13057) ***(G-4199)***
Aurora Technical Services Ltd 716 652-1463
11970 Parker Rd East Aurora (14052) ***(G-4083)***
Aurubis Buffalo Inc 716 879-6700
600 Military Rd Buffalo (14207) ***(G-2648)***
Aurubis Buffalo Inc (HQ) 716 879-6700
70 Sayre St Buffalo (14207) ***(G-2649)***
Ausco Inc 516 944-9882
425 Smith St Ste 1 Farmingdale (11735) ***(G-4588)***
Austin Air Systems Limited 716 856-3700
500 Elk St Buffalo (14210) ***(G-2650)***
Austin Industries Inc 585 589-1353
3871 Oak Orchard Rd Albion (14411) ***(G-154)***
Austin Mohawk and Company LLC 315 793-3000
2175 Beechgrove Pl Utica (13501) ***(G-15239)***
Autarkic Holdings Inc 516 371-4400
461 Doughty Blvd Inwood (11096) ***(G-6290)***
Autel North America, Farmingdale *Also called Autel US Inc* ***(G-4589)***
Autel US Inc (HQ) 631 923-2620
175 Central Ave Ste 200 Farmingdale (11735) ***(G-4589)***
Auterra Inc 518 382-9600
2135 Technology Dr Schenectady (12308) ***(G-14246)***
Authentic Brands Group LLC (PA) 212 760-2410
1411 Broadway Fl 4 New York (10018) ***(G-8680)***
Authentic Parts, Holbrook *Also called Ingham Industries Inc* ***(G-6001)***
Authority On Transportation, Dix Hills *Also called Authority Transportation Inc* ***(G-4010)***
Authority Transportation Inc 888 933-1268
167 Oakfield Ave Dix Hills (11746) ***(G-4010)***
Auto Body Services LLC 631 431-4640
400 W Hoffman Ave Lindenhurst (11757) ***(G-6941)***
Auto Data Labels, Deer Park *Also called Auto Data Systems Inc* ***(G-3843)***
Auto Data Systems Inc (PA) 631 667-2382
44 W Jefryn Blvd Ste K Deer Park (11729) ***(G-3843)***
Auto Market Publications Inc 631 667-0500
1641 Deer Park Ave Ste 5 Deer Park (11729) ***(G-3844)***
Auto Sport Designs Inc 631 425-1555
203 W Hills Rd Huntington Station (11746) ***(G-6239)***
Auto-Mat Company Inc 516 938-7373
69 Hazel St Hicksville (11801) ***(G-5886)***
Auto-Mate Technologies LLC 631 727-8886
34 Hinda Blvd Riverhead (11901) ***(G-13171)***
Autodyne Manufacturing Co Inc 631 957-5858
200 N Strong Ave Lindenhurst (11757) ***(G-6942)***
Autokiniton US Holdings Inc (PA) 212 338-5100
485 Lexington Ave Fl 31 New York (10017) ***(G-8681)***
Automated & MGT Solutions LLC 518 833-0315
743 Columbia Tpke East Greenbush (12061) ***(G-4113)***
Automated Biomass Systems LLC 607 849-7800
2235 Clarks Corners Rd Marathon (13803) ***(G-7556)***
Automated Bldg MGT Systems Inc (PA) 516 216-5603
54 Cherry Ln Floral Park (11001) ***(G-4808)***
Automated Cells & Eqp Inc 607 936-1341
9699 Enterprise Dr Painted Post (14870) ***(G-12471)***
Automated Control Logic Inc 914 769-8880
578 Commerce St Thornwood (10594) ***(G-15067)***
Automated Dynamics, Niskayuna *Also called ADC Acquisition Company* ***(G-11994)***
Automated Elevator Systems 845 595-1063
659 Jersey Ave Greenwood Lake (10925) ***(G-5478)***
Automated Office Systems Inc 516 396-5555
71 S Central Ave Valley Stream (11580) ***(G-15334)***
Automated Systems Group, Rochester *Also called Micro Instrument Corp* ***(G-13545)***
Automatic Connector Inc 631 543-5000
375 Oser Ave Hauppauge (11788) ***(G-5598)***
Automation Correct LLC 315 299-3589
405 Parrish Ln Syracuse (13205) ***(G-14821)***
Automation Evolution LLC 585 241-6010
800 Salt Rd Webster (14580) ***(G-15631)***
Automation Papers Inc 315 432-0565
6361 Thompson Rd Stop 1 Syracuse (13206) ***(G-14822)***
Automation Source Technologies (PA) 631 643-1678
21 Otis St Unit B West Babylon (11704) ***(G-15691)***
Automationcorrect.com, Syracuse *Also called Automation Correct LLC* ***(G-14821)***
Automecha International Ltd (PA) 607 843-2235
48 S Canal St Oxford (13830) ***(G-12441)***
Automotion Parking Systems LLC 516 565-5600
411 Hempstead Tpke # 200 West Hempstead (11552) ***(G-15767)***
Automotive Accessories Group 212 736-8100
505 8th Ave Rm 12a05 New York (10018) ***(G-8682)***
Automotive Leather Group LLC 516 627-4000
17 Barstow Rd Ste 206 Great Neck (11021) ***(G-5368)***
Automotive, LLC, Batavia *Also called Aludyne New York LLC* ***(G-600)***
Automtive Uphl Cnvertible Tops 914 961-4242
170 Marbledale Rd Tuckahoe (10707) ***(G-15203)***
Autostat Corporation 516 379-9447
209 Nassau Rd 11 Roosevelt (11575) ***(G-14030)***
Autronic Plastics Inc 516 333-7577
1150 Motor Pkwy Central Islip (11722) ***(G-3263)***
Auven Therapeutics MGT LP 212 616-4000
1325 Avenue Of The Americ New York (10019) ***(G-8683)***
AV Therapeutics Inc 917 497-5523
20 E 68th St Ste 204 New York (10065) ***(G-8684)***
Avalanche Fabrication Inc 585 545-4000
6314 Dean Pkwy Ontario (14519) ***(G-12285)***
Avalanche Studios New York Inc 212 993-6447
536 Broadway New York (10012) ***(G-8685)***
Avalin LLC 212 842-2286
221 W 37th St Fl 3 New York (10018) ***(G-8686)***
Avalon Copy Centers Amer Inc (PA) 315 471-3333
901 N State St Syracuse (13208) ***(G-14823)***
Avalon Copy Centers Amer Inc 716 995-7777
741 Main St Buffalo (14203) ***(G-2651)***
Avalon Document Services, Syracuse *Also called Avalon Copy Centers Amer Inc* ***(G-14823)***
Avalon Document Services, Buffalo *Also called Avalon Copy Centers Amer Inc* ***(G-2651)***
Avanel Industries Inc 516 333-0990
121 Hopper St Westbury (11590) ***(G-15871)***
Avant Garde Screen Printing Co, Flushing *Also called Albert Siy* ***(G-4836)***
Avante 516 782-4888
35 Hicks Ln Great Neck (11024) ***(G-5369)***
Avanti Advanced Mfg Corp 716 791-9001
673 Ontario St Buffalo (14207) ***(G-2652)***
Avanti Control Systems Inc 518 921-4368
1 Hamilton St Fl 2 Gloversville (12078) ***(G-5278)***
Avanti Furniture Corp 516 293-8220
497 Main St Farmingdale (11735) ***(G-4590)***
Avanti Press Inc 212 414-1025
6 W 18th St Ste 6l New York (10011) ***(G-8687)***
Avanti U S A Ltd 716 695-5800
412 Young St Tonawanda (14150) ***(G-15087)***
Avaya Services Inc 866 462-8292
2 Penn Plz Rm 702 New York (10121) ***(G-8688)***
Avco Industries Inc 631 851-1555
120 Windsor Pl Central Islip (11722) ***(G-3264)***
Avcom of Virginia Inc 585 924-4560
590 Fishers Station Dr Victor (14564) ***(G-15392)***
Aventura Technologies Inc (PA) 631 300-4000
48 Mall Dr Commack (11725) ***(G-3577)***
Avenue Magazine, New York *Also called Manhattan Media LLC* ***(G-10344)***
Avenue Therapeutics Inc 781 652-4500
2 Gansevoort St Fl 9 New York (10014) ***(G-8689)***
Avery Biomedical Devices Inc 631 864-1600
61 Mall Dr Ste 1 Commack (11725) ***(G-3578)***
Avery Dennison Corporation 626 304-2000
218 W 40th St Fl 8 New York (10018) ***(G-8690)***
Avf Group Inc (HQ) 951 360-7111
2775 Broadway St Ste 200 Cheektowaga (14227) ***(G-3339)***
AVI, Plainview *Also called Audio Video Invasion Inc* ***(G-12664)***
AVI-Spl Employee 212 840-4801
8 W 38th St Rm 1101 New York (10018) ***(G-8691)***
Avid Technology Inc 212 983-2424
90 Park Ave New York (10016) ***(G-8692)***
Avitto Leather Goods Inc 212 219-7501
424 W Broadway Frnt A New York (10012) ***(G-8693)***
Avm Printing Inc 631 351-1331
43 Corporate Dr Hauppauge (11788) ***(G-5599)***
AVM Software Inc (HQ) 646 381-2468
122 E 42nd St Rm 2600 New York (10168) ***(G-8694)***
Avoomo Power LLC 718 344-0404
1317 Avenue J Brooklyn (11230) ***(G-1553)***
Avr Optics, Rochester *Also called Avro Inc* ***(G-13254)***
Avro Inc 585 445-7588
3635 Buffalo Rd Ste 2 Rochester (14624) ***(G-13254)***
Avs Gem Stone Corp 212 944-6380
48 W 48th St Ste 1010 New York (10036) ***(G-8695)***
AVS Laminates Inc 631 286-2136
99 Bellport Ave Bellport (11713) ***(G-794)***
Avstar Fuel Systems Inc 315 255-1955
15 Brookfield Pl Auburn (13021) ***(G-465)***
AVX Corporation 716 372-6611
1695 Seneca Ave Olean (14760) ***(G-12223)***
AW Mack Manufacturing Co Inc 845 452-4050
1098 Dutchess Tpke Poughkeepsie (12603) ***(G-12947)***
Award Publishing Limited 212 246-0405
40 W 55th St Apt 9b New York (10019) ***(G-8696)***
Awe Technologies LLC 631 747-8448
261 W Main St Bay Shore (11706) ***(G-654)***
Awning Man, The, Yonkers *Also called Fabric Concepts For Industry* ***(G-16308)***
Awning Mart Inc 315 699-5928
5665 State Route 31 Cicero (13039) ***(G-3416)***
Awnings By Rainbow, Niagara Falls *Also called Rainbow Awning Co Inc* ***(G-11970)***
Awr Energy Inc 585 469-7750
35 Melody Ln Plattsburgh (12901) ***(G-12733)***
Awt Supply Corp 516 437-9105
153 Meacham Ave Elmont (11003) ***(G-4383)***
Axim Biotechnologies Inc 212 751-0001
5 Rockefeller Plz Fl 20 Flr 20 New York (10111) ***(G-8697)***
Axiom Software Ltd 914 769-8800
115 E Stevens Ave Ste 320 Valhalla (10595) ***(G-15302)***
Axis Denim, New York *Also called Axis Na LLC* ***(G-8698)***
Axis Na LLC (PA) 212 302-1959
70 W 40th St Fl 11 New York (10018) ***(G-8698)***

Axle Express.....518 347-2220
729 Broadway Schenectady (12305) *(G-14247)*
Axtell Bradtke Lumber Co.....607 265-3850
113 Beals Pond Rd Masonville (13804) *(G-7583)*
Aycan Medical Systems LLC.....585 271-3078
693 East Ave Ste 102 Rochester (14607) *(G-13255)*
Aydata Management LLC.....585 271-6133
693 East Ave Ste 102 Rochester (14607) *(G-13256)*
Ayehu Inc.....408 930-5823
1441 Broadway New York (10018) *(G-8699)*
AZ Yashir Bapaz Inc.....212 947-7357
134 W 37th St New York (10018) *(G-8700)*
Azibi Ltd.....212 869-6550
152 W 36th St Rm 403 New York (10018) *(G-8701)*
Aztec Industries Inc.....631 585-1331
200 13th Ave Unit 5 Ronkonkoma (11779) *(G-13910)*
Aztec Mfg of Rochester.....585 352-8152
19 Hickory Ln Spencerport (14559) *(G-14552)*
Aztec Tool Co Inc.....631 243-1144
180 Rodeo Dr Edgewood (11717) *(G-4262)*
Azurrx Biopharma Inc.....646 699-7855
760 Parkside Ave Ste 304 Brooklyn (11226) *(G-1554)*
B & B Forest Products Ltd.....518 622-0811
251 Route 145 Cairo (12413) *(G-3063)*
B & B Jewelry Mfg Co, New York *Also called Barber Brothers Jewelry Mfg (G-8726)*
B & B Lumber Company Inc (PA).....866 282-0582
4800 Solvay Rd Jamesville (13078) *(G-6555)*
B & B Precision Components Inc.....631 273-3321
301 Christopher St # 303 Ronkonkoma (11779) *(G-13911)*
B & B Precision Mfg Inc (PA).....585 226-6226
310 W Main St Avon (14414) *(G-511)*
B & B Sheet Metal Inc.....718 433-2501
2540 50th Ave Long Island City (11101) *(G-7173)*
B & B Sweater Mills Inc (PA).....718 456-8693
1160 Flushing Ave Brooklyn (11237) *(G-1555)*
B & D Enterprises Utica Inc (PA).....315 735-3311
2 Campion Rd Ste 7 New Hartford (13413) *(G-8236)*
B & F Architectural Support Gr.....212 279-6488
450 7th Ave Ste 307 New York (10123) *(G-8702)*
B & H Electronics Corp.....845 782-5000
308 Museum Village Rd Monroe (10950) *(G-8015)*
B & H Precision Fabricators.....631 563-9620
95 Davinci Dr Bohemia (11716) *(G-977)*
B & J Lumber Co Inc.....518 677-3845
1075 State Route 22 Cambridge (12816) *(G-3091)*
B & K Components Ltd.....323 776-4277
2100 Old Union Rd Buffalo (14227) *(G-2653)*
B & K Dye Cutting Inc.....718 497-5216
245 Varet St Brooklyn (11206) *(G-1556)*
B & P Jays Inc.....716 668-8408
19 N Hill Dr Buffalo (14224) *(G-2654)*
B & R Industries Inc.....631 736-2275
12 Commercial Blvd Medford (11763) *(G-7698)*
B & R Promotional Products.....212 563-0040
34 W 120th St Apt 1 New York (10027) *(G-8703)*
B & R Sheet.....718 558-5544
10652 157th St Jamaica (11433) *(G-6428)*
B & R Tool Inc.....718 948-2729
955 Rensselaer Ave Staten Island (10309) *(G-14622)*
B & W Heat Treating Company.....716 876-8184
2780 Kenmore Ave Tonawanda (14150) *(G-15088)*
B & Z Technologies LLC.....631 675-9666
7 Technology Dr East Setauket (11733) *(G-4176)*
B C America, New York *Also called Intertex USA Inc (G-9925)*
B C Manufacturing Inc.....585 482-1080
100 Thruway Park Dr West Henrietta (14586) *(G-15786)*
B D B Typewriter Supply Works.....718 232-4800
6215 14th Ave Brooklyn (11219) *(G-1557)*
B F G Elcpltg and Mfg Co.....716 362-0888
3949 Jeffrey Blvd Blasdell (14219) *(G-917)*
B H Aircraft Company Inc (PA).....631 580-9747
2230 Smithtown Ave Ronkonkoma (11779) *(G-13912)*
B H M Metal Products Co.....845 292-5297
Horseshoe Lake Rd Kauneonga Lake (12749) *(G-6640)*
B J Long Co, Rochester *Also called R V Dow Enterprises Inc (G-13667)*
B K Integrity, New York *Also called Golden Integrity Inc (G-9642)*
B K Jewelry Contractor Inc.....212 398-9093
71 W 47th St Fl 11 New York (10036) *(G-8704)*
B M P, Medina *Also called Bmp America Inc (G-7730)*
B M Printing, Brooklyn *Also called Bestmade Printing LLC (G-1580)*
B P I, West Henrietta *Also called Brinkman Precision Inc (G-15788)*
B Q P Inc.....518 793-4999
6 Collins Dr Queensbury (12804) *(G-13034)*
B S C, Binghamton *Also called Binghamton Simulator Co Inc (G-860)*
B Smith Furs Inc.....212 967-5290
224 W 30th St Rm 402 New York (10001) *(G-8705)*
B Tween LLC.....212 819-9040
1412 Broadway Rm 1400 New York (10018) *(G-8706)*
B V M Associates.....631 254-6220
999-32 Montrell 414 Shirley (11967) *(G-14416)*
B W A, New York *Also called Ben Wachter Associates Inc (G-8754)*

B&B Albany Pallet Company LLC.....315 492-1786
4800 Solvay Rd Jamesville (13078) *(G-6556)*
B&B Sports Nutrition LLC.....520 869-5434
244 W 72nd St Unit Phr New York (10023) *(G-8707)*
B&K Precision Corporation.....631 369-2665
31 Oakwood Dr Manorville (11949) *(G-7551)*
B-Reel Films Inc.....917 388-3836
401 Broadway Fl 24 New York (10013) *(G-8708)*
B.E.S. Publishing, Hauppauge *Also called Barrons Educational Series Inc (G-5602)*
B/E Aerospace Inc.....631 563-6400
355 Knickerbocker Ave Bohemia (11716) *(G-978)*
B2b Cleaning Services, Yonkers *Also called Rumsey Corp (G-16347)*
B3cg Interconnect Usa Inc.....518 324-4800
18 Northern Ave Ste 100 Plattsburgh (12903) *(G-12734)*
B601 V2 Inc.....646 391-6431
315 5th Ave Rm 903 New York (10016) *(G-8709)*
Ba Sports Nutrition LLC.....718 357-7402
1720 Whitestone Expy # 101 Whitestone (11357) *(G-16089)*
Baar & Beards, New York *Also called Gce International Inc (G-9581)*
Babbit Bearings, Syracuse *Also called Babbitt Bearings Inc (G-14824)*
Babbitt Bearings Inc (PA).....315 479-6603
734 Burnet Ave Syracuse (13203) *(G-14824)*
Babbitt Bearings Incorporated.....315 479-6603
734 Burnet Ave Syracuse (13203) *(G-14825)*
Babcock Co Inc.....607 776-3341
36 Delaware Ave Bath (14810) *(G-630)*
Babula Construction Inc.....716 681-0886
5136 William St Lancaster (14086) *(G-6797)*
Baby Central LLC.....718 372-2229
2436 Mcdonald Ave Brooklyn (11223) *(G-1558)*
Baby Signature Inc (PA).....212 686-1700
251 5th Ave Fl 2l New York (10016) *(G-8710)*
Babydoll, New York *Also called Mag Brands LLC (G-10319)*
Babyfair Inc.....212 736-7989
34 W 33rd St Rm 818 New York (10001) *(G-8711)*
Babyganics, Westbury *Also called Kas Direct LLC (G-15901)*
Babylon Iron Works Inc.....631 643-3311
205 Edison Ave West Babylon (11704) *(G-15692)*
Babysafe Usa LLC.....877 367-4141
251 County Road 17 Afton (13730) *(G-6)*
Backstage LLC (PA).....212 493-4243
45 Main St Ste 416 Brooklyn (11201) *(G-1559)*
Backtech Inc.....973 279-0838
2 Peter Cooper Rd Apt Mf New York (10010) *(G-8712)*
Baco Controls Inc (PA).....315 635-2500
8431 Loop Rd Baldwinsville (13027) *(G-543)*
Baco Enterprises Inc.....718 589-6225
1190 Longwood Ave Bronx (10474) *(G-1209)*
Bactolac Pharmaceutical Inc (PA).....631 951-4908
7 Oser Ave Ste 1 Hauppauge (11788) *(G-5600)*
Bactolac Pharmaceutical Inc.....631 951-4908
620 Old Willets Path Hauppauge (11788) *(G-5601)*
Bad Seed Cider Co LLC.....914 474-4422
465 Pancake Hollow Rd Highland (12528) *(G-5957)*
Bader Enterprise Inc.....718 965-9434
115 27th St Brooklyn (11232) *(G-1560)*
Badge Machine Products Inc.....585 394-0330
2491 Brickyard Rd Canandaigua (14424) *(G-3125)*
Badger Technologies Inc.....585 869-7101
5829 County Road 41 Farmington (14425) *(G-4768)*
Badgley Mischka Licensing LLC.....212 921-1585
133 W 52nd St 5 New York (10019) *(G-8713)*
Bae Systems Controls Inc (HQ).....607 770-2000
1098 Clark St Endicott (13760) *(G-4445)*
Bae Systems Info & Elec Sys.....603 885-4321
581 Phoenix Dr Rome (13441) *(G-13842)*
Bae Systems Info & Elec Sys.....631 912-1525
450 Pulaski Rd Greenlawn (11740) *(G-5452)*
Bae Systems PLC.....631 261-7000
1 Hazeltine Way Greenlawn (11740) *(G-5453)*
Baffler Foundation Inc.....203 362-8147
19 W 21st St Rm 1001 New York (10010) *(G-8714)*
Bag Arts Ltd.....212 684-7020
20 W 36th St Rm 5l New York (10018) *(G-8715)*
Bag Arts The Art Packaging LLC.....212 684-7020
20 W 36th St Fl 5 New York (10018) *(G-8716)*
Bag Bazaar Ltd.....212 689-3508
1 E 33rd St Fl 6 New York (10016) *(G-8717)*
Bagel Club, Bayside *Also called A T A Bagel Shoppe Inc (G-733)*
Bagel Club Inc.....718 423-6106
20521 35th Ave Bayside (11361) *(G-735)*
Bagel Grove Inc.....315 724-8015
7 Burrstone Rd Utica (13502) *(G-15240)*
Bagel Land.....585 442-3080
1896 Monroe Ave Rochester (14618) *(G-13257)*
Bagel Oasis, Flushing *Also called Triboro Bagel Co Inc (G-4901)*
Bagel Shoppe, The, Fishkill *Also called Enterprise Bagels Inc (G-4799)*
Bagelovers Inc.....607 844-3683
42 Elm St Dryden (13053) *(G-4037)*
Bagelry, Cedarhurst *Also called M & M Bagel Corp (G-3240)*
Bagels On The Square, Staten Island *Also called Carmine Street Bagels Inc (G-14637)*

ALPHABETIC

Bags Unlimited Inc 585 436-6282
7 Canal St Rochester (14608) *(G-13258)*

Bagznyc Corp 212 643-8202
19 W 34th St Rm 318 New York (10001) *(G-8718)*

Baikal Inc (PA) 212 239-4650
341 W 38th St Fl 3 New York (10018) *(G-8719)*

Bailey Boonville Mills Inc 315 942-2131
123 Mill St Boonville (13309) *(G-1103)*

Bailey Elc Mtr & Pump Sup LLC 585 418-5051
2186 Main Rd Corfu (14036) *(G-3701)*

Bailey Manufacturing Co LLC 716 965-2731
10987 Bennett State Rd Forestville (14062) *(G-4930)*

Bainbridge & Knight LLC 212 986-5100
801 2nd Ave Fl 19 New York (10017) *(G-8720)*

Baird Mold Making Inc 631 667-0322
195 N Fehr Way Ste C Bay Shore (11706) *(G-655)*

Bairnco Corporation (HQ) 914 461-1300
1133 Westchester Ave N-222 White Plains (10604) *(G-15977)*

Bake-Rite International Inc 518 395-3340
412 Warren St Schenectady (12305) *(G-14248)*

Baker Commodities Inc 585 482-1880
2268 Browncroft Blvd Rochester (14625) *(G-13259)*

Baker Logging & Firewood 585 374-5733
8781 Grlnghuse Atlanta Rd Naples (14512) *(G-8206)*

Baker Products Inc 212 459-2323
5 Oakley Rd White Plains (10606) *(G-15978)*

Baker Tool & Die 716 694-2025
48 Industrial Dr North Tonawanda (14120) *(G-12056)*

Baker Tool & Die & Die 716 694-2025
48 Industrial Dr North Tonawanda (14120) *(G-12057)*

Bakery & Coffee Shop 315 287-1829
274 W Main St Gouverneur (13642) *(G-5316)*

Bakery Innovative Tech Corp 631 758-3081
139 N Ocean Ave Patchogue (11772) *(G-12496)*

Balajee Enterprises Inc 212 629-6150
150 W 30th St Frnt 2 New York (10001) *(G-8721)*

Balance Enterprises Inc 516 822-3183
12 W Cherry St Hicksville (11801) *(G-5887)*

Balanced Tech Corp 212 768-8330
37 W 37th St Fl 10 New York (10018) *(G-8722)*

Balchem Corporation (PA) 845 326-5600
52 Sunrise Park Rd New Hampton (10958) *(G-8232)*

Baldwin Machine Works Inc 631 842-9110
20 Grant Ave 2040 Copiague (11726) *(G-3649)*

Baldwin Ribbon & Stamping Corp 718 335-6700
3956 63rd St Woodside (11377) *(G-16196)*

Baldwin Richardson Foods Co 315 986-2727
3268 Blue Heron Dr Macedon (14502) *(G-7461)*

Balint Tool, Brooklyn *Also called Tools & Stamping Corp (G-2510)*

Baliva Concrete Products Inc 585 328-8442
245 Paul Rd Rochester (14624) *(G-13260)*

Ball Chain Mfg Co Inc (PA) 914 664-7500
741 S Fulton Ave Mount Vernon (10550) *(G-8123)*

Ball Metal Beverage Cont Corp 845 692-3800
95 Ballard Rd Middletown (10941) *(G-7894)*

Ball Metal Beverage Cont Corp 518 587-6030
11 Adams Rd Saratoga Springs (12866) *(G-14165)*

Ball Metal Beverage Cont Div, Middletown *Also called Ball Metal Beverage Cont Corp (G-7894)*

Ball Metal Beverage Cont Div, Saratoga Springs *Also called Ball Metal Beverage Cont Corp (G-14165)*

Ballantrae Lithographers Inc 914 592-3275
96 Wayside Dr White Plains (10607) *(G-15979)*

Balticare Inc (PA) 646 380-9470
501 Fashion Ave Rm 414 New York (10018) *(G-8723)*

Bam Enterprises Inc (PA) 716 773-7634
2937 Alt Blvd Grand Island (14072) *(G-5326)*

Bam Sales LLC (PA) 212 781-3000
1407 Broadway Rm 2018 New York (10018) *(G-8724)*

Bamberger Polymers Inc (HQ) 516 622-3600
2 Jericho Plz Ste 109 Jericho (11753) *(G-6571)*

Bandaroos, New York *Also called L D Weiss Inc (G-10150)*

Bandec LLC 516 627-1971
366 N Broadway Ste 410 Jericho (11753) *(G-6572)*

Bandit International Ltd 718 402-2100
600 E 132nd St Bronx (10454) *(G-1210)*

Bands N Bows 718 984-4316
34 Fieldway Ave Staten Island (10308) *(G-14623)*

Bangla Patrika Inc 718 482-9923
3806 31st St 2 Long Island City (11101) *(G-7174)*

Bank Displays.com, Deer Park *Also called L Miller Design Inc (G-3894)*

Bank-Miller Co Inc 914 227-9357
333 Fifth Ave Pelham (10803) *(G-12565)*

Banner Metalcraft Inc 631 563-7303
300 Trade Zone Dr Ronkonkoma (11779) *(G-13913)*

Banner Smoked Fish Inc 718 449-1992
2715 W 15th St Brooklyn (11224) *(G-1561)*

Banner Transmission & Eng Co 516 221-9459
4 Cabriolet Ln Melville (11747) *(G-7762)*

Banner Transmissions, Melville *Also called Banner Transmission & Eng Co (G-7762)*

Bannerboy Corporation 646 691-6524
424 3rd Ave A Brooklyn (11215) *(G-1562)*

Baoma Industrial Inc 631 218-6515
840 Lincoln Ave Ste 6 Bohemia (11716) *(G-979)*

Bara Fashions, Brooklyn *Also called Matchables Inc (G-2123)*

Baralan Usa Inc (HQ) 718 849-5768
12019 89th Ave Richmond Hill (11418) *(G-13109)*

Barbara Matera Ltd 212 475-5006
890 Broadway Fl 5 New York (10003) *(G-8725)*

Barber & Deline Enrgy Svcs LLC 315 696-8961
10 Community Dr Tully (13159) *(G-15208)*

Barber & Deline LLC 607 749-2619
995 State Route 11a Tully (13159) *(G-15209)*

Barber Brothers Jewelry Mfg 212 819-0666
580 5th Ave Ste 725 New York (10036) *(G-8726)*

Barber Welding Inc 315 834-6645
2517 Rte 31 W Weedsport (13166) *(G-15665)*

Barbera Transduser Systems 718 816-3025
21 Louis St Staten Island (10304) *(G-14624)*

Barc Usa Inc 516 719-1052
5 Delaware Dr Ste 2 New Hyde Park (11042) *(G-8253)*

Barclay Brown Corp 718 376-7166
47 Lancaster Ave Brooklyn (11223) *(G-1563)*

Barclay Tagg Racing 631 404-8269
86 Geranium Ave Floral Park (11001) *(G-4809)*

Bardwil Industries Inc (PA) 212 944-1870
4 Bryant Park Fl 4 Flr 4 New York (10018) *(G-8727)*

Bardwil Linens, New York *Also called Bardwil Industries Inc (G-8727)*

Bare Beauty Laser Hair Removal 718 278-2273
5 E 57th St Fl 18 New York (10022) *(G-8728)*

Bare Wire Div, Jordan *Also called Omega Wire Inc (G-6630)*

Bare Wire Div, Camden *Also called Omega Wire Inc (G-3104)*

Bare Wire Division, Camden *Also called Owi Corporation (G-3105)*

Bare Wire Division, Camden *Also called International Wire Group Inc (G-3102)*

Bargold Storage Systems LLC 718 247-7000
4141 38th St Long Island City (11101) *(G-7175)*

Bari Engineering Corp 212 966-2080
240 Bowery New York (10012) *(G-8729)*

Bari-Jay Fashions Inc (PA) 212 921-1551
230 W 38th St Fl 12 New York (10018) *(G-8730)*

Barilla America Ny Inc 585 226-5600
100 Horseshoe Blvd Avon (14414) *(G-512)*

Barker Brothers Incorporated 718 456-6400
1666 Summerfield St Ste 1 Ridgewood (11385) *(G-13140)*

Barker Steel LLC 518 465-6221
126 S Port Rd Albany (12202) *(G-44)*

Barnaby Prints Inc (PA) 845 477-2501
673 Jersey Ave Greenwood Lake (10925) *(G-5479)*

Barnes Group Inc 315 457-9200
1225 State Fair Blvd Syracuse (13209) *(G-14826)*

Barnes Metal Finishing Inc 585 798-4817
3932 Salt Works Rd Medina (14103) *(G-7728)*

Barney & Dickenson Inc (PA) 607 729-1536
520 Prentice Rd Vestal (13850) *(G-15370)*

Baroka Creations Inc 212 768-0527
36 W 47th St Ste 1402 New York (10036) *(G-8731)*

Baron Packaging, Hauppauge *Also called J & M Packaging Inc (G-5679)*

Barone Offset Printing Corp 212 989-5500
89 Lake Ridge Cv Mohegan Lake (10547) *(G-8008)*

Barra & Trumbore Inc 845 626-5442
40 Old Mine Rd Kerhonkson (12446) *(G-6658)*

Barrage 212 586-9390
401 W 47th St Frnt A New York (10036) *(G-8732)*

Barrasso & Sons Trucking Inc 631 581-0360
160 Floral Park St Islip Terrace (11752) *(G-6358)*

Barrera Jose & Maria Co Ltd 212 239-1994
29 W 36th St Fl 8 New York (10018) *(G-8733)*

Barrett Paving Materials Inc 315 353-6611
Rr 56 Norwood (13668) *(G-12131)*

Barrett Paving Materials Inc 315 652-4585
4530 Wetzel Rd Liverpool (13090) *(G-7000)*

Barrett Paving Materials Inc 315 737-9471
363 Rasbach Rd Clayville (13322) *(G-3454)*

Barrett Paving Materials Inc 607 723-5367
14 Brandywine St Binghamton (13901) *(G-856)*

Barrett Paving Materials Inc 315 788-2037
26572 State Route 37 Watertown (13601) *(G-15559)*

Barrie House Coffee & Tea, Elmsford *Also called Bh Coffee Company LLC (G-4396)*

Barrier Brewing Company LLC 516 316-4429
612 W Walnut St Long Beach (11561) *(G-7135)*

Barron Games Intl Co LLC 716 630-0054
84 Aero Dr Ste 5 Buffalo (14225) *(G-2655)*

Barron Metal Products Inc 914 965-1232
286 Nepperhan Ave Yonkers (10701) *(G-16289)*

Barrons Educational Series Inc (PA) 631 434-3311
250 Wireless Blvd Hauppauge (11788) *(G-5602)*

Barry Industries Inc 212 242-5200
36 W 17th St Frnt 1 New York (10011) *(G-8734)*

Barry Steel Fabrication Inc (PA) 716 433-2144
30 Simonds St Lockport (14094) *(G-7061)*

Barry Supply Co Div, New York *Also called Barry Industries Inc (G-8734)*

Barson Composites Corporation (PA) 516 752-7882
160 Bethpage Sweet Old Bethpage (11804) *(G-12215)*

Bart Ostrander Trckg Log Corp..................518 661-6535
  1556 State Highway 30 Mayfield (12117) *(G-7681)*
Bartell Machinery Systems LLC (HQ)..........315 336-7600
  6321 Elmer Hill Rd Rome (13440) *(G-13843)*
Bartholomew Mazza Ltd Inc.....................212 935-4530
  22 W 48th St Ste 805 New York (10036) *(G-8735)*
Bartizan Data Systems LLC......................914 965-7977
  217 Riverdale Ave Yonkers (10705) *(G-16290)*
Bartolomeo Publishing Inc......................631 420-4949
  100 Cabot St Unit A West Babylon (11704) *(G-15693)*
Bartolotta Furniture, Auburn *Also called Matteo & Antonio Bartolotta (G-485)*
Barton International, Glens Falls *Also called Barton Mines Company LLC (G-5242)*
Barton Mines Company LLC (PA).............518 798-5462
  6 Warren St Glens Falls (12801) *(G-5242)*
Barton Tool Inc...................................716 665-2801
  1864 Lyndon Blvd Falconer (14733) *(G-4535)*
Base Systems Inc.................................845 278-1991
  1606 Route 22 Brewster (10509) *(G-1142)*
BASF Corporation................................914 737-2554
  1057 Lower South St Peekskill (10566) *(G-12548)*
BASF Corporation................................914 785-2000
  500 White Plains Rd Tarrytown (10591) *(G-15041)*
BASF Corporation................................518 465-6534
  70 Riverside Ave Rensselaer (12144) *(G-13087)*
BASF Corporation................................631 689-0200
  361 Sheep Pasture Rd East Setauket (11733) *(G-4177)*
BASF The Chemical Company, East Setauket *Also called BASF Corporation (G-4177)*
Basil S Kadhim..................................888 520-5192
  280 Madison Ave Rm 912 New York (10016) *(G-8736)*
Basileus Company LLC.........................315 963-3516
  8104 Cazenovia Rd Manlius (13104) *(G-7543)*
Basilio's, Canastota *Also called Salarinos Italian Foods Inc (G-3156)*
Basiloff LLC.....................................646 671-0353
  179 Bennett Ave Apt 7f New York (10040) *(G-8737)*
Basin Holdings LLC (PA).........................212 695-7376
  200 Park Ave Fl 58b New York (10166) *(G-8738)*
Bass Oil & Chemical Llc.........................718 628-4444
  136 Morgan Ave Brooklyn (11237) *(G-1564)*
Bass Oil Company Inc..........................718 628-4444
  136 Morgan Ave Brooklyn (11237) *(G-1565)*
Bastide Inc......................................646 356-0460
  300 Park Ave Fl 12 New York (10022) *(G-8739)*
Batampte Pickle Products Inc (PA)............718 251-2100
  77 Brooklyn Terminal Mkt Brooklyn (11236) *(G-1566)*
Batavia Enclosures Inc..........................585 344-1797
  636 Main St Arcade (14009) *(G-369)*
Batavia Legal Printing Inc......................585 768-2100
  7 Bank St Le Roy (14482) *(G-6896)*
Batavia Precision Glass LLC.....................585 343-6050
  231 Currier Ave Buffalo (14212) *(G-2656)*
Batavia Press LLC..............................585 343-4429
  3817 W Main Street Rd Batavia (14020) *(G-603)*
Bates Industries, South Glens Falls *Also called Mdi East Inc (G-14514)*
Bates Jackson Engraving Co Inc................716 854-3000
  17 Elm St 21 Buffalo (14203) *(G-2657)*
Bator Bintor Inc.................................347 546-6503
  42 Delevan St Brooklyn (11231) *(G-1567)*
Battenfeld Grease Oil Corp NY..................716 695-2100
  1174 Erie Ave North Tonawanda (14120) *(G-12058)*
Battenfeld-American Inc.......................716 822-8410
  1575 Clinton St Buffalo (14206) *(G-2658)*
Battery Research and Tstg Inc..................315 342-2373
  1313 County Route 1 Oswego (13126) *(G-12408)*
Batteryminder, Huntington *Also called Vdc Electronics Inc (G-6232)*
Battsco LLC....................................516 586-6544
  190 Lauman Ln Unit A Hicksville (11801) *(G-5888)*
Bauble Bar Inc.................................646 846-2044
  16 Madison Sq W Fl 5 New York (10010) *(G-8740)*
Bauerschmidt & Sons Inc......................718 528-3500
  11920 Merrick Blvd Jamaica (11434) *(G-6429)*
Baum Christine and John Corp..................585 621-8910
  1577 W Ridge Rd Rochester (14615) *(G-13261)*
Baum Essex, New York *Also called Essex Manufacturing Inc (G-9404)*
Baums Castorine Company Inc................315 336-8154
  200 Matthew St Rome (13440) *(G-13844)*
Bausch & Lomb Holdings Inc (HQ)..............585 338-6000
  450 Lexington Ave New York (10017) *(G-8741)*
Bausch & Lomb Incorporated....................585 338-6000
  1 Bausch And Lomb Pl Rochester (14604) *(G-13262)*
Bausch & Lomb Incorporated....................585 338-6000
  1400 N Goodman St Rochester (14609) *(G-13263)*
Baxter Healthcare Corporation.................800 356-3454
  711 Park Ave Medina (14103) *(G-7729)*
Bay Horse Innovations Nyinc...................607 898-3337
  130 Cayuga St Groton (13073) *(G-5480)*
Bay Sales Company, New York *Also called Salmco Jewelry Corp (G-11120)*
Bayit Home Automation Corp...................973 988-2638
  2906 Shell Rd Fl 2 Brooklyn (11224) *(G-1568)*
Bayshore Electric Motors........................631 475-1397
  33 Suffolk Ave Patchogue (11772) *(G-12497)*
Bayshore Motors, Patchogue *Also called Bayshore Electric Motors (G-12497)*

Bayshore Wire Products Corp...................631 451-8825
  480 Mill Rd Coram (11727) *(G-3692)*
Bayside Beepers & Cellular......................718 343-3888
  25607 Hillside Ave Glen Oaks (11004) *(G-5214)*
Bazaar...212 903-5497
  300 W 57th St Fl 25 New York (10019) *(G-8742)*
BC Communications Inc.........................631 549-8833
  211 Depot Rd Huntington Station (11746) *(G-6240)*
BC Systems Inc..................................631 751-9370
  200 N Belle Mead Rd Ste 2 Setauket (11733) *(G-14377)*
BCM, Mount Vernon *Also called Ball Chain Mfg Co Inc (G-8123)*
BCM Electronics Manuf Services................631 580-9516
  3279 Veterans Memorial Ronkonkoma (11779) *(G-13914)*
Bco Industries Western NY Inc.................716 877-2800
  77 Oriskany Dr Tonawanda (14150) *(G-15089)*
Bcp Ingredients Inc (HQ)........................845 326-5600
  52 Sunrise Park Rd New Hampton (10958) *(G-8233)*
Bcs Access Systems Us LLC....................315 258-3469
  2150 Crane Brook Dr Auburn (13021) *(G-466)*
Bd Initiative-Hlthcare Wrkr SA, Nyack *Also called Becton Dickinson and Company (G-12136)*
Bd Projects, New York *Also called Architects Newspaper LLC (G-8618)*
Bdg Media Inc (PA)..............................917 551-6510
  315 Park Ave S Fl 12 New York (10010) *(G-8743)*
Bdm, Syosset *Also called Buffalo Dental Mfg Co Inc (G-14780)*
Bdp Industries Inc (PA).........................518 695-6851
  354 State Route 29 Greenwich (12834) *(G-5468)*
BDR Creative Concepts Inc.....................516 942-7768
  141 Central Ave Ste B Farmingdale (11735) *(G-4591)*
Bdtrims, Brooklyn *Also called Rus Auto Parts Inc (G-2365)*
Be The Media, New Hyde Park *Also called Natural E Creative LLC (G-8283)*
Beaba USA, New York *Also called Peek A Boo USA Inc (G-10784)*
Beacon, Babylon *Also called A C J Communications Inc (G-517)*
Beacon Adhesives Inc..........................914 699-3400
  125 S Macquesten Pkwy Mount Vernon (10550) *(G-8124)*
Beacon Chemical, Mount Vernon *Also called Beacon Adhesives Inc (G-8124)*
Beacon Newspapers, Hempstead *Also called Nassau County Publications (G-5846)*
Beacon Press Inc................................212 691-5050
  32 Cushman Rd White Plains (10606) *(G-15980)*
Beacon Press News, Wappingers Falls *Also called Wappingers Falls Shopper Inc (G-15501)*
Beacon Spch Lnge Pthlgy Phys..................516 626-1635
  1441 Old Northern Blvd Roslyn (11576) *(G-14039)*
Beacon Therapy Services, Roslyn *Also called Beacon Spch Lnge Pthlgy Phys (G-14039)*
Beal Blocks, New York *Also called B & R Promotional Products (G-8703)*
BEAM Manufacturing Corp......................631 253-2724
  107 Otis St Unit A West Babylon (11704) *(G-15694)*
Bean King International LLC.....................845 268-3135
  36 N Route 9w Congers (10920) *(G-3609)*
Bear Metal Works Inc..........................716 824-4350
  39 Scoville Ave Buffalo (14206) *(G-2659)*
Beardslee Realty.................................516 747-5557
  290 E Jericho Tpke Mineola (11501) *(G-7960)*
Bears Management Group Inc....................585 624-5694
  7577 E Main St Lima (14485) *(G-6929)*
Bears Playgrounds, Lima *Also called Bears Management Group Inc (G-6929)*
Beastons Budget Printing Inc...................585 244-2721
  1260 Scttsvlle Rd Ste 300 Rochester (14624) *(G-13264)*
Beauty America LLC.............................917 744-1430
  10 Bond St Ste 296 Great Neck (11021) *(G-5370)*
Beaver Creek Industries Inc.....................607 545-6382
  11530 White Rd Canaseraga (14822) *(G-3147)*
Beaver Mountain Log Homes Inc................607 467-2700
  200 Beaver Mountain Dr Hancock (13783) *(G-5534)*
Bebitz USA Inc..................................516 280-8378
  2 Reiter Ave Hicksville (11801) *(G-5889)*
Bebop Books, New York *Also called Lee & Low Books Incorporated (G-10189)*
BEC Acquisition Co, Melville *Also called Tech Software LLC (G-7829)*
Becca Inc.......................................646 568-6250
  142 W 36th St Fl 15 New York (10018) *(G-8744)*
Becca Cosmetics, New York *Also called Becca Inc (G-8744)*
Beck Vault Company.............................315 337-7590
  6648 Shank Ave Rome (13440) *(G-13845)*
Beck, Don, Corfu *Also called Delaval Inc (G-3702)*
Becker Electronics Inc...........................631 619-9100
  50 Alexander Ct Ste 2 Ronkonkoma (11779) *(G-13915)*
Beckmann Converting Inc (PA)..................518 842-0073
  14 Park Dr Amsterdam (12010) *(G-318)*
Becks Classic Mfg Inc...........................631 435-3800
  50 Emjay Blvd Ste 14 Brentwood (11717) *(G-1116)*
Becton Dickinson and Company................845 353-3371
  1 Main St Apt 3307 Nyack (10960) *(G-12136)*
Bedessee Imports Ltd...........................718 272-1300
  140 Varick Ave Brooklyn (11237) *(G-1569)*
Bedford Freeman & Worth (HQ)................212 576-9400
  1 New York Plz Ste 4500 New York (10004) *(G-8745)*
Bedford Freeman & Worth......................212 375-7000
  1 New York Plz Ste 4500 New York (10004) *(G-8746)*
Bedford Communications Inc....................212 807-8220
  1410 Broadway Frnt 2 New York (10018) *(G-8747)*
Bedford Downing Glass..........................718 418-6409
  220 Ingraham St Ste 2 Brooklyn (11237) *(G-1570)*

A
L
P
H
A
B
E
T
I
C

Bedford Precision Parts Corp 914 241-2211
  290 Adams St Bedford Hills (10507) (G-765)
Bedford Pund Rdge Rcord Review, Katonah Also called Record Review LLC (G-6638)
Bedford Wdwrk Instllations Inc 914 764-9434
  200 Pound Ridge Rd Bedford (10506) (G-762)
Bedrock Communications 212 532-4150
  55 E 59th St Fl 20 New York (10022) (G-8748)
Bedrock Industries (PA) 202 400-0839
  45 Rockefeller Plz 2950a New York (10111) (G-8749)
Bedrock Landscaping Mtls Corp 631 587-4950
  454 Sunrise Hwy Babylon (11704) (G-518)
Bedrock Plus, Babylon Also called Bedrock Landscaping Mtls Corp (G-518)
Bee Green Industries Inc 516 334-3525
  322 Westbury Ave Carle Place (11514) (G-3171)
Bee Publications Inc 716 632-4700
  5564 Main St Williamsville (14221) (G-16121)
Beebie Printing & Art Agcy Inc 518 725-4528
  40 E Pine St Gloversville (12078) (G-5279)
Beech Grove Technology Inc 845 223-6844
  11 Sandy Pines Blvd Hopewell Junction (12533) (G-6091)
Beech-Nut Nutrition Company (HQ) 518 839-0300
  1 Nutritious Pl Amsterdam (12010) (G-319)
Beecher Emssn Sltn Tchnlgs LLC (PA) 607 796-0149
  1250 Schweizer Rd Horseheads (14845) (G-6113)
Beehive Press Inc 718 654-1200
  3742 Boston Rd Bronx (10469) (G-1211)
Beer Marketers Insights Inc 845 507-0040
  49 E Maple Ave Suffern (10901) (G-14758)
Beetins Wholesale Inc 718 524-0899
  125 Ravenhurst Ave Staten Island (10310) (G-14625)
Beetnpath LLC 607 319-5585
  950 Danby Rd Ste 150 Ithaca (14850) (G-6364)
Beets Love Production LLC 585 270-2471
  1150 Lee Rd Sectiona Rochester (14606) (G-13265)
Behance, New York Also called Adobe Systems Incorporated (G-8463)
Beila Group Inc 212 260-1948
  285 Mott St New York (10012) (G-8750)
Beis Moshiach Inc 718 778-8000
  744 Eastern Pkwy Brooklyn (11213) (G-1571)
Beitals Aquarium Sales & Svc, Pearl River Also called C B Management Services
Inc (G-12529)
Beka World LP 716 685-3717
  258 Sonwil Dr Buffalo (14225) (G-2660)
Bekaert Corporation 716 830-1321
  6000 N Bailey Ave Ste 9 Amherst (14226) (G-212)
Bektrom Foods Inc (PA) 516 802-3800
  6800 Jericho Tpke 207w Syosset (11791) (G-14778)
Bel Aire Offset Corp 718 539-8333
  1853 College Point Blvd College Point (11356) (G-3537)
Bel Aire Printing, College Point Also called Bel Aire Offset Corp (G-3537)
Bel Transformer Inc (HQ) 516 239-5777
  128 Atlantic Ave Lynbrook (11563) (G-7426)
Bel-Bee Products Incorporated 845 353-0300
  100 Snake Hill Rd Ste 1 West Nyack (10994) (G-15817)
Belangers Gravel & Stone Inc 585 728-3906
  10184 State Route 21 Wayland (14572) (G-15625)
Belden Inc 607 796-5600
  224 N Main St Ste 4 Horseheads (14845) (G-6114)
Belden Manufacturing Inc 607 238-0998
  1813 Us Route 11 Kirkwood (13795) (G-6730)
Belfair Draperies, Long Island City Also called Anthony Lawrence of New York (G-7159)
Belgian Boys USA, Brooklyn Also called Merb LLC (G-2139)
Bella Figura Letterpress 866 699-6040
  509 W Fayette St Syracuse (13204) (G-14827)
Bella International Inc 716 484-0102
  111 W 2nd St Ste 4000 Jamestown (14701) (G-6496)
Bellataire Diamonds Inc 212 687-8881
  19 W 44th St Fl 15 New York (10036) (G-8751)
Belle Maison USA Ltd 718 805-0200
  8950 127th St Richmond Hill (11418) (G-13110)
Bellerophon Publications Inc 212 627-9977
  205 Lexington Ave Fl 17 New York (10016) (G-8752)
Bellini Collections, New York Also called Formart Corp (G-9516)
Bellmore Steel Products Corp 516 785-9667
  2282 Bellmore Ave Bellmore (11710) (G-780)
Bello LLC 516 623-8800
  178 Hanse Ave Freeport (11520) (G-4987)
Belmay Holding Corporation 914 376-1515
  1 Odell Plz Ste 123 Yonkers (10701) (G-16291)
Belmet Products Inc (PA) 718 542-8220
  1350 Garrison Ave Bronx (10474) (G-1212)
Belrix Industries Inc 716 821-5964
  3590 Jeffrey Blvd Buffalo (14219) (G-2661)
Belsito Communications Inc 845 534-9700
  1 Ardmore St New Windsor (12553) (G-8360)
BELT DEWATERING PRESS, Greenwich Also called Bdp Industries Inc (G-5468)
Belt Maintenance Systems, Buffalo Also called Rlp Holdings Inc (G-2956)
Belton Industries, Brooklyn Also called Filta Clean Co Inc (G-1843)
Beltone Corporation 716 565-1015
  7474 Transit Rd Williamsville (14221) (G-16122)

Beltran Associates Inc 718 252-2996
  1133 E 35th St Ste 1 Brooklyn (11210) (G-1572)
Beltran Technologies Inc 718 338-3311
  1133 E 35th St Brooklyn (11210) (G-1573)
Beltron Products Inc 888 423-5876
  80 State St Albany (12207) (G-45)
Beluga Inc (PA) 212 594-5511
  463 7th Ave Fl 4 New York (10018) (G-8753)
Ben Wachter Associates Inc (PA) 212 736-4064
  36 W 44th St Ste 700 New York (10036) (G-8754)
Ben Weitsman of Albany LLC 518 462-4444
  300 Smith Blvd Albany (12202) (G-46)
Benartex LLC 212 840-3250
  132 W 36th St Rm 401 New York (10018) (G-8755)
Benchemark Printing Inc 518 393-1361
  1890 Maxon Rd Ext Schenectady (12308) (G-14249)
Benchers Unlimited, Brooklyn Also called Issacs Yisroel (G-1971)
Benchmark Books, Rye Brook Also called Marshall Cavendish Corp (G-14091)
Benchmark Education Co LLC (PA) 914 637-7200
  145 Huguenot St Fl 8 New Rochelle (10801) (G-8320)
Benchmark Furniture Mfg 718 257-4707
  300 Dewitt Ave Brooklyn (11236) (G-1574)
Benchmark Graphics Ltd 212 683-1711
  9 E 37th St Fl 5 New York (10016) (G-8756)
Benchmark Media Systems Inc 315 437-6300
  203 E Hampton Pl Ste 2 Syracuse (13206) (G-14828)
Benedictine Hospital, Kingston Also called Healthalliance Hospital (G-6693)
Benemy Welding & Fabrication 315 548-8500
  8 Pleasant Ave Phelps (14532) (G-12602)
Benetton Services, New York Also called Ramsbury Property Us Inc (G-10976)
Benetton Trading Usa Inc (PA) 212 593-0290
  601 5th Ave Fl 4 New York (10017) (G-8757)
Benfield Control Systems Inc 914 948-3231
  55 Lafayette Ave White Plains (10603) (G-15981)
Benishty Brothers Corp 646 339-9991
  233 Mosher Ave Woodmere (11598) (G-16190)
Benjamin Moore & Co 518 736-1723
  Union Ave Ext Johnstown (12095) (G-6611)
Benjamin Moore Authorized Ret, Brooklyn Also called Park Ave Bldg & Roofg Sups
LLC (G-2247)
Benjamin Sheridan Corporation (HQ) 585 657-6161
  7629 State Route 5 And 20 Bloomfield (14469) (G-940)
Benlee Enterprises LLC 212 730-7330
  3100 47th Ave Ste 2130 Long Island City (11101) (G-7176)
Bennett Die & Tool Inc 607 739-5629
  130 Wygant Rd Horseheads (14845) (G-6115)
Bennett Die & Tool Inc 607 273-2836
  113 Brewery Ln Ithaca (14850) (G-6365)
Bennett Manufacturing Co Inc 716 937-9161
  13315 Railroad St Alden (14004) (G-166)
Bennett Multimedia Inc 718 629-1454
  1087 Utica Ave Brooklyn (11203) (G-1575)
Bennett Stair Company Inc 518 384-1554
  1021 State Route 50 Ballston Lake (12019) (G-558)
Benson Industries Inc 212 779-3230
  192 Lexington Ave Rm 502 New York (10016) (G-8758)
Benson Mills Inc (PA) 718 236-6743
  140 58th St Ste 7j Brooklyn (11220) (G-1576)
Benson Steel Fabricators, Saugerties Also called Kenbenco Inc (G-14203)
Bentley Cravats, New York Also called W B Bow Tie Corp (G-11712)
Bentley Manufacturing Inc (PA) 212 714-1800
  10 W 33rd St Rm 220 New York (10001) (G-8759)
Bento Box LLC 718 260-8200
  254 36th St Unit 6 Brooklyn (11232) (G-1577)
Bentones Enterprises, New York Also called Hjn Inc (G-9795)
Benway-Haworth-Lwlr-Iacosta He 518 432-4070
  21 Everett Rd Albany (12205) (G-47)
Benzsay & Harrison Inc 518 895-2311
  Railroad Ave Delanson (12053) (G-3958)
Bereza Iron Works Inc 585 254-6311
  87 Dewey Ave Rochester (14608) (G-13266)
Berjen Metal Industries Ltd 631 673-7979
  645 New York Ave Unit 1 Huntington (11743) (G-6201)
Berkshire Business Forms Inc 518 828-2600
  829 Route 66 Hudson (12534) (G-6150)
Berkshire Transformer (PA) 631 467-5328
  77 Windsor Pl Ste 18 Central Islip (11722) (G-3265)
Berkshire Weaving, New York Also called Richloom Fabrics Group Inc (G-11043)
Bernan Associates, New York Also called Kraus Organization Limited (G-10138)
Bernard Chaus Inc (HQ) 212 354-1280
  530 7th Ave Fl 18 New York (10018) (G-8760)
Bernard Chaus Inc 646 562-4700
  515 7th Ave Ste 18 New York (10018) (G-8761)
Bernard Hall 585 425-3340
  10 Perinton Hills Mall Fairport (14450) (G-4489)
Bernette Apparel LLC 212 279-5526
  42 W 39th St Fl 2 New York (10018) (G-8762)
Bernhard Arnold & Company Inc (PA) 212 907-1500
  551 5th Ave Fl 3 New York (10176) (G-8763)
Bernstein Display, New York Also called Leo D Bernstein & Sons Inc (G-10198)

Berry Global Inc..315 986-2161
112 Main St Macedon (14502) *(G-7462)*

Berry Global Inc..315 484-0397
1500 Milton Ave Solvay (13209) *(G-14494)*

Berry Industrial Group Inc (PA).........................845 353-8338
30 Main St Nyack (10960) *(G-12137)*

Berry Plastics Corporation...............................315 986-6270
200 Main St Macedon (14502) *(G-7463)*

Berry Specialty Tapes LLC...............................631 727-6000
1852 Old Country Rd Riverhead (11901) *(G-13172)*

Berryfield Bottling LLC.....................................315 781-2749
3655 Berry Fields Rd Geneva (14456) *(G-5146)*

Bertelsmann Inc (HQ)......................................212 782-1000
1745 Broadway Fl 20 New York (10019) *(G-8764)*

Bertelsmann Pubg Group Inc (HQ).....................212 782-1000
1540 Broadway Fl 24 New York (10036) *(G-8765)*

Beryllium Manufacturing, Copiague Also called Worldwide Arntcal Cmpnents Inc *(G-3691)*

Besam Entrance Solutions, East Syracuse Also called Assa Abloy Entrance Systems US *(G-4198)*

Bescor Video Accessories Ltd..........................631 420-1717
244 Route 109 Farmingdale (11735) *(G-4592)*

Besicorp Ltd (PA)..845 336-7700
1151 Flatbush Rd Kingston (12401) *(G-6680)*

Bespoke Software Inc......................................518 618-0746
5 Sand Creek Rd Albany (12205) *(G-48)*

Best Adhesives Co Inc.....................................718 417-3800
4702 Metropolitan Ave Ridgewood (11385) *(G-13141)*

Best Boilers Inc..718 372-4210
2402 Neptune Ave Brooklyn (11224) *(G-1578)*

Best Brands Consumer Pdts Inc (PA).................212 684-7456
20 W 33rd St Fl 5 New York (10001) *(G-8766)*

Best Bread, Port Chester Also called Good Bread Bakery *(G-12822)*

Best Concrete Mix Corp...................................718 463-5500
3510 College Point Blvd Flushing (11354) *(G-4841)*

Best Foods Baking Group, Tonawanda Also called Bimbo Bakeries Usa Inc *(G-15090)*

Best Mdlr HMS Afrbe P Q& S In........................631 204-0049
495 County Road 39 Southampton (11968) *(G-14527)*

Best Medical Wear Ltd.....................................718 858-5544
34 Franklin Ave Ste 301 Brooklyn (11205) *(G-1579)*

Best Pallet & Crate LLC...................................518 438-2945
22 Railroad Ave Albany (12205) *(G-49)*

Best Priced Products Inc.................................914 345-3800
250 Clearbrook Rd Ste 240 Elmsford (10523) *(G-4395)*

Best Tinsmith Supply Inc.................................518 863-2541
4 Zetta Dr Northville (12134) *(G-12113)*

Best Way Tools By Anderson Inc.......................631 586-4702
171 Brook Ave Deer Park (11729) *(G-3845)*

Bestmade Printing LLC....................................718 384-0719
205 Keap St Apt 2 Brooklyn (11211) *(G-1580)*

Bestype Digital Imaging LLC.............................212 966-6886
285 W Broadway Frnt A New York (10013) *(G-8767)*

Beta Transformer Tech Corp (HQ).....................631 244-7393
40 Orville Dr Ste 2 Bohemia (11716) *(G-980)*

Betapast Holdings LLC....................................631 582-6740
110 Nicon Ct Hauppauge (11788) *(G-5603)*

Betatronix Inc..631 582-6740
125 Comac St Ronkonkoma (11779) *(G-13916)*

Beth Kobliner Company LLC..............................212 501-8407
1995 Broadway Ste 1800 New York (10023) *(G-8768)*

Beth Ward Studios LLC.....................................646 922-7575
133 W 25th St Rm 8e New York (10001) *(G-8769)*

Beths Farm Kitchen...518 799-3414
504 Rte 46 Stuyvesant Falls (12174) *(G-14755)*

Betmar, New York Also called Bollman Hat Company *(G-8831)*

Betsy & Adam Ltd (PA).....................................212 302-3750
525 Fashion Ave Fl 21 New York (10018) *(G-8770)*

Better Baked Foods LLC...................................716 326-4651
25 Jefferson St Westfield (14787) *(G-15945)*

Better Candy Company, Brooklyn Also called Bader Enterprise Inc *(G-1560)*

Better Power Inc...585 475-1321
508 White Spruce Blvd Rochester (14623) *(G-13267)*

Better Wire Products Inc.................................716 883-3377
680 New Babcock St Buffalo (14206) *(G-2662)*

Betterbee, Greenwich Also called Northast Ctr For Bekeeping LLC *(G-5474)*

Betterbee Inc...518 314-0575
8 Meader Rd Greenwich (12834) *(G-5469)*

Bettertex Inc...212 431-3373
450 Broadway New York (10013) *(G-8771)*

Bettertex Interioirs, New York Also called Bettertex Inc *(G-8771)*

Beverage Media Group Inc (PA)..........................212 571-3232
152 Madison Ave Rm 600 New York (10016) *(G-8772)*

Beverage Works Incorporated...........................718 834-0500
70 Hamilton Ave 8 Brooklyn (11231) *(G-1581)*

Beverage Works Nj Inc.....................................631 293-3501
16 Dubon Ct Farmingdale (11735) *(G-4593)*

Beverage Works Ny Inc.....................................718 812-2034
70 Hamilton Ave 8 Brooklyn (11231) *(G-1582)*

Beverages Foods & Service Inds........................914 253-2000
700 Anderson Hill Rd Purchase (10577) *(G-13002)*

Beyer Graphics Inc...631 543-3900
30 Austin Blvd Ste A Commack (11725) *(G-3579)*

Beyond Air Inc..516 665-8200
825 E Gate Blvd Ste 320 Garden City (11530) *(G-5091)*

Beyond Beauty Basics LLC...............................516 731-7100
3359 Hempstead Tpke Levittown (11756) *(G-6913)*

Beyond Better Foods LLC.................................212 888-1120
101 Lincoln Ave Frnt 2 Bronx (10454) *(G-1213)*

Beyond Design Inc..607 865-7487
807 Pines Brook Rd Walton (13856) *(G-15474)*

Beyond Loom Inc (PA)......................................212 575-3100
262 W 38th St Rm 203 New York (10018) *(G-8773)*

Beyondly Inc..646 658-3665
20 W 20th St Ste 1004 New York (10011) *(G-8774)*

Beyondspring Inc..646 305-6387
28 Liberty St Fl 39 New York (10005) *(G-8775)*

Beyondspring Phrmceuticals Inc.......................646 305-6387
28 Liberty St Fl 39 New York (10005) *(G-8776)*

Bfg Manufacturing Services Inc........................716 362-0888
3949 Jeffrey Blvd Buffalo (14219) *(G-2663)*

Bfg Marine Inc..631 586-5500
200 Candlewood Rd Bay Shore (11706) *(G-656)*

Bfgg Investors Group LLC.................................585 424-3456
1900 University Ave Rochester (14610) *(G-13268)*

Bfma Holding Corporation................................607 753-6746
37 Huntington St Cortland (13045) *(G-3755)*

Bg Bindery Inc..631 767-4242
5877 57th St Maspeth (11378) *(G-7595)*

Bga Technology LLC...631 750-4600
116 Wilbur Pl Bohemia (11716) *(G-981)*

Bh Brand Inc..212 239-1635
10 W 33rd St Rm 218 New York (10001) *(G-8777)*

Bh Coffee Company LLC (PA).............................914 377-2500
4 Warehouse Ln Elmsford (10523) *(G-4396)*

BH Multi Com Corp (PA)....................................212 944-0020
15 W 46th St Fl 6 New York (10036) *(G-8778)*

Bharat Electronics Limited...............................516 248-4021
53 Hilton Ave Garden City (11530) *(G-5092)*

Bhi Elevator Cabs Inc......................................516 431-5665
74 Alabama Ave Island Park (11558) *(G-6315)*

Bhv Sheet Mtal Fabricators Inc (PA).................607 797-1196
505 Prentice Rd 507 Vestal (13850) *(G-15371)*

Bi Nutraceuticals Inc......................................631 533-4924
85 Hoffman Ln Islandia (11749) *(G-6325)*

Bi Nutraceuticals Inc......................................631 232-1105
120 Hoffman Ln Central Islip (11749) *(G-3266)*

Bianca Burgers LLC...516 764-9591
15 S Long Beach Rd Rockville Centre (11570) *(G-13826)*

Bianca Group Ltd..212 768-3011
244 W 39th St Fl 4 New York (10018) *(G-8779)*

Bibo International LLC......................................617 304-2242
130 Water St Apt 4g New York (10005) *(G-8780)*

Bick & Heintz Inc..315 733-7577
1101 Stark St Utica (13502) *(G-15241)*

Bicker Inc..212 688-0085
50 Broad St Ste 301 New York (10004) *(G-8781)*

Bidpress LLC..267 973-8876
659 Washington St Apt 5r New York (10014) *(G-8782)*

Bielecky Bros Inc (PA).....................................718 424-4764
5022 72nd St Woodside (11377) *(G-16197)*

Bielka Inc..212 980-6841
141 E 56th St Apt 6f New York (10022) *(G-8783)*

Bien Cuit LLC..718 852-0200
120 Smith St Brooklyn (11201) *(G-1583)*

Big Apple Elevtr Srv & Consult.........................212 279-0700
247 W 30th St New York (10001) *(G-8784)*

Big Apple Sign Corp...631 342-0303
3 Oval Dr Islandia (11749) *(G-6326)*

Big Apple Sign Corp (PA)..................................212 629-3650
247 W 35th St Rm 400 New York (10001) *(G-8785)*

Big Apple Visual Group, Islandia Also called Big Apple Sign Corp *(G-6326)*

BIG APPLE VISUAL GROUP, New York Also called Big Apple Sign Corp *(G-8785)*

Big Bear, Buffalo Also called Stephen M Kiernan *(G-2992)*

Big Data Bizviz LLC...716 803-2367
1075 East And West Rd West Seneca (14224) *(G-15844)*

Big Fish Entertainment LLC..............................646 797-4955
5 Times Sq Fl 9 New York (10036) *(G-8786)*

Big Geyser Inc (PA)...718 821-2200
5765 48th St Maspeth (11378) *(G-7596)*

Big Heart Pet Brands.......................................716 891-6566
243 Urban St Buffalo (14211) *(G-2664)*

Big Idea Brands LLC..212 938-0270
1410 Broadway Frnt 4 New York (10018) *(G-8787)*

Big Indie - Beautiful Boy LLC (PA).....................917 464-5599
41 Plochmann Ln Woodstock (12498) *(G-16234)*

Big John's Beef Jerky, Saratoga Springs Also called Big Johns Adirondack Inc *(G-14166)*

Big Johns Adirondack Inc.................................518 587-3680
45 N Milton Rd Saratoga Springs (12866) *(G-14166)*

Big Shine Energy, Newburgh Also called Big Shine Worldwide Inc *(G-11859)*

Big Shine Worldwide Inc...................................845 444-5255
300 Corporate Blvd Newburgh (12550) *(G-11859)*

Big White Wall Holding Inc...............................917 281-2649
41 E 11th St Fl 11 New York (10003) *(G-8788)*

Bigbee Steel and Tank Company........................518 273-0801
958 19th St Watervliet (12189) *(G-15597)*

Bignay Inc 786 346-1673
315 E 86th St Apt 21ge New York (10028) *(G-8789)*

Bigposters.com, Deer Park *Also called Creative Juices Prtg Graphics* *(G-3855)*

Bigrow Paper Mfg Corp 718 624-4439
930 Bedford Ave Brooklyn (11205) *(G-1584)*

Bigrow Paper Product, Brooklyn *Also called Bigrow Paper Mfg Corp* *(G-1584)*

Bigsky Technologies LLC 585 270-5282
1600 N Clinton Ave Ste 11 Rochester (14621) *(G-13269)*

Bigwood Systems Inc 607 257-0915
35 Thornwood Dr Ste 400 Ithaca (14850) *(G-6366)*

Bike Shopcom LLC 716 236-7500
2045 Niagara Falls Blvd Niagara Falls (14304) *(G-11908)*

Bilbee Controls Inc 518 622-3033
628 Main St Cairo (12413) *(G-3064)*

Bilco Industries Inc 917 783-5008
214 W 39th St Rm 301 New York (10018) *(G-8790)*

Bilinski Sausage Mfg Co, Cohoes *Also called Schonwetter Enterprises Inc* *(G-3515)*

Bill Lake Homes Construction 518 673-2424
188 Flanders Rd Sprakers (12166) *(G-14564)*

Bill Shea Enterprises Inc 585 343-2284
8825 Alexander Rd Batavia (14020) *(G-604)*

Billanti Casting Co Inc 516 775-4800
299 S 11th St New Hyde Park (11040) *(G-8254)*

Billanti Jewelry Casting, New Hyde Park *Also called Billanti Casting Co Inc* *(G-8254)*

Billie-Ann Plastics Pkg Corp 718 497-3409
360 Troutman St Brooklyn (11237) *(G-1585)*

Billing Blocks Inc 718 442-5006
147 North Ave Staten Island (10314) *(G-14626)*

Billing Coding and Prtg Inc 718 827-9409
455 Grant Ave Brooklyn (11208) *(G-1586)*

Billings Sheet Metal Inc 716 372-6165
1002 S Union St Olean (14760) *(G-12224)*

Billion Tower Intl LLC 212 220-0608
989 6th Ave Fl 8 New York (10018) *(G-8791)*

Billion Tower USA LLC 212 220-0608
989 Avenue Of The America New York (10018) *(G-8792)*

Billsboro Winery 315 789-9538
4760 State Route 14 Geneva (14456) *(G-5147)*

Billy Beez LLC 315 741-5099
9090 Destiy Usa Dr L301 Syracuse (13204) *(G-14829)*

Billy Beez Usa LLC (PA) 646 606-2249
3 W 35th St Fl 3 # 3 New York (10001) *(G-8793)*

Billy Beez Usa LLC 845 915-4709
1282 Palisades Center Dr West Nyack (10994) *(G-15818)*

Billy Beez Usa LLC 315 235-3121
1 Sangertown Sq Ste 107 New Hartford (13413) *(G-8237)*

Billykirk 212 217-0679
16a Orchard St New York (10002) *(G-8794)*

Biltron Automotive Products 631 928-8613
509 Bicycle Path Unit Q Port Jeff STA (11776) *(G-12833)*

Bimbo Bakeries 631 274-4906
955 Grand Blvd Deer Park (11729) *(G-3846)*

Bimbo Bakeries 518 463-2221
78 N Manning Blvd Albany (12206) *(G-50)*

Bimbo Bakeries Usa Inc 716 692-9140
1960 Niagara Falls Blvd Tonawanda (14150) *(G-15090)*

Bimbo Bakeries Usa Inc 718 601-1561
5625 Broadway Frnt 2 Bronx (10463) *(G-1214)*

Bimbo Bakeries Usa Inc 718 545-0291
4011 34th Ave Long Island City (11101) *(G-7177)*

Bimbo Bakeries Usa Inc 845 255-4345
27 N Putt Corners Rd New Paltz (12561) *(G-8305)*

Bimbo Bakeries Usa Inc 516 877-2850
12 E Jericho Tpke Mineola (11501) *(G-7961)*

Bimbo Bakeries Usa Inc 716 372-8444
111 N 2nd St Olean (14760) *(G-12225)*

Bimbo Bakeries Usa Inc 631 951-5183
14 Spence St Bay Shore (11706) *(G-657)*

Bimbo Bakeries Usa Inc 516 887-1024
669 Sunrise Hwy Spc 4 Lynbrook (11563) *(G-7427)*

Bimbo Bakeries Usa Inc 315 379-9069
19 Miner St Ste D Canton (13617) *(G-3163)*

Bimbo Bakeries Usa Inc 518 563-1320
67 S Peru St Plattsburgh (12901) *(G-12735)*

Bimbo Bakeries Usa Inc 718 463-6300
5754 Page Pl Maspeth (11378) *(G-7597)*

Bimbo Bakeries Usa Inc 518 489-4053
40 Fuller Rd Albany (12205) *(G-51)*

Bimbo Bakeries Usa Inc 203 531-2311
30 Inez Dr Bay Shore (11706) *(G-658)*

Bimbo Bakeries Usa Inc 315 253-9782
11 Corcoran Dr Auburn (13021) *(G-467)*

Bimbo Bakeries Usa Inc 716 706-0450
2900 Commerce Pkwy Lancaster (14086) *(G-6798)*

Bimbo Bakeries Usa Inc 845 568-0943
98 Scobie Dr Newburgh (12550) *(G-11860)*

Bimbo Bakeries Usa Inc 800 856-8544
1624 Castle Gardens Rd Vestal (13850) *(G-15372)*

Bimbo Bakeries Usa Inc 315 782-4189
1100 Water St Watertown (13601) *(G-15560)*

Bimbo Bakeries Usa Inc 845 294-5282
9 Police Dr Goshen (10924) *(G-5305)*

Bin Optics 604 257-3200
20 Thornwood Dr Ste 100 Ithaca (14850) *(G-6367)*

Binah Magazines Corp 718 305-5200
207 Foster Ave Brooklyn (11230) *(G-1587)*

Bindle and Keep 917 740-5002
47 Hall St Ste 109 Brooklyn (11205) *(G-1588)*

Binghamton Burial Vault Co Inc 607 722-4931
1114 Porter Ave Binghamton (13901) *(G-857)*

Binghamton Knitting Co Inc 607 722-6941
11 Alice St Binghamton (13904) *(G-858)*

Binghamton Precast & Sup Corp 607 722-0334
18 Phelps St Binghamton (13901) *(G-859)*

Binghamton Press, Vestal *Also called Gannett Co Inc* *(G-15377)*

Binghamton Simulator Co Inc 607 321-2980
151 Court St Binghamton (13901) *(G-860)*

Bino Products LLC 212 886-6899
236 5th Ave Fl 8 New York (10001) *(G-8795)*

Binoptics LLC (HQ) 607 257-3200
9 Brown Rd Ithaca (14850) *(G-6368)*

Bio Nutrition, Oceanside *Also called Only Natural Inc* *(G-12183)*

Bio Service, Woodside *Also called Firecom Inc* *(G-16206)*

Bio-Botanica Inc (PA) 631 231-0987
75 Commerce Dr Hauppauge (11788) *(G-5604)*

Bio-Chem Barrier Systems LLC 631 261-2682
11 W Scudder Pl Northport (11768) *(G-12099)*

Bio-Nutritional Products, White Plains *Also called Meta-Therm Corp* *(G-16029)*

Biobat Inc (PA) 718 270-1011
450 Clarkson Ave Msc129 Brooklyn (11203) *(G-1589)*

Biochemical Diagnostics Inc 631 595-9200
180 Heartland Blvd Edgewood (11717) *(G-4263)*

Biocontinuum Group Inc 212 406-1060
116 Chambers St New York (10007) *(G-8796)*

Biodesign Inc of New York (PA) 845 454-6610
1 Sunset Rdg Carmel (10512) *(G-3184)*

Biodex Medical Systems Inc (PA) 631 924-9000
20 Ramsey Rd Shirley (11967) *(G-14417)*

Biodex Medical Systems Inc 631 924-3146
49 Natcon Dr Shirley (11967) *(G-14418)*

Biodigital, New Hyde Park *Also called Arnouse Digital Devices Corp* *(G-8251)*

Biofeedback Instrument Corp 212 222-5665
255 W 98th St Apt 3d New York (10025) *(G-8797)*

Bioivt LLC (PA) 516 483-1196
123 Frost St Ste 115 Westbury (11590) *(G-15872)*

Biolitec Inc 413 525-0600
110 E 42nd St Rm 1800 New York (10017) *(G-8798)*

Biologique Recherche, New York *Also called Distribio USA LLC* *(G-9240)*

Biomed Pharmaceuticals Inc 914 592-0525
4 Skyline Dr Ste 5 Hawthorne (10532) *(G-5810)*

Biomedical & Industrial, Farmingdale *Also called Netech Corporation* *(G-4694)*

Biomup Usa Inc 800 436-6266
412 W 15th St Ste 1000 New York (10011) *(G-8799)*

Bionic Eye Technologies Inc 845 505-5254
239 Cherry St Ste 1b Ithaca (14850) *(G-6369)*

Biopool Us Inc 716 483-3851
2823 Girts Rd Jamestown (14701) *(G-6497)*

Biorem Environmental Inc 585 924-2220
100 Rawson Rd Ste 230 Victor (14564) *(G-15393)*

Bioresearch Inc (PA) 212 734-5315
4 Sunset Ln Pound Ridge (10576) *(G-12991)*

Biosoil Farm Inc 518 344-4920
204 Glenville Industrial Glenville (12302) *(G-5270)*

Biospecifics Technologies Corp (PA) 516 593-7000
35 Wilbur St Lynbrook (11563) *(G-7428)*

Biospherix Ltd 315 387-3414
25 Union St Parish (13131) *(G-12495)*

Biospherix Medical, Parish *Also called Biospherix Ltd* *(G-12495)*

Biotech Energy Inc 800 340-1387
100 Clinton Point Dr Plattsburgh (12901) *(G-12736)*

Biotech Energy Systems, Plattsburgh *Also called Biotech Energy Inc* *(G-12736)*

Biotemper 516 302-7985
516 Mineola Ave Carle Place (11514) *(G-3172)*

Biotemper Plus, Carle Place *Also called Biotemper* *(G-3172)*

Biotie Therapies Inc 650 244-4850
420 Saw Mill River Rd Ardsley (10502) *(G-386)*

Bioworks Inc (PA) 585 924-4362
100 Rawson Rd Ste 205 Victor (14564) *(G-15394)*

Birch Coffee, Long Island City *Also called Birch Guys LLC* *(G-7178)*

Birch Guys LLC 917 763-0751
4035 23rd St Long Island City (11101) *(G-7178)*

Birch Machine & Tool Inc 716 735-9802
80 Telegraph Rd Middleport (14105) *(G-7887)*

Birdair Inc (HQ) 716 633-9500
65 Lawrence Bell Dr # 100 Amherst (14221) *(G-213)*

Birds Eye Foods Inc 716 988-3218
Mechanic St South Dayton (14138) *(G-14505)*

Birdsigns Inc 201 388-7613
16 W 19th St Apt 3e New York (10011) *(G-8800)*

Birkett Mills (PA) 315 536-3311
163 Main St Ste 2 Penn Yan (14527) *(G-12578)*

Birkett Mills 315 536-4112
163 Main St Ste 3 Penn Yan (14527) *(G-12579)*

Birnbaum & Bullock Ltd......212 242-2914
151 W 25th St Rm 2a New York (10001) *(G-8801)*
Birthstone Enterprises, New York *Also called Alchemy Simya Inc (G-8508)*
Bishop Print Shop Inc......607 965-8155
9 East St Edmeston (13335) *(G-4294)*
Bisley Inc......212 675-3055
1140 Broadway Rm 902 New York (10001) *(G-8802)*
Bisley North America, New York *Also called Bisley Inc (G-8802)*
Bison Iron & Step, Buffalo *Also called M K Ulrich Construction Inc (G-2855)*
Bison Products, Buffalo *Also called Upstate Niagara Coop Inc (G-3032)*
Bison Steel Incorporated......716 683-0900
2 Main St Ste 103 Depew (14043) *(G-3971)*
Bissel-Babcock Millwork Inc......716 761-6976
3866 Kendrick Rd Sherman (14781) *(G-14399)*
Bistate Oil Management Corp......212 935-4110
10 E 40th St Rm 2710 New York (10016) *(G-8803)*
Bistrian Cement Corporation......631 324-1123
225 Springs Fireplace Rd East Hampton (11937) *(G-4117)*
Bittner Company LLC......585 214-1790
75 Goodway Dr Ste 3 Rochester (14623) *(G-13270)*
Bitzer Scroll Inc......315 463-2101
6055 Court Street Rd Syracuse (13206) *(G-14830)*
Bizbash Masterplanner, New York *Also called Bizbash Media Inc (G-8804)*
Bizbash Media Inc (PA)......646 638-3602
115 W 27th St Fl 8 New York (10001) *(G-8804)*
BJ Magazines Inc......212 367-9705
200 Varick St New York (10014) *(G-8805)*
BK Associates Intl Inc......607 432-1499
127 Commerce Rd Oneonta (13820) *(G-12259)*
Bk Printing Inc......315 565-5396
6507 Basile Rowe East Syracuse (13057) *(G-4200)*
Bklynfavors Party Print......718 277-0233
49 Sheridan Ave Brooklyn (11208) *(G-1590)*
Bkny Printing Corp......718 875-4219
105 Jamaica Ave Brooklyn (11207) *(G-1591)*
Black & Decker (us) Inc......914 235-6300
2 Powers Ln Brewster (10509) *(G-1143)*
Black & Decker (us) Inc......631 952-2008
180 Oser Ave Ste 100 Hauppauge (11788) *(G-5605)*
Black & Decker Corporation......718 335-1042
5615 Queens Blvd Woodside (11377) *(G-16198)*
Black Bear Company Inc......718 784-7330
90 E Hawthorne Ave Valley Stream (11580) *(G-15335)*
Black Book Photography Inc......212 979-6700
740 Broadway Ste 202 New York (10003) *(G-8806)*
Black Book, The, New York *Also called Black Book Photography Inc (G-8806)*
Black Enterprise, New York *Also called Earl G Graves Pubg Co Inc (G-9299)*
Black Hound, Brooklyn *Also called Amiram Dror Inc (G-1504)*
Black Prince, Syosset *Also called Prince Black Distillery Inc (G-14799)*
Black River Generations LLC......315 773-2314
4515 2nd St Fort Drum (13602) *(G-4935)*
Black River Woodworking LLC......315 376-8405
4773 State Route 410 Castorland (13620) *(G-3206)*
Blackbirds Brooklyn LLC......917 362-4080
597 Sackett St Brooklyn (11217) *(G-1592)*
Blackbook Media Corp......212 334-1800
32 Union Sq E Ste 4l New York (10003) *(G-8807)*
Blackbox Biometrics Inc......585 329-3399
125 Tech Park Dr Ste 1131 Rochester (14623) *(G-13271)*
Blackburn Truck Bodies LLC......315 448-3236
6216 Thompson Rd Ste 3 Syracuse (13206) *(G-14831)*
Blackheart Records, Brooklyn *Also called Lagunatic Music & Filmworks (G-2044)*
Blackstone Advanced Tech LLC......716 665-5410
86 Blackstone Ave Jamestown (14701) *(G-6498)*
Blackstone Group, New York *Also called Grand Slam Holdings LLC (G-9660)*
Blackstone International Inc......631 289-5490
180 Long Island Ave Holtsville (11742) *(G-6045)*
Blades......212 477-1059
659 Broadway New York (10012) *(G-8808)*
Blading Services Unlimited LLC......315 875-5313
40 Madison Blvd Canastota (13032) *(G-3149)*
Blair Industries Inc (PA)......631 924-6600
3671 Horseblock Rd Medford (11763) *(G-7699)*
Blair-Hsm, Medford *Also called HSM Machine Works Inc (G-7712)*
Blanche P Field LLC......212 355-6616
155 E 56th St Ph New York (10022) *(G-8809)*
Blasch Precision Ceramics Inc (PA)......518 436-1263
580 Broadway Ste 1 Menands (12204) *(G-7841)*
Blaser Production Inc......845 294-3200
31 Hatfield Ln Goshen (10924) *(G-5306)*
Blaser Swisslube Holding Corp (HQ)......845 294-3200
31 Hatfield Ln Goshen (10924) *(G-5307)*
Blatt Searle & Company Ltd (PA)......212 730-7717
4121 28th St Long Island City (11101) *(G-7179)*
Blc Textiles Inc......844 500-7900
330 Old Country Rd # 201 Mineola (11501) *(G-7962)*
Bleecker Pastry Tartufo Inc......718 937-9830
3722 13th St Long Island City (11101) *(G-7180)*
Bleezarde Publishing Inc......518 756-2030
164 Main St Ravena (12143) *(G-13067)*
Blend Smoothie Bar......845 568-7366
25 Creamery Dr New Windsor (12553) *(G-8361)*
Bli International Inc......631 940-9000
75 N Industry Ct Deer Park (11729) *(G-3847)*
Blinc Group LLC......212 879-2329
40 Fulton St Fl 6 New York (10038) *(G-8810)*
Blinds To Go, Hartsdale *Also called TLC Vision (usa) Corporation (G-5570)*
Blinds To Go (us) Inc......718 477-9523
2845 Richmond Ave Staten Island (10314) *(G-14627)*
Blindtek Designer Systems Inc......914 347-7100
466 Saw Mill River Rd 2 Ardsley (10502) *(G-387)*
Bliss Foods Inc......212 732-8888
275 Greenwich St Frnt 2 New York (10007) *(G-8811)*
Bliss Foods Inc......212 732-8888
275 Greenwich St Frnt 2 New York (10007) *(G-8812)*
Bliss Machine Inc......585 492-5128
260 North St Arcade (14009) *(G-370)*
Bliss-Poston The Second Wind......212 481-1055
928 Broadway Ste 403 New York (10010) *(G-8813)*
Bloch Industries LLC......585 334-9600
140 Commerce Dr Rochester (14623) *(G-13272)*
Blondie S Bakeshop Inc......631 424-4545
90 Washington Dr Centerport (11721) *(G-3254)*
Blood Moon Productions Ltd......718 556-9410
75 Saint Marks Pl Staten Island (10301) *(G-14628)*
Blooming Grove Stair Co (PA)......845 783-4245
1 Stair Way Monroe (10950) *(G-8016)*
Blooming Grove Stair Co......845 791-4016
309 E Broadway Monticello (12701) *(G-8069)*
Bloomsburg Carpet Inds Inc......212 688-7447
11 E 26th St Frnt New York (10010) *(G-8814)*
Bloomsbury Publishing Inc......212 419-5300
1385 Brdwy Fl 5 Flr 5 New York (10018) *(G-8815)*
Bloomsbury USA, New York *Also called Bloomsbury Publishing Inc (G-8815)*
Blu Pharmaceuticals, Laurelton *Also called Puracap Laboratories LLC (G-6885)*
Blu Sand LLC......212 564-1147
26 Broadway Fl 8 New York (10004) *(G-8816)*
Blue and White Publishing Inc......215 431-3339
425 Riverside Dr Apt 3c New York (10025) *(G-8817)*
Blue Box, Brooklyn *Also called Pink Box Accessories LLC (G-2260)*
Blue Boy, Staten Island *Also called Rgm Signs Inc (G-14703)*
Blue Chip Mold Inc......585 647-1790
95 Lagrange Ave Rochester (14613) *(G-13273)*
Blue Duck Trading Ltd......212 268-3122
463 7th Ave Rm 806 New York (10018) *(G-8818)*
Blue Horizon Media Inc (PA)......212 661-7878
11 Park Pl Rm 1508 New York (10007) *(G-8819)*
Blue Manufacturing Co Inc......607 796-2463
3852 Watkins Rd Millport (14864) *(G-7950)*
Blue Marble Ice Cream LLC......718 858-5551
220 36th St Unit 33 Brooklyn (11232) *(G-1593)*
Blue Ocean Food Trading LLC......718 689-4291
154 42nd St Brooklyn (11232) *(G-1594)*
Blue Pig Ice Cream Factory......914 271-3850
121 Maple St Croton On Hudson (10520) *(G-3806)*
Blue Ridge Tea & Herb Co Ltd......718 625-3100
22 Woodhull St Fl 2 Brooklyn (11231) *(G-1595)*
Blue Skies......631 392-1140
859 Long Island Ave Deer Park (11729) *(G-3848)*
Blue Star Beverages Corp......718 381-3535
1099 Flushing Ave Brooklyn (11237) *(G-1596)*
Blue Star Products Inc......631 952-3204
355 Marcus Blvd Ste 2 Hauppauge (11788) *(G-5606)*
Blue Stone Press, High Falls *Also called Ulster County Press Office (G-5956)*
Blue Tee Corp (PA)......212 598-0880
387 Park Ave S Fl 5 New York (10016) *(G-8820)*
Blue Toad Hard Cider......585 424-5508
120 Mushroom Blvd Rochester (14623) *(G-13274)*
Blue Wolf Group LLC (HQ)......866 455-9653
11 E 26th St Fl 21 New York (10010) *(G-8821)*
Bluebar Oil Co Inc......315 245-4328
8446 Mill Pond Way Blossvale (13308) *(G-955)*
Blueberry Knitting Inc (PA)......718 599-6520
138 Ross St Brooklyn (11211) *(G-1597)*
Bluebird Mobility, Williamsville *Also called Bluebird Transportation LLC (G-16123)*
Bluebird Transportation LLC......716 395-0000
5477 Main St Williamsville (14221) *(G-16123)*
Bluesoho (PA)......646 805-2583
160 Varick St Fl 2 New York (10013) *(G-8822)*
Blum & Fink Inc......212 695-2606
158 W 29th St Fl 12 New York (10001) *(G-8823)*
BMA Media Services Inc......585 385-2060
1655 Lyell Ave Rochester (14606) *(G-13275)*
BMC, Broadalbin *Also called Broadalbin Manufacturing Corp (G-1172)*
BMC LLC......716 681-7755
3155 Broadway St Buffalo (14227) *(G-2665)*
Bmg Chrysalis, New York *Also called Bmg Rights Management (us) LLC (G-8824)*
Bmg Printing and Promotion LLC......631 231-9200
170 Wilbur Pl Ste 700 Bohemia (11716) *(G-982)*
Bmg Rights Management (us) LLC (HQ)......212 561-3000
1 Park Ave Ste 1800 New York (10016) *(G-8824)*

ALPHABETIC

Bmg Systems...716 432-5160
4779 Transit Rd 169 Depew (14043) ***(G-3972)***
Bmp America Inc (HQ)...585 798-0950
11625 Maple Ridge Rd Medina (14103) ***(G-7730)***
Bms Manufacturing Co Inc...607 535-2426
2857 County Line Rd Watkins Glen (14891) ***(G-15613)***
BNC Innovative Woodworking...718 277-2800
555 Liberty Ave Brooklyn (11207) ***(G-1598)***
Bnei Aram Soba Inc...718 645-4460
1616 Ocean Pkwy Brooklyn (11223) ***(G-1599)***
BNH Lead Examiner Corp...718 807-1365
199 Lee Ave Ste 481 Brooklyn (11211) ***(G-1600)***
Bnm Product Service...631 750-1586
1561 Lincoln Ave Holbrook (11741) ***(G-5986)***
Bnns Co Inc...212 302-1844
71 W 47th St Ste 600-601 New York (10036) ***(G-8825)***
BNo Intl Trdg Co Inc...716 487-1900
505 Chautauqua Ave Jamestown (14701) ***(G-6499)***
BNP Media Inc...646 849-7100
350 5th Ave Fl 60 New York (10118) ***(G-8826)***
Bnz Tech, East Setauket *Also called B & Z Technologies LLC* ***(G-4176)***
Bo-Mer Plastics LLC...315 252-7216
13 Pulaski St Auburn (13021) ***(G-468)***
Boa Handcuff Company, Huntington *Also called Boa Security Technologies Corp* ***(G-6202)***
Boa Security Technologies Corp...516 480-6822
586 New York Ave Unit 3 Huntington (11743) ***(G-6202)***
Boardman Simons Publishing (PA)...212 620-7200
88 Pine St Fl 23 New York (10005) ***(G-8827)***
Bob Murphy Inc (PA)...607 729-3553
3127 Vestal Rd Vestal (13850) ***(G-15373)***
Bob's Signs, Syracuse *Also called Wizard Equipment Inc* ***(G-15028)***
Bobley-Harmann Corporation...516 433-3800
200 Trade Zone Dr Unit 2 Ronkonkoma (11779) ***(G-13917)***
Bobrick Washroom Equipment Inc...518 877-7444
200 Commerce Dr Clifton Park (12065) ***(G-3463)***
Boces Business Office...607 763-3300
435 Glenwood Rd Binghamton (13905) ***(G-861)***
Bocks Inc...833 437-3363
195 Chrystie St Rm 502h New York (10002) ***(G-8828)***
Body Builders Inc...718 492-7997
5518 3rd Ave Brooklyn (11220) ***(G-1601)***
Bodyarmor, Whitestone *Also called Ba Sports Nutrition LLC* ***(G-16089)***
Bodycote Syracuse Heat Treatin...315 451-0000
4629 Crossroads Park Dr Liverpool (13088) ***(G-7001)***
Bodycote Thermal Proc Inc...585 436-7876
620 Buffalo Rd Rochester (14611) ***(G-13276)***
Boehm Surgical Instrument Corp...585 436-6584
966 Chili Ave Ste 3 Rochester (14611) ***(G-13277)***
Boeing Company...201 259-9400
304 Park Ave S New York (10010) ***(G-8829)***
Boeing Digital Solutions Inc...212 478-1200
444 Park Ave S Fl 10 New York (10016) ***(G-8830)***
Boeing Distribution Svcs Inc...845 534-0401
45 Quaker Ave Ste 203 Cornwall (12518) ***(G-3727)***
Boeing Medcl Trtmnt Mltry Arcr, Norwich *Also called Chenango Concrete Corp* ***(G-12115)***
Boilermatic Welding Inds Inc (PA)...631 654-1341
17 Peconic Ave Medford (11763) ***(G-7700)***
Boileroom Fabrication LLC...516 488-4848
62 Oak Dr Syosset (11791) ***(G-14779)***
Boka Printing Inc...607 725-3235
12 Hall St Binghamton (13903) ***(G-862)***
Bollman Hat Company...212 981-9836
411 5th Ave Fl 2 New York (10016) ***(G-8831)***
Bolton Point Wtr Trtmnt Plant...607 277-0660
1402 E Shore Dr Ithaca (14850) ***(G-6370)***
Bomac Inc...315 433-9181
6477 Ridings Rd Syracuse (13206) ***(G-14832)***
BOMB MAGAZINE, Brooklyn *Also called New Art Publications Inc* ***(G-2200)***
Bombardier Corp Track, Plattsburgh *Also called Bombardier Trnsp Holdings USA* ***(G-12738)***
Bombardier Mass Transit Corp...518 566-0150
71 Wall St Plattsburgh (12901) ***(G-12737)***
Bombardier Transportation...607 324-0216
1 William K Jackson Ln Hornell (14843) ***(G-6102)***
Bombardier Trnsp Holdings USA...607 776-4791
7940 State Route 415 Bath (14810) ***(G-631)***
Bombardier Trnsp Holdings USA...518 566-5067
71 Wall St Plattsburgh (12901) ***(G-12738)***
Bombas LLC...800 314-0980
37 E 18th St Fl 4 New York (10003) ***(G-8832)***
Bombay Kitchen Foods Inc...516 767-7401
76 S Bayles Ave Port Washington (11050) ***(G-12865)***
Bomber LLC (PA)...212 980-2442
681 5th Ave Ph 13 New York (10022) ***(G-8833)***
Bomber Ski, New York *Also called Bomber LLC* ***(G-8833)***
Bon Bons Chocolatier, Huntington *Also called Lady-N-Th-wndow Chocolates Inc* ***(G-6210)***
Boncraft Inc...716 662-9720
777 E Park Dr Tonawanda (14150) ***(G-15091)***
Bonded Concrete Inc (PA)...518 273-5800
303 Watervliet Shaker Rd Watervliet (12189) ***(G-15598)***
Bonded Concrete Inc...518 674-2854
Rr 43 West Sand Lake (12196) ***(G-15835)***
Bondy Printing Corp...631 242-1510
267 W Main St Bay Shore (11706) ***(G-659)***
Bonelli Foods LLC...212 346-0942
139 Fulton St Rm 314 New York (10038) ***(G-8834)***
Bonide Products LLC...315 736-8231
6301 Sutliff Rd Oriskany (13424) ***(G-12384)***
Bonjour For Kids, New York *Also called Consolidated Childrens AP Inc* ***(G-9085)***
Bonk Sam Unforms Civilian Cap...718 585-0665
131 Rose Feiss Blvd Fl 2 Bronx (10454) ***(G-1215)***
Bonnie J, New York *Also called Sanoy Inc* ***(G-11133)***
Bonnier Publishing Usa, Inc., New York *Also called Little Bee Books Inc* ***(G-10228)***
Bono Sawdust Co, Corona *Also called Bono Sawdust Supply Co Inc* ***(G-3734)***
Bono Sawdust Supply Co Inc...718 446-1374
3330 127th Pl Corona (11368) ***(G-3734)***
Bonsal American Inc...585 343-4741
102 Cedar St Batavia (14020) ***(G-605)***
Bonsal American Inc...631 208-8073
931 Burman Blvd Calverton (11933) ***(G-3077)***
Bonura and Sons Iron Works...718 381-4100
957 Lorraine Dr Franklin Square (11010) ***(G-4959)***
Book1one LLC...585 458-2101
655 Driving Park Ave Rochester (14613) ***(G-13278)***
Booklinks Publishing Svcs LLC...718 852-2116
55 Washington St Ste 253c Brooklyn (11201) ***(G-1602)***
Booklyn Artists Alliance Inc...718 383-9621
140 58th St Bldg B-7g Brooklyn (11220) ***(G-1603)***
Boom Creative Development, New York *Also called Boom LLC* ***(G-8835)***
Boom LLC...646 218-0752
800 3rd Ave Fl 2 New York (10022) ***(G-8835)***
Boonville Herald Inc...315 942-4449
105 E Schuyler St Boonville (13309) ***(G-1104)***
Boonville Manufacturing Corp...315 942-4368
13485 State Route 12 Boonville (13309) ***(G-1105)***
Boonvlle Hrald Adrndack Turist, Boonville *Also called Boonville Herald Inc* ***(G-1104)***
Boosey and Hawkes Inc (PA)...212 358-5300
229 W 28th St Fl 11 New York (10001) ***(G-8836)***
Borabora Fruit Juices Inc...914 438-8744
255 Milton Xrds Highland (12528) ***(G-5958)***
Borden & Riley Paper Co Inc...718 454-9494
18410 Jamaica Ave Ste W3 Hollis (11423) ***(G-6040)***
Borgattis Ravioli Egg Noodles...718 367-3799
632 E 187th St Bronx (10458) ***(G-1216)***
Borghese Inc (PA)...212 659-5318
3 E 54th St Fl 20 New York (10022) ***(G-8837)***
Borgwarner Inc...607 257-1800
780 Warren Rd Ithaca (14850) ***(G-6371)***
Borgwarner Morse TEC Inc...607 266-5111
780 Warren Rd Ithaca (14850) ***(G-6372)***
Borgwarner Morse TEC LLC...607 257-6700
3690 Luker Rd Cortland (13045) ***(G-3756)***
Boro Park Cutting Tool Corp...718 720-0610
106b Wakefield Ave Staten Island (10314) ***(G-14629)***
Boro Park Signs, Brooklyn *Also called Sign Group Inc* ***(G-2408)***
Bos-Hatten Inc...716 662-7030
50 Cobham Dr Orchard Park (14127) ***(G-12339)***
Boss Precision Ltd...585 352-7070
2440 S Union St Spencerport (14559) ***(G-14553)***
Boss Sauce, Rochester *Also called American Specialty Mfg Co* ***(G-13231)***
Boston Valley Pottery Inc (PA)...716 649-7490
6860 S Abbott Rd Orchard Park (14127) ***(G-12340)***
Boston Valley Terra Cotta, Orchard Park *Also called Boston Valley Pottery Inc* ***(G-12340)***
Botkier Ny LLC...212 343-2782
19 W 34th St Fl 7 New York (10001) ***(G-8838)***
Bottling Group LLC...315 788-6751
1035 Bradley St Watertown (13601) ***(G-15561)***
Bottling Group LLC...800 789-2626
1111 Westchester Ave White Plains (10604) ***(G-15982)***
Bottling Group LLC (HQ)...914 253-2000
1111 Westchester Ave White Plains (10604) ***(G-15983)***
Boucheron Joaillerie USA Inc...212 715-7330
460 Park Ave Fl 12 New York (10022) ***(G-8839)***
Boulay Fabrication Inc...315 677-5247
Rr 20 Box West La Fayette (13084) ***(G-6736)***
Boulevard Arts Inc...917 968-8693
1133 Broadway Ste 1523 New York (10010) ***(G-8840)***
Boulevard Printing...716 837-3800
1330 Niagara Falls Blvd # 2 Tonawanda (14150) ***(G-15092)***
Boundless Technologies, Phelps *Also called Z-Axis Inc* ***(G-12611)***
Bourghol Brothers Inc...845 268-9752
73 Lake Rd Congers (10920) ***(G-3610)***
Bourne Co, New York *Also called Bourne Music Publishers* ***(G-8841)***
Bourne Music Publishers...212 391-4300
35 W 45th St Fl 2 New York (10036) ***(G-8841)***
Bow Industrial Corporation...518 561-0190
178 W Service Rd Champlain (12919) ***(G-3309)***
Bowe Industries Inc (PA)...718 441-6464
8836 77th Ave Glendale (11385) ***(G-5219)***
Bowe Industries Inc...718 441-6464
8836 77th Ave Glendale (11385) ***(G-5220)***
Bowen Products Corporation...315 498-4481
5084 S Onondaga Rd Nedrow (13120) ***(G-8214)***

818
2020 Harris
New York Manufacturers Directory
(G-0000) Company's Geographic Section entry number

Bowne Business Solutions, New York *Also called Donnelley Financial LLC* **(G-9252)**
Boxcar Press Incorporated....315 473-0930
509 W Fayette St Ste 135 Syracuse (13204) **(G-14833)**
Boyd Printing Company, Latham *Also called William Boyd Printing Co Inc* **(G-6881)**
Boydell & Brewer Inc....585 275-0419
668 Mount Hope Ave Rochester (14620) **(G-13279)**
Boylan Bottling Co Inc....800 289-7978
6 E 43rd St Fl 18 New York (10017) **(G-8842)**
BP, North Babylon *Also called Quality Fuel 1 Corporation* **(G-12002)**
BP, New York *Also called Nagle Fuel Corporation* **(G-10530)**
BP Beyond Printing Inc....516 328-2700
117 Fulton Ave Hempstead (11550) **(G-5834)**
BP Digital Imaging LLC....607 753-0022
87 Main St Cortland (13045) **(G-3757)**
BP Magazine, Buffalo *Also called Green Apple Courage Inc* **(G-2785)**
Bpe Studio Inc....212 868-9896
270 W 38th St Rm 702 New York (10018) **(G-8843)**
Bqp, Glens Falls *Also called Brennans Quick Print Inc* **(G-5243)**
Bracci Ironworks Inc....718 629-2374
1440 Utica Ave Brooklyn (11203) **(G-1604)**
Brach Knitting Mills Inc....845 651-4450
12 Roosevelt Ave Florida (10921) **(G-4821)**
Brach Machine Inc....585 343-9134
4814 Ellicott Street Rd Batavia (14020) **(G-606)**
Bradford Publications Inc....716 373-2500
639 W Norton Dr Olean (14760) **(G-12226)**
Bradley Marketing Group Inc....212 967-6100
1431 Broadway Fl 12 New York (10018) **(G-8844)**
Brads Organic LLC....845 429-9080
7 Hoover Ave Haverstraw (10927) **(G-5804)**
Braga Woodworks....845 342-4636
19 Montgomery St Middletown (10940) **(G-7895)**
Bragley Mfg Co Inc....718 622-7469
924 Bergen St Brooklyn (11238) **(G-1605)**
Bragley Shipg Carrying Cases, Brooklyn *Also called Bragley Mfg Co Inc* **(G-1605)**
Braided Oak Spirits LLC....845 381-1525
12 Roberts St Middletown (10940) **(G-7896)**
Brainpop Group, New York *Also called Brainpop LLC* **(G-8845)**
Brainpop LLC....212 574-6017
71 W 23rd St Fl 17 New York (10010) **(G-8845)**
Brainwave Toys-New York, New York *Also called Vogel Applied Technologies* **(G-11702)**
Brainworks Software Dev Corp (PA)....631 563-5000
100 S Main St Ste 102 Sayville (11782) **(G-14223)**
Brakewell Stl Fabricators Inc....845 469-9131
55 Leone Ln Chester (10918) **(G-3371)**
Bral Nader Fine Jewelry Inc....800 493-1222
576 5th Ave New York (10036) **(G-8846)**
Bramson House Inc....516 764-5006
151 Albany Ave Freeport (11520) **(G-4988)**
Brand Box USA LLC....607 584-7682
1 Chamberlain St Binghamton (13904) **(G-863)**
Brands Within Reach LLC....847 720-9090
141 Halstead Ave Ste 201 Mamaroneck (10543) **(G-7499)**
Brandt Equipment LLC....718 994-0800
4461 Bronx Blvd Bronx (10470) **(G-1217)**
Brandt Industries, Bronx *Also called Brandt Equipment LLC* **(G-1217)**
Brandys Mold and Tool Ctr Ltd (PA)....585 334-8333
10 Riverton Way West Henrietta (14586) **(G-15787)**
Brannkey Inc (PA)....212 371-1515
1385 Broadway Fl 14 New York (10018) **(G-8847)**
Brannock Device Co Inc....315 475-9862
116 Luther Ave Liverpool (13088) **(G-7002)**
Branson Ultrasonics Corp....585 624-8000
475 Quaker Meeting Hse Rd Honeoye Falls (14472) **(G-6070)**
Brasilans Press Pblcations Inc....212 764-6161
60 W 46th St Rm 302 New York (10036) **(G-8848)**
Brauen Constrution....585 492-0042
1087 Chaffee Rd Arcade (14009) **(G-371)**
Braun Bros Brushes Inc....631 667-2179
35 4th St Valley Stream (11581) **(G-15336)**
Braun Brush Company, Albertson *Also called Braun Industries Inc* **(G-145)**
Braun Horticulture Inc....716 282-6101
3302 Highland Ave Niagara Falls (14305) **(G-11909)**
Braun Industries Inc (PA)....516 741-6000
43 Albertson Ave Albertson (11507) **(G-145)**
Brayley Tool & Machine Inc....585 342-7190
1685 Lyell Ave Rochester (14606) **(G-13280)**
Braze Inc....504 327-7269
330 W 34th St Fl 18 New York (10001) **(G-8849)**
Braze Alloy Inc....718 815-5757
3075 Richmond Ter Staten Island (10303) **(G-14630)**
Brazen Street LLC....516 305-7951
734 Pennsylvania Ave Brooklyn (11207) **(G-1606)**
Bread Factory LLC....914 637-8150
30 Grove Ave New Rochelle (10801) **(G-8321)**
Breal Time, New York *Also called Emx Digital LLC* **(G-9366)**
Breather Products US Inc (PA)....800 471-8704
455 Broadway Fl 3 New York (10013) **(G-8850)**
Breed Enterprises Inc....585 388-0126
34 Water St Fairport (14450) **(G-4490)**
Bren-Trnics Batteries Intl Inc....631 499-5155
10 Brayton Ct Commack (11725) **(G-3580)**
Bren-Trnics Batteries Intl LLC....631 499-5155
10 Brayton Ct Commack (11725) **(G-3581)**
Bren-Tronics Inc....631 499-5155
10 Brayton Ct Commack (11725) **(G-3582)**
Brennans Quick Print Inc....518 793-4999
6 Collins Dr Glens Falls (12804) **(G-5243)**
Brenseke George Wldg Ir Works....631 271-4870
915 Long Island Ave Ste A Deer Park (11729) **(G-3849)**
Brenseke's, Deer Park *Also called Brenseke George Wldg Ir Works* **(G-3849)**
Breton Industries Inc (PA)....518 842-3030
1 Sam Stratton Rd Amsterdam (12010) **(G-320)**
Brewer & Newell Printing, Rochester *Also called Forward Enterprises Inc* **(G-13421)**
Brewerton Special Tee's, Brewerton *Also called Irene Cerone* **(G-1136)**
Brewery Ommegang Ltd....607 286-4144
656 County Highway 33 Cooperstown (13326) **(G-3638)**
Brewster Coachworks, Lagrangeville *Also called Graphics Slution Providers Inc* **(G-6748)**
Brewster Transit Mix Corp (PA)....845 279-3738
31 Fields Ln Brewster (10509) **(G-1144)**
Brewster Transit Mix Corp....845 279-3738
Fields Ln Brewster (10509) **(G-1145)**
Brick & Ballerstein Inc....718 497-1400
1085 Irving Ave Ridgewood (11385) **(G-13142)**
Brick-It Inc....631 244-3993
17 Central Ave Hauppauge (11788) **(G-5607)**
Brickit....631 727-8977
17 Central Ave Hauppauge (11788) **(G-5608)**
Bridal Guide, New York *Also called Rfp LLC* **(G-11032)**
Bridge Components Inc....716 731-1184
2122 Cory Dr Sanborn (14132) **(G-14136)**
Bridge Enterprises Inc....718 625-6622
544 Park Ave Brooklyn (11205) **(G-1607)**
Bridge Fulfillment Inc....718 625-6622
445 Park Ave 204 Brooklyn (11205) **(G-1608)**
Bridge Metal Industries LLC....914 663-9200
717 S 3rd Ave Mount Vernon (10550) **(G-8125)**
Bridge Printing Inc....212 243-5390
4710 32nd Pl Fl 2 Long Island City (11101) **(G-7181)**
Bridge Records Inc....914 654-9270
200 Clinton Ave New Rochelle (10801) **(G-8322)**
Bridgehampton Steel & Wldg Inc....631 537-2486
27 Foster Ave Bridgehampton (11932) **(G-1164)**
Bridgeport Metalcraft Inc....315 623-9597
567 County Route 23 Constantia (13044) **(G-3635)**
Bridgestone APM Company....419 423-9552
6350 Inducon Dr E Sanborn (14132) **(G-14137)**
Brigadoon Software Inc (PA)....845 624-0909
119 Rockland Ctr 250 Nanuet (10954) **(G-8196)**
Brigantine Inc....212 354-8550
225 W 37th St New York (10018) **(G-8851)**
Brigar X-Press Solutions Inc....518 438-7817
5 Sand Creek Rd Ste 100 Albany (12205) **(G-52)**
Brigden Memorials, Albion *Also called Woodside Granite Industries* **(G-162)**
Briggs & Stratton Corporation....315 495-0100
4245 Highbridge Rd Sherrill (13461) **(G-14402)**
Bright Chair Co, Middletown *Also called Princeton Upholstery Co Inc* **(G-7928)**
Bright Kids Nyc Inc....917 539-4575
177 E 87th St 402 New York (10128) **(G-8852)**
Bright Line Eting Slutions LLC....585 245-2956
41 Lake Lacoma Dr Pittsford (14534) **(G-12637)**
Bright Way Supply Inc....718 833-2882
6302 Fort Hamilton Pkwy Brooklyn (11219) **(G-1609)**
Brightidea Incorporated....212 594-4500
1040 Ave Of The Ameri 18a New York (10018) **(G-8853)**
Brighton Design, Tonawanda *Also called Brighton Tool & Die Designers* **(G-15093)**
Brighton Tool & Die Designers (PA)....716 876-0879
463 Brighton Rd Tonawanda (14150) **(G-15093)**
Brijon, Ronkonkoma *Also called Lanco Corporation* **(G-13964)**
Brilliant Jewelers/Mjj Inc....212 353-2326
902 Broadway Fl 18 New York (10010) **(G-8854)**
Brilliant Stars Collection Inc....516 365-9000
150 Great Neck Rd Ste 400 Great Neck (11021) **(G-5371)**
Brinkman Intl Group Inc (PA)....585 429-5000
167 Ames St Rochester (14611) **(G-13281)**
Brinkman Precision Inc....585 429-5001
100 Park Centre Dr West Henrietta (14586) **(G-15788)**
Brinkman Products Inc....585 235-4545
167 Ames St Rochester (14611) **(G-13282)**
Bristol Boarding Inc....585 271-7860
1149 Highland Ave Rochester (14620) **(G-13283)**
Bristol Core Inc....585 919-0302
5310 North St Canandaigua (14424) **(G-3126)**
Bristol Gift Co Inc....845 496-2821
8 North St Washingtonville (10992) **(G-15523)**
Bristol Instruments Inc....585 924-2620
770 Canning Pkwy Victor (14564) **(G-15395)**
Bristol Metals Inc....585 657-7665
7817 State Route 5 And 20 Bloomfield (14469) **(G-941)**
Bristol Seamless Ring Corp....212 874-2645
209 W 86th St Apt 817 New York (10024) **(G-8855)**

A L P H A B E T I C

Bristol-Myers Squibb Company (PA) 212 546-4000
430 E 29th St Fl 14 New York (10016) *(G-8856)*
Bristol-Myers Squibb Company 315 432-2000
6000 Thompson Rd East Syracuse (13057) *(G-4201)*
Bristol-Myers Squibb Company 516 832-2191
1000 Stewart Ave Garden City (11530) *(G-5093)*
Bristol-Myers Squibb Intl Corp (HQ) 212 546-4000
430 E 29th St New York (10016) *(G-8857)*
Bristol/White Plains 914 681-1800
305 North St White Plains (10605) *(G-15984)*
British American Publishing 518 786-6000
19 British American Blvd Latham (12110) *(G-6849)*
British Science Corporation (PA) 212 980-8700
2550 Victory Blvd Ste 305 Staten Island (10314) *(G-14631)*
Brittish American Envmtl, Clifton Park *Also called Microb Phase Services (G-3468)*
Bro Laboratories, New York *Also called B&B Sports Nutrition LLC (G-8707)*
Broadalbin Manufacturing Corp 518 883-5313
8 Pine St Broadalbin (12025) *(G-1172)*
Broadcast Manager Inc 212 509-1200
65 Broadway Ste 602 New York (10006) *(G-8858)*
Broadnet Technologies Inc 315 443-3694
2-212 Center For Science Syracuse (13244) *(G-14834)*
Broadway Knitting Mills Inc 716 692-4421
1333 Strad Ave Ste 216 North Tonawanda (14120) *(G-12059)*
Broadway National, Ronkonkoma *Also called Broadway Neon Sign Corp (G-13918)*
Broadway Neon Sign Corp 908 241-4177
1900 Ocean Ave Ronkonkoma (11779) *(G-13918)*
Broadway Technology LLC (PA) 646 912-6450
28 Liberty St Fl 50 New York (10005) *(G-8859)*
Brock Awnings Ltd 631 765-5200
211 E Montauk Hwy Ste 1 Hampton Bays (11946) *(G-5533)*
Broda Machine Co Inc 716 297-3221
8745 Packard Rd Niagara Falls (14304) *(G-11910)*
Broder Mfg Inc 718 366-1667
566 Johnson Ave Brooklyn (11237) *(G-1610)*
Brodock Press Inc (PA) 315 735-9577
502 Court St Ste G Utica (13502) *(G-15242)*
Broetje Automation-Usa Inc 716 204-8640
165 Lawrence Bell Dr # 116 Williamsville (14221) *(G-16124)*
Broken Threads Inc 212 730-4351
147 W 35th St Ste 1401 New York (10001) *(G-8860)*
Bronx New Way Corp 347 431-1385
113 E Kingsbridge Rd Bronx (10468) *(G-1218)*
Bronx Times Reporter, Brooklyn *Also called Community News Group LLC (G-1680)*
Bronx Wstchester Tempering Inc 914 663-9400
160 S Macquesten Pkwy Mount Vernon (10550) *(G-8126)*
Bronxville Review, New Rochelle *Also called Gannett Co Inc (G-8333)*
Brook & Whittle Limited 716 691-4348
215 John Glenn Dr Amherst (14228) *(G-214)*
Brook & Whittle Limited 716 853-1688
215 John Glenn Dr Buffalo (14228) *(G-2666)*
Brook North Farms Inc 315 834-9390
89 York St Auburn (13021) *(G-469)*
Brooke Maya Inc 212 268-2626
124 W 36th St Fl 7 New York (10018) *(G-8861)*
Brookhaven Instruments Corp 631 758-3200
750 Blue Point Rd Holtsville (11742) *(G-6046)*
Brooklyn Bangers LLC 718 875-3535
111 Atlantic Ave Ste 1r Brooklyn (11201) *(G-1611)*
Brooklyn Brew Shop LLC 718 874-0119
81 Prospect St Brooklyn (11201) *(G-1612)*
Brooklyn Casing Co Inc 718 522-0866
412 3rd St Brooklyn (11215) *(G-1613)*
Brooklyn Circus (PA) 718 858-0919
150 Nevins St Brooklyn (11217) *(G-1614)*
Brooklyn Cstm Met Fbrction Inc 718 499-1573
48 Prospect Park Sw Brooklyn (11215) *(G-1615)*
Brooklyn Denim Co 718 782-2600
85 N 3rd St Brooklyn (11249) *(G-1616)*
Brooklyn Heights Press, Brooklyn *Also called Brooklyn Journal Publications (G-1618)*
Brooklyn Industries LLC 718 788-5250
328 7th Ave Brooklyn (11215) *(G-1617)*
Brooklyn Journal Publications 718 422-7400
16 Court St 30 Brooklyn (11241) *(G-1618)*
Brooklyn Printers Inc 718 511-7994
1661 Nostrand Ave Brooklyn (11226) *(G-1619)*
Brooklyn Rail Inc 718 349-8427
99 Commercial St Apt 15 Brooklyn (11222) *(G-1620)*
Brooklyn Roasting Works LLC 718 855-1000
45 Washington St Brooklyn (11201) *(G-1621)*
Brooklyn Sweet Spot Inc 718 522-2577
366 Myrtle Ave Ste A Brooklyn (11205) *(G-1622)*
Brooklyn Winery LLC (PA) 347 763-1506
213 N 8th St Brooklyn (11211) *(G-1623)*
Brooklyns Best Pasta Co Inc 917 881-3007
7520 Avenue V Brooklyn (11234) *(G-1624)*
Brooklynwrap Fresh Wraps, Brooklyn *Also called Brooklynwrap Inc (G-1625)*
Brooklynwrap Inc 718 258-8088
4714 Avenue N Brooklyn (11234) *(G-1625)*
Brooks Bottling Co LLC 607 432-1782
5560 State Highway 7 Oneonta (13820) *(G-12260)*

Brooks Litho Digital Group Inc 631 789-4500
35 W Jefryn Blvd Ste A Deer Park (11729) *(G-3850)*
Brooks Woodworking Inc 914 666-2029
15 Kensico Dr Mount Kisco (10549) *(G-8088)*
Brookside Lumber Inc 315 497-0937
4191 Duryea St Moravia (13118) *(G-8081)*
Brookvale Records Inc 631 587-7722
31 Brookvale Ave West Babylon (11704) *(G-15695)*
Broom Tioga Boces, Binghamton *Also called Boces Business Office (G-861)*
Bross Quality Paving 845 532-7116
4 Kossar Pl Ellenville (12428) *(G-4305)*
Brotherhood Americas 845 496-3661
100 Brotherhood Plaza Dr Washingtonville (10992) *(G-15524)*
Brothers Roofing Supplies Co 718 779-0280
10514 Astoria Blvd East Elmhurst (11369) *(G-4104)*
Brothers-In-Lawn Property 716 279-6191
176 Vulcan Tonawanda (14150) *(G-15094)*
Brown Publishing LLC 585 484-0432
323 Aldine St Rochester (14619) *(G-13284)*
Brown Publishing Network Inc 212 682-3330
122 E 42nd St Rm 2810 New York (10168) *(G-8862)*
Brownstone Publishers Inc 212 473-8200
149 5th Ave Fl 10 New York (10010) *(G-8863)*
Brucci Ltd 914 965-0707
861 Nepperhan Ave Yonkers (10703) *(G-16292)*
Bruce Pierce 716 731-9310
2386 Lockport Rd Sanborn (14132) *(G-14138)*
Brumis Imports Inc 646 845-6000
42 W 39th St Fl 4 New York (10018) *(G-8864)*
Brunner International Inc 585 798-6000
3959 Bates Rd Medina (14103) *(G-7731)*
Bruno & Canio Ltd 845 624-3060
130 Blauvelt Rd Nanuet (10954) *(G-8197)*
Bruno Associates, Altamont *Also called Rsb Associates Inc (G-199)*
Bruno Associates, Fort Edward *Also called Rfb Associates Inc (G-4943)*
Brunschwig & Fils LLC (HQ) 800 538-1880
245 Central Ave Bethpage (11714) *(G-833)*
Brushtech (disc) Inc 518 563-8420
4 Matt Ave Plattsburgh (12901) *(G-12739)*
Bryant Machine & Development 716 894-8282
63 Stanley St Buffalo (14206) *(G-2667)*
Bryant Machine Co Inc 716 894-8282
63 Stanley St Buffalo (14206) *(G-2668)*
Bryant Manufacturing Wny Inc 716 894-8282
63 Stanley St Buffalo (14206) *(G-2669)*
Brzozka Industries Inc 631 588-8164
790 Broadway Ave Holbrook (11741) *(G-5987)*
BSC Associates LLC 607 321-2980
151 Court St Binghamton (13901) *(G-864)*
BSD Aluminum Foil LLC 347 689-3875
260 Hewest St Brooklyn (11211) *(G-1626)*
BSD Top Direct Inc 646 468-0156
68 Route 109 West Babylon (11704) *(G-15696)*
Bso Energy Corp 212 520-1827
125 Park Ave Ste 2507 New York (10017) *(G-8865)*
Bst United Corp 631 777-2110
185 Marine St Farmingdale (11735) *(G-4594)*
Bsu Inc 607 272-8100
445 E State St Ithaca (14850) *(G-6373)*
Bsv Enterprises, Rochester *Also called BSV Metal Finishers Inc (G-13285)*
BSV Metal Finishers Inc 585 747-7070
750 Saint Paul St Rochester (14605) *(G-13285)*
Bti, Depew *Also called Buffalo Tungsten Inc (G-3975)*
Btween US, New York *Also called B Tween LLC (G-8706)*
Buckeye Corrugated Inc 585 924-1600
797 Old Dutch Rd Victor (14564) *(G-15396)*
Buckle Down, Farmingdale *Also called Custom Sitecom LLC (G-4611)*
Buckley Qc Fasteners Inc 716 662-1490
3874 California Rd Orchard Park (14127) *(G-12341)*
Bud Barger Assoc Inc 631 696-6703
3 Mount Mckinley Ave Farmingville (11738) *(G-4781)*
Bud Ravioli Center Inc 718 356-4600
3817 Richmond Ave Staten Island (10312) *(G-14632)*
Budd Woodwork Inc 718 389-1110
54 Franklin St Brooklyn (11222) *(G-1627)*
Buffalo Abrasives Inc (HQ) 716 693-3856
960 Erie Ave North Tonawanda (14120) *(G-12060)*
Buffalo Armory LLC 716 935-6346
1050 Military Rd Buffalo (14217) *(G-2670)*
Buffalo Blends Inc (PA) 716 825-4422
1400 William St Buffalo (14206) *(G-2671)*
Buffalo Circuits Inc 716 662-2113
105 Mid County Dr Orchard Park (14127) *(G-12342)*
Buffalo Compressed Air Inc 716 783-8673
2727 Broadway St Ste 3a Cheektowaga (14227) *(G-3340)*
Buffalo Crushed Stone Inc (HQ) 716 826-7310
500 Como Park Blvd Buffalo (14227) *(G-2672)*
Buffalo Crushed Stone Inc 716 566-9636
Rr 16 Franklinville (14737) *(G-4965)*
Buffalo Crushed Stone Inc 607 587-8102
638 State Route 244 Alfred Station (14803) *(G-184)*

Buffalo Crushed Stone Inc 716 632-6963
91 Barton Rd Clarence (14031) *(G-3427)*
Buffalo Dental Mfg Co Inc 516 496-7200
159 Lafayette Dr Syosset (11791) *(G-14780)*
Buffalo Envelope Company, Depew *Also called Buffalo Envelope Inc (G-3973)*
Buffalo Envelope Inc 716 686-0100
2914 Walden Ave Ste 300 Depew (14043) *(G-3973)*
Buffalo Filter LLC 716 835-7000
5900 Genesee St Lancaster (14086) *(G-6799)*
Buffalo Finishing Company, Ithaca *Also called F M Abdulky Inc (G-6381)*
Buffalo Finishing Works Inc 716 893-5266
1255 Niagara St Buffalo (14213) *(G-2673)*
Buffalo Games LLC 716 827-8393
220 James E Casey Dr Buffalo (14206) *(G-2674)*
Buffalo Gear Inc 716 731-2100
3635 Lockport Rd Sanborn (14132) *(G-14139)*
Buffalo Hearg & Speech 716 558-1105
1026 Union Rd West Seneca (14224) *(G-15845)*
Buffalo Jeans, New York *Also called Centric Denim Usa LLC (G-8956)*
Buffalo Law Journal 716 541-1600
465 Main St Ste 100 Buffalo (14203) *(G-2675)*
Buffalo Lining & Fabricating 716 883-6500
73 Gillette Ave Buffalo (14214) *(G-2676)*
Buffalo Machine Tls of Niagara 716 201-1310
4935 Lockport Rd Lockport (14094) *(G-7062)*
Buffalo Metal Casting Co Inc 716 874-6211
1875 Elmwood Ave Buffalo (14207) *(G-2677)*
Buffalo Metal Fabricating Corp 716 892-7800
50 Wecker St Buffalo (14215) *(G-2678)*
Buffalo Metal Finishing Co 716 883-2751
135 Dart St Buffalo (14213) *(G-2679)*
Buffalo News Inc 716 849-4401
1 News Plz Buffalo (14203) *(G-2680)*
Buffalo Newspress Inc 716 852-1600
200 Broadway St Buffalo (14204) *(G-2681)*
Buffalo Polymer Processors Inc 716 537-3153
42 Edgewood Dr Holland (14080) *(G-6028)*
Buffalo Power Electronics Ctr 716 651-1600
166 Taylor Dr Ste 1 Depew (14043) *(G-3974)*
Buffalo Provisions Co Inc 718 292-4300
4009 76th St Elmhurst (11373) *(G-4332)*
Buffalo Rocket, Buffalo *Also called Rocket Communications Inc (G-2959)*
Buffalo Scale and Sup Co Inc 716 847-2880
280 Seneca St Buffalo (14204) *(G-2682)*
Buffalo Snowmelter, North Tonawanda *Also called Roemac Industrial Sales Inc (G-12088)*
Buffalo Spree Publishing Inc (PA) 716 783-9119
1738 Elmwood Ave Ste 103 Buffalo (14207) *(G-2683)*
Buffalo Standard Printing Corp 716 835-9454
3620 Harlem Rd Ste 5 Buffalo (14215) *(G-2684)*
Buffalo Structural Steel Inc 814 827-1350
213 Teall Ave Syracuse (13210) *(G-14835)*
Buffalo Tungsten Inc 716 683-9170
2 Main St Depew (14043) *(G-3975)*
Buflovak LLC (PA) 716 895-2100
750 E Ferry St Buffalo (14211) *(G-2685)*
Builders Firstsource Inc 860 528-2293
30 Golf Links Rd Middletown (10940) *(G-7897)*
Building Management Assoc Inc 718 542-4779
998 E 167th St Ofc Bronx (10459) *(G-1219)*
Building New Bridges LLC 315 960-1242
202 State Route 365 Remsen (13438) *(G-13083)*
Bulkley Dunton (HQ) 212 863-1800
1 Penn Plz Ste 2814 New York (10119) *(G-8866)*
Bull Street LLC 212 495-9855
19 W 69th St Apt 201 New York (10023) *(G-8867)*
Bullet Industries Inc 585 352-0836
7 Turner Dr Spencerport (14559) *(G-14554)*
Bullex Inc 518 689-2023
20 Corporate Cir Ste 3 Albany (12203) *(G-53)*
Bullex Digital Safety, Albany *Also called Bullex Inc (G-53)*
Bullitt Group, Bohemia *Also called Bullitt Mobile LLC (G-983)*
Bullitt Mobile LLC 631 424-1749
80 Orville Dr Ste 100 Bohemia (11716) *(G-983)*
Bullock Boys LLC 518 783-6161
400 Old Loudon Rd Latham (12110) *(G-6850)*
Buna Besta Tortillas 347 987-3995
219 Johnson Ave Brooklyn (11206) *(G-1628)*
Buncee LLC 631 591-1390
170 Montauk Hwy Speonk Speonk (11972) *(G-14561)*
Bunge Limited Finance Corp 914 684-2800
50 Main St White Plains (10606) *(G-15985)*
Bunger Sayville, Sayville *Also called Bungers Surf Shop (G-14224)*
Bungers Surf Shop 631 244-3646
247 W Main St Sayville (11782) *(G-14224)*
Buperiod PBC 917 406-9804
8 Brighton 15th St Brooklyn (11235) *(G-1629)*
Burdick Publications Inc 315 685-9500
2352 E Lake Rd Skaneateles (13152) *(G-14447)*
Bureau of National Affairs Inc 212 687-4530
25 W 43rd St Ste 1007 New York (10036) *(G-8868)*
Burgess Products Division, New York Mills *Also called Fountainhead Group Inc (G-11832)*
Burgess-Manning Inc (HQ) 716 662-6540
50 Cobham Dr Orchard Park (14127) *(G-12343)*
Burke & Bannayan 585 723-1010
2465 W Ridge Rd Ste 2 Rochester (14626) *(G-13286)*
Burke Frging Heat Treating Inc 585 235-6060
30 Sherer St Rochester (14611) *(G-13287)*
Burlen Corp 212 684-0052
6 E 32nd St Fl 10 New York (10016) *(G-8869)*
Burnett Process Inc (HQ) 585 254-8080
545 Colfax St Rochester (14606) *(G-13288)*
Burnett Process Inc 585 277-1623
545 Colfax St Rochester (14606) *(G-13289)*
Burnham Polymeric Inc 518 792-3040
1408 Route 9 Fort Edward (12828) *(G-4937)*
Burnhams, The, Fort Edward *Also called Burnham Polymeric Inc (G-4937)*
Burns Archive Phtgraphic Distr 212 889-1938
140 E 38th St Frnt 1 New York (10016) *(G-8870)*
Burnt Hills Fabricators Inc 518 885-1115
318 Charlton Rd B Ballston Spa (12020) *(G-570)*
Burnt Mill Smithing 585 293-2380
127 Burnt Mill Rd Churchville (14428) *(G-3409)*
Burr & Son Inc 315 446-1550
119 Seeley Rd Syracuse (13224) *(G-14836)*
Burrows Paper Corporation 315 823-2300
730 E Mill St Little Falls (13365) *(G-6987)*
Burrows Paper Corporation 315 823-2300
489 W Main St Little Falls (13365) *(G-6988)*
Burrows Paper Mill, Little Falls *Also called Burrows Paper Corporation (G-6987)*
Burt Millwork Corporation 718 257-4601
85 Fairview Dr Albertson (11507) *(G-146)*
Burt Rigid Box Inc 607 433-2510
58 Browne St Oneonta (13820) *(G-12261)*
Burt Rigid Box Inc (PA) 607 433-2510
58 Browne St Oneonta (13820) *(G-12262)*
Burton Corporation 802 862-4500
21 Lawrence Paquette Dr Champlain (12919) *(G-3310)*
Burton Industries Inc 631 643-6660
243 Wyandanch Ave Ste A West Babylon (11704) *(G-15697)*
Burton Snowboards, Champlain *Also called Burton Corporation (G-3310)*
Busch Products Inc 315 474-8422
110 Baker St Syracuse (13206) *(G-14837)*
Bush Industries Inc (PA) 716 665-2000
1 Mason Dr Jamestown (14701) *(G-6500)*
Bushwick Bottling LLC 929 666-3618
465 Johnson Ave Brooklyn (11237) *(G-1630)*
Bushwick Kitchen LLC 917 297-1045
630 Flushing Ave Fl 5 Brooklyn (11206) *(G-1631)*
Business Advisory Services 718 337-3740
1104 Bay 25th St Far Rockaway (11691) *(G-4562)*
Business Card Express Inc 631 669-3400
300 Farmingdale Rd West Babylon (11704) *(G-15698)*
Business Directory Inc 718 486-8099
137 Division Ave Ste A Brooklyn (11211) *(G-1632)*
Business Expert Press LLC 212 661-8810
222 E 46th St Rm 203 New York (10017) *(G-8871)*
Business First of New York (HQ) 716 854-5822
465 Main St Ste 100 Buffalo (14203) *(G-2686)*
Business First of New York 518 640-6800
2 Winners Cir 104 Albany (12205) *(G-54)*
Business Integrity Inc (HQ) 718 238-2008
79 Madison Ave Fl 2 New York (10016) *(G-8872)*
Business Journal, Syracuse *Also called CNY Business Review Inc (G-14853)*
Business Journals 212 790-5100
1166 Ave Of The America New York (10036) *(G-8873)*
Business Management Systems 914 245-8558
1675 W 9th St Apt 4d Brooklyn (11223) *(G-1633)*
Business Never Stops LLC 888 479-3111
13404 97th Ave Ste 2 South Richmond Hill (11419) *(G-14522)*
Business Review, Albany *Also called Business First of New York (G-54)*
Bust Inc 212 675-1707
253 36th St Unit 3 Brooklyn (11232) *(G-1634)*
Bust Magazine, Brooklyn *Also called Bust Inc (G-1634)*
Bustle Digital Group, New York *Also called Bdg Media Inc (G-8743)*
Butterck McCall Vogue Pattern, New York *Also called McCall Pattern Company (G-10396)*
Butterwood Desserts Inc 716 652-0131
1863 Davis Rd West Falls (14170) *(G-15761)*
Buttons & Trimcom Inc 212 868-1971
519 8th Ave Rm 26 New York (10018) *(G-8874)*
Buxton Machine and Tool Co Inc 716 876-2312
2181 Elmwood Ave Buffalo (14216) *(G-2687)*
Buxton Medical Equipment Corp 631 957-4500
1178 Route 109 Lindenhurst (11757) *(G-6943)*
Buzzoole Inc 347 964-0120
450 Park Ave S Fl 3 New York (10016) *(G-8875)*
BW Elliott Mfg Co LLC 607 772-0404
11 Beckwith Ave Binghamton (13901) *(G-865)*
Bwo of NY, Binghamton *Also called Masonite International Corp (G-895)*
Bwog, New York *Also called Blue and White Publishing Inc (G-8817)*
Bws Specialty Fabrication, Orchard Park *Also called Quality Industrial Services (G-12376)*
By Robert James 212 253-2121
74 Orchard St New York (10002) *(G-8876)*

ALPHABETIC

Bycmac Corp 845 255-0884
144 Main St Gardiner (12525) ***(G-5127)***
Byelocorp Scientific Inc (PA) 212 785-2580
76 Perry St New York (10014) ***(G-8877)***
Byer California 212 944-8989
1407 Broadway Rm 807 New York (10018) ***(G-8878)***
Byk USA Inc 845 469-5800
48 Leone Ln Chester (10918) ***(G-3372)***
Bylada Foods LLC 845 623-1300
250 W Nyack Rd Ste 110 West Nyack (10994) ***(G-15819)***
Byliner Inc 415 680-3608
27 W 24th St Ste 202 New York (10010) ***(G-8879)***
Byram Concrete & Supply LLC 914 682-4477
145 Virginia Rd White Plains (10603) ***(G-15986)***
Byrne Dairy Inc (PA) 315 475-2121
2394 Us Route 11 La Fayette (13084) ***(G-6737)***
Bys Publishing LLC 315 655-9431
118 Albany St Cazenovia (13035) ***(G-3224)***
Bystronic Inc 631 231-1212
185 Commerce Dr Hauppauge (11788) ***(G-5609)***
Byte Consulting Inc 646 500-8606
295 Madison Ave Fl 35 New York (10017) ***(G-8880)***
Bytheway Publishing Services 607 334-8365
365 Follett Hill Rd Norwich (13815) ***(G-12114)***
Bz Media LLC 631 421-4158
225 Broadhollow Rd 211e Melville (11747) ***(G-7763)***
C & A Atelier, Richmond Hill *Also called Carlos & Alex Atelier Inc* ***(G-13111)***
C & A Service Inc (PA) 516 354-1200
65 S Tyson Ave Floral Park (11001) ***(G-4810)***
C & C Athletic Inc 845 713-4670
11 Myrtle Ave Walden (12586) ***(G-15457)***
C & C Bindery Co Inc 631 752-7078
25 Central Ave Unit B Farmingdale (11735) ***(G-4595)***
C & C Custom Metal Fabricators 631 235-9646
2 N Hoffman Ln Hauppauge (11788) ***(G-5610)***
C & C Metal Fabrications Inc 315 598-7607
159 Hubbard St Fulton (13069) ***(G-5055)***
C & C Ready-Mix Corporation (PA) 607 797-5108
3112 Vestal Rd Vestal (13850) ***(G-15374)***
C & C Ready-Mix Corporation 607 687-1690
3818 Rt 17 C Owego (13827) ***(G-12429)***
C & D Assembly Inc 607 898-4275
107 Corona Ave Groton (13073) ***(G-5481)***
C & F Iron Works Inc 914 592-2450
14 N Payne St Ste 1 Elmsford (10523) ***(G-4397)***
C & F Steel Design 914 592-3928
14 N Payne St Ste 2 Elmsford (10523) ***(G-4398)***
C & G of Kingston Inc 845 331-0148
25 Cornell St Kingston (12401) ***(G-6681)***
C & G Video Systems Inc (PA) 315 452-1490
7778 Tirrell Hill Cir Liverpool (13090) ***(G-7003)***
C & H Machining Inc 631 582-6737
281 Knickerbocker Ave Bohemia (11716) ***(G-984)***
C & H Precision Tools Inc 631 758-3806
194 Morris Ave Ste 20 Holtsville (11742) ***(G-6047)***
C & M Circuits Inc 631 589-0208
50 Orville Dr Bohemia (11716) ***(G-985)***
C & M Products Inc 315 471-3303
1209 N Salina St Ste 1 Syracuse (13208) ***(G-14838)***
C & R De Santis Inc 718 447-5076
2645 Forest Ave Ste 2 Staten Island (10303) ***(G-14633)***
C & T Tool & Instrument Co 718 429-1253
4125 58th St Woodside (11377) ***(G-16199)***
C B I, Oriskany *Also called Caldwell Bennett Inc* ***(G-12385)***
C B Management Services Inc 845 735-2300
73 S Pearl St Pearl River (10965) ***(G-12529)***
C B S Food Products Corp 718 452-2500
770 Chauncey St Brooklyn (11207) ***(G-1635)***
C C Industries Inc 518 581-7633
344 Burgoyne Rd Saratoga Springs (12866) ***(G-14167)***
C C M, Wolcott *Also called Carballo Contract Machining* ***(G-16162)***
C E King & Sons Inc 631 324-4944
10 Saint Francis Pl East Hampton (11937) ***(G-4118)***
C F Peters Corp 718 416-7800
7030 80th St Ste 2 Glendale (11385) ***(G-5221)***
C G & Son Machining Inc 315 964-2430
87 Nichols Rd Williamstown (13493) ***(G-16115)***
C H Thompson Company Inc 607 724-1094
69-93 Eldredge St Binghamton (13902) ***(G-866)***
C Howard Company Inc 631 286-7940
1007 Station Rd Bellport (11713) ***(G-795)***
C I G, New York *Also called Cambridge Info Group Inc* ***(G-8896)***
C J & C Sheet Metal Corp 631 376-9425
433 Falmouth Rd West Babylon (11704) ***(G-15699)***
C J Logging Equipment Inc 315 942-5431
8730 Industrial Dr Boonville (13309) ***(G-1106)***
C J Winter Machine Tech (HQ) 585 429-5000
167 Ames St Rochester (14611) ***(G-13290)***
C L Precision Machine & Tl Co 718 651-8475
5015 70th St Woodside (11377) ***(G-16200)***
C M E Corp 315 451-7101
1005 W Fayette St Ste 3c Syracuse (13204) ***(G-14839)***
C M Insurance Company Inc 716 689-5409
205 Crosspoint Pkwy Getzville (14068) ***(G-5173)***
C O P R A Inc 917 224-1727
215 E Broadway Apt 2r New York (10002) ***(G-8881)***
C P Chemical Co Inc 914 428-2517
25 Home St White Plains (10606) ***(G-15987)***
C Q Communications Inc 516 681-2922
17 W John St Unit 1 Hicksville (11801) ***(G-5890)***
C R Bard Inc 518 793-2531
289 Bay Rd Queensbury (12804) ***(G-13035)***
C R Bard Inc 518 793-2531
289 Bay Rd Glens Falls (12804) ***(G-5244)***
C R Bard Inc 518 793-2531
30 Collins Dr Queensbury (12804) ***(G-13036)***
C R C Manufacturing Inc 585 254-8820
37 Curlew St Rochester (14606) ***(G-13291)***
C S Business Systems Inc (PA) 716 886-6521
1236 Main St Buffalo (14209) ***(G-2688)***
C S I G Inc 845 383-3800
721 Broadway Ste 270 Kingston (12401) ***(G-6682)***
C S L, North Creek *Also called Creative Stage Lighting Co Inc* ***(G-12031)***
C S Welding, Ontario *Also called Cs Automation Inc* ***(G-12286)***
C Speed LLC (PA) 315 453-1043
316 Commerce Blvd Liverpool (13088) ***(G-7004)***
C T A Digital Inc 718 963-9845
36 Taaffe Pl Brooklyn (11205) ***(G-1636)***
C T A Digital Inc (PA) 845 513-0433
326 State Route 208 Monroe (10950) ***(G-8017)***
C To C Design & Print Inc 631 885-4020
1850 Pond Rd Unit B Ronkonkoma (11779) ***(G-13919)***
C V D, Central Islip *Also called Cvd Equipment Corporation* ***(G-3271)***
C W Sheet Metal, Maspeth *Also called Nelson Air Device Corporation* ***(G-7629)***
C&A Aromatics, Floral Park *Also called Citrus and Allied Essences Ltd* ***(G-4812)***
C&C Automatics Inc 315 331-1436
127 W Shore Blvd Newark (14513) ***(G-11838)***
C&C Diecuts, Farmingdale *Also called C & C Bindery Co Inc* ***(G-4595)***
C&T Tool & Instrmnt, Woodside *Also called C & T Tool & Instrument Co* ***(G-16199)***
C-Air International, Valley Stream *Also called Parnasa International Inc* ***(G-15351)***
C-Flex Bearing Co Inc 315 895-7454
104 Industrial Dr Frankfort (13340) ***(G-4948)***
C.H. Thompson Finishing, Binghamton *Also called Tcmf Inc* ***(G-912)***
C/O Court Sq Capitl Partners, New York *Also called Mdi Holdings LLC* ***(G-10404)***
C/O M&M Fowarding, Tonawanda *Also called Fiber Laminations Limited* ***(G-15104)***
C/O Pdell Ndell Fine Winberger, New York *Also called Mom Dad Publishing Inc* ***(G-10495)***
Ca Inc (HQ) 800 225-5224
520 Madison Ave New York (10022) ***(G-8882)***
Ca Inc 800 225-5224
1 Ca Plz Ste 100 Islandia (11749) ***(G-6327)***
Cab Plastics, Brooklyn *Also called Cab Signs Inc* ***(G-1637)***
Cab Signs Inc 718 479-2424
38 Livonia Ave Brooklyn (11212) ***(G-1637)***
Cab-Network Inc 516 334-8666
1500 Shames Dr Unit B Westbury (11590) ***(G-15873)***
Cabba Printing Incorporated 212 319-4747
133 E 55th St New York (10022) ***(G-8883)***
Cabezon Design Group Inc 718 488-9868
197 Waverly Ave Brooklyn (11205) ***(G-1638)***
Cabinet Factory Inc 718 351-8922
2333 Highland Blvd Staten Island (10306) ***(G-14634)***
Cabinet Shapes Corp 718 784-6255
3721 12th St Long Island City (11101) ***(G-7182)***
Cabinetry By Tbr Inc 516 365-8500
1492 Northern Blvd Manhasset (11030) ***(G-7531)***
Cabinets By Stanley Inc 718 222-5861
46 Hall St Brooklyn (11205) ***(G-1639)***
Cable Management Solutions Inc 631 674-0004
291 Skip Ln Bay Shore (11706) ***(G-660)***
Cables Unlimited Inc 631 563-6363
3 Old Dock Rd Yaphank (11980) ***(G-16256)***
Caboodle Printing Inc 716 693-6000
1975 Wehrle Dr Ste 120 Williamsville (14221) ***(G-16125)***
Cabot Coach Builders Inc 516 625-4000
77 Carriage Ln Roslyn Heights (11577) ***(G-14048)***
Cabriole Designs Inc 212 593-4528
315 E 91st St Ste 3 New York (10128) ***(G-8884)***
Cachet Industries Inc 212 944-2188
463 Fashion Ave Rm 601 New York (10018) ***(G-8885)***
Caddell Burns Manufacturing Co 631 757-1772
247 Asharoken Ave Northport (11768) ***(G-12100)***
Caddell Dry Dock & Repr Co Inc 718 442-2112
1515 Richmond Ter Staten Island (10310) ***(G-14635)***
Caddell Ship Yards, Staten Island *Also called Caddell Dry Dock & Repr Co Inc* ***(G-14635)***
Caddy Concepts Inc 516 570-6279
15 Cuttermill Rd Great Neck (11021) ***(G-5372)***
CAF Usa Inc 607 737-3004
300 E 18th St Elmira Heights (14903) ***(G-4375)***
Cafe Spice Gct Inc 845 863-0910
677 Little Britain Rd New Windsor (12553) ***(G-8362)***
Cahoon Farms Inc 315 594-8081
10951 Lummisville Rd Wolcott (14590) ***(G-16161)***

Cai Inc (PA) 212 819-0008
  430 E 56th St New York (10022) *(G-8886)*
Cai Design Inc 212 401-9973
  240 W 37th St Rm 303 New York (10018) *(G-8887)*
Caire Inc 716 691-0202
  260 Creekside Dr Amherst (14228) *(G-215)*
Caithness Equities Corporation (PA) 212 599-2112
  565 5th Ave Fl 29 New York (10017) *(G-8888)*
Calchem Corporation (PA) 631 423-5696
  2001 Ocean Ave Ronkonkoma (11779) *(G-13920)*
Caldwell Bennett Inc 315 337-8540
  6152 County Seat Rd Oriskany (13424) *(G-12385)*
Calfonex Company 845 778-2212
  121 Orchard St Walden (12586) *(G-15458)*
Calgon Carbon Corporation 716 531-9113
  830 River Rd North Tonawanda (14120) *(G-12061)*
Calia Consultants, Staten Island Also called Calia Technical Inc *(G-14636)*
Calia Technical Inc 718 447-3928
  420 Jefferson Blvd Staten Island (10312) *(G-14636)*
Caliber Imging Diagnostics Inc (PA) 585 239-9800
  50 Methodist Hill Dr # 100 Rochester (14623) *(G-13292)*
Calibrated Instruments Inc 914 741-5700
  306 Aerie Ct Manhasset (11030) *(G-7532)*
Calibration Technologies Inc 631 676-6133
  30 Woodland Blvd Centereach (11720) *(G-3250)*
Calico Cottage Inc 631 841-2100
  210 New Hwy Amityville (11701) *(G-257)*
California Fragrance Company 631 424-4023
  171 E 2nd St Huntington Station (11746) *(G-6241)*
California Petro Trnspt Corp 212 302-5151
  114 W 47th St New York (10036) *(G-8889)*
California US Holdings Inc 212 726-6500
  417 5th Ave Lbby 7th New York (10016) *(G-8890)*
Caligor Rx Inc 212 988-0590
  1226 Lexington Ave Frnt 1 New York (10028) *(G-8891)*
Caliper Studio Inc 718 302-2427
  75 Scott Ave Brooklyn (11237) *(G-1640)*
Call Forwarding Technologies 516 621-3600
  55 Northern Blvd Ste 3b Greenvale (11548) *(G-5460)*
Callahan & Nannini Quarry Inc 845 496-4323
  276 Clove Rd Salisbury Mills (12577) *(G-14134)*
Callanan Industries Inc 315 697-9569
  6375 Tuttle Rd Canastota (13032) *(G-3150)*
Callanan Industries Inc (HQ) 518 374-2222
  8 Southwoods Blvd Ste 4 Albany (12211) *(G-55)*
Callanan Industries Inc 845 457-3158
  215 Montgomery Rd Montgomery (12549) *(G-8058)*
Callanan Industries Inc 845 331-6868
  737 Flatbush Rd Kingston (12401) *(G-6683)*
Callanan Industries Inc 518 785-5666
  9 Fonda Rd Latham (12110) *(G-6851)*
Callanan Industries Inc 518 382-5354
  145 Cordell Rd Schenectady (12303) *(G-14250)*
Callaway Arts & Entrmt Inc 646 465-4667
  41 Union Sq W Ste 1101 New York (10003) *(G-8892)*
Callaway Digital Arts Inc 212 675-3050
  41 Union Sq W Ste 1101 New York (10003) *(G-8893)*
Callaway Golf Ball Oprtons Inc 518 725-5744
  115 Corporate Dr Johnstown (12095) *(G-6612)*
Callaway Golf Ball Oprtons Inc 518 773-2255
  Crossroads Industrial Par Gloversville (12078) *(G-5280)*
Calmetrics, Holbrook Also called Micromatter Tech Inc USA *(G-6012)*
Calspan Corporation (HQ) 716 631-6955
  4455 Genesee St Buffalo (14225) *(G-2689)*
Calspan Corporation 716 236-1040
  2041 Niagara Falls Blvd Niagara Falls (14304) *(G-11911)*
Calspan Flight Research Center, Niagara Falls Also called Calspan Corporation *(G-11911)*
Calspan Holdings LLC (PA) 716 631-6955
  4455 Genesee St Buffalo (14225) *(G-2690)*
Caltex International Ltd 315 425-1040
  60 Presidential Plz # 1405 Syracuse (13202) *(G-14840)*
Calvary Design Team Inc (PA) 585 347-6127
  855 Publishers Pkwy Webster (14580) *(G-15632)*
Calvary Robotics, Webster Also called Calvary Design Team Inc *(G-15632)*
Calvin Klein Inc 212 292-9000
  654 Madison Ave New York (10065) *(G-8894)*
Calvin Klein Eyewear, Melville Also called Allure Eyewear LLC *(G-7759)*
Calypso Technology Inc 212 905-0735
  99 Park Ave New York (10016) *(G-8895)*
CAM Machinery Co, Brooklyn Also called S & S Machinery Corp *(G-2370)*
CAM Touchview Products Inc 631 842-3400
  51 Division St Sag Harbor (11963) *(G-14096)*
CAM-Tech Industries Inc 585 425-2090
  95 Estates Dr W Fairport (14450) *(G-4491)*
Cama Graphics Inc 718 707-9747
  3200 Skillman Ave Ste B Long Island City (11101) *(G-7183)*
Cambridge Info Group Inc (PA) 301 961-6700
  888 7th Ave Ste 1701 New York (10106) *(G-8896)*
Cambridge Kitchens Mfg Inc 516 935-5100
  280 Duffy Ave Unit 1 Hicksville (11801) *(G-5891)*
Cambridge Manufacturing LLC 516 326-1350
  1700 Jericho Tpke New Hyde Park (11040) *(G-8255)*

Cambridge Security Seals LLC 845 520-4111
  1 Cambridge Plz Pomona (10970) *(G-12806)*
Cambridge University Press 212 337-5000
  165 Broadway Fl 20 New York (10006) *(G-8897)*
Cambridge Whos Who Pubg Inc (PA) 516 833-8440
  498 Rxr Plz Fl 4 Uniondale (11556) *(G-15224)*
Cambridge-Pacific Inc 518 677-5988
  891 State Rd 22 Cambridge (12816) *(G-3092)*
Camco, Ronkonkoma Also called Gliptone Manufacturing Inc *(G-13942)*
Camden House, Rochester Also called Boydell & Brewer Inc *(G-13279)*
Camden News Inc 315 245-1849
  39 Main St Camden (13316) *(G-3098)*
Camden Wire Co Inc 315 245-3800
  12 Masonic Ave Camden (13316) *(G-3099)*
Camellia Foods, Buffalo Also called Camellia General Provision Co *(G-2691)*
Camellia General Provision Co 716 893-5352
  1333 Genesee St Buffalo (14211) *(G-2691)*
Camelot Print & Copy Centers, Latham Also called Kjckd Inc *(G-6862)*
Cameo Metal Products Inc 718 788-1106
  127 12th St Brooklyn (11215) *(G-1641)*
Cameo Process Corp 914 948-0082
  15 Stewart Pl Apt 7g White Plains (10603) *(G-15988)*
Cameron Bridge Works LLC 607 734-9456
  727 Blostein Blvd Horseheads (14845) *(G-6116)*
Cameron Mfg & Design Inc (PA) 607 739-3606
  727 Blostein Blvd Horseheads (14845) *(G-6117)*
Camfil Usa Inc 315 468-3849
  6060 Tarbell Rd Syracuse (13206) *(G-14841)*
Caminus Corporation (HQ) 212 515-3600
  340 Madison Ave Fl 8 New York (10173) *(G-8898)*
Campanellis Poultry Farm Inc 845 482-2222
  4 Perry Rd Bethel (12720) *(G-828)*
Campbell Alliance Group Inc 212 377-2740
  335 Madison Ave Fl 17 New York (10017) *(G-8899)*
Campbell's Print Shop, Bronx Also called Linda Campbell *(G-1303)*
Campus Course Paks Inc 516 877-3967
  1 South Ave Fl 1 # 1 Garden City (11530) *(G-5094)*
Camso Manufacturing Usa Ltd (HQ) 518 561-7528
  1 Martina Cir Plattsburgh (12901) *(G-12740)*
Canaan Printing Inc 718 729-3100
  20007 46th Ave Bayside (11361) *(G-736)*
Canada Dry Bottling Co NY LP (PA) 718 358-2000
  11202 15th Ave College Point (11356) *(G-3538)*
Canada Dry Bottling Co NY LP 718 786-8550
  5035 56th Rd Maspeth (11378) *(G-7598)*
Canada Dry Bottling Co NY LP 631 694-7575
  135 Baylis Rd Melville (11747) *(G-7764)*
Canada Dry Bottling Co of NY, Melville Also called Canada Dry Bottling Co NY LP *(G-7764)*
Canada Goose Inc 888 276-6297
  601 W 26th St Rm 1745 New York (10001) *(G-8900)*
Canada Goose Us Inc (HQ) 888 276-6297
  300 International Dr Williamsville (14221) *(G-16126)*
Canal Asphalt Inc 914 667-8500
  645 S Columbus Ave Mount Vernon (10550) *(G-8127)*
Canali USA Inc (HQ) 212 767-0205
  415 W 13th St Fl 2 New York (10014) *(G-8901)*
Canandaigua Msgnr Incorporated (PA) 585 394-0770
  73 Buffalo St Canandaigua (14424) *(G-3127)*
Canandaigua Quick Print, Canandaigua Also called Carges Entps of Canandaigua *(G-3128)*
Canandaigua Technology Center, Canandaigua Also called Pactiv LLC *(G-3139)*
Canarm Ltd 800 267-4427
  808 Commerce Park Dr Ogdensburg (13669) *(G-12203)*
Canarsie Courier Inc 718 257-0600
  1142 E 92nd St 44 Brooklyn (11236) *(G-1642)*
Canastota Publishing Co Inc 315 697-9010
  130 E Center St Canastota (13032) *(G-3151)*
Canbiola Inc (PA) 954 253-4443
  960 S Broadway Ste 120 Hicksville (11801) *(G-5892)*
Candex Solutions Inc 215 650-3214
  420 Lexington Ave Rm 300 New York (10170) *(G-8902)*
Candid Litho Printing Ltd (PA) 212 431-3800
  210 Route 109 Farmingdale (11735) *(G-4596)*
Candid Worldwide LLC (HQ) 212 799-5300
  210 Route 109 Farmingdale (11735) *(G-4597)*
Candle In The Window Inc 718 852-5743
  19 Vanderbilt Ave Brooklyn (11205) *(G-1643)*
Candlelight Cabinetry Inc 716 434-2114
  24 Michigan St Lockport (14094) *(G-7063)*
Candles By Foster 914 739-9226
  810 South St Peekskill (10566) *(G-12549)*
Candlesticks Inc 212 947-8900
  112 W 34th St Fl 18 New York (10120) *(G-8903)*
Candy Kraft, Altamont Also called Robert Pikcilingis *(G-198)*
Candy Land, Rome Also called Noras Candy Shop *(G-13860)*
Candy Man, Wilmington Also called Adirondack Chocolate Co Ltd *(G-16152)*
Candy Planet Division, New York Also called Toymax Inc *(G-11525)*
Cane Simple, New York Also called Cane Sugar LLC *(G-8904)*
Cane Sugar LLC 212 329-2695
  950 3rd Ave Ste 2200 New York (10022) *(G-8904)*
Canfield & Tack Inc 585 235-7710
  925 Exchange St Rochester (14608) *(G-13293)*

A
L
P
H
A
B
E
T
I
C

Canfield Aerospace & Mar Inc.....631 648-1050
90 Remington Blvd Ronkonkoma (11779) *(G-13921)*
Canfield Electronics Inc (PA).....631 585-4100
6 Burton Pl Lindenhurst (11757) *(G-6944)*
Canfield Machine & Tool LLC.....315 593-8062
121 Howard Rd Fulton (13069) *(G-5056)*
Cannizzaro Seal & Engraving Co.....718 513-6125
435 Avenue U Brooklyn (11223) *(G-1644)*
Cannoli Factory Inc.....631 643-2700
75 Wyandanch Ave Wyandanch (11798) *(G-16243)*
Cannon Co, Brooklyn *Also called Attias Oven Corp (G-1550)*
Cannon Industries Inc (PA).....585 254-8080
525 Lee Rd Rochester (14606) *(G-13294)*
Cannonsville Lumber Inc.....607 467-3380
199 Old Route 10 Deposit (13754) *(G-3998)*
Canopy Books LLC (PA).....516 354-4888
28 N Wisconsin Ave 2-1 Massapequa (11758) *(G-7645)*
Canopy Canopy Canopy Inc.....347 529-5182
264 Canal St Ste 3w New York (10013) *(G-8905)*
Cant Live Without It LLC.....844 517-9355
28 W 23rd St Fl 5 New York (10010) *(G-8906)*
Canton Bio-Medical Inc (PA).....518 283-5963
11 Sicho Rd Poestenkill (12140) *(G-12801)*
Canton Noodle Corporation.....212 226-3276
101 Mott St New York (10013) *(G-8907)*
Canvas Products Company Inc.....516 742-1058
234 Herricks Rd Mineola (11501) *(G-7963)*
Canyon Publishing Inc.....212 334-0227
55 John St Ste 6 New York (10038) *(G-8908)*
Cap USA Jerseyman Harlem Inc (PA).....212 222-7942
112 W 125th St New York (10027) *(G-8909)*
Capco Marketing.....315 699-1687
8417 Oswego Rd 177 Baldwinsville (13027) *(G-544)*
Capco Wai Shing LLC.....212 268-1976
132 W 36th St Rm 509 New York (10018) *(G-8910)*
Capital Concrete Inc.....716 648-8001
5690 Camp Rd Hamburg (14075) *(G-5502)*
Capital District Stairs Inc.....518 383-2449
45 Dunsbach Rd Halfmoon (12065) *(G-5491)*
Capital Dst Print & Imaging.....518 456-6773
2075 Central Ave Schenectady (12304) *(G-14251)*
Capital E Financial Group.....212 319-6550
598 Madison Ave Fl 9 New York (10022) *(G-8911)*
Capital Gold Corporation (PA).....212 668-0842
601 Lexington Ave Fl 36 New York (10022) *(G-8912)*
Capital Kit Cab & Door Mfrs.....718 886-0303
1425 128th St College Point (11356) *(G-3539)*
Capital Ktchens Cab Doors Mfrs, College Point *Also called Capital Kit Cab & Door Mfrs (G-3539)*
Capital Mercury Shirtmakers Co, New York *Also called Gce International Inc (G-9582)*
Capital Partners LLC.....212 935-4990
390 Park Ave 13th New York (10022) *(G-8913)*
Capital Programs Inc.....212 842-4640
420 Lexington Ave Lbby 6 New York (10170) *(G-8914)*
Capital Reg Wkly Newsppr Group.....518 674-2841
29 Sheer Rd Averill Park (12018) *(G-506)*
Capital Region Wkly Newspapers.....518 877-7160
645 Albany Shaker Rd Albany (12211) *(G-56)*
Capital Sawmill Service.....518 479-0729
4119 Us Highway 20 Nassau (12123) *(G-8212)*
Capital Stone LLC.....518 382-7588
2241 Central Ave Schenectady (12304) *(G-14252)*
Capital Stone Saratoga LLC.....518 226-8677
4295 Route 50 Saratoga Springs (12866) *(G-14168)*
Capitol Awning & Shade Co, Jamaica *Also called Capitol Awning Co Inc (G-6430)*
Capitol Awning Co Inc.....212 505-1717
10515 180th St Jamaica (11433) *(G-6430)*
Capitol City Specialties Co.....518 486-8935
10 Burdick Dr Albany (12205) *(G-57)*
Capitol Cups Inc.....518 627-0051
1030 Riverfront Ctr Amsterdam (12010) *(G-321)*
Capitol Newspaper, Albany *Also called Newspaper Times Union (G-105)*
Capitol Plastic Products Inc.....518 627-0051
1030 Riverfront Ctr Amsterdam (12010) *(G-322)*
Capitol Restoration Corp.....516 783-1425
2473 Belmond Ave North Bellmore (11710) *(G-12014)*
Caplugs, Buffalo *Also called Protective Industries Inc (G-2936)*
Caps Teamwear Inc.....585 663-1750
65 Milburn St Rochester (14607) *(G-13295)*
Capstone Printing, New York *Also called Kallen Corp (G-10061)*
Capstream Technologies LLC.....716 945-7100
1204 Vine St Olean (14760) *(G-12227)*
Captain USA, New York *Also called CPT Usa LLC (G-9114)*
Caputo Bakery Inc.....718 875-6871
329 Court St Ste 1 Brooklyn (11231) *(G-1645)*
Caputo's Bake Shop, Brooklyn *Also called Caputo Bakery Inc (G-1645)*
Capy Machine Shop Inc (PA).....631 694-6916
114 Spagnoli Rd Melville (11747) *(G-7765)*
Car Doctor Motor Sports LLC.....631 537-1548
610 Scuttle Hole Rd Water Mill (11976) *(G-15528)*
Car Doctor, The, Water Mill *Also called Car Doctor Motor Sports LLC (G-15528)*
Car Engineering and Mfg, Victor *Also called Charles A Rogers Entps Inc (G-15397)*
Car-Freshner Corporation (HQ).....315 788-6250
21205 Little Tree Dr Watertown (13601) *(G-15562)*
Car-Freshner Corporation.....315 788-6250
22569 Fisher Cir Watertown (13601) *(G-15563)*
Car-Go Industries Inc (PA).....718 472-1443
5007 49th St Woodside (11377) *(G-16201)*
Caraustar Industries Inc.....716 874-0393
25 Dewberry Ln Buffalo (14227) *(G-2692)*
Caravan International Corp.....212 223-7190
641 Lexington Ave Fl 13 New York (10022) *(G-8915)*
Caravella Food Corp.....646 552-0455
16611 Cryders Ln Whitestone (11357) *(G-16090)*
Carballo Contract Machining.....315 594-2511
6205 Lake Ave Wolcott (14590) *(G-16162)*
Carbaugh Tool Company Inc.....607 739-3293
126 Philo Rd W Elmira (14903) *(G-4341)*
Carbide-Usa LLC.....607 331-9353
100 Home St Elmira (14904) *(G-4342)*
Carbon Activated Corporation.....716 662-2005
336 Stonehenge Dr Orchard Park (14127) *(G-12344)*
Carbon Activated Corporation.....716 677-6661
3774 Hoover Rd Blasdell (14219) *(G-918)*
Carbon Copies, Cortland *Also called BP Digital Imaging LLC (G-3757)*
Carbon Graphite Materials Inc.....716 792-7979
115 Central Ave Brocton (14716) *(G-1180)*
Carbon6 LLC.....607 229-3611
989 Pacific St Brooklyn (11238) *(G-1646)*
Carbonfree Chemicals Spe I LLC.....914 421-4900
1 N Lexington Ave White Plains (10601) *(G-15989)*
Card Pak Start Up, East Hampton *Also called Luria Communications Inc (G-4125)*
Card Printing.us, Monsey *Also called Tele-Pak Inc (G-8053)*
Cardinal Boiler and Tank, Brooklyn *Also called Cardinal Tank Corp (G-1647)*
Cardinal Data/Lark Graphics, Albany *Also called Andrew J George (G-40)*
Cardinal Tank Corp.....718 625-4350
700 Hicks St Brooklyn (11231) *(G-1647)*
Cardinali Bakery, Carle Place *Also called Gennaris Itln French Bky Inc (G-3174)*
Cardish Machine Works Inc.....518 273-2329
7 Elm St Watervliet (12189) *(G-15599)*
Cardona Industries USA Ltd (PA).....516 466-5200
505 Northern Blvd Ste 213 Great Neck (11021) *(G-5373)*
Cardullo, J Iron Works, Bay Shore *Also called Jerry Cardullo Iron Works Inc (G-685)*
Carduner Sales Company, Farmingville *Also called Bud Barger Assoc Inc (G-4781)*
Care Enterprises Inc.....631 472-8155
435 Renee Dr Bayport (11705) *(G-726)*
Careconnector.....919 360-2987
177 Concord St Apt 2a Brooklyn (11201) *(G-1648)*
Careers and The Disabled, Melville *Also called Equal Opprtnity Pblcations Inc (G-7778)*
Carefree Kitchens Inc.....631 567-2120
925 Lincoln Ave Ste 1 Holbrook (11741) *(G-5988)*
Carestream Health Inc.....585 627-1800
1669 Lake Ave Rochester (14652) *(G-13296)*
Carges Entps of Canandaigua.....585 394-2600
330 S Main St Canandaigua (14424) *(G-3128)*
Cargill Incorporated.....585 345-1160
8849 Wortendyke Rd Batavia (14020) *(G-607)*
Cargill Incorporated.....716 665-6570
1029 Poland Center Rd Kennedy (14747) *(G-6657)*
Cargill Incorporated.....315 287-0241
19 Starbuck St Gouverneur (13642) *(G-5317)*
Cargill Incorporated.....315 622-3533
7700 Maltage Dr Liverpool (13090) *(G-7005)*
Caribbean Fashion Group Inc.....212 706-8851
1410 Broadway Rm 3202 New York (10018) *(G-8916)*
Caribbean Foods Delight Inc.....845 398-3000
117 Route 303 Ste B Tappan (10983) *(G-15034)*
Caribe Bakery, Bronx *Also called 527 Franco Bakery Corporation (G-1182)*
Carl Fischer LLC (PA).....212 777-0900
48 Wall St 28 New York (10005) *(G-8917)*
Carl Safina Center Inc.....808 888-9440
80 N Country Rd Setauket (11733) *(G-14378)*
Carl Zeiss Inc (HQ).....914 747-1800
1 N Broadway Ste 401 White Plains (10601) *(G-15990)*
Carl Zeiss Microscopy LLC.....914 681-7840
1 N Broadway Ste 15 White Plains (10601) *(G-15991)*
Carl Zeiss Sbe LLC.....914 747-1132
1 N Broadway Ste 401 White Plains (10601) *(G-15992)*
Carlara Group Ltd.....914 769-2020
467 Bedford Rd Pleasantville (10570) *(G-12795)*
Carlisle Construction Mtls LLC.....386 753-0786
9 Hudson Crossing Dr Montgomery (12549) *(G-8059)*
Carlo Monte Designs Inc.....212 935-5611
17 E 48th St Fl 8 New York (10017) *(G-8918)*
Carlos & Alex Atelier Inc.....718 441-8911
10010 91st Ave Fl 2 Richmond Hill (11418) *(G-13111)*
Carlson Wood Products Inc.....716 287-2923
1705 Bates Rd Sinclairville (14782) *(G-14444)*
Carlson, L A Co, East Greenbush *Also called Leonard Carlson (G-4115)*
Carlton Ice Cream Co, Brooklyn *Also called Macedonia Ltd (G-2100)*
Carmen Mark Valvo Swimwear, Farmingdale *Also called Swimwear Anywhere Inc (G-4746)*

Carmine Street Bagels Inc.....212 691-3041
107 Park Dr N Staten Island (10314) ***(G-14637)***
Carnel Printing and Copying, Great Neck *Also called Carnels Printing Inc* ***(G-5374)***
Carnels Printing Inc.....516 883-3355
21 Schenck Ave Apt 3ba Great Neck (11021) ***(G-5374)***
Carnival, New York *Also called Cookies Inc* ***(G-9095)***
Carob Industries Inc.....631 225-0900
215 W Hoffman Ave Lindenhurst (11757) ***(G-6945)***
Caroda Inc.....212 630-9986
254 W 35th St New York (10001) ***(G-8919)***
Carol For Eva Graham Inc.....212 889-8686
366 5th Ave Rm 815 New York (10001) ***(G-8920)***
Carol Group Ltd.....212 505-2030
150 W 30th St Rm 902 New York (10001) ***(G-8921)***
Carol Peretz.....516 248-6300
49 Windsor Ave Ste 103 Mineola (11501) ***(G-7964)***
Carol Peretz Workshop, Mineola *Also called Carol Peretz* ***(G-7964)***
Carol Vail, Salem *Also called Carolina Eastern-Vail Inc* ***(G-14132)***
Carolina Amato Inc.....212 768-9095
350 7th Ave Rm 501 New York (10001) ***(G-8922)***
Carolina Eastern-Crocker LLC (PA).....585 345-4141
8610 Route 237 Stafford (14143) ***(G-14602)***
Carolina Eastern-Vail Inc.....518 854-9785
4134 State Route 22 Salem (12865) ***(G-14132)***
Carolina Herrera Ltd (HQ).....212 944-5757
501 Fashion Ave Fl 17 New York (10018) ***(G-8923)***
Carolina Precision Plas LLC.....631 981-0743
115 Comac St Ronkonkoma (11779) ***(G-13922)***
Carolinas Desserts Inc.....914 779-4000
1562 Central Park Ave Yonkers (10710) ***(G-16293)***
Carols Polar Parlor.....315 468-3404
3800 W Genesee St Syracuse (13219) ***(G-14842)***
Carolyn Ray Inc.....914 476-0619
578 Nepperhan Ave Ste C10 Yonkers (10701) ***(G-16294)***
Caron Distribution Center, New York *Also called National Spinning Co Inc* ***(G-10546)***
Carousel ADS, Brooklyn *Also called Drns Corp* ***(G-1763)***
Carpenter Industries Inc.....315 463-4284
1 General Motors Dr # 10 Syracuse (13206) ***(G-14843)***
Carpenter Manufacturing Co.....315 682-9176
110 Fairgrounds Dr Manlius (13104) ***(G-7544)***
Carpentier Industries LLC.....585 385-5550
119 Despatch Dr East Rochester (14445) ***(G-4160)***
Carpet Fabrications Intl.....914 381-6060
628 Waverly Ave Ste 1 Mamaroneck (10543) ***(G-7500)***
Carr Communications Group LLC.....607 748-0481
513 Prentice Rd Vestal (13850) ***(G-15375)***
Carr Jewelers, Latham *Also called Carr Manufacturing Jewelers* ***(G-6852)***
Carr Manufacturing Jewelers.....518 783-6093
22 West Ln Latham (12110) ***(G-6852)***
Carr Printing, Vestal *Also called Carr Communications Group LLC* ***(G-15375)***
Carrera Casting Corp.....212 382-3296
64 W 48th St Fl 2 New York (10036) ***(G-8924)***
Carrier Corporation.....315 432-6000
Carrier Pkwy Tr 20 Syracuse (13221) ***(G-14844)***
Carrier Corporation.....315 432-6000
Carrier Global Account Syracuse (13221) ***(G-14845)***
Carrier Corporation.....315 432-6000
1201 Kinne St East Syracuse (13057) ***(G-4202)***
Carrier Corporation.....315 432-3844
Carrier Pkwy Bldg Tr 20 East Syracuse (13057) ***(G-4203)***
Carrier News, Hicksville *Also called All Island Media Inc* ***(G-5880)***
Carry Hot Inc.....212 279-7535
545 W 45th St Rm 501 New York (10036) ***(G-8925)***
Carry Hot USA, New York *Also called Carry Hot Inc* ***(G-8925)***
Carry-All Canvas Bag Co Inc.....718 375-4230
1983 Coney Island Ave Brooklyn (11223) ***(G-1649)***
Carta Usa LLC.....585 436-3012
1600 Lexington Ave # 116 Rochester (14606) ***(G-13297)***
Carter Enterprises LLC (PA).....718 853-5052
4610 12th Ave Brooklyn (11219) ***(G-1650)***
Carter Street Bakery Inc.....585 749-7104
580 Child St Rochester (14606) ***(G-13298)***
Carthage Fibre Drum Inc (PA).....315 493-2730
14 Hewitt Dr Carthage (13619) ***(G-3194)***
Cartridge Evolution Inc.....718 788-0678
140 58th St Bldg Bu4e Brooklyn (11220) ***(G-1651)***
Carts Mobile Food Eqp Corp.....718 788-5540
113 8th St Brooklyn (11215) ***(G-1652)***
Carvart Glass Inc (PA).....212 675-0030
1441 Broadway Fl 28 New York (10018) ***(G-8926)***
Carver Creek Enterprises Inc.....585 657-7511
2524 Cannan Rd Bloomfield (14469) ***(G-942)***
Carver Sand & Gravel, Schoharie *Also called Masick Soil Conservation Co* ***(G-14322)***
Carver Sand & Gravel LLC (PA).....518 355-6034
494 Western Tpke Ste 1 Altamont (12009) ***(G-193)***
Carville National Leather Corp.....518 762-1634
10 Knox Ave Johnstown (12095) ***(G-6613)***
Carvin French Jewelers Inc.....212 755-6474
515 Madison Ave Rm 5c New York (10022) ***(G-8927)***
Cas, Cheektowaga *Also called Culinary Arts Specialties Inc* ***(G-3343)***
Cas Biosciences LLC.....844 227-2467
1501 Broadway Fl 12 New York (10036) ***(G-8928)***
Casa Collection Inc.....718 694-0272
106 Ferris St Brooklyn (11231) ***(G-1653)***
Casa Innovations Inc.....718 965-6600
155 Bay Ridge Ave Brooklyn (11220) ***(G-1654)***
Casa Larga Vineyards (PA).....585 223-4210
27 Emerald Hill Cir Fairport (14450) ***(G-4492)***
Casa Larga Vineyards.....585 223-4210
2287 Turk Hill Rd Fairport (14450) ***(G-4493)***
Casa Redimix Concrete Corp.....718 589-1555
886 Edgewater Rd Bronx (10474) ***(G-1220)***
Casablanca Records, New York *Also called Tm Music Inc* ***(G-11502)***
Cascade Helmets Holdings Inc.....315 453-3073
4697 Crssrads Pk Dr Ste 1 Liverpool (13088) ***(G-7006)***
Cascade Mountain Winery & Rest.....845 373-9021
835 Cascade Rd Amenia (12501) ***(G-201)***
Cascade Technical Services LLC (HQ).....516 596-6300
30 N Prospect Ave Lynbrook (11563) ***(G-7429)***
Cascade Technical Services LLC.....518 355-2201
2846 Curry Rd Ste B Schenectady (12303) ***(G-14253)***
Cascades New York Inc.....716 285-3681
4001 Packard Rd Niagara Falls (14303) ***(G-11912)***
Cascades New York Inc (HQ).....585 527-8110
1845 Emerson St Rochester (14606) ***(G-13299)***
Cascades New York Inc.....518 346-6151
801 Corporation Park Schenectady (12302) ***(G-14254)***
Cascades New York Inc.....716 681-1560
3241 Walden Ave Depew (14043) ***(G-3976)***
Cascades New York Inc.....518 689-1020
71 Fuller Rd Albany (12205) ***(G-58)***
Cascades Tssue Group-Sales Inc.....518 238-1900
148 Hudson River Rd Waterford (12188) ***(G-15533)***
Cascades Tssue Group-Sales Inc (HQ).....819 363-5100
148 Hudson River Rd Waterford (12188) ***(G-15534)***
Cascades USA Inc.....518 880-3600
148 Hudson River Rd Waterford (12188) ***(G-15535)***
Casco Security, Rochester *Also called Custom Sound and Video* ***(G-13334)***
Case Brothers Inc.....716 925-7172
370 Quinn Rd Limestone (14753) ***(G-6937)***
Case Group LLC.....518 720-3100
195 Cohoes Ave Green Island (12183) ***(G-5433)***
Case Window and Door, Green Island *Also called Case Group LLC* ***(G-5433)***
Casey Machine Co Inc.....716 651-0150
74 Ward Rd Lancaster (14086) ***(G-6800)***
Cassinelli Food Products Inc.....718 274-4881
3112 23rd Ave Long Island City (11105) ***(G-7184)***
Cassini Parfums Ltd.....212 753-7540
3 W 57th St Fl 8 New York (10019) ***(G-8929)***
Cast-All Corporation.....516 741-4025
229 Liberty Ave Mineola (11501) ***(G-7965)***
Castek Inc (HQ).....914 636-1000
20 Jones St New Rochelle (10801) ***(G-8323)***
Castel Grisch Winery, Montour Falls *Also called Malina Management Company Inc* ***(G-8075)***
Castella Imports Inc.....631 231-5500
60 Davids Dr Hauppauge (11788) ***(G-5611)***
Castella Imports Inc (PA).....631 231-5500
120 Wilshire Blvd Ste A Edgewood (11717) ***(G-4264)***
Castelli America LLC.....716 782-2101
5151 Fairbanks Rd Ashville (14710) ***(G-408)***
Casters Custom Sawing.....315 387-5104
6323 Us Route 11 Sandy Creek (13145) ***(G-14154)***
Castino Corporation.....845 229-0341
1300 Route 9g Hyde Park (12538) ***(G-6270)***
Castle Brands Inc (PA).....646 356-0200
122 E 42nd St Rm 5000 New York (10168) ***(G-8930)***
Castle Connolly Medical Ltd.....212 367-8400
42 W 24th St Fl 2 New York (10010) ***(G-8931)***
Castle Fuels Corporation.....914 381-6600
440 Mamaroneck Ave Harrison (10528) ***(G-5548)***
Castle Harvester Co Inc.....585 526-5884
3165 Seneca Castle Rd Seneca Castle (14547) ***(G-14361)***
Castle Harvstr Met Fabricators, Seneca Castle *Also called Castle Harvester Co Inc* ***(G-14361)***
Castle Power Solutions LLC.....518 743-1000
5 Depot St Hudson Falls (12839) ***(G-6183)***
Castle Reagh Print Craft, Freeport *Also called Castlereagh Printcraft Inc* ***(G-4989)***
Castlereagh Printcraft Inc.....516 623-1728
320 Buffalo Ave Freeport (11520) ***(G-4989)***
Castoleum Corporation.....914 664-5877
240 E 7th St Mount Vernon (10550) ***(G-8128)***
Casttle Harbor, Bellmore *Also called Hot Line Industries Inc* ***(G-783)***
Casual Friday Inc.....585 544-9470
1561 Lyell Ave Rochester (14606) ***(G-13300)***
Casuals Etc Inc.....212 838-1319
16 E 52nd St Fl 4 New York (10022) ***(G-8932)***
Caswell Inc.....315 946-1213
7696 State Route 31 Lyons (14489) ***(G-7447)***
Catalina Products Corp (PA).....718 336-8288
2455 Mcdonald Ave Brooklyn (11223) ***(G-1655)***
Catalyst Group Design, New York *Also called Catalyst Group Inc* ***(G-8933)***

Catalyst Group Inc..212 243-7777
 345 7th Ave Rm 1100 New York (10001) *(G-8933)*
Catapult..323 839-6204
 1140 Broadway Rm 704 New York (10001) *(G-8934)*
Catapult LLC (PA)..303 717-0334
 1140 Broadway Rm 704 New York (10001) *(G-8935)*
Cataract Hose Co..914 941-9019
 6 Waller Ave Ossining (10562) *(G-12402)*
Cataract Hose Co No 2, Ossining *Also called Cataract Hose Co (G-12402)*
Cataract Steel Industries, Niagara Falls *Also called Costanzos Welding Inc (G-11917)*
Catch Ventures Inc..347 620-4351
 30 W 63rd St Apt 14o New York (10023) *(G-8936)*
Cathay Global Co Inc..718 229-0920
 5815 215th St Bayside Hills (11364) *(G-746)*
Cathay Home Inc (PA)..212 213-0988
 230 5th Ave Ste 215 New York (10001) *(G-8937)*
Cathedral Candle Co..315 422-9119
 510 Kirkpatrick St Syracuse (13208) *(G-14846)*
Cathedral Corporation (PA)..................................315 338-0021
 632 Ellsworth Rd Rome (13441) *(G-13846)*
Catherine Stein Designs Inc................................212 840-1188
 411 5th Ave Rm 600 New York (10016) *(G-8938)*
Catholic Courier, Rochester *Also called Rochester Catholic Press (G-13684)*
Catholic New York, New York *Also called Ecclesiastical Communications (G-9314)*
Catholic News Publishing Co................................914 632-7771
 420 Railroad Way Mamaroneck (10543) *(G-7501)*
Catholic Sun, The, Syracuse *Also called Syracuse Catholic Press Assn (G-15004)*
Cathy Daniels Ltd (PA)..212 354-8000
 11 Orchard Ln Old Westbury (11568) *(G-12222)*
Catskill Castings Co, Bloomville *Also called G Haynes Holdings Inc (G-953)*
Catskill Craftsmen Inc..607 652-7321
 15 W End Ave Stamford (12167) *(G-14607)*
Catskill Delaware Publications (PA)......................845 887-5200
 5 Lower Main St Callicoon (12723) *(G-3075)*
Catskill Mountain News, Arkville *Also called Catskill Mountain Publishing (G-394)*
Catskill Mountain Publishing................................845 586-2601
 43414 State Hwy 28 Arkville (12406) *(G-394)*
Catsmo LLC..845 895-2296
 25 Myers Rd Wallkill (12589) *(G-15468)*
Cattaraugus Containers Inc................................716 676-2000
 21 Elm St 23 Franklinville (14737) *(G-4966)*
Cava Spiliadis USA..212 247-8214
 200 W 57th St Ste 908 New York (10019) *(G-8939)*
Cayuga Crushed Stone Inc..................................607 533-4273
 87 Portland Point Rd Lansing (14882) *(G-6840)*
Cayuga Press Cortland Inc..................................888 229-8421
 4707 Dey Rd Liverpool (13088) *(G-7007)*
Cayuga Tool and Die Inc......................................607 533-7400
 182 Newman Rd Groton (13073) *(G-5482)*
Cayuga Wooden Boatworks Inc............................315 253-7447
 381 Enfield Main Rd Ithaca (14850) *(G-6374)*
Cazar Printing & Advertising................................718 446-4606
 4215 102nd St Corona (11368) *(G-3735)*
CB Minerals LLC..914 777-3330
 875 Mamaroneck Ave Mamaroneck (10543) *(G-7502)*
CB Products, Floral Park *Also called CB Publishing LLC (G-4811)*
CB Publishing LLC..516 354-4888
 50 Carnation Ave Bldg 2-1 Floral Park (11001) *(G-4811)*
CBA Group LLC..607 779-7522
 33 Broome Corporate Pkwy Conklin (13748) *(G-3622)*
Cbe/New York, Plainview *Also called Conrad Blasius Equipment Co (G-12672)*
CBM Fabrications Inc..518 399-8023
 15 Westside Dr Ballston Lake (12019) *(G-559)*
Cbord Group Inc (HQ)..607 257-2410
 950 Danby Rd Ste 100c Ithaca (14850) *(G-6375)*
CCA Holding Inc..716 446-8800
 300 Corporate Pkwy Amherst (14226) *(G-216)*
CCC Publications Inc..718 306-1008
 12020 Flatlands Ave Brooklyn (11207) *(G-1656)*
CCL Label Inc..716 852-2155
 685 Howard St Buffalo (14206) *(G-2693)*
Ccmi Inc..315 781-3270
 88 Middle St Geneva (14456) *(G-5148)*
Ccn International Inc..315 789-4400
 200 Lehigh St Geneva (14456) *(G-5149)*
CCS North America LLC..312 834-2165
 1360 Sunny Ridge Rd Mohegan Lake (10547) *(G-8009)*
Cct Inc..212 532-3355
 60 Madison Ave Ste 1209 New York (10010) *(G-8940)*
CCT (us) Inc..716 297-7509
 2221 Niagara Falls Blvd # 5 Niagara Falls (14304) *(G-11913)*
Ccz Ready Mix Concrete Corp..............................516 579-7352
 2 Loring Rd Levittown (11756) *(G-6914)*
Cda Machine Inc..585 671-5959
 514 Vosburg Rd Webster (14580) *(G-15633)*
CDF Indstrial Pckg Sltions Inc............................716 672-2984
 134 Clinton Ave Fredonia (14063) *(G-4968)*
Cdj Stamping Inc..585 224-8120
 146 Halstead St Ste 123 Rochester (14610) *(G-13301)*
Cdl Manufacturing Inc..585 589-2533
 15661 Telegraph Rd Albion (14411) *(G-155)*

Cdml Computer Services Ltd................................718 428-9063
 5343 198th St Fresh Meadows (11365) *(G-5038)*
CEC Elevator Cab Corp..718 328-3632
 540 Manida St Bronx (10474) *(G-1221)*
Cedar Graphics Inc..631 467-1444
 1700 Ocean Ave Ste 1 Ronkonkoma (11779) *(G-13923)*
Cedar West Inc (PA)..631 467-1444
 1700 Ocean Ave Ste 1 Ronkonkoma (11779) *(G-13924)*
Cegid Corporation..212 757-9038
 274 Madison Ave Rm 1404 New York (10016) *(G-8941)*
Cego Custom Shirts, New York *Also called Sifonya Inc (G-11229)*
Ceipal LLC..585 351-2934
 722 Weiland Rd Rochester (14626) *(G-13302)*
Ceipal LLC..585 584-1316
 687 Lee Rd Ste 208a Rochester (14606) *(G-13303)*
CEIT Corp..518 825-0649
 625 State Route 3 Unit 2 Plattsburgh (12901) *(G-12741)*
Cell-Nique Corporation..203 856-8550
 22 Hamilton Way Castleton On Hudson (12033) *(G-3200)*
Cellec Technologies Inc......................................585 454-9166
 125 Tech Park Dr Ste 2111 Rochester (14623) *(G-13304)*
Cellectis Inc..347 809-5980
 430 E 29th St Ste 810 New York (10016) *(G-8942)*
Cellgen Inc..516 889-9300
 55 Commercial St Freeport (11520) *(G-4990)*
Cellu Tissue - Long Island LLC............................631 232-2626
 555 N Research Pl Central Islip (11722) *(G-3267)*
Celmet Co..585 647-1760
 105 Norton St Newark (14513) *(G-11839)*
Celonis Inc..941 615-9670
 1820 Avenue M Unit 544 Brooklyn (11230) *(G-1657)*
Celonis Inc..973 652-8821
 114 W 41st St Fl 16 New York (10036) *(G-8943)*
Celtic Industries, Congers *Also called Celtic Sheet Metal Inc (G-3611)*
Celtic Sheet Metal Inc..845 267-3400
 100 Brenner Dr Unit C Congers (10920) *(G-3611)*
Cem Machine Inc (PA)..315 493-4258
 571 W End Ave Carthage (13619) *(G-3195)*
Cemac Foods Corp..914 835-0526
 8 Cayuga Trl Harrison (10528) *(G-5549)*
Cemecon Inc..607 562-2363
 315 Daniel Zenker Dr Horseheads (14845) *(G-6118)*
Cementex Latex Corp..212 741-1770
 121 Varick St Frnt 2 New York (10013) *(G-8944)*
Cemento,, West Monroe *Also called Robinson Concrete Inc (G-15814)*
Cemex Cement Inc..212 317-6000
 590 Madison Ave Fl 41 New York (10022) *(G-8945)*
Cemoi Inc (PA)..212 583-4920
 5 Penn Plz Ste 2325 New York (10001) *(G-8946)*
Cenere, New York *Also called Precision International Co Inc (G-10875)*
Cenibra Inc..212 818-8242
 1251 Ave Of The Americas New York (10020) *(G-8947)*
Ceno Technologies Inc..716 885-5050
 1234 Delaware Ave Buffalo (14209) *(G-2694)*
Centar Fuel Co Inc..516 538-2424
 700 Nassau Blvd West Hempstead (11552) *(G-15768)*
Centennial Media LLC..646 527-7320
 10th Floor 40 Worth St Flr 10 New York (10013) *(G-8948)*
Center For Comprehensive Care, New York *Also called Northwell Health Inc (G-10646)*
Center For Inquiry Inc (PA)..................................716 636-4869
 3965 Rensch Rd Amherst (14228) *(G-217)*
Center For Orthotic & Prosthet............................607 215-0847
 1141 Broadway St Elmira (14904) *(G-4343)*
Center For Prosthetic..845 336-7762
 144 Pine St Ste 110 Kingston (12401) *(G-6684)*
Center Sheet Metal Inc..718 378-4476
 1371 E Bay Ave Bronx (10474) *(G-1222)*
Center State Propane LLC (PA)............................315 841-4044
 1130 Mason Rd Ste 2 Waterville (13480) *(G-15594)*
Centerless Technology Inc..................................585 436-2240
 45 Wells St Rochester (14611) *(G-13305)*
Centinel Spine LLC (PA)......................................212 583-9700
 505 Park Ave Fl 14 New York (10022) *(G-8949)*
Central Adirondack Textiles, Boonville *Also called S M S C Inc (G-1110)*
Central Apparel Group Ltd..................................212 868-6505
 16 W 36th St Rm 1202 New York (10018) *(G-8950)*
Central Asphalt, Oriskany *Also called Suit-Kote Corporation (G-12396)*
Central Asphalt, Watkins Glen *Also called Suit-Kote Corporation (G-15616)*
Central Cnfrnce of Amrcn Rbbis............................212 972-3636
 355 Lexington Ave Fl 18 New York (10017) *(G-8951)*
Central Coca-Cola Btlg Co Inc (HQ)......................914 789-1100
 555 Taxter Rd Ste 550 Elmsford (10523) *(G-4399)*
Central Dover Development....................................917 709-3266
 247 Dover Furnace Rd Dover Plains (12522) *(G-4031)*
Central Garden & Pet Company............................631 451-8021
 1100 Middle Country Rd Selden (11784) *(G-14350)*
Central Islip Pharmacy Inc..................................631 234-6039
 1629 Islip Ave Central Islip (11722) *(G-3268)*
Central Kitchen Corp..631 283-1029
 871 County Road 39 Southampton (11968) *(G-14528)*
Central Marking Equipment, Syracuse *Also called C M E Corp (G-14839)*

Central Mills Inc 212 764-9011
  1400 Broadway Rm 1605 New York (10018) *(G-8952)*
Central Nat Pulp & Ppr Sls Inc 914 696-9000
  3 Manhattanville Rd Purchase (10577) *(G-13003)*
Central Park Active Wear, New York Also called Central Apparel Group Ltd *(G-8950)*
Central Rede Sign Co Inc 716 213-0797
  317 Wheeler St Tonawanda (14150) *(G-15095)*
Central Semiconductor Corp 631 435-1110
  145 Adams Ave Hauppauge (11788) *(G-5612)*
Central Textiles Inc 212 213-8740
  10 E 40th St Rm 3410 New York (10016) *(G-8953)*
Central Timber Co Inc 518 638-6338
  9088 State Route 22 Granville (12832) *(G-5348)*
Central Timber Research/Devt, Granville Also called Central Timber Co Inc *(G-5348)*
Centre De Conformite ICC Inc 716 283-0002
  2150 Liberty Dr Ste 1 Niagara Falls (14304) *(G-11914)*
Centre Interiors Wdwkg Co Inc 718 323-1343
  10001 103rd Ave Ozone Park (11417) *(G-12458)*
Centric Brands Inc 212 925-5727
  77 Mercer St New York (10012) *(G-8954)*
Centric Brands Inc (PA) 646 582-6000
  350 5th Ave Fl 6 New York (10118) *(G-8955)*
Centric Denim Usa LLC (HQ) 646 839-7000
  350 5th Ave Fl 6 New York (10118) *(G-8956)*
Centric Socks LLC 646 839-7000
  350 5th Ave Lbby 9 New York (10118) *(G-8957)*
Centric West LLC (HQ) 646 839-7000
  350 5th Ave Fl 5 New York (10118) *(G-8958)*
Centrisource Inc 716 871-1105
  777 E Park Dr Tonawanda (14150) *(G-15096)*
Centro Inc 212 791-9450
  841 Broadway Fl 6 New York (10003) *(G-8959)*
Centroid Inc 516 349-0070
  111 E Ames Ct Unit 1 Plainview (11803) *(G-12667)*
Century Awning Concepts, Mount Vernon Also called Kingston Building Products LLC *(G-8156)*
Century Direct LLC 212 763-0600
  15 Enter Ln Islandia (11749) *(G-6328)*
Century Grand Inc 212 925-3838
  302 Grand St New York (10002) *(G-8960)*
Century Metal Parts Corp 631 667-0800
  230 S Fehr Way Bay Shore (11706) *(G-661)*
Century Mold Company Inc (PA) 585 352-8600
  25 Vantage Point Dr Rochester (14624) *(G-13306)*
Century Mold Mexico LLC (HQ) 585 352-8600
  25 Vantage Point Dr Rochester (14624) *(G-13307)*
Century Pharmacy Three, New York Also called Century Grand Inc *(G-8960)*
Century Ready Mix Inc 631 888-2200
  615 Cord Ave West Babylon (11704) *(G-15700)*
Century Tom Inc 347 654-3179
  10416 150th St Jamaica (11435) *(G-6431)*
Century-Tech Inc 718 326-9400
  32 Intersection St Hempstead (11550) *(G-5835)*
Ceo Cast Inc 212 732-4300
  211 E 43rd St Rm 400 New York (10017) *(G-8961)*
Ceoentano, Buffalo Also called Rosina Food Products Inc *(G-2962)*
Cep Technologies Corporation (PA) 914 968-4100
  763 Saw Mill River Rd Yonkers (10710) *(G-16295)*
Ceramica V. A. R. M., New Rochelle Also called Ceramica Varm *(G-8324)*
Ceramica Varm (PA) 914 381-6215
  479 5th Ave New Rochelle (10801) *(G-8324)*
Ceres Technologies Inc 845 247-4701
  5 Tower Dr Saugerties (12477) *(G-14198)*
Cerion Energy Inc 585 271-5630
  1 Blossom Rd Rochester (14610) *(G-13308)*
Cerion LLC 585 271-5630
  1 Blossom Rd Rochester (14610) *(G-13309)*
Ceros Inc (PA) 347 744-9250
  40 W 25th St Fl 12 New York (10010) *(G-8962)*
Cerovene Inc 845 359-1101
  10 Corporate Dr Orangeburg (10962) *(G-12308)*
Cerovene Inc (PA) 845 267-2055
  612 Corporate Way Ste 10 Valley Cottage (10989) *(G-15314)*
Certainteed Corporation 716 823-3684
  231 Ship Canal Pkwy Lackawanna (14218) *(G-6740)*
Certainteed Corporation 716 827-7560
  231 Ship Canal Pkwy Buffalo (14218) *(G-2695)*
Certified Flameproofing Corp 631 265-4824
  17 N Ingelore Ct Smithtown (11787) *(G-14474)*
Certified Health Products Inc 718 339-7498
  67 35th St Unit C533 Brooklyn (11232) *(G-1658)*
Certified Prcsion McHining Inc 631 244-3671
  70 Knickerbocker Ave # 4 Bohemia (11716) *(G-986)*
Ces Industries Inc 631 782-7088
  95 Hoffman Ln Ste S Islandia (11749) *(G-6329)*
Cetek Inc 845 452-3510
  19 Commerce St Poughkeepsie (12603) *(G-12948)*
Cettel Studio of New York Inc 518 494-3622
  636 Atateka Dr Chestertown (12817) *(G-3393)*
Ceylan & Co LLC 646 858-3022
  24 W 46th St Apt 3 New York (10036) *(G-8963)*
Cfe, Brooklyn Also called Carts Mobile Food Eqp Corp *(G-1652)*

Cffco USA Inc 718 747-1118
  55 Jericho Tpke Ste 302 Jericho (11753) *(G-6573)*
Cfg Group, New York Also called Caribbean Fashion Group Inc *(G-8916)*
CFI, Perry Also called Creative Food Ingredients Inc *(G-12596)*
Cfo Publishing LLC (PA) 212 459-3004
  50 Broad St Frnt New York (10004) *(G-8964)*
CFS Enterprises Inc 718 585-0500
  650 E 132nd St Bronx (10454) *(G-1223)*
CFS Steel Company, Bronx Also called CFS Enterprises Inc *(G-1223)*
Cgi Technologies Solutions Inc 212 682-7411
  655 3rd Ave Ste 700 New York (10017) *(G-8965)*
Cgm, Brocton Also called Carbon Graphite Materials Inc *(G-1180)*
Cgs Fabrication LLC 585 347-6127
  855 Publishers Pkwy Webster (14580) *(G-15634)*
Cgw Corp (PA) 631 472-6600
  102 S Gillette Ave Bayport (11705) *(G-727)*
Chad Pierson 518 251-0186
  Chad Pierson Bakers Mills (12811) *(G-529)*
Chad Pierson Logging & Trckg, Bakers Mills Also called Chad Pierson *(G-529)*
Chain Store Age Magazine 212 756-5000
  425 Park Ave New York (10022) *(G-8966)*
Chaindom Enterprises Inc 212 719-4778
  48 W 48th St Ste 200 New York (10036) *(G-8967)*
Chakra Communications Inc 607 748-7491
  32 Washington Ave Endicott (13760) *(G-4446)*
Challenge Graphics Svcs Inc (PA) 631 586-0171
  22 Connor Ln Deer Park (11729) *(G-3851)*
Chalmers Medical Group, Wilson Also called Lynx Product Group LLC *(G-16153)*
Cham Cold Brew LLC 646 926-0206
  300 Park Ave Fl 12 New York (10022) *(G-8968)*
Chambord LLC 718 859-1110
  4302 Farragut Rd Brooklyn (11203) *(G-1659)*
Chameleon Color Cards Ltd 716 625-9452
  6530 S Transit Rd Lockport (14094) *(G-7064)*
Chameleon Gems Inc 516 829-3333
  98 Cuttermill Rd Ste 398n Great Neck (11021) *(G-5375)*
Champion Home Builders Inc 315 841-4122
  951 Rte 12 S Sangerfield (13455) *(G-14155)*
Champion Materials Inc (PA) 315 493-2654
  502 S Washington St Carthage (13619) *(G-3196)*
Champion Millwork Inc 315 463-0711
  140 Hiawatha Pl Syracuse (13208) *(G-14847)*
Champion Photochemistry Inc 585 760-6444
  1669 Lake Ave Rochester (14615) *(G-13310)*
Champion Zipper Corp 212 239-0414
  447 W 36th St Fl 2 New York (10018) *(G-8969)*
Champlain Hanger, Rouses Point Also called Champlain Plastics Inc *(G-14065)*
Champlain Hudson Power Ex Inc 518 465-0710
  600 Broadway Fl 3 Albany (12207) *(G-59)*
Champlain Plastics Inc 518 297-3700
  87 Pillsbury Rd Rouses Point (12979) *(G-14065)*
Champs Sports, Hicksville Also called Foot Locker Retail Inc *(G-5908)*
Chams, New York Also called North American Mills Inc *(G-10642)*
Chamtek Mfg Inc 585 328-4900
  123 Louise St Rochester (14606) *(G-13311)*
Chan Kee Dried Bean Curd Inc 718 622-0820
  71 Steuben St Brooklyn (11205) *(G-1660)*
Changdu Technology (usa) Co 917 340-1976
  1417 Horseshoe Dr North Bellmore (11710) *(G-12015)*
Changes, Glendale Also called Bowe Industries Inc *(G-5219)*
Channel Manufacturing Inc (PA) 516 944-6271
  55 Channel Dr Port Washington (11050) *(G-12866)*
Chanse Petroleum Corporation (PA) 212 682-3789
  828 5th Ave Apt 1f New York (10065) *(G-8970)*
Chapin International Inc 585 343-3140
  700 Ellicott St Batavia (14020) *(G-608)*
Chapin Manufacturing Inc (PA) 585 343-3140
  700 Ellicott St Ste 3 Batavia (14020) *(G-609)*
Chapman Skateboard Co Inc 631 321-4773
  87 N Industry Ct Ste A Deer Park (11729) *(G-3852)*
Charing Cross Music Inc 212 541-7571
  3 Columbus Cir Ste 1720 New York (10019) *(G-8971)*
Charis & Mae Inc 212 641-0816
  31 W 34th St Fl 8 New York (10001) *(G-8972)*
Charl Industries Inc 631 234-0100
  225 Engineers Rd Hauppauge (11788) *(G-5613)*
Charles A Rogers Entps Inc 585 924-6400
  51 Victor Heights Pkwy Victor (14564) *(G-15397)*
Charles Freihofer Baking Co 518 463-2221
  1 Prospect Rd Albany (12206) *(G-60)*
Charles H Beckley Inc (PA) 718 665-2218
  749 E 137th St Bronx (10454) *(G-1224)*
Charles Henricks Inc 212 243-5800
  70 W 36th St Rm 500 New York (10018) *(G-8973)*
Charles Krypell Inc 212 752-3313
  22 W 48th St Ste 801-803 New York (10036) *(G-8974)*
Charles P Rogers Brass Beds (PA) 212 675-4400
  26 W 17th St New York (10011) *(G-8975)*
Charles P Rogers Brass Ir Bed, New York Also called Charles P Rogers Brass Beds *(G-8975)*
Charles Perrella Inc 845 348-4777
  78 S Broadway Nyack (10960) *(G-12138)*

Charles Richter, Wallkill *Also called Richter Metalcraft Corporation* **(G-15472)**

Charles Ross & Son Company (PA)............................631 234-0500
710 Old Willets Path Hauppauge (11788) *(G-5614)*

Charlotte Neuville Design LLC..................................646 530-4570
882 3rd Ave Brooklyn (11232) *(G-1661)*

Charlton Precision Products....................................845 338-2351
461 Sawkill Rd Kingston (12401) *(G-6685)*

Charm Mfg Co Inc...607 565-8161
251 State Route 17c Waverly (14892) *(G-15619)*

Charm Pools, Waverly *Also called Charm Mfg Co Inc* **(G-15619)**

Charming Fashion Inc...212 730-2872
247 W 38th St Rm 1400 New York (10018) *(G-8976)*

Chart Industries Inc...716 691-0202
260 Creekside Dr Ste 100 Amherst (14228) *(G-218)*

Charter Ventures LLC...212 868-0222
135 W 36th St Rm 1800 New York (10018) *(G-8977)*

Chartwell Pharma Nda B2 Holdin................................845 268-5000
77 Brenner Dr Congers (10920) *(G-3612)*

Chartwell Pharmaceuticals LLC..................................845 268-5000
77 Brenner Dr Congers (10920) *(G-3613)*

Chase Corporation..631 827-0476
7 Harbour Point Dr Northport (11768) *(G-12101)*

Chase Instrument Co, West Babylon *Also called Peyser Instrument Corporation* **(G-15736)**

Chase Partners, Northport *Also called Chase Corporation* **(G-12101)**

Chassix Automotive Corp...585 815-1700
4320 Federal Dr Batavia (14020) *(G-610)*

Chateau Imports Ltd..516 841-6343
8 Maple St Ste 10 Port Washington (11050) *(G-12867)*

Chateau La Fayette Reneau, Hector *Also called Lafayette Chateau* **(G-5826)**

Chatham Courier, The, Hudson *Also called Johnson Acquisition Corp* **(G-6167)**

Chautauqua Circuits Inc...716 366-5771
855 Main St Dunkirk (14048) *(G-4050)*

Chautauqua Iron Works, Mayville *Also called Kleinfelder John* **(G-7683)**

Chautauqua Machine Spc LLC......................................716 782-3276
1880 Open Meadows Rd Ashville (14710) *(G-409)*

Chautauqua Sign Co Inc..716 665-2222
2164 Allen Street Ext Falconer (14733) *(G-4536)*

Chautauqua Wine Company Inc....................................716 934-9463
2627 Chapin Rd Silver Creek (14136) *(G-14440)*

Chautauqua Woods Corporation....................................716 366-3808
134 Franklin Ave Dunkirk (14048) *(G-4051)*

Chautqua Prcsion Machining Inc..................................716 763-3752
1287 Hunt Rd Ashville (14710) *(G-410)*

Check Group LLC..212 221-4700
1385 Broadway Fl 16 New York (10018) *(G-8978)*

Check-Mate Industries Inc......................................631 491-1777
370 Wyandanch Ave West Babylon (11704) *(G-15701)*

Check-O-Matic Inc..845 781-7675
13 D A Weider Blvd # 101 Monroe (10950) *(G-8018)*

Checklist Boards Corporation....................................585 586-0152
763 Linden Ave Ste 2 Rochester (14625) *(G-13312)*

Checkpoint Therapeutics Inc....................................781 652-4500
2 Gansevoort St Fl 9 New York (10014) *(G-8979)*

Chefs Delight Packing Co...718 388-8581
94 N 8th St Brooklyn (11249) *(G-1662)*

Chelsea Plastics Inc...212 924-4530
200 Lexington Ave Rm 914 New York (10016) *(G-8980)*

Chem-Tainer Industries Inc (PA).................................631 422-8300
361 Neptune Ave West Babylon (11704) *(G-15702)*

Chem-Tek Systems Inc...631 253-3010
208 S Fehr Way Bay Shore (11706) *(G-662)*

Chembio Diagnostic Systems Inc..................................631 924-1135
3661 Horseblock Rd Ste A Medford (11763) *(G-7701)*

Chembio Diagnostics Inc (PA)...................................631 924-1135
3661 Horseblock Rd Ste C Medford (11763) *(G-7702)*

Chemclean Corporation...718 525-4500
13045 180th St Jamaica (11434) *(G-6432)*

Chemicolloid Laboratories Inc..................................516 747-2666
55 Herricks Rd New Hyde Park (11040) *(G-8256)*

Chemistry Department, Oswego *Also called Energy Nuclear Operations* **(G-12410)**

Chemlube International LLC..914 381-5800
500 Mmaroneck Ave Ste 306 Harrison (10528) *(G-5550)*

Chemlube Marketing Inc..914 381-5800
500 Mamaroneck Ave Harrison (10528) *(G-5551)*

Chemprene Inc...845 831-2800
483 Fishkill Ave Beacon (12508) *(G-749)*

Chemprene Holding Inc...845 831-2800
483 Fishkill Ave Beacon (12508) *(G-750)*

Chemtrade Chemicals US LLC......................................315 430-7650
1421 Willis Ave Syracuse (13204) *(G-14848)*

Chemtrade Chemicals US LLC......................................315 478-2323
344 W Genesee St Ste 100 Syracuse (13202) *(G-14849)*

Chenango Concrete Corp..607 334-2545
County Rd 32 E River Rd Norwich (13815) *(G-12115)*

Chenango Concrete Corp (PA).....................................518 294-9964
145 Podpadic Rd Richmondville (12149) *(G-13129)*

Chenango Union Printing Inc.....................................607 334-2112
15 American Ave Norwich (13815) *(G-12116)*

Chenango Valley Tech Inc...607 674-4115
328 Route 12b Sherburne (13460) *(G-14388)*

Chentronics LLC...607 334-5531
50 Ohara Dr Norwich (13815) *(G-12117)*

Chepaume Industries LLC..315 829-6400
6201 Cooper St Vernon (13476) *(G-15364)*

Chequedcom Inc..888 412-0699
513 Broadway Ste 1 Saratoga Springs (12866) *(G-14169)*

Cheri Mon Baby LLC...212 354-5511
1412 Broadway Rm 1608 New York (10018) *(G-8981)*

Cheribundi Inc (PA)...800 699-0460
1 Montorency Way Geneva (14456) *(G-5150)*

Cherry Creek Woodcraft Inc (PA).................................716 988-3211
1 Cherry St South Dayton (14138) *(G-14506)*

Cherry Lane Lithographing Corp..................................516 293-9294
15 E Bethpage Rd Unit A Plainview (11803) *(G-12668)*

Cherry Lane Magazine LLC...212 561-3000
1745 Broadway 19 New York (10019) *(G-8982)*

Chesky Records Inc..212 586-7799
1650 Broadway Ste 900 New York (10019) *(G-8983)*

Chester Printing Service, Middletown *Also called Triad Printing Inc* **(G-7936)**

Chester West County Press..914 684-0006
29 W 4th St Mount Vernon (10550) *(G-8129)*

Chester-Jensen Company...610 876-6276
124 S Main St Cattaraugus (14719) *(G-3220)*

Chesu Inc...239 564-2803
81 Newtown Ln East Hampton (11937) *(G-4119)*

Chf Industries Inc (PA)...212 951-7800
1 Park Ave Fl 9 New York (10016) *(G-8984)*

Chia Company, New York *Also called Chia Usa LLC* **(G-8985)**

Chia Usa LLC..212 226-7512
379 W Broadway New York (10012) *(G-8985)*

Chicago Watermark Company, New York *Also called Donald Bruhnke* **(G-9247)**

Chicken Hawk Racing Inc...845 758-0700
54 Elizabeth St Ste 10 Red Hook (12571) *(G-13072)*

Chicone Builders LLC..607 535-6540
302 W South St Montour Falls (14865) *(G-8074)*

Chief, The, New York *Also called New York Cvl Srvc Emplys Pblsh* **(G-10593)**

Child Nutrition Prog Dept Ed....................................212 371-1000
1011 1st Ave Fl 6 New York (10022) *(G-8986)*

Child's Work-Child's Play, Melville *Also called Guidance Group Inc* **(G-7788)**

Chim-Cap Corp..800 262-9622
120 Schmitt Blvd Farmingdale (11735) *(G-4598)*

Chimney Doctors Americas Corp...................................631 868-3586
738a Montauk Hwy Bayport (11705) *(G-728)*

China Daily Distribution Corp (HQ)..............................212 537-8888
1500 Broadway Ste 2800 New York (10036) *(G-8987)*

China Huaren Organic Pdts Inc...................................212 232-0120
100 Wall St Fl 15 New York (10005) *(G-8988)*

China Imprint LLC...585 563-3391
750 Saint Paul St Rochester (14605) *(G-13313)*

China Industrial Steel Inc.......................................646 328-1502
110 Wall St Fl 11 New York (10005) *(G-8989)*

China Lithium Technologies (PA).................................212 391-2688
15 W 39th St Fl 14 New York (10018) *(G-8990)*

China N E Petro Holdings Ltd.....................................212 307-3568
445 Park Ave New York (10022) *(G-8991)*

China Newsweek Corporation.......................................212 481-2510
15 E 40th St Fl 11 New York (10016) *(G-8992)*

China Ruitai Intl Holdings Ltd..................................718 740-2278
8710 Clover Pl Hollis (11423) *(G-6041)*

China Ting Fshion Group USA LL (HQ).............................212 716-1600
525 7th Ave Rm 1606 New York (10018) *(G-8993)*

Chinese Medical Report Inc.......................................718 359-5676
3907 Prince St Ste 5b Flushing (11354) *(G-4842)*

Chip It All Inc..631 473-2040
366 Sheep Pasture Rd Port Jefferson (11777) *(G-12840)*

Chipita America Inc...845 292-2540
1243 Old Route 17 Ferndale (12734) *(G-4787)*

Chiplogic Inc..631 617-6317
14a Old Dock Rd Yaphank (11980) *(G-16257)*

Chiptek, Arcade *Also called Gowanda - Bti LLC* **(G-375)**

Chlor Alkali Products & Vinyls, Niagara Falls *Also called Olin Chlor Alkali Logistics* **(G-11961)**

Chobani LLC...646 998-3800
200 Lafayette St Fl 6 New York (10012) *(G-8994)*

Chobani LLC (HQ)..607 337-1246
147 State Highway 320 Norwich (13815) *(G-12118)*

Chobani LLC...607 847-6181
669 County Road 25 New Berlin (13411) *(G-8221)*

Chobani Idaho LLC...208 432-2248
147 State Highway 320 Norwich (13815) *(G-12119)*

Chocnyc LLC..917 804-4848
4996 Broadway New York (10034) *(G-8995)*

Choco-Logo, Buffalo *Also called Dilese International Inc* **(G-2729)**

Chocolat Moderne LLC...212 229-4797
27 W 20th St Ste 904 New York (10011) *(G-8996)*

Chocolate Delivery Systems, Buffalo *Also called N Make Mold Inc* **(G-2878)**

Chocolate Delivery Systems Inc (PA).............................716 877-3146
1800 Elmwood Ave Buffalo (14207) *(G-2696)*

Chocolate Lady LLC...516 532-0551
14 Blue Heron Ln Port Jervis (12771) *(G-12845)*

Chocolate Pizza Company Inc......................................315 673-4098
3774 Lee Mulroy Rd Marcellus (13108) *(G-7561)*

Chocolatier Magazine, New York *Also called Haymarket Group Ltd* **(G-9737)**

Chocolations LLC 914 777-3600
607 E Boston Post Rd Mamaroneck (10543) *(G-7503)*

Chocovision Corporation (PA) 845 473-8003
331 Main St Poughkeepsie (12601) *(G-12949)*

Chohehco LLC 315 420-4624
78 State St Skaneateles (13152) *(G-14448)*

Choice Magazine Listening Inc 516 883-8280
85 Channel Dr Ste 3 Port Washington (11050) *(G-12868)*

Chomerics Div, Fairport Also called Parker-Hannifin Corporation *(G-4512)*

Christi Plastics Inc 585 436-8510
215 Tremont St Rochester (14608) *(G-13314)*

Christian Bus Endeavors Inc (PA) 315 788-8560
210 Court St Ste 10 Watertown (13601) *(G-15564)*

Christian Casey LLC (PA) 212 500-2200
1440 Broadway Frnt 3 New York (10018) *(G-8997)*

Christian Casey LLC 212 500-2200
1440 Broadway Frnt 3 New York (10018) *(G-8998)*

Christian Dior Perfumes LLC (HQ) 212 931-2200
19 E 57th St New York (10022) *(G-8999)*

Christian Fabrication LLC 315 822-0135
122 South St West Winfield (13491) *(G-15857)*

Christian Press Inc 718 886-4400
14317 Franklin Ave Flushing (11355) *(G-4843)*

Christian Siriano Holdings LLC 212 695-5494
5 W 54th St New York (10019) *(G-9000)*

Christiana Millwork Inc (PA) 315 492-9099
4755 Jamesville Rd Jamesville (13078) *(G-6557)*

Christina Sales Inc 212 391-0710
1441 Broadway New York (10018) *(G-9001)*

Christiny, Wantagh Also called Christopher Anthony Pubg Co *(G-15483)*

Christo Vac, Cornwall Also called Costume Armour Inc *(G-3728)*

Christophe Danhier, New York Also called Danhier Co LLC *(G-9164)*

Christopher Anthony Pubg Co 516 826-9205
2151 Spruce St Wantagh (11793) *(G-15483)*

Christopher Designs Inc 212 382-1013
50 W 47th St Ste 1507 New York (10036) *(G-9002)*

Christos Inc 212 921-0025
318 W 39th St Fl 12 New York (10018) *(G-9003)*

Chroma Communications Inc 631 289-8871
2030 Route 112 Medford (11763) *(G-7703)*

Chroma Logic 716 736-2458
6651 Wiley Rd Ripley (14775) *(G-13169)*

Chromagraphics Press Inc 631 367-6160
3 Martha Dr Melville (11747) *(G-7766)*

Chromalloy American LLC (HQ) 845 230-7355
330 Blaisdell Rd Orangeburg (10962) *(G-12309)*

Chromalloy Gas Turbine LLC 845 359-2462
330 Blaisdell Rd Orangeburg (10962) *(G-12310)*

Chromalloy Gas Turbine LLC 845 692-8912
105 Tower Dr Middletown (10941) *(G-7898)*

Chromalloy Middletown, Middletown Also called Chromalloy Gas Turbine LLC *(G-7898)*

Chromalloy New York, Orangeburg Also called Chromalloy Gas Turbine LLC *(G-12310)*

Chromosense LLC 646 541-2302
476 N Ridge St Rye Brook (10573) *(G-14087)*

Chronicle Express 315 536-4422
138 Main St Penn Yan (14527) *(G-12580)*

Chronicle, The, Glens Falls Also called Oak Lone Publishing Co Inc *(G-5262)*

Chronicles Systems Inc 516 992-2553
840 Newton Ave North Baldwin (11510) *(G-12003)*

Chudnow Manufacturing Co Inc 516 593-4222
3055 New St Oceanside (11572) *(G-12167)*

Chula Girls, New York Also called Detour Apparel Inc *(G-9211)*

Church & Dwight Co Inc 518 887-5109
706 Ennis Rd Schenectady (12306) *(G-14255)*

Church Bulletin Inc 631 249-4994
200 Dale St West Babylon (11704) *(G-15703)*

Church Communities NY Inc 518 589-5103
2255 Platte Clove Rd Elka Park (12427) *(G-4302)*

Church Communities NY Inc 518 589-5103
Platte Clove Rd Elka Park (12427) *(G-4303)*

Church Publishing Incorporated (HQ) 212 592-1800
445 5th Ave Frnt 1 New York (10016) *(G-9004)*

Chutes and Compactors of NY 718 494-2247
1011 Westwood Ave Staten Island (10314) *(G-14638)*

CHv Printed Company 516 997-1101
1905 Hempstead Tpke B East Meadow (11554) *(G-4132)*

Chyronhego Corporation (HQ) 631 845-2000
5 Hub Dr Melville (11747) *(G-7767)*

Cianfarani Armando 518 393-7755
114 Van Guysling Ave Schenectady (12305) *(G-14256)*

CIC International Ltd 212 213-0089
1118 42nd St Brooklyn (11219) *(G-1663)*

Ciccarelli Custom Taylor, Long Island City Also called Primo Coat Corp *(G-7329)*

Cid Technologies, Liverpool Also called Thermo Cidtec Inc *(G-7045)*

CIDC Corp 718 342-5820
5605 Cooper Ave Glendale (11385) *(G-5222)*

Cidega American Trim, Durham Also called Advanced Yarn Technologies Inc *(G-4069)*

Cigar Box Studios Inc 845 236-9283
24 Riverview Dr Marlboro (12542) *(G-7579)*

Cigar Oasis LLC 516 520-5258
79 Heisser Ct Farmingdale (11735) *(G-4599)*

Cilyox Inc 716 853-3809
345 Broadway St Buffalo (14204) *(G-2697)*

Ciment St-Laurent Inc 518 943-4040
6446 Route 9w Catskill (12414) *(G-3210)*

Cinch Technologies Inc 212 266-0022
7 World Trade Ctr New York (10007) *(G-9005)*

Cinderella Press Ltd 212 431-3130
327 Canal St 3 New York (10013) *(G-9006)*

Cine Design Group LLC 646 747-0734
15 Park Row Lbby L New York (10038) *(G-9007)*

Cine Magnetics Inc 914 667-6707
524 S Columbus Ave Mount Vernon (10550) *(G-8130)*

Cinedeck, New York Also called Cine Design Group LLC *(G-9007)*

Cinedigm Software 212 206-9001
45 W 36th St Fl 7 New York (10018) *(G-9008)*

Ciner Manufacturing Co Inc 212 947-3770
20 W 37th St Fl 10 New York (10018) *(G-9009)*

Cintube Ltd 518 324-3333
139 Distribution Way Plattsburgh (12901) *(G-12742)*

Circle 5 Deli Corp 718 525-5687
13440 Guy R Brewer Blvd Jamaica (11434) *(G-6433)*

Circle Peak Capital MGT LLC (PA) 646 230-8812
1325 Ave Of The Americas New York (10019) *(G-9010)*

Circle Press, New York Also called 1 800 Postcards Inc *(G-8387)*

Circle Press Inc (PA) 212 924-4277
121 Varick St Fl 4 New York (10013) *(G-9011)*

Circo File Corp 516 922-1848
69 Hamilton Ave Ste 1 Oyster Bay (11771) *(G-12445)*

Circor Aerospace Inc 631 737-1900
425 Rabro Dr Ste 1 Hauppauge (11788) *(G-5615)*

Circuits & Systems Inc 516 593-4301
59 2nd St East Rockaway (11518) *(G-4171)*

Cirrus Healthcare Products LLC (PA) 631 692-7600
60 Main St Ste A Cold Spring Harbor (11724) *(G-3526)*

Cisco Systems Inc 212 714-4000
1 Penn Plz Ste 3306 New York (10119) *(G-9012)*

CIT Aerospace LLC 212 461-5200
11 W 42nd St New York (10036) *(G-9013)*

Citation Healthcare Labels LLC (HQ) 631 293-4646
55 Engineers Rd Hauppauge (11788) *(G-5616)*

Citic Intl (usa) Travel Inc 718 888-9577
13633 37th Ave Ste 2a Flushing (11354) *(G-4844)*

Citigroup Inc 212 816-6000
388 Greenwich St New York (10013) *(G-9014)*

Citisource Industries Inc 212 683-1033
244 5th Ave Ste 229 New York (10001) *(G-9015)*

Citizen , The, Auburn Also called Auburn Publishing Co *(G-462)*

Citizen Publishing Corp 845 627-1414
119 Main St Ste 2 Nanuet (10954) *(G-8198)*

Citros Building Materials Co 718 779-0727
10514 Astoria Blvd East Elmhurst (11369) *(G-4105)*

Citrus and Allied Essences, Floral Park Also called C & A Service Inc *(G-4810)*

Citrus and Allied Essences Ltd (PA) 516 354-1200
65 S Tyson Ave Floral Park (11001) *(G-4812)*

City and State Ny LLC 212 268-0442
61 Broadway Rm 1315 New York (10006) *(G-9016)*

City Casting Corp 212 938-0511
151 W 46th St Fl 5 New York (10036) *(G-9017)*

City Cooling Enterprises Inc 718 331-7400
1624 61st St Brooklyn (11204) *(G-1664)*

City Evolutionary 718 861-7585
336 Barretto St Bronx (10474) *(G-1225)*

City Fashion, The, Brooklyn Also called Amj DOT LLC *(G-1505)*

City Gear Inc 914 450-4746
213 Taxter Rd Irvington (10533) *(G-6306)*

City Hats, New York Also called Beila Group Inc *(G-8750)*

City Jeans Inc 718 239-5353
845 White Plins Rd Frnt 1 Bronx (10473) *(G-1226)*

City Mason Corp 718 658-3796
10417 148th St Jamaica (11435) *(G-6434)*

City Newspaper 585 244-3329
250 N Goodman St Ste 1 Rochester (14607) *(G-13315)*

City of Jamestown 716 483-7545
200 E 3rd St Ste 4 Jamestown (14701) *(G-6501)*

City of Kingston 845 331-2490
91 E Strand St Kingston (12401) *(G-6686)*

City of New York 718 965-8787
4014 1st Ave Unit 3 Brooklyn (11232) *(G-1665)*

City of New York 718 236-2693
5602 19th Ave Brooklyn (11204) *(G-1666)*

City of Olean 716 376-5694
174 S 19th St Olean (14760) *(G-12228)*

City of Oneonta 607 433-3470
110 East St Oneonta (13820) *(G-12263)*

City Pattern Shop Inc 315 463-5239
4052 New Court Ave Syracuse (13206) *(G-14850)*

City Post Express Inc 718 995-8690
17518 147th Ave Jamaica (11434) *(G-6435)*

City Real Estate Book Inc 516 593-2949
9831 S Franklin Ave Valley Stream (11580) *(G-15337)*

City Signs Inc 718 375-5933
1940 Mcdonald Ave Brooklyn (11223) *(G-1667)*

A
L
P
H
A
B
E
T
I
C

City Sites Sportswear Inc (PA)...718 375-2990
2421 Mcdonald Ave Brooklyn (11223) ***(G-1668)***
City Sports Inc...212 730-2009
64 W 48th St Frnt B New York (10036) ***(G-9018)***
City Sports Imaging Inc...212 481-3600
20 E 46th St Rm 200 New York (10017) ***(G-9019)***
City Store Gates Mfg Corp...718 939-9700
1520 129th St College Point (11356) ***(G-3540)***
Citypharma Inc...917 832-6035
7316 Roosevelt Ave Jackson Heights (11372) ***(G-6419)***
Cityscape Ob/Gyn PLLC...212 683-3595
38 E 32nd St Fl 4 New York (10016) ***(G-9020)***
Citywire Americas, New York *Also called Citywire LLC* ***(G-9021)***
Citywire LLC...646 503-2216
1350 Ave Of The Am Frnt 4 New York (10019) ***(G-9021)***
Cives Corporation...315 287-2200
8 Church St Gouverneur (13642) ***(G-5318)***
Cives Corporation...315 543-2321
14331 Mill St Harrisville (13648) ***(G-5565)***
Cives Steel Company Nthrn Div, Gouverneur *Also called Cives Corporation* ***(G-5318)***
Civil Svc Rtred Employees Assn...718 937-0290
3427 Steinway St Ste 1 Long Island City (11101) ***(G-7185)***
CJ Component Products LLC...631 567-3733
624 Tower Mews Oakdale (11769) ***(G-12149)***
CJ Indstries A Div Smrset Inds, Gloversville *Also called Somerset Industries Inc* ***(G-5292)***
CJ Jewelry Inc...212 719-2464
2 W 47th St Ste 1106 New York (10036) ***(G-9022)***
CJ Motor Sports, Boonville *Also called C J Logging Equipment Inc* ***(G-1106)***
Cjk Manufacturing LLC...585 663-6370
160 Commerce Dr Rochester (14623) ***(G-13316)***
Cjn Machinery Corp...631 244-8030
917 Lincoln Ave Ste 13 Holbrook (11741) ***(G-5989)***
CK Coatings...585 502-0425
57 North St Ste 150 Le Roy (14482) ***(G-6897)***
CK Printing Corp...718 965-0388
267 41st St Brooklyn (11232) ***(G-1669)***
Clad Industries LLC...585 413-4359
1704 Wayneport Rd Ste 1 Macedon (14502) ***(G-7464)***
Clad Metal Specialties Inc...631 666-7750
1516 5th Industrial Ct Bay Shore (11706) ***(G-663)***
Claddagh Electronics Ltd...718 784-0571
1032 47th Rd Long Island City (11101) ***(G-7186)***
Clapper Hollow Designs Inc...518 234-9561
369 N Grand St Cobleskill (12043) ***(G-3497)***
Clara Papa...315 733-2660
1323 Blandina St 1 Utica (13501) ***(G-15243)***
Clarence Resins and Chemicals...716 406-9804
9585 Keller Rd Clarence Center (14032) ***(G-3444)***
Clark Botanicals Inc...914 826-4319
81 Pondfield Rd Ste 263 Bronxville (10708) ***(G-1400)***
Clark Concrete Co Inc (PA)...315 478-4101
434 E Brighton Ave Syracuse (13210) ***(G-14851)***
Clark Specialty Co Inc...607 776-3193
36 Delaware Ave Bath (14810) ***(G-632)***
Clark Trucking Co Div, Syracuse *Also called Clark Concrete Co Inc* ***(G-14851)***
Clarke Hess Communication RES...631 698-3350
3243 Route 112 Ste 1 Medford (11763) ***(G-7704)***
Clarsons Corp...585 235-8775
215 Tremont St Ste 8 Rochester (14608) ***(G-13317)***
Classic & Performance Spc...716 759-1800
80 Rotech Dr Lancaster (14086) ***(G-6801)***
Classic Album...718 388-2818
343 Lorimer St Brooklyn (11206) ***(G-1670)***
Classic Album LLC...718 388-2818
343 Lorimer St Brooklyn (11206) ***(G-1671)***
Classic Auto Crafts Inc...518 966-8003
6501 State Route 32 Greenville (12083) ***(G-5467)***
Classic Automation LLC (PA)...585 241-6010
800 Salt Rd Webster (14580) ***(G-15635)***
Classic Awnings Inc...716 649-0390
1 Elmview Ave Hamburg (14075) ***(G-5503)***
Classic Awnings and Tent Co, Hamburg *Also called Classic Awnings Inc* ***(G-5503)***
Classic Brass Inc...716 763-1400
2051 Stoneman Cir Lakewood (14750) ***(G-6780)***
Classic Business Solutions...212 563-9100
42 W 38th St Rm 1204 New York (10018) ***(G-9023)***
Classic Cabinets...845 357-4331
375 Spook Rock Rd Suffern (10901) ***(G-14759)***
Classic Collections Fine Art...914 591-4500
20 Haarlem Ave Ste 408 White Plains (10603) ***(G-15993)***
Classic Color Graphics Inc (PA)...516 822-9090
268 N Broadway Unit 8 Hicksville (11801) ***(G-5893)***
Classic Color Graphics Inc...516 822-9090
87 Broadway Hicksville (11801) ***(G-5894)***
Classic Creations Inc...516 498-1991
1 Linden Pl Ste 409 Great Neck (11021) ***(G-5376)***
Classic Designer Workshop Inc...212 730-8480
265 W 37th St Rm 703 New York (10018) ***(G-9024)***
Classic Flavors Fragrances Inc...212 777-0004
878 W End Ave Apt 12b New York (10025) ***(G-9025)***
Classic Hosiery Inc...845 342-6661
33 Mulberry St Ste 4 Middletown (10940) ***(G-7899)***
Classic Labels Inc...631 467-2300
217 River Ave Patchogue (11772) ***(G-12498)***
Classic Medallics Inc...718 392-5410
520 S Fulton Ave Mount Vernon (10550) ***(G-8131)***
Classic Sofa Ltd...212 620-0485
130 E 63rd St Ph B New York (10065) ***(G-9026)***
Classic Tool Design Inc...845 562-8700
31 Walnut St New Windsor (12553) ***(G-8363)***
Classic Tube, Lancaster *Also called Classic & Performance Spc* ***(G-6801)***
Classified Advertising, Troy *Also called Want-Ad Digest Inc* ***(G-15196)***
Classique Perfumes Inc...718 657-8200
139 01 Archer Ave Jamaica (11435) ***(G-6436)***
Classpass Inc (PA)...888 493-5953
275 7th Ave Fl 11 New York (10001) ***(G-9027)***
Classroom Inc...212 545-8400
123 William St 1201 New York (10038) ***(G-9028)***
Clayton Dubilier & Rice Fun (PA)...212 407-5200
375 Park Ave Fl 18 New York (10152) ***(G-9029)***
Clayville Ice Co Inc...315 839-5405
2514 Foundry Pl Clayville (13322) ***(G-3455)***
Clean All of Syracuse LLC...315 472-9189
838 Erie Blvd W Syracuse (13204) ***(G-14852)***
Clean Beauty Collective Inc...212 269-1387
45 W 45th St Fl 2 New York (10036) ***(G-9030)***
Clean Gas Systems Inc...631 467-1600
368 Veterans Memorial Hwy 3a Commack (11725) ***(G-3583)***
Clean Room Depot Inc...631 589-3033
1730 Church St Holbrook (11741) ***(G-5990)***
Cleancult, New York *Also called Bocks Inc* ***(G-8828)***
Cleaning Tech Group LLC...716 665-2340
9 N Main St Jamestown (14701) ***(G-6502)***
Cleanroom Systems Inc...315 452-7400
7000 Performance Dr North Syracuse (13212) ***(G-12038)***
Cleanse TEC...718 346-9111
360 Oser Ave Hauppauge (11788) ***(G-5617)***
Clear Cast Technologies Inc (PA)...914 945-0848
99 N Water St Ossining (10562) ***(G-12403)***
Clear View Bag Company Inc...518 458-7153
5 Burdick Dr Albany (12205) ***(G-61)***
Clearcove Systems Inc...585 734-3012
7910 Rae Blvd Victor (14564) ***(G-15398)***
Clearstep Technologies LLC...315 952-3628
213 Emann Dr Camillus (13031) ***(G-3108)***
Clearview Glass & Mirror, Monroe *Also called G & M Clearview Inc* ***(G-8021)***
Clearview Social Inc...801 414-7675
77 Goodell St Ste 430 Buffalo (14203) ***(G-2698)***
Clearwater Paper Corporation...315 287-1200
4921 State Highway 58 Gouverneur (13642) ***(G-5319)***
Clearwood Custom Carpentry and...315 432-8422
617 W Manlius St Ste 1 East Syracuse (13057) ***(G-4204)***
Cleary Custom Cabinets Inc...516 939-2475
794 S Broadway Hicksville (11801) ***(G-5895)***
Clemente Latham Concrete, Latham *Also called Callanan Industries Inc* ***(G-6851)***
Clemente Latham Concrete Corp...518 374-2222
1245 Kings Rd Schenectady (12303) ***(G-14257)***
Clemente Latham North Div, Schenectady *Also called Clemente Latham Concrete Corp* ***(G-14257)***
Clements Burrville Sawmill...315 782-4549
18181 Van Allen Rd N Watertown (13601) ***(G-15565)***
Clerio Vision Inc (PA)...617 216-7881
312 Susquehanna Rd Rochester (14618) ***(G-13318)***
Cleveland Biolabs Inc...716 849-6810
73 High St Buffalo (14203) ***(G-2699)***
Clever Devices Ltd (PA)...516 433-6100
300 Crossways Park Dr Woodbury (11797) ***(G-16167)***
Clever Goats Media LLC...917 512-0340
40 Exchange Pl Ste 1602 New York (10005) ***(G-9031)***
Click It Inc...631 686-2900
85 Corporate Dr Hauppauge (11788) ***(G-5618)***
Clifford H Jones Inc...716 693-2444
608 Young St Tonawanda (14150) ***(G-15097)***
Cliffstar LLC (HQ)...716 366-6100
1 Cliffstar Dr Dunkirk (14048) ***(G-4052)***
Climatronics Corp (HQ)...541 471-7111
606 Johnson Ave Ste 28 Bohemia (11716) ***(G-987)***
Climax Packaging Inc...315 376-8000
7840 State Route 26 Lowville (13367) ***(G-7414)***
Clinique Laboratories LLC (HQ)...212 572-4200
767 5th Ave Fl 41 New York (10153) ***(G-9032)***
Clinique Laboratories, Inc., New York *Also called Clinique Laboratories LLC* ***(G-9032)***
Clinique Services Inc (HQ)...212 572-4200
767 5th Ave Fl Conc6 New York (10153) ***(G-9033)***
Clinton Signs Inc...585 482-1620
1407 Empire Blvd Webster (14580) ***(G-15636)***
Clinton Vineyards Inc...845 266-5372
450 Schultzville Rd Clinton Corners (12514) ***(G-3487)***
Clintons Ditch Coop Co Inc...315 699-2695
8478 Pardee Rd Cicero (13039) ***(G-3417)***
Clintrak Clinical Labeling S (PA)...888 479-3900
2800 Veterans Hwy Bohemia (11716) ***(G-988)***
Clo-Shure Intl Inc (PA)...212 268-5029
224 W 35th St Ste 1000 New York (10001) ***(G-9034)***

Clopay Ames True Temper (HQ) 212 957-5096
712 5th Ave New York (10019) *(G-9035)*
Closet Systems Group, The, Brooklyn *Also called Designs By Robert Scott Inc (G-1738)*
Cloud Printing 212 775-0888
66 W Broadway Frnt E New York (10007) *(G-9036)*
Cloud Rock Group LLC 516 967-6023
525 Bryant Ave Roslyn (11576) *(G-14040)*
Cloud Toronto Inc 408 569-4542
1967 Wehrle Dr Ste 1 Williamsville (14221) *(G-16127)*
Cloudscale365 Inc (PA) 888 608-6245
30 Jericho Executive Plz Jericho (11753) *(G-6574)*
Cloudsense Inc 917 880-6195
295 Madison Ave Fl 39 New York (10017) *(G-9037)*
Clover Wire Forming Co Inc 914 375-0400
1021 Saw Mill River Rd Yonkers (10710) *(G-16296)*
Clovis Point, Queens Village *Also called East End Vineyards LLC (G-13019)*
Clp Holdings LLC (PA) 917 846-5094
575 Madison Ave Ste 1006 New York (10022) *(G-9038)*
Clp Pb LLC (PA) 212 340-8100
1290 Ave Of The Amrcas New York (10104) *(G-9039)*
Clyde Duneier Inc (PA) 212 398-1122
415 Madison Ave Fl 6 New York (10017) *(G-9040)*
Cmb Wireless Group LLC (PA) 631 750-4700
116 Wilbur Pl Bohemia (11716) *(G-989)*
Cmc-Kuhnke Inc 518 694-3310
90 State St Ste 601 Albany (12207) *(G-62)*
Cmnty Corporation 646 712-9949
228 E 45th St Rm 9e New York (10017) *(G-9041)*
Cmp Advnced Mech Sltons NY LLC 607 352-1712
90 Bevier St Binghamton (13904) *(G-867)*
Cmp Export Co Inc 518 434-3147
413 N Pearl St Albany (12207) *(G-63)*
Cmp Industries LLC (PA) 518 434-3147
413 N Pearl St Albany (12207) *(G-64)*
Cmp Industries LLC 518 434-3147
413 N Pearl St Albany (12207) *(G-65)*
Cmp Media, New York *Also called Ubm LLC (G-11575)*
Cmp New York, Binghamton *Also called Cmp Advnced Mech Sltons NY LLC (G-867)*
CMS Heat Transfer Division Inc 631 968-0084
273 Knickerbocker Ave Bohemia (11716) *(G-990)*
CMX Media LLC 917 793-5831
1271 Av Of The Americas New York (10020) *(G-9042)*
CN Group Incorporated 914 358-5690
76 Mamaroneck Ave White Plains (10601) *(G-15994)*
Cnc Manufacturing Corp 718 728-6800
3214 49th St Long Island City (11103) *(G-7187)*
Cnhi LLC 585 798-1400
541-543 Main St Medina (14103) *(G-7732)*
Cnhi LLC 716 693-1000
473 3rd St Ste 201 Niagara Falls (14301) *(G-11915)*
Cnhi LLC 716 282-2311
473 3rd St Ste 201 Niagara Falls (14301) *(G-11916)*
Cnhi LLC 716 439-9222
135 Main St Ste 1 Lockport (14094) *(G-7065)*
Cni Meat & Produce Inc 516 599-5929
500 W Merrick Rd Valley Stream (11580) *(G-15338)*
Cntry Cross Communications LLC 386 758-9696
106 W 3rd St Ste 106 # 106 Jamestown (14701) *(G-6503)*
Cnv Architectural Coatings Inc 718 418-9584
538 Johnson Ave Brooklyn (11237) *(G-1672)*
CNY Business Review Inc 315 472-3104
211 W Jefferson St Ste 1 Syracuse (13202) *(G-14853)*
CNy Business Solutions 315 733-5031
502 Court St Ste 206 Utica (13502) *(G-15244)*
Cnyshirts 315 432-1789
6392 Deere Rd Ste 1 Syracuse (13206) *(G-14854)*
Co-Op City News, New Rochelle *Also called Hagedorn Communications Inc (G-8336)*
Co-Optics America Lab Inc 607 432-0557
297 River Street Svc Rd Service Oneonta (13820) *(G-12264)*
Co-Optics Groups, The, Oneonta *Also called Co-Optics America Lab Inc (G-12264)*
Coach Inc 718 760-0624
90 Queens Blvd Elmhurst (11373) *(G-4333)*
Coach Services Inc (HQ) 212 594-1850
10 Hudson Yards New York (10001) *(G-9043)*
Coalition On Positive Health 212 633-2500
1751 Park Ave Fl 4 New York (10035) *(G-9044)*
Coast To Coast Circuits Inc 585 254-2980
205 Lagrange Ave Rochester (14613) *(G-13319)*
Coastal Pipeline Products Corp 631 369-4000
55 Twomey Ave Calverton (11933) *(G-3078)*
Coastal Publications Inc 631 725-1700
22 Division St Sag Harbor (11963) *(G-14097)*
Coastel Cable Tools Inc 315 471-5361
344 E Brighton Ave Syracuse (13210) *(G-14855)*
Coastel Cable Tools Intl, Syracuse *Also called Coastel Cable Tools Inc (G-14855)*
Coated Abrasive Division, Watervliet *Also called Saint-Gobain Abrasives Inc (G-15605)*
Coating Technology Inc 585 546-7170
800 Saint Paul St Rochester (14605) *(G-13320)*
Cobbe Industries Inc 716 287-2661
1397 Harris Hollow Rd Gerry (14740) *(G-5170)*
Cobblestone Frm Winery Vinyrd 315 549-1004
5102 State Route 89 Romulus (14541) *(G-13878)*
Cobey Inc (PA) 716 362-9550
1 Ship Canal Pkwy Buffalo (14218) *(G-2700)*
Cobham Holdings Inc (HQ) 716 662-0006
10 Cobham Dr Orchard Park (14127) *(G-12345)*
Cobham Holdings US Inc., Orchard Park *Also called Cobham Holdings Inc (G-12345)*
Cobham Long Island Inc (HQ) 516 694-6700
35 S Service Rd Plainview (11803) *(G-12669)*
Cobham Long Island Inc 631 231-9100
350 Kennedy Dr Hauppauge (11788) *(G-5619)*
Cobham Management Services Inc 716 662-0006
10 Centre Dr Orchard Park (14127) *(G-12346)*
Cobham Mission Systems (HQ) 716 662-0006
10 Centre Dr Orchard Park (14127) *(G-12347)*
Cobham Mission Systems Div, Orchard Park *Also called Cobham Management Services Inc (G-12346)*
Cobham Semiconductor Solutions, Plainview *Also called Aeroflex Incorporated (G-12660)*
Cobico Productions Inc 347 417-5883
344 E 50th St Apt 1b New York (10022) *(G-9045)*
Cobleskill Stone Products Inc 518 295-7121
163 Eastern Ave Schoharie (12157) *(G-14321)*
Cobleskill Stone Products Inc (PA) 518 234-0221
112 Rock Rd Cobleskill (12043) *(G-3498)*
Cobleskill Stone Products Inc 607 432-8321
57 Ceperley Ave Oneonta (13820) *(G-12265)*
Cobleskill Stone Products Inc 607 637-4271
1565 Green Flats Rd Hancock (13783) *(G-5535)*
Cobra Manufacturing Corp 845 514-2505
68 Leggs Mills Rd Lake Katrine (12449) *(G-6763)*
Cobra Operating Industries LLC 607 639-1700
37 Main St Afton (13730) *(G-7)*
Cobra Systems Inc 845 338-6675
2669 New York 32 Bloomington (12411) *(G-951)*
Coca-Cola, Horseheads *Also called Rochester Coca Cola Bottling (G-6135)*
Coca-Cola, Rochester *Also called Rochester Coca Cola Bottling (G-13685)*
Coca-Cola Bottling Company 518 483-0422
15 Ida Pkwy Malone (12953) *(G-7484)*
Coca-Cola Btlg Co Buffalo Inc 716 874-4610
200 Milens Rd Tonawanda (14150) *(G-15098)*
Coca-Cola Btlg Co of NY Inc 845 562-3037
10 Heampstead Rd New Windsor (12553) *(G-8364)*
Coca-Cola Btlg Co of NY Inc 914 789-1572
111 Fairview Pk Dr Ste 1 Elmsford (10523) *(G-4400)*
Coca-Cola Btlg Co of NY Inc 518 459-2010
38 Warehouse Row Albany (12205) *(G-66)*
Coca-Cola Btlg Co of NY Inc 718 416-7575
5840 Borden Ave Maspeth (11378) *(G-7599)*
Coca-Cola Btlg Co of NY Inc 315 457-9221
298 Farrell Rd Syracuse (13209) *(G-14856)*
Coca-Cola Btlg Co of NY Inc 631 434-3535
375 Wireless Blvd Hauppauge (11788) *(G-5620)*
Coca-Cola Btlg Co of NY Inc 718 420-6800
400 Western Ave Staten Island (10303) *(G-14639)*
Coca-Cola Btlg Co of NY Inc 914 789-1580
115 Fairview Pk Dr Ste 1 Elmsford (10523) *(G-4401)*
Coca-Cola Refreshments USA Inc 718 401-5200
977 E 149th St Bronx (10455) *(G-1227)*
Coca-Cola Refreshments USA Inc 315 785-8907
22614 County Route 51 Watertown (13601) *(G-15566)*
Coca-Cola Refreshments USA Inc 914 592-0806
3 Skyline Dr Hawthorne (10532) *(G-5811)*
Coccadotts Inc 518 438-4937
1179 Central Ave Albany (12205) *(G-67)*
Cochecton Mills Inc (PA) 845 932-8282
30 Depot Rd Cochecton (12726) *(G-3501)*
Cockpit Usa Inc 212 575-1616
15 W 39th St Fl 12 New York (10018) *(G-9046)*
Cocktail Crate LLC 718 316-2033
2323 Borden Ave Long Island City (11101) *(G-7188)*
Coco Architectureal Grilles 631 482-9449
173 Allen Blvd Farmingdale (11735) *(G-4600)*
Coco Rico Southeast, Bronx *Also called Good-O-Beverage Inc (G-1268)*
Coda Media Inc 917 478-2565
108 W 39th St Rm 1000 New York (10018) *(G-9047)*
Coda Story, New York *Also called Coda Media Inc (G-9047)*
Code Red Trading LLC 347 782-2608
995 E 8th St Fl 3 Brooklyn (11230) *(G-1673)*
Codesters Inc 646 232-1025
900 Broadway Ste 903 New York (10003) *(G-9048)*
Codinos Limited Inc 518 372-3308
704 Corporation Park # 5 Schenectady (12302) *(G-14258)*
Cody Printing Corp 718 651-8854
3728 56th St Woodside (11377) *(G-16202)*
Coe Displays Inc 718 937-5658
4301 22nd St Ste 603 Long Island City (11101) *(G-7189)*
Coecles Hbr Marina & Boat Yard 631 749-0856
68 Cartwright Rd Shelter Island (11964) *(G-14385)*
Coffee Holding Co Inc (PA) 718 832-0800
3475 Victory Blvd Ste 4 Staten Island (10314) *(G-14640)*
Coffee Holding Company Inc 718 832-0800
4425 1st Ave Brooklyn (11232) *(G-1674)*
Coffing, Getzville *Also called Columbus McKinnon Corporation (G-5175)*

ALPHABETIC

Cofire Paving Corporation...............718 463-1403
  12030 28th Ave Flushing (11354) *(G-4845)*

Cognigen Acquisition, Buffalo *Also called Cognigen Corporation (G-2701)*

Cognigen Corporation...............716 633-3463
  1780 Wehrle Dr Ste 110 Buffalo (14221) *(G-2701)*

Cognitiveflow Sensor Tech...............631 513-9369
  9 Melville Ct Stony Brook (11790) *(G-14737)*

Cognition Inc...............347 692-0640
  1407 Broadway Fl 24 New York (10018) *(G-9049)*

Cohber Press Inc (PA)...............585 475-9100
  1000 John St West Henrietta (14586) *(G-15789)*

Cohens Bakery Inc...............716 892-8149
  1132 Broadway St Buffalo (14212) *(G-2702)*

Coil Craft Inc (PA)...............718 369-1210
  10324 99th St Ozone Park (11417) *(G-12459)*

Coil Stamping Inc...............631 588-3040
  1340 Lincoln Ave Ste 1 Holbrook (11741) *(G-5991)*

Coinmach Service Corp...............516 349-8555
  303 Sunnyside Blvd # 70 Plainview (11803) *(G-12670)*

Colad Group LLC...............716 961-1776
  693 Seneca St Fl 5 Buffalo (14210) *(G-2703)*

Colarusso Blacktop Co, Hudson *Also called A Colarusso and Son Inc (G-6146)*

Colburns AC Rfrgn...............716 569-3695
  17 White Dr Frewsburg (14738) *(G-5050)*

Cold Mix Manufacturing Corp...............718 463-1444
  65 Edison Ave Mount Vernon (10550) *(G-8132)*

Cold Point Corporation...............315 339-2331
  7500 Cold Point Dr Rome (13440) *(G-13847)*

Cold Springs R & D Inc...............315 413-1237
  1207 Van Vleck Rd Ste A Syracuse (13209) *(G-14857)*

Colden Closet LLC...............716 713-6125
  1375 Boies Rd East Aurora (14052) *(G-4084)*

Coldstream Group Inc (PA)...............914 698-5959
  420 Railroad Way Mamaroneck (10543) *(G-7504)*

Colgat-Plmolive Centl Amer Inc (HQ)...............212 310-2000
  300 Park Ave New York (10022) *(G-9050)*

Colgate-Palmolive Company (PA)...............212 310-2000
  300 Park Ave Fl 3 New York (10022) *(G-9051)*

Colgate-Palmolive Company...............718 506-3961
  21818 100th Ave Queens Village (11429) *(G-13018)*

Colgate-Palmolive Nj Inc...............212 310-2000
  300 Park Ave Fl 8 New York (10022) *(G-9052)*

Coliseum, New York *Also called Plugg LLC (G-10857)*

Collaborative Coffee Source, Mohegan Lake *Also called CCS North America LLC (G-8009)*

Collection Xiix Ltd (PA)...............212 686-8990
  1370 Broadway Fl 17 New York (10018) *(G-9053)*

College Calendar Company...............315 768-8242
  148 Clinton St Whitesboro (13492) *(G-16079)*

Collegebound Teen Magazine, Staten Island *Also called Ramholtz Publishing Inc (G-14699)*

Collegeville Imagineering, Bay Shore *Also called Rubies Costume Company Inc (G-711)*

Collinite Corporation...............315 732-2282
  1520 Lincoln Ave Utica (13502) *(G-15245)*

Collinite Wax, Utica *Also called Collinite Corporation (G-15245)*

Collins Pet & Garden Center, Malone *Also called Scotts Feed Inc (G-7489)*

Colonial Electric, Farmingdale *Also called Colonial Precision Machinery (G-4601)*

Colonial Group LLC...............516 349-8010
  150 Express St Ste 2 Plainview (11803) *(G-12671)*

Colonial Label, Patchogue *Also called Depot Label Company Inc (G-12499)*

Colonial Label Systems Inc...............631 254-0111
  50 Corbin Ave Ste L Bay Shore (11706) *(G-664)*

Colonial Precision Machinery...............631 249-0738
  134 Rome St Farmingdale (11735) *(G-4601)*

Colonial Rapid, Bay Shore *Also called Colonial Label Systems Inc (G-664)*

Colonial Redi Record Corp...............718 972-7433
  1225 36th St Brooklyn (11218) *(G-1675)*

Colonial Tag & Label Co Inc...............516 482-0508
  425 Northern Blvd Ste 36 Great Neck (11021) *(G-5377)*

Colonial Tanning Corporation (PA)...............518 725-7171
  8 Wilson St 810 Gloversville (12078) *(G-5281)*

Colonial Wire & Cable Co Inc (PA)...............631 234-8500
  40 Engineers Rd Hauppauge (11788) *(G-5621)*

Colonial Wire Cable Co NJ (PA)...............631 234-8500
  40 Engineers Rd Hauppauge (11788) *(G-5622)*

Colonie Block and Supply Co...............518 869-8411
  124 Lincoln Ave Colonie (12205) *(G-3573)*

Colonie Plastics Corp...............631 434-6969
  188 Candlewood Rd Bay Shore (11706) *(G-665)*

Colony Holdings Intl LLC...............212 868-2800
  131 W 35th St Fl 6 New York (10001) *(G-9054)*

Color Card LLC...............631 232-1300
  1065 Islip Ave Central Islip (11722) *(G-3269)*

Color Carton Corp...............718 665-0840
  341 Canal Pl Bronx (10451) *(G-1228)*

Color Fx, New York *Also called Joseph Industries Inc (G-10027)*

Color Industries LLC...............718 392-8301
  3002 48th Ave Ste H Long Island City (11101) *(G-7190)*

Color Pro Sign, Schenectady *Also called Ray Sign Inc (G-14298)*

Color Story, Yonkers *Also called Leser Enterprises Ltd (G-16327)*

Color Unlimited Inc...............212 802-7547
  244 5th Ave Frnt New York (10001) *(G-9055)*

Color-Aid Corporation...............212 673-5500
  38 La Fayette St Ste 2 Hudson Falls (12839) *(G-6184)*

Colorfast...............212 929-2440
  121 Varick St Fl 9 New York (10013) *(G-9056)*

Colorfully Yours Inc...............631 242-8600
  11 Grant Ave Bay Shore (11706) *(G-666)*

Colorpak, Melville *Also called Poly-Pak Industries Inc (G-7816)*

Colors In Optics Ltd...............718 845-0300
  120 Broadway G New Hyde Park (11040) *(G-8257)*

Colorspec Coatings Intl Inc...............631 472-8251
  1716 Church St Holbrook (11741) *(G-5992)*

Colortex Inc...............212 564-2000
  1202 Lexington Ave 115 New York (10028) *(G-9057)*

Columbia, Macedon *Also called Water Technologies Inc (G-7471)*

Columbia Button Nailhead Corp...............718 386-3414
  306 Stagg St 316 Brooklyn (11206) *(G-1676)*

Columbia Cabinets LLC (PA)...............212 972-7550
  20 Maple Ave Ste F Armonk (10504) *(G-396)*

Columbia Cabinets LLC...............518 283-1700
  489 Broadway Ste 2 Saratoga Springs (12866) *(G-14170)*

Columbia Daily Spectator...............212 854-9550
  2875 Broadway Ste 303 New York (10025) *(G-9058)*

Columbia Pool Accessories Inc...............718 993-0389
  111 Bruckner Blvd Bronx (10454) *(G-1229)*

Columbia Records Inc...............212 833-8000
  25 Madison Ave Fl 19 New York (10010) *(G-9059)*

Columbia Seal N Sew, Brooklyn *Also called Dlx Industries Inc (G-1753)*

Columbia Univ Publications, New York *Also called Trust of Colum Unive In The Ci (G-11552)*

Columbia University Press (HQ)...............212 459-0600
  61 W 62nd St Fl 3 New York (10023) *(G-9060)*

Columbia University Press...............212 459-0600
  61 W 62nd St Fl 3 New York (10023) *(G-9061)*

Columbia University Press...............212 459-0600
  61 W 62nd St Fl 3 New York (10023) *(G-9062)*

Columbus Accessories, New York *Also called Columbus Trading Corp (G-9063)*

Columbus Baking Co, Syracuse *Also called George Retzos (G-14904)*

Columbus McKinnon, Getzville *Also called C M Insurance Company Inc (G-5173)*

Columbus McKinnon Corporation (PA)...............716 689-5400
  205 Crosspoint Pkwy Getzville (14068) *(G-5174)*

Columbus McKinnon Corporation...............716 689-5400
  205 Crosspoint Pkwy Getzville (14068) *(G-5175)*

Columbus McKinnon Corporation...............716 689-5400
  205 Crosspoint Pkwy Getzville (14068) *(G-5176)*

Columbus Trading Corp...............212 564-1780
  120 W 31st St Rm 600 New York (10001) *(G-9063)*

Columbus Woodworking Inc...............607 674-4546
  164 Casey Cheese Fctry Rd Sherburne (13460) *(G-14389)*

Comairco Equipment Inc (HQ)...............716 656-0211
  3250 Union Rd Cheektowaga (14227) *(G-3341)*

Comander Terminals LLC...............516 922-7600
  1 Commander Sq Oyster Bay (11771) *(G-12446)*

Comax Aromatics Corporation...............631 249-0505
  130 Baylis Rd Melville (11747) *(G-7768)*

Comax Flavors, Melville *Also called Comax Manufacturing Corp (G-7769)*

Comax Manufacturing Corp (PA)...............631 249-0505
  130 Baylis Rd Melville (11747) *(G-7769)*

Combe Incorporated (PA)...............914 694-5454
  1101 Westchester Ave White Plains (10604) *(G-15995)*

Combine Graphics Corp...............212 695-4044
  10714 Queens Blvd Forest Hills (11375) *(G-4918)*

Comboland Packing Corp...............718 858-4200
  2 Cumberland St Brooklyn (11205) *(G-1677)*

Comco Plastics Inc...............718 849-9000
  11 Stepar Pl Huntington Station (11746) *(G-6242)*

Comely International Trdg Inc...............212 683-1240
  303 5th Ave Rm 1903 New York (10016) *(G-9064)*

Comerford Collection, Bridgehampton *Also called Comerford Hennessy At Home Inc (G-1165)*

Comerford Hennessy At Home Inc...............631 537-6200
  2442 Main St Bridgehampton (11932) *(G-1165)*

Comet Flasher Inc (PA)...............716 821-9595
  1 Babcock St Buffalo (14210) *(G-2704)*

Comfort Care Textiles Inc (HQ)...............631 543-0531
  368 Veterans Memorial Hwy # 5 Commack (11725) *(G-3584)*

Comfortex Corporation (HQ)...............518 273-3333
  21 Elm St Watervliet (12189) *(G-15600)*

Comfortex Window Fashions, Watervliet *Also called Comfortex Corporation (G-15600)*

Comgraph Sales Service...............716 601-7243
  7491 Clinton St Elma (14059) *(G-4317)*

Comint Apparel Group LLC...............212 947-7474
  463 7th Ave Fl 4 New York (10018) *(G-9065)*

Command Components Corporation...............631 666-4411
  6 Cherry St Bay Shore (11706) *(G-667)*

Command Systems Division, Farmingdale *Also called Telephonics Corporation (G-4753)*

Comme-Ci Comme-CA AP Group...............631 300-1035
  380 Rabo Dr Hauppauge (11788) *(G-5623)*

Commentary Inc...............212 891-1400
  165 E 56th St Fl 16 New York (10022) *(G-9066)*

Commentary Magazine, New York *Also called American Jewish Committee (G-8553)*

Commerce Offset Ltd...............914 769-6671
  657 Commerce St Thornwood (10594) *(G-15068)*

Commerce Spring Corp 631 293-4844
  143 Allen Blvd Farmingdale (11735) *(G-4602)*
Commercehub Inc (HQ) 518 810-0700
  201 Fuller Rd Fl 6 Albany (12203) *(G-68)*
Commercial Communications LLC 845 343-9078
  14 Montgomery St Middletown (10940) *(G-7900)*
Commercial Concrete, Westbury *Also called New York Ready Mix Inc (G-15912)*
Commercial Display Design LLC 607 336-7353
  58 Browne St Oneonta (13820) *(G-12266)*
Commercial Fabrics Inc 716 694-0641
  908 Niagara Falls Blvd North Tonawanda (14120) *(G-12062)*
Commercial Gaskets New York 212 244-8130
  247 W 38th St Rm 409 New York (10018) *(G-9067)*
Commercial Lubricants Moove 718 720-3434
  229 Arlington Ave Staten Island (10303) *(G-14641)*
Commercial Press Inc 315 274-0028
  6589 Us Highway 11 Canton (13617) *(G-3164)*
Commercial Print & Imaging 716 597-0100
  4778 Main St Buffalo (14226) *(G-2705)*
Commitment 2000 Inc 716 439-1206
  105 Msgr Valente Dr Buffalo (14206) *(G-2706)*
Committee For Color & Trends, New York *Also called Cct Inc (G-8940)*
Commodity Resource Corporation 585 538-9500
  2773 Caledonia Leroy Rd Caledonia (14423) *(G-3069)*
Commodore, Bloomfield *Also called Dolco LLC (G-946)*
Commodore Chocolatier USA Inc 845 561-3960
  482 Broadway Newburgh (12550) *(G-11861)*
Commodore Machine Co Inc 585 657-6916
  26 Maple Ave Bloomfield (14469) *(G-943)*
Commodore Manufacutring Corp 718 788-2600
  3913 2nd Ave Brooklyn (11232) *(G-1678)*
Commodore Tool, Brooklyn *Also called Commodore Manufacutring Corp (G-1678)*
Common Good LLC 646 246-1441
  135 Kent Ave Brooklyn (11249) *(G-1679)*
Common Sense Natural Soap, Cambridge *Also called Robert Racine (G-3096)*
Common Sense Natural Soap 518 677-0224
  7 Pearl St Cambridge (12816) *(G-3093)*
Commonweal Foundation Inc 212 662-4200
  475 Riverside Dr Rm 405 New York (10115) *(G-9068)*
Commonweal Magazine, New York *Also called Commonweal Foundation Inc (G-9068)*
Commonwealth Home Fashion Inc 514 384-8290
  31 Station Rd Willsboro (12996) *(G-16150)*
Commonwealth Toy Novelty Inc (PA) 212 242-4070
  875 6th Ave Rm 910 New York (10001) *(G-9069)*
Communication Power Corp 631 434-7306
  80 Davids Dr Ste 3 Hauppauge (11788) *(G-5624)*
Communications Systems Div, Farmingdale *Also called Telephonics Corporation (G-4751)*
Community Cpons Frnchising Inc 516 277-1968
  100 Carney St Ste 2 Glen Cove (11542) *(G-5190)*
Community Directory, Brooklyn *Also called Business Directory Inc (G-1632)*
Community Glass Inc 607 737-8860
  139 W 17th St Elmira (14903) *(G-4344)*
Community Magazine, Brooklyn *Also called Bnei Aram Soba Inc (G-1599)*
Community Media Group Inc 315 789-3333
  218 Genesee St Geneva (14456) *(G-5151)*
Community Media Group LLC (PA) 518 439-4949
  125 Adams St Delmar (12054) *(G-3968)*
Community Media LLC 212 229-1890
  515 Canal St Fl 1 New York (10013) *(G-9070)*
Community News Group LLC (PA) 718 260-2500
  1 Metrotech Ctr Fl 10 Brooklyn (11201) *(G-1680)*
Community Newspaper Group LLC 607 432-1000
  102 Chestnut St Oneonta (13820) *(G-12267)*
Community Newspaper Group LLC 518 565-4114
  170 Margaret St Plattsburgh (12901) *(G-12743)*
Community Newspapers, Moravia *Also called Republican Registrar Inc (G-8083)*
Community Playthings, Chester *Also called Community Products LLC (G-3373)*
Community Playthings, Elka Park *Also called Church Communities NY Inc (G-4302)*
Community Playthings, Elka Park *Also called Church Communities NY Inc (G-4303)*
COMMUNITY PLAYTHINGS AND RIFTO, Rifton *Also called Community Products LLC (G-13167)*
Community Products LLC (PA) 845 658-8799
  101 Woodcrest Dr Rifton (12471) *(G-13167)*
Community Products LLC 845 658-7720
  359 Gibson Hill Rd Chester (10918) *(G-3373)*
Community Products LLC 845 572-3433
  24 Elizabeth Dr Chester (10918) *(G-3374)*
Community Products LLC 845 658-8351
  2032 Route 213 St Rifton (12471) *(G-13168)*
Community Products LLC 518 589-5103
  2255 Platte Clove Rd Elka Park (12427) *(G-4304)*
Compac Development Corporation 631 881-4903
  91 Heartland Blvd Edgewood (11717) *(G-4265)*
Compar Manufacturing Corp 212 304-2777
  308 Dyckman St New York (10034) *(G-9071)*
Compass Printing Plus 518 523-3308
  42 Main St Saranac Lake (12983) *(G-14157)*
Compelld Inc 917 494-4462
  57 Reade St Apt 10f New York (10007) *(G-9072)*

Competicion Mower Repair 516 280-6584
  75 Windsor Ave Mineola (11501) *(G-7966)*
Complemar Print LLC 716 875-7238
  3034 Genesee St Buffalo (14225) *(G-2707)*
Complete Fiber Solutions Inc 718 828-8900
  1459 Bassett Ave Bronx (10461) *(G-1230)*
Complete Orthopedic Svcs Inc 516 357-9113
  325 Merrick Ave Ste 1 East Meadow (11554) *(G-4133)*
Complete Publishing Solutions 212 242-7321
  350 W 51st St Apt 13b New York (10019) *(G-9073)*
Complete SEC & Contrls Inc 631 421-7200
  100 Hillwood Dr Huntington Station (11746) *(G-6243)*
Complex Biosystems Inc 315 464-8007
  8417 Oswego Rd 201 Baldwinsville (13027) *(G-545)*
Complex Magazine, New York *Also called CMX Media LLC (G-9042)*
Complex Media Inc (PA) 917 793-5831
  229 W 43rd St Fl 10 New York (10036) *(G-9074)*
Composite Forms Inc 914 937-1808
  7 Merritt St Port Chester (10573) *(G-12815)*
Composite Materials Division, New York *Also called Mitsubishi Chemical Amer Inc (G-10484)*
Compositech Ltd 516 835-1458
  4 Fairbanks Blvd Woodbury (11797) *(G-16168)*
Compoz A Puzzle Inc 516 883-2311
  2 Secatoag Ave Port Washington (11050) *(G-12869)*
Comprehensive Dental Tech 607 467-4456
  Rr 1 Box 69 Hancock (13783) *(G-5536)*
Comps Inc 516 676-0400
  3 School St Ste 101b Glen Cove (11542) *(G-5191)*
Compucolor Associates Inc 516 358-0000
  2200 Marcus Ave Ste C New Hyde Park (11042) *(G-8258)*
Computer Conversions Corp 631 261-3300
  6 Dunton Ct East Northport (11731) *(G-4143)*
Computer Instruments Corp 516 876-8400
  963a Brush Hollow Rd Westbury (11590) *(G-15874)*
Computerized Metal Bending Ser 631 249-1177
  91 Cabot St Unit A West Babylon (11704) *(G-15704)*
Comsec Ventures International 518 523-1600
  17 Tamarack Ave Lake Placid (12946) *(G-6766)*
Comstock Food, Leicester *Also called Seneca Foods Corporation (G-6911)*
Comstock Foods Division, South Dayton *Also called Birds Eye Foods Inc (G-14505)*
Comtech PST Corp (HQ) 631 777-8900
  105 Baylis Rd Melville (11747) *(G-7770)*
Comtech Telecom Corp (PA) 631 962-7000
  68 S Service Rd Ste 230 Melville (11747) *(G-7771)*
Con Rel Auto Electric Inc 518 356-1646
  3637 Carman Rd Schenectady (12303) *(G-14259)*
Con-Tees Custom Printing Ltd 914 664-0251
  514 Union Ave Mount Vernon (10550) *(G-8133)*
Conax Technologies LLC (PA) 716 684-4500
  2300 Walden Ave Buffalo (14225) *(G-2708)*
Concealed Baseboard Htg Co LLC 212 378-6710
  48 Wall St Ste 1100 New York (10005) *(G-9075)*
Concept Components, Bohemia *Also called McGuigan Inc (G-1045)*
Concept Nyc, New York *Also called Concepts Nyc Inc (G-9076)*
Concept One Accessories, New York *Also called Uspa Accessories LLC (G-11631)*
Concept Printing and Promotion, Nyack *Also called Concept Printing Inc (G-12139)*
Concept Printing Inc 845 353-4040
  40 Lydecker St Nyack (10960) *(G-12139)*
Conceptronic, Central Islip *Also called Cvd Equipment Corporation (G-3272)*
Concepts In Wood of CNY 315 463-8084
  4021 New Court Ave Syracuse (13206) *(G-14858)*
Concepts Nyc Inc 212 244-1033
  25 W 39th St Lbby A New York (10018) *(G-9076)*
Conco Division, Lynbrook *Also called Russell Industries Inc (G-7437)*
Concord Express Cargo Inc 718 276-7200
  17214 119th Ave Jamaica (11434) *(G-6437)*
Concord Jewelry Mfg Co LLC 212 719-4030
  64 W 48th St Ste 1004 New York (10036) *(G-9077)*
Concord Jwlry Mfrs, New York *Also called Concord Jewelry Mfg Co LLC (G-9077)*
Concord Settings, New York *Also called Kaprielian Enterprises Inc (G-10068)*
Concorde Apparel Company LLC (PA) 212 307-7848
  55 W 39th St Fl 11 New York (10018) *(G-9078)*
Concrete Designs Inc 607 738-0309
  2770 County Route 60 Elmira (14901) *(G-4345)*
Concrete Mixer Supplycom Inc (PA) 716 375-5565
  1721 Cornell Dr Olean (14760) *(G-12229)*
Conde Nast Entertainment LLC 212 286-2860
  1 World Trade Ctr New York (10007) *(G-9079)*
Conde Nast Publications, New York *Also called Advance Magazine Publs Inc (G-8470)*
Conde Nast Publications Div, New York *Also called Advance Magazine Publs Inc (G-8471)*
Conde Pumps Div, Sherrill *Also called Westmoor Ltd (G-14409)*
Condeco Software Inc 408 508-7330
  1350 Broadway Rm 1712 New York (10018) *(G-9080)*
Condor Electronics Corp 585 235-1500
  295 Mount Read Blvd Rochester (14611) *(G-13321)*
Cone Buddy System Inc 585 427-9940
  3495 Winton Pl Ste E290 Rochester (14623) *(G-13322)*
Conesus Lake Association Inc 585 346-6864
  5828 Big Tree Rd Lakeville (14480) *(G-6774)*

Confer Plastics Inc 800 635-3213
97 Witmer Rd North Tonawanda (14120) ***(G-12063)***
Conference Board Inc (PA) 212 759-0900
845 3rd Ave Fl 2 New York (10022) ***(G-9081)***
Confiant Inc 646 397-4198
72 Madison Ave Fl 2 New York (10016) ***(G-9082)***
Conformer Products Inc 516 504-6300
60 Cuttermill Rd Ste 411 Great Neck (11021) ***(G-5378)***
Confrtrnity of Prescious Blood 718 436-1120
5300 Fort Hamilton Pkwy Brooklyn (11219) ***(G-1681)***
Congress For Jewish Culture 212 505-8040
1133 Broadway Ste 1019 New York (10010) ***(G-9083)***
Conic Systems Inc 845 856-4053
11 Rebel Ln Port Jervis (12771) ***(G-12846)***
Conmed Andover Medical Inc (HQ) 315 797-8375
525 French Rd Ste 3 Utica (13502) ***(G-15246)***
Conmed Corporation 315 797-8375
525 French Rd Utica (13502) ***(G-15247)***
Conmed Corporation (PA) 315 797-8375
525 French Rd Utica (13502) ***(G-15248)***
Connection Mold Inc 585 458-6463
585 Ling Rd Rochester (14612) ***(G-13323)***
Connectiva Systems Inc (PA) 646 722-8741
19 W 44th St Ste 611 New York (10036) ***(G-9084)***
Connex Grinding & Machining 315 946-4340
65 Clyde Rd Lyons (14489) ***(G-7448)***
Connie Cleaners, Great Neck *Also called Connie French Cleaners Inc* ***(G-5379)***
Connie French Cleaners Inc 516 487-1343
801 Middle Neck Rd Great Neck (11024) ***(G-5379)***
Connie's T Shirt Shop, East Northport *Also called Island Silkscreen Inc* ***(G-4147)***
Connies Laundry 716 822-2800
1494 S Park Ave Buffalo (14220) ***(G-2709)***
Conopco Inc 585 647-8322
28 Mansfield St Rochester (14606) ***(G-13324)***
Conrad Blasius Equipment Co 516 753-1200
199 Newtown Rd Plainview (11803) ***(G-12672)***
Consoldted Precision Pdts Corp 315 687-0014
901 E Genesee St Chittenango (13037) ***(G-3404)***
Consolidated Barricades Inc 518 922-7944
179 Dillenbeck Rd Fultonville (12072) ***(G-5078)***
Consolidated Childrens AP Inc (HQ) 212 239-8615
100 W 33rd St Ste 1105 New York (10001) ***(G-9085)***
Consolidated Color Press Inc 212 929-8197
307 7th Ave Rm 904 New York (10001) ***(G-9086)***
Consolidated Container Co LLC 585 262-6470
18 Champeney Ter Rochester (14605) ***(G-13325)***
Consolidated Container Co LLC 585 343-9351
14 Hall St Batavia (14020) ***(G-611)***
Consolidated Edison Co NY Inc 914 933-2936
511 Theodore Fremd Ave Rye (10580) ***(G-14076)***
Consolidated Loose Leaf Inc (PA) 212 924-5800
989 Avnue Of The Americas New York (10018) ***(G-9087)***
Consolidated Spring LLC 845 391-8855
11 Spring St Newburgh (12550) ***(G-11862)***
Constas Printing Corporation 315 474-2176
1120 Burnet Ave Syracuse (13203) ***(G-14859)***
Constellation Brands Inc (PA) 585 678-7100
207 High Point Dr # 100 Victor (14564) ***(G-15399)***
Constellation Brands Inc 585 393-4880
3325 Marvin Sands Dr Canandaigua (14424) ***(G-3129)***
Constellation Brands Smo LLC 585 396-7161
111 8th Ave New York (10011) ***(G-9088)***
Construction Robotics LLC 585 742-2004
795 Canning Pkwy Victor (14564) ***(G-15400)***
Construction Technology Inc (PA) 914 747-8900
17 Green Ln Chappaqua (10514) ***(G-3323)***
Consumer Flavoring Extract Co 718 435-0201
921 Mcdonald Ave Brooklyn (11218) ***(G-1682)***
Consumer Reports Inc (PA) 914 378-2000
101 Truman Ave Yonkers (10703) ***(G-16297)***
CONSUMERS UNION, Yonkers *Also called Consumer Reports Inc* ***(G-16297)***
Contactive Inc 646 476-9059
137 Varick St Ste 605 New York (10013) ***(G-9089)***
Container Tstg Solutions LLC 716 487-3300
17 Tiffany Ave Jamestown (14701) ***(G-6504)***
Container Tstg Solutions LLC (PA) 716 487-3300
17 Lester St Sinclairville (14782) ***(G-14445)***
Contech Engnered Solutions LLC 716 870-9091
34 Birdsong Pkwy Orchard Park (14127) ***(G-12348)***
Contemporary Visions LLC (PA) 845 926-5469
151 Airport Dr Wappingers Falls (12590) ***(G-15490)***
Contempra Design Inc 718 984-8586
20 Grille Ct Staten Island (10309) ***(G-14642)***
Conti Auto Body Corp 516 921-6435
44 Jericho Tpke Syosset (11791) ***(G-14781)***
Continental Access, Amityville *Also called Continental Instruments LLC* ***(G-258)***
Continental Buchanan LLC 703 480-3800
350 Broadway Buchanan (10511) ***(G-2608)***
Continental Cordage Corp (HQ) 315 655-9800
75 Burton St Cazenovia (13035) ***(G-3225)***
Continental Instruments LLC 631 842-9400
355 Bayview Ave Amityville (11701) ***(G-258)***
Continental Jewelry, Long Island City *Also called J C Continental Inc* ***(G-7250)***
Continental Knitting Mills 631 242-5330
156 Brook Ave Deer Park (11729) ***(G-3853)***
Continental Kraft Corp 516 681-9090
100 Jericho Quadrangle # 219 Jericho (11753) ***(G-6575)***
Continental Latex Corp 718 783-7883
1489 Shore Pkwy Apt 1g Brooklyn (11214) ***(G-1683)***
Continental Lift Truck Inc 718 738-4738
12718 Foch Blvd South Ozone Park (11420) ***(G-14521)***
Continental Quilting Co Inc 718 499-9100
3000 Marcus Ave Ste 3e6 New Hyde Park (11042) ***(G-8259)***
Continuity Publishing Inc 212 869-4170
15 W 39th St Fl 9 New York (10018) ***(G-9090)***
Continuity Software Inc 646 216-8628
5 Penn Plz Fl 23 New York (10001) ***(G-9091)***
Continuum Intl Pubg Group Inc 646 649-4215
15 W 26th St Fl 8 New York (10010) ***(G-9092)***
Contract Pharmacal Corp 631 231-4610
110 Plant Ave Ste 3 Hauppauge (11788) ***(G-5625)***
Contract Pharmacal Corp 631 231-4610
1324 Motor Pkwy Hauppauge (11749) ***(G-5626)***
Contract Pharmacal Corp 631 231-4610
250 Kennedy Dr Hauppauge (11788) ***(G-5627)***
Contract Pharmacal Corp 631 231-4610
145 Oser Ave Hauppauge (11788) ***(G-5628)***
Contract Pharmacal Corp 631 231-4610
160 Commerce Dr Hauppauge (11788) ***(G-5629)***
Contract Pharmacal Corp 631 231-4610
150 Commerce Dr Hauppauge (11788) ***(G-5630)***
Contractors Sheet Metal LLC 718 786-2505
3406 Skillman Ave Long Island City (11101) ***(G-7191)***
Control Elec Div Fil-Coil, Sayville *Also called Esc Control Electronics LLC* ***(G-14225)***
Control Electropolishing Corp 718 858-6634
109 Walworth St Brooklyn (11205) ***(G-1684)***
Control Global Solutions, Halfmoon *Also called Ebeling Associates Inc* ***(G-5492)***
Control Logic Corporation 607 965-6423
2533 State Highway 80 West Burlington (13482) ***(G-15758)***
Control Research Inc 631 225-1111
385 Bayview Ave Unit C Amityville (11701) ***(G-259)***
Controlled Castings Corp 516 349-1718
31 Commercial Ct Plainview (11803) ***(G-12673)***
Convenience Store News 214 217-7800
770 Broadway Fl 5 New York (10003) ***(G-9093)***
Convergent Audio Tech Inc 585 359-2700
85 High Tech Dr Rush (14543) ***(G-14069)***
Convergent Cnnctivity Tech Inc 845 651-5250
1751 State Route 17a Florida (10921) ***(G-4822)***
Convergent Med MGT Svcs LLC 718 921-6159
7513 3rd Ave Brooklyn (11209) ***(G-1685)***
Conversion Labs Inc (PA) 866 351-5907
800 3rd Ave Ste 2800 New York (10022) ***(G-9094)***
Converter Design Inc (PA) 518 745-7138
25 Murdock Ave Glens Falls (12801) ***(G-5245)***
Conway Dressing For Success, Elmsford *Also called Conway Import Co Inc* ***(G-4402)***
Conway Import Co Inc 914 592-1312
4 Warehouse Ln Ste 142 Elmsford (10523) ***(G-4402)***
Coocoo SMS Inc 646 459-4260
356 New York Ave Ste 1 Huntington (11743) ***(G-6203)***
Cookie Connection Inc 315 422-2253
705 Park Ave Syracuse (13204) ***(G-14860)***
Cookie Factory, Bronx *Also called Golden Glow Cookie Co Inc* ***(G-1267)***
Cookiebaker LLC 716 878-8000
1 Robert Rich Way Buffalo (14213) ***(G-2710)***
Cookies Inc 917 261-4981
143 Madison Ave Fl 6 New York (10016) ***(G-9095)***
Cookies United LLC 631 581-4000
141 Freeman Ave Islip (11751) ***(G-6351)***
Cooking With Chef Michelle LLC 516 662-2324
4603 Middle Country Rd Calverton (11933) ***(G-3079)***
Cooks Intl Ltd Lblty Co 212 741-4407
7 World Trade Ctr Fl 46 New York (10007) ***(G-9096)***
Cooper & Clement Inc 315 454-8135
1840 Lemoyne Ave Syracuse (13208) ***(G-14861)***
Cooper Crouse Hinds Elec Pdts, Syracuse *Also called Cooper Crouse-Hinds LLC* ***(G-14862)***
Cooper Crouse-Hinds LLC (HQ) 315 477-7000
1201 Wolf St Syracuse (13208) ***(G-14862)***
Cooper Crouse-Hinds Mtl Inc 315 477-7000
1201 Wolf St Syracuse (13208) ***(G-14863)***
Cooper Industries LLC 315 477-7000
Wolf & 7th North St Syracuse (13208) ***(G-14864)***
Cooper Lighting LLC 516 470-1000
100 Andrews Rd Ste 1 Hicksville (11801) ***(G-5896)***
Cooper Molded Products, Syracuse *Also called Cooper Industries LLC* ***(G-14864)***
Cooper Power Systems LLC 716 375-7100
1648 Dugan Rd Olean (14760) ***(G-12230)***
Cooper Turbocompressor Inc (HQ) 716 896-6600
3101 Broadway St Buffalo (14227) ***(G-2711)***
Cooperfriedman Elc Sup Co Inc 718 269-4906
2219 41st Ave Long Island City (11101) ***(G-7192)***
Coopers Cave Ale Co S-Corp 518 792-0007
2 Sagamore St Glens Falls (12801) ***(G-5246)***
Cooperstown Bat Company Inc 607 547-2415
118 Main St Cooperstown (13326) ***(G-3639)***

Cooperstown Brewing Co LLC....607 286-9330
41 Browne St Oneonta (13820) ***(G-12268)***
Coopersurgical Inc....716 693-6230
825 Wurlitzer Dr North Tonawanda (14120) ***(G-12064)***
Coopervision Inc....585 385-6810
180 Thruway Park Dr West Henrietta (14586) ***(G-15790)***
Coopervision Inc....585 889-3301
711 North Rd Scottsville (14546) ***(G-14339)***
Coopervision Inc....585 385-6810
209 High Point Dr Victor (14564) ***(G-15401)***
Coopervision Inc (HQ)....585 385-6810
209 High Point Dr Ste 100 Victor (14564) ***(G-15402)***
Copeland Coating Company Inc....518 766-2932
3600 Us Highway 20 Nassau (12123) ***(G-8213)***
Copen International Limited, New York *Also called Cai Inc* ***(G-8886)***
Copen United LLC....212 819-0008
37 W 39th St Fl 6 New York (10018) ***(G-9097)***
Copesetic Inc....315 684-7780
62 E Main St Morrisville (13408) ***(G-8085)***
Copia Interactive LLC....212 481-0520
105 Madison Ave New York (10016) ***(G-9098)***
Copper John Corporation....315 258-9269
173 State St Auburn (13021) ***(G-470)***
Copper Ridge Oil Inc....716 372-4021
111 W 2nd St Ste 404 Jamestown (14701) ***(G-6505)***
Copra, New York *Also called C O P R A Inc* ***(G-8881)***
Copy Cat....718 934-2192
3177 Coney Island Ave A Brooklyn (11235) ***(G-1686)***
Copy Corner Inc....718 388-4545
200 Division Ave Brooklyn (11211) ***(G-1687)***
Copy Room Inc....212 371-8600
885 3rd Ave Lowr 2ll New York (10022) ***(G-9099)***
Copy Stop Inc....914 428-5188
50 Main St Ste 32 White Plains (10606) ***(G-15996)***
Copy X/Press Ltd....631 585-2200
700 Union Pkwy Ste 5 Ronkonkoma (11779) ***(G-13925)***
Copy4les Inc....212 487-9778
146 W 29th St Rm 9w New York (10001) ***(G-9100)***
Copyright Reprographics, New York *Also called Cabba Printing Incorporated* ***(G-8883)***
Cora Materials Corp....516 488-6300
30 Nassau Terminal Rd New Hyde Park (11040) ***(G-8260)***
Cora Matrls, New Hyde Park *Also called Cora Materials Corp* ***(G-8260)***
Coral Blood Service....800 483-4888
525 Executive Blvd # 285 Elmsford (10523) ***(G-4403)***
Coral Cast LLC....516 349-1300
31 Commercial Ct Plainview (11803) ***(G-12674)***
Coral Color Process Ltd....631 543-5200
50 Mall Dr Commack (11725) ***(G-3585)***
Coral Graphic Services Inc (HQ)....516 576-2100
840 S Broadway Hicksville (11801) ***(G-5897)***
Coral Graphic Svce, Hicksville *Also called Coral Graphic Services Inc* ***(G-5897)***
Coral Management Corp....718 893-9286
923 Bryant Ave Bronx (10474) ***(G-1231)***
Corbertex LLC....212 971-0008
1412 Broadway Rm 1100 New York (10018) ***(G-9101)***
Corbett Stves Pttern Works Inc....585 546-7109
80 Lowell St Rochester (14605) ***(G-13326)***
Cordis Solutions Inc....917 909-2002
380 Lexington Ave Fl 17 New York (10168) ***(G-9102)***
Core Group Displays Inc....845 876-5109
41 Pitcher Rd Rhinebeck (12572) ***(G-13098)***
Core Home, New York *Also called Brumis Imports Inc* ***(G-8864)***
Core Swx LLC....516 595-7488
91b Commercial St Plainview (11803) ***(G-12675)***
Core Welding, Sanborn *Also called Bruce Pierce* ***(G-14138)***
Coremet Trading Inc....212 964-3600
160 Brdwy Ste 1107 New York (10038) ***(G-9103)***
Corey Rugs, Great Neck *Also called Rosecore Division* ***(G-5418)***
Corinne McCormack Inc....212 868-7919
7 W 36th St Fl 9 New York (10018) ***(G-9104)***
Corinthian Cast Stone Inc....631 920-2340
115 Wyandanch Ave Wyandanch (11798) ***(G-16244)***
Corium Corporation (PA)....914 381-0100
147 Palmer Ave Mamaroneck (10543) ***(G-7505)***
Corkhill Grp, Jamaica *Also called Corkhill Manufacturing Co Inc* ***(G-6438)***
Corkhill Manufacturing Co Inc....718 528-7413
13121 Merrick Blvd Jamaica (11434) ***(G-6438)***
Corman USA Inc....718 727-7455
1140 Bay St Ste 2c Staten Island (10305) ***(G-14643)***
Corneal Design Corporation....301 670-7076
3288 Plank Rd Lima (14485) ***(G-6930)***
Cornell Beverages Inc....718 381-3000
105 Harrison Pl Brooklyn (11237) ***(G-1688)***
Cornell Laboratory Ornithology, Ithaca *Also called Cornell University* ***(G-6377)***
Cornell University....607 277-2338
512 E State St Ithaca (14850) ***(G-6376)***
Cornell University....607 254-2473
159 Sapsucker Woods Rd Ithaca (14850) ***(G-6377)***
Cornell University Press, Ithaca *Also called Cornell University* ***(G-6376)***
Corning Consumer Products Co, Corning *Also called Corning Vitro Corporation* ***(G-3714)***
Corning Incorporated (PA)....607 974-9000
1 Riverfront Plz Corning (14831) ***(G-3705)***
Corning Incorporated....607 974-9000
Decker Bldg Corning (14831) ***(G-3706)***
Corning Incorporated....607 974-1274
905 Addison Rd Painted Post (14870) ***(G-12472)***
Corning Incorporated....607 974-9000
1 Riverfront Plz Corning (14831) ***(G-3707)***
Corning Incorporated....315 379-3200
334 County Route 16 Canton (13617) ***(G-3165)***
Corning Incorporated....607 433-3100
275 River St Oneonta (13820) ***(G-12269)***
Corning Incorporated....607 248-1200
Hp-Ab-01-A9b Corning (14831) ***(G-3708)***
Corning Incorporated....646 521-9600
767 5th Ave Ste 2301 New York (10153) ***(G-9105)***
Corning Incorporated....607 974-9000
890 Addison Rd Painted Post (14870) ***(G-12473)***
Corning Incorporated....607 974-4488
1 W Market St Ste 601 Corning (14830) ***(G-3709)***
Corning Incorporated....607 974-8496
1 Museum Way Corning (14830) ***(G-3710)***
Corning International Corp (HQ)....607 974-9000
1 Riverfront Plz Corning (14831) ***(G-3711)***
Corning Optcal Cmmncations LLC....607 974-7543
22 W 3rd St Corning (14830) ***(G-3712)***
Corning Rubber Company Inc....631 738-0041
1744 Julia Goldbach Ave Ronkonkoma (11779) ***(G-13926)***
Corning Specialty Mtls Inc....607 974-9000
1 Riverfront Plz Corning (14831) ***(G-3713)***
Corning Tropel Corporation....585 377-3200
60 Oconnor Rd Fairport (14450) ***(G-4494)***
Corning Vitro Corporation....607 974-8605
1 Riverfront Plz Corning (14830) ***(G-3714)***
Corning Wax, Ronkonkoma *Also called Corning Rubber Company Inc* ***(G-13926)***
Cornwall Local, Cornwall *Also called News of The Highlands Inc* ***(G-3731)***
Corona Plumbing & Htg Sup Inc....718 424-4133
10466 Roosevelt Ave Corona (11368) ***(G-3736)***
Corona Ready Mix Inc....718 271-5940
5025 97th Pl Corona (11368) ***(G-3737)***
Coronet Kitchen & Bath, Ronkonkoma *Also called Dak Mica and Wood Products* ***(G-13929)***
Coronet Parts Mfg Co Inc (PA)....718 649-1750
883 Elton St Brooklyn (11208) ***(G-1689)***
Coronet Parts Mfg Co Inc....718 649-1750
901 Elton St Fl 1 Brooklyn (11208) ***(G-1690)***
Corpkit Legal Supplies, Islip *Also called Rike Enterprises Inc* ***(G-6356)***
Corporate Loss Preven....516 409-0002
38 Brooklyn Ave Massapequa (11758) ***(G-7646)***
Cort Contracting....845 758-1190
188 W Market St Red Hook (12571) ***(G-13073)***
Cortland, Cortland *Also called Actuant Corporation* ***(G-3753)***
Cortland Asphalt Products, Cortland *Also called McConnaughay Technologies* ***(G-3778)***
Cortland Cable Company Inc....607 753-8276
44 River St Cortland (13045) ***(G-3758)***
Cortland Company Inc (HQ)....607 753-8276
44 River St Cortland (13045) ***(G-3759)***
Cortland Line Mfg LLC....607 756-2851
3736 Kellogg Rd Cortland (13045) ***(G-3760)***
Cortland Machine and Tool Co....607 756-5852
60 Grant St Cortland (13045) ***(G-3761)***
Cortland Plastics Intl LLC....607 662-0120
211 S Main St Cortland (13045) ***(G-3762)***
Cortland Ready Mix, Cortland *Also called Saunders Concrete Co Inc* ***(G-3787)***
Cortland Ready Mix Inc....607 753-3063
6 Locust Ave Ofc Rte 13 Cortland (13045) ***(G-3763)***
Cortland Standard Printing Co....607 756-5665
110 Main St Cortland (13045) ***(G-3764)***
Cortland-Ithaca Subn Shopper, Freeville *Also called Freeville Publishing Co Inc* ***(G-5033)***
Corzane Cabinets, Farmingdale *Also called Kazac Inc* ***(G-4662)***
Cosa Xentaur Corporation....631 345-3434
84 Horseblock Rd Unit G Yaphank (11980) ***(G-16258)***
Cosco Enterprises Inc....718 383-4488
1930 Troutman St Ridgewood (11385) ***(G-13143)***
Cosco Interprises Inc....718 417-8995
1930 Troutman St Ste 1 Ridgewood (11385) ***(G-13144)***
Cosco Soap & Detergent, Ridgewood *Also called Cosco Enterprises Inc* ***(G-13143)***
Cosco Soap and Detergent, Ridgewood *Also called Cosco Interprises Inc* ***(G-13144)***
Cosense Inc....516 364-9161
125 Coachman Pl W Syosset (11791) ***(G-14782)***
Cosmic Enterprise....718 342-6257
147 Rockaway Ave Ste A Brooklyn (11233) ***(G-1691)***
Cosmo Electronic Machine Corp....631 249-2535
113 Gazza Blvd Farmingdale (11735) ***(G-4603)***
Cosmo Optics, Albany *Also called Ion Optics Inc* ***(G-89)***
Cosmopolitan Magazine....212 649-2000
300 W 57th St Fl 38 New York (10019) ***(G-9106)***
Cosmos Communications Inc....718 482-1800
1105 44th Dr Long Island City (11101) ***(G-7193)***
Cosmos Electronic Machine Corp (PA)....631 249-2535
140 Schmitt Blvd Farmingdale (11735) ***(G-4604)***

ALPHABETIC

Cossitt Concrete Products Inc 315 824-2700
  6543 Middleport Rd Hamilton (13346) *(G-5526)*
Costanza Ready Mix Inc 516 783-4444
  1345 Newbridge Rd North Bellmore (11710) *(G-12016)*
Costanzos Welding Inc (PA) 716 282-0845
  22nd Allen St Niagara Falls (14302) *(G-11917)*
Costello Bros Petroleum Corp (PA) 914 237-3189
  990 Mclean Ave Ste 3 Yonkers (10704) *(G-16298)*
Costello Tagliapietra, New York *Also called CTS LLC (G-9128)*
Costume Armour Inc 845 534-9120
  2 Mill St Stop 1 Cornwall (12518) *(G-3728)*
Cote Hardwood Products Inc (PA) 607 898-5737
  4725 Cat Path Rd Locke (13092) *(G-7057)*
Cote Wood Products, Locke *Also called Cote Hardwood Products Inc (G-7057)*
Coto Technology, New York *Also called Kearney-National Inc (G-10087)*
Cotswolt Industries, New York *Also called Central Textiles Inc (G-8953)*
Cott Beverages, Dunkirk *Also called Cliffstar LLC (G-4052)*
Cotton Emporium Inc (PA) 718 894-3365
  8000 Cooper Ave Ste 8 Glendale (11385) *(G-5223)*
Cotton Well Drilling Co Inc 716 672-2788
  Center Rd Sheridan (14135) *(G-14398)*
Cottonwood Metals Inc 646 807-8674
  1625 Sycamore Ave Ste A Bohemia (11716) *(G-991)*
Cottrell Paper Company Inc 518 885-1702
  1135 Rock City Rd Rock City Falls (12863) *(G-13817)*
Coty Inc (PA) 212 389-7300
  350 5th Ave New York (10118) *(G-9107)*
Coty US LLC (HQ) 212 389-7000
  350 5th Ave New York (10118) *(G-9108)*
Coty US LLC 212 389-7000
  726 Eab Plz Uniondale (11556) *(G-15225)*
Coughlin Printing Group, Watertown *Also called Christian Bus Endeavors Inc (G-15564)*
COUNCEL FOR SECULAR HUMANISM &, Amherst *Also called Center For Inquiry Inc (G-217)* .
Counter Evolution 212 647-7505
  37 W 17th St New York (10011) *(G-9109)*
Countertop Creations, Rochester *Also called Frank J Martello (G-13423)*
Countertops & Cabinets Inc 315 433-1038
  4073 New Court Ave Syracuse (13206) *(G-14865)*
Countess Corporation 212 869-7070
  225 W 37th St Fl 12 New York (10018) *(G-9110)*
Countess Mara Inc 212 768-7300
  120 W 45th St Fl 37 New York (10036) *(G-9111)*
Country Coin-Op, Newport *Also called Reynolds Drapery Service Inc (G-11899)*
Country Folks 585 343-9721
  123 N Spruce St Batavia (14020) *(G-612)*
Country Living, New York *Also called Hearst Corporation (G-9753)*
Country Printer, The, Huntington *Also called Photo Agents Ltd (G-6217)*
Country Side Sand & Gravel (HQ) 716 988-3271
  Taylor Hollow Rd Collins (14034) *(G-3569)*
Country Side Sand & Gravel 716 988-3271
  8458 Route 62 South Dayton (14138) *(G-14507)*
Countryside Truss LLC 315 985-0643
  360 County Highway 151 Saint Johnsville (13452) *(G-14116)*
County Draperies Inc 845 342-9009
  64 Genung St Middletown (10940) *(G-7901)*
County Energy Corp 718 626-7000
  65 S 11th St Apt 1e Brooklyn (11249) *(G-1692)*
County Fabricators 914 741-0219
  175 Marble Ave Pleasantville (10570) *(G-12796)*
County Line Stone Co Inc 716 542-5435
  4515 Crittenden Rd Akron (14001) *(G-16)*
Courbee, Westbury *Also called Lotus Apparel Designs Inc (G-15906)*
Courier Life Publications, Brooklyn *Also called Courier-Life Inc (G-1693)*
Courier Observer, Canton *Also called St Lawrence County Newspapers (G-3167)*
Courier Printing Corp 607 467-2191
  24 Laurel Bank Ave Ste 2 Deposit (13754) *(G-3999)*
Courier-Life Inc 718 260-2500
  1 Metrotech Ctr Brooklyn (11201) *(G-1693)*
Courser Inc 607 739-3861
  802 County Road 64 # 100 Elmira (14903) *(G-4346)*
Courtlandt Boot Jack Co Inc 718 445-6200
  3334 Prince St Flushing (11354) *(G-4846)*
Cousin's Furniture, Deer Park *Also called Cousins Furniture & Hm Imprvs (G-3854)*
Cousins Furniture & Hm Imprvs 631 254-3752
  515 Acorn St Deer Park (11729) *(G-3854)*
Couture Inc 212 921-1166
  16 W 37th St Frnt 1 New York (10018) *(G-9112)*
Couture Timber Harvesting 607 836-4719
  2760 Phelps Rd Mc Graw (13101) *(G-7687)*
Cove Point Holdings LLC (PA) 212 599-3388
  60 E 42nd St Rm 3210 New York (10165) *(G-9113)*
Coventry Manufacturing Co Inc (PA) 914 668-2212
  115 E 3rd St Mount Vernon (10550) *(G-8134)*
Coventya Inc (HQ) 216 351-1500
  132 Clear Rd Oriskany (13424) *(G-12386)*
Coventya Inc 315 768-6635
  132 Clear Rd Oriskany (13424) *(G-12387)*
Coverall Manufacturing 315 622-2852
  3653 Hayes Rd Baldwinsville (13027) *(G-546)*

Covergrip Corporation 855 268-3747
  16 Douglas Ln Manorville (11949) *(G-7552)*
Covington Sound 646 256-7486
  2705 Kingsbridge Ter Bronx (10463) *(G-1232)*
Cowee Forest Products Inc 518 658-2233
  28 Taylor Ave Berlin (12022) *(G-823)*
Cox & Company Inc 212 366-0200
  1664 Old Country Rd Plainview (11803) *(G-12676)*
Coyote Moon LLC (PA) 315 686-5600
  17371 County Route 3 Clayton (13624) *(G-3453)*
Coyote Moon Vineyards, Clayton *Also called Coyote Moon LLC (G-3453)*
Coyote Motorsports, Spencerport *Also called Bullet Industries Inc (G-14554)*
Cpac Inc (HQ) 585 382-3223
  2364 State Route 20a Leicester (14481) *(G-6908)*
Cpac Equipment Inc 585 382-3223
  2364 State Route 20a Leicester (14481) *(G-6909)*
CPI, New York *Also called Capital Programs Inc (G-8914)*
CPI Aerostructures Inc (PA) 631 586-5200
  91 Heartland Blvd Edgewood (11717) *(G-4266)*
CPI of Falconer Inc 716 664-4444
  1890 Lyndon Blvd Falconer (14733) *(G-4537)*
Cpp - Guaymas 315 687-0014
  901 E Genesee St Chittenango (13037) *(G-3405)*
Cpp - Steel Treaters 315 736-3081
  100 Furnace St Oriskany (13424) *(G-12388)*
Cpp Global, Ronkonkoma *Also called Carolina Precision Plas LLC (G-13922)*
Cpp-Syracuse Inc (HQ) 315 687-0014
  901 E Genesee St Chittenango (13037) *(G-3406)*
CPS Creative, New York *Also called Complete Publishing Solutions (G-9073)*
CPT Usa LLC (PA) 212 575-1616
  15 W 39th St Fl 12 New York (10018) *(G-9114)*
Cq Magazine, Hicksville *Also called C Q Communications Inc (G-5890)*
Cq Traffic Control Devices LLC 518 767-0057
  1521 Us Rte 9w Selkirk (12158) *(G-14356)*
Cq Traffic Control Products, Selkirk *Also called Cq Traffic Control Devices LLC (G-14356)*
Crabtree Publishing Inc 212 496-5040
  350 5th Ave Ste 3304 New York (10118) *(G-9115)*
Craft Atlantic, New York *Also called Craftatlantic LLC (G-9117)*
Craft Clerical Clothes Inc 212 764-6122
  247 W 37th St Rm 1700 New York (10018) *(G-9116)*
Craft Collective, Brooklyn *Also called Fresh Ice Cream Company LLC (G-1869)*
Craft Custom Woodwork Co Inc 718 821-2162
  5949 56th Ave Maspeth (11378) *(G-7600)*
Craft Packaging Inc 718 633-4045
  1274 49th St Ste 350 Brooklyn (11219) *(G-1694)*
Craft Robe Co., New York *Also called Craft Clerical Clothes Inc (G-9116)*
Craft-Tech Mfg Corp 631 563-4949
  1750 Artic Ave Bohemia (11716) *(G-992)*
Craftatlantic LLC 646 726-4205
  115 Greenwich Ave New York (10014) *(G-9117)*
Craftech 518 828-5011
  5 Dock St Chatham (12037) *(G-3330)*
Craftech Industries Inc 518 828-5001
  8 Dock St Hudson (12534) *(G-6151)*
Crafters Workshop Inc 914 345-2838
  116 S Central Ave Ste 1 Elmsford (10523) *(G-4404)*
Craftmaster Flavor Technology 631 789-8607
  23 Albany Ave Amityville (11701) *(G-260)*
Craftsman Manufacturing Co In 585 426-5780
  1279 Mount Read Blvd Rochester (14606) *(G-13327)*
Craftsmen Woodworkers Ltd 718 326-3350
  5865 Maspeth Ave Maspeth (11378) *(G-7601)*
Craftsmen/Access Unlimited, Binghamton *Also called Thomas F Egan (G-913)*
Craig Envelope Corp 718 786-4277
  220 Miller Pl Hicksville (11801) *(G-5898)*
Craigs Station Cheese, Pavilion *Also called Wny Cheese Enterprise LLC (G-12524)*
Crain Communications Inc 212 210-0100
  685 3rd Ave New York (10017) *(G-9118)*
Crainville Block Co, Queensbury *Also called Glens Falls Ready Mix Inc (G-13041)*
Crandall Filling Machinery Inc 716 897-3486
  80 Gruner Rd Buffalo (14227) *(G-2712)*
Crane Equipment & Service Inc (HQ) 716 689-5400
  140 John Jmes Adubon Pkwy Amherst (14228) *(G-219)*
Cranesville Block Co Inc (PA) 518 684-6154
  1250 Riverfront Ctr Amsterdam (12010) *(G-323)*
Cranesville Block Co Inc 315 732-2135
  895 Catherine St Utica (13501) *(G-15249)*
Cranesville Block Co Inc 845 896-5687
  70 Route 9 Fishkill (12524) *(G-4798)*
Cranesville Block Co Inc 315 773-2296
  23903 Cemetery Rd Felts Mills (13638) *(G-4786)*
Cranesville Block Co Inc 845 331-1775
  637 E Chester St Kingston (12401) *(G-6687)*
Cranesville Block Co Inc 315 384-4000
  8405 State Highway 56 Norfolk (13667) *(G-11998)*
Cranesville Concrete, Norfolk *Also called Cranesville Block Co Inc (G-11998)*
Cranesville Concrete Co, Utica *Also called Cranesville Block Co Inc (G-15249)*
Cranesville Ready-Mix, Amsterdam *Also called Cranesville Block Co Inc (G-323)*
Cranial Technologies Inc 914 472-0975
  495 Central Park Ave Scarsdale (10583) *(G-14234)*

Crater Service Group Inc 585 482-7770
111 Humboldt St Rochester (14609) *(G-13328)*
Crawford Print Shop Inc 607 359-4970
6120 Herrington Rd Addison (14801) *(G-4)*
Craz Woodworking Assoc Inc 631 205-1890
24 Sawgrass Dr Bellport (11713) *(G-796)*
Crazy Cowboy Brewing Co LLC 516 812-0576
60 Crossways Park Dr W # 400 Woodbury (11797) *(G-16169)*
Crazy Hatter, Holtsville *Also called Screen The World Inc (G-6052)*
Cream Bebe 917 578-2088
694 Myrtle Ave Ste 220 Brooklyn (11205) *(G-1695)*
Create Prosthetics, Cohoes *Also called Peak Performance Design LLC (G-3512)*
Create-A-Card Inc 631 584-2273
16 Brasswood Rd Saint James (11780) *(G-14108)*
Creation Baumann USA Inc 516 764-7431
114 N Centre Ave Rockville Centre (11570) *(G-13827)*
Creations In Canvas, Croton On Hudson *Also called Dalee Bookbinding Co Inc (G-3807)*
Creations In Lucite Inc 718 871-2000
165 Franklin Ave Apt 5 Brooklyn (11205) *(G-1696)*
Creative Compositions, Amityville *Also called Jeffrey John (G-281)*
Creative Costume Co 212 564-5552
3804 Rivers Pointe Way Liverpool (13090) *(G-7008)*
Creative Counter Tops Inc 845 471-6480
17 Van Kleeck Dr Poughkeepsie (12601) *(G-12950)*
Creative Custom Shades, Brooklyn *Also called Custom Lampshades Inc (G-1711)*
Creative Design and Mch Inc 845 778-9001
197 Stone Castle Rd Rock Tavern (12575) *(G-13820)*
Creative Food Ingredients Inc 585 237-2213
1 Lincoln Ave Perry (14530) *(G-12596)*
Creative Forms Inc 212 431-7540
80 Varick St Apt 10a New York (10013) *(G-9119)*
Creative Gold LLC 718 686-2225
1425 37th St Ste 5 Brooklyn (11218) *(G-1697)*
Creative Home Furnishings (PA) 631 582-8000
250 Creative Dr Central Islip (11722) *(G-3270)*
Creative Images & Applique 718 821-8700
5208 Grand Ave Ste 2 Maspeth (11378) *(G-7602)*
Creative Juices Prtg Graphics 631 249-2211
35 W Jefryn Blvd Ste A Deer Park (11729) *(G-3855)*
Creative Kids Far East Inc 844 252-7263
750 Chestnut Ridge Rd # 301 Spring Valley (10977) *(G-14565)*
Creative Laminates Inc 315 463-7580
4003 Eastbourne Dr Syracuse (13206) *(G-14866)*
Creative Magazine Inc 516 378-0800
31 Merrick Ave Ste 60 Merrick (11566) *(G-7853)*
Creative Metal Fabricators 631 567-2266
360 Knickerbocker Ave # 13 Bohemia (11716) *(G-993)*
Creative Models & Prototypes 516 433-6828
160 Lauman Ln Unit A Hicksville (11801) *(G-5899)*
Creative Orthotics & Prosthet (HQ) 607 734-7215
1300 College Ave Ste 1 Elmira (14901) *(G-4347)*
Creative Orthotics & Prosthet 607 431-2526
37 Associate Dr Oneonta (13820) *(G-12270)*
Creative Orthotics Prosthetics, Ithaca *Also called Hanger Prsthetcs & Ortho Inc (G-6384)*
Creative Orthotics Prosthetics 607 771-4672
65 Pennsylvania Ave 207 Binghamton (13903) *(G-868)*
Creative Printing Corp 212 226-3870
70 W 36th St Rm 500 New York (10018) *(G-9120)*
Creative Prntng, New York *Also called Creative Printing Corp (G-9120)*
Creative Scents USA Inc 718 522-5901
183 Wilson St Ste 106 Brooklyn (11211) *(G-1698)*
Creative Solutions Group Inc (PA) 914 771-4200
555 Tuckahoe Rd Yonkers (10710) *(G-16299)*
Creative Stage Lighting Co Inc 518 251-3302
149 State Route 28n North Creek (12853) *(G-12031)*
Creative Stone & Cabinets Corp 631 772-6548
448 Middle Country Rd # 1 Selden (11784) *(G-14351)*
Creative Stone Mfg Inc 718 386-7425
349 Covert St Brooklyn (11237) *(G-1699)*
Creative Tools & Supply Inc 212 279-7077
135 W 29th St Rm 205 New York (10001) *(G-9121)*
Creative Yard Designs Inc 315 706-6143
8329 Us Route 20 Manlius (13104) *(G-7545)*
Creatron Services Inc 516 437-5119
504 Cherry Ln Floral Park (11001) *(G-4813)*
Credit Union Journal Inc 212 803-8200
1 State St Fl 26 New York (10004) *(G-9122)*
Crescent Duck Farm Inc 631 722-8700
10 Edgar Ave Aquebogue (11931) *(G-365)*
Crescent Manufacturing, North Collins *Also called Crescent Marketing Inc (G-12024)*
Crescent Marketing Inc (PA) 716 337-0145
10285 Eagle Dr North Collins (14111) *(G-12024)*
Crescent Tank Mfg, Bloomfield *Also called Cresent Services Inc (G-944)*
Cresent Services Inc 585 657-4104
2557 Cannan Rd Bloomfield (14469) *(G-944)*
Crest Haven Precast Inc 518 483-4750
4925 State Route 11 Burke (12917) *(G-3059)*
Crest Lock Co Inc 718 345-9898
342 Herzl St Brooklyn (11212) *(G-1700)*
Creston Electronics, Orangeburg *Also called Crestron Electronics Inc (G-12311)*
Crestron Electronics Inc 201 894-0670
88 Ramland Rd S Orangeburg (10962) *(G-12311)*

Crhmdu Isulations LLC 516 353-7749
1 Soundview Gdns Apt C Port Washington (11050) *(G-12870)*
Cri Graphic, Amityville *Also called Control Research Inc (G-259)*
Crisada Inc 718 729-9730
3913 23rd St Long Island City (11101) *(G-7194)*
Crisray Printing Corp 631 293-3770
50 Executive Blvd Ste A Farmingdale (11735) *(G-4605)*
Cristina, Hempstead *Also called King Cracker Corp (G-5842)*
Criterion Bell & Specialty 718 788-2600
4312 2nd Ave Brooklyn (11232) *(G-1701)*
Critical Link LLC 315 425-4045
6712 Brooklawn Pkwy # 203 Syracuse (13211) *(G-14867)*
Cromwell Group, Mamaroneck *Also called Corium Corporation (G-7505)*
Cromwell Leather Company Inc 914 381-0100
147 Palmer Ave Mamaroneck (10543) *(G-7506)*
Cromwellgroup, Mamaroneck *Also called Cromwell Leather Company Inc (G-7506)*
Cronin Enterprises Inc 914 345-9600
70 E Main St Ste 2 Elmsford (10523) *(G-4405)*
Crosby Company 716 852-3522
183 Pratt St Buffalo (14204) *(G-2713)*
Croscill Home Fashions, New York *Also called Mistdoda Inc (G-10483)*
Crosman Corporation (HQ) 585 657-6161
7629 State Route 5 And 20 Bloomfield (14469) *(G-945)*
Crosman Corporation 585 398-3920
1360 Rural Rte 8 Farmington (14425) *(G-4769)*
Cross Border Transactions LLC (PA) 646 767-7342
580 White Plains Rd # 660 Tarrytown (10591) *(G-15042)*
Cross Bronx Optical 917 667-6611
961 E 174th St Bronx (10460) *(G-1233)*
Cross Country Mfg Inc 607 656-4103
2355 Rte 206 Greene (13778) *(G-5444)*
Cross Filtration Ltd Lblty Co 315 412-1539
87 W Cayuga St Moravia (13118) *(G-8082)*
Crosstex International Inc (HQ) 631 582-6777
10 Ranick Rd Hauppauge (11788) *(G-5631)*
Crosstex International Inc 631 582-6777
2095 Express Dr N Hauppauge (11788) *(G-5632)*
Crosswinds Farm & Creamery 607 327-0363
6762 Log City Rd Ovid (14521) *(G-12423)*
Croton River Center, Brewster *Also called Akzo Nobel Chemicals LLC (G-1139)*
Croton Watch Co Inc 800 443-7639
250 W Nyack Rd Ste 114 West Nyack (10994) *(G-15820)*
Crowley Fabg Machining Co Inc (PA) 607 484-0299
403 N Nanticoke Ave Endicott (13760) *(G-4447)*
Crowley Foods, Binghamton *Also called HP Hood LLC (G-882)*
Crowley Foods Inc (HQ) 800 637-0019
93 Pennsylvania Ave Binghamton (13903) *(G-869)*
Crowley Tar Products Co Inc (PA) 212 682-1200
305 Madison Ave Ste 1035 New York (10165) *(G-9123)*
Crown Aircraft Lighting Inc 718 767-3410
1021 Clintonville St # 4 Whitestone (11357) *(G-16091)*
Crown Cork & Seal Usa Inc 845 343-9586
21 Industrial Pl Middletown (10940) *(G-7902)*
Crown Delta Corporation 914 245-8910
1550 Front St Yorktown Heights (10598) *(G-16363)*
Crown Die Casting Corp 914 667-5400
268 W Lincoln Ave Mount Vernon (10550) *(G-8135)*
Crown Equipment Corporation 516 822-5100
5 Charlotte Ave Ste 1 Hicksville (11801) *(G-5900)*
Crown Jewelers Intl Inc 212 420-7800
168 7th Ave S New York (10014) *(G-9124)*
Crown Lift Trucks, Hicksville *Also called Crown Equipment Corporation (G-5900)*
Crown Medical Products, Suffern *Also called Advanced Medical Mfg Corp (G-14756)*
Crown Mill Work Corp 845 371-2200
33 Murray Hill Dr Nanuet (10954) *(G-8199)*
Crown Novelty Works Inc 631 253-0949
42 Elkland Rd Melville (11747) *(G-7772)*
Crown Sign Systems Inc 914 375-2118
2 South St Mount Vernon (10550) *(G-8136)*
Crown Tank Company LLC 855 276-9682
60 Electric Pkwy Horseheads (14845) *(G-6119)*
Crown Woodworking Corp 718 974-6415
583 Montgomery St Brooklyn (11225) *(G-1702)*
Crownbrook ACC LLC (PA) 718 626-0760
478 Albany Ave 113 Brooklyn (11203) *(G-1703)*
CRS Nuclear Services LLC 716 810-0688
840 Aero Dr Ste 150 Cheektowaga (14225) *(G-3342)*
CRS Remanufacturing Co Inc 718 739-1720
9440 158th St Jamaica (11433) *(G-6439)*
Crucible Industries LLC 800 365-1180
575 State Fair Blvd Solvay (13209) *(G-14495)*
Cruise Industry News, New York *Also called Mathisen Ventures Inc (G-10384)*
Crumbrubber Technology Inc 718 468-3988
18740 Hollis Ave Hollis (11423) *(G-6042)*
Crunched Inc 415 484-9909
41 E 11th St New York (10003) *(G-9125)*
Crusader Candle Co Inc 718 625-0005
325 Nevins St Ste 327329 Brooklyn (11215) *(G-1704)*
Cruzin Management Inc (HQ) 212 641-8700
401 Park Ave S Fl 7 New York (10016) *(G-9126)*
Crye Precision LLC 718 246-3838
63 Flushing Ave Brooklyn (11205) *(G-1705)*

ALPHABETIC

(PA)=Parent Co (HQ)=Headquarters (DH)=Div Headquarters

Cryomech Inc 315 455-2555
  113 Falso Dr Syracuse (13211) *(G-14868)*

Cryovac Inc 585 436-3211
  1525 Brooks Ave Rochester (14624) *(G-13329)*

Crystal Ceres Industries Inc 716 283-0445
  2250 Liberty Dr Niagara Falls (14304) *(G-11918)*

Crystal Fusion Tech Inc 631 253-9800
  185 W Montauk Hwy Lindenhurst (11757) *(G-6946)*

Crystal Is Inc (HQ) 518 271-7375
  70 Cohoes Ave Ste 1b Green Island (12183) *(G-5434)*

Crystal Linton Technologies 585 444-8784
  2180 Brigh Henri Town Lin Rochester (14623) *(G-13330)*

Crystal Rock LLC 716 626-7460
  100 Stradtman St Ste 1 Buffalo (14206) *(G-2714)*

Crystalizations Systems Inc 631 467-0090
  1401 Lincoln Ave Holbrook (11741) *(G-5993)*

Crystalonics 631 981-6140
  2805 Veterans Mem Hwy 14 Ronkonkoma (11779) *(G-13927)*

Crystalonics of New York Inc 631 981-6140
  2805 Vets Memorial Ronkonkoma (11779) *(G-13928)*

Cs Automation Inc 315 524-5123
  518 Berg Rd Ontario (14519) *(G-12286)*

CSC Serviceworks, Inc., Plainview *Also called CSC SW Holdco Inc (G-12677)*

CSC SW Holdco Inc (HQ) 516 349-8555
  303 Sunnyside Blvd # 70 Plainview (11803) *(G-12677)*

Csco LLC 212 375-6180
  1407 Broadway Rm 1503 New York (10018) *(G-9127)*

Csi, Falconer *Also called Reynolds Packaging McHy Inc (G-4554)*

Csi International Inc 800 441-2895
  1001 Main St Niagara Falls (14301) *(G-11919)*

CSP Technologies Inc (HQ) 518 627-0051
  1031 Riverfront Ctr Amsterdam (12010) *(G-324)*

Csrea, Long Island City *Also called Civil Svc Rtred Employees Assn (G-7185)*

Csw Inc 585 247-4010
  70 Pixley Industrial Pkwy Rochester (14624) *(G-13331)*

CT Industrial Supply Co Inc 718 417-3226
  305 Ten Eyck St Brooklyn (11206) *(G-1706)*

CT Publications Co 718 592-2196
  1120 154th St Whitestone (11357) *(G-16092)*

Ctac Holdings LLC 212 924-2280
  68 35th Street Brooklyn Brooklyn (11232) *(G-1707)*

CTB Enterprise LLC 631 563-0088
  1170 Lincoln Ave Unit 7 Holbrook (11741) *(G-5994)*

CTI Software Inc 631 253-3550
  44 W Jefryn Blvd Ste P Deer Park (11729) *(G-3856)*

CTS LLC 212 278-0058
  211 E 18th St Apt 4d New York (10003) *(G-9128)*

CTX Printing, Cambridge *Also called Cambridge-Pacific Inc (G-3092)*

Cuan Corp 917 579-3774
  16 Jessica Pl Roslyn Heights (11577) *(G-14049)*

Cuba Specialty Mfg Co Inc 585 567-4176
  81 S Genesee St Cuba (14735) *(G-4793)*

Cubic Trnsp Systems Inc 212 255-1810
  245 W 17th St Fl 8 New York (10011) *(G-9129)*

Cubitek Inc 631 665-6900
  95 Emjay Blvd Ste 2 Brentwood (11717) *(G-1117)*

Cuccio-Zanetti Inc 518 587-1363
  455 Middle Grove Rd Middle Grove (12850) *(G-7872)*

Cuddeback Machining Inc 585 392-5889
  18 Draffin Rd Hilton (14468) *(G-5972)*

Cuebid Technologies Inc (PA) 302 380-3910
  40 Exchange Pl Ste 1602 New York (10005) *(G-9130)*

Cuffs Planning & Models Ltd 914 632-1883
  317 Beechmont Dr New Rochelle (10804) *(G-8325)*

Culin/Colella Inc 914 698-7727
  632 Center Ave Mamaroneck (10543) *(G-7507)*

Culinary Arts Specialties Inc 716 656-8943
  2268 Union Rd Cheektowaga (14227) *(G-3343)*

Cult Records LLC 718 395-2077
  263 Bowery Apt 3 New York (10002) *(G-9131)*

Culture Clash Corporation 631 933-8179
  393 Bayview Ave Amityville (11701) *(G-261)*

Cultureiq Inc (PA) 212 755-8633
  7 Penn Plz Ste 1112 New York (10001) *(G-9132)*

Cumberland Packing Corp (PA) 718 858-4200
  2 Cumberland St Brooklyn (11205) *(G-1708)*

Cummins - Allison Corp 718 263-2482
  8002 Kew Gardens Rd # 402 Kew Gardens (11415) *(G-6662)*

Cummins Inc 716 456-2111
  4720 Baker St Lakewood (14750) *(G-6781)*

Cummins Northeast LLC 315 437-2296
  6193 Eastern Ave Syracuse (13211) *(G-14869)*

Cummins-Wagner-Siewert LLC (HQ) 585 482-9640
  175 Akron St Rochester (14609) *(G-13332)*

Cupcake Contessas Corporation 516 307-1222
  1242 Julia Ln North Bellmore (11710) *(G-12017)*

Curaegis Technologies Inc (PA) 585 254-1100
  1999 Mount Read Blvd # 3 Rochester (14615) *(G-13333)*

Curbell Medical Products Inc 716 667-2520
  20 Centre Dr Orchard Park (14127) *(G-12349)*

Curbell Medical Products Inc (HQ) 716 667-2520
  7 Cobham Dr Orchard Park (14127) *(G-12350)*

Cureatr Inc 212 203-3927
  222 Broadway Fl 20 New York (10038) *(G-9133)*

Curemdcom Inc 212 509-6200
  120 Broadway Fl 35 New York (10271) *(G-9134)*

Curiously Creative Candles 631 586-1700
  1067 Long Island Ave Deer Park (11729) *(G-3857)*

Curran Manufacturing Corp (PA) 631 273-1010
  200 Oser Ave Hauppauge (11788) *(G-5633)*

Curran Manufacturing Corp 631 273-1010
  210 Oser Ave Hauppauge (11788) *(G-5634)*

Curran Renewable Energy LLC 315 769-2000
  20 Commerce Dr Massena (13662) *(G-7667)*

Currant Company LLC 845 266-8999
  59 Walnut Ln Staatsburg (12580) *(G-14598)*

Currantc, Staatsburg *Also called Currant Company LLC (G-14598)*

Current Applications Inc 315 788-4689
  275 Bellew Ave S Watertown (13601) *(G-15567)*

Current Controls Inc 585 593-1544
  353 S Brooklyn Ave Wellsville (14895) *(G-15668)*

Curriculum Associates LLC 978 313-1355
  55 Prospect St Brooklyn (11201) *(G-1709)*

Currier Plastics Inc 315 255-1779
  101 Columbus St Auburn (13021) *(G-471)*

Curtin-Hebert Co Inc 518 725-7157
  11 Forest St Gloversville (12078) *(G-5282)*

Curtin-Hebert Machines, Gloversville *Also called Curtin-Hebert Co Inc (G-5282)*

Curtis Furniture Company, Evans Mills *Also called Peter S Curtis (G-4487)*

Curtis Instruments Inc (PA) 914 666-2971
  200 Kisco Ave Mount Kisco (10549) *(G-8089)*

Curtis L Maclean L C (HQ) 716 898-7800
  50 Thielman Dr Buffalo (14206) *(G-2715)*

Curtis PMC Division, Mount Kisco *Also called Curtis Instruments Inc (G-8089)*

Curtis Prtg Co The Del Press 518 477-4820
  1528 Columbia Tpke Castleton On Hudson (12033) *(G-3201)*

Curtis Screw Co Inc 716 898-7800
  50 Thielman Dr Buffalo (14206) *(G-2716)*

Curtis/Palmer Hydroelectric LP 518 654-6297
  15 Pine St Corinth (12822) *(G-3704)*

Curtiss-Wrght Intgrted Sensing, Farmingdale *Also called Curtiss-Wright Controls (G-4606)*

Curtiss-Wright Controls 631 756-4740
  175 Central Ave Ste 100 Farmingdale (11735) *(G-4606)*

Curtiss-Wright Electro- 585 596-3482
  37 Coats St Ste 200 Wellsville (14895) *(G-15669)*

Curtiss-Wright Flow Control (HQ) 631 293-3800
  1966 Broadhollow Rd Ste E Farmingdale (11735) *(G-4607)*

Curtiss-Wright Flow Ctrl Corp 631 293-3800
  1966 Broadhollow Rd Ste E Farmingdale (11735) *(G-4608)*

Cusimano, Michael, Rochester *Also called Empire Fabricators Inc (G-13387)*

Custom 101 Prints Inc 718 708-4425
  3601 Bronxwood Ave Bronx (10469) *(G-1234)*

Custom Bags Unlimited, Hamburg *Also called Kragel Co Inc (G-5512)*

Custom Canvas Manufacturing Co 716 852-6372
  775 Seneca St Buffalo (14210) *(G-2717)*

Custom CAS Inc 718 726-3575
  2631 1st St Long Island City (11102) *(G-7195)*

Custom Coatings, Farmingdale *Also called Time-Cap Laboratories Inc (G-4756)*

Custom Controls 315 253-4785
  2804 Skillett Rd Scipio Center (13147) *(G-14326)*

Custom Cool, Bronx *Also called S & V Restaurants Corp (G-1357)*

Custom Cool, Bronx *Also called S & V Restaurant Eqp Mfrs Inc (G-1356)*

Custom Countertops Inc (PA) 716 685-2871
  3192 Walden Ave Depew (14043) *(G-3977)*

Custom Design Kitchens Inc 518 355-4446
  1700 Duanesburg Rd Duanesburg (12056) *(G-4044)*

Custom Design Metals Inc 631 563-2444
  1612 Locust Ave Ste C Bohemia (11716) *(G-994)*

Custom Display Manufacture 516 783-6491
  1686 Logan St North Bellmore (11710) *(G-12018)*

Custom Door & Mirror Inc 631 414-7725
  148 Milbar Blvd Farmingdale (11735) *(G-4609)*

Custom Eco Friendly Bags, Roslyn *Also called Custom Eco Friendly LLC (G-14041)*

Custom Eco Friendly LLC (PA) 347 227-0229
  50 Spruce Dr Roslyn (11576) *(G-14041)*

Custom European Imports Inc 845 357-5718
  100 Sterling Mine Rd Sloatsburg (10974) *(G-14470)*

Custom Fixtures Inc 718 965-1141
  129 13th St Brooklyn (11215) *(G-1710)*

Custom Frame & Molding Co 631 491-9091
  97 Lamar St 101 West Babylon (11704) *(G-15705)*

Custom House Engravers Inc 631 567-3004
  104 Keyland Ct Bohemia (11716) *(G-995)*

Custom Klean Corp 315 865-8101
  8890 Boak Rd E Holland Patent (13354) *(G-6033)*

Custom Lampshades Inc 718 254-0500
  544 Park Ave Ste 503 Brooklyn (11205) *(G-1711)*

Custom Laser Inc (PA) 716 434-8600
  6747 Akron Rd Lockport (14094) *(G-7066)*

Custom Lucite Creations Inc 718 871-2000
  165 Franklin Ave Apt 5 Brooklyn (11205) *(G-1712)*

Custom Metal Fabrication, Farmingdale *Also called Custom Metal Incorporated (G-4610)*

Custom Metal Incorporated 631 643-4075
59 Central Ave Ste 8 Farmingdale (11735) *(G-4610)*

Custom Mix Inc 516 797-7090
31 Clark Blvd Massapequa Park (11762) *(G-7654)*

Custom Molding Solutions Inc 585 293-1702
456 Sanford Rd N Churchville (14428) *(G-3410)*

Custom Nutraceuticals LLC (PA) 631 755-1388
80 Orville Dr Ste 112 Bohemia (11716) *(G-996)*

Custom Patches Inc 845 679-6320
1760 Glasco Tpke Woodstock (12498) *(G-16235)*

Custom Pins Inc 888 922-9378
150 Clearbrook Rd Ste 139 Elmsford (10523) *(G-4406)*

Custom Power System, Sayville Also called Fil-Coil (fc) Corp *(G-14226)*

Custom Power Systems, Central Islip Also called Berkshire Transformer *(G-3265)*

Custom Prtrs Guilderland Inc 518 456-2811
2210 Western Ave Guilderland (12084) *(G-5485)*

Custom Service Solutions Inc 585 637-3760
1900 Transit Way Brockport (14420) *(G-1175)*

Custom Sheet Metal Corp 315 463-9105
1 General Motors Dr Ste 5 Syracuse (13206) *(G-14870)*

Custom Shipping Products Inc 716 355-4437
8661 Knowlton Rd Clymer (14724) *(G-3496)*

Custom Sitecom LLC 631 420-4238
470 Smith St Farmingdale (11735) *(G-4611)*

Custom Sound and Video 585 424-5000
40 Rutter St Rochester (14606) *(G-13334)*

Custom Sports Lab Inc 212 832-1648
515 Madison Ave Rm 1204 New York (10022) *(G-9135)*

Custom Sportswear Corp 914 666-9200
375 Adams St Bedford Hills (10507) *(G-766)*

Custom Stair & Millwork Co 315 839-5793
6 Gridley Pl Sauquoit (13456) *(G-14218)*

Custom Studio Division, Tappan Also called Nationwide Custom Services *(G-15036)*

Custom Wood Inc 718 927-4700
770 E 94th St Brooklyn (11236) *(G-1713)*

Custom Woodcraft LLC 315 843-4234
2525 Perry Schumaker Rd Munnsville (13409) *(G-8195)*

Custom Woodwork Ltd 631 727-5260
205 Marcy Ave Riverhead (11901) *(G-13173)*

Customize Elite Socks LLC 212 533-8551
156 2nd Ave Apt 2c New York (10003) *(G-9136)*

Customshow Inc 800 255-5303
216 E 45th St Fl 17 New York (10017) *(G-9137)*

Cutting Edge Metal Works 631 981-8333
12 Long Island Ave Holtsville (11742) *(G-6048)*

Cuzins Duzin Corp 347 724-6200
8420 Austin St Apt 3a Kew Gardens (11415) *(G-6663)*

Cvd Equipment Corporation 845 246-3631
1117 Kings Hwy Saugerties (12477) *(G-14199)*

Cvd Equipment Corporation (PA) 631 981-7081
355 S Technology Dr Central Islip (11722) *(G-3271)*

Cvd Equipment Corporation 631 582-4365
355 S Technology Dr Central Islip (11722) *(G-3272)*

Cville Yoghurt Inc 315 430-4966
3156 Byrne Hollow Xing Cortland (13045) *(G-3765)*

Cw Fasteners & Zippers Corp 212 594-3203
142 W 36th St Fl 5 New York (10018) *(G-9138)*

Cw Metals Inc 917 416-7906
3421 Greenpoint Ave Long Island City (11101) *(G-7196)*

Cws Powder Coatings Company LP 845 398-2911
2234 Bradley Hill Rd # 12 Blauvelt (10913) *(G-927)*

Cy Fashion Corp 212 730-8600
525 7th Ave Rm 811 New York (10018) *(G-9139)*

Cy Plastics Works Inc 585 229-2555
8601 Main St Honeoye (14471) *(G-6068)*

Cyber Knit, New York Also called Lifestyle Design Usa Ltd *(G-10214)*

Cyber Swag Merchandise of NY, Maspeth Also called Creative Images & Applique *(G-7602)*

Cyberlimit Inc 212 840-9597
257 W 38th St Fl 6 New York (10018) *(G-9140)*

Cybersports Inc (PA) 315 737-7150
11 Avery Pl Utica (13502) *(G-15250)*

Cyclotherm of Watertown Inc 315 782-1100
787 Pearl St Watertown (13601) *(G-15568)*

Cygnet Studio Inc 646 450-4550
319 W 118th St 1b New York (10026) *(G-9141)*

Cygnus Automation Inc 631 981-0909
1605 9th Ave Bohemia (11716) *(G-997)*

Cyncal Steel Fabricators Inc 631 254-5600
225 Pine Aire Dr Bay Shore (11706) *(G-668)*

Cynthia Rowley Inc (PA) 212 242-3803
376 Bleecker St New York (10014) *(G-9142)*

Cynthia Steffe, New York Also called Bernard Chaus Inc *(G-8761)*

Cypress Bioscience Inc 858 452-2323
110 E 59th St Fl 33 New York (10022) *(G-9143)*

Cypress Semiconductor Corp 631 261-1358
34 Rowley Dr Northport (11768) *(G-12102)*

Cytec Industries Inc 716 372-9650
1405 Buffalo St Olean (14760) *(G-12231)*

Cytec Solvay Group, Olean Also called Cytec Industries Inc *(G-12231)*

Cz USA Dwf Dan Wesson Firearm, Norwich Also called Dan Wesson Corp *(G-12120)*

D & A Offset Services Inc 212 924-0612
185 Varick St Ste 3 New York (10014) *(G-9144)*

D & A Sand & Gravel Inc 516 248-9444
335 Sagamore Ave Ste 1 Mineola (11501) *(G-7967)*

D & C Cleaning Inc 631 789-5659
1095 Campagnoli Ave Copiague (11726) *(G-3650)*

D & D Elc Mtrs & Cmpsr Inc 631 991-3001
127 E Hoffman Ave Lindenhurst (11757) *(G-6947)*

D & D Motor Systems Inc 315 701-0861
215 Park Ave Syracuse (13204) *(G-14871)*

D & D Printing, Buffalo Also called Dan Trent Company Inc *(G-2720)*

D & D Window Tech Inc (PA) 212 308-2822
979 3rd Ave Lbby 132 New York (10022) *(G-9145)*

D & E Industrial, Akron Also called Re-Al Industrial Corp *(G-21)*

D & G Sheet Metal Co Inc 718 326-9111
5400 Grand Ave Maspeth (11378) *(G-7603)*

D & G Welding Inc 716 873-3088
249 Hertel Ave Buffalo (14207) *(G-2718)*

D & H Amazing Deals Inc (PA) 347 318-3805
1233 39th St Brooklyn (11218) *(G-1714)*

D & I Finishing Inc 631 471-3034
1560 Ocean Ave Ste 7 Bohemia (11716) *(G-998)*

D & L Electronic Die, Farmingdale Also called Cosmo Electronic Machine Corp *(G-4603)*

D & L Manufacturing, Bronx Also called L & D Manufacturing Corp *(G-1295)*

D & M Custom Cabinets Inc 516 678-2818
2994 Long Beach Rd Oceanside (11572) *(G-12168)*

D & M Enterprises Incorporated 914 937-6430
1 Mill St Ste 2 Port Chester (10573) *(G-12816)*

D & S Supplies Inc 718 721-5256
2067 21st St Astoria (11105) *(G-415)*

D & W Design Inc 845 343-3366
62 Industrial Pl Middletown (10940) *(G-7903)*

D & W Diesel Inc 518 437-1300
51 Sicker Rd Ste 3 Latham (12110) *(G-6853)*

D & W Enterprises LLC 585 590-6727
10775 W Shelby Rd Medina (14103) *(G-7733)*

D and D Sheet Metal Corp 718 465-7585
9510 218th St Ste 4 Jamaica (11429) *(G-6440)*

D B F Associates 718 328-0005
1150 E 156th St Bronx (10474) *(G-1235)*

D Bag Lady Inc 585 425-8095
183 Perinton Pkwy Fairport (14450) *(G-4495)*

D Best Glass & Mirror, Brooklyn Also called D Best Service Co Inc *(G-1715)*

D Best Service Co Inc 718 972-6133
729 Church Ave Brooklyn (11218) *(G-1715)*

D C C, New York Also called Digital Color Concepts Inc *(G-9226)*

D C I Plasma Center Inc (PA) 914 241-1646
71 S Bedford Rd Mount Kisco (10549) *(G-8090)*

D C I Technical Inc 516 355-0464
475 Franklin Ave Fl 2 Franklin Square (11010) *(G-4960)*

D C M, West Babylon Also called Display Components Mfg Inc *(G-15707)*

D D & L Inc 607 729-9131
3 Alice St Binghamton (13904) *(G-870)*

D F Stauffer Biscuit Co Inc 585 968-2700
8670 Farnsworth Rd Cuba (14727) *(G-3811)*

D G M Graphics Inc 516 223-2220
55 Merrick Ave Merrick (11566) *(G-7854)*

D J Crowell Co Inc 716 684-3343
2815 Town Line Rd Alden (14004) *(G-167)*

D K Machine Inc 518 747-0626
48 Sullivan Pkwy Fort Edward (12828) *(G-4938)*

D K P Wood Railings & Stairs 631 665-8656
1971 Union Blvd Bay Shore (11706) *(G-669)*

D M J Casting Inc 212 719-1951
62 W 47th St Ste 508 New York (10036) *(G-9146)*

D Maldari & Sons Inc 718 499-3555
287 Natick St Staten Island (10306) *(G-14644)*

D N Gannon Fabricating Inc 315 463-7466
404 Wavel St Syracuse (13206) *(G-14872)*

D R Cornue Woodworks 315 655-9463
3206 Us Route 20 Cazenovia (13035) *(G-3226)*

D R M Management Inc (PA) 716 668-0333
3430 Transit Rd Depew (14043) *(G-3978)*

D R S Inc (PA) 212 819-0237
64 W 48th St Ste 1302 New York (10036) *(G-9147)*

D R S Watch Materials 212 819-0470
64 W 48th St Ste 1302 New York (10036) *(G-9148)*

D S I, Poestenkill Also called Dynamic Systems Inc *(G-12802)*

D T B, Bohemia Also called Dayton T Brown Inc *(G-1001)*

D T I, Rochester Also called Dimension Technologies Inc *(G-13347)*

D V S Iron & Aluminum Works 718 768-7961
117 14th St Brooklyn (11215) *(G-1716)*

D W S Associates Inc 631 667-6666
89 N Industry Ct Deer Park (11729) *(G-3858)*

D W S Printing, Deer Park Also called D W S Associates Inc *(G-3858)*

D&A Trans Mix, Mineola Also called D & A Sand & Gravel Inc *(G-7967)*

D&H, Brooklyn Also called D & H Amazing Deals Inc *(G-1714)*

D&V Electronics USA, Binghamton Also called Mechanical Pwr Conversion LLC *(G-896)*

D'Addario & Company Inc, Brooklyn Also called DAddario & Company Inc *(G-1717)*

D-Best Equipment Corp 516 358-0965
77 Hempstead Gardens Dr West Hempstead (11552) *(G-15769)*

A
L
P
H
A
B
E
T
I
C

D-C Theatricks 716 847-0180
  747 Main St Buffalo (14203) *(G-2719)*
D-K Manufacturing Corp 315 592-4327
  551 W 3rd St S Fulton (13069) *(G-5057)*
D-Lite Donuts 718 626-5953
  4519 Broadway Astoria (11103) *(G-416)*
D.A.M. Construction, Company, Arverne *Also called Darrell Mitchell (G-407)*
D3 Led LLC 917 757-9671
  566 7th Ave Rm 504 New York (10018) *(G-9149)*
D3 NY, New York *Also called D3 Led LLC (G-9149)*
D3 Repro Group Inc 347 507-1075
  3825 Greenpoint Ave Long Island City (11101) *(G-7197)*
Dab-O-Matic Corp (PA) 914 699-7070
  896 S Columbus Ave Mount Vernon (10550) *(G-8137)*
Dabby-Reid Ltd 212 356-0040
  347 W 36th St Rm 701 New York (10018) *(G-9150)*
Dacobe Enterprises LLC 315 368-0093
  901 Broad St Ste 10 Utica (13501) *(G-15251)*
DAddario & Company Inc 631 439-3300
  99 Marcus Dr Melville (11747) *(G-7773)*
DAddario & Company Inc 718 599-6660
  1000 Dean St Ste 410 Brooklyn (11238) *(G-1717)*
DAddario & Company Inc (PA) 631 439-3300
  595 Smith St Farmingdale (11735) *(G-4612)*
DAF Office Networks Inc 315 699-7070
  6121 Jemola Runne Cicero (13039) *(G-3418)*
DAgostino Iron Works Inc 585 235-8850
  10 Deep Rock Rd Rochester (14624) *(G-13335)*
Daheshist Publishing Co Ltd 212 581-8360
  1775 Broadway 501 New York (10019) *(G-9151)*
Dahill Distributors Inc 347 371-9453
  975 Dahill Rd Brooklyn (11204) *(G-1718)*
Dahlstrom Roll Form, Jamestown *Also called Lakeside Capital Corporation (G-6528)*
Daige Products Inc 516 621-2100
  1 Albertson Ave Ste 3 Albertson (11507) *(G-147)*
Daikin Applied Americas Inc 315 253-2771
  4900 Technology Park Blvd Auburn (13021) *(G-472)*
Dail Cornell Sun, The, Ithaca *Also called Daily Cornell Sun (G-6378)*
Daily Beast Company LLC (HQ) 212 445-4600
  7 Hanover Sq New York (10004) *(G-9152)*
Daily Cornell Sun 607 273-0746
  139 W State St Ithaca (14850) *(G-6378)*
Daily Freeman 845 331-5000
  79 Hurley Ave Kingston (12401) *(G-6688)*
Daily Gazette Company (PA) 518 374-4141
  2345 Maxon Rd Ext Schenectady (12308) *(G-14260)*
Daily Mail & Greene Cnty News (HQ) 518 943-2100
  1 Hudson City Ctr Ste 202 Hudson (12534) *(G-6152)*
Daily Media, Rochester *Also called Daily Record (G-13336)*
Daily Messenger, Canandaigua *Also called Canandaigua Msgnr Incorported (G-3127)*
Daily Muse Inc (PA) 646 357-3201
  1375 Broadway Fl 20 New York (10018) *(G-9153)*
Daily News LP (HQ) 212 210-2100
  4 New York Plz Fl 6 New York (10004) *(G-9154)*
Daily Newsppr For Torah Jewry, Brooklyn *Also called Hamodia Corp (G-1922)*
Daily Orange Corporation 315 443-2314
  744 Ostrom Ave Syracuse (13244) *(G-14873)*
Daily Racing Form Inc (HQ) 212 366-7600
  708 3rd Ave Fl 12 New York (10017) *(G-9155)*
Daily Racing Form LLC 212 514-2180
  75 Broad St New York (10004) *(G-9156)*
Daily Record (PA) 585 232-2035
  16 W Main St Ste G9 Rochester (14614) *(G-13336)*
Daily Sun New York, New York *Also called Daily World Press Inc (G-9157)*
Daily Voice, Armonk *Also called Main Street Connect LLC (G-400)*
Daily Wear Sportswear Corp (PA) 718 972-0533
  2308 Mcdonald Ave Brooklyn (11223) *(G-1719)*
Daily World Press Inc 212 922-9201
  228 E 45th St Rm 700 New York (10017) *(G-9157)*
Dailycandy Inc 646 230-8719
  584 Broadway Rm 510 New York (10012) *(G-9158)*
Daimler Buses North Amer Inc 315 768-8101
  165 Base Rd Oriskany (13424) *(G-12389)*
Dainty Home, New York *Also called Baby Signature Inc (G-8710)*
Dairy Conveyor Corp (PA) 845 278-7878
  38 Mount Ebo Rd S Brewster (10509) *(G-1146)*
Dairy Delite, Farmingdale *Also called Noga Dairies Inc (G-4695)*
Dairy Farmers America Inc 816 801-6440
  5001 Brittonfield Pkwy East Syracuse (13057) *(G-4205)*
Daisy Brand Confectionery, Bronx *Also called Scaccianoce Inc (G-1362)*
Daisy Memory Products, Roslyn *Also called Dynamic Photography Inc (G-14042)*
Dak Mica and Wood Products 631 467-0749
  2147 5th Ave Ronkonkoma (11779) *(G-13929)*
Dakota Software Corporation 216 765-7100
  1082 Chapelhill Dr Victor (14564) *(G-15403)*
Dakota Systems Mfg Corp 631 249-5811
  1885 New Hwy Ste 2 Farmingdale (11735) *(G-4613)*
Dakota Wall, Farmingdale *Also called Dakota Systems Mfg Corp (G-4613)*
Dakotah, Central Islip *Also called Creative Home Furnishings (G-3270)*

Dakott LLC 888 805-6795
  244 Madison Ave Ste 211 New York (10016) *(G-9159)*
Dal-Tile Corporation 718 894-9574
  5840 55th Dr Maspeth (11378) *(G-7604)*
Dal-Tile Corporation 914 835-1801
  31 Oakland Ave Harrison (10528) *(G-5552)*
Dalcom USA Ltd 516 466-7733
  11 Middle Neck Rd Ste 301 Great Neck (11021) *(G-5380)*
Dale Press Inc 718 543-6200
  5676 Riverdale Ave # 311 Bronx (10471) *(G-1236)*
Dalee Bookbinding Co Inc 914 965-1660
  10 Croton Lake Rd Croton On Hudson (10520) *(G-3807)*
Dalfon, Great Neck *Also called Dalcom USA Ltd (G-5380)*
Dalma Dress Mfg Co Inc 212 391-8296
  3 Carman Rd Greenvale (11548) *(G-5461)*
Dalrymple Grav & Contg Co Inc (HQ) 607 739-0391
  2105 S Broadway Pine City (14871) *(G-12627)*
Dalrymple Holding Corp (PA) 607 737-6200
  2105 S Broadway Pine City (14871) *(G-12628)*
Daly Meghan 347 699-3259
  78 5th Ave Brooklyn (11217) *(G-1720)*
Damascus Bakery Inc (PA) 718 855-1456
  56 Gold St Brooklyn (11201) *(G-1721)*
Damiani Wine Cellars LLC 607 546-5557
  4704 State Route 414 Burdett (14818) *(G-3056)*
Damianou Sportswear Inc 718 204-5600
  6001 31st Ave Ste 2 Woodside (11377) *(G-16203)*
Dampits International Inc 212 581-3047
  425 W 57th St New York (10019) *(G-9160)*
Dan Ann Associates, Kirkwood *Also called Belden Manufacturing Inc (G-6730)*
Dan Trent Company Inc 716 822-1422
  1728 Clinton St Buffalo (14206) *(G-2720)*
Dan Wesson Corp 607 336-1174
  65 Borden Ave Norwich (13815) *(G-12120)*
Dana Michele LLC 917 757-7777
  3 E 84th St New York (10028) *(G-9161)*
Danaher Corporation 516 443-9432
  445 E 14th St Apt 3f New York (10009) *(G-9162)*
Dancing Deer Baking Co LLC 617 442-7300
  22 Hamilton Way Castleton On Hudson (12033) *(G-3202)*
Dandelion Energy Inc 603 781-2663
  335 Madison Ave Fl 4 New York (10017) *(G-9163)*
DAndrea Inc 516 496-2200
  115 Eileen Way Ste 106 Syosset (11791) *(G-14783)*
Danet Inc 718 266-4444
  8518 17th Ave Fl 2 Brooklyn (11214) *(G-1722)*
Danfoss Silicon Power LLC 515 239-6376
  330 Technology Dr Utica (13502) *(G-15252)*
DAngelo Home Collections Inc 917 267-8920
  39 Warwick Tpke Warwick (10990) *(G-15511)*
Danhier Co LLC 212 563-7683
  380 Rector Pl Apt 3d New York (10280) *(G-9164)*
Dani Accessories Inc 631 692-4505
  204 Lawrence Hill Rd Cold Spring Harbor (11724) *(G-3527)*
Dani II Inc (PA) 212 869-5999
  1 River Pl Apt 2410 New York (10036) *(G-9165)*
Danice Stores Inc 212 665-0389
  305 W 125th St New York (10027) *(G-9166)*
Daniel & Lois Lyndaker Logging 315 346-6527
  10460 Monnat School Rd Castorland (13620) *(G-3207)*
Daniel Demarco and Assoc Inc 631 598-7000
  25 Greene Ave Amityville (11701) *(G-262)*
Daniel M Friedman & Assoc Inc 212 695-5545
  19w W 34th St Fl 4 New York (10001) *(G-9167)*
Daniel O Reich Incorporated 718 748-6000
  7518 3rd Ave Brooklyn (11209) *(G-1723)*
Daniels Bath & Beyond 718 765-1915
  57 49th St Brooklyn (11232) *(G-1724)*
Danisco US Inc 585 256-5200
  3490 Winton Pl Rochester (14623) *(G-13337)*
Danisco US Inc 585 277-4300
  1700 Lexington Ave Rochester (14606) *(G-13338)*
Danner, Eg Mfg, Central Islip *Also called Eugene G Danner Mfg Inc (G-3273)*
Danny & Nicole, New York *Also called Kelly Grace Corp (G-10088)*
Danny Macaroons Inc 260 622-8463
  2191 3rd Ave Ste 3 New York (10035) *(G-9168)*
Danone Nutricia Early 914 872-8556
  100 Hillside Ave White Plains (10603) *(G-15997)*
Danone Us LLC (HQ) 914 872-8400
  1 Maple Ave White Plains (10605) *(G-15998)*
Danray Textiles Corp (PA) 212 354-5213
  270 W 39th St Fl 5 New York (10018) *(G-9169)*
Dans Paper Inc 631 537-0500
  158 County Road 39 Southampton (11968) *(G-14529)*
Dansville Logging & Lumber 585 335-5879
  10903 State Route 36 Dansville (14437) *(G-3818)*
Dantec Dynamics Inc 631 654-1290
  750 Blue Point Rd Holtsville (11742) *(G-6049)*
Dantex Trimming & Textile Co, New York *Also called Danray Textiles Corp (G-9169)*
Dapper Dads Inc 917 903-8045
  45 Rochester Ave Brooklyn (11233) *(G-1725)*
Darby Dental Supply 516 688-6421
  105 Executive Ct Jericho (11753) *(G-6576)*

Darco Manufacturing Inc 315 432-8905
6756 Thompson Rd Syracuse (13211) *(G-14874)*
Dark Star Lithograph Corp 845 634-3780
9 Perth Ln New City (10956) *(G-8224)*
Dark Storm Industries LLC 631 967-3170
4116 Sunrise Hwy Oakdale (11769) *(G-12150)*
Darkpulse Inc (PA) 800 436-1436
350 5th Ave Fl 59 New York (10118) *(G-9170)*
Darling Ingredients Inc 716 895-0655
2000 William St Buffalo (14206) *(G-2721)*
Darman Manufacturing Coinc 315 724-9632
1410 Lincoln Ave Utica (13502) *(G-15253)*
Darrell Mitchell 646 659-7075
704 Beach 67th St Arverne (11692) *(G-407)*
Dart Awning Inc 516 544-2082
365 S Main St Freeport (11520) *(G-4991)*
Dart Communications, New Hartford *Also called Dartcom Incorporated (G-8238)*
Dartcom Incorporated 315 790-5456
2 Oxford Xing Ste 1 New Hartford (13413) *(G-8238)*
Das Yidishe Licht Inc 718 387-3166
66 Middleton St Apt 1 Brooklyn (11206) *(G-1726)*
Dash Printing Inc 212 643-8534
153 W 27th St New York (10001) *(G-9171)*
Dashlane Inc 212 596-7510
44 W 18th St Fl 4 New York (10011) *(G-9172)*
Dason Company Div, New York *Also called D R S Inc (G-9147)*
Data Control Inc 585 265-2980
277 David Pkwy Ontario (14519) *(G-12287)*
Data Device Corporation (HQ) 631 567-5600
105 Wilbur Pl Bohemia (11716) *(G-999)*
Data Display USA Inc 631 218-2130
1330 Lincoln Ave Ste 2 Holbrook (11741) *(G-5995)*
Data Flow Inc 631 436-9200
6 Balsam Dr Medford (11763) *(G-7705)*
Data Implementation Inc 212 979-2015
5 E 22nd St Apt 14t New York (10010) *(G-9173)*
Data Key Communication LLC 315 445-2347
7573 Hunt Ln Fayetteville (13066) *(G-4783)*
Data Max, New York *Also called Datamax International Inc (G-9175)*
Data Palette Info Svcs LLC 718 433-1060
35 Marino Ave Port Washington (11050) *(G-12871)*
Data-Pac Mailing Systems Corp 585 671-0210
1217 Bay Rd Ste 12 Webster (14580) *(G-15637)*
Datacom Systems Inc 315 463-9541
9 Adler Dr East Syracuse (13057) *(G-4206)*
Datadog Inc (PA) 866 329-4466
620 8th Ave Fl 45 New York (10018) *(G-9174)*
Datagraphic Business Systems 516 485-9069
79 Emjay Blvd Brentwood (11717) *(G-1118)*
Datalink Computer Products 914 666-2358
165 E Main St 175 Mount Kisco (10549) *(G-8091)*
Datamax International Inc 212 693-0933
132 Nassau St Rm 511 New York (10038) *(G-9175)*
Datasonic Inc 516 248-7330
1413 Cleveland Ave East Meadow (11554) *(G-4134)*
Datatran Labs Inc 845 856-4313
11 Rebel Ln Port Jervis (12771) *(G-12847)*
Datesweiser, Buffalo *Also called Knoll Inc (G-2836)*
Datorib Inc 631 698-6222
974 Middle Country Rd Selden (11784) *(G-14352)*
Datum Alloys Inc 607 239-6274
407 Airport Rd Endicott (13760) *(G-4448)*
Dave Sandel Cranes Inc 631 325-5588
56 S Country Rd Westhampton (11977) *(G-15954)*
Davel Systems Inc 718 382-6024
1314 Avenue M Brooklyn (11230) *(G-1727)*
Davenport, Rochester *Also called Brinkman Products Inc (G-13282)*
Daves Cbd LLC 917 833-7306
28 Locust St Apt 202 Brooklyn (11206) *(G-1728)*
Daves Electric Motors & Pumps 212 982-2930
282 E 7th St Apt 1 New York (10009) *(G-9176)*
Daves Precision Machine Shop 845 626-7263
56 Webster Ave Kerhonkson (12446) *(G-6659)*
David & Young Co Inc 212 594-6034
366 5th Ave Rm 707 New York (10001) *(G-9177)*
David F De Marco 315 536-0882
929 Davy Rd Penn Yan (14527) *(G-12581)*
David Fehlman 315 455-8888
6729 Pickard Dr Syracuse (13211) *(G-14875)*
David Flatt Furniture Ltd 718 937-7944
3842 Review Ave Ste 2 Long Island City (11101) *(G-7198)*
David Friedman and Sons, New York *Also called David Friedman Chain Co Inc (G-9178)*
David Friedman Chain Co Inc 212 684-1760
10 E 38th St Fl 6 New York (10016) *(G-9178)*
David Helsing 607 796-2681
2077 Grand Central Ave Horseheads (14845) *(G-6120)*
David Howell & Company, Bedford Hills *Also called David Howell Product Design (G-767)*
David Howell Product Design 914 666-4080
405 Adams St Bedford Hills (10507) *(G-767)*
David Isseks & Sons Inc 212 966-8694
298 Broome St New York (10002) *(G-9179)*
David Johnson 315 493-4735
Deer River Rd Carthage (13619) *(G-3197)*
David King Linen Inc 718 241-7298
295 5th Ave Ste 1202 New York (10016) *(G-9180)*
David Kucera Inc 845 255-1044
42 Steves Ln Gardiner (12525) *(G-5128)*
David Peyser Sportswear Inc (PA) 631 231-7788
90 Spence St Bay Shore (11706) *(G-670)*
David Peyser Sportswear Inc 212 695-7716
4 Bryant Park Fl 12 Flr 12 New York (10018) *(G-9181)*
David S Diamonds Inc 212 921-8029
546 5th Ave Fl 7 New York (10036) *(G-9182)*
David Sutherland Showrooms - N (PA) 212 871-9717
D&D Building 979 3rd New York (10022) *(G-9183)*
David Weeks Studio 212 966-3433
38 Walker St Frnt 1 New York (10013) *(G-9184)*
David Weisz & Sons USA LLC 212 840-4747
20 W 47th St Ste 601 New York (10036) *(G-9185)*
David Yurman Enterprises LLC 914 539-4444
125 Westchester Ave # 1060 White Plains (10601) *(G-15999)*
David Yurman Enterprises LLC (PA) 212 896-1550
24 Vestry St New York (10013) *(G-9186)*
David Yurman Enterprises LLC 845 928-8660
484 Evergreen Ct Central Valley (10917) *(G-3298)*
David Yurman Retail LLC 877 226-1400
712 Madison Ave New York (10065) *(G-9187)*
Davidson Publishing, New York *Also called Boardman Simons Publishing (G-8827)*
Davies Office Refurbishing Inc (PA) 518 449-2040
40 Loudonville Rd Albany (12204) *(G-69)*
Davinci Designs Inc 631 595-1095
20 Lucon Dr Unit A Deer Park (11729) *(G-3859)*
Davinci Dsgns Distinctive Furn, Deer Park *Also called Davinci Designs Inc (G-3859)*
Davis 716 833-4678
283 Minnesota Ave Buffalo (14215) *(G-2722)*
Davis Aircraft Products Co Inc 631 563-1500
1150 Walnut Ave Ste 1 Bohemia (11716) *(G-1000)*
Davis International Inc 585 421-8175
388 Mason Rd Fairport (14450) *(G-4496)*
Davis Logging & Lumber 315 245-1040
1450 Curtiss Rd Camden (13316) *(G-3100)*
Davis Trailer World LLC 585 538-6640
1640 Main St York (14592) *(G-16362)*
Davis Trlr World & Cntry Mall, York *Also called Davis Trailer World LLC (G-16362)*
Davis Vision Inc (HQ) 800 328-4728
711 Troy Schenectady Rd # 301 Latham (12110) *(G-6854)*
Davler Media Group LLC (PA) 212 315-0800
213 W 35th St Rm 1201 New York (10001) *(G-9188)*
Davos Brands LLC 212 779-1911
381 Park Ave S Rm 1015 New York (10016) *(G-9189)*
Dawn Food Products Inc 716 830-8214
160 Lawrence Bell Dr # 120 Williamsville (14221) *(G-16128)*
Dawn Paper Co Inc (PA) 516 596-9110
4 Leonard Dr East Rockaway (11518) *(G-4172)*
Dawn Printing Company, East Rockaway *Also called Dawn Paper Co Inc (G-4172)*
Dawnex Industries Inc 718 384-0199
861 Park Ave Brooklyn (11206) *(G-1729)*
Dawson Doors, Jamestown *Also called Dawson Metal Company Inc (G-6506)*
Dawson Metal Company Inc 716 664-3811
825 Allen St Jamestown (14701) *(G-6506)*
Daxor Corporation (PA) 212 330-8500
350 5th Ave Ste 4740 New York (10118) *(G-9190)*
Day Automation Systems Inc (PA) 585 924-4630
7931 Rae Blvd Victor (14564) *(G-15404)*
Day One Lighting, Suffern *Also called E-Finnergy Group LLC (G-14760)*
Dayleen Intimates Inc 914 969-5900
540 Nepperhan Ave Yonkers (10701) *(G-16300)*
Daylight Technology USA Inc 973 255-8100
5971 59th St Maspeth (11378) *(G-7605)*
Dayton Industries Inc 718 542-8144
1350 Garrison Ave Bronx (10474) *(G-1237)*
Dayton Rogers New York LLC 585 349-4040
150 Fedex Way Rochester (14624) *(G-13339)*
Dayton T Brown Inc (PA) 631 589-6300
1175 Church St Bohemia (11716) *(G-1001)*
Dbase LLC 607 729-0234
100 Emerson Pkwy Binghamton (13905) *(G-871)*
Dbg Media 718 599-6828
358 Classon Ave Brooklyn (11238) *(G-1730)*
Dbs Interiors Corp 631 491-3013
81 Otis St West Babylon (11704) *(G-15706)*
DC Contracting & Building Corp 631 385-1117
136 Railroad St Huntington Station (11746) *(G-6244)*
DC Fabrication & Welding Inc 845 295-0215
17 Radcliff Rd Ferndale (12734) *(G-4788)*
Dcl Furniture Manufacturing 516 248-2683
96 Windsor Ave Mineola (11501) *(G-7968)*
Ddc Technologies Inc 516 594-1533
311 Woods Ave Unit B Oceanside (11572) *(G-12169)*
De Ans Pork Products Inc (PA) 718 788-2464
899 4th Ave Brooklyn (11232) *(G-1731)*
De Iorio's Bakery, Utica *Also called Deiorio Foods Inc (G-15254)*

ALPHABETIC

De Luxe Packaging Corp 416 754-4633
63 North St Saugerties (12477) *(G-14200)*

De Marco Vineyards, Penn Yan *Also called David F De Marco (G-12581)*

De Matteis Food Corp 646 629-8554
5 W 19th St Fl 10 New York (10011) *(G-9191)*

De Meo Brothers Hair, New York *Also called De Meo Brothers Inc (G-9192)*

De Meo Brothers Inc (PA) 212 268-1400
129 W 29th St Fl 5 New York (10001) *(G-9192)*

De Santis Holster and Lea Gds, Amityville *Also called Helgen Industries Inc (G-269)*

Dead Ringer LLC 585 355-4685
2100 Brghton Hnrtta St375 Rochester (14623) *(G-13340)*

Deakon Homes and Interiors 518 271-0342
16 Industrial Park Rd Troy (12180) *(G-15165)*

Deal, New York *Also called Dnp Electronics America LLC (G-9242)*

Deal International Inc 585 288-4444
110 Halstead St Ste 1 Rochester (14610) *(G-13341)*

Deal To Win Inc 718 609-1165
575 Unerhill Blvd Ste 325 Syosset (11791) *(G-14784)*

Dean Foods Company 315 452-5001
6867 Schuyler Rd East Syracuse (13057) *(G-4207)*

Dean Trading Corp 718 485-0600
200 Junius St Brooklyn (11212) *(G-1732)*

Deanco Digital Printing LLC 212 371-2025
4545 39th St Sunnyside (11104) *(G-14771)*

Deangelis Ltd 212 348-8225
262 Glen Head Rd Glen Head (11545) *(G-5205)*

Deans Paving Inc 315 736-7601
6002 Cavanaugh Rd Marcy (13403) *(G-7564)*

Dearfoams Div, New York *Also called RG Barry Corporation (G-11033)*

Death Wish Coffee Company LLC (PA) 518 400-1050
100 Saratoga Village Blvd # 3 Ballston Spa (12020) *(G-571)*

Deb El Food Products LLC 845 295-8050
88 Rock Hill Dr Rock Hill (12775) *(G-13818)*

Deb El Food Products LLC 607 203-5600
35 W State St Sherburne (13460) *(G-14390)*

Debmar-Mercury 212 669-5025
75 Rockefeller Plz # 1600 New York (10019) *(G-9193)*

Deborah Connolly & Associates, New York *Also called Arabella Textiles LLC (G-8616)*

Debra Fisher, Valley Stream *Also called Ready To Assemble Company Inc (G-15356)*

Debrucque Cleveland Tramrail S 315 697-5160
3 Technology Blvd Canastota (13032) *(G-3152)*

Decal Makers Inc 516 221-7200
2477 Merrick Rd Bellmore (11710) *(G-781)*

Decal Techniques Inc 631 491-1800
40 Corbin Ave Ste I Bay Shore (11706) *(G-671)*

Deck Bros Inc 716 852-0262
88 Beacon St Buffalo (14220) *(G-2723)*

Decker Forest Products Inc 607 563-2345
New York State Rte 8 Sidney (13838) *(G-14433)*

Decorative Hardware 914 238-5251
180 Hunts Ln Chappaqua (10514) *(G-3324)*

Decree Signs & Graphics Inc 973 278-3603
91 Tulip Ave Apt Kd1 Floral Park (11001) *(G-4814)*

Dedeco International Sales Inc (PA) 845 887-4840
11617 State Route 97 Long Eddy (12760) *(G-7139)*

Deejays, Pomona *Also called DJS Nyc Inc (G-12807)*

Deephaven Data Labs LLC (PA) 855 828-8445
79 Madison Ave New York (10016) *(G-9194)*

Deer Park Driveshaft & Hose 631 667-4091
85 Brook Ave Ste C Deer Park (11729) *(G-3860)*

Deer Park Drv Shaft & Hose Co, Deer Park *Also called Deer Park Driveshaft & Hose (G-3860)*

Deer Park Macaroni Co Inc (PA) 631 667-4600
1882 Deer Park Ave Deer Park (11729) *(G-3861)*

Deer Park Macaroni Co Inc 631 667-4600
1882 Deer Park Ave Deer Park (11729) *(G-3862)*

Deer Park Ravioli & Macaroni, Deer Park *Also called Deer Park Macaroni Co Inc (G-3862)*

Deer Park Sand & Gravel Corp 631 586-2323
145 S 4th St Bay Shore (11706) *(G-672)*

Deer Pk Stair Bldg Mllwk Inc 631 363-5000
51 Kennedy Ave Blue Point (11715) *(G-956)*

Deer Run Enterprises Inc 585 346-0850
3772 W Lake Rd Geneseo (14454) *(G-5143)*

Deer Run Winery, Geneseo *Also called Deer Run Enterprises Inc (G-5143)*

Deerfield Millwork Inc 631 726-9663
58 Deerfield Rd Unit 2 Water Mill (11976) *(G-15529)*

Dees Audio & Vision 585 719-9256
347 Seneca Pkwy Rochester (14613) *(G-13342)*

Defelsko Corporation 315 393-4450
800 Proctor Ave Ogdensburg (13669) *(G-12204)*

Definition Press Inc 212 777-4490
141 Greene St New York (10012) *(G-9195)*

Defran Systems Inc 212 727-8342
1 Penn Plz Ste 1700 New York (10119) *(G-9196)*

Degennaro Fuel Service LLC 518 239-6350
242 County Route 357 Medusa (12120) *(G-7750)*

Deiorio Foods Inc (PA) 315 732-7612
2200 Bleecker St Utica (13501) *(G-15254)*

Dejana Trck Utility Eqp Co LLC (HQ) 631 544-9000
490 Pulaski Rd Kings Park (11754) *(G-6672)*

Dejana Trck Utility Eqp Co LLC 631 549-0944
743 Park Ave Huntington (11743) *(G-6204)*

Dejana Truck & Utility Eqp Co, Huntington *Also called Dejana Trck Utility Eqp Co LLC (G-6204)*

Delaney Books Inc 516 921-8888
212 Michael Dr Syosset (11791) *(G-14785)*

Delaney Machine Products Ltd 631 225-1032
150 S Alleghany Ave Ste A Lindenhurst (11757) *(G-6948)*

Delaval Inc 585 599-4696
850 Main Rd Corfu (14036) *(G-3702)*

Delaware County Times Inc 607 746-2176
56 Main St Delhi (13753) *(G-3963)*

Delaware Manufacturing Inds, North Tonawanda *Also called Dmic Inc (G-12065)*

Delaware Valley Forge Co Inc 716 447-9140
247 Rano St Buffalo (14207) *(G-2724)*

Delaware Valley Forge Inc 716 447-9140
241 Rano St Buffalo (14207) *(G-2725)*

Delbia Do Company Inc (PA) 718 585-2226
2550 Park Ave Bronx (10451) *(G-1238)*

Delbia Do Company Inc 718 585-2226
11 Canal Pl Bronx (10451) *(G-1239)*

Delcath Systems Inc (PA) 212 489-2100
1633 Broadway Fl 22c New York (10019) *(G-9197)*

Delectable, New York *Also called Vinous Group LLC (G-11685)*

Delfingen Us-New York Inc 716 215-0300
2221 Niagara Falls Blvd # 12 Niagara Falls (14304) *(G-11920)*

Delford Industries Inc 845 342-3901
82 Washington St 84 Middletown (10940) *(G-7904)*

Delft Printing Inc 716 683-1100
1000 Commerce Pkwy Lancaster (14086) *(G-6802)*

Delicias Andinas Food Corp 718 416-2922
5750 Maspeth Ave Flushing (11378) *(G-4847)*

Delicioso Coco Helado Inc 718 292-1930
849 Saint Anns Ave Bronx (10456) *(G-1240)*

Delicious Foods Inc 718 446-9352
11202 Roosevelt Ave Corona (11368) *(G-3738)*

Dell Communications Inc 212 989-3434
109 W 27th St Frnt 2 New York (10001) *(G-9198)*

Dell Graphics, New York *Also called Dell Communications Inc (G-9198)*

Dell's Maraschino Cherries Co, Brooklyn *Also called Dells Cherries LLC (G-1734)*

Della Systems Inc 631 580-0010
951 S 2nd St Ronkonkoma (11779) *(G-13930)*

Dellas Graphics, Rochester *Also called Canfield & Tack Inc (G-13293)*

Dellet Industries Inc 718 965-0101
1 43rd St Ste L8 Brooklyn (11232) *(G-1733)*

Dells Cherries LLC 718 624-4380
175 Dikeman St Ste 177 Brooklyn (11231) *(G-1734)*

Dells Cherries LLC 718 624-4380
81 Ferris St Brooklyn (11231) *(G-1735)*

Delocon Wholesale Inc 716 592-2711
270 W Main St Springville (14141) *(G-14589)*

Deloka LLC 315 946-6910
150 Dunn Rd Lyons (14489) *(G-7449)*

Delphi Amherst Test Operations, Amherst *Also called Delphi Automotive LLP (G-220)*

Delphi Automotive LLP 716 438-4886
4326 Ridge Lea Rd Amherst (14226) *(G-220)*

Delphi Powertrain Systems LLC 585 359-6000
5500 W Henrietta Rd West Henrietta (14586) *(G-15791)*

Delphi Powertrain Systems LLC 585 359-6000
5500 W Henrietta Rd West Henrietta (14586) *(G-15792)*

Delphi Powertrain Systems LLC 585 359-6000
5500 W Henrietta Rd West Henrietta (14586) *(G-15793)*

Delphi Thermal Systems 716 439-2454
350 Upper Mountain Rd Lockport (14094) *(G-7067)*

Delphi Thrmal Lckport Model Sp, Lockport *Also called Mahle Behr USA Inc (G-7089)*

Delphi-T Compressor Engrg Ctr, Amherst *Also called Mahle Indstrbeteiligungen GMBH (G-231)*

Delroyd Worm Gear, Niagara Falls *Also called Nuttall Gear L L C (G-11958)*

Delsur Parts 631 630-1606
112 Pheasant Cir Brentwood (11717) *(G-1119)*

Delta Galil USA Inc 212 710-6440
6 E 32nd St Fl 9 New York (10016) *(G-9199)*

Delta Lock Company LLC 631 238-7035
366 Central Ave Bohemia (11716) *(G-1002)*

Delta Polymers Inc 631 254-6240
130 S 2nd St Bay Shore (11706) *(G-673)*

Delta Press Inc 212 989-3445
2426 Lucas Tpke High Falls (12440) *(G-5955)*

Delta Sheet Metal Corp 718 429-5805
940 S Oyster Bay Rd Hicksville (11801) *(G-5901)*

Deluxe Corporation 845 362-4054
9 Lincoln Ave Spring Valley (10977) *(G-14566)*

Deluxe Machine & Tool Co, Batavia *Also called Bill Shea Enterprises Inc (G-604)*

Deluxe Packaging Corp 845 246-6090
63 North St Saugerties (12477) *(G-14201)*

Deluxe Passport Express, Brooklyn *Also called Deluxe Travel Store Inc (G-1736)*

Deluxe Travel Store Inc 718 435-8111
5014 12th Ave Brooklyn (11219) *(G-1736)*

Demartini Oil Equipment Svc 518 463-5752
214 River Rd Glenmont (12077) *(G-5236)*

Deming Electro-Plating Corp...................................585 968-2355
  5 Woodruff St Cuba (14727) *(G-3812)*

Democrat & Chronicle, Rochester *Also called Gannett Co Inc (G-13428)*

Demos Medical Publishing LLC..............................516 889-1791
  11 W 42nd St Ste 15c New York (10036) *(G-9200)*

Denim King Depot LLC..917 477-0550
  1350 6th Ave Ste 1004 New York (10019) *(G-9201)*

Deniz Information Systems......................................212 750-5199
  208 E 51st St Ste 129 New York (10022) *(G-9202)*

Dennies Manufacturing Inc...................................585 393-4646
  2543 State Route 21 Canandaigua (14424) *(G-3130)*

Dennis Basso Couture Inc.....................................212 794-4500
  825 Madison Ave New York (10065) *(G-9203)*

Dennis Basso Furs, New York *Also called Dennis Basso Couture Inc (G-9203)*

Dennis Metals Inc..516 487-5747
  33 Edgewood Pl Great Neck (11024) *(G-5381)*

Dennis Publishing Inc..646 717-9500
  55 W 39th St Fl 5 New York (10018) *(G-9204)*

Denny Machine Co Inc...716 873-6865
  20 Norris St Buffalo (14207) *(G-2726)*

Dennys Drive Shaft Service....................................716 875-6640
  1189 Military Rd Kenmore (14217) *(G-6649)*

Dental Tribune America LLC...................................212 244-7181
  11835 Queens Blvd Ste 400 Forest Hills (11375) *(G-4919)*

DenTek Oral Care Inc (HQ)......................................865 983-1300
  660 White Plains Rd # 250 Tarrytown (10591) *(G-15043)*

Denton Printing Corporation...................................631 586-4333
  1650 Sycamore Ave Ste 28 Bohemia (11716) *(G-1003)*

Denton Publications Inc (PA).................................518 873-6368
  14 Hand Ave Elizabethtown (12932) *(G-4299)*

Denton Publications Inc..518 561-9680
  21 Mckinley Ave Ste 3 Plattsburgh (12901) *(G-12744)*

Denton Stoneworks Inc...516 746-1500
  94 Denton Ave Garden City Park (11040) *(G-5120)*

Department of Sanitation, Brooklyn *Also called City of New York (G-1666)*

Depco Inc..631 582-1995
  20 Newton Pl Hauppauge (11788) *(G-5635)*

Dependable Acme Threaded Pdts............................516 338-4700
  167 School St Westbury (11590) *(G-15875)*

Dependable Lithographers Inc.................................718 472-4200
  3200 Skillman Ave Long Island City (11101) *(G-7199)*

Dependable Tool & Die Co Inc................................315 453-5696
  129 Dwight Park Cir # 2 Syracuse (13209) *(G-14876)*

Depot Label Company Inc.......................................631 467-2952
  217 River Ave Patchogue (11772) *(G-12499)*

Depp Glass Inc...718 784-8500
  4140 38th St Long Island City (11101) *(G-7200)*

Der Blatt Inc...845 783-1148
  6 Taitch Ct Unit 112 Monroe (10950) *(G-8019)*

Der Yid Inc..718 797-3900
  84 Bay St Brooklyn (11231) *(G-1737)*

Der Yid Publication, Brooklyn *Also called Der Yid Inc (G-1737)*

Deraffele Mfg Co Inc...914 636-6850
  2525 Palmer Ave Ste 4 New Rochelle (10801) *(G-8326)*

Derby Fashion Center, Conklin *Also called S & T Knitting Co Inc (G-3628)*

Derecktor Shipyards, Mamaroneck *Also called Robert E Derecktor Inc (G-7522)*

Dereon/24 K Style, New York *Also called Rvc Enterprises LLC (G-11101)*

Derm-Buro Inc (PA)..516 694-8300
  229 Newtown Rd Plainview (11803) *(G-12678)*

Dermatech Labs Inc..631 225-1700
  165 S 10th St Lindenhurst (11757) *(G-6949)*

Dern Moore Machine Company Inc...........................716 433-6243
  151 S Niagara St Lockport (14094) *(G-7068)*

Derosa Fabrications Inc...631 563-0640
  250 Knickerbocker Ave Bohemia (11716) *(G-1004)*

Derrick Corporation (PA)..716 683-9010
  590 Duke Rd Buffalo (14225) *(G-2727)*

Derrick Corporation...716 685-4892
  2540 Walden Ave Cheektowaga (14225) *(G-3344)*

Derrick Equipment, Buffalo *Also called Derrick Corporation (G-2727)*

Design Archives Inc..212 768-0617
  1460 Broadway New York (10036) *(G-9205)*

Design Craft Division, Jamestown *Also called Larson Metal Manufacturing Co (G-6529)*

Design Distributors Inc..631 242-2000
  300 Marcus Blvd Deer Park (11729) *(G-3863)*

Design Interiors, Brooklyn *Also called Atlantic Stairs Corp (G-1548)*

Design Lithographers Inc..212 645-8900
  519 8th Ave Ste 3 New York (10018) *(G-9206)*

Design Solutions LI Inc..631 656-8700
  711 Middle Country Rd Saint James (11780) *(G-14109)*

Design Source By Lg Inc..212 274-0022
  115 Bowery Frnt 1 New York (10002) *(G-9207)*

Design Works Craft Inc (PA)....................................631 244-5749
  70 Orville Dr Ste 1 Bohemia (11716) *(G-1005)*

Design/OI Inc..631 474-2134
  200 Wilson St Unit D2 Port Jeff STA (11776) *(G-12834)*

Designatronics Incorporated...................................516 328-3300
  250 Duffy Ave Unit A Hicksville (11801) *(G-5902)*

Designatronics Incorporated...................................516 328-3300
  55 Denton Ave S New Hyde Park (11040) *(G-8261)*

Designer Epoxy Finishes Inc...................................646 943-6044
  445 Broadhollow Rd Ste 25 Melville (11747) *(G-7774)*

Designer Glass, College Point *Also called Gmd Industries Inc (G-3543)*

Designers Folding Box Corp.....................................716 853-5141
  84 Tennessee St Buffalo (14204) *(G-2728)*

Designlogocom Inc..212 564-0200
  15 W 37th St Lbby A New York (10018) *(G-9208)*

Designplex LLC...845 358-6647
  107 Cedar Hill Ave Nyack (10960) *(G-12140)*

Designs By Hc, New York *Also called Horo Creations LLC (G-9813)*

Designs By Novello Inc...914 934-7711
  505 N Main St Port Chester (10573) *(G-12817)*

Designs By Robert Scott Inc....................................718 609-2535
  810 Humboldt St Ste 3 Brooklyn (11222) *(G-1738)*

Designs For Vision Inc..631 585-3300
  4000 Veterans Mem Hwy Bohemia (11716) *(G-1006)*

Designway Ltd..212 254-2220
  27 E 21st St Fl 7 New York (10010) *(G-9209)*

Desiron, New York *Also called F&M Ornamental Designs LLC (G-9456)*

Desktop Publishing Concepts...................................631 752-1934
  855 Conklin St Ste T Farmingdale (11735) *(G-4614)*

Desmi-Afti Inc..716 662-0632
  227 Thorn Ave Bldg C Orchard Park (14127) *(G-12351)*

Dessy Creations, New York *Also called A & M Rosenthal Entps Inc (G-8411)*

Desu Machinery Corporation....................................716 681-5798
  200 Gould Ave Depew (14043) *(G-3979)*

Detekion Security Systems Inc.................................607 729-7179
  200 Plaza Dr Ste 1 Vestal (13850) *(G-15376)*

Detny Footwear Inc...212 423-1040
  1 River Pl Apt 1224 New York (10036) *(G-9210)*

Detour Apparel Inc (PA)...212 221-3265
  530 7th Ave Rm 608 New York (10018) *(G-9211)*

Deutsch Relays...631 342-1700
  55 Engineers Rd Hauppauge (11788) *(G-5636)*

Deva Concepts LLC...212 343-0344
  75 Spring St Fl 8 New York (10012) *(G-9212)*

Devacurl, New York *Also called Deva Concepts LLC (G-9212)*

Devil Dog Manufacturing Co Inc (PA).........................845 647-4411
  23 Market St Ellenville (12428) *(G-4306)*

Devin Mfg Inc...585 496-5770
  40 Edward St Arcade (14009) *(G-372)*

Devonian Stone New York Inc..................................607 655-2600
  463 Atwell Hill Rd Windsor (13865) *(G-16157)*

Devos Ltd (PA)..800 473-2138
  100 Colin Dr Holbrook (11741) *(G-5996)*

Dew Graphics, New York *Also called DEW Graphics Inc (G-9213)*

DEW Graphics Inc..212 727-8820
  519 8th Ave Fl 18 New York (10018) *(G-9213)*

Dewey Machine & Tool Inc.......................................607 749-3930
  49 James St Homer (13077) *(G-6061)*

Dewitt Plastics Inc..315 255-1209
  28 Aurelius Ave Auburn (13021) *(G-473)*

Dezawy LLC...917 436-8820
  55 W 116th St Ste 327 New York (10026) *(G-9214)*

Df Mavens Inc...347 813-4705
  2420 49th St Astoria (11103) *(G-417)*

DFA New York LLC..212 523-0021
  318 W 39th St Fl 10 New York (10018) *(G-9215)*

Dga Energy, New York *Also called DTI Financial Inc (G-9274)*

DH Machine Tool Services, Marathon *Also called Gallery of Machines LLC (G-7557)*

Dhs Systems LLC (HQ)..845 359-6066
  560 Route 303 Ste 206 Orangeburg (10962) *(G-12312)*

Di Borghese Castello LLC.......................................631 734-5111
  17150 County Road 48 Cutchogue (11935) *(G-3815)*

Di Domenico Packaging Co Inc.................................718 727-5454
  304 Bertram Ave Staten Island (10312) *(G-14645)*

Di Fiore and Sons Custom Wdwkg..............................718 278-1663
  4202 Astoria Blvd Long Island City (11103) *(G-7201)*

Di Highway Sign Structure Corp................................315 736-8312
  40 Greenman Ave New York Mills (13417) *(G-11831)*

Di Sanos Creative Canvas Inc..................................315 894-3137
  113 W Main St Frankfort (13340) *(G-4949)*

DI ZUKUNFT, New York *Also called Congress For Jewish Culture (G-9083)*

Dia..212 675-4097
  535 W 22nd St Fl 4 New York (10011) *(G-9216)*

Dialase Inc...212 575-8833
  36 W 47th St Ste 709 New York (10036) *(G-9217)*

Diam International, Yonkers *Also called Creative Solutions Group Inc (G-16299)*

Diamex Inc..212 575-8145
  580 5th Ave Ste 625 New York (10036) *(G-9218)*

Diamond Boutique...516 444-3373
  77 Main St Port Washington (11050) *(G-12872)*

Diamond Constellation Corp....................................212 819-0324
  37 W 47th St Ste 506 New York (10036) *(G-9219)*

Diamond Coring & Cutting Inc..................................718 381-4545
  5919 55th St Maspeth (11378) *(G-7606)*

Diamond Dimensions, Mount Vernon *Also called Aaron Group LLC (G-8119)*

Diamond Distributors Inc (PA).................................212 921-9188
  608 5th Ave Fl 10 New York (10020) *(G-9220)*

Diamond Inscription Tech..646 366-7944
  36 W 47th St Ste 1008 New York (10036) *(G-9221)*

Diamond Packaging, Rochester *Also called Diamond Paper Box Company (G-13344)*

A
L
P
H
A
B
E
T
I
C

Diamond Packaging Holdings LLC...................585 334-8030
  111 Commerce Dr Rochester (14623) *(G-13343)*
Diamond Paper Box Company.........................585 334-8030
  111 Commerce Dr Rochester (14623) *(G-13344)*
Diamond Precast Products Inc........................631 874-3777
  170 Railroad Ave Center Moriches (11934) *(G-3245)*
Diamond Saw Works Inc (PA).........................716 496-7417
  12290 Olean Rd Chaffee (14030) *(G-3305)*
Diamond Seafoods Inc....................................503 351-3240
  366 Amsterdam Ave Ste 234 New York (10024) *(G-9222)*
Diana Kane Incorporated.................................718 638-6520
  229 5th Ave Ste B Brooklyn (11215) *(G-1739)*
Diane Artemis Studios, Brooklyn *Also called Artemis Studios Inc (G-1536)*
Diane Studios Inc (PA)....................................718 788-6007
  34 35th St Ste 2b Brooklyn (11232) *(G-1740)*
Diane Von Furstenberg The Shop, New York *Also called Dvf Studio LLC (G-9283)*
Dianos Kathryn Designs.................................212 267-1584
  150 W 55th St New York (10019) *(G-9223)*
Dib Managmnt Inc..718 439-8190
  251 53rd St Brooklyn (11220) *(G-1741)*
Dicamillo Marble and Granite.........................845 878-0078
  20 Jon Barrett Rd Patterson (12563) *(G-12515)*
Dice America Inc...585 869-6200
  7676 Netlink Dr Victor (14564) *(G-15405)*
Dick Bailey Printers, Brooklyn *Also called Dick Bailey Service Inc (G-1742)*
Dick Bailey Service Inc...................................718 522-4363
  25 Chapel St Ste 602 Brooklyn (11201) *(G-1742)*
Dicks Concrete Co Inc (PA)............................845 374-5966
  1053 County Route 37 New Hampton (10958) *(G-8234)*
Dico Products, Utica *Also called Divine Brothers Company (G-15259)*
Dico Products Corporation.............................315 797-0470
  200 Seward Ave Utica (13502) *(G-15255)*
Didco Inc..212 997-5022
  8570 67th Ave Rego Park (11374) *(G-13076)*
Die-Matic Products LLC..................................516 433-7900
  130 Express St Plainview (11803) *(G-12679)*
Diegraphics Group, Rochester *Also called Csw Inc (G-13331)*
Diehl Development Inc.....................................585 494-2920
  5922 N Lake Rd Bergen (14416) *(G-813)*
Diehl Sand & Gravel, Bergen *Also called Diehl Development Inc (G-813)*
Diemax of Rochester Inc.................................585 288-3912
  1555 Lyell Ave Ste 141 Rochester (14606) *(G-13345)*
Diemolding Corporation..................................315 363-4710
  100 Donald Hicks Dew Dr Wampsville (13163) *(G-15480)*
Diemolding Corporation..................................315 363-4710
  N Court St Wampsville (13163) *(G-15481)*
Dietooling, Wampsville *Also called Diemolding Corporation (G-15481)*
Dieu Donne, Brooklyn *Also called Donne Dieu Paper Mill Inc (G-1757)*
Digicom International Inc................................631 249-8999
  145 Rome St Farmingdale (11735) *(G-4615)*
Digiday Media LLC..646 419-4357
  1 Liberty Plz Fl 9 New York (10006) *(G-9224)*
Digifab Systems Inc.......................................212 944-9882
  1412 Broadway Ste 2100 New York (10018) *(G-9225)*
Digiorange Inc..718 801-8244
  5620 1st Ave Ste 4 Brooklyn (11220) *(G-1743)*
Digitac Inc (PA)...732 215-4020
  2076 Ocean Pkwy Brooklyn (11223) *(G-1744)*
Digitac LLC..732 669-7637
  2076 Ocean Pkwy 2 Brooklyn (11223) *(G-1745)*
Digital Analysis Corporation...........................315 685-0760
  716 Visions Dr Skaneateles (13152) *(G-14449)*
Digital Associates LLC...................................631 983-6075
  50 Karl Ave Ste 303 Smithtown (11787) *(G-14475)*
Digital Color Concepts Inc (PA).....................212 989-4888
  30 W 21st St Fl 5 New York (10010) *(G-9226)*
Digital Evolution Inc (PA)...............................212 732-2722
  200 N End Ave Apt 20e New York (10282) *(G-9227)*
Digital Fabrication Wkshp Inc.........................518 249-6500
  99 S 3rd St Ste 2 Hudson (12534) *(G-6153)*
Digital Home Creations Inc.............................585 576-7070
  350 Shadowbrook Dr Webster (14580) *(G-15638)*
Digital Imiging Technologies, Ballston Spa *Also called Dit Prints Incorporated (G-572)*
Digital Instruments Inc...................................716 874-5848
  580 Ensminger Rd Tonawanda (14150) *(G-15099)*
Digital Matrix Corp...516 481-7990
  34 Sarah Dr Ste B Farmingdale (11735) *(G-4616)*
Digital One USA Inc...718 396-4890
  7230 Roosevelt Ave Flushing (11372) *(G-4848)*
Digital Page LLC..518 446-9129
  75 Benjamin St Albany (12202) *(G-70)*
Digital United Color Prtg Inc...........................845 986-9846
  33 South St Warwick (10990) *(G-15512)*
Digital X-Press, Albany *Also called Brigar X-Press Solutions Inc (G-52)*
Digitech Printers, New York *Also called Balajee Enterprises Inc (G-8721)*
Digitronik Labs Inc...585 360-0043
  1344 University Ave # 6100 Rochester (14607) *(G-13346)*
Dijifi LLC...646 519-2447
  1166 Manhattan Ave # 100 Brooklyn (11222) *(G-1746)*
Dilese International Inc....................................716 855-3500
  141 Broadway St Buffalo (14203) *(G-2729)*

Diligent Board Member Svcs LLC....................212 741-8181
  310 5th Ave Fl 7 New York (10001) *(G-9228)*
Diligent Corporation (HQ)...............................212 741-8181
  111 W 33rd St 16 New York (10001) *(G-9229)*
Dillmeier Enterprises Inc................................800 325-0596
  106 7th St Ste 201 Garden City (11530) *(G-5095)*
Dillner Precast Inc (PA)..................................631 421-9130
  14 Meadow Ln Lloyd Harbor (11743) *(G-7055)*
Dillner Precast Inc..631 421-9130
  200 W 9th St Huntington Station (11746) *(G-6245)*
Dimaio Millwork Corporation..........................914 476-1937
  12 Bright Pl Yonkers (10705) *(G-16301)*
Dimanco Inc (PA)...315 797-0470
  200 Seward Ave Utica (13502) *(G-15256)*
Dimar Manufacturing Corp..............................716 759-0351
  10123 Main St Clarence (14031) *(G-3428)*
Dimarzio Inc..718 442-6655
  1388 Richmond Ter Ste 1 Staten Island (10310) *(G-14646)*
Dime Trading Inc..718 797-0303
  787 Kent Ave Brooklyn (11205) *(G-1747)*
Dimension Development Corp..........................718 361-8825
  3630 37th St Fl 1 Long Island City (11101) *(G-7202)*
Dimension Fabricators Inc..............................518 374-1936
  2000 7th St Scotia (12302) *(G-14329)*
Dimension Technologies Inc...........................585 436-3530
  315 Mount Read Blvd Ste 5 Rochester (14611) *(G-13347)*
Dimensional Mills, Hudson Falls *Also called Dwa Pallet Inc (G-6186)*
Dimensional Mills Inc.....................................518 746-1047
  337 Main St Hudson Falls (12839) *(G-6185)*
Dimoda Designs Inc.......................................212 355-8166
  48 W 48th St Ste 403 New York (10036) *(G-9230)*
Dine Rite Seating Products Inc.......................631 226-8899
  165 E Hoffman Ave Unit 3 Lindenhurst (11757) *(G-6950)*
Dinette Depot Ltd...516 515-9623
  350 Dewitt Ave Brooklyn (11207) *(G-1748)*
Dinewise Inc..631 694-1111
  500 B Cuntry Blvd Ste 400 Farmingdale (11735) *(G-4617)*
Dining Furniture, Brooklyn *Also called Dinette Depot Ltd (G-1748)*
Dinos Sausage & Meat Co Inc........................315 732-2661
  722 Catherine St Utica (13501) *(G-15257)*
Dinosaw Inc (PA)...518 828-9942
  340 Power Ave Hudson (12534) *(G-6154)*
Dionics-Usa Inc...516 997-7474
  96b Urban Ave Westbury (11590) *(G-15876)*
Dipaolo Baking Co Inc....................................585 303-5013
  598 Plymouth Ave N Rochester (14608) *(G-13348)*
Direct 2 Market Solutions, Rochester *Also called Selby Marketing Associates Inc (G-13722)*
Direct Mktg Edctl Fndation Inc.......................212 790-1512
  1333 Broadway Rm 301 New York (10018) *(G-9231)*
Direct Print Inc (PA).......................................212 987-6003
  77 E 125th St New York (10035) *(G-9232)*
Directory Major Malls Inc...............................845 348-7000
  20 N Broadway Ste 2 Nyack (10960) *(G-12141)*
Direkt Force LLC..716 652-3022
  455 Olean Rd Ste 3 East Aurora (14052) *(G-4085)*
Dirt T Shirts Inc...845 336-4230
  444 Old Neighborhood Rd Kingston (12401) *(G-6689)*
Dirty Lemon Beverages LLC (PA)...................877 897-7784
  95 Grand St Apt 5 New York (10013) *(G-9233)*
Dis, Islandia *Also called Duetto Integrated Systems Inc (G-6331)*
Dis, New York *Also called Deniz Information Systems (G-9202)*
Disc Graphics Inc...631 300-1129
  30 Gilpin Ave Hauppauge (11788) *(G-5637)*
Disc Graphics Inc (HQ)...................................631 234-1400
  10 Gilpin Ave Hauppauge (11788) *(G-5638)*
Disc-Lock LLC...310 560-9940
  400 Rverwalk Pkwy Ste 600 Tonawanda (14150) *(G-15100)*
Discover Casting Inc......................................212 398-5050
  17 W 45th St New York (10036) *(G-9234)*
Discover Magazine, New York *Also called Discover Media LLC (G-9235)*
Discover Media LLC..212 624-4800
  90 5th Ave Ste 1100 New York (10011) *(G-9235)*
Dispatch Graphics Inc....................................212 307-5943
  344 W 38th St Fl 4r New York (10018) *(G-9236)*
Dispatch Letter Service, New York *Also called Dispatch Graphics Inc (G-9236)*
Dispersion Technology Inc.............................914 241-4777
  364 Adams St Bedford Hills (10507) *(G-768)*
Display Components Mfg Inc...........................631 420-0600
  267 Edison Ave West Babylon (11704) *(G-15707)*
Display Fireworks, Canandaigua *Also called Young Explosives Corp (G-3146)*
Display Logic USA Inc.....................................631 406-1922
  40 Oser Ave Ste 4 Hauppauge (11788) *(G-5639)*
Display Marketing Group Inc...........................631 348-4450
  170 Oval Dr Ste B Islandia (11749) *(G-6330)*
Display Presentations Ltd...............................631 951-4050
  16 Court St Fl 14 Brooklyn (11241) *(G-1749)*
Display Producers Inc.....................................718 904-1200
  40 Winding Brook Rd New Rochelle (10804) *(G-8327)*
Display Shop Inc (PA).....................................646 202-9494
  261 Madison Ave Fl 9 New York (10016) *(G-9237)*
Display Technologies LLC (HQ).......................718 321-3100
  1111 Marcus Ave Ste M68 New Hyde Park (11042) *(G-8262)*

Displays By Rioux Inc 315 458-3639
6090 E Taft Rd North Syracuse (13212) **(G-12039)**
Dissent Magazine 212 316-3120
120 Wall St Fl 31 New York (10005) **(G-9238)**
Distech Systems Inc (HQ) 585 254-7020
1000 University Ave # 400 Rochester (14607) **(G-13349)**
Distinction Magazine Inc 631 843-3522
235 Pinelawn Rd Melville (11747) **(G-7775)**
Distinctive Printing Inc 212 727-3000
225 W 37th St Fl 16 New York (10018) **(G-9239)**
Distribio USA LLC 212 989-6077
261 5th Ave Rm 2000 New York (10016) **(G-9240)**
Distributors Vending Corp 914 472-8981
2 Lawrence St Ardsley (10502) **(G-388)**
Dit Prints Incorporated 518 885-4400
27 Kent St Ste 53 Ballston Spa (12020) **(G-572)**
Diva Farms Ltd 315 735-4397
1301 Broad St Utica (13501) **(G-15258)**
Diversified Air Products Sales, Orangeburg *Also called Ruskin Company* **(G-12330)**
Diversified Envelope Ltd 585 615-4697
95 Mount Read Blvd # 103 Rochester (14611) **(G-13350)**
Diversified Manufacturing Inc 716 681-7670
4401 Walden Ave Lancaster (14086) **(G-6803)**
Diversify Apparel, New York *Also called Babyfair Inc* **(G-8711)**
Diversion Magazine, New York *Also called Hearst Business Publishing Inc* **(G-9742)**
Diversity Best Practices, New York *Also called Working Mother Media Inc* **(G-11778)**
Divine Bros, Utica *Also called Dimanco Inc* **(G-15256)**
Divine Brothers Company 315 797-0470
200 Seward Ave Utica (13502) **(G-15259)**
Divine Phoenix LLC 585 737-1482
2985 Benson Rd Skaneateles (13152) **(G-14450)**
Divine Phoenix Books, Skaneateles *Also called Divine Phoenix LLC* **(G-14450)**
Division Den-Bar Enterprises 914 381-2220
745 W Boston Post Rd Mamaroneck (10543) **(G-7508)**
Division of Emergency Services, Holbrook *Also called M C Products* **(G-6008)**
Dixie Foam Ltd 212 645-8999
1205 Manhattan Ave # 311 Brooklyn (11222) **(G-1750)**
Dixiefoam Beds, Brooklyn *Also called Dixie Foam Ltd* **(G-1750)**
Dixon Tool and Manufacturing 585 235-1352
240 Burrows St Rochester (14606) **(G-13351)**
Diyzeitung, Brooklyn *Also called News Report Inc* **(G-2213)**
Dj Acquisition Management Corp (PA) 585 265-3000
6364 Dean Pkwy Ontario (14519) **(G-12288)**
Dj Expression, Brooklyn *Also called Fuzion Creations Intl LLC* **(G-1873)**
Dj Publishing Inc 516 767-2500
25 Willowdale Ave Port Washington (11050) **(G-12873)**
DJS Nyc Inc 845 445-8618
3 Laura Ln Pomona (10970) **(G-12807)**
DK, Fulton *Also called D-K Manufacturing Corp* **(G-5057)**
DK Publishing 212 366-2000
345 Hudson St New York (10014) **(G-9241)**
Dkm Ad Art, Buffalo *Also called Dkm Sales LLC* **(G-2730)**
Dkm Sales LLC 716 893-7777
1352 Genesee St Buffalo (14211) **(G-2730)**
Dkn Ready Mix LLC 718 218-6418
362 Maspeth Ave Brooklyn (11211) **(G-1751)**
Dkny, Niagara Falls *Also called AM Retail Group Inc* **(G-11902)**
Dkny Underwear, New York *Also called Wacoal America Inc* **(G-11715)**
Dl Manufacturing Inc 315 432-8977
340 Gateway Park Dr North Syracuse (13212) **(G-12040)**
Dlc Comprehensive Medical PC 718 857-1200
979 Fulton St Brooklyn (11238) **(G-1752)**
Dlh Energy Service LLC 716 410-0028
4422 W Fairmount Ave Lakewood (14750) **(G-6782)**
Dli, Cazenovia *Also called Knowles Cazenovia Inc* **(G-3228)**
Dlr Enterprises LLC 315 813-2911
104 E Seneca St Sherrill (13461) **(G-14403)**
Dlx Industries Inc 718 272-9420
225 25th St Brooklyn (11232) **(G-1753)**
Dlz Holdings South Inc 607 723-1727
27 Link Dr Ste D Binghamton (13904) **(G-872)**
DMD Machining Technology Inc 585 659-8180
17231 Roosevelt Hwy Kendall (14476) **(G-6647)**
Dmef/Edge, New York *Also called Direct Mktg Edctl Fndation Inc* **(G-9231)**
Dmic Inc 716 743-4360
3776 Commerce Ct North Tonawanda (14120) **(G-12065)**
Dnp Electronics America LLC 212 503-1060
335 Madison Ave Fl 3 New York (10017) **(G-9242)**
Do Over LLC 212 302-2336
1410 Broadway Rm 301 New York (10018) **(G-9243)**
Doar Inc 516 872-8140
170 Earle Ave Lynbrook (11563) **(G-7430)**
Dobrin Industries Inc (PA) 800 353-2229
210 Walnut St Ste 22 Lockport (14094) **(G-7069)**
Dock Hardware Incorporated 585 266-7920
24 Seneca Ave Ste 4 Rochester (14621) **(G-13352)**
Doco Quick Print Inc 315 782-6623
808 Huntington St Watertown (13601) **(G-15569)**
Doctor Pavers 516 342-6016
34 Redleaf Ln Commack (11725) **(G-3586)**
Doctor Print Inc (PA) 631 873-4560
18 Commerce Dr Ste 1 Hauppauge (11788) **(G-5640)**
Doctorow Communications Inc 845 708-5166
180 Phillips Hill Rd # 5 New City (10956) **(G-8225)**
Document Journal Inc 646 586-3099
264 Canal St New York (10013) **(G-9244)**
Document Strategies LLC 585 506-9000
185 Gibbs St Rochester (14605) **(G-13353)**
Docuware Corporation (HQ) 845 563-9045
4 Crotty Ln Ste 200 New Windsor (12553) **(G-8365)**
Doery Awning Co, Lawrence *Also called TG Peppe Inc* **(G-6893)**
Dog Guard, Troy *Also called Sunward Electronics Inc* **(G-15191)**
Doheny Nice and Easy 518 793-1733
150 Broad St Glens Falls (12801) **(G-5247)**
Doheny's Mobil, Glens Falls *Also called Doheny Nice and Easy* **(G-5247)**
Dohnsco Inc 516 773-4800
19 Gracewood Dr Manhasset (11030) **(G-7533)**
Dolby Laboratories Inc 212 767-1700
1350 6th Ave Fl 28 New York (10019) **(G-9245)**
Dolce Vite International LLC 713 962-5767
386 12th St Brooklyn (11215) **(G-1754)**
Dolco LLC 585 657-7777
26 Maple Ave Bloomfield (14469) **(G-946)**
Dollar Popular Inc 914 375-0361
473 S Broadway Yonkers (10705) **(G-16302)**
Dolmen 912 596-1537
216 Broome Corporate Pkwy Conklin (13748) **(G-3623)**
Dolomite Group, Walworth *Also called Rochester Asphalt Materials* **(G-15478)**
Dolomite Products Company Inc (HQ) 315 524-1998
1150 Penfield Rd Rochester (14625) **(G-13354)**
Dolomite Products Company Inc 607 324-3636
7610 County Road 65 Hornell (14843) **(G-6103)**
Dolomite Products Company Inc 585 586-2568
746 Whalen Rd Penfield (14526) **(G-12570)**
Dolomite Products Company Inc 585 768-7295
8250 Golf Rd Le Roy (14482) **(G-6898)**
Dolomite Products Company Inc 585 352-0460
2540 S Union St Spencerport (14559) **(G-14555)**
Dolphin Data Capture LLC 516 429-5663
45 Rockefeller Plz # 2000 New York (10111) **(G-9246)**
Doma Marketing Inc 516 684-1111
28 Haven Ave Ste 226 Port Washington (11050) **(G-12874)**
Domain, Brooklyn *Also called Sweater Brand Inc* **(G-2482)**
Domani Fashions Corp 718 797-0505
86 S 1st St Brooklyn (11249) **(G-1755)**
Domestic Casing Co 718 522-1902
410 3rd Ave Brooklyn (11215) **(G-1756)**
Dominic De Nigris Inc 718 597-4460
3255 E Tremont Ave Frnt Bronx (10461) **(G-1241)**
Dominique Intimate Apparel, Yonkers *Also called Dayleen Intimates Inc* **(G-16300)**
Domino Foods Inc 800 729-4840
1 Federal St Yonkers (10705) **(G-16303)**
Domino Sugar, Yonkers *Also called Domino Foods Inc* **(G-16303)**
Domoteck Interiors Inc 718 433-4300
2430 Brooklyn Queens Expy # 1 Woodside (11377) **(G-16204)**
Don Alleson Athletic, Geneva *Also called Alleson of Rochester Inc* **(G-5145)**
Don Beck Inc 585 493-3040
5249 State Route 39 Castile (14427) **(G-3198)**
Donald Bruhnke 212 600-1260
455 W 37th St Apt 1018 New York (10018) **(G-9247)**
Donald Snyder Jr 315 265-4485
528 Allen Falls Rd Potsdam (13676) **(G-12936)**
Donald Snyder Jr Logging, Potsdam *Also called Donald Snyder Jr* **(G-12936)**
Donald Stefan 716 492-1110
3428 W Yorkshire Rd Chaffee (14030) **(G-3306)**
Donmar Printing Co 516 280-2239
90 2nd St Ste 2 Mineola (11501) **(G-7969)**
Donna Degan, New York *Also called Leslie Stuart Co Inc* **(G-10204)**
Donna Distefano Ltd (PA) 212 594-3757
37 W 20th St Ste 1106 New York (10011) **(G-9248)**
Donna Karan International Inc (HQ) 212 789-1500
240 W 40th St New York (10018) **(G-9249)**
Donna Karan International Inc 212 768-5800
240 W 40th St Bsmt New York (10018) **(G-9250)**
Donna Morgan LLC 212 575-2550
225 W 37th St New York (10018) **(G-9251)**
Donne Dieu Paper Mill Inc 212 226-0573
63 Flushing Ave Unit 112 Brooklyn (11205) **(G-1757)**
Donnelley Financial LLC 212 351-9000
555 5th Ave Fl 4 New York (10017) **(G-9252)**
Donorwall Inc 212 766-9670
125 Maiden Ln Rm 205 New York (10038) **(G-9253)**
Donver Incorporated 716 945-1910
4185 Killbuck Rd Kill Buck (14748) **(G-6669)**
Door Dam, Wassaic *Also called Presray Corporation* **(G-15526)**
Doortec Archtctural Met GL LLC 718 567-2730
234 46th St Brooklyn (11220) **(G-1758)**
Dor-A-Mar Canvas Products Co 631 750-9202
182 Cherry Ave West Sayville (11796) **(G-15839)**
Doral Apparel Group Inc 917 208-5652
498 Fashion Ave Fl 10 New York (10018) **(G-9254)**

ALPHABETIC

Doral Refining Corp...516 223-3684
533 Atlantic Ave Freeport (11520) *(G-4992)*
Dorel Hat Co (PA)...845 831-5231
1 Main St Beacon (12508) *(G-751)*
Doremus FP LLC...212 366-3800
228 E 45th St Fl 10 New York (10017) *(G-9255)*
Dorgan Welding Service...315 462-9030
1378 White Rd Phelps (14532) *(G-12603)*
Doris Panos Designs Ltd...631 245-0580
130 Old East Neck Rd Melville (11747) *(G-7776)*
Dorm Co., Cheektowaga *Also called Dorm Company Corporation (G-3345)*
Dorm Company Corporation...502 551-6195
575 Kennedy Rd Ste 2 Cheektowaga (14227) *(G-3345)*
Dormitory Authority - State NY...631 434-1487
998 Crooked Hill Rd # 26 Brentwood (11717) *(G-1120)*
Dorose Albums, East Elmhurst *Also called Dorose Novelty Co Inc (G-4106)*
Dorose Novelty Co Inc...718 451-3088
3107 103rd St East Elmhurst (11369) *(G-4106)*
Dorset Farms Inc...631 734-6010
38355 Main Rd Peconic (11958) *(G-12545)*
Dorsey Metrology Intl Inc...845 229-2929
53 Oakley St Poughkeepsie (12601) *(G-12951)*
Dortronics Systems Inc...631 725-0505
1668 Bhmpton Sag Hbr Tpke Sag Harbor (11963) *(G-14098)*
Dory Enterprises Inc...607 565-7079
184 Sr 17c Waverly (14892) *(G-15620)*
DOT Publishing...315 593-2510
117 Cayuga St Fulton (13069) *(G-5058)*
Dotto Wagner...315 342-8020
185 E Seneca St Oswego (13126) *(G-12409)*
Double Helix Optics Inc...917 689-6490
260 E Main St Ste 6367 Rochester (14604) *(G-13355)*
Double Take Fashions Inc...718 832-9000
1407 Broadway Rm 712 New York (10018) *(G-9256)*
Doug Lambertson Od...718 698-9300
2555 Richmond Ave Ste 4 Staten Island (10314) *(G-14647)*
Douglas Patterson & Sons Inc...716 433-8100
1 Oakhurst St Lockport (14094) *(G-7070)*
Dougs Machine Shop Inc...585 905-0004
2304 Brickyard Rd Canandaigua (14424) *(G-3131)*
Dover Enterprises, Syracuse *Also called Burr & Son Inc (G-14836)*
Dover Global Holdings Inc (HQ)...212 922-1640
280 Park Ave New York (10017) *(G-9257)*
Dover Marine Mfg & Sup Co Inc...631 667-4300
98 N Industry Ct Deer Park (11729) *(G-3864)*
Dow Jones & Company Inc (HQ)...609 627-2999
1211 Avenue Of The Americ New York (10036) *(G-9258)*
Dow Jones & Company Inc...212 597-5983
1211 Avenue Of The Americ New York (10036) *(G-9259)*
Dow Jones Aer Company Inc...212 416-2000
1211 Av Of The Am Lwr C3r New York (10036) *(G-9260)*
Dowa International Corp...212 697-3217
370 Lexington Ave Rm 1002 New York (10017) *(G-9261)*
Dowd - Witbeck Printing Corp...518 274-2421
599 Pawling Ave Troy (12180) *(G-15166)*
Downright Printing Corp...516 619-7200
8829 238th St Bellerose (11426) *(G-774)*
Downtown Express Newspaper, New York *Also called Community Media LLC (G-9070)*
Downtown Interiors Inc...212 337-0230
250 Hudson St Lbby 1 New York (10013) *(G-9262)*
Downtown Media Group LLC...646 723-4510
12 W 27th St Ste 1000 New York (10001) *(G-9263)*
Doyle Sails, Huntington Station *Also called Melbourne C Fisher Yacht Sails (G-6253)*
DP Murphy Co Inc...631 673-9400
945 Grand Blvd Deer Park (11729) *(G-3865)*
DPM of Western New York LLC (HQ)...716 775-8001
3235 Grand Island Blvd Grand Island (14072) *(G-5327)*
DPM of Western New York LLC...716 684-3825
340 Nagel Dr Cheektowaga (14225) *(G-3346)*
Dpr Food Service, Deer Park *Also called Deer Park Macaroni Co Inc (G-3861)*
Dr Jacobs Naturals LLC...718 265-1522
2615 Coney Island Ave 2nd Brooklyn (11223) *(G-1759)*
Dr Jayscom...888 437-5297
853 Broadway Ste 1900 New York (10003) *(G-9264)*
Dr Print, Hauppauge *Also called Doctor Print Inc (G-5640)*
Dr Reddys Laboratories NY Inc...518 827-7702
1974 State Route 145 Middleburgh (12122) *(G-7886)*
Dra Imaging PC...845 296-1057
169 Myers Corners Rd # 250 Wappingers Falls (12590) *(G-15491)*
Drag Specialties, Ballston Spa *Also called Lemans Corporation (G-580)*
DRAGON STEEL PRODUCTS, New York *Also called Dragon Trading Inc (G-9265)*
Dragon Trading Inc...212 717-1496
211 E 70th St Apt 20d New York (10021) *(G-9265)*
Draper Associates Incorporated...212 255-2727
121 Varick St Rm 203 New York (10013) *(G-9266)*
Drapery Industries Inc...585 232-2992
175 Humboldt St Ste 222 Rochester (14610) *(G-13356)*
Drasgow Inc...585 786-3603
4150 Poplar Tree Rd Gainesville (14066) *(G-5081)*
Dray Enterprises Inc...585 768-2201
1 Church St Le Roy (14482) *(G-6899)*
Dream Fabric Printing, Warwick *Also called Dream Green Productions (G-15513)*
Dream Green Productions...917 267-8920
39 Warwick Tpke Warwick (10990) *(G-15513)*
Dream Statuary Inc...718 647-2024
251 Cleveland St Brooklyn (11208) *(G-1760)*
Dreams To Print...718 483-8020
10101 Foster Ave Brooklyn (11236) *(G-1761)*
Dreamwave LLC...212 594-4250
34 W 33rd St Fl 2 New York (10001) *(G-9267)*
Drescher Paper Box Inc...716 854-0288
10425 Keller Rd Clarence (14031) *(G-3429)*
Dresdiam Inc...212 819-2217
36 W 47th St Ste 1008 New York (10036) *(G-9268)*
Dresser-Argus Inc...718 643-1540
36 Bridge St Brooklyn (11201) *(G-1762)*
Dresser-Rand (delaware) LLC (HQ)...607 937-2011
100 E Chemung St Painted Post (14870) *(G-12474)*
Dresser-Rand Company...585 596-3100
37 Coats St Wellsville (14895) *(G-15670)*
Dresser-Rand Group Inc...716 375-3000
500 Paul Clark Dr Olean (14760) *(G-12232)*
Dressy Tessy Inc (PA)...212 869-0750
1410 Broadway Rm 502 New York (10018) *(G-9269)*
Drew Philips Corp (PA)...212 354-0095
231 W 39th St New York (10018) *(G-9270)*
Dreyfus Ashby Inc (HQ)...212 818-0770
630 3rd Ave Fl 15 New York (10017) *(G-9271)*
DRG New York Holdings Corp (PA)...914 668-9000
700 S Fulton Ave Mount Vernon (10550) *(G-8138)*
Dri Relays Inc (HQ)...631 342-1700
60 Commerce Dr Hauppauge (11788) *(G-5641)*
Drillco Equipment Co Inc...718 777-5986
3452 11th St Long Island City (11106) *(G-7203)*
Drillco National Group Inc (PA)...718 726-9801
2432 44th St Long Island City (11103) *(G-7204)*
Drimark...516 484-6200
999 S Oyster Bay Rd Bethpage (11714) *(G-834)*
Drive Devilbiss Healthcare, Port Washington *Also called Drive Medical Spv LLC (G-12875)*
Drive Devilbiss Healthcare, Port Washington *Also called Medical Depot Inc (G-12905)*
Drive Medical Spv LLC...516 998-4600
99 Seaview Blvd Port Washington (11050) *(G-12875)*
Drive Shaft Shop Inc...631 348-1818
210 Blydenburg Rd Unit A Hauppauge (11749) *(G-5642)*
Drns Corp...718 369-4530
140 58th St Ste 3f Brooklyn (11220) *(G-1763)*
Dropcar Operating Company Inc (HQ)...646 342-1595
1412 Broadway Ste 2100 New York (10018) *(G-9272)*
Drt Aerospace LLC...585 247-5940
500 Mile Crossing Blvd Rochester (14624) *(G-13357)*
Drum Ready-Mix, Felts Mills *Also called Cranesville Block Co Inc (G-4786)*
Drummond Framing Inc...212 647-1701
38 W 21st St Fl 10 New York (10010) *(G-9273)*
Dryden & Palmer Co, Canajoharie *Also called Gravymaster Inc (G-3120)*
Dryve LLC...646 279-3648
4515 Waldo Ave Bronx (10471) *(G-1242)*
DSI Group Inc...800 553-2202
5713 49th St Maspeth (11378) *(G-7607)*
DSM Nutritional Products LLC...518 372-5155
2105 Technology Dr Schenectady (12308) *(G-14261)*
DSM Nutritional Products LLC...518 372-5155
300 Tech Park Glenville (12302) *(G-5271)*
Dsr International Corp...631 427-2600
107 Northern Blvd Ste 401 Great Neck (11021) *(G-5382)*
Dt Industry, New York *Also called Dressy Tessy Inc (G-9269)*
DTI Financial Inc...212 661-7673
1148 5th Ave Ste 1b New York (10128) *(G-9274)*
Du Monde Trading Inc...212 944-1306
1407 Brrdwy Rm 1905 New York (10018) *(G-9275)*
Du Serv Development Co, Troy *Also called George M Dujack (G-15169)*
Dual Print & Mail, LLC, Grand Island *Also called DPM of Western New York LLC (G-5327)*
Duall Finishing Inc...716 827-1707
53 Hopkins St Buffalo (14220) *(G-2731)*
Dualtron Manufacturing, West Babylon *Also called Vandilay Industries Inc (G-15755)*
Ducduc LLC (PA)...212 226-1868
200 Lexington Ave Rm 715 New York (10016) *(G-9276)*
Ducduc Nyc, New York *Also called Ducduc LLC (G-9276)*
Duck Flats Pharma...315 689-3407
245 E Main St Elbridge (13060) *(G-4297)*
Duck River Textiles Inc (PA)...212 679-2980
295 5th Ave New York (10016) *(G-9277)*
Duck Walk Vinyards...631 726-7555
231 Montauk Hwy Water Mill (11976) *(G-15530)*
Ducommun Aerostructures NY Inc...518 731-2791
171 Stacey Rd Coxsackie (12051) *(G-3800)*
Ducon Technologies Inc (PA)...631 694-1700
5 Penn Plz New York (10001) *(G-9278)*
Ducon Technologies Inc...631 420-4900
110 Bi County Blvd # 124 Farmingdale (11735) *(G-4618)*
Duetto Integrated Systems Inc...631 851-0102
85 Hoffman Ln Ste Q Islandia (11749) *(G-6331)*
Dufour Pastry Kitchens Inc...718 402-8800
251 Locust Ave Bronx (10454) *(G-1243)*

Duke Company 607 347-4455
  7 Hall Rd Ithaca (14850) *(G-6379)*
Duke Concrete Products Inc 518 793-7743
  50 Duke Dr Queensbury (12804) *(G-13037)*
Duke of Iron Inc 631 543-3600
  1039 W Jericho Tpke Smithtown (11787) *(G-14476)*
Dulcette Technologies LLC 631 752-8700
  2 Hicks St Lindenhurst (11757) *(G-6951)*
Dun-Rite Spclized Carriers LLC 718 991-1100
  1561 Southern Blvd Bronx (10460) *(G-1244)*
Duncan & Son Carpentry Inc 914 664-4311
  1 W Prospect Ave Mount Vernon (10550) *(G-8139)*
Dundas-Jafine Inc 716 681-9690
  11099 Broadway St Alden (14004) *(G-168)*
Dundeespirits, Fairport *Also called Lidestri Beverages LLC (G-4503)*
Dundy Glass & Mirror Corp 718 723-5800
  12252 Montauk St Springfield Gardens (11413) *(G-14588)*
Dune Inc 212 925-6171
  200 Lexington Ave Rm 200 # 200 New York (10016) *(G-9279)*
Dunkirk Construction Products 716 366-5220
  852 Main St Dunkirk (14048) *(G-4053)*
Dunkirk Metal Products Wny LLC (PA) 716 366-2555
  3575 Chadwick Dr Dunkirk (14048) *(G-4054)*
Dunkirk Specialty Steel LLC 716 366-1000
  830 Brigham Rd Dunkirk (14048) *(G-4055)*
Dunlap Machine LLC 315 926-1013
  4205 Sunset Dr Marion (14505) *(G-7568)*
Dunlea Whl GL & Mirror Inc 914 664-5277
  147 S Macquesten Pkwy Mount Vernon (10550) *(G-8140)*
Dunmore Corporation 845 279-5061
  3633 Danbury Rd Brewster (10509) *(G-1147)*
Dunn Paper - Natural Dam Inc 315 287-1200
  4921 St Rt 58 Gouverneur (13642) *(G-5320)*
Dupli Envelope & Graphics, Syracuse *Also called Dupli Graphics Corporation (G-14877)*
Dupli Graphics Corporation (HQ) 315 234-7286
  6761 Thompson Rd Syracuse (13211) *(G-14877)*
Dupli Graphics Corporation 315 422-4732
  Dupli Park Dr Syracuse (13218) *(G-14878)*
Dupont, Buffalo *Also called E I Du Pont De Nemours & Co (G-2734)*
Duquettes Steel & Structural F 518 563-3161
  193 Sharron Ave Plattsburgh (12901) *(G-12745)*
Dura Architectural Signage, Long Island City *Also called Dura Engraving Corporation (G-7205)*
Dura Engraving Corporation 718 706-6400
  4815 32nd Pl Long Island City (11101) *(G-7205)*
Dura Foam Inc 718 894-2488
  6302 59th Ave Maspeth (11378) *(G-7608)*
Dura Spec Inc 718 526-3053
  1239 Village Ct North Baldwin (11510) *(G-12004)*
Dura-Mill Inc 518 899-2255
  16 Stonebreak Rd Ballston Spa (12020) *(G-573)*
Dural Door Company Inc 718 729-1333
  3128 Greenpoint Ave Long Island City (11101) *(G-7206)*
Durall Dolly LLC 802 728-7122
  48 Spencer St Brooklyn (11205) *(G-1764)*
Duran Jewelry Inc 212 431-1959
  36 W 47th St Ste 1205 New York (10036) *(G-9280)*
Duranm Inc 914 774-3367
  101 Dale Ave Cortlandt Manor (10567) *(G-3793)*
Durasol Systems Inc (HQ) 845 610-1100
  445 Bellvale Rd Chester (10918) *(G-3375)*
Durata Therapeutics Inc 646 871-6400
  7 Times Sq Ste 3502 New York (10036) *(G-9281)*
Duravent Inc 518 463-7284
  10 Jupiter Ln Albany (12205) *(G-71)*
Durez Corporation 716 286-0100
  5000 Packard Rd Niagara Falls (14304) *(G-11921)*
Duro Business Solutions Inc 646 577-9537
  2417 3rd Ave Ste 806 Bronx (10451) *(G-1245)*
Duro Dyne Corporation (HQ) 631 249-9000
  81 Spence St Bay Shore (11706) *(G-674)*
Duro Dyne Machinery Corp 631 249-9000
  81 Spence St Bay Shore (11706) *(G-675)*
Duro Dyne National Corp (PA) 631 249-9000
  81 Spence St Bay Shore (11706) *(G-676)*
Duro UAS, Bronx *Also called Duro Business Solutions Inc (G-1245)*
Duro-Shed Inc (PA) 585 344-0800
  721 Center Rd Buffalo (14224) *(G-2732)*
Dutch Spirits LLC 518 398-1022
  98 Ryan Rd Pine Plains (12567) *(G-12633)*
Dutch's Spirits, Pine Plains *Also called Dutch Spirits LLC (G-12633)*
Dutchess Plumbing & Heating 845 889-8255
  28 Reservoir Rd Staatsburg (12580) *(G-14599)*
Dutchess Wines LLC 845 876-1319
  39 Lorraine Dr Rhinebeck (12572) *(G-13099)*
Dutchland Plastics Inc 315 280-0247
  102 E Seneca St Sherrill (13461) *(G-14404)*
Dutchtreat, Buffalo *Also called Pdi Cone Co Inc (G-2909)*
Duvel Mortgage USA Inc 607 267-6121
  656 County Highway 33 Cooperstown (13326) *(G-3640)*
Duxiana Dux Bed 212 755-2600
  235 E 58th St New York (10022) *(G-9282)*

Duzmor Painting Inc 585 768-4760
  7959 E Main Rd Le Roy (14482) *(G-6900)*
Dvash Foods Inc 845 578-1959
  2 Brewer Rd Monsey (10952) *(G-8037)*
DVC Vending, Ardsley *Also called Distributors Vending Corp (G-388)*
Dvf Studio LLC (PA) 212 741-6607
  440 W 14th St New York (10014) *(G-9283)*
Dvf Studio LLC (PA) 646 576-8009
  252 W 37th St Fl 14 New York (10018) *(G-9284)*
Dvmax, New York *Also called Sneakers Software Inc (G-11279)*
Dwa Pallet Inc 518 746-1047
  337 Main St Hudson Falls (12839) *(G-6186)*
Dweck Industries Inc (PA) 718 615-1695
  2455 Mcdonald Ave Fl 2 Brooklyn (11223) *(G-1765)*
Dweck Industries Inc 718 615-1695
  2247 E 16th St Fl 2 Brooklyn (11229) *(G-1766)*
Dwell Life Inc 212 382-2010
  60 Broad St Fl 24 New York (10004) *(G-9285)*
Dwell Store The, New York *Also called Dwell Life Inc (G-9285)*
DWH&s Inc 718 993-6405
  825 E 140th St Bronx (10454) *(G-1246)*
Dwm International Inc 646 290-7448
  37-18 Nthrn Blvd Ste 516 Long Island City (11101) *(G-7207)*
Dwnld Inc 484 483-6572
  601394 Broadway Fl 6 Flr 6 New York (10013) *(G-9286)*
Dwyer Farm LLC 914 456-2742
  40 Bowman Ln Walden (12586) *(G-15459)*
Dyco Electronics, Hornell *Also called Dyco Manufacturing LLC (G-6105)*
Dyco Electronics Inc 607 324-2030
  7775 Industrial Park Rd Hornell (14843) *(G-6104)*
Dyco Manufacturing LLC 607 324-2030
  7775 Industrial Park Rd Hornell (14843) *(G-6105)*
Dyenamix Inc 212 941-6642
  359 Broadway Frnt 2 New York (10013) *(G-9287)*
Dylix Corporation 716 773-2985
  347 Lang Blvd Grand Island (14072) *(G-5328)*
Dyna-Empire Inc 516 222-2700
  1075 Stewart Ave Garden City (11530) *(G-5096)*
Dyna-Tech Quality Inc 585 458-9970
  1570 Emerson St Rochester (14606) *(G-13358)*
Dyna-Vac Equipment Inc 315 865-8084
  8963 State Route 365 Stittville (13469) *(G-14734)*
Dynabrade Inc (PA) 716 631-0100
  8989 Sheridan Dr Clarence (14031) *(G-3430)*
Dynak Inc 585 271-2255
  530 Savage Rd Churchville (14428) *(G-3411)*
Dynamasters Inc 585 458-9970
  1570 Emerson St Rochester (14606) *(G-13359)*
Dynamic Applications Inc 518 283-4654
  120 Defreest Dr Ste 255 Troy (12180) *(G-15167)*
Dynamic Decisions Inc (PA) 908 755-5000
  18519 64th Ave Fresh Meadows (11365) *(G-5039)*
Dynamic Dies Inc 585 247-4010
  70 Pixley Industrial Pkwy Rochester (14624) *(G-13360)*
Dynamic Health Labs Inc 718 858-0100
  110 Bridge St Ste 2 Brooklyn (11201) *(G-1767)*
Dynamic Hybirds Inc 315 426-8110
  1201 E Fayette St Ste 11 Syracuse (13210) *(G-14879)*
Dynamic Laboratories Inc 631 231-7474
  30 Haynes Ct Ronkonkoma (11779) *(G-13931)*
Dynamic Labs, Ronkonkoma *Also called Dynamic Laboratories Inc (G-13931)*
Dynamic Packaging Inc 718 388-0800
  1567 39th St Brooklyn (11218) *(G-1768)*
Dynamic Pak, Syracuse *Also called Weather Products Corporation (G-15024)*
Dynamic Photography Inc 516 381-2951
  48 Flamingo Rd N Roslyn (11576) *(G-14042)*
Dynamic Printing, Central Islip *Also called Richard Ruffner (G-3287)*
Dynamic Products Inc 631 270-4833
  500 Eastern Pkwy Ste 2 Farmingdale (11735) *(G-4619)*
Dynamic Screenprinting 518 487-4256
  12 Vatrano Rd Albany (12205) *(G-72)*
Dynamic Sealing Tech Inc 716 376-0708
  301 W Franklin St Olean (14760) *(G-12233)*
Dynamic Systems Inc (PA) 518 283-5350
  323 Rte 355 Poestenkill (12140) *(G-12802)*
Dynamica Inc 212 818-1900
  930 5th Ave Apt 3f New York (10021) *(G-9288)*
Dynasty Chemical Corp 518 463-1146
  444 N Pearl St Menands (12204) *(G-7842)*
Dynatabs LLC 718 376-6084
  1600 Ocean Pkwy Apt 1f Brooklyn (11230) *(G-1769)*
Dynax Corporation 914 764-0202
  79 Westchester Ave Pound Ridge (10576) *(G-12992)*
Dyno Nobel Inc 845 338-2144
  161 Ulster Ave Ulster Park (12487) *(G-15218)*
Dynocoat Inc 631 244-9344
  1738 Church St Holbrook (11741) *(G-5997)*
Dyson-Kissner-Moran Corp (PA) 212 661-4600
  2515 South Rd Ste 5 Poughkeepsie (12601) *(G-12952)*
Dz9 Power LLC 877 533-5530
  408 Wayne St Olean (14760) *(G-12234)*

A
L
P
H
A
B
E
T
I
C

E & D Specialty Stands Inc 716 337-0161
2081 Franklin St North Collins (14111) ***(G-12025)***
E & F Home Fashions Inc (PA) 718 968-9719
2154 E 71st St Brooklyn (11234) ***(G-1770)***
E & J Iron Works Inc 718 665-6040
801 E 136th St Bronx (10454) ***(G-1247)***
E & O Mari Inc 845 562-4400
256 Broadway Newburgh (12550) ***(G-11863)***
E & R Machine Inc 716 434-6639
211 Grand St Lockport (14094) ***(G-7071)***
E & T Plastic Mfg Co Inc (PA) 718 729-6226
4545 37th St Long Island City (11101) ***(G-7208)***
E & W Manufacturing Co Inc 516 367-8571
15 Pine Dr Woodbury (11797) ***(G-16170)***
E B Atlas Steel Corp 716 876-0900
120 Tonawanda St Buffalo (14207) ***(G-2733)***
E B B Graphics Inc 516 750-5510
75 State St Westbury (11590) ***(G-15877)***
E B Industries LLC (PA) 631 293-8565
90 Carolyn Blvd Farmingdale (11735) ***(G-4620)***
E B Industries LLC 631 293-8565
90 Carolyn Blvd Farmingdale (11735) ***(G-4621)***
E B Trottnow Machine Spc 716 694-0600
8955 Woodside Dr Eden (14057) ***(G-4254)***
E C C Corp 518 873-6494
7 Church St Elizabethtown (12932) ***(G-4300)***
E C Lyons, Bronx *Also called Edward C Lyons Company Inc* ***(G-1250)***
E C Publications Inc 212 728-1844
1700 Broadway Fl 5 New York (10019) ***(G-9289)***
E C Sumereau & Sons, Huntington Station *Also called John Larocca & Son Inc* ***(G-6251)***
E D I, Yonkers *Also called Electronic Devices Inc* ***(G-16306)***
E D I Window Systems, Binghamton *Also called D D & L Inc* ***(G-870)***
E F Iron Works & Construction 631 242-4766
241 N Fehr Way Ste 3 Bay Shore (11706) ***(G-677)***
E F Lippert Co Inc 716 373-1100
4451 S Nine Mile Rd Allegany (14706) ***(G-187)***
E F Thresh Inc 315 437-7301
6000 Galster Rd East Syracuse (13057) ***(G-4208)***
E G M Restaurant Equipment Mfg 718 782-9800
688 Flushing Ave Brooklyn (11206) ***(G-1771)***
E G S, Port Washington *Also called E Global Solutions Inc* ***(G-12876)***
E Global Solutions Inc 516 767-5138
8 Haven Ave Ste 221 Port Washington (11050) ***(G-12876)***
E Gluck Corporation (PA) 718 784-0700
6015 Little Neck Pkwy Little Neck (11362) ***(G-6997)***
E Graphics Corporation 718 486-9767
160 Havemeyer St Brooklyn (11211) ***(G-1772)***
E H Hurwitz & Associates 718 884-3766
3000 Kingsbridge Ave Bronx (10463) ***(G-1248)***
E I Du Pont De Nemours & Co 716 876-4420
3115 River Rd Buffalo (14207) ***(G-2734)***
E I Du Pont De Nemours & Co 718 761-0043
10 Teleport Dr Staten Island (10311) ***(G-14648)***
E J E Research Div, Buffalo *Also called Adco Circuits Inc* ***(G-2620)***
E J Manufacturing Inc (PA) 516 313-9380
2648 Grand Ave Bellmore (11710) ***(G-782)***
E J Willis Company Inc 315 891-7602
37 N Main St Middleville (13406) ***(G-7940)***
E M I, Rome *Also called Enviromaster International LLC* ***(G-13848)***
E P Sewing Pleating Inc 212 967-2575
327 W 36th St Frnt 2 New York (10018) ***(G-9290)***
E S M, Amherst *Also called Esm Group Inc* ***(G-222)***
E S P Metal Crafts Inc 718 381-2443
379 Harman St Brooklyn (11237) ***(G-1773)***
E Schreiber Inc 212 382-0280
580 5th Ave Fl 32a New York (10036) ***(G-9291)***
E T C, New York *Also called Casuals Etc Inc* ***(G-8932)***
E Tetz & Sons Inc (PA) 845 692-4486
130 Crotty Rd Middletown (10941) ***(G-7905)***
E W Smith Publishing Co Inc 845 562-1218
36 Meriline Ave New Windsor (12553) ***(G-8366)***
E W Williams Publications 212 661-1516
370 Lexington Ave Rm 1409 New York (10017) ***(G-9292)***
E Z Entry Doors Inc 716 434-3440
5299 Enterprise Dr Lockport (14094) ***(G-7072)***
E&I Printing 212 206-0506
145 W 55th St Apt 12a New York (10019) ***(G-9293)***
E&T Plastics, Long Island City *Also called E & T Plastic Mfg Co Inc* ***(G-7208)***
E-Beam Services Inc (PA) 516 622-1422
270 Duffy Ave Ste H Hicksville (11801) ***(G-5903)***
E-Finnergy Group LLC 845 547-2424
355 Spook Rock Rd Suffern (10901) ***(G-14760)***
E-Front, New York *Also called Efront Financial Solutions Inc* ***(G-9326)***
E-One Inc 716 646-6790
4760 Camp Rd Hamburg (14075) ***(G-5504)***
E-Play Brands LLC 212 563-2646
25 W 39th St Lbby A New York (10018) ***(G-9294)***
E-Quest Lighting, East Setauket *Also called Vision Quest Lighting Inc* ***(G-4190)***
E-Systems Group LLC 607 775-1100
100 Progress Pkwy Conklin (13748) ***(G-3624)***
E-Won Industrial Co Inc 212 750-9610
625 Main St Apt 1532 New York (10044) ***(G-9295)***
E-Z Global Wholesale Inc 888 769-7888
925 E 14th St Brooklyn (11230) ***(G-1774)***
E-Z Red Co, Deposit *Also called Walter R Tucker Entps Ltd* ***(G-4004)***
E-Z-Em Inc (HQ) 609 524-2864
155 Pinelawn Rd Ste 230n Melville (11747) ***(G-7777)***
E-Zoil Products Inc 716 213-0106
234 Fillmore Ave Tonawanda (14150) ***(G-15101)***
E.J. McKenica & Sons, Buffalo *Also called Edwin J McKenica & Sons Inc* ***(G-2739)***
E/One Utility Systems, Schenectady *Also called Environment-One Corporation* ***(G-14264)***
EAC Holdings of NY Corp 716 822-2500
701 Willet Rd Buffalo (14218) ***(G-2735)***
Ead Cases 845 343-2111
43 Smith St Middletown (10940) ***(G-7906)***
Eag Electric Inc 201 376-5103
496 Mosel Ave Staten Island (10304) ***(G-14649)***
Eagle Art Publishing Inc 212 685-7411
475 Park Ave S Rm 2800 New York (10016) ***(G-9296)***
Eagle Bridge Machine & Tl Inc 518 686-4541
135 State Route 67 Eagle Bridge (12057) ***(G-4071)***
Eagle Business Systems, Bohemia *Also called Clintrak Clinical Labeling S* ***(G-988)***
Eagle Comtronics Inc 315 451-3313
7665 Henry Clay Blvd Liverpool (13088) ***(G-7009)***
Eagle Crest Vineyard LLC 585 346-5760
7107 Vineyard Rd Conesus (14435) ***(G-3605)***
Eagle Envelope Company (HQ) 607 387-3195
8091 Trumansburg Rd Trumansburg (14886) ***(G-15199)***
Eagle Graphics Inc 585 244-5006
149 Anderson Ave Rochester (14607) ***(G-13361)***
Eagle Instruments Inc 914 939-6843
35 Grove St Port Chester (10573) ***(G-12818)***
Eagle Lace Dyeing Corp 212 947-2712
335 W 35th St Fl 2 New York (10001) ***(G-9297)***
Eagle Media Partners LP (PA) 315 434-8889
2501 James St Ste 100 Syracuse (13206) ***(G-14880)***
Eagle Metals Corp 516 338-5100
134 Linden Ave Westbury (11590) ***(G-15878)***
Eagle Newspapers, Syracuse *Also called Eagle Media Partners LP* ***(G-14880)***
Eagle Regalia Co Inc 845 425-2245
747 Chestnut Ridge Rd # 101 Spring Valley (10977) ***(G-14567)***
Eagle Telephonics Inc 631 471-3600
3880 Veterans Mem Hwy Bohemia (11716) ***(G-1007)***
Eagle Welding Machine 315 594-1845
13458 Ridge Rd Wolcott (14590) ***(G-16163)***
Eagle Zinc Co Div, New York *Also called T L Diamond & Company Inc* ***(G-11416)***
Eagles Nest Holdings LLC (PA) 513 874-5270
455 E 86th St New York (10028) ***(G-9298)***
Earl G Graves Pubg Co Inc (HQ) 212 242-8000
260 Madison Ave Ste 11 New York (10016) ***(G-9299)***
Earlville Paper Box Co Inc 315 691-2131
19 Clyde St Earlville (13332) ***(G-4076)***
Earring King Jewelry Mfg Inc 718 544-7947
62 W 47th St Ste 1202 New York (10036) ***(G-9300)***
Earth Enterprises Inc 212 741-3999
250 W 40th St Fl 15 New York (10018) ***(G-9301)***
Earth Spectrum, New York *Also called Spectrum Prtg Lithography Inc* ***(G-11316)***
Easco Boiler, Bronx *Also called A L Eastmond & Sons Inc* ***(G-1186)***
Easco Boiler Corp 718 378-3000
1175 Leggett Ave Bronx (10474) ***(G-1249)***
Easel, New York *Also called Ksk International Inc* ***(G-10143)***
Easi, Flushing *Also called Easy Analytic Software Inc* ***(G-4849)***
Easm Machine Works LLC 518 747-5326
35 Sullivan Pkwy Fort Edward (12828) ***(G-4939)***
East Aurora Advertiser, East Aurora *Also called Grant Hamilton* ***(G-4089)***
East Branch Winery Inc (PA) 607 292-3999
5503 Dutch St Dundee (14837) ***(G-4045)***
East Cast Clor Compounding Inc 631 491-9000
15 Kean St West Babylon (11704) ***(G-15708)***
East Cast Envlope Graphics LLC 718 326-2424
5615 55th Dr Maspeth (11378) ***(G-7609)***
East Cast Envmtl Rstration Inc 631 600-2000
136 Allen Blvd Farmingdale (11735) ***(G-4622)***
East Cast Orthtics Prosthetics 716 856-5192
505 Delaware Ave Buffalo (14202) ***(G-2736)***
East Coast Business Forms Inc 631 231-9300
320 Lake Ave Ste 2 Saint James (11780) ***(G-14110)***
East Coast Copacking, Brooklyn *Also called Pressed Juice LLC* ***(G-2281)***
East Coast Cultures LLC 917 261-3010
906 State Route 28 Kingston (12401) ***(G-6690)***
East Coast Embroidery Ltd 631 254-3878
74 Brook Ave Ste 1 Deer Park (11729) ***(G-3866)***
East Coast Intl Tire Group Inc 718 386-9088
5746 Flushing Ave Maspeth (11378) ***(G-7610)***
East Coast Intl Tire Inc 718 386-9088
5746 Flushing Ave Bldg C Maspeth (11378) ***(G-7611)***
East Coast Mines & Material, East Quogue *Also called East Coast Mines Ltd* ***(G-4156)***
East Coast Mines Ltd 631 653-5445
2 Lewis Rd East Quogue (11942) ***(G-4156)***
East Coast Molders Inc 516 240-6000
3001 New St Ste F Oceanside (11572) ***(G-12170)***

East Coast Orthoic & Pros Cor (PA) 516 248-5566
  75 Burt Dr Deer Park (11729) *(G-3867)*
East Coast Orthoic & Pros Cor 212 923-2161
  3927 Broadway New York (10032) *(G-9302)*
East Coast Pita Bakery, Brooklyn *Also called Aladdin Bakers Inc* *(G-1475)*
East Coast Spring Mix Inc 845 355-1215
  211 Lynch Ave New Hampton (10958) *(G-8235)*
East Coast Thermographers Inc 718 321-3211
  1558 127th St Ste 1 College Point (11356) *(G-3541)*
East End 716 532-2622
  1995 Lenox Rd Collins (14034) *(G-3570)*
East End Country Kitchens Inc 631 727-2258
  121 Edwards Ave Calverton (11933) *(G-3080)*
East End Sign Design Inc 631 399-2574
  1425 Montauk Hwy Mastic (11950) *(G-7674)*
East End Vineyards LLC 718 468-0500
  21548 Jamaica Ave Queens Village (11428) *(G-13019)*
East Hampton Ind News Inc 631 324-2500
  74 Montauk Hwy Unit 19 East Hampton (11937) *(G-4120)*
East Hampton Independent The, East Hampton *Also called East Hampton Ind News
Inc (G-4120)*
East Hampton Star Inc 631 324-0002
  153 Main St East Hampton (11937) *(G-4121)*
East Hill Creamery LLC 585 237-3622
  346 Main St S Perry (14530) *(G-12597)*
East Hills Instrument Inc 516 621-8686
  60 Shames Dr Westbury (11590) *(G-15879)*
East Hudson Watershed Corp 845 319-6349
  2 Route 164 Patterson (12563) *(G-12516)*
East Main Associates 585 624-1990
  7520 E Main St Lima (14485) *(G-6931)*
East Meet East Inc 646 481-0033
  32 W 39th St Fl 4 New York (10018) *(G-9303)*
East Pattern & Model Corp (PA) 585 461-3240
  769 Trabold Rd Rochester (14624) *(G-13362)*
East Pattern & Model Corp 585 461-3240
  80 Saginaw Dr Rochester (14623) *(G-13363)*
East Penn Manufacturing Co. 631 321-7161
  790 Railroad Ave Babylon (11704) *(G-519)*
East Ridge Quick Print 585 266-4911
  1249 Ridgeway Ave Ste Y Rochester (14615) *(G-13364)*
East Side Machine Inc 585 265-4560
  625 Phillips Rd Webster (14580) *(G-15639)*
East To West Architectral Pdts 631 433-9690
  103 Tinton Pl Ste 1a East Northport (11731) *(G-4144)*
East West Global Sourcing Inc 917 887-2286
  425 Neptune Ave Apt 22a Brooklyn (11224) *(G-1775)*
East/West Industries Inc 631 981-5900
  2002 Orville Dr N Ronkonkoma (11779) *(G-13932)*
Eastco Manufacturing Corp 914 738-5667
  38 Wilmot Cir Scarsdale (10583) *(G-14235)*
Eastend Enforcement Products 631 878-8424
  50 Dillmont Dr Smithtown (11787) *(G-14477)*
Eastern Air Products LLC 716 391-1866
  41 Ward Rd Lancaster (14086) *(G-6804)*
Eastern Castings Co 518 677-5610
  2 Pearl St Cambridge (12816) *(G-3094)*
Eastern Color Imaging, Bohemia *Also called Eastern Color Stripping Inc (G-1008)*
Eastern Color Stripping Inc 631 563-3700
  666 Lanson St Bohemia (11716) *(G-1008)*
Eastern Company 315 468-6251
  3000 Milton Ave Solvay (13209) *(G-14496)*
Eastern Concepts Ltd 718 472-3377
  4125 39th St Sunnyside (11104) *(G-14772)*
Eastern Enterprise Corp 718 727-8600
  465 Bay St Ste 2 Staten Island (10304) *(G-14650)*
Eastern Exterior Wall 631 589-3880
  869 Lincoln Ave Bohemia (11716) *(G-1009)*
Eastern Feather & Down Corp. 718 387-4100
  1027 Metropolitan Ave Brooklyn (11211) *(G-1776)*
Eastern Finding Corp 516 747-6640
  116 County Courthouse Rd New Hyde Park (11040) *(G-8263)*
Eastern Hills Printing (PA) 716 741-3300
  9195 Main St Clarence (14031) *(G-3431)*
Eastern Industrial Steel Corp (PA) 845 639-9749
  4 Fringe Ct New City (10956) *(G-8226)*
Eastern Jewelry Mfg Co Inc 212 840-0001
  48 W 48th St Ste 707 New York (10036) *(G-9304)*
Eastern Jungle Gym Inc (PA) 845 878-9800
  30 Commerce Dr Carmel (10512) *(G-3185)*
Eastern Machine and Electric 716 284-8271
  1041 Niagara Ave Niagara Falls (14305) *(G-11922)*
Eastern Manufacturing Inc 716 741-4572
  9530 Cobblestone Dr Clarence (14031) *(G-3432)*
Eastern Metal of Elmira Inc (PA) 607 734-2295
  1430 Sullivan St Elmira (14901) *(G-4348)*
Eastern Niagra Radiology 716 882-6544
  899 Main St Buffalo (14203) *(G-2737)*
Eastern Offset, Albany *Also called Northeast Commercial Prtg Inc (G-107)*
Eastern Precision Machining 631 286-4758
  11 Farber Dr Ste I Bellport (11713) *(G-797)*
Eastern Precision Mfg 845 358-1951
  76 S Franklin St 78 Nyack (10960) *(G-12142)*

Eastern Silk Mills Inc 212 730-1300
  148 W 37th St Fl 3 New York (10018) *(G-9305)*
Eastern Silver of Boro Park 718 854-5600
  4901 16th Ave Brooklyn (11204) *(G-1777)*
Eastern Storefronts & Mtls Inc 631 471-7065
  1739 Julia Goldbach Ave Ronkonkoma (11779) *(G-13933)*
Eastern Strategic Materials 212 332-1619
  45 Rockefeller Plz # 2000 New York (10111) *(G-9306)*
Eastern Trading Partners Corp 212 202-1451
  866 Eastern Pkwy Apt 2f Brooklyn (11213) *(G-1778)*
Eastern Unit Exch Rmnfacturing 718 739-7113
  186 Beech St Floral Park (11001) *(G-4815)*
Eastern Welding Inc 631 727-0306
  274 Mill Rd Riverhead (11901) *(G-13174)*
Eastern.cctv (usa) LLC (PA) 516 870-3779
  50 Commercial St Plainview (11803) *(G-12680)*
Eastland Electronics Co Inc 631 580-3800
  999 Montauk Hwy 402 Shirley (11967) *(G-14419)*
Eastman Chemical Company 585 722-2905
  2255 Mount Read Blvd Rochester (14615) *(G-13365)*
Eastman Kodak Company 585 722-2187
  233 Olde Harbour Trl Rochester (14612) *(G-13366)*
Eastman Kodak Company (PA) 585 724-4000
  343 State St Rochester (14650) *(G-13367)*
Eastman Kodak Company 585 724-5600
  1669 Lake Ave Bldg 31-4 Rochester (14652) *(G-13368)*
Eastman Kodak Company 585 722-9695
  1818 W Jefferson Rd Pittsford (14534) *(G-12638)*
Eastman Kodak Company 585 726-6261
  39 Kaywood Dr Rochester (14626) *(G-13369)*
Eastman Kodak Company 585 724-4000
  2600 Manitou Rd Rochester (14650) *(G-13370)*
Eastman Kodak Company 800 698-3324
  343 State St Rochester (14650) *(G-13371)*
Eastman Kodak Company 585 722-4385
  1999 Lake Ave 6/83/RI Rochester (14650) *(G-13372)*
Eastman Kodak Company 585 588-5598
  300 Weiland Road Rochester (14650) *(G-13373)*
Eastman Kodak Company 585 726-7000
  343 State St Rochester (14650) *(G-13374)*
Eastman Kodak Company 585 722-4007
  336 Initiative Dr Rochester (14624) *(G-13375)*
Eastman Kodak Company 585 588-3896
  100 Latona Rd Gate 340 Rochester (14652) *(G-13376)*
Eastman Kodak Company 585 724-4000
  343 State St Rochester (14650) *(G-13377)*
Eastman Machine Company 716 856-2200
  779 Washington St Buffalo (14203) *(G-2738)*
Eastman Park Micrographics Inc 866 934-4376
  100 Latona Rd Bldg 318 Rochester (14652) *(G-13378)*
Eastnets Americas Corp 212 631-0666
  450 7th Ave 1509 New York (10123) *(G-9307)*
Easton Pharmaceuticals Inc 347 284-0192
  736 Center St Ste 5 Lewiston (14092) *(G-6920)*
Eastport Feeds Inc 631 325-0077
  140 E Moriches Blvd Eastport (11941) *(G-4251)*
Eastside Orthotics Prosthetics, New York *Also called Manhattan Eastside Dev
Corp (G-10343)*
Eastside Oxide Co 607 734-1253
  211 Judson St Elmira (14901) *(G-4349)*
Eastwood Litho Impressions LLC 315 437-2626
  4020 New Court Ave Syracuse (13206) *(G-14881)*
Easy Aerial Inc 646 639-4410
  63 Flushing Ave Brooklyn (11205) *(G-1779)*
Easy Analytic Software Inc (PA) 718 740-7930
  7359 196th St Flushing (11366) *(G-4849)*
Easy Book Publishing Inc 518 459-6281
  260 Osborne Rd Ste 3 Albany (12211) *(G-73)*
Easy H2b, Hudson *Also called Micosta Enterprises Inc (G-6171)*
Eataly Net Usa LLC (PA) 212 897-2895
  2 W 24th St New York (10010) *(G-9308)*
Eaten Lightened, Bronx *Also called Beyond Better Foods LLC (G-1213)*
Eating Evolved Inc 516 510-2601
  135 Ricefield Ln Hauppauge (11788) *(G-5643)*
Eatingevolved LLC 631 675-2440
  10 Technology Dr Unit 4 Setauket (11733) *(G-14379)*
Eaton Brothers Corp 716 649-8250
  3530 Lakeview Rd Hamburg (14075) *(G-5505)*
Eaton Corporation 516 353-3017
  280 Bellmore Rd East Meadow (11554) *(G-4135)*
Eaton Corporation 315 579-2872
  125 E Jefferson St Syracuse (13202) *(G-14882)*
Eaton Crouse-Hinds, Syracuse *Also called Cooper Crouse-Hinds Mtl Inc (G-14863)*
Eatons Crouse Hinds Business 315 477-7000
  1201 Wolf St Syracuse (13208) *(G-14883)*
Eaw Electronic Systems Inc 845 471-5290
  900 Dutchess Tpke Ste 3 Poughkeepsie (12603) *(G-12953)*
Eazy Locks LLC 718 327-7770
  1914 Mott Ave Far Rockaway (11691) *(G-4563)*
Eazylift Albany LLC 518 452-6929
  836 Troy Schenectady Rd Latham (12110) *(G-6855)*
EB Acquisitions LLC 212 355-3310
  444 Madison Ave Ste 501 New York (10022) *(G-9309)*

A
L
P
H
A
B
E
T
I
C

Eb Couture Ltd 212 912-0190
110 W 34th St Rm 1002 New York (10001) *(G-9310)*

EB&I Marketing, Skaneateles *Also called Burdick Publications Inc* *(G-14447)*

Ebc Technologies LLC 631 729-8182
200 Motor Pkwy Ste D26 Hauppauge (11788) *(G-5644)*

Ebeling Associates Inc (PA) 518 688-8700
9 Corporate Dr Ste 1 Halfmoon (12065) *(G-5492)*

Ebenezer Railcar Services Inc 716 674-5650
1005 Indian Church Rd West Seneca (14224) *(G-15846)*

Eberhardt Enterprises Inc 585 458-7681
1325 Mount Read Blvd Rochester (14606) *(G-13379)*

EBM, Westbury *Also called Executive Business Media Inc* *(G-15883)*

Ebner Publishing International 646 742-0740
37 W 26th St Rm 412 New York (10010) *(G-9311)*

Eboost, New York *Also called Vitalize Labs LLC* *(G-11696)*

Ebrevia Inc 203 870-3000
12 E 49th St Fl 11 New York (10017) *(G-9312)*

Ebsco Industries Inc 585 398-2000
5815 County Road 41 Farmington (14425) *(G-4770)*

EBY Electro Inc 516 576-7777
210 Express St Plainview (11803) *(G-12681)*

EC Wood & Company Inc 718 388-2287
110 E Industry Ct Deer Park (11729) *(G-3868)*

Eccella Corporation 718 612-0451
75 Broad St Rm 2900 New York (10004) *(G-9313)*

Ecclesiastical Communications 212 688-2399
1011 1st Ave Fl 6 New York (10022) *(G-9314)*

Ecclesiastical Press, Edmeston *Also called Bishop Print Shop Inc* *(G-4294)*

Ecco Bay Sportswear, Old Westbury *Also called Cathy Daniels Ltd* *(G-12222)*

Echo Appellate Press Inc (PA) 516 432-3601
30 W Park Ave Ste 200 Long Beach (11561) *(G-7136)*

Echo Group Inc 917 608-7440
62 W 39th St Ste 1005 New York (10018) *(G-9315)*

Eci, Norwich *Also called Electron Coil Inc* *(G-12121)*

Eck Plastic Arts Inc 607 722-3227
87 Prospect Ave Binghamton (13901) *(G-873)*

Ecker Window Corp 914 776-0000
1 Odell Plz Yonkers (10701) *(G-16304)*

Ecko Fin & Tooling Inc 716 487-0200
221 Hopkins Ave Ste 2 Jamestown (14701) *(G-6507)*

Eclectic Cntract Furn Inds Inc 212 967-5504
450 Fashion Ave Ste 2710 New York (10123) *(G-9316)*

Eclipse Collection Jewelers (PA) 212 764-6883
6 E 45th St Rm 1206 New York (10017) *(G-9317)*

Ecolab Inc 716 683-6298
3719 Union Rd Ste 121 Cheektowaga (14225) *(G-3347)*

Ecological Laboratories Inc (PA) 516 823-3441
4 Waterford Rd Island Park (11558) *(G-6316)*

Econocraft Worldwide Mfg Inc 914 966-2280
56 Worth St Frnt Unit Yonkers (10701) *(G-16305)*

Econometric Software Inc 516 938-5254
15 Gloria Pl Plainview (11803) *(G-12682)*

Economist Intelligence Unit NA 212 554-0600
750 3rd Ave Fl 5 New York (10017) *(G-9318)*

Economist Magazine, The, New York *Also called Economist Newspaper NA Inc* *(G-9319)*

Economist Newspaper NA Inc (HQ) 212 554-0676
750 3rd Ave Fl 5 New York (10017) *(G-9319)*

Economy Pump & Motor Repr Inc 718 433-2600
3652 36th St Astoria (11106) *(G-418)*

Ecoquality Inc 718 887-7876
7608 Bay Pkwy Brooklyn (11214) *(G-1780)*

Ecosmartplastics, Bohemia *Also called Repellem Consumer Pdts Corp* *(G-1070)*

ECR International Inc (PA) 315 797-1310
2201 Dwyer Ave Utica (13501) *(G-15260)*

ECR International Inc 716 366-5500
85 Middle Rd Dunkirk (14048) *(G-4056)*

Ecs Global Solutions, Brooklyn *Also called Energy Conservation & Sup Inc* *(G-1805)*

Ecto Tech Automation, Buffalo *Also called Multisorb Technologies Inc* *(G-2876)*

Ecuador News Inc 718 205-7014
6403 Roosevelt Ave Fl 2 Woodside (11377) *(G-16205)*

Ed Beach Forest Management 607 538-1745
2042 Scott Rd Bloomville (13739) *(G-952)*

Ed Levin Inc 518 677-8595
52 W Main St Cambridge (12816) *(G-3095)*

Ed Levin Jewelry, Cambridge *Also called Ed Levin Inc* *(G-3095)*

Ed Negron Fine Woodworking 718 246-1016
43 Hall St Fl 5 Brooklyn (11205) *(G-1781)*

Edco Sales, Syracuse *Also called Camfil Usa Inc* *(G-14841)*

Edco Supply Corporation 718 788-8108
323 36th St Brooklyn (11232) *(G-1782)*

Eden Tool & Die Inc 716 992-4240
2721 Hemlock Rd Eden (14057) *(G-4255)*

Edesia World Wide LLC 646 705-3505
1485 5th Ave New York (10035) *(G-9320)*

Edge Display Group Entp Inc 631 498-1373
35 Sawgrass Dr Ste 2 Bellport (11713) *(G-798)*

Edgewood Industries Inc 516 227-2447
635 Commercial Ave Garden City (11530) *(G-5097)*

Edison Power & Light Co Inc 718 522-0002
204 Van Dyke St 207 Brooklyn (11231) *(G-1783)*

Edison Price Lighting Inc (PA) 718 685-0700
4150 22nd St Long Island City (11101) *(G-7209)*

Edison Price Lighting Inc 718 685-0700
4105 21st St Long Island City (11101) *(G-7210)*

Editions De Prfums Madison LLC (HQ) 646 666-0527
654 Madison Ave Rm 1609 New York (10065) *(G-9321)*

Edlaw Pharmaceuticals Inc 631 454-6888
195 Central Ave Ste B Farmingdale (11735) *(G-4623)*

EDM Mfg 631 669-1966
141 John St Ste 600 Babylon (11702) *(G-520)*

EDP Renewables North Amer LLC 518 426-1650
1971 Western Ave 230 Albany (12203) *(G-74)*

Edr Industries Inc 516 868-1928
100 Commercial St Freeport (11520) *(G-4993)*

Edrington Group Usa LLC (PA) 212 352-6000
27 W 23rd St Fl 4 New York (10010) *(G-9322)*

Edroy Products Co Inc 845 358-6600
245 N Midland Ave Nyack (10960) *(G-12143)*

Edsal Machine Products Inc (PA) 718 439-9163
126 56th St Brooklyn (11220) *(G-1784)*

Edsim Leather Co Inc (PA) 212 695-8500
131 W 35th St Fl 14 New York (10001) *(G-9323)*

Educational Networks Inc 866 526-0200
104 W 40th St Rm 1810 New York (10018) *(G-9324)*

Edward C Lyons Company Inc 718 515-5361
3646 White Plains Rd Frnt Bronx (10467) *(G-1250)*

Edward C Muller Corp 718 881-7270
3646 White Plains Rd Frnt Bronx (10467) *(G-1251)*

Edward C. Lyons, Bronx *Also called Edward C Muller Corp* *(G-1251)*

Edwards Graphic Co Inc 718 548-6858
3801 Hudson Manor Ter 4s Bronx (10463) *(G-1252)*

Edwards Vacuum LLC (HQ) 800 848-9800
6400 Inducon Corporate Dr Sanborn (14132) *(G-14140)*

Edwin J McKenica & Sons Inc 716 823-4646
1200 Clinton St Buffalo (14206) *(G-2739)*

Edwin Mellen Press Inc 716 754-2796
442 Center St Lewiston (14092) *(G-6921)*

Eeboo Corporation 212 222-0823
170 W 74th St Apt 102 New York (10023) *(G-9325)*

Eeg Enterprises Inc 516 293-7472
586 Main St Farmingdale (11735) *(G-4624)*

Efam Enterprises LLC 718 204-1760
3731 29th St Long Island City (11101) *(G-7211)*

Effective Slling Solutions LLC 716 771-8503
1898 Hanley Dr Lake View (14085) *(G-6772)*

Efficiency Printing Co Inc 914 949-8611
126 S Lexington Ave White Plains (10606) *(G-16000)*

Effy, New York *Also called BH Multi Com Corp* *(G-8778)*

Efj Inc 518 234-4799
128 Macarthur Ave Cobleskill (12043) *(G-3499)*

Efron Designs Ltd 718 482-8440
2121 41st Ave Ste 5b Long Island City (11101) *(G-7212)*

Efront Financial Solutions Inc 212 220-0660
11 E 44th St Rm 1502 New York (10017) *(G-9326)*

Efs Designs LLC 718 852-9511
610 Smith St Ste 3 Brooklyn (11231) *(G-1785)*

Eft Analytics Inc (HQ) 212 290-2300
350 5th Ave Ste 4810 New York (10118) *(G-9327)*

Eg Indsturies, Rochester *Also called Ernie Green Industries Inc* *(G-13400)*

Eg Industries, Rochester *Also called Ernie Green Industries Inc* *(G-13398)*

Eg Industries, Rochester *Also called Ernie Green Industries Inc* *(G-13399)*

Egli Machine Company Inc 607 563-3663
240 State Highway 7 Sidney (13838) *(G-14434)*

Egm Mfg Inc 718 782-9800
688 Flushing Ave Brooklyn (11206) *(G-1786)*

Egmont US Inc 212 685-0102
443 Park Ave S Rm 806 New York (10016) *(G-9328)*

Ehrlich Enterprises Inc 631 956-0690
82 Wyandanch Ave Unit C Wyandanch (11798) *(G-16245)*

Ehs Group LLC 914 937-6162
69 Townsend St Port Chester (10573) *(G-12819)*

Ei, Endicott *Also called Endicott Interconnect Tech Inc* *(G-4450)*

El Electronics Inc 516 334-0870
1800 Shames Dr Westbury (11590) *(G-15880)*

Eidosmedia Inc 646 795-2100
14 Wall St Ste 6c New York (10005) *(G-9329)*

Eileens Special Cheesecake 212 966-5585
17 Cleveland Pl Frnt A New York (10012) *(G-9330)*

Eis Legacy LLC 585 426-5330
40 Hytec Cir Rochester (14606) *(G-13380)*

Eiseman-Ludmar Co Inc 516 932-6990
56 Bethpage Dr Hicksville (11801) *(G-5904)*

Eisen Bros, Brooklyn *Also called National Die & Button Mould Co* *(G-2189)*

Ej Group Inc 315 699-2601
6177 S Bay Rd Cicero (13039) *(G-3419)*

Eko-Blu, New York *Also called N Y Winstons Inc* *(G-10529)*

Ekostinger Inc 585 739-0450
140 Despatch Dr East Rochester (14445) *(G-4161)*

Eks Manufacturing Inc 917 217-0784
577 Wortman Ave Brooklyn (11208) *(G-1787)*

El Diario LLC 212 807-4600
15 Metrotech Ctr Ste 7 Brooklyn (11201) *(G-1788)*

EL Erman International Ltd.............................212 444-9440
  1205 E 29th St Brooklyn (11210) *(G-1789)*

El Greco Woodworking Inc (PA)......................716 483-0315
  106 E 1st St Ste 1 Jamestown (14701) *(G-6508)*

El-Don Battery Post Inc...............................716 627-3697
  4109 Saint Francis Dr Hamburg (14075) *(G-5506)*

El-Gen LLC...631 218-3400
  7 Shirley St Unit 1 Bohemia (11716) *(G-1010)*

El-La Design Inc.....................................212 382-1080
  209 W 38th St Rm 901 New York (10018) *(G-9331)*

Ela, New York *Also called Electric Lighting Agencies (G-9334)*

Elab Smokers Boutique................................585 865-4513
  4373 Lake Ave Rochester (14612) *(G-13381)*

Elam Materials Inc..................................585 658-2248
  1 Conlon Ave Mount Morris (14510) *(G-8113)*

Elan Upholstery Inc..................................631 563-0650
  120b Wilbur Pl Ste B Bohemia (11716) *(G-1011)*

Elana Laderos Ltd....................................212 764-0840
  230 W 38th St Fl 15 New York (10018) *(G-9332)*

Elanco Animal Health, New Hyde Park *Also called Eli Lilly and Company (G-8265)*

Elantas Pdg Inc.....................................716 372-9650
  1405 Buffalo St Olean (14760) *(G-12235)*

Elara Brands, Jericho *Also called Elara Fdsrvice Disposables LLC (G-6577)*

Elara Fdsrvice Disposables LLC.......................877 893-3244
  420 Jericho Tpke Ste 320 Jericho (11753) *(G-6577)*

Elastomers Inc.......................................716 633-4883
  2095 Wehrle Dr Williamsville (14221) *(G-16129)*

Elco Manufacturing Co Inc (PA).......................516 767-3577
  26 Ivy Way Port Washington (11050) *(G-12877)*

Eldeen Clothing Inc..................................212 719-9190
  250 W 39th St New York (10018) *(G-9333)*

Elderlee Incorporated (HQ)..........................315 789-6670
  729 Cross Rd Oaks Corners (14518) *(G-12161)*

Eldorado Coffee Distributors, Maspeth *Also called Eldorado Coffee Roasters Ltd (G-7612)*

Eldorado Coffee Roasters Ltd.........................718 418-4100
  5675 49th St Maspeth (11378) *(G-7612)*

Electomechanical Componets, Auburn *Also called Emcom Inc (G-474)*

Electrcal Instrumentation Ctrl.......................518 861-5789
  1253 Youngs Rd Delanson (12053) *(G-3959)*

Electric City Concrete Co Inc (HQ)...................518 887-5560
  774 State Highway 5s Amsterdam (12010) *(G-325)*

Electric Lighting Agencies (PA)......................212 645-4580
  36 W 25th St Fl 6 New York (10010) *(G-9334)*

Electric Motor Specialties, Jamestown *Also called Electric Motor Specialty Inc (G-6509)*

Electric Motor Specialty, Jamestown *Also called Sunset Ridge Holdings Inc (G-6546)*

Electric Motor Specialty Inc.........................716 487-1458
  490 Crescent St Jamestown (14701) *(G-6509)*

Electric Motors and Pumps Inc........................718 935-9118
  466 Carroll St Brooklyn (11215) *(G-1790)*

Electric Swtchbard Sltions LLC.......................718 643-1105
  270 Park Ave New Hyde Park (11040) *(G-8264)*

Electrical Controls Link.............................585 924-7010
  100 Rawson Rd Ste 220 Victor (14564) *(G-15406)*

Electricsolenoidvalves.com, Islandia *Also called Jeg Online Ventures LLC (G-6337)*

Electro Abrasives LLC...............................716 822-2500
  701 Willet Rd Buffalo (14218) *(G-2740)*

Electro Alloy Recovery Inc...........................631 879-7530
  130 Knickerbocker Ave M Bohemia (11716) *(G-1012)*

Electro Form Corp....................................607 722-6404
  128 Bevier St Binghamton (13904) *(G-874)*

Electro Industries, Westbury *Also called El Electronics Inc (G-15880)*

Electro Plating Service Inc..........................914 948-3777
  127 Oakley Ave White Plains (10601) *(G-16001)*

Electro Waste Systems, Bohemia *Also called Electro Alloy Recovery Inc (G-1012)*

ELECTRO-HARMONIX, Long Island City *Also called New Sensor Corporation (G-7308)*

Electro-Metrics Corporation..........................518 762-2600
  231 Enterprise Rd Johnstown (12095) *(G-6614)*

Electro-Optical Products Corp........................718 456-6000
  6240 Forest Ave Fl 2 Ridgewood (11385) *(G-13145)*

Electrochem Solutions Inc (HQ)......................716 759-5800
  10000 Wehrle Dr Clarence (14031) *(G-3433)*

Electron Coil Inc...................................607 336-7414
  141 Barr Rd Norwich (13815) *(G-12121)*

Electron Top Mfg Co Inc..............................718 846-7400
  12615 89th Ave Richmond Hill (11418) *(G-13112)*

Electronic Arts Inc..................................212 672-0722
  1515 Broadway Rm 3601 New York (10036) *(G-9335)*

Electronic Coating Tech Inc (PA).....................518 688-2048
  1 Mustang Dr Ste 4 Cohoes (12047) *(G-3506)*

Electronic Devices Inc (HQ).........................914 965-4400
  21 Gray Oaks Ave Yonkers (10710) *(G-16306)*

Electronic Die Corp..................................718 455-3200
  19th St Fl 2 Flr 2 Brooklyn (11232) *(G-1791)*

Electronic Machine Parts LLC........................631 434-3700
  400 Oser Ave Ste 2050 Hauppauge (11788) *(G-5645)*

Electronic Printing Inc..............................631 218-2200
  1200 Prime Pl Hauppauge (11788) *(G-5646)*

Electronic Systems Inc...............................631 589-4389
  1742 Church St Holbrook (11741) *(G-5998)*

Electronic Tech Briefs, New York *Also called Abp International Inc (G-8433)*

Electronics & Innovation Ltd........................585 214-0598
  150 Research Blvd Rochester (14623) *(G-13382)*

Electronics Systems Division, Hauppauge *Also called Parker-Hannifin Corporation (G-5736)*

Electrosurgical Instrument Co, Rochester *Also called Ftt Medical Inc (G-13425)*

Electrotech Service Eqp Corp.........................718 626-7700
  2450 46th St Astoria (11103) *(G-419)*

Elegance Coating Ltd.................................518 298-2888
  33 W Service Rd Ste 100 Champlain (12919) *(G-3311)*

Elegant Desserts By Metro Inc........................718 388-1323
  868 Kent Ave Brooklyn (11205) *(G-1792)*

Elegant Headwear Co Inc..............................212 695-8520
  10 W 33rd St Rm 1122 New York (10001) *(G-9336)*

Elegant Jewelers Mfg Co Inc..........................212 869-4951
  31 W 47th St Ste 301 New York (10036) *(G-9337)*

Elegant Linen Inc....................................718 492-0297
  200 60th St Brooklyn (11220) *(G-1793)*

Elegant Sportswear, Brooklyn *Also called K & S Childrens Wear Inc (G-2016)*

Element K, Rochester *Also called Skillsoft Corporation (G-13732)*

Element St Johns Corp................................917 349-2139
  764 Saint Johns Pl Brooklyn (11216) *(G-1794)*

Elementar Americas Inc...............................856 787-0022
  119 Comac St Ronkonkoma (11779) *(G-13934)*

Elementis Srl Inc (HQ)..............................845 692-3914
  15 Big Pond Rd Huguenot (12746) *(G-6193)*

Eleni's Cookies, Long Island City *Also called Elenis Nyc Inc (G-7213)*

Elenis Nyc Inc (PA)..................................718 361-8136
  4725 34th St Ste 305 Long Island City (11101) *(G-7213)*

Elepath Inc...347 417-4975
  110 Kent Ave 9 Brooklyn (11249) *(G-1795)*

Elephants Custom Furniture Inc.......................917 509-3581
  67 Van Dam St Brooklyn (11222) *(G-1796)*

Elevator Accessories Mfg.............................914 739-7004
  1035 Howard St 37 Peekskill (10566) *(G-12550)*

Elevator Interiors Inc...............................315 218-7186
  1116 S Salina St Syracuse (13202) *(G-14884)*

Elevator Ventures Corporation........................212 375-1900
  9720 99th St Ozone Park (11416) *(G-12460)*

Elevondata Labs Inc..................................470 222-5438
  1350 Ave Of The Amrcs 2nd New York (10019) *(G-9338)*

Elgreco Gt Inc.......................................718 777-7922
  2035 18th St Apt 2c Astoria (11105) *(G-420)*

Eli Consumer Healthcare LLC..........................914 943-3107
  90 N Broadway Irvington (10533) *(G-6307)*

Eli Lilly and Company................................516 622-2244
  1979 Marcus Ave New Hyde Park (11042) *(G-8265)*

Elias Artmetal Inc...................................516 873-7501
  70 E 2nd St Mineola (11501) *(G-7970)*

Elias Fragrances Inc (PA)............................718 693-6400
  3 Hunter Dr Rye Brook (10573) *(G-14088)*

Elie Balleh Couture, New York *Also called Eb Couture Ltd (G-9310)*

Elie Tahari Ltd......................................212 763-2000
  501 5th Ave Fl 2 New York (10017) *(G-9339)*

Elie Tahari Ltd......................................631 329-8883
  1 Main St East Hampton (11937) *(G-4122)*

Elie Tahari Ltd......................................212 763-2000
  1114 Ave Of The Americas New York (10036) *(G-9340)*

Elie Tahari Ltd......................................973 671-6300
  510 5th Ave Lbby A New York (10036) *(G-9341)*

Elima-Draft Incorporated.............................631 375-2830
  20 Hopewell Dr Stony Brook (11790) *(G-14738)*

Elis Bread (eli Zabar) Inc (PA).....................212 772-2011
  403 E 91st St New York (10128) *(G-9342)*

Elite Cellular Accessories Inc.......................877 390-2502
  61 E Industry Ct Deer Park (11729) *(G-3869)*

Elite Coffee Roasters, East Amherst *Also called Elite Roasters Inc (G-4077)*

Elite Daily Inc......................................212 402-9097
  53 W 23rd St Fl 12 New York (10010) *(G-9343)*

Elite Glass Fabrication LLC..........................201 333-8100
  14 Wall St Ste 3a New York (10005) *(G-9344)*

Elite Machine Inc....................................585 289-4733
  3 Merrick Cir Manchester (14504) *(G-7527)*

Elite Parfums Ltd (HQ)...............................212 983-2640
  551 5th Ave Rm 1500 New York (10176) *(G-9345)*

Elite Precise Manufacturer LLC.......................518 993-3040
  55 Willett St Fort Plain (13339) *(G-4946)*

Elite Roasters Inc (PA).............................716 626-0307
  8600 Transit Rd Ste 1b East Amherst (14051) *(G-4077)*

Elite Semi Conductor Products........................631 884-8400
  860 N Richmond Ave Lindenhurst (11757) *(G-6952)*

Elite Steel Fabricators Inc..........................631 285-1008
  2165 5th Ave Ronkonkoma (11779) *(G-13935)*

Elite Traveler LLC...................................646 430-7900
  441 Lexington Ave Fl 3 New York (10017) *(G-9346)*

Elite Traveler Magazine, New York *Also called Universal Cmmncations of Miami (G-11604)*

Elite Turning & Machining Corp.......................585 445-8765
  42 Marway Cir Rochester (14624) *(G-13383)*

Elite Woodworking, Brooklyn *Also called Ragnatelli Inc (G-2321)*

Elizabeth Arden, New York *Also called Unilever United States Inc (G-11589)*

Elizabeth Arden Inc..................................845 810-2175
  214 Red Apple Ct Central Valley (10917) *(G-3299)*

Elizabeth Fillmore LLC...............................212 647-0863
  27 W 20th St Ste 705 New York (10011) *(G-9347)*

Elizabeth Gillett Ltd 212 629-7993
   260 W 36th St Rm 802 New York (10018) *(G-9348)*
Elizabeth Gillett Designs, New York *Also called Elizabeth Gillett Ltd (G-9348)*
Elizabeth Wilson 516 486-2157
   579 Edgemere Ave Uniondale (11553) *(G-15226)*
Elizabeth Wood 315 492-5470
   4900 Broad Rd Syracuse (13215) *(G-14885)*
Elizabeth's, Uniondale *Also called Elizabeth Wilson (G-15226)*
Ella Design, New York *Also called Lai Apparel Design Inc (G-10165)*
Elle Magazine, New York *Also called Hearst Corporation (G-9748)*
Ellicottville Distillery LLC 716 597-6121
   5462 Robbins Rd Ellicottville (14731) *(G-4313)*
Ellicottville Kitchen Eqp, Salamanca *Also called Strategies North America Inc (G-14130)*
Elliot Industries Inc 716 287-3100
   Leach Rd Ellington (14732) *(G-4316)*
Elliot Lauren, New York *Also called I S C A Corp (G-9847)*
Elliot Lucca, New York *Also called Indonesian Imports (G-9882)*
Elliot Mann Nyc Inc 212 260-0658
   324 E 9th St Frnt A New York (10003) *(G-9349)*
Elliquence LLC 516 277-9000
   2455 Grand Ave Baldwin (11510) *(G-530)*
Ellis Products Corp (PA) 516 791-3732
   628 Golf Dr Valley Stream (11581) *(G-15339)*
Ellison Bronze Inc 716 665-6522
   125 W Main St Falconer (14733) *(G-4538)*
Ellusa, Baldwin *Also called Soniquence LLC (G-535)*
Elm Graphics Inc 315 737-5984
   9694 Mallory Rd New Hartford (13413) *(G-8239)*
Elm Ready Mix, Westbury *Also called Elm Transit Mix Corporation (G-15881)*
Elm Transit Mix Corporation 516 333-6144
   482 Grand Blvd Westbury (11590) *(G-15881)*
Elma Press, Elma *Also called Frederick Coon Inc (G-4318)*
Elmar Industries Inc 716 681-5650
   200 Gould Ave Depew (14043) *(G-3980)*
Elmgang Enterprises I Inc 212 868-4142
   354 W 38th St Frnt New York (10018) *(G-9350)*
Elmgrove Technologies Div, Rochester *Also called Photonamics Inc (G-13622)*
Elmira Heat Treating Inc 607 734-1577
   407 S Kinyon St Elmira (14904) *(G-4350)*
Elmira Star-Gazette, Elmira *Also called Star-Gazette Fund Inc (G-4368)*
Elmont North Little League 516 775-8210
   1532 Clay St Elmont (11003) *(G-4384)*
Elmsford Sheet Metal Works Inc 914 739-6300
   23 Arlo Ln Cortlandt Manor (10567) *(G-3794)*
Elo Touch Solutions Inc 585 427-2802
   2245 Brdgtn Hnrtta Twn Ln Rochester (14623) *(G-13384)*
Elodina Inc 646 402-5202
   222 Broadway Fl 19 New York (10038) *(G-9351)*
Elramida Holdings Inc 646 280-0503
   2555 E 29th St Brooklyn (11235) *(G-1797)*
Elrene Home Fashions, New York *Also called Josie Accessories Inc (G-10029)*
Elsag North America LLC 877 773-5724
   7 Sutton Pl Ste A Brewster (10509) *(G-1148)*
Elsener Organ Works Inc 631 254-2744
   120 E Jefryn Blvd Ste A Deer Park (11729) *(G-3870)*
Elsevier Inc (HQ) 212 989-5800
   230 Park Ave Fl 8 New York (10169) *(G-9352)*
Eltee Tool & Die Co 607 748-4301
   404 E Franklin St Endicott (13760) *(G-4449)*
Elton El Mantle Inc 315 432-9067
   6072 Court Street Rd Syracuse (13206) *(G-14886)*
Eluminocity US Inc 651 528-1165
   80 Pine St Fl 24 New York (10005) *(G-9353)*
Elvo, Mount Kisco *Also called Zumbach Electronics Corp (G-8109)*
Elwood International Inc 631 842-6600
   89 Hudson St Copiague (11726) *(G-3651)*
Elwood Specialty Products Inc 716 877-6622
   2180 Elmwood Ave Buffalo (14216) *(G-2741)*
Ely Beach Solar LLC 718 796-9400
   5030 Broadway Ste 819 New York (10034) *(G-9354)*
EM Pfaff & Son Inc 607 739-3691
   204 E Franklin St Horseheads (14845) *(G-6121)*
Em-Kay Molds Inc 716 895-6180
   398 Ludington St Buffalo (14206) *(G-2742)*
Ema Jewelry Inc 212 575-8989
   246 W 38th St Fl 6 New York (10018) *(G-9355)*
Emagin Corporation (PA) 845 838-7900
   700 South Dr Ste 201 Hopewell Junction (12533) *(G-6092)*
Embassy Apparel Inc 212 768-8330
   37 W 37th St Fl 10 New York (10018) *(G-9356)*
Embassy Dinettes Inc 631 253-2292
   78 E Industry Ct Deer Park (11729) *(G-3871)*
Embassy Industries Inc 631 435-0209
   315 Oser Ave Ste 1 Hauppauge (11788) *(G-5647)*
Embassy Millwork Inc 518 839-0965
   3 Sam Stratton Rd Amsterdam (12010) *(G-326)*
Ember Media Corporation 212 695-1919
   224 W 35th St 1502 New York (10001) *(G-9357)*
Emblaze Systems Inc (HQ) 212 371-1100
   424 Madison Ave Fl 16 New York (10017) *(G-9358)*

Embroidery Screen Prtg Netwrk, Vestal *Also called Spst Inc (G-15383)*
EMC Corporation 212 564-6866
   2 Penn Plz Fl 24 New York (10121) *(G-9359)*
EMC Tech Inc 716 488-9071
   1984 Allen Street Ext Falconer (14733) *(G-4539)*
Emco Electric Services LLC 212 420-9766
   526 W 26th St Rm 1012 New York (10001) *(G-9360)*
Emco Finishing Products Inc 716 483-1176
   470 Crescent St Jamestown (14701) *(G-6510)*
Emcom Inc (PA) 315 255-5300
   62 Columbus St Ste 4 Auburn (13021) *(G-474)*
Emcom Industries Inc 716 852-3711
   235 Genesee St Buffalo (14204) *(G-2743)*
Emcs LLC 716 523-2002
   4414 Manor Ln Hamburg (14075) *(G-5507)*
Emda Inc 631 243-6363
   81 Westbury Ave Plainview (11803) *(G-12683)*
Emdroidme, Poughkeepsie *Also called Sciane Enterprises Inc (G-12982)*
Emerald Holdings Inc 718 797-4404
   63 Flushing Ave Unit 201 Brooklyn (11205) *(G-1798)*
Emerald Knitting, Brooklyn *Also called Emerald Holdings Inc (G-1798)*
Emergency Beacon Corp 914 576-2700
   2564 Park Ave 1 Bronx (10451) *(G-1253)*
Emergent Power Inc (HQ) 201 441-3590
   968 Albany Shaker Rd Latham (12110) *(G-6856)*
Emerson & Oliver LLC 585 775-9929
   44 Elton St Rochester (14607) *(G-13385)*
Emerson Control Techniques, Grand Island *Also called Nidec Indus Automtn USA LLC (G-5338)*
Emerson Electric Co 212 244-2490
   1250 Broadway Ste 2300 New York (10001) *(G-9361)*
Emerson Process MGT Lllp 585 214-8340
   3559 Winton Pl Ste 1 Rochester (14623) *(G-13386)*
Emes Motor Inc 718 387-2445
   876 Metropolitan Ave Brooklyn (11211) *(G-1799)*
Emhart Glass Manufacturing Inc 607 734-3671
   74 Kahler Rd Horseheads (14845) *(G-6122)*
EMI Music Publishing, New York *Also called Screen Gems-EMI Music Inc (G-11170)*
Emilia Interiors Inc (PA) 718 629-4202
   867 E 52nd St Brooklyn (11203) *(G-1800)*
Emilior Phrm Compounding Inc 646 350-0033
   3619 Provost Ave Fl 1 Bronx (10466) *(G-1254)*
Emily and Ashley, New York *Also called Greenbeads Llc (G-9673)*
Emitled Inc 516 531-3533
   2300 Shames Dr Westbury (11590) *(G-15882)*
Emkay Bordeaux, Arcade *Also called Emkay Trading Corp (G-373)*
Emkay Candle Company, Syracuse *Also called Muench-Kreuzer Candle Company (G-14947)*
Emkay Trading Corp (PA) 914 592-9000
   250 Clearbrook Rd Ste 127 Elmsford (10523) *(G-4407)*
Emkay Trading Corp 585 492-3800
   58 Church St Arcade (14009) *(G-373)*
Emmi USA Inc 845 268-9990
   100 Dutch Hill Rd Ste 220 Orangeburg (10962) *(G-12313)*
Emoji, New York *Also called Leng Universal Inc (G-10196)*
Emory Machine & Tool Co Inc 585 436-9610
   6176 Hunters Dr Farmington (14425) *(G-4771)*
Emp, Hauppauge *Also called Electronic Machine Parts LLC (G-5645)*
Emphascience 585 348-9415
   115 Sullys Trl Ste 6 Pittsford (14534) *(G-12639)*
Empire Air Hvac, West Babylon *Also called Empire Air Systems LLC (G-15709)*
Empire Air Specialties Inc 518 689-4440
   40 Kraft Ave Albany (12205) *(G-75)*
Empire Air Systems LLC 718 377-1549
   80 Kean St Ste 1 West Babylon (11704) *(G-15709)*
Empire Archtctural Systems Inc 518 773-5109
   125 Belzano Rd Johnstown (12095) *(G-6615)*
Empire Brewing Company Inc 315 925-8308
   120 Walton St Syracuse (13202) *(G-14887)*
Empire Building Products Inc 518 695-6094
   12 Spring St Schuylerville (12871) *(G-14323)*
Empire Business Forms Inc (PA) 845 562-7780
   128 S Robinson Ave 2 Newburgh (12550) *(G-11864)*
Empire Cheese Inc 585 968-1552
   4520 County Road 6 Cuba (14727) *(G-3813)*
Empire Coachworks Intl LLC 732 257-7981
   475 Haverstraw Rd Suffern (10901) *(G-14761)*
Empire Coffee Company Inc 914 934-1100
   106 Purdy Ave Port Chester (10573) *(G-12820)*
Empire Devleopment 716 789-2097
   5889 Magnolia Stedman Rd Mayville (14757) *(G-7682)*
Empire Division Inc 315 476-6273
   201 Kirkpatrick St # 207 Syracuse (13208) *(G-14888)*
Empire Emergency Apparatus Inc 716 348-3473
   3995 Lockport Rd Niagara Falls (14305) *(G-11923)*
Empire Emulsions LLC 845 610-5350
   1297 Craigville Rd Chester (10918) *(G-3376)*
Empire Fabricators Inc 585 235-3050
   95 Saginaw Dr Rochester (14623) *(G-13387)*
Empire Industrial Burner Svc 631 242-4619
   550 Brook Ave Deer Park (11729) *(G-3872)*

Empire Industrial Systems Corp (PA) 631 242-4619
  40 Corbin Ave Bay Shore (11706) *(G-678)*
Empire Innovation Group LLC 716 852-5000
  410 Main St Ste 5 Buffalo (14202) *(G-2744)*
Empire Metal Fabricators Inc 585 288-2140
  1385 Empire Blvd Ste 3 Rochester (14609) *(G-13388)*
Empire Metal Finishing Inc 718 545-6700
  2469 46th St Astoria (11103) *(G-421)*
Empire National, Brooklyn Also called A To Z Kosher Meat Products Co *(G-1436)*
Empire Open Mri 914 961-1777
  1915 Central Park Ave # 25 Yonkers (10710) *(G-16307)*
Empire Plastics Inc 607 754-9132
  2011 E Main St Endwell (13760) *(G-4479)*
Empire Precision Plastics, Rochester Also called Epp Team Inc *(G-13396)*
Empire Press Co (PA) 718 756-9500
  550 Empire Blvd Brooklyn (11225) *(G-1801)*
Empire Publishing Inc 516 829-4000
  1525 Central Ave Ste 1 Far Rockaway (11691) *(G-4564)*
Empire Signs, East Elmhurst Also called Liberty Awnings & Signs Inc *(G-4109)*
Empire State Metal Pdts Inc 718 847-1617
  10110 Jamaica Ave Richmond Hill (11418) *(G-13113)*
Empire State Weeklies Inc 585 671-1533
  46 North Ave Webster (14580) *(G-15640)*
Empire Steel Works Inc 516 561-3500
  110a New South Rd Hicksville (11801) *(G-5905)*
Empire Transit Mix Inc 718 384-3000
  430 Maspeth Ave Brooklyn (11211) *(G-1802)*
Empire Ventilation Eqp Co Inc (PA) 718 728-2143
  9 Industrial Dr Florida (10921) *(G-4823)*
Empirical Resolution Inc 510 671-0222
  41 E 11th St Fl 11 New York (10003) *(G-9362)*
Empro Niagara Inc 716 433-2769
  5027 Ridge Rd Lockport (14094) *(G-7073)*
Ems Development Corporation (HQ) 631 924-4736
  95 Horseblock Rd Unit 2 Yaphank (11980) *(G-16259)*
Ems Development Corporation 631 345-6200
  95 Horseblock Rd Unit 2a Yaphank (11980) *(G-16260)*
Ems Technologies Inc 607 723-3676
  71 Frederick St Binghamton (13901) *(G-875)*
Emsaru USA Corp 212 459-9355
  608 5th Ave Ste 500 New York (10020) *(G-9363)*
Emsig Manufacturing Corp (PA) 718 784-7717
  263 W 38th St Fl 5 New York (10018) *(G-9364)*
Emsig Manufacturing Corp. 518 828-7301
  160 Fairview Ave Ste 915 Hudson (12534) *(G-6155)*
Emtron Hybrids Inc 631 924-9668
  86 Horseblock Rd Unit G Yaphank (11980) *(G-16261)*
Emulso Corp 716 854-2889
  2750 Kenmore Ave Tonawanda (14150) *(G-15102)*
Emunas Sales Inc 718 621-3138
  947 E 27th St Brooklyn (11210) *(G-1803)*
Emusiccom Inc 212 201-9240
  215 Lexington Ave Fl 18 New York (10016) *(G-9365)*
Emvi Chocolate, Broadalbin Also called Emvi Inc *(G-1173)*
Emvi Inc 518 883-5111
  111 Bellen Rd Ste 2 Broadalbin (12025) *(G-1173)*
Emx Digital LLC (PA) 212 792-6810
  261 Madison Ave Fl 4 New York (10016) *(G-9366)*
En Foil LLC 516 466-9500
  1 Hollow Ln Ste 200 New Hyde Park (11042) *(G-8266)*
En Tech Corp 845 398-0776
  375 Western Hwy Tappan (10983) *(G-15035)*
Enbi Indiana Inc 585 647-1627
  1661 Lyell Ave Rochester (14606) *(G-13389)*
Enbi Rochester Inc 585 647-1651
  465 Paul Rd Ste A Rochester (14624) *(G-13390)*
Enchante Lites LLC (HQ) 212 602-1818
  15 W 34th St Fl 8 New York (10001) *(G-9367)*
Encore Electronics Inc 518 584-5354
  4400 Route 50 Saratoga Springs (12866) *(G-14171)*
Encore Refining and Recycleing 631 319-1910
  1120 Lincoln Ave Holbrook (11741) *(G-5999)*
Encore Retail Systems Inc (PA) 718 385-3443
  180 E Prospect Ave Mamaroneck (10543) *(G-7509)*
Encysive Pharmaceuticals Inc (HQ) 212 733-2323
  235 E 42nd St New York (10017) *(G-9368)*
Endava Inc (HQ) 212 920-7240
  757 3rd Ave Ste 1901 New York (10017) *(G-9369)*
Endeavor Printing LLC 718 570-2720
  3704 29th St Long Island City (11101) *(G-7214)*
Endicott Interconnect Tech Inc 866 820-4820
  1701 North St Endicott (13760) *(G-4450)*
Endicott Precision Inc 607 754-7076
  1328-30 Campville Rd Endicott (13760) *(G-4451)*
Endicott Research Group Inc 607 754-9187
  2601 Wayne St Endicott (13760) *(G-4452)*
Endoscopic Procedure Center, Syracuse Also called Elizabeth Wood *(G-14885)*
Endovor Inc 214 679-7385
  1330 1st Ave Apt 1119 New York (10021) *(G-9370)*
Endovor LLC 214 679-7385
  525 E 68th St A1027 New York (10065) *(G-9371)*
Endurance LLC 212 719-2500
  530 7th Ave Rm 902 New York (10018) *(G-9372)*

Endurart Inc 212 473-7000
  132 Nassau St Rm 1100 New York (10038) *(G-9373)*
Enecon Corporation (PA) 516 349-0022
  6 Platinum Ct Medford (11763) *(G-7706)*
Eneflux Armtek Magnetics Inc (HQ) 516 576-3434
  6 Platinum Ct Medford (11763) *(G-7707)*
Ener-G-Rotors Inc 518 372-2608
  17 Fern Ave Schenectady (12306) *(G-14262)*
Energy Ahead Inc 718 813-7338
  693 E 2nd St Brooklyn (11218) *(G-1804)*
Energy Brands Inc (HQ) 212 545-6000
  260 Madison Ave Fl 10 New York (10016) *(G-9374)*
Energy Conservation & Sup Inc 718 855-5888
  55 Washington St Ste 324 Brooklyn (11201) *(G-1805)*
Energy Harvesters LLC 617 325-9852
  63 Garden Dr Rochester (14609) *(G-13391)*
Energy Intelligence Group Inc (PA) 212 532-1112
  270 Madison Ave Fl 19 New York (10016) *(G-9375)*
Energy Materials Corporation 315 247-0880
  1999 Lk Ave B82 Ste B304 Rochester (14650) *(G-13392)*
Energy Nuclear Operations 315 342-0055
  268 Lake Rd Oswego (13126) *(G-12410)*
Energy Panel Structures Inc 315 923-7777
  10269 Old Route 31 Clyde (14433) *(G-3489)*
Energy Panel Structures Inc 585 343-1777
  10269 Old Route 31 Clyde (14433) *(G-3490)*
Energy Panel Structures Inc 518 355-6708
  864 Burdeck St Schenectady (12306) *(G-14263)*
Enertiv Inc 646 350-3525
  320 W 37th St Ste 1500 New York (10018) *(G-9376)*
Enetics Inc 585 924-5010
  830 Canning Pkwy Victor (14564) *(G-15407)*
Engagement Technology LLC 914 591-7600
  33 W Main St Ste 303 Elmsford (10523) *(G-4408)*
Engelack Gem Corporation 212 719-3094
  36 W 47th St Ste 601 New York (10036) *(G-9377)*
Engineered Air Products, Lancaster Also called Eastern Air Products LLC *(G-6804)*
Engineered Composites Inc 716 362-0295
  55 Roberts Ave Buffalo (14206) *(G-2745)*
Engineered Lifting Tech, Orchard Park Also called Kinedyne Inc *(G-12360)*
Engineered Metal Products Inc 631 842-3780
  10 Reith St Copiague (11726) *(G-3652)*
Engineered Plastics Inc 800 682-2525
  300 International Dr # 100 Williamsville (14221) *(G-16130)*
Engineered Polymer Systems Div, Marion Also called Parker-Hannifin Corporation *(G-7572)*
Engineered Products Oper Epo, Rochester Also called Pulsafeeder Inc *(G-13653)*
Engineering Educational Eqp Co, New Paltz Also called Kevco Industries *(G-8308)*
Engineering Maint Pdts Inc 516 624-9774
  250 Berry Hill Rd Oyster Bay (11771) *(G-12447)*
Engineering Mfg Tech LLC 607 754-7111
  101 Delaware Ave Endicott (13760) *(G-4453)*
English Computer Consulting 212 764-1717
  404 5th Ave Fl 3 New York (10018) *(G-9378)*
Englishcomp, New York Also called English Computer Consulting *(G-9378)*
Engrav-O-Type Press Inc 585 262-7590
  30 Bermar Park Ste 2 Rochester (14624) *(G-13393)*
Enhance A Colour Corp 212 490-3620
  211 E 43rd St Rm 700 New York (10017) *(G-9379)*
Enhanced Tool Inc 716 691-5200
  90 Pineview Dr Amherst (14228) *(G-221)*
Eni Mks Products Group 585 427-8300
  100 Highpower Rd Rochester (14623) *(G-13394)*
Eni Technology Inc (HQ) 585 427-8300
  100 Highpower Rd Rochester (14623) *(G-13395)*
Enivate - Aerospace Division, Orchard Park Also called ITT Enidine Inc *(G-12356)*
Enjoy, Scarsdale Also called Japan America Learning Ctr Inc *(G-14237)*
Enjoy City North Inc 607 584-5061
  100 Emerson Pkwy Binghamton (13905) *(G-876)*
Enlighten Air Inc 917 656-1248
  23 E 81st St Apt 10 New York (10028) *(G-9380)*
Enplas America Inc 646 892-7811
  299 Park Ave Fl 41a New York (10171) *(G-9381)*
Enrg Inc 716 873-2939
  155 Chandler St 5 Buffalo (14207) *(G-2746)*
Ensil Technical Services Inc 716 282-1020
  1901 Maryland Ave Niagara Falls (14305) *(G-11924)*
Entermarket 914 437-7268
  280 N Bedford Rd Ste 305 Mount Kisco (10549) *(G-8092)*
Enterprise Bagels Inc 845 896-3823
  986 Main St Ste 3 Fishkill (12524) *(G-4799)*
Enterprise Folding Box Co Inc 716 876-6421
  75 Isabelle St Buffalo (14207) *(G-2747)*
Enterprise Press Inc 212 741-2111
  627 Greenwich St New York (10014) *(G-9382)*
Enterprise Tech Group Inc 914 588-0327
  3 Church St New Rochelle (10801) *(G-8328)*
Enterprise Wood Products Inc 718 853-9243
  4710 18th Ave Brooklyn (11204) *(G-1806)*
Entertron Industries Inc 716 772-7216
  99 Robinson Pl Lockport (14094) *(G-7074)*
Entrepreneur Media Inc. 646 502-5463
  462 Fashion Ave Fl 11 New York (10018) *(G-9383)*

A
L
P
H
A
B
E
T
I
C

Entrepreneur Ventures Inc 631 261-1111
652 Bread Chese Hollow Rd Northport (11768) ***(G-12103)***
Enumeral Biomedical Corp 347 227-4787
1370 Broadway Fl 5 New York (10018) ***(G-9384)***
Enviro Service & Supply Corp 347 838-6500
45b Marble Loop Staten Island (10309) ***(G-14651)***
Enviroform Recycled Pdts Inc 315 789-1810
287 Gambee Rd Geneva (14456) ***(G-5152)***
Enviromaster International LLC 315 336-3716
5780 Success Dr Rome (13440) ***(G-13848)***
Environment-One Corporation 518 346-6161
2773 Balltown Rd Schenectady (12309) ***(G-14264)***
Environmental Closures, Mineola *Also called Geotechnical Drilling Inc* ***(G-7977)***
Environmental Temp Systems LLC 516 640-5818
111 Roosevelt Ave Ste C Mineola (11501) ***(G-7971)***
Envy Publishing Group Inc 212 253-9874
118 E 25th St Bsmt Ll New York (10010) ***(G-9385)***
Enyce, New York *Also called 5 Star Apparel LLC* ***(G-8404)***
Enzo Diagnostics, Farmingdale *Also called Enzo Life Sciences Inc* ***(G-4625)***
Enzo Life Sciences Inc (HQ) 631 694-7070
10 Executive Blvd Farmingdale (11735) ***(G-4625)***
Enzo Life Sciences Intl Inc 610 941-0430
10 Executive Blvd Farmingdale (11735) ***(G-4626)***
Enzo Manzoni LLC 212 464-7000
2896 W 12th St Brooklyn (11224) ***(G-1807)***
Eon Labs Inc (HQ) 516 478-9700
1999 Marcus Ave Ste 300 New Hyde Park (11042) ***(G-8267)***
Eos Products LLC 212 929-6367
19 W 44th St Ste 811 New York (10036) ***(G-9386)***
Ephesus Lighting, Syracuse *Also called Eaton Corporation* ***(G-14882)***
Epi Printing & Finishing, Rochester *Also called Engrav-O-Type Press Inc* ***(G-13393)***
Epic Beauty Co LLC 212 327-3059
929 Park Ave 5 New York (10028) ***(G-9387)***
Epic Pharma LLC 718 276-8600
22715 N Conduit Ave Laurelton (11413) ***(G-6882)***
Epicor Software Corporation 805 496-6789
2165 Technology Dr Schenectady (12308) ***(G-14265)***
Epl, Long Island City *Also called Edison Price Lighting Inc* ***(G-7209)***
Epner Technology Incorporated (PA) 718 782-5948
25 Division Pl Brooklyn (11222) ***(G-1808)***
Epner Technology Incorporated 718 782-8722
78 Kingsland Ave Brooklyn (11222) ***(G-1809)***
Epoch Microelectronics Inc 914 332-8570
420 Columbus Ave Ste 204 Valhalla (10595) ***(G-15303)***
Epost International Inc 212 352-9390
483 10th Ave New York (10018) ***(G-9388)***
Epp Team Inc 585 454-4995
500 Lee Rd Ste 400 Rochester (14606) ***(G-13396)***
Eps Iron Works Inc 516 294-5840
38 Windsor Ave Ste 101 Mineola (11501) ***(G-7972)***
Equal Opprtnity Pblcations Inc 631 421-9421
445 Broadhollow Rd # 425 Melville (11747) ***(G-7778)***
Equicenter Inc 585 742-2522
3247 Rush Mendon Rd Honeoye Falls (14472) ***(G-6071)***
Equicheck LLC 631 987-6356
20 Medford Ave Ste 7 Patchogue (11772) ***(G-12500)***
Equilend Holdings LLC (PA) 212 901-2200
225 Liberty St Fl 10 New York (10281) ***(G-9389)***
Equilibrium Brewery LLC 201 245-0292
22 Henry St Middletown (10940) ***(G-7907)***
Equine Imaging LLC (PA) 414 326-0665
169 Middle Neck Rd Port Washington (11050) ***(G-12878)***
Equipment Apparel LLC 212 502-1890
19 W 34th St Fl 8 New York (10001) ***(G-9390)***
Equivital Inc 646 513-4169
19 W 34th St Rm 1018 New York (10001) ***(G-9391)***
Equus Power I LP 847 908-2878
380 Patton Ave West Babylon (11704) ***(G-15710)***
ER Butler & Co Inc (PA) 212 925-3565
55 Prince St Frnt A New York (10012) ***(G-9392)***
Erbessd Reliability LLC 518 874-2700
2c Glens Falls Tech Park Glens Falls (12801) ***(G-5248)***
Erbessd Reliability Instrs, Glens Falls *Also called Erbessd Reliability LLC* ***(G-5248)***
Ercole Nyc Inc (PA) 212 675-2218
142 26th St Brooklyn (11232) ***(G-1810)***
Erdle Perforating Holdings Inc (PA) 585 247-4700
100 Pixley Indus Pkwy Rochester (14624) ***(G-13397)***
Ergun Inc 631 721-0049
10 Mineola Ave Unit B Roslyn Heights (11577) ***(G-14050)***
Erhard & Gilcher Inc 315 474-1072
235 Cortland Ave Syracuse (13202) ***(G-14889)***
Eric S Turner & Company Inc 914 235-7114
3335 Centre Ave New Rochelle (10801) ***(G-8329)***
Eric Signature, New York *Also called Harrison Sportswear Inc* ***(G-9730)***
Eric Winterling Inc 212 629-7686
20 W 20th St Fl 5 New York (10011) ***(G-9393)***
Erickson Beamon Ltd 212 643-4810
498 Fashion Ave Rm 2406 New York (10018) ***(G-9394)***
Erie Engineered Products Inc 716 206-0204
3949 Walden Ave Lancaster (14086) ***(G-6805)***
Erika T Schwartz MD PC 212 873-3420
724 5th Ave Fl 10 New York (10019) ***(G-9395)***

Ernie Green Industries Inc 585 295-8951
85 Pixley Industrial Pkwy Rochester (14624) ***(G-13398)***
Ernie Green Industries Inc 585 647-2300
1667 Emerson St Rochester (14606) ***(G-13399)***
Ernie Green Industries Inc 585 647-2300
460 Buffalo Rd Ste 220 Rochester (14611) ***(G-13400)***
Ernst Publishing Co, Albany *Also called Ucc Guide Inc* ***(G-139)***
Ert Software Inc 845 358-5721
4 Pine Glen Dr Blauvelt (10913) ***(G-928)***
Ertel Alsop, Kingston *Also called Stavo Industries Inc* ***(G-6712)***
Ertel Engineering Co, Kingston *Also called Stavo Industries Inc* ***(G-6713)***
Es Beta Inc 631 582-6740
125 Comac St Ronkonkoma (11779) ***(G-13936)***
Esc Control Electronics LLC 631 467-5328
98 Lincoln Ave Sayville (11782) ***(G-14225)***
Eschen Prosthetic & Orthotic L 212 606-1262
510 E 73rd St Ste 201 New York (10021) ***(G-9396)***
Eschen Prsthetic Orthotic Labs 516 871-0029
299 Duffy Ave Hicksville (11801) ***(G-5906)***
Escholar LLC 914 989-2900
222 Bloomingdale Rd # 107 White Plains (10605) ***(G-16002)***
Esense LLC 718 887-9779
4402 23rd St Ste 114 Long Island City (11101) ***(G-7215)***
Esensors Inc 716 837-8719
4240 Ridge Lea Rd Ste 37 Buffalo (14226) ***(G-2748)***
Eser Realty Corp (PA) 718 383-0565
62 Greenpoint Ave 64 Brooklyn (11222) ***(G-1811)***
Esi, Holbrook *Also called Electronic Systems Inc* ***(G-5998)***
ESi Cases & Accessories Inc 212 883-8838
44 E 32nd St Rm 601 New York (10016) ***(G-9397)***
Eskay Metal Fabricating, Buffalo *Also called Schuler-Subra Inc* ***(G-2975)***
Eskayel Inc 347 703-8084
75 S 6th St Brooklyn (11249) ***(G-1812)***
Esm Group Inc (HQ) 716 446-8914
300 Corporate Pkwy 118n Amherst (14226) ***(G-222)***
Esm Group Inc 724 265-1766
300 Corporate Pkwy 118n Buffalo (14226) ***(G-2749)***
Esm II Inc (HQ) 716 446-8888
300 Corporate Pkwy 118n Amherst (14226) ***(G-223)***
Esm Special Metals & Tech Inc 716 446-8914
300 Corporate Pkwy 118n Amherst (14226) ***(G-224)***
Espey Mfg & Electronics Corp (PA) 518 584-4100
233 Ballston Ave Saratoga Springs (12866) ***(G-14172)***
Espostos Fnest Qlty Ssage Pdts, New York *Also called Elmgang Enterprises I Inc* ***(G-9350)***
Esquire Magazine, New York *Also called Hearst Corporation* ***(G-9750)***
Esquire Mechanical Corp 718 625-4006
79 Sandford St Brooklyn (11205) ***(G-1813)***
Ess Bee Industries Inc 718 894-5202
95 Evergreen Ave Brooklyn (11206) ***(G-1814)***
Essar Americas 212 292-2600
277 Park Ave 47th New York (10172) ***(G-9398)***
Essar Steel Minnesota LLC (PA) 212 292-2600
150 E 52nd St Fl 27 New York (10022) ***(G-9399)***
Essence Communications Inc (PA) 212 522-1212
241 37th St Fl 1 Brooklyn (11232) ***(G-1815)***
Essence Magazine, Brooklyn *Also called Essence Communications Inc* ***(G-1815)***
Essence Ventures LLC 212 522-1212
225 Liberty St Fl 9 New York (10281) ***(G-9400)***
Essential Homme Magazine, New York *Also called Essential Publications US LLC* ***(G-9401)***
Essential Publications US LLC 646 707-0898
14 E 4th St Rm 604 New York (10012) ***(G-9401)***
Essential Ribbons Inc 212 967-4173
53 W 36th St Rm 405 New York (10018) ***(G-9402)***
Essequattro USA Inc 917 862-0005
1 Little West 12th St New York (10014) ***(G-9403)***
Essex Box & Pallet Co Inc 518 834-7279
49 Industrial Park Rd Keeseville (12944) ***(G-6641)***
Essex Industries 518 942-6671
17 Pilfershire Rd Mineville (12956) ***(G-8004)***
Essex Manufacturing Inc 212 239-0080
350 5th Ave Ste 2400 New York (10118) ***(G-9404)***
Essex Works Ltd 718 495-4575
446 Riverdale Ave Brooklyn (11207) ***(G-1816)***
Essie Cosmetics Ltd 212 818-1500
575 5th Ave New York (10017) ***(G-9405)***
Essilor Laboratories Amer Inc 845 365-6700
165 Route 303 Orangeburg (10962) ***(G-12314)***
Essity Prof Hygiene N Amer LLC 518 692-8434
72 County Route 53 Greenwich (12834) ***(G-5470)***
Essity Prof Hygiene N Amer LLC 518 583-2785
49 Geyser Rd Saratoga Springs (12866) ***(G-14173)***
ESSITY PROFESSIONAL HYGIENE NORTH AMERICA LLC, Saratoga Springs *Also called Essity Prof Hygiene N Amer LLC* ***(G-14173)***
Estebania Enterprises Inc 585 529-9330
15 Mcardle St Ste A Rochester (14611) ***(G-13401)***
Estee Lauder, New York *Also called Prescriptives Inc* ***(G-10882)***
Estee Lauder Companies Inc 917 606-3240
9 W 22nd St New York (10010) ***(G-9406)***
Estee Lauder Companies Inc 212 572-4200
110 E 59th St Fl 37 New York (10022) ***(G-9407)***

Estee Lauder Companies Inc 212 756-4800
655 Madison Ave Fl 15 New York (10065) ***(G-9408)***
Estee Lauder Companies Inc 646 762-7718
28 W 23rd St New York (10010) ***(G-9409)***
Estee Lauder Companies Inc 631 694-2601
80 Ruland Rd Ste 3 Melville (11747) ***(G-7779)***
Estee Lauder Companies Inc (PA) 212 572-4200
767 5th Ave Fl 1 New York (10153) ***(G-9410)***
Estee Lauder Companies Inc 212 572-4200
7 Corporate Center Dr Melville (11747) ***(G-7780)***
Estee Lauder Companies Inc 646 602-7590
65 Bleecker St Frnt 1 New York (10012) ***(G-9411)***
Estee Lauder Inc 631 531-1000
125 Pinelawn Rd Melville (11747) ***(G-7781)***
Estiator, New York *Also called Interhellenic Publishing Inc* ***(G-9916)***
ET Oakes Corporation 631 232-0002
686 Old Willets Path Hauppauge (11788) ***(G-5648)***
ET Precision Optics Inc 585 254-2560
33 Curlew St Rochester (14606) ***(G-13402)***
Etcetera Wallpapers, Glen Cove *Also called Sunnyside Decorative Prints Co* ***(G-5203)***
Eternal Fortune Fashion LLC (PA) 212 965-5322
135 W 36th St Fl 3 New York (10018) ***(G-9412)***
Eternal Line 845 856-1999
1237 State Route 42 Sparrow Bush (12780) ***(G-14547)***
Eternal Love Parfums Corp 516 921-6100
485 Underhill Blvd # 207 Syosset (11791) ***(G-14786)***
Eternal Love Perfumes, Syosset *Also called Eternal Love Parfums Corp* ***(G-14786)***
Ethis Communications Inc 212 791-1440
44 Church St Ste 200 White Plains (10601) ***(G-16003)***
Etna Products Co Inc (PA) 212 989-7591
99 Madison Ave Fl 11 New York (10016) ***(G-9413)***
Etna Tool & Die Corporation 212 475-4350
42 Bond St Frnt A New York (10012) ***(G-9414)***
Eton Institute 855 334-3688
1 Rockefeller Plz Fl 11 New York (10020) ***(G-9415)***
Eton International, New York *Also called Basil S Kadhim* ***(G-8736)***
Ets, Mineola *Also called Environmental Temp Systems LLC* ***(G-7971)***
Eu Design LLC 212 420-7788
73 Spring St Rm 506 New York (10012) ***(G-9416)***
Eugene Biro Corp 212 997-0146
581 5th Ave Fl 3 New York (10017) ***(G-9417)***
Eugene G Danner Mfg Inc 631 234-5261
160 Oval Dr Central Islip (11749) ***(G-3273)***
Eugenia Selective Living Inc 631 277-1461
122 Freeman Ave Islip (11751) ***(G-6352)***
Euphorbia Productions Ltd 212 533-1700
632 Broadway Fl 9 New York (10012) ***(G-9418)***
Euphrates Inc 518 762-3488
230 Enterprise Rd Johnstown (12095) ***(G-6616)***
Eur-Pac Corporation 203 756-0102
1460 5th Ave Bay Shore (11706) ***(G-679)***
Euro Bands Inc 212 719-9777
247 W 37th St Ste 700 New York (10018) ***(G-9419)***
Euro Fine Paper Inc 516 238-5253
220 Nassau Blvd Garden City (11530) ***(G-5098)***
Euro Gear (usa) Inc 518 578-1775
1 Cumberland Ave Plattsburgh (12901) ***(G-12746)***
Euro Woodworking Inc 718 246-9172
303 Park Ave Fl 8 Brooklyn (11205) ***(G-1817)***
Euroco Costumes Inc 212 629-9665
306 W 38th St Rm 1600 New York (10018) ***(G-9420)***
Euromed Inc 845 359-4039
25 Corporate Dr Orangeburg (10962) ***(G-12315)***
Europadisk LLC 718 407-7300
2402 Queens Plz S Long Island City (11101) ***(G-7216)***
European Marble Works Co Inc 718 387-9778
54 Nassau Blvd Garden City (11530) ***(G-5099)***
Europrojects Intl Inc 917 262-0795
152 W 25th St Fl 8b New York (10001) ***(G-9421)***
Eurotex Inc 716 205-8861
4600 Witmer Rd Niagara Falls (14305) ***(G-11925)***
Eurotex North America, Niagara Falls *Also called Eurotex Inc* ***(G-11925)***
Ev-Box North America Inc 646 930-6305
335 Madison Ave Fl 4 New York (10017) ***(G-9422)***
Eva Fehren, New York *Also called Gorga Fehren Fine Jewelry LLC* ***(G-9646)***
Evado Filip 917 774-8666
159 Bleecker St New York (10012) ***(G-9423)***
EVANGELIST, THE, Albany *Also called Albany Catholic Press Assoc* ***(G-31)***
Evans & Paul LLC 516 576-0800
140 Dupont St Plainview (11803) ***(G-12684)***
Evans Chemetics LP 315 539-9221
228 E Main St Waterloo (13165) ***(G-15550)***
Evans Manufacturing LLC 631 439-3300
595 Smith St Farmingdale (11735) ***(G-4627)***
Eve Sales Corp 718 589-6800
945 Close Ave Bronx (10473) ***(G-1255)***
Evelo Inc 917 251-8743
327 Beach 101st St Rockaway Park (11694) ***(G-13824)***
Evenhouse Printing 716 649-2666
4783 Southwestern Blvd Hamburg (14075) ***(G-5508)***
Evening Telegram, Utica *Also called Gatehouse Media LLC* ***(G-15268)***
Evening Tribune, Hornell *Also called Gatehouse Media LLC* ***(G-6107)***

Event Journal Inc 516 470-1811
366 N Broadway Ste 209 Jericho (11753) ***(G-6578)***
Event Services Corporation 315 488-9357
6171 Airport Rd Solvay (13209) ***(G-14497)***
Ever-Nu-Metal Products Inc 646 423-5833
471 20th St Brooklyn (11215) ***(G-1818)***
Everblock Systems LLC (PA) 844 422-5625
790 Madison Ave Rm 506 New York (10065) ***(G-9424)***
Evercore Partners Svcs E LLC 212 857-3100
55 E 52nd St New York (10055) ***(G-9425)***
Everest Bbn Inc 212 268-7979
42 Broadway Ste 1736 New York (10004) ***(G-9426)***
Everfab Inc 716 655-1550
12928 Big Tree Rd East Aurora (14052) ***(G-4086)***
Evergreen, New York *Also called Integrated Copyright Group* ***(G-9907)***
Evergreen Corp Central NY 315 454-4175
235 Cortland Ave Syracuse (13202) ***(G-14890)***
Evergreen Manufacturing, Syracuse *Also called Evergreen Corp Central NY* ***(G-14890)***
Evergreen Slate Company Inc 518 642-2530
2027 County Route 23 Middle Granville (12849) ***(G-7867)***
Everlast Sports Mfg Corp (HQ) 212 239-0990
42 W 39th St New York (10018) ***(G-9427)***
Everlast Worldwide Inc (HQ) 212 239-0990
42 W 39th St Fl 3 New York (10018) ***(G-9428)***
Everplans, New York *Also called Beyondly Inc* ***(G-8774)***
Eversan Inc 315 736-3967
34 Main St Ste 3 Whitesboro (13492) ***(G-16080)***
Everstone Industries LLC 347 777-8150
242 W 122nd St Apt 4b New York (10027) ***(G-9429)***
Everybodys Carribbean Magazine, Brooklyn *Also called Herman Hall Communications* ***(G-1933)***
Evocate Media LLC 646 361-3014
100 W 139th St Apt 34a New York (10030) ***(G-9430)***
Evoke Neuroscience Inc 917 261-6096
11 W 25th St Fl 10 New York (10010) ***(G-9431)***
Evolution Spirits Inc 917 543-7880
401 Park Ave S New York (10016) ***(G-9432)***
Evonik Corporation 518 233-7090
7 Schoolhouse Ln Waterford (12188) ***(G-15536)***
Ew, Ronkonkoma *Also called East/West Industries Inc* ***(G-13932)***
Ewatchfactory Corp (PA) 212 564-8318
390 5th Ave Rm 910 New York (10018) ***(G-9433)***
Ex El Enterprises Ltd 212 489-4500
630 Fort Washington Ave New York (10040) ***(G-9434)***
Ex-Cell Home Fashions Inc (HQ) 919 735-7111
1333 Broadway Fl 8 New York (10018) ***(G-9435)***
Ex-It Medical Devices Inc 212 653-0637
1330 Ave Of The Americas New York (10019) ***(G-9436)***
Exact Machining & Mfg 585 334-7090
305 Commerce Dr Ste 7 Rochester (14623) ***(G-13403)***
Exact Solutions Inc 212 707-8627
139 Fulton St Rm 511 New York (10038) ***(G-9437)***
Exacta LLC 716 406-2303
8955 Williams Ct Clarence Center (14032) ***(G-3445)***
Exc Holdings I Corp (HQ) 212 644-5900
666 5th Ave Fl 36 New York (10103) ***(G-9438)***
Exc Holdings II Corp (HQ) 212 644-5900
666 5th Ave Fl 36 New York (10103) ***(G-9439)***
Exc Holdings LP (PA) 212 644-5900
666 5th Ave Fl 36 New York (10103) ***(G-9440)***
Excel Aluminum Products Inc 315 471-0925
563 N Salina St Syracuse (13208) ***(G-14891)***
Excel Conveyor LLC 718 474-0001
350 Beach 79th St Ste 1 Rockaway Beach (11693) ***(G-13822)***
Excel Graphics Services Inc 212 929-2183
519 8th Ave Fl 18 New York (10018) ***(G-9441)***
Excel Industries Inc 716 542-5468
11737 Main St Clarence (14031) ***(G-3434)***
Excel Machine Technologies Inc 585 426-1911
50 Bermar Park Ste 5&6 Rochester (14624) ***(G-13404)***
Excel Paint Applicators Inc 347 221-1968
555 Doughty Blvd Inwood (11096) ***(G-6291)***
Excel Technology Inc 718 423-7262
5317 Hollis Court Blvd Fresh Meadows (11365) ***(G-5040)***
Excel Technology Inc 212 355-3400
780 3rd Ave New York (10017) ***(G-9442)***
Excelco Developments Inc 716 934-2651
65 Main St Silver Creek (14136) ***(G-14441)***
Excelco/Newbrook Inc 716 934-2644
16 Mechanic St Silver Creek (14136) ***(G-14442)***
Exceleratedѕ2p, New York *Also called Cordis Solutions Inc* ***(G-9102)***
Excell Print & Promotions Inc 914 437-8668
50 Main St Ste 100 White Plains (10606) ***(G-16004)***
Excelled Sheepskin & Lea Coat (PA) 212 594-5843
1359 Broadway Fl 9 New York (10018) ***(G-9443)***
Excellent Art Mfg Corp 718 388-7075
531 Bayview Ave Inwood (11096) ***(G-6292)***
Excellent Photo Copies (PA) 718 384-7272
165 Hooper St Brooklyn (11211) ***(G-1819)***
Excellent Photocopies, Brooklyn *Also called Excellent Printing Inc* ***(G-1821)***
Excellent Poly Inc 718 768-6555
820 4th Ave Brooklyn (11232) ***(G-1820)***

ALPHABETIC

Excellent Printing Inc 718 384-7272
 165 Hooper St Brooklyn (11211) *(G-1821)*
Excelsior Graphics Inc 212 730-6200
 485 Madison Ave Fl 13 New York (10022) *(G-9444)*
Excelsior Mlt-Cltural Inst Inc 706 627-4285
 13340 Roosevelt Ave 7g Flushing (11354) *(G-4850)*
Excelsior Publications 607 746-7600
 133 Main St Delhi (13753) *(G-3964)*
Excelsus Solutions LLC 585 533-0003
 12 Pixley Industrial Pkwy # 40 Rochester (14624) *(G-13405)*
Exchange My Mail Inc 516 605-1835
 30 Jericho Executive Plz 100c Jericho (11753) *(G-6579)*
Executive Business Media Inc 516 334-3030
 825 Old Country Rd Westbury (11590) *(G-15883)*
Executive Machines Inc 718 965-6600
 882 3rd Ave Unit 8 Brooklyn (11232) *(G-1822)*
Executive Mirror Doors Inc 631 234-1090
 1 Comac Loop Unit 7 Ronkonkoma (11779) *(G-13937)*
Executive Sign Corp 212 397-4050
 43 Boulevard Cornwall On Hudson (12520) *(G-3733)*
Executive Sign Corporation 212 397-4050
 347 W 36th St Rm 902 New York (10018) *(G-9445)*
Exergy LLC 516 832-9300
 320 Endo Blvd Unit 1 Garden City (11530) *(G-5100)*
Exhibit Corporation America 718 937-2600
 4623 Crane St Ste 3 Long Island City (11101) *(G-7217)*
Exhibit Portables, Long Island City *Also called Exhibit Corporation America* *(G-7217)*
Exhibits & More 585 924-4040
 7615 Omnitech Pl Ste 4a Victor (14564) *(G-15408)*
Exide Batteries, Batavia *Also called Exide Technologies* *(G-613)*
Exide Technologies 585 344-0656
 4330 Commerce Dr Batavia (14020) *(G-613)*
Exigo Precision Inc 585 254-5818
 190 Murray St Rochester (14606) *(G-13406)*
Exotic Print and Paper Inc 212 807-0465
 15 E 13th St New York (10003) *(G-9446)*
Expedi-Printing Inc 516 513-0919
 41 Red Brook Rd Great Neck (11024) *(G-5383)*
Expedient Heat Treating Corp 716 433-1177
 61 Dale Dr North Tonawanda (14120) *(G-12066)*
Experiment LLC 212 889-1659
 260 5th Ave Fl 3 New York (10001) *(G-9447)*
Experiment Publishing LLC 212 889-1273
 220 E 23rd St Ste 600 New York (10010) *(G-9448)*
Expert Industries Inc 718 434-6060
 848 E 43rd St Brooklyn (11210) *(G-1823)*
Expert Machine Services Inc 718 786-1200
 3944a 28th St Long Island City (11101) *(G-7218)*
Expert Metal Slitters Corp 718 361-2735
 3740 12th St Long Island City (11101) *(G-7219)*
Expo Furniture Designs Inc 516 674-1420
 1 Garvies Point Rd Glen Cove (11542) *(G-5192)*
Expo Lighting Design, Glen Cove *Also called Expo Furniture Designs Inc* *(G-5192)*
Expositor Newspapers Inc 585 427-2468
 2535 Brighton Henrietta Rochester (14623) *(G-13407)*
Express Building Supply Inc 516 608-0379
 3550 Lawson Blvd Oceanside (11572) *(G-12171)*
Express Checkout LLC 646 512-2068
 110 E 1st St Apt 20 New York (10009) *(G-9449)*
Express Concrete Inc 631 273-4224
 1250 Suffolk Ave Brentwood (11717) *(G-1121)*
Express Mart, Watertown *Also called Petre Alii Petroleum* *(G-15587)*
Express Press, Rochester *Also called Clarsons Corp* *(G-13317)*
Express Seal Div, Lancaster *Also called Apple Rubber Products Inc* *(G-6795)*
Express Tag & Label, Brooklyn *Also called Jerry Tomaselli* *(G-1991)*
Expresseal, Lancaster *Also called Apple Rubber Products Inc* *(G-6796)*
Expression Embroidery, Jamaica *Also called Expressions Punching & Digitiz* *(G-6441)*
Expressions Punching & Digitiz 718 291-1177
 9315 179th Pl Jamaica (11433) *(G-6441)*
Expressive Scent, Brooklyn *Also called Jacmax Industries LLC* *(G-1984)*
Exquisite Glass & Stone Inc 718 937-9266
 3117 12th St Astoria (11106) *(G-422)*
Extek Inc 585 533-1672
 7500 W Henrietta Rd Rush (14543) *(G-14070)*
Exten II LLC 716 895-2214
 127 Elm St East Aurora (14052) *(G-4087)*
Extreme Auto Accessories Corp (PA) 718 978-6722
 235 Liberty Ave Mineola (11501) *(G-7973)*
Extreme Group Holdings LLC (HQ) 212 833-8000
 25 Madison Ave Fl 19 New York (10010) *(G-9450)*
Extreme Molding LLC 518 326-9319
 25 Gibson St Ste 2 Watervliet (12189) *(G-15601)*
Extreme Spices Inc (PA) 917 496-4081
 5634 56th St Ste 36 Maspeth (11378) *(G-7613)*
Extreme Streetwear, Batavia *Also called Alicia F Herdlein* *(G-599)*
Exxelia-Raf Tabtronics LLC 585 243-4331
 2854 Genesee St Piffard (14533) *(G-12624)*
EY Industries Inc 718 624-9122
 63 Flushing Ave Unit 331 Brooklyn (11205) *(G-1824)*
Eye Shadow, New York *Also called Stony Apparel Corp* *(G-11367)*

Eyeglass Service Industries 914 666-3150
 777 Bedford Rd Bedford Hills (10507) *(G-769)*
Eyelock Corporation 855 393-5625
 321 W 44th St Ste 702 New York (10036) *(G-9451)*
Eyelock LLC (HQ) 855 393-5625
 321 W 44th St Ste 702 New York (10036) *(G-9452)*
Eyenovia Inc 917 289-1117
 295 Madison Ave Fl 24 New York (10017) *(G-9453)*
EZ Lift Garage Door Service, Spring Valley *Also called EZ Lift Operator Corp* *(G-14568)*
EZ Lift Operator Corp 845 356-1676
 111 S Main St Spring Valley (10977) *(G-14568)*
EZ Newsletter LLC 412 943-7777
 1449 Bay Ridge Ave 2 Brooklyn (11219) *(G-1825)*
EZ Systems US Inc 929 295-0699
 215 Water St Gf Brooklyn (11201) *(G-1826)*
Ezconcept, Webster *Also called Studco Building Systems US LLC* *(G-15655)*
Ezcontacts.com, Brooklyn *Also called Provision Supply LLC* *(G-2303)*
F & B Photo Offset Co Inc (PA) 516 431-5433
 4 California Pl N Island Park (11558) *(G-6317)*
F & D Printing, Staten Island *Also called F & D Services Inc* *(G-14652)*
F & D Services Inc 718 984-1635
 34 E Augusta Ave Staten Island (10308) *(G-14652)*
F & H Metal Finishing Co Inc 585 798-2151
 700 Genesee St Medina (14103) *(G-7734)*
F & J Designs Inc 212 302-8755
 526 Fashion Ave Fl 8 New York (10018) *(G-9454)*
F & M Precise Metals Co, Farmingdale *Also called Pirnat Precise Metals Inc* *(G-4709)*
F & R Enterprises Inc (PA) 315 841-8189
 1594 State Route 315 Waterville (13480) *(G-15595)*
F & V Distribution Company LLC 516 812-0393
 1 Arizona Plz Woodbury (11797) *(G-16171)*
F A Alpine Windows Mfg 845 469-5700
 1683 State Route 17m Chester (10918) *(G-3377)*
F C W Division, Uniondale *Also called Hearst Business Media* *(G-15230)*
F E Hale Mfg Co 315 894-5490
 120 Benson Pl Frankfort (13340) *(G-4950)*
F H Stickles & Son Inc 518 851-9048
 2590 Rr 9 Livingston (12541) *(G-7052)*
F I S, Oriskany *Also called Fiber Instrument Sales Inc* *(G-12390)*
F J Remey Co Inc 516 741-5112
 121 Willis Ave Mineola (11501) *(G-7974)*
F K Williams Division, North Tonawanda *Also called Gardei Industries LLC* *(G-12069)*
F L Demeter Inc 516 487-5187
 12 N Gate Rd Great Neck (11023) *(G-5384)*
F Logic, Hastings On Hudson *Also called Flogic Inc* *(G-5572)*
F M Abdulky Inc (PA) 607 272-7373
 527 W Seneca St Ithaca (14850) *(G-6380)*
F M Abdulky Inc 607 272-7373
 527 W Seneca St Ithaca (14850) *(G-6381)*
F M C Aricultural Chem Group, Middleport *Also called FMC Corporation* *(G-7888)*
F M C Peroxygen Chemicals Div, Tonawanda *Also called FMC Corporation* *(G-15105)*
F M EDM Inc 716 655-1784
 210 Pennsylvania Ave East Aurora (14052) *(G-4088)*
F M Group Inc 845 589-0102
 100 Wells Ave Congers (10920) *(G-3614)*
F M Howell & Company (PA) 607 734-6291
 79 Pennsylvania Ave Elmira (14904) *(G-4351)*
F M L Industries Inc 607 749-7273
 10 Hudson St Homer (13077) *(G-6062)*
F P H Communications 212 528-1728
 225 Broadway Ste 2008 New York (10007) *(G-9455)*
F R A M Technologies Inc 718 338-6230
 3048 Bedford Ave Brooklyn (11210) *(G-1827)*
F X Graphix Inc 716 871-1511
 3043 Delaware Ave Buffalo (14217) *(G-2750)*
F&M Ornamental Designs LLC 908 241-7776
 200 Lexington Ave Rm 1316 New York (10016) *(G-9456)*
F-O-R Software LLC 212 231-9506
 757 3rd Ave Fl 20 New York (10017) *(G-9457)*
F-O-R Software LLC (PA) 914 220-8800
 10 Bank St Ste 880 White Plains (10606) *(G-16005)*
F2nyc, New York *Also called Fiesta Jewelry Corporation* *(G-9492)*
F3 Foods, New York *Also called Freshly Inc* *(G-9540)*
F5 Networks Inc 888 882-7535
 600 Lexington Ave Fl 5 New York (10022) *(G-9458)*
Fab Industries Corp (HQ) 516 498-3200
 98 Cuttermill Rd Ste 412 Great Neck (11021) *(G-5385)*
Fabbian USA Corp 973 882-3824
 307 W 38th St Rm 1103 New York (10018) *(G-9459)*
Fabco Industries Inc 631 393-6024
 24 Central Dr Farmingdale (11735) *(G-4628)*
Fabric Concepts For Industry 914 375-2565
 354 Ashburton Ave Yonkers (10701) *(G-16308)*
Fabric Quilters Unlimited Inc 516 333-2866
 1400 Shames Dr Westbury (11590) *(G-15884)*
Fabric Resources Intl Ltd (PA) 516 829-4550
 9 Park Pl Great Neck (11021) *(G-5386)*
Fabrication Enterprises Inc 914 591-9300
 250 Clearbrook Rd Ste 240 Elmsford (10523) *(G-4409)*
Fabtechny LLC 845 338-2000
 401 Sawkill Rd Blgda Kingston (12401) *(G-6691)*

Faces Magazine Inc (PA)................................201 843-4004
  46 Violet Ave Poughkeepsie (12601) *(G-12954)*
Faces Magazine Inc.....................................845 454-7420
  40 Violet Ave Poughkeepsie (12601) *(G-12955)*
Facilamatic Instrument Corp..........................516 825-6300
  39 Clinton Ave Valley Stream (11580) *(G-15340)*
Facilities, New York *Also called Bedrock Communications (G-8748)*
Facilities Exchange, New York *Also called FX INC (G-9556)*
Facsimile Cmmncations Inds Inc (PA)...............212 741-6400
  134 W 26th St Fl 3 New York (10001) *(G-9460)*
Factory East..718 280-1558
  723 Kent Ave Brooklyn (11249) *(G-1828)*
Factory Nyc, Brooklyn *Also called Factory East (G-1828)*
Factory Wheel Warehouse Inc.........................516 605-2131
  57 Mall Dr Commack (11725) *(G-3587)*
Fad Inc...631 385-2460
  630 New York Ave Ste B Huntington (11743) *(G-6205)*
Fad Treasures, Huntington *Also called Fad Inc (G-6205)*
Fadec Alliance LLC.....................................607 770-3342
  1098 Clark St Endicott (13760) *(G-4454)*
Fader Inc...212 741-7100
  71 W 23rd St Ste 1300 New York (10010) *(G-9461)*
Fage USA Holdings (HQ)...............................518 762-5912
  1 Opportunity Dr Johnstown (12095) *(G-6617)*
Fahrenheit NY Inc.......................................212 354-6554
  315 W 39th St Rm 803 New York (10018) *(G-9462)*
Fahy-Williams Publishing Inc.........................315 781-6820
  171 Reed St Geneva (14456) *(G-5153)*
Fair-Rite Products Corp (PA)..........................845 895-2055
  1 Commercial Row Wallkill (12589) *(G-15469)*
Fairbanks Mfg LLC......................................845 341-0002
  79 Industrial Pl Middletown (10940) *(G-7908)*
Fairchild Publications Inc (HQ).......................212 630-4000
  475 5th Ave New York (10017) *(G-9463)*
Fairchild Publishing LLC..............................212 286-3897
  4 Times Sq Fl 17 New York (10036) *(G-9464)*
Fairmount Press...212 255-2300
  70 W 36th St Rm 500 New York (10018) *(G-9465)*
Fairview Bell and Intercom............................718 627-8621
  502 Gravesend Neck Rd B Brooklyn (11223) *(G-1829)*
Fairview Paper Box Corp...............................585 786-5230
  200 Allen St Warsaw (14569) *(G-15507)*
Falcon Chair and Table Inc...........................716 664-7136
  121 S Work St Falconer (14733) *(G-4540)*
Falcon Perspectives Inc..............................718 706-9168
  28 Vernon Blvd Ste 45 Long Island City (11101) *(G-7220)*
Falcone Food Distribution, Brooklyn *Also called Falcones Cookie Land Ltd (G-1830)*
Falconer Electronics Inc..............................716 665-4176
  421 W Everett St Falconer (14733) *(G-4541)*
Falcones Cookie Land Ltd (PA)......................718 236-4200
  1648 61st St Brooklyn (11204) *(G-1830)*
Falk Precision Inc.....................................315 437-4545
  5917 Fisher Rd East Syracuse (13057) *(G-4209)*
Fallon Inc..718 326-7226
  5930 56th Rd Maspeth (11378) *(G-7614)*
Falls Manufacturing Inc (PA).........................518 672-7189
  95 Main St Philmont (12565) *(G-12613)*
Falso Industries Inc...................................315 463-0266
  4100 New Court Ave Syracuse (13206) *(G-14892)*
Falso Metal Fabricating, Syracuse *Also called Falso Industries Inc (G-14892)*
Falvo Manufacturing Co Inc...........................315 724-7925
  20 Harbor Point Rd Utica (13502) *(G-15261)*
Fam Creations...212 869-4833
  7 W 45th St Ste 1404 New York (10036) *(G-9466)*
Fambus Inc..607 785-3700
  2800 Watson Blvd Endicott (13760) *(G-4455)*
Fame Construction Inc.................................718 626-1000
  2388 Brklyn Queens Expy W Astoria (11103) *(G-423)*
Family Fuel Co Inc......................................718 232-2009
  1571 W 10th St Brooklyn (11204) *(G-1831)*
Family Hearing Center.................................845 897-3059
  18 Westage Dr Ste 16 Fishkill (12524) *(G-4800)*
Family Printing, Bronx *Also called Figueroa Claribell (G-1256)*
Family Publications Ltd.................................212 947-2177
  325 W 38th St Rm 804 New York (10018) *(G-9467)*
Family Publishing Group Inc..........................914 381-7474
  141 Halstead Ave Mamaroneck (10543) *(G-7510)*
Famous Box Scooter Co...............................631 943-2013
  75 Rogers Ct West Babylon (11704) *(G-15711)*
Famous Doughnuts Inc.................................716 834-6356
  3043 Main St Buffalo (14214) *(G-2751)*
Fancy, New York *Also called Thing Daemon Inc (G-11466)*
Fancy Flamingo LLC....................................516 209-7306
  450 W 17th St Apt 528 New York (10011) *(G-9468)*
Fancy Window & Door, Brooklyn *Also called Fancy Windows & Doors Mfg Corp (G-1832)*
Fancy Windows & Doors Mfg Corp...................718 366-7800
  312 Ten Eyck St Brooklyn (11206) *(G-1832)*
Fanshawe Foods LLC..................................212 757-3130
  5 Columbus Cir New York (10019) *(G-9469)*
Fantasia International LLC.............................212 869-0432
  1384 Broadway Ste 1101 New York (10018) *(G-9470)*

Fantasia Jewelry Inc....................................212 921-9590
  42 W 39th St Fl 14 New York (10018) *(G-9471)*
Fantasy Glass Compan..................................845 786-5818
  61 Beach Rd Stony Point (10980) *(G-14743)*
Fantasy Sports Media Group Inc......................416 917-6002
  27 W 20th St Ste 900 New York (10011) *(G-9472)*
Fantasy Sports Network, New York *Also called Fantasy Sports Media Group Inc (G-9472)*
Fao Printing, Brooklyn *Also called Phillip Tissicher (G-2255)*
Far East Industries Inc (PA)..........................718 687-2482
  118 Stephan Marc Ln New Hyde Park (11040) *(G-8268)*
Far Eastern Coconut Company.........................631 851-8800
  200 Corporate Plz 201a Central Islip (11749) *(G-3274)*
Far Rockaway Drugs Inc...............................718 471-2500
  1727 Seagirt Blvd Far Rockaway (11691) *(G-4565)*
Faradyne Motors LLC..................................315 331-5985
  2077 Division St Palmyra (14522) *(G-12485)*
Farber Plastics Inc....................................516 378-4860
  162 Hanse Ave Freeport (11520) *(G-4994)*
Farber Trucking Corp...................................516 378-4860
  162 Hanse Ave Freeport (11520) *(G-4995)*
Farm Bridge, The, Kingston *Also called Farm To Table Community Inc (G-6692)*
Farm To Table Community Inc (PA)...................845 383-1761
  750 Enterprise Dr Kingston (12401) *(G-6692)*
Farmers Dog Inc..646 780-7957
  214 Sullivan St Fl 5 New York (10012) *(G-9473)*
Farmers Hub LLC (HQ).................................914 380-2945
  8 Francine Ct White Plains (10607) *(G-16006)*
Farmingdale Iron Works Inc...........................631 249-5995
  105 Florida St Farmingdale (11735) *(G-4629)*
Farmtobottle LLC......................................631 944-8422
  4 Valley Rd Locust Valley (11560) *(G-7122)*
Farney Lumber Corporation............................315 346-6013
  7194 Brewery Rd Lowville (13367) *(G-7415)*
Faro Industries Inc....................................585 647-6000
  340 Lyell Ave Rochester (14606) *(G-13408)*
Farrand Controls Division, Valhalla *Also called Ruhle Companies Inc (G-15309)*
Farrant Screw Machine Products.......................585 457-3213
  Gulf Rd Java Village (14083) *(G-6564)*
Farrington Packaging Company........................315 733-4600
  2007 Beechgrove Pl Utica (13501) *(G-15262)*
Fashion Accents LLC..................................401 331-6626
  366 5th Ave Rm 802 New York (10001) *(G-9474)*
Fashion Ave Sweater Knits LLC........................212 302-8282
  525 7th Ave Fl 4 New York (10018) *(G-9475)*
Fashion Avenue Knits Inc..............................718 456-9000
  1400 Broadway Rm 2401 New York (10018) *(G-9476)*
Fashion Calendar International.........................212 289-0420
  153 E 87th St Apt 6a New York (10128) *(G-9477)*
Fashion Chef, The, Brooklyn *Also called Charlotte Neuville Design LLC (G-1661)*
Fashion Ribbon Co Inc (PA)...........................718 482-0100
  3401 38th Ave Long Island City (11101) *(G-7221)*
Fashiondex Inc..914 271-6121
  153 W 27th St Ste 701 New York (10001) *(G-9478)*
Fasprint...518 483-4631
  20 Finney Blvd Malone (12953) *(G-7485)*
Fast By Gast Inc..716 773-1536
  120 Industrial Dr Grand Island (14072) *(G-5329)*
Fast Company Magazine, New York *Also called Mansueto Ventures LLC (G-10353)*
Fastener Dimensions Inc..............................718 847-6321
  9403 104th St Ozone Park (11416) *(G-12461)*
Faster-Form Corp.......................................800 327-3676
  1 Faster Form Cir Ste 1 # 1 New Hartford (13413) *(G-8240)*
Fastnet Software Intl Inc..............................888 740-7790
  459 Elwood Rd East Northport (11731) *(G-4145)*
Fastsigns, Saratoga Springs *Also called First Signs Saratoga Springs (G-14174)*
Fastsigns, Staten Island *Also called Vez Inc (G-14726)*
Fastsigns..518 456-7446
  1593 Central Ave Albany (12205) *(G-76)*
Father Sam's Bakery, Buffalo *Also called Commitment 2000 Inc (G-2706)*
Fatwire Corporation....................................516 247-4500
  330 Old Country Rd # 303 Mineola (11501) *(G-7975)*
Faucets and More Incorporated.......................734 328-2387
  5318a 16th Ave Ste 106 Brooklyn (11204) *(G-1833)*
Faulkner Truss Company Inc..........................315 536-8894
  1830 King Hill Rd Dresden (14441) *(G-4035)*
Faviana International Inc (PA).........................212 594-4422
  320 W 37th St Fl 10 New York (10018) *(G-9479)*
Favorite Plastic Corp...................................718 253-7000
  1465 Utica Ave Brooklyn (11234) *(G-1834)*
Fay Da Mott St, Brooklyn *Also called Fayda Manufacturing Corp (G-1835)*
Fayda Manufacturing Corp.............................718 456-9331
  259 Meserole St Brooklyn (11206) *(G-1835)*
Faye Bernard Loungewear.............................718 951-7245
  2604 Avenue M Brooklyn (11210) *(G-1836)*
Fayette Street Coatings Inc............................315 488-5401
  1 Burr Dr Liverpool (13088) *(G-7010)*
FB Laboratories Inc.....................................631 963-6450
  70 Commerce Dr Hauppauge (11788) *(G-5649)*
FB Sale LLC...315 986-9999
  1688 Wayneport Rd Macedon (14502) *(G-7465)*
FBC Chemical Corporation.............................716 681-1581
  4111 Walden Ave Lancaster (14086) *(G-6806)*

Fbm Galaxy Inc...315 463-5144
6741 Old Collamer Rd East Syracuse (13057) **(G-4210)**
Fcmp Inc...716 692-4623
230 Fire Tower Dr Tonawanda (14150) **(G-15103)**
Fcr LLC...845 926-1071
508 Fishkill Ave Beacon (12508) **(G-752)**
Fearby Enterprises, Medina *Also called F & H Metal Finishing Co Inc* **(G-7734)**
Federal Contract MGT Svcs, Brooklyn *Also called It Commodity Sourcing Inc* **(G-1972)**
Federal Envelope Inc...212 243-8380
22 W 32nd St New York (10001) **(G-9480)**
Federal Pump Corporation...718 451-2000
250 E 73rd St Apt 18c New York (10021) **(G-9481)**
Federal Sample Card Corp...718 458-1344
4520 83rd St Elmhurst (11373) **(G-4334)**
Federal Sheet Metal Works Inc...315 735-4730
1416 Dudley Ave Utica (13501) **(G-15263)**
Fedex Ground Package Sys Inc...800 463-3339
82 Gateway Dr Plattsburgh (12901) **(G-12747)**
Fedex Office & Print Svcs Inc...718 982-5223
2456 Richmond Ave Ste C Staten Island (10314) **(G-14653)**
Fei Communications Inc...516 794-4500
55 Charles Lindbergh Blvd Uniondale (11553) **(G-15227)**
Fei Products LLC (PA)...716 693-6230
825 Wurlitzer Dr North Tonawanda (14120) **(G-12067)**
Fei-Zyfer Inc...714 933-4045
55 Charles Lindbergh Blvd Uniondale (11553) **(G-15228)**
Feinkind Inc...800 289-6136
17 Algonquin Dr Irvington (10533) **(G-6308)**
Feinstein Iron Works Inc...516 997-8300
990 Brush Hollow Rd Westbury (11590) **(G-15885)**
Felber Metal Fabricators, Holbrook *Also called Brzozka Industries Inc* **(G-5987)**
Felchar Manufacturing Corp (HQ)...607 723-4076
196 Corporate Dr Binghamton (13904) **(G-877)**
Feldheim Publishers, Nanuet *Also called Philipp Feldheim Inc* **(G-8203)**
Feldman Company Inc...212 966-1303
241 W 37th St Rm 1001 New York (10018) **(G-9482)**
Feldman Jewelry Creations Inc...718 438-8895
4821 16th Ave Brooklyn (11204) **(G-1837)**
Feldman Manufacturing Corp...718 433-1700
3010 41st Ave Ste 3fl Long Island City (11101) **(G-7222)**
Feldmeier Equipment Inc (PA)...315 823-2000
6800 Townline Rd Syracuse (13211) **(G-14893)**
Felene Inc...716 276-3583
5522 Main St Apt 3 Williamsville (14221) **(G-16131)**
Felicetti Concrete Products...716 284-5740
4129 Hyde Park Blvd Niagara Falls (14305) **(G-11926)**
Felix Roma & Sons Inc...607 748-3336
2 S Page Ave Endicott (13760) **(G-4456)**
Felix Schoeller North Amer Inc...315 298-8425
179 County Route 2a Pulaski (13142) **(G-12994)**
Felton Machine Co Inc...716 215-9001
2221 Niagara Falls Blvd Niagara Falls (14304) **(G-11927)**
Feminist Press Inc...212 817-7915
365 5th Ave Ste 5406 New York (10016) **(G-9483)**
Fenbar Prcision Machinists Inc...914 769-5506
633 Commerce St Thornwood (10594) **(G-15069)**
Fence Plaza Corp...718 469-2200
1601 Nostrand Ave Brooklyn (11226) **(G-1838)**
Fennell Industries LLC (PA)...607 733-6693
108 Stephens Pl Elmira (14901) **(G-4352)**
Fennell Spring Company LLC...607 739-3541
295 Hemlock St Horseheads (14845) **(G-6123)**
Fenton Mobility Products Inc...716 484-7014
26 Center St Randolph (14772) **(G-13062)**
Fera Pharmaceuticals LLC...516 277-1449
134 Birch Hill Rd Locust Valley (11560) **(G-7123)**
Ferguson Enterprises Inc...800 437-1146
200 Atlantic Ave New Hyde Park (11040) **(G-8269)**
Fermer Precision Inc...315 822-6371
114 Johnson Rd Ilion (13357) **(G-6277)**
Ferrara Bakery & Cafe Inc (PA)...212 226-6150
195 Grand St New York (10013) **(G-9484)**
Ferrara Bros LLC (HQ)...718 939-3030
12005 31st Ave Flushing (11354) **(G-4851)**
Ferrara Manufacturing, New York *Also called Rogers Group Inc* **(G-11075)**
Ferrara Manufacturing Company, New York *Also called HC Contracting Inc* **(G-9740)**
Ferraro Manufacturing Company...631 752-1509
150 Central Ave Farmingdale (11735) **(G-4630)**
Ferris USA LLC...617 895-8102
18 W 108th St Apt 4a New York (10025) **(G-9485)**
Ferro Corporation...585 586-8770
603 W Commercial St East Rochester (14445) **(G-4162)**
Ferro Corporation...315 536-3357
1789 Transelco Dr Penn Yan (14527) **(G-12582)**
Ferro Electronic Mtl Systems, Penn Yan *Also called Ferro Electronics Materials* **(G-12583)**
Ferro Electronics Materials...716 278-9400
4511 Hyde Park Blvd Niagara Falls (14305) **(G-11928)**
Ferro Electronics Materials (HQ)...315 536-3357
1789 Transelco Dr Penn Yan (14527) **(G-12583)**
Ferro Fabricators Inc...718 703-0007
1117 38th St Brooklyn (11218) **(G-1839)**
Ferro Machine Co Inc...845 398-3641
70 S Greenbush Rd Orangeburg (10962) **(G-12316)**
Festival Bakers, Bronx *Also called Waldorf Bakers Inc* **(G-1394)**
Fevertree USA Inc...718 852-5577
37 W 26th St Ph New York (10010) **(G-9486)**
Feyem USA Inc...845 363-6253
7 Sutton Pl Brewster (10509) **(G-1149)**
Ffc Holding Corp Subsidiaries...716 366-5400
1 Ice Cream Dr Dunkirk (14048) **(G-4057)**
FG Galassi Moulding Co Inc...845 258-2100
699 Pulaski Hwy Goshen (10924) **(G-5308)**
Fgi, Amsterdam *Also called Fiber Glass Industries Inc* **(G-327)**
Fha Firedoor Corp...718 366-1700
32 Windsor Pl Central Islip (11722) **(G-3275)**
Fiber Foot Appliances Inc...631 465-9199
34 Sarah Dr Ste A Farmingdale (11735) **(G-4631)**
Fiber Glass Industries Inc (PA)...518 842-4000
69 Edson St Amsterdam (12010) **(G-327)**
Fiber Instrument Sales Inc (PA)...315 736-2206
161 Clear Rd Oriskany (13424) **(G-12390)**
Fiber Laminations Limited...716 692-1825
600 Main St Tonawanda (14150) **(G-15104)**
Fiber Optics Schott America, Auburn *Also called Schott Corporation* **(G-494)**
Fiber USA Corp...718 888-1512
13620 38th Ave Ste 11f Flushing (11354) **(G-4852)**
Fiber-Seal of New York Inc (PA)...212 888-5580
979 3rd Ave Ste 903 New York (10022) **(G-9487)**
Fiberall Corp...516 371-5200
449 Sheridan Blvd Inwood (11096) **(G-6293)**
Fibercel Packaging LLC (HQ)...716 933-8703
46 Brooklyn St Portville (14770) **(G-12934)**
Fiberdyne Labs Inc...315 895-8470
127 Business Park Dr Frankfort (13340) **(G-4951)**
Fiberone LLC...315 434-8877
5 Technology Pl Ste 4 East Syracuse (13057) **(G-4211)**
Fiberwave Corporation...718 802-9011
140 58th St Ste 37 Brooklyn (11220) **(G-1840)**
Fibre Case & Novelty Co Inc (PA)...212 254-6060
270 Lafayette St Ste 1510 New York (10012) **(G-9488)**
Fibre Materials Corp...516 349-1660
40 Dupont St Plainview (11803) **(G-12685)**
Fibrix LLC...716 683-4100
3307 Walden Ave Depew (14043) **(G-3981)**
Fibron Products Inc...716 886-2378
170 Florida St Buffalo (14208) **(G-2752)**
Fidelus Technologies LLC...212 616-7800
240 W 35th St Fl 6 New York (10001) **(G-9489)**
Fidesa US Corporation...212 269-9000
17 State St Unit 122 New York (10004) **(G-9490)**
Field Company, Brooklyn *Also called Field Wares LLC* **(G-1841)**
Field Trip Jerky, Brooklyn *Also called Provisionaire & Co LLC* **(G-2304)**
Field Wares LLC...508 380-6545
53 Bridge St Apt 410 Brooklyn (11201) **(G-1841)**
Fieldbrook Foods Corporation (HQ)...716 366-5400
1 Ice Cream Dr Dunkirk (14048) **(G-4058)**
Fieldtex Products Inc...585 427-2940
3055 Brighton Henrietta Rochester (14623) **(G-13409)**
Fierce Fun Toys LLC...646 322-7172
100 Riverside Dr Ste 2 New York (10024) **(G-9491)**
Fiesta Jewelry Corporation (PA)...212 564-6847
8 W 38th St Rm 801 New York (10018) **(G-9492)**
Fifty Door Partners LLC (PA)...845 562-3332
509 Temple Hill Rd New Windsor (12553) **(G-8367)**
Figueroa Claribell...718 772-8521
613 E Fordham Rd Bronx (10458) **(G-1256)**
Fika, New York *Also called Pachanga Inc* **(G-10737)**
Fil Doux Inc...212 202-1459
227 5th Ave Brooklyn (11215) **(G-1842)**
Fil-Coil (fc) Corp (PA)...631 467-5328
98 Lincoln Ave Sayville (11782) **(G-14226)**
Fil-Coil International LLC...631 467-5328
98 Lincoln Ave Sayville (11782) **(G-14227)**
Filestream Inc...516 759-4100
257 Buckram Rd Locust Valley (11560) **(G-7124)**
Filling Equipment Co Inc...718 445-2111
1539 130th St College Point (11356) **(G-3542)**
Fillmore Greenhouses Inc...585 567-2678
11589 State Route 19a Portageville (14536) **(G-12932)**
Filmpak Extrusion LLC...631 293-6767
125 Spagnoli Rd Melville (11747) **(G-7782)**
Films Media Group, New York *Also called Infobase Publishing Company* **(G-9887)**
Filta Clean Co Inc...718 495-3800
107 Georgia Ave Brooklyn (11207) **(G-1843)**
Filter Tech Inc (PA)...315 682-8815
113 Fairgrounds Dr Manlius (13104) **(G-7546)**
Filtros Ltd...585 586-8770
603 W Commercial St East Rochester (14445) **(G-4163)**
Filtros Plant, East Rochester *Also called Filtros Ltd* **(G-4163)**
Fin-Tech360, Whitestone *Also called Financial Technologies 360 Inc* **(G-16093)**
Fina Cabinet Corp...718 409-2900
20 N Macquesten Pkwy Mount Vernon (10550) **(G-8141)**

ALPHABETIC SECTION
Flagpoles Incorporated

Final Dimension Inc 718 786-0100
57-401 59th St Fl 1 Flr 1 Maspeth (11378) *(G-7615)*

Final Touch Printing Inc 845 352-2677
29 Decatur Ave Unit 1 Spring Valley (10977) *(G-14569)*

Finals, The, Port Jervis *Also called Swimwear Anywhere Inc (G-12858)*

Finance Manager, East Setauket *Also called Mml Software Ltd (G-4182)*

Financial Technologies 360 Inc 646 588-8853
15436 24th Ave Whitestone (11357) *(G-16093)*

Financial Times Newspaper, New York *Also called FT Publications Inc (G-9548)*

Financial Times, The, New York *Also called FT Publications Inc (G-9547)*

Findmine Inc 925 787-6181
33 E 33rd St Rm 807 New York (10016) *(G-9493)*

Fine and Raw Chocolate 718 366-3633
288 Seigel St Brooklyn (11206) *(G-1844)*

Fine Cut Diamonds Corporation 212 575-8780
50 W 47th St Ste 1101 New York (10036) *(G-9494)*

Fine Sheer Industries Inc (PA) 212 594-4224
350 5th Ave Ste 4710 New York (10118) *(G-9495)*

Fine Sounds Group Inc (PA) 212 364-0219
214 Lafayette St New York (10012) *(G-9496)*

Fineline Thermographers Inc 718 643-1100
544 Park Ave Ste 308 Brooklyn (11205) *(G-1845)*

Finer Touch Printing Corp 516 944-8000
4 Yennicock Ave Port Washington (11050) *(G-12879)*

Finesse Accessories, Plainview *Also called Mgd Brands Inc (G-12702)*

Finesse Creations Inc 718 692-2100
3004 Avenue J Brooklyn (11210) *(G-1846)*

Finest Cc Corp 917 574-4525
3111 E Tremont Ave Bronx (10461) *(G-1257)*

Finestar, Long Island City *Also called Efam Enterprises LLC (G-7211)*

Finger Food Products Inc 716 297-4888
6400 Inducon Dr W Sanborn (14132) *(G-14141)*

Finger Lakes Cheese Trail 607 857-5726
4970 County Road 14 Odessa (14869) *(G-12200)*

Finger Lakes Chemicals Inc (PA) 585 454-4760
420 Saint Paul St Rochester (14605) *(G-13410)*

Finger Lakes Conveyors Inc 315 539-9246
2359 State Route 414 E Waterloo (13165) *(G-15551)*

Finger Lakes Distilling 607 546-5510
4676 State Route 414 Burdett (14818) *(G-3057)*

Finger Lakes Extrusion Corp 585 905-0632
2437 State Route 21 Canandaigua (14424) *(G-3132)*

Finger Lakes Lea Crafters LLC 315 252-4107
42 Washington St Ste 1 Auburn (13021) *(G-475)*

Finger Lakes Media Inc 607 243-7600
45 Water St Dundee (14837) *(G-4046)*

Finger Lakes Radiology LLC 315 787-5399
196 North St Geneva (14456) *(G-5154)*

Finger Lakes Timber Co Inc 585 346-2990
6274 Decker Rd Livonia (14487) *(G-7054)*

Finger Lakes Times, Geneva *Also called Community Media Group Inc (G-5151)*

Finger Lakes Traffic Ctrl LLC 607 795-7458
160 E 14th St Elmira Heights (14903) *(G-4376)*

Finger Lakes/Castle, Rochester *Also called Finger Lakes Chemicals Inc (G-13410)*

Finger Lkes Stirs Cabinets LLC 315 638-3150
7496 Kingdom Rd Baldwinsville (13027) *(G-547)*

Fingerlakes Construction, Clyde *Also called Energy Panel Structures Inc (G-3489)*

Fingerlakes Construction, Clyde *Also called Energy Panel Structures Inc (G-3490)*

Fingerlakes Construction, Schenectady *Also called Energy Panel Structures Inc (G-14263)*

Fingerprint America Inc 518 435-1609
1843 Central Ave Albany (12205) *(G-77)*

Finish Line Technologies Inc (PA) 631 666-7300
50 Wireless Blvd Hauppauge (11788) *(G-5650)*

Finishing Line, The, Le Roy *Also called Duzmor Painting Inc (G-6900)*

Finzer Holding LLC 315 597-1147
2085 Division St Palmyra (14522) *(G-12486)*

Finzer Roller New York, Palmyra *Also called Finzer Holding LLC (G-12486)*

Fire Apparatus Service Tech 716 753-3538
7895 Lyons Rd Sherman (14781) *(G-14400)*

Fire Curtain Technologies, Canandaigua *Also called Murcadom Corporation (G-3137)*

Fire Fox Security Corp 917 981-9280
2070 72nd St Apt B1 Brooklyn (11204) *(G-1847)*

Fire Island Fuel 631 772-1482
106 Parkwood Dr Shirley (11967) *(G-14420)*

Fire Island News, Bronx *Also called Five Islands Publishing Inc (G-1258)*

Fire Island Sea Clam Co Inc 631 589-2199
132 Atlantic Ave West Sayville (11796) *(G-15840)*

Firecom Inc (PA) 718 899-6100
3927 59th St Woodside (11377) *(G-16206)*

Firefighters Journal 718 391-0283
2420 Jackson Ave Long Island City (11101) *(G-7223)*

Firemaxx Systems Corp 212 645-7414
307 7th Ave Rm 507 New York (10001) *(G-9497)*

Fireside Holdings LLC 718 564-4335
59 Route 59 Monsey (10952) *(G-8038)*

Firetronics Inc (PA) 516 997-5151
50 Jericho Tpke Jericho (11753) *(G-6580)*

Fireworks By Grucci Inc 631 286-0088
20 Pinehurst Dr Bellport (11713) *(G-799)*

First Brands LLC 646 432-4366
25 Merrick Ave Ste 2 Merrick (11566) *(G-7855)*

First Choice News Inc 212 477-2044
639 1/2 Broadway New York (10012) *(G-9498)*

First Displays Inc 347 642-5972
2415 43rd Ave Fl 2 Long Island City (11101) *(G-7224)*

First Due Fire Equipment Inc 845 222-1329
130 W Ramapo Rd Garnerville (10923) *(G-5134)*

First Games Publr Netwrk Inc 212 983-0501
420 Lexington Ave Rm 412 New York (10170) *(G-9499)*

First Image Design Corp 212 221-8282
98 Cuttrmill Rd Ste 231 New York (10036) *(G-9500)*

First Impressions Finishing 631 467-2244
132 Remington Blvd Ronkonkoma (11779) *(G-13938)*

First Light Farm & Creamery, East Bethany *Also called Sandvoss Farms LLC (G-4099)*

First Line Printing Inc 718 606-0860
3728 56th St Woodside (11377) *(G-16207)*

First Love Fashions LLC 212 256-1089
1407 Broadway Rm 2010 New York (10018) *(G-9501)*

First Manufacturing Co Inc (HQ) 516 763-0400
3800 Oceanside Rd W Oceanside (11572) *(G-12172)*

First Qlty Packg Solutions LLC (PA) 516 829-3030
80 Cuttermill Rd Ste 500 Great Neck (11021) *(G-5387)*

First Quality Products Inc (HQ) 516 829-4949
80 Cuttermill Rd Ste 500 Great Neck (11021) *(G-5388)*

First Sbf Holding Inc (PA) 845 425-9882
9 Pinecrest Rd Ste 101 Valley Cottage (10989) *(G-15315)*

First Signs Saratoga Springs 518 306-4449
30 Gick Rd Saratoga Springs (12866) *(G-14174)*

First Switchtech, Hauppauge *Also called Dri Relays Inc (G-5641)*

First View, New York *Also called Viewfinder Inc (G-11681)*

First2print Inc 212 868-6886
494 8th Ave Fl 12 New York (10001) *(G-9502)*

Firth Rixson Inc (HQ) 585 328-1383
181 Mckee Rd Rochester (14611) *(G-13411)*

Firth Rixson Monroe, Rochester *Also called Firth Rixson Inc (G-13411)*

Fisau, Brooklyn *Also called Business Management Systems (G-1633)*

Fischer Diamonds Inc 212 869-1990
580 5th Ave Ste 613 New York (10036) *(G-9503)*

Fischler Diamonds Inc 212 921-8196
580 5th Ave Ste 3100 New York (10036) *(G-9504)*

Fischler Hockey Service 212 749-4152
200 W 109th St Apt C5 New York (10025) *(G-9505)*

Fish & Crown Ltd (PA) 212 707-9603
42 W 39th St New York (10018) *(G-9506)*

Fisher-Price, East Aurora *Also called Mattel Inc (G-4092)*

Fishers Storage Sheds 585 382-9580
7854 Alverson Rd Leicester (14481) *(G-6910)*

Fishing Valley LLC 716 523-6158
7217 N Canal Rd Lockport (14094) *(G-7075)*

Fisonic Corp 212 732-3777
4402 23rd St Long Island City (11101) *(G-7225)*

Fisonic Corp (PA) 716 763-0295
31-00 47th Ave Ste 106 New York (10023) *(G-9507)*

Fisonic Technology, New York *Also called Fisonic Corp (G-9507)*

Fitch Group, New York *Also called Francis Emory Fitch Inc (G-9529)*

Fitsmo LLC 585 519-1956
108 Packetts Gln Fairport (14450) *(G-4497)*

Fitzgerald Publishing Co Inc 914 793-5016
1853 Central Park Ave # 8 Yonkers (10710) *(G-16309)*

Fitzpatrick and Weller Inc 716 699-2393
12 Mill St Ellicottville (14731) *(G-4314)*

Fitzsimmons Systems Inc 315 214-7010
53 Nelson St Cazenovia (13035) *(G-3227)*

Five Boro Doors Mouldings Inc 718 865-9371
3569 Maple Ct Oceanside (11572) *(G-12173)*

Five Boro Holding LLC 718 431-9500
1425 37th St Bsmt 3 Brooklyn (11218) *(G-1848)*

Five Corners Repair Inc 585 322-7369
6653 Hardys Rd Bliss (14024) *(G-939)*

Five Islands Publishing Inc 631 583-5345
8 Fort Charles Pl Bronx (10463) *(G-1258)*

Five Star Creations Inc 845 783-1187
4 Preshburg Blvd Unit 302 Monroe (10950) *(G-8020)*

Five Star Industries Inc 716 674-2589
114 Willowdale Dr West Seneca (14224) *(G-15847)*

Five Star Millwork LLC 845 920-0247
6 E Dexter Plz Pearl River (10965) *(G-12530)*

Five Star Printing, Jamaica *Also called Ssrja LLC (G-6474)*

Five Star Prtg & Mailing Svcs 212 929-0300
225 W 37th St Fl 16 New York (10018) *(G-9508)*

Five Star Tool Co Inc 585 328-9580
125 Elmgrove Park Rochester (14624) *(G-13412)*

Fixtures 2000 Inc 631 236-4100
400 Oser Ave Ste 350 Hauppauge (11788) *(G-5651)*

Fiz Beverages, Rochester *Also called Load/N/Go Beverage Corp (G-13521)*

Fk Safety Gear Inc 516 233-9628
736 Stranton Ave East Rockaway (11518) *(G-4173)*

Flado Enterprises Inc 716 668-6400
1380 French Rd Ste 6 Depew (14043) *(G-3982)*

Flagpoles Incorporated 631 751-5500
95 Gnarled Hollow Rd East Setauket (11733) *(G-4178)*

ALPHABETIC

Flagship One Inc......516 766-2223
19 Wilbur St Lynbrook (11563) *(G-7431)*
Flair Display Inc......718 324-9330
3920 Merritt Ave Bronx (10466) *(G-1259)*
Flair Printers, Brooklyn *Also called Printing Sales Group Limited (G-2293)*
Flame Control Coatings LLC......716 282-1399
4120 Hyde Park Blvd Niagara Falls (14305) *(G-11929)*
Flanagans Creative Disp Inc......845 858-2542
55 Jersey Ave Port Jervis (12771) *(G-12848)*
Flanders Precisionaire NY......518 751-5640
1 Vapor Trl Hudson (12534) *(G-6156)*
Flare Multi Copy, Brooklyn *Also called Flare Multicopy Corp (G-1849)*
Flare Multicopy Corp......718 258-8860
1840 Flatbush Ave Brooklyn (11210) *(G-1849)*
Flashflo Manufacturing Inc......716 826-9500
88 Hopkins St Buffalo (14220) *(G-2753)*
Flatcut LLC......212 542-5732
68 Jay St Ste 901 Brooklyn (11201) *(G-1850)*
Flaum Appetizing, Brooklyn *Also called M & M Food Products Inc (G-2093)*
Flavor League, Brooklyn *Also called Flavor Paper Ltd (G-1851)*
Flavor Paper Ltd (PA)......718 422-0230
216 Pacific St Brooklyn (11201) *(G-1851)*
Flavormatic Industries LLC......845 297-9100
90 Brentwood Dr Wappingers Falls (12590) *(G-15492)*
Flavors Holdings Inc (HQ)......212 572-8677
35 E 62nd St New York (10065) *(G-9509)*
Fleaheart Inc......718 521-4958
61 Greenpoint Ave Ste 403 Brooklyn (11222) *(G-1852)*
Fleetcom Inc......914 776-5582
1081 Yonkers Ave Yonkers (10704) *(G-16310)*
Fleetwood Cabinet Co Inc (PA)......516 379-2139
673 Livonia Ave Brooklyn (11207) *(G-1853)*
Fleischman Vinegar, North Rose *Also called Fleischmanns Vinegar Co Inc (G-12034)*
Fleischmanns Vinegar Co Inc......315 587-4414
4754 State Route 414 North Rose (14516) *(G-12034)*
Fleurette, New York *Also called Blum & Fink Inc (G-8823)*
Flex Enterprises Inc......585 742-1000
820 Canning Pkwy Victor (14564) *(G-15409)*
Flex Supply, Farmingdale *Also called Custom Door & Mirror Inc (G-4609)*
Flex Tubing, Canandaigua *Also called Finger Lakes Extrusion Corp (G-3132)*
Flexbar Machine Corporation......631 582-8440
250 Gibbs Rd Islandia (11749) *(G-6332)*
Flexfit Llc......516 932-8800
350 Karin Ln Unit A Hicksville (11801) *(G-5907)*
Flexible Lifeline Systems Inc......716 896-4949
100 Stradtman St Buffalo (14206) *(G-2754)*
Flexim Americas Corporation (HQ)......631 492-2300
250 Executive Dr Ste V Edgewood (11717) *(G-4267)*
Flexlume Sign Corporation......716 884-2020
1464 Main St Buffalo (14209) *(G-2755)*
Flextrade Systems Inc (PA)......516 627-8993
111 Great Neck Rd Ste 314 Great Neck (11021) *(G-5389)*
Flickinger Glassworks Inc......718 875-1531
175 Van Dyke St Ste 321ap Brooklyn (11231) *(G-1854)*
Flightline Electronics Inc (HQ)......585 924-4000
7625 Omnitech Pl Victor (14564) *(G-15410)*
Flik International/Compass......212 450-4750
450 Lexington Ave New York (10017) *(G-9510)*
Flint Group US LLC......585 458-1223
73 Cook Dr Rochester (14623) *(G-13413)*
Flint Ink North America Div, Rochester *Also called Flint Group US LLC (G-13413)*
Flirtatious, New York *Also called Soho Apparel Ltd (G-11285)*
Flo-Tech Orthotic & Prosthetic......607 387-3070
7325 Halseyville Rd Trumansburg (14886) *(G-15200)*
Float Tech Inc......518 266-0964
216 River St Ste 1 Troy (12180) *(G-15168)*
Flogic Inc......914 478-1352
25 Chestnut Dr Hastings On Hudson (10706) *(G-5572)*
Flomatic Corporation......518 761-9797
15 Pruyns Island Dr Glens Falls (12801) *(G-5249)*
Flomatic Valves, Glens Falls *Also called Flomatic Corporation (G-5249)*
Florelle Tissue Corporation......647 997-7405
1 Bridge St Brownville (13615) *(G-2607)*
Florida North Inc (PA)......518 868-2888
134 Vanderwerken Rd Sloansville (12160) *(G-14469)*
Flour City Growlers Inc......585 360-8709
125 Amsterdam Rd Rochester (14610) *(G-13414)*
Flour Power Bakery Cafe......917 747-6895
87 Debruce Rd Livingston Manor (12758) *(G-7053)*
Flow Control LLC (HQ)......914 323-5700
1 International Dr Rye Brook (10573) *(G-14089)*
Flow Dental, Deer Park *Also called Flow X Ray Corporation (G-3873)*
Flow Society, New York *Also called Big Idea Brands LLC (G-8787)*
Flow X Ray Corporation......631 242-9729
100 W Industry Ct Deer Park (11729) *(G-3873)*
Flow-Safe Inc......716 662-2585
3865 Taylor Rd Orchard Park (14127) *(G-12352)*
Flower City Printing Inc (PA)......585 663-9000
1725 Mount Read Blvd Rochester (14606) *(G-13415)*
Flower City Printing Inc......585 512-1235
1001 Lee Rd Rochester (14606) *(G-13416)*
Flower Cy Tissue Mills Co Inc (PA)......585 458-9200
700 Driving Park Ave Rochester (14613) *(G-13417)*
Flowmedica Inc......800 772-6446
603 Queensbury Ave Queensbury (12804) *(G-13038)*
Flownet LLC......716 685-4036
580 Lake Ave Lancaster (14086) *(G-6807)*
Floymar Manufacturing, Wyandanch *Also called Ehrlich Enterprises Inc (G-16245)*
Flp Group LLC......315 252-7583
301 Clark St Auburn (13021) *(G-476)*
Fluid Handling LLC......716 897-2800
175 Standard Pkwy Cheektowaga (14227) *(G-3348)*
Fluid Handling LLC (HQ)......716 897-2800
175 Standard Pkwy Cheektowaga (14227) *(G-3349)*
Fluid Mechanisms Hauppauge Inc......631 234-0100
225 Engineers Rd Hauppauge (11788) *(G-5652)*
Fluid Metering Inc (HQ)......516 922-6050
5 Aerial Way Ste 500 Syosset (11791) *(G-14787)*
Fluidampr......716 592-1000
180 Zoar Valley Rd Springville (14141) *(G-14590)*
Fluorologic Inc......585 248-2796
33 Bishops Ct Pittsford (14534) *(G-12640)*
Flushing Boiler & Welding Co......718 463-1266
8720 Ditmas Ave Brooklyn (11236) *(G-1855)*
Flushing Iron Weld Inc......718 359-2208
13125 Maple Ave Flushing (11355) *(G-4853)*
Flushing Pharmacy Inc......718 260-8999
414 Flushing Ave Ste 1 Brooklyn (11205) *(G-1856)*
Flushing Terminal, Flushing *Also called Tilcon New York Inc (G-4899)*
Fluxdata Incorporated......800 425-0176
176 Anderson Ave Ste F304 Rochester (14607) *(G-13418)*
Fly Creek Cder Mill Orchrd Inc......607 547-9692
288 Goose St Fly Creek (13337) *(G-4909)*
Fly-Tyers Carry-All LLC......607 821-1460
112 Meade Rd Charlotteville (12036) *(G-3328)*
Flycell Inc......212 400-1212
80 Pine St Fl 29 New York (10005) *(G-9511)*
Flynn's Xerox, New York *Also called Flynns Inc (G-9512)*
Flynns Inc (PA)......212 339-8700
115 W 30th St New York (10001) *(G-9512)*
FM Brush Co Inc......718 821-5939
7002 72nd Pl Glendale (11385) *(G-5224)*
FMC Corporation......716 735-3761
100 Niagara St Middleport (14105) *(G-7888)*
FMC Corporation......716 879-0400
78 Sawyer Ave Ste 1 Tonawanda (14150) *(G-15105)*
FMC Fashion Division, Oceanside *Also called First Manufacturing Co Inc (G-12172)*
Foam Products Inc......718 292-4830
360 Southern Blvd Bronx (10454) *(G-1260)*
Focus Point Windows & Doors, Long Beach *Also called Air Tite Manufacturing Inc (G-7134)*
Folam Tool Co Inc......716 688-1347
35 Burgundy Ter Buffalo (14228) *(G-2756)*
Folder Factory Inc......540 477-3852
105 Maxess Rd Melville (11747) *(G-7783)*
Folders.com, Melville *Also called Folder Factory Inc (G-7783)*
Folene Packaging LLC......917 626-6740
2509 Avenue M Brooklyn (11210) *(G-1857)*
Foleon Inc......347 727-6809
228 E 45th St Rm 9e New York (10017) *(G-9513)*
Foley Graphics, Yorktown Heights *Also called Foleys Graphic Center Inc (G-16364)*
Foleys Graphic Center Inc......914 245-3625
1661 Front St Ste 3 Yorktown Heights (10598) *(G-16364)*
Folia Water Inc......412 802-5083
175 Varick St New York (10014) *(G-9514)*
Folstaf Company, The, Charlotteville *Also called Fly-Tyers Carry-All LLC (G-3328)*
Fonar Corporation (PA)......631 694-2929
110 Marcus Dr Melville (11747) *(G-7784)*
Fontrick Door Inc......585 345-6032
9 Apollo Dr Batavia (14020) *(G-614)*
Foo Yuan Food Products Co Inc......212 925-2840
2301 Borden Ave Long Island City (11101) *(G-7226)*
Food Basket USA Company Ltd......631 231-8999
30 Inez Dr Bay Shore (11706) *(G-680)*
Food Gems Ltd......718 296-7788
8423 Rockaway Blvd Ozone Park (11416) *(G-12462)*
Foot Locker Retail Inc......516 827-5306
358 Broadway Mall Hicksville (11801) *(G-5908)*
Forbes Precision Inc......585 865-7069
100 Boxart St Ste 105 Rochester (14612) *(G-13419)*
Forbes Products, Dansville *Also called GPM Associates LLC (G-3819)*
Force Digital Media Inc......631 243-0243
39 W Jefryn Blvd Ste 2 Deer Park (11729) *(G-3874)*
Force Dynamics Inc......607 546-5023
4995 Voorheis Rd Trumansburg (14886) *(G-15201)*
Ford Gum & Machine Company Inc (PA)......716 542-4561
18 Newton Ave Akron (14001) *(G-17)*
Ford Regulator Valve Corp......718 497-3255
199 Varet St Brooklyn (11206) *(G-1858)*
Fordham Marble Company Inc......914 682-6699
45 Crane Ave White Plains (10603) *(G-16007)*
Forecast Consoles Inc......631 253-9000
681 Old Willets Path Hauppauge (11788) *(G-5653)*

Forerunner Technologies Inc (PA) 631 337-2100
150 Executive Dr Ste M Edgewood (11717) *(G-4268)*

Forest Hills Courier, Bayside *Also called Schneps Publications Inc* *(G-742)*

Forest Iron Works Inc 516 671-4229
3 Elm St Ste A Locust Valley (11560) *(G-7125)*

Forest Laboratories LLC 212 421-7850
45 Adams Ave Hauppauge (11788) *(G-5654)*

Forest Labs 631 755-1185
210 Sea Ln Farmingdale (11735) *(G-4632)*

Forest Research Institute Inc 631 858-5200
49 Mall Dr Commack (11725) *(G-3588)*

Forest Uniforms, New York *Also called Urban Textiles Inc* *(G-11617)*

Forever Grown Diamonds Inc 917 261-4511
20 W 47th St Ste 1006 New York (10036) *(G-9515)*

Forge Metal Finishing Inc 585 730-7340
383 Buell Rd Rochester (14624) *(G-13420)*

Forkey Construction & Fabg Inc 607 849-4879
3690 Luker Rd Cortland (13045) *(G-3766)*

Form A Rockland Plastics Inc 315 848-3300
7152 Main St Cranberry Lake (12927) *(G-3801)*

Form-Tec Inc 516 867-0200
216 N Main St Ste E Freeport (11520) *(G-4996)*

Formac Welding Inc 631 421-5525
42 W Hills Rd Huntington Station (11746) *(G-6246)*

Formaggio Italian Cheese, Hurleyville *Also called Mongiellos Itln Cheese Spc LLC* *(G-6269)*

Formart Corp 212 819-1819
312 5th Ave Fl 6 New York (10001) *(G-9516)*

Formatix Corp (PA) 631 467-3399
9 Colt Ct Ronkonkoma (11779) *(G-13939)*

Formats Unlimited Inc 631 249-9200
19 W Jefryn Blvd Ste 2 Deer Park (11729) *(G-3875)*

Formcraft Display Products 914 632-1410
42 Beverly Rd New Rochelle (10804) *(G-8330)*

Formed Plastics Inc 516 334-2300
207 Stonehinge Ln Carle Place (11514) *(G-3173)*

Formosa Polymer Corporation 718 326-1769
5641 55th Ave Maspeth (11378) *(G-7616)*

Forms For You Division, Newburgh *Also called Empire Business Forms Inc* *(G-11864)*

Formula 4 Media LLC 516 305-4709
17 Barstow Ste 305 Great Neck (11021) *(G-5390)*

Foro Marble Co Inc 718 852-2322
166 2nd Ave Brooklyn (11215) *(G-1859)*

Forrest Engravg, New Rochelle *Also called Forrest Engraving Co Inc* *(G-8331)*

Forrest Engraving Co Inc 845 228-0200
92 1st St New Rochelle (10801) *(G-8331)*

Forsyth Industries Inc 716 652-1070
1195 Colvin Blvd Buffalo (14223) *(G-2757)*

Forsythe Cosmetic Group Ltd 516 239-4200
10 Niagara Ave Freeport (11520) *(G-4997)*

Forsythe Licensing, Freeport *Also called Forsythe Cosmetic Group Ltd* *(G-4997)*

Fort Miller Group Inc 518 695-5000
688 Wilbur Ave Greenwich (12834) *(G-5471)*

Fort Miller Service Corp (PA) 518 695-5000
688 Wilbur Ave Greenwich (12834) *(G-5472)*

Fort Orange Press Inc 518 489-3233
11 Sand Creek Rd Albany (12205) *(G-78)*

Forte Network 631 390-9050
75 Lockfield Rd East Northport (11731) *(G-4146)*

Forte Security Group, East Northport *Also called Forte Network* *(G-4146)*

Fortech Inc 315 478-2048
223 4th North St Syracuse (13208) *(G-14894)*

Fortech Div, Syracuse *Also called Fortech Inc* *(G-14894)*

Forteq North America Inc 585 427-9410
150 Park Centre Dr West Henrietta (14586) *(G-15794)*

Fortitude Industries Inc 607 324-1500
7200 County Route 70a Hornell (14843) *(G-6106)*

Fortress Biotech Inc (PA) 781 652-4500
2 Gansevoort St Fl 9 New York (10014) *(G-9517)*

Fortuna Visual Group Inc 646 383-8682
1334 39th St Brooklyn (11218) *(G-1860)*

Fortune Magazine, New York *Also called TI Gotham Inc* *(G-11480)*

Fortune Media USA Corporation 212 522-1212
225 Liberty St New York (10281) *(G-9518)*

Fortune Poly Products Inc 718 361-0767
17910 93rd Ave Jamaica (11433) *(G-6442)*

Fortune Sign, Brooklyn *Also called Fortuna Visual Group Inc* *(G-1860)*

Forum Publishing Co 631 754-5000
383 E Main St Centerport (11721) *(G-3255)*

Forum South, The, Howard Beach *Also called Vpj Publication Inc* *(G-6143)*

Forward Enterprises Inc 585 235-7670
250 Cumberland St Ste 100 Rochester (14605) *(G-13421)*

Forwear, New York *Also called A and J Apparel Corp* *(G-8413)*

Foseco Inc 914 345-4760
777 Old Saw Mill River Rd Tarrytown (10591) *(G-15044)*

Fossil Industries Inc 631 254-9200
44 W Jefryn Blvd Ste A Deer Park (11729) *(G-3876)*

Foster - Gordon Manufacturing 631 589-6776
55 Knickerbocker Ave G Bohemia (11716) *(G-1013)*

Foster Reeve & Associates Inc (PA) 718 609-0090
1155 Manhattan Ave # 1011 Brooklyn (11222) *(G-1861)*

Foster Refrigerators Entp 518 671-6036
300 Fairview Ave Hudson (12534) *(G-6157)*

Fotis Oneonta Italian Bakery 607 432-3871
42 River St Oneonta (13820) *(G-12271)*

Fotofiles, Vestal *Also called Truebite Inc* *(G-15386)*

Fougera Pharmaceuticals Inc (HQ) 631 454-7677
60 Baylis Rd Melville (11747) *(G-7785)*

Fougera Pharmaceuticals Inc 631 454-7677
55 Cantiague Rock Rd Hicksville (11801) *(G-5909)*

Foundation Center Inc (PA) 212 620-4230
1 Financial Sq Fl 24 New York (10005) *(G-9519)*

Foundtion For A Mndful Soc Inc (PA) 902 431-8062
228 Park Ave S New York (10003) *(G-9520)*

Fountain Tile Outlet Inc 718 927-4555
609 Fountain Ave Ste A Brooklyn (11208) *(G-1862)*

Fountainhead Group Inc (PA) 315 736-0037
23 Garden St New York Mills (13417) *(G-11832)*

Fountainhead Group Inc 708 598-7100
3 Graden St New York Mills (13417) *(G-11833)*

Four &TWenty Blackbirds, Brooklyn *Also called Blackbirds Brooklyn LLC* *(G-1592)*

Four Brothers Italian Bakery 914 741-5434
332 Elwood Ave Hawthorne (10532) *(G-5812)*

Four Directions Inc 315 829-8388
4677 State Route 5 Vernon (13476) *(G-15365)*

Four Fat Fowl Inc 518 733-5230
473 State Route 43 Stephentown (12168) *(G-14731)*

Four K Machine Shop Inc 516 997-0752
54 Brooklyn Ave Westbury (11590) *(G-15886)*

Four M Studios 212 557-6600
125 Park Ave Fl 20 New York (10017) *(G-9521)*

Four M Studios 212 499-2000
805 3rd Ave Fl 22 New York (10022) *(G-9522)*

Four M Studios 515 284-2157
805 3rd Ave Fl 29 New York (10022) *(G-9523)*

Four Paws Products Ltd 631 436-7421
3125 Vtrans Mem Hwy Ste 1 Ronkonkoma (11779) *(G-13940)*

Four Quarter, Westbury *Also called Cab-Network Inc* *(G-15873)*

Four S Showcase Manufacturing 718 649-4900
1044 Linwood St Brooklyn (11208) *(G-1863)*

Four Sasons Multi-Services Inc 347 843-6262
3525 Decatur Ave Apt 2k Bronx (10467) *(G-1261)*

Four Seasons Sunrooms Windows, Holbrook *Also called Latium USA Trading LLC* *(G-6004)*

Four Square Tool, Conklin *Also called Toolroom Express Inc* *(G-3630)*

Four Star, New York *Also called Vanity Room Inc* *(G-11642)*

Four-Way Pallet Corp 631 351-3401
191 E 2nd St Huntington Station (11746) *(G-6247)*

Fourteen Arnold Ave Corp 315 272-1700
14 Arnold Ave Utica (13502) *(G-15264)*

Fourtys Ny Inc 212 382-0301
231 W 39th St Rm 806 New York (10018) *(G-9524)*

Fowler Route Co Inc 917 653-4640
25 Sunnyside Dr Yonkers (10705) *(G-16311)*

Fownes Brothers & Co Inc (PA) 800 345-6837
16 E 34th St Fl 5 New York (10016) *(G-9525)*

Fownes Brothers & Co Inc 518 752-4411
204 County Highway 157 Gloversville (12078) *(G-5283)*

Fox 416 Corp 718 385-4600
416 Thatford Ave Brooklyn (11212) *(G-1864)*

Fox Run Vineyards Inc 315 536-4616
670 State Route 14 Penn Yan (14527) *(G-12584)*

Fox Unlimited Inc 212 736-3071
345 7th Ave Rm 2b New York (10001) *(G-9526)*

Fox's U-Bet Syrups, Brooklyn *Also called Fox 416 Corp* *(G-1864)*

Foxhill Press Inc 212 995-9620
37 E 7th St Ste 2 New York (10003) *(G-9527)*

FPL Fbrctors Erctors Group LLC 917 334-6968
15633 88th St Howard Beach (11414) *(G-6139)*

Fppf Chemical Co Inc (PA) 716 856-9607
117 W Tupper St Ste 1 Buffalo (14201) *(G-2758)*

Fra-Rik Formica Fabg Co Inc 718 597-3335
1464 Blondell Ave Fl 2 Bronx (10461) *(G-1262)*

Fradan Manufacturing Corp 914 632-3653
499 5th Ave New Rochelle (10801) *(G-8332)*

Fragrance Acquisitions LLC 845 534-9172
1900 Corporate Blvd Newburgh (12550) *(G-11865)*

Fralo, Syracuse *Also called Roth Global Plastics Inc* *(G-14979)*

Frame Shoppe & Art Gallery 516 365-6014
447 Plandome Rd Manhasset (11030) *(G-7534)*

Frame Shoppe & Gallery, Manhasset *Also called Frame Shoppe & Art Gallery* *(G-7534)*

Frame Works America Inc 631 288-1300
146 Mill Rd Westhampton Beach (11978) *(G-15956)*

Framing Technology Inc 585 464-8470
137 Syke St Rochester (14611) *(G-13422)*

Francepress LLC (PA) 646 202-9828
115 E 57th St Fl 11 New York (10022) *(G-9528)*

Franchet Metal Craft Inc 718 658-6400
17832 93rd Ave Jamaica (11433) *(G-6443)*

Francis Emory Fitch Inc (HQ) 212 619-3800
229 W 28th St New York (10001) *(G-9529)*

Franco Apparel Group Inc 212 967-7272
1407 Broadway New York (10018) *(G-9530)*

Franco Apparel Group Team, New York *Also called Franco Apparel Group Inc* *(G-9530)*

ALPHABETIC

Franetta, New York *Also called Beyond Loom Inc (G-8773)*

Frank Billanti Casting Co Inc............................212 221-0440
  42 W 38th St Rm 204 New York (10018) *(G-9531)*

Frank Blancato Inc..212 768-1495
  64 W 48th St Fl 16 New York (10036) *(G-9532)*

Frank J Martello..585 235-2780
  1227 Maple St Rochester (14611) *(G-13423)*

Frank Lowe Rbr & Gasket Co Inc.......................631 777-2707
  44 Ramsey Rd Shirley (11967) *(G-14421)*

Frank Merriwell Inc..516 921-8888
  212 Michael Dr Syosset (11791) *(G-14788)*

Frank Murken Products, Schenectady *Also called Tattersall Industries LLC (G-14311)*

Frank Wardynski & Sons Inc.............................716 854-6083
  336 Peckham St Buffalo (14206) *(G-2759)*

Franklin Manufacturing Div, Hauppauge *Also called Embassy Industries Inc (G-5647)*

Franklin Packaging Inc (PA)............................631 582-8900
  96 Sea Cove Rd Northport (11768) *(G-12104)*

Franklin Poly Film Inc......................................718 492-3523
  1149 56th St Brooklyn (11219) *(G-1865)*

Franklin Report LLC...212 639-9100
  201 E 69th St Apt 14j New York (10021) *(G-9533)*

Franklin's Printing, Cheektowaga *Also called Hugh F McPherson Inc (G-3354)*

Franklin-Douglas Inc...516 883-0121
  52 Main St Side Port Washington (11050) *(G-12880)*

Franks Cushions Inc...718 848-1216
  6302 59th Ave Maspeth (11378) *(G-7617)*

Frasier and Jones, Syracuse *Also called Frazer & Jones Co (G-14895)*

Fratellis LLC..607 722-5663
  20 Campbell Rd Binghamton (13905) *(G-878)*

Frazer & Jones Co...315 468-6251
  3000 Milton Ave Syracuse (13209) *(G-14895)*

Frazer & Jones Division, Solvay *Also called Eastern Company (G-14496)*

Frazer Computing Inc...315 379-3500
  6196 Us Highway 11 Canton (13617) *(G-3166)*

Frazier Industrial Company...............................315 539-9256
  1291 Waterloo Geneva Rd Waterloo (13165) *(G-15552)*

Fred A Nudd Corporation (PA)..........................315 524-2531
  1743 State Route 104 Ontario (14519) *(G-12289)*

Fred Lawrence Co, Bay Shore *Also called Lanwood Industries Inc (G-688)*

Fred M Lawrence Co Inc (PA)............................631 617-6853
  45 Drexel Dr Bay Shore (11706) *(G-681)*

Fred M Velepec Co Inc..718 821-6636
  7172 70th St Glendale (11385) *(G-5225)*

Fred Santucci Inc...716 483-1411
  121 Jackson Ave E Jamestown (14701) *(G-6511)*

Frederick Coon Inc...716 683-6812
  5751 Clinton St Elma (14059) *(G-4318)*

Frederick Cowan & Company Inc.......................631 369-0360
  144 Beach Rd Wading River (11792) *(G-15449)*

Frederick Machine Repair Inc...........................716 332-0104
  405 Ludington St Buffalo (14206) *(G-2760)*

Fredonia Pennysaver Inc (PA)...........................716 679-1509
  276 W Main St Ste 1 Fredonia (14063) *(G-4969)*

Free Trader, Elizabethtown *Also called Denton Publications Inc (G-4299)*

Free Trader, Plattsburgh *Also called Denton Publications Inc (G-12744)*

Freedom Mfg LLC..518 584-0441
  3 Duplainville Rd Apt C Saratoga Springs (12866) *(G-14175)*

Freedom Rains Inc...646 710-4512
  230 W 39th St Fl 7 New York (10018) *(G-9534)*

Freedom Run Winery Inc....................................716 433-4136
  5138 Lower Mountain Rd Lockport (14094) *(G-7076)*

Freeman Technology Inc.....................................732 829-8345
  2355 Bell Apt 2h Bayside (11360) *(G-737)*

Freeport Baldwin Leader, Garden City *Also called L & M Publications Inc (G-5103)*

Freeport Paper Industries Inc............................631 851-1555
  120 Windsor Pl Central Islip (11722) *(G-3276)*

Freeport Screen & Stamping.............................516 379-0330
  31 Hanse Ave Freeport (11520) *(G-4998)*

Freeville Publishing Co Inc................................607 844-9119
  9 Main St Freeville (13068) *(G-5033)*

Freeze Divisional Centl Mills, New York *Also called Central Mills Inc (G-8952)*

Freeze-Dry Foods Inc., Albion *Also called 3021743 Holdings Inc (G-152)*

Freihofer's Bakery Outlet, New Paltz *Also called Bimbo Bakeries Usa Inc (G-8305)*

French & Itln Furn Craftsmen............................718 599-5000
  999 Grand St Brooklyn (11211) *(G-1866)*

French Accnt Rugs & Tapestries........................212 686-6097
  36 E 31st St Frnt B New York (10016) *(G-9535)*

French Associates Inc...718 387-9880
  7339 172nd St Fresh Meadows (11366) *(G-5041)*

French Atmosphere Inc (PA)..............................516 371-9100
  421 7th Ave 525 New York (10001) *(G-9536)*

French Itln Furn Craftsmen Cor, Brooklyn *Also called French & Itln Furn Craftsmen (G-1866)*

French Morning LLC..646 290-7463
  27 W 20th St Ste 800 New York (10011) *(G-9537)*

French Pdts Frnch Pickle Works, Fresh Meadows *Also called French Associates Inc (G-5041)*

French Publishers Agency Inc............................212 254-4540
  853 Broadway Ste 1509 New York (10003) *(G-9538)*

Frequency Electronics Inc (PA)........................516 794-4500
  55 Charles Lindbergh Blvd # 2 Uniondale (11553) *(G-15229)*

Frequency Selective Networks...........................718 424-7500
  12 N Cottage St Valley Stream (11580) *(G-15341)*

Fresenius Kabi Usa LLC....................................716 773-0053
  3159 Staley Rd Grand Island (14072) *(G-5330)*

Fresenius Kabi USA LLC.....................................716 773-0800
  3159 Staley Rd Grand Island (14072) *(G-5331)*

Fresh Bake Pizza Co, Depew *Also called D R M Management Inc (G-3978)*

Fresh Fanatic Inc..516 521-6574
  88 Washington Ave Brooklyn (11205) *(G-1867)*

Fresh Ice Cream Company LLC..........................347 603-6021
  630 Flushing Ave 4 Brooklyn (11206) *(G-1868)*

Fresh Ice Cream Company LLC (PA)..................347 603-6021
  278 6th St Apt 3b Brooklyn (11215) *(G-1869)*

Fresh Prints LLC...917 826-2752
  134 E 70th St New York (10021) *(G-9539)*

Freshly Inc (PA)..844 373-7459
  115 E 23rd St Fl 7 New York (10010) *(G-9540)*

Freshop Inc..585 738-6035
  3246 Monroe Ave Ste 1 Rochester (14618) *(G-13424)*

Freshway Distributors, Hicksville *Also called Kozy Shack Enterprises LLC (G-5920)*

Frey Concrete Inc..716 213-5832
  3949 Frest Pk Way Ste 400 North Tonawanda (14120) *(G-12068)*

Frey Concrete Incoporated, Orchard Park *Also called United Materials LLC (G-12381)*

Frey Sand & Gravel, North Tonawanda *Also called Frey Concrete Inc (G-12068)*

Fridge Magazine Inc..212 997-7673
  108 W 39th St Fl 4 New York (10018) *(G-9541)*

Friendly Fuel Incorporated.................................518 581-7036
  54 Church St Saratoga Springs (12866) *(G-14176)*

Friendly Star Fuel Inc..718 369-8801
  889 3rd Ave Brooklyn (11232) *(G-1870)*

Friendship Dairies LLC.....................................585 973-3031
  6701 County Road 20 Friendship (14739) *(G-5052)*

FriesIndcmpina Ingrdnts N Amer.......................607 746-0196
  40196 State Hwy 10 Delhi Delhi (13753) *(G-3965)*

Frigo Design, Brewerton *Also called Ae Fund Inc (G-1134)*

Frito-Lay North America Inc................................607 775-7000
  10 Spud Ln Binghamton (13904) *(G-879)*

Fritters & Buns Inc...845 227-6609
  236 Blue Hill Rd Hopewell Junction (12533) *(G-6093)*

Froebe Group LLC..646 649-2150
  154 W 27th St Rm 4 New York (10001) *(G-9542)*

Fronhofer Tool Company Inc..............................518 692-2496
  4197 County Rd 48 Cossayuna (12823) *(G-3799)*

Frontier Ht-Dip Glvanizing Inc..........................716 875-2091
  1740 Elmwood Ave Buffalo (14207) *(G-2761)*

Frontier Hydraulics Corp....................................716 694-2070
  1738 Elmwood Ave Ste 2 Buffalo (14207) *(G-2762)*

Frontiers Unlimited Inc......................................631 283-4663
  52 Jagger Ln Southampton (11968) *(G-14530)*

Fross Industries Inc..716 297-0652
  3315 Haseley Dr Niagara Falls (14304) *(G-11930)*

Frost Publications Inc...845 726-3232
  55 Laurel Hill Dr Westtown (10998) *(G-15965)*

Frozen Food Digest Inc......................................212 557-8600
  271 Madison Ave Ste 805 New York (10016) *(G-9543)*

Frozen Pastry Products Corp.............................845 364-9833
  41 Lincoln Ave Spring Valley (10977) *(G-14570)*

Frp Apparel Group LLC.....................................212 695-8000
  110 W 40th St Fl 26 New York (10018) *(G-9544)*

Fruit Fresh Up Inc..716 683-3200
  2928 Walden Ave Ste 2 Depew (14043) *(G-3983)*

Fruit St Hlth Pub Beneft Corp............................347 960-6400
  85 Broad St Fl 18 New York (10004) *(G-9545)*

Fruitcrown Products Corp (PA)..........................631 694-5800
  250 Adams Blvd Farmingdale (11735) *(G-4633)*

Fsr Beauty Ltd...212 447-0036
  411 5th Ave Rm 804 New York (10016) *(G-9546)*

FT Publications Inc (HQ)....................................212 641-6500
  330 Hudson St New York (10013) *(G-9547)*

FT Publications Inc...212 641-2420
  330 Hudson St New York (10013) *(G-9548)*

Fts Systems Inc (HQ)..845 687-5300
  3538 Main St Stone Ridge (12484) *(G-14735)*

Ftt Manufacturing, Rochester *Also called Ppi Corp (G-13632)*

Ftt Medical Inc...585 444-0980
  275 Commerce Dr Rochester (14623) *(G-13425)*

Ftt Mfg, Rochester *Also called Ppi Corp (G-13633)*

Fuda Group (usa) Corporation...........................646 751-7488
  48 Wall St Fl 11 New York (10005) *(G-9549)*

Fuel Data Systems Inc..800 447-7870
  772 Greenville Tpke Middletown (10940) *(G-7909)*

Fuel Efficiency LLC..315 923-2511
  101 Davis Pkwy Clyde (14433) *(G-3491)*

Fuel Energy Services USA Ltd............................607 846-2650
  250 Ltta Brook Indus Pkwy Horseheads (14845) *(G-6124)*

Fuel Soul...516 379-0810
  188 Merrick Rd Merrick (11566) *(G-7856)*

Fuel Watchman Sales & Service.........................718 665-6100
  364 Jackson Ave Bronx (10454) *(G-1263)*

Fujitsu Ntwrk Cmmnications Inc........................845 731-2000
  2 Blue Hill Plz Ste 1609 Pearl River (10965) *(G-12531)*

Fulcrum Acoustic LLC 866 234-0678
25 Circle St Ste 104 Rochester (14607) *(G-13426)*
Fulcrum Promos, New York *Also called Fulcrum Promotions & Prtg LLC (G-9550)*
Fulcrum Promotions & Prtg LLC 203 909-6362
135 W 41st St New York (10036) *(G-9550)*
Full Circle Home LLC 212 432-0001
131 W 35th St Fl 8 New York (10001) *(G-9551)*
Full Circle Studios LLC 716 875-7740
710 Main St Buffalo (14202) *(G-2763)*
Full Motion Beverage Inc (PA) 631 585-1100
998 Old Country Rd Plainview (11803) *(G-12686)*
Full Timer, Bronx *Also called Fuel Watchman Sales & Service (G-1263)*
Fuller Sportswear Co Inc 516 773-3353
10 Grenfell Dr Great Neck (11020) *(G-5391)*
Fuller Tool Incorporated 315 891-3183
225 Platform Rd Newport (13416) *(G-11898)*
Fulmont Ready-Mix Company Inc (PA) 518 887-5560
774 State Highway 5s Amsterdam (12010) *(G-328)*
Fulton Boiler Works Inc (PA) 315 298-5121
3981 Port St Pulaski (13142) *(G-12995)*
Fulton Boiler Works Inc 315 298-5121
972 Centerville Rd Pulaski (13142) *(G-12996)*
Fulton China LLC 315 298-0112
3981 Port St Pulaski (13142) *(G-12997)*
Fulton Companies, Pulaski *Also called Fulton Volcanic Inc (G-12999)*
Fulton Daily News, Fulton *Also called DOT Publishing (G-5058)*
Fulton Heating Solutions Inc 315 298-5121
972 Centerville Rd Pulaski (13142) *(G-12998)*
Fulton Newspapers Inc 315 598-6397
67 S 2nd St Fulton (13069) *(G-5059)*
Fulton Patriot, Fulton *Also called Fulton Newspapers Inc (G-5059)*
Fulton Screen Printing 315 593-2220
2 Harris St Fulton (13069) *(G-5060)*
Fulton Tool Co Inc 315 598-2900
802 W Broadway Ste 1 Fulton (13069) *(G-5061)*
Fulton Volcanic Inc (PA) 315 298-5121
3981 Port St Pulaski (13142) *(G-12999)*
Fultonville Machine & Tool Co 518 853-4441
73 Union St Fultonville (12072) *(G-5079)*
Fun Industries of NY 631 845-3805
111 Milbar Blvd Farmingdale (11735) *(G-4634)*
Fun Media Inc 646 472-0135
1001 Ave Of The Americas New York (10018) *(G-9552)*
Fung Wong Bakery Inc 212 267-4037
30 Mott St Frnt New York (10013) *(G-9553)*
Fung Wong Bakery Shop, New York *Also called Fung Wong Bakery Inc (G-9553)*
Fungilab Inc 631 750-6361
89 Cabot Ct Ste K Hauppauge (11788) *(G-5655)*
Furniture By Craftmaster Ltd 631 750-0658
1595 Ocean Ave Ste A9 Bohemia (11716) *(G-1014)*
Furniture Doctor Inc 585 657-6941
7007 State Route 5 And 20 Bloomfield (14469) *(G-947)*
Furniture World, New Rochelle *Also called Towse Publishing Co (G-8355)*
Fuse Electronics Inc 607 352-3222
1223 Us Route 11 Kirkwood (13795) *(G-6731)*
Fusion Brands America Inc., New York *Also called Clean Beauty Collective Inc (G-9030)*
Fusion Pro Performance Ltd 917 833-0761
16 W 36th St Rm 1205 New York (10018) *(G-9554)*
Futon City Discounters Inc 315 437-1328
6361 Thompson Rd Syracuse (13206) *(G-14896)*
Future Diagnostics LLC 347 434-6700
266 47th St Brooklyn (11220) *(G-1871)*
Future Media Group Inc 646 854-1375
1 World Trade Ctr Fl 39 New York (10007) *(G-9555)*
Future Screw Machine Pdts Inc 631 765-1610
41155 County Road 48 Southold (11971) *(G-14543)*
Future Spray Finishing Co 631 242-6252
78 Brook Ave Ste A Deer Park (11729) *(G-3877)*
Future Star Digatech 718 666-0350
713 Monroe St Brooklyn (11221) *(G-1872)*
Futurebiotics, Hauppauge *Also called FB Laboratories Inc (G-5649)*
Futurebiotics LLC 631 273-6300
70 Commerce Dr Hauppauge (11788) *(G-5656)*
Fuzion Creations Intl LLC 718 369-8800
140 58th St Ste A Brooklyn (11220) *(G-1873)*
FX INC 212 244-2240
1 Penn Plz Ste 6238 New York (10119) *(G-9556)*
G & C Welding Co Inc 516 883-3228
39 Annette Dr Port Washington (11050) *(G-12881)*
G & G C Machine & Tool Co Inc 516 873-0999
18 Sylvester St Westbury (11590) *(G-15887)*
G & H Wood Products LLC 716 372-0341
2427 N Union Street Ext Olean (14760) *(G-12236)*
G & J Rdymx & Masnry Sup Inc 718 454-0800
18330 Jamaica Ave Hollis (11423) *(G-6043)*
G & M Clearview Inc 845 781-4877
112 Spring St Monroe (10950) *(G-8021)*
G & M Dege Inc 631 475-1450
147 West Ave Patchogue (11772) *(G-12501)*
G & P Printing Inc 212 274-8092
142 Baxter St New York (10013) *(G-9557)*
G A Braun Inc (PA) 315 475-3123
79 General Irwin Blvd North Syracuse (13212) *(G-12041)*
G A Braun Inc 315 475-3123
461 E Brighton Ave Syracuse (13210) *(G-14897)*
G A Richards & Co Inc 516 334-5412
717 Main St Westbury (11590) *(G-15888)*
G and G Service 518 785-9247
21 Nelson Ave Latham (12110) *(G-6857)*
G B International Trdg Co Ltd 607 785-0938
408 Airport Rd Endicott (13760) *(G-4457)*
G Bopp USA Inc 845 296-1065
4 Bill Horton Way Wappingers Falls (12590) *(G-15493)*
G C Casting, Oneonta *Also called American Blade Mfg LLC (G-12256)*
G C Controls Inc 607 656-4117
1408 County Road 2 Greene (13778) *(G-5445)*
G C Hanford Manufacturing Co (PA) 315 476-7418
304 Oneida St Syracuse (13202) *(G-14898)*
G C Mobile Svces, Cortlandt Manor *Also called Gc Mobile Services Inc (G-3795)*
G E Inspection Technologies LP 315 554-2000
721 Visions Dr Skaneateles (13152) *(G-14451)*
G F Labels LLC 518 798-6643
10 Ferguson Ln Queensbury (12804) *(G-13039)*
G Fuel LLC (PA) 877 426-6262
113 Alder St West Babylon (11704) *(G-15712)*
G Haynes Holdings Inc 607 538-1160
51971 State Highway 10 Bloomville (13739) *(G-953)*
G I Certified Inc 212 397-1945
623 W 51st St New York (10019) *(G-9558)*
G J Olney Inc 315 827-4208
9057 Dopp Hill Rd Westernville (13486) *(G-15942)*
G M I, Hornell *Also called Gray Manufacturing Inds LLC (G-6108)*
G Marks Hdwr Liquidating Corp 631 225-5400
333 Bayview Ave Amityville (11701) *(G-263)*
G N R Co, Smithtown *Also called G N R Plastics Inc (G-14478)*
G N R Plastics Inc 631 724-8758
11 Wandering Way Smithtown (11787) *(G-14478)*
G Pesso & Sons Inc 718 224-9130
20320 35th Ave Bayside (11361) *(G-738)*
G R M, Bellmore *Also called Rush Gold Manufacturing Ltd (G-788)*
G S Communications USA Inc 718 389-7371
179 Greenpoint Ave Brooklyn (11222) *(G-1874)*
G Schirmer Inc (HQ) 212 254-2100
180 Madison Ave Ste 2400 New York (10016) *(G-9559)*
G Schirmer Inc 845 469-4699
2 Old Rt 17 Chester (10918) *(G-3378)*
G Sicuranza Ltd 516 759-0259
4 East Ave Glen Cove (11542) *(G-5193)*
G T Machine & Tool, Long Island City *Also called Theodosiou Inc (G-7380)*
G W Canfield & Son Inc 315 735-5522
600 Plant St Utica (13502) *(G-15265)*
G W Manufacturing, Poughkeepsie *Also called Gw Manufacturing (G-12960)*
G Z G Rest & Kit Met Works 718 788-8621
120 13th St Brooklyn (11215) *(G-1875)*
G&G Led LLC 800 285-6780
10 Corprate Dr Clifton Pa Clifton Park Clifton Park (12065) *(G-3464)*
G&W Industries, New York *Also called Gw Acquisition LLC (G-9700)*
G-Forces, Plainview *Also called Derm-Buro Inc (G-12678)*
G-III Apparel Group, New York *Also called G-III Leather Fashions Inc (G-9563)*
G-III Apparel Group Ltd (PA) 212 403-0500
512 7th Ave Fl 35 New York (10018) *(G-9560)*
G-III Apparel Group Ltd 212 403-0500
512 Fashion Ave Fl 35 New York (10018) *(G-9561)*
G-III Apparel Group Ltd 212 840-7272
512 7th Ave Fl 35 New York (10018) *(G-9562)*
G-III Leather Fashions Inc 212 403-0500
512 7th Ave Fl 35 New York (10018) *(G-9563)*
G-S Plastic Optics, Rochester *Also called Germanow-Simon Corporation (G-13438)*
G18 Corporation 212 869-0010
250 W 93rd St Apt 9h New York (10025) *(G-9564)*
G4i, Rensselaer *Also called Great 4 Image Inc (G-13088)*
Gabani Inc 631 283-4930
81 Lee Ave Southampton (11968) *(G-14531)*
Gabila & Sons Mfg Inc 631 789-2220
100 Wartburg Ave Copiague (11726) *(G-3653)*
Gabila Food Products Inc 631 789-2220
100 Wartburg Ave Copiague (11726) *(G-3654)*
Gabila's Knishes, Copiague *Also called Gabila & Sons Mfg Inc (G-3653)*
Gabrielle Andra 212 366-9624
305 W 21st St New York (10011) *(G-9565)*
Gac Express Inc 718 438-2227
1310 52nd St Brooklyn (11219) *(G-1876)*
Gad Systems, Lawrence *Also called John J Richardson (G-6886)*
Gadabout USA Wheelchairs Inc 585 338-2110
892 E Ridge Rd Rochester (14621) *(G-13427)*
Gaddis Engineering, Glen Cove *Also called Gaddis Industrial Equipment (G-5194)*
Gaddis Industrial Equipment 516 759-3100
140 Pratt Oval Glen Cove (11542) *(G-5194)*
Gaebel Enterprises, East Syracuse *Also called Gei International Inc (G-4212)*
Gagne Associates Inc 800 800-5954
41 Commercial Dr Johnson City (13790) *(G-6599)*

ALPHABETIC

Gailer Stamping Diecutting LLC 212 243-5662
3718 Nthrn Blvd 324 Fl 3 Long Island City (11101) ***(G-7227)***
GAI Manufacturing Co LLC (HQ) 718 292-9000
50 E 153rd St Bronx (10451) ***(G-1264)***
Galas Framing Services 718 706-0007
4224 Orchard St Fl 4 Long Island City (11101) ***(G-7228)***
Galax, Monsey *Also called Ta Chen International Inc* ***(G-8051)***
Galaxy Knitting Mills, Long Island City *Also called In Toon Amkor Fashions Inc* ***(G-7247)***
Galaxy Nutritional Foods Inc 401 667-5000
90 State St Ste 700 Albany (12207) ***(G-79)***
Galaxy Software LLC 631 244-8405
927 Montauk Hwy Unit 229 Oakdale (11769) ***(G-12151)***
Galian Handbags, New York *Also called Rodem Incorporated* ***(G-11070)***
Galison Publishing LLC 212 354-8840
70 W 36th St Fl 11 New York (10018) ***(G-9566)***
Gallagher Printing Inc 716 873-2434
2518 Delaware Ave Buffalo (14216) ***(G-2764)***
Gallant Graphics Ltd 845 868-1166
242 Attlebury Hill Rd Stanfordville (12581) ***(G-14610)***
Galle & Zinter Inc 716 833-4212
3405 Harlem Rd Buffalo (14225) ***(G-2765)***
Galle Mamorial, Buffalo *Also called Galle & Zinter Inc* ***(G-2765)***
Gallery 57 Dental 212 246-8700
24 W 57th St Ste 701 New York (10019) ***(G-9567)***
Gallery of Machines LLC 607 849-6028
20 Front St Marathon (13803) ***(G-7557)***
Galli Shirts and Sports AP 845 226-7305
246 Judith Dr Stormville (12582) ***(G-14751)***
Galmer Ltd 718 392-4609
4301 21st St Ste 130b Long Island City (11101) ***(G-7229)***
Galmer Silversmiths, Long Island City *Also called Galmer Ltd* ***(G-7229)***
Galt Industries Inc 212 758-0770
121 E 71st St Frnt A New York (10021) ***(G-9568)***
Gamble & Gamble Inc (PA) 716 731-3239
5890 West St Sanborn (14132) ***(G-14142)***
GAME Sportswear Ltd 914 962-1701
1401 Front St Yorktown Heights (10598) ***(G-16365)***
Game Time LLC 914 557-9662
1407 Broadway Rm 400 New York (10018) ***(G-9569)***
Gameclub Inc 415 359-5742
46 W 65th St Apt 1a New York (10023) ***(G-9570)***
Games For Change Inc 212 242-4922
205 E 42nd St Fl 20 New York (10017) ***(G-9571)***
Gametime Sportswear Plus LLC 315 724-5893
1206 Belle Ave Utica (13501) ***(G-15266)***
Gamma Instrument Co Inc 516 486-5526
34 Sarah Dr Ste B Farmingdale (11735) ***(G-4635)***
Gamma Lab, West Babylon *Also called G Fuel LLC* ***(G-15712)***
Gamma North Corporation 716 902-5100
13595 Broadway St Alden (14004) ***(G-169)***
Gamma Products Inc 845 562-3332
509 Temple Hill Rd New Windsor (12553) ***(G-8368)***
Gan Kavod Inc 716 633-2820
300 International Dr Buffalo (14221) ***(G-2766)***
Ganesh Foods, Waterloo *Also called Gharana Industries LLC* ***(G-15553)***
Gangi Distributors Inc 718 442-5745
135 Mcclean Ave Staten Island (10305) ***(G-14654)***
Gannett Co Inc 585 232-7100
245 E Main St Rochester (14604) ***(G-13428)***
Gannett Co Inc 914 278-9315
92 North Ave New Rochelle (10801) ***(G-8333)***
Gannett Co Inc 607 798-1234
4421 Vestal Pkwy E Vestal (13850) ***(G-15377)***
Gannett Co Inc 607 352-2702
10 Gannett Dr Johnson City (13790) ***(G-6600)***
Gannett NY Production Facility, Johnson City *Also called Gannett Co Inc* ***(G-6600)***
Gannett Stllite Info Ntwrk Inc 914 965-5000
1 Odell Plz Yonkers (10701) ***(G-16312)***
Gannett Stllite Info Ntwrk Inc 585 798-1400
413 Main St Medina (14103) ***(G-7735)***
Gannett Stllite Info Ntwrk LLC 845 578-2300
1 Crosfield Ave West Nyack (10994) ***(G-15821)***
Gannett Stllite Info Ntwrk LLC 845 454-2000
85 Civic Center Plz Poughkeepsie (12601) ***(G-12956)***
Gannett Stllite Info Ntwrk LLC 914 381-3400
700 Waverly Ave Mamaroneck (10543) ***(G-7511)***
Gannett Suburban Newspapers, Mamaroneck *Also called Gannett Stllite Info Ntwrk LLC* ***(G-7511)***
Gappa Textiles Inc 212 481-7100
295 5th Ave Ste 1021 New York (10016) ***(G-9572)***
Gar Wood Custom Boats 518 494-2966
20 Duell Hill Rd Brant Lake (12815) ***(G-1112)***
Garan Incorporated (HQ) 212 563-1292
200 Madison Ave Fl 4 New York (10016) ***(G-9573)***
Garan Manufacturing Corp (HQ) 212 563-2000
200 Madison Ave Fl 4 New York (10016) ***(G-9574)***
Garb-El Products Co, Buffalo *Also called 240 Michigan Street Inc* ***(G-2611)***
Garb-O-Liner Inc 914 235-1585
64 Drake Ave New Rochelle (10805) ***(G-8334)***
Garco, Penfield *Also called Robinson Tools LLC* ***(G-12573)***
Garco Manufacturing Corp Inc 718 287-3330
4802 Farragut Rd Brooklyn (11203) ***(G-1877)***
Gardall Safe Corporation 315 432-9115
219 Lamson St Ste 1 Syracuse (13206) ***(G-14899)***
Gardei Industries LLC (PA) 716 693-7100
1087 Erie Ave North Tonawanda (14120) ***(G-12069)***
Gardei Manufacturing, North Tonawanda *Also called Pioneer Printers Inc* ***(G-12082)***
Garden State Shavings Inc 845 544-2835
16 Almond Tree Ln Warwick (10990) ***(G-15514)***
Gardner Dnver Oberdorfer Pumps 315 437-0361
5900 Firestone Dr Syracuse (13206) ***(G-14900)***
Gardner The Train Doctor, North Rose *Also called Gargraves Trackage Corporation* ***(G-12035)***
Garelick Farms LLC 518 283-0820
504 Third Avenue Ext East Greenbush (12061) ***(G-4114)***
Gargraves Trackage Corporation 315 483-6577
8967 Ridge Rd North Rose (14516) ***(G-12035)***
Garland Technology LLC (PA) 716 242-8500
199 Delaware Ave Buffalo (14202) ***(G-2767)***
Garlock Sealing Tech LLC 315 597-4811
1666 Division St Palmyra (14522) ***(G-12487)***
Garment Care Systems LLC 518 674-1826
55 Blue Heron Dr Averill Park (12018) ***(G-507)***
Garrett J Cronin 914 761-9299
1 Stuart Way White Plains (10607) ***(G-16008)***
Gary Gelbfish MD 718 258-3004
2502 Avenue I Brooklyn (11210) ***(G-1878)***
Gary Roth & Associates Ltd 516 333-1000
1400 Old Country Rd # 305 Westbury (11590) ***(G-15889)***
Gary Stock Corporation 914 276-2700
597 Rte 22 Croton Falls (10519) ***(G-3805)***
Garys Loft 212 244-0970
28 W 36th St New York (10018) ***(G-9575)***
Gas Field Specialists Inc 716 378-6422
224 N Main St Horseheads (14845) ***(G-6125)***
Gas Recovery Systems LLC (HQ) 914 421-4903
1 N Lexington Ave Ste 620 White Plains (10601) ***(G-16009)***
Gas Recovery Systems Illinois, White Plains *Also called Gas Recovery Systems LLC* ***(G-16009)***
Gas Turbine Controls Corp 914 693-0830
6 Skyline Dr Ste 150 Hawthorne (10532) ***(G-5813)***
Gasoft Equipment Inc 845 863-1010
231 Dubois St Newburgh (12550) ***(G-11866)***
Gasport Welding & Fabg Inc 716 772-7205
8430 Telegraph Rd Gasport (14067) ***(G-5137)***
Gasser & Sons Inc (PA) 631 543-6600
440 Moreland Rd Commack (11725) ***(G-3589)***
Gassho Body & Mind Inc 518 695-9991
76 Broad St Schuylerville (12871) ***(G-14324)***
Gatecomusa, Flushing *Also called Yellow E House Inc* ***(G-4907)***
Gatehouse Media LLC (HQ) 585 598-0030
175 Sullys Trl Fl 3 Pittsford (14534) ***(G-12641)***
Gatehouse Media LLC 315 792-5000
350 Willowbrook Office Pa Utica (13501) ***(G-15267)***
Gatehouse Media LLC 607 776-2121
10 W Steuben St Bath (14810) ***(G-633)***
Gatehouse Media LLC 315 866-2220
221 Oriskany St E Utica (13501) ***(G-15268)***
Gatehouse Media LLC 607 936-4651
34 W Pulteney St Corning (14830) ***(G-3715)***
Gatehouse Media LLC 585 394-0770
73 Buffalo St Canandaigua (14424) ***(G-3133)***
Gatehouse Media LLC 607 324-1425
32 Broadway Mall Hornell (14843) ***(G-6107)***
Gatehuse Media PA Holdings Inc (HQ) 585 598-0030
175 Sullys Trl Fl 3 Pittsford (14534) ***(G-12642)***
Gateway Prtg & Graphics Inc 716 823-3873
3970 Big Tree Rd Hamburg (14075) ***(G-5509)***
Gatherer's Gourmet Granola, Delmar *Also called Sanzdranz LLC* ***(G-3969)***
Gatti Tool & Mold Inc 585 328-1350
997 Beahan Rd Rochester (14624) ***(G-13429)***
Gaughan Construction Corp 718 850-9577
13034 90th Ave Richmond Hill (11418) ***(G-13114)***
Gavin Mfg Corp 631 467-0040
25 Central Ave Unit A Farmingdale (11735) ***(G-4636)***
Gay Sheet Metal Dies Inc 716 877-0208
301 Hinman Ave Buffalo (14216) ***(G-2768)***
Gaylord Archival, North Syracuse *Also called Gaylord Bros Inc* ***(G-12042)***
Gaylord Bros Inc 315 457-5070
7282 William Barry Blvd North Syracuse (13212) ***(G-12042)***
Gaymar Industries Inc 800 828-7341
10 Centre Dr Orchard Park (14127) ***(G-12353)***
Gazette Press Inc 914 963-8300
2 Clinton Ave Rye (10580) ***(G-14077)***
Gb Aero Engine LLC 914 925-9600
555 Theodore Fremd Ave Rye (10580) ***(G-14078)***
Gb Group Inc 212 594-3748
Umpire State Bldg 1808 New York (10021) ***(G-9576)***
Gbf, Tonawanda *Also called Green Buffalo Fuel LLC* ***(G-15108)***
Gbg National Brands Group LLC 646 839-7000
350 5th Ave Lbby 9 New York (10118) ***(G-9577)***

Gbg USA Inc 646 839-7083
  350 5th Ave Fl 7 New York (10118) *(G-9578)*
Gbg USA Inc 212 615-3400
  261 W 35th St Fl 15 New York (10001) *(G-9579)*
Gc Mobile Services Inc 914 736-9730
  32 William Puckey Dr Cortlandt Manor (10567) *(G-3795)*
Gce International Inc (PA) 212 704-4800
  1385 Broadway Fl 21 New York (10018) *(G-9580)*
Gce International Inc 212 868-0500
  350 5th Ave Ste 616 New York (10118) *(G-9581)*
Gce International Inc 773 263-1210
  1359 Broadway Rm 2000 New York (10018) *(G-9582)*
GCM Metal Industries Inc 718 386-4059
  454 Troutman St Brooklyn (11237) *(G-1879)*
Gcns Technology Group Inc (PA) 347 713-8160
  597 Rutland Rd Brooklyn (11203) *(G-1880)*
Gdi, Brooklyn *Also called GDi Custom Marble & Gran Inc (G-1881)*
GDi Custom Marble & Gran Inc 718 996-9100
  134 Avenue T Brooklyn (11223) *(G-1881)*
Gds Publishing Inc 212 796-2000
  40 Wall St Fl 5 New York (10005) *(G-9583)*
GE Aviation Systems LLC 631 467-5500
  1000 Macarthur Mem Hwy Bohemia (11716) *(G-1015)*
GE Aviation Systems LLC 513 243-9104
  1000 Macarthur Mem Hwy Bohemia (11716) *(G-1016)*
GE Global Research 518 387-5000
  1 Research Cir Niskayuna (12309) *(G-11995)*
GE Healthcare Fincl Svcs Inc 212 713-2000
  299 Park Ave Fl 3 New York (10171) *(G-9584)*
GE Mds LLC (HQ) 585 242-9600
  175 Science Pkwy Rochester (14620) *(G-13430)*
GE Plastics 518 475-5011
  1 Noryl Ave Selkirk (12158) *(G-14357)*
GE Polymershapes 516 433-4092
  120 Andrews Rd Hicksville (11801) *(G-5910)*
Gear Motions Incorporated 716 885-1080
  1120 Niagara St Buffalo (14213) *(G-2769)*
Gear Motions Incorporated (PA) 315 488-0100
  1750 Milton Ave Syracuse (13209) *(G-14901)*
Geddes Bakery Co Inc 315 437-8084
  421 S Main St North Syracuse (13212) *(G-12043)*
Gefa Instrument Corp 516 420-4419
  205 Bethpage Sweet Old Bethpage (11804) *(G-12216)*
Gehring Textiles, Dolgeville *Also called Gehring Tricot Corporation (G-4022)*
Gehring Tricot Corporation (PA) 315 429-8551
  68 Ransom St Dolgeville (13329) *(G-4022)*
Gehring Tricot Corporation 315 429-8551
  68 Ransom St Ste 272 Dolgeville (13329) *(G-4023)*
Gei International Inc 315 463-9261
  100 Ball St East Syracuse (13057) *(G-4212)*
Geliko LLC 212 876-5620
  1601 3rd Ave Apt 16a New York (10128) *(G-9585)*
Gem, Schenectady *Also called Green Enviro Machine LLC (G-14276)*
Gem Manufacturing Inc 585 235-1670
  853 West Ave Bldg 17a Rochester (14611) *(G-13431)*
Gem Metal Spinning & Stamping 718 729-7014
  517 47th Rd Long Island City (11101) *(G-7230)*
Gem Reproduction Services Corp 845 298-0172
  1299 Route 9 Ste 105 Wappingers Falls (12590) *(G-15494)*
Gemcor Automation LLC 716 674-9300
  100 Gemcor Dr West Seneca (14224) *(G-15848)*
Gemini Manufactures 716 633-0306
  160 Holtz Dr Cheektowaga (14225) *(G-3350)*
Gemini Pharmaceuticals Inc 631 543-3334
  87 Modular Ave Ste 1 Commack (11725) *(G-3590)*
Gemoro Inc 212 768-8844
  98 Cuttermill Rd Ste 446s Great Neck (11021) *(G-5392)*
Gemprint Corporation 212 997-0007
  580 5th Ave Bsmt Ll05 New York (10036) *(G-9586)*
Gemtrol Inc 716 894-0716
  1800 Broadway St Bldg 1c Buffalo (14212) *(G-2770)*
Gemveto Jewelry Company Inc 212 755-2522
  18 E 48th St Rm 501 New York (10017) *(G-9587)*
Gen Publishing Inc 914 834-3880
  140 Huguenot St Fl 3 New Rochelle (10801) *(G-8335)*
Gen-West Associates LLC 315 255-1779
  101 Columbus St Auburn (13021) *(G-477)*
Genco John 716 483-5446
  71 River St Jamestown (14701) *(G-6512)*
Genencor Division Danisco US, Rochester *Also called Danisco US Inc (G-13337)*
Genencor International, Rochester *Also called Danisco US Inc (G-13338)*
Genencor International Inc 585 256-5200
  3490 Winton Pl Rochester (14623) *(G-13432)*
General Art Company Inc 212 255-1298
  14 E 38th St Fl 6 New York (10016) *(G-9588)*
General Art Framing, New York *Also called General Art Company Inc (G-9588)*
General Bearing Corporation (HQ) 845 358-6000
  44 High St West Nyack (10994) *(G-15822)*
General Business Supply Inc 518 720-3939
  2550 9th Ave Watervliet (12189) *(G-15602)*
General Chemical, Syracuse *Also called Chemtrade Chemicals US LLC (G-14848)*

General Coatings Tech Inc (PA) 718 821-1232
  24 Woodward Ave Ridgewood (11385) *(G-13146)*
General Composites Inc 518 963-7333
  39 Myers Way Willsboro (12996) *(G-16151)*
General Control Systems Inc 518 270-8045
  60 Cohoes Ave Ste 101 Green Island (12183) *(G-5435)*
General Cryogenic Tech LLC 516 334-8200
  400 Shames Dr Westbury (11590) *(G-15890)*
General Cutting Inc 631 580-5011
  90 13th Ave Unit 10 Ronkonkoma (11779) *(G-13941)*
General Diaries Corporation 516 371-2244
  56 John St Inwood (11096) *(G-6294)*
General Die and Die Cutng Inc 516 665-3584
  11 Finch Ct Massapequa Park (11762) *(G-7655)*
General Electric Company 315 456-3304
  5990 E Molloy Rd Syracuse (13211) *(G-14902)*
General Electric Company 315 554-2000
  721 Visions Dr Skaneateles (13152) *(G-14452)*
General Electric Company 518 385-4022
  1 River Rd Bldg 55 Schenectady (12305) *(G-14266)*
General Electric Company 518 385-2211
  1 River Rd Bldg 33 Schenectady (12305) *(G-14267)*
General Electric Company 518 459-4110
  11 Anderson Dr Albany (12205) *(G-80)*
General Electric Company 203 373-2756
  1 River Rd Bldg 43 Schenectady (12345) *(G-14268)*
General Electric Company 518 385-3716
  1 River Rd Schenectady (12345) *(G-14269)*
General Electric Company 518 746-5750
  446 Lock 8 Way 8th Hudson Falls (12839) *(G-6187)*
General Electric Company 518 385-2211
  1 River Rd Bldg 37 Schenectady (12345) *(G-14270)*
General Electric Company 518 387-5000
  1 Research Cir Schenectady (12309) *(G-14271)*
General Electric Company 518 385-7620
  2690 Balltown Rd Bldg 600 Niskayuna (12309) *(G-11996)*
General Electric Company 518 385-3439
  705 Corporation Park Schenectady (12302) *(G-14272)*
General Electric Intl Inc 518 385-2211
  1 River Rd Bldg 53202j Schenectady (12345) *(G-14273)*
General Fibre Products Corp 516 358-7500
  170 Nassau Terminal Rd New Hyde Park (11040) *(G-8270)*
General Fire-Proof Door Corp 718 893-5500
  913 Edgewater Rd Bronx (10474) *(G-1265)*
General Galvanizing Sup Co Inc (PA) 718 589-4300
  652 Whittier St Fl Mezz Bronx (10474) *(G-1266)*
General Led Corp 516 280-2854
  206 E Jericho Tpke Mineola (11501) *(G-7976)*
General Led Holdings LLC 212 629-6830
  19 W 36th St Fl 6 New York (10018) *(G-9589)*
General Media Strategies Inc 212 586-4141
  521 5th Ave Fl 17 New York (10175) *(G-9590)*
General Microwave Corporation (HQ) 516 802-0900
  227a Michael Dr Syosset (11791) *(G-14789)*
General Mills Inc 716 856-6060
  54 S Michigan Ave Buffalo (14203) *(G-2771)*
General Mills Inc 716 856-6060
  315 Ship Canal Pkwy Buffalo (14218) *(G-2772)*
General Motors LLC 716 879-5000
  2995 River Rd 2 Buffalo (14207) *(G-2773)*
General Mtr Cmponents Holdings, Lockport *Also called GM Components Holdings LLC (G-7080)*
General Oil Equipment Co Inc (PA) 716 691-7012
  60 John Glenn Dr Amherst (14228) *(G-225)*
General Plating LLC 585 423-0830
  850 Saint Paul St Ste 10 Rochester (14605) *(G-13433)*
General Refining & Semlt Corp 516 538-4747
  59 Madison Ave Hempstead (11550) *(G-5836)*
General Refining Corporation 516 538-4747
  59 Madison Ave Hempstead (11550) *(G-5837)*
General Semiconductor Inc 631 300-3818
  150 Motor Pkwy Ste 101 Hauppauge (11788) *(G-5657)*
General Specialties, Shokan *Also called Mack Wood Working (G-14429)*
General Splice Corporation 914 271-5131
  Hwy 129 Croton On Hudson (10520) *(G-3808)*
General Sportwear Company Inc (PA) 212 764-5820
  230 W 38th St Fl 4 New York (10018) *(G-9591)*
General Trade Mark La 718 979-7261
  31 Hylan Blvd Apt 14c Staten Island (10305) *(G-14655)*
General Vy-Coat LLC 718 266-6002
  1636 Coney Island Ave 2b Brooklyn (11230) *(G-1882)*
General Welding & Fabg Inc (PA) 716 652-0033
  991 Maple Rd Elma (14059) *(G-4319)*
General Welding & Fabg Inc 585 697-7660
  60 Saginaw Dr Ste 4 Rochester (14623) *(G-13434)*
Generation Power LLC 315 234-2451
  238 W Division St Syracuse (13204) *(G-14903)*
Generic Compositors, Stamford *Also called Stone Crest Industries Inc (G-14609)*
Generic Pharmaceutical Svcs 631 348-6900
  1324 Motor Pkwy Ste 114 Hauppauge (11749) *(G-5658)*
Genesee Building Products LLC 585 548-2726
  7982 Byron Stafford Rd Stafford (14143) *(G-14603)*
Genesee County Express, Hornell *Also called Seneca Media Inc (G-6110)*

Genesee Manufacturing Co Inc................................585 266-3201
  566 Hollenbeck St Rochester (14621) *(G-13435)*
Genesee Metal Products Inc................................585 968-6000
  106 Railroad Ave Wellsville (14895) *(G-15671)*
Genesee Metal Stampings Inc................................585 475-0450
  975 John St West Henrietta (14586) *(G-15795)*
Genesee Plant, Piffard *Also called Arkema Inc (G-12623)*
Genesee Reserve Buffalo LLC................................716 824-3116
  300 Bailey Ave Buffalo (14210) *(G-2774)*
Genesis Digital Imaging Inc................................310 305-7358
  150 Verona St Rochester (14608) *(G-13436)*
Genesis Electl Motor, Woodside *Also called Genesis Electrical Motors (G-16208)*
Genesis Electrical Motors................................718 274-7030
  6010 32nd Ave Woodside (11377) *(G-16208)*
Genesis Machining Corp................................516 377-1197
  725 Brooklyn Ave North Baldwin (11510) *(G-12005)*
Genesis Mannequins USA II Inc................................212 505-6600
  413 W 14th St Ste 209 New York (10014) *(G-9592)*
Genetic Engineering News, New Rochelle *Also called Gen Publishing Inc (G-8335)*
Geneva Granite Co Inc (PA)................................315 789-8142
  272 Border City Rd Geneva (14456) *(G-5155)*
Geneva Healthcare LLC (HQ)................................646 665-2044
  3 Columbus Cir Fl 15 New York (10019) *(G-9593)*
Geneva Printing Company Inc................................315 789-8191
  40 Castle St Geneva (14456) *(G-5156)*
Geneva Watch Company Inc (HQ)................................212 221-1177
  1407 Broadway Rm 400 New York (10018) *(G-9594)*
Genie Fastener Mfg Co, Bohemia *Also called Treo Industries Inc (G-1087)*
Genie Instant Printing Center, New York *Also called Genie Instant Printing Co Inc (G-9595)*
Genie Instant Printing Co Inc................................212 575-8258
  37 W 43rd St New York (10036) *(G-9595)*
Genius Media Group Inc................................509 670-7502
  92 3rd St Brooklyn (11231) *(G-1883)*
Gennaris Itln French Bky Inc................................516 997-8968
  465 Westbury Ave Carle Place (11514) *(G-3174)*
Genoa Sand & Gravel Lnsg................................607 533-4551
  390 Peruville Rd Freeville (13068) *(G-5034)*
Genpak Industries Inc................................518 798-9511
  26 Republic Plz Middletown (10940) *(G-7910)*
Genpak LLC................................845 343-7971
  Republic Plz Middletown (10940) *(G-7911)*
Gentner Precision Components................................315 597-5734
  406 Stafford Rd Palmyra (14522) *(G-12488)*
Genzyme Corporation................................212 698-0300
  521 W 57th St Fl 5 New York (10019) *(G-9596)*
Genzyme Genetics, New York *Also called Genzyme Corporation (G-9596)*
Geo Publishing, New York *Also called Emblaze Systems Inc (G-9358)*
Geoffrey Beene Inc................................212 371-5570
  37 W 57th St Frnt 2 New York (10019) *(G-9597)*
Geometric Circuits Inc................................631 249-0230
  10 Technology Dr Unit 7 East Setauket (11733) *(G-4179)*
Geon Performance Solutions LLC................................888 910-0536
  430 Park Ave Fl 18 New York (10022) *(G-9598)*
Geonex International Corp................................212 473-4555
  200 Park Ave S Ste 920 New York (10003) *(G-9599)*
Geopump Inc................................585 798-6666
  213 State St Medina (14103) *(G-7736)*
Geordie Magee Uphl & Canvas................................315 676-7679
  Weber Rd Brewerton (13029) *(G-1135)*
George Basch Co Inc................................516 378-8100
  1554 Peapond Rd North Bellmore (11710) *(G-12019)*
George Chilson Logging................................607 732-1558
  54 Franklin St Elmira (14904) *(G-4353)*
George Industries LLC (PA)................................607 748-3371
  1 S Page Ave Endicott (13760) *(G-4458)*
George Knitting Mills Corp................................212 242-3300
  116 W 23rd St Fl 4 New York (10011) *(G-9600)*
George Lake Distilling Company................................518 639-1025
  2 Pinecroft Dr Queensbury (12804) *(G-13040)*
George Lederman Inc................................212 753-4556
  515 Madison Ave Rm 1218 New York (10022) *(G-9601)*
George M Dujack................................518 279-1303
  80 Town Office Rd Troy (12180) *(G-15169)*
George Ponte Inc (PA)................................914 243-4202
  500 E Main St Jefferson Valley (10535) *(G-6567)*
George Raum Manufacturing, Central Islip *Also called Gmr Manufacturing Inc (G-3277)*
George Retzos................................315 422-2913
  502 Pearl St Syracuse (13203) *(G-14904)*
Georgia-Pacific Corrugared LLC................................585 343-3800
  4 Etreadeasy Ave Batavia (14020) *(G-615)*
Georgia-Pacific LLC................................518 561-3500
  327 Margaret St Plattsburgh (12901) *(G-12748)*
Georgia-Pacific LLC................................631 924-7401
  319 Yaphank Ave Yaphank (11980) *(G-16262)*
Georgie Kaye, New York *Also called Georgy Creative Fashions Inc (G-9602)*
Georgy Creative Fashions Inc................................212 279-4885
  249 W 29th St New York (10001) *(G-9602)*
Geospatial Systems (HQ)................................585 427-8310
  150 Lucius Gordon Dr # 211 West Henrietta (14586) *(G-15796)*
Geosync Microwave Inc................................631 760-5567
  320 Oser Ave Hauppauge (11788) *(G-5659)*
Geotec, Westbury *Also called Tishcon Corp (G-15931)*

Geotech Associates Ltd................................631 286-0251
  20 Stiriz Rd Brookhaven (11719) *(G-1408)*
Geotechnical Drilling Inc................................516 616-6055
  75 E 2nd St Mineola (11501) *(G-7977)*
Geoweb3d Inc................................607 323-1114
  4104 Vestal Rd Ste 202 Vestal (13850) *(G-15378)*
Gerald McGlone................................518 482-2613
  17 Zoar Ave Colonie (12205) *(G-3574)*
Geritrex LLC................................914 668-4003
  40 Commercial Ave Middletown (10941) *(G-7912)*
Geritrex Holdings Inc (PA)................................914 668-4003
  144 E Kingsbridge Rd Mount Vernon (10550) *(G-8142)*
Gerli & Co Inc................................212 213-1919
  41 Madison Ave Ste 4101 New York (10010) *(G-9603)*
German Machine & Assembly Inc................................585 546-4200
  226 Jay St Rochester (14608) *(G-13437)*
Germanium Corp America Inc................................315 853-4900
  34 Robinson Rd Clinton (13323) *(G-3482)*
Germanow-Simon Corporation................................585 232-1440
  408 Saint Paul St Rochester (14605) *(G-13438)*
Gernatt Asphalt Products Inc (PA)................................716 532-3371
  13870 Taylor Hollow Rd Collins (14034) *(G-3571)*
Gernatt Asphalt Products Inc................................716 496-5111
  Benz Dr Springville (14141) *(G-14591)*
Gernatt Companies, Collins *Also called Gernatt Asphalt Products Inc (G-3571)*
Gerome Technologies Inc................................518 463-1324
  85 Broadway Ste 1 Menands (12204) *(G-7843)*
Gerson & Gerson Inc (PA)................................212 244-6775
  100 W 33rd St Ste 911 New York (10001) *(G-9604)*
Gertrude Hawk Chocolates Inc................................
  21182 Salmon Run Mall Loo Watertown (13601) *(G-15570)*
Ges Ges................................631 291-9624
  89 Cabot Ct Ste A Hauppauge (11788) *(G-5660)*
Get Real Surfaces Inc (PA)................................845 337-4483
  121 Washington St Poughkeepsie (12601) *(G-12957)*
Getec Inc................................845 292-0800
  624 Harris Rd Ferndale (12734) *(G-4789)*
Getinge Group Logistics Ameri................................585 475-1400
  1777 E Henrietta Rd Rochester (14623) *(G-13439)*
Getting The Word Out Inc................................518 891-9352
  36 Church St Apt 106 Saranac Lake (12983) *(G-14158)*
Gevril, Valley Cottage *Also called First Sbf Holding Inc (G-15315)*
GF Packaging LLC (PA)................................716 692-2705
  2727 Broadway Ste 3 Cheektowaga (14227) *(G-3351)*
Gfb Fashions Ltd................................212 239-9230
  463 Fashion Ave Rm 1502 New York (10018) *(G-9605)*
Gfh Orthotic & Prosthetic Labs................................631 467-3725
  161 Keyland Ct Bohemia (11716) *(G-1017)*
Gg Design and Printing................................718 321-3220
  93 Henry St Frnt 1 New York (10002) *(G-9606)*
Ggp Publishing Inc................................914 834-8896
  105 Calvert St Ste 201 Harrison (10528) *(G-5553)*
GH Bass & Co (HQ)................................646 768-4600
  512 7th Ave Fl 28 New York (10018) *(G-9607)*
Gh Induction Atmospheres LLC................................585 368-2120
  35 Industrial Park Cir Rochester (14624) *(G-13440)*
Ghani Textiles Inc................................718 859-4561
  2459 Coyle St Fl 2 Brooklyn (11235) *(G-1884)*
Gharana Industries LLC................................315 651-4004
  61 Swift St Waterloo (13165) *(G-15553)*
Ghostek LLC................................855 310-3439
  140 58th St Ste 2g Brooklyn (11220) *(G-1885)*
Giagni Enterprises LLC................................914 699-6500
  550 S Columbus Ave Mount Vernon (10550) *(G-8143)*
Gianni's Chicken Burgers, Huntington *Also called Moretta Cilento Ltd Lblty Co (G-6214)*
Gibar Inc................................315 452-5656
  7838 Brewerton Rd Cicero (13039) *(G-3420)*
Gibraltar Industries Inc (PA)................................716 826-6500
  3556 Lake Shore Rd # 100 Buffalo (14219) *(G-2775)*
Giclee Unique Apparel, New York *Also called Salsa Professional Apparel LLC (G-11122)*
Gift Valleys.com, Ronkonkoma *Also called Bobley-Harmann Corporation (G-13917)*
Gifts Software Inc................................904 438-6000
  360 Lexington Ave Rm 601 New York (10017) *(G-9608)*
Gild-Rite Inc................................631 752-9000
  51 Carolyn Blvd Farmingdale (11735) *(G-4637)*
Gildan Apparel USA Inc (HQ)................................212 476-0341
  48 W 38th St Fl 8 New York (10018) *(G-9609)*
Gilded Otter Brewing Co................................845 256-1700
  3 Main St New Paltz (12561) *(G-8306)*
Giliberto Designs Inc................................212 695-0216
  142 W 36th St Fl 8 New York (10018) *(G-9610)*
Gillette Creamery, Albany *Also called Phyljohn Distributors Inc (G-115)*
Gillies Coffee Company................................718 499-7766
  150 19th St Brooklyn (11232) *(G-1886)*
Gillinder Brothers Inc................................845 856-5375
  39 Erie St 55 Port Jervis (12771) *(G-12849)*
Gillinder Glass, Port Jervis *Also called Gillinder Brothers Inc (G-12849)*
Gilmores Sound Advice Inc................................212 265-4445
  599 11th Ave Fl 5 New York (10036) *(G-9611)*
Gim Electronics Corp................................516 942-3382
  270 Duffy Ave Ste H Hicksville (11801) *(G-5911)*
Gimbel & Associates, Garden City *Also called H&E Service Corp (G-5101)*

Gina Group LLC..212 947-2445
  10 W 33rd St Ph 3 New York (10001) *(G-9612)*

Gina Hosiery, New York *Also called Gina Group LLC (G-9612)*

Ginny Lee Cafe, Lodi *Also called Wagner Vineyards & Brewing Co (G-7133)*

Giovane Ltd..212 332-7373
  592 5th Ave Ste L New York (10036) *(G-9613)*

Giovane Piranesi, New York *Also called Giovane Ltd (G-9613)*

Giovanni Bakery Corp.......................................212 695-4296
  476 9th Ave New York (10018) *(G-9614)*

Giovanni Food Co Inc (PA)................................315 457-2373
  8800 Sixty Rd Baldwinsville (13027) *(G-548)*

Giuliante Machine Tool Inc...............................914 835-0008
  12 John Walsh Blvd Peekskill (10566) *(G-12551)*

Giulietta LLC..212 334-1859
  649 Morgan Ave Ste 3h Brooklyn (11222) *(G-1887)*

Giumenta Corp (PA)...718 832-1200
  42 2nd Ave Brooklyn (11215) *(G-1888)*

Giumenta Corp...718 832-1200
  42 2nd Ave Brooklyn (11215) *(G-1889)*

Givaudan Fragrances Corp...............................212 649-8800
  40 W 57th St Fl 11 New York (10019) *(G-9615)*

Givi Inc..212 586-5029
  16 W 56th St Fl 4 New York (10019) *(G-9616)*

Gizmo Products Inc..585 301-0970
  2257 County Road 4 Bldg 3 Stanley (14561) *(G-14611)*

GKN Aerospace Monitor Inc.............................562 619-8558
  1000 New Horizons Blvd Amityville (11701) *(G-264)*

GL & RL Logging Inc...518 883-3936
  713 Union Mills Rd Broadalbin (12025) *(G-1174)*

GL&v USA Inc...518 747-2444
  27 Allen St Hudson Falls (12839) *(G-6188)*

Glaceau, New York *Also called Energy Brands Inc (G-9374)*

Glacee Skincare LLC..212 690-7632
  611 W 136th St Apt 4 New York (10031) *(G-9617)*

Gladding Braided Products LLC.......................315 653-7211
  110 County Road 13a South Otselic (13155) *(G-14520)*

Glamour Magazine...212 286-2860
  4 Times Sq Fl 16 New York (10036) *(G-9618)*

Glaro Inc..631 234-1717
  735 Calebs Path Ste 1 Hauppauge (11788) *(G-5661)*

Glasbau Hahn America LLC..............................845 566-3331
  15 Little Brook Ln Ste 2 Newburgh (12550) *(G-11867)*

Glasgow Products Inc.......................................516 374-5937
  886 Lakeside Dr Woodmere (11598) *(G-16191)*

Glass Menagerie Inc...845 754-8344
  1756 Rte 209 Westbrookville (12785) *(G-15859)*

Glassfab Inc..585 262-4000
  257 Ormond St Rochester (14605) *(G-13441)*

Glasson Sculpture Works.................................845 255-2969
  23 Shaft Rd Gardiner (12525) *(G-5129)*

Glassview LLC (PA)...646 844-4922
  25 E 67th St Ph A New York (10065) *(G-9619)*

Glasteel Parts & Services Inc (HQ)..................585 235-1010
  1000 West Ave Rochester (14611) *(G-13442)*

Glaxosmithkline LLC..845 341-7590
  3 Tyler St Montgomery (12549) *(G-8060)*

Glaxosmithkline LLC..845 797-3259
  6 Alpert Dr Wappingers Falls (12590) *(G-15495)*

Glaxosmithkline LLC..585 738-9025
  1177 Winton Rd S Rochester (14618) *(G-13443)*

Glaxosmithkline LLC..716 913-5679
  17 Mahogany Dr Buffalo (14221) *(G-2776)*

Glaxosmithkline LLC..518 239-6901
  3169 Route 145 East Durham (12423) *(G-4102)*

Glaxosmithkline LLC..518 852-9637
  108 Woodfield Blvd Mechanicville (12118) *(G-7692)*

Glaxosmthkline Cnsmr Heathcare, East Durham *Also called Glaxosmithkline LLC (G-4102)*

Gleaner Company Ltd.......................................718 657-0788
  9205 172nd St Fl 2 Jamaica (11433) *(G-6444)*

Gleason Corporation (PA).................................585 473-1000
  1000 University Ave Rochester (14607) *(G-13444)*

Gleason Works (HQ)...585 473-1000
  1000 University Ave Rochester (14607) *(G-13445)*

GLEASON-AVERY, Auburn *Also called John G Rubino Inc (G-482)*

Glen Plaza Marble & Gran Inc...........................516 671-1100
  75 Glen Cove Ave Ste A Glen Cove (11542) *(G-5195)*

Glenda Inc...718 442-8981
  1732 Victory Blvd Staten Island (10314) *(G-14656)*

Glendale Architectural WD Pdts.......................718 326-2700
  7102 80th St Glendale (11385) *(G-5226)*

Glendale Products, Glendale *Also called Glendale Architectural WD Pdts (G-5226)*

Glenn Foods Inc (PA).......................................516 377-1400
  371 S Main St Ste 119-405 Freeport (11520) *(G-4999)*

Glenn Horowitz Bookseller Inc.........................212 691-9100
  20 W 55th St Ph New York (10019) *(G-9620)*

Glenn Wayne Bakery, Bohemia *Also called Glenn Wayne Wholesale Bky Inc (G-1018)*

Glenn Wayne Wholesale Bky Inc......................631 289-9200
  1800 Artic Ave Bohemia (11716) *(G-1018)*

Glenny's, Freeport *Also called Glenn Foods Inc (G-4999)*

Glenridge Fabricators Inc...............................718 456-2297
  7945 77th Ave Glendale (11385) *(G-5227)*

Glens Falls Newspapers Inc.............................518 792-3131
  76 Lawrence St Glens Falls (12801) *(G-5250)*

Glens Falls Printing LLC.................................518 793-0555
  51 Hudson Ave Glens Falls (12801) *(G-5251)*

Glens Falls Ready Mix Inc................................518 793-1695
  112 Big Boom Rd Queensbury (12804) *(G-13041)*

Glenwood Masonry Products, Brooklyn *Also called Superior Block Corp (G-2473)*

Gli-Dex Sales Corp...716 692-6501
  855 Wurlitzer Dr North Tonawanda (14120) *(G-12070)*

Glidden Machine & Tool, North Tonawanda *Also called Gli-Dex Sales Corp (G-12070)*

Gliptone Manufacturing Inc..............................631 285-7250
  1740 Julia Goldbach Ave Ronkonkoma (11779) *(G-13942)*

Glissade New York LLC....................................631 756-4800
  399 Smith St Farmingdale (11735) *(G-4638)*

Glissen Chemical Co Inc (PA)..........................718 436-4200
  1321 58th St Brooklyn (11219) *(G-1890)*

Glitch Inc...866 364-2733
  75 Broad St Ste 1904 New York (10004) *(G-9621)*

Glitner Ticketing, Levittown *Also called Glitnir Ticketing Inc (G-6915)*

Glitnir Ticketing Inc...516 390-5168
  3 Snapdragon Ln Levittown (11756) *(G-6915)*

Glitter, New York *Also called Magic Numbers Inc (G-10326)*

Glitter Slimes LLC..845 772-1113
  51 Greenwich Ave Goshen (10924) *(G-5309)*

Gllusa, Farmingdale *Also called Green Logic Led Elec Sup Inc (G-4641)*

Global Abrasive Products Inc (PA)....................716 438-0047
  62 Mill St Lockport (14094) *(G-7077)*

Global Alliance For Tb.......................................212 227-7540
  40 Wall St Fl 24 New York (10005) *(G-9622)*

Global Alumina Services Co..............................212 309-8060
  277 Park Ave Fl 40 New York (10172) *(G-9623)*

Global Applctions Solution LLC........................212 741-9595
  125 Park Ave Fl 25 New York (10017) *(G-9624)*

Global Brands Inc...845 358-1212
  1031 Route 9w S Nyack (10960) *(G-12144)*

Global Creations, New York *Also called Global Gem Corporation (G-9628)*

Global Entity Media Inc..................................631 580-7772
  2090 5th Ave Ste 2 Ronkonkoma (11779) *(G-13943)*

Global Finance Magazine...................................212 524-3223
  7 E 20th St New York (10003) *(G-9625)*

Global Finance Magazine., New York *Also called Global Finance Media Inc (G-9626)*

Global Finance Magazine., New York *Also called Global Finance Magazine (G-9625)*

Global Finance Media Inc...............................212 447-7900
  7 E 20th St Fl 2 New York (10003) *(G-9626)*

Global Financial Shared Svcs, Seneca Falls *Also called Xylem Inc (G-14375)*

Global Fire Corporation....................................888 320-1799
  244 5th Ave Ste 2238 New York (10001) *(G-9627)*

Global Food Source & Co Inc............................914 320-9615
  114 Carpenter Ave Tuckahoe (10707) *(G-15204)*

Global Gem Corporation....................................212 350-9936
  425 Madison Ave Rm 400 New York (10017) *(G-9628)*

Global Glass Corp...516 681-2309
  134 Woodbury Rd Hicksville (11801) *(G-5912)*

Global Gold Inc (PA)..212 239-4657
  500 7th Ave Fl 17a New York (10018) *(G-9629)*

Global Gold Corporation (PA)...........................914 925-0020
  555 Theodore Fremd Ave C208 Rye (10580) *(G-14079)*

Global Graphics Inc...718 939-4967
  3711 Prince St Ste D Flushing (11354) *(G-4854)*

Global Grind Digital...212 840-9399
  512 Fashion Ave Fl 42 New York (10018) *(G-9630)*

Global Hanger & Display Inc.............................631 475-5900
  14 Hewlett Ave East Patchogue (11772) *(G-4153)*

Global Instrumentation LLC............................315 682-0272
  8104 Cazenovia Rd Ste 2/3 Manlius (13104) *(G-7547)*

Global Lighting Inc..914 591-4095
  201 Saw Mill River Rd 3 Yonkers (10701) *(G-16313)*

Global Marine Power Inc...................................631 208-2933
  221 Scott Ave Calverton (11933) *(G-3081)*

Global Market Development Inc.........................631 667-1000
  200 Executive Dr Ste G Edgewood (11717) *(G-4269)*

Global Packaging Services LLC.........................646 648-0355
  67 Kissam Ln Glen Head (11545) *(G-5206)*

Global Payment Tech Inc..................................516 887-0700
  20 E Sunrise Hwy Valley Stream (11581) *(G-15342)*

Global Payment Tech Inc (PA)..........................631 563-2500
  170 Wilbur Pl Ste 600 Bohemia (11716) *(G-1019)*

Global Plastics LLC..800 417-4605
  21 Downing St Frnt 1 New York (10014) *(G-9631)*

Global Point Technology, Farmington *Also called Hoff Associates Mfg Reps Inc (G-4773)*

Global Precision Inds Inc.................................585 254-0010
  955 Millstead Way Rochester (14624) *(G-13446)*

Global Precision Products, Rush *Also called Gpp Post-Closing Inc (G-14072)*

Global Resources Sg Inc..................................212 686-1411
  267 5th Ave Rm 506 New York (10016) *(G-9632)*

Global Security Tech LLC..................................917 838-4507
  123 Grove Ave Ste 222 Cedarhurst (11516) *(G-3239)*

Global Steel Products Corp (HQ)......................631 586-3455
  95 Marcus Blvd Deer Park (11729) *(G-3878)*

Global Textile, New York *Also called Himatsingka America Inc (G-9788)*

A
L
P
H
A
B
E
T
I
C

Global Tissue Group Inc (PA) 631 924-3019
870 Expressway Dr S Medford (11763) *(G-7708)*
Global Video LLC (HQ) 516 222-2600
1000 Woodbury Rd Ste 1 Woodbury (11797) *(G-16172)*
Globalfoundries US 2 LLC (HQ) 512 457-3900
2070 Route 52 Hopewell Junction (12533) *(G-6094)*
Globalfoundries US Inc 512 457-3900
2070 Route 52 Hopewell Junction (12533) *(G-6095)*
Globalfoundries US Inc 518 305-9013
400 Stone Break Rd Ext Malta (12020) *(G-7495)*
Globalfoundries US Inc 408 462-3900
107 Hermes Rd Ballston Spa (12020) *(G-574)*
Globalquest Solutions Inc 716 601-3524
2813 Wehrle Dr Ste 3 Buffalo (14221) *(G-2777)*
Globe Electronic Hardware Inc 718 457-0303
3424 56th St Woodside (11377) *(G-16209)*
Globe Grinding Corp 631 694-1970
1365 Akron St Copiague (11726) *(G-3655)*
Globe Metallurgical Inc 716 804-0862
3807 Highland Ave Niagara Falls (14305) *(G-11931)*
Globe Specialty Metals, Niagara Falls *Also called Globe Metallurgical Inc (G-11931)*
Globe-Tex, New Rochelle *Also called HB Athletic Inc (G-8340)*
Globe-Tex Apparal, New York *Also called Tbhl International LLC (G-11438)*
Globmarble LLC 347 717-4088
2201 Neptune Ave Ste 5 Brooklyn (11224) *(G-1891)*
Globus Cork Inc 347 963-4059
141 Flushing Ave Brooklyn (11205) *(G-1892)*
Gloede Neon Signs Ltd Inc 845 471-4366
97 N Clinton St Poughkeepsie (12601) *(G-12958)*
Glopak USA Corp (PA) 844 445-6725
35 Engel St Ste B Hicksville (11801) *(G-5913)*
Gloria Apparel Inc 212 947-0869
500 Fashion Ave 8 New York (10018) *(G-9633)*
Glowa Manufacturing Inc 607 770-0811
6 Emma St Binghamton (13905) *(G-880)*
Gluck Orgelbau Inc 212 233-2684
170 Park Row Apt 20a New York (10038) *(G-9634)*
Gluten Free Bake Shop Inc 845 782-5307
19 Industry Dr Mountainville (10953) *(G-8193)*
Glycobia Inc 607 339-0051
33 Thornwood Dr Ste 104 Ithaca (14850) *(G-6382)*
Glyph Production Technologies, Cortland *Also called Technologies Application LLC (G-3790)*
GM Components Holdings LLC 716 439-2237
200 Upper Mountain Rd Lockport (14094) *(G-7078)*
GM Components Holdings LLC 585 647-7000
1000 Lexington Ave Rochester (14606) *(G-13447)*
GM Components Holdings LLC 716 439-2463
200 Upper Mountain Rd Lockport (14094) *(G-7079)*
GM Components Holdings LLC 716 439-2011
200 Upper Mountain Rd # 7 Lockport (14094) *(G-7080)*
GM Components Holdings LLC 716 439-2402
200 Upper Mountain Rd # 10 Lockport (14094) *(G-7081)*
GM Insulation Corp 516 354-6000
1345 Rosser Ave Elmont (11003) *(G-4385)*
GM Palmer Inc 585 492-2990
51 Edward St Arcade (14009) *(G-374)*
GM Pre Cast Products, Jamestown *Also called Suhor Industries Inc (G-6544)*
GM Printing, Maspeth *Also called Grand Meridian Printing Inc (G-7619)*
Gmch Lockport, Lockport *Also called GM Components Holdings LLC (G-7079)*
Gmch Lockport Ptc, Lockport *Also called GM Components Holdings LLC (G-7078)*
Gmch Rochester, Rochester *Also called GM Components Holdings LLC (G-13447)*
Gmd Industries Inc 718 445-8779
12920 18th Ave College Point (11356) *(G-3543)*
Gmd Shipyard Corp (PA) 718 260-9202
Brooklyn Navy Yard 276 Brooklyn (11205) *(G-1893)*
Gmp LLC 914 939-0571
47 Purdy Ave Port Chester (10573) *(G-12821)*
Gmr Manufacturing Inc 631 582-2600
101 Windsor Pl Unit D Central Islip (11722) *(G-3277)*
Gms Hicks Street Corporation 718 858-1010
214 Hicks St Brooklyn (11201) *(G-1894)*
Gn Printing 718 784-1713
4216 34th Ave Long Island City (11101) *(G-7231)*
Gncc Capital Inc (PA) 702 951-9793
244 5th Ave Ste 2525 New York (10001) *(G-9635)*
Go Blue Technologies Ltd 631 404-6285
325 August Rd North Babylon (11703) *(G-12001)*
Go Go Apple Inc 646 264-8909
4126 Benham St Elmhurst (11373) *(G-4335)*
Go Mobo, New York *Also called Mobo Systems Inc (G-10487)*
Go Veggie, Albany *Also called Galaxy Nutritional Foods Inc (G-79)*
Gocare247, Brooklyn *Also called Mdcare911 LLC (G-2128)*
Goddard Design Co 718 599-0170
51 Nassau Ave Ste 1b Brooklyn (11222) *(G-1895)*
Godiva Chocolatier Inc (HQ) 212 984-5900
333 W 34th St Fl 6 New York (10001) *(G-9636)*
Goergen-Mackwirth Co Inc 716 874-4800
765 Hertel Ave Buffalo (14207) *(G-2778)*
Gogo Jeans Inc 212 944-2391
1407 Broadway Rm 1801 New York (10018) *(G-9637)*
Gogo Squeez, New York *Also called Materne North America Corp (G-10383)*
Gold & Diamonds Wholesale Outl 718 438-7888
4417 5th Ave Brooklyn (11220) *(G-1896)*
Gold Mark Mfg Co, Brooklyn *Also called Goldmark Inc (G-1899)*
Gold Medal Packing Inc 315 337-1911
8301 Old River Rd Oriskany (13424) *(G-12391)*
Gold Pride Press Inc 585 224-8800
12 Pixley Industrial Pkwy # 40 Rochester (14624) *(G-13448)*
Goldarama Company Inc 212 730-7299
56 W 45th St Ste 1504 New York (10036) *(G-9638)*
Goldberger Company LLC (PA) 212 924-1194
36 W 25th St Fl 17 New York (10010) *(G-9639)*
Goldberger International, New York *Also called Goldberger Company LLC (G-9639)*
Golden Argosy LLC (PA) 212 268-0003
225 W 34th St Ste 1106 New York (10122) *(G-9640)*
Golden Artist Colors Inc 607 847-6154
188 Bell Rd New Berlin (13411) *(G-8222)*
Golden Chocolate Inc 718 330-1000
590 Smith St Brooklyn (11231) *(G-1897)*
Golden Eagle Marketing LLC 212 726-1242
244 5th Ave New York (10001) *(G-9641)*
Golden Egret LLC 516 922-2839
38 Cord Pl East Norwich (11732) *(G-4152)*
Golden Glow Cookie Co Inc 718 379-6223
1844 Givan Ave Bronx (10469) *(G-1267)*
Golden Group International Ltd 845 440-1025
305 Quaker Rd Patterson (12563) *(G-12517)*
Golden Integrity Inc 212 764-6753
37 W 47th St Ste 1601 New York (10036) *(G-9642)*
Golden Leaves Knitwear Inc 718 875-8235
43 Hall St Ste B3 Brooklyn (11205) *(G-1898)*
Golden Legacy Ilstrd Histry, Yonkers *Also called Fitzgerald Publishing Co Inc (G-16309)*
Golden Renewable Energy LLC 914 920-9800
430 Nepperhan Ave Yonkers (10701) *(G-16314)*
Golden Taste Inc 845 356-4133
318 Roosevelt Ave Spring Valley (10977) *(G-14571)*
Goldmark Inc 718 438-0295
3611 14th Ave Ste B01 Brooklyn (11218) *(G-1899)*
Goldmark Products Inc 631 777-3343
855 Conklin St Ste D Farmingdale (11735) *(G-4639)*
Goldmont Enterprises Inc 212 947-3633
7603 Caldwell Ave Middle Village (11379) *(G-7878)*
Goldsmith, Binghamton *Also called Mellem Corporation (G-897)*
Goldstar Lighting LLC 646 543-6811
1407 Broadway Fl 30 New York (10018) *(G-9643)*
Golf Directories USA Inc 516 365-5351
39 Orchard St Ste 7 Manhasset (11030) *(G-7535)*
Golf Odyssey, New York *Also called Maven Marketing LLC (G-10387)*
Golfing Magazine 516 822-5446
22 W Nicholai St Ste 200 Hicksville (11801) *(G-5914)*
Golos Printing Inc 607 732-1896
110 E 9th St Elmira Heights (14903) *(G-4377)*
Golub Corporation 518 943-3903
320 W Bridge St Catskill (12414) *(G-3211)*
Golub Corporation 518 899-6063
3 Hemphill Pl Ste 116 Malta (12020) *(G-7496)*
Golub Corporation 315 363-0679
142 Genesee St Oneida (13421) *(G-12244)*
Golub Corporation 607 336-2588
5631 State Highway 12 Norwich (13815) *(G-12122)*
Golub Corporation 518 583-3697
3045 Route 50 Saratoga Springs (12866) *(G-14177)*
Golub Corporation 518 822-0076
351 Fairview Ave Ste 3 Hudson (12534) *(G-6158)*
Golub Corporation 845 344-0327
511 Schutt Road Ext Middletown (10940) *(G-7913)*
Gone South Concrete Block Inc 315 598-2141
2809 State Route 3 Fulton (13069) *(G-5062)*
Good Bread Bakery 914 939-3900
33 New Broad St Ste 1 Port Chester (10573) *(G-12822)*
Good Earth Inc 716 684-8111
5960 Broadway St Lancaster (14086) *(G-6808)*
Good Earth Organics Corp (PA) 716 684-8111
5960 Broadway St Lancaster (14086) *(G-6809)*
Good Health Healthcare Newsppr 585 421-8109
106 Cobblestone Court Dr Victor (14564) *(G-15411)*
Good Home Co Inc 212 352-1509
132 W 24th St New York (10011) *(G-9644)*
Good Noodles Inc 518 731-7278
25 Vermilyea Ln West Coxsackie (12192) *(G-15759)*
Good Show Sportswear, New York *Also called Good Show Sportwear Inc (G-9645)*
Good Show Sportwear Inc 212 334-8751
132 Mulberry St 3 New York (10013) *(G-9645)*
Good-O-Beverage Inc 718 328-6400
1801 Boone Ave Bronx (10460) *(G-1268)*
Gooding & Associates Inc 631 749-3313
15 Dinah Rock Rd Shelter Island (11964) *(G-14386)*
Gooding Co Inc 716 266-6252
5568 Davison Rd Lockport (14094) *(G-7082)*
Goodman Main Stopper Mfg Co 718 875-5140
523 Atlantic Ave Brooklyn (11217) *(G-1900)*
Goodnature Products Inc 800 875-3381
149 Bud Mil Dr Buffalo (14206) *(G-2779)*

Goodrich Corporation 315 838-1200
104 Otis St Rome (13441) *(G-13849)*

Goodwill Inds of Greater NY 914 621-0781
80 Route 6 Unit 605 Baldwin Place (10505) *(G-538)*

Gorbel Inc (PA) 585 924-6262
600 Fishers Run Fishers (14453) *(G-4796)*

Gorden Automotive Equipment 716 674-2700
60 N America Dr West Seneca (14224) *(G-15849)*

Gordon Fire Equipment LLC 845 691-5700
3199 Us Highway 9w Highland (12528) *(G-5959)*

Gordon S Anderson Mfg Co 845 677-3304
215 N Mabbettsville Rd Millbrook (12545) *(G-7942)*

Gorga Fehren Fine Jewelry LLC 646 861-3595
153 E 88th St New York (10128) *(G-9646)*

Goshen Quarry, Goshen Also called Tilcon New York Inc *(G-5314)*

Got Power Inc 631 767-9493
5 Campus Ln Ronkonkoma (11779) *(G-13944)*

Got Wood 315 405-3384
5748 W Main St Constableville (13325) *(G-3634)*

Gotenna Inc 718 360-4988
81 Willoughby St Fl 4 Brooklyn (11201) *(G-1901)*

Gotham City Industries Inc (PA) 914 713-3449
372 Fort Hill Rd Scarsdale (10583) *(G-14236)*

Gotham Diamonds, New York Also called American Originals Corporation *(G-8557)*

Gotham Energy 360 LLC 917 338-1023
48 Wall St Fl 5 New York (10005) *(G-9647)*

Gotham Ink & Color Co Inc 845 947-4000
19 Holt Dr Stony Point (10980) *(G-14744)*

Gotham T-Shirt Corp 516 676-0900
211 Glen Cove Ave Unit 5 Sea Cliff (11579) *(G-14345)*

Gotham Veterinary Center PC 212 222-1900
700 Columbus Ave Frnt 5 New York (10025) *(G-9648)*

Gothic Cabinet Craft Inc (PA) 347 881-1420
5877 57th St Maspeth (11378) *(G-7618)*

Gottlieb & Sons Inc 212 575-1907
21 W 47th St Fl 4 New York (10036) *(G-9649)*

Gottlieb Jewelery Mfg, New York Also called Gottlieb & Sons Inc *(G-9649)*

Gottlieb Schwartz Family 718 761-2010
724 Collfield Ave Staten Island (10314) *(G-14657)*

Goulds Pumps Incorporated, Seneca Falls Also called Goulds Pumps LLC *(G-14362)*

Goulds Pumps LLC (HQ) 315 568-2811
240 Fall St Seneca Falls (13148) *(G-14362)*

Goulds Pumps LLC 315 568-2811
280 Fall St Seneca Falls (13148) *(G-14363)*

Gourmet Boutique LLC (PA) 718 977-1200
14402 158th St Jamaica (11434) *(G-6445)*

Gourmet Connection, Baldwinsville Also called Capco Marketing *(G-544)*

Gourmet Crafts Inc 718 372-0505
152 Highlawn Ave Brooklyn (11223) *(G-1902)*

Gourmet Factory Inc 631 231-4548
55 Corporate Dr Hauppauge (11788) *(G-5662)*

Gourmet Toast Corp 718 852-4536
345 Park Ave Brooklyn (11205) *(G-1903)*

Gourmia, Brooklyn Also called Steelstone Group LLC *(G-2459)*

Government Data Publication 347 789-8719
1661 Mcdonald Ave Brooklyn (11230) *(G-1904)*

Gowanda - Bti LLC 716 492-4081
7426a Tanner Pkwy Arcade (14009) *(G-375)*

Goya Foods Inc 716 549-0076
200 S Main St Angola (14006) *(G-359)*

Goya Foods Great Lakes, Angola Also called Goya Foods Inc *(G-359)*

Goyard Inc (HQ) 212 813-0005
20 E 63rd St New York (10065) *(G-9650)*

Goyard Miami LLC (HQ) 212 813-0005
20 E 63rd St New York (10065) *(G-9651)*

Goyard NM Beverly Hills LLC 212 355-3872
20 E 63rd St New York (10065) *(G-9652)*

Goyard US, New York Also called Goyard Inc *(G-9650)*

Gpc International Inc (PA) 631 752-9600
510 Broadhollow Rd # 205 Melville (11747) *(G-7786)*

Gpi Equipment Company, Jefferson Valley Also called George Ponte Inc *(G-6567)*

GPM Associates LLC 585 335-3940
10 Forbes St Dansville (14437) *(G-3819)*

GPM Associates LLC 585 359-1770
45 High Tech Dr Ste 100 Rush (14543) *(G-14071)*

Gpp Post-Closing Inc 585 334-4640
90 High Tech Dr Rush (14543) *(G-14072)*

Gpsi, Hauppauge Also called Generic Pharmaceutical Svcs *(G-5658)*

Gpt, Bohemia Also called Global Payment Tech Inc *(G-1019)*

Gq Magazine 212 286-2860
4 Times Sq Fl 9 New York (10036) *(G-9653)*

Grace Associates Inc 718 767-9000
470 West St Harrison (10528) *(G-5554)*

Grace Love Inc 646 402-4325
202 Atlantic Ave Ste C Garden City Park (11040) *(G-5121)*

Grace Ryan & Magnus Mllwk LLC 914 665-0902
17 N Bleeker St Mount Vernon (10550) *(G-8144)*

Grace Wheeler 716 483-1254
118 E 1st St Jamestown (14701) *(G-6513)*

Gradian Health Systems Inc 212 537-0340
915 Broadway Ste 1001 New York (10010) *(G-9654)*

Gradient Lens Corporation 585 235-2620
207 Tremont St Ste 1 Rochester (14608) *(G-13449)*

Grado Group Inc 718 556-4200
66 Willow Ave Staten Island (10305) *(G-14658)*

Grado Laboratories Inc 718 435-5340
4614 7th Ave Ste 1 Brooklyn (11220) *(G-1905)*

Gradual LLC 347 293-0974
1040 46th Ave Fl 2 Long Island City (11101) *(G-7232)*

Grafconect Corp 212 714-1795
575 8th Ave Rm 1902 New York (10018) *(G-9655)*

Graham Corporation (PA) 585 343-2216
20 Florence Ave Batavia (14020) *(G-616)*

Grainful, Ithaca Also called Beetnpath LLC *(G-6364)*

Gramco Inc (PA) 716 592-2845
299 Waverly St Springville (14141) *(G-14592)*

Gramercy Designs Inc 201 919-8570
287 Park Ave S Fl 2 New York (10010) *(G-9656)*

Gramercy Jewelry Mfg Corp 212 268-0461
35 W 45th St Fl 5 New York (10036) *(G-9657)*

Granada Electronics Inc 718 387-1157
485 Kent Ave Brooklyn (11249) *(G-1906)*

Grand Central Publishing (HQ) 212 364-1200
1290 Ave Of The Americas New York (10104) *(G-9658)*

Grand Island Animal Hospital 716 773-7645
2323 Whitehaven Rd Grand Island (14072) *(G-5332)*

Grand Island Research & Dev, Grand Island Also called Grand Island Animal Hospital *(G-5332)*

Grand Knitting Mills Inc (PA) 631 226-5000
7050 New Horizons Blvd # 1 Amityville (11701) *(G-265)*

Grand Maes Cntry Naturals LLC 212 348-8171
340 E 93rd St Apt 30h New York (10128) *(G-9659)*

Grand Meridian Printing Inc 718 937-3888
5877 57th St Maspeth (11378) *(G-7619)*

Grand Prix Litho Inc 631 242-4182
400 Oser Ave Ste 2300 Hauppauge (11788) *(G-5663)*

Grand Slam Holdings LLC (HQ) 212 583-5000
345 Park Ave Bsmt Lb4 New York (10154) *(G-9660)*

Grand Slam Safety LLC 315 301-4039
9793 Bridge St Croghan (13327) *(G-3802)*

Grand Visual LLC 912 529-6215
188 Broadway Brooklyn (11211) *(G-1907)*

Grandeur Creations Inc 212 643-1277
146 W 29th St Rm 9e New York (10001) *(G-9661)*

Grandma Browns Beans Inc 315 963-7221
5837 Scenic Ave Mexico (13114) *(G-7866)*

Grandview Block & Supply Co 518 346-7981
1705 Hamburg St Schenectady (12304) *(G-14274)*

Grandview Concrete Corp 518 346-7981
1705 Hamburg St Schenectady (12304) *(G-14275)*

Granite Shop, Newburgh Also called Affordble Gran Cbntry Outl Inc *(G-11857)*

Granite Tops Inc 914 699-2909
716 S Columbus Ave Mount Vernon (10550) *(G-8145)*

Granite Works LLC 607 565-7012
133 William Donnelly Waverly (14892) *(G-15621)*

Granny's Kitchens, Frankfort Also called Maplehurst Bakeries LLC *(G-4953)*

Grant Graphics LLC 518 583-2818
610 Maple Ave Saratoga Springs (12866) *(G-14178)*

Grant Hamilton (PA) 716 652-0320
710 Main St East Aurora (14052) *(G-4089)*

Grant's Interest Rate Observer, New York Also called Grants Financial Publishing *(G-9663)*

Grant-Noren 845 726-4281
83 Ridge Rd Westtown (10998) *(G-15966)*

Grantoo LLC 646 356-0460
60 Broad St Ste 3502 New York (10004) *(G-9662)*

Grants Financial Publishing 212 809-7994
233 Broadway Fl 24 New York (10279) *(G-9663)*

Granville Glass & Granite 518 812-0492
131 Revere Rd Hudson Falls (12839) *(G-6189)*

Graph-Tex Inc 607 756-7791
46 Elm St Cortland (13045) *(G-3767)*

Graph-Tex Inc (PA) 607 756-1875
24 Court St Cortland (13045) *(G-3768)*

Graphalloy, Yonkers Also called Graphite Metallizing Corp *(G-16315)*

Graphic Cntrls Acqisition Corp (HQ) 716 853-7500
400 Exchange St Buffalo (14204) *(G-2780)*

Graphic Concepts, Plainview Also called Steval Graphics Concepts Inc *(G-12716)*

Graphic Connections, Geneva Also called Tramwell Inc *(G-5164)*

Graphic Controls Holdings Inc (HQ) 716 853-7500
400 Exchange St Buffalo (14204) *(G-2781)*

Graphic Design U S A, New York Also called American Graphic Design Awards *(G-8550)*

Graphic Fabrications Inc 516 763-3222
488a Sunrise Hwy Rockville Centre (11570) *(G-13828)*

Graphic For Industry, New York Also called Graphics For Industry Inc *(G-9665)*

Graphic Image Associates LLC 631 249-9600
305 Spagnoli Rd Melville (11747) *(G-7787)*

Graphic Lab Inc 212 682-1815
228 E 45th St Fl 4 New York (10017) *(G-9664)*

Graphic Management Partners, Port Chester Also called Gmp LLC *(G-12821)*

Graphic Printing 718 701-4433
2376 Jerome Ave Bronx (10468) *(G-1269)*

A
L
P
H
A
B
E
T
I
C

Graphic Signs & Awnings Ltd..........718 227-6000
165 Industrial Loop Ste 1 Staten Island (10309) ***(G-14659)***
Graphicomm Inc..........716 283-0830
7703 Niagara Falls Blvd Niagara Falls (14304) ***(G-11932)***
Graphics 247 Corp..........718 729-2470
4402 23rd St Ste 113 Long Island City (11101) ***(G-7233)***
Graphics For Industry Inc..........212 889-6202
307 W 36th St Fl 10 New York (10018) ***(G-9665)***
Graphics Plus Printing Inc..........607 299-0500
215 S Main St Cortland (13045) ***(G-3769)***
Graphics Service Bureau Inc (PA)..........212 684-3600
3030 47th Ave Ste 535 Long Island City (11101) ***(G-7234)***
Graphics Slution Providers Inc (PA)..........845 677-5088
115 Barmore Rd Lagrangeville (12540) ***(G-6748)***
Graphis Inc..........212 532-9387
389 5th Ave Rm 1105 New York (10016) ***(G-9666)***
Graphite Metallizing Corp (PA)..........914 968-8400
1050 Nepperhan Ave Yonkers (10703) ***(G-16315)***
Graphitek Inc..........518 686-5966
4883 State Route 67 Hoosick Falls (12090) ***(G-6083)***
Graphtex A Div of Htc, Utica *Also called Human Technologies Corporation* ***(G-15273)***
Grass Roots Juicery..........718 486-2838
336a Graham Ave Brooklyn (11211) ***(G-1908)***
Gratitude & Company Inc..........607 277-3188
215 N Cayuga St Ste 71 Ithaca (14850) ***(G-6383)***
Graver Technologies LLC..........585 624-1330
300 W Main St Honeoye Falls (14472) ***(G-6072)***
Gravity East Village Inc..........212 388-9788
515 E 5th St New York (10009) ***(G-9667)***
Gravymaster Inc..........203 453-1893
101 Erie Blvd Canajoharie (13317) ***(G-3120)***
Gray Glass Inc..........718 217-2943
21744 98th Ave Ste C Queens Village (11429) ***(G-13020)***
Gray Manufacturing Inds LLC..........607 281-1325
6258 Ice House Rd Hornell (14843) ***(G-6108)***
Grayers America Inc..........310 953-2742
304 Bleecker St Frnt 1 New York (10014) ***(G-9668)***
Grayhawk Leasing LLC (HQ)..........914 767-6000
1 Pepsi Way Somers (10589) ***(G-14498)***
Graymont Materials Inc..........518 561-5200
111 Quarry Rd Plattsburgh (12901) ***(G-12749)***
Graywood Companies Inc..........585 738-8889
1001 Lexington Ave Ste 3 Rochester (14606) ***(G-13450)***
Grc, Hempstead *Also called General Refining & Semlt Corp* ***(G-5836)***
Great 4 Image Inc..........518 424-2058
5 Forest Hills Blvd Rensselaer (12144) ***(G-13088)***
Great Adirondack Yarn Company..........518 843-3381
950 County Highway 126 Amsterdam (12010) ***(G-329)***
Great American Awning & Patio..........518 899-2300
43 Round Lake Rd Ballston Spa (12020) ***(G-575)***
Great American Bicycle LLC..........518 584-8100
41 Geyser Rd Saratoga Springs (12866) ***(G-14179)***
Great American Dessert Co LLC..........718 894-3494
5842 Maurice Ave Maspeth (11378) ***(G-7620)***
Great American Industries Inc (HQ)..........607 729-9331
300 Plaza Dr Vestal (13850) ***(G-15379)***
Great Arrow Graphics, Buffalo *Also called Massimo Friedman Inc* ***(G-2862)***
Great ATL Pr-Cast Con Statuary..........718 948-5677
225 Ellis St Staten Island (10307) ***(G-14660)***
Great Brands of Europe Inc..........914 872-8804
100 Hillside Ave Fl 3 White Plains (10603) ***(G-16010)***
Great China Empire, New York *Also called Gce International Inc* ***(G-9580)***
Great Dane Parent LLC (PA)..........518 810-0700
201 Fuller Rd Fl 6 Albany (12203) ***(G-81)***
Great Eastern Color Lith (PA)..........845 454-7420
46 Violet Ave Poughkeepsie (12601) ***(G-12959)***
Great Eastern Pasta Works LLC..........631 956-0889
385 Sheffield Ave West Babylon (11704) ***(G-15713)***
Great Impressions, South Dayton *Also called Cherry Creek Woodcraft Inc* ***(G-14506)***
Great Lakes Cheese NY Inc..........315 232-4511
23 Phelps St Adams (13605) ***(G-2)***
Great Lakes Gear Co Inc..........716 694-0715
126 E Niagara St Ste 2 Tonawanda (14150) ***(G-15106)***
Great Lakes Metal Treating..........716 694-1240
300 E Niagara St Tonawanda (14150) ***(G-15107)***
Great Lakes Orthpd Labs Inc..........716 893-4116
1031 Main St Buffalo (14203) ***(G-2782)***
Great Lakes Plastics Co Inc..........716 896-3100
2371 Broadway St Buffalo (14212) ***(G-2783)***
Great Lakes Pressed Steel Corp..........716 885-4037
1400 Niagara St Buffalo (14213) ***(G-2784)***
Great Lakes Specialites..........716 672-4622
9491 Route 60 Fredonia (14063) ***(G-4970)***
Great Lakes Technologies, Liverpool *Also called Scapa North America* ***(G-7039)***
Great Life Elixirs LLC..........332 204-1953
244 5th Ave Unit F177 New York (10001) ***(G-9669)***
Great Northern Printing Co, Potsdam *Also called Randy Sixberry* ***(G-12940)***
Great Rock Automation Inc..........631 270-1508
99 Rome St Farmingdale (11735) ***(G-4640)***
Great Shoes Inc..........718 813-1945
72 Bridge Rd Islandia (11749) ***(G-6333)***
Great Universal Corp..........917 302-0065
1441 Broadway Ste 6066 New York (10018) ***(G-9670)***
Great Wall Corp..........212 704-4372
4727 36th St Long Island City (11101) ***(G-7235)***
Great Western Malting Co..........800 496-7732
16 Beeman Way Champlain (12919) ***(G-3312)***
Greatbatch Medical, Alden *Also called Integer Holdings Corporation* ***(G-171)***
Greatbatch Medical, Clarence *Also called Precimed Inc* ***(G-3440)***
Greater Niagara Newspaper, Medina *Also called Gannett Stllite Info Ntwrk Inc* ***(G-7735)***
Greek Nat Hrald Dily Nwsppr In, Long Island City *Also called National Herald Inc* ***(G-7303)***
Green Amazon LLC..........585 300-1319
75 S Clinton Ave Ste 510 Rochester (14604) ***(G-13451)***
Green Apple Courage Inc..........716 614-4673
374 Delaware Ave Ste 240 Buffalo (14202) ***(G-2785)***
Green Beacon Solutions LLC..........617 485-5000
875 Ave Of The Amer Fl 20 New York (10001) ***(G-9671)***
Green Buffalo Fuel LLC..........716 768-0600
720 Riverview Blvd Tonawanda (14150) ***(G-15108)***
Green Conveyor & Mch Group LLC..........607 692-7050
8300 State Route 79 Whitney Point (13862) ***(G-16106)***
Green Earth Enterprise, New York *Also called Earth Enterprises Inc* ***(G-9301)***
Green Energy Concepts Inc..........845 238-2574
37 Elkay Dr Ste 51 Chester (10918) ***(G-3379)***
Green Enviro Machine LLC..........407 461-6412
2366 Algonquin Rd Schenectady (12309) ***(G-14276)***
Green Girl Prtg & Msgnr Inc..........212 575-0357
44 W 39th St New York (10018) ***(G-9672)***
Green Island Power Authority..........518 273-0661
20 Clinton St Green Island (12183) ***(G-5436)***
Green Logic Led Elec Sup Inc (PA)..........516 280-2854
75 Marine St Farmingdale (11735) ***(G-4641)***
Green Mountain Graphics, Sunnyside *Also called Eastern Concepts Ltd* ***(G-14772)***
Green Prosthetics & Orthotics..........716 484-1088
1290 E 2nd St Jamestown (14701) ***(G-6514)***
Green Renewable Inc..........518 658-2233
28 Taylor Ave Berlin (12022) ***(G-824)***
Green Valley Foods LLC..........315 926-4280
3736 S Main St Marion (14505) ***(G-7569)***
Green Wave International Inc..........718 499-3371
5423 1st Ave Brooklyn (11220) ***(G-1909)***
Green Zone Food Service Inc..........917 709-1728
9906 Christie Ave 3a Corona (11368) ***(G-3739)***
Greenbeads Llc..........212 327-2765
220 E 72nd St Apt 17d New York (10021) ***(G-9673)***
Greenbush Tape & Label Inc..........518 465-2389
40 Broadway Unit 31 Albany (12202) ***(G-82)***
Greene Brass & Alum Fndry LLC..........607 656-4204
51971 State Highway 10 Bloomville (13739) ***(G-954)***
Greene Brass & Aluminum Fndry, Greene *Also called American Blade Mfg LLC* ***(G-5443)***
Greene Lumber Co LP..........607 278-6101
16991 State Highway 23 Davenport (13750) ***(G-3821)***
Greene Technologies Inc..........607 656-4166
Grand & Clinton St Greene (13778) ***(G-5446)***
Greenebuild LLC..........917 562-0556
390a Lafayette Ave Brooklyn (11238) ***(G-1910)***
Greenfield Die Casting Corp..........516 623-9230
99 Doxsee Dr Freeport (11520) ***(G-5000)***
Greenfield Industries Inc..........516 623-9230
99 Doxsee Dr Freeport (11520) ***(G-5001)***
Greenfield Manufacturing Inc..........518 581-2368
25 Freedom Way Saratoga Springs (12866) ***(G-14180)***
Greenfield Martin Clothiers, Brooklyn *Also called Martin Greenfield Clothiers* ***(G-2120)***
Greengale Publishing, New York *Also called Niche Media Holdings LLC* ***(G-10621)***
Greenkissny Inc..........914 304-4323
75 S Broadway White Plains (10601) ***(G-16011)***
Greenleaf Cabinet Makers LLC..........315 432-4600
6691 Pickard Dr Syracuse (13211) ***(G-14905)***
Greenpac Mill LLC (HQ)..........716 299-0560
4400 Royal Ave Niagara Falls (14303) ***(G-11933)***
Greentree Pharmacy Inc..........718 768-2700
291 7th Ave Brooklyn (11215) ***(G-1911)***
Greenvale Bagel Inc..........516 221-8221
3060 Merrick Rd Wantagh (11793) ***(G-15484)***
Greenville Local, Ravena *Also called Bleezarde Publishing Inc* ***(G-13067)***
Greenway Cabinetry Inc..........516 877-0009
485 Willis Ave Williston Park (11596) ***(G-16147)***
Greenwood Winery LLC..........315 432-8132
6475 Collamer Rd East Syracuse (13057) ***(G-4213)***
Gregg Sadwick, Rochester *Also called Jml Optical Industries LLC* ***(G-13492)***
Gregson-Clark, Caledonia *Also called Rhett M Clark Inc* ***(G-3072)***
Greif Inc..........716 836-4200
2122 Colvin Blvd Tonawanda (14150) ***(G-15109)***
Greno Industries Inc..........518 393-4195
2820 Amsterdam Rd Scotia (12302) ***(G-14330)***
Gresham Technologies (us) Inc..........646 943-5955
11 Park Pl Fl 3 New York (10007) ***(G-9674)***
Grey House Publishing Inc (PA)..........518 789-8700
4919 Route 22 Amenia (12501) ***(G-202)***
Grey State Apparel LLC..........212 255-4216
305 7th Ave Rm 13a New York (10001) ***(G-9675)***

Greyline Signs Inc 716 947-4526
6681 Schuyler Dr Derby (14047) **(G-4005)**
Greyston Bakery Inc 914 375-1510
104 Alexander St Yonkers (10701) **(G-16316)**
Griffin Chemical Company LLC 716 693-2465
889 Erie Ave Ste 1 North Tonawanda (14120) **(G-12071)**
Griffin Manufacturing Company 585 265-1991
1656 Ridge Rd Webster (14580) **(G-15641)**
Griffon Corporation (PA) 212 957-5000
712 5th Ave Fl 18 New York (10019) **(G-9676)**
Grillbot LLC 646 258-5639
401 E 81st St Ste Ph-A New York (10028) **(G-9677)**
Grillmaster Inc 718 272-9191
15314 83rd St Apt 1 Howard Beach (11414) **(G-6140)**
Grimble Bakery, Bronx Also called Miss Grimble Associates Inc **(G-1316)**
Grind 646 558-3250
1216 Broadway Fl 2 New York (10001) **(G-9678)**
Grinnell Designs Ltd 212 391-5277
260 W 39th St Rm 302 New York (10018) **(G-9679)**
Grit Energy Services Inc (PA) 212 701-4500
100 Wall St Fl 11 New York (10005) **(G-9680)**
Grohe America Inc 212 206-8820
160 5th Ave Fl 4 New York (10010) **(G-9681)**
Grolier International Inc (HQ) 212 343-6100
557 Broadway New York (10012) **(G-9682)**
Grom Columbus LLC 212 974-3444
1796 Broadway New York (10019) **(G-9683)**
Grossglockner Inc 585 266-4960
2640 Brickyard Rd Canandaigua (14424) **(G-3134)**
Grosso Materials Inc 845 361-5211
90 Collabar Rd Montgomery (12549) **(G-8061)**
Group Commerce Inc (PA) 646 346-0598
902 Broadway Fl 6 New York (10010) **(G-9684)**
Group International LLC 718 475-8805
14711 34th Ave Flushing (11354) **(G-4855)**
Groupe 16sur20 LLC (PA) 212 625-1620
198 Bowery New York (10012) **(G-9685)**
Grover Cleveland Press Inc 716 564-2222
2676 Sweet Home Rd Amherst (14228) **(G-226)**
Grow Computer Inc 646 535-2037
448 15th St Apt 1r Brooklyn (11215) **(G-1912)**
Grownbeans Inc 212 989-3486
110 Bank St Apt 2j New York (10014) **(G-9686)**
Growtech Industries LLC (PA) 315 335-9692
3100 Lake Shore Rd Buffalo (14219) **(G-2786)**
Grphics Grafek, Syracuse Also called Matt Industries Inc **(G-14938)**
Gruber Display Co Inc 718 882-8220
3920g Merritt Ave Bronx (10466) **(G-1270)**
Grumman Field Support Services 516 575-0574
S Oyster Bay Rd Bethpage (11714) **(G-835)**
Gruner + Jahr Prtg & Pubg Co 212 463-1000
110 5th Ave Fl 7 New York (10011) **(G-9687)**
Gruner + Jahr USA Group Inc (PA) 866 323-9336
1745 Broadway Fl 16 New York (10019) **(G-9688)**
Gruner Jahr USA Publishing Div, New York Also called Gruner + Jahr USA Group Inc **(G-9688)**
Grunt Apparel Inc 646 878-6171
105 Duane St Apt 7c New York (10007) **(G-9689)**
Gryphon Sensors LLC 315 452-8882
5801 E Taft Rd North Syracuse (13212) **(G-12044)**
Gs Communications USA, Brooklyn Also called G S Communications USA Inc **(G-1874)**
Gsa Upstate NY (PA) 631 244-5744
755 Montauk Hwy Oakdale (11769) **(G-12152)**
Gsb Digital, Long Island City Also called Graphics Service Bureau Inc **(G-7234)**
Gschwind Group, Patchogue Also called Suffolk McHy & Pwr Tl Corp **(G-12512)**
Gscp Emax Acquisition LLC 212 902-1000
85 Broad St New York (10004) **(G-9690)**
GSE Composites Inc 631 389-1300
110 Oser Ave Hauppauge (11788) **(G-5664)**
Gsn Government Security News, Massapequa Park Also called World Business Media LLC **(G-7662)**
Gsp Components Inc 585 436-3377
1190 Brooks Ave Rochester (14624) **(G-13452)**
Gt Innovations LLC 585 739-7659
7674 Swamp Rd Bergen (14416) **(G-814)**
Gt Machine & Tool, Long Island City Also called Cnc Manufacturing Corp **(G-7187)**
Gt Parts & Services, Clifton Park Also called Worldwide Gas Turbine Pdts Inc **(G-3478)**
GTM Alap Inc 833 345-2748
2835 86th St Brooklyn (11223) **(G-1913)**
Guaranteed Printing Svc Co Inc 212 929-2410
4710 33rd St Long Island City (11101) **(G-7236)**
Guaranteed Returns, Holbrook Also called Devos Ltd **(G-5996)**
Guardian Booth LLC (PA) 844 992-6684
527 Route 303 Orangeburg (10962) **(G-12317)**
Guardian Booth LLC 844 992-6684
527 Ny 303 Orangeburg (10962) **(G-12318)**
Guardian Concrete Products Inc 518 372-0080
2140 Maxon Rd Ext Schenectady (12308) **(G-14277)**
Guardian Concrete Steps, Schenectady Also called Guardian Concrete Products Inc **(G-14277)**

Guardian Industries LLC 315 787-7000
50 Forge Ave Geneva (14456) **(G-5157)**
Guardian News & Media LLC 917 900-4663
61 Broadway Rm 1425 New York (10006) **(G-9691)**
Guardian Systems Tech Inc 716 481-5597
659 Oakwood Ave East Aurora (14052) **(G-4090)**
Guernica 646 327-7138
157 Columbus Ave Ste 424 New York (10023) **(G-9692)**
Guernica Magazine, New York Also called Guernica Inc **(G-9692)**
Guess Inc 716 298-3561
1826 Military Rd Spc 113 Niagara Falls (14304) **(G-11934)**
Guest Informat LLC 212 557-3010
110 E 42nd St Rm 1714 New York (10017) **(G-9693)**
Guest of A Guest Inc 212 206-0397
113 Jane St New York (10014) **(G-9694)**
Guidance Channel, Woodbury Also called Global Video LLC **(G-16172)**
Guidance Group Inc (PA) 631 756-4618
1 Huntington Quad 1n03 Melville (11747) **(G-7788)**
Guild Diamond Products Inc (PA) 212 871-0007
1212 Avenue Of The Americ New York (10036) **(G-9695)**
Guilderland Printing, Guilderland Also called Custom Prtrs Guilderland Inc **(G-5485)**
Guilford Press, New York Also called Guilford Publications Inc **(G-9696)**
Guilford Press, New York Also called Guilford Publications Inc **(G-9697)**
Guilford Publications Inc 212 431-9800
7 Penn Plz Ste 1200 New York (10001) **(G-9696)**
Guilford Publications Inc 800 365-7006
370 7th Ave Ste 1200 New York (10001) **(G-9697)**
Guitar Specialist Inc 914 401-9052
307 Rte 22 Goldens Bridge (10526) **(G-5303)**
Guldenschuh Logging & Lbr LLC 585 538-4750
143 Wheatland Center Rd Caledonia (14423) **(G-3070)**
Gumbusters of New York, Brooklyn Also called Metro Products & Services LLC **(G-2148)**
Gumuchian Fils Ltd 212 588-7084
16 E 52nd St Ste 701 New York (10022) **(G-9698)**
Gun Week, Buffalo Also called Second Amendment Foundation **(G-2978)**
Gunlocke Company LLC (HQ) 585 728-5111
1 Gunlocke Dr Wayland (14572) **(G-15626)**
Guosa Life Sciences Inc 718 813-7806
708 3rd Ave Fl 6 New York (10017) **(G-9699)**
Gupp Signs Inc 585 244-5070
340 Lake Ave Rochester (14608) **(G-13453)**
Gurley Precision Instrs Inc 518 272-6300
514 Fulton St Troy (12180) **(G-15170)**
Gustbuster Ltd 631 391-9000
855 Conklin St Ste O Farmingdale (11735) **(G-4642)**
Gutchess Freedom Inc 716 492-2824
10699 Maple Grove Rd Freedom (14065) **(G-4974)**
Gutchess Hardwoods Inc 607 753-3393
890 Mclean Rd Cortland (13045) **(G-3770)**
Gutchess Lumber Co Inc (PA) 607 753-3393
890 Mclean Rd Cortland (13045) **(G-3771)**
Gutchess Lumber Co Inc 716 492-2824
10699 Maple Grove Rd Freedom (14065) **(G-4975)**
Guthrie Heli-Arc Inc 585 548-5053
6276 Clinton Street Rd Bergen (14416) **(G-815)**
Guthrie Sales & Service, Bergen Also called Guthrie Heli-Arc Inc **(G-815)**
Gutts Corporation of America, Irvington Also called Guttz Corporation of America **(G-6309)**
Guttz Corporation of America 914 591-9600
50 S Buckhout St Ste 104 Irvington (10533) **(G-6309)**
Gw Acquisition LLC 212 736-4848
1370 Broadway Rm 1100 New York (10018) **(G-9700)**
Gw Manufacturing 718 386-8078
46 Violet Ave Poughkeepsie (12601) **(G-12960)**
Gym Store Inc 718 366-7804
5889 57th St Maspeth (11378) **(G-7621)**
GYM STORE.COM, Maspeth Also called Gym Store Inc **(G-7621)**
H & H Furniture Co 718 850-5252
11420 101st Ave Jamaica (11419) **(G-6446)**
H & H Hulls Inc 518 828-1339
35 Industrial Tract Anx Hudson (12534) **(G-6159)**
H & H Laboratories Inc (PA) 718 624-8041
61 4th St Brooklyn (11231) **(G-1914)**
H & H Laboratories Inc 718 624-8041
409 Hoyt St Brooklyn (11231) **(G-1915)**
H & M Leasing Corp 631 225-5246
1245 Marconi Blvd Copiague (11726) **(G-3656)**
H & R Precision, Farmingdale Also called Precision Envelope Co Inc **(G-4715)**
H & S Edible Products Corp 914 413-3489
119 Fulton Ln Mount Vernon (10550) **(G-8146)**
H A Guden Company Inc 631 737-2900
99 Raynor Ave Ronkonkoma (11779) **(G-13945)**
H and B Digital, New York Also called A & M LLC **(G-8410)**
H Arnold Wood Turning Inc 914 381-0801
220 White Plins Rd Ste 24 Tarrytown (10591) **(G-15045)**
H B Millwork Inc (PA) 631 289-8086
500 Long Island Ave Medford (11763) **(G-7709)**
H B Millwork Inc 631 924-4195
9 Old Dock Rd Yaphank (11980) **(G-16263)**
H Best Ltd 212 354-2400
1411 Broadway Fl 8 New York (10018) **(G-9701)**

A L P H A B E T I C

H C Kionka & Co Inc....212 227-3155
15 Maiden Ln Ste 908 New York (10038) ***(G-9702)***
H C Young Tool & Machine Co....315 463-0663
3700 New Court Ave Syracuse (13206) ***(G-14906)***
H D M Labs Inc....516 431-8357
153 Kingston Blvd Island Park (11558) ***(G-6318)***
H F Brown Machine Co Inc....315 732-6129
708 State St Utica (13502) ***(G-15269)***
H F Cary & Sons....607 598-2563
70 Reniff Rd Lockwood (14859) ***(G-7120)***
H F W Communications Inc (HQ)....315 703-7979
6437 Collamer Rd Ste 1 East Syracuse (13057) ***(G-4214)***
H Freund Woodworking Co Inc....516 334-3774
589 Main St Westbury (11590) ***(G-15891)***
H G Maybeck Co Inc....718 297-4410
17930 93rd Ave Ste 2 Jamaica (11433) ***(G-6447)***
H Group LLC....212 719-5500
462 7th Ave Fl 9 New York (10018) ***(G-9703)***
H Group, The, New York *Also called H Group LLC* ***(G-9703)***
H H B Bakery of Little Neck....718 631-7004
24914 Horace Harding Expy Flushing (11362) ***(G-4856)***
H K Technologies Inc....718 255-1898
4332 22nd St Ste 405 Long Island City (11101) ***(G-7237)***
H Klein & Sons Inc....516 746-0163
95 Searing Ave Ste 2 Mineola (11501) ***(G-7978)***
H L Robinson Sand & Gravel (PA)....607 659-5153
535 Ithaca Rd Candor (13743) ***(G-3161)***
H M W, Brewster *Also called Hudson Machine Works Inc* ***(G-1152)***
H P E, New York *Also called Hpe Clothing Corporation* ***(G-9829)***
H Rindustries....516 487-3825
393 Jericho Tpke Mineola (11501) ***(G-7979)***
H Risch Inc....585 442-0110
44 Saginaw Dr Rochester (14623) ***(G-13454)***
H S Assembly Inc....585 266-4287
570 Hollandback Rochester (14605) ***(G-13455)***
H T L & S Ltd....718 435-4474
5820 Fort Hamilton Pkwy Brooklyn (11219) ***(G-1916)***
H T Specialty Inc....585 458-4060
70 Bermar Park Rochester (14624) ***(G-13456)***
H THEOPHILE, New York *Also called Kathmando Valley Preservation* ***(G-10078)***
H W Naylor Co Inc....607 263-5145
121 Main St Morris (13808) ***(G-8084)***
H W Wilson Company Inc....718 588-8635
950 University Ave Bronx (10452) ***(G-1271)***
H&E Service Corp....646 472-1936
400 Garden Cy Plz Ste 405 Garden City (11530) ***(G-5101)***
H&F Products Inc....845 651-6100
12 Roosevelt Ave Florida (10921) ***(G-4824)***
H&L Computers Inc....516 873-8088
13523 Northern Blvd Flushing (11354) ***(G-4857)***
H2 At Hammerman, New York *Also called Hammerman Bros Inc* ***(G-9715)***
H2gear Fashions LLC....347 787-7508
1065 Shepherd Ave Brooklyn (11208) ***(G-1917)***
Haanen Packard Machinery Inc (PA)....518 747-2330
16 Allen St Hudson Falls (12839) ***(G-6190)***
Haba USA....800 468-6873
4407 Jordan Rd Skaneateles (13152) ***(G-14453)***
Habasit America Inc....716 824-8484
1400 Clinton St Buffalo (14206) ***(G-2787)***
Habco Corp....631 789-1400
41 Ranick Dr E Amityville (11701) ***(G-266)***
Habco Sales, Amityville *Also called Habco Corp* ***(G-266)***
Habermaass Corporation....315 729-0070
4407 Jordan Rd Skaneateles (13152) ***(G-14454)***
Habitat Magazine, New York *Also called Carol Group Ltd* ***(G-8921)***
Hachette Book Group Inc (HQ)....800 759-0190
1290 Ave Of The Americas New York (10104) ***(G-9704)***
Hachette Book Group USA....212 364-1200
237 Park Ave New York (10017) ***(G-9705)***
Haculla Nyc Inc....718 886-3163
6805 Fresh Meadow Ln Fresh Meadows (11365) ***(G-5042)***
Haddad Bros Inc (PA)....212 563-2117
28 W 36th St Rm 1026 New York (10018) ***(G-9706)***
Haddad Hosiery LLC....212 251-0022
34 W 33rd St Rm 401 New York (10001) ***(G-9707)***
Hadfield Inc....631 981-4314
49 Fifty Acre Rd Saint James (11780) ***(G-14111)***
Hadley Exhibits Inc (PA)....716 874-3666
1700 Elmwood Ave Buffalo (14207) ***(G-2788)***
Hadleys Fab-Weld Inc....315 926-5101
4202 Sunset Dr Marion (14505) ***(G-7570)***
Hadp LLC....518 831-6824
602 Potential Pkwy Scotia (12302) ***(G-14331)***
Hagadah Passover Bakery....718 638-1589
814 Bergen St Brooklyn (11238) ***(G-1918)***
Hagedorn Communications Inc (PA)....914 636-7400
662 Main St Ste 1 New Rochelle (10801) ***(G-8336)***
Hagedorn Communications Inc....914 636-7400
20 W 22nd St Ste 906 New York (10010) ***(G-9708)***
Hagner Industries Inc....716 873-5720
95 Botsford Pl Buffalo (14216) ***(G-2789)***

Hahns Old Fashioned Cake Co....631 249-3456
75 Allen Blvd Farmingdale (11735) ***(G-4643)***
Haig Graphic Communications, Hauppauge *Also called Haig Press Inc* ***(G-5665)***
Haig Press Inc....631 582-5800
690 Old Willets Path Hauppauge (11788) ***(G-5665)***
Hailo Network Usa Inc....646 561-8552
568 Broadway Fl 11 New York (10012) ***(G-9709)***
Hain Blueprint Inc....212 414-5741
1111 Marcus Ave Ste 100 New Hyde Park (11042) ***(G-8271)***
Hain Celestial Group Inc (PA)....516 587-5000
1111 Marcus Ave Ste 100 New Hyde Park (11042) ***(G-8272)***
Haines Equipment Inc....607 566-8531
20 Carrington St Avoca (14809) ***(G-510)***
Hair Color Research Group Inc....718 445-6026
13320 Whitestone Expy Flushing (11354) ***(G-4858)***
Hair Ventures LLC (PA)....718 664-7689
94 Fargo Ln Irvington (10533) ***(G-6310)***
Hairstory, Irvington *Also called Hair Ventures LLC* ***(G-6310)***
Haitian Times Inc....718 230-8700
80 Lakeside Dr New Rochelle (10801) ***(G-8337)***
Hakson Safety Wears Inc....613 667-3015
111 Colgate Ave Buffalo (14220) ***(G-2790)***
Halabieh Group Inc....347 987-8263
209 W 38th St Fl 5 New York (10018) ***(G-9710)***
Halcyon Business Publications....800 735-2732
400 Post Ave Ste 304 Westbury (11590) ***(G-15892)***
Haldey Phrm Compounding, Bronx *Also called Emilior Phrm Compounding Inc* ***(G-1254)***
Hale Electrical Dist Svcs Inc....716 818-7595
12088 Big Tree Rd Wales Center (14169) ***(G-15466)***
Haley Concrete Inc (PA)....716 492-0849
10413 Delevan Elton Rd Delevan (14042) ***(G-3961)***
Haleys Comet Seafood Corp....212 571-1828
605 3rd Ave Fl 34 New York (10158) ***(G-9711)***
Halfmoon Town Water Department....518 233-7489
8 Brookwood Rd Waterford (12188) ***(G-15537)***
Halfway House LLC....518 873-2198
7158 Us Route 9 Elizabethtown (12932) ***(G-4301)***
Hallagan Manufacturing Co Inc....315 331-4640
500 Hoffman St Newark (14513) ***(G-11840)***
Hallmark Hlth Care Sltions LLC....516 513-0959
200 Motor Pkwy Ste D26 Hauppauge (11788) ***(G-5666)***
Halm Instrument Co Inc....516 676-6700
180 Glen Head Rd Glen Head (11545) ***(G-5207)***
Halmark Architectural Finshg....718 272-1831
353 Stanley Ave Brooklyn (11207) ***(G-1919)***
Halmode Apparel Inc....212 819-9114
1400 Brdwy 11th & Fl 16 New York (10018) ***(G-9712)***
Halmode Petite Div, New York *Also called Halmode Apparel Inc* ***(G-9712)***
Halo Associates....212 691-9549
289 Bleecker St Fl 5 New York (10014) ***(G-9713)***
Halo Innovations Inc....952 259-1500
134 N 4th St Brooklyn (11249) ***(G-1920)***
Halo Optical Products Inc....518 773-4256
9 Phair St Ste 1 Gloversville (12078) ***(G-5284)***
Halo Sleep Systems, Brooklyn *Also called Halo Innovations Inc* ***(G-1920)***
Halpern Tool Corp (PA)....914 633-0038
111 Plain Ave New Rochelle (10801) ***(G-8338)***
Hamburg Finishing Works Inc....716 362-0888
3949 Jeffrey Blvd Buffalo (14219) ***(G-2791)***
Hamil America Inc....212 244-2645
42 W 39th St Fl 15 New York (10018) ***(G-9714)***
Hamilton County News, Amsterdam *Also called William J Kline & Son Inc* ***(G-354)***
Hamilton Design Kit Homes, Queensbury *Also called Northern Design & Bldg Assoc* ***(G-13050)***
Hamilton Marketing Corporation....585 395-0678
5211 Lake Rd S Brockport (14420) ***(G-1176)***
Hamilton Printing Company Inc....518 732-2161
22 Hamilton Ave Troy (12180) ***(G-15171)***
Hamlet Products Inc....914 665-0307
221 N Macquesten Pkwy # 1 Mount Vernon (10550) ***(G-8147)***
Hamlin Bottle & Can Return Inc....585 259-1301
3423 Redman Rd Brockport (14420) ***(G-1177)***
Hammer Packaging Corp (PA)....585 424-3880
200 Lucius Gordon Dr West Henrietta (14586) ***(G-15797)***
Hammerman Bros Inc....212 956-2800
50 W 57th St Fl 12 New York (10019) ***(G-9715)***
Hammond & Irving Inc (PA)....315 253-6265
254 North St Auburn (13021) ***(G-478)***
Hammond Manufacturing Co Inc....716 630-7030
475 Cayuga Rd Cheektowaga (14225) ***(G-3352)***
Hamodia Corp....718 338-5637
324 Avenue I Brooklyn (11230) ***(G-1921)***
Hamodia Corp....718 853-9094
207 Foster Ave Brooklyn (11230) ***(G-1922)***
Hampshire Chemical Corp....315 539-9221
228 E Main St Waterloo (13165) ***(G-15554)***
Hampshire Jewels, New York *Also called Emsaru USA Corp* ***(G-9363)***
Hampshire Lithographers, New York *Also called Advantage Quick Print Inc* ***(G-8483)***
Hampshire Sub II Inc (HQ)....631 321-0923
114 W 41st St Fl 5 New York (10036) ***(G-9716)***
Hampton Art LLC....631 924-1335
19 Scouting Blvd Medford (11763) ***(G-7710)***

Hampton Press Incorporated 646 638-3800
  307 7th Ave Rm 506 New York (10001) *(G-9717)*
Hampton Sand Corp 631 325-5533
  1 High St Westhampton (11977) *(G-15955)*
Hampton Shipyards Inc 631 653-6777
  7 Carter Ln East Quogue (11942) *(G-4157)*
Hampton Technologies LLC 631 924-1335
  19 Scouting Blvd Medford (11763) *(G-7711)*
Hampton Transport Inc 631 716-4445
  3655 Route 112 Coram (11727) *(G-3693)*
Hamptons Magazine, Southampton *Also called Hamptons Media LLC (G-14532)*
Hamptons Media LLC 631 283-6900
  67 Hampton Rd Unit 5 Southampton (11968) *(G-14532)*
Hamtronics Inc 585 392-9430
  39 Willnick Cir Rochester (14626) *(G-13457)*
Han-Kraft Uniform Headwear, Buffalo *Also called Hankin Brothers Cap Co (G-2792)*
Hana Pastries Inc 718 369-7593
  34 35th St Unit 9 Brooklyn (11232) *(G-1923)*
Hana Sheet Metal Inc 914 377-0773
  9 Celli Pl 11 Yonkers (10701) *(G-16317)*
Hanan Products Company Inc 516 938-1000
  196 Miller Pl Hicksville (11801) *(G-5915)*
Hanco Metal Products Inc 212 787-5992
  25 Jay St Brooklyn (11201) *(G-1924)*
Hancock Quarry/Asphalt, Hancock *Also called Cobleskill Stone Products Inc (G-5535)*
Hancor Inc 607 565-3033
  1 Wm Donnelly Ind Pkwy Waverly (14892) *(G-15622)*
Hand Care Inc 516 747-5649
  42 Sugar Maple Dr Roslyn (11576) *(G-14043)*
Handcraft Cabinetry Inc 914 681-9437
  230 Ferris Ave Ste 1 White Plains (10603) *(G-16012)*
Handcraft Manufacturing Corp (PA) 212 251-0022
  34 W 33rd St Rm 401 New York (10001) *(G-9718)*
Handmade Frames Inc 718 782-8364
  1013 Grand St Ste 2 Brooklyn (11211) *(G-1925)*
Handone Studios Inc 585 421-8175
  388 Mason Rd Fairport (14450) *(G-4498)*
Handsome Dans LLC (PA) 917 965-2499
  186 1st Ave New York (10009) *(G-9719)*
Handy & Harman Holding Corp 914 461-1300
  1133 Westchester Ave N-222 White Plains (10604) *(G-16013)*
Handy & Harman Ltd (HQ) 212 520-2300
  590 Madison Ave Rm 3202 New York (10022) *(G-9720)*
Handy Laundry Products Corp (PA) 845 701-1111
  382 Route 59 Ste 318 Airmont (10952) *(G-11)*
Handy Tool & Mfg Co Inc 718 478-9203
  1205 Rockaway Ave Brooklyn (11236) *(G-1926)*
Hanes Supply Inc 518 438-0139
  156 Railroad Ave Ste 3 Albany (12205) *(G-83)*
Hanesbrands Inc 212 576-9300
  260 Madison Ave Fl 6 New York (10016) *(G-9721)*
Hanet Plastics Usa Inc 518 324-5850
  139 Distribution Way Plattsburgh (12901) *(G-12750)*
Hanford Pharmaceuticals, Syracuse *Also called G C Hanford Manufacturing Co (G-14898)*
Hanger Inc 518 435-0840
  1315 Central Ave Albany (12205) *(G-84)*
Hanger Inc 607 431-2526
  37 Associate Dr Oneonta (13820) *(G-12272)*
Hanger Inc 518 438-4546
  6620 Fly Rd Ste 203 East Syracuse (13057) *(G-4215)*
Hanger Inc 718 575-5504
  11835 Queens Blvd Ste LI3 Forest Hills (11375) *(G-4920)*
Hanger Clinic, Syracuse *Also called Hanger Prosthetics & (G-14907)*
Hanger Clinic, Elmira *Also called Hanger Prsthetcs & Ortho Inc (G-4354)*
Hanger Clinic, Oneonta *Also called Creative Orthotics & Prosthet (G-12270)*
Hanger Prosthectics Orthotics, Forest Hills *Also called Hanger Inc (G-4920)*
Hanger Prosthetics & 315 492-6608
  522 Liberty St 1 Syracuse (13204) *(G-14907)*
Hanger Prsthetcs & Ortho Inc 516 338-4466
  5502 Brush Hollow Rd Westbury (11590) *(G-15893)*
Hanger Prsthetcs & Ortho Inc 718 892-1103
  1250 Waters Pl Bronx (10461) *(G-1272)*
Hanger Prsthetcs & Ortho Inc 607 277-6620
  310 Taughannock Blvd 1a Ithaca (14850) *(G-6384)*
Hanger Prsthetcs & Ortho Inc 607 776-8013
  47 W Steuben St Bath (14810) *(G-634)*
Hanger Prsthetcs & Ortho Inc 607 771-4672
  65 Pennsylvania Ave Binghamton (13903) *(G-881)*
Hanger Prsthetcs & Ortho Inc 315 472-5200
  910 Erie Blvd E Ste 3 Syracuse (13210) *(G-14908)*
Hanger Prsthetcs & Ortho Inc 607 795-1220
  1300 College Ave Ste 1 Elmira (14901) *(G-4354)*
Hanger Prsthetcs & Ortho Inc 315 789-4810
  787 State Route 5 And 20 Geneva (14456) *(G-5158)*
Hania By Anya Cole LLC 212 302-3550
  16 W 56th St Fl 4 New York (10019) *(G-9722)*
Hankin Brothers Cap Co 716 892-8840
  1910 Genesee St Buffalo (14211) *(G-2792)*
Hanna Altinis Co Inc 718 706-1134
  3601 48th Ave Long Island City (11101) *(G-7238)*
Hannay Reels Inc 518 797-3791
  553 State Route 143 Westerlo (12193) *(G-15941)*

Hansa Plastics Inc 631 269-9050
  8 Meadow Glen Rd Kings Park (11754) *(G-6673)*
Hansa Usa LLC 646 412-6407
  18 E 48th St New York (10017) *(G-9723)*
Hansae Co Ltd 212 354-6690
  501 Fashion Ave Rm 208 New York (10018) *(G-9724)*
Hansen & Hansen Qulty Prtg Div, Syracuse *Also called Syracuse Computer Forms Inc (G-15005)*
Hansen Metal Fabrications, Farmington *Also called Hansen Steel (G-4772)*
Hansen Steel 585 398-2020
  6021 County Road 41 Farmington (14425) *(G-4772)*
Hanson Aggregates East LLC 716 372-1574
  4419 S Nine Mile Rd Allegany (14706) *(G-188)*
Hanson Aggregates East LLC 585 798-0762
  Glenwood Ave Medina (14103) *(G-7737)*
Hanson Aggregates East LLC 716 372-1574
  4419 S 9 Mile Rd Falconer (14733) *(G-4542)*
Hanson Aggregates East LLC 585 343-1787
  5870 Main Rd Stafford (14143) *(G-14604)*
Hanson Aggregates East LLC 315 536-9391
  131 Garfield Ave Penn Yan (14527) *(G-12585)*
Hanson Aggregates East LLC 315 548-4913
  392 State Route 96 Phelps (14532) *(G-12604)*
Hanson Aggregates East LLC 315 493-3721
  County Rt 47 Great Bend (13643) *(G-5358)*
Hanson Aggregates New York LLC 716 665-4620
  2237 Allen St Jamesville (13078) *(G-6558)*
Hanson Aggregates New York LLC 716 665-4620
  2237 Allen Street Ext Jamestown (14701) *(G-6515)*
Hanson Aggregates New York LLC 585 638-5841
  6895 Ellicott Street Rd Pavilion (14525) *(G-12523)*
Hanson Aggregates New York LLC 315 469-5501
  4800 Jamesville Rd Jamesville (13078) *(G-6559)*
Hanson Aggregates New York LLC 607 776-7945
  7235 Sandpit Rd Bath (14810) *(G-635)*
Hanson Aggregates New York LLC 607 276-5881
  546 Clark Rd Almond (14804) *(G-191)*
Hanson Aggregates PA Inc 315 858-1100
  237 Kingdom Rd Jordanville (13361) *(G-6632)*
Hanson Aggregates PA Inc 518 568-2444
  7904 St Hwy 5 Saint Johnsville (13452) *(G-14117)*
Hanson Aggregates PA LLC 585 624-3800
  2049 County Rd 6 Honeoye Falls (14472) *(G-6073)*
Hanson Aggregates PA LLC 585 624-1220
  2049 Honeoye Falls 6 Rd Honeoye Falls (14472) *(G-6074)*
Hanson Aggregates PA LLC 315 469-5501
  4800 Jamesville Rd Jamesville (13078) *(G-6560)*
Hanson Aggregates PA LLC 315 685-3321
  Rr 321 Skaneateles (13152) *(G-14455)*
Hanson Aggregates PA LLC 315 782-2300
  25133 Nys Rt 3 Watertown (13601) *(G-15571)*
Hanson Aggregates PA LLC 315 821-7222
  1780 State Route 12b Oriskany Falls (13425) *(G-12400)*
Hanson Aggregates PA LLC 315 393-3743
  701 Cedar St Ogdensburg (13669) *(G-12205)*
Hanson Aggregates PA LLC 315 789-6202
  2026 County Rd Ste 6 Oaks Corners (14518) *(G-12162)*
Hanson Aggregates PA LLC 585 436-3250
  1535 Scottsville Rd Rochester (14623) *(G-13458)*
Hanson Ready Mix Concrete, Almond *Also called Hanson Aggregates New York LLC (G-191)*
Hanson Sign Companies, Falconer *Also called Hanson Sign Screen Prcess Corp (G-4543)*
Hanson Sign Screen Prcess Corp 716 661-3900
  82 Carter St Falconer (14733) *(G-4543)*
Hanzlian Sausage Deli, Cheektowaga *Also called Hanzlian Sausage Incorporated (G-3353)*
Hanzlian Sausage Incorporated 716 891-5247
  2351 Genesee St Cheektowaga (14225) *(G-3353)*
Happy Fella, New York *Also called Hf Mfg Corp (G-9777)*
Happy Sock, New York *Also called United Retail II (G-11599)*
Happy Software LLC 518 584-4668
  11 Federal St Saratoga Springs (12866) *(G-14181)*
Harbec Inc 585 265-0010
  358 Timothy Ln Ontario (14519) *(G-12290)*
Harbor Elc Fabrication Tls Inc 914 636-4400
  29 Portman Rd New Rochelle (10801) *(G-8339)*
Harbor Point Mineral Pdts Inc 315 797-1300
  71 Wurz Ave Utica (13502) *(G-15270)*
Harbor Wldg & Fabrication Corp 631 667-1880
  30 Railroad Ave Copiague (11726) *(G-3657)*
Harborside Press 631 470-4967
  94 N Woodhull Rd Huntington (11743) *(G-6206)*
Harbour Roads, Albany *Also called Kal-Harbour Inc (G-93)*
Hard Ten, Brooklyn *Also called Dreams To Print (G-1761)*
Hard Ten Clothing Inc 212 302-1321
  231 W 39th St Rm 606 New York (10018) *(G-9725)*
Harden Furniture LLC (PA) 315 675-3600
  8550 Mill Pond Way Mc Connellsville (13401) *(G-7686)*
Hardinge Inc (HQ) 607 734-2281
  1 Hardinge Dr Elmira (14903) *(G-4355)*
Hargrave Development 716 877-7880
  84 Shepard Ave Kenmore (14217) *(G-6650)*
Hargraves Bus MGT Consulting, Kenmore *Also called Hargrave Development (G-6650)*

A L P H A B E T I C

Haring, J V & Son, Staten Island *Also called J V Haring & Son* **(G-14669)**
Harmac Medical Products Inc (PA) 716 897-4500
2201 Bailey Ave Buffalo (14211) **(G-2793)**
Harmon and Castella Printing 845 471-9163
29 Travis Rd Hyde Park (12538) **(G-6271)**
Harmonic Drive LLC 631 231-6630
89 Cabot Ct Ste A Hauppauge (11788) **(G-5667)**
Harney & Sons Tea Corp (PA) 518 789-2100
5723 Route 22 Millerton (12546) **(G-7947)**
Harold Wood Co Inc 716 873-1535
329 Hinman Ave Buffalo (14216) **(G-2794)**
Harome Designs LLC 631 864-1900
75 Modular Ave Commack (11725) **(G-3591)**
Harper International Corp 716 276-9900
4455 Genesee St Ste 123 Buffalo (14225) **(G-2795)**
Harper International Corp 716 276-9900
99 Sheldon Ave Depew (14043) **(G-3984)**
Harper Products Ltd 516 997-2330
117 State St Westbury (11590) **(G-15894)**
Harper's Bazaar, New York *Also called Hearst Corporation* **(G-9752)**
Harpercollins 212 207-7000
195 Broadway New York (10007) **(G-9726)**
Harpercollins Publishers LLC (HQ) 212 207-7000
195 Broadway New York (10007) **(G-9727)**
Harpercollins Publishers LLC 212 553-4200
233 Broadway Rm 1001 New York (10279) **(G-9728)**
Harpers Magazine Foundation 212 420-5720
666 Broadway Fl 11 New York (10012) **(G-9729)**
Harris Assembly Group, Binghamton *Also called Arnold-Davis LLC* **(G-855)**
Harris Corporation, Rochester *Also called L3harris Technologies Inc* **(G-13508)**
Harris Corporation, Rochester *Also called L3harris Technologies Inc* **(G-13509)**
Harris Corporation 413 263-6200
800 Lee Rd Rochester (14606) **(G-13459)**
Harris Globl Cmmunications Inc 585 244-5830
1350 Jefferson Rd Rochester (14623) **(G-13460)**
Harris Logging Inc 518 792-1083
39 Mud Pond Rd Queensbury (12804) **(G-13042)**
Harris Machine, Newark *Also called Van Laeken Richard* **(G-11856)**
Harris Rf Communications, Rochester *Also called L3harris Technologies Inc* **(G-13513)**
Harrison Bakery West 315 422-1468
1306 W Genesee St Syracuse (13204) **(G-14909)**
Harrison Sportswear Inc 212 391-1051
260 W 39th St Fl 7 New York (10018) **(G-9730)**
Harry N Abrams Incorporated 212 206-7715
195 Broadway Fl 9 New York (10007) **(G-9731)**
Harry Winston Inc (HQ) 212 399-1000
717 5th Ave Fl 9 New York (10022) **(G-9732)**
Harry's Razor Company, New York *Also called Harrys Inc* **(G-9733)**
Harrys Inc (PA) 888 212-6855
75 Varick St Fl 9 New York (10013) **(G-9733)**
Hart Energy Publishing Lllp 212 621-4621
110 William St Fl 18 New York (10038) **(G-9734)**
Hart Rifle Barrel Inc 315 677-9841
1680 Jamesville Ave Syracuse (13210) **(G-14910)**
Hart Specialties Inc 631 226-5600
5000 New Horizons Blvd Amityville (11701) **(G-267)**
Hart Sports Inc 631 385-1805
4 Roxanne Ct Huntington Station (11746) **(G-6248)**
Hart To Hart Industries Inc 716 492-2709
13520 Chaffee Curriers Rd Chaffee (14030) **(G-3307)**
Hartchrom Inc 518 880-0411
25 Gibson St Ste 1 Watervliet (12189) **(G-15603)**
Hartford Town Park System, New Hartford *Also called Town of Hartford* **(G-8247)**
Hartman Enterprises Inc 315 363-7300
455 Elizabeth St Oneida (13421) **(G-12245)**
Harvard Woven Label, New York *Also called Imperial-Harvard Label Co* **(G-9869)**
Harvest Homes Inc 518 895-2341
1331 Cole Rd Delanson (12053) **(G-3960)**
Harvest Technologies Inc 518 899-7124
36 Featherfoil Way Ballston Spa (12020) **(G-576)**
Harwitt Industries Inc 516 623-9787
61 S Main St Unit A Freeport (11520) **(G-5002)**
Hasco Componets 516 328-9292
906 Jericho Tpke New Hyde Park (11040) **(G-8273)**
Haskell Jewels Ltd (PA) 212 764-3332
390 5th Ave Fl 2 New York (10018) **(G-9735)**
Haskell Machine & Tool Inc 607 749-2421
5 S Fulton St Homer (13077) **(G-6063)**
Hastings Hide Inc 516 295-2400
372 Doughty Blvd Inwood (11096) **(G-6295)**
Hastings Tile & Bath Inc (PA) 631 285-3330
711 Koehler Ave Ste 8 Ronkonkoma (11779) **(G-13946)**
Hat Attack I Bujibaja, Bronx *Also called Hat Attack Inc* **(G-1273)**
Hat Attack Inc (PA) 718 994-1000
4643 Bullard Ave Ste A Bronx (10470) **(G-1273)**
Hat Factory Furniture Co 914 788-6288
1000 N Division St Ste 8 Peekskill (10566) **(G-12552)**
Hatfield Metal Fab Inc 845 454-9078
16 Hatfield Ln Poughkeepsie (12603) **(G-12961)**
Hathaway Prcess Instrmentation, Amherst *Also called Allied Motion Systems Corp* **(G-206)**

Hatherleigh Company Ltd 607 538-1092
62545 State Highway 10 Hobart (13788) **(G-5978)**
Haun Welding Supply Inc 607 846-2289
1100 Sullivan St Elmira (14901) **(G-4356)**
Haun Welding Supply Inc 315 592-5012
214 N 4th St Fulton (13069) **(G-5063)**
Hauppauge Computer Works Inc (HQ) 631 434-1600
909 Motor Pkwy Hauppauge (11788) **(G-5668)**
Hauppauge Digital Inc (PA) 631 434-1600
909 Motor Pkwy Hauppauge (11788) **(G-5669)**
Hauppuge Cmpt Dgtal Erope Sarl, Hauppauge *Also called Hauppauge Computer Works Inc* **(G-5668)**
Haute By Blair Stanley LLC 212 557-7868
330 E 38th St Apt 23e New York (10016) **(G-9736)**
Have Your Cake Kitchen LLC 646 820-8074
291 Union St Phb Brooklyn (11231) **(G-1927)**
Haverstraw Quarry, Haverstraw *Also called Tilcon New York Inc* **(G-5808)**
Hawkins Fabrics Inc (PA) 518 773-9550
328 N Perry St Johnstown (12095) **(G-6618)**
Hawthorne Garden Company (HQ) 516 883-6550
800 Port Washington Blvd Port Washington (11050) **(G-12882)**
Hawthorne Gardening Co., Port Washington *Also called Hawthorne Garden Company* **(G-12882)**
Hawver Display Inc (PA) 585 544-2290
140 Carter St Rochester (14621) **(G-13461)**
Haymarket Group Ltd 212 239-0855
12 W 37th St 9 New York (10018) **(G-9737)**
Haymarket Media Inc (HQ) 646 638-6000
275 7th Ave Fl 10 New York (10001) **(G-9738)**
Haynes Roberts Inc 212 989-1901
601 W 26th St Rm 1655 New York (10001) **(G-9739)**
Hazen Holdings LLC 607 542-9365
425 N Broadway Unit 700 Jericho (11753) **(G-6581)**
Hazlitt 1852 Vineyards, Hector *Also called Hazlitts 1852 Vineyards Inc* **(G-5825)**
Hazlitts 1852 Vineyards Inc 607 546-9463
5712 State Route 414 Hector (14841) **(G-5825)**
Hazlow Electronics Inc 585 325-5323
49 Saint Bridgets Dr Rochester (14605) **(G-13462)**
HB Athletic Inc (PA) 914 560-8422
56 Harrison St Ste 305 New Rochelle (10801) **(G-8340)**
Hbs, Great Neck *Also called Toni Industries Inc* **(G-5428)**
Hc Brill Co Inc 716 685-4000
3765 Walden Ave Lancaster (14086) **(G-6810)**
HC Contracting Inc 212 643-9292
318 W 39th St Fl 4 New York (10018) **(G-9740)**
Hci Engineering 315 336-3450
5880 Bartlett Rd Rome (13440) **(G-13850)**
Hdm Hydraulics LLC 716 694-8004
125 Fire Tower Dr Tonawanda (14150) **(G-15110)**
Health Care Compliance (HQ) 516 478-4100
30 Jericho Executive Plz 400c Jericho (11753) **(G-6582)**
Health Care Originals Inc 585 471-8215
1 Pleasant St Ste 442 Rochester (14604) **(G-13463)**
Health Care Products 631 789-8228
369 Bayview Ave Amityville (11701) **(G-268)**
Health Day, Melville *Also called Scoutnews LLC* **(G-7821)**
Health Matters America Inc 716 235-8772
2501 Broadway St Ste 2 Buffalo (14227) **(G-2796)**
Healthalliance Hospital 845 338-2500
105 Marys Ave Kingston (12401) **(G-6693)**
Healthee Endeavors Inc 718 653-5499
3565c Boston Rd Bronx (10469) **(G-1274)**
Healthix Inc (PA) 877 695-4749
40 Worth St Fl 5 New York (10013) **(G-9741)**
Healthone Pharmacy Inc 718 495-9015
119 Pennsylvania Ave Brooklyn (11207) **(G-1928)**
Healthway Home Products Inc 315 298-2904
3420 Maple Ave Pulaski (13142) **(G-13000)**
Healthway Products Company 315 207-1410
249a Mitchell St Oswego (13126) **(G-12411)**
Healthy Brand Oil Corp (PA) 718 937-0806
5215 11th St Ste A Long Island City (11101) **(G-7239)**
Healthy N Fit Intl Inc (PA) 800 338-5200
7 Sutton Pl Ste A Brewster (10509) **(G-1150)**
Healthy Way of Life Magazine 718 616-1681
1529 Voorhies Ave Brooklyn (11235) **(G-1929)**
Heany Industries Inc 585 889-2700
249 Briarwood Ln Scottsville (14546) **(G-14340)**
Hearing Aid Office, The, Albany *Also called Benway-Haworth-Lwlr-Iacosta He* **(G-47)**
Hearos LLC 844 432-7327
968 Albany Shaker Rd Latham (12110) **(G-6858)**
Hearst Business Media (HQ) 516 227-1300
50 Charles Lindbergh Blvd # 103 Uniondale (11553) **(G-15230)**
Hearst Business Publishing Inc 212 969-7500
888 7th Ave Fl 2 New York (10106) **(G-9742)**
Hearst Communications Inc (HQ) 212 649-2000
300 W 57th St New York (10019) **(G-9743)**
Hearst Communications Inc 212 247-1014
828 9th Ave New York (10019) **(G-9744)**
Hearst Communications Inc (HQ) 212 649-2000
300 W 57th St New York (10019) **(G-9745)**

Hearst Corporation..212 649-3100
300 W 57th St Fl 29 New York (10019) *(G-9746)*

Hearst Corporation..212 903-5366
224 W 57th St Frnt 1 New York (10019) *(G-9747)*

Hearst Corporation..212 767-5800
1633 Broadway Fl 44 New York (10019) *(G-9748)*

Hearst Corporation..516 382-4580
810 7th Ave New York (10019) *(G-9749)*

Hearst Corporation..518 454-5694
645 Albany Shaker Rd Albany (12211) *(G-85)*

Hearst Corporation..212 649-4271
300 W 57th St Fl 21 New York (10019) *(G-9750)*

Hearst Corporation..212 204-4300
1440 Broadway Fl 13 New York (10018) *(G-9751)*

Hearst Corporation..212 903-5000
1700 Broadway New York (10019) *(G-9752)*

Hearst Corporation..212 649-3204
300 W 57th St Fl 32 New York (10019) *(G-9753)*

Hearst Corporation..212 649-2275
300 W 57th St Fl 42 New York (10019) *(G-9754)*

Hearst Digital Studios Inc................................212 969-7552
300 W 57th St Fl 18 New York (10019) *(G-9755)*

Hearst Entertainment, New York Also called Hearst Digital Studios Inc *(G-9755)*

Hearst Holdings Inc (HQ)......................................212 649-2000
300 W 57th St New York (10019) *(G-9756)*

Hearst Interactive Media, New York Also called Hearst Communications Inc *(G-9745)*

Heart & Hands Wine Company Inc.......................315 889-8500
4162 State Route 90 Union Springs (13160) *(G-15222)*

Heart of Tea...917 725-3164
419 Lafayette St Fl 2f New York (10003) *(G-9757)*

Hearth Cabinets and More Ltd.............................315 641-1197
4483 Buckley Rd Liverpool (13088) *(G-7011)*

Hearts of Palm LLC...212 944-6660
1411 Broadway Fl 23 New York (10018) *(G-9758)*

Hearts of Palm LLC (PA)......................................212 944-6660
1411 Broadway Fl 25 New York (10018) *(G-9759)*

Heartwood Specialties Inc....................................607 654-0102
10249 Gibson Rd Hammondsport (14840) *(G-5529)*

Heary Bros Lghtning Protection...........................716 941-6141
11291 Moore Rd Springville (14141) *(G-14593)*

Heat USA II LLC...212 564-4328
35 E 21st St New York (10010) *(G-9760)*

Heath Manufacturing Company............................800 444-3140
700 Ellicott St Batavia (14020) *(G-617)*

Heath Outdoors Products, Batavia Also called Heath Manufacturing Company *(G-617)*

Heatherdell RB Hammers, Blauvelt Also called Rbhammers Corp *(G-932)*

Heating & Burner Supply Inc................................718 665-0006
479 Walton Ave Bronx (10451) *(G-1275)*

Hebeler LLC (PA)..716 873-9300
2000 Military Rd Tonawanda (14150) *(G-15111)*

Hebeler Process Solutions LLC..........................716 873-9300
2000 Military Rd Tonawanda (14150) *(G-15112)*

Hecht & Sohn Glass Co Inc.................................718 782-8295
406 Willoughby Ave Brooklyn (11205) *(G-1930)*

Hedaya Home Fashions Inc (PA).........................212 889-1111
295 5th Ave Ste 1503 New York (10016) *(G-9761)*

Hedges and Gardens, East Hampton Also called Irony Limited Inc *(G-4123)*

Heed LLC...646 708-7111
462 Fashion Ave Fl 5 New York (10018) *(G-9762)*

Hefti, New Rochelle Also called Harbor Elc Fabrication Tls Inc *(G-8339)*

Heidelberg Group Inc..315 866-0999
3056 State Hwy Rte 28 N Herkimer (13350) *(G-5863)*

Heindl Printers, Rochester Also called Louis Heindl & Son Inc *(G-13523)*

Heineck Associates Inc..631 207-2347
28 Curtis Ave Bellport (11713) *(G-800)*

Heintz & Weber Co Inc..716 852-7171
150 Reading St Buffalo (14220) *(G-2797)*

Heleo.com, New York Also called Helium Media Inc *(G-9763)*

Helgen Industries Inc...631 841-6300
431 Bayview Ave Amityville (11701) *(G-269)*

Helio Precision Products Inc................................585 697-5434
200 Tech Park Dr Rochester (14623) *(G-13464)*

Helium Media Inc..917 596-4081
165 Duane St Apt 7b New York (10013) *(G-9763)*

Hellas Stone Inc...718 545-4716
3550 10th St Astoria (11106) *(G-424)*

Heller Performance Polymers, New York Also called Atc Plastics LLC *(G-8660)*

Helmel Engineering Pdts Inc................................716 297-8644
6520 Lockport Rd Niagara Falls (14305) *(G-11935)*

Helmer Avenue, West Winfield Also called Precisionmatics Co Inc *(G-15858)*

Helmont Mills Inc (HQ)..518 568-7913
15 Lion Ave Saint Johnsville (13452) *(G-14118)*

Helvetica Press Incorporated..............................212 737-1857
244 5th Ave New York (10001) *(G-9764)*

Hemisphere Novelties Inc.....................................914 378-4100
167 Saw Mill River Rd 3c Yonkers (10701) *(G-16318)*

Hempstead Sentinel Inc.......................................516 486-5000
55 Chasner St Hempstead (11550) *(G-5838)*

Hemstrought's Bakeries, New Hartford Also called B & D Enterprises Utica Inc *(G-8236)*

Henderson Products Inc..315 785-0994
22686 Fisher Rd Ste A Watertown (13601) *(G-15572)*

Henderson Truck Equipment, Watertown Also called Henderson Products Inc *(G-15572)*

Hennig Custom Woodwork Corp...........................516 536-3460
2497 Long Beach Rd Oceanside (11572) *(G-12174)*

Hennig Custom Woodworking, Oceanside Also called Hennig Custom Woodwork Corp *(G-12174)*

Henpecked Husband Farms Corp..........................631 728-2800
1212 Speonk Riverhead Rd Speonk (11972) *(G-14562)*

Henry Design Studios Inc.....................................516 801-2760
129 Birch Hill Rd Ste 2 Locust Valley (11560) *(G-7126)*

Henry Dunay Designs Inc.....................................212 768-9700
10 W 46th St Ste 1200 New York (10036) *(G-9765)*

Henry Holt and Company LLC...............................646 307-5095
175 5th Ave Ste 400 New York (10010) *(G-9766)*

Henry Newman LLC...607 273-8512
39 Elm St Rear Bldg Dryden (13053) *(G-4038)*

Henry Schein Fincl Svcs LLC (HQ)........................631 843-5500
135 Duryea Rd Melville (11747) *(G-7789)*

Henry Schein International Inc, Melville Also called Henry Schein Fincl Svcs LLC *(G-7789)*

Henry Segal Co, Woodmere Also called Shane Tex Inc *(G-16193)*

Henrys Deals Inc..347 821-4685
1002 Quentin Rd Ste 2009 Brooklyn (11223) *(G-1931)*

Hepa-Hat Incorporated...914 271-9747
31 Park Trl Croton On Hudson (10520) *(G-3809)*

Her Money Media Inc...917 882-3284
4 Justine Ct Briarcliff Manor (10510) *(G-1161)*

Herald Newspapers Company Inc (HQ).................315 470-0011
220 S Warren St Syracuse (13202) *(G-14911)*

Herald Publishing Company LLC..........................315 470-2022
4 Times Sq Fl 23 New York (10036) *(G-9767)*

Herald Statesman, Yonkers Also called Gannett Stllite Info Ntwrk Inc *(G-16312)*

Herbert Jaffe Inc..718 392-1956
4011 Skillman Ave Long Island City (11104) *(G-7240)*

Herbert Wolf Corp...718 392-2424
3658 37th St Ste 3 Long Island City (11101) *(G-7241)*

Hercules, Huntington Station Also called I A S National Inc *(G-6249)*

Hercules Candy Co..315 463-4339
720 W Manlius St East Syracuse (13057) *(G-4216)*

Hercules Gift & Gourmet, East Syracuse Also called Hercules Candy Co *(G-4216)*

Hercules Group Inc...212 813-8000
27 Seaview Blvd Port Washington (11050) *(G-12883)*

Hercules Heat Treating Corp.................................718 625-1266
101 Classon Ave 113 Brooklyn (11205) *(G-1932)*

Herff Jones LLC...607 936-2366
262 W 2nd St Corning (14830) *(G-3716)*

Hergo Ergonomic Support Syst (PA).....................888 222-7270
3530 Lawson Blvd Oceanside (11572) *(G-12175)*

Heritage Packaging, Victor Also called W Stuart Smith Inc *(G-15441)*

Heritage Printing Center.......................................518 563-8240
94 Margaret St Plattsburgh (12901) *(G-12751)*

Heritage Wide Plank Flooring, Riverhead Also called Custom Woodwork Ltd *(G-13173)*

Herkimer Cheese, Ilion Also called Original Hrkmer Cnty Chese Inc *(G-6280)*

Herkimer Diamond Mines Inc..............................315 891-7355
800 Mohawk St Herkimer (13350) *(G-5864)*

Herkimer Tool & Equipment Co, Herkimer Also called Herkimer Tool & Machining Corp *(G-5865)*

Herkimer Tool & Machining Corp..........................315 866-2110
125 Marginal Rd Herkimer (13350) *(G-5865)*

Herman Hall Communications................................718 941-1879
1630 Nostrand Ave Brooklyn (11226) *(G-1933)*

Herman Kay, New York Also called Mystic Inc *(G-10528)*

Herman Kay Company Ltd......................................212 239-2025
463 7th Ave Fl 12 New York (10018) *(G-9768)*

Herman Miller Inc..212 753-3022
1177 Ave Of The Amrcs 1 New York (10036) *(G-9769)*

Hermann Gerdens Inc...631 841-3132
1725 N Strongs Rd Copiague (11726) *(G-3658)*

Hermann J Wiemer Vineyard.................................607 243-7971
3962 Rte 14 Dundee (14837) *(G-4047)*

Hermosa Corp..315 768-4320
102 Main St New York Mills (13417) *(G-11834)*

Heron Hill Vineyards Inc (PA)................................607 868-4241
9301 County Route 76 Hammondsport (14840) *(G-5530)*

Heron Hill Winery, Hammondsport Also called Heron Hill Vineyards Inc *(G-5530)*

Herr Manufacturing Co Inc....................................716 754-4341
17 Pearce Ave Tonawanda (14150) *(G-15113)*

Herris Gourmet Inc...917 578-2308
536 Grand St Brooklyn (11211) *(G-1934)*

Herrmann Group LLC...716 876-9798
2320 Elmwood Ave Kenmore (14217) *(G-6651)*

Hersco-Arch Products, Long Island City Also called Hersco-Orthotic Labs Corp *(G-7242)*

Hersco-Orthotic Labs Corp...................................718 391-0416
3928 Crescent St Long Island City (11101) *(G-7242)*

Hershel Horowitz Corp..212 719-1710
50 W 47th St Ste 2011 New York (10036) *(G-9770)*

Hertling Trousers Inc...718 784-6100
236 Greenpoint Ave Brooklyn (11222) *(G-1935)*

Hes Inc...607 359-2974
6303 Symonds Hill Rd Addison (14801) *(G-5)*

Hess Corporation (PA)..212 997-8500
1185 Avenue Of The Americ New York (10036) *(G-9771)*

A
L
P
H
A
B
E
T
I
C

Hess Energy Exploration Ltd (HQ)............732 750-6500
  1185 Ave Of The Americas New York (10036) *(G-9772)*

Hess Explrtion Prod Hldngs Ltd (HQ)......732 750-6000
  1185 Ave Of The Americas New York (10036) *(G-9773)*

Hess Oil Virgin Island Corp.....................212 997-8500
  1185 Ave Of The Amer 39 New York (10036) *(G-9774)*

Hess Pipeline Corporation.......................212 997-8500
  1185 Ave Of The Amer 39 New York (10036) *(G-9775)*

Hess Tioga Gas Plant LLC.......................212 997-8500
  1185 Ave Of The Americas New York (10036) *(G-9776)*

Hexion Inc..518 792-8040
  64 Fernan Rd South Glens Falls (12803) *(G-14513)*

Hf Mfg Corp (PA)..................................212 594-9142
  1460 Broadway New York (10036) *(G-9777)*

HFC Prestige Intl US LLC........................212 389-7800
  350 5th Ave New York (10118) *(G-9778)*

Hfi, New York *Also called Home Fashions Intl LLC* *(G-9808)*

Hgi Skydyne, Port Jervis *Also called Hornet Group Inc* *(G-12850)*

Hh Liquidating Corp...............................646 282-2500
  110 E 59th St Fl 34 New York (10022) *(G-9779)*

Hi Speed Envelope Co Inc.......................718 617-1600
  560 S 3rd Ave Ste 1 Mount Vernon (10550) *(G-8148)*

Hi Tech Signs of NY Inc.........................516 794-7880
  415 E Meadow Ave East Meadow (11554) *(G-4136)*

Hi-Lites, Watkins Glen *Also called Skylark Publications Ltd* *(G-15615)*

Hi-Med, Old Bethpage *Also called Hitemco Med Applications Inc* *(G-12217)*

Hi-Tech Advanced Solutions Inc...............718 926-3488
  10525 65th Ave Apt 4h Forest Hills (11375) *(G-4921)*

Hi-Tech Cnc Machining Corp....................914 668-5090
  13 Elm Ave Mount Vernon (10550) *(G-8149)*

Hi-Tech Industries NY Inc........................607 217-7361
  23 Ozalid Rd Johnson City (13790) *(G-6601)*

Hi-Tech Metals Inc.................................718 894-1212
  5920 56th Ave Maspeth (11378) *(G-7622)*

Hi-Tech Packg World-Wide LLC................845 947-1912
  110 Corporate Dr New Windsor (12553) *(G-8369)*

Hi-Tech Pharmacal - An Akorn, Amityville *Also called Hi-Tech Pharmacal Co Inc* *(G-270)*

Hi-Tech Pharmacal - An Akorn, Amityville *Also called Hi-Tech Pharmacal Co Inc* *(G-272)*

Hi-Tech Pharmacal - An Akorn, Amityville *Also called Hi-Tech Pharmacal Co Inc* *(G-273)*

Hi-Tech Pharmacal Co Inc (HQ)...............631 789-8228
  369 Bayview Ave Amityville (11701) *(G-270)*

Hi-Tech Pharmacal Co Inc......................631 789-8228
  219 Dixon Ave Amityville (11701) *(G-271)*

Hi-Tech Pharmacal Co Inc......................631 789-8228
  26 Edison St Amityville (11701) *(G-272)*

Hi-Tech Pharmacal Co Inc......................631 789-8228
  225 Dixon Ave Amityville (11701) *(G-273)*

Hi-Temp Brazing Inc..............................631 491-4917
  539 Acorn St Deer Park (11729) *(G-3879)*

Hi-Temp Fabrication Inc..........................716 852-5655
  15 Lawrence Bell Dr Buffalo (14221) *(G-2798)*

Hi-Tron Semiconductor Corp....................631 231-1500
  85 Engineers Rd Hauppauge (11788) *(G-5670)*

Hibert Publishing LLC.............................914 381-7474
  222 Purchase St Rye (10580) *(G-14080)*

Hibu Inc (HQ).......................................516 730-1900
  90 Merrick Ave Ste 530 East Meadow (11554) *(G-4137)*

Hickory Hollow Wind Cellars, Dundee *Also called Hickory Road Land Co LLC* *(G-4048)*

Hickory Road Land Co LLC......................607 243-9114
  5289 Route 14 Dundee (14837) *(G-4048)*

Hicksville Machine Works Corp.................516 931-1524
  761 S Broadway Hicksville (11801) *(G-5916)*

Hig Capital, Williamsville *Also called Ashton-Potter USA Ltd* *(G-16120)*

Higgins Supl Co, Mc Graw *Also called Higgins Supply Company Inc* *(G-7688)*

Higgins Supply Company Inc...................607 836-6474
  18-25 South St Mc Graw (13101) *(G-7688)*

High Alchemy LLC..................................212 224-9600
  584 Broadway Rm 1008 New York (10012) *(G-9780)*

High End Print Solutions Inc...................585 325-5320
  250 Cumberland St Ste 100 Rochester (14605) *(G-13465)*

High Energy U. S. A., New York *Also called Kidz World Inc* *(G-10098)*

High Falls Brewing Company LLC (HQ).......585 263-9318
  445 Saint Paul St Rochester (14605) *(G-13466)*

High Falls Operating Co LLC...................585 546-1030
  445 Saint Paul St Rochester (14605) *(G-13467)*

High Performance Sftwr USA Inc...............866 616-4958
  145 Hook Creek Blvd Valley Stream (11581) *(G-15343)*

High Point Design LLC............................212 354-2400
  1411 Broadway Fl 8 New York (10018) *(G-9781)*

High Prfmce Plymr Cmposits Div, Medford *Also called Enecon Corporation* *(G-7706)*

High Quality Video Inc (PA).....................212 686-9534
  12 W 27th St Fl 7 New York (10001) *(G-9782)*

High Ridge News LLC.............................718 548-7412
  5818 Broadway Bronx (10463) *(G-1276)*

High Speed Hammer Company Inc..............585 266-4287
  313 Norton St Rochester (14621) *(G-13468)*

High Voltage Inc..................................518 329-3275
  31 County Route 7a Copake (12516) *(G-3642)*

Highcrest Investors LLC (HQ)...................212 702-4323
  445 Hamilton Ave Ste 1210 New York (10153) *(G-9783)*

Higher Power Industries Inc.....................914 709-9800
  11 Sunny Slope Ter Yonkers (10703) *(G-16319)*

Highland Organization Corp......................631 991-3240
  435 Unit 23 Brook Ave Deer Park (11729) *(G-3880)*

Highland Valley Supply Inc......................845 849-2863
  30 Airport Dr Wappingers Falls (12590) *(G-15496)*

Highlander Realty Inc..............................914 235-8073
  70 Church St New Rochelle (10805) *(G-8341)*

Highline Media LLC................................859 692-2100
  375 Park Ave New York (10152) *(G-9784)*

Highrange Fuels Inc...............................914 930-8300
  96 Oregon Rd Cortlandt Manor (10567) *(G-3796)*

Highway Garage....................................518 568-2837
  110 State Highway 331 Saint Johnsville (13452) *(G-14119)*

Highway Toll ADM LLC...........................516 684-9584
  66 Powerhouse Rd Ste 301 Roslyn Heights (11577) *(G-14051)*

Hill Knitting Mills Inc..............................718 846-5000
  10005 92nd Ave Ste Mgmt Richmond Hill (11418) *(G-13115)*

Hillary Merchant Inc...............................646 575-9242
  2 Wall St Ste 807 New York (10005) *(G-9785)*

Hilliard Corporation................................607 733-7121
  100 W 4th St Elmira (14901) *(G-4357)*

Hilliard Corporation................................607 733-7121
  1420 College Ave Elmira (14901) *(G-4358)*

Hills Pet Products Inc (HQ)....................212 310-2000
  300 Park Ave New York (10022) *(G-9786)*

Hillside Iron Works, Waterford *Also called Maximum Security Products Corp* *(G-15538)*

Hillside Printing Inc...............................718 658-6719
  16013 Hillside Ave Jamaica (11432) *(G-6448)*

Hilltop Slate Inc....................................518 642-1453
  Rr 22 Box A Middle Granville (12849) *(G-7868)*

Hilltown Pork Inc (PA)............................518 781-4050
  12948 State Route 22 Canaan (12029) *(G-3119)*

Hilord Chemical Corporation.....................631 234-7373
  70 Engineers Rd Hauppauge (11788) *(G-5671)*

Himatsingka America Inc (HQ)..................212 824-2949
  261 5th Ave Rm 1400 New York (10016) *(G-9787)*

Himatsingka America Inc.........................212 252-0802
  261 5th Ave Rm 501 New York (10016) *(G-9788)*

Himatsingka Holdings NA Inc (HQ)............212 824-2949
  261 5th Ave Rm 1400 New York (10016) *(G-9789)*

Hinge Inc...214 576-9352
  508 Laguardia Pl New York (10012) *(G-9790)*

Hinspergers Poly Industries.....................585 798-6625
  430 W Oak Orchard St Medina (14103) *(G-7738)*

Hipotronics Inc (HQ)..............................845 279-8091
  1650 Route 22 Brewster (10509) *(G-1151)*

Hippo Industries, Oyster Bay *Also called Engineering Maint Pdts Inc* *(G-12447)*

Hippo International LLC..........................617 230-0599
  333 W 86th St Apt 1207 New York (10024) *(G-9791)*

Hippocrene Books Inc (PA)......................212 685-4371
  171 Madison Ave Rm 1605 New York (10016) *(G-9792)*

Hipshot Products Inc..............................607 532-9404
  8248 State Route 96 Interlaken (14847) *(G-6284)*

Hirsch Optical Corp...............................516 752-2211
  91 Carolyn Blvd Farmingdale (11735) *(G-4644)*

His Productions USA Inc.........................212 594-3737
  15 Broad St Apt 3030 New York (10005) *(G-9793)*

His Vision Inc.......................................585 254-0022
  1260 Lyell Ave Rochester (14606) *(G-13469)*

Historic TW Inc (HQ).............................212 484-8000
  75 Rockefeller Plz New York (10019) *(G-9794)*

History Publishing Company LLC...............845 398-8161
  173 Route 9w Palisades (10964) *(G-12481)*

Hisun Led, Flushing *Also called Hisun Optoelectronics Co Ltd* *(G-4859)*

Hisun Optoelectronics Co Ltd...................718 886-6966
  4109 College Point Blvd Flushing (11355) *(G-4859)*

Hitachi Cable America Inc (HQ).................914 694-9200
  2 Manhattanville Rd # 301 Purchase (10577) *(G-13004)*

Hitachi Metals America Ltd (HQ)..............914 694-9200
  2 Manhattanville Rd # 301 Purchase (10577) *(G-13005)*

Hitech Pharm..631 789-8228
  369 Bayview Ave Amityville (11701) *(G-274)*

Hitemco, Old Bethpage *Also called Barson Composites Corporation* *(G-12215)*

Hitemco Med Applications Inc...................516 752-7882
  160 Sweet Hollow Rd Old Bethpage (11804) *(G-12217)*

Hje Company Inc...................................518 792-8733
  820 Quaker Rd Queensbury (12804) *(G-13043)*

Hjn Inc (PA)...212 398-9564
  16 W 46th St Fl 9 New York (10036) *(G-9795)*

HK Metal Trading Ltd.............................212 868-3333
  450 Fashion Ave Ste 2300 New York (10123) *(G-9796)*

Hks Printing Company Inc.......................212 675-2529
  115 E 27th St New York (10016) *(G-9797)*

Hlw Acres LLC....................................585 591-0795
  1727 Exchange Street Rd Attica (14011) *(G-457)*

Hlw Acres Poultry Processing, Attica *Also called Hlw Acres LLC* *(G-457)*

Hmh, New York *Also called Houghton Mifflin Harcourt Co* *(G-9819)*

Hmi Metal Powders, Clayville *Also called Homogeneous Metals Inc* *(G-3457)*

Hmi Metal Powders................................315 839-5421
  2395 Main St Clayville (13322) *(G-3456)*

Hmo Beverage Corporation 917 371-6100
68 33rd St Unit 4 Brooklyn (11232) ***(G-1936)***
Hn Precision, Rochester *Also called Helio Precision Products Inc* ***(G-13464)***
Hn Precision-Ny, Rochester *Also called Nationwide Precision Pdts Corp* ***(G-13567)***
Hnc Enterprises LLC 904 448-9387
10624 Avenue D Brooklyn (11236) ***(G-1937)***
Hnh, New York *Also called Handy & Harman Ltd* ***(G-9720)***
Hni Corporation 212 683-2232
200 Lexington Ave Rm 1112 New York (10016) ***(G-9798)***
HNST Mold Inspections LLC (PA) 845 215-9258
15 Johnsontown Rd Sloatsburg (10974) ***(G-14471)***
Hobart Corporation 631 864-3440
71 Mall Dr Ste 1 Commack (11725) ***(G-3592)***
Hobart Corporation 585 427-9000
3495 Winton Pl Rochester (14623) ***(G-13470)***
Hockey Facility 518 452-7396
830 Albany Shaker Rd Albany (12211) ***(G-86)***
Hodgins Engraving Co Inc 585 343-4444
3817 W Main Street Rd Batavia (14020) ***(G-618)***
Hoehn Inc 518 463-8900
159 Chestnut St Albany (12210) ***(G-87)***
Hoehn.us, Albany *Also called Hoehn Inc* ***(G-87)***
Hoercher Industries Inc 585 398-2982
A1 Country Club Rd Ste 1 East Rochester (14445) ***(G-4164)***
Hoff Associates Mfg Reps Inc 585 398-2000
5815 County Road 41 Farmington (14425) ***(G-4773)***
Hoffman & Hoffman 315 536-4773
489 State Route 54 Penn Yan (14527) ***(G-12586)***
Hoffmann-La Roche Inc 973 890-2291
430 E 29th St New York (10016) ***(G-9799)***
Hogan Flavors & Fragrances 212 598-4310
130 E 18th St Frnt New York (10003) ***(G-9800)***
Hogan Fragrances International, New York *Also called Hogan Flavors & Fragrances* ***(G-9800)***
Hogil Pharmaceutical Corp 914 681-1800
237 Mmaroneck Ave Ste 207 White Plains (10605) ***(G-16014)***
Hohenforst Splitting Co Inc 518 725-0012
152 W Fulton St Gloversville (12078) ***(G-5285)***
Hohl Machine & Conveyor Co Inc 716 882-7210
1580 Niagara St Buffalo (14213) ***(G-2799)***
Hohlveyor, Buffalo *Also called Hohl Machine & Conveyor Co Inc* ***(G-2799)***
Hohmann & Barnard Inc (HQ) 631 234-0600
30 Rasons Ct Hauppauge (11788) ***(G-5672)***
Hohmann & Barnard Inc 518 357-9757
310 Wayto Rd Schenectady (12303) ***(G-14278)***
Hola Publishing Co 718 424-3129
2932 Northern Blvd Long Island City (11101) ***(G-7243)***
Holbrooke By Sberry, New York *Also called Holbrooke Inc* ***(G-9801)***
Holbrooke Inc 646 397-4674
444 E 20th St Apt 1b New York (10009) ***(G-9801)***
Holcim (us) Inc 518 828-8478
4303 Us Route 9 Hudson (12534) ***(G-6160)***
Holdens Screen Supply Corp 212 627-2727
121 Varick St New York (10013) ***(G-9802)***
Holiday House Publishing, New York *Also called Bicker Inc* ***(G-8781)***
Holland & Sherry Inc (PA) 212 542-8410
330 E 59th St Ph New York (10022) ***(G-9803)***
Holland & Sherry Intr Design, New York *Also called Holland & Sherry Inc* ***(G-9803)***
Hollander HM Fshons Hldngs LLC 212 575-0400
440 Park Ave S Fl 10 New York (10016) ***(G-9804)***
Hollander Sleep Products LLC 212 575-0400
440 Park Ave S New York (10016) ***(G-9805)***
Hollingsworth & Vose Company 518 695-8000
3235 County Rte 113 Greenwich (12834) ***(G-5473)***
Holloween Adventures, New York *Also called Masquerade LLC* ***(G-10379)***
Hollywood Advg Banners Inc 631 842-3000
539 Oak St Copiague (11726) ***(G-3659)***
Hollywood Banners, Copiague *Also called Hollywood Advg Banners Inc* ***(G-3659)***
Hollywood Banners Inc 631 842-3000
539 Oak St Copiague (11726) ***(G-3660)***
Hollywood Signs Inc 917 577-7333
388 3rd Ave Brooklyn (11215) ***(G-1938)***
Holmes Group The Inc 212 333-2300
271 W 47th St Apt 23a New York (10036) ***(G-9806)***
Holstein World, East Syracuse *Also called H F W Communications Inc* ***(G-4214)***
Holyoke Fittings Inc 718 649-0710
850 Stanley Ave Brooklyn (11208) ***(G-1939)***
Home Fashions Intl LLC (PA) 212 689-3579
295 5th Ave Ste 1520 New York (10016) ***(G-9807)***
Home Fashions Intl LLC 212 684-0091
295 5th Ave Ste 1520 New York (10016) ***(G-9808)***
Home Ideal Inc 718 762-8998
4528 159th St Flushing (11358) ***(G-4860)***
Home Lighting & Accessories, New City *Also called Doctorow Communications Inc* ***(G-8225)***
Home Maide Incorporated 845 837-1700
1 Short St Harriman (10926) ***(G-5544)***
Home Reporter & Sunset News, Brooklyn *Also called Home Reporter Inc* ***(G-1940)***
Home Reporter Inc 718 238-6600
8723 3rd Ave Brooklyn (11209) ***(G-1940)***

Home Tech LLC 914 301-5408
13 Catherine Pl Katonah (10536) ***(G-6633)***
Home4u Inc 347 262-7214
152 Skillman St Apt 8 Brooklyn (11205) ***(G-1941)***
Homegrown For Good LLC 857 540-6361
29 Beechwood Ave New Rochelle (10801) ***(G-8342)***
Homer Iron Works LLC 607 749-3963
5130 Us Route 11 Homer (13077) ***(G-6064)***
Homer Logging Contractor 607 753-8553
6176 Sunnyside Dr Homer (13077) ***(G-6065)***
Homes Land Eastrn Long Island, Southampton *Also called Frontiers Unlimited Inc* ***(G-14530)***
Homesell Inc 718 514-0346
4010 Hylan Blvd Staten Island (10308) ***(G-14661)***
Homogeneous Metals Inc 315 839-5421
2395 Main St Clayville (13322) ***(G-3457)***
Honeoye Falls Distillery LLC (PA) 201 780-4618
168 W Main St Honeoye Falls (14472) ***(G-6075)***
Honeybee Rbtics Cft Mechanisms, Brooklyn *Also called Honeybee Robotics Ltd* ***(G-1942)***
Honeybee Robotics Ltd (HQ) 212 966-0661
Suit Bldg 128 Brooklyn (11205) ***(G-1942)***
Honeywell Authorized Dealer, Floral Park *Also called Automated Bldg MGT Systems Inc* ***(G-4808)***
Honeywell International Inc 518 270-0200
3 Tibbits Ave Troy (12183) ***(G-15158)***
Honeywell International Inc 516 577-2661
2 Corporate Center Dr # 100 Melville (11747) ***(G-7790)***
Honeywell International Inc 516 577-2000
2 Corporate Center Dr # 100 Melville (11747) ***(G-7791)***
Honeywell International Inc 845 342-4400
13 Bedford Ave Middletown (10940) ***(G-7914)***
Honeywell International Inc 516 302-9401
5 Dakota Dr Ste 120 New Hyde Park (11042) ***(G-8274)***
Honeywell International Inc 212 964-5111
263 Old Country Rd Melville (11747) ***(G-7792)***
Honeywell International Inc 516 577-2000
2 Corporate Center Dr # 100 Melville (11747) ***(G-7793)***
Honeywell International Inc 315 463-7208
7000 Airways Park Dr # 4 East Syracuse (13057) ***(G-4217)***
Honeywell International Inc 631 471-2202
1859 Lakeland Ave Lake Ronkonkoma (11779) ***(G-6770)***
Honor Brand Feeds, Narrowsburg *Also called Narrowsburg Feed & Grain Co* ***(G-8210)***
Honora, New York *Also called Brannkey Inc* ***(G-8847)***
Hood Industries Inc 716 836-0301
580 Tifft St Buffalo (14220) ***(G-2800)***
Hooek Produktion Inc 212 367-9111
307 7th Ave Rm 1204 New York (10001) ***(G-9809)***
Hookipa Pharma Inc 431 890-6360
350 5th Ave Ste 7240 New York (10118) ***(G-9810)***
Hoosier Magnetics Inc 315 323-5832
110 Denny St Ogdensburg (13669) ***(G-12206)***
Hope International Productions 212 247-3188
315 W 57th St Apt 6h New York (10019) ***(G-9811)***
Hopes Windows Inc 716 665-5124
84 Hopkins Ave Jamestown (14701) ***(G-6516)***
Hopewell Precision Inc 845 221-2737
19 Ryan Rd Hopewell Junction (12533) ***(G-6096)***
Hopscotch Technologies Inc 313 408-4285
81 Prospect St Brooklyn (11201) ***(G-1943)***
Hoptron Brewtique 631 438-0296
22 W Main St Ste 11 Patchogue (11772) ***(G-12502)***
Horace J Metz 716 873-9103
2385 Elmwood Ave Kenmore (14217) ***(G-6652)***
Horizon Apparel Mfg Inc 516 361-4878
115 Bayside Dr Atlantic Beach (11509) ***(G-453)***
Horizon Floors I LLC 212 509-9686
11 Broadway Lbby 5 New York (10004) ***(G-9812)***
Horizons Magazine, Brooklyn *Also called Targum Press USA Inc* ***(G-2493)***
Horne Organization Inc (PA) 914 572-1330
15 Arthur Pl Yonkers (10701) ***(G-16320)***
Horne Products Inc 631 293-0773
144 Verdi St Farmingdale (11735) ***(G-4645)***
Hornet Group Inc 845 858-6400
100 River Rd Port Jervis (12771) ***(G-12850)***
Horning Greenhouses, Penn Yan *Also called Ivan Horning* ***(G-12587)***
Horns & Halos Cft Brewing LLC 585 507-7248
3154 State St Caledonia (14423) ***(G-3071)***
Horo Creations LLC 212 719-4818
71 W 47th St Ste 404 New York (10036) ***(G-9813)***
Horseheads Printing, Horseheads *Also called David Helsing* ***(G-6120)***
Hosel & Ackerson Inc (PA) 212 575-1490
570 Fashion Ave Rm 805 New York (10018) ***(G-9814)***
Hoshizaki Nrtheastern Dist Ctr 516 605-1411
150 Dupont St Ste 100 Plainview (11803) ***(G-12687)***
Hoskie Co Inc 718 628-8672
132 Harrison Pl Brooklyn (11237) ***(G-1944)***
Hosmer Inc 888 467-9463
6999 State Route 89 Ovid (14521) ***(G-12424)***
Hosmer's Winery, Ovid *Also called Hosmer Inc* ***(G-12424)***
Hospira Inc 716 684-9400
2501 Walden Ave Buffalo (14225) ***(G-2801)***

A L P H A B E T I C

Hospitality Graphic Systems 212 563-9334
  500 10th Ave New York (10018) *(G-9815)*
Hospitality Graphics Inc 212 643-6700
  545 8th Ave Rm 401 New York (10018) *(G-9816)*
Hospitality Inc 212 268-1930
  247 W 35th St Fl 4 New York (10001) *(G-9817)*
Hot Cashews, New York Also called Just Bottoms & Tops Inc *(G-10044)*
Hot Line Industries Inc (PA) 516 764-0400
  2648 Grand Ave Bellmore (11710) *(G-783)*
Hot Sox Company Incorporated (PA) 212 957-2000
  95 Madison Ave Fl 15 New York (10016) *(G-9818)*
Hotel Business, Islandia Also called Icd Publications Inc *(G-6335)*
Hotelexpert, New York Also called Tyme Global Technologies LLC *(G-11568)*
Houghton Mifflin Clarion Books, New York Also called Houghton Mifflin Harcourt
Pubg *(G-9820)*
Houghton Mifflin Harcourt Co 212 420-5800
  3 Park Ave Fl 18 New York (10016) *(G-9819)*
Houghton Mifflin Harcourt Pubg 212 420-5800
  3 Park Ave Fl 18 New York (10016) *(G-9820)*
Houghton Mifflin Harcourt Pubg 914 747-2709
  28 Claremont Ave Thornwood (10594) *(G-15070)*
Houles USA Inc 212 935-3900
  979 3rd Ave Ste 1200 New York (10022) *(G-9821)*
Hound & Gatos Pet Foods Corp 212 618-1917
  14 Wall St Fl 20 New York (10005) *(G-9822)*
Hourglass Interactive LLC 954 254-2853
  1 Union Sq S Apt 20j New York (10003) *(G-9823)*
House O'Weenies, Bronx Also called Marathon Enterprises Inc *(G-1306)*
House of Heydenryk, The, Long Island City Also called New Heydenryk LLC *(G-7307)*
House of Portfolios Co Inc (PA) 212 206-7323
  37 W 26th St Rm 305 New York (10010) *(G-9824)*
House of Portfolios Co Inc 212 206-7323
  48 W 21st St New York (10010) *(G-9825)*
House of Serengeti, White Plains Also called Farmers Hub LLC *(G-16006)*
House of Stone Inc 845 782-7271
  1015 State Route 17m Monroe (10950) *(G-8022)*
House of The Foaming Case Inc 718 454-0101
  110 08 Dunkirk St Saint Albans (11412) *(G-14105)*
House Pearl Fashions (us) Ltd 212 840-3183
  1410 Broadway Rm 1501 New York (10018) *(G-9826)*
House Ur Home Inc 347 585-3308
  6 Teverya Way Unit 103 Monroe (10950) *(G-8023)*
Hovee Inc 646 249-6200
  722 Saint Nicholas Ave New York (10031) *(G-9827)*
Hover-Davis Inc (HQ) 585 352-9590
  100 Paragon Dr Rochester (14624) *(G-13471)*
Howard Charles Inc 917 902-6934
  180 Froehlich Farm Blvd Woodbury (11797) *(G-16173)*
Howard Formed Steel Pdts Div, Bronx Also called Truxton Corp *(G-1383)*
Howard J Moore Company Inc 631 351-8467
  210 Terminal Dr Ste B Plainview (11803) *(G-12688)*
Howden Fan Company, Williamsville Also called Howden North America Inc *(G-16132)*
Howden North America Inc (PA) 330 867-8540
  2475 George Urban Blvd # 120 Depew (14043) *(G-3985)*
Howden North America Inc 716 817-6900
  1775 Wehrle Dr Williamsville (14221) *(G-16132)*
Howdens, Depew Also called Howden North America Inc *(G-3985)*
Howe Machine & Tool Corp 516 931-5687
  236 Park Ave Bethpage (11714) *(G-836)*
Howell Packaging, Elmira Also called F M Howell & Company *(G-4351)*
Howmedica Osteonics Corp 518 783-1880
  2 Northway Ln Latham (12110) *(G-6859)*
Howmedica Osteonics Corp 516 484-0897
  95 Seaview Blvd Ste 201 Port Washington (11050) *(G-12884)*
HP Hood LLC 607 295-8134
  25 Hurlbut St Arkport (14807) *(G-393)*
HP Hood LLC 315 363-3870
  252 Genesee St Oneida (13421) *(G-12246)*
HP Hood LLC 315 658-2132
  20700 State Route 411 La Fargeville (13656) *(G-6733)*
HP Hood LLC 518 218-9097
  816 Burdeck St Schenectady (12306) *(G-14279)*
HP Hood LLC 315 829-3339
  19 Ward St Vernon (13476) *(G-15366)*
HP Hood LLC 607 772-6580
  93 Pennsylvania Ave Binghamton (13903) *(G-882)*
HP Inc 650 857-1501
  5 Computer Dr S Albany (12205) *(G-88)*
HP Inc 650 857-1501
  556 W 22nd St Fl 8 New York (10011) *(G-9828)*
Hpce, Pearl River Also called Hunts Point Clean Energy LLC *(G-12534)*
Hpe Clothing Corporation 946 356-0474
  60 Broad St Ste 3502 New York (10004) *(G-9829)*
Hpi Co Inc (PA) 718 851-2753
  1656 41st St Brooklyn (11218) *(G-1945)*
Hpk Industries LLC 315 724-0196
  1208 Broad St Utica (13501) *(G-15271)*
HRA Poster Project, Brooklyn Also called City of New York *(G-1665)*
Hrd Metal Products Inc 631 243-6700
  120 E Jefryn Blvd Ste A Deer Park (11729) *(G-3881)*

Hri Metals LLC 518 822-1013
  1233 Us Route 9 Hudson (12534) *(G-6161)*
Hs Grant, Saratoga Springs Also called Grant Graphics LLC *(G-14178)*
Hs Homeworx LLC 646 870-0406
  18 E 74th St Fl 5 New York (10021) *(G-9830)*
HSM Machine Works Inc (PA) 631 924-6600
  3671 Horseblock Rd Medford (11763) *(G-7712)*
HSM Packaging Corporation 315 476-7996
  4529 Crown Rd Liverpool (13090) *(G-7012)*
HSN, New York Also called Macfadden Cmmnctions Group LLC *(G-10306)*
Hti Recycling LLC (PA) 716 433-9294
  490 Ohio St Lockport (14094) *(G-7083)*
Hubbard Tool and Die Corp 315 337-7840
  Rome Indus Ctr Bldg 5 Rome (13440) *(G-13851)*
Hubbell Inc 845 586-2707
  46124 State Highway 30 # 2 Margaretville (12455) *(G-7566)*
Hubbell Galvanising, Yorkville Also called O W Hubbell & Sons Inc *(G-16376)*
Hubbell Galvanizing Inc 315 736-8311
  5124 Commercial Dr Yorkville (13495) *(G-16375)*
Hubco Inc 716 683-5940
  2885 Commerce Dr Alden (14004) *(G-170)*
Hubray Inc 800 645-2855
  2045 Grand Ave North Baldwin (11510) *(G-12006)*
Huck International Inc 845 331-7300
  1 Corporate Dr Kingston (12401) *(G-6694)*
Huckleberry Inc 631 630-5450
  655 Old Willets Path Hauppauge (11788) *(G-5673)*
Hudson Cabinetry Design, Peekskill Also called Hat Factory Furniture Co *(G-12552)*
Hudson Dying & Finishing LLC 518 752-4389
  68 Harrison St Gloversville (12078) *(G-5286)*
Hudson Eastern Industries Inc 917 295-5818
  1118 143rd Pl Whitestone (11357) *(G-16094)*
Hudson Envelope Corporation (PA) 212 473-6666
  135 3rd Ave New York (10003) *(G-9831)*
Hudson Fabrics LLC 518 671-6100
  128 2nd Street Ext Hudson (12534) *(G-6162)*
Hudson Group (hg) Inc 212 971-6800
  250 Greenwich St New York (10007) *(G-9832)*
Hudson Industries Corporation 518 762-4638
  100 Maple Ave Johnstown (12095) *(G-6619)*
Hudson Machine Works Inc 845 279-1413
  30 Branch Rd Brewster (10509) *(G-1152)*
Hudson Mirror LLC 914 930-8906
  710 Washington St Peekskill (10566) *(G-12553)*
Hudson Park Press Inc 212 929-8898
  232 Madison Ave Rm 1400 New York (10016) *(G-9833)*
Hudson Power Transmission Co 718 622-3869
  241 Halsey St Brooklyn (11216) *(G-1946)*
Hudson Printing Co Inc 718 937-8600
  747 3rd Ave Lbby 3 New York (10017) *(G-9834)*
Hudson Software Corporation 914 773-0400
  3 W Main St Ste 106 Elmsford (10523) *(G-4410)*
Hudson Technologies Company (HQ) 845 735-6000
  1 Blue Hill Plz Ste 1541 Pearl River (10965) *(G-12532)*
Hudson Valley Baking Co, Mamaroneck Also called Richard Engdal Baking Corp *(G-7521)*
Hudson Valley Black Press 845 562-1313
  343 Broadway Newburgh (12550) *(G-11868)*
Hudson Valley Chocolatier Inc (PA) 845 831-8240
  269 Main St Beacon (12508) *(G-753)*
Hudson Valley Coatings LLC 845 398-1778
  175 N Route 9w Ste 12 Congers (10920) *(G-3615)*
Hudson Valley Creamery LLC 518 851-2570
  2986 Us Route 9 Hudson (12534) *(G-6163)*
Hudson Valley Foie Gras LLC 845 292-2500
  80 Brooks Rd Ferndale (12734) *(G-4790)*
Hudson Valley Lighting Inc 845 561-0300
  151 Airport Dr Wappingers Falls (12590) *(G-15497)*
Hudson Valley Magazine, Fishkill Also called Suburban Publishing Inc *(G-4804)*
Hudson Valley Office Furn Inc 845 565-6673
  7 Wisner Ave Newburgh (12550) *(G-11869)*
Hudson Valley Paper Works Inc 845 569-8883
  8 Lander St 15 Newburgh (12550) *(G-11870)*
Hudson Valley Steel Products 845 565-2270
  5231 Route 9w Newburgh (12550) *(G-11871)*
Hudson Valley Tech Dev Ctr Inc 845 391-8214
  180 South St Highland (12528) *(G-5960)*
Huersch Marketing Group LLC 518 874-1045
  70 Cohoes Ave Ste 4 Green Island (12183) *(G-5437)*
Huffington Post, The, New York Also called Thehuffingtonpostcom Inc *(G-11460)*
Hugh F McPherson Inc 716 668-6107
  70 Innsbruck Dr Cheektowaga (14227) *(G-3354)*
Hugo Boss Usa Inc (HQ) 212 940-0600
  55 Water St Fl 48 New York (10041) *(G-9835)*
Huhtamaki Inc 315 593-5311
  100 State St Fulton (13069) *(G-5064)*
Hulley Holding Company Inc (PA) 716 332-3982
  2500 Elmwood Ave Kenmore (14217) *(G-6653)*
Hulley Woodworking Company, Kenmore Also called Hulley Holding Company Inc *(G-6653)*
Hum Limited Liability Corp 631 525-2174
  70 Deer Valley Dr Nesconset (11767) *(G-8218)*
Human Condition Safety Inc 646 867-0644
  61 Broadway Fl 31 New York (10006) *(G-9836)*

Human Electronics Inc...315 724-9850
155 Genesee St Utica (13501) ***(G-15272)***
Human Life Foundation Inc...212 685-5210
271 Madison Ave Ste 1005 New York (10016) ***(G-9837)***
Human Technologies Corporation...315 735-3532
2260 Dwyer Ave Utica (13501) ***(G-15273)***
Humana Press Inc...212 460-1500
233 Spring St Fl 6 New York (10013) ***(G-9838)***
Humanscale Corporation (PA)...212 725-4749
1114 Avenue Of The Americ New York (10036) ***(G-9839)***
Humanware USA Inc (PA)...800 722-3393
1 Ups Way Champlain (12919) ***(G-3313)***
Humboldt Woodworking...718 707-0022
3836 11th St Long Island City (11101) ***(G-7244)***
Humor Rainbow Inc...646 402-9113
555 W 18th St New York (10011) ***(G-9840)***
Hunt Country Furniture Inc (PA)...845 832-6601
19 Dog Tail Corners Rd Wingdale (12594) ***(G-16159)***
Hunt Country Vineyards...315 595-2812
4021 Italy Hill Rd Branchport (14418) ***(G-1111)***
Hunter Displays, East Patchogue *Also called Hunter Metal Industries Inc* ***(G-4154)***
Hunter Douglas Inc (HQ)...845 664-7000
1 Blue Hill Plz Ste 1569 Pearl River (10965) ***(G-12533)***
Hunter Machine Inc...585 924-7480
6551 Anthony Dr Victor (14564) ***(G-15412)***
Hunter Metal Industries Inc...631 475-5900
14 Hewlett Ave East Patchogue (11772) ***(G-4154)***
Huntington Ice & Cube Corp (PA)...718 456-2013
335 Moffat St Brooklyn (11237) ***(G-1947)***
Huntington Ingalls Inc...518 884-3834
33 Cady Hill Blvd Saratoga Springs (12866) ***(G-14182)***
Huntington Woodworking Inc...631 271-7897
4 Fox Hollow Ridings Ct Northport (11768) ***(G-12105)***
Hunts Point Clean Energy LLC...203 451-5143
401 N Middletown Rd Pearl River (10965) ***(G-12534)***
Huron Tl Cutter Grinding Inc...631 420-7000
2045 Wellwood Ave Farmingdale (11735) ***(G-4646)***
Hurryworks LLC...516 998-4600
990 Seaview Blvd Port Washington (11050) ***(G-12885)***
Hustler Powerboats, Calverton *Also called Global Marine Power Inc* ***(G-3081)***
Hutchinson Industries Inc...716 852-1435
92 Msgr Valente Dr Buffalo (14206) ***(G-2802)***
Hutnick Rehab, Bohemia *Also called Gfh Orthotic & Prosthetic Labs* ***(G-1017)***
Hvr Mso LLC...833 345-6974
2678 South Rd Ste 202 Poughkeepsie (12601) ***(G-12962)***
Hw Holdings Inc (HQ)...212 399-1000
718 5th Ave New York (10019) ***(G-9841)***
Hw Specialties Co Inc...631 589-0745
210 Knickerbocker Ave B Bohemia (11716) ***(G-1020)***
Hy Cert Services Inc...631 231-7005
122 Cain Dr Brentwood (11717) ***(G-1122)***
Hy-Grade Metal Products Corp...315 475-4221
906 Burnet Ave Syracuse (13203) ***(G-14912)***
Hy-Tech Mold Inc...585 247-2450
60 Elmgrove Park Rochester (14624) ***(G-13472)***
Hybrid Cases, Holbrook *Also called Roadie Products Inc* ***(G-6018)***
Hyde Park Brewing Co Inc...845 229-8277
4076 Albany Post Rd Hyde Park (12538) ***(G-6272)***
Hydramec Inc...585 593-5190
4393 River St Scio (14880) ***(G-14325)***
Hydrive Energy...914 925-9100
350 Theodore Fremd Ave Rye (10580) ***(G-14081)***
Hydro-Air Components Inc...716 827-6510
100 Rittling Blvd Buffalo (14220) ***(G-2803)***
Hydroacoustics Inc...585 359-1000
999 Lehigh Station Rd # 100 Henrietta (14467) ***(G-5856)***
Hydrogen Technology Corp...800 315-9554
915 Broadway Ste 801 New York (10010) ***(G-9842)***
Hygrade...718 488-9000
30 Warsoff Pl Brooklyn (11205) ***(G-1948)***
Hygrade Fuel Inc...516 741-0723
260 Columbus Pkwy Mineola (11501) ***(G-7980)***
Hyman Podrusnick Co Inc...718 853-4502
212 Foster Ave Brooklyn (11230) ***(G-1949)***
Hyperbaric Technologies Inc...518 842-3030
1 Sam Stratton Rd Amsterdam (12010) ***(G-330)***
Hyperlaw Inc...212 873-6982
17 W 70th St Apt 4 New York (10023) ***(G-9843)***
Hypoxico Inc...212 972-1009
50 Lexington Ave Ste 249 New York (10010) ***(G-9844)***
Hypres Inc (PA)...914 592-1190
175 Clearbrook Rd Elmsford (10523) ***(G-4411)***
Hytech Tool & Die Inc...716 488-2796
2202 Washington St Jamestown (14701) ***(G-6517)***
I & I Systems...845 753-9126
66 Table Rock Rd Tuxedo Park (10987) ***(G-15216)***
I & S of NY Inc...716 373-7001
4174 Route 417 Allegany (14706) ***(G-189)***
I 2 Print Inc...718 937-8800
3819 24th St Long Island City (11101) ***(G-7245)***
I 3 Manufacturing Services Inc...607 238-7077
100 Eldredge St Binghamton (13901) ***(G-883)***
I A S National Inc...631 423-6900
95 W Hills Rd Huntington Station (11746) ***(G-6249)***
I C S, New York *Also called Integrated Graphics Inc* ***(G-9908)***
I D E Processes Corporation (PA)...718 544-1177
106 81st Ave Kew Gardens (11415) ***(G-6664)***
I D Machine Inc...607 796-2549
1580 Lake St Elmira (14901) ***(G-4359)***
I D Tel Corp...718 876-6000
55 Canal St Staten Island (10304) ***(G-14662)***
I Do Machining, Elmira *Also called I D Machine Inc* ***(G-4359)***
I E D Corp...631 348-0424
88 Bridge Rd Islandia (11749) ***(G-6334)***
I E M, Troy *Also called Interntnal Elctronic Mchs Corp* ***(G-15173)***
I Fix Screen...631 421-1938
203 Centereach Mall Centereach (11720) ***(G-3251)***
I J White Corporation...631 293-3788
20 Executive Blvd Farmingdale (11735) ***(G-4647)***
I L C, Bohemia *Also called Ilc Industries LLC* ***(G-1023)***
I Love Accessories Inc...212 239-1875
10 W 33rd St Rm 210 New York (10001) ***(G-9845)***
I Meglio Corp...631 617-6900
1140 Motor Pkwy Ste C Hauppauge (11788) ***(G-5674)***
I N K T Inc...212 957-2700
250 W 54th St Fl 9 New York (10019) ***(G-9846)***
I On Youth...716 832-6509
115 Godfrey St Buffalo (14215) ***(G-2804)***
I Rauchs Sons Inc...718 507-8844
3220 112th St East Elmhurst (11369) ***(G-4107)***
I S C A Corp (PA)...212 719-5123
512 7th Ave Fl 7 New York (10018) ***(G-9847)***
I Shalom & Co Inc...212 532-7911
411 5th Ave Fl 4 New York (10016) ***(G-9848)***
I Spiewak & Sons Inc...212 695-1620
225 W 37th St Fl 15l New York (10018) ***(G-9849)***
I Trade Technology Ltd...615 348-7233
3 Rustic Dr Airmont (10952) ***(G-12)***
I Triple E Spectrum, New York *Also called Magazine I Spectrum E* ***(G-10320)***
I W M, Dryden *Also called Integrated Water Management* ***(G-4039)***
I'M Nuts, Hewlett *Also called Yes Were Nuts Ltd* ***(G-5877)***
I-Tem Brand LLC...718 790-6927
675 E 213th St Apt 1 Bronx (10467) ***(G-1277)***
I3 Assembly LLC...607 238-7077
100 Eldredge St Binghamton (13901) ***(G-884)***
I3 Electronics Inc (PA)...607 238-7077
100 Eldredge St Binghamton (13901) ***(G-885)***
I3 Electronics Inc...607 238-7077
Huron Campus 1500 1700 Endicott (13760) ***(G-4459)***
IA Construction Corporation...716 933-8787
Rr 305 Box S Portville (14770) ***(G-12935)***
Iaas , The, Flushing *Also called Intercultural Alliance Artists* ***(G-4862)***
IAC Search LLC (HQ)...212 314-7300
555 W 18th St New York (10011) ***(G-9850)***
Iac/Interactivecorp (PA)...212 314-7300
555 W 18th St New York (10011) ***(G-9851)***
Iadc Inc...718 238-0623
845 Father Capodanno Blvd Staten Island (10305) ***(G-14663)***
IaMmaliamills LLC...805 845-2137
32 33rd St Unit 13 Brooklyn (11232) ***(G-1950)***
Iat Interactive LLC...914 273-2233
333 N Bedford Rd Ste 110 Mount Kisco (10549) ***(G-8093)***
Iba Industrial Inc...631 254-6800
151 Heartland Blvd Edgewood (11717) ***(G-4270)***
IBC/ Worldwide, New Hyde Park *Also called Interntnal Bus Cmmncations Inc* ***(G-8275)***
Ibio Inc...302 355-0650
600 Madison Ave Ste 1601 New York (10022) ***(G-9852)***
IBM, Poughkeepsie *Also called International Bus Mchs Corp* ***(G-12963)***
IBM, Hopewell Junction *Also called International Bus Mchs Corp* ***(G-6097)***
IBM, Armonk *Also called International Bus Mchs Corp* ***(G-398)***
IBM World Trade Corporation (HQ)...914 765-1900
1 New Orchard Rd Ste 1 # 1 Armonk (10504) ***(G-397)***
Ibrands International LLC...212 354-1330
230 W 39th St New York (10018) ***(G-9853)***
Ic Optics, New Hyde Park *Also called Colors In Optics Ltd* ***(G-8257)***
Icarus Enterprises Inc...917 969-4461
568 Broadway Fl 11 New York (10012) ***(G-9854)***
Icd Publications Inc (PA)...631 246-9300
1377 Motor Pkwy Ste 410 Islandia (11749) ***(G-6335)***
Ice Air LLC...914 668-4700
80 Hartford Ave Mount Vernon (10553) ***(G-8150)***
Ice Cube Inc (PA)...613 254-0071
171 E Industry Ct Ste B Deer Park (11729) ***(G-3882)***
Icell Incorporated...516 590-0007
133 Fulton Ave Hempstead (11550) ***(G-5839)***
Icer Sports LLC...212 221-4700
1385 Broadway Fl 16 New York (10018) ***(G-9855)***
Ices Queen, Brooklyn *Also called Primo Frozen Desserts Inc* ***(G-2285)***
Icestone LLC...718 624-4900
63 Flushing Ave Unit 283b Brooklyn (11205) ***(G-1951)***
Ichor Therapeutics Inc...315 677-8400
2521 Us Route 11 La Fayette (13084) ***(G-6738)***

A L P H A B E T I C

ICM, North Syracuse *Also called Interntnal Cntrls Msrmnts Corp* ***(G-12046)***
ICM Controls Corp....315 233-5266
7313 William Barry Blvd North Syracuse (13212) ***(G-12045)***
Icon Design LLC....585 768-6040
9 Lent Ave Le Roy (14482) ***(G-6901)***
Icon Enterprises Intl Inc....718 752-9764
2653 Stony St Mohegan Lake (10547) ***(G-8010)***
Icon-TV, Mohegan Lake *Also called Icon Enterprises Intl Inc* ***(G-8010)***
Iconix Inc....516 513-1420
40 Oser Ave Ste 4 Hauppauge (11788) ***(G-5675)***
ICP, Depew *Also called Pcb Group Inc* ***(G-3992)***
Icpme-Ithaca Center, Ithaca *Also called International Center For Postg* ***(G-6387)***
Icy Hot Lingerie, New York *Also called Sensual Inc* ***(G-11192)***
Icynene US Acquisition Corp....800 758-7325
438 Main St Ste 100 Buffalo (14202) ***(G-2805)***
ID Signsystems Inc....585 266-5750
410 Atlantic Ave Rochester (14609) ***(G-13473)***
Idalia Solar Technologies LLC....212 792-3913
270 Lafayette St Ste 1402 New York (10012) ***(G-9856)***
Idc, Farmingdale *Also called Isolation Dynamics Corp* ***(G-4653)***
Ideal Accessories, New York *Also called Ideal Fastener Corporation* ***(G-9858)***
Ideal Burial Vault Company....585 599-2242
1166 Vision Pkwy Corfu (14036) ***(G-3703)***
Ideal Creations Inc....212 563-5928
10 W 33rd St Rm 708 New York (10001) ***(G-9857)***
Ideal Fastener Corporation....212 244-0260
246 W 38th St Rm 502 New York (10018) ***(G-9858)***
Ideal Manufacturing Inc....585 872-7190
80 Bluff Dr East Rochester (14445) ***(G-4165)***
Ideal Signs Inc....718 292-9196
538 Wales Ave Bronx (10455) ***(G-1278)***
Ideal Snacks Corporation....845 292-7000
89 Mill St Liberty (12754) ***(G-6924)***
Ideal Stair Parts, Little Falls *Also called Ideal Wood Products Inc* ***(G-6989)***
Ideal Wood Products Inc....315 823-1124
225 W Main St Little Falls (13365) ***(G-6989)***
Identfication Data Imaging LLC....516 484-6500
26 Harbor Park Dr Port Washington (11050) ***(G-12886)***
Identity Ink & Custom Tee, Kenmore *Also called Herrmann Group LLC* ***(G-6651)***
Ideoli Group Inc....212 705-8769
20w Vanderventer Ave Ll Port Washington (11050) ***(G-12887)***
Idg, New York *Also called International Direct Group Inc* ***(G-9919)***
Idg LLC....315 797-1000
31 Faass Ave Utica (13502) ***(G-15274)***
Idg Technetwork, New York *Also called International Data Group Inc* ***(G-9918)***
IDI, Port Washington *Also called Identfication Data Imaging LLC* ***(G-12886)***
Idl, Ronkonkoma *Also called Ingenious Designs LLC* ***(G-13948)***
Idonethis, New York *Also called West Internet Trading Company* ***(G-11744)***
IEC Electronics Corp (PA)....315 331-7742
105 Norton St Newark (14513) ***(G-11841)***
IEC Electronics Corp....585 647-1760
1365 Emerson St Rochester (14606) ***(G-13474)***
IEC Electronics Wire Cable Inc....585 924-9010
105 Norton St Newark (14513) ***(G-11842)***
IEC Holden Corporation....518 213-3991
51 Distribution Way Plattsburgh (12901) ***(G-12752)***
Ieh Corporation....718 492-4440
140 58th St Ste 8e Brooklyn (11220) ***(G-1952)***
Iep Energy Holding LLC....212 702-4300
767 5th Ave Ste 4600 New York (10153) ***(G-9859)***
Iet Labs Inc (PA)....516 334-5959
1 Expressway Plz Ste 120 Roslyn Heights (11577) ***(G-14052)***
Iff, New York *Also called Interntnal Flvors Frgrnces Inc* ***(G-9924)***
Ifg Corp....212 629-9600
1372 Brdwy 12ae 12 Ae New York (10018) ***(G-9860)***
Ifg Corp....212 239-8615
463 7th Ave Fl 4 New York (10018) ***(G-9861)***
Igambit Inc (PA)....631 670-6777
1050 W Jericho Tpke Ste A Smithtown (11787) ***(G-14479)***
Igk Equestrian, Auburn *Also called Brook North Farms Inc* ***(G-469)***
Ignelzi Interiors Inc....718 464-0279
9805 217th St Queens Village (11429) ***(G-13021)***
Igt Global Solutions Corp....518 382-2900
1 Broadway Ctr Fl 2 Schenectady (12305) ***(G-14280)***
Ihd Motorsports LLC....979 690-1669
1152 Upper Front St Binghamton (13905) ***(G-886)***
Iheartcommunications Inc....585 454-4884
100 Chestnut St Ste 1700 Rochester (14604) ***(G-13475)***
Ihi Inc (HQ)....212 599-8100
150 E 52nd St Fl 24 New York (10022) ***(G-9862)***
Iim Global, Long Beach *Also called Innovation In Motion Inc* ***(G-7137)***
Iimak, Amherst *Also called International Imaging Mtls Inc* ***(G-227)***
Ik Supply, Farmingdale *Also called International Key Supply LLC* ***(G-4652)***
Ikeddi Enterprises Inc (PA)....212 302-7644
1407 Brdwy Ste 1600 New York (10018) ***(G-9863)***
Ikeddi Enterprises Inc....212 302-7644
1407 Broadway Rm 1805 New York (10018) ***(G-9864)***
Ilab America Inc....631 615-5053
45 Hemlock St Selden (11784) ***(G-14353)***
Ilc Holdings Inc (HQ)....631 567-5600
105 Wilbur Pl Bohemia (11716) ***(G-1021)***
Ilc Industries Inc....631 567-5600
105 Wilbur Pl Bohemia (11716) ***(G-1022)***
Ilc Industries LLC (HQ)....631 567-5600
105 Wilbur Pl Bohemia (11716) ***(G-1023)***
Iles Formula Inc (PA)....315 834-2478
40 Harrison St Apt 17h New York (10013) ***(G-9865)***
Ilico Jewelry Inc....516 482-0201
98 Cuttermill Rd Ste 396 Great Neck (11021) ***(G-5393)***
Ilion Plastics Inc....315 894-4868
27 Pleasant Ave Ilion (13357) ***(G-6278)***
Illinois Tool Works Inc....860 435-2574
5979 N Elm Ave Millerton (12546) ***(G-7948)***
Illinois Tool Works Inc....716 681-8222
4471 Walden Ave Lancaster (14086) ***(G-6811)***
Illinois Tool Works Inc....607 770-4945
33 Lewis Rd Binghamton (13905) ***(G-887)***
Illumination Technologies Inc....315 463-4673
4172 Choke Cherry Way Liverpool (13090) ***(G-7013)***
Iluv, Port Washington *Also called Jwin Electronics Corp* ***(G-12894)***
Ima Life North America Inc....716 695-6354
2175 Military Rd Tonawanda (14150) ***(G-15114)***
Imacor Inc....516 393-0970
50 Jericho Tpke Ste 105 Jericho (11753) ***(G-6583)***
Image Iron Works Inc....718 592-8276
5050 98th St Corona (11368) ***(G-3740)***
Image Press, The, Cicero *Also called Add Associates Inc* ***(G-3415)***
Image Sales & Marketing Inc....516 238-7023
106 Thornwood Rd Massapequa Park (11762) ***(G-7656)***
Image Tech....716 635-0167
96 Donna Lea Blvd Buffalo (14221) ***(G-2806)***
Image Typography Inc....631 218-6932
751 Coates Ave Ste 31 Holbrook (11741) ***(G-6000)***
Image360....585 272-1234
275 Marketplace Dr Rochester (14623) ***(G-13476)***
Images Scientific Instruments, Staten Island *Also called Images Si Inc* ***(G-14664)***
Images Si Inc....718 966-3694
109 Woods Of Arden Rd Staten Island (10312) ***(G-14664)***
Imaginant Inc....585 264-0480
3800 Monroe Ave Ste 29 Pittsford (14534) ***(G-12643)***
Imaging and Sensing Technology, Horseheads *Also called Mirion Technologies Ist Corp* ***(G-6128)***
Imakr Store New York, Brooklyn *Also called Macadame Inc* ***(G-2099)***
Imbibitive Tech Amer Corp....888 843-2323
1623 Military Rd Ste 1011 Niagara Falls (14304) ***(G-11936)***
Imbibitive Technologies Corp (PA)....888 843-2323
1623 Military Rd Ste 1011 Niagara Falls (14304) ***(G-11937)***
Imbtec America, Niagara Falls *Also called Imbibitive Tech Amer Corp* ***(G-11936)***
IMC Teddy Food Service....631 789-8881
50 Ranick Dr E Amityville (11701) ***(G-275)***
Imco Inc....585 352-7810
15 Turner Dr Spencerport (14559) ***(G-14556)***
Imek Media LLC....212 422-9000
32 Broadway Ste 511 New York (10004) ***(G-9866)***
Imena Jewelry Manufacturer Inc....212 827-0073
2 W 45th St Ste 1000 New York (10036) ***(G-9867)***
Imerys Fsed Mnrl Ngara FLS Inc....716 286-1234
3455 Hyde Park Blvd Niagara Falls (14305) ***(G-11938)***
Imerys Fsed Mnrl Ngara FLS Inc....716 286-1250
4901 Hyde Park Blvd Niagara Falls (14305) ***(G-11939)***
Imerys Fsed Mnrl Ngara FLS Inc (HQ)....716 286-1250
2000 College Ave Niagara Falls (14305) ***(G-11940)***
Imerys Usa Inc....315 287-0780
16a Main St Hailesboro Rd Gouverneur (13642) ***(G-5321)***
IMG The Daily....212 541-5640
432 W 45th St Fl 5 New York (10036) ***(G-9868)***
Immco Diagnostics Inc....716 691-0091
640 Ellicott St Fl 3 Buffalo (14203) ***(G-2807)***
Impact Journals LLC....800 922-0957
6666 E Quaker St Ste 1 Orchard Park (14127) ***(G-12354)***
Impact Tech A Skrsky Innvtions, Rochester *Also called Sikorsky Aircraft Corporation* ***(G-13731)***
Impala Press Ltd....631 588-4262
931 S 2nd St Ronkonkoma (11779) ***(G-13947)***
Imperia Masonry Supply Corp (PA)....914 738-0900
57 Canal Rd Pelham (10803) ***(G-12566)***
Imperial Damper & Louver Co....718 731-3800
907 E 141st St Bronx (10454) ***(G-1279)***
Imperial Frames & Albums LLC....718 832-9793
8200 21st Ave Brooklyn (11214) ***(G-1953)***
Imperial Instrmnt & Mach, Westbury *Also called Imperial Instrument Corp* ***(G-15895)***
Imperial Instrument Corp....516 739-6644
18 Sylvester St Westbury (11590) ***(G-15895)***
Imperial Pools Inc (PA)....518 786-1200
33 Wade Rd Latham (12110) ***(G-6860)***
Imperial-Harvard Label Co....212 736-8420
236 W 40th St Fl 3 New York (10018) ***(G-9869)***
Imperium Partners Group LLC (PA)....212 433-1360
509 Madison Ave New York (10022) ***(G-9870)***
Impladent Ltd (PA)....718 465-1810
19845 Foothill Ave Jamaica (11423) ***(G-6449)***

Import-Export Corporation......718 707-0880
3814 30th St Long Island City (11101) *(G-7246)*
Impremedia LLC (PA)......212 807-4600
1 Metrotech Ctr Fl 18 Brooklyn (11201) *(G-1954)*
Impress Graphic Technologies......516 781-0845
141 Linden Ave Westbury (11590) *(G-15896)*
Impressart......631 940-9530
100 Executive Dr Ste D Edgewood (11717) *(G-4271)*
Impressions Inc......212 594-5954
36 W 37th St Rm 400 New York (10018) *(G-9871)*
Impressions International Inc......585 442-5240
410 Alexander St Ste 2 Rochester (14607) *(G-13477)*
Impressions Prtg & Graphics, New York *Also called Designlogocom Inc (G-9208)*
Impressive Imprints Inc......631 293-6161
195 Central Ave Ste N Farmingdale (11735) *(G-4648)*
Imprint Branded Content LLC......212 888-8073
34 W 27th St Rm 501 New York (10001) *(G-9872)*
Imprinted Sportswear, Camillus *Also called Steve Poli Sales (G-3110)*
IMR Test Labs, Lansing *Also called Metal Improvement Company LLC (G-6841)*
Imrex LLC (PA)......516 479-3675
55 Sandy Hill Rd Oyster Bay (11771) *(G-12448)*
In Mocean Group LLC (PA)......212 944-0317
463 Fashion Ave Fl 21 New York (10018) *(G-9873)*
In Room Plus Inc......716 838-9433
2495 Main St Ste 217 Buffalo (14214) *(G-2808)*
In Toon Amkor Fashions Inc......718 937-4546
4809 34th St Long Island City (11101) *(G-7247)*
In-House Inc......718 445-9007
1535 126th St Ste 3 College Point (11356) *(G-3544)*
In-Step Marketing Inc (PA)......212 797-3450
39 Broadway Fl 32 New York (10006) *(G-9874)*
In2green LLC......914 693-5054
14 Bellair Dr Hastings On Hudson (10706) *(G-5573)*
Incentivate Health LLC......518 469-8491
60 Railroad Pl Ste 101 Saratoga Springs (12866) *(G-14183)*
Incodema Inc......607 277-7070
407 Cliff St Ithaca (14850) *(G-6385)*
Incodema3d LLC......607 269-4390
330 Main St Freeville (13068) *(G-5035)*
Incon Gems Inc......212 221-8560
2 W 46th St Ste 603 New York (10036) *(G-9875)*
Incredible Scents Inc......516 656-3300
1 Plaza Rd Ste 202 Greenvale (11548) *(G-5462)*
Incro Marketing USA Corp (PA)......917 365-5552
157 Columbus Ave New York (10023) *(G-9876)*
Incycle Software Corp (PA)......212 626-2608
1120 Ave Of The Americas New York (10036) *(G-9877)*
Indegy Inc......866 801-5394
1460 Broadway New York (10036) *(G-9878)*
Independence Harley-Davidson, Binghamton *Also called Ihd Motorsports LLC (G-886)*
Independent Baptist Voice, Conklin *Also called Newspaper Publisher LLC (G-3626)*
Independent Field Svc LLC (PA)......315 559-9243
6744 Pickard Dr Syracuse (13211) *(G-14913)*
Independent Home Products LLC......718 541-1256
59 Hempstead Gardens Dr West Hempstead (11552) *(G-15770)*
Index Incorporated......440 632-5400
415 Concord Ave Bronx (10455) *(G-1280)*
Index Magazine......212 243-1428
526 W 26th St Rm 920 New York (10001) *(G-9879)*
India Abroad Publications Inc......212 929-1727
102 Madison Ave Frnt B New York (10016) *(G-9880)*
Indian Ladder Farmstead Brewer......518 577-1484
287 Altamont Rd Altamont (12009) *(G-194)*
Indian Larry Legacy......718 609-9184
400 Union Ave Brooklyn (11211) *(G-1955)*
Indian Springs Mfg Co Inc......315 635-6101
2095 W Genesee Rd Baldwinsville (13027) *(G-549)*
Indian Valley, Binghamton *Also called Ivi Services Inc (G-889)*
Indian Water Treatment Plant, Ossining *Also called Ossining Village of Inc (G-12406)*
Indigo Home Inc......212 684-4146
230 5th Ave Ste 1916 New York (10001) *(G-9881)*
Indigo Rein, New York *Also called Jrg Apparel Group Company Ltd (G-10034)*
Indikon Company, New Hartford *Also called Riverhawk Company LP (G-8244)*
Indira Cesarine, New York *Also called Untitled Media (G-11611)*
Indira Foods Inc......718 343-1500
25503 Hillside Ave # 255 Floral Park (11004) *(G-4819)*
Indium Corporation of America (PA)......800 446-3486
34 Robinson Rd Clinton (13323) *(G-3483)*
Indium Corporation of America......315 793-8200
1676 Lincoln Ave Utica (13502) *(G-15275)*
Indium Corporation of America......315 381-2330
111 Business Park Dr Utica (13502) *(G-15276)*
Indonesian Imports Inc (PA)......855 725-5656
339 5th Ave Fl 2 New York (10016) *(G-9882)*
Indulge Desserts Holdings LLC (PA)......212 231-8600
666 5th Ave Fl 27 New York (10103) *(G-9883)*
Indus Precision Manufacturing......845 268-0782
50 N Harrison Ave Ste 9 Congers (10920) *(G-3616)*
Industrial Cables, Chester *Also called Nexans Energy USA Inc (G-3381)*
Industrial Electronic Hardware......718 492-4440
140 58th St Ste 8e Brooklyn (11220) *(G-1956)*
Industrial Fabricating Corp (PA)......315 437-3353
6201 E Molloy Rd East Syracuse (13057) *(G-4218)*
Industrial Fabricating Corp......315 437-8234
4 Collamer Cir East Syracuse (13057) *(G-4219)*
Industrial Indxing Systems Inc......585 924-9181
626 Fishers Run Victor (14564) *(G-15413)*
Industrial Machine Repair......607 272-0717
1144 Taughannock Blvd Ithaca (14850) *(G-6386)*
Industrial Mch Gear Works LLC......516 695-4442
77 Woodland Ave Rockville Centre (11570) *(G-13829)*
Industrial Municipal Equipment (PA)......631 665-6712
146 Concourse E Brightwaters (11718) *(G-1171)*
Industrial Oil Tank Service......315 736-6080
120 Dry Rd Oriskany (13424) *(G-12392)*
Industrial Paint Services Corp......607 687-0107
60 W Main St 62 Owego (13827) *(G-12430)*
Industrial Paper Tube Inc......718 893-5000
1335 E Bay Ave Bronx (10474) *(G-1281)*
Industrial Precision Pdts Inc......315 343-4421
350 Mitchell St Oswego (13126) *(G-12412)*
Industrial Raw Materials LLC......212 688-8080
39 West Mall Plainview (11803) *(G-12689)*
Industrial SEC Systems Contrls, Garden City *Also called Issco Corporation (G-5102)*
Industrial Services of Wny......716 799-7788
7221 Niagara Falls Blvd Niagara Falls (14304) *(G-11941)*
Industrial Support Inc......716 662-2954
36 Depot St Buffalo (14206) *(G-2809)*
Industrial Test Eqp Co Inc......516 883-6423
2 Manhasset Ave Port Washington (11050) *(G-12888)*
Industrial Tool & Die Co Inc......518 273-7383
14 Industrial Park Rd Troy (12180) *(G-15172)*
Industrial Wax, Plainview *Also called Industrial Raw Materials LLC (G-12689)*
Industrial Welding & Fabg Co, Jamestown *Also called Wilston Enterprises Inc (G-6554)*
Industrial Welding & Fabg Co, Jamestown *Also called Fred Santucci Inc (G-6511)*
Industry Forecast, Mount Kisco *Also called Jerome Levy Forecasting Center (G-8094)*
Inertia Switch Inc......845 359-8300
70 S Greenbush Rd Orangeburg (10962) *(G-12319)*
Inex Inc......716 537-2270
9229 Olean Rd Holland (14080) *(G-6029)*
Infant Formula Laboratory Svc......718 257-3000
711 Livonia Ave Brooklyn (11207) *(G-1957)*
Inficon Inc (HQ)......315 434-1100
2 Technology Pl East Syracuse (13057) *(G-4220)*
Inficon Holding AG......315 434-1100
2 Technology Pl East Syracuse (13057) *(G-4221)*
Infimed Inc (PA)......315 453-4545
121 Metropolitan Park Dr Liverpool (13088) *(G-7014)*
Infimed Inc......585 383-1710
15 Fisher Rd Pittsford (14534) *(G-12644)*
Infinite Software Solutions......718 982-1315
1110 South Ave Ste 303 Staten Island (10314) *(G-14665)*
Infinity Augmented Reality Inc......917 677-2084
228 Park Ave S 61130 New York (10003) *(G-9884)*
Infirmary Nyc......504 606-6280
1720 2nd Ave New York (10128) *(G-9885)*
Infitec Inc......315 433-1150
6500 Badgley Rd East Syracuse (13057) *(G-4222)*
Inflation Systems Inc......914 381-8070
500 Ogden Ave Mamaroneck (10543) *(G-7512)*
Influence Graphics, Long Island City *Also called Sizzal LLC (G-7359)*
Info Label Inc......518 664-0791
12 Enterprise Ave Halfmoon (12065) *(G-5493)*
Info Quick Solutions......315 463-1400
7460 Morgan Rd Liverpool (13090) *(G-7015)*
Infobase Holdings Inc (HQ)......212 967-8800
132 W 31st St Fl 17 New York (10001) *(G-9886)*
Infobase Publishing Company (PA)......212 967-8800
132 W 31st St Fl 17 New York (10001) *(G-9887)*
Inform Studio Inc......718 401-6149
480 Austin Pl Frnt E Bronx (10455) *(G-1282)*
Informa Business Media Inc (HQ)......212 204-4200
605 3rd Ave New York (10158) *(G-9888)*
Informa Business Media Inc......914 949-8500
707 Westchester Ave # 101 White Plains (10604) *(G-16015)*
Informa Media Inc (HQ)......212 204-4200
605 3rd Ave Fl 22 New York (10158) *(G-9889)*
Informa Media Inc......212 204-4200
1166 Ave Of The Americas New York (10036) *(G-9890)*
Informa Solutions Inc......516 543-3733
45 Rockefeller Plz # 2000 New York (10111) *(G-9891)*
Informa Uk Ltd......646 957-8966
52 Vanderbilt Ave Fl 7 New York (10017) *(G-9892)*
Informatica LLC......212 845-7650
810 7th Ave Ste 1100c New York (10019) *(G-9893)*
Informerly Inc......646 238-7137
35 Essex St New York (10002) *(G-9894)*
Infrared Components Corp......315 732-1544
2306 Bleecker St Utica (13501) *(G-15277)*
Ingenious Designs LLC......631 254-3376
2060 9th Ave Ronkonkoma (11779) *(G-13948)*
Ingenious Ingenuity Inc......800 834-5279
1804 Tebor Rd Ste 2 Webster (14580) *(G-15642)*

ALPHABETIC

Ingersoll-Rand Company 716 896-6600
  3101 Broadway St Buffalo (14227) *(G-2810)*
Ingham Industries Inc 631 242-2493
  1363 Lincoln Ave Ste 1 Holbrook (11741) *(G-6001)*
Ingleside Machine Co Inc 585 924-3046
  1120 Hook Rd Farmington (14425) *(G-4774)*
Ink Publishing Corporation 347 294-1220
  68 Jay St Ste 315 Brooklyn (11201) *(G-1958)*
Ink Well 718 253-9736
  1440 Coney Island Ave Brooklyn (11230) *(G-1959)*
Ink Well Press, Orchard Park Also called Waterhouse Publications Inc *(G-12383)*
Ink-It Printing Inc 718 229-5590
  1535 126th St Ste 1 College Point (11356) *(G-3545)*
Ink-It Prtg Inc/Angle Offset, College Point Also called Ink-It Printing Inc *(G-3545)*
Inkkas LLC 646 845-9803
  38 E 29th St Rm 6r New York (10016) *(G-9895)*
Inland Paper Products Corp 718 827-8150
  444 Liberty Ave Brooklyn (11207) *(G-1960)*
Inland Printing Company Inc 516 367-4700
  36 Orchard Dr Woodbury (11797) *(G-16174)*
Inland Vacuum Industries Inc (PA) 585 293-3330
  35 Howard Ave Churchville (14428) *(G-3412)*
Innex Industries Inc 585 247-3575
  6 Marway Dr Rochester (14624) *(G-13478)*
Innofun Digital Entrmt LLC 347 708-0078
  19 W 34th St Rm 1018 New York (10001) *(G-9896)*
Innogenix Inc 631 450-4704
  8200 New Horizons Blvd Amityville (11701) *(G-276)*
Innotech Graphic Eqp Corp 845 268-6900
  614 Corporate Way Ste 5 Valley Cottage (10989) *(G-15316)*
Innova Interiors Inc 718 401-2122
  780 E 134th St Fl 2 Bronx (10454) *(G-1283)*
Innovant Inc (PA) 212 929-4883
  37 W 20th St Ste 1101 Islandia (11749) *(G-6336)*
Innovant Group, Islandia Also called Innovant Inc *(G-6336)*
Innovation Associates Inc 607 798-9376
  711 Innovation Way Johnson City (13790) *(G-6602)*
Innovation By Temi, Bronx Also called I-Tem Brand LLC *(G-1277)*
Innovation In Motion Inc 407 878-7561
  780 Long Beach Blvd Long Beach (11561) *(G-7137)*
Innovation MGT Group Inc 800 889-0987
  999 Montauk Hwy Shirley (11967) *(G-14422)*
Innovative Automation Inc 631 439-3300
  595 Smith St Farmingdale (11735) *(G-4649)*
Innovative Cleaning Solutions 716 731-4408
  2990 Carney Dr Sanborn (14132) *(G-14143)*
Innovative Designs LLC 212 695-0892
  141 W 36th St Fl 8 New York (10018) *(G-9897)*
Innovative Industries LLC 718 784-7300
  4322 22nd St Ste 205 Long Island City (11101) *(G-7248)*
Innovative Labs LLC 631 231-5522
  85 Commerce Dr Hauppauge (11788) *(G-5676)*
Innovative Municipal Pdts US 800 387-5777
  454 River Rd Glenmont (12077) *(G-5237)*
Innovative Plastics Corp (PA) 845 359-7500
  400 Route 303 Orangeburg (10962) *(G-12320)*
Innovative Power Products Inc 631 563-0088
  1170 Lincoln Ave Unit 7 Holbrook (11741) *(G-6002)*
Innovative Signage Systems Inc 315 469-7783
  6321 S Salina St Nedrow (13120) *(G-8215)*
Innovative Surface Solutions, Glenmont Also called Innovative Municipal Pdts US *(G-5237)*
Innovative Systems of New York 516 541-7410
  201 Rose St Massapequa Park (11762) *(G-7657)*
Innovative Video Tech Inc 631 388-5700
  355 Oser Ave Hauppauge (11788) *(G-5677)*
Innroad Inc 631 458-1437
  519 8th Ave Fl 15 New York (10018) *(G-9898)*
Ino-Tex LLC 212 400-2205
  135 W 36th St Fl 6 New York (10018) *(G-9899)*
Inori Jewels 347 703-5078
  580 5th Ave New York (10036) *(G-9900)*
Inova LLC 866 528-2804
  2 Van Buren Blvd Bldg 19 Guilderland Center (12085) *(G-5486)*
Inova LLC 518 861-3400
  6032 Depot Rd Altamont (12009) *(G-195)*
Inpro Corporation 716 332-4699
  250 Cooper Ave Ste 102 Tonawanda (14150) *(G-15115)*
Inprotopia Corporation 917 338-7501
  401 W 110th St Apt 2001 New York (10025) *(G-9901)*
Inquiring Minds Inc (PA) 845 246-5775
  65 S Partition St Saugerties (12477) *(G-14202)*
Inscape (new York) Inc (HQ) 716 665-6210
  221 Lister Ave 1 Falconer (14733) *(G-4544)*
Inscape Archtectural Interiors, Falconer Also called Inscape (new York) Inc *(G-4544)*
Inscape Inc 716 665-6210
  221 Lister Ave Falconer (14733) *(G-4545)*
Insert Outsert Experts, The, Lockport Also called Gooding Co Inc *(G-7082)*
Insight Unlimited Inc 914 861-2090
  660 Quaker Rd Chappaqua (10514) *(G-3325)*
Insight Venture Partners IV 212 230-9200
  1114 Avenue Of The Americ New York (10036) *(G-9902)*
Insomnia Cookies On The Hill, New York Also called U Serve Brands Inc *(G-11572)*

Inspired Entertainment Inc (PA) 646 565-3861
  250 W 57th St Ste 2223 New York (10107) *(G-9903)*
Instant Again LLC 585 436-8003
  1277 Mount Read Blvd # 2 Rochester (14606) *(G-13479)*
Instant Monogramming Inc 585 654-5550
  1150 University Ave Ste 5 Rochester (14607) *(G-13480)*
Instant Printing Service, Ithaca Also called Madison Printing Corp *(G-6394)*
Instant Stream Inc 917 438-7182
  1271 Ave Of The Americas New York (10020) *(G-9904)*
Instant Verticals Inc 631 501-0001
  330 Broadhollow Rd Farmingdale (11735) *(G-4650)*
Instantwhip of Buffalo Inc 716 892-7031
  2117 Genesee St Buffalo (14211) *(G-2811)*
Institute of Electrical and El 212 705-8900
  3 Park Ave Fl 17 New York (10016) *(G-9905)*
Instrumentation Laboratory Co 845 680-0028
  526 Route 303 Orangeburg (10962) *(G-12321)*
Insty Trints, Kenmore Also called Horace J Metz *(G-6652)*
Insty-Prints, Niagara Falls Also called Graphicomm Inc *(G-11932)*
Insty-Prints of Buffalo Inc (PA) 716 853-6483
  265 Franklin St Buffalo (14202) *(G-2812)*
Insultech, North Tonawanda Also called Shannon Global Enrgy Solutions *(G-12090)*
Int Trading USA LLC 212 760-2338
  261 W 35th St Ste 1100 New York (10001) *(G-9906)*
Intech 21 Inc 516 626-7221
  21 Harbor Park Dr Port Washington (11050) *(G-12889)*
Inteco Intimates, New York Also called Intimateco LLC *(G-9928)*
Integer Holdings Corporation 716 937-5100
  11900 Walden Ave Alden (14004) *(G-171)*
Integer Holdings Corporation 716 759-5200
  4098 Barton Rd Clarence (14031) *(G-3435)*
Integra Microsystem 1988 Inc 718 609-6099
  61 Greenpoint Ave Ste 412 Brooklyn (11222) *(G-1961)*
Integrated Control Corp 631 673-5100
  748 Park Ave Huntington (11743) *(G-6207)*
Integrated Copyright Group 615 329-3999
  1745 Broadway 19 New York (10019) *(G-9907)*
Integrated Graphics Inc (PA) 212 592-5600
  7 W 36th St Fl 12 New York (10018) *(G-9908)*
Integrated Indus Resources, Lockport Also called GM Components Holdings LLC *(G-7081)*
Integrated Liner Tech Inc (PA) 518 621-7422
  45 Discovery Dr Rensselaer (12144) *(G-13089)*
Integrated Medical Devices 315 457-4200
  549 Electronics Pkwy # 200 Liverpool (13088) *(G-7016)*
Integrated Solar Tech LLC 914 249-9364
  120 Hawley St Ste 123 Binghamton (13901) *(G-888)*
Integrated Tech Support Svcs 718 454-2497
  18616 Jordan Ave Saint Albans (11412) *(G-14106)*
Integrated Water Management 607 844-4276
  289 Cortland Rd Dryden (13053) *(G-4039)*
Integrated Wood Components Inc 607 467-1739
  791 Airport Rd Deposit (13754) *(G-4000)*
Integrity Tool Incorporated 315 524-4409
  6485 Furnace Rd Ontario (14519) *(G-12291)*
Integrted Work Envronments LLC 716 725-5088
  6346 Everwood Ct N East Amherst (14051) *(G-4078)*
Integument Technologies Inc 716 873-1199
  72 Pearce Ave Tonawanda (14150) *(G-15116)*
Intek Precision 585 293-0853
  539 Attridge Rd Churchville (14428) *(G-3413)*
INTEL Corporation 408 765-8080
  55 Dodge Rd Getzville (14068) *(G-5177)*
Intelibs Inc 877 213-2640
  1500 Stony Brook Rd Ste 3 Stony Brook (11794) *(G-14739)*
Intellicheck Inc (PA) 516 992-1900
  535 Broadhollow Rd B51 Melville (11747) *(G-7794)*
Intellidyne LLC 516 676-0777
  303 Sunnyside Blvd # 75 Plainview (11803) *(G-12690)*
Intelligen Power Systems LLC 212 750-0373
  301 Winding Rd Old Bethpage (11804) *(G-12218)*
Intelligence Newsletter, New York Also called Intellignc The Ftr Cmptng Nwsl *(G-9909)*
Intelligent Ctrl Systems LLC 516 340-1011
  208 Route 109 Ste 211 Farmingdale (11735) *(G-4651)*
Intelligent Traffic Systems 631 567-5994
  140 Keyland Ct Unit 1 Bohemia (11716) *(G-1024)*
Intellignc The Ftr Cmptng Nwsl 212 222-1123
  360 Central Park W New York (10025) *(G-9909)*
Intellimetal Inc 585 424-3260
  2025 Brighton Henrietta Rochester (14623) *(G-13481)*
Intellitravel Media Inc (HQ) 646 695-6700
  530 Fashion Ave Rm 201 New York (10018) *(G-9910)*
Intentions Jewelry LLC 845 226-4650
  83 Miller Hill Dr Lagrangeville (12540) *(G-6749)*
Inter Craft Custom Furniture 718 278-2573
  1431 Astoria Blvd Astoria (11102) *(G-425)*
Inter Metal Fabricators Inc 718 852-4000
  161 Dikeman St Brooklyn (11231) *(G-1962)*
Inter Molds Inc 631 667-8580
  26 Cleveland Ave Bay Shore (11706) *(G-682)*
Inter Pacific Consulting Corp 718 460-2787
  14055 34th Ave Apt 3n Flushing (11354) *(G-4861)*

Inter Parfums Inc (PA) 212 983-2640
551 5th Ave New York (10176) *(G-9911)*
Inter Parfums Usa LLC 212 983-2640
551 5th Ave Rm 1500 New York (10176) *(G-9912)*
Inter State Laminates Inc 518 283-8355
44 Main St Poestenkill (12140) *(G-12803)*
Inter-Fence Co Inc 718 939-9700
1520 129th St College Point (11356) *(G-3546)*
Interactive Instruments Inc 518 347-0955
704 Corporation Park # 1 Scotia (12302) *(G-14332)*
Interbrand LLC 212 840-9595
1 W 37th St Fl 9 New York (10018) *(G-9913)*
Intercept Pharmaceuticals Inc (PA) 646 747-1000
10 Hudson Yards Fl 37 New York (10001) *(G-9914)*
Intercos America Inc 845 732-3900
11 Centerock Rd West Nyack (10994) *(G-15823)*
Intercos America Inc 845 732-3910
120 Brookhill Dr West Nyack (10994) *(G-15824)*
Intercultural Alliance Artists 917 406-1202
4510 165th St Flushing (11358) *(G-4862)*
Interdgital Communications LLC 631 622-4000
2 Huntington Quad Ste 4s Melville (11747) *(G-7795)*
Interface Performance Mtls, Beaver Falls *Also called Lydall Performance Mtls US Inc (G-760)*
Interface Products Co Inc 631 242-4605
215 N Fehr Way Ste C Bay Shore (11706) *(G-683)*
Interfaceflor LLC 212 686-8284
330 5th Ave Fl 12 New York (10001) *(G-9915)*
Interhellenic Publishing Inc 212 967-5016
421 7th Ave Ste 810 New York (10001) *(G-9916)*
Interior Metals 718 439-7324
255 48th St Brooklyn (11220) *(G-1963)*
Interior Solutions of Wny LLC 716 332-0372
472 Franklin St Buffalo (14202) *(G-2813)*
Interiors By Robert, Richmond Hill *Also called Terbo Ltd (G-13127)*
Interiors-Pft Inc 212 244-9600
3200 Skillman Ave Fl 3 Long Island City (11101) *(G-7249)*
International Aids Vaccine Ini 646 381-8066
140 58th St Brooklyn (11220) *(G-1964)*
International Aids Vccne Inttv (PA) 212 847-1111
125 Broad St Fl 9th New York (10004) *(G-9917)*
International Bus Mchs Corp 914 945-3000
1101 Kitchawan Rd Yorktown Heights (10598) *(G-16366)*
International Bus Mchs Corp 845 433-1234
2455 South Rd Poughkeepsie (12601) *(G-12963)*
International Bus Mchs Corp 800 426-4968
10 North Dr Hopewell Junction (12533) *(G-6097)*
International Bus Mchs Corp 914 499-2000
20 Old Post Rd Armonk (10504) *(G-398)*
International Business Times, New York *Also called Newsweek Media Group Inc (G-10617)*
International Casein Corp Cal 516 466-4363
111 Great Neck Rd Ste 218 Great Neck (11021) *(G-5394)*
International Center For Postg 607 257-5860
179 Graham Rd Ste E Ithaca (14850) *(G-6387)*
International Climbing Mchs 607 288-4001
630 Elmira Rd Ithaca (14850) *(G-6388)*
International Data Group Inc 212 331-7883
117 E 55th St Ste 204 New York (10022) *(G-9918)*
International Direct Group Inc 212 921-9036
525 7th Ave Rm 208 New York (10018) *(G-9919)*
International Fire-Shield Inc 315 255-1006
194 Genesee St Auburn (13021) *(G-479)*
International Identity LLC 787 864-0379
824 Park Ave Apt 1c Brooklyn (11206) *(G-1965)*
International Imaging Mtls Inc (PA) 716 691-6333
310 Commerce Dr Amherst (14228) *(G-227)*
International Inspirations LLC (PA) 212 465-8500
358 5th Ave Rm 501 New York (10001) *(G-9920)*
International Key Supply LLC 631 983-6096
224 Sherwood Ave Farmingdale (11735) *(G-4652)*
International Leisure Pdts Inc 631 254-2155
191 Rodeo Dr Edgewood (11717) *(G-4272)*
International Merch Svcs Inc 914 699-4000
336 S Fulton Ave Fl 1 Mount Vernon (10553) *(G-8151)*
International Metals Trdg LLC 866 923-0182
25 Melville Park Rd # 114 Melville (11747) *(G-7796)*
International MGT Netwrk 646 401-0032
445 Park Ave Fl 9 New York (10022) *(G-9921)*
International Mtls & Sups Inc 518 834-9899
56 Industrial Park Rd Keeseville (12944) *(G-6642)*
International Newspaper Prntng, Glen Head *Also called International Newsppr Prtg Co (G-5208)*
International Newsppr Prtg Co 516 626-6095
18 Carlisle Dr Glen Head (11545) *(G-5208)*
International Office 212 334-4617
110 Greene St Ste 1206 New York (10012) *(G-9922)*
International Ord Tech Inc 716 664-1100
101 Harrison St Jamestown (14701) *(G-6518)*
International Paper Company 518 585-6761
568 Shore Airport Rd Ticonderoga (12883) *(G-15074)*
International Paper Company 585 663-1000
200 Boxart St Rochester (14612) *(G-13482)*
International Paper Company 845 986-6409
1422 Long Meadow Rd Tuxedo Park (10987) *(G-15217)*
International Paper Company 607 775-1550
1240 Conklin Rd Conklin (13748) *(G-3625)*
International Paper Company 315 797-5120
50 Harbor Point Rd Utica (13502) *(G-15278)*
International Paper Company 716 852-2144
100 Bud Mil Dr Buffalo (14206) *(G-2814)*
International Paper Company 518 372-6461
803 Corporation Park Glenville (12302) *(G-5272)*
International Society For Medl 520 820-8594
520 White Plains Rd Tarrytown (10591) *(G-15046)*
International Stone Accessrs 718 522-5399
703 Myrtle Ave Brooklyn (11205) *(G-1966)*
International Time Products 516 931-0005
410 Jericho Tpke Ste 110 Jericho (11753) *(G-6584)*
International Wire Group, Camden *Also called Camden Wire Co Inc (G-3099)*
International Wire Group (HQ) 315 245-3800
12 Masonic Ave Camden (13316) *(G-3101)*
International Wire Group Inc (HQ) 315 245-2000
12 Masonic Ave Camden (13316) *(G-3102)*
Internationl Studios Inc 212 819-1616
108 W 39th St Rm 1300 New York (10018) *(G-9923)*
Internodal International Inc 631 765-0037
54800 Route 25 Southold (11971) *(G-14544)*
Interntional Fireprof Door Inc 718 783-1310
1005 Greene Ave Brooklyn (11221) *(G-1967)*
Interntnal Auto Voluntary Untd 718 743-8732
1956 Bay Ridge Ave Fl 2 Brooklyn (11204) *(G-1968)*
Interntnal Bus Cmmncations Inc (PA) 516 352-4505
1981 Marcus Ave Ste C105 New Hyde Park (11042) *(G-8275)*
Interntnal Cntrls Msrmnts Corp (PA) 315 233-5266
7313 William Barry Blvd North Syracuse (13212) *(G-12046)*
Interntnal Elctronic Mchs Corp 518 268-1636
850 River St Troy (12180) *(G-15173)*
Interntnal Flvors Frgrnces Inc (PA) 212 765-5500
521 W 57th St New York (10019) *(G-9924)*
Interntonal Consmr Connections 516 481-3438
5 Terminal Rd Unit A West Hempstead (11552) *(G-15771)*
Interparts International Inc (PA) 516 576-2000
190 Express St Plainview (11803) *(G-12691)*
Interplex Nas Electronics, College Point *Also called Nas CP Corp (G-3556)*
Intersource Management Group (PA) 518 372-6798
7 Corporate Dr Ste 3 Halfmoon (12065) *(G-5494)*
Intersource Management Group 518 372-6798
144 Erie Blvd Schenectady (12305) *(G-14281)*
Interstate Window Corporation 631 231-0800
345 Crooked Hill Rd Ste 1 Brentwood (11717) *(G-1123)*
Interstate Wood & Vinyl Pdts, Amityville *Also called Interstate Wood Products Inc (G-277)*
Interstate Wood Products Inc 631 842-4488
1084 Sunrise Hwy Amityville (11701) *(G-277)*
Intertex USA Inc 212 279-3601
131 W 35th St Fl 10 New York (10001) *(G-9925)*
Interview New York 857 928-4120
77 Bleecker St New York (10012) *(G-9926)*
Inteva Products LLC 248 655-8886
30 Rockefeller Plz New York (10112) *(G-9927)*
Intex Company Inc (PA) 516 223-0200
80 Commercial St Freeport (11520) *(G-5003)*
Intimateco LLC 212 239-4411
463 7th Ave Rm 602 New York (10018) *(G-9928)*
Intra-Cellular Therapies Inc (PA) 646 440-9333
430 E 29th St Ste 900 New York (10016) *(G-9929)*
Intralinks Holdings Inc (HQ) 212 543-7700
685 3rd Ave Fl 9 New York (10017) *(G-9930)*
Intrapac International Corp 518 561-2030
4 Plant St Plattsburgh (12901) *(G-12753)*
Intraworlds Inc 631 602-5333
222 Broadway Fl 19 New York (10038) *(G-9931)*
Intrepid Control Service Inc 718 886-8771
2904 Francis Lewis Blvd Flushing (11358) *(G-4863)*
Intrinsiq Materials Inc 585 301-4432
1200 Ridgeway Ave Ste 110 Rochester (14615) *(G-13483)*
Intstrux LLC 646 688-2782
15 W 39th St Fl 13 New York (10018) *(G-9932)*
Intuition Publishing Limited 212 838-7115
40 E 34th St Rm 1101 New York (10016) *(G-9933)*
Inturn 212 639-9675
22 W 19th St Ste 5l New York (10011) *(G-9934)*
Invagen Pharmaceuticals Inc 631 949-6367
550 S Research Pl Central Islip (11722) *(G-3278)*
Invagen Pharmaceuticals Inc (HQ) 631 231-3233
7 Oser Ave Ste 4 Hauppauge (11788) *(G-5678)*
Investars, New York *Also called Netologic Inc (G-10569)*
Investmentnews LLC 212 210-0100
685 3rd Ave New York (10017) *(G-9935)*
Investors Business Daily Inc 212 626-7676
140 E 45th St Ste 19b New York (10017) *(G-9936)*
Invid Tech, Hauppauge *Also called Innovative Video Tech Inc (G-5677)*
Invision Inc (HQ) 212 557-5554
25 W 43rd St Ste 609 New York (10036) *(G-9937)*
Invitrogen Corp 716 774-6700
3175 Staley Rd Grand Island (14072) *(G-5333)*
Inwood Material 516 371-1842
1 Sheridan Blvd Inwood (11096) *(G-6296)*

ALPHABETIC

INX International Ink Co 716 366-6010
  3257 Middle Rd Dunkirk (14048) *(G-4059)*

Ioc, New York *Also called International Office* *(G-9922)*

Ion Optics Inc 518 339-6853
  75 Benjamin St Albany (12202) *(G-89)*

Ion-Tof Usa Inc 845 352-8082
  100 Red Schoolhouse Rd A-1 Spring Valley (10977) *(G-14572)*

Ip Med Inc 516 766-3800
  3571 Hargale Rd Oceanside (11572) *(G-12176)*

IPC/Razor LLC (PA) 212 551-4500
  277 Park Ave Fl 39 New York (10172) *(G-9938)*

Ipcc, Flushing *Also called Inter Pacific Consulting Corp* *(G-4861)*

Ipe, Orchard Park *Also called Bos-Hatten Inc* *(G-12339)*

Ippolita, New York *Also called Ale Viola LLC* *(G-8510)*

Ipsidy Inc (PA) 516 274-8700
  670 Long Beach Blvd Long Beach (11561) *(G-7138)*

Iquit Cig LLC 718 475-1422
  4014 13th Ave Brooklyn (11218) *(G-1969)*

Ir Media Group (usa) Inc 212 425-9649
  25 Broadway Fl 9 New York (10004) *(G-9939)*

Irene Cerone 315 668-2899
  9600 Brewerton Rd Brewerton (13029) *(G-1136)*

Iridesse Inc 212 230-6000
  600 Madison Ave Fl 5 New York (10022) *(G-9940)*

Iridium Industries Inc 516 504-9700
  17 Barstow Rd Ste 302 Great Neck (11021) *(G-5395)*

Iriniri Designs Ltd 845 469-7934
  1358 Kings Hwy Sugar Loaf (10981) *(G-14769)*

Irish America Inc 212 725-2993
  875 Americas Rm 2100 New York (10001) *(G-9941)*

Irish America Magazine, New York *Also called Irish America Inc* *(G-9941)*

Irish Echo Newspaper Corp 212 482-4818
  165 Madison Ave Rm 302 New York (10016) *(G-9942)*

Irish Tribune Inc 212 684-3366
  875 Avenue Of The Amerrm2 Rm 2100 New York (10001) *(G-9943)*

Irish Voice Newspaper, New York *Also called Irish Tribune Inc* *(G-9943)*

Iron Art Inc 914 592-7977
  14 N Payne St Elmsford (10523) *(G-4412)*

Iron Horse Graphics Ltd 631 537-3400
  112 Maple Ln Bridgehampton (11932) *(G-1166)*

Iron Smoke Whiskey LLC 585 388-7584
  111 Parce Ave Ste 5 Fairport (14450) *(G-4499)*

Ironshore Holdings Inc 315 457-1052
  290 Elwood Davis Rd Liverpool (13088) *(G-7017)*

Irony Limited Inc (PA) 631 329-4065
  53 Sag Harbor Tpke East Hampton (11937) *(G-4123)*

Iroquois Rock Products Inc (HQ) 585 381-7010
  1150 Penfield Rd Rochester (14625) *(G-13484)*

Irtronics Instruments Inc 914 693-6291
  132 Forest Blvd Ardsley (10502) *(G-389)*

Irv Inc 212 334-4507
  475 Park Ave S Fl 11 New York (10016) *(G-9944)*

Irv & Vic Sportswear Co, Yonkers *Also called Robert Viggiani* *(G-16346)*

Irv Schroder & Sons Inc 518 828-0194
  .2906 Atlantic Ave Stottville (12172) *(G-14753)*

Irving Consumer Products Inc (HQ) 518 747-4151
  1 Eddy St Fort Edward (12828) *(G-4940)*

Irving Tissue Div, Fort Edward *Also called Irving Consumer Products Inc* *(G-4940)*

Irwin Futures LLC 518 884-9008
  608 Rock City Rd Ballston Spa (12020) *(G-577)*

Irx Therapuetics Inc 347 442-0640
  140 58th St Brooklyn (11220) *(G-1970)*

Iscream, Cortlandt Manor *Also called Mines Press Inc* *(G-3797)*

Isfel Co Inc (PA) 212 736-6216
  110 W 34th St Rm 1101 New York (10001) *(G-9945)*

Isimulate LLC 877 947-2831
  43 New Scotland Ave Albany (12208) *(G-90)*

Isine Inc (PA) 631 913-4400
  105 Maxess Rd Ste 124 Melville (11747) *(G-7797)*

Island Audio Engineering 631 543-2372
  7 Glenmere Ct Commack (11725) *(G-3593)*

Island Automated Gate Co LLC 631 425-0196
  125 W Hills Rd Huntington Station (11746) *(G-6250)*

Island Chimney Service, Bohemia *Also called Ace Cntracting Consulting Corp* *(G-964)*

Island Circuits International 516 625-5555
  1318 130th St Fl 2 College Point (11356) *(G-3547)*

Island Components Group Inc 631 563-4224
  101 Colin Dr Unit 4 Holbrook (11741) *(G-6003)*

Island Custom Stairs Inc 631 205-5335
  23 Scouting Blvd Unit C Medford (11763) *(G-7713)*

Island Industries Corp 631 451-8825
  480 Mill Rd Coram (11727) *(G-3694)*

Island Instrument Corporation 631 243-0550
  65 Burt Dr Deer Park (11729) *(G-3883)*

Island Interiors, West Babylon *Also called Dbs Interiors Corp* *(G-15706)*

Island Lite Louvers Inc 631 608-4250
  35 Albany Ave Amityville (11701) *(G-278)*

Island Machine Inc 518 562-1232
  86 Boynton Ave Plattsburgh (12901) *(G-12754)*

Island Marketing Corp 516 739-0500
  95 Searing Ave Ste 2 Mineola (11501) *(G-7981)*

Island Nameplate Inc 845 651-4005
  124 S Main St Florida (10921) *(G-4825)*

Island Ordnance Systems LLC 516 746-2100
  267 E Jericho Tpke Ste 2 Mineola (11501) *(G-7982)*

Island Precision, Ronkonkoma *Also called Roger Latari* *(G-14004)*

Island Publications, Melville *Also called Distinction Magazine Inc* *(G-7775)*

Island Pyrochemical Inds Corp (PA) 516 746-2100
  267 E Jericho Tpke Ste 2 Mineola (11501) *(G-7983)*

Island Ready Mix Inc 631 874-3777
  170 Railroad Ave Center Moriches (11934) *(G-3246)*

Island Recycling Corp 631 234-6688
  228 Blydenburg Rd Central Islip (11749) *(G-3279)*

Island Research and Dev Corp 631 471-7100
  200 13th Ave Unit 12 Ronkonkoma (11779) *(G-13949)*

Island Silkscreen Inc 631 757-4567
  328 Larkfield Rd East Northport (11731) *(G-4147)*

Island Stairs Corp 347 645-0560
  178 Industrial Loop Staten Island (10309) *(G-14666)*

Island Street Lumber Co Inc 716 692-4127
  11 Felton St North Tonawanda (14120) *(G-12072)*

Island Technology, Ronkonkoma *Also called Island Research and Dev Corp* *(G-13949)*

Islandaire, Saint James *Also called RE Hansen Industries Inc* *(G-14113)*

Islandia Mri Associates PC 631 234-2828
  200 Corporate Plz Ste 203 Central Islip (11749) *(G-3280)*

Islechem LLC 716 773-8401
  2801 Long Rd Grand Island (14072) *(G-5334)*

Islip Bulletin, Patchogue *Also called John Lor Publishing Ltd* *(G-12504)*

Islip Miniture Golf 631 940-8900
  500 E Main St Bay Shore (11706) *(G-684)*

ISO Plastics Corp 914 663-8300
  160 E 1st St Mount Vernon (10550) *(G-8152)*

Isolation Dynamics Corp 631 491-5670
  50 Boening Plz Farmingdale (11735) *(G-4653)*

Isolation Systems Inc 716 694-6390
  889 Erie Ave Ste 1 North Tonawanda (14120) *(G-12073)*

Isolation Technology Inc 631 253-3314
  73 Nancy St Unit A West Babylon (11704) *(G-15714)*

Isonics Corporation 212 356-7400
  535 8th Ave Fl 3 New York (10018) *(G-9946)*

Israeli Yellow Pages 718 520-1000
  12510 Queens Blvd Ste 14 Kew Gardens (11415) *(G-6665)*

Issacs Yisroel 718 851-7430
  4424 18th Ave Brooklyn (11204) *(G-1971)*

Issco Corporation (PA) 212 732-8748
  111 Cherry Valley Ave # 410 Garden City (11530) *(G-5102)*

Ist Conax Nuclear, Buffalo *Also called Mirion Tech Conax Nuclear Inc* *(G-2867)*

It Commodity Sourcing Inc 718 677-1577
  1640 E 22nd St Brooklyn (11210) *(G-1972)*

It Windows & Doors Inc 646 220-8398
  245 Treetop Cres Rye Brook (10573) *(G-14090)*

It's About Time, Mount Kisco *Also called Iat Interactive LLC* *(G-8093)*

It's About Time Publishing, Mount Kisco *Also called Laurtom Inc* *(G-8098)*

Itac Label & Tag Corp 718 625-2148
  179 Lexington Ave Brooklyn (11216) *(G-1973)*

Itc Mfg Group Inc 212 684-3696
  109 W 38th St Rm 701 New York (10018) *(G-9947)*

Ithaca Ice Company, The, Dryden *Also called Henry Newman LLC* *(G-4038)*

Ithaca Journal News Co Inc 607 272-2321
  123 W State St Ste 1 Ithaca (14850) *(G-6389)*

Ithaca Peripherals, Ithaca *Also called Transact Technologies Inc* *(G-6414)*

Ithaca Pregancy Center 607 753-3909
  4 Church St Cortland (13045) *(G-3772)*

Ithaca Times, Ithaca *Also called New Ski Inc* *(G-6401)*

Itin Scale Co Inc 718 336-5900
  4802 Glenwood Rd Brooklyn (11234) *(G-1974)*

Itochu Prominent USA LLC 212 827-5715
  1411 Broadway Fl 7 New York (10018) *(G-9948)*

ITR Industries Inc (PA) 914 964-7063
  441 Saw Mill River Rd Yonkers (10701) *(G-16321)*

Its Our Time, New York *Also called Fashion Avenue Knits Inc* *(G-9476)*

Itss, Saint Albans *Also called Integrated Tech Support Svcs* *(G-14106)*

ITT Accounts Payable, Seneca Falls *Also called Goulds Pumps LLC* *(G-14363)*

ITT Aerospace Controls LLC 914 641-2000
  4 W Red Oak Ln White Plains (10604) *(G-16016)*

ITT Corp 716 662-1900
  7 Centre Dr Orchard Park (14127) *(G-12355)*

ITT Corporation 585 269-7109
  4847 Main St Hemlock (14466) *(G-5830)*

ITT Corporation 315 568-2811
  240 Fall St Seneca Falls (13148) *(G-14364)*

ITT Engineered Valves LLC (HQ) 662 257-6982
  240 Fall St Seneca Falls (13148) *(G-14365)*

ITT Enidine Inc (HQ) 716 662-1900
  7 Centre Dr Orchard Park (14127) *(G-12356)*

ITT Goulds Pumps Inc (HQ) 914 641-2129
  240 Fall St Seneca Falls (13148) *(G-14366)*

ITT Inc (PA) 914 641-2000
  1133 Westchester Ave N-100 White Plains (10604) *(G-16017)*

ITT Industries Holdings Inc (HQ) 914 641-2000
  1133 Westchester Ave N-100 White Plains (10604) *(G-16018)*

ITT International Holdings Inc (HQ) 914 641-2000
1133 Westchester Ave White Plains (10604) *(G-16019)*

ITT LLC (HQ) 914 641-2000
1133 Westchester Ave N-100 White Plains (10604) *(G-16020)*

ITT LLC 315 568-4733
240 Fall St Seneca Falls (13148) *(G-14367)*

ITT LLC 315 258-4904
1 Goulds Dr Auburn (13021) *(G-480)*

ITT LLC 914 641-2000
2881 E Bayard Street Ext Seneca Falls (13148) *(G-14368)*

ITT Monitoring Control, Seneca Falls Also called ITT LLC *(G-14367)*

ITT Water Technology, Auburn Also called ITT LLC *(G-480)*

Itts Industrial Inc 718 605-6934
165 Industrial Loop C Staten Island (10309) *(G-14667)*

ITW Deltar 860 435-2574
5979 N Elm Ave Millerton (12546) *(G-7949)*

Ivalua Inc 650 930-9710
195 Montague St Brooklyn (11201) *(G-1975)*

Ivan Horning 315 536-3028
848 State Route 14a Penn Yan (14527) *(G-12587)*

Iver Printing Inc 718 275-2070
124 N 12th St New Hyde Park (11040) *(G-8276)*

Iveric Bio Inc (PA) 212 845-8200
1 Penn Plz Fl 35 New York (10119) *(G-9949)*

Ives Farm Market 315 592-4880
2652 Rr 176 Fulton (13069) *(G-5065)*

Ives Slaughterhouse, Fulton Also called Ives Farm Market *(G-5065)*

Ivi Services Inc 607 729-5111
5 Pine Camp Dr Binghamton (13904) *(G-889)*

Ivy Classic Industries Inc 914 632-8200
40 Plain Ave New Rochelle (10801) *(G-8343)*

Ivy Enterprises Inc (HQ) 516 621-9779
25 Harbor Park Dr Port Washington (11050) *(G-12890)*

Iwc New York Btq, New York Also called Richemont North America Inc *(G-11037)*

Iwci, Deposit Also called Integrated Wood Components Inc *(G-4000)*

Iwe, East Amherst Also called Integrted Work Envronments LLC *(G-4078)*

Iweb Design Inc 805 243-8305
1491 Metro Ave Ste 3i Bronx (10462) *(G-1284)*

Izi Creations, New York Also called Adamor Inc *(G-8454)*

Izquierdo Studios Ltd 212 807-9757
122 W 30th St New York (10001) *(G-9950)*

Izun Pharmaceuticals Corp (PA) 212 618-6357
1 Rockefeller Plz Fl 11 New York (10020) *(G-9951)*

J & A Usa Inc 631 243-3336
335 Crooked Hill Rd Brentwood (11717) *(G-1124)*

J & C Finishing 718 456-1087
1067 Wyckoff Ave Ridgewood (11385) *(G-13147)*

J & D Walter Distributors Inc 518 449-1606
6 Old River Rd Glenmont (12077) *(G-5238)*

J & D Walter Wholesale Distrg, Glenmont Also called J & D Walter Distributors Inc *(G-5238)*

J & E Talit Inc 718 850-1333
13011 Atlantic Ave Fl 2 Richmond Hill (11418) *(G-13116)*

J & F Advertising, Carle Place Also called Market Place Publications *(G-3178)*

J & G Machine & Tool Co Inc 315 310-7130
4510 Smith Rd Marion (14505) *(G-7571)*

J & H Creations Inc 212 465-0962
19 W 36th St Fl 3 New York (10018) *(G-9952)*

J & J Bronze & Aluminum Cast 718 383-2111
249 Huron St Brooklyn (11222) *(G-1976)*

J & J Log & Lumber Corp 845 832-6535
528 Old State Route 22 Dover Plains (12522) *(G-4032)*

J & J Printing Inc (PA) 315 458-7411
500 Cambridge Ave Syracuse (13208) *(G-14914)*

J & J Swiss Precision Inc 631 243-5584
160 W Industry Ct Ste F Deer Park (11729) *(G-3884)*

J & J TI Die Mfg & Stampg Corp 845 228-0242
594 Horsepound Rd Carmel (10512) *(G-3186)*

J & M Packaging Inc 631 608-3069
21 Newton Rd Hauppauge (11788) *(G-5679)*

J & M Textile Co Inc 212 268-8000
505 8th Ave Rm 701 New York (10018) *(G-9953)*

J & N Computer Services Inc 585 388-8780
1387 Fairport Rd Ste 900j Fairport (14450) *(G-4500)*

J & S Licata Bros Inc 718 805-6924
8931 129th St Richmond Hill (11418) *(G-13117)*

J & S Logging Inc 315 262-2112
3860 State Highway 56 South Colton (13687) *(G-14503)*

J & T Metal Products Co Inc 631 226-7400
89 Eads St West Babylon (11704) *(G-15715)*

J & X Production Inc 718 200-1228
327 W 36th St 7f New York (10018) *(G-9954)*

J A T Printing Inc 631 427-1155
46 Gerard St Unit 2 Huntington (11743) *(G-6208)*

J A Yansick Lumber Co Inc 585 492-4312
16 Rule Dr Arcade (14009) *(G-376)*

J B S, Scotia Also called Jbs LLC *(G-14333)*

J B Tool & Die Co Inc 516 333-1480
629 Main St Westbury (11590) *(G-15897)*

J C Continental Inc 212 643-2051
3100 47th Ave Long Island City (11101) *(G-7250)*

J C Industries Inc 631 420-1920
89 Eads St West Babylon (11704) *(G-15716)*

J D Calato Manufacturing Co (PA) 716 285-3546
4501 Hyde Park Blvd Niagara Falls (14305) *(G-11942)*

J D Cousins Inc 716 824-1098
667 Tifft St Buffalo (14220) *(G-2815)*

J D Handling Systems Inc 518 828-9676
1346 State Route 9h Ghent (12075) *(G-5185)*

J D Steward Inc 718 358-0169
4537 162nd St Flushing (11358) *(G-4864)*

J Davis Manufacturing Co Inc 315 337-7574
222 Erie Blvd E Rome (13440) *(G-13852)*

J E T, Ronkonkoma Also called Jet Redi Mix Concrete Inc *(G-13954)*

J Edlin Interiors Ltd 212 243-2111
122 W 27th St Fl 2 New York (10001) *(G-9955)*

J F B & Sons Lithographers 631 467-1444
1700 Ocean Ave Lake Ronkonkoma (11779) *(G-6771)*

J F M Sheet Metal Inc 631 737-8494
2090 Pond Rd Ronkonkoma (11779) *(G-13950)*

J F Machining Company Inc 716 791-3910
2382 Balmer Rd Ransomville (14131) *(G-13066)*

J Gimbel Inc 718 296-5200
275 Hempstead Tpke Ste A West Hempstead (11552) *(G-15772)*

J H Buhrmaster Company Inc 518 843-1700
164 W Main St Amsterdam (12010) *(G-331)*

J H Buscher Inc 716 667-2003
227 Thorn Ave Ste 30 Orchard Park (14127) *(G-12357)*

J H C Fabrications Inc (PA) 718 649-0065
595 Berriman St Brooklyn (11208) *(G-1977)*

J H M Engineering 718 871-1810
4014 8th Ave Brooklyn (11232) *(G-1978)*

J H Rhodes Company Inc 315 829-3600
10 Ward St Vernon (13476) *(G-15367)*

J H Robotics Inc 607 729-3758
109 Main St Johnson City (13790) *(G-6603)*

J I Intrntnal Contact Lens Lab 718 997-1212
6352 Saunders St Ste A Rego Park (11374) *(G-13077)*

J Ironwork, Brooklyn Also called Railings By New Star Brass *(G-2324)*

J J Creations Inc 718 392-2828
4742 37th St Long Island City (11101) *(G-7251)*

J Jamner Surgical Instrs Inc 914 592-9051
40 Saw Mill River Rd # 12 Hawthorne (10532) *(G-5814)*

J K Fertility, Yonkers Also called J Kendall LLC *(G-16322)*

J Kendall LLC 646 739-4956
71 Belvedere Dr Yonkers (10705) *(G-16322)*

J Lowy Co 718 338-7324
940 E 19th St Brooklyn (11230) *(G-1979)*

J Lowy Lea Skullcaps Mfg Co, Brooklyn Also called J Lowy Co *(G-1979)*

J M Canty Inc 716 625-4227
6100 Donner Rd Lockport (14094) *(G-7084)*

J M Haley Corp 631 845-5200
151 Toledo St Ste 1 Farmingdale (11735) *(G-4654)*

J M L Productions Inc 718 643-1674
162 Spencer St Brooklyn (11205) *(G-1980)*

J M P Display Fixture Co Inc 718 649-0333
760 E 96th St Brooklyn (11236) *(G-1981)*

J M R Plastics Corporation 718 898-9825
5847 78th St Middle Village (11379) *(G-7879)*

J Mackenzie Ltd 585 321-1770
234 Wallace Way Rochester (14624) *(G-13485)*

J N White Associates Inc 585 237-5191
129 N Center St Perry (14530) *(G-12598)*

J P Installations Warehouse 914 576-3188
29 Portman Rd New Rochelle (10801) *(G-8344)*

J P Printing Inc (PA) 516 293-6110
331 Main St Farmingdale (11735) *(G-4655)*

J P R Pharmacy Inc 718 327-0600
529 Beach 20th St Far Rockaway (11691) *(G-4566)*

J Pahura Contractors 585 589-5793
415 East Ave Albion (14411) *(G-156)*

J Percoco Industries Inc 631 312-4572
1546 Ocean Ave Ste 4 Bohemia (11716) *(G-1025)*

J Percy For Mrvin Rchards Ltd (HQ) 212 944-5300
512 Fashion Ave New York (10018) *(G-9956)*

J Petrocelli Wine Cellars LLC 631 765-1100
39390 Route 25 Peconic (11958) *(G-12546)*

J R Cooperage Co Inc 718 387-1664
125 Division Pl Brooklyn (11222) *(G-1982)*

J R Dill Winery LLC 607 546-5757
4922 State Route 414 Burdett (14818) *(G-3058)*

J R Gold Designs Ltd 212 922-9292
555 5th Ave Fl 19 New York (10017) *(G-9957)*

J R Nites (PA) 212 354-9670
1400 Broadway Fl 6 New York (10018) *(G-9958)*

J R Products Inc 716 633-7565
9680 County Rd Clarence Center (14032) *(G-3446)*

J R S Precision Machining 631 737-1330
40 Raynor Ave Ste 2 Ronkonkoma (11779) *(G-13951)*

J Rettenmaier USA LP 716 693-4040
50 Bridge St North Tonawanda (14120) *(G-12074)*

J Rettenmaier USA LP 716 693-4009
4 Detroit St North Tonawanda (14120) *(G-12075)*

J Rivera, Bohemia Also called Pro Torque *(G-1067)*

J Sussman Inc 718 297-0228
10910 180th St Jamaica (11433) *(G-6450)*

J T D Stamping Co Inc 631 643-4144
403 Wyandanch Ave West Babylon (11704) ***(G-15717)***

J T Printing 21 718 484-3939
165 Industrial Loop Ste 5 Staten Island (10309) ***(G-14668)***

J T Systematic 607 754-0929
39 Valley St Endwell (13760) ***(G-4480)***

J V Haring & Son 718 720-1947
1277 Clove Rd Ste 2 Staten Island (10301) ***(G-14669)***

J V Precision Inc 518 851-3200
3031 Us Route 9 Hudson (12534) ***(G-6164)***

J Vogler Enterprise LLC 585 247-1625
15 Evelyn St Rochester (14606) ***(G-13486)***

J W Stevens Co Inc 315 472-6311
6059 Corporate Dr East Syracuse (13057) ***(G-4223)***

J&R Fuel of LI Inc 631 234-1959
97 W Suffolk Ave Central Islip (11722) ***(G-3281)***

J&T Macquesten Realty, Mount Vernon *Also called Dunlea Whl GL & Mirror Inc* ***(G-8140)***

J&T Metal Inc 631 471-5335
38 Raynor Ave Ste 3 Ronkonkoma (11779) ***(G-13952)***

J-K Prosthetics & Orthotics 914 699-2077
699 N Macquesten Pkwy Mount Vernon (10552) ***(G-8153)***

J.hoaglund, New York *Also called THE Design Group Inc* ***(G-11459)***

J.N. White Designs, Perry *Also called J N White Associates Inc* ***(G-12598)***

J3 Printing Inc 516 304-6103
11214 Colfax St Queens Village (11429) ***(G-13022)***

J9 Technologies Inc 412 586-5038
25 Broadway Fl 9 New York (10004) ***(G-9959)***

Jaab Precision Inc 631 218-3725
180 Gary Way Ronkonkoma (11779) ***(G-13953)***

Jabo Agricultural Inc 631 475-1800
9 Northwood Ln Patchogue (11772) ***(G-12503)***

Jac Usa Inc 212 841-7430
45 Broadway Ste 1810 New York (10006) ***(G-9960)***

Jack J Florio Jr 716 434-9123
36b Main St Lockport (14094) ***(G-7085)***

Jack L Popkin & Co Inc 718 361-6700
12510 84th Rd Kew Gardens (11415) ***(G-6666)***

Jack Luckner Steel Shelving Co 718 363-0500
5454 43rd St Maspeth (11378) ***(G-7623)***

Jack Merkel Inc 631 234-2600
1720 Express Dr S Hauppauge (11788) ***(G-5680)***

Jack W Miller 585 538-2399
2339 North Rd Scottsville (14546) ***(G-14341)***

Jackel International, New York *Also called Meiyume USA Inc* ***(G-10425)***

Jackie's Girls, New York *Also called Waterbury Garment LLC* ***(G-11730)***

Jacks and Jokers 52 LLC 917 740-2595
215 E 68th St Apt 5o New York (10065) ***(G-9961)***

Jacks Gourmet LLC 718 954-4681
1000 Dean St Ste 214 Brooklyn (11238) ***(G-1983)***

Jackson Dakota Inc (PA) 212 838-9444
979 3rd Ave Ste 503 New York (10022) ***(G-9962)***

Jacksons Welding LLC 607 756-2725
215 N Homer Ave Cortland (13045) ***(G-3773)***

Jacksons Welding Service & Sls, Cortland *Also called Jacksons Welding LLC* ***(G-3773)***

Jaclyn LLC (HQ) 201 909-6000
500 7th Ave New York (10018) ***(G-9963)***

Jacmax Industries LLC 718 439-3743
473 Wortman Ave Brooklyn (11208) ***(G-1984)***

Jacmel Jewelry Inc (PA) 718 349-4300
1385 Broadway Fl 8 New York (10018) ***(G-9964)***

Jacob Dresdner Co, New York *Also called Dresdiam Inc* ***(G-9268)***

Jacob Hidary Foundation Inc 212 736-6540
10 W 33rd St Rm 900 New York (10001) ***(G-9965)***

Jacob Inc 646 450-3067
287 Keap St Brooklyn (11211) ***(G-1985)***

Jacobi Industries, Medford *Also called Jacobi Tool & Die Mfg Inc* ***(G-7714)***

Jacobi Tool & Die Mfg Inc 631 736-5394
131 Middle Island Rd Medford (11763) ***(G-7714)***

Jacobs & Cohen Inc 212 714-2702
255 W 36th St Fl 9 New York (10018) ***(G-9966)***

Jacobs Juice Corp 646 255-2860
388 Avenue X Apt 2h Brooklyn (11223) ***(G-1986)***

Jacobs Manufacturing, Hogansburg *Also called Jacobs Tobacco Company* ***(G-5980)***

Jacobs Press Inc 315 252-4861
87 Columbus St Auburn (13021) ***(G-481)***

Jacobs Tobacco Company 518 358-4948
344 Frogtown Rd Hogansburg (13655) ***(G-5980)***

Jacobs Woodworking LLC 315 427-8999
801 W Fayette St Syracuse (13204) ***(G-14915)***

Jacoby Enterprises LLC 718 435-0289
1615 54th St Brooklyn (11204) ***(G-1987)***

Jacques Torres Chocolate, Brooklyn *Also called Mrchocolatecom LLC* ***(G-2179)***

Jad Corp of America 718 762-8900
2048 119th St College Point (11356) ***(G-3548)***

Jadak Technologies Inc 315 701-0678
7279 William Barry Blvd North Syracuse (13212) ***(G-12047)***

Jado Sewing Machines Inc 718 784-2314
4008 22nd St Long Island City (11101) ***(G-7252)***

Jaf Converters Inc 631 842-3131
60 Marconi Blvd Copiague (11726) ***(G-3661)***

Jag Footwear ACC & Ret Corp 800 999-1877
1411 Broadway Fl 20 New York (10018) ***(G-9967)***

Jag Lighting 917 226-3575
6105 56th Dr Maspeth (11378) ***(G-7624)***

Jag Manufacturing Inc 518 762-9558
26 Grecco Dr Johnstown (12095) ***(G-6620)***

Jaguar Casting Co Inc 212 869-0197
100 United Nations Plz 38a New York (10017) ***(G-9968)***

Jaguar Industries Inc 845 947-1800
89 Broadway Haverstraw (10927) ***(G-5805)***

Jaguar Jewelry Casting NY Inc 212 768-4848
48 W 48th St Ste 500 New York (10036) ***(G-9969)***

Jaguars, Yonkers *Also called Peter Racing* ***(G-16341)***

Jaidan Industries Inc 516 944-3650
16 Capi Ln Port Washington (11050) ***(G-12891)***

Jain Irrigation Inc 315 755-4400
740 Water St Watertown (13601) ***(G-15573)***

Jakes Sneakers Inc 718 233-1132
845 Classon Ave Brooklyn (11238) ***(G-1988)***

Jakob Schlaepfer Inc 212 221-2323
37 W 26th St Rm 208 New York (10010) ***(G-9970)***

Jal Signs Inc 516 536-7280
540 Merrick Rd Baldwin (11510) ***(G-531)***

Jalex Industries Ltd 631 491-5072
86 Nancy St West Babylon (11704) ***(G-15718)***

Jam Industries Inc 585 458-9830
9 Marway Cir Rochester (14624) ***(G-13487)***

Jam Paper, New York *Also called Hudson Envelope Corporation* ***(G-9831)***

Jam Printing Publishing Inc 914 345-8400
11 Clearbrook Rd Ste 133 Elmsford (10523) ***(G-4413)***

Jamaica Electroplating, North Baldwin *Also called Dura Spec Inc* ***(G-12004)***

Jamaica Iron Works Inc 718 657-4849
10847 Merrick Blvd Jamaica (11433) ***(G-6451)***

Jamaica Lamp Corp 718 776-5039
21220 Jamaica Ave Queens Village (11428) ***(G-13023)***

Jamaican Weekly Gleaner, Jamaica *Also called Gleaner Company Ltd* ***(G-6444)***

Jamar Precision Products Co 631 254-0234
5 Lucon Dr Deer Park (11729) ***(G-3885)***

Jamco Aerospace Inc 631 586-7900
121a E Industry Ct Deer Park (11729) ***(G-3886)***

James A Staley Co Inc 845 878-3344
5 Bowen Ct Carmel (10512) ***(G-3187)***

James B Crowell & Sons Inc 845 895-3464
242 Lippincott Rd Wallkill (12589) ***(G-15470)***

James Conolly Printing Co 585 426-4150
72 Marway Cir Rochester (14624) ***(G-13488)***

James D Rubino Inc 631 244-8730
20 Jules Ct Ste 5 Bohemia (11716) ***(G-1026)***

James King Woodworking Inc 518 761-6091
656 County Line Rd Queensbury (12804) ***(G-13044)***

James L Taylor Mfg Co (PA) 845 452-3780
130 Salt Point Tpke Poughkeepsie (12603) ***(G-12964)***

James L Taylor Mfg Co 845 452-3780
130 Salt Point Tpke Poughkeepsie (12603) ***(G-12965)***

James L. Taylor Mfg., Poughkeepsie *Also called James L Taylor Mfg Co* ***(G-12964)***

James Morgan Publishing (PA) 212 655-5470
5 Penn Plz Ste 2300 New York (10001) ***(G-9971)***

James Morris 315 824-8519
6697 Airport Rd Hamilton (13346) ***(G-5527)***

James Reed Sales, Athens *Also called Peckham Asphalt Resale Corp* ***(G-449)***

James Richard Specialty Chem 914 478-7500
24 Ridge St Hastings On Hudson (10706) ***(G-5574)***

James Thompson & Company Inc (PA) 212 686-4242
463 7th Ave Rm 1603 New York (10018) ***(G-9972)***

James Town Macadam Inc 716 665-4504
1946 New York Ave Falconer (14733) ***(G-4546)***

James Wire Die Co 315 894-3233
138 West St Ilion (13357) ***(G-6279)***

James Woerner Inc 631 454-9330
130 Allen Blvd Farmingdale (11735) ***(G-4656)***

Jamesport Vineyards, Jamesport *Also called North House Vineyards Inc* ***(G-6490)***

Jamestown Advanced Pdts Corp 716 483-3406
2855 Girts Rd Jamestown (14701) ***(G-6519)***

Jamestown Awning Inc 716 483-1435
313 Steele St Jamestown (14701) ***(G-6520)***

Jamestown Bronze Works Inc 716 665-2302
174 Hopkins Ave Jamestown (14701) ***(G-6521)***

Jamestown Cont of Rochester 585 254-9190
82 Edwards Deming Dr Rochester (14606) ***(G-13489)***

Jamestown Container Corp (PA) 716 665-4623
14 Deming Dr Falconer (14733) ***(G-4547)***

Jamestown Fab Stl & Sup Inc 716 665-2227
1034 Allen St Jamestown (14701) ***(G-6522)***

Jamestown Iron Works Inc 716 665-2818
2022 Allen Street Ext Falconer (14733) ***(G-4548)***

Jamestown Kitchen & Bath Inc 716 665-2299
1085 E 2nd St Jamestown (14701) ***(G-6523)***

Jamestown Metal Products LLC 716 665-5313
178 Blackstone Ave Jamestown (14701) ***(G-6524)***

Jamestown Plastics Inc (PA) 716 792-4144
8806 Highland Ave Brocton (14716) ***(G-1181)***

Jamestown Public Works, Jamestown *Also called City of Jamestown* ***(G-6501)***

Jamestown Scientific Inds LLC 716 665-3224
1300 E 2nd St Jamestown (14701) ***(G-6525)***

Janco Press Inc 631 563-3003
  20 Floyds Run Bohemia (11716) (G-1027)
Jane Bakes Inc 845 920-1100
  40 S Main St Pearl River (10965) (G-12535)
Jane Bohan Inc 212 529-6090
  611 Broadway New York (10012) (G-9973)
Jane Knitting Kit, New York Also called Janes Designer Yrn Pttrns Inc (G-9974)
Jane Lewis 607 722-0584
  82 Castle Creek Rd Binghamton (13901) (G-890)
Janed Enterprises 631 694-4494
  48 Allen Blvd Unit B Farmingdale (11735) (G-4657)
Janel Corporation (PA) 516 256-8143
  303 Merrick Rd Ste 400 Lynbrook (11563) (G-7432)
Janes Designer Yrn Pttrns Inc 347 260-3071
  1745 Broadway Ste 1750 New York (10019) (G-9974)
Janice Moses Represents 212 898-4898
  99 Battery Pl Apt 10d New York (10280) (G-9975)
Janlynn Corporation, The, Bohemia Also called Spectrum Crafts Inc (G-1081)
Janowski Hamburger, Rockville Centre Also called Bianca Burgers LLC (G-13826)
Japan America Learning Ctr Inc (PA) 914 723-7600
  81 Montgomery Ave Scarsdale (10583) (G-14237)
Japan Printing & Graphics Inc 212 406-2905
  48 Wall St Fl 5 New York (10005) (G-9976)
Jaquith Industries Inc 315 478-5700
  600 E Brighton Ave Syracuse (13210) (G-14916)
Jar Metals Inc 845 425-8901
  50 2nd Ave Nanuet (10954) (G-8200)
Jaracz Jr Joseph Paul 716 533-1377
  64 Ferndale Dr Orchard Park (14127) (G-12358)
Jarets Stuffed Cupcakes 607 658-9096
  116 Oak Hill Ave Endicott (13760) (G-4460) .
Jarit Surgical Instruments, Hawthorne Also called J Jamner Surgical Instrs Inc (G-5814)
Jarvik Heart Inc 212 397-3911
  333 W 52nd St Ste 700 New York (10019) (G-9977)
Jasani Designs Usa Inc 212 257-6465
  28 W 44th St Ste 1014 New York (10036) (G-9978)
Jasco Heat Treating Inc 585 388-0071
  75 Macedon Center Rd Fairport (14450) (G-4501)
Jasco Tools LLC 585 254-7000
  1390 Mount Read Blvd Rochester (14606) (G-13490)
Jason & Jean Products Inc 718 271-8300
  104 Corona Ave Corona (11368) (G-3741)
Jason Ladanye Guitar Piano & H 518 527-3973
  605 Park Ave Albany (12208) (G-91)
Jasper Transport LLC 315 729-5760
  1680 Flat St Penn Yan (14527) (G-12588)
Javcon Machine Inc 631 586-1890
  255 Skidmore Rd Deer Park (11729) (G-3887)
Javin Machine Corp 631 643-3322
  31 Otis St West Babylon (11704) (G-15719)
Javlyn Process Systems LLC 585 424-5580
  3136 Winton Rd S Ste 102 Rochester (14623) (G-13491)
Jax Coco USA LLC 347 688-8198
  5 Penn Plz Ste 2300 New York (10001) (G-9979)
Jax Signs and Neon Inc 607 727-3420
  108 Odell Ave Endicott (13760) (G-4461)
Jaxi's Sportswear, Brooklyn Also called Jaxis Inc (G-1989)
Jaxis Inc (PA) 212 302-7611
  1365 38th St Brooklyn (11218) (G-1989)
Jaxson LLC 631 842-7775
  145 Dixon Ave Ste 1 Amityville (11701) (G-279)
Jaxson Rollforming Inc 631 842-7775
  145 Dixon Ave Ste 1 Amityville (11701) (G-280)
Jay Bags Inc 845 459-6500
  55 Union Rd Ste 104 Spring Valley (10977) (G-14573)
Jay Little Oil Well Servi 716 925-8905
  5460 Nichols Run Limestone (14753) (G-6938)
Jay Moulding Corporation 518 237-4200
  7 Bridge Ave Ste 1 Cohoes (12047) (G-3507)
Jay Strongwater Holdings LLC (HQ) 646 657-0558
  12 W 21st St Fl 11 New York (10010) (G-9980)
Jay Turoff 718 856-7300
  681 Coney Island Ave Brooklyn (11218) (G-1990)
Jay-Aimee Designs Inc 718 609-0333
  1 Great Neck Rd Ste 1 # 1 Great Neck (11021) (G-5396)
Jay-Art Nvelties/Tower Grafics, Brooklyn Also called Jay Turoff (G-1990)
Jaya Apparel Group LLC 212 764-4980
  1384 Broadway Fl 18 New York (10018) (G-9981)
Jayden Star LLC 212 686-0400
  385 5th Ave Rm 507 New York (10016) (G-9982)
Jaymar Jewelry Co Inc 212 564-4788
  69 5th Ave Apt 8d New York (10003) (G-9983)
Jays Furniture Products Inc 716 876-8854
  321 Ramsdell Ave Buffalo (14216) (G-2816)
JB Star, New York Also called Jewels By Star Ltd (G-9996)
Jbf Stainless LLC 315 569-2800
  1963 Country Mile Frankfort (13340) (G-4952)
Jbren Corp 716 332-5928
  107 Dorothy St Buffalo (14206) (G-2817)
JBS Limited 212 764-4600
  1400 Broadway Rm 1703 New York (10018) (G-9984)

JBS Limited (PA) 212 221-8403
  1375 Broadway Fl 4 New York (10018) (G-9985)
Jbs LLC 518 346-0001
  6 Maple Ave Scotia (12302) (G-14333)
JC California Inc 212 334-4380
  359 Broadway Fl 3 New York (10013) (G-9986)
JC Crystal Inc 212 594-0858
  260 W 35th St Fl 10 New York (10001) (G-9987)
Jcco Enterprises 716 626-0892
  348 Cayuga Rd Buffalo (14225) (G-2818)
Jcdecaux Mallscape LLC (HQ) 646 834-1200
  350 5th Ave Fl 73 New York (10118) (G-9988)
JD Granary LLC 607 627-6294
  7 Railroad St Smyrna (13464) (G-14490)
JD Tool Inc 607 786-3129
  205 Harrison Ave Endicott (13760) (G-4462)
Jds Graphics, New York Also called JDS Graphics Inc (G-9989)
JDS Graphics Inc 973 330-3300
  226 W 37th St Fl 10 New York (10018) (G-9989)
JE Miller Inc 315 437-6811
  747 W Manlius St East Syracuse (13057) (G-4224)
JE Monahan Fabrications LLC 518 761-0414
  559 Queensbury Ave 1/2 Queensbury (12804) (G-13045)
Jeam Imports, Brooklyn Also called Executive Machines Inc (G-1822)
Jean Philippe Fragrances LLC 212 983-2640
  551 5th Ave Rm 1500 New York (10176) (G-9990)
Jeanjer LLC 212 944-1330
  1400 Broadway Fl 15 New York (10018) (G-9991)
Jed Lights Inc (HQ) 516 812-5001
  10 Connor Ln Deer Park (11729) (G-3888)
Jeff Cooper Inc 516 333-8200
  15 W 47th St Ste 1602 New York (10036) (G-9992)
Jefferson Concrete Corp 315 788-4171
  22850 County Route 51 Watertown (13601) (G-15574)
Jeffersonville Volunteer 845 482-3110
  49 Callicoon Center Rd Jeffersonville (12748) (G-6570)
Jeffrey D Menoff DDS PC 716 665-1468
  785 Fairmount Ave Jamestown (14701) (G-6526)
Jeffrey John 631 842-2850
  25 Elm Pl Amityville (11701) (G-281)
Jeffrey Spring Modern Art, Astoria Also called Modern Art Foundry Inc (G-430)
Jeg Online Ventures LLC 800 983-8230
  85 Hoffman Ln Ste B Islandia (11749) (G-6337)
Jekerda Sales, East Williston Also called North American Pipe Corp (G-4249)
Jem Container Corp 800 521-0145
  151 Fairchild Ave Ste 1 Plainview (11803) (G-12692)
Jem Sign Corp (PA) 516 867-4466
  470 S Franklin St Hempstead (11550) (G-5840)
Jem Threading Specialties Inc 718 665-3341
  1059 Washington Ave Bronx (10456) (G-1285)
Jem Tool & Die Corp 631 539-8734
  81 Paris Ct West Islip (11795) (G-15811)
JEm Wdwkg & Cabinets Inc 518 828-5361
  250 Falls Rd Hudson (12534) (G-6165)
Jemcap Servicing LLC 212 213-9353
  360 Madison Ave Rm 1902 New York (10017) (G-9993)
Jenalex Creative Marketing Inc 212 935-2266
  116 E 57th St Fl 3 New York (10022) (G-9994)
Jenlor Ltd 315 637-9080
  523 E Genesee St Fayetteville (13066) (G-4784)
Jenmar Door & Glass Inc 718 767-7900
  15038 12th Ave Whitestone (11357) (G-16095)
Jenna Concrete Corporation 718 842-5250
  1465 Bronx River Ave Bronx (10472) (G-1286)
Jenna Harlem River Inc 718 842-5997
  1465 Bronx River Ave Bronx (10472) (G-1287)
Jentsch & Co Inc 716 852-4111
  107 Dorothy St Buffalo (14206) (G-2819)
Jeric Knit Wear 631 979-8827
  61 Hofstra Dr Smithtown (11787) (G-14480)
Jerome Levy Forecasting Center 914 244-8617
  69 S Moger Ave Ste 202 Mount Kisco (10549) (G-8094)
Jerome Stvens Phrmcuticals Inc 631 567-1113
  60 Davinci Dr Bohemia (11716) (G-1028)
Jerry Cardullo Iron Works Inc 631 242-8881
  101 Spence St Bay Shore (11706) (G-685)
Jerry Miller I.D. Shoes, Buffalo Also called Jerry Miller Molded Shoes Inc (G-2820)
Jerry Miller Molded Shoes Inc (PA) 716 881-3920
  36 Mason St Buffalo (14213) (G-2820)
Jerry Sorbara Furs Inc 212 594-3897
  39 W 32nd St Rm 1400 New York (10001) (G-9995)
Jerry Tomaselli 718 965-1400
  37 3rd St Brooklyn (11232) (G-1991)
Jerry's Bagels & Bakery, Valley Stream Also called Jerrys Bagels (G-15344)
Jerrys Bagels 516 791-0063
  951 Rosedale Rd Valley Stream (11581) (G-15344)
Jersey Express Inc 716 834-6151
  3080 Main St Buffalo (14214) (G-2821)
Jescar Enterprises Inc 845 352-5850
  213 Airport Executive Par Nanuet (10954) (G-8201)
Jesco Lighting Inc 718 366-3211
  15 Harbor Park Dr Port Washington (11050) (G-12892)

Jesco Lighting Group LLC (PA).....718 366-3211
15 Harbor Park Dr Port Washington (11050) ***(G-12893)***
Jesse Joeckel.....631 668-2772
65 Tuthill Rd Montauk (11954) ***(G-8054)***
Jessel Marking Equipment, Syracuse *Also called New York Marking Devices Corp* ***(G-14951)***
Jessica Michelle, New York *Also called Orchid Manufacturing Co Inc* ***(G-10708)***
Jet Redi Mix Concrete Inc.....631 580-3640
2101 Pond Rd Ste 1 Ronkonkoma (11779) ***(G-13954)***
Jet Sew Corporation.....315 896-2683
8119 State Route 12 Barneveld (13304) ***(G-592)***
Jet-Black Sealers Inc.....716 891-4197
555 Ludwig Ave Buffalo (14227) ***(G-2822)***
Jets Lefrois Corp.....585 637-5003
56 High St Brockport (14420) ***(G-1178)***
Jets Lefrois Foods, Brockport *Also called Jets Lefrois Corp* ***(G-1178)***
Jette Group, Bay Shore *Also called Cable Management Solutions Inc* ***(G-660)***
Jetwrx Rotable Services, Elmira *Also called Jrsmm LLC* ***(G-4360)***
Jewelers Machinist Co Inc.....631 661-5020
400 Columbus Ave Babylon (11704) ***(G-521)***
Jewelers Solder Supply Inc.....718 637-1256
1362 54th St Brooklyn (11219) ***(G-1992)***
Jewelry By Sarah Belle.....518 793-1626
10394 State Route 149 Fort Ann (12827) ***(G-4933)***
Jewels By Star Ltd.....212 308-3490
555 5th Ave Fl 7 New York (10017) ***(G-9996)***
Jeweltex Mfg Corp.....212 921-8188
48 W 48th St Ste 507 New York (10036) ***(G-9997)***
Jewish Heritage For Blind.....718 338-4999
1655 E 24th St Brooklyn (11229) ***(G-1993)***
Jewish Journal.....718 630-9350
7014 13th Ave Brooklyn (11228) ***(G-1994)***
Jewish Press Inc.....718 330-1100
4915 16th Ave Brooklyn (11204) ***(G-1995)***
Jewish Week Inc (PA).....212 921-7822
1501 Broadway Ste 505 New York (10036) ***(G-9998)***
Jewler's Solder Sheet & Wire, Brooklyn *Also called Jewelers Solder Supply Inc* ***(G-1992)***
Jeypore Group, New York *Also called Incon Gems Inc* ***(G-9875)***
JF Machine Shop Inc.....631 491-7273
89 Otis St Unit A West Babylon (11704) ***(G-15720)***
Jf Rafter The Lexington Co, Eden *Also called John F Rafter Inc* ***(G-4256)***
Jfe Engineering Corporation.....212 310-9320
350 Park Ave Fl 27th New York (10022) ***(G-9999)***
Jfe Steel America Inc (HQ).....212 310-9320
600 3rd Ave Fl 12 New York (10016) ***(G-10000)***
Jfs Inc (HQ).....646 264-1200
531 W 26th St Unit 531 # 531 New York (10001) ***(G-10001)***
JG Innovative Industries Inc.....718 784-7300
8002 Kew Gardens Rd # 5002 Kew Gardens (11415) ***(G-6667)***
JGM Wholesale Bakery Inc.....631 396-0131
26 Elm Pl Amityville (11701) ***(G-282)***
Jgx LLC.....212 575-1244
1407 Broadway Rm 1416 New York (10018) ***(G-10002)***
Jhc Labresin, Brooklyn *Also called J H C Fabrications Inc* ***(G-1977)***
Jill Fagin Enterprises Inc (PA).....212 674-9383
39 E 12th St Apt 612 New York (10003) ***(G-10003)***
Jillery, New York *Also called Jill Fagin Enterprises Inc* ***(G-10003)***
Jim Henson Company Inc.....212 794-2400
3718 Northern Blvd # 400 Long Island City (11101) ***(G-7253)***
Jim Henson Productions, Long Island City *Also called Jim Henson Company Inc* ***(G-7253)***
Jim Quinn.....518 356-0398
12 Morningside Dr Schenectady (12303) ***(G-14282)***
Jim Quinn and Associates, Schenectady *Also called Jim Quinn* ***(G-14282)***
Jim Romas Bakery Inc.....607 748-7425
202 N Nanticoke Ave Endicott (13760) ***(G-4463)***
Jim Wachtler Inc.....212 755-4367
1212 Avenue Of The New York (10036) ***(G-10004)***
Jimco Lamp & Manufacturing Co.....631 218-2152
181 Freeman Ave Islip (11751) ***(G-6353)***
Jimco Lamp Company, Islip *Also called Jimco Lamp & Manufacturing Co* ***(G-6353)***
Jimeale Incorporated.....917 686-5383
130 Church St Ste 163 New York (10007) ***(G-10005)***
Jimmy Crystal New York Co Ltd.....212 594-0858
47 W 37th St Fl 3 New York (10018) ***(G-10006)***
Jimmy Sales, Brooklyn *Also called Tie King Inc* ***(G-2504)***
Jinglebell Inc.....914 219-5395
190 Byram Lake Rd Armonk (10504) ***(G-399)***
JINGLENOG DBA, Armonk *Also called Jinglebell Inc* ***(G-399)***
Jiranimo Industries Ltd.....212 921-5106
49a W 37th St New York (10018) ***(G-10007)***
Jit International Inc.....631 761-5551
62 Bridge Rd Islandia (11749) ***(G-6338)***
Jj Basics LLC (PA).....212 768-4779
1400 Broadway 14 New York (10018) ***(G-10008)***
JJ Cassone Bakery Inc.....914 939-1568
202 S Regent St Port Chester (10573) ***(G-12823)***
Jj Fantasia Inc.....212 868-1198
38 W 32nd St New York (10001) ***(G-10009)***
JK Manufacturing Inc.....212 683-3535
115 Forest Ave Unit 22 Locust Valley (11560) ***(G-7127)***
Jl Parc LLC (PA).....718 271-0703
9015 Queens Blvd Rego Park (11374) ***(G-13078)***
Jlt Lancaster Clamps Div, Poughkeepsie *Also called James L Taylor Mfg Co* ***(G-12965)***
JM Manufacturer Inc.....212 869-0626
241 W 37th St Rm 924 New York (10018) ***(G-10010)***
JM Murray Center Inc (PA).....607 756-9913
823 State Route 13 Ste 1 Cortland (13045) ***(G-3774)***
JM Originals Inc.....845 647-3003
70 Berme Rd Ellenville (12428) ***(G-4307)***
JM Studio Inc.....646 546-5514
247 W 35th St Fl 3 New York (10001) ***(G-10011)***
Jma Wireless, Liverpool *Also called John Mezzalingua Assoc LLC* ***(G-7018)***
Jmg Fuel Inc.....631 579-4319
3 Fowler Ave Ronkonkoma (11779) ***(G-13955)***
Jml Optical Industries LLC.....585 248-8900
820 Linden Ave Rochester (14625) ***(G-13492)***
Jml Quarries Inc.....845 932-8206
420 Bernas Rd Cochecton (12726) ***(G-3502)***
JMS Ices Inc.....718 448-0853
501 Port Richmond Ave Staten Island (10302) ***(G-14670)***
Jn Marina, New York *Also called Marina Jewelry Co Inc* ***(G-10361)***
Jo Mart Chocolates, Brooklyn *Also called Jo-Mart Candies Corp* ***(G-1996)***
Jo-Mart Candies Corp.....718 375-1277
2917 Avenue R Brooklyn (11229) ***(G-1996)***
Jo-Vin Decorators Inc.....718 441-9350
9423 Jamaica Ave Woodhaven (11421) ***(G-16187)***
Joan Boyce Ltd (PA).....212 867-7474
19 W 44th St Ste 417 New York (10036) ***(G-10012)***
Joanna Mastroianni, New York *Also called Elana Laderos Ltd* ***(G-9332)***
Jobs Weekly Inc.....716 648-5627
31 Buffalo St Ste 2 Hamburg (14075) ***(G-5510)***
Jobson Medical Information LLC (HQ).....212 274-7000
395 Hudson St Fl 3 New York (10014) ***(G-10013)***
Joe Benbasset Inc (PA).....212 594-8440
213 W 35th St Fl 11 New York (10001) ***(G-10014)***
Joe Fresh, New York *Also called Jfs Inc* ***(G-10001)***
Joe Moro.....607 272-0591
214 Fayette St Ithaca (14850) ***(G-6390)***
Joe Pietryka Incorporated (PA).....845 855-1201
85 Charles Colman Blvd Pawling (12564) ***(G-12526)***
Joe's Jerky, Sherrill *Also called Patla Enterprises Inc* ***(G-14405)***
Joed Press.....212 243-3620
242 W 36th St Fl 8 New York (10018) ***(G-10015)***
Joes Jeans, New York *Also called Centric West LLC* ***(G-8958)***
John A Eberly Inc.....315 449-3034
136 Beattie St Syracuse (13224) ***(G-14917)***
John A Vassilaros & Son Inc.....718 886-4140
2905 120th St Flushing (11354) ***(G-4865)***
John and Kiras, New York *Also called Aethera LLC* ***(G-8489)***
John Auguliaro Printing Co.....718 382-5283
2533 Mcdonald Ave Brooklyn (11223) ***(G-1997)***
John Bossone, Glendale *Also called New Day Woodwork Inc* ***(G-5229)***
John C Dolph Company.....732 329-2333
200 Von Roll Dr Schenectady (12306) ***(G-14283)***
John Crane Inc.....315 593-6237
2314 County Route 4 Fulton (13069) ***(G-5066)***
John Deere Authorized Dealer, Fulton *Also called Gone South Concrete Block Inc* ***(G-5062)***
John E Potente & Sons Inc.....516 935-8585
114 Woodbury Rd Unit 1 Hicksville (11801) ***(G-5917)***
John F Krell Jr.....315 492-3201
4046 W Seneca Trpk Syracuse (13215) ***(G-14918)***
John F Rafter Inc.....716 992-3425
2746 W Church St Eden (14057) ***(G-4256)***
John G Rubino Inc.....315 253-7396
45 Aurelius Ave Auburn (13021) ***(G-482)***
John Gailer Inc.....212 243-5662
3718 Northern Blvd Ste 3 Long Island City (11101) ***(G-7254)***
John Hassall LLC (HQ).....516 334-6200
609 Cantiague Rock Rd # 1 Westbury (11590) ***(G-15898)***
John Hassall LLC.....323 869-0150
609 Cantiague Rock Rd # 1 Westbury (11590) ***(G-15899)***
John J Mazur Inc.....631 242-4554
94 E Jefryn Blvd Ste K Deer Park (11729) ***(G-3889)***
John J Richardson.....516 538-6339
12 Bernard St Lawrence (11559) ***(G-6886)***
John Kochis Custom Designs.....212 244-6046
237 W 35th St Ste 502 New York (10001) ***(G-10016)***
John Kristiansen New York Inc.....212 388-1097
665 Broadway Frnt New York (10012) ***(G-10017)***
John Langenbacher Co Inc.....718 328-0141
888 Longfellow Ave Bronx (10474) ***(G-1288)***
John Larocca & Son Inc.....631 423-5256
290 Broadway Huntington Station (11746) ***(G-6251)***
John Lor Publishing Ltd.....631 475-1000
20 Medford Ave Ste 1 Patchogue (11772) ***(G-12504)***
John Mezzalingua Assoc LLC (PA).....315 431-7100
7645 Henry Clay Blvd Liverpool (13088) ***(G-7018)***
John N Fehlinger Co Inc (PA).....212 233-5656
20 Vesey St Rm 1000 New York (10007) ***(G-10018)***
John Patrick, Germantown *Also called On The Double Inc* ***(G-5169)***

John Prior......516 520-9801
2545 Hempstead Tpke # 402 East Meadow (11554) ***(G-4138)***
John R Robinson Inc......718 786-6088
3805 30th St Long Island City (11101) ***(G-7255)***
John Ramsey Elec Svcs LLC......585 298-9596
7940 Rae Blvd Victor (14564) ***(G-15414)***
John Szoke Editions, New York *Also called John Szoke Graphics Inc* ***(G-10019)***
John Szoke Graphics Inc......212 219-8300
24 W 57th St Ste 304 New York (10019) ***(G-10019)***
John T Montecalvo Inc......631 325-1492
1233 Speonk Riverhead Rd Speonk (11972) ***(G-14563)***
John V Agugliaro Printing, Brooklyn *Also called John Auguliaro Printing Co* ***(G-1997)***
John Vespa Inc (PA)......315 788-6330
19626 Overlook Dr Watertown (13601) ***(G-15575)***
Johnnie Ryan Co Inc......716 282-1606
3084 Niagara St Niagara Falls (14303) ***(G-11943)***
Johnny Mica Inc......631 225-5213
116 E Hoffman Ave Lindenhurst (11757) ***(G-6953)***
Johnny's Ideal Prntng Co, Hudson *Also called Johnnys Ideal Printing Co* ***(G-6166)***
Johnnys Ideal Printing Co......518 828-6666
17 Kline St Hudson (12534) ***(G-6166)***
Johnnys Machine Shop......631 338-9733
81 Mahan St West Babylon (11704) ***(G-15721)***
Johns Manville Corporation......518 565-3000
1 Kaycee Loop Rd Plattsburgh (12901) ***(G-12755)***
Johns Ravioli Company Inc......914 576-7030
15 Drake Ave New Rochelle (10805) ***(G-8345)***
Johnson & Hoffman LLC......516 742-3333
40 Voice Rd Carle Place (11514) ***(G-3175)***
Johnson Acquisition Corp (HQ)......518 828-1616
364 Warren St Hudson (12534) ***(G-6167)***
Johnson Bros Lumber, Cazenovia *Also called PDJ Inc* ***(G-3232)***
Johnson Contrls Authorized Dlr, Bronx *Also called Pronto Gas Heating Sups Inc* ***(G-1345)***
Johnson Contrls Authorized Dlr, North Baldwin *Also called Split Systems Corp* ***(G-12008)***
Johnson Controls......585 288-6200
90 Goodway Dr Ste 1 Rochester (14623) ***(G-13493)***
Johnson Controls......518 952-6040
1399 Vischer Ferry Rd Clifton Park (12065) ***(G-3465)***
Johnson Controls......845 774-4120
4 Commerce Dr S Ste 3 Harriman (10926) ***(G-5545)***
Johnson Controls Inc......585 924-9346
90 Goodway Dr Ste 1 Rochester (14623) ***(G-13494)***
Johnson Controls Inc......518 884-8313
339 Brownell Rd Ballston Spa (12020) ***(G-578)***
Johnson Controls Inc......518 694-4822
130 Railroad Ave Albany (12205) ***(G-92)***
Johnson Controls Inc......585 671-1930
237 Birch Ln Webster (14580) ***(G-15643)***
Johnson Controls Inc......914 593-5200
8 Skyline Dr Ste 115 Hawthorne (10532) ***(G-5815)***
Johnson Controls Inc......716 688-7340
130 John Muir Dr Ste 100 Buffalo (14228) ***(G-2823)***
Johnson Controls Inc......585 724-2232
1669 Lake Ave Bldg 333 Rochester (14652) ***(G-13495)***
Johnson Manufacturing Company......716 881-3030
1489 Niagara St Buffalo (14213) ***(G-2824)***
Johnson Mch & Fibr Pdts Co Inc......716 665-2003
142 Hopkins Ave Jamestown (14701) ***(G-6527)***
Johnson Newspaper Corporation......518 483-4700
469 E Main St Ste 2 Malone (12953) ***(G-7486)***
Johnson Outdoors Inc......607 779-2200
625 Conklin Rd Binghamton (13903) ***(G-891)***
Johnson S Sand Gravel Inc......315 771-1450
23284 County Route 3 La Fargeville (13656) ***(G-6734)***
Johnston Dandy Company......315 455-5773
100 Dippold Ave Syracuse (13208) ***(G-14919)***
Johnston Precision Inc......315 253-4181
7 Frank Smith St Auburn (13021) ***(G-483)***
Jointa Lime Company......518 580-0300
269 Ballard Rd Wilton (12831) ***(G-16156)***
Joldeson One Aerospace Inds, Ozone Park *Also called Joldeson One Aerospace Inds* ***(G-12463)***
Joldeson One Aerospace Inds......718 848-7396
10002 103rd Ave Ozone Park (11417) ***(G-12463)***
Jolibe Atelier LLC......917 319-5908
325 W 38th St Studio New York (10018) ***(G-10020)***
Jolin Machining Corp......631 589-1305
1561 Smithtown Ave Bohemia (11716) ***(G-1029)***
Jomar Industries Inc......845 357-5773
382 Route 59 Ste 352 Airmont (10952) ***(G-13)***
Jomart Associates Inc......212 627-2153
170 Oval Dr Ste A Islandia (11749) ***(G-6339)***
Jomat New York Inc......718 369-7641
4100 1st Ave Ste 3 Brooklyn (11232) ***(G-1998)***
Jon Barry Company Division, Brooklyn *Also called Kwik Ticket Inc* ***(G-2038)***
Jon Lyn Ink Inc......516 546-2312
255 Sunrise Hwy Ste 1 Merrick (11566) ***(G-7857)***
Jon Teri Sports Inc (PA)......212 398-0657
241 W 37th St Frnt 2 New York (10018) ***(G-10021)***
Jonas Louis Paul Studios Inc......518 851-2211
304 Miller Rd Hudson (12534) ***(G-6168)***
Jonathan Brose......716 417-8978
51 Canal St Lockport (14094) ***(G-7086)***
Jonathan David Publishers Inc......718 456-8611
6822 Eliot Ave Middle Village (11379) ***(G-7880)***
Jonathan Lord Corp......631 563-4445
87 Carlough Rd Unit A Bohemia (11716) ***(G-1030)***
Jonathan Meizler LLC......212 213-2977
57 Orchard St New York (10002) ***(G-10022)***
Jonathan Metal & Glass Ltd......718 846-8000
17816 104th Ave Jamaica (11433) ***(G-6452)***
Jonathan Michael Coat Corp......212 239-9230
463 Fashion Ave Rm 1502 New York (10018) ***(G-10023)***
Jonathan Michael Coats, New York *Also called Gfb Fashions Ltd* ***(G-9605)***
Jones Humdinger......607 771-6501
204 Hayes Rd Binghamton (13905) ***(G-892)***
Jones Jeanswear Group, New York *Also called One Jeanswear Group LLC* ***(G-10690)***
Jones New York, New York *Also called Premier Brnds Group Hldngs LLC* ***(G-10878)***
Jones New York, New York *Also called Premier Brnds Group Hldngs LLC* ***(G-10879)***
Jones New York, New York *Also called Authentic Brands Group LLC* ***(G-8680)***
Jonice Industires......516 640-4283
95 Angevine Ave Hempstead (11550) ***(G-5841)***
Jordache Enterprises Inc......212 944-1330
1400 Broadway Rm 1415 New York (10018) ***(G-10024)***
Jordache Enterprises Inc (PA)......212 643-8400
1400 Broadway Rm 1400 # 1400 New York (10018) ***(G-10025)***
Jordache Woodworking Corp......718 349-3373
276 Greenpoint Ave # 1303 Brooklyn (11222) ***(G-1999)***
Jordan Box Co, Syracuse *Also called Jordon Box Company Inc* ***(G-14920)***
Jordan Machine Inc......585 647-3585
1241 Ridgeway Ave Ste I Rochester (14615) ***(G-13496)***
Jordan Panel Systems Corp (PA)......631 754-4900
196 Laurel Rd Unit 2 East Northport (11731) ***(G-4148)***
Jordon Box Company Inc......315 422-3419
140 Dickerson St Syracuse (13202) ***(G-14920)***
Jordon Controls, Rochester *Also called Rotork Controls Inc* ***(G-13707)***
Jos H Lowenstein and Sons Inc (PA)......718 388-5410
420 Morgan Ave Brooklyn (11222) ***(G-2000)***
Joseph (uk) Inc......212 570-0077
1061 Madison Ave Grnd New York (10028) ***(G-10026)***
Joseph A Filippazzo Software......718 987-1626
106 Lovell Ave Staten Island (10314) ***(G-14671)***
Joseph Fedele......718 448-3658
1950b Richmond Ter Staten Island (10302) ***(G-14672)***
Joseph Industries Inc (PA)......212 764-0010
1410 Broadway Rm 1201 New York (10018) ***(G-10027)***
Joseph Paul......718 693-4269
1064 Rogers Ave Apt 5 Brooklyn (11226) ***(G-2001)***
Joseph Shalhoub & Son Inc......718 871-6300
1258 Prospect Ave Brooklyn (11218) ***(G-2002)***
Joseph Struhl Co Inc......516 741-3660
195 Atlantic Ave New Hyde Park (11040) ***(G-8277)***
Joseph Treu Successors Inc......212 691-7026
104 W 27th St Rm 5b New York (10001) ***(G-10028)***
Joseph Zakon Winery Ltd......718 604-1430
586 Montgomery St Brooklyn (11225) ***(G-2003)***
Joseph's Cloak, New York *Also called Americo Group Inc* ***(G-8561)***
Josh Packaging Inc......631 822-1660
245 Marcus Blvd Ste 1 Hauppauge (11788) ***(G-5681)***
Josie Accessories Inc......212 889-6376
261 5th Ave Fl 10 New York (10016) ***(G-10029)***
Jotaly Inc......212 886-6000
1385 Broadway Fl 12 New York (10018) ***(G-10030)***
Journal and Republican, Lowville *Also called Lowville Newspaper Corporation* ***(G-7418)***
Journal News......914 694-5000
1133 Westchester Ave N-110 White Plains (10604) ***(G-16021)***
Journal News......845 578-2324
200 N Route 303 West Nyack (10994) ***(G-15825)***
Journal Register Company......518 584-4242
20 Lake Ave Saratoga Springs (12866) ***(G-14184)***
Jovani Fashion Ltd......212 279-0222
1370 Broadway Fl 4 New York (10018) ***(G-10031)***
Joy Edward Company......315 474-3360
105 Enderberry Cir Syracuse (13224) ***(G-14921)***
Joy of Learning......718 443-6463
992 Gates Ave Brooklyn (11221) ***(G-2004)***
Joy Process Mechanical, Syracuse *Also called Joy Edward Company* ***(G-14921)***
Joya LLC......718 852-6979
19 Vanderbilt Ave Brooklyn (11205) ***(G-2005)***
Joya Studio, Brooklyn *Also called Joya LLC* ***(G-2005)***
Joyce Center, Manhasset *Also called Advanced Prosthetics Orthotics* ***(G-7530)***
Joyva Corp (PA)......718 497-0170
53 Varick Ave Brooklyn (11237) ***(G-2006)***
JP Filling Inc......845 534-4793
20 Industry Dr Mountainville (10953) ***(G-8194)***
JP Signs......518 569-3907
9592 State Route 9 Ste 1 Chazy (12921) ***(G-3334)***
Jpl Designs Ltd......212 689-7096
343 E 30th St Apt 3k New York (10016) ***(G-10032)***
Jpmorgan Chase Bank Nat Assn......718 767-3592
13207 14th Ave College Point (11356) ***(G-3549)***
Jpw Riggers & Erectors, Syracuse *Also called Jpw Structural Contracting Inc* ***(G-14922)***

ALPHABETIC

Jpw Structural Contracting Inc 315 432-1111
6376 Thompson Rd Syracuse (13206) *(G-14922)*

Jq Woodworking Inc 516 766-3424
3085 New St Oceanside (11572) *(G-12177)*

Jr Engineering Enterprise LLC 716 909-2693
2141 Bedell Rd Grand Island (14072) *(G-5335)*

Jr Licensing LLC 212 244-1230
1333 Broadway Fl 10 New York (10018) *(G-10033)*

Jrb Machine-Tool Inc 716 206-0355
5647 Seneca St Buffalo (14224) *(G-2825)*

Jre Test, Victor *Also called John Ramsey Elec Svcs LLC (G-15414)*

Jrg Apparel Group Company Ltd (HQ) 212 997-0900
1407 Broadway Rm 817 New York (10018) *(G-10034)*

Jrlon Inc 315 597-4067
4344 Fox Rd Palmyra (14522) *(G-12489)*

JRs Fuels Inc 518 622-9939
8037 Route 32 Cairo (12413) *(G-3065)*

JRS Pharma LP (HQ) 845 878-8300
2981 Route 22 Ste 1 Patterson (12563) *(G-12518)*

Jrsmm LLC 607 331-1549
1316 College Ave Elmira (14901) *(G-4360)*

JS Blank & Co Inc 212 689-4835
112 Madison Ave Fl 7 New York (10016) *(G-10035)*

Js Coating Solutions Inc 585 471-8354
12 Pixley Industrial Pkwy Rochester (14624) *(G-13497)*

JSA Jewelry Inc 212 764-4504
38 W 48th St Ste 801 New York (10036) *(G-10036)*

Jsc Design, New York *Also called Badgley Mischka Licensing LLC (G-8713)*

JSD Communications Inc 914 588-1841
10 Colonel Thomas Ln Bedford (10506) *(G-763)*

JSM Vinyl Products Inc 516 775-4520
44 Orchid Ln New Hyde Park (11040) *(G-8278)*

Jsp, Bohemia *Also called Jerome Stvens Phrmcuticals Inc (G-1028)*

Jsr Ultrasonics Division, Pittsford *Also called Imaginant Inc (G-12643)*

Jt Precision Inc 716 795-3860
8701 Haight Rd Barker (14012) *(G-591)*

Jt Roselle Lighting & Sup Inc 914 666-3700
333 N Bedford Rd Ste 120 Mount Kisco (10549) *(G-8095)*

JT Systems Inc 315 622-1980
8132 Oswego Rd Liverpool (13090) *(G-7019)*

Jta USA Inc 718 722-0902
63 Flushing Ave Unit 339 Brooklyn (11205) *(G-2007)*

Jtekt Torsen North America 585 464-5000
2 Jetview Dr Rochester (14624) *(G-13498)*

Juan Motors, Palmyra *Also called Faradyne Motors LLC (G-12485)*

Judaica Press Inc 718 972-6202
123 Ditmas Ave Brooklyn (11218) *(G-2008)*

Judi Boisson American Country, Southampton *Also called American Country Quilts & Lin (G-14526)*

Judis Lampshades Inc 917 561-3921
1495 E 22nd St Brooklyn (11210) *(G-2009)*

Judith Lewis Printer Inc 516 997-7777
1915 Ladenburg Dr Westbury (11590) *(G-15900)*

Judith N Graham Inc 914 921-5446
64 Halls Ln Rye (10580) *(G-14082)*

Judith Ripka Fine Jewelry, New York *Also called Jr Licensing LLC (G-10033)*

Judys Group Inc 212 921-0515
226 W 37th St Fl 7 New York (10018) *(G-10037)*

Juices Enterprises Inc 718 953-1860
1142 Nostrand Ave Brooklyn (11225) *(G-2010)*

Julia Knit Inc 718 848-1900
8050 Pitkin Ave Ozone Park (11417) *(G-12464)*

Julian A McDermott Corporation 718 456-3606
1639 Stephen St Ridgewood (11385) *(G-13148)*

Julian Freirich Company Inc (PA) 718 361-9111
4601 5th St Long Island City (11101) *(G-7256)*

Julians Recipe LLC 888 640-8880
42 West St Ste 2 Brooklyn (11222) *(G-2011)*

Julius Cohen Jewelers Inc 212 371-3050
169 Richardson St Brooklyn (11222) *(G-2012)*

Julius Klein Group 212 719-1811
580 5th Ave Ste 500 New York (10036) *(G-10038)*

Julius Lowy Frame Restoring Co 212 861-8585
232 E 59th St 4fn New York (10022) *(G-10039)*

Jumo, New York *Also called Medikidz Usa Inc (G-10418)*

Jump Design Group Inc (PA) 212 869-3300
1400 Broadway Fl 2 New York (10018) *(G-10040)*

Jump Design Group, The, New York *Also called Jump Design Group Inc (G-10040)*

Jumprope Inc 347 927-5867
121 W 27th St Ste 1204 New York (10001) *(G-10041)*

June Jacobs Labs LLC 212 471-4830
460 Park Ave Fl 16 New York (10022) *(G-10042)*

Juniors Cheesecake Inc (PA) 718 852-5257
386 Flatbush Avenue Ext Brooklyn (11201) *(G-2013)*

Juniper Elbow Co Inc (PA) 718 326-2546
7215 Metropolitan Ave Middle Village (11379) *(G-7881)*

Juniper Industries, Middle Village *Also called Juniper Elbow Co Inc (G-7881)*

Juniper Industries Florida Inc 718 326-2546
7215 Metropolitan Ave Middle Village (11379) *(G-7882)*

Junk In My Trunk Inc 631 420-5865
266 Route 109 Farmingdale (11735) *(G-4658)*

Juno Chefs 845 294-5400
1 6 1/2 Station Rd Goshen (10924) *(G-5310)*

Jupiter Creations Inc 917 493-9393
252 W 38th St Rm 603 New York (10018) *(G-10043)*

Juris Publishing Inc 631 351-5430
52 Elm St Ste 7 Huntington (11743) *(G-6209)*

Jurist Company Inc 212 243-8008
1105 44th Dr Long Island City (11101) *(G-7257)*

Jus By Julie LLC (PA) 718 266-3906
2184 Mcdonald Ave Brooklyn (11223) *(G-2014)*

Just Beverages LLC 480 388-1133
31 Broad St Glens Falls (12801) *(G-5252)*

Just Bottoms & Tops Inc (PA) 212 564-3202
1412 Broadway Rm 1808 New York (10018) *(G-10044)*

Just Brass Inc 212 724-5447
215 W 90th St Apt 9a New York (10024) *(G-10045)*

Just For Men Div, New York *Also called Jeanjer LLC (G-9991)*

Just Goods Inc 855 282-5878
311 W 43rd St Fl 12 New York (10036) *(G-10046)*

Just In Time Cnc Machinin 585 247-3850
13 Marway Dr Rochester (14624) *(G-13499)*

Just In Time Cnc Machining 585 335-2010
88 Ossian St Dansville (14437) *(G-3820)*

Just In Time Company, Endwell *Also called J T Systematic (G-4480)*

Just In Time Electronics, Islandia *Also called Jit International Inc (G-6338)*

Just Lamps of New York Inc 716 626-2240
334 Harris Hill Rd Apt 1 Buffalo (14221) *(G-2826)*

Just Press Print LLC 585 783-1300
304 Whitney St Rochester (14606) *(G-13500)*

Just Right Carbines LLC 585 261-5331
231 Saltonstall St Canandaigua (14424) *(G-3135)*

Just Wood Pallets Inc 718 644-7013
78 Vails Gate Heights Dr New Windsor (12553) *(G-8370)*

Justa Company 718 932-6139
3464 9th St Long Island City (11106) *(G-7258)*

Justin Ashley Designs Inc 718 707-0200
4301 21st St Ste 212a Long Island City (11101) *(G-7259)*

Justin Gregory Inc 631 249-5187
94 E Jefryn Blvd Ste E Deer Park (11729) *(G-3890)*

Justperfectmsp Ltd 877 201-0005
48 W 48th St Ste 401 New York (10036) *(G-10047)*

Justyna Kaminska NY Inc 917 423-5527
1261 Broadway Rm 406 New York (10001) *(G-10048)*

Juvly Aesthetics Inc 614 686-3627
18 E 41st St Rm 406 New York (10017) *(G-10049)*

Jvl Ventures LLC 212 365-7555
230 Park Ave Rm 2829 New York (10169) *(G-10050)*

JW Burg Machine & Tool Inc 716 434-0015
7430 Rapids Rd Clarence Center (14032) *(G-3447)*

JW Consulting Inc 845 325-7070
20 Chevron Rd Unit 201 Monroe (10950) *(G-8024)*

Jwin Electronics Corp (PA) 516 626-7188
2 Harbor Park Dr Port Washington (11050) *(G-12894)*

K & B Signs, Mount Vernon *Also called K & B Stamping Co Inc (G-8154)*

K & B Stamping Co Inc 914 664-8555
29 Mount Vernon Ave Mount Vernon (10550) *(G-8154)*

K & B Woodworking Inc 518 634-7253
133 Rolling Meadow Rd Cairo (12413) *(G-3066)*

K & E Fabricating Company Inc 716 829-1829
40 Stanley St Buffalo (14206) *(G-2827)*

K & H Industries Inc 716 312-0088
160 Elmview Ave Hamburg (14075) *(G-5511)*

K & H Precision Products Inc 585 624-4894
45 Norton St Honeoye Falls (14472) *(G-6076)*

K & R Allied Inc 718 625-6610
39 Pearl St Fl 2 Brooklyn (11201) *(G-2015)*

K & S & East, Scarsdale *Also called Eastco Manufacturing Corp (G-14235)*

K & S Childrens Wear Inc 718 624-0006
204 Wallabout St Brooklyn (11206) *(G-2016)*

K Barthelmes Mfg Co Inc 585 328-8140
61 Brooklea Dr Rochester (14624) *(G-13501)*

K D Dance, Bronx *Also called KD Dids Inc (G-1289)*

K D M Die Company Inc 716 828-9000
620 Elk St Buffalo (14210) *(G-2828)*

K Displays 718 854-6045
1363 47th St Brooklyn (11219) *(G-2017)*

K Dymond Industries Inc 631 828-0826
16 Commercial Blvd Medford (11763) *(G-7715)*

K F I Inc 516 546-2904
33 Debevoise Ave Roosevelt (11575) *(G-14031)*

K Hein Machines Inc 607 748-1546
341 Vestal Pkwy E Vestal (13850) *(G-15380)*

K Industries Inc (PA) 631 897-2125
1107 Station Rd Ste 5a Bellport (11713) *(G-801)*

K M Drive Line Inc 718 599-0628
966 Grand St Brooklyn (11211) *(G-2018)*

K P I Plastics, Howes Cave *Also called W Kintz Plastics Inc (G-6144)*

K P Signs, North Bellmore *Also called KP Industries Inc (G-12020)*

K Road Power Management LLC (PA) 212 351-0535
330 Madison Ave Fl 25 New York (10017) *(G-10051)*

K Sidrane Inc 631 393-6974
24 Baiting Place Rd Farmingdale (11735) *(G-4659)*

K T A V Publishing House Inc 201 963-9524
527 Empire Blvd Brooklyn (11225) *(G-2019)*

K T P Design Co Inc 212 481-6613
118 E 28th St Rm 707 New York (10016) *(G-10052)*

K Z Precision, Lancaster *Also called Kz Precision Inc (G-6812)*

K&G of Syracuse Inc 315 446-1921
2500 Erie Blvd E Syracuse (13224) *(G-14923)*

K&Ns Foods Usa LLC 315 598-8080
607 Phillips St Fulton (13069) *(G-5067)*

K-Binet Inc 845 348-1149
624 Route 303 Blauvelt (10913) *(G-929)*

K-D Stone Inc 518 642-2082
Rr 22 Middle Granville (12849) *(G-7869)*

K-Technologies Inc 716 828-4444
4090 Jeffrey Blvd Buffalo (14219) *(G-2829)*

K.E.Y.S. Publishers, Brooklyn *Also called Kwesi Legesse LLC (G-2037)*

K2 International Corp 212 947-1734
22 W 32nd St Fl 9 New York (10001) *(G-10053)*

K2 Plastics Inc 585 494-2727
8210 Buffalo Rd Bergen (14416) *(G-816)*

Kaazing Corporation 212 572-4859
250 Park Ave Fl 7 New York (10177) *(G-10054)*

Kabar Manufacturing Corp (HQ) 631 694-6857
140 Schnitt Blvd Farmingdale (11735) *(G-4660)*

Kabar Manufacturing Corp 631 694-1036
113 Gazza Blvd Farmingdale (11735) *(G-4661)*

Kabbalah Centre, Richmond Hill *Also called Research Centre of Kabbalah (G-13121)*

Kabco Pharmaceuticals Inc 631 842-3600
2000 New Horizons Blvd Amityville (11701) *(G-283)*

Kabrics 607 962-6344
2737 Forest Hill Dr Corning (14830) *(G-3717)*

Kadant Inc 518 793-8801
436 Quaker Rd Glens Falls (12804) *(G-5253)*

Kaddis Manufacturing Corp 585 624-3070
1175 Bragg St Honeoye Falls (14472) *(G-6077)*

Kadmon Corporation LLC (PA) 212 308-6000
450 E 29th St Fl 5 New York (10016) *(G-10055)*

Kadmon Holdings Inc 212 308-6000
450 E 29th St New York (10016) *(G-10056)*

Kafko (us) Corp 877 721-7665
787 Watervliet Shaker Rd Latham (12110) *(G-6861)*

Kahn-Lucas-Lancaster Inc 212 239-2407
112 W 34th St Ste 600 New York (10120) *(G-10057)*

Kaitery Furs Ltd 718 204-1396
2529 49th St Long Island City (11103) *(G-7260)*

Kal Manufacturing Corporation 585 265-4310
657 Basket Rd Webster (14580) *(G-15644)*

Kal-Harbour Inc 518 266-0690
11 Villa Rd Albany (12204) *(G-93)*

Kalati Company Inc 516 423-9132
10 Bond St Ste 1 Great Neck (11021) *(G-5397)*

Kale Factory Inc 917 363-6361
790 Washington Ave Brooklyn (11238) *(G-2020)*

Kaleidoscope Imaging Inc 212 631-9947
251 W 39th St Fl 4 New York (10018) *(G-10058)*

Kaleko Bros 212 819-0100
62 W 47th St Ste 1504 New York (10036) *(G-10059)*

Kalel Partners LLC 347 561-7804
7012 170th St Ste 101 Flushing (11365) *(G-4866)*

Kalikow Brothers LP 212 643-0315
34 W 33rd St Fl 4n New York (10001) *(G-10060)*

Kallen Corp 212 242-1470
99 Hudson St New York (10013) *(G-10061)*

Kaltec Food Packaging Inc 845 856-9888
36 Center St 40 Port Jervis (12771) *(G-12851)*

Kaltech Food Packaging Inc 845 856-1210
3640 Center St Port Jervis (12771) *(G-12852)*

Kaltex America Inc 212 971-0575
350 5th Ave Ste 7100 New York (10118) *(G-10062)*

Kaltex North America Inc (HQ) 212 894-3200
350 5th Ave Ste 7100 New York (10118) *(G-10063)*

Kamali Automotive Group Inc 516 627-4000
17 Barstow Rd Ste 206 Great Neck (11021) *(G-5398)*

Kamali Group Inc 516 627-4000
17 Barstow Rd Ste 206 Great Neck (11021) *(G-5399)*

Kamali Leather LLC 518 762-2522
204 Harrison St Johnstown (12095) *(G-6621)*

Kamerys Wholesale Meats Inc 716 372-6756
322 E Riverside Dr Olean (14760) *(G-12237)*

Kamwo Meridian Herbs LLC 212 966-6370
211 Grand St New York (10013) *(G-10064)*

Kan Pak LLC 620 440-2319
105 Horizon Park Dr Penn Yan (14527) *(G-12589)*

Kane-M Inc 973 777-2797
135 W 29th St Rm 1003 New York (10001) *(G-10065)*

Kaneka America LLC 212 705-4340
546 5th Ave Fl 21 New York (10036) *(G-10066)*

Kangaroo Crossing, Manlius *Also called Mayberry Shoe Company Inc (G-7549)*

Kannalife Sciences Inc 516 669-3219
4 Knoll Ct Lloyd Harbor (11743) *(G-7056)*

Kantek Inc 516 594-4600
3460a Hampton Rd Oceanside (11572) *(G-12178)*

Kantian Skincare LLC 631 780-4711
496 Smithtown Byp Smithtown (11787) *(G-14481)*

Kaplan Inc 212 752-1840
444 Madison Ave Ste 803 New York (10022) *(G-10067)*

Kaprielian Enterprises Inc 212 645-6623
207 W 25th St Fl 8 New York (10001) *(G-10068)*

Kaps-All Packaging Systems 631 574-8778
200 Mill Rd Riverhead (11901) *(G-13175)*

Karbra Company 212 736-9300
460 Park Ave Rm 401 New York (10022) *(G-10069)*

Karey Kassl Corp 516 349-8484
180 Terminal Dr Plainview (11803) *(G-12693)*

Karey Products, Plainview *Also called Karey Kassl Corp (G-12693)*

Karishma Fashions Inc 718 565-5404
3708 74th St Jackson Heights (11372) *(G-6420)*

Karlyn Industries Inc 845 351-2249
16 Spring St Southfields (10975) *(G-14541)*

Karo Sheet Metal Inc 718 542-8420
229 Russell St Brooklyn (11222) *(G-2021)*

Karosheet Metal, Brooklyn *Also called Karo Sheet Metal Inc (G-2021)*

Karp Associates Inc (PA) 631 768-8300
260 Spagnoli Rd Melville (11747) *(G-7798)*

Karp Overseas Corporation 718 784-2105
5454 43rd St Maspeth (11378) *(G-7625)*

Karr Graphics Corp 212 645-6000
2219 41st Ave Ste 2a Long Island City (11101) *(G-7261)*

Kart, Maspeth *Also called Jack Luckner Steel Shelving Co (G-7623)*

Kartell Us Inc 212 966-6665
39 Greene St New York (10013) *(G-10070)*

Kas Direct LLC 516 934-0541
1600 Stewart Ave Ste 411 Westbury (11590) *(G-15901)*

Kas-Kel, Fonda *Also called Kasson & Keller Inc (G-4910)*

Kas-Ray Industries Inc 212 620-3144
122 W 26th St New York (10001) *(G-10071)*

Kaseya US LLC (PA) 415 694-5700
26 W 17th St Fl 9 New York (10011) *(G-10072)*

Kasisto Inc 917 734-4750
43 W 24th St Fl 8 New York (10010) *(G-10073)*

Kasper Group LLC (HQ) 212 354-4311
1412 Broadway Fl 5 New York (10018) *(G-10074)*

Kasper Group LLC (HQ) 212 354-4311
1412 Broadway Fl 5 New York (10018) *(G-10075)*

Kassis Superior Sign Co Inc 315 463-7446
6699 Old Thompson Rd Syracuse (13211) *(G-14924)*

Kasson & Keller Inc 518 853-3421
60 School St Fonda (12068) *(G-4910)*

Kastor Consulting Inc 718 224-9109
3919 218th St Bayside (11361) *(G-739)*

Kat Nap Products, Brooklyn *Also called Steinbock-Braff Inc (G-2460)*

Kate Spade & Company LLC, New York *Also called Kate Spade Holdings LLC (G-10076)*

Kate Spade Holdings LLC (HQ) 212 354-4900
2 Park Ave Fl 8 New York (10016) *(G-10076)*

Kates Paperie Ltd 212 966-3904
188 Lafayette St Frnt A New York (10013) *(G-10077)*

Katherine Blizniak (PA) 716 674-8545
525 Bullis Rd West Seneca (14224) *(G-15850)*

Kathmando Valley Preservation 212 727-0074
36 W 25th St Fl 17 New York (10010) *(G-10078)*

Katikati Inc 585 678-1764
150 Lucius Gordon Dr West Henrietta (14586) *(G-15798)*

Katz Americas, Sanborn *Also called Katz Group Americas Inc (G-14144)*

Katz Gluten Free, Mountainville *Also called Gluten Free Bake Shop Inc (G-8193)*

Katz Group Americas Inc (HQ) 716 995-3059
3685 Lockport Rd Sanborn (14132) *(G-14144)*

Kaufman Brothers Printing 212 563-1854
327 W 36th St Rm 403 New York (10018) *(G-10079)*

Kawasaki Rail Car Inc (HQ) 914 376-4700
29 Wells Ave Bldg 4 Yonkers (10701) *(G-16323)*

Kawasho Foods USA Inc 212 841-7400
45 Broadway Fl 18 New York (10006) *(G-10080)*

Kay See Dental Mfg Co 816 842-2817
777 Avenue Of The New York (10001) *(G-10081)*

Kay-Ray Industries, New York *Also called Kas-Ray Industries Inc (G-10071)*

Kaylon Industries LLC 315 303-2119
15 Downer St Baldwinsville (13027) *(G-550)*

Kaymil Printing Company Inc 212 594-3718
140 W 30th St Frnt New York (10001) *(G-10082)*

Kaymil Ticket Company, New York *Also called Kaymil Printing Company Inc (G-10082)*

Kayo of California 212 354-6336
525 Fashion Ave Rm 309 New York (10018) *(G-10083)*

Kays Caps Inc (PA) 518 273-6079
65 Arch St Troy (12183) *(G-15159)*

Kazac Inc 631 249-7299
55 Allen Blvd Ste C Farmingdale (11735) *(G-4662)*

KB Millwork Inc 516 280-2183
36 Grey Ln Levittown (11756) *(G-6916)*

Kbc, Bronx *Also called Kirschner Brush LLC (G-1293)*

Kbl Healthcare LP 212 319-5555
757 3rd Ave Fl 20 New York (10017) *(G-10084)*

Kbs Communications LLC 212 765-7124
331 W 57th St Ste 148 New York (10019) *(G-10085)*

A
L
P
H
A
B
E
T
I
C

Kc Tag Co 518 842-6666
  108 Edson St Amsterdam (12010) *(G-332)*
Kcp Holdco Inc (PA) 212 265-1500
  603 W 50th St New York (10019) *(G-10086)*
KD Dids Inc 718 402-2012
  140 E 144th St Bronx (10451) *(G-1289)*
Kd Panels, Jericho *Also called Bandec LLC (G-6572)*
KDI Paragon, Lagrangeville *Also called Paragon Aquatics (G-6752)*
KDO Industries Inc 631 608-4612
  32 Ranick Dr W Amityville (11701) *(G-284)*
Ke Durasol Awnings Inc 845 610-1100
  445 Bellvale Rd Chester (10918) *(G-3380)*
Kearney-National Inc (HQ) 212 661-4600
  565 5th Ave Fl 4 New York (10017) *(G-10087)*
Keck Group Inc (PA) 845 988-5757
  314 State Route 94 S Warwick (10990) *(G-15515)*
Kedco Inc 516 454-7800
  564 Smith St Farmingdale (11735) *(G-4663)*
Kedco Wine Storage Systems, Farmingdale *Also called Kedco Inc (G-4663)*
Keebler Company 585 948-8010
  2999 Judge Rd Oakfield (14125) *(G-12157)*
Keegan Ales LLC 845 331-2739
  20 Saint James St Kingston (12401) *(G-6695)*
Keeler Services 607 776-5757
  47 W Steuben St Ste 4 Bath (14810) *(G-636)*
Keemotion LLC 914 458-3900
  81 Prospect St Fl 5 Brooklyn (11201) *(G-2022)*
Keeners East End Litho Inc 631 324-8565
  10 Prospect Blvd East Hampton (11937) *(G-4124)*
Keep Healthy Inc 631 651-9090
  1019 Fort Salonga Rd Northport (11768) *(G-12106)*
Kefa Industries Group Inc 718 568-9297
  9219 63rd Dr Rego Park (11374) *(G-13079)*
Kehr-Buffalo Wire Frame Co Inc 716 897-2288
  127 Kehr St Buffalo (14211) *(G-2830)*
Keith Grimes, Bridgehampton *Also called Sagaponack Sand & Gravel Corp (G-1167)*
Keith Lewis Studio Inc 845 339-5629
  64 Jewels Ct New Paltz (12561) *(G-8307)*
Keller Bros & Miller Inc 716 854-2374
  401 Franklin St Buffalo (14202) *(G-2831)*
Keller Technology Corporation (PA) 716 693-3840
  2320 Military Rd Tonawanda (14150) *(G-15117)*
Kelly Foundry & Machine Co 315 732-8313
  300 Hubbell St Ste 308 Utica (13501) *(G-15279)*
Kelly Grace Corp (PA) 212 704-9603
  49 W 37th St Fl 10 New York (10018) *(G-10088)*
Kelly Sheet Metal Shop, Brooklyn *Also called Kellys Sheet Metal Inc (G-2023)*
Kelly Window Systems Inc 631 420-8500
  460 Smith St Farmingdale (11735) *(G-4664)*
Kellys Sheet Metal Inc 718 774-4750
  367 Kosciuszko St Brooklyn (11221) *(G-2023)*
Kelmar Systems Inc 631 421-1230
  284 Broadway Huntington Station (11746) *(G-6252)*
Kelson Products Inc 716 825-2585
  3300 N Benzing Rd Orchard Park (14127) *(G-12359)*
Kelta Inc (PA) 631 789-5000
  141 Rodeo Dr Edgewood (11717) *(G-4273)*
Keltron Connector Co., Ronkonkoma *Also called Keltron Electronics (de Corp) (G-13956)*
Keltron Electronics (de Corp) 631 567-6300
  3385 Vtrans Mem Hwy Ste E Ronkonkoma (11779) *(G-13956)*
Kem Medical Products Corp (PA) 631 454-6565
  400 Broadhollow Rd Ste 2 Farmingdale (11735) *(G-4665)*
Kemet Properties LLC 718 654-8079
  1179 E 224th St Bronx (10466) *(G-1290)*
Kemp Metal Products Inc 516 997-8860
  2300 Shames Dr Westbury (11590) *(G-15902)*
Kemper System America Inc (HQ) 716 558-2971
  1200 N America Dr West Seneca (14224) *(G-15851)*
Ken-Ton Open Mri PC 716 876-7000
  2882 Elmwood Ave Kenmore (14217) *(G-6654)*
Kenal Services Corp 315 788-9226
  1109 Water St Watertown (13601) *(G-15576)*
Kenan International Trading 718 672-4922
  10713 Northern Blvd Corona (11368) *(G-3742)*
Kenbenco Inc 845 246-3066
  437 Route 212 Saugerties (12477) *(G-14203)*
Kendall Circuits Inc 631 473-3636
  5507-10 Nesconset Hwy 105 Mount Sinai (11766) *(G-8115)*
Kendi Iron Works Inc 718 821-2722
  236 Johnson Ave Brooklyn (11206) *(G-2024)*
Kendor Music Inc 716 492-1254
  21 Grove St Delevan (14042) *(G-3962)*
Kenmar Shirts Inc (PA) 718 824-3880
  1415 Blondell Ave Bronx (10461) *(G-1291)*
Kennedy Valve Division, Elmira *Also called McWane Inc (G-4362)*
Kennel Klub, Utica *Also called Clara Papa (G-15243)*
Kenneth Cole Productions Inc (HQ) 212 265-1500
  603 W 50th St New York (10019) *(G-10089)*
Kenneth J Lane Inc 212 868-1780
  20 W 37th St Fl 9 New York (10018) *(G-10090)*
Kenney Manufacturing Displays 631 231-5563
  1062 Bay Shore Ave Bay Shore (11706) *(G-686)*

Kenny Mfg, Bay Shore *Also called Kenney Manufacturing Displays (G-686)*
Kennyetto Graphics Inc 518 883-6360
  137 E State St Ext Gloversville (12078) *(G-5287)*
Kens Service & Sales Inc 716 683-1155
  11500 Clinton St Elma (14059) *(G-4320)*
Kensington & Sons LLC 646 430-8298
  270 Lafayette St Ste 200 New York (10012) *(G-10091)*
Kensington Publishing Corp 212 407-1500
  119 W 40th St Fl 21 New York (10018) *(G-10092)*
Kenstan Lock & Hardware Co Inc 631 423-1977
  101 Commercial St Ste 100 Plainview (11803) *(G-12694)*
Kenstan Lock Co., Plainview *Also called Kenstan Lock & Hardware Co Inc (G-12694)*
Kent Associates Inc 212 675-0722
  99 Battery Pl Apt 11p New York (10280) *(G-10093)*
Kent Chemical Corporation 212 521-1700
  460 Park Ave Fl 7 New York (10022) *(G-10094)*
Kent Gage & Tool Company, Poughkeepsie *Also called Stanfordville Mch & Mfg Co Inc (G-12984)*
Kent Nutrition Group Inc 315 788-0032
  810 Waterman Dr Watertown (13601) *(G-15577)*
Kenwell Corporation 315 592-4263
  871 Hannibal St Fulton (13069) *(G-5068)*
Kenwin Sales Corp 516 933-7553
  86 W Industry Ct Deer Park (11729) *(G-3891)*
Kenyon Press Inc 607 674-9066
  1 Kcnyon Prcss Dr Sherburne (13460) *(G-14391)*
Keon Optics Inc 845 429-7103
  30 John F Kennedy Dr Stony Point (10980) *(G-14745)*
Kepco Inc 718 461-7000
  13140 Maple Ave Flushing (11355) *(G-4867)*
Kerner and Merchant 315 463-8023
  104 Johnson St East Syracuse (13057) *(G-4225)*
Kernow North America 585 586-3590
  5 Park Forest Dr Pittsford (14534) *(G-12645)*
Kerns Manufacturing Corp (PA) 718 784-4044
  3714 29th St Long Island City (11101) *(G-7262)*
Kerry Bfnctnal Ingredients Inc (HQ) 608 363-1200
  158 State Highway 320 Norwich (13815) *(G-12123)*
Kerry Bio-Science, Norwich *Also called Kerry Bfnctnal Ingredients Inc (G-12123)*
Keryakos Inc 518 344-7092
  1080 Catalyn St Fl 2 Schenectady (12303) *(G-14284)*
Kesser Wine, Brooklyn *Also called Joseph Zakon Winery Ltd (G-2003)*
Kessler Thermometer Corp 631 841-5500
  40 Gleam St West Babylon (11704) *(G-15722)*
Kesso Foods Inc 718 777-5303
  7720 21st Ave East Elmhurst (11370) *(G-4108)*
Ketcham Medicine Cabinets 631 615-6151
  3505 Vtrans Mem Hwy Ste L Ronkonkoma (11779) *(G-13957)*
Ketcham Pump Co Inc 718 457-0800
  3420 64th St Woodside (11377) *(G-16210)*
Ketchum Manufacturing Co Inc 518 696-3331
  11 Town Shed Rd Lake Luzerne (12846) *(G-6765)*
Keuka Brewing Co LLC 607 868-4648
  8572 Briglin Rd Hammondsport (14840) *(G-5531)*
Keuka Studios Inc 585 624-5960
  1011 Rush Henrietta Townl Rush (14543) *(G-14073)*
Keurig Dr Pepper Inc 315 589-4911
  4363 State Route 104 Williamson (14589) *(G-16110)*
Keurig Dr Pepper Inc 914 846-2300
  55 Hunter Ln Elmsford (10523) *(G-4414)*
Keurig Dr Pepper Inc 718 246-6200
  212 Wolcott St Brooklyn (11231) *(G-2025)*
Kevco Industries 845 255-7407
  6 Millbrook Rd New Paltz (12561) *(G-8308)*
Kevin Freeman 631 447-5321
  414 S Service Rd Ste 119 Patchogue (11772) *(G-12505)*
Kevin J Kassman 585 529-4245
  1408 Buffalo Rd Rochester (14624) *(G-13502)*
Kevin Regan Logging Ltd 315 245-3890
  1011 Hillsboro Rd Camden (13316) *(G-3103)*
Key Brand Entertainment Inc 212 966-5400
  104 Franklin St New York (10013) *(G-10095)*
Key Cast Stone Company Inc 631 789-2145
  113 Albany Ave Amityville (11701) *(G-285)*
Key Container Corp 631 582-3847
  135 Hollins Ln East Islip (11730) *(G-4129)*
Key Digital Systems Inc 914 667-9700
  521 E 3rd St Mount Vernon (10553) *(G-8155)*
Key Foods, Valley Stream *Also called Cni Meat & Produce Inc (G-15338)*
Key High Vacuum Products Inc 631 584-5959
  36 Southern Blvd Nesconset (11767) *(G-8219)*
Key Tech Finishing 716 832-1232
  2929 Main St Ste 2 Buffalo (14214) *(G-2832)*
Keyes Machine Works Inc 585 426-5059
  147 Park Ave Gates (14606) *(G-5141)*
Keymark Corporation 518 853-3421
  1188 Cayadutta St Fonda (12068) *(G-4911)*
Keynote Systems Corporation 716 564-1332
  2810 Sweet Home Rd Buffalo (14228) *(G-2833)*
Keystone Corporation (PA) 800 880-9747
  144 Milton St Buffalo (14210) *(G-2834)*

KG Motors Inc..607 562-2877
  202 Daniel Zenker Dr Big Flats (14814) *(G-847)*

Khk Usa Inc...516 248-3850
  259 Elm Pl Ste 2 Mineola (11501) *(G-7984)*

Ki Pro Performance, New York *Also called Fusion Pro Performance Ltd (G-9554)*

Kicks Closet Sportswear Inc...............................347 577-0857
  1031 Southern Blvd Frnt 2 Bronx (10459) *(G-1292)*

Kids, New York *Also called Bagznyc Corp (G-8718)*

Kids Discover, New York *Also called Mark Levine (G-10364)*

Kids Discover LLC...212 677-4457
  192 Lexington Ave Rm 1003 New York (10016) *(G-10096)*

Kidz Concepts LLC..212 398-1110
  1412 Broadway Fl 3 New York (10018) *(G-10097)*

Kidz Toyz Inc..914 261-4453
  280 N Bedford Rd Ste 203 Mount Kisco (10549) *(G-8096)*

Kidz World Inc...212 563-4949
  226 W 37th St Fl 12 New York (10018) *(G-10098)*

Kik Us Inc...519 505-7616
  161 Bowery Apt 6 New York (10002) *(G-10099)*

Kilian Manufacturing Corp (HQ)...........................315 432-0700
  1728 Burnet Ave Syracuse (13206) *(G-14925)*

Killer Motor Sports, New York *Also called Vertana Group LLC (G-11666)*

Kiltronx Enviro Systems Corp.............................917 971-7177
  330 Motor Pkwy 15thfl Hauppauge (11788) *(G-5682)*

Kim Eugenia Inc..212 674-1345
  347 W 36th St Rm 502 New York (10018) *(G-10100)*

Kim Jae Printing Co Inc..................................212 691-6289
  249 Parkside Dr Roslyn Heights (11577) *(G-14053)*

Kim Seybert Inc (PA).....................................212 564-7850
  37 W 37th St Fl 9 New York (10018) *(G-10101)*

Kimball Office Inc.......................................212 753-6161
  215 Park Ave S Fl 3 New York (10003) *(G-10102)*

Kimber Mfg Inc (PA)......................................888 243-4522
  1120 Saw Mill River Rd Yonkers (10710) *(G-16324)*

Kimber Mfg Inc...406 758-2222
  1 Lawton St Yonkers (10705) *(G-16325)*

Kimberley Diamond, New York *Also called H C Kionka & Co Inc (G-9702)*

Kimberly-Clark Corporation...............................212 554-4252
  1285 Ave Of The Americas New York (10019) *(G-10103)*

Kimbri Liquor, Mohegan Lake *Also called Shopping Center Wine & Liquor (G-8011)*

Kimdu Corporation..516 723-1339
  1662 Old Country Rd # 9 Plainview (11803) *(G-12695)*

Kinaneco Inc (PA)..315 468-6201
  2925 Milton Ave Syracuse (13209) *(G-14926)*

Kinaneco Printing Systems, Syracuse *Also called Kinaneco Inc (G-14926)*

Kind Group LLC (PA)......................................212 645-0800
  19 W 44th St Ste 811 New York (10036) *(G-10104)*

Kindling Inc...212 400-6296
  440 Park Ave S Fl 14 New York (10016) *(G-10105)*

Kinecosystem, New York *Also called Kik Us Inc (G-10099)*

Kinedyne Inc...716 667-6833
  3566 S Benzing Rd Orchard Park (14127) *(G-12360)*

Kineflow Division, Rochester *Also called Cummins-Wagner-Siewert LLC (G-13332)*

Kinemotive Corporation...................................631 249-6440
  222 Central Ave Ste 1 Farmingdale (11735) *(G-4666)*

Kinetic Fuel Technology Inc..............................716 745-1461
  1205 Balmer Rd Youngstown (14174) *(G-16384)*

Kinetic Laboratories, Youngstown *Also called Kinetic Fuel Technology Inc (G-16384)*

Kinetic Marketing Inc....................................212 620-0600
  1133 Broadway Ste 221 New York (10010) *(G-10106)*

Kinfolk Store, Brooklyn *Also called Kinfolk Studios Inc (G-2027)*

Kinfolk Store, The, Brooklyn *Also called Kinfolk Studios Inc (G-2026)*

Kinfolk Studios Inc......................................770 617-5592
  94 Wythe Ave Brooklyn (11249) *(G-2026)*

Kinfolk Studios Inc (PA).................................347 799-2946
  90 Wythe Ave Brooklyn (11249) *(G-2027)*

King Album Inc...631 253-9500
  20 Kean St West Babylon (11704) *(G-15723)*

King Cracker Corp..516 539-9251
  307 Peninsula Blvd Hempstead (11550) *(G-5842)*

King Displays Inc..212 629-8455
  333 W 52nd St New York (10019) *(G-10107)*

King Paving, Albany *Also called King Road Materials Inc (G-94)*

King Research Inc..718 788-0122
  114 12th St Ste 1 Brooklyn (11215) *(G-2028)*

King Road Materials Inc (HQ).............................518 381-9995
  8 Southwoods Blvd Albany (12211) *(G-94)*

King Road Materials Inc..................................518 382-5354
  145 Cordell Rd Schenectady (12303) *(G-14285)*

King Road Materials Inc..................................518 382-5354
  Cordell Rd Albany (12212) *(G-95)*

King Sales Inc...718 301-9862
  284 Wallabout St Brooklyn (11206) *(G-2029)*

King Sheraz Trading Corp.................................646 944-2800
  245 Little Clove Rd Staten Island (10301) *(G-14673)*

King Steel Iron Work Corp................................718 384-7500
  2 Seneca Ave Brooklyn (11237) *(G-2030)*

Kingboard Holdings Limited...............................705 844-1993
  120 Broadway Fl 32 New York (10271) *(G-10108)*

Kingform Cap Company Inc.................................516 822-2501
  121 New South Rd Hicksville (11801) *(G-5918)*

Kingold Jewelry Inc (PA).................................212 509-1700
  888c 8th Ave 106 New York (10019) *(G-10109)*

Kings Cnty Brwers Cllctive LLC...........................917 207-2739
  381 Troutman St Brooklyn (11237) *(G-2031)*

Kings Film & Sheet Inc...................................718 624-7510
  482 Baltic St Brooklyn (11217) *(G-2032)*

Kings Material, Brooklyn *Also called US Concrete Inc (G-2548)*

Kings Park Asphalt Corporation...........................631 269-9774
  201 Moreland Rd Ste 2 Hauppauge (11788) *(G-5683)*

Kings Park Ready Mix Corp................................631 269-4330
  140 Old Northport Rd E Kings Park (11754) *(G-6674)*

Kings Quarry, Adams Center *Also called R G King General Construction (G-3)*

Kings Quartet Corp.......................................845 986-9090
  270 Kings Hwy Warwick (10990) *(G-15516)*

Kings Ready Mix, Roslyn Heights *Also called US Concrete Inc (G-14059)*

Kings Ready Mix Inc......................................718 853-4644
  703 3rd Ave Fl 2 Flr 2 Roslyn Heights (11577) *(G-14054)*

Kings Specialty Co, Brooklyn *Also called Kings Film & Sheet Inc (G-2032)*

Kingsbury Printing Co Inc................................518 747-6606
  813 Bay Rd Queensbury (12804) *(G-13046)*

Kingston Building Products LLC...........................914 665-0707
  11 Brookdale Pl Ste 101 Mount Vernon (10550) *(G-8156)*

Kingston Hoops Summer...................................845 401-6830
  68 Glen St Kingston (12401) *(G-6696)*

Kingston Operations, Kingston *Also called Arconic Fstening Systems Rings (G-6678)*

Kingston Pharma LLC......................................315 705-4019
  5 County Route 42 Massena (13662) *(G-7668)*

Kingston Pharmaceuticals, Massena *Also called Kingston Pharma LLC (G-7668)*

Kingston Wste Wtr Trment Plant, Kingston *Also called City of Kingston (G-6686)*

Kingstreet Sounds, New York *Also called His Productions USA Inc (G-9793)*

Kinplex Corp (PA)..631 242-4800
  325 Wireless Blvd Ste 1 Hauppauge (11788) *(G-5684)*

Kinplex Corp...631 242-4800
  200 Heartland Blvd Edgewood (11717) *(G-4274)*

Kinro Manufacturing Inc (HQ).............................817 483-7791
  200 Mmaroneck Ave Ste 301 White Plains (10601) *(G-16022)*

Kinshofer Usa Inc..716 731-4333
  6420 Inducon Dr W Ste G Sanborn (14132) *(G-14145)*

Kintex Inc...716 297-0652
  3315 Haseley Dr Niagara Falls (14304) *(G-11944)*

Kionix Inc...607 257-1080
  36 Thornwood Dr Ithaca (14850) *(G-6391)*

Kirschner Brush LLC......................................718 292-1809
  605 E 132nd St Frnt 3 Bronx (10454) *(G-1293)*

Kirtas Inc...585 924-5999
  749 Phillips Rd Ste 300 Victor (14564) *(G-15415)*

Kirtas Inc...585 924-2420
  7620 Omnitech Pl Victor (14564) *(G-15416)*

Kiss My Face, Gardiner *Also called Bycmac Corp (G-5127)*

Kissle, Jamaica *Also called Whitney Foods Inc (G-6488)*

Kistler Instrument Corporation...........................716 691-5100
  75 John Glenn Dr Amherst (14228) *(G-228)*

Kitcheco Inc...917 388-7479
  50 W 34th St Apt 16b7 New York (10001) *(G-10110)*

Kitchen Cabinet Co, Poughkeepsie *Also called Modern Cabinet Company Inc (G-12971)*

Kitchen Design Center, Sauquoit *Also called Custom Stair & Millwork Co (G-14218)*

Kitchen Specialty Craftsmen.............................607 739-0833
  2366 Corning Rd Elmira (14903) *(G-4361)*

Kitchen Technology, Huntington *Also called Integrated Control Corp (G-6207)*

Kiton Building Corp......................................212 486-3224
  4 E 54th St New York (10022) *(G-10111)*

Kittinger Company Inc....................................716 876-1000
  4675 Transit Rd Buffalo (14221) *(G-2835)*

Kittywalk Systems Inc....................................516 627-8418
  10 Farmview Rd Port Washington (11050) *(G-12895)*

Kj Astoria Gourmet Inc...................................718 545-6900
  3720 Broadway Astoria (11103) *(G-426)*

KJ MEAT DIRECT, Monroe *Also called JW Consulting Inc (G-8024)*

Kjckd Inc (PA)...518 435-9696
  630 Columbia St Ext Ste 2 Latham (12110) *(G-6862)*

Kk International Trading Corp.............................516 801-4741
  219 Lafayette Dr Syosset (11791) *(G-14790)*

KKR Millennium GP LLC....................................212 750-8300
  9 W 57th St Ste 4150 New York (10019) *(G-10112)*

KKR Ntral Rsources Fund I-A LP...........................212 750-8300
  9 W 57th St Ste 4200 New York (10019) *(G-10113)*

Kkw Corp..631 589-5454
  90 Bourne Blvd Sayville (11782) *(G-14228)*

KLA Corporation...845 897-1723
  20 Corporate Park Rd C Hopewell Junction (12533) *(G-6098)*

Klauber Brothers Inc (PA)................................212 686-2531
  253 W 35th St Fl 11 New York (10001) *(G-10114)*

Kld Labs Inc..631 549-4222
  55 Cabot Ct Hauppauge (11788) *(G-5685)*

Klearbar Inc..516 684-9892
  8 Graywood Rd Port Washington (11050) *(G-12896)*

Klee Corp...585 272-0320
  340 Jefferson Rd Rochester (14623) *(G-13503)*

Kleen Stik Industries Inc................................718 984-5031
  44 Lenzie St Staten Island (10312) *(G-14674)*

A
L
P
H
A
B
E
T
I
C

Kleer-Fax Inc 631 225-1100
   750 New Horizons Blvd Amityville (11701) *(G-286)*

Klees Car Wash and Detailing, Rochester *Also called Klee Corp (G-13503)*

Klein & Company, Massapequa *Also called R Klein Jewelry Co Inc (G-7649)*

Klein & Sons Logging Inc 845 292-6682
   3114 State Route 52 Wht Sphr Spgs (12787) *(G-16108)*

Klein Cutlery LLC 585 928-2500
   7971 Refinery Rd Bolivar (14715) *(G-1101)*

Klein Reinforcing Services Inc 585 352-9433
   11 Turner Dr Spencerport (14559) *(G-14557)*

Kleinfelder John 716 753-3163
   5239 W Lake Rd Mayville (14757) *(G-7683)*

Klemmt Orthopaedic Services, Johnson City *Also called Klemmt Orthotics &
Prosthetics (G-6604)*

Klemmt Orthotics & Prosthetics 607 770-4400
   130 Oakdale Rd Johnson City (13790) *(G-6604)*

Klg Usa LLC 845 856-5311
   20 W King St Port Jervis (12771) *(G-12853)*

Kling Magnetics Inc 518 392-4000
   343 State Route 295 Chatham (12037) *(G-3331)*

Klutz (HQ) 650 687-2600
   568 Broadway Rm 503 New York (10012) *(G-10115)*

Klutz Store, New York *Also called Klutz (G-10115)*

Kluwer Academic Publishers, New York *Also called Springer Nature (G-11335)*

Klx Aerospace Solutions, Cornwall *Also called Boeing Distribution Svcs Inc (G-3727)*

KMA Corporation 518 743-1330
   153 Maple St Ste 5 Glens Falls (12801) *(G-5254)*

Kms Contracting Inc 718 495-6500
   86 Georgia Ave Brooklyn (11207) *(G-2033)*

Knf Clean Room Products Corp 631 588-7000
   1800 Ocean Ave Ronkonkoma (11779) *(G-13958)*

Kng Construction Co Inc 212 595-1451
   19 Silo Ln Warwick (10990) *(G-15517)*

Knickerbocker Partition Corp (PA) 516 546-0550
   260 Spagnoli Rd Melville (11747) *(G-7799)*

Knight Sttlement Sand Grav LLC 607 776-2048
   7291 County Route 15 Bath (14810) *(G-637)*

Knightly Endeavors 845 340-0949
   319 Wall St Ste 2 Kingston (12401) *(G-6697)*

Knise & Krick Inc 315 422-3516
   324 Pearl St Syracuse (13203) *(G-14927)*

Knit Illustrated Inc 212 268-9054
   247 W 37th St Frnt 3 New York (10018) *(G-10116)*

Knitty City, New York *Also called A Thousand Cranes Inc (G-8419)*

Knj Fabricators LLC 347 234-6985
   4341 Wickham Ave Bronx (10466) *(G-1294)*

Knoa Software Inc (PA) 212 807-9608
   41 E 11th St Fl 11 New York (10003) *(G-10117)*

Knogo, Ronkonkoma *Also called Sentry Technology Corporation (G-14006)*

Knoll Inc 716 891-1700
   1700 Broadway St Buffalo (14212) *(G-2836)*

Knoll Inc 212 343-4124
   1330 Ave Of The A New York (10019) *(G-10118)*

Knoll Printing & Packaging Inc 516 621-0100
   149 Eileen Way Syosset (11791) *(G-14791)*

Knoll Textile, New York *Also called Knoll Inc (G-10118)*

Knoll Worldwide, Syosset *Also called Knoll Printing & Packaging Inc (G-14791)*

Knorr Brake Company LLC 518 561-1387
   613 State Route 3 Unit 1 Plattsburgh (12901) *(G-12756)*

Knorr Brake Holding Corp (HQ) 315 786-5356
   748 Starbuck Ave Watertown (13601) *(G-15578)*

Knorr Brake Truck Systems Co (HQ) 315 786-5200
   748 Starbuck Ave Watertown (13601) *(G-15579)*

Knothe Apparel Group, New York *Also called Sleepwear Holdings Inc (G-11268)*

Knowles Cazenovia Inc (HQ) 315 655-8710
   2777 Us Route 20 Cazenovia (13035) *(G-3228)*

Knowlton Technologies LLC 315 782-0600
   213 Factory St Watertown (13601) *(G-15580)*

Knucklehead Embroidery Inc 607 797-2725
   800 Valley Plz Ste 4 Johnson City (13790) *(G-6605)*

Ko-Sure Food Distributors, Brooklyn *Also called Taam Tov Foods Inc (G-2488)*

Kobalt Music Pubg Amer Inc (HQ) 212 247-6204
   2 Gansevoort St Fl 6 New York (10014) *(G-10119)*

Kobe Steel USA Holdings Inc (HQ) 212 751-9400
   535 Madison Ave Fl 5 New York (10022) *(G-10120)*

Koch Metal Spinning Co Inc 716 835-3631
   74 Jewett Ave Buffalo (14214) *(G-2837)*

Koch Supply & Trading LP 212 319-4895
   350 5th Ave Ste 4810 New York (10118) *(G-10121)*

Kodak Alaris Inc (HQ) 888 242-2424
   336 Initiative Dr Rochester (14624) *(G-13504)*

Kodak Gallery - Cohber, West Henrietta *Also called Cohber Press Inc (G-15789)*

Kodak Graphic Communications 585 724-4000
   343 State St Rochester (14650) *(G-13505)*

Kodansha USA Inc 917 322-6200
   451 Park Ave S Fl 7 New York (10016) *(G-10122)*

Kodiak Cutting Tools LLC 800 892-1006
   2700 Bellevue Ave Syracuse (13219) *(G-14928)*

Kodiak Studios Inc 718 769-5399
   3030 Emmons Ave Apt 3t Brooklyn (11235) *(G-2034)*

Koehler Instrument Company Inc (PA) 631 589-3800
   85 Corporate Dr Holtsville (11742) *(G-6050)*

Koehler-Gibson Mkg & Graphics, Buffalo *Also called Koehlr-Gibson Mkg Graphics
Inc (G-2838)*

Koehlr-Gibson Mkg Graphics Inc 716 838-5960
   875 Englewood Ave Buffalo (14223) *(G-2838)*

Koenig Iron Works Inc 718 433-0900
   814 37th Ave Long Island City (11101) *(G-7263)*

Kohlberg Sports Group Inc (HQ) 914 241-7430
   111 Radio Circle Dr Mount Kisco (10549) *(G-8097)*

Kohler Awning Inc 716 685-3333
   2600 Walden Ave Buffalo (14225) *(G-2839)*

Koke Inc 800 535-5303
   582 Queensbury Ave Queensbury (12804) *(G-13047)*

Kokin Inc 212 643-8225
   270 W 38th St Rm 1500 New York (10018) *(G-10123)*

Kokoroko Bakery, Woodside *Also called Kokoroko Corporation (G-16211)*

Kokoroko Corporation 718 433-4321
   4755 47th St Woodside (11377) *(G-16211)*

Komar Layering LLC (HQ) 212 725-1500
   16 E 34th St Fl 10 New York (10016) *(G-10124)*

Komar Luxury Brands 646 472-0060
   16 E 34th St Fl 10 New York (10016) *(G-10125)*

Kon Tat Group Corporation 718 207-5022
   1491 E 34th St Brooklyn (11234) *(G-2035)*

Konar Precision Mfg Inc 631 242-4466
   62 S 2nd St Ste F Deer Park (11729) *(G-3892)*

Kondor Technologies Inc 631 471-8832
   206 Christopher St Ronkonkoma (11779) *(G-13959)*

Konecranes Inc 585 359-4450
   1020 Lehigh Station Rd # 4 Henrietta (14467) *(G-5857)*

Kong Kee Food Corp 718 937-2746
   4831 Van Dam St Long Island City (11101) *(G-7264)*

Konrad Design, Farmingdale *Also called T A Tool & Molding Inc (G-4748)*

Konrad Prosthetics & Orthotics (PA) 516 485-9164
   596 Jennings Ave West Hempstead (11552) *(G-15773)*

Konstantin D FRAnk& Sons Vini 607 868-4884
   9749 Middle Rd Hammondsport (14840) *(G-5532)*

Koon Enterprises LLC 718 886-3163
   6805 Fresh Madow Ln Ste B Fresh Meadows (11365) *(G-5043)*

Koonichi Inc 718 886-8338
   6805 Fresh Madow Ln Ste B Fresh Meadows (11365) *(G-5044)*

Koppers Choclat Specialty Inc 917 834-2290
   501 Madison Ave Rm 402 New York (10022) *(G-10126)*

Koppert Cress USA LLC 631 779-3640
   2975 Sound Ave Riverhead (11901) *(G-13176)*

Korangy Publishing Inc (PA) 212 260-1332
   450 W 31st St Fl 4 New York (10001) *(G-10127)*

Kore Infrastructure LLC (PA) 646 532-9060
   4 High Pine Glen Cove (11542) *(G-5196)*

Korea Central Daily News Inc (HQ) 718 361-7700
   4331 36th St Long Island City (11101) *(G-7265)*

Korea Times New York Inc (HQ) 718 784-4526
   3710 Skillman Ave Long Island City (11101) *(G-7266)*

Korea Times New York Inc 718 961-7979
   15408 Nthrn Blvd Ste 2b Flushing (11354) *(G-4868)*

Korean New York Daily, The, Flushing *Also called New York IL Bo Inc (G-4878)*

Korean Yellow Pages 718 461-0073
   14809 Northern Blvd Flushing (11354) *(G-4869)*

Koregon Enterprises Inc 450 218-6836
   102 W Service Rd Champlain (12919) *(G-3314)*

Korin Inc 212 587-7021
   233 Broadway Rm 1801 New York (10279) *(G-10128)*

Koring Bros Inc 888 233-1292
   30 Pine St New Rochelle (10801) *(G-8346)*

Koshii Maxelum America Inc 845 471-0500
   12 Van Kleeck Dr Poughkeepsie (12601) *(G-12966)*

Kossars On Grand LLC 212 473-4810
   367 Grand St New York (10002) *(G-10129)*

Koster Keunen Waxes, Sayville *Also called Kkw Corp (G-14228)*

Koster Keunen Waxes Ltd 631 589-0400
   90 Bourne Blvd Sayville (11782) *(G-14229)*

Kotel Importers Inc 212 245-6200
   22 W 48th St Ste 607 New York (10036) *(G-10130)*

Kourosh, College Point *Also called Lahoya Enterprise Inc (G-3550)*

Kovatch Mobile Equipment Corp 518 785-0900
   68 Sicker Rd Latham (12110) *(G-6863)*

Kowa American Corporation (HQ) 212 303-7800
   55 E 59th St Fl 19 New York (10022) *(G-10131)*

Kozinn+sons Merchant Tailors 212 643-1916
   150 W 55th St Frnt 3 New York (10019) *(G-10132)*

Kozy Shack Enterprises LLC (HQ) 516 870-3000
   83 Ludy St Hicksville (11801) *(G-5919)*

Kozy Shack Enterprises LLC 516 870-3000
   50 Ludy St Hicksville (11801) *(G-5920)*

KP Industries Inc 516 679-3161
   2481 Charles Ct Ste 1 North Bellmore (11710) *(G-12020)*

KPP Ltd 516 338-5201
   200 Robbins Ln Unit C2 Jericho (11753) *(G-6585)*

Kps Capital Partners LP (PA) 212 338-5100
   485 Lexington Ave Fl 31 New York (10017) *(G-10133)*

Kraft Foods, Walton *Also called Kraft Heinz Foods Company (G-15475)*

Kraft Foods, Avon *Also called Kraft Heinz Foods Company* **(G-513)**
Kraft Hat Manufacturers Inc 845 735-6200
7 Veterans Pkwy Pearl River (10965) **(G-12536)**
Kraft Heinz Foods Company 607 865-7131
261 Delaware St Walton (13856) **(G-15475)**
Kraft Heinz Foods Company 315 376-6575
7388 Utica Blvd Lowville (13367) **(G-7416)**
Kraft Heinz Foods Company 607 527-4584
8596 Main St Campbell (14821) **(G-3116)**
Kraft Heinz Foods Company 585 226-4400
140 Spring St Avon (14414) **(G-513)**
Kraftees, Oswego *Also called Patrick Kraft* **(G-12419)**
Kragel Co Inc 716 648-1344
23 Lake St Hamburg (14075) **(G-5512)**
Krainz Creations Inc 212 583-1555
589 5th Ave New York (10017) **(G-10134)**
Kraman Iron Works Inc 212 460-8400
410 E 10th St New York (10009) **(G-10135)**
Kramartron Precision Inc 845 368-3668
2 Spook Rock Rd Unit 107 Tallman (10982) **(G-15031)**
Krasner Group Inc (PA) 212 268-4100
40 W 37th St Ph A New York (10018) **(G-10136)**
Kraus & Sons Inc 212 620-0408
355 S End Ave Apt 10j New York (10280) **(G-10137)**
Kraus Organization Limited (PA) 212 686-5411
181 Hudson St Ste 2a New York (10013) **(G-10138)**
Kraus USA Inc 800 775-0703
12 Harbor Park Dr Port Washington (11050) **(G-12897)**
Kravitz Design Inc (PA) 212 625-1644
13 Crosby St Rm 401 New York (10013) **(G-10139)**
Krengel Manufacturing Co Inc 212 227-1901
121 Fulton Ave Fl 2 Fulton (13069) **(G-5069)**
Kreon Inc 516 470-9522
999 S Oyster Bay Rd # 105 Bethpage (11714) **(G-837)**
Krieger Defense Group LLC 716 485-1970
4329 Oakwood Ave Blasdell (14219) **(G-919)**
Kris-Tech Wire Company Inc (PA) 315 339-5268
80 Otis St Rome (13441) **(G-13853)**
Kronenberger Mfg Corp 585 385-2340
115 Despatch Dr East Rochester (14445) **(G-4166)**
Kronos Incorporated 518 459-5545
16 Sage Est Ste 206 Albany (12204) **(G-96)**
Krug Precision Inc 516 944-9350
42 Webster Ave Manhasset (11030) **(G-7536)**
Krux Digital Inc 646 476-6261
155 Ave Of The Amer Fl 12 New York (10013) **(G-10140)**
Kryon Systems Inc 800 618-4318
135 E 57th St New York (10022) **(G-10141)**
Kryten Iron Works Inc 914 345-0990
3 Browns Ln Ste 201 Hawthorne (10532) **(G-5816)**
KSA Manufacturing LLC 315 488-0809
5050 Smoral Rd Camillus (13031) **(G-3109)**
Kse Sportsman Media Inc (PA) 212 852-6600
1040 Ave Of The Americas New York (10018) **(G-10142)**
Ksk International Inc (PA) 212 354-7770
450 Park Ave Ste 2703 New York (10022) **(G-10143)**
Ksm Group Ltd 716 751-6006
2905 Beebe Rd Newfane (14108) **(G-11894)**
Kt Group Inc 212 760-2500
13 W 36th St Fl 3 New York (10018) **(G-10144)**
Ktk Thermal Technologies Inc 585 678-9025
1657 E Park Dr Macedon (14502) **(G-7466)**
Kubota Authorized Dealer, Mendon *Also called Saxby Implement Corp* **(G-7852)**
Kuno Steel Products Corp 516 938-8500
132 Duffy Ave Hicksville (11801) **(G-5921)**
Kurt Gaum Inc 212 719-2836
580 5th Ave Ste 303 New York (10036) **(G-10145)**
Kurtskraft Inc 516 944-4449
437 Port Washington Blvd Port Washington (11050) **(G-12898)**
Kurtz Truck Equipment Inc 607 849-3468
1085 Mcgraw Marathon Rd Marathon (13803) **(G-7558)**
Kurz and Zobel Inc 585 254-9060
688 Colfax St Rochester (14606) **(G-13506)**
Kush Oasis Enterprises LLC 516 513-1316
228 Martin Dr Syosset (11791) **(G-14792)**
Kussmaul Electronics Co Inc 631 218-0298
170 Cherry Ave West Sayville (11796) **(G-15841)**
Kustom Collabo, Brooklyn *Also called Vsg International LLC* **(G-2571)**
Kustom Korner 716 646-0173
5140 Camp Rd Hamburg (14075) **(G-5513)**
Kw Distributors Group Inc 718 843-3500
9018 Liberty Ave Ozone Park (11417) **(G-12465)**
Kw Kitchen Design, Ozone Park *Also called Kw Distributors Group Inc* **(G-12465)**
Kwadair LLC 646 824-2511
137 Kent St Brooklyn (11222) **(G-2036)**
Kwesi Legesse LLC 347 581-9872
203 Remsen Ave Brooklyn (11212) **(G-2037)**
Kwik Kut Manufacturing Co, Mohawk *Also called Mary F Morse* **(G-8006)**
Kwik Ticket Inc (PA) 718 421-3800
4101 Glenwood Rd Brooklyn (11210) **(G-2038)**
Kwong CHI Metal Fabrication 718 369-6429
166 41st St Brooklyn (11232) **(G-2039)**
Kybod Group LLC 408 306-1657
305 E 40th St Apt 5k New York (10016) **(G-10146)**
Kyle Editing LLC 212 675-3464
48 W 25th St Fl 5 New York (10010) **(G-10147)**
Kyntec Corporation 716 810-6956
2100 Old Union Rd Buffalo (14227) **(G-2840)**
Kyocera Precision Tools Inc 607 687-0012
1436 Taylor Rd Owego (13827) **(G-12431)**
Kyra Communications Corp 516 783-6244
3864 Bayberry Ln Seaford (11783) **(G-14349)**
Kz Precision Inc 716 683-3202
1 Mason Pl Lancaster (14086) **(G-6812)**
L & D Acquisition LLC 585 531-9000
1 Lake Niagara Ln Naples (14512) **(G-8207)**
L & D Manufacturing Corp 718 665-5226
366 Canal Pl Frnt Bronx (10451) **(G-1295)**
L & J Interiors Inc 631 218-0838
35 Orville Dr Ste 3 Bohemia (11716) **(G-1031)**
L & K Graphics Inc 631 667-2269
1917 Deer Park Ave Deer Park (11729) **(G-3893)**
L & L Overhead Garage Doors (PA) 718 721-2518
3125 45th St Long Island City (11103) **(G-7267)**
L & M Optical Disc LLC 718 649-3500
65 W 36th St Fl 11 New York (10018) **(G-10148)**
L & M Publications Inc 516 378-3133
2 Endo Blvd Garden City (11530) **(G-5103)**
L & M Uniserv Corp 718 854-3700
4416 18th Ave Pmb 133 Brooklyn (11204) **(G-2040)**
L & M West, New York *Also called L & M Optical Disc LLC* **(G-10148)**
L & S Metals Inc 716 692-6865
111 Witmer Rd North Tonawanda (14120) **(G-12076)**
L A Burdick Chocolates 212 796-0143
5 E 20th St New York (10003) **(G-10149)**
L A R Electronics Corp 716 285-0555
2733 Niagara St Niagara Falls (14303) **(G-11945)**
L A S Replacement Parts Inc 718 583-4700
1645 Webster Ave Bronx (10457) **(G-1296)**
L American Ltd 716 372-9480
222 Homer St Olean (14760) **(G-12238)**
L and S Packing Co 631 845-1717
7000 New Horizons Blvd Amityville (11701) **(G-287)**
L D Flecken Inc 631 777-4881
11 Old Dock Rd Unit 11 # 11 Yaphank (11980) **(G-16264)**
L D Weiss Inc (PA) 212 697-3023
320 E 42nd St Apt 3106 New York (10017) **(G-10150)**
L F Fashion Orient Intl Co Ltd 917 667-3398
32 W 40th St Apt 2l New York (10018) **(G-10151)**
L I C Screen Printing Inc 516 546-7289
2949 Joyce Ln Merrick (11566) **(G-7858)**
L I F Publishing Corp (PA) 631 345-5200
14 Ramsey Rd Shirley (11967) **(G-14423)**
L I Stamp, Ridgewood *Also called Long Island Stamp & Seal Co* **(G-13150)**
L J Valente Inc 518 674-3750
8957 Ny Highway 66 Averill Park (12018) **(G-508)**
L K Manufacturing Corp 631 243-6910
56 Eads St West Babylon (11704) **(G-15724)**
L K Printing, White Plains *Also called Copy Stop Inc* **(G-15996)**
L K Printing Corp 914 761-1944
50 Main St Ste 32 White Plains (10606) **(G-16023)**
L LLC 716 885-3918
106 Soldiers Pl Buffalo (14222) **(G-2841)**
L M N Printing Company Inc 516 285-8526
23 W Merrick Rd Ste A Valley Stream (11580) **(G-15345)**
L M R, New York *Also called Lefrak Entertainment Co Ltd* **(G-10192)**
L Miller Design Inc 631 242-1163
100 E Jefryn Blvd Ste F Deer Park (11729) **(G-3894)**
L N D Incorporated 516 678-6141
3230 Lawson Blvd Oceanside (11572) **(G-12179)**
L P R Precision Parts & Tls Co 631 293-7334
108 Rome St Ste 1 Farmingdale (11735) **(G-4667)**
L P Transportation, Selkirk *Also called Palpross Incorporated* **(G-14359)**
L S I, East Aurora *Also called Luminescent Systems Inc* **(G-4091)**
L S Sign Co Inc 718 469-8600
1030 Wyckoff Ave Ridgewood (11385) **(G-13149)**
L S Z Inc 914 948-4040
30 Glenn St Ste 309 White Plains (10603) **(G-16024)**
L V D, Akron *Also called Strippit Inc* **(G-22)**
L Vii Resilient LLC 631 987-5819
108 Cherry Ln Medford (11763) **(G-7716)**
L W S Inc 631 580-0472
125 Gary Way Ste 1 Ronkonkoma (11779) **(G-13960)**
L& JG Stickley Incorporated (PA) 315 682-5500
1 Stickley Dr Manlius (13104) **(G-7548)**
L&B Fabricators LLC 585 265-2731
6285 Dean Prwy Ontario (14519) **(G-12292)**
L&M Specialty Fabrication 585 283-4847
3816 Oak Orchard Rd Albion (14411) **(G-157)**
L-3 Cmmnctons Ntronix Holdings 212 697-1111
600 3rd Ave Fl 34 New York (10016) **(G-10152)**
L-3 Narda-Miteq, Hauppauge *Also called L3 Technologies Inc* **(G-5687)**
L-3 Narda-Miteq, Hauppauge *Also called L3 Technologies Inc* **(G-5689)**
L3 Communication, New York *Also called L3 Foreign Holdings Inc* **(G-10153)**

ALPHABETIC

L3 Foreign Holdings Inc (HQ).......212 697-1111
600 3rd Ave Fl 32 New York (10016) ***(G-10153)***
L3 Technologies Inc (HQ).......212 697-1111
600 3rd Ave Fl 34 New York (10016) ***(G-10154)***
L3 Technologies Inc.......631 231-1700
435 Moreland Rd Hauppauge (11788) ***(G-5686)***
L3 Technologies Inc.......631 436-7400
100 Davids Dr Hauppauge (11788) ***(G-5687)***
L3 Technologies Inc.......631 289-0363
49 Rider Ave Patchogue (11772) ***(G-12506)***
L3 Technologies Inc.......631 231-1700
435 Moreland Rd Hauppauge (11788) ***(G-5688)***
L3 Technologies Inc.......631 436-7400
330 Oser Ave Hauppauge (11788) ***(G-5689)***
L3harris Technologies Inc.......585 244-5830
1680 University Ave Rochester (14610) ***(G-13507)***
L3harris Technologies Inc.......585 269-6600
400 Initiative Dr Rochester (14624) ***(G-13508)***
L3harris Technologies Inc.......585 269-5001
800 Lee Rd Bldg 601 Rochester (14606) ***(G-13509)***
L3harris Technologies Inc.......631 630-4200
1500 New Horizons Blvd Amityville (11701) ***(G-288)***
L3harris Technologies Inc.......585 269-5000
2696 Manitou Rd Bldg 101 Rochester (14624) ***(G-13510)***
L3harris Technologies Inc.......631 630-4000
1500 New Horizons Blvd Amityville (11701) ***(G-289)***
L3harris Technologies Inc.......585 244-5830
570 Culver Rd Rochester (14609) ***(G-13511)***
L3harris Technologies Inc.......585 244-5830
50 Carlson Rd Rochester (14610) ***(G-13512)***
L3harris Technologies Inc.......718 767-1100
1902 Whitestone Expy # 204 Whitestone (11357) ***(G-16096)***
L3harris Technologies Inc.......585 244-5830
1350 Jefferson Rd Rochester (14623) ***(G-13513)***
La Bella Strings, Newburgh *Also called E & O Mari Inc* ***(G-11863)***
La Cola 1 Inc.......917 509-6669
529 W 42nd St Apt 5b New York (10036) ***(G-10155)***
La Cremeria.......212 226-6758
178 Mulberry St New York (10012) ***(G-10156)***
La Escondida Inc.......845 562-1387
129 Lake St Newburgh (12550) ***(G-11872)***
La Fina Design Inc.......212 689-6725
42 W 38th St Rm 1200 New York (10018) ***(G-10157)***
La Flor Products Company Inc (PA).......631 851-9601
25 Hoffman Ave Hauppauge (11788) ***(G-5690)***
La Flor Spices, Hauppauge *Also called La Flor Products Company Inc* ***(G-5690)***
La Forge Francaise Ltd Inc.......631 591-0572
100 Kroemer Ave Riverhead (11901) ***(G-13177)***
La Lame Inc.......212 921-9770
215 W 40th St Fl 5 New York (10018) ***(G-10158)***
La Lame Importers, New York *Also called La Lame Inc* ***(G-10158)***
La Maison Du Chocolat, Long Island City *Also called LMC 49th Inc* ***(G-7277)***
La Maison Du Chocolat, New York *Also called LMC 49th Inc* ***(G-10237)***
La Mar Lighting Co Inc.......631 777-7700
485 Smith St Farmingdale (11735) ***(G-4668)***
La Newyorkina LLC.......917 669-4591
231 Court St Brooklyn (11201) ***(G-2041)***
La Prima Bakery Inc (PA).......718 584-4442
765 E 182nd St Bronx (10460) ***(G-1297)***
La Raza, Brooklyn *Also called Impremedia LLC* ***(G-1954)***
La Strada Dance Footwear Inc.......631 242-1401
770 Grand Blvd Ste 1 Deer Park (11729) ***(G-3895)***
La Torre Orthopedic Laboratory (PA).......518 786-8655
960 Troy Schenectady Rd Latham (12110) ***(G-6864)***
La Voz Hispana, New York *Also called Nick Lugo Inc* ***(G-10623)***
La-Mar Fashions, Deer Park *Also called Continental Knitting Mills* ***(G-3853)***
Lab Crafters Inc.......631 471-7755
2085 5th Ave Ronkonkoma (11779) ***(G-13961)***
Lab-Aids Inc.......631 737-1133
17 Colt Ct Ronkonkoma (11779) ***(G-13962)***
Labarba-Q LLC.......845 806-6227
32 Highland Ave Warwick (10990) ***(G-15518)***
Labatt USA LLC.......716 604-1050
79 Perry St Ste 1 Buffalo (14203) ***(G-2842)***
Labco of Palmyra Inc.......315 597-5202
904 Canandaigua Rd Palmyra (14522) ***(G-12490)***
Label Gallery Inc.......607 334-3244
1 Lee Ave 11 Norwich (13815) ***(G-12124)***
Label Source Inc.......212 244-1403
321 W 35th St New York (10001) ***(G-10159)***
Labella Pasta Inc.......845 331-9130
906 State Route 28 Kingston (12401) ***(G-6698)***
Labels I-G, New York *Also called Labels Inter-Global Inc* ***(G-10160)***
Labels Inter-Global Inc.......212 398-0006
109 W 38th St Rm 701 New York (10018) ***(G-10160)***
Labels X Press, Buffalo *Also called Magazines & Brochures Inc* ***(G-2857)***
Labels, Stickers and More, Bayport *Also called Stickershopcom Inc* ***(G-731)***
Labeltex Mills Inc.......212 279-6165
1430 Broadway Rm 1510 New York (10018) ***(G-10161)***
Labgrafix Printing Inc.......516 280-8300
43 Rocklyn Ave Unit B Lynbrook (11563) ***(G-7433)***
Labortory For Laser Energetics, Rochester *Also called University of Rochester* ***(G-13786)***
Labrador Stone Inc.......570 465-2120
11 Dutchess Rd Binghamton (13901) ***(G-893)***
Lackawanna Hot Rolled Plant, Blasdell *Also called Republic Steel Inc* ***(G-920)***
Lactalis American Group Inc.......716 827-2622
2375 S Park Ave Buffalo (14220) ***(G-2843)***
Lactalis American Group Inc (HQ).......716 823-6262
2376 S Park Ave Buffalo (14220) ***(G-2844)***
Lady Brass Co Inc.......516 887-8040
1717 Broadway Unit 2 Hewlett (11557) ***(G-5870)***
Lady Burd Exclusive Cosmt Inc (PA).......631 454-0444
44 Executive Blvd Ste 1 Farmingdale (11735) ***(G-4669)***
Lady Burd Private Label Cosmt, Farmingdale *Also called Lady Burd Exclusive Cosmt Inc* ***(G-4669)***
Lady Ester Lingerie Corp.......212 689-1729
33 E 33rd St Rm 800 New York (10016) ***(G-10162)***
Lady Linda Cakes, Bronx *Also called Operative Cake Corp* ***(G-1329)***
Lady-N-Th-wndow Chocolates Inc.......631 549-1059
319 Main St Huntington (11743) ***(G-6210)***
Ladybird Bakery Inc.......718 499-8108
1112 8th Ave Brooklyn (11215) ***(G-2042)***
Lafarge Building Materials Inc.......518 756-5000
Rr Ravena (12143) ***(G-13068)***
Lafarge North America Inc.......716 651-9235
6125 Genesee St Lancaster (14086) ***(G-6813)***
Lafarge North America Inc.......716 854-5791
575 Ohio St Buffalo (14203) ***(G-2845)***
Lafarge North America Inc.......716 772-2621
400 Hinman Rd Lockport (14094) ***(G-7087)***
Lafarge North America Inc.......914 930-3027
350 Broadway Buchanan (10511) ***(G-2609)***
Lafarge North America Inc.......518 756-5000
1916 Route 9 W Ravena (12143) ***(G-13069)***
Lafarge North America Inc.......716 876-8788
4001 River Rd Tonawanda (14150) ***(G-15118)***
Lafayette Chateau.......607 546-2062
Rr 414 Hector (14841) ***(G-5826)***
Lafayette Mirror & Glass Co.......718 768-0660
2300 Marcus Ave New Hyde Park (11042) ***(G-8279)***
Lafayette Pub Inc.......212 925-4242
332 Lafayette St New York (10012) ***(G-10163)***
Lagardere North America Inc (HQ).......212 477-7373
60 E 42nd St Ste 1940 New York (10165) ***(G-10164)***
Lagasse Works Inc.......315 946-9202
5 Old State Route 31 Lyons (14489) ***(G-7450)***
Lage Industries Corporation.......718 342-3400
9814 Ditmas Ave Brooklyn (11236) ***(G-2043)***
Lagoner Farms Inc.......315 904-4109
6895 Lake Ave Williamson (14589) ***(G-16111)***
Lagunatic Music & Filmworks.......212 353-9600
456 Johnson Ave 202 Brooklyn (11237) ***(G-2044)***
Lahoya Enterprise Inc.......718 886-8799
1842 College Point Blvd College Point (11356) ***(G-3550)***
Lahr Plastics, Fairport *Also called Lahr Recycling & Resins Inc* ***(G-4502)***
Lahr Recycling & Resins Inc.......585 425-8608
164 Daley Rd Fairport (14450) ***(G-4502)***
Lai Apparel Design Inc.......212 382-1075
209 W 38th St Rm 901 New York (10018) ***(G-10165)***
Lai International Inc.......763 780-0060
1 Tibbits Ave Green Island (12183) ***(G-5438)***
Laird Telemedia.......845 339-9555
2000 Sterling Rd Mount Marion (12456) ***(G-8110)***
Lake Country Media, Albion *Also called Albion-Holley Pennysaver Inc* ***(G-153)***
Lake Country Woodworkers Ltd.......585 374-6353
12 Clark St Naples (14512) ***(G-8208)***
Lake Image Systems Inc.......585 321-3630
205 Summit Point Dr Ste 2 Henrietta (14467) ***(G-5858)***
Lake Immunogenics Inc.......585 265-1973
348 Berg Rd Ontario (14519) ***(G-12293)***
Lake Placid Advertisers Wkshp.......518 523-3359
Cold Brook Plz Lake Placid (12946) ***(G-6767)***
Lake Region Medical Inc.......716 662-5025
3902 California Rd Orchard Park (14127) ***(G-12361)***
Lake View Graphics Inc.......607 687-7033
2771 Waits Rd Ste 101 Owego (13827) ***(G-12432)***
Lake View Manufacturing LLC.......315 364-7892
1690 State Route 90 N King Ferry (13081) ***(G-6671)***
Lakeland Industries Inc (PA).......631 981-9700
3555 Vtrans Mem Hwy Ste C Ronkonkoma (11779) ***(G-13963)***
Lakelands Concrete, Lima *Also called East Main Associates* ***(G-6931)***
Lakelands Concrete Pdts Inc.......585 624-1990
7520 E Main St Lima (14485) ***(G-6932)***
Lakeshore Carbide Inc.......716 462-4349
1959 Maple Rd Buffalo (14221) ***(G-2846)***
Lakeshore Pennysaver, Fredonia *Also called Fredonia Pennysaver Inc* ***(G-4969)***
Lakeside Capital Corporation.......716 664-2555
402 Chandler St Ste 2 Jamestown (14701) ***(G-6528)***
Lakeside Cider Mill Farm Inc.......518 399-8359
336 Schauber Rd Ballston Lake (12019) ***(G-560)***
Lakeside Container Corp (PA).......518 561-6150
299 Arizona Ave Plattsburgh (12903) ***(G-12757)***

Lakeside Industries Inc 716 386-3031
2 Lakeside Dr Bemus Point (14712) *(G-812)*

Lakeside Precision Inc 716 366-5030
208 Dove St Dunkirk (14048) *(G-4060)*

Lakewood Vineyards Inc 607 535-9252
4024 State Route 14 Watkins Glen (14891) *(G-15614)*

Lali Jewelry Inc 212 944-2277
50 W 47th St Ste 1610 New York (10036) *(G-10166)*

Lali Jewels, New York *Also called Lali Jewelry Inc (G-10166)*

Lalique Boutique, New York *Also called Lalique North America Inc (G-10167)*

Lalique North America Inc 212 355-6550
609 Madison Ave New York (10022) *(G-10167)*

Lam-Tek Millwork Fabricators, Cold Spring *Also called Old Souls Inc (G-3522)*

Lamar Plastics Packaging Ltd 516 378-2500
216 N Main St Ste F Freeport (11520) *(G-5004)*

Lambro Industries (PA) 631 842-8088
115 Albany Ave Amityville (11701) *(G-290)*

Laminated Window Products Inc 631 242-6883
211 N Fehr Way Bay Shore (11706) *(G-687)*

Lamm Industries Inc 718 368-0181
2513 E 21st St Brooklyn (11235) *(G-2045)*

Lamontage, New York *Also called Mgk Group Inc (G-10448)*

Lamoreaux Landing WI 607 582-6162
9224 State Route 414 Lodi (14860) *(G-7131)*

Lamothermic Corp 845 278-6118
391 Route 312 Brewster (10509) *(G-1153)*

Lams Foods Inc 718 217-0476
9723 218th St Queens Village (11429) *(G-13024)*

Lancaster Knives Inc (PA) 716 683-5050
165 Court St Lancaster (14086) *(G-6814)*

Lancaster Quality Pork Inc 718 439-8822
5600 1st Ave Ste 6 Brooklyn (11220) *(G-2046)*

Lancaster Tanks and Steel Pdts, Buffalo *Also called Jbren Corp (G-2817)*

Lance Valves 716 681-5825
15 Enterprise Dr Lancaster (14086) *(G-6815)*

Lanco Corporation 631 231-2300
2905 Vtrans Mem Hwy Ste 3 Ronkonkoma (11779) *(G-13964)*

Lanco Manufacturing Co 516 292-8953
384 Hempstead Tpke West Hempstead (11552) *(G-15774)*

Land n Sea Inc (PA) 212 444-6000
1440 Broadway Frnt 3 New York (10018) *(G-10168)*

Land OLakes Inc 516 681-2980
50 Ludy St Hicksville (11801) *(G-5922)*

Land Packaging Corp 914 472-5976
7 Black Birch Ln Scarsdale (10583) *(G-14238)*

Land Self Prtction Systems Div, Buffalo *Also called Northrop Grumman Intl Trdg Inc (G-2892)*

Landies Candies Co Inc 716 834-8212
2495 Main St Ste 350 Buffalo (14214) *(G-2847)*

Landlord Guard Inc 212 695-6505
1 Maiden Ln Fl 7 New York (10038) *(G-10169)*

Landmark Group Inc 845 358-0350
709 Executive Blvd Ste A Valley Cottage (10989) *(G-15317)*

Landmark Signs Elec Maint Corp (PA) 212 262-3699
1501 Broadway Ste 501 New York (10036) *(G-10170)*

Landmark Signs Elec Maint Corp 212 354-7551
1 Times Sq Frnt New York (10036) *(G-10171)*

Landpro Equipment LLC (PA) 716 665-3110
1756 Lindquist Dr Falconer (14733) *(G-4549)*

Lane Enterprises Inc 607 776-3366
16 May St Bath (14810) *(G-638)*

Lane Enterprises Inc 518 885-4385
825 State Route 67 Ballston Spa (12020) *(G-579)*

Lane Metal Products, Bath *Also called Lane Enterprises Inc (G-638)*

Lanel, Floral Park *Also called Creatron Services Inc (G-4813)*

Langer Biomechanics Inc 800 645-5520
2905 Vtrans Mem Hwy Ste 2 Ronkonkoma (11779) *(G-13965)*

Language and Graphics Inc 212 315-5266
350 W 57th St Apt 14i New York (10019) *(G-10172)*

Lanier Clothes, New York *Also called Oxford Industries Inc (G-10725)*

Lanoves Inc 718 384-1880
72 Anthony St Brooklyn (11222) *(G-2047)*

Lanwood Industries Inc 718 786-3000
45 Drexel Dr Bay Shore (11706) *(G-688)*

Lanza Corp 914 937-6360
404 Willett Ave Port Chester (10573) *(G-12824)*

Laphams Quarterly, New York *Also called American Agora Foundation Inc (G-8543)*

Lapp Insulator Company LLC 585 768-6221
130 Gilbert St Le Roy (14482) *(G-6902)*

Lapp Management Corp 607 243-5141
3700 Route 14 Himrod (14842) *(G-5976)*

Larcent Enterprises Inc 845 562-3332
509 Temple Hill Rd New Windsor (12553) *(G-8371)*

Laregence Inc 212 736-2548
34 W 27th St Fl 2 New York (10001) *(G-10173)*

Larkin Anya Ltd 718 361-1827
4310 23rd St Ste 2b Long Island City (11101) *(G-7268)*

Larosa Cupcakes 347 866-3920
314 Lake Ave Staten Island (10303) *(G-14675)*

Larry Kings Corporation 718 481-8741
13708 250th St Rosedale (11422) *(G-14036)*

Larson Metal Manufacturing Co 716 665-6807
1831 Mason Dr Jamestown (14701) *(G-6529)*

LArte Del Gelato Gruppo Inc 718 383-6600
3100 47th Ave Long Island City (11101) *(G-7269)*

Larte Del Gelato Inc 212 366-0570
75 9th Ave Frnt 38 New York (10011) *(G-10174)*

Laseoptics Corp 716 462-5078
300 International Dr # 100 Buffalo (14221) *(G-2848)*

Laser & Electron Beam Inc 603 626-6080
77 7th Ave Apt 3h New York (10011) *(G-10175)*

Laser and Varicose Vein Trtmnt 718 667-1777
500 Seaview Ave Ste 240 Staten Island (10305) *(G-14676)*

Laser Printer Checks Corp 845 782-5837
7 Vayoel Moshe Ct # 101 Monroe (10950) *(G-8025)*

Lasermaxdefense, Rochester *Also called LMD Power of Light Corp (G-13519)*

Lasertech Crtridge RE-Builders 518 373-1246
7 Longwood Dr Clifton Park (12065) *(G-3466)*

Last N Last, New Rochelle *Also called Paint Over Rust Products Inc (G-8348)*

Last Resort, The, Rouses Point *Also called Sandys Deli Inc (G-14068)*

Lasticks Aerospace Inc 631 242-8484
35 Washington Ave Ste E Bay Shore (11706) *(G-689)*

Latchable Inc 917 338-3915
450 W 33rd St Fl 12 New York (10001) *(G-10176)*

Latham International Inc (PA) 518 783-7776
787 Watervliet Shaker Rd Latham (12110) *(G-6865)*

Latham International Inc 518 346-5292
706 Corporation Park 1 Schenectady (12302) *(G-14286)*

Latham International Mfg Corp 800 833-3800
787 Watervliet Shaker Rd Latham (12110) *(G-6866)*

Latham Manufacturing, Schenectady *Also called Latham International Inc (G-14286)*

Latham Manufacturing, Latham *Also called Latham Pool Products Inc (G-6868)*

Latham Pool Products, Latham *Also called Latham International Mfg Corp (G-6866)*

Latham Pool Products Inc (HQ) 518 951-1000
787 Watervliet Shaker Rd Latham (12110) *(G-6867)*

Latham Pool Products Inc 260 432-8731
787 Watervliet Shaker Rd Latham (12110) *(G-6868)*

Latina Media Ventures LLC (PA) 212 642-0200
114 E 25th St Fl 11 New York (10010) *(G-10177)*

Latium USA Trading LLC (PA) 631 563-4000
5005 Veterans Mem Hwy Holbrook (11741) *(G-6004)*

Latorre Orthopedic Laboratory 518 786-8655
960 Troy Schenectady Rd Latham (12110) *(G-6869)*

Laufer Wind Group LLC 212 792-3912
270 Lafayette St Ste 1402 New York (10012) *(G-10178)*

Laundrylux, Inwood *Also called Autarkic Holdings Inc (G-6290)*

Laura Star Service Center, Averill Park *Also called Garment Care Systems LLC (G-507)*

Laurtom Inc 914 273-2233
333 N Bedford Rd Ste 100 Mount Kisco (10549) *(G-8098)*

Lavanya, Jackson Heights *Also called Karishma Fashions Inc (G-6420)*

Lavish Layette Inc (PA) 347 962-9955
876 Woodmere Pl Woodmere (11598) *(G-16192)*

Law360, New York *Also called Portfolio Media Inc (G-10868)*

Lawdy Miss Clawdy, Pound Ridge *Also called Lloyd Price Icon Food Brands (G-12993)*

Lawn Elements Inc 631 656-9711
1150 Lincoln Ave Ste 4 Holbrook (11741) *(G-6005)*

Lawrece Frames, Bay Shore *Also called Fred M Lawrence Co Inc (G-681)*

Lawson M Whiting Inc 315 986-3064
15 State Route 350 Macedon (14502) *(G-7467)*

Lawton Electric Co, Ogdensburg *Also called Lawtons Electric Motor Service (G-12207)*

Lawtons Electric Motor Service 315 393-2728
148 Cemetery Rd Ogdensburg (13669) *(G-12207)*

Layton Manufacturing Corp (PA) 718 498-6000
864 E 52nd St Brooklyn (11203) *(G-2048)*

Lazare Kaplan Intl Inc (PA) 212 972-9700
580 5th Ave Ste 701 New York (10036) *(G-10179)*

Lazarek Inc 315 343-1242
209 Erie St Oswego (13126) *(G-12413)*

Lazer Incorporated (PA) 336 744-8047
1465 Jefferson Rd Ste 110 Rochester (14623) *(G-13514)*

Lazer Marble & Granite Corp 718 859-9644
1053 Dahill Rd Brooklyn (11204) *(G-2049)*

Lazer Photo Engraving, Rochester *Also called Lazer Incorporated (G-13514)*

Lazo Setter Company, New York *Also called Mataci Inc (G-10381)*

Lb Furniture Industries LLC 518 828-1501
99 S 3rd St Hudson (12534) *(G-6169)*

Lb Graph-X & Printing Inc 212 246-2600
227 E Main St Smithtown (11787) *(G-14482)*

Lc Drives, Potsdam *Also called Lcdrives Corp (G-12937)*

Lcdrives Corp 860 712-8926
67 Main St Potsdam (13676) *(G-12937)*

Lco Destiny LLC 315 782-3302
1 Fisher Cir Watertown (13601) *(G-15581)*

LD McCauley LLC 716 662-6744
3875 California Rd Orchard Park (14127) *(G-12362)*

LDB Interior Textiles, New York *Also called E W Williams Publications (G-9292)*

LDI Lighting Inc (PA) 718 384-4490
240 Broadway Ste C Brooklyn (11211) *(G-2050)*

LDI Lighting Inc 718 384-4490
193 Williamsburg St W A Brooklyn (11211) *(G-2051)*

Le Book Publishing Inc (HQ) 212 334-5252
580 Broadway Rm 912 New York (10012) ***(G-10180)***
Le Bureau Du Livre Francais, New York *Also called French Publishers Agency Inc* ***(G-9538)***
Le Chocolate of Rockland LLC 845 533-4125
1 Ramapo Ave Suffern (10901) ***(G-14762)***
Le Creuset, Riverhead *Also called Schiller Stores Inc* ***(G-13188)***
Le Hook Rouge LLC 212 947-6272
275 Conover St Ste 3q-3p Brooklyn (11231) ***(G-2052)***
Le Lab, Valley Stream *Also called Lelab Dental Laboratory Inc* ***(G-15346)***
Le Labo Fragrances, Brooklyn *Also called Le Labo Holding LLC* ***(G-2053)***
Le Labo Holding LLC (HQ) 646 490-6200
122 N 6th St Fl 2 Brooklyn (11249) ***(G-2053)***
Le Labo Holding LLC 646 719-1740
80 39th St Fl Ground Brooklyn (11232) ***(G-2054)***
Le Roy Pennysaver, Le Roy *Also called Dray Enterprises Inc* ***(G-6899)***
Le Vian Corp (PA) 516 466-7200
235 Great Neck Rd Great Neck (11021) ***(G-5400)***
Lea & Viola Inc 646 918-6866
525 Fashion Ave Rm 1401 New York (10018) ***(G-10181)***
Leader Herald, The, Gloversville *Also called William B Collins Company* ***(G-5300)***
Leader Printing Inc 516 546-1544
2272 Babylon Tpke Merrick (11566) ***(G-7859)***
Leader Sheet Metal Inc 347 271-4961
759 E 133rd St Apt 2 Bronx (10454) ***(G-1298)***
Leader, The, Corning *Also called Gatehouse Media LLC* ***(G-3715)***
Leadership Connect Inc (PA) 212 627-4140
1407 Broadway Rm 318 New York (10018) ***(G-10182)***
Leadertex Group, New York *Also called Leadertex Intl Inc* ***(G-10183)***
Leadertex Intl Inc 212 563-2242
135 W 36th St Fl 12 New York (10018) ***(G-10183)***
Leading Element LLC 315 479-8790
247 W Fayette St Ste 302 Syracuse (13202) ***(G-14929)***
Leanne Marshall Designs Inc 646 918-6349
39 W 38th St Fl 12 New York (10018) ***(G-10184)***
Leape Resources,, Alexander *Also called Lenape Energy Inc* ***(G-177)***
Learn360, New York *Also called Infobase Holdings Inc* ***(G-9886)***
Learningateway LLC 212 920-7969
106 Saint James Pl Brooklyn (11238) ***(G-2055)***
Learningexpress LLC 646 274-6454
224 W 29th St Fl 3 New York (10001) ***(G-10185)***
Leather Artisan 518 359-3102
9740 State Highway 3 Childwold (12922) ***(G-3401)***
Leather Craftsmen Inc (PA) 631 752-9000
6 Dubon Ct Farmingdale (11735) ***(G-4670)***
Leather Hub Worldwide LLC 310 386-2247
264 W 40th St Fl 17 New York (10018) ***(G-10186)***
Leather Indexes Corp 516 827-1900
174a Miller Pl Hicksville (11801) ***(G-5923)***
Leather Outlet 518 668-0328
1656 State Route 9 Lake George (12845) ***(G-6757)***
Leatherstocking Mobile Home PA 315 839-5691
2089 Doolittle Rd Sauquoit (13456) ***(G-14219)***
Leblon Holdings LLC 212 741-2675
33 Irving Pl Fl 3 New York (10003) ***(G-10187)***
Leblon LLC 786 281-5672
266 W 26th St Ste 801 New York (10001) ***(G-10188)***
Lebron Equipment Supply, New York *Also called 3835 Lebron Rest Eqp & Sup Inc* ***(G-8402)***
Lechler Laboratories Inc 845 426-6800
100 Red Schoolhse Rd C2 Spring Valley (10977) ***(G-14574)***
Lechler Labs, Chestnut Ridge *Also called Mehron Inc* ***(G-3395)***
Lechler Labs, Spring Valley *Also called Lechler Laboratories Inc* ***(G-14574)***
Lecreuset of America, Central Valley *Also called Schiller Stores Inc* ***(G-3300)***
Lecroy Corporation (PA) 845 425-2000
700 Chestnut Ridge Rd Spring Valley (10977) ***(G-14575)***
Led Lumina USA LLC 631 750-4433
116 Wilbur Pl Bohemia (11716) ***(G-1032)***
Led Next, Westbury *Also called Emitled Inc* ***(G-15882)***
Led Waves, Brooklyn *Also called Light Waves Concept Inc* ***(G-2072)***
Led Waves Inc 347 416-6182
4100 1st Ave Ste 3n Brooklyn (11232) ***(G-2056)***
Ledan Inc 631 239-1226
6 Annetta Ave Northport (11768) ***(G-12107)***
Ledan Design Group, Northport *Also called Ledan Inc* ***(G-12107)***
Lee & Low Books Incorporated 212 779-4400
95 Madison Ave Rm 1205 New York (10016) ***(G-10189)***
Lee Dyeing Company NC Inc 518 736-5232
328 N Perry St Johnstown (12095) ***(G-6622)***
Lee Enterprises Incorporated 518 792-3131
76 Lawrence St Glens Falls (12801) ***(G-5255)***
Lee Newspapers Inc 518 673-3237
6113 State Highway 5 Palatine Bridge (13428) ***(G-12477)***
Lee Printing Inc 718 237-1651
188 Lee Ave Brooklyn (11211) ***(G-2057)***
Lee Publications Inc (PA) 518 673-3237
6113 State Highway 5 Palatine Bridge (13428) ***(G-12478)***
Lee Spring Company LLC (HQ) 888 777-4647
140 58th St Ste 3c Brooklyn (11220) ***(G-2058)***
Lee World Industries LLC (PA) 212 265-8866
150 Broadway Ste 1608 New York (10038) ***(G-10190)***
Lee Yuen Fung Trading Co Inc (PA) 212 594-9595
125 W 29th St Fl 5 New York (10001) ***(G-10191)***
Leesa Designs Ltd 631 261-3991
31 Glenn Cres Centerport (11721) ***(G-3256)***
Leetech Manufacturing Inc 631 563-1442
105 Carlough Rd Unit C Bohemia (11716) ***(G-1033)***
Lefrak Entertainment Co Ltd 212 586-3600
40 W 57th St Fl 4 New York (10019) ***(G-10192)***
Legacy Manufacturing, Bronx *Also called Legacy USA LLC* ***(G-1299)***
Legacy USA LLC 718 292-5333
415 Concord Ave Bronx (10455) ***(G-1299)***
Legacy Valve LLC 914 403-5075
14 Railroad Ave Valhalla (10595) ***(G-15304)***
Legal Servicing LLC 716 565-9300
2801 Wehrle Dr Ste 5 Williamsville (14221) ***(G-16133)***
Legal Strategies Inc 516 377-3940
1795 Harvard Ave Merrick (11566) ***(G-7860)***
Legendary Auto Interiors Ltd 315 331-1212
121 W Shore Blvd Newark (14513) ***(G-11843)***
Legge System, Peekskill *Also called Walter G Legge Company Inc* ***(G-12560)***
Leggiadro International Inc (PA) 212 997-8766
65 Main St 2 Yonkers (10701) ***(G-16326)***
Legion Lighting Co Inc 718 498-1770
221 Glenmore Ave Brooklyn (11207) ***(G-2059)***
Legno Veneto USA 716 651-9169
3283 Walden Ave Depew (14043) ***(G-3986)***
Lehigh Cement Company (HQ) 518 792-1137
313 Warren St Glens Falls (12801) ***(G-5256)***
Lehigh Cement Company 518 943-5940
120 Alpha Rd Catskill (12414) ***(G-3212)***
Lehigh Cement Company LLC 518 792-1137
313 Lower Warren St Glens Falls (12804) ***(G-5257)***
Lehigh Cement Company LLC 718 522-0800
63 Flushing Ave Unit 295 Brooklyn (11205) ***(G-2060)***
Lehigh Northeast Cement, Glens Falls *Also called Lehigh Cement Company* ***(G-5256)***
Lehigh Northeast Cement Co 518 792-1137
120 Alpha Rd Catskill (12414) ***(G-3213)***
Lehmann Printing Company Inc 212 929-2395
247 W 37th St Rm 2a New York (10018) ***(G-10193)***
Lehneis Orthotics Prosthetic 516 790-1897
517 Route 111 Ste 300 Hauppauge (11788) ***(G-5691)***
Lehneis Orthotics Prosthetic 631 369-3115
518 E Main St Riverhead (11901) ***(G-13178)***
Leica Microsystems Inc 716 686-3000
3362 Walden Ave Depew (14043) ***(G-3987)***
Leidel Corporation (PA) 631 244-0900
95 Orville Dr Bohemia (11716) ***(G-1034)***
Leigh Scott Enterprises Inc 718 343-5440
24802 Union Tpke Bellerose (11426) ***(G-775)***
Leiter Sukkahs Inc 718 436-0303
1346 39th St Brooklyn (11218) ***(G-2061)***
Lela Rose, New York *Also called Stitch & Couture Inc* ***(G-11364)***
Lelab Dental Laboratory Inc 516 561-5050
550 W Merrick Rd Ste 8 Valley Stream (11580) ***(G-15346)***
Lemans Corporation 518 885-7500
10 Mccrea Hill Rd Ballston Spa (12020) ***(G-580)***
Lemetric Hair Centers Inc 212 986-5620
124 E 40th St Rm 601 New York (10016) ***(G-10194)***
Lemode Concepts Inc 631 841-0796
19 Elm Pl Amityville (11701) ***(G-291)***
Lemode Plumbing & Heating 718 545-3336
3455 11th St Astoria (11106) ***(G-427)***
Lemon Brothers Foundation Inc 347 920-2749
23b Debs Pl Bronx (10475) ***(G-1300)***
Lemoyne Machine Products Corp 315 454-0708
106 Evelyn Ter Syracuse (13208) ***(G-14930)***
Lenape Energy Inc (PA) 585 344-1200
9489 Alexander Rd Alexander (14005) ***(G-177)***
Lenape Resources Inc 585 344-1200
9489 Alexander Rd Alexander (14005) ***(G-178)***
Lenaro Paper Co Inc 631 439-8800
31 Windsor Pl Central Islip (11722) ***(G-3282)***
Lenco, Amityville *Also called Saraga Industries Corp* ***(G-306)***
Lencore Acoustics Corp (PA) 516 682-9292
1 Crossways Park Dr W Woodbury (11797) ***(G-16175)***
Lencore Acoustics Corp 315 384-9114
1 S Main St Norfolk (13667) ***(G-11999)***
Lending Trimming Co Inc 212 242-7502
179 Christopher St New York (10014) ***(G-10195)***
Leng Universal Inc 212 398-6800
530 7th Ave Rm 1101 New York (10018) ***(G-10196)***
Lennons Litho Inc 315 866-3156
234 Kast Hill Rd Herkimer (13350) ***(G-5866)***
Lenny & Bill LLC 516 997-5757
717 Main St Westbury (11590) ***(G-15903)***
Lenon Models Inc 212 229-1581
300 W 245th St Bronx (10471) ***(G-1301)***
Lenore Marshall Inc 212 947-5945
231 W 29th St Frnt 1 New York (10001) ***(G-10197)***
Lens Lab 718 379-2020
2124 Bartow Ave Bronx (10475) ***(G-1302)***
Lens Lab Express 718 921-5488
482 86th St Brooklyn (11209) ***(G-2062)***

Lens Lab Express Southern Blvd 718 626-5184
  3097 Steinway St Ste 301 Astoria (11103) *(G-428)*
Lens Triptar Co Inc 585 473-4470
  439 Monroe Ave Ste 1 Rochester (14607) *(G-13515)*
Lenz, Peconic *Also called Dorset Farms Inc (G-12545)*
Leo D Bernstein & Sons Inc (PA) 212 337-9578
  151 W 25th St Frnt 1 New York (10001) *(G-10198)*
Leo Diamond, The, New York *Also called Leo Schachter Diamonds LLC (G-10202)*
Leo Ingwer Inc 212 719-1342
  62 W 47th St Ste 1004 New York (10036) *(G-10199)*
Leo International Inc 718 290-8005
  471 Sutter Ave Brooklyn (11207) *(G-2063)*
Leo P Callahan Inc 607 797-7314
  229 Lwer Stlla Ireland Rd Binghamton (13905) *(G-894)*
Leo Paper Inc 917 305-0708
  286 5th Ave Fl 6 New York (10001) *(G-10200)*
Leo Schachter & Co Inc 212 688-2000
  529 5th Ave New York (10017) *(G-10201)*
Leo Schachter Diamonds LLC 212 688-2000
  50 W 47th St Ste 2100 New York (10036) *(G-10202)*
Leon Mege Inc 212 768-3868
  151 W 46th St Ste 901 New York (10036) *(G-10203)*
Leonard Bus Sales Inc 607 467-3100
  730 Ellsworth Rd Rome (13441) *(G-13854)*
Leonard Carlson 518 477-4710
  90 Waters Rd East Greenbush (12061) *(G-4115)*
Leonard Oakes Estate Winery 585 318-4418
  10609 Ridge Rd Medina (14103) *(G-7739)*
Leonardo Printing Corp 914 664-7890
  529 E 3rd St Mount Vernon (10553) *(G-8157)*
Leonardo Prntng, Mount Vernon *Also called Leonardo Printing Corp (G-8157)*
Lep, Hawthorne *Also called Ludl Electronic Products Ltd (G-5818)*
Leprino Foods Company 570 888-9658
  400 Leprino Ave Waverly (14892) *(G-15623)*
Leroux Fuels 518 563-3653
  994 Military Tpke Plattsburgh (12901) *(G-12758)*
Leroy Plastics Inc 585 768-8158
  20 Lent Ave Le Roy (14482) *(G-6903)*
Les Ateliers Tamalet, New York *Also called Ateliers Tamalet Corp (G-8661)*
Les Chateaux De France Inc 516 239-6795
  1 Craft Ave Inwood (11096) *(G-6297)*
Lesanne Life Sciences LLC 914 234-0860
  47 Brook Farm Rd Bedford (10506) *(G-764)*
Leser Enterprises Ltd 212 832-8013
  1767 Central Park Ave # 514 Yonkers (10710) *(G-16327)*
Lesieur Cristal Inc 646 604-4314
  1034 44th Dr Fl 2 Long Island City (11101) *(G-7270)*
Leslie Stuart Co Inc 212 629-4551
  149 W 36th St Fl 8 New York (10018) *(G-10204)*
Lesly Enterprise & Associates 631 988-1301
  29 Columbo Dr Deer Park (11729) *(G-3896)*
Lessoilcom 516 319-5052
  672 Dogwood Ave Franklin Square (11010) *(G-4961)*
Letigre, New York *Also called Lt2 LLC (G-10277)*
Letterama Inc (PA) 516 349-0800
  111 Cabot St West Babylon (11704) *(G-15725)*
Lettergraphics, Bridgeport *Also called Syracuse Letter Company Inc (G-1169)*
Level Wear, Cheektowaga *Also called Accolade USA Inc (G-3336)*
Levi Shabtai 212 302-7393
  1 W 47th St New York (10036) *(G-10205)*
Levi Strauss & Co 917 213-6263
  13432 Blossom Ave Flushing (11355) *(G-4870)*
Leviton Manufacturing Co Inc (PA) 631 812-6000
  201 N Service Rd Melville (11747) *(G-7800)*
Levitt Industrial Textile, Deer Park *Also called Kenwin Sales Corp (G-3891)*
Levolor Inc (HQ) 845 664-7000
  1 Blue Hill Plz Pearl River (10965) *(G-12537)*
Levon Graphics Corp 631 753-2022
  301 Suburban Ave Deer Park (11729) *(G-3897)*
Levy Group Inc (PA) 212 398-0707
  1333 Broadway Fl 9 New York (10018) *(G-10206)*
Lewis Avenue LLC 718 669-0579
  172 5th Ave 111 Brooklyn (11217) *(G-2064)*
Lewis Machine Co Inc 718 625-0799
  209 Congress St Brooklyn (11201) *(G-2065)*
Lewis Sand & Gravel, Lewis *Also called Upstone Materials Inc (G-6918)*
Lewis, S J Machine Co, Brooklyn *Also called Lewis Machine Co Inc (G-2065)*
Lexan Industries Inc 631 434-7586
  15 Harold Ct Bay Shore (11706) *(G-690)*
Lexar Global LLC 845 352-9700
  711 Executive Blvd Ste K Valley Cottage (10989) *(G-15318)*
Lexington Machining LLC 585 235-0880
  677 Buffalo Rd Rochester (14611) *(G-13516)*
Lexington Machining LLC (PA) 585 235-0880
  677 Buffalo Rd Rochester (14611) *(G-13517)*
Lf Outerwear LLC 212 239-2025
  463 7th Ave Fl 12 New York (10018) *(G-10207)*
Lf Sourcing (millwork) LLC 212 827-3352
  1359 Broadway Fl 18 New York (10018) *(G-10208)*
Lgn Materials & Solutions 888 414-0005
  149 Esplanade Mount Vernon (10553) *(G-8158)*

Lhv Precast Inc 845 336-8880
  540 Ulster Landing Rd Kingston (12401) *(G-6699)*
LI Community Newspapers Inc 516 747-8282
  132 E 2nd St Mineola (11501) *(G-7985)*
LI Fireproof Door, Whitestone *Also called Lif Industries Inc (G-16097)*
LI Pipe Supply, Garden City *Also called Miles Moss of New York Inc (G-5109)*
LI Script LLC 631 321-3850
  333 Crossways Park Dr Woodbury (11797) *(G-16176)*
Libbys Bakery Cafe LLC 603 918-8825
  92 Montcalm St Ticonderoga (12883) *(G-15075)*
Liberty Apparel Company Inc (PA) 718 625-4000
  1407 Broadway Rm 1500 New York (10018) *(G-10209)*
Liberty Awnings & Signs Inc 347 203-1470
  7705 21st Ave East Elmhurst (11370) *(G-4109)*
Liberty Brass Turning Co Inc 718 784-2911
  1200 Shames Dr Unit C Westbury (11590) *(G-15904)*
Liberty Controls Inc 718 461-0600
  1505 132nd St Fl 2 College Point (11356) *(G-3551)*
Liberty Displays Inc 716 743-1757
  4230b Ridge Lea Rd # 110 Amherst (14226) *(G-229)*
Liberty Fabrication Inc 718 495-5735
  226 Glenmore Ave Brooklyn (11207) *(G-2066)*
Liberty Food and Fuel 315 299-4039
  1131 N Salina St Syracuse (13208) *(G-14931)*
Liberty Install Inc 631 651-5655
  27 W Neck Rd Huntington (11743) *(G-6211)*
Liberty Iron Works, Liberty *Also called Neversink Steel Corp (G-6926)*
Liberty Label Mfg Inc 631 737-2365
  21 Peachtree Ct Holbrook (11741) *(G-6006)*
Liberty Machine & Tool 315 699-3242
  7908 Ontario Ave Cicero (13039) *(G-3421)*
Liberty Panel & Home Center, Brooklyn *Also called Liberty Panel Center Inc (G-2067)*
Liberty Panel Center Inc (PA) 718 647-2763
  1009 Liberty Ave Brooklyn (11208) *(G-2067)*
Liberty Pipe Incorporated 516 747-2472
  128 Liberty Ave Mineola (11501) *(G-7986)*
Liberty Pumps Inc 800 543-2550
  7000 Appletree Ave Bergen (14416) *(G-817)*
Liberty Ready Mix Inc 718 526-1700
  9533 150th St Jamaica (11435) *(G-6453)*
Library of America, New York *Also called Literary Classics of US (G-10226)*
Lic Beer Project, Long Island City *Also called Lic Brewery LLC (G-7271)*
Lic Brewery LLC 917 832-6840
  3928 23rd St Long Island City (11101) *(G-7271)*
Licenders (PA) 212 759-5200
  939 8th Ave New York (10019) *(G-10210)*
Lickity Splits 585 345-6091
  238 East Ave Batavia (14020) *(G-619)*
Liddabit Sweets 917 912-1370
  330 Wythe Ave Apt 2g Brooklyn (11249) *(G-2068)*
Liddell Corporation 716 297-8557
  4600 Witmer Ind Est 5 Niagara Falls (14305) *(G-11946)*
Lidestri Beverages LLC (PA) 585 377-7700
  815 Whitney Rd W Fairport (14450) *(G-4503)*
Lidestri Food and Drink, Fairport *Also called Lidestri Foods Inc (G-4504)*
Lidestri Foods Inc (PA) 585 377-7700
  815 Whitney Rd W Fairport (14450) *(G-4504)*
Lids Corporation 518 459-7060
  131 Colonie Ctr Spc 429 Albany (12205) *(G-97)*
Lieb Cellars LLC 631 298-1942
  35 Cox Neck Rd Mattituck (11952) *(G-7677)*
Lieb Cellars Tasting Room, Mattituck *Also called Lieb Cellars LLC (G-7677)*
Liebe NY, Perry *Also called American Clssic Outfitters Inc (G-12595)*
Lif Industries Inc (PA) 516 390-6800
  5 Harbor Park Dr Ste 1 Port Washington (11050) *(G-12899)*
Lif Industries Inc 718 767-8800
  1105 Clintonville St Whitestone (11357) *(G-16097)*
Lifc Corp 516 426-5737
  101 Haven Ave Port Washington (11050) *(G-12900)*
Life Earth Company 310 751-0627
  200 W 113th St Apt 2d New York (10026) *(G-10211)*
Life Juice Brands LLC 585 944-7982
  115 Brook Rd Pittsford (14534) *(G-12646)*
Life Medical Technologies LLC 845 894-2121
  2070 Rte 52 21a Bldg 320a Hopewell Junction (12533) *(G-6099)*
Life On Earth Inc (PA) 646 844-9897
  575 Lexington Ave Fl 4 New York (10022) *(G-10212)*
Life Pill Laboratories LLC 914 682-2146
  50 Main St Ste 100 White Plains (10606) *(G-16025)*
Life Style Design Group 212 391-8666
  1441 Broadway Fl 7 New York (10018) *(G-10213)*
Life Technologies Corporation 716 774-6700
  3175 Staley Rd Grand Island (14072) *(G-5336)*
Life Watch Technology Inc 917 669-2428
  42-10 Polen St Ste 412 Flushing (11355) *(G-4871)*
Lifegas, Cohoes *Also called Linde Gas North America LLC (G-3508)*
Lifegas, Syracuse *Also called Linde Gas North America LLC (G-14933)*
Lifelink Monitoring Corp (PA) 845 336-2098
  3201 Route 212 Bearsville (12409) *(G-758)*
Lifesake Division, New Hartford *Also called Faster-Form Corp (G-8240)*

Lifescan Inc 516 557-2693
15 Tardy Ln N Wantagh (11793) *(G-15485)*

Lifestyle Design Usa Ltd 212 279-9400
315 W 39th St Rm 1400 New York (10018) *(G-10214)*

Lifestyle-Trimco (PA) 718 257-9101
323 Malta St Brooklyn (11207) *(G-2069)*

Lifestyle-Trimco Viaggo, Brooklyn *Also called Lifestyle-Trimco (G-2069)*

Lifetime Brands Inc (PA) 516 683-6000
1000 Stewart Ave Garden City (11530) *(G-5104)*

Lifetime Chimney Supply LLC 516 576-8144
171 E Ames Ct Plainview (11803) *(G-12696)*

Lifetime Stainless Steel Corp 585 924-9393
7387 Ny 96 850 Victor (14564) *(G-15417)*

Lifewatch Inc 800 716-1433
1344 Broadway Ste 106 Hewlett (11557) *(G-5871)*

Lifewatch Personal Mergency, Hewlett *Also called Lifewatch Inc (G-5871)*

Liffey Sheet Metal Corp 347 381-1134
4555 36th St Long Island City (11101) *(G-7272)*

Lift Safe - Fuel Safe Inc 315 423-7702
515 E Brighton Ave Syracuse (13210) *(G-14932)*

Liftforward Inc (PA) 917 693-4993
180 Maiden Ln Fl 10 New York (10038) *(G-10215)*

Light Inc 917 803-3323
42 Quicks Ln Katonah (10536) *(G-6634)*

Light Blue USA LLC 718 475-2515
1421 Locust Ave Brooklyn (11230) *(G-2070)*

Light Fabrications, Rochester *Also called Eis Legacy LLC (G-13380)*

Light House Hill Marketing 212 354-1338
38 W 39th St Fl 4l New York (10018) *(G-10216)*

Light Inc 212 629-3255
530 Fashion Ave Rm 1002 New York (10018) *(G-10217)*

Light Phone Inc (PA) 415 595-0044
49 Bogart St Apt 44 Brooklyn (11206) *(G-2071)*

Light Waves Concept Inc 212 677-6400
4100 1st Ave Brooklyn (11232) *(G-2072)*

Lightbulb Press Inc 212 485-8800
39 W 28th St New York (10001) *(G-10218)*

Lightforce Technology Inc 585 292-5610
1057 E Henrietta Rd Rochester (14623) *(G-13518)*

Lighthouse Components 917 993-6820
14 Wall St New York (10005) *(G-10219)*

Lighting By Dom Yonkers Inc 914 968-8700
253 S Broadway Yonkers (10705) *(G-16328)*

Lighting Holdings Intl LLC (PA) 845 306-1850
4 Manhattanville Rd Purchase (10577) *(G-13006)*

Lighting N Beyond LLC 718 669-9142
628 Ste 303 Blauvelt (10913) *(G-930)*

Lighting Products Division, Skaneateles Falls *Also called Welch Allyn Inc (G-14461)*

Lighting Sculptures Inc 631 242-3387
66 N Industry Ct Deer Park (11729) *(G-3898)*

Lighting Services Inc (PA) 845 942-2800
2 Holt Dr Stony Point (10980) *(G-14746)*

Lightspin Technologies Inc 301 656-7600
616 Lowell Dr Endwell (13760) *(G-4481)*

Lik LLC 516 848-5135
6 Bluff Point Rd Northport (11768) *(G-12108)*

Lilac Quarries LLC 607 867-4016
1702 State Highway 8 Mount Upton (13809) *(G-8118)*

Lilibrand LLC 212 239-8230
157 13th St 202 Brooklyn (11215) *(G-2073)*

Lilly Collection, New York *Also called Lily & Taylor Inc (G-10220)*

Lillys Homestyle Bakeshop Inc 718 491-2904
6210 9th Ave Brooklyn (11220) *(G-2074)*

Lily & Taylor Inc 212 564-5459
247 W 37th St Frnt 6 New York (10018) *(G-10220)*

Lime Energy Co 704 892-4442
1a Elk Terminal Buffalo (14204) *(G-2849)*

Limo-Print.com, Central Islip *Also called Color Card LLC (G-3269)*

Lincdoc LLC 585 563-1669
401 Main St East Rochester (14445) *(G-4167)*

Linco Printing Inc 718 937-5141
5022 23rd St Long Island City (11101) *(G-7273)*

Lincware, East Rochester *Also called Lincdoc LLC (G-4167)*

Linda Campbell 718 994-4026
4420 Richardson Ave Bronx (10470) *(G-1303)*

Linda Tool & Die Corporation 718 522-2066
163 Dwight St Brooklyn (11231) *(G-2075)*

Linde Gas North America LLC 518 713-2015
10 Arrowhead Ln Cohoes (12047) *(G-3508)*

Linde Gas North America LLC 315 431-4081
147 Midler Park Dr Syracuse (13206) *(G-14933)*

Linden Cookies Inc 845 268-5050
25 Brenner Dr Congers (10920) *(G-3617)*

Linden Forms & Systems Inc 212 219-1100
40 S 6th St Brooklyn (11249) *(G-2076)*

Lindenhurst Fabricators Inc 631 226-3737
117 S 13th St Lindenhurst (11757) *(G-6954)*

Linder New York LLC 646 678-5819
195 Chrystie St Rm 900 New York (10002) *(G-10221)*

Lindley Wood Works Inc 607 523-7786
9625 Morgan Creek Rd Lindley (14858) *(G-6986)*

Line Ward Corporation 716 675-7373
157 Seneca Creek Rd Buffalo (14224) *(G-2850)*

Linear Lighting Corporation 718 361-7552
3130 Hunters Point Ave Long Island City (11101) *(G-7274)*

Linear Signs Inc 631 532-5330
275 W Hoffman Ave Ste 1 Lindenhurst (11757) *(G-6955)*

Linita Design & Mfg Corp 716 566-7753
1951 Hamburg Tpke Ste 24 Lackawanna (14218) *(G-6741)*

Link Control Systems Inc 631 471-3950
16 Colt Ct Ronkonkoma (11779) *(G-13966)*

Linli Color, West Babylon *Also called East Cast Clor Compounding Inc (G-15708)*

Lino International Inc 516 482-7100
111 Great Neck Rd 300a Great Neck (11021) *(G-5401)*

Lino Metal, Great Neck *Also called Lino International Inc (G-5401)*

Lino Press Inc 718 665-2625
652 Southern Blvd Bronx (10455) *(G-1304)*

Lintex Linens Inc 212 679-8046
295 5th Ave Ste 1703 New York (10016) *(G-10222)*

Linzer Products Corp (HQ) 631 253-3333
248 Wyandanch Ave West Babylon (11704) *(G-15726)*

Lion Die-Cutting Co Inc 718 383-8841
95 Dobbin St Ste 1 Brooklyn (11222) *(G-2077)*

Lion E-Mobility North Amer Inc 917 345-6365
6 Sherman Ave Bronxville (10708) *(G-1401)*

Lion In The Sun Park Slope Ltd 718 369-4006
232 7th Ave Brooklyn (11215) *(G-2078)*

Lionel Habas Associates Inc 212 860-8454
1601 3rd Ave Apt 22d New York (10128) *(G-10223)*

Lipe Automation, Liverpool *Also called Ironshore Holdings Inc (G-7017)*

Lippincott Massie McQuilkin L 212 352-2055
27 W 20th St Ste 305 New York (10011) *(G-10224)*

Liptis Pharmaceuticals USA Inc 845 627-0260
110 Red Schoolhouse Rd Spring Valley (10977) *(G-14576)*

Liquid Industries Inc 716 628-2999
7219 New Jersey Ave Niagara Falls (14305) *(G-11947)*

Liquid Knits Inc 718 706-6600
3200 Skillman Ave Fl 2 Long Island City (11101) *(G-7275)*

Liquid Management Partners LLC 516 775-5050
3000 Marcus Ave Ste 1w9 New Hyde Park (11042) *(G-8280)*

Liquid State Brewing Co Inc 607 319-6209
620 W Green St Ithaca (14850) *(G-6392)*

Liquitane, Rochester *Also called Consolidated Container Co LLC (G-13325)*

Liquitane, Batavia *Also called Consolidated Container Co LLC (G-611)*

List & Beisler GMBH 646 866-6960
311 W 43rd St Fl 12 New York (10036) *(G-10225)*

Listec Video Corp (PA) 631 273-3029
90 Oser Ave Hauppauge (11788) *(G-5692)*

Liston Manufacturing Inc 716 695-2111
421 Payne Ave North Tonawanda (14120) *(G-12077)*

Litchfield Fabrics of NC (PA) 518 773-9500
111 Woodside Ave Gloversville (12078) *(G-5288)*

Lite Brite Manufacturing Inc 718 855-9797
575 President St Brooklyn (11215) *(G-2079)*

Lite-Makers Inc 718 739-9300
10715 180th St Jamaica (11433) *(G-6454)*

Litelab Corp 718 361-6829
540 54th Ave Long Island City (11101) *(G-7276)*

Litelab Corp (PA) 716 856-4300
251 Elm St Buffalo (14203) *(G-2851)*

Literary Classics of US 212 308-3360
14 E 60th St Ste 1101 New York (10022) *(G-10226)*

Litho Dynamics Inc 914 769-1759
17 Saw Mill River Rd Hawthorne (10532) *(G-5817)*

Lithomatic Business Forms Inc 212 255-6700
233 W 18th St Frnt A New York (10011) *(G-10227)*

Litmor Publications, Garden City *Also called Litmor Publishing Corp (G-5105)*

Litmor Publishing Corp (PA) 516 931-0012
821 Franklin Ave Ste 208 Garden City (11530) *(G-5105)*

Little Bee Books Inc 212 321-0237
251 Park Ave S Fl 12 New York (10010) *(G-10228)*

Little Bird Chocolates Inc 646 620-6395
25 Fairchild Ave Ste 200 Plainview (11803) *(G-12697)*

Little Bird Kitchen, Plainview *Also called Little Bird Chocolates Inc (G-12697)*

Little Eric Shoes On Madison 212 717-1513
1118 Madison Ave New York (10028) *(G-10229)*

Little Trees, Watertown *Also called Car-Freshner Corporation (G-15562)*

Little Valley Sand & Gravel 716 938-6676
8984 New Albion Rd Little Valley (14755) *(G-6999)*

Little Wolf Cabinet Shop Inc 212 734-1116
1583 1st Ave Frnt 1 New York (10028) *(G-10230)*

Littlebits Electronics Inc (HQ) 917 464-4577
601 W 26th St Rm M274 New York (10001) *(G-10231)*

Live Oak Media, Pine Plains *Also called ABRA Media Inc (G-12632)*

Live Up Top Inc 866 333-1332
1460 Broadway New York (10036) *(G-10232)*

Live Vote II Inc 646 343-9053
105 W 86th St 322 New York (10024) *(G-10233)*

Liveright Publishing Corp 212 354-5500
500 5th Ave Fl 6 New York (10110) *(G-10234)*

Livetiles Corp (PA) 917 472-7887
137 W 25th St Fl 6 New York (10001) *(G-10235)*

Livid Magazine 929 340-7123
1055 Bedford Ave Apt 4c Brooklyn (11216) *(G-2080)*

Living Doors Inc 631 924-5393
22 Scouting Blvd Ste 3 Medford (11763) *(G-7717)*

Living Media, Long Island City *Also called Thomson Press (india) Limited* *(G-7382)*

Living Well Innovations Inc 646 517-3200
115 Engineers Rd Hauppauge (11788) *(G-5693)*

Livingston County News 585 243-1234
122 Main St Geneseo (14454) *(G-5144)*

Livingston Lighting and Power, Scottsville *Also called Power and Cnstr Group
Inc* *(G-14342)*

Liz Claiborne Coats, New York *Also called Levy Group Inc* *(G-10206)*

Lizotte Logging Inc 518 359-2200
5 White Pine Ln Tupper Lake (12986) *(G-15210)*

Ljmm Inc 845 454-5876
188 Washington St Poughkeepsie (12601) *(G-12967)*

Lk Industries Inc 716 941-9202
9731 Center St Glenwood (14069) *(G-5274)*

LLC Major Major 212 354-8550
1407 Broadway Fl 10 New York (10018) *(G-10236)*

Llcs Publishing Corp 718 569-2703
2071 Flatbush Ave Ste 189 Brooklyn (11234) *(G-2081)*

Lloyd Price Icon Food Brands 914 764-8624
95 Horseshoe Hill Rd Pound Ridge (10576) *(G-12993)*

Lloyds Fashions Inc (PA) 631 435-3353
335 Crooked Hill Rd Brentwood (11717) *(G-1125)*

LMC 49th Inc (HQ) 718 361-9161
4707 30th Pl Long Island City (11101) *(G-7277)*

LMC 49th Inc 212 744-7117
1018 Madison Ave New York (10075) *(G-10237)*

LMD Power of Light Corp 585 272-5420
3495 Winton Pl Ste A37 Rochester (14623) *(G-13519)*

Lmg National Publishing Inc (HQ) 585 598-6874
350 Willowbrook Office Pa Fairport (14450) *(G-4505)*

Lmgi, Liverpool *Also called Lockheed Martin Global Inc* *(G-7022)*

Lmr Group Inc 212 730-9221
463 7th Ave Fl 4 New York (10018) *(G-10238)*

Lmt Technology Solutions 585 784-7470
4 Commercial St Ste 400 Rochester (14614) *(G-13520)*

Lnd, Oceanside *Also called L N D Incorporated* *(G-12179)*

LNK International Inc 631 435-3500
22 Arkay Dr Hauppauge (11788) *(G-5694)*

LNK International Inc 631 435-3500
100 Ricefield Ln Hauppauge (11788) *(G-5695)*

LNK International Inc 631 435-3500
325 Kennedy Dr Hauppauge (11788) *(G-5696)*

LNK International Inc 631 543-3787
145 Ricefield Ln Hauppauge (11788) *(G-5697)*

LNK International Inc 631 435-3500
40 Arkay Dr Hauppauge (11788) *(G-5698)*

LNK International Inc 631 231-4020
55 Arkay Dr Hauppauge (11788) *(G-5699)*

Lo & Sons Inc 917 775-4025
55 Prospect St Brooklyn (11201) *(G-2082)*

Lo-Co Fuel Corp 631 929-5086
10 Stephen Dr Wading River (11792) *(G-15450)*

Load/N/Go Beverage Corp (PA) 585 218-4019
355 Portland Ave Rochester (14605) *(G-13521)*

Loar Group Inc (PA) 212 210-9348
450 Lexington Ave Fl 31 New York (10017) *(G-10239)*

Local Media Group Inc 845 341-1100
40 Mulberry St Middletown (10940) *(G-7915)*

Local Media Group Inc (HQ) 845 341-1100
40 Mulberry St Middletown (10940) *(G-7916)*

Local Media Group Inc 845 341-1100
60 Brookline Ave Middletown (10940) *(G-7917)*

Local Media Group Inc 845 794-3712
479 Broadway Monticello (12701) *(G-8070)*

Local Media Group Inc 845 340-4910
34 John St Kingston (12401) *(G-6700)*

Local Media Group Holdings LLC (HQ) 585 598-0030
175 Sullys Trl Ste 300 Pittsford (14534) *(G-12647)*

Local News, Oswego *Also called Dotto Wagner* *(G-12409)*

Locations Magazine 212 288-4745
124 E 79th St New York (10075) *(G-10240)*

Lock 1 Distilling Company LLC 315 934-4376
17 Culvert St Phoenix (13135) *(G-12616)*

Locker Masters Inc 518 288-3203
10329 State Route 22 Granville (12832) *(G-5349)*

Lockheed Martin Corporation 716 297-1000
2221 Niagara Falls Blvd Niagara Falls (14304) *(G-11948)*

Lockheed Martin Corporation 212 953-1510
420 Lexington Ave Rm 2601 New York (10170) *(G-10241)*

Lockheed Martin Corporation 315 456-3386
497 Electronics Pkwy Liverpool (13088) *(G-7020)*

Lockheed Martin Corporation 315 793-5800
8373 Seneca Tpke New Hartford (13413) *(G-8241)*

Lockheed Martin Corporation 516 228-2000
55 Charles Lindbergh Blvd # 1 Uniondale (11553) *(G-15231)*

Lockheed Martin Corporation 607 751-2000
1801 State Route 17 Owego (13827) *(G-12433)*

Lockheed Martin Corporation 315 456-0123
497 Electronics Pkwy # 5 Liverpool (13088) *(G-7021)*

Lockheed Martin Corporation 315 456-6604
6060 Tarbell Rd Syracuse (13206) *(G-14934)*

Lockheed Martin Corporation 212 697-1105
600 3rd Ave Fl 35 New York (10016) *(G-10242)*

Lockheed Martin Global Inc (HQ) 315 456-2982
497 Electronics Pkwy # 5 Liverpool (13088) *(G-7022)*

Lockheed Martin Integrtd Systm 315 456-3333
497 Electronics Pkwy Syracuse (13221) *(G-14935)*

Lockheed Martin Overseas 315 456-0123
497 Electronics Pkwy # 7 Liverpool (13088) *(G-7023)*

Lockhouse Distillery 716 768-4898
41 Columbia St Ste 3 Buffalo (14204) *(G-2852)*

Lockwood Trade Journal Co Inc 212 391-2060
3743 Crescent St Ste 2 Long Island City (11101) *(G-7278)*

Lodi Down & Feather, New York *Also called Sleepable Sofas Ltd* *(G-11267)*

Lodolce Machine Co Inc 845 246-7017
196 Malden Tpke Saugerties (12477) *(G-14204)*

Logical Control Solutions Inc 585 424-5340
829 Phillips Rd Ste 100 Victor (14564) *(G-15418)*

Logical Operations Inc 585 350-7000
3535 Winton Pl Rochester (14623) *(G-13522)*

Logitek Inc 631 567-1100
110 Wilbur Pl Bohemia (11716) *(G-1035)*

Logo 212 846-2568
1515 Broadway New York (10036) *(G-10243)*

Logo Print Company 607 324-5403
135 Seneca St Hornell (14843) *(G-6109)*

Logomax Inc 631 420-0484
242 Route 109 Ste B Farmingdale (11735) *(G-4671)*

Lois Kitchen LLC 216 308-9335
206 Avenue A Apt 2a New York (10009) *(G-10244)*

Lokai Holdings LLC 646 979-3474
180 Varick St Rm 504 New York (10014) *(G-10245)*

Lola, New York *Also called Alyk Inc* *(G-8535)*

Lollytogs Ltd (PA) 212 502-6000
100 W 33rd St Ste 1012 New York (10001) *(G-10246)*

Lomak Petroleum, Mayville *Also called Range Rsurces - Appalachia LLC* *(G-7684)*

Lombardi Design & Mfg, Freeport *Also called Anna Young Assoc Ltd* *(G-4985)*

Lomin Construction Company 516 759-5734
328 Glen Cove Rd Glen Head (11545) *(G-5209)*

Lomir Inc 518 483-7697
213 W Main St Malone (12953) *(G-7487)*

Lomir Biomedical Inc, Malone *Also called Lomir Inc* *(G-7487)*

London Paris Ltd 718 564-4793
4211 13th Ave Brooklyn (11219) *(G-2083)*

London Theater News Ltd 212 517-8608
12 E 86th St Apt 620 New York (10028) *(G-10247)*

Long Blockchain Corp (PA) 855 542-2832
12 Dubon Ct Ste 1 Farmingdale (11735) *(G-4672)*

Long Ireland Brewing LLC 631 403-4303
723 Pulaski St Riverhead (11901) *(G-13179)*

Long Island Advance, Patchogue *Also called Patchogue Advance Inc* *(G-12509)*

Long Island Analytical Labs 631 472-3400
110 Colin Dr Holbrook (11741) *(G-6007)*

Long Island Brand Bevs LLC 855 542-2832
3788 Review Ave Long Island City (11101) *(G-7279)*

Long Island Business News 631 737-1700
2150 Smithtown Ave Ste 7 Ronkonkoma (11779) *(G-13967)*

Long Island Cmnty Nwsppers Inc (PA).............516 482-4490
132 E 2nd St Mineola (11501) *(G-7987)*

Long Island Cmnty Nwsppers Inc 631 427-7000
322 Main St Huntington (11743) *(G-6212)*

Long Island Compost Corp 516 334-6600
100 Urban Ave Westbury (11590) *(G-15905)*

Long Island Fireproof Door, Port Washington *Also called Lif Industries Inc* *(G-12899)*

Long Island Geotech 631 473-1044
6 Berkshire Ct Port Jefferson (11777) *(G-12841)*

Long Island Golfer Magazine, Hicksville *Also called Golfing Magazine* *(G-5914)*

Long Island Green Guys 631 664-4306
26 Silverbrook Dr Riverhead (11901) *(G-13180)*

Long Island Metalform Inc 631 242-9088
12 Lucon Dr Deer Park (11729) *(G-3899)*

Long Island Pipe Supply Inc 718 456-7877
5858 56th St Flushing (11378) *(G-4872)*

Long Island Pipe Supply Inc 518 270-2159
75 Cohoes Ave Troy (12183) *(G-15160)*

LONG ISLAND PIPE SUPPLY OF ALBANY, INC., Flushing *Also called Long Island Pipe
Supply Inc* *(G-4872)*

Long Island Precast Inc 631 286-0240
20 Stiriz Rd Brookhaven (11719) *(G-1409)*

Long Island Press, Farmingdale *Also called Morey Publishing* *(G-4689)*

Long Island Radiant Heat, Mastic Beach *Also called Vincent Genovese* *(G-7675)*

Long Island Ready Mix 516 485-5260
75 Chasner St Hempstead (11550) *(G-5843)*

Long Island Stamp & Seal Co 718 628-8550
5431 Myrtle Ave Ste 2 Ridgewood (11385) *(G-13150)*

Long Island Tool & Die Inc 631 225-0600
1445 S Strong Ave Copiague (11726) *(G-3662)*

Long Islander Newspapers LLC............................631 427-7000
  46 Green St Ste A Huntington (11743) *(G-6213)*
Long Islands Best Inc.....................................855 542-3785
  1650 Sycamore Ave Ste 4b Bohemia (11716) *(G-1036)*
Long Islndr Nrth/Sth Pblctns, Huntington *Also called Long Island Cmnty Nwsppers*
Inc (G-6212)
Long Lumber and Supply Corp...........................518 439-1661
  2100 New Scotland Rd Slingerlands (12159) *(G-14466)*
Long Paige, New York *Also called Jiranimo Industries Ltd (G-10007)*
Longevity Brands LLC.....................................212 231-7877
  250 W 39th St Rm 405 New York (10018) *(G-10248)*
Longo Cabinets, Lindenhurst *Also called Longo Commercial Cabinets Inc (G-6956)*
Longo Commercial Cabinets Inc..........................631 225-4290
  829 N Richmond Ave Lindenhurst (11757) *(G-6956)*
Longo New York Inc.......................................212 929-7128
  444 W 17th St New York (10011) *(G-10249)*
Longstem Organizers Inc..................................914 777-2174
  380 E Main St Jefferson Valley (10535) *(G-6568)*
Longtail Studios Inc......................................646 443-8146
  180 Varick St Rm 820 New York (10014) *(G-10250)*
Lonza, Rochester *Also called Arch Chemicals Inc (G-13243)*
Loobrica International Corp...............................347 997-0296
  41 Darnell Ln Staten Island (10309) *(G-14677)*
Look By M Inc..212 213-4019
  838 Avenue Of The America New York (10001) *(G-10251)*
Lookbooks Media Inc......................................646 737-3360
  208 W 30th St Rm 802 New York (10001) *(G-10252)*
Loom Concepts LLC.......................................212 813-9586
  767 Lexington Ave Rm 405 New York (10065) *(G-10253)*
Loominus Handwoven, Woodstock *Also called Marsha Fleisher (G-16236)*
Loomis Root Inc..716 564-7668
  135 Pineview Dr Amherst (14228) *(G-230)*
Loomstate LLC...212 219-2300
  270 Bowery Fl 3 New York (10012) *(G-10254)*
Looney Tunes CD Store, West Babylon *Also called Brookvale Records Inc (G-15695)*
Looseleaf Law Publications Inc...........................718 359-5559
  4308 162nd St Flushing (11358) *(G-4873)*
Loosesleeve Law Publications, Flushing *Also called Warodean Corporation (G-4905)*
Lopez Restorations Inc (PA)..............................718 383-1555
  394 Mcguinness Blvd Ste 4 Brooklyn (11222) *(G-2084)*
Lopopolo Iron Works Inc.................................718 339-0572
  2495 Mcdonald Ave Brooklyn (11223) *(G-2085)*
Loral Space & Commnctns Holdng.........................212 697-1105
  600 5th Ave Fl 16 New York (10020) *(G-10255)*
Loral Space Communications Inc (PA).....................212 697-1105
  600 5th Ave Fl 16 New York (10020) *(G-10256)*
Loral Spacecom Corporation (HQ).........................212 697-1105
  565 5th Ave Fl 19 New York (10017) *(G-10257)*
LOreal Usa Inc...212 818-1500
  575 5th Ave Bsmt New York (10017) *(G-10258)*
LOreal Usa Inc...917 606-9554
  435 Hudson St New York (10014) *(G-10259)*
LOreal Usa Inc...212 389-4201
  10 Hudson Yards Fl 27 New York (10001) *(G-10260)*
LOreal Usa Inc...646 658-5477
  1485 5th Ave New York (10035) *(G-10261)*
LOreal USA Products Inc (HQ)............................212 818-1500
  10 Hudson Yards New York (10001) *(G-10262)*
Lorelei Orthotics Prosthetics............................212 727-2011
  30 E 40th St Rm 905 New York (10016) *(G-10263)*
Loreman's, Keeseville *Also called Loremanss Embroidery Engrav (G-6643)*
Loremanss Embroidery Engrav............................518 834-9205
  1599 Front St Keeseville (12944) *(G-6643)*
Lorena Canals USA Inc...................................844 567-3622
  104 Burnside Dr Hastings On Hudson (10706) *(G-5575)*
Lori Silverman Shoes, White Plains *Also called Lsil & Co Inc (G-16026)*
Lornamead Inc...646 745-3643
  175 Cooper Ave Tonawanda (14150) *(G-15119)*
Lornamead Inc (HQ)......................................716 874-7190
  1359 Broadway Fl 17 New York (10018) *(G-10264)*
Los Angles Tmes Cmmnctions LLC.........................212 692-7170
  711 3rd Ave New York (10017) *(G-10265)*
Los Angles Tmes Cmmnctions LLC.........................212 418-9600
  780 3rd Ave Fl 40 New York (10017) *(G-10266)*
Los Olivos Ltd...631 773-6439
  105 Bi County Blvd Farmingdale (11735) *(G-4673)*
Lost Worlds Inc...212 923-3423
  920 Riverside Dr Apt 68 New York (10032) *(G-10267)*
Losurdo Creamery, Heuvelton *Also called Losurdo Foods Inc (G-5867)*
Losurdo Foods Inc.......................................518 842-1500
  78 Sam Stratton Rd Amsterdam (12010) *(G-333)*
Losurdo Foods Inc.......................................315 344-2444
  34 Union St Heuvelton (13654) *(G-5867)*
Lots O' Luv, Syosset *Also called Bektrom Foods Inc (G-14778)*
Lotta Luv Beauty LLC....................................646 786-2847
  1359 Broadway Fl 17 New York (10018) *(G-10268)*
Lotus Apparel Designs Inc...............................646 236-9363
  661 Oakwood Ct Westbury (11590) *(G-15906)*
Lotus Awnings Enterprises Inc...........................718 965-4824
  157 11th St Brooklyn (11215) *(G-2086)*
Lotus Thread, New York *Also called Nasserati Inc (G-10535)*

Lou Sally Fashions Corp (HQ)............................212 354-9670
  1400 Broadway Fl 6 New York (10018) *(G-10269)*
Lou Sally Fashions Corp.................................212 354-1283
  1400 Broadway Frnt 3 New York (10018) *(G-10270)*
Loudon Ltd..631 757-4447
  281 Larkfield Rd East Northport (11731) *(G-4149)*
Loughlin Manufacturing Corp.............................631 585-4422
  1601 9th Ave Bohemia (11716) *(G-1037)*
Louis Heindl & Son Inc...................................585 454-5080
  306 Central Ave Rochester (14605) *(G-13523)*
Louis Iannettoni..315 454-3231
  1841 Lemoyne Ave Syracuse (13208) *(G-14936)*
Louis Schwartz..845 356-6624
  28 Lawrence St Spring Valley (10977) *(G-14577)*
Louis Vuitton North Amer Inc............................212 644-2574
  1000 3rd Ave New York (10022) *(G-10271)*
Louise Blouin Media, New York *Also called Ltb Media (usa) Inc (G-10278)*
Loungehouse LLC..646 524-2965
  34 W 33rd St Fl 11 New York (10001) *(G-10272)*
Lourdes Industries Inc (PA).............................631 234-6600
  65 Hoffman Ave Hauppauge (11788) *(G-5700)*
Lourdes Systems Inc.....................................631 234-7077
  21 Newton Pl Hauppauge (11788) *(G-5701)*
Love & Quiches Desserts, Freeport *Also called Saj of Freeport Corp (G-5021)*
Love Bright Jewelry Inc..................................516 620-2509
  3446 Frederick St Oceanside (11572) *(G-12180)*
Love Charm Clothing, Melville *Also called 18 Rocks LLC (G-7752)*
Love Unlimited NY Inc...................................718 359-8500
  762 Summa Ave Westbury (11590) *(G-15907)*
Lovebrightjewelry.com, Oceanside *Also called Love Bright Jewelry Inc (G-12180)*
Lovee Doll & Toy Co Inc.................................212 242-1545
  39 W 38th St Rm 4w New York (10018) *(G-10273)*
Lovejoy Chaplet Corporation.............................518 686-5232
  12 River St Hoosick Falls (12090) *(G-6084)*
Low-Cost Mfg Co Inc....................................516 627-3282
  318 Westbury Ave Carle Place (11514) *(G-3176)*
Lowel-Light Manufacturing Inc...........................718 921-0600
  140 58th St Ste 8c Brooklyn (11220) *(G-2087)*
Lowville Farmers Coop Inc...............................315 376-6587
  5500 Shady Ave Lowville (13367) *(G-7417)*
Lowville Newspaper Corporation..........................315 376-3525
  7840 State Route 26 Lowville (13367) *(G-7418)*
Loy L Press Inc...716 634-5966
  3959 Union Rd Buffalo (14225) *(G-2853)*
Loyaltyplant Inc (PA)....................................551 221-2701
  70 23 Juno St Forest Hills (11375) *(G-4922)*
LPI Envelope, Bay Shore *Also called 3dflam Inc (G-641)*
Lr Acquisition LLC.......................................212 301-8765
  1407 Broadway Rm 1207 New York (10018) *(G-10274)*
Lr Paris LLC (PA).......................................845 709-8013
  345 7th Ave Fl 19th New York (10001) *(G-10275)*
Lrc Electronics, Horseheads *Also called Belden Inc (G-6114)*
Ls Power Equity Partners LP (PA)........................212 615-3456
  1700 Broadway Fl 35 New York (10019) *(G-10276)*
Lsc Peripherals Incorporated............................631 244-0707
  415 Central Ave Ste F Bohemia (11716) *(G-1038)*
LSI Computer Systems...................................631 271-0400
  1235 Walt Whitman Rd Melville (11747) *(G-7801)*
Lsil & Co Inc..914 761-0998
  2 Greene Ln White Plains (10605) *(G-16026)*
Lt Apparel Group, New York *Also called Lollytogs Ltd (G-10246)*
Lt2 LLC...212 684-1510
  250 Park Ave S Fl 10 New York (10003) *(G-10277)*
Ltb Media (usa) Inc.....................................212 447-9555
  77 Water St Ste 702 New York (10005) *(G-10278)*
Ltdm Incorporated.......................................718 965-1339
  129 48th St Brooklyn (11232) *(G-2088)*
LTS Inc...845 494-2940
  37 Ramland Rd 2 Orangeburg (10962) *(G-12322)*
LTS Ny Inc..646 558-3888
  99 Seaview Blvd Ste 1b Port Washington (11050) *(G-12901)*
Lu Biscuits, White Plains *Also called Great Brands of Europe Inc (G-16010)*
Lubbu Inc...917 693-9600
  20 Payne Ave Sag Harbor (11963) *(G-14099)*
Lucas Dental Equipment Co Inc..........................631 244-2807
  360 Knickerbocker Ave # 4 Bohemia (11716) *(G-1039)*
Lucas Vineyards Inc.....................................607 532-4825
  3862 County Road 150 Interlaken (14847) *(G-6285)*
Lucia Group Inc...631 392-4900
  45 W Jefryn Blvd Ste 108 Deer Park (11729) *(G-3900)*
Lucida Surfaces USA, Tallman *Also called Lucida Usa LLC (G-15032)*
Lucida Usa LLC...845 877-7008
  321 Route 59 Unit 327 Tallman (10982) *(G-15032)*
Lucideon...518 382-0082
  2210 Technology Dr Schenectady (12308) *(G-14287)*
Lucinas Gourmet Food Inc...............................646 835-9784
  3646 37th St Long Island City (11101) *(G-7280)*
Lucky Lous Inc..631 672-1932
  24 State St Lake Grove (11755) *(G-6759)*
Lucky Magazine...212 286-6220
  4 Times Sq Fl 22 New York (10036) *(G-10279)*

Lucky Peach LLC	212 228-0031
60 E 11th St Fl 5 New York (10003) *(G-10280)*	
Ludl Electronic Products Ltd	914 769-6111
171 Brady Ave Ste 2 Hawthorne (10532) *(G-5818)*	
Ludlow Music Inc	212 594-9795
266 W 37th St Fl 17 New York (10018) *(G-10281)*	
Ludwig and Larsen	718 369-0999
4655 Metro Ave Ste 201 Ridgewood (11385) *(G-13151)*	
Lugo Nutrition Inc	302 573-2503
51 N Broadway Ste 2 Nyack (10960) *(G-12145)*	
Lukas Lighting Inc	800 841-4011
4020 22nd St Ste 11 Long Island City (11101) *(G-7281)*	
Luke's Copy Shop, Staten Island *Also called R & L Press of SI Inc (G-14697)*	
Lukoil Americas Corporation (HQ)	212 421-4141
505 5th Ave Fl 9 New York (10017) *(G-10282)*	
Luluvise Inc	914 309-7812
229 W 116th St Apt 5a New York (10026) *(G-10283)*	
Lumazu LLC	518 623-3372
141 Garnet Lake Rd Warrensburg (12885) *(G-15503)*	
Lumazu LLC (PA)	518 623-3372
484 S Johnsburg Rd Warrensburg (12885) *(G-15504)*	
Lumetrics Inc	585 214-2455
1565 Jefferson Rd Ste 420 Rochester (14623) *(G-13524)*	
Luminary Publishing Inc	845 334-8600
314 Wall St Kingston (12401) *(G-6701)*	
Luminati Aerospace LLC	631 574-2616
400 David Ct Calverton (11933) *(G-3082)*	
Luminatta Inc	914 664-3600
717 S 3rd Ave Mount Vernon (10550) *(G-8159)*	
Luminescent Systems Inc (HQ)	716 655-0800
130 Commerce Way East Aurora (14052) *(G-4091)*	
Luna Luz, New York *Also called Azibi Ltd (G-8701)*	
Lunzer Inc	201 794-2800
305 E 86th St New York (10028) *(G-10284)*	
Luria Communications Inc	631 329-4922
31 Shorewood Dr Fl 1 East Hampton (11937) *(G-4125)*	
Lutz Feed Co Inc	607 432-7984
80 Lower River St Oneonta (13820) *(G-12273)*	
Luvente, Long Island City *Also called Benlee Enterprises LLC (G-7176)*	
Lux Mundi Corp	631 244-4596
1595 Ocean Ave Ste B12 Bohemia (11716) *(G-1040)*	
Luxcore Networks Inc (PA)	212 618-1724
14 Wall St Fl 20 New York (10005) *(G-10285)*	
Luxe Imagine Consulting LLC	212 273-9770
261 W 35th St Ste 404 New York (10001) *(G-10286)*	
Luxerdame Co Inc	718 752-9800
4315 Queens St Ste A Long Island City (11101) *(G-7282)*	
Luxfer Magtech Inc	631 727-8600
680 Elton St Riverhead (11901) *(G-13181)*	
Luxottica of America Inc	516 484-3800
44 Harbor Park Dr Port Washington (11050) *(G-12902)*	
Luxury Daily, New York *Also called Napean LLC (G-10533)*	
Lvl Xiii Brands Inc	646 530-2795
315 W 39th St Rm 1201 New York (10018) *(G-10287)*	
Lwa Works Inc	518 271-8360
2622 7th Ave Ste 50s Watervliet (12189) *(G-15604)*	
Lycian Stage Lighting, Chester *Also called Ric-Lo Productions Ltd (G-3384)*	
Lydall Performance Mtls Inc	518 273-6320
68 George St Green Island (12183) *(G-5439)*	
Lydall Performance Mtls US Inc	315 592-8100
2885 State Route 481 Fulton (13069) *(G-5070)*	
Lydall Performance Mtls US Inc	315 346-3100
9635 Main St Beaver Falls (13305) *(G-760)*	
Lydall Performance Mtls US Inc	518 686-3400
12 Davis St Hoosick Falls (12090) *(G-6085)*	
Lydall Thermal/Acoustical Inc	518 273-6320
68 George St Green Island (12183) *(G-5440)*	
Lyn Jo Enterprises Ltd	716 753-2776
136 Fredrick Blvd Jamestown (14701) *(G-6530)*	
Lyn Jo Kitchens Inc	718 336-6060
1679 Mcdonald Ave Brooklyn (11230) *(G-2089)*	
Lynch Knitting Mills Inc	718 821-3436
538 Johnson Ave Brooklyn (11237) *(G-2090)*	
Lyndaker Timber Harvesting LLC	315 346-1328
10204 State Route 812 Castorland (13620) *(G-3208)*	
Lynmar Printing Corp	631 957-8500
8600 New Horizons Blvd Amityville (11701) *(G-292)*	
Lynn Brands LLC	212 921-5495
230 W 38th St Fl 12 New York (10018) *(G-10288)*	
Lynn Brands LLC	626 376-8948
729 Seventh Ave New York (10019) *(G-10289)*	
Lynne B Enterprises Inc	631 254-6975
593 Acorn St Ste B Deer Park (11729) *(G-3901)*	
Lyntronics Inc	631 205-1061
7 Old Dock Rd Unit 1 Yaphank (11980) *(G-16265)*	
Lynx Product Group LLC	716 751-3100
650 Lake St Wilson (14172) *(G-16153)*	
Lyophilization Systems Inc	845 338-0456
14 Hickory Hill Rd New Paltz (12561) *(G-8309)*	
Lyteline LLC	657 333-5983
175 Varick St Fl 8 New York (10014) *(G-10290)*	
M & C Furniture	718 422-2136
375 Park Ave Brooklyn (11205) *(G-2091)*	

M & D Fire Door, Brooklyn *Also called M & D Installers Inc (G-2092)*	
M & D Installers Inc (PA)	718 782-6978
70 Flushing Ave Ste 1 Brooklyn (11205) *(G-2092)*	
M & E Mfg Co Inc	845 331-7890
19 Progress St Kingston (12401) *(G-6702)*	
M & H Research and Dev Corp	607 734-2346
471 Post Creek Rd Beaver Dams (14812) *(G-759)*	
M & J Custom Lampshade Company, Brooklyn *Also called Mjk Enterprises LLC (G-2163)*	
M & L Steel & Ornamental Iron	718 816-8660
27 Housman Ave Staten Island (10303) *(G-14678)*	
M & M Bagel Corp	516 295-1222
507 Central Ave Cedarhurst (11516) *(G-3240)*	
M & M Food Products Inc	718 821-1970
286 Scholes St Brooklyn (11206) *(G-2093)*	
M & M Molding Corp	631 582-1900
250 Creative Dr Central Islip (11722) *(G-3283)*	
M & R Design, New York *Also called Mrinalini Inc (G-10513)*	
M & R Woodworking & Finishing	718 486-5480
49 Withers St Brooklyn (11211) *(G-2094)*	
M & S Precision Machine Co LLC	518 747-1193
27 Casey Rd Queensbury (12804) *(G-13048)*	
M & S Quality Co Ltd	212 302-8757
26 W 47th St Ste 502 New York (10036) *(G-10291)*	
M & S Schmalberg Inc	212 244-2090
242 W 36th St Rm 700 New York (10018) *(G-10292)*	
M & W Aluminum Products Inc	315 414-0005
321 Wavel St Syracuse (13206) *(G-14937)*	
M &L Industry of NY Inc	845 827-6255
583 State Route 32 Ste 1u Highland Mills (10930) *(G-5968)*	
M A C, Elmsford *Also called Magnetic Analysis Corporation (G-4415)*	
M A Moslow & Bros Inc	716 896-2950
375 Norfolk Ave Buffalo (14215) *(G-2854)*	
M A R A Metals Ltd	718 786-7868
2520 40th Ave Long Island City (11101) *(G-7283)*	
M and J Hair Connection Inc	516 872-1010
1103 Stewart Ave Ste 100 Garden City (11530) *(G-5106)*	
M B C Metal Inc	718 384-6713
68 Lombardy St Brooklyn (11222) *(G-2095)*	
M B M Manufacturing Inc	718 769-4148
331 Rutledge St Ste 203 Brooklyn (11211) *(G-2096)*	
M C Kitchen & Bath, Brooklyn *Also called M & C Furniture (G-2091)*	
M C Packaging Corp Plant, Babylon *Also called M C Packaging Corporation (G-522)*	
M C Packaging Corporation (PA)	631 694-3012
120-200 Adams Blvd Farmingdale (11735) *(G-4674)*	
M C Packaging Corporation	631 643-3763
300 Governor Ave Babylon (11704) *(G-522)*	
M C Products	631 471-4070
1330 Lincoln Ave Ste 2 Holbrook (11741) *(G-6008)*	
M D I, Shirley *Also called Modular Devices Inc (G-14425)*	
M D I Industries, Deer Park *Also called MD International Industries (G-3906)*	
M D L, New York *Also called Meryl Diamond Ltd (G-10439)*	
M F L B Inc	631 254-8300
38 Eastgate Rd Massapequa Park (11762) *(G-7658)*	
M F Manufacturing Enterprises	516 822-5135
2 Ballad Ln Hicksville (11801) *(G-5924)*	
M Factory USA Inc	917 410-7878
147 41st St Unit 8 Brooklyn (11232) *(G-2097)*	
M G New York Inc	212 371-5566
14 E 60th St Ste 400 New York (10022) *(G-10293)*	
M H Mandelbaum Orthotic	631 473-8668
116 Oakland Ave Port Jefferson (11777) *(G-12842)*	
M H Manufacturing Incorporated	212 461-6900
50 W 47th St New York (10036) *(G-10294)*	
M H Stryke Co Inc	631 242-2660
181 E Industry Ct Ste A Deer Park (11729) *(G-3902)*	
M Heskia Company Inc	212 768-1845
98 Cutter Rd Ste 125 New York (10036) *(G-10295)*	
M Hidary & Co Inc	212 736-6540
10 W 33rd St Rm 900 New York (10001) *(G-10296)*	
M I, Hauppauge *Also called Mason Industries Inc (G-5708)*	
M I I, Mamaroneck *Also called Marval Industries Inc (G-7514)*	
M I T Poly-Cart Corp	212 724-7290
211 Central Park W New York (10024) *(G-10297)*	
M J K, Brooklyn *Also called Mjk Cutting Inc (G-2162)*	
M J M Tooling Corp	718 292-3590
1059 Washington Ave Bronx (10456) *(G-1305)*	
M K S, Rochester *Also called Mks Medical Electronics (G-13555)*	
M K Ulrich Construction Inc	716 893-5777
1601 Harlem Rd Buffalo (14206) *(G-2855)*	
M L A, New York *Also called Modern Language Assn Amer Inc (G-10488)*	
M L Design Inc (PA)	212 233-0213
77 Ludlow St Frnt 1 New York (10002) *(G-10298)*	
M M Tool and Manufacturing	845 691-4140
175 Chapel Hill Rd Highland (12528) *(G-5961)*	
M M Welding	315 363-3980
558 Lenox Ave Oneida (13421) *(G-12247)*	
M Manastrip-M Corporation	518 664-2089
821 Main St Clifton Park (12065) *(G-3467)*	
M O S S Communications, Franklin Square *Also called Movin On Sounds and SEC Inc (G-4962)*	

ALPHABETIC

M P I, Tarrytown *Also called Micro Powders Inc* ***(G-15048)***
M P X, Melville *Also called Military Parts Exchange LLC* ***(G-7805)***
M R C, Buffalo *Also called Tchnologies N MRC Ameerica LLC* ***(G-3003)***
M R C Industries Inc 516 328-6900
99 Seaview Blvd Ste 210 Port Washington (11050) ***(G-12903)***
M S B International Ltd (PA) 212 302-5551
1412 Broadway Rm 1210 New York (10018) ***(G-10299)***
M S Riviera Inc 212 391-0206
42 W 48th St Fl 4 New York (10036) ***(G-10300)***
M Santoliquido Corp 914 375-6674
925 Saw Mill River Rd Yonkers (10710) ***(G-16329)***
M Shanken Communications Inc (PA) 212 684-4224
825 8th Ave Fl 33 New York (10019) ***(G-10301)***
M Squared Graphics, Oyster Bay *Also called Miroddi Imaging Inc* ***(G-12450)***
M T D Corporation 631 491-3905
41 Otis St West Babylon (11704) ***(G-15727)***
M T M Printing Co Inc 718 353-3297
2321 College Point Blvd College Point (11356) ***(G-3552)***
M V Sport, Bay Shore *Also called Mv Corp Inc* ***(G-695)***
M W Microwave Corp 516 295-1814
45 Auerbach Ln Lawrence (11559) ***(G-6887)***
M&A Metals, Brooklyn *Also called Interior Metals* ***(G-1963)***
M&C Associates LLC 631 467-8760
700 Vets Memrl Hwy 335 Hauppauge (11788) ***(G-5702)***
M&F Stringing LLC 914 664-1600
2 Cortlandt St Mount Vernon (10550) ***(G-8160)***
M&H Soaring, Beaver Dams *Also called M & H Research and Dev Corp* ***(G-759)***
M&M Printing Inc 516 796-3020
245 Westbury Ave Carle Place (11514) ***(G-3177)***
M/Wbe, Brooklyn *Also called Active World Solutions Inc* ***(G-1459)***
M2 Apparel, New York *Also called M2 Fashion Group Holdings Inc* ***(G-10302)***
M2 Fashion Group Holdings Inc 917 208-2948
153 E 87th St Apt 10d New York (10128) ***(G-10302)***
M2 Race Systems Inc 607 882-9078
53 Enfield Main Rd Ithaca (14850) ***(G-6393)***
Mac Artspray Finishing Corp 718 649-3800
799 Sheffield Ave Brooklyn (11207) ***(G-2098)***
Mac Crete Corporation 718 932-1803
3412 10th St Long Island City (11106) ***(G-7284)***
Mac Donuts of New York, Long Island City *Also called Mac Crete Corporation* ***(G-7284)***
Mac Fadden Holdings Inc (PA) 212 979-4805
333 7th Ave Fl 11 New York (10001) ***(G-10303)***
Mac Swed Inc 212 684-7730
20 W 36th St Rm 5l New York (10018) ***(G-10304)***
Mac-Artspray Finshg, Brooklyn *Also called Mac Artspray Finishing Corp* ***(G-2098)***
Macabee Foods LLC 845 623-1300
250 W Nyack Rd Ste 110 West Nyack (10994) ***(G-15826)***
Macadame Inc 212 477-1930
68 34th St Unit 6 Brooklyn (11232) ***(G-2099)***
Macadoodles 607 652-9019
26 River St Stamford (12167) ***(G-14608)***
Macandrews & Forbes Inc (PA) 212 572-8600
35 E 62nd St New York (10065) ***(G-10305)***
Macaran Printed Products, Cohoes *Also called W N Vanalstine & Sons Inc* ***(G-3520)***
Macauto Usa Inc (HQ) 585 342-2060
80 Excel Dr Rochester (14621) ***(G-13525)***
Macedonia Ltd 718 462-3596
34 E 29th St Brooklyn (11226) ***(G-2100)***
Macfadden Cmmnctions Group LLC 212 979-4800
333 7th Ave Fl 11 New York (10001) ***(G-10306)***
Machias Furniture Factory Inc (PA) 716 353-8687
3638 Route 242 Machias (14101) ***(G-7472)***
Machida Incorporated 845 365-0600
40 Ramland Rd S Ste 1 Orangeburg (10962) ***(G-12323)***
Machina Deus Lex Inc 917 577-0972
15921 Grand Central Pkwy Jamaica (11432) ***(G-6455)***
Machine Clothing Company, New York *Also called Billion Tower Intl LLC* ***(G-8791)***
Machine Components Corp 516 694-7222
70 Newtown Rd Plainview (11803) ***(G-12698)***
Machine Technology Inc 845 454-4030
104 Bushwick Rd Poughkeepsie (12603) ***(G-12968)***
Machinecraft Inc 585 436-1070
1645 Lyell Ave Ste 125 Rochester (14606) ***(G-13526)***
Machinery Mountings Inc 631 851-0480
41 Sarah Dr Hauppauge (11788) ***(G-5703)***
Machinit Inc 631 454-9297
400 Smith St Farmingdale (11735) ***(G-4675)***
Macinnes Tool Corporation 585 467-1920
1700 Hudson Ave Ste 3 Rochester (14617) ***(G-13527)***
Mack Studios Displays Inc 315 252-7542
5500 Technology Park Blvd Auburn (13021) ***(G-484)***
Mack Wood Working 845 657-6625
2792 State Route 28 Shokan (12481) ***(G-14429)***
Mackenzie-Childs LLC (PA) 315 364-6118
3260 State Route 90 Aurora (13026) ***(G-504)***
Maclean Curtis, Buffalo *Also called Curtis L Maclean L C* ***(G-2715)***
Macmillan College Pubg Co Inc 212 702-2000
866 3rd Ave Frnt 2 New York (10022) ***(G-10307)***
Macmillan Holdings LLC 212 576-9428
1 New York Plz Ste 4500 New York (10004) ***(G-10308)***
Macmillan Publishers Inc 646 307-5151
175 5th Ave Ste 400 New York (10010) ***(G-10309)***
Macmillan Publishing Group LLC (HQ) 212 674-5145
175 5th Ave New York (10010) ***(G-10310)***
Macneil Polymers Inc (PA) 716 681-7755
3155 Broadway St Buffalo (14227) ***(G-2856)***
Maco Bag Corporation 315 226-1000
412 Van Buren St Newark (14513) ***(G-11844)***
Macro Tool & Machine Company 845 223-3824
1397 Route 55 Lagrangeville (12540) ***(G-6750)***
Macrolink Inc 631 924-8200
25 Industrial Blvd Ste 1 Medford (11763) ***(G-7718)***
Mad Scntsts Brwing Prtners LLC 347 766-2739
40 Van Dyke St Brooklyn (11231) ***(G-2101)***
Madame Alexander Doll 2018 LLC 917 576-8381
600 3rd Ave Fl 2 New York (10016) ***(G-10311)***
Madame Alexander Doll Co LLC 212 244-4500
112 W 34th St Ste 1410 New York (10120) ***(G-10312)***
Made Close LLC 917 837-1357
141 Meserole Ave Brooklyn (11222) ***(G-2102)***
Made Fresh Daily 212 285-2253
226 Front St New York (10038) ***(G-10313)***
Madhat Inc 518 947-0732
149 Sullivan St Apt 3e New York (10012) ***(G-10314)***
Madison & Dunn 585 563-7760
850 Saint Paul St Ste 29 Rochester (14605) ***(G-13528)***
Madison County Distillery LLC 315 391-6070
2420 Rte 20 Cazenovia (13035) ***(G-3229)***
Madison Lifestyle Ny LLC (PA) 212 725-4002
1412 Broadway Rm 1610 New York (10018) ***(G-10315)***
Madison Manufacturing, Hamilton *Also called James Morris* ***(G-5527)***
Madison Mfg & Mch Inc 315 922-4476
3882 Sanderson Rd Erieville (13061) ***(G-4484)***
Madison Printing Corp 607 273-3535
704 W Buffalo St Ithaca (14850) ***(G-6394)***
Madison Square Press, New York *Also called Annuals Publishing Co Inc* ***(G-8594)***
Madjek Inc 631 842-4475
185 Dixon Ave Amityville (11701) ***(G-293)***
Madoff Energy III LLC 212 744-1918
319 Lafayette St New York (10012) ***(G-10316)***
Madonna, New York *Also called Haddad Bros Inc* ***(G-9706)***
Maehr Industries Inc 631 924-1661
14 Sawgrass Dr Bellport (11713) ***(G-802)***
Maesa Engineering Beauty, New York *Also called Maesa LLC* ***(G-10317)***
Maesa LLC (HQ) 212 674-5555
40 Worth St Rm 705 New York (10013) ***(G-10317)***
Mafco Consolidated Group Inc (HQ) 212 572-8600
35 E 62nd St New York (10065) ***(G-10318)***
Mag Brands LLC 212 629-9600
463 7th Ave Fl 4 New York (10018) ***(G-10319)***
Mag Inc 607 257-6970
20 Eastlake Rd Ithaca (14850) ***(G-6395)***
Magazine Group, New York *Also called Thomas Publishing Company LLC* ***(G-11470)***
Magazine I Spectrum E 212 419-7555
3 Park Ave Fl 17 New York (10016) ***(G-10320)***
Magazines & Brochures Inc 716 875-9699
2205 Kenmore Ave Ste 107 Buffalo (14207) ***(G-2857)***
Magcrest Packaging Inc 845 425-0451
5 Highview Rd Monsey (10952) ***(G-8039)***
Mageba USA LLC 212 317-1991
575 Lexington Ave Fl 4 New York (10022) ***(G-10321)***
Magee Canvas & Trailer Sales, Brewerton *Also called Geordie Magee Uphl & Canvas* ***(G-1135)***
Magellan Aerospace Bethel Inc 203 798-9373
9711 50th Ave Corona (11368) ***(G-3743)***
Magellan Aerospace NY Inc (HQ) 718 699-4000
9711 50th Ave Corona (11368) ***(G-3744)***
Magellan Aerospace NY Inc 631 589-2440
25 Aero Rd Bohemia (11716) ***(G-1041)***
Magellan Aerospace Processing 631 694-1818
165 Field St West Babylon (11704) ***(G-15728)***
Mager & Gougelman Inc (PA) 212 661-3939
345 E 37th St Rm 316 New York (10016) ***(G-10322)***
Mager & Gougelman Inc 212 661-3939
230 Hilton Ave Ste 112 Hempstead (11550) ***(G-5844)***
Maggio Data Forms 631 348-0343
1735 Express Dr S Hauppauge (11788) ***(G-5704)***
Maggy London Blouse Div, New York *Also called Maggy London International Ltd* ***(G-10323)***
Maggy London International Ltd (PA) 212 944-7199
225 W 37th St Fl 7 New York (10018) ***(G-10323)***
Magic Brands International LLC 212 563-4999
31 W 34th St Rm 401 New York (10001) ***(G-10324)***
Magic Maestro Music, New York *Also called Simon & Simon LLC* ***(G-11245)***
Magic Novelty Co Inc (PA) 212 304-2777
308 Dyckman St New York (10034) ***(G-10325)***
Magic Numbers Inc 646 839-8578
29 Little West 12th St New York (10014) ***(G-10326)***
Magic Reed 914 630-4006
723 Larchmont Acres Apt D Larchmont (10538) ***(G-6842)***
Magic Software Inc 646 827-9788
1 Penn Plz Ste 2412 New York (10119) ***(G-10327)***

Magic Tank LLC 877 646-2442
80 Maiden Ln Rm 2204 New York (10038) *(G-10328)*
Magic Tech Co Ltd 516 539-7944
401 Hempstead Tpke West Hempstead (11552) *(G-15775)*
Magic Touch Icewares Intl 212 794-2852
220 E 72nd St Apt 11g New York (10021) *(G-10329)*
Magna Products Corp 585 647-2280
777 Mount Read Blvd Rochester (14606) *(G-13529)*
Magnaworks Technology Inc 631 218-3431
36 Carlough Rd Unit H Bohemia (11716) *(G-1042)*
Magnesium Technologies Corp 905 689-7361
266 Elmwood Ave Buffalo (14222) *(G-2858)*
Magnet Wire Division, Edgewood *Also called Weico Wire & Cable Inc (G-4292)*
Magnet-Ndctive Systems Ltd USA 585 924-4000
7625 Omnitech Pl Victor (14564) *(G-15419)*
Magnetic Aids Inc 845 863-1400
1160 Route 9w Marlboro (12542) *(G-7580)*
Magnetic Analysis Corporation (PA) 914 530-2000
103 Fairview Pk Dr Ste 2 Elmsford (10523) *(G-4415)*
Magnetic Technologies Corp (HQ) 585 385-9010
770 Linden Ave Rochester (14625) *(G-13530)*
Magnetic Technology, Rochester *Also called Arnold Magnetic Tech Corp (G-13246)*
Magnificat Inc 914 502-1820
86 Main St Ste 303 Yonkers (10701) *(G-16330)*
Magniflood Inc 631 226-1000
7200 New Horizons Blvd Amityville (11701) *(G-294)*
Magnum Creation Inc 212 869-2600
23 W 47th St Fl 5 New York (10036) *(G-10330)*
Magnum Shielding Corporation 585 381-9957
3800 Monroe Ave Ste 14f Pittsford (14534) *(G-12648)*
Magnus Precision Mfg Inc 315 548-8032
1912 State Route 96 Phelps (14532) *(G-12605)*
Magnus Sands Point Shop, Port Washington *Also called Robert Bartholomew Ltd (G-12919)*
Magtrol Inc 716 668-5555
70 Gardenville Pkwy W Buffalo (14224) *(G-2859)*
Maharlika Holdings LLC 631 319-6203
111 Trade Zone Ct Unit A Ronkonkoma (11779) *(G-13968)*
Mahin Impressions Inc 212 871-9777
30 W Main St Ste 301 Riverhead (11901) *(G-13182)*
Mahle Behr Troy Inc 716 439-3039
350 Upper Mountain Rd Lockport (14094) *(G-7088)*
Mahle Behr USA Inc 716 439-2011
350 Upper Mountain Rd Lockport (14094) *(G-7089)*
Mahle Indstrbeteiligungen GMBH 716 319-6700
4236 Ridge Lea Rd Amherst (14226) *(G-231)*
Mahle Manufacturing MGT Inc (HQ) 248 735-3623
4236 Ridge Lea Rd Amherst (14226) *(G-232)*
Maia Systems LLC 718 206-0100
8344 Parsons Blvd Ste 101 Jamaica (11432) *(G-6456)*
Maidenform LLC 201 436-9200
260 Madison Ave Fl 6 New York (10016) *(G-10331)*
Mailers-Pblsher Wlfare Tr Fund 212 869-5986
1501 Broadway New York (10036) *(G-10332)*
Main Street Connect LLC 203 803-4110
200 Business Park Dr # 209 Armonk (10504) *(G-400)*
Mainly Monograms Inc 845 624-4923
260 W Nyack Rd Ste 1 West Nyack (10994) *(G-15827)*
Maio Fuel Company LP 914 683-1154
46 Fairview Ave White Plains (10603) *(G-16027)*
Maison Goyard, New York *Also called Goyard Miami LLC (G-9651)*
Maiyet Inc (PA) 212 343-9999
16 Crosby St Apt Corp New York (10013) *(G-10333)*
Maizteca Foods Inc 718 641-3933
13005 Liberty Ave South Richmond Hill (11419) *(G-14523)*
Majestic Curtains LLC 718 898-0774
4410 Ketcham St Apt 2g Elmhurst (11373) *(G-4336)*
Majestic Home Imprvs Distr 718 853-5079
5902 Fort Hamilton Pkwy Brooklyn (11219) *(G-2103)*
Majestic Mold & Tool Inc 315 695-2079
177 Volney St Phoenix (13135) *(G-12617)*
Majestic Rayon Corporation 212 929-6443
54 W 21st St Rm 1005 New York (10010) *(G-10334)*
Majesty Brands LLC 212 283-3400
469 7th Ave Rm 1301 New York (10018) *(G-10335)*
Major-IPC Inc 845 292-2200
53 Webster Ave Liberty (12754) *(G-6925)*
Makamah Enterprises Inc 631 231-0200
89 Cabot Ct Ste C Hauppauge (11788) *(G-5705)*
Makarenko Studios Inc 914 968-7673
2984 Saddle Ridge Dr Yorktown Heights (10598) *(G-16367)*
Makari, New York *Also called Victoria Albi International (G-11677)*
Make-Waves Instrument Corp (PA) 716 681-7524
4172 Vinewood Dr Buffalo (14221) *(G-2860)*
Makerbot Industries LLC (HQ) 347 334-6800
1 Metrotech Ctr Fl 21 Brooklyn (11201) *(G-2104)*
Makers Nutrition LLC (PA) 631 456-5397
315 Oser Ave Ste 1 Hauppauge (11788) *(G-5706)*
Makers Nutrition LLC 844 625-3771
71s Mall Dr Commack (11725) *(G-3594)*
Makiplastic 716 772-2222
4904 Gasport Rd Gasport (14067) *(G-5138)*
Maks Pharma & Diagnostics Inc 631 270-1528
2365 Milburn Ave Bldg 2 Baldwin (11510) *(G-532)*

Malcon Inc 914 666-7146
405 Adams St Bedford Hills (10507) *(G-770)*
Male Power Apparel, Hauppauge *Also called Comme-Ci Comme-CA AP Group (G-5623)*
Malhame Publs & Importers Inc 631 694-8600
180 Orville Dr Unit A Bohemia (11716) *(G-1043)*
Malia Mills, Brooklyn *Also called IaMmaliamills LLC (G-1950)*
Malia Mills Inc 212 354-4200
32 33rd St Unit 13 Brooklyn (11232) *(G-2105)*
Malibu Cabinets, Suffern *Also called American Best Cabinets Inc (G-14757)*
Malin + Goetz Inc (PA) 212 244-7771
330 7th Ave Ste 2100 New York (10001) *(G-10336)*
Malina Management Company Inc 607 535-9614
3620 County Road 16 Montour Falls (14865) *(G-8075)*
Malisa Branko Inc 631 225-9741
95 Garfield Ave Copiague (11726) *(G-3663)*
Mall Inc 315 751-9490
4876 Bethel Rd Cazenovia (13035) *(G-3230)*
Mallery Lumber LLC 607 637-2236
158 Labarre St Hancock (13783) *(G-5537)*
Mallinckrodt Pharmaceuticals, Hobart *Also called Specgx LLC (G-5979)*
Mallory & Church LLC 212 868-7888
552 Fashion Ave Rm 202 New York (10018) *(G-10337)*
Malone Concrete Products Div, Malone *Also called Upstone Materials Inc (G-7493)*
Malone Industrial Press Inc 518 483-5880
10 Stevens St Malone (12953) *(G-7488)*
Malone News, Malone *Also called Johnson Newspaper Corporation (G-7486)*
Malone Welding, Montour Falls *Also called Robert M Brown (G-8076)*
Malouf Colette Inc 212 941-9588
27 E 28th St New York (10016) *(G-10338)*
Maloya Laser Inc 631 543-2327
65a Mall Dr Ste 1 Commack (11725) *(G-3595)*
Malyn Industrial Ceramics Inc 716 741-1510
8640 Roll Rd Clarence Center (14032) *(G-3448)*
Mam Molding Inc 607 433-2121
147 River St Oneonta (13820) *(G-12274)*
Mam USA Corporation 914 269-2500
2700 Westchester Ave # 315 Purchase (10577) *(G-13007)*
Mamco, Oneonta *Also called Mold-A-Matic Corporation (G-12276)*
Mamma Says, Ferndale *Also called Chipita America Inc (G-4787)*
Man of World 212 915-0017
25 W 39th St Fl 5 New York (10018) *(G-10339)*
Man Products Inc 631 789-6500
99 Milbar Blvd Unit 1 Farmingdale (11735) *(G-4676)*
Mana Products Inc (PA) 718 361-2550
3202 Queens Blvd Fl 6 Long Island City (11101) *(G-7285)*
Mana Products Inc 718 361-5204
3202 Queens Blvd Fl 6 Long Island City (11101) *(G-7286)*
Manacraft Precision Inc 914 654-0967
945 Spring Rd Pelham (10803) *(G-12567)*
Manchester Newspaper Inc (PA) 518 642-1234
14 E Main St Granville (12832) *(G-5350)*
Manchester Wood Inc 518 642-9518
1159 County Route 24 Granville (12832) *(G-5351)*
Manchu New York Inc 212 921-5050
530 Fashion Ave Rm 1906 New York (10018) *(G-10340)*
Manchu Times Fashion Inc 212 921-5050
530 Sventh Ave Ste 1906 New York (10018) *(G-10341)*
Mancum Graphics, New York *Also called Mc Squared Nyc Inc (G-10395)*
Mandarin Soy Sauce Inc 845 343-1505
4 Sands Station Rd Middletown (10940) *(G-7918)*
MANE Enterprises Inc 718 472-4955
4929 30th Pl Long Island City (11101) *(G-7287)*
Mango Usa Inc 718 998-6050
5620 1st Ave Ste 1 Brooklyn (11220) *(G-2106)*
Manhasset Tool & Die Co Inc 716 684-6066
4270 Walden Ave Lancaster (14086) *(G-6816)*
Manhattan Cabinets Inc 212 548-2436
1349 2nd Ave New York (10021) *(G-10342)*
Manhattan Comfort Inc (PA) 908 888-0818
1482 Carroll St Brooklyn (11213) *(G-2107)*
Manhattan Cooling Towers Inc 212 279-1045
1142 46th Rd Ste 2 Long Island City (11101) *(G-7288)*
Manhattan Display Inc 718 392-1365
1215 Jackson Ave Ste B Long Island City (11101) *(G-7289)*
Manhattan Eastside Dev Corp 212 305-3275
622 W 168th St Ste Vc333 New York (10032) *(G-10343)*
Manhattan Map Co, New York *Also called Yale Robbins Inc (G-11805)*
Manhattan Media LLC (PA) 212 268-8600
535 5th Ave Fl 23 New York (10017) *(G-10344)*
Manhattan Milling & Drying Co 516 496-1041
78 Pond Rd Woodbury (11797) *(G-16177)*
Manhattan Poly Bag Corporation 917 689-7549
1228 47th St Brooklyn (11219) *(G-2108)*
Manhattan Scientifics Inc (PA) 212 541-2405
405 Lexington Ave Fl 26 New York (10174) *(G-10345)*
Manhattan Shade & Glass Co Inc (PA) 212 288-5616
37 Pond Park Rd Great Neck (11023) *(G-5402)*
Manhattan Shade & Glass Co Inc 212 288-5616
135 Ricefield Ln Hauppauge (11788) *(G-5707)*
Manhattan Signs, Floral Park *Also called Decree Signs & Graphics Inc (G-4814)*

ALPHABETIC

Manhattan Special Bottling....718 388-4144
342 Manhattan Ave Brooklyn (11211) *(G-2109)*
Manhattan Times Inc....212 569-5800
5030 Broadway Ste 801 New York (10034) *(G-10346)*
Manhole Brrier SEC Systems Inc....516 741-1032
8002 Kew Gardens Rd # 901 Kew Gardens (11415) *(G-6668)*
Manifestation-Glow Press Inc....718 380-5259
8471 Parsons Blvd Jamaica (11432) *(G-6457)*
Manifold Center, The, Medford *Also called B & R Industries Inc (G-7698)*
Manitou Concrete....585 424-6040
1260 Jefferson Rd Rochester (14623) *(G-13531)*
Mann Consultants LLC....914 763-0512
67 Chapel Rd Waccabuc (10597) *(G-15446)*
Mann Publications Inc....212 840-6266
450 Fashion Ave Ste 2306 New York (10123) *(G-10347)*
Mannesmann Corporation....212 258-4000
601 Lexington Ave Fl 56 New York (10022) *(G-10348)*
Manning Lewis Div Rubicon Inds....908 687-2400
848 E 43rd St Brooklyn (11210) *(G-2110)*
Mannix, Brentwood *Also called Interstate Window Corporation (G-1123)*
Manny Grunberg Inc....212 302-6173
62 W 47th St Ste 703 New York (10036) *(G-10349)*
Mannys Cheesecake Inc....315 732-0639
1221 Pleasant St Utica (13501) *(G-15280)*
Manrico Cashmere, New York *Also called Manrico Usa Inc (G-10350)*
Manrico Usa Inc....212 794-4200
922 Madison Ave New York (10021) *(G-10350)*
Manrico Usa Inc (PA)....212 794-4200
922 Madison Ave New York (10021) *(G-10351)*
Mansfield Press Inc....212 265-5411
599 11th Ave Fl 3 New York (10036) *(G-10352)*
Mansueto Ventures LLC....212 389-5300
7 World Trade Ctr Fl 29 New York (10007) *(G-10353)*
Mantel & Mantel Stamping Corp....631 467-1916
802 S 4th St Ronkonkoma (11779) *(G-13969)*
Manth Mfg Inc....716 693-6525
131 Fillmore Ave Tonawanda (14150) *(G-15120)*
Manth-Brownell Inc....315 687-7263
1120 Fyler Rd Kirkville (13082) *(G-6724)*
Manufacturers Indexing Pdts....631 271-0956
53 Gristmill Ln Halesite (11743) *(G-5488)*
Manufacturers Tool & Die Co....585 352-1080
3 Turner Dr Spencerport (14559) *(G-14558)*
Manufacturing, Lockport *Also called Hti Recycling LLC (G-7083)*
Manufacturing & Tech Entp Ctr, Highland *Also called Hudson Valley Tech Dev Ctr Inc (G-5960)*
Manufacturing Facility, Middletown *Also called President Cont Group II LLC (G-7927)*
Manufacturing Resources Inc....631 481-0041
2392 Innovation Way # 4 Rochester (14624) *(G-13532)*
Manufacturing Solutions Inc....585 235-3320
850 Saint Paul St Ste 11 Rochester (14605) *(G-13533)*
Manzella Knitting....716 825-0808
3345 N Benzing Rd Orchard Park (14127) *(G-12363)*
Manzione Enterprises, Brooklyn *Also called Manzione Ready Mix Corp (G-2111)*
Manzione Ready Mix Corp....718 628-3837
46 Knickerbocker Ave Brooklyn (11237) *(G-2111)*
Mapeasy Inc....631 537-6213
54 Industrial Rd Wainscott (11975) *(G-15455)*
Maple Grove and Enterprises, Arcade *Also called Maple Grove Corp (G-377)*
Maple Grove Corp....585 492-5286
7075 Route 98 Arcade (14009) *(G-377)*
Maple Hill Creamery LLC (PA)....518 758-7777
285 Allendale Rd W Stuyvesant (12173) *(G-14754)*
Maple Tree Kitchen & Bath Inc....845 236-3660
1108 Route 9w Marlboro (12542) *(G-7581)*
Maplehurst Bakeries LLC....315 735-5000
178 Industrial Park Dr Frankfort (13340) *(G-4953)*
Mapleland Farms LLC....518 854-7669
647 Bunker Hill Rd Salem (12865) *(G-14133)*
Maplewood Ice Co Inc....518 499-2345
9785 State Route 4 Whitehall (12887) *(G-16076)*
Mar-A-Thon Filters Inc....631 957-4774
369 41st St Lindenhurst (11757) *(G-6957)*
Maracle Industrial Finshg Co....585 387-9077
93 Kilbourn Rd Rochester (14618) *(G-13534)*
Maramont Corporation (PA)....718 439-8900
5600 1st Ave Brooklyn (11220) *(G-2112)*
Marathon Boat Group Inc....607 849-3211
1 Grumman Way Marathon (13803) *(G-7559)*
Marathon Enterprises Inc....718 665-2560
787 E 138th St Bronx (10454) *(G-1306)*
Marathon Roofing Products Inc....716 685-3340
3310 N Benzing Rd Orchard Park (14127) *(G-12364)*
Marble Works Inc....914 376-3653
681 Saw Mill River Rd Yonkers (10710) *(G-16331)*
Marc Kaufman Furs, New York *Also called Mksf Inc (G-10485)*
Marcal Printing Inc....516 942-9500
85 N Broadway Hicksville (11801) *(G-5925)*
Marcasiano Inc....212 614-9412
296 Elizabeth St Apt 2f New York (10012) *(G-10354)*
Marcel Finishing Corp....718 381-2889
4 David Ct Plainview (11803) *(G-12699)*
Marcellus Energy Services LLC....607 236-0038
3 Mill St Ste 6 Candor (13743) *(G-3162)*
Marco Hi-Tech JV LLC (PA)....212 798-8100
475 Park Ave S Fl 10 New York (10016) *(G-10355)*
Marco Industries Ltd (PA)....212 798-8100
475 Park Ave S 10f New York (10016) *(G-10356)*
Marco Manufacturing Inc....845 485-1571
55 Page Park Dr Poughkeepsie (12603) *(G-12969)*
Marcon Electronic Systems LLC....516 633-6396
152 Westend Ave Freeport (11520) *(G-5005)*
Marcon Services....516 223-8019
152 Westend Ave Freeport (11520) *(G-5006)*
Marconi Intl USA Co Ltd....212 391-2626
214 W 39th St Rm 703 New York (10018) *(G-10357)*
Marcovicci-Wenz Engineering....631 467-9040
33 Comac Loop Unit 10 Ronkonkoma (11779) *(G-13970)*
Marcus Goldman Inc....212 431-0707
37 W 39th St Rm 1201 New York (10018) *(G-10358)*
Marcy Business Forms Inc....718 935-9100
1468 40th St Brooklyn (11218) *(G-2113)*
Marcy Printing Inc....718 935-9100
777 Kent Ave Ste A Brooklyn (11205) *(G-2114)*
Mardek LLC....585 735-9333
73 N Wilmarth Rd Pittsford (14534) *(G-12649)*
Mardon Tool & Die Co Inc....585 254-4545
19 Lois St Rochester (14606) *(G-13535)*
Marex Aquisition Corp....585 458-3940
1385 Emerson St Rochester (14606) *(G-13536)*
Mari Strings Inc....212 799-6781
14 W 71st St New York (10023) *(G-10359)*
Maria Dionisio Welding Inc....631 956-0815
71 W Montauk Hwy Lindenhurst (11757) *(G-6958)*
Mariah Metal Products Inc....516 938-9783
89 Tec St Hicksville (11801) *(G-5926)*
Marie Claire Magazine, New York *Also called Marie Claire USA (G-10360)*
Marie Claire USA....212 841-8493
300 W 57th St Fl 34 New York (10019) *(G-10360)*
Marietta Corporation (HQ)....607 753-6746
37 Huntington St Cortland (13045) *(G-3775)*
Marietta Corporation....607 753 0982
106 Central Ave Cortland (13045) *(G-3776)*
Marietta Corporation....323 589-8181
37 Huntington St Cortland (13045) *(G-3777)*
Marietta Hospitality, Cortland *Also called Marietta Corporation (G-3775)*
Marigold Signs Inc....516 433-7446
485 S Broadway Ste 34 Hicksville (11801) *(G-5927)*
Marina Holding Corp....718 646-9283
3939 Emmons Ave Brooklyn (11235) *(G-2115)*
Marina Jewelry Co Inc....212 354-5027
42 W 48th St Ste 804 New York (10036) *(G-10361)*
Marine & Indus Hydraulics Inc....914 698-2036
329 Center Ave Mamaroneck (10543) *(G-7513)*
Marinos Italian Ices, Richmond Hill *Also called Olympic Ice Cream Co Inc (G-13118)*
Maripharm Laboratories....716 984-6520
2045 Niagara Falls Blvd Niagara Falls (14304) *(G-11949)*
Maritime Activity Reports (PA)....212 477-6700
118 E 25th St Fl 2 New York (10010) *(G-10362)*
Mark - 10 Corporation....631 842-9200
11 Dixon Ave Copiague (11726) *(G-3664)*
Mark Dri Products Inc....516 484-6200
999 S Oyster Bay Rd # 312 Bethpage (11714) *(G-838)*
Mark Ecko Enterprises, New York *Also called Mee Accessories LLC (G-10421)*
Mark F Rosenhaft N A O....516 374-1010
538 Central Ave Cedarhurst (11516) *(G-3241)*
Mark Goldberg Prosthetic....631 689-6606
9 Technology Dr East Setauket (11733) *(G-4180)*
Mark I Publications Inc....718 205-8000
7119 80th St Ste 8201 Glendale (11385) *(G-5228)*
Mark King Jewelry Inc....212 921-0746
62 W 47th St Ste 310r New York (10036) *(G-10363)*
Mark Levine....212 677-4457
149 5th Ave Fl 10 New York (10010) *(G-10364)*
Mark Nelson Designs LLC....646 422-7020
174 5th Ave Ste 501 New York (10010) *(G-10365)*
Mark Peri International....516 208-6824
3516 Hargale Rd Oceanside (11572) *(G-12181)*
Mark Robinson Inc....212 223-3515
18 E 48th St Rm 1102 New York (10017) *(G-10366)*
Mark T Westinghouse....518 678-3262
138 Grandview Ave Catskill (12414) *(G-3214)*
Markar Architectural Products....716 685-4104
68 Ward Rd Lancaster (14086) *(G-6817)*
Market Factory Inc....212 625-9988
45 W 27th St Frnt 1 New York (10001) *(G-10367)*
Market Logic Software Inc....646 405-1041
80 Pine St Fl 24 New York (10005) *(G-10368)*
Market Partners International....212 447-0855
232 Madison Ave Rm 1400 New York (10016) *(G-10369)*
Market Place Publications....516 997-7909
234 Silverlake Blvd Ste 2 Carle Place (11514) *(G-3178)*
Marketer's Forum Magazine, Centerport *Also called Forum Publishing Co (G-3255)*

Marketfax Information Services, Hastings On Hudson *Also called Alternative Technology Corp* *(G-5571)*

Marketing Action Xecutives Inc 212 971-9155
50 W 96th St Apt 7b New York (10025) *(G-10370)*

Marketing Group International 631 754-8095
1 Stargazer Ct Northport (11768) *(G-12109)*

Marketplace Slutions Group LLC 631 868-0111
48 Nimbus Rd Ste 303 Holbrook (11741) *(G-6009)*

Marketplace, The, Chester *Also called Advertiser Publications Inc* *(G-3369)*

Marketresearchcom Inc 212 807-2600
641 Ave Of The America New York (10011) *(G-10371)*

Markin Tubing LP (PA) 585 495-6211
1 Markin Ln Wyoming (14591) *(G-16250)*

Markin Tubing LP 585 495-6211
400 Ingham Ave Buffalo (14218) *(G-2861)*

Markin Tubing Division, Buffalo *Also called Markin Tubing LP* *(G-2861)*

Markin Tubing Inc 585 495-6211
Pearl Creek Rd Wyoming (14591) *(G-16251)*

Markowitz Jewelry Co Inc 845 774-1175
53 Forest Rd Ste 104 Monroe (10950) *(G-8026)*

Markpericom 516 208-6824
3516 Hargale Rd Oceanside (11572) *(G-12182)*

Marks USA, Amityville *Also called G Marks Hdwr Liquidating Corp* *(G-263)*

Marksmen Manufacturing Corp 800 305-6942
355 Marcus Blvd Deer Park (11729) *(G-3903)*

Marktech International Corp (PA) 518 956-2980
3 Northway Ln N Ste 1 Latham (12110) *(G-6870)*

Marktech Optoelectronics, Latham *Also called Marktech International Corp* *(G-6870)*

Markwik Corp 516 470-1990
309 W John St Hicksville (11801) *(G-5928)*

Marlborough Jewels Inc 718 768-2000
67 35th St Unit B516 Brooklyn (11232) *(G-2116)*

Marley Spoon Inc 866 228-4513
601 W 26th St Rm 900 New York (10001) *(G-10372)*

Marlou Garments Inc 516 739-7100
2115 Jericho Tpke New Hyde Park (11040) *(G-8281)*

Marlow Printing Co Inc 718 625-4948
667 Kent Ave Brooklyn (11249) *(G-2117)*

Marly Home Industries USA Inc 718 388-3030
181 Lombardy St Brooklyn (11222) *(G-2118)*

Marmach Machine Inc 585 768-8800
11 Lent Ave Le Roy (14482) *(G-6904)*

Marotta Dental Studio Inc 631 249-7520
130 Finn Ct Farmingdale (11735) *(G-4677)*

Marovato Industries Inc 718 389-0800
108 Dobbin St Brooklyn (11222) *(G-2119)*

Marplex Furniture Corporation 914 969-7755
167 Saw Mill Rver Rd Fl 1 Flr 1 Yonkers (10701) *(G-16332)*

Marquardt Switches Inc (HQ) 315 655-8050
2711 Us Route 20 Cazenovia (13035) *(G-3231)*

Marretti USA Inc 212 255-5565
101 Ave Of The Amrcas 9th New York (10013) *(G-10373)*

Marros Equipment & Trucks 315 539-8702
2354 State Route 414 Waterloo (13165) *(G-15555)*

Marsal & Sons, Lindenhurst *Also called Middleby Corporation* *(G-6960)*

Marsha Fleisher 845 679-6500
18 Tinker St Woodstock (12498) *(G-16236)*

Marshall Cavendish Corp 914 332-8888
800 Westchester Ave N641 Rye Brook (10573) *(G-14091)*

Marshall Ingredients LLC 800 796-9353
5786 Limekiln Rd Wolcott (14590) *(G-16164)*

Marsid Group Ltd 516 334-1603
245 Westbury Ave Carle Place (11514) *(G-3179)*

Marsid Press, Carle Place *Also called Marsid Group Ltd* *(G-3179)*

MARsid-M&m Group, The, Carle Place *Also called M&M Printing Inc* *(G-3177)*

Mart-Tex Athletics Inc 631 454-9583
180 Allen Blvd Farmingdale (11735) *(G-4678)*

Martens Country Kit Pdts LLC 315 776-8821
1323 Towpath Rd Port Byron (13140) *(G-12809)*

Martha & Marley Spoon, New York *Also called Marley Spoon Inc* *(G-10372)*

Martha Stewart Living (HQ) 212 827-8000
601 W 26th St Rm 900 New York (10001) *(G-10374)*

Martha Stewart Living Omni LLC 212 827-8000
20 W 43rd St New York (10036) *(G-10375)*

Martin Dental Studio, Watertown *Also called Martins Dental Studio* *(G-15582)*

Martin Flyer Incorporated 212 840-8899
29 Woodcliff Ct Manhasset (11030) *(G-7537)*

Martin Greenfield Clothiers 718 497-5480
239 Varet St Brooklyn (11206) *(G-2120)*

Martin Orna Ir Works Ii Inc 516 354-3923
266 Elmont Rd Elmont (11003) *(G-4386)*

Martinelli Holdings LLC 302 504-1361
4 Ellsworth Ave Apt 2 Harrison (10528) *(G-5555)*

Martinelli Publications, Yonkers *Also called Yonkers Time Publishing Co* *(G-16360)*

Martinez Specialties Inc 607 898-3053
205 Bossard Rd Groton (13073) *(G-5483)*

Martins Dental Studio 315 788-0800
162 Sterling St Watertown (13601) *(G-15582)*

Marval Industries Inc 914 381-2400
315 Hoyt Ave Mamaroneck (10543) *(G-7514)*

Marvel Dairy Whip Inc 516 889-4232
258 Lido Blvd Lido Beach (11561) *(G-6928)*

Marvellissima Intl Ltd 212 682-7306
333 E 46th St Apt 20a New York (10017) *(G-10376)*

Marx Myles Graphic Services, New York *Also called X Myles Mar Inc* *(G-11795)*

Mary Ann Liebert Inc 914 740-2100
140 Huguenot St Fl 3 New Rochelle (10801) *(G-8347)*

Mary Bright Inc 212 677-1970
269 E 10th St Apt 7 New York (10009) *(G-10377)*

Mary F Morse 315 866-2741
125 Columbia St Ste 1 Mohawk (13407) *(G-8006)*

Mas Cutting Inc 212 869-0826
257 W 39th St Rm 11e New York (10018) *(G-10378)*

Masick Soil Conservation Co 518 827-5354
4860 State Route 30 Schoharie (12157) *(G-14322)*

Mason Carvings Inc 716 484-7884
2871 Ivystone Dr Jamestown (14701) *(G-6531)*

Mason Contract Products LLC 516 328-6900
85 Denton Ave New Hyde Park (11040) *(G-8282)*

Mason Industries Inc (PA) 631 348-0282
350 Rabro Dr Hauppauge (11788) *(G-5708)*

Mason Industries Inc 631 348-0282
33 Ranick Rd Ste 1 Hauppauge (11788) *(G-5709)*

Mason Medical Products, Port Washington *Also called M R C Industries Inc* *(G-12903)*

Mason Transparent Package Inc 718 792-6000
1180 Commerce Ave Bronx (10462) *(G-1307)*

Mason Woodworks LLC 917 363-7052
127 Chester Ave Brooklyn (11218) *(G-2121)*

Masonite International Corp 607 775-0615
28 Track Dr Binghamton (13904) *(G-895)*

Masonville Stone Incorporated 607 265-3597
12999 State Highway 8 Masonville (13804) *(G-7584)*

Maspeth Press Inc 718 429-2363
6620 Grand Ave Maspeth (11378) *(G-7626)*

Maspeth Welding Inc 718 497-5430
5930 54th St Maspeth (11378) *(G-7627)*

Masquerade LLC 212 673-4546
104 4th Ave New York (10003) *(G-10379)*

Mass Appeal Magazine 718 858-0979
261 Vandervoort Ave Brooklyn (11211) *(G-2122)*

Mass Mdsg Self Selection Eqp 631 234-3300
35 Orville Dr Ste 2 Bohemia (11716) *(G-1044)*

Massapequa Post 516 798-5100
1045b Park Blvd Massapequa Park (11762) *(G-7659)*

Massapqua Prcsion McHining Ltd 631 789-1485
30 Seabro Ave Amityville (11701) *(G-295)*

Massena Ready Mix, Massena *Also called Upstone Materials Inc* *(G-7673)*

Massimo Friedman Inc 716 836-0408
2495 Main St Ste 457 Buffalo (14214) *(G-2862)*

Masten Enterprises LLC (PA) 845 932-8206
420 Bernas Rd Cochecton (12726) *(G-3503)*

Master & Dynamics, New York *Also called New Audio LLC* *(G-10576)*

Master Craft Finishers Inc 631 586-0540
30 W Jefryn Blvd Ste 1 Deer Park (11729) *(G-3904)*

Master Image Printing Inc 914 347-4400
75 N Central Ave Ste 202 Elmsford (10523) *(G-4416)*

Master Juvenile Products Inc 845 647-8400
70 Berme Rd Ellenville (12428) *(G-4308)*

Master Machine Incorporated 716 487-2555
155 Blackstone Ave Jamestown (14701) *(G-6532)*

Master Printing USA Inc 718 456-0962
192 New York Ave Island Park (11558) *(G-6319)*

Master-Halco Inc 631 585-8150
19 Zorn Blvd Yaphank (11980) *(G-16266)*

Mastercraft Decorators Inc 585 223-5150
320 Macedon Center Rd Fairport (14450) *(G-4506)*

Mastercraft Manufacturing Co 718 729-5620
3715 11th St Long Island City (11101) *(G-7290)*

Masterdisk Corporation 212 541-5022
134 S Central Ave Ste C Elmsford (10523) *(G-4417)*

Masterlibrarycom LLC 585 270-6676
1160 Pittsford Victor Rd J Pittsford (14534) *(G-12650)*

Mastro Concrete Inc 718 528-6788
15433 Brookville Blvd Rosedale (11422) *(G-14037)*

Mastro Graphic Arts Inc 585 436-7570
67 Deep Rock Rd Rochester (14624) *(G-13537)*

Mata Fashions LLC 917 716-7894
222 W 37th St Fl 4 New York (10018) *(G-10380)*

Mataci Inc 212 502-1899
247 W 35th St Fl 15 New York (10001) *(G-10381)*

Match Eyewear LLC 516 877-0170
1600 Shames Dr Westbury (11590) *(G-15908)*

Matchables Inc 718 389-9318
106 Green St Ste G1 Brooklyn (11222) *(G-2123)*

Matel LLC 646 825-6760
90 Park Ave Fl 18 New York (10016) *(G-10382)*

Material Measuring Corporation 516 334-6167
121 Hopper St Westbury (11590) *(G-15909)*

Material Process Systems Inc 718 302-3081
613 Berriman St Brooklyn (11208) *(G-2124)*

Materials Design Workshop 718 893-1954
830 Barry St Bronx (10474) *(G-1308)*

A
L
P
H
A
B
E
T
I
C

Materion Advanced Materials 800 327-1355
42 Mount Ebo Rd S Brewster (10509) **(G-1154)**
Materion Brewster LLC 845 279-0900
42 Mount Ebo Rd S Brewster (10509) **(G-1155)**
Materne North America Corp (HQ) 212 675-7881
20 W 22nd St Fl 12 New York (10010) **(G-10383)**
Matheson Tri-Gas Inc 518 203-5003
15 Green Mountain Dr Cohoes (12047) **(G-3509)**
Mathisen Ventures Inc 212 986-1025
441 Lexington Ave Rm 809 New York (10017) **(G-10384)**
Matic Industries Inc 718 886-5470
1540 127th St College Point (11356) **(G-3553)**
Matov Industries Inc 718 392-5060
1011 40th Ave Long Island City (11101) **(G-7291)**
Matrix Machining Corp 631 643-6690
69 B Nancy St Unitb West Babylon (11704) **(G-15729)**
Matrix Railway Corp 631 643-1483
69 Nancy St Unit A West Babylon (11704) **(G-15730)**
Matrix Steel Company Inc 718 381-6800
50 Bogart St Brooklyn (11206) **(G-2125)**
Matrixcare Inc 518 583-6400
575 8th Ave Fl 15 New York (10018) **(G-10385)**
Matt Industries Inc (PA) 315 472-1316
6761 Thompson Rd Syracuse (13211) **(G-14938)**
Mattel Inc 310 252-2000
636 Girard Ave East Aurora (14052) **(G-4092)**
Matteo & Antonio Bartolotta 315 252-2220
282 State St Auburn (13021) **(G-485)**
Matteson Logging Inc 585 593-3037
2808 Beech Hill Rd Wellsville (14895) **(G-15672)**
Mattessich Iron LLC 315 409-8496
1484 New State Route 31 Memphis (13112) **(G-7835)**
Matthew Shively LLC 914 937-3531
40 Merritt St Port Chester (10573) **(G-12825)**
Matthew-Lee Corporation 631 226-0100
149 Pennsylvania Ave Lindenhurst (11757) **(G-6959)**
Matthews Hats 718 859-4683
99 Kenilworth Pl Fl 1 Brooklyn (11210) **(G-2126)**
Matys Healthy Products LLC 585 218-0507
140 Office Pkwy Pittsford (14534) **(G-12651)**
Mauceri Sign & Awning Co, Jamaica *Also called Mauceri Sign Inc* **(G-6458)**
Mauceri Sign Inc 718 656-7700
16725 Rockaway Blvd Jamaica (11434) **(G-6458)**
Maurice Max Inc 212 334-6573
49 W 27th St Fl 5 New York (10001) **(G-10386)**
Mausner Equipment Co Inc 631 689-7358
8 Heritage Ln Setauket (11733) **(G-14380)**
Maven Marketing LLC (PA) 615 510-3248
349 5th Ave Fl 8 New York (10016) **(G-10387)**
Maverik Lacrosse LLC 516 213-3050
535 W 24th St Fl 5 New York (10011) **(G-10388)**
Maviano Corp 845 494-2598
21 Robert Pitt Dr Ste 207 Monsey (10952) **(G-8040)**
Max Header 680 888-9786
12 Pinehurst Ave Apt 1h New York (10033) **(G-10389)**
Max 200 Performance Dog Eqp 315 776-9588
2113 State Route 31 Port Byron (13140) **(G-12810)**
Max Brenner Union Square LLC 646 467-8803
841 Broadway New York (10003) **(G-10390)**
Max Kahan Inc 212 575-4646
20 W 47th St Ste 300 New York (10036) **(G-10391)**
Maxam North America Inc 315 322-8651
3 Cemetary Dr Ogdensburg (13669) **(G-12208)**
Maxi Companies Inc 315 446-1002
4317 E Genesee St De Witt (13214) **(G-3824)**
Maxim Hygiene Products Inc (PA) 516 621-3323
121 E Jericho Tpke Mineola (11501) **(G-7988)**
Maximum Security Products Corp 518 233-1800
3 Schoolhouse Ln Waterford (12188) **(G-15538)**
Maxine Denker Inc (PA) 212 689-1440
212 Manhattan St Staten Island (10307) **(G-14679)**
Maxsecure Systems Inc 800 657-4336
300 International Dr # 100 Buffalo (14221) **(G-2863)**
Maxsun Corporation (PA) 718 418-6800
5711 49th St Maspeth (11378) **(G-7628)**
Maxsun Furnishings, Maspeth *Also called Maxsun Corporation* **(G-7628)**
Maxwell Bakery Inc 718 498-2200
2700 Atlantic Ave Brooklyn (11207) **(G-2127)**
May Ship Repair Contg Corp 718 442-9700
3075 Richmond Ter Ste 3 Staten Island (10303) **(G-14680)**
May Tool & Die Inc 716 695-1033
9 Hackett Dr Tonawanda (14150) **(G-15121)**
Maybelline Inc 212 885-1310
575 5th Ave Fl Mezz New York (10017) **(G-10392)**
Mayberry Shoe Company Inc 315 692-4086
131 W Seneca St Ste B Manlius (13104) **(G-7549)**
Maybrook Asphalt, Montgomery *Also called Tilcon New York Inc* **(G-8067)**
Mayer Bros Apple Products Inc (PA) 716 668-1787
3300 Transit Rd West Seneca (14224) **(G-15852)**
Mayfair Machine Company Inc 631 981-6644
128 Remington Blvd Ronkonkoma (11779) **(G-13971)**
Mayflower Splint Co 631 549-5131
16 Arbor Ln Dix Hills (11746) **(G-4011)**
Mayim Chaim Beverages, Bronx *Also called New York Bottling Co Inc* **(G-1323)**
Maz Systems Inc (PA) 855 629-3444
109 W 27th St Fl 7 New York (10001) **(G-10393)**
Mazerna USA, Nanuet *Also called Jescar Enterprises Inc* **(G-8201)**
Mazza Chautauqua Cellars LLC 716 793-9463
8398 W Route 20 Westfield (14787) **(G-15946)**
Mazza Classics Incorporated 631 390-9060
117 Gazza Blvd Farmingdale (11735) **(G-4679)**
Mazza Co, The, North Baldwin *Also called W & B Mazza & Sons Inc* **(G-12012)**
Mazzella Blasting Mat Co, Bronx *Also called T M International LLC* **(G-1377)**
MB Food Processing Inc 845 436-5001
5190 S Fallsburg Main St South Fallsburg (12779) **(G-14509)**
MB Plastics Inc (PA) 718 523-1180
130 Stony Hollow Rd Greenlawn (11740) **(G-5454)**
MBA Orthotics Inc 631 392-4755
60 Corbin Ave Unit 60g Bay Shore (11706) **(G-691)**
Mbh Furniture Innovations Inc 845 354-8202
28 Lincoln Ave Spring Valley (10977) **(G-14578)**
Mbny LLC (PA) 646 467-8810
260 5th Ave Fl 9 New York (10001) **(G-10394)**
Mbss, Kew Gardens *Also called Manhole Brrier SEC Systems Inc* **(G-6668)**
Mc Coy Tops and Covers, Woodside *Also called Mc Coy Tops and Interiors Inc* **(G-16212)**
Mc Coy Tops and Interiors Inc 718 458-5800
6914 49th Ave Woodside (11377) **(G-16212)**
Mc Gregor Vineyard Winery, Dundee *Also called East Branch Winery Inc* **(G-4045)**
Mc Ivor Manufacturing Inc 716 825-1808
400 Ingham Ave Buffalo (14218) **(G-2864)**
Mc Squared Nyc Inc 212 947-2260
121 Varick St Frnt B New York (10013) **(G-10395)**
McAllisters Precision Wldg Inc 518 221-3455
47 Broadway Menands (12204) **(G-7844)**
McAlpin Industries Inc (PA) 585 266-3060
255 Hollenbeck St Rochester (14621) **(G-13538)**
McAlpin Industries Inc 585 544-5335
265 Hollenbeck St Rochester (14621) **(G-13539)**
McArdle Solutions, New York *Also called McPc Inc* **(G-10403)**
McAuliffe Paper Inc 315 453-2222
100 Commerce Blvd Liverpool (13088) **(G-7024)**
McCall Pattern Company (HQ) 212 465-6800
120 Broadway Fl 34 New York (10271) **(G-10396)**
McCarthy Tire and Auto Ctr, Menands *Also called McCarthy Tire Svc Co NY Inc* **(G-7845)**
McCarthy Tire Svc Co NY Inc 518 449-5185
980 Broadway Menands (12204) **(G-7845)**
McClary Media Inc 800 453-6397
1 Venner Rd Amsterdam (12010) **(G-334)**
McConnaughay Technologies 607 753-1100
1911 Lorings Crossing Rd Cortland (13045) **(G-3778)**
McCullagh Coffee, Buffalo *Also called S J McCullagh Inc* **(G-2970)**
McD Metals LLC 518 456-9694
20 Corporate Cir Ste 2 Albany (12203) **(G-98)**
McDermott Light & Signal, Ridgewood *Also called Julian A McDermott Corporation* **(G-13148)**
McDonough Hardwoods Ltd 315 829-3449
6426 Skinner Rd Vernon Center (13477) **(G-15368)**
McDowell Research Co Inc (HQ) 315 332-7100
2000 Technology Pkwy Newark (14513) **(G-11845)**
McEwan Trucking & Grav Produc 716 609-1828
11696 Route 240 East Concord (14055) **(G-4100)**
McG Electronics Inc 631 586-5125
12 Burt Dr Deer Park (11729) **(G-3905)**
McG Graphics Inc 631 499-0730
101 Village Hill Dr Dix Hills (11746) **(G-4012)**
McG Surge Protection, Deer Park *Also called McG Electronics Inc* **(G-3905)**
McGraw Hill Education, New York *Also called McGraw-Hill Globl Edcatn Hldng* **(G-10398)**
McGraw Wood Products LLC (PA) 607 836-6465
1 Charles St Mc Graw (13101) **(G-7689)**
McGraw-Hill Education Inc (PA) 646 766-2000
2 Penn Plz Fl 20 New York (10121) **(G-10397)**
McGraw-Hill Globl Edcatn Hldng (PA) 800 338-3987
2 Penn Plz Fl 20 New York (10121) **(G-10398)**
McGraw-Hill School Education H (HQ) 646 766-2000
2 Penn Plz Fl 20 New York (10121) **(G-10399)**
McGraw-Hill School Educatn LLC 646 766-2060
2 Penn Plz Fl 20 New York (10121) **(G-10400)**
McGuigan Inc 631 750-6222
210 Knickerbocker Ave Bohemia (11716) **(G-1045)**
McHone Industries Inc 716 945-3380
110 Elm St Salamanca (14779) **(G-14122)**
McIntosh Box & Pallet Co Inc 315 789-8750
40 Doran Ave Geneva (14456) **(G-5159)**
McIntosh Box & Pallet Co Inc 315 675-8511
741 State Route 49 Bernhards Bay (13028) **(G-826)**
McIntosh Box & Pallet Co Inc 315 446-9350
200 6th St Rome (13440) **(G-13855)**
McKee Foods Corporation 631 979-9364
111 Serene Pl Hauppauge (11788) **(G-5710)**
McKeon Rolling Stl Door Co Inc (PA) 631 803-3000
44 Sawgrass Dr Bellport (11713) **(G-803)**
MCM Natural Stone Inc 585 586-6510
860 Linden Ave Ste 1 Rochester (14625) **(G-13540)**

McM Products USA Inc (PA)..........646 756-4090
681 5th Ave Fl 10 New York (10022) *(G-10401)*
McMahon Group LLC (PA)..........212 957-5300
545 W 45th St New York (10036) *(G-10402)*
McMahon Publishing Group, New York *Also called McMahon Group LLC (G-10402)*
McNeilly Wood Products Inc..........845 457-9651
120 Neelytown Rd Campbell Hall (10916) *(G-3118)*
McPc Inc..........212 583-6000
731 Lexington Ave New York (10022) *(G-10403)*
McQuilling Partners Inc (PA)..........516 227-5718
1035 Stewart Ave Ste 100 Garden City (11530) *(G-5107)*
McWane Inc..........607 734-2211
1021 E Water St Elmira (14901) *(G-4362)*
MD International Industries..........631 254-3100
120 E Jefryn Blvd Ste Aa Deer Park (11729) *(G-3906)*
Md-Reports, Staten Island *Also called Infinite Software Solutions (G-14665)*
Mdcare911 LLC..........917 640-4869
30 Main St Apt 5c Brooklyn (11201) *(G-2128)*
Mdi, Hauppauge *Also called Metal Dynamics Intl Corp (G-5715)*
Mdi East Inc..........518 747-8730
22 Hudson Falls Rd Ste 6 South Glens Falls (12803) *(G-14514)*
Mdi Holdings LLC..........212 559-1127
399 Park Ave Fl 14 New York (10022) *(G-10404)*
Mdj Sales Associates Inc..........914 420-5897
27 Doris Rd Mamaroneck (10543) *(G-7515)*
Mdr Printing Corp..........516 627-3221
125 Plandome Rd Manhasset (11030) *(G-7538)*
Mds Hot Bagels Deli Inc..........718 438-5650
127 Church Ave Brooklyn (11218) *(G-2129)*
ME & Ro Inc..........212 431-8744
241 Elizabeth St Frnt A New York (10012) *(G-10405)*
Meade Machine Co Inc..........315 923-1703
31 Ford St Clyde (14433) *(G-3492)*
Meades Welding and Fabricating..........631 581-1555
331 Islip Ave Islip (11751) *(G-6354)*
Mealplan Corp..........909 706-8398
203 E 4th St Apt 6 New York (10009) *(G-10406)*
Measupro Inc (PA)..........845 425-8777
1 Alpine Ct Spring Valley (10977) *(G-14579)*
Measurement Incorporated..........914 682-1969
34 S Broadway Ste 601 White Plains (10601) *(G-16028)*
Mecca Printing, Buffalo *Also called B & P Jays Inc (G-2654)*
Mechanical Displays Inc..........718 258-5588
4420 Farragut Rd Brooklyn (11203) *(G-2130)*
Mechanical Pwr Conversion LLC..........607 766-9620
6 Emma St Binghamton (13905) *(G-896)*
Mechanical Rubber Pdts Co Inc..........845 986-2271
77 Forester Ave Ste 1 Warwick (10990) *(G-15519)*
Mechanical Specialties Co, Binghamton *Also called Ms Machining Inc (G-900)*
Mechanical Technology Inc (PA)..........518 218-2550
325 Washington Avenue Ext Albany (12205) *(G-99)*
Mechon Beiss Uvas..........718 436-1489
1130 40th St Brooklyn (11218) *(G-2131)*
Mechoshade Systems Inc (HQ)..........718 729-2020
4203 35th St Long Island City (11101) *(G-7292)*
Med Reviews LLC..........212 239-5860
1370 Broadway Fl 5 New York (10018) *(G-10407)*
Med Services Inc..........631 218-6450
100 Knickerbocker Ave C Bohemia (11716) *(G-1046)*
Med-Eng LLC..........315 713-0130
103 Tulloch Dr Ogdensburg (13669) *(G-12209)*
Medallion Associates Inc..........212 929-9130
37 W 20th St Fl 4 New York (10011) *(G-10408)*
Medallion Security Door & Win, New Hyde Park *Also called Texas Home Security Inc (G-8296)*
Medaptive Health Inc..........646 541-7389
235 W 22nd St Apt 7d New York (10011) *(G-10409)*
Medco, Edgewood *Also called Merit Electronic Design Co Inc (G-4275)*
Medco Machine LLC..........315 986-2109
2320 Walworth Marion Rd Walworth (14568) *(G-15477)*
Medek Laboratories Inc..........845 943-4988
63 First Ave Monroe (10950) *(G-8027)*
Meder Textile Co Inc..........516 883-0409
20 Lynn Rd Port Washington (11050) *(G-12904)*
Medi-Ray Inc..........877 898-3003
150 Marbledale Rd Tuckahoe (10707) *(G-15205)*
Medi-Tech International Corp (PA)..........800 333-0109
26 Court St Ste 1301 Brooklyn (11242) *(G-2132)*
Media Press Corp..........212 791-6347
55 John St 520 New York (10038) *(G-10410)*
Media Technologies Ltd..........631 467-7900
220 Sonata Ct Eastport (11941) *(G-4252)*
Media Transcripts Inc..........212 362-1481
41 W 83rd St Apt 2b New York (10024) *(G-10411)*
Media Trust LLC (PA)..........212 802-1162
404 Park Ave S Fl 2 New York (10016) *(G-10412)*
Mediamorph Inc (HQ)..........212 643-0762
205 Lexington Ave Fl 7 New York (10016) *(G-10413)*
Mediaplanet Publishing Hse Inc (HQ)..........646 922-1400
350 7th Ave Fl 18 New York (10001) *(G-10414)*
Mediapost Communications LLC..........212 204-2000
1460 Broadway Fl 12 New York (10036) *(G-10415)*
Medical Action Industries Inc..........631 231-4600
150 Motor Pkwy Ste 205 Hauppauge (11788) *(G-5711)*
Medical Coaches Incorporated..........607 432-1333
399 County Highway 58 Oneonta (13820) *(G-12275)*
Medical Daily Inc..........646 867-7100
7 Hanover Sq Fl 6 New York (10004) *(G-10416)*
Medical Depot Inc (PA)..........516 998-4600
99 Seaview Blvd Ste 210 Port Washington (11050) *(G-12905)*
Medical Information Systems..........516 621-7200
28 Patricia Ln Syosset (11791) *(G-14793)*
Medical Technology Products..........631 285-6640
33a Smith St Greenlawn (11740) *(G-5455)*
Medidata Solutions Inc (HQ)..........212 918-1800
350 Hudson St Fl 9 New York (10014) *(G-10417)*
Mediflex, Islandia *Also called Flexbar Machine Corporation (G-6332)*
Medikidz Usa Inc..........646 895-9319
205 Lexington Ave Rm 1601 New York (10016) *(G-10418)*
Medima LLC..........716 741-0400
5727 Strickler Rd Clarence (14031) *(G-3436)*
Medima Metals, Clarence *Also called Medima LLC (G-3436)*
Medina Journal Register, Medina *Also called Cnhi LLC (G-7732)*
Medina Millworks LLC..........585 798-2969
10694 Ridge Rd Medina (14103) *(G-7740)*
Medipoint Inc..........516 294-8822
72 E 2nd St Mineola (11501) *(G-7989)*
Medipoint International,, Mineola *Also called Medipoint Inc (G-7989)*
Medisonic Inc..........516 653-2345
57 Watermill Ln Ste 296 Great Neck (11021) *(G-5403)*
Mediterranean Thick Yogurt, East Elmhurst *Also called Kesso Foods Inc (G-4108)*
Mediterrean Dyro Company..........718 786-4888
1102 38th Ave Long Island City (11101) *(G-7293)*
Meditub Incorporated..........866 633-4882
11 Wedgewood Ln Lawrence (11559) *(G-6888)*
Medius North America, New York *Also called Medius Software Inc (G-10419)*
Medius Software Inc..........877 295-0058
12 E 49th St Fl 11 New York (10017) *(G-10419)*
Medline Industries Inc..........845 344-3301
3301 Route 6 Middletown (10940) *(G-7919)*
Medpod Inc..........631 863-8090
324 S Service Rd Ste 112 Melville (11747) *(G-7802)*
Medsafe Systems Inc..........516 883-8222
46 Orchard Farm Rd Port Washington (11050) *(G-12906)*
Medscale Plus LLC..........212 218-4070
152 W 57th St Fl 52 New York (10019) *(G-10420)*
Medsim-Eagle Simulation Inc..........607 658-9354
811 North St Endicott (13760) *(G-4464)*
Medsource Technologies LLC..........716 662-5025
3902 California Rd Orchard Park (14127) *(G-12365)*
Medsurg Direct, Plainview *Also called Peter Digioia (G-12707)*
Medtech Products Inc (HQ)..........914 524-6810
660 White Plains Rd Tarrytown (10591) *(G-15047)*
Medtek Skin Care Inc (PA)..........518 745-7264
206 Glen St Ste 5 Glens Falls (12801) *(G-5258)*
Mee Accessories LLC (PA)..........917 262-1000
475 10th Ave Fl 9 New York (10018) *(G-10421)*
Meeco Sullivan LLC..........800 232-3625
3 Chancellor Ln Warwick (10990) *(G-15520)*
Meegenius Inc..........212 283-7285
151 W 25th St Fl 3 New York (10001) *(G-10422)*
Meeker Sales Corp..........718 384-5400
551 Sutter Ave Brooklyn (11207) *(G-2133)*
Mega Apparel International, Merrick *Also called Mega Sourcing Inc (G-7861)*
Mega Graphics Inc..........914 962-1402
1725 Front St Ste 1 Yorktown Heights (10598) *(G-16368)*
Mega Plastic Group Inc..........347 737-8444
2667 Coney Island Ave Brooklyn (11223) *(G-2134)*
Mega Power Sports Corporation..........212 627-3380
1123 Broadway Ph New York (10010) *(G-10423)*
Mega Sourcing Inc (PA)..........646 682-0304
1929 Edward Ln Merrick (11566) *(G-7861)*
Mega Tool & Mfg Corp..........607 734-8398
1023 Caton Ave Elmira (14904) *(G-4363)*
Mehr Foil Corp..........631 648-9742
200 13th Ave Unit 10 Ronkonkoma (11779) *(G-13972)*
Mehron Inc..........845 426-1700
100 Red Schoolhouse Rd C2 Chestnut Ridge (10977) *(G-3395)*
Meiragtx Holdings PLC (PA)..........646 490-2965
430 E 29th St Fl 10 New York (10016) *(G-10424)*
Meisel-Peskin Co Inc (PA)..........718 497-1840
349 Scholes St 353 Brooklyn (11206) *(G-2135)*
Meiyume USA Inc..........646 927-2370
1359 Broadway Fl 17 New York (10018) *(G-10425)*
Mekanism Inc..........212 226-2772
250 Hudson St Rm 200 New York (10013) *(G-10426)*
Mekatronics Incorporated..........516 883-6805
85 Channel Dr Ste 2 Port Washington (11050) *(G-12907)*
Mel Bernie and Company Inc..........212 889-8570
384 5th Ave Fl 4 New York (10018) *(G-10427)*
Melbourne C Fisher Yacht Sails..........631 673-5055
1345 New York Ave Ste 2 Huntington Station (11746) *(G-6253)*
Melcher Media Inc..........212 727-2322
124 W 13th St New York (10011) *(G-10428)*

ALPHABETIC

Meliorum Technologies Inc 585 313-0616
  620 Park Ave 145 Rochester (14607) *(G-13541)*

Melissa, Interlaken *Also called Hipshot Products Inc (G-6284)*

Melita Corp 718 392-7280
  3330 14th St Astoria (11106) *(G-429)*

Melland Gear Instr of Huppauge 631 234-0100
  225 Engineers Rd Hauppauge (11788) *(G-5712)*

Mellem Corporation 607 723-0001
  31 Lewis St Ste 1 Binghamton (13901) *(G-897)*

Mellen Press, The, Lewiston *Also called PSR Press Ltd (G-6923)*

Mellen Pressroom & Bindery, Lewiston *Also called 450 Ridge St Inc (G-6919)*

Melmont Fine Pringng/Graphics 516 939-2253
  6 Robert Ct Ste 24 Bethpage (11714) *(G-839)*

Meloon Foundries LLC 315 454-3231
  1841 Lemoyne Ave Syracuse (13208) *(G-14939)*

Melto Metal Products Co Inc 516 546-8866
  37 Hanse Ave Freeport (11520) *(G-5007)*

Meltz Lumber Co of Mellenville 518 672-7021
  483 Route 217 Hudson (12534) *(G-6170)*

Melwood Partners Inc 631 923-0134
  102 Marcus Dr Melville (11747) *(G-7803)*

Memo America Inc 646 356-0460
  60 Broad St Ste 3502 New York (10004) *(G-10429)*

Memory Md Inc (PA) 917 318-0215
  205 E 42nd St Fl 14 New York (10017) *(G-10430)*

Memory Protection Devices Inc 631 249-0001
  200 Broadhollow Rd Ste 4 Farmingdale (11735) *(G-4680)*

Menpin Supply Corp 718 415-4168
  1229 60th St Brooklyn (11219) *(G-2136)*

Menrose USA LLC 718 221-5540
  605 Montgomery St Brooklyn (11225) *(G-2137)*

Mens Journal, New York *Also called Straight Arrow Publishing Co (G-11368)*

Mens Journal LLC 212 484-1616
  1290 Ave Of The Americas New York (10104) *(G-10431)*

Mensch Mill & Lumber Corp (PA) 718 359-7500
  1261 Commerce Ave Bronx (10462) *(G-1309)*

Mensch Supply, Bronx *Also called Mensch Mill & Lumber Corp (G-1309)*

Mentholatum Company (HQ) 716 677-2500
  707 Sterling Dr Orchard Park (14127) *(G-12366)*

Menucha Publishers Inc 718 232-0856
  1221 38th St Brooklyn (11218) *(G-2138)*

Mer Gems Corp 212 714-9129
  62 W 47th St Ste 614 New York (10036) *(G-10432)*

Merb LLC 631 393-3621
  240 Kent Ave Brooklyn (11249) *(G-2139)*

Mercado Global Inc 718 838-9908
  254 36th St Unit 41 Brooklyn (11232) *(G-2140)*

Mercer Milling Co 315 701-1334
  4698 Crossroads Park Dr Liverpool (13088) *(G-7025)*

Mercer Rubber Co 631 348-0282
  350 Rabro Dr Hauppauge (11788) *(G-5713)*

Mercer's Dairy, Boonville *Also called Quality Dairy Farms Inc (G-1109)*

Merchandiser Inc 315 462-6411
  70 Stephens St Clifton Springs (14432) *(G-3479)*

Merchant Service Pymnt Access 212 561-5516
  626 Rxr Plz Uniondale (11556) *(G-15232)*

Merco Hackensack Inc 845 357-3699
  201 Route 59 Ste D2 Hillburn (10931) *(G-5970)*

Merco Tape, Hillburn *Also called Merco Hackensack Inc (G-5970)*

Mercury Apparel, West Nyack *Also called Mainly Monograms Inc (G-15827)*

Mercury Envelope Co Inc 516 678-6744
  100 Merrick Rd Ste 204e Rockville Centre (11570) *(G-13830)*

Mercury Envelope Printing, Rockville Centre *Also called Mercury Envelope Co Inc (G-13830)*

Mercury Lock and Door Service 718 542-7048
  529 C Wortham St Bronx (10474) *(G-1310)*

Mercury Paint Corporation (PA) 718 469-8787
  4808 Farragut Rd Brooklyn (11203) *(G-2141)*

Mercury Pen Company Inc 518 899-9653
  245 Eastline Rd Ballston Lake (12019) *(G-561)*

Mercury Plastics Corp 718 498-5400
  989 Utica Ave 995 Brooklyn (11203) *(G-2142)*

Mercury Print Productions Inc (PA) 585 458-7900
  2332 Innovation Way 4 Rochester (14624) *(G-13542)*

Meredith Corporate Solutions, New York *Also called Four M Studios (G-9522)*

Meredith Hispanic Ventures, New York *Also called Four M Studios (G-9523)*

Mergence Studios Ltd 212 288-5616
  135 Ricefield Ln Hauppauge (11788) *(G-5714)*

Mergent Inc 212 413-7700
  444 Madison Ave Ste 502 New York (10022) *(G-10433)*

Meridian Adhesives Group LLC (PA) 212 771-1717
  100 Park Ave Fl 31 New York (10017) *(G-10434)*

Meridian Manufacturing Inc 518 885-0450
  27 Kent St Ste 103a Ballston Spa (12020) *(G-581)*

Merit Electronic Design Co Inc 631 667-9699
  190 Rodeo Dr Edgewood (11717) *(G-4275)*

Meritool LLC 716 699-6005
  4496 Route 353 Salamanca (14779) *(G-14123)*

Merkos Bookstore, Brooklyn *Also called Merkos Llnyonei Chinuch Inc (G-2143)*

Merkos Llnyonei Chinuch Inc 718 778-0226
  291 Kingston Ave Brooklyn (11213) *(G-2143)*

Merrill Communications, New York *Also called Merrill New York Company Inc (G-10438)*

Merrill Communications LLC 212 620-5600
  1345 Ave Of The Amrcs 1 New York (10105) *(G-10435)*

Merrill Corporation 917 934-7300
  25 W 45th St Ste 900 New York (10036) *(G-10436)*

Merrill Corporation 212 620-5600
  1345 Ave Of The Ave Fl 17 Flr 17 New York (10105) *(G-10437)*

Merrill New York Company Inc 212 229-6500
  246 W 54th St New York (10019) *(G-10438)*

Merrill Press, Buffalo *Also called Complemar Print LLC (G-2707)*

Merrimac Leasing, Johnstown *Also called Lee Dyeing Company NC Inc (G-6622)*

Merritt Estate Winery Inc 716 965-4800
  2264 King Rd Forestville (14062) *(G-4931)*

Merritt Machinery LLC 716 434-5558
  10 Simonds St Lockport (14094) *(G-7090)*

Meryl Diamond Ltd (PA) 212 730-0333
  1375 Broadway Fl 9 New York (10018) *(G-10439)*

Merzon Leather Co Inc 718 782-6260
  810 Humboldt St Ste 2 Brooklyn (11222) *(G-2144)*

Mesh LLC 646 839-7000
  350 5th Ave Lbby 9 New York (10118) *(G-10440)*

Mesoblast Inc 212 880-2060
  505 5th Ave Fl 3 New York (10017) *(G-10441)*

Mesorah Publications Ltd 718 921-9000
  4401 2nd Ave Brooklyn (11232) *(G-2145)*

Messenger Post Media, Canandaigua *Also called Wolfe Publications Inc (G-3145)*

Messenger Press 518 885-9231
  1826 Amsterdam Rd Ballston Spa (12020) *(G-582)*

Messer LLC 716 847-0748
  101 Katherine St Buffalo (14210) *(G-2865)*

Messer LLC 518 439-8187
  76 W Yard Rd Feura Bush (12067) *(G-4791)*

Messer LLC 716 773-7552
  3279 Grand Island Blvd Grand Island (14072) *(G-5337)*

Messer Merchant Production LLC 315 593-1360
  370 Owens Rd Fulton (13069) *(G-5071)*

Messex Group Inc 646 229-2582
  244 5th Ave Ste D256 New York (10001) *(G-10442)*

Mestel Brothers Stairs & Rails 516 496-4127
  11 Gary Rd Ste 102 Syosset (11791) *(G-14794)*

Met Weld International LLC 518 765-2318
  5727 Ostrander Rd Altamont (12009) *(G-196)*

Meta-Therm Corp 914 697-4840
  70 W Red Oak Ln White Plains (10604) *(G-16029)*

Metadure Parts & Sales Inc 631 249-2141
  165 Gazza Blvd Farmingdale (11735) *(G-4681)*

Metal Cladding Inc 716 434-5513
  230 S Niagara St Lockport (14094) *(G-7091)*

Metal Coated Fibers Inc 518 280-8514
  679 Mariaville Rd Schenectady (12306) *(G-14288)*

Metal Container Corporation 845 567-1500
  1000 Breunig Rd New Windsor (12553) *(G-8372)*

Metal Crafts Inc 718 443-3333
  650 Berriman St Brooklyn (11208) *(G-2146)*

Metal Dynamics Intl Corp 631 231-1153
  25 Corporate Dr Hauppauge (11788) *(G-5715)*

Metal Fab LLC 607 775-3200
  13 Spud Ln Binghamton (13904) *(G-898)*

Metal Improvement Company LLC 607 533-7000
  131 Woodsedge Dr Lansing (14882) *(G-6841)*

Metal Man Restoration 914 662-4218
  254 E 3rd St Fl 1 Mount Vernon (10553) *(G-8161)*

Metal Man Services, Watertown *Also called Kenal Services Corp (G-15576)*

Metal Parts Manufacturing Inc 315 831-2530
  119 Remsen Rd Barneveld (13304) *(G-593)*

Metal Products Intl LLC 716 215-1930
  7510 Porter Rd Ste 4 Niagara Falls (14304) *(G-11950)*

Metal Solutions Inc 315 732-6271
  1821 Broad St Ste 5 Utica (13501) *(G-15281)*

Metal Stampings, Honeoye Falls *Also called Stever-Locke Industries Inc (G-6081)*

Metal Tek Products 516 586-4514
  100 Express St Plainview (11803) *(G-12700)*

Metal Works of NY Inc 718 525-9440
  11603 Merrick Blvd Jamaica (11434) *(G-6459)*

Metalcraft By N Barzel, Brooklyn *Also called Metal Crafts Inc (G-2146)*

Metalcraft Marine Us Inc 315 501-4015
  583 E Broadway St Cape Vincent (13618) *(G-3168)*

Metalico Aluminum Recovery Inc 315 463-9500
  6223 Thompson Rd Syracuse (13206) *(G-14940)*

Metalico Syracuse, Syracuse *Also called Metalico Aluminum Recovery Inc (G-14940)*

Metallic Ladder Mfg Corp 716 358-6201
  41 S Washington St Randolph (14772) *(G-13063)*

Metalline Fire Door Co Inc (PA) 718 583-2320
  4110 Park Ave Bronx (10457) *(G-1311)*

Metallized Carbon Corporation (PA) 914 941-3738
  19 S Water St Ossining (10562) *(G-12404)*

Metallogix Design Fabrication 315 738-4554
  1305 Conkling Ave Utica (13501) *(G-15282)*

Metalocke Industries Inc 718 267-9200
  3202 57th St Woodside (11377) *(G-16213)*

Metals Building Products 844 638-2527
  5005 Veterans Mem Hwy Holbrook (11741) *(G-6010)*

Metalsigma Usa Inc 212 731-4346
  350 5th Ave New York (10118) *(G-10443)*
Metalsmith Inc 631 467-1500
  1340 Lincoln Ave Ste 13 Holbrook (11741) *(G-6011)*
Metalworks Inc 718 319-0011
  1303 Herschell St Bronx (10461) *(G-1312)*
Metcar Products, Ossining *Also called Metallized Carbon Corporation* *(G-12404)*
Meteor Express Inc 718 551-9177
  16801 Rockaway Blvd # 202 Jamaica (11434) *(G-6460)*
Methods Tooling & Mfg Inc 845 246-7100
  635 Glasco Tpke Mount Marion (12456) *(G-8111)*
Metpar Corp 516 333-2600
  95 State St Westbury (11590) *(G-15910)*
Metro Center Western New York, Buffalo *Also called William S Hein & Co Inc* *(G-3049)*
Metro City Group Inc 516 781-2500
  2283 Bellmore Ave Bellmore (11710) *(G-784)*
Metro Creative Graphics Inc (PA) 212 947-5100
  519 8th Ave Fl 18 New York (10018) *(G-10444)*
Metro Door Inc (HQ) 800 669-3667
  2929 Express Dr N 300b Islandia (11749) *(G-6340)*
Metro Duct Systems Inc 718 278-4294
  1219 Astoria Blvd Apt 2 Long Island City (11102) *(G-7294)*
Metro Dynamics Scie 631 842-4300
  20 Nancy St Unit A West Babylon (11704) *(G-15731)*
Metro Fuel LLC 212 836-9608
  800 3rd Ave Fl 28 New York (10022) *(G-10445)*
Metro Group Inc (PA) 718 729-7200
  5023 23rd St Long Island City (11101) *(G-7295)*
Metro Group Inc 716 434-4055
  8 South St Lockport (14094) *(G-7092)*
Metro Grouping, Long Island City *Also called Metro Group Inc* *(G-7295)*
Metro Iron Corp 631 842-5929
  4 Seabro Ave Amityville (11701) *(G-296)*
Metro Kitchens Corp 718 434-1166
  1040 E 45th St Brooklyn (11203) *(G-2147)*
Metro Lube (PA) 718 947-1167
  9110 Metropolitan Ave Rego Park (11374) *(G-13080)*
Metro Machining & Fabricating 718 545-0104
  3234 61st St Woodside (11377) *(G-16214)*
Metro Mattress Corp 716 205-2300
  2212 Military Rd Niagara Falls (14304) *(G-11951)*
Metro Nespaper, New York *Also called Seabay Media Holdings LLC* *(G-11172)*
Metro New York, New York *Also called Sb New York Inc* *(G-11144)*
Metro Products & Services LLC (PA) 866 846-8486
  1424 74th St Brooklyn (11228) *(G-2148)*
Metro Service Center, Elmsford *Also called Westinghouse A Brake Tech Corp* *(G-4440)*
Metro Service Solutions, Islandia *Also called Metro Door Inc* *(G-6340)*
METRO STORAGE CENTER, Getzville *Also called William S Hein & Co Inc* *(G-5184)*
Metro Tel Communications, Staten Island *Also called I D Tel Corp* *(G-14662)*
Metrofab Pipe Incorporated 516 349-7373
  15 Fairchild Ct Plainview (11803) *(G-12701)*
Metropltan Data Sltons MGT Inc 516 586-5520
  279 Conklin St Farmingdale (11735) *(G-4682)*
Metropolis Magazine, New York *Also called Bellerophon Publications Inc* *(G-8752)*
Metropolitan Granite & MBL Inc 585 342-7020
  860 Maple St Ste 100 Rochester (14611) *(G-13543)*
Metropolitan Packg Mfg Corp 718 383-2700
  68 Java St Brooklyn (11222) *(G-2149)*
Metropolitan Signs Inc 315 638-1448
  3760 Patchett Rd Baldwinsville (13027) *(G-551)*
Metrosource Publishing Inc 212 691-5127
  498 Fashion Ave Fl 10 New York (10018) *(G-10446)*
Mettowee Lumber & Plastics Co 518 642-1100
  82 Church St Granville (12832) *(G-5352)*
Meyco Products Inc (PA) 631 421-9800
  1225 Walt Whitman Rd Melville (11747) *(G-7804)*
Mezmeriz Inc 607 216-8140
  33 Thornwood Dr Ste 100 Ithaca (14850) *(G-6396)*
Mezzoprint LLC (PA) 347 480-9199
  201 E Merrick Rd Ste 3 Valley Stream (11580) *(G-15347)*
Mf Digital, Deer Park *Also called Formats Unlimited Inc* *(G-3875)*
Mg Imaging 212 704-4073
  229 W 28th St Rm 300 New York (10001) *(G-10447)*
Mgd Brands Inc 516 545-0150
  30 Commercial Ct Plainview (11803) *(G-12702)*
Mgi, Hauppauge *Also called Mini Graphics Inc* *(G-5720)*
Mgi, Northport *Also called Marketing Group International* *(G-12109)*
Mgk Group Inc 212 989-2732
  979 3rd Ave Ste 1811 New York (10022) *(G-10448)*
MGM, Buffalo *Also called Tyson Deli Inc* *(G-3024)*
Mgr Equipment Corp 516 239-3030
  22 Gates Ave Inwood (11096) *(G-6298)*
Mgs Group, The, Rome *Also called MGS Manufacturing Inc* *(G-13856)*
MGS Manufacturing Inc (PA) 315 337-3350
  122 Otis St Rome (13441) *(G-13856)*
Mhg Studio Inc 212 674-7610
  175 Rivington St Frnt 2 New York (10002) *(G-10449)*
Mht Lighting, Staten Island *Also called North American Mfg Entps Inc* *(G-14684)*
Mhxco Foam Company LLC 518 843-8400
  120 Edson St Amsterdam (12010) *(G-335)*

Miami Media LLC (HQ) 212 268-8600
  72 Madison Ave Fl 11 New York (10016) *(G-10450)*
Mica International Ltd 516 378-3400
  126 Albany Ave Freeport (11520) *(G-5008)*
Mica World, Northport *Also called Huntington Woodworking Inc* *(G-12105)*
Micatu Inc 888 705-8836
  315 Daniel Zenker Dr # 202 Horseheads (14845) *(G-6126)*
Micelli Chocalate Mold Co, West Babylon *Also called Sweet Tooth Enterprises LLC* *(G-15752)*
Michael Andrews Bespoke, New York *Also called Michael Andrews LLC* *(G-10451)*
Michael Andrews LLC 212 677-1755
  680 Broadway Fl Mezz New York (10012) *(G-10451)*
Michael Benalt Inc 845 628-1008
  100 Buckshollow Rd Mahopac (10541) *(G-7474)*
Michael Bernstein Design Assoc 718 456-9277
  361 Stagg St Fl 4 Brooklyn (11206) *(G-2150)*
Michael Bondanza Inc 212 869-0043
  10 E 38th St Fl 6 New York (10016) *(G-10452)*
Michael Feldman Inc 718 433-1700
  3010 41st Ave Ste 3 Long Island City (11101) *(G-7296)*
Michael Fiore Ltd 516 561-8238
  126 E Fairview Ave Valley Stream (11580) *(G-15348)*
Michael K Lennon Inc 631 288-5200
  851 Riverhead Rd Westhampton Beach (11978) *(G-15957)*
Michael Karp Music Inc 212 840-3285
  59 W 71st St Apt 7a New York (10023) *(G-10453)*
Michael Kors, New York *Also called Herman Kay Company Ltd* *(G-9768)*
Michael Neuman, Rye *Also called Western Oil and Gas JV Inc* *(G-14086)*
Michael P Mmarr 315 623-9380
  1358 State Route 49 Constantia (13044) *(G-3636)*
Michael Stuart Inc 718 821-0704
  199 Cook St Brooklyn (11206) *(G-2151)*
Michael Todd Stevens 585 436-9957
  95 Mount Read Blvd # 125 Rochester (14611) *(G-13544)*
Michaelian & Kohlberg Inc 212 431-9009
  225 E 59th St New York (10022) *(G-10454)*
Michbi Doors Inc 631 231-9050
  175 Marine St Farmingdale (11735) *(G-4683)*
Michel Design Works Ltd 914 763-2244
  41 Katonah Ave Ste 209 Katonah (10536) *(G-6635)*
Michel Design Works USA, Katonah *Also called Michel Design Works Ltd* *(G-6635)*
Mickelberry Communications Inc (PA) 212 832-0303
  405 Park Ave New York (10022) *(G-10455)*
Micosta Enterprises Inc 518 822-9708
  3007 County Route 20 Hudson (12534) *(G-6171)*
Micro Contacts Inc (PA) 516 433-4830
  1 Enterprise Pl Unit E Hicksville (11801) *(G-5929)*
Micro Contract Manufacturing 631 738-7874
  27 Scouting Blvd Unit E Medford (11763) *(G-7719)*
Micro Essential Laboratory 718 338-3618
  4224 Avenue H Brooklyn (11210) *(G-2152)*
Micro Graphics, Lockport *Also called Jack J Florio Jr* *(G-7085)*
Micro Instrument Corp 585 458-3150
  1199 Emerson St Rochester (14606) *(G-13545)*
Micro Photo Acoustics Inc 631 750-6035
  105 Comac St Ronkonkoma (11779) *(G-13973)*
Micro Powders Inc (PA) 914 332-6400
  580 White Plains Rd # 400 Tarrytown (10591) *(G-15048)*
Micro Publishing Inc 212 533-9180
  71 W 23rd St Lbby A New York (10010) *(G-10456)*
Micro Semicdtr Researches LLC (PA) 646 863-6070
  310 W 52nd St Apt 12b New York (10019) *(G-10457)*
Micro Systems Specialists Inc 845 677-6150
  3280 Franklin Ave Fl 2 Millbrook (12545) *(G-7943)*
Micro Threaded Products Inc 585 288-0080
  325 Mount Read Blvd Ste 4 Rochester (14611) *(G-13546)*
Micro-Tech Machine Inc 315 331-6671
  301 W Shore Blvd Newark (14513) *(G-11846)*
Microb Phase Services 518 877-8948
  14 Nottingham Way S Clifton Park (12065) *(G-3468)*
Microcad Trning Consulting Inc 617 923-0500
  1110 Route 55 Ste 209 Lagrangeville (12540) *(G-6751)*
Microcad Trning Consulting Inc 631 291-9484
  77 Arkay Dr Ste C2 Hauppauge (11788) *(G-5716)*
Microchip Technology Inc 631 233-3280
  80 Arkay Dr Ste 100 Hauppauge (11788) *(G-5717)*
Microchip Technology Inc 607 785-5992
  3301 Country Club Rd Endicott (13760) *(G-4465)*
Microera Printers Inc 585 783-1300
  304 Whitney St Rochester (14606) *(G-13547)*
Microfoam, Utica *Also called Idg LLC* *(G-15274)*
Microgen Systems Inc 585 214-2426
  3 Railroad St Ste D Fairport (14450) *(G-4507)*
Micromatter Tech Inc USA 631 580-2522
  1340 Lincoln Ave Ste 6 Holbrook (11741) *(G-6012)*
Micromem Technologies 212 672-1806
  245 Park Ave Fl 24 New York (10167) *(G-10458)*
Micromold Products Inc 914 969-2850
  7 Odell Plz 133 Yonkers (10701) *(G-16333)*
Micron Inds Rochester Inc 585 247-6130
  31 Industrial Park Cir Rochester (14624) *(G-13548)*
Micropage, New York *Also called Micro Publishing Inc* *(G-10456)*

ALPHABETIC

MICROPEN DIVISION, Honeoye Falls *Also called Micropen Technologies Corp* ***(G-6078)***
Micropen Technologies Corp....585 624-2610
93 Papermill St Honeoye Falls (14472) ***(G-6078)***
Microsoft Corporation....914 323-2150
125 Westchester Ave White Plains (10601) ***(G-16030)***
Microsoft Corporation....631 760-2340
160 Walt Whitman Rd 1006b Huntington Station (11746) ***(G-6254)***
Microsoft Corporation....212 245-2100
11 Times Sq Fl 9 New York (10036) ***(G-10459)***
Microsoft Corporation....516 380-1531
2929 Expressway Dr N # 300 Hauppauge (11749) ***(G-5718)***
Microstrategy Incorporated....888 537-8135
5 Penn Plz Ste 901 New York (10001) ***(G-10460)***
Microwave Filter Company Inc (PA)....315 438-4700
6743 Kinne St East Syracuse (13057) ***(G-4226)***
Mid Atlantic Graphics Corp....631 345-3800
14 Ramsey Rd Shirley (11967) ***(G-14424)***
Mid Enterprise Inc....631 924-3933
809 Middle Country Rd Middle Island (11953) ***(G-7875)***
Mid Hdson Wkshp For The Dsbled....845 471-3820
188 Washington St Poughkeepsie (12601) ***(G-12970)***
Mid York Weekly & Pennysaver....315 792-4990
221 Oriskany St E Utica (13501) ***(G-15283)***
Mid-Hudson Concrete Pdts Inc....845 265-3141
3504 Route 9 Cold Spring (10516) ***(G-3521)***
Mid-State Ready Mix, Central Square *Also called Torrington Industries Inc* ***(G-3296)***
Mid-York Press Inc....607 674-4491
2808 State Highway 80 Sherburne (13460) ***(G-14392)***
Midas Mdici Group Holdings Inc (PA)....212 792-0920
445 Park Ave Frnt 5 New York (10022) ***(G-10461)***
Midbury Industries Inc....516 868-0600
86 E Merrick Rd Freeport (11520) ***(G-5009)***
Middle Ages Brewing Company....315 476-4250
120 Wilkinson St Ste 1 Syracuse (13204) ***(G-14941)***
Middleby Corporation....631 226-6688
175 E Hoffman Ave Lindenhurst (11757) ***(G-6960)***
Middletown Press (PA)....845 343-1895
20 W Main St 26 Middletown (10940) ***(G-7920)***
Midgley Printing Corp....315 475-1864
433 W Onondaga St Syracuse (13202) ***(G-14942)***
Midland Farms Inc (PA)....518 436-7038
375 Broadway Menands (12204) ***(G-7846)***
Midland Machinery Co Inc....716 692-1200
101 Cranbrook Road Ext Exd Tonawanda (14150) ***(G-15122)***
Midstate Printing Corp....315 475-4101
4707 Dey Rd Liverpool (13088) ***(G-7026)***
Midstate Spring Inc....315 437-2623
4054 New Court Ave Syracuse (13206) ***(G-14943)***
Midura Jewels Inc....213 265-8090
36 W 47th St Ste 809i New York (10036) ***(G-10462)***
Mikael Aghal LLC....212 596-4010
49 W 38th St Fl 4 New York (10018) ***(G-10463)***
Mikam Graphics LLC....212 684-9393
1440 Broadway Fl 22 New York (10018) ***(G-10464)***
Mike's Custom Cabinets, Constantia *Also called Michael P Mmarr* ***(G-3636)***
Mikkeller Nyc....917 572-0357
12001 Roosevelt Ave Flushing (11368) ***(G-4874)***
Mil & Mir Steel Pdts Co Inc....718 328-7596
1210 Randall Ave Bronx (10474) ***(G-1313)***
Mil-Spec. Enterprises, Brooklyn *Also called Carter Enterprises LLC* ***(G-1650)***
Milaaya Embroideries, New York *Also called Milaaya Inc* ***(G-10465)***
Milaaya Inc....212 764-6386
147 W 35th St Ste 602 New York (10001) ***(G-10465)***
Milan Provision Co Inc....718 899-7678
10815 Roosevelt Ave Corona (11368) ***(G-3745)***
Milanese Commercial Door LLC....518 658-0398
28 Taylor Ave Berlin (12022) ***(G-825)***
Milburn Printing, Bohemia *Also called Mpe Graphics Inc* ***(G-1048)***
Miles Machine Inc....716 484-6026
85 Jones And Gifford Ave Jamestown (14701) ***(G-6533)***
Miles Moss of Albany Inc (HQ)....516 222-8008
586 Commercial Ave Garden City (11530) ***(G-5108)***
Miles Moss of New York Inc (PA)....516 222-8008
586 Commercial Ave Garden City (11530) ***(G-5109)***
Milestone Construction Corp....718 459-8500
13620 38th Ave Ste 11j Flushing (11354) ***(G-4875)***
Milex Precision Inc....631 595-2393
66 S 2nd St Ste G Bay Shore (11706) ***(G-692)***
Milgo Industrial, Brooklyn *Also called M B C Metal Inc* ***(G-2095)***
Milgo Industrial Inc (PA)....718 388-6476
68 Lombardy St Brooklyn (11222) ***(G-2153)***
Milgo Industrial Inc....718 387-0406
514 Varick Ave Brooklyn (11222) ***(G-2154)***
Milgo/Bufkin, Brooklyn *Also called Milgo Industrial Inc* ***(G-2153)***
Military Parts Exchange LLC....631 243-1700
145 Pinelawn Rd Ste 240n Melville (11747) ***(G-7805)***
Milkboy, Brooklyn *Also called Menrose USA LLC* ***(G-2137)***
Mill Services, Cobleskill *Also called Efj Inc* ***(G-3499)***
Mill, The, Corning *Also called Ryers Creek Corp* ***(G-3720)***
Mill-Max Mfg Corp....516 922-6000
190 Pine Hollow Rd Oyster Bay (11771) ***(G-12449)***

Millbrook Vineyard, Millbrook *Also called Millbrook Winery Inc* ***(G-7944)***
Millbrook Winery Inc....845 677-8383
26 Wing Rd Millbrook (12545) ***(G-7944)***
Millco Woodworking LLC....585 526-6844
1710 Railroad Pl Hall (14463) ***(G-5500)***
Millennium Antenna Corp....315 798-9374
1001 Broad St Ste 401 Utica (13501) ***(G-15284)***
Millennium Medical Publishing....212 995-2211
611 Broadway Rm 310 New York (10012) ***(G-10466)***
Millennium Productions Inc....212 944-6203
265 W 37th St 11 New York (10018) ***(G-10467)***
Millennium Rmnfctred Toner Inc....718 585-9887
7 Bruckner Blvd Bronx (10454) ***(G-1314)***
Millennium Signs & Display Inc....516 292-8000
90 W Graham Ave Hempstead (11550) ***(G-5845)***
Millennium Stl Rack Rntals Inc (PA)....718 965-4736
253 Bond St Brooklyn (11217) ***(G-2155)***
Miller & Berkowitz Ltd....212 244-5459
345 7th Ave Fl 20 New York (10001) ***(G-10468)***
Miller & Veit Inc....212 247-2275
22 W 48th St Ste 703 New York (10036) ***(G-10469)***
Miller Blaker Inc....718 665-0500
620 E 132nd St Bronx (10454) ***(G-1315)***
Miller Mechanical Services Inc....518 792-0430
55-57 Walnut St Glens Falls (12801) ***(G-5259)***
Miller Metal Fabricating Inc....585 359-3400
315 Commerce Dr Rochester (14623) ***(G-13549)***
Miller Mohr Display Inc....631 941-2769
12 Technology Dr Unit 6 East Setauket (11733) ***(G-4181)***
Miller Place Printing Inc....631 473-1158
451 Route 25a Unit 11 Miller Place (11764) ***(G-7945)***
Miller Printing & Litho Inc....518 842-0001
97 Guy Park Ave Amsterdam (12010) ***(G-336)***
Miller Stuart, Edgewood *Also called Compac Development Corporation* ***(G-4265)***
Miller Technology Inc....631 694-2224
61 Gazza Blvd Farmingdale (11735) ***(G-4684)***
Miller Truck Rental, Scottsville *Also called Jack W Miller* ***(G-14341)***
Miller's Ready Mix, Gloversville *Also called Stephen Miller Gen Contrs Inc* ***(G-5293)***
Millercoors LLC....585 385-0670
1000 Pittsford Victor Rd Pittsford (14534) ***(G-12652)***
Millers Bulk Food and Bakery....585 798-9700
10858 Ridge Rd Medina (14103) ***(G-7741)***
Millers Millworks Inc....585 494-1420
29 N Lake Ave Bergen (14416) ***(G-818)***
Millers Presentation Furniture, Bergen *Also called Millers Millworks Inc* ***(G-818)***
Milli Home, New York *Also called Global Resources Sg Inc* ***(G-9632)***
Milligan & Higgins Div, Johnstown *Also called Hudson Industries Corporation* ***(G-6619)***
Millivac Instruments Inc....518 355-8300
2818 Curry Rd Schenectady (12303) ***(G-14289)***
Millman's, Poughkeepsie *Also called T-Shirt Factory Inc* ***(G-12987)***
Millrock Technology Inc....845 339-5700
39 Kieffer Ln Ste 2 Kingston (12401) ***(G-6703)***
Mills, William J & Company, Greenport *Also called 125-127 Main Street Corp* ***(G-5456)***
Millwood Inc....518 233-1475
430 Hudson River Rd Waterford (12188) ***(G-15539)***
Millwright Wdwrk Installetion....631 587-2635
991 Peconic Ave West Babylon (11704) ***(G-15732)***
Milmar Food Group, Goshen *Also called Juno Chefs* ***(G-5310)***
Milmar Food Group II LLC....845 294-5400
1 6 1/2 Station Rd Goshen (10924) ***(G-5311)***
Milne Mfg Inc....716 772-2536
8411 State St Gasport (14067) ***(G-5139)***
Milnot Holding Corporation....518 839-0300
1 Nutritious Pl Amsterdam (12010) ***(G-337)***
Milso Industries Inc....631 234-1133
25 Engineers Rd Hauppauge (11788) ***(G-5719)***
Milton Merl & Associates Inc....212 634-9292
647 W 174th St Bsmt B New York (10033) ***(G-10470)***
Miltons of New York Inc....212 997-3359
110 W 40th St Rm 1001 New York (10018) ***(G-10471)***
Milward Alloys Inc....716 434-5536
500 Mill St Lockport (14094) ***(G-7093)***
Mima S Bakery, Brooklyn *Also called Vito & Sons Bakery* ***(G-2566)***
Mimeocom Inc (PA)....212 847-3000
3 Park Ave Fl 22 New York (10016) ***(G-10472)***
Mimi So International LLC....212 300-8600
22 W 48th St Ste 902 New York (10036) ***(G-10473)***
Mimi So New York, New York *Also called Mimi So International LLC* ***(G-10473)***
Min Ho Designs Inc....212 838-3667
425 Madison Ave Rm 1703 New York (10017) ***(G-10474)***
Min New York, New York *Also called Salonclick LLC* ***(G-11121)***
Min-Max Machine Ltd....631 585-4378
1971 Pond Rd Ronkonkoma (11779) ***(G-13974)***
Mind Designs Inc (PA)....631 563-3644
5 Gregory Ct Farmingville (11738) ***(G-4782)***
Mindbodygreen LLC....347 529-6952
45 Main St Ste 422 Brooklyn (11201) ***(G-2156)***
Mindful Foods Inc....646 708-0454
246 5th Ave Fl 3 New York (10001) ***(G-10475)***
Mineo & Sapio Meats Inc....716 884-2398
410 Connecticut St Buffalo (14213) ***(G-2866)***

Minerals Technologies Inc (PA) 212 878-1800
622 3rd Ave Rm 3800 New York (10017) *(G-10476)*

Minero & Sapio Sausage, Buffalo *Also called Mineo & Sapio Meats Inc (G-2866)*

Mines Press Inc 888 559-2634
231 Croton Ave Cortlandt Manor (10567) *(G-3797)*

Ming Pao (new York) Inc 212 334-2220
265 Canal St Ste 403 New York (10013) *(G-10477)*

Mini Circuits, Brooklyn *Also called Scientific Components Corp (G-2391)*

Mini Circuits Lab, Deer Park *Also called Scientific Components Corp (G-3934)*

Mini Graphics Inc 516 223-6464
140 Commerce Dr Hauppauge (11788) *(G-5720)*

Mini-Circuits, Brooklyn *Also called Scientific Components Corp (G-2390)*

Mini-Circuits Fort Wayne LLC 718 934-4500
13 Neptune Ave Brooklyn (11235) *(G-2157)*

Minico Industries Inc 631 595-1455
66a S 2nd St Ste A Bay Shore (11706) *(G-693)*

Minimill Technologies Inc 315 692-4557
5792 Widewaters Pkwy # 1 Syracuse (13214) *(G-14944)*

Minisink Rubber, Warwick *Also called Mechanical Rubber Pdts Co Inc (G-15519)*

Minitec Framing Systems LLC 585 924-4690
5602 County Road 41 Farmington (14425) *(G-4775)*

Mink Mart Inc 212 868-2785
345 7th Ave Fl 9 New York (10001) *(G-10478)*

Minority Reporter Inc (PA) 585 225-3628
19 Borrowdale Dr Rochester (14626) *(G-13550)*

Minority Reporter Inc 585 301-4199
506 W Broad St Rochester (14608) *(G-13551)*

Mint-X Products Corporation 877 646-8224
2048 119th St College Point (11356) *(G-3554)*

Minted Green Inc 845 458-1845
85 Regina Rd Airmont (10952) *(G-14)*

Minute Man Printing Company, White Plains *Also called Garrett J Cronin (G-16008)*

Minuteman Press, Manhasset *Also called Mdr Printing Corp (G-7538)*

Minuteman Press, Port Washington *Also called Kurtskraft Inc (G-12898)*

Minuteman Press, Hewlett *Also called Torsaf Printers Inc (G-5873)*

Minuteman Press, Glen Oaks *Also called Wynco Press One Inc (G-5215)*

Minuteman Press, Deer Park *Also called L & K Graphics Inc (G-3893)*

Minuteman Press, Huntington *Also called J A T Printing Inc (G-6208)*

Minuteman Press, East Syracuse *Also called Seaboard Graphic Services LLC (G-4237)*

Minuteman Press, Hauppauge *Also called Huckleberry Inc (G-5673)*

Minuteman Press, Bellerose *Also called Leigh Scott Enterprises Inc (G-775)*

Minuteman Press, Rockville Centre *Also called Graphic Fabrications Inc (G-13828)*

Minuteman Press, Elmsford *Also called Cronin Enterprises Inc (G-4405)*

Minuteman Press, Rochester *Also called Baum Christine and John Corp (G-13261)*

Minuteman Press, Selden *Also called Datorib Inc (G-14352)*

Minuteman Press, Rochester *Also called Multiple Imprssons of Rchester (G-13563)*

Minuteman Press, Fairport *Also called Bernard Hall (G-4489)*

Minuteman Press, Farmingdale *Also called J P Printing Inc (G-4655)*

Minuteman Press, Merrick *Also called Jon Lyn Ink Inc (G-7857)*

Minuteman Press, East Northport *Also called Loudon Ltd (G-4149)*

Minuteman Press Inc 845 623-2277
121 W Nyack Rd Ste 3 Nanuet (10954) *(G-8202)*

Minuteman Press Intl Inc (PA) 631 249-1370
61 Executive Blvd Farmingdale (11735) *(G-4685)*

Minuteman Press Inc 718 343-5440
24814 Union Tpke Jamaica (11426) *(G-6461)*

Minutemen Precision Mch & TI, Ronkonkoma *Also called Minutemen Precsn McHning Tool (G-13975)*

Minutemen Precsn McHning Tool 631 467-4900
135 Raynor Ave Ronkonkoma (11779) *(G-13975)*

Miny Group Inc 212 925-6722
148 Lafayette St Fl 2 New York (10013) *(G-10479)*

Minyanville Media Inc 212 991-6200
708 3rd Ave Fl 6 New York (10017) *(G-10480)*

Mip, Halesite *Also called Manufacturers Indexing Pdts (G-5488)*

Mirage Moulding & Supply, Farmingdale *Also called Mirage Moulding Mfg Inc (G-4686)*

Mirage Moulding Mfg Inc 631 843-6168
160 Milbar Blvd Farmingdale (11735) *(G-4686)*

Mirion Tech Conax Nuclear Inc 716 681-1973
402 Sonwil Dr Buffalo (14225) *(G-2867)*

Mirion Tech Imaging LLC 607 562-4300
315 Daniel Zenker Dr Horseheads (14845) *(G-6127)*

Mirion Tech Imging Systems Div, Horseheads *Also called Mirion Tech Imaging LLC (G-6127)*

Mirion Technologies Ist Corp (HQ) 607 562-4300
315 Daniel Zenker Dr # 204 Horseheads (14845) *(G-6128)*

Miroddi Imaging Inc (PA) 516 624-6898
27 Centre View Dr Oyster Bay (11771) *(G-12450)*

Mirror Show Management Inc 585 232-4020
855 Hard Rd Webster (14580) *(G-15645)*

Mirror-Tech Manufacturing Co 914 965-1232
286 Nepperhan Ave Yonkers (10701) *(G-16334)*

Mirrorlite Superscript, Peekskill *Also called Hudson Mirror LLC (G-12553)*

Miscellnous Ir Fabricators Inc 518 355-1822
1404 Dunnsville Rd Schenectady (12306) *(G-14290)*

Mishpacha Magazine Inc 718 686-9339
5809 16th Ave Brooklyn (11204) *(G-2158)*

Mison Concepts Inc 516 933-8000
485 S Broadway Ste 33 Hicksville (11801) *(G-5930)*

Misonix Opco Inc (PA) 631 694-9555
1938 New Hwy Farmingdale (11735) *(G-4687)*

Miss Grimble Associates Inc 718 665-2253
909 E 135th St Bronx (10454) *(G-1316)*

Miss Group (PA) 212 391-2535
1410 Broadway Rm 703 New York (10018) *(G-10481)*

Miss Group, The, New York *Also called MISS Sportswear Inc (G-10482)*

Miss Group, The, Brooklyn *Also called MISS Sportswear Inc (G-2160)*

MISS Sportswear Inc 212 391-2535
117 9th St Brooklyn (11215) *(G-2159)*

MISS Sportswear Inc (PA) 212 391-2535
1410 Broadway Rm 703 New York (10018) *(G-10482)*

MISS Sportswear Inc 718 369-6012
117 9th St Brooklyn (11215) *(G-2160)*

Mission Crane Service Inc (PA) 718 937-3333
4700 33rd St Long Island City (11101) *(G-7297)*

Mission Critical Energy Inc 716 276-8465
1801 N French Rd Getzville (14068) *(G-5178)*

Missiontex Inc 718 532-9053
236 Greenpoint Ave Ste 12 Brooklyn (11222) *(G-2161)*

Mistdoda Inc (HQ) 919 735-7111
261 5th Ave Fl 25 New York (10016) *(G-10483)*

Mitchell Electronics Corp 914 699-3800
85 W Grand St Mount Vernon (10552) *(G-8162)*

Mitchell Machine Tool LLC 585 254-7520
190 Murray St Rochester (14606) *(G-13552)*

Mitchell Prtg & Mailing Inc (PA) 315 343-3531
1 Burkle St Oswego (13126) *(G-12414)*

Mitchell Stone Products LLC 518 359-7029
161 Main St Tupper Lake (12986) *(G-15211)*

Mitchell's Speedway Press, Oswego *Also called Speedway Press Inc (G-12421)*

Mitco Manufacturing 516 745-9236
605 Locust St Garden City (11530) *(G-5110)*

Mitegen LLC 607 266-8877
95 Brown Rd Ste 1034 Ithaca (14850) *(G-6397)*

Mitel Networks Inc 877 654-3573
300 State St Ste 100 Rochester (14614) *(G-13553)*

Mitsubishi Chemical Amer Inc (HQ) 212 223-3043
655 3rd Ave Fl 15 New York (10017) *(G-10484)*

Mitsubishi Elc Pwr Pdts Inc 516 962-2813
55 Marcus Dr Melville (11747) *(G-7806)*

Mitsui Chemicals America Inc (HQ) 914 253-0777
800 Westchester Ave N607 Rye Brook (10573) *(G-14092)*

Mitsui Plastics Inc (HQ) 914 287-6800
10 Bank St Ste 1010 White Plains (10606) *(G-16031)*

Mitten Manufacturing Inc (PA) 315 437-7564
5960 Court Street Rd Syracuse (13206) *(G-14945)*

Mix N Mac LLC 845 381-5536
280 Route 211 E Middletown (10940) *(G-7921)*

Mixture Screen Printing 845 561-2857
1607 Route 300 100 Newburgh (12550) *(G-11873)*

Mizkan America Inc 585 798-5720
711 Park Ave Medina (14103) *(G-7742)*

Mizkan America Inc 585 765-9171
247 West Ave Lyndonville (14098) *(G-7445)*

Mizkan Americas Inc 315 483-6944
7673 Sodus Center Rd Sodus (14551) *(G-14491)*

MJB Printing Corp 631 581-0177
280 Islip Ave Islip (11751) *(G-6355)*

Mjj Brilliant, New York *Also called Brilliant Jewelers/Mjj Inc (G-8854)*

Mjk Cutting Inc 718 384-7613
117 9th St Brooklyn (11215) *(G-2162)*

Mjk Enterprises LLC 917 653-9042
34 35th St Brooklyn (11232) *(G-2163)*

Mjs Woodworking, Bohemia *Also called J Percoco Industries Inc (G-1025)*

Mkj Communications Inc 212 206-0072
850 3rd Ave Ste 402 Brooklyn (11232) *(G-2164)*

Mks Instruments Inc 585 292-7472
100 Highpower Rd Rochester (14623) *(G-13554)*

Mks Medical Electronics 585 292-7400
100 Highpower Rd Rochester (14623) *(G-13555)*

Mksf Inc 212 563-3877
212 W 30th St New York (10001) *(G-10485)*

Mkt329 Inc 631 249-5500
565 Broadhollow Rd Ste 5 Farmingdale (11735) *(G-4688)*

MLS Sales 516 681-2736
226 10th St Bethpage (11714) *(G-840)*

MMC Enterprises Corp 800 435-1088
175 Commerce Dr Ste E Hauppauge (11788) *(G-5721)*

Mmj Apparel LLC 212 354-8550
1407 Broadway Fl 10 New York (10018) *(G-10486)*

Mml Software Ltd. 631 941-1313
45 Research Way Ste 207 East Setauket (11733) *(G-4182)*

Mnn Holding Company LLC 404 558-5251
155 Water St Ste 616 Brooklyn (11201) *(G-2165)*

MNS Fuel Corp. 516 735-3835
2154 Pond Rd Ronkonkoma (11779) *(G-13976)*

Mobile Fleet Inc (PA) 631 206-2920
10 Commerce Dr Hauppauge (11788) *(G-5722)*

Mobile Media Inc (PA) 845 744-8080
24 Center St Pine Bush (12566) *(G-12625)*

A
L
P
H
A
B
E
T
I
C

Mobile Mini Inc 315 732-4555
2222 Oriskany St W Ste 3 Utica (13502) *(G-15285)*
Mobileapp Systems LLC 716 667-2780
4 Grand View Trl Buffalo (14217) *(G-2868)*
Mobius Labs Inc 518 961-2600
37 Vischer Ferry Rd Rexford (12148) *(G-13095)*
Mobo Systems Inc 212 260-0895
26 Broadway Fl 24 New York (10004) *(G-10487)*
Mod Printing, Islip Also called MJB Printing Corp *(G-6355)*
Mod-A-Can Inc (PA) 516 931-8545
178 Miller Pl Hicksville (11801) *(G-5931)*
Mod-Pac Corp (PA) 716 898-8480
1801 Elmwood Ave Ste 1 Buffalo (14207) *(G-2869)*
Mod-Pac Corp 716 447-9013
1801 Elmwood Ave Ste 1 Buffalo (14207) *(G-2870)*
Modern Art Foundry Inc 718 728-2030
1870 41st St Astoria (11105) *(G-430)*
Modern Block LLC 315 923-7443
2440 Wyne Zandra Rose Vly Clyde (14433) *(G-3493)*
Modern Cabinet Company Inc 845 473-4900
17 Van Kleeck Dr Poughkeepsie (12601) *(G-12971)*
Modern Coating & Research, Palmyra Also called Modern Coating and Research *(G-12491)*
Modern Coating and Research 315 597-3517
400 E Main St Palmyra (14522) *(G-12491)*
Modern Coating and Research (PA) 315 597-3517
400 E Main St Palmyra (14522) *(G-12492)*
Modern Craft Bar Rest Equip, Lindenhurst Also called Modern Craft Bar Rest
Equip *(G-6961)*
Modern Craft Bar Rest Equip 631 226-5647
165 E Hoffman Ave Unit 3 Lindenhurst (11757) *(G-6961)*
Modern Decal Co 315 622-2778
8146 Soule Rd Liverpool (13090) *(G-7027)*
Modern Farmer Media Inc 518 828-7447
403 Warren St Hudson (12534) *(G-6172)*
Modern Itln Bky of W Babylon 631 589-7300
301 Locust Ave Oakdale (11769) *(G-12153)*
Modern Language Assn Amer Inc 646 576-5000
85 Broad St Fl 5 New York (10004) *(G-10488)*
Modern Mechanical Fab Inc 518 298-5177
100 Walnut St Ste 7 Champlain (12919) *(G-3315)*
Modern Metal Fabricators Inc 518 966-4142
799 Cr 111 Hannacroix (12087) *(G-5541)*
Modern Packaging Inc 631 595-2437
505 Acorn St Deer Park (11729) *(G-3907)*
Modern Plastic Bags Mfg Inc 718 237-2985
63 Flushing Ave Unit 303 Brooklyn (11205) *(G-2166)*
Modern Publishing, New York Also called Unisystems Inc *(G-11596)*
Modern-TEC Manufacturing Inc 716 625-8700
4935 Lockport Rd Lockport (14094) *(G-7094)*
Modo Eyewear, New York Also called Modo Retail LLC *(G-10489)*
Modo Retail LLC 212 965-4900
252 Mott St New York (10012) *(G-10489)*
Modu-Craft Inc (PA) 716 694-0709
276 Creekside Dr Tonawanda (14150) *(G-15123)*
Modu-Craft Inc 716 694-0709
337 Payne Ave North Tonawanda (14120) *(G-12078)*
Modular Devices Inc 631 345-3100
1 Roned Rd Shirley (11967) *(G-14425)*
Modular Medical Corp 718 829-2626
1513 Olmstead Ave Bronx (10462) *(G-1317)*
Modulex New York Inc 646 742-1320
192 Lexington Ave Rm 1002 New York (10016) *(G-10490)*
Modulightor Inc 212 371-0336
246 E 58th St New York (10022) *(G-10491)*
Modutank Inc 718 392-1112
4104 35th Ave Long Island City (11101) *(G-7298)*
Moelis Capital Partners LLC (PA) 212 883-3800
399 Park Ave Fl 5 New York (10022) *(G-10492)*
Moes Wear Apparel Inc 718 940-1597
1020 E 48th St Ste 8 Brooklyn (11203) *(G-2167)*
Moga Trading Company Inc 718 760-2966
57 Granger St Corona (11368) *(G-3746)*
Mogen David Winegroup, Westfield Also called Wine Group Inc *(G-15953)*
Mohawk Electro Techniques Inc 315 896-2661
7677 Cameron Hill Rd Barneveld (13304) *(G-594)*
Mohawk Fabric Company Inc 518 842-3090
96 Guy Park Ave Amsterdam (12010) *(G-338)*
Mohawk Fine Papers Inc (PA) 518 237-1740
465 Saratoga St Cohoes (12047) *(G-3510)*
Mohawk Group Holdings Inc (PA) 347 676-1681
37 E 18th St Fl 7 New York (10003) *(G-10493)*
Mohawk Innovative Tech Inc (PA) 518 862-4290
1037 Watervliet Shaker Rd Albany (12205) *(G-100)*
Mohawk Metal Mfg & Sls 315 853-7663
4901 State Route 233 Westmoreland (13490) *(G-15960)*
Mohawk Resources Ltd 518 842-1431
65 Vrooman Ave Amsterdam (12010) *(G-339)*
Mohawk River Leather Works 518 853-3900
32 Broad St Fultonville (12072) *(G-5080)*
Mohawk Sign Systems Inc 518 842-5303
5 Dandreano Dr Amsterdam (12010) *(G-340)*

Mohawk Valley Knt McHy Co Inc 315 736-3038
561 Main St New York Mills (13417) *(G-11835)*
Mohawk Valley Manufacturing 315 797-0851
2237 Broad St Frankfort (13340) *(G-4954)*
Mohawk Valley Mill, Little Falls Also called Burrows Paper Corporation *(G-6988)*
Mohawk Valley Printing Co, Herkimer Also called Lennons Litho Inc *(G-5866)*
Moira New Hope Food Pantry 518 529-6524
2341 County Route 5 Moira (12957) *(G-8012)*
Mokai Manufacturing Inc 845 566-8287
13 Jeanne Dr Newburgh (12550) *(G-11874)*
Molabs Inc 310 721-6828
32 Little West 12th St New York (10014) *(G-10494)*
Mold-A-Matic Corporation 607 433-2121
147 River St Oneonta (13820) *(G-12276)*
Mold-Rite Plastics LLC 518 561-1812
1 Plant St Plattsburgh (12901) *(G-12759)*
Moldcraft Inc 716 684-1126
240 Gould Ave Depew (14043) *(G-3988)*
Moldedtanks.com, Bay Shore Also called Chem-Tek Systems Inc *(G-662)*
Moldova Pickles & Salads Inc 718 284-2220
1060 E 46th St Brooklyn (11203) *(G-2168)*
Moldtech Inc 716 685-3344
1900 Commerce Pkwy Lancaster (14086) *(G-6818)*
Molecular Glasses Inc 585 210-2861
1667 Lake Ave Ste 278b Rochester (14615) *(G-13556)*
Moley Magnetics Inc 716 434 4023
5202 Commerce Dr Lockport (14094) *(G-7095)*
Mom Dad Publishing Inc 646 476-9170
59 Maiden Ln Fl 27 New York (10038) *(G-10495)*
Mom Holding Company (PA) 518 233-3330
260 Hudson River Rd Waterford (12188) *(G-15540)*
Momentive, Waterford Also called Mpm Holdings Inc *(G-15543)*
Momentive, Waterford Also called Mpm Silicones LLC *(G-15545)*
Momentive Performance LLC (HQ) 281 325-3536
260 Hudson River Rd Waterford (12188) *(G-15541)*
Momentive Performance Mtls Inc 914 784-4807
769 Old Saw Mill River Rd Tarrytown (10591) *(G-15049)*
Momentive Performance Mtls Inc (HQ) 518 233-3330
260 Hudson River Rd Waterford (12188) *(G-15542)*
Momentummedia Sports Pubg, Ithaca Also called Mag Inc *(G-6395)*
Momn Pops Inc 845 567-0640
13 Orr Hatch Cornwall (12518) *(G-3729)*
Momofuku 171 First Avenue LLC 212 777-7773
171 1st Ave New York (10003) *(G-10496)*
Monacelli Press LLC 212 229-9925
6 W 18th St Ste 2c New York (10011) *(G-10497)*
Monaghan Medical Corporation (PA) 518 561-7330
5 Latour Ave Ste 1600 Plattsburgh (12901) *(G-12760)*
Monaghan Medical Corporation 315 472-2136
327 W Fayette St Ste 214 Syracuse (13202) *(G-14946)*
Monarch Electric Products Inc 718 583-7996
4077 Park Ave Fl 5 Bronx (10457) *(G-1318)*
Monarch Graphics Inc 631 232-1300
1065 Islip Ave Central Islip (11722) *(G-3284)*
Monarch Metal Fabrication Inc 631 563-8967
1625 Sycamore Ave Ste A Bohemia (11716) *(G-1047)*
Monarch Plastics Inc 716 569-2175
225 Falconer St Frewsburg (14738) *(G-5051)*
Monasani Signs Inc 631 266-2635
22 Compton St East Northport (11731) *(G-4150)*
Mondelez Global LLC 845 567-4701
800 Corporate Blvd Newburgh (12550) *(G-11875)*
Mondelez Global LLC 585 345-3300
4303 Federal Dr Batavia (14020) *(G-620)*
Mondo Publishing Inc (PA) 212 268-3560
980 Avenue Of The America New York (10018) *(G-10498)*
Moneast LLC 845 298-8898
1708 Route 9 Ste 3 Wappingers Falls (12590) *(G-15498)*
Monelle Jewelry 212 977-9535
608 5th Ave Ste 504 New York (10020) *(G-10499)*
Moneypaper Inc 914 925-0022
411 Theodore Fremd Ave # 132 Rye (10580) *(G-14083)*
Monfefo LLC 347 779-2600
630 Flushing Ave 5q Brooklyn (11206) *(G-2169)*
Mongiello Sales Inc 845 436-4200
250 Hilldale Rd Hurleyville (12747) *(G-6268)*
Mongiellos Itln Cheese Spc LLC 845 436-4200
250 Hilldale Rd Hurleyville (12747) *(G-6269)*
Mongodb Inc (PA) 646 727-4092
1633 Broadway Fl 38 New York (10019) *(G-10500)*
Mongru Neckwear Inc 718 706-0406
1010 44th Ave Fl 2 Long Island City (11101) *(G-7299)*
Monitor Controls, Hauppauge Also called Monitor Elevator Products LLC *(G-5723)*
Monitor Elevator Products LLC 631 543-4334
125 Ricefield Ln Hauppauge (11788) *(G-5723)*
Monkey Rum, New York Also called Evolution Spirits Inc *(G-9432)*
Mono-Systems Inc 716 821-1344
180 Hopkins St Buffalo (14220) *(G-2871)*
Monofrax LLC 716 483-7200
1870 New York Ave Falconer (14733) *(G-4550)*
Monogram Online, Syosset Also called Deal To Win Inc *(G-14784)*

Monolithic Coatings Inc..............................914 621-2765
 916 Highway Route 20 Sharon Springs (13459) *(G-14383)*
Monroe Cable Company Inc..........................845 692-2800
 14 Commercial Ave Middletown (10941) *(G-7922)*
Monroe Cnty Chapter Nysarc Inc...................585 698-1320
 1651 Lyell Ave Rochester (14606) *(G-13557)*
Monroe Fluid Technology Inc.......................585 392-3434
 36 Draffin Rd Hilton (14468) *(G-5973)*
Monroe Industries Inc.................................585 226-8230
 5611 Tec Dr Avon (14414) *(G-514)*
Monroe Piping & Shtmtl LLC (PA)..................585 482-0200
 68 Humboldt St Rochester (14609) *(G-13558)*
Monroe Plating Div, Rochester *Also called McAlpin Industries Inc (G-13539)*
Monroe Sign & Awning, Cicero *Also called Awning Mart Inc (G-3416)*
Monroe Stair Products Inc (PA).....................845 783-4245
 1 Stair Way Monroe (10950) *(G-8028)*
Monroe Stair Products Inc...........................845 791-4016
 309 E Broadway Monticello (12701) *(G-8071)*
Monroe Table Company Inc..........................716 945-7700
 255 Rochester St Ste 15 Salamanca (14779) *(G-14124)*
Montauk Brewing Company Inc.....................631 668-8471
 62 S Erie Ave Montauk (11954) *(G-8055)*
Montauk Inlet Seafood Inc...........................631 668-3419
 E Lake Dr Ste 540-541 Montauk (11954) *(G-8056)*
Monte Press Inc......................................718 325-4999
 4808 White Plains Rd Bronx (10470) *(G-1319)*
Monteforte Bakery, Richmond Hill *Also called J & S Licata Bros Inc (G-13117)*
Montero International Inc.............................212 695-1787
 155 Sullivan Ln 1 Westbury (11590) *(G-15911)*
Montezuma Winery LLC...............................315 568-8190
 2981 Us Route 20 Seneca Falls (13148) *(G-14369)*
Montfort Brothers Inc................................845 896-6694
 44 Elm St Fishkill (12524) *(G-4801)*
Monthly Gift Inc......................................888 444-9661
 401 Park Ave S New York (10016) *(G-10501)*
Monticello Black Top Corp............................845 434-7280
 80 Patio Dr Thompsonville (12784) *(G-15066)*
Montly Gift, New York *Also called Monthly Gift Inc (G-10501)*
Montrose Equipment Sales Inc......................718 388-7446
 202 N 10th St Brooklyn (11211) *(G-2170)*
Moo Goong Hwa, Corona *Also called Kenan International Trading (G-3742)*
Moog - Isp, Niagara Falls *Also called Moog Inc (G-11952)*
Moog Inc (PA)..716 805-2604
 400 Jamison Rd Elma (14059) *(G-4321)*
Moog Inc..716 687-4954
 300 Jamison Rd East Aurora (14052) *(G-4093)*
Moog Inc..716 805-8100
 7021 Seneca St East Aurora (14052) *(G-4094)*
Moog Inc..716 731-6300
 6686 Walmore Rd Niagara Falls (14304) *(G-11952)*
Moog Inc..716 687-4778
 160 Jamison Rd Elma (14059) *(G-4322)*
Moog Inc..716 687-7825
 6860 Seneca St Elma (14059) *(G-4323)*
Moog Inc..716 687-5486
 500 Jamison Rd Plt20 Elma (14059) *(G-4324)*
Moog Industrial Group, East Aurora *Also called Moog Inc (G-4093)*
Moog Space and Defense Group, Elma *Also called Moog Inc (G-4324)*
MOOG-FTS, Elma *Also called Moog Inc (G-4321)*
Moogs Medical Devices Group......................716 652-2000
 251 Seneca St Buffalo (14204) *(G-2872)*
Moon Gates Company.................................718 426-0023
 3243 104th St East Elmhurst (11369) *(G-4110)*
Moon, Wm, Catskill *Also called William Moon Iron Works Inc (G-3217)*
Mooney-Keehley Inc..................................585 271-1573
 38 Saginaw Dr Rochester (14623) *(G-13559)*
Mooradian Hydraulics & Eqp Co (PA)..............518 766-3866
 1190 Route 9 Castleton On Hudson (12033) *(G-3203)*
Moore Business Forms, Lakewood *Also called R R Donnelley & Sons Company (G-6784)*
Moore Business Forms, Grand Island *Also called R R Donnelley & Sons Company (G-5341)*
Moore Printing Company Inc.........................585 394-1533
 9 Coy St Canandaigua (14424) *(G-3136)*
Moore Research Center, Grand Island *Also called R R Donnelley & Sons Company (G-5342)*
Mooseberry Soap Co LLC.............................315 332-8913
 513 W Union St Ste B Newark (14513) *(G-11847)*
Moran Shipyard Corporation (HQ)...................718 981-5600
 2015 Richmond Ter Staten Island (10302) *(G-14681)*
Morco, Plainview *Also called Howard J Moore Company Inc (G-12688)*
Morco Products Corp.................................718 853-4005
 556 39th St Brooklyn (11232) *(G-2171)*
Morcon Inc (PA).....................................518 677-8511
 62 Owlkill Rd Eagle Bridge (12057) *(G-4072)*
Morcon Tissue, Eagle Bridge *Also called Morcon Inc (G-4072)*
Mordechai Collection, New York *Also called Ada Gems Corp (G-8452)*
More Good..845 765-0115
 383 Main St Beacon (12508) *(G-754)*
Morehouse Publishing, New York *Also called Church Publishing Incorporated (G-9004)*
Moreland Hose & Belting Corp.......................631 563-7071
 4118 Sunrise Hwy Oakdale (11769) *(G-12154)*

Morelle Products Ltd.................................212 391-8070
 211 E 18th St Apt 4d New York (10003) *(G-10502)*
Moresca Clothing and Costume......................845 331-6012
 361 Union Center Rd Ulster Park (12487) *(G-15219)*
Moretta Cilento Ltd Lblty Co..........................631 386-8654
 80 W Neck Rd Huntington (11743) *(G-6214)*
Morey Publishing.....................................516 284-3300
 20 Hempstead Tpke Unit B Farmingdale (11735) *(G-4689)*
Morgik Metal Designs................................212 463-0304
 145 Hudson St Frnt 4 New York (10013) *(G-10503)*
Morgood Tools Inc...................................585 436-8828
 940 Millstead Way Rochester (14624) *(G-13560)*
Morito/Kane-M, New York *Also called Kane-M Inc (G-10065)*
Morningstar Concrete Products......................716 693-4020
 528 Young St Tonawanda (14150) *(G-15124)*
Morningstar Foods, Delhi *Also called Saputo Dairy Foods Usa LLC (G-3966)*
Moro Corporation....................................607 724-4241
 23 Griswold St Binghamton (13904) *(G-899)*
Moro Design, Ithaca *Also called Joe Moro (G-6390)*
Morris Brothers Sign Svc Inc........................212 675-9130
 37 W 20th St Ste 708 New York (10011) *(G-10504)*
Morris Fine Furniture Workshop, Brooklyn *Also called Walter P Sauer LLC (G-2574)*
Morris Golf Ventures.................................631 283-0559
 Sebonac Inlet Rd Southampton (11968) *(G-14533)*
Morris Products Inc.................................518 743-0523
 53 Carey Rd Queensbury (12804) *(G-13049)*
Mortech Industries Inc...............................845 628-6138
 961 Route 6 Mahopac (10541) *(G-7475)*
Mortgage Press Ltd..................................516 409-1400
 1220 Wantagh Ave Wantagh (11793) *(G-15486)*
Morton Buildings Inc................................585 786-8191
 5616 Route 20a E Warsaw (14569) *(G-15508)*
Morton Salt Inc......................................585 493-2511
 45 Ribaud Ave Silver Springs (14550) *(G-14443)*
Mosaic Microsystems LLC...........................585 314-7441
 500 Lee Rd Ste 200 Rochester (14606) *(G-13561)*
Mosby Holdings Corp (HQ)..........................212 309-8100
 125 Park Ave New York (10017) *(G-10505)*
Moschos Furs Inc...................................212 244-0255
 345 7th Ave Rm 1501 New York (10001) *(G-10506)*
Moscot Wholesale Corp (PA)........................212 647-1550
 69 W 14th St Fl 2 New York (10011) *(G-10507)*
Moser Baer Technologies Inc........................585 749-0480
 6 Camborne Cir Fairport (14450) *(G-4508)*
Mostly Mica Inc......................................631 586-4200
 77 Cleveland Ave Ste A Bay Shore (11706) *(G-694)*
Motema Music LLC..................................212 860-6969
 8 W 127th St Apt 2 New York (10027) *(G-10508)*
Mother Nature & Partners, Brooklyn *Also called Mnn Holding Company LLC (G-2165)*
Moti Inc...718 436-4280
 4118 13th Ave Brooklyn (11219) *(G-2172)*
Motion Message Inc.................................631 924-9500
 22 Sawgrass Dr Ste 4 Bellport (11713) *(G-804)*
Motiva Enterprises LLC..............................516 371-4780
 74 East Ave Lawrence (11559) *(G-6889)*
Motiva Sales Terminal, Lawrence *Also called Motiva Enterprises LLC (G-6889)*
Motivair Corporation.................................716 691-9222
 85 Woodridge Dr Amherst (14228) *(G-233)*
Motor Components LLC...............................607 737-8011
 2243 Corning Rd Elmira Heights (14903) *(G-4378)*
Motorola Solutions Inc..............................518 348-0833
 7 Deer Run Holw Halfmoon (12065) *(G-5495)*
Motorola Solutions Inc..............................518 869-9517
 251 New Karner Rd Albany (12205) *(G-101)*
Motorola Solutions Sls & Svcs.......................716 633-5022
 4990 Meadowbrook Rd Williamsville (14221) *(G-16134)*
Mott's, Williamson *Also called Keurig Dr Pepper Inc (G-16110)*
Motts, Elmsford *Also called Motts LLP (G-4418)*
Motts LLP (HQ).......................................972 673-8088
 55 Hunter Ln Elmsford (10523) *(G-4418)*
Mount Vernon Iron Works Inc........................914 668-7064
 130 Miller Pl Mount Vernon (10550) *(G-8163)*
Mountain and Isles LLC.............................212 354-1890
 525 7th Ave Fl 22 New York (10018) *(G-10509)*
Mountain Forest Products Inc........................518 597-3674
 3281 Nys Route 9n Crown Point (12928) *(G-3810)*
Mountain Side Farms Inc.............................718 526-3442
 15504 Liberty Ave Jamaica (11433) *(G-6462)*
Mountain T-Shirts Inc...............................518 943-4533
 8 W Bridge St Catskill (12414) *(G-3215)*
Mountain T-Shirts & Sign Works, Catskill *Also called Mountain T-Shirts Inc (G-3215)*
Movin On Sounds and SEC Inc.......................516 489-2350
 636 Hempstead Tpke Franklin Square (11010) *(G-4962)*
Movinads & Signs LLC..............................518 378-3000
 1771 Route 9 Halfmoon (12065) *(G-5496)*
Moznaim Co, Brooklyn *Also called Moznaim Publishing Co Inc (G-2173)*
Moznaim Publishing Co Inc..........................718 853-0525
 4304 12th Ave Brooklyn (11219) *(G-2173)*
MP Caroll Inc...716 683-8520
 4822 Genesee St Cheektowaga (14225) *(G-3355)*
Mp Displays LLC....................................845 268-4113
 704 Executive Blvd Ste 1 Valley Cottage (10989) *(G-15319)*

ALPHABETIC

Mp Studio Inc 212 302-5666
147 W 35th St Ste 1603 New York (10001) *(G-10510)*

MP&sm, Rochester *Also called Monroe Piping & Shtmtl LLC (G-13558)*

Mpdraw LLC 212 228-8383
109 Ludlow St New York (10002) *(G-10511)*

Mpdw Inc (PA) 925 631-6878
158 W 29th St Fl 12 New York (10001) *(G-10512)*

Mpe Graphics Inc 631 582-8900
120 Wilbur Pl Ste A Bohemia (11716) *(G-1048)*

Mpi Consulting Incorporated 631 253-2377
87 Jersey St West Babylon (11704) *(G-15733)*

Mpi Incorporated (PA) 845 471-7630
165 Smith St Stop 3 Poughkeepsie (12601) *(G-12972)*

Mpl Inc 607 266-0480
41 Dutch Mill Rd Ithaca (14850) *(G-6398)*

Mpl Metal Inc 718 338-4952
1560 Troy Ave Brooklyn (11203) *(G-2174)*

Mpm, Waterford *Also called Momentive Performance Mtls Inc (G-15542)*

Mpm AR LLC 518 233-3397
22 Corporate Woods Blvd Albany (12211) *(G-102)*

Mpm Holdings Inc (HQ) 518 233-3330
260 Hudson River Rd Waterford (12188) *(G-15543)*

Mpm Intermediate Holdings Inc (HQ) 518 237-3330
260 Hudson River Rd Waterford (12188) *(G-15544)*

Mpm Silicones LLC 518 233-3330
260 Hudson River Rd Waterford (12188) *(G-15545)*

Mr Disposable Inc 718 388 8574
101 Richardson St Ste 2 Brooklyn (11211) *(G-2175)*

Mr Glass Tempering LLC 718 576-3826
38 15th St Brooklyn (11215) *(G-2176)*

Mr Pierogi LLC 718 499-7821
126 12th St Brooklyn (11215) *(G-2177)*

Mr Sign, Yonkers *Also called Wings For Wheels Inc (G-16357)*

Mr Sign, East Northport *Also called Monasani Signs Inc (G-4150)*

Mr Sign Usa Inc 718 218-3321
1920 Atlantic Ave Brooklyn (11233) *(G-2178)*

Mr Smoothie 845 296-1686
207 South Ave Ste F102 Poughkeepsie (12601) *(G-12973)*

Mr Steam, Long Island City *Also called Sussman-Automatic Corporation (G-7376)*

MRC Bearings, Falconer *Also called SKF USA Inc (G-4556)*

MRC Global (us) Inc 607 739-8575
224 N Main St Bldg 13-1 Horseheads (14845) *(G-6129)*

Mrchocolatecom LLC 718 875-9772
66 Water St Ste 2 Brooklyn (11201) *(G-2179)*

Mri Northtowns Group PC 716 836-4646
199 Park Club Ln Ste 300 Buffalo (14221) *(G-2873)*

Mrinalini Inc 646 510-2747
469 7th Ave Rm 1254 New York (10018) *(G-10513)*

Mrp Supports LLC 716 332-7673
3310 N Benzing Rd Orchard Park (14127) *(G-12367)*

Mrs Baking Distribution Corp 718 460-6700
1825 127th St College Point (11356) *(G-3555)*

Mrs John L Strong & Co LLC 212 838-3775
699 Madison Ave Fl 5 New York (10065) *(G-10514)*

Mrt Textile Inc 800 674-1073
350 5th Ave New York (10118) *(G-10515)*

Ms Machining Inc 607 723-1105
2 William St Binghamton (13904) *(G-900)*

Ms Paper Products Co Inc 718 624-0248
930 Bedford Ave Brooklyn (11205) *(G-2180)*

Ms Spares LLC 607 223-3024
8055 Evesborough Dr Clay (13041) *(G-3451)*

Ms. Michelles, Calverton *Also called Cooking With Chef Michelle LLC (G-3079)*

Msdivisions, Middletown *Also called Commercial Communications LLC (G-7900)*

Msi Inc 845 639-6683
329 Strawtown Rd New City (10956) *(G-8227)*

Msi-Molding Solutions Inc 315 736-2412
6247 State Route 233 Rome (13440) *(G-13857)*

Msm Designz Inc 914 909-5900
505 White Plains Rd # 204 Tarrytown (10591) *(G-15050)*

MSP Technologycom LLC 631 424-7542
77 Bankside Dr Centerport (11721) *(G-3752)*

MSQ Corporation 718 465-0900
21504 Hempstead Ave Queens Village (11429) *(G-13025)*

Mssi, Millbrook *Also called Micro Systems Specialists Inc (G-7943)*

Mt Fuel Corp 631 445-2047
9 Bayles Ave Stony Brook (11790) *(G-14740)*

Mt Morris Shopper Inc 585 658-3520
85 N Main St Mount Morris (14510) *(G-8114)*

Mtc Industries Inc (PA) 631 274-4818
255 Oser Ave Ste 1 Hauppauge (11788) *(G-5724)*

MTI, Albany *Also called Mechanical Technology Inc (G-99)*

MTI Instruments Inc 518 218-2550
325 Washington Ave 3 Albany (12206) *(G-103)*

MTK Electronics Inc 631 924-7666
1 National Blvd Medford (11763) *(G-7720)*

Mtm Publishing Inc 212 242-6930
435 W 23rd St Apt 8c New York (10011) *(G-10516)*

Mtwli Precision Corp 631 244-3767
1605 Sycamore Ave Unit B Bohemia (11716) *(G-1049)*

Mtz Enterprises Inc 347 834-2716
870 39th St Brooklyn (11232) *(G-2181)*

Mud Puddle Books Inc 212 647-9168
36 W 25th St Fl 5 New York (10010) *(G-10517)*

Muddy Trail Jerky Co 518 642-2194
85 Quaker St Granville (12832) *(G-5353)*

Mudpuppy, New York *Also called Galison Publishing LLC (G-9566)*

Muench-Kreuzer Candle Company (PA) 315 471-4515
617 Hiawatha Blvd E Syracuse (13208) *(G-14947)*

Mulitex Usa Inc 212 398-0440
215 W 40th St Fl 7 New York (10018) *(G-10518)*

Muller Tool Inc 716 895-3658
74 Anderson Rd Buffalo (14225) *(G-2874)*

Mullers Cider House LLC 585 287-5875
1344 University Ave # 180 Rochester (14607) *(G-13562)*

Multi Packaging Solutions Inc 516 488-2000
325 Duffy Ave Unit 1 Hicksville (11801) *(G-5932)*

Multi Packaging Solutions Inc (HQ) 646 885-0005
885 3rd Ave Fl 28 New York (10022) *(G-10519)*

Multi Packg Solutions Intl Ltd (HQ) 646 885-0005
885 3rd Ave Fl 28 New York (10022) *(G-10520)*

Multi-Health Systems Inc 800 456-3003
Indus Pkwy Ste 70660 60 Cheektowaga (14227) *(G-3356)*

Multifold Die Ctng Finshg Corp 631 232-1235
555 Raymond Dr Islandia (11749) *(G-6341)*

Multimatic Products Inc 800 767-7633
900 Marconi Ave Ronkonkoma (11779) *(G-13977)*

Multimedia Services Inc 607 936-3186
11136 River Rd 40 Corning (14830) *(G-3718)*

Multiple Imprssons of Rchester (PA) 585 546-1160
41 Chestnut St Rochester (14604) *(G-13563)*

Multisorb Tech Intl LLC (PA) 716 824-8900
325 Harlem Rd Buffalo (14224) *(G-2875)*

Multisorb Technologies Inc 716 656-1402
10 French Rd Buffalo (14227) *(G-2876)*

Multitone Finishing Co Inc 516 485-1043
56 Hempstead Gardens Dr West Hempstead (11552) *(G-15776)*

Multiwire Laboratories Ltd 607 257-3378
95 Brown Rd 1018266a Ithaca (14850) *(G-6399)*

Munn Works LLC 914 665-6100
150 N Macquesten Pkwy Mount Vernon (10550) *(G-8164)*

Munschauer Inc 716 895-8888
330 Greene St Buffalo (14206) *(G-2877)*

Munson Machinery Company Inc 315 797-0090
210 Seward Ave Utica (13502) *(G-15286)*

Murcadom Corporation 585 412-2176
5711 Thomas Rd Canandaigua (14424) *(G-3137)*

Murphs Famous Inc 516 398-0417
200 Raymond St Rockville Centre (11570) *(G-13831)*

Murphy Manufacturing Co Inc 585 223-0100
38 West Ave Fairport (14450) *(G-4509)*

Murray Bresky Consultants Ltd (PA) 845 436-5001
5190 Main St South Fallsburg (12779) *(G-14510)*

Murray Logging LLC 518 834-7372
1535 Route 9 Keeseville (12944) *(G-6644)*

Murray's Chicken, South Fallsburg *Also called Murray Bresky Consultants Ltd (G-14510)*

Muse, The, New York *Also called Daily Muse Inc (G-9153)*

Music & Sound Retailer Inc 516 767-2500
25 Willowdale Ave Port Washington (11050) *(G-12908)*

Music Sales, New York *Also called G Schirmer Inc (G-9559)*

Music Sales, Chester *Also called G Schirmer Inc (G-3378)*

Music Sales Corporation (PA) 212 254-2100
180 Madison Ave Ste 2400 New York (10016) *(G-10521)*

Mustang Bio Inc 781 652-4500
2 Gansevoort St Fl 9 New York (10014) *(G-10522)*

Mustang-Major Tool & Die Co 716 992-9200
3243 N Boston Rd Eden (14057) *(G-4257)*

Mustard Tin 315 769-8409
6100 Saint Lawrence Ctr Massena (13662) *(G-7669)*

Mutual Engraving Company Inc 516 489-0534
497 Hempstead Ave West Hempstead (11552) *(G-15777)*

Mutual Harware, Long Island City *Also called Mutual Sales Corp (G-7300)*

Mutual Library Bindery Inc 315 455-6638
6295 E Molloy Rd Ste 3 East Syracuse (13057) *(G-4227)*

Mutual Sales Corp 718 361-8373
545 49th Ave Long Island City (11101) *(G-7300)*

Muzet Inc 315 452-0050
104 S Main St Syracuse (13212) *(G-14948)*

Mv Corp Inc 631 273-8020
88 Spence St Ste 90 Bay Shore (11706) *(G-695)*

Mwi Inc (PA) 585 424-4200
1269 Brighton Henrietta T Rochester (14623) *(G-13564)*

Mwsi Inc (PA) 914 347-4200
12 Skyline Dr Ste 230 Hawthorne (10532) *(G-5819)*

Mx Solar USA LLC 732 356-7300
100 Wall St Ste 1000 New York (10005) *(G-10523)*

My Apparel, New York *Also called El-La Design Inc (G-9331)*

My Hanky Inc 646 321-0869
680 81st St Apt 4d Brooklyn (11228) *(G-2182)*

My Life My Health, Flushing *Also called Life Watch Technology Inc (G-4871)*

My Most Favorite Food 212 580-5130
247 W 72nd St Frnt 1 New York (10023) *(G-10524)*

Myers Group LLC (PA) 973 761-6414
257 W 38th St New York (10018) *(G-10525)*

Mylan Health Management LLC 917 262-2950
  405 Lexington Ave New York (10174) *(G-10526)*
Myles Tool Company Inc 716 731-1300
  6300 Inducon Corporate Dr Sanborn (14132) *(G-14146)*
Mymee Inc 917 476-4122
  101 Avenue Of Flr 3 New York (10013) *(G-10527)*
Mystery Scene Magazine, New York *Also called Kbs Communications LLC (G-10085)*
Mystic Display Co Inc 718 485-2651
  909 Remsen Ave Brooklyn (11236) *(G-2183)*
Mystic Inc (PA) 212 239-2025
  463 7th Ave Fl 12 New York (10018) *(G-10528)*
Myx Beverage LLC 585 978-3542
  39 E Main St Unit 101 Oyster Bay (11771) *(G-12451)*
Myx Fusions, Oyster Bay *Also called Myx Beverage LLC (G-12451)*
MZB Accessories LLC 718 472-7500
  2976 Northern Blvd Fl 4 Long Island City (11101) *(G-7301)*
N & G of America Inc 516 428-3414
  28 W Lane Dr Plainview (11803) *(G-12703)*
N & L Fuel Corp 718 863-3538
  2014 Blackrock Ave Bronx (10472) *(G-1320)*
N & L Instruments Inc 631 471-4000
  90 13th Ave Unit 1 Ronkonkoma (11779) *(G-13978)*
N A Alumil Corporation 718 355-9393
  4401 21st St Ste 203 Long Island City (11101) *(G-7302)*
N A P, Brooklyn *Also called Nap Industries Inc (G-2187)*
N A R Associates Inc 845 557-8713
  128 Rte 55 Barryville (12719) *(G-598)*
N A S C O, Watertown *Also called Northern Awning & Sign Company (G-15585)*
N C Iron Works Inc 718 633-4660
  1117 60th St Brooklyn (11219) *(G-2184)*
N E Controls LLC 315 626-2480
  7048 Interstate Island Rd Syracuse (13209) *(G-14949)*
N I Boutique, Long Island City *Also called Nazim Izzak Inc (G-7304)*
N I T, New York *Also called Network Infrstructure Tech Inc (G-10571)*
N Make Mold Inc 716 877-3146
  85 River Rock Dr Ste 202 Buffalo (14207) *(G-2878)*
N R S I, Syosset *Also called National Rding Styles Inst Inc (G-14797)*
N Sketch Build Inc 800 975-0597
  982 Main St Ste 4-130 Fishkill (12524) *(G-4802)*
N V Magazine, New York *Also called Envy Publishing Group Inc (G-9385)*
N Y B P Inc 585 624-2541
  1355 Pittsford Mendon Rd Mendon (14506) *(G-7851)*
N Y Bijoux Corp 212 244-9585
  33 Sands Point Rd Port Washington (11050) *(G-12909)*
N Y Elli Design Corp 718 228-0014
  5001 Metropolitan Ave 1 Ridgewood (11385) *(G-13152)*
N Y Western Concrete Corp 585 343-6850
  638 E Main St Batavia (14020) *(G-621)*
N Y Winstons Inc 212 665-3166
  5 W 86th St Apt 9e New York (10024) *(G-10529)*
N3a Corporation 516 284-6799
  345 Doughty Blvd Inwood (11096) *(G-6299)*
Nabisco, Newburgh *Also called Mondelez Global LLC (G-11875)*
Nabisco, Batavia *Also called Mondelez Global LLC (G-620)*
Nafco, Newark *Also called North American Filter Corp (G-11848)*
Nagad Cabinets Inc 718 382-7200
  1039 Mcdonald Ave Brooklyn (11230) *(G-2185)*
Nagle Fuel Corporation 212 304-4618
  265 Nagle Ave New York (10034) *(G-10530)*
Naito International Corp 718 309-2425
  100 Merrick Rd Ste 400e Rockville Centre (11570) *(G-13832)*
Nak International Corp (PA) 516 334-6245
  108 Forest Ave Ste 1 Locust Valley (11560) *(G-7128)*
Nakano Foods, Medina *Also called Mizkan America Inc (G-7742)*
Nakano Foods, Lyndonville *Also called Mizkan America Inc (G-7445)*
Naked Brand Group Inc 212 851-8050
  225 5th Ave Apt 2d New York (10010) *(G-10531)*
Nalco Company LLC 518 796-1985
  6 Butler Pl 2 Saratoga Springs (12866) *(G-14185)*
Nalge Nunc International Corp (HQ) 585 498-2661
  1600 Lexington Ave # 107 Rochester (14606) *(G-13565)*
Nameplate Mfrs of Amer 631 752-0055
  65 Toledo St Farmingdale (11735) *(G-4690)*
Namsnet, Long Island City *Also called Toweriq Inc (G-7384)*
Nanette Lepore, Brooklyn *Also called Nlhe LLC (G-2217)*
Nanette Lepore Showroom, New York *Also called Robespierre Inc (G-11063)*
Nano Vibronix Inc (PA) 516 374-8330
  601 Chestnut St Cedarhurst (11516) *(G-3242)*
Nanobionovum LLC 518 581-1171
  117 Grand Ave Saratoga Springs (12866) *(G-14186)*
Nanoprobes Inc 631 205-9490
  95 Horseblock Rd Unit 1 Yaphank (11980) *(G-16267)*
Nanopv Corporation 609 851-3666
  7526 Morgan Rd Liverpool (13090) *(G-7028)*
Nanorx Inc 914 671-0224
  6 Devoe Pl Chappaqua (10514) *(G-3326)*
Nanotronics Imaging Inc 212 401-6209
  63 Flushing Ave Unit 128 Brooklyn (11205) *(G-2186)*
Nanovibronix Inc 914 233-3004
  525 Executive Blvd Elmsford (10523) *(G-4419)*

Nantier Ball Minoustchine Pubg, New York *Also called NBM Publishing Inc (G-10558)*
Nanz Company, The, New York *Also called Nanz Custom Hardware Inc (G-10532)*
Nanz Custom Hardware Inc (PA) 212 367-7000
  20 Vandam St Fl 5l New York (10013) *(G-10532)*
Nanz Custom Hardware Inc 212 367-7000
  105 E Jefryn Blvd Deer Park (11729) *(G-3908)*
Naomi Manufacturing, Island Park *Also called Nathan Berrie & Sons Inc (G-6320)*
Nap Industries, Brooklyn *Also called Marlow Printing Co Inc (G-2117)*
Nap Industries Inc 718 625-4948
  667 Kent Ave Brooklyn (11249) *(G-2187)*
Napco Security Tech Inc (PA) 631 842-9400
  333 Bayview Ave Amityville (11701) *(G-297)*
Napean LLC 917 968-6757
  401 Broadway Ste 1408 New York (10013) *(G-10533)*
Naples Vly Mrgers Acqstons LLC 585 490-1339
  154 N Main St Naples (14512) *(G-8209)*
Narda Satellite Networks, Hauppauge *Also called L3 Technologies Inc (G-5688)*
Narratively Inc 203 536-0332
  30 John St Brooklyn (11201) *(G-2188)*
Narrowsburg Feed & Grain Co 845 252-3936
  Fifth And Main St Narrowsburg (12764) *(G-8210)*
Nas CP Corp (HQ) 718 961-6757
  1434 110th St Apt 4a College Point (11356) *(G-3556)*
Nas Quick Sign Inc 716 876-7599
  1628 Elmwood Ave Buffalo (14207) *(G-2879)*
Nas-Tra Automotive Inds Inc 631 225-1225
  3 Sidney Ct Lindenhurst (11757) *(G-6962)*
Nasco Enterprises Inc 516 921-9696
  95 Woodcrest Dr Syosset (11791) *(G-14795)*
Nasco Printing Corporation 212 229-2462
  121 Varick St Rm 201 New York (10013) *(G-10534)*
Nasdaq Omx, New York *Also called Omx (us) Inc (G-10688)*
Nash Metalware Co Inc 315 339-5794
  200 Railroad St Rome (13440) *(G-13858)*
Nash Printing Inc 516 935-4567
  101 Dupont St Ste 2 Plainview (11803) *(G-12704)*
Nasiff Associates Inc 315 676-2346
  841 County Route 37 Central Square (13036) *(G-3295)*
Nassau Candy Distributors Inc (HQ) 516 433-7100
  530 W John St Hicksville (11801) *(G-5933)*
Nassau Candy Specialty, Hicksville *Also called Nassau Candy Distributors Inc (G-5933)*
Nassau Chromium Plating Co Inc 516 746-6666
  122 2nd St Mineola (11501) *(G-7990)*
Nassau County Publications 516 481-5400
  5 Centre St Hempstead (11550) *(G-5846)*
Nassau Suffolk Brd of Womens 631 666-8835
  145 New York Ave Bay Shore (11706) *(G-696)*
Nassau Tool Works Inc 631 328-7031
  1479 N Clinton Ave Bay Shore (11706) *(G-697)*
Nasserati Inc 212 947-8100
  225 W 39th St Fl 6 New York (10018) *(G-10535)*
Nastra Automotive, Lindenhurst *Also called Nas-Tra Automotive Inds Inc (G-6962)*
Nat Nast Company Inc (PA) 212 575-1186
  1370 Broadway Rm 900 New York (10018) *(G-10536)*
Natech Plastics Inc 631 580-3506
  85 Remington Blvd Ronkonkoma (11779) *(G-13979)*
Nathan Berrie & Sons Inc 516 432-8500
  3956 Long Beach Rd Island Park (11558) *(G-6320)*
Nathan Love LLC 212 925-7111
  407 Broome St Rm 6r New York (10013) *(G-10537)*
Nathan Printing Express Inc 914 472-0914
  740 Central Park Ave Scarsdale (10583) *(G-14239)*
Nathan Steel Corp 315 797-1335
  36 Wurz Ave Utica (13502) *(G-15287)*
Nation Company LLC 212 209-5400
  520 8th Ave Rm 2100 New York (10018) *(G-10538)*
Nation Magazine 212 209-5400
  33 Irving Pl Fl 8 New York (10003) *(G-10539)*
Nation, The, New York *Also called Nation Company LLC (G-10538)*
National Advertising & Prtg 212 629-7650
  231 W 29th St Rm 1408 New York (10001) *(G-10540)*
National Catholic Wkly Review, New York *Also called America Press Inc (G-8542)*
National Computer & Electronic 631 242-7222
  367 Bay Shore Rd Ste D Deer Park (11729) *(G-3909)*
National Contract Industries 212 249-0045
  510 E 86th St Apt 16b New York (10028) *(G-10541)*
National Die & Button Mould Co 201 939-7800
  1 Kent Ave Brooklyn (11249) *(G-2189)*
National Elev Cab & Door Corp 718 478-5900
  5315 37th Ave Woodside (11377) *(G-16215)*
National Energy Audits LLC 631 883-3407
  1069 Main St 321 Holbrook (11741) *(G-6013)*
National Equipment Corporation (PA) 718 585-0200
  600 Mmaroneck Ave Ste 400 Harrison (10528) *(G-5556)*
National Equipment Corporation 718 585-0200
  801 E 141st St Bronx (10454) *(G-1321)*
National Flag & Display Co Inc (PA) 212 228-6600
  30 E 21st St Apt 2b New York (10010) *(G-10542)*
National Ggraphic Partners LLC 212 656-0726
  485 Lexington Ave Fl 3 New York (10017) *(G-10543)*
National Grape Coop Assn Inc (PA) 716 326-5200
  80 State St Westfield (14787) *(G-15947)*

ALPHABETIC

National Health Prom Assoc...914 421-2525
711 Westchester Ave # 301 White Plains (10604) **(G-16032)**
National Herald Inc...718 784-5255
3710 30th St Long Island City (11101) **(G-7303)**
National Learning Corp (PA)...516 921-8888
212 Michael Dr Syosset (11791) **(G-14796)**
National Maint Contg Corp...716 285-1583
5600 Niagara Falls Blvd Niagara Falls (14304) **(G-11953)**
National Pad & Paper, Syracuse *Also called Automation Papers Inc* **(G-14822)**
National Paper Converting Inc...607 687-6049
207 Corporate Dr Owego (13827) **(G-12434)**
National Parachute Industries...908 782-1646
78 White Rd Extensio Palenville (12463) **(G-12479)**
National Parachute Industry, Palenville *Also called National Parachute Industries* **(G-12479)**
National Pipe & Plastics Inc (PA)...607 729-9381
3421 Vestal Rd Vestal (13850) **(G-15381)**
National Prfmce Solutions Inc...718 833-4767
1043 78th St Brooklyn (11228) **(G-2190)**
National Prosthetic Orthot...718 767-8400
21441 42nd Ave Ste 3a Bayside (11361) **(G-740)**
National Ramp, Valley Cottage *Also called Landmark Group Inc* **(G-15317)**
National Rding Styles Inst Inc...516 921-5500
179 Lafayette Dr Syosset (11791) **(G-14797)**
National Reproductions Inc...212 619-3800
229 W 28th St Fl 9 New York (10001) **(G-10544)**
National RES Mktg Council Inc...914 591-4297
1 Bridge St Ste 44 Irvington (10533) **(G-6311)**
National Review Inc (PA)...212 679-7330
19 W 44th St Ste 1701 New York (10036) **(G-10545)**
NATIONAL REVIEW ONLINE, New York *Also called National Review Inc* **(G-10545)**
National Security Systems Inc...516 627-2222
511 Manhasset Woods Rd Manhasset (11030) **(G-7539)**
National Spinning Co Inc...212 382-6400
1212 Ave Of The Americ St New York (10036) **(G-10546)**
National Steel Rule Die Inc...718 402-1396
441 Southern Blvd Bronx (10455) **(G-1322)**
National Time Recording Eqp Co...212 227-3310
64 Reade St Fl 2 New York (10007) **(G-10547)**
National Tobacco Company LP...212 253-8185
257 Park Ave S Fl 7 New York (10010) **(G-10548)**
National Vac Envmtl Svcs Corp...518 743-0563
80 Park Rd Glens Falls (12804) **(G-5260)**
National Wire & Metal Tech Inc...716 661-9180
22 Carolina St Jamestown (14701) **(G-6534)**
Nationwide Circuits Inc...585 328-0791
1444 Emerson St Rochester (14606) **(G-13566)**
Nationwide Coils Inc (PA)...914 277-7396
24 Foxwood Cir Mount Kisco (10549) **(G-8099)**
Nationwide Custom Services...845 365-0414
77 Main St Tappan (10983) **(G-15036)**
Nationwide Dairy Inc...347 689-8148
792 E 93rd St Brooklyn (11236) **(G-2191)**
Nationwide Displays, Central Islip *Also called Nationwide Exhibitor Svcs Inc* **(G-3285)**
Nationwide Exhibitor Svcs Inc...631 467-2034
110 Windsor Pl Central Islip (11722) **(G-3285)**
Nationwide Lifts, Queensbury *Also called S & H Enterprises Inc* **(G-13055)**
Nationwide Precision Pdts Corp...585 272-7100
200 Tech Park Dr Rochester (14623) **(G-13567)**
Nationwide Sales and Service...631 491-6625
303 Smith St Ste 4 Farmingdale (11735) **(G-4691)**
Nationwide Tarps Incorporated (PA)...518 843-1545
50 Willow St Amsterdam (12010) **(G-341)**
Native Amercn Enrgy Group Inc...718 408-2323
7211 Austin St Ste 288 Forest Hills (11375) **(G-4923)**
Native Textiles Inc (PA)...212 951-5100
411 5th Ave Rm 901 New York (10016) **(G-10549)**
Natori Company Incorporated (PA)...212 532-7796
180 Madison Ave Fl 18 New York (10016) **(G-10550)**
Natori Company Incorporated...212 532-7796
180 Madison Ave Fl 19 New York (10016) **(G-10551)**
Natori Company, The, New York *Also called Natori Company Incorporated* **(G-10551)**
Natural Dreams LLC...718 760-4202
5312 104th St Corona (11368) **(G-3747)**
Natural E Creative LLC...516 488-1143
1110 Jericho Tpke New Hyde Park (11040) **(G-8283)**
Natural Image Hair Concepts, Garden City *Also called M and J Hair Center Inc* **(G-5106)**
Natural Lab Inc...718 321-8848
13538 39th Ave Ste 4 Flushing (11354) **(G-4876)**
Natural Matters Inc...212 337-3077
300 W 12th St New York (10014) **(G-10552)**
Natural Organics Labs Inc...631 957-5600
548 Broadhollow Rd Melville (11747) **(G-7807)**
Natural Stone & Cabinet Inc...718 388-2988
1365 Halsey St Brooklyn (11237) **(G-2192)**
Naturally Serious, New York *Also called Peter Thomas Roth Labs LLC* **(G-10816)**
Nature Only Inc...917 922-6539
10420 Queens Blvd Apt 3b Forest Hills (11375) **(G-4924)**
Nature Publishing Co...212 726-9200
345 Park Ave S New York (10010) **(G-10553)**
Nature Publishing Group, New York *Also called Springer Nature America Inc* **(G-11336)**
Natures Bounty Co...631 472-2817
10 Vitamin Dr Bayport (11705) **(G-729)**
Natures Bounty Co...631 244-2021
2100 Smithtown Ave Ronkonkoma (11779) **(G-13980)**
Natures Bounty Inc...631 567-9500
90 Orville Dr Bohemia (11716) **(G-1050)**
Natures Bounty Inc (HQ)...631 200-2000
2100 Smithtown Ave Ronkonkoma (11779) **(G-13981)**
Natures Value Inc (PA)...631 846-2500
468 Mill Rd Coram (11727) **(G-3695)**
Natures Warehouse...800 215-4372
55 Main St Philadelphia (13673) **(G-12612)**
Naturpathica Holistic Hlth Inc...631 329-8792
74 Montauk Hwy Unit 23 East Hampton (11937) **(G-4126)**
Natus Medical Incorporated...631 457-4430
150 Motor Pkwy Ste 106 Hauppauge (11788) **(G-5725)**
Nautical Marine Paint Corp...718 462-7000
4802 Farragut Rd Brooklyn (11203) **(G-2193)**
Nautical Paint, Brooklyn *Also called Nautical Marine Paint Corp* **(G-2193)**
Nautilus Controls Corp...917 676-7005
99 Madison Ave Fl 5 New York (10016) **(G-10554)**
Nautilusthink Inc...646 239-6858
360 W 36th St Apt 7s New York (10018) **(G-10555)**
Nava Global Partners Inc...516 737-7127
347 Great Neck Rd Great Neck (11021) **(G-5404)**
Navas Designs Inc...818 988-9050
200 E 58th St Apt 17b New York (10022) **(G-10556)**
Navatar Group Inc (HQ)...212 863-9655
90 Broad St Ste 1703 New York (10004) **(G-10557)**
Navilyst Medical Inc...800 833-9973
10 Glens Fls Technical Pa Glens Falls (12801) **(G-5261)**
Navitar Inc...585 359-4000
200 Commerce Dr Rochester (14623) **(G-13568)**
Navy Plum LLC...845 641-7441
47 Plum Rd Monsey (10952) **(G-8041)**
Nazim Izzak Inc...212 920-5546
4402 23rd St Ste 517 Long Island City (11101) **(G-7304)**
Nb Elctrcal Enclsures Mfrs Inc...718 272-8792
902 903 Shepherd Ave Brooklyn (11208) **(G-2194)**
Nbets Corporation...516 785-1259
1901 Wantagh Ave Wantagh (11793) **(G-15487)**
NBM Publishing Inc...646 559-4681
160 Brdway Ste 700 E Wing New York (10038) **(G-10558)**
Nbn Technologies LLC...585 355-5556
136 Wilshire Rd Rochester (14618) **(G-13569)**
Nbs, Amityville *Also called New Business Solutions Inc* **(G-298)**
Nbty Inc...631 200-2062
4320 Veterans Mem Hwy Holbrook (11741) **(G-6014)**
Nbty Manufacturing LLC (HQ)...631 567-9500
2100 Smithtown Ave Ronkonkoma (11779) **(G-13982)**
NC Audience Exchange LLC...212 416-3400
1211 Ave Of The Americas New York (10036) **(G-10559)**
Ncc Ny LLC...718 943-7000
1840 Mcdonald Ave Brooklyn (11223) **(G-2195)**
Nceec, Deer Park *Also called National Computer & Electronic* **(G-3909)**
Nci, New York *Also called National Contract Industries* **(G-10541)**
Nci Group Inc...315 339-1245
6168 State Route 233 Rome (13440) **(G-13859)**
Nci Panel Systems, Montgomery *Also called Northeast Cnstr Inds Inc* **(G-8062)**
NCM Publishers Inc...212 691-9100
200 Varick St Rm 608 New York (10014) **(G-10560)**
NCR Corporation...607 273-5310
950 Danby Rd Ithaca (14850) **(G-6400)**
NCR Corporation...516 876-7200
30 Jericho Executive Plz Jericho (11753) **(G-6586)**
ND Labs Inc...516 612-4900
202 Merrick Rd Lynbrook (11563) **(G-7434)**
NEa Manufacturing Corp...516 371-4200
345 Doughty Blvd Inwood (11096) **(G-6300)**
Nea Naturals Inc...845 522-8042
815 Blooming Grove Tpke # 505 New Windsor (12553) **(G-8373)**
Necd, Woodside *Also called National Elev Cab & Door Corp* **(G-16215)**
Necessary Objects Ltd (PA)...212 334-9888
3030 47th Ave Fl 6 Long Island City (11101) **(G-7305)**
Necessity Systems LLC...907 322-4084
203 Creek View Path Kirkville (13082) **(G-6725)**
Neenah Northeast LLC...315 376-3571
5492 Bostwick St Lowville (13367) **(G-7419)**
Nefab Packaging North East LLC...518 346-9105
203 Glenville Indus Park Scotia (12302) **(G-14334)**
Nefco, Copiague *Also called North East Finishing Co Inc* **(G-3666)**
Negys New Land Vinyrd Winery...315 585-4432
623 Lerch Rd Ste 1 Geneva (14456) **(G-5160)**
Neighbor Newspapers...631 226-2636
565 Broadhollow Rd Ste 3 Farmingdale (11735) **(G-4692)**
Neighbor To Neighbor News Inc...585 492-2525
223 Main St Arcade (14009) **(G-378)**
Neil Savalia Inc...212 869-0123
15 W 47th St Ste 903 New York (10036) **(G-10561)**
Neilson International Inc...631 454-0400
144 Allen Blvd Ste B Farmingdale (11735) **(G-4693)**
Nelco Laboratories Inc...631 242-0082
154 Brook Ave Deer Park (11729) **(G-3910)**

Nell-Joy Industries Inc (PA) 631 842-8989
8 Reith St Ste 10 Copiague (11726) *(G-3665)*
Nelson Air Device Corporation 718 729-3801
4628 54th Ave Maspeth (11378) *(G-7629)*
Nelson Holdings Ltd (PA) 607 772-1794
71 Frederick St Binghamton (13901) *(G-901)*
Nelson Prsthtics Orthotics Lab, Cheektowaga *Also called Prosthetics By Nelson Inc (G-3359)*
Nemaris Inc 646 794-8648
475 Park Ave S Fl 11 New York (10016) *(G-10562)*
Neo Cabinetry LLC 718 403-0456
400 Liberty Ave Brooklyn (11207) *(G-2196)*
Neo Plastics LLC 646 542-1499
1007 Sheffield Ave Brooklyn (11207) *(G-2197)*
Neo Ray Lighting Products, Hicksville *Also called Cooper Lighting LLC (G-5896)*
Neometrics, Hauppauge *Also called Natus Medical Incorporated (G-5725)*
Neon 212 727-5628
1400 Broadway Rm 300 New York (10018) *(G-10563)*
Neopost USA Inc 631 435-9100
415 Oser Ave Ste K Hauppauge (11788) *(G-5726)*
Nepco, Warrensburg *Also called Northeastern Products Corp (G-15505)*
Neptune Machine Inc 718 852-4100
521 Carroll St Brooklyn (11215) *(G-2198)*
Neptune Soft Water Inc 315 446-5151
1201 E Fayette St Ste 6 Syracuse (13210) *(G-14950)*
Nerak Systems Inc 914 763-8259
4 Stage Door Rd Fishkill (12524) *(G-4803)*
Nervve Technologies Inc (PA) 716 800-2250
450 Park Ave Fl 30 New York (10022) *(G-10564)*
Nes Bearing Company Inc 716 372-6532
1601 Johnson St Olean (14760) *(G-12239)*
Nes Costume, New York *Also called Nes Jewelry Inc (G-10565)*
Nes Jewelry Inc (PA) 212 502-0025
10 W 33rd St Fl 9 New York (10001) *(G-10565)*
Nesher Printing Inc 212 760-2521
30 E 33rd St Frnt A New York (10016) *(G-10566)*
Ness Legwear LLC 212 335-0777
1407 Broadway Rm 2010 New York (10018) *(G-10567)*
Nessen Lighting, The, Mamaroneck *Also called Coldstream Group Inc (G-7504)*
Nestle Purina Factory, Dunkirk *Also called Nestle Purina Petcare Company (G-4061)*
Nestle Purina Petcare Company 716 366-8080
3800 Middle Rd Dunkirk (14048) *(G-4061)*
Nestle Usa Inc 914 272-4021
1311 Mmroneck Ave Ste 350 White Plains (10605) *(G-16033)*
Nestle Usa Inc 212 688-2490
520 Madison Ave New York (10022) *(G-10568)*
NET & Die Inc 315 592-4311
24 Foster St Fulton (13069) *(G-5072)*
Netech Corporation 631 531-0100
110 Toledo St Farmingdale (11735) *(G-4694)*
Netologic Inc 212 269-3796
17 State St Fl 38 New York (10004) *(G-10569)*
Netsuite Inc 646 652-5700
8 W 40th St Fl 8 # 8 New York (10018) *(G-10570)*
Nettle Meadow Farm, Warrensburg *Also called Lumazu LLC (G-15504)*
Network Infrstructure Tech Inc 212 404-7340
90 John St Fl 7 New York (10038) *(G-10571)*
Neu Group Inc (PA) 914 232-4068
135 Katonah Ave Ste 2 Katonah (10536) *(G-6636)*
Neumann Jutta New York Inc 212 982-7048
355 E 4th St New York (10009) *(G-10572)*
Neurosteer Inc 401 837-0351
375 S End Ave Apt 26c New York (10280) *(G-10573)*
Neurotrope Inc 973 242-0005
1185 Ave Of The Amrcas Fl New York (10036) *(G-10574)*
Neva Slip, Inwood *Also called Excellent Art Mfg Corp (G-6292)*
Neversink Steel Corp 845 292-4611
12 Asthalter Rd Liberty (12754) *(G-6926)*
Neverware Inc (PA) 516 302-3223
112 W 27th St Ste 201 New York (10001) *(G-10575)*
Neville Mfg Svc & Dist Inc (PA) 716 834-3038
2320 Clinton St Cheektowaga (14227) *(G-3357)*
New Age Ironworks Inc 718 277-1895
183 Van Siclen Ave Brooklyn (11207) *(G-2199)*
New Age Precision Tech Inc 631 471-4000
151 Remington Blvd Ronkonkoma (11779) *(G-13983)*
New American, Brooklyn *Also called Afro Times Newspaper (G-1470)*
New Art Publications Inc 718 636-9100
80 Hanson Pl Ste 703 Brooklyn (11217) *(G-2200)*
New Art Signs Co Inc 718 443-0900
78 Plymouth Dr N Glen Head (11545) *(G-5210)*
New Audio LLC 212 213-6060
132 W 31st St Rm 701 New York (10001) *(G-10576)*
New Avon LLC 716 572-4842
433 Thorncliff Rd Buffalo (14223) *(G-2880)*
New Avon LLC (HQ) 212 282-6000
1 Liberty Plz Fl 25 New York (10006) *(G-10577)*
New Balance Underwear, New York *Also called Balanced Tech Corp (G-8722)*
New Bgnnngs Win Door Dstrs LLC 845 214-0698
28 Willowbrook Hts Poughkeepsie (12603) *(G-12974)*

New Buffalo Shirt Factory Inc 716 436-5839
1979 Harlem Rd Buffalo (14212) *(G-2881)*
New Business Solutions Inc 631 789-1500
31 Sprague Ave Amityville (11701) *(G-298)*
New City Press Inc 845 229-0335
202 Comforter Blvd Hyde Park (12538) *(G-6273)*
New Classic Inc 718 609-1100
4143 37th St Long Island City (11101) *(G-7306)*
New Concepts of New York LLC 212 695-4999
89 19th St 91 Brooklyn (11232) *(G-2201)*
New Cov Manufacturing, West Henrietta *Also called Semans Enterprises Inc (G-15803)*
New Day Woodwork Inc 718 275-1721
8861 76th Ave Glendale (11385) *(G-5229)*
New Deal Printing Corp (PA) 718 729-5800
420 E 55th St Apt Grdp New York (10022) *(G-10578)*
New Dimension Awards Inc (PA) 718 236-8200
6505 11th Ave Brooklyn (11219) *(G-2202)*
New Dimensions Office Group 718 387-0995
540 Morgan Ave Brooklyn (11222) *(G-2203)*
New Directions Publishing 212 255-0230
80 8th Ave Fl 19 New York (10011) *(G-10579)*
New Dynamics Corporation 845 692-0022
15 Fortune Rd W Middletown (10941) *(G-7923)*
New Eagle Silo Corp 585 492-1300
7648 Hurdville Rd Arcade (14009) *(G-379)*
New Energy Systems Group 917 573-0302
116 W 23rd St Fl 5 New York (10011) *(G-10580)*
New England Barns Inc 631 445-1461
45805 Route 25 Southold (11971) *(G-14545)*
New England Orthotic & Prost 212 682-9313
235 E 38th St New York (10016) *(G-10581)*
New England Reclamation Inc 914 949-2000
20 Haarlem Ave White Plains (10603) *(G-16034)*
New ERA Cap Co Inc 716 604-9000
160 Delaware Ave Buffalo (14202) *(G-2882)*
New ERA Cap Co Inc (PA) 716 604-9000
160 Delaware Ave Buffalo (14202) *(G-2883)*
New ERA Cap Co Inc 716 549-0445
8061 Erie Rd Derby (14047) *(G-4006)*
New Fine Chemicals Inc 631 321-8151
35 W Hoffman Ave Lindenhurst (11757) *(G-6963)*
New Generation Lighting Inc 212 966-0328
144 Bowery Frnt 1 New York (10013) *(G-10582)*
New Goldstar 1 Printing Corp 212 343-3909
63 Orchard St New York (10002) *(G-10583)*
New Hampton Creations Inc 212 244-7474
237 W 35th St Ste 502 New York (10001) *(G-10584)*
New Heydenryk LLC 212 206-9611
3727 10th St Long Island City (11101) *(G-7307)*
New Hope Media LLC 646 366-0830
108 W 39th St Rm 805 New York (10018) *(G-10585)*
New Hope Mills Inc 315 252-2676
181 York St Auburn (13021) *(G-486)*
New Hope Mills Mfg Inc (PA) 315 252-2676
181 York St Auburn (13021) *(G-487)*
New Horizon Graphics Inc 631 231-8055
1200 Prime Pl Hauppauge (11788) *(G-5727)*
New Horizons Bakery, Binghamton *Also called Fratellis LLC (G-878)*
New Jersey Pulverizing Co Inc (PA) 516 921-9595
4 Rita St Syosset (11791) *(G-14798)*
New Kit On The Block 631 757-5655
100 Knickerbocker Ave K Bohemia (11716) *(G-1051)*
New Living Inc 631 751-8819
99 Waverly Ave Apt 6d Patchogue (11772) *(G-12507)*
New Market Products LLC 607 292-6226
9671 Back St Wayne (14893) *(G-15628)*
New Media Investment Group Inc (PA) 212 479-3160
1345 Avenue Of The Americ New York (10105) *(G-10586)*
New Mount Pleasant Bakery 518 374-7577
941 Crane St Schenectady (12303) *(G-14291)*
New Mountain Capital LLC (PA) 212 720-0300
787 7th Ave Fl 49 New York (10019) *(G-10587)*
New Paltz Times, New Paltz *Also called Ulster Publishing Co Inc (G-8313)*
New Press 212 629-8802
120 Wall St Fl 31 New York (10005) *(G-10588)*
New Primecare 516 822-4031
1184 Broadway Hewlett (11557) *(G-5872)*
New Republic 212 989-8200
1 Union Sq W Fl 6 New York (10003) *(G-10589)*
New Rosen Printing, Buffalo *Also called Cilyox Inc (G-2697)*
New Scale Technologies Inc 585 924-4450
121 Victor Heights Pkwy Victor (14564) *(G-15420)*
New Sensor Corporation (PA) 718 937-8300
5501 2nd St Long Island City (11101) *(G-7308)*
New Ski Inc 607 277-7000
109 N Cayuga St Ste A Ithaca (14850) *(G-6401)*
New Skin, Tarrytown *Also called Medtech Products Inc (G-15047)*
New Star Bakery 718 961-8868
4121a Kissena Blvd Flushing (11355) *(G-4877)*
New Style Signs Limited Inc 212 242-7848
171 Madison Ave Rm 204 New York (10016) *(G-10590)*
New Top Sales Company, Baldwinsville *Also called Coverall Manufacturing (G-546)*

New Triad For Collaborative 212 873-9610
  205 W 86th St Apt 911 New York (10024) *(G-10591)*
New Vision Industries Inc 607 687-7700
  1239 Campville Rd Endicott (13760) *(G-4466)*
New Windsor Waste Water Plant 845 561-2550
  145 Caesars Ln New Windsor (12553) *(G-8374)*
New Wop Records 631 617-9732
  317 W 14th St Deer Park (11729) *(G-3911)*
New World Records, Brooklyn *Also called Recorded Anthology of Amrcn Mus (G-2333)*
New York Accessory Group Inc (PA) 212 532-7911
  411 5th Ave Fl 4 New York (10016) *(G-10592)*
New York Air Brake, Watertown *Also called Knorr Brake Truck Systems Co (G-15579)*
New York Air Brake LLC 315 786-5576
  781 Pearl St Watertown (13601) *(G-15583)*
New York Air Brake LLC (HQ) 315 786-5219
  748 Starbuck Ave Watertown (13601) *(G-15584)*
New York Barbell, Elmira *Also called TDS Fitness Equipment Corp (G-4370)*
New York Binding Co Inc 718 729-2454
  2121 41st Ave Ste A Long Island City (11101) *(G-7309)*
New York Blood Pressure, Mendon *Also called N Y B P Inc (G-7851)*
New York Bottling Co Inc 718 963-3232
  626 Whittier St Bronx (10474) *(G-1323)*
New York Christan Times Inc 718 638-6397
  1061 Atlantic Ave Brooklyn (11238) *(G-2204)*
New York Computer Consulting 516 921-1932
  14 Pheasant Ln Woodbury (11797) *(G-16178)*
New York Cutting & Gumming Co 212 563-4146
  265 Ballard Rd Middletown (10941) *(G-7924)*
New York Cvl Srvc Emplys Pblsh 212 962-2690
  277 Broadway Ste 1506 New York (10007) *(G-10593)*
New York Daily Challenge Inc (PA) 718 636-9500
  1195 Atlantic Ave Fl 2 Brooklyn (11216) *(G-2205)*
New York Daily News, New York *Also called Daily News LP (G-9154)*
New York Daily News 212 248-2100
  4 New York Plz Fl 6 New York (10004) *(G-10594)*
New York Digital Corporation 631 630-9798
  33 Walt Whitman Rd # 117 Huntington Station (11746) *(G-6255)*
New York Digital Print Ctr Inc 718 767-1953
  15050 14th Rd Ste 1 Whitestone (11357) *(G-16098)*
New York Distilling Co LLC 718 473-2955
  405 Leonard St Brooklyn (11222) *(G-2206)*
New York Distilling Co LLC (PA) 917 893-7519
  511 8th St Apt 1I Brooklyn (11215) *(G-2207)*
New York Division, Owego *Also called Kyocera Precision Tools Inc (G-12431)*
New York Elegance Entps Inc 212 685-3088
  385 5th Ave Rm 709 New York (10016) *(G-10595)*
New York Embroidery & Monogram, Hicksville *Also called NY Embroidery Inc (G-5934)*
New York Enrgy Synthetics Inc 212 634-4787
  375 Park Ave Ste 2607 New York (10152) *(G-10596)*
New York Enterprise Report, New York *Also called Rsl Media LLC (G-11094)*
New York Eye, Amityville *Also called Hart Specialties Inc (G-267)*
New York Familypublications, Mamaroneck *Also called Family Publishing Group Inc (G-7510)*
New York Fan Coil LLC 646 580-1344
  7 Chesapeake Bay Rd Coram (11727) *(G-3696)*
New York Findings Corp 212 925-5745
  70 Bowery Unit 8 New York (10013) *(G-10597)*
New York Fshion Week Guide LLC 646 757-9119
  387 Park Ave S Fl 5 New York (10016) *(G-10598)*
New York Hospital Disposable 718 384-1620
  101 Richardson St Ste 1 Brooklyn (11211) *(G-2208)*
New York IL Bo Inc 718 961-1538
  4522 162nd St Fl 2 Flushing (11358) *(G-4878)*
New York Imaging Service Inc 716 834-8022
  255 Cooper Ave Tonawanda (14150) *(G-15125)*
New York Laser & Aestheticks 516 627-7777
  1025 Nthrn Blvd Ste 206 Roslyn (11576) *(G-14044)*
New York Law Journal, New York *Also called Alm Media LLC (G-8524)*
New York Legal Publishing 518 459-1100
  120 Broadway Ste 1a Menands (12204) *(G-7847)*
New York Manufactured Products 585 254-9353
  6 Cairn St Rochester (14611) *(G-13570)*
New York Manufacturing Corp 585 254-9353
  6 Cairn St Rochester (14611) *(G-13571)*
New York Marking Devices Corp 585 454-5188
  700 Clinton Ave S Ste 2 Rochester (14620) *(G-13572)*
New York Marking Devices Corp (PA) 315 463-8641
  2207 Teall Ave Syracuse (13206) *(G-14951)*
New York Media LLC (PA) 212 508-0700
  75 Varick St Ste 1404 New York (10013) *(G-10599)*
New York Moves Magazine LLC 212 396-2394
  393 Broadway Fl 2 New York (10013) *(G-10600)*
New York Packaging Corp 516 746-0600
  135 Fulton Ave New Hyde Park (11040) *(G-8284)*
New York Packaging II LLC 516 746-0600
  135 Fulton Ave Garden City Park (11040) *(G-5122)*
New York Pasta Authority Inc 347 787-2130
  640 Parkside Ave Brooklyn (11226) *(G-2209)*
New York Poplin LLC 718 768-3296
  4611 1st Ave Brooklyn (11232) *(G-2210)*
New York Post, Brooklyn *Also called Nyp Holdings Inc (G-2227)*

New York Post, New York *Also called Nyp Holdings Inc (G-10666)*
New York Press Inc 212 268-8600
  72 Madison Ave Fl 11 New York (10016) *(G-10601)*
New York Qrtrly Foundation Inc 917 843-8825
  322 76th St Brooklyn (11209) *(G-2211)*
New York Quarries Inc 518 756-3138
  305 Rte 111 Alcove (12007) *(G-163)*
New York Ravioli Pasta Co Inc 516 270-2852
  12 Denton Ave S New Hyde Park (11040) *(G-8285)*
New York Ready Mix Inc 516 338-6969
  120 Rushmore St Westbury (11590) *(G-15912)*
New York Review of Books, New York *Also called Nyrev Inc (G-10667)*
New York Rhbilitative Svcs LLC 516 239-0990
  214 E Sunrise Hwy Valley Stream (11581) *(G-15349)*
New York Running Co, New York *Also called PRC Liquidating Company (G-10873)*
New York Skateboards, Deer Park *Also called Chapman Skateboard Co Inc (G-3852)*
New York Spring Water Inc 212 777-4649
  517 W 36th St New York (10018) *(G-10602)*
New York State Assoc 518 434-2281
  453 New Karner Rd Albany (12205) *(G-104)*
New York State Foam Enrgy LLC 845 534-4656
  2 Commercial Dr Cornwall (12518) *(G-3730)*
New York State Tool Co Inc 315 737-8985
  3343 Oneida St Chadwicks (13319) *(G-3303)*
New York Steel Services Co 718 291-7770
  18009 Liberty Ave Jamaica (11433) *(G-6463)*
New York Sugars LLC 585 500-0155
  2301 Mount Read Blvd Rochester (14615) *(G-13573)*
New York Sweater Company Inc 845 629-9533
  141 W 36th St Rm 17 New York (10018) *(G-10603)*
New York Tank Co, Watervliet *Also called Bigbee Steel and Tank Company (G-15597)*
New York Times Co Mag Group, New York *Also called Gruner + Jahr Prtg & Pubg Co (G-9687)*
New York Times Company (PA) 212 556-1234
  620 8th Ave Bsmt 1 New York (10018) *(G-10604)*
New York Times Company 718 281-7000
  1 New York Times Plz Flushing (11354) *(G-4879)*
New York Times Company 212 556-1200
  620 8th Ave Bsmt 1 New York (10018) *(G-10605)*
New York Times Company 212 556-4300
  620 8th Ave Bsmt 1 New York (10018) *(G-10606)*
New York Trading Co, New York *Also called E-Won Industrial Co Inc (G-9295)*
New York Typing & Printing Co 718 268-7900
  10816 72nd Ave Forest Hills (11375) *(G-4925)*
New York University 212 998-4300
  7 E 12th St Ste 800 New York (10003) *(G-10607)*
New York Vanity and Mfg Co 718 417-1010
  10 Henry St Freeport (11520) *(G-5010)*
New York1 News Operations 212 379-3311
  75 9th Ave Frnt 6 New York (10011) *(G-10608)*
Newbay Media LLC (HQ) 212 378-0400
  28 E 28th St Fl 12 New York (10016) *(G-10609)*
Newburgh Asphalt, New Windsor *Also called Tilcon New York Inc (G-8384)*
Newburgh Brewing Company LLC 845 569-2337
  88 S Colden St Newburgh (12550) *(G-11876)*
Newburgh Distribution Corp (PA) 845 561-6330
  463 Temple Hill Rd New Windsor (12553) *(G-8375)*
Newburgh Envelope Corp 845 566-4211
  1720 Route 300 Newburgh (12550) *(G-11877)*
Newcastle Fabrics Corp 718 388-6600
  86 Beadel St Brooklyn (11222) *(G-2212)*
Newchem Inc 315 331-7680
  407 Cliff St Ithaca (14850) *(G-6402)*
Newcut, Ithaca *Also called Newchem Inc (G-6402)*
Newline Products Inc 972 881-3318
  509 Temple Hill Rd New Windsor (12553) *(G-8376)*
Newmat Northeast Corp 631 253-9277
  81b Mahan St West Babylon (11704) *(G-15734)*
Newport Corporation 585 248-4246
  705 Saint Paul St Rochester (14605) *(G-13574)*
Newport Graphics Inc 212 924-2600
  121 Varick St Rm 302 New York (10013) *(G-10610)*
Newport Rochester Inc 585 262-1325
  705 Saint Paul St Rochester (14605) *(G-13575)*
News Communications Inc (PA) 212 689-2500
  501 Madison Ave Fl 23 New York (10022) *(G-10611)*
News Corporation (PA) 212 416-3400
  1211 Avenue Of The Americ New York (10036) *(G-10612)*
News India Times, New York *Also called News India USA Inc (G-10614)*
News India Times, New York *Also called News India Usa LLC (G-10613)*
News India Usa LLC 212 675-7515
  37 W 20th St Ste 1109 New York (10011) *(G-10613)*
News India USA Inc 212 675-7515
  37 W 20th St Ste 1109 New York (10011) *(G-10614)*
News Now Waverly 607 296-6769
  446 Broad St Apt 2 Waverly (14892) *(G-15624)*
News of The Highlands Inc (PA) 845 534-7771
  35 Hasbrouck Ave Cornwall (12518) *(G-3731)*
News Report Inc 718 851-6607
  1281 49th St Ste 3 Brooklyn (11219) *(G-2213)*
News Review, The, Mattituck *Also called Times Review Newspaper Corp (G-7680)*

(G-0000) Company's Geographic Section entry number

News/Sprts Microwave Rentl Inc 619 670-0572
415 Madison Ave Fl 11 New York (10017) *(G-10615)*
Newsday LLC (PA) 631 843-4050
6 Corporate Center Dr Melville (11747) *(G-7808)*
Newsday LLC 631 843-3135
25 Deshon Dr Melville (11747) *(G-7809)*
Newsday Media Group, Melville *Also called Newsday LLC (G-7808)*
Newspaper Delivery Solutions 718 370-1111
309 Bradley Ave Staten Island (10314) *(G-14682)*
Newspaper Publisher LLC 607 775-0472
1035 Conklin Rd Conklin (13748) *(G-3626)*
Newspaper Times Union 518 454-5676
645 Albany Shaker Rd Albany (12211) *(G-105)*
Newsweek LLC 646 867-7100
7 Hanover Sq Fl 5 New York (10004) *(G-10616)*
Newsweek Media Group Inc (PA) 646 867-7100
7 Hanover Sq Fl 5 New York (10004) *(G-10617)*
Newtex Industries Inc (PA) 585 924-9135
8050 Victor Mendon Rd Victor (14564) *(G-15421)*
Newtown Finishing, Brooklyn *Also called Newcastle Fabrics Corp (G-2212)*
Newyork Pedorthic Associates 718 236-7700
2102 63rd St Brooklyn (11204) *(G-2214)*
Nex-Gen Ready Mix Corp 347 231-0073
530 Faile St Bronx (10474) *(G-1324)*
Nexans Energy USA Inc 845 469-2141
25 Oakland Ave Chester (10918) *(G-3381)*
Nexbev Industries LLC (PA) 646 648-1255
600 Bradley Hill Rd Ste 2 Blauvelt (10913) *(G-931)*
Nexgen Enviro Systems Inc 631 226-2930
190 E Hoffman Ave Ste D Lindenhurst (11757) *(G-6964)*
Nexis 3 LLC 585 285-4120
1681 Lyell Ave Rochester (14606) *(G-13576)*
Nexstar Holding Corp 716 929-9000
275 Northpointe Pkwy Amherst (14228) *(G-234)*
Next Advance Inc (PA) 518 674-3510
2113 Ny 7 Ste 1 Troy (12180) *(G-15174)*
Next Big Sound Inc 646 657-9837
125 Park Ave Fl 19 New York (10017) *(G-10618)*
Next Magazine, New York *Also called Rnd Enterprises Inc (G-11056)*
Next Potential LLC 401 742-5190
278 E 10th St Apt 5b New York (10009) *(G-10619)*
Next Step Magazine, The, Victor *Also called Next Step Publishing Inc (G-15422)*
Next Step Publishing Inc 585 742-1260
2 W Main St Ste 200 Victor (14564) *(G-15422)*
Nextgen Building Components 585 924-7171
6080 Collett Rd Farmington (14425) *(G-4776)*
Nextpotential, New York *Also called Next Potential LLC (G-10619)*
Nfe Management LLC 212 798-6100
1345 Avenue Of The Americ New York (10105) *(G-10620)*
Nfk International, Brooklyn *Also called Slava Industries Incorporated (G-2425)*
Niabraze LLC 716 447-1082
675 Ensminger Rd Tonawanda (14150) *(G-15126)*
Niagara Blower Company, Tonawanda *Also called Alfa Laval Niagara Inc (G-15084)*
Niagara Chocolates, Buffalo *Also called Sweetworks Inc (G-2998)*
Niagara Cooler Inc 716 434-1235
6605 Slyton Settlement Rd Lockport (14094) *(G-7096)*
Niagara Development & Mfg Div, Niagara Falls *Also called Fross Industries Inc (G-11930)*
Niagara Falls Plant, Niagara Falls *Also called Richardson Molding LLC (G-11973)*
Niagara Fiberboard Inc 716 434-8881
140 Van Buren St Lockport (14094) *(G-7097)*
Niagara Fiberglass Inc 716 822-3921
88 Okell St Buffalo (14220) *(G-2884)*
Niagara Gazette, Niagara Falls *Also called Cnhi LLC (G-11916)*
Niagara Gear Corporation 716 874-3131
941 Military Rd Buffalo (14217) *(G-2885)*
Niagara Label Company Inc 716 542-3000
12715 Lewis Rd Akron (14001) *(G-18)*
Niagara Precision Inc 716 439-0956
233 Market St Lockport (14094) *(G-7098)*
Niagara Punch & Die Corp 716 896-7619
176 Gruner Rd Buffalo (14227) *(G-2886)*
Niagara Refining LLC 716 706-1400
5661 Transit Rd Depew (14043) *(G-3989)*
Niagara Sample Book Co Inc 716 284-6151
1717 Mackenna Ave Niagara Falls (14303) *(G-11954)*
Niagara Scientific Inc 315 437-0821
6743 Kinne St East Syracuse (13057) *(G-4228)*
Niagara Sheets LLC 716 692-1129
7393 Shawnee Rd North Tonawanda (14120) *(G-12079)*
Niagara Specialty Metals Inc 716 542-5552
12600 Clarence Center Rd Akron (14001) *(G-19)*
Niagara Thermo Products, Niagara Falls *Also called Kintex Inc (G-11944)*
Niagara Transformer Corp 716 896-6500
1747 Dale Rd Buffalo (14225) *(G-2887)*
Niagara Tying Service Inc 716 825-0066
176 Dingens St Buffalo (14206) *(G-2888)*
Nibble Inc Baking Co 518 334-3950
451 Broadway Apt 5 Troy (12180) *(G-15175)*
Nibmor Project LLC 718 374-5091
11 Middle Neck Rd Great Neck (11021) *(G-5405)*

Nice-Pak Products Inc (PA) 845 365-1700
2 Nice Pak Park Orangeburg (10962) *(G-12324)*
Nice-Pak Products Inc. 845 353-6090
100 Brookhill Dr West Nyack (10994) *(G-15828)*
Niche Design Inc 212 777-2101
310 Fishkill Ave Unit 11 Beacon (12508) *(G-755)*
Niche Media Holdings LLC (HQ) 702 990-2500
257 Park Ave S Fl 5 New York (10010) *(G-10621)*
Niche Modern, Beacon *Also called Niche Design Inc (G-755)*
Nicholas Kirkwood LLC (PA) 646 559-5239
598 Madison Ave New York (10022) *(G-10622)*
Nicholson Steam Trap, Walden *Also called Spence Engineering Company Inc (G-15462)*
Nick Lugo Inc 212 348-2100
159 E 116th St Fl 2 New York (10029) *(G-10623)*
Nickel City Studios Photo Jour 716 200-0956
45 Linwood Ave Buffalo (14209) *(G-2889)*
Nickelodeon Magazines Inc (HQ) 212 541-1949
1633 Broadway Fl 7 New York (10019) *(G-10624)*
Nicoform Inc. 585 454-5530
72 Cascade Dr Ste 12 Rochester (14614) *(G-13577)*
Nicolia Concrete Products Inc 631 669-0700
640 Muncy St Lindenhurst (11757) *(G-6965)*
Nicolia of Long Island, Lindenhurst *Also called Nicolia Concrete Products Inc (G-6965)*
Nicolia Ready Mix Inc (PA) 631 669-7000
615 Cord Ave Lindenhurst (11757) *(G-6966)*
Nicolia Ready Mix Inc. 631 669-7000
615 Cord Ave Lindenhurst (11757) *(G-6967)*
Nicolo Raineri 212 925-6128
82 Bowery New York (10013) *(G-10625)*
Nicolo Raineri Jeweler, New York *Also called Nicolo Raineri (G-10625)*
Nicolock Paving Stones LLC (HQ) 631 669-0700
612 Muncy St Lindenhurst (11757) *(G-6968)*
Nidec Indus Automtn USA LLC 716 774-1193
359 Lang Blvd Bldg B Grand Island (14072) *(G-5338)*
Nidec Motor Corporation 315 434-9303
6268 E Molloy Rd East Syracuse (13057) *(G-4229)*
Niebylski Bakery Inc 718 721-5152
2364 Steinway St Astoria (11105) *(G-431)*
Nielsen Hardware Corporation (PA) 607 821-1475
71 Frederick St Binghamton (13901) *(G-902)*
Nielsen/Sessions, Binghamton *Also called Nielsen Hardware Corporation (G-902)*
Nift Group Inc 504 505-1144
14 Woodbine St Brooklyn (11221) *(G-2215)*
Nifty Bar Grinding & Cutting 585 381-0450
450 Whitney Rd Penfield (14526) *(G-12571)*
Nightingale Corp 905 896-3434
750 Ensminger Rd Ste 108 Tonawanda (14150) *(G-15127)*
Nightingale Food Entps Inc 347 577-1630
2306 1st Ave New York (10035) *(G-10626)*
Nigun Music 718 977-5700
4116 13th Ave Brooklyn (11219) *(G-2216)*
Nijon Tool Co Inc 631 242-3434
12 Evergreen Pl 12 # 12 Deer Park (11729) *(G-3912)*
Nike Inc 631 960-0184
2675 Sunrise Hwy Islip Terrace (11752) *(G-6359)*
Nike Inc. 716 298-5615
1886 Military Rd Niagara Falls (14304) *(G-11955)*
Nikish Software Corp 631 754-1618
12 Whispering Fields Dr Northport (11768) *(G-12110)*
Nikkei America Inc (HQ) 212 261-6200
1325 Avenue Of The Americ New York (10019) *(G-10627)*
Nikkei America Holdings Inc (HQ) 212 261-6200
1325 Ave Of The Usa New York (10019) *(G-10628)*
Nikon Instruments Inc (HQ) 631 547-4200
1300 Walt Whitman Rd Fl 2 Melville (11747) *(G-7810)*
Nikon Instruments Inc 631 845-7620
200 Executive Dr Ste A Edgewood (11717) *(G-4276)*
Nilda Desserts, Poughkeepsie *Also called Ljmm Inc (G-12967)*
Nildas Desserts Limited 845 454-5876
188 Washington St Poughkeepsie (12601) *(G-12975)*
Nimbletv Inc 646 502-7010
450 Fashion Ave Fl 43 New York (10123) *(G-10629)*
Ninas Custard 716 636-0345
2577 Millersport Hwy Getzville (14068) *(G-5179)*
Nine Pin Ciderworks LLC 518 449-9999
929 Broadway Albany (12207) *(G-106)*
Nine West Holdings Inc. 212 391-5000
1411 Broadway Fl 15 New York (10018) *(G-10630)*
Ninth Wave Inc 212 401-6381
115 Broadway Rm 1705 New York (10006) *(G-10631)*
Nireco America, Port Jervis *Also called Datatran Labs Inc (G-12847)*
Nirvana Inc 315 942-4900
1 Nirvana Plz Forestport (13338) *(G-4928)*
Nirx Medical Technologies LLC 516 676-6479
15 Cherry Ln Glen Head (11545) *(G-5211)*
Nite Train R, Champlain *Also called Koregon Enterprises Inc (G-3314)*
Nitram Energy Inc 716 662-6540
50 Cobham Dr Orchard Park (14127) *(G-12368)*
Nitro Manufacturing LLC 716 646-9900
440 Shirley Rd North Collins (14111) *(G-12026)*
Nitro Manufacturing LLC 716 646-9900
106 Evans St Ste E Hamburg (14075) *(G-5514)*

Nitro Wheels Inc 716 337-0709
4440 Shirley Rd North Collins (14111) *(G-12027)*

Nixon Gear, Syracuse *Also called Gear Motions Incorporated* *(G-14901)*

Njf Publishing Corp 631 345-5200
14 Ramsey Rd Shirley (11967) *(G-14426)*

Njr Medical Devices 440 258-8204
390 Oak Ave Cedarhurst (11516) *(G-3243)*

NK Medical Products Inc (PA) 716 759-7200
80 Creekside Dr Amherst (14228) *(G-235)*

Nlhe LLC 212 594-0012
141 Flushing Ave 906 Brooklyn (11205) *(G-2217)*

Nlr Counter Tops LLC 347 295-0410
902 E 92nd St New York (10128) *(G-10632)*

Nmcc, Niagara Falls *Also called National Maint Contg Corp* *(G-11953)*

No Longer Empty Inc 202 413-4262
122 W 27th St Fl 10 New York (10001) *(G-10633)*

Noah Enterprises Ltd (PA) 212 736-2888
520 8th Ave Lbby 2 New York (10018) *(G-10634)*

Nobilium, Albany *Also called Cmp Industries LLC* *(G-65)*

Noble Checks Inc 212 537-6241
1682 43rd St Apt 2 Brooklyn (11204) *(G-2218)*

Noble Pine Products Co Inc 914 664-5877
240 E 7th St Mount Vernon (10550) *(G-8165)*

Noble Vintages, Fredonia *Also called Woodbury Vineyards Inc* *(G-4973)*

Noble Wood Shavings, Sherrill *Also called Dlr Enterprises LLC* *(G-14403)*

Nochairs Inc 917 748 8731
325 W 38th St Rm 310 New York (10018) *(G-10635)*

Nodus Noodle Corporation 718 309-3725
4504 Queens Blvd Sunnyside (11104) *(G-14773)*

Noel Assoc 516 371-5420
114 Henry St Ste A Inwood (11096) *(G-6301)*

Noetic Partners Inc 212 836-4351
445 Park Ave Frnt 1 New York (10022) *(G-10636)*

Noga Dairies Inc 516 293-5448
175 Price Pkwy Farmingdale (11735) *(G-4695)*

Noir Jewelry LLC 212 465-8500
358 5th Ave Rm 501 New York (10001) *(G-10637)*

Nola Speaker, Holbrook *Also called Accent Speaker Technology Ltd* *(G-5982)*

Nomad Editions LLC 212 918-0992
123 Ellison Ave Bronxville (10708) *(G-1402)*

None, College Point *Also called City Store Gates Mfg Corp* *(G-3540)*

Nook Media LLC 212 633-3300
122 5th Ave New York (10011) *(G-10638)*

Norampac New York City Inc 718 340-2100
5515 Grand Ave Maspeth (11378) *(G-7630)*

Noras Candy Shop 315 337-4530
321 N Doxtator St Rome (13440) *(G-13860)*

Norazza Inc 716 706-1160
3938 Broadway St Buffalo (14227) *(G-2890)*

Norcorp Inc 914 666-1310
400 E Main St Mount Kisco (10549) *(G-8100)*

Nordic Interior Inc 718 456-7000
26 Court St Ste 2211 Brooklyn (11242) *(G-2219)*

Nordic Press Inc 212 686-3356
243 E 34th St New York (10016) *(G-10639)*

Nordon Inc (PA) 585 546-6200
691 Exchange St Rochester (14608) *(G-13578)*

Nordon Inc. 585 546-6200
1600 Lexington Ave 235a Rochester (14606) *(G-13579)*

Nordon Inc. 585 546-6200
711 Exchange St Rochester (14608) *(G-13580)*

Noresco Industrial Group Inc 516 759-3355
3 School St Ste 103 Glen Cove (11542) *(G-5197)*

Norfalco LLC 416 775-1431
330 Madison Ave Fl 7 New York (10017) *(G-10640)*

Norlite LLC 518 235-0030
628 Saratoga St Cohoes (12047) *(G-3511)*

Norlite Corporation, Cohoes *Also called Norlite LLC* *(G-3511)*

Noroc Enterprises Inc 718 585-3230
415 Concord Ave Bronx (10455) *(G-1325)*

Norse Energy Corp USA 716 568-2048
3556 Lake Shore Rd # 700 Buffalo (14219) *(G-2891)*

Norsk Titanium US Inc (HQ) 518 324-4010
44 Martina Cir Plattsburgh (12901) *(G-12761)*

Nortek Powder Coating LLC 315 337-2339
5900 Success Dr Rome (13440) *(G-13861)*

North America Pastel Artists 718 463-4701
13303 41st Ave Apt 1a Flushing (11355) *(G-4880)*

North American Breweries Inc (HQ) 585 546-1030
445 Saint Paul St Rochester (14605) *(G-13581)*

North American Carbide, Orchard Park *Also called Transport National Dev Inc* *(G-12379)*

North American Carbide of NY, Orchard Park *Also called Transport National Dev Inc* *(G-12380)*

North American DF Inc (PA) 718 698-2500
4591 Hylan Blvd Staten Island (10312) *(G-14683)*

North American Filter Corp (PA) 800 265-8943
200 W Shore Blvd Newark (14513) *(G-11848)*

North American Graphics Inc 212 725-2200
150 Varick St Rm 303 New York (10013) *(G-10641)*

North American Hoganas Inc 716 285-3451
5950 Packard Rd Niagara Falls (14304) *(G-11956)*

North American MBL Systems Inc 718 898-8700
31 Lafayette Ave Sea Cliff (11579) *(G-14346)*

North American Mfg Entps Inc 718 524-4370
1961 Richmond Ter Staten Island (10302) *(G-14684)*

North American Mills Inc. 212 695-6146
1370 Broadway Rm 1101 New York (10018) *(G-10642)*

North American Pipe Corp 516 338-2863
156 High St East Williston (11596) *(G-4249)*

North American Service Group, Ballston Spa *Also called North American Svcs Group LLC* *(G-583)*

North American Signs Buffalo, Buffalo *Also called Nas Quick Sign Inc* *(G-2879)*

North American Slate Inc 518 642-1702
50 Columbus St Granville (12832) *(G-5354)*

North American Supply LLC (PA) 607 432-1480
62 Roundhouse Rd Oneonta (13820) *(G-12277)*

North American Svcs Group LLC (HQ) 518 885-1820
1240 Saratoga Rd Ballston Spa (12020) *(G-583)*

North Americas Breweries, Rochester *Also called High Falls Brewing Company LLC* *(G-13466)*

North Amrcn Brwries Hldngs LLC (PA) 585 546-1030
445 Saint Paul St Rochester (14605) *(G-13582)*

North Atlantic Industries Inc 631 567-1100
50 Orville Dr Ste 3 Bohemia (11716) *(G-1052)*

North Atlantic Industries Inc (PA) 631 567-1100
110 Wilbur Pl Bohemia (11716) *(G-1053)*

North Atlantic Tradlng Co, New York *Also called National Tobacco Company LP* *(G-10548)*

North Bronx Retinal & Ophthlmi 347 535-4932
3725 Henry Hudson Pkwy Bronx (10463) *(G-1326)*

North Coast Outfitters Ltd 631 727-5580
1015 E Main St Ste 1 Riverhead (11901) *(G-13183)*

NORTH COUNTRY BEHAVIORAL HEALT, Saranac Lake *Also called Northern New York Rural* *(G-14159)*

North Country Books Inc 315 735-4877
220 Lafayette St Utica (13502) *(G-15288)*

North Country Dairy, North Lawrence *Also called Upstate Niagara Coop Inc* *(G-12033)*

North Country This Week Inc 315 265-1000
4 Clarkson Ave Potsdam (13676) *(G-12938)*

North County News, Yorktown Heights *Also called Northern Tier Publishing Corp* *(G-16369)*

North Delaware Printing Inc 716 692-0576
645 Delaware St Ste 1 Tonawanda (14150) *(G-15128)*

North E Rggers Erectors NY Inc 518 842-6377
178 Clizbe Ave Amsterdam (12010) *(G-342)*

North East Finishing Co Inc 631 789-8000
245 Ralph Ave Copiague (11726) *(G-3666)*

North East Fuel Group Inc 718 984-6774
51 Stuyvesant Ave Staten Island (10312) *(G-14685)*

North End Paper Co Inc 315 593-8100
702 Hannibal St Fulton (13069) *(G-5073)*

North Face, Central Valley *Also called Vf Outdoor LLC* *(G-3301)*

NORTH FIELD, Island Park *Also called Northfeld Precision Instr Corp* *(G-6321)*

North Hills Signal Proc Corp 631 244-7393
40 Orville Dr Bohemia (11716) *(G-1054)*

North House Vineyards Inc 631 779-2817
1216 Main Rd Rte 25a Jamesport (11947) *(G-6490)*

North Hudson Woodcraft Corp 315 429-3105
152 N Helmer Ave Dolgeville (13329) *(G-4024)*

North Pk Innovations Group Inc 716 699-2031
6442 Route 242 E Ellicottville (14731) *(G-4315)*

North Point Technologies 607 238-1114
520 Columbia Dr Ste 105 Johnson City (13790) *(G-6606)*

North Point Technology LLC 866 885-3377
816 Buffalo St Endicott (13760) *(G-4467)*

North Salina Cigar Store, Syracuse *Also called Saakshi Inc* *(G-14982)*

North Shore Farms Two Ltd 516 280-6880
330 E Jericho Tpke Mineola (11501) *(G-7991)*

North Shore Home Improver 631 474-2824
200 Wilson St Port Jeff STA (11776) *(G-12835)*

North Shore Monuments Inc 516 759-2156
667 Cedar Swamp Rd Ste 5 Glen Head (11545) *(G-5212)*

North Shore Neon Sign Co Inc 718 937-4848
4649 54th Ave Flushing (11378) *(G-4881)*

North Shore News Group, Smithtown *Also called Smithtown News Inc* *(G-14487)*

North Shore Orthtics Prsthtics 631 928-3040
591 Bicycle Path Ste D Port Jeff STA (11776) *(G-12836)*

North Shore Pallet Inc 631 673-4700
191 E 2nd St Huntington Station (11746) *(G-6256)*

North Six Inc 212 463-7227
159 Bleecker St Frnt A New York (10012) *(G-10643)*

North Star Knitting Mills Inc 718 894-4848
7030 80th St Glendale (11385) *(G-5230)*

North Sunshine LLC 307 027-1634
616 Corporate Way Ste 2-3 Valley Cottage (10989) *(G-15320)*

North-East Machine Inc 518 746-1837
4160 State Route 4 Hudson Falls (12839) *(G-6191)*

Northamerican Breweries, Rochester *Also called North American Breweries Inc* *(G-13581)*

Northast Coml Win Trtments Inc 845 331-0148
25 Cornell St Kingston (12401) *(G-6704)*

Northast Ctr For Bekeeping LLC 800 632-3379
8 Meader Rd Greenwich (12834) *(G-5474)*

Northcountrynow.com, Potsdam *Also called North Country This Week Inc* *(G-12938)*

Northeast Cnstr Inds Inc 845 565-1000
  657 Rte 17 K S St Ste 2 Montgomery (12549) *(G-8062)*
Northeast Commercial Prtg Inc (PA) 518 459-5047
  1237 Central Ave Ste 3 Albany (12205) *(G-107)*
Northeast Concrete Pdts Inc 518 563-0700
  1024 Military Tpke Plattsburgh (12901) *(G-12762)*
Northeast Conveyors Inc 585 768-8912
  7620 Evergreen St Lima (14485) *(G-6933)*
Northeast Data 845 331-5554
  619 State Route 28 Kingston (12401) *(G-6705)*
Northeast Doulas 845 621-0654
  23 Hilltop Dr Mahopac (10541) *(G-7476)*
Northeast Fabricators LLC 607 865-4031
  30-35 William St Walton (13856) *(G-15476)*
Northeast Group 518 563-8214
  12 Nepco Way Plattsburgh (12903) *(G-12763)*
Northeast Group, The, Plattsburgh *Also called Northeast Prtg & Dist Co Inc (G-12765)*
Northeast Hardware Specialties 516 487-6868
  393 Jericho Tpke Ste 103 Mineola (11501) *(G-7992)*
Northeast Mesa LLC (PA) 845 878-9344
  10 Commerce Dr Carmel (10512) *(G-3188)*
Northeast Metrology Corp 716 827-3770
  4490 Broadway Depew (14043) *(G-3990)*
Northeast Pallet & Cont Co Inc 518 271-0535
  1 Mann Ave Bldg 300 Troy (12180) *(G-15176)*
Northeast Promotional Group In 518 793-1024
  75 Main St South Glens Falls (12803) *(G-14515)*
Northeast Prtg & Dist Co Inc 514 577-3545
  163 Idaho Ave Plattsburgh (12903) *(G-12764)*
Northeast Prtg & Dist Co Inc (PA) 518 563-8214
  12 Nepco Way Plattsburgh (12903) *(G-12765)*
Northeast Solite Corporation (PA) 845 246-2646
  1135 Kings Hwy Saugerties (12477) *(G-14205)*
Northeast Solite Corporation 845 246-2177
  962 Kings Hwy Mount Marion (12456) *(G-8112)*
Northeast Stitches & Ink Inc 518 798-5549
  95 Main St South Glens Falls (12803) *(G-14516)*
Northeast Toner Inc 518 899-5545
  26 Walden Gln Fl 2 Ballston Lake (12019) *(G-562)*
Northeast Treaters Inc 518 945-2660
  796 Schoharie Tpke Athens (12015) *(G-447)*
Northeast Treaters NY LLC 518 945-2660
  796 Schoharie Tpke Athens (12015) *(G-448)*
Northeast Windows Usa Inc 516 378-6577
  1 Kees Pl Merrick (11566) *(G-7862)*
Northeastern Air Quality Inc 518 857-3641
  730 3rd St Albany (12206) *(G-108)*
Northeastern Fuel Corp 917 560-6241
  51 Stuyvesant Ave Staten Island (10312) *(G-14686)*
Northeastern Products Corp (PA) 518 623-3161
  115 Sweet Rd Warrensburg (12885) *(G-15505)*
Northeastern Sealcoat Inc 585 544-4372
  470 Hollenbeck St Ste 3 Rochester (14621) *(G-13583)*
Northeastern Sign Corp 315 265-6657
  102 Cold Brook Dr South Colton (13687) *(G-14504)*
Northeastern Water Jet Inc 518 843-4988
  4 Willow St Amsterdam (12010) *(G-343)*
Northern Air Systems Inc (PA) 585 594-5050
  3605 Buffalo Rd Rochester (14624) *(G-13584)*
Northern Air Technology Inc (PA) 585 594-5050
  3605 Buffalo Rd Rochester (14624) *(G-13585)*
Northern Awning & Sign Company 315 782-8515
  22891 County Route 51 Watertown (13601) *(G-15585)*
Northern Biodiesel Inc 585 545-4534
  317 State Route 104 Ontario (14519) *(G-12294)*
Northern Bituminous Mix Inc 315 598-2141
  32 Silk Rd Fulton (13069) *(G-5074)*
Northern Crushing LLC 518 365-8452
  167 Totem Lodge Rd Averill Park (12018) *(G-509)*
Northern Design & Bldg Assoc 518 747-2200
  100 Park Rd Queensbury (12804) *(G-13050)*
Northern Design Inc 716 652-7071
  12990 Old Big Tree Rd East Aurora (14052) *(G-4095)*
Northern Explorng/Timeless T, Plattsburgh *Also called Studley Prtg Publications Inc (G-12782)*
Northern Forest Pdts Co Inc 315 942-6955
  9833 Crolius Dr Boonville (13309) *(G-1107)*
Northern Goose Polar Project, New York *Also called Freedom Rains Inc (G-9534)*
Northern King Lures Inc (PA) 585 865-3373
  167 Armstrong Rd Rochester (14616) *(G-13586)*
Northern Lights Candles, Wellsville *Also called Northern Lights Entps Inc (G-15673)*
Northern Lights Entps Inc 800 836-8797
  3474 Andover Rd Wellsville (14895) *(G-15673)*
Northern Machining Inc 315 384-3189
  2a N Main St Norfolk (13667) *(G-12000)*
Northern Metalworks Corp 646 523-1689
  15 King Ave Selden (11784) *(G-14354)*
Northern New York Rural 518 891-9460
  126 Kiwassa Rd Saranac Lake (12983) *(G-14159)*
Northern NY Newspapers Corp 315 782-1000
  260 Washington St Watertown (13601) *(G-15586)*
Northern Ready Mix LLC (HQ) 315 336-7900
  6131 E Taft Rd North Syracuse (13212) *(G-12048)*

Northern Tier Cnc Inc (PA) 518 236-4702
  733 Woods Falls Rd Mooers Forks (12959) *(G-8080)*
Northern Tier Publishing Corp 914 962-4748
  1520 Front St Yorktown Heights (10598) *(G-16369)*
Northern Timber Harvesting LLC 585 233-7330
  6042 State Route 21 Alfred Station (14803) *(G-185)*
NORTHERN WESTCHESTER HOSPITAL, Mount Kisco *Also called Norcorp Inc (G-8100)*
Northfeld Precision Instr Corp 516 431-1112
  4400 Austin Blvd Island Park (11558) *(G-6321)*
Northknight Logistics Inc 716 283-3090
  7724 Buffalo Ave Niagara Falls (14304) *(G-11957)*
Northland Filter Intl LLC 315 207-1410
  249a Mitchell St Oswego (13126) *(G-12415)*
Northpoint Digital LLC 212 819-1700
  1540 Broadway Fl 41 New York (10036) *(G-10644)*
Northpoint Trading Inc (PA) 212 481-8001
  347 5th Ave New York (10016) *(G-10645)*
Northport Printing, West Babylon *Also called Bartolomeo Publishing Inc (G-15693)*
Northrock Industries Inc 631 924-6130
  31 Crossway E Bohemia (11716) *(G-1055)*
Northrop Grumman Corporation, Bethpage *Also called Northrop Grumman Systems Corp (G-842)*
Northrop Grumman Corporation 703 280-2900
  660 Grumman Rd W Bethpage (11714) *(G-841)*
Northrop Grumman Intl Trdg Inc 716 626-7233
  1740 Wehrle Dr Buffalo (14221) *(G-2892)*
Northrop Grumman Systems Corp 516 575-0574
  925 S Oyster Bay Rd Bethpage (11714) *(G-842)*
Northrop Grumman Systems Corp 716 626-4600
  1740 Wehrle Dr Buffalo (14221) *(G-2893)*
Northrop Grumman Systems Corp 631 423-1014
  70 Dewey St Huntington (11743) *(G-6215)*
Northrop Grumman Systems Corp 516 346-7100
  925 S Oyster Bay Rd Bethpage (11714) *(G-843)*
Northside Media Group LLC 917 318-6513
  55 Washington St Ste 652 Brooklyn (11201) *(G-2220)*
Northtown Imaging, Buffalo *Also called Mri Northtowns Group PC (G-2873)*
Northwell Health Inc 646 665-6000
  30 7th Ave New York (10011) *(G-10646)*
Northwest Company LLC (PA) 516 484-6996
  49 Bryant Ave Roslyn (11576) *(G-14045)*
Northwest Wine Services, Riverhead *Also called Railex Wine Services LLC (G-13186)*
Northwind Graphics 518 899-9651
  2453 State Route 9 Ballston Spa (12020) *(G-584)*
Norton Pulpstones Incorporated 716 433-9400
  120 Church St Lockport (14094) *(G-7099)*
Norton, Ww & Company,, New York *Also called Liveright Publishing Corp (G-10234)*
Norton-Smith Hardwoods Inc (PA) 716 945-0346
  25 Morningside Ave Salamanca (14779) *(G-14125)*
Nortonlifelock Inc 646 487-6000
  1 Penn Plz Ste 5420 New York (10119) *(G-10647)*
Norwesco Inc 607 687-8081
  263 Corporate Dr Owego (13827) *(G-12435)*
Norwich Manufacturing Division, Binghamton *Also called Felchar Manufacturing Corp (G-877)*
Norwich Pharma Services, Norwich *Also called Norwich Pharmaceuticals Inc (G-12125)*
Norwich Pharmaceuticals Inc 607 335-3000
  6826 State Highway 12 Norwich (13815) *(G-12125)*
Norwood Quar Btmnous Con Plnts, Norwood *Also called Barrett Paving Materials Inc (G-12131)*
Norwood Screw Machine Parts 516 481-6644
  200 E 2nd St Ste 2 Mineola (11501) *(G-7993)*
Not For Profit Chari, Bronx *Also called Lemon Brothers Foundation Inc (G-1300)*
Noteworthy Company, The, Amsterdam *Also called Noteworthy Industries Inc (G-344)*
Noteworthy Industries Inc 518 842-2662
  336 Forest Ave Amsterdam (12010) *(G-344)*
Noticia Hispanoamericana Inc 516 223-5678
  3815 Bell Blvd Bayside (11361) *(G-741)*
Noto Industrial Corp 631 736-7600
  11 Thomas St Coram (11727) *(G-3697)*
Notubes.com, Big Flats *Also called KG Motors Inc (G-847)*
Nouryon Functional Chem LLC 845 276-8200
  281 Fields Ln Brewster (10509) *(G-1156)*
Nouryon Surface Chemistry 914 674-5008
  7 Livingstone Ave Dobbs Ferry (10522) *(G-4018)*
Nouryon Surface Chemistry 716 778-8554
  2153 Lockport Olcott Rd Burt (14028) *(G-3060)*
Nova Inc 212 967-1139
  362 5th Ave Ste 1001 New York (10001) *(G-10648)*
Nova Optical, Orangeburg *Also called Essilor Laboratories Amer Inc (G-12314)*
Nova Pack, Philmont *Also called Pvc Container Corporation (G-12614)*
Nova Packaging Ltd Inc 914 232-8406
  7 Sunrise Ave Katonah (10536) *(G-6637)*
Nova Science Publishers Inc 631 231-7269
  415 Oser Ave Ste N Hauppauge (11788) *(G-5728)*
Novamed-Usa Inc 914 789-2100
  4 Westchester Plz Ste 137 Elmsford (10523) *(G-4420)*
Novartis Corporation 718 276-8600
  22715 N Conduit Ave Laurelton (11413) *(G-6883)*

Novartis Pharmaceuticals Corp 888 669-6682
230 Park Ave New York (10169) ***(G-10649)***
Novartis Pharmaceuticals Corp 718 276-8600
22715 N Conduit Ave Laurelton (11413) ***(G-6884)***
Novatech Inc 716 892-6682
190 Gruner Rd Cheektowaga (14227) ***(G-3358)***
Novel Box Company Ltd 718 965-2222
5620 1st Ave Ste 4 Brooklyn (11220) ***(G-2221)***
Novelis Corporation 315 342-1036
448 County Route 1a Oswego (13126) ***(G-12416)***
Novelis Corporation 315 349-0121
72 Alcan W Entrance Rd Oswego (13126) ***(G-12417)***
Novelis Inc 315 349-0121
448 County Route 1a Oswego (13126) ***(G-12418)***
Novelty Crystal Corp (PA) 718 458-6700
3015 48th Ave Long Island City (11101) ***(G-7310)***
Novelty Scenic Studios Inc, Monroe *Also called Associated Drapery & Equipment* ***(G-8014)***
Noven Pharmaceuticals Inc 212 682-4420
350 5th Ave Ste 3700 New York (10118) ***(G-10650)***
Novita Fabrics Furnishing Corp 516 299-4500
207 Elm Pl Ste 2 Mineola (11501) ***(G-7994)***
Novoye Rsskoye Slovo Pubg Corp 646 460-4566
2614 Voorhies Ave Brooklyn (11235) ***(G-2222)***
Novum Medical Products Ny LLC 716 759-7200
80 Creekside Dr Amherst (14228) ***(G-236)***
Nppi, Vestal *Also called National Pipe & Plastics Inc* ***(G-15381)***
Nr Fragrances & Cosmetics Inc 212 686-4006
1220 Broadway Rm 700 New York (10001) ***(G-10651)***
Nrd LLC 716 773-7634
2937 Alt Blvd Grand Island (14072) ***(G-5339)***
Nsgv Inc 212 367-3100
90 5th Ave New York (10011) ***(G-10652)***
Nsh, Menands *Also called Simmons Machine Tool Corp* ***(G-7848)***
Nsi Industries LLC 800 841-2505
50 S Macquesten Pkwy Mount Vernon (10550) ***(G-8166)***
NSM Surveillance, New York *Also called News/Sprts Microwave Rentl Inc* ***(G-10615)***
Nsusa, Deer Park *Also called Nutra Solutions USA Inc* ***(G-3914)***
NTI Global, Amsterdam *Also called Nationwide Tarps Incorporated* ***(G-341)***
Nu Ways Inc 585 254-7510
655 Pullman Ave Rochester (14615) ***(G-13587)***
Nu-Chem Laboratories, Bellport *Also called Optisource International Inc* ***(G-805)***
Nu2 Systems LLC 914 719-7272
155 Lafayette Ave White Plains (10603) ***(G-16035)***
Nubian Heritage 631 265-3551
367 Old Willets Path Hauppauge (11788) ***(G-5729)***
Nucare Pharmacy & Surgical, New York *Also called Nucare Pharmacy West LLC* ***(G-10654)***
Nucare Pharmacy & Surgical, New York *Also called Nucare Pharmacy Inc* ***(G-10653)***
Nucare Pharmacy Inc 212 426-9300
1789 1st Ave New York (10128) ***(G-10653)***
Nucare Pharmacy West LLC 212 462-2525
250 9th Ave New York (10001) ***(G-10654)***
Nuclear Diagnostic Pdts NY Inc 516 575-4201
130 Commercial St Plainview (11803) ***(G-12705)***
Nucor Steel Auburn Inc 315 253-4561
25 Quarry Rd Auburn (13021) ***(G-488)***
Nulux Inc 718 383-1112
1717 Troutman St Ridgewood (11385) ***(G-13153)***
Numed, Brooklyn *Also called Ys Marketing Inc* ***(G-2603)***
Numerix LLC (PA) 212 302-2220
99 Park Ave Fl 5 New York (10016) ***(G-10655)***
Nutec Components Inc 631 242-1224
81 E Jefryn Blvd Ste A Deer Park (11729) ***(G-3913)***
Nutech Biosciences Inc 315 505-6500
537 Fitch St Oneida (13421) ***(G-12248)***
Nutek Disposables Inc 516 829-3030
80 Cuttermill Rd Ste 500 Great Neck (11021) ***(G-5406)***
Nutra Solutions USA Inc 631 392-1900
1019 Grand Blvd Deer Park (11729) ***(G-3914)***
Nutra-Vet Research Corp 845 473-1900
201 Smith St Poughkeepsie (12601) ***(G-12976)***
Nutraceutical Wellness Inc 888 454-3320
136 Madison Ave Fl 10 New York (10016) ***(G-10656)***
Nutrafol, New York *Also called Nutraceutical Wellness Inc* ***(G-10656)***
Nutraqueen LLC 347 368-6568
138 E 34th St Apt 2f New York (10016) ***(G-10657)***
Nutrascience Labs Inc 631 247-0660
70 Carolyn Blvd Farmingdale (11735) ***(G-4696)***
Nutratech Labs Inc 315 695-2256
406 State Route 264 Phoenix (13135) ***(G-12618)***
Nutrifast LLC 347 671-3181
244 5th Ave Ste W249 New York (10001) ***(G-10658)***
Nutritional Designs, Lynbrook *Also called ND Labs Inc* ***(G-7434)***
Nuttall Gear L L C (HQ) 716 298-4100
2221 Niagara Falls Blvd # 17 Niagara Falls (14304) ***(G-11958)***
Nuvite Chemical Compounds Corp 718 383-8351
213 Freeman St 215 Brooklyn (11222) ***(G-2223)***
NY Cabinet Factory Inc 718 256-6541
6901 14th Ave Brooklyn (11228) ***(G-2224)***
NY Cutting Inc 646 434-1355
3 Chestnut St Ste 1 Suffern (10901) ***(G-14763)***
NY Denim Inc 212 764-6668
1407 Broadway Rm 1021 New York (10018) ***(G-10659)***
NY Embroidery Inc 516 822-6456
25 Midland Ave Hicksville (11801) ***(G-5934)***
NY Froyo LLC 516 312-4588
324 W 19th St Deer Park (11729) ***(G-3915)***
NY Iron Inc 718 302-9000
3131 48th Ave Ste 2 Long Island City (11101) ***(G-7311)***
NY Orthopedic Usa Inc 718 852-5330
63 Flushing Ave Unit 333 Brooklyn (11205) ***(G-2225)***
NY Phrmacy Compounding Ctr Inc 201 403-5151
3715 23rd Ave Astoria (11105) ***(G-432)***
NY Print Partners, Sunnyside *Also called Deanco Digital Printing LLC* ***(G-14771)***
NY Tempering LLC 718 326-8989
6021 Flushing Ave Maspeth (11378) ***(G-7631)***
Nyahb Inc 845 352-5300
161 Route 59 Ste 101 Monsey (10952) ***(G-8042)***
Nyb Distributors Inc (PA) 516 937-0666
37 17th St Jericho (11753) ***(G-6587)***
Nyc Bronx Inc 917 417-0509
2490 Grand Concourse Bronx (10458) ***(G-1327)***
Nyc Community Media LLC 212 229-1890
1 Metrotech Ctr N Fl 10 Brooklyn (11201) ***(G-2226)***
Nyc Design Co, New York *Also called M S B International Ltd* ***(G-10299)***
Nyc District Council Ubcja 212 366-7500
395 Hudson St Lbby 3 New York (10014) ***(G-10660)***
Nyc Idol Apparel Inc 212 997-9797
214 W 39th St Rm 807 New York (10018) ***(G-10661)***
Nyc Knitwear Inc 212 840-1313
525 Fashion Ave Rm 701 New York (10018) ***(G-10662)***
Nyc Trade Printers Corp 718 606-0610
3245 62nd St Woodside (11377) ***(G-16216)***
Nyc Vinyl Screen Printing Inc (PA) 718 784-1360
204 Lawrence Hill Rd Cold Spring Harbor (11724) ***(G-3528)***
Nyc Vinyl Screen Printing Inc 718 784-1360
4436 21st St Long Island City (11101) ***(G-7312)***
Nycom Business Solutions Inc 516 345-6000
804 Hempstead Tpke Franklin Square (11010) ***(G-4963)***
Nycon Diamond & Tools Corp 855 937-6922
55 Knickerbocker Ave A Bohemia (11716) ***(G-1056)***
Nycon Supply, Long Island City *Also called US Concrete Inc* ***(G-7390)***
Nyemac Inc 631 668-1303
Paradise Ln Montauk (11954) ***(G-8057)***
Nyi Building Products Inc (PA) 518 458-7500
5 Southside Dr Ste 204 Clifton Park (12065) ***(G-3469)***
Nykon Inc 315 483-0504
8175 Stell Rd Sodus (14551) ***(G-14492)***
Nylon LLc 212 226-6454
110 Greene St Ste 607 New York (10012) ***(G-10663)***
Nylon Magazine, New York *Also called Nylon LLc* ***(G-10663)***
Nylon Media Inc (PA) 212 226-6454
110 Greene St Ste 607 New York (10012) ***(G-10664)***
Nylonshop, New York *Also called Nylon Media Inc* ***(G-10664)***
Nyman Jewelry Inc (PA) 212 944-1976
66 W 9th St New York (10011) ***(G-10665)***
Nyp Holdings Inc 718 260-2500
1 Metrotech Ctr N Fl 10 Brooklyn (11201) ***(G-2227)***
Nyp Holdings Inc (HQ) 212 997-9272
1211 Ave Of The Americas New York (10036) ***(G-10666)***
Nyrev Inc 212 757-8070
435 Hudson St Rm 300 New York (10014) ***(G-10667)***
Nys Nyu-Cntr Intl Cooperation 212 998-3680
418 Lafayette St New York (10003) ***(G-10668)***
NYSASBO, Albany *Also called New York State Assoc* ***(G-104)***
Nysco Products LLC 718 792-9000
211 Saw Mill River Rd Hawthorne (10532) ***(G-5820)***
Nyt Capital LLC (HQ) 212 556-1234
620 8th Ave New York (10018) ***(G-10669)***
Nytimes Corporate 212 556-1234
620 8th Ave Fl 17 New York (10018) ***(G-10670)***
O & S Machine & Tool Co Inc 716 941-5542
8143 State Rd Colden (14033) ***(G-3530)***
O C Choppers, Newburgh *Also called Orange County Choppers Inc* ***(G-11878)***
O P I Industries, Ronkonkoma *Also called Paramount Equipment Inc* ***(G-13991)***
O Rama Light Inc 518 539-9000
22 Hudson Falls Rd Ste 52 South Glens Falls (12803) ***(G-14517)***
O Tex, Rochester *Also called Robert J Faraone* ***(G-13677)***
O Val Nick Music Co Inc 212 873-2179
254 W 72nd St Apt 1a New York (10023) ***(G-10671)***
O W Hubbell & Sons Inc 315 736-8311
5124 Commercial Dr Yorkville (13495) ***(G-16376)***
O'Bryan Bros, New York *Also called Komar Layering LLC* ***(G-10124)***
O'Neil Construction, Glen Head *Also called Lomin Construction Company* ***(G-5209)***
O-At-Ka Milk Products Coop Inc (PA) 585 343-0536
700 Ellicott St Batavia (14020) ***(G-622)***
O-Neh-Da Vineyard, Conesus *Also called Eagle Crest Vineyard LLC* ***(G-3605)***
Oak Lone Publishing Co Inc 518 792-1126
15 Ridge St Glens Falls (12801) ***(G-5262)***
Oak Valley Logging Inc 518 622-8249
558 Frank Hitchcock Rd Cairo (12413) ***(G-3067)***

Oak-Bark Corporation 518 372-5691
37 Maple Ave Scotia (12302) **(G-14335)**
Oak-Mitsui Inc 518 686-8060
1 Mechanic St Bldg 2 Hoosick Falls (12090) **(G-6086)**
Oak-Mitsui Technologies LLC 518 686-4961
80 1st St Hoosick Falls (12090) **(G-6087)**
Oakdale Industrial Elec Corp 631 737-4092
1995 Pond Rd Ronkonkoma (11779) **(G-13984)**
Oakhurst Partners LLC 212 502-3220
148 Madison Ave Fl 13 New York (10016) **(G-10672)**
Oaklee International Inc 631 436-7900
125 Raynor Ave Ronkonkoma (11779) **(G-13985)**
Oakwood Publishing Co 516 482-7720
10 Bond St Ste 1 Great Neck (11021) **(G-5407)**
Oasis Cosmetic Labs Inc 631 758-0038
182 Long Island Ave Holtsville (11742) **(G-6051)**
Oatly Inc 646 625-4633
220 E 42nd St Rm 409a New York (10017) **(G-10673)**
Oberdorfer Pumps Inc 315 437-0361
5900 Firestone Dr Syracuse (13206) **(G-14952)**
Oberon, New York *Also called Tabrisse Collections Inc* **(G-11422)**
Observer Daily Sunday Newsppr 716 366-3000
10 E 2nd St Dunkirk (14048) **(G-4062)**
Observer Dispatch, Utica *Also called Gatehouse Media LLC* **(G-15267)**
Observer Media LLC 212 755-2400
1 Whitehall St Fl 7 New York (10004) **(G-10674)**
Ocala Group LLC 516 233-2750
1981 Marcus Ave Ste 227 New Hyde Park (11042) **(G-8286)**
Occidental Chemical Corp 716 278-7795
4700 Buffalo Ave Niagara Falls (14304) **(G-11959)**
Occidental Chemical Corp 716 773-8100
2801 Long Rd Grand Island (14072) **(G-5340)**
Occidental Chemical Corp 716 278-7794
56 Street & Energy Blvd Niagara Falls (14302) **(G-11960)**
Occidental Chemical Corp 716 694-3827
3780 Commerce Ct Ste 600 North Tonawanda (14120) **(G-12080)**
Occidental Energy Mktg Inc 212 632-4950
1230 Av Of The Amrcs 80 New York (10020) **(G-10675)**
Occunomix International LLC 631 741-1940
585 Bicycle Path Ste 52 Port Jeff STA (11776) **(G-12837)**
Ocean Cardiac Monitoring 631 777-3700
38 W 17th St Deer Park (11729) **(G-3916)**
Ocean Park Drugs & Surgical, Far Rockaway *Also called Far Rockaway Drugs Inc* **(G-4565)**
Ocean Printing, Ronkonkoma *Also called Copy X/Press Ltd* **(G-13925)**
Ocean Stone and Fireplace, Holtsville *Also called Blackstone International Inc* **(G-6045)**
Ocean Waves Swim LLC 212 967-4481
19 W 34th St Fl 11 New York (10001) **(G-10676)**
Oceanside-Island Park Herald, Lawrence *Also called Richner Communications Inc* **(G-6891)**
Oci USA Inc (PA) 646 589-6180
660 Madison Ave Fl 19 New York (10065) **(G-10677)**
Ocip Holding LLC 646 589-6180
660 Madison Ave Fl 19 New York (10065) **(G-10678)**
Ocs Industries, Glendale *Also called CIDC Corp* **(G-5222)**
Octave Music Group Inc (HQ) 212 991-6540
850 3rd Ave Ste 15th New York (10022) **(G-10679)**
Octopus Advanced Systems Inc 914 771-6110
27 Covington Rd Yonkers (10710) **(G-16335)**
Odegard Inc 212 545-0069
3030 47th Ave Ste 700 Long Island City (11101) **(G-7313)**
Oden Machinery Inc (PA) 716 874-3000
600 Ensminger Rd Tonawanda (14150) **(G-15129)**
ODY Accessories Inc 212 239-0580
1239 Broadway New York (10001) **(G-10680)**
Odyssey Controls Inc 585 548-9800
6256 Clinton Street Rd Bergen (14416) **(G-819)**
Odyssey Mag Pubg Group Inc 212 545-4800
4 New York Plz New York (10004) **(G-10681)**
Oehlers Wldg & Fabrication Inc 716 821-1800
242 Elk St Buffalo (14210) **(G-2894)**
OEM Solutions Inc 716 864-9324
4995 Rockhaven Dr Clarence (14031) **(G-3437)**
Oerlikon Blzers Cating USA Inc 716 270-2228
6000 N Bailey Ave Ste 9 Amherst (14226) **(G-237)**
Oerlikon Blzers Cating USA Inc 716 564-8557
6000 N Bailey Ave Ste 3 Buffalo (14226) **(G-2895)**
Oerlikon Metco (us) Inc 716 270-2228
6000 N Bailey Ave Amherst (14226) **(G-238)**
Oestreich Metal Works Inc 315 463-4268
6131 Court Street Rd Syracuse (13206) **(G-14953)**
Office Grabs LLC 347 678-3993
1245 50th St Apt 4d Brooklyn (11219) **(G-2228)**
Office Grabs NY Inc 212 444-1331
1303 53rd St 105 Brooklyn (11219) **(G-2229)**
Officegrabscom, Brooklyn *Also called Office Grabs LLC* **(G-2228)**
Official Offset Corporation 631 957-8500
8600 New Horizons Blvd Amityville (11701) **(G-299)**
Official Press, The, New York *Also called Hks Printing Company Inc* **(G-9797)**
Ogd V-Hvac Inc 315 858-1002
174 Pumkinhook Rd Van Hornesville (13475) **(G-15363)**
Ogden Newspapers Inc 716 487-1111
15 W 2nd St Jamestown (14701) **(G-6535)**
Ogilvie Press, Lancaster *Also called Rmf Printing Technologies Inc* **(G-6830)**
Ogulnick Uniforms, New York *Also called Tailored Sportsman LLC* **(G-11425)**
OH How Cute Inc 347 838-6031
38 Androvette St Staten Island (10309) **(G-14687)**
Ohana Metal & Iron Works Inc 845 344-7520
60 Miller Rd Montgomery (12549) **(G-8063)**
Ohio Baking Company Inc 315 724-2033
10585 Cosby Manor Rd Utica (13502) **(G-15289)**
Ohserase Manufacturing LLC 518 358-9309
26 Eagle Dr Akwesasne (13655) **(G-25)**
Ohserase Manufacturing LLC 518 358-9309
393 Frogtown Rd Hogansburg (13655) **(G-5981)**
Oil and Lubricant Depot LLC 631 841-5000
44 Island Container Plz Wyandanch (11798) **(G-16246)**
Oil Depot, The, Wyandanch *Also called Oil and Lubricant Depot LLC* **(G-16246)**
Oil Solutions Intl Inc 631 608-8889
35 Mill St Amityville (11701) **(G-300)**
Okcupid, New York *Also called Humor Rainbow Inc* **(G-9840)**
Okey Enterprises Inc 212 213-2640
347 5th Ave Rm 1005 New York (10016) **(G-10682)**
Okra Energy LLC 206 495-7574
99 Jane St Apt 5d New York (10014) **(G-10683)**
Olan Laboratories Inc 631 582-2082
20 Newton Pl Hauppauge (11788) **(G-5730)**
Olb Group Inc 212 278-0900
200 Park Ave Ste 1700 New York (10166) **(G-10684)**
Old Castle Precast, Middle Island *Also called Afco Precast Sales Corp* **(G-7873)**
Old Dutch Mustard Co Inc (PA) 516 466-0522
98 Cuttermill Rd Ste 260s Great Neck (11021) **(G-5408)**
Old Dutchmans Wrough Iron Inc 716 688-2034
2800 Millersport Hwy Getzville (14068) **(G-5180)**
Old Souls Inc 845 809-5886
63 Main St Cold Spring (10516) **(G-3522)**
Old Williamsburgh Corp 631 952-0100
100 Wireless Blvd Hauppauge (11788) **(G-5731)**
Old World Mouldings Inc 631 563-8660
821 Lincoln Ave Bohemia (11716) **(G-1057)**
Oldcastle Building Envelope 212 957-5400
1350 Ave Of The Americas New York (10019) **(G-10685)**
Oldcastle Buildingenvelope Inc 631 234-2200
895 Motor Pkwy Hauppauge (11788) **(G-5732)**
Oldcastle Infrastructure Inc 518 767-2116
100 S County Rte 101 South Bethlehem (12161) **(G-14502)**
Oldcastle Infrastructure Inc 518 767-2112
123 County Route 101 Selkirk (12158) **(G-14358)**
Oldcastle Materials Inc 585 424-6410
1260 Jefferson Rd Rochester (14623) **(G-13588)**
Oldcastle Precast Bldg Systems, Selkirk *Also called Oldcastle Infrastructure Inc* **(G-14358)**
Olde Chtqua Vneyards Ltd Lblty 716 792-2749
6654 W Main Rd Portland (14769) **(G-12933)**
Olean Advanced Products, Olean *Also called AVX Corporation* **(G-12223)**
Olean Waste Water Treatment, Olean *Also called City of Olean* **(G-12228)**
Oledworks LLC (PA) 585 287-6802
1645 Lyell Ave Ste 140 Rochester (14606) **(G-13589)**
Olin Chlor Alkali Logistics 716 278-6411
2400 Buffalo Ave Niagara Falls (14303) **(G-11961)**
Olive Branch Foods LLC 631 343-7070
3124 Express Dr S Islandia (11749) **(G-6342)**
Olive Led Lighting Inc 718 746-0830
1310 111th St College Point (11356) **(G-3557)**
OLIVEA MATHEWS, New York *Also called Pride & Joys Inc* **(G-10888)**
Oliver Disc, Hauppauge *Also called Disc Graphics Inc* **(G-5638)**
Oliver Gear, Buffalo *Also called Gear Motions Incorporated* **(G-2769)**
Oliver Gear Inc 716 885-1080
1120 Niagara St Buffalo (14213) **(G-2896)**
Olmstead Machine Inc 315 587-9864
10399 Warehouse Ave North Rose (14516) **(G-12036)**
Olmstead Products Corp 516 681-3700
1 Jefry Ln Hicksville (11801) **(G-5935)**
Olollo Inc 877 701-0110
43 Hall St Ste B8 Brooklyn (11205) **(G-2230)**
Olson Sign Company Inc 518 370-2118
1750 Valley Rd Ext Schenectady (12302) **(G-14292)**
Olson Signs & Graphics, Schenectady *Also called Olson Sign Company Inc* **(G-14292)**
Olympia Company, Elmsford *Also called Olympia Sports Company Inc* **(G-4421)**
Olympia Sports Company Inc 914 347-4737
500 Executive Blvd # 170 Elmsford (10523) **(G-4421)**
Olympic Ice Cream Co Inc 718 849-6200
12910 91st Ave Richmond Hill (11418) **(G-13118)**
Olympic Jewelry Inc 212 768-7004
62 W 47th St Ste 810 New York (10036) **(G-10686)**
Olympic Manufacturing Inc 631 231-8900
195 Marcus Blvd Hauppauge (11788) **(G-5733)**
Olympic Software & Consulting 631 351-0655
290 Broadhollow Rd 130e Melville (11747) **(G-7811)**
Omc Inc 718 731-5001
4010 Park Ave Bronx (10457) **(G-1328)**
Omc2 LLC 415 580-0262
1000 N Division St Ste 15 Peekskill (10566) **(G-12554)**
Omega Consolidated Corporation 585 392-9262
101 Heinz St Hilton (14468) **(G-5974)**

ALPHABETIC

Omega Furniture Manufacturing............................315 463-7428
　102 Wavel St Syracuse (13206) *(G-14954)*
Omega Heater Company Inc.................................631 588-8820
　2059 9th Ave Ronkonkoma (11779) *(G-13986)*
Omega Tool Measuring Mchs Inc (PA)...................585 598-7800
　101 Perinton Pkwy Fairport (14450) *(G-4510)*
Omega Wire Inc..315 337-4300
　900 Railroad St Rome (13440) *(G-13862)*
Omega Wire Inc...315 689-7115
　24 N Beaver St Jordan (13080) *(G-6630)*
Omega Wire Inc (HQ)...315 245-3800
　12 Masonic Ave Camden (13316) *(G-3104)*
Omg Cleaners Inc..718 282-2011
　565 Coney Island Ave Brooklyn (11218) *(G-2231)*
Omg Desserts Inc..585 698-1561
　1227 Ridgeway Ave Ste J Rochester (14615) *(G-13590)*
Omicron Technologies Inc..................................631 434-7697
　1736 Church St Holbrook (11741) *(G-6015)*
Omni Turbine Parts LLC....................................607 564-9922
　12 Seely Hill Rd Newfield (14867) *(G-11897)*
Omni-ID Usa Inc..585 299-5990
　333 W Cmmrcl St 333-150 East Rochester (14445) *(G-4168)*
Omniafiltra LLC...315 346-7300
　9567 Main St Beaver Falls (13305) *(G-761)*
Omnicare Anesthesia PC (PA)............................718 433-0044
　3636 33rd St Ste 211 Astoria (11106) *(G-433)*
Omnimusic, Port Washington *Also called Franklin-Douglas Inc (G-12880)*
Omntec Mfg Inc...631 981-2001
　1993 Pond Rd Ronkonkoma (11779) *(G-13987)*
Omp Printing & Graphics, Clinton *Also called Tenney Media Group (G-3486)*
Omrix Biopharmaceuticals Inc............................908 218-0707
　1 Rckfller Ctr Ste 2322 New York (10020) *(G-10687)*
Omt, Yorkville *Also called Oriskany Mfg Tech LLC (G-16378)*
Omx (us) Inc...646 428-2800
　140 Broadway Fl 25 New York (10005) *(G-10688)*
On Demand Books LLC..212 966-2222
　939 Lexington Ave New York (10065) *(G-10689)*
On Line Power Technologies................................914 968-4440
　113 Sunnyside Dr Yonkers (10705) *(G-16336)*
On Montauk, Montauk *Also called Nyemac Inc (G-8057)*
On The Double Inc...518 431-3571
　178 Viewmont Rd Germantown (12526) *(G-5169)*
On The Job Embroidery & AP...............................914 381-3556
　154 E Boston Post Rd # 1 Mamaroneck (10543) *(G-7516)*
On The Mark Digital Printing &.............................716 823-3373
　5758 S Park Ave Hamburg (14075) *(G-5515)*
On The Spot Binding Inc.....................................718 497-2200
　4805 Metropolitan Ave Ridgewood (11385) *(G-13154)*
On Time Plastics Inc...516 442-4280
　121 Henry St Freeport (11520) *(G-5011)*
Once Again Nut Butter Collectv (PA)....................585 468-2535
　12 S State St Nunda (14517) *(G-12133)*
Ondrivesus Corp...516 771-6777
　216 N Main St Bldg B2 Freeport (11520) *(G-5012)*
One In A Million Inc..516 829-1111
　51 Franklin Ave Valley Stream (11580) *(G-15350)*
One Jeanswear Group LLC (HQ)...........................212 575-2571
　1441 Broadway Fl 11 New York (10018) *(G-10690)*
One Jeanswear Group, LLC, New York *Also called Premier Brnds Group Hldngs LLC (G-10876)*
One Step Up Kids, New York *Also called Kidz Concepts LLC (G-10097)*
One Step Up Ltd (PA)..212 398-1110
　1412 Broadway Fl 3 New York (10018) *(G-10691)*
One Story Inc...917 816-3659
　232 3rd St Ste A108 Brooklyn (11215) *(G-2232)*
One Tree Dist...315 701-2924
　200 Midler Park Dr Syracuse (13206) *(G-14955)*
One-Blue LLC..212 223-4380
　1350 Broadway Rm 1406 New York (10018) *(G-10692)*
Oneder, New York *Also called Specialneedsware Inc (G-11312)*
Oneida Air Systems Inc......................................315 476-5151
　1001 W Fayette St Ste 2a Syracuse (13204) *(G-14956)*
Oneida Concrete Products, Buffalo *Also called Oneida Sales & Service Inc (G-2897)*
Oneida Dispatch, Oneida *Also called Oneida Publications Inc (G-12251)*
Oneida International Inc.....................................315 361-3000
　163-181 Kenwood Ave Oneida (13421) *(G-12249)*
Oneida Molded Plastics LLC (PA)........................315 363-7980
　104 S Warner St Oneida (13421) *(G-12250)*
Oneida Publications Inc......................................315 363-5100
　730 Lenox Ave Oneida (13421) *(G-12251)*
Oneida Sales & Service Inc...............................716 822-8205
　155 Commerce Dr Buffalo (14218) *(G-2897)*
Oneida Silversmiths Inc......................................315 361-3000
　163 Kenwood Ave 181 Oneida (13421) *(G-12252)*
Oneonta Asphalt, Oneonta *Also called Cobleskill Stone Products Inc (G-12265)*
Oneonta City Wtr Trtmnt Plant, Oneonta *Also called City of Oneonta (G-12263)*
Oneonta Fence..607 433-6707
　2 Washburn St Oneonta (13820) *(G-12278)*
Ongweoweh Corp (PA).......................................607 266-7070
　5 Barr Rd Ithaca (14850) *(G-6403)*

Onia LLC (PA)...646 701-0008
　10 E 40th St Fl 37 New York (10016) *(G-10693)*
Onia Com, New York *Also called Onia LLC (G-10693)*
Only Hearts Ltd (PA)..212 268-0886
　134 W 37th St Fl 9 New York (10018) *(G-10694)*
Only Natural Inc...516 897-7001
　3580 Oceanside Rd Unit 5 Oceanside (11572) *(G-12183)*
Onondaga Nation..315 469-3230
　3951 State Route 11 Nedrow (13120) *(G-8216)*
Ontario Knife Company......................................716 676-5527
　26 Empire St Franklinville (14737) *(G-4967)*
Ontario Label Graphics Inc.................................716 434-8505
　6444 Ridge Rd Lockport (14094) *(G-7100)*
Ontario Plastics Inc...585 663-2644
　2503 Dewey Ave Rochester (14616) *(G-13591)*
Ony Biotech Inc...716 636-9096
　1576 Sweet Home Rd Amherst (14228) *(G-239)*
Ony Inc Baird Researchpark...............................716 636-9096
　1576 Sweet Home Rd Buffalo (14228) *(G-2898)*
Onyx Solar Group LLC..917 951-9732
　79 Madison Ave Fl 8 New York (10016) *(G-10695)*
Oova Inc...215 880-3125
　152 W 57th St New York (10019) *(G-10696)*
Opd, Depew *Also called Leica Microsystems Inc (G-3987)*
Open & Shut Doors, Farmingdale *Also called Michbi Doors Inc (G-4683)*
Openfin Inc...917 450-8822
　80 Broad St Fl 35 New York (10004) *(G-10697)*
Openroad Integrated Media Inc............................212 691-0900
　180 Maiden Ln Ste 2803 New York (10038) *(G-10698)*
Operateit Inc...631 259-4777
　2805 Vtrans Mem Hwy Ste 2 Ronkonkoma (11779) *(G-13988)*
Operative Cake Corp...718 278-5600
　711 Brush Ave Bronx (10465) *(G-1329)*
Operative Media Inc (HQ).................................212 994-8930
　6 E 32nd St Fl 3 New York (10016) *(G-10699)*
Opposuits USA Inc..917 438-8878
　228 E 45th St Rm 9e New York (10017) *(G-10700)*
Oprah Magazine, New York *Also called Hearst Corporation (G-9747)*
Optical Gaging Products Div, Rochester *Also called Quality Vision Intl Inc (G-13660)*
Opticool Solutions LLC.....................................585 347-6127
　855 Publishers Pkwy Webster (14580) *(G-15646)*
Opticool Technologies, Webster *Also called Opticool Solutions LLC (G-15646)*
Optics Technology Inc.......................................585 586-0950
　3800 Monroe Ave Ste 3 Pittsford (14534) *(G-12653)*
Optika Eyes Ltd...631 567-8852
　153 Main St Unit 1 Sayville (11782) *(G-14230)*
Optimax Systems Inc (PA).................................585 265-1020
　6367 Dean Pkwy Ontario (14519) *(G-12295)*
Optimized Devices Inc......................................914 769-6100
　220 Marble Ave Pleasantville (10570) *(G-12797)*
Optimum Applied Systems Inc............................845 471-3333
　16 Victory Ln Ste 5 Poughkeepsie (12603) *(G-12977)*
Optimum Semiconductor Tech.............................914 287-8500
　120 White Plains Rd Fl 4 Tarrytown (10591) *(G-15051)*
Optimum Window Mfg Corp..................................845 647-1900
　28 Canal St Ellenville (12428) *(G-4309)*
Optionline LLC...516 218-3225
　100 Hilton Ave Apt 23 Garden City (11530) *(G-5111)*
Options Publishing, New York *Also called Triumph Learning LLC (G-11549)*
Optipro Systems LLC...585 265-0160
　6368 Dean Pkwy Ontario (14519) *(G-12296)*
Optisource International Inc................................631 924-8360
　40 Sawgrass Dr Ste 1 Bellport (11713) *(G-805)*
Optogenics of Syracuse Inc..............................315 446-3000
　2840 Erie Blvd E Syracuse (13224) *(G-14957)*
Opus Technology Corporation (PA).......................631 271-1883
　10 Gwynne Rd Melville (11747) *(G-7812)*
Oracle, Mineola *Also called Fatwire Corporation (G-7975)*
Oracle America Inc..518 427-9353
　7 Southwoods Blvd Ste 1 Albany (12211) *(G-109)*
Oracle America Inc..585 317-4648
　345 Woodcliff Dr Ste 1 Fairport (14450) *(G-4511)*
Oracle Corporation...212 508-7700
　120 Park Ave Fl 26 New York (10017) *(G-10701)*
Orafol Americas Inc..585 272-0309
　200 Park Centre Dr Henrietta (14467) *(G-5859)*
Oramaax Dental Products Inc..............................516 771-8514
　216 N Main St Ste A Freeport (11520) *(G-5013)*
Orange County Choppers Inc...............................845 522-5200
　14 Crossroads Ct Newburgh (12550) *(G-11878)*
Orange County Ironworks LLC.............................845 769-3000
　36 Maybrook Rd Montgomery (12549) *(G-8064)*
Orange Die Cutting Corp.....................................845 562-0900
　1 Favoriti Ave Newburgh (12550) *(G-11879)*
Orange Packaging, Newburgh *Also called Orange Die Cutting Corp (G-11879)*
Orangenius Inc...631 742-0648
　79 Madison Ave Fl 4 New York (10016) *(G-10702)*
Orbcomm Inc..703 433-6396
　125 Business Park Dr Utica (13502) *(G-15290)*
Orbis Brynmore Lithographics............................212 987-2100
　1735 2nd Ave Frnt 1 New York (10128) *(G-10703)*

Orbit Industries LLC..........914 244-1500
116 Radio Circle Dr # 302 Mount Kisco (10549) *(G-8101)*
Orbit International Corp (PA)..........631 435-8300
80 Cabot Ct Hauppauge (11788) *(G-5734)*
Orbit International Corp..........631 435-8300
80 Cabot Ct Hauppauge (11788) *(G-5735)*
Orbital Holdings Inc..........951 360-7100
2775 Broadway St Ste 200 Buffalo (14227) *(G-2899)*
Orcam Inc..........800 713-3741
16 Madison Sq W Fl 11 New York (10010) *(G-10704)*
Orchard App Inc..........888 217-2718
101 5th Ave Fl 4 New York (10003) *(G-10705)*
Orchard Apparel Group Ltd..........212 268-8701
212 W 35th St Fl 7 New York (10001) *(G-10706)*
Orchard Platform Advisors LLC..........888 217-2718
55 W 21st St Fl 2 New York (10010) *(G-10707)*
Orchard Sausages Inc..........718 381-9388
340 Johnson Ave Brooklyn (11206) *(G-2233)*
Orchard Way, Port Jeff STA *Also called Ahmazing Boutique Inc (G-12832)*
Orchid Manufacturing Co Inc..........212 840-5700
77 W 55th St Apt 4k New York (10019) *(G-10708)*
Orcon Industries Corp (PA)..........585 768-7000
8715 Lake Rd Le Roy (14482) *(G-6905)*
Ordergroove Inc..........866 253-1261
75 Broad St Fl 23 New York (10004) *(G-10709)*
Orenova Group LLC..........914 517-3000
10 New King St Ste 106 White Plains (10604) *(G-16036)*
Orens Daily Roast Inc (PA)..........212 348-5400
12 E 46th St Fl 6 New York (10017) *(G-10710)*
Orffeo Printing & Imaging Inc..........716 681-5757
99 Cambria St Lancaster (14086) *(G-6819)*
Organic Nectars Inc..........845 246-0506
162 Malden Tpke Bldg 5 Saugerties (12477) *(G-14206)*
Organic Peak, Mineola *Also called Maxim Hygiene Products Inc (G-7988)*
Orics Industries Inc..........718 461-8613
240 Smith St Farmingdale (11735) *(G-4697)*
Original Crunch Roll Fctry LLC..........716 402-5030
90 Sylvan Pkwy Amherst (14228) *(G-240)*
Original Dream Statuary, Brooklyn *Also called Dream Statuary Inc (G-1760)*
Original Hrkmer Cnty Chese Inc..........315 895-7428
2745 State Route 51 Ilion (13357) *(G-6280)*
Original Tube Tshirt..........845 291-7031
185 Ridge Rd Goshen (10924) *(G-5312)*
Oriskany Arms Inc..........315 737-2196
175 Clear Rd Oriskany (13424) *(G-12393)*
Oriskany Manufacturing LLC..........315 732-4962
2 Wurz Ave Yorkville (13495) *(G-16377)*
Oriskany Mfg Tech LLC..........315 732-4962
2 Wurz Ave Yorkville (13495) *(G-16378)*
Orlandi Inc (PA)..........631 756-0110
131 Executive Blvd Farmingdale (11735) *(G-4698)*
Orlandi Inc..........631 756-0110
121 Executive Blvd Farmingdale (11735) *(G-4699)*
Orlandi Scented Products, Farmingdale *Also called Orlandi Inc (G-4698)*
Orleans Custom Packing Inc..........585 314-8227
101 Cadbury Way Holley (14470) *(G-6036)*
Orleans Pallet Company Inc..........585 589-0781
227 West Ave Albion (14411) *(G-158)*
Ormec Systems Corp (PA)..........585 385-3520
19 Linden Park Rochester (14625) *(G-13592)*
Ornametal Inc..........845 562-5151
216 S William St Newburgh (12550) *(G-11880)*
Oro Avanti Inc (PA)..........516 487-5185
250 Kings Point Rd Great Neck (11024) *(G-5409)*
Orolia Usa Inc (HQ)..........585 321-5800
1565 Jefferson Rd Ste 460 Rochester (14623) *(G-13593)*
Orpheo USA Corp..........212 464-8255
353 Lexington Ave Lbby 1 New York (10016) *(G-10711)*
Ortex Home Textile Inc..........718 241-7298
523 E 82nd St Brooklyn (11236) *(G-2234)*
Ortex Home Textiles, Brooklyn *Also called Ortex Home Textile Inc (G-2234)*
Ortho Medical Products (PA)..........212 879-3700
315 E 83rd St New York (10028) *(G-10712)*
Ortho Rite Inc..........914 235-9100
434 Waverly Ave Mamaroneck (10543) *(G-7517)*
Ortho-Clinical Diagnostics Inc..........585 453-3000
513 Technology Blvd Rochester (14626) *(G-13594)*
Ortho-Clinical Diagnostics Inc..........585 453-4771
100 Latona Rd Bldg 313 Rochester (14626) *(G-13595)*
Ortho-Clinical Diagnostics Inc..........585 453-5200
2402 Innovation Way # 3 Rochester (14624) *(G-13596)*
Ortho-Clinical Diagnostics Inc..........716 631-1281
15 Limestone Dr Williamsville (14221) *(G-16135)*
Ortho-Clinical Diagnostics Inc..........585 453-3000
1000 Lee Rd Rochester (14626) *(G-13597)*
Ortho/Rochester Tech, Rochester *Also called Ortho-Clinical Diagnostics Inc (G-13596)*
Orthocon Inc..........914 357-2600
1 Bridge St Ste 121 Irvington (10533) *(G-6312)*
Orthocraft Inc..........718 951-1700
1477 E 27th St Brooklyn (11210) *(G-2235)*
Orthogonal..........585 254-2775
1999 Lake Ave Rochester (14650) *(G-13598)*
Orthopedic Arts Laboratory Inc..........718 858-2400
141 Atlantic Ave Apt 1 Brooklyn (11201) *(G-2236)*
Orthopedic Treatment Facility..........718 898-7326
4906 Queens Blvd Woodside (11377) *(G-16217)*
Orthotics & Prosthetics Dept..........585 341-9299
4901 Lac De Ville Blvd Rochester (14618) *(G-13599)*
Orthstar Enterprises Inc..........607 562-2100
119 Sing Sing Rd Horseheads (14845) *(G-6130)*
Os33 Inc..........708 336-3466
16 W 22nd St Fl 6 New York (10010) *(G-10713)*
Osaka Gas Energy America Corp..........914 253-5500
1 N Lexington Ave Ste 504 White Plains (10601) *(G-16037)*
Oscar Heyman & Bros Inc (PA)..........212 593-0400
501 Madison Ave Fl 15 New York (10022) *(G-10714)*
OSI Pharmaceuticals LLC..........631 847-0175
500 Bi County Blvd # 118 Farmingdale (11735) *(G-4700)*
OSI Pharmaceuticals LLC (HQ)..........631 962-2000
1 Bioscience Way Dr Farmingdale (11735) *(G-4701)*
OSI Specialties, Tarrytown *Also called Momentive Performance Mtls Inc (G-15049)*
Osmose Holdings Inc..........716 882-5905
2475 George Urban Blvd Depew (14043) *(G-3991)*
Oso Industries Inc..........917 709-2050
1205 Manhattan Ave Brooklyn (11222) *(G-2237)*
Osprey Boat..........631 331-4153
96 Mount Sinai Ave Mount Sinai (11766) *(G-8116)*
Osprey Publishing Inc..........212 419-5300
1385 Broadway Fl 5 New York (10018) *(G-10715)*
Ossining Bakery Lmp Inc..........914 941-2654
50 N Highland Ave Ossining (10562) *(G-12405)*
Ossining Village of Inc..........914 202-9668
25 Fowler Ave Ossining (10562) *(G-12406)*
Osteohealth, Shirley *Also called American Regent Inc (G-14410)*
Osu NJ Distribution, New York *Also called One Step Up Ltd (G-10691)*
Oswald Manufacturing Co Inc..........516 883-8850
65 Channel Dr Port Washington (11050) *(G-12910)*
Otex Protective Inc..........585 232-7160
2180 Brighton Henrietta Rochester (14623) *(G-13600)*
Other Press LLC..........212 414-0054
267 5th Ave Fl 6 New York (10016) *(G-10716)*
Otis Bedding Mfg Co Inc (PA)..........716 825-2599
80 James E Casey Dr Buffalo (14206) *(G-2900)*
Otis Elevator Company..........315 736-0167
5172 Commercial Dr Yorkville (13495) *(G-16379)*
Otis Elevator Company..........917 339-9600
1 Penn Plz Frnt 6 New York (10119) *(G-10717)*
Otis Products Inc (PA)..........315 348-4300
6987 Laura St Lyons Falls (13368) *(G-7455)*
Otis Technology, Lyons Falls *Also called Otis Products Inc (G-7455)*
Otiwti, Fairport *Also called Qualitrol Company LLC (G-4516)*
Otsego Ready Mix Inc..........607 432-3400
2 Wells Ave Oneonta (13820) *(G-12279)*
Ottaway Newspapers Inc..........845 343-2181
40 Mulberry St Middletown (10940) *(G-7925)*
Ougra Inc..........646 342-4575
3100 47th Ave Unit 4 Long Island City (11101) *(G-7314)*
Our Daily Eats LLC..........518 810-8412
10 Burdick Dr Ste 1 Albany (12205) *(G-110)*
Our Own Candle Company Inc (PA)..........716 769-5000
10349 Main St Findley Lake (14736) *(G-4795)*
Our Terms Fabricators Inc..........631 752-1517
48 Cabot St West Babylon (11704) *(G-15735)*
Ourem Iron Works Inc..........914 476-4856
498 Nepperhan Ave Ste 5 Yonkers (10701) *(G-16337)*
Out of Print, New York *Also called Sputnick 84 LLC (G-11340)*
Outdoor Group LLC..........877 503-5483
1325 John St West Henrietta (14586) *(G-15799)*
Outdoor Sportsman Group..........323 791-7190
1040 6th Ave Rm 12 New York (10018) *(G-10718)*
Outer Image LLC..........914 420-3097
226 42nd St Brooklyn (11232) *(G-2238)*
Outreach Publishing Corp..........718 773-0525
546 Montgomery St Brooklyn (11225) *(G-2239)*
Ovation Instore, Maspeth *Also called DSI Group Inc (G-7607)*
Oved Mens LLC..........212 563-4999
31 W 34th St Fl 4 New York (10001) *(G-10719)*
Overhead Door Corporation..........518 828-7652
1 Hudson Ave Hudson (12534) *(G-6173)*
Overlook Press, The, New York *Also called Peter Mayer Publishers Inc (G-10815)*
Overnight Mountings Inc..........516 865-3000
1400 Plaza Ave New Hyde Park (11040) *(G-8287)*
Overture Media Inc..........917 446-7455
411 Lafayette St Ste 638 New York (10003) *(G-10720)*
Ovid Therapeutics Inc..........646 661-7661
1460 Broadway Fl 4 New York (10036) *(G-10721)*
Ovitz Corporation..........585 967-2114
260 E Main St Rochester (14604) *(G-13601)*
OWayne Enterprises Inc..........718 326-2200
4901 Maspeth Ave Maspeth (11378) *(G-7632)*
Owego Pennysaver Press Inc..........607 687-2434
181 Front St Owego (13827) *(G-12436)*
Owens Corning Sales LLC..........518 475-3600
1277 Feura Bush Rd Feura Bush (12067) *(G-4792)*

ALPHABETIC

Owens Table Mixers LLC 650 303-7342
250 Mercer St Apt C616 New York (10012) ***(G-10722)***
Owens-Brockway Glass Cont Inc 315 258-3211
7134 County House Rd Auburn (13021) ***(G-489)***
Owi Corporation 315 245-4305
12 Masonic Ave Camden (13316) ***(G-3105)***
Owl Books Div, New York *Also called Henry Holt and Company LLC* ***(G-9766)***
Owl Wire & Cable LLC 315 697-2011
3127 Seneca Tpke Canastota (13032) ***(G-3153)***
Owletts Saw Mills 607 525-6340
4214 Cook Rd Woodhull (14898) ***(G-16189)***
Own Instrument Inc 914 668-6546
250 E 7th St Mount Vernon (10550) ***(G-8167)***
Oxair Ltd 716 298-8288
8320 Quarry Rd Niagara Falls (14304) ***(G-11962)***
Oxbo International Corporation (HQ) 585 548-2665
7275 Batavia Byron Rd Byron (14422) ***(G-3062)***
Oxford Book Company Inc 212 227-2120
9 Pine St New York (10005) ***(G-10723)***
Oxford Cleaners 212 734-0006
847 Lexington Ave Frnt New York (10065) ***(G-10724)***
Oxford Industries Inc 212 247-7712
600 5th Ave Fl 12 New York (10020) ***(G-10725)***
Oxford Industries Inc 212 840-2288
25 W 39th St New York (10018) ***(G-10726)***
Oxford University Press LLC (HQ) 212 726-6000
198 Madison Ave Fl 8 New York (10016) ***(G-10727)***
Oxford University Press LLC 212 726-6000
198 Madison Ave Fl 8 New York (10016) ***(G-10728)***
Oxford University Press USA, New York *Also called Oxford University Press LLC* ***(G-10727)***
Oxo International Inc 212 242-3333
601 W 26th St Rm 950 New York (10001) ***(G-10729)***
Oxygen Inc (PA) 516 433-1144
6 Midland Ave Hicksville (11801) ***(G-5936)***
Oxygen Generating Systems Intl, North Tonawanda *Also called Audubon Machinery Corporation* ***(G-12055)***
Oyster Bay Brewing Company 516 802-5546
36 Audrey Ave Oyster Bay (11771) ***(G-12452)***
Oyster Bay Publications LLC 516 922-1300
146 Cove Rd Oyster Bay (11771) ***(G-12453)***
Oyster Bay Pump Works Inc 516 933-4500
78 Midland Ave Unit 1 Hicksville (11801) ***(G-5937)***
Oz Baking Company Ltd 516 466-5114
114 Middle Neck Rd Great Neck (11021) ***(G-5410)***
Ozipko Enterprises Inc 585 424-6740
125 White Spruce Blvd Rochester (14623) ***(G-13602)***
Ozmodyl Ltd 212 226-0622
233 Broadway Rm 707 New York (10279) ***(G-10730)***
Ozteck Industries Inc 516 883-8857
65 Channel Dr Port Washington (11050) ***(G-12911)***
P & B Woodworking Inc 845 744-2508
2415 State Route 52 Pine Bush (12566) ***(G-12626)***
P & C Gas Measurements Service 716 257-3412
9505 Tannery Rd Cattaraugus (14719) ***(G-3221)***
P & C Insurance Systems, New York *Also called P&C Group Inc* ***(G-10734)***
P & C Service, Cattaraugus *Also called P & C Gas Measurements Service* ***(G-3221)***
P & F Bakers Inc 516 931-6821
640 S Broadway Hicksville (11801) ***(G-5938)***
P & F Industries Inc (PA) 631 694-9800
445 Broadhollow Rd # 100 Melville (11747) ***(G-7813)***
P & F Industries of NY Corp 718 894-3501
6006 55th Dr Maspeth (11378) ***(G-7633)***
P & G Steel Products Co Inc 716 896-7900
54 Gruner Rd Buffalo (14227) ***(G-2901)***
P & H Machine Shop Inc 585 247-5500
40 Industrial Park Cir Rochester (14624) ***(G-13603)***
P & H Thermotech Inc 585 624-1310
1883 Heath Markham Rd Lima (14485) ***(G-6934)***
P & I Sportswear Inc 718 934-4587
384 5th Ave New York (10018) ***(G-10731)***
P & L Development LLC 516 986-1700
200 Hicks St Westbury (11590) ***(G-15913)***
P & L Development LLC 631 693-8000
33 Ralph Ave Copiague (11726) ***(G-3667)***
P & L Development LLC 516 986-1700
275 Grand Blvd Unit 1 Westbury (11590) ***(G-15914)***
P & L Development LLC (PA) 516 986-1700
609 Cantiague Rock Rd 2a Westbury (11590) ***(G-15915)***
P & M LLC 631 842-2200
50 Ranick Dr E Amityville (11701) ***(G-301)***
P & R Industries Inc (PA) 585 266-6725
1524 N Clinton Ave Rochester (14621) ***(G-13604)***
P & W Press Inc 646 486-3417
20 W 22nd St Ste 710 New York (10010) ***(G-10732)***
P and F Machine Industries, Maspeth *Also called P & F Industries of NY Corp* ***(G-7633)***
P B & H Moulding Corporation 315 455-1756
7121 Woodchuck Hill Rd Fayetteville (13066) ***(G-4785)***
P C I, Bohemia *Also called Precision Charts Inc* ***(G-1064)***
P C I Manufacturing Div, Westbury *Also called Procomponents Inc* ***(G-15921)***
P C I Paper Conversions Inc (HQ) 315 437-1641
3584 Walters Rd Syracuse (13209) ***(G-14958)***
P C I Paper Conversions Inc 315 703-8300
6761 Thompson Rd Syracuse (13211) ***(G-14959)***
P C I Paper Conversions Inc 315 634-3317
6761 Thompson Rd Syracuse (13211) ***(G-14960)***
P C I Paper Conversions Inc 315 437-1641
6761 Thompson Rd Syracuse (13211) ***(G-14961)***
P C Rfrs Radiology 212 586-5700
3630 37th St Frnt Long Island City (11101) ***(G-7315)***
P C T, Amsterdam *Also called Power and Composite Tech LLC* ***(G-345)***
P D A Panache, Bohemia *Also called Pda Panache Corp* ***(G-1060)***
P D I, Brooklyn *Also called Promotional Development Inc* ***(G-2301)***
P D R Inc 516 829-5300
101 Dupont St Plainview (11803) ***(G-12706)***
P E Guerin (PA) 212 243-5270
23 Jane St New York (10014) ***(G-10733)***
P E Machine Works, Plainview *Also called Port Everglades Machine Works* ***(G-12708)***
P G I, Forest Hills *Also called Preston Glass Industries Inc* ***(G-4926)***
P G Media, New York *Also called Parents Guide Network Corp* ***(G-10757)***
P H Custom Woodworking Corp 917 801-1444
830 Barry St Fl 2nd Bronx (10474) ***(G-1330)***
P J D Publications Ltd 516 626-0650
1315 Jericho Tpke New Hyde Park (11040) ***(G-8288)***
P J R Industries Inc 716 825-9300
1951 Hamburg Tpke Ste 17 Buffalo (14218) ***(G-2902)***
P K G Equipment Incorporated 585 436-4650
367 Paul Rd Rochester (14624) ***(G-13605)***
P L X, Deer Park *Also called Plx Inc* ***(G-3919)***
P M Belts Usa Inc 800 762-3580
131 32nd St Brooklyn (11232) ***(G-2240)***
P M I, Saint James *Also called Polymers Merona Inc* ***(G-14112)***
P M Plastics Inc 716 662-1255
1 Bank St Ste 1 # 1 Orchard Park (14127) ***(G-12369)***
P P I Business Forms Inc 716 825-1241
94 Spaulding St Buffalo (14220) ***(G-2903)***
P Pascal Coffee Roasters, Yonkers *Also called P Pascal Inc* ***(G-16338)***
P Pascal Inc 914 969-7933
960 Nepperhan Ave Yonkers (10703) ***(G-16338)***
P R B Metal Products Inc 631 467-1800
200 Christopher St Ronkonkoma (11779) ***(G-13989)***
P S M Group Inc 716 532-6686
17 Main St Forestville (14062) ***(G-4932)***
P S Pibbs Inc 718 445-8046
13315 32nd Ave Flushing (11354) ***(G-4882)***
P T E Inc 516 775-3839
36 Ontario Rd Floral Park (11001) ***(G-4816)***
P Tool & Die Co Inc 585 889-1340
3535 Union St North Chili (14514) ***(G-12022)***
P V C Molding Technologies 315 331-1212
122 W Shore Blvd Newark (14513) ***(G-11849)***
P&C Group Inc (PA) 212 425-9200
111 Broadway Rm 1703 New York (10006) ***(G-10734)***
P&F, Melville *Also called P & F Industries Inc* ***(G-7813)***
P&I, Pper P I Daily P I People, New York *Also called Pensions & Investments* ***(G-10796)***
P-Ryton Corp 718 937-7052
504 50th Ave Long Island City (11101) ***(G-7316)***
P.A.t, Bohemia *Also called Precision Assembly Tech Inc* ***(G-1063)***
P1 Generator Windings LLC (PA) 518 930-2879
2165 Technology Dr Schenectady (12308) ***(G-14293)***
P8h Inc 212 343-1142
81 Prospect St 7 Brooklyn (11201) ***(G-2241)***
PA Pellets LLC (HQ) 814 848-9970
1 Fischers Rd Ste 160 Pittsford (14534) ***(G-12654)***
Paal Technologies Inc 631 319-6262
152 Remington Blvd Ste 1 Ronkonkoma (11779) ***(G-13990)***
Pac Plastics LLC 631 545-0382
455 Tarrytown Rd Ste 1266 White Plains (10607) ***(G-16038)***
Pace Editions Inc (PA) 212 421-3237
32 E 57th St Fl 3 New York (10022) ***(G-10735)***
Pace Editions Inc 212 643-6353
44 W 18th St Fl 5 New York (10011) ***(G-10736)***
Pace Polyethylene Mfg Co Inc (PA) 914 381-3000
46 Calvert St Harrison (10528) ***(G-5557)***
Pace Prints, New York *Also called Pace Editions Inc* ***(G-10735)***
Pace Up Pharmaceuticals LLC 631 450-4495
200 Bangor St Lindenhurst (11757) ***(G-6969)***
Pace Walkers of America Inc 631 444-2147
105 Washington Ave Port Jefferson (11777) ***(G-12843)***
Pace Window & Door, Victor *Also called Pace Window and Door Corp* ***(G-15423)***
Pace Window and Door Corp (PA) 585 924-8350
7224 State Route 96 Victor (14564) ***(G-15423)***
Pacemaker Packaging Corp 718 458-1188
7200 51st Rd Woodside (11377) ***(G-16218)***
Pachanga Inc 212 832-0022
824 10th Ave New York (10019) ***(G-10737)***
Pacific Alliance Usa Inc 336 500-8184
350 5th Ave Lbby 9 New York (10118) ***(G-10738)***
Pacific Alliance Usa Inc (HQ) 646 839-7000
1450 Broadway Fl 21 New York (10018) ***(G-10739)***
Pacific Concepts, New York *Also called Ewatchfactory Corp* ***(G-9433)***

Pacific Designs Intl Inc 718 364-2867
  2743 Webster Ave Bronx (10458) *(G-1331)*

Pacific Die Cast Inc 845 778-6374
  827 Route 52 Ste 2 Walden (12586) *(G-15460)*

Pacific Poly Product Corp 718 786-7129
  3934 Crescent St Long Island City (11101) *(G-7317)*

Pack America Corp (HQ) 212 508-6666
  108 W 39th St Fl 16 New York (10018) *(G-10740)*

Package One Inc 518 344-5425
  414 Union St Schenectady (12305) *(G-14294)*

Package Pavement Company Inc (PA) 845 221-2224
  3530 Route 52 Stormville (12582) *(G-14752)*

Package Print Technologies 716 871-9905
  1831 Niagara St Buffalo (14207) *(G-2904)*

Packaging Avantage/Marietta La, Cortland *Also called Marietta Corporation (G-3777)*

Packaging Corporation America 315 457-6780
  4471 Steelway Blvd S Liverpool (13090) *(G-7029)*

Packaging Dynamics Ltd 631 563-4499
  35 Carlough Rd Ste 2 Bohemia (11716) *(G-1058)*

Pactiv Corporation 518 743-3100
  6 Haskell Ave Glens Falls (12801) *(G-5263)*

Pactiv LLC 518 562-6101
  74 Weed St Plattsburgh (12901) *(G-12766)*

Pactiv LLC 315 457-6780
  4471 Steelway Blvd S Liverpool (13090) *(G-7030)*

Pactiv LLC 585 394-5125
  2651 Brickyard Rd Canandaigua (14424) *(G-3138)*

Pactiv LLC 518 793-2524
  18 Peck Ave Glens Falls (12801) *(G-5264)*

Pactiv LLC 585 248-1213
  1169 Pittsford Victor Rd Pittsford (14534) *(G-12655)*

Pactiv LLC 585 393-3149
  5250 North St Canandaigua (14424) *(G-3139)*

Paddle8, Brooklyn *Also called P8h Inc (G-2241)*

Paddock Chevrolet Golf Dome 716 504-4059
  175 Brompton Rd Tonawanda (14150) *(G-15130)*

Paddy Lee Fashions Inc 718 786-6020
  4709 36th St Fl 2 Long Island City (11101) *(G-7318)*

Paesana, Amityville *Also called L and S Packing Co (G-287)*

Page Front Group Inc 716 823-8222
  2703 S Park Ave Lackawanna (14218) *(G-6742)*

Paint Over Rust Products Inc 914 636-0700
  38 Portman Rd New Rochelle (10801) *(G-8348)*

Pak 21, Brooklyn *Also called Apex Real Holdings Inc (G-1517)*

Paklab, Hauppauge *Also called Universal Packg Systems Inc (G-5792)*

Pal Aluminum Inc (PA) 516 937-1990
  230 Duffy Ave Unit B Hicksville (11801) *(G-5939)*

Pal Industries, Hicksville *Also called Pal Aluminum Inc (G-5939)*

Pal Manufacturing Corp 516 937-1990
  230 Duffy Ave Unit B Hicksville (11801) *(G-5940)*

Paladino Prtg & Graphics Inc 718 279-6000
  20009 32nd Ave Flushing (11361) *(G-4883)*

Palagonia Bakery Co Inc 718 272-5400
  508 Junius St Brooklyn (11212) *(G-2242)*

Palagonia Italian Bread, Brooklyn *Also called Palagonia Bakery Co Inc (G-2242)*

Palagrave Macmillan, New York *Also called Macmillan Publishing Group LLC (G-10310)*

Paleteria Fernandez Inc 914 315-1598
  350 Mamaroneck Ave Mamaroneck (10543) *(G-7518)*

Paleteria Fernandez Inc (PA) 914 939-3694
  33 N Main St Port Chester (10573) *(G-12826)*

Paletot Ltd 212 268-3774
  499 Fashion Ave Rm 25s New York (10018) *(G-10741)*

Palgrave Macmillan Ltd 646 307-5028
  175 5th Ave Frnt 4 New York (10010) *(G-10742)*

Palisades Paper Inc 845 354-0333
  13 Jackson Ave Spring Valley (10977) *(G-14580)*

Pall Aerospace, Port Washington *Also called Pall Corporation (G-12913)*

Pall Biomedical Inc 516 484-3600
  25 Harbor Park Dr Port Washington (11050) *(G-12912)*

Pall Corporation (HQ) 516 484-5400
  25 Harbor Park Dr Port Washington (11050) *(G-12913)*

Pall Corporation 607 753-6041
  3643 State Route 281 Cortland (13045) *(G-3779)*

Pall Corporation 607 753-6041
  3669 State Route 281 Cortland (13045) *(G-3780)*

Pall Corporation 516 484-2818
  25 Harbor Park Dr Port Washington (11050) *(G-12914)*

Pall Corporation 607 753-6041
  839 State Route 13 Ste 12 Cortland (13045) *(G-3781)*

Pall Life Sciences, Port Washington *Also called Pall Corporation (G-12914)*

Pall Medical, Port Washington *Also called Pall Biomedical Inc (G-12912)*

Pall Trinity Micro, Cortland *Also called Pall Corporation (G-3779)*

Pall's Advnced Sprtons Systems, Cortland *Also called Pall Corporation (G-3781)*

Palladia Inc 212 206-3669
  105 W 17th St New York (10011) *(G-10743)*

Palladium Times, Oswego *Also called Sample News Group LLC (G-12420)*

Pallet Division Inc 585 328-3780
  40 Silver St Rochester (14611) *(G-13606)*

Pallet Services Inc (PA) 716 873-7700
  4055 Casillio Pkwy Clarence (14031) *(G-3438)*

Pallet Services Inc 585 647-4020
  1681 Lyell Ave Ste 100 Rochester (14606) *(G-13607)*

Pallets Inc 518 747-4177
  99 1/2 East St Fort Edward (12828) *(G-4941)*

Pallets Plus, Olean *Also called G & H Wood Products LLC (G-12236)*

Pallets R US Inc (PA) 631 758-2360
  555 Woodside Ave Bellport (11713) *(G-806)*

Pallette Stone Corporation 518 584-2421
  269 Ballard Rd Gansevoort (12831) *(G-5084)*

Palma Tool & Die Company Inc 716 681-4464
  40 Ward Rd Lancaster (14086) *(G-6820)*

Palmbay Ltd 718 424-3388
  4459 Kissena Blvd Apt 6h Flushing (11355) *(G-4884)*

Palmer Industries Inc 607 754-8741
  2320 Lewis St Endicott (13760) *(G-4468)*

Palmer Industries Inc (PA) 607 754-2957
  509 Paden St Endicott (13760) *(G-4469)*

Palmer Industries Inc 607 754-8741
  1 Heath St Endicott (13760) *(G-4470)*

Palogloss Fashions, New York *Also called Max Header (G-10389)*

Palpross Incorporated 845 469-2188
  Maple Ave Rr 396 Selkirk (12158) *(G-14359)*

Paltalk, New York *Also called AVM Software Inc (G-8694)*

Palumbo Block Co Inc 845 832-6100
  365 Dover Furnace Rd Dover Plains (12522) *(G-4033)*

Pama Enterprises Inc 516 504-6300
  60 Cuttermill Rd Ste 411 Great Neck (11021) *(G-5411)*

Pan American Leathers Inc (PA) 978 741-4150
  347 W 36th St Rm 1204 New York (10018) *(G-10744)*

Pan American Roller Inc 914 762-8700
  5 Broad Ave Ossining (10562) *(G-12407)*

Panagraphics Inc 716 312-8088
  30 Quail Run Orchard Park (14127) *(G-12370)*

Panda Plates Inc (PA) 888 997-6623
  1450 Broadway Fl 40 New York (10018) *(G-10745)*

Pane DOro 914 964-0043
  166 Ludlow St Yonkers (10705) *(G-16339)*

Panelogic Inc 607 962-6319
  366 Baker Street Ext Corning (14830) *(G-3719)*

Pangea Brands LLC (PA) 617 638-0001
  6 W 20th St Fl 3 New York (10011) *(G-10746)*

Panther Graphics Inc (PA) 585 546-7163
  465 Central Ave Rochester (14605) *(G-13608)*

Panzarella Prtg & Packg Inc 716 853-4480
  310 Creekside Dr Ste 324 Amherst (14228) *(G-241)*

Pap Chat Inc 516 350-1888
  3105 Quentin Rd Brooklyn (11234) *(G-2243)*

Papa Bubble 212 966-2599
  380 Broome St Frnt A New York (10013) *(G-10747)*

Paper Box Corp 212 226-7490
  1751 2nd Ave Apt 10a New York (10128) *(G-10748)*

Paper Comics, New York *Also called Papercutz Inc (G-10751)*

Paper House Productions Inc 845 246-7261
  160 Malden Tpke Bldg 2 Saugerties (12477) *(G-14207)*

Paper Magazine, New York *Also called Paper Publishing Company Inc (G-10750)*

Paper Magic Group Inc 631 521-3682
  345 7th Ave Fl 6 New York (10001) *(G-10749)*

Paper Publishing Company Inc 212 226-4405
  15 E 32nd St New York (10016) *(G-10750)*

Paper Solutions Inc 718 499-4666
  342 37th St Brooklyn (11232) *(G-2244)*

Papercutz Inc 646 559-4681
  160 Broadway Rm 700e New York (10038) *(G-10751)*

Paperstreet Technology Inc 704 773-5689
  240 Kent Ave Brooklyn (11249) *(G-2245)*

Paperworks, Baldwinsville *Also called Specialized Packg Group Inc (G-553)*

Paperworks Industries Inc 315 638-4355
  2900 Mclane Rd Baldwinsville (13027) *(G-552)*

Paperworld Inc 516 221-2702
  3054 Lee Pl Bellmore (11710) *(G-785)*

Par Pharmaceutical Inc (HQ) 845 573-5500
  1 Ram Ridge Rd Chestnut Ridge (10977) *(G-3396)*

Par Phrmceutical Companies Inc (HQ) 845 573-5500
  1 Ram Ridge Rd Chestnut Ridge (10977) *(G-3397)*

Par Sterile Products LLC (HQ) 845 573-5500
  6 Ram Ridge Rd Chestnut Ridge (10977) *(G-3398)*

Par Technology Corporation (PA) 315 738-0600
  8383 Seneca Tpke Ste 2 New Hartford (13413) *(G-8242)*

Par-Foam Products Inc 716 855-2066
  239 Van Rensselaer St Buffalo (14210) *(G-2905)*

Parabit Systems Inc 516 378-4800
  2677 Grand Ave Bellmore (11710) *(G-786)*

PARABOLA, New York *Also called Society For The Study (G-11283)*

Parace Bionics LLC 877 727-2231
  100 Park Ave Rm 1600 New York (10017) *(G-10752)*

Parachute Publishing LLC 212 337-6743
  322 8th Ave Ste 702 New York (10001) *(G-10753)*

Parade Magazine, New York *Also called Parade Publications Inc (G-10754)*

Parade Publications Inc (HQ) 212 450-7000
  711 3rd Ave New York (10017) *(G-10754)*

Paradigm Spine LLC 888 273-9897
  505 Park Ave Fl 14 New York (10022) *(G-10755)*

A L P H A B E T I C

Paradise Plastics LLC 718 788-3733
116 39th St Brooklyn (11232) ***(G-2246)***
Paradiso Cnsld Entps LLC 585 924-3937
1115 E Main St Unit 58 Rochester (14609) ***(G-13609)***
Paragon Aquatics 845 452-5500
1351 Route 55 Unit 1 Lagrangeville (12540) ***(G-6752)***
Paragon Steel Rule Dies Inc 585 254-3395
979 Mount Read Blvd Rochester (14606) ***(G-13610)***
Paramount Cord & Brackets 212 325-9100
6 Tournament Dr White Plains (10605) ***(G-16039)***
Paramount Equipment Inc 631 981-4422
201 Christopher St Ronkonkoma (11779) ***(G-13991)***
Paramount Graphix 845 367-5003
26 Hill St Port Jervis (12771) ***(G-12854)***
Paramount Textiles Inc 212 966-1040
34 Walker St New York (10013) ***(G-10756)***
Paratore Signs Inc 315 455-5551
1551 Brewerton Rd Syracuse (13208) ***(G-14962)***
Paratus Industries Inc 716 826-2000
6659 E Quaker St Orchard Park (14127) ***(G-12371)***
Pardazzio Uomo, Westbury *Also called Montero International Inc* ***(G-15911)***
Parents Guide Network Corp 212 213-8840
419 Park Ave S Rm 505 New York (10016) ***(G-10757)***
Pareteum Corporation (PA) 212 984-1096
1185 Ave Of The Amrcas Fl New York (10036) ***(G-10758)***
Parfums Boucheron Jewelry, New York *Also called Boucheron Joaillerie USA Inc* ***(G-8839)***
Parfuse Corp 516 997-8888
65 Kinkel St Westbury (11590) ***(G-15916)***
Parijat Jewels Inc 212 302-2549
36 W 47th St Ste 809i New York (10036) ***(G-10759)***
Paris Art Label Co Inc 631 467-2300
217 River Ave Patchogue (11772) ***(G-12508)***
Paris Review Foundation Inc 212 343-1333
544 W 27th St Fl 3 New York (10001) ***(G-10760)***
Paris Wedding Center Corp (PA) 347 368-4085
42-53 42 55 Main St Flushing (11355) ***(G-4885)***
Paris Wedding Center Corp 212 267-8088
45 E Broadway Fl 2 New York (10002) ***(G-10761)***
Park Aerospace Corp (PA) 631 465-3600
48 S Service Rd Melville (11747) ***(G-7814)***
Park Assist LLC 646 666-7525
57 W 38th St Fl 11 New York (10018) ***(G-10762)***
Park Ave Bldg & Roofg Sups LLC 718 403-0100
2120 Atlantic Ave Brooklyn (11233) ***(G-2247)***
Park Avenue Imprints LLC (PA) 716 822-5737
2955 S Park Ave Buffalo (14218) ***(G-2906)***
Park Avenue Nutrition, Richmond Hill *Also called Womens Health Care PC* ***(G-13128)***
Park Avenue Sportswear Ltd (PA) 718 369-0520
820 4th Ave Brooklyn (11232) ***(G-2248)***
Park Enterprises Rochester Inc 585 546-4200
226 Jay St Rochester (14608) ***(G-13611)***
Park Slope Copy Center 718 783-0268
123 7th Ave Brooklyn (11215) ***(G-2249)***
Park West Jewelery Inc 646 329-6145
565 W End Ave Apt 8b New York (10024) ***(G-10763)***
Park's Department, Williamsville *Also called Town of Amherst* ***(G-16144)***
Park-Ohio Inds Trsry Co Inc (HQ) 212 966-3310
80 State St Albany (12207) ***(G-111)***
Parkchester Dps LLC 718 823-4411
2000 E Tremont Ave Bronx (10462) ***(G-1332)***
Parker Machine Company Inc 518 747-0675
28 Sullivan Pkwy Fort Edward (12828) ***(G-4942)***
Parker Warby Retail Inc (PA) 646 517-5223
161 Ave Of The Amrcs Fl 6 New York (10013) ***(G-10764)***
Parker-Hannifin Aerospace, Clyde *Also called Parker-Hannifin Corporation* ***(G-3494)***
Parker-Hannifin Corporation 716 686-6400
4087 Walden Ave Lancaster (14086) ***(G-6821)***
Parker-Hannifin Corporation 631 231-3737
124 Columbia St Clyde (14433) ***(G-3494)***
Parker-Hannifin Corporation 716 685-4040
4087 Walden Ave Lancaster (14086) ***(G-6822)***
Parker-Hannifin Corporation 631 231-3737
300 Marcus Blvd Hauppauge (11788) ***(G-5736)***
Parker-Hannifin Corporation 585 425-7000
83 Estates Dr W Fairport (14450) ***(G-4512)***
Parker-Hannifin Corporation 315 926-4211
3967 Buffalo St Marion (14505) ***(G-7572)***
Parker-Hannifin Corporation 716 685-4040
4087 Walden Ave Lancaster (14086) ***(G-6823)***
Parkmatic Car Prkg Systems LLC (PA) 516 224-7700
47-10 A 32nd Pl Long Island City (11101) ***(G-7319)***
Parkmatic Car Prkg Systems LLC 800 422-5438
2025 130th St College Point (11356) ***(G-3558)***
Parkside Candy Co Inc (PA) 716 833-7540
3208 Main St Ste 1 Buffalo (14214) ***(G-2907)***
Parkside Printing Co Inc 516 933-5423
4 Tompkins Ave Jericho (11753) ***(G-6588)***
Parlec LLC 585 425-4400
101 Perinton Pkwy Fl 1 Fairport (14450) ***(G-4513)***
Parlor City Paper Box Co Inc 607 772-0600
2 Eldredge St Binghamton (13901) ***(G-903)***
Parlor Labs Inc 866 801-7323
515 W 19th St New York (10011) ***(G-10765)***
Parmed Pharmaceuticals LLC (HQ) 716 773-1113
4220 Hyde Park Blvd Niagara Falls (14305) ***(G-11963)***
Parnasa International Inc 516 394-0400
181 S Franklin Ave # 400 Valley Stream (11581) ***(G-15351)***
Parrinello Printing Inc 716 633-7780
84 Aero Dr Buffalo (14225) ***(G-2908)***
Parrington Instruments 518 373-8420
12 Droms Rd Rexford (12148) ***(G-13096)***
Parsley Apparel Corp 631 981-7181
2153 Pond Rd Ronkonkoma (11779) ***(G-13992)***
Parsons & Whittemore Inc 914 937-9009
4 International Dr # 300 Port Chester (10573) ***(G-12827)***
Parsons Whittemore Entps Corp (PA) 914 937-9009
4 International Dr # 300 Port Chester (10573) ***(G-12828)***
Parsons-Meares Ltd 212 242-3378
2107 41st Ave Ste 1l Long Island City (11101) ***(G-7320)***
Partech Inc (HQ) 315 738-0600
8383 Seneca Tpke Ste 2 New Hartford (13413) ***(G-8243)***
Pasabahce USA 212 683-1600
41 Madison Ave Fl 7 New York (10010) ***(G-10766)***
Pascale Madonna, Long Island City *Also called Fashion Ribbon Co Inc* ***(G-7221)***
Pass & Seymour Inc (HQ) 315 468-6211
50 Boyd Ave Syracuse (13209) ***(G-14963)***
Pass Em-Entries Inc (PA) 718 392-0100
3914 Crescent St Long Island City (11101) ***(G-7321)***
Passive-Plus Inc 631 425-0938
48 Elm St Huntington (11743) ***(G-6216)***
Passport Brands Inc (PA) 646 459-2625
240 Madison Ave Fl 8 New York (10016) ***(G-10767)***
Passport Magazine, New York *Also called Q Communications Inc* ***(G-10940)***
Passur Aerospace Inc 631 589-6800
35 Orville Dr Ste 1 Bohemia (11716) ***(G-1059)***
Pasta People, West Babylon *Also called Great Eastern Pasta Works LLC* ***(G-15713)***
Pastosa Ravioli, Staten Island *Also called Bud Ravioli Center Inc* ***(G-14632)***
Pat & Rose Dress Inc 212 279-1357
327 W 36th St Rm 3a New York (10018) ***(G-10768)***
Patchogue Advance Inc 631 475-1000
20 Medford Ave Ste 1 Patchogue (11772) ***(G-12509)***
Patco Group, Maspeth *Also called Patco Tapes Inc* ***(G-7634)***
Patco Tapes Inc 718 497-1527
5927 56th St Maspeth (11378) ***(G-7634)***
Patdan Fuel Corporation 718 326-3668
7803 68th Rd Middle Village (11379) ***(G-7883)***
Paterson, Douglas G & Sons, Lockport *Also called Douglas Patterson & Sons Inc* ***(G-7070)***
Pathfinder 103 Inc 315 363-4260
229 Park Ave Oneida (13421) ***(G-12253)***
Pathfinder Industries Inc 315 593-2483
117 N 3rd St Fulton (13069) ***(G-5075)***
Pati Inc 718 244-6788
Jfk Intl Airprt Hngar 16 Jamaica (11430) ***(G-6464)***
Patient-Wear LLC 914 740-7770
3940 Merritt Ave Bronx (10466) ***(G-1333)***
Patla Enterprises Inc 315 367-0237
190 E State St Sherrill (13461) ***(G-14405)***
Patmian LLC 212 758-0770
655 Madison Ave Fl 24 New York (10065) ***(G-10769)***
Patricia Underwood, New York *Also called Paletot Ltd* ***(G-10741)***
Patrick Rohan 718 781-2573
9 Green St Monticello (12701) ***(G-8072)***
Patrick Kraft (PA) 315 343-9376
262 W Seneca St Oswego (13126) ***(G-12419)***
Patrick Mackin Custom Furn 718 237-2592
612 Degraw St Brooklyn (11217) ***(G-2250)***
Patrick Ryans Modern Press 518 434-2921
1 Colonie St Albany (12207) ***(G-112)***
Patsy Strocchia & Sons Iron Wo 516 625-8800
175 I U Willets Rd Ste 4 Albertson (11507) ***(G-148)***
Patterson Blacktop Corp 845 628-3425
1181 Route 6 Carmel (10512) ***(G-3189)***
Patterson Blacktop Corp (HQ) 914 949-2000
20 Haarlem Ave White Plains (10603) ***(G-16040)***
Patterson Materials Corp 845 832-6000
322 Walsh Ave New Windsor (12553) ***(G-8377)***
Patterson Materials Corp (HQ) 914 949-2000
20 Haarlem Ave White Plains (10603) ***(G-16041)***
Patuga LLC 716 204-7220
7954 Transit Rd 316 Williamsville (14221) ***(G-16136)***
Paul Bunyan Products Inc 315 696-6164
890 Mclean Rd Cortland (13045) ***(G-3782)***
Paul David Enterprises Inc 646 667-5530
19 W 34th St Rm 1018 New York (10001) ***(G-10770)***
Paul De Lima Coffee Company, Liverpool *Also called Paul De Lima Company Inc* ***(G-7031)***
Paul De Lima Company Inc (PA) 315 457-3725
7546 Morgan Rd Ste 1 Liverpool (13090) ***(G-7031)***
Paul De Lima Company Inc 315 457-3725
8550 Pardee Rd Cicero (13039) ***(G-3422)***
Paul J Mitchell Logging Inc 518 359-7029
15 Mitchell Ln Tupper Lake (12986) ***(G-15212)***
Paul Michael Group Inc 631 585-5700
460 Hawkins Ave Ronkonkoma (11779) ***(G-13993)***
Paul T Freund Corporation (PA) 315 597-4873
216 Park Dr Palmyra (14522) ***(G-12493)***

Paula Dorf Cosmetics Inc 212 582-0073
850 7th Ave Ste 801 New York (10019) *(G-10771)*

Paula Varsalona Ltd 212 570-9100
552 Fashion Ave Rm 602 New York (10018) *(G-10772)*

Paulin Investment Company 631 957-8500
8600 New Horizons Blvd Amityville (11701) *(G-302)*

Paulpac LLC 631 283-7610
104 Foster Xing Southampton (11968) *(G-14534)*

Pauls Rods & Restos Inc 631 665-7637
131 Brook Ave Ste 13 Deer Park (11729) *(G-3917)*

Paulson & Co Inc (PA) 212 956-2221
1133 Ave Of The Americas New York (10036) *(G-10773)*

Paumanok Vineyards Ltd 631 722-8800
1074 Main Rd Rte 25 Aquebogue (11931) *(G-366)*

Pavana USA Inc 646 833-8811
10 W 33rd St Rm 408 New York (10001) *(G-10774)*

Pavmed Inc 212 949-4319
60 E 42nd St Fl 46 New York (10165) *(G-10775)*

Pawling Corporation (PA) 845 373-9300
32 Nelson Hill Rd Wassaic (12592) *(G-15525)*

Pawling Engineered Pdts Inc 845 855-1000
157 Charles Colman Blvd Pawling (12564) *(G-12527)*

Paxton Metal Craft Division, Peekskill *Also called Elevator Accessories Mfg (G-12550)*

Paya Printing of NY Inc 516 625-8346
87 Searingtown Rd Albertson (11507) *(G-149)*

Pb Industries, Homer *Also called Solidus Industries Inc (G-6067)*

Pb Mapinfo Corporation 518 285-6000
1 Global Vw Troy (12180) *(G-15177)*

Pb08 Inc 347 866-7353
40 Bloomingdale Rd Hicksville (11801) *(G-5941)*

Pbi Media Inc., New York *Also called Access Intelligence LLC (G-8440)*

PBL Industries Corp 631 979-4266
49 Dillmont Dr Smithtown (11787) *(G-14483)*

PBR Graphics Inc 518 458-2909
20 Railroad Ave Ste 1 Albany (12205) *(G-113)*

PC Solutions & Consulting 607 735-0466
407 S Walnut St Elmira (14904) *(G-4364)*

Pca/Syracuse, 384, Liverpool *Also called Packaging Corporation America (G-7029)*

Pcamerica, Pearl River *Also called Xenial Inc (G-12544)*

Pcb Group Inc 716 684-0001
3425 Walden Ave Depew (14043) *(G-3992)*

Pcb Piezotronics Inc 716 684-0001
3425 Walden Ave Depew (14043) *(G-3993)*

Pcb Piezotronics Inc 716 684-0003
3425 Walden Ave Depew (14043) *(G-3994)*

PCI Industries Corp 914 662-2700
550 Franklin Ave Mount Vernon (10550) *(G-8168)*

Pcx Aerostructures LLC 631 467-2632
60 Milbar Blvd Farmingdale (11735) *(G-4702)*

Pda Panache Corp 631 776-0523
70 Knickerbocker Ave # 7 Bohemia (11716) *(G-1060)*

Pdf Seal Incorporated 631 595-7035
280 Oser Ave Hauppauge (11788) *(G-5737)*

Pdi, New York *Also called Props Displays & Interiors (G-10915)*

Pdi Cone Co Inc 716 825-8750
69 Leddy St Buffalo (14210) *(G-2909)*

Pdi Fashion, New York *Also called Product Development Intl LLC (G-10903)*

Pdj Components Inc 845 469-9191
35 Brookside Ave Chester (10918) *(G-3382)*

PDJ Inc 315 655-8824
2550 E Ballina Rd Cazenovia (13035) *(G-3232)*

PDM Studios Inc 716 694-8337
510 Main St Tonawanda (14150) *(G-15131)*

PDQ Manufacturing Co Inc 845 889-3123
29 Hilee Rd Rhinebeck (12572) *(G-13100)*

PDQ Printing, New Paltz *Also called PDQ Shipping Services (G-8310)*

PDQ Shipping Services 845 255-5500
8 New Paltz Plz 299 New Paltz (12561) *(G-8310)*

Peace Times Weekly Inc 718 762-6500
14527 33rd Ave Flushing (11354) *(G-4886)*

Peaceful Valley Maple Farm (PA) 518 762-0491
116 Lagrange Rd Johnstown (12095) *(G-6623)*

Peachtree Enterprises Inc 212 989-3445
2219 41st Ave Ste 4a Long Island City (11101) *(G-7322)*

Peak Motion Inc 716 534-4925
11190 Main St Clarence (14031) *(G-3439)*

Peak Performance Design LLC 518 302-9198
1 Mustang Dr Ste 2 Cohoes (12047) *(G-3512)*

Peaks Coffee Company 315 565-1900
3264 Rte 20 Cazenovia (13035) *(G-3233)*

Peanut Butter & Co Inc 212 757-3130
119 W 57th St Ste 300 New York (10019) *(G-10776)*

Pearl Erwin Inc (PA) 212 889-7410
389 5th Ave Rm 1100 New York (10016) *(G-10777)*

Pearl Leather Finishers Inc (PA) 518 762-4543
11 Industrial Pkwy 21 Johnstown (12095) *(G-6624)*

Pearl Leather Group LLC 516 627-4047
17 Barstow Rd Ste 206 Great Neck (11021) *(G-5412)*

Pearl River Textiles Inc 212 629-5490
57 W 38th St Rm 1202 New York (10018) *(G-10778)*

Pearl Technologies Inc 315 365-3742
13297 Seneca St Savannah (13146) *(G-14220)*

Pearltek, New York *Also called Robin Stanley Inc (G-11064)*

Pearson Education Inc 845 340-8700
317 Wall St Kingston (12401) *(G-6706)*

Pearson Education Inc 212 782-3337
1185 Avenue Of The Americ New York (10036) *(G-10779)*

Pearson Education Inc 212 366-2000
375 Hudson St New York (10014) *(G-10780)*

Pearson Education Inc 201 236-7000
59 Brookhill Dr West Nyack (10994) *(G-15829)*

Pearson Education Holdings Inc (HQ) 201 236-6716
330 Hudson St Fl 9 New York (10013) *(G-10781)*

Pearson Inc (HQ) 212 641-2400
1330 Hudson St New York (10013) *(G-10782)*

Pearson Longman LLC 917 981-2200
51 Madison Ave Fl 27 New York (10010) *(G-10783)*

Pearson Longman LLC (HQ) 212 641-2400
10 Bank St Ste 1030 White Plains (10606) *(G-16042)*

Peck & Hale LLC 631 589-2510
180 Division Ave West Sayville (11796) *(G-15842)*

Peckham Asphalt Resale Corp (HQ) 914 949-2000
20 Haarlem Ave Ste 200 White Plains (10603) *(G-16043)*

Peckham Asphalt Resale Corp 518 945-1120
2 Union St Athens (12015) *(G-449)*

Peckham Industries Inc (PA) 914 949-2000
20 Haarlem Ave Ste 200 White Plains (10603) *(G-16044)*

Peckham Industries Inc 518 943-0155
7065 Us Highway 9w Catskill (12414) *(G-3216)*

Peckham Industries Inc 518 893-2176
430 Coy Rd Greenfield Center (12833) *(G-5450)*

Peckham Industries Inc 518 945-1120
Uninn St Athens (12015) *(G-450)*

Peckham Materials, Carmel *Also called Patterson Blacktop Corp (G-3189)*

Peckham Materials Corp 845 562-5370
322 Walsh Ave Newburgh (12553) *(G-11881)*

Peckham Materials Corp (HQ) 914 686-2045
20 Haarlem Ave Ste 200 White Plains (10603) *(G-16045)*

Peckham Materials Corp 518 747-3353
438 Vaughn Rd Hudson Falls (12839) *(G-6192)*

Peckham Materials Corp 518 945-1120
2 Union St Ext Athens (12015) *(G-451)*

Peckham Materials Corp 518 494-2313
5983 State Route 9 Chestertown (12817) *(G-3394)*

Peckham Road Corp 518 792-3157
375 Bay Rd Ste 101 Queensbury (12804) *(G-13051)*

Peco Conduit Fittings, Orangeburg *Also called Producto Electric Corp (G-12328)*

Peco Pallet Inc (HQ) 914 376-5444
50 S Buckhout St Ste 301 Irvington (10533) *(G-6313)*

Peconic B Shopper, Southold *Also called Academy Printing Services Inc (G-14542)*

Peconic Ironworks Ltd 631 204-0323
33 Flying Point Rd # 108 Southampton (11968) *(G-14535)*

Peconic Plastics Inc 631 653-3676
6062 Old Country Rd Quogue (11959) *(G-13061)*

Pecoraro Dairy Products Inc (PA) 718 388-2379
287 Leonard St Brooklyn (11211) *(G-2251)*

Pedifix Inc 845 277-2850
301 Fields Ln Brewster (10509) *(G-1157)*

Pedinol Pharmacal Inc 800 733-4665
30 Banfi Plz N Farmingdale (11735) *(G-4703)*

Pedre Corp (PA) 212 868-2935
270 Duffy Ave Ste G Hicksville (11801) *(G-5942)*

Pedre Watch, Hicksville *Also called Pedre Corp (G-5942)*

Peek A Boo USA Inc 201 533-8700
555 8th Ave Rm 403 New York (10018) *(G-10784)*

Peelle Company (PA) 631 231-6000
373 Smithtown Byp 311 Hauppauge (11788) *(G-5738)*

Peer International Corp (HQ) 212 265-3910
152 W 57th St Fl 10 New York (10019) *(G-10785)*

Peer Software Incorporated (PA) 631 979-1770
1363 Veterans Hwy Ste 44 Hauppauge (11788) *(G-5739)*

Peer-Southern Productions Inc (HQ) 212 265-3910
152 W 57th St Fl 10 New York (10019) *(G-10786)*

Peerless Envelopes & Prtg Co, Brooklyn *Also called H T L & S Ltd (G-1916)*

Peerless Instrument Co Inc 631 396-6500
1966 Broadhollow Rd Ste D Farmingdale (11735) *(G-4704)*

Peerless-Winsmith Inc 716 592-9311
172 Eaton St Springville (14141) *(G-14594)*

Peermusic III Ltd (PA) 212 265-3910
152 W 57th St Fl 10 New York (10019) *(G-10787)*

Peermusic Ltd (HQ) 212 265-3910
152 W 57th St Fl 10 New York (10019) *(G-10788)*

Pegasus Books NY Ltd 646 343-9502
148 W 37th St Fl 13 New York (10018) *(G-10789)*

Pegasystems Inc 212 626-6550
1120 Ave Of The Americas New York (10036) *(G-10790)*

Peking Food LLC 718 628-8080
47 Stewart Ave Brooklyn (11237) *(G-2252)*

Peko Precision Products Inc 585 301-1386
70 Holworthy St Rochester (14606) *(G-13612)*

Pelican Bay Ltd 718 729-9300
3901 22nd St Long Island City (11101) *(G-7323)*

Pelican Products Co Inc (PA) 718 860-3220
1049 Lowell St Bronx (10459) *(G-1334)*

Pelkowski Precast Corp...631 269-5727
294a Old Northport Rd Kings Park (11754) ***(G-6675)***
Pella Corporation...607 223-2023
800 Valley Plz Ste 5 Johnson City (13790) ***(G-6607)***
Pella Corporation...516 385-3622
77 Albertson Ave Ste 2 Albertson (11507) ***(G-150)***
Pella Corporation...516 385-3622
77 Albertson Ave Ste 2 Albertson (11507) ***(G-151)***
Pella Corporation...631 208-0710
901 Burman Blvd Calverton (11933) ***(G-3083)***
Pella Window Door, Johnson City *Also called Pella Corporation* ***(G-6607)***
Pella Window Door, Albertson *Also called Pella Corporation* ***(G-150)***
Pella Window Door, Albertson *Also called Pella Corporation* ***(G-151)***
Pellegrini Vineyards LLC...631 734-4111
23005 Main Rd Cutchogue (11935) ***(G-3816)***
Pellets LLC...716 693-1750
63 Industrial Dr Ste 3 North Tonawanda (14120) ***(G-12081)***
Pellicano Specialty Foods Inc...716 822-2366
195 Reading St Buffalo (14220) ***(G-2910)***
Pems Tool & Machine Inc...315 823-3595
125 Southern Ave Little Falls (13365) ***(G-6990)***
Pemystifying Diital, Woodbury *Also called Photo Industry Inc* ***(G-16179)***
Penasack Machine Company Inc...585 589-7044
49 Sanford St Albion (14411) ***(G-159)***
Pencoa, Westbury *Also called Harper Products Ltd* ***(G-15894)***
Penetradar Corporation...716 731-2629
2509 Niagara Falls Blvd Niagara Falls (14304) ***(G-11964)***
Penetron International Ltd...631 941-9700
45 Research Way Ste 203 East Setauket (11733) ***(G-4183)***
Penfli Industries Inc...212 947-6080
11 Woodland Pl Great Neck (11021) ***(G-5413)***
Penguin Putnam Inc...212 366-2000
375 Hudson St Bsmt 1 New York (10014) ***(G-10791)***
Penguin Random House LLC...212 782-1000
1540 Broadway New York (10036) ***(G-10792)***
Penguin Random House LLC (HQ)...212 782-9000
1745 Broadway Frnt 1 New York (10019) ***(G-10793)***
Penguin Random House LLC...212 572-6162
1745 Broadway Frnt 3 New York (10019) ***(G-10794)***
Penguin Random House LLC...212 366-2377
80 State St Albany (12207) ***(G-114)***
Penhouse Media Group Inc (PA)...212 702-6000
11 Penn Plz Fl 12 New York (10001) ***(G-10795)***
Peninsula Plastics Ltd...716 854-3050
161 Marine Dr Apt 6e Buffalo (14202) ***(G-2911)***
Penn & Fletcher Inc...212 239-6868
2107 41st Ave Fl 5 Long Island City (11101) ***(G-7324)***
Penn Can Asphalt Materials, Lyons *Also called Penn Can Equipment Corporation* ***(G-7451)***
Penn Can Equipment Corporation...315 378-0337
300 Cole Rd Lyons (14489) ***(G-7451)***
Penn Enterprises Inc...845 446-0765
845 Washington Rd West Point (10996) ***(G-15834)***
Penn State Mtal Fbrctors No 2...718 786-8814
810 Humboldt St Ste 1-B Brooklyn (11222) ***(G-2253)***
Pennant Foods, Rochester *Also called Aryzta LLC* ***(G-13251)***
Pennant Ingredients Inc (HQ)...585 235-8160
64 Chester St Rochester (14611) ***(G-13613)***
Penner Elbow Company Inc...718 526-9000
4700 76th St Elmhurst (11373) ***(G-4337)***
Pennsauken Packing Company LLC...585 377-7700
815 Whitney Rd W Fairport (14450) ***(G-4514)***
Penny Express, Avon *Also called Penny Lane Printing Inc* ***(G-515)***
Penny Lane Printing Inc...585 226-8111
1471 Rte 15 Avon (14414) ***(G-515)***
Penny Saver News, Edgewood *Also called S G New York LLC* ***(G-4281)***
Pennysaver Group Inc...914 966-1400
80 Alexander St Yonkers (10701) ***(G-16340)***
Pennysaver Group Inc...845 627-3600
39 S Main St Ste 1 New City (10956) ***(G-8228)***
Pennysaver News, Bohemia *Also called S G New York LLC* ***(G-1072)***
Pennysaver/Town Crier, Edgewood *Also called All Island Media Inc* ***(G-4261)***
Pennysavers Rw Publications, Elma *Also called R W Publications Div of Wtrhs* ***(G-4326)***
Pensions & Investments...212 210-0763
711 3rd Ave New York (10017) ***(G-10796)***
Penta-Tech Coated Products LLC...315 986-4098
1610 Commons Pkwy Macedon (14502) ***(G-7468)***
Pentair Water Pool and Spa Inc...845 452-5500
341 Route 55 Lagrangeville (12540) ***(G-6753)***
Pentaplastics, Bohemia *Also called Leidel Corporation* ***(G-1034)***
Penthouse Group, The, Freeport *Also called Penthouse Manufacturing Co Inc* ***(G-5014)***
Penthouse Manufacturing Co Inc...516 379-1300
225 Buffalo Ave Freeport (11520) ***(G-5014)***
Penton Information Services, New York *Also called Informa Business Media Inc* ***(G-9888)***
Penton Media - Aviation Week, New York *Also called Informa Media Inc* ***(G-9889)***
Peoples Choice M R I...716 681-7377
125 Galileo Dr Buffalo (14221) ***(G-2912)***
Pep Realty, New York *Also called Atlas Recycling LLC* ***(G-8672)***
Pepe Creations Inc...212 391-1514
2 W 45th St Ste 1003 New York (10036) ***(G-10797)***
Peppermints Salon Inc...718 357-6304
15722 Powells Cove Blvd Whitestone (11357) ***(G-16099)***
Pepsi Beverages Co...518 782-2150
421 Old Niskayuna Rd Latham (12110) ***(G-6871)***
Pepsi Beverages Company, Watertown *Also called Bottling Group LLC* ***(G-15561)***
Pepsi Beverages Company, White Plains *Also called Bottling Group LLC* ***(G-15982)***
Pepsi Beverages Company, White Plains *Also called Bottling Group LLC* ***(G-15983)***
Pepsi Bottling Ventures LLC...631 226-9000
550 New Horizons Blvd Amityville (11701) ***(G-303)***
Pepsi Btlg Group Globl Fin LLC (HQ)...914 767-6000
1 Pepsi Way Ste 1 # 1 Somers (10589) ***(G-14499)***
Pepsi-Cola Bottling Co NY Inc...914 699-2600
601 S Fulton Ave Mount Vernon (10550) ***(G-8169)***
Pepsi-Cola Bottling Co NY Inc (HQ)...718 392-1000
11202 15th Ave College Point (11356) ***(G-3559)***
Pepsi-Cola Bottling Co NY Inc...718 892-1570
650 Brush Ave Bronx (10465) ***(G-1335)***
Pepsi-Cola Bottling Group (HQ)...914 767-6000
1111 Westchester Ave White Plains (10604) ***(G-16046)***
Pepsi-Cola Metro Btlg Co Inc (HQ)...914 767-6000
1111 Westchester Ave White Plains (10604) ***(G-16047)***
Pepsi-Cola Metro Btlg Co Inc...914 253-2000
700 Anderson Hill Rd Purchase (10577) ***(G-13008)***
Pepsi-Cola Metro Btlg Co Inc...607 795-2122
140 Wygant Rd Horseheads (14845) ***(G-6131)***
Pepsi-Cola Metro Btlg Co Inc...585 454-5220
400 Creative Dr Rochester (14624) ***(G-13614)***
Pepsi-Cola Metro Btlg Co Inc...518 834-7811
1524 Route 9 Keeseville (12944) ***(G-6645)***
Pepsi-Cola Newburgh Btlg Inc...845 562-5400
1 Pepsi Way Newburgh (12550) ***(G-11882)***
Pepsi-Cola Operating Company (HQ)...914 767-6000
1111 Westchester Ave White Plains (10604) ***(G-16048)***
Pepsi-Cola Sales and Dist Inc (HQ)...914 253-2000
700 Anderson Hill Rd Purchase (10577) ***(G-13009)***
Pepsico, White Plains *Also called Pepsi-Cola Metro Btlg Co Inc* ***(G-16047)***
Pepsico, Newburgh *Also called Pepsi-Cola Newburgh Btlg Inc* ***(G-11882)***
Pepsico, Purchase *Also called Beverages Foods & Service Inds* ***(G-13002)***
Pepsico, Latham *Also called Pepsi Beverages Co* ***(G-6871)***
Pepsico, Horseheads *Also called Pepsi-Cola Metro Btlg Co Inc* ***(G-6131)***
Pepsico, Keeseville *Also called Pepsi-Cola Metro Btlg Co Inc* ***(G-6645)***
Pepsico, White Plains *Also called Pepsi-Cola Bottling Group* ***(G-16046)***
Pepsico, Amityville *Also called Pepsi Bottling Ventures LLC* ***(G-303)***
Pepsico...419 252-0247
3 Skyline Dr Hawthorne (10532) ***(G-5821)***
Pepsico...914 801-1500
100 Summit Lake Dr # 103 Valhalla (10595) ***(G-15305)***
Pepsico Inc (PA)...914 253-2000
700 Anderson Hill Rd Purchase (10577) ***(G-13010)***
Pepsico Inc...914 253-2000
350 Hudson St New York (10014) ***(G-10798)***
Pepsico Inc...914 253-2000
1111 Westchester Ave White Plains (10604) ***(G-16049)***
Pepsico Inc...914 742-4500
100 E Stevens Ave Valhalla (10595) ***(G-15306)***
Pepsico Inc...914 253-2000
Anderson Hill Rd Purchase (10577) ***(G-13011)***
Pepsico Inc...914 253-3474
150 Airport Rd Hngr V White Plains (10604) ***(G-16050)***
Pepsico Inc...914 253-2713
700 Anderson Hill Rd Purchase (10577) ***(G-13012)***
Pepsico Capital Resources Inc...914 253-2000
700 Anderson Hill Rd Purchase (10577) ***(G-13013)***
Pepsico Design & Innovation...917 405-9307
350 Hudson St New York (10014) ***(G-10799)***
Pepsico Sales Inc...914 253-2000
700 Anderson Hill Rd Purchase (10577) ***(G-13014)***
Per Annum Inc...212 647-8700
555 8th Ave Rm 202 New York (10018) ***(G-10800)***
Peraflex Hose Inc...716 876-8806
155 Great Arrow Ave Ste 4 Buffalo (14207) ***(G-2913)***
Peralta Metal Works Inc...718 649-8661
602 Atkins Ave Brooklyn (11208) ***(G-2254)***
Peraton Inc...315 838-7000
474 Phoenix Dr Rome (13441) ***(G-13863)***
Peregrine Industries Inc...631 838-2870
40 Wall St New York (10005) ***(G-10801)***
Pereira & ODell LLC...212 897-1000
5 Crosby St Rm 5h New York (10013) ***(G-10802)***
Perfect Form Manufacturing LLC...585 500-5923
1325 John St West Henrietta (14586) ***(G-15800)***
Perfect Forms and Systems Inc...631 462-1100
35 Riverview Ter Smithtown (11787) ***(G-14484)***
Perfect Gear & Instrument (HQ)...516 328-3330
250 Duffy Ave Hicksville (11801) ***(G-5943)***
Perfect Gear & Instrument...516 873-6122
125 Railroad Ave Garden City Park (11040) ***(G-5123)***
Perfect Poly Inc...631 265-0539
1 Gina Ct Nesconset (11767) ***(G-8220)***
Perfect Publications, Brooklyn *Also called Joseph Paul* ***(G-2001)***

Perfect Shoulder Company Inc 914 699-8100
2 Cortlandt St Mount Vernon (10550) *(G-8170)*

Perfection Gear Inc 716 592-9310
172 Eaton St Springville (14141) *(G-14595)*

Perforated Screen Surfaces 866 866-8690
216 Broome Corporate Pkwy Conklin (13748) *(G-3627)*

Performance Advantage Co Inc 716 683-7413
6 W Main St Lowr Rear Lancaster (14086) *(G-6824)*

Performance Custom Trailer 518 504-4021
230 Lockhart Mountain Rd Lake George (12845) *(G-6758)*

Performance Designed By Peters 585 223-9062
7 Duxbury Hts Fairport (14450) *(G-4515)*

Performance Diesel Service LLC 315 854-5269
24 Latour Ave Plattsburgh (12901) *(G-12767)*

Performance Lacrosse Group Inc (HQ) 315 453-3073
4697 Crossroads Park Dr Liverpool (13088) *(G-7032)*

Performance Mfg Inc 716 735-3500
80 Telegraph Rd Middleport (14105) *(G-7889)*

Performance Precision Mfg LLC 518 993-3033
55 Willett St Fort Plain (13339) *(G-4947)*

Performance Sourcing Group Inc (PA) 914 636-2100
109 Montgomery Ave Scarsdale (10583) *(G-14240)*

Performance Systems Contg Inc 607 277-6240
124 Brindley St Ithaca (14850) *(G-6404)*

Performance Technologies Inc (HQ) 585 256-0200
3500 Winton Pl Ste 4 Rochester (14623) *(G-13615)*

Performance Wire & Cable Inc 315 245-2594
9482 State Route 13 Camden (13316) *(G-3106)*

Perfumers Workshop Intl Ltd (PA) 212 644-8950
350 7th Ave Rm 802 New York (10001) *(G-10803)*

Peri-Facts Academy 585 275-6037
601 Elmwood Ave Rochester (14642) *(G-13616)*

Perimondo LLC 212 749-0721
331 W 84th St Apt 2 New York (10024) *(G-10804)*

Periodical Services Co Inc 518 822-9300
351 Fairview Ave Ste 300 Hudson (12534) *(G-6174)*

Perkins International Inc (HQ) 309 675-1000
672 Delaware Ave Buffalo (14209) *(G-2914)*

Perma Glow Ltd Inc 212 575-9677
48 W 48th St Ste 301 New York (10036) *(G-10805)*

Perma Tech Inc 716 854-0707
363 Hamburg St Buffalo (14204) *(G-2915)*

Permanent Observer Mission 212 883-0140
320 E 51st St New York (10022) *(G-10806)*

Permanent Press, Sag Harbor *Also called Second Chance Press Inc (G-14102)*

Permit Fashion Group Inc 212 912-0988
111 Forster Pl Melville (11747) *(G-7815)*

Peroxychem LLC 716 873-0812
35 Sawyer Ave Tonawanda (14150) *(G-15132)*

Perretta Graphics Corp 845 473-0550
46 Violet Ave Poughkeepsie (12601) *(G-12978)*

Perrigo Company 718 960-9900
1625 Bathgate Ave Bronx (10457) *(G-1336)*

Perrigo New York Inc 718 901-2800
455 Claremont Pkwy Bronx (10457) *(G-1337)*

Perrigo New York Inc (HQ) 718 960-9900
1700 Bathgate Ave Bronx (10457) *(G-1338)*

Perrottas Bakery Inc 518 283-4711
766 Pawling Ave Troy (12180) *(G-15178)*

Perry Ellis America, New York *Also called Perry Ellis Menswear LLC (G-10809)*

Perry Ellis International Inc 212 536-5400
1126 Avenue Of The Americ New York (10036) *(G-10807)*

Perry Ellis International Inc 212 536-5499
42 W 39th St Fl 4 New York (10018) *(G-10808)*

Perry Ellis Menswear LLC (HQ) 212 221-7500
1120 Avenue Of The Americ New York (10036) *(G-10809)*

Perry Plastics Inc 718 747-5600
3050 Whitestone Expy # 300 Flushing (11354) *(G-4887)*

Perry Street Software Inc 415 935-1429
489 5th Ave Rm 29a New York (10017) *(G-10810)*

Perrys Ice Cream Company Inc 716 542-5492
1 Ice Cream Plz Akron (14001) *(G-20)*

Persch Service Print Inc (PA) 716 366-2677
11 W 3rd St Dunkirk (14048) *(G-4063)*

Perseus Books Group, New York *Also called Clp Pb LLC (G-9039)*

Personal Graphics Corporation 315 853-3421
5123 State Route 233 Westmoreland (13490) *(G-15961)*

Perugina Div, New York *Also called Nestle Usa Inc (G-10568)*

Pervi Precision Company Inc 631 589-5557
220 Knickerbocker Ave # 1 Bohemia (11716) *(G-1061)*

PES Group, Brooklyn *Also called Project Energy Savers LLC (G-2300)*

Pesce Bakery, Saugerties *Also called Pesces Bakery Inc (G-14208)*

Pesces Bakery Inc 845 246-4730
20 Pesce Ct Saugerties (12477) *(G-14208)*

Pesselnik & Cohen Inc 212 925-0287
82 Bowery Unit 10 New York (10013) *(G-10811)*

Pet Authority, Brooklyn *Also called Dynamic Health Labs Inc (G-1767)*

Pet Proteins LLC 888 293-1029
347 W 36th St Rm 1204 New York (10018) *(G-10812)*

Pete Levin Music Inc 845 247-9211
598 Schoolhouse Rd Saugerties (12477) *(G-14209)*

Peter Atman Inc 212 644-8882
6 E 45th St Rm 1100 New York (10017) *(G-10813)*

Peter C Herman Inc 315 926-4100
5395 Skinner Rd Marion (14505) *(G-7573)*

Peter Digioia 516 644-5517
7 Sherwood Dr Plainview (11803) *(G-12707)*

Peter Kwasny Inc 727 641-1462
400 Oser Ave Ste 1650 Hauppauge (11788) *(G-5740)*

Peter Lang Publishing Inc (HQ) 212 647-7700
29 Broadway Rm 1800 New York (10006) *(G-10814)*

Peter Mayer Publishers Inc 212 673-2210
195 Broadway Fl 9 New York (10007) *(G-10815)*

Peter Papastrat 607 723-8112
193 Main St Binghamton (13905) *(G-904)*

Peter Pauper Press Inc 914 681-0144
202 Mmaroneck Ave Ste 400 White Plains (10601) *(G-16051)*

Peter Productions Devivi Inc 315 568-8484
2494 Kingdom Rd Waterloo (13165) *(G-15556)*

Peter Racing 914 968-4150
73 Market St Yonkers (10710) *(G-16341)*

Peter S Curtis 315 782-7363
25465 Ny State Rt 342 Evans Mills (13637) *(G-4487)*

Peter Thomas Roth Labs LLC (PA) 212 581-5800
460 Park Ave Fl 16 New York (10022) *(G-10816)*

Peters LLC 607 637-5470
5259 Peas Eddy Rd Hancock (13783) *(G-5538)*

Petit Printing Corp 716 871-9490
42 Hunters Gln Getzville (14068) *(G-5181)*

Petnet Solutions Inc 865 218-2000
660 1st Ave Rm 140 New York (10016) *(G-10817)*

Petre Alii Petroleum 315 785-1037
1268 Arsenal St Watertown (13601) *(G-15587)*

Petrillo's Bakery, Fairport *Also called Scaife Enterprises Inc (G-4519)*

Petro Inc 516 686-1900
477 W John St Hicksville (11801) *(G-5944)*

Petro River Oil Corp (PA) 469 828-3900
205 E 42nd St Fl 14 New York (10017) *(G-10818)*

Petrune, Ithaca *Also called Petrunia LLC (G-6405)*

Petrunia LLC 607 277-1930
126 E State St Ithaca (14850) *(G-6405)*

Petteys Lumber 518 792-5943
10247 State Route 149 Fort Ann (12827) *(G-4934)*

Pexip Inc (HQ) 703 338-3544
240 W 35th St Ste 400 New York (10001) *(G-10819)*

Peyser Instrument Corporation 631 841-3600
40 Gleam St West Babylon (11704) *(G-15736)*

Pezera Associates, Calverton *Also called East End Country Kitchens Inc (G-3080)*

Pfannenberg Inc 716 685-6866
68 Ward Rd Lancaster (14086) *(G-6825)*

Pfannenberg Manufacturing LLC 716 685-6866
68 Ward Rd Lancaster (14086) *(G-6826)*

Pfaudler Inc (HQ) 585 235-1000
1000 West Ave Rochester (14611) *(G-13617)*

Pfaudler US Inc 585 235-1000
1000 West Ave Rochester (14611) *(G-13618)*

Pfaudler USA, Rochester *Also called Pfaudler Inc (G-13617)*

Pfeil & Holing Inc 718 545-4600
5815 Northern Blvd Woodside (11377) *(G-16219)*

Pfisterer Lapp LLC 585 768-6221
130 Gilbert St Le Roy (14482) *(G-6906)*

Pfizer HCP Corporation (HQ) 212 733-2323
235 E 42nd St New York (10017) *(G-10820)*

Pfizer Inc (PA) 212 733-2323
235 E 42nd St New York (10017) *(G-10821)*

Pfizer Inc 518 297-6611
64 Maple St Rouses Point (12979) *(G-14066)*

Pfizer Inc 914 437-5868
4 Martine Ave White Plains (10606) *(G-16052)*

Pfizer Inc 937 746-3603
150 E 42nd St Fl 38 New York (10017) *(G-10822)*

Pfizer Inc 212 733-6276
150 E 42nd St Bsmt 2 New York (10017) *(G-10823)*

Pfizer Overseas LLC 212 733-2323
235 E 42nd St New York (10017) *(G-10824)*

PGM, Rochester *Also called Precision Grinding & Mfg Corp (G-13636)*

Pgs Millwork Inc (PA) 518 828-2608
32 Hickory Ln Hudson (12534) *(G-6175)*

PH David J Rossi 585 455-1160
50 Celtic Ln Rochester (14626) *(G-13619)*

Phaidon Press Inc 212 652-5400
65 Bleecker St Fl 8 New York (10012) *(G-10825)*

Phantom Laboratory Inc 518 692-1190
2727 State Route 29 Greenwich (12834) *(G-5475)*

Phantom Laboratory, The, Greenwich *Also called Phantom Laboratory Inc (G-5475)*

Pharbest Pharmaceuticals Inc 631 249-5130
14 Engineers Ln Ste 1 Farmingdale (11735) *(G-4705)*

Pharmaderm, Melville *Also called Fougera Pharmaceuticals Inc (G-7785)*

Pharmadva LLC 585 469-1410
36 King St Rochester (14608) *(G-13620)*

Pharmalife Inc 631 249-4040
130 Gazza Blvd Farmingdale (11735) *(G-4706)*

A
L
P
H
A
B
E
T
I
C

Pharmavantage LLC 631 321-8171
15 Lakeland Ave Babylon (11702) **(G-523)**
PHASE IL MARKETING DBA, Amherst *Also called Nexstar Holding Corp* **(G-234)**
Phelinger Tool & Die Corp 716 685-1780
1254 Town Line Rd Alden (14004) **(G-172)**
Phelps Cement Products Inc 315 548-9415
5 S Newark St Phelps (14532) **(G-12606)**
Pheonix Custom Furniture Ltd 212 727-2648
2107 41st Ave Fl 2 Long Island City (11101) **(G-7325)**
Philadelphia Coatings LLC 917 929-4738
780 3rd Ave Fl 22 New York (10017) **(G-10826)**
Philcom Ltd 716 875-8005
1144 Military Rd Buffalo (14217) **(G-2916)**
Philip Morris Globl Brands Inc (HQ) 917 663-2000
120 Park Ave Fl 6 New York (10017) **(G-10827)**
Philip Morris Intl Inc (PA) 917 663-2000
120 Park Ave Fl 6 New York (10017) **(G-10828)**
Philipp Feldheim Inc (PA) 845 356-2282
208 Airport Executive Par Nanuet (10954) **(G-8203)**
Philippe Adec Paris, New York *Also called Morelle Products Ltd* **(G-10502)**
Philips Elec N Amer Corp 607 776-3692
7265 State Route 54 Bath (14810) **(G-639)**
Philips Healthcare, Latham *Also called Philips Medical Systems Mr* **(G-6872)**
Philips Medical Systems Mr (HQ) 518 782-1122
450 Old Niskayuna Rd Latham (12110) **(G-6872)**
Phillip J Ortiz Manufacturing 845 226-7030
44 Railroad Ave Hopewell Junction (12533) **(G-6100)**
Phillip Tissicher 718 282-3310
1688 Utica Ave Brooklyn (11234) **(G-2255)**
Phillips-Van Heusen Europe 212 381-3500
200 Madison Ave Bsmt 1 New York (10016) **(G-10829)**
Philpac Corporation (PA) 716 875-8005
1144 Military Rd Buffalo (14217) **(G-2917)**
Phoenix Envmtl Svcs Corp 718 381-8100
7314 88th St Glendale (11385) **(G-5231)**
Phoenix Graphics Inc 585 232-4040
464 State St 470 Rochester (14608) **(G-13621)**
Phoenix Laboratories Inc 516 822-1230
200 Adams Blvd Farmingdale (11735) **(G-4707)**
Phoenix Material Handling, Phoenix *Also called Phoenix Welding & Fabg Inc* **(G-12619)**
Phoenix Metal Designs Inc 516 597-4100
100 Hinsdale St Brooklyn (11207) **(G-2256)**
Phoenix Metal Products Inc 516 546-4200
100 Bennington Ave Freeport (11520) **(G-5015)**
Phoenix Usa LLC 646 351-6598
315 W 33rd St Apt 30h New York (10001) **(G-10830)**
Phoenix Venture Fund LLC 212 759-1909
70 E 55th St Fl 10 New York (10022) **(G-10831)**
Phoenix Welding & Fabg Inc 315 695-2223
10 County Route 6 Phoenix (13135) **(G-12619)**
Phoenix Wood Wrights Ltd 631 727-9691
132 Kroemer Ave 3 Riverhead (11901) **(G-13184)**
Photo Agents Ltd 631 421-0258
716 New York Ave Huntington (11743) **(G-6217)**
Photo Industry Inc 516 364-0016
7600 Jericho Tpke Ste 301 Woodbury (11797) **(G-16179)**
Photo Medic Equipment Inc 631 242-6600
3 Saxwood St Ste E Deer Park (11729) **(G-3918)**
Photograve Corporation 718 667-4825
1140 S Railroad Ave Staten Island (10306) **(G-14688)**
Photon Gear Inc 585 265-3360
245 David Pkwy Ontario (14519) **(G-12297)**
Photon Vision Systems Inc (PA) 607 749-2689
1 Technology Pl Homer (13077) **(G-6066)**
Photonamics Inc 585 247-8990
558 Elmgrove Rd Rochester (14606) **(G-13622)**
Photonic Controls LLC 607 562-4585
500 1st Ctr Ste 2 Horseheads (14845) **(G-6132)**
Photonics Industries Intl Inc (PA) 631 218-2240
1800 Ocean Ave Unit A Ronkonkoma (11779) **(G-13994)**
Photonix Technologies Inc 607 786-4600
48 Washington Ave Endicott (13760) **(G-4471)**
Photonstring Inc 917 966-5717
35 Shore Dr Godeffroy (12729) **(G-5302)**
Phototherapeutix, Glens Falls *Also called Medtek Skin Care Inc* **(G-5258)**
Phyljohn Distributors Inc 518 459-2775
6 Interstate Ave Albany (12205) **(G-115)**
Phymetrix Inc 631 627-3950
28 Scouting Blvd Ste C Medford (11763) **(G-7721)**
Physical Review, Ridge *Also called American Physical Society* **(G-13132)**
Physicalmind Institute 212 343-2150
84 Wooster St Ste 605 New York (10012) **(G-10832)**
Phytofilter Technologies Inc 518 507-6399
9 Kirby Rd Apt 19 Saratoga Springs (12866) **(G-14187)**
Piaggio Group Americas Inc 212 380-4400
257 Park Ave S Fl 4 New York (10010) **(G-10833)**
Piano Software Inc (PA) 646 350-1999
1 World Trade Ctr Ste 46d New York (10007) **(G-10834)**
Piazzas Ice Cream Ice Hse Inc 718 818-8811
41 Housman Ave Staten Island (10303) **(G-14689)**
Pibbs Industries, Flushing *Also called P S Pibbs Inc* **(G-4882)**
Pic A Poc Enterprises Inc 631 981-2094
53 Union Ave Ronkonkoma (11779) **(G-13995)**
Pic Nic LLC 914 245-6500
51 Mahopac Ave Amawalk (10501) **(G-200)**
Picador USA 646 307-5629
175 5th Ave New York (10010) **(G-10835)**
Piccini Industries Ltd 845 365-0614
37 Ramland Rd Orangeburg (10962) **(G-12325)**
Piccini Mnm Inc 845 741-6770
35 Highland Ave West Nyack (10994) **(G-15830)**
Pickett Building Materials, Oneonta *Also called Arnan Development Corp* **(G-12257)**
Picone Meat Specialties Ltd 914 381-3002
180 Jefferson Ave Mamaroneck (10543) **(G-7519)**
Picone's Sausage, Mamaroneck *Also called Picone Meat Specialties Ltd* **(G-7519)**
Pictoure Inc 212 641-0098
110 Wall St New York (10005) **(G-10836)**
Picture Perfect Framing 718 851-1884
1758 50th St Brooklyn (11204) **(G-2257)**
Pidyon Controls Inc (PA) 212 683-9523
141 W 24th St Apt 4 New York (10011) **(G-10837)**
Piemonte Company, Woodside *Also called Piemonte Home Made Ravioli Co* **(G-16220)**
Piemonte Home Made Ravioli Co (PA) 718 429-1972
3436 65th St Woodside (11377) **(G-16220)**
Piemonte Home Made Ravioli Co 212 226-0475
190 Grand St New York (10013) **(G-10838)**
Pier-Tech Inc 516 442-5420
7 Hampton Rd Oceanside (11572) **(G-12184)**
Pierce Arrow Draperies, Buffalo *Also called Pierce Arrow Drapery Mfg* **(G-2918)**
Pierce Arrow Drapery Mfg 716 876-3023
1685 Elmwood Ave Ste 312 Buffalo (14207) **(G-2918)**
Pierce Industries LLC 585 458-0888
465 Paul Rd Ste A Rochester (14624) **(G-13623)**
Pierce Steel Fabricators 716 372-7652
430 N 7th St Olean (14760) **(G-12240)**
Pierrepont Visual Graphics 585 305-9672
15 Elser Ter Rochester (14611) **(G-13624)**
Pietro Demarco Importers Inc 914 969-3201
1185 Saw Mill River Rd Yonkers (10710) **(G-16342)**
Pietryka Plastics LLC 845 855-1201
85 Charles Colman Blvd Pawling (12564) **(G-12528)**
Pii Holdings Inc (HQ) 716 876-9951
2150 Elmwood Ave Buffalo (14207) **(G-2919)**
Pilates Designs LLC 718 721-5929
3517 31st St Astoria (11106) **(G-434)**
Pilgrim Foods Co, Great Neck *Also called Old Dutch Mustard Co Inc* **(G-5408)**
Pilgrim Surf & Supply 718 218-7456
68 N 3rd St Brooklyn (11249) **(G-2258)**
Pilkington North America Inc 315 438-3341
6412 Deere Rd Ste 1 Syracuse (13206) **(G-14964)**
Piller Power Systems Inc (HQ) 845 695-6658
45 Wes Warren Dr Middletown (10941) **(G-7926)**
Pillow Perfections Ltd Inc 718 383-2259
252 Norman Ave Ste 101 Brooklyn (11222) **(G-2259)**
Pilot Inc (PA) 212 951-1133
421 W 24th St Apt 4c New York (10011) **(G-10839)**
Pilot Inc 212 951-1133
110 E 25th St New York (10010) **(G-10840)**
Pilot Products Inc 718 728-2141
2413 46th St Long Island City (11103) **(G-7326)**
Pin Pharma Inc 212 543-2583
55 Broadway Ste 315 New York (10006) **(G-10841)**
Pindar Vineyards LLC 631 734-6200
37645 Route 25 Peconic (11958) **(G-12547)**
Pinder International Inc (PA) 631 273-0324
1140 Motor Pkwy Ste A Hauppauge (11788) **(G-5741)**
Pine Barrens Printing, Westhampton Beach *Also called Michael K Lennon Inc* **(G-15957)**
Pine Bush Printing Co Inc 518 456-2431
2005 Western Ave Albany (12203) **(G-116)**
Pine Tree Farms Inc 607 532-4312
3714 Cayuga St Interlaken (14847) **(G-6286)**
Pingmd Inc 212 632-2665
136 Madison Ave Fl 6 New York (10016) **(G-10842)**
Pink Inc 212 352-8282
23 E 10th St Apt 1b New York (10003) **(G-10843)**
Pink and Palmer, Rye *Also called Judith N Graham Inc* **(G-14082)**
Pink Box Accessories LLC 718 435-2821
940 40th St Brooklyn (11219) **(G-2260)**
Pink Crush LLC 718 788-6978
1410 Broadway Rm 1002 New York (10018) **(G-10844)**
Pinnacle Manufacturing Co Inc 585 343-5664
56 Harvester Ave Batavia (14020) **(G-623)**
Pinos Press Inc 315 935-0110
201 E Jefferson St Syracuse (13202) **(G-14965)**
Pins and Lanes, Lowville *Also called Qubicaamf Worldwide LLC* **(G-7420)**
Pins N Needles 212 535-6222
1045 Lexington Ave Apt 2n New York (10021) **(G-10845)**
Pintail Coffee Inc 631 396-0808
1776 New Hwy Farmingdale (11735) **(G-4708)**
Pintrill LLC 718 782-1000
185 Wythe Ave Brooklyn (11249) **(G-2261)**
Pioneer Printers Inc 716 693-7100
1087 Erie Ave North Tonawanda (14120) **(G-12082)**

Pioneer Window Holdings Inc (PA).........................516 822-7000
3 Expressway Plz Ste 221 Roslyn Heights (11577) *(G-14055)*
Pioneer Window Holdings Inc................................518 762-5526
200 Union Ave Johnstown (12095) *(G-6625)*
Pioneer Windows Manufacturing, Roslyn Heights Also called Pioneer Window Holdings Inc *(G-14055)*
PIP Inc...518 861-0133
968 Albany Shaker Rd Latham (12110) *(G-6873)*
PIP Printing, Oceanside Also called Ahw Printing Corp *(G-12165)*
PIP Printing, Latham Also called PIP Inc *(G-6873)*
PIP Printing, Lynbrook Also called Pro Printing *(G-7435)*
PIP Printing, Syosset Also called Vivona Business Printers Inc *(G-14805)*
PIP Printing, White Plains Also called Alamar Printing Inc *(G-15969)*
PIP Printing, Hicksville Also called Marcal Printing Inc *(G-5925)*
Piper Plastics Corp (PA).....................................631 842-6889
102 Ralph Ave Copiague (11726) *(G-3668)*
Piper Plastics Corp..631 842-6889
105 Ralph Ave Copiague (11726) *(G-3669)*
Piping Solutions Inc...646 258-5381
4601c 1st Ave Brooklyn (11232) *(G-2262)*
Pirnat Precise Metals Inc...................................631 293-9169
127 Marine St Farmingdale (11735) *(G-4709)*
Pirod Inc...631 231-7660
15 Oser Ave Hauppauge (11788) *(G-5742)*
Piroke Trade Inc...646 515-1537
1430 35th St Fl 2 Brooklyn (11218) *(G-2263)*
Pisarro Nights, New York Also called JBS Limited *(G-9985)*
Pit Stop Motorsports, Forestville Also called P S M Group Inc *(G-4932)*
Pitney Bowes Inc...212 564-7548
637 W 27th St Fl 8 New York (10001) *(G-10846)*
Pitney Bowes Inc...203 356-5000
90 Park Ave Rm 1110 New York (10016) *(G-10847)*
Pitney Bowes Inc...516 822-0900
200 Robbins Ln Unit B2 Jericho (11753) *(G-6589)*
Pitney Bowes Software Inc...................................518 285-6000
350 Jordan Rd Ste 1 Troy (12180) *(G-15179)*
Pivot Punch Corporation......................................716 625-8000
6550 Campbell Blvd Lockport (14094) *(G-7101)*
Pivot Records LLC..718 417-1213
600 Johnson Ave Brooklyn (11237) *(G-2264)*
Piwik Pro LLC..888 444-0049
222 Broadway Fl 19 New York (10038) *(G-10848)*
Pixacore, New York Also called Intstrux LLC *(G-9932)*
Pixos Print..585 500-4600
75 Goodway Dr Rochester (14623) *(G-13625)*
Pizza Blends LLC...518 356-6650
1411 Rottrdm Indstl Park Schenectady (12306) *(G-14295)*
Pj Decorators Inc..516 735-9693
257 Pontiac Pl East Meadow (11554) *(G-4139)*
Pk Metals, Coram Also called Suffolk Indus Recovery Corp *(G-3700)*
Pk30 System LLC..212 473-8050
3607 Atwood Rd Stone Ridge (12484) *(G-14736)*
Pkg Group..212 965-0112
560 Broadway Rm 406 New York (10012) *(G-10849)*
Pl Developments, Copiague Also called P & L Development LLC *(G-3667)*
Pl Developments, Westbury Also called P & L Development LLC *(G-15915)*
Pl Developments New York, Westbury Also called P & L Development LLC *(G-15914)*
Place Vendome Holding Co Inc................................212 696-0765
230 5th Ave Ste 1112 New York (10001) *(G-10850)*
Placid Baker...518 326-2657
250 Broadway Troy (12180) *(G-15180)*
Placid Industries, Elmira Also called Sepac Inc *(G-4367)*
Planar Optics Inc..585 671-0100
858 Hard Rd Webster (14580) *(G-15647)*
Planet Embroidery..718 381-4827
6695 Forest Ave Ridgewood (11385) *(G-13155)*
Planet Gold Clothing Co Inc.................................646 432-5100
500 Fashion Ave Fl 17a New York (10018) *(G-10851)*
Planet Motherhood, Brooklyn Also called Zoomers Inc *(G-2606)*
Plant Office, Wyoming Also called Texas Brine Company LLC *(G-16252)*
Plant Science Laboratories LLC..............................716 228-4553
649 Wyoming Ave Buffalo (14215) *(G-2920)*
Plant-Tech2o Inc...516 483-7845
30 Chasner St Hempstead (11550) *(G-5847)*
Plascal Corp...516 249-2200
361 Eastern Pkwy Farmingdale (11735) *(G-4710)*
Plascoline Inc...917 410-5754
275 Madison Ave Fl 14th New York (10016) *(G-10852)*
Plaslok Corp...716 681-7755
3155 Broadway St Buffalo (14227) *(G-2921)*
Plastic & Reconstructive Svcs...............................914 584-5605
333 N Bedford Rd Mount Kisco (10549) *(G-8102)*
Plastic Solutions Inc..631 234-9013
158 Schenck Ave Bayport (11705) *(G-730)*
Plastic Sys/Gr Bflo Inc......................................716 835-7555
465 Cornwall Ave Buffalo (14215) *(G-2922)*
Plastic Works..914 576-2050
26 Garden St New Rochelle (10801) *(G-8349)*
Plastic-Craft Products Corp.................................845 358-3010
744 W Nyack Rd West Nyack (10994) *(G-15831)*

Plasticware LLC (PA)...845 267-0790
13 Wilsher Dr Monsey (10952) *(G-8043)*
Plasticweld Systems, Newfane Also called Vante Inc *(G-11896)*
Plasticycle Corporation (PA).................................914 997-6882
245 Main St Ste 430 White Plains (10601) *(G-16053)*
Plastifold Industries Division, Brooklyn Also called Visitainer Corp *(G-2564)*
Plastirun Corporation..631 273-2626
70 Emjay Blvd Bldg A Brentwood (11717) *(G-1126)*
Plastitel Usa Inc..800 667-2313
641 Ridge Rd Bldg 7 Chazy (12921) *(G-3335)*
Plastpac Inc...908 272-7200
32 Walton St Brooklyn (11206) *(G-2265)*
Platform Experts Inc...646 843-7100
2938 Quentin Rd Brooklyn (11229) *(G-2266)*
Platina, New York Also called Alexander Primak Jewelry Inc *(G-8513)*
Platinum Printing & Graphics................................631 249-3325
70 Carolyn Blvd Ste C Farmingdale (11735) *(G-4711)*
Platinum Sales Promotion Inc................................718 361-0200
3514a Crescent St Long Island City (11106) *(G-7327)*
Plattco Corporation (PA).....................................518 563-4640
7 White St Plattsburgh (12901) *(G-12768)*
Plattco Corporation..518 563-4640
18 White St Plattsburgh (12901) *(G-12769)*
Platter's Chocolates, North Tonawanda Also called Roger L Urban Inc *(G-12089)*
Plattsburgh Press-Republican, Plattsburgh Also called Community Newspaper Group LLC *(G-12743)*
Plattsburgh Quarry, Plattsburgh Also called Graymont Materials Inc *(G-12749)*
Plattsburgh Sheet Metal Inc.................................518 561-4930
95 Sailly Ave Plattsburgh (12901) *(G-12770)*
Playbill Incorporated (PA)...................................212 557-5757
729 7th Ave Fl 4 New York (10019) *(G-10853)*
Playbill Incorporated..718 335-4033
3715 61st St Woodside (11377) *(G-16221)*
Playfitness Corp...917 497-5443
27 Palisade St Staten Island (10305) *(G-14690)*
Plaza Braceltte Mounting, New Hyde Park Also called Satco Castings Service Inc *(G-8291)*
Pleasure Chest Sales Ltd.....................................212 242-2158
156 7th Ave S New York (10014) *(G-10854)*
Pleatco LLC..516 609-0200
28 Garvies Point Rd Glen Cove (11542) *(G-5198)*
Plectica LLC...646 941-8822
25 Broadway Fl 9 New York (10004) *(G-10855)*
Plexi Craft Quality Products................................212 924-3244
200 Lexington Ave Rm 914 New York (10016) *(G-10856)*
Pliant LLC...315 986-6286
200 Main St Macedon (14502) *(G-7469)*
Pliotron Company America LLC................................716 298-4457
4650 Witmer Indus Est Niagara Falls (14305) *(G-11965)*
Plt, Rochester Also called Precision Laser Technology LLC *(G-13637)*
Plug Power Inc...585 474-3993
1200 Ridgeway Ave Ste 123 Rochester (14615) *(G-13626)*
Plug Power Inc (PA)..518 782-7700
968 Albany Shaker Rd Latham (12110) *(G-6874)*
Plugg LLC..212 840-6655
1410 Broadway Frnt 2 New York (10018) *(G-10857)*
Plura Broadcast Inc (PA).....................................516 997-5675
67 Grand Ave Massapequa (11758) *(G-7647)*
Plures Technologies Inc (PA)................................585 905-0554
4070 County Road 16 Canandaigua (14424) *(G-3140)*
Pluribus Products Inc..718 852-1614
1 Overlook Ave Bayville (11709) *(G-747)*
Pluslux LLC..516 371-4400
461 Doughty Blvd Inwood (11096) *(G-6302)*
Plx Inc..631 586-4190
40 W Jefryn Blvd Deer Park (11729) *(G-3919)*
PM Spirits LLC...347 689-4414
505 Johnson Ave Apt 17 Brooklyn (11237) *(G-2267)*
Pmb Precision Products Inc...................................631 491-6753
725 Mount Ave West Babylon (11704) *(G-15737)*
Pmd, Victor Also called Progressive Mch & Design LLC *(G-15425)*
PMF, Brooklyn Also called Precision Mtal Fabricators Inc *(G-2277)*
PMG, Ronkonkoma Also called Paul Michael Group Inc *(G-13993)*
PMI Global Services Inc......................................917 663-2000
120 Park Ave Fl 6 New York (10017) *(G-10858)*
PMI Industries LLC...585 464-8050
350 Buell Rd Rochester (14624) *(G-13627)*
Pmrnyc, Brooklyn Also called Total Metal Resource *(G-2513)*
PNC Sports...516 665-2244
1880 Deer Park Ave Deer Park (11729) *(G-3920)*
Pneumercator Company Inc....................................631 293-8450
1785 Express Dr N Hauppauge (11788) *(G-5743)*
Pni Capital Partners...516 466-7120
1400 Old Country Rd # 103 Westbury (11590) *(G-15917)*
Podravka International USA...................................212 661-0125
420 Lexington Ave Rm 2034 New York (10170) *(G-10859)*
Poerformance Design, Fairport Also called Performance Designed By Peters *(G-4515)*
Poetry Mailing List Marsh Hawk..............................516 766-1891
2823 Rockaway Ave Oceanside (11572) *(G-12185)*
Poets House Inc..212 431-7920
10 River Ter New York (10282) *(G-10860)*

A
L
P
H
A
B
E
T
I
C

Point Canvas Company Inc 607 692-4381
5952 State Route 26 Whitney Point (13862) **(G-16107)**
Point Electric Div, Blauvelt *Also called Swivelier Company Inc* **(G-934)**
Point Industrial, Bemus Point *Also called Lakeside Industries Inc* **(G-812)**
Point of Sale Outfitters, Geneva *Also called R M Reynolds* **(G-5161)**
Pointman LLC (PA) 716 842-1439
403 Main St Ste 200 Buffalo (14203) **(G-2923)**
Pointwise Information Service 315 457-4111
223 1st St Liverpool (13088) **(G-7033)**
Pol-Tek Industries Ltd 716 823-1502
2300 Clinton St Buffalo (14227) **(G-2924)**
Pole-Tech Co Inc 631 689-5525
97 Gnarled Hollow Rd East Setauket (11733) **(G-4184)**
Poletech Flagpole Manufaturer, East Setauket *Also called Pole-Tech Co Inc* **(G-4184)**
Polich Tallix Inc 845 567-9464
453 State Route 17k Rock Tavern (12575) **(G-13821)**
Policy ADM Solutions Inc 914 332-4320
505 White Plains Rd Tarrytown (10591) **(G-15052)**
Polish American Journal, Orchard Park *Also called Panagraphics Inc* **(G-12370)**
Political Risk Services, The, East Syracuse *Also called The PRS Group Inc* **(G-4242)**
POLITICAL SCIENCE QUARTERLY, New York *Also called Academy of Political Science* **(G-8437)**
Polkadot Usa Inc 914 835-3697
33 Country Rd Mamaroneck (10543) **(G-7520)**
Pollack Graphics Inc 212 727-8400
601 W 26th St Ste M204 New York (10001) **(G-10861)**
Pollardwater, New Hyde Park *Also called Ferguson Enterprises Inc* **(G-8269)**
Polly Treating, New York *Also called Xinya International Trading Co* **(G-11799)**
Polo Ralph Lauren Hosiery Div, New York *Also called Hot Sox Company Incorporated* **(G-9818)**
Poly Can, Carthage *Also called David Johnson* **(G-3197)**
Poly Craft Industries Corp 631 630-6731
40 Ranick Rd Hauppauge (11788) **(G-5744)**
Poly Scientific R&D Corp 631 586-0400
70 Cleveland Ave Bay Shore (11706) **(G-698)**
Poly-Flex Corp (PA) 631 586-9500
250 Executive Dr Ste S Edgewood (11717) **(G-4277)**
Poly-Pak Industries Inc (PA) 800 969-1933
125 Spagnoli Rd Melville (11747) **(G-7816)**
Polycast Industries Inc 631 595-2530
130 S 2nd St Bay Shore (11706) **(G-699)**
Polycom Inc 212 372-6960
1 Penn Plz Fl 48 New York (10119) **(G-10862)**
Polygen Pharmaceuticals Inc 631 392-4044
41 Mercedes Way Unit 17 Edgewood (11717) **(G-4278)**
Polymag Inc 631 286-4111
685 Station Rd Ste 2 Bellport (11713) **(G-807)**
Polymag Tek Inc 585 235-8390
215 Tremont St Ste 2 Rochester (14608) **(G-13628)**
Polymer Conversions Inc 716 662-8550
5732 Big Tree Rd Orchard Park (14127) **(G-12372)**
Polymer Engineered Pdts Inc 585 426-1811
23 Moonlanding Rd Rochester (14624) **(G-13629)**
Polymer Slutions Group Fin LLC (PA) 212 771-1717
100 Park Ave Fl 31 New York (10017) **(G-10863)**
Polymers Merona Inc 631 862-8010
347 Lake Ave Ste 4 Saint James (11780) **(G-14112)**
Polyplastic Forms Inc 631 249-5011
49 Gazza Blvd Farmingdale (11735) **(G-4712)**
Polyset Company Inc 518 664-6000
65 Hudson Ave Mechanicville (12118) **(G-7693)**
Polyshot Corporation 585 292-5010
75 Lucius Gordon Dr West Henrietta (14586) **(G-15801)**
Polytech Pool Mfg Inc 718 492-8991
262 48th St 262 Brooklyn (11220) **(G-2268)**
Polytex Inc 716 549-5100
1305 Eden Evans Center Rd Angola (14006) **(G-360)**
Pom Industries LLC 800 695-4791
251 W 39th St Fl 2 New York (10018) **(G-10864)**
Pompian Manufacturing Co Inc 914 476-7076
280 Nepperhan Ave Yonkers (10701) **(G-16343)**
Poncio Signs 718 543-4851
3007 Albany Cres Bronx (10463) **(G-1339)**
Ponder, New York *Also called Parlor Labs Inc* **(G-10765)**
Ponti Rossi Inc 347 506-9616
186 Franklin St Apt C16 Brooklyn (11222) **(G-2269)**
Pony Farm Press & Graphics 607 432-9020
330 Pony Farm Rd Oneonta (13820) **(G-12280)**
Pooran Pallet Inc 718 938-7970
319 Barretto St Bronx (10474) **(G-1340)**
Pop A2z, New York *Also called Sky Frame & Art Inc* **(G-11263)**
Pop Nyc, New York *Also called Popnyc 1 LLC* **(G-10865)**
Pop Printing Incorporated 212 808-7800
299 24th St Brooklyn (11232) **(G-2270)**
Popnyc 1 LLC 646 684-4600
75 Saint Nicholas Pl 2e New York (10032) **(G-10865)**
Poppin Inc 212 391-7200
16 Madison Sq W Fl 3 New York (10010) **(G-10866)**
Popular Mechanics, New York *Also called Hearst Corporation* **(G-9749)**
Popular Pattern, New York *Also called Stephen Singer Pattern Co Inc* **(G-11359)**
Pork King Sausage Inc 718 542-2810
F22 Hunts Point Co Op Mkt Bronx (10474) **(G-1341)**
Porous Materials Inc 607 257-5544
20 Dutch Mill Rd Ithaca (14850) **(G-6406)**
Port Authority of NY & NJ 718 390-2534
2777 Goethals Rd N Fl 2 Staten Island (10303) **(G-14691)**
Port Everglades Machine Works 516 367-2280
57 Colgate Dr Plainview (11803) **(G-12708)**
Port Jackson Media, Amsterdam *Also called McClary Media Inc* **(G-334)**
Port Jervis Machine Corp 845 856-6210
176 1/2 Jersey Ave Port Jervis (12771) **(G-12855)**
Portequip Work Stations, Niagara Falls *Also called Stephenson Custom Case Company* **(G-11982)**
Portfolio Decisionware Inc 212 947-1326
235 W 48th St New York (10036) **(G-10867)**
Portfolio Media Inc 646 783-7100
111 W 19th St Fl 5 New York (10011) **(G-10868)**
Portville Sand & Gravel Div, Portville *Also called IA Construction Corporation* **(G-12935)**
Portware LLC (HQ) 212 425-5233
233 Broadway Fl 24 New York (10279) **(G-10869)**
Poseidon Systems LLC 585 239-6025
200 Canal View Blvd # 300 Rochester (14623) **(G-13630)**
Posillico Materials LLC 631 249-1872
1750 New Hwy Farmingdale (11735) **(G-4713)**
Posimech Inc 631 924-5959
15 Scouting Blvd Unit 3 Medford (11763) **(G-7722)**
Positive Print Litho Offset 212 431-4850
121 Varick St Rm 204 New York (10013) **(G-10870)**
Positive Promotions Inc (PA) 631 648-1200
15 Gilpin Ave Hauppauge (11788) **(G-5745)**
Post Heritage Inc 646 286-7579
266 90th St Brooklyn (11209) **(G-2271)**
Post Journal 716 487-1111
412 Murray Ave Jamestown (14701) **(G-6536)**
Post Road 203 545-2122
101 E 16th St Apt 4b New York (10003) **(G-10871)**
Post Standard, The, Syracuse *Also called Herald Newspapers Company Inc* **(G-14911)**
Post Star, Glens Falls *Also called Lee Enterprises Incorporated* **(G-5255)**
Post-Journal, The, Jamestown *Also called Ogden Newspapers Inc* **(G-6535)**
Post-Standard CNY Department 315 470-2188
101 N Salina St Syracuse (13202) **(G-14966)**
Potential Poly Bag Inc 718 258-0800
1253 Coney Island Ave Brooklyn (11230) **(G-2272)**
Potsdam Specialty Paper Inc 315 265-4000
547a Sissonville Rd Potsdam (13676) **(G-12939)**
Potsdam Stone Concrete, Plattsburgh *Also called Upstone Materials Inc* **(G-12788)**
Potter Lumber Co Inc 716 373-1260
3786 Potter Rd Allegany (14706) **(G-190)**
Potters Industries LLC 315 265-4920
56 Reynolds Rd Norwood (13668) **(G-12132)**
Poughkeepsie Journal, Poughkeepsie *Also called Gannett Stllite Info Ntwrk LLC* **(G-12956)**
Poultry Dist, Brooklyn *Also called Vineland Kosher Poultry Inc* **(G-2560)**
Powa Technologies Inc 347 344-7848
1 Bryant Park Ste 39 New York (10036) **(G-10872)**
Power and Cnstr Group Inc 585 889-6020
86 River Rd Scottsville (14546) **(G-14342)**
Power and Composite Tech LLC 518 843-6825
200 Wallins Corners Rd Amsterdam (12010) **(G-345)**
Power Connector Inc 631 563-7878
140 Wilbur Pl Ste 4 Bohemia (11716) **(G-1062)**
Power Gneration Indus Engs Inc 315 633-9389
8927 Tyler Rd Bridgeport (13030) **(G-1168)**
Power Line Constructors Inc 315 853-6183
24 Robinson Rd Clinton (13323) **(G-3484)**
Power Metrics Intl Inc 718 524-4370
1961 Richmond Ter Staten Island (10302) **(G-14692)**
Power Scrub It Inc 516 997-2500
75 Urban Ave Westbury (11590) **(G-15918)**
Power Up Manufacturing Inc 716 876-4890
275 N Pointe Pkwy Ste 100 Buffalo (14228) **(G-2925)**
Power-Flo Technologies Inc 315 399-5801
6500 New Venture Gear Dr East Syracuse (13057) **(G-4230)**
Power-Flo Technologies Inc 585 426-4607
62 Marway Cir Rochester (14624) **(G-13631)**
Powerflow Inc 716 892-1014
1714 Broadway St Buffalo (14212) **(G-2926)**
Powerhouse Books, Brooklyn *Also called Powerhouse Cultural Entrmt Inc* **(G-2273)**
Powerhouse Cultural Entrmt Inc 212 604-9074
126a Front St Brooklyn (11201) **(G-2273)**
Powermate Cellular 718 833-9400
140 58th St Ste 1d Brooklyn (11220) **(G-2274)**
Powers Fasteners, Brewster *Also called Black & Decker (us) Inc* **(G-1143)**
Powertex Inc (PA) 518 297-4000
1 Lincoln Blvd Ste 101 Rouses Point (12979) **(G-14067)**
Powertex Bulk Shipg Solutions, Rouses Point *Also called Powertex Inc* **(G-14067)**
Powr-UPS Corp 631 345-5700
1 Roned Rd Shirley (11967) **(G-14427)**
Poz Publishing, New York *Also called Smart & Strong LLC* **(G-11271)**
Ppc Broadband Inc (HQ) 315 431-7200
6176 E Molloy Rd East Syracuse (13057) **(G-4231)**

Ppi Corp 585 880-7277
275 Commerce Dr Rochester (14623) *(G-13632)*
Ppi Corp 585 243-0300
275 Commerce Dr Rochester (14623) *(G-13633)*
Ppr Direct Marketing LLC (PA) 718 965-8600
74 20th St Brooklyn (11232) *(G-2275)*
PR & Stone & Tile Inc 718 383-1115
17 Beadel St Brooklyn (11222) *(G-2276)*
Pragmatics Technology Inc 845 795-5071
14 Old Indian Trl Milton (12547) *(G-7951)*
Pratt With ME Hmi Met Powders, Clayville *Also called Hmi Metal Powders (G-3456)*
Praxair Inc 716 879-2000
175 E Park Dr Tonawanda (14150) *(G-15133)*
Praxair Inc 716 649-1600
5322 Scranton Rd Hamburg (14075) *(G-5516)*
Praxair Inc 518 482-4360
120 Railroad Ave Albany (12205) *(G-117)*
Praxair Inc 716 286-4600
4501 Royal Ave Niagara Falls (14303) *(G-11966)*
Praxair Inc 845 359-4200
542 Route 303 Orangeburg (10962) *(G-12326)*
Praxair Inc 716 879-4000
135 E Park Dr Tonawanda (14150) *(G-15134)*
Praxair Distribution Inc 315 457-5821
4560 Morgan Pl Liverpool (13090) *(G-7034)*
Praxair Distribution Inc 716 879-2185
345 Evans St Apt A Buffalo (14221) *(G-2927)*
Praxair Distribution Inc 315 735-6153
9432 State Route 49 Marcy (13403) *(G-7565)*
Praxair Surface Tech Inc 845 398-8322
560 Route 303 Orangeburg (10962) *(G-12327)*
Praxis Powder Technology Inc 518 812-0112
604 Queensbury Ave Queensbury (12804) *(G-13052)*
PRC Liquidating Company 212 823-9626
10 Columbus Cir New York (10019) *(G-10873)*
Pre Cycled Inc 845 278-7611
1689 Route 22 Brewster (10509) *(G-1158)*
Pre-Tech Plastics Inc 518 942-5950
3085 Plank Rd Mineville (12956) *(G-8005)*
Precare Corp (PA) 631 667-1055
150 Marcus Blvd Hauppauge (11788) *(G-5746)*
Precimed Inc 716 759-5600
10000 Wehrle Dr Clarence (14031) *(G-3440)*
Precious Plate Inc 716 283-0690
2124 Liberty Dr Niagara Falls (14304) *(G-11967)*
Precipart Corporation (HQ) 631 694-3100
120 Finn Ct Ste 2 Farmingdale (11735) *(G-4714)*
Precise Optics, Deer Park *Also called Photo Medic Equipment Inc (G-3918)*
Precise Punch Corporation 716 625-8000
6550 Campbell Blvd Lockport (14094) *(G-7102)*
Precise Tool & Mfg Inc 585 247-0700
9 Coldwater Cres Rochester (14624) *(G-13634)*
Preciseled Inc 516 418-5337
52 Railroad Ave Valley Stream (11580) *(G-15352)*
Precision Abrasives Corp 716 826-5833
3176 Abbott Rd Orchard Park (14127) *(G-12373)*
Precision Apparel Mfg LLC 201 805-2664
3 Hanover Sq Apt 14g New York (10004) *(G-10874)*
Precision Arms Inc 845 225-1130
421 Route 52 Carmel (10512) *(G-3190)*
Precision Assembly Tech Inc 631 699-9400
160 Wilbur Pl Ste 500 Bohemia (11716) *(G-1063)*
Precision Built Tops LLC 607 336-5417
89 Borden Ave Norwich (13815) *(G-12126)*
Precision Charts Inc 631 244-8295
130 Wilbur Pl Bohemia (11716) *(G-1064)*
Precision Cnc 631 847-3999
71 E Jefryn Blvd Deer Park (11729) *(G-3921)*
Precision Co., Menands *Also called McAllisters Precision Wldg Inc (G-7844)*
Precision Cosmetics Mfg Co 914 667-1200
519 S 5th Ave Ste 6 Mount Vernon (10550) *(G-8171)*
Precision Dental Cabinets Inc (PA) 631 543-3870
900 W Jericho Tpke Smithtown (11787) *(G-14485)*
Precision Design Systems Inc 585 426-4500
1645 Lyell Ave Ste 136 Rochester (14606) *(G-13635)*
Precision Diecutting Inc 315 776-8465
1381 Spring Lake Rd Port Byron (13140) *(G-12811)*
Precision Eforming LLC 607 753-7730
839 State Route 13 Ste 1 Cortland (13045) *(G-3783)*
Precision Elctro Mnrl Pmco Inc 716 284-2484
150 Portage Rd Niagara Falls (14303) *(G-11968)*
Precision Electronics Inc 631 842-4900
1 Di Tomas Ct Copiague (11726) *(G-3670)*
Precision Engraving Company, Amityville *Also called Precision Signscom Inc (G-304)*
Precision Envelope Co Inc 631 694-3990
110 Schmitt Blvd 7a Farmingdale (11735) *(G-4715)*
Precision Extrusion Inc 518 792-1199
12 Glens Fls Technical Pa Glens Falls (12801) *(G-5265)*
Precision Fabrication LLC 585 591-3449
40 S Pearl St Attica (14011) *(G-458)*
Precision Filters Inc (PA) 607 277-3550
240 Cherry St Ithaca (14850) *(G-6407)*
Precision Furniture, Bronx *Also called Precision Orna Ir Works Inc (G-1342)*
Precision Gear Incorporated 718 321-7200
11207 14th Ave College Point (11356) *(G-3560)*
Precision Grinding & Mfg Corp (PA) 585 458-4300
1305 Emerson St Rochester (14606) *(G-13636)*
Precision Index Equipment Inc 631 468-8776
1555 Ocean Ave Ste A Bohemia (11716) *(G-1065)*
Precision International Co Inc 212 268-9090
201 E 28th St 9n New York (10016) *(G-10875)*
Precision Label Corporation 631 270-4490
50 Marcus Blvd Hauppauge (11788) *(G-5747)*
Precision Laser Technology LLC 585 458-6208
1001 Lexington Ave Ste 4 Rochester (14606) *(G-13637)*
Precision Locker, Jamestown *Also called Rollform of Jamestown Inc (G-6539)*
Precision Machine Parts, Valatie *Also called Weiss Industries Inc (G-15301)*
Precision Machine Tech LLC 585 467-1840
85 Excel Dr Rochester (14621) *(G-13638)*
Precision Magnetics LLC 585 385-9010
770 Linden Ave Rochester (14625) *(G-13639)*
Precision Mechanisms Corp 516 333-5955
50 Bond St Westbury (11590) *(G-15919)*
Precision Metals Corp 631 586-5032
221 Skip Ln Bay Shore (11706) *(G-700)*
Precision Mtal Fabricators Inc 718 832-9805
236 39th St Brooklyn (11232) *(G-2277)*
Precision N Amer Fd McHy LLC 518 462-3387
60 Commerce Ave Ste 42 Albany (12206) *(G-118)*
Precision Orna Ir Works Inc 718 379-5200
1838 Adee Ave Bronx (10469) *(G-1342)*
Precision Packaging Pdts Inc 585 638-8200
88 Nesbitt Dr Holley (14470) *(G-6037)*
Precision Pharma Services Inc 631 752-7314
155 Duryea Rd Melville (11747) *(G-7817)*
Precision Photo-Fab Inc 716 821-9393
4020 Jeffrey Blvd Buffalo (14219) *(G-2928)*
Precision Plus Vacuum Parts 716 297-2039
6416 Inducon Dr W Sanborn (14132) *(G-14147)*
Precision Polish LLC 315 894-3792
144 Adams St Frankfort (13340) *(G-4955)*
Precision Process Inc (PA) 716 731-1587
2111 Liberty Dr Niagara Falls (14304) *(G-11969)*
Precision Product Inc 718 852-7127
18 Steuben St Brooklyn (11205) *(G-2278)*
Precision Ready Mix Inc 718 658-5600
14707 Liberty Ave Jamaica (11435) *(G-6465)*
Precision Signscom Inc 631 841-7500
243 Dixon Ave Amityville (11701) *(G-304)*
Precision Spclty Fbrctions LLC 716 824-2108
51 N Gates Ave Buffalo (14218) *(G-2929)*
Precision Systems Mfg Inc 315 451-3480
4855 Executive Dr Liverpool (13088) *(G-7035)*
Precision Techniques Inc 718 991-1440
25 Holt Dr Stony Point (10980) *(G-14747)*
Precision Tool and Mfg 518 678-3130
314 Pennsylvania Ave Palenville (12463) *(G-12480)*
Precision Valve & Automtn Inc (PA) 518 371-2684
1 Mustang Dr Ste 3 Cohoes (12047) *(G-3513)*
Precisionmatics Co Inc 315 822-6324
1 Helmer Ave West Winfield (13491) *(G-15858)*
Predator Mountainwear Inc 315 727-3241
324 Fire Lane 15 Auburn (13021) *(G-490)*
Preebro Printing 718 633-7300
5319 Fort Hamilton Pkwy Brooklyn (11219) *(G-2279)*
Preferred Fragrance, Newburgh *Also called Fragrance Acquisitions LLC (G-11865)*
Preferred Wholesale, New York *Also called R-S Restaurant Eqp Mfg Corp (G-10969)*
Prejean Winery Inc 315 536-7524
2634 State Route 14 Penn Yan (14527) *(G-12590)*
Preload Concrete Structures 631 231-8100
60 Commerce Dr Hauppauge (11788) *(G-5748)*
Premco Inc 914 636-7095
11 Beechwood Ave New Rochelle (10801) *(G-8350)*
Premier Brands America Inc 718 325-3000
555 E 242nd St Bronx (10470) *(G-1343)*
Premier Brands America Inc (PA) 914 667-6200
170 Hamilton Ave Ste 201 White Plains (10601) *(G-16054)*
Premier Brands America Inc 718 325-3000
120 Pearl St Mount Vernon (10550) *(G-8172)*
Premier Brnds Group Hldngs LLC (HQ) 215 785-4000
1441 Broadway New York (10018) *(G-10876)*
Premier Brnds Group Hldngs LLC 212 642-3860
1411 Broadway New York (10018) *(G-10877)*
Premier Brnds Group Hldngs LLC 212 575-2571
1441 Broadway Fl 20 New York (10018) *(G-10878)*
Premier Brnds Group Hldngs LLC 212 642-3860
575 Fashion Ave Frnt 1 New York (10018) *(G-10879)*
Premier Cabinet Wholesalers, Rochester *Also called Rochester Countertop Inc (G-13687)*
Premier Care Industries, Hauppauge *Also called Precare Corp (G-5746)*
Premier Finishing Inc 716 484-6271
85 Jones And Gifford Ave Jamestown (14701) *(G-6537)*
Premier Glass New York Inc 718 967-7179
22 Brienna Ct Staten Island (10309) *(G-14693)*
Premier Glass Services, Staten Island *Also called Premier Glass New York Inc (G-14693)*

ALPHABETIC

Premier Hardwood Products Inc.....315 492-1786
4800 Solvay Rd Jamesville (13078) ***(G-6561)***
Premier Heart LLC.....516 883-3383
110 Main St Port Washington (11050) ***(G-12915)***
Premier Ingridients Inc.....516 641-6763
3 Johnstone Rd Great Neck (11021) ***(G-5414)***
Premier Ink Systems Inc.....845 782-5802
2 Commerce Dr S Harriman (10926) ***(G-5546)***
Premier Knits Ltd.....718 323-8264
9735 133rd Ave Ozone Park (11417) ***(G-12466)***
Premier Machining Tech Inc.....716 608-1311
2100 Old Union Rd Buffalo (14227) ***(G-2930)***
Premier Packaging Corporation.....585 924-8460
6 Framark Dr Victor (14564) ***(G-15424)***
Premier Paint Roller Co LLC.....718 441-7700
13111 Atlantic Ave Richmond Hill (11418) ***(G-13119)***
Premier Paint Roller Co LLC (PA).....718 441-7700
13111 Atlantic Ave Richmond Hill (11418) ***(G-13120)***
Premier Prcision Machining LLC.....716 665-5217
2072 Allen Street Ext Falconer (14733) ***(G-4551)***
Premier Sign Systems LLC.....585 235-0390
10 Excel Dr Rochester (14621) ***(G-13640)***
Premier Skirting Products Inc.....516 239-6581
241 Mill St Lawrence (11559) ***(G-6890)***
Premier Skrting Tblecloths Too, Lawrence *Also called Premier Skirting Products Inc* ***(G-6890)***
Premier Store Fixtures, Hauppauge *Also called Fixtures 2000 Inc* ***(G-5651)***
Premier Systems LLC.....631 587-9700
41 John St Ste 6 Babylon (11702) ***(G-524)***
Premier Woodcraft Ltd.....610 383-6624
277 Martine Ave 214 White Plains (10601) ***(G-16055)***
Premier Woodworking Inc.....631 236-4100
400 Oser Ave Hauppauge (11788) ***(G-5749)***
Premiere Living Products LLC.....631 873-4337
22 Branwood Dr Dix Hills (11746) ***(G-4013)***
Premium 5 Kids LLC.....212 563-4999
31 W 34th St New York (10001) ***(G-10880)***
Premium Assure Inc.....605 252-9999
1726 Mcdonald Ave Ste 201 Brooklyn (11230) ***(G-2280)***
Premium Bldg Components Inc.....518 885-0194
831 Rt 67 Bldg 46 Ballston Spa (12020) ***(G-585)***
Premium Mulch & Materials Inc.....631 320-3666
482 Mill Rd Coram (11727) ***(G-3698)***
Premium Ocean LLC.....917 231-1061
1271 Ryawa Ave Bronx (10474) ***(G-1344)***
Premium Processing Corp.....631 232-1105
30 Kittiwake Ln Babylon (11702) ***(G-525)***
Premium Sweets USA Inc.....718 739-6000
16803 Hillside Ave Jamaica (11432) ***(G-6466)***
Premium Wine Group LLC.....631 298-1900
35 Cox Neck Rd Mattituck (11952) ***(G-7678)***
Premium Woodworking LLC.....631 485-3133
108 Lamar St West Babylon (11704) ***(G-15738)***
Prepac Designs Inc.....914 524-7800
25 Abner Pl Yonkers (10704) ***(G-16344)***
Preparatory Magazine Group.....718 761-4800
1200 South Ave Ste 202 Staten Island (10314) ***(G-14694)***
Presbrey- Leland Memorials, Valhalla *Also called Presbrey-Leland Inc* ***(G-15307)***
Presbrey-Leland Inc.....914 949-2264
250 Lakeview Ave Valhalla (10595) ***(G-15307)***
Prescribing Reference Inc.....646 638-6000
275 7th Ave Fl 10 New York (10001) ***(G-10881)***
Prescriptives Inc (HQ).....212 572-4400
767 5th Ave New York (10153) ***(G-10882)***
Preserving Chrstn Publications (PA).....315 942-6617
12614 State Route 46 Boonville (13309) ***(G-1108)***
President Cont Group II LLC.....845 516-1600
290 Ballard Rd Middletown (10941) ***(G-7927)***
Presray Corporation.....845 373-9300
32 Nelson Hill Rd Wassaic (12592) ***(G-15526)***
Press Express.....914 592-3790
400 Executive Blvd # 146 Elmsford (10523) ***(G-4422)***
Press Glass Na Inc (PA).....212 631-3044
1345 Ave Of The Flr 2 New York (10105) ***(G-10883)***
Press of Manorville & Moriches, Southampton *Also called Southampton Town Newspapers* ***(G-14538)***
Press Room New York Division, New York *Also called Circle Press Inc* ***(G-9011)***
Pressed Juice LLC (PA).....646 573-9157
205 Clinton Ave Apt 12a Brooklyn (11205) ***(G-2281)***
Presser Kosher Baking Corp.....718 375-5088
1720 Avenue M Brooklyn (11230) ***(G-2282)***
Presstek Printing.....585 266-2770
20 Balfour Dr Rochester (14621) ***(G-13641)***
Presstek Printing LLC.....585 467-8140
521 E Ridge Rd Rochester (14621) ***(G-13642)***
Presstek Printing LLC.....585 266-2770
20 Balfour Dr Rochester (14621) ***(G-13643)***
Pressure Washer Sales, Holland Patent *Also called Custom Klean Corp* ***(G-6033)***
Prestacycle Llc.....518 588-5546
689 Riverview Rd Rexford (12148) ***(G-13097)***
Prestel Publishing LLC.....212 995-2720
900 Broadway Ste 603 New York (10003) ***(G-10884)***
Presti Ready Mix Concrete Inc.....516 378-6006
210 E Merrick Rd Freeport (11520) ***(G-5016)***
Presti Stone and Mason, Freeport *Also called Presti Ready Mix Concrete Inc* ***(G-5016)***
Prestige Box Corporation (PA).....516 773-3115
115 Cuttermill Rd Great Neck (11021) ***(G-5415)***
PRESTIGE BRANDS, Tarrytown *Also called Prestige Consmr Healthcare Inc* ***(G-15054)***
Prestige Brands Intl LLC.....914 524-6800
660 White Plains Rd Tarrytown (10591) ***(G-15053)***
Prestige Consmr Healthcare Inc (PA).....914 524-6800
660 White Plains Rd Tarrytown (10591) ***(G-15054)***
Prestige Envelope & Lithograph.....631 521-7043
1745 Merrick Ave Ste 2 Merrick (11566) ***(G-7863)***
Prestige Global NY Sls Corp.....212 776-4322
42 W 38th St Rm 802 New York (10018) ***(G-10885)***
Prestige Hangers Str Fixs Corp.....718 522-6777
1026 55th St Brooklyn (11219) ***(G-2283)***
Prestige Litho & Graphics, Merrick *Also called Prestige Envelope & Lithograph* ***(G-7863)***
Prestige Printing Company, Brooklyn *Also called 6727 11th Ave Corp* ***(G-1421)***
Prestigeline Inc.....631 273-3636
5 Inez Dr Bay Shore (11706) ***(G-701)***
Prestolite Electric Inc.....585 492-2278
400 Main St Arcade (14009) ***(G-380)***
Preston Glass Industries Inc.....718 997-8888
10420 Queens Blvd Apt 17a Forest Hills (11375) ***(G-4926)***
Pretty Fuel Inc.....315 823-4063
29 W Lansing St Little Falls (13365) ***(G-6991)***
Prevail Therapeutics Inc.....917 336-9310
430 E 29th St Ste 940 New York (10016) ***(G-10886)***
Prevost Car (us) Inc.....518 957-2052
260 Banker Rd Plattsburgh (12901) ***(G-12771)***
Prg Integrated Solutions, Armonk *Also called Production Resource Group LLC* ***(G-401)***
Price Chopper Pharmacy, Catskill *Also called Golub Corporation* ***(G-3211)***
Price Chopper Pharmacy, Oneida *Also called Golub Corporation* ***(G-12244)***
Price Chopper Pharmacy, Norwich *Also called Golub Corporation* ***(G-12122)***
Price Chopper Pharmacy, Hudson *Also called Golub Corporation* ***(G-6158)***
Price Chopper Pharmacy, Middletown *Also called Golub Corporation* ***(G-7913)***
Price Chopper Pharmacy 184, Malta *Also called Golub Corporation* ***(G-7496)***
Pricet Printing.....315 655-0369
3852 Charles Rd Cazenovia (13035) ***(G-3234)***
Pricing Engine Inc.....917 549-3289
175 Varick St Fl 4 New York (10014) ***(G-10887)***
Pride & Joys Inc.....212 594-9820
1400 Broadway Rm 503 New York (10018) ***(G-10888)***
Pride Lines Ltd.....631 225-0033
651 W Hoffman Ave Lindenhurst (11757) ***(G-6970)***
Pride Pak Inc.....905 828-2149
11531 Maple Ridge Rd Medina (14103) ***(G-7743)***
Prim Hall Enterprises Inc.....518 561-7408
11 Spellman Rd Plattsburgh (12901) ***(G-12772)***
Prima Satchel Inc.....929 367-7770
51 Forest Rd Ste 302 Monroe (10950) ***(G-8029)***
Primary Wave Publishing LLC.....212 661-6990
116 E 16th St Fl 9 New York (10003) ***(G-10889)***
Prime Cook (wttc) Inc (PA).....646 881-0068
15038 Jewel Ave Flushing (11367) ***(G-4888)***
Prime Electric Motors Inc.....718 784-1124
4850 33rd St Long Island City (11101) ***(G-7328)***
Prime Food Processing Corp.....718 963-2323
300 Vandervoort Ave Brooklyn (11211) ***(G-2284)***
Prime Garments Inc.....212 354-7294
66 Randall Ave Rockville Centre (11570) ***(G-13833)***
Prime Materials Recovery Inc.....315 697-5251
51 Madison Blvd Canastota (13032) ***(G-3154)***
Prime Pack LLC.....732 253-7734
303 5th Ave Rm 1007 New York (10016) ***(G-10890)***
Prime Pharmaceutical, New York *Also called Prime Pack LLC* ***(G-10890)***
Prime Research Solutions LLC.....917 836-7941
7328 136th St Flushing (11367) ***(G-4889)***
Prime Time, Garden City *Also called Richner Communications Inc* ***(G-5113)***
Prime Tool & Die LLC.....607 334-5435
6277 County Road 32 Norwich (13815) ***(G-12127)***
Prime Turbine Parts LLC.....518 306-7306
77 Railroad Pl Saratoga Springs (12866) ***(G-14188)***
Prime View USA Inc.....212 730-4905
36 W 44th St Ste 812 New York (10036) ***(G-10891)***
Prime Wood Products.....518 792-1407
1288 Vaughn Rd Queensbury (12804) ***(G-13053)***
Primelite Manufacturing Corp.....516 868-4411
407 S Main St Freeport (11520) ***(G-5017)***
Primesouth Inc.....585 567-4191
11537 Route 19 Fillmore (14735) ***(G-4794)***
Primo Coat Corp.....718 349-2070
4315 Queens St Fl 3 Long Island City (11101) ***(G-7329)***
Primo Frozen Desserts Inc.....718 252-2312
1633 Utica Ave Brooklyn (11234) ***(G-2285)***
Primo Plastics Inc.....718 349-1000
162 Russell St Brooklyn (11222) ***(G-2286)***
Primoplast Inc.....631 750-0680
1555 Ocean Ave Ste E Bohemia (11716) ***(G-1066)***
Prince Black Distillery Inc.....212 695-6187
425 Underhill Blvd Unit 4 Syosset (11791) ***(G-14799)***

Prince Minerals, New York *Also called American Minerals Inc (G-8556)*
Prince Rubber & Plas Co Inc (PA)....225 272-1653
137 Arthur St Buffalo (14207) *(G-2931)*
Prince Seating Corp....718 363-2300
1355 Atlantic Ave Brooklyn (11216) *(G-2287)*
Princess Marcella Borghese, New York *Also called Borghese Inc (G-8837)*
Princess Music Publishing Co....212 586-0240
1650 Broadway Ste 701 New York (10019) *(G-10892)*
Princetel Inc....914 579-2410
200 Saw Mill River Rd Hawthorne (10532) *(G-5822)*
Princeton Label & Packaging....609 490-0800
217 River Ave Patchogue (11772) *(G-12510)*
Princeton Upholstery Co Inc (PA)....845 343-2196
51 Railroad Ave Middletown (10940) *(G-7928)*
Principia Partners LLC....212 480-2270
140 Broadway Fl 46 New York (10005) *(G-10893)*
Princton Archtctural Press LLC (HQ)....518 671-6100
202 Warren St Hudson (12534) *(G-6176)*
Print & Graphics Group....518 371-4649
12 Fire Rd Ste 3 Clifton Park (12065) *(G-3470)*
Print Better Inc....347 348-1841
5939 Myrtle Ave Ridgewood (11385) *(G-13156)*
Print Center Inc....718 643-9559
3 Harbor Rd Ste 21 Cold Spring Harbor (11724) *(G-3529)*
Print City Corp....212 487-9778
165 W 29th St New York (10001) *(G-10894)*
Print Cottage LLC....516 369-1749
1138 Lakeshore Dr Massapequa Park (11762) *(G-7660)*
Print Early LLC....718 915-7368
821 Prospect Ave Apt 1a Westbury (11590) *(G-15920)*
Print House Inc....718 443-7500
538 Johnson Ave Brooklyn (11237) *(G-2288)*
Print It Here....516 308-7785
185 Jerusalem Ave Massapequa (11758) *(G-7648)*
Print It Inc....845 371-2227
59 Route 59 Ste 141 Monsey (10952) *(G-8044)*
Print Mall....718 437-7700
4122 16th Ave Brooklyn (11204) *(G-2289)*
Print Management Group Inc....212 213-1555
31 W 34th St Fl 7 New York (10001) *(G-10895)*
Print Market Inc....631 940-8181
66 E Jefryn Blvd Ste 1 Deer Park (11729) *(G-3922)*
Print Masters, Mount Vernon *Also called Con-Tees Custom Printing Ltd (G-8133)*
Print Media Inc....212 563-4040
350 7th Ave Fl 12 New York (10001) *(G-10896)*
Print On Demand Initiative Inc....585 239-6044
1240 Jefferson Rd Rochester (14623) *(G-13644)*
Print Seforim Bzul Inc....718 679-1011
8 Lynch St Apt 6r Brooklyn (11206) *(G-2290)*
Print Shoppe....315 792-9585
311 Turner St Ste 310 Utica (13501) *(G-15291)*
Print Solutions Plus Inc....315 234-3801
7325 Oswego Rd Liverpool (13090) *(G-7036)*
Print Tech Inc....585 202-3888
11 Stablegate Dr Webster (14580) *(G-15648)*
Print-O-Rama Copy Center, Merrick *Also called Leader Printing Inc (G-7859)*
Printcorp Inc....631 696-0641
2050 Ocean Ave Ronkonkoma (11779) *(G-13996)*
Printech Business Systems Inc....212 290-2542
519 8th Ave Fl 3 New York (10018) *(G-10897)*
Printed Deals, Rochester *Also called Valassis Communications Inc (G-13793)*
Printed Image....716 821-1880
1906 Clinton St Buffalo (14206) *(G-2932)*
Printers 3, Hauppauge *Also called Avm Printing Inc (G-5599)*
Printers 3 Inc....631 351-1331
43 Corporate Dr Ste 2 Hauppauge (11788) *(G-5750)*
Printery....516 922-3250
43 W Main St Oyster Bay (11771) *(G-12454)*
Printery....315 253-7403
55 Arterial W Auburn (13021) *(G-491)*
Printex Packaging Corporation....631 234-4300
555 Raymond Dr Islandia (11749) *(G-6343)*
Printfacility Inc....212 349-4009
225 Broadway Fl 3 New York (10007) *(G-10898)*
Printhouse, The, Brooklyn *Also called Print House Inc (G-2288)*
Printing, Hempstead *Also called Reliable Press II Inc (G-5849)*
Printing Emporium, Merrick *Also called D G M Graphics Inc (G-7854)*
Printing Express, Jamaica *Also called Hillside Printing Inc (G-6448)*
Printing Factory LLC....718 451-0500
1940 Utica Ave Brooklyn (11234) *(G-2291)*
Printing House of W S Miller, Oyster Bay *Also called Printery (G-12454)*
Printing Max New York Inc....718 692-1400
2282 Flatbush Ave Brooklyn (11234) *(G-2292)*
Printing Plus, Rochester *Also called Ozipko Enterprises Inc (G-13602)*
Printing Prep Inc....716 852-5011
707 Washington St Buffalo (14203) *(G-2933)*
Printing Prmtnal Solutions LLC....315 474-1110
2320 Milton Ave Ste 5 Syracuse (13209) *(G-14967)*
Printing Promotional Solutions, Syracuse *Also called Printing Prmtnal Solutions LLC (G-14967)*
Printing Resources Inc....518 482-2470
100 Fuller Rd Ste 1 Albany (12205) *(G-119)*
Printing Sales Group Limited....718 258-8860
1856 Flatbush Ave Brooklyn (11210) *(G-2293)*
Printing Spectrum Inc....631 689-1010
12 Research Way Ste 1 East Setauket (11733) *(G-4185)*
Printing X Press Ions....631 242-1992
5 Dix Cir Dix Hills (11746) *(G-4014)*
Printinghouse Press Ltd....212 719-0990
10 E 39th St Rm 700 New York (10016) *(G-10899)*
Printout Copy Corp....718 855-4040
829 Bedford Ave Brooklyn (11205) *(G-2294)*
Printroc Inc....585 461-2556
620 South Ave Rochester (14620) *(G-13645)*
Printutopia....718 788-1545
393 Prospect Ave Brooklyn (11215) *(G-2295)*
Printworks Printing & Design....315 433-8587
5982 E Molloy Rd Syracuse (13211) *(G-14968)*
Printz and Patternz LLC....518 944-6020
1550 Altamont Ave Schenectady (12303) *(G-14296)*
Printz Pttrnz Scrn-Prnting EMB, Schenectady *Also called Printz and Patternz LLC (G-14296)*
Priscilla Quart Co Firts....516 365-2755
160 Plandome Rd Ste 2 Manhasset (11030) *(G-7540)*
Prism Solar Technologies Inc (HQ)....845 883-4200
180 South St Highland (12528) *(G-5962)*
Prismatic Dyeing & Finshg Inc....845 561-1800
40 Wisner Ave Newburgh (12550) *(G-11883)*
Private Lbel Fods Rchester Inc....585 254-9205
1686 Lyell Ave Rochester (14606) *(G-13646)*
Private Portfolio, New York *Also called Coty US LLC (G-9108)*
Pro Drones Usa LLC....718 530-3558
115 E 57th St Fl 11 New York (10022) *(G-10900)*
Pro Metal of NY Corp....516 285-0440
814 W Merrick Rd Valley Stream (11580) *(G-15353)*
Pro Pack, Eagle Bridge *Also called Professional Packg Svcs Inc (G-4073)*
Pro Printers of Greene County, Catskill *Also called Mark T Westinghouse (G-3214)*
Pro Printing....516 561-9700
359 Merrick Rd Lynbrook (11563) *(G-7435)*
Pro Publica Inc....212 514-5250
155 Ave Of The Americas New York (10013) *(G-10901)*
Pro Torque....631 218-8700
1440 Church St Bohemia (11716) *(G-1067)*
Pro-Gear Co Inc....716 684-3811
1120 Niagara St Buffalo (14213) *(G-2934)*
Pro-Line Solutions Inc....914 664-0002
18 Sargent Pl Mount Vernon (10550) *(G-8173)*
Pro-TEC V I P, Gloversville *Also called Protech (llc) (G-5289)*
Pro-Tech Catings Solutions Inc....631 707-9400
250 Executive Dr Ste H Edgewood (11717) *(G-4279)*
Pro-Tech Sno Pusher, Rochester *Also called Pro-Tech Wldg Fabrication Inc (G-13647)*
Pro-Tech Wldg Fabrication Inc....585 436-9855
711 West Ave Rochester (14611) *(G-13647)*
Pro-Teck Coating Inc....716 537-2619
7785 Olean Rd Holland (14080) *(G-6030)*
Pro-Tek Packaging Group, Ronkonkoma *Also called Oaklee International Inc (G-13985)*
Pro-Value Distribution Inc....585 783-1461
1547 Lyell Ave Ste 3 Rochester (14606) *(G-13648)*
Proactive Medical Products LLC....845 205-6004
270 Washington St Mount Vernon (10553) *(G-8174)*
Procab, Woodridge *Also called Professional Cab Detailing Co (G-16194)*
Processing Foundation Inc....415 748-2679
400 Jay St 175 Brooklyn (11201) *(G-2296)*
Procomponents Inc (PA)....516 683-0909
900 Merchants Concourse Westbury (11590) *(G-15921)*
Procter & Gamble Company....646 885-4201
120 W 45th St Fl 3 New York (10036) *(G-10902)*
Product Development Intl LLC....212 279-6170
215 W 40th St Fl 8 New York (10018) *(G-10903)*
Product Integration & Mfg Inc....585 436-6260
55 Fessenden St Rochester (14611) *(G-13649)*
Product Station Inc....516 942-4220
366 N Broadway Ste 410 Jericho (11753) *(G-6590)*
Productand Design Inc....718 858-2440
63 Flushing Ave Unit 322 Brooklyn (11205) *(G-2297)*
Production Metal Cutting Inc....585 458-7136
1 Curlew St Rochester (14606) *(G-13650)*
Production Milling Company....914 666-0792
364 Adams St Ste 5 Bedford Hills (10507) *(G-771)*
Production Resource Group LLC (PA)....877 774-7088
200 Business Park Dr # 109 Armonk (10504) *(G-401)*
Production Resource Group LLC....845 567-5700
539 Temple Hill Rd New Windsor (12553) *(G-8378)*
Producto Corporation....716 484-7131
2980 Turner Rd Jamestown (14701) *(G-6538)*
Producto Electric Corp....845 359-4900
11 Kings Hwy Orangeburg (10962) *(G-12328)*
Professional Cab Detailing Co....845 436-7282
Navogrярsky Rd Woodridge (12789) *(G-16194)*
Professional Health Imaging, Wantagh *Also called R M F Health Management L L C (G-15488)*
Professional Manufacturers....631 586-2440
475 Brook Ave Deer Park (11729) *(G-3923)*

ALPHABETIC

Professional Medical Devices 914 835-0614
10 Century Trl Harrison (10528) *(G-5558)*
Professional Packg Svcs Inc 518 677-5100
62 Owlkill Rd Eagle Bridge (12057) *(G-4073)*
Professional Pavers Corp 718 784-7853
6605 Woodhaven Blvd Bsmt Rego Park (11374) *(G-13081)*
Professional Remodelers Inc 516 565-9300
340 Hempstead Ave Unit A West Hempstead (11552) *(G-15778)*
Professional Solutions Print 631 231-9300
543 Hunter Ave 3 West Islip (11795) *(G-15812)*
Professional Tape Corporation 516 656-5519
100 Pratt Oval Glen Cove (11542) *(G-5199)*
Professional Technologies, Rome *Also called Professional Technology Inc* *(G-13864)*
Professional Technology Inc 315 337-4156
5433 Lowell Rd Rome (13440) *(G-13864)*
Professnal Dsposables Intl Inc (PA) 800 999-6423
2 Nice Pak Park Orangeburg (10962) *(G-12329)*
Professnal Spt Pblications Inc 212 697-1460
519 8th Ave New York (10018) *(G-10904)*
Professnal Spt Pblications Inc 516 327-9500
570 Elmont Rd Elmont (11003) *(G-4387)*
Professnal Spt Pblications Inc 516 327-9500
570 Elmont Rd Ste 202 Elmont (11003) *(G-4388)*
Proficient Surgical Eqp Inc 516 487-1175
99 Seaview Blvd Ste 1c Port Washington (11050) *(G-12916)*
Profile Nyc, New York *Also called Eternal Fortune Fashion LLC* *(G-9412)*
Profile Printing & Graphics (PA) 631 273-2727
275 Marcus Blvd Hauppauge (11788) *(G-5751)*
Profoot Inc (PA) 718 965-8600
74 20th St Fl 2 Brooklyn (11232) *(G-2298)*
Proforma, Westfield *Also called A Trusted Name Inc* *(G-15944)*
Proformance Foods Inc 703 869-3413
42 West St Apt 316 Brooklyn (11222) *(G-2299)*
Progenics Pharmaceuticals Inc (PA) 646 975-2500
1 World Trade Ctr Fl 47 New York (10007) *(G-10905)*
PROGRESS INDUSTRIES SALES, Utica *Also called Fourteen Arnold Ave Corp* *(G-15264)*
Progressive Color Graphics 212 292-8787
122 Station Rd Great Neck (11023) *(G-5416)*
Progressive Fibre Products Co 212 566-2720
160 Broadway Rm 1105 New York (10038) *(G-10906)*
Progressive Graphics & Prtg. 315 331-3635
415 West Ave Newark (14513) *(G-11850)*
Progressive Mch & Design LLC (PA) 585 924-5250
727 Rowley Rd Victor (14564) *(G-15425)*
Progressive Orthotics Ltd (PA) 631 732-5556
280 Middle Country Rd G Selden (11784) *(G-14355)*
Progressive Orthotics Ltd 631 447-3860
285 Sills Rd Bldg 8c East Patchogue (11772) *(G-4155)*
Progressive Products LLC 914 417-6022
4 International Dr # 224 Rye Brook (10573) *(G-14093)*
Progressive Tool Company Inc 607 748-8294
3221 Lawndale St Endwell (13760) *(G-4482)*
Progressus Company Inc 516 255-0245
100 Merrick Rd Ste 510w Rockville Centre (11570) *(G-13834)*
Prohibition Distillery LLC 917 685-8989
10 Union St Roscoe (12776) *(G-14035)*
Project Energy Savers LLC 718 596-6448
68 Jay St Ste 517 Brooklyn (11201) *(G-2300)*
Project Visual, Islandia *Also called Zahk Sales Inc* *(G-6347)*
Projected, Brooklyn *Also called Amplify Education Inc* *(G-1509)*
Prokosch and Sonn Sheet Metal 845 562-4211
772 South St Newburgh (12550) *(G-11884)*
Prolink Industries Inc 212 354-5690
1407 Broadway Rm 3605 New York (10018) *(G-10907)*
Prolocksusa, Hauppauge *Also called Olan Laboratories Inc* *(G-5730)*
Promats Athletics, Delhi *Also called Sportsfield Specialties Inc* *(G-3967)*
Promenade Magazines Inc 212 888-3500
246 W 38th St F10 New York (10018) *(G-10908)*
Prometheus Books Inc 716 691-0133
25 Chapel Woods Buffalo (14221) *(G-2935)*
Prometheus International Inc 718 472-0700
3717 74th St Ste 2f Jackson Heights (11372) *(G-6421)*
Promosuite, New York *Also called Broadcast Manager Inc* *(G-8858)*
Promotional Development Inc 718 485-8550
909 Remsen Ave Brooklyn (11236) *(G-2301)*
Promotional Sales Books LLC 212 675-0364
30 W 26th St Frnt New York (10010) *(G-10909)*
Prompt Bindery Co Inc 212 675-5181
350 W 38th St New York (10018) *(G-10910)*
Prompt Printing Inc 631 454-6524
160 Rome St Farmingdale (11735) *(G-4716)*
Pronovias USA Inc 212 897-6393
45 E 58th St New York (10022) *(G-10911)*
Pronto Gas Heating Sups Inc 718 292-0707
431 E 165th St Fl 2 Bronx (10456) *(G-1345)*
Pronto Jewelry Inc 212 719-9455
23 W 47th St New York (10036) *(G-10912)*
Pronto Printer 914 737-0800
2085 E Main St Ste 3 Cortlandt Manor (10567) *(G-3798)*
Pronto Tool & Die Co Inc 631 981-8920
50 Remington Blvd Ronkonkoma (11779) *(G-13997)*

Proof 7 Ltd 212 680-1843
149 W 27th St Fl 4 New York (10001) *(G-10913)*
Proof Industries Inc 631 694-7663
125 Rome St Farmingdale (11735) *(G-4717)*
Proof Magazine, New York *Also called Rough Draft Publishing LLC* *(G-11087)*
Propak Inc 518 677-5100
70 Owlkill Rd Eagle Bridge (12057) *(G-4074)*
Proper Chemical Ltd 631 420-8000
280 Smith St Farmingdale (11735) *(G-4718)*
Proper Cloth LLC 646 964-4221
495 Broadway Fl 6 New York (10012) *(G-10914)*
Props Displays & Interiors 212 620-3840
132 W 18th St New York (10011) *(G-10915)*
Props For Today, Long Island City *Also called Interiors-Pft Inc* *(G-7249)*
Prospect News Inc 212 374-2800
6 Maiden Ln Fl 9 New York (10038) *(G-10916)*
Prosthetic Rehabilitation Ctr (PA) 845 565-8255
2 Winding Ln Newburgh (12550) *(G-11885)*
Prosthetics By Nelson Inc (PA) 716 894-6666
2959 Genesee St Cheektowaga (14225) *(G-3359)*
Protec Friction Supply, Mount Kisco *Also called Rpb Distributors LLC* *(G-8105)*
Protech (llc) 518 725-7785
11 Cayadutta St Gloversville (12078) *(G-5289)*
Protective Industries Inc (HQ) 716 876-9951
2150 Elmwood Ave Buffalo (14207) *(G-2936)*
Protective Industries Inc. 716 876-9951
2510 Elmwood Ave Buffalo (14217) *(G-2937)*
Protective Lining Corp 718 854-3838
601 39th St Brooklyn (11232) *(G-2302)*
Protective Power Systms & Cntr 845 721-1875
2092 Rt 9 G Staatsburg Staatsburg (12580) *(G-14600)*
Protein Sciences Corporation 203 686-0800
401 N Middletown Rd Pearl River (10965) *(G-12538)*
Protex International Corp 631 563-4250
366 Central Ave Bohemia (11716) *(G-1068)*
Proto Machine Inc 631 392-1159
60 Corbin Ave Ste D Bay Shore (11706) *(G-702)*
Protocase Incorporated 866 849-3911
210 S 8th St Lewiston (14092) *(G-6922)*
Protofast Holding Corp 631 753-2549
182 N Oak St Copiague (11726) *(G-3671)*
Prototype Manufacturing Corp 716 695-1700
836 Wurlitzer Dr North Tonawanda (14120) *(G-12083)*
Provident Fuel Inc 516 224-4427
4 Stillwell Ln Woodbury (11797) *(G-16180)*
Provider Ally, Slingerlands *Also called Technology Partners Inc* *(G-14468)*
Provision Supply LLC (PA) 347 623-0237
1153 55th St Brooklyn (11219) *(G-2303)*
Provisionaire & Co LLC 646 681-8600
630 Flushing Ave Fl 4 Brooklyn (11206) *(G-2304)*
PRSA, New York *Also called Public Relations Soc Amer Inc* *(G-10922)*
Prweek/Prescribing Reference, New York *Also called Haymarket Media Inc* *(G-9738)*
Pry Care Products, Mount Vernon *Also called Pro-Line Solutions Inc* *(G-8173)*
Prym Fashion Americas LLC (HQ) 212 760-9660
470 7th Ave New York (10018) *(G-10917)*
Prz Technologies Inc 716 683-1300
5490 Broadway St Lancaster (14086) *(G-6827)*
Ps38 LLC 212 302-1108
209 W 38th St Fl 5 New York (10018) *(G-10918)*
Psb Ltd 585 654-7078
543 Atlantic Ave Ste 2 Rochester (14609) *(G-13651)*
Psg Innovations Inc 917 299-8986
924 Kilmer Ln Valley Stream (11581) *(G-15354)*
PSI Transit Mix Corp 631 382-7930
34 E Main St Smithtown (11787) *(G-14486)*
Pspi, Potsdam *Also called Potsdam Specialty Paper Inc* *(G-12939)*
Pspi, Elmont *Also called Professnal Spt Pblications Inc* *(G-4388)*
PSR Press Ltd 716 754-2266
415 Ridge St Lewiston (14092) *(G-6923)*
Psychology Today, New York *Also called Sussex Publishers LLC* *(G-11402)*
Psychonomic Society Inc 512 381-1494
233 Spring St Fl 7 New York (10013) *(G-10919)*
Ptc Precision LLC 607 748-8294
3221 Lawndale St Endwell (13760) *(G-4483)*
Pti-Pacific Inc 212 414-8495
16 W 32nd St Rm 306 New York (10001) *(G-10920)*
Pts Financial Technology LLC 844 825-7634
1001 Ave Of The Americas New York (10018) *(G-10921)*
Public Relations Soc Amer Inc (PA) 212 460-1400
120 Wall St Fl 21 New York (10005) *(G-10922)*
Public School, New York *Also called Ps38 LLC* *(G-10918)*
Publicis Health LLC 212 771-5500
2701 Queens Plz N Long Island City (11101) *(G-7330)*
Publimax Printing Corp. 718 366-7133
6615 Traffic Ave Ridgewood (11385) *(G-13157)*
Publishers Clearing House LLC 516 249-4063
265 Spagnoli Rd Ste 1 Melville (11747) *(G-7818)*
Publishers Weekly, New York *Also called Pwxyz LLC* *(G-10939)*
Publishing Group America Inc 646 658-0550
60 E 42nd St Ste 1146 New York (10165) *(G-10923)*
Publishing Medical Journals, Orchard Park *Also called Impact Journals LLC* *(G-12354)*

Publishing Synthesis Ltd......................................212 219-0135
39 Crosby St Apt 2n New York (10013) *(G-10924)*
Publishing Trends, New York *Also called Market Partners International (G-10369)*
Puccio Design International...................................516 248-6426
54 Nassau Blvd Garden City (11530) *(G-5112)*
Puccio European Marble & Onyx, Garden City *Also called Puccio Design International (G-5112)*
Puccio Marble and Onyx, Garden City *Also called European Marble Works Co Inc (G-5099)*
Pugliese Vineyards Inc.......................................631 734-4057
34515 Main Rd Rte 25 Cutchogue (11935) *(G-3817)*
Puglisi & Co..212 300-2285
800 3rd Ave Ste 902 New York (10022) *(G-10925)*
Puig Usa Inc (HQ)...917 208-3219
183 Madison Ave Fl 19 New York (10016) *(G-10926)*
Pullman Mfg Corporation....................................585 334-1350
77 Commerce Dr Rochester (14623) *(G-13652)*
Pulmuone Foods Usa Inc.....................................845 365-3300
30 Rockland Park Ave Tappan (10983) *(G-15037)*
Pulsafeeder Inc (HQ)...585 292-8000
2883 Brghton Hnrietta Twn Rochester (14623) *(G-13653)*
Pulsar Technology Systems Inc..............................718 361-9292
2720 42nd Rd Long Island City (11101) *(G-7331)*
Pulse Plastics Products Inc..................................718 328-5224
1156 E 165th St Bronx (10459) *(G-1346)*
Pumilia's Pizza Shell, Waterville *Also called F & R Enterprises Inc (G-15595)*
Pumpcrete Corporation.......................................716 667-7867
7126 Ellicott Rd Orchard Park (14127) *(G-12374)*
Pura Fruta LLC...415 279-5727
2323 Borden Ave Long Island City (11101) *(G-7332)*
Puracap Laboratories LLC....................................270 586-6386
22715 N Conduit Ave Laurelton (11413) *(G-6885)*
Pure Acoustics Inc..718 788-4411
18 Fuller Pl Brooklyn (11215) *(G-2305)*
Pure Functional Foods Inc...................................315 294-0733
267 State Route 89 Savannah (13146) *(G-14221)*
Pure Ghee Inc (PA)...917 214-5431
33 Cherry St Glen Head (11545) *(G-5213)*
Pure Golds Family Corp......................................516 483-5600
1 Brooklyn Rd Hempstead (11550) *(G-5848)*
Pure Green Holdings Inc.....................................917 209-8811
121 Nassau St New York (10038) *(G-10927)*
Pure Green LLC..800 306-9122
439 Centre Island Rd Oyster Bay (11771) *(G-12455)*
Pure Kemika LLC..718 745-2200
2156 Legion St Bellmore (11710) *(G-787)*
Pure Planet Waters LLC......................................718 676-7900
4809 Avenue N Ste 185 Brooklyn (11234) *(G-2306)*
Pure Trade Us Inc...212 256-1600
347 5th Ave Rm 604 New York (10016) *(G-10928)*
Purebase Networks Inc.......................................646 670-8964
37 Wall St Apt 9a New York (10005) *(G-10929)*
Puregrab LLC...718 935-1959
294 Hoyt St Brooklyn (11231) *(G-2307)*
Purely Maple LLC..203 997-9309
902 Broadway Fl 6 New York (10010) *(G-10930)*
Pureology Research LLC......................................212 984-4360
565 5th Ave New York (10017) *(G-10931)*
Purity Ice Cream Co Inc......................................607 272-1545
700 Cascadilla St Ste A Ithaca (14850) *(G-6408)*
Purity Products Inc...516 767-1967
200 Terminal Dr Plainview (11803) *(G-12709)*
Purvi Enterprises Incorporated..............................347 808-9448
5556 44th St Maspeth (11378) *(G-7635)*
Putnam Cnty News Recorder LLC............................845 265-2468
3 Stone St Cold Spring (10516) *(G-3523)*
Putnam Rolling Ladder Co Inc (PA).........................212 226-5147
32 Howard St New York (10013) *(G-10932)*
Putnam Rolling Ladder Co Inc...............................718 381-8219
444 Jefferson St Brooklyn (11237) *(G-2308)*
PVA, Cohoes *Also called Precision Valve & Automtn Inc (G-3513)*
Pvc Container Corporation...................................518 672-7721
370 Stevers Crossing Rd Philmont (12565) *(G-12614)*
Pvc Industries Inc...518 877-8670
107 Pierce Rd Clifton Park (12065) *(G-3471)*
Pvh Corp (PA)..212 381-3500
200 Madison Ave Bsmt 1 New York (10016) *(G-10933)*
Pvh Corp..845 561-0233
1073 State Route 94 New Windsor (12553) *(G-8379)*
Pvh Corp..631 254-8200
1358 The Arches Cir Deer Park (11729) *(G-3924)*
Pvh Corp..212 549-6000
285 Madison Ave Fl 2 New York (10017) *(G-10934)*
Pvh Corp..212 381-3800
200 Madison Ave Bsmt 1 New York (10016) *(G-10935)*
Pvh Corp..212 502-6300
404 5th Ave Fl 4 New York (10018) *(G-10936)*
Pvh Corp..212 719-2600
205 W 39th St Fl 4 New York (10018) *(G-10937)*
Pvh Europe, New York *Also called Phillips-Van Heusen Europe (G-10829)*
Pvi Solar Inc..212 280-2100
599 11th Ave Bby New York (10036) *(G-10938)*

PVS Chemical Solutions Inc..................................716 825-5762
55 Lee St Buffalo (14210) *(G-2938)*
Pwf Enterprise LLC..315 695-2223
19 County Route 6 B Phoenix (13135) *(G-12620)*
Pwxyz LLC..212 377-5500
71 W 23rd St Ste 1608 New York (10010) *(G-10939)*
Pylantis New York LLC..310 429-5911
102 E Cortland St Groton (13073) *(G-5484)*
Pyragon Inc...585 697-0444
95 Mount Read Blvd Ste 14 Rochester (14611) *(G-13654)*
Pyrotek Incorporated...607 756-3050
641 State Route 13 Cortland (13045) *(G-3784)*
Pyrotek Incorporated...716 731-3221
2040 Cory Dr Sanborn (14132) *(G-14148)*
Q Communications Inc..212 594-6520
247 W 35th St Rm 1200 New York (10001) *(G-10940)*
Q Ed Creations..212 391-1155
2 W 46th St Ste 1408 New York (10036) *(G-10941)*
Q Omni Inc...914 962-2726
1994 Commerce St Yorktown Heights (10598) *(G-16370)*
Q Squared Design LLC..212 686-8860
1133 Broadway Ste 1424 New York (10010) *(G-10942)*
Q.E.d, Rochester *Also called QED Technologies Intl Inc (G-13655)*
Qca, Rochester *Also called Quality Contract Assemblies (G-13659)*
QED Technologies Intl Inc....................................585 256-6540
1040 University Ave Rochester (14607) *(G-13655)*
Qes Solutions Inc (PA)..585 783-1455
1547 Lyell Ave Rochester (14606) *(G-13656)*
Qhi Group Incorporated.......................................646 512-5727
40 Wall St Ste 2866 New York (10005) *(G-10943)*
Qlc, Long Island City *Also called Quadlogic Controls Corporation (G-7334)*
Qlogix Entertainment LLC....................................215 459-6315
600 W 113th St 7b4 New York (10025) *(G-10944)*
Qls Solutions Group Inc......................................716 852-2203
701 Seneca St Ste 600 Buffalo (14210) *(G-2939)*
Qmc Technologies Inc...716 681-0810
4388 Broadway Depew (14043) *(G-3995)*
Qmetis Inc..212 500-5000
57 W 57th St Fl 4 New York (10019) *(G-10945)*
Qmi, Mount Vernon *Also called Giagni Enterprises LLC (G-8143)*
Qna Tech, Ridge *Also called Quality and Asrn Tech Corp (G-13133)*
Qos Enterprises LLC..585 454-0550
282 Hollenbeck St Rochester (14621) *(G-13657)*
Qpbc Inc..718 685-1900
1306 38th Ave Long Island City (11101) *(G-7333)*
Qps Die Cutters Finishers Corp..............................718 966-1811
140 Alverson Ave Staten Island (10309) *(G-14695)*
Qrs Technologies Inc..315 457-5300
549 Electronics Pkwy Liverpool (13088) *(G-7037)*
Qsr Medical Communications, Westhampton Beach *Also called Shugar Publishing (G-15958)*
Qssi, Walden *Also called Pacific Die Cast Inc (G-15460)*
Qta Machining Inc...716 862-8108
876 Bailey Ave Buffalo (14206) *(G-2940)*
Qtalk Publishing LLC..877 549-1841
1 E Broadway Fl 4 New York (10038) *(G-10946)*
Quad/Graphics Inc...518 581-4000
56 Duplainville Rd Saratoga Springs (12866) *(G-14189)*
Quad/Graphics Inc...212 672-1300
3 Times Sq New York (10036) *(G-10947)*
Quad/Graphics Inc...212 206-5535
60 5th Ave Lowr Level New York (10011) *(G-10948)*
Quad/Graphics Inc...212 741-1001
375 Hudson St New York (10014) *(G-10949)*
Quadlogic Controls Corporation.............................212 930-9300
3300 Northern Blvd Fl 2 Long Island City (11101) *(G-7334)*
Quadra Flex Corp..607 758-7066
1955 State Route 13 Cortland (13045) *(G-3785)*
Quadra Flex Quality Labels, Cortland *Also called Quadra Flex Corp (G-3785)*
Quadrant Biosciences Inc.....................................315 614-2325
505 Irving Ave Ste 3100ab Syracuse (13210) *(G-14969)*
Quadristi LLC...585 279-3318
275 Mount Read Blvd Rochester (14611) *(G-13658)*
Quaker Bonnet Inc..716 885-7208
54 Irving Pl Buffalo (14201) *(G-2941)*
Quaker Boy Inc (PA)...716 662-3979
195 W Main St Springville (14141) *(G-14596)*
Quaker Boy Turkey Calls, Springville *Also called Quaker Boy Inc (G-14596)*
Quaker Millwork & Lumber Inc...............................716 662-3388
77 S Davis St Orchard Park (14127) *(G-12375)*
Qualbuys LLC..855 884-3274
6800 Jericho Tpke 120w Syosset (11791) *(G-14800)*
Qualicoat Inc...585 293-2650
14 Sanford Rd N Churchville (14428) *(G-3414)*
Qualified Manufacturing Corp................................631 249-4440
15 Amber Ct East Islip (11730) *(G-4130)*
Qualitea Imports Inc..917 624-6750
74 Lafayette Ave Suffern (10901) *(G-14764)*
Qualitrol Company LLC (HQ).................................586 643-3717
1385 Fairport Rd Fairport (14450) *(G-4516)*
Quality and Asrn Tech Corp (PA)............................646 450-6762
18 Marginwood Dr Ridge (11961) *(G-13133)*

Quality Bindery Service Inc 716 883-5185
501 Amherst St Buffalo (14207) *(G-2942)*
Quality Candle Mfg Co Inc 631 842-8475
121 Cedar St Copiague (11726) *(G-3672)*
Quality Castings Inc 732 409-3203
3100 47th Ave Ste 2120b Long Island City (11101) *(G-7335)*
Quality Circle Products Inc 914 736-6600
2108 Albany Post Rd Montrose (10548) *(G-8078)*
Quality Components Framing Sys 315 768-1167
44 Mohawk St Bldg 10 Whitesboro (13492) *(G-16081)*
Quality Contract Assemblies 585 663-9030
100 Boxart St Ste 251 Rochester (14612) *(G-13659)*
Quality Dairy Farms Inc 315 942-2611
13584 State Route 12 Boonville (13309) *(G-1109)*
Quality Embedments Mfg Co, New York *Also called Endurart Inc (G-9373)*
Quality Enclosures Inc (PA) 631 234-0115
101 Windsor Pl Unit H Central Islip (11722) *(G-3286)*
Quality Fence, Merrick *Also called Quality Lineals Usa Inc (G-7864)*
Quality Foam Inc 718 381-3644
137 Gardner Ave Brooklyn (11237) *(G-2309)*
Quality Fuel 1 Corporation 631 392-4090
1235 Deer Park Ave North Babylon (11703) *(G-12002)*
Quality Graphics Tri State 845 735-2523
171 Center St Pearl River (10965) *(G-12539)*
Quality Grinding Inc 716 480-3766
7223 Boston State Rd Hamburg (14075) *(G-5517)*
Quality Guides 716 326-3163
39 E Main St Westfield (14787) *(G-15948)*
Quality HM Brands Holdings LLC (PA) 718 292-2024
125 Rose Feiss Blvd Bronx (10454) *(G-1347)*
Quality Impressions Inc 646 613-0002
4334 32nd Pl Ste 3 Long Island City (11101) *(G-7336)*
Quality Industrial Services 716 667-7703
75 Bank St Orchard Park (14127) *(G-12376)*
Quality King Distributors Inc 631 439-2027
201 Comac St Ronkonkoma (11779) *(G-13998)*
Quality Life Inc 718 939-5787
2047 129th St College Point (11356) *(G-3561)*
Quality Lineals Usa Inc 516 378-6577
105 Bennington Ave Ste 1 Freeport (11520) *(G-5018)*
Quality Lineals Usa Inc (PA) 516 378-6577
1 Kees Pl Merrick (11566) *(G-7864)*
Quality Machining Service Inc 315 736-5774
70 Sauquoit St New York Mills (13417) *(G-11836)*
Quality Manufacturing Sys LLC 716 763-0988
1995 Stoneman Cir Lakewood (14750) *(G-6783)*
Quality Metal Stamping LLC (PA) 516 255-9000
100 Merrick Rd Ste 310w Rockville Centre (11570) *(G-13835)*
Quality Millwork Corp 718 892-2250
425 Devoe Ave Bronx (10460) *(G-1348)*
Quality Nature Inc 718 484-4666
8225 5th Ave Ste 215 Brooklyn (11209) *(G-2310)*
Quality Offset LLC 347 342-4660
4750 30th St Long Island City (11101) *(G-7337)*
Quality One Wireless LLC 631 233-3337
2127 Lakeland Ave Unit 2 Ronkonkoma (11779) *(G-13999)*
Quality Patterns Inc 212 704-0355
246 W 38th St Fl 9 New York (10018) *(G-10950)*
Quality Plus, Rochester *Also called Rapid Precision Machining Inc (G-13669)*
Quality Quick Signs, Depew *Also called Flado Enterprises Inc (G-3982)*
Quality Ready Mix Inc 516 437-0100
1824 Gilford Ave New Hyde Park (11040) *(G-8289)*
Quality Saw & Knife Inc 631 491-4747
115 Otis St West Babylon (11704) *(G-15739)*
Quality Stainless Steel NY Inc (PA) 718 748-1785
865 63rd St Brooklyn (11220) *(G-2311)*
Quality Stair Builders Inc 631 694-0711
95 Schmitt Blvd Farmingdale (11735) *(G-4719)*
Quality Strapping Inc 718 418-1111
55 Meadow St Brooklyn (11206) *(G-2312)*
Quality Vision International, Rochester *Also called Quality Vision Services Inc (G-13662)*
Quality Vision Intl Inc (PA) 585 544-0450
850 Hudson Ave Rochester (14621) *(G-13660)*
Quality Vision Intl Inc 585 544-0400
850 Hudson Ave Rochester (14621) *(G-13661)*
Quality Vision Services Inc 585 544-0450
1175 North St Rochester (14621) *(G-13662)*
Quality Woodworking Corp 718 875-3437
260 Butler St Brooklyn (11217) *(G-2313)*
Qualtech Tool & Machine Inc 585 223-9227
1000 Turk Hill Rd Ste 292 Fairport (14450) *(G-4517)*
Quanta Electronics Inc 631 961-9953
48 Fran Ln Centereach (11720) *(G-3252)*
Quantify Energy LLC 917 268-1234
3 Columbus Cir Fl 15 New York (10019) *(G-10951)*
Quantum Knowledge LLC 631 727-6111
356 Reeves Ave Riverhead (11901) *(G-13185)*
Quantum Logic Corp 516 746-1380
91 5th Ave New Hyde Park (11040) *(G-8290)*
Quantum Mechanics Ny LLC 917 519-7077
40 Hennessey Dr Huntington (11743) *(G-6218)*
Quantum Medical Imaging LLC 631 567-5800
150 Verona St Rochester (14608) *(G-13663)*
Quantum Sails Rochester LLC 585 342-5200
1461 Hudson Ave Rochester (14621) *(G-13664)*
Quartet Financial Systems Inc (PA) 845 358-6071
1412 Broadway Rm 2300 New York (10018) *(G-10952)*
Quarto Group Inc (HQ) 212 779-0700
276 5th Ave Rm 205 New York (10001) *(G-10953)*
Quartz Media LLC 646 539-6604
675 6th Ave Ste 410 New York (10010) *(G-10954)*
Quattro Frameworks Inc 718 361-2620
4414 Astoria Blvd Fl 4 Astoria (11103) *(G-435)*
Qubicaamf Worldwide LLC 315 376-6541
7412 Utica Blvd Lowville (13367) *(G-7420)*
Queen Ann Macaroni Mfg Co Inc 718 256-1061
7205 18th Ave Brooklyn (11204) *(G-2314)*
Queen Ann Ravioli, Brooklyn *Also called Queen Ann Macaroni Mfg Co Inc (G-2314)*
Queen City Malting LLC 716 481-1313
644 N Forest Rd Buffalo (14221) *(G-2943)*
Queen City Manufacturing Inc 716 877-1102
333 Henderson Ave Buffalo (14217) *(G-2944)*
Queenaire Technologies Inc 315 393-5454
9483 State Highway 37 Ogdensburg (13669) *(G-12210)*
Queens Central News, Camden *Also called Camden News Inc (G-3098)*
Queens Chronicle, Glendale *Also called Mark I Publications Inc (G-5228)*
Queens Ldgr/Grenpoint Star Inc 718 639-7000
6960 Grand Ave Fl 2 Maspeth (11378) *(G-7636)*
Queens Ready Mix Inc 718 526-4919
14901 95th Ave Jamaica (11435) *(G-6467)*
Queens Times, Whitestone *Also called CT Publications Co (G-16092)*
Queens Tribune, Whitestone *Also called Tribco LLC (G-16102)*
Quest Bead & Cast Inc 212 354-1737
49 W 37th St Fl 16 New York (10018) *(G-10955)*
Quest Beads, New York *Also called Quest Bead & Cast Inc (G-10955)*
Quest Magazine, New York *Also called Quest Media Llc (G-10956)*
Quest Manufacturing Inc 716 312-8000
5600 Camp Rd Hamburg (14075) *(G-5518)*
Quest Manufacturing Inc 716 312-8000
5600 Camp Rd Hamburg (14075) *(G-5519)*
Quest Media Llc 646 840-3404
920 3rd Ave Fl 6 New York (10022) *(G-10956)*
Queue Solutions LLC 631 750-6440
155 Knickerbocker Ave # 1 Bohemia (11716) *(G-1069)*
Quick Frzen Foods Annual Prcss, New York *Also called Frozen Food Digest Inc (G-9543)*
Quick Guide, New York *Also called Guest Informat LLC (G-9693)*
Quick Roll Leaf Mfg Co Inc (PA) 845 457-1500
118 Bracken Rd Montgomery (12549) *(G-8065)*
Quick Sign F X 516 249-6531
6 Powell St Farmingdale (11735) *(G-4720)*
Quick Turn Around Machining, Buffalo *Also called Qta Machining Inc (G-2940)*
Quicker Printer Inc 607 734-8622
210 W Gray St Elmira (14901) *(G-4365)*
Quickpouch Packaging Automtn, Ronkonkoma *Also called Adaptive Mfg Tech Inc (G-13888)*
Quickprint 585 394-2600
330 S Main St Canandaigua (14424) *(G-3141)*
Quikrete Companies LLC 716 213-2027
11 N Steelawanna Ave Lackawanna (14218) *(G-6743)*
Quikrete Companies LLC 315 673-2020
4993 Limeledge Rd Ste 560 Marcellus (13108) *(G-7562)*
Quikrete-Buffalo, Lackawanna *Also called Quikrete Companies LLC (G-6743)*
Quill.org, New York *Also called Empirical Resolution Inc (G-9362)*
Quilted Koala Ltd 800 223-5678
1384 Broadway Ste 15 New York (10018) *(G-10957)*
Quinn and Co of NY Ltd 212 868-1900
48 W 38th St Ph New York (10018) *(G-10958)*
Quintel Usa Inc 585 420-8364
1200 Ridgeway Ave Ste 132 Rochester (14615) *(G-13665)*
Quip Nyc Inc 917 331-3993
45 Main St Ste 616 Brooklyn (11201) *(G-2315)*
Quist Industries Ltd 718 243-2800
204 Van Dyke St Ste 320a Brooklyn (11231) *(G-2316)*
Quogue Capital LLC 212 554-4475
1285 Ave Of The Ave Fl 35 Flr 35 New York (10019) *(G-10959)*
Quoin LLC 914 967-9400
555 Theodore Fremd Ave B302 Rye (10580) *(G-14084)*
Quoizel Inc 631 436-4402
590 Old Willets Path # 1 Hauppauge (11788) *(G-5752)*
Quorum Group LLC 585 798-8888
11601 Maple Ridge Rd Medina (14103) *(G-7744)*
Quotable Cards Inc 212 420-7552
611 Broadway Rm 615 New York (10012) *(G-10960)*
Quovo Inc (PA) 212 643-0695
54 W 21st St Frnt 1 New York (10010) *(G-10961)*
Qworldstar Inc 212 768-4500
200 Park Ave S Fl 8 New York (10003) *(G-10962)*
R & A Industrial Products 716 823-4300
30 Cornelia St Buffalo (14210) *(G-2945)*
R & B Fabrication Inc 315 640-9901
7282 State Route 31 Cicero (13039) *(G-3423)*
R & B Machinery Corp 716 894-3332
400 Kennedy Rd Ste 3 Buffalo (14227) *(G-2946)*
R & F Boards & Dividers Inc 718 331-1529
1678 57th St Brooklyn (11204) *(G-2317)*

R & F Handmade Paints Inc 845 331-3112
  84 Ten Broeck Ave Kingston (12401) **(G-6707)**

R & F Marketing, New York *Also called Place Vendome Holding Co Inc* **(G-10850)**

R & H Baking Co Inc 718 852-1768
  19 5th St Brooklyn (11231) **(G-2318)**

R & J Displays Inc 631 491-3500
  96 Otis St West Babylon (11704) **(G-15740)**

R & J Graphics Inc 631 293-6611
  45 Central Ave Farmingdale (11735) **(G-4721)**

R & J Sheet Metal Distributors 518 433-1525
  156 Orange St Albany (12210) **(G-120)**

R & L Press Inc 718 447-8557
  896 Forest Ave Staten Island (10310) **(G-14696)**

R & L Press of SI Inc 718 667-3258
  2461 Hylan Blvd Staten Island (10306) **(G-14697)**

R & M Graphics of New York 212 929-0294
  121 Varick St Fl 9 New York (10013) **(G-10963)**

R & M Industries Inc 212 366-6414
  111 Broadway Rm 1112 New York (10006) **(G-10964)**

R & M Richards Inc (PA) 212 921-8820
  10 Times Sq Fl 4 New York (10018) **(G-10965)**

R & M Thermofoil Doors Inc 718 206-4991
  14830 94th Ave Jamaica (11435) **(G-6468)**

R & R Grosbard Inc 212 575-0077
  1156 Avenue Of The Amrcs New York (10036) **(G-10966)**

R & S Machine Center Inc 518 563-4016
  4398 Route 22 Plattsburgh (12901) **(G-12773)**

R and J Sheet Metal, Albany *Also called R & J Sheet Metal Distributors* **(G-120)**

R C Henderson Stair Builders 516 876-9898
  100 Summa Ave Westbury (11590) **(G-15922)**

R C Kolstad Water Corp 585 216-2230
  73 Lake Rd Ontario (14519) **(G-12298)**

R D A Container Corporation 585 247-2323
  70 Cherry Rd Gates (14624) **(G-5142)**

R D Drive and Shop, Little Falls *Also called R D S Mountain View Trucking* **(G-6992)**

R D Printing Associates Inc 631 390-5964
  1865 New Hwy Ste 1 Farmingdale (11735) **(G-4722)**

R D R Industries Inc 315 866-5020
  146 W Main St Mohawk (13407) **(G-8007)**

R D S Mountain View Trucking 315 823-4265
  1600 State Route 5s Little Falls (13365) **(G-6992)**

R D Specialties Inc 585 265-0220
  560 Salt Rd Webster (14580) **(G-15649)**

R E F Precision Products 631 242-4471
  517 Acorn St Ste A Deer Park (11729) **(G-3925)**

R F Giardina Co 516 922-1364
  200 Lexington Ave Apt 3a Oyster Bay (11771) **(G-12456)**

R G Flair Co Inc 631 586-7311
  199 S Fehr Way Bay Shore (11706) **(G-703)**

R G Glass, New York *Also called RG Glass Creations Inc* **(G-11034)**

R G King General Construction 315 583-3560
  13018 County Route 155 Adams Center (13606) **(G-3)**

R Goldsmith 718 239-1396
  1974 Mayflower Ave Bronx (10461) **(G-1349)**

R H Crown Co Inc 518 762-4589
  100 N Market St Johnstown (12095) **(G-6626)**

R H Guest Inc 718 675-7600
  1300 Church Ave Brooklyn (11226) **(G-2319)**

R Hadley Corporation 607 589-4415
  89 Tompkins St Spencer (14883) **(G-14549)**

R Hochman Papers Incorporated 516 466-6414
  68 35th St Brooklyn (11232) **(G-2320)**

R I C, Ontario *Also called Rochester Industrial Ctrl Inc* **(G-12301)**

R I R Communications Systems 718 706-9957
  20 Nuvern Ave Mount Vernon (10550) **(G-8175)**

R J Reynolds Tobacco Company 716 871-1553
  275 Cooper Ave Ste 116 Tonawanda (14150) **(G-15135)**

R J Valente Gravel Inc (PA) 518 432-4470
  1 Madison St Troy (12180) **(G-15181)**

R J Valente Gravel Inc 518 279-1001
  3349 Rte 2 Cropseyville (12052) **(G-3803)**

R J Valente Gravel Inc 518 432-4470
  315 Partition St Ext Rensselaer (12144) **(G-13090)**

R K B Opto-Electronics Inc (PA) 315 455-6636
  6677 Moore Rd Syracuse (13211) **(G-14970)**

R Klein Jewelry Co Inc 516 482-3260
  39 Brockmeyer Dr Massapequa (11758) **(G-7649)**

R L C Electronics Inc 914 241-1334
  83 Radio Circle Dr Mount Kisco (10549) **(G-8103)**

R M F Health Management L L C 718 854-5400
  3361 Park Ave Wantagh (11793) **(G-15488)**

R M Reynolds 315 789-7365
  504 Exchange St Geneva (14456) **(G-5161)**

R P Fedder Corp (PA) 585 288-1600
  740 Driving Park Ave B Rochester (14613) **(G-13666)**

R P M, Deer Park *Also called Rinaldi Precision Machine* **(G-3928)**

R P M Industries Inc 315 255-1105
  26 Aurelius Ave Auburn (13021) **(G-492)**

R P O, West Henrietta *Also called Rochester Precision Optics LLC* **(G-15802)**

R R Donnelley & Sons Company 716 763-2613
  112 Winchester Rd Lakewood (14750) **(G-6784)**

R R Donnelley & Sons Company 716 773-0647
  300 Lang Blvd Grand Island (14072) **(G-5341)**

R R Donnelley & Sons Company 518 438-9722
  4 Executive Park Dr Ste 2 Albany (12203) **(G-121)**

R R Donnelley & Sons Company 646 755-8125
  250 W 26th St Rm 402 New York (10001) **(G-10967)**

R R Donnelley & Sons Company 716 773-0300
  3235 Grand Island Blvd Grand Island (14072) **(G-5342)**

R S T Cable and Tape Inc 631 981-0096
  2130 Pond Rd Ste B Ronkonkoma (11779) **(G-14000)**

R Schleider Contracting Corp 631 269-4249
  135 Old Northport Rd Kings Park (11754) **(G-6676)**

R Steiner Technologies Inc 585 425-5912
  180 Perinton Pkwy Fairport (14450) **(G-4518)**

R T C A, Elmsford *Also called Radon Testing Corp of America* **(G-4423)**

R T F Manufacturing, Hudson *Also called Atmost Refrigeration Co Inc* **(G-6149)**

R V Dow Enterprises Inc 585 454-5862
  466 Central Ave Rochester (14605) **(G-13667)**

R V H Estates Inc 914 664-9888
  138 Mount Vernon Ave Mount Vernon (10550) **(G-8176)**

R W Publications Div of Wtrhs (PA) 716 714-5620
  6091 Seneca St Bldg C Elma (14059) **(G-4325)**

R W Publications Div of Wtrhs 716 714-5620
  6091 Seneca St Bldg C Elma (14059) **(G-4326)**

R&A Prods, Buffalo *Also called R & A Industrial Products* **(G-2945)**

R&S Machine, Plattsburgh *Also called R & S Machine Center Inc* **(G-12773)**

R&S Steel LLC 315 281-0123
  412 Canal St Rome (13440) **(G-13865)**

R-Co Products Corporation 800 854-7657
  1855 Big Tree Rd Lakewood (14750) **(G-6785)**

R-Pac International Corp (PA) 212 465-1818
  132 W 36th St Fl 7 New York (10018) **(G-10968)**

R-S Restaurant Eqp Mfg Corp (PA) 212 925-0335
  272 Bowery New York (10012) **(G-10969)**

R-Tronics, Rome *Also called J Davis Manufacturing Co Inc* **(G-13852)**

RA Newhouse Inc (PA) 516 248-6670
  110 Liberty Ave Mineola (11501) **(G-7995)**

Racing Industries Inc 631 905-0100
  901 Scott Ave Calverton (11933) **(G-3084)**

RAD Soap Co LLC 518 461-9667
  8 Wolfert Ave Albany (12204) **(G-122)**

Radax Industries Inc 585 265-2055
  700 Basket Rd Ste A Webster (14580) **(G-15650)**

Radiant Pro Ltd 516 763-5678
  245 Merrick Rd Oceanside (11572) **(G-12186)**

Radiation Shielding Systems 888 631-2278
  415 Spook Rock Rd Suffern (10901) **(G-14765)**

Radicle Farm Company, New York *Also called Radicle Farm LLC* **(G-10970)**

Radicle Farm LLC 315 226-3294
  394 Broadway Fl 5 New York (10013) **(G-10970)**

Radiology Film Reading Svcs, Long Island City *Also called P C Rfrs Radiology* **(G-7315)**

Radloop, Poughkeepsie *Also called Hvr Mso LLC* **(G-12962)**

Radnor-Wallace (PA) 516 767-2131
  921 Port Washington Blvd # 1 Port Washington (11050) **(G-12917)**

Radon Testing Corp of America (PA) 914 345-3380
  2 Hayes St Elmsford (10523) **(G-4423)**

Raff Enterprises 518 218-7883
  12 Petra Ln Ste 6 Albany (12205) **(G-123)**

Rag & Bone Industries LLC (PA) 212 278-8214
  425 W 13th St Fl 3 New York (10014) **(G-10971)**

Ragnatelli Inc 718 765-4050
  300 Dewitt Ave Brooklyn (11236) **(G-2321)**

Rago Foundations LLC (PA) 718 728-8436
  1815 27th Ave Astoria (11102) **(G-436)**

Ragozin Data 212 674-3123
  4402 11th St Ste 613 Long Island City (11101) **(G-7338)**

Rags Knitwear Ltd 718 782-8417
  850 Metropolitan Ave Brooklyn (11211) **(G-2322)**

Raharney Capital LLC 212 220-9084
  325 Gold St Fl 502 Brooklyn (11201) **(G-2323)**

Railex Wine Services LLC (PA) 631 369-7000
  889 Harrison Ave Riverhead (11901) **(G-13186)**

Railings By New Star Brass 516 358-1153
  26 Cobeck Ct Brooklyn (11223) **(G-2324)**

Railworks Corporation 904 296-5055
  83 Central Ave Farmingdale (11735) **(G-4723)**

Railworks Transit Systems Inc (HQ) 212 502-7900
  5 Penn Plz New York (10001) **(G-10972)**

Rain Catchers Seamless Gutters 516 520-1956
  39 Park Ln Bethpage (11714) **(G-844)**

Rainbeau Ridge Farm 914 234-2197
  49 Davids Way Bedford Hills (10507) **(G-772)**

Rainbow Awning Co Inc 716 297-3939
  9025 Niagara Falls Blvd Niagara Falls (14304) **(G-11970)**

Rainbow Custom Counter Tops, Staten Island *Also called Joseph Fedele* **(G-14672)**

Rainbow Leather Inc 718 939-8762
  1415 112th St College Point (11356) **(G-3562)**

Rainbow Lettering 607 732-5751
  1329 College Ave Elmira (14901) **(G-4366)**

Rainbow Plastics Inc 718 218-7288
  371 Vandervoort Ave Brooklyn (11211) **(G-2325)**

Rainbow Poly Bag Co Inc 718 386-3500
179 Morgan Ave Brooklyn (11237) ***(G-2326)***
Rainbow Powder Coating Corp 631 586-4019
86 E Industry Ct Deer Park (11729) ***(G-3926)***
Rainforest Apothecary, Long Island City *Also called Anima Mundi Herbals LLC* ***(G-7158)***
Rainforest Inc 212 575-7620
54 W 40th St New York (10018) ***(G-10973)***
Raith America Inc 518 874-3000
300 Jordan Rd Troy (12180) ***(G-15182)***
RAK Finishing Corp 718 416-4242
15934 83rd St Howard Beach (11414) ***(G-6141)***
Raleigh & Drake Pbc (PA) 212 625-8212
110 E 25th St Fl 3 New York (10010) ***(G-10974)***
Raloid Tool Co Inc 518 664-4261
Hc 146 Mechanicville (12118) ***(G-7694)***
Ralph Lauren Corporation (PA) 212 318-7000
650 Madison Ave Fl C1 New York (10022) ***(G-10975)***
Ralph Martinelli 914 345-3055
100 Clearbrook Rd Ste 170 Elmsford (10523) ***(G-4424)***
Ralph's Ices, Staten Island *Also called JMS Ices Inc* ***(G-14670)***
Ralphs Famous Italian Ices 718 605-5052
4212c Hylan Blvd Staten Island (10308) ***(G-14698)***
Ram Fabricating LLC 315 437-6654
412 Wavel St Syracuse (13206) ***(G-14971)***
Ram Machining LLC 585 426-1007
1645 Lyell Ave Ste 158 Rochester (14606) ***(G-13668)***
Ram Precision Tool Inc 716 759-8722
139 Gunnville Rd Lancaster (14086) ***(G-6828)***
Ram Transformer Technologies 914 632-3988
11 Beechwood Ave New Rochelle (10801) ***(G-8351)***
Ramco Arts, Sodus *Also called Nykon Inc* ***(G-14492)***
Ramen & Yakitori Okidoki Inc 718 806-1677
3405 30th Ave Astoria (11103) ***(G-437)***
Ramholtz Publishing Inc 718 761-4800
1200 South Ave Ste 202 Staten Island (10314) ***(G-14699)***
Ramick Welding, Farmingdale *Also called W R P Welding Ltd* ***(G-4763)***
Ramler International Ltd 516 353-3106
471 N Broadway 132 Jericho (11753) ***(G-6591)***
Ramsbury Property Us Inc (HQ) 212 223-6250
601 5th Ave Fl 4 New York (10017) ***(G-10976)***
Ramsey Electronics, Victor *Also called Avcom of Virginia Inc* ***(G-15392)***
Ramsey Electronics LLC 585 924-4560
590 Fishers Station Dr Victor (14564) ***(G-15426)***
Ramsey Solutions LLC 888 329-1055
228 Park Ave S Ste 29075 New York (10003) ***(G-10977)***
Ramy Brook LLC 212 744-2789
231 W 39th St Rm 720 New York (10018) ***(G-10978)***
Ran Mar Enterprises Ltd 631 666-4754
143 Anchor Ln Bay Shore (11706) ***(G-704)***
Rand & Paseka Mfg Co Inc 516 867-1500
10 Hanse Ave Freeport (11520) ***(G-5019)***
Rand Machine Products, Falconer *Also called Premier Prcision Machining LLC* ***(G-4551)***
Rand Machine Products, Inc. 716 665-5217
2072 Allen Street Ext Falconer (14733) ***(G-4552)***
Rand Mfg, Schenectady *Also called Rand Products Manufacturing Co* ***(G-14297)***
Rand Products Manufacturing Co 518 374-9871
1602 Van Vranken Ave Schenectady (12308) ***(G-14297)***
Randa Accessories Lea Gds LLC 212 354-5100
417 5th Ave Fl 11 New York (10016) ***(G-10979)***
Randall Loeffler Inc 212 226-8787
588 Broadway Rm 1203 New York (10012) ***(G-10980)***
Randob Labs Ltd 845 534-2197
45 Quaker Ave Ste 207 Cornwall (12518) ***(G-3732)***
Randolph Dimension Corporation 716 358-6901
216 Main St Ste 216 Randolph (14772) ***(G-13064)***
Randy Sixberry 315 265-6211
6 Main St Ste 101 Potsdam (13676) ***(G-12940)***
Range Repair Warehouse 585 235-0980
421 Penbrooke Dr Ste 2 Penfield (14526) ***(G-12572)***
Range Rsurces - Appalachia LLC 716 753-3385
100 E Chautauqua St Mayville (14757) ***(G-7684)***
Ranger Design Us Inc 800 565-5321
6377 Dean Pkwy Ontario (14519) ***(G-12299)***
Ranney Precision 716 731-6418
6421 Wendt Dr Niagara Falls (14304) ***(G-11971)***
Ranney Precision Machining, Niagara Falls *Also called Ranney Precision* ***(G-11971)***
Rap Genius, Brooklyn *Also called Genius Media Group Inc* ***(G-1883)***
Rapa Independent North America 518 561-0513
124 Connecticut Rd Plattsburgh (12903) ***(G-12774)***
Raphael, Peconic *Also called J Petrocelli Wine Cellars LLC* ***(G-12546)***
Rapid Fan & Blower Inc 718 786-2060
2314 39th Ave Long Island City (11101) ***(G-7339)***
Rapid Intellect Group Inc 518 929-3210
77 Church St Apt B Chatham (12037) ***(G-3332)***
Rapid Precision Machining Inc 585 467-0780
50 Lafayette Rd Rochester (14609) ***(G-13669)***
Rapid Print and Marketing Inc 585 924-1520
8 High St Victor (14564) ***(G-15427)***
Rapid Rays Printing & Copying 716 852-0550
300 Broadway St Buffalo (14204) ***(G-2947)***
Rapid Removal LLC 716 665-4663
1599 Route 394 Falconer (14733) ***(G-4553)***
Rapid Reproductions LLC 607 843-2221
4511 State Hwy 12 Oxford (13830) ***(G-12442)***
Rapid Service Engraving Co 716 896-4555
1593 Genesee St Buffalo (14211) ***(G-2948)***
Rapid-Lite Fixture Corporation 347 599-2600
249 Huron St Brooklyn (11222) ***(G-2327)***
Rapistak Corporation 716 822-2804
1 Alliance Dr Buffalo (14218) ***(G-2949)***
Rapp Signs Inc 607 656-8167
3979 State Route 206 Greene (13778) ***(G-5447)***
Rare Editions, New York *Also called Star Childrens Dress Co Inc* ***(G-11348)***
Rare Form Brewing Company 518 313-9256
90 Congress St Troy (12180) ***(G-15183)***
Rasco Graphics Inc 212 206-0447
519 8th Ave Fl 18 New York (10018) ***(G-10981)***
Rasna Therapeutics Inc 646 396-4087
420 Lexington Ave # 2525 New York (10170) ***(G-10982)***
Rasp Incorporated 518 747-8020
8 Dukes Way Gansevoort (12831) ***(G-5085)***
Ratan Ronkonkoma 631 588-6800
3055 Veterans Mem Hwy Ronkonkoma (11779) ***(G-14001)***
Rational Enterprises, Albany *Also called Rational Retention LLC* ***(G-124)***
Rational Retention LLC (PA) 518 489-3000
2 Tower Pl Ste 13 Albany (12203) ***(G-124)***
Rauch Industries Inc 704 867-5333
828 S Broadway Tarrytown (10591) ***(G-15055)***
Raulli and Sons Inc (PA) 315 479-6693
213 Teall Ave Syracuse (13210) ***(G-14972)***
Raulli and Sons Inc 315 474-1370
660 Burnet Ave Syracuse (13203) ***(G-14973)***
Raulli and Sons Inc 315 479-2515
920 Canal St Syracuse (13210) ***(G-14974)***
Raulli Iron Works Inc 315 337-8070
133 Mill St Rome (13440) ***(G-13866)***
Rave Inc 716 695-1110
940 River Rd North Tonawanda (14120) ***(G-12084)***
Raven New York LLC 212 584-9690
450 W 15th St New York (10011) ***(G-10983)***
Ravioli Store Inc 718 729-9300
4344 21st St Long Island City (11101) ***(G-7340)***
Ravioli Store, The, Long Island City *Also called Pelican Bay Ltd* ***(G-7323)***
Raw Indulgence Ltd 866 498-4671
44 Executive Blvd Ste 205 Elmsford (10523) ***(G-4425)***
Raw Revolution, Elmsford *Also called Raw Indulgence Ltd* ***(G-4425)***
Rawlings Sporting Goods Co Inc 315 429-8511
52 Mckinley Ave Dolgeville (13329) ***(G-4025)***
Rawpothecary Inc 917 783-7770
630 Flushing Ave Brooklyn (11206) ***(G-2328)***
Raxon Fabrics Corp (HQ) 212 532-6816
261 5th Ave New York (10016) ***(G-10984)***
Ray Gold Shade Inc 718 377-8892
16 Wellington Ct Brooklyn (11230) ***(G-2329)***
Ray Griffiths Inc 212 689-7209
303 5th Ave Rm 1901 New York (10016) ***(G-10985)***
Ray Medica Inc 952 885-0500
505 Park Ave Ste 1400 New York (10022) ***(G-10986)***
Ray Sign Inc 518 377-1371
28 Colonial Ave Schenectady (12304) ***(G-14298)***
Ray Theta Inc 646 757-4956
31 W 34th St Fl 7 New York (10001) ***(G-10987)***
Rayana Designs Inc 718 786-2040
288 Westbury Ave Carle Place (11514) ***(G-3180)***
Rayco of Schenectady Inc 518 212-5113
4 Sam Stratton Rd Amsterdam (12010) ***(G-346)***
Raydon Precision Bearing Co 516 887-2582
75 Merrick Rd Lynbrook (11563) ***(G-7436)***
Raydoor Inc 212 421-0641
134 W 29th St Rm 909 New York (10001) ***(G-10988)***
Raymond Corporation (HQ) 607 656-2311
22 S Canal St Greene (13778) ***(G-5448)***
Raymond Corporation 315 643-5000
6533 Chrysler Ln East Syracuse (13057) ***(G-4232)***
Raymond Sales Corporation (HQ) 607 656-2311
22 S Canal St Greene (13778) ***(G-5449)***
Rays Italian Bakery Inc 516 825-9170
45 Railroad Ave Valley Stream (11580) ***(G-15355)***
Rays Restaurant & Bakery Inc 718 441-7707
12325 Jamaica Ave Jamaica (11418) ***(G-6469)***
Raytech Corp Asbestos Personal 516 747-0300
190 Willis Ave Mineola (11501) ***(G-7996)***
RB Converting Inc 607 777-1325
28 Track Dr Binghamton (13904) ***(G-905)***
RB Diamond Inc 212 398-4560
22 W 48th St Ste 904 New York (10036) ***(G-10989)***
RB Woodcraft Inc 315 474-2429
1860 Erie Blvd E Ste 1 Syracuse (13210) ***(G-14975)***
RB Wyatt Mfg Co Inc 718 209-9682
2518 Ralph Ave Brooklyn (11234) ***(G-2330)***
Rbhammers Corp 845 353-5042
500 Bradley Hill Rd Blauvelt (10913) ***(G-932)***
Rbw Studio LLC 212 388-1621
67 34th St Unit 5 Brooklyn (11232) ***(G-2331)***

RC Entps Bus & Trck Inc 518 568-5753
5895 State Highway 29 Saint Johnsville (13452) *(G-14120)*
Rce Manufacturing LLC 631 856-9005
110 Nicon Ct Hauppauge (11788) *(G-5753)*
RCM Design Division, New York *Also called S Rothschild & Co Inc (G-11110)*
Rd2 Construction & Dem LLC 718 980-1650
63 Trossach Rd Staten Island (10304) *(G-14700)*
Rda Holding Co (PA) 914 238-1000
750 3rd Ave New York (10017) *(G-10990)*
Rdd Pharma Inc 302 319-9970
3 Columbus Cir Fl 15 New York (10019) *(G-10991)*
Rdi, Edgewood *Also called Iba Industrial Inc (G-4270)*
Rdi Inc (PA) 914 773-1000
333 N Bedford Rd Ste 135 Mount Kisco (10549) *(G-8104)*
Rdi Electronics, Mount Kisco *Also called Rdi Inc (G-8104)*
RE 99 Cents Inc 718 639-2325
4905 Roosevelt Ave Woodside (11377) *(G-16222)*
RE Hansen Industries Inc (PA) 631 471-2900
500 Middle Country Rd A Saint James (11780) *(G-14113)*
Re-Al Industrial Corp 716 542-4556
5391 Crittenden Rd Akron (14001) *(G-21)*
Reactivecore LLC 631 944-1618
79 Madison Ave Fl 8 New York (10016) *(G-10992)*
Read Manufacturing Company Inc 631 567-4487
330 Dante Ct Holbrook (11741) *(G-6016)*
Reader's Digest, New York *Also called Trusted Media Brands Inc (G-11553)*
Readers Dgest Yung Fmilies Inc 914 238-1000
Readers Digest Rd Pleasantville (10570) *(G-12798)*
Readers Digest Assn Incthe 414 423-0100
16 E 34th St Fl 14 New York (10016) *(G-10993)*
Readers Digest Sls & Svcs Inc 914 238-1000
Readers Digest Rd Pleasantville (10570) *(G-12799)*
Ready Check Glo Inc 516 547-1849
23 Bruce Ln Ste E East Northport (11731) *(G-4151)*
Ready To Assemble Company Inc 516 825-4397
115 S Corona Ave Valley Stream (11580) *(G-15356)*
Real Co Inc 347 433-8549
616 Corporate Way Valley Cottage (10989) *(G-15321)*
Real Deal, The, New York *Also called Korangy Publishing Inc (G-10127)*
Real Design Inc 315 429-3071
187 S Main St Dolgeville (13329) *(G-4026)*
Real Est Book of Long Island 516 364-5000
575 Underhill Blvd # 110 Syosset (11791) *(G-14801)*
Real Estate Media Inc 212 929-6976
120 Broadway Fl 5 New York (10271) *(G-10994)*
Real Factors Inc 206 963-6661
3049 Crescent St Apt H1b5 Astoria (11102) *(G-438)*
Real Wood Tiles, Buffalo *Also called Fibron Products Inc (G-2752)*
Reality Ai, New York *Also called Reality Analytics Inc (G-10995)*
Reality Analytics Inc (PA) 347 363-2200
157 Columbus Ave New York (10023) *(G-10995)*
Realtimetraderscom 716 632-6600
1325 N Forest Rd Ste 240 Buffalo (14221) *(G-2950)*
Rear View Safety Inc 855 815-3842
1797 Atlantic Ave Brooklyn (11233) *(G-2332)*
Reason Software Company Inc 646 664-1038
228 Park Ave S Unit 74122 New York (10003) *(G-10996)*
REB Lybss Inc 845 238-5633
44 Virginia Ave Monroe (10950) *(G-8030)*
Recommunity, Beacon *Also called Fcr LLC (G-752)*
Record 518 270-1200
20 Lake Ave Saratoga Springs (12866) *(G-14190)*
Record Advertiser 716 693-1000
435 River Rd North Tonawanda (14120) *(G-12085)*
Record Review LLC 914 244-0533
16 The Pkwy Fl 3 Katonah (10536) *(G-6638)*
Recorded Anthlogy of Amrcn Mus 212 290-1695
20 Jay St Ste 1001 Brooklyn (11201) *(G-2333)*
Recorder, The, Amsterdam *Also called Tri-Village Publishers Inc (G-349)*
Recycled Brooklyn Group LLC 917 902-0662
236 Van Brunt St Brooklyn (11231) *(G-2334)*
Red Hawk Fire & Security LLC 518 877-7616
14 Jetway Dr Albany (12211) *(G-125)*
Red Line Networx Screen Prtg, Brooklyn *Also called Body Builders Inc (G-1601)*
Red Newt Cellars Inc 607 546-4100
3675 Tichenor Rd Hector (14841) *(G-5827)*
Red Oak Software Inc 585 454-3170
3349 Monroe Ave Ste 175 Rochester (14618) *(G-13670)*
Red Onyx Industrial Pdts LLC 516 459-6035
23 Green St Ste 310 Huntington (11743) *(G-6219)*
Red Tail Moulding & Mllwk LLC 516 852-4613
23 Frowein Rd Ste 1 Center Moriches (11934) *(G-3247)*
Red Tail Ridge Inc 315 536-4580
846 State Route 14 Penn Yan (14527) *(G-12591)*
Red Tail Ridge Winery, Penn Yan *Also called Red Tail Ridge Inc (G-12591)*
Red White & Blue Entps Corp 718 565-8080
3443 56th St Woodside (11377) *(G-16223)*
Redbook Magazine 212 649-3331
224 W 57th St Lbby Fl22 New York (10019) *(G-10997)*
Redcom Laboratories Inc (PA) 585 924-6567
1 Redcom Ctr Victor (14564) *(G-15428)*

Reddi Car Corp 631 589-3141
174 Greeley Ave Sayville (11782) *(G-14231)*
Redding Reloading Equipment, Cortland *Also called Redding-Hunter Inc (G-3786)*
Redding-Hunter Inc 607 753-3331
1089 Starr Rd Cortland (13045) *(G-3786)*
Redi Bag USA, Garden City Park *Also called New York Packaging II LLC (G-5122)*
Redi Records Payroll 718 854-6990
1225 36th St Brooklyn (11218) *(G-2335)*
Redi-Bag USA, New Hyde Park *Also called New York Packaging Corp (G-8284)*
Redken 5th Avenue NYC LLC 212 818-1500
575 5th Ave Fl 23 New York (10017) *(G-10998)*
Redland Foods Corp 716 288-9061
40 Sonwil Dr Cheektowaga (14225) *(G-3360)*
Redspring Communications Inc 518 587-0547
125 High Rock Ave Saratoga Springs (12866) *(G-14191)*
Reed Business Information, New York *Also called Relx Inc (G-11005)*
Reed Systems Ltd 845 647-3660
17 Edwards Pl Ellenville (12428) *(G-4310)*
Reefer Tek Llc 347 590-1067
885a E 149th St Fl 2 Bronx (10455) *(G-1350)*
Reelcology Inc 845 258-1880
39 Transport Ln Pine Island (10969) *(G-12630)*
Reelex Packaging Solutions Inc 845 878-7878
39 Jon Barrett Rd Patterson (12563) *(G-12519)*
Reenergy Black River, Fort Drum *Also called Black River Generations LLC (G-4935)*
Reentry Games Inc 646 421-0080
215 E 5th St New York (10003) *(G-10999)*
Reese Manufacturing Inc 631 842-3780
16 Reith St Copiague (11726) *(G-3673)*
Refill Services LLC 607 369-5864
16 Winkler Rd Sidney (13838) *(G-14435)*
Refined Sugars Inc 914 963-2400
1 Federal St Yonkers (10705) *(G-16345)*
REFINEDKIND PET PRODUCTS, Irvington *Also called Feinkind Inc (G-6308)*
Refinery 29 Inc (PA) 212 966-3112
225 Broadway Fl 23 New York (10007) *(G-11000)*
Reflective Image 631 477-3368
74605 Main Rd Greenport (11944) *(G-5457)*
Reflex Offset Inc 516 746-4142
305 Suburban Ave Deer Park (11729) *(G-3927)*
Reflexite Precision Tech Ctr, Henrietta *Also called Orafol Americas Inc (G-5859)*
Regal Commodities, Purchase *Also called Regal Trading Inc (G-13015)*
Regal Emblem Co Inc 212 925-8833
250 W Broadway Fl 2 New York (10013) *(G-11001)*
Regal Screen Printing Intl 845 356-8181
515 Route 304 Ste 1a New City (10956) *(G-8229)*
Regal Tip, Niagara Falls *Also called J D Calato Manufacturing Co (G-11942)*
Regal Trading Inc 914 694-6100
2975 Westchester Ave # 210 Purchase (10577) *(G-13015)*
Rege Inc 845 565-7772
110 Corporate Dr New Windsor (12553) *(G-8380)*
Regeneron Pharmaceuticals Inc (PA) 914 847-7000
777 Old Saw Mill River Rd # 10 Tarrytown (10591) *(G-15056)*
Regeneron Pharmaceuticals Inc 518 488-6000
81 Columbia Tpke Rensselaer (12144) *(G-13091)*
Regenron Hlthcare Slutions Inc 914 847-7000
745 Old Saw Mill River Rd Tarrytown (10591) *(G-15057)*
Regina Press, Bohemia *Also called Malhame Publs & Importers Inc (G-1043)*
Regional MGT & Consulting Inc 718 599-3718
79 Bridgewater St Brooklyn (11222) *(G-2336)*
Register Graphics Inc 716 358-2921
220 Main St Randolph (14772) *(G-13065)*
Rehab Tech, Syracuse *Also called Rehabilitation Tech of Syracuse (G-14976)*
Rehabilitation International 212 420-1500
15350 89th Ave Apt 1101 Jamaica (11432) *(G-6470)*
Rehablitation Tech of Syracuse 315 426-9920
1101 Erie Blvd E Ste 209 Syracuse (13210) *(G-14976)*
Reich Paper, Brooklyn *Also called Daniel O Reich Incorporated (G-1723)*
Reichert Inc 716 686-4500
3362 Walden Ave Ste 100 Depew (14043) *(G-3996)*
Reichert Technologies, Depew *Also called Reichert Inc (G-3996)*
Reilly Windows & Doors, Calverton *Also called Pella Corporation (G-3083)*
Reimann & Georger Corporation 716 895-1156
1849 Harlem Rd Buffalo (14212) *(G-2951)*
Reinhold Brothers Inc 212 867-8310
799 Park Ave New York (10021) *(G-11002)*
Reino Manufacturing Co Inc 914 636-8990
34 Circuit Rd New Rochelle (10805) *(G-8352)*
Reis D Furniture Mfg 516 248-5676
327 Sagamore Ave Ste 2 Mineola (11501) *(G-7997)*
Reisman Bros Bakery Inc 718 331-1975
110 Avenue O Brooklyn (11204) *(G-2337)*
Reismans Bros. Bakery, Brooklyn *Also called Reisman Bros Bakery Inc (G-2337)*
Release Coatings New York Inc 585 593-2335
125 S Brooklyn Ave Wellsville (14895) *(G-15674)*
Reliable Autmtc Sprnklr Co Inc (PA) 800 431-1588
103 Fairview Pk Dr Ste 1 Elmsford (10523) *(G-4426)*
Reliable Brothers Inc 518 273-6732
185 Cohoes Ave Green Island (12183) *(G-5441)*

ALPHABETIC

Reliable Elec Mt Vernon Inc 914 668-4440
  519 S 5th Ave Mount Vernon (10550) *(G-8177)*
Reliable Press II Inc 718 840-5812
  73 Sealey Ave Hempstead (11550) *(G-5849)*
Reliable Welding & Fabrication 631 758-2637
  214 W Main St Patchogue (11772) *(G-12511)*
Reliance Fluid Tech LLC 716 332-0988
  3943 Buffalo Ave Niagara Falls (14303) *(G-11972)*
Reliance Gayco, Kingston *Also called Universal Metal Fabricators (G-6719)*
Reliance Machining Inc 718 784-0314
  4335 Vernon Blvd Long Island City (11101) *(G-7341)*
Reliance Mica Co Inc 718 788-0282
  336 Beach 149th St Rockaway Park (11694) *(G-13825)*
Reliant Security 917 338-2200
  450 Fashion Ave Ste 503 New York (10123) *(G-11003)*
Relmada Therapeutics Inc 646 677-3853
  750 3rd Ave Fl 9 New York (10017) *(G-11004)*
Relx Inc (HQ) 212 309-8100
  230 Park Ave Ste 700 New York (10169) *(G-11005)*
Relx Inc 212 463-6644
  249 W 17th St New York (10011) *(G-11006)*
Relx Inc 212 633-3900
  655 6th Ave New York (10010) *(G-11007)*
REM Printing Inc 518 438-7338
  55 Railroad Ave Albany (12205) *(G-126)*
Rem-Tronics Inc 716 934-2697
  659 Brigham Rd Dunkirk (14048) *(G-4064)*
Remains Lighting, Brooklyn *Also called Aesthonics Inc (G-1469)*
Remains Lighting 212 675-8051
  130 W 28th St Frnt 1 New York (10001) *(G-11008)*
Remarkable Liquids LLC 518 861-5351
  6032 Depot Rd Altamont (12009) *(G-197)*
Remarkety Inc (PA) 800 570-7564
  81 Prospect St Brooklyn (11201) *(G-2338)*
Rembar Company LLC 914 693-2620
  67 Main St Dobbs Ferry (10522) *(G-4019)*
Remcoda LLC 212 354-1330
  230 W 39th St Fl 10 New York (10018) *(G-11009)*
Remedies Surgical Supplies 718 599-5301
  331 Rutledge St Ste 204 Brooklyn (11211) *(G-2339)*
Remee Products Corp (PA) 845 651-4431
  1751 State Route 17a Florida (10921) *(G-4826)*
Remfo, Florida *Also called Remee Products Corp (G-4826)*
Remington Arms Company LLC 315 895-3482
  14 Hoefler Ave Ilion (13357) *(G-6281)*
Remodeling News, Bedford *Also called JSD Communications Inc (G-763)*
Remsen Fuel Inc 718 984-9551
  4668 Amboy Rd Staten Island (10312) *(G-14701)*
Remsen Graphics Corp 718 643-7500
  52 Court St 2 Brooklyn (11201) *(G-2340)*
Ren Tool & Manufacturing Co 518 377-2123
  1801 Chrisler Ave Schenectady (12303) *(G-14299)*
Renaissance Bijou Ltd 212 869-1969
  20 W 47th St Ste 18 New York (10036) *(G-11010)*
Renaissance Global, New York *Also called Renaissnce Crpt Tapestries Inc (G-11011)*
Renaissance Import, Lockport *Also called Candlelight Cabinetry Inc (G-7063)*
Renaissnce Crpt Tapestries Inc 212 696-0080
  200 Lexington Ave Rm 1006 New York (10016) *(G-11011)*
Renaldos Sales & Service Ctr 716 337-3760
  1770 Milestrip Rd North Collins (14111) *(G-12028)*
Renanssance The Book, Port Chester *Also called Albumx Corp (G-12813)*
Renco Group Inc (PA) 212 541-6000
  1 Rockefeller Plz Fl 29 New York (10020) *(G-11012)*
Renco Group of Companies, Inc., New York *Also called Renco Group Inc (G-11012)*
Renco Manufacturing Inc 718 392-8877
  1040 45th Ave Fl 2 Long Island City (11101) *(G-7342)*
Rene Portier Inc 718 853-7896
  3611 14th Ave Ste 6 Brooklyn (11218) *(G-2341)*
Renegade Nation Ltd 212 868-9000
  434 Ave Of The Amer Fl 6 New York (10011) *(G-11013)*
Renegade Nation Online LLC 212 868-9000
  434 Ave Of The Americas # 6 New York (10011) *(G-11014)*
Renewable Energy Inc 718 690-2691
  6 Cornell Ln Little Neck (11363) *(G-6998)*
Renmatix Inc 315 356-4780
  679 Ellsworth Rd Rome (13441) *(G-13867)*
Rennen International, Mineola *Also called Extreme Auto Accessories Corp (G-7973)*
Renold Inc 716 326-3121
  100 Bourne St Westfield (14787) *(G-15949)*
Renovatio Med & Surgical Sups, Buffalo *Also called Yr Blanc & Co LLC (G-3053)*
Rentschler Biotechnologie GMBH 631 656-7137
  400 Oser Ave Ste 1650 Hauppauge (11788) *(G-5754)*
REO Welding Inc 518 238-1022
  5 New Cortland St Cohoes (12047) *(G-3514)*
Repapers Corporation (PA) 305 691-1635
  268 N Broadway Unit 9 Hicksville (11801) *(G-5945)*
Repellem Consumer Pdts Corp 631 273-3992
  1626 Locust Ave Ste 6 Bohemia (11716) *(G-1070)*
Repertoire International De LI 212 817-1990
  365 5th Ave Fl 3 New York (10016) *(G-11015)*
Repro Med Systems Inc 845 469-2042
  24 Carpenter Rd Ste 1 Chester (10918) *(G-3383)*

Repsol Oil & Gas Usa LLC 607 562-4000
  337 Daniel Zenker Dr Horseheads (14845) *(G-6133)*
Republic Clothing Corporation 212 719-3000
  1411 Broadway Fl 37 New York (10018) *(G-11016)*
Republic Clothing Group, New York *Also called Republic Clothing Corporation (G-11016)*
Republic Clothing Group Inc 212 719-3000
  1411 Broadway Fl 37 New York (10018) *(G-11017)*
Republic Construction Co Inc 914 235-3654
  305 North Ave New Rochelle (10801) *(G-8353)*
Republic Steel Inc 716 827-2800
  3049 Lake Shore Rd Blasdell (14219) *(G-920)*
Republican Registrar Inc 315 497-1551
  6 Central St Moravia (13118) *(G-8083)*
Request Inc 518 899-1254
  14 Corporate Dr Ste 6 Halfmoon (12065) *(G-5497)*
Request Jeans, New York *Also called US Design Group Ltd (G-11623)*
Request Multimedia, Halfmoon *Also called Request Inc (G-5497)*
Request Serious Play LLC 518 899-1254
  14 Corporate Dr Halfmoon (12065) *(G-5498)*
Rescuestuff Inc 718 318-7570
  962 Washington St Peekskill (10566) *(G-12555)*
Research Centre of Kabbalah 718 805-0380
  8384 115th St Richmond Hill (11418) *(G-13121)*
Research Frontiers Inc (PA) 516 364-1902
  240 Crossways Park Dr Woodbury (11797) *(G-16181)*
Research Report For Food Svc, Irvington *Also called National RES Mktg Council
Inc (G-6311)*
Reserve Confections Chocolate, Spring Valley *Also called Reserve Confections
Inc (G-14581)*
Reserve Confections Inc 845 371-7744
  3 Perlman Dr Ste 105 Spring Valley (10977) *(G-14581)*
Reserve Gas Company, Alden *Also called Alden Aurora Gas Company Inc (G-165)*
Reserve Gas Company Inc 716 937-9484
  13441 Railroad St Alden (14004) *(G-173)*
Reservoir Media Management Inc (PA) 212 675-0541
  75 Varick St Fl 9a New York (10013) *(G-11018)*
Residential Fences Corp 631 205-9758
  1760 Middle Country Rd Ridge (11961) *(G-13134)*
Resonance Technologies Inc 631 237-4901
  109 Comac St Ronkonkoma (11779) *(G-14002)*
Resonant Legal Media LLC (PA) 800 781-3591
  1 Penn Plz Ste 1514 New York (10119) *(G-11019)*
Resource Capital Funds LP 631 692-9111
  2 Jericho Plz Ste 103 Jericho (11753) *(G-6592)*
Resource PTRlm&ptrochmcl Intl 212 537-3856
  3 Columbus Cir Fl 15 New York (10019) *(G-11020)*
Response Care Inc 585 671-4144
  38 Commercial St Webster (14580) *(G-15651)*
Responselink Inc 518 424-7776
  31 Dussault Dr Latham (12110) *(G-6875)*
Responselink of Albany, Latham *Also called Responselink Inc (G-6875)*
Restaurant 570 8th Avenue LLC 646 722-8191
  213 W 40th St Fl 3 New York (10018) *(G-11021)*
Restonic, Buffalo *Also called Royal Bedding Co Buffalo Inc (G-2966)*
Restorsea LLC 212 828-8878
  641 Lexington Ave Fl 27 New York (10022) *(G-11022)*
Retailer, Lockport *Also called Metro Group Inc (G-7092)*
Retailer, The, Port Washington *Also called Music & Sound Retailer Inc (G-12908)*
Retia Medical LLC (PA) 914 594-1986
  7 Dana Rd Ste 121 Valhalla (10595) *(G-15308)*
Retina Labs (usa) Inc 866 344-2692
  165 Broadway Ste 2301 New York (10006) *(G-11023)*
Retrophin LLC 646 564-3680
  777 3rd Ave Fl 22 New York (10017) *(G-11024)*
Reuse Action Incorporated 716 949-0900
  279 Northampton St Buffalo (14208) *(G-2952)*
Reuter Pallet Pkg Sys Inc 845 457-9937
  272 Neelytown Rd Montgomery (12549) *(G-8066)*
Revival Industries Inc 315 868-1085
  126 Old Forge Rd Ilion (13357) *(G-6282)*
Revival Sash & Door LLC (PA) 973 500-4242
  135 E 57th St Bldg 15125 New York (10022) *(G-11025)*
Revivn Public Benefit Corp 347 762-8193
  63 Flushing Ave Unit 231 Brooklyn (11205) *(G-2342)*
Revlon Inc (PA) 212 527-4000
  1 New York Plz Fl 49 New York (10004) *(G-11026)*
Revlon Consumer Products Corp (HQ) 212 527-4000
  1 New York Plz New York (10004) *(G-11027)*
Revman Distribution Center, New York *Also called Revman International Inc (G-11028)*
Revman International Inc (HQ) 212 894-3100
  350 5th Ave Fl 70 New York (10118) *(G-11028)*
Revol Usa LLC 678 456-8671
  41 Madison Ave Ste 1904 New York (10010) *(G-11029)*
Revolution Lighting LLC 518 779-3655
  211 Warren St Ste 1 Glens Falls (12801) *(G-5266)*
Revolutionwear Inc 617 669-9191
  1745 Broadway Fl 17 New York (10019) *(G-11030)*
Rexford Services Inc 716 366-6671
  4849 W Lake Rd Dunkirk (14048) *(G-4065)*
Reynolds Book Bindery LLC 607 772-8937
  37 Milford St Binghamton (13904) *(G-906)*

Reynolds Drapery Service Inc.................................315 845-8632
  7440 Main St Newport (13416) *(G-11899)*
Reynolds Manufacturing Inc..................................607 562-8936
  3298 State Rte 352 Big Flats (14814) *(G-848)*
Reynolds Metals Company LLC (HQ)........................212 518-5400
  390 Park Ave New York (10022) *(G-11031)*
Reynolds Packaging McHy Inc...............................716 358-6451
  2632 S Work St 24 Falconer (14733) *(G-4554)*
Reynolds Shipyard Corporation..............................718 981-2800
  200 Edgewater St Staten Island (10305) *(G-14702)*
Reynolds Tech Fabricators Inc................................315 437-0532
  6895 Kinne St East Syracuse (13057) *(G-4233)*
Rf Communications, Rochester *Also called L3harris Technologies Inc (G-13511)*
Rf Inter Science Co, Patchogue *Also called Kevin Freeman (G-12505)*
Rfb Associates Inc..518 271-0551
  35 Sullivan Pkwy Fort Edward (12828) *(G-4943)*
Rfg, New York *Also called M S Riviera Inc (G-10300)*
Rfn Inc...516 764-5100
  44 Drexel Dr Bay Shore (11706) *(G-705)*
Rfp LLC...212 838-7733
  228 E 45th St Fl 11 New York (10017) *(G-11032)*
Rft, New York *Also called Rainforest Inc (G-10973)*
RG, Buffalo *Also called Roberts-Gordon LLC (G-2957)*
RG Apparel Group, New York *Also called Excelled Sheepskin & Lea Coat (G-9443)*
RG Barry Corporation...212 244-3145
  9 E 37th St Fl 11 New York (10016) *(G-11033)*
RG Glass Creations Inc.......................................212 675-0030
  1441 Broadway Ste 28 New York (10018) *(G-11034)*
RGH Associates Inc..631 643-1111
  86 Nancy St West Babylon (11704) *(G-15741)*
Rgm Signs Inc..718 442-0598
  1234 Castleton Ave Staten Island (10310) *(G-14703)*
Rheonix Inc (PA)..607 257-1242
  10 Brown Rd Ste 103 Ithaca (14850) *(G-6409)*
Rhett M Clark Inc...585 538-9570
  3213 Lehigh St Caledonia (14423) *(G-3072)*
Rhino Rugby, Tarrytown *Also called Rhino Sports & Leisure LLC (G-15058)*
Rhino Sports & Leisure LLC..................................844 877-4466
  303 S Broadway Ste 450 Tarrytown (10591) *(G-15058)*
Rhino Trunk & Case Inc......................................585 244-4553
  565 Blossom Rd Ste J Rochester (14610) *(G-13671)*
Rhoda Lee Inc..212 840-5700
  77 W 55th St Apt 4k New York (10019) *(G-11035)*
Rhosey LLC...718 382-1226
  1677 Mcdonald Ave Brooklyn (11230) *(G-2343)*
Ribble Lumber Inc..315 536-6221
  249 1/2 Lake St Penn Yan (14527) *(G-12592)*
Ribz LLC..212 764-9595
  1407 Broadway Rm 1402 New York (10018) *(G-11036)*
Ric-Lo Productions Ltd.......................................845 469-2285
  1144 Kings Hwy Chester (10918) *(G-3384)*
Rich Brilliant Willing, Brooklyn *Also called Rbw Studio LLC (G-2331)*
Rich Holdings Inc...716 878-8000
  1 Robert Rich Way Buffalo (14213) *(G-2953)*
Rich Products Corporation (PA)..............................716 878-8000
  1 Robert Rich Way Buffalo (14213) *(G-2954)*
Richard Anthony Corp...914 922-7141
  1500 Front St Ste 12 Yorktown Heights (10598) *(G-16371)*
Richard Anthony Custom Mllwk, Yorktown Heights *Also called Richard Anthony
Corp (G-16371)*
Richard Bauer Logging.......................................585 343-4149
  3936 Cookson Rd Alexander (14005) *(G-179)*
Richard C Owen Publishers Inc..............................914 232-3903
  243 Route 100 Somers (10589) *(G-14500)*
Richard Engdal Baking Corp..................................914 777-9600
  421 Waverly Ave Mamaroneck (10543) *(G-7521)*
Richard Manno & Company Inc..............................631 643-2200
  42 Lamar St West Babylon (11704) *(G-15742)*
Richard Manufacturing Co Inc...............................718 254-0958
  63 Flushing Ave Unit 327 Brooklyn (11205) *(G-2344)*
Richard Rothbard Inc...845 355-2300
  1866 Route 284 Slate Hill (10973) *(G-14463)*
Richard Ruffner..631 234-4600
  69 Carleton Ave Central Islip (11722) *(G-3287)*
Richard Stacey Rs Automation, Albion *Also called Rs Automation (G-160)*
Richard Stewart...518 632-5363
  4495 State Rte 149 Hartford (12838) *(G-5566)*
Richards & West Inc...585 461-4088
  501 W Commercial St Ste 1 East Rochester (14445) *(G-4169)*
Richards Logging LLC..518 359-2775
  201 State Route 3 Tupper Lake (12986) *(G-15213)*
Richards Machine Tool Co Inc................................716 683-3380
  36 Nichter Rd Lancaster (14086) *(G-6829)*
Richards Screw Machine, West Babylon *Also called RGH Associates Inc (G-15741)*
Richardson Brands Company (HQ)...........................800 839-8938
  101 Erie Blvd Canajoharie (13317) *(G-3121)*
Richardson Foods, Canajoharie *Also called Richardson Brands Company (G-3121)*
Richardson Molding LLC.....................................716 282-1261
  3123 Highland Ave Niagara Falls (14305) *(G-11973)*
Richemont North America Inc................................212 355-7052
  535 Madison Ave New York (10022) *(G-11037)*

Richemont North America Inc................................212 644-9500
  729 Madison Ave New York (10065) *(G-11038)*
Richer's Bakery, Flushing *Also called H H B Bakery of Little Neck (G-4856)*
Richlar Custom Foam Div, East Syracuse *Also called Richlar Industries Inc (G-4234)*
Richlar Industries Inc...315 463-5144
  6741 Old Collamer Rd East Syracuse (13057) *(G-4234)*
Richline Group Inc...212 643-2908
  245 W 29th St Rm 900 New York (10001) *(G-11039)*
Richline Group Inc...212 764-8454
  1385 Broadway Fl 12 New York (10018) *(G-11040)*
Richline Group Inc...914 699-0000
  1385 Broadway Fl 12 New York (10018) *(G-11041)*
Richloom Fabrics Corp (PA)..................................212 685-5400
  261 5th Ave Fl 12 New York (10016) *(G-11042)*
Richloom Fabrics Group Inc (PA)............................212 685-5400
  261 5th Ave Fl 12 New York (10016) *(G-11043)*
Richmar Printing Inc...631 617-6915
  44 Drexel Dr Bay Shore (11706) *(G-706)*
Richmond Ready Mix Corp....................................917 731-8400
  328 Park St Staten Island (10306) *(G-14704)*
Richmond Ready Mix Corp II.................................917 731-8400
  291 Chelsea Rd Staten Island (10314) *(G-14705)*
Richner Communications Inc (PA)...........................516 569-4000
  2 Endo Blvd Garden City (11530) *(G-5113)*
Richner Communications Inc.................................516 569-4000
  379 Central Ave Lawrence (11559) *(G-6891)*
Richs Stitches EMB Screenprint..............................845 621-2175
  407 Route 6 Mahopac (10541) *(G-7477)*
Richter Charles Metal STMp&sp..............................845 895-2025
  80 Cottage St Wallkill (12589) *(G-15471)*
Richter Metalcraft Corporation...............................845 895-2025
  80 Cottage St Wallkill (12589) *(G-15472)*
Rid Lom Precision Mfg..585 594-8600
  50 Regency Oaks Blvd Rochester (14624) *(G-13672)*
Ridge Cabinet & Showcase Inc..............................585 663-0560
  1545 Mount Read Blvd # 2 Rochester (14606) *(G-13673)*
Ridgewood Times Prtg & Pubg................................718 821-7500
  6071 Woodbine St Fl 1 Ridgewood (11385) *(G-13158)*
Rigicon Inc...631 676-3376
  2805 Veterans Memo Ronkonkoma (11779) *(G-14003)*
Rigidized Metals Corporation.................................716 849-4703
  658 Ohio St Buffalo (14203) *(G-2955)*
Rigidized-Metal, Buffalo *Also called Rigidized Metals Corporation (G-2955)*
Rij Pharmaceutical Corporation...............................845 692-5799
  40 Commercial Ave Middletown (10941) *(G-7929)*
Rike Enterprises Inc...631 277-8338
  46 Taft Ave Islip (11751) *(G-6356)*
Riley Gear Corporation.......................................716 694-0900
  61 Felton St North Tonawanda (14120) *(G-12086)*
RILM, New York *Also called Repertoire International De LI (G-11015)*
Rimco Plastics Corp..607 739-3864
  316 Colonial Dr Horseheads (14845) *(G-6134)*
Rimowa Inc (PA)...214 360-4268
  598 Madison Ave Fl 8 New York (10022) *(G-11044)*
Rimowa Distribution, New York *Also called Rimowa Inc (G-11044)*
Rims Like New Inc..845 537-0396
  507 Union School Rd Middletown (10941) *(G-7930)*
Rina, Plattsburgh *Also called Rapa Independent North America (G-12774)*
Rinaldi Precision Machine....................................631 242-4141
  43 Crossway Dr Deer Park (11729) *(G-3928)*
Ring Division Producto Machine, Jamestown *Also called Producto Corporation (G-6538)*
Ringlead Inc..310 906-0545
  200 Broadhollow Rd # 400 Melville (11747) *(G-7819)*
Rings Wire Inc..212 741-9779
  246 W 38th St Rm 501 New York (10018) *(G-11045)*
Rini Tank & Truck Service.....................................718 384-6606
  327 Nassau Ave Brooklyn (11222) *(G-2345)*
Riot New Media Group Inc.....................................604 700-4896
  147 Prince St Ste 1 Brooklyn (11201) *(G-2346)*
Rip-It Rip-It Shred-It Corp....................................516 818-5825
  920 Lincoln Ave Unit 8 Holbrook (11741) *(G-6017)*
Ripak Aerospace Processing, West Babylon *Also called Magellan Aerospace
Processing (G-15728)*
Ripi Precision Co Inc (PA)....................................631 694-2453
  92 Toledo St Farmingdale (11735) *(G-4724)*
Ripley Machine & Tool Co Inc................................716 736-3205
  9825 E Main Rd Ripley (14775) *(G-13170)*
Riri USA Inc..212 268-3866
  350 5th Ave Ste 6700 New York (10118) *(G-11046)*
Risa Management Corp..718 361-2606
  5501 43rd St Fl 3 Maspeth (11378) *(G-7637)*
Risa's, Maspeth *Also called Risa Management Corp (G-7637)*
Rising Stars Soccer Club CNY...............................315 381-3096
  4980 State Route 233 Westmoreland (13490) *(G-15962)*
Rising Tide Fuel LLC...631 374-7361
  2 S Bay Ave Amityville (11701) *(G-305)*
Rision Inc..212 987-2628
  306 E 78th St Apt 1b New York (10075) *(G-11047)*
Risk Management Magazine, New York *Also called Risk Society Management
Pubg (G-11048)*

A
L
P
H
A
B
E
T
I
C

Risk Society Management Pubg 212 286-9364
  655 3rd Ave Fl 2 New York (10017) *(G-11048)*

RIT Printing Corp 631 586-6220
  250 N Fairway Bay Shore (11706) *(G-707)*

Ritani LLC 888 974-8264
  30 Dr Martin Luther White Plains (10601) *(G-16056)*

Ritchie Corp 212 768-0083
  263 W 38th St Fl 13 New York (10018) *(G-11049)*

Ritnoa Inc 212 660-2148
  24019 Jamaica Ave Ste 2 Bellerose (11426) *(G-776)*

Rittlewood Holding Co, New York *Also called Rda Holding Co (G-10990)*

Riva Jewelry Manufacturing Inc 718 361-3100
  140 58th St Ste 8b Brooklyn (11220) *(G-2347)*

River Valley Paper Co, Syracuse *Also called Rvc Inc (G-14981)*

Riverdale Press, The, Bronx *Also called Dale Press Inc (G-1236)*

Riverfront Costume Design 716 693-2501
  200 River Rd North Tonawanda (14120) *(G-12087)*

Riverhawk Company LP 315 624-7171
  215 Clinton Rd New Hartford (13413) *(G-8244)*

Riverside Automation, Rochester *Also called Riverview Associates Inc (G-13674)*

Riverside Iron LLC 315 535-4864
  26 Water St Gouverneur (13642) *(G-5322)*

Riverside Machinery Company (PA) 718 492-7400
  140 53rd St Brooklyn (11232) *(G-2348)*

Riverside Machinery Company 718 492-7400
  132 54th St Brooklyn (11220) *(G-2349)*

Rivertowns Enterprise, Dobbs Ferry *Also called W H White Publications Inc (G-4021)*

Riverview Associates Inc 585 235-5980
  1040 Jay St Rochester (14611) *(G-13674)*

Riverview Industries Inc 845 265-5284
  3012 Route 9 Ste 1 Cold Spring (10516) *(G-3524)*

Riverwood Signs By Dandev Desi 845 229-0282
  7 Maple Ln Hyde Park (12538) *(G-6274)*

Riviera Sun Inc 212 546-9220
  512 Fashion Ave Fl 30 New York (10018) *(G-11050)*

Rizzoli Intl Publications Inc (HQ) 212 387-3400
  300 Park Ave S Fl 4 New York (10010) *(G-11051)*

Rizzoli Intl Publications Inc 212 387-3572
  300 Park Ave S Fl 3 New York (10010) *(G-11052)*

Rizzoli Intl Publications Inc 212 308-2000
  300 Park Ave Frnt 4 New York (10022) *(G-11053)*

RJ Harvey Instrument Corp 845 359-3943
  11 Jane St Tappan (10983) *(G-15038)*

Rj Millworkers Inc 607 433-0525
  12 Lewis St Oneonta (13820) *(G-12281)*

RJ Precision LLC 585 768-8030
  6662 Main Rd Stafford (14143) *(G-14605)*

Rj Welding & Fabricating Inc 315 523-1288
  2300 Wheat Rd Clifton Springs (14432) *(G-3480)*

Rjd Associates, New York *Also called Robert J Deluca Associates (G-11061)*

Rjm2 Ltd 212 944-1660
  241 W 37th St Rm 926 New York (10018) *(G-11054)*

Rjs Machine Works Inc 716 826-1778
  1611 Electric Ave Lackawanna (14218) *(G-6744)*

Rk Pharma Inc (PA) 646 884-3765
  401 N Middletown Rd Pearl River (10965) *(G-12540)*

Rle Industries LLC 973 276-1444
  1175 York Ave Apt 15e New York (10065) *(G-11055)*

Rli Schlgel Specialty Pdts LLC (HQ) 585 627-5919
  1555 Jefferson Rd Rochester (14623) *(G-13675)*

Rlp Holdings Inc 716 852-0832
  1049 Military Rd Buffalo (14217) *(G-2956)*

Rls Holdings Inc 716 418-7274
  11342 Main St Clarence (14031) *(G-3441)*

Rm Bakery LLC 718 472-3036
  220 Coster St Bronx (10474) *(G-1351)*

Rmb Embroidery Service 585 271-5560
  176 Anderson Ave Ste F110 Rochester (14607) *(G-13676)*

Rmd Holding Inc 845 628-0030
  593 Route 6 Mahopac (10541) *(G-7478)*

Rmf Print Management Group 716 683-4351
  786 Terrace Blvd Ste 3 Depew (14043) *(G-3997)*

Rmf Printing Technologies Inc 716 683-7500
  50 Pearl St Lancaster (14086) *(G-6830)*

Rmi Printing, New York *Also called Rosen Mandell & Immerman Inc (G-11083)*

RMS Medical Products, Chester *Also called Repro Med Systems Inc (G-3383)*

RMS Packaging Inc 914 205-2070
  1050 Lower South St Peekskill (10566) *(G-12556)*

Rmw Filtration Products Co LLC 631 226-9412
  230 Lambert Ave Copiague (11726) *(G-3674)*

Rnd Enterprises Inc 212 627-0165
  446 W 33rd St New York (10001) *(G-11056)*

Rnd Food Service Inc 917 291-0061
  88 W Broadway New York (10007) *(G-11057)*

Road Cases USA Inc 631 563-0633
  1625 Sycamore Ave Ste A Bohemia (11716) *(G-1071)*

Roadie Products Inc 631 567-8588
  1121 Lincoln Ave Unit 20 Holbrook (11741) *(G-6018)*

Roadrunner Records Inc (PA) 212 274-7500
  1290 Ave Of The Americas New York (10104) *(G-11058)*

Roanwell Corporation 718 401-0288
  2564 Park Ave Bronx (10451) *(G-1352)*

Roar Beverages LLC 631 683-5565
  2 Seaview Blvd Fl 3 Port Washington (11050) *(G-12918)*

Roar Biomedical Inc 631 591-2749
  4603 Middle Country Rd Calverton (11933) *(G-3085)*

Rob Herschenfeld Design Inc 718 456-6801
  304 Boerum St Brooklyn (11206) *(G-2350)*

Rob Salamida Company Inc 607 729-4868
  71 Pratt Ave Ste 1 Johnson City (13790) *(G-6608)*

Robeco/Ascot Products Inc 516 248-1521
  100 Ring Rd W Garden City (11530) *(G-5114)*

Robell Research Inc 212 755-6577
  655 Madison Ave Fl 24 New York (10065) *(G-11059)*

Robert & William Inc (PA) 631 727-5780
  224 Griffing Ave Riverhead (11901) *(G-13187)*

Robert Abady Dog Food Co Ltd 845 473-1900
  201 Smith St Poughkeepsie (12601) *(G-12979)*

Robert Bartholomew Ltd 516 767-2970
  15 Main St Port Washington (11050) *(G-12919)*

Robert Bosch LLC 315 733-3312
  2118 Beechgrove Pl Utica (13501) *(G-15292)*

Robert Cohen 718 789-0996
  10540 Rockaway Blvd Ste A Ozone Park (11417) *(G-12467)*

Robert Danes Danes Inc (PA) 212 226-1351
  481 Greenwich St Apt 5b New York (10013) *(G-11060)*

Robert E Derecktor Inc 914 698-0962
  311 E Boston Post Rd Mamaroneck (10543) *(G-7522)*

Robert Greenburg (PA) 845 586-2226
  Cross Rd Margaretville (12455) *(G-7567)*

Robert J Deluca Associates 845 357-3212
  260 Riverside Dr Apt 8a New York (10025) *(G-11061)*

Robert J Faraone 585 232-7160
  1600 N Clinton Ave Rochester (14621) *(G-13677)*

Robert King Music, New York *Also called Alphonse Lduc - Rbert King Inc (G-8527)*

Robert Lighting & Energy, New York *Also called Rle Industries LLC (G-11055)*

Robert M Brown 607 426-6250
  150 Mill St Montour Falls (14865) *(G-8076)*

Robert Miller Associates LLC 718 392-1640
  2219 41st Ave Ste 505 Long Island City (11101) *(G-7343)*

Robert Pikcilingis 518 355-1860
  2575 Western Ave Altamont (12009) *(G-198)*

Robert Racine (PA) 518 677-0224
  41 N Union St Cambridge (12816) *(G-3096)*

Robert Tabatznik Assoc Inc (PA) 845 336-4555
  867 Flatbush Rd Kingston (12401) *(G-6708)*

Robert Viggiani 914 423-4046
  37 Vredenburgh Ave Ste B Yonkers (10704) *(G-16346)*

Robert-Masters Corp 718 545-1030
  3217 61st St Woodside (11377) *(G-16224)*

Roberto Coin Inc (PA) 212 486-4545
  579 5th Ave Fl 17 New York (10017) *(G-11062)*

Roberts Office Furn Cncpts Inc 315 451-9185
  7327 Henry Clay Blvd Liverpool (13088) *(G-7038)*

Roberts-Gordon LLC (HQ) 716 852-4400
  1250 William St Buffalo (14206) *(G-2957)*

Robespierre Inc 212 764-8810
  214 W 39th St Ph Ste 602 New York (10018) *(G-11063)*

Robin Industries Ltd 718 218-9616
  56 N 3rd St Brooklyn (11249) *(G-2351)*

Robin Stanley Inc 212 871-0007
  1212 Avenue Of The Americ New York (10036) *(G-11064)*

Robinson Concrete Inc (PA) 315 253-6666
  3486 Franklin Street Rd Auburn (13021) *(G-493)*

Robinson Concrete Inc 315 676-4333
  2735 State Route 49 West Monroe (13167) *(G-15814)*

Robinson Concrete Inc 315 492-6200
  3537 Apulia Rd Jamesville (13078) *(G-6562)*

Robinson Concrete Inc 315 676-4662
  7020 Corporate Park Dr Brewerton (13029) *(G-1137)*

Robinson Knife 716 685-6300
  2615 Walden Ave Buffalo (14225) *(G-2958)*

Robinson Tools LLC 585 586-5432
  477 Whitney Rd Penfield (14526) *(G-12573)*

Robly Digital Marketing LLC 917 238-0730
  93 Leonard St Apt 6 New York (10013) *(G-11065)*

Robo Self Serve, Williamsville *Also called Schmitt Sales Inc (G-16137)*

Robocom Systems International, Farmingdale *Also called Robocom Us LLC (G-4725)*

Robocom Us LLC (HQ) 631 861-2045
  1111 Broadhollow Rd # 100 Farmingdale (11735) *(G-4725)*

Roboshop Inc 315 437-6454
  226 Midler Park Dr Syracuse (13206) *(G-14977)*

Robot Fruit Inc 631 423-7250
  40 Radcliff Dr Huntington (11743) *(G-6220)*

Robs Cycle Supply 315 292-6878
  613 Wolf St Syracuse (13208) *(G-14978)*

Robs Really Good LLC 516 671-4411
  100 Roslyn Ave Sea Cliff (11579) *(G-14347)*

Roccera LLC 585 426-0887
  771 Elmgrove Rd Bldg No2 Rochester (14624) *(G-13678)*

Rocco Bormioli Glass Co Inc (PA) 212 719-0606
  41 Madison Ave Ste 1603 New York (10010) *(G-11066)*

Roche Tcrc Inc 800 626-3553
  420 E 29th St Fl 15 Flr 15 New York (10016) *(G-11067)*

Rochester 100 Inc..585 475-0200
40 Jefferson Rd Rochester (14623) *(G-13679)*

Rochester Area Mdia Prtners LL....................585 244-3329
280 State St Rochester (14614) *(G-13680)*

Rochester Asphalt Materials (HQ)....................585 381-7010
1150 Penfield Rd Rochester (14625) *(G-13681)*

Rochester Asphalt Materials.........................315 524-4619
1200 Atlantic Ave Walworth (14568) *(G-15478)*

Rochester Asphalt Materials.........................585 924-7360
5929 Loomis Rd Farmington (14425) *(G-4777)*

Rochester Atomated Systems Inc..................585 594-3222
40 Regency Oaks Blvd Rochester (14624) *(G-13682)*

Rochester Business Journal.........................585 546-8303
16 W Main St Ste 341 Rochester (14614) *(G-13683)*

Rochester Catholic Press (PA).....................585 529-9530
1150 Buffalo Rd Rochester (14624) *(G-13684)*

Rochester Coca Cola Bottling.......................607 739-5678
210 Industrial Park Rd Horseheads (14845) *(G-6135)*

Rochester Coca Cola Bottling.......................585 546-3900
123 Upper Falls Blvd Rochester (14605) *(G-13685)*

Rochester Colonial Mfg Corp (PA)..................585 254-8191
1794 Lyell Ave Rochester (14606) *(G-13686)*

Rochester Countertop Inc (PA).....................585 338-2260
3300 Monroe Ave Ste 212 Rochester (14618) *(G-13687)*

Rochester Democrat & Chronicle....................585 232-7100
55 Exchange Blvd Rochester (14614) *(G-13688)*

Rochester Gear Inc..................................585 254-5442
213 Norman St Rochester (14613) *(G-13689)*

Rochester Golf Week, Rochester Also called Expositor Newspapers Inc *(G-13407)*

Rochester Industrial Ctrl Inc (PA)..................315 524-4555
6400 Furnace Rd Ontario (14519) *(G-12300)*

Rochester Industrial Ctrl Inc.......................315 524-4555
6345 Furnace Rd Ontario (14519) *(G-12301)*

Rochester Insulated Glass Inc......................585 289-3611
73 Merrick Cir Manchester (14504) *(G-7528)*

Rochester Lumber Company.........................585 924-7171
6080 Collett Rd Farmington (14425) *(G-4778)*

Rochester Magnet, East Rochester Also called Carpentier Industries LLC *(G-4160)*

Rochester Midland Corporation (PA)...............585 336-2200
155 Paragon Dr Rochester (14624) *(G-13690)*

Rochester Orthopedic Labs (PA)....................585 272-1060
300 Airpark Dr Ste 100 Rochester (14624) *(G-13691)*

Rochester Overnight Pltg LLC.......................585 328-4590
2 Cairn St Rochester (14611) *(G-13692)*

Rochester Personal Defense LLC....................585 406-6758
115 Redwood Rd Rochester (14615) *(G-13693)*

Rochester Photonics Corp...........................585 387-0674
115 Canal Landing Blvd Rochester (14626) *(G-13694)*

Rochester Precision Optics LLC.....................585 292-5450
850 John St West Henrietta (14586) *(G-15802)*

Rochester Screen Printing, Rochester Also called Michael Todd Stevens *(G-13544)*

Rochester Seal Pro LLC.............................585 594-3818
155 W Hill Est Rochester (14626) *(G-13695)*

Rochester Silver Works LLC.........................585 477-9501
100 Latona Rd Bldg 110 Rochester (14652) *(G-13696)*

Rochester Silver Works LLC.........................585 743-1610
240 Aster St Rochester (14615) *(G-13697)*

Rochester Stampings Inc...........................585 467-5241
400 Trade Ct Rochester (14624) *(G-13698)*

Rochester Steel Treating Works.....................585 546-3348
962 E Main St Rochester (14605) *(G-13699)*

Rochester Structural LLC...........................585 436-1250
961 Lyell Ave Bldg 5 Rochester (14606) *(G-13700)*

Rochester Technology Park, Rochester Also called Tech Park Food Services LLC *(G-13762)*

Rochester Tool and Mold Inc........................585 464-9336
515 Lee Rd Rochester (14606) *(G-13701)*

Rock Hill Bakehouse Ltd............................518 743-1627
21 Saratoga Rd Gansevoort (12831) *(G-5086)*

Rock Iroquois Products Inc..........................585 637-6834
5251 Sweden Walker Rd Brockport (14420) *(G-1179)*

Rock Mountain Farms Inc...........................845 647-9084
11 Spring St Ellenville (12428) *(G-4311)*

Rock Stream Vineyards..............................607 243-8322
162 Fir Tree Point Rd Rock Stream (14878) *(G-13819)*

Rockaloid, Piermont Also called Rockland Colloid Corp *(G-12622)*

Rockaway Stairs Ltd................................718 945-0047
1011 Bay 24th St Far Rockaway (11691) *(G-4567)*

Rocket Communications, Buffalo Also called Gallagher Printing Inc *(G-2764)*

Rocket Communications Inc.........................716 873-2594
2507 Delaware Ave Buffalo (14216) *(G-2959)*

Rocket Fuel, New York Also called Sizmek Dsp Inc *(G-11253)*

Rocket Pharmaceuticals Inc (PA)....................646 440-9100
350 5th Ave Ste 7530 New York (10118) *(G-11068)*

Rocket Tech Fuel Corp..............................516 810-8947
20 Corbin Ave Bay Shore (11706) *(G-708)*

Rocking The Boat Inc................................718 466-5799
812 Edgewater Rd Bronx (10474) *(G-1353)*

Rockland Colloid Corp (PA)..........................845 359-5559
44 Franklin St Piermont (10968) *(G-12622)*

Rockland County Times, Nanuet Also called Citizen Publishing Corp *(G-8198)*

Rockland Insulated Wire Cable......................845 429-3103
87 Broadway Haverstraw (10927) *(G-5806)*

Rockland Manufacturing Co.........................845 358-6000
44 High St West Nyack (10994) *(G-15832)*

Rockland Review Publishing, West Nyack Also called Angel Media and Publishing *(G-15816)*

Rockmills Steel Products Corp.......................718 366-8300
3 Hayden Ave Great Neck (11024) *(G-5417)*

Rockport Pa LLC (PA)...............................212 482-8580
505 5th Ave Fl 26 New York (10017) *(G-11069)*

Rockville Pro, Inwood Also called Audiosavings Inc *(G-6289)*

Rockwell Automation Inc............................585 487-2700
1000 Pittsford Victor Rd # 17 Pittsford (14534) *(G-12656)*

Rockwell Industries Intl Corp........................516 927-8300
80 Newtown Rd Plainview (11803) *(G-12710)*

Rockwell Video Solutions LLC.......................631 745-0582
10 Koral Dr Southampton (11968) *(G-14536)*

Rodac USA Corp....................................716 741-3931
5605 Kraus Rd Clarence (14031) *(G-3442)*

Rodan, Hicksville Also called Oxygen Inc *(G-5936)*

Rodem Incorporated................................212 779-7122
120 W 29th St Frnt A New York (10001) *(G-11070)*

Rodgard Corporation................................716 852-1435
92 Msgr Valente Dr Buffalo (14206) *(G-2960)*

Roechling Medical Rochester LP (HQ)...............585 254-2000
999 Ridgeway Ave Rochester (14615) *(G-13702)*

Roemac Industrial Sales Inc........................716 692-7332
27 Fredericka St North Tonawanda (14120) *(G-12088)*

Roessel & Co Inc...................................585 458-5560
199 Lagrange Ave Rochester (14613) *(G-13703)*

Roffe Accessories Inc..............................212 213-1440
833 Broadway Apt 4 New York (10003) *(G-11071)*

Rogan LLC..212 680-1407
330 Bowery New York (10012) *(G-11072)*

Rogan LLC (PA).....................................646 496-9339
270 Bowery 3 New York (10012) *(G-11073)*

Roger & Sons Inc...................................212 226-4734
268 Bowery Frnt 6 New York (10012) *(G-11074)*

Roger L Urban Inc (PA).............................716 693-5391
908 Niagara Falls Blvd # 107 North Tonawanda (14120) *(G-12089)*

Roger Latari.......................................631 580-2422
30 Raynor Ave Ste 1 Ronkonkoma (11779) *(G-14004)*

Roger Michael Press Inc (PA).......................732 752-0800
499 Van Brunt St Ste 6b Brooklyn (11231) *(G-2352)*

Rogers Enterprises, Rochester Also called Dock Hardware Incorporated *(G-13352)*

Rogers Group Inc...................................212 643-9292
318 W 39th St Fl 4 New York (10018) *(G-11075)*

Rogers Industrial Spring, Buffalo Also called Kehr-Buffalo Wire Frame Co Inc *(G-2830)*

Rohlfs Stined Leaded GL Studio.....................914 699-4848
783 S 3rd Ave Mount Vernon (10550) *(G-8178)*

Rohrbach Brewing Company Inc......................585 594-9800
3859 Buffalo Rd Rochester (14624) *(G-13704)*

Rokon Tech LLC....................................718 429-0729
5223 74th St Elmhurst (11373) *(G-4338)*

Roli Retreads Inc..................................631 694-7670
212 E Carmans Rd Unit A Farmingdale (11735) *(G-4726)*

Roli Tire and Auto Repair, Farmingdale Also called Roli Retreads Inc *(G-4726)*

Roli USA Inc.......................................412 600-4840
100 5th Ave New York (10011) *(G-11076)*

Rolite Mfg Inc.....................................716 683-0259
10 Wendling Ct Lancaster (14086) *(G-6831)*

Roll Lock Truss, Waddington Also called Structural Wood Corporation *(G-15447)*

Rollers Inc..716 837-0700
2495 Main St Bldg 359 Buffalo (14214) *(G-2961)*

Rollers Unlimited, Syracuse Also called David Fehlman *(G-14875)*

Rollform of Jamestown Inc.........................716 665-5310
181 Blackstone Ave Jamestown (14701) *(G-6539)*

Rollhaus Seating Products Inc......................718 729-9111
4310 21st St Long Island City (11101) *(G-7344)*

Rolling Gate Supply Corp...........................718 366-5258
7919 Cypress Ave Glendale (11385) *(G-5232)*

Rolling Star Manufacturing Inc......................315 896-4767
125 Liberty Ln Barneveld (13304) *(G-595)*

Rolling Stone, New York Also called Wenner Media LLC *(G-11743)*

Rolling Stone Magazine..............................212 484-1616
1290 Ave Of The Amer Fl 2 New York (10104) *(G-11077)*

Rollo Mio Artisan Bakery, Bronx Also called Rm Bakery LLC *(G-1351)*

Rollson Inc..631 423-9578
10 Smugglers Cv Huntington (11743) *(G-6221)*

Roly Door Sales Inc................................716 877-1515
5659 Herman Hill Rd Hamburg (14075) *(G-5520)*

Roma Bakery Inc...................................516 825-9170
45 Railroad Ave Valley Stream (11580) *(G-15357)*

Roma Industries LLC................................212 268-0723
12 W 37th St Fl 10 New York (10018) *(G-11078)*

Roma Ray Bakery, Valley Stream Also called Rays Italian Bakery Inc *(G-15355)*

Romac Electronics Inc..............................516 349-7900
155 E Ames Ct Unit 1 Plainview (11803) *(G-12711)*

Roman Iron Works Inc..............................516 621-1103
15 Plaza Rd Greenvale (11548) *(G-5463)*

Roman Stone Construction Co.......................631 667-0566
85 S 4th St Bay Shore (11706) *(G-709)*

Romance & Co Inc..................................212 382-0337
2 W 47th St Ste 1111 New York (10036) *(G-11079)*

Romantic Times Inc 718 237-1097
9 Ridgewood Pl Brooklyn (11237) *(G-2353)*

Romantic Times Magazine, Brooklyn *Also called Romantic Times Inc (G-2353)*

Romar Contracting Inc 845 778-2737
630 State Route 52 Walden (12586) *(G-15461)*

Romark Diagnostics, Tappan *Also called RJ Harvey Instrument Corp (G-15038)*

Rome Fastener, New York *Also called Rings Wire Inc (G-11045)*

Rome Main Street Alliance Inc 315 271-8356
506 N James St Rome (13440) *(G-13868)*

Rome Sign & Display Co 315 336-0550
510 Erie Blvd W Rome (13440) *(G-13869)*

Rome Specialty Company Inc 315 337-8200
501 W Embargo St Rome (13440) *(G-13870)*

Romir Enterprises, New York *Also called Mer Gems Corp (G-10432)*

Romold Inc 585 529-4440
5 Moonlanding Rd Rochester (14624) *(G-13705)*

Rona Precision Inc 631 737-4034
142 Remington Blvd Ste 2 Ronkonkoma (11779) *(G-14005)*

Rona Precision Mfg, Ronkonkoma *Also called Rona Precision Inc (G-14005)*

Ronan Paints, Bronx *Also called T J Ronan Paint Corp (G-1376)*

Ronbar Laboratories Inc 718 937-6755
5202 Van Dam St Long Island City (11101) *(G-7345)*

Roner Inc (PA) 718 392-6020
3553 24th St Long Island City (11106) *(G-7346)*

Roner Inc 718 392-6020
1433 31st Ave Long Island City (11106) *(G-7347)*

Ronmar, Flushing *Also called United Steel Products Inc (G-4904)*

Ronni Nicole Group LLC 212 764-1000
1400 Broadway Rm 2102 New York (10018) *(G-11080)*

Roo Inc 212 905-6100
41 E 11th St Fl 11 New York (10003) *(G-11081)*

Roode Hoek & Co Inc 718 522-5921
55 Ferris St Brooklyn (11231) *(G-2354)*

Roofing Consultant, Buffalo *Also called Tiedemann Waldemar Inc (G-3010)*

Roome Technologies Inc 585 229-4437
4796 Honeoye Business Par Honeoye (14471) *(G-6069)*

Rooster Hill Vineyards, Penn Yan *Also called Hoffman & Hoffman (G-12586)*

Ropack USA Inc 631 482-7777
49 Mall Dr Commack (11725) *(G-3596)*

Rosco Inc (PA) 718 526-2601
9021 144th Pl Jamaica (11435) *(G-6471)*

Rosco Collision Avoidance Inc 718 526-2601
9021 144th Pl Jamaica (11435) *(G-6472)*

Rosco Div, Rome *Also called Rome Specialty Company Inc (G-13870)*

Rosco Vision Systems, Jamaica *Also called Rosco Inc (G-6471)*

Roscoe Brothers Inc 607 844-3750
15 Freeville Rd Dryden (13053) *(G-4040)*

Rose Fence Inc 516 790-2308
356 Bay Ave Halesite (11743) *(G-5489)*

Rose Fence Inc 516 223-0777
345 Sunrise Hwy Baldwin (11510) *(G-533)*

Rose Gourmet, Brooklyn *Also called Rhosey LLC (G-2343)*

Rose Graphics LLC 516 547-6142
109 Kean St West Babylon (11704) *(G-15743)*

Rose Solomon Co 718 855-1788
63 Flushing Ave Unit 330 Brooklyn (11205) *(G-2355)*

Rose Trunk Mfg Co Inc 516 766-6686
3935 Sally Ln Oceanside (11572) *(G-12187)*

Rose-Ann Division, New York *Also called Texport Fabrics Corp (G-11456)*

Rosecore Division 516 504-4530
11 Grace Ave Ste 100 Great Neck (11021) *(G-5418)*

Rosedub, South Fallsburg *Also called Allied Wine Corp (G-14508)*

Rosemont Press Incorporated (PA) 212 239-4770
253 Church St Apt 2 New York (10013) *(G-11082)*

Rosemont Press Incorporated 212 239-4770
35 W Jefryn Blvd Ste A Deer Park (11729) *(G-3929)*

Rosemount Inc. 585 424-2460
3559 Winton Pl Ste 1 Rochester (14623) *(G-13706)*

Rosen Mandell & Immerman Inc 212 691-2277
121 Varick St Rm 301 New York (10013) *(G-11083)*

Rosen Publishing Group Inc 212 777-3017
29 E 21st St Fl 2 New York (10010) *(G-11084)*

Rosenbaum Foot, Brooklyn *Also called Newyork Pedorthic Associates (G-2214)*

Rosenwach Group, The, Astoria *Also called Rosenwach Tank Co Inc (G-439)*

Rosenwach Tank Co, Astoria *Also called Sitecraft Inc (G-441)*

Rosenwach Tank Co Inc (PA) 212 972-4411
4302 Ditmars Blvd Astoria (11105) *(G-439)*

Rosetti Handbags and ACC (HQ) 646 839-7945
350 5th Ave Lbby 9 New York (10118) *(G-11085)*

Rosina Food Products Inc (HQ) 716 668-0123
170 French Rd Buffalo (14227) *(G-2962)*

Rosina Holding Inc (PA) 716 668-0123
170 French Rd Buffalo (14227) *(G-2963)*

Roslyn Bread Company Inc 516 625-1470
190 Mineola Ave Roslyn Heights (11577) *(G-14056)*

Ross Communications Associates 631 393-5089
200 Broadhollow Rd # 207 Melville (11747) *(G-7820)*

Ross Electronics Ltd 718 569-6643
12 Maple Ave Haverstraw (10927) *(G-5807)*

Ross JC Inc 716 439-1161
6722 Lincoln Ave Lockport (14094) *(G-7103)*

Ross L Sports Screening Inc 716 824-5350
2756 Seneca St Buffalo (14224) *(G-2964)*

Ross Metal Fabricators Div, Hauppauge *Also called Charles Ross & Son Company (G-5614)*

Ross Metal Fabricators Inc 631 586-7000
225 Marcus Blvd Deer Park (11729) *(G-3930)*

Ross Precision Mfg Inc 518 273-3912
1 Tibbits Ave Green Island (12183) *(G-5442)*

Ross Valve Mfg 518 274-0961
75 102nd St Troy (12180) *(G-15184)*

Rossi Tool & Dies Inc 845 267-8246
161 Route 303 Valley Cottage (10989) *(G-15322)*

Rosy Blue Inc (HQ) 212 687-8838
529 5th Ave Fl 12 New York (10017) *(G-11086)*

Rota File Corporation 516 496-7200
159 Lafayette Dr Syosset (11791) *(G-14802)*

Rota Pack Inc 631 274-1037
34 Sarah Dr Ste B Farmingdale (11735) *(G-4727)*

Rota Tool, Syosset *Also called Rota File Corporation (G-14802)*

Rotation Dynamics Corporation 585 352-9023
3581 Big Ridge Rd Spencerport (14559) *(G-14559)*

Roth Clothing Co Inc (PA) 718 384-4927
300 Penn St Brooklyn (11211) *(G-2356)*

Roth Design & Consulting Inc 718 209-0193
132 Bogart St Brooklyn (11206) *(G-2357)*

Roth Global Plastics Inc 315 475-0100
1 General Motors Dr Syracuse (13206) *(G-14979)*

Roth's Metal Works, Brooklyn *Also called Roth Design & Consulting Inc (G-2357)*

Rothe Welding Inc 845 246-3051
1455 Route 212 Saugerties (12477) *(G-14210)*

Roto Salt Company Inc 315 536-3742
118 Monell St Penn Yan (14527) *(G-12593)*

Rotork Controls Inc 585 328-1550
675 Mile Crossing Blvd Rochester (14624) *(G-13707)*

Rotron Incorporated (HQ) 845 679-2401
55 Hasbrouck Ln Woodstock (12498) *(G-16237)*

Rotron Incorporated 845 679-2401
9 Hasbrouck Ln Woodstock (12498) *(G-16238)*

Rotronic Instrument Corp 631 427-3898
160 E Main St Ste 1 Huntington (11743) *(G-6222)*

Rotronic Instrument Corp (HQ) 631 348-6844
135 Engineers Rd Ste 150 Hauppauge (11788) *(G-5755)*

Rottkamp Tennis Inc 631 421-0040
100 Broadway Huntington Station (11746) *(G-6257)*

Rough Brothers Holding Co (HQ) 716 826-6500
3556 Lake Shore Rd # 100 Buffalo (14219) *(G-2965)*

Rough Draft Publishing LLC 212 741-4773
1916 Old Chelsea Sta New York (10113) *(G-11087)*

Rough Guides US Ltd 212 414-3635
345 Hudson St Fl 4 New York (10014) *(G-11088)*

Round Top Knit & Screening 518 622-3600
Rr 31 Round Top (12473) *(G-14064)*

Roust USA, New York *Also called Russian Standard Vodka USA Inc (G-11100)*

Rovel Manufacturing Co Inc 516 365-2752
52 Wimbledon Dr Roslyn (11576) *(G-14046)*

Row, The, New York *Also called Tr Apparel LLC (G-11526)*

Roxanne Assoulin, New York *Also called Maurice Max Inc (G-10386)*

Roxter Lighting, Long Island City *Also called Matov Industries Inc (G-7291)*

Royal Adhesives & Sealants LLC 315 451-1755
3584 Walters Rd Rsd Syracuse (13209) *(G-14980)*

Royal Apparel, Hauppauge *Also called Summit Apparel Inc (G-5777)*

Royal Bedding Co Buffalo Inc 716 895-1414
201 James E Casey Dr Buffalo (14206) *(G-2966)*

Royal Clothing Corp 718 436-5841
1316 48th St Apt 1 Brooklyn (11219) *(G-2358)*

Royal Copenhagen Inc (PA) 845 454-4442
63 Page Park Dr Poughkeepsie (12603) *(G-12980)*

Royal Crown Financial 718 234-7237
1028 Dahill Rd Brooklyn (11204) *(G-2359)*

Royal Custom Cabinets 315 376-6042
6149 Patty St Lowville (13367) *(G-7421)*

Royal Engraving, Brooklyn *Also called Tripi Engraving Co Inc (G-2522)*

Royal Fireworks Prtg Co Inc 845 726-3333
First Ave Unionville (10988) *(G-15234)*

Royal Jewelry Mfg Inc (PA) 212 302-2500
825 Northern Blvd Fl 2 Great Neck (11021) *(G-5419)*

Royal Kedem Wine, Marlboro *Also called Royal Wine Corporation (G-7582)*

Royal Kosher Foods LLC 347 221-1867
1464 45th St Ste 1a Brooklyn (11219) *(G-2360)*

Royal Marble & Granite Inc 516 536-5900
3295 Royal Ave Oceanside (11572) *(G-12188)*

Royal Media Group, New York *Also called Royal News Corp (G-11090)*

Royal Metal Products Inc 518 966-4442
463 West Rd Surprise (12176) *(G-14776)*

Royal Miracle Corp 212 921-5797
2 W 46th St Ste 909 New York (10036) *(G-11089)*

Royal Molds Inc 718 382-7686
1634 Marine Pkwy Brooklyn (11234) *(G-2361)*

Royal News Corp 212 564-8972
8 W 38th St Rm 901 New York (10018) *(G-11090)*

ALPHABETIC SECTION Ryba Software Inc

Royal Paint Roller Corp 516 367-4370
1 Harvard Dr Woodbury (11797) *(G-16182)*
Royal Paint Roller Mfg, Woodbury *Also called Royal Paint Roller Corp (G-16182)*
Royal Press, Staten Island *Also called C & R De Santis Inc (G-14633)*
Royal Press, White Plains *Also called L K Printing Corp (G-16023)*
Royal Products, Hauppauge *Also called Curran Manufacturing Corp (G-5633)*
Royal Products, Hauppauge *Also called Curran Manufacturing Corp (G-5634)*
Royal Promotion Group Inc 212 246-3780
119 W 57th St Ste 906 New York (10019) *(G-11091)*
Royal Sweet Bakery Inc 718 567-7770
119 49th St Brooklyn (11232) *(G-2362)*
Royal Tees Inc 845 357-9448
29 Lafayette Ave Suffern (10901) *(G-14766)*
Royal Windows and Doors, Bay Shore *Also called Royal Windows Mfg Corp (G-710)*
Royal Windows Mfg Corp 631 435-8888
1769 5th Ave Unit A Bay Shore (11706) *(G-710)*
Royal Wine Corporation 845 236-4000
1519 Route 9w Marlboro (12542) *(G-7582)*
Royale Limousine Manufacturers, Roslyn Heights *Also called Cabot Coach Builders Inc (G-14048)*
Royalton Millwork & Design 716 439-4092
7526 Tonawanda Creek Rd Lockport (14094) *(G-7104)*
Royalty Network Inc (PA) 212 967-4300
224 W 30th St Rm 1007 New York (10001) *(G-11092)*
ROYCE ASSOCIATES A LIMITED PARTNERSHIP, Jericho *Also called Royce Associates A Ltd Partnr (G-6593)*
Royce Associates A Ltd Partnr 516 367-6298
366 N Broadway Ste 400 Jericho (11753) *(G-6593)*
Rozal Industries Inc 631 420-4277
151 Marine St Farmingdale (11735) *(G-4728)*
Rp55 Inc 212 840-4035
230 W 39th St Fl 7 New York (10018) *(G-11093)*
Rpb Distributors LLC 914 244-3600
45 Kensico Dr Mount Kisco (10549) *(G-8105)*
RPC Photonics Inc 585 272-2840
330 Clay Rd Rochester (14623) *(G-13708)*
Rpf Associates Inc 631 462-7446
2155 Jericho Tpke Ste A Commack (11725) *(G-3597)*
Rpg, New York *Also called Royal Promotion Group Inc (G-11091)*
RPI of Indiana Inc 330 279-2421
123 Varick Ave Brooklyn (11237) *(G-2363)*
RPM Displays, Auburn *Also called R P M Industries Inc (G-492)*
RPS Holdings Inc 607 257-7778
99 Eastlake Rd Ithaca (14850) *(G-6410)*
Rs Automation 585 589-0199
4015 Oak Orchard Rd Albion (14411) *(G-160)*
RS Precision Industries Inc 631 420-0424
295 Adams Blvd Farmingdale (11735) *(G-4729)*
Rsb Associates Inc 518 281-5067
488 Picard Rd Altamont (12009) *(G-199)*
RSC Molding Inc 516 351-9871
75 Hanse Ave Freeport (11520) *(G-5020)*
Rsl Media LLC 212 307-6760
1001 Ave Of The Ave Fl 11 Flr 11 New York (10018) *(G-11094)*
RSM Electron Power Inc (PA) 631 586-7600
221 W Industry Ct Deer Park (11729) *(G-3931)*
RSM Electron Power Inc 631 586-7600
100 Engineers Rd Ste 100 # 100 Hauppauge (11788) *(G-5756)*
Rsquared Ny Inc 631 521-8700
100 Heartland Blvd Edgewood (11717) *(G-4280)*
Rt Machined Specialties 716 731-2055
2221 Niagara Falls Blvd Niagara Falls (14304) *(G-11974)*
Rt Solutions LLC 585 245-3456
80 Linden Oaks Ste 210 Rochester (14625) *(G-13709)*
RTD Manufacturing Inc 315 337-3151
6273 State Route 233 Rome (13440) *(G-13871)*
Rtr Bag & Co Ltd 212 620-0011
127 W 26th St Rm 301 New York (10001) *(G-11095)*
Rubber Stamp X Press 631 423-1322
7 Bradford Pl Huntington Station (11747) *(G-6258)*
Rubber Stamps Inc 212 675-1180
174 Herricks Rd Mineola (11501) *(G-7998)*
Rubberform Recycled Pdts LLC 716 478-0404
75 Michigan St Lockport (14094) *(G-7105)*
Rubicon Industries Corp (PA) 718 434-4700
848 E 43rd St Brooklyn (11210) *(G-2364)*
Rubie's Distribution Center, Bay Shore *Also called Rubies Costume Company Inc (G-712)*
Rubies Costume Company Inc (PA) 718 846-1008
12008 Jamaica Ave Richmond Hill (11418) *(G-13122)*
Rubies Costume Company Inc 631 777-3300
158 Candlewood Rd Bay Shore (11706) *(G-711)*
Rubies Costume Company Inc 718 441-0834
12017 Jamaica Ave Richmond Hill (11418) *(G-13123)*
Rubies Costume Company Inc 631 951-3688
1 Holloween Hwy Bay Shore (11706) *(G-712)*
Rubies Costume Company Inc 516 333-3473
601 Cantiague Rock Rd Westbury (11590) *(G-15923)*
Rubies Costume Company Inc 631 435-7912
158 Candlewood Rd Bay Shore (11706) *(G-713)*
Rubies Costume Company Inc 718 846-1008
1 Rubie Plz Richmond Hill (11418) *(G-13124)*
Rubies Masquerade Company LLC (HQ) 718 846-1008
1 Rubie Plz Richmond Hill (11418) *(G-13125)*
Rubinstein Jewelry Mfg Co 718 784-8650
3100 47th Ave Long Island City (11101) *(G-7348)*
Ruby Automation LLC 585 254-8840
1000 University Ave # 800 Rochester (14607) *(G-13710)*
Ruby Newco LLC 212 852-7000
1211 Ave Of The Americas New York (10036) *(G-11096)*
Ruby Road, New York *Also called Hearts of Palm LLC (G-9758)*
Ruby Road, New York *Also called Hearts of Palm LLC (G-9759)*
Ruckel Manufacturing Co, Brooklyn *Also called EY Industries Inc (G-1824)*
Rudolf Friedman Inc 212 869-5070
42 W 48th St Ste 1102 New York (10036) *(G-11097)*
Rudy Stempel & Family Sawmill 518 872-0431
73 Stempel Ln East Berne (12059) *(G-4098)*
Ruga Grinding & Mfg Corp 631 924-5067
84 Horseblock Rd Unit A Yaphank (11980) *(G-16268)*
Rugby Magazine, White Plains *Also called American Intl Media LLC (G-15973)*
Ruggeri Manufacturing, Rochester *Also called Van Thomas Inc (G-13795)*
Ruhle Companies Inc 914 287-4000
99 Wall St Valhalla (10595) *(G-15309)*
Rule Breaker Snacks, Brooklyn *Also called Have Your Cake Kitchen LLC (G-1927)*
Rumsey Corp 914 751-3640
15 Rumsey Rd Yonkers (10705) *(G-16347)*
Rumson Acquisition LLC 718 349-4300
1385 Broadway Fl 9 New York (10018) *(G-11098)*
Run It Systems, New York *Also called Marcus Goldman Inc (G-10358)*
Runs Inc 212 618-1201
14 Wall St Fl 203420 New York (10005) *(G-11099)*
Rural Hill Sand and Grav Corp 315 846-5212
10262 County Route 79 Woodville (13650) *(G-16239)*
Rus Auto Parts Inc 800 410-2669
508 Coney Island Ave Brooklyn (11218) *(G-2365)*
Rus Industries Inc 716 284-7828
3255 Lockport Rd Niagara Falls (14305) *(G-11975)*
Rush Gold Manufacturing Ltd 516 781-3155
2400 Merrick Rd Bellmore (11710) *(G-788)*
Rush Gravel Corp 585 533-1740
130 Kavanaugh Rd Honeoye Falls (14472) *(G-6079)*
Rush Machinery Inc 585 554-3070
4761 State Route 364 Rushville (14544) *(G-14075)*
Ruskin Company 845 767-4100
1 Corporate Dr Orangeburg (10962) *(G-12330)*
Russco Metal Spinning Co Inc 516 872-6055
1020 Archer Pl Baldwin (11510) *(G-534)*
Russell Bass 607 637-5253
59 Saw Mill Rd Hancock (13783) *(G-5539)*
Russell Bass & Son Lumber, Hancock *Also called Russell Bass (G-5539)*
Russell Industries Inc 516 536-5000
40 Horton Ave Lynbrook (11563) *(G-7437)*
Russell Plastics Tech Co Inc 631 963-8602
521 W Hoffman Ave Lindenhurst (11757) *(G-6971)*
Russian Bazaar, Brooklyn *Also called Danet Inc (G-1722)*
Russian Daily, Brooklyn *Also called Novoye Rsskoye Slovo Pubg Corp (G-2222)*
Russian Mix Inc 347 385-7198
2225 Benson Ave Apt 74 Brooklyn (11214) *(G-2366)*
Russian Standard Vodka USA Inc (PA) 212 679-1894
232 Madison Ave Fl 16 New York (10016) *(G-11100)*
Russkaya Reklama Inc 718 769-3000
2699 Coney Island Ave Brooklyn (11235) *(G-2367)*
Russo's Gluten Free Gourmet, Shirley *Also called Anthony Gigi Inc (G-14413)*
Rutcarele Inc 347 830-5353
3449 110th St Corona (11368) *(G-3748)*
Rv Printing 631 567-8658
39 Portside Dr Holbrook (11741) *(G-6019)*
Rvc Enterprises LLC (PA) 212 391-4600
1384 Broadway Fl 17 New York (10018) *(G-11101)*
Rvc Inc 330 631-8320
2801 Court St Syracuse (13208) *(G-14981)*
Rw Gate Company (PA) 518 874-4750
79 102nd St Troy (12180) *(G-15185)*
Rw Gate Company 518 874-4750
75 102nd St Troy (12180) *(G-15186)*
Rw Manufacturing Company, East Rochester *Also called Richards & West Inc (G-4169)*
Rwb Controls Inc 716 897-4341
471 Connecticut St Buffalo (14213) *(G-2967)*
RWS Manufacturing Inc 518 361-1657
22 Ferguson Ln Queensbury (12804) *(G-13054)*
Ry-Gan Printing, Rochester *Also called Whitestone Dev Group LLC (G-13804)*
Ryan Gems Inc 212 697-0149
20 E 46th St Rm 500 New York (10017) *(G-11102)*
Ryan Printing, Hilton *Also called William J Ryan (G-5975)*
Ryan Printing Inc 845 535-3235
300 Corporate Dr Ste 6 Blauvelt (10913) *(G-933)*
Ryans Mobile Welding Svc LLC 315 769-5699
59 Bishop Ave Massena (13662) *(G-7670)*
Ryba General Merchandise Inc 718 522-2028
63 Flushing Ave Unit 332 Brooklyn (11205) *(G-2368)*
Ryba Software Inc 718 264-9352
7359 186th St Fresh Meadows (11366) *(G-5045)*

ALPHABETIC

Rye Record...914 713-3213
14 Elm Pl Ste 200 Rye (10580) *(G-14085)*
Ryers Creek Corp...607 523-6617
1330 Mill Dr Corning (14830) *(G-3720)*
Ryland Peters & Small Inc...646 791-5410
341 E 116th St New York (10029) *(G-11103)*
S & B Fashion Inc...718 482-1386
4315 Queens St Ste B Long Island City (11101) *(G-7349)*
S & B Machine Works Inc...516 997-2666
111 New York Ave Westbury (11590) *(G-15924)*
S & C Bridal LLC (PA)...212 789-7000
1407 Broadway Fl 41 New York (10018) *(G-11104)*
S & C Bridals LLC...213 624-4477
1407 Broadway Fl 41 New York (10018) *(G-11105)*
S & D Welding Corp...631 454-0383
229 Edison Ave Ste A West Babylon (11704) *(G-15744)*
S & H Enterprises Inc...888 323-8755
10b Holden Ave Queensbury (12804) *(G-13055)*
S & H Machine Company Inc...716 834-1194
83 Clyde Ave Buffalo (14215) *(G-2968)*
S & H Uniform Corp...914 937-6800
1 Aqueduct Rd White Plains (10606) *(G-16057)*
S & J Sheet Metal Supply...718 384-0800
70 Grand Ave Brooklyn (11205) *(G-2369)*
S & J Trading Inc...718 347-1323
8030 263rd St Floral Park (11004) *(G-4820)*
S & R Tool Inc...585 346-2029
6066 Stone Hill Rd Lakeville (14480) *(G-6775)*
S & S Enterprises, Jamestown *Also called Genco John (G-6512)*
S & S Fashions Inc...718 328-0001
941 Longfellow Ave Bronx (10474) *(G-1354)*
S & S Machinery Corp (PA)...718 492-7400
140 53rd St Brooklyn (11232) *(G-2370)*
S & S Machinery Corp...718 492-7400
132 54th St Brooklyn (11220) *(G-2371)*
S & S Manufacturing Co Inc (PA)...212 444-6000
1375 Broadway Fl 2 New York (10018) *(G-11106)*
S & S Prtg Die-Cutting Co Inc...718 388-8990
488 Morgan Ave Ste A Brooklyn (11222) *(G-2372)*
S & S Soap Co Inc...718 585-2900
815 E 135th St Bronx (10454) *(G-1355)*
S & T Knitting Co Inc (PA)...607 722-7558
1010 Conklin Rd Conklin (13748) *(G-3628)*
S & T Machine Inc...718 272-2484
970 E 92nd St Fl 1 Brooklyn (11236) *(G-2373)*
S & V Custom Furniture Mfg...516 746-8299
75 Windsor Ave Unit E Mineola (11501) *(G-7999)*
S & V Knits Inc...631 752-1595
117 Marine St Farmingdale (11735) *(G-4730)*
S & V Restaurant Eqp Mfrs Inc...718 220-1140
4320 Park Ave Bronx (10457) *(G-1356)*
S & V Restaurants Corp...718 220-1140
4320 Park Ave Bronx (10457) *(G-1357)*
S & W Ladies Wear...718 431-2800
3611 14th Ave Ste 601 Brooklyn (11218) *(G-2374)*
S & W Metal Trading Corp...212 719-5070
1601 E 7th St Brooklyn (11230) *(G-2375)*
S A Baxter LLC (PA)...845 469-7995
37 Elkay Dr Ste 33 Chester (10918) *(G-3385)*
S A W, Kingston *Also called Spiegel Woodworks Inc (G-6710)*
S and G Imaging, Walworth *Also called Software & General Services Co (G-15479)*
S B B, East Syracuse *Also called Sullivan Bazinet Bongio Inc (G-4240)*
S B Manufacturing LLC...845 352-3700
161 Route 59 Monsey (10952) *(G-8045)*
S B Whistler & Sons Inc...585 798-3000
11023 W Center Street Ext Medina (14103) *(G-7745)*
S Broome and Co Inc...718 663-6800
3300 47th Ave Fl 1 Long Island City (11101) *(G-7350)*
S C Magazine...646 638-6018
275 7th Ave Fl 10 New York (10001) *(G-11107)*
S D C, Armonk *Also called Surgical Design Corp (G-403)*
S D I, Binghamton *Also called Sensor & Decontamination Inc (G-908)*
S D S of Long Island, Massapequa Park *Also called M F L B Inc (G-7658)*
S D Z Metal Spinning Stamping...718 778-3600
1807 Pacific St Brooklyn (11233) *(G-2376)*
S Donadic Inc...718 361-9888
4525 39th St Sunnyside (11104) *(G-14774)*
S E A Supls, Plainview *Also called S E A Supplies Ltd (G-12712)*
S E A Supplies Ltd...516 694-6677
1670 Old Country Rd # 104 Plainview (11803) *(G-12712)*
S G I...917 386-0385
40 E 52nd St Frnt A New York (10022) *(G-11108)*
S G New York LLC...631 698-8400
1 Rodeo Dr Edgewood (11717) *(G-4281)*
S G New York LLC (PA)...631 665-4000
2950 Vtrans Mem Hwy Ste 1 Bohemia (11716) *(G-1072)*
S Hellerman Inc (PA)...718 622-2995
242 Green St Brooklyn (11222) *(G-2377)*
S I Communications Inc...914 725-2500
8 Harwood Ct Scarsdale (10583) *(G-14241)*
S J B Fabrication...716 895-0281
430 Kennedy Rd Buffalo (14227) *(G-2969)*
S J McCullagh Inc (PA)...716 856-3473
245 Swan St Buffalo (14204) *(G-2970)*
S K Circuits Inc (PA)...703 376-8718
340 Rosewood Cir Canastota (13032) *(G-3155)*
S Kashi & Sons Inc...212 869-9393
175 Great Neck Rd Ste 204 Great Neck (11021) *(G-5420)*
S L C Industries Incorporated...607 775-2299
63 Barlow Rd Binghamton (13904) *(G-907)*
S L Fashions Group, New York *Also called Lou Sally Fashions Corp (G-10269)*
S M S C Inc...315 942-4394
101 Water St Boonville (13309) *(G-1110)*
S P Books Inc...212 431-5011
99 Spring St Fl 3 New York (10012) *(G-11109)*
S P Industries Inc...845 255-5000
815 Rte 208 Gardiner (12525) *(G-5130)*
S R & R Industries Inc...845 692-8329
45 Enterprise Pl Middletown (10941) *(G-7931)*
S R Instruments Inc (PA)...716 693-5977
600 Young St Tonawanda (14150) *(G-15136)*
S R Sloan Inc (PA)...315 736-7730
8111 Halsey Rd Whitesboro (13492) *(G-16082)*
S Rothschild & Co Inc (PA)...212 354-8550
1407 Broadway Fl 10 New York (10018) *(G-11110)*
S S I, Rochester *Also called Schlegel Systems Inc (G-13718)*
S S Precision Gear & Instr...718 457-7474
4512 104th St Corona (11368) *(G-3749)*
S Scharf Inc...516 541-9552
278 N Richmond Ave Massapequa (11758) *(G-7650)*
S T J Orthotic Svces, Lindenhurst *Also called Stj Orthotic Services Inc (G-6975)*
S&D Welding, West Babylon *Also called S & D Welding Corp (G-15744)*
S&G Optical, Long Island City *Also called 21st Century Optics Inc (G-7140)*
S&L Aerospace Metals LLC...718 326-1821
12012 28th Ave Flushing (11354) *(G-4890)*
S'Well Bottle, New York *Also called Cant Live Without It LLC (G-8906)*
S.W.H. Precision Industries, Hauppauge *Also called Makamah Enterprises Inc (G-5705)*
S2 Sportswear Inc...347 335-0713
4100 1st Ave Ste 5n Brooklyn (11232) *(G-2378)*
S3j Electronics LLC...716 206-1309
2000 Commerce Pkwy Lancaster (14086) *(G-6832)*
SA Day Buffalo Flux Facility, Buffalo *Also called Johnson Manufacturing Company (G-2824)*
Saab Defense and SEC USA LLC...315 445-5009
5717 Enterprise Pkwy East Syracuse (13057) *(G-4235)*
Saad Collection Inc (PA)...212 937-0341
1165 Broadway Ste 305 New York (10001) *(G-11111)*
Saakshi Inc...315 475-3988
851 N Salina St Syracuse (13208) *(G-14982)*
Sabbsons International Inc...718 360-1947
474 50th St Brooklyn (11220) *(G-2379)*
Sabic Innovative Plas US LLC...518 475-5011
1 Noryl Ave Selkirk (12158) *(G-14360)*
Sabic Innovative Plastics...713 448-7474
1 Gail Ct East Greenbush (12061) *(G-4116)*
Sabila Corp (PA)...845 981-7128
480 Liberty Corners Rd Pine Island (10969) *(G-12631)*
Sabin Metal Corporation (PA)...631 329-1695
300 Pantigo Pl Ste 102 East Hampton (11937) *(G-4127)*
Sabin Metal Corporation...585 538-2194
1647 Wheatland Center Rd Scottsville (14546) *(G-14343)*
Sabin Robbins, New York *Also called Eagles Nest Holdings LLC (G-9298)*
Sabin Robbins Paper Company...513 874-5270
455 E 86th St New York (10028) *(G-11112)*
Sabra Dipping Company LLC (PA)...914 372-3900
777 Westchester Ave Fl 3 White Plains (10604) *(G-16058)*
Sabre Energy Services LLC...518 514-1572
1891 New Scotland Rd Slingerlands (12159) *(G-14467)*
Sabre Enterprises Inc...315 430-3127
6799 Townline Rd Syracuse (13211) *(G-14983)*
Saccomize Inc...818 287-3000
1554 Stillwell Ave Bronx (10461) *(G-1358)*
Sacks and Company New York (PA)...212 741-1000
119 W 57th St Ste 512 New York (10019) *(G-11113)*
Sadowsky Guitars Ltd...718 433-1990
2107 41st Ave Fl 4 Long Island City (11101) *(G-7351)*
Saes Memry, New Hartford *Also called Saes Smart Materials Inc (G-8245)*
Saes Smart Materials Inc...315 266-2026
4355 Middle Settlement Rd New Hartford (13413) *(G-8245)*
Safavieh Inc...516 945-1900
40 Harbor Park Dr Port Washington (11050) *(G-12920)*
Safcore LLC...917 627-5263
23 Van Dam St Brooklyn (11222) *(G-2380)*
Safe Flight Instrument Corp...914 946-9500
20 New King St White Plains (10604) *(G-16059)*
Safe Passage International Inc...585 292-4910
333 Metro Park Ste F204 Rochester (14623) *(G-13711)*
Safe Seat USA Inc...516 586-8240
1670 Old Country Rd # 116 Plainview (11803) *(G-12713)*
Safe Skies LLC (PA)...888 632-5027
954 3rd Ave Ste 504 New York (10022) *(G-11114)*
Safe-Dent Enterprises LLC...845 362-0141
4 Orchard Hill Dr Monsey (10952) *(G-8046)*
Safeguard Inc...631 929-3273
578 Sound Ave Wading River (11792) *(G-15451)*

Safespan Platform Systems Inc 716 694-1100
  237 Fillmore Ave Tonawanda (14150) *(G-15137)*

Safetec of America Inc 716 895-1822
  887 Kensington Ave Buffalo (14215) *(G-2971)*

Safety-Kleen Systems Inc 716 855-2212
  60 Katherine St Buffalo (14210) *(G-2972)*

Sag Harbor, New York *Also called Life Style Design Group (G-10213)*

Sag Harbor Express 631 725-1700
  22 Division St Sag Harbor (11963) *(G-14100)*

Sag Harbor Industries Inc (PA) 631 725-0440
  1668 Bhmpton Sag Hbr Tpke Sag Harbor (11963) *(G-14101)*

Sagaponack Sand & Gravel Corp 631 537-2424
  Haines Path Bridgehampton (11932) *(G-1167)*

Sage Audio Video Tech LLC 212 213-1523
  53 W 36th St Rm 605 New York (10018) *(G-11115)*

Sage Knitwear Inc 718 628-7902
  103 Jersey St Unit D West Babylon (11704) *(G-15745)*

Sagelife Parenting LLC 315 299-5713
  235 Harrison St Ste 2 Syracuse (13202) *(G-14984)*

Sagemylife, Syracuse *Also called Sagelife Parenting LLC (G-14984)*

Sahadi Fine Foods Inc 718 369-0100
  4215 1st Ave Brooklyn (11232) *(G-2381)*

Sahlen Packing Company Inc 716 852-8677
  318 Howard St Buffalo (14206) *(G-2973)*

Sailorbags, Rochester *Also called Paradiso Cnsld Entps LLC (G-13609)*

Saint Gobain Grains & Powders 716 731-8200
  6600 Walmore Rd Niagara Falls (14304) *(G-11976)*

Saint Honore Pastry Shop Inc 516 767-2555
  993 Port Washington Blvd Port Washington (11050) *(G-12921)*

Saint Laurie, New York *Also called Kozinn+sons Merchant Tailors (G-10132)*

Saint Martins Press, New York *Also called Bedford Freeman & Worth (G-8746)*

Saint-Gbain Advnced Crmics LLC 716 691-2000
  168 Creekside Dr Amherst (14228) *(G-242)*

Saint-Gbain Advnced Crmics LLC (HQ) 716 278-6066
  23 Acheson Dr Niagara Falls (14303) *(G-11977)*

Saint-Gobain Abrasives Inc 518 266-2200
  2600 10th Ave Watervliet (12189) *(G-15605)*

Saint-Gobain Adfors Amer Inc (HQ) 716 775-3900
  1795 Baseline Rd Grand Island (14072) *(G-5343)*

Saint-Gobain Adfors Amer Inc 585 589-4401
  14770 East Ave Albion (14411) *(G-161)*

Saint-Gobain Dynamics Inc 716 278-6007
  23 Acheson Dr Niagara Falls (14303) *(G-11978)*

Saint-Gobain Performance Plas, Poestenkill *Also called Canton Bio-Medical Inc (G-12801)*

Saint-Gobain Prfmce Plas Corp 518 642-2200
  1 Sealants Park Granville (12832) *(G-5355)*

Saint-Gobain Prfmce Plas Corp 518 686-7301
  14 Mccaffrey St Hoosick Falls (12090) *(G-6088)*

Saint-Gobain Prfmce Plas Corp 518 283-5963
  11 Sicho Rd Poestenkill (12140) *(G-12804)*

Saint-Gobain Prfmce Plas Corp 518 686-7301
  1 Liberty St Hoosick Falls (12090) *(G-6089)*

Saint-Gobain Strl Ceramics 716 278-6233
  23 Acheson Dr Niagara Falls (14303) *(G-11979)*

Saint-Gobain-Paris France, Grand Island *Also called Saint-Gobain Adfors Amer Inc (G-5343)*

Saj of Freeport Corp 516 623-8800
  178 Hanse Ave Freeport (11520) *(G-5021)*

Sakonnet Technology LLC 212 849-9267
  11 E 44th St Fl 1000 New York (10017) *(G-11116)*

Salamanca Daily Reporter, Salamanca *Also called Sun-Times Media Group Inc (G-14131)*

Salamanca Lumber Company Inc 716 945-4810
  59 Rochester St Salamanca (14779) *(G-14126)*

Salamanca Penny Saver, Salamanca *Also called Salamanca Press Penny Saver (G-14127)*

Salamanca Press Penny Saver 716 945-1500
  36 River St Salamanca (14779) *(G-14127)*

Salarinos Italian Foods Inc 315 697-9766
  110 James St Canastota (13032) *(G-3156)*

Sale 121 Corp 240 855-8988
  1324 Lexington Ave # 111 New York (10128) *(G-11117)*

Salerno Packaging Inc (HQ) 518 563-3636
  14 Gus Lapham Ln Plattsburgh (12901) *(G-12775)*

Salerno Plastic Film and Bags, Plattsburgh *Also called Salerno Packaging Inc (G-12775)*

Sales & Marketing Office, Syracuse *Also called Monaghan Medical Corporation (G-14946)*

Sales Department, Floral Park *Also called Allomatic Products Company (G-4807)*

Sales Hacker Inc 516 660-2836
  505 E 14th St Apt 5h New York (10009) *(G-11118)*

Sales Office, Northport *Also called Cypress Semiconductor Corp (G-12102)*

Sales Tax Asset Rceivable Corp 212 788-5874
  255 Greenwich St Fl 6 New York (10007) *(G-11119)*

Salisbury Sportswear Inc 516 221-9519
  2523 Marine Pl Bellmore (11710) *(G-789)*

Salit Specialty Rebar Inc 716 299-1990
  1050 Military Rd Buffalo (14217) *(G-2974)*

Salko Kitchens Inc 845 565-4420
  256 Walsh Ave New Windsor (12553) *(G-8381)*

Sally Sherman Foods, Mount Vernon *Also called UFS Industries Inc (G-8190)*

Salmco Jewelry Corp 212 695-8792
  22 W 32nd St Fl 16 New York (10001) *(G-11120)*

Salmon Crek Cabinetry Inc 315 589-5419
  6687 Salmon Creek Rd Williamson (14589) *(G-16112)*

Salonclick LLC 718 643-6793
  117 Crosby St New York (10012) *(G-11121)*

Salsa Professional Apparel LLC 212 575-6565
  1441 Broadway Fl 3 New York (10018) *(G-11122)*

Salty Road Inc 347 673-3925
  190 Bedford Ave 404 Brooklyn (11249) *(G-2382)*

Salutem Group LLC 347 620-2640
  44 Wall St Fl 12 New York (10005) *(G-11123)*

Salvador Colletti Blank 718 217-6725
  25141 Van Zandt Ave Douglaston (11362) *(G-4028)*

Salvin Company, Kingston *Also called Vincent Conigliaro (G-6722)*

Sam A Lupo & Sons Inc (PA) 800 388-5352
  1219 Campville Rd Endicott (13760) *(G-4472)*

Sam Bonk Uniform, Bronx *Also called Bonk Sam Unforms Civilian Cap (G-1215)*

Sam NY, New York *Also called Andrew M Schwartz LLC (G-8580)*

Sam Salem & Son LLC 212 695-6020
  302 5th Ave Fl 4 New York (10001) *(G-11124)*

Samaki Inc 845 858-1012
  62 Jersey Ave Port Jervis (12771) *(G-12856)*

Samco LLC 518 725-4705
  122 S Main St Gloversville (12078) *(G-5290)*

Samco Scientific LLC 800 625-4327
  75 Panorama Creek Dr Rochester (14625) *(G-13712)*

Samoss Group Ltd (PA) 212 239-6677
  213 W 35th St Rm 1301 New York (10001) *(G-11125)*

Sampla Belting North Amer LLC 716 667-7450
  61 N Gates Ave Lackawanna (14218) *(G-6745)*

Sample News Group LLC 315 343-3800
  140 W 1st St Oswego (13126) *(G-12420)*

Sampsons Prsthtic Orthotic Lab, Schenectady *Also called Sampsons Prsthtic Orthotic Lab (G-14300)*

Sampsons Prsthtic Orthotic Lab 518 374-6011
  1737 State St Schenectady (12304) *(G-14300)*

Samson Technologies Corp (HQ) 631 784-2200
  278 Duffy Ave Unit B Hicksville (11801) *(G-5946)*

Samuel Son & Co (usa) Inc 716 856-6500
  250 Lake Ave Blasdell (14219) *(G-921)*

Samuel B Collection Inc 516 466-1826
  98 Cuttermill Rd Ste 234s Great Neck (11021) *(G-5421)*

Samuel Broome Uniform ACC, Long Island City *Also called S Broome and Co Inc (G-7350)*

Samuel French Inc (PA) 212 206-8990
  235 Park Ave S Fl 5 New York (10003) *(G-11126)*

Samuel H Moss, New York *Also called Samoss Group Ltd (G-11125)*

Samuel Schulman Furs Inc 212 736-5550
  150 W 30th St Fl 13 New York (10001) *(G-11127)*

Samzong Inc 718 475-1843
  46 Main St Ste 258 Monsey (10952) *(G-8047)*

San Esters Corporation 212 223-0020
  55 E 59th St Fl 1900a New York (10022) *(G-11128)*

San Francisco Chronicle, New York *Also called Hearst Communications Inc (G-9743)*

San Jae Educational Resou 845 364-5458
  9 Chamberlain Ct Pomona (10970) *(G-12808)*

San Signs & Awnings, Yonkers *Also called M Santoliquido Corp (G-16329)*

Sanaa Spices, Maspeth *Also called Extreme Spices Inc (G-7613)*

Sanctuary Brands LLC (PA) 212 704-4014
  70 W 40th St Fl 5 New York (10018) *(G-11129)*

Sand Hill Industries Inc 518 885-7991
  12 Grove St Ballston Spa (12020) *(G-586)*

Sandberg & Sikorski, New York *Also called A Jaffe Inc (G-8418)*

Sandbox Brands Inc 212 647-8877
  26 W 17th St Lbby New York (10011) *(G-11130)*

Sandle Custom Bearing Corp 585 593-7000
  1110 State Route 19 Wellsville (14895) *(G-15675)*

Sandow Media LLC 646 805-0200
  101 Park Ave Fl 4 New York (10178) *(G-11131)*

Sandstone Technologies Corp (PA) 585 785-5537
  2117 Buffalo Rd 245 Rochester (14624) *(G-13713)*

Sandstone Technologies Corp 585 785-5537
  2117 Buffalo Rd Unit 245 Rochester (14624) *(G-13714)*

Sandvoss Farms LLC 585 297-7044
  10198 East Rd East Bethany (14054) *(G-4099)*

Sandy Duftler Designs Ltd 516 379-3084
  775 Brooklyn Ave Ste 105 North Baldwin (11510) *(G-12007)*

Sandy Littman Inc 845 562-1112
  420 N Montgomery St Newburgh (12550) *(G-11886)*

Sandys Bumper Mart Inc 315 472-8149
  120 Wall St Syracuse (13204) *(G-14985)*

Sandys Deli Inc 518 297-6951
  90 Montgomery St Rouses Point (12979) *(G-14068)*

Sanford Printing Inc 718 461-1202
  13335 41st Rd Flushing (11355) *(G-4891)*

Sanford Stone LLC 607 467-1313
  185 Latham Rd Deposit (13754) *(G-4001)*

Sangster Foods Inc 212 993-9129
  225 Parkside Ave Apt 3p Brooklyn (11226) *(G-2383)*

Sanguine Gas Exploration LLC 212 582-8555
  152 W 57th St Fl 4100 New York (10019) *(G-11132)*

Sanjay Pallets Inc 347 590-2485
  424 Coster St Bronx (10474) *(G-1359)*

Sanmina Corporation 607 689-5000
  1200 Taylor Rd Owego (13827) *(G-12437)*

Sanoy Inc..212 695-6384
  19 W 36th St Fl 11 New York (10018) *(G-11133)*

Sanrex Corporation.......................................516 625-1313
  50 Seaview Blvd Ste 2 Port Washington (11050) *(G-12922)*

Santa Fe Manufacturing Corp........................631 234-0100
  225 Engineers Rd Hauppauge (11788) *(G-5757)*

Santee Print Works (PA)................................212 997-1570
  58 W 40th St Fl 11 New York (10018) *(G-11134)*

Santucci Custom Lighting.............................866 853-1929
  2943 Lumbard Rd Clinton (13323) *(G-3485)*

Sanzdranz LLC (PA).....................................518 894-8625
  83 Dumbarton Dr Delmar (12054) *(G-3969)*

Sanzdranz LLC..518 894-8625
  388 Broadway Schenectady (12305) *(G-14301)*

Sapienza Bake Shop, Elmont *Also called Sapienza Pastry Inc (G-4389)*

Sapienza Pastry Inc......................................516 352-5232
  1376 Hempstead Tpke Elmont (11003) *(G-4389)*

Sapphire Systems Inc (HQ)..........................212 905-0100
  405 Lexington Ave Fl 49 New York (10174) *(G-11135)*

Sappi North America Inc...............................914 696-5544
  925 Westchester Ave # 115 White Plains (10604) *(G-16060)*

Saptalil Pharmacueticals Inc........................631 231-2751
  45 Davids Dr Hauppauge (11788) *(G-5758)*

Saptalis Pharmaceuticals LLC (PA)..............631 231-2751
  45 Davids Dr Hauppauge (11788) *(G-5759)*

Saputo Dairy Foods Usa LLC........................607 746-2141
  40236 State Highway 10 Delhi (13753) *(G-3966)*

Sarabeth's Bakery, Bronx *Also called Sbk Preserves Inc (G-1361)*

Sarabeths Kitchen LLC.................................718 589-2900
  1161 E 156th St Bronx (10474) *(G-1360)*

Saraga Industries Corp.................................631 842-4049
  690 Albany Ave Unit D Amityville (11701) *(G-306)*

Saratoga Chips LLC......................................877 901-6950
  63 Putnam St Ste 202 Saratoga Springs (12866) *(G-14192)*

Saratoga Horseworks Ltd..............................518 843-6756
  57 Edson St Amsterdam (12010) *(G-347)*

Saratoga Lighting Holdings LLC (PA).............212 906-7800
  535 Madison Ave Fl 4 New York (10022) *(G-11136)*

Saratoga Spring Water Company....................518 584-6363
  11 Geyser Rd Saratoga Springs (12866) *(G-14193)*

Saratogian USA Today, Saratoga Springs *Also called Journal Register Company (G-14184)*

Sargent Manufacturing Inc............................212 722-7000
  120 E 124th St New York (10035) *(G-11137)*

Sargento Foods Inc.......................................920 893-8484
  498 7th Ave New York (10018) *(G-11138)*

Sarina Accessories LLC................................212 239-8106
  469 Fashion Ave Rm 1301 New York (10018) *(G-11139)*

Sartek Industries Inc....................................631 473-3555
  17 N Belle Mead Ave Ste 1 East Setauket (11733) *(G-4186)*

Sarug Inc...718 339-2791
  2055 Mcdonald Ave Brooklyn (11223) *(G-2384)*

SAS Industries Inc.......................................631 727-1441
  939 Wading River Manor Rd Manorville (11949) *(G-7553)*

Sas Maintenance Services Inc......................718 837-2124
  8435 Bay 16th St Ste A Brooklyn (11214) *(G-2385)*

Satco Castings Service Inc...........................516 354-1500
  1400 Plaza Ave New Hyde Park (11040) *(G-8291)*

Satco Lighting, Edgewood *Also called Satco Products Inc (G-4282)*

Satco Products Inc (PA)................................631 243-2022
  110 Heartland Blvd Edgewood (11717) *(G-4282)*

Satellite Incorporated...................................212 221-6687
  43 W 46th St Ste 503 New York (10036) *(G-11140)*

Satin Fine Foods Inc.....................................845 469-1034
  32 Leone Ln Chester (10918) *(G-3386)*

Satispie LLC..716 982-4600
  155 Balta Dr Rochester (14623) *(G-13715)*

Saturn Industries Inc (PA).............................518 828-9956
  157 Union Tpke Hudson (12534) *(G-6177)*

Satya Jewelry, New York *Also called Sube Inc (G-11383)*

Saugerties Delicioso Inc...............................845 217-5072
  3218 Route 9w Saugerties (12477) *(G-14211)*

Saunders Concrete, Etna *Also called W F Saunders & Sons Inc (G-4486)*

Saunders Concrete Co Inc............................607 756-7905
  6 Locust Ave Cortland (13045) *(G-3787)*

Sausbiers Awning Shop Inc...........................518 828-3748
  43 8th St Hudson (12534) *(G-6178)*

SAV Thermo Inc...631 249-9444
  133 Cabot St West Babylon (11704) *(G-15746)*

Savaco Inc...716 751-9455
  2905 Beebe Rd Newfane (14108) *(G-11895)*

Savage & Son Installations LLC....................585 342-7533
  676 Pullman Ave Rochester (14615) *(G-13716)*

Save Around, Binghamton *Also called Enjoy City North Inc (G-876)*

Save Mor Copy Center, Brooklyn *Also called At Copy Inc (G-1543)*

Save More Beverage Corp.............................518 371-2520
  1512 Route 9 Ste 1 Halfmoon (12065) *(G-5499)*

Save O Seal Corporation Inc.........................914 592-3031
  90 E Main St Elmsford (10523) *(G-4427)*

Saveur Magazine..212 219-7400
  304 Park Ave S Fl 8 New York (10010) *(G-11141)*

Savoritefactory, New York *Also called Q Ed Creations (G-10941)*

Savwatt Usa Inc (PA)....................................646 478-2676
  475 Park Ave S Fl 30 New York (10016) *(G-11142)*

Saxby Implement Corp (PA)..........................585 624-2938
  180 Mendon Victor Rd Mendon (14506) *(G-7852)*

Saxon Glass Technologies Inc......................607 587-9630
  200 N Main St Ste 114 Alfred (14802) *(G-182)*

Saxton Corporation......................................518 732-7705
  1320 Route 9 Castleton On Hudson (12033) *(G-3204)*

Sayeda Manufacturing Corp..........................631 345-2525
  20 Scouting Blvd Medford (11763) *(G-7723)*

Sb Corporation...212 822-3166
  114 W 41st St Fl 4 New York (10036) *(G-11143)*

Sb Molds LLC..845 352-3700
  161 Route 59 Ste 203a Monsey (10952) *(G-8048)*

Sb New York Inc (HQ)...................................212 457-7790
  120 Broadway New York (10271) *(G-11144)*

Sbb Inc...315 422-2376
  1 Gm Dr Ste 5 East Syracuse (13057) *(G-4236)*

Sbcontract.com, Farmingdale *Also called Metadure Parts & Sales Inc (G-4681)*

Sbi Enterprises, Ellenville *Also called Master Juvenile Products Inc (G-4308)*

Sbi Enterprises, Ellenville *Also called JM Originals Inc (G-4307)*

Sbk Preserves Inc..800 773-7378
  1161 E 156th St Bronx (10474) *(G-1361)*

SC Building Solutions LLC............................800 564-1152
  53 W 23rd St Fl 12 New York (10010) *(G-11145)*

SC Supply Chain Management LLC.................212 344-3322
  90 Broad St Ste 1504 New York (10004) *(G-11146)*

SC Textiles Inc..631 944-6262
  434 New York Ave Huntington (11743) *(G-6223)*

Scaccianoce Inc...718 991-4462
  1165 Burnett Pl Bronx (10474) *(G-1362)*

Scaife Enterprises Inc..................................585 454-5231
  4 Chillon Ct Fairport (14450) *(G-4519)*

Scalamandre Silks, Hauppauge *Also called Scalamandre Wallpaper Inc (G-5760)*

Scalamandre Silks Inc (PA)..........................212 980-3888
  979 3rd Ave Ste 202 New York (10022) *(G-11147)*

Scalamandre Wallpaper Inc...........................631 467-8800
  350 Wireless Blvd Hauppauge (11788) *(G-5760)*

Scale-Tronix Inc..914 948-8117
  4341 State Street Rd Skaneateles (13152) *(G-14456)*

Scan-A-Chrome Color Inc.............................631 532-6146
  555 Oak St Copiague (11726) *(G-3675)*

Scancorp Inc...315 454-5596
  1840 Lemoyne Ave Syracuse (13208) *(G-14986)*

Scanga Woodworking Corp...........................845 265-9115
  22 Corporate Park W Cold Spring (10516) *(G-3525)*

Scapa North America.....................................315 413-1111
  1111 Vine St Liverpool (13088) *(G-7039)*

Scara-Mix Inc..718 442-7357
  2537 Richmond Ter Staten Island (10303) *(G-14706)*

Scarano Boat Building Inc.............................518 463-3401
  194 S Port Rd Albany (12202) *(G-127)*

Scarano Boatbuilding Inc..............................518 463-3401
  194 S Port Rd Albany (12202) *(G-128)*

Scarguard Labs LLC.....................................516 482-8050
  15 Barstow Rd Great Neck (11021) *(G-5422)*

Scarsdale Inquirer, Scarsdale *Also called S I Communications Inc (G-14241)*

Scehenvus Fire Dist......................................607 638-9017
  40 Main St Schenevus (12155) *(G-14320)*

Scehenvus Gram Hose Co, Schenevus *Also called Scehenvus Fire Dist (G-14320)*

Scent 2 Market, Yonkers *Also called Belmay Holding Corporation (G-16291)*

Scent-A-Vision Inc.......................................631 424-4905
  171 E 2nd St Huntington Station (11746) *(G-6259)*

Sch Dpx Corporation....................................917 405-5377
  22 W 21st St Ste 700 New York (10010) *(G-11148)*

Schaefer Entps Deposit Inc (PA)...................607 467-4990
  315 Old Route 10 Deposit (13754) *(G-4002)*

Schaefer Logging Inc...................................607 467-4990
  315 Old Route 10 Deposit (13754) *(G-4003)*

Schaefer Machine Co Inc.............................516 248-6880
  100 Hudson St Mineola (11501) *(G-8000)*

Schaller & Webber, New York *Also called Schaller Manufacturing Corp (G-11150)*

Schaller & Weber, New York *Also called Schaller Manufacturing Corp (G-11149)*

Schaller Manufacturing Corp (PA)..................718 721-5480
  1654 2nd Ave Apt 2n New York (10028) *(G-11149)*

Schaller Manufacturing Corp.........................212 879-3047
  1654 2nd Ave Apt 2n New York (10028) *(G-11150)*

Scharf and Breit Inc.....................................516 282-0287
  2 Hillside Ave Ste F Williston Park (11596) *(G-16148)*

Schatz Bearing Corporation..........................845 452-6000
  10 Fairview Ave Poughkeepsie (12601) *(G-12981)*

Schenck Corporation (HQ)............................631 242-4010
  535 Acorn St Deer Park (11729) *(G-3932)*

Schenck USA Corp (HQ)...............................631 242-4010
  535 Acorn St Deer Park (11729) *(G-3933)*

Schenectady Steel Co Inc.............................518 355-3220
  18 Mariaville Rd Schenectady (12306) *(G-14302)*

Schiller Stores Inc.......................................845 928-4316
  869 Adirondack Way Central Valley (10917) *(G-3300)*

Schiller Stores Inc (PA)................................631 208-9400
  509 Tanger Mall Dr Riverhead (11901) *(G-13188)*

Schilling Forge Inc 315 454-4421
606 Factory Ave Syracuse (13208) *(G-14987)*

Schindler Elevator Corporation 212 708-1000
620 12th Ave Fl 4 New York (10036) *(G-11151)*

Schindler Elevator Corporation 800 225-3123
1211 6th Ave Ste 2950 New York (10036) *(G-11152)*

Schlegel Electronic Mtls Inc (PA) 585 295-2030
1600 Lexington Ave # 236 Rochester (14606) *(G-13717)*

Schlegel Systems Inc (HQ) 585 427-7200
1555 Jefferson Rd Rochester (14623) *(G-13718)*

Schless Bottles Inc (PA) 718 236-2790
4616 16th Ave Brooklyn (11204) *(G-2386)*

Schlumberger Technology Corp 607 378-0105
224 N Main St Bldg S Horseheads (14845) *(G-6136)*

Schmersal Inc 914 347-4775
15 Skyline Dr Ste 230 Hawthorne (10532) *(G-5823)*

Schmitt Sales Inc 716 632-8595
5095 Main St Williamsville (14221) *(G-16137)*

Schneeman Studio Limited 212 244-3330
330 W 38th St Rm 505 New York (10018) *(G-11153)*

Schneider Amalco Inc 917 470-9674
600 3rd Ave Fl 2 New York (10016) *(G-11154)*

Schneider Brothers Corporation 315 458-8369
7371 Eastman Rd Syracuse (13212) *(G-14988)*

Schneider Elc Systems USA Inc 214 527-3099
7 E 8th St New York (10003) *(G-11155)*

Schneider Electric 124, Albany Also called Schneider Electric Usa Inc *(G-129)*

Schneider Electric It Corp 646 335-0216
520 8th Ave Rm 2103 New York (10018) *(G-11156)*

Schneider Electric Usa Inc 646 335-0220
112 W 34th St Ste 908 New York (10120) *(G-11157)*

Schneider Electric Usa Inc 585 377-1313
441 Penbrooke Dr Ste 9 Penfield (14526) *(G-12574)*

Schneider Electric Usa Inc 631 567-5710
1430 Church St Unit H Bohemia (11716) *(G-1073)*

Schneider Electric Usa Inc 518 452-2590
501 New Karner Rd Ste 5 Albany (12205) *(G-129)*

Schneider M Soap & Chemical Co 718 389-1000
1930 Troutman St Ridgewood (11385) *(G-13159)*

Schneider Mills Inc 828 632-0801
1430 Broadway Rm 1202 New York (10018) *(G-11158)*

Schneider Optics Inc (HQ) 631 761-5000
285 Oser Ave Hauppauge (11788) *(G-5761)*

Schneps Media LLC (PA) 718 224-5863
1 Metrotech Ctr Brooklyn (11201) *(G-2387)*

Schneps Publications Inc (PA) 718 260-2500
3815 Bell Blvd Ste 38 Bayside (11361) *(G-742)*

Schoen Trimming & Cord Co Inc 212 255-3949
151 W 25th St Fl 10 New York (10001) *(G-11159)*

Schoharie Quarry/Asphalt, Schoharie Also called Cobleskill Stone Products Inc *(G-14321)*

Scholastic Copy Center, New York Also called Scholastic Inc *(G-11162)*

Scholastic Corporation (PA) 212 343-6100
557 Broadway Lbby 1 New York (10012) *(G-11160)*

Scholastic Inc (HQ) 212 343-6100
557 Broadway Lbby 1 New York (10012) *(G-11161)*

Scholastic Inc 212 343-6100
120 Mercer St New York (10012) *(G-11162)*

Scholastic Inc 212 343-7100
568 Broadway Rm 809 New York (10012) *(G-11163)*

Scholastic U.S.A., New York Also called Scholastic Inc *(G-11161)*

Scholium International Inc 516 883-8032
151 Cow Neck Rd Port Washington (11050) *(G-12923)*

Schonbek, Plattsburgh Also called Swarovski Lighting Ltd *(G-12783)*

Schonbek Shipping Bldg, Plattsburgh Also called Swarovski Lighting Ltd *(G-12784)*

Schonwetter Enterprises Inc 518 237-0171
41 Lark St Cohoes (12047) *(G-3515)*

School Guide Publications, Mamaroneck Also called Catholic News Publishing Co *(G-7501)*

School News Nationwide Inc 718 753-9920
490 E 28th St Brooklyn (11226) *(G-2388)*

School of Management, Binghamton Also called Suny At Binghamton *(G-910)*

Schoolnet Inc (HQ) 646 496-9000
525 Fashion Ave Fl 4 New York (10018) *(G-11164)*

Schott Corporation (HQ) 914 831-2200
555 Taxter Rd Ste 470 Elmsford (10523) *(G-4428)*

Schott Corporation 315 255-2791
62 Columbus St Auburn (13021) *(G-494)*

Schott Gemtron Corporation 423 337-3522
555 Taxter Rd Ste 470 Elmsford (10523) *(G-4429)*

Schott Lithotec USA Corp 845 463-5300
555 Taxter Rd Ste 470 Elmsford (10523) *(G-4430)*

Schott North America Inc (HQ) 914 831-2200
555 Taxter Rd Ste 470 Elmsford (10523) *(G-4431)*

Schott Solar Pv LLC 888 457-6527
555 Taxter Rd Ste 470 Elmsford (10523) *(G-4432)*

Schott Solar Pv, Inc., Elmsford Also called Schott Solar Pv LLC *(G-4432)*

Schrader Meat Market 607 869-6328
1937 Summerville Rd Romulus (14541) *(G-13879)*

Schroeder Machine Div, East Syracuse Also called Niagara Scientific Inc *(G-4228)*

Schuler-Haas Electric Corp 607 936-3514
598 Ritas Way Painted Post (14870) *(G-12475)*

Schuler-Subra Inc 716 893-3100
83 Doat St Buffalo (14211) *(G-2975)*

Schulze Vineyards & Winery LLC 716 778-8090
2090 Coomer Rd Burt (14028) *(G-3061)*

Schuster & Richard Lab, College Point Also called Schuster & Richard Labortories *(G-3563)*

Schuster & Richard Labortories 718 358-8607
1420 130th St College Point (11356) *(G-3563)*

Schutt Cider Mill 585 872-2924
1063 Plank Rd Webster (14580) *(G-15652)*

Schutte-Buffalo Hammer Mill, Buffalo Also called Schutte-Buffalo Hammermill LLC *(G-2976)*

Schutte-Buffalo Hammermill LLC 716 855-1202
61 Depot St Buffalo (14206) *(G-2976)*

Schwabel Fabricating Co Inc (PA) 716 876-2086
349 Sawyer Ave Tonawanda (14150) *(G-15138)*

Schwartz Textile LLC 718 499-8243
160 7th St Brooklyn (11215) *(G-2389)*

Schweitzer-Mauduit Intl Inc 518 329-4222
2424 Route 82 Ancram (12502) *(G-355)*

SCI Bore Inc 212 674-7128
70 Irving Pl Apt 5c New York (10003) *(G-11165)*

Sciane Enterprises Inc 845 452-2400
2600 South Rd Ste 37 Poughkeepsie (12601) *(G-12982)*

Sciarra Laboratories Inc 516 933-7853
48509 S Broadway Hicksville (11801) *(G-5947)*

Sciegen Pharmaceuticals Inc (HQ) 631 951-4908
7 Oser Ave Hauppauge (11788) *(G-5762)*

Scienta Pharmaceuticals LLC 845 589-0774
612 Corporate Way Ste 9 Valley Cottage (10989) *(G-15323)*

Scientific American Library, New York Also called Bedford Freeman & Worth *(G-8745)*

Scientific Components Corp (PA) 718 934-4500
13 Neptune Ave Brooklyn (11235) *(G-2390)*

Scientific Components Corp 631 243-4901
161 E Industry Ct Deer Park (11729) *(G-3934)*

Scientific Components Corp 718 368-2060
2450 Knapp St Brooklyn (11235) *(G-2391)*

Scientific Industries Inc (PA) 631 567-4700
80 Orville Dr Ste 102 Bohemia (11716) *(G-1074)*

Scientific Plastics Inc 212 967-1199
243 W 30th St Fl 8 New York (10001) *(G-11166)*

Scientific Polymer Products 585 265-0413
6265 Dean Pkwy Ontario (14519) *(G-12302)*

Scientific Solutions Globl LLC 516 543-3376
326 Westbury Ave Carle Place (11514) *(G-3181)*

Scientific Tool Co Inc 315 431-4243
101 Arterial Rd Syracuse (13206) *(G-14989)*

Scientifics Direct Inc 716 773-7500
532 Main St Tonawanda (14150) *(G-15139)*

Scissor Online, Bolivar Also called Klein Cutlery LLC *(G-1101)*

Sciterra LLC 646 883-3724
244 5th Ave Ste L280 New York (10001) *(G-11167)*

Scj Associates Inc 585 359-0600
60 Commerce Dr Rochester (14623) *(G-13719)*

SCM, New York Also called SC Supply Chain Management LLC *(G-11146)*

SCM, Suffern Also called Super Conductor Materials Inc *(G-14767)*

Scomac Inc 585 494-2200
8629 Buffalo Rd Bergen (14416) *(G-820)*

Scooby Dog Food, Utica Also called Scooby Rendering & Inc *(G-15293)*

Scooby Rendering & Inc 315 793-1014
1930 Oriskany St W Utica (13502) *(G-15293)*

Scoops R US Incorporated 212 730-7959
1514 Broadway New York (10036) *(G-11168)*

Scorpion Security Products Inc 607 724-9999
330 N Jensen Rd Vestal (13850) *(G-15382)*

Scotia Beverages Inc 518 370-3621
701 Corporation Park Schenectady (12302) *(G-14303)*

Scott Rotary Seals, Olean Also called Dynamic Sealing Tech Inc *(G-12233)*

Scott Silverstein Llc 212 781-1818
242 W 38th St New York (10018) *(G-11169)*

Scotti Graphics Inc 212 367-9602
3200 Skillman Ave Fl 1 Long Island City (11101) *(G-7352)*

Scotts Company LLC 631 478-6843
65 Engineers Rd Hauppauge (11788) *(G-5763)*

Scotts Company LLC 631 816-2831
445 Horseblock Rd Yaphank (11980) *(G-16269)*

Scotts Feed Inc 518 483-3110
245 Elm St Malone (12953) *(G-7489)*

Scoutnews LLC 203 855-1400
150 Broadhollow Rd # 302 Melville (11747) *(G-7821)*

SCR Group NY Inc 516 601-3174
2799 Coney Island Ave 2f Brooklyn (11235) *(G-2392)*

Screen Gems Inc 845 561-0036
41 Windsor Hwy New Windsor (12553) *(G-8382)*

Screen Gems-EMI Music Inc (HQ) 212 786-8000
150 5th Ave Fl 7 New York (10011) *(G-11170)*

Screen Team Inc 718 786-2424
3402c Review Ave Long Island City (11101) *(G-7353)*

Screen The World Inc 631 475-0023
658 Blue Point Rd Holtsville (11742) *(G-6052)*

Screw Compressor Tech Inc 716 827-6600
158 Ridge Rd Buffalo (14218) *(G-2977)*

Scriven Duplicating Service 518 233-8180
100 Eastover Rd Troy (12182) *(G-15187)*

Scriven Press, Troy Also called Scriven Duplicating Service *(G-15187)*

A
L
P
H
A
B
E
T
I
C

Scroll Media Inc 617 395-8904
  235 W 102nd St Apt 14i New York (10025) *(G-11171)*

Scully Sanitation 315 899-8996
  11146 Skaneateles Tpke West Edmeston (13485) *(G-15760)*

Scy Manufacturing Inc 516 986-3083
  600 Bayview Ave Ste 200 Inwood (11096) *(G-6303)*

SD Christie Associates Inc 914 734-1800
  424 Central Ave Ste 5 Peekskill (10566) *(G-12557)*

SD Eagle Global Inc 516 822-1778
  2 Kay St Jericho (11753) *(G-6594)*

SD Times, Melville *Also called Bz Media LLC (G-7763)*

SDC, Saugerties *Also called Stainless Design Concepts Ltd (G-14213)*

Sdi, Sunnyside *Also called S Donadic Inc (G-14774)*

Sdi Cable, Bohemia *Also called Security Dynamics Inc (G-1075)*

SDJ Machine Shop Inc 585 458-1236
  1215 Mount Read Blvd # 1 Rochester (14606) *(G-13720)*

Sdp/Si, Hicksville *Also called Designatronics Incorporated (G-5902)*

Sdr Technology Inc 716 583-1249
  1613 Lindan Dr Alden (14004) *(G-174)*

Se-Mar Electric Co Inc 716 674-7404
  101 South Ave West Seneca (14224) *(G-15853)*

Sea, Garden City *Also called Software Engineering Amer Inc (G-5116)*

Sea Breeze Fish & Seafood of S (PA) 718 984-0447
  240 Page Ave Staten Island (10307) *(G-14707)*

Sea Isle Custom Rod Builders 516 868-8855
  495 Guy Lombardo Ave Freeport (11520) *(G-5022)*

Sea Mats, Malone *Also called Seaway Mats Inc (G-7490)*

Sea Waves Inc (PA) 516 766-4201
  2425 Long Beach Rd Oceanside (11572) *(G-12189)*

Seabay Media Holdings LLC (PA) 212 457-7790
  120 Broadway Fl 6 New York (10271) *(G-11172)*

Seaboard Electronics, New Rochelle *Also called Highlander Realty Inc (G-8341)*

Seaboard Graphic Services LLC 315 652-4200
  6881 Schuyler Rd East Syracuse (13057) *(G-4237)*

Seal & Design Inc 315 432-8021
  6741 Thompson Rd Syracuse (13211) *(G-14990)*

Seal Reinforced Fiberglass Inc (PA) 631 842-2230
  19 Bethpage Rd Copiague (11726) *(G-3676)*

Seal Reinforced Fiberglass Inc 631 842-2230
  23 Bethpage Rd Copiague (11726) *(G-3677)*

Sealmaster, Buffalo *Also called Jet-Black Sealers Inc (G-2822)*

Sealtest Dairy Products, Rochester *Also called Upstate Niagara Coop Inc (G-13789)*

Sealy Mattress Co Albany Inc 518 880-1600
  30 Veterans Memorial Dr Troy (12183) *(G-15161)*

Seaman Schepps, New York *Also called Trianon Collection Inc (G-11542)*

Sean John, New York *Also called Christian Casey LLC (G-8997)*

Sean John Clothing, New York *Also called Christian Casey LLC (G-8998)*

Sean John Clothing Inc 212 500-2200
  1710 Broadway Frnt 1 New York (10019) *(G-11173)*

Sean John Clothing Inc (PA) 212 500-2200
  1440 Broadway Frnt 3 New York (10018) *(G-11174)*

Seanair Machine Co Inc 631 694-2820
  95 Verdi St Farmingdale (11735) *(G-4731)*

Searles Graphics Inc (PA) 631 345-2202
  56 Old Dock Rd Yaphank (11980) *(G-16270)*

Seasons Soyfood Inc 718 797-9896
  605 Degraw St Brooklyn (11217) *(G-2393)*

Seating Inc 800 468-2475
  60 N State St Nunda (14517) *(G-12134)*

Seaward Candies 585 638-6761
  3588 N Main Street Rd Holley (14470) *(G-6038)*

Seaway Mats Inc 518 483-2560
  252 Park St Malone (12953) *(G-7490)*

Seaway Timber Harvesting Inc (PA) 315 769-5970
  15121 State Highway 37 Massena (13662) *(G-7671)*

Sebby Clothing, New York *Also called Comint Apparel Group LLC (G-9065)*

Second Amendment Foundation 716 885-6408
  267 Linwood Ave Ste A Buffalo (14209) *(G-2978)*

Second Chance Press Inc 631 725-1101
  4170 Noyac Rd Sag Harbor (11963) *(G-14102)*

Second Generation Wood Stairs 718 370-0085
  2581 Richmond Ter Ste 3 Staten Island (10303) *(G-14708)*

Secret Celebrity Licensing LLC 212 812-9277
  1431 Broadway Fl 10 New York (10018) *(G-11175)*

Secs Inc 914 667-5600
  550 S Columbus Ave Mount Vernon (10550) *(G-8179)*

Sector Microwave Inds Inc 631 242-2245
  999 Grand Blvd Deer Park (11729) *(G-3935)*

Securax, Bohemia *Also called Protex International Corp (G-1068)*

Secure International 716 206-2500
  100 W Drullard Ave Ste 3 Lancaster (14086) *(G-6833)*

Secured Services Inc (PA) 866 419-3900
  110 William St Fl 14 New York (10038) *(G-11176)*

Secureit Tactical Inc (PA) 800 651-8835
  6691 Commerce Blvd Syracuse (13211) *(G-14991)*

Security Defense System 718 769-7900
  15038 12th Ave Whitestone (11357) *(G-16100)*

Security Dynamics Inc 631 392-1701
  217 Knickerbocker Ave # 4 Bohemia (11716) *(G-1075)*

Security Letter 212 348-1553
  166 E 96th St Apt 3b New York (10128) *(G-11177)*

Seedlngs Lf Scnce Ventures LLC 917 913-8511
  230 E 15th St Apt 1a New York (10003) *(G-11178)*

Seeley Machine Inc 518 798-9510
  75 Big Boom Rd Queensbury (12804) *(G-13056)*

Seeley Machine & Fabrication, Queensbury *Also called Seeley Machine Inc (G-13056)*

Seelos Corporation 646 998-6475
  300 Park Ave New York (10022) *(G-11179)*

Seelos Therapeutics Inc (PA) 646 998-6475
  300 Park Ave Fl 12 New York (10022) *(G-11180)*

Sefaira Inc 855 733-2472
  135 E 57th St Fl 6 New York (10022) *(G-11181)*

Sefi Fabricator, Amityville *Also called IMC Teddy Food Service (G-275)*

Sefi Fabricators, Amityville *Also called P & M LLC (G-301)*

Segovia Technology Co 212 868-4412
  33 Irving Pl Fl 7 New York (10003) *(G-11182)*

Seibel Modern Mfg & Wldg Corp 716 683-1536
  38 Palmer Pl Lancaster (14086) *(G-6834)*

Seidlin Consulting 212 496-2043
  580 W End Ave New York (10024) *(G-11183)*

Seifert Graphics Inc 315 736-2744
  6133 Judd Rd Oriskany (13424) *(G-12394)*

Seifert Transit Graphics, Oriskany *Also called Seifert Graphics Inc (G-12394)*

Seisenbacher Inc 585 730-4960
  175 Humboldt St Ste 250 Rochester (14610) *(G-13721)*

Seize Sur Vingt, New York *Also called Groupe 16sur20 LLC (G-9685)*

Sekas International Ltd 212 629-6095
  345 7th Ave Fl 9 New York (10001) *(G-11184)*

Selby Marketing Associates Inc (PA) 585 377-0750
  1001 Lexington Aveste 800 Rochester (14606) *(G-13722)*

Select Controls Inc 631 567-9010
  45 Knickerbocker Ave # 3 Bohemia (11716) *(G-1076)*

Select Door, North Java *Also called Select Interior Door Ltd (G-12032)*

Select Fabricators Inc 585 393-0650
  5310 North St Ste 5 Canandaigua (14424) *(G-3142)*

Select Industries New York Inc 800 723-5333
  450 Fashion Ave Ste 3002 New York (10123) *(G-11185)*

Select Information Exchange 212 496-6435
  175 W 79th St 3a New York (10024) *(G-11186)*

Select Interior Door Ltd 585 535-9900
  2074 Perry Rd North Java (14113) *(G-12032)*

Select Jewelry Inc 718 784-3626
  4728 37th St Fl 3 Long Island City (11101) *(G-7354)*

Select Products Holdings LLC (PA) 631 421-6000
  1 Arnold Dr Unit 3 Huntington (11743) *(G-6224)*

Select-A-Form Inc 631 981-3076
  4717 Veterans Mem Hwy Holbrook (11741) *(G-6020)*

Select-Tech Inc 845 895-8111
  3050 State Route 208 Wallkill (12589) *(G-15473)*

Selective Beauty Corporation 585 336-7600
  315 Bleecker St 109 New York (10014) *(G-11187)*

Selectrode Industries Inc (PA) 631 547-5470
  230 Broadway Huntington Station (11746) *(G-6260)*

Selflock Screw Products Co Inc 315 541-4464
  461 E Brighton Ave Syracuse (13210) *(G-14992)*

Sellas Life Sciences Group Inc (PA) 917 438-4353
  15 W 38th St Fl 10 New York (10018) *(G-11188)*

Sellco Industries Inc 607 756-7594
  58 Grant St Cortland (13045) *(G-3788)*

Selux Corporation 845 691-7723
  5 Lumen Ln Highland (12528) *(G-5963)*

Semans Enterprises Inc 585 444-0097
  25 Hendrix Rd Ste E West Henrietta (14586) *(G-15803)*

Semco Ceramics Inc 315 782-3000
  363 Eastern Blvd Watertown (13601) *(G-15588)*

Semec Corp 518 825-0160
  20 Gateway Dr Plattsburgh (12901) *(G-12776)*

Semi-Linear Inc 212 243-2108
  1123 Broadway Ste 718 New York (10010) *(G-11189)*

Semitronics Corp (HQ) 516 223-0200
  80 Commercial St Freeport (11520) *(G-5023)*

Semrock, Rochester *Also called Semrok Inc (G-13723)*

Semrok Inc 585 594-7050
  3625 Buffalo Rd Ste 6 Rochester (14624) *(G-13723)*

Semtex Industrial, Freeport *Also called Intex Company Inc (G-5003)*

Sendec Corp 585 425-5965
  151 Perinton Pkwy Fairport (14450) *(G-4520)*

Seneca Ceramics Corp 315 781-0100
  835 Mcivor Rd Phelps (14532) *(G-12607)*

Seneca County Area Shopper 607 532-4333
  1885 State Route 96a Ovid (14521) *(G-12425)*

Seneca Falls Capital Inc (PA) 315 568-5804
  314 Fall St Seneca Falls (13148) *(G-14370)*

Seneca Falls Machine, Seneca Falls *Also called Seneca Falls Capital Inc (G-14370)*

Seneca Falls Machine Tool Co 315 568-5804
  314 Fall St Seneca Falls (13148) *(G-14371)*

Seneca Falls Technology Group, Seneca Falls *Also called Seneca Falls Machine Tool Co (G-14371)*

Seneca FLS Spc & Logistics Co (PA) 315 568-4139
  50 Johnston St Seneca Falls (13148) *(G-14372)*

Seneca Foods Corporation (PA) 315 926-8100
  3736 S Main St Marion (14505) *(G-7574)*

Seneca Foods Corporation 315 781-8733
  100 Gambee Rd Geneva (14456) *(G-5162)*

Seneca Foods Corporation 315 926-4277
  3732 S Main St Marion (14505) *(G-7575)*

Seneca Foods Corporation 585 658-2211
  5705 Rte 36 Leicester (14481) *(G-6911)*

Seneca Manufacturing Company 716 945-4400
  175 Rochester St Salamanca (14779) *(G-14128)*

Seneca Media Inc (PA) 607 324-1425
  32 Broadway Mall Hornell (14843) *(G-6110)*

Seneca Nation Enterprise 716 934-7430
  11482 Route 20 Irving (14081) *(G-6304)*

Seneca Resources Company LLC 716 630-6750
  165 Lawrence Bell Dr Williamsville (14221) *(G-16138)*

Seneca Signs LLC 315 446-9420
  102 Headson Dr Syracuse (13214) *(G-14993)*

Seneca Stone Corporation (HQ) 607 737-6200
  2105 S Broadway Pine City (14871) *(G-12629)*

Seneca TEC Inc 585 381-2645
  73 Country Corner Ln Fairport (14450) *(G-4521)*

Seneca Truck & Trailer Inc 315 781-1100
  2200 State Route 14 Geneva (14456) *(G-5163)*

Seneca West Printing Inc 716 675-8010
  860 Center Rd West Seneca (14224) *(G-15854)*

Senera Co Inc 516 639-3774
  834 Glenridge Ave Valley Stream (11581) *(G-15358)*

Senior Brands LLC 212 213-5100
  347 5th Ave Rm 506 New York (10016) *(G-11190)*

Sensational Collection Inc (PA) 212 840-7388
  1410 Broadway Rm 505 New York (10018) *(G-11191)*

Sensio America 877 501-5337
  800 Route 146 Ste 175 Clifton Park (12065) *(G-3472)*

Sensio America LLC (PA) 877 501-5337
  800 Route 146 Ste 175 Clifton Park (12065) *(G-3473)*

Sensitron Semiconductor, Deer Park Also called RSM Electron Power Inc *(G-3931)*

Sensitron Semiconductor, Hauppauge Also called RSM Electron Power Inc *(G-5756)*

Sensodx II LLC 585 202-4552
  600 Fishers Station Dr # 124 Victor (14564) *(G-15429)*

Sensor & Decontamination Inc 301 526-8389
  892 Powderhouse Rd Binghamton (13903) *(G-908)*

Sensor Films Incorporated 585 738-3500
  687 Rowley Rd Victor (14564) *(G-15430)*

Sensormatic Electronics LLC 845 365-3125
  10 Corporate Dr Orangeburg (10962) *(G-12331)*

Sensual Inc 212 869-1450
  463 7th Ave Rm 1101 New York (10018) *(G-11192)*

Sentine Printing Inc 516 334-7400
  75 State St Westbury (11590) *(G-15925)*

Sentinel Printing, Hempstead Also called Hempstead Sentinel Inc *(G-5838)*

Sentinel, The, New Windsor Also called E W Smith Publishing Co Inc *(G-8366)*

Sentry Automatic Sprinkler 631 723-3095
  735 Flanders Rd Riverhead (11901) *(G-13189)*

Sentry Devices Corp 631 491-3191
  33 Rustic Gate Ln Dix Hills (11746) *(G-4015)*

Sentry Funding Partnership, Ronkonkoma Also called Sentry Technology
Corporation *(G-14007)*

Sentry Metal Blast Inc 716 285-5241
  553 West Ave Lockport (14094) *(G-7106)*

Sentry Metal Services, Lockport Also called Sentry Metal Blast Inc *(G-7106)*

Sentry Technology Corporation 631 739-2000
  1881 Lakeland Ave Ronkonkoma (11779) *(G-14006)*

Sentry Technology Corporation (PA) 800 645-4224
  1881 Lakeland Ave Ronkonkoma (11779) *(G-14007)*

Seoul Shopping Bag Inc 718 439-9226
  10001 Avenue D Brooklyn (11236) *(G-2394)*

Sepac Inc 607 732-2030
  1580 Lake St Ste 1 Elmira (14901) *(G-4367)*

Sepco-Sturges Electronics, Dryden Also called Sturges Elec Pdts Co Inc *(G-4041)*

Sephardic Yellow Pages 718 998-0299
  2150 E 4th St Brooklyn (11223) *(G-2395)*

Sepsa North America, Ballston Spa Also called Albatros North America Inc *(G-567)*

September Associates, Oakdale Also called Steel-Brite Ltd *(G-12156)*

Sequa Corporation 201 343-1122
  330 Blaisdell Rd Orangeburg (10962) *(G-12332)*

Serge Duct Designs Inc 718 783-7799
  535 Dean St Apt 124 Brooklyn (11217) *(G-2396)*

Seri Systems Inc 585 272-5515
  172 Metro Park Rochester (14623) *(G-13724)*

Seriesone Inc 212 385-1552
  860 Broadway Fl 5 New York (10003) *(G-11193)*

Sermoneta Gloves, New York Also called Shadal LLC *(G-11200)*

Serraview America Inc 800 903-3716
  2 Wall St Fl 10 New York (10005) *(G-11194)*

Service Advertising Group Inc 718 361-6161
  4216 34th Ave Long Island City (11101) *(G-7355)*

Service Canvas Co Inc 716 853-0558
  149 Swan St Unit 155 Buffalo (14203) *(G-2979)*

Service Education Incorporated 585 264-9240
  790 Canning Pkwy Ste 1 Victor (14564) *(G-15431)*

Service Filtration Corp 716 877-2608
  225 E Park Dr Tonawanda (14150) *(G-15140)*

Service Machine & Tool Company 607 732-0413
  206 E Mccanns Blvd Elmira Heights (14903) *(G-4379)*

Service Mfg Group Inc (PA) 716 893-1482
  400 Scajaquada St Buffalo (14211) *(G-2980)*

Service Mfg Group Inc 716 893-1482
  400 Scajaquada St Buffalo (14211) *(G-2981)*

Servicenow Inc 914 318-1168
  60 E 42nd St Ste 1230 New York (10165) *(G-11195)*

Servo Reeler System, Queens Village Also called Xedit Corp *(G-13028)*

Servotec Usa LLC 518 671-6120
  1 Industrial Tract Anx # 3 Hudson (12534) *(G-6179)*

Servotronics Inc (PA) 716 655-5990
  1110 Maple Rd Elma (14059) *(G-4327)*

Serway Bros Inc (PA) 315 337-0601
  Plant 2 Rome Indus Ctr Rome (13440) *(G-13872)*

Serway Cabinet Trends, Rome Also called Serway Bros Inc *(G-13872)*

Setauket Manufacturing Co 631 231-7272
  202 Christopher St Ronkonkoma (11779) *(G-14008)*

Seton Identification Products, Williamsville Also called Tricor Direct Inc *(G-16145)*

Settapani Bakery, Brooklyn Also called Settepani Inc *(G-2397)*

Settepani Inc (PA) 718 349-6524
  602 Lorimer St Brooklyn (11211) *(G-2397)*

Setterstix Inc 716 257-3451
  261 S Main St Cattaraugus (14719) *(G-3222)*

Setton Brothers Inc 646 902-6011
  326 Troy Ave Brooklyn (11213) *(G-2398)*

Setton Farms, Commack Also called Settons Intl Foods Inc *(G-3598)*

Settons Intl Foods Inc (PA) 631 543-8090
  85 Austin Blvd Commack (11725) *(G-3598)*

Seven Springs Gravel Pdts LLC 585 343-4336
  8479 Seven Springs Rd Batavia (14020) *(G-624)*

Seven Stories Press Inc 212 226-8760
  140 Watts St New York (10013) *(G-11196)*

Seventeen Magazine, New York Also called Hearst Corporation *(G-9751)*

Seville Central Mix Corp (PA) 516 868-3000
  157 Albany Ave Freeport (11520) *(G-5024)*

Seville Central Mix Corp 516 293-6190
  495 Wining Rd Old Bethpage (11804) *(G-12219)*

Seville Central Mix Corp 516 239-8333
  101 Johnson Rd Lawrence (11559) *(G-6892)*

Seviroli Foods Inc (PA) 516 222-6220
  385 Oak St Garden City (11530) *(G-5115)*

Sew True, New York Also called Champion Zipper Corp *(G-8969)*

Sextet Fabrics Inc 516 593-0608
  145 Babylon Tpke Roosevelt (11575) *(G-14032)*

Sfoglini Pasta, West Coxsackie Also called Good Noodles Inc *(G-15759)*

Sg Blocks Inc (PA) 646 240-4235
  195 Montague St Fl 14 Brooklyn (11201) *(G-2399)*

Sg Nyc LLC 310 210-1837
  28 W 27th St Fl 12 New York (10001) *(G-11197)*

SGD North America 212 753-4200
  900 3rd Ave Fl 4 New York (10022) *(G-11198)*

SGD Pharma Packaging Inc 212 223-7100
  900 3rd Ave Fl 4 New York (10022) *(G-11199)*

Sgg, Long Island City Also called Stanley Creations Inc *(G-7365)*

SGS, Phoenix Also called Southern Graphic Systems LLC *(G-12621)*

Sgt Dresser-Rand, Wellsville Also called Siemens Government Tech Inc *(G-15676)*

Sh Leather Novelty Company 718 387-7742
  123 Clymer St Bsmt Brooklyn (11249) *(G-2400)*

Shaant Industries Inc 716 366-3654
  134 Franklin Ave Dunkirk (14048) *(G-4066)*

Shad Industries Inc 631 504-6028
  7 Old Dock Rd Unit 1 Yaphank (11980) *(G-16271)*

Shadal LLC 212 319-5946
  609 Madison Ave Ste 611 New York (10022) *(G-11200)*

Shade & Shutter Systems of NY 631 208-0275
  260 Hampton Rd Southampton (11968) *(G-14537)*

Shade Tree Greetings Inc 585 442-4580
  704 Clinton Ave S Rochester (14620) *(G-13725)*

Shadow Lake Golf & Racquet CLB, Rochester Also called Dolomite Products Company
Inc *(G-13354)*

Shadowtv Inc 212 445-2540
  630 9th Ave Ste 202 New York (10036) *(G-11201)*

Shafer & Sons 315 853-5285
  4932 State Route 233 Westmoreland (13490) *(G-15963)*

Shah Diamonds Inc 212 888-9393
  22 W 48th St Ste 600 New York (10036) *(G-11202)*

Shahin Designs Ltd 212 737-7225
  766 Madison Ave Fl 3 New York (10065) *(G-11203)*

Shake Inc 650 544-5479
  175 Varick St Fl 4 New York (10014) *(G-11204)*

Shake-N-Go Fashion Inc 516 944-7777
  83 Harbor Rd Port Washington (11050) *(G-12924)*

Shake-N-Go Fashion Inc (PA) 516 944-7777
  85 Harbor Rd Port Washington (11050) *(G-12925)*

Shako Inc 315 437-1294
  6191 E Molloy Rd East Syracuse (13057) *(G-4238)*

Shakuff LLC 212 675-0383
  34 35th St Unit 29 Brooklyn (11232) *(G-2401)*

A
L
P
H
A
B
E
T
I
C

Shalam Imports Inc (PA) 718 686-6271
1552 Dahill Rd Ste B Brooklyn (11204) *(G-2402)*

Shalamex, Brooklyn *Also called Shalam Imports Inc* *(G-2402)*

Shamrock Materials LLC 718 273-9223
100 Signal Hill Rd Staten Island (10301) *(G-14709)*

Shamrock Plastic Corporation 585 328-6040
95 Mount Read Blvd Rochester (14611) *(G-13726)*

Shamrock Plastics & Tool Inc 585 328-6040
95 Mount Read Blvd # 149 Rochester (14611) *(G-13727)*

Shamron Mills Ltd 212 354-0430
484 River St Troy (12180) *(G-15188)*

Shane & Shawn, New York *Also called Detny Footwear Inc* *(G-9210)*

Shane Tex Inc 516 486-7522
717 Longacre Ave Woodmere (11598) *(G-16193)*

Shanghai Harmony AP Intl LLC 646 569-5680
3 Wykagyl Ter New Rochelle (10804) *(G-8354)*

Shanghai Stove Inc 718 599-4583
78 Gerry St 82 Brooklyn (11206) *(G-2403)*

Shannon Global Enrgy Solutions 716 693-7954
75 Main St North Tonawanda (14120) *(G-12090)*

Shanu Gems Inc 212 921-4470
1212 Ave Of The Americas New York (10036) *(G-11205)*

Shapeways Inc (PA) 914 356-5816
44 W 28th St Fl 12 New York (10001) *(G-11206)*

Shapeways Inc 646 470-3576
3002 48th Ave Ste 2 Long Island City (11101) *(G-7356)*

Shapiro Bernstein & Co Inc 212 588-0878
488 Madison Ave Fl 1201 New York (10022) *(G-11207)*

Shapiro Wlliam NY Univ Med Ctr, New York *Also called William H Shapiro* *(G-11758)*

Shar-Mar Machine Company 631 567-8040
1648 Locust Ave Ste F Bohemia (11716) *(G-1077)*

Sharedbook Inc 646 442-8840
110 William St Fl 30 New York (10038) *(G-11208)*

Sharemethods LLC 877 742-7366
1 N 4th Pl Apt 19i Brooklyn (11249) *(G-2404)*

Sharodine Inc 516 767-3548
18 Haven Ave Frnt 2 Port Washington (11050) *(G-12926)*

Sharon Manufacturing Co Inc 631 242-8870
540 Brook Ave Deer Park (11729) *(G-3936)*

Sharonana Enterprises Inc 631 875-5619
52 Sharon Dr Coram (11727) *(G-3699)*

Sharp Printing Inc 716 731-3994
3477 Lockport Rd Sanborn (14132) *(G-14149)*

Shawmut Woodworking & Sup Inc 212 920-8900
3 E 54th St Fl 8 New York (10022) *(G-11209)*

Shawmutdesign and Construction, New York *Also called Shawmut Woodworking & Sup Inc* *(G-11209)*

Sheets, The, Long Island City *Also called Ragozin Data* *(G-7338)*

Shehawken Archery Co Inc 607 967-8333
40 S Main St Bainbridge (13733) *(G-526)*

Shelby Crushed Stone Inc 585 798-4501
10830 Blair Rd Medina (14103) *(G-7746)*

Sheldon Slate Products Co Inc 518 642-1280
Fox Rd Middle Granville (12849) *(G-7870)*

Sheldrake Point Vineyard LLC 607 532-8967
7448 County Road 153 Ovid (14521) *(G-12426)*

Sheldrake Point Winery, Ovid *Also called Sheldrake Point Vineyard LLC* *(G-12426)*

Shell Ann Printing, Stony Point *Also called Stony Point Graphics Ltd* *(G-14748)*

Shell Containers Inc 516 352-4505
1981 Marcus Ave Ste C105 New Hyde Park (11042) *(G-8292)*

Shelley Promotions Inc 212 924-4987
87 5th Ave New York (10003) *(G-11210)*

Shelter Enterprises Inc 518 237-4100
8 Saratoga St Cohoes (12047) *(G-3516)*

Shelter Island Cmnty Nwspapers, Shelter Island *Also called Shelter Island Reporter Inc* *(G-14387)*

Shelter Island Reporter Inc 631 749-1000
50 N Ferry Rd Shelter Island (11964) *(G-14387)*

Shenfeld Studio Tile, Syracuse *Also called Shenfield Studio LLC* *(G-14994)*

Shenfield Studio LLC 315 436-8869
6361 Thompson Rd Stop 12 Syracuse (13206) *(G-14994)*

Shengkun North America Inc 212 217-2460
262 W 38th St Rm 903 New York (10018) *(G-11211)*

Shenzhen Xnhdingsheng Tech Ltd 510 506-5753
4112a Main St 2fd09 Flushing (11355) *(G-4892)*

Shepherds Flat, New York *Also called Caithness Equities Corporation* *(G-8888)*

Shepherds Pl LLC 516 647-8151
31 Keller St Valley Stream (11580) *(G-15359)*

Sheppard Grain Enterprises LLC 315 548-9271
1615 Maryland Rd Phelps (14532) *(G-12608)*

Sher Plastics, New York *Also called Prym Fashion Americas LLC* *(G-10917)*

Sherburne Metal Sales Inc (PA) 607 674-4441
40 S Main St Sherburne (13460) *(G-14393)*

Sherco Services LLC 516 676-3028
2 Park Pl Ste A Glen Cove (11542) *(G-5200)*

Sheridan House Inc 914 725-5431
230 Nelson Rd Scarsdale (10583) *(G-14242)*

Sherrill Manufacturing Inc 315 280-0727
102 E Seneca St Sherrill (13461) *(G-14406)*

Sherwin Commerce, New York *Also called AT&T Corp* *(G-8659)*

Sherwood Group Inc 240 731-8573
166 E 96th St Apt 5a New York (10128) *(G-11212)*

Shhhmouse, Brooklyn *Also called Digiorange Inc* *(G-1743)*

Shield Press Inc 212 431-7489
9 Lispenard St Fl 1 New York (10013) *(G-11213)*

Shield Security Doors Ltd 202 468-3308
300 Cadman Plz W Fl 12 Brooklyn (11201) *(G-2405)*

Shieldex Trading-US, Palmyra *Also called V Technical Textiles Inc* *(G-12494)*

Shimada Shoji (hk) Limited 212 268-0465
165 W 46th St Ste 709 New York (10036) *(G-11214)*

Shindo Usa Inc 212 868-9311
162 W 36th St New York (10018) *(G-11215)*

Shining Creations Inc 845 358-4911
40 S Main St Ste 1 New City (10956) *(G-8230)*

Shinn Vineyard, Mattituck *Also called Shinn Winery LLC* *(G-7679)*

Shinn Winery LLC 631 804-0367
2000 Oregon Rd Mattituck (11952) *(G-7679)*

Shipman Print Solutions, Niagara Falls *Also called Shipman Printing Inds Inc* *(G-11980)*

Shipman Printing Inds Inc (PA) 716 504-7700
2424 Niagara Falls Blvd Niagara Falls (14304) *(G-11980)*

Shipman Printing Inds Inc 716 504-7700
6120 Lendell Dr Sanborn (14132) *(G-14150)*

Shipmtes/Printmates Holdg Corp (PA) 518 370-1158
705 Corporation Park # 2 Scotia (12302) *(G-14336)*

Shiprite Services Inc 315 427-2422
1312 Genesee St Utica (13502) *(G-15294)*

Shiprite Software, Utica *Also called Shiprite Services Inc* *(G-15294)*

Shira Accessories Ltd 212 594-4455
28 W 36th St Fl 6 New York (10018) *(G-11216)*

Shirl-Lynn of New York (PA) 315 363-5898
266 Wilson St Oneida (13421) *(G-12254)*

Shiro Limited 212 780-0007
928 Broadway Ste 806 New York (10010) *(G-11217)*

Shirt Shack, New City *Also called Regal Screen Printing Intl* *(G-8229)*

Shiseido Americas Corporation (HQ) 212 805-2300
900 3rd Ave Fl 15 New York (10022) *(G-11218)*

Shiseido Cosmetics, New York *Also called Shiseido Americas Corporation* *(G-11218)*

Shmaltz Brewing Company 518 406-5430
6 Fairchild Sq 1 Clifton Park (12065) *(G-3474)*

Shop Sky Inc 347 686-4616
10471 128th St South Richmond Hill (11419) *(G-14524)*

Shoppers Weekly Newspapers, Melville *Also called Star Community Publishing* *(G-7824)*

Shopping Center Wine & Liquor 914 528-1600
3008 E Main St Mohegan Lake (10547) *(G-8011)*

Shore Line Momogramming & EMB, Mamaroneck *Also called Shore Line Monogramming Inc* *(G-7523)*

Shore Line Monogramming Inc 914 698-8000
115 Hoyt Ave Mamaroneck (10543) *(G-7523)*

Shore Products Co, Auburn *Also called T Shore Products Ltd* *(G-497)*

Shoreline Fruit LLC 585 765-2639
10190 Route 18 Lyndonville (14098) *(G-7446)*

Shoreline Publishing Inc 914 738-7869
629 Fifth Ave Ste B01 Pelham (10803) *(G-12568)*

Short Jj Associates Inc (PA) 315 986-3511
1645 Wayneport Rd Macedon (14502) *(G-7470)*

Short Run Forms Inc 631 567-7171
171 Keyland Ct Bohemia (11716) *(G-1078)*

Showeray Co 718 965-3633
1857 E 8th St Brooklyn (11223) *(G-2406)*

Shred Center 716 664-3052
20 Carroll St Jamestown (14701) *(G-6540)*

Shredder Essentials, Brooklyn *Also called Casa Innovations Inc* *(G-1654)*

Shrineeta Pharmacy 212 234-7959
1749 Amsterdam Ave Frnt New York (10031) *(G-11219)*

Shrineeta Pharmacy Inc 212 234-7959
1743 Amsterdam Ave New York (10031) *(G-11220)*

Shugar Publishing 631 288-4404
99b Main St Westhampton Beach (11978) *(G-15958)*

Shyam Ahuja Limited 212 644-5910
201 E 56th St Frnt A New York (10022) *(G-11221)*

Shyk International Corp 212 663-3302
258 Riverside Dr Apt 7b New York (10025) *(G-11222)*

Si Funeral Services, Fairport *Also called Suhor Industries Inc* *(G-4526)*

Si Group Inc (HQ) 518 347-4200
2750 Balltown Rd Schenectady (12309) *(G-14304)*

Si Group Inc 518 347-4200
1000 Main St Rotterdam Junction (12150) *(G-14060)*

Si Group Inc 518 347-4200
Rr 5 Box South Rotterdam Junction (12150) *(G-14061)*

Si Group Global Manufacturing, Rotterdam Junction *Also called Si Group Inc* *(G-14060)*

SI Partners Inc 516 433-1415
15 E Carl St Unit 1 Hicksville (11801) *(G-5948)*

Sick Inc 585 347-2000
855 Publishers Pkwy Webster (14580) *(G-15653)*

Sidco Filter Corporation 585 289-3100
58 North Ave Manchester (14504) *(G-7529)*

Sidco Food Distribution Corp 718 733-3939
2324 Webster Ave Bronx (10458) *(G-1363)*

Side Hill Farmers Coop Inc 315 697-9862
8275 State Route 13 Canastota (13032) *(G-3157)*

Side Hustle Music Group LLC....800 219-4003
600 3rd Ave Fl 2 New York (10016) ***(G-11223)***
Sidney Favorite Printing Div, Sidney *Also called Tri-Town News Inc **(G-14436)***
Siegel & Stockman Inc....212 633-1508
126 W 25th St Frnt 1 New York (10001) ***(G-11224)***
Siegfrieds Call Inc....845 765-2275
20 Kent St 109 Beacon (12508) ***(G-756)***
Siemens AG....212 946-2440
1 Penn Plz New York (10119) ***(G-11225)***
Siemens Corporation....202 434-7800
527 Madison Ave Fl 8 New York (10022) ***(G-11226)***
Siemens Government Tech Inc....585 593-1234
37 Coats St Wellsville (14895) ***(G-15676)***
Siemens Hlthcare Dgnostics Inc....914 631-0475
511 Benedict Ave Tarrytown (10591) ***(G-15059)***
Siemens Industry Inc....716 568-0983
85 Northpointe Pkwy Amherst (14228) ***(G-243)***
Siemens Industry Inc....716 568-0983
85 Northpointe Pkwy Ste 8 Buffalo (14228) ***(G-2982)***
Siemens Industry Inc....585 797-2300
50 Methodist Hill Dr # 1500 Rochester (14623) ***(G-13728)***
Siemens Mobility Inc (HQ)....212 672-4000
1 Penn Plz Ste 1100 New York (10119) ***(G-11227)***
Siemens Product Life Mgmt Sftw....585 389-8699
345 Woodcliff Dr Fairport (14450) ***(G-4522)***
Siemens Product Life Mgmt Sftw....631 549-2300
60 Broadhollow Rd Melville (11747) ***(G-7822)***
Siemens USA Holdings Inc....212 258-4000
527 Madison Ave Fl 8 New York (10022) ***(G-11228)***
Sierra Processing LLC....518 433-0020
2 Moyer Ave Schenectady (12306) ***(G-14305)***
Sierson Crane Inc....315 723-6914
4822 State Route 233 Westmoreland (13490) ***(G-15964)***
Sifonya Inc....212 620-4512
303 Park Ave S Frnt 2 New York (10010) ***(G-11229)***
Siga Technologies Inc (PA)....212 672-9100
31 E 62nd St New York (10065) ***(G-11230)***
Sigelock Systems LLC (PA)....888 744-3562
3205 Lawson Blvd Oceanside (11572) ***(G-12190)***
Sigma Intl Gen Med Apprtus LLC....585 798-3901
711 Park Ave Medina (14103) ***(G-7747)***
Sigma Manufacturing Inds Inc....718 842-9180
1361 E Bay Ave Bronx (10474) ***(G-1364)***
Sigma Worldwide LLC (PA)....646 217-0629
65 W 83rd St Apt 5 New York (10024) ***(G-11231)***
Sigmacare, New York *Also called Matrixcare Inc **(G-10385)***
Sigmamotor Inc....716 735-3115
3 N Main St Middleport (14105) ***(G-7890)***
Sigmund Cohn Corp....914 664-5300
121 S Columbus Ave Mount Vernon (10553) ***(G-8180)***
Sign & Signs....718 941-6200
783 Coney Island Ave Brooklyn (11218) ***(G-2407)***
Sign A Rama Inc....631 952-3324
663 Old Willets Path C Hauppauge (11788) ***(G-5764)***
Sign Center Inc....212 967-2113
127 W 26th St Rm 401 New York (10001) ***(G-11232)***
Sign City of New York Inc....718 661-1118
13212 11th Ave College Point (11356) ***(G-3564)***
Sign Company....212 967-2113
15 W 39th St Fl 7 New York (10018) ***(G-11233)***
Sign Company, The, New York *Also called Sign Center Inc **(G-11232)***
Sign Depot Distribution, Huntington Station *Also called BC Communications Inc **(G-6240)***
Sign Design, Port Chester *Also called Lanza Corp **(G-12824)***
Sign Design Group New York Inc....718 392-0779
47 Wireless Blvd Hauppauge (11788) ***(G-5765)***
Sign Expo, New York *Also called Signexpo Enterprises Inc **(G-11236)***
Sign Group Inc....718 438-7103
5215 New Utrecht Ave Brooklyn (11219) ***(G-2408)***
Sign Guys New York City Inc (PA)....718 414-2310
237 Oak St West Hempstead (11552) ***(G-15779)***
Sign Guys Nyc, West Hempstead *Also called Sign Guys New York City Inc **(G-15779)***
Sign Heaven Corp....718 499-4423
160 25th St Brooklyn (11232) ***(G-2409)***
Sign Here Enterprises LLC....914 328-3111
28 N Central Ave Rear Hartsdale (10530) ***(G-5568)***
Sign Impressions Inc....585 723-0420
2590 W Ridge Rd Ste 6 Rochester (14626) ***(G-13729)***
Sign Language Custom WD Signs, Perry *Also called Sign Language Inc **(G-12599)***
Sign Language Inc....585 237-2620
6491 State Route 20a Perry (14530) ***(G-12599)***
Sign Men....718 227-7446
389 Wild Ave Ste G Staten Island (10314) ***(G-14710)***
Sign Shop Inc....631 226-4145
1272 Montauk Hwy Ste A Copiague (11726) ***(G-3678)***
Sign Studio Inc....518 266-0877
98 Niver St Ste 3 Cohoes (12047) ***(G-3517)***
Sign Works Incorporated....914 592-0700
150 Clearbrook Rd Ste 118 Elmsford (10523) ***(G-4433)***
Sign World Inc....212 619-9000
1194 Utica Ave Brooklyn (11203) ***(G-2410)***
Sign-A-Rama, Hartsdale *Also called Sign Here Enterprises LLC **(G-5568)***
Sign-A-Rama, Baldwin *Also called Jal Signs Inc **(G-531)***
Sign-A-Rama, Mount Kisco *Also called Westchester Signs Inc **(G-8106)***
Sign-A-Rama, Syracuse *Also called Seneca Signs LLC **(G-14993)***
Sign-A-Rama, Huntington Station *Also called Z-Car-D Corp **(G-6267)***
Sign-A-Rama, Bellmore *Also called Speedy Sign A Rama USA Inc **(G-790)***
Sign-A-Rama, Hicksville *Also called Marigold Signs Inc **(G-5927)***
Sign-A-Rama, New Hyde Park *Also called Three Gems Inc **(G-8297)***
Sign-A-Rama, Hauppauge *Also called Sign A Rama Inc **(G-5764)***
Signa Chemistry Inc (PA)....212 933-4101
400 Madison Ave Fl 21 New York (10017) ***(G-11234)***
Signal Graphics Printing, Wappingers Falls *Also called Gem Reproduction Services Corp **(G-15494)***
Signal Transformer, Lynbrook *Also called Bel Transformer Inc **(G-7426)***
Signature Diamond Entps LLC....212 869-5115
15 W 47th St Ste 203 New York (10036) ***(G-11235)***
Signature Industries Inc....516 771-8182
32 Saint Johns Pl Freeport (11520) ***(G-5025)***
Signature Metal MBL Maint LLC....718 292-8280
791 E 132nd St Bronx (10454) ***(G-1365)***
Signature Name Plate Co Inc....585 321-9960
292 Commerce Dr Rochester (14623) ***(G-13730)***
Signatures Group, New York *Also called Light House Hill Marketing **(G-10216)***
Signexpo Enterprises Inc (PA)....212 925-8585
127 W 26th St Rm 401 New York (10001) ***(G-11236)***
Signify North America Corp....646 265-7170
267 5th Ave New York (10016) ***(G-11237)***
Signpost Inc....877 334-2837
127 W 26th St Fl 2 New York (10001) ***(G-11238)***
Signs & Decal Corp....718 486-6400
410 Morgan Ave Brooklyn (11211) ***(G-2411)***
Signs By Sunrise, Jamaica *Also called Tru-Art Sign Co Inc **(G-6482)***
Signs By Tomorrow, Commack *Also called Rpf Associates Inc **(G-3597)***
Signs Inc....518 483-4759
2 Boyer Ave Malone (12953) ***(G-7491)***
Signs Ink Ltd....914 739-9059
3255 Crompond Rd Yorktown Heights (10598) ***(G-16372)***
Signs Now, Rochester *Also called Image360 **(G-13476)***
Signs of Success Ltd....516 295-6000
247 Merrick Rd Ste 101 Lynbrook (11563) ***(G-7438)***
Signworks....518 745-0700
22 Hudson Falls Rd 54 South Glens Falls (12803) ***(G-14518)***
Sigro Precision, West Babylon *Also called BEAM Manufacturing Corp **(G-15694)***
Sikorsky Aircraft Corporation....585 424-1990
300 Canal View Blvd Rochester (14623) ***(G-13731)***
Silar Laboratories Division, Scotia *Also called Oak-Bark Corporation **(G-14335)***
Silgan Containers Mfg Corp....315 946-4826
8673 Lyons Marengo Rd Lyons (14489) ***(G-7452)***
Silgan Plastics LLC....315 536-5690
40 Powell Ln Penn Yan (14527) ***(G-12594)***
Silicon Carbide Products Inc....607 562-8599
361 Daniel Zenker Dr Horseheads (14845) ***(G-6137)***
Silicone Products & Technology....716 684-1155
4471 Walden Ave Lancaster (14086) ***(G-6835)***
Silipos Holding LLC (PA)....716 283-0700
7049 Williams Rd Niagara Falls (14304) ***(G-11981)***
Silk Screen Art Inc....518 762-8423
1 School St Johnstown (12095) ***(G-6627)***
Silky Tones Inc....718 218-5598
777 Kent Ave Ste 213 Brooklyn (11205) ***(G-2412)***
Silly Feet, New York *Also called Bh Brand Inc **(G-8777)***
Silly Phillie Creations Inc....718 492-6300
140 58th St Ste 6f Brooklyn (11220) ***(G-2413)***
Silva Cabinetry Inc....914 737-7697
12 White St Ste C Buchanan (10511) ***(G-2610)***
Silvatrim Corp....212 675-0933
324 W 22nd St New York (10011) ***(G-11239)***
Silvatrim Corporation America, New York *Also called Silvatrim Corp **(G-11239)***
Silver Bell Baking Co....718 335-9539
6406 Admiral Ave Middle Village (11379) ***(G-7884)***
Silver City Group Inc....315 363-0344
27577 W Seneca St Sherrill (13461) ***(G-14407)***
Silver City Metals, Sherrill *Also called Silver City Group Inc **(G-14407)***
Silver Creek Carpet, New York *Also called Bloomsburg Carpet Inds Inc **(G-8814)***
Silver Griffin Inc....518 272-7771
691 Hoosick Rd Troy (12180) ***(G-15189)***
Silver Oak Pharmacy Inc....718 922-3400
5105 Church Ave Brooklyn (11203) ***(G-2414)***
Silverlight Digital LLC....646 650-5330
15 E 32nd St Fl 3 New York (10016) ***(G-11240)***
Silverman & Gorf Inc....718 625-1309
60 Franklin Ave Brooklyn (11205) ***(G-2415)***
Silverstone Shtmtl Fbrications....718 422-0380
66 Huntington St Brooklyn (11231) ***(G-2416)***
Silvertique Fine Jewelry, New York *Also called Goldarama Company Inc **(G-9638)***
Sima Technologies LLC....412 828-9130
345 Oser Ave Hauppauge (11788) ***(G-5766)***
Simcha Candle Co Inc....845 783-0406
244 Mac Arthur Ave New Windsor (12553) ***(G-8383)***
Simco Leather Corporation....518 762-7100
99 Pleasant Ave Johnstown (12095) ***(G-6628)***

ALPHABETIC

Similarweb Inc 347 685-5422
35 E 21st St Fl 9 New York (10010) *(G-11241)*

Simka Diamond Corp 212 921-4420
580 5th Ave Ste 523 New York (10036) *(G-11242)*

Simmons Fabricating Svc Inc 845 635-3755
1558 Main St Pleasant Valley (12569) *(G-12794)*

Simmons Machine Tool Corp (PA) 518 462-5431
1700 Broadway Menands (12204) *(G-7848)*

Simmons-Boardman Pubg Corp (HQ) 212 620-7200
55 Broad St 26 New York (10004) *(G-11243)*

Simon & Schuster Inc 212 698-7000
1230 Ave Of The Americas New York (10020) *(G-11244)*

Simon & Simon LLC 202 419-0490
1745 Broadway Fl 17 New York (10019) *(G-11245)*

Simon Defense Inc 516 217-6000
1 Trade Zone Dr Unit 15 Ronkonkoma (11779) *(G-14009)*

Simon Liu Inc 718 567-2011
280 24th St Brooklyn (11232) *(G-2417)*

Simon S Decorating Inc 718 339-2931
911 Avenue N Brooklyn (11230) *(G-2418)*

Simon Schuster Digital Sls Inc 212 698-4391
51 W 52d St New York (10019) *(G-11246)*

Simple Brewer 845 490-0182
346 Route 202 Somers (10589) *(G-14501)*

Simple Elegance New York, Brooklyn Also called Sabbsons International Inc *(G-2379)*

Simple Elegance New York Inc 718 360-1947
474 50th St Brooklyn (11220) *(G-2419)*

Simplex Manufacturing Co Inc 315 252-7524
105 Dunning Ave Auburn (13021) *(G-495)*

Simply Active Cosmetics Inc 646 554-6421
433 W 21st St Apt 2c New York (10011) *(G-11247)*

Simply Amazing Enterprises Inc 631 503-6452
68 S Service Rd Ste 1 Melville (11747) *(G-7823)*

Simply Lite Foods, Commack Also called Simply Natural Foods LLC *(G-3599)*

Simply Natural Foods LLC 631 543-9600
74 Mall Dr Commack (11725) *(G-3599)*

Simpore Inc 585 748-5980
150 Lucius Gordon Dr # 110 West Henrietta (14586) *(G-15804)*

Simrex Corporation 716 206-0174
1223 William St Buffalo (14206) *(G-2983)*

Sims Group USA Holdings Corp 718 786-6031
3027 Greenpoint Ave Long Island City (11101) *(G-7357)*

Sims Metal Management, New York Also called Smm - North America Trade Corp *(G-11275)*

Sims Steel Corporation 631 587-8670
650 Muncy St Lindenhurst (11757) *(G-6972)*

Simtec Industries Corporation 631 293-0080
65 Marine St Ste A Farmingdale (11735) *(G-4732)*

Simulaids Inc 845 679-2475
16 Simulaids Dr Saugerties (12477) *(G-14212)*

Sinapi's Italian Ice, Hawthorne Also called Four Brothers Italian Bakery *(G-5812)*

Sincerus LLC 800 419-2804
2478 Mcdonald Ave Brooklyn (11223) *(G-2420)*

Sinclair International Company (PA) 518 798-2361
85 Boulevard Queensbury (12804) *(G-13057)*

Sinclair Technologies Inc (HQ) 716 874-3682
5811 S Park Ave 3 Hamburg (14075) *(G-5521)*

Sing Ah Poultry 718 625-7253
114 Sackett St Brooklyn (11231) *(G-2421)*

Sing Tao Daily, New York Also called Sing Tao Newspapers NY Ltd *(G-11248)*

Sing Tao Newspapers NY Ltd 212 431-9030
5317 8th Ave Brooklyn (11220) *(G-2422)*

Sing Tao Newspapers NY Ltd 718 821-0123
905 Flushing Ave Fl 2 Brooklyn (11206) *(G-2423)*

Sing Tao Newspapers NY Ltd (PA) 212 699-3800
188 Lafayette St New York (10013) *(G-11248)*

Sing Trix 212 352-1500
118 W 22nd St Fl 3 New York (10011) *(G-11249)*

Singlecut Beersmiths LLC (PA) 718 606-0788
1933 37th St Astoria (11105) *(G-440)*

Sinn- Tech Industries Inc 631 643-1171
125 Wilbur Pl Ste 210 Bohemia (11716) *(G-1079)*

Sinnara, Maspeth Also called Purvi Enterprises Incorporated *(G-7635)*

Sino Printing Inc 212 334-6896
30 Allen St Frnt A New York (10002) *(G-11250)*

Sir Industries Inc 631 234-2444
208 Blydenburg Rd Unit C Hauppauge (11749) *(G-5767)*

Sir Kensington's, New York Also called Kensington & Sons LLC *(G-10091)*

Sir Speedy, Bay Shore Also called Bondy Printing Corp *(G-659)*

Sir Speedy, Rochester Also called Beastons Budget Printing Inc *(G-13264)*

Sir Speedy, Westbury Also called E B B Graphics Inc *(G-15877)*

Sir Speedy, Plainview Also called Nash Printing Inc *(G-12704)*

Sir Speedy, Wappingers Falls Also called Moneast Inc *(G-15498)*

Sir Speedy, Pleasantville Also called Carlara Group Ltd *(G-12795)*

Sir Speedy, Westbury Also called Sentine Printing Inc *(G-15925)*

Sir Speedy, Lake Placid Also called Lake Placid Advertisers Wkshp *(G-6767)*

Sir Speedy, Plainview Also called P D R Inc *(G-12706)*

Sirianni Hardwoods Inc 607 962-4688
912 Addison Rd Painted Post (14870) *(G-12476)*

Siskind Group Inc 212 840-0880
1385 Broadway Fl 24 New York (10018) *(G-11251)*

Sister Sister Inc (PA) 212 629-9600
463 7th Ave Fl 4 New York (10018) *(G-11252)*

Sita Finishing Inc 718 417-5295
207 Starr St Ste 1 Brooklyn (11237) *(G-2424)*

Sita Knitting, Brooklyn Also called Sita Finishing Inc *(G-2424)*

Sitecraft Inc 718 729-4900
4302 Ditmars Blvd Astoria (11105) *(G-441)*

Sitewatch Technology LLC 207 778-3246
22 Sunset Ave East Quogue (11942) *(G-4158)*

Siw Inc 631 888-0130
271 Skip Ln Bay Shore (11706) *(G-714)*

Six15 Technologies, Henrietta Also called Tdg Acquistion Co LLC *(G-5860)*

Sixnet LLC 518 877-5173
331 Ushers Rd Ste 14 Ballston Lake (12019) *(G-563)*

Sixnet Holdings LLC 518 877-5173
331 Ushers Rd Ste 10 Ballston Lake (12019) *(G-564)*

Sixpoint Brewery, Brooklyn Also called Mad Scntsts Brwing Prtners LLC *(G-2101)*

Sixthscents Paper Products Ltd 212 627-5066
37-18 Nthrn Blvd Ste 418 Long Island City (11101) *(G-7358)*

Sixthscents Products, Long Island City Also called Sixthscents Paper Products Ltd *(G-7358)*

Sizmek Dsp Inc 212 594-8888
401 Park Ave S Fl 5 New York (10016) *(G-11253)*

Sizzal LLC 212 354-6123
1105 44th Rd Fl 2 Long Island City (11101) *(G-7359)*

Sj Associates Inc (PA) 516 942-3232
500 N Broadway Ste 159 Jericho (11753) *(G-6595)*

Sjm Interface, New York Also called Sign Company *(G-11233)*

Sk Capital Partners II LP (PA) 212 826-2700
430 Park Ave Fl 18 New York (10022) *(G-11254)*

Sk Titan Holdings LLC (HQ) 212 826-2700
400 Park Ave New York (10022) *(G-11255)*

Skae Power Solutions LLC (PA) 845 365-9103
348 Route 9w Palisades (10964) *(G-12482)*

Skaffles Group LLC 212 944-9494
1400 Broadway Fl 26 New York (10018) *(G-11256)*

Skandacor Direct Inc 585 265-9020
545 Basket Rd Webster (14580) *(G-15654)*

Skd Distribution Corp 718 525-6000
28 Westchester Ave Jericho (11753) *(G-6596)*

Skd Tactical Inc 845 897-2889
291 Main St Highland Falls (10928) *(G-5966)*

Skelton Screw Products Co, Westbury Also called All Type Screw Machine Pdts *(G-15866)*

Sketch Studio Trading Inc 212 244-2875
218 W 37th St Rm 600 New York (10018) *(G-11257)*

SKF Aeroengine North America, Falconer Also called SKF USA Inc *(G-4555)*

SKF Aeroengine North America, Falconer Also called SKF USA Inc *(G-4557)*

SKF USA Inc 716 661-2869
1 Maroco St Falconer (14733) *(G-4555)*

SKF USA Inc 716 661-2600
1 Maroco St Falconer (14733) *(G-4556)*

SKF USA Inc 716 661-2600
1 Maroco St Falconer (14733) *(G-4557)*

Skil-Care Corporation 914 963-2040
29 Wells Ave Bldg 4 Yonkers (10701) *(G-16348)*

Skills Alliance Inc 646 492-5300
135 W 29th St Rm 201 New York (10001) *(G-11258)*

Skillsoft Corporation 585 240-7500
500 Canal View Blvd Rochester (14623) *(G-13732)*

Skimovex USA, Orchard Park Also called Burgess-Manning Inc *(G-12343)*

Skin Atelier Inc 845 294-1202
1997 Route 17m Goshen (10924) *(G-5313)*

Skin Dynamic, Long Island City Also called P-Ryton Corp *(G-7316)*

Skin Prints Inc 845 920-8756
63 Walter St Pearl River (10965) *(G-12541)*

Skincare Products Inc 917 837-5255
5933 Main St Apt 208 Williamsville (14221) *(G-16139)*

Skinprint, Goshen Also called Skin Atelier Inc *(G-5313)*

Skip Hop Inc 646 902-9874
50 W 23rd St Fl 10 New York (10010) *(G-11259)*

Skip Hop Holdings Inc (HQ) 212 868-9850
50 W 23rd St Fl 10 New York (10010) *(G-11260)*

Skiva International Inc (PA) 212 736-9520
1407 Broadway Frnt 5 New York (10018) *(G-11261)*

Skooba Design, Rochester Also called Three Point Ventures LLC *(G-13767)*

Sky Aerospace Products, Westbury Also called John Hassall LLC *(G-15899)*

Sky Art Media Inc 917 355-9022
132 Bowery Apt 2f New York (10013) *(G-11262)*

Sky Frame & Art Inc 212 925-7856
141 W 28th St Fl 12 New York (10001) *(G-11263)*

Sky Geek, Lagrangeville Also called Styles Aviation Inc *(G-6754)*

Sky Laundromat Inc 718 639-7070
8615 Ava Pl Apt 4e Jamaica (11432) *(G-6473)*

Skydyne Company 845 858-6400
100 River Rd Port Jervis (12771) *(G-12857)*

Skye's The Limit, New York Also called Alfred Dunner Inc *(G-8515)*

Skyguard, Hauppauge Also called Vehicle Manufacturers Inc *(G-5795)*

Skyhorse Publishing Inc (PA) 212 643-6816
307 W 36th St Fl 11 New York (10018) *(G-11264)*

Skyko International LLC 518 562-9696
35 Gateway Dr Ste 201 Plattsburgh (12901) *(G-12777)*

Skylark Publications Ltd 607 535-9866
  217 N Franklin St Watkins Glen (14891) *(G-15615)*
Skyler Brand Ventures LLC 646 979-5904
  150 W 56th St Apt 5301 New York (10019) *(G-11265)*
Skyline Custom Cabinetry Inc 631 393-2983
  200 Verdi St Unit A Farmingdale (11735) *(G-4733)*
Skyline LLC 631 403-4131
  16 Hulse Rd Ste 1 East Setauket (11733) *(G-4187)*
Skyline New York, Hauppauge *Also called Watson Productions LLC (G-5799)*
Skyop LLC 585 598-4737
  5297 Parkside Dr Ste 440c Canandaigua (14424) *(G-3143)*
Skystem LLC 877 778-3320
  100 W 92nd St Apt 20d New York (10025) *(G-11266)*
Skytravel (usa) LLC 518 888-2610
  20 Talon Dr Schenectady (12309) *(G-14306)*
Slant/Fin Corporation (PA) 516 484-2600
  100 Forest Dr Greenvale (11548) *(G-5464)*
Slantco Manufacturing Inc (HQ) 516 484-2600
  100 Forest Dr Greenvale (11548) *(G-5465)*
Slanto Manufacturing Inc 516 759-5721
  40 Garvies Point Rd Glen Cove (11542) *(G-5201)*
Slava Industries Incorporated (PA) 718 499-4850
  555 16th St Brooklyn (11215) *(G-2425)*
SLC, Auburn *Also called Auburn Custom Millwork Inc (G-460)*
Sleep Improvement Center Inc 516 536-5799
  178 Sunrise Hwy Fl 2 Rockville Centre (11570) *(G-13836)*
Sleep Master, Syracuse *Also called Futon City Discounters Inc (G-14896)*
Sleepable Sofas Ltd 973 546-4502
  600 3rd Ave Fl 15 New York (10016) *(G-11267)*
Sleeping Partners Home Fashion, Brooklyn *Also called Sleeping Partners Intl Inc (G-2426)*
Sleeping Partners Intl Inc 212 254-1515
  140 58th St Ste 3e Brooklyn (11220) *(G-2426)*
Sleepwear Holdings Inc 516 466-4738
  1372 Broadway Fl 18 New York (10018) *(G-11268)*
Sleepy Head Inc 718 237-9655
  230 3rd St Brooklyn (11215) *(G-2427)*
Slidebean Incorporated 866 365-0588
  25 Broadway New York (10004) *(G-11269)*
Slim Line Case Co Inc 585 546-3639
  64 Spencer St Rochester (14608) *(G-13733)*
Slims Bagels Unlimited Inc (PA) 718 229-1140
  22118 Horace Harding Expy Oakland Gardens (11364) *(G-12160)*
Sliperfection, New York *Also called Lady Ester Lingerie Corp (G-10162)*
Sln Group Inc 718 677-5969
  2172 E 26th St Brooklyn (11229) *(G-2428)*
Sloane Design Inc 212 539-0184
  226 52nd St Brooklyn (11220) *(G-2429)*
Slosson Eductl Publications 716 652-0930
  538 Buffalo Rd East Aurora (14052) *(G-4096)*
Slyde Inc 917 331-2114
  474 48th Ave Apt 18a Long Island City (11109) *(G-7360)*
SM News Plus Incorporated 212 888-0153
  346 E 59th St Frnt 1 New York (10022) *(G-11270)*
Small Business Advisors Inc 516 374-1387
  2005 Park St Atlantic Beach (11509) *(G-454)*
Smart & Strong LLC 212 938-2051
  212 W 35th St Fl 8 New York (10001) *(G-11271)*
Smart High Voltage Solutions 631 563-6724
  390 Knickerbocker Ave # 6 Bohemia (11716) *(G-1080)*
Smart Space Products LLC (PA) 877 777-2441
  244 5th Ave Ste 2487 New York (10001) *(G-11272)*
Smart Systems Inc 607 776-5380
  320 E Washington St Bath (14810) *(G-640)*
Smart USA Inc (PA) 631 969-1111
  1440 5th Ave Bay Shore (11706) *(G-715)*
Smart Weigh, Spring Valley *Also called Measupro Inc (G-14579)*
Smartoners Inc (PA) 718 975-0197
  289 Keap St Ste A Brooklyn (11211) *(G-2430)*
Smartpill Corporation 716 882-0701
  847 Main St Buffalo (14203) *(G-2984)*
Smartys Corner 607 239-5276
  501 W Main St Endicott (13760) *(G-4473)*
SMC, Conklin *Also called E-Systems Group LLC (G-3624)*
SMC Diode Solutions LLC 631 965-0869
  101 Sunnyside Blvd Plainview (11803) *(G-12714)*
Smg Control Systems, Buffalo *Also called Service Mfg Group Inc (G-2981)*
Smg Metal Products LLC 716 633-6439
  390 Cayuga Rd Cheektowaga (14225) *(G-3361)*
SMI, Salamanca *Also called Snyder Manufacturing Inc (G-14129)*
Smidgens Inc 585 624-1486
  7336 Community Dr Lima (14485) *(G-6935)*
Smile Specialists 877 337-6135
  236 E 36th St New York (10016) *(G-11273)*
Smith & Watson 212 686-6444
  200 Lexington Ave Rm 805 New York (10016) *(G-11274)*
Smith Control Systems Inc 518 828-7646
  1839 Route 9h Hudson (12534) *(G-6180)*
Smith Graphics Inc 631 420-4180
  40 Florida St Farmingdale (11735) *(G-4734)*
Smith International Inc 585 265-2330
  1915 Lake Rd Ontario (14519) *(G-12303)*

Smith Metal Works Newark Inc 315 331-1651
  1000 E Union St Newark (14513) *(G-11851)*
Smith Sand & Gravel Inc 315 673-4124
  4782 Shepard Rd Marcellus (13108) *(G-7563)*
Smith Service Corps, Ontario *Also called Smith International Inc (G-12303)*
Smith Street Bread Co LLC 718 797-9712
  17 5th St Brooklyn (11231) *(G-2431)*
Smithers Tools & Mch Pdts Inc 845 876-3063
  3718 Route 9g Rhinebeck (12572) *(G-13101)*
Smithtown Concrete Products 631 265-1815
  441 Middle Country Rd Saint James (11780) *(G-14114)*
Smithtown News Inc 631 265-2100
  1 Brooksite Dr Smithtown (11787) *(G-14487)*
Sml Acquisition LLC 914 592-3130
  33 W Main St Ste 505 Elmsford (10523) *(G-4434)*
Sml Brothers Holding Corp 718 402-2000
  820 E 140th St Bronx (10454) *(G-1366)*
Smm - North America Trade Corp 212 604-0710
  16 W 22nd St Fl 10 New York (10010) *(G-11275)*
Smokey Joes, Oceanside *Also called Yale Trouser Corporation (G-12199)*
Smooth Industries Incorporated 212 869-1080
  1411 Broadway Rm 3000 New York (10018) *(G-11276)*
Smooth Magazine 212 925-1150
  55 John St Ste 800 New York (10038) *(G-11277)*
Smoothbore International Inc 315 754-8124
  13881 Westbury Cutoff Rd Red Creek (13143) *(G-13070)*
Smoothies Strawberry Nysf 315 406-4250
  581 State Fair Blvd Syracuse (13209) *(G-14995)*
SMS, Huntington Station *Also called Super Sweep Inc (G-6261)*
Smsc, Hauppauge *Also called Standard Microsystems Corp (G-5774)*
Snake Tray, Bay Shore *Also called Snake Tray International LLC (G-716)*
Snake Tray International LLC 631 674-0004
  291 Skip Ln Bay Shore (11706) *(G-716)*
Snapp Too Enterprise 718 224-5252
  3312 211th St Flushing (11361) *(G-4893)*
Snapple Beverage Corp (HQ) 914 612-4000
  900 King St Rye Brook (10573) *(G-14094)*
Snapple Distributors, Staten Island *Also called Gangi Distributors Inc (G-14654)*
Snapple Distributors, Ronkonkoma *Also called American Bottling Company (G-13902)*
Sneaker News Inc 347 687-1588
  41 Elizabeth St Ste 301 New York (10013) *(G-11278)*
Sneakers Software Inc 800 877-9221
  519 8th Ave Rm 812 New York (10018) *(G-11279)*
Sneaky Chef Foods LLC 914 301-3277
  520 White Plains Rd Tarrytown (10591) *(G-15060)*
Snow Craft 216 Inc 718 757-6121
  216 N Main St Ste F Freeport (11520) *(G-5026)*
Snow Craft Co Inc 516 739-1399
  200 Fulton Ave New Hyde Park (11040) *(G-8293)*
Snowman 212 239-8818
  350 5th Ave Fl 59 New York (10118) *(G-11280)*
Snr Cctv Systems Division, East Setauket *Also called Sartek Industries Inc (G-4186)*
Sns Machinery, Brooklyn *Also called Riverside Machinery Company (G-2348)*
Snyder Industries Inc (PA) 716 694-1240
  340 Wales Ave Tonawanda (14150) *(G-15141)*
Snyder Logging 315 265-1462
  528 Allen Falls Rd Potsdam (13676) *(G-12941)*
Snyder Manufacturing Inc 716 945-0354
  255 Rochester St Unit 1 Salamanca (14779) *(G-14129)*
Snyder Neon & Plastic Signs, Colonie *Also called Snyders Neon Displays Inc (G-3575)*
Snyders Neon Displays Inc 518 857-4100
  5 Highland Ave Colonie (12205) *(G-3575)*
Sobi, Brooklyn *Also called Social Bicycles LLC (G-2432)*
Soc America Inc 631 472-6666
  3505 Veterans Memorial Hw Ronkonkoma (11779) *(G-14010)*
Social Bicycles LLC 917 746-7624
  55 Prospect St Ste 304 Brooklyn (11201) *(G-2432)*
Social Register Association 646 612-7314
  14 Wall St Ste 3f New York (10005) *(G-11281)*
Social Science Electronic Pubg 585 442-8170
  1239 University Ave Rochester (14607) *(G-13734)*
Socialed Inc 516 297-2172
  335 Madison Ave Rm 5f2 New York (10017) *(G-11282)*
Society Awards, Long Island City *Also called Dwm International Inc (G-7207)*
Society For The Study 212 822-8806
  20 W 20th St Fl 2 New York (10011) *(G-11283)*
Sockbin 917 519-1119
  718 Avenue U Brooklyn (11223) *(G-2433)*
Socket Products Mfg Corp 631 232-9870
  175 Bridge Rd Islandia (11749) *(G-6344)*
Socks and More of NY Inc 718 769-1785
  1605 Avenue Z Fl 1 Brooklyn (11235) *(G-2434)*
Sofanou, Niagara Falls *Also called Delfingen Us-New York Inc (G-11920)*
Soft Sheen Products Inc (HQ) 212 818-1500
  10 Hudson Yards Fl 27 New York (10001) *(G-11284)*
Soft-Noze Usa Inc 315 732-2726
  2216 Broad St Frankfort (13340) *(G-4956)*
Soft-Tex International Inc 800 366-2324
  428 Hudson River Rd Waterford (12188) *(G-15546)*
Soft-Tex Manufacturing Co, Waterford *Also called Soft-Tex International Inc (G-15546)*

Softcard, New York *Also called Jvl Ventures LLC* ***(G-10050)***
Softlink International 914 574-8197
297 Knollwood Rd Ste 301 White Plains (10607) ***(G-16061)***
Software & General Services Co 315 986-4184
1365 Fairway 5 Cir Walworth (14568) ***(G-15479)***
Software Engineering Amer Inc (PA) 516 328-7000
1325 Franklin Ave Ste 545 Garden City (11530) ***(G-5116)***
Soggy Doggy Productions LLC 877 504-4811
50 Chestnut Ave Larchmont (10538) ***(G-6843)***
Sogimex, New York *Also called Myers Group LLC* ***(G-10525)***
Soho and Tribeca Map, New York *Also called Ozmodyl Ltd* ***(G-10730)***
Soho Apparel Ltd 212 840-1109
525 7th Ave Fl 6 New York (10018) ***(G-11285)***
Soho Guilds, Kew Gardens *Also called A & B Color Corp* ***(G-6660)***
Soho Letterpress Inc 718 788-2518
68 35th St Unit 6 Brooklyn (11232) ***(G-2435)***
Soho Press Inc 212 260-1900
79 Madison Ave Fl 8 New York (10016) ***(G-11286)***
Sokolin LLC (PA) 631 537-4434
445 Sills Rd Unit K Yaphank (11980) ***(G-16272)***
Sokolin Wine, Yaphank *Also called Sokolin LLC* ***(G-16272)***
Sol Markowitz, Monroe *Also called C T A Digital Inc* ***(G-8017)***
Sol Savransky Diamonds Inc 212 730-4700
25 W 43rd St Ste 802 New York (10036) ***(G-11287)***
Sola Home Expo Inc 718 646-3383
172 Neptune Ave Brooklyn (11235) ***(G-2436)***
Solabia USA Inc 212 847-2397
28 W 44th St New York (10036) ***(G-11288)***
Solar Energy Systems LLC (PA) 718 389-1545
1205 Manhattan Ave # 1210 Brooklyn (11222) ***(G-2437)***
Solar Metrology LLC 845 247-4701
1340 Lincoln Ave Ste 6 Holbrook (11741) ***(G-6021)***
Solar Screen Co Inc 718 592-8222
5311 105th St Corona (11368) ***(G-3750)***
Solar Thin Films Inc (PA) 212 629-8260
445 Central Ave Unit 366 Cedarhurst (11516) ***(G-3244)***
Solarelectricway, Brooklyn *Also called Solarwaterway Inc* ***(G-2438)***
Solarpath Inc 201 490-4499
415 Madison Ave Fl 14 New York (10017) ***(G-11289)***
Solarpath Sun Solutions, New York *Also called Solarpath Inc* ***(G-11289)***
Solarwaterway Inc 888 998-5337
254 36th St Ste C453 Brooklyn (11232) ***(G-2438)***
Solarz Bros Printing Corp 718 383-1330
231 Norman Ave Ste 105 Brooklyn (11222) ***(G-2439)***
Solenis LLC 718 383-1717
761 Humboldt St Brooklyn (11222) ***(G-2440)***
Solenis LLC 315 461-4730
911 Old Liverpool Rd Liverpool (13088) ***(G-7040)***
Soleo Health, Hawthorne *Also called Biomed Pharmaceuticals Inc* ***(G-5810)***
Solepoxy Inc 716 372-6300
211 W Franklin St Olean (14760) ***(G-12241)***
Solex Catsmo Fine Foods, Wallkill *Also called Catsmo LLC* ***(G-15468)***
Solid Cell Inc 585 426-5000
771 Elmgrove Rd Rochester (14624) ***(G-13735)***
Solid Sealing Technology Inc 518 874-3600
44 Dalliba Ave Ste 240 Watervliet (12189) ***(G-15606)***
Solid Surface Acrylics LLC 716 743-1870
800 Walck Rd Ste 14 North Tonawanda (14120) ***(G-12091)***
Solid Surfaces Inc 585 292-5340
1 Townline Cir Rochester (14623) ***(G-13736)***
Solidus Industries Inc 607 749-4540
6849 N Glen Haven Rd Homer (13077) ***(G-6067)***
Solmac Inc 716 630-7061
1975 Wehrle Dr Ste 130 Williamsville (14221) ***(G-16140)***
Solo, Brooklyn *Also called Air Skate & Air Jump Corp* ***(G-1473)***
Solstarny, New York *Also called Solstars Inc* ***(G-11290)***
Solstars Inc 212 605-0430
575 Madison Ave Ste 1006 New York (10022) ***(G-11290)***
Solstiss Inc 212 719-9194
561 Fashion Ave Fl 16 New York (10018) ***(G-11291)***
Soludos LLC 212 219-1101
520 Broadway Fl 5 New York (10012) ***(G-11292)***
Solutia Business Entps Inc 314 674-1000
111 8th Ave New York (10011) ***(G-11293)***
Solve Advisors Inc 646 699-5041
265 Sunrise Hwy Ste 22 Rockville Centre (11570) ***(G-13837)***
Solvents Company Inc 631 595-9300
9 Cornell St Kingston (12401) ***(G-6709)***
Somar North America Corp 716 458-0742
211 W Franklin St Olean (14760) ***(G-12242)***
Somers Stain Glass Inc 631 586-7772
108 Brook Ave Ste A Deer Park (11729) ***(G-3937)***
Somerset Dyeing & Finishing 518 773-7383
68 Harrison St Gloversville (12078) ***(G-5291)***
Somerset Industries Inc (PA) 518 773-7383
68 Harrison St Gloversville (12078) ***(G-5292)***
Somerset Manufacturers Inc 516 626-3832
36 Glen Cove Rd Roslyn Heights (11577) ***(G-14057)***
Somerset Production Co LLC 716 932-6480
338 Harris Hill Rd # 102 Buffalo (14221) ***(G-2985)***
Somerville Acquisitions Co Inc 845 856-5261
15 Big Pond Rd Huguenot (12746) ***(G-6194)***
Somerville Tech Group Inc 908 782-9500
15 Big Pond Rd Huguenot (12746) ***(G-6195)***
Sommer and Sons Printing Inc 716 822-4311
2222 S Park Ave Buffalo (14220) ***(G-2986)***
Somml Health Inc 518 880-2170
43 New Scotland Ave Mc25 Albany (12208) ***(G-130)***
Sonaal Industries Inc 718 383-3860
210 Kingsland Ave Brooklyn (11222) ***(G-2441)***
Sonaer Inc 631 756-4780
68 Lamar St Unit D West Babylon (11704) ***(G-15747)***
Sonicor Inc 631 920-6555
82 Otis St West Babylon (11704) ***(G-15748)***
Soniquence LLC 516 267-6400
2473 Grand Ave Baldwin (11510) ***(G-535)***
Sonneman-A Way of Light, Wappingers Falls *Also called Contemporary Visions LLC* ***(G-15490)***
Sono-Tek Corporation (PA) 845 795-2020
2012 Route 9w Stop 3 Milton (12547) ***(G-7952)***
Sonoco-Crellin Intl Inc (HQ) 518 392-2000
87 Center St Chatham (12037) ***(G-3333)***
Sonomed Inc 516 354-0900
1979 Marcus Ave Ste C105 New Hyde Park (11042) ***(G-8294)***
Sonomed Escalon, New Hyde Park *Also called Sonomed Inc* ***(G-8294)***
Sonotec US Inc 631 415-4758
190 Blydenburg Rd Islandia (11749) ***(G-6345)***
Sony Broadband Entertainment (HQ) 212 833-6800
550 Madison Ave Fl 6 New York (10022) ***(G-11294)***
Sony Corporation of America (HQ) 212 833-8000
25 Madison Ave Fl 27 New York (10010) ***(G-11295)***
Sony Dadc US Inc 212 833-8800
550 Madison Ave New York (10022) ***(G-11296)***
Sony Music Entertainment, New York *Also called Sony Music Holdings Inc* ***(G-11299)***
Sony Music Entertainment, New York *Also called Sony Corporation of America* ***(G-11295)***
Sony Music Entertainment 212 833-8000
25 Madison Ave Fl 19 New York (10010) ***(G-11297)***
Sony Music Entertainment Inc (HQ) 212 833-8000
25 Madison Ave Fl 19 New York (10010) ***(G-11298)***
Sony Music Holdings, New York *Also called Sony Music Entertainment* ***(G-11297)***
Sony Music Holdings Inc (HQ) 212 833-8000
25 Madison Ave Fl 26 New York (10010) ***(G-11299)***
Sony Style, New York *Also called Sony Dadc US Inc* ***(G-11296)***
Sony Wonder, New York *Also called Sony Music Entertainment Inc* ***(G-11298)***
Sony/Atv Music Publishing LLC (HQ) 212 833-7730
25 Madison Ave Fl 24 New York (10010) ***(G-11300)***
Soozy's Grain-Free, New York *Also called Mindful Foods Inc* ***(G-10475)***
Sopark Corp (PA) 716 822-0434
3300 S Park Ave Buffalo (14218) ***(G-2987)***
Soper Designs, New York *Also called Kurt Gaum Inc* ***(G-10145)***
Sorfin Yoshimura Ltd 516 802-4600
100 Crossways Park Dr W # 215 Woodbury (11797) ***(G-16183)***
Soroc Technology Corp 716 849-5913
1051 Clinton St Buffalo (14206) ***(G-2988)***
Sorrento Lactalis, Buffalo *Also called Lactalis American Group Inc* ***(G-2844)***
Sorrento Lactalis Inc 716 823-6262
2376 S Park Ave Buffalo (14220) ***(G-2989)***
SOS Chefs New York Inc 212 505-5813
104 Avenue B Apt 1 New York (10009) ***(G-11301)***
SOS International LLC 212 742-2410
426 W Broadway Apt 6a New York (10012) ***(G-11302)***
Sotek Inc 716 821-5961
3590 Jeffrey Blvd Blasdell (14219) ***(G-922)***
Soterix Medical Inc 888 990-8327
237 W 35th St Ste 1401 New York (10001) ***(G-11303)***
Soterix Medical Technologies, New York *Also called Soterix Medical Inc* ***(G-11303)***
Soto Sake Corporation 305 781-3906
18 Bridge St Ste 4i Brooklyn (11201) ***(G-2442)***
Sound & Communication, Port Washington *Also called Testa Communications Inc* ***(G-12929)***
Sound Communications Inc 516 767-2500
25 Willowdale Ave Port Washington (11050) ***(G-12927)***
Sound Source Inc 585 271-5370
161 Norris Dr Rochester (14610) ***(G-13737)***
Sound Video Systems Wny LLC 716 684-8200
1720 Military Rd Buffalo (14217) ***(G-2990)***
Soundcoat Company Inc (HQ) 631 242-2200
1 Burt Dr Deer Park (11729) ***(G-3938)***
Source Envelope Inc 866 284-0707
104 Allen Blvd Ste I Farmingdale (11735) ***(G-4735)***
Source Media, New York *Also called Credit Union Journal Inc* ***(G-9122)***
Source Media LLC (HQ) 212 803-8200
1 State St Fl 27 New York (10004) ***(G-11304)***
Source Technologies 718 708-0305
9728 3rd Ave Brooklyn (11209) ***(G-2443)***
South Bridge Press Inc 212 233-4047
122 W 26th St Fl 3 New York (10001) ***(G-11305)***
South Brooklyn Book Company, New York *Also called Welcome Rain Publishers LLC* ***(G-11738)***

South Central Boyz ... 718 496-7270
2568 Bedford Ave Apt 1a Brooklyn (11226) ***(G-2444)***
South of The Highway, Southampton *Also called Dans Paper Inc* ***(G-14529)***
South Seneca Vinyl LLC ... 315 585-6050
1585 Yale Farm Rd Romulus (14541) ***(G-13880)***
South Shore Ice Co Inc ... 516 379-2056
89 E Fulton Ave Roosevelt (11575) ***(G-14033)***
South Shore Ready Mix Inc ... 516 872-3049
116 E Hawthorne Ave Valley Stream (11580) ***(G-15360)***
South Shore Tribune Inc ... 516 431-5628
4 California Pl N Island Park (11558) ***(G-6322)***
Southampton Town Newspapers (PA) ... 631 283-4100
135 Windmill Ln Southampton (11968) ***(G-14538)***
Southampton Town Newspapers ... 631 288-1100
12 Mitchell Rd Westhampton Beach (11978) ***(G-15959)***
Southbay Fuel Injectors ... 516 442-4707
566 Merrick Rd Ste 3 Rockville Centre (11570) ***(G-13838)***
Southco Inc ... 585 624-2545
250 East St Honeoye Falls (14472) ***(G-6080)***
Southern Adirondack Honey Co., Greenwich *Also called Betterbee Inc* ***(G-5469)***
Southern Adrndck Fbr Prdcrs CP ... 518 692-2700
2532 State Route 40 Greenwich (12834) ***(G-5476)***
Southern Graphic Systems LLC ... 315 695-7079
67 County Route 59 Phoenix (13135) ***(G-12621)***
Southern Standard Cartons, Great Neck *Also called Standard Group* ***(G-5424)***
Southern Standard Cartoons, Great Neck *Also called Standard Group LLC* ***(G-5425)***
Southern Tier Pennysaver, Jamestown *Also called Spartan Publishing Inc* ***(G-6541)***
Southern Tier Pet Ntrtn LLC ... 607 674-2121
8 W State St Sherburne (13460) ***(G-14394)***
Southern Tier Plastics Inc ... 607 723-2601
Kirkwood Industrial Park Binghamton (13902) ***(G-909)***
Southside Precast Products, Buffalo *Also called P J R Industries Inc* ***(G-2902)***
Soutine Inc ... 212 496-1450
104 W 70th St Frnt 1 New York (10023) ***(G-11306)***
Sovereign Brands LLC (PA) ... 212 343-8366
383 W Broadway Apt 5 New York (10012) ***(G-11307)***
Sovereign Servicing System LLC ... 914 779-1400
1 Stone Pl Ste 200 Bronxville (10708) ***(G-1403)***
Sp Scientific, Gardiner *Also called S P Industries Inc* ***(G-5130)***
Spa Sciara, Mount Kisco *Also called Plastic & Reconstructive Svcs* ***(G-8102)***
Space 150 ... 612 332-6458
20 Jay St Ste 928 Brooklyn (11201) ***(G-2445)***
Space Age Plstic Fbrcators Inc ... 718 324-4062
8522 218th St Queens Village (11427) ***(G-13026)***
Space Coast Semiconductor Inc ... 631 414-7131
1111 Broadhollow Rd Fl 3 Farmingdale (11735) ***(G-4736)***
Space Sign ... 718 961-1112
1525 132nd St College Point (11356) ***(G-3565)***
Space-Craft Worldwide Inc ... 631 603-3000
47 Wireless Blvd Hauppauge (11788) ***(G-5768)***
Spaeth Design Inc ... 718 606-9685
6006 37th Ave Woodside (11377) ***(G-16225)***
Spalding Sports Worldwide, Johnstown *Also called Callaway Golf Ball Oprtons Inc* ***(G-6612)***
Spalding Sports Worldwide, Gloversville *Also called Callaway Golf Ball Oprtons Inc* ***(G-5280)***
Spandage, Brooklyn *Also called Medi-Tech International Corp* ***(G-2132)***
Spanish Artisan Wine Group LLC ... 914 414-6982
370 Cushman Rd Patterson (12563) ***(G-12520)***
Spanish Artisan Wine Group Ltd, Patterson *Also called Spanish Artisan Wine Group LLC* ***(G-12520)***
Spanish Tele Dirctry Hola 912, Long Island City *Also called Hola Publishing Co* ***(G-7243)***
Spanjer Corp ... 347 448-8033
3856 11th St Long Island City (11101) ***(G-7361)***
Spanjer Signs, Long Island City *Also called Spanjer Corp* ***(G-7361)***
Spano's Bread, Utica *Also called Ohio Baking Company Inc* ***(G-15289)***
Sparclean MBL Refinishing Inc ... 718 445-2351
6915 64th Pl Ridgewood (11385) ***(G-13160)***
Spark Creations Inc ... 212 575-8385
10 W 46th St Fl 9 New York (10036) ***(G-11308)***
Sparkcharge Inc ... 315 480-3645
304 S Franklin St Ste 200 Syracuse (13202) ***(G-14996)***
Sparkle Light Manufacturing, Yonkers *Also called Lighting By Dom Yonkers Inc* ***(G-16328)***
Sparrow Mining Co (PA) ... 718 519-6600
3743 White Plains Rd Bronx (10467) ***(G-1367)***
Sparta Commercial Services Inc (PA) ... 212 239-2666
555 5th Ave Fl 14 New York (10017) ***(G-11309)***
Spartacist Publishing Co ... 212 732-7860
48 Warren St New York (10007) ***(G-11310)***
Spartan Brands Inc (PA) ... 212 340-0320
451 Park Ave S Fl 5 New York (10016) ***(G-11311)***
Spartan Instruments, West Babylon *Also called Pmb Precision Products Inc* ***(G-15737)***
Spartan Publishing Inc ... 716 664-7373
2 Harding Ave Jamestown (14701) ***(G-6541)***
Spaulding & Rogers Mfg Inc ... 518 768-2070
3252 New Scotland Rd Voorheesville (12186) ***(G-15445)***
Spaulding Law Printing Inc ... 315 422-4805
231 Walton St Ste 103 Syracuse (13202) ***(G-14997)***
Speaqua Corp ... 858 334-9042
46 W Jefryn Blvd Deer Park (11729) ***(G-3939)***
Specgx LLC ... 607 538-9124
172 Railroad Ave Hobart (13788) ***(G-5979)***
Special Circle Inc ... 516 595-9988
123 Shelter Rock Rd New Hyde Park (11040) ***(G-8295)***
Special Metals Corporation ... 716 366-5663
100 Willowbrook Ave Dunkirk (14048) ***(G-4067)***
Special Metals Corporation ... 315 798-2900
4317 Middle Settlement Rd New Hartford (13413) ***(G-8246)***
Special Tees ... 718 980-0987
250 Buel Ave Staten Island (10305) ***(G-14711)***
Specialists Ltd ... 212 941-7696
4740 Metropolitan Ave Ridgewood (11385) ***(G-13161)***
Speciality Quality Packaging, Schenectady *Also called Sqp Inc* ***(G-14307)***
Specialized Packg Group Inc (HQ) ... 315 638-4355
2900 Mclane Rd Baldwinsville (13027) ***(G-553)***
Specialized Packg Radisson LLC ... 315 638-4355
8800 Sixty Rd Baldwinsville (13027) ***(G-554)***
Specialized Printed Forms Inc ... 585 538-2381
352 Center St Caledonia (14423) ***(G-3073)***
Specialneedsware Inc ... 646 278-9959
1 Irving Pl Apt V9c New York (10003) ***(G-11312)***
Specialty Conveyor Corp ... 347 707-0490
132 Gazza Blvd Farmingdale (11735) ***(G-4737)***
Specialty Fabricators ... 631 433-0258
4120 Sunrise Hwy Oakdale (11769) ***(G-12155)***
Specialty Ink Co Inc (PA) ... 631 586-3666
40 Harbour Dr Blue Point (11715) ***(G-957)***
Specialty Microwave Corp ... 631 737-1919
120 Raynor Ave Ronkonkoma (11779) ***(G-14011)***
Specialty Minerals Inc ... 518 585-7982
35 Highland St Ticonderoga (12883) ***(G-15076)***
Specialty Model & Mold Inc ... 631 475-0840
2231 5th Ave Ste 22 Ronkonkoma (11779) ***(G-14012)***
Specialty Products Inc ... 866 869-4335
15 Frowein Rd Bldg E2 Center Moriches (11934) ***(G-3248)***
Specialty Quality Packg LLC ... 914 580-3200
602 Potential Pkwy Scotia (12302) ***(G-14337)***
Specialty Services ... 585 728-5650
2631e Naples St Wayland (14572) ***(G-15627)***
Specialty Signs Co Inc ... 212 243-8521
15 W 39th St Fl 7 New York (10018) ***(G-11313)***
Specialty Silicone Pdts Inc ... 518 885-8826
3 Mccrea Hill Rd Ballston Spa (12020) ***(G-587)***
Specialty Steel Fabg Corp ... 718 893-6326
544 Casanova St Bronx (10474) ***(G-1368)***
Specialty Steel of America., Bronx *Also called Specialty Steel Fabg Corp* ***(G-1368)***
Specialty Wldg & Fabg NY Inc (PA) ... 315 426-1807
1025 Hiawatha Blvd E Syracuse (13208) ***(G-14998)***
Specified Air Solutions LLC (HQ) ... 716 852-4400
1250 William St Buffalo (14206) ***(G-2991)***
Specilty Bus Mchs Holdings LLC ... 212 587-9600
260 W 35th St Fl 11 New York (10001) ***(G-11314)***
Spectacle Brewing LLC ... 845 942-8776
55 W Rr Ave Ste 25 Garnerville (10923) ***(G-5135)***
Spectacle Optical Inc ... 646 706-1015
9801 67th Ave Apt 7f Rego Park (11374) ***(G-13082)***
Spectaculars, Westhampton Beach *Also called Frame Works America Inc* ***(G-15956)***
Spectra Polymers & Color Spc ... 631 694-6943
77 Marine St Farmingdale (11735) ***(G-4738)***
Spectra Vista Corporation ... 845 471-7007
29 Firemens Way Stop 3 Poughkeepsie (12603) ***(G-12983)***
Spectral Systems LLC (PA) ... 845 896-2200
35 Corporate Park Rd Hopewell Junction (12533) ***(G-6101)***
Spectron Glass & Electronics ... 631 582-5600
595 Old Willets Path A Hauppauge (11788) ***(G-5769)***
Spectron Systems Technology (PA) ... 631 582-5600
595 Old Willets Path A Hauppauge (11788) ***(G-5770)***
Spectronics Corporation ... 516 333-4840
956 Brush Hollow Rd Westbury (11590) ***(G-15926)***
Spectrum, Oceanside *Also called Kantek Inc* ***(G-12178)***
Spectrum Apparel Inc ... 212 239-2025
463 Fashion Ave Fl 12 New York (10018) ***(G-11315)***
Spectrum Brands Inc ... 631 232-1200
2100 Pacific St Hauppauge (11788) ***(G-5771)***
Spectrum Cable Corporation ... 585 235-7714
295 Mount Read Blvd Ste 2 Rochester (14611) ***(G-13738)***
Spectrum Catalysts Inc ... 631 560-3683
69 Windsor Pl Central Islip (11722) ***(G-3288)***
Spectrum Crafts Inc ... 631 244-5749
70 Orville Dr Ste 1 Bohemia (11716) ***(G-1081)***
Spectrum On Broadway ... 718 932-5388
6106 34th Ave Woodside (11377) ***(G-16226)***
Spectrum Prtg Lithography Inc ... 212 255-3131
505 8th Ave Rm 1802 New York (10018) ***(G-11316)***
Spectrum Signs Inc ... 631 756-1010
6106 34th Ave Woodside (11377) ***(G-16227)***
Spectrum Thin Films Inc ... 631 901-1010
135 Marcus Blvd Hauppauge (11788) ***(G-5772)***
Speedpro Imaging, East Syracuse *Also called Bk Printing Inc* ***(G-4200)***
Speedway LLC ... 631 738-2536
2825 Middle Country Rd Lake Grove (11755) ***(G-6760)***
Speedway Press Inc (HQ) ... 315 343-3531
1 Burkle St Oswego (13126) ***(G-12421)***
Speedy Enterprise USA Corp (PA) ... 718 463-3000
4111 162nd St Flushing (11358) ***(G-4894)***

ALPHABETIC

Speedy Sign A Rama USA Inc 516 783-1075
2956 Merrick Rd Bellmore (11710) *(G-790)*
Spektrix Inc 646 741-5110
115 W 30th St Rm 501 New York (10001) *(G-11317)*
Spellman Hgh-Voltage Elec Corp (PA) 631 630-3000
475 Wireless Blvd Hauppauge (11788) *(G-5773)*
Spellman High Vltage Elec Corp 914 686-3600
1 Commerce Park Valhalla (10595) *(G-15310)*
Spence Engineering Company Inc 845 778-5566
150 Coldenham Rd Walden (12586) *(G-15462)*
Spencer AB Inc 646 831-3728
265 W 37th St Rm 2388 New York (10018) *(G-11318)*
Sperry Advertising, South Glens Falls *Also called Northeast Stitches & Ink Inc (G-14516)*
Spex, Rochester *Also called Precision Machine Tech LLC (G-13638)*
Speyside Foundry Holdings LLC (PA) 212 994-0308
430 E 86th St New York (10028) *(G-11319)*
Speyside Holdings LLC 845 928-2221
911 State Route 32 Highland Mills (10930) *(G-5969)*
Spf Holdings II LLC 212 750-8300
9 W 57th St Ste 4200 New York (10019) *(G-11320)*
Spfm Corp (PA) 718 788-6800
162 2nd Ave Brooklyn (11215) *(G-2446)*
Spforms, Caledonia *Also called Specialized Printed Forms Inc (G-3073)*
Sph Group Holdings LLC (HQ) 212 520-2300
590 Madison Ave Fl 32 New York (10022) *(G-11321)*
Sphere Cables & Chips Inc (PA) 212 619-3132
121 Fulton St Fl 4 New York (10038) *(G-11322)*
Spic and Span Company 914 524-6823
660 White Plains Rd # 250 Tarrytown (10591) *(G-15061)*
Spiegel Woodworks Inc 845 336-8090
418 Old Neighborhood Rd Kingston (12401) *(G-6710)*
Spin Holdco Inc (HQ) 516 349-8555
303 Sunnyside Blvd # 70 Plainview (11803) *(G-12715)*
Spin Magazine Media 212 231-7400
276 5th Ave Rm 800 New York (10001) *(G-11323)*
Spin-Rite Corporation 585 266-5200
30 Dubelbeiss Ln Rochester (14622) *(G-13739)*
Spinco Metal Products Inc 315 331-6285
1 Country Club Dr Newark (14513) *(G-11852)*
Spinergy, Rochester *Also called BMA Media Services Inc (G-13275)*
Spirit Music Group Inc (HQ) 212 533-7672
235 W 23rd St Fl 4 New York (10011) *(G-11324)*
Spitale Cnstr Resources Inc 914 352-6366
2025 Crompond Rd Yorktown Heights (10598) *(G-16373)*
Splacer Inc 646 853-9789
33 W 17th St Fl 6 New York (10011) *(G-11325)*
Splice Technologies Inc 631 924-8108
625 North St Manorville (11949) *(G-7554)*
Split Rock Trading Co Inc 631 929-3261
22 Creek Rd Wading River (11792) *(G-15452)*
Split Systems Corp (PA) 516 223-5511
1593 Grand Ave North Baldwin (11510) *(G-12008)*
Sports Depot Inc 516 965-4668
891 Hayes St Baldwin (11510) *(G-536)*
Sports Illustrated For Kids 212 522-1212
1271 Ave Of The Americas New York (10020) *(G-11326)*
Sports Pblications Prod NY LLC 212 366-7700
708 3rd Ave Fl 12 New York (10017) *(G-11327)*
Sports Products America LLC 212 594-5511
34 W 33rd St Fl 2 New York (10001) *(G-11328)*
Sports Reporter Inc 212 737-2750
527 3rd Ave Ste 327 New York (10016) *(G-11329)*
Sportsfield Specialties Inc (PA) 607 746-8911
41155 State Highway 10 Delhi (13753) *(G-3967)*
Sportsgrid Inc 646 849-4085
404 5th Ave Fl 3 New York (10018) *(G-11330)*
Sportsmaster Apparel, Troy *Also called Standard Manufacturing Co Inc (G-15190)*
Sportswear Unlimited, Bedford Hills *Also called Custom Sportswear Corp (G-766)*
Spotlight Newspaper, Delmar *Also called Community Media Group LLC (G-3968)*
Spotlight Publications LLC 914 345-9473
100 Clearbrook Rd Ste 170 Elmsford (10523) *(G-4435)*
Spray Market, The, Brooklyn *Also called Spfm Corp (G-2446)*
Spray Moret LLC 917 213-9592
1411 Broadway Fl 8 New York (10018) *(G-11331)*
Spray Nine Corporation 800 477-7299
309 W Montgomery St Johnstown (12095) *(G-6629)*
Spray-Tech Finishing Inc 716 664-6317
443 Buffalo St Jamestown (14701) *(G-6542)*
Sprayground, New York *Also called Spray Moret LLC (G-11331)*
Spread-Mmms LLC 917 727-8116
545 Prospect Pl Apt 10d Brooklyn (11238) *(G-2447)*
Spring Inc 646 732-0323
41 E 11th St Fl 11 New York (10003) *(G-11332)*
Spring Lake Winery LLC 716 439-5253
7373 Rochester Rd Lockport (14094) *(G-7107)*
Spring Street Design Group, New York *Also called Vetta Jewelry Inc (G-11669)*
Springer Adis Us LLC (HQ) 212 460-1500
233 Spring St Fl 6 New York (10013) *(G-11333)*
Springer Business Media, New York *Also called Springer Scnce + Bus Media LLC (G-11339)*
Springer Customer Svc Ctr LLC, New York *Also called Springer Nature Cust Serv Cent (G-11337)*
Springer Healthcare LLC 212 460-1500
233 Spring St New York (10013) *(G-11334)*
Springer Nature 212 460-1500
233 Spring St New York (10013) *(G-11335)*
Springer Nature America Inc (HQ) 212 726-9200
1 New York Plz Ste 4500 New York (10004) *(G-11336)*
Springer Nature Cust Serv Cent 212 460-1500
233 Spring St New York (10013) *(G-11337)*
Springer Publishing Co LLC 212 431-4370
11 W 42nd St Ste 15a New York (10036) *(G-11338)*
Springer Scnce + Bus Media LLC (HQ) 212 460-1500
233 Spring St Fl 6 New York (10013) *(G-11339)*
Springfield Control Systems 718 631-0870
4056 Douglaston Pkwy Douglaston (11363) *(G-4029)*
Springfield Oil Services Inc (PA) 914 315-6812
550 Mmaroneck Ave Ste 503 Harrison (10528) *(G-5559)*
Springville Mfg Co Inc 716 592-4957
8798 North St Springville (14141) *(G-14597)*
SPS Medical Supply Corp (HQ) 585 359-0130
6789 W Henrietta Rd Rush (14543) *(G-14074)*
SPS Medical Supply Corp 585 968-2377
31 Water St Ste 1 Cuba (14727) *(G-3814)*
Spst Inc 607 798-6952
119b Rano Blvd Vestal (13850) *(G-15383)*
Sputnick 84 LLC 844 667-7468
1745 Broadway Frnt 3 New York (10019) *(G-11340)*
SPX Cooling Technologies Inc 914 697-5030
50 S Buckhout St Ste 204 Irvington (10533) *(G-6314)*
SPX Corporation 914 366-7402
220 White Plains Rd Tarrytown (10591) *(G-15062)*
SPX Corporation 585 436-5550
1000 Millstead Way Rochester (14624) *(G-13740)*
SPX Corporation 631 467-2632
70 Raynor Ave Ronkonkoma (11779) *(G-14013)*
SPX Corporation 585 436-5550
135 Mount Read Blvd Rochester (14611) *(G-13741)*
SPX Flow Technology, Rochester *Also called SPX Flow Us LLC (G-13742)*
SPX Flow Us LLC (HQ) 585 436-5550
135 Mount Read Blvd Rochester (14611) *(G-13742)*
SPX Flow Us LLC 716 692-3000
105 Crosspoint Pkwy Getzville (14068) *(G-5182)*
SPX Precision Components, Ronkonkoma *Also called SPX Corporation (G-14013)*
Sqp, Scotia *Also called Specialty Quality Packg LLC (G-14337)*
Sqp Inc 518 831-6800
602 Potential Pkwy Schenectady (12302) *(G-14307)*
Square One Coating Systems LLC 315 790-5921
170 Base Rd Oriskany (13424) *(G-12395)*
Square One Publishers Inc 516 535-2010
115 Herricks Rd Garden City Park (11040) *(G-5124)*
Square Stamping Mfg Corp 315 896-2641
108 Old Remsen Rd Barneveld (13304) *(G-596)*
Squeaky Clean, Brooklyn *Also called National Prfmce Solutions Inc (G-2190)*
SRC Liquidation Company 716 631-3900
435 Lawrence Bell Dr # 4 Williamsville (14221) *(G-16141)*
SRC Ventures Inc (HQ) 315 452-8000
7502 Round Pond Rd North Syracuse (13212) *(G-12049)*
Srctec LLC 315 452-8700
5801 E Taft Rd Ste 6 Syracuse (13212) *(G-14999)*
Sriracha2go, New York *Also called Kybod Group LLC (G-10146)*
Srlh Holdings Inc (HQ) 929 529-7951
15 Big Pond Rd Huguenot (12746) *(G-6196)*
SRP, New York *Also called Structured Retail Products (G-11375)*
SRP Apparel Group Inc 212 764-4810
525 7th Ave Rm 1808 New York (10018) *(G-11341)*
Srtech Industry Corp 718 496-7001
12019 Ketch Ct College Point (11356) *(G-3566)*
SS&c Financial Services LLC (HQ) 914 670-3600
1 South Rd Harrison (10528) *(G-5560)*
Ssa Trading Ltd 646 465-9500
226 W 37th St Fl 6l New York (10018) *(G-11342)*
Ssac Inc 800 843-8848
8242 Loop Rd Baldwinsville (13027) *(G-555)*
Ssf Production LLC 518 324-3407
194 Pleasant Ridge Rd Plattsburgh (12901) *(G-12778)*
SSG Fashions Ltd 212 221-0933
27 E 37th St Frnt 1 New York (10016) *(G-11343)*
Ssjjj Manufacturing LLC (PA) 516 498-3200
98 Cuttermill Rd Ste 412 Great Neck (11021) *(G-5423)*
SSP, Syracuse *Also called Selflock Screw Products Co Inc (G-14992)*
Ssrja LLC 718 725-7020
10729 180th St Jamaica (11433) *(G-6474)*
St James Printing Inc 631 981-2095
656 Rosevale Ave Ronkonkoma (11779) *(G-14014)*
St John 718 720-8367
229 Morrison Ave Staten Island (10310) *(G-14712)*
St John 718 771-4541
1700 Saint Johns Pl Brooklyn (11233) *(G-2448)*
St Killians America Inc 917 648-4351
614 Corporate Way Ste 3 Valley Cottage (10989) *(G-15324)*
St Lawrence Cement Co, Catskill *Also called Ciment St-Laurent Inc (G-3210)*
St Lawrence County Newspapers (HQ) 315 393-1003
1 Main St Ste 103 Canton (13617) *(G-3167)*

St Lawrence Lumber Inc......315 649-2990
27140 County Route 57 Three Mile Bay (13693) ***(G-15072)***
St Raymond Monument Co......718 824-3600
2727 Lafayette Ave Bronx (10465) ***(G-1369)***
St Silicones Corporation......518 406-3208
821 Main St Clifton Park (12065) ***(G-3475)***
St Silicones Inc......518 664-0745
95 N Central Ave Mechanicville (12118) ***(G-7695)***
Stack Electronics, Deer Park *Also called Veja Electronics Inc* ***(G-3949)***
Stafford Labs Orthotics/Prosth......845 692-5227
189 Monhagen Ave Middletown (10940) ***(G-7932)***
Stag Brothers Cast Stone Co......718 629-0975
909 E 51st St Brooklyn (11203) ***(G-2449)***
Stainless Design Concepts Ltd......845 246-3631
1117 Kings Hwy Saugerties (12477) ***(G-14213)***
Stainless Metals Inc......718 784-1454
6001 31st Ave Ste 1 Woodside (11377) ***(G-16228)***
Stairworld Inc......718 441-9722
5635 175th Pl B Fresh Meadows (11365) ***(G-5046)***
Stallion Inc (PA)......718 706-0111
3620 34th St Long Island City (11106) ***(G-7362)***
Stallion Technologies Inc......315 622-1176
4324 Loveland Dr Liverpool (13090) ***(G-7041)***
Stamp, Rhinebeck *Also called Smithers Tools & Mch Pdts Inc* ***(G-13101)***
Stamp Rite Tool & Die Inc......718 752-0334
4311 35th St Long Island City (11101) ***(G-7363)***
Stampcrete Decorative Concrete, Liverpool *Also called Stampcrete International Ltd* ***(G-7042)***
Stampcrete International Ltd......315 451-2837
325 Commerce Blvd Liverpool (13088) ***(G-7042)***
Stamped Fittings Inc......607 733-9988
217 Lenox Ave Elmira Heights (14903) ***(G-4380)***
Stamper Technology Inc......585 247-8370
232 Wallace Way Rochester (14624) ***(G-13743)***
Stamps & Signs Online Corp......718 218-0050
622 Broadway Brooklyn (11206) ***(G-2450)***
Standard Analytics Io Inc......917 882-5422
7 World Trade Ctr 46th New York (10007) ***(G-11344)***
Standard Bots Company......646 876-2687
18 Pomeroy Ln Locust Valley (11560) ***(G-7129)***
Standard Diversified Inc (PA)......302 248-1100
155 Mineola Blvd Mineola (11501) ***(G-8001)***
Standard Group (PA)......718 335-5500
1010 Nthrn Blvd Ste 236 Great Neck (11021) ***(G-5424)***
Standard Group LLC (HQ)......718 507-6430
1010 Nthrn Blvd Ste 236 Great Neck (11021) ***(G-5425)***
Standard Industrial Works Inc......631 888-0130
271 Skip Ln Bay Shore (11706) ***(G-717)***
Standard Industries Inc......212 821-1600
9 W 57th St Fl 30 New York (10019) ***(G-11345)***
Standard Manufacturing Co Inc (PA)......518 235-2200
750 2nd Ave Troy (12182) ***(G-15190)***
Standard Microsystems Corp (HQ)......631 435-6000
80 Arkay Dr Ste 100 Hauppauge (11788) ***(G-5774)***
Standard Motor Products Inc (PA)......718 392-0200
3718 Northern Blvd # 600 Long Island City (11101) ***(G-7364)***
Standard Paper Box Machine Co......718 328-3300
347 Coster St Fl 2 Bronx (10474) ***(G-1370)***
Standard Portable, Jamestown *Also called Lyn Jo Enterprises Ltd* ***(G-6530)***
Standard Screen Supply Corp (PA)......212 627-2727
121 Varick St Rm 200 New York (10013) ***(G-11346)***
Standard Wedding Band Co......516 294-0954
951 Franklin Ave Garden City (11530) ***(G-5117)***
Standing Stone Vineyards......607 582-6051
9934 State Route 414 Hector (14841) ***(G-5828)***
Standwill Packaging Inc......631 752-1236
220 Sherwood Ave Farmingdale (11735) ***(G-4739)***
Stanfordville Mch & Mfg Co Inc (PA)......845 868-2266
29 Victory Ln Poughkeepsie (12603) ***(G-12984)***
Stanley Creations Inc......718 361-6100
3100 47th Ave Ste 4105 Long Island City (11101) ***(G-7365)***
Stanley Home Products, Leicester *Also called Cpac Inc* ***(G-6908)***
Stanley Industrial Eqp LLC......315 656-8733
8094 Saintsville Rd Kirkville (13082) ***(G-6726)***
Stanley Paper Co Inc......518 489-1131
1 Terminal St Albany (12206) ***(G-131)***
Stanmark Jewelry Inc......212 730-2557
64 W 48th St Ste 1303 New York (10036) ***(G-11347)***
Stanson Automated LLC......866 505-7826
145 Saw Mill River Rd # 2 Yonkers (10701) ***(G-16349)***
Staplex Company Inc......718 768-3333
777 5th Ave Brooklyn (11232) ***(G-2451)***
Star Childrens Dress Co Inc (PA)......212 279-1524
1250 Broadway Fl 18 New York (10001) ***(G-11348)***
Star Communications, Hauppauge *Also called Star Quality Printing Inc* ***(G-5775)***
Star Community Publishing......631 843-4050
6 Corporate Center Dr Melville (11747) ***(G-7824)***
Star Composition Services Inc......212 684-4001
170 Hewes St Brooklyn (11211) ***(G-2452)***
Star Desk Pad Co Inc......914 963-9400
60 Mclean Ave Yonkers (10705) ***(G-16350)***
Star Headlight Lantern Co Inc (PA)......585 226-9500
455 Rochester St Avon (14414) ***(G-516)***
Star Kay White Inc (PA)......845 268-2600
151 Wells Ave Congers (10920) ***(G-3618)***
Star Mold Co Inc......631 694-2283
125 Florida St Farmingdale (11735) ***(G-4740)***
Star Mountain Coffee, Jamaica *Also called Star Mountain JFK Inc* ***(G-6475)***
Star Mountain JFK Inc......718 553-6787
Federal Cir Bldg 141 Jamaica (11430) ***(G-6475)***
Star Press Pearl River Inc......845 268-2294
614 Corporate Way Ste 8 Valley Cottage (10989) ***(G-15325)***
Star Quality Printing Inc......631 273-1900
270 Oser Ave Hauppauge (11788) ***(G-5775)***
Star Ready Mix East Inc......631 289-8787
225 Springs Fireplace Rd East Hampton (11937) ***(G-4128)***
Star Ready-Mix Inc......631 289-8787
172 Peconic Ave Medford (11763) ***(G-7724)***
Star Sports Corp......516 773-4075
747 Middle Neck Rd # 103 Great Neck (11024) ***(G-5426)***
Star Tubing Corp......716 483-1703
53 River St Jamestown (14701) ***(G-6543)***
Star Wire Mesh Fabricators......212 831-4133
518 E 119th St New York (10035) ***(G-11349)***
Star-Gazette Fund Inc......607 734-5151
310 E Church St Elmira (14901) ***(G-4368)***
Starcraft Press Inc......718 383-6700
4402 11th St Ste 311 Long Island City (11101) ***(G-7366)***
Starcyl USA Corp......877 782-7295
348 State Route 11 Champlain (12919) ***(G-3316)***
Starfire Holding Corporation (PA)......914 614-7000
767 5th Ave Fl 47 New York (10153) ***(G-11350)***
Starfire Printing, Holbrook *Also called Image Typography Inc* ***(G-6000)***
Starfire Printing Inc......631 736-1495
28 Washington Ave Holtsville (11742) ***(G-6053)***
Starfire Swords Ltd Inc......607 589-7244
74 Railroad Ave Spencer (14883) ***(G-14550)***
Starfire Systems Inc......518 899-9336
8 Sarnowski Dr Glenville (12302) ***(G-5273)***
Starfuels Inc (HQ)......914 289-4800
50 Main St White Plains (10606) ***(G-16062)***
Stargate Computer Corp......516 474-4799
24 Harmony Dr Port Jeff STA (11776) ***(G-12838)***
Stark Aquarium Products Co Inc......718 445-5357
2914 122nd St Flushing (11354) ***(G-4895)***
Stark Fish, Flushing *Also called Stark Aquarium Products Co Inc* ***(G-4895)***
Starkey & Henricks, New York *Also called Charles Henricks Inc* ***(G-8973)***
Starlight Paint Factory, Bronx *Also called Starlite Pnt & Varnish Co Inc* ***(G-1371)***
Starline Usa Inc......716 773-0100
3036 Alt Blvd Grand Island (14072) ***(G-5344)***
Starliner Shipping & Travel......718 385-1515
5305 Church Ave Ste 1 Brooklyn (11203) ***(G-2453)***
Starlite Media LLC (PA)......212 909-7700
118 E 28th St Rm 601 New York (10016) ***(G-11351)***
Starlite Pnt & Varnish Co Inc......718 292-6420
724 E 140th St Bronx (10454) ***(G-1371)***
Staroba Plastics Inc......716 537-3153
42 Edgewood Dr Holland (14080) ***(G-6031)***
Stasi Industries Inc......516 334-2742
501 Winding Rd Old Bethpage (11804) ***(G-12220)***
Statebook LLC......845 383-1991
185 Fair St Ste 2 Kingston (12401) ***(G-6711)***
Staten Island Advance, New York *Also called Advance Publications Inc* ***(G-8475)***
Staten Island Parent Magazine......718 761-4800
16 Shenandoah Ave Ste 2 Staten Island (10314) ***(G-14713)***
Staten Island Stair Inc......718 317-9276
439 Sharrotts Rd Staten Island (10309) ***(G-14714)***
Statewide Fireproof Door Co......845 268-6043
178 Charles Blvd Valley Cottage (10989) ***(G-15326)***
Static Coatings Inc (PA)......516 764-0040
3585 Lawson Blvd Unit B Oceanside (11572) ***(G-12191)***
Static Coatings Inc......646 296-0754
344 Hendrickson Ave Lynbrook (11563) ***(G-7439)***
Station Hill of Barrytown......845 758-5293
120 Station Hill Rd Barrytown (12507) ***(G-597)***
Stature Electric, Watertown *Also called Allied Motion Technologies Inc* ***(G-15558)***
Stature Electric Inc......716 242-7535
495 Commerce Dr Amherst (14228) ***(G-244)***
Staub Machine Company Inc......716 649-4211
206 Lake St Hamburg (14075) ***(G-5522)***
Staub Square, Hamburg *Also called Staub Machine Company Inc* ***(G-5522)***
Stavo Industries Inc (PA)......845 331-4552
132 Flatbush Ave Kingston (12401) ***(G-6712)***
Stavo Industries Inc......845 331-5389
132 Flatbush Ave Kingston (12401) ***(G-6713)***
Stealth Archtctral Windows Inc......718 821-6666
232 Varet St Brooklyn (11206) ***(G-2454)***
Stealth Inc......718 252-7900
1129 E 27th St Brooklyn (11210) ***(G-2455)***
Stealth Window, Brooklyn *Also called Stealth Archtctral Windows Inc* ***(G-2454)***
Steamline Machine, Fairport *Also called Streamline Precision Inc* ***(G-4525)***
Steamworks, Lockport *Also called Jonathan Brose* ***(G-7086)***

ALPHABETIC

Stebe Shcjhjff 839 383-9833
  18 Lynbrook Rd Poughkeepsie (12603) *(G-12985)*

Stedman Energy Inc 716 789-3018
  4411 Canterbury Dr Mayville (14757) *(G-7685)*

Steel & Obrien Mfg Inc 585 492-5800
  7869 Route 98 Arcade (14009) *(G-381)*

Steel City Salt LLC 716 532-0000
  13870 Taylor Hollow Rd Collins (14034) *(G-3572)*

Steel Craft, Brooklyn *Also called Steelcraft Manufacturing Co* *(G-2456)*

Steel Craft Rolling Door 631 608-8662
  5 Di Tomas Ct Copiague (11726) *(G-3679)*

Steel Excel Inc (HQ) 914 461-1300
  1133 Westchester Ave White Plains (10604) *(G-16063)*

Steel Partners Holdings LP (PA) 212 520-2300
  590 Madison Ave Rm 3202 New York (10022) *(G-11352)*

Steel Sales Inc 607 674-6363
  8085 State Hwy 12 Sherburne (13460) *(G-14395)*

Steel Tech SA LLC 845 786-3691
  7 Hillside Dr Thiells (10984) *(G-15065)*

Steel Work Inc 585 232-1555
  340 Oak St Rochester (14608) *(G-13744)*

Steel-Brite Ltd 631 589-4044
  2 Dawn Dr Oakdale (11769) *(G-12156)*

Steelcraft Manufacturing Co 718 277-2404
  352 Pine St Brooklyn (11208) *(G-2456)*

Steeldeck Ny Inc 718 599-3700
  141 Banker St Brooklyn (11222) *(G-2457)*

Steele Truss and Panel LLC 518 562-4663
  112 Trade Rd Plattsburgh (12901) *(G-12779)*

Steele Truss Company Inc 518 562-4663
  118 Trade Rd Plattsburgh (12901) *(G-12780)*

Steelflex Electro Corp 516 226-4466
  145 S 13th St Lindenhurst (11757) *(G-6973)*

Steelmasters Inc 718 498-2854
  135 Liberty Ave Brooklyn (11212) *(G-2458)*

Steelstone Group LLC 888 552-0033
  3611 14th Ave Ste 540 Brooklyn (11218) *(G-2459)*

Steelways Inc 845 562-0860
  401 S Water St Newburgh (12553) *(G-11887)*

Steelways Shipyard, Newburgh *Also called Steelways Inc* *(G-11887)*

Steering Columns Galore Inc 845 278-5762
  8 Vine Rd Mahopac (10541) *(G-7479)*

Steezys LLC 646 276-5333
  80 8th Ave 202 New York (10011) *(G-11353)*

Stefan & Sons Welding, Chaffee *Also called Donald Stefan* *(G-3306)*

Stefan Furs Inc 212 594-2788
  150 W 30th St Fl 15 New York (10001) *(G-11354)*

Stefan Sydor Optics Inc 585 271-7300
  31 Jetview Dr Rochester (14624) *(G-13745)*

Steffen Publishing Inc 315 865-4100
  9584 Main St Holland Patent (13354) *(G-6034)*

Steigercraft, Bellport *Also called AVS Laminates Inc* *(G-794)*

Stein Fibers Ltd (PA) 518 489-5700
  4 Computer Dr W Ste 200 Albany (12205) *(G-132)*

Stein Industries Inc 631 789-2222
  22 Sprague Ave Amityville (11701) *(G-307)*

Steinbock-Braff Inc 718 972-6500
  3611 14th Ave Brooklyn (11218) *(G-2460)*

Steindl Cast Stone Co Inc 718 296-8530
  9107 76th St Woodhaven (11421) *(G-16188)*

Steiner Doors, Brooklyn *Also called A G M Deco Inc* *(G-1434)*

Steiner Technologies Inc 585 425-5910
  180 Perinton Pkwy Fairport (14450) *(G-4523)*

Steinway Inc (HQ) 718 721-2600
  1 Steinway Pl Long Island City (11105) *(G-7367)*

Steinway and Sons (HQ) 718 721-2600
  1 Steinway Pl Long Island City (11105) *(G-7368)*

Steinway Awning II LLC (PA) 718 729-2965
  4230 24th St Astoria (11101) *(G-442)*

Steinway Awnings, Astoria *Also called Steinway Awning II LLC* *(G-442)*

Steinway Hall, Long Island City *Also called Steinway Inc* *(G-7367)*

Steinway Musical Instrs Inc (HQ) 781 894-9770
  1133 Avenue Of The Americ New York (10036) *(G-11355)*

Steinway Pasta & Gelati Inc 718 246-5414
  146 Steinway Ave Lindenhurst (11757) *(G-6974)*

Stellar Alliance, New York *Also called Alen Sands York Associates Ltd* *(G-8511)*

Stellar Printing Inc 718 361-1600
  3838 9th St Long Island City (11101) *(G-7369)*

Stemcultures LLC 518 621-0848
  1 Discovery Dr Rensselaer (12144) *(G-13092)*

Stemline Therapeutics Inc (PA) 646 502-2311
  750 Lexington Ave Fl 11 New York (10022) *(G-11356)*

Stensul Inc (PA) 212 380-8620
  150 W 25th St Fl 3 New York (10001) *(G-11357)*

Stephan & Company ACC Ltd (PA) 212 481-3888
  251 W 19th St Apt 1f New York (10011) *(G-11358)*

Stephen Bader Company Inc 518 753-4456
  10 Charles St Valley Falls (12185) *(G-15331)*

Stephen Dweck, New York *Also called Rumson Acquisition LLC* *(G-11098)*

Stephen Dweck Industries, Brooklyn *Also called Dweck Industries Inc* *(G-1765)*

Stephen J Lipkins Inc 631 249-8866
  855 Conklin St Ste A Farmingdale (11735) *(G-4741)*

Stephen M Kiernan 716 836-6300
  701 Seneca St Ste 300 Buffalo (14210) *(G-2992)*

Stephen Miller Gen Contrs Inc 518 661-5601
  301 Riceville Rd Gloversville (12078) *(G-5293)*

Stephen Singer Pattern Co Inc 212 947-2902
  340 W 39th St Fl 4 New York (10018) *(G-11359)*

Stephenson Custom Case Company 905 542-8762
  1623 Military Rd Niagara Falls (14304) *(G-11982)*

Stephenson Lumber Company Inc 518 548-7521
  Rr 8 Speculator (12164) *(G-14548)*

Stepping Stones One Day Signs 518 237-5774
  105 Broad St Waterford (12188) *(G-15547)*

Steps Plus Inc 315 432-0885
  6375 Thompson Rd Syracuse (13206) *(G-15000)*

Stereo Advantage Inc 716 656-7161
  45 Boxwood Ln Cheektowaga (14227) *(G-3362)*

Steri-Pharma LLC 315 473-7180
  429 S West St Syracuse (13202) *(G-15001)*

Sterilator Company, Cuba *Also called SPS Medical Supply Corp* *(G-3814)*

Steriliz LLC 585 415-5411
  150 Linden Oaks Ste B Rochester (14625) *(G-13746)*

Steris Corporation 845 469-4087
  23 Elizabeth Dr Chester (10918) *(G-3387)*

Sterling Digital Print, Hauppauge *Also called Sterling North America Inc* *(G-5776)*

Sterling Industries Inc 631 753-3070
  410 Eastern Pkwy Farmingdale (11735) *(G-4742)*

Sterling McFadden, New York *Also called Mac Fadden Holdings Inc* *(G-10303)*

Sterling Molded Products Inc 845 344-4546
  9-17 Oliver Ave Middletown (10940) *(G-7933)*

Sterling North America Inc 631 243-6933
  270 Oser Ave Hauppauge (11788) *(G-5776)*

Sterling Pierce Company Inc 516 593-1170
  395 Atlantic Ave East Rockaway (11518) *(G-4174)*

Sterling Shelf Liners Inc 631 676-5175
  836 Grundy Ave Holbrook (11741) *(G-6022)*

Sterling Sound Inc 212 604-9433
  88 10th Ave Frnt 6 New York (10011) *(G-11360)*

Sterling Toggle Inc 631 491-0500
  99 Mahan St West Babylon (11704) *(G-15749)*

Stern & Stern Industries Inc 607 324-4485
  188 Thacher St Hornell (14843) *(G-6111)*

Sterrx LLC 518 324-7879
  141 Idaho Ave Plattsburgh (12903) *(G-12781)*

Stetron International Inc (PA) 716 854-3443
  90 Broadway St Ste 1 Buffalo (14203) *(G-2993)*

Steuben Courier Advocate, Bath *Also called Gatehouse Media LLC* *(G-633)*

Steuben Foods Incorporated (PA) 718 291-3333
  1150 Maple Rd Elma (14059) *(G-4328)*

Steuben Foods Incorporated 716 655-4000
  1150 Maple Rd Elma (14059) *(G-4329)*

Steval Graphics Concepts Inc 516 576-0220
  7 Fairchild Ct Ste 200 Plainview (11803) *(G-12716)*

Steve Madden, Long Island City *Also called Steven Madden Ltd* *(G-7370)*

Steve Poli Sales 315 487-0394
  102 Farmington Dr Camillus (13031) *(G-3110)*

Steven Coffey Pallet S Inc 585 261-6783
  3376 Edgemere Dr Rochester (14612) *(G-13747)*

Steven John Opticians 718 543-3336
  5901 Riverdale Ave Bronx (10471) *(G-1372)*

Steven Kraus Associates Inc 631 923-2033
  9 Private Rd Huntington (11743) *(G-6225)*

Steven Madden Ltd (PA) 718 446-1800
  5216 Barnett Ave Long Island City (11104) *(G-7370)*

Stevens Bandes Graphics Corp 212 675-1128
  333 Hudson St Fl 3 New York (10013) *(G-11361)*

Stevenson Printing Co Inc 516 676-1233
  1 Brewster St Ste 2 Glen Cove (11542) *(G-5202)*

Stever-Locke Industries Inc 585 624-3450
  179 N Main St Honeoye Falls (14472) *(G-6081)*

Steves Original Furs Inc 212 967-8007
  345 7th Ave Fl 9 New York (10001) *(G-11362)*

Stewart Tobori & Chang Div, New York *Also called Harry N Abrams Incorporated* *(G-9731)*

Stewarts Processing Corp (PA) 518 581-1200
  2907 State Route 9 Ballston Spa (12020) *(G-588)*

Stewarts Shops Corp 518 499-9376
  60 Poultney St Whitehall (12887) *(G-16077)*

Stf, Cedarhurst *Also called Solar Thin Films Inc* *(G-3244)*

STf Services Inc 315 463-8506
  26 Corporate Cir Ste 2 East Syracuse (13057) *(G-4239)*

STI-Co Industries Inc 716 662-2680
  11 Cobham Dr Ste A Orchard Park (14127) *(G-12377)*

Stickershopcom Inc 631 563-4323
  582 Middle Rd Bayport (11705) *(G-731)*

Sticky Socks LLC 212 541-5927
  200 W 60th St Apt 7g New York (10023) *(G-11363)*

Stidd Systems Inc 631 477-2400
  220 Carpenter St Greenport (11944) *(G-5458)*

Stiegelbauer Associates Inc (PA) 718 624-0835
  63 Flushing Ave Unit 280 Brooklyn (11205) *(G-2461)*

Stilltheone Distillery LLC 914 217-0347
  500 Mmaroneck Ave Ste 205 Harrison (10528) *(G-5561)*

2020 Harris
New York Manufacturers Directory

(G-0000) Company's Geographic Section entry number

Stillwater Wood & Iron 518 664-4501
114 N Hudson Ave Stillwater (12170) *(G-14733)*
Stitch & Couture Inc (PA) 212 947-9204
224 W 30th St Fl 14 New York (10001) *(G-11364)*
Stj Orthotic Services Inc (PA) 631 956-0181
920 Wellwood Ave Ste B Lindenhurst (11757) *(G-6975)*
Stk Electronics Inc 315 655-8476
2747 Rte 20 Cazenovia (13035) *(G-3235)*
Stock Drive Products Div, New Hyde Park *Also called Designatronics Incorporated (G-8261)*
Stoffel Polygon Systems Inc 914 961-2000
199 Marbledale Rd Tuckahoe (10707) *(G-15206)*
Stone & Terrazzo World Inc 718 361-6899
5132 35th St Long Island City (11101) *(G-7371)*
Stone and Bath Gallery 718 438-4500
868 39th St Brooklyn (11232) *(G-2462)*
Stone Boss Industries Inc 718 278-2677
2604 Borough Pl Woodside (11377) *(G-16229)*
Stone Bridge Iron and Stl Inc 518 695-3752
426 Purinton Rd Gansevoort (12831) *(G-5087)*
Stone Crafters International, Brooklyn *Also called PR & Stone & Tile Inc (G-2276)*
Stone Crest Industries Inc 607 652-2665
152 Starheim Rd Stamford (12167) *(G-14609)*
Stone Expo & Cabinetry LLC 516 292-2988
7 Terminal Rd West Hempstead (11552) *(G-15780)*
Stone Glo Products, Bronx *Also called TWI-Laq Industries Inc (G-1385)*
Stone House Associates Inc 212 221-7447
37 W 47th St Ste 910 New York (10036) *(G-11365)*
Stone Well Bodies & Mch Inc 315 497-3512
625 Sill Rd Genoa (13071) *(G-5168)*
Stonegate Stabless 518 746-7133
106 Reynolds Rd Fort Edward (12828) *(G-4944)*
Stones Homemade Candies Inc 315 343-8401
23 W Seneca St Oswego (13126) *(G-12422)*
Stonesong Press LLC 212 929-4600
270 W 39th St Rm 201 New York (10018) *(G-11366)*
Stoney Croft Converters Inc 718 608-9800
364 Sharrotts Rd Staten Island (10309) *(G-14715)*
Stony Apparel Corp 212 391-0022
1407 Broadway Rm 3300 New York (10018) *(G-11367)*
Stony Brook Mfg Co Inc (PA) 631 369-9530
652 Scott Ave Calverton (11933) *(G-3086)*
Stony Brook University 631 632-6434
310 Administration Bldg Stony Brook (11794) *(G-14741)*
Stony Manufacturing Inc 716 652-6730
591 Pound Rd Elma (14059) *(G-4330)*
Stony Point Graphics Ltd 845 786-3322
79 S Liberty Dr Stony Point (10980) *(G-14748)*
Stop Entertainment Inc 212 242-7867
408 Rye Hill Rd Monroe (10950) *(G-8031)*
Stop N Shop LLC 518 512-9657
911 Central Ave Ste 149 Albany (12206) *(G-133)*
Storage Sheds, Westmoreland *Also called Shafer & Sons (G-15963)*
Storflex Fixture, Corning *Also called Storflex Holdings Inc (G-3721)*
Storflex Holdings Inc 607 962-2137
392 Pulteney St Corning (14830) *(G-3721)*
Stork H & E Turbo Blading Inc 607 277-4968
334 Comfort Rd Ithaca (14850) *(G-6411)*
Stormberg Brand, Valley Cottage *Also called Stromberg Brand Corporation (G-15327)*
Storybooks Forever 716 822-7845
4 Magnolia Ave Buffalo (14220) *(G-2994)*
Strada Soft Inc 718 556-6940
20 Clifton Ave Staten Island (10305) *(G-14716)*
Strahl & Pitsch Inc 631 669-0175
230 Great East Neck Rd West Babylon (11704) *(G-15750)*
Straight Arrow Publishing Co 212 484-1616
1290 Ave Of The Amer Fl 2 New York (10104) *(G-11368)*
Strassburg Medical LLC 800 452-0631
525 Wheatfield St North Tonawanda (14120) *(G-12092)*
Stratconglobal Inc 212 989-2355
685 3rd Ave Fl 4 New York (10017) *(G-11369)*
Strategic Signage Sourcing LLC 518 450-1093
2 Gilbert Rd Saratoga Springs (12866) *(G-14194)*
Strategies North America Inc 716 945-6053
150 Elm St Salamanca (14779) *(G-14130)*
Strativa Pharmaceuticals 201 802-4000
1 Ram Ridge Rd Spring Valley (10977) *(G-14582)*
Strato Transit Components LLC 518 686-4541
155 State Route 67 Eagle Bridge (12057) *(G-4075)*
Stratusoft, Great Neck *Also called Application Resources Inc (G-5365)*
Straus Communications 845 782-4000
20 West Ave Ste 201 Chester (10918) *(G-3388)*
Straus Newspaper, Chester *Also called Straus Communications (G-3388)*
Straus Newspapers Inc 845 782-4000
20 West Ave Chester (10918) *(G-3389)*
Strauss Eye Prosthetics Inc 585 424-1350
360 White Spruce Blvd Rochester (14623) *(G-13748)*
Strawtown Jewelry, New City *Also called Shining Creations Inc (G-8230)*
Stream Police, New York *Also called Instant Stream Inc (G-9904)*
Streamline Precision Inc 585 421-9050
205 Turk Hill Park Fairport (14450) *(G-4524)*
Streamline Precision Inc 585 421-9050
1000 Turk Hill Rd Ste 205 Fairport (14450) *(G-4525)*
Streck's Machinery, Watervliet *Also called Strecks Inc (G-15607)*
Strecks Inc 518 273-4410
800 1st St Watervliet (12189) *(G-15607)*
Street Beat Sportswear Inc (PA) 718 302-1500
462 Kent Ave Fl 2 Brooklyn (11249) *(G-2463)*
Street Smart Designs Inc 646 865-0056
29 W 35th St Fl 6 New York (10001) *(G-11370)*
Street Smarts Vr Inc 413 438-7787
116 Nassau St Ste 523 New York (10038) *(G-11371)*
Streetcred Nyc LLC 646 675-0073
1006 6th Ave Fl 3 New York (10018) *(G-11372)*
Streit Matzoh Co, Orangeburg *Also called Aron Streit Inc (G-12307)*
Striata Inc 212 918-4677
48 Wall St Ste 1100 New York (10005) *(G-11373)*
Strictly Business, Plattsburgh *Also called Northeast Group (G-12763)*
Strider Global LLC 212 726-1302
261 W 28th St Apt 6a New York (10001) *(G-11374)*
Striker Orthopedics 585 381-1773
7 Linden Park Rochester (14625) *(G-13749)*
Strippit Inc (HQ) 716 542-4511
12975 Clarence Center Rd Akron (14001) *(G-22)*
Strocchia Iron Works, Albertson *Also called Patsy Strocchia & Sons Iron Wo (G-148)*
Stroehmann Bakeries 33, Maspeth *Also called Bimbo Bakeries Usa Inc (G-7597)*
Stroehmann Bakeries 56, Olean *Also called Bimbo Bakeries Usa Inc (G-12225)*
Stroehmann Bakeries 72, Goshen *Also called Bimbo Bakeries Usa Inc (G-5305)*
Stroehmann Bakeries 90, Vestal *Also called Bimbo Bakeries Usa Inc (G-15372)*
Stromberg Brand Corporation 914 739-7410
12 Ford Products Rd Valley Cottage (10989) *(G-15327)*
Strong Forge & Fabrication 585 343-5251
20 Liberty St Batavia (14020) *(G-625)*
Strong Group Inc 516 766-6300
222 Atlantic Ave Unit B Oceanside (11572) *(G-12192)*
Strong Hospital, Rochester *Also called Orthotics & Prosthetics Dept (G-13599)*
Strong Ventures, New York *Also called Mrs John L Strong & Co LLC (G-10514)*
Structural Ceramics Division, Niagara Falls *Also called Saint-Gbain Advnced Crmics LLC (G-11977)*
Structural Ceramics Group, Niagara Falls *Also called Saint-Gobain Dynamics Inc (G-11978)*
Structural Industries Inc 631 471-5200
2950 Veterans Memorial Hw Bohemia (11716) *(G-1082)*
Structural Wood Corporation 315 388-4442
243 Lincoln Ave Waddington (13694) *(G-15447)*
Structured 3d Inc 346 704-2614
188 Dixon Ave Amityville (11701) *(G-308)*
Structured Retail Products 212 224-3692
225 Park Ave S Fl 8 New York (10003) *(G-11375)*
Structuredweb Inc 201 325-3110
20 W 20th St Ste 402 New York (10011) *(G-11376)*
Struthers Electronics, Bay Shore *Also called Lexan Industries Inc (G-690)*
Strux Corp 516 768-3969
100 Montauk Hwy Lindenhurst (11757) *(G-6976)*
STS Refill America LLC 516 934-8008
399 W John St Unit A Hicksville (11801) *(G-5949)*
STS Steel Inc 518 370-2693
301 Nott St Bldg 304 Schenectady (12305) *(G-14308)*
Stu-Art Supplies, North Baldwin *Also called Hubray Inc (G-12006)*
Stuart Communications Inc 845 252-7414
93 Erie Ave Narrowsburg (12764) *(G-8211)*
Stuart Mold & Manufacturing 716 488-9765
560 N Work St Falconer (14733) *(G-4558)*
Stuart Spector Designs Ltd 845 246-6124
1450 Route 212 Saugerties (12477) *(G-14214)*
Stuart Tool & Die Inc 716 488-1975
600 N Work St Falconer (14733) *(G-4559)*
Stuart-Dean Co Inc 718 472-1326
4350 10th St Long Island City (11101) *(G-7372)*
Stubbs Printing Inc 315 769-8641
271 E Orvis St Ste B Massena (13662) *(G-7672)*
Stucki Embroidery Works Inc (PA) 845 657-2308
Rr 28 Box W Boiceville (12412) *(G-1100)*
Studco Building Systems US LLC 585 545-3000
1700 Boulter Indus Pkwy Webster (14580) *(G-15655)*
Student Lifeline Inc 516 327-0800
922 Hempstead Tpke Franklin Square (11010) *(G-4964)*
Student Safety Books, Franklin Square *Also called Student Lifeline Inc (G-4964)*
Studio 21 LA Inc 718 965-6579
13 42nd St Fl 5 Brooklyn (11232) *(G-2464)*
Studio 22 Print 212 679-2656
20 Park Ave New York (10016) *(G-11377)*
Studio 26, New York *Also called R R Donnelley & Sons Company (G-10967)*
Studio 40 Inc 212 420-8631
810 Humboldt St Ste 4 Brooklyn (11222) *(G-2465)*
Studio Associates of New York 212 268-1163
242 W 30th St Rm 604 New York (10001) *(G-11378)*
Studio Fun International Inc 914 238-1000
44 S Broadway Fl 7 White Plains (10601) *(G-16064)*
Studio Glass Batch LLC 585 924-9579
7491 Modock Rd Victor (14564) *(G-15432)*
Studio One Leather Design Inc 212 760-1701
270 W 39th St Rm 505 New York (10018) *(G-11379)*

ALPHABETIC

Studio Silversmiths Inc..............718 418-6785
6315 Traffic Ave Ridgewood (11385) ***(G-13162)***
Studley Prtg Publications Inc..............518 563-1414
4701 State Route 9 Plattsburgh (12901) ***(G-12782)***
Stuff Magazine..............212 302-2626
1040 Ave Of The Amrcas New York (10018) ***(G-11380)***
Stuhrling Original LLC..............718 840-5760
449 20th St Brooklyn (11215) ***(G-2466)***
Sturdy Store Displays Inc..............718 389-9919
110 Beard St Brooklyn (11231) ***(G-2467)***
Sturges Elec Pdts Co Inc..............607 844-8604
23 North St Dryden (13053) ***(G-4041)***
Sturges Electronics LLC..............607 844-8604
23 North St Dryden (13053) ***(G-4042)***
Sturges Manufacturing Co Inc..............315 732-6159
2030 Sunset Ave Utica (13502) ***(G-15295)***
Stutzman Management Corp..............800 735-2013
11 Saint Joseph St Lancaster (14086) ***(G-6836)***
Style Plus Hosiery Mills, Valley Stream *Also called Ellis Products Corp* ***(G-15339)***
Stylebuilt Accessories Inc (PA)..............917 439-0578
45 Rose Ln East Rockaway (11518) ***(G-4175)***
Stylebuilt Acesries, East Rockaway *Also called Stylebuilt Accessories Inc* ***(G-4175)***
Styleclick Inc (HQ)..............212 329-0300
810 7th Ave Fl 18 New York (10019) ***(G-11381)***
Stylecraft Interiors Inc..............516 487-2133
22 Watermill Ln Great Neck (11021) ***(G-5427)***
Stylemaster, Richmond Hill *Also called Belle Maison USA Ltd* ***(G-13110)***
Styles Aviation Inc (PA)..............845 677-8185
30 Airway Dr Ste 2 Lagrangeville (12540) ***(G-6754)***
Styles Manufacturing Corp..............516 763-5303
3571 Hargale Rd Oceanside (11572) ***(G-12193)***
Stylist Pleating Corp..............718 384-8181
107 Vanderveer St Apt 3b Brooklyn (11207) ***(G-2468)***
Stylistic Press Inc..............212 675-0797
99 Battery Pl Apt 11p New York (10280) ***(G-11382)***
Sube Inc..............212 243-6930
146 W 29th St Rm 4e New York (10001) ***(G-11383)***
Substrate LLC..............212 913-9600
539 46th Ave Long Island City (11101) ***(G-7373)***
Suburban Marketing Assoc, Elmsford *Also called Ralph Martinelli* ***(G-4424)***
Suburban News, Spencerport *Also called Westside News Inc* ***(G-14560)***
Suburban Publishing Inc (PA)..............845 463-0542
1 Summit Ct Ste 200a Fishkill (12524) ***(G-4804)***
Success Apparel LLC..............212 502-1890
19 W 34th St Fl 7 New York (10001) ***(G-11384)***
Successware Inc..............716 565-2338
8860 Main St 102 Williamsville (14221) ***(G-16142)***
Suffolk Cement Precast Inc (PA)..............631 727-4432
1813 Middle Rd Calverton (11933) ***(G-3087)***
Suffolk Cement Products Inc..............631 727-2317
1843 Middle Rd Calverton (11933) ***(G-3088)***
Suffolk Community Council Inc (PA)..............631 434-9277
819 Grand Blvd Ste 1 Deer Park (11729) ***(G-3940)***
Suffolk Copy Center Inc..............631 665-0570
26 W Main St Bay Shore (11706) ***(G-718)***
Suffolk Granite Manufacturing..............631 226-4774
25 Gear Ave Lindenhurst (11757) ***(G-6977)***
Suffolk Indus Recovery Corp..............631 732-6403
3542 Route 112 Coram (11727) ***(G-3700)***
Suffolk McHy & Pwr Tl Corp (PA)..............631 289-7153
12 Waverly Ave Patchogue (11772) ***(G-12512)***
Suffolk Monument Mfg, Lindenhurst *Also called Suffolk Granite Manufacturing* ***(G-6977)***
Suffolk Printing, Bay Shore *Also called Suffolk Copy Center Inc* ***(G-718)***
Sugar Foods Corporation (PA)..............212 753-6900
950 3rd Ave Fl 21 New York (10022) ***(G-11385)***
Sugar Shack Desert Company Inc..............518 523-7540
2567 Main St Lake Placid (12946) ***(G-6768)***
Sugarbear Cupcakes..............917 698-9005
14552 159th St Jamaica (11434) ***(G-6476)***
Suhor Industries Inc (PA)..............585 377-5100
72 Oconnor Rd Fairport (14450) ***(G-4526)***
Suhor Industries Inc..............716 483-6818
584 Buffalo St Jamestown (14701) ***(G-6544)***
Suit-Kote Corporation (PA)..............607 753-1100
1911 Lorings Crossing Rd Cortland (13045) ***(G-3789)***
Suit-Kote Corporation..............315 735-8501
191 Dry Rd Oriskany (13424) ***(G-12396)***
Suit-Kote Corporation..............607 535-2743
20 Fairgrounds Ln Watkins Glen (14891) ***(G-15616)***
Suit-Kote Corporation..............585 268-7127
5628 Tuckers Corners Rd Belmont (14813) ***(G-811)***
Suit-Kote Corporation..............716 664-3750
57 Lister St Jamestown (14701) ***(G-6545)***
Suit-Kote Corporation..............716 683-8850
505 Como Park Blvd Buffalo (14227) ***(G-2995)***
Suite Solutions Inc..............716 929-3050
100 Corporate Pkwy # 338 Amherst (14226) ***(G-245)***
Sukkah Center, Brooklyn *Also called Y & A Trading Inc* ***(G-2598)***
Sullivan Bazinet Bongio Inc..............315 437-6500
6295 E Molloy Rd Ste 3 East Syracuse (13057) ***(G-4240)***
Sullivan Concrete Inc..............845 888-2235
420 Bernas Rd Cochecton (12726) ***(G-3504)***
Sullivan County Democrat, Callicoon *Also called Catskill Delaware Publications* ***(G-3075)***
Sullivan St Bky - Hlls Kit Inc..............212 265-5580
533 W 47th St New York (10036) ***(G-11386)***
Sullivan Structures, Cochecton *Also called Sullivan Concrete Inc* ***(G-3504)***
Suma Industries Inc..............646 436-5202
345 E 52nd St Apt 9d New York (10022) ***(G-11387)***
Sumax Cycle Products Inc..............315 768-1058
122 Clear Rd Oriskany (13424) ***(G-12397)***
Sumer Gold Ltd..............212 354-8677
33 W 46th St Fl 4 New York (10036) ***(G-11388)***
Sumitomo Elc USA Holdings Inc (HQ)..............212 490-6610
600 5th Ave Fl 18 New York (10020) ***(G-11389)***
Summit Aerospace Inc..............718 433-1326
4301 21st St Ste 203 Long Island City (11101) ***(G-7374)***
Summit Apparel Inc (PA)..............631 213-8299
91 Cabot Ct Hauppauge (11788) ***(G-5777)***
Summit Communications..............914 273-5504
28 Half Mile Rd Armonk (10504) ***(G-402)***
Summit Fincl Disclosure LLC..............212 913-0510
216 E 45th St Fl 15 New York (10017) ***(G-11390)***
Summit Laser Products, Holbrook *Also called Summit Technologies LLC* ***(G-6023)***
Summit Lubricants Inc..............585 815-0798
4d Treadeasy Ave Batavia (14020) ***(G-626)***
Summit Manufacturing LLC (HQ)..............631 952-1570
100 Spence St Bay Shore (11706) ***(G-719)***
Summit MSP LLC..............716 433-1014
6042 Old Beattie Rd Lockport (14094) ***(G-7108)***
Summit MSP LLC..............716 433-1014
6042 Old Beattie Rd Lockport (14094) ***(G-7109)***
Summit Plastics, Bay Shore *Also called Summit Manufacturing LLC* ***(G-719)***
Summit Professional Networks..............212 557-7480
469 Fashion Ave Fl 10 New York (10018) ***(G-11391)***
Summit Research Laboratories, Huguenot *Also called Somerville Acquisitions Co Inc* ***(G-6194)***
Summit Technologies LLC..............631 590-1040
723 Broadway Ave Holbrook (11741) ***(G-6023)***
Summit Vitamins, Hauppauge *Also called American Hlth Formulations Inc* ***(G-5590)***
Summitreheis, Huguenot *Also called Elementis Srl Inc* ***(G-6193)***
Sumner Industries Inc..............631 666-7290
309 Orinoco Dr Bay Shore (11706) ***(G-720)***
Sun Microsystems, Albany *Also called Oracle America Inc* ***(G-109)***
Sun Ming Jan Inc..............718 418-8221
145 Noll St Brooklyn (11206) ***(G-2469)***
Sun Printing Incorporated..............607 337-3034
57 Borden Ave 65 Norwich (13815) ***(G-12128)***
Sun Scientific Inc..............914 479-5108
145 Palisade St Dobbs Ferry (10522) ***(G-4020)***
Sun Source, New York *Also called Jacobs & Cohen Inc* ***(G-9966)***
Sun Valley Printing, Binghamton *Also called Jane Lewis* ***(G-890)***
Sun-Times Media Group Inc..............716 945-1644
36 River St Salamanca (14779) ***(G-14131)***
Suna Bros Inc..............212 869-5670
10 W 46th St Fl 5 New York (10036) ***(G-11392)***
Sunbelt Industries Inc (PA)..............315 823-2947
540 E Mill St Little Falls (13365) ***(G-6993)***
Sunbilt Solar Pdts By Sussman..............718 297-0228
10910 180th St Jamaica (11433) ***(G-6477)***
Sunburst Studios Inc..............718 768-6360
584 3rd Ave Brooklyn (11215) ***(G-2470)***
Sunbuster, Farmingdale *Also called Gustbuster Ltd* ***(G-4642)***
Sundance Industries Inc..............845 795-5809
36 Greentree Ln Milton (12547) ***(G-7953)***
Sunday Record, The, Saratoga Springs *Also called Record* ***(G-14190)***
Sundial Brands..............631 842-8800
1 Adams Blvd Farmingdale (11735) ***(G-4743)***
Sundial Brands LLC..............631 842-8800
11 Ranick Dr S Amityville (11701) ***(G-309)***
Sundial Creations, Amityville *Also called Sundial Group LLC* ***(G-311)***
Sundial Fragrances & Flavors..............631 842-8800
11 Ranick Dr S Amityville (11701) ***(G-310)***
Sundial Group LLC..............631 842-8800
11 Ranick Dr S Amityville (11701) ***(G-311)***
Sundown Ski & Sport Shop Inc (PA)..............631 737-8600
3060 Middle Country Rd Lake Grove (11755) ***(G-6761)***
Sunfeather Herbal Soap, Potsdam *Also called Sunfeather Natural Soap Co Inc* ***(G-12942)***
Sunfeather Natural Soap Co Inc..............315 265-1776
1551 State Highway 72 Potsdam (13676) ***(G-12942)***
Sunham Home Fashions LLC (PA)..............212 695-1218
136 Madison Ave Fl 16 New York (10016) ***(G-11393)***
Sunlight US Co., Inc., Buffalo *Also called Rough Brothers Holding Co* ***(G-2965)***
Sunny Names, Roslyn Heights *Also called Sunynams Fashions Ltd* ***(G-14058)***
Sunnycrest Inc (PA)..............315 252-7214
58 Prospect St Auburn (13021) ***(G-496)***
Sunnyside Decorative Prints Co..............516 671-1935
67 Robinson Ave Glen Cove (11542) ***(G-5203)***
Sunquest Pharmaceuticals Inc..............855 478-6779
385 W John St Ste 1 Hicksville (11801) ***(G-5950)***
Sunrise Door Solutions..............631 464-4139
1215 Sunrise Hwy Copiague (11726) ***(G-3680)***
Sunrise Installation, Copiague *Also called Sunrise Door Solutions* ***(G-3680)***

Sunrise Jewelers of NY Inc................................516 541-1302
1220 Sunrise Hwy Massapequa (11758) *(G-7651)*

Sunrise Snacks Rockland Inc (PA)................845 352-2676
3 Sunrise Dr Monsey (10952) *(G-8049)*

Sunrise Tile Inc...718 939-0538
13309 35th Ave Flushing (11354) *(G-4896)*

Sunset Ridge Holdings Inc............................716 487-1458
490-496 Crescent St Jamestown (14701) *(G-6546)*

Sunshine Diamond Cutter Inc........................212 221-1028
38 W 48th St Ste 905 New York (10036) *(G-11394)*

Suntegra, Binghamton *Also called Integrated Solar Tech LLC (G-888)*

Sunward Electronics Inc.................................518 687-0030
258 Broadway Ste 2a Troy (12180) *(G-15191)*

Sunwin Global Industry Inc............................646 370-6196
295 5th Ave Ste 515 New York (10016) *(G-11395)*

Suny At Binghamton..607 777-2316
Vestal Pkwy E Binghamton (13901) *(G-910)*

Sunynams Fashions Ltd..................................212 268-5200
170 Westwood Cir Roslyn Heights (11577) *(G-14058)*

Supdates, New York *Also called Bull Street LLC (G-8867)*

Super Conductor Materials Inc......................845 368-0240
391 Spook Rock Rd Suffern (10901) *(G-14767)*

Super Express USA Pubg Corp.......................212 227-5800
8410 101st St Apt 4l Richmond Hill (11418) *(G-13126)*

Super Millwork Inc..631 293-5025
125 Spagnoli Rd Melville (11747) *(G-7825)*

Super Moderna/Magic Master, New Hyde Park *Also called Joseph Struhl Co Inc (G-8277)*

Super Neon Light Co Inc.................................718 236-5667
7813 16th Ave Brooklyn (11214) *(G-2471)*

Super Price Chopper Inc.................................716 893-3323
1580 Genesee St Buffalo (14211) *(G-2996)*

Super Sauces Inc...347 497-2537
553 Prospect Ave Brooklyn (11215) *(G-2472)*

Super Stud Building Products, Long Island City *Also called Superior Metals & Processing (G-7375)*

Super Sweep Inc (PA)......................................631 223-8205
20 Railroad St Unit 1 Huntington Station (11746) *(G-6261)*

Super Web Inc..631 643-9100
97 Lamar St West Babylon (11704) *(G-15751)*

Super-Trim Inc...212 255-2370
30 W 24th St Fl 4 New York (10010) *(G-11396)*

Superboats Inc...631 226-1761
694 Roosevelt Ave Lindenhurst (11757) *(G-6978)*

Supergen Products LLC..................................315 573-7887
320 Hoffman St Newark (14513) *(G-11853)*

Superior Aggragates Supply LLC...................516 333-2923
612 Muncy St Lindenhurst (11757) *(G-6979)*

Superior Bat Company, Jamestown *Also called Grace Wheeler (G-6513)*

Superior Block Corp..718 421-0900
761 E 42nd St Brooklyn (11210) *(G-2473)*

Superior Confections Inc................................718 698-3300
1150 South Ave Staten Island (10314) *(G-14717)*

Superior Elec Enclosure Inc...........................718 797-9090
16 Spencer St Brooklyn (11205) *(G-2474)*

Superior Energy Services Inc.........................716 483-0100
1720 Foote Avenue Ext Jamestown (14701) *(G-6547)*

Superior Exteriors of Buffalo........................716 873-1000
57 Insbrook Ct East Amherst (14051) *(G-4079)*

Superior Fiber Mills Inc..................................718 782-7500
181 Lombardy St Brooklyn (11222) *(G-2475)*

Superior Furs Inc..516 365-4123
1697 Northern Blvd Manhasset (11030) *(G-7541)*

Superior Glove Works USA Ltd.......................716 626-9500
2345 Walden Ave Ste 600 Cheektowaga (14225) *(G-3363)*

Superior Interiors NY Corp.............................845 274-7600
25 Robert Pitt Dr Ste 208 Monsey (10952) *(G-8050)*

Superior Metal & Woodwork Inc....................631 465-9004
70 Central Ave Farmingdale (11735) *(G-4744)*

Superior Metals & Processing.......................718 545-7500
801 26th Ave Long Island City (11102) *(G-7375)*

Superior Model Form Co, Middle Village *Also called Goldmont Enterprises Inc (G-7878)*

Superior Motion Controls Inc.........................516 420-2921
40 Smith Rd Farmingdale (11735) *(G-4745)*

Superior Packaging, Farmingdale *Also called Mkt329 Inc (G-4688)*

Superior Print On Demand..............................607 240-5231
165 Charles St Vestal (13850) *(G-15384)*

Superior Printing Ink Co Inc...........................716 877-0250
777 E Park Dr Tonawanda (14150) *(G-15142)*

Superior Stl Door Trim Co Inc.........................716 665-3256
154 Fairmount Ave Jamestown (14701) *(G-6548)*

Superior Technology Inc.................................585 352-6556
200 Paragon Dr Rochester (14624) *(G-13750)*

Superior Tool Company, North Tonawanda *Also called Ameri-Cut Tool Grinding Inc (G-12051)*

Superior Walls of Hudson Vly, Poughkeepsie *Also called Superior Wlls of Hdson Vly Inc (G-12986)*

Superior Walls Upstate NY Inc (PA)...............585 624-9390
7574 E Main St Lima (14485) *(G-6936)*

Superior Washer & Gasket Corp (PA)............631 273-8282
170 Adams Ave Hauppauge (11788) *(G-5778)*

Superior Welding..631 676-2751
331 Dante Ct Ste G Holbrook (11741) *(G-6024)*

Superior Wlls of Hdson Vly Inc......................845 485-4033
68 Violet Ave Poughkeepsie (12601) *(G-12986)*

Superior Wood Turnings.................................716 483-1254
118 E 1st St Jamestown (14701) *(G-6549)*

Superite Gear Instr of Hppauge (PA).............631 234-0100
225 Engineers Rd Hauppauge (11788) *(G-5779)*

Supermarket Equipment Depo Inc.................718 665-6200
1135 Bronx River Ave Bronx (10472) *(G-1373)*

Supermedia LLC..212 513-9700
2 Penn Plz Fl 22 New York (10121) *(G-11397)*

Superpower Inc..518 346-1414
450 Duane Ave Ste 1 Schenectady (12304) *(G-14309)*

Supersmile, New York *Also called Robell Research Inc (G-11059)*

Supplement Mfg Partner Inc...........................516 368-2656
250 Executive Dr Ste L Edgewood (11717) *(G-4283)*

Supply & Demand, New York *Also called Drew Philips Corp (G-9270)*

Supply Technologies NY , Inc., Albany *Also called Park-Ohio Inds Trsry Co Inc (G-111)*

Supplynet Inc (PA)..800 826-0279
706 Executive Blvd Ste B Valley Cottage (10989) *(G-15328)*

Suppositoria Laboratory, Bronx *Also called Perrigo New York Inc (G-1338)*

Supreme Boilers Inc..718 342-2220
9221 Ditmas Ave Brooklyn (11236) *(G-2476)*

Supreme Chocolatier LLC...............................718 761-9600
1150 South Ave Fl 1 Staten Island (10314) *(G-14718)*

Supreme Fire Proof Door Co..........................718 665-4224
391 Rider Ave Bronx (10451) *(G-1374)*

Supreme Leather Products, Spring Valley *Also called Louis Schwartz (G-14577)*

Supreme Lighting Design LLC.........................718 812-3347
5308 13th Ave Brooklyn (11219) *(G-2477)*

Supreme Poly Plastics Inc..............................718 456-9300
299 Meserole St Brooklyn (11206) *(G-2478)*

Supreme Screw Products Inc..........................718 293-6600
10 Skyline Dr Unit B Plainview (11803) *(G-12717)*

Supresta US LLC (HQ).....................................914 674-9434
420 Saw Mill River Rd Ardsley (10502) *(G-390)*

Sure Fit Inc..212 395-9340
58 W 40th St Rm 2a New York (10018) *(G-11398)*

Sure Flow Equipment Inc................................800 263-8251
250 Cooper Ave Ste 102 Tonawanda (14150) *(G-15143)*

Sure Iron Works, Brooklyn *Also called Kms Contracting Inc (G-2033)*

Sure-Kol Refrigerator Co Inc...........................718 625-0601
490 Flushing Ave Brooklyn (11205) *(G-2479)*

Surepure Inc..917 368-8480
405 Lexington Ave Fl 25 New York (10174) *(G-11399)*

Surescan Corporation.....................................607 321-0042
100 Eldredge St Binghamton (13901) *(G-911)*

Surf-Tech Manufacturing Corp.......................631 589-1194
28 Colt Ct Ronkonkoma (11779) *(G-14015)*

Surface Finish Technology.............................607 732-2909
215 Judson St Elmira (14901) *(G-4369)*

Surface Magazine...646 805-0200
134 W 26th St Frnt 1 New York (10001) *(G-11400)*

Surface Media LLC..212 229-1500
1 World Trade Ctr Fl 32 New York (10007) *(G-11401)*

Surface Publishing, New York *Also called Surface Magazine (G-11400)*

Surgical Design Corp.......................................914 273-2445
3 Macdonald Ave Armonk (10504) *(G-403)*

Surmet Ceramics Corporation.......................716 875-4091
699 Hertel Ave Ste 290 Buffalo (14207) *(G-2997)*

Surmotech LLC..585 742-1220
7676 Netlink Dr Victor (14564) *(G-15433)*

Surprise Plastics Inc......................................718 492-6355
124 57th St Brooklyn (11220) *(G-2480)*

Surtic Mining Company LLC...........................718 434-0477
1825 Foster Ave Brooklyn (11230) *(G-2481)*

Surving Studios...845 355-1430
17 Millsburg Rd Middletown (10940) *(G-7934)*

Survival Inc...631 385-5060
90 Washington Dr Ste C Centerport (11721) *(G-3258)*

Suslo, New York *Also called Halabieh Group Inc (G-9710)*

Sussex Publishers LLC (PA)...........................212 260-7210
115 E 23rd St Fl 9 New York (10010) *(G-11402)*

Sussman-Automatic Corporation (PA)...........718 937-4500
4320 34th St Long Island City (11101) *(G-7376)*

Sutter Machine Tool and Die, Bronx *Also called M J M Tooling Corp (G-1305)*

Sutton Place Software Inc...............................631 421-1737
13 Tappen Dr Melville (11747) *(G-7826)*

Svyz Trading Corp...718 220-1140
4320 Park Ave Bronx (10457) *(G-1375)*

Swagelok Western NY......................................585 359-8470
10 Thruway Park Dr West Henrietta (14586) *(G-15805)*

Swain Technology Inc......................................585 889-2786
963 North Rd Scottsville (14546) *(G-14344)*

Swamp Island Dessert Co, West Falls *Also called Butterwood Desserts Inc (G-15761)*

Swank Inc...212 867-2600
90 Park Ave Rm 1302 New York (10016) *(G-11403)*

Swanson Lumber...716 499-1726
5273 N Hill Rd Gerry (14740) *(G-5171)*

Swaps Monitor Publications Inc.....................212 742-8550
29 Broadway Rm 1510 New York (10006) *(G-11404)*

A L P H A B E T I C

Swarovski Lighting Ltd (PA).......518 563-7500
61 Industrial Blvd Plattsburgh (12901) ***(G-12783)***
Swarovski Lighting Ltd.......518 324-6378
1483 Military Tpke Ste B Plattsburgh (12901) ***(G-12784)***
Swarovski North America Ltd.......212 695-1502
1 Penn Plz Frnt 4 New York (10119) ***(G-11405)***
Swatfame Inc.......212 944-8022
530 Fashion Ave Rm 1204 New York (10018) ***(G-11406)***
Swatt Baking Co, Olean *Also called L American Ltd* ***(G-12238)***
Sweater Brand Inc.......718 797-0505
86 S 1st St Brooklyn (11249) ***(G-2482)***
Swedish Hill Vineyard Inc.......607 403-0029
4565 State Route 414 Romulus (14541) ***(G-13881)***
Swedish Hill Winery, Romulus *Also called Swedish Hill Vineyard Inc* ***(G-13881)***
Sweet Melodys LLC.......716 580-3227
8485 Transit Rd East Amherst (14051) ***(G-4080)***
Sweet Mouth Inc.......800 433-7758
244 5th Ave Ste L243 New York (10001) ***(G-11407)***
Sweet Tooth Enterprises LLC.......631 752-2888
135 Dale St West Babylon (11704) ***(G-15752)***
Sweeteners Plus LLC.......585 728-3770
5768 Sweeteners Blvd Lakeville (14480) ***(G-6776)***
Sweetwater Energy Inc.......585 647-5760
500 Lee Rd Ste 200 Rochester (14606) ***(G-13751)***
Sweetworks Inc (PA).......716 634-4545
3500 Genesee St Buffalo (14225) ***(G-2998)***
Swell LLC.......646 738-8981
28 W 23rd St Fl 5 New York (10010) ***(G-11408)***
Swift Fulfillment Services.......516 593-1198
290 Broadway Lynbrook (11563) ***(G-7440)***
Swift Glass Co Inc.......607 733-7166
131 22nd St Elmira Heights (14903) ***(G-4381)***
Swift Multigraphics LLC.......585 442-8000
55 Southwood Ln Rochester (14618) ***(G-13752)***
Swift River Associates Inc.......716 875-0902
4051 River Rd Tonawanda (14150) ***(G-15144)***
Swim USA, New York *Also called Longevity Brands LLC* ***(G-10248)***
Swimline Corp (PA).......631 254-2155
191 Rodeo Dr Edgewood (11717) ***(G-4284)***
Swimline International Corp.......631 254-2155
191 Rodeo Dr Edgewood (11717) ***(G-4285)***
Swimways Corp.......757 460-1156
3030 47th Ave Ste 680 Long Island City (11101) ***(G-7377)***
Swimwear Anywhere Inc (PA).......631 420-1400
85 Sherwood Ave Farmingdale (11735) ***(G-4746)***
Swimwear Anywhere Inc.......845 858-4141
21 Minisink Ave Port Jervis (12771) ***(G-12858)***
Swing Frame, Freeport *Also called Access Display Group Inc* ***(G-4979)***
Swirl Bliss LLC.......516 867-9475
1777 Grand Ave North Baldwin (11510) ***(G-12009)***
Swirls Twirls Incorporated.......516 541-9400
4116 Sunrise Hwy Massapequa (11758) ***(G-7652)***
Swiss Specialties Inc.......631 567-8800
15 Crescent Ct Wading River (11792) ***(G-15453)***
Swiss Tool Corporation.......631 842-7766
100 Court St Copiague (11726) ***(G-3681)***
Swissbit Na Inc.......914 935-1400
18 Willett Ave 202 Port Chester (10573) ***(G-12829)***
Swisse Cheeks, Brooklyn *Also called Silly Phillie Creations Inc* ***(G-2413)***
Swissmar Inc.......905 764-1121
6391 Walmore Rd Niagara Falls (14304) ***(G-11983)***
Swissway Inc.......631 351-5350
123 W Hills Rd Huntington Station (11746) ***(G-6262)***
Switch Beverage Company LLC.......203 202-7383
2 Seaview Blvd Fl 3 Port Washington (11050) ***(G-12928)***
Switched Source LLC.......708 207-1479
85 Murray Hl Rd Ste 2225 Vestal (13850) ***(G-15385)***
Switches and Sensors Inc.......631 924-2167
86 Horseblock Rd Unit J Yaphank (11980) ***(G-16273)***
Switching Power Inc.......631 981-7231
3601 Veterans Mem Hwy Ronkonkoma (11779) ***(G-14016)***
Switzer, Buffalo *Also called Precision Photo-Fab Inc* ***(G-2928)***
Swivelier Company Inc.......845 353-1455
600 Bradley Hill Rd Ste 3 Blauvelt (10913) ***(G-934)***
Swremote, Buffalo *Also called Pointman LLC* ***(G-2923)***
Sycamore Hill Designs Inc.......585 820-7322
7585 Modock Rd Victor (14564) ***(G-15434)***
Sylhan LLC (PA).......631 243-6600
210 Rodeo Dr Edgewood (11717) ***(G-4286)***
Symantec, New York *Also called Nortonlifelock Inc* ***(G-10647)***
Symbio Technologies LLC.......914 576-1205
333 Mamaroneck Ave White Plains (10605) ***(G-16065)***
Symbol Technologies LLC (HQ).......631 737-6851
1 Zebra Plz Holtsville (11742) ***(G-6054)***
Symbol Technologies LLC.......631 738-2400
110 Orville Dr Bohemia (11716) ***(G-1083)***
Symbol Technologies LLC.......631 218-3907
25 Andrea Rd Holbrook (11741) ***(G-6025)***
Symbol Technologies Delaware, Holtsville *Also called Symbol Technologies LLC* ***(G-6054)***
Symmetry Medical Inc.......845 368-4573
201 Route 59 Bldg E Hillburn (10931) ***(G-5971)***
Symphony Talent LLC (PA).......212 999-9000
19 W 34th St Rm 1000 New York (10001) ***(G-11409)***
Symrise Inc.......646 459-5000
505 Park Ave Fl 15 New York (10022) ***(G-11410)***
Symwave Inc (HQ).......949 542-4400
80 Arkay Dr Hauppauge (11788) ***(G-5780)***
Synced Inc.......917 565-5591
120 Walker St Ste 4 New York (10013) ***(G-11411)***
Synco Technologies Inc.......212 255-2031
54 W 21st St Rm 602 New York (10010) ***(G-11412)***
Synergx Systems Inc (HQ).......516 433-4700
3927 59th St Woodside (11377) ***(G-16230)***
Synergy Digital.......718 643-2742
43 Hall St Brooklyn (11205) ***(G-2483)***
Synergy Flavors NY Company LLC.......585 232-6647
86 White St Rochester (14608) ***(G-13753)***
Synergy Pharmaceuticals Inc (HQ).......212 227-8611
420 Lexington Ave Rm 2500 New York (10170) ***(G-11413)***
Synergy Resources Inc.......631 665-2050
320 Carleton Ave Ste 6200 Central Islip (11722) ***(G-3289)***
Synergy Tooling Systems Inc (PA).......716 834-4457
287 Commerce Dr Amherst (14228) ***(G-246)***
Syntec Optics, Rochester *Also called Syntec Technologies Inc* ***(G-13754)***
Syntec Technologies Inc.......585 768-2513
515 Lee Rd Rochester (14606) ***(G-13754)***
Synthes Usa LLC.......607 271-2500
35 Airport Rd Horseheads (14845) ***(G-6138)***
Synthetic Textiles Inc (PA).......716 842-2598
398 Broadway St Buffalo (14204) ***(G-2999)***
Syntho Pharmaceuticals Inc.......631 755-9898
230 Sherwood Ave Farmingdale (11735) ***(G-4747)***
Syraco Products Inc.......315 476-5306
1054 S Clinton St Syracuse (13202) ***(G-15002)***
Syracusa Sand and Gravel Inc.......585 924-7146
1389 Malone Rd Victor (14564) ***(G-15435)***
Syracuse Casing Co Inc.......315 475-0309
528 Erie Blvd W Syracuse (13204) ***(G-15003)***
Syracuse Catholic Press Assn.......315 422-8153
421 S Warren St Fl 2 Syracuse (13202) ***(G-15004)***
Syracuse Computer Forms Inc.......315 478-0108
216 Burnet Ave Syracuse (13203) ***(G-15005)***
Syracuse Corrugated Box Corp.......315 437-9901
302 Stoutenger St East Syracuse (13057) ***(G-4241)***
Syracuse Cultural Workers Prj.......315 474-1132
400 Lodi St Syracuse (13203) ***(G-15006)***
Syracuse Hvac, Syracuse *Also called John F Krell Jr* ***(G-14918)***
Syracuse Industrial Sls Co Ltd.......315 478-5751
1850 Lemoyne Ave Syracuse (13208) ***(G-15007)***
Syracuse Label & Surround Prtg, Syracuse *Also called Syracuse Label Co Inc* ***(G-15008)***
Syracuse Label Co Inc.......315 422-1037
200 Stewart Dr Syracuse (13212) ***(G-15008)***
Syracuse Letter Company Inc.......315 476-8328
1179 Oak Ln Bridgeport (13030) ***(G-1169)***
Syracuse Midstate Spring, Syracuse *Also called Midstate Spring Inc* ***(G-14943)***
Syracuse New Times, Syracuse *Also called All Times Publishing LLC* ***(G-14809)***
Syracuse New Times, Syracuse *Also called A Zimmer Ltd* ***(G-14808)***
Syracuse Plastics LLC.......315 637-9881
7400 Morgan Rd Liverpool (13090) ***(G-7043)***
Syracuse Prosthetic Center Inc.......315 476-9697
1124 E Fayette St Syracuse (13210) ***(G-15009)***
Syracuse Stamping Company, Syracuse *Also called Syraco Products Inc* ***(G-15002)***
Syracuse Technical Center, Syracuse *Also called Chemtrade Chemicals US LLC* ***(G-14849)***
Syracuse University Press Inc.......315 443-5534
621 Skytop Rd Ste 110 Syracuse (13244) ***(G-15010)***
Syrasoft LLC.......315 708-0341
6 Canton St Baldwinsville (13027) ***(G-556)***
System of AME Binding.......631 390-8560
95 Hoffman Ln Central Islip (11749) ***(G-3290)***
Systems Drs C3 Inc (HQ).......716 631-6200
485 Cayuga Rd Buffalo (14225) ***(G-3000)***
Systems Trading Inc.......718 261-8900
48 S Svc Rd Ste Ll90 Melville (11747) ***(G-7827)***
T & C Power Conversion Inc.......585 482-5551
132 Humboldt St Rochester (14610) ***(G-13755)***
T & K Printing, Brooklyn *Also called T&K Printing Inc* ***(G-2487)***
T & L Automatics Inc.......585 647-3717
770 Emerson St Rochester (14613) ***(G-13756)***
T & L Trading Co.......718 782-5550
17 Meserole St Brooklyn (11206) ***(G-2484)***
T & M Plating Inc.......212 967-1110
357 W 36th St Fl 7 New York (10018) ***(G-11414)***
T & R Knitting Mills Inc (PA).......718 497-4017
8000 Cooper Ave Ste 6 Glendale (11385) ***(G-5233)***
T & R Knitting Mills Inc.......212 840-8665
1410 Broadway Rm 401 New York (10018) ***(G-11415)***
T & Smoothie Inc.......631 804-6653
499 N Service Rd Ste 83 Patchogue (11772) ***(G-12513)***
T A S Sales Service LLC.......518 234-4919
105 Kenyon Rd Cobleskill (12043) ***(G-3500)***
T A Tool & Molding Inc.......631 293-0172
185 Marine St Farmingdale (11735) ***(G-4748)***

970 2020 Harris New York Manufacturers Directory (G-0000) Company's Geographic Section entry number

T C Dunham Paint Company Inc 914 969-4202
761 Nepperhan Ave Yonkers (10703) *(G-16351)*

T C I, Whitesboro *Also called Telecommunication Concepts (G-16083)*

T C Peters Printing Co Inc 315 724-4149
2336 W Whitesboro St Utica (13502) *(G-15296)*

T C Timber, Skaneateles *Also called Habermaass Corporation (G-14454)*

T E Q, Huntington Station *Also called Tequipment Inc (G-6264)*

T G M Products Inc 631 491-0515
90 Wyandanch Ave Unit E Wyandanch (11798) *(G-16247)*

T G S Inc 516 629-6905
6 Wildwood Ct Locust Valley (11560) *(G-7130)*

T J Ronan Paint Corp 718 292-1100
749 E 135th St Bronx (10454) *(G-1376)*

T J Signs Unlimited LLC (PA) 631 273-4800
327 New S Rd Islip (11751) *(G-6357)*

T L Diamond & Company Inc (PA) 212 249-6660
116 E 68th St Apt 5a New York (10065) *(G-11416)*

T L F Graphics Inc (PA) 585 272-5500
235 Metro Park Rochester (14623) *(G-13757)*

T L X, Plainview *Also called Xpress Printing Inc (G-12729)*

T Lemme Mechanical Inc 518 436-4136
1074 Broadway Menands (12204) *(G-7849)*

T M Design Screen Printing, Rochester *Also called Todd Walbridge (G-13768)*

T M I of New York, Brooklyn *Also called Technipoly Manufacturing Inc (G-2496)*

T M I Plastics Industries Inc 718 383-0363
28 Wythe Ave Brooklyn (11249) *(G-2485)*

T M International LLC 718 842-0949
413 Faile St 15 Bronx (10474) *(G-1377)*

T M Machine Inc 716 822-0817
176 Reading St Buffalo (14220) *(G-3001)*

T M W Diamonds Mfg Co (PA) 212 869-8444
15 W 47th St Ste 302 New York (10036) *(G-11417)*

T Mix Inc 646 379-6814
6217 5th Ave Brooklyn (11220) *(G-2486)*

T O Dey Service Corp 212 683-6300
151 W 46th St Fl 3 New York (10036) *(G-11418)*

T O Gronlund Company Inc 212 679-3535
200 Lexington Ave Rm 1515 New York (10016) *(G-11419)*

T R P Machine Inc 631 567-9620
35 Davinci Dr Ste B Bohemia (11716) *(G-1084)*

T Rj Shirts Inc 347 642-3071
3050 90th St East Elmhurst (11369) *(G-4111)*

T RS Great American Rest 516 294-1680
17 Hillside Ave Williston Park (11596) *(G-16149)*

T S B A Group Inc (PA) 718 565-6000
3830 Woodside Ave Sunnyside (11104) *(G-14775)*

T S O General Corp 631 952-5320
81 Emjay Blvd Unit 1 Brentwood (11717) *(G-1127)*

T S P Corp 585 768-6769
78 One Half Lake St Le Roy (14482) *(G-6907)*

T S Pink Corp 607 432-1100
139 Pony Farm Rd Oneonta (13820) *(G-12282)*

T Shore Products Ltd 315 252-9174
5 Eagle Dr Auburn (13021) *(G-497)*

T T I, Oriskany *Also called Terahertz Technologies Inc (G-12398)*

T V Trade Media Inc 212 288-3933
216 E 75th St Apt 1w New York (10021) *(G-11420)*

T&B Bakery Corp 646 642-4300
5870 56th St Maspeth (11378) *(G-7638)*

T&K Printing Inc 718 439-9454
262 44th St Brooklyn (11232) *(G-2487)*

T-Base Communications USA Inc 315 713-0013
806 Commerce Park Dr Ogdensburg (13669) *(G-12211)*

T-Company LLC 646 290-6365
16 Monitor Rd Smithtown (11787) *(G-14488)*

T-Rex Supply Corporation 516 308-0505
1 Fulton Ave Ste 120 Hempstead (11550) *(G-5850)*

T-S-K Electronics Inc 716 693-3916
908 Niagara Falls Blvd # 201 North Tonawanda (14120) *(G-12093)*

T-Shirt Factory Inc 845 454-2255
12 Fowler Ave Poughkeepsie (12603) *(G-12987)*

T-Shirt Graphics, Ballston Spa *Also called Sand Hill Industries Inc (G-586)*

Ta Chen International Inc 845 352-5300
17 Main St Ste 217 Monsey (10952) *(G-8051)*

Taam Tov Foods Inc 718 788-8880
188 28th St Brooklyn (11232) *(G-2488)*

Taazu Inc 212 618-1201
14 Wall St Fl 203420 New York (10005) *(G-11421)*

Taber Acquisition Corp 716 694-4000
455 Bryant St North Tonawanda (14120) *(G-12094)*

Taber Industries, North Tonawanda *Also called Taber Acquisition Corp (G-12094)*

Tabi Inc 347 701-1051
488 Onderdonk Ave Apt 1l Flushing (11385) *(G-4897)*

Table Tops Paper Corp 718 831-6440
47 Hall St Ste C-2 Brooklyn (11205) *(G-2489)*

Tablecloths For Granted Ltd 518 370-5481
510 Union St Schenectady (12305) *(G-14310)*

Tables Manufacturing, Edgewood *Also called Kinplex Corp (G-4274)*

Tablet Newspaper, The, Brooklyn *Also called Tablet Publishing Company Inc (G-2490)*

Tablet Publishing Company Inc 718 965-7333
1712 10th Ave Brooklyn (11215) *(G-2490)*

Tabrisse Collections Inc 212 921-1014
1412 Broadway New York (10018) *(G-11422)*

TAC Screw Products Inc 585 663-5840
170 Bennington Dr Rochester (14616) *(G-13758)*

Tackle Factory, Fillmore *Also called Cuba Specialty Mfg Co Inc (G-4793)*

Taconic, Petersburg *Also called Tonoga Inc (G-12600)*

Tactair Fluid Controls Inc 315 451-3928
4806 W Taft Rd Liverpool (13088) *(G-7044)*

Tactica International Inc (PA) 212 575-0500
11 W 42nd St New York (10036) *(G-11423)*

Tag Dental Implant Solutions, Valley Stream *Also called Total Dntl Implant Sltions LLC (G-15361)*

Tag Envelope Co Inc 718 389-6844
1419 128th St College Point (11356) *(G-3567)*

Tag Flange & Machining Inc 516 536-1300
3375 Royal Ave Oceanside (11572) *(G-12194)*

Tag Manufacturing, Brooklyn *Also called Schwartz Textile LLC (G-2389)*

Tahari Arthur S Levine, New York *Also called Tahari ASL LLC (G-11424)*

Tahari ASL LLC 212 763-2800
525 Fashion Ave Rm 701 New York (10018) *(G-11424)*

Tai Seng 718 399-6311
106 Lexington Ave Brooklyn (11238) *(G-2491)*

Tailorbyrd, New York *Also called Sanctuary Brands LLC (G-11129)*

Tailored Coatings Inc 716 893-4869
1800 Brdwy St Bldg 2a Buffalo (14212) *(G-3002)*

Tailored Sportsman LLC 646 366-8733
230 W 38th St Fl 6 New York (10018) *(G-11425)*

Takasago Intl Corp USA 845 751-0622
114 Commerce Dr S Harriman (10926) *(G-5547)*

Takeform Archtectural Graphics, Medina *Also called Quorum Group LLC (G-7744)*

Takeout Printing LLC 845 564-2609
610 Broadway Ste 222 Newburgh (12550) *(G-11888)*

Talas, Brooklyn *Also called Technical Library Service Inc (G-2495)*

Talisman Industries LLC 908 433-7116
237 Flatbush Ave Apt 3 New York (10007) *(G-11426)*

Talmu NY LLC 347 434-6700
266 47th St Brooklyn (11220) *(G-2492)*

Tam Ceramics Group of Ny LLC 716 278-9400
4511 Hyde Park Blvd Niagara Falls (14305) *(G-11984)*

Tam Ceramics LLC 716 278-9480
4511 Hyde Park Blvd Niagara Falls (14305) *(G-11985)*

Tambetti Inc 212 751-9584
48 W 48th St Ste 501 New York (10036) *(G-11427)*

Tami Great Food Corp 845 352-7901
22 Briarcliff Dr Monsey (10952) *(G-8052)*

Tamka Sport LLC 718 224-7820
225 Beverly Rd Douglaston (11363) *(G-4030)*

Tamperproof Screw Company Inc 516 931-1616
30 Laurel St Hicksville (11801) *(G-5951)*

Tamsen Z LLC 212 292-6412
350 Park Ave Fl 4 New York (10022) *(G-11428)*

Tanagro Jewelry Corp 212 753-2817
36 W 44th St Ste 1101 New York (10036) *(G-11429)*

Tandy Leather Factory Inc 845 480-3588
298 Main St Nyack (10960) *(G-12146)*

Tangent Machine & Tool Corp 631 249-3088
108 Gazza Blvd Farmingdale (11735) *(G-4749)*

Tango Publishing Corporation 646 773-3060
101 W 79th St Apt 2g New York (10024) *(G-11430)*

Tangram Company LLC 631 758-0460
125 Corporate Dr Holtsville (11742) *(G-6055)*

Tannens 718 292-4646
363 E 149th St Bronx (10455) *(G-1378)*

Tao Group LLC 646 625-4818
355 W 16th St New York (10011) *(G-11431)*

Tap2play LLC 914 960-6232
110 W 40th St Rm 1902 New York (10018) *(G-11432)*

Tape Printers Inc 631 249-5585
155 Allen Blvd Ste A Farmingdale (11735) *(G-4750)*

Tape Systems Inc 914 668-3700
630 S Columbus Ave Mount Vernon (10550) *(G-8181)*

Tape-It Inc 631 243-4100
233 N Fehr Way Bay Shore (11706) *(G-721)*

Tapemaker Supply Company LLC 914 693-3407
22 Sherbrooke Rd Hartsdale (10530) *(G-5569)*

Tapestries Etc, New York *Also called Vander Heyden Woodworking (G-11639)*

Tapestry Inc 212 615-2082
515 W 33rd St New York (10001) *(G-11433)*

Tapestry Inc (PA) 212 594-1850
10 Hudson Yards New York (10001) *(G-11434)*

Tapinator Inc (PA) 914 930-6232
110 W 40th St Rm 1902 New York (10018) *(G-11435)*

Tappan Wire & Cable Inc (HQ) 845 353-9000
100 Bradley Hill Rd Blauvelt (10913) *(G-935)*

Tara Rific Screen Printing Inc 718 583-6864
4197 Park Ave Bronx (10457) *(G-1379)*

Target Rock, Farmingdale *Also called Curtiss-Wright Flow Control (G-4607)*

Targetprocess Inc (PA) 877 718-2617
1325 Millersport Hwy Amherst (14221) *(G-247)*

Targum Press USA Inc 248 355-2266
1946 59th St Brooklyn (11204) *(G-2493)*

Taro Manufacturing Company Inc......315 252-9430
114 Clark St Auburn (13021) ***(G-498)***
Tarrytown Bakery Inc......914 631-0209
150 Wildey St Tarrytown (10591) ***(G-15063)***
Tarsia Technical Industries......631 231-8322
93 Marcus Blvd Hauppauge (11788) ***(G-5781)***
Tarsier Ltd......646 880-8680
1365 York Ave Apt 23e New York (10021) ***(G-11436)***
Tate's Bake Shop, East Moriches *Also called Tates Wholesale LLC* ***(G-4140)***
Tates Wholesale LLC......631 780-6511
62 Pine St East Moriches (11940) ***(G-4140)***
Tatra Mfg Corporation......631 691-1184
30 Railroad Ave Copiague (11726) ***(G-3682)***
Tattersall Industries LLC......518 381-4270
2125 Technology Dr Schenectady (12308) ***(G-14311)***
Taumel Assembly Systems, Patterson *Also called Taumel Metalforming Corp* ***(G-12521)***
Taumel Metalforming Corp......845 878-3100
25 Jon Barrett Rd Patterson (12563) ***(G-12521)***
Taylor & Francis Group LLC......212 216-7800
52 Vanderbilt Ave Fl 11 New York (10017) ***(G-11437)***
Taylor Brothers Inc......607 625-2828
6 Jacobs Rd Apalachin (13732) ***(G-362)***
Taylor Communications Inc......937 221-1303
155 Pinelawn Rd Ste 120s Melville (11747) ***(G-7828)***
Taylor Communications Inc......718 361-1000
3200 Skillman Ave Fl 3 Long Island City (11101) ***(G-7378)***
Taylor Communications Inc......718 352-0220
1600 Stewart Ave Ste 301 Westbury (11590) ***(G-15927)***
Taylor Concrete Products Inc......315 788-2191
20475 Old Rome Rd Watertown (13601) ***(G-15589)***
Taylor Copy Services, Syracuse *Also called Constas Printing Corporation* ***(G-14859)***
Taylor Devices Inc (PA)......716 694-0800
90 Taylor Dr North Tonawanda (14120) ***(G-12095)***
Taylor Made Group LLC......518 725-0681
93 South Blvd Gloversville (12078) ***(G-5294)***
Taylor Metalworks Inc......716 662-3113
3925 California Rd Orchard Park (14127) ***(G-12378)***
Taylor Precision Machining......607 535-3101
3921 Dug Rd Montour Falls (14865) ***(G-8077)***
Taylor Products Inc (PA)......518 773-9312
66 Kingsboro Ave Gloversville (12078) ***(G-5295)***
Taylor Tank Company Inc......718 434-1300
848 E 43rd St Brooklyn (11210) ***(G-2494)***
Tb, Rochester *Also called Turner Bellows Inc* ***(G-13778)***
Tbhl International LLC......212 799-2007
252 W 38th St Fl 11 New York (10018) ***(G-11438)***
Tc Transcontinental USA Inc......818 993-4767
67 Irving Pl Fl 2 New York (10003) ***(G-11439)***
Tchnologies N MRC Ameerica LLC......716 822-4300
25 Roberts Ave Buffalo (14206) ***(G-3003)***
Tcmf Inc......607 724-1094
69-93 Eldredge St Binghamton (13901) ***(G-912)***
TCS Electronics Inc......585 337-4301
1124 Corporate Dr Farmington (14425) ***(G-4779)***
TCS Industries Inc......585 426-1160
400 Trabold Rd Rochester (14624) ***(G-13759)***
Tdg Acquistion Co LLC (PA)......585 500-4625
336 Summit Point Dr Ste 1 Henrietta (14467) ***(G-5860)***
Tdg Operations LLC......212 779-4300
200 Lexington Ave Rm 1314 New York (10016) ***(G-11440)***
Tdk USA Corporation (HQ)......516 535-2600
455 Rxr Plz Uniondale (11556) ***(G-15233)***
Tdo Sandblasting, Roosevelt *Also called Tropical Driftwood Originals* ***(G-14034)***
TDS Fitness Equipment Corp......607 733-6789
160 Home St Elmira (14904) ***(G-4370)***
TDS Foundry Corporation......607 733-6789
160 Home St Elmira (14904) ***(G-4371)***
TDS Woodcraft, Staten Island *Also called TDS Woodworking Inc* ***(G-14719)***
TDS Woodworking Inc......718 442-5298
104 Port Richmond Ave Staten Island (10302) ***(G-14719)***
Tdy Industries LLC......716 433-4411
695 Ohio St Lockport (14094) ***(G-7110)***
Te Connectivity Corporation......585 785-2500
2245 Brighton Henrta Twn Rochester (14623) ***(G-13760)***
Te Neues Publishing Co LP (PA)......212 627-9090
350 7th Ave Rm 301 New York (10001) ***(G-11441)***
Tea & Coffee Trade Journal, Long Island City *Also called Lockwood Trade Journal Co Inc* ***(G-7278)***
Tea Life LLC......516 365-7711
73 Plandome Rd Manhasset (11030) ***(G-7542)***
Teachergaming LLC......866 644-9323
809 W 181st St 231 New York (10033) ***(G-11442)***
Teachley LLC......347 552-1272
25 Broadway Fl 13 New York (10004) ***(G-11443)***
Teale Machine Company Inc......585 244-6700
1425 University Ave Rochester (14607) ***(G-13761)***
Tealeafs......716 688-8022
5416 Main St Williamsville (14221) ***(G-16143)***
Team Builders Inc......718 979-1005
88 New Dorp Plz S Ste 303 Staten Island (10306) ***(G-14720)***
Team Builders Management, Staten Island *Also called Team Builders Inc* ***(G-14720)***
Team Fabrication Inc......716 655-4038
1055 Davis Rd West Falls (14170) ***(G-15762)***
Tebbens Steel LLC......631 208-8330
800 Burman Blvd Calverton (11933) ***(G-3089)***
TEC - Crete Transit Mix Corp......718 657-6880
4673 Metropolitan Ave Ridgewood (11385) ***(G-13163)***
TEC Glass & Inst LLC......315 926-7639
4211 Sunset Dr Marion (14505) ***(G-7576)***
Tech Lube, Yaphank *Also called Tribology Inc* ***(G-16275)***
Tech Park Food Services LLC......585 295-1250
789 Elmgrove Rd Rochester (14624) ***(G-13762)***
Tech Products Inc......718 442-4900
105 Willow Ave Staten Island (10305) ***(G-14721)***
Tech Software LLC......516 986-3050
270 Spagnoli Rd Ste 102 Melville (11747) ***(G-7829)***
Tech Times LLC......646 599-7201
61 Broadway Ste A New York (10006) ***(G-11444)***
Tech Valley Printing, Watervliet *Also called General Business Supply Inc* ***(G-15602)***
Techgrass......646 719-2000
77 Water St New York (10005) ***(G-11445)***
Technic Inc......516 349-0700
111 E Ames Ct Unit 2 Plainview (11803) ***(G-12718)***
Technical Library Service Inc......212 219-0770
330 Morgan Ave Brooklyn (11211) ***(G-2495)***
Technical Packaging Inc......516 223-2300
2365 Milburn Ave Baldwin (11510) ***(G-537)***
Technical Precision Corp......845 473-0548
1 Vanderbilt Ave Pleasantville (10570) ***(G-12800)***
Technical Service Industries......212 719-9800
17506 Devonshire Rd 5n Jamaica (11432) ***(G-6478)***
Technical Wldg Fabricators LLC......518 463-2229
27 Thatcher St Albany (12207) ***(G-134)***
Techniflo Corporation......716 741-3500
9730 County Rd Clarence Center (14032) ***(G-3449)***
Technimetal Precision Inds......631 231-8900
195 Marcus Blvd Hauppauge (11788) ***(G-5782)***
Technipoly Manufacturing Inc......718 383-0363
20 Wythe Ave Brooklyn (11249) ***(G-2496)***
Technologies Application LLC......607 275-0345
3736 Kellogg Rd Cortland (13045) ***(G-3790)***
Technology Desking Inc......212 257-6998
39 Broadway Rm 1640 New York (10006) ***(G-11446)***
Technology Partners Inc......518 621-2993
1399 New Scotland Rd # 499 Slingerlands (12159) ***(G-14468)***
Technopaving New York Inc......631 351-6472
270 Broadway Huntington Station (11746) ***(G-6263)***
Tecmotiv (usa) Inc......716 282-1211
1500 James Ave Niagara Falls (14305) ***(G-11986)***
Tecnofil Chenango SAC......607 674-4441
40 S Main St Sherburne (13460) ***(G-14396)***
Tecnolux Incorporated......718 369-3900
103 14th St Brooklyn (11215) ***(G-2497)***
Tecsys US Inc (HQ)......800 922-8649
1001 Ave Of The Amricas 4 New York (10018) ***(G-11447)***
Tectonic Flooring USA LLC......212 686-2700
1140 1st Ave Frnt 1 New York (10065) ***(G-11448)***
Tectran Inc......800 776-5549
2345 Walden Ave Ste 100 Cheektowaga (14225) ***(G-3364)***
Tectran Mfg Inc (HQ)......800 776-5549
2345 Walden Ave Ste 1 Buffalo (14225) ***(G-3004)***
Ted Westbrook......716 625-4443
4736 Mapleton Rd Lockport (14094) ***(G-7111)***
Tee Pee Auto Sales Corp......516 338-9333
52 Swan St Westbury (11590) ***(G-15928)***
Tee Pee Fence & Rail, Jamaica *Also called Tee Pee Fence and Railing* ***(G-6479)***
Tee Pee Fence and Railing......718 658-8323
9312 179th Pl Jamaica (11433) ***(G-6479)***
Tee Pee Signs, Hempstead *Also called Jem Sign Corp* ***(G-5840)***
Teen Vogue, New York *Also called Conde Nast Entertainment LLC* ***(G-9079)***
Teena Creations Inc......516 867-1500
10 Hanse Ave Freeport (11520) ***(G-5027)***
Tegna Inc......716 849-2222
259 Delaware Ave Buffalo (14202) ***(G-3005)***
Tek Precision Co Ltd......631 242-0330
205 W Industry Ct Deer Park (11729) ***(G-3941)***
Teka Fine Line Brushes Inc......718 692-2928
3691 Bedford Ave Brooklyn (11229) ***(G-2498)***
Teka Precision Inc......845 753-1900
251 Mountainview Ave Nyack (10960) ***(G-12147)***
Teknic Inc......585 784-7454
115 Victor Heights Pkwy Victor (14564) ***(G-15436)***
Tel Tech International......516 393-5174
200 Broadhollow Rd # 207 Melville (11747) ***(G-7830)***
Tel Technology Center Amer LLC (HQ)......512 424-4200
255 Fuller Rd Ste 244 Albany (12203) ***(G-135)***
Tel-Tru Inc (PA)......585 295-0225
408 Saint Paul St Rochester (14605) ***(G-13763)***
Tel-Tru Manufacturing Company, Rochester *Also called Tel-Tru Inc* ***(G-13763)***
Tele-Pak Inc......845 426-2300
421 Route 59 Ste 7 Monsey (10952) ***(G-8053)***
Tele-Vue Optics Inc......845 469-4551
32 Elkay Dr Chester (10918) ***(G-3390)***

Telebyte Inc (PA) 631 423-3232
355 Marcus Blvd Ste 2 Hauppauge (11788) *(G-5783)*

Telechemische Inc 845 561-3237
222 Dupont Ave Newburgh (12550) *(G-11889)*

Telecommunication Concepts 315 736-8523
329 Oriskany Blvd Whitesboro (13492) *(G-16083)*

Teledyne Lecroy Inc (HQ) 845 425-2000
700 Chestnut Ridge Rd Chestnut Ridge (10977) *(G-3399)*

Telemergency Ltd 914 629-4222
3 Quincy Ln White Plains (10605) *(G-16066)*

Telephone Sales & Service Co (PA) 212 233-8505
132 W Broadway New York (10013) *(G-11449)*

Telephonics Corporation 631 755-7659
815 Broadhollow Rd Farmingdale (11735) *(G-4751)*

Telephonics Corporation 631 549-6000
770 Park Ave Huntington (11743) *(G-6226)*

Telephonics Corporation (HQ) 631 755-7000
815 Broadhollow Rd Farmingdale (11735) *(G-4752)*

Telephonics Corporation 631 755-7000
815 Broadhollow Rd Farmingdale (11735) *(G-4753)*

Telephonics Corporation 631 470-8800
780 Park Ave Huntington (11743) *(G-6227)*

Telephonics Tlsi Corp 631 470-8854
780 Park Ave Huntington (11743) *(G-6228)*

Telesca-Heyman Inc 212 534-3442
304 E 94th St 6 New York (10128) *(G-11450)*

Teller Printing Corp 718 486-3662
317 Division Ave Brooklyn (11211) *(G-2499)*

Telmar Information Services (PA) 212 725-3000
711 3rd Ave Rm 1500 New York (10017) *(G-11451)*

Telog Instruments Inc 585 742-3000
830 Canning Pkwy Victor (14564) *(G-15437)*

Telxon Corporation (HQ) 631 738-2400
1 Zebra Plz Holtsville (11742) *(G-6056)*

Tempco Glass Fabrication LLC 718 461-6888
13110 Maple Ave Flushing (11355) *(G-4898)*

Temper Corporation (PA) 518 853-3467
544 Persse Rd Fonda (12068) *(G-4912)*

Temper Corporation 518 853-3467
544 Persse Rd Fonda (12068) *(G-4913)*

Temple Bar, New York *Also called Lafayette Pub Inc (G-10163)*

Temple St Clair LLC 212 219-8664
594 Broadway Rm 306 New York (10012) *(G-11452)*

Tempo Industries Inc 516 334-6900
90 Hopper St Westbury (11590) *(G-15929)*

Tempo Paris, New York *Also called 6th Avenue Showcase Inc (G-8407)*

Temptu Inc 718 937-9503
522 46th Ave Ste B Long Island City (11101) *(G-7379)*

Temrex Corporation (PA) 516 868-6221
300 Buffalo Ave Freeport (11520) *(G-5028)*

Temrick Inc 631 567-8860
1605 Sycamore Ave Unit B Bohemia (11716) *(G-1085)*

Tenney Media Group (PA) 315 853-5569
28 Robinson Rd Clinton (13323) *(G-3486)*

Tennyson Machine Co Inc 914 668-5468
535 S 5th Ave Mount Vernon (10550) *(G-8182)*

Tens Machine Company Inc 631 981-3321
800 Grundy Ave Holbrook (11741) *(G-6026)*

Tensator Group, Bay Shore *Also called Tensator Inc (G-722)*

Tensator Inc 631 666-0300
260 Spur Dr S Bay Shore (11706) *(G-722)*

Tent and Table Com LLC 716 570-0258
2845 Bailey Ave Buffalo (14215) *(G-3006)*

Tentina Window Fashions Inc 631 957-9585
1186 Route 109 Lindenhurst (11757) *(G-6980)*

Tepco, Pleasantville *Also called Technical Precision Corp (G-12800)*

Tequipment Inc 516 922-3508
7 Norden Ln Huntington Station (11746) *(G-6264)*

Terahertz Technologies Inc 315 736-3642
169 Clear Rd Oriskany (13424) *(G-12398)*

Terani Couture, New York *Also called Countess Corporation (G-9110)*

Terbo Ltd 718 847-2860
8905 130th St Richmond Hill (11418) *(G-13127)*

Termatec Molding Inc 315 483-4150
28 Foley Dr Sodus (14551) *(G-14493)*

Terphane Holdings LLC (HQ) 585 657-5800
2754 W Park Dr Bloomfield (14469) *(G-948)*

Terphane LLC 585 657-5800
2754 W Park Dr Bloomfield (14469) *(G-949)*

Terra Enrgy Resource Tech Inc (PA) 212 286-9197
99 Park Ave Ph A New York (10016) *(G-11453)*

Terrabilt Inc 914 341-1500
619 Center Ave Mamaroneck (10543) *(G-7524)*

Terrance Brown 716 648-6171
4625 Ironwood Dr Hamburg (14075) *(G-5523)*

Terranua US Corp 212 852-9028
535 5th Ave Fl 4 New York (10017) *(G-11454)*

Terrapin Station Ltd 716 874-6677
1172 Hertel Ave Buffalo (14216) *(G-3007)*

Terrells Potato Chip Co Inc 315 437-2786
218 Midler Park Dr Syracuse (13206) *(G-15011)*

Tesla Motors Inc 212 206-1204
10 Columbus Cir Ste 102d New York (10019) *(G-11455)*

Tessy Plastics Corp (PA) 315 689-3924
700 Visions Dr Skaneateles (13152) *(G-14457)*

Tessy Plastics Corp 315 689-3924
488 State Route 5 Elbridge (13060) *(G-4298)*

Testa Communications 516 767-2500
25 Willowdale Ave Port Washington (11050) *(G-12929)*

Testori Interiors Inc 518 298-4400
107 Lwrnce Paqtte Indstrl Champlain (12919) *(G-3317)*

Texas Brine Company LLC 585 495-6228
1346 Saltvale Rd Wyoming (14591) *(G-16252)*

Texas Home Security Inc (PA) 516 747-2100
50 Rose Pl New Hyde Park (11040) *(G-8296)*

Texport Fabrics Corp 212 226-6066
495 Broadway Fl 7 New York (10012) *(G-11456)*

Texray, New York *Also called Z-Ply Corp (G-11814)*

Textured Fd Innvations Tfi LLC 515 731-3663
552 Westbury Ave Carle Place (11514) *(G-3182)*

TG Peppe Inc 516 239-7852
299 Rockaway Pqtte Tpke Unit B Lawrence (11559) *(G-6893)*

Tg Polymers Inc 585 670-9427
667 Hills Pond Rd Webster (14580) *(G-15656)*

Tg Therapeutics Inc 212 554-4484
2 Gansevoort St Fl 9 New York (10014) *(G-11457)*

Tgp Flying Cloud Holdings LLC 646 829-3900
565 5th Ave Fl 27 New York (10017) *(G-11458)*

Thales Laser SA 585 223-2370
78 Schuyler Baldwin Dr Fairport (14450) *(G-4527)*

Thalian, New York *Also called F & J Designs Inc (G-9454)*

Thalle Industries Inc (PA) 914 762-3415
51 Route 100 Briarcliff Manor (10510) *(G-1162)*

Thatcher Company New York Inc 315 589-9330
4135 Rte 104 Williamson (14589) *(G-16113)*

Thats My Girl Inc (PA) 212 695-0020
80 39th St Ste 501 Brooklyn (11232) *(G-2500)*

Thayer Tool & Die Inc 716 782-4841
1718 Blckvlle Watts Flts Ashville (14710) *(G-411)*

The Caldwell Manufacturing Co (PA) 585 352-3790
2605 Manitou Rd Ste 100 Rochester (14624) *(G-13764)*

The Caldwell Manufacturing Co 585 352-2803
Holland Industrial Park Victor (14564) *(G-15438)*

The Centro Company Inc 914 533-2200
215 Silver Spring Rd South Salem (10590) *(G-14525)*

The Chocolate Shop 716 882-5055
871 Niagara St Buffalo (14213) *(G-3008)*

THE Design Group Inc 212 681-1548
240 Madison Ave Fl 8 New York (10016) *(G-11459)*

The Earth Times Foundation 718 297-0488
195 Adams St Apt 6j Brooklyn (11201) *(G-2501)*

The Fisherman, Shirley *Also called L I F Publishing Corp (G-14423)*

The Fisherman, Shirley *Also called Njf Publishing Corp (G-14426)*

The Gramecy Group 518 348-1325
4 Gramecy Ct Clifton Park (12065) *(G-3476)*

The Hacker Quarterly, Saint James *Also called 2600 Enterprises Inc (G-14107)*

The Kingsbury Printing Co Inc 518 747-6606
632 County Line Rd Queensbury (12804) *(G-13058)*

The Observer, Dundee *Also called Finger Lakes Media Inc (G-4046)*

The Observer, Dunkirk *Also called Observer Daily Sunday Newsppr (G-4062)*

The Printing Company, Albany *Also called Printing Resources Inc (G-119)*

The PRS Group Inc (PA) 315 431-0511
5010 Campuswood Dr # 204 East Syracuse (13057) *(G-4242)*

The River Reporter, Narrowsburg *Also called Stuart Communications Inc (G-8211)*

The Sandhar Corp 718 523-0819
16427 Highland Ave Jamaica (11432) *(G-6480)*

The Smoke House of Catskills 845 246-8767
724 Route 212 Saugerties (12477) *(G-14215)*

The Spirited Shipper, Long Island City *Also called Platinum Sales Promotion Inc (G-7327)*

Theautopartsshop.com, Hauppauge *Also called Ebc Technologies LLC (G-5644)*

Thego, Calverton *Also called Acme Marine Hoist Inc (G-3076)*

Thego Corporation 631 776-2472
2 Mooring Dr Bellport (11713) *(G-808)*

Thehuffingtonpostcom Inc (HQ) 212 245-7844
770 Broadway Fl 4 New York (10003) *(G-11460)*

Theirapp LLC 212 896-1255
950 3rd Ave Ste 190 New York (10022) *(G-11461)*

Themis Chimney Inc 718 937-4716
190 Morgan Ave Brooklyn (11237) *(G-2502)*

Theodore A Rapp Associates 845 469-2100
728 Craigville Rd Chester (10918) *(G-3391)*

Theodosiou Inc 718 728-6800
3214 49th St Long Island City (11103) *(G-7380)*

Theory LLC 212 762-2300
1114 Avenue Of The Americ New York (10036) *(G-11462)*

Theory LLC 212 879-0265
1157 Madison Ave New York (10028) *(G-11463)*

Therm Incorporated 607 272-8500
1000 Hudson Street Ext Ithaca (14850) *(G-6412)*

Thermacon Tank Insulation, Jericho *Also called Vertarib Inc (G-6597)*

Thermal Foams/Syracuse Inc (PA) 716 874-6474
2101 Kenmore Ave Buffalo (14207) *(G-3009)*

Thermal Foams/Syracuse Inc 315 699-8734
6173 S Bay Rd Cicero (13039) *(G-3424)*

A
L
P
H
A
B
E
T
I
C

Thermal Process Cnstr Co 631 293-6400
  19 Engineers Ln Farmingdale (11735) *(G-4754)*
Thermal Tech Doors Inc (PA) 516 745-0100
  576 Brook St Garden City (11530) *(G-5118)*
Thermo Cidtec Inc 315 451-9410
  101 Commerce Blvd Liverpool (13088) *(G-7045)*
Thermo Fisher Scientific Inc 585 899-7780
  1935 Penfield Rd Penfield (14526) *(G-12575)*
Thermo Fisher Scientific Inc 716 774-6700
  3175 Staley Rd Grand Island (14072) *(G-5345)*
Thermo Fisher Scientific Inc 585 458-8008
  1999 Mnt Rd Blvd 1-3 Rochester (14615) *(G-13765)*
Thermo Fisher Scientific Inc 585 899-7610
  75 Panorama Creek Dr Rochester (14625) *(G-13766)*
Thermoaura Inc 518 813-4997
  132b Railroad Ave Ste B Albany (12205) *(G-136)*
Thermold Corporation 315 697-3924
  7059 Harp Rd Canastota (13032) *(G-3158)*
Thermopatch Corporation (PA) 315 446-8110
  2204 Erie Blvd E Syracuse (13224) *(G-15012)*
Theskimm Inc 646 213-4754
  50 W 23rd St Ste 501 New York (10010) *(G-11464)*
Thestreet Inc (HQ) 212 321-5000
  14 Wall St Fl 15 New York (10005) *(G-11465)*
Thewritedeal, New York *Also called Dezawy LLC (G-9214)*
Thing Daemon Inc 917 746-9895
  57 Bond St Frnt A New York (10012) *(G-11466)*
Think Green Junk Removal Inc 845 297-7771
  29 Meadow Wood Ln Wappingers Falls (12590) *(G-15499)*
Think Tank, New York *Also called City and State Ny LLC (G-9016)*
Thirsty Owl Wine Company Inc 607 869-5805
  6861 State Route 89 Ovid (14521) *(G-12427)*
Thistle Hill Weavers 518 284-2729
  143 Baxter Rd Cherry Valley (13320) *(G-3368)*
Thom McGinnes Excavating Plbg, Le Roy *Also called T S P Corp (G-6907)*
Thomas C Wilson, Long Island City *Also called Thomas C Wilson LLC (G-7381)*
Thomas C Wilson LLC 718 729-3360
  2111 44th Ave Long Island City (11101) *(G-7381)*
Thomas Electronics Inc (PA) 315 923-2051
  208 Davis Pkwy Clyde (14433) *(G-3495)*
Thomas Enterprise Solutions, New York *Also called Thomas Publishing Company
LLC (G-11468)*
Thomas F Egan 607 669-4822
  570 Hance Rd Binghamton (13903) *(G-913)*
Thomas Group Inc 212 947-6400
  131 Varick St Rm 1016 New York (10013) *(G-11467)*
Thomas Group, The, New York *Also called Thomas Group Inc (G-11467)*
Thomas Jefferson Press, Port Jefferson *Also called Pace Walkers of America Inc (G-12843)*
Thomas Matthews Wdwkg Ltd 631 287-3657
  15 Powell Ave Southampton (11968) *(G-14539)*
Thomas Matthews Wdwkg Ltd (PA) 631 287-2023
  225 Ocean View Pkwy Southampton (11968) *(G-14540)*
Thomas Publishing Company LLC (PA) 212 695-0500
  5 Penn Plz Fl 8 New York (10001) *(G-11468)*
Thomas Publishing Company LLC 212 695-0500
  5 Penn Plz Fl 9 New York (10001) *(G-11469)*
Thomas Publishing Company LLC 212 695-0500
  5 Penn Plz Fl 8 New York (10001) *(G-11470)*
Thomas Publishing Company LLC 212 695-0500
  5 Penn Plz Fl 8 New York (10001) *(G-11471)*
Thomas R Schul TEC GL & Inst, Marion *Also called TEC Glass & Inst LLC (G-7576)*
Thomas Sasson Co Inc 212 697-4998
  555 5th Ave Rm 1900 New York (10017) *(G-11472)*
Thompson Ferrier LLC 212 244-2212
  230 5th Ave Ste 1004 New York (10001) *(G-11473)*
Thompson Group, Troy *Also called Pitney Bowes Software Inc (G-15179)*
Thompson Overhead Door Co Inc 718 788-2470
  47 16th St Brooklyn (11215) *(G-2503)*
Thomson Industries Inc (PA) 716 691-9100
  45 Hazelwood Dr Amherst (14228) *(G-248)*
Thomson Press (india) Limited 646 318-0369
  4 Court Sq Ste 3 Long Island City (11101) *(G-7382)*
Thomson Reuters Corporation 212 393-9461
  500 Pearl St New York (10007) *(G-11474)*
Thomson Reuters Corporation (HQ) 646 223-4000
  3 Times Sq New York (10036) *(G-11475)*
Thornwillow Press Ltd 212 980-0738
  57 W 58th St Ste 11e New York (10019) *(G-11476)*
Thornwood Products Ltd 914 769-9161
  401 Claremont Ave Ste 7 Thornwood (10594) *(G-15071)*
Thousand Island Diamond Center, Watertown *Also called Watertown 1785 LLC (G-15591)*
Thousand Island Ready Mix Con 315 686-3203
  38760 State Route 180 La Fargeville (13656) *(G-6735)*
Thousand Islands Printing Co. 315 482-2581
  45501 St Rt 12 Alexandria Bay (13607) *(G-180)*
Thousand Islands Sun, Alexandria Bay *Also called Thousand Islands Printing Co (G-180)*
Thousand Islands Winery LLC 315 482-9306
  43298 Seaway Ave Ste 1 Alexandria Bay (13607) *(G-181)*
Thread Check Inc 631 231-1515
  390 Oser Ave Ste 2 Hauppauge (11788) *(G-5784)*

Thread LLC (PA) 212 414-8844
  26 W 17th St Rm 301 New York (10011) *(G-11477)*
Three Brothers Winery, Geneva *Also called Negys New Land Vinyrd Winery (G-5160)*
Three Five III-V Materials Inc 212 213-8290
  19 W 21st St Rm 203 New York (10010) *(G-11478)*
Three Gems Inc 516 248-0388
  2201 Hillside Ave New Hyde Park (11040) *(G-8297)*
Three Point Ventures LLC 585 697-3444
  3495 Winton Pl Ste E120 Rochester (14623) *(G-13767)*
Three Star Offset Printing 516 867-8223
  188 N Main St Freeport (11520) *(G-5029)*
Three Star Supply, Jamaica *Also called City Mason Corp (G-6434)*
Three V, Brooklyn *Also called 3v Company Inc (G-1417)*
Three Village Times, Mineola *Also called Westbury Times (G-8003)*
Thuro Metal Products Inc (PA) 631 435-0444
  21-25 Grand Blvd N Brentwood (11717) *(G-1128)*
Thyssenkrupp Materials NA Inc 585 279-0000
  19 Ransier Dr West Seneca (14224) *(G-15855)*
TI Gotham Inc 212 522-1212
  1271 Ave Of The Americas New York (10020) *(G-11479)*
TI Gotham Inc 212 522-1633
  135 W 50th St New York (10020) *(G-11480)*
TI Gotham Inc (HQ) 212 522-1212
  225 Liberty St New York (10281) *(G-11481)*
TI Gotham Inc 212 522-0361
  1271 Ave Of The Amer Sb7 New York (10020) *(G-11482)*
TI Group Auto Systems LLC 315 568-7042
  240 Fall St Seneca Falls (13148) *(G-14373)*
Tia Lattrell 845 373-9494
  13 Powder House Rd Amenia (12501) *(G-203)*
Tibana Finishing Inc 718 417-5375
  7107 65th Pl Apt 1l Glendale (11385) *(G-5234)*
Tibco Software Inc 646 495-2600
  120 W 45th St Fl 18 New York (10036) *(G-11483)*
Tibro Water Technologies Ltd 647 426-3415
  106 E Seneca St Unit 25 Sherrill (13461) *(G-14408)*
Tic TAC Toes Mfg Corp 518 773-8187
  1 Hamilton St Gloversville (12078) *(G-5296)*
Tickle Hill Winery 607 546-7740
  3831 Ball Diamond Rd Hector (14841) *(G-5829)*
Ticonderoga Mch & Wldg Corp 518 585-7444
  55 Race Track Rd Ticonderoga (12883) *(G-15077)*
Ticonium Division, Albany *Also called Cmp Industries LLC (G-64)*
Ticoniun, Albany *Also called Cmp Export Co Inc (G-63)*
Tie King Inc (PA) 718 768-8484
  243 44th St Brooklyn (11232) *(G-2504)*
Tie King Inc 212 714-9611
  42 W 38th St Rm 1200 New York (10018) *(G-11484)*
Tiedemann Waldemar Inc 716 875-5665
  1720 Military Rd Ste 2 Buffalo (14217) *(G-3010)*
Tien Wah Press, New York *Also called Twp America Inc (G-11567)*
Tiffen Co, The, Hauppauge *Also called Tiffen Company LLC (G-5785)*
Tiffen Company LLC 631 273-2500
  80 Oser Ave Hauppauge (11788) *(G-5785)*
Tiffen Company LLC (PA) 631 273-2500
  90 Oser Ave Hauppauge (11788) *(G-5786)*
Tiga Holdings Inc 845 838-3000
  74 Dennings Ave Beacon (12508) *(G-757)*
Tiger 21 LLC 212 360-1700
  1995 Broadway Fl 6 New York (10023) *(G-11485)*
Tiger J LLC 212 465-9300
  1430 Broadway Rm 1900 New York (10018) *(G-11486)*
Tiger Supply Inc 631 293-2700
  99 Sherwood Ave Farmingdale (11735) *(G-4755)*
Tii Industries Inc 631 789-5000
  1385 Akron St Copiague (11726) *(G-3683)*
Tii Technologies Inc (HQ) 516 364-9300
  141 Rodeo Dr Edgewood (11717) *(G-4287)*
Tika Mobile Inc (PA) 646 650-5545
  902 Broadway Fl 6 New York (10010) *(G-11487)*
Tikamobile, New York *Also called Tika Mobile Inc (G-11487)*
Tiki Industries Inc 516 779-3629
  8 Tree Haven Ln Riverhead (11901) *(G-13190)*
Tilcon New York Inc 845 778-5591
  272 Berea Rd Walden (12586) *(G-15463)*
Tilcon New York Inc 845 638-3594
  66 Scratchup Rd Haverstraw (10927) *(G-5808)*
Tilcon New York Inc 845 480-3249
  3466 College Point Blvd Flushing (11354) *(G-4899)*
Tilcon New York Inc 845 615-0216
  2 Quarry Rd Goshen (10924) *(G-5314)*
Tilcon New York Inc 845 457-3158
  215 Montgomery Rd Montgomery (12549) *(G-8067)*
Tilcon New York Inc 845 942-0602
  Fort Of Elm Tomkins Cove (10986) *(G-15079)*
Tilcon New York Inc 845 358-3100
  1 Crusher Rd West Nyack (10994) *(G-15833)*
Tilcon New York Inc 845 562-3240
  50 Ruscitti Rd New Windsor (12553) *(G-8384)*
Tillsonburg Company USA Inc 267 994-8096
  37 W 39th St Rm 1101 New York (10018) *(G-11488)*

Tim Cretin Logging & Sawmill ... 315 946-4476
3607 Wayne Center Rd Lyons (14489) *(G-7453)*
Timber Frames Inc ... 585 374-6405
5557 State Route 64 Canandaigua (14424) *(G-3144)*
Timberbuilt Inc ... 716 337-0012
10821 Schaffstall Dr North Collins (14111) *(G-12029)*
Time Base Consoles, Edgewood *Also called Time Base Corporation* *(G-4288)*
Time Base Corporation (PA) ... 631 293-4068
170 Rodeo Dr Edgewood (11717) *(G-4288)*
Time Home Entertainment Inc ... 212 522-1212
1271 Ave Of The Americas New York (10020) *(G-11489)*
Time Inc Affluent Media Group (HQ) ... 212 382-5600
1120 Ave Of The Americas New York (10036) *(G-11490)*
Time Inc., New York *Also called TI Gotham Inc* *(G-11481)*
Time Out America LLC ... 646 432-3000
1540 Broadway Fl 42 New York (10036) *(G-11491)*
Time Out New York, New York *Also called Time Out America LLC* *(G-11491)*
Time Out New York Partners LP ... 646 432-3000
475 10th Ave Fl 12 New York (10018) *(G-11492)*
Time Precision, Carmel *Also called Precision Arms Inc* *(G-3190)*
Time Release Sciences Inc ... 716 823-4580
205 Dingens St Buffalo (14206) *(G-3011)*
Time Square Lighting, Stony Point *Also called Times Square Stage Ltg Co Inc* *(G-14749)*
Time To Know Inc ... 212 230-1210
655 3rd Ave Fl 21 New York (10017) *(G-11493)*
Time Warner Companies Inc (HQ) ... 212 484-8000
1 Time Warner Ctr Bsmt B New York (10019) *(G-11494)*
Time-Cap Laboratories Inc ... 631 753-9090
7 Michael Ave Farmingdale (11735) *(G-4756)*
Timeless Decor LLC ... 315 782-5759
22419 Fisher Rd Watertown (13601) *(G-15590)*
Timeless Fashions LLC ... 212 730-9328
100 United Nations Plz 28e New York (10017) *(G-11495)*
Timeless Frames, Watertown *Also called Lco Destiny LLC* *(G-15581)*
Timely Signs Inc ... 516 285-5339
2135 Linden Blvd Ste C Elmont (11003) *(G-4390)*
Timely Signs of Kingston Inc (PA) ... 845 331-8710
154 Clinton Ave Fl 1 Kingston (12401) *(G-6714)*
Times Beacon Record Newspapers (PA) ... 631 331-1154
185 Route 25a Ste 4 East Setauket (11733) *(G-4188)*
Times Center, The, New York *Also called New York Times Company* *(G-10606)*
Times Herald, The, Olean *Also called Bradford Publications Inc* *(G-12226)*
Times Herald-Record, Middletown *Also called Local Media Group Inc* *(G-7917)*
Times Herald-Record, Monticello *Also called Local Media Group Inc* *(G-8070)*
Times Herald-Record, Kingston *Also called Local Media Group Inc* *(G-6700)*
Times News Weekly, Ridgewood *Also called Ridgewood Times Prtg & Pubg* *(G-13158)*
Times One Inc ... 718 686-8988
5415 8th Ave Brooklyn (11220) *(G-2505)*
Times Review Newspaper Corp ... 631 354-8031
7780 Main Rd Mattituck (11952) *(G-7680)*
Times Square Stage Ltg Co Inc ... 845 947-3034
5 Holt Dr Stony Point (10980) *(G-14749)*
Times Square Studios Ltd ... 212 930-7720
1500 Broadway Fl 2 New York (10036) *(G-11496)*
Timesdigest, New York *Also called New York Times Company* *(G-10605)*
Timing Group LLC ... 646 878-2600
237 W 37th St Ste 1100 New York (10018) *(G-11497)*
Timothy L Simpson ... 518 234-1401
5819 State Route 145 Sharon Springs (13459) *(G-14384)*
Timtronics LLC ... 631 345-6509
35 Old Dock Rd Yaphank (11980) *(G-16274)*
Tin Box Company of America Inc (PA) ... 631 845-1600
216 Sherwood Ave Farmingdale (11735) *(G-4757)*
Tin Inc ... 607 775-1550
1240 Conklin Rd Conklin (13748) *(G-3629)*
Tin Rage Productions Inc ... 718 398-0787
123 7th Ave Brooklyn (11215) *(G-2506)*
Tint World ... 631 458-1999
3165 Route 112 Medford (11763) *(G-7725)*
Tio Foods LLC ... 917 946-1160
120 E 23rd St Fl 5 New York (10010) *(G-11498)*
Tio Gazpacho, New York *Also called Tio Foods LLC* *(G-11498)*
Tioga County Courier ... 607 687-0108
59 Church St Owego (13827) *(G-12438)*
Tioga County Waste Wood Recycl, Owego *Also called Wholesale Mulch & Sawdust Inc* *(G-12440)*
Tioga Hardwoods Inc (PA) ... 607 657-8686
12685 State Route 38 Berkshire (13736) *(G-821)*
Tioga Tool Inc (PA) ... 607 785-6005
160 Glendale Dr Endicott (13760) *(G-4474)*
Tips & Dies Inc ... 315 337-4161
505 Rome Industrial Park Rome (13440) *(G-13873)*
Tire Conversion Tech Inc ... 518 372-1600
874 Albany Shaker Rd Latham (12110) *(G-6876)*
Tis Ansonia LLC ... 518 272-4920
70 Cohoes Rd Watervliet (12189) *(G-15608)*
Tishcon Corp (PA) ... 516 333-3056
30 New York Ave Westbury (11590) *(G-15930)*
Tishcon Corp ... 516 333-3056
37 Brooklyn Ave Westbury (11590) *(G-15931)*
Tishcon Corp ... 516 333-3050
41 New York Ave Westbury (11590) *(G-15932)*
Tishcon Corp ... 516 333-3050
36 New York Ave Westbury (11590) *(G-15933)*
Titan Controls Inc ... 516 358-2407
122 W 27th St Fl 5 New York (10001) *(G-11499)*
Titan Steel Corp ... 315 656-7046
6333 N Kirkville Rd Kirkville (13082) *(G-6727)*
Titan Technology Group, New York *Also called Ttg LLC* *(G-11556)*
Titanium Dem Remediation Group ... 716 433-4100
4907 I D A Park Dr Lockport (14094) *(G-7112)*
Titanx Engine Cooling Inc ... 716 665-7129
2258 Allen Street Ext Jamestown (14701) *(G-6550)*
Titchener Iron Works Division, Binghamton *Also called Moro Corporation* *(G-899)*
Titherington Design & Mfg ... 518 324-2205
102 Sharron Ave Unit 1 Plattsburgh (12901) *(G-12785)*
Title of Work, New York *Also called Jonathan Meizler LLC* *(G-10022)*
Tito Moldmaker Co, New York *Also called Vasquez Tito* *(G-11648)*
Titus Mountain Sand & Grav LLC ... 518 483-3740
17 Junction Rd Malone (12953) *(G-7492)*
Tiziana Therapeutics Inc ... 646 396-4970
420 Lexington Ave # 2525 New York (10170) *(G-11500)*
Tj Signs Unlimited LLC ... 631 273-4800
327 New South Rd Hicksville (11801) *(G-5952)*
Tjb Sunshine Enterprises ... 518 384-6483
6 Redwood Dr Ballston Lake (12019) *(G-565)*
Tkm Technologies Inc ... 631 474-4700
623 Bicycle Path Ste 5 Port Jeff STA (11776) *(G-12839)*
TLC Industries Inc ... 718 596-2842
600 Smith St Brooklyn (11231) *(G-2507)*
TLC Vision (usa) Corporation ... 914 395-3949
150 Central Park Ave Hartsdale (10530) *(G-5570)*
TLC-Lc Inc (PA) ... 212 756-8900
115 E 57th St Bsmt New York (10022) *(G-11501)*
TLC-The Light Connection Inc ... 315 736-7384
132 Base Rd Oriskany (13424) *(G-12399)*
Tlf Graphics, Rochester *Also called T L F Graphics Inc* *(G-13757)*
Tli Import Inc ... 917 578-4568
151 2nd Ave Brooklyn (11215) *(G-2508)*
Tlsi Incorporated ... 631 470-8880
780 Park Ave Huntington (11743) *(G-6229)*
Tm Music Inc ... 212 471-4000
9 E 63rd St Apt 2-3 New York (10065) *(G-11502)*
Tmp Technologies Inc (PA) ... 716 895-6100
1200 Northland Ave Buffalo (14215) *(G-3012)*
Tmp Technologies Inc ... 585 495-6231
6110 Lamb Rd Wyoming (14591) *(G-16253)*
Tms Development, Westbury *Also called Vescom Structural Systems Inc* *(G-15938)*
Tms International LLC ... 315 253-8925
25 Quarry Rd Auburn (13021) *(G-499)*
Tms Structures Inc ... 646 740-7646
1745 Broadway Fl 17 New York (10019) *(G-11503)*
Tntpaving ... 607 372-4911
1077 Taft Ave Endicott (13760) *(G-4475)*
To Dey, New York *Also called T O Dey Service Corp* *(G-11418)*
Tobay Printing Co Inc ... 631 842-3300
1361 Marconi Blvd Copiague (11726) *(G-3684)*
Tobeyco Manufacturing Co Inc ... 607 962-2446
165 Cedar St Corning (14830) *(G-3722)*
Tocare LLC ... 718 767-0618
15043b 14th Ave Fl 1 Whitestone (11357) *(G-16101)*
Today Media, Harrison *Also called Martinelli Holdings LLC* *(G-5555)*
Todaysgentleman.com, Oceanside *Also called Adf Accessories Inc* *(G-12164)*
Todd Enterprises, West Babylon *Also called Chem-Tainer Industries Inc* *(G-15702)*
Todd Systems Inc ... 914 963-3400
50 Ash St Yonkers (10701) *(G-16352)*
Todd Walbridge ... 585 254-3018
1916 Lyell Ave Rochester (14606) *(G-13768)*
Todt Hill Audiological Svcs ... 718 816-1952
78 Todt Hill Rd Ste 202 Staten Island (10314) *(G-14722)*
Toga Manufacturing Inc (HQ) ... 631 242-4800
200 Heartland Blvd Edgewood (11717) *(G-4289)*
Toho Company Limited ... 212 391-9058
1501 Broadway Ste 2005 New York (10036) *(G-11504)*
Toho Shoji (new York) Inc ... 212 868-7466
990 Avenue Of The America New York (10018) *(G-11505)*
Token, Brooklyn *Also called 3phase Industries LLC* *(G-1415)*
Tokenize Inc ... 585 981-9919
125 Tech Park Dr 2137b Rochester (14623) *(G-13769)*
Tokens, Staten Island *Also called Maxine Denker Inc* *(G-14679)*
Tokenworks Inc ... 914 704-3100
26 Milburn St Fl 2 Bronxville (10708) *(G-1404)*
Tokion Magazine, New York *Also called Downtown Media Group LLC* *(G-9263)*
Tokyo Electron America Inc ... 518 289-3100
2 Bayberry Dr Malta (12020) *(G-7497)*
Tokyo Electron America Inc ... 518 292-4200
255 Fuller Rd Ste 214 Albany (12203) *(G-137)*
Toledo Graphics Group, Farmingdale *Also called Desktop Publishing Concepts* *(G-4614)*
Toltec Fabrics Inc ... 212 706-9310
437 5th Ave Fl 10 New York (10016) *(G-11506)*

ALPHABETIC

Tom & Jerry Printcraft Forms (PA)..............914 777-7468
960 Mamaroneck Ave Mamaroneck (10543) *(G-7525)*
Tom & Linda Platt Inc..............212 221-7208
55 W 39th St Rm 1701 New York (10018) *(G-11507)*
Tom Doherty Associates Inc..............212 388-0100
175 5th Ave Frnt 1 New York (10010) *(G-11508)*
Tom James Company..............212 593-0204
717 5th Ave New York (10022) *(G-11509)*
Tomahawk Welding Svcs & Insptn..............903 249-4451
30 Midland Dr Apt W16 Norwich (13815) *(G-12129)*
Tomas Maier..............212 988-8686
956 Madison Ave Frnt 1 New York (10021) *(G-11510)*
Tomkins USA, Syracuse *Also called Tompkins Srm LLC* *(G-15013)*
Tommy Boy Entertainment LLC..............212 388-8300
220 E 23rd St Ste 509 New York (10010) *(G-11511)*
Tommy Hilfiger, New York *Also called Pvh Corp* *(G-10934)*
Tommy John Inc..............800 708-3490
100 Broadway Ste 1101 New York (10005) *(G-11512)*
Tompkins Metal Finishing Inc..............585 344-2600
6 Apollo Dr Batavia (14020) *(G-627)*
Tompkins Srm LLC..............315 422-8763
623 Oneida St Syracuse (13202) *(G-15013)*
Tompkins Weekly Inc..............607 539-7100
36 Besemer Rd Ithaca (14850) *(G-6413)*
Tomric Systems Inc..............716 854-6050
85 River Rock Dr Buffalo (14207) *(G-3013)*
Tonanwanda News, Niagara Falls *Also called Cnhi LLC* *(G-11915)*
Tonawanda Coke Corporation..............716 876-6222
3875 River Rd Tonawanda (14150) *(G-15145)*
Tonawanda Limb & Brace Inc..............716 695-1131
545 Delaware St Ste 2 Tonawanda (14150) *(G-15146)*
Tonche Timber LLC..............845 389-3489
3959 State Highway 30 Amsterdam (12010) *(G-348)*
Toner-N-More Inc..............718 232-6200
2220 65th St Ste 103 Brooklyn (11204) *(G-2509)*
Tongli Pharmaceuticals USA Inc (PA)..............212 842-8837
4260 Main St Apt 6f Flushing (11355) *(G-4900)*
Toni Industries Inc..............212 921-0700
111 Great Neck Rd Ste 305 Great Neck (11021) *(G-5428)*
Tonix Pharmaceuticals Inc (HQ)..............917 288-8908
509 Madison Ave Rm 1608 New York (10022) *(G-11513)*
Tonix Phrmceuticals Holdg Corp (PA)..............212 980-9155
509 Madison Ave Rm 1608 New York (10022) *(G-11514)*
Tonoga Inc (PA)..............518 658-3202
95-136 Coonbrook Rd Petersburg (12138) *(G-12600)*
Tony Baird Electronics Inc..............315 422-4430
461 E Brighton Ave Syracuse (13210) *(G-15014)*
Tonys Ornamental Ir Works Inc..............315 337-3730
6757 Martin St Rome (13440) *(G-13874)*
Tooling Enterprises Inc..............716 842-0445
680 New Babcock St Ste 1 Buffalo (14206) *(G-3014)*
Toolroom Express Inc..............607 723-5373
1010 Conklin Rd Conklin (13748) *(G-3630)*
Tools & Stamping Corp..............718 392-4040
48 Eagle St Brooklyn (11222) *(G-2510)*
Top Fortune Usa Ltd..............516 608-2694
100 Atlantic Ave Ste 2 Lynbrook (11563) *(G-7441)*
Top Seedz LLC..............716 380-2612
247 Cayuga Rd Buffalo (14225) *(G-3015)*
Top Stuff, New York *Also called Isfel Co Inc* *(G-9945)*
Topaz Industries Inc..............631 207-0700
130 Corporate Dr Holtsville (11742) *(G-6057)*
Topiderm Inc (PA)..............631 226-7979
5200 New Horizons Blvd Amityville (11701) *(G-312)*
Topix Pharmaceuticals Inc (PA)..............631 226-7979
5200 New Horizons Blvd Amityville (11701) *(G-313)*
Topoo Industries Incorporated..............718 331-3755
2847 W 21st St Brooklyn (11224) *(G-2511)*
Toppan Merrill USA Inc (HQ)..............212 596-7747
747 3rd Ave Fl 7 New York (10017) *(G-11515)*
Topps-All Products of Yonkers..............914 968-4226
148 Ludlow St Ste 2 Yonkers (10705) *(G-16353)*
Toprint Ltd..............718 439-0469
6110 7th Ave Brooklyn (11220) *(G-2512)*
Toptec Products LLC..............631 421-9800
1225 Walt Whitman Rd Melville (11747) *(G-7831)*
Tor Books, New York *Also called Tom Doherty Associates Inc* *(G-11508)*
Toray Holding (usa) Inc (HQ)..............212 697-8150
461 5th Ave Fl 9 New York (10017) *(G-11516)*
Toray Industries Inc...............212 697-8150
600 3rd Ave Fl 5 New York (10016) *(G-11517)*
Torino Indus Fabrication Inc..............631 509-1640
4 Pinehurst Dr Bellport (11713) *(G-809)*
Torino Industrial Inc..............631 509-1640
4 Pinehurst Dr Bellport (11713) *(G-810)*
Torino Industrial Fabrication, Bellport *Also called Torino Industrial Inc* *(G-810)*
Tork Inc (PA)..............914 664-3542
50 S Macquesten Pkwy Mount Vernon (10550) *(G-8183)*
Torotron Corporation..............718 428-6992
18508 Union Tpke Ste 101 Fresh Meadows (11366) *(G-5047)*
Torre Products Co Inc..............212 925-8989
10 Beach St Mount Vernon (10550) *(G-8184)*

Torrent Ems LLC..............716 312-4099
190 Walnut St Lockport (14094) *(G-7113)*
Torrey Pines Research, Fairport *Also called Xactiv Inc* *(G-4531)*
Torrington Industries Inc..............315 676-4662
90 Corporate Park Dr Central Square (13036) *(G-3296)*
Torsaf Printers Inc..............516 569-5577
1313 Broadway Hewlett (11557) *(G-5873)*
Tortilla Heaven Inc..............845 339-1550
97 Abeel St Kingston (12401) *(G-6715)*
Tortilleria Oaxaca..............347 355-7336
121 Port Richmond Ave Staten Island (10302) *(G-14723)*
Tosch Products Ltd..............315 672-3040
25 Main St Camillus (13031) *(G-3111)*
Toshiba Amer Info Systems Inc (HQ)..............949 583-3000
1251 Ave Of The Amrcas St New York (10020) *(G-11518)*
Toshiba America Inc (HQ)..............212 596-0600
1251 Ave Of Ameri New York (10020) *(G-11519)*
Total Concept Graphic Inc..............212 229-2626
519 8th Ave Rm 805a New York (10018) *(G-11520)*
Total Defense Inc..............631 257-3258
1393 Veterans Memorial Hw Hauppauge (11788) *(G-5787)*
Total Dntl Implant Sltions LLC..............212 877-3777
260 W Sunrise Hwy Valley Stream (11581) *(G-15361)*
Total Energy Fabrication Corp..............580 363-1500
2 Hardscrabble Rd North Salem (10560) *(G-12037)*
Total Machine and Welding, Bronx *Also called Coral Management Corp* *(G-1231)*
Total Metal Resource..............718 384-7818
175 Bogart St Brooklyn (11206) *(G-2513)*
Total Piping Solutions Inc..............716 372-0160
1760 Haskell Rd Olean (14760) *(G-12243)*
Total Solution Graphics Inc..............718 706-1540
2511 49th Ave Long Island City (11101) *(G-7383)*
Total Webcasting Inc..............845 883-0909
8 Bruce St New Paltz (12561) *(G-8311)*
Toto USA Inc..............917 237-0665
20 W 22nd St Frnt 2 New York (10010) *(G-11521)*
Touch Adjust Clip Co Inc..............631 589-3077
1687 Roosevelt Ave Bohemia (11716) *(G-1086)*
Touch Tunes, New York *Also called Touchtunes Music Corporation* *(G-11523)*
Touchcare P LLC..............646 824-5373
135 Madison Ave Fl 5 New York (10016) *(G-11522)*
Touchdown, New York *Also called Professnal Spt Pblications Inc* *(G-10904)*
Touchstone Technology Inc..............585 458-2690
350 Mile Crossing Blvd Rochester (14624) *(G-13770)*
Touchtunes Music Corporation (HQ)..............847 419-3300
850 3rd Ave Ste 15c New York (10022) *(G-11523)*
Toura LLC..............646 652-8668
392 2nd St Apt 2 Brooklyn (11215) *(G-2514)*
Tovie Asarese Royal Prtg Co..............716 885-7692
351 Grant St Buffalo (14213) *(G-3016)*
Tower Computers, Brewster *Also called Base Systems Inc* *(G-1142)*
Tower Isles Frozen Foods Ltd..............718 495-2626
2025 Atlantic Ave Brooklyn (11233) *(G-2515)*
Tower Isles Patties, Brooklyn *Also called Tower Isles Frozen Foods Ltd* *(G-2515)*
Tower Sales Co, Brooklyn *Also called Turoff Tower Graphics Inc* *(G-2529)*
Toweriq Inc (PA)..............844 626-7638
37-18 Nthm Blvd Ste 421 Long Island City (11101) *(G-7384)*
Town Line Auto, Greenville *Also called Classic Auto Crafts Inc* *(G-5467)*
Town of Amherst..............716 631-7113
450 Maple Rd Williamsville (14221) *(G-16144)*
Town of Hartford..............315 724-0654
Rr 12 New Hartford (13413) *(G-8247)*
Town of Ohio..............315 392-2055
N Lake Rd Forestport (13338) *(G-4929)*
Town of Ohio Highway Garage, Forestport *Also called Town of Ohio* *(G-4929)*
Towne House Restorations Inc..............718 497-9200
4309 Vernon Blvd Long Island City (11101) *(G-7385)*
Townley Inc..............212 779-0544
10 W 33rd St Rm 418 New York (10001) *(G-11524)*
Townley Cosmetics, New York *Also called Townley Inc* *(G-11524)*
Townline Machine Co Inc..............315 462-3413
3151 Manchester Clifton Springs (14432) *(G-3481)*
Towpath Machine Corp..............315 252-0112
31 Allen St Auburn (13021) *(G-500)*
Towse Publishing Co..............914 235-3095
1333 North Ave Ste A New Rochelle (10804) *(G-8355)*
Toymax Inc (HQ)..............212 633-6611
200 5th Ave New York (10010) *(G-11525)*
Tpa Computer Corp..............877 866-6044
531 Route 52 Apt 4 Carmel (10512) *(G-3191)*
TPC Inc..............315 438-8605
6780 Nthrn Blvd Ste 401 East Syracuse (13057) *(G-4243)*
Tpi Arcade Inc..............585 492-0122
7888 Route 98 Arcade (14009) *(G-382)*
Tpi Industries LLC (HQ)..............845 692-2820
265 Ballard Rd Middletown (10941) *(G-7935)*
Tpti, Stony Brook *Also called Transistor Power Tech Inc* *(G-14742)*
Tr Apparel LLC (HQ)..............646 358-3888
609 Greenwich St Fl 3 New York (10014) *(G-11526)*
TR Designs Inc..............212 398-9300
260 W 39th St Fl 19 New York (10018) *(G-11527)*

Trac Medical Solutions Inc 518 346-7799
2165 Technology Dr Schenectady (12308) *(G-14312)*
Trac Regulators Inc 914 699-9352
160 S Terrace Ave Mount Vernon (10550) *(G-8185)*
Tracco LLC 516 938-4588
6800 Jericho Tpke 101w Syosset (11791) *(G-14803)*
Tracey Welding Co Inc 518 756-6309
29 Riverview Dr Coeymans (12045) *(G-3505)*
Track 7 Inc 845 544-1810
3 Forester Ave Warwick (10990) *(G-15521)*
Traco Manufacturing Inc 585 343-2434
4300 Commerce Dr Batavia (14020) *(G-628)*
Tracy Reese, New York *Also called TR Designs Inc* *(G-11527)*
Traddle LLC 646 330-0436
165 Broadway New York (10006) *(G-11528)*
Trade Mark Graphics Inc 718 306-0001
3982 Amboy Rd Staten Island (10308) *(G-14724)*
Tradeblock Inc 212 231-8353
156 5th Ave Fl 7 New York (10010) *(G-11529)*
Trader Interntnal Publications 914 631-6856
50 Fremont Rd Sleepy Hollow (10591) *(G-14464)*
Tradewins Publishing Corp 631 361-6916
528 Route 25a Ste A Saint James (11780) *(G-14115)*
Trading Edge Ltd 347 699-7079
1923 Bleecker St Apt 1r Ridgewood (11385) *(G-13164)*
Trading Services International 212 501-0142
133 W 72nd St Rm 601 New York (10023) *(G-11530)*
Tradition Leather Inc 518 725-2555
41 W 11th Ave Gloversville (12078) *(G-5297)*
Tradition Leather Co, Gloversville *Also called Tradition Leather Inc* *(G-5297)*
Trafalgar Company LLC (HQ) 212 768-8800
417 5th Ave Fl 11 New York (10016) *(G-11531)*
Traffic Lane Closures LLC 845 228-6100
1214 Route 52 Ste 1 Carmel (10512) *(G-3192)*
Traffic Logix Corporation 866 915-6449
3 Harriet Ln Spring Valley (10977) *(G-14583)*
Tramwell Inc 315 789-2762
70 State St Geneva (14456) *(G-5164)*
Trane US Inc 718 721-8844
4518 Court Sq Ste 100 Long Island City (11101) *(G-7386)*
Trane US Inc 914 593-0303
3 Westchester Plz Ste 198 Elmsford (10523) *(G-4436)*
Trane US Inc 315 234-1500
15 Technology Pl East Syracuse (13057) *(G-4244)*
Trane US Inc 518 785-1315
301 Old Niskayuna Rd # 1 Latham (12110) *(G-6877)*
Trane US Inc 585 256-2500
75 Town Centre Dr Ste I Rochester (14623) *(G-13771)*
Trane US Inc 716 626-1260
45 Earhart Dr Ste 103 Buffalo (14221) *(G-3017)*
Trane US Inc 631 952-9477
245 Newtown Rd Ste 500 Plainview (11803) *(G-12719)*
Trans Tech Bus, Warwick *Also called Transprttion Collaborative Inc* *(G-15522)*
Trans-High Corporation 212 387-0500
250 W 57th St Ste 920 New York (10107) *(G-11532)*
Trans-Lux Corporation (HQ) 800 243-5544
135 E 57th St Unit 100 New York (10022) *(G-11533)*
Transact Technologies Inc 607 257-8901
20 Bomax Dr Ithaca (14850) *(G-6414)*
Transaction Printer Group 607 274-2500
108 Woodcrest Ter Ithaca (14850) *(G-6415)*
Transcat Inc (PA) 585 352-7777
35 Vantage Point Dr Rochester (14624) *(G-13772)*
Transcntinental Ultra Flex Inc 718 272-9100
975 Essex St Brooklyn (11208) *(G-2516)*
Transco Railway Products Inc 716 825-1663
Milestrip Rd Rr 179 Buffalo (14219) *(G-3018)*
Transco Railway Products Inc 716 824-1219
Milestrip Rd Blasdell (14219) *(G-923)*
Transcontinental Printing GP 716 626-3078
300 International Dr # 200 Amherst (14221) *(G-249)*
Transcontinental Ross-Ellis, New York *Also called Tc Transcontinental USA Inc* *(G-11439)*
Transistor Devices Inc 631 471-7492
125 Comac St Ronkonkoma (11779) *(G-14017)*
Transistor Power Tech Inc (PA) 631 491-0265
38 Robert Cres Stony Brook (11790) *(G-14742)*
Transit Air Inc 607 324-0216
1 William K Jackson Ln Hornell (14843) *(G-6112)*
Transitair Systems, Hornell *Also called Transit Air Inc* *(G-6112)*
Transland Sourcing LLC 718 596-5704
5 Lynch St Brooklyn (11249) *(G-2517)*
Transpo Industries Inc (PA) 914 636-1000
20 Jones St Ste 3 New Rochelle (10801) *(G-8356)*
Transport National Dev Inc (PA) 716 662-0270
5720 Ellis Rd Orchard Park (14127) *(G-12379)*
Transport National Dev Inc 716 662-0270
5720 Ellis Rd Orchard Park (14127) *(G-12380)*
Transportation Department, Bay Shore *Also called Bimbo Bakeries Usa Inc* *(G-657)*
Transportgistics Inc 631 567-4100
28 N Country Rd Ste 103 Mount Sinai (11766) *(G-8117)*
Transprttion Collaborative Inc 845 988-2333
7 Lake Station Rd Warwick (10990) *(G-15522)*
Transtech Systems Inc (PA) 518 370-5558
900 Albany Shaker Rd Latham (12110) *(G-6878)*
Trash and Vaudeville Inc 212 777-1727
96 E 7th St Frnt A New York (10009) *(G-11534)*
Travel Leisure Magazine, New York *Also called Time Inc Affluent Media Group* *(G-11490)*
Treauu Inc 703 731-0196
60 E 120th St Fl 2 New York (10035) *(G-11535)*
Trebor Instrument Corp 631 423-7026
39 Balsam Dr Dix Hills (11746) *(G-4016)*
Treehouse Private Brands Inc 716 693-4715
570 Fillmore Ave Tonawanda (14150) *(G-15147)*
Treiman Publications Corp 607 657-8473
12724 State Route 38 Berkshire (13736) *(G-822)*
Trek Inc (PA) 716 438-7555
190 Walnut St Lockport (14094) *(G-7114)*
Tremont Offset Inc 718 892-7333
1500 Ericson Pl Bronx (10461) *(G-1380)*
Trench, New York *Also called Gramercy Designs Inc* *(G-9656)*
Trench & Marine Pump Co Inc 212 423-9098
3466 Park Ave Bronx (10456) *(G-1381)*
Trend Pot Inc 212 431-9970
40 Exchange Pl Ste 1902 New York (10005) *(G-11536)*
Trendsformers Ltd Liability Co 888 700-2423
150 W 56th St Apt 6406 New York (10019) *(G-11537)*
Trensdformers, New York *Also called Trendsformers Ltd Liability Co* *(G-11537)*
Trentset Originals, New York *Also called Skiva International Inc* *(G-11261)*
Treo Brands LLC 914 341-1850
106 Calvert St Harrison (10528) *(G-5562)*
Treo Industries Inc 631 737-4022
35 Carlough Rd Ste 1 Bohemia (11716) *(G-1087)*
Treyco Products Corp 716 693-6525
131 Fillmore Ave Tonawanda (14150) *(G-15148)*
Tri City Highway Products Inc 607 722-2967
111 Bevier St Binghamton (13904) *(G-914)*
Tri County Custom Vacuum 845 774-7595
653 State Route 17m Monroe (10950) *(G-8032)*
Tri Kolor Printing & Sty 315 474-6753
1035 Montgomery St Syracuse (13202) *(G-15015)*
Tri Star, Maspeth *Also called Asn Inc* *(G-7593)*
Tri Star Label Inc 914 237-4800
630 S Columbus Ave Mount Vernon (10550) *(G-8186)*
Tri State Awnings, Sloatsburg *Also called Custom European Imports Inc* *(G-14470)*
Tri State Hardwoods Ltd 845 687-7814
54 Breezy Hill Rd Kingston (12401) *(G-6716)*
Tri State Media Group, New City *Also called Pennysaver Group Inc* *(G-8228)*
Tri State Shearing Bending Inc 718 485-2200
366 Herzl St Brooklyn (11212) *(G-2518)*
Tri Supreme Optical, Farmingdale *Also called Tri-Supreme Optical LLC* *(G-4759)*
Tri Valley Iron Inc 845 365-1013
700 Oak Tree Rd Palisades (10964) *(G-12483)*
Tri-Boro Shelving Inc 718 782-8527
1940 Flushing Ave Ridgewood (11385) *(G-13165)*
Tri-City Highway Products Inc 518 294-9964
145 Podpadic Rd Richmondville (12149) *(G-13130)*
Tri-Flex Label Corp 631 293-0411
48 Allen Blvd Unit A Farmingdale (11735) *(G-4758)*
Tri-Force Sales LLC 732 261-5507
767 3rd Ave Rm 35b New York (10017) *(G-11538)*
Tri-Metal Industries Inc 716 691-3323
100 Pineview Dr Amherst (14228) *(G-250)*
Tri-Plex Packaging Corporation 212 481-6070
307 5th Ave Fl 7 New York (10016) *(G-11539)*
Tri-Seal Holdings Inc 845 353-3300
900 Bradley Hill Rd Blauvelt (10913) *(G-936)*
Tri-Seal International Inc (HQ) 845 353-3300
900 Bradley Hill Rd Blauvelt (10913) *(G-937)*
Tri-Star Offset Corp 718 894-5555
6020 59th Pl Ste 3 Maspeth (11378) *(G-7639)*
Tri-State Brick & Stone NY Inc (PA) 212 366-0300
333 7th Ave Fl 5 New York (10001) *(G-11540)*
Tri-State Envelope Corporation 212 736-3110
1 W 34th St Rm 704 New York (10001) *(G-11541)*
Tri-State Food Jobbers Inc 718 921-1211
5600 1st Ave Unit A5 Brooklyn (11220) *(G-2519)*
Tri-State Metals LLC 914 347-8157
41 N Lawn Ave Elmsford (10523) *(G-4437)*
Tri-State Towing Equipment NY, Westbury *Also called Tee Pee Auto Sales Corp* *(G-15928)*
Tri-State Window Factory Corp 631 667-8600
360 Marcus Blvd Deer Park (11729) *(G-3942)*
Tri-Supreme Optical LLC 631 249-2020
91 Carolyn Blvd Farmingdale (11735) *(G-4759)*
Tri-Technologies Inc 914 699-2001
40 Hartford Ave Mount Vernon (10553) *(G-8187)*
Tri-Town News Inc (PA) 607 561-3515
74 Main St Sidney (13838) *(G-14436)*
Tri-Town Packing Corp 315 389-5101
Helena Rd Brasher Falls (13613) *(G-1113)*
Tri-Village Publishers Inc 518 843-1100
1 Venner Rd Amsterdam (12010) *(G-349)*
Triad Counter Corp 631 750-0615
1225 Church St Bohemia (11716) *(G-1088)*

ALPHABETIC

Triad Network Technologies 585 924-8505
75b Victor Heights Pkwy Victor (14564) *(G-15439)*

Triad Printing Inc 845 343-2722
7 Prospect St Middletown (10940) *(G-7936)*

Trialgraphix, New York Also called *Resonant Legal Media LLC (G-11019)*

Triangle Grinding Machine Corp 631 643-3636
66 Nancy St Unit A West Babylon (11704) *(G-15753)*

Triangle Rubber Co Inc 631 589-9400
50 Aero Rd Bohemia (11716) *(G-1089)*

Trianon Collection Inc 212 921-9450
16 W 46th St Fl 10 New York (10036) *(G-11542)*

Tribco LLC 718 357-7400
15050 14th Rd Ste 2 Whitestone (11357) *(G-16102)*

Tribology Inc 631 345-3000
35 Old Dock Rd Yaphank (11980) *(G-16275)*

Triboro Bagel Co Inc 718 359-9245
18312 Horace Harding Expy Flushing (11365) *(G-4901)*

Tribune Entertainment Co Del 203 866-2204
220 E 42nd St Fl 26 New York (10017) *(G-11543)*

Tribune Media Services Inc (HQ) 518 792-9914
40 Media Dr Queensbury (12804) *(G-13059)*

Trico Holding Corporation (HQ) 716 852-5700
50 Thielman Dr Buffalo (14206) *(G-3019)*

Trico Manufacturing Corp 718 349-6565
196 Dupont St Brooklyn (11222) *(G-2520)*

Trico Products, Buffalo Also called *Trico Holding Corporation (G-3019)*

Tricon Machine LLC 585 671-0679
820 Coventry Dr Webster (14580) *(G-15657)*

Tricon Piping Systems Inc 315 697-8787
2 Technology Blvd Canastota (13032) *(G-3159)*

Tricor Direct Inc (HQ) 716 626-1616
2491 Wehrle Dr Williamsville (14221) *(G-16145)*

Tricycle Foundation Inc 800 873-9871
89 5th Ave Ste 301 New York (10003) *(G-11544)*

Trident Partners III, Victor Also called *Newtex Industries Inc (G-15421)*

Trident Precision Mfg Inc 585 265-2010
734 Salt Rd Webster (14580) *(G-15658)*

Trident Valve Actuator Co 914 698-2650
329 Center Ave Mamaroneck (10543) *(G-7526)*

Trihex Manufacturing Inc 315 589-9331
6708 Pound Rd Williamson (14589) *(G-16114)*

Tril Inc 631 645-7989
320 Pioxi St Copiague (11726) *(G-3685)*

Trilake Three Press Corp 518 359-2462
136 Park St Tupper Lake (12986) *(G-15214)*

Trimac Molding Services 607 967-2900
13 Pruyn St Bainbridge (13733) *(G-527)*

Trimaster/Htech Holding LLC (HQ) 212 257-6772
590 Madison Ave Fl 27 New York (10022) *(G-11545)*

Trimet Coal LLC 718 951-3654
1615 Avenue I Apt 420 Brooklyn (11230) *(G-2521)*

Trimfit Inc (PA) 215 245-1122
463 7th Ave Rm 1501 New York (10018) *(G-11546)*

Trimfit Global, New York Also called *Trimfit Inc (G-11546)*

Trimmer Capacitor Company, The, Cazenovia Also called *Voltronics LLC (G-3237)*

Trimworld Inc 212 354-8973
247 W 37th St Rm 11e New York (10018) *(G-11547)*

Trinic LLC 607 775-1948
40 Grossett Dr Kirkwood (13795) *(G-6732)*

Trinity Biotech Distribution, Jamestown Also called *Biopool Us Inc (G-6497)*

Trinity Packaging Corporation 716 668-3111
55 Innsbruck Dr Buffalo (14227) *(G-3020)*

Trinity Packaging Corporation (HQ) 914 273-4111
357 Main St Unit 1 Armonk (10504) *(G-404)*

Trinity Tools Inc 716 694-1111
261 Main St North Tonawanda (14120) *(G-12096)*

Trio Clean LLC 518 627-4055
1451 State Highway 5s Amsterdam (12010) *(G-350)*

Trio French Bakery, New York Also called *Giovanni Bakery Corp (G-9614)*

Tripar Manufacturing Co Inc 631 563-0855
2050 Artic Ave Ste A Bohemia (11716) *(G-1090)*

Tripi Engraving Co Inc 718 383-6500
60 Meserole Ave Brooklyn (11222) *(G-2522)*

Triple Canopy, New York Also called *Canopy Canopy Canopy Inc (G-8905)*

Triple E Manufacturing 716 761-6996
117 Osborn St Sherman (14781) *(G-14401)*

Triple H Construction Inc 516 280-8252
10737 180th St Jamaica (11433) *(G-6481)*

Triple J Bedding LLC 718 643-8005
63 Flushing Ave Unit 331 Brooklyn (11205) *(G-2523)*

Triple Point Manufacturing 631 218-4988
1371 Church St Ste 6 Bohemia (11716) *(G-1091)*

Triplett Machine Inc 315 548-3198
1374 Phelps Junction Rd Phelps (14532) *(G-12609)*

Triplex Industries Inc 585 621-6920
100 Boxart St Ste 27 Rochester (14612) *(G-13773)*

Tripp Plating Works Inc 716 894-2424
1491 William St Buffalo (14206) *(G-3021)*

Tristate Contract Sales LLC 845 782-2614
164 Dug Rd Chester (10918) *(G-3392)*

Triton Builders Inc 631 841-2534
645 Broadway Ste T Amityville (11701) *(G-314)*

Triumph Actuation Systems LLC 516 378-0162
417 S Main St Freeport (11520) *(G-5030)*

Triumph Apparel Corporation (PA) 212 302-2606
530 Fashion Ave Ste M1 New York (10018) *(G-11548)*

Triumph Group Inc 516 997-5757
717 Main St Westbury (11590) *(G-15934)*

Triumph Learning LLC (HQ) 212 652-0200
212 W 35th St Fl 2 New York (10001) *(G-11549)*

Triumph Structures-Long Island, Westbury Also called *Triumph Group Inc (G-15934)*

TRM Linen Inc 718 686-6075
1546 59th St Brooklyn (11219) *(G-2524)*

Trojan Metal Fabrication Inc (PA) 631 968-5040
2215 Union Blvd Bay Shore (11706) *(G-723)*

Trojan Powder Coating, Bay Shore Also called *Trojan Metal Fabrication Inc (G-723)*

Tronic Plating Co Inc 516 293-7883
37 Potter St Farmingdale (11735) *(G-4760)*

Tronser Inc 315 655-9528
3066 John Trush Jr Blvd Cazenovia (13035) *(G-3236)*

Tropical Driftwood Originals 516 623-0980
499 Nassau Rd Roosevelt (11575) *(G-14034)*

Trove Inc 212 268-2046
20 Jay St Ste 846 Brooklyn (11201) *(G-2525)*

Troy Belting and Supply Co (PA) 518 272-4920
70 Cohoes Rd Watervliet (12189) *(G-15609)*

Troy Boiler Works Inc 518 274-2650
2800 7th Ave Troy (12180) *(G-15192)*

Troy Cabinet Manufacturing Div, Troy Also called *Deakon Homes and Interiors (G-15165)*

Troy Industrial Solutions 518 272-4920
70 Cohoes Rd Watervliet (12189) *(G-15610)*

Troy Sand & Gravel Co Inc (PA) 518 203-5115
34 Grange Rd West Sand Lake (12196) *(G-15836)*

Troy Sand & Gravel Co Inc 518 674-2854
Rr 43 West Sand Lake (12196) *(G-15837)*

Troy Sign & Printing 718 994-4482
4827 White Plains Rd Bronx (10470) *(G-1382)*

Troy Sign Printing Center, Bronx Also called *Troy Sign & Printing (G-1382)*

Troyer Inc 585 352-5590
4555 Lyell Rd Rochester (14606) *(G-13774)*

Troys Landscape Supply Co Inc 518 785-1526
1266 Loudon Rd Cohoes (12047) *(G-3518)*

Trs Packaging, Buffalo Also called *Time Release Sciences Inc (G-3011)*

Tru Mold Shoes Inc 716 881-4484
42 Breckenridge St Buffalo (14213) *(G-3022)*

Tru-Art Sign Co Inc 718 658-5068
10515 180th St Jamaica (11433) *(G-6482)*

Tru-Tone Metal Products Inc 718 386-5960
1261 Willoughby Ave Brooklyn (11237) *(G-2526)*

Truarc Fabrication 518 691-0430
1 Commerce Park Dr Gansevoort (12831) *(G-5088)*

Truck-Lite Co LLC (HQ) 716 665-6214
310 E Elmwood Ave Falconer (14733) *(G-4560)*

Truck-Lite Sub Inc 800 888-7095
310 E Elmwood Ave Falconer (14733) *(G-4561)*

True Type Printing Co Inc 718 706-6900
8600 New Horizons Blvd Amityville (11701) *(G-315)*

Truebite Inc 607 785-7664
2590 Glenwood Rd Vestal (13850) *(G-15386)*

Truebite Inc 607 786-3184
129 Squires Ave Endicott (13760) *(G-4476)*

Trueex LLC 646 786-8526
162 5th Ave Ste 900 New York (10010) *(G-11550)*

Trueforge Global McHy Corp 516 825-7040
100 Merrick Rd Ste 208e Rockville Centre (11570) *(G-13839)*

Truemade Products Inc 631 981-4755
910 Marconi Ave Ronkonkoma (11779) *(G-14018)*

Truesense Imaging Inc 585 784-5500
1964 Lake Ave Rochester (14615) *(G-13775)*

Truform Manufacturing Corp 585 458-1090
1500 N Clinton Ave Rochester (14621) *(G-13776)*

Truly Tubular Fitting Corp 914 664-8686
115 E 3rd St Mount Vernon (10550) *(G-8188)*

Trunk & Trolley LLC 212 947-9001
15 W 34th St New York (10001) *(G-11551)*

Trunk Outlet, Rochester Also called *Rhino Trunk & Case Inc (G-13671)*

Trusses & Trim Division, Farmington Also called *Rochester Lumber Company (G-4778)*

Trust of Colum Unive In The Ci 212 854-2793
2929 Broadway Fl 3 New York (10025) *(G-11552)*

Trusted Media Brands Inc (HQ) 914 238-1000
750 3rd Ave Fl 3 New York (10017) *(G-11553)*

Trusted Media Brands Inc 914 244-5244
44 S Broadway Fl 7 White Plains (10601) *(G-16067)*

Trustfort LLC 781 787-0906
4250 Veterans Memorial Hw Holbrook (11741) *(G-6027)*

Truth Hardware Corporation 585 627-5964
1555 Jefferson Rd Rochester (14623) *(G-13777)*

Truxton Corp 718 842-6000
1357 Lafayette Ave Bronx (10474) *(G-1383)*

Trylon Wire & Metal Works Inc 718 542-4472
526 Tiffany St Bronx (10474) *(G-1384)*

Tryp Times Square 212 246-8800
234 W 48th St New York (10036) *(G-11554)*

TS Manufacturing, New York Also called *Alpine Creations Ltd (G-8531)*

TS Pink, Oneonta *Also called T S Pink Corp* **(G-12282)**
TSA Luggage Locks, New York *Also called Safe Skies LLC* **(G-11114)**
Tsar USA LLC....646 415-7968
99 Madison Ave Fl 5 New York (10016) **(G-11555)**
Tsi Technologies, New York *Also called Trading Services International* **(G-11530)**
Tsm, Elmsford *Also called Tri-State Metals LLC* **(G-4437)**
TSS Foam Industries Corp....585 538-2321
2770 W Main St Caledonia (14423) **(G-3074)**
Tss-Transport Simulation, New York *Also called Aimsun Inc* **(G-8501)**
Tte Filters LLC (HQ)....716 532-2234
1 Magnetic Pkwy Gowanda (14070) **(G-5323)**
Ttg LLC....917 777-0959
115 W 30th St Rm 209 New York (10001) **(G-11556)**
TTI, Hauppauge *Also called Tarsia Technical Industries* **(G-5781)**
Tube Fabrication Company Inc....716 673-1871
183 E Main St Ste 10 Fredonia (14063) **(G-4971)**
Tucano Usa Inc....212 966-9211
77 Bleecker St Apt C212 New York (10012) **(G-11557)**
Tucker Jones House Inc....631 642-9092
1 Enterprise Dr East Setauket (11733) **(G-4189)**
Tucker Printers Inc....585 359-3030
270 Middle Rd Henrietta (14467) **(G-5861)**
Tudor Electrical Supply Co Inc....212 867-7550
137 W 24th St New York (10011) **(G-11558)**
Tug Hill Vineyards....315 376-4336
4051 Yancey Rd Lowville (13367) **(G-7422)**
Tully Products Inc....716 773-3166
2065 Baseline Rd Grand Island (14072) **(G-5346)**
Tulmar Manufacturing Inc....315 393-7191
101 Tulloch Dr Ogdensburg (13669) **(G-12212)**
Tumble Forms Inc (PA)....315 429-3101
1013 Barker Rd Dolgeville (13329) **(G-4027)**
Tumblehome Boatshop....518 623-5050
684 State Route 28 Warrensburg (12885) **(G-15506)**
Tummyzen, Irvington *Also called Eli Consumer Healthcare LLC* **(G-6307)**
Tunaverse Media Inc....631 778-8350
750 Veterans Hwy Ste 200 Hauppauge (11788) **(G-5788)**
Tunecore Inc (PA)....646 651-1060
45 Main St Ste 705 Brooklyn (11201) **(G-2527)**
Tunecore Inc....646 651-1060
63 Pearl St Brooklyn (11201) **(G-2528)**
Tupper Lake Hardwoods Inc....518 359-8248
167 Pitchfork Pond Rd Tupper Lake (12986) **(G-15215)**
Turbine Engine Comp Utica....315 768-8070
8273 Halsey Rd Whitesboro (13492) **(G-16084)**
Turbo Express Inc....718 723-3686
16019 Rockaway Blvd Ste D Jamaica (11434) **(G-6483)**
Turbo Machined Products LLC....315 895-3010
102 Industrial Dr Frankfort (13340) **(G-4957)**
Turbofil Packaging Mchs LLC....914 239-3878
30 Beach St Mount Vernon (10550) **(G-8189)**
Turbopro Inc....716 681-8651
1284 Town Line Rd Alden (14004) **(G-175)**
Turkprime, Flushing *Also called Prime Research Solutions LLC* **(G-4889)**
Turn On Products Inc (PA)....212 764-2121
48 W 37th St Fl 5 New York (10018) **(G-11559)**
Turn On Products Inc....212 764-4545
525 7th Ave Rm 1403 New York (10018) **(G-11560)**
Turner Bellows Inc....585 235-4456
526 Child St Ste 1 Rochester (14606) **(G-13778)**
Turner Plating, New Rochelle *Also called Eric S Turner & Company Inc* **(G-8329)**
Turner Undgrd Instllations Inc....585 359-2531
1233 Lehigh Station Rd Henrietta (14467) **(G-5862)**
Turning Point Tool LLC....585 288-7380
135 Dodge St Rochester (14606) **(G-13779)**
Turoff Tower Graphics Inc....718 856-7300
681 Coney Island Ave Brooklyn (11218) **(G-2529)**
Tusk Manufacturing Inc....631 567-3349
1371 Church St Ste 1 Bohemia (11716) **(G-1092)**
Tuthill Corporation....631 727-1097
75 Kings Dr Riverhead (11901) **(G-13191)**
Tuthilltown Spirits LLC....845 255-1527
14 Gristmill Ln Gardiner (12525) **(G-5131)**
Tuv Taam Corp....718 855-2207
502 Flushing Ave Brooklyn (11205) **(G-2530)**
TV Data, Queensbury *Also called Tribune Media Services Inc* **(G-13059)**
TV Executive, New York *Also called T V Trade Media Inc* **(G-11420)**
TV Guide Magazine LLC (HQ)....800 866-1400
50 Rockefeller Plz Fl 14 New York (10020) **(G-11561)**
TV Guide Magazine Group Inc (HQ)....212 852-7500
1211 Ave Of The Americas New York (10036) **(G-11562)**
TV Guilfoil & Associates Inc (PA)....315 453-0920
121 Dwight Park Cir Syracuse (13209) **(G-15016)**
TVI Imports LLC....631 793-3077
178 Abbey St Massapequa Park (11762) **(G-7661)**
Twcc Product and Sales....212 614-9364
122 5th Ave New York (10011) **(G-11563)**
Twenty-First Century Press Inc....716 837-0800
501 Cornwall Ave Buffalo (14215) **(G-3023)**
Twentyone Brix Winery, Portland *Also called Olde Chtqua Vneyards Ltd Lblty* **(G-12933)**
TWI Watches LLC....718 663-3969
4014 1st Ave Unit 10 Brooklyn (11232) **(G-2531)**
TWI-Laq Industries Inc....718 638-5860
1345 Seneca Ave Bronx (10474) **(G-1385)**
Twin Counties Pro Printers Inc....518 828-3278
59 Fairview Ave Hudson (12534) **(G-6181)**
Twin County Recycling Corp (PA)....516 827-6900
113 Magnolia Ave Westbury (11590) **(G-15935)**
Twin Lake Chemical Inc....716 433-3824
520 Mill St Lockport (14094) **(G-7115)**
Twin Marquis Inc (HQ)....718 386-6868
7 Bushwick Pl Brooklyn (11206) **(G-2532)**
Twin Pane Insulated GL Co Inc....631 924-1060
86 Horseblock Rd Unit D Yaphank (11980) **(G-16276)**
Twin Rivers Paper Company LLC....315 348-8491
Lyonsdale Rd Lyons Falls (13368) **(G-7456)**
Twin Rivers Paper Company LLC....315 823-2300
501 W Main St Ste 1 Little Falls (13365) **(G-6994)**
Twinco Mfg Co Inc (PA)....631 231-0022
30 Commerce Dr Hauppauge (11788) **(G-5789)**
Twinkle Lighting Inc....718 225-0939
13114 40th Rd Flushing (11354) **(G-4902)**
Twist Intimate Apparel, New York *Also called Twist Intimate Group LLC* **(G-11564)**
Twist Intimate Group LLC (PA)....212 695-5990
35 W 35th St Rm 903 New York (10001) **(G-11564)**
Two Bills Machine & Tool Co....516 437-2585
17 Concord St Floral Park (11001) **(G-4817)**
Two Palms Press Inc....212 965-8598
476 Broadway Ste 3f New York (10013) **(G-11565)**
Two Worlds Arts Ltd....212 929-2210
307 Kingsland Ave Brooklyn (11222) **(G-2533)**
Two Worlds Arts Ltd (PA)....212 929-2210
122 W 18th St New York (10011) **(G-11566)**
Two-Four Software, New York *Also called F-O-R Software LLC* **(G-9457)**
Two-Four Software, White Plains *Also called F-O-R Software LLC* **(G-16005)**
Twp America Inc (HQ)....212 274-8090
299 Broadway Ste 720 New York (10007) **(G-11567)**
TX Rx Systems Inc....716 549-4700
8625 Industrial Pkwy Angola (14006) **(G-361)**
Tyco Simplexgrinnell....315 437-9664
6731 Collamer Rd Ste 4 East Syracuse (13057) **(G-4245)**
Tyme Global Technologies LLC....212 796-1950
60 W 66th St Apt 15a New York (10023) **(G-11568)**
Tyme Technologies Inc (PA)....212 461-2315
17 State St Fl 7 New York (10004) **(G-11569)**
Tymetal Corp....518 692-9930
1109 State Route 4 Fort Edward (12828) **(G-4945)**
Tymetal Corp (HQ)....518 692-9930
678 Wilbur Ave Greenwich (12834) **(G-5477)**
Tymor Park....845 724-5691
249 Duncan Rd Lagrangeville (12540) **(G-6755)**
Tyson Deli Inc (HQ)....716 566-3189
665 Perry St Buffalo (14210) **(G-3024)**
U All Inc....518 438-2558
9 Interstate Ave Albany (12205) **(G-138)**
U B J, New York *Also called United Brothers Jewelry Inc* **(G-11597)**
U E Systems Incorporated (PA)....914 592-1220
14 Hayes St Elmsford (10523) **(G-4438)**
U Invite Limited....212 739-0620
17 State St Ste 4000 New York (10004) **(G-11570)**
U K Sailmakers, Port Chester *Also called Ulmer Sales LLC* **(G-12830)**
U S Air Tool Co Inc (PA)....631 471-3300
60 Fleetwood Ct Ronkonkoma (11779) **(G-14019)**
U S Air Tool International, Ronkonkoma *Also called U S Air Tool Co Inc* **(G-14019)**
U S Energy Development Corp (PA)....716 636-0401
2350 N Forest Rd Getzville (14068) **(G-5183)**
U S Japan Publication NY Inc....212 252-8833
147 W 35th St Ste 1705 New York (10001) **(G-11571)**
U S Orthotic Center, New York *Also called Custom Sports Lab Inc* **(G-9135)**
U S Plychmical Overseas Corp....845 356-5530
584 Chestnut Ridge Rd # 586 Chestnut Ridge (10977) **(G-3400)**
U S Sugar Co Inc....716 828-1170
692 Bailey Ave Buffalo (14206) **(G-3025)**
U S TEC, Victor *Also called 331 Holding Inc* **(G-15389)**
U S Tech Corporation....315 437-7207
6 Hawthorne Woods Ct Skaneateles (13152) **(G-14458)**
U Serve Brands Inc....877 632-6654
345 7th Ave Rm 501 New York (10001) **(G-11572)**
U T C, Newburgh *Also called Urethane Technology Co Inc* **(G-11892)**
U X World Inc....914 375-6167
245 Saw Mill River Rd # 106 Hawthorne (10532) **(G-5824)**
U-Cut Enterprises Inc....315 492-9316
4800 Solvay Rd Jamesville (13078) **(G-6563)**
U2o Usa LLC....516 813-9500
206 Terminal Dr Plainview (11803) **(G-12720)**
Uat, Troy *Also called United Aircraft Tech Inc* **(G-15193)**
Ub Welding Corp....347 688-5196
2230 Dr Martin L King Jr Bronx (10453) **(G-1386)**
Ubees Inc....916 505-8470
575 5th Ave 21 New York (10017) **(G-11573)**
Ubm Inc....212 600-3000
605 3rd Ave Fl 22 New York (10158) **(G-11574)**

Ubm LLC (HQ)....516 562-7800
1983 Marcus Ave Ste 250 New Hyde Park (11042) *(G-8298)*
Ubm LLC....516 562-5000
605 3rd Ave Fl 22 New York (10158) *(G-11575)*
Ubm Tech, New Hyde Park *Also called Ubm LLC (G-8298)*
Uc Coatings LLC (PA)....716 833-9366
2250 Fillmore Ave Buffalo (14214) *(G-3026)*
Ucc Guide Inc (HQ)....518 434-0909
99 Washington Ave Albany (12210) *(G-139)*
Ucr Steel Group LLC....718 764-3414
90 Trade Zone Ct Ronkonkoma (11779) *(G-14020)*
Ue Music, New York *Also called Universal Edition Inc (G-11605)*
Ufc Biotechnology Inc....716 603-3652
435 Creekside Dr Ste 1 Amherst (14228) *(G-251)*
Ufo Contemporary Inc....212 226-5400
42 W 38th St Rm 1204 New York (10018) *(G-11576)*
Ufp New York LLC....716 496-5484
13989 E Schutt Rd Chaffee (14030) *(G-3308)*
Ufp New York LLC....518 828-2888
11 Falls Industrial Pk Rd Hudson (12534) *(G-6182)*
Ufp New York LLC (HQ)....315 253-2758
11 Allen St Auburn (13021) *(G-501)*
Ufp New York LLC....607 563-1556
13 Winkler Rd Sidney (13838) *(G-14437)*
UFS Industries Inc....914 664-6262
300 N Macquesten Pkwy Mount Vernon (10550) *(G-8190)*
Ufx Holding I Corporation (HQ)....212 644-5900
55 E 52nd St Fl 35 New York (10055) *(G-11577)*
Ufx Holding II Corporation (HQ)....212 644-5900
55 E 52nd St Fl 35 New York (10055) *(G-11578)*
UGI, Brooklyn *Also called United Gemdiam Inc (G-2538)*
Uhmac Inc....716 537-2343
136 N Main St Holland (14080) *(G-6032)*
Ui Acquisition Holding Co (PA)....607 779-7522
33 Broome Corporate Pkwy Conklin (13748) *(G-3631)*
Ui Holding Company (HQ)....607 779-7522
33 Broome Corporate Pkwy Conklin (13748) *(G-3632)*
Ul Corp....201 203-4453
3812 Corporal Stone St # 2 Bayside (11361) *(G-743)*
Ul Information & Insights Inc (HQ)....518 640-9200
23 British American Blvd # 2 Latham (12110) *(G-6879)*
Ullink Inc (HQ)....646 565-6675
11 Times Sq Ste 31d New York (10036) *(G-11579)*
Ulmer Sales LLC....718 885-1700
10 Midland Ave Ste 1 Port Chester (10573) *(G-12830)*
Ulrich Planfiling Eqp Corp....716 763-1815
2120 4th Ave Lakewood (14750) *(G-6786)*
Ulrich Sign Co Inc....716 434-0167
177 Oakhurst St Lockport (14094) *(G-7116)*
Ulster County Iron Works LLC....845 255-0003
64 N Putt Corners Rd New Paltz (12561) *(G-8312)*
Ulster County Press Office....845 687-4480
1209 State Route 213 High Falls (12440) *(G-5956)*
Ulster Precision Inc....845 338-0995
100 Lipton St Kingston (12401) *(G-6717)*
Ulster Publishing Co Inc (PA)....845 334-8205
322 Wall St Fl 1 Kingston (12401) *(G-6718)*
Ulster Publishing Co Inc....845 255-7005
29 S Chestnut St Ste 101 New Paltz (12561) *(G-8313)*
Ultimate Signs & Designs Inc....516 481-0800
86 Sewell St Hempstead (11550) *(G-5851)*
Ultimate Styles of America....631 254-0219
27 Garfield Ave Unit A Bay Shore (11706) *(G-724)*
Ultra Clarity Corp....719 470-1010
3101 Parkview Dr Spring Valley (10977) *(G-14584)*
Ultra Elec Flightline Systems, Victor *Also called Flightline Electronics Inc (G-15410)*
Ultra Electronics Inc, Victor *Also called Magnet-Ndctive Systems Ltd USA (G-15419)*
Ultra Electronics, Ems, Yaphank *Also called Ems Development Corporation (G-16259)*
Ultra Fine Jewelry Mfg....516 349-2848
180 Dupont St Unit C Plainview (11803) *(G-12721)*
Ultra Thin Pzza Shlls Fltbrads, Deer Park *Also called Ultra Thin Ready To Bake Pizza (G-3943)*
Ultra Thin Ready To Bake Pizza....516 679-6655
151 E Industry Ct Deer Park (11729) *(G-3943)*
Ultra Tool and Manufacturing....585 467-3700
159 Lagrange Ave Rochester (14613) *(G-13780)*
Ultra-Scan Corporation....716 832-6269
4240 Ridge Lea Rd Ste 10 Amherst (14226) *(G-252)*
Ultra-Tab Laboratories Inc....845 691-8361
50 Toc Dr Highland (12528) *(G-5964)*
Ultradian Diagnostics LLC....518 618-0046
5 University Pl A324 Rensselaer (12144) *(G-13093)*
Ultraflex Power Technologies....631 467-6814
158 Remington Blvd Ste 2 Ronkonkoma (11779) *(G-14021)*
Ultralife Corporation (PA)....315 332-7100
2000 Technology Pkwy Newark (14513) *(G-11854)*
Ultrapedics Ltd (PA)....718 748-4806
355 Ovington Ave Ste 104 Brooklyn (11209) *(G-2534)*
Ultratab, Brooklyn *Also called Digitac LLC (G-1745)*
Ultravolt Inc....631 471-4444
1800 Ocean Ave Unit A Ronkonkoma (11779) *(G-14022)*
Ultrepet LLC....781 275-6400
136c Fuller Rd Albany (12205) *(G-140)*
Umbro Machine & Tool Co Inc....845 876-4669
3811 Route 9g Rhinebeck (12572) *(G-13102)*
Umi, New York *Also called Urban Mapping Inc (G-11616)*
Umicore Elec Mtls USA Inc....518 792-7700
9 Pruyns Island Dr Glens Falls (12801) *(G-5267)*
Umicore USA Inc....919 874-7171
9 Pruyns Island Dr Glens Falls (12801) *(G-5268)*
Ums Manufacturing LLC....518 562-2410
194 Pleasant Ridge Rd Plattsburgh (12901) *(G-12786)*
Unacast Inc (PA)....917 670-7852
245 5th Ave Rm 1101 New York (10016) *(G-11580)*
Unadilla Laminated Products, Sidney *Also called Unadilla Silo Company Inc (G-14438)*
Unadilla Silo Company Inc....607 369-9341
100 West Rd Sidney (13838) *(G-14438)*
Unbroken Rtr Usa Inc....541 640-9457
110 Airport Dr Wappingers Falls (12590) *(G-15500)*
Uncle Wallys LLC....631 205-0455
41 Natcon Dr Shirley (11967) *(G-14428)*
Underline Communications LLC....212 994-4340
12 W 27th St Fl 14 New York (10001) *(G-11581)*
Uneeda Enterprizes Inc....800 431-2494
640 Chestnut Ridge Rd Spring Valley (10977) *(G-14585)*
UNI Jewelry Inc....212 398-1818
48 W 48th St Ste 1401 New York (10036) *(G-11582)*
UNI Source Technology....514 748-8888
1320 Rt 9 Champlain (12919) *(G-3318)*
Unicel Corporation....760 741-3912
235 W Industry Ct Deer Park (11729) *(G-3944)*
Unicell Body Company Inc (PA)....716 853-8628
571 Howard St Buffalo (14206) *(G-3027)*
Unicell Body Company Inc....716 853-8628
170 Cordell Rd Schenectady (12303) *(G-14313)*
Unicell Body Company Inc....585 424-2660
1319 Brighton Henrietta Rochester (14623) *(G-13781)*
Unicenter Millwork Inc....716 741-8201
9605 Clarence Center Rd Clarence Center (14032) *(G-3450)*
Unico Special Products Inc....845 562-9255
25 Renwick St Newburgh (12550) *(G-11890)*
Unicorn Graphics, Garden City *Also called Won & Lee Inc (G-5119)*
Unifab Inc....585 235-1760
215 Tremont St Ste 31 Rochester (14608) *(G-13782)*
Unified Inc led....646 370-4650
35 W 36th St New York (10018) *(G-11583)*
Unified Media Inc....917 595-2710
180 Madison Ave New York (10016) *(G-11584)*
Unified Solutions For Clg Inc....718 782-8800
1829 Pacific St Brooklyn (11233) *(G-2535)*
Uniflex Holdings LLC (PA)....516 932-2000
1600 Caleds Ext Ste 135 Hauppauge (11788) *(G-5790)*
Unifor Inc....212 673-3434
149 5th Ave Ste 3r New York (10010) *(G-11585)*
Uniform Express, Rochester *Also called Kevin J Kassman (G-13502)*
Uniform Namemakers Inc....716 626-5474
55 Amherst Villa Rd Buffalo (14225) *(G-3028)*
Uniformed Fire Officer Assoiat....212 293-9300
125 Maiden Ln New York (10038) *(G-11586)*
Uniforms By Park Coats Inc....718 499-1182
790 3rd Ave Brooklyn (11232) *(G-2536)*
Unifrax Corporation....716 278-3800
2351 Whirlpool St Niagara Falls (14305) *(G-11987)*
Unifrax Holding Co (HQ)....212 644-5900
55 E 52nd St Fl 35 New York (10055) *(G-11587)*
Unifrax I LLC....716 696-3000
360 Fire Tower Dr Tonawanda (14150) *(G-15149)*
Unifrax I LLC (PA)....716 768-6500
600 Rverwalk Pkwy Ste 120 Tonawanda (14150) *(G-15150)*
Unifuse LLC....845 889-4000
2092 Route 9g Staatsburg (12580) *(G-14601)*
Unike Products Inc....347 686-4616
18230 Wexford Ter Apt 2m Jamaica (11432) *(G-6484)*
Unilever United States Inc....212 546-0200
390 Park Ave New York (10022) *(G-11588)*
Unilever United States Inc....212 546-0200
663 5th Ave Fl 8 New York (10022) *(G-11589)*
Unilock Ltd....716 822-6074
510 Smith St Buffalo (14210) *(G-3029)*
Unilock New York Inc (HQ)....845 278-6700
51 International Blvd Brewster (10509) *(G-1159)*
Unilumin North America Inc (PA)....732 904-2037
254 W 31st St New York (10001) *(G-11590)*
Unimar Inc....315 699-4400
3195 Vickery Rd Syracuse (13212) *(G-15017)*
Unimex Corporation (PA)....800 886-0390
54 E 64th St New York (10065) *(G-11591)*
Unimex Corporation....718 236-2222
1462 62nd St Brooklyn (11219) *(G-2537)*
Union Standard & Un Conf McHy, Bronx *Also called National Equipment Corporation (G-1321)*
Union Standard Eqp Co Div, Harrison *Also called National Equipment Corporation (G-5556)*
Union Sun & Journal, Lockport *Also called Cnhi LLC (G-7065)*

Unipharm Inc 212 594-3260
  350 5th Ave Ste 6701 New York (10118) *(G-11592)*

Uniqlo USA LLC 877 486-4756
  546 Broadway New York (10012) *(G-11593)*

Unique Designs Inc 212 575-7701
  521 5th Ave Rm 820 New York (10175) *(G-11594)*

Unique Display Mfg Corp (PA) 516 546-3800
  216 N Main St Ste D Freeport (11520) *(G-5031)*

Unique MBL Gran Orgnztion Corp 718 482-0440
  3831 9th St Long Island City (11101) *(G-7387)*

Unique Overseas Inc 516 466-9792
  425 Northern Blvd Ste 22 Great Neck (11021) *(G-5429)*

Unique Packaging Corporation 514 341-5872
  11320 State Route 9 # 3807 Champlain (12919) *(G-3319)*

Unique Petz LLC 212 714-1800
  10 W 33rd St Rm 220 New York (10001) *(G-11595)*

Unisend LLC 585 414-9575
  249 Gallant Fox Ln Webster (14580) *(G-15659)*

Unison Industries LLC 607 335-5000
  5345 State Highway 12 Norwich (13815) *(G-12130)*

Unistel LLC 585 341-4600
  860 Hard Rd Webster (14580) *(G-15660)*

Unisystems Inc (PA) 212 826-0850
  155 E 55th St Apt 203 New York (10022) *(G-11596)*

Unit Step Company, Sanborn *Also called Gamble & Gamble Inc (G-14142)*

United Aircraft Tech Inc 518 286-8867
  30 3rd St Troy (12180) *(G-15193)*

United Baking Co Inc 631 413-5116
  16 Bronx Ave Central Islip (11722) *(G-3291)*

United Biochemicals LLC 716 731-5161
  6351 Inducon Dr E Sanborn (14132) *(G-14151)*

United Brothers Jewelry Inc 212 921-2558
  48 W 48th St Ste 700 New York (10036) *(G-11597)*

United Business Forms, Woodside *Also called United Print Group Inc (G-16231)*

United Data Systems Inc 631 549-6900
  202 E Main St Ste 302 Huntington (11743) *(G-6230)*

United Dividers, Elmira *Also called Fennell Industries LLC (G-4352)*

United Farm Processing Corp (PA) 718 933-6060
  4366 Park Ave Bronx (10457) *(G-1387)*

United Gemdiam Inc 718 851-5083
  1537 52nd St Brooklyn (11219) *(G-2538)*

United Iron Inc 914 667-5700
  6 Roslyn Pl Mount Vernon (10550) *(G-8191)*

United Knitwear International (PA) 212 354-2920
  379 W Broadway Fl 3 New York (10012) *(G-11598)*

United Machining Inc 631 589-6751
  1595 Smithtown Ave Ste D Bohemia (11716) *(G-1093)*

United Materials LLC (PA) 716 683-1432
  3949 Frest Pk Way Ste 400 North Tonawanda (14120) *(G-12097)*

United Materials LLC 716 731-2332
  2186 Cory Dr Sanborn (14132) *(G-14152)*

United Materials LLC 716 662-0564
  75 Bank St Orchard Park (14127) *(G-12381)*

United Metal Industries Inc 516 354-6800
  1008 3rd Ave New Hyde Park (11040) *(G-8299)*

United Pet Group, Hauppauge *Also called Spectrum Brands Inc (G-5771)*

United Pickle Products Corp 718 933-6060
  4366 Park Ave Bronx (10457) *(G-1388)*

United Pipe Nipple Co Inc 516 295-2468
  1602 Lakeview Dr Hewlett (11557) *(G-5874)*

United Plastics Inc 718 389-2255
  640 Humboldt St Ste 1 Brooklyn (11222) *(G-2539)*

United Print Group Inc 718 392-4242
  4523 47th St Woodside (11377) *(G-16231)*

United Retail II 212 966-9692
  436 W Broadway New York (10012) *(G-11599)*

United Richter Electrical Mtrs 716 855-1945
  106 Michigan Ave Buffalo (14204) *(G-3030)*

United Rockland Holding Co Inc 845 357-1900
  9 N Airmont Rd Suffern (10901) *(G-14768)*

United Rubber Supply Co Inc 212 233-6650
  54 Warren St New York (10007) *(G-11600)*

United Satcom Inc 718 359-4100
  4555 Robinson St Flushing (11355) *(G-4903)*

United Sheet Metal Corp 718 482-1197
  4602 28th St Long Island City (11101) *(G-7388)*

United Silicone Inc 716 681-8222
  4471 Walden Ave Lancaster (14086) *(G-6837)*

United States Gypsum Company 585 948-5221
  2750 Maple Ave Oakfield (14125) *(G-12158)*

United Steel Products Inc 914 968-7782
  3340 127th Pl Flushing (11368) *(G-4904)*

United Steel Products Inc 718 478-5330
  3340 127th Pl Corona (11368) *(G-3751)*

United Structure Solution Inc 347 227-7526
  240 W 65th St Apt 26c New York (10023) *(G-11601)*

United Sttes Brnze Sign of Fla 516 352-5155
  811 2nd Ave New Hyde Park (11040) *(G-8300)*

United Synggue Cnsrvtive Jdism (PA) 212 533-7800
  3080 Broadway New York (10027) *(G-11602)*

United Technologies Corp 315 432-7849
  6304 Carrier Pkwy East Syracuse (13057) *(G-4246)*

United Technologies Corp 866 788-5095
  1212 Pittsford Victor Rd Pittsford (14534)` *(G-12657)*

United Thread Mills Corp (PA) 516 536-3900
  3530 Lawson Blvd Gf Oceanside (11572) *(G-12195)*

United Transit Mix Inc 718 416-3400
  318 Boerum St Brooklyn (11206) *(G-2540)*

United Wind Inc 888 313-3353
  155 Water St Brooklyn (11201) *(G-2541)*

United Wire Technologies Inc 315 623-7203
  1804 State Route 49 Constantia (13044) *(G-3637)*

United-Guardian Inc (PA) 631 273-0900
  230 Marcus Blvd Hauppauge (11788) *(G-5791)*

Unither Manufacturing LLC (HQ) 585 475-9000
  755 Jefferson Rd Rochester (14623) *(G-13783)*

Unither Manufacturing LLC 585 274-5430
  331 Clay Rd Rochester (14623) *(G-13784)*

Unitone Communication Systems 212 777-9090
  220 E 23rd St Ste 411 New York (10010) *(G-11603)*

Universal 3d Innovation Inc 516 837-9423
  1085 Rockaway Ave Valley Stream (11581) *(G-15362)*

Universal Armor Systems Corp 631 838-1836
  9 Tanners Ln Levittown (11756) *(G-6917)*

Universal Builders Supply Inc 845 758-8801
  45 Ocallaghan Ln Red Hook (12571) *(G-13074)*

Universal Cmmncations of Miami 212 986-5100
  801 2nd Ave Lbby New York (10017) *(G-11604)*

Universal Coolers Inc 718 788-8621
  120 13th St Brooklyn (11215) *(G-2542)*

Universal Custom Millwork Inc 518 330-6622
  3 Sam Stratton Rd Amsterdam (12010) *(G-351)*

Universal Designs Inc 718 721-1111
  3517 31st St Long Island City (11106) *(G-7389)*

Universal Edition Inc 917 213-2177
  331 W 57th St Ste 380 New York (10019) *(G-11605)*

Universal Elliot Corp 212 736-8877
  327 W 36th St Rm 700 New York (10018) *(G-11606)*

Universal Fire Proof Door 718 455-8442
  1171 Myrtle Ave Brooklyn (11206) *(G-2543)*

Universal Forest Products, Chaffee *Also called Ufp New York LLC (G-3308)*

Universal Forest Products, Hudson *Also called Ufp New York LLC (G-6182)*

Universal Forest Products, Auburn *Also called Ufp New York LLC (G-501)*

Universal Instruments Corp (HQ) 800 842-9732
  33 Broome Corporate Pkwy Conklin (13748) *(G-3633)*

Universal Interiors LLC 518 298-4400
  107 Lawrence Paquette Dr Champlain (12919) *(G-3320)*

Universal Luxury Brands Inc (PA) 646 248-5700
  452 W Broadway New York (10012) *(G-11607)*

Universal Metal Fabricators 845 331-8248
  27 Emerick St Kingston (12401) *(G-6719)*

Universal Metal Works LLC 315 598-7607
  159 Hubbard St Fulton (13069) *(G-5076)*

Universal Metals Inc 516 829-0896
  98 Cuttermill Rd Ste 428 Great Neck (11021) *(G-5430)*

Universal Mus Group Hldngs Inc (HQ) 212 333-8000
  1755 Broadway Fl 6 New York (10019) *(G-11608)*

Universal Music Group Inc 212 333-8237
  825 8th Ave Fl C2b New York (10019) *(G-11609)*

Universal Packg Systems Inc (PA) 631 543-2277
  380 Townline Rd Ste 130 Hauppauge (11788) *(G-5792)*

Universal Parent and Youth 917 754-2426
  1530 Pa Ave Apt 17e Brooklyn (11239) *(G-2544)*

Universal Precision Corp 585 321-9760
  40 Commerce Dr Rochester (14623) *(G-13785)*

Universal Proteins, Melville *Also called Natural Organics Labs Inc (G-7807)*

Universal Ready Mix Inc 516 746-4535
  197 Atlantic Ave New Hyde Park (11040) *(G-8301)*

Universal Remote Control Inc (PA) 914 835-4484
  500 Mmaroneck Ave Ste 502 Harrison (10528) *(G-5563)*

Universal Screening Associates 718 232-2744
  6509 11th Ave Brooklyn (11219) *(G-2545)*

Universal Shielding Corp 631 667-7900
  20 W Jefryn Blvd Deer Park (11729) *(G-3945)*

Universal Signs and Svc Inc 631 446-1121
  435 Brook Ave Unit 2 Deer Park (11729) *(G-3946)*

Universal Steel Fabricators 718 342-0782
  90 Junius St Brooklyn (11212) *(G-2546)*

Universal Step Inc 315 437-7611
  5970 Butternut Dr East Syracuse (13057) *(G-4247)*

Universal Thin Film Lab Corp 845 562-0601
  232 N Plank Rd Newburgh (12550) *(G-11891)*

Universal Tooling Corporation 716 985-4691
  4533 Route 60 Gerry (14740) *(G-5172)*

Universal Water Technology, Far Rockaway *Also called Business Advisory Services (G-4562)*

Universe Publishing, New York *Also called Rizzoli Intl Publications Inc (G-11052)*

University Advertising Agency, Stony Brook *Also called Stony Brook University (G-14741)*

University of Rochester 585 275-3483
  250 E River Rd Rochester (14623) *(G-13786)*

University Table Cloth Company 845 371-3876
  10 Centre St Spring Valley (10977) *(G-14586)*

Uniware Houseware Corp (PA) 631 242-7400
  120 Wilshire Blvd Ste B Brentwood (11717) *(G-1129)*

Unlimited Industries Inc..................................631 665-5800
44 W Jefryn Blvd Ste Q2 Deer Park (11729) (G-3947)
Unlimited Ink Inc...631 582-0696
595 Old Willets Path B Hauppauge (11788) (G-5793)
Unqork Inc..844 486-7675
85 5th Ave Fl 6 New York (10003) (G-11610)
Untitled Media...212 780-0960
45 Lispenard St Apt 1w New York (10013) (G-11611)
Untuckit LLC (PA)..347 524-9111
110 Greene St Ste 400 New York (10012) (G-11612)
Untuckit LLC..646 724-1857
379 W Broadway Fl 2 New York (10012) (G-11613)
UOP LLC...716 879-7600
175 E Park Dr Tonawanda (14150) (G-15151)
Up Country, New York Also called Du Monde Trading Inc (G-9275)
Upayori, Brooklyn Also called Universal Parent and Youth (G-2544)
Upbeat Upholstery & Design LLC.......................347 480-3980
344 Stagg St Brooklyn (11206) (G-2547)
Uppercut, Suffern Also called NY Cutting Inc (G-14763)
Upstate Cabinet Company Inc.........................585 429-5090
32 Marway Cir Rochester (14624) (G-13787)
Upstate Door Inc (PA)..................................585 786-3880
26 Industrial St Warsaw (14569) (G-15509)
Upstate Farms Cheese LLC............................607 527-4584
8600 Main St Campbell (14821) (G-3117)
Upstate Farms Dairy LLC..............................716 892-3156
25 Anderson Rd Buffalo (14225) (G-3031)
Upstate Increte Incorporated..........................585 254-2010
1029 Lyell Ave Ste A Rochester (14606) (G-13788)
Upstate Insulated Glass Inc............................315 475-4960
47 Weber Rd Central Square (13036) (G-3297)
Upstate Milk Co-Operatives, Buffalo Also called Upstate Niagara Coop Inc (G-3033)
Upstate Niagara Coop Inc (PA).........................716 892-3156
25 Anderson Rd Buffalo (14225) (G-3032)
Upstate Niagara Coop Inc..............................716 892-2121
1730 Dale Rd Buffalo (14225) (G-3033)
Upstate Niagara Coop Inc..............................585 458-1880
45 Fulton Ave Rochester (14608) (G-13789)
Upstate Niagara Coop Inc..............................716 484-7178
223 Fluvanna Ave Jamestown (14701) (G-6551)
Upstate Niagara Coop Inc..............................315 389-5111
22 County Route 52 North Lawrence (12967) (G-12033)
Upstate Office Furniture, Johnson City Also called Upstate Office Liquidators Inc (G-6609)
Upstate Office Liquidators Inc........................607 722-9234
718 Azon Way Johnson City (13790) (G-6609)
Upstate Piping Products Inc...........................518 238-3457
95 Hudson River Rd Waterford (12188) (G-15548)
Upstate Printing Inc.....................................315 475-6140
433 W Onondaga St Syracuse (13202) (G-15018)
Upstate Records Management LLC.....................518 834-1144
1729 Front St Keeseville (12944) (G-6646)
Upstate Refractory Svcs Inc...........................315 331-2955
100 Erie Blvd Newark (14513) (G-11855)
Upstate Tube Inc...315 488-5636
5050 Smoral Rd Camillus (13031) (G-3112)
Upstone Materials Inc...................................518 873-2275
Rr 9 Lewis (12950) (G-6918)
Upstone Materials Inc...................................518 891-0236
909 State Route 3 Saranac Lake (12983) (G-14160)
Upstone Materials Inc (HQ).............................518 561-5321
111 Quarry Rd Plattsburgh (12901) (G-12787)
Upstone Materials Inc...................................518 483-2671
359 Elm St Malone (12953) (G-7493)
Upstone Materials Inc...................................315 265-8036
111 Quarry Rd Plattsburgh (12901) (G-12788)
Upstone Materials Inc...................................315 764-0251
539 S Main St Massena (13662) (G-7673)
Uptek Solutions Corp....................................631 256-5565
130 Knickerbocker Ave A Bohemia (11716) (G-1094)
Uptown, Halfmoon Also called Save More Beverage Corp (G-5499)
Uptown Media Group LLC...............................212 360-5073
113 E 125th St Frnt 1 New York (10035) (G-11614)
Upturn Industries Inc..................................607 967-2923
2-4 Whitney Way Bainbridge (13733) (G-528)
Urban Apparel Group Inc...............................212 947-7009
226 W 37th St Fl 6l New York (10018) (G-11615)
Urban Mapping Inc......................................415 946-8170
295 Madison Ave Rm 1010 New York (10017) (G-11616)
Urban Precast LLC......................................845 331-6299
6 Kieffer Ln Kingston (12401) (G-6720)
Urban Rose, New York Also called French Atmosphere Inc (G-9536)
Urban Technologies Inc.................................716 672-2709
3451 Stone Quarry Rd Fredonia (14063) (G-4972)
Urban Textiles Inc.......................................212 777-1900
254 W 35th St Unit 13 New York (10001) (G-11617)
Urbandaddy Inc...212 929-7905
900 Broadway Ste 1003 New York (10003) (G-11618)
Urc, Harrison Also called Universal Remote Control Inc (G-5563)
Urdu Times...718 297-8700
16920 Hillside Ave Jamaica (11432) (G-6485)
Urethane Technology Co Inc............................845 561-5500
59 Temple Ave Newburgh (12550) (G-11892)

Urogen Ltd...646 768-9780
689 5th Ave Fl 14 New York (10022) (G-11619)
Urogen Pharma Inc......................................646 506-4663
499 Park Ave Ste 1200 New York (10022) (G-11620)
Ursula Company Store, Waterford Also called Ursula of Switzerland Inc (G-15549)
Ursula of Switzerland Inc (PA).........................518 237-2580
31 Mohawk Ave Waterford (12188) (G-15549)
Urthworx Inc..646 373-7535
320 W 106th St Apt 2f New York (10025) (G-11621)
US Airports Flight Support Svc, Rochester Also called Usairports Services Inc (G-13790)
US Allegro Inc...347 408-6601
5430 44th St Maspeth (11378) (G-7640)
US Alliance Paper Inc...................................631 254-3030
101 Heartland Blvd Edgewood (11717) (G-4290)
US Angels, New York Also called S & C Bridals LLC (G-11105)
US Authentic LLC...914 767-0295
11 Mt Holly Rd E Katonah (10536) (G-6639)
US Beverage Net Inc......................................315 579-2025
225 W Jefferson St Syracuse (13202) (G-15019)
US China Magazine..212 663-4333
200 W 95th St Apt 21 New York (10025) (G-11622)
US Concrete Inc..718 433-0111
4717 27th St Long Island City (11101) (G-7390)
US Concrete Inc..718 853-4644
10 Powerhouse Rd Roslyn Heights (11577) (G-14059)
US Concrete Inc..718 438-6800
692 Mcdonald Ave Brooklyn (11218) (G-2548)
US Design Group Ltd.....................................212 354-4070
1385 Broadway Rm 1905 New York (10018) (G-11623)
US Diagnostics Inc.......................................866 216-5308
711 3rd Ave Rm 1502 New York (10017) (G-11624)
US Drives Inc..716 731-1606
2221 Niagara Falls Blvd # 41 Niagara Falls (14304) (G-11988)
US Electroplating Corp...................................631 293-1998
100 Field St Unit A West Babylon (11704) (G-15754)
US Energy Group, New Hyde Park Also called Use Acquisition LLC (G-8302)
US Epoxy Inc..800 332-3883
11 Old Dock Rd Unit 7 Yaphank (11980) (G-16277)
US Global Lubricants Inc................................845 271-4277
22 Hudson Dr Stony Point (10980) (G-14750)
US Hoists Corp...631 472-3030
800 Burman Blvd Calverton (11933) (G-3090)
US Home Textiles Group LLC............................212 768-3030
1400 Broadway Fl 18 New York (10018) (G-11625)
US Juice Partners LLC (HQ).............................516 621-1122
2 Seaview Blvd Port Washington (11050) (G-12930)
US News & World Report Inc (PA)........................212 716-6800
120 5th Ave Fl 7 New York (10011) (G-11626)
US Nonwovens Corp.......................................631 236-4491
105 Emjay Blvd Brentwood (11717) (G-1130)
US Nonwovens Corp.......................................631 232-0001
85 Nicon Ct Hauppauge (11788) (G-5794)
US Nonwovens Corp.......................................631 952-0100
360 Moreland Rd Commack (11725) (G-3600)
US Nonwovens Corp.......................................631 952-0100
110 Emjay Blvd Brentwood (11717) (G-1131)
US Nonwovens Corp (PA).................................631 952-0100
100 Emjay Blvd Brentwood (11717) (G-1132)
US Peroxide..716 775-5585
1815 Love Rd Ste 1 Grand Island (14072) (G-5347)
US Polychemical Holding Corp...........................845 356-5530
584 Chestnut Ridge Rd Spring Valley (10977) (G-14587)
US Pump Corp..516 303-7799
707 Woodfield Rd West Hempstead (11552) (G-15781)
US Salt LLC..607 535-2721
3580 Salt Point Rd Watkins Glen (14891) (G-15617)
US Salt LLC (HQ)...888 872-7258
3580 Salt Point Rd Watkins Glen (14891) (G-15618)
US Sander LLC..518 875-9157
4131 Rte 20 Esperance (12066) (G-4485)
US Space LLC...646 278-0371
1212 Avenue Of The New York (10036) (G-11627)
US Sweeteners Corp.....................................718 854-8714
133-48 St Brooklyn (11232) (G-2549)
US Weekly..212 484-1616
1290 Ave Of The Americas New York (10104) (G-11628)
USA Body Inc...315 852-6123
994 Middle Lake Rd De Ruyter (13052) (G-3823)
USA Custom Pad Corp (PA).............................607 563-9550
16 Winkler Rd Sidney (13838) (G-14439)
USA Furs By George Inc.................................212 643-1415
212 W 30th St New York (10001) (G-11629)
USA Illumination Inc....................................845 565-8500
1126 River Rd New Windsor (12553) (G-8385)
USA Sewing Inc..315 792-8017
901 Broad St Ste 2 Utica (13501) (G-15297)
USA Signs of America Inc...............................631 254-6900
172 E Industry Ct Deer Park (11729) (G-3948)
USA Tees.com, Brooklyn Also called Universal Screening Associates (G-2545)
USA Today International Corp............................703 854-3400
535 Madison Ave Fl 27 New York (10022) (G-11630)
Usai, New Windsor Also called USA Illumination Inc (G-8385)

Usairports Services Inc......585 527-6835
1295 Scottsville Rd Rochester (14624) *(G-13790)*
Use Acquisition LLC......516 812-6800
270 Park Ave New Hyde Park (11040) *(G-8302)*
Used Equipment Directory, New York *Also called Informa Media Inc (G-9890)*
Usheco Inc......845 658-9200
138 Maple Hill Rd Kingston (12401) *(G-6721)*
Ushers Machine and Tool Co Inc......518 877-5501
180 Ushers Rd Round Lake (12151) *(G-14062)*
Uspa Accessories LLC......212 868-2590
1411 Broadway Fl 7 New York (10018) *(G-11631)*
Usq Group LLC......212 777-7751
222 Broadway Fl 19 New York (10038) *(G-11632)*
UTC Aerospace Systems......315 838-1200
104 Otis St Rome (13441) *(G-13875)*
Utica Boilers, Utica *Also called ECR International Inc (G-15260)*
Utica Cutlery Company......315 733-4663
820 Noyes St Utica (13502) *(G-15298)*
Utica Metal Products Inc......315 732-6163
1526 Lincoln Ave Utica (13502) *(G-15299)*
Utility Brass & Bronze Div, Brooklyn *Also called Giumenta Corp (G-1888)*
Utility Canvas Inc (PA)......845 255-9290
2686 Route 44 55 Gardiner (12525) *(G-5132)*
Utility Engineering Co......845 735-8900
40 Walter St Pearl River (10965) *(G-12542)*
Utility Manufacturing Co Inc......516 997-6300
700 Main St Westbury (11590) *(G-15936)*
Utility Systems Tech Inc......518 326-4142
70 Cohoes Rd Watervliet (12189) *(G-15611)*
Utleys Incorporated......718 956-1661
3123 61st St Woodside (11377) *(G-16232)*
V & E Kohnstamm & Co Div, Brooklyn *Also called Virginia Dare Extract Co Inc (G-2561)*
V & J Graphics Inc......315 363-1933
153 Phelps St Oneida (13421) *(G-12255)*
V A I, Ronkonkoma *Also called Vormittag Associates Inc (G-14024)*
V A P Tool & Dye......631 587-5262
436 W 4th St West Islip (11795) *(G-15813)*
V C N Group Ltd Inc......516 223-4812
1 Clifton St North Baldwin (11510) *(G-12010)*
V E Power Door Co Inc......631 231-4500
140 Emjay Blvd Brentwood (11717) *(G-1133)*
V E W, New York *Also called Vera Wang Group LLC (G-11657)*
V Lake Industries Inc......716 885-9141
1555 Niagara St Buffalo (14213) *(G-3034)*
V Magazine, New York *Also called Visionaire Publishing LLC (G-11693)*
V Technical Textiles Inc......315 597-1674
4502 State Route 31 Palmyra (14522) *(G-12494)*
Va Inc......585 385-5930
803 Linden Ave Ste 1 Rochester (14625) *(G-13791)*
Vaad LHafotzas Sichoes......718 778-5436
788 Eastern Pkwy Brooklyn (11213) *(G-2550)*
Vac Air Service Inc......716 665-2206
1295 E 2nd St Jamestown (14701) *(G-6552)*
Vaccinex Inc......585 271-2700
1895 Mount Hope Ave Rochester (14620) *(G-13792)*
Vacheron New York Btq, New York *Also called Richemont North America Inc (G-11038)*
Vactronics, Bayside Hills *Also called Cathay Global Co Inc (G-746)*
Vacuum Instrument Corporation (PA)......631 737-0900
2101 9th Ave Ste A Ronkonkoma (11779) *(G-14023)*
Vaire LLC......631 271-4933
200 E 2nd St Ste 34 Huntington Station (11746) *(G-6265)*
Valad Electric Heating Corp......888 509-4927
65 Leonards Dr Montgomery (12549) *(G-8068)*
Valair Inc......716 751-9480
87 Harbor St Wilson (14172) *(G-16154)*
Valassis Communications Inc......585 627-4138
5 Marway Cir Ste 8 Rochester (14624) *(G-13793)*
Valcour Brewing Company LLC......518 324-2337
49 Ohio Rd Plattsburgh (12903) *(G-12789)*
Valenti Distributing......716 824-2304
84 Maple Ave Blasdell (14219) *(G-924)*
Valenti Neckwear Co Inc......914 969-0700
540 Nepperhan Ave Ste 564 Yonkers (10701) *(G-16354)*
Valentin & Kalich Jwly Mfg Ltd......212 575-9044
42 W 48th St Ste 903 New York (10036) *(G-11633)*
Valentin Magro, New York *Also called Valentin & Kalich Jwly Mfg Ltd (G-11633)*
Valentine Jewelry Mfg Co Inc......212 382-0606
31 W 47th St Ste 602 New York (10036) *(G-11634)*
Valentine Packaging Corp......718 418-6000
6020 59th Pl Ste 7 Maspeth (11378) *(G-7641)*
Valerie Bohigian......914 631-8866
225 Hunter Ave Sleepy Hollow (10591) *(G-14465)*
Valian Associates, Sleepy Hollow *Also called Valerie Bohigian (G-14465)*
Valiant Entertainment LLC......212 972-0361
350 7th Ave Rm 300 New York (10001) *(G-11635)*
Valle Signs and Awnings......516 408-3440
55 Decker St Copiague (11726) *(G-3686)*
Valley Creek Side Inc......315 839-5526
1960 State Route 8 Clayville (13322) *(G-3458)*
Valley Industrial Products Inc......631 385-9300
152 New York Ave Huntington (11743) *(G-6231)*
Valley Industries, Gerry *Also called Cobbe Industries Inc (G-5170)*
Valley Signs, Clayville *Also called Valley Creek Side Inc (G-3458)*
Valley Stream Sporting Gds Inc......516 593-7800
325 Hendrickson Ave Lynbrook (11563) *(G-7442)*
Valmont Inc (PA)......212 685-1653
1 W 34th St Rm 303 New York (10001) *(G-11636)*
Valmont Site Pro 1, Hauppauge *Also called Pirod Inc (G-5742)*
Valois of America Inc......845 639-3700
250 N Route 303 Congers (10920) *(G-3619)*
Valplast International Corp......516 442-3923
200 Shames Dr Westbury (11590) *(G-15937)*
Value Fragrances & Flavors Inc......845 294-5726
7 Musket Ct Goshen (10924) *(G-5315)*
Value Line Inc (HQ)......212 907-1500
551 5th Ave Fl 3 New York (10176) *(G-11637)*
Value Line Publishing LLC......201 842-8054
551 5th Ave Fl 3 New York (10176) *(G-11638)*
Value Spring Technology Inc......917 705-4658
521 Harrison Ave Harrison (10528) *(G-5564)*
Valvetech Inc......315 548-4551
1391 Phelps Junction Rd Phelps (14532) *(G-12610)*
Van Blarcom Closures Inc (PA)......718 855-3810
156 Sanford St Brooklyn (11205) *(G-2551)*
Van Cpeters Logging Inc......607 637-3574
4480 Peas Eddy Rd Hancock (13783) *(G-5540)*
Van Heusen, New Windsor *Also called Pvh Corp (G-8379)*
Van Heusen, Deer Park *Also called Pvh Corp (G-3924)*
Van Heusen, New York *Also called Pvh Corp (G-10936)*
Van Heusen, New York *Also called Pvh Corp (G-10937)*
Van Laeken Richard......315 331-0289
2680 Parker Rd Newark (14513) *(G-11856)*
Van Leeuwen Artisan Ice Cream......718 701-1630
56 Dobbin St Brooklyn (11222) *(G-2552)*
Van Reenen Tool & Die Inc......585 288-6000
350 Commerce Dr Ste 4 Rochester (14623) *(G-13794)*
Van Rip Inc......415 529-5403
67 West St Ste 705 Brooklyn (11222) *(G-2553)*
Van Slyke Belting LLC......518 283-5479
606 Snyders Corners Rd Poestenkill (12140) *(G-12805)*
Van Thomas Inc......585 426-1414
740 Driving Park Ave G1 Rochester (14613) *(G-13795)*
Vanberg & Dewulf Co Inc......607 547-8184
52 Pioneer St Ste 4 Cooperstown (13326) *(G-3641)*
Vance Metal Fabricators Inc......315 789-5626
251 Gambee Rd Geneva (14456) *(G-5165)*
Vanchlor Company Inc (PA)......716 434-2624
45 Main St Lockport (14094) *(G-7117)*
Vanchlor Company Inc......716 434-2624
555 W Jackson St Lockport (14094) *(G-7118)*
Vandam Inc......212 929-0416
1111 44th Rd Fl 403 Long Island City (11101) *(G-7391)*
Vandemark Chemical Inc (PA)......716 433-6764
1 N Transit Rd Lockport (14094) *(G-7119)*
Vander Heyden Woodworking......212 242-0525
151 W 25th St Fl 8 New York (10001) *(G-11639)*
Vandilay Industries Inc......631 226-3064
60 Bell St Unit A West Babylon (11704) *(G-15755)*
Vanec, Orchard Park *Also called Vibration & Noise Engrg Corp (G-12382)*
Vanguard Graphics LLC......607 272-1212
17 Hallwoods Rd Ithaca (14850) *(G-6416)*
Vanguard Metals Inc......631 234-6500
135 Brightside Ave Central Islip (11722) *(G-3292)*
Vanguard Printing, Ithaca *Also called Vanguard Graphics LLC (G-6416)*
Vanhouten Motorsports......315 387-6312
27 Center Rd Lacona (13083) *(G-6747)*
Vanilla Sky LLC......347 738-4195
3318 Broadway Long Island City (11106) *(G-7392)*
Vanity Fair......212 286-7919
285 Fulton St New York (10007) *(G-11640)*
Vanity Fair Bathmart Inc......718 584-6700
2971 Webster Ave Bronx (10458) *(G-1389)*
Vanity Fair Brands LP......212 548-1548
25 W 39th St New York (10018) *(G-11641)*
Vanity Room Inc......212 921-7154
230 W 39th St Rm 900 New York (10018) *(G-11642)*
Vanlab, Rochester *Also called Synergy Flavors NY Company LLC (G-13753)*
Vans Inc......631 724-1011
313 Smith Haven Mall Lake Grove (11755) *(G-6762)*
Vansantis Development Inc......315 461-0113
4595 Morgan Pl Liverpool (13090) *(G-7046)*
Vansridge Dairy LLC......315 364-8569
2831 Black St Scipio Center (13147) *(G-14327)*
Vantage Elevator Solutions, Bronx *Also called GAI Manufacturing Co LLC (G-1264)*
Vantage Mfg & Assembly LLC......845 471-5290
900 Dutchess Tpke Poughkeepsie (12603) *(G-12988)*
Vante Inc......716 778-7691
3600 Coomer Rd Newfane (14108) *(G-11896)*
Varflex Corporation......315 336-4400
512 W Court St Rome (13440) *(G-13876)*
Variable Graphics LLC......212 691-2323
15 W 36th St Rm 601 New York (10018) *(G-11643)*

ALPHABETIC

Varian Medical Systems, Liverpool *Also called Infimed Inc* ***(G-7014)***
Varick Street Litho Inc....646 843-0800
149 W 27th St Fl 4 New York (10001) ***(G-11644)***
Varnish Software Inc....201 857-2832
85 Broad St Fl 18 New York (10004) ***(G-11645)***
Varonis Systems Inc (PA)....877 292-8787
1250 Broadway Fl 29 New York (10001) ***(G-11646)***
Varsity Monitor LLC....212 691-6292
50 5th Ave Fl 3 Flr 3 New York (10011) ***(G-11647)***
Vaso Corporation (PA)....516 997-4600
137 Commercial St Ste 200 Plainview (11803) ***(G-12722)***
Vasomedical Solutions Inc....516 997-4600
137 Commercial St Ste 200 Plainview (11803) ***(G-12723)***
Vasquez Tito....212 944-0441
36 W 47th St Ste 206 New York (10036) ***(G-11648)***
Vassilaros Coffee, Flushing *Also called John A Vassilaros & Son Inc* ***(G-4865)***
Vaughan Designs Inc (HQ)....212 319-7070
979 3rd Ave Ste 1511 New York (10022) ***(G-11649)***
Vault.com, Vault Media, New York *Also called Vaultcom Inc* ***(G-11650)***
Vaultcom Inc (PA)....212 366-4212
132 W 31st St Rm 1501 New York (10001) ***(G-11650)***
Vcp Mobility Inc....718 356-7827
4131 Richmond Ave Staten Island (10312) ***(G-14725)***
Vdc Electronics Inc....631 423-8220
155 W Carver St Ste 2 Huntington (11743) ***(G-6232)***
Vector Group Ltd....212 409-2800
712 5th Ave New York (10019) ***(G-11651)***
Vector Magnetics LLC....607 273-8351
236 Cherry St Ithaca (14850) ***(G-6417)***
Vectra Visual, Long Island City *Also called Taylor Communications Inc* ***(G-7378)***
Veea Inc....212 535-6050
164 E 83rd St New York (10028) ***(G-11652)***
Veeapay, New York *Also called Veea Inc* ***(G-11652)***
Veeco Instruments Inc....516 677-0200
100 Sunnyside Blvd Ste B Woodbury (11797) ***(G-16184)***
Veeco Instruments Inc....516 349-8300
1 Terminal Dr Plainview (11803) ***(G-12724)***
Veeco Instruments Inc (PA)....516 677-0200
1 Terminal Dr Plainview (11803) ***(G-12725)***
Veeco Process Equipment, Plainview *Also called Veeco Instruments Inc* ***(G-12724)***
Veeco Process Equipment Inc (HQ)....516 677-0200
1 Terminal Dr Plainview (11803) ***(G-12726)***
Vega Coffee Inc....415 881-7969
325 N End Ave Apt 4b New York (10282) ***(G-11653)***
Vegetable Operations, Geneva *Also called Seneca Foods Corporation* ***(G-5162)***
Vegetable Operations, Marion *Also called Seneca Foods Corporation* ***(G-7575)***
Vehicle Manufacturers Inc....631 851-1700
1300 Veterans Hwy Ste 110 Hauppauge (11788) ***(G-5795)***
Vehicle Safety Dept....315 458-6683
5801 E Taft Rd Ste 4 Syracuse (13212) ***(G-15020)***
Vehicle Tracking Solutions LLC....631 586-7400
152 Veterans Memorial Hwy Commack (11725) ***(G-3601)***
Veja Electronics Inc (PA)....631 321-6086
46 W Jefryn Blvd Ste A Deer Park (11729) ***(G-3949)***
Velis Associates Inc (PA)....631 225-4220
151 S 14th St Lindenhurst (11757) ***(G-6981)***
Vell Company Inc....845 365-1013
700 Oak Tree Rd Palisades (10964) ***(G-12484)***
Velmex Inc....585 657-6151
7550 State Route 5 And 20 Bloomfield (14469) ***(G-950)***
Velocity Pharma LLC....631 393-2905
210-220 Sea Ln Farmingdale (11735) ***(G-4761)***
Velocity Print Solutions, Scotia *Also called Shipmtes/Printmates Holdg Corp* ***(G-14336)***
Velp Scientific Inc....631 573-6002
155 Keyland Ct Bohemia (11716) ***(G-1095)***
Velvet Healing By Alma Corp....347 271-4220
645 Melrose Ave Frnt 1 Bronx (10455) ***(G-1390)***
Velvetop Products, Huntington Station *Also called Walsh & Hughes Inc* ***(G-6266)***
Venco Sales Inc....631 754-0782
755 Park Ave Ste 300 Huntington (11743) ***(G-6233)***
Vending Times Inc....516 442-1850
55 Maple Ave Ste 304 Rockville Centre (11570) ***(G-13840)***
Vendome Group LLC....646 795-3899
237 W 35th St Fl 16 New York (10001) ***(G-11654)***
Vendome Press, New York *Also called Helvetica Press Incorporated* ***(G-9764)***
Veneer One Inc....516 536-6480
3415 Hampton Rd Oceanside (11572) ***(G-12196)***
Vengo Inc....866 526-7054
999 S Oyster Bay Rd # 407 Bethpage (11714) ***(G-845)***
Venice Marina, Brooklyn *Also called Marina Holding Corp* ***(G-2115)***
Vent-A-Fume, Buffalo *Also called Vent-A-Kiln Corporation* ***(G-3035)***
Vent-A-Kiln Corporation....716 876-2023
51 Botsford Pl Ste 1 Buffalo (14216) ***(G-3035)***
Ventosa Vineyards LLC....315 719-0000
3440 State Route 96a Geneva (14456) ***(G-5166)***
Ventrus Biosciences Inc....646 706-5208
99 Hudson St New York (10013) ***(G-11655)***
Ventura Enterprise Co Inc....212 391-0170
512 Fashion Ave Fl 38 New York (10018) ***(G-11656)***
Venue Graphics Supply Inc....718 361-1690
1120 46th Rd Long Island City (11101) ***(G-7393)***
Venus, New York *Also called Shah Diamonds Inc* ***(G-11202)***
Venus Manufacturing Co Inc (PA)....315 639-3100
349 Lakeview Dr Dexter (13634) ***(G-4007)***
Venus Printing Company....212 967-8900
1420 Kew Ave Hewlett (11557) ***(G-5875)***
Vepo Solutions LLC....914 384-2121
3 Fairview Ct Cross River (10518) ***(G-3804)***
Ver-Tech Elevator, Ozone Park *Also called Elevator Ventures Corporation* ***(G-12460)***
Vera Wang Group LLC (PA)....212 575-6400
15 E 26th St Fl 4 New York (10010) ***(G-11657)***
Veranda Magazine, New York *Also called Veranda Publications Inc* ***(G-11658)***
Veranda Publications Inc....212 903-5206
300 W 57th St Fl 28 New York (10019) ***(G-11658)***
Veratex Inc (PA)....212 683-9300
534 W 42nd St Apt 8 New York (10036) ***(G-11659)***
Verdonette Inc....212 719-2003
270 W 39th St Fl 5 New York (10018) ***(G-11660)***
Veriled Inc....877 521-5520
100 Church St Ste 871 New York (10007) ***(G-11661)***
Verilogue, Long Island City *Also called Publicis Health LLC* ***(G-7330)***
Verint Americas Inc (HQ)....631 962-9334
175 Broadhollow Rd # 100 Melville (11747) ***(G-7832)***
Verint SEC Intelligence Inc....631 962-9300
175 Broadhollow Rd # 100 Melville (11747) ***(G-7833)***
Verint Systems Inc (PA)....631 962-9600
175 Broadhollow Rd # 100 Melville (11747) ***(G-7834)***
Verizon, New York *Also called Supermedia LLC* ***(G-11397)***
Verla International Ltd....845 561-2440
463 Temple Hill Rd New Windsor (12553) ***(G-8386)***
Vermed, Buffalo *Also called Vermont Medical Inc* ***(G-3036)***
Vermont Medical Inc....802 463-9976
400 Exchange St Buffalo (14204) ***(G-3036)***
Vermont Multicolor Slate....518 642-2400
146 State Route 22a Middle Granville (12849) ***(G-7871)***
Vermont Structural Slate Co....518 499-1912
Buckley Rd Whitehall (12887) ***(G-16078)***
Vernon Devices, New Rochelle *Also called Halpern Tool Corp* ***(G-8338)***
Vernon Plating Works Inc....718 639-1124
3318 57th St Woodside (11377) ***(G-16233)***
Vernon Wine & Liquor Inc....718 784-5096
5006 Vernon Blvd Long Island City (11101) ***(G-7394)***
Verns Machine Co Inc....315 926-4223
4929 Steel Point Rd Marion (14505) ***(G-7577)***
Verona Pharma Inc....914 797-5007
50 Main St Ste 1000 White Plains (10606) ***(G-16068)***
Verragio Ltd (PA)....212 868-8181
132 W 36th St Bsmt New York (10018) ***(G-11662)***
Verris Inc....201 565-1648
99 Wall St Unit 236 New York (10005) ***(G-11663)***
Versailles Drapery Upholstery....212 533-2059
4709 30th St Ste 200 Long Island City (11101) ***(G-7395)***
Versailles Industries LLC....212 792-9615
485 Fashion Ave Rm 500 New York (10018) ***(G-11664)***
Versant Health, Latham *Also called Davis Vision Inc* ***(G-6854)***
Versaponents, Deer Park *Also called Lighting Sculptures Inc* ***(G-3898)***
Versaponents Inc....631 242-3387
66 N Industry Ct Deer Park (11729) ***(G-3950)***
Verso Inc....718 246-8160
20 Jay St Ste 1010 Brooklyn (11201) ***(G-2554)***
Verso Corporation....212 599-2700
370 Lexington Ave Rm 802 New York (10017) ***(G-11665)***
Vertaloc, New York *Also called US Diagnostics Inc* ***(G-11624)***
Vertana Group LLC (PA)....646 430-8226
450 Lexington Ave Fl 4 New York (10017) ***(G-11666)***
Vertarib Inc....561 683-0888
471 N Broadway Ste 196 Jericho (11753) ***(G-6597)***
Vertex Innovative Solutions....315 437-6711
6671 Commerce Blvd Syracuse (13211) ***(G-15021)***
Vertical Apparel, New York *Also called American Apparel Trading Corp* ***(G-8544)***
Vertical Research Partners LLC....212 257-6499
52 Vanderbilt Ave Rm 200 New York (10017) ***(G-11667)***
Vertigo Drones, Webster *Also called Ingenious Ingenuity Inc* ***(G-15642)***
Vertiv Corporation....516 349-8500
79 Express St Fl 14 Plainview (11803) ***(G-12727)***
Vescom Structural Systems Inc....516 876-8100
1327 Roosevelt Way Westbury (11590) ***(G-15938)***
Vespa Sand & Stone, Watertown *Also called John Vespa Inc* ***(G-15575)***
Vestal Asphalt Inc....607 785-3393
201 Stage Rd Vestal (13850) ***(G-15387)***
Vestal Electronic Devices LLC....607 773-8461
635 Dickson St Endicott (13760) ***(G-4477)***
Veteran Air LLC....315 720-1101
7174 State Fair Blvd Syracuse (13209) ***(G-15022)***
Veteran Air Filtration, Syracuse *Also called Veteran Air LLC* ***(G-15022)***
Veteran Offset Printing, Rochester *Also called Veterans Offset Printing Inc* ***(G-13796)***
Veterans Offset Printing Inc....585 288-2900
500 N Goodman St Rochester (14609) ***(G-13796)***
Veterinary Biochemical Ltd....845 473-1900
201 Smith St Poughkeepsie (12601) ***(G-12989)***
Vetra Systems Corporation....631 434-3185
275 Marcus Blvd Unit J Hauppauge (11788) ***(G-5796)***

Vetroelite Inc 925 724-7900
  115 W 30th St Rm 402 New York (10001) *(G-11668)*

Vetta Jewelry Inc (PA) 212 564-8250
  989 Avenue Of The America New York (10018) *(G-11669)*

Vexos Inc (HQ) 855 711-3227
  60 E 42nd St Ste 1250 New York (10165) *(G-11670)*

Vez Inc 718 273-7002
  3801 Victory Blvd Ste 5 Staten Island (10314) *(G-14726)*

Vf Imagewear Inc 718 352-2363
  333 Pratt Ave Bayside (11359) *(G-744)*

Vf Outdoor Inc 718 698-6215
  2655 Richmond Ave # 1570 Staten Island (10314) *(G-14727)*

Vf Outdoor LLC 845 928-4900
  461 Dune Rd Central Valley (10917) *(G-3301)*

Vf Services LLC 212 575-7820
  25 W 39th St New York (10018) *(G-11671)*

Vgg Holding LLC 212 415-6700
  590 Madison Ave Fl 41 New York (10022) *(G-11672)*

Vhx Corporation 347 689-1446
  555 W 18th St New York (10011) *(G-11673)*

Via America Fine Jewelry Inc 212 302-1218
  578 5th Ave Unit 26 New York (10036) *(G-11674)*

Viamedia Corporation 718 485-7792
  2610 Atlantic Ave Brooklyn (11207) *(G-2555)*

Viana Signs Corp 516 887-2000
  3520 Lawson Blvd Oceanside (11572) *(G-12197)*

Viatran Corporation (HQ) 716 564-7813
  199 Fire Tower Dr Tonawanda (14150) *(G-15152)*

Vibe Magazine, New York *Also called Vibe Media Group LLC* *(G-11675)*

Vibe Media Group LLC 212 448-7300
  120 Wall St Fl 21 New York (10005) *(G-11675)*

Vibra Tech Industries Inc 914 946-1916
  126 Oakley Ave White Plains (10601) *(G-16069)*

Vibration & Noise Engrg Corp 716 827-4959
  3374 N Benzing Rd Orchard Park (14127) *(G-12382)*

Vibration Eliminator Co Inc (PA) 631 841-4000
  15 Dixon Ave Copiague (11726) *(G-3687)*

Vibro-Laser Instrs Corp LLC 518 874-2700
  2c Glens Falls Tech Park Glens Falls (12801) *(G-5269)*

Vic Demayos Inc 845 626-4343
  4967 Us Highway 209 Accord (12404) *(G-1)*

Vic Leak Detection, Ronkonkoma *Also called Vacuum Instrument Corporation* *(G-14023)*

Vick Construction Inc 718 313-7625
  1489014 90th Ave Apt 1f Jamaica (11435) *(G-6486)*

Vickers Stock Research Corp 212 425-7500
  61 Broadway Rm 1910 New York (10006) *(G-11676)*

Vicks Lithograph & Prtg Corp (PA) 315 272-2401
  5166 Commercial Dr Yorkville (13495) *(G-16380)*

Vicks Lithograph & Prtg Corp 315 736-9344
  5210 Commercial Dr Yorkville (13495) *(G-16381)*

Vicron Electronic Mfg, Bronx *Also called Monarch Electric Products Inc* *(G-1318)*

Victoire Latam Asset MGT LLC, New York *Also called Capital E Financial Group* *(G-8911)*

Victor Insulators Inc 585 924-2127
  280 Maple Ave Victor (14564) *(G-15440)*

Victoria Albi International 212 689-2600
  1178 Broadway Fl 5 New York (10001) *(G-11677)*

Victoria Dngelo Intr Cllctions, Warwick *Also called DAngelo Home Collections Inc* *(G-15511)*

Victoria Fine Foods LLC (HQ) 718 649-1635
  443 E 100th St Brooklyn (11236) *(G-2556)*

Victoria Fine Foods Holding Co (HQ) 718 649-1635
  443 E 100th St Brooklyn (11236) *(G-2557)*

Victoria Plating Co Inc 718 589-1550
  650 Tiffany St Bronx (10474) *(G-1391)*

Victoria Precision Inc 845 473-9309
  78 Travis Rd Hyde Park (12538) *(G-6275)*

Victory Garden 212 206-7273
  31 Carmine St Frnt A New York (10014) *(G-11678)*

Victory Signs Inc 315 762-0220
  8915 Old State Route 13 Canastota (13032) *(G-3160)*

Victory Sports, Staten Island *Also called Glenda Inc* *(G-14656)*

Vida-Blend LLC 518 627-4138
  1430 State Highway 5s Amsterdam (12010) *(G-352)*

Vidal Candies USA Inc 609 781-8169
  845 3rd Ave Fl 6 New York (10022) *(G-11679)*

Videk Inc 585 377-0377
  1387 Fairport Rd 1000c Fairport (14450) *(G-4528)*

Video Technology Services Inc 516 937-9700
  5 Aerial Way Ste 300 Syosset (11791) *(G-14804)*

Viducci, Great Neck *Also called Classic Creations Inc* *(G-5376)*

Viele Manufacturing Corp 718 893-2200
  1340 Viele Ave Bronx (10474) *(G-1392)*

View Collections Inc 212 944-4030
  265 W 37th St Rm 5w New York (10018) *(G-11680)*

Viewfinder Inc 212 831-0939
  101 W 23rd St Ste 2303 New York (10011) *(G-11681)*

Viewsport International Inc 585 259-1562
  11 Feathery Cir Penfield (14526) *(G-12576)*

Vigliotti's Great Garden, Yaphank *Also called Scotts Company LLC* *(G-16269)*

Vigneri Chocolate Inc 585 254-6160
  810 Emerson St Rochester (14613) *(G-13797)*

Vigo Industries LLC (PA) 866 591-7792
  138 W 25th St Fl 3 New York (10001) *(G-11682)*

Viking Athletics Ltd 631 957-8000
  80 Montauk Hwy Ste 1 Lindenhurst (11757) *(G-6982)*

Viking Industries Inc 845 883-6325
  89 S Ohioville Rd New Paltz (12561) *(G-8314)*

Viking Iron Works Inc 845 471-5010
  37 Hatfield Ln Poughkeepsie (12603) *(G-12990)*

Viking Jackets & Athletic Wear, Walden *Also called C & C Athletic Inc* *(G-15457)*

Viking Mar Wldg Ship Repr LLC 718 758-4116
  14 Raleigh Pl Brooklyn (11226) *(G-2558)*

Viking Technologies Ltd 631 957-8000
  80 E Montauk Hwy Lindenhurst (11757) *(G-6983)*

Viking-Cives, Harrisville *Also called Cives Corporation* *(G-5565)*

Viktor Gold Enterprise Corp 212 768-8885
  58 W 47th St Unit 36 New York (10036) *(G-11683)*

Vilebrequin, New York *Also called Riviera Sun Inc* *(G-11050)*

Village Decoration Ltd 315 437-2522
  20 Corporate Cir East Syracuse (13057) *(G-4248)*

Village Herald 516 569-4403
  379 Central Ave Lawrence (11559) *(G-6894)*

Village Lantern Baking Corp 631 225-1690
  155 N Wellwood Ave Lindenhurst (11757) *(G-6984)*

Village Plaquesmith, Ththe, Bohemia *Also called Custom House Engravers Inc* *(G-995)*

Village Print Room, Oneonta *Also called Pony Farm Press & Graphics* *(G-12280)*

Village Printing, Endicott *Also called Fambus Inc* *(G-4455)*

Village Times, The, East Setauket *Also called Times Beacon Record Newspapers* *(G-4188)*

Village Video News, West Babylon *Also called Village Video Productions Inc* *(G-15756)*

Village Video Productions Inc 631 752-9311
  107 Alder St West Babylon (11704) *(G-15756)*

Village Wrought Iron Inc 315 683-5589
  7756 Main St Fabius (13063) *(G-4488)*

Villager, The, Brooklyn *Also called Nyc Community Media LLC* *(G-2226)*

Villeroy & Boch Usa Inc 212 213-8149
  41 Madison Ave Ste 1801 New York (10010) *(G-11684)*

Vin Mar Precision Metals Inc 631 563-6608
  1465 S Strong Ave Copiague (11726) *(G-3688)*

Vin-Clair Bindery, West Haverstraw *Also called Vin-Clair Inc* *(G-15764)*

Vin-Clair Inc 845 429-4998
  132 E Railroad Ave West Haverstraw (10993) *(G-15764)*

Vincent Associates, Rochester *Also called Va Inc* *(G-13791)*

Vincent Conigliaro 845 340-0489
  308 State Route 28 Kingston (12401) *(G-6722)*

Vincent Genovese 631 281-8170
  19 Woodmere Dr Mastic Beach (11951) *(G-7675)*

Vincent Manufacturing Co Inc 315 823-0280
  560 E Mill St Little Falls (13365) *(G-6995)*

Vincent Martino Dental Lab 716 674-7800
  74 Ransier Dr Buffalo (14224) *(G-3037)*

Vincents Food Corp 516 481-3544
  179 Old Country Rd Carle Place (11514) *(G-3183)*

Vincys Printing Ltd 518 355-4363
  1832 Curry Rd Schenectady (12306) *(G-14314)*

Vinegar Hill Asset LLC 718 469-0342
  436 E 34th St Brooklyn (11203) *(G-2559)*

Vineland Kosher Poultry Inc 718 921-1347
  5600 1st Ave A7 Brooklyn (11220) *(G-2560)*

Vinevrest Co, Washingtonville *Also called Brotherhood Americas* *(G-15524)*

Vinifera Wine Cellard, Hammondsport *Also called Konstantin D FRAnk& Sons Vini* *(G-5532)*

Vinous Group LLC 917 275-5184
  54 W 40th St New York (10018) *(G-11685)*

Vinyl Materials Inc 631 586-9444
  365 Bay Shore Rd Deer Park (11729) *(G-3951)*

Vinyl Tech Window, Staten Island *Also called Eastern Enterprise Corp* *(G-14650)*

Vinyl Works Inc 518 786-1200
  33 Wade Rd Latham (12110) *(G-6880)*

Vinyline Window and Door Inc 914 476-3500
  636 Saw Mill River Rd Yonkers (10710) *(G-16355)*

Viola Cabinet Corporation 716 284-6327
  4205 Hyde Park Blvd Niagara Falls (14305) *(G-11989)*

Viola Construction, Niagara Falls *Also called Viola Cabinet Corporation* *(G-11989)*

Violettes Cellar LLC 718 650-5050
  2271 Hylan Blvd Staten Island (10306) *(G-14728)*

VIP Foods Inc 718 821-5330
  1080 Wyckoff Ave Ridgewood (11385) *(G-13166)*

VIP Printing 718 641-9361
  16040 95th St Howard Beach (11414) *(G-6142)*

Viraj - USA Inc (HQ) 516 280-8380
  2 Reiter Ave Hicksville (11801) *(G-5953)*

Virgil Mountain Inc (PA) 212 378-0007
  1 E 28th St Fl 4 New York (10016) *(G-11686)*

Virginia Dare Extract Co Inc (PA) 718 788-6320
  882 3rd Ave Unit 2 Brooklyn (11232) *(G-2561)*

Viridis Learning Inc 347 420-9181
  2 Gold St Apt 4005 New York (10038) *(G-11687)*

Viropro Inc 650 300-5190
  49 W 38th St Fl 11 New York (10018) *(G-11688)*

Virtual Facility Inc 646 891-4861
  39 W 37th St Fl 17 New York (10018) *(G-11689)*

Virtual Frameworks Inc (PA) 646 690-8207
  115 5th Ave Frnt 2 New York (10003) *(G-11690)*

Virtual Super LLC 212 685-6400
116 E 27th St Fl 3 New York (10016) ***(G-11691)***
Virtualapt Corp 917 293-3173
45 Main St Ste 613 Brooklyn (11201) ***(G-2562)***
Virtusphere Inc 607 760-2207
7 Hillside Ave Binghamton (13903) ***(G-915)***
Virtuvent Inc 855 672-8677
81 Prospect St Fl 7 Brooklyn (11201) ***(G-2563)***
Visant Secondary Holdings Corp (HQ) 914 595-8200
357 Main St Armonk (10504) ***(G-405)***
Vishay Thin Film LLC 716 283-4025
2160 Liberty Dr Niagara Falls (14304) ***(G-11990)***
Visimetrics Corporation 716 871-7070
2290 Kenmore Ave Buffalo (14207) ***(G-3038)***
Vision Logic Inc 212 729-4606
300 Park Ave Fl 12 New York (10022) ***(G-11692)***
Vision Quest, Brooklyn *Also called Lens Lab Express* ***(G-2062)***
Vision Quest Lighting Inc 631 737-4800
12 Satterly Rd East Setauket (11733) ***(G-4190)***
Vision World, Bedford Hills *Also called Eyeglass Service Industries* ***(G-769)***
Vision-Sciences, Orangeburg *Also called Machida Incorporated* ***(G-12323)***
Visionaire Publishing LLC 646 434-6091
30 W 24th St New York (10010) ***(G-11693)***
Visiontron Corp 631 582-8600
720 Old Willets Path Hauppauge (11788) ***(G-5797)***
Visitainer Corp 718 636-0300
148 Classon Ave Brooklyn (11205) ***(G-2564)***
Vista Pharmacy & Surgical, Far Rockaway *Also called J P R Pharmacy Inc* ***(G-4566)***
Vista Visual Group, Lindenhurst *Also called Linear Signs Inc* ***(G-6955)***
Vistalab Technologies Inc 914 244-6226
2 Geneva Rd Brewster (10509) ***(G-1160)***
Vistec Lithography, Troy *Also called Raith America Inc* ***(G-15182)***
Visual Citi Inc (PA) 631 482-3030
305 Henry St Lindenhurst (11757) ***(G-6985)***
Visual F-X, Brooklyn *Also called Street Beat Sportswear Inc* ***(G-2463)***
Visual ID Source Inc 516 307-9759
65 E 2nd St Mineola (11501) ***(G-8002)***
Visual Impact Graphics Inc 585 548-7118
653 Ellicott St Ste 6 Batavia (14020) ***(G-629)***
Visual Millwork & Fix Mfg Inc 718 267-7800
95 Marcus Blvd Deer Park (11729) ***(G-3952)***
Vita-Gen Laboratories LLC 631 450-4357
71s Mall Dr Commack (11725) ***(G-3602)***
Vita-Nat Inc 631 293-6000
298 Adams Blvd Farmingdale (11735) ***(G-4762)***
Vitafede (PA) 646 869-4003
25 W 26th St Fl 5 New York (10010) ***(G-11694)***
Vitakem Nutraceutical Inc 631 956-8343
811 W Jericho Tpke Smithtown (11787) ***(G-14489)***
Vital Signs & Graphics Co Inc 518 237-8372
251 Saratoga St Cohoes (12047) ***(G-3519)***
Vital Vio Inc 914 245-6048
185 Jordan Rd Ste 1 Troy (12180) ***(G-15194)***
Vitale Ready Mix Concrete, Auburn *Also called Robinson Concrete Inc* ***(G-493)***
Vitalis LLC 646 831-7338
902 Broadway Fl 6 New York (10010) ***(G-11695)***
Vitalize Labs LLC 212 966-6130
134 Spring St Ste 502 New York (10012) ***(G-11696)***
Vitamix Laboratories, Commack *Also called Wellmill LLC* ***(G-3603)***
Vitane Pharmaceuticals Inc 845 267-6700
125 Wells Ave Congers (10920) ***(G-3620)***
Vitarose Corp of America 718 951-9700
2615 Nostrand Ave Ste 1 Brooklyn (11210) ***(G-2565)***
Viterion Corporation 914 333-6033
565 Taxter Rd Ste 175 Elmsford (10523) ***(G-4439)***
Vitiprints LLC 646 591-4343
630 9th Ave Ste 208 New York (10036) ***(G-11697)***
Vito & Sons Bakery 201 617-8501
1423 72nd St Brooklyn (11228) ***(G-2566)***
Vitobob Furniture Inc 516 676-1696
3879 13th St Long Island City (11101) ***(G-7396)***
Vitra Inc (HQ) 212 463-5700
95 Madison Ave Frnt 1 New York (10016) ***(G-11698)***
Vitrix Hot Glass and Crafts, Corning *Also called Vitrix Inc* ***(G-3723)***
Vitrix Inc 607 936-8707
77 W Market St Corning (14830) ***(G-3723)***
Vits International Inc 845 353-5000
200 Corporate Dr Blauvelt (10913) ***(G-938)***
Vivid Rgb Lighting LLC 718 635-0817
824 Main St Ste 1 Peekskill (10566) ***(G-12558)***
Vivona Business Printers Inc 516 496-3453
343 Jackson Ave Syosset (11791) ***(G-14805)***
Vivus Technologies LLC 585 798-6658
591 Mahar St Medina (14103) ***(G-7748)***
Viwit Pharmaceuticals Inc 201 701-9787
1600 Brookview Station Rd Castleton On Hudson (12033) ***(G-3205)***
Vizbee Inc 650 787-1424
120 E 23rd St Fl 5 New York (10010) ***(G-11699)***
Vizio Medical Devices LLC 646 845-7382
200 Chambers St Apt 28a New York (10007) ***(G-11700)***
VJ Technologies Inc (PA) 631 589-8800
89 Carlough Rd Bohemia (11716) ***(G-1096)***
Vjt, Bohemia *Also called VJ Technologies Inc* ***(G-1096)***
Vline Inc 512 222-5464
81 Prospect St Brooklyn (11201) ***(G-2567)***
VM Choppy & Sons LLC 518 266-1444
4 Van Buren St Troy (12180) ***(G-15195)***
Vma, Poughkeepsie *Also called Vantage Mfg & Assembly LLC* ***(G-12988)***
Vnovom Svete 212 302-9480
55 Broad St Fl 20 New York (10004) ***(G-11701)***
Vogel Applied Technologies 212 677-3136
36 E 12th St Fl 7 New York (10003) ***(G-11702)***
Vogue China, New York *Also called Advance Magazine Publs Inc* ***(G-8474)***
Vogue Too Plting Stitching EMB 212 354-1022
265 W 37th St Fl 14 New York (10018) ***(G-11703)***
Voices For All LLC 518 261-1664
29 Moreland Dr Mechanicville (12118) ***(G-7696)***
Volckening Inc (PA) 718 748-0294
6700 3rd Ave Brooklyn (11220) ***(G-2568)***
Volkert Precision Tech Inc 718 464-9500
22240 96th Ave Ste 3 Queens Village (11429) ***(G-13027)***
Volpi Manufacturing USA Co Inc 315 255-1737
5 Commerce Way Auburn (13021) ***(G-502)***
Volt Tek Inc 585 377-2050
111 Parce Ave Fairport (14450) ***(G-4529)***
Voltronics LLC 410 749-2424
2777 Us Route 20 Cazenovia (13035) ***(G-3237)***
Von Musulin Patricia 212 206-8345
148 W 24th St Fl 10 New York (10011) ***(G-11704)***
Von Pok & Chang New York Inc 212 599-0556
4 E 43rd St Fl 7 New York (10017) ***(G-11705)***
Von Roll Usa Inc 203 562-2171
200 Von Roll Dr Schenectady (12306) ***(G-14315)***
Von Roll Usa Inc (HQ) 518 344-7100
200 Von Roll Dr Schenectady (12306) ***(G-14316)***
Von Roll USA Holding Inc 518 344-7200
1 W Campbell Rd Schenectady (12306) ***(G-14317)***
Vondom LLC 212 207-3252
979 3rd Ave Ste 1532 New York (10022) ***(G-11706)***
Voodoo Manufacturing Inc 646 893-8366
361 Stagg St Ste 408 Brooklyn (11206) ***(G-2569)***
Vormittag Associates Inc (PA) 800 824-7776
120 Comac St Ste 1 Ronkonkoma (11779) ***(G-14024)***
Vortex Ventures Inc 516 946-8345
857 Newton Ave North Baldwin (11510) ***(G-12011)***
Vosky Precision Machining Corp 631 737-3200
70 Air Park Dr Ronkonkoma (11779) ***(G-14025)***
Voss Manufacturing Inc 716 731-5062
2345 Lockport Rd Sanborn (14132) ***(G-14153)***
Voss Signs LLC 315 682-6418
112 Fairgrounds Dr Ste 2 Manlius (13104) ***(G-7550)***
Voss Usa Inc 212 995-2255
236 W 30th St Rm 900 New York (10001) ***(G-11707)***
Voyager Custom Products, Buffalo *Also called Voyager Emblems Inc* ***(G-3039)***
Voyager Emblems Inc 416 255-3421
701 Seneca St Ste D Buffalo (14210) ***(G-3039)***
Vpj Publication Inc 718 845-3221
15519 Lahn St Howard Beach (11414) ***(G-6143)***
Vps Control Systems Inc 518 686-0019
19 Hill Rd Hoosick (12089) ***(G-6082)***
Vpulse Inc 646 729-5675
191 Nassau Ave Brooklyn (11222) ***(G-2570)***
Vr Bags Inc 212 714-1494
637 E 132nd St Bronx (10454) ***(G-1393)***
Vr Containment LLC 917 972-3441
17625 Union Tpke Ste 175 Fresh Meadows (11366) ***(G-5048)***
Vr Food Equipment Inc 315 531-8133
5801 County Road 41 Farmington (14425) ***(G-4780)***
Vsg International LLC 718 300-8171
196 Clinton Ave Apt A2 Brooklyn (11205) ***(G-2571)***
Vship Co 718 706-8566
3636 33rd St Ste 207 Astoria (11106) ***(G-443)***
Vsii, Melville *Also called Verint SEC Intelligence Inc* ***(G-7833)***
VSM Investors LLC (PA) 212 351-1600
245 Park Ave Fl 41 New York (10167) ***(G-11708)***
Vtb Holdings Inc (HQ) 914 345-2255
100 Summit Lake Dr Valhalla (10595) ***(G-15311)***
Vulcan Iron Works Inc 631 395-6846
190 Weeks Ave Manorville (11949) ***(G-7555)***
Vulcan Steam Forging Co 716 875-3680
247 Rano St Buffalo (14207) ***(G-3040)***
Vulcraft of New York Inc (HQ) 607 529-9000
621 M St Chemung (14825) ***(G-3366)***
Vuniverse Inc 212 206-1041
575 5th Ave Fl 17 New York (10017) ***(G-11709)***
Vuzix Corporation (PA) 585 359-5900
25 Hendrix Rd Ste A West Henrietta (14586) ***(G-15806)***
Vvs International Inc 212 302-5410
2 W 46th St New York (10036) ***(G-11710)***
Vyera Pharmaceuticals LLC 646 356-5577
600 3rd Ave Fl 10 New York (10016) ***(G-11711)***
Vytek Inc 631 750-1770
271 Knickerbocker Ave Bohemia (11716) ***(G-1097)***
W & B Mazza & Sons Inc 516 379-4130
2145 Marion Pl North Baldwin (11510) ***(G-12012)***

986

2020 Harris
New York Manufacturers Directory

(G-0000) Company's Geographic Section entry number

W & H Stampings Inc 631 234-6161
45 Engineers Rd Hauppauge (11788) *(G-5798)*

W A American, New York *Also called San Esters Corporation (G-11128)*

W A Baum Co Inc 631 226-3940
620 Oak St Copiague (11726) *(G-3689)*

W B Bow Tie Corp 212 683-6130
521 W 26th St Fl 6 New York (10001) *(G-11712)*

W By Worth, New York *Also called Worth Collection Ltd (G-11785)*

W D Technology Inc 914 779-8738
42 Water St Ste B Eastchester (10709) *(G-4250)*

W Designe Inc 914 736-1058
5 John Walsh Blvd Peekskill (10566) *(G-12559)*

W E W Container Corporation 718 827-8150
189 Wyona St Brooklyn (11207) *(G-2572)*

W F Saunders & Sons Inc (PA) 315 469-3217
5126 S Onondaga Rd Nedrow (13120) *(G-8217)*

W F Saunders & Sons Inc 607 257-6930
30 Pinckney Rd Etna (13062) *(G-4486)*

W G R Z - T V Channel 2, Buffalo *Also called Tegna Inc (G-3005)*

W H Jones & Son Inc 716 875-8233
1208 Military Rd Kenmore (14217) *(G-6655)*

W H White Publications Inc 914 725-2500
95 Main St Dobbs Ferry (10522) *(G-4021)*

W Hubbell & Sons Inc (PA) 315 736-8311
5124 Commercial Dr Yorkville (13495) *(G-16382)*

W J Albro Machine Works Inc 631 345-0657
86 Horseblock Rd Unit L Yaphank (11980) *(G-16278)*

W K Z A 106.9 K I S S-F M, Jamestown *Also called Cntry Cross Communications LLC (G-6503)*

W Kintz Plastics Inc (HQ) 518 296-8513
165 Caverns Rd Howes Cave (12092) *(G-6144)*

W M T Publications Inc 585 244-3329
280 State St Rochester (14614) *(G-13798)*

W M W, Buffalo *Also called West Metal Works Inc (G-3045)*

W N R Pattern & Tool Inc 716 681-9334
21 Pavement Rd Lancaster (14086) *(G-6838)*

W N Vanalstine & Sons Inc (PA) 518 237-1436
18 New Cortland St Cohoes (12047) *(G-3520)*

W R P Welding Ltd 631 249-8859
126 Toledo St Farmingdale (11735) *(G-4763)*

W Stuart Smith Inc 585 742-3310
625 Fishers Run Victor (14564) *(G-15441)*

W W Custom Clad Inc (PA) 518 673-3322
337 E Main St Canajoharie (13317) *(G-3122)*

W W Custom Clad Inc 518 673-3322
75 Creek St Canajoharie (13317) *(G-3123)*

W W Norton & Company Inc (PA) 212 354-5500
500 5th Ave Fl 5 New York (10110) *(G-11713)*

W W Norton & Company Inc 212 354-5500
500 5th Ave Lbby 1 New York (10110) *(G-11714)*

W W Trading Co Inc 718 935-1085
50 Franklin Ave Brooklyn (11205) *(G-2573)*

W.O.w Brand Products, North Tonawanda *Also called Griffin Chemical Company LLC (G-12071)*

Wacf Enterprise Inc 631 745-5841
275 Asharoken Ave Northport (11768) *(G-12111)*

Wacoal America Inc 212 743-9600
136 Madison Ave Fl 15 New York (10016) *(G-11715)*

Wadadda.com, Monticello *Also called Patrick Rohan (G-8072)*

Waddington North America Inc 585 638-8200
88 Nesbitt Dr Holley (14470) *(G-6039)*

Wadsworth Logging Inc 518 863-6870
3095 State Highway 30 Gloversville (12078) *(G-5298)*

Waffenbauch USA 716 326-4508
165 Academy St Westfield (14787) *(G-15950)*

Wagner Farms, Lodi *Also called Lamoreaux Landing Wl (G-7131)*

Wagner Hardwoods LLC 607 594-3321
6307 St Route 224 Cayuta (14824) *(G-3223)*

Wagner Hardwoods LLC (PA) 607 229-8198
6052 County Road 20 Friendship (14739) *(G-5053)*

Wagner Lumber, Owego *Also called Wagner Millwork Inc (G-12439)*

Wagner Millwork Inc 607 687-5362
4060 Gaskill Rd Owego (13827) *(G-12439)*

Wagner Nineveh Inc 607 693-2689
224 County Rd 26 Afton (13730) *(G-8)*

Wagner Vineyards LLC 607 582-6976
9322 State Route 414 Lodi (14860) *(G-7132)*

Wagner Vineyards & Brewing Co. 607 582-6574
9322 State Route 414 Lodi (14860) *(G-7133)*

Wagners LLC (PA) 516 933-6580
366 N Broadway Ste 402 Jericho (11753) *(G-6598)*

Waguya News, Wolcott *Also called Wayuga Community Newspapers (G-16165)*

Wainland Inc 718 626-2233
2460 47th St Astoria (11103) *(G-444)*

Wal Machine, West Babylon *Also called Mpi Consulting Incorporated (G-15733)*

Walco Stainless, Utica *Also called Utica Cutlery Company (G-15298)*

Waldman Publishing Corporation (PA) 212 730-9590
570 Fashion Ave Rm 800 New York (10018) *(G-11716)*

Waldorf Bakers Inc 718 665-2253
909 E 135th St Bronx (10454) *(G-1394)*

Walking Charger, The, Rochester *Also called Energy Harvesters LLC (G-13391)*

Wall Protection Products LLC 877 943-6826
32 Nelson Hill Rd Wassaic (12592) *(G-15527)*

Wall Street Reporter Magazine 212 363-2600
419 Lafayette St Fl 2 New York (10003) *(G-11717)*

Wall Tool & Tape Corp 718 641-6813
8111 101st Ave Ozone Park (11416) *(G-12468)*

Wall Tool Manufacturing, Ozone Park *Also called Wall Tool & Tape Corp (G-12468)*

Wallace Home Design Ctr 631 765-3890
44500 County Road 48 Southold (11971) *(G-14546)*

Wallace Refiners Inc 212 391-2649
15 W 47th St Ste 808 New York (10036) *(G-11718)*

Wallguard.com, Wassaic *Also called Wall Protection Products LLC (G-15527)*

Wallkill Lodge No 627 F&Am 845 778-7148
61 Main St Walden (12586) *(G-15464)*

Wallkill Valley Publications 845 561-0170
300 Stony Brook Ct Ste B Newburgh (12550) *(G-11893)*

Wallkill Valley Times, Newburgh *Also called Wallkill Valley Publications (G-11893)*

Wally Packaging, Monsey *Also called Magcrest Packaging Inc (G-8039)*

Walnut Packaging Inc 631 293-3836
450 Smith St Farmingdale (11735) *(G-4764)*

Walnut Printing Inc (PA) 718 707-0100
2812 41st Ave Long Island City (11101) *(G-7397)*

Walpole Woodworkers Inc 631 726-2859
779 Montauk Hwy Water Mill (11976) *(G-15531)*

Walsh & Hughes Inc (PA) 631 427-5904
1455 New York Ave Huntington Station (11746) *(G-6266)*

Walsh & Sons Machine Inc 845 526-0301
15 Secor Rd Ste 5 Mahopac (10541) *(G-7480)*

Walter G Legge Company Inc 914 737-5040
444 Central Ave Peekskill (10566) *(G-12560)*

Walter P Sauer LLC 718 937-0600
276 Grndpint Ave Ste 8400 Brooklyn (11222) *(G-2574)*

Walter R Tucker Entps Ltd 607 467-2866
8 Leonard Way Deposit (13754) *(G-4004)*

Walters & Walters Inc 347 202-8535
961 E 224th St Bronx (10466) *(G-1395)*

Wan Ja Shan, Middletown *Also called Mandarin Soy Sauce Inc (G-7918)*

Wanjashan International LLC 845 343-1505
4 Sands Station Rd Middletown (10940) *(G-7937)*

Want-Ad Digest Inc 518 279-1181
870 Hoosick Rd Ste 1 Troy (12180) *(G-15196)*

Wantagh 5 & 10, Wantagh *Also called Nbets Corporation (G-15487)*

Wantagh Computer Center 516 826-2189
10 Stanford Ct Wantagh (11793) *(G-15489)*

Wapons Specialists, Ridgewood *Also called Specialists Ltd (G-13161)*

Wappingers Falls Shopper Inc 845 297-3723
84 E Main St Wappingers Falls (12590) *(G-15501)*

Warby Parker Eyewear, New York *Also called Parker Warby Retail Inc (G-10764)*

Ward Diesel Filter Systems, Horseheads *Also called Beecher Emssn Sltn Tchnlgs LLC (G-6113)*

Ward Industrial Equipment Inc (PA) 716 856-6966
1051 Clinton St Buffalo (14206) *(G-3041)*

Ward Iron Works Limited, Buffalo *Also called Ward Industrial Equipment Inc (G-3041)*

Ward Lafrance Truck Corp 518 893-1865
26 Congress St Ste 259f Saratoga Springs (12866) *(G-14195)*

Ward Sales Co Inc 315 476-5276
1117 W Fayette St Ste 1 Syracuse (13204) *(G-15023)*

Ward Steel Company Inc 315 451-4566
4591 Morgan Pl Liverpool (13090) *(G-7047)*

Warm 212 925-1200
181 Mott St Frnt 1 New York (10012) *(G-11719)*

Warnaco Group Inc (HQ) 212 287-8000
501 Fashion Ave New York (10018) *(G-11720)*

Warnaco Inc (HQ) 212 287-8000
501 Fashion Ave Fl 14 New York (10018) *(G-11721)*

Warnaco Inc 718 722-3000
70 Washington St Fl 10 Brooklyn (11201) *(G-2575)*

Warner Energy LLC (PA) 315 457-3828
7526 Morgan Rd Liverpool (13090) *(G-7048)*

Warner Music Group Corp (HQ) 212 275-2000
1633 Broadway Fl 11 New York (10019) *(G-11722)*

Warner Music Inc (HQ) 212 275-2000
1633 Broadway Fl 11 New York (10019) *(G-11723)*

Warner S, New York *Also called Warnaco Inc (G-11721)*

Warodean Corporation 718 359-5559
4308 162nd St Flushing (11358) *(G-4905)*

Warren Corporation (HQ) 917 379-3434
711 5th Ave Fl 11 New York (10022) *(G-11724)*

Warren Cutlery Corp 845 876-3444
3584 Route 9g Rhinebeck (12572) *(G-13103)*

Warren Energy Services LLC 212 697-9660
1114 Ave Of The Americas New York (10036) *(G-11725)*

Warren Printing Inc 212 627-5000
3718 Northern Blvd # 418 Long Island City (11101) *(G-7398)*

Warshaw Jacobson Group, New York *Also called Irv Inc (G-9944)*

Warwick Press, Warwick *Also called Digital United Color Prtg Inc (G-15512)*

Wascomat of America, Inwood *Also called Pluslux LLC (G-6302)*

Washburn Litho Envirgo Prtg, Rochester *Also called Presstek Printing LLC (G-13643)*

Washburn Manufacturing Tech 607 387-3991
9828 State Route 96 Trumansburg (14886) ***(G-15202)***
Washburns Dairy Inc 518 725-0629
145 N Main St Gloversville (12078) ***(G-5299)***
Washer Solutions Inc 585 742-6388
760 Canning Pkwy Ste A Victor (14564) ***(G-15442)***
Washingtom Mills Elec Mnrls (HQ) 716 278-6600
1801 Buffalo Ave Niagara Falls (14303) ***(G-11991)***
Washington Foundries Inc 516 374-8447
1434 Vian Ave Hewlett (11557) ***(G-5876)***
Washington Mills Tonawanda Inc (HQ) 716 693-4550
1000 E Niagara St Tonawanda (14150) ***(G-15153)***
Washington Post Advg Sls Ofc, New York *Also called Wp Company LLC* ***(G-11789)***
Washington Square News, New York *Also called New York University* ***(G-10607)***
Waste Management, Palatine Bridge *Also called Lee Publications Inc* ***(G-12478)***
Wastecorp Pumps LLC (PA) 888 829-2783
345 W 85th St Apt 23 New York (10024) ***(G-11726)***
Wastequip - Consolidated, New Lebanon *Also called Wastequip Manufacturing Co LLC* ***(G-8304)***
Wastequip Manufacturing Co LLC 800 235-0734
1079 Route 20 New Lebanon (12125) ***(G-8304)***
Watch Journal LLC 212 229-1500
110 E 25th St Fl 4 New York (10010) ***(G-11727)***
Watchanish LLC 917 558-0404
1 Rockefeller Plz Fl 11 New York (10020) ***(G-11728)***
Watchcraft Inc 347 531-0382
2214 40th Ave Ste 4 Long Island City (11101) ***(G-7399)***
Watchtime Magazine, New York *Also called Ebner Publishing International* ***(G-9311)***
Watec America Corporation 702 434-6111
720 Route 17m Ste 4 Middletown (10940) ***(G-7938)***
Water Cooling Corp 718 723-6500
24520 Merrick Blvd Rosedale (11422) ***(G-14038)***
Water Energy Systems LLC 844 822-7665
1 Maiden Ln New York (10038) ***(G-11729)***
Water Lilies, Astoria *Also called Wlf Founders Corporation* ***(G-446)***
Water Oracle 845 876-8327
41 E Market St Ste 4 Rhinebeck (12572) ***(G-13104)***
Water Splash Inc 800 936-3430
25 Locust St Ste 421 Champlain (12919) ***(G-3321)***
Water Street Brass Corporation 716 763-0059
4515 Gleason Rd Lakewood (14750) ***(G-6787)***
Water Technologies Inc (PA) 315 986-0000
1635 Commons Pkwy Macedon (14502) ***(G-7471)***
Water Wise of America Inc 585 232-1210
75 Bermar Park Ste 5 Rochester (14624) ***(G-13799)***
Waterbury Garment LLC 212 725-1500
16 E 34th St Fl 10 New York (10016) ***(G-11730)***
Waterhouse Publications Inc 716 662-4200
3770 Transit Rd Orchard Park (14127) ***(G-12383)***
Watermans Distillery LLC 607 258-0274
6172 State Route 434 Apalachin (13732) ***(G-363)***
Watermark Designs Holdings Ltd 718 257-2800
350 Dewitt Ave Brooklyn (11207) ***(G-2576)***
Watertown 1785 LLC 315 785-0062
21875 Towne Center Dr Watertown (13601) ***(G-15591)***
Watertown Concrete Inc 315 788-1040
24471 State Route 12 Watertown (13601) ***(G-15592)***
Watertown Daily Times, Watertown *Also called Northern NY Newspapers Corp* ***(G-15586)***
Watkins Welding and Mch Sp Inc 914 949-6168
87 Westmoreland Ave White Plains (10606) ***(G-16070)***
Watson Adventures LLC 212 564-8293
330 W 38th St Rm 407 New York (10018) ***(G-11731)***
Watson Bowman Acme Corp 716 691-8162
95 Pineview Dr Amherst (14228) ***(G-253)***
Watson Productions LLC 516 334-9766
740 Old Willets Path # 400 Hauppauge (11788) ***(G-5799)***
Wave Float Rooms LLC 844 356-2876
4817 Kraus Rd Clarence (14031) ***(G-3443)***
Wave of Long Island, The, Rockaway Beach *Also called Wave Publishing Co Inc* ***(G-13823)***
Wave Publishing Co Inc 718 634-4000
8808 Rockaway Beach Blvd Rockaway Beach (11693) ***(G-13823)***
Waverly Iron Corp 631 732-2800
25 Commercial Blvd Medford (11763) ***(G-7726)***
Wavodyne Therapeutics Inc 954 632-6630
150 Lucius Gordon Dr West Henrietta (14586) ***(G-15807)***
Wax Jams LLC 914 834-7886
66 E Brookside Dr Larchmont (10538) ***(G-6844)***
Way Out Toys Inc 212 689-9094
230 5th Ave Ste 800 New York (10001) ***(G-11732)***
Waymor1 Inc 518 677-8511
Hc 22 Cambridge (12816) ***(G-3097)***
Wayne County Mail, Webster *Also called Empire State Weeklies Inc* ***(G-15640)***
Wayne Decorators Inc 718 529-4200
14409 Rockaway Blvd Apt 1 Jamaica (11436) ***(G-6487)***
Wayne Integrated Tech Corp 631 242-0213
160 Rodeo Dr Edgewood (11717) ***(G-4291)***
Wayne Printing Inc 914 761-2400
70 W Red Oak Ln Fl 4 White Plains (10604) ***(G-16071)***
Wayne Printing & Lithographic, White Plains *Also called Wayne Printing Inc* ***(G-16071)***
Waynes Welding Inc 315 768-6146
66 Calder Ave Yorkville (13495) ***(G-16383)***
Wayuga Community Newspapers (PA) 315 754-6229
6784 Main St Red Creek (13143) ***(G-13071)***
Wayuga Community Newspapers 315 594-2506
12039 E Main St Wolcott (14590) ***(G-16165)***
Wayuga News, Red Creek *Also called Wayuga Community Newspapers* ***(G-13071)***
Wazer Inc 201 580-6486
141 Flushing Ave Brooklyn (11205) ***(G-2577)***
Wcd Window Coverings Inc 845 336-4511
1711 Ulster Ave Lake Katrine (12449) ***(G-6764)***
WD Certified Contracting LLC 516 493-9319
112 Magnolia Ave 101-A Westbury (11590) ***(G-15939)***
We Work 877 673-6628
1 Little West 12th St New York (10014) ***(G-11733)***
Wea International Inc (HQ) 212 275-1300
75 Rockefeller Plz New York (10019) ***(G-11734)***
Weather Products Corporation 315 474-8593
102 W Division St Fl 1 Syracuse (13204) ***(G-15024)***
Weather Tight Exteriors 631 375-5108
8 Woodbrook Dr Ridge (11961) ***(G-13135)***
Weatherproof, Bay Shore *Also called David Peyser Sportswear Inc* ***(G-670)***
Weaver Machine & Tool Co Inc 315 253-4422
44 York St Auburn (13021) ***(G-503)***
Weaver Wind Energy LLC 607 379-9463
7 Union St Freeville (13068) ***(G-5036)***
Web Associates Inc 716 883-3377
1255 Niagara St Buffalo (14213) ***(G-3042)***
Web Seal Inc (PA) 585 546-1320
15 Oregon St Rochester (14605) ***(G-13800)***
Web-Tech Packaging Inc 716 684-4520
500 Commerce Pkwy Lancaster (14086) ***(G-6839)***
Webb-Mason Inc 716 276-8792
300 Airborne Pkwy Ste 210 Buffalo (14225) ***(G-3043)***
Weber Intl Packg Co LLC 518 561-8282
318 Cornelia St Plattsburgh (12901) ***(G-12790)***
Weber-Knapp Company (PA) 716 484-9135
441 Chandler St Jamestown (14701) ***(G-6553)***
Webinfinity Americas Inc (PA) 516 331-5180
315 Main St Unit 4 Huntington (11743) ***(G-6234)***
Webster Ontrio Wlwrth Pnnysver 585 265-3620
164 E Main St Webster (14580) ***(G-15661)***
Webster Printing Corporation 585 671-1533
46 North Ave Webster (14580) ***(G-15662)***
Wecare Organics LLC (PA) 315 689-1937
9293 Bonta Bridge Rd Jordan (13080) ***(G-6631)***
Weco Metal Products, Ontario *Also called Dj Acquisition Management Corp* ***(G-12288)***
Wedding Gown Preservation Co 607 748-7999
707 North St Endicott (13760) ***(G-4478)***
Wedel Sign Company Inc 631 727-4577
705 W Main St Riverhead (11901) ***(G-13192)***
Week Publications, The, New York *Also called Dennis Publishing Inc* ***(G-9204)***
Weekly Ajkal 718 565-2100
3707 74th St Ste 8 Jackson Heights (11372) ***(G-6422)***
Weekly Business News Corp 212 689-5888
274 Madison Ave Rm 1101 New York (10016) ***(G-11735)***
Weeks & Reichel Printing Inc 631 589-1443
131 Railroad Ave Sayville (11782) ***(G-14232)***
Wego International Floors LLC 516 487-3510
239 Great Neck Rd Great Neck (11021) ***(G-5431)***
Weico Wire & Cable Inc 631 254-2970
161 Rodeo Dr Edgewood (11717) ***(G-4292)***
Weicro Graphics Inc 631 253-3360
2190 Brigham St Apt 2h Brooklyn (11229) ***(G-2578)***
Weider Publications LLC 212 545-4800
1 Park Ave Fl 10 New York (10016) ***(G-11736)***
Weighing & Systems Tech Inc 518 274-2797
274 2nd St Troy (12180) ***(G-15197)***
Weinfeld Skull Cap Mfg Co Inc 718 854-3864
6022 14th Ave Brooklyn (11219) ***(G-2579)***
Weisbeck Publishing Printing 716 937-9226
13200 Broadway St Alden (14004) ***(G-176)***
Weisco Inc 212 575-8989
246 W 38th St Fl 6 New York (10018) ***(G-11737)***
Weiss Industries Inc 518 784-9643
27 Blossom Ln Valatie (12184) ***(G-15301)***
Weiss Instruments Inc 631 207-1200
905 Waverly Ave Holtsville (11742) ***(G-6058)***
Wel Made Enterprises Inc 631 752-1238
1630 New Hwy Farmingdale (11735) ***(G-4765)***
Welch Allyn Inc 315 685-4100
4341 State Street Rd Skaneateles Falls (13153) ***(G-14459)***
Welch Allyn Inc (HQ) 315 685-4100
4341 State Street Rd Skaneateles Falls (13153) ***(G-14460)***
Welch Allyn Inc 315 685-4347
4619 Jordan Rd Skaneateles Falls (13153) ***(G-14461)***
Welch Allyn Inc 503 530-7500
4341 State Street Rd Skaneateles Falls (13153) ***(G-14462)***
Welch Foods Inc A Cooperative 716 326-5252
2 S Portage St Westfield (14787) ***(G-15951)***
Welch Foods Inc A Cooperative 716 326-3131
100 N Portage St Westfield (14787) ***(G-15952)***
Welch Machine Inc 585 647-3578
961 Lyell Ave Bldg 1-6 Rochester (14606) ***(G-13801)***

Welcome Magazine Inc 716 839-3121
4511 Harlem Rd Amherst (14226) *(G-254)*
Welcome Rain Publishers LLC 212 686-1909
230 5th Ave New York (10001) *(G-11738)*
Weld-Built Body Co Inc 631 643-9700
276 Long Island Ave Wyandanch (11798) *(G-16248)*
Weldcomputer Corporation 518 283-2897
105 Jordan Rd Ste 1 Troy (12180) *(G-15198)*
Welded Tube Usa Inc 716 828-1111
2537 Hamburg Tpke Lackawanna (14218) *(G-6746)*
Welding and Brazing Svcs Inc 607 397-1009
2761 County Highway 26 Richfield Springs (13439) *(G-13106)*
Welding Chapter of New York 212 481-1496
44 W 28th St Fl 12 New York (10001) *(G-11739)*
Welding Guy, The, Menands *Also called Welding Guys LLC* *(G-7850)*
Welding Guys LLC 518 898-8323
47 Broadway Bldg C Menands (12204) *(G-7850)*
Welding Metallurgy Inc (HQ) 631 586-5200
91 Heartland Blvd Edgewood (11717) *(G-4293)*
Well-Made Toy Mfg Corporation 718 381-4225
146 Soundview Dr Port Washington (11050) *(G-12931)*
Wellmill LLC 631 465-9245
69 Mall Dr Ste 1 Commack (11725) *(G-3603)*
Wellquest International Inc (PA) 212 689-9094
230 5th Ave Ste 800 New York (10001) *(G-11740)*
Wells Rugs Inc 516 676-2056
44 Sea Cliff Ave Glen Cove (11542) *(G-5204)*
Wells, George Ruggery, Glen Cove *Also called Wells Rugs Inc* *(G-5204)*
Wellspring Corp (PA) 212 529-5454
54a Ludlow St New York (10002) *(G-11741)*
Wellspring Omni Holdings Corp 212 318-9800
390 Park Ave New York (10022) *(G-11742)*
Wemco Casting LLC 631 563-8050
20 Jules Ct Ste 2 Bohemia (11716) *(G-1098)*
Wen Hwa Printing, Flushing *Also called Global Graphics Inc* *(G-4854)*
Wendels Poultry Farm 716 592-2299
12466 Vaughn St East Concord (14055) *(G-4101)*
Wendon Engineering, Hawthorne *Also called Princetel Inc* *(G-5822)*
Wendt Corporation 716 391-1200
2555 Walden Ave Buffalo (14225) *(G-3044)*
Wendys Auto Express Inc 845 624-6100
121 Main St Nanuet (10954) *(G-8204)*
Wenig Corporation 718 542-3600
230 Manida St Fl 2 Bronx (10474) *(G-1396)*
Wenner Bakery, Ronkonkoma *Also called Wenner Bread Products Inc* *(G-14027)*
Wenner Bakery, Bayport *Also called Wenner Bread Products Inc* *(G-732)*
Wenner Bread Products Inc (PA) 800 869-6262
2001 Orville Dr N Ronkonkoma (11779) *(G-14026)*
Wenner Bread Products Inc 800 869-6262
2001 Orville Dr N Ronkonkoma (11779) *(G-14027)*
Wenner Bread Products Inc 800 869-6262
33 Rajon Rd Bayport (11705) *(G-732)*
Wenner Media LLC (PA) 212 484-1616
1290 Ave Of The Amer Fl 2 New York (10104) *(G-11743)*
Were Forms Inc 585 482-4400
500 Helendale Rd Ste 190 Rochester (14609) *(G-13802)*
Werlatone Inc 845 278-2220
17 Jon Barrett Rd Patterson (12563) *(G-12522)*
Werok LLC 845 675-7710
18 Ford Products Rd Valley Cottage (10989) *(G-15329)*
Weslor Enterprises, Lyons *Also called Weslor Industries Inc* *(G-7454)*
Weslor Industries Inc 315 871-4405
924 Sohn Alloway Rd Lyons (14489) *(G-7454)*
Wessie Machine Inc 315 926-4060
5229 Steel Point Rd Marion (14505) *(G-7578)*
West End Iron Works Inc 518 456-1105
4254 Albany St Albany (12205) *(G-141)*
West End Journal, Far Rockaway *Also called Empire Publishing Inc* *(G-4564)*
West Falls Machine Co Inc 716 655-0440
11692 E Main Rd East Aurora (14052) *(G-4097)*
West Falls Machine Co 1, East Aurora *Also called West Falls Machine Co Inc* *(G-4097)*
West Herr Automotive Group, Hamburg *Also called Kustom Korner* *(G-5513)*
West Internet Trading Company 415 484-5848
47 Great Jones St Fl 5 New York (10012) *(G-11744)*
West Metal Works Inc 716 895-4900
68 Hayes Pl Buffalo (14210) *(G-3045)*
West Seneca Bee Inc 716 632-4700
5564 Main St Williamsville (14221) *(G-16146)*
Westbrook Machinery, Lockport *Also called Ted Westbrook* *(G-7111)*
Westbury Times 516 747-8282
132 E 2nd St Mineola (11501) *(G-8003)*
Westchester County Bus Jurnl, West Harrison *Also called Westfair Communications Inc* *(G-15763)*
Westchester Law Journal Inc 914 948-0715
199 Main St Ste 301 White Plains (10601) *(G-16072)*
Westchester Mailing Service 914 948-1116
39 Westmoreland Ave Fl 2 White Plains (10606) *(G-16073)*
Westchester Modular Homes Inc 845 832-9400
30 Reagans Mill Rd Wingdale (12594) *(G-16160)*
Westchester Signs Inc 914 666-7446
145 Kisco Ave Mount Kisco (10549) *(G-8106)*
Westchester Technologies Inc 914 736-1034
8 John Walsh Blvd Ste 311 Peekskill (10566) *(G-12561)*
Westchester Valve & Fitting Co 914 762-6600
741 Pierce Rd Clifton Park (12065) *(G-3477)*
Westchester Wine Warehouse LLC 914 824-1400
53 Tarrytown Rd Ste 1 White Plains (10607) *(G-16074)*
Westchster Crankshaft Grinding, East Elmhurst *Also called Westchstr Crnkshft Grndng* *(G-4112)*
Westchstr Crnkshft Grndng 718 651-3900
3263 110th St East Elmhurst (11369) *(G-4112)*
Westcode Incorporated 607 766-9881
2226 Airport Rd Binghamton (13905) *(G-916)*
Western Edition, Westhampton Beach *Also called Southampton Town Newspapers* *(G-15959)*
Western New York Energy LLC 585 798-9693
4141 Bates Rd Medina (14103) *(G-7749)*
Western New York Family Mag 716 836-3486
3147 Delaware Ave Ste B Buffalo (14217) *(G-3046)*
Western Oil and Gas JV Inc 914 967-4758
7 Mccullough Pl Rye (10580) *(G-14086)*
Western Queens Gazette, Long Island City *Also called Service Advertising Group Inc* *(G-7355)*
Western Slate Inc (PA) 802 287-2210
33 Dekalb Rd Granville (12832) *(G-5356)*
Westfair Communications Inc 914 694-3600
701 Westchester Ave 100w West Harrison (10604) *(G-15763)*
Westfield Publication, Westfield *Also called Quality Guides* *(G-15948)*
Westinghouse A Brake Tech Corp 518 561-0044
72 Arizona Ave Plattsburgh (12903) *(G-12791)*
Westinghouse A Brake Tech Corp 914 347-8650
4 Warehouse Ln Ste 144 Elmsford (10523) *(G-4440)*
Westmail Press, White Plains *Also called Westchester Mailing Service* *(G-16073)*
Westman Atelier LLC 917 297-0842
135 Central Park W 10s New York (10023) *(G-11745)*
Westmoor Ltd 315 363-1500
906 W Hamilton Ave Sherrill (13461) *(G-14409)*
Westmore Litho Corp 718 361-9403
4017 22nd St Long Island City (11101) *(G-7400)*
Westmore Litho Printing Co, Long Island City *Also called Westmore Litho Corp* *(G-7400)*
Westpoint Home LLC (HQ) 212 930-2000
777 3rd Ave Fl 7 New York (10017) *(G-11746)*
Westpoint International Inc 212 930-2000
28 E 28th St Bsmt 2 New York (10016) *(G-11747)*
Westrock - Solvay Llc (HQ) 315 484-9050
53 Indl Dr Syracuse (13204) *(G-15025)*
Westrock - Southern Cont LLC 315 487-6111
100 Southern Dr Camillus (13031) *(G-3113)*
Westrock Container LLC 518 842-2450
28 Park Dr Amsterdam (12010) *(G-353)*
Westrock Cp LLC 315 484-9050
53 Industrial Dr Syracuse (13204) *(G-15026)*
Westrock Cp LLC 716 694-1000
51 Robinson St North Tonawanda (14120) *(G-12098)*
Westrock Cp LLC 770 448-2193
45 Campion Rd New Hartford (13413) *(G-8248)*
Westrock Mwv LLC 212 688-5000
299 Park Ave Fl 13 New York (10171) *(G-11748)*
Westrock Rkt LLC 631 586-6000
140 W Industry Ct Deer Park (11729) *(G-3953)*
Westrock Rkt LLC 315 487-6111
100 Southern Dr Camillus (13031) *(G-3114)*
Westrock Rkt LLC 770 448-2193
4914 W Genesee St Camillus (13031) *(G-3115)*
Westrock Rkt Company 770 448-2193
53 Indl Dr Syracuse (13204) *(G-15027)*
Westside News Inc 585 352-3411
1835 N Union St Spencerport (14559) *(G-14560)*
Westypo Printers Inc 914 737-7394
540 Harrison Ave Peekskill (10566) *(G-12562)*
Wet & Wild Pools & Spas, Brooklyn *Also called Polytech Pool Mfg Inc* *(G-2268)*
Wet Paint, Floral Park *Also called Wetpaintcom Inc* *(G-4818)*
Wetherall Contracting NY Inc 718 894-7011
8312 Penelope Ave Ste 101 Middle Village (11379) *(G-7885)*
Wetlook Detailing Inc 212 390-8877
1125 Banner Ave Apt 11a Brooklyn (11235) *(G-2580)*
Wetpaintcom Inc 206 859-6300
9523 242nd St Floral Park (11001) *(G-4818)*
Wew Container, Brooklyn *Also called Inland Paper Products Corp* *(G-1960)*
WF Lake Corp 518 798-9934
65 Park Rd Queensbury (12804) *(G-13060)*
Wg Sheet Metal Corp 718 235-3093
341 Amber St Brooklyn (11208) *(G-2581)*
Whalebone Creative, Montauk *Also called Jesse Joeckel* *(G-8054)*
Whalens Horseradish Products 518 587-6404
1710 Route 29 Galway (12074) *(G-5082)*
Wham 1180 AM, Rochester *Also called Iheartcommunications Inc* *(G-13475)*
Whentech LLC (PA) 212 571-0042
55 E 52nd St Fl 40 New York (10055) *(G-11749)*
Where Is Utica Cof Rasting Inc 315 269-8898
92 Genesee St Utica (13502) *(G-15300)*

ALPHABETIC

Whirlwind Music Distrs Inc 800 733-9473
99 Ling Rd Rochester (14612) **(G-13803)**
Whispr Group Inc 212 924-3979
6 Saint Johns Ln New York (10013) **(G-11750)**
Whitacre Engineering Company 315 622-1075
4522 Wetzel Rd Liverpool (13090) **(G-7049)**
White Coffee Corp 718 204-7900
1835 38th St Astoria (11105) **(G-445)**
White Eagle Packing Co Inc 518 374-4366
922 Congress St Schenectady (12303) **(G-14318)**
White House Cabinet Shop LLC 607 674-9358
11 Knapp St Sherburne (13460) **(G-14397)**
White Plains Coat Apron Co Inc 914 736-2610
4 John Walsh Blvd Peekskill (10566) **(G-12563)**
White Plains Linen, Peekskill *Also called White Plains Coat Apron Co Inc* **(G-12563)**
White Plains Marble Inc 914 347-6000
186 E Main St Elmsford (10523) **(G-4441)**
Whiteboard Ventures Inc 855 972-6346
315 W 36th St Fl 10 New York (10018) **(G-11751)**
Whitehall Times, Granville *Also called Manchester Newspaper Inc* **(G-5350)**
Whitesboro Spring & Alignment (PA) 315 736-4441
247 Oriskany Blvd Whitesboro (13492) **(G-16085)**
Whitesboro Spring Svce, Whitesboro *Also called Whitesboro Spring & Alignment* **(G-16085)**
Whitestone Dev Group LLC 585 482-7770
111 Humboldt St Rochester (14609) **(G-13804)**
Whitestone Panetteria LLC 516 543-9788
15045 12th Rd Whitestone (11357) **(G-16103)**
Whitestone Pharmacy, Whitestone *Also called Tocare LLC* **(G-16101)**
Whitewall Magazine, New York *Also called Sky Art Media Inc* **(G-11262)**
Whitford Development Inc 631 471-7711
646 Main St Ste 301 Port Jefferson (11777) **(G-12844)**
Whiting Door Mfg Corp (PA) 716 542-5427
113 Cedar St Akron (14001) **(G-23)**
Whiting Door Mfg Corp 716 542-3070
13550 Bloomingdale Rd Akron (14001) **(G-24)**
Whitley East LLC 718 403-0050
Brooklyn Navy Yd Bg 2 Fl Brooklyn (11205) **(G-2582)**
Whitney Foods Inc 718 291-3333
15504 Liberty Ave Jamaica (11433) **(G-6488)**
Whitsons Food Svc Bronx Corp 631 424-2700
1800 Motor Pkwy Islandia (11749) **(G-6346)**
Whittall & Shon (PA) 212 594-2626
1201 Broadway Ste 904a New York (10001) **(G-11752)**
Wholesale, New York *Also called Ashko Group LLC* **(G-8645)**
Wholesale Mulch & Sawdust Inc 607 687-2637
3711 Waverly Rd Owego (13827) **(G-12440)**
Wholesale Window Warehouse, Oceanside *Also called Express Building Supply Inc* **(G-12171)**
Wicked Smart LLC 518 459-2855
700 5th Ave Watervliet (12189) **(G-15612)**
Wicked Spoon Inc 646 335-2890
127 W 24th St Fl 6 New York (10011) **(G-11753)**
Wickers Performance Wear, Commack *Also called Wickers Sportswear Inc* **(G-3604)**
Wickers Sportswear Inc (PA) 631 543-1640
88 Wyandanch Blvd Commack (11725) **(G-3604)**
Wide Flange Inc 718 492-8705
176 27th St Brooklyn (11232) **(G-2583)**
Widex International, Hauppauge *Also called Widex Usa Inc* **(G-5800)**
Widex Usa Inc (HQ) 718 360-1000
185 Commerce Dr Hauppauge (11788) **(G-5800)**
Widgetworks Unlimited LLC 914 666-6395
395 Millwood Rd Chappaqua (10514) **(G-3327)**
Widmer Time Recorder Company 212 227-0405
27 Park Pl Rm 219 New York (10007) **(G-11754)**
Wiggby Precision Machine Corp 718 439-6900
140 58th St Ste 56 Brooklyn (11220) **(G-2584)**
Wikoff Color Corporation 585 458-0653
686 Pullman Ave Rochester (14615) **(G-13805)**
Wil-Nic, Freeport *Also called Edr Industries Inc* **(G-4993)**
Wilbar International Inc 631 951-9800
50 Cabot Ct Hauppauge (11788) **(G-5801)**
Wilbedone Inc 607 756-8813
1133 State Route 222 Cortland (13045) **(G-3791)**
Wilco Industries Inc 631 676-2593
788 Marconi Ave Ronkonkoma (11779) **(G-14028)**
Wilcro Inc 716 632-4204
90 Earhart Dr Ste 19 Buffalo (14221) **(G-3047)**
Wild Works Incorporated 716 891-4197
30 Railroad Ave Albany (12205) **(G-142)**
Wilda, Long Island City *Also called Import-Export Corporation* **(G-7246)**
Wilkesboro Road, New York *Also called Schneider Mills Inc* **(G-11158)**
Willard Machine 716 885-1630
73 Forest Ave Buffalo (14213) **(G-3048)**
Willco Fine Art Ltd 718 935-9567
145 Nassau St Apt 9c New York (10038) **(G-11755)**
William B Collins Company 518 773-8272
8 E Fulton St Gloversville (12078) **(G-5300)**
William Boyd Printing Co Inc 518 339-5832
4 Weed Rd Ste 1 Latham (12110) **(G-6881)**
William Brooks Woodworking 718 495-9767
856 Saratoga Ave Brooklyn (11212) **(G-2585)**
William Charles Prtg Co Inc 516 349-0900
7 Fairchild Ct Ste 100 Plainview (11803) **(G-12728)**
William E William Valve Corp 718 392-1660
3852 Review Ave Long Island City (11101) **(G-7401)**
William E Williams Valve Corp 718 392-1660
3850 Review Ave Long Island City (11101) **(G-7402)**
William Goldberg Diamond Corp 212 980-4343
589 5th Ave Fl 14 New York (10017) **(G-11756)**
William H Jackson Company 718 784-4482
3629 23rd St Long Island City (11106) **(G-7403)**
William H Sadlier Inc (PA) 212 233-3646
9 Pine St New York (10005) **(G-11757)**
William H Shapiro 212 263-7037
530 1st Ave Ste 3e New York (10016) **(G-11758)**
William Harvey Studio Inc 718 599-4343
214 N 8th St Brooklyn (11211) **(G-2586)**
William J Kline & Son Inc (PA) 518 843-1100
1 Venner Rd Amsterdam (12010) **(G-354)**
William J Ryan 585 392-6200
1365 Hamlin Parma Townlne Hilton (14468) **(G-5975)**
William Kanes Mfg Corp 718 346-1515
23 Alabama Ave Brooklyn (11207) **(G-2587)**
William Moon Iron Works Inc 518 943-3861
80 Main St Catskill (12414) **(G-3217)**
William Morrow Publishing, New York *Also called Harpercollins Publishers LLC* **(G-9727)**
William R Shoemaker Inc 716 649-0511
399 Pleasant Ave Hamburg (14075) **(G-5524)**
William S Hein & Co Inc (PA) 716 882-2600
2350 N Forest Rd Ste 14a Getzville (14068) **(G-5184)**
William S Hein & Co Inc 716 882-2600
1575 Main St Buffalo (14209) **(G-3049)**
William Somerville Maintenance 212 534-4600
129 E 124th St New York (10035) **(G-11759)**
Williams Tool Inc 315 737-7226
9372 Elm St Chadwicks (13319) **(G-3304)**
Williams-Sonoma Store 154, New York *Also called Williams-Sonoma Stores Inc* **(G-11760)**
Williams-Sonoma Stores Inc 212 633-2203
110 7th Ave New York (10011) **(G-11760)**
Williamsburg Bulletin 718 387-0123
136 Ross St Brooklyn (11211) **(G-2588)**
Williamson Law Book Co 585 924-3400
790 Canning Pkwy Ste 2 Victor (14564) **(G-15443)**
Willis Mc Donald Co Inc 212 366-1526
44 W 62nd St Ph A New York (10023) **(G-11761)**
Willow Creek Winery, Silver Creek *Also called Chautauqua Wine Company Inc* **(G-14440)**
Wilmax Usa LLC 917 388-2790
315 5th Ave Rm 505 New York (10016) **(G-11762)**
Wilmington Products USA, Roslyn *Also called Northwest Company LLC* **(G-14045)**
Wilson & Wilson Group 212 729-4736
6514 110th St Forest Hills (11375) **(G-4927)**
Wilson Beef Farms LLC 607 545-8308
10751 Hess Rd Canaseraga (14822) **(G-3148)**
Wilson N Wilson Group & RES, Forest Hills *Also called Wilson & Wilson Group* **(G-4927)**
Wilson Picture Frames, West Hempstead *Also called Interntonal Consmr Connections* **(G-15771)**
Wilson Press LLC 315 568-9693
56 Miller St Seneca Falls (13148) **(G-14374)**
Wilsonart Intl Holdings LLC 516 935-6980
999 S Oyster Bay Rd # 3305 Bethpage (11714) **(G-846)**
Wilston Enterprises Inc 716 483-1411
121 Jackson Ave Jamestown (14701) **(G-6554)**
Wilt Industries Inc 518 548-4961
2452 State Route 8 Lake Pleasant (12108) **(G-6769)**
Win Set Technologies LLC 631 234-7077
2364 Middle Country Rd Centereach (11720) **(G-3253)**
Win Wood Cabinetry Inc 516 304-2216
200 Forest Dr Ste 7 Greenvale (11548) **(G-5466)**
Win-Holt Equipment Corp (PA) 516 222-0335
20 Crossways Park Dr N # 205 Woodbury (11797) **(G-16185)**
Win-Holt Equipment Group, Woodbury *Also called Win-Holt Equipment Corp* **(G-16185)**
Winchester Optical Company (HQ) 607 734-4251
1935 Lake St Elmira (14901) **(G-4372)**
Windiam Usa Inc 212 542-0949
580 5th Ave Ste 2907 New York (10036) **(G-11763)**
Window Tech Systems Inc 518 899-9000
15 Old Stonebreak Rd Ballston Spa (12020) **(G-589)**
Window-Fix Inc 718 854-3475
331 37th St Fl 1 Brooklyn (11232) **(G-2589)**
Windowcraft Inc 516 294-3580
77 2nd Ave Garden City Park (11040) **(G-5125)**
Windowman Inc (usa) 718 246-2626
460 Kingsland Ave Brooklyn (11222) **(G-2590)**
Windows Media Publishing LLC 917 732-7892
369 Remsen Ave Brooklyn (11212) **(G-2591)**
Windowtex Inc 877 294-3580
77 2nd Ave New Hyde Park (11040) **(G-8303)**
Windsor Technology LLC 585 461-2500
1527 Lyell Ave Rochester (14606) **(G-13806)**
Windsor United Industries LLC 607 655-3300
10 Park St Windsor (13865) **(G-16158)**
Wine & Spirits Magazine Inc (PA) 212 695-4660
2 W 32nd St Ste 601 New York (10001) **(G-11764)**

Wine Group Inc 716 326-3151
85 Bourne St Westfield (14787) *(G-15953)*

Wine Services Inc 631 722-3800
1129 Cross River Dr Ste A Riverhead (11901) *(G-13193)*

Winerackscom Inc 845 658-7181
819 Route 32 Tillson (12486) *(G-15078)*

Winesoft International Corp 914 400-6247
503 S Broadway Ste 220 Yonkers (10705) *(G-16356)*

Wing Heung Noodle Inc 212 966-7496
144 Baxter St New York (10013) *(G-11765)*

Wing Kei Noodle Inc 212 226-1644
102 Canal St New York (10002) *(G-11766)*

Wings For Wheels Inc 914 961-0276
590 Tuckahoe Rd Yonkers (10710) *(G-16357)*

Wink Inc 212 389-1382
606 W 28th St Fl 6 New York (10001) *(G-11767)*

Wink Labs Inc (HQ) 844 946-5277
606 W 28th St Fl 7 New York (10001) *(G-11768)*

Winn Manufacturing Inc 518 642-3515
12 Burtis Ave Granville (12832) *(G-5357)*

Winner Press Inc 718 937-7715
4331 33rd St 1 Long Island City (11101) *(G-7404)*

Winsight LLC 646 708-7309
90 Broad St Ste 402 New York (10004) *(G-11769)*

Winson Surnamer Inc 718 729-8787
4402 11th St Ste 601 Long Island City (11101) *(G-7405)*

Winter Water Factory 646 387-3247
191 33rd St Brooklyn (11232) *(G-2592)*

Winterling, Eric Costumes, New York *Also called Eric Winterling Inc (G-9393)*

Winters Instruments, Buffalo *Also called Winters Instruments Inc (G-3050)*

Winters Instruments Inc (HQ) 281 880-8607
455 Cayuga Rd Ste 650 Buffalo (14225) *(G-3050)*

Winters Railroad Service Inc 716 337-2668
11309 Sisson Hwy North Collins (14111) *(G-12030)*

Wired Coffee and Bagel Inc 518 506-3194
Rr 9 Malta (12020) *(G-7498)*

Wireless Communications Inc 845 353-5921
4 Chemong Ct Nyack (10960) *(G-12148)*

With You Designs LLC 800 413-0670
23a E Mkt St Red Hook Red Hook (12571) *(G-13075)*

With You Lockets, Red Hook *Also called With You Designs LLC (G-13075)*

Witt Preparations LLC 716 948-4002
65 Inns Brook Rd Cheektowaga (14227) *(G-3365)*

Wizard Equipment Inc 315 414-9999
10 Dwight Park Dr Ste 3 Syracuse (13209) *(G-15028)*

Wizer Equipment, Rochester *Also called Woerner Industries Inc (G-13807)*

Wizq Inc 586 381-9048
307 5th Ave Fl 8 New York (10016) *(G-11770)*

WI Concepts & Production Inc 516 565-5151
1 Bennington Ave Freeport (11520) *(G-5032)*

Wlf Founders Corporation 718 777-8899
4510 19th Ave Astoria (11105) *(G-446)*

Wlj Printers, White Plains *Also called Westchester Law Journal Inc (G-16072)*

Wm E Martin and Sons Co Inc 516 605-2444
55 Bryant Ave Ste 300 Roslyn (11576) *(G-14047)*

Wmg Acquisition Corp (HQ) 212 275-2000
1633 Broadway Fl 7 New York (10019) *(G-11771)*

Wmw Machinery Company, Deer Park *Also called World LLC (G-3956)*

Wna-Holley, Holley *Also called Waddington North America Inc (G-6039)*

Wny Cheese Enterprise LLC 585 243-6516
1842 Craig Rd Pavilion (14525) *(G-12524)*

Wny Enterprise LLC 585 243-6514
1840 Craig Rd Pavilion (14525) *(G-12525)*

Wny Jobs.com, Hamburg *Also called Jobs Weekly Inc (G-5510)*

Wobbleworks Inc (PA) 718 618-9904
89 5th Ave Ste 602 New York (10003) *(G-11772)*

Wochlt Inc (PA) 212 979-8343
12 E 33rd St Fl 4 New York (10016) *(G-11773)*

Woerner Industries Inc 585 436-1934
485 Hague St Rochester (14606) *(G-13807)*

Wok To Walk, New York *Also called Restaurant 570 8th Avenue LLC (G-11021)*

Wolak Inc 315 839-5366
2360 King Rd Clayville (13322) *(G-3459)*

Wolf X-Ray Corporation 631 242-9729
100 W Industry Ct Deer Park (11729) *(G-3954)*

Wolfe Lumber Mill Inc 716 772-7750
8416 Ridge Rd Gasport (14067) *(G-5140)*

Wolfe Publications Inc (PA) 585 394-0770
73 Buffalo St Canandaigua (14424) *(G-3145)*

Wolff & Dungey Inc 315 475-2105
325 Temple St Syracuse (13202) *(G-15029)*

Wolffer Estate Vineyard Inc 631 537-5106
139 Sagg Rd Sagaponack (11962) *(G-14103)*

Wolffer Estate Winery, Sagaponack *Also called Wolffer Estate Vineyard Inc (G-14103)*

Wolfgang B Gourmet Foods Inc 518 719-1727
117 Cauterskill Ave Catskill (12414) *(G-3218)*

Wolo Mfg Corp 631 242-0333
1 Saxwood St Ste 1 # 1 Deer Park (11729) *(G-3955)*

Wolski Wood Works Inc 718 577-9816
14134 78th Rd Apt 3c Flushing (11367) *(G-4906)*

Wolters Kluwer US Inc 212 894-8920
28 Liberty St Fl 26 New York (10005) *(G-11774)*

Womens E News Inc 212 244-1720
6 Barclay St Fl 6 # 6 New York (10007) *(G-11775)*

Womens Health Care PC (PA) 718 850-0009
11311 Jamaica Ave Ste C Richmond Hill (11418) *(G-13128)*

Womens Wear Daily, New York *Also called Fairchild Publications Inc (G-9463)*

Won & Lee Inc 516 222-0712
971 Stewart Ave Garden City (11530) *(G-5119)*

Wonder Natural Foods Corp (PA) 631 726-4433
670 Montauk Hwy Unit 2 Water Mill (11976) *(G-15532)*

Wonder Products, Middletown *Also called Advanced Enterprises Inc (G-7892)*

Wonderly Company, The, Kingston *Also called Northast Coml Win Trtments Inc (G-6704)*

Wonton Food Inc 718 784-8178
5210 37th St Long Island City (11101) *(G-7406)*

Wonton Food Inc (PA) 718 628-6868
220 Moore St 222 Brooklyn (11206) *(G-2593)*

Wonton Food Inc 212 677-8865
183 E Broadway New York (10002) *(G-11776)*

Woo Audio Inc 917 324-5284
2219 41st Ave Ste 502 Long Island City (11101) *(G-7407)*

Wood & Hyde Leather Co Inc 518 725-7105
68 Wood St Gloversville (12078) *(G-5301)*

Wood Design, Peekskill *Also called W Designe Inc (G-12559)*

Wood Etc Inc 315 484-9663
1175 State Fair Blvd # 2 Syracuse (13209) *(G-15030)*

Wood Innovations of Suffolk 631 698-2345
100 Daly Blvd Apt 3218 Oceanside (11572) *(G-12198)*

Wood Talk 631 940-3085
203 N Fehr Way Ste C Bay Shore (11706) *(G-725)*

Wood Tex Products LLC 607 243-5141
3700 Route 14 Himrod (14842) *(G-5977)*

Wood-Mizer Holdings Inc 315 564-5722
8604 State Route 104 Hannibal (13074) *(G-5543)*

Wood-Tex Products, Himrod *Also called Lapp Management Corp (G-5976)*

Woodards Concrete Products Inc 845 361-3471
629 Lybolt Rd Bullville (10915) *(G-3054)*

Woodbine Products Inc 631 586-3770
110 Plant Ave Hauppauge (11788) *(G-5802)*

Woodbury Printing Plus + Inc 845 928-6610
96 Turner Rd Central Valley (10917) *(G-3302)*

Woodbury Systems Group Inc 516 364-2653
30 Glenn Dr Woodbury (11797) *(G-16186)*

Woodbury Vineyards Inc 716 679-9463
3215 S Roberts Rd Fredonia (14063) *(G-4973)*

Woodcock Brothers Brewing Comp 716 333-4000
638 Lake St Wilson (14172) *(G-16155)*

Wooden Boatworks 631 477-6507
190 Sterling St Unit 2 Greenport (11944) *(G-5459)*

Woodfalls Industries 518 236-7201
434 Burke Rd Plattsburgh (12901) *(G-12792)*

Woodmaster Industries, Jamaica *Also called Abbott Industries Inc (G-6423)*

Woodmotif Inc 516 564-8325
42 Chasner St Hempstead (11550) *(G-5852)*

Woodmotif Cabinetry, Hempstead *Also called Woodmotif Inc (G-5852)*

Woods Knife Corporation 516 798-4972
19 Brooklyn Ave Massapequa (11758) *(G-7653)*

Woods Machine and Tool LLC 607 699-3253
150 Howell St Nichols (13812) *(G-11993)*

Woodside Decorator, Staten Island *Also called All Signs (G-14618)*

Woodside Granite Industries 585 589-6500
13890 Ridge Rd W Albion (14411) *(G-162)*

Woodstock Times, Kingston *Also called Ulster Publishing Co Inc (G-6718)*

Woodtalk Stairs & Rails, Bay Shore *Also called Wood Talk (G-725)*

Woodtronics Inc 914 962-5205
1661 Front St Ste 3 Yorktown Heights (10598) *(G-16374)*

Woodward Industries Inc 716 692-2242
233 Fillmore Ave Ste 23 Tonawanda (14150) *(G-15154)*

Woodward/White Inc 718 509-6082
45 Main St Ste 820 Brooklyn (11201) *(G-2594)*

Woodworks 845 677-3960
2559 Route 44 Salt Point (12578) *(G-14135)*

Woolmark Americas Inc 347 767-3160
110 E 25th St Fl 3 New York (10010) *(G-11777)*

Woolmark Company, The, New York *Also called Woolmark Americas Inc (G-11777)*

Wordingham Machine Co Inc 585 924-2294
515 Lee Rd Rochester (14606) *(G-13808)*

Wordingham Technologies, Rochester *Also called Wordingham Machine Co Inc (G-13808)*

Working Family Solutions Inc 845 802-6182
359 Washington Avenue Ext Saugerties (12477) *(G-14216)*

Working Mother Media Inc 212 351-6400
2 Park Ave Fl 27 New York (10016) *(G-11778)*

Workman Publishing Co Inc (PA) 212 254-5900
225 Varick St Fl 9 New York (10014) *(G-11779)*

Workman Publishing Co Inc 212 254-5900
708 Broadway Fl 6 New York (10003) *(G-11780)*

Workplace Interiors LLC 585 425-7420
400 Packetts Lndg Fairport (14450) *(G-4530)*

Workshop Art Fabrication 845 331-0385
117 Tremper Ave Kingston (12401) *(G-6723)*

Worksman Cycles, Ozone Park *Also called Worksman Trading Corp (G-12469)*

Worksman Trading Corp (PA) 718 322-2000
9415 100th St Ozone Park (11416) *(G-12469)*

World Best Sporting Goods Inc 800 489-0908
225 Post Ave Westbury (11590) **(G-15940)**
World Business Media LLC 212 344-0759
4770 Sunrise Hwy Ste 105 Massapequa Park (11762) **(G-7662)**
World Cheese Co Inc 718 965-1700
178 28th St Brooklyn (11232) **(G-2595)**
World Guide Publishing 800 331-7840
1271 Ave Of The Americas New York (10020) **(G-11781)**
World Journal LLC (HQ) 718 746-8889
14107 20th Ave Fl 2 Whitestone (11357) **(G-16104)**
World Journal LLC 718 871-5000
6007 8th Ave Brooklyn (11220) **(G-2596)**
World LLC 631 940-9121
513 Acorn St Ste B Deer Park (11729) **(G-3956)**
World Maritime News 212 477-6700
118 E 25th St Fl 2 New York (10010) **(G-11782)**
World of McIntosh, New York *Also called Fine Sounds Group Inc* **(G-9496)**
World Screen News, New York *Also called Wsn Inc* **(G-11792)**
World Trading Center Inc 631 273-3330
115 Engineers Rd Ste 200 Hauppauge (11788) **(G-5803)**
Worlds Best Cookie Dough Inc 347 592-3422
164 Bleecker St New York (10012) **(G-11783)**
Worldwide Arntcal Cmpnents Inc (PA) 631 842-3780
10 Reith St Copiague (11726) **(G-3690)**
Worldwide Arntcal Cmpnents Inc 631 842-3780
10 Reith St Copiague (11726) **(G-3691)**
Worldwide Electric Corp LLC 800 808-2131
3540 Winton Pl Rochester (14623) **(G-13809)**
Worldwide Gas Turbine Pdts Inc 518 877-7200
300 Commerce Dr Clifton Park (12065) **(G-3478)**
Worldwide Media Svcs Group Inc 212 545-4800
4 New York Plz New York (10004) **(G-11784)**
Worldwide Protective Pdts LLC 877 678-4568
4255 Mckinley Pkwy Hamburg (14075) **(G-5525)**
Worldwide Resources Inc 718 760-5000
1908 Avenue O Brooklyn (11230) **(G-2597)**
Worldwide Ticket Craft 516 538-6200
1390 Jerusalem Ave Merrick (11566) **(G-7865)**
Worm Power, Rochester *Also called Rt Solutions LLC* **(G-13709)**
Worth Collection Ltd (PA) 212 268-0312
520 8th Ave Rm 2301 New York (10018) **(G-11785)**
Worth Imports LLC 212 398-5410
93 Worth St Ste 201 New York (10013) **(G-11786)**
Worth Publishers Inc 212 475-6000
1 New York Plz Ste 4500 New York (10004) **(G-11787)**
Worthington Industries Inc 315 336-5500
530 Henry St Rome (13440) **(G-13877)**
Worzalla Publishing Company 212 967-7909
222 W 37th St Fl 10 New York (10018) **(G-11788)**
Wp Company LLC 212 445-5050
395 Hudson St Lbby 1 New York (10014) **(G-11789)**
Wp Lavori USA Inc (HQ) 212 244-6074
597 Broadway Fl 2 New York (10012) **(G-11790)**
WR Design Corp 212 354-9000
230 W 39th St Fl 5f New York (10018) **(G-11791)**
WR Smith & Sons Inc 845 620-9400
121 W Nyack Rd Nanuet (10954) **(G-8205)**
Wr9000, New York *Also called WR Design Corp* **(G-11791)**
Wrightcut EDM & Machine Inc 607 733-5018
951 Carl St Elmira (14904) **(G-4373)**
Writing Sculptures, Deer Park *Also called Versaponents Inc* **(G-3950)**
Wrkbook LLC 914 355-1293
19 Brookdale Ave White Plains (10603) **(G-16075)**
Wsf Industries Inc 716 692-4930
7 Hackett Dr Tonawanda (14150) **(G-15155)**
Wsn Inc 212 924-7620
1123 Broadway Ste 1207 New York (10010) **(G-11792)**
Wt Shade, New Hyde Park *Also called Windowtex Inc* **(G-8303)**
Www.dynatabs.com, Brooklyn *Also called Dynatabs LLC* **(G-1769)**
Www.picturesongold.com, Staten Island *Also called Photogrove Corporation* **(G-14688)**
Wyde Lumber 845 513-5571
419 State Route 17b Monticello (12701) **(G-8073)**
Wyeth, Rouses Point *Also called Pfizer Inc* **(G-14066)**
Wyeth Holdings LLC 845 602-5000
401 N Middletown Rd Pearl River (10965) **(G-12543)**
Wyeth LLC (HQ) 212 733-2323
235 E 42nd St New York (10017) **(G-11793)**
Wyeth Pharmaceutical Division, Pearl River *Also called Wyeth Holdings LLC* **(G-12543)**
Wynco Press One Inc 516 354-6145
7839 268th St Glen Oaks (11004) **(G-5215)**
Wyrestorm Technologies LLC 518 289-1293
23 Wood Rd Round Lake (12151) **(G-14063)**
X Brand Editions 718 482-7646
4020 22nd St Ste 1 Long Island City (11101) **(G-7408)**
X Function Inc (PA) 212 231-0092
45 W 89th St Apt 4a New York (10024) **(G-11794)**
X Myles Mar Inc 212 683-2015
875 Ave Of The Am Rm 1715 New York (10001) **(G-11795)**
X Press Screen Printing 716 679-7788
4867 W Lake Rd Dunkirk (14048) **(G-4068)**
X Vision Inc 917 412-3570
209 W 38th St Rm 1003 New York (10018) **(G-11796)**
X-Gen Pharmaceuticals Inc (PA) 607 562-2700
300 Daniel Zenker Dr Big Flats (14814) **(G-849)**
X-Gen Pharmaceuticals Inc 631 261-8188
4 York Ct Northport (11768) **(G-12112)**
X-L Envelope and Printing Inc 716 852-2135
701 Seneca St Ste 100 Buffalo (14210) **(G-3051)**
X-Press Printing & Office Sup, Mahopac *Also called Rmd Holding Inc* **(G-7478)**
X-Treme Ready Mix Inc 718 739-3384
17801 Liberty Ave Jamaica (11433) **(G-6489)**
X1000, Binghamton *Also called Surescan Corporation* **(G-911)**
Xactiv Inc 585 288-7220
71 Perinton Pkwy Fairport (14450) **(G-4531)**
Xactra Technologies Inc 585 426-2030
105 Mclaughlin Rd Ste F Rochester (14615) **(G-13810)**
Xanadu 212 465-0580
150 W 30th St Rm 702 New York (10001) **(G-11797)**
Xania Labs Inc 718 361-2550
3202 Queens Blvd Fl 6 Long Island City (11101) **(G-7409)**
Xborder Entertainment LLC 518 726-7036
568 State Route 3 Plattsburgh (12901) **(G-12793)**
Xedit Corp 718 380-1592
21831 97th Ave Queens Village (11429) **(G-13028)**
Xeku Corporation 607 761-1447
2520 Vestal Pkwy E222 Vestal (13850) **(G-15388)**
Xeleum Lighting LLC 954 617-8170
333 N Bedford Rd Ste 135 Mount Kisco (10549) **(G-8107)**
Xelic Incorporated 585 415-2764
1250 Pittsford Victor Rd # 370 Pittsford (14534) **(G-12658)**
Xenial Inc 845 920-0800
1 Blue Hill Plz Ste 16 Pearl River (10965) **(G-12544)**
Xentaur Corporation 631 345-3434
84 Horseblock Rd Unit G Yaphank (11980) **(G-16279)**
Xerox Corporation 585 422-4564
800 Phillips Rd Ste 20599 Webster (14580) **(G-15663)**
Xerox Corporation 585 264-5584
80 Linden Oaks Rochester (14625) **(G-13811)**
Xing Lin USA Intl Corp 212 947-4846
1410 Broadway Rm 3201 New York (10018) **(G-11798)**
Xinya International Trading Co 212 216-9681
115 W 30th St Rm 1109 New York (10001) **(G-11799)**
Xl Graphics Inc 212 929-8700
121 Varick St Rm 300 New York (10013) **(G-11800)**
Xli Manufacturing LLC 585 436-2250
55 Vanguard Pkwy Rochester (14606) **(G-13812)**
Xomox Jewelry Inc 212 944-8428
151 W 46th St Fl 15 New York (10036) **(G-11801)**
Xpand, New York *Also called Whiteboard Ventures Inc* **(G-11751)**
Xpress Printing Inc 516 605-1000
7 Fairchild Ct Ste 100 Plainview (11803) **(G-12729)**
Xstelos Holdings Inc 212 729-4962
630 5th Ave Ste 2600 New York (10111) **(G-11802)**
Xto Incorporated (PA) 315 451-7807
110 Wrentham Dr Liverpool (13088) **(G-7050)**
Xylem, Cheektowaga *Also called Fluid Handling LLC* **(G-3349)**
Xylem Inc 315 239-2499
2881 E Bayard Street Ext Seneca Falls (13148) **(G-14375)**
Xylem Inc (PA) 914 323-5700
1 International Dr Rye Brook (10573) **(G-14095)**
Xylon Industries Inc 631 293-4717
79 Florida St Farmingdale (11735) **(G-4766)**
Y & A Trading Inc 718 436-6333
1365 38th St Brooklyn (11218) **(G-2598)**
Y & Z Precision Inc 516 349-8243
155 E Ames Ct Unit 4 Plainview (11803) **(G-12730)**
Y & Z Precision Machine Shop, Plainview *Also called Y & Z Precision Inc* **(G-12730)**
Y-Mabs Therapeutics Inc (PA) 917 817-2992
230 Park Ave Rm 3350 New York (10169) **(G-11803)**
Yacoubian Jewelers Inc 212 302-6729
2 W 45th St Ste 1104 New York (10036) **(G-11804)**
Yale, Getzville *Also called Columbus McKinnon Corporation* **(G-5176)**
Yale Robbins Inc 212 683-5700
205 Lexington Ave Fl 12 New York (10016) **(G-11805)**
Yale Trouser Corporation 516 255-0700
3670 Oceanside Rd W Ste 6 Oceanside (11572) **(G-12199)**
Yaloz Mold & Die, Brooklyn *Also called Yaloz Mould & Die Co Inc* **(G-2599)**
Yaloz Mould & Die Co Inc 718 389-1131
239 Java St Fl 2 Brooklyn (11222) **(G-2599)**
Yam TV LLC 917 932-5418
144 W 23rd St Apt 8e New York (10011) **(G-11806)**
Yankee Corp 718 589-1377
1180 Randall Ave Bronx (10474) **(G-1397)**
Yankee Fuel Inc 631 880-8810
780 Sunrise Hwy West Babylon (11704) **(G-15757)**
Yankee Wiping Cloth, Bronx *Also called Yankee Corp* **(G-1397)**
Yarnz International Inc 212 868-5883
260 W 36th St Rm 201 New York (10018) **(G-11807)**
Yellow E House Inc 718 888-2000
18812 Northern Blvd Flushing (11358) **(G-4907)**
Yellow Pages Inc (PA) 845 639-6060
222 N Main St New City (10956) **(G-8231)**
Yellowpagecitycom 585 410-6688
280 Kenneth Dr Ste 300 Rochester (14623) **(G-13813)**

Yeohlee Inc 212 631-8099
12 W 29th St New York (10001) *(G-11808)*

Yepes Fine Furniture 718 383-0221
72 Van Dam St Brooklyn (11222) *(G-2600)*

Yes Were Nuts Ltd 516 374-1940
1215 Broadway Hewlett (11557) *(G-5877)*

Yesteryears Vintage Doors LLC 315 324-5250
66 S Main St Hammond (13646) *(G-5528)*

Yewtree Millworks Corp 914 320-5851
372 Ashburton Ave Yonkers (10701) *(G-16358)*

Yfd Cabinetry, West Haverstraw Also called *Your Furniture Designers Inc (G-15765)*

Yiamas Dairy Farms LLC 347 766-7177
2 Bay Club Dr Bayside (11360) *(G-745)*

Yigal-Azrouel Inc (PA) 212 302-1194
500 7th Ave Fl 8 New York (10018) *(G-11809)*

Ying Ke Youth Age Group Inc 929 402-8458
1 Campbell Dr Dix Hills (11746) *(G-4017)*

Yiwen Usa Inc 212 370-0828
60 E 42nd St Ste 1030 New York (10165) *(G-11810)*

Yofah Religious Articles Inc 718 435-3288
2001 57th St Ste 1 Brooklyn (11204) *(G-2601)*

Yogibo LLC 518 456-1762
120 Washington Avenue Ext # 23 Albany (12203) *(G-143)*

Yogolicious Inc 914 236-3455
516 N State Rd Briarcliff Manor (10510) *(G-1163)*

Yoman Madeo Fano 631 438-0246
1 S Ocean Ave Patchogue (11772) *(G-12514)*

Yomiuri International Inc 212 752-2196
747 3rd Ave Fl 28 New York (10017) *(G-11811)*

Yong Ji Productions Inc 917 559-4616
10219 44th Ave Corona (11368) *(G-3752)*

Yonkers Cabinet Inc 914 668-2133
1179 Yonkers Ave Yonkers (10704) *(G-16359)*

Yonkers Time Publishing Co 914 965-4000
40 Larkin Plz Yonkers (10701) *(G-16360)*

Yonkers Whl Beer Distrs Inc 914 963-8600
424 Riverdale Ave Yonkers (10705) *(G-16361)*

Yorganic, New York Also called *Bliss Foods Inc (G-8811)*

Yorganic, New York Also called *Bliss Foods Inc (G-8812)*

York Fuel Incorporated 718 951-0202
1760 Flatbush Ave Brooklyn (11210) *(G-2602)*

York Industries Inc 516 746-3736
303 Nassau Blvd Garden City Park (11040) *(G-5126)*

York International Corporation 718 389-4152
1130 45th Rd Long Island City (11101) *(G-7410)*

York Ladder Inc 718 784-6666
3720 12th St Long Island City (11101) *(G-7411)*

York Ladders, Long Island City Also called *AAAA York Inc (G-7142)*

Yorkville Sound Inc 716 297-2920
4625 Witmer Indus Est Niagara Falls (14305) *(G-11992)*

Yost Neon Displays Inc 716 674-6780
20 Ransier Dr West Seneca (14224) *(G-15856)*

You and ME Legwear LLC 212 279-9292
10 W 33rd St Rm 300 New York (10001) *(G-11812)*

Young & Franklin Inc (HQ) 315 457-3110
942 Old Liverpool Rd Liverpool (13088) *(G-7051)*

Young & Swartz Inc 716 852-2171
39 Cherry St Buffalo (14204) *(G-3052)*

Young Explosives Corp 585 394-1783
2165 New Michigan Rd Canandaigua (14424) *(G-3146)*

Younique Clothing, New York Also called *Turn On Products Inc (G-11560)*

Your Furniture Designers Inc 845 947-3046
118 E Railroad Ave West Haverstraw (10993) *(G-15765)*

Your Name Professional Brand, Long Island City Also called *Mana Products Inc (G-7285)*

Your Way Custom Cabinets Inc 914 371-1870
20 N Macquesten Pkwy Mount Vernon (10550) *(G-8192)*

Ypis of Staten Island Inc 718 815-4557
130 Stuyvesant Pl Ste 5 Staten Island (10301) *(G-14729)*

Yr Blanc & Co LLC 716 800-3999
25 Eltham Dr Buffalo (14226) *(G-3053)*

Ys Marketing Inc (PA) 718 778-6080
2004 Mcdonald Ave Brooklyn (11223) *(G-2603)*

YS Publishing Co Inc 212 682-9360
228 E 45th St Rm 700 New York (10017) *(G-11813)*

Yugo Landau, Brooklyn Also called *Eastern Feather & Down Corp (G-1776)*

Yula Corporation 718 991-0900
330 Bryant Ave Bronx (10474) *(G-1398)*

Yumble Kids, New York Also called *Panda Plates Inc (G-10745)*

Yummy Fabric, New York Also called *Planet Gold Clothing Co Inc (G-10851)*

Yurman Retail, New York Also called *David Yurman Enterprises LLC (G-9186)*

Z Card North America, New York Also called *In-Step Marketing Inc (G-9874)*

Z Works Inc 631 750-0612
1395 Lakeland Ave Ste 10 Bohemia (11716) *(G-1099)*

Z-Axis Inc 315 548-5000
1916 State Route 96 Phelps (14532) *(G-12611)*

Z-Car-D Corp 631 424-2077
403 Oakwood Rd Huntington Station (11746) *(G-6267)*

Z-Ply Corp 212 398-7011
213 W 35th St Ste 5w New York (10001) *(G-11814)*

Z-Studios Dsign Fbrication LLC 347 512-4210
30 Haven Pl Brooklyn (11233) *(G-2604)*

Zacks Enterprises Inc 800 366-4924
33 Corporate Dr Orangeburg (10962) *(G-12333)*

Zacmel Graphics LLC 631 944-6031
500 Brook Ave Ste B Deer Park (11729) *(G-3957)*

Zadig and Voltaire, New York Also called *Arteast LLC (G-8633)*

Zagwear, Orangeburg Also called *Zacks Enterprises Inc (G-12333)*

Zahk Sales Inc 631 851-0851
75 Hoffman Ln Ste A Islandia (11749) *(G-6347)*

Zaika Flavors of India, New Windsor Also called *Cafe Spice Gct Inc (G-8362)*

Zak Jewelry Tools Inc 212 768-8122
55 W 47th St Fl 2 New York (10036) *(G-11815)*

Zanetti Millwork, Middle Grove Also called *Cuccio-Zanetti Inc (G-7872)*

Zanzano Woodworking Inc 914 725-6025
91 Locust Ave Scarsdale (10583) *(G-14243)*

Zappala Farms AG Systems Inc 315 626-6293
11404 Schuler Rd Cato (13033) *(G-3209)*

Zar Apparel Group, New York Also called *Zar Group LLC (G-11816)*

Zar Group LLC (PA) 212 944-2510
1450 Broadway Fl 17 New York (10018) *(G-11816)*

Zastech Inc 516 496-4777
15 Ryan St Syosset (11791) *(G-14806)*

Zazoom LLC (PA) 212 321-2100
1 Exchange Plz Ste 801 New York (10006) *(G-11817)*

Zazoom Media Group, New York Also called *Zazoom LLC (G-11817)*

Zebra Books, New York Also called *Kensington Publishing Corp (G-10092)*

Zebra Environmental Corp (PA) 516 596-6300
30 N Prospect Ave Lynbrook (11563) *(G-7443)*

Zebra Technologies Entp Corp 800 722-6234
1 Zebra Plz Holtsville (11742) *(G-6059)*

Zedge Inc 330 577-3424
22 Cortlandt St Fl 11 New York (10007) *(G-11818)*

Zeeba Jewelry Manufacturing, New York Also called *Zeeba Jewelry Mfg Inc (G-11819)*

Zeeba Jewelry Mfg Inc 212 997-1009
36 W 47th St Ste 902a New York (10036) *(G-11819)*

Zehnder Rittling, Buffalo Also called *Hydro-Air Components Inc (G-2803)*

Zela International Co 518 436-1833
13 Manor St Albany (12207) *(G-144)*

Zelman & Friedman Jwly Mfg Co 718 349-3400
4722 37th St Long Island City (11101) *(G-7412)*

Zenger Group Inc 716 871-1058
777 E Park Dr Tonawanda (14150) *(G-15156)*

Zenger Partners LLC 716 876-2284
1881 Kenmore Ave Kenmore (14217) *(G-6656)*

Zenith Autoparts Corp 845 344-1382
20 Industrial Pl Middletown (10940) *(G-7939)*

Zenith Color Comm Group Inc (PA) 212 989-4400
4710 33rd St Long Island City (11101) *(G-7413)*

Zenith Energy US Logistics (PA) 212 993-1280
725 5th Ave Fl 19 New York (10022) *(G-11820)*

Zenith Solutions 718 575-8570
23 Robinson St Saugerties (12477) *(G-14217)*

Zeo Health Ltd 845 353-5185
159 Route 303 Valley Cottage (10989) *(G-15330)*

Zeppelin Electric Company Inc 631 928-9467
26 Deer Ln East Setauket (11733) *(G-4191)*

Zered Inc (PA) 718 353-7464
12717 20th Ave College Point (11356) *(G-3568)*

Zerovalent Nanometals Inc 585 298-8592
693 East Ave Ste 103 Rochester (14607) *(G-13814)*

Zeta Machine Corp 631 471-8832
206 Christopher St Ronkonkoma (11779) *(G-14029)*

Zeteck, New York Also called *Zetek Corporation (G-11821)*

Zetek Corporation 212 668-1485
13 E 37th St Ste 701 New York (10016) *(G-11821)*

Zg Apparel Group LLC 212 944-2510
1450 Broadway Fl 17 New York (10018) *(G-11822)*

Zia Power Inc 845 661-8388
116 E 27th St New York (10016) *(G-11823)*

Ziegler Truck & Diesl Repr Inc 315 782-7278
22249 Fabco Rd Watertown (13601) *(G-15593)*

Zielinskis Asphalt Inc 315 306-4057
4989 State Route 12b Oriskany Falls (13425) *(G-12401)*

Zierick Manufacturing Corp (PA) 800 882-8020
131 Radio Circle Dr Mount Kisco (10549) *(G-8108)*

Ziff Davis Publishing LLC (HQ) 212 503-3500
28 E 28th St Fl 10 New York (10016) *(G-11824)*

Ziff-Davis Publishing, New York Also called *Ziff Davis Publishing LLC (G-11824)*

Zinc Corporation America Div, New York Also called *Hh Liquidating Corp (G-9779)*

Zinepak LLC 212 706-8621
349 5th Ave New York (10016) *(G-11825)*

Zings Company LLC 631 454-0339
250 Adams Blvd Farmingdale (11735) *(G-4767)*

Zinnias Inc 718 746-8551
24520 Grand Central Pkwy 4l Bellerose (11426) *(G-777)*

Zip Jack Custom Umbrellas, Tarrytown Also called *Zip-Jack Industries Ltd (G-15064)*

Zip Products Inc 585 482-0044
565 Blossom Rd Ste E Rochester (14610) *(G-13815)*

Zip-Jack Industries Ltd 914 592-2000
73 Carrollwood Dr Tarrytown (10591) *(G-15064)*

Zipari Inc 855 558-7884
45 Main St Ste 406 Brooklyn (11201) *(G-2605)*

Ziptswitch, Bay Shore *Also called Adeptronics Incorporated* *(G-643)*

Zircar Ceramics Inc (PA) 845 651-6600
  100 N Main St Ste 2 Florida (10921) *(G-4827)*

Zircar Refr Composites Inc 845 651-2200
  14 Golden Hill Ter Florida (10921) *(G-4828)*

Zircar Refr Composites Inc (PA) 845 651-4481
  46 Jayne St Florida (10921) *(G-4829)*

Zircar Zirconia Inc 845 651-3040
  87 Meadow Rd Florida (10921) *(G-4830)*

Zirconia Creations Intl 212 239-3730
  134 W 29th St Rm 801 New York (10001) *(G-11826)*

Zitomer LLC 212 737-5560
  969 Madison Ave Fl 1 New York (10021) *(G-11827)*

Zmz Mfg Inc 518 234-4336
  300 Mickle Hollow Rd Warnerville (12187) *(G-15502)*

Zographos Designs Ltd 212 545-0227
  300 E 33rd St Apt 9m New York (10016) *(G-11828)*

Zomega Terahertz Corporation 585 347-4337
  806 Admiralty Way Webster (14580) *(G-15664)*

Zone Fabricators Inc 718 272-0200
  10780 101st St Ozone Park (11417) *(G-12470)*

Zoomers Inc (PA) 718 369-2656
  32 33rd St Brooklyn (11232) *(G-2606)*

Zoomifier Corporation 800 255-5303
  216 E 45th St Fl 17 New York (10017) *(G-11829)*

Zorlu USA Inc (PA) 212 689-4622
  295 5th Ave Ste 503 New York (10016) *(G-11830)*

Zotos International Inc 315 781-3207
  300 Forge Ave Geneva (14456) *(G-5167)*

Zuant, Valley Stream *Also called High Performance Sftwr USA Inc* *(G-15343)*

Zumbach Electronics Corp 914 241-7080
  140 Kisco Ave Mount Kisco (10549) *(G-8109)*

Zumtobel Lighting Inc (HQ) 845 691-6262
  3300 Route 9w Highland (12528) *(G-5965)*

Zwack Incorporated 518 733-5135
  15875 Ny 22 Stephentown (12168) *(G-14732)*

Zweigles Inc 585 546-1740
  651 Plymouth Ave N Rochester (14608) *(G-13816)*

Zwuits Inc 929 387-2323
  2005 Palmer Ave Larchmont (10538) *(G-6845)*

Zydoc Med Transcription LLC 631 273-1963
  1455 Veterans Memorial Hw Islandia (11749) *(G-6348)*

Zyloware Corporation (PA) 914 708-1200
  8 Slater St Ste 1 Port Chester (10573) *(G-12831)*

Zyloware Eyewear, Port Chester *Also called Zyloware Corporation* *(G-12831)*

Zymtrnix Catalytic Systems Inc 607 351-2639
  526 N Campus Ithaca (14853) *(G-6418)*

Zyp Precision LLC 315 539-3667
  1098 Birdsey Rd Waterloo (13165) *(G-15557)*

PRODUCT INDEX

- **Product categories are listed in alphabetical order.**

A

ABRASIVES
ABRASIVES: Aluminum Oxide Fused
ABRASIVES: Coated
ABRASIVES: Grains
ACADEMIC TUTORING SVCS
ACCELERATION INDICATORS & SYSTEM COMPONENTS: Aerospace
ACCELERATORS: Electron Linear
ACID RESIST: Etching
ACIDS
ACIDS: Sulfuric, Oleum
ACOUSTICAL BOARD & TILE
ACRYLIC RESINS
ACTUATORS: Indl, NEC
ADDITIVE BASED PLASTIC MATERIALS: Plasticizers
ADHESIVES
ADHESIVES & SEALANTS
ADHESIVES & SEALANTS WHOLESALERS
ADHESIVES: Epoxy
ADVERTISING AGENCIES
ADVERTISING AGENCIES: Consultants
ADVERTISING DISPLAY PRDTS
ADVERTISING MATERIAL DISTRIBUTION
ADVERTISING REPRESENTATIVES: Electronic Media
ADVERTISING REPRESENTATIVES: Magazine
ADVERTISING REPRESENTATIVES: Media
ADVERTISING REPRESENTATIVES: Newspaper
ADVERTISING REPRESENTATIVES: Printed Media
ADVERTISING SPECIALTIES, WHOLESALE
ADVERTISING SVCS: Direct Mail
ADVERTISING SVCS: Display
ADVERTISING SVCS: Sample Distribution
ADVERTISING SVCS: Transit
AERIAL WORK PLATFORMS
AEROSOLS
AGENTS, BROKERS & BUREAUS: Personal Service
AGRICULTURAL EQPT: BARN, SILO, POULTRY, DAIRY/LIVESTOCK MACH
AGRICULTURAL EQPT: Fertilizng, Sprayng, Dustng/Irrigatn Mach
AGRICULTURAL EQPT: Milking Machines
AGRICULTURAL EQPT: Planting Machines
AGRICULTURAL EQPT: Spreaders, Fertilizer
AGRICULTURAL EQPT: Trailers & Wagons, Farm
AGRICULTURAL EQPT: Turf & Grounds Eqpt
AIR CLEANING SYSTEMS
AIR CONDITIONERS, AUTOMOTIVE: Wholesalers
AIR CONDITIONING & VENTILATION EQPT & SPLYS: Wholesales
AIR CONDITIONING EQPT
AIR CONDITIONING UNITS: Complete, Domestic Or Indl
AIR DUCT CLEANING SVCS
AIR MATTRESSES: Plastic
AIR POLLUTION MEASURING SVCS
AIR PREHEATERS: Nonrotating, Plate Type
AIR PURIFICATION EQPT
AIRCRAFT & AEROSPACE FLIGHT INSTRUMENTS & GUIDANCE SYSTEMS
AIRCRAFT & HEAVY EQPT REPAIR SVCS
AIRCRAFT ASSEMBLY PLANTS
AIRCRAFT CONTROL SYSTEMS: Electronic Totalizing Counters
AIRCRAFT ENGINES & ENGINE PARTS: Research & Development, Mfr
AIRCRAFT ENGINES & PARTS
AIRCRAFT EQPT & SPLYS WHOLESALERS
AIRCRAFT FLIGHT INSTRUMENT REPAIR SVCS
AIRCRAFT FLIGHT INSTRUMENTS
AIRCRAFT LIGHTING
AIRCRAFT PARTS & AUXILIARY EQPT: Assemblies, Fuselage
AIRCRAFT PARTS & AUXILIARY EQPT: Assys, Subassemblies/Parts
AIRCRAFT PARTS & AUXILIARY EQPT: Body & Wing Assys & Parts
AIRCRAFT PARTS & AUXILIARY EQPT: Body Assemblies & Parts

AIRCRAFT PARTS & AUXILIARY EQPT: Gears, Power Transmission
AIRCRAFT PARTS & AUXILIARY EQPT: Landing Assemblies & Brakes
AIRCRAFT PARTS & AUXILIARY EQPT: Military Eqpt & Armament
AIRCRAFT PARTS & AUXILIARY EQPT: Refueling Eqpt, In Flight
AIRCRAFT PARTS & AUXILIARY EQPT: Seat Ejector Devices
AIRCRAFT PARTS & EQPT, NEC
AIRCRAFT SEATS
AIRCRAFT UPHOLSTERY REPAIR SVCS
AIRCRAFT: Airplanes, Fixed Or Rotary Wing
AIRCRAFT: Autogiros
AIRCRAFT: Gliders
AIRCRAFT: Motorized
AIRCRAFT: Research & Development, Manufacturer
ALARM SYSTEMS WHOLESALERS
ALARMS: Burglar
ALARMS: Fire
ALCOHOL, GRAIN: For Beverage Purposes
ALCOHOL: Ethyl & Ethanol
ALCOHOL: Methyl & Methanol, Synthetic
ALKALIES & CHLORINE
ALKALOIDS & OTHER BOTANICAL BASED PRDTS
ALLERGENS & ALLERGENIC EXTRACTS
ALTERNATORS & GENERATORS: Battery Charging
ALTERNATORS: Automotive
ALUMINUM
ALUMINUM ORE MINING
ALUMINUM PRDTS
ALUMINUM: Coil & Sheet
ALUMINUM: Rolling & Drawing
AMMONIUM NITRATE OR AMMONIUM SULFATE
AMMUNITION
AMMUNITION: Components
AMMUNITION: Pellets & BB's, Pistol & Air Rifle
AMMUNITION: Small Arms
AMPLIFIERS
AMPLIFIERS: Parametric
AMPLIFIERS: Pulse Amplifiers
AMPLIFIERS: RF & IF Power
AMUSEMENT & RECREATION SVCS: Amusement Ride
AMUSEMENT & RECREATION SVCS: Arcades
AMUSEMENT & RECREATION SVCS: Art Gallery, Commercial
AMUSEMENT & RECREATION SVCS: Arts & Crafts Instruction
AMUSEMENT & RECREATION SVCS: Exposition Operation
AMUSEMENT & RECREATION SVCS: Gambling & Lottery Svcs
AMUSEMENT & RECREATION SVCS: Game Machines
AMUSEMENT & RECREATION SVCS: Golf Club, Membership
AMUSEMENT & RECREATION SVCS: Physical Fitness Instruction
AMUSEMENT & RECREATION SVCS: Tennis & Professionals
AMUSEMENT MACHINES: Coin Operated
AMUSEMENT PARK DEVICES & RIDES
ANALGESICS
ANALYZERS: Moisture
ANALYZERS: Network
ANESTHESIA EQPT
ANIMAL FEED & SUPPLEMENTS: Livestock & Poultry
ANIMAL FEED: Wholesalers
ANIMAL FOOD & SUPPLEMENTS: Bird Food, Prepared
ANIMAL FOOD & SUPPLEMENTS: Cat
ANIMAL FOOD & SUPPLEMENTS: Dog
ANIMAL FOOD & SUPPLEMENTS: Dog & Cat
ANIMAL FOOD & SUPPLEMENTS: Feed Concentrates
ANIMAL FOOD & SUPPLEMENTS: Feed Premixes
ANIMAL FOOD & SUPPLEMENTS: Feed Supplements
ANIMAL FOOD & SUPPLEMENTS: Livestock
ANIMAL FOOD & SUPPLEMENTS: Mineral feed supplements
ANIMAL FOOD & SUPPLEMENTS: Pet, Exc Dog & Cat, Canned
ANIMAL FOOD & SUPPLEMENTS: Poultry

ANODIZING SVC
ANTENNAS: Radar Or Communications
ANTENNAS: Receiving
ANTIBIOTICS
ANTIBIOTICS, PACKAGED
ANTIFREEZE
ANTIQUE FURNITURE RESTORATION & REPAIR
ANTIQUE REPAIR & RESTORATION SVCS, EXC FURNITURE & AUTOS
ANTIQUE SHOPS
ANTIQUES, WHOLESALE
APPAREL ACCESS STORES
APPAREL DESIGNERS: Commercial
APPLIANCE CORDS: Household Electrical Eqpt
APPLIANCES, HOUSEHOLD: Kitchen, Major, Exc Refrigs & Stoves
APPLIANCES, HOUSEHOLD: Laundry Machines, Incl Coin-Operated
APPLIANCES, HOUSEHOLD: Refrigerator Cabinets, Metal Or Wood
APPLIANCES, HOUSEHOLD: Refrigs, Mechanical & Absorption
APPLIANCES, HOUSEHOLD: Sewing Machines & Attchmnts, Domestic
APPLIANCES: Household, Refrigerators & Freezers
APPLIANCES: Major, Cooking
APPLIANCES: Small, Electric
APPLICATIONS SOFTWARE PROGRAMMING
AQUARIUM ACCESS, METAL
AQUARIUM DESIGN & MAINTENANCE SVCS
AQUARIUMS & ACCESS: Glass
AQUARIUMS & ACCESS: Plastic
ARCHITECTURAL SVCS
ARMATURE REPAIRING & REWINDING SVC
AROMATIC CHEMICAL PRDTS
ARRESTERS & COILS: Lightning
ART & ORNAMENTAL WARE: Pottery
ART DEALERS & GALLERIES
ART DESIGN SVCS
ART GOODS & SPLYS WHOLESALERS
ART MARBLE: Concrete
ART NEEDLEWORK, MADE FROM PURCHASED MATERIALS
ART RELATED SVCS
ART RESTORATION SVC
ART SPLY STORES
ARTISTS' EQPT
ARTISTS' MATERIALS, WHOLESALE
ARTISTS' MATERIALS: Frames, Artists' Canvases
ARTISTS' MATERIALS: Ink, Drawing, Black & Colored
ARTISTS' MATERIALS: Paints, Exc Gold & Bronze
ARTISTS' MATERIALS: Pastels
ARTISTS' MATERIALS: Wax
ARTS & CRAFTS SCHOOL
ARTWORK: Framed
ASBESTOS PRODUCTS
ASPHALT & ASPHALT PRDTS
ASPHALT COATINGS & SEALERS
ASPHALT MIXTURES WHOLESALERS
ASPHALT PLANTS INCLUDING GRAVEL MIX TYPE
ASSOCIATIONS: Engineering
ASSOCIATIONS: Scientists'
ATOMIZERS
ATTENUATORS
AUDIO & VIDEO EQPT, EXC COMMERCIAL
AUDIO COMPONENTS
AUDIO ELECTRONIC SYSTEMS
AUDIO-VISUAL PROGRAM PRODUCTION SVCS
AUDIOLOGISTS' OFFICES
AUDITING SVCS
AUTO & HOME SUPPLY STORES: Auto & Truck Eqpt & Parts
AUTO & HOME SUPPLY STORES: Automotive Access
AUTO & HOME SUPPLY STORES: Speed Shops, Incl Race Car Splys
AUTO & HOME SUPPLY STORES: Trailer Hitches, Automotive
AUTO & HOME SUPPLY STORES: Truck Eqpt & Parts
AUTOCLAVES: Indl

AUTOCLAVES: Laboratory
AUTOMATIC REGULATING CONTROL: Building Svcs Monitoring, Auto
AUTOMATIC REGULATING CONTROLS: AC & Refrigeration
AUTOMATIC REGULATING CONTROLS: Elect Air Cleaner, Automatic
AUTOMATIC REGULATING CONTROLS: Energy Cutoff, Residtl/Comm
AUTOMATIC REGULATING CONTROLS: Ice Maker
AUTOMATIC REGULATING CONTROLS: Pneumatic Relays, Air-Cond
AUTOMATIC REGULATING CONTROLS: Refrig/Air-Cond Defrost
AUTOMATIC REGULATING CTRLS: Damper, Pneumatic Or Electric
AUTOMATIC TELLER MACHINES
AUTOMATIC VENDING MACHINES: Mechanisms & Parts
AUTOMOBILE RECOVERY SVCS
AUTOMOBILES: Off-Highway, Electric
AUTOMOBILES: Wholesalers
AUTOMOTIVE & TRUCK GENERAL REPAIR SVC
AUTOMOTIVE BODY, PAINT & INTERIOR REPAIR & MAINTENANCE SVC
AUTOMOTIVE PARTS, ACCESS & SPLYS
AUTOMOTIVE PARTS: Plastic
AUTOMOTIVE PRDTS: Rubber
AUTOMOTIVE REPAIR SHOPS: Brake Repair
AUTOMOTIVE REPAIR SHOPS: Diesel Engine Repair
AUTOMOTIVE REPAIR SHOPS: Electrical Svcs
AUTOMOTIVE REPAIR SHOPS: Engine Repair
AUTOMOTIVE REPAIR SHOPS: Machine Shop
AUTOMOTIVE REPAIR SHOPS: Springs, Rebuilding & Repair
AUTOMOTIVE REPAIR SHOPS: Trailer Repair
AUTOMOTIVE REPAIR SVC
AUTOMOTIVE SPLYS & PARTS, NEW, WHOL: Testing Eqpt, Electric
AUTOMOTIVE SPLYS & PARTS, NEW, WHOLESALE: Brakes
AUTOMOTIVE SPLYS & PARTS, NEW, WHOLESALE: Clutches
AUTOMOTIVE SPLYS & PARTS, NEW, WHOLESALE: Splys
AUTOMOTIVE SPLYS & PARTS, NEW, WHOLESALE: Trim
AUTOMOTIVE SPLYS & PARTS, NEW, WHOLESALE: Wheels
AUTOMOTIVE SPLYS & PARTS, USED, WHOLESALE: Wheels
AUTOMOTIVE SPLYS & PARTS, WHOLESALE, NEC
AUTOMOTIVE SPLYS/PARTS, NEW, WHOL: Body Rpr/Paint Shop Splys
AUTOMOTIVE SVCS, EXC REPAIR & CARWASHES: Maintenance
AUTOMOTIVE SVCS, EXC REPAIR: Washing & Polishing
AUTOMOTIVE SVCS, EXC RPR/CARWASHES: High Perf Auto Rpr/Svc
AUTOMOTIVE TOPS INSTALLATION OR REPAIR: Canvas Or Plastic
AUTOMOTIVE TOWING & WRECKING SVC
AUTOMOTIVE UPHOLSTERY SHOPS
AUTOMOTIVE WELDING SVCS
AUTOMOTIVE: Bodies
AUTOMOTIVE: Seating
AUTOTRANSFORMERS: Electric
AWNING REPAIR SHOP
AWNINGS & CANOPIES
AWNINGS & CANOPIES: Awnings, Fabric, From Purchased Matls
AWNINGS & CANOPIES: Canopies, Fabric, From Purchased Matls
AWNINGS & CANOPIES: Fabric
AWNINGS: Fiberglass
AWNINGS: Metal
AXLES

B

BABY FORMULA
BABY PACIFIERS: Rubber
BADGES: Identification & Insignia
BAGS & BAGGING: Knit
BAGS & CONTAINERS: Textile, Exc Sleeping
BAGS & SACKS: Shipping & Shopping
BAGS: Canvas
BAGS: Cellophane
BAGS: Duffle, Canvas, Made From Purchased Materials
BAGS: Food Storage & Frozen Food, Plastic
BAGS: Food Storage & Trash, Plastic

BAGS: Garment Storage Exc Paper Or Plastic Film
BAGS: Grocers', Made From Purchased Materials
BAGS: Knapsacks, Canvas, Made From Purchased Materials
BAGS: Laundry, Garment & Storage
BAGS: Paper
BAGS: Paper, Made From Purchased Materials
BAGS: Plastic
BAGS: Plastic & Pliofilm
BAGS: Plastic, Made From Purchased Materials
BAGS: Rubber Or Rubberized Fabric
BAGS: Shipping
BAGS: Shopping, Made From Purchased Materials
BAGS: Tea, Fabric, Made From Purchased Materials
BAGS: Textile
BAGS: Trash, Plastic Film, Made From Purchased Materials
BAGS: Wardrobe, Closet Access, Made From Purchased Materials
BAKERIES, COMMERCIAL: On Premises Baking Only
BAKERIES: On Premises Baking & Consumption
BAKERY FOR HOME SVC DELIVERY
BAKERY PRDTS, FROZEN: Wholesalers
BAKERY PRDTS: Bagels, Fresh Or Frozen
BAKERY PRDTS: Bakery Prdts, Partially Cooked, Exc frozen
BAKERY PRDTS: Bread, All Types, Fresh Or Frozen
BAKERY PRDTS: Buns, Sweet, Frozen
BAKERY PRDTS: Cakes, Bakery, Exc Frozen
BAKERY PRDTS: Cakes, Bakery, Frozen
BAKERY PRDTS: Cones, Ice Cream
BAKERY PRDTS: Cookies
BAKERY PRDTS: Cookies & crackers
BAKERY PRDTS: Cracker Meal & Crumbs
BAKERY PRDTS: Doughnuts, Exc Frozen
BAKERY PRDTS: Doughnuts, Frozen
BAKERY PRDTS: Dry
BAKERY PRDTS: Frozen
BAKERY PRDTS: Matzoth
BAKERY PRDTS: Pastries, Exc Frozen
BAKERY PRDTS: Pies, Bakery, Frozen
BAKERY PRDTS: Pretzels
BAKERY PRDTS: Rolls, Bread Type, Fresh Or Frozen
BAKERY PRDTS: Wholesalers
BAKERY: Wholesale Or Wholesale & Retail Combined
BANDAGES
BANDS: Copper & Copper Alloy
BANNERS: Fabric
BANQUET HALL FACILITIES
BAR FIXTURES: Wood
BARBECUE EQPT
BARRICADES: Metal
BARS & BAR SHAPES: Steel, Hot-Rolled
BARS: Concrete Reinforcing, Fabricated Steel
BARS: Extruded, Aluminum
BARS: Iron, Made In Steel Mills
BASEBOARDS: Metal
BASES, BEVERAGE
BASKETS: Steel Wire
BATCHING PLANTS: Cement Silos
BATH SALTS
BATHING SUIT STORES
BATHMATS, COTTON
BATHROOM ACCESS & FITTINGS: Vitreous China & Earthenware
BATHTUBS: Concrete
BATTERIES, EXC AUTOMOTIVE: Wholesalers
BATTERIES: Alkaline, Cell Storage
BATTERIES: Lead Acid, Storage
BATTERIES: Rechargeable
BATTERIES: Storage
BATTERIES: Wet
BATTERY CASES: Plastic Or Plastics Combination
BATTERY CHARGERS
BATTERY CHARGERS: Storage, Motor & Engine Generator Type
BATTERY CHARGING GENERATORS
BATTS & BATTING: Cotton
BEARINGS & PARTS Ball
BEARINGS: Ball & Roller
BEAUTY & BARBER SHOP EQPT
BEAUTY SALONS
BED & BREAKFAST INNS
BEDDING, BEDSPREADS, BLANKETS & SHEETS
BEDDING, BEDSPREADS, BLANKETS & SHEETS: Comforters & Quilts
BEDDING, FROM SILK OR MANMADE FIBER
BEDS & ACCESS STORES

BEDS: Hospital
BEDSPREADS & BED SETS, FROM PURCHASED MATERIALS
BEDSPREADS, COTTON
BEEKEEPERS' SPLYS
BEEKEEPERS' SPLYS: Bee Smokers
BEER & ALE, WHOLESALE: Beer & Other Fermented Malt Liquors
BEER, WINE & LIQUOR STORES
BEER, WINE & LIQUOR STORES: Beer, Packaged
BEER, WINE & LIQUOR STORES: Wine
BELLOWS
BELTING: Rubber
BELTS: Conveyor, Made From Purchased Wire
BENCHES: Seating
BEVERAGE BASES & SYRUPS
BEVERAGE PRDTS: Brewers' Grain
BEVERAGE, NONALCOHOLIC: Iced Tea/Fruit Drink, Bottled/Canned
BEVERAGES, ALCOHOLIC: Ale
BEVERAGES, ALCOHOLIC: Applejack
BEVERAGES, ALCOHOLIC: Beer
BEVERAGES, ALCOHOLIC: Beer & Ale
BEVERAGES, ALCOHOLIC: Bourbon Whiskey
BEVERAGES, ALCOHOLIC: Brandy
BEVERAGES, ALCOHOLIC: Brandy Spirits
BEVERAGES, ALCOHOLIC: Cocktails
BEVERAGES, ALCOHOLIC: Cordials & Premixed Cocktails
BEVERAGES, ALCOHOLIC: Distilled Liquors
BEVERAGES, ALCOHOLIC: Gin
BEVERAGES, ALCOHOLIC: Liquors, Malt
BEVERAGES, ALCOHOLIC: Near Beer
BEVERAGES, ALCOHOLIC: Neutral Spirits, Fruit
BEVERAGES, ALCOHOLIC: Rum
BEVERAGES, ALCOHOLIC: Vodka
BEVERAGES, ALCOHOLIC: Wines
BEVERAGES, MALT
BEVERAGES, MILK BASED
BEVERAGES, NONALCOHOLIC: Bottled & canned soft drinks
BEVERAGES, NONALCOHOLIC: Carbonated
BEVERAGES, NONALCOHOLIC: Carbonated, Canned & Bottled, Etc
BEVERAGES, NONALCOHOLIC: Cider
BEVERAGES, NONALCOHOLIC: Flavoring extracts & syrups, nec
BEVERAGES, NONALCOHOLIC: Fruit Drnks, Under 100% Juice, Can
BEVERAGES, NONALCOHOLIC: Lemonade, Bottled & Canned, Etc
BEVERAGES, NONALCOHOLIC: Soft Drinks, Canned & Bottled, Etc
BEVERAGES, NONALCOHOLIC: Tea, Iced, Bottled & Canned, Etc
BEVERAGES, WINE & DISTILLED ALCOHOLIC, WHOLESALE: Liquor
BEVERAGES, WINE & DISTILLED ALCOHOLIC, WHOLESALE: Neutral Sp
BEVERAGES, WINE & DISTILLED ALCOHOLIC, WHOLESALE: Wine
BEVERAGES, WINE WHOLESALE : Wine Coolers
BICYCLE SHOPS
BICYCLES, PARTS & ACCESS
BILLETS: Steel
BILLFOLD INSERTS: Plastic
BILLIARD & POOL TABLES & SPLYS
BINDING SVC: Books & Manuals
BINDING SVC: Magazines
BINDING SVC: Trade
BINS: Prefabricated, Sheet Metal
BIOLOGICAL PRDTS: Bacterial Vaccines
BIOLOGICAL PRDTS: Blood Derivatives
BIOLOGICAL PRDTS: Exc Diagnostic
BIOLOGICAL PRDTS: Extracts
BIOLOGICAL PRDTS: Vaccines
BIOLOGICAL PRDTS: Vaccines & Immunizing
BIOLOGICAL PRDTS: Veterinary
BLADES: Knife
BLADES: Saw, Chain Type
BLADES: Saw, Hand Or Power
BLANKBOOKS
BLANKBOOKS & LOOSELEAF BINDERS
BLANKBOOKS: Albums
BLANKBOOKS: Albums, Record
BLANKBOOKS: Memorandum, Printed

BLANKETS & BLANKETING, COTTON
BLASTING SVC: Sand, Metal Parts
BLINDS & SHADES: Vertical
BLINDS : Window
BLOCK & BRICK: Sand Lime
BLOCKS & BRICKS: Concrete
BLOCKS: Chimney Or Fireplace, Concrete
BLOCKS: Landscape Or Retaining Wall, Concrete
BLOCKS: Paving, Asphalt, Not From Refineries
BLOCKS: Paving, Concrete
BLOCKS: Paving, Cut Stone
BLOCKS: Radiation-Proof, Concrete
BLOCKS: Standard, Concrete Or Cinder
BLOWERS & FANS
BLOWERS & FANS
BLUEPRINTING SVCS
BOAT BUILDING & REPAIR
BOAT BUILDING & REPAIRING: Fiberglass
BOAT BUILDING & REPAIRING: Kayaks
BOAT BUILDING & REPAIRING: Motorized
BOAT BUILDING & REPAIRING: Non-Motorized
BOAT BUILDING & RPRG: Fishing, Small, Lobster, Crab, Oyster
BOAT DEALERS
BOAT DEALERS: Canoe & Kayak
BOAT LIFTS
BOAT REPAIR SVCS
BOAT YARD: Boat yards, storage & incidental repair
BOATS & OTHER MARINE EQPT: Plastic
BODIES: Truck & Bus
BODY PARTS: Automobile, Stamped Metal
BOILER REPAIR SHOP
BOILERS & BOILER SHOP WORK
BOILERS: Low-Pressure Heating, Steam Or Hot Water
BOLTS: Metal
BONDERIZING: Bonderizing, Metal Or Metal Prdts
BOOK STORES
BOOK STORES: College
BOOKS, WHOLESALE
BOOTHS: Spray, Sheet Metal, Prefabricated
BOOTS: Women's
BORING MILL
BOTTLE CAPS & RESEALERS: Plastic
BOTTLED WATER DELIVERY
BOTTLES: Plastic
BOTTLES: Vacuum
BOUTIQUE STORES
BOWLING EQPT & SPLYS
BOX & CARTON MANUFACTURING EQPT
BOXES & CRATES: Rectangular, Wood
BOXES & SHOOK: Nailed Wood
BOXES: Corrugated
BOXES: Filing, Paperboard Made From Purchased Materials
BOXES: Mail Or Post Office, Collection/Storage, Sheet Metal
BOXES: Packing & Shipping, Metal
BOXES: Paperboard, Folding
BOXES: Paperboard, Set-Up
BOXES: Plastic
BOXES: Solid Fiber
BOXES: Stamped Metal
BOXES: Switch, Electric
BOXES: Wooden
BRAKES & BRAKE PARTS
BRAKES: Electromagnetic
BRASS FOUNDRY, NEC
BRAZING SVCS
BRAZING: Metal
BRIC-A-BRAC
BRICK, STONE & RELATED PRDTS WHOLESALERS
BRICKS & BLOCKS: Structural
BRICKS: Concrete
BRIDAL SHOPS
BRIDGE COMPONENTS: Bridge sections, prefabricated, highway
BROADCASTING & COMMS EQPT: Antennas, Transmitting/Comms
BROADCASTING & COMMS EQPT: Rcvr-Transmitter Unt, Transceiver
BROADCASTING & COMMUNICATIONS EQPT: Cellular Radio Telephone
BROADCASTING & COMMUNICATIONS EQPT: Studio Eqpt, Radio & TV
BROADCASTING & COMMUNICATIONS EQPT: Transmitting, Radio/TV
BROKERS' SVCS

BROKERS: Business
BROKERS: Food
BROKERS: Loan
BROKERS: Printing
BRONZE FOUNDRY, NEC
BROOMS
BROOMS & BRUSHES
BROOMS & BRUSHES: Hair Pencils Or Artists' Brushes
BROOMS & BRUSHES: Household Or Indl
BROOMS & BRUSHES: Paint & Varnish
BROOMS & BRUSHES: Paint Rollers
BROOMS & BRUSHES: Paintbrushes
BRUSHES
BRUSHES & BRUSH STOCK CONTACTS: Electric
BUCKLES & PARTS
BUILDING & OFFICE CLEANING SVCS
BUILDING & STRUCTURAL WOOD MBRS: Timbers, Struct, Lam Lumber
BUILDING & STRUCTURAL WOOD MEMBERS
BUILDING & STRUCTURAL WOOD MEMBERS: Arches, Laminated Lumber
BUILDING BOARD & WALLBOARD, EXC GYPSUM
BUILDING BOARD: Gypsum
BUILDING CLEANING & MAINTENANCE SVCS
BUILDING COMPONENTS: Structural Steel
BUILDING ITEM REPAIR SVCS, MISCELLANEOUS
BUILDING PRDTS & MATERIALS DEALERS
BUILDING PRDTS: Concrete
BUILDING PRDTS: Stone
BUILDINGS & COMPONENTS: Prefabricated Metal
BUILDINGS, PREFABRICATED: Wholesalers
BUILDINGS: Portable
BUILDINGS: Prefabricated, Metal
BUILDINGS: Prefabricated, Wood
BUILDINGS: Prefabricated, Wood
BULLETIN BOARDS: Wood
BUMPERS: Motor Vehicle
BURIAL VAULTS: Concrete Or Precast Terrazzo
BURLAP & BURLAP PRDTS
BURNERS: Gas, Indl
BUS BARS: Electrical
BUSES: Wholesalers
BUSHINGS & BEARINGS: Copper, Exc Machined
BUSINESS ACTIVITIES: Non-Commercial Site
BUSINESS FORMS WHOLESALERS
BUSINESS FORMS: Printed, Continuous
BUSINESS FORMS: Printed, Manifold
BUSINESS MACHINE REPAIR, ELECTRIC
BUSINESS SUPPORT SVCS
BUSINESS TRAINING SVCS
BUTADIENE: Indl, Organic, Chemical
BUTTER WHOLESALERS
BUTTONS

C

CABINETS & CASES: Show, Display & Storage, Exc Wood
CABINETS: Bathroom Vanities, Wood
CABINETS: Entertainment
CABINETS: Entertainment Units, Household, Wood
CABINETS: Factory
CABINETS: Filing, Wood
CABINETS: Kitchen, Metal
CABINETS: Kitchen, Wood
CABINETS: Office, Metal
CABINETS: Office, Wood
CABINETS: Radio & Television, Metal
CABINETS: Show, Display, Etc, Wood, Exc Refrigerated
CABLE TELEVISION
CABLE TELEVISION PRDTS
CABLE: Fiber
CABLE: Fiber Optic
CABLE: Nonferrous, Shipboard
CABLE: Noninsulated
CABLE: Ropes & Fiber
CABLE: Steel, Insulated Or Armored
CAGES: Wire
CALCULATING & ACCOUNTING EQPT
CALIBRATING SVCS, NEC
CAMERAS & RELATED EQPT: Photographic
CANDLE SHOPS
CANDLES
CANDLES: Wholesalers
CANDY & CONFECTIONS: Cake Ornaments
CANDY & CONFECTIONS: Candy Bars, Including Chocolate Covered

CANDY & CONFECTIONS: Chocolate Candy, Exc Solid Chocolate
CANDY & CONFECTIONS: Halvah
CANDY, NUT & CONFECTIONERY STORES: Candy
CANDY: Chocolate From Cacao Beans
CANNED SPECIALTIES
CANOPIES: Sheet Metal
CANS: Aluminum
CANS: Metal
CANVAS PRDTS
CANVAS PRDTS, WHOLESALE
CANVAS PRDTS: Convertible Tops, Car/Boat, Fm Purchased Mtrl
CANVAS PRDTS: Shades, Made From Purchased Materials
CAPACITORS: Fixed Or Variable
CAPACITORS: NEC
CAPS & PLUGS: Electric, Attachment
CAR WASH EQPT
CARBIDES
CARBON & GRAPHITE PRDTS, NEC
CARBONS: Electric
CARDBOARD PRDTS, EXC DIE-CUT
CARDBOARD: Waterproof, Made From Purchased Materials
CARDIOVASCULAR SYSTEM DRUGS, EXC DIAGNOSTIC
CARDS: Beveled
CARDS: Color
CARDS: Greeting
CARDS: Identification
CARPET DYEING & FINISHING
CARPETS & RUGS: Tufted
CARPETS, RUGS & FLOOR COVERING
CARPETS: Hand & Machine Made
CARPETS: Textile Fiber
CARRIAGES: Horse Drawn
CARRYING CASES, WHOLESALE
CARTONS: Egg, Molded Pulp, Made From Purchased Materials
CASEMENTS: Aluminum
CASES, WOOD
CASES: Attache'
CASES: Carrying
CASES: Carrying, Clothing & Apparel
CASES: Jewelry
CASES: Nonrefrigerated, Exc Wood
CASES: Packing, Nailed Or Lock Corner, Wood
CASES: Plastic
CASES: Sample Cases
CASES: Shipping, Nailed Or Lock Corner, Wood
CASH REGISTER REPAIR SVCS
CASINGS: Sheet Metal
CASKETS & ACCESS
CASKETS WHOLESALERS
CAST STONE: Concrete
CASTERS
CASTINGS GRINDING: For The Trade
CASTINGS: Aerospace Investment, Ferrous
CASTINGS: Aerospace, Aluminum
CASTINGS: Aerospace, Nonferrous, Exc Aluminum
CASTINGS: Aluminum
CASTINGS: Bronze, NEC, Exc Die
CASTINGS: Die, Aluminum
CASTINGS: Die, Lead
CASTINGS: Die, Nonferrous
CASTINGS: Die, Zinc
CASTINGS: Ductile
CASTINGS: Gray Iron
CASTINGS: Machinery, Aluminum
CASTINGS: Machinery, Copper Or Copper-Base Alloy
CASTINGS: Machinery, Nonferrous, Exc Die or Aluminum Copper
CASTINGS: Precision
CASTINGS: Steel
CATALOG & MAIL-ORDER HOUSES
CATALOG SHOWROOMS
CATALYSTS: Chemical
CATAPULTS
CATERERS
CEMENT & CONCRETE RELATED PRDTS & EQPT: Bituminous
CEMENT ROCK: Crushed & Broken
CEMENT: Heat Resistant
CEMENT: High Temperature, Refractory, Nonclay
CEMENT: Hydraulic
CEMENT: Masonry
CEMENT: Natural

INDEX

CEMENT: Portland
CEMETERY MEMORIAL DEALERS
CERAMIC FIBER
CERAMIC FLOOR & WALL TILE WHOLESALERS
CHAIN: Welded, Made From Purchased Wire
CHAINS: Forged
CHAMBERS & CAISSONS
CHANDELIERS: Commercial
CHANDELIERS: Residential
CHARCOAL: Activated
CHART & GRAPH DESIGN SVCS
CHASSIS: Motor Vehicle
CHEESE WHOLESALERS
CHEMICAL ELEMENTS
CHEMICAL INDICATORS
CHEMICAL PROCESSING MACHINERY & EQPT
CHEMICAL: Sodm Compnds/Salts, Inorg, Exc Rfnd Sodm Chloride
CHEMICALS & ALLIED PRDTS WHOLESALERS, NEC
CHEMICALS & ALLIED PRDTS, WHOLESALE: Alkalines & Chlorine
CHEMICALS & ALLIED PRDTS, WHOLESALE: Anti-Corrosion Prdts
CHEMICALS & ALLIED PRDTS, WHOLESALE: Aromatic
CHEMICALS & ALLIED PRDTS, WHOLESALE: Chemical Additives
CHEMICALS & ALLIED PRDTS, WHOLESALE: Chemicals, Indl
CHEMICALS & ALLIED PRDTS, WHOLESALE: Detergent/Soap
CHEMICALS & ALLIED PRDTS, WHOLESALE: Dry Ice
CHEMICALS & ALLIED PRDTS, WHOLESALE: Essential Oils
CHEMICALS & ALLIED PRDTS, WHOLESALE: Oxygen
CHEMICALS & ALLIED PRDTS, WHOLESALE: Plastics Materials, NEC
CHEMICALS & ALLIED PRDTS, WHOLESALE: Plastics Prdts, NEC
CHEMICALS & ALLIED PRDTS, WHOLESALE: Plastics Sheets & Rods
CHEMICALS & ALLIED PRDTS, WHOLESALE: Polyurethane Prdts
CHEMICALS & ALLIED PRDTS, WHOLESALE: Salts & Polishes, Indl
CHEMICALS & ALLIED PRDTS, WHOLESALE: Spec Clean/Sanitation
CHEMICALS & ALLIED PRDTS, WHOLESALE: Syn Resin, Rub/Plastic
CHEMICALS & ALLIED PRDTS, WHOLESALE: Waxes, Exc Petroleum
CHEMICALS/ALLIED PRDTS, WHOL: Coal Tar Prdts, Prim/Intermdt
CHEMICALS: Agricultural
CHEMICALS: Alcohols
CHEMICALS: Aluminum Chloride
CHEMICALS: Aluminum Compounds
CHEMICALS: Aluminum Oxide
CHEMICALS: Brine
CHEMICALS: Calcium & Calcium Compounds
CHEMICALS: Compounds Or Salts, Iron, Ferric Or Ferrous
CHEMICALS: Fire Retardant
CHEMICALS: Formaldehyde
CHEMICALS: Fuel Tank Or Engine Cleaning
CHEMICALS: High Purity Grade, Organic
CHEMICALS: High Purity, Refined From Technical Grade
CHEMICALS: Hydrogen Peroxide
CHEMICALS: Inorganic, NEC
CHEMICALS: Isotopes, Radioactive
CHEMICALS: Lithium Compounds, Inorganic
CHEMICALS: Medicinal
CHEMICALS: Medicinal, Organic, Uncompounded, Bulk
CHEMICALS: NEC
CHEMICALS: Organic, NEC
CHEMICALS: Phenol
CHEMICALS: Silica Compounds
CHEMICALS: Sodium Bicarbonate
CHEMICALS: Sodium/Potassium Cmpnds,Exc Bleach,Alkalies/Alum
CHEMICALS: Sulfur Chloride
CHEMICALS: Water Treatment
CHEWING GUM
CHILD DAY CARE SVCS
CHILDREN'S & INFANTS' CLOTHING STORES
CHILDREN'S WEAR STORES
CHIMES: Electric
CHIMNEY CAPS: Concrete

CHIMNEYS & FITTINGS
CHINA COOKWARE
CHLORINE
CHOCOLATE, EXC CANDY FROM BEANS: Chips, Powder, Block, Syrup
CHOCOLATE, EXC CANDY FROM PURCH CHOC: Chips, Powder, Block
CHRISTMAS TREE LIGHTING SETS: Electric
CHUCKS
CHURCHES
CHUTES & TROUGHS
CHUTES: Coal, Sheet Metal, Prefabricated
CIGAR LIGHTERS EXC PRECIOUS METAL
CIGARETTE & CIGAR PRDTS & ACCESS
CIRCUIT BOARDS, PRINTED: Television & Radio
CIRCUIT BOARDS: Wiring
CIRCUIT BREAKERS
CIRCUITS, INTEGRATED: Hybrid
CIRCUITS: Electronic
CIRCULAR KNIT FABRICS DYEING & FINISHING
CLAMPS & COUPLINGS: Hose
CLAY PRDTS: Architectural
CLAYS, EXC KAOLIN & BALL
CLEANING EQPT: Blast, Dustless
CLEANING EQPT: Carpet Sweepers, Exc Household Elec Vacuum
CLEANING EQPT: Commercial
CLEANING EQPT: High Pressure
CLEANING OR POLISHING PREPARATIONS, NEC
CLEANING PRDTS: Automobile Polish
CLEANING PRDTS: Degreasing Solvent
CLEANING PRDTS: Deodorants, Nonpersonal
CLEANING PRDTS: Disinfectants, Household Or Indl Plant
CLEANING PRDTS: Drycleaning Preparations
CLEANING PRDTS: Laundry Preparations
CLEANING PRDTS: Metal Polish
CLEANING PRDTS: Polishing Preparations & Related Prdts
CLEANING PRDTS: Sanitation Preparations
CLEANING PRDTS: Sanitation Preps, Disinfectants/Deodorants
CLEANING PRDTS: Shoe Polish Or Cleaner
CLEANING PRDTS: Specialty
CLEANING PRDTS: Window Cleaning Preparations
CLEANING SVCS: Industrial Or Commercial
CLIPPERS: Fingernail & Toenail
CLIPS & FASTENERS, MADE FROM PURCHASED WIRE
CLOSURES: Closures, Stamped Metal
CLOSURES: Plastic
CLOTHING & ACCESS, WOMEN, CHILD & INFANT, WHOL: Scarves
CLOTHING & ACCESS, WOMEN, CHILD & INFANT, WHOLESALE: Under
CLOTHING & ACCESS, WOMEN, CHILD & INFANT, WHSLE: Sportswear
CLOTHING & ACCESS, WOMEN, CHILDREN & INFANT, WHOL: Access
CLOTHING & ACCESS, WOMEN, CHILDREN & INFANT, WHOL: Gloves
CLOTHING & ACCESS, WOMEN, CHILDREN & INFANT, WHOL: Handbags
CLOTHING & ACCESS, WOMEN, CHILDREN & INFANT, WHOL: Sweaters
CLOTHING & ACCESS, WOMEN, CHILDREN & INFANTS, WHOL: Purses
CLOTHING & ACCESS, WOMEN, CHILDREN/INFANT, WHOL: Baby Goods
CLOTHING & ACCESS, WOMEN, CHILDREN/INFANT, WHOL: Nightwear
CLOTHING & ACCESS, WOMEN, CHILDREN/INFANT, WHOL: Swimsuits
CLOTHING & ACCESS, WOMENS, CHILDREN & INFANTS, WHOL: Hats
CLOTHING & ACCESS: Costumes, Masquerade
CLOTHING & ACCESS: Costumes, Theatrical
CLOTHING & ACCESS: Cummerbunds
CLOTHING & ACCESS: Footlets
CLOTHING & ACCESS: Handicapped
CLOTHING & ACCESS: Handkerchiefs, Exc Paper
CLOTHING & ACCESS: Hospital Gowns
CLOTHING & ACCESS: Men's Miscellaneous Access
CLOTHING & ACCESS: Suspenders
CLOTHING & APPAREL STORES: Custom
CLOTHING & FURNISHINGS, MEN & BOY, WHOLESALE: Suits/Trousers

CLOTHING & FURNISHINGS, MEN'S & BOYS', WHOLESALE: Caps
CLOTHING & FURNISHINGS, MEN'S & BOYS', WHOLESALE: Fur
CLOTHING & FURNISHINGS, MEN'S & BOYS', WHOLESALE: Gloves
CLOTHING & FURNISHINGS, MEN'S & BOYS', WHOLESALE: Hats
CLOTHING & FURNISHINGS, MEN'S & BOYS', WHOLESALE: Neckwear
CLOTHING & FURNISHINGS, MEN'S & BOYS', WHOLESALE: Scarves
CLOTHING & FURNISHINGS, MEN'S & BOYS', WHOLESALE: Shirts
CLOTHING & FURNISHINGS, MEN'S & BOYS', WHOLESALE: Umbrellas
CLOTHING & FURNISHINGS, MEN'S & BOYS', WHOLESALE: Uniforms
CLOTHING & FURNISHINGS, MEN/BOY, WHOL: Hats, Scarves/Gloves
CLOTHING & FURNISHINGS, MENS & BOYS, WHOL: Sportswear/Work
CLOTHING & FURNISHINGS, MENS & BOYS, WHOLESALE: Apprl Belts
CLOTHING ACCESS STORES: Umbrellas
CLOTHING STORES, NEC
CLOTHING STORES: Caps & Gowns
CLOTHING STORES: Dancewear
CLOTHING STORES: Designer Apparel
CLOTHING STORES: Jeans
CLOTHING STORES: Leather
CLOTHING STORES: T-Shirts, Printed, Custom
CLOTHING STORES: Uniforms & Work
CLOTHING STORES: Unisex
CLOTHING STORES: Work
CLOTHING, WOMEN & CHILD, WHLSE: Dress, Suit, Skirt & Blouse
CLOTHING/ACCESS, WOMEN, CHILDREN/INFANT, WHOL: Apparel Belt
CLOTHING/FURNISHINGS, MEN/BOY, WHOL: Furnishings, Exc Shoes
CLOTHING: Academic Vestments
CLOTHING: Access
CLOTHING: Access, Women's & Misses'
CLOTHING: Anklets & Socks
CLOTHING: Aprons, Exc Rubber/Plastic, Women, Misses, Junior
CLOTHING: Aprons, Harness
CLOTHING: Aprons, Work, Exc Rubberized & Plastic, Men's
CLOTHING: Athletic & Sportswear, Men's & Boys'
CLOTHING: Athletic & Sportswear, Women's & Girls'
CLOTHING: Baker, Barber, Lab/Svc Ind Apparel, Washable, Men
CLOTHING: Bathing Suits & Beachwear, Children's
CLOTHING: Bathing Suits & Swimwear, Girls, Children & Infant
CLOTHING: Bathing Suits & Swimwear, Knit
CLOTHING: Bathrobes, Mens & Womens, From Purchased Materials
CLOTHING: Belts
CLOTHING: Blouses & Shirts, Girls' & Children's
CLOTHING: Blouses, Boys', From Purchased Materials
CLOTHING: Blouses, Women's & Girls'
CLOTHING: Blouses, Womens & Juniors, From Purchased Mtrls
CLOTHING: Brassieres
CLOTHING: Bridal Gowns
CLOTHING: Burial
CLOTHING: Capes & Jackets, Women's & Misses'
CLOTHING: Capes, Exc Fur/Rubber, Womens, Misses & Juniors
CLOTHING: Chemises, Camisoles/Teddies, Women, Misses/Junior
CLOTHING: Children & Infants'
CLOTHING: Children's, Girls'
CLOTHING: Clergy Vestments
CLOTHING: Coats & Jackets, Leather & Sheep-Lined
CLOTHING: Coats & Suits, Men's & Boys'
CLOTHING: Coats, Leatherette, Oiled Fabric, Etc, Mens & Boys
CLOTHING: Coats, Tailored, Mens/Boys, From Purchased Mtls
CLOTHING: Corset Access, Clasps & Stays
CLOTHING: Costumes

CLOTHING: Diaper Covers, Waterproof, From Purchased Material
CLOTHING: Disposable
CLOTHING: Down-Filled, Men's & Boys'
CLOTHING: Dresses
CLOTHING: Dresses & Skirts
CLOTHING: Dresses, Knit
CLOTHING: Dressing Gowns, Mens/Womens, From Purchased Matls
CLOTHING: Foundation Garments, Women's
CLOTHING: Furs
CLOTHING: Garments, Indl, Men's & Boys
CLOTHING: Girdles & Other Foundation Garments, Knit
CLOTHING: Girdles & Panty Girdles
CLOTHING: Gloves, Knit, Exc Dress & Semidress
CLOTHING: Gowns & Dresses, Wedding
CLOTHING: Gowns, Formal
CLOTHING: Hats & Caps, Leather
CLOTHING: Hats & Caps, NEC
CLOTHING: Hats & Caps, Uniform
CLOTHING: Hats & Headwear, Knit
CLOTHING: Hosiery, Men's & Boys'
CLOTHING: Hosiery, Pantyhose & Knee Length, Sheer
CLOTHING: Hospital, Men's
CLOTHING: Housedresses
CLOTHING: Jackets & Vests, Exc Fur & Leather, Women's
CLOTHING: Jackets, Knit
CLOTHING: Jeans, Men's & Boys'
CLOTHING: Knit Underwear & Nightwear
CLOTHING: Leather
CLOTHING: Leather & Sheep-Lined
CLOTHING: Leather & sheep-lined clothing
CLOTHING: Maternity
CLOTHING: Men's & boy's clothing, nec
CLOTHING: Men's & boy's underwear & nightwear
CLOTHING: Mens & Boys Jackets, Sport, Suede, Leatherette
CLOTHING: Millinery
CLOTHING: Neckties, Knit
CLOTHING: Neckwear
CLOTHING: Outerwear, Knit
CLOTHING: Outerwear, Lthr, Wool/Down-Filled, Men, Youth/Boy
CLOTHING: Outerwear, Women's & Misses' NEC
CLOTHING: Overcoats & Topcoats, Men/Boy, Purchased Materials
CLOTHING: Pants, Work, Men's, Youths' & Boys'
CLOTHING: Panty Hose
CLOTHING: Raincoats, Exc Vulcanized Rubber, Purchased Matls
CLOTHING: Robes & Dressing Gowns
CLOTHING: Robes & Housecoats, Children's
CLOTHING: Scarves & Mufflers, Knit
CLOTHING: Service Apparel, Women's
CLOTHING: Shawls, Knit
CLOTHING: Sheep-Lined
CLOTHING: Shirts
CLOTHING: Shirts, Dress, Men's & Boys'
CLOTHING: Shirts, Knit
CLOTHING: Shirts, Sports & Polo, Men & Boy, Purchased Mtrl
CLOTHING: Shirts, Sports & Polo, Men's & Boys'
CLOTHING: Shirts, Women's & Juniors', From Purchased Mtrls
CLOTHING: Skirts
CLOTHING: Slacks & Shorts, Dress, Men's, Youths' & Boys'
CLOTHING: Slacks, Girls' & Children's
CLOTHING: Sleeping Garments, Men's & Boys'
CLOTHING: Sleeping Garments, Women's & Children's
CLOTHING: Slipper Socks
CLOTHING: Socks
CLOTHING: Sportswear, Women's
CLOTHING: Suits & Skirts, Women's & Misses'
CLOTHING: Suits, Men's & Boys', From Purchased Materials
CLOTHING: Sweaters & Sweater Coats, Knit
CLOTHING: Sweaters, Men's & Boys'
CLOTHING: Sweatshirts & T-Shirts, Men's & Boys'
CLOTHING: Swimwear, Men's & Boys'
CLOTHING: Swimwear, Women's & Misses'
CLOTHING: T-Shirts & Tops, Knit
CLOTHING: T-Shirts & Tops, Women's & Girls'
CLOTHING: Tailored Suits & Formal Jackets
CLOTHING: Ties, Handsewn, From Purchased Materials
CLOTHING: Ties, Neck & Bow, Men's & Boys'
CLOTHING: Ties, Neck, Men's & Boys', From Purchased Material
CLOTHING: Tights & Leg Warmers

CLOTHING: Trousers & Slacks, Men's & Boys'
CLOTHING: Underwear, Knit
CLOTHING: Underwear, Men's & Boys'
CLOTHING: Underwear, Women's & Children's
CLOTHING: Uniforms & Vestments
CLOTHING: Uniforms, Ex Athletic, Women's, Misses' & Juniors'
CLOTHING: Uniforms, Firemen's, From Purchased Materials
CLOTHING: Uniforms, Men's & Boys'
CLOTHING: Uniforms, Military, Men/Youth, Purchased Materials
CLOTHING: Uniforms, Policemen's, From Purchased Materials
CLOTHING: Uniforms, Team Athletic
CLOTHING: Uniforms, Work
CLOTHING: Warm Weather Knit Outerwear, Including Beachwear
CLOTHING: Waterproof Outerwear
CLOTHING: Work Apparel, Exc Uniforms
CLOTHING: Work, Men's
CLUTCHES OR BRAKES: Electromagnetic
CLUTCHES, EXC VEHICULAR
COAL MINING SERVICES
COAL MINING SVCS: Bituminous, Contract Basis
COAL MINING: Anthracite
COATING COMPOUNDS: Tar
COATING SVC
COATING SVC: Aluminum, Metal Prdts
COATING SVC: Electrodes
COATING SVC: Metals & Formed Prdts
COATING SVC: Metals, With Plastic Or Resins
COATING SVC: Rust Preventative
COATING SVC: Silicon
COATINGS: Air Curing
COATINGS: Epoxy
COATINGS: Polyurethane
COFFEE SVCS
COILS & TRANSFORMERS
COILS: Electric Motors Or Generators
COILS: Pipe
COIN OPERATED LAUNDRIES & DRYCLEANERS
COIN-OPERATED LAUNDRY
COKE: Calcined Petroleum, Made From Purchased Materials
COKE: Produced In Chemical Recovery Coke Ovens
COLLECTION AGENCY, EXC REAL ESTATE
COLLEGES, UNIVERSITIES & PROFESSIONAL SCHOOLS
COLLETS
COLOGNES
COLOR SEPARATION: Photographic & Movie Film
COLORS: Pigments, Inorganic
COLORS: Pigments, Organic
COMFORTERS & QUILTS, FROM MANMADE FIBER OR SILK
COMMERCIAL & INDL SHELVING WHOLESALERS
COMMERCIAL & OFFICE BUILDINGS RENOVATION & REPAIR
COMMERCIAL ART & GRAPHIC DESIGN SVCS
COMMERCIAL CONTAINERS WHOLESALERS
COMMERCIAL EQPT WHOLESALERS, NEC
COMMERCIAL EQPT, WHOLESALE: Bakery Eqpt & Splys
COMMERCIAL EQPT, WHOLESALE: Comm Cooking & Food Svc Eqpt
COMMERCIAL EQPT, WHOLESALE: Display Eqpt, Exc Refrigerated
COMMERCIAL EQPT, WHOLESALE: Mannequins
COMMERCIAL EQPT, WHOLESALE: Restaurant, NEC
COMMERCIAL EQPT, WHOLESALE: Scales, Exc Laboratory
COMMERCIAL EQPT, WHOLESALE: Store Fixtures & Display Eqpt
COMMERCIAL LAUNDRY EQPT
COMMERCIAL PRINTING & NEWSPAPER PUBLISHING COMBINED
COMMON SAND MINING
COMMUNICATION HEADGEAR: Telephone
COMMUNICATIONS CARRIER: Wired
COMMUNICATIONS EQPT & SYSTEMS, NEC
COMMUNICATIONS EQPT REPAIR & MAINTENANCE
COMMUNICATIONS EQPT WHOLESALERS
COMMUNICATIONS EQPT: Microwave
COMMUNICATIONS SVCS
COMMUNICATIONS SVCS: Cellular
COMMUNICATIONS SVCS: Data
COMMUNICATIONS SVCS: Facsimile Transmission
COMMUNICATIONS SVCS: Internet Host Svcs
COMMUNICATIONS SVCS: Online Svc Providers

COMMUNICATIONS SVCS: Proprietary Online Svcs Networks
COMMUNICATIONS SVCS: Satellite Earth Stations
COMMUNICATIONS SVCS: Signal Enhancement Network Svcs
COMMUNICATIONS SVCS: Telephone, Data
COMMUNICATIONS SVCS: Telephone, Local
COMMUNICATIONS SVCS: Telephone, Voice
COMMUTATORS: Electronic
COMPACT DISCS OR CD'S, WHOLESALE
COMPACT LASER DISCS: Prerecorded
COMPACTORS: Trash & Garbage, Residential
COMPARATORS: Optical
COMPOSITION STONE: Plastic
COMPOST
COMPRESSORS, AIR CONDITIONING: Wholesalers
COMPRESSORS: Air & Gas
COMPRESSORS: Air & Gas, Including Vacuum Pumps
COMPRESSORS: Refrigeration & Air Conditioning Eqpt
COMPRESSORS: Wholesalers
COMPUTER & COMPUTER SOFTWARE STORES
COMPUTER & COMPUTER SOFTWARE STORES: Peripheral Eqpt
COMPUTER & COMPUTER SOFTWARE STORES: Software, Bus/Non-Game
COMPUTER & COMPUTER SOFTWARE STORES: Software, Computer Game
COMPUTER & OFFICE MACHINE MAINTENANCE & REPAIR
COMPUTER DISKETTES WHOLESALERS
COMPUTER FORMS
COMPUTER GRAPHICS SVCS
COMPUTER HARDWARE REQUIREMENTS ANALYSIS
COMPUTER INTERFACE EQPT: Indl Process
COMPUTER PERIPHERAL EQPT, NEC
COMPUTER PERIPHERAL EQPT, WHOLESALE
COMPUTER PERIPHERAL EQPT: Decoders
COMPUTER PERIPHERAL EQPT: Encoders
COMPUTER PERIPHERAL EQPT: Film Reader Devices
COMPUTER PERIPHERAL EQPT: Graphic Displays, Exc Terminals
COMPUTER PERIPHERAL EQPT: Input Or Output
COMPUTER PROGRAMMING SVCS
COMPUTER PROGRAMMING SVCS: Custom
COMPUTER RELATED MAINTENANCE SVCS
COMPUTER SERVICE BUREAU
COMPUTER SOFTWARE DEVELOPMENT
COMPUTER SOFTWARE DEVELOPMENT & APPLICATIONS
COMPUTER SOFTWARE SYSTEMS ANALYSIS & DESIGN: Custom
COMPUTER STORAGE DEVICES, NEC
COMPUTER TERMINALS
COMPUTER TERMINALS: CRT
COMPUTER-AIDED DESIGN SYSTEMS SVCS
COMPUTER-AIDED ENGINEERING SYSTEMS SVCS
COMPUTERS, NEC
COMPUTERS, PERIPHERALS & SOFTWARE, WHOLESALE: Disk Drives
COMPUTERS, PERIPHERALS & SOFTWARE, WHOLESALE: Software
COMPUTERS: Indl, Process, Gas Flow
COMPUTERS: Mainframe
COMPUTERS: Personal
CONCENTRATES, DRINK
CONCENTRATES, FLAVORING, EXC DRINK
CONCRETE CURING & HARDENING COMPOUNDS
CONCRETE MIXERS
CONCRETE PLANTS
CONCRETE PRDTS
CONCRETE PRDTS, PRECAST, NEC
CONCRETE: Asphaltic, Not From Refineries
CONCRETE: Bituminous
CONCRETE: Ready-Mixed
CONDENSERS & CONDENSING UNITS: Air Conditioner
CONDENSERS: Fixed Or Variable
CONDENSERS: Heat Transfer Eqpt, Evaporative
CONDENSERS: Motors Or Generators
CONDUITS & FITTINGS: Electric
CONDUITS: Pressed Pulp Fiber, Made From Purchased Materials
CONFECTIONERY PRDTS WHOLESALERS
CONFECTIONS & CANDY
CONFINEMENT SURVEILLANCE SYS MAINTENANCE & MONITORING SVCS

INDEX

CONNECTORS & TERMINALS: Electrical Device Uses
CONNECTORS: Cord, Electric
CONNECTORS: Electrical
CONNECTORS: Electronic
CONNECTORS: Solderless, Electric-Wiring Devices
CONSTRUCTION & MINING MACHINERY WHOLESALERS
CONSTRUCTION & ROAD MAINTENANCE EQPT: Drags, Road
CONSTRUCTION EQPT: Attachments
CONSTRUCTION EQPT: Attachments, Snow Plow
CONSTRUCTION EQPT: Crane Carriers
CONSTRUCTION EQPT: Cranes
CONSTRUCTION EQPT: Dozers, Tractor Mounted, Material Moving
CONSTRUCTION EQPT: Hammer Mills, Port, Incl Rock/Ore Crush
CONSTRUCTION EQPT: Rollers, Sheepsfoot & Vibratory
CONSTRUCTION EQPT: SCRAPERS, GRADERS, ROLLERS & SIMILAR EQPT
CONSTRUCTION EQPT: Wrecker Hoists, Automobile
CONSTRUCTION MATERIALS, WHOLESALE: Aggregate
CONSTRUCTION MATERIALS, WHOLESALE: Awnings
CONSTRUCTION MATERIALS, WHOLESALE: Block, Concrete & Cinder
CONSTRUCTION MATERIALS, WHOLESALE: Blocks, Building, NEC
CONSTRUCTION MATERIALS, WHOLESALE: Building Stone, Granite
CONSTRUCTION MATERIALS, WHOLESALE: Building Stone, Marble
CONSTRUCTION MATERIALS, WHOLESALE: Building, Exterior
CONSTRUCTION MATERIALS, WHOLESALE: Building, Interior
CONSTRUCTION MATERIALS, WHOLESALE: Cement
CONSTRUCTION MATERIALS, WHOLESALE: Clay, Exc Refractory
CONSTRUCTION MATERIALS, WHOLESALE: Concrete Mixtures
CONSTRUCTION MATERIALS, WHOLESALE: Door Frames
CONSTRUCTION MATERIALS, WHOLESALE: Glass
CONSTRUCTION MATERIALS, WHOLESALE: Gravel
CONSTRUCTION MATERIALS, WHOLESALE: Limestone
CONSTRUCTION MATERIALS, WHOLESALE: Masons' Materials
CONSTRUCTION MATERIALS, WHOLESALE: Millwork
CONSTRUCTION MATERIALS, WHOLESALE: Molding, All Materials
CONSTRUCTION MATERIALS, WHOLESALE: Paving Materials
CONSTRUCTION MATERIALS, WHOLESALE: Paving Mixtures
CONSTRUCTION MATERIALS, WHOLESALE: Prefabricated Structures
CONSTRUCTION MATERIALS, WHOLESALE: Roof, Asphalt/Sheet Metal
CONSTRUCTION MATERIALS, WHOLESALE: Roofing & Siding Material
CONSTRUCTION MATERIALS, WHOLESALE: Sand
CONSTRUCTION MATERIALS, WHOLESALE: Septic Tanks
CONSTRUCTION MATERIALS, WHOLESALE: Siding, Exc Wood
CONSTRUCTION MATERIALS, WHOLESALE: Stone, Crushed Or Broken
CONSTRUCTION MATERIALS, WHOLESALE: Tile & Clay Prdts
CONSTRUCTION MATERIALS, WHOLESALE: Tile, Clay/Other Ceramic
CONSTRUCTION MATERIALS, WHOLESALE: Windows
CONSTRUCTION MATLS, WHOL: Lumber, Rough, Dressed/Finished
CONSTRUCTION MATLS, WHOLESALE: Soil Erosion Cntrl Fabrics
CONSTRUCTION SAND MINING
CONSTRUCTION SITE PREPARATION SVCS
CONSTRUCTION: Bridge
CONSTRUCTION: Commercial & Institutional Building
CONSTRUCTION: Concrete Patio
CONSTRUCTION: Dry Cleaning Plant
CONSTRUCTION: Food Prdts Manufacturing or Packing Plant
CONSTRUCTION: Guardrails, Highway
CONSTRUCTION: Heavy Highway & Street
CONSTRUCTION: Indl Building & Warehouse
CONSTRUCTION: Indl Building, Prefabricated
CONSTRUCTION: Indl Buildings, New, NEC

CONSTRUCTION: Pharmaceutical Manufacturing Plant
CONSTRUCTION: Power & Communication Transmission Tower
CONSTRUCTION: Power Plant
CONSTRUCTION: Religious Building
CONSTRUCTION: Residential, Nec
CONSTRUCTION: Single-Family Housing
CONSTRUCTION: Single-family Housing, New
CONSTRUCTION: Steel Buildings
CONSTRUCTION: Street Sign Installation & Mntnce
CONSTRUCTION: Street Surfacing & Paving
CONSTRUCTION: Tennis Court
CONSTRUCTION: Warehouse
CONSULTING SVC: Business, NEC
CONSULTING SVC: Computer
CONSULTING SVC: Educational
CONSULTING SVC: Engineering
CONSULTING SVC: Financial Management
CONSULTING SVC: Human Resource
CONSULTING SVC: Management
CONSULTING SVC: Marketing Management
CONSULTING SVC: Online Technology
CONSULTING SVC: Sales Management
CONSULTING SVCS, BUSINESS: Communications
CONSULTING SVCS, BUSINESS: Energy Conservation
CONSULTING SVCS, BUSINESS: Publishing
CONSULTING SVCS, BUSINESS: Safety Training Svcs
CONSULTING SVCS, BUSINESS: Sys Engnrg, Exc Computer/Prof
CONSULTING SVCS, BUSINESS: Systems Analysis Or Design
CONSULTING SVCS, BUSINESS: Test Development & Evaluation
CONSULTING SVCS, BUSINESS: Testing, Educational Or Personnel
CONSULTING SVCS: Oil
CONSULTING SVCS: Scientific
CONTACT LENSES
CONTACTS: Electrical
CONTAINERS, GLASS: Cosmetic Jars
CONTAINERS, GLASS: Food
CONTAINERS, GLASS: Medicine Bottles
CONTAINERS: Cargo, Wood & Metal Combination
CONTAINERS: Cargo, Wood & Wood With Metal
CONTAINERS: Corrugated
CONTAINERS: Foil, Bakery Goods & Frozen Foods
CONTAINERS: Food & Beverage
CONTAINERS: Food, Folding, Made From Purchased Materials
CONTAINERS: Food, Liquid Tight, Including Milk
CONTAINERS: Food, Metal
CONTAINERS: Glass
CONTAINERS: Laminated Phenolic & Vulcanized Fiber
CONTAINERS: Liquid Tight Fiber, From Purchased Materials
CONTAINERS: Metal
CONTAINERS: Plastic
CONTAINERS: Sanitary, Food
CONTAINERS: Shipping & Mailing, Fiber
CONTAINERS: Shipping, Bombs, Metal Plate
CONTAINERS: Shipping, Wood
CONTAINERS: Wood
CONTRACT FOOD SVCS
CONTRACTOR: Framing
CONTRACTORS: Acoustical & Ceiling Work
CONTRACTORS: Acoustical & Insulation Work
CONTRACTORS: Antenna Installation
CONTRACTORS: Awning Installation
CONTRACTORS: Boiler & Furnace
CONTRACTORS: Boiler Maintenance Contractor
CONTRACTORS: Building Eqpt & Machinery Installation
CONTRACTORS: Building Sign Installation & Mntnce
CONTRACTORS: Carpentry Work
CONTRACTORS: Carpentry, Cabinet & Finish Work
CONTRACTORS: Carpentry, Cabinet Building & Installation
CONTRACTORS: Carpentry, Finish & Trim Work
CONTRACTORS: Ceramic Floor Tile Installation
CONTRACTORS: Closed Circuit Television Installation
CONTRACTORS: Commercial & Office Building
CONTRACTORS: Communications Svcs
CONTRACTORS: Concrete
CONTRACTORS: Concrete Pumping
CONTRACTORS: Concrete Repair
CONTRACTORS: Construction Site Cleanup
CONTRACTORS: Countertop Installation
CONTRACTORS: Demountable Partition Installation

CONTRACTORS: Directional Oil & Gas Well Drilling Svc
CONTRACTORS: Drywall
CONTRACTORS: Electrical
CONTRACTORS: Electronic Controls Installation
CONTRACTORS: Energy Management Control
CONTRACTORS: Excavating
CONTRACTORS: Excavating Slush Pits & Cellars Svcs
CONTRACTORS: Exterior Wall System Installation
CONTRACTORS: Fence Construction
CONTRACTORS: Fiber Optic Cable Installation
CONTRACTORS: Fire Detection & Burglar Alarm Systems
CONTRACTORS: Fire Escape Installation
CONTRACTORS: Fire Sprinkler System Installation Svcs
CONTRACTORS: Floor Laying & Other Floor Work
CONTRACTORS: Garage Doors
CONTRACTORS: Gas Field Svcs, NEC
CONTRACTORS: Gasoline Condensation Removal Svcs
CONTRACTORS: Glass, Glazing & Tinting
CONTRACTORS: Heating & Air Conditioning
CONTRACTORS: Highway & Street Construction, General
CONTRACTORS: Highway & Street Paving
CONTRACTORS: Highway Sign & Guardrail Construction & Install
CONTRACTORS: Home & Office Intrs Finish, Furnish/Remodel
CONTRACTORS: Hydraulic Eqpt Installation & Svcs
CONTRACTORS: Hydronics Heating
CONTRACTORS: Insulation Installation, Building
CONTRACTORS: Kitchen & Bathroom Remodeling
CONTRACTORS: Lighting Syst
CONTRACTORS: Machinery Installation
CONTRACTORS: Marble Installation, Interior
CONTRACTORS: Masonry & Stonework
CONTRACTORS: Mechanical
CONTRACTORS: Multi-Family Home Remodeling
CONTRACTORS: Office Furniture Installation
CONTRACTORS: Oil & Gas Building, Repairing & Dismantling Svc
CONTRACTORS: Oil & Gas Field Fire Fighting Svcs
CONTRACTORS: Oil & Gas Field Geological Exploration Svcs
CONTRACTORS: Oil & Gas Field Geophysical Exploration Svcs
CONTRACTORS: Oil & Gas Well Casing Cement Svcs
CONTRACTORS: Oil & Gas Well Drilling Svc
CONTRACTORS: Oil & Gas Well Foundation Grading Svcs
CONTRACTORS: Oil & Gas Wells Svcs
CONTRACTORS: Oil Field Haulage Svcs
CONTRACTORS: Oil Field Lease Tanks: Erectg, Clng/Rprg Svcs
CONTRACTORS: Oil Sampling Svcs
CONTRACTORS: Oil/Gas Well Construction, Rpr/Dismantling Svcs
CONTRACTORS: On-Site Welding
CONTRACTORS: Ornamental Metal Work
CONTRACTORS: Painting & Wall Covering
CONTRACTORS: Parking Facility Eqpt Installation
CONTRACTORS: Patio & Deck Construction & Repair
CONTRACTORS: Pipe Laying
CONTRACTORS: Plastering, Plain or Ornamental
CONTRACTORS: Plumbing
CONTRACTORS: Power Generating Eqpt Installation
CONTRACTORS: Prefabricated Fireplace Installation
CONTRACTORS: Prefabricated Window & Door Installation
CONTRACTORS: Roofing
CONTRACTORS: Roustabout Svcs
CONTRACTORS: Safety & Security Eqpt
CONTRACTORS: Sandblasting Svc, Building Exteriors
CONTRACTORS: Screening, Window & Door
CONTRACTORS: Seismograph Survey Svcs
CONTRACTORS: Sheet Metal Work, NEC
CONTRACTORS: Sheet metal Work, Architectural
CONTRACTORS: Siding
CONTRACTORS: Single-family Home General Remodeling
CONTRACTORS: Solar Energy Eqpt
CONTRACTORS: Sound Eqpt Installation
CONTRACTORS: Stone Masonry
CONTRACTORS: Store Fixture Installation
CONTRACTORS: Store Front Construction
CONTRACTORS: Structural Iron Work, Structural
CONTRACTORS: Structural Steel Erection
CONTRACTORS: Svc Station Eqpt Installation, Maint & Repair
CONTRACTORS: Svc Well Drilling Svcs
CONTRACTORS: Textile Warping

CONTRACTORS: Tile Installation, Ceramic
CONTRACTORS: Ventilation & Duct Work
CONTRACTORS: Water Intake Well Drilling Svc
CONTRACTORS: Water Well Drilling
CONTRACTORS: Water Well Servicing
CONTRACTORS: Waterproofing
CONTRACTORS: Well Chemical Treating Svcs
CONTRACTORS: Well Logging Svcs
CONTRACTORS: Window Treatment Installation
CONTRACTORS: Windows & Doors
CONTRACTORS: Wood Floor Installation & Refinishing
CONTROL CIRCUIT DEVICES
CONTROL EQPT: Electric
CONTROL EQPT: Noise
CONTROL PANELS: Electrical
CONTROLS & ACCESS: Indl, Electric
CONTROLS & ACCESS: Motor
CONTROLS: Access, Motor
CONTROLS: Automatic Temperature
CONTROLS: Electric Motor
CONTROLS: Environmental
CONTROLS: Marine & Navy, Auxiliary
CONTROLS: Numerical
CONTROLS: Relay & Ind
CONTROLS: Thermostats
CONTROLS: Thermostats, Exc Built-in
CONTROLS: Voice
CONVENIENCE STORES
CONVENTION & TRADE SHOW SVCS
CONVERTERS: Data
CONVERTERS: Frequency
CONVERTERS: Phase Or Rotary, Electrical
CONVERTERS: Power, AC to DC
CONVERTERS: Rotary, Electrical
CONVERTERS: Torque, Exc Auto
CONVEYOR SYSTEMS: Belt, General Indl Use
CONVEYOR SYSTEMS: Bulk Handling
CONVEYOR SYSTEMS: Pneumatic Tube
CONVEYORS & CONVEYING EQPT
COOKING & FOOD WARMING EQPT: Commercial
COOKING & FOODWARMING EQPT: Coffee Brewing
COOKING & FOODWARMING EQPT: Commercial
COOKING WARE, EXC PORCELAIN ENAMELED
COOKING WARE: Cooking Ware, Porcelain Enameled
COOKWARE, STONEWARE: Coarse Earthenware & Pottery
COOKWARE: Fine Earthenware
COOLING TOWERS: Metal
COPPER ORES
COPPER: Rolling & Drawing
COPYRIGHT BUYING & LICENSING
CORD & TWINE
CORE WASH OR WAX
CORES: Magnetic
CORK & CORK PRDTS: Tiles
CORRESPONDENCE SCHOOLS
CORRUGATED PRDTS: Boxes, Partition, Display Items, Sheet/Pad
COSMETIC PREPARATIONS
COSMETICS & TOILETRIES
COSMETICS WHOLESALERS
COSTUME JEWELRY & NOVELTIES: Apparel, Exc Precious Metals
COSTUME JEWELRY & NOVELTIES: Bracelets, Exc Precious Metals
COSTUME JEWELRY & NOVELTIES: Costume Novelties
COSTUME JEWELRY & NOVELTIES: Earrings, Exc Precious Metals
COSTUME JEWELRY & NOVELTIES: Exc Semi & Precious
COSTUME JEWELRY & NOVELTIES: Pins, Exc Precious Metals
COUNTER & SINK TOPS
COUNTERS & COUNTING DEVICES
COUNTERS OR COUNTER DISPLAY CASES, EXC WOOD
COUNTERS OR COUNTER DISPLAY CASES, WOOD
COUNTERS: Mechanical
COUNTING DEVICES: Controls, Revolution & Timing
COUNTING DEVICES: Electromechanical
COUNTING DEVICES: Speed Indicators & Recorders, Vehicle
COUPLINGS: Shaft
COUPON REDEMPTION SVCS
COURIER SVCS: Ground
COVERS: Automobile Seat
COVERS: Automotive, Exc Seat & Tire
COVERS: Canvas
COVERS: Hot Tub & Spa

CRANE & AERIAL LIFT SVCS
CRANES & MONORAIL SYSTEMS
CRANES: Indl Plant
CRANKSHAFTS & CAMSHAFTS: Machining
CRATES: Fruit, Wood Wirebound
CREDIT BUREAUS
CROWNS & CLOSURES
CRUDE PETROLEUM & NATURAL GAS PRODUCTION
CRUDE PETROLEUM & NATURAL GAS PRODUCTION
CRUDE PETROLEUM PRODUCTION
CRUDES: Cyclic, Organic
CRYOGENIC COOLING DEVICES: Infrared Detectors, Masers
CRYSTALS
CULTURE MEDIA
CULVERTS: Metal Plate
CUPS: Paper, Made From Purchased Materials
CUPS: Plastic Exc Polystyrene Foam
CURBING: Granite Or Stone
CURTAIN & DRAPERY FIXTURES: Poles, Rods & Rollers
CURTAINS & CURTAIN FABRICS: Lace
CURTAINS: Cottage Sets, From Purchased Materials
CURTAINS: Shower
CURTAINS: Window, From Purchased Materials
CUSHIONS & PILLOWS
CUSHIONS & PILLOWS: Bed, From Purchased Materials
CUSHIONS: Textile, Exc Spring & Carpet
CUSTOM COMPOUNDING OF RUBBER MATERIALS
CUT STONE & STONE PRODUCTS
CUTLERY
CUTLERY WHOLESALERS
CUTOUTS: Cardboard, Die-Cut, Made From Purchased Materials
CUTOUTS: Distribution
CUTTING SVC: Paper, Exc Die-Cut
CYCLIC CRUDES & INTERMEDIATES
CYLINDER & ACTUATORS: Fluid Power
CYLINDERS: Pressure

D

DAIRY EQPT
DAIRY PRDTS STORE: Cheese
DAIRY PRDTS STORE: Ice Cream, Packaged
DAIRY PRDTS STORES
DAIRY PRDTS WHOLESALERS: Fresh
DAIRY PRDTS: Bakers' Cheese
DAIRY PRDTS: Bottled Baby Formula
DAIRY PRDTS: Butter
DAIRY PRDTS: Butter Oil
DAIRY PRDTS: Canned Baby Formula
DAIRY PRDTS: Cheese
DAIRY PRDTS: Cheese, Cottage
DAIRY PRDTS: Concentrated Skim Milk
DAIRY PRDTS: Cream Substitutes
DAIRY PRDTS: Cream, Sweet
DAIRY PRDTS: Dairy Based Desserts, Frozen
DAIRY PRDTS: Dietary Supplements, Dairy & Non-Dairy Based
DAIRY PRDTS: Dips & Spreads, Cheese Based
DAIRY PRDTS: Dried & Powdered Milk & Milk Prdts
DAIRY PRDTS: Evaporated Milk
DAIRY PRDTS: Farmers' Cheese
DAIRY PRDTS: Fermented & Cultured Milk Prdts
DAIRY PRDTS: Frozen Desserts & Novelties
DAIRY PRDTS: Ice Cream & Ice Milk
DAIRY PRDTS: Ice Cream, Bulk
DAIRY PRDTS: Ice Cream, Packaged, Molded, On Sticks, Etc.
DAIRY PRDTS: Milk & Cream, Cultured & Flavored
DAIRY PRDTS: Milk, Chocolate
DAIRY PRDTS: Milk, Condensed & Evaporated
DAIRY PRDTS: Milk, Fluid
DAIRY PRDTS: Milk, Processed, Pasteurized, Homogenized/Btld
DAIRY PRDTS: Natural Cheese
DAIRY PRDTS: Processed Cheese
DAIRY PRDTS: Sherbets, Dairy Based
DAIRY PRDTS: Spreads, Cheese
DAIRY PRDTS: Whipped Topping, Exc Frozen Or Dry Mix
DAIRY PRDTS: Yogurt, Exc Frozen
DAIRY PRDTS: Yogurt, Frozen
DATA PROCESSING & PREPARATION SVCS
DATA PROCESSING SVCS
DECORATIVE WOOD & WOODWORK
DEFENSE SYSTEMS & EQPT

DEGREASING MACHINES
DEHUMIDIFIERS: Electric
DEHYDRATION EQPT
DELAY LINES
DENTAL EQPT
DENTAL EQPT & SPLYS
DENTAL EQPT & SPLYS WHOLESALERS
DENTAL EQPT & SPLYS: Cabinets
DENTAL EQPT & SPLYS: Compounds
DENTAL EQPT & SPLYS: Cutting Instruments
DENTAL EQPT & SPLYS: Dental Materials
DENTAL EQPT & SPLYS: Enamels
DENTAL EQPT & SPLYS: Laboratory
DENTAL EQPT & SPLYS: Orthodontic Appliances
DENTAL EQPT & SPLYS: Sterilizers
DENTAL EQPT & SPLYS: Teeth, Artificial, Exc In Dental Labs
DENTAL EQPT & SPLYS: Wax
DENTISTS' OFFICES & CLINICS
DEODORANTS: Personal
DEPILATORIES, COSMETIC
DERMATOLOGICALS
DERRICKS: Oil & Gas Field
DESALTER KITS: Sea Water
DESIGN SVCS, NEC
DESIGN SVCS: Commercial & Indl
DESIGN SVCS: Computer Integrated Systems
DESIGN SVCS: Shoe
DETECTION APPARATUS: Electronic/Magnetic Field, Light/Heat
DIAGNOSTIC SUBSTANCES
DIAGNOSTIC SUBSTANCES OR AGENTS: Blood Derivative
DIAGNOSTIC SUBSTANCES OR AGENTS: In Vivo
DIAGNOSTIC SUBSTANCES OR AGENTS: Microbiology & Virology
DIAGNOSTIC SUBSTANCES OR AGENTS: Veterinary
DIAMOND MINING SVCS: Indl
DIAMOND SETTER SVCS
DIAMONDS, GEMS, WHOLESALE
DIAMONDS: Cutting & Polishing
DIAPERS: Cloth
DIAPERS: Disposable
DIE CUTTING SVC: Paper
DIE SETS: Presses, Metal Stamping
DIES & TOOLS: Special
DIES: Cutting, Exc Metal
DIES: Extrusion
DIES: Paper Cutting
DIES: Plastic Forming
DIES: Steel Rule
DIODES & RECTIFIERS
DIODES: Light Emitting
DIODES: Solid State, Germanium, Silicon, Etc
DIRECT SELLING ESTABLISHMENTS: Beverage Svcs
DIRECT SELLING ESTABLISHMENTS: Food Svcs
DISCOUNT DEPARTMENT STORES
DISCS & TAPE: Optical, Blank
DISHWASHING EQPT: Commercial
DISINFECTING SVCS
DISK & DRUM DRIVES & COMPONENTS: Computers
DISK DRIVES: Computer
DISPENSING EQPT & PARTS, BEVERAGE: Fountain/Other Beverage
DISPENSING EQPT & SYSTEMS, BEVERAGE: Liquor
DISPLAY FIXTURES: Showcases, Wood, Exc Refrigerated
DISPLAY FIXTURES: Wood
DISPLAY ITEMS: Corrugated, Made From Purchased Materials
DISPLAY STANDS: Merchandise, Exc Wood
DISTILLATES: Hardwood
DOCK OPERATION SVCS, INCL BLDGS, FACILITIES, OPERS & MAINT
DOCKS: Floating, Wood
DOCKS: Prefabricated Metal
DOCUMENT EMBOSSING SVCS
DOLLIES: Mechanics'
DOLOMITE: Crushed & Broken
DOLOMITIC MARBLE: Crushed & Broken
DOMESTIC HELP SVCS
DOOR & WINDOW REPAIR SVCS
DOOR FRAMES: Wood
DOOR OPERATING SYSTEMS: Electric
DOORS & WINDOWS WHOLESALERS: All Materials
DOORS & WINDOWS: Screen & Storm
DOORS & WINDOWS: Storm, Metal
DOORS: Dormers, Wood

INDEX

DOORS: Fire, Metal
DOORS: Folding, Plastic Or Plastic Coated Fabric
DOORS: Garage, Overhead, Metal
DOORS: Garage, Overhead, Wood
DOORS: Glass
DOORS: Rolling, Indl Building Or Warehouse, Metal
DOORS: Wooden
DOWN FEATHERS
DRAPERIES & CURTAINS
DRAPERIES & DRAPERY FABRICS, COTTON
DRAPERIES: Plastic & Textile, From Purchased Materials
DRAPERY & UPHOLSTERY STORES: Draperies
DRAPES & DRAPERY FABRICS, FROM MANMADE FIBER
DRIED FRUITS WHOLESALERS
DRILLING MACHINERY & EQPT: Water Well
DRINK MIXES, NONALCOHOLIC: Cocktail
DRINKING PLACES: Alcoholic Beverages
DRINKING PLACES: Night Clubs
DRINKING PLACES: Wine Bar
DRINKING WATER COOLERS WHOLESALERS: Mechanical
DRIVE SHAFTS
DRIVES: High Speed Indl, Exc Hydrostatic
DRONES: Target, Used By Ships, Metal
DROP CLOTHS: Fabric
DRUG TESTING KITS: Blood & Urine
DRUGS & DRUG PROPRIETARIES, WHOL: Biologicals/Allied Prdts
DRUGS & DRUG PROPRIETARIES, WHOLESALE
DRUGS & DRUG PROPRIETARIES, WHOLESALE: Pharmaceuticals
DRUGS & DRUG PROPRIETARIES, WHOLESALE: Vitamins & Minerals
DRUGS ACTING ON THE CENTRAL NERVOUS SYSTEM & SENSE ORGANS
DRUGS AFFECTING NEOPLASMS & ENDOCRINE SYSTEMS
DRUGS/DRUG PROPRIETARIES, WHOL: Proprietary/Patent Medicines
DRUGS: Parasitic & Infective Disease Affecting
DRUMS: Fiber
DRYCLEANING EQPT & SPLYS: Commercial
DRYCLEANING SVC: Drapery & Curtain
DUCTING: Plastic
DUCTS: Sheet Metal
DUMPSTERS: Garbage
DYES & PIGMENTS: Organic
DYES: Synthetic Organic

E

EATING PLACES
EDUCATIONAL PROGRAMS ADMINISTRATION SVCS
EDUCATIONAL SVCS
EDUCATIONAL SVCS, NONDEGREE GRANTING: Continuing Education
ELASTOMERS
ELECTRIC MOTOR REPAIR SVCS
ELECTRIC SERVICES
ELECTRIC SVCS, NEC Power Transmission
ELECTRIC SVCS, NEC: Power Generation
ELECTRICAL APPARATUS & EQPT WHOLESALERS
ELECTRICAL APPLIANCES, TELEVISIONS & RADIOS WHOLESALERS
ELECTRICAL CONSTRUCTION MATERIALS WHOLESALERS
ELECTRICAL CURRENT CARRYING WIRING DEVICES
ELECTRICAL DISCHARGE MACHINING, EDM
ELECTRICAL EQPT & SPLYS
ELECTRICAL EQPT FOR ENGINES
ELECTRICAL EQPT REPAIR & MAINTENANCE
ELECTRICAL EQPT REPAIR SVCS
ELECTRICAL EQPT: Automotive, NEC
ELECTRICAL EQPT: Household
ELECTRICAL GOODS, WHOL: Vid Camera-Aud Recorders/Camcorders
ELECTRICAL GOODS, WHOLESALE: Batteries, Dry Cell
ELECTRICAL GOODS, WHOLESALE: Burglar Alarm Systems
ELECTRICAL GOODS, WHOLESALE: Capacitors
ELECTRICAL GOODS, WHOLESALE: Connectors
ELECTRICAL GOODS, WHOLESALE: Electronic Parts
ELECTRICAL GOODS, WHOLESALE: Facsimile Or Fax Eqpt
ELECTRICAL GOODS, WHOLESALE: Fans, Household
ELECTRICAL GOODS, WHOLESALE: Fittings & Construction Mat
ELECTRICAL GOODS, WHOLESALE: Intercommunication Eqpt

ELECTRICAL GOODS, WHOLESALE: Light Bulbs & Related Splys
ELECTRICAL GOODS, WHOLESALE: Lighting Fittings & Access
ELECTRICAL GOODS, WHOLESALE: Lighting Fixtures, Comm & Indl
ELECTRICAL GOODS, WHOLESALE: Lighting Fixtures, Residential
ELECTRICAL GOODS, WHOLESALE: Mobile telephone Eqpt
ELECTRICAL GOODS, WHOLESALE: Motors
ELECTRICAL GOODS, WHOLESALE: Semiconductor Devices
ELECTRICAL GOODS, WHOLESALE: Signaling, Eqpt
ELECTRICAL GOODS, WHOLESALE: Sound Eqpt
ELECTRICAL GOODS, WHOLESALE: Telephone Eqpt
ELECTRICAL GOODS, WHOLESALE: Transformers
ELECTRICAL GOODS, WHOLESALE: VCR & Access
ELECTRICAL GOODS, WHOLESALE: Vacuum Cleaners, Household
ELECTRICAL GOODS, WHOLESALE: Video Eqpt
ELECTRICAL GOODS, WHOLESALE: Wire & Cable
ELECTRICAL GOODS, WHOLESALE: Wire & Cable, Electronic
ELECTRICAL INDL APPARATUS, NEC
ELECTRICAL SPLYS
ELECTRICAL SUPPLIES: Porcelain
ELECTRODES: Fluorescent Lamps
ELECTRODES: Indl Process
ELECTRODES: Thermal & Electrolytic
ELECTROMEDICAL EQPT
ELECTRON TUBES
ELECTRON TUBES: Cathode Ray
ELECTRONIC COMPONENTS
ELECTRONIC DETECTION SYSTEMS: Aeronautical
ELECTRONIC DEVICES: Solid State, NEC
ELECTRONIC EQPT REPAIR SVCS
ELECTRONIC LOADS & POWER SPLYS
ELECTRONIC PARTS & EQPT WHOLESALERS
ELECTRONIC SHOPPING
ELECTRONIC TRAINING DEVICES
ELECTROPLATING & PLATING SVC
ELEVATORS & EQPT
ELEVATORS WHOLESALERS
ELEVATORS: Installation & Conversion
ELEVATORS: Stair, Motor Powered
EMBLEMS: Embroidered
EMBOSSING SVC: Paper
EMBROIDERING & ART NEEDLEWORK FOR THE TRADE
EMBROIDERING SVC
EMBROIDERING SVC: Schiffli Machine
EMBROIDERING: Swiss Loom
EMBROIDERY ADVERTISING SVCS
EMERGENCY ALARMS
EMPLOYMENT AGENCY SVCS
ENAMELING SVC: Metal Prdts, Including Porcelain
ENAMELS
ENCLOSURES: Electronic
ENCODERS: Digital
ENERGY MEASUREMENT EQPT
ENGINE REBUILDING: Diesel
ENGINE REBUILDING: Gas
ENGINEERING SVCS
ENGINEERING SVCS: Building Construction
ENGINEERING SVCS: Electrical Or Electronic
ENGINEERING SVCS: Heating & Ventilation
ENGINEERING SVCS: Industrial
ENGINEERING SVCS: Marine
ENGINEERING SVCS: Mechanical
ENGINEERING SVCS: Pollution Control
ENGINEERING SVCS: Professional
ENGINEERING SVCS: Sanitary
ENGINEERING SVCS: Structural
ENGINES: Internal Combustion, NEC
ENGRAVING SVC, NEC
ENGRAVING SVC: Jewelry & Personal Goods
ENGRAVING SVCS
ENGRAVING: Steel line, For The Printing Trade
ENGRAVINGS: Plastic
ENTERTAINERS & ENTERTAINMENT GROUPS
ENVELOPES
ENVELOPES WHOLESALERS
ENVIRONMENTAL QUALITY PROGS ADMIN, GOVT: Waste Management
ENZYMES
EPOXY RESINS

EQUIPMENT: Pedestrian Traffic Control
EQUIPMENT: Rental & Leasing, NEC
ESCALATORS: Passenger & Freight
ETCHING & ENGRAVING SVC
ETCHING SVC: Metal
ETCHING SVC: Photochemical
ETHANOLAMINES
ETHYLENE-PROPYLENE RUBBERS: EPDM Polymers
EXCAVATING EQPT
EXERCISE EQPT STORES
EXHAUST HOOD OR FAN CLEANING SVCS
EXHAUST SYSTEMS: Eqpt & Parts
EXPANSION JOINTS: Rubber
EXPLOSIVES
EXPLOSIVES, EXC AMMO & FIREWORKS WHOLESALERS
EXTENSION CORDS
EXTRACTS, FLAVORING
EXTRACTS: Dying Or Tanning, Natural
EYEGLASS CASES
EYEGLASSES
EYEGLASSES: Sunglasses
EYES: Artificial

F

FABRIC FINISHING: Mending, Wool
FABRIC STORES
FABRICATED METAL PRODUCTS, NEC
FABRICS & CLOTH: Quilted
FABRICS: Alpacas, Mohair, Woven
FABRICS: Apparel & Outerwear, Broadwoven
FABRICS: Apparel & Outerwear, Cotton
FABRICS: Apparel & Outerwear, From Manmade Fiber Or Silk
FABRICS: Bags & Bagging, Cotton
FABRICS: Broad Woven, Goods, Cotton
FABRICS: Broadwoven, Cotton
FABRICS: Broadwoven, Synthetic Manmade Fiber & Silk
FABRICS: Broadwoven, Wool
FABRICS: Brocade, Cotton
FABRICS: Canvas
FABRICS: Chemically Coated & Treated
FABRICS: Coated Or Treated
FABRICS: Cords
FABRICS: Corduroys, Cotton
FABRICS: Denims
FABRICS: Elastic, From Manmade Fiber Or Silk
FABRICS: Fiberglass, Broadwoven
FABRICS: Glass, Narrow
FABRICS: Glove, Lining
FABRICS: Hand Woven
FABRICS: Handkerchief, Cotton
FABRICS: Jean
FABRICS: Jersey Cloth
FABRICS: Lace & Decorative Trim, Narrow
FABRICS: Lace & Lace Prdts
FABRICS: Lace, Knit, NEC
FABRICS: Laminated
FABRICS: Linings & Interlinings, Cotton
FABRICS: Long Cloth, Cotton
FABRICS: Nonwoven
FABRICS: Nylon, Broadwoven
FABRICS: Paper, Broadwoven
FABRICS: Pile Warp or Flat Knit
FABRICS: Pile, Circular Knit
FABRICS: Pocketing Twill, Cotton
FABRICS: Polyester, Broadwoven
FABRICS: Print, Cotton
FABRICS: Resin Or Plastic Coated
FABRICS: Rubberized
FABRICS: Shoe
FABRICS: Silk, Broadwoven
FABRICS: Silk, Narrow
FABRICS: Spandex, Broadwoven
FABRICS: Specialty Including Twisted Weaves, Broadwoven
FABRICS: Stretch, Cotton
FABRICS: Surgical Fabrics, Cotton
FABRICS: Tapestry, Cotton
FABRICS: Tricot
FABRICS: Trimmings
FABRICS: Trimmings, Textile
FABRICS: Upholstery, Cotton
FABRICS: Varnished Glass & Coated Fiberglass
FABRICS: Wall Covering, From Manmade Fiber Or Silk
FABRICS: Warp & Flat Knit Prdts
FABRICS: Warp Knit, Lace & Netting
FABRICS: Weft Or Circular Knit

FABRICS: Woven, Narrow Cotton, Wool, Silk
FACILITIES SUPPORT SVCS
FACSIMILE COMMUNICATION EQPT
FAMILY CLOTHING STORES
FANS, BLOWING: Indl Or Commercial
FANS, EXHAUST: Indl Or Commercial
FANS, VENTILATING: Indl Or Commercial
FARM & GARDEN MACHINERY WHOLESALERS
FARM PRDTS, RAW MATERIALS, WHOLESALE: Bristles
FARM PRDTS, RAW MATERIALS, WHOLESALE: Hides
FARM SPLY STORES
FARM SPLYS, WHOLESALE: Beekeeping Splys, Nondurable
FASTENERS: Metal
FASTENERS: Metal
FASTENERS: Notions, NEC
FASTENERS: Notions, Snaps
FASTENERS: Notions, Zippers
FAUCETS & SPIGOTS: Metal & Plastic
FEATHERS: Renovating
FELT: Acoustic
FELT: Automotive
FENCE POSTS: Iron & Steel
FENCES & FENCING MATERIALS
FENCES OR POSTS: Ornamental Iron Or Steel
FENCING DEALERS
FENCING MATERIALS: Docks & Other Outdoor Prdts, Wood
FENCING MATERIALS: Plastic
FENCING MATERIALS: Wood
FENCING: Chain Link
FERRITES
FERROALLOYS
FERROMANGANESE, NOT MADE IN BLAST FURNACES
FERTILIZERS: NEC
FERTILIZERS: Nitrogenous
FERTILIZERS: Phosphatic
FIBER & FIBER PRDTS: Acrylic
FIBER & FIBER PRDTS: Fluorocarbon
FIBER & FIBER PRDTS: Organic, Noncellulose
FIBER & FIBER PRDTS: Polyester
FIBER & FIBER PRDTS: Synthetic Cellulosic
FIBER & FIBER PRDTS: Vinyl
FIBER OPTICS
FIBERS: Carbon & Graphite
FILLERS & SEALERS: Wood
FILM & SHEET: Unsuppported Plastic
FILM BASE: Cellulose Acetate Or Nitrocellulose Plastics
FILM: Motion Picture
FILTERS
FILTERS & SOFTENERS: Water, Household
FILTERS: Air
FILTERS: Air Intake, Internal Combustion Engine, Exc Auto
FILTERS: General Line, Indl
FILTERS: Motor Vehicle
FILTERS: Paper
FILTRATION DEVICES: Electronic
FINANCIAL INVESTMENT ACTIVITIES, NEC: Financial Reporting
FINANCIAL INVESTMENT ADVICE
FINDINGS & TRIMMINGS Fabric, NEC
FINDINGS & TRIMMINGS Waistbands, Trouser
FINDINGS & TRIMMINGS: Apparel
FINDINGS & TRIMMINGS: Fabric
FINGERNAILS, ARTIFICIAL
FINGERPRINT EQPT
FINISHING AGENTS: Leather
FIRE ARMS, SMALL: Guns Or Gun Parts, 30 mm & Below
FIRE ARMS, SMALL: Pellet & BB guns
FIRE ARMS, SMALL: Rifles Or Rifle Parts, 30 mm & below
FIRE CONTROL OR BOMBING EQPT: Electronic
FIRE DETECTION SYSTEMS
FIRE ESCAPES
FIRE EXTINGUISHERS: Portable
FIRE OR BURGLARY RESISTIVE PRDTS
FIRE PROTECTION EQPT
FIREARMS & AMMUNITION, EXC SPORTING, WHOLESALE
FIREARMS: Small, 30mm or Less
FIREFIGHTING APPARATUS
FIREPLACE & CHIMNEY MATERIAL: Concrete
FIREPLACE EQPT & ACCESS
FIREPLACES: Concrete
FIREWORKS
FIREWORKS DISPLAY SVCS
FISH & SEAFOOD PROCESSORS: Canned Or Cured
FISH & SEAFOOD PROCESSORS: Fresh Or Frozen
FISHING EQPT: Lures

FISHING EQPT: Nets & Seines
FITTINGS & ASSEMBLIES: Hose & Tube, Hydraulic Or Pneumatic
FITTINGS: Pipe
FITTINGS: Pipe, Fabricated
FIXTURES & EQPT: Kitchen, Metal, Exc Cast Aluminum
FIXTURES: Bank, Metal, Ornamental
FIXTURES: Cut Stone
FLAGPOLES
FLAGS: Fabric
FLAT GLASS: Antique
FLAT GLASS: Building
FLAT GLASS: Construction
FLAT GLASS: Plate, Polished & Rough
FLAT GLASS: Strengthened Or Reinforced
FLAT GLASS: Tempered
FLAT GLASS: Window, Clear & Colored
FLATWARE, STAINLESS STEEL
FLAVORS OR FLAVORING MATERIALS: Synthetic
FLOOR COMPOSITION: Magnesite
FLOOR COVERING STORES
FLOOR COVERING STORES: Carpets
FLOOR COVERING: Plastic
FLOOR COVERINGS WHOLESALERS
FLOOR COVERINGS: Tile, Support Plastic
FLOORING & GRATINGS: Open, Construction Applications
FLOORING: Hard Surface
FLOORING: Hardwood
FLORISTS
FLOWER POTS Plastic
FLOWERS: Artificial & Preserved
FLUID METERS & COUNTING DEVICES
FLUID POWER PUMPS & MOTORS
FLUID POWER VALVES & HOSE FITTINGS
FLUORO RUBBERS
FLUXES
FOAM CHARGE MIXTURES
FOAM RUBBER
FOIL & LEAF: Metal
FOIL, ALUMINUM, HOUSEHOLD, WHOLESALE
FOIL: Aluminum
FOIL: Copper
FOIL: Laminated To Paper Or Other Materials
FOOD CASINGS: Plastic
FOOD PRDTS CANNED: Fruit Nectars
FOOD PRDTS, BREAKFAST: Cereal, Infants' Food
FOOD PRDTS, BREAKFAST: Cereal, Wheat Flakes
FOOD PRDTS, CANNED OR FRESH PACK: Fruit Juices
FOOD PRDTS, CANNED OR FRESH PACK: Vegetable Juices
FOOD PRDTS, CANNED OR FRESH PACK: Vegetable Juices
FOOD PRDTS, CANNED: Baby Food
FOOD PRDTS, CANNED: Barbecue Sauce
FOOD PRDTS, CANNED: Beans & Bean Sprouts
FOOD PRDTS, CANNED: Broth, Chicken
FOOD PRDTS, CANNED: Catsup
FOOD PRDTS, CANNED: Ethnic
FOOD PRDTS, CANNED: Fruit Juices, Concentrated
FOOD PRDTS, CANNED: Fruit Juices, Fresh
FOOD PRDTS, CANNED: Fruits
FOOD PRDTS, CANNED: Fruits
FOOD PRDTS, CANNED: Fruits & Fruit Prdts
FOOD PRDTS, CANNED: Italian
FOOD PRDTS, CANNED: Jams, Including Imitation
FOOD PRDTS, CANNED: Jams, Jellies & Preserves
FOOD PRDTS, CANNED: Maraschino Cherries
FOOD PRDTS, CANNED: Mexican, NEC
FOOD PRDTS, CANNED: Olives
FOOD PRDTS, CANNED: Puddings, Exc Meat
FOOD PRDTS, CANNED: Ravioli
FOOD PRDTS, CANNED: Sauerkraut
FOOD PRDTS, CANNED: Spaghetti & Other Pasta Sauce
FOOD PRDTS, CANNED: Tomato Sauce.
FOOD PRDTS, CANNED: Tomatoes
FOOD PRDTS, CANNED: Vegetables
FOOD PRDTS, CONFECTIONERY, WHOLESALE: Candy
FOOD PRDTS, CONFECTIONERY, WHOLESALE: Nuts, Salted/Roasted
FOOD PRDTS, CONFECTIONERY, WHOLESALE: Snack Foods
FOOD PRDTS, FISH & SEAFOOD, WHOLESALE: Fresh
FOOD PRDTS, FISH & SEAFOOD: Canned & Jarred, Etc
FOOD PRDTS, FISH & SEAFOOD: Fish, Fresh, Prepared
FOOD PRDTS, FISH & SEAFOOD: Fish, Smoked

FOOD PRDTS, FISH & SEAFOOD: Salmon, Smoked
FOOD PRDTS, FISH & SEAFOOD: Seafood, Frozen, Prepared
FOOD PRDTS, FROZEN: Breakfasts, Packaged
FOOD PRDTS, FROZEN: Dinners, Packaged
FOOD PRDTS, FROZEN: Ethnic Foods, NEC
FOOD PRDTS, FROZEN: Fruits & Vegetables
FOOD PRDTS, FROZEN: Fruits, Juices & Vegetables
FOOD PRDTS, FROZEN: NEC
FOOD PRDTS, FROZEN: Pizza
FOOD PRDTS, FROZEN: Snack Items
FOOD PRDTS, FROZEN: Soups
FOOD PRDTS, FROZEN: Vegetables, Exc Potato Prdts
FOOD PRDTS, FROZEN: Waffles
FOOD PRDTS, FROZEN: Whipped Topping
FOOD PRDTS, MEAT & MEAT PRDTS, WHOLESALE: Brokers
FOOD PRDTS, MEAT & MEAT PRDTS, WHOLESALE: Fresh
FOOD PRDTS, WHOL: Canned Goods, Fruit, Veg, Seafood/Meats
FOOD PRDTS, WHOLESALE: Beverage Concentrates
FOOD PRDTS, WHOLESALE: Beverages, Exc Coffee & Tea
FOOD PRDTS, WHOLESALE: Chocolate
FOOD PRDTS, WHOLESALE: Coffee & Tea
FOOD PRDTS, WHOLESALE: Coffee, Green Or Roasted
FOOD PRDTS, WHOLESALE: Condiments
FOOD PRDTS, WHOLESALE: Flour
FOOD PRDTS, WHOLESALE: Grains
FOOD PRDTS, WHOLESALE: Health
FOOD PRDTS, WHOLESALE: Juices
FOOD PRDTS, WHOLESALE: Organic & Diet
FOOD PRDTS, WHOLESALE: Pasta & Rice
FOOD PRDTS, WHOLESALE: Salad Dressing
FOOD PRDTS, WHOLESALE: Sandwiches
FOOD PRDTS, WHOLESALE: Sausage Casings
FOOD PRDTS, WHOLESALE: Specialty
FOOD PRDTS, WHOLESALE: Tea
FOOD PRDTS: Almond Pastes
FOOD PRDTS: Animal & marine fats & oils
FOOD PRDTS: Bran, Rice
FOOD PRDTS: Bread Crumbs, Exc Made In Bakeries
FOOD PRDTS: Breakfast Bars
FOOD PRDTS: Cane Syrup, From Purchased Raw Sugar
FOOD PRDTS: Cereals
FOOD PRDTS: Cheese Curls & Puffs
FOOD PRDTS: Chicken, Processed, Frozen
FOOD PRDTS: Chocolate Bars, Solid
FOOD PRDTS: Chocolate Coatings & Syrup
FOOD PRDTS: Coconut Oil
FOOD PRDTS: Coconut, Desiccated & Shredded
FOOD PRDTS: Coffee
FOOD PRDTS: Coffee Extracts
FOOD PRDTS: Coffee Roasting, Exc Wholesale Grocers
FOOD PRDTS: Coffee, Ground, Mixed With Grain Or Chicory
FOOD PRDTS: Cole Slaw, Bulk
FOOD PRDTS: Cooking Oils, Refined Vegetable, Exc Corn
FOOD PRDTS: Corn Chips & Other Corn-Based Snacks
FOOD PRDTS: Corn Oil Prdts
FOOD PRDTS: Cottonseed Lecithin
FOOD PRDTS: Dessert Mixes & Fillings
FOOD PRDTS: Desserts, Ready-To-Mix
FOOD PRDTS: Dough, Pizza, Prepared
FOOD PRDTS: Doughs & Batters From Purchased Flour
FOOD PRDTS: Doughs, Frozen Or Refrig From Purchased Flour
FOOD PRDTS: Dressings, Salad, Raw & Cooked Exc Dry Mixes
FOOD PRDTS: Dried & Dehydrated Fruits, Vegetables & Soup Mix
FOOD PRDTS: Ducks, Processed, Fresh
FOOD PRDTS: Ducks, Processed, NEC
FOOD PRDTS: Edible Oil Prdts, Exc Corn Oil
FOOD PRDTS: Edible fats & oils
FOOD PRDTS: Eggs, Processed
FOOD PRDTS: Emulsifiers
FOOD PRDTS: Flavored Ices, Frozen
FOOD PRDTS: Flour & Other Grain Mill Products
FOOD PRDTS: Flour Mixes & Doughs
FOOD PRDTS: Fruit Juices
FOOD PRDTS: Fruits & Vegetables, Pickled
FOOD PRDTS: Fruits, Dehydrated Or Dried
FOOD PRDTS: Fruits, Dried Or Dehydrated, Exc Freeze-Dried
FOOD PRDTS: Gelatin Dessert Preparations
FOOD PRDTS: Gluten Meal

INDEX

FOOD PRDTS: Granulated Cane Sugar
FOOD PRDTS: Horseradish, Exc Sauce
FOOD PRDTS: Ice, Blocks
FOOD PRDTS: Ice, Cubes
FOOD PRDTS: Instant Coffee
FOOD PRDTS: Jelly, Corncob
FOOD PRDTS: Juice Pops, Frozen
FOOD PRDTS: Macaroni Prdts, Dry, Alphabet, Rings Or Shells
FOOD PRDTS: Macaroni, Noodles, Spaghetti, Pasta, Etc
FOOD PRDTS: Malt
FOOD PRDTS: Mayonnaise & Dressings, Exc Tomato Based
FOOD PRDTS: Mixes, Bread & Roll From Purchased Flour
FOOD PRDTS: Mixes, Cake, From Purchased Flour
FOOD PRDTS: Mixes, Doughnut From Purchased Flour
FOOD PRDTS: Mixes, Pancake From Purchased Flour
FOOD PRDTS: Mixes, Seasonings, Dry
FOOD PRDTS: Mustard, Prepared
FOOD PRDTS: Nuts & Seeds
FOOD PRDTS: Oils & Fats, Marine
FOOD PRDTS: Olive Oil
FOOD PRDTS: Oriental Noodles
FOOD PRDTS: Pasta, Rice/Potatoes, Uncooked, Pkgd
FOOD PRDTS: Pasta, Uncooked, Packaged With Other Ingredients
FOOD PRDTS: Peanut Butter
FOOD PRDTS: Pickles, Vinegar
FOOD PRDTS: Pizza, Refrigerated
FOOD PRDTS: Popcorn, Popped
FOOD PRDTS: Popcorn, Unpopped
FOOD PRDTS: Potato & Corn Chips & Similar Prdts
FOOD PRDTS: Potato Chips & Other Potato-Based Snacks
FOOD PRDTS: Potatoes, Dried, Packaged With Other Ingredients
FOOD PRDTS: Poultry, Processed, NEC
FOOD PRDTS: Poultry, Slaughtered & Dressed
FOOD PRDTS: Preparations
FOOD PRDTS: Prepared Meat Sauces Exc Tomato & Dry
FOOD PRDTS: Prepared Sauces, Exc Tomato Based
FOOD PRDTS: Raw cane sugar
FOOD PRDTS: Relishes, Vinegar
FOOD PRDTS: Rice, Milled
FOOD PRDTS: Salads
FOOD PRDTS: Sandwiches
FOOD PRDTS: Seasonings & Spices
FOOD PRDTS: Soup Mixes
FOOD PRDTS: Soy Sauce
FOOD PRDTS: Spices, Including Ground
FOOD PRDTS: Sugar
FOOD PRDTS: Sugar, Beet
FOOD PRDTS: Sugar, Cane
FOOD PRDTS: Sugar, Corn
FOOD PRDTS: Sugar, Granulated Cane, Purchd Raw Sugar/Syrup
FOOD PRDTS: Sugar, Liquid Sugar Beet
FOOD PRDTS: Syrup, Maple
FOOD PRDTS: Syrups
FOOD PRDTS: Tea
FOOD PRDTS: Tofu Desserts, Frozen
FOOD PRDTS: Tofu, Exc Frozen Desserts
FOOD PRDTS: Tortillas
FOOD PRDTS: Vegetables, Dried or Dehydrated Exc Freeze-Dried
FOOD PRDTS: Vegetables, Pickled
FOOD PRDTS: Vinegar
FOOD PRODUCTS MACHINERY
FOOD STORES: Delicatessen
FOOD STORES: Supermarkets
FOOTWEAR, WHOLESALE: Athletic
FOOTWEAR, WHOLESALE: Shoe Access
FOOTWEAR, WHOLESALE: Shoes
FOOTWEAR: Cut Stock
FORGINGS
FORGINGS: Aircraft, Ferrous
FORGINGS: Aluminum
FORGINGS: Gear & Chain
FORGINGS: Machinery, Ferrous
FORGINGS: Nonferrous
FORGINGS: Pump & compressor, Nonferrous
FORMS: Concrete, Sheet Metal
FOUNDRIES: Aluminum
FOUNDRIES: Brass, Bronze & Copper
FOUNDRIES: Gray & Ductile Iron
FOUNDRIES: Iron
FOUNDRIES: Nonferrous

FOUNDRIES: Steel
FOUNDRIES: Steel Investment
FRAMES & FRAMING WHOLESALE
FRANCHISES, SELLING OR LICENSING
FREIGHT CONSOLIDATION SVCS
FREIGHT FORWARDING ARRANGEMENTS
FRICTION MATERIAL, MADE FROM POWDERED METAL
FRUIT & VEGETABLE MARKETS
FUEL ADDITIVES
FUEL BRIQUETTES & WAXES
FUEL BRIQUETTES OR BOULETS, MADE WITH PETROLEUM BINDER
FUEL CELL FORMS: Cardboard, Made From Purchased Materials
FUEL CELLS: Solid State
FUEL DEALERS: Wood
FUEL OIL DEALERS
FUELS: Diesel
FUELS: Ethanol
FUELS: Oil
FUNDRAISING SVCS
FUNERAL HOMES & SVCS
FUNGICIDES OR HERBICIDES
FUR APPAREL STORES
FUR CLOTHING WHOLESALERS
FUR FINISHING & LINING: For The Fur Goods Trade
FUR: Apparel
FUR: Coats
FUR: Coats & Other Apparel
FUR: Hats
FUR: Jackets
FURNACES & OVENS: Indl
FURNACES: Indl, Electric
FURNITURE & CABINET STORES: Cabinets, Custom Work
FURNITURE & CABINET STORES: Custom
FURNITURE & FIXTURES Factory
FURNITURE PARTS: Metal
FURNITURE REFINISHING SVCS
FURNITURE STOCK & PARTS: Carvings, Wood
FURNITURE STOCK & PARTS: Dimension Stock, Hardwood
FURNITURE STOCK & PARTS: Frames, Upholstered Furniture, Wood
FURNITURE STOCK & PARTS: Hardwood
FURNITURE STORES
FURNITURE STORES: Cabinets, Kitchen, Exc Custom Made
FURNITURE STORES: Custom Made, Exc Cabinets
FURNITURE STORES: Juvenile
FURNITURE STORES: Office
FURNITURE STORES: Outdoor & Garden
FURNITURE STORES: Unfinished
FURNITURE WHOLESALERS
FURNITURE, HOUSEHOLD: Wholesalers
FURNITURE, OFFICE: Wholesalers
FURNITURE, WHOLESALE: Beds & Bedding
FURNITURE, WHOLESALE: Racks
FURNITURE, WHOLESALE: Tables, Occasional
FURNITURE: Bed Frames & Headboards, Wood
FURNITURE: Bedroom, Wood
FURNITURE: Beds, Household, Incl Folding & Cabinet, Metal
FURNITURE: Bookcases, Office, Wood
FURNITURE: Box Springs, Assembled
FURNITURE: Cabinets & Filing Drawers, Office, Exc Wood
FURNITURE: Cabinets & Vanities, Medicine, Metal
FURNITURE: Chairs & Couches, Wood, Upholstered
FURNITURE: Chairs, Household Upholstered
FURNITURE: Chairs, Household Wood
FURNITURE: Chairs, Office Exc Wood
FURNITURE: Chairs, Office Wood
FURNITURE: China Closets
FURNITURE: Church
FURNITURE: Console Tables, Wood
FURNITURE: Couches, Sofa/Davenport, Upholstered Wood Frames
FURNITURE: Cribs, Metal
FURNITURE: Cut Stone
FURNITURE: Desks & Tables, Office, Wood
FURNITURE: Desks, Metal
FURNITURE: Desks, Wood
FURNITURE: Dinette Sets, Metal
FURNITURE: Dining Room, Wood
FURNITURE: Fiberglass & Plastic
FURNITURE: Foundations & Platforms
FURNITURE: Game Room
FURNITURE: Game Room, Wood
FURNITURE: Garden, Exc Wood, Metal, Stone Or Concrete

FURNITURE: Hospital
FURNITURE: Hotel
FURNITURE: Household, Metal
FURNITURE: Household, NEC
FURNITURE: Household, Upholstered On Metal Frames
FURNITURE: Household, Upholstered, Exc Wood Or Metal
FURNITURE: Household, Wood
FURNITURE: Hydraulic Barber & Beauty Shop Chairs
FURNITURE: Institutional, Exc Wood
FURNITURE: Juvenile, Wood
FURNITURE: Kitchen & Dining Room
FURNITURE: Kitchen & Dining Room, Metal
FURNITURE: Laboratory
FURNITURE: Living Room, Upholstered On Wood Frames
FURNITURE: Mattresses & Foundations
FURNITURE: Mattresses, Box & Bedsprings
FURNITURE: Mattresses, Innerspring Or Box Spring
FURNITURE: NEC
FURNITURE: Novelty, Wood
FURNITURE: Office Panel Systems, Exc Wood
FURNITURE: Office Panel Systems, Wood
FURNITURE: Office, Exc Wood
FURNITURE: Office, Wood
FURNITURE: Outdoor, Wood
FURNITURE: Pews, Church
FURNITURE: Picnic Tables Or Benches, Park
FURNITURE: Rattan
FURNITURE: Restaurant
FURNITURE: School
FURNITURE: Ship
FURNITURE: Silverware Chests, Wood
FURNITURE: Sleep
FURNITURE: Sofa Beds Or Convertible Sofas)
FURNITURE: Storage Chests, Household, Wood
FURNITURE: Tables & Table Tops, Wood
FURNITURE: Theater
FURNITURE: Unfinished, Wood
FURNITURE: Upholstered
FURNITURE: Vehicle
FURRIERS
FUSES: Electric

G

GAMES & TOYS: Airplanes
GAMES & TOYS: Baby Carriages & Restraint Seats
GAMES & TOYS: Banks
GAMES & TOYS: Child Restraint Seats, Automotive
GAMES & TOYS: Craft & Hobby Kits & Sets
GAMES & TOYS: Doll Hats
GAMES & TOYS: Dolls & Doll Clothing
GAMES & TOYS: Dolls, Exc Stuffed Toy Animals
GAMES & TOYS: Electronic
GAMES & TOYS: Game Machines, Exc Coin-Operated
GAMES & TOYS: Puzzles
GAMES & TOYS: Scooters, Children's
GAMES & TOYS: Trains & Eqpt, Electric & Mechanical
GARBAGE CONTAINERS: Plastic
GARBAGE DISPOSERS & COMPACTORS: Commercial
GARNET MINING SVCS
GAS & OIL FIELD EXPLORATION SVCS
GAS & OIL FIELD SVCS, NEC
GAS STATIONS
GASES & LIQUIFIED PETROLEUM GASES
GASES: Carbon Dioxide
GASES: Flourinated Hydrocarbon
GASES: Indl
GASES: Neon
GASES: Nitrogen
GASES: Oxygen
GASKET MATERIALS
GASKETS
GASKETS & SEALING DEVICES
GASOLINE FILLING STATIONS
GASOLINE WHOLESALERS
GATES: Dam, Metal Plate
GATES: Ornamental Metal
GAUGES
GEARS
GEARS & GEAR UNITS: Reduction, Exc Auto
GEARS: Power Transmission, Exc Auto
GELATIN
GEM STONES MINING, NEC: Natural
GEMSTONE & INDL DIAMOND MINING SVCS
GENERAL & INDUSTRIAL LOAN INSTITUTIONS
GENERAL MERCHANDISE, NONDURABLE, WHOLESALE

GENERATING APPARATUS & PARTS: Electrical
GENERATION EQPT: Electronic
GENERATORS: Electric
GENERATORS: Electrochemical, Fuel Cell
GENERATORS: Gas
GIFT SHOP
GIFT, NOVELTY & SOUVENIR STORES: Artcraft & carvings
GIFT, NOVELTY & SOUVENIR STORES: Gifts & Novelties
GIFTS & NOVELTIES: Wholesalers
GIFTWARE: Brass
GLASS FABRICATORS
GLASS PRDTS, FROM PURCHASED GLASS: Art
GLASS PRDTS, FROM PURCHASED GLASS: Glass Beads, Reflecting
GLASS PRDTS, FROM PURCHASED GLASS: Glassware
GLASS PRDTS, FROM PURCHASED GLASS: Insulating
GLASS PRDTS, FROM PURCHASED GLASS: Mirrored
GLASS PRDTS, FROM PURCHASED GLASS: Mirrors, Framed
GLASS PRDTS, FROM PURCHASED GLASS: Ornaments, Christmas Tree
GLASS PRDTS, FROM PURCHASED GLASS: Sheet, Bent
GLASS PRDTS, FROM PURCHASED GLASS: Watch Crystals
GLASS PRDTS, FROM PURCHASED GLASS: Windshields
GLASS PRDTS, FROM PURCHD GLASS: Strengthened Or Reinforced
GLASS PRDTS, PRESSED OR BLOWN: Bulbs, Electric Lights
GLASS PRDTS, PRESSED OR BLOWN: Glassware, Art Or Decorative
GLASS PRDTS, PRESSED OR BLOWN: Glassware, Novelty
GLASS PRDTS, PRESSED OR BLOWN: Lens Blanks, Optical
GLASS PRDTS, PRESSED OR BLOWN: Lighting Eqpt Parts
GLASS PRDTS, PRESSED OR BLOWN: Optical
GLASS PRDTS, PRESSED OR BLOWN: Ornaments, Christmas Tree
GLASS PRDTS, PRESSED OR BLOWN: Scientific Glassware
GLASS PRDTS, PRESSED/BLOWN: Glassware, Art, Decor/Novelty
GLASS PRDTS, PURCHASED GLASS: Glassware, Scientific/Tech
GLASS PRDTS, PURCHASED GLASS: Insulating, Multiple-Glazed
GLASS PRDTS, PURCHD GLASS: Furniture Top, Cut, Beveld/Polshd
GLASS PRDTS, PURCHSD GLASS: Ornamental, Cut, Engraved/Décor
GLASS STORE: Leaded Or Stained
GLASS STORES
GLASS: Fiber
GLASS: Flat
GLASS: Leaded
GLASS: Pressed & Blown, NEC
GLASS: Safety
GLASS: Stained
GLASS: Structural
GLASS: Tempered
GLASSWARE STORES
GLASSWARE WHOLESALERS
GLASSWARE: Laboratory
GLASSWARE: Laboratory & Medical
GLOBAL POSITIONING SYSTEMS & EQPT
GLOVES: Fabric
GLOVES: Leather
GLOVES: Leather, Dress Or Semidress
GLOVES: Leather, Work
GLOVES: Plastic
GLOVES: Safety
GLOVES: Work
GLOVES: Woven Or Knit, From Purchased Materials
GLUE
GOLD ORE MINING
GOLD ORES
GOLD RECOVERY FROM TAILINGS
GOLD STAMPING, EXC BOOKS
GOLF EQPT
GOURMET FOOD STORES
GOVERNMENT, EXECUTIVE OFFICES: Mayors'
GOVERNMENT, GENERAL: Administration
GRANITE: Crushed & Broken
GRANITE: Cut & Shaped
GRANITE: Dimension
GRANITE: Dimension

GRAPHIC ARTS & RELATED DESIGN SVCS
GRAPHIC LAYOUT SVCS: Printed Circuitry
GRASSES: Artificial & Preserved
GRATINGS: Tread, Fabricated Metal
GRAVE MARKERS: Concrete
GRAVEL MINING
GREASE CUPS: Metal
GREASE TRAPS: Concrete
GREENHOUSES: Prefabricated Metal
GREETING CARDS WHOLESALERS
GRINDING BALLS: Ceramic
GRINDING SVC: Precision, Commercial Or Indl
GRINDS: Electric
GRIT: Steel
GRITS: Crushed & Broken
GROCERIES WHOLESALERS, NEC
GROCERIES, GENERAL LINE WHOLESALERS
GUARDRAILS
GUIDANCE SYSTEMS & EQPT: Space Vehicle
GUIDED MISSILES & SPACE VEHICLES
GUM & WOOD CHEMICALS
GUN STOCKS: Wood
GUNSMITHS
GUTTERS: Sheet Metal
GYPSUM PRDTS

H

HAIR & HAIR BASED PRDTS
HAIR ACCESS WHOLESALERS
HAIR CARE PRDTS
HAIR CARE PRDTS: Hair Coloring Preparations
HAIRPIN MOUNTINGS
HANDBAG STORES
HANDBAGS
HANDBAGS: Women's
HANDCUFFS & LEG IRONS
HANDLES: Brush Or Tool, Plastic
HANDLES: Wood
HANGERS: Garment, Plastic
HANGERS: Garment, Wire
HARDBOARD & FIBERBOARD PRDTS
HARDWARE
HARDWARE & BUILDING PRDTS: Plastic
HARDWARE & EQPT: Stage, Exc Lighting
HARDWARE CLOTH: Woven Wire, Made From Purchased Wire
HARDWARE STORES
HARDWARE STORES: Builders'
HARDWARE STORES: Pumps & Pumping Eqpt
HARDWARE STORES: Tools
HARDWARE WHOLESALERS
HARDWARE, WHOLESALE: Bolts
HARDWARE, WHOLESALE: Builders', NEC
HARDWARE, WHOLESALE: Security Devices, Locks
HARDWARE: Aircraft
HARDWARE: Aircraft & Marine, Incl Pulleys & Similar Items
HARDWARE: Builders'
HARDWARE: Cabinet
HARDWARE: Door Opening & Closing Devices, Exc Electrical
HARDWARE: Furniture
HARDWARE: Furniture, Builders' & Other Household
HARDWARE: Luggage
HARNESS ASSEMBLIES: Cable & Wire
HARNESSES, HALTERS, SADDLERY & STRAPS
HEADPHONES: Radio
HEALTH AIDS: Exercise Eqpt
HEARING AIDS
HEAT EXCHANGERS
HEAT EXCHANGERS: After Or Inter Coolers Or Condensers, Etc
HEAT TREATING: Metal
HEATERS: Space, Exc Electric
HEATERS: Unit, Domestic
HEATING & AIR CONDITIONING EQPT & SPLYS WHOLESALERS
HEATING & AIR CONDITIONING UNITS, COMBINATION
HEATING EQPT & SPLYS
HEATING EQPT: Complete
HEATING EQPT: Induction
HEATING SYSTEMS: Radiant, Indl Process
HEATING UNITS & DEVICES: Indl, Electric
HELICOPTERS
HELMETS: Athletic
HIGH ENERGY PARTICLE PHYSICS EQPT
HIGHWAY SIGNALS: Electric

HOBBY & CRAFT SPLY STORES
HOBBY, TOY & GAME STORES: Ceramics Splys
HOBBY, TOY & GAME STORES: Toys & Games
HOISTS
HOLDING COMPANIES: Banks
HOLDING COMPANIES: Investment, Exc Banks
HOLDING COMPANIES: Personal, Exc Banks
HOME DELIVERY NEWSPAPER ROUTES
HOME ENTERTAINMENT EQPT: Electronic, NEC
HOME FURNISHINGS WHOLESALERS
HOME HEALTH CARE SVCS
HOMEBUILDERS & OTHER OPERATIVE BUILDERS
HOMEFURNISHING STORES: Beddings & Linens
HOMEFURNISHING STORES: Lighting Fixtures
HOMEFURNISHING STORES: Mirrors
HOMEFURNISHING STORES: Towels
HOMEFURNISHING STORES: Vertical Blinds
HOMEFURNISHING STORES: Wicker, Rattan, Or Reed
HOMEFURNISHING STORES: Window Furnishings
HOMEFURNISHINGS & SPLYS, WHOLESALE: Decorative
HOMEFURNISHINGS, WHOLESALE: Bedspreads
HOMEFURNISHINGS, WHOLESALE: Blinds, Venetian
HOMEFURNISHINGS, WHOLESALE: Blinds, Vertical
HOMEFURNISHINGS, WHOLESALE: Carpets
HOMEFURNISHINGS, WHOLESALE: Curtains
HOMEFURNISHINGS, WHOLESALE: Draperies
HOMEFURNISHINGS, WHOLESALE: Fireplace Eqpt & Access
HOMEFURNISHINGS, WHOLESALE: Kitchenware
HOMEFURNISHINGS, WHOLESALE: Linens, Table
HOMEFURNISHINGS, WHOLESALE: Pillowcases
HOMEFURNISHINGS, WHOLESALE: Rugs
HOMEFURNISHINGS, WHOLESALE: Stainless Steel Flatware
HOMEFURNISHINGS, WHOLESALE: Window Covering Parts & Access
HOMEFURNISHINGS, WHOLESALE: Wood Flooring
HOMES, MODULAR: Wooden
HOMES: Log Cabins
HONES
HORMONE PREPARATIONS
HORSE & PET ACCESSORIES: Textile
HORSE ACCESS: Harnesses & Riding Crops, Etc, Exc Leather
HOSE: Automobile, Plastic
HOSE: Fire, Rubber
HOSE: Flexible Metal
HOSE: Plastic
HOSE: Pneumatic, Rubber Or Rubberized Fabric, NEC
HOSE: Rubber
HOSE: Vacuum Cleaner, Rubber
HOSES & BELTING: Rubber & Plastic
HOSIERY KITS: Sewing & Mending
HOSPITALS: Cancer
HOSPITALS: Medical & Surgical
HOT TUBS
HOT TUBS: Plastic & Fiberglass
HOUSEHOLD APPLIANCE STORES: Air Cond Rm Units, Self-Contnd
HOUSEHOLD APPLIANCE STORES: Fans, Electric
HOUSEHOLD ARTICLES: Metal
HOUSEHOLD FURNISHINGS, NEC
HOUSEWARE STORES
HOUSEWARES, ELECTRIC, EXC COOKING APPLIANCES & UTENSILS
HOUSEWARES, ELECTRIC: Cooking Appliances
HOUSEWARES, ELECTRIC: Extractors, Juice
HOUSEWARES, ELECTRIC: Fryers
HOUSEWARES, ELECTRIC: Heaters, Space
HOUSEWARES, ELECTRIC: Heating, Bsbrd/Wall, Radiant Heat
HOUSEWARES, ELECTRIC: Humidifiers, Household
HOUSEWARES, ELECTRIC: Massage Machines, Exc Beauty/Barber
HOUSEWARES: Dishes, China
HOUSEWARES: Dishes, Earthenware
HOUSEWARES: Dishes, Plastic
HOUSEWARES: Kettles & Skillets, Cast Iron
HUMIDIFIERS & DEHUMIDIFIERS
HYDRAULIC EQPT REPAIR SVC
Hard Rubber & Molded Rubber Prdts

I

ICE
ICE CREAM & ICES WHOLESALERS

INDEX

IDENTIFICATION TAGS, EXC PAPER
IGNEOUS ROCK: Crushed & Broken
IGNITION APPARATUS & DISTRIBUTORS
IGNITION SYSTEMS: High Frequency
IGNITION SYSTEMS: Internal Combustion Engine
INCINERATORS
INDICATORS: Cabin Environment
INDL & PERSONAL SVC PAPER WHOLESALERS
INDL & PERSONAL SVC PAPER, WHOL: Bags, Paper/Disp Plastic
INDL & PERSONAL SVC PAPER, WHOL: Boxes, Corrugtd/Solid Fiber
INDL & PERSONAL SVC PAPER, WHOL: Container, Paper/Plastic
INDL & PERSONAL SVC PAPER, WHOL: Cups, Disp, Plastic/Paper
INDL & PERSONAL SVC PAPER, WHOLESALE: Paperboard & Prdts
INDL & PERSONAL SVC PAPER, WHOLESALE: Press Sensitive Tape
INDL & PERSONAL SVC PAPER, WHOLESALE: Sanitary Food
INDL EQPT SVCS
INDL GASES WHOLESALERS
INDL MACHINERY & EQPT WHOLESALERS
INDL MACHINERY REPAIR & MAINTENANCE
INDL PATTERNS: Foundry Patternmaking
INDL PROCESS INSTRUMENT: Potentiomtrc Self-Bal, Exc XY Plot
INDL PROCESS INSTRUMENTS: Analyzers
INDL PROCESS INSTRUMENTS: Control
INDL PROCESS INSTRUMENTS: Controllers, Process Variables
INDL PROCESS INSTRUMENTS: Digital Display, Process Variables
INDL PROCESS INSTRUMENTS: Elements, Primary
INDL PROCESS INSTRUMENTS: Fluidic Devices, Circuit & Systems
INDL PROCESS INSTRUMENTS: Indl Flow & Measuring
INDL PROCESS INSTRUMENTS: Level & Bulk Measuring
INDL PROCESS INSTRUMENTS: On-Stream Gas Or Liquid Analysis
INDL PROCESS INSTRUMENTS: Temperature
INDL PROCESS INSTRUMENTS: Water Quality Monitoring/Cntrl Sys
INDL SALTS WHOLESALERS
INDL SPLYS WHOLESALERS
INDL SPLYS, WHOL: Fasteners, Incl Nuts, Bolts, Screws, Etc
INDL SPLYS, WHOLESALE: Abrasives
INDL SPLYS, WHOLESALE: Adhesives, Tape & Plasters
INDL SPLYS, WHOLESALE: Bearings
INDL SPLYS, WHOLESALE: Bins & Containers, Storage
INDL SPLYS, WHOLESALE: Brushes, Indl
INDL SPLYS, WHOLESALE: Clean Room Splys
INDL SPLYS, WHOLESALE: Fasteners & Fastening Eqpt
INDL SPLYS, WHOLESALE: Gears
INDL SPLYS, WHOLESALE: Knives, Indl
INDL SPLYS, WHOLESALE: Mill Splys
INDL SPLYS, WHOLESALE: Rubber Goods, Mechanical
INDL SPLYS, WHOLESALE: Seals
INDL SPLYS, WHOLESALE: Sewing Thread
INDL SPLYS, WHOLESALE: Tools
INDL SPLYS, WHOLESALE: Valves & Fittings
INDUCTORS
INFORMATION RETRIEVAL SERVICES
INFRARED OBJECT DETECTION EQPT
INGOT: Aluminum
INK OR WRITING FLUIDS
INK: Letterpress Or Offset
INK: Printing
INK: Screen process
INSECTICIDES
INSECTICIDES & PESTICIDES
INSPECTION & TESTING SVCS
INSTR, MEASURE & CONTROL: Gauge, Oil Pressure & Water Temp
INSTRUMENTS & METERS: Measuring, Electric
INSTRUMENTS, LABORATORY: Differential Thermal Analysis
INSTRUMENTS, LABORATORY: Magnetic/Elec Properties Measuring
INSTRUMENTS, LABORATORY: Mass Spectrometers
INSTRUMENTS, LABORATORY: Protein Analyzers
INSTRUMENTS, LABORATORY: Spectrometers
INSTRUMENTS, MEASURING & CNTRL: Radiation & Testing, Nuclear

INSTRUMENTS, MEASURING & CNTRL: Testing, Abrasion, Etc
INSTRUMENTS, MEASURING & CNTRLG: Aircraft & Motor Vehicle
INSTRUMENTS, MEASURING & CNTRLG: Stress, Strain & Measure
INSTRUMENTS, MEASURING & CNTRLG: Tensile Strength Testing
INSTRUMENTS, MEASURING & CNTRLG: Thermometers/Temp Sensors
INSTRUMENTS, MEASURING & CONTROLLING: Gas Detectors
INSTRUMENTS, MEASURING & CONTROLLING: Magnetometers
INSTRUMENTS, MEASURING & CONTROLLING: Photogrammetrical
INSTRUMENTS, MEASURING & CONTROLLING: Toll Booths, Automatic
INSTRUMENTS, MEASURING & CONTROLLING: Ultrasonic Testing
INSTRUMENTS, MEASURING/CNTRL: Hydrometers, Exc Indl Process
INSTRUMENTS, MEASURING/CNTRLG: Fare Registers, St Cars/Buses
INSTRUMENTS, MEASURING/CNTRLNG: Med Diagnostic Sys, Nuclear
INSTRUMENTS, OPTICAL: Borescopes
INSTRUMENTS, OPTICAL: Elements & Assemblies, Exc Ophthalmic
INSTRUMENTS, OPTICAL: Gratings, Diffraction
INSTRUMENTS, OPTICAL: Grinding, Lens Exc Ophthalmic
INSTRUMENTS, OPTICAL: Lenses, All Types Exc Ophthalmic
INSTRUMENTS, OPTICAL: Mirrors
INSTRUMENTS, OPTICAL: Prisms
INSTRUMENTS, OPTICAL: Spyglasses
INSTRUMENTS, OPTICAL: Test & Inspection
INSTRUMENTS, SURGICAL & MEDICAL: Blood & Bone Work
INSTRUMENTS, SURGICAL & MEDICAL: Blood Pressure
INSTRUMENTS, SURGICAL & MEDICAL: Catheters
INSTRUMENTS, SURGICAL & MEDICAL: IV Transfusion
INSTRUMENTS, SURGICAL & MEDICAL: Inhalation Therapy
INSTRUMENTS, SURGICAL & MEDICAL: Inhalators
INSTRUMENTS, SURGICAL & MEDICAL: Knives
INSTRUMENTS, SURGICAL & MEDICAL: Lasers, Surgical
INSTRUMENTS, SURGICAL & MEDICAL: Muscle Exercise, Ophthalmic
INSTRUMENTS, SURGICAL & MEDICAL: Ophthalmic
INSTRUMENTS, SURGICAL & MEDICAL: Physiotherapy, Electrical
INSTRUMENTS, SURGICAL & MEDICAL: Skin Grafting
INSTRUMENTS, SURGICAL & MEDICAL: Suction Therapy
INSTRUMENTS: Analytical
INSTRUMENTS: Colonoscopes, Electromedical
INSTRUMENTS: Combustion Control, Indl
INSTRUMENTS: Electrocardiographs
INSTRUMENTS: Electrolytic Conductivity, Indl
INSTRUMENTS: Endoscopic Eqpt, Electromedical
INSTRUMENTS: Flow, Indl Process
INSTRUMENTS: Function Generators
INSTRUMENTS: Generators Tachometer
INSTRUMENTS: Indl Process Control
INSTRUMENTS: Laser, Scientific & Engineering
INSTRUMENTS: Measurement, Indl Process
INSTRUMENTS: Measuring & Controlling
INSTRUMENTS: Measuring Electricity
INSTRUMENTS: Measuring, Electrical Energy
INSTRUMENTS: Measuring, Electrical Power
INSTRUMENTS: Medical & Surgical
INSTRUMENTS: Meteorological
INSTRUMENTS: Microwave Test
INSTRUMENTS: Optical, Analytical
INSTRUMENTS: Oscillographs & Oscilloscopes
INSTRUMENTS: Pressure Measurement, Indl
INSTRUMENTS: Radar Testing, Electric
INSTRUMENTS: Radio Frequency Measuring
INSTRUMENTS: Standards & Calibration, Electrical Measuring
INSTRUMENTS: Telemetering, Indl Process
INSTRUMENTS: Temperature Measurement, Indl
INSTRUMENTS: Test, Electronic & Electric Measurement
INSTRUMENTS: Test, Electronic & Electrical Circuits
INSTRUMENTS: Testing, Semiconductor
INSTRUMENTS: Thermal Conductive, Indl
INSTRUMENTS: Vibration

INSTRUMENTS: Viscometer, Indl Process
INSULATION & CUSHIONING FOAM: Polystyrene
INSULATION MATERIALS WHOLESALERS
INSULATION: Felt
INSULATION: Fiberglass
INSULATORS & INSULATION MATERIALS: Electrical
INSULATORS, PORCELAIN: Electrical
INTEGRATED CIRCUITS, SEMICONDUCTOR NETWORKS, ETC
INTERCOMMUNICATIONS SYSTEMS: Electric
INTERIOR DECORATING SVCS
INTERIOR DESIGNING SVCS
INTERIOR REPAIR SVCS
INTRAVENOUS SOLUTIONS
INVERTERS: Nonrotating Electrical
INVERTERS: Rotating Electrical
INVESTMENT ADVISORY SVCS
INVESTMENT FUNDS: Open-Ended
INVESTORS: Security Speculators For Own Account
IRON & STEEL PRDTS: Hot-Rolled
IRON & STEEL: Corrugating, Cold-Rolled
IRON ORE MINING
IRON OXIDES
IRONING BOARDS
IRRADIATION EQPT: Nuclear
IRRIGATION SYSTEMS, NEC Water Distribution Or Sply Systems

J

JANITORIAL & CUSTODIAL SVCS
JANITORIAL EQPT & SPLYS WHOLESALERS
JEWELERS' FINDINGS & MATERIALS
JEWELERS' FINDINGS & MATERIALS: Castings
JEWELERS' FINDINGS & MATERIALS: Parts, Unassembled
JEWELERS' FINDINGS & MTLS: Jewel Prep, Instr, Tools, Watches
JEWELERS' FINDINGS/MTRLS: Gem Prep, Settings, Real/Imitation
JEWELRY & PRECIOUS STONES WHOLESALERS
JEWELRY APPAREL
JEWELRY FINDINGS & LAPIDARY WORK
JEWELRY FINDINGS WHOLESALERS
JEWELRY REPAIR SVCS
JEWELRY STORES
JEWELRY STORES: Precious Stones & Precious Metals
JEWELRY STORES: Silverware
JEWELRY STORES: Watches
JEWELRY, PREC METAL: Mountings, Pens, Lthr, Etc, Gold/Silver
JEWELRY, PRECIOUS METAL: Bracelets
JEWELRY, PRECIOUS METAL: Cases
JEWELRY, PRECIOUS METAL: Cigar & Cigarette Access
JEWELRY, PRECIOUS METAL: Earrings
JEWELRY, PRECIOUS METAL: Medals, Precious Or Semiprecious
JEWELRY, PRECIOUS METAL: Mountings & Trimmings
JEWELRY, PRECIOUS METAL: Necklaces
JEWELRY, PRECIOUS METAL: Pearl, Natural Or Cultured
JEWELRY, PRECIOUS METAL: Pins
JEWELRY, PRECIOUS METAL: Rings, Finger
JEWELRY, PRECIOUS METAL: Rosaries/Other Sm Religious Article
JEWELRY, PRECIOUS METAL: Settings & Mountings
JEWELRY, PRECIOUS METAL: Trimmings, Canes, Umbrellas, Etc
JEWELRY, WHOLESALE
JEWELRY: Decorative, Fashion & Costume
JEWELRY: Precious Metal
JIGS & FIXTURES
JOB PRINTING & NEWSPAPER PUBLISHING COMBINED
JOB TRAINING & VOCATIONAL REHABILITATION SVCS
JOINTS: Ball Except aircraft & Auto
JOINTS: Expansion
JOINTS: Expansion, Pipe

K

KEYS, KEY BLANKS
KITCHEN CABINET STORES, EXC CUSTOM
KITCHEN CABINETS WHOLESALERS
KITCHEN TOOLS & UTENSILS WHOLESALERS
KITCHEN UTENSILS: Bakers' Eqpt, Wood
KITCHEN UTENSILS: Food Handling & Processing Prdts, Wood
KITCHEN UTENSILS: Wooden
KITCHENWARE STORES

KITCHENWARE: Plastic
KNIT GOODS, WHOLESALE
KNIVES: Agricultural Or indl

L

LABELS: Paper, Made From Purchased Materials
LABELS: Woven
LABORATORIES, TESTING: Forensic
LABORATORIES, TESTING: Product Testing, Safety/Performance
LABORATORIES: Biological Research
LABORATORIES: Biotechnology
LABORATORIES: Commercial Nonphysical Research
LABORATORIES: Dental
LABORATORIES: Dental Orthodontic Appliance Production
LABORATORIES: Electronic Research
LABORATORIES: Medical
LABORATORIES: Noncommercial Research
LABORATORIES: Physical Research, Commercial
LABORATORIES: Testing
LABORATORIES: Testing
LABORATORY APPARATUS & FURNITURE
LABORATORY APPARATUS: Furnaces
LABORATORY APPARATUS: Pipettes, Hemocytometer
LABORATORY APPARATUS: Shakers & Stirrers
LABORATORY EQPT, EXC MEDICAL: Wholesalers
LABORATORY EQPT: Chemical
LABORATORY EQPT: Clinical Instruments Exc Medical
LABORATORY EQPT: Measuring
LABORATORY EQPT: Sterilizers
LACE GOODS & WARP KNIT FABRIC DYEING & FINISHING
LADDERS: Metal
LADDERS: Portable, Metal
LADDERS: Wood
LAMINATED PLASTICS: Plate, Sheet, Rod & Tubes
LAMINATING SVCS
LAMP & LIGHT BULBS & TUBES
LAMP BULBS & TUBES, ELECTRIC: For Specialized Applications
LAMP BULBS & TUBES, ELECTRIC: Light, Complete
LAMP BULBS & TUBES/PARTS, ELECTRIC: Generalized Applications
LAMP FRAMES: Wire
LAMP SHADES: Glass
LAMP SHADES: Metal
LAMP STORES
LAMPS: Arc Units, Electrotherapeutic
LAMPS: Floor, Residential
LAMPS: Fluorescent
LAMPS: Table, Residential
LAMPS: Ultraviolet
LAND SUBDIVIDERS & DEVELOPERS: Commercial
LANGUAGE SCHOOLS
LANTERNS
LAPIDARY WORK & DIAMOND CUTTING & POLISHING
LAPIDARY WORK: Contract Or Other
LAPIDARY WORK: Jewel Cut, Drill, Polish, Recut/Setting
LARD: From Slaughtering Plants
LASER SYSTEMS & EQPT
LASERS: Welding, Drilling & Cutting Eqpt
LAUNDRY & GARMENT SVCS, NEC: Fur Cleaning, Repairing/Storage
LAUNDRY & GARMENT SVCS, NEC: Garment Alteration & Repair
LAUNDRY EQPT: Commercial
LAUNDRY EQPT: Household
LAUNDRY SVC: Wiping Towel Sply
LAWN & GARDEN EQPT
LAWN & GARDEN EQPT STORES
LAWN & GARDEN EQPT: Tractors & Eqpt
LAWN & GARDEN EQPT: Trimmers
LAWN MOWER REPAIR SHOP
LEAD & ZINC
LEAD PENCILS & ART GOODS
LEASING & RENTAL SVCS: Cranes & Aerial Lift Eqpt
LEASING & RENTAL SVCS: Earth Moving Eqpt
LEASING & RENTAL: Computers & Eqpt
LEASING & RENTAL: Construction & Mining Eqpt
LEASING & RENTAL: Other Real Estate Property
LEASING: Laundry Eqpt
LEASING: Shipping Container
LEATHER GOODS, EXC FOOTWEAR, GLOVES, LUGGAGE/BELTING, WHOL
LEATHER GOODS: Belt Laces
LEATHER GOODS: Belting & Strapping

LEATHER GOODS: Boxes
LEATHER GOODS: Cases
LEATHER GOODS: Corners, Luggage
LEATHER GOODS: Cosmetic Bags
LEATHER GOODS: Desk Sets
LEATHER GOODS: Garments
LEATHER GOODS: Holsters
LEATHER GOODS: Key Cases
LEATHER GOODS: NEC
LEATHER GOODS: Personal
LEATHER GOODS: Wallets
LEATHER TANNING & FINISHING
LEATHER, LEATHER GOODS & FURS, WHOLESALE
LEATHER: Accessory Prdts
LEATHER: Artificial
LEATHER: Bag
LEATHER: Bookbinders'
LEATHER: Case
LEATHER: Colored
LEATHER: Cut
LEATHER: Die-cut
LEATHER: Embossed
LEATHER: Finished
LEATHER: Glove
LEATHER: Handbag
LEATHER: Indl Prdts
LEATHER: Processed
LEATHER: Upholstery
LEGAL & TAX SVCS
LEGAL OFFICES & SVCS
LEGITIMATE LIVE THEATER PRODUCERS
LENS COATING: Ophthalmic
LENSES: Plastic, Exc Optical
LESSORS: Landholding Office
LIFESAVING & SURVIVAL EQPT, EXC MEDICAL, WHOLESALE
LIGHT SENSITIVE DEVICES
LIGHTING EQPT: Flashlights
LIGHTING EQPT: Motor Vehicle, Headlights
LIGHTING EQPT: Motor Vehicle, NEC
LIGHTING EQPT: Outdoor
LIGHTING EQPT: Reflectors, Metal, For Lighting Eqpt
LIGHTING EQPT: Streetcar Fixtures
LIGHTING EQPT: Strobe Lighting Systems
LIGHTING FIXTURES WHOLESALERS
LIGHTING FIXTURES, NEC
LIGHTING FIXTURES: Airport
LIGHTING FIXTURES: Decorative Area
LIGHTING FIXTURES: Fluorescent, Commercial
LIGHTING FIXTURES: Fluorescent, Residential
LIGHTING FIXTURES: Indl & Commercial
LIGHTING FIXTURES: Motor Vehicle
LIGHTING FIXTURES: Ornamental, Commercial
LIGHTING FIXTURES: Public
LIGHTING FIXTURES: Residential
LIGHTING FIXTURES: Residential, Electric
LIGHTING FIXTURES: Street
LIGHTS: Trouble lights
LIME
LIME: Agricultural
LIMESTONE & MARBLE: Dimension
LIMESTONE: Crushed & Broken
LIMESTONE: Cut & Shaped
LIMESTONE: Dimension
LIMESTONE: Ground
LINEN SPLY SVC: Apron
LINEN SPLY SVC: Coat
LINENS & TOWELS WHOLESALERS
LINENS: Napkins, Fabric & Nonwoven, From Purchased Materials
LINENS: Tablecloths, From Purchased Materials
LINERS & COVERS: Fabric
LINERS & LINING
LINERS: Indl, Metal Plate
LINGERIE WHOLESALERS
LINIMENTS
LININGS: Apparel, Made From Purchased Materials
LININGS: Fabric, Apparel & Other, Exc Millinery
LIP BALMS
LIPSTICK
LIQUEFIED PETROLEUM GAS DEALERS
LIQUID CRYSTAL DISPLAYS
LOCK & KEY SVCS
LOCKERS
LOCKERS: Refrigerated

LOCKS
LOCKS: Coin-Operated
LOCKS: Safe & Vault, Metal
LOCKSMITHS
LOCOMOTIVES & PARTS
LOG LOADING & UNLOADING SVCS
LOGGING
LOGGING CAMPS & CONTRACTORS
LOGGING: Timber, Cut At Logging Camp
LOGGING: Wood Chips, Produced In The Field
LOGGING: Wooden Logs
LOOSELEAF BINDERS
LOTIONS OR CREAMS: Face
LOTIONS: SHAVING
LOUDSPEAKERS
LOUVERS: Ventilating
LUBRICANTS: Corrosion Preventive
LUBRICATING EQPT: Indl
LUBRICATING OIL & GREASE WHOLESALERS
LUBRICATION SYSTEMS & EQPT
LUGGAGE & BRIEFCASES
LUGGAGE & LEATHER GOODS STORES: Leather, Exc Luggage & Shoes
LUGGAGE WHOLESALERS
LUGGAGE: Traveling Bags
LUGGAGE: Wardrobe Bags
LUMBER & BLDG MATLS DEALER, RET: Garage Doors, Sell/Install
LUMBER & BLDG MATRLS DEALERS, RET: Bath Fixtures, Eqpt/Sply
LUMBER & BLDG MTRLS DEALERS, RET: Windows, Storm, Wood/Metal
LUMBER & BUILDING MATERIAL DEALERS, RETAIL: Roofing Material
LUMBER & BUILDING MATERIALS DEALER, RET: Door & Window Prdts
LUMBER & BUILDING MATERIALS DEALER, RET: Masonry Matls/Splys
LUMBER & BUILDING MATERIALS DEALERS, RETAIL: Brick
LUMBER & BUILDING MATERIALS DEALERS, RETAIL: Countertops
LUMBER & BUILDING MATERIALS DEALERS, RETAIL: Paving Stones
LUMBER & BUILDING MATERIALS DEALERS, RETAIL: Sand & Gravel
LUMBER & BUILDING MATERIALS DEALERS, RETAIL: Tile, Ceramic
LUMBER & BUILDING MATERIALS RET DEALERS: Millwork & Lumber
LUMBER & BUILDING MATLS DEALERS, RET: Concrete/Cinder Block
LUMBER: Dimension, Hardwood
LUMBER: Fiberboard
LUMBER: Fuelwood, From Mill Waste
LUMBER: Furniture Dimension Stock, Softwood
LUMBER: Hardwood Dimension
LUMBER: Hardwood Dimension & Flooring Mills
LUMBER: Kiln Dried
LUMBER: Plywood, Hardwood
LUMBER: Plywood, Hardwood or Hardwood Faced
LUMBER: Plywood, Prefinished, Hardwood
LUMBER: Plywood, Softwood
LUMBER: Poles, Wood, Untreated
LUMBER: Siding, Dressed
LUMBER: Silo Stock, Sawn
LUMBER: Treated
LUNCHROOMS & CAFETERIAS

M

MACHINE PARTS: Stamped Or Pressed Metal
MACHINE SHOPS
MACHINE TOOL ACCESS: Balancing Machines
MACHINE TOOL ACCESS: Cams
MACHINE TOOL ACCESS: Cutting
MACHINE TOOL ACCESS: Diamond Cutting, For Turning, Etc
MACHINE TOOL ACCESS: Dies, Thread Cutting
MACHINE TOOL ACCESS: Dressing/Wheel Crushing Attach, Diamond
MACHINE TOOL ACCESS: Drills
MACHINE TOOL ACCESS: Knives, Shear
MACHINE TOOL ACCESS: Sockets
MACHINE TOOL ACCESS: Tool Holders
MACHINE TOOL ACCESS: Tools & Access
MACHINE TOOL ATTACHMENTS & ACCESS
MACHINE TOOLS & ACCESS

INDEX

MACHINE TOOLS, METAL CUTTING: Centering
MACHINE TOOLS, METAL CUTTING: Exotic, Including Explosive
MACHINE TOOLS, METAL CUTTING: Grind, Polish, Buff, Lapp
MACHINE TOOLS, METAL CUTTING: Lathes
MACHINE TOOLS, METAL CUTTING: Numerically Controlled
MACHINE TOOLS, METAL CUTTING: Tool Replacement & Rpr Parts
MACHINE TOOLS, METAL FORMING: Die Casting & Extruding
MACHINE TOOLS, METAL FORMING: Electroforming
MACHINE TOOLS, METAL FORMING: Forging Machinery & Hammers
MACHINE TOOLS, METAL FORMING: Headers
MACHINE TOOLS, METAL FORMING: High Energy Rate
MACHINE TOOLS, METAL FORMING: Presses, Hyd & Pneumatic
MACHINE TOOLS, METAL FORMING: Pressing
MACHINE TOOLS, METAL FORMING: Punching & Shearing
MACHINE TOOLS, METAL FORMING: Rebuilt
MACHINE TOOLS, METAL FORMING: Spinning, Spline Rollg/Windg
MACHINE TOOLS: Metal Cutting
MACHINE TOOLS: Metal Forming
MACHINERY & EQPT, AGRICULTURAL, WHOLESALE: Dairy
MACHINERY & EQPT, AGRICULTURAL, WHOLESALE: Landscaping Eqpt
MACHINERY & EQPT, AGRICULTURAL, WHOLESALE: Lawn & Garden
MACHINERY & EQPT, INDL, WHOL: Controlling Instruments/Access
MACHINERY & EQPT, INDL, WHOL: Recording Instruments/Access
MACHINERY & EQPT, INDL, WHOLESALE: Conveyor Systems
MACHINERY & EQPT, INDL, WHOLESALE: Countersinks
MACHINERY & EQPT, INDL, WHOLESALE: Fans
MACHINERY & EQPT, INDL, WHOLESALE: Food Manufacturing
MACHINERY & EQPT, INDL, WHOLESALE: Food Product Manufacturng
MACHINERY & EQPT, INDL, WHOLESALE: Heat Exchange
MACHINERY & EQPT, INDL, WHOLESALE: Hydraulic Systems
MACHINERY & EQPT, INDL, WHOLESALE: Indl Machine Parts
MACHINERY & EQPT, INDL, WHOLESALE: Instruments & Cntrl Eqpt
MACHINERY & EQPT, INDL, WHOLESALE: Machine Tools & Access
MACHINERY & EQPT, INDL, WHOLESALE: Measure/Test, Electric
MACHINERY & EQPT, INDL, WHOLESALE: Packaging
MACHINERY & EQPT, INDL, WHOLESALE: Pneumatic Tools
MACHINERY & EQPT, INDL, WHOLESALE: Power Plant Machinery
MACHINERY & EQPT, INDL, WHOLESALE: Processing & Packaging
MACHINERY & EQPT, INDL, WHOLESALE: Robots
MACHINERY & EQPT, INDL, WHOLESALE: Safety Eqpt
MACHINERY & EQPT, INDL, WHOLESALE: Textile
MACHINERY & EQPT, INDL, WHOLESALE: Tire Recapping Machinery
MACHINERY & EQPT, INDL, WHOLESALE: Water Pumps
MACHINERY & EQPT, INDL, WHOLESALE: Woodworking
MACHINERY & EQPT, WHOLESALE: Construction, General
MACHINERY & EQPT, WHOLESALE: Crushing, Pulverizng & Screeng
MACHINERY & EQPT, WHOLESALE: Masonry
MACHINERY & EQPT, WHOLESALE: Road Construction & Maintenance
MACHINERY & EQPT: Electroplating
MACHINERY & EQPT: Farm
MACHINERY & EQPT: Gas Producers, Generators/Other Rltd Eqpt
MACHINERY & EQPT: Liquid Automation
MACHINERY & EQPT: Metal Finishing, Plating Etc
MACHINERY BASES
MACHINERY, COMMERCIAL LAUNDRY: Dryers, Incl Coin-Operated
MACHINERY, COMMERCIAL LAUNDRY: Washing, Incl Coin-Operated
MACHINERY, EQPT & SUPPLIES: Parking Facility
MACHINERY, FLOOR SANDING: Commercial

MACHINERY, FOOD PRDTS: Beverage
MACHINERY, FOOD PRDTS: Choppers, Commercial
MACHINERY, FOOD PRDTS: Confectionery
MACHINERY, FOOD PRDTS: Cutting, Chopping, Grinding, Mixing
MACHINERY, FOOD PRDTS: Dairy & Milk
MACHINERY, FOOD PRDTS: Dairy, Pasteurizing
MACHINERY, FOOD PRDTS: Food Processing, Smokers
MACHINERY, FOOD PRDTS: Juice Extractors, Fruit & Veg, Comm
MACHINERY, FOOD PRDTS: Milk Processing, NEC
MACHINERY, FOOD PRDTS: Mixers, Commercial
MACHINERY, FOOD PRDTS: Oilseed Crushing & Extracting
MACHINERY, FOOD PRDTS: Ovens, Bakery
MACHINERY, FOOD PRDTS: Packing House
MACHINERY, FOOD PRDTS: Presses, Cheese, Beet, Cider & Sugar
MACHINERY, FOOD PRDTS: Roasting, Coffee, Peanut, Etc.
MACHINERY, MAILING: Canceling
MACHINERY, MAILING: Postage Meters
MACHINERY, METALWORKING: Assembly, Including Robotic
MACHINERY, METALWORKING: Cutting & Slitting
MACHINERY, OFFICE: Perforators
MACHINERY, OFFICE: Stapling, Hand Or Power
MACHINERY, OFFICE: Time Clocks &Time Recording Devices
MACHINERY, PACKAGING: Canning, Food
MACHINERY, PACKAGING: Carton Packing
MACHINERY, PACKAGING: Packing & Wrapping
MACHINERY, PAPER INDUSTRY: Converting, Die Cutting & Stampng
MACHINERY, PAPER INDUSTRY: Paper Mill, Plating, Etc
MACHINERY, PRINTING TRADES: Copy Holders
MACHINERY, PRINTING TRADES: Plates
MACHINERY, PRINTING TRADES: Plates, Offset
MACHINERY, PRINTING TRADES: Presses, Envelope
MACHINERY, PRINTING TRADES: Printing Trade Parts & Attchts
MACHINERY, PRINTING TRADES: Sticks
MACHINERY, SEWING: Sewing & Hat & Zipper Making
MACHINERY, TEXTILE: Card Cutting, Jacquard
MACHINERY, TEXTILE: Embroidery
MACHINERY, TEXTILE: Silk Screens
MACHINERY, TEXTILE: Thread Making Or Spinning
MACHINERY, WOODWORKING: Bandsaws
MACHINERY, WOODWORKING: Cabinet Makers'
MACHINERY, WOODWORKING: Furniture Makers
MACHINERY, WOODWORKING: Lathes, Wood Turning Includes Access
MACHINERY, WOODWORKING: Pattern Makers'
MACHINERY, WOODWORKING: Sanding, Exc Portable Floor Sanders
MACHINERY: Ammunition & Explosives Loading
MACHINERY: Assembly, Exc Metalworking
MACHINERY: Automotive Maintenance
MACHINERY: Automotive Related
MACHINERY: Billing
MACHINERY: Brewery & Malting
MACHINERY: Bridge Or Gate, Hydraulic
MACHINERY: Concrete Prdts
MACHINERY: Construction
MACHINERY: Cryogenic, Industrial
MACHINERY: Custom
MACHINERY: Drill Presses
MACHINERY: Electronic Component Making
MACHINERY: Engraving
MACHINERY: Extruding
MACHINERY: Gear Cutting & Finishing
MACHINERY: General, Industrial, NEC
MACHINERY: Glassmaking
MACHINERY: Grinding
MACHINERY: Ice Cream
MACHINERY: Ice Crushers
MACHINERY: Ice Making
MACHINERY: Industrial, NEC
MACHINERY: Jewelers
MACHINERY: Marking, Metalworking
MACHINERY: Metalworking
MACHINERY: Milling
MACHINERY: Mining
MACHINERY: Optical Lens
MACHINERY: Ozone
MACHINERY: Packaging
MACHINERY: Paper Industry Miscellaneous
MACHINERY: Pharmaciutical

MACHINERY: Photographic Reproduction
MACHINERY: Plastic Working
MACHINERY: Printing Presses
MACHINERY: Recycling
MACHINERY: Riveting
MACHINERY: Road Construction & Maintenance
MACHINERY: Rubber Working
MACHINERY: Screening Eqpt, Electric
MACHINERY: Semiconductor Manufacturing
MACHINERY: Separation Eqpt, Magnetic
MACHINERY: Sheet Metal Working
MACHINERY: Specialty
MACHINERY: Textile
MACHINERY: Tire Shredding
MACHINERY: Wire Drawing
MACHINERY: Woodworking
MACHINES: Forming, Sheet Metal
MACHINISTS' TOOLS: Measuring, Precision
MACHINISTS' TOOLS: Precision
MAGAZINES, WHOLESALE
MAGNETIC INK & OPTICAL SCANNING EQPT
MAGNETIC RESONANCE IMAGING DEVICES: Nonmedical
MAGNETIC TAPE, AUDIO: Prerecorded
MAGNETOHYDRODYNAMIC DEVICES OR MHD
MAGNETS: Ceramic
MAGNETS: Permanent
MAIL-ORDER BOOK CLUBS
MAIL-ORDER HOUSE, NEC
MAIL-ORDER HOUSES: Book & Record Clubs
MAIL-ORDER HOUSES: Books, Exc Book Clubs
MAIL-ORDER HOUSES: Cards
MAIL-ORDER HOUSES: Clothing, Exc Women's
MAIL-ORDER HOUSES: Computer Eqpt & Electronics
MAIL-ORDER HOUSES: Cosmetics & Perfumes
MAIL-ORDER HOUSES: Fitness & Sporting Goods
MAIL-ORDER HOUSES: Food
MAIL-ORDER HOUSES: Furniture & Furnishings
MAIL-ORDER HOUSES: Gift Items
MAIL-ORDER HOUSES: Jewelry
MAIL-ORDER HOUSES: Magazines
MAILING LIST: Brokers
MAILING LIST: Compilers
MAILING SVCS, NEC
MANAGEMENT CONSULTING SVCS: Automation & Robotics
MANAGEMENT CONSULTING SVCS: Business
MANAGEMENT CONSULTING SVCS: Construction Project
MANAGEMENT CONSULTING SVCS: Distribution Channels
MANAGEMENT CONSULTING SVCS: Food & Beverage
MANAGEMENT CONSULTING SVCS: Industrial
MANAGEMENT CONSULTING SVCS: Industrial & Labor
MANAGEMENT CONSULTING SVCS: Industry Specialist
MANAGEMENT CONSULTING SVCS: New Products & Svcs
MANAGEMENT CONSULTING SVCS: Real Estate
MANAGEMENT CONSULTING SVCS: Training & Development
MANAGEMENT SERVICES
MANAGEMENT SVCS: Administrative
MANAGEMENT SVCS: Circuit, Motion Picture Theaters
MANAGEMENT SVCS: Construction
MANAGEMENT SVCS: Restaurant
MANDRELS
MANHOLES COVERS: Concrete
MANICURE PREPARATIONS
MANIFOLDS: Pipe, Fabricated From Purchased Pipe
MANNEQUINS
MANUFACTURING INDUSTRIES, NEC
MAPS
MARBLE BOARD
MARBLE, BUILDING: Cut & Shaped
MARBLE: Crushed & Broken
MARINAS
MARINE HARDWARE
MARINE RELATED EQPT
MARINE SVC STATIONS
MARKERS
MARKETS: Meat & fish
MARKING DEVICES
MARKING DEVICES: Date Stamps, Hand, Rubber Or Metal
MARKING DEVICES: Embossing Seals & Hand Stamps
MARKING DEVICES: Embossing Seals, Corporate & Official
MARKING DEVICES: Figures, Metal
MARKING DEVICES: Letters, Metal
MARKING DEVICES: Numbering Machines
MARKING DEVICES: Pads, Inking & Stamping

MARKING DEVICES: Postmark Stamps, Hand, Rubber Or Metal
MARKING DEVICES: Screens, Textile Printing
MASKS: Gas
MASQUERADE OR THEATRICAL COSTUMES STORES
MASTIC ROOFING COMPOSITION
MATERIALS HANDLING EQPT WHOLESALERS
MATS & MATTING, MADE FROM PURCHASED WIRE
MATS OR MATTING, NEC: Rubber
MATS, MATTING & PADS: Auto, Floor, Exc Rubber Or Plastic
MATS, MATTING & PADS: Nonwoven
MATS: Blasting, Rope
MATTRESS STORES
MEAT & FISH MARKETS: Fish
MEAT & MEAT PRDTS WHOLESALERS
MEAT CUTTING & PACKING
MEAT MARKETS
MEAT PRDTS: Boneless Meat, From Purchased Meat
MEAT PRDTS: Dried Beef, From Purchased Meat
MEAT PRDTS: Frankfurters, From Purchased Meat
MEAT PRDTS: Frozen
MEAT PRDTS: Meat By-Prdts, From Slaughtered Meat
MEAT PRDTS: Meat Extracts, From Purchased Meat
MEAT PRDTS: Pork, From Slaughtered Meat
MEAT PRDTS: Prepared Beef Prdts From Purchased Beef
MEAT PRDTS: Prepared Pork Prdts, From Purchased Meat
MEAT PRDTS: Sausage Casings, Natural
MEAT PRDTS: Sausages & Related Prdts, From Purchased Meat
MEAT PRDTS: Sausages, From Purchased Meat
MEAT PRDTS: Sausages, From Slaughtered Meat
MEAT PRDTS: Snack Sticks, Incl Jerky, From Purchased Meat
MEAT PROCESSED FROM PURCHASED CARCASSES
MED, DENTAL & HOSPITAL EQPT, WHOL: Incontinent Prdts/Splys
MEDIA BUYING AGENCIES
MEDIA: Magnetic & Optical Recording
MEDICAL & HOSPITAL EQPT WHOLESALERS
MEDICAL & HOSPITAL SPLYS: Radiation Shielding Garments
MEDICAL & SURGICAL SPLYS: Bandages & Dressings
MEDICAL & SURGICAL SPLYS: Braces, Orthopedic
MEDICAL & SURGICAL SPLYS: Clothing, Fire Resistant & Protect
MEDICAL & SURGICAL SPLYS: Cotton & Cotton Applicators
MEDICAL & SURGICAL SPLYS: Ear Plugs
MEDICAL & SURGICAL SPLYS: Foot Appliances, Orthopedic
MEDICAL & SURGICAL SPLYS: Gynecological Splys & Appliances
MEDICAL & SURGICAL SPLYS: Limbs, Artificial
MEDICAL & SURGICAL SPLYS: Orthopedic Appliances
MEDICAL & SURGICAL SPLYS: Personal Safety Eqpt
MEDICAL & SURGICAL SPLYS: Prosthetic Appliances
MEDICAL & SURGICAL SPLYS: Respiratory Protect Eqpt, Personal
MEDICAL & SURGICAL SPLYS: Sponges
MEDICAL & SURGICAL SPLYS: Suspensories
MEDICAL & SURGICAL SPLYS: Technical Aids, Handicapped
MEDICAL EQPT REPAIR SVCS, NON-ELECTRIC
MEDICAL EQPT: Diagnostic
MEDICAL EQPT: Electromedical Apparatus
MEDICAL EQPT: Electrotherapeutic Apparatus
MEDICAL EQPT: Heart-Lung Machines, Exc Iron Lungs
MEDICAL EQPT: Laser Systems
MEDICAL EQPT: MRI/Magnetic Resonance Imaging Devs, Nuclear
MEDICAL EQPT: PET Or Position Emission Tomography Scanners
MEDICAL EQPT: Patient Monitoring
MEDICAL EQPT: Sterilizers
MEDICAL EQPT: Ultrasonic Scanning Devices
MEDICAL EQPT: Ultrasonic, Exc Cleaning
MEDICAL EQPT: X-Ray Apparatus & Tubes, Radiographic
MEDICAL EQPT: X-Ray Apparatus & Tubes, Therapeutic
MEDICAL PHOTOGRAPHY & ART SVCS
MEDICAL, DENTAL & HOSPITAL EQPT, WHOL: Dentists' Prof Splys
MEDICAL, DENTAL & HOSPITAL EQPT, WHOL: Hosptl Eqpt/Furniture
MEDICAL, DENTAL & HOSPITAL EQPT, WHOL: Surgical Eqpt & Splys
MEDICAL, DENTAL & HOSPITAL EQPT, WHOLESALE: Diagnostic, Med

MEDICAL, DENTAL & HOSPITAL EQPT, WHOLESALE: Med Eqpt & Splys
MEDICAL, DENTAL & HOSPITAL EQPT, WHOLESALE: Medical Lab
MELAMINE RESINS: Melamine-Formaldehyde
MEMBERSHIP ORGANIZATIONS, PROFESSIONAL: Health Association
MEMBERSHIP ORGS, BUSINESS: Growers' Marketing Advisory Svc
MEMBERSHIP ORGS, CIVIC, SOCIAL/FRAT: Educator's Assoc
MEMORY DEVICES: Magnetic Bubble
MEN'S & BOYS' CLOTHING ACCESS STORES
MEN'S & BOYS' CLOTHING STORES
MEN'S & BOYS' CLOTHING WHOLESALERS, NEC
MEN'S & BOYS' SPORTSWEAR CLOTHING STORES
MEN'S & BOYS' SPORTSWEAR WHOLESALERS
MEN'S SUITS STORES
MERCHANDISING MACHINE OPERATORS: Vending
MESSAGE CONCENTRATORS
METAL & STEEL PRDTS: Abrasive
METAL COMPONENTS: Prefabricated
METAL CUTTING SVCS
METAL FABRICATORS: Architechtural
METAL FABRICATORS: Plate
METAL FABRICATORS: Sheet
METAL FABRICATORS: Structural, Ship
METAL FINISHING SVCS
METAL RESHAPING & REPLATING SVCS
METAL SERVICE CENTERS & OFFICES
METAL SPINNING FOR THE TRADE
METAL STAMPING, FOR THE TRADE
METAL STAMPINGS: Patterned
METAL STAMPINGS: Perforated
METAL STAMPINGS: Rigidized
METAL TREATING COMPOUNDS
METAL, TITANIUM: Sponge & Granules
METAL: Heavy, Perforated
METALLIC ORES WHOLESALERS
METALS SVC CENTERS & WHOL: Structural Shapes, Iron Or Steel
METALS SVC CENTERS & WHOLESALERS: Cable, Wire
METALS SVC CENTERS & WHOLESALERS: Iron & Steel Prdt, Ferrous
METALS SVC CENTERS & WHOLESALERS: Misc Nonferrous Prdts
METALS SVC CENTERS & WHOLESALERS: Nonferrous Sheets, Etc
METALS SVC CENTERS & WHOLESALERS: Pipe & Tubing, Steel
METALS SVC CENTERS & WHOLESALERS: Sheets, Metal
METALS SVC CENTERS & WHOLESALERS: Steel
METALS SVC CENTERS & WHOLESALERS: Tin & Tin Base Metals
METALS SVC CENTERS & WHOLESALERS: Tubing, Metal
METALS: Honeycombed
METALS: Precious NEC
METALS: Precious, Secondary
METALS: Primary Nonferrous, NEC
METALWORK: Miscellaneous
METALWORK: Ornamental
METALWORKING MACHINERY WHOLESALERS
METER READERS: Remote
METERING DEVICES: Flow Meters, Impeller & Counter Driven
METERING DEVICES: Water Quality Monitoring & Control Systems
METERS: Elasped Time
METERS: Liquid
METHANOL: Natural
MICA PRDTS
MICROCIRCUITS, INTEGRATED: Semiconductor
MICROFILM EQPT
MICROPHONES
MICROPROCESSORS
MICROWAVE COMPONENTS
MICROWAVE OVENS: Household
MILITARY INSIGNIA
MILITARY INSIGNIA, TEXTILE
MILL PRDTS: Structural & Rail
MILLINERY SUPPLIES: Veils & Veiling, Bridal, Funeral, Etc
MILLING: Grains, Exc Rice
MILLWORK
MINE DEVELOPMENT SVCS: Nonmetallic Minerals
MINERAL ABRASIVES MINING SVCS

MINERAL MINING: Nonmetallic
MINERAL PRODUCTS
MINERAL WOOL
MINERAL WOOL INSULATION PRDTS
MINERALS: Ground Or Otherwise Treated
MINERALS: Ground or Treated
MINIATURES
MINING EXPLORATION & DEVELOPMENT SVCS
MINING SVCS, NEC: Lignite
MIRROR REPAIR SHOP
MIRRORS: Motor Vehicle
MIXING EQPT
MIXTURES & BLOCKS: Asphalt Paving
MOBILE COMMUNICATIONS EQPT
MOBILE HOMES
MOBILE HOMES WHOLESALERS
MODELS
MODELS: General, Exc Toy
MODULES: Computer Logic
MODULES: Solid State
MOLDED RUBBER PRDTS
MOLDING COMPOUNDS
MOLDINGS, ARCHITECTURAL: Plaster Of Paris
MOLDINGS: Picture Frame
MOLDS: Indl
MOLDS: Plastic Working & Foundry
MONUMENTS & GRAVE MARKERS, EXC TERRAZZO
MONUMENTS: Concrete
MONUMENTS: Cut Stone, Exc Finishing Or Lettering Only
MOPS: Floor & Dust
MORTGAGE BANKERS
MOTION PICTURE & VIDEO PRODUCTION SVCS
MOTION PICTURE & VIDEO PRODUCTION SVCS: Non-Theatrical, TV
MOTION PICTURE PRODUCTION & DISTRIBUTION
MOTION PICTURE PRODUCTION & DISTRIBUTION: Television
MOTION PICTURE PRODUCTION ALLIED SVCS
MOTION PICTURE PRODUCTION SVCS
MOTOR & GENERATOR PARTS: Electric
MOTOR HOMES
MOTOR REPAIR SVCS
MOTOR SCOOTERS & PARTS
MOTOR VEHICLE ASSEMBLY, COMPLETE: Autos, Incl Specialty
MOTOR VEHICLE ASSEMBLY, COMPLETE: Buses, All Types
MOTOR VEHICLE ASSEMBLY, COMPLETE: Cars, Armored
MOTOR VEHICLE ASSEMBLY, COMPLETE: Fire Department Vehicles
MOTOR VEHICLE ASSEMBLY, COMPLETE: Military Motor Vehicle
MOTOR VEHICLE ASSEMBLY, COMPLETE: Motor Buses
MOTOR VEHICLE ASSEMBLY, COMPLETE: Snow Plows
MOTOR VEHICLE ASSEMBLY, COMPLETE: Truck & Tractor Trucks
MOTOR VEHICLE ASSEMBLY, COMPLETE: Trucks, Pickup
MOTOR VEHICLE DEALERS: Automobiles, New & Used
MOTOR VEHICLE PARTS & ACCESS: Acceleration Eqpt
MOTOR VEHICLE PARTS & ACCESS: Air Conditioner Parts
MOTOR VEHICLE PARTS & ACCESS: Axel Housings & Shafts
MOTOR VEHICLE PARTS & ACCESS: Bearings
MOTOR VEHICLE PARTS & ACCESS: Body Components & Frames
MOTOR VEHICLE PARTS & ACCESS: Cylinder Heads
MOTOR VEHICLE PARTS & ACCESS: Electrical Eqpt
MOTOR VEHICLE PARTS & ACCESS: Engines & Parts
MOTOR VEHICLE PARTS & ACCESS: Fuel Systems & Parts
MOTOR VEHICLE PARTS & ACCESS: Gears
MOTOR VEHICLE PARTS & ACCESS: Power Steering Eqpt
MOTOR VEHICLE PARTS & ACCESS: Propane Conversion Eqpt
MOTOR VEHICLE PARTS & ACCESS: Sanders, Safety
MOTOR VEHICLE PARTS & ACCESS: Tops
MOTOR VEHICLE PARTS & ACCESS: Transmissions
MOTOR VEHICLE PARTS & ACCESS: Wheel rims
MOTOR VEHICLE PARTS & ACCESS: Wiring Harness Sets
MOTOR VEHICLE SPLYS & PARTS WHOLESALERS: New
MOTOR VEHICLE: Hardware
MOTOR VEHICLE: Radiators
MOTOR VEHICLE: Steering Mechanisms
MOTOR VEHICLES & CAR BODIES
MOTOR VEHICLES, WHOLESALE: Recreational, All-Terrain
MOTOR VEHICLES, WHOLESALE: Truck bodies
MOTORCYCLE ACCESS

MOTORCYCLE DEALERS
MOTORCYCLE DEALERS: Bicycles, Motorized
MOTORCYCLE PARTS: Wholesalers
MOTORCYCLES & RELATED PARTS
MOTORS: Electric
MOTORS: Generators
MOTORS: Torque
MOVIE THEATERS, EXC DRIVE-IN
MOWERS & ACCESSORIES
MULTIPLEXERS: Telephone & Telegraph
MUSEUMS
MUSEUMS & ART GALLERIES
MUSIC BROADCASTING SVCS
MUSIC COPYING SVCS
MUSIC DISTRIBUTION APPARATUS
MUSIC LICENSING & ROYALTIES
MUSIC LICENSING TO RADIO STATIONS
MUSIC RECORDING PRODUCER
MUSICAL ENTERTAINERS
MUSICAL INSTRUMENT PARTS & ACCESS, WHOLESALE
MUSICAL INSTRUMENT REPAIR
MUSICAL INSTRUMENTS & ACCESS: Carrying Cases
MUSICAL INSTRUMENTS & ACCESS: NEC
MUSICAL INSTRUMENTS & ACCESS: Pianos
MUSICAL INSTRUMENTS & ACCESS: Pipe Organs
MUSICAL INSTRUMENTS & PARTS: Brass
MUSICAL INSTRUMENTS & PARTS: String
MUSICAL INSTRUMENTS & SPLYS STORES
MUSICAL INSTRUMENTS & SPLYS STORES: Pianos
MUSICAL INSTRUMENTS WHOLESALERS
MUSICAL INSTRUMENTS: Electric & Electronic
MUSICAL INSTRUMENTS: Guitars & Parts, Electric & Acoustic
MUSICAL INSTRUMENTS: Harmonicas
MUSICAL INSTRUMENTS: Heads, Drum
MUSICAL INSTRUMENTS: Organs
MUSICAL INSTRUMENTS: Strings, Instrument

N

NAIL SALONS
NAME PLATES: Engraved Or Etched
NAMEPLATES
NATIONAL SECURITY FORCES
NATURAL BUTANE PRODUCTION
NATURAL GAS COMPRESSING SVC, On-Site
NATURAL GAS LIQUIDS PRODUCTION
NATURAL GAS PRODUCTION
NATURAL GAS TRANSMISSION & DISTRIBUTION
NATURAL GASOLINE PRODUCTION
NAVIGATIONAL SYSTEMS & INSTRUMENTS
NET & NETTING PRDTS
NETS: Laundry
NEW & USED CAR DEALERS
NEWS DEALERS & NEWSSTANDS
NEWS FEATURE SYNDICATES
NEWS PICTURES GATHERING & DISTRIBUTING SVCS
NEWS SYNDICATES
NEWSPAPERS & PERIODICALS NEWS REPORTING SVCS
NEWSPAPERS, WHOLESALE
NICKEL ALLOY
NONCURRENT CARRYING WIRING DEVICES
NONFERROUS: Rolling & Drawing, NEC
NONMETALLIC MINERALS: Support Activities, Exc Fuels
NOTARIES PUBLIC
NOTEBOOKS, MADE FROM PURCHASED MATERIALS
NOTIONS: Button Blanks & Molds
NOTIONS: Pins, Straight, Steel Or Brass
NOTIONS: Studs, Shirt, Exc Precious/Semi Metal/Stone
NOVELTIES
NOVELTIES & SPECIALTIES: Metal
NOVELTIES: Paper, Made From Purchased Materials
NOVELTIES: Plastic
NOVELTY SHOPS
NOZZLES & SPRINKLERS Lawn Hose
NOZZLES: Spray, Aerosol, Paint Or Insecticide
NUCLEAR REACTORS: Military Or Indl
NURSERIES & LAWN & GARDEN SPLY STORES, RETAIL: Fertilizer
NURSERIES & LAWN & GARDEN SPLY STORES, RETAIL: Sod
NURSERIES & LAWN & GARDEN SPLY STORES, RETAIL: Top Soil
NURSERY & GARDEN CENTERS
NUTS: Metal
NYLON RESINS

O

OFFICE EQPT WHOLESALERS
OFFICE EQPT, WHOLESALE: Duplicating Machines
OFFICE FIXTURES: Exc Wood
OFFICE FIXTURES: Wood
OFFICE FURNITURE REPAIR & MAINTENANCE SVCS
OFFICE SPLY & STATIONERY STORES
OFFICE SPLY & STATIONERY STORES: Office Forms & Splys
OFFICE SPLYS, NEC, WHOLESALE
OFFICES & CLINICS OF DENTISTS: Prosthodontist
OFFICES & CLINICS OF DRS, MED: Specialized Practitioners
OFFICES & CLINICS OF HEALTH PRACTITIONERS: Nutrition
OFFICES & CLINICS OF HEALTH PRACTITIONERS: Nutritionist
OIL & GAS FIELD MACHINERY
OIL FIELD MACHINERY & EQPT
OIL FIELD SVCS, NEC
OIL ROYALTY TRADERS
OILS & GREASES: Blended & Compounded
OILS & GREASES: Lubricating
OILS: Anise
OILS: Essential
OILS: Lubricating
OILS: Lubricating
OILS: Orange
OINTMENTS
ON-LINE DATABASE INFORMATION RETRIEVAL SVCS
OPEN PIT GOLD MINING
OPERATOR: Apartment Buildings
OPHTHALMIC GOODS
OPHTHALMIC GOODS WHOLESALERS
OPHTHALMIC GOODS, NEC, WHOLESALE: Frames
OPHTHALMIC GOODS: Eyewear, Protective
OPHTHALMIC GOODS: Frames & Parts, Eyeglass & Spectacle
OPHTHALMIC GOODS: Frames, Lenses & Parts, Eyeglasses
OPHTHALMIC GOODS: Lenses, Ophthalmic
OPHTHALMIC GOODS: Spectacles
OPHTHALMIC GOODS: Temples & Fronts, Ophthalmic
OPTICAL GOODS STORES
OPTICAL GOODS STORES: Opticians
OPTICAL INSTRUMENTS & APPARATUS
OPTICAL INSTRUMENTS & LENSES
OPTICAL SCANNING SVCS
ORAL PREPARATIONS
ORDNANCE
ORGAN TUNING & REPAIR SVCS
ORGANIZATIONS, NEC
ORGANIZATIONS: Medical Research
ORGANIZATIONS: Professional
ORGANIZATIONS: Religious
ORGANIZATIONS: Research Institute
ORGANIZATIONS: Scientific Research Agency
ORGANIZERS, CLOSET & DRAWER Plastic
ORNAMENTS: Christmas Tree, Exc Electrical & Glass
ORTHOPEDIC SUNDRIES: Molded Rubber
OUTLETS: Electric, Convenience
OVENS: Paint Baking & Drying

P

PACKAGE DESIGN SVCS
PACKAGED FROZEN FOODS WHOLESALERS, NEC
PACKAGING & LABELING SVCS
PACKAGING MATERIALS, INDL: Wholesalers
PACKAGING MATERIALS, WHOLESALE
PACKAGING MATERIALS: Paper
PACKAGING MATERIALS: Paper, Coated Or Laminated
PACKAGING MATERIALS: Paper, Thermoplastic Coated
PACKAGING MATERIALS: Plastic Film, Coated Or Laminated
PACKAGING MATERIALS: Polystyrene Foam
PACKAGING MATERIALS: Resinous Impregnated Paper
PACKAGING: Blister Or Bubble Formed, Plastic
PACKING & CRATING SVC
PACKING & CRATING SVCS: Containerized Goods For Shipping
PACKING MATERIALS: Mechanical
PACKING: Metallic
PADDING: Foamed Plastics
PADS: Desk, Exc Paper
PADS: Desk, Paper, Made From Purchased Materials
PADS: Mattress

PAGERS: One-way
PAINT STORE
PAINTING SVC: Metal Prdts
PAINTS & ADDITIVES
PAINTS & ALLIED PRODUCTS
PAINTS, VARNISHES & SPLYS, WHOLESALE: Paints
PALLET REPAIR SVCS
PALLETS
PALLETS & SKIDS: Wood
PALLETS: Wood & Metal Combination
PALLETS: Wooden
PANEL & DISTRIBUTION BOARDS: Electric
PANELS: Building, Wood
PANELS: Cardboard, Die-Cut, Made From Purchased Materials
PAPER & BOARD: Die-cut
PAPER CONVERTING
PAPER MANUFACTURERS: Exc Newsprint
PAPER PRDTS: Feminine Hygiene Prdts
PAPER PRDTS: Infant & Baby Prdts
PAPER PRDTS: Napkin Stock
PAPER PRDTS: Napkins, Sanitary, Made From Purchased Material
PAPER PRDTS: Pattern Tissue
PAPER PRDTS: Pressed Pulp Prdts
PAPER PRDTS: Sanitary
PAPER PRDTS: Sanitary Tissue Paper
PAPER PRDTS: Tampons, Sanitary, Made From Purchased Material
PAPER PRDTS: Toilet Paper, Made From Purchased Materials
PAPER PRDTS: Toweling Tissue
PAPER PRDTS: Towels, Napkins/Tissue Paper, From Purchd Mtrls
PAPER, WHOLESALE: Fine
PAPER, WHOLESALE: Printing
PAPER: Absorbent
PAPER: Adding Machine Rolls, Made From Purchased Materials
PAPER: Adhesive
PAPER: Art
PAPER: Bristols
PAPER: Building, Insulating & Packaging
PAPER: Business Form
PAPER: Card
PAPER: Chemically Treated, Made From Purchased Materials
PAPER: Cigarette
PAPER: Cloth, Lined, Made From Purchased Materials
PAPER: Coated & Laminated, NEC
PAPER: Coated, Exc Photographic, Carbon Or Abrasive
PAPER: Corrugated
PAPER: Envelope
PAPER: Filter
PAPER: Kraft
PAPER: Packaging
PAPER: Parchment
PAPER: Printer
PAPER: Specialty
PAPER: Tissue
PAPER: Wrapping
PAPER: Wrapping & Packaging
PAPER: Writing
PAPERBOARD
PAPERBOARD CONVERTING
PAPERBOARD PRDTS: Building Insulating & Packaging
PAPERBOARD PRDTS: Container Board
PAPERBOARD PRDTS: Folding Boxboard
PAPERBOARD PRDTS: Kraft Linerboard
PAPERBOARD PRDTS: Packaging Board
PAPERBOARD: Boxboard
PAPERBOARD: Liner Board
PAPIER-MACHE PRDTS, EXC STATUARY & ART GOODS
PARACHUTES
PARKING LOTS
PARTITIONS & FIXTURES: Except Wood
PARTITIONS: Nonwood, Floor Attached
PARTITIONS: Wood & Fixtures
PARTITIONS: Wood, Floor Attached
PARTS: Metal
PARTY & SPECIAL EVENT PLANNING SVCS
PATENT OWNERS & LESSORS
PATTERNS: Indl
PAVERS
PAVING MATERIALS: Prefabricated, Concrete
PAVING MIXTURES

PENCILS & PENS WHOLESALERS
PENS & PARTS: Ball Point
PENS & PARTS: Cartridges, Refill, Ball Point
PENS & PENCILS: Mechanical, NEC
PENS: Fountain, Including Desk Sets
PERFUME: Concentrated
PERFUME: Perfumes, Natural Or Synthetic
PERFUMES
PERLITE: Processed
PERSONAL APPEARANCE SVCS
PERSONAL CREDIT INSTITUTIONS: Consumer Finance
    Companies
PEST CONTROL SVCS
PET COLLARS, LEASHES, MUZZLES & HARNESSES:
    Leather
PET SPLYS
PET SPLYS WHOLESALERS
PETROLEUM & PETROLEUM PRDTS, WHOLESALE Engine
    Fuels & Oils
PETROLEUM & PETROLEUM PRDTS, WHOLESALE Fuel
    Oil
PETROLEUM & PETROLEUM PRDTS, WHOLESALE: Bulk
    Stations
PETROLEUM PRDTS WHOLESALERS
PEWTER WARE
PHARMACEUTICAL PREPARATIONS: Adrenal
PHARMACEUTICAL PREPARATIONS: Barbituric Acid
PHARMACEUTICAL PREPARATIONS: Digitalis
PHARMACEUTICAL PREPARATIONS: Druggists' Prepara-
    tions
PHARMACEUTICAL PREPARATIONS: Medicines, Capsule
    Or Ampule
PHARMACEUTICAL PREPARATIONS: Penicillin
PHARMACEUTICAL PREPARATIONS: Pills
PHARMACEUTICAL PREPARATIONS: Powders
PHARMACEUTICAL PREPARATIONS: Procaine
PHARMACEUTICAL PREPARATIONS: Proprietary Drug
    PRDTS
PHARMACEUTICAL PREPARATIONS: Solutions
PHARMACEUTICAL PREPARATIONS: Tablets
PHARMACEUTICALS
PHARMACEUTICALS: Mail-Order Svc
PHARMACEUTICALS: Medicinal & Botanical Prdts
PHARMACIES & DRUG STORES
PHONOGRAPH NEEDLES
PHONOGRAPH RECORDS WHOLESALERS
PHONOGRAPH RECORDS: Prerecorded
PHOSPHATES
PHOTOCOPY MACHINES
PHOTOCOPYING & DUPLICATING SVCS
PHOTOELECTRIC DEVICES: Magnetic
PHOTOENGRAVING SVC
PHOTOFINISHING LABORATORIES
PHOTOGRAPHIC EQPT & CAMERAS, WHOLESALE
PHOTOGRAPHIC EQPT & SPLY: Sound Recordg/Reprod
    Eqpt, Motion
PHOTOGRAPHIC EQPT & SPLYS
PHOTOGRAPHIC EQPT & SPLYS WHOLESALERS
PHOTOGRAPHIC EQPT & SPLYS, WHOLESALE: Motion
    Picture
PHOTOGRAPHIC EQPT & SPLYS: Cameras, Aerial
PHOTOGRAPHIC EQPT & SPLYS: Editing Eqpt, Motion Pic-
    ture
PHOTOGRAPHIC EQPT & SPLYS: Film, Sensitized
PHOTOGRAPHIC EQPT & SPLYS: Graphic Arts Plates, Sen-
    sitized
PHOTOGRAPHIC EQPT & SPLYS: Plates, Sensitized
PHOTOGRAPHIC EQPT & SPLYS: Printing Eqpt
PHOTOGRAPHIC EQPT & SPLYS: Shutters, Camera
PHOTOGRAPHIC EQPT & SPLYS: Toners, Prprd, Not Chem
    Plnts
PHOTOGRAPHIC EQPT/SPLYS, WHOL: Cameras/Projec-
    tors/Eqpt/Splys
PHOTOGRAPHIC LIBRARY SVCS
PHOTOGRAPHIC PEOCESSING CHEMICALS
PHOTOGRAPHIC PROCESSING EQPT & CHEMICALS
PHOTOGRAPHIC SENSITIZED GOODS, NEC
PHOTOGRAPHIC SVCS
PHOTOGRAPHY SVCS: Commercial
PHOTOGRAPHY SVCS: Portrait Studios
PHOTOGRAPHY SVCS: Still Or Video
PHOTOTYPESETTING SVC
PHOTOVOLTAIC Solid State
PHYSICAL FITNESS CENTERS
PHYSICIANS' OFFICES & CLINICS: Medical doctors

PICTURE FRAMES: Metal
PICTURE FRAMES: Wood
PICTURE FRAMING SVCS, CUSTOM
PICTURE PROJECTION EQPT
PIECE GOODS & NOTIONS WHOLESALERS
PIECE GOODS, NOTIONS & DRY GOODS, WHOL: Textile
    Converters
PIECE GOODS, NOTIONS & DRY GOODS, WHOL: Textiles,
    Woven
PIECE GOODS, NOTIONS & DRY GOODS, WHOL: Trim-
    mings, Apparel
PIECE GOODS, NOTIONS & DRY GOODS, WHOLESALE:
    Fabrics, Knit
PIECE GOODS, NOTIONS & DRY GOODS, WHOLESALE:
    Fabrics, Lace
PIECE GOODS, NOTIONS & DRY GOODS, WHOLESALE:
    Sewing Access
PIECE GOODS, NOTIONS & OTHER DRY GOODS,
    WHOLESALE: Bridal
PIECE GOODS, NOTIONS & OTHER DRY GOODS,
    WHOLESALE: Buttons
PIECE GOODS, NOTIONS & OTHER DRY GOODS,
    WHOLESALE: Fabrics
PIECE GOODS, NOTIONS & OTHER DRY GOODS,
    WHOLESALE: Woven
PIECE GOODS, NOTIONS/DRY GOODS, WHOL: Drapery
    Mtrl, Woven
PIECE GOODS, NOTIONS/DRY GOODS, WHOL: Linen
    Piece, Woven
PIECE GOODS, NOTIONS/DRY GOODS, WHOL: Sewing
    Splys/Notions
PILLOW FILLING MTRLS: Curled Hair, Cotton Waste, Moss
PILLOWS: Sponge Rubber
PINS
PIPE & FITTING: Fabrication
PIPE & FITTINGS: Cast Iron
PIPE & FITTINGS: Pressure, Cast Iron
PIPE CLEANERS
PIPE JOINT COMPOUNDS
PIPE: Concrete
PIPE: Extruded, Aluminum
PIPE: Plastic
PIPE: Sheet Metal
PIPES & TUBES: Steel
PIPES & TUBES: Welded
PIPES: Steel & Iron
PIPES: Tobacco
PISTONS & PISTON RINGS
PLACEMATS: Plastic Or Textile
PLANING MILLS: Independent, Exc Millwork
PLANING MILLS: Millwork
PLANT CARE SVCS
PLAQUES: Clay, Plaster/Papier-Mache, Factory Production
PLAQUES: Picture, Laminated
PLASMAS
PLASTER WORK: Ornamental & Architectural
PLASTIC PRDTS
PLASTIC PRDTS REPAIR SVCS
PLASTICIZERS, ORGANIC: Cyclic & Acyclic
PLASTICS FILM & SHEET
PLASTICS FILM & SHEET: Polyethylene
PLASTICS FILM & SHEET: Polyvinyl
PLASTICS FILM & SHEET: Vinyl
PLASTICS FINISHED PRDTS: Laminated
PLASTICS MATERIAL & RESINS
PLASTICS MATERIALS, BASIC FORMS & SHAPES
    WHOLESALERS
PLASTICS PROCESSING
PLASTICS SHEET: Packing Materials
PLASTICS: Blow Molded
PLASTICS: Cast
PLASTICS: Extruded
PLASTICS: Finished Injection Molded
PLASTICS: Injection Molded
PLASTICS: Molded
PLASTICS: Polystyrene Foam
PLASTICS: Thermoformed
PLATE WORK: Metalworking Trade
PLATEMAKING SVC: Color Separations, For The Printing
    Trade
PLATEMAKING SVC: Gravure, Plates Or Cylinders
PLATES
PLATES: Paper, Made From Purchased Materials
PLATES: Plastic Exc Polystyrene Foam
PLATES: Truss, Metal

PLATING & FINISHING SVC: Decorative, Formed Prdts
PLATING & POLISHING SVC
PLATING COMPOUNDS
PLATING SVC: Chromium, Metals Or Formed Prdts
PLATING SVC: Electro
PLATING SVC: Gold
PLATING SVC: NEC
PLAYGROUND EQPT
PLEATING & STITCHING FOR THE TRADE: Decorative &
    Novelty
PLEATING & STITCHING FOR TRADE: Permanent Pleat-
    ing/Pressing
PLEATING & STITCHING SVC
PLEATING & TUCKING FOR THE TRADE
PLUGS: Electric
PLUMBING & HEATING EQPT & SPLY, WHOL: Htg
    Eqpt/Panels, Solar
PLUMBING & HEATING EQPT & SPLY, WHOLESALE: Hy-
    dronic Htg Eqpt
PLUMBING & HEATING EQPT & SPLYS WHOLESALERS
PLUMBING & HEATING EQPT & SPLYS, WHOL: Fireplaces,
    Prefab
PLUMBING & HEATING EQPT & SPLYS, WHOL: Plumbing
    Fitting/Sply
PLUMBING & HEATING EQPT & SPLYS, WHOL:
    Plumbng/Heatng Valves
PLUMBING & HEATING EQPT & SPLYS, WHOL: Water Purif
    Eqpt
PLUMBING & HEATING EQPT & SPLYS, WHOLESALE: Boil-
    ers, Steam
PLUMBING & HEATING EQPT & SPLYS, WHOLESALE:
    Brass/Fittings
PLUMBING FIXTURES
PLUMBING FIXTURES: Brass, Incl Drain Cocks,
    Faucets/Spigots
PLUMBING FIXTURES: Plastic
POINT OF SALE DEVICES
POLISHING SVC: Metals Or Formed Prdts
POLYESTERS
POLYETHYLENE CHLOROSULFONATED RUBBER
POLYETHYLENE RESINS
POLYTETRAFLUOROETHYLENE RESINS
POLYVINYL CHLORIDE RESINS
POPCORN & SUPPLIES WHOLESALERS
PORCELAIN ENAMELED PRDTS & UTENSILS
POSTERS
POTTERY: Laboratory & Indl
POULTRY & POULTRY PRDTS WHOLESALERS
POULTRY & SMALL GAME SLAUGHTERING & PROCESS-
    ING
POULTRY SLAUGHTERING & PROCESSING
POWDER PUFFS & MITTS
POWDER: Aluminum Atomized
POWDER: Metal
POWDER: Silver
POWER GENERATORS
POWER SPLY CONVERTERS: Static, Electronic Applications
POWER SUPPLIES: All Types, Static
POWER SUPPLIES: Transformer, Electronic Type
POWER SWITCHING EQPT
POWER TOOLS, HAND: Grinders, Portable, Electric Or Pneu-
    matic
POWER TOOLS, HAND: Hammers, Portable, Elec/Pneu-
    matic, Chip
POWER TRANSMISSION EQPT WHOLESALERS
POWER TRANSMISSION EQPT: Aircraft
POWER TRANSMISSION EQPT: Mechanical
PRECAST TERRAZZO OR CONCRETE PRDTS
PRECIOUS METALS
PRECIOUS METALS WHOLESALERS
PRECIOUS STONES & METALS, WHOLESALE
PRECIOUS STONES WHOLESALERS
PRECIPITATORS: Electrostatic
PRERECORDED TAPE, CD & RECORD STORES: Video
    Discs/Tapes
PRERECORDED TAPE, CD/RECORD STORES: Video
    Tapes, Prerecorded
PRERECORDED TAPE, COMPACT DISC & RECORD
    STORES: Records
PRESSED FIBER & MOLDED PULP PRDTS, EXC FOOD
    PRDTS
PRESSES
PRIMARY METAL PRODUCTS
PRINT CARTRIDGES: Laser & Other Computer Printers
PRINTED CIRCUIT BOARDS

INDEX

PRINTERS & PLOTTERS
PRINTERS' SVCS: Folding, Collating, Etc
PRINTERS: Computer
PRINTERS: Magnetic Ink, Bar Code
PRINTING & BINDING: Book Music
PRINTING & BINDING: Books
PRINTING & BINDING: Pamphlets
PRINTING & EMBOSSING: Plastic Fabric Articles
PRINTING & ENGRAVING: Card, Exc Greeting
PRINTING & ENGRAVING: Financial Notes & Certificates
PRINTING & ENGRAVING: Invitation & Stationery
PRINTING & ENGRAVING: Plateless
PRINTING & ENGRAVING: Poster & Decal
PRINTING & STAMPING: Fabric Articles
PRINTING & WRITING PAPER WHOLESALERS
PRINTING EQPT & SUPPLIES: Illustration & Poster Wood-
cuts
PRINTING INKS WHOLESALERS
PRINTING MACHINERY
PRINTING MACHINERY, EQPT & SPLYS: Wholesalers
PRINTING TRADES MACHINERY & EQPT REPAIR SVCS
PRINTING, COMMERCIAL Newspapers, NEC
PRINTING, COMMERCIAL: Announcements, NEC
PRINTING, COMMERCIAL: Bags, Plastic, NEC
PRINTING, COMMERCIAL: Business Forms, NEC
PRINTING, COMMERCIAL: Calendars, NEC
PRINTING, COMMERCIAL: Cards, Visiting, Incl Business,
NEC
PRINTING, COMMERCIAL: Circulars, NEC
PRINTING, COMMERCIAL: Coupons, NEC
PRINTING, COMMERCIAL: Decals, NEC
PRINTING, COMMERCIAL: Envelopes, NEC
PRINTING, COMMERCIAL: Imprinting
PRINTING, COMMERCIAL: Invitations, NEC
PRINTING, COMMERCIAL: Labels & Seals, NEC
PRINTING, COMMERCIAL: Letterpress & Screen
PRINTING, COMMERCIAL: Literature, Advertising, NEC
PRINTING, COMMERCIAL: Magazines, NEC
PRINTING, COMMERCIAL: Periodicals, NEC
PRINTING, COMMERCIAL: Post Cards, Picture, NEC
PRINTING, COMMERCIAL: Promotional
PRINTING, COMMERCIAL: Publications
PRINTING, COMMERCIAL: Screen
PRINTING, COMMERCIAL: Stamps, Trading, NEC
PRINTING, COMMERCIAL: Tags, NEC
PRINTING, LITHOGRAPHIC: Advertising Posters
PRINTING, LITHOGRAPHIC: Calendars
PRINTING, LITHOGRAPHIC: Color
PRINTING, LITHOGRAPHIC: Decals
PRINTING, LITHOGRAPHIC: Forms & Cards, Business
PRINTING, LITHOGRAPHIC: Forms, Business
PRINTING, LITHOGRAPHIC: Letters, Circular Or Form
PRINTING, LITHOGRAPHIC: Menus
PRINTING, LITHOGRAPHIC: Offset & photolithographic print-
ing
PRINTING, LITHOGRAPHIC: On Metal
PRINTING, LITHOGRAPHIC: Post Cards, Picture
PRINTING, LITHOGRAPHIC: Promotional
PRINTING, LITHOGRAPHIC: Publications
PRINTING, LITHOGRAPHIC: Tags
PRINTING, LITHOGRAPHIC: Tickets
PRINTING, LITHOGRAPHIC: Transfers, Decalcomania Or Dry
PRINTING: Books
PRINTING: Books
PRINTING: Broadwoven Fabrics. Cotton
PRINTING: Checkbooks
PRINTING: Commercial, NEC
PRINTING: Engraving & Plate
PRINTING: Flexographic
PRINTING: Gravure, Business Form & Card
PRINTING: Gravure, Color
PRINTING: Gravure, Forms, Business
PRINTING: Gravure, Imprinting
PRINTING: Gravure, Job
PRINTING: Gravure, Labels
PRINTING: Gravure, Rotogravure
PRINTING: Gravure, Stamps, Trading
PRINTING: Gravure, Stationery
PRINTING: Laser
PRINTING: Letterpress
PRINTING: Lithographic
PRINTING: Offset
PRINTING: Pamphlets
PRINTING: Photo-Offset
PRINTING: Photogravure

PRINTING: Photolithographic
PRINTING: Rotary Photogravure
PRINTING: Rotogravure
PRINTING: Screen, Broadwoven Fabrics, Cotton
PRINTING: Screen, Fabric
PRINTING: Screen, Manmade Fiber & Silk, Broadwoven Fab-
ric
PRINTING: Thermography
PROFESSIONAL EQPT & SPLYS, WHOLESALE: Analytical
Instruments
PROFESSIONAL EQPT & SPLYS, WHOLESALE: Engineers',
NEC
PROFESSIONAL EQPT & SPLYS, WHOLESALE: Optical
Goods
PROFESSIONAL EQPT & SPLYS, WHOLESALE: Scientific &
Engineerg
PROFESSIONAL EQPT & SPLYS, WHOLESALE: Theatrical
PROFILE SHAPES: Unsupported Plastics
PROGRAM ADMIN, GOVT: Air, Water & Solid Waste Mgmt,
Local
PROTECTION EQPT: Lightning
PUBLIC RELATIONS & PUBLICITY SVCS
PUBLISHERS: Art Copy
PUBLISHERS: Art Copy & Poster
PUBLISHERS: Atlases
PUBLISHERS: Book
PUBLISHERS: Book Clubs, No Printing
PUBLISHERS: Books, No Printing
PUBLISHERS: Catalogs
PUBLISHERS: Comic Books, No Printing
PUBLISHERS: Directories, NEC
PUBLISHERS: Directories, Telephone
PUBLISHERS: Guides
PUBLISHERS: Magazines, No Printing
PUBLISHERS: Maps
PUBLISHERS: Miscellaneous
PUBLISHERS: Music Book
PUBLISHERS: Music Book & Sheet Music
PUBLISHERS: Music, Book
PUBLISHERS: Music, Sheet
PUBLISHERS: Newsletter
PUBLISHERS: Newspaper
PUBLISHERS: Newspapers, No Printing
PUBLISHERS: Pamphlets, No Printing
PUBLISHERS: Periodical, With Printing
PUBLISHERS: Periodicals, Magazines
PUBLISHERS: Periodicals, No Printing
PUBLISHERS: Posters
PUBLISHERS: Sheet Music
PUBLISHERS: Shopping News
PUBLISHERS: Technical Manuals
PUBLISHERS: Technical Manuals & Papers
PUBLISHERS: Technical Papers
PUBLISHERS: Telephone & Other Directory
PUBLISHERS: Textbooks, No Printing
PUBLISHERS: Trade journals, No Printing
PUBLISHING & BROADCASTING: Internet Only
PUBLISHING & PRINTING: Art Copy
PUBLISHING & PRINTING: Book Clubs
PUBLISHING & PRINTING: Book Music
PUBLISHING & PRINTING: Books
PUBLISHING & PRINTING: Catalogs
PUBLISHING & PRINTING: Comic Books
PUBLISHING & PRINTING: Directories, NEC
PUBLISHING & PRINTING: Magazines: publishing & printing
PUBLISHING & PRINTING: Music, Book
PUBLISHING & PRINTING: Newsletters, Business Svc
PUBLISHING & PRINTING: Newspapers
PUBLISHING & PRINTING: Patterns, Paper
PUBLISHING & PRINTING: Posters
PUBLISHING & PRINTING: Shopping News
PUBLISHING & PRINTING: Technical Manuals
PUBLISHING & PRINTING: Textbooks
PUBLISHING & PRINTING: Trade Journals
PUBLISHING & PRINTING: Yearbooks
PULP MILLS
PULP MILLS: Mech Pulp, Incl Groundwood & Thermome-
chanical
PULP MILLS: Mechanical & Recycling Processing
PULP MILLS: Soda Pulp
PUMICE
PUMP GOVERNORS: Gas Machines
PUMPS
PUMPS & PARTS: Indl
PUMPS & PUMPING EQPT REPAIR SVCS

PUMPS & PUMPING EQPT WHOLESALERS
PUMPS, HEAT: Electric
PUMPS: Domestic, Water Or Sump
PUMPS: Fluid Power
PUMPS: Measuring & Dispensing
PUMPS: Vacuum, Exc Laboratory
PUNCHES: Forming & Stamping
PURIFICATION & DUST COLLECTION EQPT
PURSES: Women's
PUSHCARTS & WHEELBARROWS

Q

QUICKLIME

R

RACE TRACK OPERATION
RACKS & SHELVING: Household, Wood
RACKS: Garment, Exc Wood
RACKS: Garment, Wood
RACKS: Pallet, Exc Wood
RADAR SYSTEMS & EQPT
RADIO & TELEVISION COMMUNICATIONS EQUIPMENT
RADIO & TELEVISION REPAIR
RADIO BROADCASTING & COMMUNICATIONS EQPT
RADIO BROADCASTING STATIONS
RADIO RECEIVER NETWORKS
RADIO, TELEVISION & CONSUMER ELECTRONICS
STORES: Eqpt, NEC
RADIO, TV & CONSUMER ELEC STORES: Automotive
Sound Eqpt
RADIO, TV & CONSUMER ELECTRONICS: VCR & Access
RADIO, TV/CONSUMER ELEC STORES: Antennas, Satellite
Dish
RAILINGS: Prefabricated, Metal
RAILINGS: Wood
RAILROAD CAR RENTING & LEASING SVCS
RAILROAD CAR REPAIR SVCS
RAILROAD CARGO LOADING & UNLOADING SVCS
RAILROAD EQPT
RAILROAD EQPT & SPLYS WHOLESALERS
RAILROAD EQPT, EXC LOCOMOTIVES
RAILROAD EQPT: Brakes, Air & Vacuum
RAILROAD EQPT: Cars & Eqpt, Dining
RAILROAD EQPT: Cars & Eqpt, Rapid Transit
RAILROAD EQPT: Cars, Maintenance
RAILROAD EQPT: Cars, Motor
RAILROAD EQPT: Locomotives & Parts, Indl
RAILROAD RELATED EQPT: Railway Track
RAILS: Steel Or Iron
RAMPS: Prefabricated Metal
RAZORS, RAZOR BLADES
RAZORS: Electric
REAL ESTATE AGENCIES & BROKERS
REAL ESTATE AGENTS & MANAGERS
REAL ESTATE OPERATORS, EXC DEVELOPERS: Apart-
ment Hotel
REAL ESTATE OPERATORS, EXC DEVELOPERS: Commer-
cial/Indl Bldg
RECEIVERS: Radio Communications
RECLAIMED RUBBER: Reworked By Manufacturing Process
RECORD BLANKS: Phonographic
RECORDING HEADS: Speech & Musical Eqpt
RECORDS & TAPES: Prerecorded
RECORDS OR TAPES: Masters
RECOVERY SVC: Iron Ore, From Open Hearth Slag
RECOVERY SVCS: Metal
RECREATIONAL & SPORTING CAMPS
RECTIFIERS: Electrical Apparatus
RECTIFIERS: Solid State
RECYCLABLE SCRAP & WASTE MATERIALS WHOLE-
SALERS
RECYCLING: Paper
REELS: Cable, Metal
REFINERS & SMELTERS: Aluminum
REFINERS & SMELTERS: Antimony, Primary
REFINERS & SMELTERS: Cobalt, Primary
REFINERS & SMELTERS: Copper
REFINERS & SMELTERS: Copper, Secondary
REFINERS & SMELTERS: Gold
REFINERS & SMELTERS: Nonferrous Metal
REFINERS & SMELTERS: Platinum Group Metal Refining,
Primary
REFINERS & SMELTERS: Silicon, Primary, Over 99% Pure
REFINERS & SMELTERS: Silver

REFINERS & SMELTERS: Zinc, Primary, Including Slabs & Dust
REFINING LUBRICATING OILS & GREASES, NEC
REFINING: Petroleum
REFRACTORIES: Alumina Fused
REFRACTORIES: Brick
REFRACTORIES: Brick
REFRACTORIES: Clay
REFRACTORIES: Graphite, Carbon Or Ceramic Bond
REFRACTORIES: Nonclay
REFRACTORY MATERIALS WHOLESALERS
REFRIGERATION & HEATING EQUIPMENT
REFRIGERATION EQPT & SPLYS WHOLESALERS
REFRIGERATION EQPT: Complete
REFRIGERATION REPAIR SVCS
REFRIGERATION SVC & REPAIR
REFUSE SYSTEMS
REGULATORS: Power
REGULATORS: Transmission & Distribution Voltage
REGULATORS: Transmission & Distribution Voltage
RELAYS & SWITCHES: Indl, Electric
RELAYS: Electronic Usage
RELIGIOUS SPLYS WHOLESALERS
REMOVERS & CLEANERS
RENTAL CENTERS: General
RENTAL SVCS: Business Machine & Electronic Eqpt
RENTAL SVCS: Costume
RENTAL SVCS: Electronic Eqpt, Exc Computers
RENTAL SVCS: Eqpt, Theatrical
RENTAL SVCS: Invalid Splys
RENTAL SVCS: Live Plant
RENTAL SVCS: Pallet
RENTAL SVCS: Tent & Tarpaulin
RENTAL SVCS: Work Zone Traffic Eqpt, Flags, Cones, Etc
RENTAL: Video Tape & Disc
REPEATERS: Passive
REPRODUCTION SVCS: Video Tape Or Disk
RESEARCH, DEV & TESTING SVCS, COMM: Chem Lab, Exc Testing
RESEARCH, DEVELOPMENT & TEST SVCS, COMM: Business Analysis
RESEARCH, DEVELOPMENT & TEST SVCS, COMM: Cmptr Hardware Dev
RESEARCH, DEVELOPMENT & TEST SVCS, COMM: Research, Exc Lab
RESEARCH, DEVELOPMENT & TESTING SVCS, COMM: Research Lab
RESEARCH, DEVELOPMENT & TESTING SVCS, COMMERCIAL: Medical
RESEARCH, DVLPMT & TESTING SVCS, COMM: Merger, Acq & Reorg
RESEARCH, DVLPT & TEST SVCS, COMM: Mkt Analysis or Research
RESIDENTIAL REMODELERS
RESINS: Custom Compound Purchased
RESISTORS
RESISTORS & RESISTOR UNITS
RESORT HOTELS
RESPIRATORS
RESTAURANT EQPT REPAIR SVCS
RESTAURANT EQPT: Carts
RESTAURANT EQPT: Food Wagons
RESTAURANT EQPT: Sheet Metal
RESTAURANTS:Full Svc, American
RESTAURANTS:Full Svc, Mexican
RESTAURANTS:Full Svc, Seafood
RESTAURANTS:Limited Svc, Coffee Shop
RESTAURANTS:Limited Svc, Ice Cream Stands Or Dairy Bars
RESTAURANTS:Limited Svc, Lunch Counter
RETAIL BAKERY: Bagels
RETAIL BAKERY: Bread
RETAIL BAKERY: Cookies
RETAIL FIREPLACE STORES
RETAIL LUMBER YARDS
RETAIL STORES, NEC
RETAIL STORES: Alarm Signal Systems
RETAIL STORES: Alcoholic Beverage Making Eqpt & Splys
RETAIL STORES: Aquarium Splys
RETAIL STORES: Art & Architectural Splys
RETAIL STORES: Artificial Limbs
RETAIL STORES: Audio-Visual Eqpt & Splys
RETAIL STORES: Awnings
RETAIL STORES: Cake Decorating Splys
RETAIL STORES: Canvas Prdts

RETAIL STORES: Cleaning Eqpt & Splys
RETAIL STORES: Cosmetics
RETAIL STORES: Educational Aids & Electronic Training Mat
RETAIL STORES: Electronic Parts & Eqpt
RETAIL STORES: Engine & Motor Eqpt & Splys
RETAIL STORES: Farm Eqpt & Splys
RETAIL STORES: Fiberglass Materials, Exc Insulation
RETAIL STORES: Fire Extinguishers
RETAIL STORES: Gravestones, Finished
RETAIL STORES: Hearing Aids
RETAIL STORES: Ice
RETAIL STORES: Infant Furnishings & Eqpt
RETAIL STORES: Medical Apparatus & Splys
RETAIL STORES: Mobile Telephones & Eqpt
RETAIL STORES: Monuments, Finished To Custom Order
RETAIL STORES: Motors, Electric
RETAIL STORES: Orthopedic & Prosthesis Applications
RETAIL STORES: Religious Goods
RETAIL STORES: Stones, Crystalline, Rough
RETAIL STORES: Telephone Eqpt & Systems
RETAIL STORES: Tents
RETAIL STORES: Water Purification Eqpt
RETAIL STORES: Welding Splys
REUPHOLSTERY & FURNITURE REPAIR
REUPHOLSTERY SVCS
RIBBONS & BOWS
RIBBONS, NEC
RIBBONS: Machine, Inked Or Carbon
RIDING APPAREL STORES
RIVETS: Metal
ROAD MATERIALS: Bituminous, Not From Refineries
ROBOTS: Assembly Line
ROCK SALT MINING
ROCKET LAUNCHERS
ROCKETS: Space & Military
RODS: Extruded, Aluminum
RODS: Plastic
RODS: Steel & Iron, Made In Steel Mills
RODS: Welding
ROLL COVERINGS: Rubber
ROLL FORMED SHAPES: Custom
ROLLED OR DRAWN SHAPES, NEC: Copper & Copper Alloy
ROLLERS & FITTINGS: Window Shade
ROLLING MILL MACHINERY
ROLLS & BLANKETS, PRINTERS': Rubber Or Rubberized Fabric
ROLLS: Rubber, Solid Or Covered
ROOFING MATERIALS: Asphalt
ROOFING MATERIALS: Sheet Metal
ROPE
ROTORS: Motor
RUBBER
RUBBER PRDTS: Automotive, Mechanical
RUBBER PRDTS: Mechanical
RUBBER PRDTS: Oil & Gas Field Machinery, Mechanical
RUBBER PRDTS: Reclaimed
RUBBER PRDTS: Silicone
RUBBER PRDTS: Sponge
RUBBER PRDTS: Wet Suits
RUBBER STRUCTURES: Air-Supported
RUGS : Hand & Machine Made
RULERS: Metal

S

SAFES & VAULTS: Metal
SAFETY EQPT & SPLYS WHOLESALERS
SAILBOAT BUILDING & REPAIR
SAILS
SALES PROMOTION SVCS
SALT
SAMPLE BOOKS
SAND & GRAVEL
SAND MINING
SAND: Hygrade
SANDSTONE: Crushed & Broken
SANITARY SVCS: Environmental Cleanup
SANITARY SVCS: Waste Materials, Recycling
SANITARY WARE: Metal
SANITATION CHEMICALS & CLEANING AGENTS
SASHES: Door Or Window, Metal
SATCHELS
SATELLITES: Communications
SAW BLADES
SAWDUST & SHAVINGS
SAWDUST, WHOLESALE

SAWING & PLANING MILLS
SAWING & PLANING MILLS: Custom
SCALES & BALANCES, EXC LABORATORY
SCALES: Baby
SCALP TREATMENT SVCS
SCANNING DEVICES: Optical
SCHOOLS & EDUCATIONAL SVCS, NEC
SCIENTIFIC EQPT REPAIR SVCS
SCISSORS: Hand
SCRAP & WASTE MATERIALS, WHOLESALE: Ferrous Metal
SCRAP & WASTE MATERIALS, WHOLESALE: Metal
SCRAP & WASTE MATERIALS, WHOLESALE: Plastics Scrap
SCRAP & WASTE MATERIALS, WHOLESALE: Rags
SCREENS: Projection
SCREENS: Window, Metal
SCREENS: Woven Wire
SCREW MACHINE PRDTS
SCREW MACHINES
SCREWS: Metal
SEALANTS
SEARCH & DETECTION SYSTEMS, EXC RADAR
SEARCH & NAVIGATION SYSTEMS
SEATING: Bleacher, Portable
SECRETARIAL SVCS
SECURITY CONTROL EQPT & SYSTEMS
SECURITY DEVICES
SECURITY EQPT STORES
SECURITY PROTECTIVE DEVICES MAINTENANCE & MONITORING SVCS
SECURITY SYSTEMS SERVICES
SEMICONDUCTOR & RELATED DEVICES: Read-Only Memory Or ROM
SEMICONDUCTOR DEVICES: Wafers
SEMICONDUCTORS & RELATED DEVICES
SENSORS: Temperature For Motor Windings
SENSORS: Temperature, Exc Indl Process
SEPARATORS: Metal Plate
SEPTIC TANKS: Concrete
SEPTIC TANKS: Plastic
SERVOMOTORS: Electric
SEWAGE & WATER TREATMENT EQPT
SEWAGE TREATMENT SYSTEMS & EQPT
SEWER CLEANING EQPT: Power
SEWING CONTRACTORS
SEWING MACHINES & PARTS: Indl
SEWING, NEEDLEWORK & PIECE GOODS STORE: Needlework Gds/Sply
SEWING, NEEDLEWORK & PIECE GOODS STORES: Sewing & Needlework
SHADES: Lamp & Light, Residential
SHADES: Lamp Or Candle
SHADES: Window
SHAFTS: Flexible
SHALE MINING, COMMON
SHALE: Expanded
SHAPES & PILINGS, STRUCTURAL: Steel
SHEATHING: Paper
SHEET METAL SPECIALTIES, EXC STAMPED
SHEET MUSIC STORES
SHEET MUSIC, WHOLESALE
SHEETING: Laminated Plastic
SHEETS & STRIPS: Aluminum
SHEETS: Fabric, From Purchased Materials
SHELVES & SHELVING: Wood
SHELVING: Office & Store, Exc Wood
SHERARDIZING SVC: Metals Or Metal Prdts
SHIELDS OR ENCLOSURES: Radiator, Sheet Metal
SHIMS: Metal
SHIP BUILDING & REPAIRING: Cargo Vessels
SHIP BUILDING & REPAIRING: Cargo, Commercial
SHIP BUILDING & REPAIRING: Ferryboats
SHIP BUILDING & REPAIRING: Rigging, Marine
SHIP BUILDING & REPAIRING: Tankers
SHIPBUILDING & REPAIR
SHIPPING AGENTS
SHOCK ABSORBERS: Indl
SHOE & BOOT ACCESS
SHOE MATERIALS: Counters
SHOE MATERIALS: Plastic
SHOE MATERIALS: Quarters
SHOE MATERIALS: Sole Parts
SHOE REPAIR SHOP
SHOE STORES
SHOE STORES: Children's

SHOE STORES: Orthopedic
SHOE STORES: Women's
SHOES & BOOTS WHOLESALERS
SHOES: Athletic, Exc Rubber Or Plastic
SHOES: Ballet Slippers
SHOES: Canvas, Rubber Soled
SHOES: Infants' & Children's
SHOES: Men's
SHOES: Men's, Sandals
SHOES: Men's, Work
SHOES: Orthopedic, Men's
SHOES: Orthopedic, Women's
SHOES: Plastic Or Rubber
SHOES: Plastic Or Rubber Soles With Fabric Uppers
SHOES: Women's
SHOES: Women's, Dress
SHOES: Women's, Sandals
SHOPPING CENTERS & MALLS
SHOT PEENING SVC
SHOWCASES & DISPLAY FIXTURES: Office & Store
SHOWER STALLS: Metal
SHOWER STALLS: Plastic & Fiberglass
SIDING & STRUCTURAL MATERIALS: Wood
SIDING: Precast Stone
SIGN LETTERING & PAINTING SVCS
SIGN PAINTING & LETTERING SHOP
SIGNALING APPARATUS: Electric
SIGNALING DEVICES: Sound, Electrical
SIGNALS: Railroad, Electric
SIGNALS: Traffic Control, Electric
SIGNS & ADVERTISING SPECIALTIES
SIGNS & ADVERTISING SPECIALTIES: Artwork, Advertising
SIGNS & ADVERTISING SPECIALTIES: Displays, Paint Process
SIGNS & ADVERTISING SPECIALTIES: Letters For Signs, Metal
SIGNS & ADVERTISING SPECIALTIES: Novelties
SIGNS & ADVERTISING SPECIALTIES: Scoreboards, Electric
SIGNS & ADVERTISING SPECIALTIES: Signs
SIGNS & ADVERTSG SPECIALTIES: Displays/Cutouts Window/Lobby
SIGNS, EXC ELECTRIC, WHOLESALE
SIGNS: Electrical
SIGNS: Neon
SILICA MINING
SILICON & CHROMIUM
SILICON WAFERS: Chemically Doped
SILICONE RESINS
SILICONES
SILK SCREEN DESIGN SVCS
SILVER ORES
SILVER ORES PROCESSING
SILVERSMITHS
SILVERWARE
SILVERWARE & PLATED WARE
SILVERWARE, SILVER PLATED
SIMULATORS: Flight
SINKS: Vitreous China
SKYLIGHTS
SLAB & TILE: Precast Concrete, Floor
SLABS: Steel
SLATE PRDTS
SLATE: Crushed & Broken
SLATE: Dimension
SLAUGHTERING & MEAT PACKING
SLINGS: Rope
SLIP RINGS
SLIPPERS: House
SMOKE DETECTORS
SNOW PLOWING SVCS
SOAPS & DETERGENTS
SOAPS & DETERGENTS: Textile
SOCIAL SERVICES INFORMATION EXCHANGE
SOCIAL SVCS, HANDICAPPED
SOCIAL SVCS: Individual & Family
SOFT DRINKS WHOLESALERS
SOFTWARE PUBLISHERS: Application
SOFTWARE PUBLISHERS: Business & Professional
SOFTWARE PUBLISHERS: Computer Utilities
SOFTWARE PUBLISHERS: Education
SOFTWARE PUBLISHERS: Home Entertainment
SOFTWARE PUBLISHERS: NEC
SOFTWARE PUBLISHERS: Operating Systems
SOFTWARE PUBLISHERS: Publisher's

SOFTWARE PUBLISHERS: Word Processing
SOFTWARE TRAINING, COMPUTER
SOLAR CELLS
SOLAR HEATING EQPT
SOLDERS
SOLVENTS
SONAR SYSTEMS & EQPT
SOUND EQPT: Electric
SOUND EQPT: Underwater
SOUND REPRODUCING EQPT
SPACE VEHICLE EQPT
SPARK PLUGS: Internal Combustion Engines
SPAS
SPEAKER SYSTEMS
SPECIAL EVENTS DECORATION SVCS
SPECIALTY FOOD STORES: Coffee
SPECIALTY FOOD STORES: Health & Dietetic Food
SPECIALTY FOOD STORES: Juices, Fruit Or Vegetable
SPECIALTY FOOD STORES: Tea
SPECIALTY FOOD STORES: Vitamin
SPERM BANK
SPONGES, ANIMAL, WHOLESALE
SPONGES: Plastic
SPOOLS: Fiber, Made From Purchased Materials
SPOOLS: Indl
SPORTING & ATHLETIC GOODS: Bags, Golf
SPORTING & ATHLETIC GOODS: Bowling Pins
SPORTING & ATHLETIC GOODS: Bows, Archery
SPORTING & ATHLETIC GOODS: Boxing Eqpt & Splys, NEC
SPORTING & ATHLETIC GOODS: Camping Eqpt & Splys
SPORTING & ATHLETIC GOODS: Cartridge Belts
SPORTING & ATHLETIC GOODS: Driving Ranges, Golf, Electronic
SPORTING & ATHLETIC GOODS: Dumbbells & Other Weight Eqpt
SPORTING & ATHLETIC GOODS: Fishing Bait, Artificial
SPORTING & ATHLETIC GOODS: Fishing Eqpt
SPORTING & ATHLETIC GOODS: Fishing Tackle, General
SPORTING & ATHLETIC GOODS: Game Calls
SPORTING & ATHLETIC GOODS: Hockey Eqpt & Splys, NEC
SPORTING & ATHLETIC GOODS: Lacrosse Eqpt & Splys, NEC
SPORTING & ATHLETIC GOODS: Pools, Swimming, Exc Plastic
SPORTING & ATHLETIC GOODS: Pools, Swimming, Plastic
SPORTING & ATHLETIC GOODS: Shooting Eqpt & Splys, General
SPORTING & ATHLETIC GOODS: Skateboards
SPORTING & ATHLETIC GOODS: Skates & Parts, Roller
SPORTING & ATHLETIC GOODS: Snow Skis
SPORTING & ATHLETIC GOODS: Target Shooting Eqpt
SPORTING & ATHLETIC GOODS: Team Sports Eqpt
SPORTING & ATHLETIC GOODS: Tennis Eqpt & Splys
SPORTING & REC GOODS, WHOLESALE: Camping Eqpt & Splys
SPORTING & RECREATIONAL GOODS & SPLYS WHOLESALERS
SPORTING & RECREATIONAL GOODS, WHOL: Sharpeners, Sporting
SPORTING & RECREATIONAL GOODS, WHOLESALE: Bicycle
SPORTING & RECREATIONAL GOODS, WHOLESALE: Boat Access & Part
SPORTING & RECREATIONAL GOODS, WHOLESALE: Exercise
SPORTING & RECREATIONAL GOODS, WHOLESALE: Fishing
SPORTING & RECREATIONAL GOODS, WHOLESALE: Fishing Tackle
SPORTING & RECREATIONAL GOODS, WHOLESALE: Hot Tubs
SPORTING & RECREATIONAL GOODS, WHOLESALE: Skiing
SPORTING & RECREATIONAL GOODS, WHOLESALE: Watersports
SPORTING GOODS
SPORTING GOODS STORES, NEC
SPORTING GOODS STORES: Camping Eqpt
SPORTING GOODS STORES: Fishing Eqpt
SPORTING GOODS STORES: Playground Eqpt
SPORTING GOODS STORES: Skateboarding Eqpt
SPORTING GOODS STORES: Tennis Goods & Eqpt
SPORTING GOODS: Archery
SPORTING GOODS: Fishing Nets
SPORTING GOODS: Sailboards

SPORTING GOODS: Surfboards
SPORTING/ATHLETIC GOODS: Gloves, Boxing, Handball, Etc
SPORTS APPAREL STORES
SPORTS PROMOTION SVCS
SPOUTING: Plastic & Fiberglass Reinforced
SPRAYING & DUSTING EQPT
SPRAYING EQPT: Agricultural
SPRAYS: Self-Defense
SPRINGS: Coiled Flat
SPRINGS: Leaf, Automobile, Locomotive, Etc
SPRINGS: Mechanical, Precision
SPRINGS: Precision
SPRINGS: Sash Balances
SPRINGS: Steel
SPRINGS: Wire
SPRINKLING SYSTEMS: Fire Control
STAGE LIGHTING SYSTEMS
STAINLESS STEEL
STAIRCASES & STAIRS, WOOD
STAMPED ART GOODS FOR EMBROIDERING
STAMPING SVC: Book, Gold
STAMPINGS: Automotive
STAMPINGS: Metal
STANDS & RACKS: Engine, Metal
STARTERS: Motor
STATIC ELIMINATORS: Ind
STATIONARY & OFFICE SPLYS, WHOLESALE: Blank Books
STATIONARY & OFFICE SPLYS, WHOLESALE: Stationery
STATIONER'S SUNDRIES: Rubber
STATIONERY & OFFICE SPLYS WHOLESALERS
STATIONERY PRDTS
STATIONERY: Made From Purchased Materials
STATUES: Nonmetal
STEAM SPLY SYSTEMS SVCS INCLUDING GEOTHERMAL
STEAM, HEAT & AIR CONDITIONING DISTRIBUTION SVC
STEEL & ALLOYS: Tool & Die
STEEL FABRICATORS
STEEL MILLS
STEEL, COLD-ROLLED: Sheet Or Strip, From Own Hot-Rolled
STEEL, COLD-ROLLED: Strip NEC, From Purchased Hot-Rolled
STEEL, HOT-ROLLED: Sheet Or Strip
STEEL: Cold-Rolled
STEEL: Galvanized
STEEL: Laminated
STENCIL BOARD: Die-Cut, Made From Purchased Materials
STENCILS
STONE: Cast Concrete
STONE: Crushed & Broken, NEC
STONE: Dimension, NEC
STONE: Quarrying & Processing, Own Stone Prdts
STONEWARE CLAY MINING
STORE FIXTURES, EXC REFRIGERATED: Wholesalers
STORE FIXTURES: Exc Wood
STORE FIXTURES: Wood
STORE FRONTS: Prefabricated, Metal
STORE FRONTS: Prefabricated, Wood
STORES: Auto & Home Supply
STRAPPING
STRAPS: Bindings, Textile
STRAPS: Braids, Textile
STRAPS: Cotton Webbing
STRAWS: Drinking, Made From Purchased Materials
STRINGING BEADS
STRUCTURAL SUPPORT & BUILDING MATERIAL: Concrete
STUDIOS: Artist's
STUDIOS: Sculptor's
STUDS & JOISTS: Sheet Metal
SUBSCRIPTION FULFILLMENT SVCS: Magazine, Newspaper, Etc
SUGAR SUBSTITUTES: Organic
SUNDRIES & RELATED PRDTS: Medical & Laboratory, Rubber
SUNGLASSES, WHOLESALE
SUNROOMS: Prefabricated Metal
SUPERMARKETS & OTHER GROCERY STORES
SURFACE ACTIVE AGENTS
SURFACE ACTIVE AGENTS: Oils & Greases
SURGICAL & MEDICAL INSTRUMENTS WHOLESALERS
SURGICAL APPLIANCES & SPLYS
SURGICAL APPLIANCES & SPLYS
SURGICAL EQPT: See Also Instruments
SURGICAL IMPLANTS

INDEX

TRUCKING: Local, Without Storage
TRUCKS & TRACTORS: Industrial
TRUCKS: Forklift
TRUCKS: Indl
TRUNKS
TRUSSES & FRAMING: Prefabricated Metal
TRUSSES: Wood, Roof
TUBE & TUBING FABRICATORS
TUBES: Finned, For Heat Transfer
TUBES: Generator, Electron Beam, Beta Ray
TUBES: Paper
TUBES: Paper Or Fiber, Chemical Or Electrical Uses
TUBES: Steel & Iron
TUBES: Vacuum
TUBES: Wrought, Welded Or Lock Joint
TUBING: Flexible, Metallic
TUBING: Glass
TUBING: Plastic
TUBING: Seamless
TUNGSTEN CARBIDE
TUNGSTEN CARBIDE POWDER
TURBINE GENERATOR SET UNITS: Hydraulic, Complete
TURBINES & TURBINE GENERATOR SET UNITS: Gas, Complete
TURBINES & TURBINE GENERATOR SETS
TURBINES & TURBINE GENERATOR SETS & PARTS
TURBINES: Hydraulic, Complete
TURBINES: Steam
TURBO-GENERATORS
TYPESETTING SVC
TYPESETTING SVC: Computer
TYPOGRAPHY

U

ULTRASONIC EQPT: Cleaning, Exc Med & Dental
UMBRELLAS & CANES
UMBRELLAS: Garden Or Wagon
UNIFORM STORES
UNIVERSITY
UNSUPPORTED PLASTICS: Floor Or Wall Covering
UPHOLSTERY FILLING MATERIALS
UPHOLSTERY MATERIALS, BROADWOVEN
UPHOLSTERY WORK SVCS
URANIUM ORE MINING, NEC
USED CAR DEALERS
USED MERCHANDISE STORES: Building Materials
USED MERCHANDISE STORES: Rare Books
UTENSILS: Cast Aluminum, Cooking Or Kitchen
UTENSILS: Household, Cooking & Kitchen, Metal
UTENSILS: Household, Cooking & Kitchen, Porcelain Enameled
UTENSILS: Household, Porcelain Enameled
UTILITY TRAILER DEALERS

V

VACUUM CLEANER STORES
VACUUM CLEANERS: Household
VACUUM CLEANERS: Indl Type
VACUUM SYSTEMS: Air Extraction, Indl
VALUE-ADDED RESELLERS: Computer Systems
VALVES
VALVES & PIPE FITTINGS
VALVES & REGULATORS: Pressure, Indl
VALVES Solenoid
VALVES: Aerosol, Metal
VALVES: Aircraft
VALVES: Aircraft, Control, Hydraulic & Pneumatic
VALVES: Aircraft, Fluid Power
VALVES: Control, Automatic
VALVES: Electrohydraulic Servo, Metal
VALVES: Engine
VALVES: Fluid Power, Control, Hydraulic & pneumatic
VALVES: Gas Cylinder, Compressed
VALVES: Hard Rubber
VALVES: Indl
VALVES: Plumbing & Heating
VALVES: Regulating & Control, Automatic
VALVES: Water Works
VARNISHES, NEC
VEGETABLE STANDS OR MARKETS

VEHICLES: All Terrain
VEHICLES: Recreational
VENDING MACHINES & PARTS
VENTILATING EQPT: Metal
VENTILATING EQPT: Sheet Metal
VENTURE CAPITAL COMPANIES
VETERINARY PHARMACEUTICAL PREPARATIONS
VIBRATORS: Concrete Construction
VIDEO & AUDIO EQPT, WHOLESALE
VIDEO CAMERA-AUDIO RECORDERS: Household Use
VIDEO EQPT
VIDEO PRODUCTION SVCS
VIDEO REPAIR SVCS
VIDEO TAPE PRODUCTION SVCS
VINYL RESINS, NEC
VITAMINS: Natural Or Synthetic, Uncompounded, Bulk
VITAMINS: Pharmaceutical Preparations

W

WALL COVERINGS WHOLESALERS
WALLBOARD: Decorated, Made From Purchased Materials
WALLPAPER & WALL COVERINGS
WALLS: Curtain, Metal
WAREHOUSE CLUBS STORES
WAREHOUSING & STORAGE FACILITIES, NEC
WAREHOUSING & STORAGE, REFRIGERATED: Frozen Or Refrig Goods
WAREHOUSING & STORAGE: General
WAREHOUSING & STORAGE: General
WAREHOUSING & STORAGE: Refrigerated
WARM AIR HEATING & AC EQPT & SPLYS, WHOLESALE Air Filters
WARM AIR HEATING/AC EQPT/SPLYS, WHOL Dehumidifiers, Exc Port
WARM AIR HEATING/AC EQPT/SPLYS, WHOL: Ventilating Eqpt/Sply
WASHCLOTHS
WASHERS: Metal
WASHERS: Plastic
WATCH STRAPS, EXC METAL
WATCHCASES
WATCHES
WATCHES & PARTS, WHOLESALE
WATER PURIFICATION EQPT: Household
WATER TREATMENT EQPT: Indl
WATER: Mineral, Carbonated, Canned & Bottled, Etc
WATER: Pasteurized & Mineral, Bottled & Canned
WATER: Pasteurized, Canned & Bottled, Etc
WATERPROOFING COMPOUNDS
WAVEGUIDES & FITTINGS
WAXES: Mineral, Natural
WAXES: Paraffin
WAXES: Petroleum, Not Produced In Petroleum Refineries
WEATHER STRIPS: Metal
WEAVING MILL, BROADWOVEN FABRICS: Wool Or Similar Fabric
WEDDING CHAPEL: Privately Operated
WEIGHING MACHINERY & APPARATUS
WELDING & CUTTING APPARATUS & ACCESS, NEC
WELDING EQPT
WELDING EQPT & SPLYS WHOLESALERS
WELDING EQPT: Electrical
WELDING MACHINES & EQPT: Ultrasonic
WELDING REPAIR SVC
WELDING SPLYS, EXC GASES: Wholesalers
WELDING TIPS: Heat Resistant, Metal
WELDMENTS
WHEELBARROWS
WHEELCHAIR LIFTS
WHEELCHAIRS
WHEELS & PARTS
WHEELS: Abrasive
WHEELS: Buffing & Polishing
WHEELS: Iron & Steel, Locomotive & Car
WIGS & HAIRPIECES
WIND TUNNELS
WINDINGS: Coil, Electronic
WINDMILLS: Electric Power Generation
WINDOW & DOOR FRAMES
WINDOW BLIND REPAIR SVCS

WINDOW FRAMES & SASHES: Plastic
WINDOW FRAMES, MOLDING & TRIM: Vinyl
WINDOW TRIMMING SVCS
WINDOWS: Wood
WINE & DISTILLED ALCOHOLIC BEVERAGES WHOLESALERS
WINE CELLARS, BONDED: Wine, Blended
WIRE
WIRE & CABLE: Aluminum
WIRE & CABLE: Nonferrous, Aircraft
WIRE & WIRE PRDTS
WIRE CLOTH & WOVEN WIRE PRDTS, MADE FROM PURCHASED WIRE
WIRE FABRIC: Welded Steel
WIRE FENCING & ACCESS WHOLESALERS
WIRE MATERIALS: Copper
WIRE MATERIALS: Steel
WIRE PRDTS: Ferrous Or Iron, Made In Wiredrawing Plants
WIRE PRDTS: Steel & Iron
WIRE WHOLESALERS
WIRE: Barbed
WIRE: Barbed & Twisted
WIRE: Communication
WIRE: Mesh
WIRE: Nonferrous
WIRE: Nonferrous, Appliance Fixture
WIRE: Steel, Insulated Or Armored
WOMEN'S & CHILDREN'S CLOTHING WHOLESALERS, NEC
WOMEN'S & GIRLS' SPORTSWEAR WHOLESALERS
WOMEN'S CLOTHING STORES
WOMEN'S CLOTHING STORES: Ready-To-Wear
WOMEN'S SPECIALTY CLOTHING STORES
WOMEN'S SPORTSWEAR STORES
WOOD FENCING WHOLESALERS
WOOD PRDTS: Beekeeping Splys
WOOD PRDTS: Clothespins
WOOD PRDTS: Display Forms, Boot & Shoe
WOOD PRDTS: Engraved
WOOD PRDTS: Furniture Inlays, Veneers
WOOD PRDTS: Jalousies, Glass, Wood Framed
WOOD PRDTS: Ladders & Stepladders
WOOD PRDTS: Laundry
WOOD PRDTS: Moldings, Unfinished & Prefinished
WOOD PRDTS: Mulch Or Sawdust
WOOD PRDTS: Novelties, Fiber
WOOD PRDTS: Outdoor, Structural
WOOD PRDTS: Panel Work
WOOD PRDTS: Pedestals & Statuary
WOOD PRDTS: Rulers & Rules
WOOD PRDTS: Shavings & Packaging, Excelsior
WOOD PRDTS: Shoe Trees
WOOD PRDTS: Signboards
WOOD PRDTS: Silo Staves
WOOD PRDTS: Trophy Bases
WOOD PRDTS: Window Backs, Store Or Lunchroom, Prefabricated
WOOD PRODUCTS: Reconstituted
WOOD TREATING: Creosoting
WOOD TREATING: Flooring, Block
WOOD TREATING: Structural Lumber & Timber
WOODWORK & TRIM: Interior & Ornamental
WOODWORK: Carved & Turned
WOODWORK: Interior & Ornamental, NEC
WOVEN WIRE PRDTS, NEC
WRITING FOR PUBLICATION SVCS

X

X-RAY EQPT & TUBES

Y

YARN & YARN SPINNING
YARN MILLS: Twisting
YARN WHOLESALERS
YARN: Embroidery, Spun
YARN: Natural & Animal Fiber, Spun
YARN: Specialty & Novelty
YARN: Weaving, Twisting, Winding Or Spooling
YOGURT WHOLESALERS

Indicates approximate employment figure
A = Over 500 employees, B = 251-500
C = 101-250, D = 51-100, E = 20-50
F = 10-19, G = 5-9

Product category

BOXES: Folding

Edgar & Son Paperboard ....G..... 999 999-9999
  Yourtown *(G-11480)*
Ready Box Co..E..... 999 999-9999
  Anytown *(G-7097)*

Business phone

Geographic Section entry number where full company information appears.

City

See footnotes for symbols and codes identification.

- Refer to the Industrial Product Index preceding this section to locate product headings.

ABRASIVES

American Douglas Metals Inc.............F 716 856-3170
  Buffalo *(G-2630)*
Buffalo Abrasives Inc ....E 716 693-3856
  North Tonawanda *(G-12060)*
Dedeco International Sales Inc.............D 845 887-4840
  Long Eddy *(G-7139)*
Dico Products Corporation ....F 315 797-0470
  Utica *(G-15255)*
Electro Abrasives LLC......................E 716 822-2500
  Buffalo *(G-2740)*
Imerys Fsed Mnrl Ngara FLS Inc ....G...... 716 286-1234
  Niagara Falls *(G-11938)*
Imerys Fsed Mnrl Ngara FLS Inc ....G...... 716 286-1250
  Niagara Falls *(G-11939)*
Imerys Fsed Mnrl Ngara FLS Inc ....E...... 716 286-1250
  Niagara Falls *(G-11940)*
Lunzer Inc ....G...... 201 794-2800
  New York *(G-10284)*
Meloon Foundries LLC......................E 315 454-3231
  Syracuse *(G-14939)*
Niabraze LLC..................................F 716 447-1082
  Tonawanda *(G-15126)*
Precision Elctro Mnrl Pmco Inc ....E 716 284-2484
  Niagara Falls *(G-11968)*
Saint-Gbain Advnced Crmics LLC ....E 716 691-2000
  Amherst *(G-242)*
Saint-Gobain Abrasives Inc ....B 518 266-2200
  Watervliet *(G-15605)*
Select-Tech Inc...............................G 845 895-8111
  Wallkill *(G-15473)*
Uneeda Enterprizes Inc ....C 800 431-2494
  Spring Valley *(G-14585)*
Warren Cutlery Corp.........................F 845 876-3444
  Rhinebeck *(G-13103)*

ABRASIVES: Aluminum Oxide Fused

Washington Mills Tonawanda Inc..........E 716 693-4550
  Tonawanda *(G-15153)*

ABRASIVES: Coated

Barton Mines Company LLC.................C 518 798-5462
  Glens Falls *(G-5242)*
Brick-It Inc ....G 631 244-3993
  Hauppauge *(G-5607)*
Conrad Blasius Equipment Co ....G 516 753-1200
  Plainview *(G-12672)*
Global Abrasive Products Inc ....E 716 438-0047
  Lockport *(G-7077)*
Precision Abrasives Corp ....E 716 826-5833
  Orchard Park *(G-12373)*

ABRASIVES: Grains

EAC Holdings of NY Corp ....E 716 822-2500
  Buffalo *(G-2735)*
Sunbelt Industries Inc ....F 315 823-2947
  Little Falls *(G-6993)*
Washingtom Mills Elec Mnrls ....D 716 278-6600
  Niagara Falls *(G-11991)*

ACADEMIC TUTORING SVCS

Bright Kids Nyc Inc..........................E 917 539-4575
  New York *(G-8852)*

ACCELERATION INDICATORS & SYSTEM COMPONENTS: Aerospace

Aeroflex Incorporated.......................B 516 694-6700
  Plainview *(G-12660)*

Arsenal Holdings LLC......................G..... 212 398-9139
  New York *(G-8626)*
Cobham Holdings Inc ....F 716 662-0006
  Orchard Park *(G-12345)*
Ihi Inc...E 212 599-8100
  New York *(G-9862)*
Inertia Switch Inc ....E 845 359-8300
  Orangeburg *(G-12319)*
Woodbine Products Inc ....E 631 586-3770
  Hauppauge *(G-5802)*

ACCELERATORS: Electron Linear

Iba Industrial Inc ....E 631 254-6800
  Edgewood *(G-4270)*

ACID RESIST: Etching

Greenfield Manufacturing Inc ....F 518 581-2368
  Saratoga Springs *(G-14180)*

ACIDS

Evans Chemetics LP.........................D 315 539-9221
  Waterloo *(G-15550)*

ACIDS: Sulfuric, Oleum

Norfalco LLC ....F 416 775-1431
  New York *(G-10640)*

ACOUSTICAL BOARD & TILE

Lencore Acoustics Corp ....F 315 384-9114
  Norfolk *(G-11999)*
Ssf Production LLC ....F 518 324-3407
  Plattsburgh *(G-12778)*

ACRYLIC RESINS

Creations In Lucite Inc ....G...... 718 871-2000
  Brooklyn *(G-1696)*

ACTUATORS: Indl, NEC

Makerbot Industries LLC.....................C 347 334-6800
  Brooklyn *(G-2104)*
Marine & Indus Hydraulics Inc..............F 914 698-2036
  Mamaroneck *(G-7513)*
Rotork Controls Inc ....F 585 328-1550
  Rochester *(G-13707)*
Trident Valve Actuator Co ....F 914 698-2650
  Mamaroneck *(G-7526)*
Young & Franklin Inc ....D 315 457-3110
  Liverpool *(G-7051)*

ADDITIVE BASED PLASTIC MATERIALS: Plasticizers

Dewitt Plastics Inc ....F 315 255-1209
  Auburn *(G-473)*
Fougera Pharmaceuticals Inc ....C 631 454-7677
  Melville *(G-7785)*
Mitsui Chemicals America Inc ....E 914 253-0777
  Rye Brook *(G-14092)*

ADHESIVES

Adirondack Spclty Adhsives Inc ....F 518 869-5736
  Albany *(G-28)*
Aremco Products Inc ....F 845 268-0039
  Valley Cottage *(G-15313)*
Beacon Adhesives Inc ....E 914 699-3400
  Mount Vernon *(G-8124)*

Best Adhesives Co Inc ....G...... 718 417-3800
  Ridgewood *(G-13141)*
Ran Mar Enterprises Ltd ....F 631 666-4754
  Bay Shore *(G-704)*
Saint Gobain Grains & Powders...........A 716 731-8200
  Niagara Falls *(G-11976)*

ADHESIVES & SEALANTS

Able National Corp............................E 718 386-8801
  Brooklyn *(G-1450)*
Advanced Polymer Solutions LLC ....G...... 516 621-5800
  Port Washington *(G-12860)*
All Out Die Cutting Inc ....E 718 346-6666
  Brooklyn *(G-1486)*
Angiotech Biocoatings Corp ....E 585 321-1130
  Henrietta *(G-5854)*
Astro Chemical Company Inc ....E 518 399-5338
  Ballston Lake *(G-557)*
Classic Labels Inc............................E 631 467-2300
  Patchogue *(G-12498)*
Hexion Inc......................................E 518 792-8040
  South Glens Falls *(G-14513)*
Legacy USA LLC ....F 718 292-5333
  Bronx *(G-1299)*
Meridian Adhesives Group LLC ....G...... 212 771-1717
  New York *(G-10434)*
P C I Paper Conversions Inc ....D 315 703-8300
  Syracuse *(G-14959)*
P C I Paper Conversions Inc ....E 315 634-3317
  Syracuse *(G-14960)*
Polycast Industries Inc.......................G...... 631 595-2530
  Bay Shore *(G-699)*
Polyset Company Inc..........................E 518 664-6000
  Mechanicville *(G-7693)*
Royal Adhesives & Sealants LLC ....F 315 451-1755
  Syracuse *(G-14980)*
Utility Manufacturing Co Inc ....E 516 997-6300
  Westbury *(G-15936)*
Wild Works Incorporated ....G...... 716 891-4197
  Albany *(G-142)*

ADHESIVES & SEALANTS WHOLESALERS

Nyi Building Products Inc ....F 518 458-7500
  Clifton Park *(G-3469)*

ADHESIVES: Epoxy

US Epoxy Inc ....G...... 800 332-3883
  Yaphank *(G-16277)*
Von Roll USA Holding Inc....................F 518 344-7200
  Schenectady *(G-14317)*

ADVERTISING AGENCIES

Act Communications Group Inc............F 631 669-2403
  West Islip *(G-15809)*
Ad Makers Long Island Inc ....F 631 595-9100
  Deer Park *(G-3829)*
Gatehouse Media LLC ....B 585 598-0030
  Pittsford *(G-12641)*
Gruner + Jahr Prtg & Pubg Co..............C...... 212 463-1000
  New York *(G-9687)*
Kinaneco Inc....................................E 315 468-6201
  Syracuse *(G-14926)*
Luria Communications Inc....................G...... 631 329-4922
  East Hampton *(G-4125)*
Media Trust LLC ....G...... 212 802-1162
  New York *(G-10412)*
Mickelberry Communications Inc...........G...... 212 832-0303
  New York *(G-10455)*
Middletown Press ....G...... 845 343-1895
  Middletown *(G-7920)*

PRODUCT

Msm Designz Inc................................G...... 914 909-5900
Tarrytown (G-15050)

Scholastic Corporation........................G...... 212 343-6100
New York (G-11160)

Service Advertising Group Inc ....F...... 718 361-6161
Long Island City (G-7355)

Stop Entertainment Inc.......................F...... 212 242-7867
Monroe (G-8031)

ADVERTISING AGENCIES: Consultants

Galli Shirts and Sports AP ....G...... 845 226-7305
Stormville (G-14751)

Whispr Group Inc ....G...... 212 924-3979
New York (G-11750)

ADVERTISING DISPLAY PRDTS

Arnprior Rpid Mfg Slutions Inc..........C...... 585 617-6301
Rochester (G-13247)

Arnprior Rpid Mfg Slutions Inc..........G...... 585 617-6301
Rochester (G-13248)

D3 Led LLC ....E...... 917 757-9671
New York (G-9149)

Federal Sample Card Corp.................D...... 718 458-1344
Elmhurst (G-4334)

Grand Visual LLC ....G...... 912 529-6215
Brooklyn (G-1907)

JG Innovative Industries Inc ....G...... 718 784-7300
Kew Gardens (G-6667)

Mack Studios Displays Inc ....E...... 315 252-7542
Auburn (G-484)

Nationwide Exhibitor Svcs Inc...........F...... 631 467-2034
Central Islip (G-3285)

Promotional Development Inc ....D...... 718 485-8550
Brooklyn (G-2301)

Qps Die Cutters Finishers Corp ....E...... 718 966-1811
Staten Island (G-14695)

Sherwood Group Inc............................G...... 240 731-8573
New York (G-11212)

Swift Multigraphics LLC ....G...... 585 442-8000
Rochester (G-13752)

Tri-Plex Packaging Corporation ....E...... 212 481-6070
New York (G-11539)

ADVERTISING MATERIAL DISTRIBUTION

Penny Lane Printing Inc ....D...... 585 226-8111
Avon (G-515)

Real Est Book of Long Island ....F...... 516 364-5000
Syosset (G-14801)

Shipmtes/Printmates Holdg Corp.........D...... 518 370-1158
Scotia (G-14336)

ADVERTISING REPRESENTATIVES: Electronic Media

Business Never Stops LLC...................G...... 888 479-3111
South Richmond Hill (G-14522)

World Business Media LLC..................F...... 212 344-0759
Massapequa Park (G-7662)

ADVERTISING REPRESENTATIVES: Magazine

Icd Publications Inc ....E...... 631 246-9300
Islandia (G-6335)

McClary Media Inc...............................G...... 800 453-6397
Amsterdam (G-334)

ADVERTISING REPRESENTATIVES: Media

Redbook Magazine ....F...... 212 649-3331
New York (G-10997)

ADVERTISING REPRESENTATIVES: Newspaper

Advertiser Publications Inc.................F...... 845 783-1111
Chester (G-3369)

Bradford Publications Inc ....C...... 716 373-2500
Olean (G-12226)

Community Cpons Frnchising Inc ....E...... 516 277-1968
Glen Cove (G-5190)

L & M Publications Inc........................E...... 516 378-3133
Garden City (G-5103)

Local Media Group Inc ....E...... 845 341-1100
Middletown (G-7916)

Long Island Cmnty Nwsppers Inc.......D...... 516 482-4490
Mineola (G-7987)

Market Place Publications...................E...... 516 997-7909
Carle Place (G-3178)

Service Advertising Group Inc ....F...... 718 361-6161
Long Island City (G-7355)

ADVERTISING REPRESENTATIVES: Printed Media

Informa Media Inc ....B...... 212 204-4200
New York (G-9889)

Press Express ....G...... 914 592-3790
Elmsford (G-4422)

ADVERTISING SPECIALTIES, WHOLESALE

A Trusted Name Inc ....F...... 716 326-7400
Westfield (G-15944)

Ad-Vantage Printing Inc ....F...... 718 820-0688
Kew Gardens (G-6661)

All American Awards Inc ....E...... 631 567-2025
Bohemia (G-968)

Concept Printing Inc ....G...... 845 353-4040
Nyack (G-12139)

Elco Manufacturing Co Inc..................F...... 516 767-3577
Port Washington (G-12877)

In-Step Marketing Inc.........................F...... 212 797-3450
New York (G-9874)

Middletown Press ....G...... 845 343-1895
Middletown (G-7920)

Msm Designz Inc..................................G...... 914 909-5900
Tarrytown (G-15050)

Sherwood Group Inc............................G...... 240 731-8573
New York (G-11212)

U All Inc ....E...... 518 438-2558
Albany (G-138)

Ward Sales Co Inc ....G...... 315 476-5276
Syracuse (G-15023)

Whispr Group Inc ....F...... 212 924-3979
New York (G-11750)

ADVERTISING SVCS: Direct Mail

Advertiser Publications Inc.................F...... 845 783-1111
Chester (G-3369)

Century Direct LLC ....C...... 212 763-0600
Islandia (G-6328)

Design Distributors Inc ....D...... 631 242-2000
Deer Park (G-3863)

Orffeo Printing & Imaging Inc.............G...... 716 681-5757
Lancaster (G-6819)

Shipmtes/Printmates Holdg Corp........D...... 518 370-1158
Scotia (G-14336)

Syracuse Letter Company Inc ....F...... 315 476-8328
Bridgeport (G-1169)

Thomas Publishing Company LLC ....B...... 212 695-0500
New York (G-11468)

ADVERTISING SVCS: Display

Apple Imprints Apparel Inc ....E...... 716 893-1130
Buffalo (G-2641)

Exhibits & More...................................G...... 585 924-4040
Victor (G-15408)

L Miller Design Inc ....G...... 631 242-1163
Deer Park (G-3894)

Mystic Display Co Inc..........................G...... 718 485-2651
Brooklyn (G-2183)

ADVERTISING SVCS: Sample Distribution

Instantwhip of Buffalo Inc..................E...... 716 892-7031
Buffalo (G-2811)

ADVERTISING SVCS: Transit

Danet Inc..F...... 718 266-4444
Brooklyn (G-1722)

Fun Media Inc ....E...... 646 472-0135
New York (G-9552)

AERIAL WORK PLATFORMS

Park Ave Bldg & Roofg Sups LLC ....E...... 718 403-0100
Brooklyn (G-2247)

AEROSOLS

Fountainhead Group Inc ....C...... 708 598-7100
New York Mills (G-11833)

AGENTS, BROKERS & BUREAUS: Personal Service

Superior Print On Demand...................G...... 607 240-5231
Vestal (G-15384)

T J Signs Unlimited LLC......................E...... 631 273-4800
Islip (G-6357)

AGRICULTURAL EQPT: BARN, SILO, POULTRY, DAIRY/LIVESTOCK MACH

Vansridge Dairy LLC............................E...... 315 364-8569
Scipio Center (G-14327)

AGRICULTURAL EQPT: Fertilizng, Sprayng, Dustng/Irrigatn Mach

Jain Irrigation Inc...............................G...... 315 755-4400
Watertown (G-15573)

AGRICULTURAL EQPT: Milking Machines

Westmoor Ltd.......................................F...... 315 363-1500
Sherrill (G-14409)

AGRICULTURAL EQPT: Planting Machines

Good Earth Organics Corp ....E...... 716 684-8111
Lancaster (G-6809)

AGRICULTURAL EQPT: Spreaders, Fertilizer

Chapin Manufacturing Inc...................C...... 585 343-3140
Batavia (G-609)

AGRICULTURAL EQPT: Trailers & Wagons, Farm

Renaldos Sales & Service Ctr..............G...... 716 337-3760
North Collins (G-12028)

AGRICULTURAL EQPT: Turf & Grounds Eqpt

Bdp Industries Inc...............................E...... 518 695-6851
Greenwich (G-5468)

AIR CLEANING SYSTEMS

Acme Engineering Products Inc...........E...... 518 236-5659
Mooers (G-8079)

Flanders Precisionaire NY ....G...... 518 751-5640
Hudson (G-6156)

Veteran Air LLC ....G...... 315 720-1101
Syracuse (G-15022)

AIR CONDITIONERS, AUTOMOTIVE: Wholesalers

American Comfort Direct LLC ....E...... 201 364-8309
New York (G-8548)

AIR CONDITIONING & VENTILATION EQPT & SPLYS: Wholesales

Elima-Draft Incorporated.....................G...... 631 375-2830
Stony Brook (G-14738)

Layton Manufacturing Corp..................E...... 718 498-6000
Brooklyn (G-2048)

AIR CONDITIONING EQPT

Carrier Corporation..............................B...... 315 432-6000
East Syracuse (G-4202)

Duro Dyne Corporation ....C...... 631 249-9000
Bay Shore (G-674)

Duro Dyne National Corp ....C...... 631 249-9000
Bay Shore (G-676)

Elima-Draft Incorporated.....................G...... 631 375-2830
Stony Brook (G-14738)

EMC Tech Inc..F...... 716 488-9071
Falconer (G-4539)

Empire Air Systems LLC ....F...... 718 377-1549
West Babylon (G-15709)

Layton Manufacturing Corp..................E...... 718 498-6000
Brooklyn (G-2048)

M M Tool and Manufacturing ....G...... 845 691-4140
Highland (G-5961)

RE Hansen Industries Inc.....................C...... 631 471-2900
Saint James (G-14113)

Split Systems Corp ....E...... 516 223-5511
North Baldwin (G-12008)

Transit Air Inc......................................E...... 607 324-0216
Hornell (G-6112)

AIR CONDITIONING UNITS: Complete, Domestic Or Indl

AC Air Cooling Co Inc ....F........ 718 933-1011
  Bronx (G-1190)

Alfa Laval Niagara Inc ....D........ 800 426-5169
  Tonawanda (G-15084)

Balticare Inc ....F........ 646 380-9470
  New York (G-8723)

Duro Dyne Machinery Corp ....E........ 631 249-9000
  Bay Shore (G-675)

Ice Air LLC ....E........ 914 668-4700
  Mount Vernon (G-8150)

JE Miller Inc ....F........ 315 437-6811
  East Syracuse (G-4224)

Pfannenberg Inc ....D........ 716 685-6866
  Lancaster (G-6825)

AIR DUCT CLEANING SVCS

Filta Clean Co Inc ....E........ 718 495-3800
  Brooklyn (G-1843)

AIR MATTRESSES: Plastic

Diamond Packaging Holdings LLC ......G........ 585 334-8030
  Rochester (G-13343)

Waddington North America Inc ....C........ 585 638-8200
  Holley (G-6039)

AIR POLLUTION MEASURING SVCS

Clean Gas Systems Inc ....E........ 631 467-1600
  Commack (G-3583)

AIR PREHEATERS: Nonrotating, Plate Type

Arvos Inc ....G........ 585 593-2700
  Wellsville (G-15667)

AIR PURIFICATION EQPT

Aeromed Inc ....G........ 518 843-9144
  Utica (G-15238)

Airgle Corporation ....E........ 866 501-7750
  Ronkonkoma (G-13894)

Austin Air Systems Limited ....D........ 716 856-3700
  Buffalo (G-2650)

Beecher Emssn Sltn Tchnlgs LLC .....F........ 607 796-0149
  Horseheads (G-6113)

Beltran Associates Inc ....E........ 718 252-2996
  Brooklyn (G-1572)

Clean Gas Systems Inc ....E........ 631 467-1600
  Commack (G-3583)

JT Systems Inc ....F........ 315 622-1980
  Liverpool (G-7019)

Phytofilter Technologies Inc ....G........ 518 507-6399
  Saratoga Springs (G-14187)

Sbb Inc ....G........ 315 422-2376
  East Syracuse (G-4236)

Sullivan Bazinet Bongio Inc ....E........ 315 437-6500
  East Syracuse (G-4240)

AIRCRAFT & AEROSPACE FLIGHT INSTRUMENTS & GUIDANCE SYSTEMS

Bae Systems Controls Inc ....A........ 607 770-2000
  Endicott (G-4445)

CIC International Ltd ....D........ 212 213-0089
  Brooklyn (G-1663)

Emergency Beacon Corp ....F........ 914 576-2700
  Bronx (G-1253)

Facilamatic Instrument Corp ....E........ 516 825-6300
  Valley Stream (G-15340)

Kwadair LLC ....G........ 646 824-2511
  Brooklyn (G-2036)

No Longer Empty Inc ....G........ 202 413-4262
  New York (G-10633)

Rockwell Industries Intl Corp ....E........ 516 927-8300
  Plainview (G-12710)

Select Fabricators Inc ....F........ 585 393-0650
  Canandaigua (G-3142)

AIRCRAFT & HEAVY EQPT REPAIR SVCS

Binghamton Simulator Co Inc ....E........ 607 321-2980
  Binghamton (G-860)

James A Staley Inc ....F........ 845 878-3344
  Carmel (G-3187)

AIRCRAFT ASSEMBLY PLANTS

Altius Aviation LLC ....G........ 315 455-7555
  Syracuse (G-14813)

Barclay Tagg Racing ....E........ 631 404-8269
  Floral Park (G-4809)

Bombardier Trnsp Holdings USA ....E........ 518 566-5067
  Plattsburgh (G-12738)

Easy Aerial Inc ....G........ 646 639-4410
  Brooklyn (G-1779)

Grumman Field Support Services ....D........ 516 575-0574
  Bethpage (G-835)

Ingenious Ingenuity Inc ....F........ 800 834-5279
  Webster (G-15642)

Lesly Enterprise & Associates ....G........ 631 988-1301
  Deer Park (G-3896)

Lockheed Martin Corporation ....D........ 315 793-5800
  New Hartford (G-8241)

Moog Inc ....B........ 716 687-4954
  East Aurora (G-4093)

Northrop Grumman Systems Corp .....A........ 516 575-0574
  Bethpage (G-842)

Pro Drones Usa LLC ....F........ 718 530-3558
  New York (G-10900)

Sikorsky Aircraft Corporation ....D........ 585 424-1990
  Rochester (G-13731)

AIRCRAFT CONTROL SYSTEMS: Electronic Totalizing Counters

Kimdu Corporation ....E........ 516 723-1339
  Plainview (G-12695)

Moog Inc ....A........ 716 805-2604
  Elma (G-4321)

Moog Inc ....B........ 716 687-5486
  Elma (G-4324)

AIRCRAFT ENGINES & ENGINE PARTS: Research & Development, Mfr

General Electric Company ....E........ 518 385-7620
  Niskayuna (G-11996)

General Electric Company ....A........ 518 385-4022
  Schenectady (G-14266)

AIRCRAFT ENGINES & PARTS

Ademco Inc ....G........ 716 631-2197
  Cheektowaga (G-3337)

Advanced Atomization Tech LLC ....B........ 315 923-2341
  Clyde (G-3488)

ARC Systems Inc ....E........ 631 582-8020
  Hauppauge (G-5592)

B H Aircraft Company Inc ....D........ 631 580-9747
  Ronkonkoma (G-13912)

Chromalloy American LLC ....E........ 845 230-7355
  Orangeburg (G-12309)

Chromalloy Gas Turbine LLC ....C........ 845 359-2462
  Orangeburg (G-12310)

Chromalloy Gas Turbine LLC ....E........ 845 692-8912
  Middletown (G-7898)

Colonial Group LLC ....E........ 516 349-8010
  Plainview (G-12671)

Davis Aircraft Products Co Inc ....C........ 631 563-1500
  Bohemia (G-1000)

Dyna-Empire Inc ....C........ 516 222-2700
  Garden City (G-5096)

Eur-Pac Corporation ....G........ 203 756-0102
  Bay Shore (G-679)

Fadec Alliance LLC ....C........ 607 770-3342
  Endicott (G-4454)

Gb Aero Engine LLC ....B........ 914 925-9600
  Rye (G-14078)

Honeywell International Inc ....D........ 518 270-0200
  Troy (G-15158)

Honeywell International Inc ....E........ 516 577-2661
  Melville (G-7790)

Honeywell International Inc ....E........ 516 577-2000
  Melville (G-7791)

Honeywell International Inc ....A........ 845 342-4400
  Middletown (G-7914)

Honeywell International Inc ....G........ 516 302-9401
  New Hyde Park (G-8274)

Honeywell International Inc ....A........ 212 964-5111
  Melville (G-7792)

Honeywell International Inc ....B........ 516 577-2000
  Melville (G-7793)

Honeywell International Inc ....F........ 315 463-7208
  East Syracuse (G-4217)

Honeywell International Inc ....G........ 631 471-2202
  Lake Ronkonkoma (G-6770)

ITT Enidine Inc ....B........ 716 662-1900
  Orchard Park (G-12356)

Kerns Manufacturing Corp ....C........ 718 784-4044
  Long Island City (G-7262)

Lourdes Industries Inc ....D........ 631 234-6600
  Hauppauge (G-5700)

Magellan Aerospace Bethel Inc ....C........ 203 798-9373
  Corona (G-3743)

Magellan Aerospace Processing ....G........ 631 694-1818
  West Babylon (G-15728)

McGuigan Inc ....E........ 631 750-6222
  Bohemia (G-1045)

Nell-Joy Industries Inc ....E........ 631 842-8989
  Copiague (G-3665)

SOS International LLC ....B........ 212 742-2410
  New York (G-11302)

Therm Incorporated ....C........ 607 272-8500
  Ithaca (G-6412)

Triumph Actuation Systems LLC ....C........ 516 378-0162
  Freeport (G-5030)

Triumph Group Inc ....D........ 516 997-5757
  Westbury (G-15934)

Turbine Engine Comp Utica ....A........ 315 768-8070
  Whitesboro (G-16084)

United Technologies Corp ....G........ 315 432-7849
  East Syracuse (G-4246)

AIRCRAFT EQPT & SPLYS WHOLESALERS

Fastener Dimensions Inc ....E........ 718 847-6321
  Ozone Park (G-12461)

Magellan Aerospace NY Inc ....C........ 631 589-2440
  Bohemia (G-1041)

Styles Aviation Inc ....G........ 845 677-8185
  Lagrangeville (G-6754)

Worldwide Arntcal Cmpnents Inc ....E........ 631 842-3780
  Copiague (G-3690)

AIRCRAFT FLIGHT INSTRUMENT REPAIR SVCS

Safe Flight Instrument Corp ....C........ 914 946-9500
  White Plains (G-16059)

AIRCRAFT FLIGHT INSTRUMENTS

Mod-A-Can Inc ....D........ 516 931-8545
  Hicksville (G-5931)

Safe Flight Instrument Corp ....C........ 914 946-9500
  White Plains (G-16059)

AIRCRAFT LIGHTING

Aerospace Lighting Corporation ....D........ 631 563-6400
  Bohemia (G-967)

Astronics Corporation ....C........ 716 805-1599
  East Aurora (G-4082)

B/E Aerospace Inc ....E........ 631 563-6400
  Bohemia (G-978)

Luminescent Systems Inc ....B........ 716 655-0800
  East Aurora (G-4091)

AIRCRAFT PARTS & AUXILIARY EQPT: Assemblies, Fuselage

Moelis Capital Partners LLC ....B........ 212 883-3800
  New York (G-10492)

AIRCRAFT PARTS & AUXILIARY EQPT: Assys, Subassemblies/Parts

Aero Trades Mfg Corp ....E........ 516 746-3360
  Mineola (G-7955)

Air Industries Machining Corp ....C........ 631 328-7000
  Bay Shore (G-645)

Arkwin Industries Inc ....C........ 516 333-2640
  Westbury (G-15870)

Ausco Inc ....D........ 516 944-9882
  Farmingdale (G-4588)

CPI Aerostructures Inc ....C........ 631 586-5200
  Edgewood (G-4266)

Design/OI Inc ....F........ 631 474-2134
  Port Jeff STA (G-12834)

Engineered Metal Products Inc ....G........ 631 842-3780
  Copiague (G-3652)

Excelco Developments Inc ....E........ 716 934-2651
  Silver Creek (G-14441)

Excelco/Newbrook Inc ....D........ 716 934-2644
  Silver Creek (G-14442)

GKN Aerospace Monitor Inc ....B........ 562 619-8558
  Amityville (G-264)

PRODUCT

Goodrich Corporation ....C 315 838-1200
  Rome (G-13849)
Handy Tool & Mfg Co Inc ....E 718 478-9203
  Brooklyn (G-1926)
Hicksville Machine Works Corp ....F 516 931-1524
  Hicksville (G-5916)
Lai International Inc ....E 763 780-0060
  Green Island (G-5438)
Magellan Aerospace Bethel Inc ....C 203 798-9373
  Corona (G-3743)
Magellan Aerospace NY Inc ....C 718 699-4000
  Corona (G-3744)
Min-Max Machine Ltd ....F 631 585-4378
  Ronkonkoma (G-13974)
Norsk Titanium US Inc ....E 518 324-4010
  Plattsburgh (G-12761)
Posimech Inc ....E 631 924-5959
  Medford (G-7722)
S&L Aerospace Metals LLC ....D 718 326-1821
  Flushing (G-4890)
Superior Motion Controls Inc ....E 516 420-2921
  Farmingdale (G-4745)
Tek Precision Co Ltd ....E 631 242-0330
  Deer Park (G-3941)
Wilco Industries Inc ....G 631 676-2593
  Ronkonkoma (G-14028)

AIRCRAFT PARTS & AUXILIARY EQPT: Body & Wing Assys & Parts

Aero Strctures Long Island Inc ....D 516 997-5757
  Westbury (G-15863)
Mpi Consulting Incorporated ....F 631 253-2377
  West Babylon (G-15733)

AIRCRAFT PARTS & AUXILIARY EQPT: Body Assemblies & Parts

Air Industries Group ....D 631 881-4920
  Bay Shore (G-644)
Reese Manufacturing Inc ....G 631 842-3780
  Copiague (G-3673)

AIRCRAFT PARTS & AUXILIARY EQPT: Gears, Power Transmission

Gleason Works ....A 585 473-1000
  Rochester (G-13445)
W J Albro Machine Works Inc ....G 631 345-0657
  Yaphank (G-16278)

AIRCRAFT PARTS & AUXILIARY EQPT: Landing Assemblies & Brakes

Blair Industries Inc ....E 631 924-6600
  Medford (G-7699)
Dyna-Empire Inc ....C 516 222-2700
  Garden City (G-5096)
Nassau Tool Works Inc ....E 631 328-7031
  Bay Shore (G-697)

AIRCRAFT PARTS & AUXILIARY EQPT: Military Eqpt & Armament

Dresser-Argus Inc ....G 718 643-1540
  Brooklyn (G-1762)
Metadure Parts & Sales Inc ....F 631 249-2141
  Farmingdale (G-4681)

AIRCRAFT PARTS & AUXILIARY EQPT: Refueling Eqpt, In Flight

Usairports Services Inc ....E 585 527-6835
  Rochester (G-13790)

AIRCRAFT PARTS & AUXILIARY EQPT: Seat Ejector Devices

East/West Industries Inc ....E 631 981-5900
  Ronkonkoma (G-13932)

AIRCRAFT PARTS & EQPT, NEC

AAR Allen Services Inc ....E 516 222-9000
  Garden City (G-5089)
Alken Industries Inc ....E 631 467-2000
  Ronkonkoma (G-13896)
Astronics Corporation ....C 716 805-1599
  East Aurora (G-4082)
B & B Precision Components Inc ....G 631 273-3321
  Ronkonkoma (G-13911)

B/E Aerospace Inc ....E 631 563-6400
  Bohemia (G-978)
Canfield Aerospace & Mar Inc ....E 631 648-1050
  Ronkonkoma (G-13921)
Caravan International Corp ....G 212 223-7190
  New York (G-8915)
Circor Aerospace Inc ....D 631 737-1900
  Hauppauge (G-5615)
Cox & Company Inc ....C 212 366-0200
  Plainview (G-12676)
Crown Aircraft Lighting Inc ....G 718 767-3410
  Whitestone (G-16091)
Davis Aircraft Products Co Inc ....C 631 563-1500
  Bohemia (G-1000)
Drt Aerospace LLC ....G 585 247-5940
  Rochester (G-13357)
Ducommun Aerostructures NY Inc ....B 518 731-2791
  Coxsackie (G-3800)
Eastern Precision Machining ....E 631 286-4758
  Bellport (G-797)
Fluid Mechanisms Hauppauge Inc ....E 631 234-0100
  Hauppauge (G-5652)
GE Aviation Systems LLC ....C 631 467-5500
  Bohemia (G-1015)
HSM Machine Works Inc ....E 631 924-6600
  Medford (G-7712)
Jac Usa Inc ....G 212 841-7430
  New York (G-9960)
Jamco Aerospace Inc ....E 631 586-7900
  Deer Park (G-3886)
Jaquith Industries Inc ....E 315 478-5700
  Syracuse (G-14916)
Joldeson One Aerospace Inds ....D 718 848-7396
  Ozone Park (G-12463)
Jrsmm LLC ....G 607 331-1549
  Elmira (G-4360)
Lenny & Bill LLC ....D 516 997-5757
  Westbury (G-15903)
Loar Group Inc ....C 212 210-9348
  New York (G-10239)
Magellan Aerospace NY Inc ....C 631 589-2440
  Bohemia (G-1041)
MD International Industries ....E 631 254-3100
  Deer Park (G-3906)
Metal Dynamics Intl Corp ....G 631 231-1153
  Hauppauge (G-5715)
Milex Precision Inc ....F 631 595-2393
  Bay Shore (G-692)
Military Parts Exchange LLC ....F 631 243-1700
  Melville (G-7805)
Minutemen Precsn McHning Tool ....E 631 467-4900
  Ronkonkoma (G-13975)
Moog Inc ....A 716 805-2604
  Elma (G-4321)
Parker-Hannifin Corporation ....C 631 231-3737
  Clyde (G-3494)
Precision Cnc ....E 631 847-3999
  Deer Park (G-3921)
Santa Fe Manufacturing Corp ....G 631 234-0100
  Hauppauge (G-5757)
Servotronics Inc ....C 716 655-5990
  Elma (G-4327)
Styles Aviation Inc ....G 845 677-8185
  Lagrangeville (G-6754)
Sumner Industries Inc ....F 631 666-7290
  Bay Shore (G-720)
Tangent Machine & Tool Corp ....F 631 249-3088
  Farmingdale (G-4749)
Tens Machine Company Inc ....E 631 981-3321
  Holbrook (G-6026)
TPC Inc ....G 315 438-8605
  East Syracuse (G-4243)
Triumph Actuation Systems LLC ....D 516 378-0162
  Freeport (G-5030)
Universal Armor Systems Corp ....E 631 838-1836
  Levittown (G-6917)
UTC Aerospace Systems ....E 315 838-1200
  Rome (G-13875)
Vosky Precision Machining Corp ....F 631 737-3200
  Ronkonkoma (G-14025)
Young & Franklin Inc ....D 315 457-3110
  Liverpool (G-7051)

AIRCRAFT SEATS

B/E Aerospace Inc ....E 631 563-6400
  Bohemia (G-978)
East/West Industries Inc ....E 631 981-5900
  Ronkonkoma (G-13932)

AIRCRAFT UPHOLSTERY REPAIR SVCS

Moelis Capital Partners LLC ....B 212 883-3800
  New York (G-10492)

AIRCRAFT: Airplanes, Fixed Or Rotary Wing

Boeing Company ....A 201 259-9400
  New York (G-8829)

AIRCRAFT: Autogiros

Necessity Systems LLC ....G 907 322-4084
  Kirkville (G-6725)

AIRCRAFT: Gliders

M & H Research and Dev Corp ....G 607 734-2346
  Beaver Dams (G-759)

AIRCRAFT: Motorized

Lockheed Martin Corporation ....E 716 297-1000
  Niagara Falls (G-11948)

AIRCRAFT: Research & Development, Manufacturer

Alliant Tchsystems Oprtons LLC ....E 631 737-6100
  Ronkonkoma (G-13898)
Calspan Corporation ....C 716 631-6955
  Buffalo (G-2689)
Calspan Corporation ....F 716 236-1040
  Niagara Falls (G-11911)
Calspan Holdings LLC ....F 716 631-6955
  Buffalo (G-2690)
Luminati Aerospace LLC ....F 631 574-2616
  Calverton (G-3082)
Tech Park Food Services LLC ....G 585 295-1250
  Rochester (G-13762)
Xactiv Inc ....F 585 288-7220
  Fairport (G-4531)

ALARM SYSTEMS WHOLESALERS

Lifewatch Inc ....F 800 716-1433
  Hewlett (G-5871)

ALARMS: Burglar

Datasonic Inc ....G 516 248-7330
  East Meadow (G-4134)
Harris Corporation ....A 413 263-6200
  Rochester (G-13459)
Sentry Devices Corp ....G 631 491-3191
  Dix Hills (G-4015)
Unitone Communication Systems ....G 212 777-9090
  New York (G-11603)

ALARMS: Fire

Fire Apparatus Service Tech ....G 716 753-3538
  Sherman (G-14400)
Toweriq Inc ....F 844 626-7638
  Long Island City (G-7384)

ALCOHOL, GRAIN: For Beverage Purposes

Watermans Distillery LLC ....G 607 258-0274
  Apalachin (G-363)

ALCOHOL: Ethyl & Ethanol

Attis Ethanol Fulton LLC ....D 315 593-0500
  Fulton (G-5054)

ALCOHOL: Methyl & Methanol, Synthetic

Balchem Corporation ....B 845 326-5600
  New Hampton (G-8232)
Hunts Point Clean Energy LLC ....G 203 451-5143
  Pearl River (G-12534)

ALKALIES & CHLORINE

FMC Corporation ....C 716 879-0400
  Tonawanda (G-15105)
Occidental Chemical Corp ....E 716 278-7795
  Niagara Falls (G-11959)
Occidental Chemical Corp ....E 716 773-8100
  Grand Island (G-5340)
Occidental Chemical Corp ....G 716 694-3827
  North Tonawanda (G-12080)
Olin Chlor Alkali Logistics ....C 716 278-6411
  Niagara Falls (G-11961)

Peroxychem LLC..........................D......716 873-0812
Tonawanda *(G-15132)*

ALKALOIDS & OTHER BOTANICAL BASED PRDTS

Bio-Botanica Inc..........................D......631 231-0987
Hauppauge *(G-5604)*

ALLERGENS & ALLERGENIC EXTRACTS

Nelco Laboratories Inc ....E......631 242-0082
Deer Park *(G-3910)*

ALTERNATORS & GENERATORS: Battery Charging

ARC Systems Inc ....E......631 582-8020
Hauppauge *(G-5592)*

ALTERNATORS: Automotive

Con Rel Auto Electric Inc ....E......518 356-1646
Schenectady *(G-14259)*
Eastern Unit Exch Rmnfacturing........F......718 739-7113
Floral Park *(G-4815)*
Prestolite Electric Inc ....C......585 492-2278
Arcade *(G-380)*

ALUMINUM

Alcoa USA Corp ....G......315 764-4011
Massena *(G-7664)*
Alcoa USA Corp ....E......315 764-4106
Massena *(G-7665)*
American Std Shtmtl Sup Corp ....F......718 888-9350
Flushing *(G-4839)*
Greene Brass & Alum Fndry LLC ....G......607 656-4204
Bloomville *(G-954)*

ALUMINUM ORE MINING

American Douglas Metals Inc...........F......716 856-3170
Buffalo *(G-2630)*

ALUMINUM PRDTS

A-Fab Initiatives Inc ....F......716 877-5257
Buffalo *(G-2616)*
Amt Incorporated ....E......518 284-2910
Sharon Springs *(G-14382)*
Apollo Management V LP ....E......914 467-6510
Purchase *(G-13001)*
Arconic Inc ....G......315 764-4011
Massena *(G-7666)*
Flagpoles Incorporated ....D......631 751-5500
East Setauket *(G-4178)*
J Sussman Inc ....E......718 297-0228
Jamaica *(G-6450)*
Keymark Corporation ....A......518 853-3421
Fonda *(G-4911)*
Minitec Framing Systems LLC ....E......585 924-4690
Farmington *(G-4775)*
North Coast Outfitters Ltd.................E......631 727-5580
Riverhead *(G-13183)*
Nyahb Inc ....G......845 352-5300
Monsey *(G-8042)*
Pioneer Window Holdings Inc ....E......518 762-5526
Johnstown *(G-6625)*
Super Sweep Inc ....F......631 223-8205
Huntington Station *(G-6261)*
Swiss Tool Corporation....................E......631 842-7766
Copiague *(G-3681)*

ALUMINUM: Coil & Sheet

American Custom Metals Inc............G......585 694-4893
Spencerport *(G-14551)*

ALUMINUM: Rolling & Drawing

Alcoa Corporation..........................B......412 315-2900
Massena *(G-7663)*
Arconic Inc ....G......315 764-4011
Massena *(G-7666)*
Mitsubishi Chemical Amer Inc.............E......212 223-3043
New York *(G-10484)*
N A Alumil Corporation....................G......718 355-9393
Long Island City *(G-7302)*

AMMONIUM NITRATE OR AMMONIUM SULFATE

Oci USA Inc ....G......646 589-6180
New York *(G-10677)*
Ocip Holding LLC ....G......646 589-6180
New York *(G-10678)*

AMMUNITION

Circor Aerospace Inc ....D......631 737-1900
Hauppauge *(G-5615)*

AMMUNITION: Components

CIC International Ltd........................D......212 213-0089
Brooklyn *(G-1663)*

AMMUNITION: Pellets & BB's, Pistol & Air Rifle

Benjamin Sheridan Corporation...........G......585 657-6161
Bloomfield *(G-940)*
Crosman Corporation ....E......585 657-6161
Bloomfield *(G-945)*
Crosman Corporation ....E......585 398-3920
Farmington *(G-4769)*

AMMUNITION: Small Arms

CIC International Ltd........................D......212 213-0089
Brooklyn *(G-1663)*

AMPLIFIERS

Aguilar Amplification LLC ....F......212 431-9109
New York *(G-8496)*
Amplitech Group Inc.......................G......631 521-7831
Bohemia *(G-972)*
Broadcast Manager Inc ....G......212 509-1200
New York *(G-8858)*
Ilab America Inc ....G......631 615-5053
Selden *(G-14353)*

AMPLIFIERS: Parametric

Electronics & Innovation Ltd ....F......585 214-0598
Rochester *(G-13382)*

AMPLIFIERS: Pulse Amplifiers

AMP-Line Corp ....F......845 623-3288
West Nyack *(G-15815)*
Sparkcharge Inc ....G......315 480-3645
Syracuse *(G-14996)*

AMPLIFIERS: RF & IF Power

Ametek CTS Us Inc ....E......631 467-8400
Ronkonkoma *(G-13905)*
B & H Electronics Corp ....E......845 782-5000
Monroe *(G-8015)*
Communication Power Corp ....E......631 434-7306
Hauppauge *(G-5624)*
Mks Medical Electronics ....E......585 292-7400
Rochester *(G-13555)*
Srtech Industry Corp ....E......718 496-7001
College Point *(G-3566)*

AMUSEMENT & RECREATION SVCS: Amusement Ride

Billy Beez Usa LLC ....F......315 741-5099
Syracuse *(G-14829)*
Billy Beez Usa LLC ....F......646 606-2249
New York *(G-8793)*
Billy Beez Usa LLC ....E......845 915-4709
West Nyack *(G-15818)*

AMUSEMENT & RECREATION SVCS: Arcades

Inspired Entertainment Inc.................F......646 565-3861
New York *(G-9903)*

AMUSEMENT & RECREATION SVCS: Art Gallery, Commercial

Pace Editions Inc ....E......212 421-3237
New York *(G-10735)*

AMUSEMENT & RECREATION SVCS: Arts & Crafts Instruction

Donne Dieu Paper Mill Inc.................G......212 226-0573
Brooklyn *(G-1757)*

AMUSEMENT & RECREATION SVCS: Exposition Operation

Family Publications Ltd......................F......212 947-2177
New York *(G-9467)*

AMUSEMENT & RECREATION SVCS: Gambling & Lottery Svcs

Inspired Entertainment Inc.................F......646 565-3861
New York *(G-9903)*

AMUSEMENT & RECREATION SVCS: Game Machines

Mission Crane Service Inc ....D......718 937-3333
Long Island City *(G-7297)*

AMUSEMENT & RECREATION SVCS: Golf Club, Membership

Dolomite Products Company Inc ....E......315 524-1998
Rochester *(G-13354)*

AMUSEMENT & RECREATION SVCS: Physical Fitness Instruction

Playfitness Corp..............................G......917 497-5443
Staten Island *(G-14690)*

AMUSEMENT & RECREATION SVCS: Tennis & Professionals

Paddock Chevrolet Golf Dome ....E......716 504-4059
Tonawanda *(G-15130)*

AMUSEMENT MACHINES: Coin Operated

Mission Crane Service Inc ....D......718 937-3333
Long Island City *(G-7297)*

AMUSEMENT PARK DEVICES & RIDES

Acro Industries Inc ....C......585 254-3661
Rochester *(G-13204)*
Alkemy Machine LLC ....G......585 436-8730
Rochester *(G-13217)*
Lakeside Industries Inc ....F......716 386-3031
Bemus Point *(G-812)*
Macro Tool & Machine Company..........G......845 223-3824
Lagrangeville *(G-6750)*

ANALGESICS

Mentholatum Company ....E......716 677-2500
Orchard Park *(G-12366)*
Perrigo Company ....E......718 960-9900
Bronx *(G-1336)*
Wyeth LLC ....A......212 733-2323
New York *(G-11793)*

ANALYZERS: Moisture

Phymetrix Inc ....G......631 627-3950
Medford *(G-7721)*

ANALYZERS: Network

Cgw Corp ....G......631 472-6600
Bayport *(G-727)*
Everest Bbn Inc...............................F......212 268-7979
New York *(G-9426)*
Gcns Technology Group Inc ....G......347 713-8160
Brooklyn *(G-1880)*

ANESTHESIA EQPT

Gradian Health Systems Inc ....G......212 537-0340
New York *(G-9654)*
Omnicare Anesthesia PC ....E......718 433-0044
Astoria *(G-433)*

ANIMAL FEED & SUPPLEMENTS: Livestock & Poultry

Bailey Boonville Mills Inc ....G...... 315 942-2131
　Boonville (G-1103)
Baker Commodities Inc ....E...... 585 482-1880
　Rochester (G-13259)
Cargill Incorporated............D...... 585 345-1160
　Batavia (G-607)
Cargill Incorporated............G...... 716 665-6570
　Kennedy (G-6657)
Cargill Incorporated............E...... 315 287-0241
　Gouverneur (G-5317)
Cargill Incorporated............E...... 315 622-3533
　Liverpool (G-7005)
Central Garden & Pet Company ....G...... 631 451-8021
　Selden (G-14350)
Eastport Feeds Inc ....G...... 631 325-0077
　Eastport (G-4251)
Harbor Point Mineral Pdts Inc...........F...... 315 797-1300
　Utica (G-15270)
Lowville Farmers Coop Inc ....E...... 315 376-6587
　Lowville (G-7417)
Lutz Feed Co Inc ....E...... 607 432-7984
　Oneonta (G-12273)
Scotts Feed Inc ....E...... 518 483-3110
　Malone (G-7489)

ANIMAL FEED: Wholesalers

Scotts Feed Inc ....E...... 518 483-3110
　Malone (G-7489)

ANIMAL FOOD & SUPPLEMENTS: Bird Food, Prepared

Heath Manufacturing Company ....G...... 800 444-3140
　Batavia (G-617)
Pine Tree Farms Inc ....E...... 607 532-4312
　Interlaken (G-6286)
Wagners LLC ....G...... 516 933-6580
　Jericho (G-6598)

ANIMAL FOOD & SUPPLEMENTS: Cat

American Cat Club LLC............G...... 212 779-1140
　New York (G-8546)

ANIMAL FOOD & SUPPLEMENTS: Dog

Farmers Dog Inc............G...... 646 780-7957
　New York (G-9473)
Nestle Purina Petcare Company...........B...... 716 366-8080
　Dunkirk (G-4061)
Robert Abady Dog Food Co Ltd ....F...... 845 473-1900
　Poughkeepsie (G-12979)
Scooby Rendering & Inc ....G...... 315 793-1014
　Utica (G-15293)
Southern Tier Pet Ntrtn LLC ....E...... 607 674-2121
　Sherburne (G-14394)

ANIMAL FOOD & SUPPLEMENTS: Dog & Cat

Colgate-Palmolive Company ....A...... 212 310-2000
　New York (G-9051)
Hills Pet Products Inc............G...... 212 310-2000
　New York (G-9786)
Hound & Gatos Pet Foods Corp...........G...... 212 618-1917
　New York (G-9822)
Pet Proteins LLC ....G...... 888 293-1029
　New York (G-10812)

ANIMAL FOOD & SUPPLEMENTS: Feed Concentrates

Gramco Inc ....G...... 716 592-2845
　Springville (G-14592)

ANIMAL FOOD & SUPPLEMENTS: Feed Premixes

Commodity Resource Corporation ......F...... 585 538-9500
　Caledonia (G-3069)

ANIMAL FOOD & SUPPLEMENTS: Feed Supplements

Veterinary Biochemical Ltd...........G...... 845 473-1900
　Poughkeepsie (G-12989)

ANIMAL FOOD & SUPPLEMENTS: Livestock

Carolina Eastern-Crocker LLC............E....... 585 345-4141
　Stafford (G-14602)
JD Granary LLC............G...... 607 627-6294
　Smyrna (G-14490)
Kent Nutrition Group Inc ....F...... 315 788-0032
　Watertown (G-15577)

ANIMAL FOOD & SUPPLEMENTS: Mineral feed supplements

Nutra-Vet Research Corp ....F...... 845 473-1900
　Poughkeepsie (G-12976)

ANIMAL FOOD & SUPPLEMENTS: Pet, Exc Dog & Cat, Canned

Grand Maes Cntry Naturals LLC...........G...... 212 348-8171
　New York (G-9659)

ANIMAL FOOD & SUPPLEMENTS: Poultry

Cochecton Mills Inc ....E...... 845 932-8282
　Cochecton (G-3501)
Narrowsburg Feed & Grain Co ....F...... 845 252-3936
　Narrowsburg (G-8210)

ANODIZING SVC

Able Anodizing Corp ....F...... 718 252-0660
　Brooklyn (G-1449)
C H Thompson Company Inc...........D...... 607 724-1094
　Binghamton (G-866)
Fallon Inc............E...... 718 326-7226
　Maspeth (G-7614)
Forge Metal Finishing Inc............G...... 585 730-7340
　Rochester (G-13420)
Keymark Corporation ....A...... 518 853-3421
　Fonda (G-4911)
Tru-Tone Metal Products Inc............E...... 718 386-5960
　Brooklyn (G-2526)
Utica Metal Products Inc ....D...... 315 732-6163
　Utica (G-15299)

ANTENNAS: Radar Or Communications

B & Z Technologies LLC............G...... 631 675-9666
　East Setauket (G-4176)
Gryphon Sensors LLC............F...... 315 452-8882
　North Syracuse (G-12044)
SRC Ventures Inc ....C...... 315 452-8000
　North Syracuse (G-12049)
Srctec LLC ....C...... 315 452-8700
　Syracuse (G-14999)

ANTENNAS: Receiving

Ampro International Inc............G...... 845 278-4910
　Brewster (G-1141)
Pyragon Inc ....G...... 585 697-0444
　Rochester (G-13654)
Russell Industries Inc............G...... 516 536-5000
　Lynbrook (G-7437)

ANTIBIOTICS

G C Hanford Manufacturing Co ....C...... 315 476-7418
　Syracuse (G-14898)
Pfizer Inc ....A...... 212 733-2323
　New York (G-10821)
Pfizer Overseas LLC............G...... 212 733-2323
　New York (G-10824)

ANTIBIOTICS, PACKAGED

Durata Therapeutics Inc ....G...... 646 871-6400
　New York (G-9281)

ANTIFREEZE

Bass Oil Company Inc ....E...... 718 628-4444
　Brooklyn (G-1565)
Fppf Chemical Co Inc............G...... 716 856-9607
　Buffalo (G-2758)

ANTIQUE FURNITURE RESTORATION & REPAIR

Irony Limited Inc ....G...... 631 329-4065
　East Hampton (G-4123)

ANTIQUE REPAIR & RESTORATION SVCS, EXC FURNITURE & AUTOS

A W R Group Inc ....F...... 718 729-0412
　Long Island City (G-7141)

ANTIQUE SHOPS

American Country Quilts & Lin............G...... 631 283-5466
　Southampton (G-14526)
Blanche P Field LLC ....E...... 212 355-6616
　New York (G-8809)

ANTIQUES, WHOLESALE

Two Worlds Arts Ltd ....G...... 212 929-2210
　New York (G-11566)

APPAREL ACCESS STORES

Crye Precision LLC............C...... 718 246-3838
　Brooklyn (G-1705)
Jag Footwear ACC & Ret Corp ....A...... 800 999-1877
　New York (G-9967)
Nazim Izzak LLC............G...... 212 920-5546
　Long Island City (G-7304)

APPAREL DESIGNERS: Commercial

Arteast LLC............E...... 646 859-6020
　New York (G-8633)
Dianos Kathryn Designs ....G...... 212 267-1584
　New York (G-9223)

APPLIANCE CORDS: Household Electrical Eqpt

All Shore Industries Inc............F...... 718 720-0018
　Staten Island (G-14617)

APPLIANCES, HOUSEHOLD: Kitchen, Major, Exc Refrigs & Stoves

Ajmadison Corp ....D...... 718 532-1800
　Brooklyn (G-1474)
Barrage ....E...... 212 586-9390
　New York (G-8732)
Design Solutions LI Inc ....G...... 631 656-8700
　Saint James (G-14109)
Hobart Corporation ....E...... 631 864-3440
　Commack (G-3592)
Mohawk Group Holdings Inc ....G...... 347 676-1681
　New York (G-10493)
Talmu NY LLC............G...... 347 434-6700
　Brooklyn (G-2492)

APPLIANCES, HOUSEHOLD: Laundry Machines, Incl Coin-Operated

Autarkic Holdings Inc ....D...... 516 371-4400
　Inwood (G-6290)
Pluslux LLC............G...... 516 371-4400
　Inwood (G-6302)

APPLIANCES, HOUSEHOLD: Refrigerator Cabinets, Metal Or Wood

Ae Fund Inc ....E...... 315 698-7650
　Brewerton (G-1134)

APPLIANCES, HOUSEHOLD: Refrigs, Mechanical & Absorption

General Electric Company ....A...... 518 385-4022
　Schenectady (G-14266)

APPLIANCES, HOUSEHOLD: Sewing Machines & Attchmnts, Domestic

Jado Sewing Machines Inc ....E...... 718 784-2314
　Long Island City (G-7252)

APPLIANCES: Household, Refrigerators & Freezers

Robin Industries Ltd ....F...... 718 218-9616
　Brooklyn (G-2351)
Sure-Kol Refrigerator Co Inc ....F...... 718 625-0601
　Brooklyn (G-2479)

APPLIANCES: Major, Cooking

Applince Installation Svc Corp.............E.......716 884-7425
Buffalo *(G-2642)*

Oxo International Inc.............................C......212 242-3333
New York *(G-10729)*

Steelstone Group LLC.........................G.......888 552-0033
Brooklyn *(G-2459)*

APPLIANCES: Small, Electric

A & M LLC..G......212 354-1341
New York *(G-8410)*

Algonquin Power..................................G......315 393-5595
Ogdensburg *(G-12201)*

Fulton Volcanic Inc..............................D......315 298-5121
Pulaski *(G-12999)*

General Electric Company....................G......315 554-2000
Skaneateles *(G-14452)*

Tactica International Inc.......................E......212 575-0500
New York *(G-11423)*

Uniware Houseware Corp......................E......631 242-7400
Brentwood *(G-1129)*

APPLICATIONS SOFTWARE PROGRAMMING

Galaxy Software LLC...........................G.......631 244-8405
Oakdale *(G-12151)*

Maven Marketing LLC..........................G......615 510-3248
New York *(G-10387)*

AQUARIUM ACCESS, METAL

Aquarium Pump & Piping Systems.....F......631 567-5555
Sayville *(G-14222)*

AQUARIUM DESIGN & MAINTENANCE SVCS

C B Management Services Inc..............F......845 735-2300
Pearl River *(G-12529)*

AQUARIUMS & ACCESS: Glass

C B Management Services Inc..............F......845 735-2300
Pearl River *(G-12529)*

Stark Aquarium Products Co Inc..........E......718 445-5357
Flushing *(G-4895)*

AQUARIUMS & ACCESS: Plastic

Aquarium Pump & Piping Systems.......F......631 567-5555
Sayville *(G-14222)*

Eugene G Danner Mfg Inc....................E.......631 234-5261
Central Islip *(G-3273)*

ARCHITECTURAL SVCS

B & F Architectural Support Gr............E......212 279-6488
New York *(G-8702)*

Deerfield Millwork Inc.........................F......631 726-9663
Water Mill *(G-15529)*

Productand Design Inc........................F......718 858-2440
Brooklyn *(G-2297)*

ARMATURE REPAIRING & REWINDING SVC

Ener-G-Rotors Inc...............................G......518 372-2608
Schenectady *(G-14262)*

Power-Flo Technologies Inc.................D......315 399-5801
East Syracuse *(G-4230)*

Sunset Ridge Holdings Inc..................G......716 487-1458
Jamestown *(G-6546)*

AROMATIC CHEMICAL PRDTS

C & A Service Inc................................G......516 354-1200
Floral Park *(G-4810)*

Citrus and Allied Essences Ltd............E......516 354-1200
Floral Park *(G-4812)*

ARRESTERS & COILS: Lightning

Ludwig and Larsen..............................G......718 369-0999
Ridgewood *(G-13151)*

ART & ORNAMENTAL WARE: Pottery

American Country Quilts & Lin.............G......631 283-5466
Southampton *(G-14526)*

ART DEALERS & GALLERIES

Frame Shoppe & Art Gallery................G......516 365-6014
Manhasset *(G-7534)*

Penhouse Media Group Inc..................C......212 702-6000
New York *(G-10795)*

ART DESIGN SVCS

Dwm International Inc..........................F......646 290-7448
Long Island City *(G-7207)*

Graphics Plus Printing Inc...................E......607 299-0500
Cortland *(G-3769)*

ART GOODS & SPLYS WHOLESALERS

Gei International Inc.............................E......315 463-9261
East Syracuse *(G-4212)*

Golden Group International Ltd.............G......845 440-1025
Patterson *(G-12517)*

Patrick Mackin Custom Furn................G......718 237-2592
Brooklyn *(G-2250)*

ART MARBLE: Concrete

Fordham Marble Company Inc..............F......914 682-6699
White Plains *(G-16007)*

Royal Marble & Granite Inc.................G......516 536-5900
Oceanside *(G-12188)*

ART NEEDLEWORK, MADE FROM PURCHASED MATERIALS

Corporate Loss Preven.........................G......516 409-0002
Massapequa *(G-7646)*

Jomar Industries Inc............................E......845 357-5773
Airmont *(G-13)*

Knucklehead Embroidery Inc...............G......607 797-2725
Johnson City *(G-6605)*

Screen The World Inc...........................F......631 475-0023
Holtsville *(G-6052)*

Verdonette Inc.....................................G......212 719-2003
New York *(G-11660)*

ART RELATED SVCS

Halo Associates...................................G......212 691-9549
New York *(G-9713)*

ART RESTORATION SVC

Julius Lowy Frame Restoring Co..........E......212 861-8585
New York *(G-10039)*

Sunburst Studios Inc...........................G......718 768-6360
Brooklyn *(G-2470)*

ART SPLY STORES

Simon Liu Inc.......................................F......718 567-2011
Brooklyn *(G-2417)*

ARTISTS' EQPT

Simon Liu Inc.......................................F......718 567-2011
Brooklyn *(G-2417)*

Spaulding & Rogers Mfg Inc................D......518 768-2070
Voorheesville *(G-15445)*

ARTISTS' MATERIALS, WHOLESALE

R & F Handmade Paints Inc..................F......845 331-3112
Kingston *(G-6707)*

ARTISTS' MATERIALS: Frames, Artists' Canvases

Clapper Hollow Designs Inc.................E......518 234-9561
Cobleskill *(G-3497)*

Handmade Frames Inc..........................F......718 782-8364
Brooklyn *(G-1925)*

Lopez Restorations Inc........................F......718 383-1555
Brooklyn *(G-2084)*

Timeless Decor LLC.............................C......315 782-5759
Watertown *(G-15590)*

ARTISTS' MATERIALS: Ink, Drawing, Black & Colored

Sml Brothers Holding Corp..................D......718 402-2000
Bronx *(G-1366)*

ARTISTS' MATERIALS: Paints, Exc Gold & Bronze

Golden Artist Colors Inc......................C......607 847-6154
New Berlin *(G-8222)*

ARTISTS' MATERIALS: Pastels

North America Pastel Artists...............G......718 463-4701
Flushing *(G-4880)*

ARTISTS' MATERIALS: Wax

Micro Powders Inc...............................E......914 332-6400
Tarrytown *(G-15048)*

ARTS & CRAFTS SCHOOL

Slosson Eductl Publications.................F......716 652-0930
East Aurora *(G-4096)*

ARTWORK: Framed

Handmade Frames Inc..........................F......718 782-8364
Brooklyn *(G-1925)*

ASBESTOS PRODUCTS

Andujar Asbestos and Lead.................G......716 228-6757
Buffalo *(G-2634)*

Regional MGT & Consulting Inc...........F......718 599-3718
Brooklyn *(G-2336)*

ASPHALT & ASPHALT PRDTS

A Colarusso and Son Inc.....................E......518 828-3218
Hudson *(G-6146)*

Atlas Bituminous Co Inc......................F......315 457-2394
Syracuse *(G-14820)*

Barrett Paving Materials Inc.................F......315 737-9471
Clayville *(G-3454)*

Barrett Paving Materials Inc.................G......607 723-5367
Binghamton *(G-856)*

C & C Ready-Mix Corporation..............E......607 797-5108
Vestal *(G-15374)*

Callanan Industries Inc........................E......845 457-3158
Montgomery *(G-8058)*

Cobleskill Stone Products Inc..............F......607 432-8321
Oneonta *(G-12265)*

Cobleskill Stone Products Inc..............F......607 637-4271
Hancock *(G-5535)*

Hanson Aggregates PA LLC..................E......585 624-3800
Honeoye Falls *(G-6073)*

King Road Materials Inc.......................E......518 381-9995
Albany *(G-94)*

King Road Materials Inc.......................F......518 382-5354
Schenectady *(G-14285)*

Northern Bituminous Mix Inc...............G......315 598-2141
Fulton *(G-5074)*

Package Pavement Company Inc...........D......845 221-2224
Stormville *(G-14752)*

Peckham Materials Corp.......................F......845 562-5370
Newburgh *(G-11881)*

Peckham Materials Corp.......................D......914 686-2045
White Plains *(G-16045)*

Posillico Materials LLC........................F......631 249-1872
Farmingdale *(G-4713)*

Suit-Kote Corporation..........................C......607 753-1100
Cortland *(G-3789)*

Suit-Kote Corporation..........................E......716 664-3750
Jamestown *(G-6545)*

Upstone Materials Inc..........................D......518 561-5321
Plattsburgh *(G-12787)*

Vestal Asphalt Inc...............................F......607 785-3393
Vestal *(G-15387)*

ASPHALT COATINGS & SEALERS

Barrett Paving Materials Inc.................E......315 353-6611
Norwood *(G-12131)*

Callanan Industries Inc........................E......845 457-3158
Montgomery *(G-8058)*

Empire Emulsions LLC.........................G......845 610-5350
Chester *(G-3376)*

Northeastern Sealcoat Inc...................F......585 544-4372
Rochester *(G-13583)*

Peckham Materials Corp.......................E......518 747-3353
Hudson Falls *(G-6192)*

Sheldon Slate Products Co Inc.............E......518 642-1280
Middle Granville *(G-7870)*

Suit-Kote Corporation..........................E......607 535-2743
Watkins Glen *(G-15616)*

Tntpaving..G......607 372-4911
Endicott *(G-4475)*

ASPHALT MIXTURES WHOLESALERS

A Colarusso and Son Inc.....................E......518 828-3218
Hudson *(G-6146)*

**P
R
O
D
U
C
T**

County Line Stone Co Inc ....E 716 542-5435
  Akron (G-16)

Hanson Aggregates PA LLC ....E 585 624-1220
  Honeoye Falls (G-6074)

ASPHALT PLANTS INCLUDING GRAVEL MIX TYPE

Midland Machinery Co Inc...................D 716 692-1200
  Tonawanda (G-15122)

Peckham Materials Corp ....E 518 747-3353
  Hudson Falls (G-6192)

Penn Can Equipment Corporation.......G 315 378-0337
  Lyons (G-7451)

Rochester Asphalt Materials................G 315 524-4619
  Walworth (G-15478)

ASSOCIATIONS: Engineering

American Inst Chem Engners Inc..........D 646 495-1355
  New York (G-8552)

ASSOCIATIONS: Scientists'

Association For Cmpt McHy Inc............D 212 869-7440
  New York (G-8654)

ATOMIZERS

Aloi Solutions LLC ....E 585 292-0920
  Rochester (G-13223)

Ascribe Inc ....E 585 413-0298
  Rochester (G-13252)

Boom LLC ....E 646 218-0752
  New York (G-8835)

Christian Dior Perfumes LLC ....E 212 931-2200
  New York (G-8999)

Deva Concepts LLC ....E 212 343-0344
  New York (G-9212)

Givi Inc ....F 212 586-5029
  New York (G-9616)

Hoskie Co Inc ....D 718 628-8672
  Brooklyn (G-1944)

Mitten Manufacturing Inc ....F 315 437-7564
  Syracuse (G-14945)

Shyam Ahuja Limited ....G 212 644-5910
  New York (G-11221)

Trendsformers Ltd Liability Co ....G 888 700-2423
  New York (G-11537)

ATTENUATORS

Mini-Circuits Fort Wayne LLC..............B 718 934-4500
  Brooklyn (G-2157)

Traffic Lane Closures LLC ....F 845 228-6100
  Carmel (G-3192)

AUDIO & VIDEO EQPT, EXC COMMERCIAL

Audio Video Invasion Inc ....F 516 345-2636
  Plainview (G-12664)

Audiosavings Inc ....F 888 445-1555
  Inwood (G-6289)

Avcom of Virginia Inc ....D 585 924-4560
  Victor (G-15392)

AVI-Spl Employee ....B 212 840-4801
  New York (G-8691)

B & H Electronics Corp ....E 845 782-5000
  Monroe (G-8015)

Communication Power Corp.................E 631 434-7306
  Hauppauge (G-5624)

Digital Home Creations Inc ....G 585 576-7070
  Webster (G-15638)

Fulcrum Acoustic LLC ....G 866 234-0678
  Rochester (G-13426)

G E Inspection Technologies LP ....C 315 554-2000
  Skaneateles (G-14451)

General Electric Company ....C 315 554-2000
  Skaneateles (G-14452)

Key Digital Systems Inc ....E 914 667-9700
  Mount Vernon (G-8155)

L3 Technologies Inc............................A 631 436-7400
  Hauppauge (G-5687)

Laird Telemedia ....C 845 339-9555
  Mount Marion (G-8110)

Masterdisk Corporation.......................F 212 541-5022
  Elmsford (G-4417)

Navitar Inc ....D 585 359-4000
  Rochester (G-13568)

NEa Manufacturing Corp......................E 516 371-4200
  New York (G-6300)

New Wop Records ....G 631 617-9732
  Deer Park (G-3911)

Octave Music Group Inc ....G 212 991-6540
  New York (G-10679)

Sage Audio Video Tech LLC ....E 212 213-1523
  New York (G-11115)

Scy Manufacturing Inc ....G 516 986-3083
  Inwood (G-6303)

Sima Technologies LLC ....G 412 828-9130
  Hauppauge (G-5766)

Sony Corporation of America ....C 212 833-8000
  New York (G-11295)

Sound Video Systems Wny LLC...........F 716 684-8200
  Buffalo (G-2990)

Tkm Technologies Inc ....G 631 474-4700
  Port Jeff STA (G-12839)

Touchtunes Music Corporation ....D 847 419-3300
  New York (G-11523)

Woo Audio Inc ....F 917 324-5284
  Long Island City (G-7407)

Wyrestorm Technologies LLC ....G 518 289-1293
  Round Lake (G-14063)

AUDIO COMPONENTS

Ashly Audio Inc ....E 585 872-0010
  Webster (G-15630)

AUDIO ELECTRONIC SYSTEMS

Audio Technology New York Inc............F 718 369-7528
  Brooklyn (G-1552)

B & K Components Ltd ....D 323 776-4277
  Buffalo (G-2653)

Convergent Audio Tech Inc..................G 585 359-2700
  Rush (G-14069)

Gilmores Sound Advice Inc ....F 212 265-4445
  New York (G-9611)

Granada Electronics Inc.......................G 718 387-1157
  Brooklyn (G-1906)

Lamm Industries Inc ....G 718 368-0181
  Brooklyn (G-2045)

Vincent Conigliaro ....F 845 340-0489
  Kingston (G-6722)

Whirlwind Music Distrs Inc ....G 800 733-9473
  Rochester (G-13803)

Yorkville Sound Inc ....G 716 297-2920
  Niagara Falls (G-11992)

AUDIO-VISUAL PROGRAM PRODUCTION SVCS

ABRA Media Inc ....G 518 398-1010
  Pine Plains (G-12632)

Guilford Publications Inc ....D 212 431-9800
  New York (G-9696)

Hatherleigh Company Ltd ....G 607 538-1092
  Hobart (G-5978)

AUDIOLOGISTS' OFFICES

Family Hearing Center ....G 845 897-3059
  Fishkill (G-4800)

Todt Hill Audiological Svcs ....G 718 816-1952
  Staten Island (G-14722)

AUDITING SVCS

Advance Finance Group LLC................D 212 630-5900
  New York (G-8468)

AUTO & HOME SUPPLY STORES: Auto & Truck Eqpt & Parts

K M Drive Line Inc...............................G 718 599-0628
  Brooklyn (G-2018)

AUTO & HOME SUPPLY STORES: Automotive Access

Blackburn Truck Bodies LLC................G 315 448-3236
  Syracuse (G-14831)

Legendary Auto Interiors Ltd ....E 315 331-1212
  Newark (G-11843)

Split Rock Trading Co Inc ....G 631 929-3261
  Wading River (G-15452)

Zappala Farms AG Systems Inc ....E 315 626-6293
  Cato (G-3209)

AUTO & HOME SUPPLY STORES: Speed Shops, Incl Race Car Splys

Auto Sport Designs Inc ....F 631 425-1555
  Huntington Station (G-6239)

Marcovicci-Wenz Engineering ....G 631 467-9040
  Ronkonkoma (G-13970)

Troyer Inc..F 585 352-5590
  Rochester (G-13774)

AUTO & HOME SUPPLY STORES: Trailer Hitches, Automotive

General Welding & Fabg Inc ....F 585 697-7660
  Rochester (G-13434)

AUTO & HOME SUPPLY STORES: Truck Eqpt & Parts

Agri Services Co ....G 716 937-6618
  Alden (G-164)

Bick & Heintz Inc ....F 315 733-7577
  Utica (G-15241)

Dejana Trck Utility Eqp Co LLC ....C 631 544-9000
  Kings Park (G-6672)

General Welding & Fabg Inc ....G 716 652-0033
  Elma (G-4319)

AUTOCLAVES: Indl

Wsf Industries Inc ....E 716 692-4930
  Tonawanda (G-15155)

AUTOCLAVES: Laboratory

SPS Medical Supply Corp ....F 585 968-2377
  Cuba (G-3814)

Vivus Technologies LLC ....F 585 798-6658
  Medina (G-7748)

AUTOMATIC REGULATING CONTROL: Building Svcs Monitoring, Auto

Building Management Assoc Inc...........E 718 542-4779
  Bronx (G-1219)

Johnson Controls Inc ....C 585 724-2232
  Rochester (G-13495)

Reuse Action Incorporated ....G 716 949-0900
  Buffalo (G-2952)

Unisend LLC ....G 585 414-9575
  Webster (G-15659)

Virtual Super LLC ....G 212 685-6400
  New York (G-11691)

AUTOMATIC REGULATING CONTROLS: AC & Refrigeration

Bitzer Scroll Inc ....D 315 463-2101
  Syracuse (G-14830)

Care Enterprises Inc ....G 631 472-8155
  Bayport (G-726)

Siemens Industry Inc ....D 716 568-0983
  Amherst (G-243)

AUTOMATIC REGULATING CONTROLS: Elect Air Cleaner, Automatic

Biorem Environmental Inc ....E 585 924-2220
  Victor (G-15393)

AUTOMATIC REGULATING CONTROLS: Energy Cutoff, Residtl/Comm

Black River Generations LLC ....E 315 773-2314
  Fort Drum (G-4935)

Eastern Strategic Materials..................E 212 332-1619
  New York (G-9306)

Johnson Controls Inc ....E 914 593-5200
  Hawthorne (G-5815)

AUTOMATIC REGULATING CONTROLS: Ice Maker

Henderson Products Inc ....E 315 785-0994
  Watertown (G-15572)

AUTOMATIC REGULATING CONTROLS: Pneumatic Relays, Air-Cond

A K Allen Co Inc ....C 516 747-5450
  Melville (G-7753)

AUTOMATIC REGULATING CONTROLS: Refrig/Air-Cond Defrost

Carrier Corporation .... B 315 432-6000
Syracuse (G-14844)

Svyz Trading Corp .... G 718 220-1140
Bronx (G-1375)

AUTOMATIC REGULATING CTRLS: Damper, Pneumatic Or Electric

Air Louver & Damper Inc .... F 718 392-3232
Long Island City (G-7147)

Airflex Industrial Inc .... E 631 752-1234
Farmingdale (G-4575)

Ruskin Company .... G 845 767-4100
Orangeburg (G-12330)

AUTOMATIC TELLER MACHINES

International Merch Svcs Inc .... G 914 699-4000
Mount Vernon (G-8151)

Jpmorgan Chase Bank Nat Assn ...... G 718 767-3592
College Point (G-3549)

K&G of Syracuse Inc .... G 315 446-1921
Syracuse (G-14923)

Mid Enterprise Inc .... G 631 924-3933
Middle Island (G-7875)

Parabit Systems Inc .... E 516 378-4800
Bellmore (G-786)

Stanson Automated LLC .... F 866 505-7826
Yonkers (G-16349)

AUTOMATIC VENDING MACHINES: Mechanisms & Parts

Global Payment Tech Inc .... F 516 887-0700
Valley Stream (G-15342)

Global Payment Tech Inc .... E 631 563-2500
Bohemia (G-1019)

AUTOMOBILE RECOVERY SVCS

Nova Inc .... G 212 967-1139
New York (G-10648)

AUTOMOBILES: Off-Highway, Electric

Bombardier Trnsp Holdings USA .... D 607 776-4791
Bath (G-631)

AUTOMOBILES: Wholesalers

Split Rock Trading Co Inc .... G 631 929-3261
Wading River (G-15452)

AUTOMOTIVE & TRUCK GENERAL REPAIR SVC

Dennys Drive Shaft Service .... G 716 875-6640
Kenmore (G-6649)

Homer Iron Works LLC .... G 607 749-3963
Homer (G-6064)

James Woerner Inc .... G 631 454-9330
Farmingdale (G-4656)

Whitesboro Spring & Alignment ...... F 315 736-4441
Whitesboro (G-16085)

AUTOMOTIVE BODY, PAINT & INTERIOR REPAIR & MAINTENANCE SVC

Conti Auto Body Corp .... G 516 921-6435
Syosset (G-14781)

AUTOMOTIVE PARTS, ACCESS & SPLYS

Actasys Inc .... G 914 432-2336
Watervliet (G-15596)

Allomatic Products Company .... G 516 775-0330
Floral Park (G-4807)

Alloy Metal Products LLC .... F 315 676-2405
Central Square (G-3293)

Aludyne New York LLC .... F 248 728-8642
Batavia (G-600)

American Auto ACC Incrporation ..... E 718 886-6600
Flushing (G-4838)

American Refuse Supply Inc .... G 718 893-8157
Bronx (G-1204)

Anchor Commerce Trading Corp ...... G 516 881-3485
Atlantic Beach (G-452)

Axle Express .... E 518 347-2220
Schenectady (G-14247)

Bigbee Steel and Tank Company ...... E 518 273-0801
Watervliet (G-15597)

Borgwarner Inc .... E 607 257-1800
Ithaca (G-6371)

Borgwarner Morse TEC Inc .... D 607 266-5111
Ithaca (G-6372)

Borgwarner Morse TEC LLC .... D 607 257-6700
Cortland (G-3756)

Car-Go Industries Inc .... G 718 472-1443
Woodside (G-16201)

Crestron Electronics Inc .... D 201 894-0670
Orangeburg (G-12311)

Cubic Trnsp Systems Inc .... F 212 255-1810
New York (G-9129)

Custom Sitecom LLC .... F 631 420-4238
Farmingdale (G-4611)

Delphi Automotive LLP .... G 716 438-4886
Amherst (G-220)

Delphi Powertrain Systems LLC ..... C 585 359-6000
West Henrietta (G-15791)

Delphi Powertrain Systems LLC ..... B 585 359-6000
West Henrietta (G-15792)

Delphi Powertrain Systems LLC ..... E 585 359-6000
West Henrietta (G-15793)

Delphi Thermal Systems .... F 716 439-2454
Lockport (G-7067)

Dmic Inc .... D 716 743-4360
North Tonawanda (G-12065)

Electronic Machine Parts LLC ...... F 631 434-3700
Hauppauge (G-5645)

Empire Emergency Apparatus Inc .... E 716 348-3473
Niagara Falls (G-11923)

Exten II LLC .... F 716 895-2214
East Aurora (G-4087)

Fast By Gast Inc .... G 716 773-1536
Grand Island (G-5329)

Flagship One Inc .... F 516 766-2223
Lynbrook (G-7431)

General Motors LLC .... A 716 879-5000
Buffalo (G-2773)

GM Components Holdings LLC .... B 585 647-7000
Rochester (G-13447)

GM Components Holdings LLC .... B 716 439-2463
Lockport (G-7079)

GM Components Holdings LLC .... B 716 439-2011
Lockport (G-7080)

Interntnal Auto Voluntary Untd ..... G 718 743-8732
Brooklyn (G-1968)

ITT Enidine Inc .... B 716 662-1900
Orchard Park (G-12356)

Jtekt Torsen North America .... F 585 464-5000
Rochester (G-13498)

Karlyn Industries Inc .... F 845 351-2249
Southfields (G-14541)

Kerns Manufacturing Corp .... C 718 784-4044
Long Island City (G-7262)

Lee World Industries LLC .... F 212 265-8866
New York (G-10190)

Magtrol Inc .... E 716 668-5555
Buffalo (G-2859)

Mahle Behr Troy Inc .... C 716 439-3039
Lockport (G-7088)

Mahle Behr USA Inc .... B 716 439-2011
Lockport (G-7089)

Mahle Indstrbeteiligungen GMBH ... D 716 319-6700
Amherst (G-231)

Mahle Manufacturing MGT Inc ...... G 248 735-3623
Amherst (G-232)

Nas-Tra Automotive Inds Inc .... C 631 225-1225
Lindenhurst (G-6962)

Par-Foam Products Inc .... C 716 855-2066
Buffalo (G-2905)

Parker-Hannifin Corporation .... D 716 685-4040
Lancaster (G-6822)

Performance Designed By Peters ..... F 585 223-9062
Fairport (G-4515)

Phillip J Ortiz Manufacturing ...... G 845 226-7030
Hopewell Junction (G-6100)

Powerflow Inc .... D 716 892-1014
Buffalo (G-2926)

Pro-Value Distribution Inc .... G 585 783-1461
Rochester (G-13648)

Rosco Inc .... C 718 526-2601
Jamaica (G-6471)

Specialty Silicone Pdts Inc .... D 518 885-8826
Ballston Spa (G-587)

Tesla Motors Inc .... A 212 206-1204
New York (G-11455)

Trico Holding Corporation .... A 716 852-5700
Buffalo (G-3019)

Troyer Inc .... F 585 352-5590
Rochester (G-13774)

Whiting Door Mfg Corp .... B 716 542-5427
Akron (G-23)

Wolo Mfg Corp .... E 631 242-0333
Deer Park (G-3955)

Yomiuri International Inc .... G 212 752-2196
New York (G-11811)

AUTOMOTIVE PARTS: Plastic

CN Group Incorporated .... A 914 358-5690
White Plains (G-15994)

Fiber Laminations Limited .... F 716 692-1825
Tonawanda (G-15104)

Fluidampr .... G 716 592-1000
Springville (G-14590)

Koonichi Inc .... G 718 886-8338
Fresh Meadows (G-5044)

Macauto Usa Inc .... E 585 342-2060
Rochester (G-13525)

Rus Auto Parts Inc .... G 800 410-2669
Brooklyn (G-2365)

Tint World .... G 631 458-1999
Medford (G-7725)

AUTOMOTIVE PRDTS: Rubber

Vehicle Manufacturers Inc .... E 631 851-1700
Hauppauge (G-5795)

AUTOMOTIVE REPAIR SHOPS: Brake Repair

Whitesboro Spring & Alignment ...... F 315 736-4441
Whitesboro (G-16085)

AUTOMOTIVE REPAIR SHOPS: Diesel Engine Repair

Jack W Miller .... G 585 538-2399
Scottsville (G-14341)

AUTOMOTIVE REPAIR SHOPS: Electrical Svcs

Gerome Technologies Inc .... D 518 463-1324
Menands (G-7843)

AUTOMOTIVE REPAIR SHOPS: Engine Repair

Jack Merkel Inc .... G 631 234-2600
Hauppauge (G-5680)

AUTOMOTIVE REPAIR SHOPS: Machine Shop

Bullet Industries Inc .... G 585 352-0836
Spencerport (G-14554)

Meade Machine Co Inc .... G 315 923-1703
Clyde (G-3492)

Vytek Inc .... F 631 750-1770
Bohemia (G-1097)

AUTOMOTIVE REPAIR SHOPS: Springs, Rebuilding & Repair

Andersens Spring & Wldg Corp ...... G 516 785-7337
Bellmore (G-778)

AUTOMOTIVE REPAIR SHOPS: Trailer Repair

General Welding & Fabg Inc .... F 585 697-7660
Rochester (G-13434)

AUTOMOTIVE REPAIR SVC

Banner Transmission & Eng Co ...... F 516 221-9459
Melville (G-7762)

AUTOMOTIVE SPLYS & PARTS, NEW, WHOL: Testing Eqpt, Electric

Katikati Inc .... G 585 678-1764
West Henrietta (G-15798)

AUTOMOTIVE SPLYS & PARTS, NEW, WHOLESALE: Brakes

Interparts International Inc .... E 516 576-2000
Plainview (G-12691)

PRODUCT

AUTOMOTIVE SPLYS & PARTS, NEW, WHOLESALE: Clutches

Rpb Distributors LLC..................G.... 914 244-3600
Mount Kisco *(G-8105)*

AUTOMOTIVE SPLYS & PARTS, NEW, WHOLESALE: Splys

Extreme Auto Accessories Corp ....F.... 718 978-6722
Mineola *(G-7973)*

AUTOMOTIVE SPLYS & PARTS, NEW, WHOLESALE: Trim

Legendary Auto Interiors Ltd................E.... 315 331-1212
Newark *(G-11843)*

AUTOMOTIVE SPLYS & PARTS, NEW, WHOLESALE: Wheels

Factory Wheel Warehouse Inc..............G.... 516 605-2131
Commack *(G-3587)*

AUTOMOTIVE SPLYS & PARTS, USED, WHOLESALE: Wheels

Factory Wheel Warehouse Inc..............G.... 516 605-2131
Commack *(G-3587)*

AUTOMOTIVE SPLYS & PARTS, WHOLESALE, NEC

Auto-Mat Company Inc..................E.... 516 938-7373
Hicksville *(G-5886)*
Deer Park Driveshaft & Hose ....G.... 631 667-4091
Deer Park *(G-3860)*
Depot Label Company Inc ....G.... 631 467-2952
Patchogue *(G-12499)*
Noresco Industrial Group Inc ....E.... 516 759-3355
Glen Cove *(G-5197)*
Qpbc Inc.......................E.... 718 685-1900
Long Island City *(G-7333)*
Split Rock Trading Co Inc ....G.... 631 929-3261
Wading River *(G-15452)*
Tint World ....G.... 631 458-1999
Medford *(G-7725)*

AUTOMOTIVE SPLYS/PARTS, NEW, WHOL: Body Rpr/Paint Shop Splys

Auto Body Services LLC ....F.... 631 431-4640
Lindenhurst *(G-6941)*

AUTOMOTIVE SVCS, EXC REPAIR & CARWASHES: Maintenance

Roli Retreads Inc.......................E.... 631 694-7670
Farmingdale *(G-4726)*

AUTOMOTIVE SVCS, EXC REPAIR: Washing & Polishing

Saccomize Inc ....G.... 818 287-3000
Bronx *(G-1358)*

AUTOMOTIVE SVCS, EXC RPR/CARWASHES: High Perf Auto Rpr/Svc

Riverview Industries Inc....................G.... 845 265-5284
Cold Spring *(G-3524)*

AUTOMOTIVE TOPS INSTALLATION OR REPAIR: Canvas Or Plastic

Quantum Sails Rochester LLC ....G.... 585 342-5200
Rochester *(G-13664)*

AUTOMOTIVE TOWING & WRECKING SVC

American Towman Network Inc.............F.... 845 986-4546
Warwick *(G-15510)*

AUTOMOTIVE UPHOLSTERY SHOPS

Sausbiers Awning Shop Inc...............G.... 518 828-3748
Hudson *(G-6178)*

AUTOMOTIVE WELDING SVCS

Chautauqua Machine Spc LLC ....F.... 716 782-3276
Ashville *(G-409)*
Waynes Welding Inc ....E.... 315 768-6146
Yorkville *(G-16383)*

AUTOMOTIVE: Bodies

Antiques & Collectible Autos ....G.... 716 825-3990
Buffalo *(G-2636)*
Conti Auto Body Corp ....G.... 516 921-6435
Syosset *(G-14781)*
Empire Coachworks Intl LLC ....D.... 732 257-7981
Suffern *(G-14761)*

AUTOMOTIVE: Seating

Johnson Controls Inc ....D.... 518 884-8313
Ballston Spa *(G-578)*
Johnson Controls Inc ....G.... 518 694-4822
Albany *(G-92)*
Johnson Controls Inc ....E.... 585 671-1930
Webster *(G-15643)*
Johnson Controls Inc ....C.... 585 724-2232
Rochester *(G-13495)*

AUTOTRANSFORMERS: Electric

General Electric Company ....A.... 518 385-4022
Schenectady *(G-14266)*
General Electric Company ....E.... 518 385-7620
Niskayuna *(G-11996)*

AWNING REPAIR SHOP

Kohler Awning Inc.......................E.... 716 685-3333
Buffalo *(G-2839)*
TG Peppe Inc ....G.... 516 239-7852
Lawrence *(G-6893)*

AWNINGS & CANOPIES

Hart To Hart Industries Inc ....G.... 716 492-2709
Chaffee *(G-3307)*
Lotus Awnings Enterprises Inc ....G.... 718 965-4824
Brooklyn *(G-2086)*
Superior Exteriors of Buffalo..................F.... 716 873-1000
East Amherst *(G-4079)*
Vitarose Corp of America ....G.... 718 951-9700
Brooklyn *(G-2565)*

AWNINGS & CANOPIES: Awnings, Fabric, From Purchased Matls

125-127 Main Street Corp ....F.... 631 477-1500
Greenport *(G-5456)*
Abble Awning Co Inc ....G.... 516 822-1200
Bethpage *(G-830)*
Acme Awning Co Inc ....F.... 718 409-1881
Bronx *(G-1195)*
Awning Mart Inc ....G.... 315 699-5928
Cicero *(G-3416)*
Brock Awnings Ltd ....F.... 631 765-5200
Hampton Bays *(G-5533)*
C E King & Sons Inc ....G.... 631 324-4944
East Hampton *(G-4118)*
Canvas Products Company Inc.............F.... 516 742-1058
Mineola *(G-7963)*
Capitol Awning Co Inc ....F.... 212 505-1717
Jamaica *(G-6430)*
Classic Awnings Inc ....F.... 716 649-0390
Hamburg *(G-5503)*
Di Sanos Creative Canvas Inc ....G.... 315 894-3137
Frankfort *(G-4949)*
Dor-A-Mar Canvas Products Co ....F.... 631 750-9202
West Sayville *(G-15839)*
Durasol Systems Inc.......................D.... 845 610-1100
Chester *(G-3375)*
Fabric Concepts For Industry ....F.... 914 375-2565
Yonkers *(G-16308)*
Jamestown Awning Inc ....G.... 716 483-1435
Jamestown *(G-6520)*
Kohler Awning Inc.......................E.... 716 685-3333
Buffalo *(G-2839)*
Mauceri Sign Inc ....F.... 718 656-7700
Jamaica *(G-6458)*
Northern Awning & Sign Company ....G.... 315 782-8515
Watertown *(G-15585)*
Perma Tech Inc ....F.... 716 854-0707
Buffalo *(G-2915)*
Sausbiers Awning Shop Inc...............G.... 518 828-3748
Hudson *(G-6178)*

Steinway Awning II LLC ....G.... 718 729-2965
Astoria *(G-442)*
TG Peppe Inc ....G.... 516 239-7852
Lawrence *(G-6893)*

AWNINGS & CANOPIES: Canopies, Fabric, From Purchased Matls

Service Canvas Co Inc ....F.... 716 853-0558
Buffalo *(G-2979)*

AWNINGS & CANOPIES: Fabric

Kingston Building Products LLC ....G.... 914 665-0707
Mount Vernon *(G-8156)*
Lanza Corp ....G.... 914 937-6360
Port Chester *(G-12824)*

AWNINGS: Fiberglass

Acme Awning Co Inc ....F.... 718 409-1881
Bronx *(G-1195)*
Aqua Shield Inc ....G.... 631 420-4490
West Babylon *(G-15690)*
Space Sign.......................F.... 718 961-1112
College Point *(G-3565)*
Vitarose Corp of America ....G.... 718 951-9700
Brooklyn *(G-2565)*

AWNINGS: Metal

Dart Awning Inc ....G.... 516 544-2082
Freeport *(G-4991)*
Kenan International Trading ....G.... 718 672-4922
Corona *(G-3742)*
Rainbow Awning Co Inc ....F.... 716 297-3939
Niagara Falls *(G-11970)*
Space Sign.......................F.... 718 961-1112
College Point *(G-3565)*

AXLES

Temper Corporation ....G.... 518 853-3467
Fonda *(G-4913)*

BABY FORMULA

Baby Central LLC ....G.... 718 372-2229
Brooklyn *(G-1558)*
FriesIndcmpina Ingrdnts N Amer ....E.... 607 746-0196
Delhi *(G-3965)*

BABY PACIFIERS: Rubber

Mam USA Corporation ....F.... 914 269-2500
Purchase *(G-13007)*

BADGES: Identification & Insignia

Identfication Data Imaging LLC ....G.... 516 484-6500
Port Washington *(G-12886)*

BAGS & BAGGING: Knit

Nochairs Inc ....G.... 917 748-8731
New York *(G-10635)*

BAGS & CONTAINERS: Textile, Exc Sleeping

Carry Hot Inc ....E.... 212 279-7535
New York *(G-8925)*

BAGS & SACKS: Shipping & Shopping

Seoul Shopping Bag Inc ....G.... 718 439-9226
Brooklyn *(G-2394)*
Westrock Container LLC ....D.... 518 842-2450
Amsterdam *(G-353)*

BAGS: Canvas

H G Maybeck Co Inc ....E.... 718 297-4410
Jamaica *(G-6447)*
Spray Moret LLC ....G.... 917 213-9592
New York *(G-11331)*

BAGS: Cellophane

Aladdin Packaging LLC.......................D.... 631 273-4747
Hauppauge *(G-5582)*

BAGS: Duffle, Canvas, Made From Purchased Materials

Select Fabricators Inc.................F...... 585 393-0650
Canandaigua (G-3142)

BAGS: Food Storage & Frozen Food, Plastic

Pactiv LLC.................................C...... 585 394-5125
Canandaigua (G-3138)

BAGS: Food Storage & Trash, Plastic

Bag Arts The Art Packaging LLC..........G...... 212 684-7020
New York (G-8716)

Mint-X Products Corporation ....F...... 877 646-8224
College Point (G-3554)

Pactiv LLC.................................C...... 518 793-2524
Glens Falls (G-5264)

BAGS: Garment Storage Exc Paper Or Plastic Film

Apex Real Holdings Inc.................G...... 877 725-2150
Brooklyn (G-1517)

BAGS: Grocers', Made From Purchased Materials

333 J & M Food Corp.....................F...... 718 381-1493
Ridgewood (G-13136)

Bag Arts The Art Packaging LLC..........G...... 212 684-7020
New York (G-8716)

BAGS: Knapsacks, Canvas, Made From Purchased Materials

Johnson Outdoors Inc....................C...... 607 779-2200
Binghamton (G-891)

BAGS: Laundry, Garment & Storage

Handy Laundry Products Corp............G...... 845 701-1111
Airmont (G-11)

Vr Bags Inc................................G...... 212 714-1494
Bronx (G-1393)

BAGS: Paper

American Packaging Corporation ....C...... 585 254-9500
Rochester (G-13230)

APC Paper Company Inc.................D...... 315 384-4225
Norfolk (G-11997)

R P Fedder Corp..........................E...... 585 288-1600
Rochester (G-13666)

Uniflex Holdings LLC....................F...... 516 932-2000
Hauppauge (G-5790)

BAGS: Paper, Made From Purchased Materials

Elgreco Gt Inc............................G...... 718 777-7922
Astoria (G-420)

BAGS: Plastic

American Packaging Corporation ....G...... 585 254-2002
Rochester (G-13229)

American Packaging Corporation ....C...... 585 254-9500
Rochester (G-13230)

Berry Global Inc.........................C...... 315 986-2161
Macedon (G-7462)

Centre De Conformite ICC Inc ....E...... 716 283-0002
Niagara Falls (G-11914)

Clear View Bag Company Inc ....C...... 518 458-7153
Albany (G-61)

Edco Supply Corporation...............D...... 718 788-8108
Brooklyn (G-1782)

H G Maybeck Co Inc.....................E...... 718 297-4410
Jamaica (G-6447)

Ivi Services Inc..........................D...... 607 729-5111
Binghamton (G-889)

Jay Bags Inc...............................G...... 845 459-6500
Spring Valley (G-14573)

JM Murray Center Inc...................C...... 607 756-9913
Cortland (G-3774)

Nova Packaging Ltd Inc.................E...... 914 232-8406
Katonah (G-6637)

Select Fabricators Inc..................F...... 585 393-0650
Canandaigua (G-3142)

Tai Seng....................................G...... 718 399-6311
Brooklyn (G-2491)

Tg Polymers Inc..........................G...... 585 670-9427
Webster (G-15656)

Trinity Packaging Corporation..........E...... 716 668-3111
Buffalo (G-3020)

W E W Container Corporation ....E...... 718 827-8150
Brooklyn (G-2572)

BAGS: Plastic & Pliofilm

Maco Bag Corporation ....C...... 315 226-1000
Newark (G-11844)

Uniflex Holdings LLC....................F...... 516 932-2000
Hauppauge (G-5790)

BAGS: Plastic, Made From Purchased Materials

Ace Bag & Burlap Company Inc ....F...... 718 319-9300
Bronx (G-1192)

Alco Plastics Inc.........................E...... 716 683-3020
Lancaster (G-6793)

Allied Converters Inc....................E...... 914 235-1585
New Rochelle (G-8319)

Amby International Inc....................F...... 718 645-0964
Brooklyn (G-1496)

API Industries Inc.........................B...... 845 365-2200
Orangeburg (G-12305)

API Industries Inc.........................C...... 845 365-2200
Orangeburg (G-12306)

Bags Unlimited Inc.......................E...... 585 436-6282
Rochester (G-13258)

D Bag Lady Inc............................G...... 585 425-8095
Fairport (G-4495)

Elgreco Gt Inc............................G...... 718 777-7922
Astoria (G-420)

Excellent Poly Inc........................F...... 718 768-6555
Brooklyn (G-1820)

Filmpak Extrusion LLC...................D...... 631 293-6767
Melville (G-7782)

Fortune Poly Products Inc................F...... 718 361-0767
Jamaica (G-6442)

Franklin Poly Film Inc....................E...... 718 492-3523
Brooklyn (G-1865)

Josh Packaging Inc......................E...... 631 822-1660
Hauppauge (G-5681)

Magcrest Packaging Inc.................G...... 845 425-0451
Monsey (G-8039)

Manhattan Poly Bag Corporation ....E...... 917 689-7549
Brooklyn (G-2108)

Mason Transparent Package Inc ....E...... 718 792-6000
Bronx (G-1307)

Metropolitan Packg Mfg Corp ....E...... 718 383-2700
Brooklyn (G-2149)

Modern Plastic Bags Mfg Inc ....G...... 718 237-2985
Brooklyn (G-2166)

New York Packaging Corp ....D...... 516 746-0600
New Hyde Park (G-8284)

New York Packaging II LLC ....E...... 516 746-0600
Garden City Park (G-5122)

Noteworthy Industries Inc...............C...... 518 842-2662
Amsterdam (G-344)

Pacific Poly Product Corp................F...... 718 786-7129
Long Island City (G-7317)

Pack America Corp.......................G...... 212 508-6666
New York (G-10740)

Paradise Plastics LLC....................E...... 718 788-3733
Brooklyn (G-2246)

Paramount Equipment Inc ....E...... 631 981-4422
Ronkonkoma (G-13991)

Poly Craft Industries Corp................E...... 631 630-6731
Hauppauge (G-5744)

Poly-Pak Industries Inc...................B...... 800 969-1933
Melville (G-7816)

Primo Plastics Inc........................E...... 718 349-1000
Brooklyn (G-2286)

Protective Lining Corp...................D...... 718 854-3838
Brooklyn (G-2302)

Rainbow Poly Bag Co Inc.................E...... 718 386-3500
Brooklyn (G-2326)

Rege Inc....................................F...... 845 565-7772
New Windsor (G-8380)

Rtr Bag & Co Ltd..........................G...... 212 620-0011
New York (G-11095)

Salerno Packaging Inc...................F...... 518 563-3636
Plattsburgh (G-12775)

Supreme Poly Plastics Inc ....E...... 718 456-9300
Brooklyn (G-2478)

T M I Plastics Industries Inc ....F...... 718 383-0363
Brooklyn (G-2485)

Technipoly Manufacturing Inc............G...... 718 383-0363
Brooklyn (G-2496)

Trinity Packaging Corporation..............F...... 914 273-4111
Armonk (G-404)

United Plastics Inc.........................G...... 718 389-2255
Brooklyn (G-2539)

BAGS: Rubber Or Rubberized Fabric

Adam Scott Designs Inc...................E...... 212 420-8866
New York (G-8453)

BAGS: Shipping

Shalam Imports Inc.......................F...... 718 686-6271
Brooklyn (G-2402)

BAGS: Shopping, Made From Purchased Materials

Ampac Paper LLC.........................G...... 845 713-6600
Walden (G-15456)

Custom Eco Friendly LLC ....F...... 347 227-0229
Roslyn (G-14041)

Rtr Bag & Co Ltd..........................G...... 212 620-0011
New York (G-11095)

BAGS: Tea, Fabric, Made From Purchased Materials

Health Matters America Inc..............F...... 716 235-8772
Buffalo (G-2796)

BAGS: Textile

Ace Bag & Burlap Company Inc ....F...... 718 319-9300
Bronx (G-1192)

Ace Drop Cloth Canvas Pdts Inc ....E...... 718 731-1550
Bronx (G-1193)

GPM Associates LLC ....G...... 585 359-1770
Rush (G-14071)

GPM Associates LLC ....G...... 585 335-3940
Dansville (G-3819)

Ivi Services Inc............................D...... 607 729-5111
Binghamton (G-889)

Jag Manufacturing Inc....................E...... 518 762-9558
Johnstown (G-6620)

Kragel Co Inc..............................E...... 716 648-1344
Hamburg (G-5512)

Kush Oasis Enterprises LLC ....G...... 516 513-1316
Syosset (G-14792)

Mgk Group Inc.............................E...... 212 989-2732
New York (G-10448)

Paulpac LLC...............................G...... 631 283-7610
Southampton (G-14534)

Prima Satchel Inc..........................G...... 929 367-7770
Monroe (G-8029)

BAGS: Trash, Plastic Film, Made From Purchased Materials

Garb-O-Liner Inc.........................G...... 914 235-1585
New Rochelle (G-8334)

Golden Group International Ltd...........F...... 845 440-1025
Patterson (G-12517)

Jad Corp of America......................E...... 718 762-8900
College Point (G-3548)

Repellem Consumer Pdts Corp ....F...... 631 273-3992
Bohemia (G-1070)

BAGS: Wardrobe, Closet Access, Made From Purchased Materials

Colden Closet LLC........................G...... 716 713-6125
East Aurora (G-4084)

BAKERIES, COMMERCIAL: On Premises Baking Only

40 Street Baking Inc......................G...... 212 683-4700
Brooklyn (G-1418)

A Angonoa Inc.............................C...... 718 762-4466
College Point (G-3531)

Aladdin Bakers Inc........................D...... 718 499-1818
Brooklyn (G-1475)

Aphrodities.................................G...... 718 224-1774
Whitestone (G-16087)

Aryzta LLC.................................C...... 585 235-8160
Rochester (G-13251)

Aryzta LLC.................................F...... 585 235-8160
Rochester (G-13250)

Better Baked Foods LLC ....D...... 716 326-4651
Westfield (G-15945)

P
R
O
D
U
C
T

Bimbo Bakeries .... G 631 274-4906
  Deer Park (G-3846)
Bimbo Bakeries .... F 518 463-2221
  Albany (G-50)
Bimbo Bakeries Usa Inc .... G 718 601-1561
  Bronx (G-1214)
Bimbo Bakeries Usa Inc .... G 718 545-0291
  Long Island City (G-7177)
Bimbo Bakeries Usa Inc .... F 845 255-4345
  New Paltz (G-8305)
Bimbo Bakeries Usa Inc .... E 631 951-5183
  Bay Shore (G-657)
Bimbo Bakeries Usa Inc .... F 518 563-1320
  Plattsburgh (G-12735)
Bimbo Bakeries Usa Inc .... D 315 253-9782
  Auburn (G-467)
Bimbo Bakeries Usa Inc .... F 716 706-0450
  Lancaster (G-6798)
Chambord LLC .... E 718 859-1110
  Brooklyn (G-1659)
Cohens Bakery Inc .... E 716 892-8149
  Buffalo (G-2702)
Fayda Manufacturing Corp ..... F 718 456-9331
  Brooklyn (G-1835)
Fratellis LLC .... E 607 722-5663
  Binghamton (G-878)
Gennaris Itln French Bky Inc .. G 516 997-8968
  Carle Place (G-3174)
Gourmet Toast Corp .... G 718 852-4536
  Brooklyn (G-1903)
H & S Edible Products Corp .... E 914 413-3489
  Mount Vernon (G-8146)
Hagadah Passover Bakery ...... F 718 638-1589
  Brooklyn (G-1918)
Hana Pastries Inc .... G 718 369-7593
  Brooklyn (G-1923)
J & S Licata Bros Inc .... F 718 805-6924
  Richmond Hill (G-13117)
Jarets Stuffed Cupcakes .... G 607 658-9096
  Endicott (G-4460)
King Cracker Corp .... F 516 539-9251
  Hempstead (G-5842)
Larosa Cupcakes .... G 347 866-3920
  Staten Island (G-14675)
Maplehurst Bakeries LLC .... B 315 735-5000
  Frankfort (G-4953)
Melita Corp .... G 718 392-7280
  Astoria (G-429)
Mrs Baking Distribution Corp .. G 718 460-6700
  College Point (G-3555)
New Mount Pleasant Bakery ... E 518 374-7577
  Schenectady (G-14291)
New Star Bakery .... E 718 961-8868
  Flushing (G-4877)
Nibble Inc Baking Co .... G 518 334-3950
  Troy (G-15175)
Nightingale Food Entps Inc .... G 347 577-1630
  New York (G-10626)
Operative Cake Corp .... E 718 278-5600
  Bronx (G-1329)
Ossining Bakery Lmp Inc .... G 914 941-2654
  Ossining (G-12405)
Oz Baking Company Ltd .... G 516 466-5114
  Great Neck (G-5410)
Palagonia Bakery Co Inc .... G 718 272-5400
  Brooklyn (G-2242)
Pane DOro .... F 914 964-0043
  Yonkers (G-16339)
Peking Food LLC .... E 718 628-8080
  Brooklyn (G-2252)
Rays Italian Bakery Inc .... F 516 825-9170
  Valley Stream (G-15355)
Roma Bakery Inc .... F 516 825-9170
  Valley Stream (G-15357)
Saint Honore Pastry Shop Inc . G 516 767-2555
  Port Washington (G-12921)
Saj of Freeport Corp .... C 516 623-8800
  Freeport (G-5021)
Silver Bell Baking Co .... G 718 335-9539
  Middle Village (G-7884)
Smith Street Bread Co LLC ..... F 718 797-9712
  Brooklyn (G-2431)
Sugarbear Cupcakes .... G 917 698-9005
  Jamaica (G-6476)
Sullivan St Bky - Hlls Kit Inc ... E 212 265-5580
  New York (G-11386)
Uncle Wallys LLC .... E 631 205-0455
  Shirley (G-14428)
Village Lantern Baking Corp ... G 631 225-1690
  Lindenhurst (G-6984)

Vito & Sons Bakery .... F 201 617-8501
  Brooklyn (G-2566)
Waldorf Bakers Inc .... F 718 665-2253
  Bronx (G-1394)
Wenner Bread Products Inc .... F 800 869-6262
  Bayport (G-732)
Whitestone Panetteria LLC ..... G 516 543-9788
  Whitestone (G-16103)

BAKERIES: On Premises Baking & Consumption

B & D Enterprises Utica Inc ... D 315 735-3311
  New Hartford (G-8236)
Bagel Land .... E 585 442-3080
  Rochester (G-13257)
Caputo Bakery Inc .... G 718 875-6871
  Brooklyn (G-1645)
Dipaolo Baking Co Inc .... G 585 303-5013
  Rochester (G-13348)
Ferrara Bakery & Cafe Inc ..... C 212 226-6150
  New York (G-9484)
Geddes Bakery Co Inc .... E 315 437-8084
  North Syracuse (G-12043)
Gennaris Itln French Bky Inc .. G 516 997-8968
  Carle Place (G-3174)
JJ Cassone Bakery Inc .... B 914 939-1568
  Port Chester (G-12823)
L American Ltd .... F 716 372-9480
  Olean (G-12238)
New Hope Mills Mfg Inc .... E 315 252-2676
  Auburn (G-487)
New Mount Pleasant Bakery ... E 518 374-7577
  Schenectady (G-14291)
Niebylski Bakery Inc .... G 718 721-5152
  Astoria (G-431)
Ohio Baking Company Inc ...... E 315 724-2033
  Utica (G-15289)
Perrottas Bakery Inc .... G 518 283-4711
  Troy (G-15178)
Pesces Bakery Inc .... G 845 246-4730
  Saugerties (G-14208)
Presser Kosher Baking Corp ... E 718 375-5088
  Brooklyn (G-2282)
Saint Honore Pastry Shop Inc . G 516 767-2555
  Port Washington (G-12921)
Sapienza Pastry Inc .... E 516 352-5232
  Elmont (G-4389)
Settepani Inc .... E 718 349-6524
  Brooklyn (G-2397)
T Shore Products Ltd .... G 315 252-9174
  Auburn (G-497)
Tarrytown Bakery Inc .... F 914 631-0209
  Tarrytown (G-15063)
Wenner Bread Products Inc .... B 800 869-6262
  Ronkonkoma (G-14026)
Wenner Bread Products Inc .... E 800 869-6262
  Ronkonkoma (G-14027)

BAKERY FOR HOME SVC DELIVERY

Circle 5 Deli Corp .... G 718 525-5687
  Jamaica (G-6433)

BAKERY PRDTS, FROZEN: Wholesalers

Fratellis LLC .... E 607 722-5663
  Binghamton (G-878)
Modern Itln Bky of W Babylon . C 631 589-7300
  Oakdale (G-12153)

BAKERY PRDTS: Bagels, Fresh Or Frozen

999 Bagels Inc .... G 718 915-0742
  Brooklyn (G-1426)
A T A Bagel Shoppe Inc .... G 718 352-4948
  Bayside (G-733)
Bagel Club Inc .... F 718 423-6106
  Bayside (G-735)
Bagel Grove Inc .... E 315 724-8015
  Utica (G-15240)
Bagel Land .... E 585 442-3080
  Rochester (G-13257)
Bagelovers Inc .... F 607 844-3683
  Dryden (G-4037)
Enterprise Bagels Inc .... F 845 896-3823
  Fishkill (G-4799)
FB Sale LLC .... G 315 986-9999
  Macedon (G-7465)
Greenvale Bagel Inc .... E 516 221-8221
  Wantagh (G-15484)

M & M Bagel Corp .... F 516 295-1222
  Cedarhurst (G-3240)
Mds Hot Bagels Deli Inc .... G 718 438-5650
  Brooklyn (G-2129)

BAKERY PRDTS: Bakery Prdts, Partially Cooked, Exc frozen

New Hope Mills Mfg Inc .... E 315 252-2676
  Auburn (G-487)
T&B Bakery Corp .... G 646 642-4300
  Maspeth (G-7638)

BAKERY PRDTS: Bread, All Types, Fresh Or Frozen

Addeo Bakers Inc .... F 718 367-8316
  Bronx (G-1197)
Bimbo Bakeries Usa Inc .... C 718 463-6300
  Maspeth (G-7597)
Commitment 2000 Inc .... E 716 439-1206
  Buffalo (G-2706)
Dipaolo Baking Co Inc .... D 585 303-5013
  Rochester (G-13348)
George Retzos .... G 315 422-2913
  Syracuse (G-14904)
Giovanni Bakery Corp .... F 212 695-4296
  New York (G-9614)
Harrison Bakery West .... G 315 422-1468
  Syracuse (G-14909)
L American Ltd .... F 716 372-9480
  Olean (G-12238)
La Prima Bakery Inc .... F 718 584-4442
  Bronx (G-1297)
Modern Itln Bky of W Babylon . C 631 589-7300
  Oakdale (G-12153)
Ohio Baking Company Inc ...... E 315 724-2033
  Utica (G-15289)
Rock Hill Bakehouse Ltd .... E 518 743-1627
  Gansevoort (G-5086)
Roslyn Bread Company Inc ..... E 516 625-1470
  Roslyn Heights (G-14056)
Tarrytown Bakery Inc .... F 914 631-0209
  Tarrytown (G-15063)
Wenner Bread Products Inc .... B 800 869-6262
  Ronkonkoma (G-14026)
Wenner Bread Products Inc .... E 800 869-6262
  Ronkonkoma (G-14027)

BAKERY PRDTS: Buns, Sweet, Frozen

Liddabit Sweets .... G 917 912-1370
  Brooklyn (G-2068)

BAKERY PRDTS: Cakes, Bakery, Exc Frozen

Always Baked Fresh Inc .... G 631 648-0811
  Holbrook (G-5985)
Brooklyn Sweet Spot Inc .... G 718 522-2577
  Brooklyn (G-1622)
Charlotte Neuville Design LLC . G 646 530-4570
  Brooklyn (G-1661)
Chocnyc LLC .... G 917 804-4848
  New York (G-8995)
Coccadotts Inc .... F 518 438-4937
  Albany (G-67)
Cupcake Contessas Corporation . G 516 307-1222
  North Bellmore (G-12017)
Ferrara Bakery & Cafe Inc ..... C 212 226-6150
  New York (G-9484)
Great American Dessert Co LLC . D 718 894-3494
  Maspeth (G-7620)
Hahns Old Fashioned Cake Co . F 631 249-3456
  Farmingdale (G-4643)
Herris Gourmet Inc .... G 917 578-2308
  Brooklyn (G-1934)
Jonathan Lord Corp .... F 631 563-4445
  Bohemia (G-1030)
McKee Foods Corporation ...... A 631 979-9364
  Hauppauge (G-5710)
Placid Baker .... G 518 326-2657
  Troy (G-15180)
Rm Bakery LLC .... E 718 472-3036
  Bronx (G-1351)
Scaife Enterprises Inc .... F 585 454-5231
  Fairport (G-4519)

BAKERY PRDTS: Cakes, Bakery, Frozen

Culinary Arts Specialties Inc .. D 716 656-8943
  Cheektowaga (G-3343)

LArte Del Gelato Gruppo Inc..............F....... 718 383-6600
Long Island City (G-7269)

BAKERY PRDTS: Cones, Ice Cream

Cone Buddy System Inc.........................F....... 585 427-9940
Rochester (G-13322)
Larte Del Gelato Inc.............................G....... 212 366-0570
New York (G-10174)
Pdi Cone Co Inc..................................D....... 716 825-8750
Buffalo (G-2909)

BAKERY PRDTS: Cookies

Chipita America Inc ....E....... 845 292-2540
Ferndale (G-4787)
Cooking With Chef Michelle LLC...........G....... 516 662-2324
Calverton (G-3079)
D F Stauffer Biscuit Co Inc ....E....... 585 968-2700
Cuba (G-3811)
Elenis Nyc Inc....................................E....... 718 361-8136
Long Island City (G-7213)
Falcones Cookie Land Ltd ....E....... 718 236-4200
Brooklyn (G-1830)
Golden Glow Cookie Co Inc ....E....... 718 379-6223
Bronx (G-1267)
Great Brands of Europe Inc ....G....... 914 872-8804
White Plains (G-16010)
Kaltec Food Packaging Inc ....E....... 845 856-9888
Port Jervis (G-12851)
Keebler Company ....F....... 585 948-8010
Oakfield (G-12157)
Linden Cookies Inc ....E....... 845 268-5050
Congers (G-3617)
Lloyd Price Icon Food Brands ....F....... 914 764-8624
Pound Ridge (G-12993)
Mannys Cheesecake Inc.......................G....... 315 732-0639
Utica (G-15280)
Quaker Bonnet Inc ....G....... 716 885-7208
Buffalo (G-2941)
Treehouse Private Brands Inc ....C....... 716 693-4715
Tonawanda (G-15147)
Wonton Food Inc..................................C....... 718 628-6868
Brooklyn (G-2593)

BAKERY PRDTS: Cookies & crackers

212kiddish Inc ....G....... 718 705-7227
Brooklyn (G-1411)
Butterwood Desserts Inc ....E....... 716 652-0131
West Falls (G-15761)
Cookies United LLC ....C....... 631 581-4000
Islip (G-6351)
Dancing Deer Baking Co LLC ....E....... 617 442-7300
Castleton On Hudson (G-3202)
Danny Macaroons Inc...........................G....... 260 622-8463
New York (G-9168)
Jonathan Lord Corp..............................F....... 631 563-4445
Bohemia (G-1030)
Ladybird Bakery Inc.............................G....... 718 499-8108
Brooklyn (G-2042)
New Mount Pleasant Bakery ....E....... 518 374-7577
Schenectady (G-14291)
Pepsico Inc ....A....... 914 253-2000
Purchase (G-13010)
Sapienza Pastry Inc ....E....... 516 352-5232
Elmont (G-4389)
Top Seedz LLC ....G....... 716 380-2612
Buffalo (G-3015)
United Baking Co Inc ....F....... 631 413-5116
Central Islip (G-3291)

BAKERY PRDTS: Cracker Meal & Crumbs

Wonton Food Inc..................................E....... 718 784-8178
Long Island City (G-7406)

BAKERY PRDTS: Doughnuts, Exc Frozen

3rd Avenue Doughnut Inc ....F....... 718 748-3294
Brooklyn (G-1416)
Alicias Bakery Inc................................G....... 914 235-4689
New Rochelle (G-8318)
Bimbo Bakeries Usa Inc ....E....... 203 531-2311
Bay Shore (G-658)
Cuzins Duzin Corp...............................G....... 347 724-6200
Kew Gardens (G-6663)
D-Lite Donuts ....G....... 718 626-5953
Astoria (G-416)
Famous Doughnuts Inc.........................G....... 716 834-6356
Buffalo (G-2751)

BAKERY PRDTS: Doughnuts, Frozen

Maplehurst Bakeries LLC......................B....... 315 735-5000
Frankfort (G-4953)

BAKERY PRDTS: Dry

17 Bakers LLC ....F....... 844 687-6836
Williamsville (G-16116)
Aryzta LLC ....C....... 585 235-8160
Rochester (G-13251)
Creative Food Ingredients Inc ....C....... 585 237-2213
Perry (G-12596)
Mindful Foods Inc................................G....... 646 708-0454
New York (G-10475)
My Most Favorite Food..........................G....... 212 580-5130
New York (G-10524)

BAKERY PRDTS: Frozen

Bello LLC ....E....... 516 623-8800
Freeport (G-4987)
Butterwood Desserts Inc ....E....... 716 652-0131
West Falls (G-15761)
Deiorio Foods Inc ....C....... 315 732-7612
Utica (G-15254)
Dufour Pastry Kitchens Inc ....E....... 718 402-8800
Bronx (G-1243)
Fratellis LLC ....E....... 607 722-5663
Binghamton (G-878)
Rich Holdings Inc.................................D....... 716 878-8000
Buffalo (G-2953)
Rich Products Corporation ....A....... 716 878-8000
Buffalo (G-2954)
Wenner Bread Products Inc ....B....... 800 869-6262
Ronkonkoma (G-14026)
Wenner Bread Products Inc ....E....... 800 869-6262
Ronkonkoma (G-14027)

BAKERY PRDTS: Matzoth

Aron Streit Inc ....E....... 212 475-7000
Orangeburg (G-12307)

BAKERY PRDTS: Pastries, Exc Frozen

Cannoli Factory Inc..............................E....... 631 643-2700
Wyandanch (G-16243)

BAKERY PRDTS: Pies, Bakery, Frozen

Circle Peak Capital MGT LLC..................E....... 646 230-8812
New York (G-9010)
Micosta Enterprises Inc........................G....... 518 822-9708
Hudson (G-6171)

BAKERY PRDTS: Pretzels

U Serve Brands Inc ....F....... 877 632-6654
New York (G-11572)

BAKERY PRDTS: Rolls, Bread Type, Fresh Or Frozen

Kossars On Grand LLC ....F....... 212 473-4810
New York (G-10129)

BAKERY PRDTS: Wholesalers

A & M Appel Distributing Inc..................G....... 516 735-1172
Massapequa (G-7642)
Aron Streit Inc ....E....... 212 475-7000
Orangeburg (G-12307)
B & D Enterprises Utica Inc ....D....... 315 735-3311
New Hartford (G-8236)
Cannoli Factory Inc..............................E....... 631 643-2700
Wyandanch (G-16243)
Damascus Bakery Inc...........................D....... 718 855-1456
Brooklyn (G-1721)
Fratellis LLC ....E....... 607 722-5663
Binghamton (G-878)
Hahns Old Fashioned Cake Co...............F....... 631 249-3456
Farmingdale (G-4643)
King Cracker Corp................................F....... 516 539-9251
Hempstead (G-5842)
Mac Crete Corporation ....F....... 718 932-1803
Long Island City (G-7284)
Modern Itln Bky of W Babylon................C....... 631 589-7300
Oakdale (G-12153)
Ohio Baking Company Inc ....E....... 315 724-2033
Utica (G-15289)
Operative Cake Corp............................E....... 718 278-5600
Bronx (G-1329)

Roslyn Bread Company Inc ....E....... 516 625-1470
Roslyn Heights (G-14056)
Wenner Bread Products Inc ....E....... 800 869-6262
Ronkonkoma (G-14027)

BAKERY: Wholesale Or Wholesale & Retail Combined

527 Franco Bakery Corporation ....G....... 718 993-4200
Bronx (G-1182)
A & M Appel Distributing Inc..................G....... 516 735-1172
Massapequa (G-7642)
Above The Rest Baking Corp ....D....... 718 313-9222
Bronx (G-1189)
Amiram Dror Inc..................................F....... 212 979-9505
Brooklyn (G-1504)
Andreas Protein Cakery Inc ....G....... 646 801-9826
New York (G-8579)
B & D Enterprises Utica Inc ....D....... 315 735-3311
New Hartford (G-8236)
Bakery & Coffee Shop ....G....... 315 287-1829
Gouverneur (G-5316)
Bien Cuit LLC ....E....... 718 852-0200
Brooklyn (G-1583)
Bimbo Bakeries Usa Inc ....G....... 716 692-9140
Tonawanda (G-15090)
Bimbo Bakeries Usa Inc ....E....... 516 877-2850
Mineola (G-7961)
Bimbo Bakeries Usa Inc ....C....... 716 372-8444
Olean (G-12225)
Bimbo Bakeries Usa Inc ....F....... 516 887-1024
Lynbrook (G-7427)
Bimbo Bakeries Usa Inc ....F....... 315 379-9069
Canton (G-3163)
Bimbo Bakeries Usa Inc ....F....... 518 489-4053
Albany (G-51)
Bimbo Bakeries Usa Inc ....D....... 845 568-0943
Newburgh (G-11860)
Bimbo Bakeries Usa Inc ....C....... 315 782-4189
Watertown (G-15560)
Blackbirds Brooklyn LLC ....G....... 917 362-4080
Brooklyn (G-1592)
Blondie S Bakeshop Inc ....G....... 631 424-4545
Centerport (G-3254)
Bread Factory LLC ....E....... 914 637-8150
New Rochelle (G-8321)
Caputo Bakery Inc ....G....... 718 875-6871
Brooklyn (G-1645)
Carmine Street Bagels Inc ....F....... 212 691-3041
Staten Island (G-14637)
Carolinas Desserts Inc ....G....... 914 779-4000
Yonkers (G-16293)
Carter Street Bakery Inc ....G....... 585 749-7104
Rochester (G-13298)
Cookie Connection Inc ....C....... 315 422-2253
Syracuse (G-14860)
Daly Meghan ....F....... 347 699-3259
Brooklyn (G-1720)
Damascus Bakery Inc...........................D....... 718 855-1456
Brooklyn (G-1721)
Dancing Deer Baking Co LLC ....E....... 617 442-7300
Castleton On Hudson (G-3202)
Delicias Andinas Food Corp ....E....... 718 416-2922
Flushing (G-4847)
Eileens Special Cheesecake ....G....... 212 966-5585
New York (G-9330)
Felix Roma & Sons Inc ....D....... 607 748-3336
Endicott (G-4456)
Flour Power Bakery Cafe ....F....... 917 747-6895
Livingston Manor (G-7053)
Food Gems Ltd ....E....... 718 296-7788
Ozone Park (G-12462)
Fotis Oneonta Italian Bakery ....G....... 607 432-3871
Oneonta (G-12271)
Fung Wong Bakery Inc ....E....... 212 267-4037
New York (G-9553)
Gabila & Sons Mfg Inc ....E....... 631 789-2220
Copiague (G-3653)
Geddes Bakery Co Inc...........................E....... 315 437-8084
North Syracuse (G-12043)
Glenn Wayne Wholesale Bky Inc............D....... 631 289-9200
Bohemia (G-1018)
Gluten Free Bake Shop Inc ....E....... 845 782-5307
Mountainville (G-8193)
Golden Glow Cookie Co Inc ....E....... 718 379-6223
Bronx (G-1267)
Good Bread Bakery ....F....... 914 939-3900
Port Chester (G-12822)
H H B Bakery of Little Neck....................G....... 718 631-7004
Flushing (G-4856)

PRODUCT

Have Your Cake Kitchen LLC ....G 646 820-8074
Brooklyn *(G-1927)*

Heidelberg Group Inc ....E 315 866-0999
Herkimer *(G-5863)*

Hum Limited Liability Corp ....G 631 525-2174
Nesconset *(G-8218)*

Jane Bakes Inc ....G 845 920-1100
Pearl River *(G-12535)*

Jerrys Bagels ....G 516 791-0063
Valley Stream *(G-15344)*

JGM Wholesale Bakery Inc ....G 631 396-0131
Amityville *(G-282)*

Jim Romas Bakery Inc. ....E 607 748-7425
Endicott *(G-4463)*

JJ Cassone Bakery Inc ....B 914 939-1568
Port Chester *(G-12823)*

Kokoroko Corporation.....................G 718 433-4321
Woodside *(G-16211)*

Ladybird Bakery Inc ....G 718 499-8108
Brooklyn *(G-2042)*

Lillys Homestyle Bakeshop Inc ....D 718 491-2904
Brooklyn *(G-2074)*

Ljmm Inc ....E 845 454-5876
Poughkeepsie *(G-12967)*

Made Close LLC ....G 917 837-1357
Brooklyn *(G-2102)*

Maxwell Bakery Inc ....E 718 498-2200
Brooklyn *(G-2127)*

Millers Bulk Food and Bakery ....G 585 798-9700
Medina *(G-7741)*

Miss Grimble Associates Inc ....F 718 665-2253
Bronx *(G-1316)*

Niebylski Bakery Inc ....G 718 721-5152
Astoria *(G-431)*

Nildas Desserts Limited ....F 845 454-5876
Poughkeepsie *(G-12975)*

Perrottas Bakery Inc ....G 518 283-4711
Troy *(G-15178)*

Pesces Bakery Inc ....G 845 246-4730
Saugerties *(G-14208)*

Presser Kosher Baking Corp ....E 718 375-5088
Brooklyn *(G-2282)*

Quaker Bonnet Inc ....G 716 885-7208
Buffalo *(G-2941)*

R & H Baking Co Inc ....E 718 852-1768
Brooklyn *(G-2318)*

Rays Restaurant & Bakery Inc ....G 718 441-7707
Jamaica *(G-6469)*

Reisman Bros Bakery Inc ....F 718 331-1975
Brooklyn *(G-2337)*

Richard Engdal Baking Corp ....F 914 777-9600
Mamaroneck *(G-7521)*

Rnd Food Service Inc ....F 917 291-0061
New York *(G-11057)*

Royal Sweet Bakery Inc ....F 718 567-7770
Brooklyn *(G-2362)*

Sapienza Pastry Inc ....E 516 352-5232
Elmont *(G-4389)*

Secure International ....G 716 206-2500
Lancaster *(G-6833)*

Settepani Inc ....E 718 349-6524
Brooklyn *(G-2397)*

Slims Bagels Unlimited Inc ....E 718 229-1140
Oakland Gardens *(G-12160)*

Soutine Inc ....G 212 496-1450
New York *(G-11306)*

Stebe Shcjhjff ....F 839 383-9833
Poughkeepsie *(G-12985)*

Tates Wholesale LLC ....C 631 780-6511
East Moriches *(G-4140)*

Triboro Bagel Co Inc ....E 718 359-9245
Flushing *(G-4901)*

Worlds Best Cookie Dough Inc ....G 347 592-3422
New York *(G-11783)*

BANDAGES

Medi-Tech International Corp ....G 800 333-0109
Brooklyn *(G-2132)*

BANDS: Copper & Copper Alloy

Milward Alloys Inc..........................E 716 434-5536
Lockport *(G-7093)*

BANNERS: Fabric

Ace Banner & Flag Company............F 212 620-9111
New York *(G-8445)*

Arista Flag Corporation....................F 845 246-7700
Saugerties *(G-14197)*

Big Apple Sign Corp ....D 212 629-3650
New York *(G-8785)*

Big Apple Sign Corp ....E 631 342-0303
Islandia *(G-6326)*

Dkm Sales LLC ....E 716 893-7777
Buffalo *(G-2730)*

Kraus & Sons Inc ....F 212 620-0408
New York *(G-10137)*

Sellco Industries Inc ....E 607 756-7594
Cortland *(G-3788)*

BANQUET HALL FACILITIES

Casa Larga Vineyards ....E 585 223-4210
Fairport *(G-4492)*

BAR FIXTURES: Wood

Modern Craft Bar Rest Equip............G 631 226-5647
Lindenhurst *(G-6961)*

BARBECUE EQPT

Korin Inc ....E 212 587-7021
New York *(G-10128)*

Podravka International USA................F 212 661-0125
New York *(G-10859)*

BARRICADES: Metal

Consolidated Barricades Inc ....G 518 922-7944
Fultonville *(G-5078)*

Inpro Corporation ....G 716 332-4699
Tonawanda *(G-15115)*

BARS & BAR SHAPES: Steel, Hot-Rolled

Vell Company Inc ....G 845 365-1013
Palisades *(G-12484)*

BARS: Concrete Reinforcing, Fabricated Steel

Agl Industries Inc...........................E 718 326-7597
Maspeth *(G-7585)*

Arista Steel Designs Corp.................G 718 965-7077
Brooklyn *(G-1529)*

Baco Enterprises Inc ....D 718 589-6225
Bronx *(G-1209)*

Barker Steel LLC ....E 518 465-6221
Albany *(G-44)*

City Evolutionary ....G 718 861-7585
Bronx *(G-1225)*

DAgostino Iron Works Inc ....G 585 235-8850
Rochester *(G-13335)*

Designs By Novello Inc ....G 914 934-7711
Port Chester *(G-12817)*

Dimension Fabricators Inc ....E 518 374-1936
Scotia *(G-14329)*

Ferro Fabricators Inc ....E 718 703-0007
Brooklyn *(G-1839)*

GCM Metal Industries Inc ....F 718 386-4059
Brooklyn *(G-1879)*

Harbor Wldg & Fabrication Corp..........F 631 667-1880
Copiague *(G-3657)*

Klein Reinforcing Services Inc ....F 585 352-9433
Spencerport *(G-14557)*

New York Steel Services Co ....G 718 291-7770
Jamaica *(G-6463)*

Siw Inc ....F 631 888-0130
Bay Shore *(G-714)*

Steel Sales Inc ....E 607 674-6363
Sherburne *(G-14395)*

Torino Industrial Inc ....F 631 509-1640
Bellport *(G-810)*

Wide Flange Inc..............................F 718 492-8705
Brooklyn *(G-2583)*

BARS: Extruded, Aluminum

Itts Industrial Inc ....E 718 605-6934
Staten Island *(G-14667)*

BARS: Iron, Made In Steel Mills

Crucible Industries LLC ....B 800 365-1180
Solvay *(G-14495)*

Tri Valley Iron Inc ....F 845 365-1013
Palisades *(G-12483)*

BASEBOARDS: Metal

Slanto Manufacturing Inc ....E 516 759-5721
Glen Cove *(G-5201)*

BASES, BEVERAGE

Life On Earth Inc ....F 646 844-9897
New York *(G-10212)*

Myx Beverage LLC ....F 585 978-3542
Oyster Bay *(G-12451)*

Tealeafs ....G 716 688-8022
Williamsville *(G-16143)*

BASKETS: Steel Wire

Braun Horticulture Inc ....G 716 282-6101
Niagara Falls *(G-11909)*

BATCHING PLANTS: Cement Silos

New Eagle Silo Corp ....G 585 492-1300
Arcade *(G-379)*

BATH SALTS

Aromasong Usa Inc ....F 718 838-9669
Brooklyn *(G-1533)*

BATHING SUIT STORES

Malia Mills Inc ....F 212 354-4200
Brooklyn *(G-2105)*

Shirl-Lynn of New York ....F 315 363-5898
Oneida *(G-12254)*

BATHMATS, COTTON

Michael Stuart Inc ....E 718 821-0704
Brooklyn *(G-2151)*

BATHROOM ACCESS & FITTINGS: Vitreous China & Earthenware

AMG JV LLC ....G 212 602-1818
New York *(G-8563)*

Gamma Products Inc ....D 845 562-3332
New Windsor *(G-8368)*

Larcent Enterprises Inc ....E 845 562-3332
New Windsor *(G-8371)*

Stone and Bath Gallery ....G 718 438-4500
Brooklyn *(G-2462)*

BATHTUBS: Concrete

Meditub Incorporated ....F 866 633-4882
Lawrence *(G-6888)*

BATTERIES, EXC AUTOMOTIVE: Wholesalers

El-Don Battery Post Inc ....G 716 627-3697
Hamburg *(G-5506)*

BATTERIES: Alkaline, Cell Storage

Bren-Trnics Batteries Intl LLC ....E 631 499-5155
Commack *(G-3581)*

Ultralife Corporation.........................B 315 332-7100
Newark *(G-11854)*

BATTERIES: Lead Acid, Storage

Exide Technologies ....G 585 344-0656
Batavia *(G-613)*

Johnson Controls Inc ....C 585 724-2232
Rochester *(G-13495)*

BATTERIES: Rechargeable

Bren-Trnics Batteries Intl Inc ....G 631 499-5155
Commack *(G-3580)*

Synergy Digital ....F 718 643-2742
Brooklyn *(G-2483)*

BATTERIES: Storage

Amco Intl Mfg & Design Inc ....E 718 388-8668
Brooklyn *(G-1497)*

Battery Research and Tstg Inc ....F 315 342-2373
Oswego *(G-12408)*

Battsco LLC ....G 516 586-6544
Hicksville *(G-5888)*

Bren-Tronics Inc. ....C 631 499-5155
Commack *(G-3582)*

Cellec Technologies Inc ....G 585 454-9166
Rochester *(G-13304)*

China Lithium Technologies ....G 212 391-2688
New York *(G-8990)*

El-Don Battery Post Inc........................G...... 716 627-3697
Hamburg *(G-5506)*
New Energy Systems Group................C...... 917 573-0302
New York *(G-10580)*
Sparkcharge Inc................................G...... 315 480-3645
Syracuse *(G-14996)*

BATTERIES: Wet

Bren-Tronics Inc...............................C...... 631 499-5155
Commack *(G-3582)*
Electrochem Solutions Inc................D...... 716 759-5800
Clarence *(G-3433)*
Shad Industries Inc..........................G...... 631 504-6028
Yaphank *(G-16271)*

BATTERY CASES: Plastic Or Plastics Combination

Memory Protection Devices Inc........F...... 631 249-0001
Farmingdale *(G-4680)*

BATTERY CHARGERS

Applied Energy Solutions LLC.........E...... 585 538-3270
Webster *(G-15629)*
China Lithium Technologies.............G...... 212 391-2688
New York *(G-8990)*
Eluminocity US Inc...........................G...... 651 528-1165
New York *(G-9353)*
Exide Technologies..........................G...... 585 344-0656
Batavia *(G-613)*
Kussmaul Electronics Co Inc............E...... 631 218-0298
West Sayville *(G-15841)*
Walter R Tucker Entps Ltd...............E...... 607 467-2866
Deposit *(G-4004)*

BATTERY CHARGERS: Storage, Motor & Engine Generator Type

Apogee Power Usa Inc.....................F...... 202 746-2890
Hartsdale *(G-5567)*
Vdc Electronics Inc..........................F...... 631 423-8220
Huntington *(G-6232)*

BATTERY CHARGING GENERATORS

Eluminocity US Inc...........................G...... 651 528-1165
New York *(G-9353)*

BATTS & BATTING: Cotton

Ino-Tex LLC.....................................G...... 212 400-2205
New York *(G-9899)*
Rovel Manufacturing Co Inc..............G...... 516 365-2752
Roslyn *(G-14046)*
Superior Fiber Mills Inc....................F...... 718 782-7500
Brooklyn *(G-2475)*
Vincent Manufacturing Co Inc..........F...... 315 823-0280
Little Falls *(G-6995)*

BEARINGS & PARTS Ball

A Hyatt Ball Co Ltd..........................G...... 518 747-0272
Fort Edward *(G-4936)*
General Bearing Corporation.............C...... 845 358-6000
West Nyack *(G-15822)*
Kilian Manufacturing Corp................D...... 315 432-0700
Syracuse *(G-14925)*
Mageba USA LLC.............................E...... 212 317-1991
New York *(G-10321)*
Nes Bearing Company Inc.................E...... 716 372-6532
Olean *(G-12239)*
Schatz Bearing Corporation..............D...... 845 452-6000
Poughkeepsie *(G-12981)*
SKF USA Inc....................................D...... 716 661-2869
Falconer *(G-4555)*
SKF USA Inc....................................D...... 716 661-2600
Falconer *(G-4557)*
SKF USA Inc....................................D...... 716 661-2600
Falconer *(G-4556)*

BEARINGS: Ball & Roller

American Refuse Supply Inc...............G...... 718 893-8157
Bronx *(G-1204)*
Auburn Bearing & Mfg Inc.................G...... 315 986-7600
Macedon *(G-7460)*
David Fehlman.................................G...... 315 455-8888
Syracuse *(G-14875)*
Enbi Rochester Inc...........................G...... 585 647-1651
Rochester *(G-13390)*

Lemoyne Machine Products Corp.......G...... 315 454-0708
Syracuse *(G-14930)*
Raydon Precision Bearing Co.............G...... 516 887-2582
Lynbrook *(G-7436)*
Sandle Custom Bearing Corp.............G...... 585 593-7000
Wellsville *(G-15675)*

BEAUTY & BARBER SHOP EQPT

Accurate Pnt Powdr Coating Inc.........F...... 585 235-1650
Rochester *(G-13201)*
Adults and Children With Learn.........E...... 516 593-8230
East Rockaway *(G-4170)*
Advanced Assembly Services Inc........G...... 716 217-8144
Lancaster *(G-6789)*
Blackbox Biometrics Inc....................E...... 585 329-3399
Rochester *(G-13271)*
Brooklyn Industries LLC....................G...... 718 788-5250
Brooklyn *(G-1617)*
Callanan Industries Inc.....................G...... 518 382-5354
Schenectady *(G-14250)*
Deal To Win Inc................................E...... 718 609-1165
Syosset *(G-14784)*
East Penn Manufacturing Co.............G...... 631 321-7161
Babylon *(G-519)*
Egm Mfg Inc.....................................G...... 718 782-9800
Brooklyn *(G-1786)*
Freedom Mfg LLC.............................F...... 518 584-0441
Saratoga Springs *(G-14175)*
Goodwill Inds of Greater NY..............G...... 914 621-0781
Baldwin Place *(G-538)*
Innovative Industries LLC..................G...... 718 784-7300
Long Island City *(G-7248)*
J & A Usa Inc...................................G...... 631 243-3336
Brentwood *(G-1124)*
Nitro Manufacturing LLC...................F...... 716 646-9900
Hamburg *(G-5514)*
Ohserase Manufacturing LLC............E...... 518 358-9309
Akwesasne *(G-25)*
Ohserase Manufacturing LLC............G...... 518 358-9309
Hogansburg *(G-5981)*
Oledworks LLC.................................E...... 585 287-6802
Rochester *(G-13589)*
P S Pibbs Inc...................................G...... 718 445-8046
Flushing *(G-4882)*
Paratus Industries Inc......................E...... 716 826-2000
Orchard Park *(G-12371)*
PCI Industries Corp..........................E...... 914 662-2700
Mount Vernon *(G-8168)*
Qualbuys LLC...................................G...... 855 884-3274
Syosset *(G-14800)*
S B Manufacturing LLC.....................F...... 845 352-3700
Monsey *(G-8045)*
Sayeda Manufacturing Corp..............F...... 631 345-2525
Medford *(G-7723)*

BEAUTY SALONS

Lemetric Hair Centers Inc..................F...... 212 986-5620
New York *(G-10194)*

BED & BREAKFAST INNS

Malina Management Company Inc.......E...... 607 535-9614
Montour Falls *(G-8075)*
Newspaper Publisher LLC.................F...... 607 775-0472
Conklin *(G-3626)*

BEDDING, BEDSPREADS, BLANKETS & SHEETS

Cathay Home Inc..............................E...... 212 213-0988
New York *(G-8937)*
Indigo Home Inc...............................G...... 212 684-4146
New York *(G-9881)*
Northpoint Trading Inc......................F...... 212 481-8001
New York *(G-10645)*
Richloom Fabrics Group Inc...............G...... 212 685-5400
New York *(G-11043)*
Sunham Home Fashions LLC............D...... 212 695-1218
New York *(G-11393)*

BEDDING, BEDSPREADS, BLANKETS & SHEETS: Comforters & Quilts

Alen Sands York Associates Ltd........F...... 212 563-6305
New York *(G-8511)*
EY Industries Inc..............................F...... 718 624-9122
Brooklyn *(G-1824)*
Kaltex North America Inc...................F...... 212 894-3200
New York *(G-10063)*

Revman International Inc...................E...... 212 894-3100
New York *(G-11028)*

BEDDING, FROM SILK OR MANMADE FIBER

Chf Industries Inc............................E...... 212 951-7800
New York *(G-8984)*
Westpoint Home LLC.........................A...... 212 930-2000
New York *(G-11746)*

BEDS & ACCESS STORES

Charles P Rogers Brass Beds.............F...... 212 675-4400
New York *(G-8975)*
Duxiana Dux Bed..............................G...... 212 755-2600
New York *(G-9282)*
Metro Mattress Corp.........................E...... 716 205-2300
Niagara Falls *(G-11951)*

BEDS: Hospital

NK Medical Products Inc....................G...... 716 759-7200
Amherst *(G-235)*
Novum Medical Products Ny LLC........F...... 716 759-7200
Amherst *(G-236)*
VSM Investors LLC...........................G...... 212 351-1600
New York *(G-11708)*

BEDSPREADS & BED SETS, FROM PURCHASED MATERIALS

Belle Maison USA Ltd........................E...... 718 805-0200
Richmond Hill *(G-13110)*
Bramson House Inc...........................C...... 516 764-5006
Freeport *(G-4988)*
C & G of Kingston Inc.......................D...... 845 331-0148
Kingston *(G-6681)*
County Draperies Inc........................E...... 845 342-9009
Middletown *(G-7901)*
Fabric Quilters Unlimited Inc............E...... 516 333-2866
Westbury *(G-15884)*
Himatsingka America Inc...................E...... 212 824-2949
New York *(G-9787)*
Jo-Vin Decorators Inc.......................E...... 718 441-9350
Woodhaven *(G-16187)*
Wayne Decorators Inc.......................G...... 718 529-4200
Jamaica *(G-6487)*

BEDSPREADS, COTTON

Mason Contract Products LLC............D...... 516 328-6900
New Hyde Park *(G-8282)*

BEEKEEPERS' SPLYS

Northast Ctr For Bekeeping LLC.........F...... 800 632-3379
Greenwich *(G-5474)*

BEEKEEPERS' SPLYS: Bee Smokers

Ubees Inc...F...... 916 505-8470
New York *(G-11573)*

BEER & ALE, WHOLESALE: Beer & Other Fermented Malt Liquors

Constellation Brands Inc...................D...... 585 678-7100
Victor *(G-15399)*
Load/N/Go Beverage Corp.................F...... 585 218-4019
Rochester *(G-13521)*
Save More Beverage Corp.................G...... 518 371-2520
Halfmoon *(G-5499)*

BEER, WINE & LIQUOR STORES

Lucas Vineyards Inc.........................F...... 607 532-4825
Interlaken *(G-6285)*

BEER, WINE & LIQUOR STORES: Beer, Packaged

Load/N/Go Beverage Corp.................F...... 585 218-4019
Rochester *(G-13521)*
Save More Beverage Corp.................G...... 518 371-2520
Halfmoon *(G-5499)*
Valcour Brewing Company LLC...........E...... 518 324-2337
Plattsburgh *(G-12789)*

BEER, WINE & LIQUOR STORES: Wine

Casa Larga Vineyards.......................E...... 585 223-4210
Fairport *(G-4492)*

PRODUCT

Coyote Moon LLC ....F 315 686-5600
   Clayton *(G-3453)*

J Petrocelli Wine Cellars LLC ....E 631 765-1100
   Peconic *(G-12546)*

Negys New Land Vinyrd Winery ....G 315 585-4432
   Geneva *(G-5160)*

Olde Chtqua Vneyards Ltd Lblty ....F 716 792-2749
   Portland *(G-12933)*

Standing Stone Vineyards ....G 607 582-6051
   Hector *(G-5828)*

BELLOWS

Kinemotive Corporation ....E 631 249-6440
   Farmingdale *(G-4666)*

Nicoform Inc ....E 585 454-5530
   Rochester *(G-13577)*

BELTING: Rubber

Van Slyke Belting LLC ....G 518 283-5479
   Poestenkill *(G-12805)*

BELTS: Conveyor, Made From Purchased Wire

Chemprene Inc ....C 845 831-2800
   Beacon *(G-749)*

Chemprene Holding Inc ....C 845 831-2800
   Beacon *(G-750)*

Habasit America Inc ....D 716 824-8484
   Buffalo *(G-2787)*

Sampla Belting North Amer LLC ....E 716 667-7450
   Lackawanna *(G-6745)*

BENCHES: Seating

Jays Furniture Products Inc ....E 716 876-8854
   Buffalo *(G-2816)*

Jcdecaux Mallscape LLC ....F 646 834-1200
   New York *(G-9988)*

BEVERAGE BASES & SYRUPS

Agua Enerviva LLC ....F 516 597-5440
   Bethpage *(G-832)*

Boylan Bottling Co Inc ....E 800 289-7978
   New York *(G-8842)*

Buffalo Blends Inc ....E 716 825-4422
   Buffalo *(G-2671)*

Flavormatic Industries LLC...................E 845 297-9100
   Wappingers Falls *(G-15492)*

BEVERAGE PRDTS: Brewers' Grain

Kings Cnty Brwers Cllctive LLC ....F 917 207-2739
   Brooklyn *(G-2031)*

Lic Brewery LLC ....G 917 832-6840
   Long Island City *(G-7271)*

BEVERAGE, NONALCOHOLIC: Iced Tea/Fruit Drink, Bottled/Canned

4 Star Brands Inc ....G 516 944-0472
   Elmhurst *(G-4331)*

Arizona Beverage Company LLC ....G 516 812-0300
   Woodbury *(G-16166)*

Cell-Nique Corporation.........................G 203 856-8550
   Castleton On Hudson *(G-3200)*

Cham Cold Brew LLC ....G 646 926-0206
   New York *(G-8968)*

F & V Distribution Company LLC ....G 516 812-0393
   Woodbury *(G-16171)*

Hain Celestial Group Inc ....C 516 587-5000
   New Hyde Park *(G-8272)*

Heart of Tea ....F 917 725-3164
   New York *(G-9757)*

Long Blockchain Corp...........................E 855 542-2832
   Farmingdale *(G-4672)*

Long Island Brand Bevs LLC ....D 855 542-2832
   Long Island City *(G-7279)*

BEVERAGES, ALCOHOLIC: Ale

Empire Brewing Company Inc ....D 315 925-8308
   Syracuse *(G-14887)*

BEVERAGES, ALCOHOLIC: Applejack

Honeoye Falls Distillery LLC ....F 201 780-4618
   Honeoye Falls *(G-6075)*

BEVERAGES, ALCOHOLIC: Beer

Anheuser-Busch LLC ....C 315 638-0365
   Baldwinsville *(G-542)*

Anheuser-Busch LLC ....C 212 573-8800
   New York *(G-8585)*

Anheuser-Busch Companies LLC..........G 718 589-2610
   Bronx *(G-1206)*

Anheuser-Busch Inbev Fin Inc ....F 212 573-8800
   New York *(G-8586)*

Anheuser-Busch Inbev Svcs LLC ....G 314 765-4729
   New York *(G-8587)*

Brazen Street LLC ....E 516 305-7951
   Brooklyn *(G-1606)*

Brewery Ommegang Ltd ....E 607 286-4144
   Cooperstown *(G-3638)*

Constellation Brands Inc ....D 585 678-7100
   Victor *(G-15399)*

Coopers Cave Ale Co S-Corp ....F 518 792-0007
   Glens Falls *(G-5246)*

Cooperstown Brewing Co LLC ....G 607 286-9330
   Oneonta *(G-12268)*

Gilded Otter Brewing Co ....D 845 256-1700
   New Paltz *(G-8306)*

High Falls Brewing Company LLC ....E 585 263-9318
   Rochester *(G-13466)*

Hoptron Brewtique...............................G 631 438-0296
   Patchogue *(G-12502)*

Hyde Park Brewing Co Inc ....E 845 229-8277
   Hyde Park *(G-6272)*

Indian Ladder Farmstead Brewer ....E 518 577-1484
   Altamont *(G-194)*

Keegan Ales LLC ....E 845 331-2739
   Kingston *(G-6695)*

Keuka Brewing Co LLC ....G 607 868-4648
   Hammondsport *(G-5531)*

Labatt USA LLC ....D 716 604-1050
   Buffalo *(G-2842)*

Lock 1 Distilling Company LLC ....G 315 934-4376
   Phoenix *(G-12616)*

Long Ireland Brewing LLC ....G 631 403-4303
   Riverhead *(G-13179)*

Mad Scntsts Brwing Prtners LLC ....E 347 766-2739
   Brooklyn *(G-2101)*

Middle Ages Brewing Company ....G 315 476-4250
   Syracuse *(G-14941)*

Millercoors LLC ....E 585 385-0670
   Pittsford *(G-12652)*

Montauk Brewing Company Inc ....F 631 668-8471
   Montauk *(G-8055)*

Newburgh Brewing Company LLC ....F 845 569-2337
   Newburgh *(G-11876)*

North American Breweries Inc ....F 585 546-1030
   Rochester *(G-13581)*

North Amrcn Brwries Hldngs LLC ....E 585 546-1030
   Rochester *(G-13582)*

Oyster Bay Brewing Company ....F 516 802-5546
   Oyster Bay *(G-12452)*

Rare Form Brewing Company ....G 518 313-9256
   Troy *(G-15183)*

Remarkable Liquids LLC ....E 518 861-5351
   Altamont *(G-197)*

Rohrbach Brewing Company Inc ....D 585 594-9800
   Rochester *(G-13704)*

Shmaltz Brewing Company ....E 518 406-5430
   Clifton Park *(G-3474)*

Spectacle Brewing LLC ....F 845 942-8776
   Garnerville *(G-5135)*

Vanberg & Dewulf Co Inc ....G 607 547-8184
   Cooperstown *(G-3641)*

Woodcock Brothers Brewing Comp ....F 716 333-4000
   Wilson *(G-16155)*

Yonkers Whl Beer Distrs Inc ....G 914 963-8600
   Yonkers *(G-16361)*

BEVERAGES, ALCOHOLIC: Beer & Ale

Anheuser-Busch LLC ....G 315 638-0365
   Baldwinsville *(G-541)*

Barrier Brewing Company LLC...............G 516 316-4429
   Long Beach *(G-7135)*

Duvel Mortgage USA Inc ....G 607 267-6121
   Cooperstown *(G-3640)*

Equilibrium Brewery LLC ....G 201 245-0292
   Middletown *(G-7907)*

Mikkeller Nyc ....G 917 572-0357
   Flushing *(G-4874)*

Murphs Famous Inc ....G 516 398-0417
   Rockville Centre *(G-13831)*

Simple Brewer ....E 845 490-0182
   Somers *(G-14501)*

Valcour Brewing Company LLC ....E 518 324-2337
   Plattsburgh *(G-12789)*

Wagner Vineyards & Brewing Co ....E 607 582-6574
   Lodi *(G-7133)*

BEVERAGES, ALCOHOLIC: Bourbon Whiskey

Iron Smoke Whiskey LLC.......................G 585 388-7584
   Fairport *(G-4499)*

BEVERAGES, ALCOHOLIC: Brandy

Cruzin Management Inc.........................E 212 641-8700
   New York *(G-9126)*

BEVERAGES, ALCOHOLIC: Brandy Spirits

PM Spirits LLC ....F 347 689-4414
   Brooklyn *(G-2267)*

BEVERAGES, ALCOHOLIC: Cocktails

Cocktail Crate LLC................................G 718 316-2033
   Long Island City *(G-7188)*

Dutch Spirits LLC.................................F 518 398-1022
   Pine Plains *(G-12633)*

BEVERAGES, ALCOHOLIC: Cordials & Premixed Cocktails

Infirmary Nyc ....G 504 606-6280
   New York *(G-9885)*

BEVERAGES, ALCOHOLIC: Distilled Liquors

Adirondack Distilling Company..............G 315 316-0387
   Utica *(G-15236)*

Anheusr-Bsch Coml Strategy LLC..........F 347 429-1082
   New York *(G-8588)*

Braided Oak Spirits LLC ....F 845 381-1525
   Middletown *(G-7896)*

Constellation Brands Inc.......................D 585 678-7100
   Victor *(G-15399)*

Ellicottville Distillery LLC.....................G 716 597-6121
   Ellicottville *(G-4313)*

Finger Lakes Distilling..........................F 607 546-5510
   Burdett *(G-3057)*

George Lake Distilling Company ....G 518 639-1025
   Queensbury *(G-13040)*

Leblon LLC ....E 786 281-5672
   New York *(G-10188)*

Lockhouse Distillery ....G 716 768-4898
   Buffalo *(G-2852)*

New York Distilling Co LLC ....B 718 473-2955
   Brooklyn *(G-2206)*

New York Distilling Co LLC ....G 917 893-7519
   Brooklyn *(G-2207)*

Prince Black Distillery Inc ....E 212 695-6187
   Syosset *(G-14799)*

Prohibition Distillery LLC ....G 917 685-8989
   Roscoe *(G-14035)*

Sovereign Brands LLC ....G 212 343-8366
   New York *(G-11307)*

Stilltheone Distillery LLC ....E 914 217-0347
   Harrison *(G-5561)*

Tuthilltown Spirits LLC ....F 845 255-1527
   Gardiner *(G-5131)*

BEVERAGES, ALCOHOLIC: Gin

21st Century Spirits Corp......................G 718 499-0606
   Brooklyn *(G-1412)*

Madison County Distillery LLC ....G 315 391-6070
   Cazenovia *(G-3229)*

BEVERAGES, ALCOHOLIC: Liquors, Malt

Castle Brands Inc ....E 646 356-0200
   New York *(G-8930)*

Vernon Wine & Liquor Inc ....G 718 784-5096
   Long Island City *(G-7394)*

BEVERAGES, ALCOHOLIC: Near Beer

Horns & Halos Cft Brewing LLC ....E 585 507-7248
   Caledonia *(G-3071)*

Liquid State Brewing Co Inc ....G 607 319-6209
   Ithaca *(G-6392)*

BEVERAGES, ALCOHOLIC: Neutral Spirits, Fruit

Davos Brands LLC ....F...... 212 779-1911
New York (G-9189)

Dutch Spirits LLC ....F...... 518 398-1022
Pine Plains (G-12633)

BEVERAGES, ALCOHOLIC: Rum

Castle Brands Inc ....E...... 646 356-0200
New York (G-8930)

Cruzin Management Inc ....E...... 212 641-8700
New York (G-9126)

Evolution Spirits Inc ....G...... 917 543-7880
New York (G-9432)

Leblon Holdings LLC ....E...... 212 741-2675
New York (G-10187)

BEVERAGES, ALCOHOLIC: Vodka

Felene Inc ....G...... 716 276-3583
Williamsville (G-16131)

Russian Standard Vodka USA Inc ....G...... 212 679-1894
New York (G-11100)

BEVERAGES, ALCOHOLIC: Wines

Adirondack Winery LLC ....G...... 518 668-9463
Lake George (G-6756)

Allied Wine Corp ....F...... 845 796-4160
South Fallsburg (G-14508)

Americana Vineyards & Winery ....F...... 607 387-6801
Interlaken (G-6283)

Anthony Road Wine Co Inc ....F...... 315 536-2182
Penn Yan (G-12577)

Anyelas Vineyards LLC ....F...... 315 685-3797
Skaneateles (G-14446)

Arrowhead Spring Vineyards LLC.........G...... 716 434-8030
Lockport (G-7060)

Atwater Estate Vineyards LLC ....E...... 607 546-8463
Burdett (G-3055)

Bad Seed Cider Co LLC ....G...... 914 474-4422
Highland (G-5957)

Billsboro Winery ....G...... 315 789-9538
Geneva (G-5147)

Brooklyn Winery LLC ....F...... 347 763-1506
Brooklyn (G-1623)

Brotherhood Americas ....E...... 845 496-3661
Washingtonville (G-15524)

Casa Larga Vineyards ....E...... 585 223-4210
Fairport (G-4492)

Casa Larga Vineyards ....E...... 585 223-4210
Fairport (G-4493)

Cascade Mountain Winery & Rest.........F...... 845 373-9021
Amenia (G-201)

Cava Spiliadis USA ....E...... 212 247-8214
New York (G-8939)

Chautauqua Wine Company Inc ....G...... 716 934-9463
Silver Creek (G-14440)

Clinton Vineyards Inc ....G...... 845 266-5372
Clinton Corners (G-3487)

Cobblestone Frm Winery Vinyrd ....F...... 315 549-1004
Romulus (G-13878)

Coyote Moon LLC ....F...... 315 686-5600
Clayton (G-3453)

Damiani Wine Cellars LLC ....G...... 607 546-5557
Burdett (G-3056)

David F De Marco ....G...... 315 536-0882
Penn Yan (G-12581)

Deer Run Enterprises Inc ....G...... 585 346-0850
Geneseo (G-5143)

Di Borghese Castello LLC ....F...... 631 734-5111
Cutchogue (G-3815)

Dorset Farms Inc ....F...... 631 734-6010
Peconic (G-12545)

Duck Walk Vinyards ....F...... 631 726-7555
Water Mill (G-15530)

Dutchess Wines LLC ....G...... 845 876-1319
Rhinebeck (G-13099)

Eagle Crest Vineyard LLC ....G...... 585 346-5760
Conesus (G-3605)

East Branch Winery Inc ....G...... 607 292-3999
Dundee (G-4045)

East End Vineyards LLC ....G...... 718 468-0500
Queens Village (G-13019)

Fly Creek Cder Mill Orchrd Inc ....G...... 607 547-9692
Fly Creek (G-4909)

Fox Run Vineyards Inc ....F...... 315 536-4616
Penn Yan (G-12584)

Freedom Run Winery Inc ....G...... 716 433-4136
Lockport (G-7076)

Greenwood Winery LLC ....E...... 315 432-8132
East Syracuse (G-4213)

Hazlitts 1852 Vineyards Inc ....E...... 607 546-9463
Hector (G-5825)

Heart & Hands Wine Company Inc ....G...... 315 889-8500
Union Springs (G-15222)

Hermann J Wiemer Vineyard ....G...... 607 243-7971
Dundee (G-4047)

Heron Hill Vineyards Inc ....E...... 607 868-4241
Hammondsport (G-5530)

Hickory Road Land Co LLC ....G...... 607 243-9114
Dundee (G-4048)

Hoffman & Hoffman ....G...... 315 536-4773
Penn Yan (G-12586)

Hosmer Inc ....F...... 888 467-9463
Ovid (G-12424)

Hunt Country Vineyards ....G...... 315 595-2812
Branchport (G-1111)

J Petrocelli Wine Cellars LLC ....E...... 631 765-1100
Peconic (G-12546)

J R Dill Winery LLC ....G...... 607 546-5757
Burdett (G-3058)

Joseph Zakon Winery Ltd ....G...... 718 604-1430
Brooklyn (G-2003)

Konstantin D FRAnk& Sons Vini ....E...... 607 868-4884
Hammondsport (G-5532)

L & D Acquisition LLC ....F...... 585 531-9000
Naples (G-8207)

Lafayette Chateau ....E...... 607 546-2062
Hector (G-5826)

Lakewood Vineyards Inc ....F...... 607 535-9252
Watkins Glen (G-15614)

Lamoreaux Landing WI ....D...... 607 582-6162
Lodi (G-7131)

Leonard Oakes Estate Winery ....G...... 585 318-4418
Medina (G-7739)

Lieb Cellars LLC ....E...... 631 298-1942
Mattituck (G-7677)

Lucas Vineyards Inc ....F...... 607 532-4825
Interlaken (G-6285)

Malina Management Company Inc ....E...... 607 535-9614
Montour Falls (G-8075)

Mazza Chautauqua Cellars LLC ....F...... 716 793-9463
Westfield (G-15946)

Merritt Estate Winery Inc ....F...... 716 965-4800
Forestville (G-4931)

Millbrook Winery Inc ....F...... 845 677-8383
Millbrook (G-7944)

Montezuma Winery LLC ....G...... 315 568-8190
Seneca Falls (G-14369)

Negys New Land Vinyrd Winery ....G...... 315 585-4432
Geneva (G-5160)

North House Vineyards Inc ....G...... 631 779-2817
Jamesport (G-6490)

Olde Chtqua Vneyards Ltd Lblty ....F...... 716 792-2749
Portland (G-12933)

Paumanok Vineyards Ltd ....E...... 631 722-8800
Aquebogue (G-366)

Pellegrini Vineyards LLC ....G...... 631 734-4111
Cutchogue (G-3816)

Pindar Vineyards LLC ....E...... 631 734-6200
Peconic (G-12547)

Prejean Winery Inc ....F...... 315 536-7524
Penn Yan (G-12590)

Premium Wine Group LLC ....E...... 631 298-1900
Mattituck (G-7678)

Pugliese Vineyards Inc ....G...... 631 734-4057
Cutchogue (G-3817)

Railex Wine Services LLC ....E...... 631 369-7000
Riverhead (G-13186)

Red Newt Cellars Inc ....F...... 607 546-4100
Hector (G-5827)

Red Tail Ridge Inc ....F...... 315 536-4580
Penn Yan (G-12591)

Rock Stream Vineyards ....G...... 607 243-8322
Rock Stream (G-13819)

Royal Wine Corporation ....F...... 845 236-4000
Marlboro (G-7582)

Schulze Vineyards & Winery LLC............F...... 716 778-8090
Burt (G-3061)

Sheldrake Point Vineyard LLC ....F...... 607 532-8967
Ovid (G-12426)

Shinn Winery LLC ....G...... 631 804-0367
Mattituck (G-7679)

Sokolin LLC ....G...... 631 537-4434
Yaphank (G-16272)

Spanish Artisan Wine Group LLC ....G...... 914 414-6982
Patterson (G-12520)

Standing Stone Vineyards ....G...... 607 582-6051
Hector (G-5828)

Swedish Hill Vineyard Inc ....D...... 607 403-0029
Romulus (G-13881)

Thirsty Owl Wine Company Inc ....G...... 607 869-5805
Ovid (G-12427)

Thousand Islands Winery LLC ....E...... 315 482-9306
Alexandria Bay (G-181)

Tickle Hill Winery ....G...... 607 546-7740
Hector (G-5829)

Tug Hill Vineyards ....G...... 315 376-4336
Lowville (G-7422)

Ventosa Vineyards LLC ....G...... 315 719-0000
Geneva (G-5166)

Wagner Vineyards LLC ....G...... 607 582-6976
Lodi (G-7132)

Wagner Vineyards & Brewing Co ....E...... 607 582-6574
Lodi (G-7133)

Westchester Wine Warehouse LLC.......F...... 914 824-1400
White Plains (G-16074)

Wine Group Inc ....D...... 716 326-3151
Westfield (G-15953)

Wolffer Estate Vineyard Inc ....E...... 631 537-5106
Sagaponack (G-14103)

Woodbury Vineyards Inc ....G...... 716 679-9463
Fredonia (G-4973)

BEVERAGES, MALT

Crazy Cowboy Brewing Co LLC ....E...... 516 812-0576
Woodbury (G-16169)

High Falls Operating Co LLC ....A...... 585 546-1030
Rochester (G-13467)

BEVERAGES, MILK BASED

Oatly Inc ....E...... 646 625-4633
New York (G-10673)

BEVERAGES, NONALCOHOLIC: Bottled & canned soft drinks

3v Company Inc ....E...... 718 858-7333
Brooklyn (G-1417)

American Bottling Company ....F...... 516 714-0002
Ronkonkoma (G-13902)

Beverage Works Nj Inc ....E...... 631 293-3501
Farmingdale (G-4593)

Beverage Works Ny Inc ....E...... 718 812-2034
Brooklyn (G-1582)

Big Geyser Inc ....C...... 718 821-2200
Maspeth (G-7596)

Borabora Fruit Juices Inc ....G...... 914 438-8744
Highland (G-5958)

Bottling Group LLC ....F...... 914 253-2000
White Plains (G-15983)

Brands Within Reach LLC ....E...... 847 720-9090
Mamaroneck (G-7499)

Canada Dry Bottling Co NY LP ....D...... 718 358-2000
College Point (G-3538)

Canada Dry Bottling Co NY LP ....D...... 718 786-8550
Maspeth (G-7598)

Canada Dry Bottling Co NY LP ....E...... 631 694-7575
Melville (G-7764)

Central Coca-Cola Btlg Co Inc ....B...... 914 789-1100
Elmsford (G-4399)

Cliffstar LLC ....A...... 716 366-6100
Dunkirk (G-4052)

Coca-Cola Bottling Company ....E...... 518 483-0422
Malone (G-7484)

Coca-Cola Btlg Co Buffalo Inc ....C...... 716 874-4610
Tonawanda (G-15098)

Coca-Cola Btlg Co of NY Inc ....F...... 845 562-3037
New Windsor (G-8364)

Coca-Cola Btlg Co of NY Inc ....F...... 914 789-1572
Elmsford (G-4400)

Coca-Cola Btlg Co of NY Inc ....F...... 518 459-2010
Albany (G-66)

Coca-Cola Btlg Co of NY Inc ....F...... 718 416-7575
Maspeth (G-7599)

Coca-Cola Btlg Co of NY Inc ....F...... 315 457-9221
Syracuse (G-14856)

Coca-Cola Btlg Co of NY Inc ....E...... 631 434-3535
Hauppauge (G-5620)

Coca-Cola Btlg Co of NY Inc ....E...... 718 420-6800
Staten Island (G-14639)

Coca-Cola Btlg Co of NY Inc ....F...... 914 789-1580
Elmsford (G-4401)

Coca-Cola Refreshments USA Inc ....E...... 718 401-5200
Bronx (G-1227)

Coca-Cola Refreshments USA Inc ....E...... 315 785-8907
Watertown (G-15566)

Coca-Cola Refreshments USA Inc ....G...... 914 592-0806
Hawthorne (G-5811)

BEVERAGES, NONALCOHOLIC: Bottled & canned soft drinks

Doheny Nice and Easy .... G 518 793-1733
  Glens Falls (G-5247)
Fancy Flamingo LLC .... G 516 209-7306
  New York (G-9468)
Gangi Distributors Inc .... F 718 442-5745
  Staten Island (G-14654)
Grayhawk Leasing LLC .... G 914 767-6000
  Somers (G-14498)
N Y Winstons Inc .... G 212 665-3166
  New York (G-10529)
Owens Table Mixers LLC .... G 650 303-7342
  New York (G-10722)
Pepsi-Cola Operating Company ..... E 914 767-6000
  White Plains (G-16048)
Pepsi Inc .... A 914 253-2000
  Purchase (G-13010)
Pepsico Capital Resources Inc ...... G 914 253-2000
  Purchase (G-13013)
Rochester Coca Cola Bottling .... E 607 739-5678
  Horseheads (G-6135)
Rochester Coca Cola Bottling .... D 585 546-3900
  Rochester (G-13685)
Shopping Center Wine & Liquor ..... G 914 528-1600
  Mohegan Lake (G-8011)
Snapp Too Enterprise .... G 718 224-5252
  Flushing (G-4893)
Unilever United States Inc .... F 212 546-0200
  New York (G-11588)
Unilever United States Inc .... C 212 546-0200
  New York (G-11589)

BEVERAGES, NONALCOHOLIC: Carbonated

Beverages Foods & Service Inds ... D 914 253-2000
  Purchase (G-13002)
Bottling Group LLC .... E 315 788-6751
  Watertown (G-15561)
Bottling Group LLC .... B 800 789-2626
  White Plains (G-15982)
Pepsi Beverages Co .... G 518 782-2150
  Latham (G-6871)
Pepsi Bottling Ventures LLC .... E 631 226-9000
  Amityville (G-303)
Pepsi Btlg Group Globl Fin LLC ...... G 914 767-6000
  Somers (G-14499)
Pepsi-Cola Bottling Co NY Inc .... F 914 699-2600
  Mount Vernon (G-8169)
Pepsi-Cola Bottling Co NY Inc .... A 718 392-1000
  College Point (G-3559)
Pepsi-Cola Bottling Group .... G 914 767-6000
  White Plains (G-16046)
Pepsi-Cola Metro Btlg Co Inc .... G 914 767-6000
  White Plains (G-16047)
Pepsi-Cola Metro Btlg Co Inc .... G 914 253-2000
  Purchase (G-13008)
Pepsi-Cola Metro Btlg Co Inc .... D 607 795-2122
  Horseheads (G-6131)
Pepsi-Cola Metro Btlg Co Inc .... C 585 454-5220
  Rochester (G-13614)
Pepsi-Cola Metro Btlg Co Inc .... B 518 834-7811
  Keeseville (G-6645)
Pepsi-Cola Newburgh Btlg Inc .... C 845 562-5400
  Newburgh (G-11882)
Pepsi-Cola Sales and Dist Inc .... G 914 253-2000
  Purchase (G-13009)
Pepsico .... F 419 252-0247
  Hawthorne (G-5821)
Pepsico .... E 914 801-1500
  Valhalla (G-15305)
Pepsico Inc .... G 914 253-2000
  New York (G-10798)
Pepsico Inc .... B 914 253-2000
  White Plains (G-16049)
Pepsico Inc .... B 914 742-4500
  Valhalla (G-15306)
Pepsico Inc .... A 914 253-2000
  Purchase (G-13011)
Pepsico Inc .... E 914 253-3474
  White Plains (G-16050)
Pepsico Inc .... F 914 253-2713
  Purchase (G-13012)
Pepsico Design & Innovation .... G 917 405-9307
  New York (G-10799)
Pepsico Sales Inc .... G 914 253-2000
  Purchase (G-13014)

BEVERAGES, NONALCOHOLIC: Carbonated, Canned & Bottled, Etc

Beverage Works Incorporated .... G 718 834-0500
  Brooklyn (G-1581)

Blue Star Beverages Corp .... G 718 381-3535
  Brooklyn (G-1596)
Chateau Imports Ltd .... G 516 841-6343
  Port Washington (G-12867)
Chohehco LLC .... G 315 420-4624
  Skaneateles (G-14448)
Fevertree USA Inc .... F 718 852-5577
  New York (G-9486)
Green Zone Food Service Inc .... G 917 709-1728
  Corona (G-3739)
Hmo Beverage Corporation .... G 917 371-6100
  Brooklyn (G-1936)
Hydrive Energy .... G 914 925-9100
  Rye (G-14081)
Juices Enterprises Inc .... G 718 953-1860
  Brooklyn (G-2010)
Liquid Management Partners LLC ... F 516 775-5050
  New Hyde Park (G-8280)
Nexbev Industries LLC .... F 646 648-1255
  Blauvelt (G-931)
Save More Beverage Corp .... G 518 371-2520
  Halfmoon (G-5499)
Switch Beverage Company LLC ...... F 203 202-7383
  Port Washington (G-12928)
Treo Brands LLC .... F 914 341-1850
  Harrison (G-5562)

BEVERAGES, NONALCOHOLIC: Cider

Lakeside Cider Mill Farm Inc .... G 518 399-8359
  Ballston Lake (G-560)
Mullers Cider House LLC .... G 585 287-5875
  Rochester (G-13562)
Nine Pin Ciderworks LLC .... F 518 449-9999
  Albany (G-106)
Schutt Cider Mill .... F 585 872-2924
  Webster (G-15652)

BEVERAGES, NONALCOHOLIC: Flavoring extracts & syrups, nec

Bi Nutraceuticals Inc .... G 631 533-4934
  Islandia (G-6325)
Citrus and Allied Essences Ltd ...... E 516 354-1200
  Floral Park (G-4812)
Comax Manufacturing Corp .... D 631 249-0505
  Melville (G-7769)
Danisco US Inc .... D 585 277-4300
  Rochester (G-13338)
Delbia Do Company Inc .... G 718 585-2226
  Bronx (G-1238)
Delbia Do Company Inc .... F 718 585-2226
  Bronx (G-1239)
DSM Nutritional Products LLC .... C 518 372-5155
  Schenectady (G-14261)
DSM Nutritional Products LLC .... C 518 372-5155
  Glenville (G-5271)
Interntnal Flvors Frgrnces Inc .... C 212 765-5500
  New York (G-9924)
Keurig Dr Pepper Inc .... C 315 589-4911
  Williamson (G-16110)
Natural Organics Labs Inc .... B 631 957-5600
  Melville (G-7807)
Pepsi Inc .... A 914 253-2000
  Purchase (G-13010)
Star Kay White Inc .... D 845 268-2600
  Congers (G-3618)
Synergy Flavors NY Company LLC ... G 585 232-6647
  Rochester (G-13753)
Torre Products Co Inc .... G 212 925-8989
  Mount Vernon (G-8184)

BEVERAGES, NONALCOHOLIC: Fruit Drnks, Under 100% Juice, Can

A Health Obsession LLC .... E 347 850-4587
  Brooklyn (G-1435)
Ba Sports Nutrition LLC .... C 718 357-7402
  Whitestone (G-16089)
Cheribundi Inc .... E 800 699-0460
  Geneva (G-5150)
Farmtobottle LLC .... G 631 944-8422
  Locust Valley (G-7122)
Purely Maple LLC .... F 203 997-9309
  New York (G-10930)

BEVERAGES, NONALCOHOLIC: Lemonade, Bottled & Canned, Etc

Dirty Lemon Beverages LLC .... G 877 897-7784
  New York (G-9233)

BEVERAGES, NONALCOHOLIC: Soft Drinks, Canned & Bottled, Etc

Boylan Bottling Co Inc .... E 800 289-7978
  New York (G-8842)
Clintons Ditch Coop Co Inc .... C 315 699-2695
  Cicero (G-3417)
Cornell Beverages Inc .... F 718 381-3000
  Brooklyn (G-1688)
Energy Brands Inc .... E 212 545-6000
  New York (G-9374)
Good-O-Beverage Inc .... F 718 328-6400
  Bronx (G-1268)
Johnnie Ryan Co Inc .... F 716 282-1606
  Niagara Falls (G-11943)
Keurig Dr Pepper Inc .... C 315 589-4911
  Williamson (G-16110)
Keurig Dr Pepper Inc .... D 914 846-2300
  Elmsford (G-4414)
Keurig Dr Pepper Inc .... G 718 246-6200
  Brooklyn (G-2025)
La Cola 1 Inc .... G 917 509-6669
  New York (G-10155)
Life Earth Company .... G 310 751-0627
  New York (G-10211)
Load/N/Go Beverage Corp .... F 585 218-4019
  Rochester (G-13521)
Manhattan Special Bottling .... F 718 388-4144
  Brooklyn (G-2109)
Monfefo LLC .... G 347 779-2600
  Brooklyn (G-2169)
New York Bottling Co Inc .... F 718 963-3232
  Bronx (G-1323)
Pepsi-Cola Bottling Co NY Inc .... G 718 892-1570
  Bronx (G-1335)
Royal Crown Financial .... G 718 234-7237
  Brooklyn (G-2359)
Scotia Beverages Inc .... A 518 370-3621
  Schenectady (G-14303)
Snapple Beverage Corp .... D 914 612-4000
  Rye Brook (G-14094)
Stewarts Processing Corp .... D 518 581-1200
  Ballston Spa (G-588)

BEVERAGES, NONALCOHOLIC: Tea, Iced, Bottled & Canned, Etc

East Coast Cultures LLC .... F 917 261-3010
  Kingston (G-6690)

BEVERAGES, WINE & DISTILLED ALCOHOLIC, WHOLESALE: Liquor

Cruzin Management Inc .... E 212 641-8700
  New York (G-9126)

BEVERAGES, WINE & DISTILLED ALCOHOLIC, WHOLESALE: Neutral Sp

Spanish Artisan Wine Group LLC ... G 914 414-6982
  Patterson (G-12520)

BEVERAGES, WINE & DISTILLED ALCOHOLIC, WHOLESALE: Wine

Coyote Moon LLC .... F 315 686-5600
  Clayton (G-3453)
Royal Wine Corporation .... F 845 236-4000
  Marlboro (G-7582)

BEVERAGES, WINE WHOLESALE : Wine Coolers

Hoptron Brewtique .... G 631 438-0296
  Patchogue (G-12502)

BICYCLE SHOPS

Bignay Inc .... G 786 346-1673
  New York (G-8789)
Worksman Trading Corp .... G 718 322-2000
  Ozone Park (G-12469)

BICYCLES, PARTS & ACCESS

Bignay Inc .... G 786 346-1673
  New York (G-8789)
Bike Shopcom LLC .... G 716 236-7500
  Niagara Falls (G-11908)
Evelo Inc .... G 917 251-8743
  Rockaway Park (G-13824)

Great American Bicycle LLC ....E 518 584-8100
Saratoga Springs *(G-14179)*

KG Motors Inc ....E 607 562-2877
Big Flats *(G-847)*

Prestacycle Llc ....G 518 588-5546
Rexford *(G-13097)*

Social Bicycles LLC ....E 917 746-7624
Brooklyn *(G-2432)*

BILLETS: Steel

Homogeneous Metals Inc....................D 315 839-5421
Clayville *(G-3457)*

BILLFOLD INSERTS: Plastic

Quality Lineals Usa Inc.......................D 516 378-6577
Merrick *(G-7864)*

BILLIARD & POOL TABLES & SPLYS

A Hyatt Ball Co Ltd ....G 518 747-0272
Fort Edward *(G-4936)*

International Leisure Pdts Inc................E 631 254-2155
Edgewood *(G-4272)*

BINDING SVC: Books & Manuals

514 Adams Corporation ....G 516 352-6948
Deer Park *(G-3825)*

A-Quick Bindery LLC ....G 631 491-1110
West Babylon *(G-15679)*

Agrecolor Inc ....F 516 741-8700
Mineola *(G-7957)*

Argo Lithographers Inc ....E 718 729-2700
Long Island City *(G-7166)*

Arista Innovations Inc ....E 516 746-2262
Mineola *(G-7959)*

Baum Christine and John Corp ....G 585 621-8910
Rochester *(G-13261)*

Beastons Budget Printing Inc..............G 585 244-2721
Rochester *(G-13264)*

Benchemark Printing Inc....................D 518 393-1361
Schenectady *(G-14249)*

Bernard Hall ....G 585 425-3340
Fairport *(G-4489)*

Beyer Graphics Inc ....D 631 543-3900
Commack *(G-3579)*

Bg Bindery Inc ....G 631 767-4242
Maspeth *(G-7595)*

Boncraft Inc ....D 716 662-9720
Tonawanda *(G-15091)*

Bondy Printing Corp ....G 631 242-1510
Bay Shore *(G-659)*

Brodock Press Inc ....D 315 735-9577
Utica *(G-15242)*

Brooks Litho Digital Group Inc.............G 631 789-4500
Deer Park *(G-3850)*

Carlara Group Ltd ....G 914 769-2020
Pleasantville *(G-12795)*

Carnels Printing Inc..........................G 516 883-3355
Great Neck *(G-5374)*

Castlereagh Printcraft Inc ....D 516 623-1728
Freeport *(G-4989)*

Chakra Communications Inc ....E 607 748-7491
Endicott *(G-4446)*

Challenge Graphics Svcs Inc...............E 631 586-0171
Deer Park *(G-3851)*

Classic Album ....E 718 388-2818
Brooklyn *(G-1670)*

Cohber Press Inc ....D 585 475-9100
West Henrietta *(G-15789)*

Copy Corner Inc ....G 718 388-4545
Brooklyn *(G-1687)*

Cosmos Communications Inc ....C 718 482-1800
Long Island City *(G-7193)*

D G M Graphics Inc..........................F 516 223-2220
Merrick *(G-7854)*

David Helsing..................................G 607 796-2681
Horseheads *(G-6120)*

Dependable Lithographers Inc ....F 718 472-4200
Long Island City *(G-7199)*

Dispatch Graphics Inc ....F 212 307-5943
New York *(G-9236)*

Division Den-Bar Enterprises ....G 914 381-2220
Mamaroneck *(G-7508)*

Dowd - Witbeck Printing Corp ....F 518 274-2421
Troy *(G-15166)*

DP Murphy Co Inc............................D 631 673-9400
Deer Park *(G-3865)*

E B B Graphics Inc...........................F 516 750-5510
Westbury *(G-15877)*

Eastwood Litho Impressions LLC ....F 315 437-2626
Syracuse *(G-14881)*

Erhard & Gilcher Inc ....E 315 474-1072
Syracuse *(G-14889)*

Flare Multicopy Corp ....E 718 258-8860
Brooklyn *(G-1849)*

Flp Group LLC ....F 315 252-7583
Auburn *(G-476)*

Foleys Graphic Center Inc ....E 914 245-3625
Yorktown Heights *(G-16364)*

Fulton Newspapers Inc.......................E 315 598-6397
Fulton *(G-5059)*

Gateway Prtg & Graphics Inc...............E 716 823-3873
Hamburg *(G-5509)*

Gazette Press Inc ....E 914 963-8300
Rye *(G-14077)*

Graphicomm Inc ....G 716 283-0830
Niagara Falls *(G-11932)*

Haig Press Inc ....E 631 582-5800
Hauppauge *(G-5665)*

Hudson Printing Co Inc ....E 718 937-8600
New York *(G-9834)*

In-House Inc ....F 718 445-9007
College Point *(G-3544)*

Jack J Florio Jr................................G 716 434-9123
Lockport *(G-7085)*

James Conolly Printing Co ....E 585 426-4150
Rochester *(G-13488)*

Jane Lewis ....G 607 722-0584
Binghamton *(G-890)*

Johnnys Ideal Printing Co...................E 518 828-6666
Hudson *(G-6166)*

Jon Lyn Ink Inc ....G 516 546-2312
Merrick *(G-7857)*

Kaufman Brothers Printing ....G 212 563-1854
New York *(G-10079)*

Louis Heindl & Son Inc ....G 585 454-5080
Rochester *(G-13523)*

Loy L Press Inc ....G 716 634-5966
Buffalo *(G-2853)*

Melcher Media Inc ....F 212 727-2322
New York *(G-10428)*

Mercury Print Productions Inc..............C 585 458-7900
Rochester *(G-13542)*

Midgley Printing Corp ....G 315 475-1864
Syracuse *(G-14942)*

Moneast Inc ....G 845 298-8898
Wappingers Falls *(G-15498)*

Multiple Imprssons of Rchester ....G 585 546-1160
Rochester *(G-13563)*

Newport Graphics Inc........................E 212 924-2600
New York *(G-10610)*

Prestige Envelope & Lithograph ....F 631 521-7043
Merrick *(G-7863)*

Printing Resources Inc.......................E 518 482-2470
Albany *(G-119)*

Pro Printing ....G 516 561-9700
Lynbrook *(G-7435)*

Progressive Graphics & Prtg ....G 315 331-3635
Newark *(G-11850)*

Prompt Bindery Co Inc ....F 212 675-5181
New York *(G-10910)*

Psychonomic Society Inc....................E 512 381-1494
New York *(G-10919)*

Quad/Graphics Inc ....A 518 581-4000
Saratoga Springs *(G-14189)*

Reynolds Book Bindery LLC ....F 607 772-8937
Binghamton *(G-906)*

Richard Ruffner ....F 631 234-4600
Central Islip *(G-3287)*

Rmd Holding Inc ....G 845 628-0030
Mahopac *(G-7478)*

Roger Michael Press Inc ....D 732 752-0800
Brooklyn *(G-2352)*

Rosemont Press Incorporated.............E 212 239-4770
New York *(G-11082)*

Rosen Mandell & Immerman Inc...........E 212 691-2277
New York *(G-11083)*

S L C Industries Incorporated.............F 607 775-2299
Binghamton *(G-907)*

Sentine Printing Inc ....G 516 334-7400
Westbury *(G-15925)*

Shipman Printing Inds Inc...................E 716 504-7700
Niagara Falls *(G-11980)*

Spectrum Prtg Lithography Inc ....E 212 255-3131
New York *(G-11316)*

Thomas Group Inc ....F 212 947-6400
New York *(G-11467)*

Tobay Printing Co Inc ....E 631 842-3300
Copiague *(G-3684)*

Tom & Jerry Printcraft Forms ....E 914 777-7468
Mamaroneck *(G-7525)*

Vicks Lithograph & Prtg Corp ....E 315 272-2401
Yorkville *(G-16380)*

Vin-Clair Inc ....E 845 429-4998
West Haverstraw *(G-15764)*

Webster Printing Corporation ....F 585 671-1533
Webster *(G-15662)*

Westchester Mailing Service ....E 914 948-1116
White Plains *(G-16073)*

William Charles Prtg Co Inc ....E 516 349-0900
Plainview *(G-12728)*

Wilson Press LLC ....E 315 568-9693
Seneca Falls *(G-14374)*

Won & Lee Inc ....E 516 222-0712
Garden City *(G-5119)*

Wynco Press One Inc ....G 516 354-6145
Glen Oaks *(G-5215)*

X Myles Mar Inc ....E 212 683-2015
New York *(G-11795)*

Zenger Partners LLC ....E 716 876-2284
Kenmore *(G-6656)*

BINDING SVC: Magazines

Copy Room Inc.................................F 212 371-8600
New York *(G-9099)*

BINDING SVC: Trade

Dime Trading Inc ....G 718 797-0303
Brooklyn *(G-1747)*

Gold Pride Press Inc ....E 585 224-8800
Rochester *(G-13448)*

Piroke Trade Inc ....G 646 515-1537
Brooklyn *(G-2263)*

Quality Bindery Service Inc ....E 716 883-5185
Buffalo *(G-2942)*

Whitford Development Inc ....F 631 471-7711
Port Jefferson *(G-12844)*

BINS: Prefabricated, Sheet Metal

Golden Group International Ltd.............G 845 440-1025
Patterson *(G-12517)*

H & M Leasing Corp..........................G 631 225-5246
Copiague *(G-3656)*

BIOLOGICAL PRDTS: Bacterial Vaccines

Ip Med Inc ....G 516 766-3800
Oceanside *(G-12176)*

BIOLOGICAL PRDTS: Blood Derivatives

Instrumentation Laboratory Co ....C 845 680-0028
Orangeburg *(G-12321)*

BIOLOGICAL PRDTS: Exc Diagnostic

Acorda Therapeutics Inc ....C 914 347-4300
Ardsley *(G-383)*

Advance Biofactures Corp ....E 516 593-7000
Lynbrook *(G-7423)*

Albany Molecular Research Inc.............G 518 512-2234
Albany *(G-33)*

Albany Molecular Research Inc.............B 518 512-2000
Albany *(G-34)*

Biomup Usa Inc ....G 800 436-6266
New York *(G-8799)*

Cypress Bioscience Inc......................F 858 452-2323
New York *(G-9143)*

Ecological Laboratories Inc ....D 516 823-3441
Island Park *(G-6316)*

Invitrogen Corp ....G 716 774-6700
Grand Island *(G-5333)*

Kadmon Holdings Inc ....D 212 308-6000
New York *(G-10056)*

Meiragtx Holdings PLC ....E 646 490-2965
New York *(G-10424)*

Nanoprobes Inc ....F 631 205-9490
Yaphank *(G-16267)*

Omrix Biopharmaceuticals Inc ....C 908 218-0707
New York *(G-10687)*

Prevail Therapeutics Inc.....................E 917 336-9310
New York *(G-10886)*

Renmatix Inc ....G 315 356-4780
Rome *(G-13867)*

Rentschler Biotechnologie GMBH ....G 631 656-7137
Hauppauge *(G-5754)*

Roar Biomedical Inc ....E 631 591-2749
Calverton *(G-3085)*

Synergy Pharmaceuticals Inc ....G...... 212 227-8611
New York *(G-11413)*

Vyera Pharmaceuticals LLC ....E...... 646 356-5577
New York *(G-11711)*

Wyeth Holdings LLC ....D...... 845 602-5000
Pearl River *(G-12543)*

Wyeth LLC ....A...... 212 733-2323
New York *(G-11793)*

BIOLOGICAL PRDTS: Extracts

Akshar Extracts Inc ....G...... 631 588-9727
Ronkonkoma *(G-13895)*

BIOLOGICAL PRDTS: Vaccines

AV Therapeutics Inc ....E...... 917 497-5523
New York *(G-8684)*

International Aids Vaccine Ini ....D...... 646 381-8066
Brooklyn *(G-1964)*

International Aids Vccne Inttv ....D...... 212 847-1111
New York *(G-9917)*

BIOLOGICAL PRDTS: Vaccines & Immunizing

Siga Technologies Inc ....E...... 212 672-9100
New York *(G-11230)*

BIOLOGICAL PRDTS: Veterinary

Bioivt LLC ....D...... 516 483-1196
Westbury *(G-15872)*

BLADES: Knife

Ontario Knife Company ....D...... 716 676-5527
Franklinville *(G-4967)*

BLADES: Saw, Chain Type

Quality Saw & Knife Inc ....F...... 631 491-4747
West Babylon *(G-15739)*

BLADES: Saw, Hand Or Power

Niabraze LLC ....F...... 716 447-1082
Tonawanda *(G-15126)*

BLANKBOOKS

Dalee Bookbinding Co Inc ....F...... 914 965-1660
Croton On Hudson *(G-3807)*

BLANKBOOKS & LOOSELEAF BINDERS

Classic Album ....E...... 718 388-2818
Brooklyn *(G-1670)*

Colad Group LLC ....D...... 716 961-1776
Buffalo *(G-2703)*

Folder Factory Inc ....F...... 540 477-3852
Melville *(G-7783)*

Foster - Gordon Manufacturing ....G...... 631 589-6776
Bohemia *(G-1013)*

GPM Associates LLC ....E...... 585 335-3940
Dansville *(G-3819)*

Leather Indexes Corp ....D...... 516 827-1900
Hicksville *(G-5923)*

Roger Michael Press Inc ....D...... 732 752-0800
Brooklyn *(G-2352)*

BLANKBOOKS: Albums

Albumx Corp ....D...... 914 939-6878
Port Chester *(G-12813)*

Classic Album LLC ....D...... 718 388-2818
Brooklyn *(G-1671)*

Dorose Novelty Co Inc ....F...... 718 451-3088
East Elmhurst *(G-4106)*

King Album Inc ....E...... 631 253-9500
West Babylon *(G-15723)*

Lanwood Industries Inc ....E...... 718 786-3000
Bay Shore *(G-688)*

Leather Craftsmen Inc ....D...... 631 752-9000
Farmingdale *(G-4670)*

BLANKBOOKS: Albums, Record

Brookvale Records Inc ....F...... 631 587-7722
West Babylon *(G-15695)*

Motema Music LLC ....G...... 212 860-6969
New York *(G-10508)*

Renegade Nation Ltd ....F...... 212 868-9000
New York *(G-11013)*

Simon & Simon LLC ....G...... 202 419-0490
New York *(G-11245)*

Tm Music Inc ....F...... 212 471-4000
New York *(G-11502)*

Tommy Boy Entertainment LLC ....F...... 212 388-8300
New York *(G-11511)*

Wmg Acquisition Corp ....F...... 212 275-2000
New York *(G-11771)*

BLANKBOOKS: Memorandum, Printed

General Diaries Corporation ....F...... 516 371-2244
Inwood *(G-6294)*

Quotable Cards Inc ....E...... 212 420-7552
New York *(G-10960)*

BLANKETS & BLANKETING, COTTON

In2green LLC ....G...... 914 693-5054
Hastings On Hudson *(G-5573)*

Northwest Company LLC ....C...... 516 484-6996
Roslyn *(G-14045)*

BLASTING SVC: Sand, Metal Parts

Carpenter Industries Inc ....F...... 315 463-4284
Syracuse *(G-14843)*

Tropical Driftwood Originals ....G...... 516 623-0980
Roosevelt *(G-14034)*

Witt Preparations LLC ....G...... 716 948-4002
Cheektowaga *(G-3365)*

BLINDS & SHADES: Vertical

Blindtek Designer Systems Inc ....F...... 914 347-7100
Ardsley *(G-387)*

J Gimbel Inc ....E...... 718 296-5200
West Hempstead *(G-15772)*

KPP Ltd ....G...... 516 338-5201
Jericho *(G-6585)*

Vertical Research Partners LLC ....F...... 212 257-6499
New York *(G-11667)*

BLINDS : Window

Blinds To Go (us) Inc ....E...... 718 477-9523
Staten Island *(G-14627)*

Comfortex Corporation ....C...... 518 273-3333
Watervliet *(G-15600)*

D & D Window Tech Inc ....G...... 212 308-2822
New York *(G-9145)*

Drapery Industries Inc ....F...... 585 232-2992
Rochester *(G-13356)*

Fabric Quilters Unlimited Inc ....E...... 516 333-2866
Westbury *(G-15884)*

Hunter Douglas Inc ....D...... 845 664-7000
Pearl River *(G-12533)*

Instant Verticals Inc ....F...... 631 501-0001
Farmingdale *(G-4650)*

Levolor Inc ....B...... 845 664-7000
Pearl River *(G-12537)*

Nu Ways Inc ....G...... 585 254-7510
Rochester *(G-13587)*

Tentina Window Fashions Inc ....E...... 631 957-9585
Lindenhurst *(G-6980)*

TLC Vision (usa) Corporation ....G...... 914 395-3949
Hartsdale *(G-5570)*

BLOCK & BRICK: Sand Lime

Everblock Systems LLC ....G...... 844 422-5625
New York *(G-9424)*

BLOCKS & BRICKS: Concrete

All American Concrete Corp ....G...... 718 497-3301
Brooklyn *(G-1484)*

Chenango Concrete Corp ....F...... 607 334-2545
Norwich *(G-12115)*

Dicks Concrete Co Inc ....E...... 845 374-5966
New Hampton *(G-8234)*

Dkn Ready Mix LLC ....G...... 718 218-6418
Brooklyn *(G-1751)*

Edgewood Industries Inc ....G...... 516 227-2447
Garden City *(G-5097)*

Fort Miller Service Corp ....F...... 518 695-5000
Greenwich *(G-5472)*

Grace Associates Inc ....G...... 718 767-9000
Harrison *(G-5554)*

Jenna Concrete Corporation ....E...... 718 842-5250
Bronx *(G-1286)*

Jenna Harlem River Inc ....G...... 718 842-5997
Bronx *(G-1287)*

Modern Block LLC ....G...... 315 923-7443
Clyde *(G-3493)*

Superior Block Corp ....F...... 718 421-0900
Brooklyn *(G-2473)*

Unilock New York Inc ....G...... 845 278-6700
Brewster *(G-1159)*

BLOCKS: Chimney Or Fireplace, Concrete

Ace Cntracting Consulting Corp ....G...... 631 567-4752
Bohemia *(G-964)*

Chimney Doctors Americas Corp ....G...... 631 868-3586
Bayport *(G-728)*

Great American Awning & Patio ....F...... 518 899-2300
Ballston Spa *(G-575)*

BLOCKS: Landscape Or Retaining Wall, Concrete

Creative Yard Designs Inc ....G...... 315 706-6143
Manlius *(G-7545)*

Everblock Systems LLC ....G...... 844 422-5625
New York *(G-9424)*

Northeast Mesa LLC ....G...... 845 878-9344
Carmel *(G-3188)*

Troys Landscape Supply Co Inc ....F...... 518 785-1526
Cohoes *(G-3518)*

BLOCKS: Paving, Asphalt, Not From Refineries

Kings Park Asphalt Corporation ....G...... 631 269-9774
Hauppauge *(G-5683)*

BLOCKS: Paving, Concrete

Nicolia Concrete Products Inc ....D...... 631 669-0700
Lindenhurst *(G-6965)*

Unilock Ltd ....E...... 716 822-6074
Buffalo *(G-3029)*

BLOCKS: Paving, Cut Stone

Unilock New York Inc ....G...... 845 278-6700
Brewster *(G-1159)*

BLOCKS: Radiation-Proof, Concrete

Radiation Shielding Systems ....F...... 888 631-2278
Suffern *(G-14765)*

BLOCKS: Standard, Concrete Or Cinder

Barrasso & Sons Trucking Inc ....E...... 631 581-0360
Islip Terrace *(G-6358)*

Colonie Block and Supply Co ....G...... 518 869-8411
Colonie *(G-3573)*

Cranesville Block Co Inc ....E...... 518 684-6154
Amsterdam *(G-323)*

Cranesville Block Co Inc ....G...... 315 773-2296
Felts Mills *(G-4786)*

Crest Haven Precast Inc ....G...... 518 483-4750
Burke *(G-3059)*

Duke Concrete Products Inc ....E...... 518 793-7743
Queensbury *(G-13037)*

Felicetti Concrete Products ....G...... 716 284-5740
Niagara Falls *(G-11926)*

Gone South Concrete Block Inc ....E...... 315 598-2141
Fulton *(G-5062)*

Grandview Block & Supply Co ....G...... 518 346-7981
Schenectady *(G-14274)*

Imperia Masonry Supply Corp ....E...... 914 738-0900
Pelham *(G-12566)*

Lafarge North America Inc ....E...... 518 756-5000
Ravena *(G-13069)*

Montfort Brothers Inc ....E...... 845 896-6694
Fishkill *(G-4801)*

New York Ready Mix Inc ....G...... 516 338-6969
Westbury *(G-15912)*

Palumbo Block Co Inc ....E...... 845 832-6100
Dover Plains *(G-4033)*

Phelps Cement Products Inc ....E...... 315 548-9415
Phelps *(G-12606)*

Smithtown Concrete Products ....F...... 631 265-1815
Saint James *(G-14114)*

Suffolk Cement Products Inc ....E...... 631 727-2317
Calverton *(G-3088)*

Taylor Concrete Products Inc ....E...... 315 788-2191
Watertown *(G-15589)*

BLOWERS & FANS

Air Crafters Inc ....C........ 631 471-7788
Ronkonkoma *(G-13893)*

American Filtration Tech Inc ....F 585 359-4130
West Henrietta *(G-15783)*

Applied Safety LLC ....G....... 718 608-6292
Long Island City *(G-7161)*

Buffalo Filter LLC ....D....... 716 835-7000
Lancaster *(G-6799)*

Camfil Usa Inc ....F 315 468-3849
Syracuse *(G-14841)*

Daikin Applied Americas Inc ....D....... 315 253-2771
Auburn *(G-472)*

Delphi Powertrain Systems LLC......B....... 585 359-6000
West Henrietta *(G-15792)*

Ducon Technologies Inc ....E....... 631 420-4900
Farmingdale *(G-4618)*

Ducon Technologies Inc ....B....... 631 694-1700
New York *(G-9278)*

Dundas-Jafine Inc ....E....... 716 681-9690
Alden *(G-168)*

Filtros Ltd ....E....... 585 586-8770
East Rochester *(G-4163)*

Healthway Products Company ....E....... 315 207-1410
Oswego *(G-12411)*

North American Filter Corp ....D....... 800 265-8943
Newark *(G-11848)*

Parker-Hannifin Corporation............D....... 716 685-4040
Lancaster *(G-6822)*

Standard Motor Products Inc ....B....... 718 392-0200
Long Island City *(G-7364)*

Vent-A-Kiln Corporation...................G....... 716 876-2023
Buffalo *(G-3035)*

BLOWERS & FANS

Rotron Incorporated ....B....... 845 679-2401
Woodstock *(G-16237)*

Rotron Incorporated ....E....... 845 679-2401
Woodstock *(G-16238)*

BLUEPRINTING SVCS

A Esteban & Company Inc ....E....... 212 989-7000
New York *(G-8414)*

Foleys Graphic Center Inc ....E....... 914 245-3625
Yorktown Heights *(G-16364)*

BOAT BUILDING & REPAIR

American Metalcraft Marine ....G....... 315 686-9891
Clayton *(G-3452)*

Cayuga Wooden Boatworks Inc ....E....... 315 253-7447
Ithaca *(G-6374)*

Coecles Hbr Marina & Boat Yard......F 631 749-0856
Shelter Island *(G-14385)*

Eastern Welding Inc ....G....... 631 727-0306
Riverhead *(G-13174)*

Global Marine Power Inc ....E....... 631 208-2933
Calverton *(G-3081)*

Hampton Shipyards Inc ....F 631 653-6777
East Quogue *(G-4157)*

Jag Manufacturing Inc ....E....... 518 762-9558
Johnstown *(G-6620)*

Katherine Blizniak ....G....... 716 674-8545
West Seneca *(G-15850)*

May Ship Repair Contg Corp ....E....... 718 442-9700
Staten Island *(G-14680)*

Metalcraft Marine Us Inc ....F 315 501-4015
Cape Vincent *(G-3168)*

Mokai Manufacturing Inc ....G....... 845 566-8287
Newburgh *(G-11874)*

Scarano Boat Building Inc ....E....... 518 463-3401
Albany *(G-127)*

Scarano Boatbuilding Inc ....E....... 518 463-3401
Albany *(G-128)*

Wooden Boatworks ....G....... 631 477-6507
Greenport *(G-5459)*

BOAT BUILDING & REPAIRING: Fiberglass

Fantasy Glass Compan ....G....... 845 786-5818
Stony Point *(G-14743)*

Gar Wood Custom Boats ....G....... 518 494-2966
Brant Lake *(G-1112)*

Superboats Inc ....G....... 631 226-1761
Lindenhurst *(G-6978)*

Tumblehome Boatshop ....G....... 518 623-5050
Warrensburg *(G-15506)*

BOAT BUILDING & REPAIRING: Kayaks

Ashco Management Inc ....F 212 960-8428
Brooklyn *(G-1540)*

BOAT BUILDING & REPAIRING: Motorized

Marathon Boat Group Inc ....F 607 849-3211
Marathon *(G-7559)*

BOAT BUILDING & REPAIRING: Non-Motorized

Rocking The Boat Inc ....F 718 466-5799
Bronx *(G-1353)*

BOAT BUILDING & RPRG: Fishing, Small, Lobster, Crab, Oyster

AVS Laminates Inc ....E....... 631 286-2136
Bellport *(G-794)*

Robert E Derecktor Inc ....D....... 914 698-0962
Mamaroneck *(G-7522)*

BOAT DEALERS

Global Marine Power Inc ....E....... 631 208-2933
Calverton *(G-3081)*

Marathon Boat Group Inc ....F 607 849-3211
Marathon *(G-7559)*

Marina Holding Corp ....F 718 646-9283
Brooklyn *(G-2115)*

Superboats Inc ....G....... 631 226-1761
Lindenhurst *(G-6978)*

BOAT DEALERS: Canoe & Kayak

Johnson Outdoors Inc ....C....... 607 779-2200
Binghamton *(G-891)*

BOAT LIFTS

Kleinfelder John ....G....... 716 753-3163
Mayville *(G-7683)*

T Shore Products Ltd ....G....... 315 252-9174
Auburn *(G-497)*

BOAT REPAIR SVCS

Cayuga Wooden Boatworks Inc ....E....... 315 253-7447
Ithaca *(G-6374)*

Robert E Derecktor Inc ....D....... 914 698-0962
Mamaroneck *(G-7522)*

Superboats Inc ....G....... 631 226-1761
Lindenhurst *(G-6978)*

BOAT YARD: Boat yards, storage & incidental repair

Robert E Derecktor Inc ....D....... 914 698-0962
Mamaroneck *(G-7522)*

BOATS & OTHER MARINE EQPT: Plastic

Global Marine Power Inc ....E....... 631 208-2933
Calverton *(G-3081)*

Swimways Corp ....C....... 757 460-1156
Long Island City *(G-7377)*

BODIES: Truck & Bus

Able Weldbuilt Industries Inc............F 631 643-9700
Deer Park *(G-3826)*

Bay Horse Innovations Nyinc ....G....... 607 898-3337
Groton *(G-5480)*

Blackburn Truck Bodies LLC............G....... 315 448-3236
Syracuse *(G-14831)*

Conti Auto Body Corp ....G....... 516 921-6435
Syosset *(G-14781)*

Daimler Buses North Amer Inc ....A....... 315 768-8101
Oriskany *(G-12389)*

Donver Incorporated ....F 716 945-1910
Kill Buck *(G-6669)*

Premium Bldg Components Inc ....E....... 518 885-0194
Ballston Spa *(G-585)*

BODY PARTS: Automobile, Stamped Metal

Albert Kemperle Inc ....E....... 718 629-1084
Brooklyn *(G-1476)*

Autokiniton US Holdings Inc ....G....... 212 338-5100
New York *(G-8681)*

Kustom Korner ....F 716 646-0173
Hamburg *(G-5513)*

M & W Aluminum Products Inc ....F 315 414-0005
Syracuse *(G-14937)*

Qpbc Inc ....E....... 718 685-1900
Long Island City *(G-7333)*

Racing Industries Inc ....E....... 631 905-0100
Calverton *(G-3084)*

Utica Metal Products Inc ....D....... 315 732-6163
Utica *(G-15299)*

BOILER REPAIR SHOP

A L Eastmond & Sons Inc ....D....... 718 378-3000
Bronx *(G-1186)*

Empire Industrial Systems Corp ....F 631 242-4619
Bay Shore *(G-678)*

Flushing Boiler & Welding Co ....G....... 718 463-1266
Brooklyn *(G-1855)*

Troy Boiler Works Inc ....E....... 518 274-2650
Troy *(G-15192)*

BOILERS & BOILER SHOP WORK

Supreme Boilers Inc ....G....... 718 342-2220
Brooklyn *(G-2476)*

BOILERS: Low-Pressure Heating, Steam Or Hot Water

Best Boilers Inc ....F 718 372-4210
Brooklyn *(G-1578)*

ECR International Inc ....D....... 315 797-1310
Utica *(G-15260)*

ECR International Inc ....C....... 716 366-5500
Dunkirk *(G-4056)*

Great Rock Automation Inc ....F 631 270-1508
Farmingdale *(G-4640)*

Rockmills Steel Products Corp ....F 718 366-8300
Great Neck *(G-5417)*

BOLTS: Metal

Baco Enterprises Inc ....D....... 718 589-6225
Bronx *(G-1209)*

Jem Threading Specialties Inc ....G....... 718 665-3341
Bronx *(G-1285)*

Marksmen Manufacturing Corp ....E....... 800 305-6942
Deer Park *(G-3903)*

Park-Ohio Inds Trsry Co Inc..............F 212 966-3310
Albany *(G-111)*

Simon Defense Inc ....G....... 516 217-6000
Ronkonkoma *(G-14009)*

BONDERIZING: Bonderizing, Metal Or Metal Prdts

Clad Metal Specialties Inc ....F 631 666-7750
Bay Shore *(G-663)*

BOOK STORES

Barrons Educational Series Inc.........C 631 434-3311
Hauppauge *(G-5602)*

Penguin Random House LLC ....A 212 572-6162
New York *(G-10794)*

Penguin Random House LLC ....C..... 212 366-2377
Albany *(G-114)*

Rizzoli Intl Publications Inc...............E..... 212 387-3400
New York *(G-11051)*

Romantic Times Inc ....F 718 237-1097
Brooklyn *(G-2353)*

Samuel French Inc ....E..... 212 206-8990
New York *(G-11126)*

Second Chance Press Inc ....G..... 631 725-1101
Sag Harbor *(G-14102)*

Sharedbook Inc ....E..... 646 442-8840
New York *(G-11208)*

Society For The Study ....G..... 212 822-8806
New York *(G-11283)*

Soho Press Inc ....G..... 212 260-1900
New York *(G-11286)*

Thornwillow Press Ltd........................G..... 212 980-0738
New York *(G-11476)*

William S Hein & Co Inc ....C..... 716 882-2600
Getzville *(G-5184)*

BOOK STORES: College

Patrick Kraft ....G..... 315 343-9376
Oswego *(G-12419)*

BOOKS, WHOLESALE

Anthroposophic Press Inc ....G...... 518 851-2054
Clifton Park *(G-3461)*

Columbia University Press ....E...... 212 459-0600
New York *(G-9062)*

Kensington Publishing Corp ....D...... 212 407-1500
New York *(G-10092)*

Kodansha USA Inc ....G...... 917 322-6200
New York *(G-10122)*

Living Well Innovations Inc ....G...... 646 517-3200
Hauppauge *(G-5693)*

Macmillan Publishers Inc ....A...... 646 307-5151
New York *(G-10309)*

Macmillan Publishing Group LLC ....B...... 212 674-5145
New York *(G-10310)*

Moznaim Publishing Co Inc ....G...... 718 853-0525
Brooklyn *(G-2173)*

North Country Books Inc ....G...... 315 735-4877
Utica *(G-15288)*

Rizzoli Intl Publications Inc ....E...... 212 387-3400
New York *(G-11051)*

S P Books Inc ....G...... 212 431-5011
New York *(G-11109)*

Samuel French Inc ....E...... 212 206-8990
New York *(G-11126)*

Scholium International Inc ....E...... 516 883-8032
Port Washington *(G-12923)*

Swift Fulfillment Services ....G...... 516 593-1198
Lynbrook *(G-7440)*

Te Neues Publishing Co LP ....F...... 212 627-9090
New York *(G-11441)*

W W Norton & Company Inc ....C...... 212 354-5500
New York *(G-11713)*

BOOTHS: Spray, Sheet Metal, Prefabricated

Auto Body Services LLC ....F...... 631 431-4640
Lindenhurst *(G-6941)*

BOOTS: Women's

Jag Footwear ACC & Ret Corp ....A...... 800 999-1877
New York *(G-9967)*

Lsil & Co Inc ....G...... 914 761-0998
White Plains *(G-16026)*

S & W Ladies Wear ....G...... 718 431-2800
Brooklyn *(G-2374)*

BORING MILL

Graywood Companies Inc ....A...... 585 738-8889
Rochester *(G-13450)*

RTD Manufacturing Inc ....G...... 315 337-3151
Rome *(G-13871)*

BOTTLE CAPS & RESEALERS: Plastic

Berry Global Inc ....C...... 315 986-2161
Macedon *(G-7462)*

Berry Global Inc ....C...... 315 484-0397
Solvay *(G-14494)*

BOTTLED WATER DELIVERY

Mayer Bros Apple Products Inc ....D...... 716 668-1787
West Seneca *(G-15852)*

BOTTLES: Plastic

Alphamed Bottles Inc ....E...... 631 524-5577
Central Islip *(G-3261)*

Alpla Inc ....G...... 607 250-8101
Cortland *(G-3754)*

Capitol Plastic Products Inc ....C...... 518 627-0051
Amsterdam *(G-322)*

Chapin International Inc ....C...... 585 343-3140
Batavia *(G-608)*

Chapin Manufacturing Inc ....C...... 585 343-3140
Batavia *(G-609)*

Cortland Plastics Intl LLC ....E...... 607 662-0120
Cortland *(G-3762)*

David Johnson ....F...... 315 493-4735
Carthage *(G-3197)*

Intrapac International Corp ....E...... 518 561-2030
Plattsburgh *(G-12753)*

Kybod Group LLC ....G...... 408 306-1657
New York *(G-10146)*

Monroe Cnty Chapter Nysarc Inc ....G...... 585 698-1320
Rochester *(G-13557)*

Nalge Nunc International Corp ....A...... 585 498-2661
Rochester *(G-13565)*

Pvc Container Corporation ....C...... 518 672-7721
Philmont *(G-12614)*

Samco Scientific LLC ....C...... 800 625-4327
Rochester *(G-13712)*

Schless Bottles Inc ....F...... 718 236-2790
Brooklyn *(G-2386)*

BOTTLES: Vacuum

Cant Live Without It LLC ....D...... 844 517-9355
New York *(G-8906)*

BOUTIQUE STORES

Elab Smokers Boutique ....G...... 585 865-4513
Rochester *(G-13381)*

BOWLING EQPT & SPLYS

Joe Moro ....G...... 607 272-0591
Ithaca *(G-6390)*

Mac Swed Inc ....F...... 212 684-7730
New York *(G-10304)*

BOX & CARTON MANUFACTURING EQPT

Standard Paper Box Machine Co ....E...... 718 328-3300
Bronx *(G-1370)*

BOXES & CRATES: Rectangular, Wood

J & M Packaging Inc ....F...... 631 608-3069
Hauppauge *(G-5679)*

Northeast Pallet & Cont Co Inc ....F...... 518 271-0535
Troy *(G-15176)*

R D A Container Corporation ....E...... 585 247-2323
Gates *(G-5142)*

BOXES & SHOOK: Nailed Wood

Great Lakes Specialites ....E...... 716 672-4622
Fredonia *(G-4970)*

McGraw Wood Products LLC ....E...... 607 836-6465
Mc Graw *(G-7689)*

McIntosh Box & Pallet Co Inc ....D...... 315 675-8511
Bernhards Bay *(G-826)*

McIntosh Box & Pallet Co Inc ....E...... 315 446-9350
Rome *(G-13855)*

McNeilly Wood Products Inc ....E...... 845 457-9651
Campbell Hall *(G-3118)*

Philpac Corporation ....E...... 716 875-8005
Buffalo *(G-2917)*

Reuter Pallet Pkg Sys Inc ....G...... 845 457-9937
Montgomery *(G-8066)*

BOXES: Corrugated

Action Paper Co Inc ....G...... 718 665-1652
Bronx *(G-1196)*

Arma Container Corp ....E...... 631 254-1200
Deer Park *(G-3841)*

Buckeye Corrugated Inc ....D...... 585 924-1600
Victor *(G-15396)*

Cattaraugus Containers Inc ....E...... 716 676-2000
Franklinville *(G-4966)*

Fennell Industries LLC ....E...... 607 733-6693
Elmira *(G-4352)*

General Fibre Products Corp ....D...... 516 358-7500
New Hyde Park *(G-8270)*

International Paper Company ....C...... 585 663-1000
Rochester *(G-13482)*

International Paper Company ....C...... 607 775-1550
Conklin *(G-3625)*

International Paper Company ....D...... 518 372-6461
Glenville *(G-5272)*

J & M Packaging Inc ....F...... 631 608-3069
Hauppauge *(G-5679)*

Jamestown Cont of Rochester ....D...... 585 254-9190
Rochester *(G-13489)*

Jamestown Container Corp ....E...... 716 665-4623
Falconer *(G-4547)*

Lakeside Container Corp ....F...... 518 561-6150
Plattsburgh *(G-12757)*

Mkt329 Inc ....E...... 631 249-5500
Farmingdale *(G-4688)*

Niagara Sheets LLC ....D...... 716 692-1129
North Tonawanda *(G-12079)*

Norampac New York City Inc ....E...... 718 340-2100
Maspeth *(G-7630)*

Packaging Corporation America ....C...... 315 457-6780
Liverpool *(G-7029)*

Pactiv LLC ....C...... 315 457-6780
Liverpool *(G-7030)*

Paperworks Industries Inc ....C...... 315 638-4355
Baldwinsville *(G-552)*

Philpac Corporation ....E...... 716 875-8005
Buffalo *(G-2917)*

President Cont Group II LLC ....E...... 845 516-1600
Middletown *(G-7927)*

Prestige Box Corporation ....E...... 516 773-3115
Great Neck *(G-5415)*

Professional Packg Svcs Inc ....E...... 518 677-5100
Eagle Bridge *(G-4073)*

R D A Container Corporation ....E...... 585 247-2323
Gates *(G-5142)*

Seneca FLS Spc & Logistics Co ....D...... 315 568-4139
Seneca Falls *(G-14372)*

Syracuse Corrugated Box Corp ....F...... 315 437-9901
East Syracuse *(G-4241)*

Technical Packaging Inc ....F...... 516 223-2300
Baldwin *(G-537)*

Tin Inc ....F...... 607 775-1550
Conklin *(G-3629)*

Westrock - Southern Cont LLC ....C...... 315 487-6111
Camillus *(G-3113)*

Westrock Container LLC ....E...... 518 842-2450
Amsterdam *(G-353)*

Westrock Cp LLC ....C...... 716 694-1000
North Tonawanda *(G-12098)*

Westrock Cp LLC ....C...... 770 448-2193
New Hartford *(G-8248)*

Westrock Rkt LLC ....C...... 631 586-6000
Deer Park *(G-3953)*

Westrock Rkt LLC ....C...... 770 448-2193
Camillus *(G-3115)*

BOXES: Filing, Paperboard Made From Purchased Materials

Paul T Freund Corporation ....D...... 315 597-4873
Palmyra *(G-12493)*

BOXES: Mail Or Post Office, Collection/Storage, Sheet Metal

Maloya Laser Inc ....E...... 631 543-2327
Commack *(G-3595)*

BOXES: Packing & Shipping, Metal

Alpine Paper Box Co Inc ....E...... 718 345-4040
Brooklyn *(G-1492)*

BOXES: Paperboard, Folding

Abbot & Abbot Box Corp ....F...... 888 930-5972
Long Island City *(G-7143)*

Alpha Packaging Industries Inc ....E...... 718 267-4115
Long Island City *(G-7152)*

Arkay Packaging Corporation ....E...... 631 273-2000
Hauppauge *(G-5593)*

Burt Rigid Box Inc ....D...... 607 433-2510
Oneonta *(G-12261)*

Cattaraugus Containers Inc ....E...... 716 676-2000
Franklinville *(G-4966)*

Climax Packaging Inc ....C...... 315 376-8000
Lowville *(G-7414)*

Color Carton Corp ....D...... 718 665-0840
Bronx *(G-1228)*

Designers Folding Box Corp ....E...... 716 853-5141
Buffalo *(G-2728)*

Diamond Paper Box Company ....B...... 585 334-8030
Rochester *(G-13344)*

Disc Graphics Inc ....C...... 631 300-1129
Hauppauge *(G-5637)*

Disc Graphics Inc ....D...... 631 234-1400
Hauppauge *(G-5638)*

F M Howell & Company ....D...... 607 734-6291
Elmira *(G-4351)*

Fairview Paper Box Corp ....E...... 585 786-5230
Warsaw *(G-15507)*

Flower City Printing Inc ....C...... 585 663-9000
Rochester *(G-13415)*

Gavin Mfg Corp ....E...... 631 467-0040
Farmingdale *(G-4636)*

Gaylord Bros Inc ....D...... 315 457-5070
North Syracuse *(G-12042)*

HSM Packaging Corporation ....D...... 315 476-7996
Liverpool *(G-7012)*

Knoll Printing & Packaging Inc ....E...... 516 621-0100
Syosset *(G-14791)*

M C Packaging Corporation ....E...... 631 643-3763
Babylon *(G-522)*

BOXES (continued)

Multi Packg Solutions Intl Ltd...............E....... 646 885-0005
New York (G-10520)

Novel Box Company Ltd.................E....... 718 965-2222
Brooklyn (G-2221)

Paper Box Corp.........................D....... 212 226-7490
New York (G-10748)

Premier Packaging Corporation..........E....... 585 924-8460
Victor (G-15424)

Prestige Box Corporation...............E....... 516 773-3115
Great Neck (G-5415)

Specialized Packg Group Inc............G....... 315 638-4355
Baldwinsville (G-553)

Specialized Packg Radisson LLC.........C....... 315 638-4355
Baldwinsville (G-554)

Standard Group.........................E....... 718 335-5500
Great Neck (G-5424)

Standard Group LLC.....................C....... 718 507-6430
Great Neck (G-5425)

Viking Industries Inc..................D....... 845 883-6325
New Paltz (G-8314)

Visitainer Corp........................E....... 718 636-0300
Brooklyn (G-2564)

BOXES: Paperboard, Set-Up

A Fleisig Paper Box Corp...............F....... 212 226-7490
New York (G-8415)

American Package Company Inc...........E....... 718 389-4444
Brooklyn (G-1500)

Brick & Ballerstein Inc................E....... 718 497-1400
Ridgewood (G-13142)

Burt Rigid Box Inc.....................D....... 607 433-2510
Oneonta (G-12261)

Drescher Paper Box Inc.................F....... 716 854-0288
Clarence (G-3429)

Earlville Paper Box Co Inc.............E....... 315 691-2131
Earlville (G-4076)

F M Howell & Company...................D....... 607 734-6291
Elmira (G-4351)

Jordon Box Company Inc.................E....... 315 422-3419
Syracuse (G-14920)

Lionel Habas Associates Inc............F....... 212 860-8454
New York (G-10223)

Parlor City Paper Box Co Inc...........D....... 607 772-0600
Binghamton (G-903)

Prestige Box Corporation...............E....... 516 773-3115
Great Neck (G-5415)

Propak Inc.............................G....... 518 677-5100
Eagle Bridge (G-4074)

Pure Trade Us Inc......................E....... 212 256-1600
New York (G-10928)

Seneca FLS Spc & Logistics Co..........D....... 315 568-4139
Seneca Falls (G-14372)

BOXES: Plastic

American Package Company Inc...........E....... 718 389-4444
Brooklyn (G-1500)

Hornet Group Inc.......................D....... 845 858-6400
Port Jervis (G-12850)

Novel Box Company Ltd..................E....... 718 965-2222
Brooklyn (G-2221)

Philcom Ltd............................G....... 716 875-8005
Buffalo (G-2916)

Printex Packaging Corporation..........D....... 631 234-4300
Islandia (G-6343)

R P M Industries Inc...................E....... 315 255-1105
Auburn (G-492)

BOXES: Solid Fiber

Burt Rigid Box Inc.....................D....... 607 433-2510
Oneonta (G-12261)

Specialized Packg Radisson LLC.........C....... 315 638-4355
Baldwinsville (G-554)

BOXES: Stamped Metal

Novel Box Company Ltd..................E....... 718 965-2222
Brooklyn (G-2221)

BOXES: Switch, Electric

Sphere Cables & Chips Inc..............E....... 212 619-3132
New York (G-11322)

BOXES: Wooden

Abbot & Abbot Box Corp.................F....... 888 930-5972
Long Island City (G-7143)

M &L Industry of NY Inc................G....... 845 827-6255
Highland Mills (G-5968)

BRAKES & BRAKE PARTS

Interparts International Inc...........E....... 516 576-2000
Plainview (G-12691)

Rpb Distributors LLC...................G....... 914 244-3600
Mount Kisco (G-8105)

BRAKES: Electromagnetic

Magtrol Inc............................E....... 716 668-5555
Buffalo (G-2859)

BRASS FOUNDRY, NEC

Eastern Finding Corp...................F....... 516 747-6640
New Hyde Park (G-8263)

BRAZING SVCS

Parfuse Corp...........................E....... 516 997-8888
Westbury (G-15916)

W R P Welding Ltd......................G....... 631 249-8859
Farmingdale (G-4763)

Welding and Brazing Svcs Inc...........G....... 607 397-1009
Richfield Springs (G-13106)

BRAZING: Metal

Bodycote Syracuse Heat Treatin.........E....... 315 451-0000
Liverpool (G-7001)

Hi-Temp Brazing Inc....................E....... 631 491-4917
Deer Park (G-3879)

Milgo Industrial Inc...................D....... 718 388-6476
Brooklyn (G-2153)

Milgo Industrial Inc...................G....... 718 387-0406
Brooklyn (G-2154)

BRIC-A-BRAC

Five Star Creations Inc................E....... 845 783-1187
Monroe (G-8020)

BRICK, STONE & RELATED PRDTS WHOLESALERS

Barrasso & Sons Trucking Inc...........E....... 631 581-0360
Islip Terrace (G-6358)

Clemente Latham Concrete Corp..........D....... 518 374-2222
Schenectady (G-14257)

East Coast Mines Ltd...................E....... 631 653-5445
East Quogue (G-4156)

Hampton Sand Corp......................G....... 631 325-5533
Westhampton (G-15955)

Hanson Aggregates PA LLC...............E....... 585 624-3800
Honeoye Falls (G-6073)

Imperia Masonry Supply Corp............E....... 914 738-0900
Pelham (G-12566)

Peckham Materials Corp.................F....... 518 494-2313
Chestertown (G-3394)

Phelps Cement Products Inc.............E....... 315 548-9415
Phelps (G-12606)

BRICKS & BLOCKS: Structural

Everblock Systems LLC..................G....... 844 422-5625
New York (G-9424)

Semco Ceramics Inc.....................G....... 315 782-3000
Watertown (G-15588)

BRICKS: Concrete

Brickit................................E....... 631 727-8977
Hauppauge (G-5608)

BRIDAL SHOPS

Vera Wang Group LLC....................C....... 212 575-6400
New York (G-11657)

BRIDGE COMPONENTS: Bridge sections, prefabricated, highway

Apollo Steel Corporation...............F....... 716 283-8758
Niagara Falls (G-11907)

Port Authority of NY & NJ..............D....... 718 390-2534
Staten Island (G-14691)

BROADCASTING & COMMS EQPT: Antennas, Transmitting/Comms

Century Metal Parts Corp...............E....... 631 667-0800
Bay Shore (G-661)

Fei-Zyfer Inc..........................G....... 714 933-4045
Uniondale (G-15228)

John Mezzalingua Assoc LLC.............C....... 315 431-7100
Liverpool (G-7018)

Millennium Antenna Corp................F....... 315 798-9374
Utica (G-15284)

Sinclair Technologies Inc..............E....... 716 874-3682
Hamburg (G-5521)

STI-Co Industries Inc..................E....... 716 662-2680
Orchard Park (G-12377)

BROADCASTING & COMMS EQPT: Rcvr-Transmitter Unt, Transceiver

Magnet-Ndctive Systems Ltd USA.........E....... 585 924-4000
Victor (G-15419)

BROADCASTING & COMMUNICATIONS EQPT: Cellular Radio Telephone

Advanced Comm Solutions................G....... 914 693-5076
Ardsley (G-384)

Bullitt Mobile LLC.....................D....... 631 424-1749
Bohemia (G-983)

Ghostek LLC............................F....... 855 310-3439
Brooklyn (G-1885)

Nycom Business Solutions Inc...........G....... 516 345-6000
Franklin Square (G-4963)

BROADCASTING & COMMUNICATIONS EQPT: Studio Eqpt, Radio & TV

Big Fish Entertainment LLC.............C....... 646 797-4955
New York (G-8786)

Hopewell Precision Inc.................E....... 845 221-2737
Hopewell Junction (G-6096)

Times Square Studios Ltd...............C....... 212 930-7720
New York (G-11496)

BROADCASTING & COMMUNICATIONS EQPT: Transmitting, Radio/TV

Armstrong Transmitter Corp.............F....... 315 673-1269
Marcellus (G-7560)

BROKERS' SVCS

Remsen Graphics Corp...................G....... 718 643-7500
Brooklyn (G-2340)

BROKERS: Business

Spanish Artisan Wine Group LLC.........G....... 914 414-6982
Patterson (G-12520)

BROKERS: Food

Quinn and Co of NY Ltd.................D....... 212 868-1900
New York (G-10958)

BROKERS: Loan

Mml Software Ltd.......................E....... 631 941-1313
East Setauket (G-4182)

BROKERS: Printing

Alabaster Group Inc....................G....... 516 867-8223
Freeport (G-4981)

Melmont Fine Pringng/Graphics..........G....... 516 939-2253
Bethpage (G-839)

Prestige Envelope & Lithograph.........F....... 631 521-7043
Merrick (G-7863)

Print Tech Inc.........................G....... 585 202-3888
Webster (G-15648)

BRONZE FOUNDRY, NEC

American Blade Mfg LLC.................G....... 607 656-4204
Greene (G-5443)

American Blade Mfg LLC.................F....... 607 432-4518
Oneonta (G-12256)

BROOMS

K & R Allied Inc.......................F....... 718 625-6610
Brooklyn (G-2015)

BROOMS & BRUSHES

Braun Industries Inc...................F....... 516 741-6000
Albertson (G-145)

Cpac Inc...............................E....... 585 382-3223
Leicester (G-6908)

Employee Codes: A=Over 500 employees, B=251-500
C=101-250, D=51-100, E=20-50, F=10-19, G=5-9

2020 Harris
New York Manufacturers Directory

1039

PRODUCT

Excel Paint Applicators Inc ....E...... 347 221-1968
  Inwood *(G-6291)*

Full Circle Home LLC......................G...... 212 432-0001
  New York *(G-9551)*

BROOMS & BRUSHES: Hair Pencils Or Artists' Brushes

Teka Fine Line Brushes Inc...................G...... 718 692-2928
  Brooklyn *(G-2498)*

BROOMS & BRUSHES: Household Or Indl

Abtex Corporation ....E...... 315 536-7403
  Dresden *(G-4034)*

Braun Bros Brushes Inc......................G...... 631 667-2179
  Valley Stream *(G-15336)*

Brushtech (disc) Inc ....F...... 518 563-8420
  Plattsburgh *(G-12739)*

FM Brush Co Inc ....C...... 718 821-5939
  Glendale *(G-5224)*

Volckening Inc ....E...... 718 748-0294
  Brooklyn *(G-2568)*

Young & Swartz Inc ....F...... 716 852-2171
  Buffalo *(G-3052)*

BROOMS & BRUSHES: Paint & Varnish

Linzer Products Corp ....C...... 631 253-3333
  West Babylon *(G-15726)*

BROOMS & BRUSHES: Paint Rollers

Pan American Roller Inc ....F...... 914 762-8700
  Ossining *(G-12407)*

Premier Paint Roller Co LLC................D...... 718 441-7700
  Richmond Hill *(G-13119)*

Premier Paint Roller Co LLC................F...... 718 441-7700
  Richmond Hill *(G-13120)*

Royal Paint Roller Corp ....E...... 516 367-4370
  Woodbury *(G-16182)*

BROOMS & BRUSHES: Paintbrushes

E & W Manufacturing Co Inc...............E...... 516 367-8571
  Woodbury *(G-16170)*

Kirschner Brush LLC ....F...... 718 292-1809
  Bronx *(G-1293)*

BRUSHES

Walter R Tucker Entps Ltd ....E...... 607 467-2866
  Deposit *(G-4004)*

BRUSHES & BRUSH STOCK CONTACTS: Electric

Graphite Metallizing Corp ....C...... 914 968-8400
  Yonkers *(G-16315)*

BUCKLES & PARTS

Maxine Denker Inc ....G...... 212 689-1440
  Staten Island *(G-14679)*

BUILDING & OFFICE CLEANING SVCS

Rumsey Corp..................................G...... 914 751-3640
  Yonkers *(G-16347)*

BUILDING & STRUCTURAL WOOD MBRS: Timbers, Struct, Lam Lumber

Empire Building Products Inc ....G...... 518 695-6094
  Schuylerville *(G-14323)*

New England Barns Inc ....E...... 631 445-1461
  Southold *(G-14545)*

BUILDING & STRUCTURAL WOOD MEMBERS

Architctral Mllwk Installation ....E...... 631 499-0755
  East Northport *(G-4142)*

Harvest Homes Inc...........................E...... 518 895-2341
  Delanson *(G-3960)*

Timber Frames Inc ....G...... 585 374-6405
  Canandaigua *(G-3144)*

Ufp New York LLC ....E...... 607 563-1556
  Sidney *(G-14437)*

Unadilla Silo Company Inc ....D...... 607 369-9341
  Sidney *(G-14438)*

BUILDING & STRUCTURAL WOOD MEMBERS: Arches, Laminated Lumber

Stephenson Lumber Company Inc........G...... 518 548-7521
  Speculator *(G-14548)*

BUILDING BOARD & WALLBOARD, EXC GYPSUM

Continental Buchanan LLC ....D...... 703 480-3800
  Buchanan *(G-2608)*

Superior Interiors NY Corp ....F...... 845 274-7600
  Monsey *(G-8050)*

BUILDING BOARD: Gypsum

Continental Buchanan LLC ....D...... 703 480-3800
  Buchanan *(G-2608)*

BUILDING CLEANING & MAINTENANCE SVCS

JM Murray Center Inc ....C...... 607 756-9913
  Cortland *(G-3774)*

Richard Ruffner................................F...... 631 234-4600
  Central Islip *(G-3287)*

BUILDING COMPONENTS: Structural Steel

Castle Harvester Co Inc......................G...... 585 526-5884
  Seneca Castle *(G-14361)*

D N Gannon Fabricating Inc ....G...... 315 463-7466
  Syracuse *(G-14872)*

Eastern Trading Partners Corp.............G...... 212 202-1451
  Brooklyn *(G-1778)*

International Metals Trdg LLC ....G...... 866 923-0182
  Melville *(G-7796)*

Kuno Steel Products Corp ....F...... 516 938-8500
  Hicksville *(G-5921)*

Marovato Industries Inc......................F...... 718 389-0800
  Brooklyn *(G-2119)*

Nextgen Building Components ....E...... 585 924-7171
  Farmington *(G-4776)*

R&S Steel LLC ....E...... 315 281-0123
  Rome *(G-13865)*

Schenectady Steel Co Inc ....E...... 518 355-3220
  Schenectady *(G-14302)*

Stone Bridge Iron and Stl Inc...............D...... 518 695-3752
  Gansevoort *(G-5087)*

STS Steel Inc ....D...... 518 370-2693
  Schenectady *(G-14308)*

Titan Steel Corp ....F...... 315 656-7046
  Kirkville *(G-6727)*

Torino Indus Fabrication Inc.................E...... 631 509-1640
  Bellport *(G-809)*

Ward Steel Company Inc ....E...... 315 451-4566
  Liverpool *(G-7047)*

Wilston Enterprises Inc ....F...... 716 483-1411
  Jamestown *(G-6554)*

BUILDING ITEM REPAIR SVCS, MISCELLANEOUS

ER Butler & Co Inc...........................E...... 212 925-3565
  New York *(G-9392)*

Otis Elevator Company ....E...... 917 339-9600
  New York *(G-10717)*

BUILDING PRDTS & MATERIALS DEALERS

Alvio-US Corp ....G...... 631 664-0618
  Hauppauge *(G-5586)*

Arnan Development Corp.....................D...... 607 432-8391
  Oneonta *(G-12257)*

Cossitt Concrete Products Inc ....F...... 315 824-2700
  Hamilton *(G-5526)*

Delocon Wholesale Inc.......................F...... 716 592-2711
  Springville *(G-14589)*

Gone South Concrete Block Inc ....E...... 315 598-2141
  Fulton *(G-5062)*

Imperia Masonry Supply Corp ....E...... 914 738-0900
  Pelham *(G-12566)*

Phelps Cement Products Inc ....F...... 315 548-9415
  Phelps *(G-12606)*

Structural Wood Corporation ....E...... 315 388-4442
  Waddington *(G-15447)*

BUILDING PRDTS: Concrete

Access Products Inc ....G...... 800 679-4022
  Buffalo *(G-2617)*

Apollo Management V LP....................E...... 914 467-6510
  Purchase *(G-13001)*

Duke Company ....G...... 607 347-4455
  Ithaca *(G-6379)*

Hanson Aggregates East LLC ....G...... 716 372-1574
  Allegany *(G-188)*

Murcadom Corporation ....F...... 585 412-2176
  Canandaigua *(G-3137)*

Standard Industries Inc ....F...... 212 821-1600
  New York *(G-11345)*

BUILDING PRDTS: Stone

Icestone LLC ....E...... 718 624-4900
  Brooklyn *(G-1951)*

Roto Salt Company Inc.......................E...... 315 536-3742
  Penn Yan *(G-12593)*

BUILDINGS & COMPONENTS: Prefabricated Metal

All American Building ....G...... 607 797-7123
  Binghamton *(G-851)*

Austin Mohawk and Company LLC.......E...... 315 793-3000
  Utica *(G-15239)*

Birdair Inc ....D...... 716 633-9500
  Amherst *(G-213)*

Man Products Inc ....E...... 631 789-6500
  Farmingdale *(G-4676)*

Metals Building Products ....F...... 844 638-2527
  Holbrook *(G-6010)*

Overhead Door Corporation ....D...... 518 828-7652
  Hudson *(G-6173)*

Walpole Woodworkers Inc ....G...... 631 726-2859
  Water Mill *(G-15531)*

BUILDINGS, PREFABRICATED: Wholesalers

Shafer & Sons ....G...... 315 853-5285
  Westmoreland *(G-15963)*

BUILDINGS: Portable

Deraffele Mfg Co Inc ....E...... 914 636-6850
  New Rochelle *(G-8326)*

Mobile Mini Inc ....E...... 315 732-4555
  Utica *(G-15285)*

Morton Buildings Inc ....E...... 585 786-8191
  Warsaw *(G-15508)*

Nci Group Inc ....D...... 315 339-1245
  Rome *(G-13859)*

Universal Shielding Corp ....E...... 631 667-7900
  Deer Park *(G-3945)*

BUILDINGS: Prefabricated, Metal

Energy Panel Structures Inc ....G...... 315 923-7777
  Clyde *(G-3489)*

Energy Panel Structures Inc ....G...... 585 343-1777
  Clyde *(G-3490)*

Energy Panel Structures Inc ....G...... 518 355-6708
  Schenectady *(G-14263)*

BUILDINGS: Prefabricated, Wood

Cort Contracting ....F...... 845 758-1190
  Red Hook *(G-13073)*

Duro-Shed Inc ....E...... 585 344-0800
  Buffalo *(G-2732)*

Eastern Exterior Wall ....E...... 631 589-3880
  Bohemia *(G-1009)*

Energy Panel Structures Inc ....G...... 315 923-7777
  Clyde *(G-3489)*

Energy Panel Structures Inc ....G...... 585 343-1777
  Clyde *(G-3490)*

Energy Panel Structures Inc ....G...... 518 355-6708
  Schenectady *(G-14263)*

Fishers Storage Sheds ....G...... 585 382-9580
  Leicester *(G-6910)*

Walpole Woodworkers Inc ....G...... 631 726-2859
  Water Mill *(G-15531)*

BUILDINGS: Prefabricated, Wood

Lapp Management Corp ....G...... 607 243-5141
  Himrod *(G-5976)*

Roscoe Brothers Inc ....F...... 607 844-3750
  Dryden *(G-4040)*

Shafer & Sons ....G...... 315 853-5285
  Westmoreland *(G-15963)*

Shelter Enterprises Inc ....D...... 518 237-4100
  Cohoes *(G-3516)*

Wood Tex Products LLC ....D...... 607 243-5141
Himrod (G-5977)

BULLETIN BOARDS: Wood

Aarco Products Inc ....F 631 924-5461
Yaphank (G-16254)

BUMPERS: Motor Vehicle

4bumpers Llc ....F 212 721-9600
New York (G-8403)

BURIAL VAULTS: Concrete Or Precast Terrazzo

Beck Vault Company ....G...... 315 337-7590
Rome (G-13845)
Ideal Burial Vault Company ....G...... 585 599-2242
Corfu (G-3703)
Suhor Industries Inc ....F 585 377-5100
Fairport (G-4526)
Suhor Industries Inc ....G...... 716 483-6818
Jamestown (G-6544)

BURLAP & BURLAP PRDTS

James Thompson & Company Inc ......E 212 686-4242
New York (G-9972)

BURNERS: Gas, Indl

Dyson-Kissner-Moran Corp ....E 212 661-4600
Poughkeepsie (G-12952)
Frederick Cowan & Company Inc ......F 631 369-0360
Wading River (G-15449)

BUS BARS: Electrical

Schneider Electric Usa Inc ....G...... 631 567-5710
Bohemia (G-1073)

BUSES: Wholesalers

Leonard Bus Sales Inc ....G...... 607 467-3100
Rome (G-13854)

BUSHINGS & BEARINGS: Copper, Exc Machined

Amt Incorporated ....E 518 284-2910
Sharon Springs (G-14382)

BUSINESS ACTIVITIES: Non-Commercial Site

Adirondack Leather Pdts Inc ....F 607 547-5798
Fly Creek (G-4908)
Ajmadison Corp ....D...... 718 532-1800
Brooklyn (G-1474)
American Comfort Direct LLC ....E 201 364-8309
New York (G-8548)
Anne Taintor Inc ....G...... 718 483-9312
Brooklyn (G-1512)
Arm Construction Company Inc ...G...... 646 235-6520
East Elmhurst (G-4103)
Ashley Resin Corp ....G 718 851-8111
Brooklyn (G-1541)
Aspire One Communications Inc ......G...... 845 534-6110
Cornwall (G-3726)
Aureonic ....G...... 518 791-9331
Gansevoort (G-5083)
Birdsigns Inc ....G...... 201 388-7613
New York (G-8800)
Buperiod PBC ....G...... 917 406-9804
Brooklyn (G-1629)
Catch Ventures Inc ....F 347 620-4351
New York (G-8936)
Crhmdu Isulations LLC ....G...... 516 353-7749
Port Washington (G-12870)
Dapper Dads Inc ....G...... 917 903-8045
Brooklyn (G-1725)
Dezawy LLC ....G...... 917 436-8820
New York (G-9214)
Eccella Corporation ....G...... 718 612-0451
New York (G-9313)
Edesia World Wide LLC ....G...... 646 705-3505
New York (G-9320)
Evocate Media LLC ....F 646 361-3014
New York (G-9430)
Excell Print & Promotions Inc ......G...... 914 437-8668
White Plains (G-16004)

Fitsmo LLC ....G...... 585 519-1956
Fairport (G-4497)
Fresh Prints LLC ....E 917 826-2752
New York (G-9539)
Garrett J Cronin ....G...... 914 761-9299
White Plains (G-16008)
Gorga Fehren Fine Jewelry LLC ......G...... 646 861-3595
New York (G-9646)
Green Amazon LLC ....G...... 585 300-1319
Rochester (G-13451)
Greene Brass & Alum Fndry LLC ......G...... 607 656-4204
Bloomville (G-954)
Have Your Cake Kitchen LLC ......G...... 646 820-8074
Brooklyn (G-1927)
Hepa-Hat Incorporated ....F 914 271-9747
Croton On Hudson (G-3809)
Hourglass Interactive LLC ....F 954 254-2853
New York (G-9823)
Hovee Inc ....F 646 249-6200
New York (G-9827)
Hs Homeworx LLC ....G...... 646 870-0406
New York (G-9830)
Hum Limited Liability Corp ....G...... 631 525-2174
Nesconset (G-8218)
Inscape (new York) Inc ....D...... 716 665-6210
Falconer (G-4544)
Jr Engineering Enterprise LLC ......G...... 716 909-2693
Grand Island (G-5335)
Kemper System America Inc ......D...... 716 558-2971
West Seneca (G-15851)
L VII Resilient LLC ....G...... 631 987-5819
Medford (G-7716)
Labrador Stone Inc ....G...... 570 465-2120
Binghamton (G-893)
Live Up Top Inc ....F 866 333-1332
New York (G-10232)
Magcrest Packaging Inc ....Magcrest 845 425-0451
Monsey (G-8039)
New York Qrtrly Foundation Inc ......F 917 843-8825
Brooklyn (G-2211)
On Line Power Technologies ....G...... 914 968-4440
Yonkers (G-16336)
Pap Chat Inc ....G...... 516 350-1888
Brooklyn (G-2243)
Patrick Rohan ....G...... 718 781-2573
Monticello (G-8072)
Patuga LLC ....G...... 716 204-7220
Williamsville (G-16136)
Phoenix Usa LLC ....G...... 646 351-6598
New York (G-10830)
Pilot Inc ....G...... 212 951-1133
New York (G-10839)
Pilot Inc ....G...... 212 951-1133
New York (G-10840)
Pink Box Accessories LLC ....G...... 718 435-2821
Brooklyn (G-2260)
Playfitness Corp ....G...... 917 497-5443
Staten Island (G-14690)
Ready Check Glo Inc ....G...... 516 547-1849
East Northport (G-4151)
Ready To Assemble Company Inc ......E 516 825-4397
Valley Stream (G-15356)
Rision Inc ....G...... 212 987-2628
New York (G-11047)
Roscoe Brothers Inc ....F 607 844-3750
Dryden (G-4040)
Scan-A-Chrome Color Inc ....G...... 631 532-6146
Copiague (G-3675)
Sensor & Decontamination Inc ......F 301 526-8389
Binghamton (G-908)
Slyde Inc ....F 917 331-2114
Long Island City (G-7360)
South Central Boyz ....G...... 718 496-7270
Brooklyn (G-2444)
Special Circle Inc ....F 516 595-9988
New Hyde Park (G-8295)
Streetcred Nyc LLC ....G...... 646 675-0073
New York (G-11372)
Surtic Mining Company LLC ....F 718 434-0477
Brooklyn (G-2481)
Tg Polymers Inc ....G...... 585 670-9427
Webster (G-15656)
Treauu Inc ....G...... 703 731-0196
New York (G-11535)
Urthworx Inc ....G...... 646 373-7535
New York (G-11621)
Verris Inc ....G...... 201 565-1648
New York (G-11663)
Viewsport International Inc ....G...... 585 259-1562
Penfield (G-12576)

Virtuvent Inc ....G...... 855 672-8677
Brooklyn (G-2563)
Vortex Ventures Inc ....G...... 516 946-8345
North Baldwin (G-12011)
Wazer Inc ....E 201 580-6486
Brooklyn (G-2577)
Wrkbook LLC ....F 914 355-1293
White Plains (G-16075)

BUSINESS FORMS WHOLESALERS

American Print Solutions Inc ....G...... 718 208-2309
Brooklyn (G-1502)
Composite Forms Inc ....F 914 937-1808
Port Chester (G-12815)
Empire Business Forms Inc ....F 845 562-7780
Newburgh (G-11864)

BUSINESS FORMS: Printed, Continuous

Five Boro Holding LLC ....F 718 431-9500
Brooklyn (G-1848)
Linden Forms & Systems Inc ....E 212 219-1100
Brooklyn (G-2076)
Syracuse Computer Forms Inc ......E 315 478-0108
Syracuse (G-15005)

BUSINESS FORMS: Printed, Manifold

Abra-Ka-Data Systems Ltd ....E 631 667-5550
Deer Park (G-3827)
Amsterdam Printing & Litho Inc ......F 518 842-6000
Amsterdam (G-316)
Amsterdam Printing & Litho Inc ......E 518 842-6000
Amsterdam (G-317)
Bmg Printing and Promotion LLC ......G...... 631 231-9200
Bohemia (G-982)
Gateway Prtg & Graphics Inc ......E 716 823-3873
Hamburg (G-5509)
Maggio Data Forms ....C 631 348-0343
Hauppauge (G-5704)
Marcy Business Forms Inc ....G...... 718 935-9100
Brooklyn (G-2113)
P P I Business Forms Inc ....G...... 716 825-1241
Buffalo (G-2903)
R R Donnelley & Sons Company ......D...... 716 773-0300
Grand Island (G-5342)
Resonant Legal Media LLC ....D...... 800 781-3591
New York (G-11019)
Richard Ruffner ....F 631 234-4600
Central Islip (G-3287)
Select-A-Form Inc ....D...... 631 981-3076
Holbrook (G-6020)
Taylor Communications Inc ....F 937 221-1303
Melville (G-7828)
Taylor Communications Inc ....F 718 352-0220
Westbury (G-15927)
Williamson Law Book Co ....F 585 924-3400
Victor (G-15443)

BUSINESS MACHINE REPAIR, ELECTRIC

National Time Recording Eqp Co ......F 212 227-3310
New York (G-10547)
Neopost USA Inc ....E 631 435-9100
Hauppauge (G-5726)
Yellow E House Inc ....G...... 718 888-2000
Flushing (G-4907)

BUSINESS SUPPORT SVCS

Bart Ostrander Trckg Log Corp ......G...... 518 661-6535
Mayfield (G-7681)
Cloud Rock Group LLC ....G...... 516 967-6023
Roslyn (G-14040)
Murcadom Corporation ....F 585 412-2176
Canandaigua (G-3137)

BUSINESS TRAINING SVCS

Logical Operations Inc ....C 585 350-7000
Rochester (G-13522)

BUTADIENE: Indl, Organic, Chemical

Unified Solutions For Clg Inc ....F 718 782-8800
Brooklyn (G-2535)

BUTTER WHOLESALERS

Pure Ghee Inc ....G...... 917 214-5431
Glen Head (G-5213)

BUTTONS

Buttons & Trimcom Inc..............................F......212 868-1971
New York (G-8874)

E-Won Industrial Co Inc ....E......212 750-9610
New York (G-9295)

Empire State Metal Pdts Inc....................E......718 847-1617
Richmond Hill (G-13113)

Emsig Manufacturing Corp ....F......718 784-7717
New York (G-9364)

Emsig Manufacturing Corp ....F......518 828-7301
Hudson (G-6155)

Eu Design LLC ....G......212 420-7788
New York (G-9416)

Kraus & Sons Inc ....F......212 620-0408
New York (G-10137)

National Die & Button Mould Co............E......201 939-7800
Brooklyn (G-2189)

Shimada Shoji (hk) Limited....................G......212 268-0465
New York (G-11214)

CABINETS & CASES: Show, Display & Storage, Exc Wood

260 Oak Street Inc..................................G......877 852-4676
Buffalo (G-2612)

Able Steel Equipment Co Inc ....F......718 361-9240
Long Island City (G-7144)

CABINETS: Bathroom Vanities, Wood

Glissade New York LLC ....E......631 756-4800
Farmingdale (G-4638)

Nagad Cabinets Inc................................E......718 382-7200
Brooklyn (G-2185)

New York Vanity and Mfg Co ....E......718 417-1010
Freeport (G-5010)

Tristate Contract Sales LLC ....G......845 782-2614
Chester (G-3392)

CABINETS: Entertainment

Dbs Interiors Corp ....F......631 491-3013
West Babylon (G-15706)

Time Base Corporation ....E......631 293-4068
Edgewood (G-4288)

W Designe Inc ....E......914 736-1058
Peekskill (G-12559)

CABINETS: Entertainment Units, Household, Wood

Handcraft Cabinetry Inc ....G......914 681-9437
White Plains (G-16012)

CABINETS: Factory

T O Gronlund Company Inc ....F......212 679-3535
New York (G-11419)

Thornwood Products Ltd ....E......914 769-9161
Thornwood (G-15071)

Wood Etc Inc ....F......315 484-9663
Syracuse (G-15030)

CABINETS: Filing, Wood

Red White & Blue Entps Corp................G......718 565-8080
Woodside (G-16223)

CABINETS: Kitchen, Metal

American Best Cabinets Inc ....E......845 369-6666
Suffern (G-14757)

Hellas Stone Inc ....G......718 545-4716
Astoria (G-424)

Majestic Home Imprvs Distr....................G......718 853-5079
Brooklyn (G-2103)

Manhattan Cabinets Inc..........................G......212 548-2436
New York (G-10342)

Methods Tooling & Mfg Inc ....E......845 246-7100
Mount Marion (G-8111)

Steelcraft Manufacturing Co ....F......718 277-2404
Brooklyn (G-2456)

CABINETS: Kitchen, Wood

Able Kitchen ....F......877 268-1264
Cedarhurst (G-3238)

Affordble Gran Cbntry Outl Inc...............F......845 564-0500
Newburgh (G-11857)

Aka Enterprises.......................................E......716 474-4579
Wyoming (G-16249)

Aki Cabinets Inc......................................E......718 721-2541
Astoria (G-413)

American Classic Kitchens Inc................G......212 838-9308
New York (G-8547)

Andike Millwork Inc.................................G......718 894-1796
Maspeth (G-7590)

Artone LLC ....D......716 664-2232
Jamestown (G-6495)

Auburn-Watson Corp ....F......716 876-8000
Depew (G-3970)

Aucapina Cabinets Inc............................G......718 609-9054
Maspeth (G-7594)

Bauerschmidt & Sons Inc ....D......718 528-3500
Jamaica (G-6429)

Bloch Industries LLC...............................D......585 334-9600
Rochester (G-13272)

Cabinet Factory Inc.................................F......718 351-8922
Staten Island (G-14634)

Cabinet Shapes Corp ....F......718 784-6255
Long Island City (G-7182)

Cabinetry By Tbr Inc...............................G......516 365-8500
Manhasset (G-7531)

Cabinets By Stanley Inc ....G......718 222-5861
Brooklyn (G-1639)

Cambridge Kitchens Mfg Inc ....F......516 935-5100
Hicksville (G-5891)

Candlelight Cabinetry Inc.......................C......716 434-2114
Lockport (G-7063)

Capital Kit Cab & Door Mfrs ....G......718 886-0303
College Point (G-3539)

Carefree Kitchens Inc ....G......631 567-2120
Holbrook (G-5988)

Carlos & Alex Atelier Inc ....E......718 441-8911
Richmond Hill (G-13111)

Casa Collection Inc.................................G......718 694-0272
Brooklyn (G-1653)

Catskill Craftsmen Inc ....D......607 652-7321
Stamford (G-14607)

Central Kitchen Corp ....F......631 283-1029
Southampton (G-14528)

Chicone Builders LLC ....G......607 535-6540
Montour Falls (G-8074)

Classic Cabinets ....F......845 357-4331
Suffern (G-14759)

Clearwood Custom Carpentry and........E......315 432-8422
East Syracuse (G-4204)

Cleary Custom Cabinets Inc ....F......516 939-2475
Hicksville (G-5895)

Columbia Cabinets LLC..........................G......212 972-7550
Armonk (G-396)

Columbia Cabinets LLC..........................F......518 283-1700
Saratoga Springs (G-14170)

Craft Custom Woodwork Co Inc.............F......718 821-2162
Maspeth (G-7600)

Creative Stone & Cabinets Corp............G......631 772-6548
Selden (G-14351)

Custom CAS Inc......................................E......718 726-3575
Long Island City (G-7195)

Custom Woodcraft LLC ....F......315 843-4234
Munnsville (G-8195)

D & M Custom Cabinets Inc....................F......516 678-2818
Oceanside (G-12168)

Dak Mica and Wood Products ....G......631 467-0749
Ronkonkoma (G-13929)

Dbs Interiors Corp ....F......631 491-3013
West Babylon (G-15706)

Deakon Homes and Interiors ....F......518 271-0342
Troy (G-15165)

Di Fiore and Sons Custom Wdwkg ....G......718 278-1663
Long Island City (G-7201)

East End Country Kitchens Inc ....F......631 727-2258
Calverton (G-3080)

EC Wood & Company Inc ....F......718 388-2287
Deer Park (G-3868)

EM Pfaff & Son Inc ....F......607 739-3691
Horseheads (G-6121)

Enterprise Wood Products Inc ....F......718 853-9243
Brooklyn (G-1806)

Euro Woodworking Inc............................G......718 246-9172
Brooklyn (G-1817)

Fina Cabinet Corp...................................G......718 409-2900
Mount Vernon (G-8141)

Finger Lkes Stirs Cabinets LLC ....G......315 638-3150
Baldwinsville (G-547)

Fra-Rik Formica Fabg Co Inc ....F......718 597-3335
Bronx (G-1262)

Greenway Cabinetry Inc.........................F......516 877-0009
Williston Park (G-16147)

Hearth Cabinets and More Ltd...............G......315 641-1197
Liverpool (G-7011)

Home Ideal Inc..G......718 762-8998
Flushing (G-4860)

Huntington Woodworking Inc..................G......631 271-7897
Northport (G-12105)

Ignelzi Interiors Inc................................E......718 464-0279
Queens Village (G-13021)

J Percoco Industries Inc ....G......631 312-4572
Bohemia (G-1025)

Jordache Woodworking Corp ....F......718 349-3373
Brooklyn (G-1999)

K-Binet Inc ....G......845 348-1149
Blauvelt (G-929)

Kw Distributors Group Inc ....F......718 843-3500
Ozone Park (G-12465)

Longo Commercial Cabinets Inc ....E......631 225-4290
Lindenhurst (G-6956)

Lyn Jo Kitchens Inc ....G......718 336-6060
Brooklyn (G-2089)

Maple Tree Kitchen & Bath Inc ....G......845 236-3660
Marlboro (G-7581)

Material Process Systems Inc ....F......718 302-3081
Brooklyn (G-2124)

Matteo & Antonio Bartolotta ....G......315 252-2220
Auburn (G-485)

McGraw Wood Products LLC ....E......607 836-6465
Mc Graw (G-7689)

Methods Tooling & Mfg Inc ....E......845 246-7100
Mount Marion (G-8111)

Metro Kitchens Corp...............................F......718 434-1166
Brooklyn (G-2147)

Michael Bernstein Design Assoc ....E......718 456-9277
Brooklyn (G-2150)

Michael P Mmarr ....G......315 623-9380
Constantia (G-3636)

Millco Woodworking LLC ....F......585 526-6844
Hall (G-5500)

Modern Cabinet Company Inc ....E......845 473-4900
Poughkeepsie (G-12971)

Mostly Mica Inc.......................................G......631 586-4200
Bay Shore (G-694)

N Y Elli Design Corp ....F......718 228-0014
Ridgewood (G-13152)

Neo Cabinetry LLC..................................F......718 403-0456
Brooklyn (G-2196)

Nexis 3 LLC ....E......585 285-4120
Rochester (G-13576)

NY Cabinet Factory Inc...........................G......718 256-6541
Brooklyn (G-2224)

Old Souls Inc ....G......845 809-5886
Cold Spring (G-3522)

Pgs Millwork Inc......................................D......518 828-2608
Hudson (G-6175)

Piccini Industries Ltd..............................E......845 365-0614
Orangeburg (G-12325)

Precision Built Tops LLC ....G......607 336-5417
Norwich (G-12126)

Precision Dental Cabinets Inc ....F......631 543-3870
Smithtown (G-14485)

Premier Woodcraft Ltd ....E......610 383-6624
White Plains (G-16055)

Premium Woodworking LLC.....................G......631 485-3133
West Babylon (G-15738)

R & M Thermofoil Doors Inc....................E......718 206-4991
Jamaica (G-6468)

Red White & Blue Entps Corp................G......718 565-8080
Woodside (G-16223)

Ribble Lumber Inc...................................G......315 536-6221
Penn Yan (G-12592)

Royal Custom Cabinets...........................G......315 376-6042
Lowville (G-7421)

S & V Custom Furniture Mfg....................F......516 746-8299
Mineola (G-7999)

S Donadic Inc ....D......718 361-9888
Sunnyside (G-14774)

Salko Kitchens Inc..................................F......845 565-4420
New Windsor (G-8381)

Salmon Crek Cabinetry Inc ....E......315 589-5419
Williamson (G-16112)

Serway Bros Inc......................................G......315 337-0601
Rome (G-13872)

Silva Cabinetry Inc.................................E......914 737-7697
Buchanan (G-2610)

Skyline Custom Cabinetry Inc ....G......631 393-2983
Farmingdale (G-4733)

Stone Expo & Cabinetry LLC ....F......516 292-2988
West Hempstead (G-15780)

Upbeat Upholstery & Design LLC ....G......347 480-3980
Brooklyn (G-2547)

Upstate Cabinet Company Inc ....F......585 429-5090
Rochester (G-13787)

Viola Cabinet Corporation...............G...... 716 284-6327
Niagara Falls (G-11989)

W Designe Inc................................E...... 914 736-1058
Peekskill (G-12559)

White House Cabinet Shop LLC...........G...... 607 674-9358
Sherburne (G-14397)

William Brooks Woodworking.............F...... 718 495-9767
Brooklyn (G-2585)

Win Wood Cabinetry Inc...................G...... 516 304-2216
Greenvale (G-5466)

Wood Etc Inc..................................F...... 315 484-9663
Syracuse (G-15030)

Yonkers Cabinet Inc.........................G...... 914 668-2133
Yonkers (G-16359)

Your Furniture Designers Inc.............G...... 845 947-3046
West Haverstraw (G-15765)

Your Way Custom Cabinets Inc...........G...... 914 371-1870
Mount Vernon (G-8192)

CABINETS: Office, Metal

Gothic Cabinet Craft Inc...................D...... 347 881-1420
Maspeth (G-7618)

Natural Stone & Cabinet Inc..............G...... 718 388-2988
Brooklyn (G-2192)

Riverfront Costume Design................G...... 716 693-2501
North Tonawanda (G-12087)

CABINETS: Office, Wood

Chicone Builders LLC.......................G...... 607 535-6540
Montour Falls (G-8074)

Commercial Display Design LLC..........F...... 607 336-7353
Oneonta (G-12266)

Concepts In Wood of CNY..................E...... 315 463-8084
Syracuse (G-14858)

Craft Custom Woodwork Co Inc...........F...... 718 821-2162
Maspeth (G-7600)

Culin/Colella Inc.............................G...... 914 698-7727
Mamaroneck (G-7507)

Fina Cabinet Corp............................G...... 718 409-2900
Mount Vernon (G-8141)

Gothic Cabinet Craft Inc...................D...... 347 881-1420
Maspeth (G-7618)

Materials Design Workshop................F...... 718 893-1954
Bronx (G-1308)

N Y Elli Design Corp........................F...... 718 228-0014
Ridgewood (G-13152)

Poppin Inc....................................D...... 212 391-7200
New York (G-10866)

Riverfront Costume Design................G...... 716 693-2501
North Tonawanda (G-12087)

Stylecraft Interiors Inc.....................F...... 516 487-2133
Great Neck (G-5427)

Wood Etc Inc..................................F...... 315 484-9663
Syracuse (G-15030)

CABINETS: Radio & Television, Metal

CIDC Corp.....................................F...... 718 342-5820
Glendale (G-5222)

CABINETS: Show, Display, Etc, Wood, Exc Refrigerated

Custom Design Kitchens Inc..............F...... 518 355-4446
Duanesburg (G-4044)

E F Thresh Inc................................G...... 315 437-7301
East Syracuse (G-4208)

Fleetwood Cabinet Co Inc..................G...... 516 379-2139
Brooklyn (G-1853)

Johnny Mica Inc..............................G...... 631 225-5213
Lindenhurst (G-6953)

Telesca-Heyman Inc.........................F...... 212 534-3442
New York (G-11450)

CABLE TELEVISION

Hearst Holdings Inc.........................F...... 212 649-2000
New York (G-9756)

Historic TW Inc..............................E...... 212 484-8000
New York (G-9794)

Time Warner Companies Inc...............D...... 212 484-8000
New York (G-11494)

CABLE TELEVISION PRDTS

Arcom Automatics LLC......................G...... 315 422-1230
Syracuse (G-14815)

Arrow-Communication Labs Inc..........B...... 315 422-1230
Syracuse (G-14818)

Belden Inc.....................................B...... 607 796-5600
Horseheads (G-6114)

Eagle Comtronics Inc.......................C...... 315 451-3313
Liverpool (G-7009)

Eeg Enterprises Inc.........................F...... 516 293-7472
Farmingdale (G-4624)

CABLE: Fiber

Fiber Instrument Sales Inc.................C...... 315 736-2206
Oriskany (G-12390)

Fiberone LLC..................................F...... 315 434-8877
East Syracuse (G-4211)

Laseoptics Corp..............................F...... 716 462-5078
Buffalo (G-2848)

Sphere Cables & Chips Inc................E...... 212 619-3132
New York (G-11322)

Triad Network Technologies...............E...... 585 924-8505
Victor (G-15439)

CABLE: Fiber Optic

Complete Fiber Solutions Inc.............G...... 718 828-8900
Bronx (G-1230)

Corning Incorporated.......................A...... 607 974-9000
Painted Post (G-12473)

Corning Incorporated.......................A...... 607 974-9000
Corning (G-3705)

Corning Incorporated.......................E...... 607 248-1200
Corning (G-3708)

Corning Specialty Mtls Inc................G...... 607 974-9000
Corning (G-3713)

Crhmdu Isulations LLC.....................G...... 516 353-7749
Port Washington (G-12870)

Fiberdyne Labs Inc..........................D...... 315 895-8470
Frankfort (G-4951)

TLC-The Light Connection Inc............D...... 315 736-7384
Oriskany (G-12399)

CABLE: Nonferrous, Shipboard

Monroe Cable Company Inc................C...... 845 692-2800
Middletown (G-7922)

CABLE: Noninsulated

Cortland Cable Company Inc..............E...... 607 753-8276
Cortland (G-3758)

J Davis Manufacturing Co Inc.............E...... 315 337-7574
Rome (G-13852)

Nexans Energy USA Inc.....................C...... 845 469-2141
Chester (G-3381)

Reelcology Inc...............................F...... 845 258-1880
Pine Island (G-12630)

Samzong Inc..................................G...... 718 475-1843
Monsey (G-8047)

Ultra Clarity Corp...........................G...... 719 470-1010
Spring Valley (G-14584)

Weico Wire & Cable Inc....................E...... 631 254-2970
Edgewood (G-4292)

CABLE: Ropes & Fiber

Cortland Company Inc.......................D...... 607 753-8276
Cortland (G-3759)

CABLE: Steel, Insulated Or Armored

Dragon Trading Inc..........................G...... 212 717-1496
New York (G-9265)

Dsr International Corp......................G...... 631 427-2600
Great Neck (G-5382)

CAGES: Wire

Renco Group Inc.............................G...... 212 541-6000
New York (G-11012)

CALCULATING & ACCOUNTING EQPT

Merchant Service Pymnt Access..........G...... 212 561-5516
Uniondale (G-15232)

CALIBRATING SVCS, NEC

Phymetrix Inc.................................G...... 631 627-3950
Medford (G-7721)

Quality Vision Services Inc................D...... 585 544-0450
Rochester (G-13662)

CAMERAS & RELATED EQPT: Photographic

Bescor Video Accessories Ltd.............F...... 631 420-1717
Farmingdale (G-4592)

Core Swx LLC.................................F...... 516 595-7488
Plainview (G-12675)

Easterncctv (usa) LLC......................F...... 516 870-3779
Plainview (G-12680)

Lake Image Systems Inc....................F...... 585 321-3630
Henrietta (G-12680)

Rear View Safety Inc........................E...... 855 815-3842
Brooklyn (G-2332)

Rosco Collision Avoidance Inc............G...... 718 526-2601
Jamaica (G-6472)

Watec America Corporation................E...... 702 434-6111
Middletown (G-7938)

CANDLE SHOPS

Candles By Foster...........................G...... 914 739-9226
Peekskill (G-12549)

Northern Lights Entps Inc.................C...... 800 836-8797
Wellsville (G-15673)

CANDLES

A & L Asset Management Ltd..............C...... 718 566-1500
Brooklyn (G-1428)

Astron Candle Manufacturing Co.........G...... 718 728-3330
Long Island City (G-7168)

Betterbee Inc.................................F...... 518 314-0575
Greenwich (G-5469)

Candle In The Window Inc.................F...... 718 852-5743
Brooklyn (G-1643)

Candles By Foster...........................G...... 914 739-9226
Peekskill (G-12549)

Cathedral Candle Co.........................D...... 315 422-9119
Syracuse (G-14846)

Crusader Candle Co Inc.....................E...... 718 625-0005
Brooklyn (G-1704)

Curiously Creative Candles................G...... 631 586-1700
Deer Park (G-3857)

Hs Homeworx LLC............................G...... 646 870-0406
New York (G-9830)

Joya LLC.......................................F...... 718 852-6979
Brooklyn (G-2005)

Kkw Corp......................................E...... 631 589-5454
Sayville (G-14228)

Lux Mundi Corp..............................G...... 631 244-4596
Bohemia (G-1040)

Muench-Kreuzer Candle Company.........D...... 315 471-4515
Syracuse (G-14947)

Northern Lights Entps Inc.................C...... 800 836-8797
Wellsville (G-15673)

Quality Candle Mfg Co Inc.................F...... 631 842-8475
Copiague (G-3672)

Simcha Candle Co Inc.......................G...... 845 783-0406
New Windsor (G-8383)

St Killians America Inc.....................G...... 917 648-4351
Valley Cottage (G-15324)

Thompson Ferrier LLC.......................G...... 212 244-2212
New York (G-11473)

TV Guilfoil & Associates Inc..............G...... 315 453-0920
Syracuse (G-15016)

CANDLES: Wholesalers

Candle In The Window Inc.................F...... 718 852-5743
Brooklyn (G-1643)

CANDY & CONFECTIONS: Cake Ornaments

Naples Vly Mrgers Acqstons LLC.........G...... 585 490-1339
Naples (G-8209)

OH How Cute Inc.............................G...... 347 838-6031
Staten Island (G-14687)

Pfeil & Holing Inc...........................D...... 718 545-4600
Woodside (G-16219)

CANDY & CONFECTIONS: Candy Bars, Including Chocolate Covered

Chocolate Delivery Systems Inc...........E...... 716 877-3146
Buffalo (G-2696)

Eatingevolved LLC...........................F...... 631 675-2440
Setauket (G-14379)

Fine and Raw Chocolate.....................G...... 718 366-3633
Brooklyn (G-1844)

N Make Mold Inc.............................G...... 716 877-3146
Buffalo (G-2878)

Vigneri Chocolate Inc.......................G...... 585 254-6160
Rochester (G-13797)

CANDY & CONFECTIONS: Chocolate Candy, Exc Solid Chocolate

Aigner Chocolates...........................G...... 718 544-1850
Forest Hills (G-4915)

PRODUCT

Amiram Dror Inc ....F 212 979-9505
Brooklyn (G-1504)

Chocolate Pizza Company Inc ....F 315 673-4098
Marcellus (G-7561)

Robert Pikcilingis ....F 518 355-1860
Altamont (G-198)

CANDY & CONFECTIONS: Halvah

Joyva Corp ....D 718 497-0170
Brooklyn (G-2006)

CANDY, NUT & CONFECTIONERY STORES: Candy

5th Avenue Chocolatiere Ltd ....G 212 935-5454
Freeport (G-4977)

Adirondack Chocolate Co Ltd ....F 518 946-7270
Wilmington (G-16152)

Amiram Dror Inc ....F 212 979-9505
Brooklyn (G-1504)

Commodore Chocolatier USA Inc ....F 845 561-3960
Newburgh (G-11861)

Ford Gum & Machine Company Inc ......D 716 542-4561
Akron (G-17)

Godiva Chocolatier Inc ....E 212 984-5900
New York (G-9636)

Hercules Candy Co ....G 315 463-4339
East Syracuse (G-4216)

Hudson Valley Chocolatier Inc ....F 845 831-8240
Beacon (G-753)

Jo-Mart Candies Corp ....F 718 375-1277
Brooklyn (G-1996)

Lady-N-Th-wndow Chocolates Inc ....F 631 549-1059
Huntington (G-6210)

Noras Candy Shop ....F 315 337-4530
Rome (G-13860)

Parkside Candy Co Inc ....F 716 833-7540
Buffalo (G-2907)

Roger L Urban Inc ....E 716 693-5391
North Tonawanda (G-12089)

Seaward Candies ....G 585 638-6761
Holley (G-6038)

The Chocolate Shop ....G 716 882-5055
Buffalo (G-3008)

CANDY: Chocolate From Cacao Beans

Adirondack Chocolate Co Ltd ....F 518 946-7270
Wilmington (G-16152)

Aigner Chocolates ....G 718 544-1850
Forest Hills (G-4915)

Chocolate Pizza Company Inc ....F 315 673-4098
Marcellus (G-7561)

Godiva Chocolatier Inc ....E 212 984-5900
New York (G-9636)

Roger L Urban Inc ....E 716 693-5391
North Tonawanda (G-12089)

Superior Confections Inc ....D 718 698-3300
Staten Island (G-14717)

CANNED SPECIALTIES

Global Food Source & Co Inc ....G 914 320-9615
Tuckahoe (G-15204)

Goya Foods Inc ....D 716 549-0076
Angola (G-359)

Grandma Browns Beans Inc ....F 315 963-7221
Mexico (G-7866)

Kawasho Foods USA Inc ....F 212 841-7400
New York (G-10080)

CANOPIES: Sheet Metal

Austin Mohawk and Company LLC ......E 315 793-3000
Utica (G-15239)

CANS: Aluminum

Anheuser-Busch Companies LLC ....G 718 589-2610
Bronx (G-1206)

Ball Metal Beverage Cont Corp ....C 845 692-3800
Middletown (G-7894)

Reynolds Metals Company LLC ....G 212 518-5400
New York (G-11031)

CANS: Metal

Arconic Fastening Systems ....F 585 368-5049
Rochester (G-13244)

Ardagh Metal Packaging USA Inc ....C 607 584-3300
Conklin (G-3621)

Ball Metal Beverage Cont Corp ....C 518 587-6030
Saratoga Springs (G-14165)

Brakewell Stl Fabricators Inc ....E 845 469-9131
Chester (G-3371)

Crown Cork & Seal Usa Inc ....C 845 343-9586
Middletown (G-7902)

Erie Engineered Products Inc ....E 716 206-0204
Lancaster (G-6805)

Hornet Group Inc ....D 845 858-6400
Port Jervis (G-12850)

J C Industries Inc ....E 631 420-1920
West Babylon (G-15716)

Metal Container Corporation ....C 845 567-1500
New Windsor (G-8372)

CANVAS PRDTS

Ace Canvas & Tent Corp ....F 631 981-9705
Ronkonkoma (G-13886)

Anchor Canvas LLC ....G 631 265-5602
Smithtown (G-14473)

Broadway Neon Sign Corp ....F 908 241-4177
Ronkonkoma (G-13918)

Coverall Manufacturing ....G 315 622-2852
Baldwinsville (G-546)

Custom European Imports Inc ....E 845 357-5718
Sloatsburg (G-14470)

Jag Manufacturing Inc ....F 518 762-9558
Johnstown (G-6620)

Ke Durasol Awnings Inc ....F 845 610-1100
Chester (G-3380)

Nationwide Tarps Incorporated ....D 518 843-1545
Amsterdam (G-341)

Point Canvas Company Inc ....G 607 692-4381
Whitney Point (G-16107)

Utility Canvas Inc ....G 845 255-9290
Gardiner (G-5132)

Y & A Trading Inc ....F 718 436-6333
Brooklyn (G-2598)

CANVAS PRDTS, WHOLESALE

Awning Mart Inc ....G 315 699-5928
Cicero (G-3416)

Brock Awnings Ltd ....F 631 765-5200
Hampton Bays (G-5533)

Point Canvas Company Inc ....G 607 692-4381
Whitney Point (G-16107)

CANVAS PRDTS: Convertible Tops, Car/Boat, Fm Purchased Mtrl

Automtive Uphl Cnvertible Tops ....G 914 961-4242
Tuckahoe (G-15203)

Mc Coy Tops and Interiors Inc ....G 718 458-5800
Woodside (G-16212)

Quantum Sails Rochester LLC ....G 585 342-5200
Rochester (G-13664)

CANVAS PRDTS: Shades, Made From Purchased Materials

Jo-Vin Decorators Inc ....E 718 441-9350
Woodhaven (G-16187)

Laminated Window Products Inc ....F 631 242-6883
Bay Shore (G-687)

CAPACITORS: Fixed Or Variable

General Electric Company ....B 518 746-5750
Hudson Falls (G-6187)

CAPACITORS: NEC

American Tchncal Ceramics Corp ....B 631 622-4700
Huntington Station (G-6238)

American Tchncal Ceramics Corp ....B 631 622-4700
Huntington Station (G-6237)

AVX Corporation ....D 716 372-6611
Olean (G-12223)

Electron Coil Inc ....D 607 336-7414
Norwich (G-12121)

Ems Development Corporation ....D 631 345-6200
Yaphank (G-16260)

Hipotronics Inc ....C 845 279-8091
Brewster (G-1151)

Kemet Properties LLC ....G 718 654-8079
Bronx (G-1290)

Knowles Cazenovia Inc ....C 315 655-8710
Cazenovia (G-3228)

MTK Electronics Inc ....E 631 924-7666
Medford (G-7720)

Passive-Plus Inc ....F 631 425-0938
Huntington (G-6216)

Russell Industries Inc ....G 516 536-5000
Lynbrook (G-7437)

Stk Electronics Inc ....E 315 655-8476
Cazenovia (G-3235)

Strux Corp ....E 516 768-3969
Lindenhurst (G-6976)

Tronser Inc ....G 315 655-9528
Cazenovia (G-3236)

Viking Technologies Ltd ....E 631 957-8000
Lindenhurst (G-6983)

Voltronics LLC ....E 410 749-2424
Cazenovia (G-3237)

CAPS & PLUGS: Electric, Attachment

Delfingen Us-New York Inc ....E 716 215-0300
Niagara Falls (G-11920)

Leviton Manufacturing Co Inc ....B 631 812-6000
Melville (G-7800)

CAR WASH EQPT

Cresent Services Inc ....G 585 657-4104
Bloomfield (G-944)

Econocraft Worldwide Mfg Inc ....G 914 966-2280
Yonkers (G-16305)

I A S National Inc ....E 631 423-6900
Huntington Station (G-6249)

Klee Corp ....G 585 272-0320
Rochester (G-13503)

Liquid Industries Inc ....G 716 628-2999
Niagara Falls (G-11947)

Metro Lube ....G 718 947-1167
Rego Park (G-13080)

Wetlook Detailing Inc ....G 212 390-8877
Brooklyn (G-2580)

CARBIDES

Carbide-Usa LLC ....G 607 331-9353
Elmira (G-4342)

Lakeshore Carbide Inc ....G 716 462-4349
Buffalo (G-2846)

Transport National Dev Inc ....E 716 662-0270
Orchard Park (G-12380)

CARBON & GRAPHITE PRDTS, NEC

Americarb Inc ....D 419 281-5800
Niagara Falls (G-11903)

Americarb International Corp ....G 419 281-5800
Niagara Falls (G-11904)

Carbon Graphite Materials Inc ....G 716 792-7979
Brocton (G-1180)

Carbonfree Chemicals Spe I LLC ....E 914 421-4900
White Plains (G-15989)

Go Blue Technologies Ltd ....G 631 404-6285
North Babylon (G-12001)

Hh Liquidating Corp ....A 646 282-2500
New York (G-9779)

Mwi Inc ....D 585 424-4200
Rochester (G-13564)

Pyrotek Incorporated ....E 716 731-3221
Sanborn (G-14148)

Xactiv Inc ....F 585 288-7220
Fairport (G-4531)

CARBONS: Electric

Metallized Carbon Corporation ....C 914 941-3738
Ossining (G-12404)

CARDBOARD PRDTS, EXC DIE-CUT

M C Packaging Corporation ....C 631 694-3012
Farmingdale (G-4674)

M C Packaging Corporation ....E 631 643-3763
Babylon (G-522)

CARDBOARD: Waterproof, Made From Purchased Materials

Ums Manufacturing LLC ....F 518 562-2410
Plattsburgh (G-12786)

CARDIOVASCULAR SYSTEM DRUGS, EXC DIAGNOSTIC

Mesoblast Inc ....G 212 880-2060
New York (G-10441)

Pfizer Inc ....A 212 733-2323
New York (G-10821)

CARDS: Beveled

Foster - Gordon Manufacturing ....G 631 589-6776
Bohemia (G-1013)

CARDS: Color

Mooney-Keehley Inc ....G 585 271-1573
Rochester (G-13559)
Tele-Pak Inc ....E 845 426-2300
Monsey (G-8053)

CARDS: Greeting

1/2 Off Cards Wantagh Inc ....G 516 809-9832
Wantagh (G-15482)
Anne Taintor Inc ....G 718 483-9312
Brooklyn (G-1512)
Avanti Press Inc ....E 212 414-1025
New York (G-8687)
Massimo Friedman Inc ....E 716 836-0408
Buffalo (G-2862)
Paper House Productions Inc ....E 845 246-7261
Saugerties (G-14207)
Paper Magic Group Inc ....B 631 521-3682
New York (G-10749)
Quotable Cards Inc ....G 212 420-7552
New York (G-10960)
Shade Tree Greetings Inc ....F 585 442-4580
Rochester (G-13725)

CARDS: Identification

Allsafe Technologies Inc ....D 716 691-0400
Amherst (G-208)
Alpha Incorporated ....G 718 765-1614
Brooklyn (G-1490)
Global Security Tech LLC ....F 917 838-4507
Cedarhurst (G-3239)
Iadc Inc ....F 718 238-0623
Staten Island (G-14663)
Metropltan Data Sltons MGT Inc ....E 516 586-5520
Farmingdale (G-4682)
Multi Packaging Solutions Inc ....E 646 885-0005
New York (G-10519)

CARPET DYEING & FINISHING

Eskayel Inc ....G 347 703-8084
Brooklyn (G-1812)

CARPETS & RUGS: Tufted

Interfaceflor LLC ....E 212 686-8284
New York (G-9915)

CARPETS, RUGS & FLOOR COVERING

Aladdin Manufacturing Corp ....C 212 561-8715
New York (G-8504)
Bloomsburg Carpet Inds Inc ....G 212 688-7447
New York (G-8814)
Carpet Fabrications Intl ....E 914 381-6060
Mamaroneck (G-7500)
Excellent Art Mfg Corp ....F 718 388-7075
Inwood (G-6292)
Kalati Company Inc ....G 516 423-9132
Great Neck (G-5397)
Loom Concepts LLC ....G 212 813-9586
New York (G-10253)
Lorena Canals USA Inc ....G 844 567-3622
Hastings On Hudson (G-5575)
Michaelian & Kohlberg Inc ....G 212 431-9009
New York (G-10454)
Northpoint Trading Inc ....F 212 481-8001
New York (G-10645)
Odegard Inc ....F 212 545-0069
Long Island City (G-7313)
Peter Racing ....E 914 968-4150
Yonkers (G-16341)
Rosecore Division ....F 516 504-4530
Great Neck (G-5418)
Shyam Ahuja Limited ....G 212 644-5910
New York (G-11221)
Sunrise Tile Inc ....G 718 939-0538
Flushing (G-4896)
Tdg Operations LLC ....G 212 779-4300
New York (G-11440)
Tiger 21 LLC ....G 212 360-1700
New York (G-11485)

Wells Rugs Inc ....G 516 676-2056
Glen Cove (G-5204)

CARPETS: Hand & Machine Made

Tsar USA LLC ....F 646 415-7968
New York (G-11555)

CARPETS: Textile Fiber

Scalamandre Silks Inc ....D 212 980-3888
New York (G-11147)

CARRIAGES: Horse Drawn

Tectran Inc ....G 800 776-5549
Cheektowaga (G-3364)

CARRYING CASES, WHOLESALE

Bristol Boarding Inc ....G 585 271-7860
Rochester (G-13283)
Sigma Worldwide LLC ....G 646 217-0629
New York (G-11231)

CARTONS: Egg, Molded Pulp, Made From Purchased Materials

Tri-Seal International Inc ....G 845 353-3300
Blauvelt (G-937)

CASEMENTS: Aluminum

Rohlfs Stined Leaded GL Studio ....E 914 699-4848
Mount Vernon (G-8178)

CASES, WOOD

Bragley Mfg Co Inc ....E 718 622-7469
Brooklyn (G-1605)

CASES: Attache'

Dlx Industries Inc ....D 718 272-9420
Brooklyn (G-1753)
Randa Accessories Lea Gds LLC ....D 212 354-5100
New York (G-10979)
Trafalgar Company LLC ....G 212 768-8800
New York (G-11531)

CASES: Carrying

Ead Cases ....F 845 343-2111
Middletown (G-7906)
Fieldtex Products Inc ....C 585 427-2940
Rochester (G-13409)
Merzon Leather Co Inc ....C 718 782-6260
Brooklyn (G-2144)
Sigma Worldwide LLC ....G 646 217-0629
New York (G-11231)
Three Point Ventures LLC ....F 585 697-3444
Rochester (G-13767)

CASES: Carrying, Clothing & Apparel

212 Biz LLC ....G 212 391-4444
New York (G-8393)
Calvin Klein Inc ....E 212 292-9000
New York (G-8894)
Donna Morgan LLC ....E 212 575-2550
New York (G-9251)
Rimowa Inc ....F 214 360-4268
New York (G-11044)

CASES: Jewelry

Ada Gems Corp ....G 212 719-0100
New York (G-8452)
Astucci US Ltd ....G 212 725-3171
New York (G-8658)
Bauble Bar Inc ....E 646 846-2044
New York (G-8740)
K Displays ....F 718 854-6045
Brooklyn (G-2017)
Unique Packaging Corporation ....G 514 341-5872
Champlain (G-3319)

CASES: Nonrefrigerated, Exc Wood

R H Guest Inc ....G 718 675-7600
Brooklyn (G-2319)

CASES: Packing, Nailed Or Lock Corner, Wood

Falvo Manufacturing Co Inc ....F 315 724-7925
Utica (G-15261)
Technical Packaging Inc ....F 516 223-2300
Baldwin (G-537)

CASES: Plastic

Bragley Mfg Co Inc ....E 718 622-7469
Brooklyn (G-1605)
Displays By Rioux Inc ....G 315 458-3639
North Syracuse (G-12039)
Hamlet Products Inc ....F 914 665-0307
Mount Vernon (G-8147)
Sigma Worldwide LLC ....G 646 217-0629
New York (G-11231)

CASES: Sample Cases

Fibre Case & Novelty Co Inc ....G 212 254-6060
New York (G-9488)
Progressive Fibre Products Co ....E 212 566-2720
New York (G-10906)

CASES: Shipping, Nailed Or Lock Corner, Wood

Bristol Boarding Inc ....G 585 271-7860
Rochester (G-13283)
McIntosh Box & Pallet Co Inc ....F 315 789-8750
Geneva (G-5159)

CASH REGISTER REPAIR SVCS

Precision Laser Technology LLC ....F 585 458-6208
Rochester (G-13637)
SPX Flow Us LLC ....D 585 436-5550
Rochester (G-13742)

CASINGS: Sheet Metal

Craft-Tech Mfg Corp ....G 631 563-4949
Bohemia (G-992)

CASKETS & ACCESS

Milso Industries Inc ....F 631 234-1133
Hauppauge (G-5719)
North Hudson Woodcraft Corp ....E 315 429-3105
Dolgeville (G-4024)

CASKETS WHOLESALERS

Milso Industries Inc ....F 631 234-1133
Hauppauge (G-5719)

CAST STONE: Concrete

Steindl Cast Stone Co Inc ....G 718 296-8530
Woodhaven (G-16188)

CASTERS

Dimanco Inc ....G 315 797-0470
Utica (G-15256)
Workshop Art Fabrication ....F 845 331-0385
Kingston (G-6723)

CASTINGS GRINDING: For The Trade

Grind ....G 646 558-3250
New York (G-9678)
Herbert Wolf Corp ....G 718 392-2424
Long Island City (G-7241)

CASTINGS: Aerospace Investment, Ferrous

Brinkman Precision Inc ....D 585 429-5001
West Henrietta (G-15788)
Cpp-Syracuse Inc ....E 315 687-0014
Chittenango (G-3406)
Worldwide Resources Inc ....F 718 760-5000
Brooklyn (G-2597)

CASTINGS: Aerospace, Aluminum

Broetje Automation-Usa Inc ....C 716 204-8640
Williamsville (G-16124)
Eastern Strategic Materials ....E 212 332-1619
New York (G-9306)

PRODUCT

CASTINGS: Aerospace, Nonferrous, Exc Aluminum

Summit Aerospace Inc ....G...... 718 433-1326
Long Island City *(G-7374)*

CASTINGS: Aluminum

Airflex Industrial Inc ....E...... 631 752-1234
Farmingdale *(G-4575)*

Armstrong Mold Corporation ....E...... 315 437-1517
East Syracuse *(G-4196)*

Armstrong Mold Corporation ....D...... 315 437-1517
East Syracuse *(G-4197)*

Hitachi Metals America Ltd ....E...... 914 694-9200
Purchase *(G-13005)*

J & J Bronze & Aluminum Cast ....E...... 718 383-2111
Brooklyn *(G-1976)*

Milward Alloys Inc ....E...... 716 434-5536
Lockport *(G-7093)*

Taylor Metalworks Inc ....C...... 716 662-3113
Orchard Park *(G-12378)*

CASTINGS: Bronze, NEC, Exc Die

Art Bedi-Makky Foundry Corp ....G...... 718 383-4191
Brooklyn *(G-1534)*

J & J Bronze & Aluminum Cast ....E...... 718 383-2111
Brooklyn *(G-1976)*

Modern Art Foundry Inc ....E...... 718 728-2030
Astoria *(G-430)*

CASTINGS: Die, Aluminum

Albest Metal Stamping Corp ....E...... 718 388-6000
Brooklyn *(G-1477)*

Crown Die Casting Corp ....E...... 914 667-5400
Mount Vernon *(G-8135)*

Greene Brass & Alum Fndry LLC ....G...... 607 656-4204
Bloomville *(G-954)*

Greenfield Industries Inc ....D...... 516 623-9230
Freeport *(G-5001)*

ITT Corporation ....D...... 315 568-2811
Seneca Falls *(G-14364)*

ITT LLC ....D...... 914 641-2000
Seneca Falls *(G-14368)*

Louis Iannettoni ....D...... 315 454-3231
Syracuse *(G-14936)*

Pinnacle Manufacturing Co Inc ....E...... 585 343-5664
Batavia *(G-623)*

Tpi Arcade Inc ....D...... 585 492-0122
Arcade *(G-382)*

CASTINGS: Die, Lead

American Casting and Mfg Corp ....D...... 800 342-0333
Plainview *(G-12662)*

American Casting and Mfg Corp ....G...... 516 349-7010
Plainview *(G-12663)*

CASTINGS: Die, Nonferrous

Albest Metal Stamping Corp ....E...... 718 388-6000
Brooklyn *(G-1477)*

AM Cast Inc ....F...... 631 750-1644
Bohemia *(G-970)*

Crown Die Casting Corp ....E...... 914 667-5400
Mount Vernon *(G-8135)*

Crown Novelty Works Inc ....G...... 631 253-0949
Melville *(G-7772)*

Mar-A-Thon Filters Inc ....G...... 631 957-4774
Lindenhurst *(G-6957)*

CASTINGS: Die, Zinc

Cast-All Corporation ....E...... 516 741-4025
Mineola *(G-7965)*

Greenfield Die Casting Corp ....E...... 516 623-9230
Freeport *(G-5000)*

Pinnacle Manufacturing Co Inc ....E...... 585 343-5664
Batavia *(G-623)*

CASTINGS: Ductile

Hitachi Metals America Ltd ....E...... 914 694-9200
Purchase *(G-13005)*

Jamestown Iron Works Inc ....F...... 716 665-2818
Falconer *(G-4548)*

Noresco Industrial Group Inc ....E...... 516 759-3355
Glen Cove *(G-5197)*

CASTINGS: Gray Iron

Auburn Foundry Inc ....F...... 315 253-4441
Auburn *(G-461)*

Speyside Foundry Holdings LLC ....G...... 212 994-0308
New York *(G-11319)*

CASTINGS: Machinery, Aluminum

Auto-Mate Technologies LLC ....F...... 631 727-8886
Riverhead *(G-13171)*

Corbett Stves Pttern Works Inc ....E...... 585 546-7109
Rochester *(G-13326)*

Ppi Corp ....D...... 585 243-0300
Rochester *(G-13633)*

CASTINGS: Machinery, Copper Or Copper-Base Alloy

Ross Precision Mfg Inc ....F...... 518 273-3912
Green Island *(G-5442)*

CASTINGS: Machinery, Nonferrous, Exc Die or Aluminum Copper

Plattco Corporation ....E...... 518 563-4640
Plattsburgh *(G-12768)*

Zierick Manufacturing Corp ....D...... 800 882-8020
Mount Kisco *(G-8108)*

CASTINGS: Precision

Buffalo Metal Casting Co Inc ....E...... 716 874-6211
Buffalo *(G-2677)*

Controlled Castings Corp ....E...... 516 349-1718
Plainview *(G-12673)*

Lamothermic Corp ....D...... 845 278-6118
Brewster *(G-1153)*

Miller Technology Inc ....G...... 631 694-2224
Farmingdale *(G-4684)*

Quality Castings Inc ....B...... 732 409-3203
Long Island City *(G-7335)*

CASTINGS: Steel

A & V Castings Inc ....G...... 212 997-0042
New York *(G-8412)*

Speyside Foundry Holdings LLC ....G...... 212 994-0308
New York *(G-11319)*

CATALOG & MAIL-ORDER HOUSES

Avcom of Virginia Inc ....D...... 585 924-4560
Victor *(G-15392)*

Iac/Interactivecorp ....A...... 212 314-7300
New York *(G-9851)*

Kate Spade Holdings LLC ....B...... 212 354-4900
New York *(G-10076)*

Lechler Laboratories Inc ....E...... 845 426-6800
Spring Valley *(G-14574)*

Rda Holding Co ....E...... 914 238-1000
New York *(G-10990)*

Valmont Inc ....F...... 212 685-1653
New York *(G-11636)*

CATALOG SHOWROOMS

Studio 21 LA Inc ....E...... 718 965-6579
Brooklyn *(G-2464)*

CATALYSTS: Chemical

Ames Goldsmith Corp ....F...... 518 792-7435
Glens Falls *(G-5239)*

Next Potential LLC ....G...... 401 742-5190
New York *(G-10619)*

Signa Chemistry Inc ....F...... 212 933-4101
New York *(G-11234)*

UOP LLC ....E...... 716 879-7600
Tonawanda *(G-15151)*

CATAPULTS

Catapult...G...... 323 839-6204
New York *(G-8934)*

Laser & Electron Beam Inc ....G...... 603 626-6080
New York *(G-10175)*

CATERERS

Delicious Foods Inc ....F...... 718 446-9352
Corona *(G-3738)*

Lifc Corp ....G...... 516 426-5737
Port Washington *(G-12900)*

Soutine Inc..G...... 212 496-1450
New York *(G-11306)*

Violettes Cellar LLC ....F...... 718 650-5050
Staten Island *(G-14728)*

CEMENT & CONCRETE RELATED PRDTS & EQPT: Bituminous

Presti Ready Mix Concrete Inc ....G...... 516 378-6006
Freeport *(G-5016)*

CEMENT ROCK: Crushed & Broken

Schaefer Entps Deposit Inc ....E...... 607 467-4990
Deposit *(G-4002)*

CEMENT: Heat Resistant

Roccera LLC...F...... 585 426-0887
Rochester *(G-13678)*

CEMENT: High Temperature, Refractory, Nonclay

Silicon Carbide Products Inc ....E...... 607 562-8599
Horseheads *(G-6137)*

CEMENT: Hydraulic

Lafarge North America Inc ....E...... 716 651-9235
Lancaster *(G-6813)*

Lafarge North America Inc ....E...... 716 772-2621
Lockport *(G-7087)*

Lafarge North America Inc ....D...... 914 930-3027
Buchanan *(G-2609)*

Lafarge North America Inc ....F...... 716 876-8788
Tonawanda *(G-15118)*

Upstone Materials Inc ....E...... 518 873-2275
Lewis *(G-6918)*

CEMENT: Masonry

Ciment St-Laurent Inc............................C...... 518 943-4040
Catskill *(G-3210)*

Lafarge Building Materials Inc..............F...... 518 756-5000
Ravena *(G-13068)*

CEMENT: Natural

Euro Gear (usa) Inc...............................G...... 518 578-1775
Plattsburgh *(G-12746)*

CEMENT: Portland

Holcim (us) Inc.......................................G...... 518 828-8478
Hudson *(G-6160)*

Lafarge North America Inc ....E...... 518 756-5000
Ravena *(G-13069)*

Lehigh Cement Company ....C...... 518 792-1137
Glens Falls *(G-5256)*

Lehigh Cement Company LLC................E...... 518 792-1137
Glens Falls *(G-5257)*

Pallette Stone Corporation.....................E...... 518 584-2421
Gansevoort *(G-5084)*

CEMETERY MEMORIAL DEALERS

Glen Plaza Marble & Gran Inc...............G...... 516 671-1100
Glen Cove *(G-5195)*

North Shore Monuments Inc...................G...... 516 759-2156
Glen Head *(G-5212)*

CERAMIC FIBER

Argosy Composite Advanced Mate.......F...... 212 268-0003
New York *(G-8622)*

Cetek Inc...E...... 845 452-3510
Poughkeepsie *(G-12948)*

Enrg Inc..F...... 716 873-2939
Buffalo *(G-2746)*

Heany Industries Inc ....D...... 585 889-2700
Scottsville *(G-14340)*

Starfire Systems Inc ....F...... 518 899-9336
Glenville *(G-5273)*

Ufx Holding I Corporation ....G...... 212 644-5900
New York *(G-11577)*

Ufx Holding II Corporation ....G...... 212 644-5900
New York *(G-11578)*

Unifrax Holding Co ....G...... 212 644-5900
New York *(G-11587)*

Unifrax I LLC...C...... 716 768-6500
Tonawanda *(G-15150)*

Unifrax I LLC...C...... 716 696-3000
Tonawanda *(G-15149)*

CERAMIC FLOOR & WALL TILE WHOLESALERS

Dal-Tile Corporation ....G....... 718 894-9574
Maspeth *(G-7604)*
Dal-Tile Corporation ....G....... 914 835-1801
Harrison *(G-5552)*

CHAIN: Welded, Made From Purchased Wire

All-Lifts Incorporated...................E....... 518 465-3461
Albany *(G-37)*
Columbus McKinnon Corporation ....C....... 716 689-5400
Getzville *(G-5174)*
Columbus McKinnon Corporation ....C....... 716 689-5400
Getzville *(G-5175)*
Columbus McKinnon Corporation ....C....... 716 689-5400
Getzville *(G-5176)*

CHAINS: Forged

Dragon Trading Inc ....G....... 212 717-1496
New York *(G-9265)*

CHAMBERS & CAISSONS

Hyperbaric Technologies Inc ....G....... 518 842-3030
Amsterdam *(G-330)*

CHANDELIERS: Commercial

Global Lighting Inc ....G....... 914 591-4095
Yonkers *(G-16313)*
Lite-Makers Inc...................E....... 718 739-9300
Jamaica *(G-6454)*
Sandy Littman Inc ....G 845 562-1112
Newburgh *(G-11886)*
Santucci Custom Lighting ....F....... 866 853-1929
Clinton *(G-3485)*

CHANDELIERS: Residential

Sandy Littman Inc ....G 845 562-1112
Newburgh *(G-11886)*
Swarovski Lighting Ltd ....B....... 518 324-6378
Plattsburgh *(G-12784)*

CHARCOAL: Activated

Calgon Carbon Corporation...................G....... 716 531-9113
North Tonawanda *(G-12061)*
Carbon Activated Corporation...............G....... 716 662-2005
Orchard Park *(G-12344)*

CHART & GRAPH DESIGN SVCS

Orcon Industries Corp...................D....... 585 768-7000
Le Roy *(G-6905)*

CHASSIS: Motor Vehicle

Wendys Auto Express Inc ....G....... 845 624-6100
Nanuet *(G-8204)*

CHEESE WHOLESALERS

Alps Provision Co Inc...................E....... 718 721-4477
Astoria *(G-414)*

CHEMICAL ELEMENTS

Leading Element LLC ....G....... 315 479-8790
Syracuse *(G-14929)*

CHEMICAL INDICATORS

LTS Inc...................F....... 845 494-2940
Orangeburg *(G-12322)*

CHEMICAL PROCESSING MACHINERY & EQPT

Charles Ross & Son Company ....D....... 631 234-0500
Hauppauge *(G-5614)*
Maharlika Holdings LLC ....F....... 631 319-6203
Ronkonkoma *(G-13968)*
National Equipment Corporation...........F....... 718 585-0200
Harrison *(G-5556)*
National Equipment Corporation...........E....... 718 585-0200
Bronx *(G-1321)*
Spectrum Catalysts Inc ....G....... 631 560-3683
Central Islip *(G-3288)*
Stainless Design Concepts Ltd ....E....... 845 246-3631
Saugerties *(G-14213)*

Surepure Inc...................G....... 917 368-8480
New York *(G-11399)*
West Metal Works Inc ....E....... 716 895-4900
Buffalo *(G-3045)*

CHEMICAL: Sodm Compnds/Salts, Inorg, Exc Rfnd Sodm Chloride

Chemtrade Chemicals US LLC ....G....... 315 478-2323
Syracuse *(G-14849)*

CHEMICALS & ALLIED PRDTS WHOLESALERS, NEC

Aithaca Chemical Corp...................F 516 229-2330
Uniondale *(G-15223)*
Caswell Inc ....F....... 315 946-1213
Lyons *(G-7447)*
Chemlube International LLC ....F....... 914 381-5800
Harrison *(G-5550)*
Chemlube Marketing Inc ....F....... 914 381-5800
Harrison *(G-5551)*
Ecological Laboratories Inc ....D....... 516 823-3441
Island Park *(G-6316)*
FBC Chemical Corporation ....G....... 716 681-1581
Lancaster *(G-6806)*
Finger Lakes Chemicals Inc...............E....... 585 454-4760
Rochester *(G-13410)*
Island Pyrochemical Inds Corp ....C....... 516 746-2100
Mineola *(G-7983)*
Jad Corp of America ....E....... 718 762-8900
College Point *(G-3548)*
Nalco Company LLC ....E....... 518 796-1985
Saratoga Springs *(G-14185)*
Poly Scientific R&D Corp ....E....... 631 586-0400
Bay Shore *(G-698)*
Tattersall Industries LLC ....E....... 518 381-4270
Schenectady *(G-14311)*
Thatcher Company New York Inc ....E....... 315 589-9330
Williamson *(G-16113)*
Water Wise of America Inc ....F....... 585 232-1210
Rochester *(G-13799)*

CHEMICALS & ALLIED PRDTS, WHOLESALE: Alkalines & Chlorine

Arcadia Chem Preservative LLC ....G....... 516 466-5258
Great Neck *(G-5366)*

CHEMICALS & ALLIED PRDTS, WHOLESALE: Anti-Corrosion Prdts

Engineering Maint Pdts Inc..................F 516 624-9774
Oyster Bay *(G-12447)*

CHEMICALS & ALLIED PRDTS, WHOLESALE: Aromatic

Classic Flavors Fragrances Inc.............G....... 212 777-0004
New York *(G-9025)*

CHEMICALS & ALLIED PRDTS, WHOLESALE: Chemical Additives

Mitsui Chemicals America Inc ....E....... 914 253-0777
Rye Brook *(G-14092)*

CHEMICALS & ALLIED PRDTS, WHOLESALE: Chemicals, Indl

Dynasty Chemical Corp...................E....... 518 463-1146
Menands *(G-7842)*
Umicore USA Inc...................E....... 919 874-7171
Glens Falls *(G-5268)*

CHEMICALS & ALLIED PRDTS, WHOLESALE: Detergent/Soap

US Nonwovens Corp ....D....... 631 952-0100
Brentwood *(G-1132)*

CHEMICALS & ALLIED PRDTS, WHOLESALE: Dry Ice

South Shore Ice Co Inc...................F....... 516 379-2056
Roosevelt *(G-14033)*

CHEMICALS & ALLIED PRDTS, WHOLESALE: Essential Oils

Flavormatic Industries LLC...................E....... 845 297-9100
Wappingers Falls *(G-15492)*

CHEMICALS & ALLIED PRDTS, WHOLESALE: Oxygen

Praxair Distribution Inc ....G....... 315 457-5821
Liverpool *(G-7034)*

CHEMICALS & ALLIED PRDTS, WHOLESALE: Plastics Materials, NEC

Ampac Paper LLC ....G....... 845 713-6600
Walden *(G-15456)*
Josh Packaging Inc ....E....... 631 822-1660
Hauppauge *(G-5681)*
Marval Industries Inc ....D....... 914 381-2400
Mamaroneck *(G-7514)*

CHEMICALS & ALLIED PRDTS, WHOLESALE: Plastics Prdts, NEC

Albea Cosmetics America Inc...............E....... 212 371-5100
New York *(G-8507)*
Autronic Plastics Inc ....C....... 516 333-7577
Central Islip *(G-3263)*
Broder Mfg Inc...................G....... 718 366-1667
Brooklyn *(G-1610)*
Vinyl Materials Inc ....E....... 631 586-9444
Deer Park *(G-3951)*

CHEMICALS & ALLIED PRDTS, WHOLESALE: Plastics Sheets & Rods

Astra Products Inc...................G....... 631 464-4747
Copiague *(G-3648)*

CHEMICALS & ALLIED PRDTS, WHOLESALE: Polyurethane Prdts

Vincent Manufacturing Co Inc ....F....... 315 823-0280
Little Falls *(G-6995)*

CHEMICALS & ALLIED PRDTS, WHOLESALE: Salts & Polishes, Indl

R Schleider Contracting Corp...............G....... 631 269-4249
Kings Park *(G-6676)*

CHEMICALS & ALLIED PRDTS, WHOLESALE: Spec Clean/Sanitation

Prestige Consmr Healthcare Inc...........D....... 914 524-6800
Tarrytown *(G-15054)*

CHEMICALS & ALLIED PRDTS, WHOLESALE: Syn Resin, Rub/Plastic

Clarence Resins and Chemicals...........G....... 716 406-9804
Clarence Center *(G-3444)*

CHEMICALS & ALLIED PRDTS, WHOLESALE: Waxes, Exc Petroleum

Collinite Corporation ....G....... 315 732-2282
Utica *(G-15245)*

CHEMICALS/ALLIED PRDTS, WHOL: Coal Tar Prdts, Prim/Intermdt

Castoleum Corporation...................F....... 914 664-5877
Mount Vernon *(G-8128)*

CHEMICALS: Agricultural

Agrochem Inc...................E....... 518 226-4850
Saratoga Springs *(G-14164)*
E I Du Pont De Nemours & Co ....C....... 718 761-0043
Staten Island *(G-14648)*
FMC Corporation ....E....... 716 735-3761
Middleport *(G-7888)*

CHEMICALS: Alcohols

Full Motion Beverage Inc ....G....... 631 585-1100
Plainview *(G-12686)*

PRODUCT

CHEMICALS: Aluminum Chloride

Vanchlor Company Inc ....F 716 434-2624
   Lockport (G-7117)
Vanchlor Company Inc ....F 716 434-2624
   Lockport (G-7118)

CHEMICALS: Aluminum Compounds

Benzsay & Harrison Inc ....G 518 895-2311
   Delanson (G-3958)
Somerville Acquisitions Co Inc ....F 845 856-5261
   Huguenot (G-6194)
Somerville Tech Group Inc ....D 908 782-9500
   Huguenot (G-6195)

CHEMICALS: Aluminum Oxide

Meliorum Technologies Inc ....G 585 313-0616
   Rochester (G-13541)

CHEMICALS: Brine

Texas Brine Company LLC ....G 585 495-6228
   Wyoming (G-16252)

CHEMICALS: Calcium & Calcium Compounds

Minerals Technologies Inc ....E 212 878-1800
   New York (G-10476)

CHEMICALS: Compounds Or Salts, Iron, Ferric Or Ferrous

North American Hoganas Inc ....E 716 285-3451
   Niagara Falls (G-11956)

CHEMICALS: Fire Retardant

Flame Control Coatings LLC ....E 716 282-1399
   Niagara Falls (G-11929)
Gordon Fire Equipment LLC ....G 845 691-5700
   Highland (G-5959)
International Fire-Shield Inc ....F 315 255-1006
   Auburn (G-479)
Kent Chemical Corporation ....E 212 521-1700
   New York (G-10094)
Safeguard Inc ....F 631 929-3273
   Wading River (G-15451)
Supresta US LLC ....E 914 674-9434
   Ardsley (G-390)

CHEMICALS: Formaldehyde

Hexion Inc ....E 518 792-8040
   South Glens Falls (G-14513)
Oak-Bark Corporation ....G 518 372-5691
   Scotia (G-14335)

CHEMICALS: Fuel Tank Or Engine Cleaning

Amtek Research LLC ....E 416 400-2906
   Niagara Falls (G-11905)

CHEMICALS: High Purity Grade, Organic

Molecular Glasses Inc ....G 585 210-2861
   Rochester (G-13556)

CHEMICALS: High Purity, Refined From Technical Grade

Aithaca Chemical Corp ....F 516 229-2330
   Uniondale (G-15223)
Germanium Corp America Inc ....F 315 853-4900
   Clinton (G-3482)

CHEMICALS: Hydrogen Peroxide

US Peroxide ....G 716 775-5585
   Grand Island (G-5347)

CHEMICALS: Inorganic, NEC

Amtek Research LLC ....E 416 400-2906
   Niagara Falls (G-11905)
Anchor Commerce Trading Corp ....G 516 881-3485
   Atlantic Beach (G-452)
Arch Chemicals Inc ....C 585 436-3030
   Rochester (G-13243)
Arkema Inc ....C 585 243-6359
   Piffard (G-12623)

Auterra Inc ....G 518 382-9600
   Schenectady (G-14246)
Byk USA Inc ....E 845 469-5800
   Chester (G-3372)
Carbon Activated Corporation ....E 716 677-6661
   Blasdell (G-918)
CB Minerals LLC ....F 914 777-3330
   Mamaroneck (G-7502)
Cerion Energy Inc ....E 585 271-5630
   Rochester (G-13308)
Cerion LLC ....F 585 271-5630
   Rochester (G-13309)
Chemtrade Chemicals US LLC ....E 315 430-7650
   Syracuse (G-14848)
Danisco US Inc ....D 585 277-4300
   Rochester (G-13338)
Dynasty Chemical Corp ....E 518 463-1146
   Menands (G-7842)
Element St Johns Corp ....G 917 349-2139
   Brooklyn (G-1794)
Elementis Srl Inc ....C 845 692-3914
   Huguenot (G-6193)
Esm Group Inc ....F 716 446-8914
   Amherst (G-222)
Esm Group Inc ....G 724 265-1766
   Buffalo (G-2749)
Esm Special Metals & Tech Inc ....F 716 446-8914
   Amherst (G-224)
Ferro Corporation ....E 585 586-8770
   East Rochester (G-4162)
Ferro Corporation ....C 315 536-3357
   Penn Yan (G-12582)
Ferro Electronics Materials ....E 716 278-9400
   Niagara Falls (G-11928)
FMC Corporation ....E 716 735-3761
   Middleport (G-7888)
Hampshire Chemical Corp ....D 315 539-9221
   Waterloo (G-15554)
Innovative Municipal Pdts US ....E 800 387-5777
   Glenmont (G-5237)
Kowa American Corporation ....E 212 303-7800
   New York (G-10131)
Lawn Elements Inc ....F 631 656-9711
   Holbrook (G-6005)
Moog Inc ....D 716 731-6300
   Niagara Falls (G-11952)
Multisorb Tech Intl LLC ....G 716 824-8900
   Buffalo (G-2875)
Multisorb Technologies Inc ....E 716 656-1402
   Buffalo (G-2876)
New Mountain Capital LLC ....D 212 720-0300
   New York (G-10587)
Nouryon Surface Chemistry ....C 914 674-5008
   Dobbs Ferry (G-4018)
Poly Scientific R&D Corp ....E 631 586-0400
   Bay Shore (G-698)
Polyset Company Inc ....E 518 664-6000
   Mechanicville (G-7693)
S E A Supplies Ltd ....F 516 694-6677
   Plainview (G-12712)
Scientific Polymer Products ....G 585 265-0413
   Ontario (G-12302)
Specialty Minerals Inc ....E 518 585-7982
   Ticonderoga (G-15076)
Srlh Holdings Inc ....C 929 529-7951
   Huguenot (G-6196)
Tangram Company LLC ....E 631 758-0460
   Holtsville (G-6055)
Thatcher Company New York Inc ....E 315 589-9330
   Williamson (G-14113)
Washingtom Mills Elec Mnrls ....D 716 278-6600
   Niagara Falls (G-11991)

CHEMICALS: Isotopes, Radioactive

Isonics Corporation ....G 212 356-7400
   New York (G-9946)

CHEMICALS: Lithium Compounds, Inorganic

Alpha-En Corporation ....G 914 418-2000
   Yonkers (G-16282)

CHEMICALS: Medicinal

Biobat Inc ....G 718 270-1011
   Brooklyn (G-1589)
Biotemper Inc ....G 516 302-7985
   Carle Place (G-3172)
Matys Healthy Products LLC ....G 585 218-0507
   Pittsford (G-12651)

Proper Chemical Ltd ....G 631 420-8000
   Farmingdale (G-4718)

CHEMICALS: Medicinal, Organic, Uncompounded, Bulk

Asept Pak Inc ....E 518 651-2026
   Malone (G-7483)
Good Earth Inc ....G 716 684-8111
   Lancaster (G-6808)

CHEMICALS: NEC

Anabec Inc ....G 716 759-1674
   Clarence (G-3425)
Ask Chemicals Hi-Tech LLC ....C 607 587-9146
   Alfred Station (G-183)
Balchem Corporation ....B 845 326-5600
   New Hampton (G-8232)
Barson Composites Corporation ....E 516 752-7882
   Old Bethpage (G-12215)
Bcp Ingredients Inc ....D 845 326-5600
   New Hampton (G-8233)
Bonide Products LLC ....G 315 736-8231
   Oriskany (G-12384)
C & A Service Inc ....G 516 354-1200
   Floral Park (G-4810)
Calfonex Company ....F 845 778-2212
   Walden (G-15458)
Citrus and Allied Essences Ltd ....E 516 354-1200
   Floral Park (G-4812)
Classic Flavors Fragrances Inc ....G 212 777-0004
   New York (G-9025)
Danisco US Inc ....D 585 256-5200
   Rochester (G-13337)
Fitzsimmons Systems Inc ....F 315 214-7010
   Cazenovia (G-3227)
Hampshire Chemical Corp ....D 315 539-9221
   Waterloo (G-15554)
I A S National Inc ....E 631 423-6900
   Huntington Station (G-6249)
Indium Corporation of America ....E 315 793-8200
   Utica (G-15275)
Instrumentation Laboratory Co ....C 845 680-0028
   Orangeburg (G-12321)
Kaneka America LLC ....D 212 705-4340
   New York (G-10066)
Kemper System America Inc ....D 716 558-2971
   West Seneca (G-15851)
Micro Powders Inc ....E 914 332-6400
   Tarrytown (G-15048)
Momentive Performance LLC ....G 281 325-3536
   Waterford (G-15541)
Momentive Performance Mtls Inc ....D 914 784-4807
   Tarrytown (G-15049)
Monroe Fluid Technology Inc ....E 585 392-3434
   Hilton (G-5973)
Nalco Company LLC ....G 518 796-1985
   Saratoga Springs (G-14185)
New Fine Chemicals Inc ....E 631 321-8151
   Lindenhurst (G-6963)
Nouryon Surface Chemistry ....G 716 778-8554
   Burt (G-3060)
Nouryon Surface Chemistry ....C 914 674-5008
   Dobbs Ferry (G-4018)
Pure Kemika LLC ....G 718 745-2200
   Bellmore (G-787)
PVS Chemical Solutions Inc ....D 716 825-5762
   Buffalo (G-2938)
Reddi Car Corp ....G 631 589-3141
   Sayville (G-14231)
Rochester Midland Corporation ....C 585 336-2200
   Rochester (G-13690)
Royce Associates A Ltd Partnr ....G 516 367-6298
   Jericho (G-6593)
Solenis LLC ....G 315 461-4730
   Liverpool (G-7040)
Tam Ceramics LLC ....D 716 278-9480
   Niagara Falls (G-11985)
Tangram Company LLC ....E 631 758-0460
   Holtsville (G-6055)
US Polychemical Holding Corp ....E 845 356-5530
   Spring Valley (G-14587)
Utility Manufacturing Co Inc ....E 516 997-6300
   Westbury (G-15936)
Venue Graphics Supply Inc ....F 718 361-1690
   Long Island City (G-7393)
Wyeth Holdings LLC ....D 845 602-5000
   Pearl River (G-12543)
Yiwen Usa Inc ....F 212 370-0828
   New York (G-11810)

CHEMICALS: Organic, NEC

Akzo Nobel Chemicals LLC ....G....... 845 276-8200
Brewster (G-1139)

Ames Goldsmith Corp ....F..... 518 792-7435
Glens Falls (G-5239)

Arcadia Chem Preservative LLC ....G..... 516 466-5258
Great Neck (G-5366)

Arkema Inc ....C..... 585 243-6359
Piffard (G-12623)

BASF Corporation ....B..... 914 737-2554
Peekskill (G-12548)

BASF Corporation ....F..... 914 785-2000
Tarrytown (G-15041)

BASF Corporation ....B..... 518 465-6534
Rensselaer (G-13087)

BASF Corporation ....C..... 631 689-0200
East Setauket (G-4177)

Caltex International Ltd ....E..... 315 425-1040
Syracuse (G-14840)

China Ruitai Intl Holdings Ltd.............G....... 718 740-2278
Hollis (G-6041)

Danisco US Inc ....D..... 585 256-5200
Rochester (G-13337)

Enviro Service & Supply Corp ....F 347 838-6500
Staten Island (G-14651)

Evonik Corporation ....E..... 518 233-7090
Waterford (G-15536)

Genencor International Inc ....G..... 585 256-5200
Rochester (G-13432)

Hampshire Chemical Corp ....D..... 315 539-9221
Waterloo (G-15554)

Henpecked Husband Farms Corp ....G..... 631 728-2800
Speonk (G-14562)

International Mtls & Sups Inc..............G..... 518 834-9899
Keeseville (G-6642)

Islechem LLC ....E..... 716 773-8401
Grand Island (G-5334)

Jos H Lowenstein and Sons Inc ....D..... 718 388-5410
Brooklyn (G-2000)

Marval Industries Inc ....D..... 914 381-2400
Mamaroneck (G-7514)

Nouryon Functional Chem LLC ....D..... 845 276-8200
Brewster (G-1156)

Nouryon Surface Chemistry ....G..... 716 778-8554
Burt (G-3060)

Poly Scientific R&D Corp ....E..... 631 586-0400
Bay Shore (G-698)

Polymer Slutions Group Fin LLC ....G..... 212 771-1717
New York (G-10863)

Rose Solomon Co ....E..... 718 855-1788
Brooklyn (G-2355)

Royce Associates A Ltd Partnr ....G..... 516 367-6298
Jericho (G-6593)

Solvents Company Inc ....F..... 631 595-9300
Kingston (G-6709)

Telechemische Inc ....G..... 845 561-3237
Newburgh (G-11889)

Twin Lake Chemical Inc ....F..... 716 433-3824
Lockport (G-7115)

United Biochemicals LLC....................E..... 716 731-5161
Sanborn (G-14151)

Vandemark Chemical Inc....................D..... 716 433-6764
Lockport (G-7119)

CHEMICALS: Phenol

Si Group Inc.......................................C..... 518 347-4200
Schenectady (G-14304)

Si Group Inc.......................................C..... 518 347-4200
Rotterdam Junction (G-14060)

CHEMICALS: Silica Compounds

Precision Elctro Mnrl Pmco Inc ....E..... 716 284-2484
Niagara Falls (G-11968)

CHEMICALS: Sodium Bicarbonate

Church & Dwight Co Inc.....................F..... 518 887-5109
Schenectady (G-14255)

CHEMICALS: Sodium/Potassium Cmpnds,Exc Bleach,Alkalies/Alum

Tibro Water Technologies Ltd..............F..... 647 426-3415
Sherrill (G-14408)

CHEMICALS: Sulfur Chloride

PVS Chemical Solutions Inc ....D..... 716 825-5762
Buffalo (G-2938)

Sabre Energy Services LLC ....F....... 518 514-1572
Slingerlands (G-14467)

CHEMICALS: Water Treatment

Coventya Inc ....D....... 216 351-1500
Oriskany (G-12386)

Crystal Fusion Tech Inc ....E..... 631 253-9800
Lindenhurst (G-6946)

Cytec Industries Inc ....D..... 716 372-9650
Olean (G-12231)

Ecological Laboratories Inc ....D..... 516 823-3441
Island Park (G-6316)

Halfmoon Town Water Department .....G..... 518 233-7489
Waterford (G-15537)

Solenis LLC ....G..... 718 383-1717
Brooklyn (G-2440)

Water Wise of America Inc ....F..... 585 232-1210
Rochester (G-13799)

CHEWING GUM

Ford Gum & Machine Company Inc ......D..... 716 542-4561
Akron (G-17)

Sweetworks Inc ....C..... 716 634-4545
Buffalo (G-2998)

CHILD DAY CARE SVCS

Parents Guide Network Corp ....E..... 212 213-8840
New York (G-10757)

CHILDREN'S & INFANTS' CLOTHING STORES

Slims Bagels Unlimited Inc ....E..... 718 229-1140
Oakland Gardens (G-12160)

CHILDREN'S WEAR STORES

JM Originals Inc ....C..... 845 647-3003
Ellenville (G-4307)

S & C Bridal LLC ....F..... 212 789-7000
New York (G-11104)

S & C Bridals LLC ....E..... 213 624-4477
New York (G-11105)

CHIMES: Electric

Analog Digital Technology LLC...........G..... 585 698-1845
Rochester (G-13235)

Ingham Industries Inc ....G..... 631 242-2493
Holbrook (G-6001)

CHIMNEY CAPS: Concrete

American Chimney Supplies Inc ....G..... 631 434-2020
Hauppauge (G-5588)

CHIMNEYS & FITTINGS

American Chimney Supplies Inc ....G..... 631 434-2020
Hauppauge (G-5588)

Chimney Doctors Americas Corp.........G..... 631 868-3586
Bayport (G-728)

CHINA COOKWARE

Prime Cook (wttc) Inc ....G..... 646 881-0068
Flushing (G-4888)

Swissmar Inc ....G..... 905 764-1121
Niagara Falls (G-11983)

CHLORINE

Indian Springs Mfg Co Inc ....F 315 635-6101
Baldwinsville (G-549)

Occidental Chemical Corp ....C..... 716 278-7794
Niagara Falls (G-11960)

CHOCOLATE, EXC CANDY FROM BEANS: Chips, Powder, Block, Syrup

5th Avenue Chocolatiere Ltd ....G..... 212 935-5454
Freeport (G-4977)

Associated Brands Inc ....B..... 585 798-3475
Medina (G-7727)

Big Heart Pet Brands ....E..... 716 891-6566
Buffalo (G-2664)

Eating Evolved Inc ....G..... 516 510-2601
Hauppauge (G-5643)

Jo-Mart Candies Corp ....F..... 718 375-1277
Brooklyn (G-1996)

Joyva Corp ....D..... 718 497-0170
Brooklyn (G-2006)

Lanco Corporation ....C..... 631 231-2300
Ronkonkoma (G-13964)

Momn Pops Inc ....E..... 845 567-0640
Cornwall (G-3729)

Noras Candy Shop ....F..... 315 337-4530
Rome (G-13860)

Robert Pikcilingis ....F..... 518 355-1860
Altamont (G-198)

Settons Intl Foods Inc ....D..... 631 543-8090
Commack (G-3598)

Simply Natural Foods LLC ....C..... 631 543-9600
Commack (G-3599)

The Chocolate Shop ....G..... 716 882-5055
Buffalo (G-3008)

CHOCOLATE, EXC CANDY FROM PURCH CHOC: Chips, Powder, Block

5th Avenue Chocolatiere LLC ....E..... 516 868-8070
Freeport (G-4976)

Aethera LLC ....E..... 215 324-9222
New York (G-8489)

Chocolate Lady LLC ....G..... 516 532-0551
Port Jervis (G-12845)

Commodore Chocolatier USA Inc ....F..... 845 561-3960
Newburgh (G-11861)

Ctac Holdings LLC ....E..... 212 924-2280
Brooklyn (G-1707)

Dilese International Inc ....F..... 716 855-3500
Buffalo (G-2729)

Dolce Vite International LLC ....F..... 713 962-5767
Brooklyn (G-1754)

Doma Marketing Inc ....G..... 516 684-1111
Port Washington (G-12874)

Emvi Inc ....E..... 518 883-5111
Broadalbin (G-1173)

Greenwood Winery LLC ....E..... 315 432-8132
East Syracuse (G-4213)

Lady-N-Th-wndow Chocolates Inc ....F..... 631 549-1059
Huntington (G-6210)

Le Chocolate of Rockland LLC ....E..... 845 533-4125
Suffern (G-14762)

LMC 49th Inc.....................................E..... 718 361-9161
Long Island City (G-7277)

LMC 49th Inc.....................................F..... 212 744-7117
New York (G-10237)

Menrose USA LLC ....G..... 718 221-5540
Brooklyn (G-2137)

Nibmor Project LLC ....F..... 718 374-5091
Great Neck (G-5405)

Reserve Confections Inc ....F..... 845 371-7744
Spring Valley (G-14581)

Sweetworks Inc ....C..... 716 634-4545
Buffalo (G-2998)

Van Rip Inc ....E..... 415 529-5403
Brooklyn (G-2553)

Yes Were Nuts Ltd ....G..... 516 374-1940
Hewlett (G-5877)

CHRISTMAS TREE LIGHTING SETS: Electric

Rbw Studio LLC ....E..... 212 388-1621
Brooklyn (G-2331)

CHUCKS

Northfeld Precision Instr Corp.............E..... 516 431-1112
Island Park (G-6321)

CHURCHES

Christian Press Inc ....G..... 718 886-4400
Flushing (G-4843)

CHUTES & TROUGHS

Sargent Manufacturing Inc..................G....... 212 722-7000
New York (G-11137)

CHUTES: Coal, Sheet Metal, Prefabricated

Fenton Mobility Products Inc...............G..... 716 484-7014
Randolph (G-13062)

CIGAR LIGHTERS EXC PRECIOUS METAL

Arcadia Mfg Group Inc ....E..... 518 434-6213
Green Island (G-5432)

Arcadia Mfg Group Inc ....G..... 518 434-6213
Menands (G-7840)

PRODUCT

CIGARETTE & CIGAR PRDTS & ACCESS

Iquit Cig LLC.................................G....... 718 475-1422
Brooklyn (G-1969)

Saakshi Inc..................................G....... 315 475-3988
Syracuse (G-14982)

CIRCUIT BOARDS, PRINTED: Television & Radio

Buffalo Circuits Inc......................G....... 716 662-2113
Orchard Park (G-12342)

Kendall Circuits Inc.....................E....... 631 473-3636
Mount Sinai (G-8115)

Sanmina Corporation...................B....... 607 689-5000
Owego (G-12437)

TCS Electronics Inc....................E....... 585 337-4301
Farmington (G-4779)

CIRCUIT BOARDS: Wiring

Coast To Coast Circuits Inc..........E....... 585 254-2980
Rochester (G-13319)

Nationwide Circuits Inc................E....... 585 328-0791
Rochester (G-13566)

Stever-Locke Industries Inc.........G....... 585 624-3450
Honeoye Falls (G-6081)

CIRCUIT BREAKERS

Schneider Electric Usa Inc...........G....... 631 567-5710
Bohemia (G-1073)

CIRCUITS, INTEGRATED: Hybrid

Crystalonics Inc.........................F....... 631 981-6140
Ronkonkoma (G-13927)

Emtron Hybrids Inc......................F....... 631 924-9668
Yaphank (G-16261)

General Microwave Corporation.....F....... 516 802-0900
Syosset (G-14789)

CIRCUITS: Electronic

A K Allen Co Inc.........................C....... 516 747-5450
Melville (G-7753)

A R V Precision Mfg Inc................G....... 631 293-9643
Farmingdale (G-4569)

Accessories For Electronics..........F....... 631 847-0158
South Hempstead (G-14519)

Adco Circuits Inc........................G....... 716 668-6600
Buffalo (G-2620)

Advance Circuit Technology Inc.....E....... 585 328-2000
Rochester (G-13208)

All Shore Industries Inc................F....... 718 720-0018
Staten Island (G-14617)

Alloy Machine & Tool Co Inc..........G....... 516 593-3445
Lynbrook (G-7425)

American Quality Technology.........F....... 607 777-9488
Binghamton (G-853)

Anaren Inc.................................B....... 315 432-8909
East Syracuse (G-4195)

B H M Metal Products Co...............G....... 845 292-5297
Kauneonga Lake (G-6640)

Canfield Electronics Inc...............E....... 631 585-4100
Lindenhurst (G-6944)

Celmet Co..................................G....... 585 647-1760
Newark (G-11839)

Centroid Inc...............................E....... 516 349-0070
Plainview (G-12667)

Chiplogic Inc..............................F....... 631 617-6317
Yaphank (G-16257)

Cloud Toronto Inc........................F....... 408 569-4542
Williamsville (G-16127)

Cobham Long Island Inc...............B....... 516 694-6700
Plainview (G-12669)

Cobham Long Island Inc...............C....... 631 231-9100
Hauppauge (G-5619)

Dynamic Hybirds Inc....................G....... 315 426-8110
Syracuse (G-14879)

Eastland Electronics Co Inc..........G....... 631 580-3800
Shirley (G-14419)

Espey Mfg & Electronics Corp........C....... 518 584-4100
Saratoga Springs (G-14172)

Exc Holdings I Corp.....................A....... 212 644-5900
New York (G-9438)

Exc Holdings II Corp....................A....... 212 644-5900
New York (G-9439)

Exc Holdings LP..........................G....... 212 644-5900
New York (G-9440)

Fei Communications Inc................C....... 516 794-4500
Uniondale (G-15227)

Hudson Valley Tech Dev Ctr Inc......F....... 845 391-8214
Highland (G-5960)

Hypres Inc.................................E....... 914 592-1190
Elmsford (G-4411)

IEC Electronics Corp....................B....... 315 331-7742
Newark (G-11841)

IEC Electronics Wire Cable Inc.......D....... 585 924-9010
Newark (G-11842)

Imrex LLC..................................B....... 516 479-3675
Oyster Bay (G-12448)

Island Circuits International...........G....... 516 625-5555
College Point (G-3547)

Island Research and Dev Corp........D....... 631 471-7100
Ronkonkoma (G-13949)

Jenlor Ltd..................................F....... 315 637-9080
Fayetteville (G-4784)

Keltron Electronics (de Corp)..........F....... 631 567-6300
Ronkonkoma (G-13956)

Logitek Inc.................................D....... 631 567-1100
Bohemia (G-1035)

Marcon Electronic Systems LLC......G....... 516 633-6396
Freeport (G-5005)

Mekatronics Incorporated.............E....... 516 883-6805
Port Washington (G-12907)

Merit Electronic Design Co Inc.......C....... 631 667-9699
Edgewood (G-4275)

Mid Hdson Wkshp For The Dsbled....E....... 845 471-3820
Poughkeepsie (G-12970)

Mirion Technologies Ist Corp..........D....... 607 562-4300
Horseheads (G-6128)

Nelson Holdings Ltd.....................F....... 607 772-1794
Binghamton (G-901)

Oakdale Industrial Elec Corp..........F....... 631 737-4092
Ronkonkoma (G-13984)

Opus Technology Corporation.........F....... 631 271-1883
Melville (G-7812)

Pcb Piezotronics Inc.....................B....... 716 684-0003
Depew (G-3994)

Polycast Industries Inc..................G....... 631 595-2530
Bay Shore (G-699)

Precision Assembly Tech Inc...........E....... 631 699-9400
Bohemia (G-1063)

Premier Systems LLC...................G....... 631 587-9700
Babylon (G-524)

Quality Contract Assemblies...........F....... 585 663-9030
Rochester (G-13659)

R L C Electronics Inc....................D....... 914 241-1334
Mount Kisco (G-8103)

Rdi Inc......................................F....... 914 773-1000
Mount Kisco (G-8104)

Rem-Tronics Inc..........................D....... 716 934-2697
Dunkirk (G-4064)

Rochester Industrial Ctrl Inc..........D....... 315 524-4555
Ontario (G-12301)

Rochester Industrial Ctrl Inc..........D....... 315 524-4555
Ontario (G-12300)

Scientific Components Corp............B....... 718 368-2060
Brooklyn (G-2391)

Sonaer Inc.................................G....... 631 756-4780
West Babylon (G-15747)

Sopark Corp...............................D....... 716 822-0434
Buffalo (G-2987)

Space Coast Semiconductor Inc......F....... 631 414-7131
Farmingdale (G-4736)

Stetron International Inc................F....... 716 854-3443
Buffalo (G-2993)

Surmotech LLC...........................D....... 585 742-1220
Victor (G-15433)

T-S-K Electronics Inc....................G....... 716 693-3916
North Tonawanda (G-12093)

Te Connectivity Corporation...........E....... 585 785-2500
Rochester (G-13760)

Telephonics Corporation...............E....... 631 549-6000
Huntington (G-6226)

Telephonics Corporation...............A....... 631 755-7000
Farmingdale (G-4752)

Tlsi Incorporated.........................D....... 631 470-8880
Huntington (G-6229)

Torotron Corporation....................G....... 718 428-6992
Fresh Meadows (G-5047)

Trading Services International.........F....... 212 501-0142
New York (G-11530)

Unison Industries LLC...................B....... 607 335-5000
Norwich (G-12130)

Vestal Electronic Devices LLC.........F....... 607 773-8461
Endicott (G-4477)

Xedit Corp..................................G....... 718 380-1592
Queens Village (G-13028)

CIRCULAR KNIT FABRICS DYEING & FINISHING

A-One Moving & Storage Inc..........E....... 718 266-6002
Brooklyn (G-1443)

Gehring Tricot Corporation.............C....... 315 429-8551
Dolgeville (G-4023)

Lifestyle Design Usa Ltd...............G....... 212 279-9400
New York (G-10214)

CLAMPS & COUPLINGS: Hose

United Metal Industries Inc............G....... 516 354-6800
New Hyde Park (G-8299)

CLAY PRDTS: Architectural

Jq Woodworking Inc.....................G....... 516 766-3424
Oceanside (G-12177)

Lenon Models Inc.........................G....... 212 229-1581
Bronx (G-1301)

CLAYS, EXC KAOLIN & BALL

Applied Minerals Inc.....................F....... 212 226-4265
Brooklyn (G-1520)

CLEANING EQPT: Blast, Dustless

Cleaning Tech Group LLC...............E....... 716 665-2340
Jamestown (G-6502)

CLEANING EQPT: Carpet Sweepers, Exc Household Elec Vacuum

American Comfort Direct LLC..........E....... 201 364-8309
New York (G-8548)

CLEANING EQPT: Commercial

Oxford Cleaners..........................G....... 212 734-0006
New York (G-10724)

CLEANING EQPT: High Pressure

Custom Klean Corp.......................F....... 315 865-8101
Holland Patent (G-6033)

Power Scrub It Inc........................F....... 516 997-2500
Westbury (G-15918)

CLEANING OR POLISHING PREPARATIONS, NEC

American Wax Company Inc............E....... 718 392-8080
Long Island City (G-7156)

Car-Freshner Corporation..............D....... 315 788-6250
Watertown (G-15563)

Chemclean Corporation.................E....... 718 525-4500
Jamaica (G-6432)

Clean All of Syracuse LLC..............G....... 315 472-9189
Syracuse (G-14852)

Collinite Corporation....................G....... 315 732-2282
Utica (G-15245)

FBC Chemical Corporation.............G....... 716 681-1581
Lancaster (G-6806)

George Basch Co Inc.....................F....... 516 378-8100
North Bellmore (G-12019)

Grillbot LLC................................G....... 646 258-5639
New York (G-9677)

Mdi Holdings LLC.........................A....... 212 559-1127
New York (G-10404)

Nuvite Chemical Compounds Corp....F....... 718 383-8351
Brooklyn (G-2223)

Progressive Products LLC...............G....... 914 417-6022
Rye Brook (G-14093)

Spic and Span Company................F....... 914 524-6823
Tarrytown (G-15061)

Spray Nine Corporation.................D....... 800 477-7299
Johnstown (G-6629)

Topps-All Products of Yonkers.........F....... 914 968-4226
Yonkers (G-16353)

U S Plychmical Overseas Corp.........F....... 845 356-5530
Chestnut Ridge (G-3400)

CLEANING PRDTS: Automobile Polish

Jescar Enterprises Inc...................G....... 845 352-5850
Nanuet (G-8201)

CLEANING PRDTS: Degreasing Solvent

Solvents Company Inc....................F....... 631 595-9300
Kingston (G-6709)

CLEANING PRDTS: Deodorants, Nonpersonal

Car-Freshner Corporation ....C...... 315 788-6250
Watertown (G-15562)

CLEANING PRDTS: Disinfectants, Household Or Indl Plant

Castoleum Corporation ....F...... 914 664-5877
Mount Vernon (G-8128)
King Research Inc ....E...... 718 788-0122
Brooklyn (G-2028)
Noble Pine Products Co Inc ....F...... 914 664-5877
Mount Vernon (G-8165)
Safe Seat USA Inc ....F...... 516 586-8240
Plainview (G-12713)

CLEANING PRDTS: Drycleaning Preparations

Connie French Cleaners Inc ....G...... 516 487-1343
Great Neck (G-5379)
Omg Cleaners Inc ....G...... 718 282-2011
Brooklyn (G-2231)
Wedding Gown Preservation Co ....D...... 607 748-7999
Endicott (G-4478)

CLEANING PRDTS: Laundry Preparations

Connies Laundry ....G...... 716 822-2800
Buffalo (G-2709)

CLEANING PRDTS: Metal Polish

Conrad Blasius Equipment Co ....G...... 516 753-1200
Plainview (G-12672)

CLEANING PRDTS: Polishing Preparations & Related Prdts

Royce Associates A Ltd Partnr.............G...... 516 367-6298
Jericho (G-6593)

CLEANING PRDTS: Sanitation Preparations

Adirondack Waste MGT Inc ....G...... 518 585-2224
Ticonderoga (G-15073)
City of New York...................C...... 718 236-2693
Brooklyn (G-1666)
Simply Amazing Enterprises Inc ....G...... 631 503-6452
Melville (G-7823)
TWI-Laq Industries Inc ....E...... 718 638-5860
Bronx (G-1385)

CLEANING PRDTS: Sanitation Preps, Disinfectants/Deodorants

Scully Sanitation ....G...... 315 899-8996
West Edmeston (G-15760)
Walter G Legge Company Inc ....G...... 914 737-5040
Peekskill (G-12560)

CLEANING PRDTS: Shoe Polish Or Cleaner

Premier Brands America Inc ....E...... 718 325-3000
Mount Vernon (G-8172)
Premier Brands America Inc ....F...... 718 325-3000
Bronx (G-1343)
Premier Brands America Inc ....C...... 914 667-6200
White Plains (G-16054)

CLEANING PRDTS: Specialty

Caltex International Ltd ....E...... 315 425-1040
Syracuse (G-14840)
Cpac Inc ....E...... 585 382-3223
Leicester (G-6908)
Crescent Marketing Inc ....C...... 716 337-0145
North Collins (G-12024)
Enviro Service & Supply Corp ....F...... 347 838-6500
Staten Island (G-14651)
Finger Lakes Chemicals Inc...................E...... 585 454-4760
Rochester (G-13410)
Four Sasons Multi-Services Inc ....G...... 347 843-6262
Bronx (G-1261)
Gliptone Manufacturing Inc ....F...... 631 285-7250
Ronkonkoma (G-13942)
Griffin Chemical Company LLC...................G...... 716 693-2465
North Tonawanda (G-12071)
HFC Prestige Intl US LLC ....A...... 212 389-7800
New York (G-9778)

Sensor & Decontamination Inc...................F...... 301 526-8389
Binghamton (G-908)

CLEANING PRDTS: Window Cleaning Preparations

Tjb Sunshine Enterprises...................F...... 518 384-6483
Ballston Lake (G-565)

CLEANING SVCS: Industrial Or Commercial

Wellspring Omni Holdings Corp...................A...... 212 318-9800
New York (G-11742)

CLIPPERS: Fingernail & Toenail

Revlon Consumer Products Corp ....B...... 212 527-4000
New York (G-11027)

CLIPS & FASTENERS, MADE FROM PURCHASED WIRE

Hohmann & Barnard Inc...................E...... 631 234-0600
Hauppauge (G-5672)
Hohmann & Barnard Inc...................E...... 518 357-9757
Schenectady (G-14278)

CLOSURES: Closures, Stamped Metal

Van Blarcom Closures Inc...................C...... 718 855-3810
Brooklyn (G-2551)

CLOSURES: Plastic

Industrial Paper Tube Inc ....F...... 718 893-5000
Bronx (G-1281)
Van Blarcom Closures Inc...................C...... 718 855-3810
Brooklyn (G-2551)

CLOTHING & ACCESS, WOMEN, CHILD & INFANT, WHOL: Scarves

Ace & Jig LLC...................G...... 347 227-0318
Brooklyn (G-1454)
Gce International Inc ....D...... 212 704-4800
New York (G-9580)
Lr Paris LLC...................F...... 845 709-8013
New York (G-10275)

CLOTHING & ACCESS, WOMEN, CHILD & INFANT, WHOLESALE: Under

Authentic Brands Group LLC ....C...... 212 760-2410
New York (G-8680)
Mrt Textile Inc ....G...... 800 674-1073
New York (G-10515)

CLOTHING & ACCESS, WOMEN, CHILD & INFANT, WHSLE: Sportswear

Bandit International Ltd...................F...... 718 402-2100
Bronx (G-1210)
Kidz Concepts LLC...................D...... 212 398-1110
New York (G-10097)
Sensational Collection Inc ....G...... 212 840-7388
New York (G-11191)

CLOTHING & ACCESS, WOMEN, CHILDREN & INFANT, WHOL: Access

Embassy Apparel Inc...................F...... 212 768-8330
New York (G-9356)
Fad Inc ....E...... 631 385-2460
Huntington (G-6205)
Skiva International Inc...................E...... 212 736-9520
New York (G-11261)

CLOTHING & ACCESS, WOMEN, CHILDREN & INFANT, WHOL: Gloves

Fownes Brothers & Co Inc...................E...... 800 345-6837
New York (G-9525)
Fownes Brothers & Co Inc...................E...... 518 752-4411
Gloversville (G-5283)

CLOTHING & ACCESS, WOMEN, CHILDREN & INFANT, WHOL: Handbags

Accessries Direct Intl USA Inc...................E...... 646 448-8200
New York (G-8443)
Goyard Inc ....G...... 212 813-0000
New York (G-9650)

Goyard Miami LLC...................G...... 212 813-0005
New York (G-9651)
Quilted Koala Ltd ....F...... 800 223-5678
New York (G-10957)
Street Smart Designs Inc ....G...... 646 865-0056
New York (G-11370)

CLOTHING & ACCESS, WOMEN, CHILDREN & INFANT, WHOL: Sweaters

B & B Sweater Mills Inc ....F...... 718 456-8693
Brooklyn (G-1555)
Keryakos Inc...................F...... 518 344-7092
Schenectady (G-14284)

CLOTHING & ACCESS, WOMEN, CHILDREN & INFANTS, WHOL: Purses

Formart Corp ....F...... 212 819-1819
New York (G-9516)

CLOTHING & ACCESS, WOMEN, CHILDREN/INFANT, WHOL: Baby Goods

Sunwin Global Industry Inc...................G...... 646 370-6196
New York (G-11395)

CLOTHING & ACCESS, WOMEN, CHILDREN/INFANT, WHOL: Nightwear

Komar Luxury Brands ....G...... 646 472-0060
New York (G-10125)

CLOTHING & ACCESS, WOMEN, CHILDREN/INFANT, WHOL: Swimsuits

Christina Sales Inc...................F...... 212 391-0710
New York (G-9001)

CLOTHING & ACCESS, WOMENS, CHILDREN & INFANTS, WHOL: Hats

Gramercy Designs Inc...................G...... 201 919-8570
New York (G-9656)
Mega Power Sports Corporation ....G...... 212 627-3380
New York (G-10423)

CLOTHING & ACCESS: Costumes, Masquerade

Lr Paris LLC...................F...... 845 709-8013
New York (G-10275)
Masquerade LLC...................F...... 212 673-4546
New York (G-10379)
Rubies Masquerade Company LLC......G...... 718 846-1008
Richmond Hill (G-13125)

CLOTHING & ACCESS: Costumes, Theatrical

Barbara Matera Ltd...................D...... 212 475-5006
New York (G-8725)
Costume Armour Inc ....F...... 845 534-9120
Cornwall (G-3728)
D-C Theatricks...................G...... 716 847-0180
Buffalo (G-2719)
Euroco Costumes Inc ....G...... 212 629-9665
New York (G-9420)
Izquierdo Studios Ltd ....F...... 212 807-9757
New York (G-9950)
Parsons-Meares Ltd...................D...... 212 242-3378
Long Island City (G-7320)
Schneeman Studio Limited...................G...... 212 244-3330
New York (G-11153)

CLOTHING & ACCESS: Cummerbunds

Westchester Wine Warehouse LLC......F...... 914 824-1400
White Plains (G-16074)

CLOTHING & ACCESS: Footlets

Jersey Express Inc ....F...... 716 834-6151
Buffalo (G-2821)

CLOTHING & ACCESS: Handicapped

Brooklyn Denim Co...................F...... 718 782-2600
Brooklyn (G-1616)
Eb Couture Ltd ....E...... 212 912-0190
New York (G-9310)
M2 Fashion Group Holdings Inc...................G...... 917 208-2948
New York (G-10302)

PRODUCT

Rhino Sports & Leisure LLC ....E 844 877-4466
Tarrytown *(G-15058)*

Ribz LLC ....G 212 764-9595
New York *(G-11036)*

Timeless Fashions LLC ....G 212 730-9328
New York *(G-11495)*

CLOTHING & ACCESS: Handkerchiefs, Exc Paper

Gce International Inc ....D 212 704-4800
New York *(G-9580)*

My Hanky Inc ....F 646 321-0869
Brooklyn *(G-2182)*

CLOTHING & ACCESS: Hospital Gowns

New York Hospital Disposable ....E 718 384-1620
Brooklyn *(G-2208)*

Shamron Mills Ltd ....G 212 354-0430
Troy *(G-15188)*

CLOTHING & ACCESS: Men's Miscellaneous Access

Accessries Direct Intl USA Inc ....E 646 448-8200
New York *(G-8443)*

Adf Accessories Inc ....G 516 450-5755
Oceanside *(G-12164)*

Apollo Apparel Group LLC ....F 212 398-6585
New York *(G-8604)*

Carter Enterprises LLC ....E 718 853-5052
Brooklyn *(G-1650)*

Dreamwave LLC ....E 212 594-4250
New York *(G-9267)*

Foot Locker Retail Inc ....F 516 827-5306
Hicksville *(G-5908)*

Hoehn Inc ....F 518 463-8900
Albany *(G-87)*

Hudson Dying & Finishing LLC ....E 518 752-4389
Gloversville *(G-5286)*

I Shalom & Co Inc ....C 212 532-7911
New York *(G-9848)*

Jimeale Incorporated ....G 917 686-5383
New York *(G-10005)*

Jolibe Atelier LLC ....F 917 319-5908
New York *(G-10020)*

Jonathan Meizler LLC ....G 212 213-2977
New York *(G-10022)*

Joseph Industries Inc ....E 212 764-0010
New York *(G-10027)*

L D Weiss Inc ....G 212 697-3023
New York *(G-10150)*

Linder New York LLC ....F 646 678-5819
New York *(G-10221)*

Meryl Diamond Ltd ....D 212 730-0333
New York *(G-10439)*

Mountain and Isles LLC ....F 212 354-1890
New York *(G-10509)*

New York Accessory Group Inc ....E 212 532-7911
New York *(G-10592)*

Onia LLC ....E 646 701-0008
New York *(G-10693)*

Ppr Direct Marketing LLC ....G 718 965-8600
Brooklyn *(G-2275)*

Rjm2 Ltd ....G 212 944-1660
New York *(G-11054)*

Robert Miller Associates LLC ....F 718 392-1640
Long Island City *(G-7343)*

Rosetti Handbags and ACC ....E 646 839-7945
New York *(G-11085)*

Setton Brothers Inc ....G 646 902-6011
Brooklyn *(G-2398)*

Skiva International Inc ....E 212 736-9520
New York *(G-11261)*

Swank Inc ....B 212 867-2600
New York *(G-11403)*

Trash and Vaudeville Inc ....G 212 777-1727
New York *(G-11534)*

Ufo Contemporary Inc ....F 212 226-5400
New York *(G-11576)*

Unified Inc led ....F 646 370-4650
New York *(G-11583)*

CLOTHING & ACCESS: Suspenders

Perry Ellis Menswear LLC ....C 212 221-7500
New York *(G-10809)*

Randa Accessories Lea Gds LLC ....D 212 354-5100
New York *(G-10979)*

Trafalgar Company LLC ....G 212 768-8800
New York *(G-11531)*

CLOTHING & APPAREL STORES: Custom

Crye Precision LLC ....C 718 246-3838
Brooklyn *(G-1705)*

Knucklehead Embroidery Inc ....G 607 797-2725
Johnson City *(G-6605)*

Peter Papastrat ....G 607 723-8112
Binghamton *(G-904)*

CLOTHING & FURNISHINGS, MEN & BOY, WHOLESALE: Suits/Trousers

Hugo Boss Usa Inc ....D 212 940-0600
New York *(G-9835)*

CLOTHING & FURNISHINGS, MEN'S & BOYS', WHOLESALE: Caps

Grunt Apparel Inc ....G 646 878-6171
New York *(G-9689)*

CLOTHING & FURNISHINGS, MEN'S & BOYS', WHOLESALE: Fur

Georgy Creative Fashions Inc ....G 212 279-4885
New York *(G-9602)*

CLOTHING & FURNISHINGS, MEN'S & BOYS', WHOLESALE: Gloves

Fownes Brothers & Co Inc ....E 800 345-6837
New York *(G-9525)*

Fownes Brothers & Co Inc ....E 518 752-4411
Gloversville *(G-5283)*

CLOTHING & FURNISHINGS, MEN'S & BOYS', WHOLESALE: Hats

Ideal Creations Inc ....E 212 563-5928
New York *(G-9857)*

Mega Power Sports Corporation ....G 212 627-3380
New York *(G-10423)*

CLOTHING & FURNISHINGS, MEN'S & BOYS', WHOLESALE: Neckwear

Mongru Neckwear Inc ....E 718 706-0406
Long Island City *(G-7299)*

Roffe Accessories Inc ....E 212 213-1440
New York *(G-11071)*

CLOTHING & FURNISHINGS, MEN'S & BOYS', WHOLESALE: Scarves

Gce International Inc ....D 212 704-4800
New York *(G-9580)*

CLOTHING & FURNISHINGS, MEN'S & BOYS', WHOLESALE: Shirts

Hard Ten Clothing Inc ....G 212 302-1321
New York *(G-9725)*

Just Brass Inc ....G 212 724-5447
New York *(G-10045)*

CLOTHING & FURNISHINGS, MEN'S & BOYS', WHOLESALE: Umbrellas

Adam Scott Designs Inc ....E 212 420-8866
New York *(G-8453)*

CLOTHING & FURNISHINGS, MEN'S & BOYS', WHOLESALE: Uniforms

Custom Sportswear Corp ....G 914 666-9200
Bedford Hills *(G-766)*

CLOTHING & FURNISHINGS, MEN/BOY, WHOL: Hats, Scarves/Gloves

Gramercy Designs Inc ....G 201 919-8570
New York *(G-9656)*

CLOTHING & FURNISHINGS, MENS & BOYS, WHOL: Sportswear/Work

Bilco Industries Inc ....F 917 783-5008
New York *(G-8790)*

X Vision Inc ....G 917 412-3570
New York *(G-11796)*

CLOTHING & FURNISHINGS, MENS & BOYS, WHOLESALE: Apprl Belts

New Classic Inc ....F 718 609-1100
Long Island City *(G-7306)*

CLOTHING ACCESS STORES: Umbrellas

Zip-Jack Industries Ltd ....E 914 592-2000
Tarrytown *(G-15064)*

CLOTHING STORES, NEC

1 Atelier LLC ....G 917 916-2968
New York *(G-8388)*

Fad Inc ....E 631 385-2460
Huntington *(G-6205)*

Kcp Holdco Inc ....F 212 265-1500
New York *(G-10086)*

Kenneth Cole Productions Inc ....B 212 265-1500
New York *(G-10089)*

Loungehouse LLC ....E 646 524-2965
New York *(G-10272)*

Marsha Fleisher ....F 845 679-6500
Woodstock *(G-16236)*

Tr Apparel LLC ....G 646 358-3888
New York *(G-11526)*

CLOTHING STORES: Caps & Gowns

Rhino Sports & Leisure LLC ....E 844 877-4466
Tarrytown *(G-15058)*

CLOTHING STORES: Dancewear

Shirl-Lynn of New York ....F 315 363-5898
Oneida *(G-12254)*

CLOTHING STORES: Designer Apparel

Randall Loeffler Inc ....E 212 226-8787
New York *(G-10980)*

CLOTHING STORES: Jeans

Brooklyn Denim Co ....F 718 782-2600
Brooklyn *(G-1616)*

Centric Denim Usa LLC ....G 646 839-7000
New York *(G-8956)*

Joseph (uk) Inc ....G 212 570-0077
New York *(G-10026)*

CLOTHING STORES: Leather

Leather Artisan ....G 518 359-3102
Childwold *(G-3401)*

Lost Worlds Inc ....G 212 923-3423
New York *(G-10267)*

CLOTHING STORES: T-Shirts, Printed, Custom

JP Signs ....G 518 569-3907
Chazy *(G-3334)*

Randy Sixberry ....G 315 265-6211
Potsdam *(G-12940)*

CLOTHING STORES: Uniforms & Work

All American Awards Inc ....F 631 567-2025
Bohemia *(G-968)*

Vans Inc ....F 631 724-1011
Lake Grove *(G-6762)*

CLOTHING STORES: Unisex

David Peyser Sportswear Inc ....E 212 695-7716
New York *(G-9181)*

CLOTHING STORES: Work

Protech (llc) ....E 518 725-7785
Gloversville *(G-5289)*

CLOTHING, WOMEN & CHILD, WHLSE: Dress, Suit, Skirt & Blouse

Billy Beez Usa LLC ....F 315 741-5099
Syracuse (G-14829)

Billy Beez Usa LLC ....F 646 606-2249
New York (G-8793)

Billy Beez Usa LLC ....E 845 915-4709
West Nyack (G-15818)

CLOTHING/ACCESS, WOMEN, CHILDREN/INFANT, WHOL: Apparel Belt

New Classic Inc ....F 718 609-1100
Long Island City (G-7306)

CLOTHING/FURNISHINGS, MEN/BOY, WHOL: Furnishings, Exc Shoes

Embassy Apparel Inc ....F 212 768-8330
New York (G-9356)

CLOTHING: Academic Vestments

Tr Apparel LLC ....G 646 358-3888
New York (G-11526)

CLOTHING: Access

Astor Accessories LLC ....G 212 695-6146
New York (G-8657)

David & Young Co Inc ....G 212 594-6034
New York (G-9177)

J & C Finishing ....E 718 456-1087
Ridgewood (G-13147)

JC California Inc ....G 212 334-4380
New York (G-9986)

Patient-Wear LLC ....G 914 740-7770
Bronx (G-1333)

S & B Fashion Inc ....G 718 482-1386
Long Island City (G-7349)

Twcc Product and Sales ....E 212 614-9364
New York (G-11563)

CLOTHING: Access, Women's & Misses'

1 Atelier LLC ....G 917 916-2968
New York (G-8388)

5th & Ocean Clothing Inc ....C 716 604-9000
Buffalo (G-2613)

Accessries Direct Intl USA Inc ....E 646 448-8200
New York (G-8443)

Authentic Brands Group LLC ....C 212 760-2410
New York (G-8680)

Bag Bazaar Ltd ....E 212 689-3508
New York (G-8717)

Botkier Ny LLC ....G 212 343-2782
New York (G-8838)

Carolina Amato Inc ....G 212 768-9095
New York (G-8922)

Collection Xiix Ltd ....F 212 686-8990
New York (G-9053)

DFA New York LLC ....E 212 523-0021
New York (G-9215)

Elliot Mann Nyc Inc ....G 212 260-0658
New York (G-9349)

Fad Inc ....E 631 385-2460
Huntington (G-6205)

Giulietta LLC ....G 212 334-1859
Brooklyn (G-1887)

Hoehn Inc ....F 518 463-8900
Albany (G-87)

I Shalom & Co Inc ....C 212 532-7911
New York (G-9848)

Krasner Group Inc ....G 212 268-4100
New York (G-10136)

Ksk International Inc ....E 212 354-7770
New York (G-10143)

L D Weiss Inc ....G 212 697-3023
New York (G-10150)

Naito International Corp ....F 718 309-2425
Rockville Centre (G-13832)

New Concepts of New York LLC ....E 212 695-4999
Brooklyn (G-2201)

New York Accessory Group Inc ....E 212 532-7911
New York (G-10592)

ODY Accessories Inc ....E 212 239-0580
New York (G-10680)

Petrunia LLC ....G 607 277-1930
Ithaca (G-6405)

Popnyc 1 LLC ....G 646 684-4600
New York (G-10865)

Uspa Accessories LLC ....C 212 868-2590
New York (G-11631)

CLOTHING: Anklets & Socks

Bombas LLC ....G 800 314-0980
New York (G-8832)

CLOTHING: Aprons, Exc Rubber/Plastic, Women, Misses, Junior

Elizabeth Wilson ....G 516 486-2157
Uniondale (G-15226)

Hedaya Home Fashions Inc ....C 212 889-1111
New York (G-9761)

Republic Clothing Group Inc ....C 212 719-3000
New York (G-11017)

Richard Manufacturing Co Inc ....G 718 254-0958
Brooklyn (G-2344)

CLOTHING: Aprons, Harness

Breton Industries Inc ....C 518 842-3030
Amsterdam (G-320)

CLOTHING: Aprons, Work, Exc Rubberized & Plastic, Men's

Richard Manufacturing Co Inc ....G 718 254-0958
Brooklyn (G-2344)

CLOTHING: Athletic & Sportswear, Men's & Boys'

Adpro Sports LLC ....D 716 854-5116
Buffalo (G-2622)

Bandit International Ltd ....F 718 402-2100
Bronx (G-1210)

Beluga Inc ....E 212 594-5511
New York (G-8753)

Benetton Trading Usa Inc ....G 212 593-0290
New York (G-8757)

Bilco Industries Inc ....F 917 783-5008
New York (G-8790)

Billion Tower USA LLC ....G 212 220-0608
New York (G-8792)

Broken Threads Inc ....G 212 730-4351
New York (G-8860)

Caps Teamwear Inc ....G 585 663-1750
Rochester (G-13295)

Caribbean Fashion Group Inc ....G 212 706-8851
New York (G-8916)

Central Mills Inc ....C 212 764-9011
New York (G-8952)

City Jeans Inc ....G 718 239-5353
Bronx (G-1226)

Continental Knitting Mills ....G 631 242-5330
Deer Park (G-3853)

David Peyser Sportswear Inc ....C 631 231-7788
Bay Shore (G-670)

David Peyser Sportswear Inc ....E 212 695-7716
New York (G-9181)

Endurance LLC ....E 212 719-2500
New York (G-9372)

Eternal Fortune Fashion LLC ....G 212 965-5322
New York (G-9412)

Ferris USA LLC ....G 617 895-8102
New York (G-9485)

Feyem USA Inc ....G 845 363-6253
Brewster (G-1149)

General Sportwear Company Inc ....C 212 764-5820
New York (G-9591)

Groupe 16sur20 LLC ....F 212 625-1620
New York (G-9685)

Haculla Nyc Inc ....F 718 886-3163
Fresh Meadows (G-5042)

Hansae Co Ltd ....F 212 354-6690
New York (G-9724)

Hf Mfg Corp ....D 212 594-9142
New York (G-9777)

Icer Sports LLC ....F 212 221-4700
New York (G-9855)

Jacob Hidary Foundation Inc ....F 212 736-6540
New York (G-9965)

Joseph (uk) Inc ....G 212 570-0077
New York (G-10026)

Kicks Closet Sportswear Inc ....G 347 577-0857
Bronx (G-1292)

Kidz World Inc ....F 212 563-4949
New York (G-10098)

Luxe Imagine Consulting LLC ....G 212 273-9770
New York (G-10286)

M Hidary & Co Inc ....D 212 736-6540
New York (G-10296)

Mann Consultants LLC ....E 914 763-0512
Waccabuc (G-15446)

Mee Accessories LLC ....B 917 262-1000
New York (G-10421)

Miss Group ....G 212 391-2535
New York (G-10481)

North American Mills Inc ....F 212 695-6146
New York (G-10642)

On The Double Inc ....G 518 431-3571
Germantown (G-5169)

One Step Up Ltd ....D 212 398-1110
New York (G-10691)

P & I Sportswear Inc ....G 718 934-4587
New York (G-10731)

Premier Brnds Group Hldngs LLC ....G 212 575-2571
New York (G-10878)

Pvh Corp ....G 212 381-3800
New York (G-10935)

Ralph Lauren Corporation ....B 212 318-7000
New York (G-10975)

Ramsbury Property Us Inc ....F 212 223-6250
New York (G-10976)

Rp55 Inc ....G 212 840-4035
New York (G-11093)

S & S Fashions Inc ....G 718 328-0001
Bronx (G-1354)

Sb Corporation ....G 212 822-3166
New York (G-11143)

Siskind Group Inc ....F 212 840-0880
New York (G-11251)

Sister Sister Inc ....G 212 629-9600
New York (G-11252)

Tbhl International LLC ....F 212 799-2007
New York (G-11438)

Tibana Finishing Inc ....E 718 417-5375
Glendale (G-5234)

Tillsonburg Company USA Inc ....E 267 994-8096
New York (G-11488)

Warnaco Group Inc ....E 212 287-8000
New York (G-11720)

Warnaco Inc ....B 212 287-8000
New York (G-11721)

Worth Imports LLC ....G 212 398-5410
New York (G-11786)

CLOTHING: Athletic & Sportswear, Women's & Girls'

18 Rocks LLC ....E 631 465-9990
Melville (G-7752)

Adpro Sports LLC ....D 716 854-5116
Buffalo (G-2622)

Alpha 6 Distributions LLC ....F 516 801-8290
Locust Valley (G-7121)

Amber Bever Inc ....G 212 391-4911
Brooklyn (G-1495)

Anna Sui Corp ....E 212 941-8406
New York (G-8593)

Avalin LLC ....F 212 842-2286
New York (G-8686)

B Tween LLC ....F 212 819-9040
New York (G-8706)

Bam Sales LLC ....G 212 781-3000
New York (G-8724)

Bilco Industries Inc ....F 917 783-5008
New York (G-8790)

Caribbean Fashion Group Inc ....G 212 706-8851
New York (G-8916)

Casuals Etc Inc ....D 212 838-1319
New York (G-8932)

Continental Knitting Mills ....G 631 242-5330
Deer Park (G-3853)

Dianos Kathryn Designs ....E 212 267-1584
New York (G-9223)

Doral Apparel Group Inc ....G 917 208-5652
New York (G-9254)

Dr Jayscom ....G 888 437-5297
New York (G-9264)

First Love Fashions LLC ....F 212 256-1089
New York (G-9501)

H2gear Fashions LLC ....G 347 787-7508
Brooklyn (G-1917)

Hearts of Palm LLC ....E 212 944-6660
New York (G-9758)

Hearts of Palm LLC ....D 212 944-6660
New York (G-9759)

P
R
O
D
U
C
T

Jaya Apparel Group LLC ....E 212 764-4980
New York *(G-9981)*

Kicks Closet Sportswear Inc ....G 347 577-0857
Bronx *(G-1292)*

Lai Apparel Design Inc ....E 212 382-1075
New York *(G-10165)*

Lavish Layette Inc ....G 347 962-9955
Woodmere *(G-16192)*

Leslie Stuart Co Inc ....F 212 629-4551
New York *(G-10204)*

Liquid Knits Inc ....F 718 706-6600
Long Island City *(G-7275)*

Mango Usa Inc ....E 718 998-6050
Brooklyn *(G-2106)*

Marconi Intl USA Co Ltd ....G 212 391-2626
New York *(G-10357)*

MISS Sportswear Inc ....F 212 391-2535
Brooklyn *(G-2159)*

MISS Sportswear Inc ....G 212 391-2535
New York *(G-10482)*

MISS Sportswear Inc ....F 718 369-6012
Brooklyn *(G-2160)*

On The Double Inc ....G 518 431-3571
Germantown *(G-5169)*

One Step Up Ltd ....D 212 398-1110
New York *(G-10691)*

Penfli Industries Inc ....F 212 947-6080
Great Neck *(G-5413)*

Premier Brnds Group Hldngs LLC ....G 212 575-2571
New York *(G-10878)*

Sensational Collection Inc ....G 212 840-7388
New York *(G-11191)*

Shanghai Harmony AP Intl LLC ....E 646 569-5680
New Rochelle *(G-8354)*

Shirl-Lynn of New York ....F 315 363-5898
Oneida *(G-12254)*

Stony Apparel Corp ....G 212 391-0022
New York *(G-11367)*

Swatfame Inc ....G 212 944-8022
New York *(G-11406)*

Tillsonburg Company USA Inc ....E 267 994-8096
New York *(G-11488)*

X Vision Inc ....G 917 412-3570
New York *(G-11796)*

Z-Ply Corp ....E 212 398-7011
New York *(G-11814)*

Zg Apparel Group LLC ....E 212 944-2510
New York *(G-11822)*

CLOTHING: Baker, Barber, Lab/Svc Ind Apparel, Washable, Men

HC Contracting Inc ....D 212 643-9292
New York *(G-9740)*

CLOTHING: Bathing Suits & Beachwear, Children's

Warnaco Group Inc ....E 212 287-8000
New York *(G-11720)*

CLOTHING: Bathing Suits & Swimwear, Girls, Children & Infant

6 Shore Road LLC ....G 212 274-9666
New York *(G-8406)*

Candlesticks Inc ....F 212 947-8900
New York *(G-8903)*

In Mocean Group LLC ....D 212 944-0317
New York *(G-9873)*

Longevity Brands LLC ....G 212 231-7877
New York *(G-10248)*

Oxygen Inc ....G 516 433-1144
Hicksville *(G-5936)*

CLOTHING: Bathing Suits & Swimwear, Knit

IaMmaliamills LLC ....G 805 845-2137
Brooklyn *(G-1950)*

Riviera Sun Inc ....G 212 546-9220
New York *(G-11050)*

Tomas Maier ....G 212 988-8686
New York *(G-11510)*

CLOTHING: Bathrobes, Mens & Womens, From Purchased Materials

Natori Company Incorporated ....D 212 532-7796
New Park *(G-10550)*

Sketch Studio Trading Inc ....G 212 244-2875
New York *(G-11257)*

CLOTHING: Belts

Barrera Jose & Maria Co Ltd ....E 212 239-1994
New York *(G-8733)*

Centric Brands Inc ....D 646 582-6000
New York *(G-8955)*

Courtlandt Boot Jack Co Inc ....E 718 445-6200
Flushing *(G-4846)*

Daniel M Friedman & Assoc Inc ....E 212 695-5545
New York *(G-9167)*

Gbg USA Inc ....D 646 839-7083
New York *(G-9578)*

Gbg USA Inc ....E 212 615-3400
New York *(G-9579)*

Nassau Suffolk Brd of Womens ....E 631 666-8835
Bay Shore *(G-696)*

New Classic Inc ....F 718 609-1100
Long Island City *(G-7306)*

P M Belts Usa Inc ....E 800 762-3580
Brooklyn *(G-2240)*

Perry Ellis Menswear LLC ....C 212 221-7500
New York *(G-10809)*

Randa Accessories Lea Gds LLC ....D 212 354-5100
New York *(G-10979)*

Sandy Duftler Designs Ltd ....F 516 379-3084
North Baldwin *(G-12007)*

Sh Leather Novelty Company ....G 718 387-7742
Brooklyn *(G-2400)*

Tapestry Inc ....E 212 594-1850
New York *(G-11434)*

Trafalgar Company LLC ....G 212 768-8800
New York *(G-11531)*

Universal Elliot Corp ....G 212 736-8877
New York *(G-11606)*

Xinya International Trading Co ....G 212 216-9681
New York *(G-11799)*

CLOTHING: Blouses & Shirts, Girls' & Children's

Cheri Mon Baby LLC ....G 212 354-5511
New York *(G-8981)*

Gw Acquisition LLC ....E 212 736-4848
New York *(G-9700)*

Sports Products America LLC ....E 212 594-5511
New York *(G-11328)*

CLOTHING: Blouses, Boys', From Purchased Materials

Jacks and Jokers 52 LLC ....G 917 740-2595
New York *(G-9961)*

Nat Nast Company Inc ....E 212 575-1186
New York *(G-10536)*

CLOTHING: Blouses, Women's & Girls'

Accessries Direct Intl USA Inc ....E 646 448-8200
New York *(G-8443)*

Apparel Group Ltd ....E 212 328-1200
New York *(G-8607)*

August Silk Inc ....E 212 643-2400
New York *(G-8678)*

August Silk Inc ....G 212 643-2400
New York *(G-8679)*

Ben Wachter Associates Inc ....G 212 736-4064
New York *(G-8754)*

Bernard Chaus Inc ....D 212 354-1280
New York *(G-8760)*

Bernard Chaus Inc ....C 646 562-4700
New York *(G-8761)*

Cyberlimit Inc ....F 212 840-9597
New York *(G-9140)*

Cynthia Rowley Inc ....F 212 242-3803
New York *(G-9142)*

Embassy Apparel Inc ....F 212 768-8330
New York *(G-9356)*

Feyem USA Inc ....G 845 363-6253
Brewster *(G-1149)*

Fourtys Ny Inc ....F 212 382-0301
New York *(G-9524)*

Gildan Apparel USA Inc ....D 212 476-0341
New York *(G-9609)*

Grey State Apparel LLC ....E 212 255-4216
New York *(G-9675)*

Icer Sports LLC ....F 212 221-4700
New York *(G-9855)*

JI Parc LLC ....G 718 271-0703
Rego Park *(G-13078)*

Kate Spade Holdings LLC ....B 212 354-4900
New York *(G-10076)*

Krasner Group Inc ....G 212 268-4100
New York *(G-10136)*

Ksk International Inc ....E 212 354-7770
New York *(G-10143)*

Lea & Viola Inc ....G 646 918-6866
New York *(G-10181)*

Liberty Apparel Company Inc ....E 718 625-4000
New York *(G-10209)*

Lt2 LLC ....E 212 684-1510
New York *(G-10277)*

Lynn Brands LLC ....E 212 921-5495
New York *(G-10288)*

M S B International Ltd ....F 212 302-5551
New York *(G-10299)*

Maggy London International Ltd ....D 212 944-7199
New York *(G-10323)*

Mega Sourcing Inc ....G 646 682-0304
Merrick *(G-7861)*

Mulitex Usa Inc ....G 212 398-0440
New York *(G-10518)*

Nyc Knitwear Inc ....E 212 840-1313
New York *(G-10662)*

Orchid Manufacturing Co Inc ....F 212 840-5700
New York *(G-10708)*

Plugg LLC ....F 212 840-6655
New York *(G-10857)*

Ramy Brook LLC ....E 212 744-2789
New York *(G-10978)*

Raven New York LLC ....G 212 584-9690
New York *(G-10983)*

Robert Danes Danes Inc ....E 212 226-1351
New York *(G-11060)*

Saad Collection Inc ....G 212 937-0341
New York *(G-11111)*

Soho Apparel Ltd ....G 212 840-1109
New York *(G-11285)*

Spencer AB Inc ....G 646 831-3728
New York *(G-11318)*

Tibana Finishing Inc ....E 718 417-5375
Glendale *(G-5234)*

Triumph Apparel Corporation ....E 212 302-2606
New York *(G-11548)*

Turn On Products Inc ....D 212 764-2121
New York *(G-11559)*

Ursula of Switzerland Inc ....E 518 237-2580
Waterford *(G-15549)*

Vanity Room Inc ....F 212 921-7154
New York *(G-11642)*

Ventura Enterprise Co Inc ....E 212 391-0170
New York *(G-11656)*

Yeohlee Inc ....F 212 631-8099
New York *(G-11808)*

CLOTHING: Blouses, Womens & Juniors, From Purchased Mtrls

79 Metro Ltd ....G 212 944-4030
New York *(G-8408)*

Agi Brooks Production Co Inc ....F 212 268-1533
New York *(G-8493)*

Alexander Wang Incorporated ....D 212 532-3103
New York *(G-8514)*

Amerex Corporation ....G 212 221-3151
New York *(G-8539)*

Anna Sui Corp ....E 212 941-8406
New York *(G-8593)*

Donna Karan International Inc ....F 212 789-1500
New York *(G-9249)*

Donna Karan International Inc ....G 212 768-5800
New York *(G-9250)*

Elie Tahari Ltd ....G 212 763-2000
New York *(G-9339)*

Elie Tahari Ltd ....D 212 763-2000
New York *(G-9340)*

Fuller Sportswear Co Inc ....G 516 773-3353
Great Neck *(G-5391)*

Gabrielle Andra ....G 212 366-9624
New York *(G-9565)*

Geoffrey Beene Inc ....E 212 371-5570
New York *(G-9597)*

International Direct Group Inc ....E 212 921-9036
New York *(G-9919)*

Jeanjer LLC ....A 212 944-1330
New York *(G-9991)*

Land n Sea Inc ....D 212 444-6000
New York *(G-10168)*

Necessary Objects Ltd ....E 212 334-9888
Long Island City *(G-7305)*

Orchard Apparel Group Ltd ....G 212 268-8701
New York *(G-10706)*

Paddy Lee Fashions Inc ....F 718 786-6020
Long Island City *(G-7318)*
Pat & Rose Dress Inc ....D 212 279-1357
New York *(G-10768)*
Permit Fashion Group Inc ....G 212 912-0988
Melville *(G-7815)*
Phillips-Van Heusen Europe ....F 212 381-3500
New York *(G-10829)*
Pvh Corp ....D 212 381-3500
New York *(G-10933)*
Pvh Corp ....G 212 549-6000
New York *(G-10934)*
Pvh Corp ....G 212 719-2600
New York *(G-10937)*
Rhoda Lee Inc ....D 212 840-5700
New York *(G-11035)*
S & S Manufacturing Co Inc ....D 212 444-6000
New York *(G-11106)*
Stitch & Couture Inc ....E 212 947-9204
New York *(G-11364)*
Tahari ASL LLC ....B 212 763-2800
New York *(G-11424)*
Turn On Products Inc ....F 212 764-4545
New York *(G-11560)*

CLOTHING: Brassieres

East Coast Molders Inc ....C 516 240-6000
Oceanside *(G-12170)*
New York Elegance Entps Inc ....F 212 685-3088
New York *(G-10595)*
Valmont Inc ....F 212 685-1653
New York *(G-11636)*
Warnaco Inc ....B 212 287-8000
New York *(G-11721)*
Warnaco Inc ....F 718 722-3000
Brooklyn *(G-2575)*

CLOTHING: Bridal Gowns

Anna B Inc ....G 516 680-6609
New York *(G-8592)*
JBS Limited ....E 212 764-4600
New York *(G-9984)*
JBS Limited ....E 212 221-8403
New York *(G-9985)*
Leanne Marshall Designs Inc ....F 646 918-6349
New York *(G-10184)*
Nasserati Inc ....E 212 947-8100
New York *(G-10535)*
Shane Tex Inc ....F 516 486-7522
Woodmere *(G-16193)*
Stitch & Couture Inc ....E 212 947-9204
New York *(G-11364)*
Thread LLC ....G 212 414-8844
New York *(G-11477)*
Vera Wang Group LLC ....C 212 575-6400
New York *(G-11657)*

CLOTHING: Burial

Rose Solomon Co ....E 718 855-1788
Brooklyn *(G-2355)*

CLOTHING: Capes & Jackets, Women's & Misses'

Alicia Adams Alpaca Inc ....G 845 868-3366
Millbrook *(G-7941)*
Uniqlo USA LLC ....F 877 486-4756
New York *(G-11593)*

CLOTHING: Capes, Exc Fur/Rubber, Womens, Misses & Juniors

Adrienne Landau Designs Inc ....F 212 695-8362
New York *(G-8464)*

CLOTHING: Chemises, Camisoles/Teddies, Women, Misses/Junior

Lady Ester Lingerie Corp ....E 212 689-1729
New York *(G-10162)*
Mrt Textile Inc ....G 800 674-1073
New York *(G-10515)*

CLOTHING: Children & Infants'

Andy & Evan Industries Inc ....G 212 967-7908
New York *(G-8581)*
Gce International Inc ....F 212 868-0500
New York *(G-9581)*

Grand Knitting Mills Inc ....E 631 226-5000
Amityville *(G-265)*
Great Universal Corp ....E 917 302-0065
New York *(G-9670)*
Haddad Bros Inc ....F 212 563-2117
New York *(G-9706)*
JM Originals Inc ....C 845 647-3003
Ellenville *(G-4307)*
Manchu New York Inc ....G 212 921-5050
New York *(G-10340)*
Michael Stuart Inc ....E 718 821-0704
Brooklyn *(G-2151)*
S & C Bridal LLC ....F 212 789-7000
New York *(G-11104)*
S & C Bridals LLC ....G 213 624-4477
New York *(G-11105)*
Silly Phillie Creations Inc ....E 718 492-6300
Brooklyn *(G-2413)*
Skip Hop Inc ....E 646 902-9874
New York *(G-11259)*
Skip Hop Holdings Inc ....G 212 868-9850
New York *(G-11260)*
Thats My Girl Inc ....F 212 695-0020
Brooklyn *(G-2500)*

CLOTHING: Children's, Girls'

Aerobic Wear Inc ....G 631 673-1830
Huntington Station *(G-6235)*
Domani Fashions Corp ....G 718 797-0505
Brooklyn *(G-1755)*
Franco Apparel Group Inc ....D 212 967-7272
New York *(G-9530)*
Gerson & Gerson Inc ....C 212 244-6775
New York *(G-9604)*
Gw Acquisition LLC ....E 212 736-4848
New York *(G-9700)*
Isfel Co Inc ....G 212 736-6216
New York *(G-9945)*
Jeanjer LLC ....A 212 944-1330
New York *(G-9991)*
JM Originals Inc ....C 845 647-3003
Ellenville *(G-4307)*
Jomat New York Inc ....E 718 369-7641
Brooklyn *(G-1998)*
Kahn-Lucas-Lancaster Inc ....D 212 239-2407
New York *(G-10057)*
Land n Sea Inc ....D 212 444-6000
New York *(G-10168)*
Liberty Apparel Company Inc ....E 718 625-4000
New York *(G-10209)*
Lollytogs Ltd ....D 212 502-6000
New York *(G-10246)*
M Hidary & Co Inc ....D 212 736-6540
New York *(G-10296)*
Michael Stuart Inc ....E 718 821-0704
Brooklyn *(G-2151)*
Miltons of New York Inc ....G 212 997-3359
New York *(G-10471)*
Nyc Bronx Inc ....G 917 417-0509
Bronx *(G-1327)*
Pink Crush LLC ....G 718 788-6978
New York *(G-10844)*
Pti-Pacific Inc ....G 212 414-8495
New York *(G-10920)*
Rogers Group Inc ....E 212 643-9292
New York *(G-11075)*
S Rothschild & Co Inc ....C 212 354-8550
New York *(G-11110)*
Sch Dpx Corporation ....G 917 405-5377
New York *(G-11148)*
Swatfame Inc ....G 212 944-8022
New York *(G-11406)*
Yigal-Azrouel Inc ....E 212 302-1194
New York *(G-11809)*
Z-Ply Corp ....E 212 398-7011
New York *(G-11814)*

CLOTHING: Clergy Vestments

Davis ....G 716 833-4678
Buffalo *(G-2722)*
Roth Clothing Co Inc ....E 718 384-4927
Brooklyn *(G-2356)*

CLOTHING: Coats & Jackets, Leather & Sheep-Lined

Andrew M Schwartz LLC ....G 212 391-7070
New York *(G-8580)*
Cockpit Usa Inc ....F 212 575-1616
New York *(G-9046)*

Excelled Sheepskin & Lea Coat ......F 212 594-5843
New York *(G-9443)*
J Percy For Mrvin Rchards Ltd ......E 212 944-5300
New York *(G-9956)*
Lost Worlds Inc ....G 212 923-3423
New York *(G-10267)*

CLOTHING: Coats & Suits, Men's & Boys'

Adrian Jules Ltd ....D 585 342-5886
Rochester *(G-13207)*
Advance Apparel Intl Inc ....G 212 944-0984
New York *(G-8467)*
Allytex LLC ....G 518 376-7539
Ballston Spa *(G-568)*
Centric Brands Inc ....D 646 582-6000
New York *(G-8955)*
Check Group LLC ....D 212 221-4700
New York *(G-8978)*
Christian Casey LLC ....E 212 500-2200
New York *(G-8997)*
Christian Casey LLC ....E 212 500-2200
New York *(G-8998)*
Concorde Apparel Company LLC ....G 212 307-7848
New York *(G-9078)*
Excelled Sheepskin & Lea Coat ......F 212 594-5843
New York *(G-9443)*
G-III Apparel Group Ltd ....B 212 403-0500
New York *(G-9560)*
G-III Apparel Group Ltd ....F 212 840-7272
New York *(G-9562)*
Giliberto Designs Inc ....E 212 695-0216
New York *(G-9610)*
Great 4 Image Inc ....E 518 424-2058
Rensselaer *(G-13088)*
Hugo Boss Usa Inc ....D 212 940-0600
New York *(G-9835)*
J & X Production Inc ....F 718 200-1228
New York *(G-9954)*
L F Fashion Orient Intl Co Ltd .....G 917 667-3398
New York *(G-10151)*
Lvl Xiii Brands Inc ....F 646 530-2795
New York *(G-10287)*
M Hidary & Co Inc ....D 212 736-6540
New York *(G-10296)*
Manchu New York Inc ....G 212 921-5050
New York *(G-10340)*
Mv Corp Inc ....C 631 273-8020
Bay Shore *(G-695)*
Opposuits USA Inc ....E 917 438-8878
New York *(G-10700)*
Pat & Rose Dress Inc ....D 212 279-1357
New York *(G-10768)*
Proper Cloth LLC ....G 646 964-4221
New York *(G-10914)*
Ps38 LLC ....G 212 302-1108
New York *(G-10918)*
Wp Lavori USA Inc ....G 212 244-6074
New York *(G-11790)*
Yong Ji Productions Inc ....E 917 559-4616
Corona *(G-3752)*

CLOTHING: Coats, Leatherette, Oiled Fabric, Etc, Mens & Boys

House Pearl Fashions (us) Ltd ......F 212 840-3183
New York *(G-9826)*

CLOTHING: Coats, Tailored, Mens/Boys, From Purchased Mtls

Blue Duck Trading Ltd ....G 212 268-3122
New York *(G-8818)*

CLOTHING: Corset Access, Clasps & Stays

Higgins Supply Company Inc ....D 607 836-6474
Mc Graw *(G-7688)*

CLOTHING: Costumes

Creative Costume Co ....G 212 564-5552
Liverpool *(G-7008)*
Cygnet Studio Inc ....F 646 450-4550
New York *(G-9141)*
Eric Winterling Inc ....E 212 629-7686
New York *(G-9393)*
John Kristiansen New York Inc ......F 212 388-1097
New York *(G-10017)*
Kidz Concepts LLC ....D 212 398-1110
New York *(G-10097)*

P
R
O
D
U
C
T

Kiton Building Corp ....E 212 486-3224
New York (G-10111)

Koon Enterprises LLC ....G 718 886-3163
Fresh Meadows (G-5043)

Moresca Clothing and Costume ....F 845 331-6012
Ulster Park (G-15219)

Prolink Industries Inc ....F 212 354-5690
New York (G-10907)

Rubies Costume Company Inc ....B 718 846-1008
Richmond Hill (G-13122)

Rubies Costume Company Inc ....D 631 777-3300
Bay Shore (G-711)

Rubies Costume Company Inc ....C 718 441-0834
Richmond Hill (G-13123)

Rubies Costume Company Inc ....C 631 951-3688
Bay Shore (G-712)

Rubies Costume Company Inc ....E 516 333-3473
Westbury (G-15923)

Rubies Costume Company Inc ....F 631 435-7912
Bay Shore (G-713)

Rubies Costume Company Inc ....C 718 846-1008
Richmond Hill (G-13124)

South Central Boyz ....G 718 496-7270
Brooklyn (G-2444)

CLOTHING: Diaper Covers, Waterproof, From Purchased Material

Hercules Group Inc ....E 212 813-8000
Port Washington (G-12883)

CLOTHING: Disposable

A Lunt Design Inc ....F 716 662-0781
Orchard Park (G-12334)

Dvf Studio LLC ....D 212 741-6607
New York (G-9283)

Dvf Studio LLC ....G 646 576-8009
New York (G-9284)

HB Athletic Inc ....F 914 560-8422
New Rochelle (G-8340)

Hpk Industries LLC ....F 315 724-0196
Utica (G-15271)

Lakeland Industries Inc ....C 631 981-9700
Ronkonkoma (G-13963)

CLOTHING: Down-Filled, Men's & Boys'

Nyc Idol Apparel Inc ....G 212 997-9797
New York (G-10661)

CLOTHING: Dresses

Agi Brooks Production Co Inc ....F 212 268-1533
New York (G-8493)

Allison Che Fashion Inc ....F 212 391-1433
New York (G-8519)

AM Retail Group Inc ....C 716 297-0752
Niagara Falls (G-11902)

Amj DOT LLC ....G 718 775-3288
Brooklyn (G-1505)

Anna Sui Corp ....E 212 941-8406
New York (G-8593)

Arteast LLC ....E 646 859-6020
New York (G-8633)

August Silk Inc ....E 212 643-2400
New York (G-8678)

August Silk Inc ....G 212 643-2400
New York (G-8679)

Christian Siriano Holdings LLC ....G 212 695-5494
New York (G-9000)

Csco LLC ....E 212 375-6180
New York (G-9127)

CTS LLC ....G 212 278-0058
New York (G-9128)

Cynthia Rowley Inc ....F 212 242-3803
New York (G-9142)

Dalma Dress Mfg Co Inc ....E 212 391-8296
Greenvale (G-5461)

Damianou Sportswear Inc ....D 718 204-5600
Woodside (G-16203)

Donna Karan International Inc ....F 212 789-1500
New York (G-9249)

Donna Karan International Inc ....G 212 768-5800
New York (G-9250)

Faviana International Inc ....E 212 594-4422
New York (G-9479)

G-III Apparel Group Ltd ....E 212 403-0500
New York (G-9561)

Geoffrey Beene Inc ....E 212 371-5570
New York (G-9597)

Halmode Apparel Inc ....A 212 819-9114
New York (G-9712)

Haute By Blair Stanley LLC ....G 212 557-7868
New York (G-9736)

I S C A Corp ....F 212 719-5123
New York (G-9847)

J R Nites ....G 212 354-9670
New York (G-9958)

Jiranimo Industries Ltd ....F 212 921-5106
New York (G-10007)

Jon Teri Sports Inc ....E 212 398-0657
New York (G-10021)

Judys Group Inc ....E 212 921-0515
New York (G-10037)

Jump Design Group Inc ....C 212 869-3300
New York (G-10040)

Kasper Group LLC ....C 212 354-4311
New York (G-10075)

Krasner Group Inc ....G 212 268-4100
New York (G-10136)

L F Fashion Orient Intl Co Ltd ....G 917 667-3398
New York (G-10151)

Lavish Layette Inc ....G 347 962-9955
Woodmere (G-16192)

Lmr Group Inc ....G 212 730-9221
New York (G-10238)

Lou Sally Fashions Corp ....E 212 354-9670
New York (G-10269)

Lou Sally Fashions Corp ....E 212 354-1283
New York (G-10270)

Mmj Apparel LLC ....E 212 354-8550
New York (G-10486)

Necessary Objects Ltd ....E 212 334-9888
Long Island City (G-7305)

Nine West Holdings Inc ....G 212 391-5000
New York (G-10630)

Pat & Rose Dress Inc ....D 212 279-1357
New York (G-10768)

Plugg LLC ....F 212 840-6655
New York (G-10857)

Product Development Intl LLC ....G 212 279-6170
New York (G-10903)

Quality Patterns Inc ....D 212 704-0355
New York (G-10950)

R & M Richards Inc ....C 212 921-8820
New York (G-10965)

Raven New York LLC ....G 212 584-9690
New York (G-10983)

Rogan LLC ....G 212 680-1407
New York (G-11072)

Rogan LLC ....E 646 496-9339
New York (G-11073)

Ronni Nicole Group LLC ....E 212 764-1000
New York (G-11080)

Sg Nyc LLC ....E 310 210-1837
New York (G-11197)

Spencer AB Inc ....G 646 831-3728
New York (G-11318)

SSG Fashions Ltd ....G 212 221-0933
New York (G-11343)

Tabrisse Collections Inc ....F 212 921-1014
New York (G-11422)

Tahari ASL LLC ....B 212 763-2800
New York (G-11424)

Texport Fabrics Corp ....G 212 226-6066
New York (G-11456)

Tom & Linda Platt Inc ....F 212 221-7208
New York (G-11507)

Turn On Products Inc ....F 212 764-4545
New York (G-11560)

Vanity Room Inc ....F 212 921-7154
New York (G-11642)

Worth Collection Ltd ....E 212 268-0312
New York (G-11785)

Yeohlee Inc ....F 212 631-8099
New York (G-11808)

CLOTHING: Dresses & Skirts

Betsy & Adam Ltd ....E 212 302-3750
New York (G-8770)

CLOTHING: Dresses, Knit

Summit Apparel Inc ....E 631 213-8299
Hauppauge (G-5777)

Winter Water Factory ....G 646 387-3247
Brooklyn (G-2592)

CLOTHING: Dressing Gowns, Mens/Womens, From Purchased Matls

Mata Fashions LLC ....G 917 716-7894
New York (G-10380)

CLOTHING: Foundation Garments, Women's

E P Sewing Pleating Inc ....E 212 967-2575
New York (G-9290)

Rago Foundations LLC ....E 718 728-8436
Astoria (G-436)

CLOTHING: Furs

Anastasia Furs International ....F 212 868-9241
New York (G-8574)

Avante ....G 516 782-4888
Great Neck (G-5369)

B Smith Furs Inc ....F 212 967-5290
New York (G-8705)

Dennis Basso Couture Inc ....F 212 794-4500
New York (G-9203)

Georgy Creative Fashions Inc ....G 212 279-4885
New York (G-9602)

Miller & Berkowitz Ltd ....F 212 244-5459
New York (G-10468)

Sekas International Ltd ....E 212 629-6095
New York (G-11184)

Stefan Furs Inc ....G 212 594-2788
New York (G-11354)

USA Furs By George Inc ....G 212 643-1415
New York (G-11629)

CLOTHING: Garments, Indl, Men's & Boys

Beardslee Realty ....G 516 747-5557
Mineola (G-7960)

Classic Designer Workshop Inc ....G 212 730-8480
New York (G-9024)

Kse Sportsman Media Inc ....D 212 852-6600
New York (G-10142)

Stealth Inc ....F 718 252-7900
Brooklyn (G-2455)

CLOTHING: Girdles & Other Foundation Garments, Knit

Maidenform LLC ....F 201 436-9200
New York (G-10331)

CLOTHING: Girdles & Panty Girdles

Burlen Corp ....F 212 684-0052
New York (G-8869)

CLOTHING: Gloves, Knit, Exc Dress & Semidress

Hawkins Fabrics Inc ....E 518 773-9550
Johnstown (G-6618)

CLOTHING: Gowns & Dresses, Wedding

A & M Rosenthal Entps Inc ....E 646 638-9600
New York (G-8411)

Alvina Vlenta Couture Collectn ....F 212 921-7058
New York (G-8533)

Alvina Vlenta Couture Collectn ....F 212 921-7058
New York (G-8534)

Birnbaum & Bullock Ltd ....G 212 242-2914
New York (G-8801)

Cachet Industries Inc ....E 212 944-2188
New York (G-8885)

Christos Inc ....E 212 921-0025
New York (G-9003)

Couture Inc ....G 212 921-1166
New York (G-9112)

Elana Laderos Ltd ....F 212 764-0840
New York (G-9332)

Elizabeth Fillmore LLC ....G 212 647-0863
New York (G-9347)

Kelly Grace Corp ....C 212 704-9603
New York (G-10088)

Paris Wedding Center Corp ....F 347 368-4085
Flushing (G-4885)

Paris Wedding Center Corp ....E 212 267-8088
New York (G-10761)

Parsley Apparel Corp ....E 631 981-7181
Ronkonkoma (G-13992)

Paula Varsalona Ltd ....F 212 570-9100
New York (G-10772)

CLOTHING: Gowns, Formal

Bari-Jay Fashions Inc ....E 212 921-1551
New York *(G-8730)*

Crisada Inc ....G 718 729-9730
Long Island City *(G-7194)*

Jovani Fashion Ltd ....E 212 279-0222
New York *(G-10031)*

Lily & Taylor Inc ....F 212 564-5459
New York *(G-10220)*

Pronovias USA Inc ....E 212 897-6393
New York *(G-10911)*

Ursula of Switzerland Inc ......E 518 237-2580
Waterford *(G-15549)*

CLOTHING: Hats & Caps, Leather

J Lowy Co ....G 718 338-7324
Brooklyn *(G-1979)*

CLOTHING: Hats & Caps, NEC

A-1 Skull Cap Corp ....E 718 633-9333
Brooklyn *(G-1441)*

Athletic Cap Co Inc ....E 718 398-1300
Staten Island *(G-14621)*

Flexfit Llc ....D 516 932-8800
Hicksville *(G-5907)*

Hepa-Hat Incorporated ....F 914 271-9747
Croton On Hudson *(G-3809)*

Kraft Hat Manufacturers Inc ...D 845 735-6200
Pearl River *(G-12536)*

Paletot Ltd ....F 212 268-3774
New York *(G-10741)*

Weinfeld Skull Cap Mfg Co Inc .....G 718 854-3864
Brooklyn *(G-2579)*

CLOTHING: Hats & Caps, Uniform

Bonk Sam Unforms Civilian Cap .....E 718 585-0665
Bronx *(G-1215)*

Hankin Brothers Cap Co ....F 716 892-8840
Buffalo *(G-2792)*

Kays Caps Inc ....G 518 273-6079
Troy *(G-15159)*

Kingform Cap Company Inc .....D 516 822-2501
Hicksville *(G-5918)*

New ERA Cap Co Inc ....B 716 604-9000
Buffalo *(G-2882)*

New ERA Cap Co Inc ....B 716 604-9000
Buffalo *(G-2883)*

New ERA Cap Co Inc ....F 716 549-0445
Derby *(G-4006)*

CLOTHING: Hats & Headwear, Knit

Gce International Inc ....D 212 704-4800
New York *(G-9580)*

Lids Corporation ....G 518 459-7060
Albany *(G-97)*

CLOTHING: Hosiery, Men's & Boys'

Haddad Hosiery LLC ....G 212 251-0022
New York *(G-9707)*

High Point Design LLC ....F 212 354-2400
New York *(G-9781)*

Lr Acquisition LLC ....F 212 301-8765
New York *(G-10274)*

You and ME Legwear LLC ....F 212 279-9292
New York *(G-11812)*

CLOTHING: Hosiery, Pantyhose & Knee Length, Sheer

Gina Group LLC ....E 212 947-2445
New York *(G-9612)*

Hot Sox Company Incorporated .....D 212 957-2000
New York *(G-9818)*

Silky Tones Inc ....G 718 218-5598
Brooklyn *(G-2412)*

Trimfit Inc ....E 215 245-1122
New York *(G-11546)*

CLOTHING: Hospital, Men's

Norcorp Inc ....E 914 666-1310
Mount Kisco *(G-8100)*

CLOTHING: Housedresses

Millennium Productions Inc .....F 212 944-6203
New York *(G-10467)*

CLOTHING: Jackets & Vests, Exc Fur & Leather, Women's

Donna Karan International Inc .....F 212 789-1500
New York *(G-9249)*

Donna Karan International Inc .....G 212 768-5800
New York *(G-9250)*

Levy Group Inc ....C 212 398-0707
New York *(G-10206)*

Standard Manufacturing Co Inc .....D 518 235-2200
Troy *(G-15190)*

Tiger J LLC ....E 212 465-9300
New York *(G-11486)*

CLOTHING: Jackets, Knit

Freedom Rains Inc ....G 646 710-4512
New York *(G-9534)*

J & D Walter Distributors Inc ....F 518 449-1606
Glenmont *(G-5238)*

CLOTHING: Jeans, Men's & Boys'

Denim King Depot LLC ....E 917 477-0550
New York *(G-9201)*

Guess Inc ....E 716 298-3561
Niagara Falls *(G-11934)*

Messex Group Inc ....G 646 229-2582
New York *(G-10442)*

One Jeanswear Group LLC ......B 212 575-2571
New York *(G-10690)*

CLOTHING: Knit Underwear & Nightwear

In Toon Amkor Fashions Inc .....E 718 937-4546
Long Island City *(G-7247)*

Maidenform LLC ....F 201 436-9200
New York *(G-10331)*

Native Textiles Inc ....G 212 951-5100
New York *(G-10549)*

CLOTHING: Leather

G-III Apparel Group Ltd ....B 212 403-0500
New York *(G-9560)*

Georgy Creative Fashions Inc .....G 212 279-4885
New York *(G-9602)*

Louis Schwartz ....G 845 356-6624
Spring Valley *(G-14577)*

Studio One Leather Design Inc .....F 212 760-1701
New York *(G-11379)*

CLOTHING: Leather & Sheep-Lined

Zwuits Inc ....F 929 387-2323
Larchmont *(G-6845)*

CLOTHING: Leather & sheep-lined clothing

G-III Leather Fashions Inc ....E 212 403-0500
New York *(G-9563)*

CLOTHING: Maternity

Medi-Tech International Corp .....G 800 333-0109
Brooklyn *(G-2132)*

Zoomers Inc ....E 718 369-2656
Brooklyn *(G-2606)*

CLOTHING: Men's & boy's clothing, nec

Apogee Retail NY ....G 516 731-1727
Levittown *(G-6912)*

By Robert James ....G 212 253-2121
New York *(G-8876)*

CLOTHING: Men's & boy's underwear & nightwear

Candlesticks Inc ....F 212 947-8900
New York *(G-8903)*

Christian Casey LLC ....E 212 500-2200
New York *(G-8997)*

Christian Casey LLC ....E 212 500-2200
New York *(G-8998)*

Revolutionwear Inc ....G 617 669-9191
New York *(G-11030)*

Tommy John Inc ....E 800 708-3490
New York *(G-11512)*

Waterbury Garment LLC ....E 212 725-1500
New York *(G-11730)*

CLOTHING: Mens & Boys Jackets, Sport, Suede, Leatherette

Broadway Knitting Mills Inc .....G 716 692-4421
North Tonawanda *(G-12059)*

G-III Apparel Group Ltd ....B 212 403-0500
New York *(G-9560)*

Standard Manufacturing Co Inc .....D 518 235-2200
Troy *(G-15190)*

CLOTHING: Millinery

Albrizio Inc ....G 212 719-5290
Brooklyn *(G-1479)*

Lenore Marshall Inc ....G 212 947-5945
New York *(G-10197)*

Lloyds Fashions Inc ....D 631 435-3353
Brentwood *(G-1125)*

CLOTHING: Neckties, Knit

Mongru Neckwear Inc ....E 718 706-0406
Long Island City *(G-7299)*

CLOTHING: Neckwear

Emunas Sales Inc ....F 718 621-3138
Brooklyn *(G-1803)*

JS Blank & Co Inc ....E 212 689-4835
New York *(G-10035)*

MANE Enterprises Inc ....D 718 472-4955
Long Island City *(G-7287)*

Mongru Neckwear Inc ....G 718 706-0406
Long Island City *(G-7299)*

Roffe Accessories Inc ....E 212 213-1440
New York *(G-11071)*

S Broome and Co Inc ....D 718 663-6800
Long Island City *(G-7350)*

Valenti Neckwear Co Inc ....G 914 969-0700
Yonkers *(G-16354)*

Warnaco Inc ....B 212 287-8000
New York *(G-11721)*

Wetherall Contracting NY Inc ...G 718 894-7011
Middle Village *(G-7885)*

CLOTHING: Outerwear, Knit

Alpha Knitting Mills Inc ....F 718 628-6300
Brooklyn *(G-1491)*

Andrea Strongwater ....G 212 873-0905
New York *(G-8578)*

Asian Global Trading Corp ......G 718 786-0998
New York *(G-8647)*

Dressy Tessy Inc ....G 212 869-0750
New York *(G-9269)*

E I Du Pont De Nemours & Co .....E 716 876-4420
Buffalo *(G-2734)*

Emerald Holdings Inc ....G 718 797-4404
Brooklyn *(G-1798)*

Fashion Avenue Knits Inc ....F 718 456-9000
New York *(G-9476)*

Gabani Inc ....G 631 283-4930
Southampton *(G-14531)*

GAME Sportswear Ltd ....C 914 962-1701
Yorktown Heights *(G-16365)*

Gildan Apparel USA Inc ....D 212 476-0341
New York *(G-9609)*

Hamil America Inc ....F 212 244-2645
New York *(G-9714)*

Hania By Anya Cole LLC ....G 212 302-3550
New York *(G-9722)*

Lynch Knitting Mills Inc ....E 718 821-3436
Brooklyn *(G-2090)*

Machinit Inc ....G 631 454-9297
Farmingdale *(G-4675)*

Mdj Sales Associates Inc ....G 914 420-5897
Mamaroneck *(G-7515)*

Native Textiles Inc ....G 212 951-5100
New York *(G-10549)*

North Star Knitting Mills Inc ....G 718 894-4848
Glendale *(G-5230)*

S & V Knits Inc ....E 631 752-1595
Farmingdale *(G-4730)*

T & R Knitting Mills Inc ....F 212 840-8665
New York *(G-11415)*

CLOTHING: Outerwear, Lthr, Wool/Down-Filled, Men, Youth/Boy

Brigantine Inc ....G 212 354-8550
New York *(G-8851)*

Employee Codes: A=Over 500 employees, B=251-500
C=101-250, D=51-100, F=20-50, F=10-19, G=5-9

2020 Harris
New York Manufacturers Directory

1057

PRODUCT

Herman Kay Company Ltd ....C ... 212 239-2025
New York (G-9768)
I Spiewak & Sons Inc ....E ... 212 695-1620
New York (G-9849)
Maiyet Inc ....G ... 212 343-9999
New York (G-10333)
Rainforest Inc ....F ... 212 575-7620
New York (G-10973)
Vf Outdoor Inc ....E ... 718 698-6215
Staten Island (G-14727)
Vf Outdoor LLC ....E ... 845 928-4900
Central Valley (G-3301)

CLOTHING: Outerwear, Women's & Misses' NEC

525 America LLC ....G ... 212 921-5688
New York (G-8405)
6th Avenue Showcase Inc ....G ... 212 382-0400
New York (G-8407)
A & B Finishing Inc ....E ... 718 522-4702
Brooklyn (G-1427)
Accessory Street LLC ....F ... 212 686-8990
New York (G-8442)
Ally Nyc Corp ....G ... 212 447-7277
New York (G-8523)
Angel-Made In Heaven Inc ....G ... 718 832-4778
Brooklyn (G-1510)
Bagznyc Corp ....F ... 212 643-8202
New York (G-8718)
Bank-Miller Co Inc ....E ... 914 227-9357
Pelham (G-12565)
Canada Goose Us Inc ....G ... 888 276-6297
Williamsville (G-16126)
Candlesticks Inc ....F ... 212 947-8900
New York (G-8903)
Carolina Herrera Ltd ....E ... 212 944-5757
New York (G-8923)
Central Mills Inc ....C ... 212 764-9011
New York (G-8952)
China Ting Fshion Group USA LL ....G ... 212 716-1600
New York (G-8993)
Comint Apparel Group LLC ....E ... 212 947-7474
New York (G-9065)
Cynthia Rowley Inc ....F ... 212 242-3803
New York (G-9142)
Dalma Dress Mfg Co Inc ....E ... 212 391-8296
Greenvale (G-5461)
Dana Michele LLC ....G ... 917 757-7777
New York (G-9161)
Dani II Inc ....F ... 212 869-5999
New York (G-9165)
Donna Karan International Inc ....F ... 212 789-1500
New York (G-9249)
Donna Karan International Inc ....E ... 212 768-5800
New York (G-9250)
Emerald Holdings Inc ....G ... 718 797-4404
Brooklyn (G-1798)
Emerson & Oliver LLC ....G ... 585 775-9929
Rochester (G-13385)
Falls Manufacturing Inc ....E ... 518 672-7189
Philmont (G-12613)
G-III Apparel Group Ltd ....B ... 212 403-0500
New York (G-9560)
G-III Leather Fashions Inc ....E ... 212 403-0500
New York (G-9563)
GAME Sportswear Ltd ....C ... 914 962-1701
Yorktown Heights (G-16365)
Gloria Apparel Inc ....F ... 212 947-0869
New York (G-9633)
Golden Leaves Knitwear Inc ....E ... 718 875-8235
Brooklyn (G-1898)
Herman Kay Company Ltd ....C ... 212 239-2025
New York (G-9768)
Hot Line Industries Inc ....F ... 516 764-0400
Bellmore (G-783)
House Pearl Fashions (us) Ltd ....F ... 212 840-3183
New York (G-9826)
Int Trading USA LLC ....C ... 212 760-2338
New York (G-9906)
Jesse Joeckel ....G ... 631 668-2772
Montauk (G-8054)
Jomat New York Inc ....E ... 718 369-7641
Brooklyn (G-1998)
Just Bottoms & Tops Inc ....F ... 212 564-3202
New York (G-10044)
Kasper Group LLC ....F ... 212 354-4311
New York (G-10074)
Lahoya Enterprise Inc ....E ... 718 886-8799
College Point (G-3550)

Land n Sea Inc ....D ... 212 444-6000
New York (G-10168)
Liberty Apparel Company Inc ....E ... 718 625-4000
New York (G-10209)
Light Inc ....G ... 212 629-3255
New York (G-10217)
Luxe Imagine Consulting LLC ....G ... 212 273-9770
New York (G-10286)
Maiyet Inc ....G ... 212 343-9999
New York (G-10333)
Manchu New York Inc ....G ... 212 921-5050
New York (G-10340)
Manchu Times Fashion Inc ....G ... 212 921-5050
New York (G-10341)
Marina Holding Corp ....F ... 718 646-9283
Brooklyn (G-2115)
Miltons of New York Inc ....E ... 212 997-3359
New York (G-10471)
Moes Wear Apparel Inc ....F ... 718 940-1597
Brooklyn (G-2167)
Mv Corp Inc ....G ... 631 273-8020
Bay Shore (G-695)
Mystic Inc ....C ... 212 239-2025
New York (G-10528)
Only Hearts Ltd ....E ... 212 268-0886
New York (G-10694)
Pacific Alliance Usa Inc ....G ... 336 500-8184
New York (G-10738)
Pacific Alliance Usa Inc ....D ... 646 839-7000
New York (G-10739)
Pat & Rose Dress Inc ....D ... 212 279-1357
New York (G-10768)
Primo Coat Corp ....F ... 718 349-2070
Long Island City (G-7329)
Pti-Pacific Inc ....E ... 212 414-8495
New York (G-10920)
Pvh Corp ....D ... 212 502-6300
New York (G-10936)
Republic Clothing Corporation ....E ... 212 719-3000
New York (G-11016)
Rogers Group Inc ....E ... 212 643-9292
New York (G-11075)
Rvc Enterprises LLC ....E ... 212 391-4600
New York (G-11101)
S & V Knits Inc ....S ... 631 752-1595
Farmingdale (G-4730)
Smooth Industries Incorporated ....E ... 212 869-1080
New York (G-11276)
SRP Apparel Group Inc ....G ... 212 764-4810
New York (G-11341)
Standard Manufacturing Co Inc ....D ... 518 235-2200
Troy (G-15190)
Sunynams Fashions Ltd ....G ... 212 268-5200
Roslyn Heights (G-14058)
Survival Inc ....G ... 631 385-5060
Centerport (G-3258)
Tbhl International LLC ....F ... 212 799-2007
New York (G-11438)
THE Design Group Inc ....F ... 212 681-1548
New York (G-11459)
Vf Imagewear Inc ....E ... 718 352-2363
Bayside (G-744)
Vf Outdoor LLC ....E ... 845 928-4900
Central Valley (G-3301)
Warnaco Group Inc ....E ... 212 287-8000
New York (G-11720)
Yigal-Azrouel Inc ....E ... 212 302-1194
New York (G-11809)
Zar Group LLC ....F ... 212 944-2510
New York (G-11816)
Zia Power Inc ....G ... 845 661-8388
New York (G-11823)

CLOTHING: Overcoats & Topcoats, Men/Boy, Purchased Materials

Ralph Lauren Corporation ....B ... 212 318-7000
New York (G-10975)

CLOTHING: Pants, Work, Men's, Youths' & Boys'

Ace Drop Cloth Canvas Pdts Inc ....E ... 718 731-1550
Bronx (G-1193)

CLOTHING: Panty Hose

Brach Knitting Mills Inc ....F ... 845 651-4450
Florida (G-4821)
Classic Hosiery Inc ....E ... 845 342-6661
Middletown (G-7899)

Ellis Products Corp ....G ... 516 791-3732
Valley Stream (G-15339)
Fine Sheer Industries Inc ....F ... 212 594-4224
New York (G-9495)

CLOTHING: Raincoats, Exc Vulcanized Rubber, Purchased Matls

Essex Manufacturing Inc ....D ... 212 239-0080
New York (G-9404)
Levy Group Inc ....C ... 212 398-0707
New York (G-10206)
Mpdw Inc ....G ... 925 631-6878
New York (G-10512)

CLOTHING: Robes & Dressing Gowns

Authentic Brands Group LLC ....C ... 212 760-2410
New York (G-8680)
Komar Luxury Brands ....G ... 646 472-0060
New York (G-10125)
Lady Ester Lingerie Corp ....E ... 212 689-1729
New York (G-10162)
Palmbay Ltd ....G ... 718 424-3388
Flushing (G-4884)

CLOTHING: Robes & Housecoats, Children's

Waterbury Garment LLC ....E ... 212 725-1500
New York (G-11730)

CLOTHING: Scarves & Mufflers, Knit

180s LLC ....E ... 410 534-6320
New York (G-8390)

CLOTHING: Service Apparel, Women's

Fashion Ave Sweater Knits LLC ....C ... 212 302-8282
New York (G-9475)
HC Contracting Inc ....D ... 212 643-9292
New York (G-9740)
Lotus Apparel Designs Inc ....G ... 646 236-9363
Westbury (G-15906)
Mag Brands LLC ....D ... 212 629-9600
New York (G-10319)
RAK Finishing Corp ....E ... 718 416-4242
Howard Beach (G-6141)
Salsa Professional Apparel LLC ....G ... 212 575-6565
New York (G-11122)

CLOTHING: Shawls, Knit

Lloyds Fashions Inc ....D ... 631 435-3353
Brentwood (G-1125)

CLOTHING: Sheep-Lined

US Authentic LLC ....G ... 914 767-0295
Katonah (G-6639)

CLOTHING: Shirts

Andy & Evan Industries Inc ....G ... 212 967-7908
New York (G-8581)
August Silk Inc ....E ... 212 643-2400
New York (G-8678)
August Silk Inc ....G ... 212 643-2400
New York (G-8679)
Ben Wachter Associates Inc ....G ... 212 736-4064
New York (G-8754)
Bowe Industries Inc ....D ... 718 441-6464
Glendale (G-5219)
Bowe Industries Inc ....D ... 718 441-6464
Glendale (G-5220)
Check Group LLC ....D ... 212 221-4700
New York (G-8978)
Christian Casey LLC ....E ... 212 500-2200
New York (G-8997)
Christian Casey LLC ....E ... 212 500-2200
New York (G-8998)
Colony Holdings Intl LLC ....F ... 212 868-2800
New York (G-9054)
Cyberlimit Inc ....F ... 212 840-9597
New York (G-9140)
Donna Karan International Inc ....E ... 212 789-1500
New York (G-9249)
Donna Karan International Inc ....G ... 212 768-5800
New York (G-9250)
Garan Incorporated ....E ... 212 563-1292
New York (G-9573)
Garan Manufacturing Corp ....G ... 212 563-2000
New York (G-9574)

Gbg National Brands Group LLC ....G...... 646 839-7000
New York *(G-9577)*

Grayers America Inc ....F...... 310 953-2742
New York *(G-9668)*

Groupe 16sur20 LLC ....F...... 212 625-1620
New York *(G-9685)*

Haddad Bros Inc ....F...... 212 563-2117
New York *(G-9706)*

Interbrand LLC ....G...... 212 840-9595
New York *(G-9913)*

Jordache Enterprises Inc ....D...... 212 944-1330
New York *(G-10024)*

Jordache Enterprises Inc ....C...... 212 643-8400
New York *(G-10025)*

Just Brass Inc ....G...... 212 724-5447
New York *(G-10045)*

Lt2 LLC ....E...... 212 684-1510
New York *(G-10277)*

M S B International Ltd ....F...... 212 302-5551
New York *(G-10299)*

Mega Sourcing Inc ....G...... 646 682-0304
Merrick *(G-7861)*

Miltons of New York Inc ....G...... 212 997-3359
New York *(G-10471)*

Mulitex Usa Inc ....G...... 212 398-0440
New York *(G-10518)*

Oxford Industries Inc ....F...... 212 840-2288
New York *(G-10726)*

Perry Ellis Menswear LLC ....C...... 212 221-7500
New York *(G-10809)*

Roffe Accessories Inc ....E...... 212 213-1440
New York *(G-11071)*

Saad Collection Inc ....G...... 212 937-0341
New York *(G-11111)*

Schwartz Textile LLC ....E...... 718 499-8243
Brooklyn *(G-2389)*

Sifonya Inc ....G...... 212 620-4512
New York *(G-11229)*

Whittall & Shon ....G...... 212 594-2626
New York *(G-11752)*

Yale Trouser Corporation ....F...... 516 255-0700
Oceanside *(G-12199)*

CLOTHING: Shirts, Dress, Men's & Boys'

Americo Group Inc ....E...... 212 563-2700
New York *(G-8560)*

Americo Group Inc ....E...... 212 563-2700
New York *(G-8561)*

Arthur Gluck Shirtmakers Inc ....F...... 212 755-8165
Brooklyn *(G-1537)*

Gce International Inc ....D...... 773 263-1210
New York *(G-9582)*

Great Universal Corp ....E...... 917 302-0065
New York *(G-9670)*

Phillips-Van Heusen Europe ....F...... 212 381-3500
New York *(G-10829)*

Pvh Corp ....D...... 212 381-3500
New York *(G-10933)*

Pvh Corp ....G...... 845 561-0233
New Windsor *(G-8379)*

Pvh Corp ....G...... 631 254-8200
Deer Park *(G-3924)*

Pvh Corp ....G...... 212 549-6000
New York *(G-10934)*

Pvh Corp ....G...... 212 719-2600
New York *(G-10937)*

Ralph Lauren Corporation ....B...... 212 318-7000
New York *(G-10975)*

Warnaco Inc ....B...... 212 287-8000
New York *(G-11721)*

Warnaco Inc ....F...... 718 722-3000
Brooklyn *(G-2575)*

CLOTHING: Shirts, Knit

KD Dids Inc ....E...... 718 402-2012
Bronx *(G-1289)*

Ralph Lauren Corporation ....B...... 212 318-7000
New York *(G-10975)*

Warnaco Inc ....F...... 718 722-3000
Brooklyn *(G-2575)*

CLOTHING: Shirts, Sports & Polo, Men & Boy, Purchased Mtrl

Ibrands International LLC ....F...... 212 354-1330
New York *(G-9853)*

CLOTHING: Shirts, Sports & Polo, Men's & Boys'

Grunt Apparel Inc ....G...... 646 878-6171
New York *(G-9689)*

Oved Mens LLC ....E...... 212 563-4999
New York *(G-10719)*

Perry Ellis International Inc ....F...... 212 536-5400
New York *(G-10807)*

Perry Ellis International Inc ....G...... 212 536-5499
New York *(G-10808)*

CLOTHING: Shirts, Women's & Juniors', From Purchased Mtrls

Brach Knitting Mills Inc ....F...... 845 651-4450
Florida *(G-4821)*

Jordache Enterprises Inc ....D...... 212 944-1330
New York *(G-10024)*

Jordache Enterprises Inc ....C...... 212 643-8400
New York *(G-10025)*

CLOTHING: Skirts

Alfred Dunner Inc ....B...... 212 478-4300
New York *(G-8515)*

Anna Sui Corp ....E...... 212 941-8406
New York *(G-8593)*

Bruno & Canio Ltd ....E...... 845 624-3060
Nanuet *(G-8197)*

Carolina Herrera Ltd ....E...... 212 944-5757
New York *(G-8923)*

Geoffrey Beene Inc ....E...... 212 371-5570
New York *(G-9597)*

Hampshire Sub II Inc ....D...... 631 321-0923
New York *(G-9716)*

Kayo of California ....G...... 212 354-6336
New York *(G-10083)*

Nyc Idol Apparel Inc ....G...... 212 997-9797
New York *(G-10661)*

Pat & Rose Dress Inc ....D...... 212 279-1357
New York *(G-10768)*

Permit Fashion Group Inc ....G...... 212 912-0988
Melville *(G-7815)*

Rhoda Lee Inc ....D...... 212 840-5700
New York *(G-11035)*

Turn On Products Inc ....F...... 212 764-4545
New York *(G-11560)*

CLOTHING: Slacks & Shorts, Dress, Men's, Youths' & Boys'

Montero International Inc ....G...... 212 695-1787
Westbury *(G-15911)*

CLOTHING: Slacks, Girls' & Children's

Garan Incorporated ....C...... 212 563-1292
New York *(G-9573)*

Garan Manufacturing Corp ....G...... 212 563-2000
New York *(G-9574)*

Jordache Enterprises Inc ....D...... 212 944-1330
New York *(G-10024)*

Jordache Enterprises Inc ....C...... 212 643-8400
New York *(G-10025)*

CLOTHING: Sleeping Garments, Men's & Boys'

Sleepwear Holdings Inc ....C...... 516 466-4738
New York *(G-11268)*

CLOTHING: Sleeping Garments, Women's & Children's

Allure Fashions Inc ....G...... 516 829-2470
Great Neck *(G-5363)*

Candlesticks Inc ....F...... 212 947-8900
New York *(G-8903)*

Halo Innovations Inc ....E...... 952 259-1500
Brooklyn *(G-1920)*

Kokin Inc ....E...... 212 643-8225
New York *(G-10123)*

Komar Luxury Brands ....G...... 646 472-0060
New York *(G-10125)*

Natori Company Incorporated ....D...... 212 532-7796
New York *(G-10550)*

Pearl River Textiles Inc ....G...... 212 629-5490
New York *(G-10778)*

Waterbury Garment LLC ....E...... 212 725-1500
New York *(G-11730)*

CLOTHING: Slipper Socks

Palmbay Ltd ....G...... 718 424-3388
Flushing *(G-4884)*

CLOTHING: Socks

Ace Drop Cloth Canvas Pdts Inc ....E...... 718 731-1550
Bronx *(G-1193)*

Ashko Group LLC ....F...... 212 594-6050
New York *(G-8645)*

Centric Socks LLC ....E...... 646 839-7000
New York *(G-8957)*

Customize Elite Socks LLC ....G...... 212 533-8551
New York *(G-9136)*

Fine Sheer Industries Inc ....F...... 212 594-4224
New York *(G-9495)*

Gina Group LLC ....E...... 212 947-2445
New York *(G-9612)*

La Strada Dance Footwear Inc ....G...... 631 242-1401
Deer Park *(G-3895)*

Majesty Brands LLC ....G...... 212 283-3400
New York *(G-10335)*

Ness Legwear LLC ....G...... 212 335-0777
New York *(G-10567)*

New Hampton Creations Inc ....G...... 212 244-7474
New York *(G-10584)*

Sockbin ....G...... 917 519-1119
Brooklyn *(G-2433)*

Socks and More of NY Inc ....G...... 718 769-1785
Brooklyn *(G-2434)*

Sticky Socks LLC ....G...... 212 541-5927
New York *(G-11363)*

Strassburg Medical LLC ....G...... 800 452-0631
North Tonawanda *(G-12092)*

Trimfit Inc ....E...... 215 245-1122
New York *(G-11546)*

United Retail II ....G...... 212 966-9692
New York *(G-11599)*

CLOTHING: Sportswear, Women's

31 Phillip Lim LLC ....E...... 212 354-6540
New York *(G-8401)*

American Apparel Trading Corp ....G...... 212 764-5990
New York *(G-8544)*

Angel-Made In Heaven Inc ....E...... 212 869-5678
New York *(G-8583)*

Argee America Inc ....G...... 212 768-9840
New York *(G-8621)*

AZ Yashir Bapaz Inc ....G...... 212 947-7357
New York *(G-8700)*

Bandit International Ltd ....F...... 718 402-2100
Bronx *(G-1210)*

Bernard Chaus Inc ....D...... 212 354-1280
New York *(G-8760)*

Bernard Chaus Inc ....C...... 646 562-4700
New York *(G-8761)*

Cai Design Inc ....F...... 212 401-9973
New York *(G-8887)*

Cathy Daniels Ltd ....E...... 212 354-8000
Old Westbury *(G-12222)*

Central Apparel Group Ltd ....F...... 212 868-6505
New York *(G-8950)*

City Sites Sportswear Inc ....E...... 718 375-2990
Brooklyn *(G-1668)*

Daily Wear Sportswear Corp ....G...... 718 972-0533
Brooklyn *(G-1719)*

Danice Stores Inc ....F...... 212 665-0389
New York *(G-9166)*

Double Take Fashions Inc ....F...... 718 832-9000
New York *(G-9256)*

Drew Philips Corp ....F...... 212 354-0095
New York *(G-9270)*

El-La Design Inc ....G...... 212 382-1080
New York *(G-9331)*

F & J Designs Inc ....G...... 212 302-8755
New York *(G-9454)*

French Atmosphere Inc ....F...... 516 371-9100
New York *(G-9536)*

Halmode Apparel Inc ....A...... 212 819-9114
New York *(G-9712)*

Ikeddi Enterprises Inc ....F...... 212 302-7644
New York *(G-9863)*

Ikeddi Enterprises Inc ....G...... 212 302-7644
New York *(G-9864)*

J & E Talit Inc ....G...... 718 850-1333
Richmond Hill *(G-13116)*

Jaxis Inc ....G...... 212 302-7611
Brooklyn *(G-1989)*

JI Parc LLC ....G...... 718 271-0703
Rego Park *(G-13078)*

Joe Benbasset Inc ....E 212 594-8440
  New York (G-10014)
Kayo of California ....G 212 354-6336
  New York (G-10083)
Leggiadro International Inc ....E 212 997-8766
  Yonkers (G-16326)
Life Style Design Group ....E 212 391-8666
  New York (G-10213)
Marcasiano Inc ....G 212 614-9412
  New York (G-10354)
Meryl Diamond Ltd ....D 212 730-0333
  New York (G-10439)
Millennium Productions Inc ....F 212 944-6203
  New York (G-10467)
Morelle Products Ltd ....F 212 391-8070
  New York (G-10502)
Nlhe LLC ....E 212 594-0012
  Brooklyn (G-2217)
Noah Enterprises Ltd ....E 212 736-2888
  New York (G-10634)
P & I Sportswear Inc ....G 718 934-4587
  New York (G-10731)
Park Avenue Sportswear Ltd ....F 718 369-0520
  Brooklyn (G-2248)
Planet Gold Clothing Co Inc ....C 646 432-5100
  New York (G-10851)
Premier Brnds Group Hldngs LLC ......G 212 642-3860
  New York (G-10877)
Premier Brnds Group Hldngs LLC ......E 212 642-3860
  New York (G-10879)
Pride & Joys Inc ....F 212 594-9820
  New York (G-10888)
Pvh Corp ....G 212 381-3800
  New York (G-10935)
Ramsbury Property Us Inc ....F 212 223-6250
  New York (G-10976)
Rene Portier Inc ....G 718 853-7896
  Brooklyn (G-2341)
Ritchie Corp ....F 212 768-0083
  New York (G-11049)
Robespierre Inc ....G 212 764-8810
  New York (G-11063)
S & S Manufacturing Co Inc ....D 212 444-6000
  New York (G-11106)
S2 Sportswear Inc ....F 347 335-0713
  Brooklyn (G-2378)
Salisbury Sportswear Inc ....E 516 221-9519
  Bellmore (G-789)
Siskind Group Inc ....F 212 840-0880
  New York (G-11251)
Snowman ....G 212 239-8818
  New York (G-11280)
Ssa Trading Ltd ....F 646 465-9500
  New York (G-11342)
SSG Fashions Ltd ....G 212 221-0933
  New York (G-11343)
St John ....G 718 720-8367
  Staten Island (G-14712)
St John ....G 718 771-4541
  Brooklyn (G-2448)
Street Beat Sportswear Inc ....F 718 302-1500
  Brooklyn (G-2463)
Tiger J LLC ....E 212 465-9300
  New York (G-11486)
TR Designs Inc ....E 212 398-9300
  New York (G-11527)
Turn On Products Inc ....D 212 764-2121
  New York (G-11559)
Urban Apparel Group Inc ....E 212 947-7009
  New York (G-11615)

CLOTHING: Suits & Skirts, Women's & Misses'

Bindle and Keep ....G 917 740-5002
  Brooklyn (G-1588)
Centric Brands Inc ....G 212 925-5727
  New York (G-8954)
Centric Brands Inc ....D 646 582-6000
  New York (G-8955)
Itochu Prominent USA LLC ....C 212 827-5715
  New York (G-9948)
Opposuits USA Inc ....E 917 438-8878
  New York (G-10700)
R & M Richards Inc ....C 212 921-8820
  New York (G-10965)

CLOTHING: Suits, Men's & Boys', From Purchased Materials

Bindle and Keep ....G 917 740-5002
  Brooklyn (G-1588)
Canali USA Inc ....E 212 767-0205
  New York (G-8901)
Kozinn+sons Merchant Tailors .....E 212 643-1916
  New York (G-10132)
Martin Greenfield Clothiers ....C 718 497-5480
  Brooklyn (G-2120)
Michael Andrews LLC ....F 212 677-1755
  New York (G-10451)
Primo Coat Corp ....E 718 349-2070
  Long Island City (G-7329)
Roth Clothing Co Inc ....G 718 384-4927
  Brooklyn (G-2356)
Royal Clothing Corp ....G 718 436-5841
  Brooklyn (G-2358)
Tom James Company ....F 212 593-0204
  New York (G-11509)

CLOTHING: Sweaters & Sweater Coats, Knit

79 Metro Ltd ....G 212 944-4030
  New York (G-8408)
A & B Finishing Inc ....E 718 522-4702
  Brooklyn (G-1427)
Accurate Knitting Corp ....G 646 552-2216
  Brooklyn (G-1451)
B & B Sweater Mills Inc ....F 718 456-8693
  Brooklyn (G-1555)
Binghamton Knitting Co Inc ....E 607 722-6941
  Binghamton (G-858)
Blueberry Knitting Inc ....E 718 599-6520
  Brooklyn (G-1597)
Charter Ventures LLC ....F 212 868-0222
  New York (G-8977)
Domani Fashions Corp ....G 718 797-0505
  Brooklyn (G-1755)
Golden Leaves Knitwear Inc ....E 718 875-8235
  Brooklyn (G-1898)
Great Adirondack Yarn Company ......F 518 843-3381
  Amsterdam (G-329)
Jeric Knit Wear ....G 631 979-8827
  Smithtown (G-14480)
Jj Basics LLC ....E 212 768-4779
  New York (G-10008)
Julia Knit Inc ....G 718 848-1900
  Ozone Park (G-12464)
K & S Childrens Wear Inc ....E 718 624-0006
  Brooklyn (G-2016)
Keryakos Inc ....F 518 344-7092
  Schenectady (G-14284)
Knit Illustrated Inc ....E 212 268-9054
  New York (G-10116)
M B M Manufacturing Inc ....F 718 769-4148
  Brooklyn (G-2096)
Manrico Usa Inc ....G 212 794-4200
  New York (G-10350)
Matchables Inc ....F 718 389-9318
  Brooklyn (G-2123)
New York Sweater Company Inc ......G 845 629-9533
  New York (G-10603)
Phillips-Van Heusen Europe ....F 212 381-3500
  New York (G-10829)
Premier Knits Ltd ....F 718 323-8264
  Ozone Park (G-12466)
Pvh Corp ....D 212 381-3500
  New York (G-10933)
Pvh Corp ....G 212 549-6000
  New York (G-10934)
Rags Knitwear Ltd ....F 718 782-8417
  Brooklyn (G-2322)
S & T Knitting Co Inc ....E 607 722-7558
  Conklin (G-3628)
Sage Knitwear Inc ....G 718 628-7902
  West Babylon (G-15745)
Sarug Inc ....D 718 339-2791
  Brooklyn (G-2384)
Sweater Brand Inc ....G 718 797-0505
  Brooklyn (G-2482)
T & R Knitting Mills Inc ....E 718 497-4017
  Glendale (G-5233)
United Knitwear International ....E 212 354-2920
  New York (G-11598)
WR Design Corp ....E 212 354-9000
  New York (G-11791)

CLOTHING: Sweaters, Men's & Boys'

Bernette Apparel LLC ....F 212 279-5526
  New York (G-8762)
Cotton Emporium Inc ....G 718 894-3365
  Glendale (G-5223)
Just Bottoms & Tops Inc ....F 212 564-3202
  New York (G-10044)
Komar Luxury Brands ....G 646 472-0060
  New York (G-10125)
Scharf and Breit Inc ....E 516 282-0287
  Williston Park (G-16148)
Schwartz Textile LLC ....E 718 499-8243
  Brooklyn (G-2389)
Uniqlo USA LLC ....F 877 486-4756
  New York (G-11593)

CLOTHING: Sweatshirts & T-Shirts, Men's & Boys'

Kt Group Inc ....G 212 760-2500
  New York (G-10144)

CLOTHING: Swimwear, Men's & Boys'

Comme-Ci Comme-CA AP Group ......E 631 300-1035
  Hauppauge (G-5623)
Longevity Brands LLC ....G 212 231-7877
  New York (G-10248)
Swimwear Anywhere Inc ....E 845 858-4141
  Port Jervis (G-12858)

CLOTHING: Swimwear, Women's & Misses'

Christina Sales Inc ....F 212 391-0710
  New York (G-9001)
Comme-Ci Comme-CA AP Group ......E 631 300-1035
  Hauppauge (G-5623)
Feldman Manufacturing Corp ......D 718 433-1700
  Long Island City (G-7222)
Malia Mills Inc ....F 212 354-4200
  Brooklyn (G-2105)
Michael Feldman Inc ....D 718 433-1700
  Long Island City (G-7296)
Ocean Waves Swim LLC ....G 212 967-4481
  New York (G-10676)
Sea Waves Inc ....G 516 766-4201
  Oceanside (G-12189)
Swimwear Anywhere Inc ....G 631 420-1400
  Farmingdale (G-4746)
Swimwear Anywhere Inc ....E 845 858-4141
  Port Jervis (G-12858)
Venus Manufacturing Co Inc ....D 315 639-3100
  Dexter (G-4007)

CLOTHING: T-Shirts & Tops, Knit

Central Mills Inc ....C 212 764-9011
  New York (G-8952)
Elegant Headwear Co Inc ....G 212 695-8520
  New York (G-9336)
J & E Talit Inc ....G 718 850-1333
  Richmond Hill (G-13116)
Jfs Inc ....E 646 264-1200
  New York (G-10001)
Mann Consultants LLC ....E 914 763-0512
  Waccabuc (G-15446)
Precision Apparel Mfg LLC ....G 201 805-2664
  New York (G-10874)

CLOTHING: T-Shirts & Tops, Women's & Girls'

Alfred Dunner Inc ....B 212 478-4300
  New York (G-8515)
Bowe Industries Inc ....D 718 441-6464
  Glendale (G-5219)
Garan Incorporated ....C 212 563-1292
  New York (G-9573)
Garan Manufacturing Corp ....G 212 563-2000
  New York (G-9574)
Gce International Inc ....D 212 704-4800
  New York (G-9580)
Hansae Co Ltd ....F 212 354-6690
  New York (G-9724)
T Rj Shirts Inc ....G 347 642-3071
  East Elmhurst (G-4111)

CLOTHING: Tailored Suits & Formal Jackets

Crisada Inc ....G 718 729-9730
  Long Island City (G-7194)

(G-0000) Company's Geographic Section entry number

John Kochis Custom Designs .... G 212 244-6046
New York *(G-10016)*

Shane Tex Inc .... F 516 486-7522
Woodmere *(G-16193)*

CLOTHING: Ties, Handsewn, From Purchased Materials

Ralph Lauren Corporation .... B 212 318-7000
New York *(G-10975)*

Tie King Inc .... G 212 714-9611
New York *(G-11484)*

CLOTHING: Ties, Neck & Bow, Men's & Boys'

Tie King Inc .... E 718 768-8484
Brooklyn *(G-2504)*

CLOTHING: Ties, Neck, Men's & Boys', From Purchased Material

Countess Mara Inc .... G 212 768-7300
New York *(G-9111)*

Mallory & Church LLC .... G 212 868-7888
New York *(G-10337)*

Perry Ellis Menswear LLC .... C 212 221-7500
New York *(G-10809)*

Randa Accessories Lea Gds LLC .... D 212 354-5100
New York *(G-10979)*

W B Bow Tie Corp .... F 212 683-6130
New York *(G-11712)*

CLOTHING: Tights & Leg Warmers

Look By M Inc .... G 212 213-4019
New York *(G-10251)*

CLOTHING: Trousers & Slacks, Men's & Boys'

Adrian Jules Ltd .... D 585 342-5886
Rochester *(G-13207)*

Check Group LLC .... D 212 221-4700
New York *(G-8978)*

Christian Casey LLC .... E 212 500-2200
New York *(G-8997)*

Christian Casey LLC .... E 212 500-2200
New York *(G-8998)*

Groupe 16sur20 LLC .... F 212 625-1620
New York *(G-9685)*

Hertling Trousers Inc .... E 718 784-6100
Brooklyn *(G-1935)*

Hugo Boss Usa Inc .... D 212 940-0600
New York *(G-9835)*

Int Trading USA LLC .... C 212 760-2338
New York *(G-9906)*

Jordache Enterprises Inc .... D 212 944-1330
New York *(G-10024)*

Jordache Enterprises Inc .... C 212 643-8400
New York *(G-10025)*

M Hidary & Co Inc .... D 212 736-6540
New York *(G-10296)*

M S B International Ltd .... F 212 302-5551
New York *(G-10299)*

Miltons of New York Inc .... G 212 997-3359
New York *(G-10471)*

Mulitex Usa Inc .... G 212 398-0440
New York *(G-10518)*

Pat & Rose Dress Inc .... D 212 279-1357
New York *(G-10768)*

Perry Ellis International Inc .... F 212 536-5400
New York *(G-10807)*

Primo Coat Corp .... E 718 349-2070
Long Island City *(G-7329)*

Ralph Lauren Corporation .... B 212 318-7000
New York *(G-10975)*

Sean John Clothing Inc .... E 212 500-2200
New York *(G-11173)*

Sean John Clothing Inc .... E 212 500-2200
New York *(G-11174)*

CLOTHING: Underwear, Knit

Balanced Tech Corp .... E 212 768-8330
New York *(G-8722)*

CLOTHING: Underwear, Men's & Boys'

Becks Classic Mfg Inc .... D 631 435-3800
Brentwood *(G-1116)*

Check Group LLC .... D 212 221-4700
New York *(G-8978)*

Comme-Ci Comme-CA AP Group .... E 631 300-1035
Hauppauge *(G-5623)*

Twist Intimate Group LLC .... G 212 695-5990
New York *(G-11564)*

Warnaco Group Inc .... E 212 287-8000
New York *(G-11720)*

Warnaco Inc .... B 212 287-8000
New York *(G-11721)*

Warnaco Inc .... F 718 722-3000
Brooklyn *(G-2575)*

Wickers Sportswear Inc .... G 631 543-1640
Commack *(G-3604)*

CLOTHING: Underwear, Women's & Children's

Intimateco LLC .... G 212 239-4411
New York *(G-9928)*

Luxerdame Co Inc .... E 718 752-9800
Long Island City *(G-7282)*

Natori Company Incorporated .... E 212 532-7796
New York *(G-10551)*

Only Hearts Ltd .... E 212 268-0886
New York *(G-10694)*

Wickers Sportswear Inc .... G 631 543-1640
Commack *(G-3604)*

CLOTHING: Uniforms & Vestments

Craft Clerical Clothes Inc .... G 212 764-6122
New York *(G-9116)*

JM Studio Inc .... F 646 546-5514
New York *(G-10011)*

NY Orthopedic Usa Inc .... D 718 852-5330
Brooklyn *(G-2225)*

RA Newhouse Inc .... D 516 248-6670
Mineola *(G-7995)*

White Plains Coat Apron Co Inc .... G 914 736-2610
Peekskill *(G-12563)*

CLOTHING: Uniforms, Ex Athletic, Women's, Misses' & Juniors'

Elie Tahari Ltd .... D 212 763-2000
New York *(G-9340)*

Lady Brass Co Inc .... G 516 887-8040
Hewlett *(G-5870)*

Marlou Garments Inc .... F 516 739-7100
New Hyde Park *(G-8281)*

Shane Tex Inc .... F 516 486-7522
Woodmere *(G-16193)*

Uniforms By Park Coats Inc .... E 718 499-1182
Brooklyn *(G-2536)*

CLOTHING: Uniforms, Firemen's, From Purchased Materials

Salsa Professional Apparel LLC .... G 212 575-6565
New York *(G-11122)*

CLOTHING: Uniforms, Men's & Boys'

Occunomix International LLC .... E 631 741-1940
Port Jeff STA *(G-12837)*

Otex Protective Inc .... G 585 232-7160
Rochester *(G-13600)*

Uniforms By Park Coats Inc .... E 718 499-1182
Brooklyn *(G-2536)*

Urban Textiles Inc .... F 212 777-1900
New York *(G-11617)*

Vf Imagewear Inc .... E 718 352-2363
Bayside *(G-744)*

CLOTHING: Uniforms, Military, Men/Youth, Purchased Materials

Crye Precision LLC .... C 718 246-3838
Brooklyn *(G-1705)*

Med-Eng LLC .... E 315 713-0130
Ogdensburg *(G-12209)*

CLOTHING: Uniforms, Policemen's, From Purchased Materials

Strong Group Inc .... G 516 766-6300
Oceanside *(G-12192)*

CLOTHING: Uniforms, Team Athletic

American Challenge Enterprises .... G 631 595-7171
Bay Shore *(G-648)*

American Clssic Outfitters Inc .... D 585 237-6111
Perry *(G-12595)*

Mayberry Shoe Company Inc .... G 315 692-4086
Manlius *(G-7549)*

Pti-Pacific Inc .... G 212 414-8495
New York *(G-10920)*

Tamka Sport LLC .... G 718 224-7820
Douglaston *(G-4030)*

CLOTHING: Uniforms, Work

Best Medical Wear Ltd .... G 718 858-5544
Brooklyn *(G-1579)*

Lady Brass Co Inc .... G 516 887-8040
Hewlett *(G-5870)*

Vf Imagewear Inc .... E 718 352-2363
Bayside *(G-744)*

CLOTHING: Warm Weather Knit Outerwear, Including Beachwear

Warm .... F 212 925-1200
New York *(G-11719)*

CLOTHING: Waterproof Outerwear

A W R Group Inc .... F 718 729-0412
Long Island City *(G-7141)*

Float Tech Inc .... G 518 266-0964
Troy *(G-15168)*

Top Fortune Usa Ltd .... G 516 608-2694
Lynbrook *(G-7441)*

CLOTHING: Work Apparel, Exc Uniforms

Enzo Manzoni LLC .... G 212 464-7000
Brooklyn *(G-1807)*

Salsa Professional Apparel LLC .... G 212 575-6565
New York *(G-11122)*

CLOTHING: Work, Men's

5 Star Apparel LLC .... G 212 563-1233
New York *(G-8404)*

American Apparel Ltd .... G 516 504-4559
Great Neck *(G-5364)*

Badgley Mischka Licensing LLC .... E 212 921-1585
New York *(G-8713)*

Billion Tower Intl LLC .... F 212 220-0608
New York *(G-8791)*

Broadway Knitting Mills Inc .... G 716 692-4421
North Tonawanda *(G-12059)*

Dalcom USA Ltd .... F 516 466-7733
Great Neck *(G-5380)*

Doral Apparel Group Inc .... G 917 208-5652
New York *(G-9254)*

Du Monde Trading Inc .... E 212 944-1306
New York *(G-9275)*

E J Manufacturing Inc .... G 516 313-9380
Bellmore *(G-782)*

Far East Industries Inc .... G 718 687-2482
New Hyde Park *(G-8268)*

Ferris USA LLC .... G 617 895-8102
New York *(G-9485)*

Hillary Merchant Inc .... G 646 575-9242
New York *(G-9785)*

Itochu Prominent USA LLC .... C 212 827-5715
New York *(G-9948)*

LLC Major Major .... E 212 354-8550
New York *(G-10236)*

Lynn Brands LLC .... E 626 376-8948
New York *(G-10289)*

Medline Industries Inc .... B 845 344-3301
Middletown *(G-7919)*

Mesh LLC .... E 646 839-7000
New York *(G-10440)*

New York Hospital Disposable .... E 718 384-1620
Brooklyn *(G-2208)*

Occunomix International LLC .... E 631 741-1940
Port Jeff STA *(G-12837)*

Penfli Industries Inc .... F 212 947-6080
Great Neck *(G-5413)*

Rag & Bone Industries LLC .... D 212 278-8214
New York *(G-10971)*

S & H Uniform Corp .... D 914 937-6800
White Plains *(G-16057)*

Shanghai Harmony AP Intl LLC .... E 646 569-5680
New Rochelle *(G-8354)*

Untuckit LLC .... D 347 524-9111
New York *(G-11612)*

Untuckit LLC .... C 646 724-1857
New York *(G-11613)*

PRODUCT

Ventura Enterprise Co Inc ....E 212 391-0170
New York *(G-11656)*

CLUTCHES OR BRAKES: Electromagnetic

American Precision Inds Inc ....C 716 691-9100
Amherst *(G-210)*

Fortitude Industries Inc ....D 607 324-1500
Hornell *(G-6106)*

CLUTCHES, EXC VEHICULAR

Machine Components Corp ....E 516 694-7222
Plainview *(G-12698)*

Magtrol Inc ....E 716 668-5555
Buffalo *(G-2859)*

COAL MINING SERVICES

Dowa International Corp ....F 212 697-3217
New York *(G-9261)*

Starfuels Inc ....G 914 289-4800
White Plains *(G-16062)*

Trimet Coal LLC ....E 718 951-3654
Brooklyn *(G-2521)*

COAL MINING SVCS: Bituminous, Contract Basis

Lessoilcom ....G 516 319-5052
Franklin Square *(G-4961)*

COAL MINING: Anthracite

Puglisi & Co ....E 212 300-2285
New York *(G-10925)*

COATING COMPOUNDS: Tar

Aremco Products Inc ....F 845 268-0039
Valley Cottage *(G-15313)*

Polyset Company Inc ....E 518 664-6000
Mechanicville *(G-7693)*

Spray-Tech Finishing Inc ....F 716 664-6317
Jamestown *(G-6542)*

COATING SVC

Cnv Architectural Coatings Inc ....G 718 418-9584
Brooklyn *(G-1672)*

Static Coatings Inc ....G 516 764-0040
Oceanside *(G-12191)*

COATING SVC: Aluminum, Metal Prdts

72 Steel and Aluminium Work ....G 917 667-3033
Brooklyn *(G-1422)*

Micromatter Tech Inc USA ....G 631 580-2522
Holbrook *(G-6012)*

COATING SVC: Electrodes

Chepaume Industries LLC ....G 315 829-6400
Vernon *(G-15364)*

Hilord Chemical Corporation ....E 631 234-7373
Hauppauge *(G-5671)*

COATING SVC: Metals & Formed Prdts

Advanced Surface Finishing ....E 516 876-9710
Westbury *(G-15862)*

Applause Coating LLC ....F 631 231-5223
Brentwood *(G-1115)*

Barson Composites Corporation ....E 516 752-7882
Old Bethpage *(G-12215)*

Deloka LLC ....G 315 946-6910
Lyons *(G-7449)*

Dynocoat Inc ....F 631 244-9344
Holbrook *(G-5997)*

Electronic Coating Tech Inc ....F 518 688-2048
Cohoes *(G-3506)*

Elegance Coating Ltd ....D 518 298-2888
Champlain *(G-3311)*

Future Spray Finishing Co ....G 631 242-6252
Deer Park *(G-3877)*

Greene Technologies Inc ....D 607 656-4166
Greene *(G-5446)*

Kwong CHI Metal Fabrication ....G 718 369-6429
Brooklyn *(G-2039)*

Master Craft Finishers Inc ....E 631 586-0540
Deer Park *(G-3904)*

Modern Coating and Research ....F 315 597-3517
Palmyra *(G-12492)*

Oerlikon Blzers Cating USA Inc ....E 716 270-2228
Amherst *(G-237)*

Oerlikon Blzers Cating USA Inc ....E 716 564-8557
Buffalo *(G-2895)*

Qualicoat Inc ....D 585 293-2650
Churchville *(G-3414)*

Sentry Metal Blast Inc ....E 716 285-5241
Lockport *(G-7106)*

Sequa Corporation ....E 201 343-1122
Orangeburg *(G-12332)*

Solidus Industries Inc ....D 607 749-4540
Homer *(G-6067)*

Static Coatings Inc ....G 646 296-0754
Lynbrook *(G-7439)*

Swain Technology Inc ....F 585 889-2786
Scottsville *(G-14344)*

Trojan Metal Fabrication Inc ....E 631 968-5040
Bay Shore *(G-723)*

W W Custom Clad Inc ....E 518 673-3322
Canajoharie *(G-3122)*

W W Custom Clad Inc ....E 518 673-3322
Canajoharie *(G-3123)*

COATING SVC: Metals, With Plastic Or Resins

Heany Industries Inc ....D 585 889-2700
Scottsville *(G-14340)*

Hudson Valley Coatings LLC ....G 845 398-1778
Congers *(G-3615)*

Metal Cladding Inc ....D 716 434-5513
Lockport *(G-7091)*

Piper Plastics Corp ....E 631 842-6889
Copiague *(G-3668)*

Pro-Teck Coating Inc ....F 716 537-2619
Holland *(G-6030)*

COATING SVC: Rust Preventative

Hubbell Galvanizing Inc ....G 315 736-8311
Yorkville *(G-16375)*

COATING SVC: Silicon

Mom Holding Company ....G 518 233-3330
Waterford *(G-15540)*

Momentive Performance Mtls Inc ....E 518 233-3330
Waterford *(G-15542)*

Mpm Holdings Inc ....G 518 233-3330
Waterford *(G-15543)*

Mpm Intermediate Holdings Inc ....G 518 237-3330
Waterford *(G-15544)*

COATINGS: Air Curing

Enecon Corporation ....D 516 349-0022
Medford *(G-7706)*

COATINGS: Epoxy

Delta Polymers Inc ....G 631 254-6240
Bay Shore *(G-673)*

Designer Epoxy Finishes Inc ....G 646 943-6044
Melville *(G-7774)*

Robert Greenburg ....G 845 586-2226
Margaretville *(G-7567)*

COATINGS: Polyurethane

Absolute Coatings Inc ....E 914 636-0700
New Rochelle *(G-8316)*

Paint Over Rust Products Inc ....E 914 636-0700
New Rochelle *(G-8348)*

COFFEE SVCS

Adirondack Ice & Air Inc ....E 518 483-4340
Malone *(G-7481)*

COILS & TRANSFORMERS

Aeroflex Incorporated ....B 516 694-6700
Plainview *(G-12660)*

All Shore Industries Inc ....F 718 720-0018
Staten Island *(G-14617)*

American Trans-Coil Corp ....F 516 922-9640
Oyster Bay *(G-12443)*

Bel Transformer Inc ....D 516 239-5777
Lynbrook *(G-7426)*

Electron Coil Inc ....D 607 336-7414
Norwich *(G-12121)*

Ems Development Corporation ....D 631 345-6200
Yaphank *(G-16260)*

Ems Development Corporation ....D 631 924-4736
Yaphank *(G-16259)*

Eni Technology Inc ....B 585 427-8300
Rochester *(G-13395)*

Es Beta Inc ....E 631 582-6740
Ronkonkoma *(G-13936)*

Fuse Electronics Inc ....G 607 352-3222
Kirkwood *(G-6731)*

Gowanda - Bti LLC ....D 716 492-4081
Arcade *(G-375)*

Hipotronics Inc ....C 845 279-8091
Brewster *(G-1151)*

M F L B Inc ....F 631 254-8300
Massapequa Park *(G-7658)*

Magnetic Technologies Corp ....D 585 385-9010
Rochester *(G-13530)*

Mini-Circuits Fort Wayne LLC ....B 718 934-4500
Brooklyn *(G-2157)*

Misonix Opco Inc ....D 631 694-9555
Farmingdale *(G-4687)*

Mitchell Electronics Corp ....E 914 699-3800
Mount Vernon *(G-8162)*

New York Fan Coil LLC ....G 646 580-1344
Coram *(G-3696)*

Rdi Inc ....F 914 773-1000
Mount Kisco *(G-8104)*

Sag Harbor Industries Inc ....E 631 725-0440
Sag Harbor *(G-14101)*

COILS: Electric Motors Or Generators

Electron Coil Inc ....D 607 336-7414
Norwich *(G-12121)*

P1 Generator Windings LLC ....G 518 930-2879
Schenectady *(G-14293)*

Sag Harbor Industries Inc ....E 631 725-0440
Sag Harbor *(G-14101)*

COILS: Pipe

Falcon Perspectives Inc ....G 718 706-9168
Long Island City *(G-7220)*

COIN OPERATED LAUNDRIES & DRYCLEANERS

Oxford Cleaners ....G 212 734-0006
New York *(G-10724)*

COIN-OPERATED LAUNDRY

Reynolds Drapery Service Inc ....F 315 845-8632
Newport *(G-11899)*

Sky Laundromat Inc ....E 718 639-7070
Jamaica *(G-6473)*

COKE: Calcined Petroleum, Made From Purchased Materials

Hh Liquidating Corp ....A 646 282-2500
New York *(G-9779)*

COKE: Produced In Chemical Recovery Coke Ovens

Tonawanda Coke Corporation ....C 716 876-6222
Tonawanda *(G-15145)*

COLLECTION AGENCY, EXC REAL ESTATE

Nyt Capital LLC ....F 212 556-1234
New York *(G-10669)*

COLLEGES, UNIVERSITIES & PROFESSIONAL SCHOOLS

Stony Brook University ....E 631 632-6434
Stony Brook *(G-14741)*

COLLETS

Hardinge Inc ....B 607 734-2281
Elmira *(G-4355)*

COLOGNES

Classique Perfumes Inc ....G 718 657-8200
Jamaica *(G-6436)*

COLOR SEPARATION: Photographic & Movie Film

Applied Image Inc ....E 585 482-0300
  Rochester (G-13241)
Eastern Color Stripping Inc ....F 631 563-3700
  Bohemia (G-1008)

COLORS: Pigments, Inorganic

Heany Industries Inc..........................D 585 889-2700
  Scottsville (G-14340)

COLORS: Pigments, Organic

Sml Brothers Holding Corp..................D 718 402-2000
  Bronx (G-1366)

COMFORTERS & QUILTS, FROM MANMADE FIBER OR SILK

Ess Bee Industries Inc.......................E 718 894-5202
  Brooklyn (G-1814)

COMMERCIAL & INDL SHELVING WHOLESALERS

Tri-Boro Shelving Inc.........................F 718 782-8527
  Ridgewood (G-13165)

COMMERCIAL & OFFICE BUILDINGS RENOVATION & REPAIR

Kng Construction Co Inc.....................F 212 595-1451
  Warwick (G-15517)

COMMERCIAL ART & GRAPHIC DESIGN SVCS

Art Digital Technologies LLC...............F 646 649-4820
  Brooklyn (G-1535)
Artscroll Printing Corp ....E 212 929-2413
  New York (G-8640)
Avalon Copy Centers Amer Inc ....D 315 471-3333
  Syracuse (G-14823)
Avalon Copy Centers Amer Inc ....E 716 995-7777
  Buffalo (G-2651)
Clinton Signs Inc................................G 585 482-1620
  Webster (G-15636)
David Helsing ....G 607 796-2681
  Horseheads (G-6120)
Digital Evolution Inc ....E 212 732-2722
  New York (G-9227)
Dowd - Witbeck Printing Corp ....F 518 274-2421
  Troy (G-15166)
Dynamic Photography Inc ....G 516 381-2951
  Roslyn (G-14042)
F X Graphix Inc..................................G 716 871-1511
  Buffalo (G-2750)
Jay Turoff ....F 718 856-7300
  Brooklyn (G-1990)
Kjckd Inc ....G 518 435-9696
  Latham (G-6862)
Messenger Press ....G 518 885-9231
  Ballston Spa (G-582)
Patrick Rohan ....G 718 781-2573
  Monticello (G-8072)
Riverwood Signs By Dandev Desi........G 845 229-0282
  Hyde Park (G-6274)
Scan-A-Chrome Color Inc ....G 631 532-6146
  Copiague (G-3675)
Terrabilt Inc.......................................G 914 341-1500
  Mamaroneck (G-7524)
Zacmel Graphics LLC.........................G 631 944-6031
  Deer Park (G-3957)

COMMERCIAL CONTAINERS WHOLESALERS

Carry Hot Inc ....E 212 279-7535
  New York (G-8925)

COMMERCIAL EQPT WHOLESALERS, NEC

Hamlet Products Inc ....F 914 665-0307
  Mount Vernon (G-8147)

COMMERCIAL EQPT, WHOLESALE: Bakery Eqpt & Splys

Pfeil & Holing Inc ....D 718 545-4600
  Woodside (G-16219)

COMMERCIAL EQPT, WHOLESALE: Comm Cooking & Food Svc Eqpt

Genpak LLC..C 845 343-7971
  Middletown (G-7911)
Mar-A-Thon Filters Inc........................G 631 957-4774
  Lindenhurst (G-6957)
Meades Welding and Fabricating ....G 631 581-1555
  Islip (G-6354)
Modern Craft Bar Rest Equip ....G 631 226-5647
  Lindenhurst (G-6961)
S & D Welding Corp ....G 631 454-0383
  West Babylon (G-15744)

COMMERCIAL EQPT, WHOLESALE: Display Eqpt, Exc Refrigerated

Bfma Holding Corporation ....G 607 753-6746
  Cortland (G-3755)
Marietta Corporation...........................A 323 589-8181
  Cortland (G-3777)

COMMERCIAL EQPT, WHOLESALE: Mannequins

Lifestyle-Trimco ....E 718 257-9101
  Brooklyn (G-2069)
R P M Industries Inc...........................E 315 255-1105
  Auburn (G-492)

COMMERCIAL EQPT, WHOLESALE: Restaurant, NEC

Bari Engineering Corp ....E 212 966-2080
  New York (G-8729)
R-S Restaurant Eqp Mfg Corp ....F 212 925-0335
  New York (G-10969)
Roger & Sons Inc ....G 212 226-4734
  New York (G-11074)

COMMERCIAL EQPT, WHOLESALE: Scales, Exc Laboratory

Itin Scale Co Inc................................E 718 336-5900
  Brooklyn (G-1974)

COMMERCIAL EQPT, WHOLESALE: Store Fixtures & Display Eqpt

Manhattan Display Inc.........................G 718 392-1365
  Long Island City (G-7289)

COMMERCIAL LAUNDRY EQPT

Fowler Route Co Inc ....D 917 653-4640
  Yonkers (G-16311)

COMMERCIAL PRINTING & NEWSPAPER PUBLISHING COMBINED

Aspect Printing Inc ....E 347 789-4284
  Brooklyn (G-1542)
Bleezarde Publishing Inc ....G 518 756-2030
  Ravena (G-13067)
Buffalo Standard Printing Corp ....F 716 835-9454
  Buffalo (G-2684)
Catskill Delaware Publications ....F 845 887-5200
  Callicoon (G-3075)
City Newspaper.................................G 585 244-3329
  Rochester (G-13315)
Community News Group LLC...............C 718 260-2500
  Brooklyn (G-1680)
Daily Gazette Company ....B 518 374-4141
  Schenectady (G-14260)
Daily News LP ....A 212 210-2100
  New York (G-9154)
Daily World Press Inc ....F 212 922-9201
  New York (G-9157)
Denton Publications Inc......................D 518 873-6368
  Elizabethtown (G-4299)
Denton Publications Inc......................E 518 561-9680
  Plattsburgh (G-12744)
E W Smith Publishing Co Inc ....F 845 562-1218
  New Windsor (G-8366)

Eagle Media Partners LP ....E 315 434-8889
  Syracuse (G-14880)
East Hampton Star Inc........................E 631 324-0002
  East Hampton (G-4121)
Gatehuse Media PA Holdings Inc.........E 585 598-0030
  Pittsford (G-12642)
Herald Newspapers Company Inc ....A 315 470-0011
  Syracuse (G-14911)
Home Reporter Inc.............................E 718 238-6600
  Brooklyn (G-1940)
Huersch Marketing Group LLC............F 518 874-1045
  Green Island (G-5437)
Ithaca Journal News Co Inc ....E 607 272-2321
  Ithaca (G-6389)
Johnson Acquisition Corp ....F 518 828-1616
  Hudson (G-6167)
LI Community Newspapers Inc.............G 516 747-8282
  Mineola (G-7985)
Local Media Group Inc ....D 845 341-1100
  Middletown (G-7917)
Local Media Group Holdings LLC ....G 585 598-0030
  Pittsford (G-12647)
Long Island Cmnty Nwsppers Inc ....D 516 482-4490
  Mineola (G-7987)
Lowville Newspaper Corporation ....G 315 376-3525
  Lowville (G-7418)
Mid York Weekly & Pennysaver ....G 315 792-4990
  Utica (G-15283)
Neighbor Newspapers ....G 631 226-2636
  Farmingdale (G-4692)
New York Times Company ....F 718 281-7000
  Flushing (G-4879)
News India Usa LLC...........................G 212 675-7515
  New York (G-10613)
News of The Highlands Inc ....F 845 534-7771
  Cornwall (G-3731)
Newsday LLC ....B 631 843-4050
  Melville (G-7808)
Nyc Trade Printers Corp ....F 718 606-0610
  Woodside (G-16216)
Nyp Holdings Inc................................B 212 997-9272
  New York (G-10666)
Ogden Newspapers Inc ....C 716 487-1111
  Jamestown (G-6535)
Panzarella Prtg & Packg Inc ....G 716 853-4480
  Amherst (G-241)
Post Journal ....F 716 487-1111
  Jamestown (G-6536)
Prometheus International Inc ....F 718 472-0700
  Jackson Heights (G-6421)
Record ....G 518 270-1200
  Saratoga Springs (G-14190)
Richner Communications Inc ....C 516 569-4000
  Garden City (G-5113)
Ridgewood Times Prtg & Pubg ....E 718 821-7500
  Ridgewood (G-13158)
Seneca County Area Shopper ....G 607 532-4333
  Ovid (G-12425)
Smithtown News Inc ....E 631 265-2100
  Smithtown (G-14487)
South Shore Tribune Inc ....G 516 431-5628
  Island Park (G-6322)
St Lawrence County Newspapers ....D 315 393-1003
  Canton (G-3167)
Ubm LLC...F 516 562-5000
  New York (G-11575)
Ulster County Press Office ....G 845 687-4480
  High Falls (G-5956)
Vnovom Svete ....G 212 302-9480
  New York (G-11701)
Weisbeck Publishing Printing ....G 716 937-9226
  Alden (G-176)
William B Collins Company ....D 518 773-8272
  Gloversville (G-5300)
William Boyd Printing Co Inc ....C 518 339-5832
  Latham (G-6881)
Williamsburg Bulletin ....G 718 387-0123
  Brooklyn (G-2588)
Wolfe Publications Inc........................C 585 394-0770
  Canandaigua (G-3145)
Zenith Color Comm Group Inc..............E 212 989-4400
  Long Island City (G-7413)

COMMON SAND MINING

E F Lippert Co Inc ....F 716 373-1100
  Allegany (G-187)
Hanson Aggregates East LLC ....G 315 536-9391
  Penn Yan (G-12585)
Hanson Aggregates PA Inc ....E 315 858-1100
  Jordanville (G-6632)

PRODUCT

Hanson Aggregates PA Inc ....F 518 568-2444
  Saint Johnsville *(G-14117)*
Hanson Aggregates PA LLC ....E 315 469-5501
  Jamesville *(G-6560)*
Hanson Aggregates PA LLC ....E 315 685-3321
  Skaneateles *(G-14455)*
Hanson Aggregates PA LLC ....F 315 821-7222
  Oriskany Falls *(G-12400)*
Sagaponack Sand & Gravel Corp .....E 631 537-2424
  Bridgehampton *(G-1167)*
Smith Sand & Gravel Inc ....G 315 673-4124
  Marcellus *(G-7563)*

COMMUNICATION HEADGEAR: Telephone

Rus Industries Inc ....E 716 284-7828
  Niagara Falls *(G-11975)*

COMMUNICATIONS CARRIER: Wired

Comsec Ventures International ....G 518 523-1600
  Lake Placid *(G-6766)*
Fiberdyne Labs Inc ....D 315 895-8470
  Frankfort *(G-4951)*

COMMUNICATIONS EQPT & SYSTEMS, NEC

Light Phone Inc ....G 415 595-0044
  Brooklyn *(G-2071)*
Lik LLC ....F 516 848-5135
  Northport *(G-12108)*

COMMUNICATIONS EQPT REPAIR & MAINTENANCE

Unitone Communication Systems ....G 212 777-9090
  New York *(G-11603)*
Zetek Corporation ....F 212 668-1485
  New York *(G-11821)*

COMMUNICATIONS EQPT WHOLESALERS

AES Electronics Inc ....G 212 371-8120
  New York *(G-8488)*
Caravan International Corp ....G 212 223-7190
  New York *(G-8915)*
Communication Power Corp ....E 631 434-7306
  Hauppauge *(G-5624)*
Sinclair Technologies Inc ....E 716 874-3682
  Hamburg *(G-5521)*

COMMUNICATIONS EQPT: Microwave

Amplitech Inc ....G 631 521-7738
  Bohemia *(G-971)*
Amplitech Group Inc ....G 631 521-7831
  Bohemia *(G-972)*
Comtech PST Corp ....C 631 777-8900
  Melville *(G-7770)*
Comtech Telecom Corp ....C 631 962-7000
  Melville *(G-7771)*
Specialty Microwave Corp ....F 631 737-1919
  Ronkonkoma *(G-14011)*
United Satcom Inc ....G 718 359-4100
  Flushing *(G-4903)*

COMMUNICATIONS SVCS

Aspire One Communications LLC ......F 201 281-2998
  Cornwall *(G-3725)*
Forerunner Technologies Inc ....E 631 337-2100
  Edgewood *(G-4268)*

COMMUNICATIONS SVCS: Cellular

Bayside Beepers & Cellular ....G 718 343-3888
  Glen Oaks *(G-5214)*

COMMUNICATIONS SVCS: Data

Forerunner Technologies Inc ....E 631 337-2100
  Edgewood *(G-4268)*

COMMUNICATIONS SVCS: Facsimile Transmission

Alternative Technology Corp ....G 914 478-5900
  Hastings On Hudson *(G-5571)*

COMMUNICATIONS SVCS: Internet Host Svcs

Nyemac Inc ....G 631 668-1303
  Montauk *(G-8057)*

COMMUNICATIONS SVCS: Online Svc Providers

Beauty America LLC ....E 917 744-1430
  Great Neck *(G-5370)*
Martha Stewart Living ....C 212 827-8000
  New York *(G-10374)*

COMMUNICATIONS SVCS: Proprietary Online Svcs Networks

Working Mother Media Inc ....D 212 351-6400
  New York *(G-11778)*

COMMUNICATIONS SVCS: Satellite Earth Stations

Loral Space Communications Inc ....E 212 697-1105
  New York *(G-10256)*

COMMUNICATIONS SVCS: Signal Enhancement Network Svcs

Fiberdyne Labs Inc ....D 315 895-8470
  Frankfort *(G-4951)*

COMMUNICATIONS SVCS: Telephone, Data

Akoustis Inc ....E 585 919-3073
  Canandaigua *(G-3124)*

COMMUNICATIONS SVCS: Telephone, Local

Highcrest Investors LLC ....D 212 702-4323
  New York *(G-9783)*

COMMUNICATIONS SVCS: Telephone, Voice

ABS Talkx Inc ....G 631 254-9100
  Bay Shore *(G-642)*

COMMUTATORS: Electronic

Amron Electronics Inc ....E 631 737-1234
  Ronkonkoma *(G-13907)*

COMPACT DISCS OR CD'S, WHOLESALE

Universal Mus Group Hldngs Inc ....E 212 333-8000
  New York *(G-11608)*

COMPACT LASER DISCS: Prerecorded

A To Z Media Inc ....E 212 260-0237
  New York *(G-8420)*
Atlantic Recording Corp ....B 212 707-2000
  New York *(G-8667)*
Bertelsmann Inc ....B 212 782-1000
  New York *(G-8764)*
Historic TW Inc ....E 212 484-8000
  New York *(G-9794)*
Media Technologies Ltd ....F 631 467-7900
  Eastport *(G-4252)*
Sony Corporation of America ....C 212 833-8000
  New York *(G-11295)*
Time Warner Companies Inc ....D 212 484-8000
  New York *(G-11494)*
Vaire LLC ....G 631 271-4933
  Huntington Station *(G-6265)*

COMPACTORS: Trash & Garbage, Residential

A Gatty Products Inc ....G 914 592-3903
  Elmsford *(G-4391)*

COMPARATORS: Optical

Quality Vision Services Inc ....D 585 544-0450
  Rochester *(G-13662)*

COMPOSITION STONE: Plastic

Seaway Mats Inc ....G 518 483-2560
  Malone *(G-7490)*

COMPOST

Long Island Compost Corp ....C 516 334-6600
  Westbury *(G-15905)*
Scotts Company LLC ....E 631 816-2831
  Yaphank *(G-16269)*

COMPRESSORS, AIR CONDITIONING: Wholesalers

Toshiba America Inc ....E 212 596-0600
  New York *(G-11519)*

COMPRESSORS: Air & Gas

Buffalo Compressed Air Inc ....G 716 783-8673
  Cheektowaga *(G-3340)*
Chapin International Inc ....C 585 343-3140
  Batavia *(G-608)*
Chapin Manufacturing Inc ....C 585 343-3140
  Batavia *(G-609)*
Comairco Equipment Inc ....G 716 656-0211
  Cheektowaga *(G-3341)*
Cooper Turbocompressor Inc ....B 716 896-6600
  Buffalo *(G-2711)*
Crosman Corporation ....E 585 657-6161
  Bloomfield *(G-945)*
Crosman Corporation ....E 585 398-3920
  Farmington *(G-4769)*
Dresser-Rand (delaware) LLC ....E 607 937-2011
  Painted Post *(G-12474)*
Dresser-Rand Group Inc ....D 716 375-3000
  Olean *(G-12232)*
GM Components Holdings LLC ....B 716 439-2463
  Lockport *(G-7079)*
GM Components Holdings LLC ....B 716 439-2011
  Lockport *(G-7080)*
Ingersoll-Rand Company ....B 716 896-6600
  Buffalo *(G-2810)*
Screw Compressor Tech Inc ....F 716 827-6600
  Buffalo *(G-2977)*
Turbopro Inc ....G 716 681-8651
  Alden *(G-175)*

COMPRESSORS: Air & Gas, Including Vacuum Pumps

Air Techniques Inc ....B 516 433-7676
  Melville *(G-7758)*
Atlas Copco Comptec LLC ....B 518 765-3344
  Voorheesville *(G-15444)*
Eastern Air Products LLC ....F 716 391-1866
  Lancaster *(G-6804)*

COMPRESSORS: Refrigeration & Air Conditioning Eqpt

Graham Corporation ....B 585 343-2216
  Batavia *(G-616)*
Standard Motor Products Inc ....B 718 392-0200
  Long Island City *(G-7364)*

COMPRESSORS: Wholesalers

Archrock Inc ....F 716 763-1553
  Lakewood *(G-6777)*

COMPUTER & COMPUTER SOFTWARE STORES

A I T Computers Inc ....G 518 266-9010
  Troy *(G-15162)*
Astrodyne Inc ....G 516 536-5755
  Oceanside *(G-12166)*
Biofeedback Instrument Corp ....G 212 222-5665
  New York *(G-8797)*
G S Communications USA Inc ....E 718 389-7371
  Brooklyn *(G-1874)*
J & N Computer Services Inc ....F 585 388-8780
  Fairport *(G-4500)*
Lasertech Crtridge RE-Builders ....G 518 373-1246
  Clifton Park *(G-3466)*
Maia Systems LLC ....G 718 206-0100
  Jamaica *(G-6456)*
Tpa Computer Corp ....F 877 866-6044
  Carmel *(G-3191)*

2020 Harris
New York Manufacturers Directory
(G-0000) Company's Geographic Section entry number

COMPUTER & COMPUTER SOFTWARE STORES: Peripheral Eqpt

Sphere Cables & Chips Inc ....E 212 619-3132
New York *(G-11322)*

COMPUTER & COMPUTER SOFTWARE STORES: Software, Bus/Non-Game

Noetic Partners Inc ....F 212 836-4351
New York *(G-10636)*

Pointman LLC ....G 716 842-1439
Buffalo *(G-2923)*

COMPUTER & COMPUTER SOFTWARE STORES: Software, Computer Game

Sony Broadband Entertainment ....F 212 833-6800
New York *(G-11294)*

COMPUTER & OFFICE MACHINE MAINTENANCE & REPAIR

Innovative Systems of New York ....G 516 541-7410
Massapequa Park *(G-7657)*

COMPUTER DISKETTES WHOLESALERS

Formats Unlimited Inc ....F 631 249-9200
Deer Park *(G-3875)*

COMPUTER FORMS

Boces Business Office ....F 607 763-3300
Binghamton *(G-861)*

Multi Packaging Solutions Inc ....E 646 885-0005
New York *(G-10519)*

Specialized Printed Forms Inc ....E 585 538-2381
Caledonia *(G-3073)*

COMPUTER GRAPHICS SVCS

Belsito Communications Inc ....F 845 534-9700
New Windsor *(G-8360)*

Beyer Graphics Inc ....D 631 543-3900
Commack *(G-3579)*

Christian Bus Endeavors Inc ....F 315 788-8560
Watertown *(G-15564)*

Star Composition Services Inc ....G 212 684-4001
Brooklyn *(G-2452)*

COMPUTER HARDWARE REQUIREMENTS ANALYSIS

Quality and Asrn Tech Corp ....G 646 450-6762
Ridge *(G-13133)*

COMPUTER INTERFACE EQPT: Indl Process

Anchor Commerce Trading Corp ....G 516 881-3485
Atlantic Beach *(G-452)*

Aspex Incorporated ....E 212 966-0410
New York *(G-8652)*

Industrial Machine Repair ....G 607 272-0717
Ithaca *(G-6386)*

Macrolink Inc ....E 631 924-8200
Medford *(G-7718)*

Sixnet LLC ....D 518 877-5173
Ballston Lake *(G-563)*

Veea Inc ....F 212 535-6050
New York *(G-11652)*

Vetra Systems Corporation ....G 631 434-3185
Hauppauge *(G-5796)*

COMPUTER PERIPHERAL EQPT, NEC

A I T Computers Inc ....G 518 266-9010
Troy *(G-15162)*

Aalborg Instrs & Contrls Inc ....D 845 398-3160
Orangeburg *(G-12304)*

Aero-Vision Technologies Inc ....G 631 643-8349
Melville *(G-7756)*

Andrea Electronics Corporation ....G 631 719-1800
Bohemia *(G-973)*

Anorad Corporation ....C 631 344-6600
Shirley *(G-14412)*

Aruba Networks Inc ....G 732 343-1305
New York *(G-8641)*

Atlaz International Ltd ....F 516 239-1854
Freeport *(G-4986)*

Aventura Technologies Inc ....E 631 300-4000
Commack *(G-3577)*

B V M Associates ....G 631 254-6220
Shirley *(G-14416)*

Clayton Dubilier & Rice Fun ....E 212 407-5200
New York *(G-9029)*

Cobham Long Island Inc ....C 631 231-9100
Hauppauge *(G-5619)*

Datatran Labs Inc ....G 845 856-4313
Port Jervis *(G-12847)*

Digiorange Inc ....G 718 801-8244
Brooklyn *(G-1743)*

Dolphin Data Capture LLC ....G 516 429-5663
New York *(G-9246)*

Dynamic Decisions Inc ....E 908 755-5000
Fresh Meadows *(G-5039)*

Eastman Kodak Company ....B 585 724-4000
Rochester *(G-13367)*

Ems Development Corporation ....D 631 345-6200
Yaphank *(G-16260)*

Epicor Software Corporation ....E 805 496-6789
Schenectady *(G-14265)*

Gasoft Equipment Inc ....F 845 863-1010
Newburgh *(G-11866)*

Glowa Manufacturing Inc ....E 607 770-0811
Binghamton *(G-880)*

Hauppauge Computer Works Inc ....E 631 434-1600
Hauppauge *(G-5668)*

Hauppauge Digital Inc ....E 631 434-1600
Hauppauge *(G-5669)*

Hergo Ergonomic Support Syst ....E 888 222-7270
Oceanside *(G-12175)*

Hitachi Metals America Ltd ....E 914 694-9200
Purchase *(G-13005)*

Humanscale Corporation ....E 212 725-4749
New York *(G-9839)*

IBM World Trade Corporation ....G 914 765-1900
Armonk *(G-397)*

Innovative Systems of New York ....G 516 541-7410
Massapequa Park *(G-7657)*

Kantek Inc ....E 516 594-4600
Oceanside *(G-12178)*

Luminescent Systems Inc ....B 716 655-0800
East Aurora *(G-4091)*

Macrolink Inc ....E 631 924-8200
Medford *(G-7718)*

Maia Systems LLC ....G 718 206-0100
Jamaica *(G-6456)*

Mirion Technologies Ist Corp ....D 607 562-4300
Horseheads *(G-6128)*

NCR Corporation ....C 607 273-5310
Ithaca *(G-6400)*

Norazza Inc ....F 716 706-1160
Buffalo *(G-2890)*

O Rama Light Inc ....E 518 539-9000
South Glens Falls *(G-14517)*

Office Grabs LLC ....G 347 678-3993
Brooklyn *(G-2228)*

Orbit International Corp ....D 631 435-8300
Hauppauge *(G-5734)*

Performance Technologies Inc ....E 585 256-0200
Rochester *(G-13615)*

Phoenix Venture Fund LLC ....E 212 759-1909
New York *(G-10831)*

Rdi Inc ....F 914 773-1000
Mount Kisco *(G-8104)*

Reliable Elec Mt Vernon Inc ....E 914 668-4440
Mount Vernon *(G-8177)*

Ruhle Companies Inc ....E 914 287-4000
Valhalla *(G-15309)*

S G I ....G 917 386-0385
New York *(G-11108)*

Sima Technologies LLC ....G 412 828-9130
Hauppauge *(G-5766)*

Sony Corporation of America ....C 212 833-8000
New York *(G-11295)*

Symbol Technologies LLC ....F 631 738-2400
Bohemia *(G-1083)*

Torrent Ems LLC ....F 716 312-4099
Lockport *(G-7113)*

Toshiba Amer Info Systems Inc ....B 949 583-3000
New York *(G-11518)*

Vishay Thin Film LLC ....C 716 283-4025
Niagara Falls *(G-11990)*

Vuzix Corporation ....E 585 359-5900
West Henrietta *(G-15806)*

Wantagh Computer Center ....F 516 826-2189
Wantagh *(G-15489)*

Welch Allyn Inc ....A 315 685-4100
Skaneateles Falls *(G-14459)*

Wilson & Wilson Group ....G 212 729-4736
Forest Hills *(G-4927)*

Z-Axis Inc ....D 315 548-5000
Phelps *(G-12611)*

Zebra Technologies Entp Corp ....E 800 722-6234
Holtsville *(G-6059)*

COMPUTER PERIPHERAL EQPT, WHOLESALE

Atlaz International Ltd ....F 516 239-1854
Freeport *(G-4986)*

C S Business Systems Inc ....E 716 886-6521
Buffalo *(G-2688)*

Cbord Group Inc ....C 607 257-2410
Ithaca *(G-6375)*

Digicom International Inc ....F 631 249-8999
Farmingdale *(G-4615)*

Doar Inc ....G 516 872-8140
Lynbrook *(G-7430)*

COMPUTER PERIPHERAL EQPT: Decoders

Tokenworks Inc ....G 914 704-3100
Bronxville *(G-1404)*

COMPUTER PERIPHERAL EQPT: Encoders

Iweb Design Inc ....F 805 243-8305
Bronx *(G-1284)*

COMPUTER PERIPHERAL EQPT: Film Reader Devices

P C Rfrs Radiology ....G 212 586-5700
Long Island City *(G-7315)*

COMPUTER PERIPHERAL EQPT: Graphic Displays, Exc Terminals

Binghamton Simulator Co Inc ....E 607 321-2980
Binghamton *(G-860)*

Medsim-Eagle Simulation Inc ....F 607 658-9354
Endicott *(G-4464)*

Mp Displays LLC ....G 845 268-4113
Valley Cottage *(G-15319)*

Watson Productions LLC ....F 516 334-9766
Hauppauge *(G-5799)*

COMPUTER PERIPHERAL EQPT: Input Or Output

Pda Panache Corp ....G 631 776-0523
Bohemia *(G-1060)*

COMPUTER PROGRAMMING SVCS

Atomic Information Systems ....E 716 713-5402
Unadilla *(G-15221)*

Billing Blocks Inc ....F 718 442-5006
Staten Island *(G-14626)*

Cdml Computer Services Ltd ....G 718 428-9063
Fresh Meadows *(G-5038)*

Data Key Communication LLC ....F 315 445-2347
Fayetteville *(G-4783)*

Defran Systems Inc ....E 212 727-8342
New York *(G-9196)*

Digitronik Labs Inc ....F 585 360-0043
Rochester *(G-13346)*

Doar Inc ....G 516 872-8140
Lynbrook *(G-7430)*

Fidesa US Corporation ....B 212 269-9000
New York *(G-9490)*

Fuel Data Systems Inc ....G 800 447-7870
Middletown *(G-7909)*

Glitch Inc ....G 866 364-2733
New York *(G-9621)*

Hauppauge Computer Works Inc ....E 631 434-1600
Hauppauge *(G-5668)*

Hudson Software Corporation ....E 914 773-0400
Elmsford *(G-4410)*

Infinity Augmented Reality Inc ....G 917 677-2084
New York *(G-9884)*

Irv Inc ....E 212 334-4507
New York *(G-9944)*

Lockheed Martin Corporation ....D 315 793-5800
New Hartford *(G-8241)*

Matrixcare Inc ....G 518 583-6400
New York *(G-10385)*

Openfin Inc ....G 917 450-8822
New York *(G-10697)*

PC Solutions & Consulting ....G 607 735-0466
Elmira *(G-4364)*

PRODUCT

Qlogix Entertainment LLC..............G...... 215 459-6315
New York (G-10944)

Safe Passage International Inc..........F...... 585 292-4910
Rochester (G-13711)

Suite Solutions Inc..............E...... 716 929-3050
Amherst (G-245)

Syrasoft LLC..............G...... 315 708-0341
Baldwinsville (G-556)

Wetpaintcom Inc..............E...... 206 859-6300
Floral Park (G-4818)

X Function Inc..............E...... 212 231-0092
New York (G-11794)

Ziff Davis Publishing LLC..............D...... 212 503-3500
New York (G-11824)

COMPUTER PROGRAMMING SVCS: Custom

Endava Inc..............F...... 212 920-7240
New York (G-9369)

Modern Farmer Media Inc..............F...... 518 828-7447
Hudson (G-6172)

Post Heritage Inc..............G...... 646 286-7579
Brooklyn (G-2271)

US Beverage Net Inc..............F...... 315 579-2025
Syracuse (G-15019)

COMPUTER RELATED MAINTENANCE SVCS

Century Direct LLC..............C...... 212 763-0600
Islandia (G-6328)

Global Applctions Solution LLC..........G...... 212 741-9595
New York (G-9624)

IBM World Trade Corporation..............G...... 914 765-1900
Armonk (G-397)

COMPUTER SERVICE BUREAU

Datalink Computer Products..............F...... 914 666-2358
Mount Kisco (G-8091)

Hudson Software Corporation..............E...... 914 773-0400
Elmsford (G-4410)

COMPUTER SOFTWARE DEVELOPMENT

Advanced Barcode Tech Inc..............F...... 516 570-8100
Great Neck (G-5359)

Geoweb3d Inc..............F...... 607 323-1114
Vestal (G-15378)

Lake Image Systems Inc..............F...... 585 321-3630
Henrietta (G-5858)

Os33 Inc..............G...... 708 336-3466
New York (G-10713)

Sale 121 Corp..............D...... 240 855-8988
New York (G-11117)

Standard Analytics Io Inc..............G...... 917 882-5422
New York (G-11344)

Structuredweb Inc..............E...... 201 325-3110
New York (G-11376)

Unacast Inc..............G...... 917 670-7852
New York (G-11580)

Williamson Law Book Co..............F...... 585 924-3400
Victor (G-15443)

COMPUTER SOFTWARE DEVELOPMENT & APPLICATIONS

Amcom Software Inc..............G...... 212 951-7600
New York (G-8537)

Forerunner Technologies Inc..............E...... 631 337-2100
Edgewood (G-4268)

Hearst Digital Studios Inc..............E...... 212 969-7552
New York (G-9755)

Innovation In Motion Inc..............G...... 407 878-7561
Long Beach (G-7137)

Ipsidy Inc..............F...... 516 274-8700
Long Beach (G-7138)

Kingboard Holdings Limited..............A...... 705 844-1993
New York (G-10108)

Orpheo USA Corp..............G...... 212 464-8255
New York (G-10711)

Pitney Bowes Software Inc..............F...... 518 285-6000
Troy (G-15179)

Post Road..............F...... 203 545-2122
New York (G-10871)

Randall Loeffler Inc..............E...... 212 226-8787
New York (G-10980)

Vepo Solutions LLC..............G...... 914 384-2121
Cross River (G-3804)

Worlds Best Cookie Dough Inc..............G...... 347 592-3422
New York (G-11783)

COMPUTER SOFTWARE SYSTEMS ANALYSIS & DESIGN: Custom

Complex Biosystems Inc..............G...... 315 464-8007
Baldwinsville (G-545)

Inprotopia Corporation..............F...... 917 338-7501
New York (G-9901)

Live Vote II Inc..............G...... 646 343-9053
New York (G-10233)

New York Computer Consulting..........G...... 516 921-1932
Woodbury (G-16178)

Vizbee Inc..............F...... 650 787-1424
New York (G-11699)

Vormittag Associates Inc..............G...... 800 824-7776
Ronkonkoma (G-14024)

COMPUTER STORAGE DEVICES, NEC

Datalink Computer Products..............F...... 914 666-2358
Mount Kisco (G-8091)

EMC Corporation..............C...... 212 564-6866
New York (G-9359)

Emcs LLC..............G...... 716 523-2002
Hamburg (G-5507)

Garland Technology LLC..............E...... 716 242-8500
Buffalo (G-2767)

Gim Electronics Corp..............F...... 516 942-3382
Hicksville (G-5911)

Quantum Knowledge LLC..............G...... 631 727-6111
Riverhead (G-13185)

Quantum Logic Corp..............G...... 516 746-1380
New Hyde Park (G-8290)

Quantum Mechanics Ny LLC..............G...... 917 519-7077
Huntington (G-6218)

Sony Corporation of America..............E...... 212 833-8000
New York (G-11295)

Technologies Application LLC..............F...... 607 275-0345
Cortland (G-3790)

William S Hein & Co Inc..............C...... 716 882-2600
Getzville (G-5184)

COMPUTER TERMINALS

AG Neovo Professional Inc..............F...... 212 647-9080
New York (G-8492)

Clayton Dubilier & Rice Fun..............E...... 212 407-5200
New York (G-9029)

Doar Inc..............G...... 516 872-8140
Lynbrook (G-7430)

Igt Global Solutions Corp..............D...... 518 382-2900
Schenectady (G-14280)

Orbit International Corp..............E...... 631 435-8300
Hauppauge (G-5734)

Symbio Technologies LLC..............G...... 914 576-1205
White Plains (G-16065)

COMPUTER TERMINALS: CRT

Cine Design Group LLC..............G...... 646 747-0734
New York (G-9007)

COMPUTER-AIDED DESIGN SYSTEMS SVCS

Circuits & Systems Inc..............E...... 516 593-4301
East Rockaway (G-4171)

Trident Precision Mfg Inc..............D...... 585 265-2010
Webster (G-15658)

COMPUTER-AIDED ENGINEERING SYSTEMS SVCS

Complex Biosystems Inc..............G...... 315 464-8007
Baldwinsville (G-545)

COMPUTERS, NEC

Argon Corp..............F...... 516 487-5314
Great Neck (G-5367)

Amouse Digital Devices Corp..............D...... 516 673-4444
New Hyde Park (G-8251)

Binghamton Simulator Co Inc..............E...... 607 321-2980
Binghamton (G-860)

Computer Conversions Corp..............E...... 631 261-3300
East Northport (G-4143)

Critical Link LLC..............E...... 315 425-4045
Syracuse (G-14867)

Data-Pac Mailing Systems Corp..............F...... 585 671-0210
Webster (G-15637)

Datacom Systems Inc..............G...... 315 463-9541
East Syracuse (G-4206)

Dees Audio & Vision..............G...... 585 719-9256
Rochester (G-13342)

Digicom International Inc..............F...... 631 249-8999
Farmingdale (G-4615)

Doar Inc..............G...... 516 872-8140
Lynbrook (G-7430)

Dynamic Decisions Inc..............E...... 908 755-5000
Fresh Meadows (G-5039)

E-Systems Group LLC..............E...... 607 775-1100
Conklin (G-3624)

Ebc Technologies LLC..............D...... 631 729-8182
Hauppauge (G-5644)

Electronic Systems Inc..............G...... 631 589-4389
Holbrook (G-5998)

H&L Computers Inc..............E...... 516 873-8088
Flushing (G-4857)

Hi-Tech Advanced Solutions Inc..............F...... 718 926-3488
Forest Hills (G-4921)

Human Electronics Inc..............G...... 315 724-9850
Utica (G-15272)

IBM World Trade Corporation..............G...... 914 765-1900
Armonk (G-397)

International Bus Mchs Corp..............A...... 914 945-3000
Yorktown Heights (G-16366)

International Bus Mchs Corp..............A...... 845 433-1234
Poughkeepsie (G-12963)

J & N Computer Services Inc..............F...... 585 388-8780
Fairport (G-4500)

M&C Associates LLC..............E...... 631 467-8760
Hauppauge (G-5702)

Medsim-Eagle Simulation Inc..............F...... 607 658-9354
Endicott (G-4464)

N & G of America Inc..............G...... 516 428-3414
Plainview (G-12703)

N & L Instruments Inc..............F...... 631 471-4000
Ronkonkoma (G-13978)

NCR Corporation..............C...... 516 876-7200
Jericho (G-6586)

North Atlantic Industries Inc..............C...... 631 567-1100
Bohemia (G-1053)

Photon Vision Systems Inc..............F...... 607 749-2689
Homer (G-6066)

Revivn Public Benefit Corp..............F...... 347 762-8193
Brooklyn (G-2342)

Toshiba Amer Info Systems Inc..............B...... 949 583-3000
New York (G-11518)

Transland Sourcing LLC..............G...... 718 596-5704
Brooklyn (G-2517)

Wantagh Computer Center..............F...... 516 826-2189
Wantagh (G-15489)

Yellow E House Inc..............G...... 718 888-2000
Flushing (G-4907)

COMPUTERS, PERIPHERALS & SOFTWARE, WHOLESALE: Disk Drives

Formats Unlimited Inc..............F...... 631 249-9200
Deer Park (G-3875)

COMPUTERS, PERIPHERALS & SOFTWARE, WHOLESALE: Software

Base Systems Inc..............G...... 845 278-1991
Brewster (G-1142)

Cgi Technologies Solutions Inc..............F...... 212 682-7411
New York (G-8965)

Escholar LLC..............F...... 914 989-2900
White Plains (G-16002)

Infinite Software Solutions..............F...... 718 982-1315
Staten Island (G-14665)

Kse Sportsman Media Inc..............D...... 212 852-6600
New York (G-10142)

Pointman LLC..............G...... 716 842-1439
Buffalo (G-2923)

United Data Systems Inc..............G...... 631 549-6900
Huntington (G-6230)

COMPUTERS: Indl, Process, Gas Flow

Pneumercator Company Inc..............E...... 631 293-8450
Hauppauge (G-5743)

COMPUTERS: Mainframe

Partech Inc..............C...... 315 738-0600
New Hartford (G-8243)

Policy ADM Solutions Inc..............E...... 914 332-4320
Tarrytown (G-15052)

COMPUTERS: Personal

Apple Commuter Inc..............G...... 917 299-0066
New Hyde Park (G-8250)

Digitac LLC ....G ... 732 669-7637
  Brooklyn *(G-1745)*

G S Communications USA Inc ....E ... 718 389-7371
  Brooklyn *(G-1874)*

Go Go Apple Inc ....G ... 646 264-8909
  Elmhurst *(G-4335)*

HP Inc ....E ... 650 857-1501
  Albany *(G-88)*

HP Inc ....G ... 650 857-1501
  New York *(G-9828)*

Stargate Computer Corp ....G ... 516 474-4799
  Port Jeff STA *(G-12838)*

Telxon Corporation ....E ... 631 738-2400
  Holtsville *(G-6056)*

Toshiba America Inc ....E ... 212 596-0600
  New York *(G-11519)*

Wilcro Inc ....G ... 716 632-4204
  Buffalo *(G-3047)*

CONCENTRATES, DRINK

Constellation Brands Inc ....D ... 585 678-7100
  Victor *(G-15399)*

Mr Smoothie ....G ... 845 296-1686
  Poughkeepsie *(G-12973)*

Roar Beverages LLC ....E ... 631 683-5565
  Port Washington *(G-12918)*

Sabila Corp ....G ... 845 981-7128
  Pine Island *(G-12631)*

CONCENTRATES, FLAVORING, EXC DRINK

Consumer Flavoring Extract Co ....F ... 718 435-0201
  Brooklyn *(G-1682)*

CONCRETE CURING & HARDENING COMPOUNDS

Hanson Aggregates PA LLC ....F ... 585 436-3250
  Rochester *(G-13458)*

Watson Bowman Acme Corp ....C ... 716 691-8162
  Amherst *(G-253)*

CONCRETE MIXERS

X-Treme Ready Mix Inc ....G ... 718 739-3384
  Jamaica *(G-6489)*

CONCRETE PLANTS

Oneida Sales & Service Inc ....E ... 716 822-8205
  Buffalo *(G-2897)*

Seville Central Mix Corp ....D ... 516 293-6190
  Old Bethpage *(G-12219)*

CONCRETE PRDTS

Alpine Building Supply Inc ....G ... 718 456-2522
  Ridgewood *(G-13139)*

Arnan Development Corp ....D ... 607 432-8391
  Oneonta *(G-12257)*

Baliva Concrete Products Inc ....G ... 585 328-8442
  Rochester *(G-13260)*

Barrett Paving Materials Inc ....F ... 315 737-9471
  Clayville *(G-3454)*

Bonsal American Inc ....F ... 585 343-4741
  Batavia *(G-605)*

Bonsal American Inc ....G ... 631 208-8073
  Calverton *(G-3077)*

City Mason Corp ....F ... 718 658-3796
  Jamaica *(G-6434)*

Elderlee Incorporated ....C ... 315 789-6670
  Oaks Corners *(G-12161)*

Express Concrete Inc ....G ... 631 273-4224
  Brentwood *(G-1121)*

Get Real Surfaces Inc ....E ... 845 337-4483
  Poughkeepsie *(G-12957)*

Grace Associates Inc ....G ... 718 767-9000
  Harrison *(G-5554)*

Jenna Concrete Corporation ....E ... 718 842-5250
  Bronx *(G-1286)*

Jenna Harlem River Inc ....G ... 718 842-5997
  Bronx *(G-1287)*

Lafarge North America Inc ....E ... 518 756-5000
  Ravena *(G-13069)*

Long Island Geotech ....G ... 631 473-1044
  Port Jefferson *(G-12841)*

M K Ulrich Construction Inc ....F ... 716 893-5777
  Buffalo *(G-2855)*

Nicolia Concrete Products Inc ....D ... 631 669-0700
  Lindenhurst *(G-6965)*

Nicolock Paving Stones LLC ....D ... 631 669-0700
  Lindenhurst *(G-6968)*

NY Tempering LLC ....G ... 718 326-8989
  Maspeth *(G-7631)*

Quikrete Companies LLC ....E ... 716 213-2027
  Lackawanna *(G-6743)*

Quikrete Companies LLC ....E ... 315 673-2020
  Marcellus *(G-7562)*

Stag Brothers Cast Stone Co ....G ... 718 629-0975
  Brooklyn *(G-2449)*

Taylor Concrete Products Inc ....E ... 315 788-2191
  Watertown *(G-15589)*

Towne House Restorations Inc ....G ... 718 497-9200
  Long Island City *(G-7385)*

Trinic LLC ....F ... 607 775-1948
  Kirkwood *(G-6732)*

Unilock New York Inc ....G ... 845 278-6700
  Brewster *(G-1159)*

Upstone Materials Inc ....G ... 518 873-2275
  Lewis *(G-6918)*

CONCRETE PRDTS, PRECAST, NEC

A & R Concrete Products LLC ....E ... 845 562-0640
  New Windsor *(G-8357)*

Afco Precast Sales Corp ....D ... 631 924-7114
  Middle Island *(G-7873)*

Callanan Industries Inc ....E ... 315 697-9569
  Canastota *(G-3150)*

Callanan Industries Inc ....C ... 518 374-2222
  Albany *(G-55)*

Callanan Industries Inc ....E ... 845 331-6868
  Kingston *(G-6683)*

Callanan Industries Inc ....E ... 518 785-5666
  Latham *(G-6851)*

Castek Inc ....G ... 914 636-1000
  New Rochelle *(G-8323)*

Coastal Pipeline Products Corp ....E ... 631 369-4000
  Calverton *(G-3078)*

David Kucera Inc ....E ... 845 255-1044
  Gardiner *(G-5128)*

Dillner Precast Inc ....G ... 631 421-9130
  Lloyd Harbor *(G-7055)*

Dillner Precast Inc ....G ... 631 421-9130
  Huntington Station *(G-6245)*

East Main Associates ....D ... 585 624-1990
  Lima *(G-6931)*

Fort Miller Group Inc ....F ... 518 695-5000
  Greenwich *(G-5471)*

Fort Miller Service Corp ....F ... 518 695-5000
  Greenwich *(G-5472)*

Gamble & Gamble Inc ....E ... 716 731-3239
  Sanborn *(G-14142)*

Glens Falls Ready Mix Inc ....F ... 518 793-1695
  Queensbury *(G-13041)*

Great ATL Pr-Cast Con Statuary ....G ... 718 948-5677
  Staten Island *(G-14660)*

Guardian Concrete Products Inc ....F ... 518 372-0080
  Schenectady *(G-14277)*

Island Ready Mix Inc ....E ... 631 874-3777
  Center Moriches *(G-3246)*

John E Potente & Sons Inc ....G ... 516 935-8585
  Hicksville *(G-5917)*

Lakelands Concrete Pdts Inc ....E ... 585 624-1990
  Lima *(G-6932)*

Lhv Precast Inc ....E ... 845 336-8880
  Kingston *(G-6699)*

Long Island Precast Inc ....E ... 631 286-0240
  Brookhaven *(G-1409)*

Mid-Hudson Concrete Pdts Inc ....F ... 845 265-3141
  Cold Spring *(G-3521)*

Oldcastle Infrastructure Inc ....F ... 518 767-2116
  South Bethlehem *(G-14502)*

Oldcastle Infrastructure Inc ....E ... 518 767-2112
  Selkirk *(G-14358)*

P J R Industries Inc ....E ... 716 825-9300
  Buffalo *(G-2902)*

Pelkowski Precast Corp ....F ... 631 269-5727
  Kings Park *(G-6675)*

Robinson Concrete Inc ....E ... 315 253-6666
  Auburn *(G-493)*

Sunnycrest Inc ....E ... 315 252-7214
  Auburn *(G-496)*

Transpo Industries Inc ....E ... 914 636-1000
  New Rochelle *(G-8356)*

Urban Precast LLC ....E ... 845 331-6299
  Kingston *(G-6720)*

Wel Made Enterprises Inc ....F ... 631 752-1238
  Farmingdale *(G-4765)*

Woodards Concrete Products Inc ......E ... 845 361-3471
  Bullville *(G-3054)*

CONCRETE: Asphaltic, Not From Refineries

Monticello Black Top Corp ....G ... 845 434-7280
  Thompsonville *(G-15066)*

Peckham Industries Inc ....E ... 914 949-2000
  White Plains *(G-16044)*

Peckham Industries Inc ....F ... 518 943-0155
  Catskill *(G-3216)*

Peckham Industries Inc ....F ... 518 893-2176
  Greenfield Center *(G-5450)*

PSI Transit Mix Corp ....G ... 631 382-7930
  Smithtown *(G-15986)*

Swift River Associates Inc ....G ... 716 875-0902
  Tonawanda *(G-15144)*

CONCRETE: Bituminous

Barrett Paving Materials Inc ....E ... 315 353-6611
  Norwood *(G-12131)*

Pallette Stone Corporation ....E ... 518 584-2421
  Gansevoort *(G-5084)*

CONCRETE: Ready-Mixed

Advanced Ready Mix Corp ....F ... 718 497-5020
  Brooklyn *(G-1465)*

Advanced Transit Mix Corp ....G ... 718 497-5020
  Brooklyn *(G-1466)*

All American Transit Mix Corp ....G ... 718 417-3654
  Brooklyn *(G-1485)*

Anbriella Sand & Gravel Corp ....E ... 631 586-2111
  Bay Shore *(G-650)*

Atlas Concrete Batching Corp ....D ... 718 523-3000
  Jamaica *(G-6426)*

Atlas Transit Mix Corp ....C ... 718 523-3000
  Jamaica *(G-6427)*

Barney & Dickenson Inc ....D ... 607 729-1536
  Vestal *(G-15370)*

Barrett Paving Materials Inc ....F ... 315 788-2037
  Watertown *(G-15559)*

Best Concrete Mix Corp ....E ... 718 463-5500
  Flushing *(G-4841)*

Bonded Concrete Inc ....E ... 518 273-5800
  Watervliet *(G-15598)*

Bonded Concrete Inc ....E ... 518 674-2854
  West Sand Lake *(G-15835)*

Brewster Transit Mix Corp ....D ... 845 279-3738
  Brewster *(G-1144)*

Brewster Transit Mix Corp ....E ... 845 279-3738
  Brewster *(G-1145)*

Byram Concrete & Supply LLC ....F ... 914 682-4477
  White Plains *(G-15986)*

C & C Ready-Mix Corporation ....E ... 607 797-5108
  Vestal *(G-15374)*

C & C Ready-Mix Corporation ....F ... 607 687-1690
  Owego *(G-12429)*

Capital Concrete Inc ....G ... 716 648-8001
  Hamburg *(G-5502)*

Casa Redimix Concrete Corp ....F ... 718 589-1555
  Bronx *(G-1220)*

Ccz Ready Mix Concrete Corp ....G ... 516 579-7352
  Levittown *(G-6914)*

Cemex Cement Inc ....D ... 212 317-6000
  New York *(G-8945)*

Century Ready Mix Inc ....G ... 631 888-2200
  West Babylon *(G-15700)*

Champion Materials Inc ....G ... 315 493-2654
  Carthage *(G-3196)*

Chenango Concrete Corp ....F ... 518 294-9964
  Richmondville *(G-13129)*

Clark Concrete Co Inc ....G ... 315 478-4101
  Syracuse *(G-14851)*

Clemente Latham Concrete Corp ......D ... 518 374-2222
  Schenectady *(G-14257)*

Corona Ready Mix Inc ....F ... 718 271-5940
  Corona *(G-3737)*

Cortland Ready Mix Inc ....F ... 607 753-3063
  Cortland *(G-3763)*

Cossitt Concrete Products Inc ....F ... 315 824-2700
  Hamilton *(G-5526)*

Costanza Ready Mix Inc ....G ... 516 783-4444
  North Bellmore *(G-12016)*

Cranesville Block Co Inc ....E ... 315 732-2135
  Utica *(G-15249)*

Cranesville Block Co Inc ....E ... 845 896-5687
  Fishkill *(G-4798)*

Cranesville Block Co Inc ....E ... 845 331-1775
  Kingston *(G-6687)*

Cranesville Block Co Inc ....E ... 315 384-4000
  Norfolk *(G-11998)*

Cranesville Block Co Inc ....E ... 518 684-6154
  Amsterdam *(G-323)*

PRODUCT

Cranesville Block Co Inc ....E 315 773-2296
  Felts Mills (G-4786)
Custom Mix Inc ....G 516 797-7090
  Massapequa Park (G-7654)
Dalrymple Grav & Contg Co Inc ....F 607 739-0391
  Pine City (G-12627)
Dalrymple Holding Corp ....F 607 737-6200
  Pine City (G-12628)
Deer Park Sand & Gravel Corp ....E 631 586-2323
  Bay Shore (G-672)
Dicks Concrete Co Inc ....E 845 374-5966
  New Hampton (G-8234)
Dunkirk Construction Products ....G 716 366-5220
  Dunkirk (G-4053)
E Tetz & Sons Inc ....D 845 692-4486
  Middletown (G-7905)
East Coast Spring Mix Inc ....G 845 355-1215
  New Hampton (G-8235)
Elam Materials Inc ....F 585 658-2248
  Mount Morris (G-8113)
Electric City Concrete Co Inc ....E 518 887-5560
  Amsterdam (G-325)
Elm Transit Mix Corporation ....E 516 333-6144
  Westbury (G-15881)
Empire Transit Mix Inc ....E 718 384-3000
  Brooklyn (G-1802)
F H Stickles & Son Inc ....F 518 851-9048
  Livingston (G-7052)
Ferrara Bros LLC ....F 718 939-3030
  Flushing (G-4851)
Frey Concrete Inc ....G 716 213-5832
  North Tonawanda (G-12068)
Fulmont Ready-Mix Company Inc ....F 518 887-5560
  Amsterdam (G-328)
G & J Rdymx & Masnry Sup Inc ....F 718 454-0800
  Hollis (G-6043)
Glens Falls Ready Mix Inc ....F 518 793-1695
  Queensbury (G-13041)
Grandview Concrete Corp ....E 518 346-7981
  Schenectady (G-14275)
Haley Concrete Inc ....F 716 492-0849
  Delevan (G-3961)
Hanson Aggregates East LLC ....F 585 798-0762
  Medina (G-7737)
Hanson Aggregates East LLC ....F 716 372-1574
  Falconer (G-4542)
Hanson Aggregates East LLC ....F 315 548-4913
  Phelps (G-12604)
Hanson Aggregates New York LLC ......F 716 665-4620
  Jamesville (G-6558)
Hanson Aggregates New York LLC ......F 716 665-4620
  Jamestown (G-6515)
Hanson Aggregates New York LLC ......F 585 638-5841
  Pavilion (G-12523)
Hanson Aggregates New York LLC ......C 315 469-5501
  Jamesville (G-6559)
Hanson Aggregates New York LLC ......F 607 776-7945
  Bath (G-635)
Hanson Aggregates New York LLC ......G 607 276-5881
  Almond (G-191)
Inwood Material ....F 516 371-1842
  Inwood (G-6296)
Iroquois Rock Products Inc ....F 585 381-7010
  Rochester (G-13484)
Island Ready Mix Inc ....E 631 874-3777
  Center Moriches (G-3246)
James Town Macadam Inc ....D 716 665-4504
  Falconer (G-4546)
Jenna Concrete Corporation ....E 718 842-5250
  Bronx (G-1286)
Jenna Harlem River Inc ....G 718 842-5997
  Bronx (G-1287)
Jet Redi Mix Concrete Inc ....F 631 580-3640
  Ronkonkoma (G-13954)
King Road Materials Inc ....F 518 382-5354
  Albany (G-95)
Kings Park Ready Mix Corp ....F 631 269-4330
  Kings Park (G-6674)
Kings Ready Mix Inc ....E 718 853-4644
  Roslyn Heights (G-14054)
Knight Sttlement Sand Grav LLC ....E 607 776-2048
  Bath (G-637)
Lafarge North America Inc ....G 716 854-5791
  Buffalo (G-2845)
Lafarge North America Inc ....E 518 756-5000
  Ravena (G-13069)
Lage Industries Corporation ....F 718 342-3400
  Brooklyn (G-2043)
Lazarek Inc ....G 315 343-1242
  Oswego (G-12413)

Lehigh Cement Company ....E 518 943-5940
  Catskill (G-3212)
Lehigh Cement Company LLC ....E 718 522-0800
  Brooklyn (G-2060)
Lehigh Northeast Cement Co ....G 518 792-1137
  Catskill (G-3213)
Liberty Ready Mix Inc ....F 718 526-1700
  Jamaica (G-6453)
Long Island Ready Mix ....G 516 485-5260
  Hempstead (G-5843)
Manitou Concrete ....D 585 424-6040
  Rochester (G-13531)
Manzione Ready Mix Corp ....G 718 628-3837
  Brooklyn (G-2111)
Mastro Concrete Inc ....G 718 528-6788
  Rosedale (G-14037)
Mix N Mac LLC ....G 845 381-5536
  Middletown (G-7921)
Morningstar Concrete Products ....F 716 693-4020
  Tonawanda (G-15124)
N Y Western Concrete Corp ....G 585 343-6850
  Batavia (G-621)
Nex-Gen Ready Mix Corp ....G 347 231-0073
  Bronx (G-1324)
Nicolia Ready Mix Inc ....D 631 669-7000
  Lindenhurst (G-6966)
Nicolia Ready Mix Inc ....F 631 669-7000
  Lindenhurst (G-6967)
Northern Ready Mix LLC ....F 315 336-7900
  North Syracuse (G-12048)
Oldcastle Infrastructure Inc ....F 518 767-2116
  South Bethlehem (G-14502)
Oldcastle Materials Inc ....G 585 424-6410
  Rochester (G-13588)
Otsego Ready Mix Inc ....F 607 432-3400
  Oneonta (G-12279)
Precision Ready Mix Inc ....G 718 658-5600
  Jamaica (G-6465)
Presti Ready Mix Concrete Inc ....G 516 378-6006
  Freeport (G-5016)
Quality Ready Mix Inc ....F 516 437-0100
  New Hyde Park (G-8289)
Queens Ready Mix Inc ....G 718 526-4919
  Jamaica (G-6467)
Residential Fences Corp ....E 631 205-9758
  Ridge (G-13134)
Richmond Ready Mix Corp ....G 917 731-8400
  Staten Island (G-14704)
Richmond Ready Mix Corp II ....E 917 731-8400
  Staten Island (G-14705)
Robinson Concrete Inc ....E 315 253-6666
  Auburn (G-493)
Robinson Concrete Inc ....C 315 676-4333
  West Monroe (G-15814)
Robinson Concrete Inc ....F 315 492-6200
  Jamesville (G-6562)
Robinson Concrete Inc ....F 315 676-4662
  Brewerton (G-1137)
Rochester Asphalt Materials ....D 585 924-7360
  Farmington (G-4777)
Rochester Asphalt Materials ....G 585 381-7010
  Rochester (G-13681)
Rural Hill Sand and Grav Corp ....F 315 846-5212
  Woodville (G-16239)
Russian Mix Inc ....G 347 385-7198
  Brooklyn (G-2366)
Saunders Concrete Co Inc ....F 607 756-7905
  Cortland (G-3787)
Scara-Mix Inc ....E 718 442-7357
  Staten Island (G-14706)
Seville Central Mix Corp ....G 516 868-3000
  Freeport (G-5024)
Seville Central Mix Corp ....D 516 293-6190
  Old Bethpage (G-12219)
Seville Central Mix Corp ....E 516 239-8333
  Lawrence (G-6892)
Shamrock Materials LLC ....D 718 273-9223
  Staten Island (G-14709)
South Shore Ready Mix Inc ....G 516 872-3049
  Valley Stream (G-15360)
Star Ready Mix East Inc ....F 631 289-8787
  East Hampton (G-4128)
Star Ready-Mix Inc ....F 631 289-8787
  Medford (G-7724)
Stephen Miller Gen Contrs Inc ....E 518 661-5601
  Gloversville (G-5293)
Suffolk Cement Precast Inc ....G 631 727-4432
  Calverton (G-3087)
Suffolk Cement Products Inc ....E 631 727-2317
  Calverton (G-3088)

Sullivan Concrete Inc ....F 845 888-2235
  Cochecton (G-3504)
T Mix Inc ....G 646 379-6814
  Brooklyn (G-2486)
TEC - Crete Transit Mix Corp ....E 718 657-6880
  Ridgewood (G-13163)
Thousand Island Ready Mix Con ....G 315 686-3203
  La Fargeville (G-6735)
Torrington Industries Inc ....G 315 676-4662
  Central Square (G-3296)
United Materials LLC ....D 716 683-1432
  North Tonawanda (G-12097)
United Materials LLC ....E 716 731-2332
  Sanborn (G-14152)
United Materials LLC ....G 716 662-0564
  Orchard Park (G-12381)
United Transit Mix Inc ....F 718 416-3400
  Brooklyn (G-2540)
Upstone Materials Inc ....G 518 483-2671
  Malone (G-7493)
Upstone Materials Inc ....F 315 265-8036
  Plattsburgh (G-12788)
Upstone Materials Inc ....G 315 764-0251
  Massena (G-7673)
Upstone Materials Inc ....F 518 873-2275
  Lewis (G-6918)
Upstone Materials Inc ....D 518 561-5321
  Plattsburgh (G-12787)
US Concrete Inc ....F 718 433-0111
  Long Island City (G-7390)
US Concrete Inc ....E 718 853-4644
  Roslyn Heights (G-14059)
US Concrete Inc ....F 718 438-6800
  Brooklyn (G-2548)
W F Saunders & Sons Inc ....F 315 469-3217
  Nedrow (G-8217)
W F Saunders & Sons Inc ....G 607 257-6930
  Etna (G-4486)
Watertown Concrete Inc ....F 315 788-1040
  Watertown (G-15592)

CONDENSERS & CONDENSING UNITS: Air Conditioner

Motivair Corporation ....E 716 691-9222
  Amherst (G-233)

CONDENSERS: Fixed Or Variable

Viking Technologies Ltd ....E 631 957-8000
  Lindenhurst (G-6983)

CONDENSERS: Heat Transfer Eqpt, Evaporative

Roemac Industrial Sales Inc ....G 716 692-7332
  North Tonawanda (G-12088)
Rubicon Industries Corp ....E 718 434-4700
  Brooklyn (G-2364)

CONDENSERS: Motors Or Generators

GM Components Holdings LLC ....B 716 439-2463
  Lockport (G-7079)
GM Components Holdings LLC ....B 716 439-2011
  Lockport (G-7080)

CONDUITS & FITTINGS: Electric

Highland Valley Supply Inc ....F 845 849-2863
  Wappingers Falls (G-15496)
Producto Electric Corp ....E 845 359-4900
  Orangeburg (G-12328)
Quadristi LLC ....F 585 279-3318
  Rochester (G-13658)

CONDUITS: Pressed Pulp Fiber, Made From Purchased Materials

Stanley Paper Co Inc ....F 518 489-1131
  Albany (G-131)

CONFECTIONERY PRDTS WHOLESALERS

Mrchocolatecom LLC ....E 718 875-9772
  Brooklyn (G-2179)
Roger L Urban Inc ....E 716 693-5391
  North Tonawanda (G-12089)

CONFECTIONS & CANDY

5th Avenue Chocolatiere Ltd ....G 212 935-5454
Freeport (G-4977)

Anyas Licorice Inc ....G 917 935-1916
Brooklyn (G-1515)

Bader Enterprise Inc ....G 718 965-9434
Brooklyn (G-1560)

C Howard Company Inc ....G 631 286-7940
Bellport (G-795)

Calico Cottage Inc ....E 631 841-2100
Amityville (G-257)

Chocolat Moderne LLC ....G 212 229-4797
New York (G-8996)

Chocolations LLC ....G 914 777-3600
Mamaroneck (G-7503)

Dilese International Inc ....F 716 855-3500
Buffalo (G-2729)

Fairbanks Mfg LLC ....C 845 341-0002
Middletown (G-7908)

Fruit Fresh Up Inc ....E 716 683-3200
Depew (G-3983)

Gertrude Hawk Chocolates Inc ....E .....
Watertown (G-15570)

Godiva Chocolatier Inc ....E 212 984-5900
New York (G-9636)

Golden Chocolate Inc ....G 718 330-1000
Brooklyn (G-1897)

Gravymaster Inc ....E 203 453-1893
Canajoharie (G-3120)

Handsome Dans LLC ....G 917 965-2499
New York (G-9719)

Hercules Candy Co ....G 315 463-4339
East Syracuse (G-4216)

Hudson Valley Chocolatier Inc ....F 845 831-8240
Beacon (G-753)

In Room Plus Inc ....E 716 838-9433
Buffalo (G-2808)

Jo-Mart Candies Corp ....F 718 375-1277
Brooklyn (G-1996)

Koppers Choclat Specialty Inc ....G 917 834-2290
New York (G-10126)

L A Burdick Chocolates ....G 212 796-0143
New York (G-10149)

Lady-N-Th-wndow Chocolates Inc ....F 631 549-1059
Huntington (G-6210)

Lanco Corporation ....C 631 231-2300
Ronkonkoma (G-13964)

Landies Candies Co Inc ....F 716 834-8212
Buffalo (G-2847)

Little Bird Chocolates Inc ....G 646 620-6395
Plainview (G-12697)

Momn Pops Inc ....E 845 567-0640
Cornwall (G-3729)

Mrchocolatecom LLC ....F 718 875-9772
Brooklyn (G-2179)

Nassau Candy Distributors Inc ....C 516 433-7100
Hicksville (G-5933)

Noras Candy Shop ....F 315 337-4530
Rome (G-13860)

Pachanga Inc ....F 212 832-0022
New York (G-10737)

Papa Bubble ....G 212 966-2599
New York (G-10747)

Premium Sweets USA Inc ....G 718 739-6000
Jamaica (G-6466)

Richardson Brands Company ....C 800 839-8938
Canajoharie (G-3121)

Roger L Urban Inc ....E 716 693-5391
North Tonawanda (G-12089)

Salty Road Inc ....G 347 673-3925
Brooklyn (G-2382)

Satin Fine Foods Inc ....D 845 469-1034
Chester (G-3386)

Scaccianoce Inc ....F 718 991-4462
Bronx (G-1362)

Seaward Candies ....G 585 638-6761
Holley (G-6038)

Settons Intl Foods Inc ....D 631 543-8090
Commack (G-3598)

Simply Natural Foods LLC ....C 631 543-9600
Commack (G-3599)

Stones Homemade Candies Inc ....G 315 343-8401
Oswego (G-12422)

Sweetworks Inc ....C 716 634-4545
Buffalo (G-2998)

Tomric Systems Inc ....F 716 854-6050
Buffalo (G-3013)

Valenti Distributing ....G 716 824-2304
Blasdell (G-924)

Vidal Candies USA Inc ....G 609 781-8169
New York (G-11679)

Wellspring Corp ....G 212 529-5454
New York (G-11741)

CONFINEMENT SURVEILLANCE SYS MAINTENANCE & MONITORING SVCS

Par Technology Corporation ....D 315 738-0600
New Hartford (G-8242)

CONNECTORS & TERMINALS: Electrical Device Uses

Fiber Instrument Sales Inc ....C 315 736-2206
Oriskany (G-12390)

International Key Supply LLC ....F 631 983-6096
Farmingdale (G-4652)

Zierick Manufacturing Corp ....D 800 882-8020
Mount Kisco (G-8108)

CONNECTORS: Cord, Electric

Crown Die Casting Corp ....E 914 667-5400
Mount Vernon (G-8135)

EB Acquisitions LLC ....D 212 355-3310
New York (G-9309)

CONNECTORS: Electrical

Automatic Connector Inc ....F 631 543-5000
Hauppauge (G-5598)

Command Components Corporation ....G 631 666-4411
Bay Shore (G-667)

CONNECTORS: Electronic

Accessories For Electronics ....E 631 847-0158
South Hempstead (G-14519)

Amphenol Cables On Demand Corp ....F 607 321-2115
Endicott (G-4443)

Amphenol Corporation ....B 607 563-5364
Sidney (G-14431)

Amphenol Corporation ....A 607 563-5011
Sidney (G-14432)

Automatic Connector Inc ....F 631 543-5000
Hauppauge (G-5598)

Belden Inc ....B 607 796-5600
Horseheads (G-6114)

C S Business Systems Inc ....E 716 886-6521
Buffalo (G-2688)

Casa Innovations Inc ....G 718 965-6600
Brooklyn (G-1654)

EBY Electro Inc ....E 516 576-7777
Plainview (G-12681)

Executive Machines Inc ....E 718 965-6600
Brooklyn (G-1822)

Felchar Manufacturing Corp ....A 607 723-4076
Binghamton (G-877)

I Trade Technology Ltd ....E 615 348-7233
Airmont (G-12)

Ieh Corporation ....C 718 492-4440
Brooklyn (G-1952)

Kirtas Inc ....G 585 924-5999
Victor (G-15415)

Kirtas Inc ....E 585 924-2420
Victor (G-15416)

Leviton Manufacturing Co Inc ....B 631 812-6000
Melville (G-7800)

Mason Industries Inc ....C 631 348-0282
Hauppauge (G-5708)

Mill-Max Mfg Corp ....C 516 922-6000
Oyster Bay (G-12449)

Mini-Circuits Fort Wayne LLC ....B 718 934-4500
Brooklyn (G-2157)

NEa Manufacturing Corp ....E 516 371-4200
Inwood (G-6300)

Power Connector Inc ....E 631 563-7878
Bohemia (G-1062)

Ppc Broadband Inc ....B 315 431-7200
East Syracuse (G-4231)

Princetel Inc ....F 914 579-2410
Hawthorne (G-5822)

Rdi Inc ....F 914 773-1000
Mount Kisco (G-8104)

Resonance Technologies Inc ....E 631 237-4901
Ronkonkoma (G-14002)

Sitewatch Technology LLC ....G 207 778-3246
East Quogue (G-4158)

Supplynet Inc ....G 800 826-0279
Valley Cottage (G-15328)

Taro Manufacturing Company Inc ....F 315 252-9430
Auburn (G-498)

Universal Remote Control Inc ....D 914 835-4484
Harrison (G-5563)

Whirlwind Music Distrs Inc ....D 800 733-9473
Rochester (G-13803)

CONNECTORS: Solderless, Electric-Wiring Devices

Andros Manufacturing Corp ....G 585 663-5700
Rochester (G-13237)

CONSTRUCTION & MINING MACHINERY WHOLESALERS

Gone South Concrete Block Inc ....E 315 598-2141
Fulton (G-5062)

CONSTRUCTION & ROAD MAINTENANCE EQPT: Drags, Road

Drillco National Group Inc ....E 718 726-9801
Long Island City (G-7204)

Highway Garage ....G 518 568-2837
Saint Johnsville (G-14119)

CONSTRUCTION EQPT: Attachments

Primoplast Inc ....F 631 750-0680
Bohemia (G-1066)

CONSTRUCTION EQPT: Attachments, Snow Plow

Cives Corporation ....D 315 543-2321
Harrisville (G-5565)

North American Supply LLC ....G 607 432-1480
Oneonta (G-12277)

Pro-Tech Wldg Fabrication Inc ....E 585 436-9855
Rochester (G-13647)

Town of Ohio ....E 315 392-2055
Forestport (G-4929)

CONSTRUCTION EQPT: Crane Carriers

Crane Equipment & Service Inc ....G 716 689-5400
Amherst (G-219)

CONSTRUCTION EQPT: Cranes

Dave Sandel Cranes Inc ....G 631 325-5588
Westhampton (G-15954)

Kinedyne Inc ....F 716 667-6833
Orchard Park (G-12360)

CONSTRUCTION EQPT: Dozers, Tractor Mounted, Material Moving

Rapistak Corporation ....G 716 822-2804
Buffalo (G-2949)

CONSTRUCTION EQPT: Hammer Mills, Port, Incl Rock/Ore Crush

Schutte-Buffalo Hammermill LLC ....E 716 855-1202
Buffalo (G-2976)

CONSTRUCTION EQPT: Rollers, Sheepsfoot & Vibratory

S R & R Industries Inc ....G 845 692-8329
Middletown (G-7931)

CONSTRUCTION EQPT: SCRAPERS, GRADERS, ROLLERS & SIMILAR EQPT

Gei International Inc ....E 315 463-9261
East Syracuse (G-4212)

CONSTRUCTION EQPT: Wrecker Hoists, Automobile

Pauls Rods & Restos Inc ....G 631 665-7637
Deer Park (G-3917)

Vanhouten Motorsports ....G 315 387-6312
Lacona (G-6747)

CONSTRUCTION MATERIALS, WHOLESALE: Aggregate

Twin County Recycling Corp ....F 516 827-6900
  Westbury (G-15935)

CONSTRUCTION MATERIALS, WHOLESALE: Awnings

Acme Awning Co Inc ....F 718 409-1881
  Bronx (G-1195)
Kassis Superior Sign Co Inc ....F 315 463-7446
  Syracuse (G-14924)

CONSTRUCTION MATERIALS, WHOLESALE: Block, Concrete & Cinder

Lazarek Inc ....G 315 343-1242
  Oswego (G-12413)
Taylor Concrete Products Inc ....E 315 788-2191
  Watertown (G-15589)

CONSTRUCTION MATERIALS, WHOLESALE: Blocks, Building, NEC

Sg Blocks Inc ....F 646 240-4235
  Brooklyn (G-2399)

CONSTRUCTION MATERIALS, WHOLESALE: Building Stone, Granite

Glen Plaza Marble & Gran Inc ....G 516 671-1100
  Glen Cove (G-5195)
MCM Natural Stone Inc ....F 585 586-6510
  Rochester (G-13540)

CONSTRUCTION MATERIALS, WHOLESALE: Building Stone, Marble

Stone & Terrazzo World Inc ....G 718 361-6899
  Long Island City (G-7371)

CONSTRUCTION MATERIALS, WHOLESALE: Building, Exterior

Bob Murphy Inc ....F 607 729-3553
  Vestal (G-15373)
Dolomite Products Company Inc ....E 315 524-1998
  Rochester (G-13354)
Tri-State Brick & Stone NY Inc ....D 212 366-0300
  New York (G-11540)

CONSTRUCTION MATERIALS, WHOLESALE: Building, Interior

Great American Industries Inc ....G 607 729-9331
  Vestal (G-15379)
Nanz Custom Hardware Inc ....E 212 367-7000
  New York (G-10532)
Nanz Custom Hardware Inc ....C 212 367-7000
  Deer Park (G-3908)

CONSTRUCTION MATERIALS, WHOLESALE: Cement

Dicks Concrete Co Inc ....E 845 374-5966
  New Hampton (G-8234)
Lehigh Cement Company ....E 518 943-5940
  Catskill (G-3212)

CONSTRUCTION MATERIALS, WHOLESALE: Clay, Exc Refractory

Walsh & Hughes Inc ....G 631 427-5904
  Huntington Station (G-6266)

CONSTRUCTION MATERIALS, WHOLESALE: Concrete Mixtures

Barney & Dickenson Inc ....D 607 729-1536
  Vestal (G-15370)

CONSTRUCTION MATERIALS, WHOLESALE: Door Frames

Lif Industries Inc ....D 516 390-6800
  Port Washington (G-12899)
Lif Industries Inc ....E 718 767-8800
  Whitestone (G-16097)

Milanese Commercial Door LLC ....F 518 658-0398
  Berlin (G-825)

CONSTRUCTION MATERIALS, WHOLESALE: Glass

Twin Pane Insulated GL Co Inc ....F 631 924-1060
  Yaphank (G-16276)

CONSTRUCTION MATERIALS, WHOLESALE: Gravel

Brewster Transit Mix Corp ....D 845 279-3738
  Brewster (G-1144)
Deer Park Sand & Gravel Corp ....E 631 586-2323
  Bay Shore (G-672)

CONSTRUCTION MATERIALS, WHOLESALE: Limestone

Minerals Technologies Inc ....E 212 878-1800
  New York (G-10476)

CONSTRUCTION MATERIALS, WHOLESALE: Masons' Materials

Colonie Block and Supply Co ....G 518 869-8411
  Colonie (G-3573)
Grandview Block & Supply Co ....E 518 346-7981
  Schenectady (G-14274)

CONSTRUCTION MATERIALS, WHOLESALE: Millwork

I Meglio Corp ....E 631 617-6900
  Hauppauge (G-5674)
Metalocke Industries Inc ....G 718 267-9200
  Woodside (G-16213)

CONSTRUCTION MATERIALS, WHOLESALE: Molding, All Materials

Globmarble LLC ....G 347 717-4088
  Brooklyn (G-1891)
Jaxson Rollforming Inc ....E 631 842-7775
  Amityville (G-280)

CONSTRUCTION MATERIALS, WHOLESALE: Paving Materials

Barrett Paving Materials Inc ....E 315 353-6611
  Norwood (G-12131)

CONSTRUCTION MATERIALS, WHOLESALE: Paving Mixtures

Peckham Materials Corp ....D 914 686-2045
  White Plains (G-16045)

CONSTRUCTION MATERIALS, WHOLESALE: Prefabricated Structures

Morton Buildings Inc ....E 585 786-8191
  Warsaw (G-15508)

CONSTRUCTION MATERIALS, WHOLESALE: Roof, Asphalt/Sheet Metal

Jordan Panel Systems Corp ....E 631 754-4900
  East Northport (G-4148)

CONSTRUCTION MATERIALS, WHOLESALE: Roofing & Siding Material

Marathon Roofing Products Inc ....F 716 685-3340
  Orchard Park (G-12364)
Park Ave Bldg & Roofg Sups LLC ....F 718 403-0100
  Brooklyn (G-2247)
S & J Sheet Metal Supply ....G 718 384-0800
  Brooklyn (G-2369)

CONSTRUCTION MATERIALS, WHOLESALE: Sand

F H Stickles & Son Inc ....F 518 851-9048
  Livingston (G-7052)
Monticello Black Top Corp ....G 845 434-7280
  Thompsonville (G-15066)

CONSTRUCTION MATERIALS, WHOLESALE: Septic Tanks

Guardian Concrete Products Inc ....F 518 372-0080
  Schenectady (G-14277)

CONSTRUCTION MATERIALS, WHOLESALE: Siding, Exc Wood

Pal Aluminum Inc ....G 516 937-1990
  Hicksville (G-5939)

CONSTRUCTION MATERIALS, WHOLESALE: Stone, Crushed Or Broken

Buffalo Crushed Stone Inc ....F 716 566-9636
  Franklinville (G-4965)
Callahan & Nannini Quarry Inc ....G 845 496-4323
  Salisbury Mills (G-14134)
Callanan Industries Inc ....E 845 457-3158
  Montgomery (G-8058)
Grosso Materials Inc ....F 845 361-5211
  Montgomery (G-8061)
Hanson Aggregates PA LLC ....F 315 782-2300
  Watertown (G-15571)
Pallette Stone Corporation ....E 518 584-2421
  Gansevoort (G-5084)
Troy Sand & Gravel Co Inc ....F 518 674-2854
  West Sand Lake (G-15837)

CONSTRUCTION MATERIALS, WHOLESALE: Tile & Clay Prdts

Adore Floors Inc ....G 631 843-0900
  Farmingdale (G-4573)

CONSTRUCTION MATERIALS, WHOLESALE: Tile, Clay/Other Ceramic

Foro Marble Co Inc ....E 718 852-2322
  Brooklyn (G-1859)
Kowa American Corporation ....E 212 303-7800
  New York (G-10131)

CONSTRUCTION MATERIALS, WHOLESALE: Windows

Excel Aluminum Products Inc ....G 315 471-0925
  Syracuse (G-14891)
Express Building Supply Inc ....E 516 608-0379
  Oceanside (G-12171)
New Bgnnngs Win Door Dstrs LLC ....F 845 214-0698
  Poughkeepsie (G-12974)

CONSTRUCTION MATLS, WHOL: Lumber, Rough, Dressed/Finished

Berry Industrial Group Inc ....G 845 353-8338
  Nyack (G-12137)
Georgia-Pacific LLC ....E 631 924-7401
  Yaphank (G-16262)
McNeilly Wood Products Inc ....E 845 457-9651
  Campbell Hall (G-3118)

CONSTRUCTION MATLS, WHOLESALE: Soil Erosion Cntrl Fabrics

Traffic Lane Closures LLC ....F 845 228-6100
  Carmel (G-3192)

CONSTRUCTION SAND MINING

Buffalo Crushed Stone Inc ....G 607 587-8102
  Alfred Station (G-184)
Country Side Sand & Gravel ....F 716 988-3271
  South Dayton (G-14507)
John Vespa Inc ....F 315 788-6330
  Watertown (G-15575)
Lazarek Inc ....G 315 343-1242
  Oswego (G-12413)
Little Valley Sand & Gravel ....G 716 938-6676
  Little Valley (G-6999)
Rural Hill Sand and Grav Corp ....F 315 846-5212
  Woodville (G-16239)
Syracusa Sand and Gravel Inc ....F 585 924-7146
  Victor (G-15435)

CONSTRUCTION SITE PREPARATION SVCS

Kevin Regan Logging Ltd ....G 315 245-3890
  Camden (G-3103)

CONSTRUCTION: Bridge

Dalrymple Holding Corp.................E..... 607 737-6200
Pine City (G-12628)

Tiki Industries Inc ....G..... 516 779-3629
Riverhead (G-13190)

CONSTRUCTION: Commercial & Institutional Building

Alvio-US Corp............................G..... 631 664-0618
Hauppauge (G-5586)

Stephen Miller Gen Contrs Inc.............E..... 518 661-5601
Gloversville (G-5293)

CONSTRUCTION: Concrete Patio

Concrete Designs Inc ....G..... 607 738-0309
Elmira (G-4345)

CONSTRUCTION: Dry Cleaning Plant

Genco John ....G..... 716 483-5446
Jamestown (G-6512)

CONSTRUCTION: Food Prdts Manufacturing or Packing Plant

Patla Enterprises Inc ....F..... 315 367-0237
Sherrill (G-14405)

Sidco Food Distribution Corp............F..... 718 733-3939
Bronx (G-1363)

CONSTRUCTION: Guardrails, Highway

Elderlee Incorporated ....C..... 315 789-6670
Oaks Corners (G-12161)

CONSTRUCTION: Heavy Highway & Street

A Colarusso and Son Inc ....E..... 518 828-3218
Hudson (G-6146)

Barrett Paving Materials Inc............F..... 315 788-2037
Watertown (G-15559)

Dalrymple Holding Corp.................E..... 607 737-6200
Pine City (G-12628)

Peckham Materials Corp ....E..... 518 747-3353
Hudson Falls (G-6192)

Suit-Kote Corporation ....E..... 607 535-2743
Watkins Glen (G-15616)

CONSTRUCTION: Indl Building & Warehouse

Siemens Industry Inc...................E..... 716 568-0983
Buffalo (G-2982)

CONSTRUCTION: Indl Building, Prefabricated

R & B Fabrication Inc ....F..... 315 640-9901
Cicero (G-3423)

Zebra Technologies Entp Corp............E..... 800 722-6234
Holtsville (G-6059)

CONSTRUCTION: Indl Buildings, New, NEC

Orange County Ironworks LLC............E..... 845 769-3000
Montgomery (G-8064)

Stephen Miller Gen Contrs Inc.............E..... 518 661-5601
Gloversville (G-5293)

CONSTRUCTION: Pharmaceutical Manufacturing Plant

Knf Clean Room Products Corp ....E..... 631 588-7000
Ronkonkoma (G-13958)

CONSTRUCTION: Power & Communication Transmission Tower

Ducon Technologies Inc.................B..... 631 694-1700
New York (G-9278)

CONSTRUCTION: Power Plant

Ducon Technologies Inc.................B..... 631 694-1700
New York (G-9278)

CONSTRUCTION: Religious Building

Makarenko Studios Inc..................G..... 914 968-7673
Yorktown Heights (G-16367)

CONSTRUCTION: Residential, Nec

Alvio-US Corp............................G..... 631 664-0618
Hauppauge (G-5586)

WD Certified Contracting LLC ....F..... 516 493-9319
Westbury (G-15939)

CONSTRUCTION: Single-Family Housing

Frost Publications Inc ....G..... 845 726-3232
Westtown (G-15965)

Kasson & Keller Inc ....A..... 518 853-3421
Fonda (G-4910)

CONSTRUCTION: Single-family Housing, New

Capitol Restoration Corp ....G..... 516 783-1425
North Bellmore (G-12014)

CONSTRUCTION: Steel Buildings

Steele Truss Company Inc ....E..... 518 562-4663
Plattsburgh (G-12780)

CONSTRUCTION: Street Sign Installation & Mntnce

Architectural Sign Group Inc ....G..... 516 326-1800
Elmont (G-4382)

CONSTRUCTION: Street Surfacing & Paving

Barrett Paving Materials Inc...........E..... 315 353-6611
Norwood (G-12131)

Cofire Paving Corporation ....E..... 718 463-1403
Flushing (G-4845)

John T Montecalvo Inc ....G..... 631 325-1492
Speonk (G-14563)

Lomin Construction Company ....G..... 516 759-5734
Glen Head (G-5209)

CONSTRUCTION: Tennis Court

Lomin Construction Company ....G..... 516 759-5734
Glen Head (G-5209)

CONSTRUCTION: Warehouse

Tech Park Food Services LLC ....G..... 585 295-1250
Rochester (G-13762)

CONSULTING SVC: Business, NEC

Batavia Precision Glass LLC ....G..... 585 343-6050
Buffalo (G-2656)

Cambridge Whos Who Pubg Inc ....E..... 516 833-8440
Uniondale (G-15224)

Chromagraphics Press Inc ....G..... 631 367-6160
Melville (G-7766)

Compelld Inc ....G..... 917 494-4462
New York (G-9072)

Doar Inc................................G..... 516 872-8140
Lynbrook (G-7430)

Holmes Group The Inc ....G..... 212 333-2300
New York (G-9806)

Integrated Graphics Inc.................E..... 212 592-5600
New York (G-9908)

Marketplace Slutions Group LLC ....E..... 631 868-0111
Holbrook (G-6009)

Milmar Food Group II LLC...............C..... 845 294-5400
Goshen (G-5311)

Next Step Publishing Inc................F..... 585 742-1260
Victor (G-15422)

Trendsformers Ltd Liability Co...........G..... 888 700-2423
New York (G-11537)

UI Information & Insights Inc............E..... 518 640-9200
Latham (G-6879)

CONSULTING SVC: Computer

Caminus Corporation ....D..... 212 515-3600
New York (G-8898)

Cgi Technologies Solutions Inc...........F..... 212 682-7411
New York (G-8965)

Classroom Inc ....E..... 212 545-8400
New York (G-9028)

Dohnsco Inc ....G..... 516 773-4800
Manhasset (G-7533)

Pegasystems Inc ....E..... 212 626-6550
New York (G-10790)

Reactivecore LLC.......................G..... 631 944-1618
New York (G-10992)

CONSULTING SVC: Educational

National Rding Styles Inst Inc ....F..... 516 921-5500
Syosset (G-14797)

CONSULTING SVC: Engineering

Complex Biosystems Inc ....G..... 315 464-8007
Baldwinsville (G-545)

Exergy LLC.............................E..... 516 832-9300
Garden City (G-5100)

General Composites Inc ....E..... 518 963-7333
Willsboro (G-16151)

Glasgow Products Inc ....E..... 516 374-5937
Woodmere (G-16191)

Hudson Valley Tech Dev Ctr Inc ....F..... 845 391-8214
Highland (G-5960)

Innovation Associates Inc................C..... 607 798-9376
Johnson City (G-6602)

Laser & Electron Beam Inc ....G..... 603 626-6080
New York (G-10175)

Procomponents Inc ....E..... 516 683-0909
Westbury (G-15921)

Select Controls Inc ....E..... 631 567-9010
Bohemia (G-1076)

Skae Power Solutions LLC ....E..... 845 365-9103
Palisades (G-12482)

CONSULTING SVC: Financial Management

Principia Partners LLC ....D..... 212 480-2270
New York (G-10893)

CONSULTING SVC: Human Resource

Chequedcom Inc........................E..... 888 412-0699
Saratoga Springs (G-14169)

CONSULTING SVC: Management

Altius Aviation LLC ....G..... 315 455-7555
Syracuse (G-14813)

Answermgmt LLC ....G..... 914 318-1301
Albany (G-41)

Barker Steel LLC ....E..... 518 465-6221
Albany (G-44)

Beer Marketers Insights Inc ....G..... 845 507-0040
Suffern (G-14758)

Ca Inc ....A..... 800 225-5224
New York (G-8882)

Gary Roth & Associates Ltd ....E..... 516 333-1000
Westbury (G-15889)

Marketplace Slutions Group LLC ....E..... 631 868-0111
Holbrook (G-6009)

CONSULTING SVC: Marketing Management

In-Step Marketing Inc...................F..... 212 797-3450
New York (G-9874)

Incro Marketing USA Corp ....G..... 917 365-5552
New York (G-9876)

Maven Marketing LLC...................G..... 615 510-3248
New York (G-10387)

Msm Designz Inc ....G..... 914 909-5900
Tarrytown (G-15050)

Rainforest Inc ....F..... 212 575-7620
New York (G-10973)

Ramsbury Property Us Inc ....F..... 212 223-6250
New York (G-10976)

Rfn Inc.................................F..... 516 764-5100
Bay Shore (G-705)

Sales Hacker Inc ....G..... 516 660-2836
New York (G-11118)

Takeout Printing LLC...................G..... 845 564-2609
Newburgh (G-11888)

Tri-Force Sales LLC ....E..... 732 261-5507
New York (G-11538)

Zacks Enterprises Inc...................E..... 800 366-4924
Orangeburg (G-12333)

CONSULTING SVC: Online Technology

Orthstar Enterprises Inc.................D..... 607 562-2100
Horseheads (G-6130)

CONSULTING SVC: Sales Management

Island Marketing Corp...................G..... 516 739-0500
Mineola (G-7981)

Karp Overseas Corporation ....E..... 718 784-2105
Maspeth (G-7625)

PRODUCT

CONSULTING SVCS, BUSINESS: Communications

L3 Technologies Inc................................D...... 631 231-1700
Hauppauge *(G-5688)*
Redcom Laboratories Inc.......................C...... 585 924-6567
Victor *(G-15428)*

CONSULTING SVCS, BUSINESS: Energy Conservation

Gotham Energy 360 LLC........................F...... 917 338-1023
New York *(G-9647)*
Project Energy Savers LLC....................F...... 718 596-6448
Brooklyn *(G-2300)*
Rle Industries LLC..................................E...... 973 276-1444
New York *(G-11055)*
Western Oil and Gas JV Inc...................G...... 914 967-4758
Rye *(G-14086)*

CONSULTING SVCS, BUSINESS: Publishing

Mnn Holding Company LLC.....................F...... 404 558-5251
Brooklyn *(G-2165)*
Slosson Eductl Publications...................F...... 716 652-0930
East Aurora *(G-4096)*

CONSULTING SVCS, BUSINESS: Safety Training Svcs

Bullex Inc..F...... 518 689-2023
Albany *(G-53)*

CONSULTING SVCS, BUSINESS: Sys Engnrg, Exc Computer/Prof

Parlor Labs Inc.....................................G...... 866 801-7323
New York *(G-10765)*
Sale 121 Corp.......................................D...... 240 855-8988
New York *(G-11117)*

CONSULTING SVCS, BUSINESS: Systems Analysis Or Design

Relx Inc..E...... 212 309-8100
New York *(G-11005)*

CONSULTING SVCS, BUSINESS: Test Development & Evaluation

Micro Semicdtr Researches LLC.............G...... 646 863-6070
New York *(G-10457)*

CONSULTING SVCS, BUSINESS: Testing, Educational Or Personnel

Bright Kids Nyc Inc...............................E...... 917 539-4575
New York *(G-8852)*

CONSULTING SVCS: Oil

Gotham Energy 360 LLC........................F...... 917 338-1023
New York *(G-9647)*

CONSULTING SVCS: Scientific

Cognigen Corporation............................D...... 716 633-3463
Buffalo *(G-2701)*
Guosa Life Sciences Inc.........................F...... 718 813-7806
New York *(G-9699)*
Prime Research Solutions LLC................F...... 917 836-7941
Flushing *(G-4889)*
Xactiv Inc..F...... 585 288-7220
Fairport *(G-4531)*

CONTACT LENSES

Acuity Polymers Inc...............................G...... 585 458-8409
Rochester *(G-13205)*
Coopervision Inc...................................A...... 585 385-6810
West Henrietta *(G-15790)*
Coopervision Inc...................................A...... 585 889-3301
Scottsville *(G-14339)*
Coopervision Inc...................................C...... 585 385-6810
Victor *(G-15401)*
Coopervision Inc...................................D...... 585 385-6810
Victor *(G-15402)*
Corneal Design Corporation...................F...... 301 670-7076
Lima *(G-6930)*
J I Intrntnal Contact Lens Lab................G...... 718 997-1212
Rego Park *(G-13077)*

CONTACTS: Electrical

Micro Contacts Inc................................E...... 516 433-4830
Hicksville *(G-5929)*

CONTAINERS, GLASS: Cosmetic Jars

Baralan Usa Inc.....................................E...... 718 849-5768
Richmond Hill *(G-13109)*

CONTAINERS, GLASS: Food

Pennsauken Packing Company LLC.....G...... 585 377-7700
Fairport *(G-4514)*
Saint Gobain Grains & Powders............A...... 716 731-8200
Niagara Falls *(G-11976)*

CONTAINERS, GLASS: Medicine Bottles

Velvet Healing By Alma Corp.................G...... 347 271-4220
Bronx *(G-1390)*

CONTAINERS: Cargo, Wood & Metal Combination

219 South West.....................................G...... 315 474-2065
Syracuse *(G-14807)*
Sg Blocks Inc.......................................F...... 646 240-4235
Brooklyn *(G-2399)*

CONTAINERS: Cargo, Wood & Wood With Metal

Airline Container Services.....................G...... 516 371-4125
Lido Beach *(G-6927)*
Concord Express Cargo Inc....................G...... 718 276-7200
Jamaica *(G-6437)*

CONTAINERS: Corrugated

Ares Printing and Packg Corp................C...... 718 858-8760
Brooklyn *(G-1527)*
Brand Box USA LLC...............................G...... 607 584-7682
Binghamton *(G-863)*
Color Carton Corp.................................D...... 718 665-0840
Bronx *(G-1228)*
Fiber USA Corp.....................................G...... 718 888-1512
Flushing *(G-4852)*
Gavin Mfg Corp.....................................E...... 631 467-0040
Farmingdale *(G-4636)*
International Paper Company...................F...... 716 852-2144
Buffalo *(G-2814)*
Key Container Corp................................G...... 631 582-3847
East Islip *(G-4129)*
M C Packaging Corporation....................E...... 631 643-3763
Babylon *(G-522)*
Orange Die Cutting Corp........................C...... 845 562-0900
Newburgh *(G-11879)*
Orcon Industries Corp...........................D...... 585 768-7000
Le Roy *(G-6905)*
Pactiv LLC...E...... 585 248-1213
Pittsford *(G-12655)*
Parlor City Paper Box Co Inc.................D...... 607 772-0600
Binghamton *(G-903)*
Specialized Packg Group Inc.................G...... 315 638-4355
Baldwinsville *(G-553)*
Track 7 Inc..G...... 845 544-1810
Warwick *(G-15521)*

CONTAINERS: Foil, Bakery Goods & Frozen Foods

De Luxe Packaging Corp........................E...... 416 754-4633
Saugerties *(G-14200)*
Tri-State Food Jobbers Inc.....................G...... 718 921-1211
Brooklyn *(G-2519)*

CONTAINERS: Food & Beverage

Cmc-Kuhnke Inc...................................F...... 518 694-3310
Albany *(G-62)*
Marley Spoon Inc..................................C...... 866 228-4513
New York *(G-10372)*

CONTAINERS: Food, Folding, Made From Purchased Materials

Diamond Packaging Holdings LLC.........G...... 585 334-8030
Rochester *(G-13343)*
Genpak Industries Inc............................E...... 518 798-9511
Middletown *(G-7910)*

Mod-Pac Corp.......................................C...... 716 898-8480
Buffalo *(G-2869)*
Pactiv LLC...C...... 518 562-6101
Plattsburgh *(G-12766)*

CONTAINERS: Food, Liquid Tight, Including Milk

International Paper Company...................C...... 607 775-1550
Conklin *(G-3625)*

CONTAINERS: Food, Metal

Silgan Containers Mfg Corp...................C...... 315 946-4826
Lyons *(G-7452)*

CONTAINERS: Glass

Anchor Glass Container Corp.................B...... 607 737-1933
Elmira Heights *(G-4374)*
Certainteed Corporation.........................C...... 716 823-3684
Lackawanna *(G-6740)*
Intrapac International Corp......................C...... 518 561-2030
Plattsburgh *(G-12753)*
Owens-Brockway Glass Cont Inc............C...... 315 258-3211
Auburn *(G-489)*
Rocco Bormioli Glass Co Inc..................E...... 212 719-0606
New York *(G-11066)*
Schott Corporation................................D...... 914 831-2200
Elmsford *(G-4428)*
SGD North America................................E...... 212 753-4200
New York *(G-11198)*
SGD Pharma Packaging Inc....................F...... 212 223-7100
New York *(G-11199)*

CONTAINERS: Laminated Phenolic & Vulcanized Fiber

Diemolding Corporation..........................C...... 315 363-4710
Wampsville *(G-15480)*
Skydyne Company..................................D...... 845 858-6400
Port Jervis *(G-12857)*

CONTAINERS: Liquid Tight Fiber, From Purchased Materials

Acran Spill Containment Inc...................F...... 631 841-2300
Massapequa *(G-7643)*

CONTAINERS: Metal

Abbot & Abbot Box Corp........................F...... 888 930-5972
Long Island City *(G-7143)*
Erie Engineered Products Inc.................E...... 716 206-0204
Lancaster *(G-6805)*
Hornet Group Inc...................................D...... 845 858-6400
Port Jervis *(G-12850)*
J R Cooperage Co Inc............................G...... 718 387-1664
Brooklyn *(G-1982)*
Medi-Ray Inc...D...... 877 898-3003
Tuckahoe *(G-15205)*
Mobile Mini Inc.....................................F...... 315 732-4555
Utica *(G-15285)*
Westrock - Southern Cont LLC...............C...... 315 487-6111
Camillus *(G-3113)*
Westrock Cp LLC...................................C...... 716 694-1000
North Tonawanda *(G-12098)*

CONTAINERS: Plastic

A R Arena Products Inc..........................E...... 585 277-1680
Rochester *(G-13195)*
Albea Cosmetics America Inc.................E...... 212 371-5100
New York *(G-8507)*
Amcor Rigid Packaging Usa LLC............E...... 716 366-2440
Dunkirk *(G-4049)*
Baralan Usa Inc.....................................E...... 718 849-5768
Richmond Hill *(G-13109)*
Chem-Tainer Industries Inc....................E...... 631 422-8300
West Babylon *(G-15702)*
Consolidated Container Co LLC..............F...... 585 343-9351
Batavia *(G-611)*
Erie Engineered Products Inc.................E...... 716 206-0204
Lancaster *(G-6805)*
Form A Rockland Plastics Inc.................G...... 315 848-3300
Cranberry Lake *(G-3801)*
Forteq North America Inc........................D...... 585 427-9410
West Henrietta *(G-15794)*
GSE Composites Inc..............................F...... 631 389-1300
Hauppauge *(G-5664)*
Ingenious Designs LLC..........................E...... 631 254-3376
Ronkonkoma *(G-13948)*

Iridium Industries Inc..................E...... 516 504-9700
Great Neck (G-5395)

Kenney Manufacturing Displays ....F...... 631 231-5563
Bay Shore (G-686)

Kernow North America ....F...... 585 586-3590
Pittsford (G-12645)

M I T Poly-Cart Corp ....G...... 212 724-7290
New York (G-10297)

Micromold Products Inc ....E...... 914 969-2850
Yonkers (G-16333)

Neo Plastics LLC.................F...... 646 542-1499
Brooklyn (G-2197)

Ontario Plastics Inc ....E...... 585 663-2644
Rochester (G-13591)

Pactiv LLC ....C...... 518 793-2524
Glens Falls (G-5264)

Plastic Solutions Inc ....E...... 631 234-9013
Bayport (G-730)

Plastic Sys/Gr Bflo Inc............G...... 716 835-7555
Buffalo (G-2922)

Plasticware LLC.................F...... 845 267-0790
Monsey (G-8043)

Powertex Inc ....E...... 518 297-4000
Rouses Point (G-14067)

Precision Packaging Pdts Inc ....C...... 585 638-8200
Holley (G-6037)

Quoin LLC ....A...... 914 967-9400
Rye (G-14084)

Silgan Plastics LLC...............C...... 315 536-5690
Penn Yan (G-12594)

Somar North America Corp ....G...... 716 458-0742
Olean (G-12242)

Summit Manufacturing LLC ....G...... 631 952-1570
Bay Shore (G-719)

Visitainer Corp ....E...... 718 636-0300
Brooklyn (G-2564)

Weber Intl Packg Co LLC ....D...... 518 561-8282
Plattsburgh (G-12790)

CONTAINERS: Sanitary, Food

Consolidated Container Co LLC............C...... 585 262-6470
Rochester (G-13325)

CONTAINERS: Shipping & Mailing, Fiber

American Intrmdal Cont Mfg LLC..........G...... 631 774-6790
Hauppauge (G-5591)

CONTAINERS: Shipping, Bombs, Metal Plate

828 Express Inc ....G...... 917 577-9019
Staten Island (G-14612)

Erie Engineered Products Inc..............E...... 716 206-0204
Lancaster (G-6805)

Vship Co ....F...... 718 706-8566
Astoria (G-443)

Wayne Integrated Tech Corp............E...... 631 242-0213
Edgewood (G-4291)

CONTAINERS: Shipping, Wood

Hood Industries Inc ....F...... 716 836-0301
Buffalo (G-2800)

CONTAINERS: Wood

Abbot & Abbot Box Corp ....F...... 888 930-5972
Long Island City (G-7143)

David Isseks & Sons Inc..............E...... 212 966-8694
New York (G-9179)

Essex Box & Pallet Co Inc.............E...... 518 834-7279
Keeseville (G-6641)

Great Lakes Specialites...............E...... 716 672-4622
Fredonia (G-4970)

Pluribus Products Inc...............E...... 718 852-1614
Bayville (G-747)

CONTRACT FOOD SVCS

Herris Gourmet Inc ....G...... 917 578-2308
Brooklyn (G-1934)

CONTRACTOR: Framing

Timber Frames Inc ....G...... 585 374-6405
Canandaigua (G-3144)

CONTRACTORS: Acoustical & Ceiling Work

Newmat Northeast Corp ....F...... 631 253-9277
West Babylon (G-15734)

CONTRACTORS: Acoustical & Insulation Work

New York State Foam Enrgy LLC ....G...... 845 534-4656
Cornwall (G-3730)

CONTRACTORS: Antenna Installation

Fred A Nudd Corporation ....E...... 315 524-2531
Ontario (G-12289)

CONTRACTORS: Awning Installation

Aqua Shield Inc ....G...... 631 420-4490
West Babylon (G-15690)

Awning Mart Inc ....G...... 315 699-5928
Cicero (G-3416)

Space Sign.....................F...... 718 961-1112
College Point (G-3565)

CONTRACTORS: Boiler & Furnace

Empire Industrial Systems Corp ....F...... 631 242-4619
Bay Shore (G-678)

CONTRACTORS: Boiler Maintenance Contractor

Empire Industrial Burner Svc ....G...... 631 242-4619
Deer Park (G-3872)

CONTRACTORS: Building Eqpt & Machinery Installation

Advanced Door Solutions Inc...............G...... 631 773-6100
Holbrook (G-5984)

Assa Abloy Entrance Systems US ....E...... 315 492-6600
East Syracuse (G-4198)

Bargold Storage Systems LLC ....E...... 718 247-7000
Long Island City (G-7175)

Otis Elevator Company ....E...... 917 339-9600
New York (G-10717)

Schindler Elevator Corporation ....C...... 212 708-1000
New York (G-11151)

Windowman Inc (usa)...............G...... 718 246-2626
Brooklyn (G-2590)

CONTRACTORS: Building Sign Installation & Mntnce

Adirondack Sign Company LLC ....F...... 518 409-7446
Saratoga Springs (G-14162)

Alley Cat Signs Inc................F...... 631 924-7446
Middle Island (G-7874)

Clinton Signs Inc.................G...... 585 482-1620
Webster (G-15636)

Flexlume Sign Corporation ....G...... 716 884-2020
Buffalo (G-2755)

Gloede Neon Signs Ltd Inc ....F...... 845 471-4366
Poughkeepsie (G-12958)

Jem Sign Corp ....G...... 516 867-4466
Hempstead (G-5840)

Lanza Corp ....G...... 914 937-6360
Port Chester (G-12824)

North Shore Neon Sign Co Inc ....E...... 718 937-4848
Flushing (G-4881)

Rapp Signs Inc..................F...... 607 656-8167
Greene (G-5447)

Ray Sign Inc ....F...... 518 377-1371
Schenectady (G-14298)

Rgm Signs Inc ....G...... 718 442-0598
Staten Island (G-14703)

Sign Works Incorporated ....G...... 914 592-0700
Elmsford (G-4433)

T J Signs Unlimited LLC ....E...... 631 273-4800
Islip (G-6357)

CONTRACTORS: Carpentry Work

EZ Lift Operator Corp ....F...... 845 356-1676
Spring Valley (G-14568)

Innova Interiors Inc................E...... 718 401-2122
Bronx (G-1283)

Mestel Brothers Stairs & Rails..............C...... 516 496-4127
Syosset (G-14794)

CONTRACTORS: Carpentry, Cabinet & Finish Work

Cabinet Shapes Corp...............F...... 718 784-6255
Long Island City (G-7182)

Capital Kit Cab & Door Mfrs...............G...... 718 886-0303
College Point (G-3539)

Central Kitchen Corp ....F...... 631 283-1029
Southampton (G-14528)

Dak Mica and Wood Products ....G...... 631 467-0749
Ronkonkoma (G-13929)

Eugenia Selective Living Inc ....E...... 631 277-1461
Islip (G-6352)

Hennig Custom Woodwork Corp...........G...... 516 536-3460
Oceanside (G-12174)

Johnny Mica Inc ....G...... 631 225-5213
Lindenhurst (G-6953)

Jq Woodworking Inc ....G...... 516 766-3424
Oceanside (G-12177)

M & C Furniture ....G...... 718 422-2136
Brooklyn (G-2091)

Metro Kitchens Corp................F...... 718 434-1166
Brooklyn (G-2147)

CONTRACTORS: Carpentry, Cabinet Building & Installation

Auburn-Watson Corp ....F...... 716 876-8000
Depew (G-3970)

Daniel Demarco and Assoc Inc ....E...... 631 598-7000
Amityville (G-262)

Fontrick Door Inc ....E...... 585 345-6032
Batavia (G-614)

Home Ideal Inc..................E...... 718 762-8998
Flushing (G-4860)

Manhattan Cabinets Inc ....G...... 212 548-2436
New York (G-10342)

Precision Dental Cabinets Inc ....F...... 631 543-3870
Smithtown (G-14485)

Yost Neon Displays Inc ....G...... 716 674-6780
West Seneca (G-15856)

CONTRACTORS: Carpentry, Finish & Trim Work

Millwright Wdwrk Installetion ....E...... 631 587-2635
West Babylon (G-15732)

CONTRACTORS: Ceramic Floor Tile Installation

Icestone LLC ....E...... 718 624-4900
Brooklyn (G-1951)

CONTRACTORS: Closed Circuit Television Installation

Sartek Industries Inc................G...... 631 473-3555
East Setauket (G-4186)

CONTRACTORS: Commercial & Office Building

United Steel Products Inc ....D...... 718 478-5330
Corona (G-3751)

CONTRACTORS: Communications Svcs

Professional Technology Inc ....G...... 315 337-4156
Rome (G-13864)

CONTRACTORS: Concrete

A Colarusso and Son Inc ....E...... 518 828-3218
Hudson (G-6146)

Geneva Granite Co Inc ....F...... 315 789-8142
Geneva (G-5155)

Seneca Stone Corporation.................G...... 607 737-6200
Pine City (G-12629)

CONTRACTORS: Concrete Pumping

Barney & Dickenson Inc................D...... 607 729-1536
Vestal (G-15370)

CONTRACTORS: Concrete Repair

Capitol Restoration Corp ....G...... 516 783-1425
North Bellmore (G-12014)

CONTRACTORS: Construction Site Cleanup

Darrell Mitchell ....G...... 646 659-7075
Arverne (G-407)

P
R
O
D
U
C
T

CONTRACTORS: Countertop Installation

Contempra Design Inc ....G 718 984-8586
　Staten Island (G-14642)
Countertops & Cabinets Inc ....G 315 433-1038
　Syracuse (G-14865)
FX INC ....F 212 244-2240
　New York (G-9556)
Johnny Mica Inc ....G 631 225-5213
　Lindenhurst (G-6953)
Joseph Fedele ....G 718 448-3658
　Staten Island (G-14672)
Rochester Countertop Inc ....F 585 338-2260
　Rochester (G-13687)
Thornwood Products Ltd ....E 914 769-9161
　Thornwood (G-15071)

CONTRACTORS: Demountable Partition Installation

Able Steel Equipment Co Inc ....F 718 361-9240
　Long Island City (G-7144)

CONTRACTORS: Directional Oil & Gas Well Drilling Svc

Turner Undgrd Instllations Inc ....E 585 359-2531
　Henrietta (G-5862)

CONTRACTORS: Drywall

L & J Interiors Inc ....G 631 218-0838
　Bohemia (G-1031)
Nordic Interior Inc ....C 718 456-7000
　Brooklyn (G-2219)

CONTRACTORS: Electrical

331 Holding Inc ....E 585 924-1740
　Victor (G-15389)
A & S Electric ....G 212 228-2030
　Brooklyn (G-1430)
C & G Video Systems Inc ....G 315 452-1490
　Liverpool (G-7003)
Cooperfriedman Elc Sup Co Inc ....G 718 269-4906
　Long Island City (G-7192)
Mitsubishi Elc Pwr Pdts Inc ....G 516 962-2813
　Melville (G-7806)
Schuler-Haas Electric Corp ....G 607 936-3514
　Painted Post (G-12475)
Siemens Industry Inc ....E 585 797-2300
　Rochester (G-13728)
Spectrum Cable Corporation ....G 585 235-7714
　Rochester (G-13738)

CONTRACTORS: Electronic Controls Installation

Emco Electric Services LLC ....G 212 420-9766
　New York (G-9360)
Zeppelin Electric Company Inc ....G 631 928-9467
　East Setauket (G-4191)

CONTRACTORS: Energy Management Control

Ihi Inc ....E 212 599-8100
　New York (G-9862)
T S B A Group Inc ....E 718 565-6000
　Sunnyside (G-14775)

CONTRACTORS: Excavating

Ribble Lumber Inc ....G 315 536-6221
　Penn Yan (G-12592)

CONTRACTORS: Excavating Slush Pits & Cellars Svcs

Alice Perkins ....G 716 378-5100
　Salamanca (G-14121)

CONTRACTORS: Exterior Wall System Installation

Plant-Tech2o Inc ....G 516 483-7845
　Hempstead (G-5847)

CONTRACTORS: Fence Construction

City Store Gates Mfg Corp ....E 718 939-9700
　College Point (G-3540)

Fence Plaza Corp ....G 718 469-2200
　Brooklyn (G-1838)
Fort Miller Service Corp ....F 518 695-5000
　Greenwich (G-5472)
Interstate Wood Products Inc ....E 631 842-4488
　Amityville (G-277)
Master-Halco Inc ....F 631 585-8150
　Yaphank (G-16266)
Metro Door Inc ....D 800 669-3667
　Islandia (G-6340)
Oneida Sales & Service Inc ....E 716 822-8205
　Buffalo (G-2897)
Ourem Iron Works Inc ....F 914 476-4856
　Yonkers (G-16337)
Universal Steel Fabricators ....F 718 342-0782
　Brooklyn (G-2546)
Wood Innovations of Suffolk ....G 631 698-2345
　Oceanside (G-12198)

CONTRACTORS: Fiber Optic Cable Installation

Complete Fiber Solutions Inc ....G 718 828-8900
　Bronx (G-1230)

CONTRACTORS: Fire Detection & Burglar Alarm Systems

Detekion Security Systems Inc ....F 607 729-7179
　Vestal (G-15376)
Johnson Controls ....G 845 774-4120
　Harriman (G-5545)
Sentry Devices Corp ....G 631 491-3191
　Dix Hills (G-4015)

CONTRACTORS: Fire Escape Installation

Firecom Inc ....C 718 899-6100
　Woodside (G-16206)

CONTRACTORS: Fire Sprinkler System Installation Svcs

Johnson Controls ....G 845 774-4120
　Harriman (G-5545)

CONTRACTORS: Floor Laying & Other Floor Work

Delta Polymers Inc ....G 631 254-6240
　Bay Shore (G-673)
Designer Epoxy Finishes Inc ....G 646 943-6044
　Melville (G-7774)

CONTRACTORS: Garage Doors

Griffon Corporation ....E 212 957-5000
　New York (G-9676)

CONTRACTORS: Gas Field Svcs, NEC

Schmitt Sales Inc ....G 716 632-8595
　Williamsville (G-16137)
T A S Sales Service LLC ....G 518 234-4919
　Cobleskill (G-3500)

CONTRACTORS: Gasoline Condensation Removal Svcs

Gas Recovery Systems LLC ....F 914 421-4903
　White Plains (G-16009)

CONTRACTORS: Glass, Glazing & Tinting

A&B McKeon Glass Inc ....G 718 525-2152
　Staten Island (G-14614)
Advanced Door Solutions Inc ....G 631 773-6100
　Holbrook (G-5984)
Benson Industries Inc ....F 212 779-3230
　New York (G-8758)
Global Glass Corp ....G 516 681-2309
　Hicksville (G-5912)
Jordan Panel Systems Corp ....E 631 754-4900
　East Northport (G-4148)
Lafayette Mirror & Glass Co ....G 718 768-0660
　New Hyde Park (G-8279)
Upstate Insulated Glass Inc ....G 315 475-4960
　Central Square (G-3297)

CONTRACTORS: Heating & Air Conditioning

Automated Control Logic Inc ....F 914 769-8880
　Thornwood (G-15067)
City Cooling Enterprises Inc ....G 718 331-7400
　Brooklyn (G-1664)
Layton Manufacturing Corp ....E 718 498-6000
　Brooklyn (G-2048)
Nelson Air Device Corporation ....C 718 729-3801
　Maspeth (G-7629)
Prokosch and Sonn Sheet Metal ....E 845 562-4211
　Newburgh (G-11884)
Robin Industries Ltd ....F 718 218-9616
　Brooklyn (G-2351)
Vincent Genovese ....G 631 281-8170
　Mastic Beach (G-7675)

CONTRACTORS: Highway & Street Construction, General

Tiki Industries Inc ....G 516 779-3629
　Riverhead (G-13190)

CONTRACTORS: Highway & Street Paving

Peckham Materials Corp ....D 914 686-2045
　White Plains (G-16045)
Suit-Kote Corporation ....C 607 753-1100
　Cortland (G-3789)
Suit-Kote Corporation ....E 716 664-3750
　Jamestown (G-6545)

CONTRACTORS: Highway Sign & Guardrail Construction & Install

Traffic Lane Closures LLC ....F 845 228-6100
　Carmel (G-3192)

CONTRACTORS: Home & Office Intrs Finish, Furnish/Remodel

Drapery Industries Inc ....F 585 232-2992
　Rochester (G-13356)
Griffon Corporation ....E 212 957-5000
　New York (G-9676)

CONTRACTORS: Hydraulic Eqpt Installation & Svcs

A Gatty Products Inc ....G 914 592-3903
　Elmsford (G-4391)

CONTRACTORS: Hydronics Heating

Corona Plumbing & Htg Sup Inc ....G 718 424-4133
　Corona (G-3736)

CONTRACTORS: Insulation Installation, Building

Advanced Comfort Systems Inc ....F 518 884-8444
　Ballston Spa (G-566)

CONTRACTORS: Kitchen & Bathroom Remodeling

Di Fiore and Sons Custom Wdwkg ....G 718 278-1663
　Long Island City (G-7201)
Triad Counter Corp ....E 631 750-0615
　Bohemia (G-1088)

CONTRACTORS: Lighting Syst

Light Blue USA LLC ....G 718 475-2515
　Brooklyn (G-2070)
Vincent Conigliaro ....F 845 340-0489
　Kingston (G-6722)

CONTRACTORS: Machinery Installation

Finger Lakes Conveyors Inc ....G 315 539-9246
　Waterloo (G-15551)
Re-Al Industrial Corp ....G 716 542-4556
　Akron (G-21)

CONTRACTORS: Marble Installation, Interior

Aurora Stone Group LLC ....F 315 471-6869
　East Syracuse (G-4199)

CONTRACTORS: Masonry & Stonework

Tiki Industries Inc ....G..... 516 779-3629
  Riverhead *(G-13190)*

CONTRACTORS: Mechanical

All-City Metal Inc ....E..... 718 937-3975
  Maspeth *(G-7586)*
Joy Edward Company ....E..... 315 474-3360
  Syracuse *(G-14921)*
Metro Duct Systems Inc ....F..... 718 278-4294
  Long Island City *(G-7294)*

CONTRACTORS: Multi-Family Home Remodeling

Rob Herschenfeld Design Inc ....F..... 718 456-6801
  Brooklyn *(G-2350)*

CONTRACTORS: Office Furniture Installation

Evans & Paul LLC ....E..... 516 576-0800
  Plainview *(G-12684)*

CONTRACTORS: Oil & Gas Building, Repairing & Dismantling Svc

Cotton Well Drilling Co Inc ....G..... 716 672-2788
  Sheridan *(G-14398)*
Steel Excel Inc ....G..... 914 461-1300
  White Plains *(G-16063)*

CONTRACTORS: Oil & Gas Field Fire Fighting Svcs

Uniformed Fire Officer Assoiat ....F..... 212 293-9300
  New York *(G-11586)*

CONTRACTORS: Oil & Gas Field Geological Exploration Svcs

Aquifer Drilling & Testing Inc ....D..... 516 616-6026
  Mineola *(G-7958)*
Aterra Exploration LLC ....E..... 212 315-0030
  New York *(G-8663)*

CONTRACTORS: Oil & Gas Field Geophysical Exploration Svcs

Schlumberger Technology Corp ....C..... 607 378-0105
  Horseheads *(G-6136)*

CONTRACTORS: Oil & Gas Well Casing Cement Svcs

Sabre Energy Services LLC ....F..... 518 514-1572
  Slingerlands *(G-14467)*

CONTRACTORS: Oil & Gas Well Drilling Svc

Alden Aurora Gas Company Inc ....G..... 716 937-9484
  Alden *(G-165)*
Copper Ridge Oil Inc ....G..... 716 372-4021
  Jamestown *(G-6505)*
Geotechnical Drilling Inc ....D..... 516 616-6055
  Mineola *(G-7977)*
Lenape Energy Inc ....G..... 585 344-1200
  Alexander *(G-177)*
Schneider Amalco Inc ....G..... 917 470-9674
  New York *(G-11154)*
Steel Partners Holdings LP ....D..... 212 520-2300
  New York *(G-11352)*
U S Energy Development Corp ....D..... 716 636-0401
  Getzville *(G-5183)*
Western Oil and Gas JV Inc ....G..... 914 967-4758
  Rye *(G-14086)*

CONTRACTORS: Oil & Gas Well Foundation Grading Svcs

DTI Financial Inc ....E..... 212 661-7673
  New York *(G-9274)*

CONTRACTORS: Oil & Gas Wells Svcs

I & S of NY Inc ....F..... 716 373-7001
  Allegany *(G-189)*
Superior Energy Services Inc ....G..... 716 483-0100
  Jamestown *(G-6547)*

CONTRACTORS: Oil Field Haulage Svcs

Lenape Energy Inc ....G..... 585 344-1200
  Alexander *(G-177)*

CONTRACTORS: Oil Field Lease Tanks: Erectg, Clng/Rprg Svcs

Wellspring Omni Holdings Corp ....A..... 212 318-9800
  New York *(G-11742)*

CONTRACTORS: Oil Sampling Svcs

P & C Gas Measurements Service ....F..... 716 257-3412
  Cattaraugus *(G-3221)*

CONTRACTORS: Oil/Gas Well Construction, Rpr/Dismantling Svcs

A & Mt Realty Group LLC ....F..... 718 974-5871
  Brooklyn *(G-1429)*
Arm Construction Company Inc ....G..... 646 235-6520
  East Elmhurst *(G-4103)*
Babula Construction Inc ....G..... 716 681-0886
  Lancaster *(G-6797)*
Barber & Deline Enrgy Svcs LLC ....F..... 315 696-8961
  Tully *(G-15208)*
Darrell Mitchell ....G..... 646 659-7075
  Arverne *(G-407)*
Fame Construction Inc ....E..... 718 626-1000
  Astoria *(G-423)*
Professional Remodelers Inc ....G..... 516 565-9300
  West Hempstead *(G-15778)*
Vick Construction Inc ....G..... 718 313-7625
  Jamaica *(G-6486)*

CONTRACTORS: On-Site Welding

AG Tech Welding Corp ....G..... 845 398-0005
  Tappan *(G-15033)*
Bridgehampton Steel & Wldg Inc ....F..... 631 537-2486
  Bridgehampton *(G-1164)*
Crownbrook ACC LLC ....E..... 718 626-0760
  Brooklyn *(G-1703)*
Dorgan Welding Service ....G..... 315 462-9030
  Phelps *(G-12603)*
Flushing Boiler & Welding Co ....G..... 718 463-1266
  Brooklyn *(G-1855)*
G & C Welding Co Inc ....G..... 516 883-3228
  Port Washington *(G-12881)*
Glenridge Fabricators Inc ....F..... 718 456-2297
  Glendale *(G-5227)*
Hadfield Inc ....F..... 631 981-4314
  Saint James *(G-14111)*
Hagner Industries Inc ....G..... 716 873-5720
  Buffalo *(G-2789)*
Jacksons Welding LLC ....G..... 607 756-2725
  Cortland *(G-3773)*
Kleinfelder John ....G..... 716 753-3163
  Mayville *(G-7683)*
Reliable Welding & Fabrication ....G..... 631 758-2637
  Patchogue *(G-12511)*
S & D Welding Corp ....G..... 631 454-0383
  West Babylon *(G-15744)*
Tioga Tool Inc ....F..... 607 785-6005
  Endicott *(G-4474)*
Weslor Industries Inc ....E..... 315 871-4405
  Lyons *(G-7454)*

CONTRACTORS: Ornamental Metal Work

Bonura and Sons Iron Works ....F..... 718 381-4100
  Franklin Square *(G-4959)*
E F Iron Works & Construction ....G..... 631 242-4766
  Bay Shore *(G-677)*
GCM Metal Industries Inc ....F..... 718 386-4059
  Brooklyn *(G-1879)*
Irony Limited Inc ....G..... 631 329-4065
  East Hampton *(G-4123)*
M K Ulrich Construction Inc ....F..... 716 893-5777
  Buffalo *(G-2855)*

CONTRACTORS: Painting & Wall Covering

D & I Finishing Inc ....G..... 631 471-3034
  Bohemia *(G-998)*

CONTRACTORS: Parking Facility Eqpt Installation

Parkmatic Car Prkg Systems LLC ....G..... 516 224-7700
  Long Island City *(G-7319)*

CONTRACTORS: Patio & Deck Construction & Repair

Rainbow Awning Co Inc ....G..... 716 297-3939
  Niagara Falls *(G-11970)*

CONTRACTORS: Pipe Laying

AAA Welding and Fabrication of ....G..... 585 254-2830
  Rochester *(G-13196)*

CONTRACTORS: Plastering, Plain or Ornamental

Foster Reeve & Associates Inc ....G..... 718 609-0090
  Brooklyn *(G-1861)*

CONTRACTORS: Plumbing

Aquifer Drilling & Testing Inc ....D..... 516 616-6026
  Mineola *(G-7958)*
Metro City Group Inc ....G..... 516 781-2500
  Bellmore *(G-784)*

CONTRACTORS: Power Generating Eqpt Installation

Ls Power Equity Partners LP ....G..... 212 615-3456
  New York *(G-10276)*

CONTRACTORS: Prefabricated Fireplace Installation

Chimney Doctors Americas Corp ....G..... 631 868-3586
  Bayport *(G-728)*

CONTRACTORS: Prefabricated Window & Door Installation

Pace Window and Door Corp ....E..... 585 924-8350
  Victor *(G-15423)*
Pella Corporation ....C..... 631 208-0710
  Calverton *(G-3083)*
Proof Industries Inc ....G..... 631 694-7663
  Farmingdale *(G-4717)*
Royal Windows Mfg Corp ....E..... 631 435-8888
  Bay Shore *(G-710)*
Tri-State Window Factory Corp ....D..... 631 667-8600
  Deer Park *(G-3942)*
Woodworks ....F..... 845 677-3960
  Salt Point *(G-14135)*

CONTRACTORS: Roofing

H Klein & Sons Inc ....E..... 516 746-0163
  Mineola *(G-7978)*
Tiedemann Waldemar Inc ....F..... 716 875-5665
  Buffalo *(G-3010)*

CONTRACTORS: Roustabout Svcs

Jemcap Servicing LLC ....G..... 212 213-9353
  New York *(G-9993)*
Legal Servicing LLC ....G..... 716 565-9300
  Williamsville *(G-16133)*
Sovereign Servicing System LLC ....F..... 914 779-1400
  Bronxville *(G-1403)*

CONTRACTORS: Safety & Security Eqpt

Napco Security Tech Inc ....C..... 631 842-9400
  Amityville *(G-297)*
Windowman Inc (usa) ....G..... 718 246-2626
  Brooklyn *(G-2590)*

CONTRACTORS: Sandblasting Svc, Building Exteriors

Bruce Pierce ....G..... 716 731-9310
  Sanborn *(G-14138)*
Miller Metal Fabricating Inc ....G..... 585 359-3400
  Rochester *(G-13549)*
North Shore Monuments Inc ....G..... 516 759-2156
  Glen Head *(G-5212)*

CONTRACTORS: Screening, Window & Door

Rainbow Awning Co Inc ....G..... 716 297-3939
  Niagara Falls *(G-11970)*

PRODUCT

CONTRACTORS: Seismograph Survey Svcs

Wellspring Omni Holdings Corp............A 212 318-9800
New York *(G-11742)*

CONTRACTORS: Sheet Metal Work, NEC

Aabco Sheet Metal Co Inc...................D 718 821-1166
Ridgewood *(G-13137)*
B & R Sheet ....G 718 558-5544
Jamaica *(G-6428)*
Berjen Metal Industries Ltd ....G 631 673-7979
Huntington *(G-6201)*
Broadalbin Manufacturing Corp ....E 518 883-5313
Broadalbin *(G-1172)*
Goergen-Mackwirth Co Inc ....E 716 874-4800
Buffalo *(G-2778)*
Lodolce Machine Co Inc ....E 845 246-7017
Saugerties *(G-14204)*
Pro Metal of NY Corp ....G 516 285-0440
Valley Stream *(G-15353)*

CONTRACTORS: Sheet metal Work, Architectural

A&B McKeon Glass Inc ....G 718 525-2152
Staten Island *(G-14614)*
Morgik Metal Designs ....F 212 463-0304
New York *(G-10503)*

CONTRACTORS: Siding

Tri-State Window Factory Corp ....D 631 667-8600
Deer Park *(G-3942)*

CONTRACTORS: Single-family Home General Remodeling

Bator Bintor Inc ....F 347 546-6503
Brooklyn *(G-1567)*
Deakon Homes and Interiors ....F 518 271-0342
Troy *(G-15165)*
Kng Construction Co Inc ....F 212 595-1451
Warwick *(G-15517)*
Texas Home Security Inc ....E 516 747-2100
New Hyde Park *(G-8296)*

CONTRACTORS: Solar Energy Eqpt

Solar Energy Systems LLC ....F 718 389-1545
Brooklyn *(G-2437)*

CONTRACTORS: Sound Eqpt Installation

L A R Electronics Corp ....G 716 285-0555
Niagara Falls *(G-11945)*
Telephone Sales & Service Co ....E 212 233-8505
New York *(G-11449)*

CONTRACTORS: Stone Masonry

Stuart-Dean Co Inc ....F 718 472-1326
Long Island City *(G-7372)*

CONTRACTORS: Store Fixture Installation

Mass Mdsg Self Selection Eqp ....E 631 234-3300
Bohemia *(G-1044)*

CONTRACTORS: Store Front Construction

A&B McKeon Glass Inc ....G 718 525-2152
Staten Island *(G-14614)*

CONTRACTORS: Structural Iron Work, Structural

M & L Steel & Ornamental Iron ....F 718 816-8660
Staten Island *(G-14678)*
Miscellnous Ir Fabricators Inc ....E 518 355-1822
Schenectady *(G-14290)*
Moon Gates Company ....G 718 426-0023
East Elmhurst *(G-4110)*
Neversink Steel Corp ....G 845 292-4611
Liberty *(G-6926)*
Roman Iron Works Inc ....F 516 621-1103
Greenvale *(G-5463)*

CONTRACTORS: Structural Steel Erection

Barry Steel Fabrication Inc ....E 716 433-2144
Lockport *(G-7061)*
Cives Corporation................................C 315 287-2200
Gouverneur *(G-5318)*

Elite Steel Fabricators Inc ....G 631 285-1008
Ronkonkoma *(G-13935)*
GCM Metal Industries Inc ....F 718 386-4059
Brooklyn *(G-1879)*
Irv Schroder & Sons Inc ....E 518 828-0194
Stottville *(G-14753)*
Rochester Structural LLC ....E 585 436-1250
Rochester *(G-13700)*
Roth Design & Consulting Inc ....E 718 209-0193
Brooklyn *(G-2357)*

CONTRACTORS: Svc Station Eqpt Installation, Maint & Repair

North American Svcs Group LLC ....F 518 885-1820
Ballston Spa *(G-583)*

CONTRACTORS: Svc Well Drilling Svcs

Barber & Deline LLC ....F 607 749-2619
Tully *(G-15209)*

CONTRACTORS: Textile Warping

Tli Import Inc ....G 917 578-4568
Brooklyn *(G-2508)*

CONTRACTORS: Tile Installation, Ceramic

Alp Stone Inc ....F 718 706-6166
Long Island City *(G-7151)*
GDi Custom Marble & Gran Inc ....F 718 996-9100
Brooklyn *(G-1881)*

CONTRACTORS: Ventilation & Duct Work

Aabco Sheet Metal Co Inc ....D 718 821-1166
Ridgewood *(G-13137)*
Aeroduct Inc ....E 516 248-9550
Mineola *(G-7956)*
American Std Shtmtl Sup Corp ....F 718 888-9350
Flushing *(G-4839)*
Liffey Sheet Metal Corp ....F 347 381-1134
Long Island City *(G-7272)*

CONTRACTORS: Water Intake Well Drilling Svc

Barber & Deline Enrgy Svcs LLC ....F 315 696-8961
Tully *(G-15208)*
US Pump Corp......................................G 516 303-7799
West Hempstead *(G-15781)*

CONTRACTORS: Water Well Drilling

Barber & Deline LLC ....F 607 749-2619
Tully *(G-15209)*

CONTRACTORS: Water Well Servicing

Yr Blanc & Co LLC ....G 716 800-3999
Buffalo *(G-3053)*

CONTRACTORS: Waterproofing

Tiki Industries Inc ....G 516 779-3629
Riverhead *(G-13190)*

CONTRACTORS: Well Chemical Treating Svcs

Metro Group Inc ....D 718 729-7200
Long Island City *(G-7295)*

CONTRACTORS: Well Logging Svcs

Jay Little Oil Well Servi ....G 716 925-8905
Limestone *(G-6938)*
Schlumberger Technology Corp ....C 607 378-0105
Horseheads *(G-6136)*

CONTRACTORS: Window Treatment Installation

Instant Verticals Inc ....F 631 501-0001
Farmingdale *(G-4650)*
Majestic Curtains LLC ....G 718 898-0774
Elmhurst *(G-4336)*

CONTRACTORS: Windows & Doors

Advanced Door Solutions Inc................G 631 773-6100
Holbrook *(G-5984)*

D Best Service Co Inc ....G 718 972-6133
Brooklyn *(G-1715)*
Ecker Window Corp ....D 914 776-0000
Yonkers *(G-1879)*
Triple H Construction Inc ....E 516 280-8252
Jamaica *(G-6481)*
Window-Fix Inc ....E 718 854-3475
Brooklyn *(G-2589)*
Windowman Inc (usa) ....G 718 246-2626
Brooklyn *(G-2590)*

CONTRACTORS: Wood Floor Installation & Refinishing

Stuart-Dean Co Inc ....F 718 472-1326
Long Island City *(G-7372)*
Sunrise Tile Inc ....G 718 939-0538
Flushing *(G-4896)*
Zahk Sales Inc ....G 631 851-0851
Islandia *(G-6347)*

CONTROL CIRCUIT DEVICES

Inertia Switch Inc ....E 845 359-8300
Orangeburg *(G-12319)*

CONTROL EQPT: Electric

Altronix Corp ....D 718 567-8181
Brooklyn *(G-1494)*
Calia Technical Inc ....G 718 447-3928
Staten Island *(G-14636)*
Conic Systems Inc ....F 845 856-4053
Port Jervis *(G-12846)*
Continental Instruments LLC ....E 631 842-9400
Amityville *(G-258)*
Electronic Machine Parts LLC ....F 631 434-3700
Hauppauge *(G-5645)*
Goddard Design Co ....G 718 599-0170
Brooklyn *(G-1895)*
ITT Corp ....E 716 662-1900
Orchard Park *(G-12355)*
ITT Corporation ....E 585 269-7109
Hemlock *(G-5830)*
ITT Corporation ....D 315 568-2811
Seneca Falls *(G-14364)*
ITT Inc ....C 914 641-2000
White Plains *(G-16017)*
ITT International Holdings Inc ....G 914 641-2000
White Plains *(G-16019)*
ITT LLC ....G 315 568-4733
Seneca Falls *(G-14367)*
ITT LLC ....C 315 258-4904
Auburn *(G-480)*
ITT LLC ....D 914 641-2000
Seneca Falls *(G-14368)*
ITT LLC ....B 914 641-2000
White Plains *(G-16020)*
Kussmaul Electronics Co Inc ....E 631 218-0298
West Sayville *(G-15841)*
L3harris Technologies Inc.....................C 631 630-4000
Amityville *(G-289)*
N E Controls LLC ....F 315 626-2480
Syracuse *(G-14949)*
Nitram Energy Inc ....E 716 662-6540
Orchard Park *(G-12368)*
Peraton Inc ....E 315 838-7000
Rome *(G-13863)*
Ruhle Companies Inc ....E 914 287-4000
Valhalla *(G-15309)*
Weldcomputer Corporation ....F 518 283-2897
Troy *(G-15198)*

CONTROL EQPT: Noise

Burgess-Manning Inc ....D 716 662-6540
Orchard Park *(G-12343)*
I D E Processes Corporation ....F 718 544-1177
Kew Gardens *(G-6664)*
Mason Industries Inc ....C 631 348-0282
Hauppauge *(G-5708)*
Mason Industries Inc ....G 631 348-0282
Hauppauge *(G-5709)*
Soundcoat Company Inc ....D 631 242-2200
Deer Park *(G-3938)*
Techniflo Corporation ....G 716 741-3500
Clarence Center *(G-3449)*
Vibration & Noise Engrg Corp ....G 716 827-4959
Orchard Park *(G-12382)*
Vibration Eliminator Co Inc ....E 631 841-4000
Copiague *(G-3687)*

CONTROL PANELS: Electrical

Abasco Inc ....E 716 649-4790
Hamburg (G-5501)

Avanti Control Systems Inc ....G 518 921-4368
Gloversville (G-5278)

Benfield Control Systems Inc ....F 914 948-3231
White Plains (G-15981)

Boulay Fabrication Inc ....F 315 677-5247
La Fayette (G-6736)

Custom Controls ....G 315 253-4785
Scipio Center (G-14326)

Link Control Systems Inc ....F 631 471-3950
Ronkonkoma (G-13966)

Micro Instrument Corp ....D 585 458-3150
Rochester (G-13545)

Odyssey Controls Inc ....G 585 548-9800
Bergen (G-819)

Se-Mar Electric Co Inc ....E 716 674-7404
West Seneca (G-15853)

Smith Control Systems Inc ....F 518 828-7646
Hudson (G-6180)

Transit Air Inc ....E 607 324-0216
Hornell (G-6112)

CONTROLS & ACCESS: Indl, Electric

Afi Cybernetics Corporation ....E 607 732-3244
Elmira (G-4339)

Bomac Inc ....F 315 433-9181
Syracuse (G-14832)

Entertron Industries Inc ....E 716 772-7216
Lockport (G-7074)

G C Controls Inc ....E 607 656-4117
Greene (G-5445)

Gemtrol Inc ....G 716 894-0716
Buffalo (G-2770)

General Oil Equipment Co Inc ....E 716 691-7012
Amherst (G-225)

ICM Controls Corp ....F 315 233-5266
North Syracuse (G-12045)

Interntnal Cntrls Msrmnts Corp ....C 315 233-5266
North Syracuse (G-12046)

Morris Products Inc ....F 518 743-0523
Queensbury (G-13049)

Panelogic Inc ....E 607 962-6319
Corning (G-3719)

Soft-Noze Usa Inc ....G 315 732-2726
Frankfort (G-4956)

Vps Control Systems Inc ....F 518 686-0019
Hoosick (G-6082)

CONTROLS & ACCESS: Motor

Designatronics Incorporated ....B 516 328-3300
New Hyde Park (G-8261)

Eaton Corporation ....C 516 353-3017
East Meadow (G-4135)

Eatons Crouse Hinds Business ....F 315 477-7000
Syracuse (G-14883)

ITT Aerospace Controls LLC ....G 914 641-2000
White Plains (G-16016)

Powr-UPS Corp ....E 631 345-5700
Shirley (G-14427)

Ruby Automation LLC ....D 585 254-8840
Rochester (G-13710)

Teknic Inc ....E 585 784-7454
Victor (G-15436)

CONTROLS: Access, Motor

Bakery Innovative Tech Corp ....F 631 758-3081
Patchogue (G-12496)

Schmersal Inc ....E 914 347-4775
Hawthorne (G-5823)

CONTROLS: Automatic Temperature

Advantex Solutions Inc ....G 718 278-2290
Bellerose (G-773)

Automated Bldg MGT Systems Inc ....E 516 216-5603
Floral Park (G-4808)

Day Automation Systems Inc ....D 585 924-4630
Victor (G-15404)

Intellidyne LLC ....F 516 676-0777
Plainview (G-12690)

Intrepid Control Service Inc ....G 718 886-8771
Flushing (G-4863)

Johnson Controls Inc ....E 585 924-9346
Rochester (G-13494)

Logical Control Solutions Inc ....F 585 424-5340
Victor (G-15418)

Pii Holdings Inc ....G 716 876-9951
Buffalo (G-2919)

Protective Industries Inc ....D 716 876-9951
Buffalo (G-2937)

Protective Industries Inc ....B 716 876-9951
Buffalo (G-2936)

Siemens Industry Inc ....E 585 797-2300
Rochester (G-13728)

T S B A Group Inc ....E 718 565-6000
Sunnyside (G-14775)

Use Acquisition LLC ....F 516 812-6800
New Hyde Park (G-8302)

CONTROLS: Electric Motor

Dyson-Kissner-Moran Corp ....E 212 661-4600
Poughkeepsie (G-12952)

US Drives Inc ....D 716 731-1606
Niagara Falls (G-11988)

CONTROLS: Environmental

Ademco Inc ....G 716 631-2197
Cheektowaga (G-3337)

Anderson Instrument Co Inc ....D 518 922-5315
Fultonville (G-5077)

Cascade Technical Services LLC ......F 516 596-6300
Lynbrook (G-7429)

Cascade Technical Services LLC ......G 518 355-2201
Schenectady (G-14253)

Clean Room Depot Inc ....F 631 589-3033
Holbrook (G-5990)

Cox & Company Inc ....C 212 366-0200
Plainview (G-12676)

Daikin Applied Americas Inc ....D 315 253-2771
Auburn (G-472)

E Global Solutions Inc ....G 516 767-5138
Port Washington (G-12876)

East Hudson Watershed Corp ....G 845 319-6349
Patterson (G-12516)

Fuel Watchman Sales & Service ....F 718 665-6100
Bronx (G-1263)

Grillmaster Inc ....E 718 272-9191
Howard Beach (G-6140)

Heating & Burner Supply Inc ....G 718 665-0006
Bronx (G-1275)

Infitec Inc ....D 315 433-1150
East Syracuse (G-4222)

Johnson Controls Inc ....E 716 688-7340
Buffalo (G-2823)

Long Island Analytical Labs ....F 631 472-3400
Holbrook (G-6007)

Microb Phase Services ....F 518 877-8948
Clifton Park (G-3468)

Pulsafeeder Inc ....C 585 292-2000
Rochester (G-13653)

RE Hansen Industries Inc ....C 631 471-2900
Saint James (G-14113)

Transit Air Inc ....E 607 324-0216
Hornell (G-6112)

Zebra Environmental Corp ....F 516 596-6300
Lynbrook (G-7443)

CONTROLS: Marine & Navy, Auxiliary

L-3 Cmmnctons Ntronix Holdings .....D 212 697-1111
New York (G-10152)

CONTROLS: Numerical

Teale Machine Company Inc ....D 585 244-6700
Rochester (G-13761)

CONTROLS: Relay & Ind

Air Crafters Inc ....C 631 471-7788
Ronkonkoma (G-13893)

Anderson Instrument Co Inc ....D 518 922-5315
Fultonville (G-5077)

Baco Controls Inc ....F 315 635-2500
Baldwinsville (G-543)

Con Rel Auto Electric Inc ....E 518 356-1646
Schenectady (G-14259)

Cox & Company Inc ....C 212 366-0200
Plainview (G-12676)

Crestron Electronics Inc ....D 201 894-0670
Orangeburg (G-12311)

Designatronics Incorporated ....B 516 328-3300
Hicksville (G-5902)

Deutsch Relays ....F 631 342-1700
Hauppauge (G-5636)

Enetics Inc ....G 585 924-5010
Victor (G-15407)

Gas Turbine Controls Corp ....E 914 693-0830
Hawthorne (G-5813)

I E D Corp ....F 631 348-0424
Islandia (G-6334)

Industrial Indxing Systems Inc ....E 585 924-9181
Victor (G-15413)

JE Miller Inc ....F 315 437-6811
East Syracuse (G-4224)

Kearney-National Inc ....F 212 661-4600
New York (G-10087)

Logitek Inc ....D 631 567-1100
Bohemia (G-1035)

Magnus Precision Mfg Inc ....D 315 548-8032
Phelps (G-12605)

Messer LLC ....D 716 773-7552
Grand Island (G-5337)

Moog Inc ....E 716 687-4778
Elma (G-4322)

Moog Inc ....A 716 805-2604
Elma (G-4321)

Nas-Tra Automotive Inds Inc ....C 631 225-1225
Lindenhurst (G-6962)

National Time Recording Eqp Co ....F 212 227-3310
New York (G-10547)

North Point Technology LLC ....F 866 885-3377
Endicott (G-4467)

Omntec Mfg Inc ....E 631 981-2001
Ronkonkoma (G-13987)

Peerless Instrument Co Inc ....C 631 396-6500
Farmingdale (G-4704)

Precision Mechanisms Corp ....C 516 333-5955
Westbury (G-15919)

Pulsafeeder Inc ....C 585 292-2000
Rochester (G-13653)

Rochester Industrial Ctrl Inc ....D 315 524-4555
Ontario (G-12300)

Rockwell Automation Inc ....E 585 487-2700
Pittsford (G-12656)

Schneider Electric Usa Inc ....F 631 567-5710
Bohemia (G-1073)

Service Mfg Group Inc ....F 716 893-1482
Buffalo (G-2980)

Ssac Inc ....E 800 843-8848
Baldwinsville (G-555)

Stetron International Inc ....F 716 854-3443
Buffalo (G-2993)

Unimar Inc ....F 315 699-4400
Syracuse (G-15017)

Zeppelin Electric Company Inc ....G 631 928-9467
East Setauket (G-4191)

CONTROLS: Thermostats

Darkpulse Inc ....G 800 436-1436
New York (G-9170)

CONTROLS: Thermostats, Exc Built-in

Bilbee Controls Inc ....F 518 622-3033
Cairo (G-3064)

CONTROLS: Voice

Voices For All LLC ....G 518 261-1664
Mechanicville (G-7696)

CONVENIENCE STORES

Patla Enterprises Inc ....F 315 367-0237
Sherrill (G-14405)

Schaefer Logging Inc ....F 607 467-4990
Deposit (G-4003)

Stewarts Shops Corp ....F 518 499-9376
Whitehall (G-16077)

CONVENTION & TRADE SHOW SVCS

Mechanical Displays Inc ....G 718 258-5588
Brooklyn (G-2130)

CONVERTERS: Data

Annese & Associates Inc ....G 716 972-0076
Buffalo (G-2635)

Cisco Systems Inc ....C 212 714-4000
New York (G-9012)

Data Device Corporation ....B 631 567-5600
Bohemia (G-999)

Scroll Media Inc ....G 617 395-8904
New York (G-11171)

PRODUCT

CONVERTERS: Frequency

Applied Power Systems Inc ....E ... 516 935-2230
Hicksville (G-5883)

CONVERTERS: Phase Or Rotary, Electrical

Automation Source Technologies ....F ... 631 643-1678
West Babylon (G-15691)

CONVERTERS: Power, AC to DC

Curtis/Palmer Hydroelectric LP ....F ... 518 654-6297
Corinth (G-3704)
Endicott Research Group Inc ....D ... 607 754-9187
Endicott (G-4452)
G B International Trdg Co Ltd ....C ... 607 785-0938
Endicott (G-4457)

CONVERTERS: Rotary, Electrical

Switched Source LLC ....G ... 708 207-1479
Vestal (G-15385)

CONVERTERS: Torque, Exc Auto

American Torque Inc ....F ... 718 526-2433
Jamaica (G-6425)

CONVEYOR SYSTEMS: Belt, General Indl Use

American Material Processing ....F ... 315 318-0017
Phoenix (G-12615)
Desmi-Afti Inc ....E ... 716 662-0632
Orchard Park (G-12351)
Hohl Machine & Conveyor Co Inc ....E ... 716 882-7210
Buffalo (G-2799)
Specialty Conveyor Corp ....G ... 347 707-0490
Farmingdale (G-4737)

CONVEYOR SYSTEMS: Bulk Handling

Ward Industrial Equipment Inc ....G ... 716 856-6966
Buffalo (G-3041)

CONVEYOR SYSTEMS: Pneumatic Tube

Shako Inc ....G ... 315 437-1294
East Syracuse (G-4238)

CONVEYORS & CONVEYING EQPT

Automated Biomass Systems LLC ....F ... 607 849-7800
Marathon (G-7556)
Chemprene Inc ....C ... 845 831-2800
Beacon (G-749)
Chemprene Holding Inc ....C ... 845 831-2800
Beacon (G-750)
Columbus McKinnon Corporation ....C ... 716 689-5400
Getzville (G-5174)
Columbus McKinnon Corporation ....C ... 716 689-5400
Getzville (G-5175)
Columbus McKinnon Corporation ....C ... 716 689-5400
Getzville (G-5176)
Crownbrook ACC LLC ....E ... 718 626-0760
Brooklyn (G-1703)
Dairy Conveyor Corp ....D ... 845 278-7878
Brewster (G-1146)
Excel Conveyor LLC ....F ... 718 474-0001
Rockaway Beach (G-13822)
General Splice Corporation ....G ... 914 271-5131
Croton On Hudson (G-3808)
Glasgow Products Inc ....E ... 516 374-5937
Woodmere (G-16191)
Green Conveyor & Mch Group LLC ......G ... 607 692-7050
Whitney Point (G-16106)
Haines Equipment Inc ....E ... 607 566-8531
Avoca (G-510)
I J White Corporation ....D ... 631 293-3788
Farmingdale (G-4647)
J D Handling Systems Inc ....E ... 518 828-9676
Ghent (G-5185)
Joldeson One Aerospace Inds ....D ... 718 848-7396
Ozone Park (G-12463)
Nerak Systems Inc ....F ... 914 763-8259
Fishkill (G-4803)
Northeast Conveyors Inc ....F ... 585 768-8912
Lima (G-6933)
Noto Industrial Corp ....G ... 631 736-7600
Coram (G-3697)
Raymond Corporation ....A ... 607 656-2311
Greene (G-5448)

Raymond Corporation ....E ... 315 643-5000
East Syracuse (G-4232)
Re-Al Industrial Corp ....G ... 716 542-4556
Akron (G-21)
Renold Inc ....D ... 716 326-3121
Westfield (G-15949)
Rlp Holdings Inc ....G ... 716 852-0832
Buffalo (G-2956)
Rota Pack Inc ....F ... 631 274-1037
Farmingdale (G-4727)
Troy Belting and Supply Co ....D ... 518 272-4920
Watervliet (G-15609)

COOKING & FOOD WARMING EQPT: Commercial

Advance Tabco Inc ....D ... 631 242-8270
Hauppauge (G-5578)
Attias Oven Corp ....G ... 718 499-0145
Brooklyn (G-1550)
Carts Mobile Food Eqp Corp ....E ... 718 788-5540
Brooklyn (G-1652)
Fantasia International LLC ....G ... 212 869-0432
New York (G-9470)
IMC Teddy Food Service ....E ... 631 789-8881
Amityville (G-275)
Kinplex Corp ....E ... 631 242-4800
Hauppauge (G-5684)
Kinplex Corp ....E ... 631 242-4800
Edgewood (G-4274)
Korin Inc ....E ... 212 587-7021
New York (G-10128)
R-S Restaurant Eqp Mfg Corp ....F ... 212 925-0335
New York (G-10969)
Roger & Sons Inc ....G ... 212 226-4734
New York (G-11074)
Toga Manufacturing Inc ....E ... 631 242-4800
Edgewood (G-4289)

COOKING & FOODWARMING EQPT: Coffee Brewing

Arista Coffee Inc ....F ... 347 531-0813
Maspeth (G-7592)

COOKING & FOODWARMING EQPT: Commercial

Advance Food Service Co Inc ....C ... 631 242-4800
Edgewood (G-4260)

COOKING WARE, EXC PORCELAIN ENAMELED

Allied Metal Spinning Corp ....D ... 718 893-3300
Bronx (G-1201)

COOKING WARE: Cooking Ware, Porcelain Enameled

Schiller Stores Inc ....G ... 631 208-9400
Riverhead (G-13188)
Wilmax Usa LLC ....F ... 917 388-2790
New York (G-11762)

COOKWARE, STONEWARE: Coarse Earthenware & Pottery

Schiller Stores Inc ....G ... 845 928-4316
Central Valley (G-3300)

COOKWARE: Fine Earthenware

Lifetime Stainless Steel Corp ....G ... 585 924-9393
Victor (G-15417)
Mackenzie-Childs LLC ....C ... 315 364-6118
Aurora (G-504)
Williams-Sonoma Stores Inc ....F ... 212 633-2203
New York (G-11760)

COOLING TOWERS: Metal

Manhattan Cooling Towers Inc ....F ... 212 279-1045
Long Island City (G-7288)
SPX Corporation ....E ... 631 467-2632
Ronkonkoma (G-14013)
SPX Corporation ....B ... 585 436-5550
Rochester (G-13741)

COPPER ORES

Global Gold Corporation ....F ... 914 925-0020
Rye (G-14079)

COPPER: Rolling & Drawing

Aurubis Buffalo Inc ....F ... 716 879-6700
Buffalo (G-2648)
Aurubis Buffalo Inc ....B ... 716 879-6700
Buffalo (G-2649)
Continental Cordage Corp ....D ... 315 655-9800
Cazenovia (G-3225)

COPYRIGHT BUYING & LICENSING

Abkco Music & Records Inc ....E ... 212 399-0300
New York (G-8430)
Penhouse Media Group Inc ....C ... 212 702-6000
New York (G-10795)
Scholastic Corporation ....G ... 212 343-6100
New York (G-11160)
Universal Mus Group Hldngs Inc ....E ... 212 333-8000
New York (G-11608)

CORD & TWINE

Albany International Corp ....C ... 607 749-7226
Homer (G-6060)

CORE WASH OR WAX

Beyond Beauty Basics LLC ....F ... 516 731-7100
Levittown (G-6913)

CORES: Magnetic

Fair-Rite Products Corp ....C ... 845 895-2055
Wallkill (G-15469)

CORK & CORK PRDTS: Tiles

Globus Cork Inc ....F ... 347 963-4059
Brooklyn (G-1892)

CORRESPONDENCE SCHOOLS

Boardman Simons Publishing ....E ... 212 620-7200
New York (G-8827)
Simmons-Boardman Pubg Corp ....G ... 212 620-7200
New York (G-11243)

CORRUGATED PRDTS: Boxes, Partition, Display Items, Sheet/Pad

Dory Enterprises Inc ....F ... 607 565-7079
Waverly (G-15620)
Land Packaging Corp ....F ... 914 472-5976
Scarsdale (G-14238)
Technical Library Service Inc ....F ... 212 219-0770
Brooklyn (G-2495)

COSMETIC PREPARATIONS

Ardex Cosmetics of America ....E ... 518 283-6700
Troy (G-15164)
Becca Inc ....D ... 646 568-6250
New York (G-8744)
Brucci Ltd ....E ... 914 965-0707
Yonkers (G-16292)
Bycmac Corp ....E ... 845 255-0884
Gardiner (G-5127)
California Fragrance Company ....E ... 631 424-4023
Huntington Station (G-6241)
Clark Botanicals Inc ....F ... 914 826-4319
Bronxville (G-1400)
Clean Beauty Collective Inc ....E ... 212 269-1387
New York (G-9030)
Clinique Laboratories LLC ....E ... 212 572-4200
New York (G-9032)
Clinique Services Inc ....E ... 212 572-4200
New York (G-9033)
D & H Amazing Deals Inc ....G ... 347 318-3805
Brooklyn (G-1714)
Dermatech Labs Inc ....F ... 631 225-1700
Lindenhurst (G-6949)
Epic Beauty Co LLC ....E ... 212 327-3059
New York (G-9387)
Estee Lauder Companies Inc ....E ... 212 572-4200
New York (G-9407)
Estee Lauder Companies Inc ....G ... 212 756-4800
New York (G-9408)
Estee Lauder Companies Inc ....A ... 212 572-4200
New York (G-9410)

Ex-It Medical Devices Inc ....G...... 212 653-0637
  New York **(G-9436)**

Forsythe Cosmetic Group Ltd ....E...... 516 239-4200
  Freeport **(G-4997)**

Inter Parfums Inc ....D...... 212 983-2640
  New York **(G-9911)**

Intercos America Inc ....G...... 845 732-3900
  West Nyack **(G-15823)**

June Jacobs Labs LLC ....D...... 212 471-4830
  New York **(G-10042)**

Kantian Skincare LLC ....G...... 631 780-4711
  Smithtown **(G-14481)**

Klg Usa LLC ....A...... 845 856-5311
  Port Jervis **(G-12853)**

Lady Burd Exclusive Cosmt Inc ......C...... 631 454-0444
  Farmingdale **(G-4669)**

Lechler Laboratories Inc ....E...... 845 426-6800
  Spring Valley **(G-14574)**

Liddell Corporation ....F...... 716 297-8557
  Niagara Falls **(G-11946)**

Lornamead Inc ....D...... 646 745-3643
  Tonawanda **(G-15119)**

Lornamead Inc ....D...... 716 874-7190
  New York **(G-10264)**

Malin + Goetz Inc ....F...... 212 244-7771
  New York **(G-10336)**

Mana Products Inc ....B...... 718 361-2550
  Long Island City **(G-7285)**

Mana Products Inc ....B...... 718 361-5204
  Long Island City **(G-7286)**

Marietta Corporation ....B...... 607 753-6746
  Cortland **(G-3775)**

Maybelline Inc ....A...... 212 885-1310
  New York **(G-10392)**

Mehron Inc ....E...... 845 426-1700
  Chestnut Ridge **(G-3395)**

Meiyume USA Inc ....E...... 646 927-2370
  New York **(G-10425)**

Nature Only Inc ....G...... 917 922-6539
  Forest Hills **(G-4924)**

Naturpathica Holistic Hlth Inc ....D...... 631 329-8792
  East Hampton **(G-4126)**

New Avon LLC ....B...... 212 282-6000
  New York **(G-10577)**

Newburgh Distribution Corp ....G...... 845 561-6330
  New Windsor **(G-8375)**

Oasis Cosmetic Labs Inc ....F...... 631 758-0038
  Holtsville **(G-6051)**

Olan Laboratories Inc ....G...... 631 582-2082
  Hauppauge **(G-5730)**

Peppermints Salon Inc ....F...... 718 357-6304
  Whitestone **(G-16099)**

Peter Thomas Roth Labs LLC ....E...... 212 581-5800
  New York **(G-10816)**

Plastic & Reconstructive Svcs ....G...... 914 584-5605
  Mount Kisco **(G-8102)**

Redken 5th Avenue NYC LLC ....C...... 212 818-1500
  New York **(G-10998)**

Revlon Consumer Products Corp ....B...... 212 527-4000
  New York **(G-11027)**

Scientific Solutions Globl LLC ....F...... 516 543-3376
  Carle Place **(G-3181)**

Shiseido Americas Corporation ....G...... 212 805-2300
  New York **(G-11218)**

Simply Active Cosmetics Inc ....G...... 646 554-6421
  New York **(G-11247)**

Solabia USA Inc ....G...... 212 847-2397
  New York **(G-11288)**

Sundial Brands LLC ....C...... 631 842-8800
  Amityville **(G-309)**

Sundial Group LLC ....E...... 631 842-8800
  Amityville **(G-311)**

Temptu Inc ....G...... 718 937-9503
  Long Island City **(G-7379)**

Topiderm Inc ....C...... 631 226-7979
  Amityville **(G-312)**

United-Guardian Inc ....E...... 631 273-0900
  Hauppauge **(G-5791)**

Universal Packg Systems Inc ....A...... 631 543-2277
  Hauppauge **(G-5792)**

Verla International Ltd ....B...... 845 561-2440
  New Windsor **(G-8386)**

Victoria Albi International ....F...... 212 689-2600
  New York **(G-11677)**

Westman Atelier LLC ....G...... 917 297-0842
  New York **(G-11745)**

Xania Labs Inc ....G...... 718 361-2550
  Long Island City **(G-7409)**

Zela International Co ....E...... 518 436-1833
  Albany **(G-144)**

COSMETICS & TOILETRIES

AEP Environmental LLC ....F...... 716 446-0739
  Buffalo **(G-2625)**

Alabu Inc ....G...... 518 665-0411
  Mechanicville **(G-7690)**

Alexandria Professional LLC ....F...... 716 242-8514
  Williamsville **(G-16119)**

Allan John Company ....F...... 212 940-2210
  New York **(G-8516)**

Antimony New York LLC ....G...... 917 232-1836
  New York **(G-8598)**

Bastide Inc ....D...... 646 356-0460
  New York **(G-8739)**

Bio-Botanica Inc ....D...... 631 231-0987
  Hauppauge **(G-5604)**

Borghese Inc ....E...... 212 659-5318
  New York **(G-8837)**

China Huaren Organic Pdts Inc ....G...... 212 232-0120
  New York **(G-8988)**

Common Good LLC ....G...... 646 246-1441
  Brooklyn **(G-1679)**

Common Sense Natural Soap ....E...... 518 677-0224
  Cambridge **(G-3093)**

Conopco Inc ....E...... 585 647-8322
  Rochester **(G-13324)**

Coty Inc ....D...... 212 389-7300
  New York **(G-9107)**

Elite Parfums Ltd ....D...... 212 983-2640
  New York **(G-9345)**

Elizabeth Arden Inc ....C...... 845 810-2175
  Central Valley **(G-3299)**

Eos Products LLC ....D...... 212 929-6367
  New York **(G-9386)**

Estee Lauder Companies Inc ....A...... 917 606-3240
  New York **(G-9406)**

Estee Lauder Companies Inc ....F...... 646 762-7718
  New York **(G-9409)**

Estee Lauder Companies Inc ....D...... 631 694-2601
  Melville **(G-7779)**

Estee Lauder Companies Inc ....A...... 212 572-4200
  Melville **(G-7780)**

Estee Lauder Companies Inc ....A...... 646 602-7590
  New York **(G-9411)**

Eternal Love Parfums Corp ....G...... 516 921-6100
  Syosset **(G-14786)**

Four Paws Products Ltd ....D...... 631 436-7421
  Ronkonkoma **(G-13940)**

Hain Celestial Group Inc ....C...... 516 587-5000
  New Hyde Park **(G-8272)**

HFC Prestige Intl US LLC ....A...... 212 389-7800
  New York **(G-9778)**

Hnc Enterprises LLC ....G...... 904 448-9387
  Brooklyn **(G-1937)**

Iles Formula Inc ....G...... 315 834-2478
  New York **(G-9865)**

Intercos America Inc ....G...... 845 732-3910
  West Nyack **(G-15824)**

Interntnal Flvors Frgrnces Inc ....C...... 212 765-5500
  New York **(G-9924)**

Judith N Graham Inc ....G...... 914 921-5446
  Rye **(G-14082)**

Kind Group LLC ....G...... 212 645-0800
  New York **(G-10104)**

LOreal Usa Inc ....B...... 917 606-9554
  New York **(G-10259)**

LOreal Usa Inc ....B...... 646 658-5477
  New York **(G-10261)**

Maesa LLC ....E...... 212 674-5555
  New York **(G-10317)**

Marvellissima Intl Ltd ....G...... 212 682-7306
  New York **(G-10376)**

Medisonic Inc ....F...... 516 653-2345
  Great Neck **(G-5403)**

Mentholatum Company ....E...... 716 677-2500
  Orchard Park **(G-12366)**

Michel Design Works Ltd ....F...... 914 763-2244
  Katonah **(G-6635)**

Nava Global Partners Inc ....G...... 516 737-7127
  Great Neck **(G-5404)**

New Avon LLC ....F...... 716 572-4842
  Buffalo **(G-2880)**

Old Williamsburgh Corp ....D...... 631 952-0100
  Hauppauge **(G-5731)**

Paula Dorf Cosmetics Inc ....E...... 212 582-0073
  New York **(G-10771)**

Prescriptives Inc ....G...... 212 572-4400
  New York **(G-10882)**

Puig Usa Inc ....F...... 917 208-3219
  New York **(G-10926)**

Quality King Distributors Inc ....C...... 631 439-2027
  Ronkonkoma **(G-13998)**

REB Lybss Inc ....G...... 845 238-5633
  Monroe **(G-8030)**

Revlon Inc ....B...... 212 527-4000
  New York **(G-11026)**

Robert Racine ....E...... 518 677-0224
  Cambridge **(G-3096)**

Scent-A-Vision Inc ....E...... 631 424-4905
  Huntington Station **(G-6259)**

Skin Atelier Inc ....F...... 845 294-1202
  Goshen **(G-5313)**

Sml Acquisition LLC ....C...... 914 592-3130
  Elmsford **(G-4434)**

Sundial Brands ....G...... 631 842-8800
  Farmingdale **(G-4743)**

Unilever United States Inc ....F...... 212 546-0200
  New York **(G-11588)**

Unilever United States Inc ....C...... 212 546-0200
  New York **(G-11589)**

COSMETICS WHOLESALERS

Abbe Laboratories Inc ....F...... 631 756-2223
  Farmingdale **(G-4571)**

Clean Beauty Collective Inc ....E...... 212 269-1387
  New York **(G-9030)**

Clinique Laboratories LLC ....G...... 212 572-4200
  New York **(G-9032)**

Dermatech Labs Inc ....F...... 631 225-1700
  Lindenhurst **(G-6949)**

Essie Cosmetics Ltd ....D...... 212 818-1500
  New York **(G-9405)**

Hnc Enterprises LLC ....G...... 904 448-9387
  Brooklyn **(G-1937)**

Lotta Luv Beauty LLC ....F...... 646 786-2847
  New York **(G-10268)**

Mana Products Inc ....B...... 718 361-2550
  Long Island City **(G-7285)**

Marvellissima Intl Ltd ....G...... 212 682-7306
  New York **(G-10376)**

New Avon LLC ....B...... 212 282-6000
  New York **(G-10577)**

Shiseido Americas Corporation ....G...... 212 805-2300
  New York **(G-11218)**

Xania Labs Inc ....G...... 718 361-2550
  Long Island City **(G-7409)**

Zela International Co ....E...... 518 436-1833
  Albany **(G-144)**

COSTUME JEWELRY & NOVELTIES: Apparel, Exc Precious Metals

Jj Fantasia Inc ....G...... 212 868-1198
  New York **(G-10009)**

Kenneth J Lane Inc ....F...... 212 868-1780
  New York **(G-10090)**

Mercado Global Inc ....G...... 718 838-9908
  Brooklyn **(G-2140)**

Von Musulin Patricia ....G...... 212 206-8345
  New York **(G-11704)**

COSTUME JEWELRY & NOVELTIES: Bracelets, Exc Precious Metals

Aniiwe Inc ....G...... 347 683-1891
  Brooklyn **(G-1511)**

Vitafede ....F...... 646 869-4003
  New York **(G-11694)**

COSTUME JEWELRY & NOVELTIES: Costume Novelties

Jay Turoff ....F...... 718 856-7300
  Brooklyn **(G-1990)**

COSTUME JEWELRY & NOVELTIES: Earrings, Exc Precious Metals

Fashion Accents LLC ....F...... 401 331-6626
  New York **(G-9474)**

COSTUME JEWELRY & NOVELTIES: Exc Semi & Precious

Accessory Plays LLC ....E...... 212 564-7301
  New York **(G-8441)**

Barrera Jose & Maria Co Ltd ....E...... 212 239-1994
  New York **(G-8733)**

Carol For Eva Graham Inc ....E...... 212 889-8686
  New York **(G-8920)**

Catherine Stein Designs Inc ....E 212 840-1188
New York (G-8938)

Ciner Manufacturing Co Inc ....E 212 947-3770
New York (G-9009)

Dabby-Reid Ltd ....F 212 356-0040
New York (G-9150)

Erickson Beamon Ltd ....F 212 643-4810
New York (G-9394)

Fantasia Jewelry Inc ....E 212 921-9590
New York (G-9471)

J & H Creations Inc ....E 212 465-0962
New York (G-9952)

Jaymar Jewelry Co Inc ....G 212 564-4788
New York (G-9983)

Magic Novelty Co Inc ....G 212 304-2777
New York (G-10325)

Marlborough Jewels Inc ....G 718 768-2000
Brooklyn (G-2116)

Mwsi Inc ....D 914 347-4200
Hawthorne (G-5819)

Salmco Jewelry Corp ....F 212 695-8792
New York (G-11120)

Steezys LLC ....G 646 276-5333
New York (G-11353)

Stephan & Company ACC Ltd ....E 212 481-3888
New York (G-11358)

COSTUME JEWELRY & NOVELTIES: Pins, Exc Precious Metals

Custom Pins Inc ....G 888 922-9378
Elmsford (G-4406)

COUNTER & SINK TOPS

Arcy Plastic Laminates Inc ....E 518 235-0753
Albany (G-42)

Countertops & Cabinets Inc ....G 315 433-1038
Syracuse (G-14865)

Delocon Wholesale Inc ....F 716 592-2711
Springville (G-14589)

Empire Fabricators Inc ....G 585 235-3050
Rochester (G-13387)

Frank J Martello ....G 585 235-2780
Rochester (G-13423)

Icestone LLC ....E 718 624-4900
Brooklyn (G-1951)

Joseph Fedele ....G 718 448-3658
Staten Island (G-14672)

Metropolitan Granite & MBL Inc ....G 585 342-7020
Rochester (G-13543)

Nlr Counter Tops LLC ....G 347 295-0410
New York (G-10632)

Rochester Countertop Inc ....F 585 338-2260
Rochester (G-13687)

Solid Surfaces Inc ....D 585 292-5340
Rochester (G-13736)

Triad Counter Corp ....E 631 750-0615
Bohemia (G-1088)

Wilbedone Inc ....E 607 756-8813
Cortland (G-3791)

Wolak Inc ....G 315 839-5366
Clayville (G-3459)

COUNTERS & COUNTING DEVICES

Cmp Advnced Mech Sltons NY LLC ......C 607 352-1712
Binghamton (G-867)

Designatronics Incorporated ....G 516 328-3300
Hicksville (G-5902)

Encore Electronics Inc ....E 518 584-5354
Saratoga Springs (G-14171)

Environment-One Corporation ....C 518 346-6161
Schenectady (G-14264)

COUNTERS OR COUNTER DISPLAY CASES, EXC WOOD

GF Packaging LLC ....E 716 692-2705
Cheektowaga (G-3351)

Glasbau Hahn America LLC ....G 845 566-3331
Newburgh (G-11867)

Stone Expo & Cabinetry LLC ....F 516 292-2988
West Hempstead (G-15780)

COUNTERS OR COUNTER DISPLAY CASES, WOOD

Bloch Industries LLC ....D 585 334-9600
Rochester (G-13272)

Creative Counter Tops Inc ....F 845 471-6480
Poughkeepsie (G-12950)

Serway Bros Inc ....G 315 337-0601
Rome (G-13872)

COUNTERS: Mechanical

Melland Gear Instr of Huppauge ....E 631 234-0100
Hauppauge (G-5712)

COUNTING DEVICES: Controls, Revolution & Timing

Schlumberger Technology Corp ....C 607 378-0105
Horseheads (G-6136)

COUNTING DEVICES: Electromechanical

K-Technologies Inc ....E 716 828-4444
Buffalo (G-2829)

Vantage Mfg & Assembly LLC ....E 845 471-5290
Poughkeepsie (G-12988)

COUNTING DEVICES: Speed Indicators & Recorders, Vehicle

Curtis Instruments Inc ....C 914 666-2971
Mount Kisco (G-8089)

COUPLINGS: Shaft

Howden North America Inc ....D 330 867-8540
Depew (G-3985)

Kinemotive Corporation ....E 631 249-6440
Farmingdale (G-4666)

Renold Inc ....D 716 326-3121
Westfield (G-15949)

COUPON REDEMPTION SVCS

Syracuse Letter Company Inc ....F 315 476-8328
Bridgeport (G-1169)

COURIER SVCS: Ground

Comsec Ventures International ....G 518 523-1600
Lake Placid (G-6766)

COVERS: Automobile Seat

Mc Coy Tops and Interiors Inc ....G 718 458-5800
Woodside (G-16212)

COVERS: Automotive, Exc Seat & Tire

Automtive Uphl Cnvertible Tops ....G 914 961-4242
Tuckahoe (G-15203)

Kamali Group Inc ....G 516 627-4000
Great Neck (G-5399)

COVERS: Canvas

Covergrip Corporation ....G 855 268-3747
Manorville (G-7552)

Custom Canvas Manufacturing Co ......E 716 852-6372
Buffalo (G-2717)

COVERS: Hot Tub & Spa

Commercial Fabrics Inc ....F 716 694-0641
North Tonawanda (G-12062)

Wave Float Rooms LLC ....G 844 356-2876
Clarence (G-3443)

CRANE & AERIAL LIFT SVCS

Neversink Steel Corp ....G 845 292-4611
Liberty (G-6926)

Snyders Neon Displays Inc ....G 518 857-4100
Colonie (G-3575)

CRANES & MONORAIL SYSTEMS

Debrucque Cleveland Tramrail S ....G 315 697-5160
Canastota (G-3152)

CRANES: Indl Plant

Gorbel Inc ....C 585 924-6262
Fishers (G-4796)

Konecranes Inc ....F 585 359-4450
Henrietta (G-5857)

CRANKSHAFTS & CAMSHAFTS: Machining

Peko Precision Products Inc ....F 585 301-1386
Rochester (G-13612)

Quality Grinding Inc ....G 716 480-3766
Hamburg (G-5517)

Westchstr Crnkshft Grndng ....G 718 651-3900
East Elmhurst (G-4112)

CRATES: Fruit, Wood Wirebound

Wolfe Lumber Mill Inc ....G 716 772-7750
Gasport (G-5140)

CREDIT BUREAUS

Nyt Capital LLC ....F 212 556-1234
New York (G-10669)

CROWNS & CLOSURES

Protocase Incorporated ....C 866 849-3911
Lewiston (G-6922)

Reynolds Packaging McHy Inc ....D 716 358-6451
Falconer (G-4554)

CRUDE PETROLEUM & NATURAL GAS PRODUCTION

Hess Energy Exploration Ltd ....G 732 750-6500
New York (G-9772)

Hess Explrtion Prod Hldngs Ltd ....G 732 750-6000
New York (G-9773)

CRUDE PETROLEUM & NATURAL GAS PRODUCTION

Lukoil Americas Corporation ....C 212 421-4141
New York (G-10282)

MRC Global (us) Inc ....F 607 739-8575
Horseheads (G-6129)

Petro River Oil Corp ....G 469 828-3900
New York (G-10818)

Rocket Tech Fuel Corp ....F 516 810-8947
Bay Shore (G-708)

Zenith Energy US Logistics ....G 212 993-1280
New York (G-11820)

CRUDE PETROLEUM PRODUCTION

Chanse Petroleum Corporation ....G 212 682-3789
New York (G-8970)

China N E Petro Holdings Ltd ....A 212 307-3568
New York (G-8991)

Hess Corporation ....B 212 997-8500
New York (G-9771)

Hess Pipeline Corporation ....C 212 997-8500
New York (G-9775)

Hess Tioga Gas Plant LLC ....C 212 997-8500
New York (G-9776)

Resource PTRlm&ptrochmcl Intl ....E 212 537-3856
New York (G-11020)

Speedway LLC ....F 631 738-2536
Lake Grove (G-6760)

Stedman Energy Inc ....G 716 789-3018
Mayville (G-7685)

CRUDES: Cyclic, Organic

Magic Tank LLC ....G 877 646-2442
New York (G-10328)

CRYOGENIC COOLING DEVICES: Infrared Detectors, Masers

Philips Medical Systems Mr ....B 518 782-1122
Latham (G-6872)

CRYSTALS

Crystal Is Inc ....E 518 271-7375
Green Island (G-5434)

Mom Holding Company ....G 518 233-3330
Waterford (G-15540)

Momentive Performance Mtls Inc ....E 518 233-3330
Waterford (G-15542)

Mpm Holdings Inc ....G 518 233-3330
Waterford (G-15543)

Mpm Intermediate Holdings Inc ....G 518 237-3330
Waterford (G-15544)

CULTURE MEDIA

Angus Chemical Company ....E 716 283-1434
Niagara Falls (G-11906)
Debmar-Mercury ....G 212 669-5025
New York (G-9193)
Man of World ....G 212 915-0017
New York (G-10339)
Stemcultures LLC ....G 518 621-0848
Rensselaer (G-13092)

CULVERTS: Metal Plate

Lane Enterprises Inc........................F 607 776-3366
Bath (G-638)

CUPS: Paper, Made From Purchased Materials

Ecoquality Inc..................................G 718 887-7876
Brooklyn (G-1780)

CUPS: Plastic Exc Polystyrene Foam

Capitol Cups Inc...............................E 518 627-0051
Amsterdam (G-321)
Mehr Foil Corp..................................G 631 648-9742
Ronkonkoma (G-13972)

CURBING: Granite Or Stone

Granite Works LLC ....E 607 565-7012
Waverly (G-15621)
Stone & Terrazzo World Inc ....G 718 361-6899
Long Island City (G-7371)

CURTAIN & DRAPERY FIXTURES: Poles, Rods & Rollers

Abalene Decorating Services ....E 718 782-2000
New York (G-8425)
P E Guerin...D 212 243-5270
New York (G-10733)
Pj Decorators Inc..............................E 516 735-9693
East Meadow (G-4139)
Wcd Window Coverings Inc................E 845 336-4511
Lake Katrine (G-6764)

CURTAINS & CURTAIN FABRICS: Lace

Mary Bright Inc ....G 212 677-1970
New York (G-10377)

CURTAINS: Cottage Sets, From Purchased Materials

Northast Coml Win Trtments Inc ....D 845 331-0148
Kingston (G-6704)

CURTAINS: Shower

Catalina Products Corp ....E 718 336-8288
Brooklyn (G-1655)
Daniels Bath & Beyond ....G 718 765-1915
Brooklyn (G-1724)
Showeray Co ....D 718 965-3633
Brooklyn (G-2406)

CURTAINS: Window, From Purchased Materials

Belle Maison USA Ltd........................E 718 805-0200
Richmond Hill (G-13110)
Drapery Industries Inc ....F 585 232-2992
Rochester (G-13356)

CUSHIONS & PILLOWS

Alexandra Ferguson LLC ....G 718 788-7768
New Rochelle (G-8317)
Anhui Skyworth LLC...........................D 917 940-6903
Hempstead (G-5831)
Creative Home Furnishings ....G 631 582-8000
Central Islip (G-3270)
Ex-Cell Home Fashions Inc................C 919 735-7111
New York (G-9435)
Franks Cushions Inc..........................F 718 848-1216
Maspeth (G-7617)
Hollander Sleep Products LLC ....D 212 575-0400
New York (G-9805)
Soft-Tex International Inc ....D 800 366-2324
Waterford (G-15546)

CUSHIONS & PILLOWS: Bed, From Purchased Materials

Arlee Home Fashions Inc...................D 212 689-0020
New York (G-8624)
Hollander HM Fshons Hldngs LLC......F 212 575-0400
New York (G-9804)
Home Fashions Intl LLC ....E 212 689-3579
New York (G-9807)
Home Fashions Intl LLC ....F 212 684-0091
New York (G-9808)
Place Vendome Holding Co Inc ....C 212 696-0765
New York (G-10850)
R & M Industries Inc ....F 212 366-6414
New York (G-10964)

CUSHIONS: Textile, Exc Spring & Carpet

Advanced Medical Mfg Corp...............E 845 369-7535
Suffern (G-14756)
Jakes Sneakers Inc...........................G 718 233-1132
Brooklyn (G-1988)
Wayne Decorators Inc ....G 718 529-4200
Jamaica (G-6487)

CUSTOM COMPOUNDING OF RUBBER MATERIALS

Pawling Corporation ....C 845 373-9300
Wassaic (G-15525)
Tire Conversion Tech Inc ....E 518 372-1600
Latham (G-6876)

CUT STONE & STONE PRODUCTS

Alart Inc ....G 212 840-1508
New York (G-8505)
Barra & Trumbore Inc ....G 845 626-5442
Kerhonkson (G-6658)
Busch Products Inc ....E 315 474-8422
Syracuse (G-14837)
Denton Stoneworks Inc ....F 516 746-1500
Garden City Park (G-5120)
Devonian Stone New York Inc ....E 607 655-2600
Windsor (G-16157)
Douglas Patterson & Sons Inc............F 716 433-8100
Lockport (G-7070)
European Marble Works Co Inc ....F 718 387-9778
Garden City (G-5099)
Fordham Marble Company Inc ....F 914 682-6699
White Plains (G-16007)
Hilltop Slate Inc ....E 518 642-1453
Middle Granville (G-7868)
Masonville Stone Incorporated............G 607 265-3597
Masonville (G-7584)
Pallette Stone Corporation ....E 518 584-2421
Gansevoort (G-5084)
Sanford Stone LLC ....E 607 467-1313
Deposit (G-4001)
Seneca Stone Corporation ....G 607 737-6200
Pine City (G-12629)
Vermont Structural Slate Co ....F 518 499-1912
Whitehall (G-16078)
W F Saunders & Sons Inc ....F 315 469-3217
Nedrow (G-8217)

CUTLERY

Advanced Machine Design Co Inc ....E 716 826-2000
Buffalo (G-2624)
Korin Inc ....E 212 587-7021
New York (G-10128)
Lifetime Brands Inc ....B 516 683-6000
Garden City (G-5104)
Novelty Crystal Corp ....D 718 458-6700
Long Island City (G-7310)
Oneida International Inc ....G 315 361-3000
Oneida (G-12249)
Oneida Silversmiths Inc ....G 315 361-3000
Oneida (G-12252)
Schilling Forge Inc ....G 315 454-4421
Syracuse (G-14987)
Servotronics Inc ....C 716 655-5990
Elma (G-4327)
Sherrill Manufacturing Inc ....C 315 280-0727
Sherrill (G-14406)
Warren Cutlery Corp ....F 845 876-3444
Rhinebeck (G-13103)
Woods Knife Corporation ....E 516 798-4972
Massapequa (G-7653)

CUTLERY WHOLESALERS

Utica Cutlery Company ....D 315 733-4663
Utica (G-15298)
Warren Cutlery Corp ....F 845 876-3444
Rhinebeck (G-13103)

CUTOUTS: Cardboard, Die-Cut, Made From Purchased Materials

Lion Die-Cutting Co Inc ....E 718 383-8841
Brooklyn (G-2077)

CUTOUTS: Distribution

Product Station Inc ....F 516 942-4220
Jericho (G-6590)

CUTTING SVC: Paper, Exc Die-Cut

A-1 Products Inc ....G 718 789-1818
Brooklyn (G-1440)
J Mackenzie Ltd ....E 585 321-1770
Rochester (G-13485)
Rip-It Rip-It Shred-It Corp..................G 516 818-5825
Holbrook (G-6017)

CYCLIC CRUDES & INTERMEDIATES

Durez Corporation ....F 716 286-0100
Niagara Falls (G-11921)
Micro Powders Inc ....E 914 332-6400
Tarrytown (G-15048)
Mitsui Chemicals America Inc ....G 914 253-0777
Rye Brook (G-14092)
Premier Brands America Inc................E 718 325-3000
Mount Vernon (G-8172)

CYLINDER & ACTUATORS: Fluid Power

A K Allen Co Inc ....C 516 747-5450
Melville (G-7753)
Ameritool Mfg Inc..............................E 315 668-2172
Central Square (G-3294)
ITT Enidine Inc ....B 716 662-1900
Orchard Park (G-12356)
Precision Mechanisms Corp ....E 516 333-5955
Westbury (G-15919)
Triumph Actuation Systems LLC ....D 516 378-0162
Freeport (G-5030)
Young & Franklin Inc ....D 315 457-3110
Liverpool (G-7051)

CYLINDERS: Pressure

A K Allen Co Inc ....C 516 747-5450
Melville (G-7753)

DAIRY EQPT

Richard Stewart.................................G 518 632-5363
Hartford (G-5566)

DAIRY PRDTS STORE: Cheese

Artisanal Brands Inc ....E 914 441-3591
Bronxville (G-1399)

DAIRY PRDTS STORE: Ice Cream, Packaged

Bleecker Pastry Tartufo Inc.................G 718 937-9830
Long Island City (G-7180)
Blue Marble Ice Cream LLC ....G 718 858-5551
Brooklyn (G-1593)
Delicioso Coco Helado Inc ....F 718 292-1930
Bronx (G-1240)
Marvel Dairy Whip Inc........................G 516 889-4232
Lido Beach (G-6928)

DAIRY PRDTS STORES

Crosswinds Farm & Creamery.............G 607 327-0363
Ovid (G-12423)

DAIRY PRDTS WHOLESALERS: Fresh

HP Hood LLC ....C 315 363-3870
Oneida (G-12246)
Upstate Niagara Coop Inc ....E 716 484-7178
Jamestown (G-6551)

DAIRY PRDTS: Bakers' Cheese

P & F Bakers Inc...............................F 516 931-6821
Hicksville (G-5938)

PRODUCT

DAIRY PRDTS: Bottled Baby Formula

Infant Formula Laboratory Svc............F....... 718 257-3000
Brooklyn *(G-1957)*

DAIRY PRDTS: Butter

O-At-Ka Milk Products Coop Inc ....B....... 585 343-0536
Batavia *(G-622)*

DAIRY PRDTS: Butter Oil

Pure Ghee Inc..G....... 917 214-5431
Glen Head *(G-5213)*

DAIRY PRDTS: Canned Baby Formula

Danone Nutricia Early.......................E....... 914 872-8556
White Plains *(G-15997)*

DAIRY PRDTS: Cheese

Castelli America LLC ....D....... 716 782-2101
Ashville *(G-408)*
Emkay Trading Corp ....G....... 914 592-9000
Elmsford *(G-4407)*
Emkay Trading Corp ....E....... 585 492-3800
Arcade *(G-373)*
Fly Creek Cder Mill Orchrd Inc ....G....... 607 547-9692
Fly Creek *(G-4909)*
Friendship Dairies LLC.......................C....... 585 973-3031
Friendship *(G-5052)*
Galaxy Nutritional Foods Inc ....E....... 401 667-5000
Albany *(G-79)*
Gharana Industries LLC ....G....... 315 651-4004
Waterloo *(G-15553)*
Great Lakes Cheese NY Inc ....D....... 315 232-4511
Adams *(G-2)*
HP Hood LLC ....D....... 607 295-8134
Arkport *(G-393)*
Hudson Valley Creamery LLC ....F....... 518 851-2570
Hudson *(G-6163)*
Instantwhip of Buffalo Inc ....E....... 716 892-7031
Buffalo *(G-2811)*
Kraft Heinz Foods Company ....B....... 315 376-6575
Lowville *(G-7416)*
Kraft Heinz Foods Company ....E....... 607 527-4584
Campbell *(G-3116)*
Kraft Heinz Foods Company ....C....... 607 865-7131
Walton *(G-15475)*
Mondelez Global LLC ....G....... 845 567-4701
Newburgh *(G-11875)*
Mongiellos Itln Cheese Spc LLC ....C....... 845 436-4200
Hurleyville *(G-6269)*
Rainbeau Ridge Farm ....G....... 914 234-2197
Bedford Hills *(G-772)*
Wny Cheese Enterprise LLC..................E....... 585 243-6516
Pavilion *(G-12524)*

DAIRY PRDTS: Cheese, Cottage

Garelick Farms LLC ....C....... 518 283-0820
East Greenbush *(G-4114)*
HP Hood LLC ....D....... 607 295-8134
Arkport *(G-393)*

DAIRY PRDTS: Concentrated Skim Milk

O-At-Ka Milk Products Coop Inc ....B....... 585 343-0536
Batavia *(G-622)*

DAIRY PRDTS: Cream Substitutes

Sugar Foods Corporation ....E....... 212 753-6900
New York *(G-11385)*

DAIRY PRDTS: Cream, Sweet

Emkay Trading Corp...........................E....... 585 492-3800
Arcade *(G-373)*
HP Hood LLC ....D....... 315 829-3339
Vernon *(G-15366)*

DAIRY PRDTS: Dairy Based Desserts, Frozen

Chobani Idaho LLC ....G....... 208 432-2248
Norwich *(G-12119)*
Indulge Desserts Holdings LLC............G....... 212 231-8600
New York *(G-9883)*
Sweet Melodys LLC ....E....... 716 580-3227
East Amherst *(G-4080)*

DAIRY PRDTS: Dietary Supplements, Dairy & Non-Dairy Based

America Health Corp ....G....... 800 860-1868
New York *(G-8541)*
B&B Sports Nutrition LLC ....G....... 520 869-5434
New York *(G-8707)*
Century Tom Inc.................................C....... 347 654-3179
Jamaica *(G-6431)*
Dynatabs LLC....................................F....... 718 376-6084
Brooklyn *(G-1769)*
El-Gen LLC ....C....... 631 218-3400
Bohemia *(G-1010)*
Eli Consumer Healthcare LLC ....F....... 914 943-3107
Irvington *(G-6307)*
Makers Nutrition LLC ....E....... 631 456-5397
Hauppauge *(G-5706)*
Makers Nutrition LLC ....G....... 844 625-3771
Commack *(G-3594)*
Nyb Distributors Inc ....G....... 516 937-0666
Jericho *(G-6587)*
Unbroken Rtr Usa Inc ....G....... 541 640-9457
Wappingers Falls *(G-15500)*
Vitakem Nutraceutical Inc ....C....... 631 956-8343
Smithtown *(G-14489)*

DAIRY PRDTS: Dips & Spreads, Cheese Based

East Hill Creamery LLC ....G....... 585 237-3622
Perry *(G-12597)*
Lumazu LLC ....G....... 518 623-3372
Warrensburg *(G-15503)*
Lumazu LLC ....F....... 518 623-3372
Warrensburg *(G-15504)*
Taam Tov Foods Inc............................G....... 718 788-8880
Brooklyn *(G-2488)*

DAIRY PRDTS: Dried & Powdered Milk & Milk Prdts

Hain Celestial Group Inc ....C....... 516 587-5000
New Hyde Park *(G-8272)*

DAIRY PRDTS: Evaporated Milk

Nestle Usa Inc ....C....... 914 272-4021
White Plains *(G-16033)*
Nestle Usa Inc ....C....... 212 688-2490
New York *(G-10568)*

DAIRY PRDTS: Farmers' Cheese

Dwyer Farm LLC ....G....... 914 456-2742
Walden *(G-15459)*

DAIRY PRDTS: Fermented & Cultured Milk Prdts

Crowley Foods Inc..............................E....... 800 637-0019
Binghamton *(G-869)*
HP Hood LLC ....A....... 607 772-6580
Binghamton *(G-882)*
Kong Kee Food Corp ....E....... 718 937-2746
Long Island City *(G-7264)*
Kraft Heinz Foods Company ....C....... 607 865-7131
Walton *(G-15475)*
Upstate Farms Dairy LLC ....C....... 716 892-3156
Buffalo *(G-3031)*
Upstate Niagara Coop Inc ....D....... 716 892-3156
Buffalo *(G-3032)*
Yiamas Dairy Farms LLC......................G....... 347 766-7177
Bayside *(G-745)*

DAIRY PRDTS: Frozen Desserts & Novelties

Ample Hills Creamery Inc ....E....... 347 725-4061
Brooklyn *(G-1506)*
Ample Hills Creamery Inc ....E....... 718 809-1678
Brooklyn *(G-1507)*
Ample Hills Holdings Inc ....G....... 347 725-4061
Brooklyn *(G-1508)*
Blue Pig Ice Cream Factory ....G....... 914 271-3850
Croton On Hudson *(G-3806)*
Carols Polar Parlor ....G....... 315 468-3404
Syracuse *(G-14842)*
Crowley Foods Inc ....E....... 800 637-0019
Binghamton *(G-869)*
Df Mavens Inc....................................E....... 347 813-4705
Astoria *(G-417)*

Ffc Holding Corp Subsidiaries ....B....... 716 366-5400
Dunkirk *(G-4057)*
Fresh Ice Cream Company LLC...........F....... 347 603-6021
Brooklyn *(G-1868)*
Fresh Ice Cream Company LLC...........E....... 347 603-6021
Brooklyn *(G-1869)*
HP Hood LLC ....D....... 315 829-3339
Vernon *(G-15366)*
HP Hood LLC ....A....... 607 772-6580
Binghamton *(G-882)*
Jones Humdinger...............................F....... 607 771-6501
Binghamton *(G-892)*
Kan Pak LLC ....G....... 620 440-2319
Penn Yan *(G-12589)*
Kozy Shack Enterprises LLC ....G....... 516 870-3000
Hicksville *(G-5920)*
LArte Del Gelato Gruppo Inc ....F....... 718 383-6600
Long Island City *(G-7269)*
Lickity Splits ....G....... 585 345-6091
Batavia *(G-619)*
Macadoodles ....G....... 607 652-9019
Stamford *(G-14608)*
Ninas Custard ....E....... 716 636-0345
Getzville *(G-5179)*
Nutrifast LLC ....F....... 347 671-3181
New York *(G-10658)*
Phyljohn Distributors Inc ....F....... 518 459-2775
Albany *(G-115)*
Quaker Bonnet Inc ....G....... 716 885-7208
Buffalo *(G-2941)*
Ralphs Famous Italian Ices ....G....... 718 605-5052
Staten Island *(G-14698)*
Textured Fd Innvations Tfi LLC ....G....... 515 731-3663
Carle Place *(G-3182)*
Tia Lattrell ....G....... 845 373-9494
Amenia *(G-203)*
Unilever United States Inc...................F....... 212 546-0200
New York *(G-11588)*
Unilever United States Inc...................E....... 212 546-0200
New York *(G-11589)*
Van Leeuwen Artisan Ice Cream..........G....... 718 701-1630
Brooklyn *(G-2552)*
Wicked Spoon Inc...............................F....... 646 335-2890
New York *(G-11753)*

DAIRY PRDTS: Ice Cream & Ice Milk

MSQ Corporation ....G....... 718 465-0900
Queens Village *(G-13025)*
Stewarts Processing Corp ....D....... 518 581-1200
Ballston Spa *(G-588)*
Stewarts Shops Corp...........................F....... 518 499-9376
Whitehall *(G-16077)*
TLC-Lc Inc ....E....... 212 756-8900
New York *(G-11501)*
Vanilla Sky LLC ....G....... 347 738-4195
Long Island City *(G-7392)*
Washburns Dairy Inc ....E....... 518 725-0629
Gloversville *(G-5299)*

DAIRY PRDTS: Ice Cream, Bulk

Bleecker Pastry Tartufo Inc ....G....... 718 937-9830
Long Island City *(G-7180)*
Blue Marble Ice Cream LLC ....G....... 718 858-5551
Brooklyn *(G-1593)*
Delicioso Coco Helado Inc ....F....... 718 292-1930
Bronx *(G-1240)*
Fieldbrook Foods Corporation ....C....... 716 366-5400
Dunkirk *(G-4058)*
G Pesso & Sons Inc............................G....... 718 224-9130
Bayside *(G-738)*
Grom Columbus LLC ....G....... 212 974-3444
New York *(G-9683)*
La Cremeria ....G....... 212 226-6758
New York *(G-10156)*
Macedonia Ltd ....F....... 718 462-3596
Brooklyn *(G-2100)*
Marvel Dairy Whip Inc ....G....... 516 889-4232
Lido Beach *(G-6928)*
Paleteria Fernandez Inc ....F....... 914 315-1598
Mamaroneck *(G-7518)*
Paleteria Fernandez Inc ....G....... 914 939-3694
Port Chester *(G-12826)*
Perrys Ice Cream Company Inc ....B....... 716 542-5492
Akron *(G-20)*
Piazzas Ice Cream Ice Hse Inc ....F....... 718 818-8811
Staten Island *(G-14689)*
Purity Ice Cream Co Inc ....F....... 607 272-1545
Ithaca *(G-6408)*
Quality Dairy Farms Inc ....G....... 315 942-2611
Boonville *(G-1109)*

Scoops R US Incorporated ....G....... 212 730-7959
New York *(G-11168)*

Smartys Corner ....G....... 607 239-5276
Endicott *(G-4473)*

Victory Garden ....G....... 212 206-7273
New York *(G-11678)*

DAIRY PRDTS: Ice Cream, Packaged, Molded, On Sticks, Etc.

Beyond Better Foods LLC................G....... 212 888-1120
Bronx *(G-1213)*

Byrne Dairy Inc................................B....... 315 475-2121
La Fayette *(G-6737)*

DAIRY PRDTS: Milk & Cream, Cultured & Flavored

Upstate Niagara Coop Inc ....D....... 315 389-5111
North Lawrence *(G-12033)*

DAIRY PRDTS: Milk, Chocolate

Aethera LLC ....E....... 215 324-9222
New York *(G-8489)*

DAIRY PRDTS: Milk, Condensed & Evaporated

Friendship Dairies LLC...................C....... 585 973-3031
Friendship *(G-5052)*

J Rettenmaier USA LP ....D....... 716 693-4009
North Tonawanda *(G-12075)*

Kerry Bfnctnal Ingredients Inc..........D....... 608 363-1200
Norwich *(G-12123)*

Nationwide Dairy Inc.......................G....... 347 689-8148
Brooklyn *(G-2191)*

Rich Products Corporation ....A....... 716 878-8000
Buffalo *(G-2954)*

DAIRY PRDTS: Milk, Fluid

Cville Yoghurt Inc.............................G....... 315 430-4966
Cortland *(G-3765)*

Finger Lakes Cheese Trail................F....... 607 857-5726
Odessa *(G-12200)*

HP Hood LLC ....C....... 315 363-3870
Oneida *(G-12246)*

HP Hood LLC ....B....... 315 658-2132
La Fargeville *(G-6733)*

HP Hood LLC ....B....... 518 218-9097
Schenectady *(G-14279)*

Instantwhip of Buffalo Inc ....E....... 716 892-7031
Buffalo *(G-2811)*

Kesso Foods Inc ....G....... 718 777-5303
East Elmhurst *(G-4108)*

Kraft Heinz Foods Company ....B....... 607 527-4584
Campbell *(G-3116)*

O-At-Ka Milk Products Coop Inc ....B....... 585 343-0536
Batavia *(G-622)*

Purity Ice Cream Co Inc ....F....... 607 272-1545
Ithaca *(G-6408)*

Stewarts Processing Corp ....D....... 518 581-1200
Ballston Spa *(G-588)*

Upstate Niagara Coop Inc ....C....... 716 892-2121
Buffalo *(G-3033)*

DAIRY PRDTS: Milk, Processed, Pasteurized, Homogenized/Btld

Byrne Dairy Inc................................B....... 315 475-2121
La Fayette *(G-6737)*

Dairy Farmers America Inc ....E....... 816 801-6440
East Syracuse *(G-4205)*

Dean Foods Company.......................D....... 315 452-5001
East Syracuse *(G-4207)*

Midland Farms LLC..........................D....... 518 436-7038
Menands *(G-7846)*

Mountain Side Farms Inc ....E....... 718 526-3442
Jamaica *(G-6462)*

Saputo Dairy Foods Usa LLC...........D....... 607 746-2141
Delhi *(G-3966)*

Steuben Foods Incorporated ....C....... 716 655-4000
Elma *(G-4329)*

Upstate Niagara Coop Inc ....C....... 585 458-1880
Rochester *(G-13789)*

Upstate Niagara Coop Inc ....E....... 716 484-7178
Jamestown *(G-6551)*

Wny Enterprise LLC..........................E....... 585 243-6514
Pavilion *(G-12525)*

DAIRY PRDTS: Natural Cheese

Agri-Mark Inc ....D....... 518 497-6644
Chateaugay *(G-3329)*

Artisanal Brands Inc ....E....... 914 441-3591
Bronxville *(G-1399)*

Cemac Foods Corp ....F....... 914 835-0526
Harrison *(G-5549)*

Crosswinds Farm & Creamery.............G....... 607 327-0363
Ovid *(G-12423)*

Empire Cheese Inc ....C....... 585 968-1552
Cuba *(G-3813)*

Euphrates Inc ....D....... 518 762-3488
Johnstown *(G-6616)*

Four Fat Fowl Inc ....G....... 518 733-5230
Stephentown *(G-14731)*

Lactalis American Group Inc ....D....... 716 827-2622
Buffalo *(G-2843)*

Lactalis American Group Inc ....B....... 716 823-6262
Buffalo *(G-2844)*

Leprino Foods Company....................C....... 570 888-9658
Waverly *(G-15623)*

Losurdo Foods Inc ....C....... 315 344-2444
Heuvelton *(G-5867)*

Mongiello Sales Inc.........................E....... 845 436-4200
Hurleyville *(G-6268)*

Original Hrkmer Cnty Chese Inc ....D....... 315 895-7428
Ilion *(G-6280)*

Pecoraro Dairy Products Inc.............G....... 718 388-2379
Brooklyn *(G-2251)*

Sandvoss Farms LLC.......................G....... 585 297-7044
East Bethany *(G-4099)*

Sargento Foods Inc ....C....... 920 893-8484
New York *(G-11138)*

Sorrento Lactalis Inc ....F....... 716 823-6262
Buffalo *(G-2989)*

World Cheese Co Inc ....F....... 718 965-1700
Brooklyn *(G-2595)*

DAIRY PRDTS: Processed Cheese

Habco Corp ....E....... 631 789-1400
Amityville *(G-266)*

HP Hood LLC ....D....... 315 829-3339
Vernon *(G-15366)*

Upstate Farms Cheese LLC...............C....... 607 527-4584
Campbell *(G-3117)*

DAIRY PRDTS: Sherbets, Dairy Based

Lumazu LLC ....G....... 518 623-3372
Warrensburg *(G-15503)*

Lumazu LLC ....F....... 518 623-3372
Warrensburg *(G-15504)*

DAIRY PRDTS: Spreads, Cheese

Noga Dairies Inc...............................F....... 516 293-5448
Farmingdale *(G-4695)*

DAIRY PRDTS: Whipped Topping, Exc Frozen Or Dry Mix

Hanan Products Company Inc.............E....... 516 938-1000
Hicksville *(G-5915)*

DAIRY PRDTS: Yogurt, Exc Frozen

Bliss Foods Inc ....G....... 212 732-8888
New York *(G-8811)*

Bliss Foods Inc ....F....... 212 732-8888
New York *(G-8812)*

Chobani LLC ....F....... 646 998-3800
New York *(G-8994)*

Chobani LLC ....C....... 607 337-1246
Norwich *(G-12118)*

Chobani LLC ....G....... 607 847-6181
New Berlin *(G-8221)*

Currant Company LLC........................G....... 845 266-8999
Staatsburg *(G-14598)*

Danone Us LLC ....D....... 914 872-8400
White Plains *(G-15998)*

Fage USA Holdings ....G....... 518 762-5912
Johnstown *(G-6617)*

Maple Hill Creamery LLC...................F....... 518 758-7777
Stuyvesant *(G-14754)*

Noga Dairies Inc...............................F....... 516 293-5448
Farmingdale *(G-4695)*

Steuben Foods Incorporated ....F....... 718 291-3333
Elma *(G-4328)*

Swirls Twirls Incorporated ....G....... 516 541-9400
Massapequa *(G-7652)*

Whitney Foods Inc............................F....... 718 291-3333
Jamaica *(G-6488)*

Yogolicious Inc..................................G....... 914 236-3455
Briarcliff Manor *(G-1163)*

DAIRY PRDTS: Yogurt, Frozen

NY Froyo LLC....................................G....... 516 312-4588
Deer Park *(G-3915)*

Swirl Bliss LLC ....G....... 516 867-9475
North Baldwin *(G-12009)*

DATA PROCESSING & PREPARATION SVCS

Data Palette Info Svcs LLC ....D....... 718 433-1060
Port Washington *(G-12871)*

Informa Solutions Inc ....E....... 516 543-3733
New York *(G-9891)*

Rational Retention LLC ....E....... 518 489-3000
Albany *(G-124)*

Relx Inc ....E....... 212 309-8100
New York *(G-11005)*

Standard Analytics Io Inc ....G....... 917 882-5422
New York *(G-11344)*

Vaso Corporation ....F....... 516 997-4600
Plainview *(G-12722)*

DATA PROCESSING SVCS

DP Murphy Co Inc ....D....... 631 673-9400
Deer Park *(G-3865)*

Thomas Publishing Company LLC ......B....... 212 695-0500
New York *(G-11468)*

DECORATIVE WOOD & WOODWORK

A Van Hoek Woodworking Limited........G....... 718 599-4388
Brooklyn *(G-1437)*

Adams Interior Fabrications ....F....... 631 249-8282
Massapequa *(G-7644)*

Andike Millwork Inc ....G....... 718 894-1796
Maspeth *(G-7590)*

Art Essentials of New York ....G....... 845 368-1100
Airmont *(G-10)*

Atelier Viollet Corp ....G....... 718 782-1727
Brooklyn *(G-1545)*

Brooks Woodworking Inc...................F....... 914 666-2029
Mount Kisco *(G-8088)*

Budd Woodwork Inc ....F....... 718 389-1110
Brooklyn *(G-1627)*

Cabinet Shapes Corp.........................E....... 718 784-6255
Long Island City *(G-7182)*

Craz Woodworking Assoc Inc..............F....... 631 205-1890
Bellport *(G-796)*

Daniel Demarco and Assoc Inc ....E....... 631 598-7000
Amityville *(G-262)*

Di Fiore and Sons Custom Wdwkg ....G....... 718 278-1663
Long Island City *(G-7201)*

Digital Fabrication Wkshp Inc............G....... 518 249-6500
Hudson *(G-6153)*

Ed Negron Fine Woodworking.............G....... 718 246-1016
Brooklyn *(G-1781)*

Elephants Custom Furniture Inc ....D....... 917 509-3581
Brooklyn *(G-1796)*

Hennig Custom Woodwork Corp..........G....... 516 536-3460
Oceanside *(G-12174)*

Innova Interiors Inc ....E....... 718 401-2122
Bronx *(G-1283)*

Ivan Horning ....G....... 315 536-3028
Penn Yan *(G-12587)*

Jeffrey John ....G....... 631 842-2850
Amityville *(G-281)*

Jordache Woodworking Corp................F....... 718 349-3373
Brooklyn *(G-1999)*

K & B Woodworking Inc ....G....... 518 634-7253
Cairo *(G-3066)*

M & R Woodworking & Finishing ....G....... 718 486-5480
Brooklyn *(G-2094)*

McGraw Wood Products LLC ....E....... 607 836-6465
Mc Graw *(G-7689)*

N Sketch Build Inc ....G....... 800 975-0597
Fishkill *(G-4802)*

Northern Forest Pdts Co Inc..............G....... 315 942-6955
Boonville *(G-1107)*

Pdj Components Inc ....E....... 845 469-9191
Chester *(G-3382)*

Pella Corporation ....C....... 631 208-0710
Calverton *(G-3083)*

Pgs Millwork Inc ....D....... 518 828-2608
Hudson *(G-6175)*

Piccini Mnm Inc ....G....... 845 741-6770
West Nyack *(G-15830)*

PRODUCT

Prime Wood Products ....G...... 518 792-1407
Queensbury *(G-13053)*
Richard Rothbard Inc ....G...... 845 355-2300
Slate Hill *(G-14463)*
Windsor United Industries LLC ......E...... 607 655-3300
Windsor *(G-16158)*
Wood Innovations of Suffolk ....G...... 631 698-2345
Oceanside *(G-12198)*
Woodmotif Inc ....F...... 516 564-8325
Hempstead *(G-5852)*
Woodtronics Inc ....G...... 914 962-5205
Yorktown Heights *(G-16374)*

DEFENSE SYSTEMS & EQPT

Eastern Strategic Materials ....E...... 212 332-1619
New York *(G-9306)*
Krieger Defense Group LLC ....F...... 716 485-1970
Blasdell *(G-919)*
Premier Prcision Machining LLC ......E...... 716 665-5217
Falconer *(G-4551)*
Rochester Personal Defense LLC ....G...... 585 406-6758
Rochester *(G-13693)*
UNI Source Technology ....F...... 514 748-8888
Champlain *(G-3318)*

DEGREASING MACHINES

Cleaning Tech Group LLC ....E...... 716 665-2340
Jamestown *(G-6502)*

DEHUMIDIFIERS: Electric

Mohawk Group Holdings Inc ....G...... 347 676-1681
New York *(G-10493)*

DEHYDRATION EQPT

Purvi Enterprises Incorporated ....G...... 347 808-9448
Maspeth *(G-7635)*

DELAY LINES

Esc Control Electronics LLC ....E...... 631 467-5328
Sayville *(G-14225)*

DENTAL EQPT

Air Techniques Inc ....G...... 516 433-7676
Hicksville *(G-5878)*
Boehm Surgical Instrument Corp ....F...... 585 436-6584
Rochester *(G-13277)*
Brandt Equipment LLC ....G...... 718 994-0800
Bronx *(G-1217)*
Buffalo Dental Mfg Co Inc ....E...... 516 496-7200
Syosset *(G-14780)*
J H M Engineering ....E...... 718 871-1810
Brooklyn *(G-1978)*
Kay See Dental Mfg Co ....F...... 816 842-2817
New York *(G-10081)*
Lucas Dental Equipment Co Inc ....F...... 631 244-2807
Bohemia *(G-1039)*

DENTAL EQPT & SPLYS

Air Techniques Inc ....B...... 516 433-7676
Melville *(G-7758)*
American Regent Inc ....E...... 631 924-4000
Shirley *(G-14411)*
Cmp Export Co Inc ....E...... 518 434-3147
Albany *(G-63)*
Cmp Industries LLC ....E...... 518 434-3147
Albany *(G-64)*
Crosstex International Inc ....D...... 631 582-6777
Hauppauge *(G-5631)*
Crosstex International Inc ....F...... 631 582-6777
Hauppauge *(G-5632)*
Darby Dental Supply ....G...... 516 688-6421
Jericho *(G-6576)*
Dedeco International Sales Inc ....D...... 845 887-4840
Long Eddy *(G-7139)*
DenTek Oral Care Inc ....D...... 865 983-1300
Tarrytown *(G-15043)*
Glaxosmithkline LLC ....D...... 518 239-6901
East Durham *(G-4102)*
Henry Schein Fincl Svcs LLC ....G...... 631 843-5500
Melville *(G-7789)*
Impladent Ltd ....G...... 718 465-1810
Jamaica *(G-6449)*
JM Murray Center Inc ....C...... 607 756-9913
Cortland *(G-3774)*
Lelab Dental Laboratory Inc ....G...... 516 561-5050
Valley Stream *(G-15346)*

Oramaax Dental Products Inc ....F...... 516 771-8514
Freeport *(G-5013)*
Professional Manufacturers ....F...... 631 586-2440
Deer Park *(G-3923)*
Schilling Forge Inc ....E...... 315 454-4421
Syracuse *(G-14987)*
Temrex Corporation ....E...... 516 868-6221
Freeport *(G-5028)*
Tiger Supply Inc ....G...... 631 293-2700
Farmingdale *(G-4755)*
Total Dntl Implant Sltions LLC ....G...... 212 877-3777
Valley Stream *(G-15361)*
Valplast International Corp ....F...... 516 442-3923
Westbury *(G-15937)*

DENTAL EQPT & SPLYS WHOLESALERS

Impladent Ltd ....G...... 718 465-1810
Jamaica *(G-6449)*
Oramaax Dental Products Inc ....F...... 516 771-8514
Freeport *(G-5013)*

DENTAL EQPT & SPLYS: Cabinets

Precision Dental Cabinets Inc ....F...... 631 543-3870
Smithtown *(G-14485)*
Stylecraft Interiors Inc ....F...... 516 487-2133
Great Neck *(G-5427)*

DENTAL EQPT & SPLYS: Compounds

Lornamead Inc ....D...... 716 874-7190
New York *(G-10264)*

DENTAL EQPT & SPLYS: Cutting Instruments

Smile Specialists ....G...... 877 337-6135
New York *(G-11273)*

DENTAL EQPT & SPLYS: Dental Materials

Marotta Dental Studio Inc ....E...... 631 249-7520
Farmingdale *(G-4677)*
Safe-Dent Enterprises LLC ....G...... 845 362-0141
Monsey *(G-8046)*

DENTAL EQPT & SPLYS: Enamels

Gallery 57 Dental ....E...... 212 246-8700
New York *(G-9567)*
Gan Kavod Inc ....E...... 716 633-2820
Buffalo *(G-2766)*
Jeffrey D Menoff DDS PC ....G...... 716 665-1468
Jamestown *(G-6526)*

DENTAL EQPT & SPLYS: Laboratory

Cmp Industries LLC ....G...... 518 434-3147
Albany *(G-65)*

DENTAL EQPT & SPLYS: Orthodontic Appliances

Cettel Studio of New York Inc ....G...... 518 494-3622
Chestertown *(G-3393)*
Vincent Martino Dental Lab ....F...... 716 674-7800
Buffalo *(G-3037)*

DENTAL EQPT & SPLYS: Sterilizers

Cpac Equipment Inc ....F...... 585 382-3223
Leicester *(G-6909)*

DENTAL EQPT & SPLYS: Teeth, Artificial, Exc In Dental Labs

Martins Dental Studio ....G...... 315 788-0800
Watertown *(G-15582)*

DENTAL EQPT & SPLYS: Wax

Corning Rubber Company Inc ....F...... 631 738-0041
Ronkonkoma *(G-13926)*

DENTISTS' OFFICES & CLINICS

Comprehensive Dental Tech ....E...... 607 467-4456
Hancock *(G-5536)*
Marotta Dental Studio Inc ....E...... 631 249-7520
Farmingdale *(G-4677)*

DEODORANTS: Personal

Procter & Gamble Company ....C...... 646 885-4201
New York *(G-10902)*

DEPILATORIES, COSMETIC

LOreal Usa Inc ....E...... 212 389-4201
New York *(G-10260)*
Shop Sky Inc ....F...... 347 686-4616
South Richmond Hill *(G-14524)*

DERMATOLOGICALS

Skincare Products Inc ....G...... 917 837-5255
Williamsville *(G-16139)*

DERRICKS: Oil & Gas Field

Derrick Corporation ....B...... 716 685-4892
Cheektowaga *(G-3344)*

DESALTER KITS: Sea Water

Luxfer Magtech Inc ....D...... 631 727-8600
Riverhead *(G-13181)*

DESIGN SVCS, NEC

1 Atelier LLC ....G...... 917 916-2968
New York *(G-8388)*
A To Z Media Inc ....E...... 212 260-0237
New York *(G-8420)*
Acad Design Corp ....F...... 585 254-6960
Rochester *(G-13198)*
Holland & Sherry Inc ....E...... 212 542-8410
New York *(G-9803)*
International Direct Group Inc ....E...... 212 921-9036
New York *(G-9919)*
Internodal International Inc ....E...... 631 765-0037
Southold *(G-14544)*
Jinglebell Inc ....G...... 914 219-5395
Armonk *(G-399)*
Leo D Bernstein & Sons Inc ....E...... 212 337-9578
New York *(G-10198)*
Linita Design & Mfg Corp ....E...... 716 566-7753
Lackawanna *(G-6741)*
Msm Designz Inc ....G...... 914 909-5900
Tarrytown *(G-15050)*
Northern Design & Bldg Assoc ....E...... 518 747-2200
Queensbury *(G-13050)*
Peerless Instrument Co Inc ....C...... 631 396-6500
Farmingdale *(G-4704)*
Polymag Tek Inc ....F...... 585 235-8390
Rochester *(G-13628)*
Skincare Products Inc ....G...... 917 837-5255
Williamsville *(G-16139)*
Twcc Product and Sales ....E...... 212 614-9364
New York *(G-11563)*

DESIGN SVCS: Commercial & Indl

Precision Systems Mfg Inc ....E...... 315 451-3480
Liverpool *(G-7035)*
Prim Hall Enterprises Inc ....F...... 518 561-7408
Plattsburgh *(G-12772)*
Riverwood Signs By Dandev Desi ....G...... 845 229-0282
Hyde Park *(G-6274)*
Voss Manufacturing Inc ....D...... 716 731-5062
Sanborn *(G-14153)*

DESIGN SVCS: Computer Integrated Systems

331 Holding Inc ....E...... 585 924-1740
Victor *(G-15389)*
Cisco Systems Inc ....C...... 212 714-4000
New York *(G-9012)*
Informa Solutions Inc ....E...... 516 543-3733
New York *(G-9891)*
Innovative Systems of New York ....G...... 516 541-7410
Massapequa Park *(G-7657)*
Kld Labs Inc ....E...... 631 549-4222
Hauppauge *(G-5685)*
Performance Technologies Inc ....E...... 585 256-0200
Rochester *(G-13615)*
Siemens Industry Inc ....E...... 716 568-0983
Buffalo *(G-2982)*

DESIGN SVCS: Shoe

Soludos LLC ....F...... 212 219-1101
New York *(G-11292)*

DETECTION APPARATUS:
Electronic/Magnetic Field, Light/Heat

Sensormatic Electronics LLC ....F 845 365-3125
  Orangeburg (G-12331)
Sentry Technology Corporation ....E 631 739-2000
  Ronkonkoma (G-14006)
Sentry Technology Corporation ....F 800 645-4224
  Ronkonkoma (G-14007)

DIAGNOSTIC SUBSTANCES

Bella International Inc ....G 716 484-0102
  Jamestown (G-6496)
Biochemical Diagnostics Inc ....E 631 595-9200
  Edgewood (G-4263)
Biopool Us Inc ....E 716 483-3851
  Jamestown (G-6497)
Chembio Diagnostic Systems Inc ....C 631 924-1135
  Medford (G-7701)
Danisco US Inc ....D 585 256-5200
  Rochester (G-13337)
E-Z-Em Inc ....E 609 524-2864
  Melville (G-7777)
Enzo Life Sciences Inc ....E 631 694-7070
  Farmingdale (G-4625)
Immco Diagnostics Inc ....G 716 691-0091
  Buffalo (G-2807)
Kannalife Sciences Inc ....G 516 669-3219
  Lloyd Harbor (G-7056)
Lesanne Life Sciences LLC ....G 914 234-0860
  Bedford (G-764)
Lifelink Monitoring Corp ....E 845 336-2098
  Bearsville (G-758)
Petnet Solutions Inc ....G 865 218-2400
  New York (G-10817)
Siemens Hlthcare Dgnostics Inc ....E 914 631-0475
  Tarrytown (G-15059)
US Diagnostics Inc ....E 866 216-5308
  New York (G-11624)
Welch Allyn Inc..............A 315 685-4100
  Skaneateles Falls (G-14460)

DIAGNOSTIC SUBSTANCES OR AGENTS:
Blood Derivative

Lifescan Inc ....B 516 557-2693
  Wantagh (G-15485)
Ortho-Clinical Diagnostics Inc.............E 716 631-1281
  Williamsville (G-16135)
Ortho-Clinical Diagnostics Inc.............E 585 453-3000
  Rochester (G-13597)

DIAGNOSTIC SUBSTANCES OR AGENTS: In Vivo

Ken-Ton Open Mri PC ....G 716 876-7000
  Kenmore (G-6654)

DIAGNOSTIC SUBSTANCES OR AGENTS:
Microbiology & Virology

Tiziana Therapeutics Inc ....G 646 396-4970
  New York (G-11500)
Ufc Biotechnology Inc ....F 716 603-3652
  Amherst (G-251)

DIAGNOSTIC SUBSTANCES OR AGENTS:
Veterinary

Gotham Veterinary Center PC ....E 212 222-1900
  New York (G-9648)

DIAMOND MINING SVCS: Indl

Romance & Co Inc ....G 212 382-0337
  New York (G-11079)
Signature Diamond Entps LLC ....E 212 869-5115
  New York (G-11235)

DIAMOND SETTER SVCS

Crystal Ceres Industries Inc ....D 716 283-0445
  Niagara Falls (G-11918)

DIAMONDS, GEMS, WHOLESALE

Antwerp Diamond Distributors.............F 212 319-3300
  New York (G-8599)
David Weisz & Sons USA LLC ....G 212 840-4747
  New York (G-9185)

Diamex Inc..............G 212 575-8145
  New York (G-9218)
Diamond Constellation Corp ....G 212 819-0324
  New York (G-9219)
E Schreiber Inc ....E 212 382-0280
  New York (G-9291)
Eugene Biro Corp ....E 212 997-0146
  New York (G-9417)
Fine Cut Diamonds Corporation ....G 212 575-8780
  New York (G-9494)
Fischler Diamonds Inc ....G 212 921-8196
  New York (G-9504)
Forever Grown Diamonds Inc ....G 917 261-4511
  New York (G-9515)
Global Gem Corporation ....G 212 350-9936
  New York (G-9628)
Gold & Diamonds Wholesale Outl........G 718 438-7888
  Brooklyn (G-1896)
Herkimer Diamond Mines Inc ....E 315 891-7355
  Herkimer (G-5864)
Leo Schachter & Co Inc ....E 212 688-2000
  New York (G-10201)
Miller & Veit Inc ....F 212 247-2275
  New York (G-10469)
Romance & Co Inc ....G 212 382-0337
  New York (G-11079)
Rosy Blue Inc ....E 212 687-8838
  New York (G-11086)
T M W Diamonds Mfg Co ....G 212 869-8444
  New York (G-11417)
United Gemdiam Inc ....E 718 851-5083
  Brooklyn (G-2538)

DIAMONDS: Cutting & Polishing

Ace Diamond Corp..............G 212 730-8231
  New York (G-8446)
Antwerp Diamond Distributors.............F 212 319-3300
  New York (G-8599)
Antwerp Sales Intl Inc ....F 212 354-6515
  New York (G-8600)
Baroka Creations Inc ....G 212 768-0527
  New York (G-8731)
Dialase Inc ....G 212 575-8833
  New York (G-9217)
Diamex Inc..............G 212 575-8145
  New York (G-9218)
Diamond Constellation Corp ....G 212 819-0324
  New York (G-9219)
Dresdiam Inc ....E 212 819-2217
  New York (G-9268)
E Schreiber Inc ....E 212 382-0280
  New York (G-9291)
Eugene Biro Corp ....E 212 997-0146
  New York (G-9417)
Fine Cut Diamonds Corporation ....G 212 575-8780
  New York (G-9494)
Fischler Diamonds Inc ....G 212 921-8196
  New York (G-9504)
Forever Grown Diamonds Inc ....G 917 261-4511
  New York (G-9515)
Guild Diamond Products Inc ....F 212 871-0007
  New York (G-9695)
Hershel Horowitz Corp ....G 212 719-1710
  New York (G-9770)
Julius Klein Group ....E 212 719-1811
  New York (G-10038)
Kaleko Bros ....G 212 819-0100
  New York (G-10059)
Lazare Kaplan Intl Inc ....D 212 972-9700
  New York (G-10179)
Levi Shabtai ....G 212 302-7393
  New York (G-10205)
Miller & Veit Inc ....F 212 247-2275
  New York (G-10469)
Shah Diamonds Inc..............F 212 888-9393
  New York (G-11202)
T M W Diamonds Mfg Co ....G 212 869-8444
  New York (G-11417)
United Gemdiam Inc ....E 718 851-5083
  Brooklyn (G-2538)
William Goldberg Diamond Corp.........E 212 980-4343
  New York (G-11756)
Windiam Usa Inc ....G 212 542-0949
  New York (G-11763)

DIAPERS: Cloth

Becks Classic Mfg Inc ....D 631 435-3800
  Brentwood (G-1116)

DIAPERS: Disposable

Bentley Manufacturing Inc ....G 212 714-1800
  New York (G-8759)
Mr Disposable Inc ....F 718 388-8574
  Brooklyn (G-2175)

DIE CUTTING SVC: Paper

Able National Corp..............E 718 386-8801
  Brooklyn (G-1450)

DIE SETS: Presses, Metal Stamping

Gay Sheet Metal Dies Inc ....G 716 877-0208
  Buffalo (G-2768)

DIES & TOOLS: Special

Ace Specialty Co Inc ....G 716 874-3670
  Tonawanda (G-15081)
All Out Die Cutting Inc............E 718 346-6666
  Brooklyn (G-1486)
Allstate Tool and Die Inc ....D 585 426-0400
  Rochester (G-13222)
Amada Tool America Inc ....D 585 344-3900
  Batavia (G-601)
Anka Tool & Die Inc ....E 845 268-4116
  Congers (G-3607)
Arro Tool & Die Inc ....F 716 763-6203
  Lakewood (G-6779)
Art Precision Metal Products ....E 631 842-8889
  Copiague (G-3647)
Barron Metal Products Inc ....E 914 965-1232
  Yonkers (G-16289)
Bel-Bee Products Incorporated ....F 845 353-0300
  West Nyack (G-15817)
Bennett Die & Tool Inc ....E 607 739-5629
  Horseheads (G-6115)
Brayley Tool & Machine Inc ....G 585 342-7190
  Rochester (G-13280)
Brighton Tool & Die Designers ....F 716 876-0879
  Tonawanda (G-15093)
Carbaugh Tool Company Inc ....E 607 739-3293
  Elmira (G-4341)
Chamtek Mfg Inc ....F 585 328-4900
  Rochester (G-13311)
Charles A Rogers Entps Inc ....E 585 924-6400
  Victor (G-15397)
Cosmo Electronic Machine Corp.........E 631 249-2535
  Farmingdale (G-4603)
Cuddeback Machining Inc...........G 585 392-5889
  Hilton (G-5972)
Dependable Tool & Die Co Inc ....G 315 453-5696
  Syracuse (G-14876)
Diemax of Rochester Inc ....E 585 288-3912
  Rochester (G-13345)
Diemolding Corporation ....F 315 363-4710
  Wampsville (G-15481)
Eden Tool & Die Inc ....G 716 992-4240
  Eden (G-4255)
Electronic Die Corp..............F 718 455-3200
  Brooklyn (G-1791)
Enhanced Tool Inc ....E 716 691-5200
  Amherst (G-221)
Etna Tool & Die Corporation ....F 212 475-4350
  New York (G-9414)
F M EDM Inc..............G 716 655-1784
  East Aurora (G-4088)
Intek Precision ....G 585 293-0853
  Churchville (G-3413)
James Wire Die Co ....G 315 894-3233
  Ilion (G-6279)
K D M Die Company Inc ....F 716 828-9000
  Buffalo (G-2828)
Keyes Machine Works Inc ....E 585 426-5059
  Gates (G-5141)
Long Island Tool & Die Inc ....G 631 225-0600
  Copiague (G-3662)
M J M Tooling Corp ....G 718 292-3590
  Bronx (G-1305)
Machinecraft Inc..............E 585 436-1070
  Rochester (G-13526)
Magnus Precision Mfg Inc..........D 315 548-8032
  Phelps (G-12605)
Mantel & Mantel Stamping Corp.........G 631 467-1916
  Ronkonkoma (G-13969)
Manufacturers Tool & Die Co ....G 585 352-1080
  Spencerport (G-14558)
Micron Inds Rochester Inc ....G 585 247-6130
  Rochester (G-13548)

Ms Machining Inc ....G.... 607 723-1105
Binghamton *(G-900)*

Multifold Die Ctng Finshg Corp ....G.... 631 232-1235
Islandia *(G-6341)*

Mustang-Major Tool & Die Co ....G.... 716 992-9200
Eden *(G-4257)*

Niagara Punch & Die Corp ....G.... 716 896-7619
Buffalo *(G-2886)*

Nijon Tool Co Inc ....F.... 631 242-3434
Deer Park *(G-3912)*

P & R Industries Inc ....E.... 585 266-6725
Rochester *(G-13604)*

P Tool & Die Co Inc ....E.... 585 889-1340
North Chili *(G-12022)*

Pacific Die Cast Inc ....F.... 845 778-6374
Walden *(G-15460)*

Palma Tool & Die Company Inc ......E.... 716 681-4464
Lancaster *(G-6820)*

Phelinger Tool & Die Corp ....E.... 716 685-1780
Alden *(G-172)*

Precision Grinding & Mfg Corp ....C.... 585 458-4300
Rochester *(G-13636)*

Pronto Tool & Die Co Inc ....E.... 631 981-8920
Ronkonkoma *(G-13997)*

Raloid Tool Co Inc ....F.... 518 664-4261
Mechanicville *(G-7694)*

Rid Lom Precision Mfg ....E.... 585 594-8600
Rochester *(G-13672)*

Rochester Stampings Inc ....F.... 585 467-5241
Rochester *(G-13698)*

S B Whistler & Sons Inc ....E.... 585 798-3000
Medina *(G-7745)*

Stamp Rite Tool & Die Inc ....G.... 718 752-0334
Long Island City *(G-7363)*

Synergy Tooling Systems Inc ....E.... 716 834-4457
Amherst *(G-246)*

Thayer Tool & Die Inc ....G.... 716 782-4841
Ashville *(G-411)*

Tips & Dies Inc ....F.... 315 337-4161
Rome *(G-13873)*

Tools & Stamping Corp ....G.... 718 392-4040
Brooklyn *(G-2510)*

Trinity Tools Inc ....E.... 716 694-1111
North Tonawanda *(G-12096)*

DIES: Cutting, Exc Metal

Royal Molds Inc ....F.... 718 382-7686
Brooklyn *(G-2361)*

DIES: Extrusion

D Maldari & Sons Inc ....E.... 718 499-3555
Staten Island *(G-14644)*

DIES: Paper Cutting

Evergreen Corp Central NY ....F.... 315 454-4175
Syracuse *(G-14890)*

DIES: Plastic Forming

Alliance Precision Plas Corp ....C.... 585 426-5310
Rochester *(G-13219)*

Alliance Precision Plas Corp ....D.... 585 426-5310
Rochester *(G-13220)*

Quality Lineals Usa Inc ....E.... 516 378-6577
Freeport *(G-5018)*

DIES: Steel Rule

Dixon Tool and Manufacturing ....F.... 585 235-1352
Rochester *(G-13351)*

Dynamic Dies Inc ....F.... 585 247-4010
Rochester *(G-13360)*

Great Lakes Pressed Steel Corp .....E.... 716 885-4037
Buffalo *(G-2784)*

National Steel Rule Die Inc ....F.... 718 402-1396
Bronx *(G-1322)*

Paragon Steel Rule Dies Inc ....F.... 585 254-3395
Rochester *(G-13610)*

DIODES & RECTIFIERS

Exc Holdings I Corp ....A.... 212 644-5900
New York *(G-9438)*

Exc Holdings II Corp ....A.... 212 644-5900
New York *(G-9439)*

Exc Holdings LP ....G.... 212 644-5900
New York *(G-9440)*

DIODES: Light Emitting

Acolyte Technologies Corp ....F.... 212 629-3239
New York *(G-8449)*

Emagin Corporation ....C.... 845 838-7900
Hopewell Junction *(G-6092)*

General Led Holdings LLC ....F.... 212 629-6830
New York *(G-9589)*

Green Logic Led Elec Sup Inc ....E.... 516 280-2854
Farmingdale *(G-4641)*

Hisun Optoelectronics Co Ltd ....F.... 718 886-6966
Flushing *(G-4859)*

Light Blue USA LLC ....G.... 718 475-2515
Brooklyn *(G-2070)*

Oledworks LLC ....E.... 585 287-6802
Rochester *(G-13589)*

S3j Electronics LLC ....E.... 716 206-1309
Lancaster *(G-6832)*

Tarsier Ltd ....C.... 646 880-8680
New York *(G-11436)*

Veriled Inc ....G.... 877 521-5520
New York *(G-11661)*

DIODES: Solid State, Germanium, Silicon, Etc

Leviton Manufacturing Co Inc ....B.... 631 812-6000
Melville *(G-7800)*

SMC Diode Solutions LLC ....G.... 631 965-0869
Plainview *(G-12714)*

DIRECT SELLING ESTABLISHMENTS: Beverage Svcs

Tao Group LLC ....G.... 646 625-4818
New York *(G-11431)*

DIRECT SELLING ESTABLISHMENTS: Food Svcs

New Dynamics Corporation ....E.... 845 692-0022
Middletown *(G-7923)*

DISCOUNT DEPARTMENT STORES

First Choice News Inc ....G.... 212 477-2044
New York *(G-9498)*

DISCS & TAPE: Optical, Blank

L & M Optical Disc LLC ....D.... 718 649-3500
New York *(G-10148)*

Sony Corporation of America ....C.... 212 833-8000
New York *(G-11295)*

Sony Dadc US Inc ....B.... 212 833-8800
New York *(G-11296)*

DISHWASHING EQPT: Commercial

Hobart Corporation ....E.... 585 427-9000
Rochester *(G-13470)*

Strategies North America Inc ....G.... 716 945-6053
Salamanca *(G-14130)*

DISINFECTING SVCS

Vital Vio Inc ....F.... 914 245-6048
Troy *(G-15194)*

DISK & DRUM DRIVES & COMPONENTS: Computers

Globalfoundries US Inc ....D.... 518 305-9013
Malta *(G-7495)*

DISK DRIVES: Computer

Formats Unlimited Inc ....F.... 631 249-9200
Deer Park *(G-3875)*

Sale 121 Corp ....D.... 240 855-8988
New York *(G-11117)*

Toshiba Amer Info Systems Inc ....B.... 949 583-3000
New York *(G-11518)*

DISPENSING EQPT & PARTS, BEVERAGE: Fountain/Other Beverage

Chudnow Manufacturing Co Inc ....E.... 516 593-4222
Oceanside *(G-12167)*

Klearbar Inc ....G.... 516 684-9892
Port Washington *(G-12896)*

DISPENSING EQPT & SYSTEMS, BEVERAGE: Liquor

Oyster Bay Pump Works Inc ....F.... 516 933-4500
Hicksville *(G-5937)*

DISPLAY FIXTURES: Showcases, Wood, Exc Refrigerated

R H Guest Inc ....G.... 718 675-7600
Brooklyn *(G-2319)*

DISPLAY FIXTURES: Wood

All Merchandise Display Corp ....G.... 718 257-2221
Highland Mills *(G-5967)*

David Flatt Furniture Ltd ....F.... 718 937-7944
Long Island City *(G-7198)*

Gotham City Industries Inc ....G.... 914 713-3449
Scarsdale *(G-14236)*

Hunter Metal Industries Inc ....D.... 631 475-5900
East Patchogue *(G-4154)*

J M P Display Fixture Co Inc ....G.... 718 649-0333
Brooklyn *(G-1981)*

Marplex Furniture Corporation ....G.... 914 969-7755
Yonkers *(G-16332)*

Mirror Show Management Inc ....D.... 585 232-4020
Webster *(G-15645)*

Specialty Services ....G.... 585 728-5650
Wayland *(G-15627)*

DISPLAY ITEMS: Corrugated, Made From Purchased Materials

General Die and Die Cutng Inc ....D.... 516 665-3584
Massapequa Park *(G-7655)*

Mp Displays LLC ....G.... 845 268-4113
Valley Cottage *(G-15319)*

Spaeth Design Inc ....E.... 718 606-9685
Woodside *(G-16225)*

DISPLAY STANDS: Merchandise, Exc Wood

Trylon Wire & Metal Works Inc ....E.... 718 542-4472
Bronx *(G-1384)*

DISTILLATES: Hardwood

Tioga Hardwoods Inc ....G.... 607 657-8686
Berkshire *(G-821)*

DOCK OPERATION SVCS, INCL BLDGS, FACILITIES, OPERS & MAINT

Kleinfelder John ....G.... 716 753-3163
Mayville *(G-7683)*

DOCKS: Floating, Wood

Meeco Sullivan LLC ....C.... 800 232-3625
Warwick *(G-15520)*

DOCKS: Prefabricated Metal

Guardian Booth LLC ....F.... 844 992-6684
Orangeburg *(G-12317)*

Guardian Booth LLC ....F.... 844 992-6684
Orangeburg *(G-12318)*

Metallic Ladder Mfg Corp ....F.... 716 358-6201
Randolph *(G-13063)*

T Shore Products Ltd ....G.... 315 252-9174
Auburn *(G-497)*

DOCUMENT EMBOSSING SVCS

Batavia Press LLC ....E.... 585 343-4429
Batavia *(G-603)*

DOLLIES: Mechanics'

Durall Dolly LLC ....F.... 802 728-7122
Brooklyn *(G-1764)*

DOLOMITE: Crushed & Broken

Dolomite Products Company Inc ......E.... 315 524-1998
Rochester *(G-13354)*

DOLOMITIC MARBLE: Crushed & Broken

Rock Iroquois Products Inc ....E.... 585 637-6834
Brockport *(G-1179)*

Tilcon New York Inc ....D.... 845 480-3249
Flushing *(G-4899)*

Tilcon New York Inc ....D...... 845 615-0216
Goshen (G-5314)
Tilcon New York Inc ....D...... 845 457-3158
Montgomery (G-8067)

DOMESTIC HELP SVCS

Custom Klean Corp ....F...... 315 865-8101
Holland Patent (G-6033)

DOOR & WINDOW REPAIR SVCS

Lif Industries Inc ....E...... 718 767-8800
Whitestone (G-16097)
United Steel Products Inc ....D...... 718 478-5330
Corona (G-3751)

DOOR FRAMES: Wood

Upstate Door Inc ....E...... 585 786-3880
Warsaw (G-15509)

DOOR OPERATING SYSTEMS: Electric

Assa Abloy Entrance Systems US ......E...... 315 492-6600
East Syracuse (G-4198)
EZ Lift Operator Corp ....F...... 845 356-1676
Spring Valley (G-14568)
V E Power Door Co Inc ....E...... 631 231-4500
Brentwood (G-1133)
Windowman Inc (usa) ....G...... 718 246-2626
Brooklyn (G-2590)

DOORS & WINDOWS WHOLESALERS: All Materials

Alvio-US Corp ....G...... 631 664-0618
Hauppauge (G-5586)
Pella Corporation ....C...... 631 208-0710
Calverton (G-3083)
Royal Windows Mfg Corp ....E...... 631 435-8888
Bay Shore (G-710)
Structural Wood Corporation ....E...... 315 388-4442
Waddington (G-15447)
Woodworks ....F...... 845 677-3960
Salt Point (G-14135)

DOORS & WINDOWS: Screen & Storm

I Fix Screen ....G...... 631 421-1938
Centereach (G-3251)
Optimum Window Mfg Corp ....E...... 845 647-1900
Ellenville (G-4309)

DOORS & WINDOWS: Storm, Metal

A & S Window Associates Inc ....E...... 718 275-7900
Glendale (G-5216)
Air Tite Manufacturing Inc ....C...... 516 897-0295
Long Beach (G-7134)
All United Window Corp ....E...... 718 624-0490
Brooklyn (G-1487)
Corkhill Manufacturing Co Inc ....E...... 718 528-7413
Jamaica (G-6438)
Excel Aluminum Products Inc ....G...... 315 471-0925
Syracuse (G-14891)
Karey Kassl Corp ....E...... 516 349-8484
Plainview (G-12693)
Pal Manufacturing Corp ....E...... 516 937-1990
Hicksville (G-5940)
Pioneer Window Holdings Inc ....E...... 516 822-7000
Roslyn Heights (G-14055)
Pioneer Window Holdings Inc ....E...... 518 762-5526
Johnstown (G-6625)
Texas Home Security Inc ....E...... 516 747-2100
New Hyde Park (G-8296)

DOORS: Dormers, Wood

Dorm Company Corporation ....G...... 502 551-6195
Cheektowaga (G-3345)

DOORS: Fire, Metal

Ace Fire Door Corp ....E...... 718 901-0001
Bronx (G-1194)
Altype Fire Door Corporation ....G...... 718 292-3500
Bronx (G-1203)
General Fire-Proof Door Corp ....E...... 718 893-5500
Bronx (G-1265)
Interntional Fireprof Door Inc ....F...... 718 783-1310
Brooklyn (G-1967)
Lif Industries Inc ....E...... 718 767-8800
Whitestone (G-16097)

M & D Installers Inc ....D...... 718 782-6978
Brooklyn (G-2092)
Mercury Lock and Door Service ....E...... 718 542-7048
Bronx (G-1310)
Metalline Fire Door Co Inc ....E...... 718 583-2320
Bronx (G-1311)
Statewide Fireproof Door Co ....F...... 845 268-6043
Valley Cottage (G-15326)
Supreme Fire Proof Door Co ....F...... 718 665-4224
Bronx (G-1374)
Universal Fire Proof Door ....E...... 718 455-8442
Brooklyn (G-2543)

DOORS: Folding, Plastic Or Plastic Coated Fabric

Custom Door & Mirror Inc ....E...... 631 414-7725
Farmingdale (G-4609)
Perma Tech Inc ....E...... 716 854-0707
Buffalo (G-2915)

DOORS: Garage, Overhead, Metal

Amarr Company ....F...... 585 426-8290
Rochester (G-13226)
Griffon Corporation ....E...... 212 957-5000
New York (G-9676)
L & L Overhead Garage Doors ....G...... 718 721-2518
Long Island City (G-7267)
Overhead Door Corporation ....D...... 518 828-7652
Hudson (G-6173)
Roly Door Sales Inc ....G...... 716 877-1515
Hamburg (G-5520)

DOORS: Garage, Overhead, Wood

Griffon Corporation ....E...... 212 957-5000
New York (G-9676)

DOORS: Glass

Executive Mirror Doors Inc ....G...... 631 234-1090
Ronkonkoma (G-13937)
Hecht & Sohn Glass Co Inc ....G...... 718 782-8295
Brooklyn (G-1930)
RB Wyatt Mfg Co Inc ....F...... 718 209-9682
Brooklyn (G-2330)

DOORS: Rolling, Indl Building Or Warehouse, Metal

Robert-Masters Corp ....G...... 718 545-1030
Woodside (G-16224)
Steelmasters Inc ....E...... 718 498-2854
Brooklyn (G-2458)
Thompson Overhead Door Co Inc ....F...... 718 788-2470
Brooklyn (G-2503)
United Steel Products Inc ....D...... 914 968-7782
Flushing (G-4904)

DOORS: Wooden

Ace Fire Door Corp ....E...... 718 901-0001
Bronx (G-1194)
Burt Millwork Corporation ....E...... 718 257-4601
Albertson (G-146)
Capital Kit Cab & Door Mfrs ....G...... 718 886-0303
College Point (G-3539)
Chautauqua Woods Corporation ....E...... 716 366-3808
Dunkirk (G-4051)
Cuccio-Zanetti Inc ....G...... 518 587-1363
Middle Grove (G-7872)
D R Cornue Woodworks ....G...... 315 655-9463
Cazenovia (G-3226)
Overhead Door Corporation ....D...... 518 828-7652
Hudson (G-6173)
Quality Millwork Corp ....E...... 718 892-2250
Bronx (G-1348)
Rj Millworkers Inc ....F...... 607 433-0525
Oneonta (G-12281)
Rochester Lumber Company ....E...... 585 924-7171
Farmington (G-4778)
Select Interior Door Ltd ....E...... 585 535-9900
North Java (G-12032)
Super Millwork Inc ....G...... 631 293-5025
Melville (G-7825)
Yesteryears Vintage Doors LLC ....G...... 315 324-5250
Hammond (G-5528)

DOWN FEATHERS

Eastern Feather & Down Corp ....G...... 718 387-4100
Brooklyn (G-1776)

DRAPERIES & CURTAINS

Abalene Decorating Services ....E...... 718 782-2000
New York (G-8425)
Associated Drapery & Equipment ....F...... 516 671-5245
Monroe (G-8014)
Baby Signature Inc ....G...... 212 686-1700
New York (G-8710)
Bettertex Inc ....F...... 212 431-3373
New York (G-8771)
Bramson House Inc ....C...... 516 764-5006
Freeport (G-4988)
Cabriole Designs Inc ....G...... 212 593-4528
New York (G-8884)
Commonwealth Home Fashion Inc ....D...... 514 384-8290
Willsboro (G-16150)
Daniels Bath & Beyond ....G...... 718 765-1915
Brooklyn (G-1724)
J Edlin Interiors Ltd ....F...... 212 243-2111
New York (G-9955)
Jo-Vin Decorators Inc ....E...... 718 441-9350
Woodhaven (G-16187)
Laregence Inc ....E...... 212 736-2548
New York (G-10173)
Majestic Curtains LLC ....G...... 718 898-0774
Elmhurst (G-4336)
Mason Contract Products LLC ....D...... 516 328-6900
New Hyde Park (G-8282)
Mistdoda Inc ....E...... 919 735-7111
New York (G-10483)
Mutual Sales Corp ....E...... 718 361-8373
Long Island City (G-7300)
Puregrab LLC ....G...... 718 935-1959
Brooklyn (G-2307)
Richloom Fabrics Corp ....F...... 212 685-5400
New York (G-11042)
Richloom Fabrics Group Inc ....G...... 212 685-5400
New York (G-11043)
Seaway Mats Inc ....G...... 518 483-2560
Malone (G-7490)
Showeray Co ....D...... 718 965-3633
Brooklyn (G-2406)
Shyam Ahuja Limited ....G...... 212 644-5910
New York (G-11221)
Terbo Ltd ....G...... 718 847-2860
Richmond Hill (G-13127)

DRAPERIES & DRAPERY FABRICS, COTTON

Designway Ltd ....G...... 212 254-2220
New York (G-9209)
Versailles Drapery Upholstery ....F...... 212 533-2059
Long Island City (G-7395)
Wallace Home Design Ctr ....G...... 631 765-3890
Southold (G-14546)

DRAPERIES: Plastic & Textile, From Purchased Materials

Anthony Lawrence of New York ....E...... 212 206-8820
Long Island City (G-7159)
C & G of Kingston Inc ....D...... 845 331-0148
Kingston (G-6681)
County Draperies Inc ....E...... 845 342-9009
Middletown (G-7901)
Deangelis Ltd ....E...... 212 348-8225
Glen Head (G-5205)
Fabric Quilters Unlimited Inc ....E...... 516 333-2866
Westbury (G-15884)
Laminated Window Products Inc ....F...... 631 242-6883
Bay Shore (G-687)
Revman International Inc ....E...... 212 894-3100
New York (G-11028)
Reynolds Drapery Service Inc ....F...... 315 845-8632
Newport (G-11899)
Wayne Decorators Inc ....G...... 718 529-4200
Jamaica (G-6487)
Wcd Window Coverings Inc ....E...... 845 336-4511
Lake Katrine (G-6764)

DRAPERY & UPHOLSTERY STORES: Draperies

Albert Menin Interiors Ltd ....F...... 212 876-3041
Bronx (G-1200)
Reynolds Drapery Service Inc ....F...... 315 845-8632
Newport (G-11899)

PRODUCT

Versailles Drapery Upholstery ....F 212 533-2059
Long Island City *(G-7395)*

DRAPES & DRAPERY FABRICS, FROM MANMADE FIBER

Pierce Arrow Drapery Mfg ....G 716 876-3023
Buffalo *(G-2918)*

DRIED FRUITS WHOLESALERS

Sahadi Fine Foods Inc ....E 718 369-0100
Brooklyn *(G-2381)*

DRILLING MACHINERY & EQPT: Water Well

Blue Tee Corp ....G 212 598-0880
New York *(G-8820)*

DRINK MIXES, NONALCOHOLIC: Cocktail

American Juice Company LLC ....G 347 620-0252
New York *(G-8555)*
Cocktail Crate LLC ....G 718 316-2033
Long Island City *(G-7188)*
Motts LLP ....C 972 673-8088
Elmsford *(G-4418)*

DRINKING PLACES: Alcoholic Beverages

Lafayette Pub Inc ....E 212 925-4242
New York *(G-10163)*

DRINKING PLACES: Night Clubs

Flushing Pharmacy Inc ....C 718 260-8999
Brooklyn *(G-1856)*

DRINKING PLACES: Wine Bar

Wolffer Estate Vineyard Inc ....E 631 537-5106
Sagaponack *(G-14103)*

DRINKING WATER COOLERS WHOLESALERS: Mechanical

Pure Planet Waters LLC ....F 718 676-7900
Brooklyn *(G-2306)*
Yr Blanc & Co LLC ....G 716 800-3999
Buffalo *(G-3053)*

DRIVE SHAFTS

Deer Park Driveshaft & Hose ....G 631 667-4091
Deer Park *(G-3860)*
Dennys Drive Shaft Service ....G 716 875-6640
Kenmore *(G-6649)*
Drive Shaft Shop Inc ....F 631 348-1818
Hauppauge *(G-5642)*
K M Drive Line Inc ....G 718 599-0628
Brooklyn *(G-2018)*

DRIVES: High Speed Indl, Exc Hydrostatic

Magna Products Corp ....E 585 647-2280
Rochester *(G-13529)*
Nidec Indus Automtn USA LLC ....E 716 774-1193
Grand Island *(G-5338)*

DRONES: Target, Used By Ships, Metal

Dz9 Power LLC ....G 877 533-5530
Olean *(G-12234)*

DROP CLOTHS: Fabric

Ace Drop Cloth Canvas Pdts Inc ....E 718 731-1550
Bronx *(G-1193)*

DRUG TESTING KITS: Blood & Urine

Yr Blanc & Co LLC ....G 716 800-3999
Buffalo *(G-3053)*

DRUGS & DRUG PROPRIETARIES, WHOL: Biologicals/Allied Prdts

Roar Biomedical Inc ....G 631 591-2749
Calverton *(G-3085)*

DRUGS & DRUG PROPRIETARIES, WHOLESALE

Alo Acquisition LLC ....G 518 464-0279
Albany *(G-38)*
Ip Med Inc ....G 516 766-3800
Oceanside *(G-12176)*

DRUGS & DRUG PROPRIETARIES, WHOLESALE: Pharmaceuticals

Amneal Pharmaceuticals LLC ....E 631 952-0214
Brookhaven *(G-1406)*
Amneal Pharmaceuticals NY LLC ....E 908 947-3120
Brookhaven *(G-1407)*
Derm-Buro Inc ....E 516 694-8300
Plainview *(G-12678)*
G C Hanford Manufacturing Co ....C 315 476-7418
Syracuse *(G-14898)*
Invagen Pharmaceuticals Inc ....B 631 231-3233
Hauppauge *(G-5678)*
Prestige Consmr Healthcare Inc..........D 914 524-6800
Tarrytown *(G-15054)*
Saptalil Pharmacueticals Inc ....G 631 231-2751
Hauppauge *(G-5758)*
Tocare LLC ....F 718 767-0618
Whitestone *(G-16101)*
Vyera Pharmaceuticals LLC ....G 646 356-5577
New York *(G-11711)*

DRUGS & DRUG PROPRIETARIES, WHOLESALE: Vitamins & Minerals

Bi Nutraceuticals Inc ....G 631 533-4934
Islandia *(G-6325)*
Healthy N Fit Intl Inc ....F 800 338-5200
Brewster *(G-1150)*
Natures Bounty Co ....D 631 244-2021
Ronkonkoma *(G-13980)*
Nbty Manufacturing LLC ....G 631 567-9500
Ronkonkoma *(G-13982)*
Unipharm Inc ....D 212 594-3260
New York *(G-11592)*
Wellquest International Inc ....G 212 689-9094
New York *(G-11740)*

DRUGS ACTING ON THE CENTRAL NERVOUS SYSTEM & SENSE ORGANS

Acorda Therapeutics Inc ....C 914 347-4300
Ardsley *(G-383)*

DRUGS AFFECTING NEOPLASMS & ENDOCRINE SYSTEMS

OSI Pharmaceuticals LLC ....D 631 847-0175
Farmingdale *(G-4700)*
OSI Pharmaceuticals LLC ....G 631 962-2000
Farmingdale *(G-4701)*

DRUGS/DRUG PROPRIETARIES, WHOL: Proprietary/Patent Medicines

Apothecus Pharmaceutical Corp ....F 516 624-8200
Oyster Bay *(G-12444)*

DRUGS: Parasitic & Infective Disease Affecting

Safetec of America Inc ....D 716 895-1822
Buffalo *(G-2971)*

DRUMS: Fiber

Greif Inc ....D 716 836-4200
Tonawanda *(G-15109)*

DRYCLEANING EQPT & SPLYS: Commercial

Q Omni Inc ....G 914 962-2726
Yorktown Heights *(G-16370)*
Thermopatch Corporation ....D 315 446-8110
Syracuse *(G-15012)*

DRYCLEANING SVC: Drapery & Curtain

Abalene Decorating Services ....E 718 782-2000
New York *(G-8425)*
Reynolds Drapery Service Inc ....F 315 845-8632
Newport *(G-11899)*

DUCTING: Plastic

Vpulse Inc ....G 646 729-5675
Brooklyn *(G-2570)*

DUCTS: Sheet Metal

Aabco Sheet Metal Co Inc ....D 718 821-1166
Ridgewood *(G-13137)*
Accurate Specialty Metal Fabri............E 718 418-6895
Middle Village *(G-7876)*
D and D Sheet Metal Corp ....F 718 465-7585
Jamaica *(G-6440)*
Delta Sheet Metal Corp ....C 718 429-5805
Hicksville *(G-5901)*
Karo Sheet Metal Inc ....E 718 542-8420
Brooklyn *(G-2021)*
Liffey Sheet Metal Corp ....F 347 381-1134
Long Island City *(G-7272)*
Nelson Air Device Corporation ....C 718 729-3801
Maspeth *(G-7629)*
United Sheet Metal Corp ....E 718 482-1197
Long Island City *(G-7388)*

DUMPSTERS: Garbage

RPI of Indiana Inc ....E 330 279-2421
Brooklyn *(G-2363)*
Wastequip Manufacturing Co LLC ....E 800 235-0734
New Lebanon *(G-8304)*

DYES & PIGMENTS: Organic

East Cast Clor Compounding Inc.........G 631 491-9000
West Babylon *(G-15708)*
F M Group Inc ....F 845 589-0102
Congers *(G-3614)*

DYES: Synthetic Organic

Jos H Lowenstein and Sons Inc ....D 718 388-5410
Brooklyn *(G-2000)*

EATING PLACES

A T A Bagel Shoppe Inc ....G 718 352-4948
Bayside *(G-733)*
Brooklynwrap Inc ....G 718 258-8088
Brooklyn *(G-1625)*
Capco Marketing ....F 315 699-1687
Baldwinsville *(G-544)*
Cascade Mountain Winery & Rest........F 845 373-9021
Amenia *(G-201)*
Culture Clash Corporation ....G 631 933-8179
Amityville *(G-261)*
Food Gems Ltd...................................E 718 296-7788
Ozone Park *(G-12462)*
Gilded Otter Brewing Co ....D 845 256-1700
New Paltz *(G-8306)*
Grass Roots Juicery ....E 718 486-2838
Brooklyn *(G-1908)*
Heron Hill Vineyards Inc ....E 607 868-4241
Hammondsport *(G-5530)*
Hyde Park Brewing Co Inc ....E 845 229-8277
Hyde Park *(G-6272)*
Lakeside Cider Mill Farm Inc ....G 518 399-8359
Ballston Lake *(G-560)*
Malina Management Company Inc ....E 607 535-9614
Montour Falls *(G-8075)*
Piemonte Home Made Ravioli Co ....F 718 429-1972
Woodside *(G-16220)*
Rawpothecary Inc ....G 917 783-7770
Brooklyn *(G-2328)*
Rosina Food Products Inc ....C 716 668-0123
Buffalo *(G-2962)*
Sign Company ....G 212 967-2113
New York *(G-11233)*

EDUCATIONAL PROGRAMS ADMINISTRATION SVCS

Stony Brook University ....E 631 632-6434
Stony Brook *(G-14741)*
Suny At Binghamton ....D 607 777-2316
Binghamton *(G-910)*

EDUCATIONAL SVCS

Amplify Education Inc ....B 212 213-8177
Brooklyn *(G-1509)*
Rainbeau Ridge Farm ....G 914 234-2197
Bedford Hills *(G-772)*

Social Science Electronic Pubg ....F 585 442-8170
  Rochester (G-13734)

EDUCATIONAL SVCS, NONDEGREE GRANTING: Continuing Education

Conference Board Inc ....C 212 759-0900
  New York (G-9081)

ELASTOMERS

Elastomers Inc ....G 716 633-4883
  Williamsville (G-16129)
Everfab Inc ....D 716 655-1550
  East Aurora (G-4086)
Rodgard Corporation ....E 716 852-1435
  Buffalo (G-2960)

ELECTRIC MOTOR REPAIR SVCS

A & C/Furia Electric Motors ....F 914 949-0585
  White Plains (G-15968)
Bailey Elc Mtr & Pump Sup LLC ....G 585 418-5051
  Corfu (G-3701)
Bayshore Electric Motors ....G 631 475-1397
  Patchogue (G-12497)
D & D Elc Mtrs & Cmpsr Inc ....F 631 991-3001
  Lindenhurst (G-6947)
Daves Electric Motors & Pumps ....G 212 982-2930
  New York (G-9176)
Electric Motor Specialty Inc ....G 716 487-1458
  Jamestown (G-6509)
General Electric Company ....E 315 456-3304
  Syracuse (G-14902)
General Electric Company ....E 518 459-4110
  Albany (G-80)
Genesis Electrical Motors ....G 718 274-7030
  Woodside (G-16208)
Lawtons Electric Motor Service ....G 315 393-2728
  Ogdensburg (G-12207)
Longo New York Inc ....F 212 929-7128
  New York (G-10249)
Power-Flo Technologies Inc ....E 585 426-4607
  Rochester (G-13631)
Prime Electric Motors Inc ....G 718 784-1124
  Long Island City (G-7328)
Tis Ansonia LLC ....F 518 272-4920
  Watervliet (G-15608)
Troy Belting and Supply Co ....D 518 272-4920
  Watervliet (G-15609)
Troy Industrial Solutions ....F 518 272-4920
  Watervliet (G-15610)
United Richter Electrical Mtrs ....F 716 855-1945
  Buffalo (G-3030)

ELECTRIC SERVICES

Besicorp Ltd ....F 845 336-7700
  Kingston (G-6680)
County Energy Corp ....G 718 626-7000
  Brooklyn (G-1692)

ELECTRIC SVCS, NEC Power Transmission

Hess Corporation ....B 212 997-8500
  New York (G-9771)

ELECTRIC SVCS, NEC: Power Generation

Caithness Equities Corporation ....E 212 599-2112
  New York (G-8888)

ELECTRICAL APPARATUS & EQPT WHOLESALERS

Aerospace Lighting Corporation ....D 631 563-6400
  Bohemia (G-967)
Amertac Holdings Inc ....G 610 336-1330
  Monsey (G-8034)
Bombardier Trnsp Holdings USA ....D 607 776-4791
  Bath (G-631)
Cummins Northeast LLC ....E 315 437-2296
  Syracuse (G-14869)
Edison Price Lighting Inc ....D 718 685-0700
  Long Island City (G-7210)
Ener-G-Rotors Inc ....E 518 372-2608
  Schenectady (G-14262)
Hammond Manufacturing Co Inc ....F 716 630-7030
  Cheektowaga (G-3352)
Linear Lighting Corporation ....C 718 361-7552
  Long Island City (G-7274)

Medi-Ray Inc ....D 877 898-3003
  Tuckahoe (G-15205)
On Line Power Technologies ....G 914 968-4440
  Yonkers (G-16336)
Pcb Piezotronics Inc ....B 716 684-0003
  Depew (G-3994)
Pompian Manufacturing Co Inc ....G 914 476-7076
  Yonkers (G-16343)
Powr-UPS Corp ....E 631 345-5700
  Shirley (G-14427)
S & J Trading Inc ....G 718 347-1323
  Floral Park (G-4820)
Satco Products Inc ....D 631 243-2022
  Edgewood (G-4282)
Schneider Electric Usa Inc ....G 631 567-5710
  Bohemia (G-1073)
Stk Electronics Inc ....E 315 655-8476
  Cazenovia (G-3235)

ELECTRICAL APPLIANCES, TELEVISIONS & RADIOS WHOLESALERS

AVI-Spl Employee ....B 212 840-4801
  New York (G-8691)
Sony Music Entertainment Inc ....A 212 833-8000
  New York (G-11298)

ELECTRICAL CONSTRUCTION MATERIALS WHOLESALERS

All-Lifts Incorporated ....E 518 465-3461
  Albany (G-37)
Morris Products Inc ....F 518 743-0523
  Queensbury (G-13049)

ELECTRICAL CURRENT CARRYING WIRING DEVICES

Associated Lightning Rod Co ....F 845 373-8309
  Millerton (G-7946)
Atc Plastics LLC ....E 212 375-2515
  New York (G-8660)
Belden Inc ....B 607 796-5600
  Horseheads (G-6114)
Charlton Precision Products ....G 845 338-2351
  Kingston (G-6685)
Cooper Power Systems LLC ....B 716 375-7100
  Olean (G-12230)
Cox & Company Inc ....C 212 366-0200
  Plainview (G-12676)
Exxelia-Raf Tabtronics LLC ....E 585 243-4331
  Piffard (G-12624)
Hubbell Inc ....E 845 586-2707
  Margaretville (G-7566)
Inertia Switch Inc ....E 845 359-8300
  Orangeburg (G-12319)
Jaguar Industries Inc ....F 845 947-1800
  Haverstraw (G-5805)
Joldeson One Aerospace Inds ....D 718 848-7396
  Ozone Park (G-12463)
Kelta Inc ....E 631 789-5000
  Edgewood (G-4273)
L3 Technologies Inc ....A 631 436-7400
  Hauppauge (G-5687)
Lighting Holdings Intl LLC ....A 845 306-1850
  Purchase (G-13006)
Lite Brite Manufacturing Inc ....F 718 855-9797
  Brooklyn (G-2079)
Lourdes Industries Inc ....D 631 234-6600
  Hauppauge (G-5700)
Mini-Circuits Fort Wayne LLC ....B 718 934-4500
  Brooklyn (G-2157)
Mono-Systems Inc ....E 716 821-1344
  Buffalo (G-2871)
NEa Manufacturing Corp ....E 516 371-4200
  Inwood (G-6300)
Orbit International Corp ....D 631 435-8300
  Hauppauge (G-5734)
Pass & Seymour Inc ....B 315 468-6211
  Syracuse (G-14963)
Reynolds Packaging McHy Inc ....D 716 358-6451
  Falconer (G-4554)
Saturn Industries Inc ....E 518 828-9956
  Hudson (G-6177)
Sinclair Technologies Inc ....E 716 874-3682
  Hamburg (G-5521)
Stever-Locke Industries Inc ....G 585 624-3450
  Honeoye Falls (G-6081)
Superpower Inc ....E 518 346-1414
  Schenectady (G-14309)

Switching Power Inc ....D 631 981-7231
  Ronkonkoma (G-14016)
Swivelier Company Inc ....D 845 353-1455
  Blauvelt (G-934)
Tappan Wire & Cable Inc ....C 845 353-9000
  Blauvelt (G-935)
Utility Systems Tech Inc ....F 518 326-4142
  Watervliet (G-15611)
Whirlwind Music Distrs Inc ....D 800 733-9473
  Rochester (G-13803)

ELECTRICAL DISCHARGE MACHINING, EDM

Fermer Precision Inc ....D 315 822-6371
  Ilion (G-6277)
Hoercher Industries Inc ....G 585 398-2982
  East Rochester (G-4164)
K & H Industries Inc ....E 716 312-0088
  Hamburg (G-5511)
Ppi Corp ....D 585 243-0300
  Rochester (G-13633)

ELECTRICAL EQPT & SPLYS

331 Holding Inc ....E 585 924-1740
  Victor (G-15389)
A & S Electric ....G 212 228-2030
  Brooklyn (G-1430)
Advanced Mfg Techniques ....G 518 877-8560
  Clifton Park (G-3460)
Altaquip LLC ....G 631 580-4740
  Ronkonkoma (G-13901)
Amertac Holdings Inc ....G 610 336-1330
  Monsey (G-8034)
Ametek Inc ....D 585 263-7700
  Rochester (G-13234)
Atlas Switch Co Inc ....E 516 222-6280
  Garden City (G-5090)
B & H Electronics Corp ....E 845 782-5000
  Monroe (G-8015)
Binghamton Simulator Co Inc ....E 607 321-2980
  Binghamton (G-860)
Bombardier Trnsp Holdings USA ....D 607 776-4791
  Bath (G-631)
Bren-Tronics Inc ....C 631 499-5155
  Commack (G-3582)
Buffalo Filter LLC ....D 716 835-7000
  Lancaster (G-6799)
Castle Power Solutions LLC ....F 518 743-1000
  Hudson Falls (G-6183)
Cathay Global Co Inc ....G 718 229-0920
  Bayside Hills (G-746)
Cooper Industries LLC ....F 315 477-7000
  Syracuse (G-14864)
Cooper Power Systems LLC ....E 716 375-7100
  Olean (G-12230)
Cooperfriedman Elc Sup Co Inc ....G 718 269-4906
  Long Island City (G-7192)
Dahill Distributors Inc ....G 347 371-9453
  Brooklyn (G-1718)
Dorsey Metrology Intl Inc ....E 845 229-2929
  Poughkeepsie (G-12951)
Eastco Manufacturing Corp ....F 914 738-5667
  Scarsdale (G-14235)
Emco Electric Services LLC ....G 212 420-9766
  New York (G-9360)
Emcom Inc ....D 315 255-5300
  Auburn (G-474)
General Electric Company ....E 315 554-2000
  Skaneateles (G-14452)
Gerome Technologies Inc ....D 518 463-1324
  Menands (G-7843)
Green Island Power Authority ....F 518 273-0661
  Green Island (G-5436)
Gsa Upstate NY ....G 631 244-5744
  Oakdale (G-12152)
Guardian Systems Tech Inc ....F 716 481-5597
  East Aurora (G-4090)
Hergo Ergonomic Support Syst ....E 888 222-7270
  Oceanside (G-12175)
Iconix Inc ....F 516 513-1420
  Hauppauge (G-5675)
Intelligent Ctrl Systems LLC ....E 516 340-1011
  Farmingdale (G-4651)
Itin Scale Co Inc ....E 718 336-5900
  Brooklyn (G-1974)
J H M Engineering ....E 718 871-1810
  Brooklyn (G-1978)
Knf Clean Room Products Corp ....E 631 588-7000
  Ronkonkoma (G-13958)
Koregon Enterprises Inc ....G 450 218-6836
  Champlain (G-3314)

PRODUCT

L3harris Technologies Inc................A....... 631 630-4200
  Amityville (G-288)
Manhattan Scientifics Inc................F....... 212 541-2405
  New York (G-10345)
Manufacturing Solutions Inc................E....... 585 235-3320
  Rochester (G-13533)
Mitsubishi Elc Pwr Pdts Inc................G....... 516 962-2813
  Melville (G-7806)
Nbn Technologies LLC................G....... 585 355-5556
  Rochester (G-13569)
OEM Solutions Inc................G....... 716 864-9324
  Clarence (G-3437)
Optimum Applied Systems Inc................F....... 845 471-3333
  Poughkeepsie (G-12977)
Piller Power Systems Inc................E....... 845 695-6658
  Middletown (G-7926)
Power Metrics Intl Inc................F....... 718 524-4370
  Staten Island (G-14692)
Quantify Energy LLC................G....... 917 268-1234
  New York (G-10951)
Ross Electronics Ltd................E....... 718 569-6643
  Haverstraw (G-5807)
Schneider Electric Usa Inc................F....... 518 452-2590
  Albany (G-129)
Schuler-Haas Electric Corp................G....... 607 936-3514
  Painted Post (G-12475)
Sima Technologies LLC................G....... 412 828-9130
  Hauppauge (G-5766)
Simulaids Inc................D....... 845 679-2475
  Saugerties (G-14212)
Skae Power Solutions LLC................E....... 845 365-9103
  Palisades (G-12482)
Smithers Tools & Mch Pdts Inc................D....... 845 876-3063
  Rhinebeck (G-13101)
U E Systems Incorporated................E....... 914 592-1220
  Elmsford (G-4438)
United Technologies Corp................B....... 866 788-5095
  Pittsford (G-12657)
Z-Axis Inc................D....... 315 548-5000
  Phelps (G-12611)

ELECTRICAL EQPT FOR ENGINES

Delphi Powertrain Systems LLC...........B....... 585 359-6000
  West Henrietta (G-15792)
Kearney-National Inc................F....... 212 661-4600
  New York (G-10087)
Leviton Manufacturing Co Inc................B....... 631 812-6000
  Melville (G-7800)
Nas-Tra Automotive Inds Inc................C....... 631 225-1225
  Lindenhurst (G-6962)
Sopark Corp................D....... 716 822-0434
  Buffalo (G-2987)

ELECTRICAL EQPT REPAIR & MAINTENANCE

A L Eastmond & Sons Inc................D....... 718 378-3000
  Bronx (G-1186)
Hobart Corporation................E....... 631 864-3440
  Commack (G-3592)
Strecks Inc................E....... 518 273-4410
  Watervliet (G-15607)

ELECTRICAL EQPT REPAIR SVCS

Siemens Industry Inc................E....... 585 797-2300
  Rochester (G-13728)
Zetek Corporation................F....... 212 668-1485
  New York (G-11821)

ELECTRICAL EQPT: Automotive, NEC

Autel US Inc................G....... 631 923-2620
  Farmingdale (G-4589)
Ev-Box North America Inc................G....... 646 930-6305
  New York (G-9422)
International Key Supply LLC................F....... 631 983-6096
  Farmingdale (G-4652)

ELECTRICAL EQPT: Household

Altan Robotech (usa) Inc................G....... 866 291-1101
  Goshen (G-5304)
Kinetic Marketing Inc................G....... 212 620-0600
  New York (G-10106)
World Trading Center Inc................G....... 631 273-3330
  Hauppauge (G-5803)

ELECTRICAL GOODS, WHOL: Vid Camera-Aud Recorders/Camcorders

Digitac LLC................G....... 732 669-7637
  Brooklyn (G-1745)

ELECTRICAL GOODS, WHOLESALE: Batteries, Dry Cell

Lyntronics Inc................E....... 631 205-1061
  Yaphank (G-16265)

ELECTRICAL GOODS, WHOLESALE: Burglar Alarm Systems

Altronix Corp................D....... 718 567-8181
  Brooklyn (G-1494)
Detekion Security Systems Inc................F....... 607 729-7179
  Vestal (G-15376)

ELECTRICAL GOODS, WHOLESALE: Capacitors

AVX Corporation................D....... 716 372-6611
  Olean (G-12223)

ELECTRICAL GOODS, WHOLESALE: Connectors

I Trade Technology Ltd................E....... 615 348-7233
  Airmont (G-12)
Sphere Cables & Chips Inc................E....... 212 619-3132
  New York (G-11322)

ELECTRICAL GOODS, WHOLESALE: Electronic Parts

Falconer Electronics Inc................D....... 716 665-4176
  Falconer (G-4541)
Intex Company Inc................D....... 516 223-0200
  Freeport (G-5003)
Oakdale Industrial Elec Corp................F....... 631 737-4092
  Ronkonkoma (G-13984)
Sj Associates Inc................E....... 516 942-3232
  Jericho (G-6595)
Veja Electronics Inc................D....... 631 321-6086
  Deer Park (G-3949)

ELECTRICAL GOODS, WHOLESALE: Facsimile Or Fax Eqpt

Alternative Technology Corp................G....... 914 478-5900
  Hastings On Hudson (G-5571)

ELECTRICAL GOODS, WHOLESALE: Fans, Household

Canarm Ltd................G....... 800 267-4427
  Ogdensburg (G-12203)

ELECTRICAL GOODS, WHOLESALE: Fittings & Construction Mat

Veja Electronics Inc................D....... 631 321-6086
  Deer Park (G-3949)

ELECTRICAL GOODS, WHOLESALE: Intercommunication Eqpt

Apple Core Electronics Inc................F....... 718 628-4068
  Brooklyn (G-1519)
Elite Cellular Accessories Inc................E....... 877 390-2502
  Deer Park (G-3869)
Ingham Industries Inc................G....... 631 242-2493
  Holbrook (G-6001)

ELECTRICAL GOODS, WHOLESALE: Light Bulbs & Related Splys

Led Waves Inc................F....... 347 416-6182
  Brooklyn (G-2056)
Olive Led Lighting Inc................G....... 718 746-0830
  College Point (G-3557)
Sir Industries Inc................G....... 631 234-2444
  Hauppauge (G-5767)

ELECTRICAL GOODS, WHOLESALE: Lighting Fittings & Access

Gagne Associates Inc................E....... 800 800-5954
  Johnson City (G-6599)
Jed Lights Inc................F....... 516 812-5001
  Deer Park (G-3888)

ELECTRICAL GOODS, WHOLESALE: Lighting Fixtures, Comm & Indl

Canarm Ltd................G....... 800 267-4427
  Ogdensburg (G-12203)
Creative Stage Lighting Co Inc................E....... 518 251-3302
  North Creek (G-12031)
Unimar Inc................F....... 315 699-4400
  Syracuse (G-15017)

ELECTRICAL GOODS, WHOLESALE: Lighting Fixtures, Residential

Prestigeline Inc................D....... 631 273-3636
  Bay Shore (G-701)
Rapid-Lite Fixture Corporation................F....... 347 599-2600
  Brooklyn (G-2327)

ELECTRICAL GOODS, WHOLESALE: Mobile telephone Eqpt

U2o Usa LLC................S....... 516 813-9500
  Plainview (G-12720)

ELECTRICAL GOODS, WHOLESALE: Motors

Electric Motor Specialty Inc................G....... 716 487-1458
  Jamestown (G-6509)
Empire Division Inc................D....... 315 476-6273
  Syracuse (G-14888)
Heating & Burner Supply Inc................G....... 718 665-0006
  Bronx (G-1275)

ELECTRICAL GOODS, WHOLESALE: Semiconductor Devices

Enplas America Inc................G....... 646 892-7811
  New York (G-9381)

ELECTRICAL GOODS, WHOLESALE: Signaling, Eqpt

BNo Intl Trdg Co Inc................G....... 716 487-1900
  Jamestown (G-6499)

ELECTRICAL GOODS, WHOLESALE: Sound Eqpt

L A R Electronics Corp................G....... 716 285-0555
  Niagara Falls (G-11945)
Magic Tech Co Ltd................E....... 516 539-7944
  West Hempstead (G-15775)
Samson Technologies Corp................D....... 631 784-2200
  Hicksville (G-5946)

ELECTRICAL GOODS, WHOLESALE: Telephone Eqpt

L3harris Technologies Inc................F....... 718 767-1100
  Whitestone (G-16096)

ELECTRICAL GOODS, WHOLESALE: Transformers

Buffalo Power Electronics Ctr................F....... 716 651-1600
  Depew (G-3974)

ELECTRICAL GOODS, WHOLESALE: VCR & Access

Toshiba America Inc................E....... 212 596-0600
  New York (G-11519)

ELECTRICAL GOODS, WHOLESALE: Vacuum Cleaners, Household

Empire Division Inc................D....... 315 476-6273
  Syracuse (G-14888)

ELECTRICAL GOODS, WHOLESALE: Video Eqpt

Bescor Video Accessories Ltd ....F 631 420-1717
Farmingdale (G-4592)

ELECTRICAL GOODS, WHOLESALE: Wire & Cable

Cortland Company Inc.....................D 607 753-8276
Cortland (G-3759)

Cygnus Automation Inc ....E 631 981-0909
Bohemia (G-997)

ELECTRICAL GOODS, WHOLESALE: Wire & Cable, Electronic

Cables Unlimited Inc ....E 631 563-6363
Yaphank (G-16256)

Dsr International Corp ....G 631 427-2600
Great Neck (G-5382)

Sphere Cables & Chips Inc ....E 212 619-3132
New York (G-11322)

ELECTRICAL INDL APPARATUS, NEC

Calibration Technologies Inc ....G 631 676-6133
Centereach (G-3250)

Energy Harvesters LLC ....G 617 325-9852
Rochester (G-13391)

ELECTRICAL SPLYS

Cooper Industries LLC ....F 315 477-7000
Syracuse (G-14864)

Rwb Controls Inc ....G 716 897-4341
Buffalo (G-2967)

Tudor Electrical Supply Co Inc ....G 212 867-7550
New York (G-11558)

Worldwide Electric Corp LLC ....E 800 808-2131
Rochester (G-13809)

ELECTRICAL SUPPLIES: Porcelain

Cetek Inc ....E 845 452-3510
Poughkeepsie (G-12948)

Corning Incorporated ....E 607 974-1274
Painted Post (G-12472)

Ferro Electronics Materials ....C 716 278-9400
Niagara Falls (G-11928)

Ferro Electronics Materials ....G 315 536-3357
Penn Yan (G-12583)

Filtros Ltd ....E 585 586-8770
East Rochester (G-4163)

ELECTRODES: Fluorescent Lamps

Preston Glass Industries Inc ....E 718 997-8888
Forest Hills (G-4926)

ELECTRODES: Indl Process

Vermont Medical Inc ....C 802 463-9976
Buffalo (G-3036)

ELECTRODES: Thermal & Electrolytic

J V Precision Inc ....G 518 851-3200
Hudson (G-6164)

Saturn Industries Inc ....E 518 828-9956
Hudson (G-6177)

ELECTROMEDICAL EQPT

Argon Medical Devices Inc ....G 585 321-1130
Henrietta (G-5855)

C R Bard Inc ....A 518 793-2531
Glens Falls (G-5244)

Caire Inc ....E 716 691-0202
Amherst (G-215)

Caliber Imging Diagnostics Inc ....E 585 239-9800
Rochester (G-13292)

Conmed Corporation ....D 315 797-8375
Utica (G-15247)

Evoke Neuroscience Inc ....F 917 261-6096
New York (G-9431)

Excel Technology Inc ....E 212 355-3400
New York (G-9442)

Fonar Corporation ....C 631 694-2929
Melville (G-7784)

Geneva Healthcare LLC ....G 646 665-2044
New York (G-9593)

Infimed Inc................................D 315 453-4545
Liverpool (G-7014)

Infimed Inc ....G 585 383-1710
Pittsford (G-12644)

J H M Engineering ....E 718 871-1810
Brooklyn (G-1978)

Jaracz Jr Joseph Paul ....G 716 533-1377
Orchard Park (G-12358)

Kal Manufacturing Corporation ....E 585 265-4310
Webster (G-15644)

Med Services Inc ....D 631 218-6450
Bohemia (G-1046)

Misonix Opco Inc ....D 631 694-9555
Farmingdale (G-4687)

Natus Medical Incorporated ....G 631 457-4430
Hauppauge (G-5725)

Netech Corporation ....F 631 531-0100
Farmingdale (G-4694)

Neurosteer Inc ....F 401 837-0351
New York (G-10573)

Pharmadva LLC ....G 585 469-1410
Rochester (G-13620)

Ray Medica Inc ....E 952 885-0500
New York (G-10986)

Sonomed Inc ....E 516 354-0900
New Hyde Park (G-8294)

Soterix Medical Inc ....F 888 990-8327
New York (G-11303)

Sun Scientific Inc ....G 914 479-5108
Dobbs Ferry (G-4020)

Ultradian Diagnostics LLC ....G 518 618-0046
Rensselaer (G-13093)

Vaso Corporation ....F 516 997-4600
Plainview (G-12722)

Vermont Medical Inc ....C 802 463-9976
Buffalo (G-3036)

Z-Axis Inc ....D 315 548-5000
Phelps (G-12611)

ELECTRON TUBES

Cuebid Technologies Inc ....G 302 380-3910
New York (G-9130)

L3harris Technologies Inc ....E 585 244-5830
Rochester (G-13511)

Y & Z Precision Inc ....F 516 349-8243
Plainview (G-12730)

ELECTRON TUBES: Cathode Ray

Passur Aerospace Inc ....G 631 589-6800
Bohemia (G-1059)

Thomas Electronics Inc....................C 315 923-2051
Clyde (G-3495)

ELECTRONIC COMPONENTS

Bud Barger Assoc Inc ....G 631 696-6703
Farmingville (G-4781)

Haynes Roberts Inc ....F 212 989-1901
New York (G-9739)

Lighthouse Components....................E 917 993-6820
New York (G-10219)

Lion E-Mobility North Amer Inc ....G 917 345-6365
Bronxville (G-1401)

Mezmeriz Inc ....G 607 216-8140
Ithaca (G-6396)

MLS Sales ....G 516 681-2736
Bethpage (G-840)

Sln Group Inc ....G 718 677-5969
Brooklyn (G-2428)

ELECTRONIC DETECTION SYSTEMS: Aeronautical

Accutrak Inc ....F 212 925-5330
New York (G-8444)

ELECTRONIC DEVICES: Solid State, NEC

Autodyne Manufacturing Co Inc............F 631 957-5858
Lindenhurst (G-6942)

Automated Control Logic Inc.............F 914 769-8880
Thornwood (G-15067)

Bharat Electronics Limited ....G 516 248-4021
Garden City (G-5092)

DJS Nyc Inc ....G 845 445-8618
Pomona (G-12807)

Enrg Inc ....F 716 873-2939
Buffalo (G-2746)

Orbit International Corp ....D 631 435-8300
Hauppauge (G-5734)

Sonotec US Inc............................C 631 415-4758
Islandia (G-6345)

Thermo Cidtec Inc........................E 315 451-9410
Liverpool (G-7045)

ELECTRONIC EQPT REPAIR SVCS

Ah Elctronic Test Eqp Repr Ctr ....F 631 234-8979
Central Islip (G-3260)

Alexy Associates Inc ....E 845 482-3000
Bethel (G-827)

Custom Sound and Video ....E 585 424-5000
Rochester (G-13334)

ELECTRONIC LOADS & POWER SPLYS

AMP-Line Corp ....F 845 623-3288
West Nyack (G-15815)

Berkshire Transformer ....G 631 467-5328
Central Islip (G-3265)

D & S Supplies Inc ....F 718 721-5256
Astoria (G-415)

Engagement Technology LLC ....F 914 591-7600
Elmsford (G-4408)

Eni Technology Inc ....B 585 427-8300
Rochester (G-13395)

Mechanical Pwr Conversion LLC ....F 607 766-9620
Binghamton (G-896)

New York Digital Corporation ....F 631 630-9798
Huntington Station (G-6255)

Pvi Solar Inc ....G 212 280-2100
New York (G-10938)

SC Textiles Inc..............................G 631 944-6262
Huntington (G-6223)

Spellman Hgh-Voltage Elec Corp ....B 631 630-3000
Hauppauge (G-5773)

Superior Motion Controls Inc ....E 516 420-2921
Farmingdale (G-4745)

Three Five III-V Materials Inc ....F 212 213-8290
New York (G-11478)

Ultralife Corporation ....B 315 332-7100
Newark (G-11854)

ELECTRONIC PARTS & EQPT WHOLESALERS

Apex Signal Corporation...................D 631 567-1100
Bohemia (G-974)

Apollo Display Tech Corp ....E 631 580-4360
Ronkonkoma (G-13908)

Becker Electronics Inc ....D 631 619-9100
Ronkonkoma (G-13915)

Bsu Inc ....E 607 272-8100
Ithaca (G-6373)

Canfield Electronics Inc ....E 631 585-4100
Lindenhurst (G-6944)

Claddagh Electronics Ltd...................E 718 784-0571
Long Island City (G-7186)

Cypress Semiconductor Corp ....F 631 261-1358
Northport (G-12102)

Electronic Devices Inc ....E 914 965-4400
Yonkers (G-16306)

Forerunner Technologies Inc.............E 631 337-2100
Edgewood (G-4268)

G B International Trdg Co Ltd...............C 607 785-0938
Endicott (G-4457)

General Microwave Corporation...........F 516 802-0900
Syosset (G-14789)

Iba Industrial Inc ....E 631 254-6800
Edgewood (G-4270)

Iconix Inc ....F 516 513-1420
Hauppauge (G-5675)

Jaguar Industries Inc......................F 845 947-1800
Haverstraw (G-5805)

Kinetic Marketing Inc......................G 212 620-0600
New York (G-10106)

L K Manufacturing Corp ....E 631 243-6910
West Babylon (G-15724)

Mill-Max Mfg Corp ....C 516 922-6000
Oyster Bay (G-12449)

New Sensor Corporation..................D 718 937-8300
Long Island City (G-7308)

Omntec Mfg Inc ....E 631 981-2001
Ronkonkoma (G-13987)

Ramsey Electronics LLC ....E 585 924-4560
Victor (G-15426)

Sag Harbor Industries Inc ....E 631 725-0440
Sag Harbor (G-14101)

Semitronics Corp ....E 516 223-0200
Freeport (G-5023)

Switching Power Inc ....D 631 981-7231
Ronkonkoma (G-14016)

PRODUCT

Ultravolt Inc ....D...... 631 471-4444
  Ronkonkoma (G-14022)
Ying Ke Youth Age Group Inc ....F...... 929 402-8458
  Dix Hills (G-4017)

ELECTRONIC SHOPPING

Ceylan & Co LLC ....G...... 646 858-3022
  New York (G-8963)
Lyteline LLC ....G...... 657 333-5983
  New York (G-10290)
Scientifics Direct Inc ....F...... 716 773-7500
  Tonawanda (G-15139)
Taazu Inc ....E...... 212 618-1201
  New York (G-11421)

ELECTRONIC TRAINING DEVICES

Ces Industries Inc ....E...... 631 782-7088
  Islandia (G-6329)
Full Circle Studios LLC ....G...... 716 875-7740
  Buffalo (G-2763)
Telephonics Corporation ....D...... 631 755-7000
  Farmingdale (G-4753)
Telephonics Corporation ....D...... 631 470-8800
  Huntington (G-6227)

ELECTROPLATING & PLATING SVC

General Galvanizing Sup Co Inc ....D...... 718 589-4300
  Bronx (G-1266)
Psb Ltd ....F...... 585 654-7078
  Rochester (G-13651)

ELEVATORS & EQPT

A & D Entrances LLC ....F...... 718 989-2441
  Wyandanch (G-16240)
Access Elevator & Lift Inc ....G...... 716 483-3696
  Jamestown (G-6491)
An Excelsior Elevator Corp ....F...... 516 408-3070
  Westbury (G-15869)
Bhi Elevator Cabs Inc ....F...... 516 431-5665
  Island Park (G-6315)
Big Apple Elevtr Srv & Consult ....G...... 212 279-0700
  New York (G-8784)
CEC Elevator Cab Corp ....D...... 718 328-3632
  Bronx (G-1221)
Dural Door Company Inc ....F...... 718 729-1333
  Long Island City (G-7206)
E Z Entry Doors Inc ....F...... 716 434-3440
  Lockport (G-7072)
Elevator Accessories Mfg ....F...... 914 739-7004
  Peekskill (G-12550)
Elevator Interiors Inc ....E...... 315 218-7186
  Syracuse (G-14884)
Herbert Wolf Corp ....G...... 718 392-2424
  Long Island City (G-7241)
Interface Products Co Inc ....G...... 631 242-4605
  Bay Shore (G-683)
Monitor Elevator Products LLC ....D...... 631 543-4334
  Hauppauge (G-5723)
National Elev Cab & Door Corp ....E...... 718 478-5900
  Woodside (G-16215)
Otis Elevator Company ....F...... 315 736-0167
  Yorkville (G-16379)
Otis Elevator Company ....E...... 917 339-9600
  New York (G-10717)
Schindler Elevator Corporation ....C...... 212 708-1000
  New York (G-11151)
Schindler Elevator Corporation ....E...... 800 225-3123
  New York (G-11152)
Velis Associates Inc ....G...... 631 225-4220
  Lindenhurst (G-6981)

ELEVATORS WHOLESALERS

An Excelsior Elevator Corp ....F...... 516 408-3070
  Westbury (G-15869)
EZ Lift Operator Corp ....F...... 845 356-1676
  Spring Valley (G-14568)

ELEVATORS: Installation & Conversion

Schindler Elevator Corporation ....E...... 800 225-3123
  New York (G-11152)

ELEVATORS: Stair, Motor Powered

S & H Enterprises Inc ....G...... 888 323-8755
  Queensbury (G-13055)

EMBLEMS: Embroidered

Eagle Regalia Co Inc ....F...... 845 425-2245
  Spring Valley (G-14567)
Glenda Inc ....G...... 718 442-8981
  Staten Island (G-14656)
Quist Industries Ltd ....F...... 718 243-2800
  Brooklyn (G-2316)
Voyager Emblems Inc ....C...... 416 255-3421
  Buffalo (G-3039)

EMBOSSING SVC: Paper

Gailer Stamping Diecutting LLC ....F...... 212 243-5662
  Long Island City (G-7227)

EMBROIDERING & ART NEEDLEWORK FOR THE TRADE

Active World Solutions Inc ....G...... 718 922-9404
  Brooklyn (G-1459)
All American Awards Inc ....F...... 631 567-2025
  Bohemia (G-968)
Control Research Inc ....G...... 631 225-1111
  Amityville (G-259)
Custom Patches Inc ....E...... 845 679-6320
  Woodstock (G-16235)
Design Archives Inc ....E...... 212 768-0617
  New York (G-9205)
Eiseman-Ludmar Co Inc ....F...... 516 932-6990
  Hicksville (G-5904)
Holland & Sherry Inc ....E...... 212 542-8410
  New York (G-9803)
Kabrics ....G...... 607 962-6344
  Corning (G-3717)
Karishma Fashions Inc ....G...... 718 565-5404
  Jackson Heights (G-6420)
Loremanss Embroidery Engrav ....F...... 518 834-9205
  Keeseville (G-6643)
Mrinalini Inc ....G...... 646 510-2747
  New York (G-10513)
NY Embroidery Inc ....E...... 516 822-6456
  Hicksville (G-5934)
Point Canvas Company Inc ....G...... 607 692-4381
  Whitney Point (G-16107)
Round Top Knit & Screening ....G...... 518 622-3600
  Round Top (G-14064)
Royal Tees Inc ....G...... 845 357-9448
  Suffern (G-14766)
Sand Hill Industries Inc ....E...... 518 885-7991
  Ballston Spa (G-586)
Screen Gems Inc ....G...... 845 561-0036
  New Windsor (G-8382)
Stephen M Kiernan ....E...... 716 836-6300
  Buffalo (G-2992)
Trimworld Inc ....F...... 212 354-8973
  New York (G-11547)
U All Inc ....E...... 518 438-2558
  Albany (G-138)
Uniform Namemakers Inc ....F...... 716 626-5474
  Buffalo (G-3028)
Wicked Smart LLC ....F...... 518 459-2855
  Watervliet (G-15612)

EMBROIDERING SVC

Aditiany Inc ....G...... 212 997-8440
  New York (G-8460)
All About Art Inc ....F...... 718 321-0755
  Flushing (G-4837)
American Quality Embroidery ....G...... 631 467-3200
  Ronkonkoma (G-13903)
Arena Graphics Inc ....G...... 516 767-5108
  Port Washington (G-12864)
Casual Friday Inc ....F...... 585 544-9470
  Rochester (G-13300)
East Coast Embroidery Ltd ....G...... 631 254-3878
  Deer Park (G-3866)
Expressions Punching & Digitiz ....G...... 718 291-1177
  Jamaica (G-6441)
F X Graphix Inc ....G...... 716 871-1511
  Buffalo (G-2750)
Hosel & Ackerson Inc ....G...... 212 575-1490
  New York (G-9814)
Human Technologies Corporation ......F...... 315 735-3532
  Utica (G-15273)
Instant Monogramming Inc ....G...... 585 654-5550
  Rochester (G-13480)
Kevin J Kassman ....G...... 585 529-4245
  Rochester (G-13502)
Mainly Monograms Inc ....E...... 845 624-4923
  West Nyack (G-15827)

Milaaya Inc ....G...... 212 764-6386
  New York (G-10465)
Northeast Stitches & Ink Inc ....E...... 518 798-5549
  South Glens Falls (G-14516)
On The Job Embroidery & AP ....G...... 914 381-3556
  Mamaroneck (G-7516)
Penn & Fletcher Inc ....F...... 212 239-6868
  Long Island City (G-7324)
Planet Embroidery ....F...... 718 381-4827
  Ridgewood (G-13155)
Rescuestuff Inc ....G...... 718 318-7570
  Peekskill (G-12555)
Sciane Enterprises Inc ....G...... 845 452-2400
  Poughkeepsie (G-12982)
Sports Depot Inc ....G...... 516 965-4668
  Baldwin (G-536)

EMBROIDERING SVC: Schiffli Machine

American Images Inc ....F...... 716 825-8888
  Buffalo (G-2631)
Rmb Embroidery Service ....G...... 585 271-5560
  Rochester (G-13676)

EMBROIDERING: Swiss Loom

Stucki Embroidery Works Inc ....F...... 845 657-2308
  Boiceville (G-1100)

EMBROIDERY ADVERTISING SVCS

Dray Enterprises Inc ....F...... 585 768-2201
  Le Roy (G-6899)
Drns Corp ....E...... 718 369-4530
  Brooklyn (G-1763)
Northeast Promotional Group In ....G...... 518 793-1024
  South Glens Falls (G-14515)

EMERGENCY ALARMS

Ademco Inc ....G...... 716 631-2197
  Cheektowaga (G-3337)
All Metro Emrgncy Response Sys ....G...... 516 750-9100
  Lynbrook (G-7424)
Johnson Controls ....D...... 585 288-6200
  Rochester (G-13493)
Johnson Controls ....E...... 518 952-6040
  Clifton Park (G-3465)
Johnson Controls ....G...... 845 774-4120
  Harriman (G-5545)
Lifewatch Inc ....F...... 800 716-1433
  Hewlett (G-5871)
Napco Security Tech Inc ....C...... 631 842-9400
  Amityville (G-297)
Octopus Advanced Systems Inc ....G...... 914 771-6110
  Yonkers (G-16335)
Synergx Systems Inc ....G...... 516 433-4700
  Woodside (G-16230)
Telemergency Ltd ....G...... 914 629-4222
  White Plains (G-16066)

EMPLOYMENT AGENCY SVCS

Equal Opprtnity Pblcations Inc ....F...... 631 421-9421
  Melville (G-7778)
Symphony Talent LLC ....D...... 212 999-9000
  New York (G-11409)
Vaultcom Inc ....E...... 212 366-4212
  New York (G-11650)

ENAMELING SVC: Metal Prdts, Including Porcelain

F & H Metal Finishing Co Inc ....F...... 585 798-2151
  Medina (G-7734)

ENAMELS

Si Group Inc ....C...... 518 347-4200
  Schenectady (G-14304)

ENCLOSURES: Electronic

Compac Development Corporation ......D...... 631 881-4903
  Edgewood (G-4265)
Kerns Manufacturing Corp ....C...... 718 784-4044
  Long Island City (G-7262)
National Computer & Electronic ....G...... 631 242-7222
  Deer Park (G-3909)

ENCODERS: Digital

Digifab Systems Inc ....G...... 212 944-9882
  New York (G-9225)

Silverlight Digital LLC..................G.....646 650-5330
New York (G-11240)

ENERGY MEASUREMENT EQPT

New York Enrgy Synthetics Inc ....G.......212 634-4787
New York (G-10596)

Performance Systems Contg Inc..........E.....607 277-6240
Ithaca (G-6404)

ENGINE REBUILDING: Diesel

D & W Diesel Inc...............................F.......518 437-1300
Latham (G-6853)

Jack W Miller...................................G.......585 538-2399
Scottsville (G-14341)

ENGINE REBUILDING: Gas

Washer Solutions Inc..........................F.......585 742-6388
Victor (G-15442)

ENGINEERING SVCS

Acad Design Corp...............................F.......585 254-6960
Rochester (G-13198)

Acme Engineering Products Inc..........E.....518 236-5659
Mooers (G-8079)

Atlantic Industrial Tech Inc ....E.....631 234-3131
Shirley (G-14415)

Auburn Bearing & Mfg Inc ....G.......315 986-7600
Macedon (G-7460)

Avanti Control Systems Inc ....G.......518 921-4368
Gloversville (G-5278)

Beltran Technologies Inc ....E.....718 338-3311
Brooklyn (G-1573)

Benfield Control Systems Inc..............F.......914 948-3231
White Plains (G-15981)

Bombardier Trnsp Holdings USA..........D.......607 776-4791
Bath (G-631)

Bsu Inc...E.....607 272-8100
Ithaca (G-6373)

Critical Link LLC...............................E.....315 425-4045
Syracuse (G-14867)

Dayton T Brown Inc ....B.......631 589-6300
Bohemia (G-1001)

Della Systems Inc ....F.......631 580-0010
Ronkonkoma (G-13930)

Digitronik Labs Inc ....F.......585 360-0043
Rochester (G-13346)

H S Assembly Inc..............................G.......585 266-4287
Rochester (G-13455)

Howden North America Inc ....D.......716 817-6900
Williamsville (G-16132)

Interntnal Elctronic Mchs Corp............E.....518 268-1636
Troy (G-15173)

Linita Design & Mfg Corp ....E.....716 566-7753
Lackawanna (G-6741)

Lourdes Industries Inc ....D.......631 234-6600
Hauppauge (G-5700)

Millennium Antenna Corp ....F.......315 798-9374
Utica (G-15284)

Mohawk Innovative Tech Inc...............F.......518 862-4290
Albany (G-100)

Photon Gear Inc ....F.......585 265-3360
Ontario (G-12297)

Remington Arms Company LLC..........A.......315 895-3482
Ilion (G-6281)

Rt Solutions LLC...............................G.......585 245-3456
Rochester (G-13709)

Sg Blocks Inc ....F.......646 240-4235
Brooklyn (G-2399)

Stone Well Bodies & Mch Inc..............E.....315 497-3512
Genoa (G-5168)

Xactiv Inc..F.......585 288-7220
Fairport (G-4531)

ENGINEERING SVCS: Building Construction

Roth Design & Consulting Inc ....E.....718 209-0193
Brooklyn (G-2357)

ENGINEERING SVCS: Electrical Or Electronic

Advanced Testing Tech Inc ....C.......631 231-8777
Hauppauge (G-5580)

C Speed LLC ....E.....315 453-1043
Liverpool (G-7004)

Nervve Technologies Inc.....................E.....716 800-2250
New York (G-10564)

Tkm Technologies Inc ....G.......631 474-4700
Port Jeff STA (G-12839)

ENGINEERING SVCS: Heating & Ventilation

Vincent Genovese..............................G.......631 281-8170
Mastic Beach (G-7675)

ENGINEERING SVCS: Industrial

Advanced Machine Design Co Inc ....E.....716 826-2000
Buffalo (G-2624)

ENGINEERING SVCS: Marine

L-3 Cmmnctns Ntronix Holdings........D.......212 697-1111
New York (G-10152)

ENGINEERING SVCS: Mechanical

Calvary Design Team Inc....................C.......585 347-6127
Webster (G-15632)

ENGINEERING SVCS: Pollution Control

Clean Gas Systems Inc ....E.....631 467-1600
Commack (G-3583)

ENGINEERING SVCS: Professional

Nasiff Associates Inc ....G.......315 676-2346
Central Square (G-3295)

ENGINEERING SVCS: Sanitary

Nes Bearing Company Inc ....E.....716 372-6532
Olean (G-12239)

ENGINEERING SVCS: Structural

Marovato Industries Inc......................F.......718 389-0800
Brooklyn (G-2119)

Tebbens Steel LLC.............................F.......631 208-8330
Calverton (G-3089)

ENGINES: Internal Combustion, NEC

AB Engine.......................................G.......518 557-3510
Latham (G-6846)

Briggs & Stratton Corporation..............F.......315 495-0100
Sherrill (G-14402)

Cummins - Allison Corp ....D.......718 263-2482
Kew Gardens (G-6662)

Cummins Inc ....A.......716 456-2111
Lakewood (G-6781)

Cummins Northeast LLC ....E.....315 437-2296
Syracuse (G-14869)

Cummins-Wagner-Siewert LLC ....E.....585 482-9640
Rochester (G-13332)

Mannesmann Corporation ....D.......212 258-4000
New York (G-10348)

Perkins International Inc ....G.......309 675-1000
Buffalo (G-2914)

ENGRAVING SVC, NEC

Bates Jackson Engraving Co Inc ....E.....716 854-3000
Buffalo (G-2657)

GTM Alap Inc....................................G.......833 345-2748
Brooklyn (G-1913)

Tripi Engraving Co Inc ....E.....718 383-6500
Brooklyn (G-2522)

ENGRAVING SVC: Jewelry & Personal Goods

Eastern Silver of Boro Park ....G.......718 854-5600
Brooklyn (G-1777)

Rayana Designs Inc ....E.....718 786-2040
Carle Place (G-3180)

With You Designs LLC........................G.......800 413-0670
Red Hook (G-13075)

ENGRAVING SVCS

Loremanss Embroidery Engrav............F.......518 834-9205
Keeseville (G-6643)

Mooney-Keehley Inc...........................G.......585 271-1573
Rochester (G-13559)

ENGRAVING: Steel line, For The Printing Trade

Lgn Materials & Solutions...................F.......888 414-0005
Mount Vernon (G-8158)

ENGRAVINGS: Plastic

Custom House Engravers Inc...............G.......631 567-3004
Bohemia (G-995)

ENTERTAINERS & ENTERTAINMENT GROUPS

Comsec Ventures International ....G.......518 523-1600
Lake Placid (G-6766)

G Schirmer Inc ....G.......212 254-2100
New York (G-9559)

Tele-Pak Inc ....E.....845 426-2300
Monsey (G-8053)

ENVELOPES

3dflam Inc ....F.......631 647-2694
Bay Shore (G-641)

Apec Paper Industries Ltd ....G.......212 730-0088
New York (G-8601)

Buffalo Envelope Inc ....F.......716 686-0100
Depew (G-3973)

Cambridge-Pacific Inc ....E.....518 677-5988
Cambridge (G-3092)

Conformer Products Inc......................G.......516 504-6300
Great Neck (G-5378)

East Cast Envlope Graphics LLC ....E.....718 326-2424
Maspeth (G-7609)

Jacmax Industries LLC......................G.......718 439-3743
Brooklyn (G-1984)

Kleer-Fax Inc ....D.......631 225-1100
Amityville (G-286)

Mercury Envelope Co Inc ....D.......516 678-6744
Rockville Centre (G-13830)

Poly-Pak Industries Inc ....B.......800 969-1933
Melville (G-7816)

Premier Packaging Corporation ....E.....585 924-8460
Victor (G-15424)

Rochester 100 Inc ....C.......585 475-0200
Rochester (G-13679)

Westrock Mwv LLC ....C.......212 688-5000
New York (G-11748)

X-L Envelope and Printing Inc ....F.......716 852-2135
Buffalo (G-3051)

ENVELOPES WHOLESALERS

AC Envelope Inc................................G.......516 420-0646
Farmingdale (G-4572)

Apec Paper Industries Ltd ....G.......212 730-0088
New York (G-8601)

Buffalo Envelope Inc ....F.......716 686-0100
Depew (G-3973)

Diversified Envelope Ltd ....F.......585 615-4697
Rochester (G-13350)

Matt Industries Inc ....C.......315 472-1316
Syracuse (G-14938)

Prestige Envelope & Lithograph ....F.......631 521-7043
Merrick (G-7863)

ENVIRONMENTAL QUALITY PROGS ADMIN, GOVT: Waste Management

City of New York................................C.......718 236-2693
Brooklyn (G-1666)

ENZYMES

D-Best Equipment Corp ....E.....516 358-0965
West Hempstead (G-15769)

Zymtrnix Catalytic Systems Inc............G.......607 351-2639
Ithaca (G-6418)

EPOXY RESINS

American Epoxy and Metal Inc ....G.......718 828-7828
Scarsdale (G-14233)

John C Dolph Company ....E.....732 329-2333
Schenectady (G-14283)

EQUIPMENT: Pedestrian Traffic Control

Cq Traffic Control Devices LLC ....G.......518 767-0057
Selkirk (G-14356)

Finger Lakes Traffic Ctrl LLC...............E.....607 795-7458
Elmira Heights (G-4376)

EQUIPMENT: Rental & Leasing, NEC

Beck Vault Company ....G.......315 337-7590
Rome (G-13845)

P R O D U C T

G E Inspection Technologies LP ....C 315 554-2000
Skaneateles (G-14451)
Millennium Stl Rack Rntals Inc.............G 718 965-4736
Brooklyn (G-2155)
Mobile Mini Inc ....F 315 732-4555
Utica (G-15285)
Raymond Corporation ....A 607 656-2311
Greene (G-5448)
Raymond Corporation ....E 315 643-5000
East Syracuse (G-4232)

ESCALATORS: Passenger & Freight

Allround Logistics Inc ....G 718 544-8945
Forest Hills (G-4916)

ETCHING & ENGRAVING SVC

Accurate Pnt Powdr Coating Inc ....F 585 235-1650
Rochester (G-13201)
Advanced Coating Service LLC............G 585 247-3970
Rochester (G-13209)
Ascribe Inc ....E 585 413-0298
Rochester (G-13252)
Custom House Engravers Inc ....G 631 567-3004
Bohemia (G-995)
Custom Laser Inc ....E 716 434-8600
Lockport (G-7066)
Modern Coating and Research ....F 315 597-3517
Palmyra (G-12491)
Pro-Tech Catings Solutions Inc ....G 631 707-9400
Edgewood (G-4279)
Steel Partners Holdings LP ....D 212 520-2300
New York (G-11352)
Stuart-Dean Co Inc ....F 718 472-1326
Long Island City (G-7372)

ETCHING SVC: Metal

Jamestown Bronze Works Inc ....G 716 665-2302
Jamestown (G-6521)

ETCHING SVC: Photochemical

Newchem Inc ....E 315 331-7680
Ithaca (G-6402)

ETHANOLAMINES

Western New York Energy LLC............E 585 798-9693
Medina (G-7749)

ETHYLENE-PROPYLENE RUBBERS: EPDM Polymers

Formosa Polymer Corporation ....G 718 326-1769
Maspeth (G-7616)
Geon Performance Solutions LLC ....E 888 910-0536
New York (G-9598)
Hilord Chemical Corporation ....E 631 234-7373
Hauppauge (G-5671)

EXCAVATING EQPT

Kinshofer Usa Inc ....E 716 731-4333
Sanborn (G-14145)
TLC Industries Inc ....F 718 596-2842
Brooklyn (G-2507)

EXERCISE EQPT STORES

TDS Fitness Equipment Corp ....F 607 733-6789
Elmira (G-4370)

EXHAUST HOOD OR FAN CLEANING SVCS

Jr Engineering Enterprise LLC.............G 716 909-2693
Grand Island (G-5335)

EXHAUST SYSTEMS: Eqpt & Parts

Classic & Performance Spc ....E 716 759-1800
Lancaster (G-6801)

EXPANSION JOINTS: Rubber

Mercer Rubber Co ....C 631 348-0282
Hauppauge (G-5713)

EXPLOSIVES

Dyno Nobel Inc ....D 845 338-2144
Ulster Park (G-15218)
Maxam North America Inc ....G 315 322-8651
Ogdensburg (G-12208)

EXPLOSIVES, EXC AMMO & FIREWORKS WHOLESALERS

Island Ordnance Systems LLC............F 516 746-2100
Mineola (G-7982)
Maxam North America Inc ....G 315 322-8651
Ogdensburg (G-12208)

EXTENSION CORDS

Ncc Ny LLC ....E 718 943-7000
Brooklyn (G-2195)

EXTRACTS, FLAVORING

Baldwin Richardson Foods Co ....B 315 986-2727
Macedon (G-7461)
Craftmaster Flavor Technology ....F 631 789-8607
Amityville (G-260)
Esense LLC ....F 718 887-9779
Long Island City (G-7215)
Virginia Dare Extract Co Inc ....C 718 788-6320
Brooklyn (G-2561)

EXTRACTS: Dying Or Tanning, Natural

Prismatic Dyeing & Finshg Inc ....D 845 561-1800
Newburgh (G-11883)

EYEGLASS CASES

Premier Glass New York Inc ....G 718 967-7179
Staten Island (G-14693)

EYEGLASSES

Allure Eyewear LLC ....G 631 755-2121
Melville (G-7759)
Colors In Optics Ltd ....D 718 845-0300
New Hyde Park (G-8257)
Corinne McCormack Inc ....F 212 868-7919
New York (G-9104)
Davis Vision Inc ....G 800 328-4728
Latham (G-6854)
Essilor Laboratories Amer Inc ....E 845 365-6700
Orangeburg (G-12314)
Frame Works America Inc ....E 631 288-1300
Westhampton Beach (G-15956)
Hirsch Optical Corp ....D 516 752-2211
Farmingdale (G-4644)
Humanware USA Inc ....D 800 722-3393
Champlain (G-3313)
M Factory USA Inc ....G 917 410-7878
Brooklyn (G-2097)
Optogenics of Syracuse Inc ....D 315 446-3000
Syracuse (G-14957)
Parker Warby Retail Inc ....D 646 517-5223
New York (G-10764)
SCR Group NY Inc ....G 516 601-3174
Brooklyn (G-2392)

EYEGLASSES: Sunglasses

Xinya International Trading Co ....G 212 216-9681
New York (G-11799)

EYES: Artificial

Mager & Gougelman Inc.......................G 212 661-3939
New York (G-10322)
Mager & Gougelman Inc.......................G 212 661-3939
Hempstead (G-5844)
Mark F Rosenhaft N A O ....G 516 374-1010
Cedarhurst (G-3241)
Strauss Eye Prosthetics Inc ....G 585 424-1350
Rochester (G-13748)

FABRIC FINISHING: Mending, Wool

Woolmark Americas Inc ....G 347 767-3160
New York (G-11777)

FABRIC STORES

Creation Baumann USA Inc ....E 516 764-7431
Rockville Centre (G-13827)
Missiontex Inc ....G 718 532-9053
Brooklyn (G-2161)
Shengkun North America Inc ....F 212 217-2460
New York (G-11211)

FABRICATED METAL PRODUCTS, NEC

Brooklyn Cstm Met Fbrction Inc...........G 718 499-1573
Brooklyn (G-1615)
James D Rubino Inc ....E 631 244-8730
Bohemia (G-1026)
Kwong CHI Metal Fabrication ....G 718 369-6429
Brooklyn (G-2039)
PBL Industries Corp ....F 631 979-4266
Smithtown (G-14483)
Range Repair Warehouse ....G 585 235-0980
Penfield (G-12572)
Total Metal Resource ....F 718 384-7818
Brooklyn (G-2513)

FABRICS & CLOTH: Quilted

American Country Quilts & Lin ....G 631 283-5466
Southampton (G-14526)
Pink Inc ....E 212 352-8282
New York (G-10843)

FABRICS: Alpacas, Mohair, Woven

Alicia Adams Alpaca Inc ....G 845 868-3366
Millbrook (G-7941)

FABRICS: Apparel & Outerwear, Broadwoven

Eldeen Clothing Inc ....G 212 719-9190
New York (G-9333)
Light House Hill Marketing...................F 212 354-1338
New York (G-10216)
Nazim Izzak Inc...................................G 212 920-5546
Long Island City (G-7304)
Oakhurst Partners LLC ....G 212 502-3220
New York (G-10672)
Pinder International Inc ....G 631 273-0324
Hauppauge (G-5741)
Yarnz International Inc.........................G 212 868-5883
New York (G-11807)

FABRICS: Apparel & Outerwear, Cotton

A and J Apparel Corp ....G 212 398-8899
New York (G-8413)
A3 Apparel LLC ....G 888 403-9669
New York (G-8422)
Accolade USA Inc ....F 302 257-5688
Cheektowaga (G-3336)
Advanced Fashions Technology ....G 212 221-0606
New York (G-8480)
Basileus Company LLC ....F 315 963-3516
Manlius (G-7543)
Benartex LLC ....E 212 840-3250
New York (G-8755)
Charming Fashion Inc ....G 212 730-2872
New York (G-8976)
Creation Baumann USA Inc ....E 516 764-7431
Rockville Centre (G-13827)
Cy Fashion Corp ....G 212 730-8600
New York (G-9139)
Do Over LLC ....G 212 302-2336
New York (G-9243)
Equipment Apparel LLC ....G 212 502-1890
New York (G-9390)
H Group LLC ....F 212 719-5500
New York (G-9703)
Hanesbrands Inc ....G 212 576-9300
New York (G-9721)
High Alchemy LLC ....F 212 224-9600
New York (G-9780)
Horizon Apparel Mfg Inc ....G 516 361-4878
Atlantic Beach (G-453)
Internationl Studios Inc ....G 212 819-1616
New York (G-9923)
Knightly Endeavors ....F 845 340-0949
Kingston (G-6697)
Magic Brands International LLC............F 212 563-4999
New York (G-10324)
Melwood Partners Inc ....F 631 923-0134
Melville (G-7803)
Phoenix Usa LLC ....G 646 351-6598
New York (G-10830)
Premium 5 Kids LLC ....F 212 563-4999
New York (G-10880)
Shahin Designs Ltd ....G 212 737-7225
New York (G-11203)
Success Apparel LLC ....D 212 502-1890
New York (G-11384)
US Design Group Ltd ....F 212 354-4070
New York (G-11623)

Vf Services LLC............G...... 212 575-7820
New York (G-11671)

FABRICS: Apparel & Outerwear, From Manmade Fiber Or Silk

Concepts Nyc Inc............E...... 212 244-1033
New York (G-9076)

JM Manufacturer Inc............G...... 212 869-0626
New York (G-10010)

New York Poplin LLC............G...... 718 768-3296
Brooklyn (G-2210)

FABRICS: Bags & Bagging, Cotton

Nochairs Inc............G...... 917 748-8731
New York (G-10635)

FABRICS: Broad Woven, Goods, Cotton

Beyond Loom Inc............G...... 212 575-3100
New York (G-8773)

Gerli & Co Inc............B...... 212 213-1919
New York (G-9603)

Lydall Thermal/Acoustical Inc............C...... 518 273-6320
Green Island (G-5440)

FABRICS: Broadwoven, Cotton

Joy of Learning............G...... 718 443-6463
Brooklyn (G-2004)

Marsha Fleisher............F...... 845 679-6500
Woodstock (G-16236)

Scalamandre Wallpaper Inc............B...... 631 467-8800
Hauppauge (G-5760)

Schneider Mills Inc............C...... 828 632-0801
New York (G-11158)

Westpoint International Inc............A...... 212 930-2000
New York (G-11747)

FABRICS: Broadwoven, Synthetic Manmade Fiber & Silk

Apex Texicon Inc............E...... 516 239-4400
New York (G-8602)

Creation Baumann USA Inc............E...... 516 764-7431
Rockville Centre (G-13827)

Eastern Silk Mills Inc............G...... 212 730-1300
New York (G-9305)

Fabric Resources Intl Ltd............F...... 516 829-4550
Great Neck (G-5386)

Fibrix LLC............G...... 716 683-4100
Depew (G-3981)

Gerli & Co Inc............B...... 212 213-1919
New York (G-9603)

Ivi Services Inc............D...... 607 729-5111
Binghamton (G-889)

Jag Manufacturing Inc............E...... 518 762-9558
Johnstown (G-6620)

Jakob Schlaepfer Inc............G...... 212 221-2323
New York (G-9970)

Scalamandre Wallpaper Inc............B...... 631 467-8800
Hauppauge (G-5760)

Schneider Mills Inc............C...... 828 632-0801
New York (G-11158)

Superior Fiber Mills Inc............E...... 718 782-7500
Brooklyn (G-2475)

Toltec Fabrics Inc............C...... 212 706-9310
New York (G-11506)

Toray Industries Inc............E...... 212 697-8150
New York (G-11517)

V Technical Textiles Inc............G...... 315 597-1674
Palmyra (G-12494)

FABRICS: Broadwoven, Wool

Acker & LI Mills Corporation............G...... 212 307-7247
New York (G-8448)

Citisource Industries Inc............E...... 212 683-1033
New York (G-9015)

Fabric Resources Intl Ltd............F...... 516 829-4550
Great Neck (G-5386)

Hawkins Fabrics Inc............E...... 518 773-9550
Johnstown (G-6618)

Scalamandre Wallpaper Inc............B...... 631 467-8800
Hauppauge (G-5760)

FABRICS: Brocade, Cotton

La Lame Inc............G...... 212 921-9770
New York (G-10158)

FABRICS: Canvas

Geordie Magee Uphl & Canvas............G...... 315 676-7679
Brewerton (G-1135)

Sita Finishing Inc............F...... 718 417-5295
Brooklyn (G-2424)

FABRICS: Chemically Coated & Treated

Kiltronx Enviro Systems Corp............E...... 917 971-7177
Hauppauge (G-5682)

Perry Plastics Inc............F...... 718 747-5600
Flushing (G-4887)

FABRICS: Coated Or Treated

Breton Industries Inc............C...... 518 842-3030
Amsterdam (G-320)

Chemprene Inc............C...... 845 831-2800
Beacon (G-749)

Chemprene Holding Inc............C...... 845 831-2800
Beacon (G-750)

Comfort Care Textiles Inc............E...... 631 543-0531
Commack (G-3584)

Eurotex Inc............F...... 716 205-8861
Niagara Falls (G-11925)

Fabric Resources Intl Ltd............F...... 516 829-4550
Great Neck (G-5386)

Newtex Industries Inc............E...... 585 924-9135
Victor (G-15421)

V Technical Textiles Inc............G...... 315 597-1674
Palmyra (G-12494)

FABRICS: Cords

Schoen Trimming & Cord Co Inc............F...... 212 255-3949
New York (G-11159)

FABRICS: Corduroys, Cotton

Paramount Cord & Brackets............G...... 212 325-9100
White Plains (G-16039)

FABRICS: Denims

Axis Na LLC............F...... 212 302-1959
New York (G-8698)

Brooklyn Denim Co............F...... 718 782-2600
Brooklyn (G-1616)

Jrg Apparel Group Company Ltd............E...... 212 997-0900
New York (G-10034)

SD Eagle Global Inc............G...... 516 822-1778
Jericho (G-6594)

Xing Lin USA Intl Corp............G...... 212 947-4846
New York (G-11798)

FABRICS: Elastic, From Manmade Fiber Or Silk

ABC Elastic Corp............G...... 718 388-2953
Brooklyn (G-1447)

FABRICS: Fiberglass, Broadwoven

Fiber Glass Industries Inc............D...... 518 842-4000
Amsterdam (G-327)

Newtex Industries Inc............E...... 585 924-9135
Victor (G-15421)

Polytex Inc............D...... 716 549-5100
Angola (G-360)

FABRICS: Glass, Narrow

Mergence Studios Ltd............F...... 212 288-5616
Hauppauge (G-5714)

FABRICS: Glove, Lining

J & M Textile Co Inc............F...... 212 268-8000
New York (G-9953)

FABRICS: Hand Woven

Thistle Hill Weavers............G...... 518 284-2729
Cherry Valley (G-3368)

FABRICS: Handkerchief, Cotton

Northpoint Trading Inc............F...... 212 481-8001
New York (G-10645)

FABRICS: Jean

Apollo Apparel Group LLC............F...... 212 398-6585
New York (G-8604)

FABRICS: Jersey Cloth

Cap USA Jerseyman Harlem Inc............G...... 212 222-7942
New York (G-8909)

FABRICS: Lace & Decorative Trim, Narrow

Eiseman-Ludmar Co Inc............F...... 516 932-6990
Hicksville (G-5904)

FABRICS: Lace & Lace Prdts

Orbit Industries LLC............F...... 914 244-1500
Mount Kisco (G-8101)

Solstiss Inc............G...... 212 719-9194
New York (G-11291)

Super-Trim Inc............E...... 212 255-2370
New York (G-11396)

FABRICS: Lace, Knit, NEC

Hosel & Ackerson Inc............G...... 212 575-1490
New York (G-9814)

Klauber Brothers Inc............E...... 212 686-2531
New York (G-10114)

FABRICS: Laminated

A-One Laminating Corp............G...... 718 266-6002
Brooklyn (G-1442)

A-One Moving & Storage Inc............E...... 718 266-6002
Brooklyn (G-1443)

New York Cutting & Gumming Co............E...... 212 563-4146
Middletown (G-7924)

Tpi Industries LLC............E...... 845 692-2820
Middletown (G-7935)

FABRICS: Linings & Interlinings, Cotton

Navas Designs Inc............E...... 818 988-9050
New York (G-10556)

FABRICS: Long Cloth, Cotton

Haleys Comet Seafood Corp............E...... 212 571-1828
New York (G-9711)

FABRICS: Nonwoven

Albany International Corp............C...... 518 445-2200
Rensselaer (G-13084)

Fabrication Enterprises Inc............E...... 914 591-9300
Elmsford (G-4409)

Legendary Auto Interiors Ltd............E...... 315 331-1212
Newark (G-11843)

Mgk Group Inc............E...... 212 989-2732
New York (G-10448)

Saint-Gobain Adfors Amer Inc............D...... 716 775-3900
Grand Island (G-5343)

Saint-Gobain Adfors Amer Inc............D...... 585 589-4401
Albion (G-161)

FABRICS: Nylon, Broadwoven

Kragel Co Inc............G...... 716 648-1344
Hamburg (G-5512)

FABRICS: Paper, Broadwoven

Albany International Corp............C...... 518 445-2200
Rensselaer (G-13084)

FABRICS: Pile Warp or Flat Knit

George Knitting Mills Corp............G...... 212 242-3300
New York (G-9600)

FABRICS: Pile, Circular Knit

Hill Knitting Mills Inc............E...... 718 846-5000
Richmond Hill (G-13115)

FABRICS: Pocketing Twill, Cotton

Cai Inc............G...... 212 819-0008
New York (G-8886)

FABRICS: Polyester, Broadwoven

Marly Home Industries USA Inc............F...... 718 388-3030
Brooklyn (G-2118)

FABRICS: Print, Cotton

Neilson International Inc............G...... 631 454-0400
Farmingdale (G-4693)

PRODUCT

FABRICS: Resin Or Plastic Coated

GE Polymershapes ....F 516 433-4092
  Hicksville *(G-5910)*

Kaneka America LLC ....D 212 705-4340
  New York *(G-10066)*

Tonoga Inc ....C 518 658-3202
  Petersburg *(G-12600)*

FABRICS: Rubberized

Chemprene Inc ....C 845 831-2800
  Beacon *(G-749)*

Chemprene Holding Inc ....C 845 831-2800
  Beacon *(G-750)*

Kelson Products Inc ....G 716 825-2585
  Orchard Park *(G-12359)*

FABRICS: Shoe

Avitto Leather Goods Inc ....G 212 219-7501
  New York *(G-8693)*

FABRICS: Silk, Broadwoven

Beyond Loom Inc ....G 212 575-3100
  New York *(G-8773)*

Himatsingka America Inc ....E 212 252-0802
  New York *(G-9788)*

Himatsingka Holdings NA Inc ....G 212 824-2949
  New York *(G-9789)*

FABRICS: Silk, Narrow

Solstiss Inc ....G 212 719-9194
  New York *(G-11291)*

FABRICS: Spandex, Broadwoven

La Lame Inc ....G 212 921-9770
  New York *(G-10158)*

FABRICS: Specialty Including Twisted Weaves, Broadwoven

Intertex USA Inc ....F 212 279-3601
  New York *(G-9925)*

FABRICS: Stretch, Cotton

Shindo Usa Inc ....G 212 868-9311
  New York *(G-11215)*

FABRICS: Surgical Fabrics, Cotton

Medline Industries Inc ....B 845 344-3301
  Middletown *(G-7919)*

FABRICS: Tapestry, Cotton

Renaissnce Crpt Tapestries Inc ....F 212 696-0080
  New York *(G-11011)*

FABRICS: Tricot

Hudson Fabrics LLC ....F 518 671-6100
  Hudson *(G-6162)*

Litchfield Fabrics of NC ....G 518 773-9500
  Gloversville *(G-5288)*

Veratex Inc ....F 212 683-9300
  New York *(G-11659)*

FABRICS: Trimmings

Albert Siy ....G 718 359-0389
  Flushing *(G-4836)*

American Spray-On Corp ....E 212 929-2100
  New York *(G-8559)*

Angel Textiles Inc ....G 212 532-0900
  New York *(G-8582)*

Athletic Cap Co Inc ....G 718 398-1300
  Staten Island *(G-14621)*

Barnaby Prints Inc ....F 845 477-2501
  Greenwood Lake *(G-5479)*

Bondy Printing Corp ....G 631 242-1510
  Bay Shore *(G-659)*

C H Thompson Company Inc ......D 607 724-1094
  Binghamton *(G-866)*

Coe Displays Inc ....G 718 937-5658
  Long Island City *(G-7189)*

Cooper & Clement Inc ....E 315 454-8135
  Syracuse *(G-14861)*

Decal Makers Inc ....E 516 221-7200
  Bellmore *(G-781)*

Eagle Lace Dyeing Corp ....F 212 947-2712
  New York *(G-9297)*

Emtron Hybrids Inc ....F 631 924-9668
  Yaphank *(G-16261)*

Flp Group LLC ....F 315 252-7583
  Auburn *(G-476)*

Folder Factory Inc ....F 540 477-3852
  Melville *(G-7783)*

Freeport Screen & Stamping ......E 516 379-0330
  Freeport *(G-4998)*

Ihd Motorsports LLC ....F 979 690-1669
  Binghamton *(G-886)*

Jack J Florio Jr ....G 716 434-9123
  Lockport *(G-7085)*

Kenmar Shirts Inc ....E 718 824-3880
  Bronx *(G-1291)*

L I C Screen Printing Inc ....E 516 546-7289
  Merrick *(G-7858)*

Loremanss Embroidery Engrav ....F 518 834-9205
  Keeseville *(G-6643)*

Master Craft Finishers Inc ....E 631 586-0540
  Deer Park *(G-3904)*

Master Image Printing Inc ....G 914 347-4400
  Elmsford *(G-4416)*

New York Binding Co Inc ....E 718 729-2454
  Long Island City *(G-7309)*

Northeast Stitches & Ink Inc ......E 518 798-5549
  South Glens Falls *(G-14516)*

Round Top Knit & Screening ......G 518 622-3600
  Round Top *(G-14064)*

Sellco Industries Inc ....E 607 756-7594
  Cortland *(G-3788)*

Solidus Industries Inc. ....D 607 749-4540
  Homer *(G-6067)*

Todd Walbridge ....G 585 254-3018
  Rochester *(G-13768)*

U All Inc ....E 518 438-2558
  Albany *(G-138)*

FABRICS: Trimmings, Textile

American Trim Mfg Inc ....E 518 239-8151
  Durham *(G-4070)*

Bardwil Industries Inc. ....C 212 944-1870
  New York *(G-8727)*

Champion Zipper Corp ....G 212 239-0414
  New York *(G-8969)*

Danray Textiles Corp ....F 212 354-5213
  New York *(G-9169)*

Jakob Schlaepfer Inc ....G 212 221-2323
  New York *(G-9970)*

Marketing Action Xecutives Inc ....G 212 971-9155
  New York *(G-10370)*

Scalamandre Silks Inc. ....G 212 980-3888
  New York *(G-11147)*

FABRICS: Upholstery, Cotton

Meder Textile Co Inc ....G 516 883-0409
  Port Washington *(G-12904)*

Mgk Group Inc ....E 212 989-2732
  New York *(G-10448)*

FABRICS: Varnished Glass & Coated Fiberglass

Architectural Fiberglass Corp ......E 631 842-4772
  Copiague *(G-3645)*

FABRICS: Wall Covering, From Manmade Fiber Or Silk

Art People Inc ....G 212 431-4865
  New York *(G-8629)*

Mgk Group Inc ....E 212 989-2732
  New York *(G-10448)*

National Contract Industries ......G 212 249-0045
  New York *(G-10541)*

FABRICS: Warp & Flat Knit Prdts

Fab Industries Corp ....B 516 498-3200
  Great Neck *(G-5385)*

Gehring Tricot Corporation ....C 315 429-8551
  Dolgeville *(G-4023)*

Ssjjj Manufacturing LLC ....B 516 498-3200
  Great Neck *(G-5423)*

FABRICS: Warp Knit, Lace & Netting

Apex Aridyne Corp ....G 516 239-4400
  Inwood *(G-6287)*

Helmont Mills Inc ....G 518 568-7913
  Saint Johnsville *(G-14118)*

Mohawk Fabric Company Inc ......F 518 842-3090
  Amsterdam *(G-338)*

Somerset Industries Inc ....E 518 773-7383
  Gloversville *(G-5292)*

Sunwin Global Industry Inc ....G 646 370-6196
  New York *(G-11395)*

FABRICS: Weft Or Circular Knit

Apex Aridyne Corp ....G 516 239-4400
  Inwood *(G-6287)*

Apex Texicon Inc ....G 516 239-4400
  New York *(G-8602)*

FABRICS: Woven, Narrow Cotton, Wool, Silk

Albany International Corp ....C 518 445-2200
  Rensselaer *(G-13084)*

American Canvas Binders Corp ....G 914 969-0300
  Yonkers *(G-16284)*

Breton Industries Inc ....E 518 842-3030
  Amsterdam *(G-320)*

Depot Label Company Inc ....G 631 467-2952
  Patchogue *(G-12499)*

Labeltex Mills Inc ....G 212 279-6165
  New York *(G-10161)*

Newtex Industries Inc ....E 585 924-9135
  Victor *(G-15421)*

Skil-Care Corporation ....G 914 963-2040
  Yonkers *(G-16348)*

Valley Industrial Products Inc ......E 631 385-9300
  Huntington *(G-6231)*

FACILITIES SUPPORT SVCS

Johnson Controls Inc ....C 585 724-2232
  Rochester *(G-13495)*

FACSIMILE COMMUNICATION EQPT

Alternative Technology Corp ....G 914 478-5900
  Hastings On Hudson *(G-5571)*

FAMILY CLOTHING STORES

Kate Spade Holdings LLC ....B 212 354-4900
  New York *(G-10076)*

Land n Sea Inc ....D 212 444-6000
  New York *(G-10168)*

Loungehouse LLC ....E 646 524-2965
  New York *(G-10272)*

Missiontex Inc ....G 718 532-9053
  Brooklyn *(G-2161)*

Ramsbury Property Us Inc ....F 212 223-6250
  New York *(G-10976)*

Round Top Knit & Screening ......G 518 622-3600
  Round Top *(G-14064)*

S & T Knitting Co Inc ....E 607 722-7558
  Conklin *(G-3628)*

X Vision Inc ....G 917 412-3570
  New York *(G-11796)*

FANS, BLOWING: Indl Or Commercial

Apgn Inc ....E 518 324-4150
  Plattsburgh *(G-12732)*

Canarm Ltd ....G 800 267-4427
  Ogdensburg *(G-12203)*

Oestreich Metal Works Inc ....G 315 463-4268
  Syracuse *(G-14953)*

Rapid Fan & Blower Inc ....F 718 786-2060
  Long Island City *(G-7339)*

FANS, EXHAUST: Indl Or Commercial

Howden North America Inc ....D 330 867-8540
  Depew *(G-3985)*

Jr Engineering Enterprise LLC ....G 716 909-2693
  Grand Island *(G-5335)*

FANS, VENTILATING: Indl Or Commercial

Howden North America Inc ....D 716 817-6900
  Williamsville *(G-16132)*

FARM & GARDEN MACHINERY WHOLESALERS

Oxbo International Corporation ......D 585 548-2665
  Byron *(G-3062)*

Saxby Implement Corp ....F 585 624-2938
  Mendon *(G-7852)*

FARM PRDTS, RAW MATERIALS, WHOLESALE: Bristles

Cenibra Inc...............................G........ 212 818-8242
New York *(G-8947)*

FARM PRDTS, RAW MATERIALS, WHOLESALE: Hides

Hastings Hide Inc.........................G........ 516 295-2400
Inwood *(G-6295)*

FARM SPLY STORES

Bailey Boonville Mills Inc...........G........ 315 942-2131
Boonville *(G-1103)*
Gramco Inc................................G........ 716 592-2845
Springville *(G-14592)*
Lowville Farmers Coop Inc..........E........ 315 376-6587
Lowville *(G-7417)*

FARM SPLYS, WHOLESALE: Beekeeping Splys, Nondurable

Northast Ctr For Bekeeping LLC..........F........ 800 632-3379
Greenwich *(G-5474)*

FASTENERS: Metal

John Hassall LLC.........................D........ 516 334-6200
Westbury *(G-15898)*
Pmb Precision Products Inc..........F........ 631 491-6753
West Babylon *(G-15737)*
Universal Metals Inc....................G........ 516 829-0896
Great Neck *(G-5430)*

FASTENERS: Metal

D Best Service Co Inc..................G........ 718 972-6133
Brooklyn *(G-1715)*
Southco Inc................................B........ 585 624-2545
Honeoye Falls *(G-6080)*

FASTENERS: Notions, NEC

American Pride Fasteners LLC.........E........ 631 940-8292
Bay Shore *(G-649)*
CPI of Falconer Inc.....................E........ 716 664-4444
Falconer *(G-4537)*
Cw Fasteners & Zippers Corp.........F........ 212 594-3203
New York *(G-9138)*
Jem Threading Specialties Inc.........G........ 718 665-3341
Bronx *(G-1285)*
Kenwin Sales Corp......................G........ 516 933-7553
Deer Park *(G-3891)*

FASTENERS: Notions, Snaps

M H Stryke Co Inc.......................F........ 631 242-2660
Deer Park *(G-3902)*
Rings Wire Inc............................G........ 212 741-9779
New York *(G-11045)*

FASTENERS: Notions, Zippers

Champion Zipper Corp..................G........ 212 239-0414
New York *(G-8969)*
Riri USA Inc................................G........ 212 268-3866
New York *(G-11046)*

FAUCETS & SPIGOTS: Metal & Plastic

Faucets and More Incorporated..........G........ 734 328-2387
Brooklyn *(G-1833)*
Giagni Enterprises LLC................G........ 914 699-6500
Mount Vernon *(G-8143)*
Hanco Metal Products Inc.............F........ 212 787-5992
Brooklyn *(G-1924)*

FEATHERS: Renovating

Eser Realty Corp.........................E........ 718 383-0565
Brooklyn *(G-1811)*

FELT: Acoustic

Ghani Textiles Inc.......................G........ 718 859-4561
Brooklyn *(G-1884)*
Soundcoat Company Inc................D........ 631 242-2200
Deer Park *(G-3938)*

FELT: Automotive

Rli Schlgel Specialty Pdts LLC..........G........ 585 627-5919
Rochester *(G-13675)*

FENCE POSTS: Iron & Steel

Bonura and Sons Iron Works..........F........ 718 381-4100
Franklin Square *(G-4959)*

FENCES & FENCING MATERIALS

Rose Fence Inc...........................D........ 516 790-2308
Halesite *(G-5489)*
Sunward Electronics Inc...............F........ 518 687-0030
Troy *(G-15191)*

FENCES OR POSTS: Ornamental Iron Or Steel

786 Iron Works Corp...................G........ 718 418-4808
Brooklyn *(G-1424)*
Empire Steel Works Inc................F........ 516 561-3500
Hicksville *(G-5905)*
Fence Plaza Corp........................G........ 718 469-2200
Brooklyn *(G-1838)*
Jamaica Iron Works Inc................F........ 718 657-4849
Jamaica *(G-6451)*
McAllisters Precision Wldg Inc.........F........ 518 221-3455
Menands *(G-7844)*
Ourem Iron Works Inc..................F........ 914 476-4856
Yonkers *(G-16337)*
Tee Pee Fence and Railing............F........ 718 658-8323
Jamaica *(G-6479)*
Triple H Construction Inc.............E........ 516 280-8252
Jamaica *(G-6481)*

FENCING DEALERS

A & T Iron Works Inc..................E........ 914 632-8992
New Rochelle *(G-8315)*
Fence Plaza Corp........................G........ 718 469-2200
Brooklyn *(G-1838)*
Long Lumber and Supply Corp.........F........ 518 439-1661
Slingerlands *(G-14466)*
Rose Fence Inc...........................F........ 516 223-0777
Baldwin *(G-533)*
Walpole Woodworkers Inc.............G........ 631 726-2859
Water Mill *(G-15531)*

FENCING MATERIALS: Docks & Other Outdoor Prdts, Wood

Atlas Fence & Railing Co Inc.........E........ 718 767-2200
Whitestone *(G-16088)*
Cffco USA Inc.............................G........ 718 747-1118
Jericho *(G-6573)*

FENCING MATERIALS: Plastic

Atlas Fence & Railing Co Inc.........E........ 718 767-2200
Whitestone *(G-16088)*
Oneonta Fence...........................G........ 607 433-6707
Oneonta *(G-12278)*

FENCING MATERIALS: Wood

Interstate Wood Products Inc.........E........ 631 842-4488
Amityville *(G-277)*
Long Lumber and Supply Corp.........F........ 518 439-1661
Slingerlands *(G-14466)*
Rose Fence Inc...........................F........ 516 223-0777
Baldwin *(G-533)*
Walpole Woodworkers Inc.............G........ 631 726-2859
Water Mill *(G-15531)*

FENCING: Chain Link

Master-Halco Inc........................F........ 631 585-8150
Yaphank *(G-16266)*

FERRITES

Hoosier Magnetics Inc..................E........ 315 323-5832
Ogdensburg *(G-12206)*

FERROALLOYS

CCA Holding Inc..........................C........ 716 446-8800
Amherst *(G-216)*
Medima LLC................................C........ 716 741-0400
Clarence *(G-3436)*

FERROMANGANESE, NOT MADE IN BLAST FURNACES

Globe Metallurgical Inc................D........ 716 804-0862
Niagara Falls *(G-11931)*

FERTILIZERS: NEC

Biosoil Farm Inc.........................G........ 518 344-4920
Glenville *(G-5270)*
Carolina Eastern-Vail Inc.............E........ 518 854-9785
Salem *(G-14132)*
Commodity Resource Corporation.....F........ 585 538-9500
Caledonia *(G-3069)*

FERTILIZERS: Nitrogenous

Rt Solutions LLC.........................G........ 585 245-3456
Rochester *(G-13709)*

FERTILIZERS: Phosphatic

Occidental Chemical Corp.............C........ 716 278-7794
Niagara Falls *(G-11960)*

FIBER & FIBER PRDTS: Acrylic

Solid Surface Acrylics LLC...........F........ 716 743-1870
North Tonawanda *(G-12091)*

FIBER & FIBER PRDTS: Fluorocarbon

Dynax Corporation.......................G........ 914 764-0202
Pound Ridge *(G-12992)*

FIBER & FIBER PRDTS: Organic, Noncellulose

Dal-Tile Corporation....................G........ 718 894-9574
Maspeth *(G-7604)*
Fibrix LLC...................................E........ 716 683-4100
Depew *(G-3981)*
Solutia Business Entps Inc............F........ 314 674-1000
New York *(G-11293)*

FIBER & FIBER PRDTS: Polyester

Marly Home Industries USA Inc.........F........ 718 388-3030
Brooklyn *(G-2118)*
Stein Fibers Ltd..........................E........ 518 489-5700
Albany *(G-132)*

FIBER & FIBER PRDTS: Synthetic Cellulosic

3M Company................................B........ 716 876-1596
Tonawanda *(G-15080)*
Cortland Cable Company Inc...........E........ 607 753-8276
Cortland *(G-3758)*
Cytec Industries Inc....................D........ 716 372-9650
Olean *(G-12231)*
E I Du Pont De Nemours & Co.........E........ 716 876-4420
Buffalo *(G-2734)*
J Rettenmaier USA LP..................D........ 716 693-4040
North Tonawanda *(G-12074)*
J Rettenmaier USA LP..................D........ 716 693-4009
North Tonawanda *(G-12075)*

FIBER & FIBER PRDTS: Vinyl

Jaclyn LLC..................................D........ 201 909-6000
New York *(G-9963)*

FIBER OPTICS

Biolitec Inc.................................E........ 413 525-0600
New York *(G-8798)*
Complete Fiber Solutions Inc.........G........ 718 828-8900
Bronx *(G-1230)*
Photonic Controls LLC..................F........ 607 562-4585
Horseheads *(G-6132)*

FIBERS: Carbon & Graphite

Metal Coated Fibers Inc...............E........ 518 280-8514
Schenectady *(G-14288)*

FILLERS & SEALERS: Wood

Uc Coatings LLC.........................E........ 716 833-9366
Buffalo *(G-3026)*

FILM & SHEET: Unsuppported Plastic

American Acrylic Corporation.........E........ 631 422-2200
West Babylon *(G-15687)*

PRODUCT

API Industries Inc ....B 845 365-2200
  Orangeburg *(G-12305)*
API Industries Inc ....C 845 365-2200
  Orangeburg *(G-12306)*
Berry Global Inc ....C 315 986-2161
  Macedon *(G-7462)*
Berry Global Inc ....C 315 484-0397
  Solvay *(G-14494)*
Berry Plastics Corporation ....B 315 986-6270
  Macedon *(G-7463)*
Comco Plastics Inc ....E 718 849-9000
  Huntington Station *(G-6242)*
Excellent Poly Inc ....F 718 768-6555
  Brooklyn *(G-1820)*
Franklin Poly Film Inc ....E 718 492-3523
  Brooklyn *(G-1865)*
Great Lakes Plastics Co Inc ....E 716 896-3100
  Buffalo *(G-2783)*
Kent Chemical Corporation ....E 212 521-1700
  New York *(G-10094)*
Knf Clean Room Products Corp ...E 631 588-7000
  Ronkonkoma *(G-13958)*
Msi Inc ....F 845 639-6683
  New City *(G-8227)*
Nap Industries Inc ....D 718 625-4948
  Brooklyn *(G-2187)*
Nova Packaging Ltd Inc ....E 914 232-8406
  Katonah *(G-6637)*
Oaklee International Inc ....E 631 436-7900
  Ronkonkoma *(G-13985)*
Pliant LLC ....B 315 986-6286
  Macedon *(G-7469)*
R & F Boards & Dividers Inc ....G 718 331-1529
  Brooklyn *(G-2317)*
Rainbow Poly Bag Co Inc ....E 718 386-3500
  Brooklyn *(G-2326)*
Sand Hill Industries Inc ....G 518 885-7991
  Ballston Spa *(G-586)*
Scapa North America ....E 315 413-1111
  Liverpool *(G-7039)*
Swimline Corp ....C 631 254-2155
  Edgewood *(G-4284)*
Toray Industries Inc ....G 212 697-8150
  New York *(G-11517)*
Trinity Packaging Corporation ....E 716 668-3111
  Buffalo *(G-3020)*
Turner Bellows Inc ....E 585 235-4456
  Rochester *(G-13778)*

FILM BASE: Cellulose Acetate Or Nitrocellulose Plastics

Bfgg Investors Group LLC ....G 585 424-3456
  Rochester *(G-13268)*
Island Pyrochemical Inds Corp ....C 516 746-2100
  Mineola *(G-7983)*

FILM: Motion Picture

Big Indie - Beautiful Boy LLC .....G 917 464-5599
  Woodstock *(G-16234)*
Dolby Laboratories Inc ....F 212 767-1700
  New York *(G-9245)*

FILTERS

Acme Engineering Products Inc ....E 518 236-5659
  Mooers *(G-8079)*
Burnett Process Inc ....E 585 277-1623
  Rochester *(G-13289)*
Foseco Inc ....F 914 345-4760
  Tarrytown *(G-15044)*
Hilliard Corporation ....B 607 733-7121
  Elmira *(G-4357)*
Hilliard Corporation ....G 607 733-7121
  Elmira *(G-4358)*
Lydall Performance Mtls Inc ....F 518 273-6320
  Green Island *(G-5439)*
Pall Corporation ....A 516 484-5400
  Port Washington *(G-12913)*
Pall Corporation ....A 607 753-6041
  Cortland *(G-3779)*
Parker-Hannifin Corporation ......D 716 685-4040
  Lancaster *(G-6822)*
Peregrine Industries Inc ....E 631 838-2870
  New York *(G-10801)*
Pyrotek Incorporated ....E 716 731-3221
  Sanborn *(G-14148)*
SC Supply Chain Management LLC ...G 212 344-3322
  New York *(G-11146)*
Sinclair International Company ....D 518 798-2361
  Queensbury *(G-13057)*

Stavo Industries Inc ....E 845 331-5389
  Kingston *(G-6713)*

FILTERS & SOFTENERS: Water, Household

Menpin Supply Corp ....F 718 415-4168
  Brooklyn *(G-2136)*
Pure Planet Waters LLC ....F 718 676-7900
  Brooklyn *(G-2306)*
Water Technologies Inc ....G 315 986-0000
  Macedon *(G-7471)*

FILTERS: Air

Air Engineering Filters Inc ....G 914 238-5945
  Chappaqua *(G-3322)*
Air Export Mechanical ....G 917 709-5310
  Flushing *(G-4835)*
Filta Clean Co Inc ....E 718 495-3800
  Brooklyn *(G-1843)*
Healthway Home Products Inc .....E 315 298-2904
  Pulaski *(G-13000)*
Isolation Systems Inc ....F 716 694-6390
  North Tonawanda *(G-12073)*
Nexstar Holding Corp ....E 716 929-9000
  Amherst *(G-234)*
Northland Filter Intl LLC ....E 315 207-1410
  Oswego *(G-12415)*
Pliotron Company America LLC .....E 716 298-4457
  Niagara Falls *(G-11965)*
R P Fedder Corp ....E 585 288-1600
  Rochester *(G-13666)*
Roome Technologies Inc ....E 585 229-4437
  Honeoye *(G-6069)*

FILTERS: Air Intake, Internal Combustion Engine, Exc Auto

Modern-TEC Manufacturing Inc ....G 716 625-8700
  Lockport *(G-7094)*
Pall Corporation ....A 516 484-5400
  Port Washington *(G-12913)*
Pall Corporation ....A 607 753-6041
  Cortland *(G-3779)*

FILTERS: General Line, Indl

Adams Sfc Inc ....E 716 877-2608
  Tonawanda *(G-15082)*
American Felt & Filter Co Inc ......D 845 561-3560
  New Windsor *(G-8359)*
American Filtration Tech Inc ....F 585 359-4130
  West Henrietta *(G-15783)*
Cross Filtration Ltd Lblty Co ....F 315 412-1539
  Moravia *(G-8082)*
Filter Tech Inc ....D 315 682-8815
  Manlius *(G-7546)*
Graver Technologies LLC ....E 585 624-1330
  Honeoye Falls *(G-6072)*
North American Filter Corp ....D 800 265-8943
  Newark *(G-11848)*
Service Filtration Corp ....E 716 877-2608
  Tonawanda *(G-15140)*
Sidco Filter Corporation ....E 585 289-3100
  Manchester *(G-7529)*
Stavo Industries Inc ....F 845 331-4552
  Kingston *(G-6712)*

FILTERS: Motor Vehicle

P & F Industries Inc ....E 631 694-9800
  Melville *(G-7813)*
Pall Corporation ....A 516 484-5400
  Port Washington *(G-12913)*
Pall Corporation ....A 607 753-6041
  Cortland *(G-3779)*

FILTERS: Paper

Folia Water Inc ....G 412 802-5083
  New York *(G-9514)*

FILTRATION DEVICES: Electronic

Fil-Coil (fc) Corp ....E 631 467-5328
  Sayville *(G-14226)*
Frequency Selective Networks ....F 718 424-7500
  Valley Stream *(G-15341)*
Microwave Filter Company Inc .....E 315 438-4700
  East Syracuse *(G-4226)*
MTK Electronics Inc ....E 631 924-7666
  Medford *(G-7720)*

Service Filtration Corp ....E 716 877-2608
  Tonawanda *(G-15140)*
Tte Filters LLC ....G 716 532-2234
  Gowanda *(G-5323)*

FINANCIAL INVESTMENT ACTIVITIES, NEC: Financial Reporting

Dow Jones & Company Inc ....E 212 597-5983
  New York *(G-9259)*
Ruby Newco LLC ....G 212 852-7000
  New York *(G-11096)*

FINANCIAL INVESTMENT ADVICE

Bernhard Arnold & Company Inc ...G 212 907-1500
  New York *(G-8763)*
Envy Publishing Group Inc ....G 212 253-9874
  New York *(G-9385)*
Investors Business Daily Inc ....F 212 626-7676
  New York *(G-9936)*
Moneypaper Inc ....F 914 925-0022
  Rye *(G-14083)*
Swaps Monitor Publications Inc ...F 212 742-8550
  New York *(G-11404)*

FINDINGS & TRIMMINGS Fabric, NEC

Lending Trimming Co Inc ....D 212 242-7502
  New York *(G-10195)*

FINDINGS & TRIMMINGS Waistbands, Trouser

Cai Inc ....G 212 819-0008
  New York *(G-8886)*

FINDINGS & TRIMMINGS: Apparel

Mas Cutting Inc ....G 212 869-0826
  New York *(G-10378)*

FINDINGS & TRIMMINGS: Fabric

Legendary Auto Interiors Ltd ......E 315 331-1212
  Newark *(G-11843)*
Rli Schlgel Specialty Pdts LLC .....G 585 627-5919
  Rochester *(G-13675)*

FINGERNAILS, ARTIFICIAL

Ivy Enterprises Inc ....B 516 621-9779
  Port Washington *(G-12890)*

FINGERPRINT EQPT

Fingerprint America Inc ....G 518 435-1609
  Albany *(G-77)*

FINISHING AGENTS: Leather

Androme Leather Inc ....F 518 773-7945
  Gloversville *(G-5277)*

FIRE ARMS, SMALL: Guns Or Gun Parts, 30 mm & Below

Dark Storm Industries LLC ....G 631 967-3170
  Oakdale *(G-12150)*
Oriskany Arms Inc ....F 315 737-2196
  Oriskany *(G-12393)*
Remington Arms Company LLC .....A 315 895-3482
  Ilion *(G-6281)*

FIRE ARMS, SMALL: Pellet & BB guns

Benjamin Sheridan Corporation ...G 585 657-6161
  Bloomfield *(G-940)*
Crosman Corporation ....E 585 657-6161
  Bloomfield *(G-945)*
Crosman Corporation ....E 585 398-3920
  Farmington *(G-4769)*

FIRE ARMS, SMALL: Rifles Or Rifle Parts, 30 mm & below

Hart Rifle Barrel Inc ....G 315 677-9841
  Syracuse *(G-14910)*
Kyntec Corporation ....G 716 810-6956
  Buffalo *(G-2840)*

FIRE CONTROL OR BOMBING EQPT: Electronic

Cooper Crouse-Hinds LLC .... B 315 477-7000
Syracuse (G-14862)

FIRE DETECTION SYSTEMS

Firecom Inc .... C 718 899-6100
Woodside (G-16206)
Firemaxx Systems Corp .... E 212 645-7414
New York (G-9497)
Firetronics Inc .... G 516 997-5151
Jericho (G-6580)
Zetek Corporation .... F 212 668-1485
New York (G-11821)

FIRE ESCAPES

Jamestown Fab Stl & Sup Inc .... G 716 665-2227
Jamestown (G-6522)

FIRE EXTINGUISHERS: Portable

Nubian Heritage .... G 631 265-3551
Hauppauge (G-5729)
Trove Inc .... F 212 268-2046
Brooklyn (G-2525)

FIRE OR BURGLARY RESISTIVE PRDTS

Clad Industries LLC .... G 585 413-4359
Macedon (G-7464)
Crystalizations Systems Inc .... F 631 467-0090
Holbrook (G-5993)
Empire Metal Finishing Inc .... E 718 545-6700
Astoria (G-421)
Finger Lakes Conveyors Inc .... G 315 539-9246
Waterloo (G-15551)
Maximum Security Products Corp .... E 518 233-1800
Waterford (G-15538)
Nrd LLC .... E 716 773-7634
Grand Island (G-5339)

FIRE PROTECTION EQPT

First Due Fire Equipment Inc .... F 845 222-1329
Garnerville (G-5134)
Lifc Corp .... G 516 426-5737
Port Washington (G-12900)
Sigelock Systems LLC .... G 888 744-3562
Oceanside (G-12190)

FIREARMS & AMMUNITION, EXC SPORTING, WHOLESALE

Island Ordnance Systems LLC .... F 516 746-2100
Mineola (G-7982)

FIREARMS: Small, 30mm or Less

Dan Wesson Corp .... F 607 336-1174
Norwich (G-12120)
Redding-Hunter Inc .... E 607 753-3331
Cortland (G-3786)
Sycamore Hill Designs Inc .... G 585 820-7322
Victor (G-15434)
Tri-Technologies Inc .... E 914 699-2001
Mount Vernon (G-8187)

FIREFIGHTING APPARATUS

Bullex Inc .... F 518 689-2023
Albany (G-53)
Eastern Precision Mfg .... G 845 358-1951
Nyack (G-12142)
Fountainhead Group Inc .... C 315 736-0037
New York Mills (G-11832)
William R Shoemaker Inc .... G 716 649-0511
Hamburg (G-5524)

FIREPLACE & CHIMNEY MATERIAL: Concrete

Chim-Cap Corp .... E 800 262-9622
Farmingdale (G-4598)
Chimney Doctors Americas Corp .... G 631 868-3586
Bayport (G-728)

FIREPLACE EQPT & ACCESS

William H Jackson Company .... G 718 784-4482
Long Island City (G-7403)

FIREPLACES: Concrete

Blackstone International Inc .... G 631 289-5490
Holtsville (G-6045)

FIREWORKS

Alonzo Fire Works Display Inc .... G 518 664-9994
Mechanicville (G-7691)
Fireworks By Grucci Inc .... E 631 286-0088
Bellport (G-799)
Young Explosives Corp .... D 585 394-1783
Canandaigua (G-3146)

FIREWORKS DISPLAY SVCS

Alonzo Fire Works Display Inc .... G 518 664-9994
Mechanicville (G-7691)
Young Explosives Corp .... D 585 394-1783
Canandaigua (G-3146)

FISH & SEAFOOD PROCESSORS: Canned Or Cured

Blue Ocean Food Trading LLC .... G 718 689-4291
Brooklyn (G-1594)
Incro Marketing USA Corp .... G 917 365-5552
New York (G-9876)
Sangster Foods Inc .... F 212 993-9129
Brooklyn (G-2383)

FISH & SEAFOOD PROCESSORS: Fresh Or Frozen

6th Ave Gourmet Inc .... G 845 782-9067
Monroe (G-8013)
AB Seafood Trading Inc .... G 718 353-8848
Flushing (G-4832)
Entrepreneur Ventures Inc .... G 631 261-1111
Northport (G-12103)
Rich Products Corporation .... A 716 878-8000
Buffalo (G-2954)

FISHING EQPT: Lures

Northern King Lures Inc .... G 585 865-3373
Rochester (G-13586)

FISHING EQPT: Nets & Seines

Cortland Line Mfg LLC .... E 607 756-2851
Cortland (G-3760)

FITTINGS & ASSEMBLIES: Hose & Tube, Hydraulic Or Pneumatic

KSA Manufacturing LLC .... F 315 488-0809
Camillus (G-3109)

FITTINGS: Pipe

Legacy Valve LLC .... F 914 403-5075
Valhalla (G-15304)
United Pipe Nipple Co Inc .... F 516 295-2468
Hewlett (G-5874)

FITTINGS: Pipe, Fabricated

D & G Welding Inc .... G 716 873-3088
Buffalo (G-2718)

FIXTURES & EQPT: Kitchen, Metal, Exc Cast Aluminum

Vanity Fair Bathmart Inc .... F 718 584-6700
Bronx (G-1389)
Vigo Industries LLC .... E 866 591-7792
New York (G-11682)

FIXTURES: Bank, Metal, Ornamental

Jonathan Metal & Glass Ltd .... C 718 846-8000
Jamaica (G-6452)
Ludwig and Larsen .... G 718 369-0999
Ridgewood (G-13151)

FIXTURES: Cut Stone

Jamestown Kitchen & Bath Inc .... G 716 665-2299
Jamestown (G-6523)

FLAGPOLES

Flagpoles Incorporated .... D 631 751-5500
East Setauket (G-4178)
Pole-Tech Co Inc .... F 631 689-5525
East Setauket (G-4184)

FLAGS: Fabric

AAa Amercn Flag Dctg Co Inc .... G 212 279-3524
New York (G-8423)
City Signs Inc .... G 718 375-5933
Brooklyn (G-1667)
Eagle Regalia Co Inc .... F 845 425-2245
Spring Valley (G-14567)
National Flag & Display Co Inc .... E 212 228-6600
New York (G-10542)
Sherwood Group Inc .... G 240 731-8573
New York (G-11212)

FLAT GLASS: Antique

Munn Works LLC .... E 914 665-6100
Mount Vernon (G-8164)

FLAT GLASS: Building

Lazer Marble & Granite Corp .... G 718 859-9644
Brooklyn (G-2049)
Tempco Glass Fabrication LLC .... D 718 461-6888
Flushing (G-4898)

FLAT GLASS: Construction

RG Glass Creations Inc .... E 212 675-0030
New York (G-11034)
Twin Pane Insulated GL Co Inc .... F 631 924-1060
Yaphank (G-16276)

FLAT GLASS: Plate, Polished & Rough

Lafayette Mirror & Glass Co .... G 718 768-0660
New Hyde Park (G-8279)
Zered Inc .... F 718 353-7464
College Point (G-3568)

FLAT GLASS: Strengthened Or Reinforced

Saxon Glass Technologies Inc .... F 607 587-9630
Alfred (G-182)

FLAT GLASS: Tempered

Mr Glass Tempering LLC .... F 718 576-3826
Brooklyn (G-2176)

FLAT GLASS: Window, Clear & Colored

Express Building Supply Inc .... E 516 608-0379
Oceanside (G-12171)
Manhattan Shade & Glass Co Inc .... E 212 288-5616
Great Neck (G-5402)
Manhattan Shade & Glass Co Inc .... E 212 288-5616
Hauppauge (G-5707)
South Seneca Vinyl LLC .... G 315 585-6050
Romulus (G-13880)
Window-Fix Inc .... E 718 854-3475
Brooklyn (G-2589)

FLATWARE, STAINLESS STEEL

Utica Cutlery Company .... D 315 733-4663
Utica (G-15298)

FLAVORS OR FLAVORING MATERIALS: Synthetic

Classic Flavors Fragrances Inc .... G 212 777-0004
New York (G-9025)
Comax Aromatics Corporation .... E 631 249-0505
Melville (G-7768)
Craftmaster Flavor Technology .... F 631 789-8607
Amityville (G-260)
Interntnal Flvors Frgrnces Inc .... C 212 765-5500
New York (G-9924)
Kent Chemical Corporation .... E 212 521-1700
New York (G-10094)
Mafco Consolidated Group Inc .... F 212 572-8600
New York (G-10318)

FLOOR COMPOSITION: Magnesite

Vescom Structural Systems Inc .... F 516 876-8100
Westbury (G-15938)

P
R
O
D
U
C
T

FLOOR COVERING STORES

North Sunshine LLC ....F 307 027-1634
Valley Cottage *(G-15320)*

FLOOR COVERING STORES: Carpets

Albert Menin Interiors Ltd ....F 212 876-3041
Bronx *(G-1200)*

Wallace Home Design Ctr ....G 631 765-3890
Southold *(G-14546)*

FLOOR COVERING: Plastic

Adore Floors Inc ....G 631 843-0900
Farmingdale *(G-4573)*

Engineered Composites Inc ....E 716 362-0295
Buffalo *(G-2745)*

H Risch Inc ....D 585 442-0110
Rochester *(G-13454)*

FLOOR COVERINGS WHOLESALERS

Carpet Fabrications Intl ....E 914 381-6060
Mamaroneck *(G-7500)*

FLOOR COVERINGS: Tile, Support Plastic

Engineered Plastics Inc ....E 800 682-2525
Williamsville *(G-16130)*

FLOORING & GRATINGS: Open, Construction Applications

Oldcastle Infrastructure Inc ....F 518 767-2116
South Bethlehem *(G-14502)*

FLOORING: Hard Surface

East To West Architectrl Pdts ....G 631 433-9690
East Northport *(G-4144)*

FLOORING: Hardwood

Custom Woodwork Ltd ....F 631 727-5260
Riverhead *(G-13173)*

Fountain Tile Outlet Inc ....G 718 927-4555
Brooklyn *(G-1862)*

Legno Veneto USA ....G 716 651-9169
Depew *(G-3986)*

Madison & Dunn ....G 585 563-7760
Rochester *(G-13528)*

MP Caroll Inc ....F 716 683-8520
Cheektowaga *(G-3355)*

Tectonic Flooring USA LLC ....G 212 686-2700
New York *(G-11448)*

FLORISTS

M & S Schmalberg Inc ....F 212 244-2090
New York *(G-10292)*

FLOWER POTS Plastic

TVI Imports LLC ....G 631 793-3077
Massapequa Park *(G-7661)*

FLOWERS: Artificial & Preserved

Faster-Form Corp ....D 800 327-3676
New Hartford *(G-8240)*

M & S Schmalberg Inc ....F 212 244-2090
New York *(G-10292)*

FLUID METERS & COUNTING DEVICES

Aalborg Instrs & Cntrls Inc ....D 845 398-3160
Orangeburg *(G-12304)*

Computer Instruments Corp ....E 516 876-8400
Westbury *(G-15874)*

East Hills Instrument Inc ....F 516 621-8686
Westbury *(G-15879)*

FLUID POWER PUMPS & MOTORS

Atlantic Industrial Tech Inc ....E 631 234-3131
Shirley *(G-14415)*

Huck International Inc ....C 845 331-7300
Kingston *(G-6694)*

Hydroacoustics Inc ....F 585 359-1000
Henrietta *(G-5856)*

ITT Corporation ....D 315 568-2811
Seneca Falls *(G-14364)*

ITT Inc ....C 914 641-2000
White Plains *(G-16017)*

ITT LLC ....B 914 641-2000
White Plains *(G-16020)*

Parker-Hannifin Corporation ....B 631 231-3737
Hauppauge *(G-5736)*

Parker-Hannifin Corporation ....C 585 425-7000
Fairport *(G-4512)*

Trench & Marine Pump Co Inc ....E 212 423-9098
Bronx *(G-1381)*

Triumph Actuation Systems LLC ....D 516 378-0162
Freeport *(G-5030)*

FLUID POWER VALVES & HOSE FITTINGS

A K Allen Co Inc ....C 516 747-5450
Melville *(G-7753)*

Aalborg Instrs & Cntrls Inc ....D 845 398-3160
Orangeburg *(G-12304)*

Key High Vacuum Products Inc ....D 631 584-5959
Nesconset *(G-8219)*

Kinemotive Corporation ....E 631 249-6440
Farmingdale *(G-4666)*

Lourdes Industries Inc ....D 631 234-6600
Hauppauge *(G-5700)*

Moog Inc ....B 716 687-4954
East Aurora *(G-4093)*

Own Instrument Inc ....F 914 668-6546
Mount Vernon *(G-8167)*

Steel & Obrien Mfg Inc ....D 585 492-5800
Arcade *(G-381)*

Upstate Tube Inc ....G 315 488-5636
Camillus *(G-3112)*

FLUORO RUBBERS

Dynax Corporation ....G 914 764-0202
Pound Ridge *(G-12992)*

FLUXES

Aufhauser Corporation ....F 516 694-8696
Plainview *(G-12665)*

Johnson Manufacturing Company ....F 716 881-3030
Buffalo *(G-2824)*

Pwf Enterprise LLC ....F 315 695-2223
Phoenix *(G-12620)*

FOAM CHARGE MIXTURES

C P Chemical Co Inc ....G 914 428-2517
White Plains *(G-15987)*

Concrete Designs Inc ....G 607 738-0309
Elmira *(G-4345)*

Icynene US Acquisition Corp ....G 800 758-7325
Buffalo *(G-2805)*

FOAM RUBBER

Foam Products Inc ....E 718 292-4830
Bronx *(G-1260)*

Mhxco Foam Company LLC ....F 518 843-8400
Amsterdam *(G-335)*

Par-Foam Products Inc ....C 716 855-2066
Buffalo *(G-2905)*

Turner Bellows Inc ....E 585 235-4456
Rochester *(G-13778)*

FOIL & LEAF: Metal

American Packaging Corporation ....G 585 254-2002
Rochester *(G-13229)*

American Packaging Corporation ....C 585 254-9500
Rochester *(G-13230)*

Pactiv LLC ....C 518 793-2524
Glens Falls *(G-5264)*

Quick Roll Leaf Mfg Co Inc ....G 845 457-1500
Montgomery *(G-8065)*

Thermal Process Cnstr Co ....E 631 293-6400
Farmingdale *(G-4754)*

FOIL, ALUMINUM, HOUSEHOLD, WHOLESALE

Golden Argosy LLC ....G 212 268-0003
New York *(G-9640)*

FOIL: Aluminum

Alufoil Products Co Inc ....F 631 231-4141
Hauppauge *(G-5585)*

En Foil LLC ....G 516 466-9500
New Hyde Park *(G-8266)*

FOIL: Copper

Oak-Mitsui Inc ....D 518 686-8060
Hoosick Falls *(G-6086)*

Oak-Mitsui Technologies LLC ....E 518 686-4961
Hoosick Falls *(G-6087)*

Steel Partners Holdings LP ....D 212 520-2300
New York *(G-11352)*

FOIL: Laminated To Paper Or Other Materials

Alufoil Products Co Inc ....F 631 231-4141
Hauppauge *(G-5585)*

FOOD CASINGS: Plastic

Pactiv LLC ....C 585 394-5125
Canandaigua *(G-3138)*

FOOD PRDTS CANNED: Fruit Nectars

Organic Nectars Inc ....G 845 246-0506
Saugerties *(G-14206)*

FOOD PRDTS, BREAKFAST: Cereal, Infants' Food

Group International LLC ....G 718 475-8805
Flushing *(G-4855)*

Sangster Foods Inc ....F 212 993-9129
Brooklyn *(G-2383)*

FOOD PRDTS, BREAKFAST: Cereal, Wheat Flakes

General Mills Inc ....D 716 856-6060
Buffalo *(G-2772)*

FOOD PRDTS, CANNED OR FRESH PACK: Fruit Juices

Apple & Eve LLC ....D 516 621-1122
Port Washington *(G-12863)*

Mizkan America Inc ....D 585 765-9171
Lyndonville *(G-7445)*

Motts LLP ....C 972 673-8088
Elmsford *(G-4418)*

National Grape Coop Assn Inc ....E 716 326-5200
Westfield *(G-15947)*

Pressed Juice LLC ....G 646 573-9157
Brooklyn *(G-2281)*

US Juice Partners LLC ....C 516 621-1122
Port Washington *(G-12930)*

Welch Foods Inc A Cooperative ....C 716 326-5252
Westfield *(G-15951)*

FOOD PRDTS, CANNED OR FRESH PACK: Vegetable Juices

Jus By Julie LLC ....G 718 266-3906
Brooklyn *(G-2014)*

FOOD PRDTS, CANNED OR FRESH PACK: Vegetable Juices

Life Juice Brands LLC ....G 585 944-7982
Pittsford *(G-12646)*

FOOD PRDTS, CANNED: Baby Food

Beech-Nut Nutrition Company ....B 518 839-0300
Amsterdam *(G-319)*

FOOD PRDTS, CANNED: Barbecue Sauce

Jets Lefrois Corp ....G 585 637-5003
Brockport *(G-1178)*

Labarba-Q LLC ....F 845 806-6227
Warwick *(G-15518)*

FOOD PRDTS, CANNED: Beans & Bean Sprouts

Sahadi Fine Foods Inc ....E 718 369-0100
Brooklyn *(G-2381)*

FOOD PRDTS, CANNED: Broth, Chicken

Dinewise Inc ....G 631 694-1111
Farmingdale *(G-4617)*

FOOD PRDTS, CANNED: Catsup

Kensington & Sons LLC ....E 646 430-8298
New York (G-10091)

FOOD PRDTS, CANNED: Ethnic

Delicious Foods Inc ....F 718 446-9352
Corona (G-3738)

Sangster Foods Inc ....F 212 993-9129
Brooklyn (G-2383)

FOOD PRDTS, CANNED: Fruit Juices, Concentrated

Old Dutch Mustard Co Inc ....G 516 466-0522
Great Neck (G-5408)

FOOD PRDTS, CANNED: Fruit Juices, Fresh

Cahoon Farms Inc ....E 315 594-8081
Wolcott (G-16161)

Cheribundi Inc ....E 800 699-0460
Geneva (G-5150)

Cliffstar LLC ....A 716 366-6100
Dunkirk (G-4052)

Fresh Fanatic Inc ....G 516 521-6574
Brooklyn (G-1867)

Mayer Bros Apple Products Inc ....D 716 668-1787
West Seneca (G-15852)

FOOD PRDTS, CANNED: Fruits

Andros Bowman Products LLC ....G 540 217-4100
Lyndonville (G-7444)

Lagoner Farms Inc ....D 315 904-4109
Williamson (G-16111)

FOOD PRDTS, CANNED: Fruits

Fly Creek Cider Mill Orchrd Inc ....G 607 547-9692
Fly Creek (G-4909)

Goya Foods Inc ....D 716 549-0076
Angola (G-359)

Hc Brill Co Inc ....G 716 685-4000
Lancaster (G-6810)

Lidestri Foods Inc ....B 585 377-7700
Fairport (G-4504)

Seneca Foods Corporation ....E 585 658-2211
Leicester (G-6911)

Victoria Fine Foods LLC ....D 718 649-1635
Brooklyn (G-2556)

Victoria Fine Foods Holding Co ....G 718 649-1635
Brooklyn (G-2557)

Welch Foods Inc A Cooperative ....E 716 326-3131
Westfield (G-15952)

FOOD PRDTS, CANNED: Fruits & Fruit Prdts

Amiram Dror Inc ....F 212 979-9505
Brooklyn (G-1504)

Spf Holdings II LLC ....G 212 750-8300
New York (G-11320)

FOOD PRDTS, CANNED: Italian

A & G Food Distributors LLC ....G 917 939-3457
Franklin Square (G-4958)

Antico Casale Usa LLC ....G 718 357-2000
Whitestone (G-16086)

Eataly Net Usa LLC ....G 212 897-2895
New York (G-9308)

Edesia World Wide LLC ....G 646 705-3505
New York (G-9320)

Indira Foods Inc ....F 718 343-1500
Floral Park (G-4819)

Marketplace Slutions Group LLC ....E 631 868-0111
Holbrook (G-6009)

FOOD PRDTS, CANNED: Jams, Including Imitation

Brads Organic LLC ....G 845 429-9080
Haverstraw (G-5804)

Sbk Preserves Inc ....E 800 773-7378
Bronx (G-1361)

FOOD PRDTS, CANNED: Jams, Jellies & Preserves

Sarabeths Kitchen LLC ....G 718 589-2900
Bronx (G-1360)

Wax Jams LLC ....F 914 834-7886
Larchmont (G-6844)

FOOD PRDTS, CANNED: Maraschino Cherries

Dells Cherries LLC ....E 718 624-4380
Brooklyn (G-1734)

Dells Cherries LLC ....E 718 624-4380
Brooklyn (G-1735)

FOOD PRDTS, CANNED: Mexican, NEC

Eve Sales Corp ....F 718 589-6800
Bronx (G-1255)

Fireside Holdings LLC ....G 718 564-4335
Monsey (G-8038)

FOOD PRDTS, CANNED: Olives

L and S Packing Co ....D 631 845-1717
Amityville (G-287)

Olive Branch Foods LLC ....G 631 343-7070
Islandia (G-6342)

FOOD PRDTS, CANNED: Puddings, Exc Meat

Steuben Foods Incorporated ....F 718 291-3333
Elma (G-4328)

FOOD PRDTS, CANNED: Ravioli

Borgattis Ravioli Egg Noodles ....G 718 367-3799
Bronx (G-1216)

FOOD PRDTS, CANNED: Sauerkraut

Seneca Foods Corporation ....C 315 781-8733
Geneva (G-5162)

FOOD PRDTS, CANNED: Spaghetti & Other Pasta Sauce

Brooklyns Best Pasta Co Inc ....G 917 881-3007
Brooklyn (G-1624)

Kaltech Food Packaging Inc ....E 845 856-1210
Port Jervis (G-12852)

New York Pasta Authority Inc ....F 347 787-2130
Brooklyn (G-2209)

Sneaky Chef Foods LLC ....F 914 301-3277
Tarrytown (G-15060)

Wolfgang B Gourmet Foods Inc ....F 518 719-1727
Catskill (G-3218)

FOOD PRDTS, CANNED: Tomato Sauce.

Super Sauces Inc ....G 347 497-2537
Brooklyn (G-2472)

Vincents Food Corp ....F 516 481-3544
Carle Place (G-3183)

FOOD PRDTS, CANNED: Tomatoes

Giovanni Food Co Inc ....D 315 457-2373
Baldwinsville (G-548)

FOOD PRDTS, CANNED: Vegetables

Green Valley Foods LLC ....G 315 926-4280
Marion (G-7569)

Seneca Foods Corporation ....E 315 926-8100
Marion (G-7574)

FOOD PRDTS, CONFECTIONERY, WHOLESALE: Candy

Chocolat Moderne LLC ....G 212 229-4797
New York (G-8996)

OH How Cute Inc ....G 347 838-6031
Staten Island (G-14687)

Premium Sweets USA Inc ....G 718 739-6000
Jamaica (G-6466)

FOOD PRDTS, CONFECTIONERY, WHOLESALE: Nuts, Salted/Roasted

Sahadi Fine Foods Inc ....E 718 369-0100
Brooklyn (G-2381)

FOOD PRDTS, CONFECTIONERY, WHOLESALE: Snack Foods

Materne North America Corp ....B 212 675-7881
New York (G-10383)

Perrys Ice Cream Company Inc ....B 716 542-5492
Akron (G-20)

FOOD PRDTS, FISH & SEAFOOD, WHOLESALE: Fresh

Fresh Fanatic Inc ....G 516 521-6574
Brooklyn (G-1867)

Montauk Inlet Seafood Inc ....G 631 668-3419
Montauk (G-8056)

FOOD PRDTS, FISH & SEAFOOD: Canned & Jarred, Etc

Diamond Seafoods Inc ....G 503 351-3240
New York (G-9222)

Premium Ocean LLC ....F 917 231-1061
Bronx (G-1344)

FOOD PRDTS, FISH & SEAFOOD: Fish, Fresh, Prepared

Foo Yuan Food Products Co Inc ....G 212 925-2840
Long Island City (G-7226)

Montauk Inlet Seafood Inc ....G 631 668-3419
Montauk (G-8056)

FOOD PRDTS, FISH & SEAFOOD: Fish, Smoked

Acme Smoked Fish Corp ....D 954 942-5598
Brooklyn (G-1458)

Banner Smoked Fish Inc ....D 718 449-1992
Brooklyn (G-1561)

Samaki Inc ....G 845 858-1012
Port Jervis (G-12856)

FOOD PRDTS, FISH & SEAFOOD: Salmon, Smoked

Catsmo LLC ....F 845 895-2296
Wallkill (G-15468)

FOOD PRDTS, FISH & SEAFOOD: Seafood, Frozen, Prepared

Sea Breeze Fish & Seafood of S ....F 718 984-0447
Staten Island (G-14707)

FOOD PRDTS, FROZEN: Breakfasts, Packaged

Beetnpath LLC ....G 607 319-5585
Ithaca (G-6364)

Juno Chefs ....D 845 294-5400
Goshen (G-5310)

FOOD PRDTS, FROZEN: Dinners, Packaged

Alle Processing Corp ....C 718 894-2000
Maspeth (G-7587)

FOOD PRDTS, FROZEN: Ethnic Foods, NEC

America NY RI Wang Fd Group Co ....E 631 231-8999
Bay Shore (G-647)

America NY RI Wang Fd Group Co ....F 631 231-8999
Maspeth (G-7589)

Delicious Foods Inc ....F 718 446-9352
Corona (G-3738)

Rhosey LLC ....G 718 382-1226
Brooklyn (G-2343)

FOOD PRDTS, FROZEN: Fruits & Vegetables

Atlantic Farm & Food Inc ....F 718 441-3152
Richmond Hill (G-13108)

FOOD PRDTS, FROZEN: Fruits, Juices & Vegetables

Blend Smoothie Bar ....G 845 568-7366
New Windsor (G-8361)

C O P R A Inc ....G 917 224-1727
New York (G-8881)

Cahoon Farms Inc ....E 315 594-8081
  Wolcott *(G-16161)*

Fly Creek Cder Mill Orchrd Inc ....G 607 547-9692
  Fly Creek *(G-4909)*

Grace Love Inc ....F 646 402-4325
  Garden City Park *(G-5121)*

Grass Roots Juicery ....E 718 486-2838
  Brooklyn *(G-1908)*

Kj Astoria Gourmet Inc 718 545-6900
  Astoria *(G-426)*

National Grape Coop Assn Inc ....E 716 326-5200
  Westfield *(G-15947)*

Smoothies Strawberry Nysf ....G 315 406-4250
  Syracuse *(G-14995)*

T & Smoothie Inc ....G 631 804-6653
  Patchogue *(G-12513)*

Textured Fd Innvations Tfi LLC ....G 515 731-3663
  Carle Place *(G-3182)*

FOOD PRDTS, FROZEN: NEC

3021743 Holdings Inc ....E 585 589-6399
  Albion *(G-152)*

Codinos Limited Inc ....E 518 372-3308
  Schenectady *(G-14258)*

Dufour Pastry Kitchens Inc ....E 718 402-8800
  Bronx *(G-1243)*

Dvash Foods Inc ....F 845 578-1959
  Monsey *(G-8037)*

Finger Food Products Inc ....E 716 297-4888
  Sanborn *(G-14141)*

Food Basket USA Company Ltd ....E 631 231-8999
  Bay Shore *(G-680)*

Julians Recipe LLC ....G 888 640-8880
  Brooklyn *(G-2011)*

Macabee Foods LLC ....G 845 623-1300
  West Nyack *(G-15826)*

Milmar Food Group II LLC ....C 845 294-5400
  Goshen *(G-5311)*

Moretta Cilento Ltd Lblty Co ....G 631 386-8654
  Huntington *(G-6214)*

Seviroli Foods Inc ....G 516 222-6220
  Garden City *(G-5115)*

Tami Great Food Corp ....G 845 352-7901
  Monsey *(G-8052)*

Textured Fd Innvations Tfi LLC ....G 515 731-3663
  Carle Place *(G-3182)*

Tuv Taam Corp ....E 718 855-2207
  Brooklyn *(G-2530)*

Unilever United States Inc ....F 212 546-0200
  New York *(G-11588)*

Unilever United States Inc ....C 212 546-0200
  New York *(G-11589)*

Wlf Founders Corporation ....D 718 777-8899
  Astoria *(G-446)*

FOOD PRDTS, FROZEN: Pizza

D R M Management Inc ....E 716 668-0333
  Depew *(G-3978)*

F & R Enterprises Inc ....G 315 841-8189
  Waterville *(G-15595)*

Salarinos Italian Foods Inc ....F 315 697-9766
  Canastota *(G-3156)*

FOOD PRDTS, FROZEN: Snack Items

Les Chateaux De France Inc ....E 516 239-6795
  Inwood *(G-6297)*

FOOD PRDTS, FROZEN: Soups

Tio Foods LLC ....F 917 946-1160
  New York *(G-11498)*

FOOD PRDTS, FROZEN: Vegetables, Exc Potato Prdts

Birds Eye Foods Inc ....G 716 988-3218
  South Dayton *(G-14505)*

Prime Food Processing Corp ....D 718 963-2323
  Brooklyn *(G-2284)*

Seneca Foods Corporation ....E 315 926-8100
  Marion *(G-7574)*

Tami Great Food Corp ....G 845 352-7901
  Monsey *(G-8052)*

FOOD PRDTS, FROZEN: Waffles

Van Rip Inc ....E 415 529-5403
  Brooklyn *(G-2553)*

FOOD PRDTS, FROZEN: Whipped Topping

Kraft Heinz Foods Company ....B 585 226-4400
  Avon *(G-513)*

FOOD PRDTS, MEAT & MEAT PRDTS, WHOLESALE: Brokers

Lancaster Quality Pork Inc ....F 718 439-8822
  Brooklyn *(G-2046)*

FOOD PRDTS, MEAT & MEAT PRDTS, WHOLESALE: Fresh

Alps Provision Co Inc ....E 718 721-4477
  Astoria *(G-414)*

Camellia General Provision Co ....E 716 893-5352
  Buffalo *(G-2691)*

Kamerys Wholesale Meats Inc ....E 716 372-6756
  Olean *(G-12237)*

Reliable Brothers Inc ....E 518 273-6732
  Green Island *(G-5441)*

FOOD PRDTS, WHOL: Canned Goods, Fruit, Veg, Seafood/Meats

Frank Wardynski & Sons Inc ....G 716 854-6083
  Buffalo *(G-2759)*

Spf Holdings II LLC ....G 212 750-8300
  New York *(G-11320)*

Wonton Food Inc ....C 718 628-6868
  Brooklyn *(G-2593)*

FOOD PRDTS, WHOLESALE: Beverage Concentrates

Motts LLP ....C 972 673-8088
  Elmsford *(G-4418)*

FOOD PRDTS, WHOLESALE: Beverages, Exc Coffee & Tea

A Health Obsession LLC ....E 347 850-4587
  Brooklyn *(G-1435)*

Pepsi-Cola Sales and Dist Inc ....G 914 253-2000
  Purchase *(G-13009)*

Pepsico Sales Inc ....G 914 253-2000
  Purchase *(G-13014)*

TLC-Lc Inc ....E 212 756-8900
  New York *(G-11501)*

FOOD PRDTS, WHOLESALE: Chocolate

Aethera LLC ....E 215 324-9222
  New York *(G-8489)*

Amiram Dror Inc ....F 212 979-9505
  Brooklyn *(G-1504)*

Chocolate Pizza Company Inc ....F 315 673-4098
  Marcellus *(G-7561)*

Commodore Chocolatier USA Inc ....F 845 561-3960
  Newburgh *(G-11861)*

Godiva Chocolatier Inc ....E 212 984-5900
  New York *(G-9636)*

Hercules Candy Co ....G 315 463-4339
  East Syracuse *(G-4216)*

Lanco Corporation ....C 631 231-2300
  Ronkonkoma *(G-13964)*

FOOD PRDTS, WHOLESALE: Coffee & Tea

Anandsar Inc ....E 551 556-5555
  Oakland Gardens *(G-12159)*

Cham Cold Brew LLC ....G 646 926-0206
  New York *(G-8968)*

Talmu NY LLC ....G 347 434-6700
  Brooklyn *(G-2492)*

FOOD PRDTS, WHOLESALE: Coffee, Green Or Roasted

Coffee Holding Co Inc ....D 718 832-0800
  Staten Island *(G-14640)*

Elite Roasters Inc ....E 716 626-0307
  East Amherst *(G-4077)*

Orens Daily Roast Inc ....G 212 348-5400
  New York *(G-10710)*

Paul De Lima Company Inc ....D 315 457-3725
  Liverpool *(G-7031)*

Pintail Coffee Inc ....G 631 396-0808
  Farmingdale *(G-4708)*

FOOD PRDTS, WHOLESALE: Condiments

Kensington & Sons LLC ....E 646 430-8298
  New York *(G-10091)*

FOOD PRDTS, WHOLESALE: Flour

Archer-Daniels-Midland Company ....D 518 828-4691
  Hudson *(G-6148)*

FOOD PRDTS, WHOLESALE: Grains

Chia Usa LLC ....E 212 226-7512
  New York *(G-8985)*

FOOD PRDTS, WHOLESALE: Health

Sangster Foods Inc ....F 212 993-9129
  Brooklyn *(G-2383)*

FOOD PRDTS, WHOLESALE: Juices

Schutt Cider Mill ....F 585 872-2924
  Webster *(G-15652)*

FOOD PRDTS, WHOLESALE: Organic & Diet

Natural Lab Inc ....E 718 321-8848
  Flushing *(G-4876)*

FOOD PRDTS, WHOLESALE: Pasta & Rice

Brooklyns Best Pasta Co Inc ....G 917 881-3007
  Brooklyn *(G-1624)*

Deer Park Macaroni Co Inc ....F 631 667-4600
  Deer Park *(G-3862)*

Great Eastern Pasta Works LLC ....E 631 956-0889
  West Babylon *(G-15713)*

New York Ravioli Pasta Co Inc ....E 516 270-2852
  New Hyde Park *(G-8285)*

Steinway Pasta & Gelati Inc ....F 718 246-5414
  Lindenhurst *(G-6974)*

Victoria Fine Foods LLC ....D 718 649-1635
  Brooklyn *(G-2556)*

Victoria Fine Foods Holding Co ....G 718 649-1635
  Brooklyn *(G-2557)*

FOOD PRDTS, WHOLESALE: Salad Dressing

Allied Food Products Inc ....F 718 230-4227
  Brooklyn *(G-1488)*

FOOD PRDTS, WHOLESALE: Sandwiches

Fresh Fanatic Inc ....G 516 521-6574
  Brooklyn *(G-1867)*

FOOD PRDTS, WHOLESALE: Sausage Casings

DRG New York Holdings Corp ....D 914 668-9000
  Mount Vernon *(G-8138)*

FOOD PRDTS, WHOLESALE: Specialty

Castella Imports Inc ....E 631 231-5500
  Hauppauge *(G-5611)*

Castella Imports Inc ....C 631 231-5500
  Edgewood *(G-4264)*

Fanshawe Foods LLC ....F 212 757-3130
  New York *(G-9469)*

FOOD PRDTS, WHOLESALE: Tea

Harney & Sons Tea Corp ....C 518 789-2100
  Millerton *(G-7947)*

White Coffee Corp ....D 718 204-7900
  Astoria *(G-445)*

FOOD PRDTS: Almond Pastes

Farm To Table Community Inc ....E 845 383-1761
  Kingston *(G-6692)*

R Hadley Corporation ....D 607 589-4415
  Spencer *(G-14549)*

FOOD PRDTS: Animal & marine fats & oils

Darling Ingredients Inc ....F 716 895-0655
  Buffalo *(G-2721)*

FOOD PRDTS: Bran, Rice

Gassho Body & Mind Inc ....G 518 695-9991
  Schuylerville *(G-14324)*

FOOD PRDTS: Bread Crumbs, Exc Made In Bakeries

Gourmet Toast Corp ....G....... 718 852-4536
Brooklyn *(G-1903)*

H & S Edible Products Corp ....E 914 413-3489
Mount Vernon *(G-8146)*

FOOD PRDTS: Breakfast Bars

Keep Healthy Inc ....F 631 651-9090
Northport *(G-12106)*

FOOD PRDTS: Cane Syrup, From Purchased Raw Sugar

Cane Sugar LLC ....G....... 212 329-2695
New York *(G-8904)*

FOOD PRDTS: Cereals

Associated Brands Inc ....B 585 798-3475
Medina *(G-7727)*

Chia Usa LLC ....G.... 212 226-7512
New York *(G-8985)*

Gabila Food Products Inc ....E 631 789-2220
Copiague *(G-3654)*

Pepsico Inc ....A 914 253-2000
Purchase *(G-13010)*

Sanzdranz LLC ....G.... 518 894-8625
Delmar *(G-3969)*

Sanzdranz LLC ....G.... 518 894-8625
Schenectady *(G-14301)*

FOOD PRDTS: Cheese Curls & Puffs

Emmi USA Inc ....F 845 268-9990
Orangeburg *(G-12313)*

FOOD PRDTS: Chicken, Processed, Frozen

K&Ns Foods Usa LLC ....E 315 598-8080
Fulton *(G-5067)*

FOOD PRDTS: Chocolate Bars, Solid

Amiram Dror Inc ....F 212 979-9505
Brooklyn *(G-1504)*

Cemoi Inc ....G....... 212 583-4920
New York *(G-8946)*

Max Brenner Union Square LLC ....G....... 646 467-8803
New York *(G-10390)*

Mbny LLC ....F 646 467-8810
New York *(G-10394)*

Micosta Enterprises Inc ....G....... 518 822-9708
Hudson *(G-6171)*

Parkside Candy Co Inc ....F 716 833-7540
Buffalo *(G-2907)*

FOOD PRDTS: Chocolate Coatings & Syrup

Fox 416 Corp ....E 718 385-4600
Brooklyn *(G-1864)*

FOOD PRDTS: Coconut Oil

Jax Coco USA LLC ....G....... 347 688-8198
New York *(G-9979)*

FOOD PRDTS: Coconut, Desiccated & Shredded

Far Eastern Coconut Company ....F 631 851-8800
Central Islip *(G-3274)*

FOOD PRDTS: Coffee

Arista Coffee Inc ....F 347 531-0813
Maspeth *(G-7592)*

Birch Guys LLC ....G....... 917 763-0751
Long Island City *(G-7178)*

CCS North America LLC ....G....... 312 834-2165
Mohegan Lake *(G-8009)*

Coffee Holding Co Inc ....D 718 832-0800
Staten Island *(G-14640)*

Coffee Holding Company Inc ....G....... 718 832-0800
Brooklyn *(G-1674)*

Elite Roasters Inc ....E 716 626-0307
East Amherst *(G-4077)*

Jonathan Brose ....G....... 716 417-8978
Lockport *(G-7086)*

List & Beisler GMBH ....E 646 866-6960
New York *(G-10225)*

P Pascal Inc ....E 914 969-7933
Yonkers *(G-16338)*

Paul De Lima Company Inc ....E 315 457-3725
Cicero *(G-3422)*

Star Mountain JFK Inc ....G....... 718 553-6787
Jamaica *(G-6475)*

Vega Coffee Inc ....G....... 415 881-7969
New York *(G-11653)*

FOOD PRDTS: Coffee Extracts

Brooklyn Roasting Works LLC ....G....... 718 855-1000
Brooklyn *(G-1621)*

Death Wish Coffee Company LLC ....E 518 400-1050
Ballston Spa *(G-571)*

Eldorado Coffee Roasters Ltd ....D 718 418-4100
Maspeth *(G-7612)*

FOOD PRDTS: Coffee Roasting, Exc Wholesale Grocers

Bh Coffee Company LLC ....D 914 377-2500
Elmsford *(G-4396)*

BK Associates Intl Inc ....F 607 432-1499
Oneonta *(G-12259)*

Brads Organic LLC ....G....... 845 429-9080
Haverstraw *(G-5804)*

Empire Coffee Company Inc ....E 914 934-1100
Port Chester *(G-12820)*

Gillies Coffee Company ....F 718 499-7766
Brooklyn *(G-1886)*

John A Vassilaros & Son Inc ....E 718 886-4140
Flushing *(G-4865)*

Paul De Lima Company Inc ....D 315 457-3725
Liverpool *(G-7031)*

Peaks Coffee Company ....G....... 315 565-1900
Cazenovia *(G-3233)*

Pintail Coffee Inc ....G....... 631 396-0808
Farmingdale *(G-4708)*

Regal Trading Inc ....E 914 694-6100
Purchase *(G-13015)*

S J McCullagh Inc ....F 716 856-3473
Buffalo *(G-2970)*

Where Is Utica Cof Rasting Inc ....F 315 269-8898
Utica *(G-15300)*

White Coffee Corp ....D 718 204-7900
Astoria *(G-445)*

FOOD PRDTS: Coffee, Ground, Mixed With Grain Or Chicory

Anandsar Inc ....E 551 556-5555
Oakland Gardens *(G-12159)*

FOOD PRDTS: Cole Slaw, Bulk

UFS Industries Inc ....D 914 664-6262
Mount Vernon *(G-8190)*

FOOD PRDTS: Cooking Oils, Refined Vegetable, Exc Corn

C B S Food Products Corp ....F 718 452-2500
Brooklyn *(G-1635)*

Gourmet Factory Inc ....G....... 631 231-4548
Hauppauge *(G-5662)*

Healthy Brand Oil Corp ....E 718 937-0806
Long Island City *(G-7239)*

FOOD PRDTS: Corn Chips & Other Corn-Based Snacks

Brads Organic LLC ....G....... 845 429-9080
Haverstraw *(G-5804)*

FOOD PRDTS: Corn Oil Prdts

Attis Ethanol Fulton LLC ....D 315 593-0500
Fulton *(G-5054)*

FOOD PRDTS: Cottonseed Lecithin

Perimondo LLC ....G....... 212 749-0721
New York *(G-10804)*

FOOD PRDTS: Dessert Mixes & Fillings

Allied Food Products Inc ....F 718 230-4227
Brooklyn *(G-1488)*

Brooklynwrap Inc ....G....... 718 258-8088
Brooklyn *(G-1625)*

Lucky Lous Inc ....G....... 631 672-1932
Lake Grove *(G-6759)*

Rich Products Corporation ....A 716 878-8000
Buffalo *(G-2954)*

VIP Foods Inc ....E 718 821-5330
Ridgewood *(G-13166)*

FOOD PRDTS: Desserts, Ready-To-Mix

Butterwood Desserts Inc ....E 716 652-0131
West Falls *(G-15761)*

Kozy Shack Enterprises LLC ....C 516 870-3000
Hicksville *(G-5919)*

Kozy Shack Enterprises LLC ....C 516 870-3000
Hicksville *(G-5920)*

Omg Desserts Inc ....F 585 698-1561
Rochester *(G-13590)*

FOOD PRDTS: Dough, Pizza, Prepared

Ohio Baking Company Inc ....E 315 724-2033
Utica *(G-15289)*

Pizza Blends LLC ....G.... 518 356-6650
Schenectady *(G-14295)*

FOOD PRDTS: Doughs & Batters From Purchased Flour

Cohens Bakery Inc ....E 716 892-8149
Buffalo *(G-2702)*

FOOD PRDTS: Doughs, Frozen Or Refrig From Purchased Flour

Rhosey LLC ....G.... 718 382-1226
Brooklyn *(G-2343)*

FOOD PRDTS: Dressings, Salad, Raw & Cooked Exc Dry Mixes

Mizkan America Inc ....F 585 798-5720
Medina *(G-7742)*

Unilever United States Inc ....F 212 546-0200
New York *(G-11588)*

Unilever United States Inc ....C 212 546-0200
New York *(G-11589)*

FOOD PRDTS: Dried & Dehydrated Fruits, Vegetables & Soup Mix

Goya Foods Inc ....D 716 549-0076
Angola *(G-359)*

Shoreline Fruit LLC ....D 585 765-2639
Lyndonville *(G-7446)*

FOOD PRDTS: Ducks, Processed, Fresh

Crescent Duck Farm Inc ....E 631 722-8700
Aquebogue *(G-365)*

FOOD PRDTS: Ducks, Processed, NEC

Hudson Valley Foie Gras LLC ....F 845 292-2500
Ferndale *(G-4790)*

FOOD PRDTS: Edible Oil Prdts, Exc Corn Oil

Consumer Flavoring Extract Co ....F 718 435-0201
Brooklyn *(G-1682)*

FOOD PRDTS: Edible fats & oils

Bunge Limited Finance Corp ....D 914 684-2800
White Plains *(G-15985)*

Kerry Bfnctnal Ingredients Inc ....D 608 363-1200
Norwich *(G-12123)*

FOOD PRDTS: Eggs, Processed

Deb El Food Products LLC ....F 845 295-8050
Rock Hill *(G-13818)*

Deb El Food Products LLC ....E 607 203-5600
Sherburne *(G-14390)*

Fruit Fresh Up Inc ....E 716 683-3200
Depew *(G-3983)*

FOOD PRDTS: Emulsifiers

Chemicolloid Laboratories Inc ....F 516 747-2656
New Hyde Park *(G-8256)*

Momentive Performance Mtls Inc ....D 914 784-4807
Tarrytown *(G-15049)*

PRODUCT

Redland Foods Corp................................F 716 288-9061
Cheektowaga (G-3360)

FOOD PRDTS: Flavored Ices, Frozen

Elegant Desserts By Metro Inc ....F 718 388-1323
Brooklyn (G-1792)
Four Brothers Italian Bakery....................G...... 914 741-5434
Hawthorne (G-5812)
JMS Ices Inc ....F 718 448-0853
Staten Island (G-14670)
My Most Favorite Food ....G...... 212 580-5130
New York (G-10524)
Olympic Ice Cream Co Inc ....E 718 849-6200
Richmond Hill (G-13118)
Primo Frozen Desserts Inc.......................G...... 718 252-2312
Brooklyn (G-2285)

FOOD PRDTS: Flour & Other Grain Mill Products

Archer-Daniels-Midland Company ....D...... 716 849-7333
Buffalo (G-2643)
Archer-Daniels-Midland Company ....E 518 828-4691
Hudson (G-6147)
Archer-Daniels-Midland Company ....D...... 518 828-4691
Hudson (G-6148)
Archer-Daniels-Midland Company ....G...... 585 346-2311
Lakeville (G-6773)
Ardent Mills LLC ....D...... 518 447-1700
Albany (G-43)
Aryzta LLC ....F 585 235-8160
Rochester (G-13250)
Birkett Mills ....G...... 315 536-3311
Penn Yan (G-12578)
Birkett Mills ....E 315 536-4112
Penn Yan (G-12579)
Cochecton Mills Inc ....E 845 932-8282
Cochecton (G-3501)
Sheppard Grain Enterprises LLC ....E 315 548-9271
Phelps (G-12608)

FOOD PRDTS: Flour Mixes & Doughs

Bektrom Foods Inc ....G...... 516 802-3800
Syosset (G-14778)
Pizza Blends LLC ....G...... 518 356-6650
Schenectady (G-14295)

FOOD PRDTS: Fruit Juices

Berryfield Bottling LLC ....E 315 781-2749
Geneva (G-5146)
Cheribundi Inc ....E 800 699-0460
Geneva (G-5150)
Dynamic Health Labs Inc ....E 718 858-0100
Brooklyn (G-1767)
Farmtobottle LLC ....G...... 631 944-8422
Locust Valley (G-7122)
Hain Blueprint Inc ....F 212 414-5741
New Hyde Park (G-8271)
Pepsico Inc ....A...... 914 253-2000
Purchase (G-13010)
Pura Fruta LLC ....F 415 279-5727
Long Island City (G-7332)
Pure Green Holdings Inc ....F 917 209-8811
New York (G-10927)

FOOD PRDTS: Fruits & Vegetables, Pickled

United Farm Processing Corp ....C...... 718 933-6060
Bronx (G-1387)

FOOD PRDTS: Fruits, Dehydrated Or Dried

Settons Intl Foods Inc ....D...... 631 543-8090
Commack (G-3598)

FOOD PRDTS: Fruits, Dried Or Dehydrated, Exc Freeze-Dried

Associated Brands Inc ....B...... 585 798-3475
Medina (G-7727)
Marshall Ingredients LLC ....G...... 800 796-9353
Wolcott (G-16164)

FOOD PRDTS: Gelatin Dessert Preparations

Original Hrkmer Cnty Chese Inc.........D...... 315 895-7428
Ilion (G-6280)

FOOD PRDTS: Gluten Meal

Anthony Gigi Inc ....G...... 860 984-1943
Shirley (G-14413)

FOOD PRDTS: Granulated Cane Sugar

US Sweeteners Corp.................................E 718 854-8714
Brooklyn (G-2549)

FOOD PRDTS: Horseradish, Exc Sauce

Whalens Horseradish Products...............G...... 518 587-6404
Galway (G-5082)

FOOD PRDTS: Ice, Blocks

Clayville Ice Co Inc ....G...... 315 839-5405
Clayville (G-3455)
Huntington Ice & Cube Corp ....F 718 456-2013
Brooklyn (G-1947)

FOOD PRDTS: Ice, Cubes

Henry Newman LLC ....F 607 273-8512
Dryden (G-4038)
Ice Cube Inc ....G...... 613 254-0071
Deer Park (G-3882)

FOOD PRDTS: Instant Coffee

Orens Daily Roast Inc ....G...... 212 348-5400
New York (G-10710)
Sangster Foods Inc ....F 212 993-9129
Brooklyn (G-2383)

FOOD PRDTS: Jelly, Corncob

Larte Del Gelato Inc ....G...... 212 366-0570
New York (G-10174)

FOOD PRDTS: Juice Pops, Frozen

La Newyorkina LLC...................................G...... 917 669-4591
Brooklyn (G-2041)
Zings Company LLC ....G...... 631 454-0339
Farmingdale (G-4767)

FOOD PRDTS: Macaroni Prdts, Dry, Alphabet, Rings Or Shells

Piemonte Home Made Ravioli Co ....F 718 429-1972
Woodside (G-16220)
Queen Ann Macaroni Mfg Co Inc.........G...... 718 256-1061
Brooklyn (G-2314)
Wing Kei Noodle Inc ....F 212 226-1644
New York (G-11766)

FOOD PRDTS: Macaroni, Noodles, Spaghetti, Pasta, Etc

Cassinelli Food Products Inc...................G...... 718 274-4881
Long Island City (G-7184)
Deer Park Macaroni Co Inc ....F 631 667-4600
Deer Park (G-3861)
Ravioli Store Inc......................................G...... 718 729-9300
Long Island City (G-7340)

FOOD PRDTS: Malt

Great Western Malting Co ....G...... 800 496-7732
Champlain (G-3312)
Queen City Malting LLC ....G...... 716 481-1313
Buffalo (G-2943)

FOOD PRDTS: Mayonnaise & Dressings, Exc Tomato Based

Conway Import Co Inc ....G...... 914 592-1312
Elmsford (G-4402)
Kensington & Sons LLC ....E 646 430-8298
New York (G-10091)

FOOD PRDTS: Mixes, Bread & Roll From Purchased Flour

Elis Bread (eli Zabar) Inc ....F 212 772-2011
New York (G-9342)

FOOD PRDTS: Mixes, Cake, From Purchased Flour

Allied Food Products Inc..........................F 718 230-4227
Brooklyn (G-1488)

FOOD PRDTS: Mixes, Doughnut From Purchased Flour

Dawn Food Products Inc ....C...... 716 830-8214
Williamsville (G-16128)

FOOD PRDTS: Mixes, Pancake From Purchased Flour

New Hope Mills Inc ....F 315 252-2676
Auburn (G-486)

FOOD PRDTS: Mixes, Seasonings, Dry

Kerry Bfnctnal Ingredients Inc...............D...... 608 363-1200
Norwich (G-12123)

FOOD PRDTS: Mustard, Prepared

Old Dutch Mustard Co Inc ....G...... 516 466-0522
Great Neck (G-5408)

FOOD PRDTS: Nuts & Seeds

Our Daily Eats LLC ....F 518 810-8412
Albany (G-110)
Scaccianoce Inc ....F 718 991-4462
Bronx (G-1362)
Sugar Foods Corporation ....E 212 753-6900
New York (G-11385)
Whitsons Food Svc Bronx Corp............B...... 631 424-2700
Islandia (G-6346)

FOOD PRDTS: Oils & Fats, Marine

Textured Fd Innvations Tfi LLC ....G...... 515 731-3663
Carle Place (G-3182)

FOOD PRDTS: Olive Oil

Bonelli Foods LLC ....G...... 212 346-0942
New York (G-8834)
L LLC ....E 716 885-3918
Buffalo (G-2841)
Lesieur Cristal Inc...................................G...... 646 604-4314
Long Island City (G-7270)
Pietro Demarco Importers Inc.................F 914 969-3201
Yonkers (G-16342)
Pinos Press Inc ....G...... 315 935-0110
Syracuse (G-14965)

FOOD PRDTS: Oriental Noodles

Lams Foods Inc..F 718 217-0476
Queens Village (G-13024)
Twin Marquis Inc ....D...... 718 386-6868
Brooklyn (G-2532)
Wonton Food Inc......................................E 718 784-8178
Long Island City (G-7406)
Wonton Food Inc......................................C...... 718 628-6868
Brooklyn (G-2593)
Wonton Food Inc......................................F 212 677-8865
New York (G-11776)

FOOD PRDTS: Pasta, Rice/Potatoes, Uncooked, Pkgd

Barilla America Ny Inc ....C...... 585 226-5600
Avon (G-512)
Bektrom Foods Inc ....G...... 516 802-3800
Syosset (G-14778)
New York Ravioli Pasta Co Inc ....E 516 270-2852
New Hyde Park (G-8285)
Steinway Pasta & Gelati Inc....................F 718 246-5414
Lindenhurst (G-6974)

FOOD PRDTS: Pasta, Uncooked, Packaged With Other Ingredients

Brooklyns Best Pasta Co Inc ....G...... 917 881-3007
Brooklyn (G-1624)
De Matteis Food Corp ....G...... 646 629-8554
New York (G-9191)
Good Noodles Inc ....F 518 731-7278
West Coxsackie (G-15759)

Great Eastern Pasta Works LLC...........E........631 956-0889
West Babylon *(G-15713)*
Johns Ravioli Company Inc...............F........914 576-7030
New Rochelle *(G-8345)*
Labella Pasta Inc.........................G........845 331-9130
Kingston *(G-6698)*

FOOD PRDTS: Peanut Butter

ABC Peanut Butter LLC...................B........212 661-6886
New York *(G-8427)*
Capitol City Specialties Co ....G........518 486-8935
Albany *(G-57)*
Once Again Nut Butter Collectv ....D........585 468-2535
Nunda *(G-12133)*
Peanut Butter & Co Inc...................E........212 757-3130
New York *(G-10776)*
Sneaky Chef Foods LLC...................F........914 301-3277
Tarrytown *(G-15060)*
Wonder Natural Foods Corp ....G........631 726-4433
Water Mill *(G-15532)*

FOOD PRDTS: Pickles, Vinegar

Allen Pickle Works Inc....................F........516 676-0640
Glen Cove *(G-5187)*
Batampte Pickle Products Inc ....D........718 251-2100
Brooklyn *(G-1566)*
French Associates Inc....................F........718 387-9880
Fresh Meadows *(G-5041)*
Heintz & Weber Co Inc....................G........716 852-7171
Buffalo *(G-2797)*
Moldova Pickles & Salads Inc...........G........718 284-2220
Brooklyn *(G-2168)*

FOOD PRDTS: Pizza, Refrigerated

D R M Management Inc....................E........716 668-0333
Depew *(G-3978)*
Ultra Thin Ready To Bake Pizza..........E........516 679-6655
Deer Park *(G-3943)*

FOOD PRDTS: Popcorn, Popped

Saratoga Chips LLC.......................G........877 901-6950
Saratoga Springs *(G-14192)*

FOOD PRDTS: Popcorn, Unpopped

Sunrise Snacks Rockland Inc............F........845 352-2676
Monsey *(G-8049)*

FOOD PRDTS: Potato & Corn Chips & Similar Prdts

BSD Top Direct Inc........................G........646 468-0156
West Babylon *(G-15696)*
Hain Celestial Group Inc ....C........516 587-5000
New Hyde Park *(G-8272)*
Ideal Snacks Corporation................C........845 292-7000
Liberty *(G-6924)*
Pepsico Inc................................A........914 253-2000
Purchase *(G-13010)*
Proformance Foods Inc..................G........703 869-3413
Brooklyn *(G-2299)*
Robs Really Good LLC....................F........516 671-4411
Sea Cliff *(G-14347)*
Switch Beverage Company LLC..........F........203 202-7383
Port Washington *(G-12928)*
TLC-Lc Inc.................................E........212 756-8900
New York *(G-11501)*

FOOD PRDTS: Potato Chips & Other Potato-Based Snacks

Frito-Lay North America Inc..............D........607 775-7000
Binghamton *(G-879)*
Terrells Potato Chip Co Inc..............D........315 437-2786
Syracuse *(G-15011)*

FOOD PRDTS: Potatoes, Dried, Packaged With Other Ingredients

Martens Country Kit Pdts LLC...........F........315 776-8821
Port Byron *(G-12809)*

FOOD PRDTS: Poultry, Processed, NEC

Wendels Poultry Farm....................G........716 592-2299
East Concord *(G-4101)*

FOOD PRDTS: Poultry, Slaughtered & Dressed

Sing Ah Poultry............................G........718 625-7253
Brooklyn *(G-2421)*

FOOD PRDTS: Preparations

3v Company Inc...........................E........718 858-7333
Brooklyn *(G-1417)*
Ahhmigo LLC..............................F........212 315-1818
New York *(G-8497)*
Andros Bowman Products LLC...........G........540 217-4100
Lyndonville *(G-7444)*
Armour Bearer Group Inc.................G........646 812-4487
Arverne *(G-406)*
Associated Brands Inc...................B........585 798-3475
Medina *(G-7727)*
Bainbridge & Knight LLC.................E........212 986-5100
New York *(G-8720)*
Baldwin Richardson Foods Co...........B........315 986-2727
Macedon *(G-7461)*
Beths Farm Kitchen.......................G........518 799-3414
Stuyvesant Falls *(G-14755)*
Bombay Kitchen Foods Inc..............F........516 767-7401
Port Washington *(G-12865)*
Bud Ravioli Center Inc....................G........718 356-4600
Staten Island *(G-14632)*
Bylada Foods LLC........................E........845 623-1300
West Nyack *(G-15819)*
Cafe Spice Gct Inc.......................C........845 863-0910
New Windsor *(G-8362)*
Castella Imports Inc.......................E........631 231-5500
Hauppauge *(G-5611)*
Castella Imports Inc.......................C........631 231-5500
Edgewood *(G-4264)*
Child Nutrition Prog Dept Ed.............D........212 371-1000
New York *(G-8986)*
China Huaren Organic Pdts Inc.........G........212 232-0120
New York *(G-8988)*
Cookiebaker LLC.........................G........716 878-8000
Buffalo *(G-2710)*
Event Services Corporation..............G........315 488-9357
Solvay *(G-14497)*
Fanshawe Foods LLC....................F........212 757-3130
New York *(G-9469)*
Flik International/Compass...............E........212 450-4750
New York *(G-9510)*
Frito-Lay North America Inc..............D........607 775-7000
Binghamton *(G-879)*
Fruitcrown Products Corp ....E........631 694-5800
Farmingdale *(G-4633)*
Glenn Foods Inc..........................F........516 377-1400
Freeport *(G-4999)*
Gourmet Boutique LLC ....C........718 977-1200
Jamaica *(G-6445)*
Gourmet Crafts Inc.......................F........718 372-0505
Brooklyn *(G-1902)*
Gravymaster Inc..........................E........203 453-1893
Canajoharie *(G-3120)*
H&F Products Inc.........................E........845 651-6100
Florida *(G-4824)*
HP Hood LLC.............................D........607 295-8134
Arkport *(G-393)*
Instantwhip of Buffalo Inc................E........716 892-7031
Buffalo *(G-2811)*
Joyva Corp.................................D........718 497-0170
Brooklyn *(G-2006)*
Kale Factory Inc...........................G........917 363-6361
Brooklyn *(G-2020)*
Kaneka America LLC.....................D........212 705-4340
New York *(G-10066)*
Kraft Heinz Foods Company.............B........585 226-4400
Avon *(G-513)*
Land OLakes Inc.........................G........516 681-2980
Hicksville *(G-5922)*
Lidestri Beverages LLC..................F........585 377-7700
Fairport *(G-4503)*
Losurdo Foods Inc.......................E........518 842-1500
Amsterdam *(G-333)*
Lugo Nutrition Inc........................G........302 573-2503
Nyack *(G-12145)*
Mediterrean Dyro Company.............E........718 786-4888
Long Island City *(G-7293)*
Merb LLC..................................F........631 393-3621
Brooklyn *(G-2139)*
Meta-Therm Corp........................F........914 697-4840
White Plains *(G-16029)*
Milnot Holding Corporation..............G........518 839-0300
Amsterdam *(G-337)*

Mizkan America Inc.......................D........585 765-9171
Lyndonville *(G-7445)*
Moira New Hope Food Pantry...........E........518 529-6524
Moira *(G-8012)*
Mondelez Global LLC....................G........585 345-3300
Batavia *(G-620)*
More Good................................G........845 765-0115
Beacon *(G-754)*
Natural Lab Inc...........................G........718 321-8848
Flushing *(G-4876)*
Natural Matters Inc.......................G........212 337-3077
New York *(G-10552)*
North Shore Farms Two Ltd.............G........516 280-6880
Mineola *(G-7991)*
Parnasa International Inc.................G........516 394-0400
Valley Stream *(G-15351)*
Pelican Bay Ltd...........................F........718 729-9300
Long Island City *(G-7323)*
Pellicano Specialty Foods Inc ....F........716 822-2366
Buffalo *(G-2910)*
Ponti Rossi Inc............................G........347 506-9616
Brooklyn *(G-2269)*
Private Lbel Fods Rchester Inc ....E........585 254-9205
Rochester *(G-13646)*
Pure Functional Foods Inc...............G........315 294-0733
Savannah *(G-14221)*
Pure Golds Family Corp ....D........516 483-5600
Hempstead *(G-5848)*
Qualitea Imports Inc......................G........917 624-6750
Suffern *(G-14764)*
Raw Indulgence Ltd......................F........866 498-4671
Elmsford *(G-4425)*
Rob Salamida Company Inc.............F........607 729-4868
Johnson City *(G-6608)*
Royal Kosher Foods LLC.................G........347 221-1867
Brooklyn *(G-2360)*
Sabra Dipping Company LLC............D........914 372-3900
White Plains *(G-16058)*
Salvador Colletti Blank..................G........718 217-6725
Douglaston *(G-4028)*
Sapienza Pastry Inc......................E........516 352-5232
Elmont *(G-4389)*
Seneca Foods Corporation..............F........315 926-4277
Marion *(G-7575)*
Settons Intl Foods Inc....................D........631 543-8090
Commack *(G-3598)*
Tracco LLC................................G........516 938-4588
Syosset *(G-14803)*
Whitsons Food Svc Bronx Corp..........B........631 424-2700
Islandia *(G-6346)*
Win-Holt Equipment Corp................E........516 222-0335
Woodbury *(G-16185)*

FOOD PRDTS: Prepared Meat Sauces Exc Tomato & Dry

American Specialty Mfg Co...............F........585 544-5600
Rochester *(G-13231)*

FOOD PRDTS: Prepared Sauces, Exc Tomato Based

Bushwick Kitchen LLC...................G........917 297-1045
Brooklyn *(G-1631)*
Culture Clash Corporation...............G........631 933-8179
Amityville *(G-261)*
Elwood International Inc ....F........631 842-6600
Copiague *(G-3651)*
Gravymaster Inc..........................E........203 453-1893
Canajoharie *(G-3120)*
Mandarin Soy Sauce Inc.................E........845 343-1505
Middletown *(G-7918)*
Pure Golds Family Corp ....D........516 483-5600
Hempstead *(G-5848)*
Rob Salamida Company Inc.............F........607 729-4868
Johnson City *(G-6608)*
T RS Great American Rest ....F........516 294-1680
Williston Park *(G-16149)*

FOOD PRDTS: Raw cane sugar

Supreme Chocolatier LLC................E........718 761-9600
Staten Island *(G-14718)*

FOOD PRDTS: Relishes, Vinegar

Jets Lefrois Corp..........................G........585 637-5003
Brockport *(G-1178)*

PRODUCT

FOOD PRDTS: Rice, Milled

Real Co Inc ....G 347 433-8549
Valley Cottage (G-15321)

FOOD PRDTS: Salads

Golden Taste Inc ....E 845 356-4133
Spring Valley (G-14571)
Koppert Cress USA LLC ....E 631 779-3640
Riverhead (G-13176)
M & M Food Products Inc ....F 718 821-1970
Brooklyn (G-2093)
Pride Pak Inc ....D 905 828-2149
Medina (G-7743)
Radicle Farm LLC ....G 315 226-3294
New York (G-10970)

FOOD PRDTS: Sandwiches

Spread-Mmms LLC ....G 917 727-8116
Brooklyn (G-2447)

FOOD PRDTS: Seasonings & Spices

Aromasong Usa Inc ....F 718 838-9669
Brooklyn (G-1533)
Diva Farms Ltd ....G 315 735-4397
Utica (G-15258)
La Flor Products Company Inc ....E 631 851-9601
Hauppauge (G-5690)
Pennant Ingredients Inc ....D 585 235-8160
Rochester (G-13613)
SOS Chefs New York Inc ....G 212 505-5813
New York (G-11301)
Unistel LLC ....D 585 341-4600
Webster (G-15660)

FOOD PRDTS: Soup Mixes

Allied Food Products Inc ....F 718 230-4227
Brooklyn (G-1488)

FOOD PRDTS: Soy Sauce

Wanjashan International LLC ....F 845 343-1505
Middletown (G-7937)

FOOD PRDTS: Spices, Including Ground

Extreme Spices Inc ....G 917 496-4081
Maspeth (G-7613)
Manhattan Milling & Drying Co ....E 516 496-1041
Woodbury (G-16177)
Victoria Fine Foods LLC ....D 718 649-1635
Brooklyn (G-2556)
Victoria Fine Foods Holding Co ....G 718 649-1635
Brooklyn (G-2557)
Wm E Martin and Sons Co Inc ....E 516 605-2444
Roslyn (G-14047)

FOOD PRDTS: Sugar

New York Sugars LLC ....F 585 500-0155
Rochester (G-13573)
Real Co Inc ....G 347 433-8549
Valley Cottage (G-15321)
Sugar Foods Corporation ....E 212 753-6900
New York (G-11385)
Sugar Shack Desert Company Inc ....G 518 523-7540
Lake Placid (G-6768)
U S Sugar Co Inc ....E 716 828-1170
Buffalo (G-3025)

FOOD PRDTS: Sugar, Beet

Beets Love Production LLC ....E 585 270-2471
Rochester (G-13265)

FOOD PRDTS: Sugar, Cane

American Sugar Refining Inc ....E 914 376-3386
Yonkers (G-16285)
Refined Sugars Inc ....G 914 963-2400
Yonkers (G-16345)
Sweeteners Plus LLC ....D 585 728-3770
Lakeville (G-6776)

FOOD PRDTS: Sugar, Corn

Sweetwater Energy Inc ....G 585 647-5760
Rochester (G-13751)

FOOD PRDTS: Sugar, Granulated Cane, Purchd Raw Sugar/Syrup

Domino Foods Inc ....F 800 729-4840
Yonkers (G-16303)

FOOD PRDTS: Sugar, Liquid Sugar Beet

New York Sugars LLC ....F 585 500-0155
Rochester (G-13573)

FOOD PRDTS: Syrup, Maple

Brads Organic LLC ....G 845 429-9080
Haverstraw (G-5804)
Peaceful Valley Maple Farm ....G 518 762-0491
Johnstown (G-6623)

FOOD PRDTS: Syrups

Spf Holdings II LLC ....G 212 750-8300
New York (G-11320)

FOOD PRDTS: Tea

Anandsar Inc ....E 551 556-5555
Oakland Gardens (G-12159)
Blue Ridge Tea & Herb Co Ltd ....G 718 625-3100
Brooklyn (G-1595)
Farmers Hub LLC ....G 914 380-2945
White Plains (G-16006)
Gillies Coffee Company ....F 718 499-7766
Brooklyn (G-1886)
Harney & Sons Tea Corp ....C 518 789-2100
Millerton (G-7947)
Tea Life LLC ....G 516 365-7711
Manhasset (G-7542)

FOOD PRDTS: Tofu Desserts, Frozen

Pulmuone Foods Usa Inc ....E 845 365-3300
Tappan (G-15037)

FOOD PRDTS: Tofu, Exc Frozen Desserts

Chan Kee Dried Bean Curd Inc ....G 718 622-0820
Brooklyn (G-1660)
Seasons Soyfood Inc ....G 718 797-9896
Brooklyn (G-2393)

FOOD PRDTS: Tortillas

Buna Besta Tortillas ....G 347 987-3995
Brooklyn (G-1628)
La Escondida Inc ....G 845 562-1387
Newburgh (G-11872)
Maizteca Foods Inc ....E 718 641-3933
South Richmond Hill (G-14523)
Tortilla Heaven Inc ....E 845 339-1550
Kingston (G-6715)
Tortilleria Oaxaca ....G 347 355-7336
Staten Island (G-14723)
Tuv Taam Corp ....E 718 855-2207
Brooklyn (G-2530)

FOOD PRDTS: Vegetables, Dried or Dehydrated Exc Freeze-Dried

Wm E Martin and Sons Co Inc ....E 516 605-2444
Roslyn (G-14047)

FOOD PRDTS: Vegetables, Pickled

United Pickle Products Corp ....E 718 933-6060
Bronx (G-1388)

FOOD PRDTS: Vinegar

Fleischmanns Vinegar Co Inc ....E 315 587-4414
North Rose (G-12034)
Mizkan America Inc ....F 585 798-5720
Medina (G-7742)
Mizkan Americas Inc ....F 315 483-6944
Sodus (G-14491)
Old Dutch Mustard Co Inc ....E 516 466-0522
Great Neck (G-5408)
Vinegar Hill Asset LLC ....G 718 469-0342
Brooklyn (G-2559)

FOOD PRODUCTS MACHINERY

Ag-Pak Inc ....F 716 772-2651
Gasport (G-5136)

Alard Equipment Corporation ....E 315 589-4511
Williamson (G-16109)
Bake-Rite International Inc ....G 518 395-3340
Schenectady (G-14248)
Bari Engineering Corp ....E 212 966-2080
New York (G-8729)
Buflovak LLC ....E 716 895-2100
Buffalo (G-2685)
C-Flex Bearing Co Inc ....E 315 895-7454
Frankfort (G-4948)
Carts Mobile Food Eqp Corp ....E 718 788-5540
Brooklyn (G-1652)
Chester-Jensen Company ....E 610 876-6276
Cattaraugus (G-3220)
Delsur Parts ....G 631 630-1606
Brentwood (G-1119)
Esquire Mechanical Corp ....E 718 625-4006
Brooklyn (G-1813)
G J Olney Inc ....E 315 827-4208
Westernville (G-15942)
Haines Equipment Inc ....G 607 566-8531
Avoca (G-510)
Kinplex Corp ....E 631 242-4800
Edgewood (G-4274)
Lyophilization Systems Inc ....G 845 338-0456
New Paltz (G-8309)
Olmstead Products Corp ....F 516 681-3700
Hicksville (G-5935)
P & M LLC ....E 631 842-2200
Amityville (G-301)
Precision N Amer Fd McHy LLC ....F 518 462-3387
Albany (G-118)
Sidco Food Distribution Corp ....F 718 733-3939
Bronx (G-1363)
Simply Natural Foods LLC ....C 631 543-9600
Commack (G-3599)
SPX Flow Us LLC ....A 716 692-3000
Getzville (G-5182)
Vr Food Equipment Inc ....F 315 531-8133
Farmington (G-4780)

FOOD STORES: Delicatessen

Cassinelli Food Products Inc ....G 718 274-4881
Long Island City (G-7184)
Jim Romas Bakery Inc ....E 607 748-7425
Endicott (G-4463)
Mds Hot Bagels Deli Inc ....G 718 438-5650
Brooklyn (G-2129)
Sam A Lupo & Sons Inc ....G 800 388-5352
Endicott (G-4472)

FOOD STORES: Supermarkets

Hana Pastries Inc ....G 718 369-7593
Brooklyn (G-1923)
Reisman Bros Bakery Inc ....F 718 331-1975
Brooklyn (G-2337)

FOOTWEAR, WHOLESALE: Athletic

Air Skate & Air Jump Corp ....G 212 967-1201
New York (G-8503)
Air Skate & Air Jump Corp ....F 212 967-1201
Brooklyn (G-1473)

FOOTWEAR, WHOLESALE: Shoe Access

Aniiwe Inc ....G 347 683-1891
Brooklyn (G-1511)
Bfma Holding Corporation ....G 607 753-6746
Cortland (G-3755)
Marietta Corporation ....A 323 589-8181
Cortland (G-3777)

FOOTWEAR, WHOLESALE: Shoes

Anthony L & S LLC ....E 212 386-7245
New York (G-8597)
Onia LLC ....E 646 701-0008
New York (G-10693)

FOOTWEAR: Cut Stock

Age Manufacturers Inc ....D 718 927-0048
Brooklyn (G-1471)
Premier Brands America Inc ....F 718 325-3000
Bronx (G-1343)
Premier Brands America Inc ....C 914 667-6200
White Plains (G-16054)

FORGINGS

Biltron Automotive Products ....E 631 928-8613
  Port Jeff STA *(G-12833)*
Burke Frging Heat Treating Inc ....E 585 235-6060
  Rochester *(G-13287)*
Delaware Valley Forge Co Inc ....G 716 447-9140
  Buffalo *(G-2724)*
Delaware Valley Forge Inc ....E 716 447-9140
  Buffalo *(G-2725)*
Designatronics Incorporated ....G 516 328-3300
  Hicksville *(G-5902)*
Hammond & Irving Inc ....D 315 253-6265
  Auburn *(G-478)*
Hohmann & Barnard Inc ....E 631 234-0600
  Hauppauge *(G-5672)*
Hohmann & Barnard Inc ....E 518 357-9757
  Schenectady *(G-14278)*
Jrlon Inc ....D 315 597-4067
  Palmyra *(G-12489)*
Mattessich Iron LLC ....G 315 409-8496
  Memphis *(G-7835)*
Peck & Hale LLC ....E 631 589-2510
  West Sayville *(G-15842)*
Schilling Forge Inc ....E 315 454-4421
  Syracuse *(G-14987)*
Special Metals Corporation ....D 716 366-5663
  Dunkirk *(G-4067)*
Stoffel Polygon Systems Inc ....F 914 961-2000
  Tuckahoe *(G-15206)*
Superior Motion Controls Inc ....E 516 420-2921
  Farmingdale *(G-4745)*
Viking Iron Works Inc ....F 845 471-5010
  Poughkeepsie *(G-12990)*
W J Albro Machine Works Inc ....G 631 345-0657
  Yaphank *(G-16278)*
York Industries Inc ....E 516 746-3736
  Garden City Park *(G-5126)*

FORGINGS: Aircraft, Ferrous

Firth Rixson Inc ....D 585 328-1383
  Rochester *(G-13411)*

FORGINGS: Aluminum

Arconic Inc ....G 315 764-4011
  Massena *(G-7666)*

FORGINGS: Gear & Chain

Ball Chain Mfg Co Inc ....D 914 664-7500
  Mount Vernon *(G-8123)*
Kurz and Zobel Inc ....G 585 254-9060
  Rochester *(G-13506)*

FORGINGS: Machinery, Ferrous

Alry Tool and Die Co Inc ....E 716 693-2419
  Tonawanda *(G-15085)*

FORGINGS: Nonferrous

Nak International Corp ....D 516 334-6245
  Locust Valley *(G-7128)*
Special Metals Corporation ....D 716 366-5663
  Dunkirk *(G-4067)*

FORGINGS: Pump & compressor, Nonferrous

Penn State Mtal Fbrctors No 2 ....G 718 786-8814
  Brooklyn *(G-2253)*

FORMS: Concrete, Sheet Metal

Gt Innovations LLC ....G 585 739-7659
  Bergen *(G-814)*

FOUNDRIES: Aluminum

American Blade Mfg LLC ....F 607 432-4518
  Oneonta *(G-12256)*
American Blade Mfg LLC ....G 607 656-4204
  Greene *(G-5443)*
Amt Incorporated ....E 518 284-2910
  Sharon Springs *(G-14382)*
Consoldted Precision Pdts Corp ....B 315 687-0014
  Chittenango *(G-3404)*
Crown Die Casting Corp ....E 914 667-5400
  Mount Vernon *(G-8135)*
East Pattern & Model Corp ....E 585 461-3240
  Rochester *(G-13362)*

East Pattern & Model Corp ....F 585 461-3240
  Rochester *(G-13363)*
Eastern Castings Co ....F 518 677-5610
  Cambridge *(G-3094)*
Meloon Foundries LLC ....E 315 454-3231
  Syracuse *(G-14939)*
Micro Instrument Corp ....D 585 458-3150
  Rochester *(G-13545)*
Pyrotek Incorporated ....D 607 756-3050
  Cortland *(G-3784)*
Wolff & Dungey Inc ....E 315 475-2105
  Syracuse *(G-15029)*

FOUNDRIES: Brass, Bronze & Copper

David Fehlman ....G 315 455-8888
  Syracuse *(G-14875)*
Meloon Foundries LLC ....E 315 454-3231
  Syracuse *(G-14939)*
Omega Wire Inc ....E 315 337-4300
  Rome *(G-13862)*
Omega Wire Inc ....D 315 689-7115
  Jordan *(G-6630)*

FOUNDRIES: Gray & Ductile Iron

En Tech Corp ....F 845 398-0776
  Tappan *(G-15035)*
Matrix Steel Company Inc ....G 718 381-6800
  Brooklyn *(G-2125)*
McWane Inc ....B 607 734-2211
  Elmira *(G-4362)*

FOUNDRIES: Iron

Eastern Company ....D 315 468-6251
  Solvay *(G-14496)*
Emcom Industries Inc ....G 716 852-3711
  Buffalo *(G-2743)*
Noresco Industrial Group Inc ....E 516 759-3355
  Glen Cove *(G-5197)*
Plattco Corporation ....E 518 563-4640
  Plattsburgh *(G-12768)*

FOUNDRIES: Nonferrous

Allstar Casting Corporation ....E 212 563-0909
  New York *(G-8520)*
Carrera Casting Corp ....C 212 382-3296
  New York *(G-8924)*
Cast-All Corporation ....E 516 741-4025
  Mineola *(G-7965)*
Cpp-Syracuse Inc ....E 315 687-0014
  Chittenango *(G-3406)*
Crown Die Casting Corp ....E 914 667-5400
  Mount Vernon *(G-8135)*
Globalfoundries US Inc ....D 518 305-9013
  Malta *(G-7495)*
Globalfoundries US Inc ....F 408 462-3900
  Ballston Spa *(G-574)*
Greenfield Die Casting Corp ....E 516 623-9230
  Freeport *(G-5000)*
J & J Bronze & Aluminum Cast ....E 718 383-2111
  Brooklyn *(G-1976)*
Jamestown Bronze Works Inc ....G 716 665-2302
  Jamestown *(G-6521)*
K & H Precision Products Inc ....E 585 624-4894
  Honeoye Falls *(G-6076)*
Karbra Company ....C 212 736-9300
  New York *(G-10069)*
Kelly Foundry & Machine Co ....E 315 732-8313
  Utica *(G-15279)*
Medi-Ray Inc ....D 877 898-3003
  Tuckahoe *(G-15205)*
Plattco Corporation ....F 518 563-4640
  Plattsburgh *(G-12769)*
Polich Tallix Inc ....D 845 567-9464
  Rock Tavern *(G-13821)*
Speyside Foundry Holdings LLC ....G 212 994-0308
  New York *(G-11319)*
Wemco Casting LLC ....D 631 563-8050
  Bohemia *(G-1098)*

FOUNDRIES: Steel

Amt Incorporated ....E 518 284-2910
  Sharon Springs *(G-14382)*
Brinkman Intl Group Inc ....G 585 429-5000
  Rochester *(G-13281)*
C J Winter Machine Tech ....E 585 429-5000
  Rochester *(G-13290)*
Eastern Industrial Steel Corp ....F 845 639-9749
  New City *(G-8226)*

Frazer & Jones Co ....D 315 468-6251
  Syracuse *(G-14895)*
Steel Craft Rolling Door ....F 631 608-8662
  Copiague *(G-3679)*

FOUNDRIES: Steel Investment

Consoldted Precision Pdts Corp ....B 315 687-0014
  Chittenango *(G-3404)*
Jbf Stainless LLC ....E 315 569-2800
  Frankfort *(G-4952)*
Quality Castings Inc ....E 732 409-3203
  Long Island City *(G-7335)*

FRAMES & FRAMING WHOLESALE

AC Moore Incorporated ....E 516 796-5831
  Bethpage *(G-831)*
Galas Framing Services ....F 718 706-0007
  Long Island City *(G-7228)*
General Art Company Inc ....F 212 255-1298
  New York *(G-9588)*
Inter Pacific Consulting Corp ....G 718 460-2787
  Flushing *(G-4861)*

FRANCHISES, SELLING OR LICENSING

Authentic Brands Group LLC ....C 212 760-2410
  New York *(G-8680)*
Hugo Boss Usa Inc ....D 212 940-0600
  New York *(G-9835)*
Perry Ellis International Inc ....F 212 536-5400
  New York *(G-10807)*

FREIGHT CONSOLIDATION SVCS

ITT Industries Holdings Inc ....G 914 641-2000
  White Plains *(G-16018)*

FREIGHT FORWARDING ARRANGEMENTS

Janel Corporation ....G 516 256-8143
  Lynbrook *(G-7432)*

FRICTION MATERIAL, MADE FROM POWDERED METAL

Materion Brewster LLC ....D 845 279-0900
  Brewster *(G-1155)*
Raytech Corp Asbestos Personal ....A 516 747-0300
  Mineola *(G-7996)*

FRUIT & VEGETABLE MARKETS

Lagoner Farms Inc ....D 315 904-4109
  Williamson *(G-16111)*

FUEL ADDITIVES

E-Zoil Products Inc ....E 716 213-0106
  Tonawanda *(G-15101)*
Fppf Chemical Co Inc ....G 716 856-9607
  Buffalo *(G-2758)*
Kinetic Fuel Technology Inc ....G 716 745-1461
  Youngstown *(G-16384)*

FUEL BRIQUETTES & WAXES

Costello Bros Petroleum Corp ....G 914 237-3189
  Yonkers *(G-16298)*

FUEL BRIQUETTES OR BOULETS, MADE WITH PETROLEUM BINDER

Cooks Intl Ltd Lblty Co ....G 212 741-4407
  New York *(G-9096)*

FUEL CELL FORMS: Cardboard, Made From Purchased Materials

Emergent Power Inc ....G 201 441-3590
  Latham *(G-6856)*

FUEL CELLS: Solid State

Plug Power Inc ....G 585 474-3993
  Rochester *(G-13626)*
Plug Power Inc ....B 518 782-7700
  Latham *(G-6874)*

FUEL DEALERS: Wood

B & J Lumber Co Inc ....G 518 677-3845
  Cambridge *(G-3091)*

PRODUCT

FUEL OIL DEALERS

Bluebar Oil Co Inc ....F 315 245-4328
  Blossvale *(G-955)*
Costello Bros Petroleum Corp ....G 914 237-3189
  Yonkers *(G-16298)*
Montauk Inlet Seafood Inc ....G 631 668-3419
  Montauk *(G-8056)*

FUELS: Diesel

Algafuel America ....G 516 295-2257
  Hewlett *(G-5869)*
Northern Biodiesel Inc ....G 585 545-4534
  Ontario *(G-12294)*
Performance Diesel Service LLC ....F 315 854-5269
  Plattsburgh *(G-12767)*

FUELS: Ethanol

A and L Home Fuel LLC ....G 607 638-1994
  Schenevus *(G-14319)*
Avstar Fuel Systems Inc ....G 315 255-1955
  Auburn *(G-465)*
Castle Fuels Corporation ....E 914 381-6600
  Harrison *(G-5548)*
Centar Fuel Co Inc ....G 516 538-2424
  West Hempstead *(G-15768)*
Consolidated Edison Co NY Inc ....F 914 933-2936
  Rye *(G-14076)*
Degennaro Fuel Service LLC ....F 518 239-6350
  Medusa *(G-7750)*
Dib Managmnt Inc ....F 718 439-8190
  Brooklyn *(G-1741)*
Family Fuel Co Inc ....G 718 232-2009
  Brooklyn *(G-1831)*
Fire Island Fuel ....G 631 772-1482
  Shirley *(G-14420)*
Friendly Fuel Incorporated ....G 518 581-7036
  Saratoga Springs *(G-14176)*
Friendly Star Fuel Inc ....G 718 369-8801
  Brooklyn *(G-1870)*
Fuel Energy Services USA Ltd ....E 607 846-2650
  Horseheads *(G-6124)*
Fuel Soul ....G 516 379-0810
  Merrick *(G-7856)*
Golden Renewable Energy LLC ....G 914 920-9800
  Yonkers *(G-16314)*
Highrange Fuels Inc. ....G 914 930-8300
  Cortland Manor *(G-3796)*
J&R Fuel of LI Inc ....G 631 234-1959
  Central Islip *(G-3281)*
Jmg Fuel Inc ....G 631 579-4319
  Ronkonkoma *(G-13955)*
JRs Fuels Inc ....G 518 622-9939
  Cairo *(G-3065)*
Kore Infrastructure LLC ....G 646 532-9060
  Glen Cove *(G-5196)*
Leroux Fuels ....F 518 563-3653
  Plattsburgh *(G-12758)*
Liberty Food and Fuel ....G 315 299-4039
  Syracuse *(G-14931)*
Lift Safe - Fuel Safe Inc ....G 315 423-7702
  Syracuse *(G-14932)*
Lo-Co Fuel Corp ....G 631 929-5086
  Wading River *(G-15450)*
Logo ....G 212 846-2568
  New York *(G-10243)*
Maio Fuel Company LP ....G 914 683-1154
  White Plains *(G-16027)*
Metro Fuel LLC ....C 212 836-9608
  New York *(G-10445)*
MNS Fuel Corp ....F 516 735-3835
  Ronkonkoma *(G-13976)*
Mt Fuel Corp ....G 631 445-2047
  Stony Brook *(G-14740)*
N & L Fuel Corp ....G 718 863-3538
  Bronx *(G-1320)*
Nagle Fuel Corporation ....G 212 304-4618
  New York *(G-10530)*
North East Fuel Group Inc ....G 718 984-6774
  Staten Island *(G-14685)*
Northeastern Fuel Corp ....G 917 560-6241
  Staten Island *(G-14686)*
Patdan Fuel Corporation ....G 718 326-3668
  Middle Village *(G-7883)*
Pretty Fuel Inc ....G 315 823-4063
  Little Falls *(G-6991)*
Provident Fuel Inc ....G 516 224-4427
  Woodbury *(G-16180)*
Quality Fuel 1 Corporation ....G 631 392-4090
  North Babylon *(G-12002)*

Remsen Fuel Inc ....G 718 984-9551
  Staten Island *(G-14701)*
Rising Tide Fuel LLC ....G 631 374-7361
  Amityville *(G-305)*
Southbay Fuel Injectors ....G 516 442-4707
  Rockville Centre *(G-13838)*
Yankee Fuel Inc ....G 631 880-8810
  West Babylon *(G-15757)*
York Fuel Incorporated ....G 718 951-0202
  Brooklyn *(G-2602)*

FUELS: Oil

209 Discount Oil ....E 845 386-2090
  Middletown *(G-7891)*
Ergun Inc ....G 631 721-0049
  Roslyn Heights *(G-14050)*
Fuel Energy Services USA Ltd ....E 607 846-2650
  Horseheads *(G-6124)*
Heat USA II LLC ....E 212 564-4328
  New York *(G-9760)*
Hygrade Fuel Inc ....G 516 741-0723
  Mineola *(G-7980)*
Starfuels Inc ....G 914 289-4800
  White Plains *(G-16062)*

FUNDRAISING SVCS

Consumer Reports Inc ....B 914 378-2000
  Yonkers *(G-16297)*

FUNERAL HOMES & SVCS

Sunnycrest Inc ....E 315 252-7214
  Auburn *(G-496)*

FUNGICIDES OR HERBICIDES

Bioworks Inc ....G 585 924-4362
  Victor *(G-15394)*

FUR APPAREL STORES

Missiontex Inc ....G 718 532-9053
  Brooklyn *(G-2161)*

FUR CLOTHING WHOLESALERS

Blum & Fink Inc ....F 212 695-2606
  New York *(G-8823)*
Georgy Creative Fashions Inc ....G 212 279-4885
  New York *(G-9602)*

FUR FINISHING & LINING: For The Fur Goods Trade

Steves Original Furs Inc ....E 212 967-8007
  New York *(G-11362)*

FUR: Apparel

CPT Usa LLC ....E 212 575-1616
  New York *(G-9114)*
Fox Unlimited Inc ....G 212 736-3071
  New York *(G-9526)*
Jerry Sorbara Furs Inc ....F 212 594-3897
  New York *(G-9995)*
Mink Mart Inc ....G 212 868-2785
  New York *(G-10478)*
Superior Furs Inc ....F 516 365-4123
  Manhasset *(G-7541)*
Xanadu ....G 212 465-0580
  New York *(G-11797)*

FUR: Coats

Stallion Inc ....E 718 706-0111
  Long Island City *(G-7362)*

FUR: Coats & Other Apparel

Blum & Fink Inc ....F 212 695-2606
  New York *(G-8823)*
J Percy For Mrvin Rchards Ltd ....E 212 944-5300
  New York *(G-9956)*
Mksf Inc ....F 212 563-3877
  New York *(G-10485)*
Moschos Furs Inc ....G 212 244-0255
  New York *(G-10506)*
Samuel Schulman Furs Inc ....E 212 736-5550
  New York *(G-11127)*

FUR: Hats

Best Brands Consumer Pdts Inc ....G 212 684-7456
  New York *(G-8766)*
First Brands LLC ....E 646 432-4366
  Merrick *(G-7855)*
Kaitery Furs Ltd ....G 718 204-1396
  Long Island City *(G-7260)*

FUR: Jackets

Anage Inc ....F 212 944-6533
  New York *(G-8571)*

FURNACES & OVENS: Indl

Buflovak LLC ....E 716 895-2100
  Buffalo *(G-2685)*
Cosmos Electronic Machine Corp ....E 631 249-2535
  Farmingdale *(G-4604)*
Embassy Industries Inc ....C 631 435-0209
  Hauppauge *(G-5647)*
Harper International Corp ....D 716 276-9900
  Buffalo *(G-2795)*
Harper International Corp ....G 716 276-9900
  Depew *(G-3984)*
Hpi Co Inc ....G 718 851-2753
  Brooklyn *(G-1945)*
J H Buhrmaster Company Inc ....G 518 843-1700
  Amsterdam *(G-331)*
Messer LLC ....D 716 773-7552
  Grand Island *(G-5337)*
Parker-Hannifin Corporation ....D 716 685-4040
  Lancaster *(G-6823)*
Vincent Genovese ....G 631 281-8170
  Mastic Beach *(G-7675)*

FURNACES: Indl, Electric

Cooks Intl Ltd Lblty Co ....G 212 741-4407
  New York *(G-9096)*

FURNITURE & CABINET STORES: Cabinets, Custom Work

A Van Hoek Woodworking Limited ....G 718 599-4388
  Brooklyn *(G-1437)*
Central Kitchen Corp ....F 631 283-1029
  Southampton *(G-14528)*
Custom Woodcraft LLC ....F 315 843-4234
  Munnsville *(G-8195)*
Di Fiore and Sons Custom Wdwkg ....G 718 278-1663
  Long Island City *(G-7201)*
Jamestown Kitchen & Bath Inc ....G 716 665-2299
  Jamestown *(G-6523)*
Time Base Corporation ....G 631 293-4068
  Edgewood *(G-4288)*
Ultimate Styles of America ....F 631 254-0219
  Bay Shore *(G-724)*

FURNITURE & CABINET STORES: Custom

Red White & Blue Entps Corp ....G 718 565-8080
  Woodside *(G-16223)*

FURNITURE & FIXTURES Factory

Adirondack Scenic Inc ....D 518 638-8000
  Argyle *(G-392)*
Armada New York LLC ....F 718 852-8105
  Brooklyn *(G-1531)*
Artistry In Wood of Syracuse ....F 315 431-4022
  Syracuse *(G-14819)*
Futon City Discounters Inc ....F 315 437-1328
  Syracuse *(G-14896)*
Interiors-Pft Inc ....E 212 244-9600
  Long Island City *(G-7249)*
J P Installations Warehouse ....F 914 576-3188
  New Rochelle *(G-8344)*
Modu-Craft Inc. ....G 716 694-0709
  North Tonawanda *(G-12078)*
Modu-Craft Inc. ....G 716 694-0709
  Tonawanda *(G-15123)*
T-Company LLC ....G 646 290-6365
  Smithtown *(G-14488)*

FURNITURE PARTS: Metal

Dimar Manufacturing Corp ....C 716 759-0351
  Clarence *(G-3428)*
Icestone LLC ....E 718 624-4900
  Brooklyn *(G-1951)*

(G-0000) Company's Geographic Section entry number

Protocase Incorporated................C...... 866 849-3911
Lewiston (G-6922)

FURNITURE REFINISHING SVCS

FX INC..F...... 212 244-2240
New York (G-9556)

Telesca-Heyman................................F...... 212 534-3442
New York (G-11450)

FURNITURE STOCK & PARTS: Carvings, Wood

Essequattro USA Inc ....G...... 917 862-0005
New York (G-9403)

Jim Quinn..F...... 518 356-0398
Schenectady (G-14282)

Mason Carvings Inc...........................G...... 716 484-7884
Jamestown (G-6531)

FURNITURE STOCK & PARTS: Dimension Stock, Hardwood

Fitzpatrick and Weller Inc................D...... 716 699-2393
Ellicottville (G-4314)

North Hudson Woodcraft Corp.............E...... 315 429-3105
Dolgeville (G-4024)

Randolph Dimension Corporation ....F...... 716 358-6901
Randolph (G-13064)

FURNITURE STOCK & PARTS: Frames, Upholstered Furniture, Wood

Artistic Frame Corp ....C...... 212 289-2100
New York (G-8636)

Vitobob Furniture Inc.........................G...... 516 676-1696
Long Island City (G-7396)

FURNITURE STOCK & PARTS: Hardwood

Guldenschuh Logging & Lbr LLC ....G...... 585 538-4750
Caledonia (G-3070)

FURNITURE STORES

Classic Sofa Ltd ....D...... 212 620-0485
New York (G-9026)

D & W Design Inc ....E...... 845 343-3366
Middletown (G-7903)

French & Itln Furn Craftsmen ....G...... 718 599-5000
Brooklyn (G-1866)

Furniture Doctor Inc ....G...... 585 657-6941
Bloomfield (G-947)

Futon City Discounters Inc ....F...... 315 437-1328
Syracuse (G-14896)

Gothic Cabinet Craft Inc....................D...... 347 881-1420
Maspeth (G-7618)

Little Wolf Cabinet Shop Inc ....E...... 212 734-1116
New York (G-10230)

Long Lumber and Supply Corp ....F...... 518 439-1661
Slingerlands (G-14466)

Manhattan Comfort Inc......................G...... 908 888-0818
Brooklyn (G-2107)

Omega Furniture Manufacturing ....F...... 315 463-7428
Syracuse (G-14954)

Pillow Perfections Ltd Inc ....G...... 718 383-2259
Brooklyn (G-2259)

Recycled Brooklyn Group LLC.............F...... 917 902-0662
Brooklyn (G-2334)

Safavieh Inc......................................A...... 516 945-1900
Port Washington (G-12920)

Smart Space Products LLC..................G...... 877 777-2441
New York (G-11272)

Studio 21 LA Inc ....E...... 718 965-6579
Brooklyn (G-2464)

Upstate Cabinet Company Inc ....F...... 585 429-5090
Rochester (G-13787)

Yepes Fine Furniture ....E...... 718 383-0221
Brooklyn (G-2600)

FURNITURE STORES: Cabinets, Kitchen, Exc Custom Made

Home Ideal Inc...................................G...... 718 762-8998
Flushing (G-4860)

FURNITURE STORES: Custom Made, Exc Cabinets

Atelier Viollet Corp............................G...... 718 782-1727
Brooklyn (G-1545)

Designway Ltd....................................G...... 212 254-2220
New York (G-9209)

John Langenbacher Co Inc.................E...... 718 328-0141
Bronx (G-1288)

FURNITURE STORES: Juvenile

Casa Collection Inc............................G...... 718 694-0272
Brooklyn (G-1653)

FURNITURE STORES: Office

FX INC..F...... 212 244-2240
New York (G-9556)

FURNITURE STORES: Outdoor & Garden

Walpole Woodworkers Inc ....G...... 631 726-2859
Water Mill (G-15531)

Wood Innovations of Suffolk ....G...... 631 698-2345
Oceanside (G-12198)

FURNITURE STORES: Unfinished

Universal Designs Inc.........................G...... 718 721-1111
Long Island City (G-7389)

FURNITURE WHOLESALERS

Etna Products Co Inc ....F...... 212 989-7591
New York (G-9413)

Furniture Doctor Inc ....G...... 585 657-6941
Bloomfield (G-947)

Harden Furniture LLC........................C...... 315 675-3600
Mc Connellsville (G-7686)

Holland & Sherry Inc.........................E...... 212 542-8410
New York (G-9803)

Marretti USA Inc ....G...... 212 255-5565
New York (G-10373)

FURNITURE, HOUSEHOLD: Wholesalers

Steinbock-Braff Inc ....E...... 718 972-6500
Brooklyn (G-2460)

Two Worlds Arts Ltd ....G...... 212 929-2210
New York (G-11566)

FURNITURE, OFFICE: Wholesalers

Artistic Frame Corp ....C...... 212 289-2100
New York (G-8636)

Kas-Ray Industries Inc ....F...... 212 620-3144
New York (G-10071)

Workplace Interiors LLC ....E...... 585 425-7420
Fairport (G-4530)

FURNITURE, WHOLESALE: Beds & Bedding

Wcd Window Coverings Inc ....E...... 845 336-4511
Lake Katrine (G-6764)

FURNITURE, WHOLESALE: Racks

ASAP Rack Rental Inc ....G...... 718 499-4495
Brooklyn (G-1539)

Reliable Welding & Fabrication ....G...... 631 758-2637
Patchogue (G-12511)

FURNITURE, WHOLESALE: Tables, Occasional

Vaughan Designs Inc..........................F...... 212 319-7070
New York (G-11649)

FURNITURE: Bed Frames & Headboards, Wood

Inova LLC...E...... 866 528-2804
Guilderland Center (G-5486)

FURNITURE: Bedroom, Wood

Fiber-Seal of New York Inc ....G...... 212 888-5580
New York (G-9487)

Your Furniture Designers Inc...............G...... 845 947-3046
West Haverstraw (G-15765)

FURNITURE: Beds, Household, Incl Folding & Cabinet, Metal

Charles P Rogers Brass Beds ....F...... 212 675-4400
New York (G-8975)

FURNITURE: Bookcases, Office, Wood

F E Hale Mfg Co.................................D...... 315 894-5490
Frankfort (G-4950)

FURNITURE: Box Springs, Assembled

Charles H Beckley Inc ....F...... 718 665-2218
Bronx (G-1224)

FURNITURE: Cabinets & Filing Drawers, Office, Exc Wood

Falvo Manufacturing Co Inc................F...... 315 724-7925
Utica (G-15261)

Ulrich Planfiling Eqp Corp ....E...... 716 763-1815
Lakewood (G-6786)

FURNITURE: Cabinets & Vanities, Medicine, Metal

Glissade New York LLC.......................E...... 631 756-4800
Farmingdale (G-4638)

FURNITURE: Chairs & Couches, Wood, Upholstered

Sleepable Sofas Ltd..........................D...... 973 546-4502
New York (G-11267)

FURNITURE: Chairs, Household Upholstered

Avanti Furniture Corp.........................F...... 516 293-8220
Farmingdale (G-4590)

FURNITURE: Chairs, Household Wood

Custom Display Manufacture ....G...... 516 783-6491
North Bellmore (G-12018)

El Greco Woodworking Inc ....E...... 716 483-0315
Jamestown (G-6508)

Hunt Country Furniture Inc.................D...... 845 832-6601
Wingdale (G-16159)

Manchester Wood Inc.........................C...... 518 642-9518
Granville (G-5351)

FURNITURE: Chairs, Office Exc Wood

Poppin Inc...D...... 212 391-7200
New York (G-10866)

Vitra Inc...F...... 212 463-5700
New York (G-11698)

FURNITURE: Chairs, Office Wood

Interior Solutions of Wny LLC ....G...... 716 332-0372
Buffalo (G-2813)

FURNITURE: China Closets

Raff Enterprises ....G...... 518 218-7883
Albany (G-123)

FURNITURE: Church

American Bptst Chrches Mtro NY........G...... 212 870-3195
New York (G-8545)

FURNITURE: Console Tables, Wood

Forecast Consoles Inc........................E...... 631 253-9000
Hauppauge (G-5653)

FURNITURE: Couches, Sofa/Davenport, Upholstered Wood Frames

Classic Sofa Ltd ....D...... 212 620-0485
New York (G-9026)

FURNITURE: Cribs, Metal

NK Medical Products Inc ....G...... 716 759-7200
Amherst (G-235)

Novum Medical Products Ny LLC ....F...... 716 759-7200
Amherst (G-236)

FURNITURE: Cut Stone

Puccio Design International.................F...... 516 248-6426
Garden City (G-5112)

FURNITURE: Desks & Tables, Office, Wood

Centre Interiors Wdwkg Co Inc............E...... 718 323-1343
Ozone Park (G-12458)

PRODUCT

FURNITURE: Desks, Metal

Artistic Products LLC ....E 631 435-0200
 Hauppauge (G-5595)

FURNITURE: Desks, Wood

Bush Industries Inc ....C 716 665-2000
 Jamestown (G-6500)
Ccn International Inc ....D 315 789-4400
 Geneva (G-5149)

FURNITURE: Dinette Sets, Metal

Embassy Dinettes Inc....................G 631 253-2292
 Deer Park (G-3871)

FURNITURE: Dining Room, Wood

Falcon Chair and Table Inc ....E 716 664-7136
 Falconer (G-4540)
Harden Furniture LLC ....C 315 675-3600
 Mc Connellsville (G-7686)

FURNITURE: Fiberglass & Plastic

Universal Interiors LLC ....F 518 298-4400
 Champlain (G-3320)

FURNITURE: Foundations & Platforms

Acworth Foundation ....G 631 784-7802
 Huntington (G-6197)
Ideal Manufacturing Inc ....E 585 872-7190
 East Rochester (G-4165)

FURNITURE: Game Room

Acem Corp......................................G 631 242-2440
 Deer Park (G-3828)

FURNITURE: Game Room, Wood

Acem Corp......................................G 631 242-2440
 Deer Park (G-3828)

FURNITURE: Garden, Exc Wood, Metal, Stone Or Concrete

Anandamali Inc ....F 212 343-8964
 New York (G-8573)
Holland & Sherry Inc ....E 212 542-8410
 New York (G-9803)

FURNITURE: Hospital

AFC Industries Inc ....D 718 747-0237
 College Point (G-3535)
Brandt Equipment LLC ....G 718 994-0800
 Bronx (G-1217)
Evans & Paul LLC ....E 516 576-0800
 Plainview (G-12684)

FURNITURE: Hotel

Inova LLC......................................E 866 528-2804
 Guilderland Center (G-5486)
N3a Corporation ....D 516 284-6799
 Inwood (G-6299)
Ramler International Ltd ....E 516 353-3106
 Jericho (G-6591)
Smart Space Products LLC ....G 877 777-2441
 New York (G-11272)
Timeless Decor LLC ....C 315 782-5759
 Watertown (G-15590)

FURNITURE: Household, Metal

D & W Design Inc ....E 845 343-3366
 Middletown (G-7903)
F&M Ornamental Designs LLC ....E 908 241-7776
 New York (G-9456)
Furniture Doctor Inc ....G 585 657-6941
 Bloomfield (G-947)
La Forge Francaise Ltd Inc ....G 631 591-0572
 Riverhead (G-13177)
Meeker Sales Corp.........................G 718 384-5400
 Brooklyn (G-2133)
Royal Metal Products Inc ....E 518 966-4442
 Surprise (G-14776)
Slava Industries Incorporated ....G 718 499-4850
 Brooklyn (G-2425)

FURNITURE: Household, NEC

Matthew Shively LLC ....G 914 937-3531
 Port Chester (G-12825)
Safcore LLC ....F 917 627-5263
 Brooklyn (G-2380)

FURNITURE: Household, Upholstered On Metal Frames

Precision Orna lr Works Inc ....G 718 379-5200
 Bronx (G-1342)

FURNITURE: Household, Upholstered, Exc Wood Or Metal

3phase Industries LLC ....G 347 763-2942
 Brooklyn (G-1415)
Albert Menin Interiors Ltd ....F 212 876-3041
 Bronx (G-1200)
Culin/Colella Inc ....G 914 698-7727
 Mamaroneck (G-7507)
Harome Designs LLC ....E 631 864-1900
 Commack (G-3591)
L& JG Stickley Incorporated ....A 315 682-5500
 Manlius (G-7548)
Mbh Furniture Innovations Inc ....G 845 354-8202
 Spring Valley (G-14578)
Olollo Inc.....................................G 877 701-0110
 Brooklyn (G-2230)
Ready To Assemble Company Inc ......E 516 825-4397
 Valley Stream (G-15356)
Two Worlds Arts Ltd ....G 212 929-2210
 New York (G-11566)
Yogibo LLC ....F 518 456-1762
 Albany (G-143)

FURNITURE: Household, Wood

A & S Woodworking Inc ....G 518 821-0832
 Hudson (G-6145)
Anthony Lawrence of New York ....E 212 206-8820
 Long Island City (G-7159)
Arthur Brown W Mfg Co ....F 631 243-5594
 Deer Park (G-3842)
Artisan Woodworking Ltd ....G 516 486-0818
 West Hempstead (G-15766)
Atelier Viollet Corp.....................G 718 782-1727
 Brooklyn (G-1545)
Benchmark Furniture Mfg ....D 718 257-4707
 Brooklyn (G-1574)
Black River Woodworking LLC ....G 315 376-8405
 Castorland (G-3206)
Bush Industries Inc ....C 716 665-2000
 Jamestown (G-6500)
Carlos & Alex Atelier Inc ....E 718 441-8911
 Richmond Hill (G-13111)
Carver Creek Enterprises Inc ....G 585 657-7511
 Bloomfield (G-942)
Charles H Beckley Inc ....F 718 665-2218
 Bronx (G-1224)
Comerford Hennessy At Home Inc ......G 631 537-6200
 Bridgehampton (G-1165)
Concepts In Wood of CNY ....E 315 463-8084
 Syracuse (G-14858)
Conesus Lake Association Inc ....E 585 346-6864
 Lakeville (G-6774)
Cousins Furniture & Hm Imprvs ......E 631 254-3752
 Deer Park (G-3854)
Custom Woodcraft LLC....................F 315 843-4234
 Munnsville (G-8195)
D & W Design Inc ....E 845 343-3366
 Middletown (G-7903)
David Sutherland Showrooms - N ......G 212 871-9717
 New York (G-9183)
Dbs Interiors Corp.......................F 631 491-3013
 West Babylon (G-15706)
Dcl Furniture Manufacturing ....E 516 248-2683
 Mineola (G-7968)
Deakon Homes and Interiors ....F 518 271-0342
 Troy (G-15165)
Designs By Robert Scott Inc ....E 718 609-2535
 Brooklyn (G-1738)
Dune Inc ....G 212 925-6171
 New York (G-9279)
Eclectic Cntract Furn Inds Inc ....F 212 967-5504
 New York (G-9316)
Emilia Interiors Inc ....F 718 629-4202
 Brooklyn (G-1800)
Eugenia Selective Living Inc ....F 631 277-1461
 Islip (G-6352)

Final Dimension Inc ....G 718 786-0100
 Maspeth (G-7615)
French & Itln Furn Craftsmen ....G 718 599-5000
 Brooklyn (G-1866)
Furniture Doctor Inc ....G 585 657-6941
 Bloomfield (G-947)
Glendale Architectural WD Pdts ....E 718 326-2700
 Glendale (G-5226)
Icon Design LLC ....E 585 768-6040
 Le Roy (G-6901)
Inter Craft Custom Furniture ....G 718 278-2573
 Astoria (G-425)
J Percoco Industries Inc ....G 631 312-4572
 Bohemia (G-1025)
K & B Woodworking Inc ....E 518 634-7253
 Cairo (G-3066)
Kazac Inc ....G 631 249-7299
 Farmingdale (G-4662)
Kittinger Company Inc...................E 716 876-1000
 Buffalo (G-2835)
Knoll Inc ....D 212 343-4124
 New York (G-10118)
L& JG Stickley Incorporated ....A 315 682-5500
 Manlius (G-7548)
Lanoves Inc ....G 718 384-1880
 Brooklyn (G-2047)
Little Wolf Cabinet Shop Inc ....E 212 734-1116
 New York (G-10230)
Ltdm Incorporated ....G 718 965-1339
 Brooklyn (G-2088)
M & C Furniture ....G 718 422-2136
 Brooklyn (G-2091)
M T D Corporation ....F 631 491-3905
 West Babylon (G-15727)
Mackenzie-Childs LLC.....................C 315 364-6118
 Aurora (G-504)
Mica International Ltd ....F 516 378-3400
 Freeport (G-5008)
New Day Woodwork Inc ....E 718 275-1721
 Glendale (G-5229)
Patrick Mackin Custom Furn ....G 718 237-2592
 Brooklyn (G-2250)
Peter S Curtis ....E 315 782-7363
 Evans Mills (G-4487)
Piccini Industries Ltd ....E 845 365-0614
 Orangeburg (G-12325)
Pillow Perfections Ltd Inc ....G 718 383-2259
 Brooklyn (G-2259)
Plexi Craft Quality Products ....F 212 924-3244
 New York (G-10856)
Premier Woodcraft Ltd ....E 610 383-6624
 White Plains (G-16055)
Recycled Brooklyn Group LLC............F 917 902-0662
 Brooklyn (G-2334)
Reis D Furniture Mfg.....................E 516 248-5676
 Mineola (G-7997)
Renco Group Inc ....E 212 541-6000
 New York (G-11012)
Ridge Cabinet & Showcase Inc ....E 585 663-0560
 Rochester (G-13673)
Triple J Bedding LLC ....G 718 643-8005
 Brooklyn (G-2523)
Universal Designs Inc...................G 718 721-1111
 Long Island City (G-7389)
Wallace Home Design Ctr ....G 631 765-3890
 Southold (G-14546)
Walpole Woodworkers Inc ....G 631 726-2859
 Water Mill (G-15531)
Walter P Sauer LLC ....E 718 937-0600
 Brooklyn (G-2574)
William Somerville Maintenance ....D 212 534-4600
 New York (G-11759)
Woodmotif Inc ....F 516 564-8325
 Hempstead (G-5852)
World Trading Center Inc ....G 631 273-3330
 Hauppauge (G-5803)

FURNITURE: Hydraulic Barber & Beauty Shop Chairs

Pyrotek Incorporated ....E 716 731-3221
 Sanborn (G-14148)

FURNITURE: Institutional, Exc Wood

Able Steel Equipment Co Inc ....F 718 361-9240
 Long Island City (G-7144)
Artistry In Wood of Syracuse ....F 315 431-4022
 Syracuse (G-14819)
Artone LLC ....D 716 664-2232
 Jamestown (G-6495)

Forecast Consoles Inc ....E 631 253-9000
Hauppauge (G-5653)
Maximum Security Products Corp ....E ... 518 233-1800
Waterford (G-15538)
Maxsecure Systems Inc ....G 800 657-4336
Buffalo (G-2863)
N Y Elli Design Corp ....F 718 228-0014
Ridgewood (G-13152)
Pluribus Products Inc ....E 718 852-1614
Bayville (G-747)
Rosenwach Tank Co Inc ....E 212 972-4411
Astoria (G-439)
Seating Inc ....E 800 468-2475
Nunda (G-12134)
Testori Interiors Inc ....E 518 298-4400
Champlain (G-3317)
Unifor Inc ....F 212 673-3434
New York (G-11585)
Universal Interiors LLC ....F 518 298-4400
Champlain (G-3320)

FURNITURE: Juvenile, Wood

Community Products LLC ....C 845 658-8799
Rifton (G-13167)
Ducduc LLC ....F ... 212 226-1868
New York (G-9276)

FURNITURE: Kitchen & Dining Room

Bento Box LLC ....G 718 260-8200
Brooklyn (G-1577)
Cab-Network Inc ....G 516 334-8666
Westbury (G-15873)
Catskill Craftsmen Inc ....D 607 652-7321
Stamford (G-14607)
Dinette Depot Ltd ....D 516 515-9623
Brooklyn (G-1748)
Lemode Concepts Inc ....G 631 841-0796
Amityville (G-291)
Professional Cab Detailing Co............F ... 845 436-7282
Woodridge (G-16194)

FURNITURE: Kitchen & Dining Room, Metal

Renco Group Inc ....G 212 541-6000
New York (G-11012)

FURNITURE: Laboratory

J H C Fabrications Inc ....E 718 649-0065
Brooklyn (G-1977)
Modu-Craft Inc......................G 716 694-0709
Tonawanda (G-15123)
Modu-Craft Inc......................G 716 694-0709
North Tonawanda (G-12078)

FURNITURE: Living Room, Upholstered On Wood Frames

Hallagan Manufacturing Co Inc ....D ... 315 331-4640
Newark (G-11840)

FURNITURE: Mattresses & Foundations

M R C Industries Inc ....C 516 328-6900
Port Washington (G-12903)
Steinbock-Braff Inc ....E 718 972-6500
Brooklyn (G-2460)
VSM Investors LLC ....G 212 351-1600
New York (G-11708)

FURNITURE: Mattresses, Box & Bedsprings

Brook North Farms Inc ....F 315 834-9390
Auburn (G-469)
Dixie Foam Ltd ....G 212 645-8999
Brooklyn (G-1750)
Duxiana Dux Bed ....G 212 755-2600
New York (G-9282)
Metro Mattress Corp ....E 716 205-2300
Niagara Falls (G-11951)
Natural Dreams LLC ....G 718 760-4202
Corona (G-3747)

FURNITURE: Mattresses, Innerspring Or Box Spring

KKR Millennium GP LLC ....A 212 750-8300
New York (G-10112)
Otis Bedding Mfg Co Inc ....E 716 825-2599
Buffalo (G-2900)

Royal Bedding Co Buffalo Inc ....E 716 895-1414
Buffalo (G-2966)
Sealy Mattress Co Albany Inc ....B 518 880-1600
Troy (G-15161)

FURNITURE: NEC

Dellet Industries Inc ....F ... 718 965-0101
Brooklyn (G-1733)
Inova LLC ....F ... 518 861-3400
Altamont (G-195)

FURNITURE: Novelty, Wood

Feinkind Inc ....G 800 289-6136
Irvington (G-6308)

FURNITURE: Office Panel Systems, Exc Wood

Aztec Industries Inc ....G 631 585-1331
Ronkonkoma (G-13910)
Knoll Inc ....D 212 343-4124
New York (G-10118)

FURNITURE: Office Panel Systems, Wood

New Dimensions Office Group ....D ... 718 387-0995
Brooklyn (G-2203)

FURNITURE: Office, Exc Wood

3phase Industries LLC ....G 347 763-2942
Brooklyn (G-1415)
Able Steel Equipment Co Inc ....F 718 361-9240
Long Island City (G-7144)
Allcraft Fabricators Inc...............D 631 951-4100
Hauppauge (G-5583)
Aronowitz Metal Works ....G 845 356-1660
Monsey (G-8035)
Artone LLC ....D 716 664-2232
Jamestown (G-6495)
Bisley Inc ....G 212 675-3055
New York (G-8802)
Davies Office Refurbishing Inc............C ... 518 449-2040
Albany (G-69)
Davinci Designs Inc ....F 631 595-1095
Deer Park (G-3859)
Dcl Furniture Manufacturing..............E ... 516 248-2683
Mineola (G-7968)
Deakon Homes and Interiors ....F 518 271-0342
Troy (G-15165)
E-Systems Group LLC ....E 607 775-1100
Conklin (G-3624)
Eugenia Selective Living Inc............G 631 277-1461
Islip (G-6352)
Exhibit Corporation America ....E ... 718 937-2600
Long Island City (G-7217)
Forecast Consoles Inc...............G 631 253-9000
Hauppauge (G-5653)
FX INC ....F 212 244-2240
New York (G-9556)
Hergo Ergonomic Support Syst ....E ... 888 222-7270
Oceanside (G-12175)
Herman Miller Inc ....E 212 753-3022
New York (G-9769)
Hudson Valley Office Furn Inc.............G 845 565-6673
Newburgh (G-11869)
Inscape Inc ....E 716 665-6210
Falconer (G-4545)
Integrated Tech Support Svcs ....G 718 454-2497
Saint Albans (G-14106)
International Office ....G 212 334-4617
New York (G-9922)
Larson Metal Manufacturing Co ....G 716 665-6807
Jamestown (G-6529)
Lucia Group Inc.....................G 631 392-4900
Deer Park (G-3900)
Modern Metal Fabricators Inc ....G 518 966-4142
Hannacroix (G-5541)
New Dimensions Office Group ....D 718 387-0995
Brooklyn (G-2203)
Piccini Industries Ltd..............E 845 365-0614
Orangeburg (G-12325)
Premier Woodcraft Ltd ....E 610 383-6624
White Plains (G-16055)
Roberts Office Furn Cncpts Inc............E 315 451-9185
Liverpool (G-7038)
Royal Metal Products Inc ....E 518 966-4442
Surprise (G-14776)
Workplace Interiors LLC ....E 585 425-7420
Fairport (G-4530)

Zographos Designs Ltd...............G 212 545-0227
New York (G-11828)

FURNITURE: Office, Wood

Artone LLC ....D 716 664-2232
Jamestown (G-6495)
B D B Typewriter Supply Works ....E 718 232-4800
Brooklyn (G-1557)
Bauerschmidt & Sons Inc ....D 718 528-3500
Jamaica (G-6429)
Bloch Industries LLC ....D 585 334-9600
Rochester (G-13272)
Breather Products US Inc ....E 800 471-8704
New York (G-8850)
DAF Office Networks Inc ....G 315 699-7070
Cicero (G-3418)
Davinci Designs Inc ....F 631 595-1095
Deer Park (G-3859)
Dcl Furniture Manufacturing..............E 516 248-2683
Mineola (G-7968)
Deakon Homes and Interiors ....E 518 271-0342
Troy (G-15165)
Designs By Robert Scott Inc ....E 718 609-2535
Brooklyn (G-1738)
E-Systems Group LLC ....E 607 775-1100
Conklin (G-3624)
Eugenia Selective Living Inc............E 631 277-1461
Islip (G-6352)
Exhibit Corporation America ....E 718 937-2600
Long Island City (G-7217)
Forecast Consoles Inc ....E 631 253-9000
Hauppauge (G-5653)
Furniture By Craftmaster Ltd ....G 631 750-0658
Bohemia (G-1014)
Glendale Architectural WD Pdts ....E 718 326-2700
Glendale (G-5226)
Gunlocke Company LLC ....C 585 728-5111
Wayland (G-15626)
H Freund Woodworking Co Inc ....F 516 334-3774
Westbury (G-15891)
Harden Furniture LLC ....C 315 675-3600
Mc Connellsville (G-7686)
Heartwood Specialties Inc ....G 607 654-0102
Hammondsport (G-5529)
Hni Corporation ....C 212 683-2232
New York (G-9798)
House Ur Home Inc ....G 347 585-3308
Monroe (G-8023)
Humanscale Corporation ....E 212 725-4749
New York (G-9839)
Innovant Inc ....G 212 929-4883
Islandia (G-6336)
Kazac Inc ....G 631 249-7299
Farmingdale (G-4662)
Kimball Office Inc ....E 212 753-6161
New York (G-10102)
Kittinger Company Inc ....E 716 876-1000
Buffalo (G-2835)
Knoll Inc ....D 716 891-1700
Buffalo (G-2836)
Knoll Inc ....D 212 343-4124
New York (G-10118)
Lake Country Woodworkers Ltd...........E 585 374-6353
Naples (G-8208)
Longo Commercial Cabinets Inc ....E 631 225-4290
Lindenhurst (G-6956)
M T D Corporation ....F 631 491-3905
West Babylon (G-15727)
Manhattan Comfort Inc ....G 908 888-0818
Brooklyn (G-2107)
Matteo & Antonio Bartolotta ....F 315 252-2220
Auburn (G-485)
Miller Blaker Inc ....D 718 665-0500
Bronx (G-1315)
Millers Millworks Inc ....E 585 494-1420
Bergen (G-818)
Omega Furniture Manufacturing ....F 315 463-7428
Syracuse (G-14954)
Pheonix Custom Furniture Ltd ....E 212 727-2648
Long Island City (G-7325)
Piccini Industries Ltd..............E 845 365-0614
Orangeburg (G-12325)
Premier Woodcraft Ltd ....E 610 383-6624
White Plains (G-16055)
Princeton Upholstery Co Inc............D 845 343-2196
Middletown (G-7928)
Technology Desking Inc..............E 212 257-6998
New York (G-11446)
Universal Designs Inc...............G 718 721-1111
Long Island City (G-7389)

PRODUCT

FURNITURE: Office, Wood (continued)

Upstate Office Liquidators Inc ....F 607 722-9234
　Johnson City (G-6609)
WD Certified Contracting LLC ....F 516 493-9319
　Westbury (G-15939)
Woodmotif Inc ....F 516 564-8325
　Hempstead (G-5852)
Your Furniture Designers Inc ....G 845 947-3046
　West Haverstraw (G-15765)
Zographos Designs Ltd ....G 212 545-0227
　New York (G-11828)

FURNITURE: Outdoor, Wood

Long Lumber and Supply Corp ....F 518 439-1661
　Slingerlands (G-14466)
Sitecraft Inc ....G 718 729-4900
　Astoria (G-441)
Sundown Ski & Sport Shop Inc ....D 631 737-8600
　Lake Grove (G-6761)

FURNITURE: Pews, Church

Keck Group Inc ....F 845 988-5757
　Warwick (G-15515)

FURNITURE: Picnic Tables Or Benches, Park

Studio 21 LA Inc ....E 718 965-6579
　Brooklyn (G-2464)
Town of Amherst ....E 716 631-7113
　Williamsville (G-16144)
Town of Hartford ....G 315 724-0654
　New Hartford (G-8247)
Tymor Park ....G 845 724-5691
　Lagrangeville (G-6755)

FURNITURE: Rattan

Bielecky Bros Inc ....E 718 424-4764
　Woodside (G-16197)

FURNITURE: Restaurant

Dine Rite Seating Products Inc ....E 631 226-8899
　Lindenhurst (G-6950)
Hunt Country Furniture Inc ....D 845 832-6601
　Wingdale (G-16159)
L & D Manufacturing Corp ....E 718 665-5226
　Bronx (G-1295)
Lb Furniture Industries LLC.................C 518 828-1501
　Hudson (G-6169)
Maxsun Corporation ....F 718 418-6800
　Maspeth (G-7628)
Rollhaus Seating Products Inc ....F 718 729-9111
　Long Island City (G-7344)

FURNITURE: School

Inova LLC...E 866 528-2804
　Guilderland Center (G-5486)

FURNITURE: Ship

Starliner Shipping & Travel ....G 718 385-1515
　Brooklyn (G-2453)

FURNITURE: Silverware Chests, Wood

McGraw Wood Products LLC ....E 607 836-6465
　Mc Graw (G-7689)

FURNITURE: Sleep

Sleep Improvement Center Inc ....F 516 536-5799
　Rockville Centre (G-13836)

FURNITURE: Sofa Beds Or Convertible Sofas)

Sleepable Sofas Ltd...............................D 973 546-4502
　New York (G-11267)

FURNITURE: Storage Chests, Household, Wood

Premiere Living Products LLC ....F 631 873-4337
　Dix Hills (G-4013)

FURNITURE: Tables & Table Tops, Wood

Ercole Nyc Inc ....F 212 675-2218
　Brooklyn (G-1810)

FURNITURE: Theater

Steeldeck Ny Inc ....F 718 599-3700
　Brooklyn (G-2457)

FURNITURE: Unfinished, Wood

Stillwater Wood & Iron..........................G 518 664-4501
　Stillwater (G-14733)

FURNITURE: Upholstered

Artone LLC ....D 716 664-2232
　Jamestown (G-6495)
August Studios ....G 718 706-6487
　Long Island City (G-7172)
Deangelis Ltd ....E 212 348-8225
　Glen Head (G-5205)
Elan Upholstery Inc ....F 631 563-0650
　Bohemia (G-1011)
Falvo Manufacturing Co Inc ....F 315 724-7925
　Utica (G-15261)
Fiber-Seal of New York Inc ....F 212 888-5580
　New York (G-9487)
Furniture By Craftmaster Ltd ....G 631 750-0658
　Bohemia (G-1014)
H & H Furniture Co................................G 718 850-5252
　Jamaica (G-6446)
Harden Furniture LLC ....C 315 675-3600
　Mc Connellsville (G-7686)
Jackson Dakota Inc ....G 212 838-9444
　New York (G-9962)
Jays Furniture Products Inc ....E 716 876-8854
　Buffalo (G-2816)
Kittinger Company Inc ....E 716 876-1000
　Buffalo (G-2835)
Mackenzie-Childs LLC...........................C 315 364-6118
　Aurora (G-504)
Matteo & Antonio Bartolotta ....F 315 252-2220
　Auburn (G-485)
Mazza Classics Incorporated................G 631 390-9060
　Farmingdale (G-4679)
Pheonix Custom Furniture Ltd ....E 212 727-2648
　Long Island City (G-7325)
Princeton Upholstery Co Inc.................D 845 343-2196
　Middletown (G-7928)
Rob Herschenfeld Design Inc ....F 718 456-6801
　Brooklyn (G-2350)
Simon S Decorating Inc.........................G 718 339-2931
　Brooklyn (G-2418)
Slava Industries Incorporated ....G 718 499-4850
　Brooklyn (G-2425)
Smith & Watson ....E 212 686-6444
　New York (G-11274)
Two Worlds Arts Ltd ....G 212 929-2210
　Brooklyn (G-2533)
Versailles Drapery Upholstery ....F 212 533-2059
　Long Island City (G-7395)
Wallace Home Design Ctr ....G 631 765-3890
　Southold (G-14546)
Yepes Fine Furniture ....E 718 383-0221
　Brooklyn (G-2600)

FURNITURE: Vehicle

Stidd Systems Inc ....E 631 477-2400
　Greenport (G-5458)

FURRIERS

Anastasia Furs International.................F 212 868-9241
　New York (G-8574)
Superior Furs Inc ....F 516 365-4123
　Manhasset (G-7541)

FUSES: Electric

Leviton Manufacturing Co Inc ....B 631 812-6000
　Melville (G-7800)
Soc America Inc ....F 631 472-6666
　Ronkonkoma (G-14010)

GAMES & TOYS: Airplanes

Jupiter Creations Inc ....G 917 493-9393
　New York (G-10043)

GAMES & TOYS: Baby Carriages & Restraint Seats

Babysafe Usa LLC ....G 877 367-4141
　Afton (G-6)

GAMES & TOYS: Banks

E C C Corp ....G 518 873-6494
　Elizabethtown (G-4300)

GAMES & TOYS: Child Restraint Seats, Automotive

Pidyon Controls Inc ....F 212 683-9523
　New York (G-10837)

GAMES & TOYS: Craft & Hobby Kits & Sets

Design Works Craft Inc ....F 631 244-5749
　Bohemia (G-1005)
Innovative Designs LLC ....E 212 695-0892
　New York (G-9897)
R F Giardina Co ....F 516 922-1364
　Oyster Bay (G-12456)
Spectrum Crafts Inc ....E 631 244-5749
　Bohemia (G-1081)

GAMES & TOYS: Doll Hats

Beila Group Inc ....F 212 260-1948
　New York (G-8750)

GAMES & TOYS: Dolls & Doll Clothing

Goldberger Company LLC ....F 212 924-1194
　New York (G-9639)

GAMES & TOYS: Dolls, Exc Stuffed Toy Animals

ADC Dolls Inc ....C 212 244-4500
　New York (G-8455)
Lovee Doll & Toy Co Inc ....G 212 242-1545
　New York (G-10273)
Madame Alexander Doll 2018 LLC ....G 917 576-8381
　New York (G-10311)
Madame Alexander Doll Co LLC...........D 212 244-4500
　New York (G-10312)

GAMES & TOYS: Electronic

Barron Games Intl Co LLC ....F 716 630-0054
　Buffalo (G-2655)
Code Red Trading LLC ....E 347 782-2608
　Brooklyn (G-1673)
Kidz Toyz Inc ....G 914 261-4453
　Mount Kisco (G-8096)

GAMES & TOYS: Game Machines, Exc Coin-Operated

Ellis Products Corp.................................G 516 791-3732
　Valley Stream (G-15339)

GAMES & TOYS: Puzzles

Compoz A Puzzle Inc ....G 516 883-2311
　Port Washington (G-12869)
Tucker Jones House Inc ....E 631 642-9092
　East Setauket (G-4189)

GAMES & TOYS: Scooters, Children's

Dakott LLC ....G 888 805-6795
　New York (G-9159)
Famous Box Scooter Co ....G 631 943-2013
　West Babylon (G-15711)

GAMES & TOYS: Trains & Eqpt, Electric & Mechanical

Gargraves Trackage Corporation ....G 315 483-6577
　North Rose (G-12035)
Mechanical Displays Inc ....G 718 258-5588
　Brooklyn (G-2130)
Pride Lines Ltd ....G 631 225-0033
　Lindenhurst (G-6970)

GARBAGE CONTAINERS: Plastic

CT Industrial Supply Co Inc ....F 718 417-3226
　Brooklyn (G-1706)
Rainbow Plastics Inc ....F 718 218-7288
　Brooklyn (G-2325)
Think Green Junk Removal Inc ....G 845 297-7771
　Wappingers Falls (G-15499)

GARBAGE DISPOSERS & COMPACTORS: Commercial

240 Michigan Street Inc ....F 716 434-6010
 Buffalo *(G-2611)*

Blue Tee Corp ....G...... 212 598-0880
 New York *(G-8820)*

GARNET MINING SVCS

Barton Mines Company LLC ....C....... 518 798-5462
 Glens Falls *(G-5242)*

GAS & OIL FIELD EXPLORATION SVCS

Able Environmental Services ....G...... 631 567-6585
 Bohemia *(G-961)*

Aegis Oil Limited Ventures LLC ....F 646 233-4900
 New York *(G-8487)*

America Capital Energy Corp ....G...... 212 983-8316
 New York *(G-8540)*

Bistate Oil Management Corp ....F 212 935-4110
 New York *(G-8803)*

Hess Energy Exploration Ltd ....G...... 732 750-6500
 New York *(G-9772)*

Hess Explrtion Prod Hldngs Ltd ....G...... 732 750-6000
 New York *(G-9773)*

KKR Ntral Rsources Fund I-A LP ....G...... 212 750-8300
 New York *(G-10113)*

Lenape Energy Inc ....G...... 585 344-1200
 Alexander *(G-177)*

Lenape Resources Inc ....F 585 344-1200
 Alexander *(G-178)*

Mac Fadden Holdings Inc ....E 212 979-4805
 New York *(G-10303)*

Madoff Energy III LLC ....G...... 212 744-1918
 New York *(G-10316)*

Native Amercn Enrgy Group Inc..........G...... 718 408-2323
 Forest Hills *(G-4923)*

Norse Energy Corp USA ....G...... 716 568-2048
 Buffalo *(G-2891)*

Occidental Energy Mktg Inc ....G...... 212 632-4950
 New York *(G-10675)*

Range Rsurces - Appalachia LLC ....E 716 753-3385
 Mayville *(G-7684)*

Sanguine Gas Exploration LLC ....E 212 582-8555
 New York *(G-11132)*

Seneca Resources Company LLC ....F 716 630-6750
 Williamsville *(G-16138)*

Somerset Production Co LLC ....G...... 716 932-6480
 Buffalo *(G-2985)*

Springfield Oil Services Inc ....F 914 315-6812
 Harrison *(G-5559)*

U S Energy Development Corp ....D....... 716 636-0401
 Getzville *(G-5183)*

Waffenbauch USA ....E 716 326-4508
 Westfield *(G-15950)*

Warren Energy Services LLC ....F 212 697-9660
 New York *(G-11725)*

GAS & OIL FIELD SVCS, NEC

Case Brothers Inc ....G....... 716 925-7172
 Limestone *(G-6937)*

Essar Americas ....G...... 212 292-2600
 New York *(G-9398)*

GAS STATIONS

Marina Holding Corp.........................F 718 646-9283
 Brooklyn *(G-2115)*

GASES & LIQUIFIED PETROLEUM GASES

Osaka Gas Energy America Corp.........F 914 253-5500
 White Plains *(G-16037)*

GASES: Carbon Dioxide

Messer Merchant Production LLC........G....... 315 593-1360
 Fulton *(G-5071)*

GASES: Flourinated Hydrocarbon

Hudson Technologies Company ....E 845 735-6000
 Pearl River *(G-12532)*

GASES: Indl

Praxair Inc.....................................F 716 879-2000
 Tonawanda *(G-15133)*

Praxair Inc.....................................E 716 649-1600
 Hamburg *(G-5516)*

Praxair Inc.....................................E 518 482-4360
 Albany *(G-117)*

Praxair Inc.....................................E 716 286-4600
 Niagara Falls *(G-11966)*

Praxair Inc.....................................C....... 845 359-4200
 Orangeburg *(G-12326)*

Praxair Inc.....................................E 716 879-4000
 Tonawanda *(G-15134)*

Praxair Distribution Inc ....G...... 716 879-2185
 Buffalo *(G-2927)*

GASES: Neon

Neon ....F 212 727-5628
 New York *(G-10563)*

GASES: Nitrogen

Linde Gas North America LLC ....E 518 713-2015
 Cohoes *(G-3508)*

Linde Gas North America LLC ....F 315 431-4081
 Syracuse *(G-14933)*

Matheson Tri-Gas Inc........................G...... 518 203-5003
 Cohoes *(G-3509)*

Messer LLC....................................E 716 847-0748
 Buffalo *(G-2865)*

Messer LLC....................................D....... 518 439-8187
 Feura Bush *(G-4791)*

GASES: Oxygen

Air Products and Chemicals Inc...........D....... 518 463-4273
 Glenmont *(G-5235)*

Airgas Inc ....F 518 690-0068
 Albany *(G-30)*

Oxair Ltd ....G...... 716 298-8288
 Niagara Falls *(G-11962)*

Praxair Distribution Inc ....G...... 315 457-5821
 Liverpool *(G-7034)*

Praxair Distribution Inc ....F 315 735-6153
 Marcy *(G-7565)*

GASKET MATERIALS

Hollingsworth & Vose Company...........C....... 518 695-8000
 Greenwich *(G-5473)*

Jed Lights Inc ....F 516 812-5001
 Deer Park *(G-3888)*

Noroc Enterprises Inc.......................C....... 718 585-3230
 Bronx *(G-1325)*

GASKETS

Allstate Gasket & Packing Inc ....F 631 254-4050
 Deer Park *(G-3835)*

Boonville Manufacturing Corp..............G...... 315 942-4368
 Boonville *(G-1105)*

Frank Lowe Rbr & Gasket Co Inc ....E 631 777-2707
 Shirley *(G-14421)*

SAS Industries Inc ....F 631 727-1441
 Manorville *(G-7553)*

Schlegel Electronic Mtls Inc ....F 585 295-2030
 Rochester *(G-13717)*

Seal & Design Inc ....E 315 432-8021
 Syracuse *(G-14990)*

GASKETS & SEALING DEVICES

A L Sealing.....................................G....... 315 699-6900
 Chittenango *(G-3402)*

Garlock Sealing Tech LLC ....A 315 597-4811
 Palmyra *(G-12487)*

GM Components Holdings LLC............D....... 716 439-2402
 Lockport *(G-7081)*

John Crane Inc ....D....... 315 593-6237
 Fulton *(G-5066)*

SKF USA Inc ....D....... 716 661-2600
 Falconer *(G-4556)*

Temper Corporation ....E 518 853-3467
 Fonda *(G-4912)*

Web Seal Inc ....E 585 546-1320
 Rochester *(G-13800)*

Xto Incorporated ....D....... 315 451-7807
 Liverpool *(G-7050)*

GASOLINE FILLING STATIONS

Hess Corporation ....B....... 212 997-8500
 New York *(G-9771)*

GASOLINE WHOLESALERS

Bluebar Oil Co Inc ....F 315 245-4328
 Blossvale *(G-955)*

Seneca Nation Enterprise ....F 716 934-7430
 Irving *(G-6304)*

GATES: Dam, Metal Plate

Linita Design & Mfg Corp ....E 716 566-7753
 Lackawanna *(G-6741)*

Riverside Iron LLC ....E 315 535-4864
 Gouverneur *(G-5322)*

Rw Gate Company ....F 518 874-4750
 Troy *(G-15185)*

Rw Gate Company ....D....... 518 874-4750
 Troy *(G-15186)*

GATES: Ornamental Metal

City Store Gates Mfg Corp ....E 718 939-9700
 College Point *(G-3540)*

E & J Iron Works Inc ....E 718 665-6040
 Bronx *(G-1247)*

Inter-Fence Co Inc ....E 718 939-9700
 College Point *(G-3546)*

Lopopolo Iron Works Inc ....G...... 718 339-0572
 Brooklyn *(G-2085)*

Moon Gates Company ....G...... 718 426-0023
 East Elmhurst *(G-4110)*

United Steel Products Inc ....D....... 914 968-7782
 Flushing *(G-4904)*

Vr Containment LLC ....E 917 972-3441
 Fresh Meadows *(G-5048)*

GAUGES

Dorsey Metrology Intl Inc ....E 845 229-2929
 Poughkeepsie *(G-12951)*

Trinity Tools Inc...............................E 716 694-1111
 North Tonawanda *(G-12096)*

GEARS

Gear Motions Incorporated ....E 716 885-1080
 Buffalo *(G-2769)*

Gear Motions Incorporated ....E 315 488-0100
 Syracuse *(G-14901)*

Great Lakes Gear Co Inc ....G...... 716 694-0715
 Tonawanda *(G-15106)*

Industrial Mch Gear Works LLC ....G...... 516 695-4442
 Rockville Centre *(G-13829)*

Perfect Gear & Instrument ....F 516 328-3330
 Hicksville *(G-5943)*

Perfect Gear & Instrument ....E 516 873-6122
 Garden City Park *(G-5123)*

Pro-Gear Co Inc...............................G...... 716 684-3811
 Buffalo *(G-2934)*

Riley Gear Corporation ....E 716 694-0900
 North Tonawanda *(G-12086)*

S R & R Industries Inc ....G...... 845 692-8329
 Middletown *(G-7931)*

Secs Inc ....E 914 667-5600
 Mount Vernon *(G-8179)*

Superite Gear Instr of Hppauge............G...... 631 234-0100
 Hauppauge *(G-5779)*

GEARS & GEAR UNITS: Reduction, Exc Auto

Perfection Gear Inc ....C....... 716 592-9310
 Springville *(G-14595)*

GEARS: Power Transmission, Exc Auto

Buffalo Gear Inc ....E 716 731-2100
 Sanborn *(G-14139)*

Gleason Works ....A 585 473-1000
 Rochester *(G-13445)*

Jrlon Inc ....D...... 315 597-4067
 Palmyra *(G-12489)*

Khk Usa Inc ....G...... 516 248-3850
 Mineola *(G-7984)*

McGuigan Inc ....E 631 750-6222
 Bohemia *(G-1045)*

Niagara Gear Corporation ....E 716 874-3131
 Buffalo *(G-2885)*

Nuttall Gear L L C ....E 716 298-4100
 Niagara Falls *(G-11958)*

Oliver Gear Inc ....E 716 885-1080
 Buffalo *(G-2896)*

Peerless-Winsmith Inc.......................C....... 716 592-9311
 Springville *(G-14594)*

Precipart Corporation ....C....... 631 694-3100
 Farmingdale *(G-4714)*

Precision Mechanisms Corp ....E 516 333-5955
 Westbury *(G-15919)*

P
R
O
D
U
C
T

Rochester Gear Inc..................E...... 585 254-5442
Rochester (G-13689)

GELATIN

Geliko LLC..................E...... 212 876-5620
New York (G-9585)

GEM STONES MINING, NEC: Natural

Ray Griffiths Inc..................G...... 212 689-7209
New York (G-10985)

GEMSTONE & INDL DIAMOND MINING SVCS

Avs Gem Stone Corp..................G...... 212 944-6380
New York (G-8695)
Didco Inc..................F...... 212 997-5022
Rego Park (G-13076)
Herkimer Diamond Mines Inc..................E...... 315 891-7355
Herkimer (G-5864)
Kotel Importers Inc..................F...... 212 245-6200
New York (G-10130)

GENERAL & INDUSTRIAL LOAN INSTITUTIONS

Mitsui Chemicals America Inc..................E...... 914 253-0777
Rye Brook (G-14092)

GENERAL MERCHANDISE, NONDURABLE, WHOLESALE

Dahill Distributors Inc..................G...... 347 371-9453
Brooklyn (G-1718)
French Associates Inc..................F...... 718 387-9880
Fresh Meadows (G-5041)
Lokai Holdings LLC..................F...... 646 979-3474
New York (G-10245)
Specialty Products Inc..................E...... 866 869-4335
Center Moriches (G-3248)

GENERATING APPARATUS & PARTS: Electrical

Industrial Test Eqp Co Inc..................E...... 516 883-6423
Port Washington (G-12888)
Mks Medical Electronics..................C...... 585 292-7400
Rochester (G-13555)

GENERATION EQPT: Electronic

Alliance Control Systems Inc..................G...... 845 279-4430
Brewster (G-1140)
Beltron Products Inc..................E...... 888 423-5876
Albany (G-45)
C & M Circuits Inc..................E...... 631 589-0208
Bohemia (G-985)
Curtis Instruments Inc..................C...... 914 666-2971
Mount Kisco (G-8089)
Cygnus Automation Inc..................E...... 631 981-0909
Bohemia (G-997)
General Electric Company..................E...... 518 459-4110
Albany (G-80)
Sparkcharge Inc..................G...... 315 480-3645
Syracuse (G-14996)
Tonoga Inc..................E...... 518 658-3202
Petersburg (G-12600)

GENERATORS: Electric

Cellgen Inc..................G...... 516 889-9300
Freeport (G-4990)
Getec Inc..................F...... 845 292-0800
Ferndale (G-4789)

GENERATORS: Electrochemical, Fuel Cell

Plug Power Inc..................G...... 585 474-3993
Rochester (G-13626)
Plug Power Inc..................B...... 518 782-7700
Latham (G-6874)

GENERATORS: Gas

Better Power Inc..................G...... 585 475-1321
Rochester (G-13267)

GIFT SHOP

Csi International Inc..................E...... 800 441-2895
Niagara Falls (G-11919)

Exotic Print and Paper Inc..................F...... 212 807-0465
New York (G-9446)
Fly Creek Cder Mill Orchrd Inc..................G...... 607 547-9692
Fly Creek (G-4909)
Frame Shoppe & Art Gallery..................G...... 516 365-6014
Manhasset (G-7534)

GIFT, NOVELTY & SOUVENIR STORES: Artcraft & carvings

Kleinfelder John..................G...... 716 753-3163
Mayville (G-7683)

GIFT, NOVELTY & SOUVENIR STORES: Gifts & Novelties

Issacs Yisroel..................G...... 718 851-7430
Brooklyn (G-1971)
Mainly Monograms Inc..................E...... 845 624-4923
West Nyack (G-15827)

GIFTS & NOVELTIES: Wholesalers

Cannizzaro Seal & Engraving Co..................G...... 718 513-6125
Brooklyn (G-1644)
Full Circle Home LLC..................G...... 212 432-0001
New York (G-9551)
Justa Company..................G...... 718 932-6139
Long Island City (G-7258)
Mountain T-Shirts Inc..................E...... 518 943-4533
Catskill (G-3215)
Nubian Heritage..................G...... 631 265-3551
Hauppauge (G-5729)
OH How Cute Inc..................G...... 347 838-6031
Staten Island (G-14687)
Studio Silversmiths Inc..................E...... 718 418-6785
Ridgewood (G-13162)
Trove Inc..................F...... 212 268-2046
Brooklyn (G-2525)

GIFTWARE: Brass

Lr Paris LLC..................F...... 845 709-8013
New York (G-10275)

GLASS FABRICATORS

Benson Industries Inc..................F...... 212 779-3230
New York (G-8758)
Community Glass Inc..................G...... 607 737-8860
Elmira (G-4344)
Dillmeier Enterprises Inc..................F...... 800 325-0596
Garden City (G-5095)
Glassfab Inc..................E...... 585 262-4000
Rochester (G-13441)
Global Glass Corp..................G...... 516 681-2309
Hicksville (G-5912)
Granville Glass & Granite..................G...... 518 812-0492
Hudson Falls (G-6189)
Gray Glass Inc..................E...... 718 217-2943
Queens Village (G-13020)
Kasson & Keller Inc..................A...... 518 853-3421
Fonda (G-4910)
Manhattan Shade & Glass Co Inc..................E...... 212 288-5616
Hauppauge (G-5707)
Michbi Doors Inc..................D...... 631 231-9050
Farmingdale (G-4683)
Oldcastle Building Envelope..................F...... 212 957-5400
New York (G-10685)
Pal Manufacturing Corp..................E...... 516 937-1990
Hicksville (G-5940)
Quality Enclosures Inc..................E...... 631 234-0115
Central Islip (G-3286)
Royal Metal Products Inc..................E...... 518 966-4442
Surprise (G-14776)
Select Interior Door Ltd..................E...... 585 535-9900
North Java (G-12032)
Studio Glass Batch LLC..................G...... 585 924-9579
Victor (G-15432)
Vitarose Corp of America..................G...... 718 951-9700
Brooklyn (G-2565)
Vitrix Inc..................G...... 607 936-8707
Corning (G-3723)

GLASS PRDTS, FROM PURCHASED GLASS: Art

Carvart Glass Inc..................E...... 212 675-0030
New York (G-8926)

GLASS PRDTS, FROM PURCHASED GLASS: Glass Beads, Reflecting

Potters Industries LLC..................E...... 315 265-4920
Norwood (G-12132)

GLASS PRDTS, FROM PURCHASED GLASS: Glassware

Exquisite Glass & Stone Inc..................G...... 718 937-9266
Astoria (G-422)
Flour City Growlers Inc..................F...... 585 360-8709
Rochester (G-13414)
Gmd Industries Inc..................G...... 718 445-8779
College Point (G-3543)

GLASS PRDTS, FROM PURCHASED GLASS: Insulating

Dunlea Whl GL & Mirror Inc..................G...... 914 664-5277
Mount Vernon (G-8140)
Press Glass Na Inc..................E...... 212 631-3044
New York (G-10883)
Rochester Insulated Glass Inc..................D...... 585 289-3611
Manchester (G-7528)

GLASS PRDTS, FROM PURCHASED GLASS: Mirrored

Depp Glass Inc..................F...... 718 784-8500
Long Island City (G-7200)
Dundy Glass & Mirror Corp..................E...... 718 723-5800
Springfield Gardens (G-14588)
G & M Clearview Inc..................G...... 845 781-4877
Monroe (G-8021)
Lafayette Mirror & Glass Co..................E...... 718 768-0660
New Hyde Park (G-8279)
Mirror-Tech Manufacturing Co..................F...... 914 965-1232
Yonkers (G-16334)

GLASS PRDTS, FROM PURCHASED GLASS: Mirrors, Framed

Apf Management Company LLC..................C...... 914 665-5400
Yonkers (G-16286)
Apf Manufacturing Company LLC..................E...... 914 963-6300
Yonkers (G-16287)
Munn Works LLC..................E...... 914 665-6100
Mount Vernon (G-8164)
Timeless Decor LLC..................C...... 315 782-5759
Watertown (G-15590)

GLASS PRDTS, FROM PURCHASED GLASS: Ornaments, Christmas Tree

Jinglebell Inc..................G...... 914 219-5395
Armonk (G-399)
Rauch Industries Inc..................E...... 704 867-5333
Tarrytown (G-15055)

GLASS PRDTS, FROM PURCHASED GLASS: Sheet, Bent

Flickinger Glassworks Inc..................G...... 718 875-1531
Brooklyn (G-1854)

GLASS PRDTS, FROM PURCHASED GLASS: Watch Crystals

Jimmy Crystal New York Co Ltd..................E...... 212 594-0858
New York (G-10006)
Lalique North America Inc..................E...... 212 355-6550
New York (G-10167)

GLASS PRDTS, FROM PURCHASED GLASS: Windshields

Taylor Made Group LLC..................E...... 518 725-0681
Gloversville (G-5294)

GLASS PRDTS, FROM PURCHD GLASS: Strengthened Or Reinforced

Rochester Colonial Mfg Corp..................D...... 585 254-8191
Rochester (G-13686)

GLASS PRDTS, PRESSED OR BLOWN: Bulbs, Electric Lights

Daylight Technology USA Inc ....G........ 973 255-8100
Maspeth (G-7605)
Led Lumina USA LLC ....G........ 631 750-4433
Bohemia (G-1032)

GLASS PRDTS, PRESSED OR BLOWN: Glassware, Art Or Decorative

Architectural Glass Inc ....F....... 845 831-3116
Beacon (G-748)
Bedford Downing Glass ....G....... 718 418-6409
Brooklyn (G-1570)
Jay Strongwater Holdings LLC ....A....... 646 657-0558
New York (G-9980)
King Research Inc ....E....... 718 788-0122
Brooklyn (G-2028)

GLASS PRDTS, PRESSED OR BLOWN: Glassware, Novelty

Glass Menagerie Inc ....G....... 845 754-8344
Westbrookville (G-15859)

GLASS PRDTS, PRESSED OR BLOWN: Lens Blanks, Optical

Ion Optics Inc ....F....... 518 339-6853
Albany (G-89)

GLASS PRDTS, PRESSED OR BLOWN: Lighting Eqpt Parts

Niche Design Inc ....F....... 212 777-2101
Beacon (G-755)

GLASS PRDTS, PRESSED OR BLOWN: Optical

Match Eyewear LLC ....E....... 516 877-0170
Westbury (G-15908)
Semrok Inc ....D....... 585 594-7050
Rochester (G-13723)

GLASS PRDTS, PRESSED OR BLOWN: Ornaments, Christmas Tree

Formcraft Display Products ....G....... 914 632-1410
New Rochelle (G-8330)
Jinglebell Inc ....G....... 914 219-5395
Armonk (G-399)

GLASS PRDTS, PRESSED OR BLOWN: Scientific Glassware

Scientifics Direct Inc ....F....... 716 773-7500
Tonawanda (G-15139)

GLASS PRDTS, PRESSED/BLOWN: Glassware, Art, Decor/Novelty

Bronx Wstchester Tempering Inc ....E....... 914 663-9400
Mount Vernon (G-8126)
Pasabahce USA ....G....... 212 683-1600
New York (G-10766)

GLASS PRDTS, PURCHASED GLASS: Glassware, Scientific/Tech

Swift Glass Co Inc ....D....... 607 733-7166
Elmira Heights (G-4381)

GLASS PRDTS, PURCHASED GLASS: Insulating, Multiple-Glazed

Upstate Insulated Glass Inc ....G....... 315 475-4960
Central Square (G-3297)

GLASS PRDTS, PURCHD GLASS: Furniture Top, Cut, Beveld/Polshd

Our Terms Fabricators Inc ....E....... 631 752-1517
West Babylon (G-15735)

GLASS PRDTS, PURCHSD GLASS: Ornamental, Cut, Engraved/Décor

Oneida International Inc ....G....... 315 361-3000
Oneida (G-12249)
Oneida Silversmiths Inc ....G....... 315 361-3000
Oneida (G-12252)

GLASS STORE: Leaded Or Stained

Flickinger Glassworks Inc ....G....... 718 875-1531
Brooklyn (G-1854)

GLASS STORES

Global Glass Corp ....G....... 516 681-2309
Hicksville (G-5912)
Oldcastle Buildingenvelope Inc ....C....... 631 234-2200
Hauppauge (G-5732)
Upstate Insulated Glass Inc ....G....... 315 475-4960
Central Square (G-3297)

GLASS: Fiber

Corning Incorporated ....A....... 607 974-9000
Corning (G-3705)
Corning Incorporated ....E....... 607 974-1274
Painted Post (G-12472)
Corning Incorporated ....E....... 607 248-1200
Corning (G-3708)
Corning Specialty Mtls Inc ....G....... 607 974-9000
Corning (G-3713)
New York Enrgy Synthetics Inc ....G....... 212 634-4787
New York (G-10596)
Schott Corporation ....D....... 914 831-2200
Elmsford (G-4428)
Volpi Manufacturing USA Co Inc ....E....... 315 255-1737
Auburn (G-502)

GLASS: Flat

A Sunshine Glass & Aluminum ....E....... 718 932-8080
Woodside (G-16195)
Corning Incorporated ....D....... 315 379-3200
Canton (G-3165)
Corning Incorporated ....A....... 607 974-9000
Painted Post (G-12473)
Elite Glass Fabrication LLC ....B....... 201 333-8100
New York (G-9344)
Global Glass Corp ....G....... 516 681-2309
Hicksville (G-5912)
Guardian Industries LLC ....B....... 315 787-7000
Geneva (G-5157)
Hecht & Sohn Glass Co Inc ....G....... 718 782-8295
Brooklyn (G-1930)
Pilkington North America Inc ....C....... 315 438-3341
Syracuse (G-14964)
Schott Corporation ....D....... 914 831-2200
Elmsford (G-4428)
Schott Gemtron Corporation ....C....... 423 337-3522
Elmsford (G-4429)
Schott Solar Pv LLC ....G....... 888 457-6527
Elmsford (G-4432)
Stefan Sydor Optics Inc ....E....... 585 271-7300
Rochester (G-13745)

GLASS: Leaded

Batavia Precision Glass LLC ....G....... 585 343-6050
Buffalo (G-2656)

GLASS: Pressed & Blown, NEC

Co-Optics America Lab Inc ....E....... 607 432-0557
Oneonta (G-12264)
Corning Incorporated ....D....... 607 974-9000
Corning (G-3706)
Corning Incorporated ....E....... 607 974-9000
Corning (G-3707)
Corning Incorporated ....D....... 315 379-3200
Canton (G-3165)
Corning Incorporated ....E....... 607 433-3100
Oneonta (G-12269)
Corning Incorporated ....G....... 646 521-9600
New York (G-9105)
Corning Incorporated ....G....... 607 974-4488
Corning (G-3709)
Corning Incorporated ....G....... 607 974-8496
Corning (G-3710)
Corning Incorporated ....A....... 607 974-9000
Painted Post (G-12473)
Corning International Corp ....G....... 607 974-9000
Corning (G-3711)

Corning Tropel Corporation

Corning Tropel Corporation ....C....... 585 377-3200
Fairport (G-4494)
Corning Vitro Corporation ....A....... 607 974-8605
Corning (G-3714)
Gillinder Brothers Inc ....D....... 845 856-5375
Port Jervis (G-12849)
Glasteel Parts & Services Inc ....E....... 585 235-1010
Rochester (G-13442)
Lighting Holdings Intl LLC ....A....... 845 306-1850
Purchase (G-13006)
Navitar Inc ....D....... 585 359-4000
Rochester (G-13568)
Owens Corning Sales LLC ....B....... 518 475-3600
Feura Bush (G-4792)
Schott Corporation ....D....... 315 255-2791
Auburn (G-494)
Schott North America Inc ....D....... 914 831-2200
Elmsford (G-4431)
Stefan Sydor Optics Inc ....E....... 585 271-7300
Rochester (G-13745)

GLASS: Safety

Armoured One LLC ....C....... 315 720-4186
Syracuse (G-14816)

GLASS: Stained

Adirondack Stained Glass Works ....G....... 518 725-0387
Gloversville (G-5275)
Makarenko Studios Inc ....G....... 914 968-7673
Yorktown Heights (G-16367)
Rohlfs Stined Leaded GL Studio ....E....... 914 699-4848
Mount Vernon (G-8178)
Somers Stain Glass Inc ....F....... 631 586-7772
Deer Park (G-3937)
Sunburst Studios Inc ....G....... 718 768-6360
Brooklyn (G-2470)

GLASS: Structural

Europrojects Intl Inc ....F....... 917 262-0795
New York (G-9421)

GLASS: Tempered

Oldcastle Buildingenvelope Inc ....C....... 631 234-2200
Hauppauge (G-5732)
Taylor Products Inc ....G....... 518 773-9312
Gloversville (G-5295)

GLASSWARE STORES

Vitrix Inc ....G....... 607 936-8707
Corning (G-3723)

GLASSWARE WHOLESALERS

A Sunshine Glass & Aluminum ....E....... 718 932-8080
Woodside (G-16195)

GLASSWARE: Laboratory

TEC Glass & Inst LLC ....G....... 315 926-7639
Marion (G-7576)

GLASSWARE: Laboratory & Medical

Immco Diagnostics Inc ....G....... 716 691-0091
Buffalo (G-2807)
Mri Northtowns Group PC ....F....... 716 836-4646
Buffalo (G-2873)

GLOBAL POSITIONING SYSTEMS & EQPT

Evado Filip ....F....... 917 774-8666
New York (G-9423)
Intelibs Inc ....G....... 877 213-2640
Stony Brook (G-14739)
Rehabilitation International ....G....... 212 420-1500
Jamaica (G-6470)

GLOVES: Fabric

Falls Manufacturing Inc ....G....... 518 672-7189
Philmont (G-12613)
Gce International Inc ....F....... 212 868-0500
New York (G-9581)

GLOVES: Leather

American Target Marketing Inc ....E....... 518 725-4369
Gloversville (G-5276)
Fieldtex Products Inc ....C....... 585 427-2940
Rochester (G-13409)

PRODUCT

J & D Walter Distributors Inc ....F 518 449-1606
  Glenmont (G-5238)
USA Sewing Inc ....E 315 792-8017
  Utica (G-15297)

GLOVES: Leather, Dress Or Semidress

Fownes Brothers & Co Inc ....E 800 345-6837
  New York (G-9525)
Fownes Brothers & Co Inc ....E 518 752-4411
  Gloversville (G-5283)
Samco LLC ....E 518 725-4705
  Gloversville (G-5290)

GLOVES: Leather, Work

Protech (llc) ....E 518 725-7785
  Gloversville (G-5289)

GLOVES: Plastic

Elara Fdsrvice Disposables LLC ....G 877 893-3244
  Jericho (G-6577)

GLOVES: Safety

Hand Care Inc ....G 516 747-5649
  Roslyn (G-14043)
Superior Glove Works USA Ltd ....E 716 626-9500
  Cheektowaga (G-3363)

GLOVES: Work

Manzella Knitting ....G 716 825-0808
  Orchard Park (G-12363)
Worldwide Protective Pdts LLC ....C 877 678-4568
  Hamburg (G-5525)

GLOVES: Woven Or Knit, From Purchased Materials

Fownes Brothers & Co Inc ....E 800 345-6837
  New York (G-9525)
Fownes Brothers & Co Inc ....E 518 752-4411
  Gloversville (G-5283)

GLUE

Hudson Industries Corporation ....E 518 762-4638
  Johnstown (G-6619)

GOLD ORE MINING

Andes Gold Corporation ....D 212 541-2495
  New York (G-8576)
Capital Gold Corporation ....G 212 668-0842
  New York (G-8912)

GOLD ORES

Global Gold Corporation ....F 914 925-0020
  Rye (G-14079)
Gncc Capital Inc ....G 702 951-9793
  New York (G-9635)

GOLD RECOVERY FROM TAILINGS

Fuda Group (usa) Corporation ....G 646 751-7488
  New York (G-9549)

GOLD STAMPING, EXC BOOKS

John Gailer Inc ....E 212 243-5662
  Long Island City (G-7254)

GOLF EQPT

728 Berriman LLC ....G 718 272-5000
  Brooklyn (G-1423)
Callaway Golf Ball Oprtons Inc ....F 518 725-5744
  Johnstown (G-6612)
Callaway Golf Ball Oprtons Inc ....C 518 773-2255
  Gloversville (G-5280)
Jag Manufacturing Inc ....E 518 762-9558
  Johnstown (G-6620)
Morris Golf Ventures ....E 631 283-0559
  Southampton (G-14533)

GOURMET FOOD STORES

Dinewise Inc ....G 631 694-1111
  Farmingdale (G-4617)
Herris Gourmet Inc ....G 917 578-2308
  Brooklyn (G-1934)

Johns Ravioli Company Inc ....F 914 576-7030
  New Rochelle (G-8345)
New York Ravioli Pasta Co Inc ....E 516 270-2852
  New Hyde Park (G-8285)
Queen Ann Macaroni Mfg Co Inc ....G 718 256-1061
  Brooklyn (G-2314)

GOVERNMENT, EXECUTIVE OFFICES: Mayors'

City of Olean ....G 716 376-5694
  Olean (G-12228)
City of Oneonta ....G 607 433-3470
  Oneonta (G-12263)
Town of Amherst ....E 716 631-7113
  Williamsville (G-16144)
Town of Hartford ....G 315 724-0654
  New Hartford (G-8247)

GOVERNMENT, GENERAL: Administration

City of New York ....E 718 965-8787
  Brooklyn (G-1665)

GRANITE: Crushed & Broken

MCM Natural Stone Inc ....F 585 586-6510
  Rochester (G-13540)
Suffolk Granite Manufacturing ....E 631 226-4774
  Lindenhurst (G-6977)
Tilcon New York Inc ....D 845 358-3100
  West Nyack (G-15833)

GRANITE: Cut & Shaped

6478 Ridge Road LLC ....E 716 625-8400
  Lockport (G-7058)
Adirondack Precision Cut Stone ....F 518 681-3060
  Queensbury (G-13029)
Amendola MBL & Stone Ctr Inc ....D 914 997-7968
  White Plains (G-15972)
American Bluestone LLC ....F 607 369-2235
  Sidney (G-14430)
Aurora Stone Group LLC ....G 315 471-6869
  East Syracuse (G-4199)
Capital Stone LLC ....E 518 382-7588
  Schenectady (G-14252)
Capital Stone Saratoga LLC ....G 518 226-8677
  Saratoga Springs (G-14168)
Glen Plaza Marble & Gran Inc ....G 516 671-1100
  Glen Cove (G-5195)
Granite Tops Inc ....E 914 699-2909
  Mount Vernon (G-8145)
House of Stone Inc ....G 845 782-7271
  Monroe (G-8022)
Marble Works Inc ....E 914 376-3653
  Yonkers (G-16331)
MCM Natural Stone Inc ....F 585 586-6510
  Rochester (G-13540)
New York Quarries Inc ....E 518 756-3138
  Alcove (G-163)
North Shore Monuments Inc ....G 516 759-2156
  Glen Head (G-5212)
PR & Stone & Tile Inc ....G 718 383-1115
  Brooklyn (G-2276)
Royal Marble & Granite Inc ....E 516 536-5900
  Oceanside (G-12188)

GRANITE: Dimension

Imerys Usa Inc ....F 315 287-0780
  Gouverneur (G-5321)

GRANITE: Dimension

Alice Perkins ....G 716 378-5100
  Salamanca (G-14121)

GRAPHIC ARTS & RELATED DESIGN SVCS

Accent Label & Tag Co Inc ....G 631 244-7066
  Ronkonkoma (G-13885)
Ad-Vantage Printing Inc ....F 718 820-0688
  Kew Gardens (G-6661)
Adcomm Graphics Inc ....E 212 645-1298
  West Babylon (G-15681)
Alabaster Group Inc ....G 516 867-8223
  Freeport (G-4981)
Beebie Printing & Art Agcy Inc ....G 518 725-4528
  Gloversville (G-5279)
Desktop Publishing Concepts ....F 631 752-1934
  Farmingdale (G-4614)

Eastern Metal of Elmira Inc ....D 607 734-2295
  Elmira (G-4348)
Gg Design and Printing ....G 718 321-3220
  New York (G-9606)
Horne Organization Inc ....F 914 572-1330
  Yonkers (G-16320)
Middletown Press ....G 845 343-1895
  Middletown (G-7920)
Msm Designz Inc ....G 914 909-5900
  Tarrytown (G-15050)
North American Graphics Inc ....F 212 725-2200
  New York (G-10641)
Pic A Poc Enterprises Inc ....G 631 981-2094
  Ronkonkoma (G-13995)
Proof 7 Ltd ....F 212 680-1843
  New York (G-10913)
Resonant Legal Media LLC ....D 800 781-3591
  New York (G-11019)
Tri Kolor Printing & Sty ....F 315 474-6753
  Syracuse (G-15015)
Vital Signs & Graphics Co Inc ....G 518 237-8372
  Cohoes (G-3519)

GRAPHIC LAYOUT SVCS: Printed Circuitry

J N White Associates Inc ....D 585 237-5191
  Perry (G-12598)
Post Heritage Inc ....G 646 286-7579
  Brooklyn (G-2271)

GRASSES: Artificial & Preserved

Techgrass ....F 646 719-2000
  New York (G-11445)

GRATINGS: Tread, Fabricated Metal

Eagle Metals Corp ....F 516 338-5100
  Westbury (G-15878)

GRAVE MARKERS: Concrete

Woodside Granite Industries ....G 585 589-6500
  Albion (G-162)

GRAVEL MINING

Buffalo Crushed Stone Inc ....F 716 566-9636
  Franklinville (G-4965)
Central Dover Development ....G 917 709-3266
  Dover Plains (G-4031)
Diehl Development Inc ....G 585 494-2920
  Bergen (G-813)
Hanson Aggregates PA LLC ....E 585 624-1220
  Honeoye Falls (G-6074)
Hanson Aggregates PA LLC ....F 315 782-2300
  Watertown (G-15571)
Hanson Aggregates PA LLC ....E 315 789-6202
  Oaks Corners (G-12162)
Hanson Aggregates PA LLC ....E 585 624-3800
  Honeoye Falls (G-6073)
Hanson Aggregates PA LLC ....E 585 436-3250
  Rochester (G-13458)
IA Construction Corporation ....G 716 933-8787
  Portville (G-12935)
Rock Mountain Farms Inc ....G 845 647-9084
  Ellenville (G-4311)
Seven Springs Gravel Pdts LLC ....G 585 343-4336
  Batavia (G-624)
Shelby Crushed Stone Inc ....E 585 798-4501
  Medina (G-7746)

GREASE CUPS: Metal

Blue Manufacturing Co Inc ....G 607 796-2463
  Millport (G-7950)

GREASE TRAPS: Concrete

Long Island Green Guys ....G 631 664-4306
  Riverhead (G-13180)

GREENHOUSES: Prefabricated Metal

Fillmore Greenhouses Inc ....E 585 567-2678
  Portageville (G-12932)

GREETING CARDS WHOLESALERS

Paper House Productions Inc ....E 845 246-7261
  Saugerties (G-14207)

(G-0000) Company's Geographic Section entry number

GRINDING BALLS: Ceramic

Malyn Industrial Ceramics Inc ....G....... 716 741-1510
Clarence Center (G-3448)

GRINDING SVC: Precision, Commercial Or Indl

Acme Industries of W Babylon ....F 631 737-5231
Ronkonkoma (G-13887)
Ascribe Inc...E 585 413-0298
Rochester (G-13252)
Micro Instrument Corp ....D 585 458-3150
Rochester (G-13545)
Temrick Inc ....G 631 567-8860
Bohemia (G-1085)

GRINDS: Electric

Arise At Marshall Farms Inc ....G......315 687-6727
Chittenango (G-3403)

GRIT: Steel

Smm - North America Trade Corp ....G...... 212 604-0710
New York (G-11275)

GRITS: Crushed & Broken

Hanson Aggregates PA LLC ....F 315 393-3743
Ogdensburg (G-12205)
Hanson Aggregates PA LLC ....F 315 821-7222
Oriskany Falls (G-12400)
Masten Enterprises LLC ....C 845 932-8206
Cochecton (G-3503)
Upstone Materials Inc ....D 518 561-5321
Plattsburgh (G-12787)

GROCERIES WHOLESALERS, NEC

Bimbo Bakeries Usa Inc ....C 718 463-6300
Maspeth (G-7597)
Bimbo Bakeries Usa Inc ....E 800 856-8544
Vestal (G-15372)
Bimbo Bakeries Usa Inc ....F 845 294-5282
Goshen (G-5305)
Coca-Cola Btlg Co of NY Inc ....F 518 459-2010
Albany (G-66)
Coca-Cola Refreshments USA Inc ....E 718 401-5200
Bronx (G-1227)
Cohens Bakery Inc.....................................E 716 892-8149
Buffalo (G-2702)
French Associates Inc................................F 718 387-9880
Fresh Meadows (G-5041)
Infant Formula Laboratory Svc ....F 718 257-3000
Brooklyn (G-1957)
Kozy Shack Enterprises LLC ....C 516 870-3000
Hicksville (G-5919)
Kozy Shack Enterprises LLC ....C 516 870-3000
Hicksville (G-5920)
Luxfer Magtech Inc ....D 631 727-8600
Riverhead (G-13181)
Mandarin Soy Sauce Inc ....E 845 343-1505
Middletown (G-7918)
Rochester Coca Cola Bottling ....D 585 546-3900
Rochester (G-13685)
S J McCullagh Inc ....E 716 856-3473
Buffalo (G-2970)
Wellspring Corp ....G 212 529-5454
New York (G-11741)

GROCERIES, GENERAL LINE WHOLESALERS

Kong Kee Food Corp.................................E 718 937-2746
Long Island City (G-7264)
Mondelez Global LLC ....G 585 345-3300
Batavia (G-620)

GUARDRAILS

Elderlee Incorporated................................C 315 789-6670
Oaks Corners (G-12161)

GUIDANCE SYSTEMS & EQPT: Space Vehicle

L3harris Technologies Inc........................A 585 269-6600
Rochester (G-13508)
L3harris Technologies Inc........................B 585 269-5001
Rochester (G-13509)
L3harris Technologies Inc........................C 585 269-5000
Rochester (G-13510)

GUIDED MISSILES & SPACE VEHICLES

Drt Aerospace LLC ....G 585 247-5940
Rochester (G-13357)
L3harris Technologies Inc........................A 631 630-4200
Amityville (G-288)
Lockheed Martin Corporation..................A 607 751-2000
Owego (G-12433)

GUM & WOOD CHEMICALS

Metro Products & Services LLC ....G 866 846-8486
Brooklyn (G-2148)
Westrock Mwv LLC ....C 212 688-5000
New York (G-11748)

GUN STOCKS: Wood

Revival Industries Inc ....F 315 868-1085
Ilion (G-6282)

GUNSMITHS

Precision Arms Inc ....G 845 225-1130
Carmel (G-3190)

GUTTERS: Sheet Metal

Genesee Building Products LLC ....F 585 548-2726
Stafford (G-14603)

GYPSUM PRDTS

East Pattern & Model Corp......................E 585 461-3240
Rochester (G-13362)
Lafarge North America Inc ....D 914 930-3027
Buchanan (G-2609)
United States Gypsum Company ....C 585 948-5221
Oakfield (G-12158)

HAIR & HAIR BASED PRDTS

Age Manufacturers Inc ....D 718 927-0048
Brooklyn (G-1471)
American Culture Hair Inc........................E 631 242-3142
Huntington Station (G-6236)
De Meo Brothers Inc ....G 212 268-1400
New York (G-9192)
Hair Color Research Group Inc ....E 718 445-6026
Flushing (G-4858)
Jason & Jean Products Inc ....F 718 271-8300
Corona (G-3741)
Malouf Colette Inc ....F 212 941-9588
New York (G-10338)
Mgd Brands Inc ....E 516 545-0150
Plainview (G-12702)
Premium Assure Inc ....G 605 252-9999
Brooklyn (G-2280)
Spartan Brands Inc ....F 212 340-0320
New York (G-11311)
Tactica International Inc ....E 212 575-0500
New York (G-11423)

HAIR ACCESS WHOLESALERS

Mgd Brands Inc ....E 516 545-0150
Plainview (G-12702)

HAIR CARE PRDTS

All Cultures Inc...E 631 293-3143
Greenlawn (G-5451)
Belmay Holding Corporation ....E 914 376-1515
Yonkers (G-16291)
Hair Ventures LLC....................................F 718 664-7689
Irvington (G-6310)
LOreal Usa Inc ....B 212 818-1500
New York (G-10258)
Pureology Research LLC ....F 212 984-4360
New York (G-10931)
Unike Products Inc ....G 347 686-4616
Jamaica (G-6484)
Zotos International Inc ....B 315 781-3207
Geneva (G-5167)

HAIR CARE PRDTS: Hair Coloring Preparations

LOreal USA Products Inc ....G..... 212 818-1500
New York (G-10262)
Salonclick LLC ....F 718 643-6793
New York (G-11121)

HAIRPIN MOUNTINGS

Lemetric Hair Centers Inc ....F 212 986-5620
New York (G-10194)
Shake-N-Go Fashion Inc ....E 516 944-7777
Port Washington (G-12924)
Shake-N-Go Fashion Inc ....C 516 944-7777
Port Washington (G-12925)

HANDBAG STORES

Quilted Koala Ltd ....F 800 223-5678
New York (G-10957)
Steven Madden Ltd ....B 718 446-1800
Long Island City (G-7370)

HANDBAGS

Affordable Luxury Group Inc ....G 631 523-9266
New York (G-8490)
Ahq LLC ....E 212 328-1560
New York (G-8498)
Bagznyc Corp ....F 212 643-8202
New York (G-8718)
Essex Manufacturing Inc........................D 212 239-0080
New York (G-9404)
Jag Footwear ACC & Ret Corp ....A 800 999-1877
New York (G-9967)
McM Products USA Inc.............................E 646 756-4090
New York (G-10401)
Pure Trade Us Inc ....E 212 256-1600
New York (G-10928)
Quilted Koala Ltd ....F 800 223-5678
New York (G-10957)
Rodem Incorporated..................................F 212 779-7122
New York (G-11070)

HANDBAGS: Women's

Atalla Handbags Inc.................................G 718 965-5500
Brooklyn (G-1544)
Baikal Inc ....D 212 239-4650
New York (G-8719)
Coach Inc..F 718 760-0624
Elmhurst (G-4333)
Coach Services Inc ....E 212 594-1850
New York (G-9043)
Dani Accessories Inc................................E 631 692-4505
Cold Spring Harbor (G-3527)
Kcp Holdco Inc ....F 212 265-1500
New York (G-10086)
Kenneth Cole Productions Inc................B 212 265-1500
New York (G-10089)
Paradiso Cnsld Entps LLC ....E 585 924-3937
Rochester (G-13609)
Renco Group Inc ....G 212 541-6000
New York (G-11012)
Roadie Products Inc ....E 631 567-8588
Holbrook (G-6018)
Tapestry Inc ....G 212 615-2082
New York (G-11433)
Tapestry Inc ....B 212 594-1850
New York (G-11434)

HANDCUFFS & LEG IRONS

Boa Security Technologies Corp..........G 516 480-6822
Huntington (G-6202)

HANDLES: Brush Or Tool, Plastic

Allen Field Co Inc......................................F 631 665-2782
Brightwaters (G-1170)

HANDLES: Wood

Fibron Products Inc ....E 716 886-2378
Buffalo (G-2752)

HANGERS: Garment, Plastic

Capco Wai Shing LLC...............................G 212 268-1976
New York (G-8910)
Prestige Hangers Str Fixs Corp.............G 718 522-6777
Brooklyn (G-2283)

HANGERS: Garment, Wire

Styles Manufacturing Corp ....G 516 763-5303
Oceanside (G-12193)

Employee Codes: A=Over 500 employees, B=251-500
C=101-250, D=51-100, E=20-50, F=10-19, G=5-9

2020 Harris
New York Manufacturers Directory

1117

PRODUCT

HARDBOARD & FIBERBOARD PRDTS

Hi-Temp Fabrication Inc ....F 716 852-5655
Buffalo (G-2798)

HARDWARE

Advantage Wholesale Supply LLC ....D 718 284-5346
Brooklyn (G-1467)

American Casting and Mfg Corp ....G 516 349-7010
Plainview (G-12663)

Amertac Holdings Inc ....G 610 336-1330
Monsey (G-8034)

Barry Industries Inc ....F 212 242-5200
New York (G-8734)

Cast-All Corporation ....E 516 741-4025
Mineola (G-7965)

City Store Gates Mfg Corp ....E 718 939-9700
College Point (G-3540)

Designatronics Incorporated ....B 516 328-3300
New Hyde Park (G-8261)

Dico Products Corporation ....F 315 797-0470
Utica (G-15255)

ER Butler & Co Inc ....E 212 925-3565
New York (G-9392)

Excelco Developments Inc ....E 716 934-2651
Silver Creek (G-14441)

Grow Computer Inc ....G 646 535-2037
Brooklyn (G-1912)

H A Guden Company Inc ....E 631 737-2900
Ronkonkoma (G-13945)

Industrial Electronic Hardware ....D 718 492-4440
Brooklyn (G-1956)

Ingham Industries Inc ....G 631 242-2493
Holbrook (G-6001)

ITR Industries Inc ....E 914 964-7063
Yonkers (G-16321)

Jaquith Industries Inc ....E 315 478-5700
Syracuse (G-14916)

Key High Vacuum Products Inc ....E 631 584-5959
Nesconset (G-8219)

Kilian Manufacturing Corp ....D 315 432-0700
Syracuse (G-14925)

Legendary Auto Interiors Ltd ....E 315 331-1212
Newark (G-11843)

Liberty Brass Turning Co Inc ....E 718 784-2911
Westbury (G-15904)

Lif Industries Inc ....E 718 767-8800
Whitestone (G-16097)

Metalocke Industries Inc ....G 718 267-9200
Woodside (G-16213)

Nielsen Hardware Corporation ....E 607 821-1475
Binghamton (G-902)

Orbital Holdings Inc ....E 951 360-7100
Buffalo (G-2899)

P & F Industries Inc ....E 631 694-9800
Melville (G-7813)

Rosco Inc ....C 718 526-2601
Jamaica (G-6471)

Syraco Products Inc ....F 315 476-5306
Syracuse (G-15002)

Tattersall Industries LLC ....E 518 381-4270
Schenectady (G-14311)

Taylor Made Group LLC ....E 518 725-0681
Gloversville (G-5294)

Truth Hardware Corporation ....G 585 627-5964
Rochester (G-13777)

Yaloz Mould & Die Co Inc ....E 718 389-1131
Brooklyn (G-2599)

York Industries Inc ....E 516 746-3736
Garden City Park (G-5126)

HARDWARE & BUILDING PRDTS: Plastic

Abbott Industries Inc ....B 718 291-0800
Jamaica (G-6423)

Cementex Latex Corp ....F 212 741-1770
New York (G-8944)

Dortronics Systems Inc ....E 631 725-0505
Sag Harbor (G-14098)

Gagne Associates Inc ....E 800 800-5954
Johnson City (G-6599)

Kelta Inc ....E 631 789-5000
Edgewood (G-4273)

Markwik Corp ....F 516 470-1990
Hicksville (G-5928)

Metal Cladding Inc ....D 716 434-5513
Lockport (G-7091)

Pace Window and Door Corp ....E 585 924-8350
Victor (G-15423)

Performance Advantage Co Inc ....F 716 683-7413
Lancaster (G-6824)

Schlegel Systems Inc ....C 585 427-7200
Rochester (G-13718)

Space Age Plstic Fbrcators Inc ....F 718 324-4062
Queens Village (G-13026)

Tii Technologies Inc ....E 516 364-9300
Edgewood (G-4287)

Transpo Industries Inc ....E 914 636-1000
New Rochelle (G-8356)

HARDWARE & EQPT: Stage, Exc Lighting

Props Displays & Interiors ....F 212 620-3840
New York (G-10915)

Steeldeck Ny Inc ....F 718 599-3700
Brooklyn (G-2457)

HARDWARE CLOTH: Woven Wire, Made From Purchased Wire

Dico Products Corporation ....F 315 797-0470
Utica (G-15255)

HARDWARE STORES

Interntional Fireprof Door Inc ....E 718 783-1310
Brooklyn (G-1967)

Lowville Farmers Coop Inc ....E 315 376-6587
Lowville (G-7417)

Syracuse Industrial Sls Co Ltd ....E 315 478-5751
Syracuse (G-15007)

HARDWARE STORES: Builders'

Ingham Industries Inc ....G 631 242-2493
Holbrook (G-6001)

HARDWARE STORES: Pumps & Pumping Eqpt

A & C/Furia Electric Motors ....F 914 949-0585
White Plains (G-15968)

HARDWARE STORES: Tools

Boro Park Cutting Tool Corp ....E 718 720-0610
Staten Island (G-14629)

Parker Machine Company Inc ....F 518 747-0675
Fort Edward (G-4942)

Zak Jewelry Tools Inc ....F 212 768-8122
New York (G-11815)

HARDWARE WHOLESALERS

Amertac Holdings Inc ....G 610 336-1330
Monsey (G-8034)

Barry Industries Inc ....F 212 242-5200
New York (G-8734)

Best Way Tools By Anderson Inc ....G 631 586-4702
Deer Park (G-3845)

Expo Furniture Designs Inc ....F 516 674-1420
Glen Cove (G-5192)

Globe Electronic Hardware Inc ....F 718 457-0303
Woodside (G-16209)

H A Guden Company Inc ....E 631 737-2900
Ronkonkoma (G-13945)

Metalline Fire Door Co Inc ....E 718 583-2320
Bronx (G-1311)

Steel-Brite Ltd ....F 631 589-4044
Oakdale (G-12156)

Sure Flow Equipment Inc ....E 800 263-8251
Tonawanda (G-15143)

HARDWARE, WHOLESALE: Bolts

Park-Ohio Inds Trsry Co Inc ....F 212 966-3310
Albany (G-111)

HARDWARE, WHOLESALE: Builders', NEC

ER Butler & Co Inc ....E 212 925-3565
New York (G-9392)

P E Guerin ....D 212 243-5270
New York (G-10733)

S A Baxter LLC ....G 845 469-7995
Chester (G-3385)

HARDWARE, WHOLESALE: Security Devices, Locks

Shield Security Doors Ltd ....G 202 468-3308
Brooklyn (G-2405)

HARDWARE: Aircraft

Fastener Dimensions Inc ....E 718 847-6321
Ozone Park (G-12461)

Kyntec Corporation ....G 716 810-6956
Buffalo (G-2840)

Magellan Aerospace Processing ....G 631 694-1818
West Babylon (G-15728)

HARDWARE: Aircraft & Marine, Incl Pulleys & Similar Items

United Aircraft Tech Inc ....G 518 286-8867
Troy (G-15193)

HARDWARE: Builders'

Northknight Logistics Inc ....F 716 283-3090
Niagara Falls (G-11957)

Pk30 System LLC ....F 212 473-8050
Stone Ridge (G-14736)

HARDWARE: Cabinet

Daniel Demarco and Assoc Inc ....E 631 598-7000
Amityville (G-262)

Darman Manufacturing Coinc ....F 315 724-9632
Utica (G-15253)

Kenstan Lock & Hardware Co Inc ....E 631 423-1977
Plainview (G-12694)

HARDWARE: Door Opening & Closing Devices, Exc Electrical

Nanz Custom Hardware Inc ....E 212 367-7000
New York (G-10532)

Nanz Custom Hardware Inc ....C 212 367-7000
Deer Park (G-3908)

HARDWARE: Furniture

Real Design Inc ....F 315 429-3071
Dolgeville (G-4026)

Water Street Brass Corporation ....E 716 763-0059
Lakewood (G-6787)

Weber-Knapp Company ....C 716 484-9135
Jamestown (G-6553)

HARDWARE: Furniture, Builders' & Other Household

Classic Brass Inc ....D 716 763-1400
Lakewood (G-6780)

Decorative Hardware ....F 914 238-5251
Chappaqua (G-3324)

Morgik Metal Designs ....F 212 463-0304
New York (G-10503)

HARDWARE: Luggage

Crest Lock Co Inc ....F 718 345-9898
Brooklyn (G-1700)

Tools & Stamping Corp ....G 718 392-4040
Brooklyn (G-2510)

HARNESS ASSEMBLIES: Cable & Wire

Advanced Interconnect Mfg Inc ....D 585 742-2220
Victor (G-15390)

Amphenol Intrconnect Pdts Corp ....G 607 754-4444
Endicott (G-4444)

Apx Technologies Inc ....E 516 433-1313
Hicksville (G-5884)

Arnold-Davis LLC ....C 607 772-1201
Binghamton (G-855)

B3cg Interconnect Usa Inc ....G 518 324-4800
Plattsburgh (G-12734)

Becker Electronics Inc ....D 631 619-9100
Ronkonkoma (G-13915)

Cables Unlimited Inc ....E 631 563-6363
Yaphank (G-16256)

Condor Electronics Corp ....E 585 235-1500
Rochester (G-13321)

Hazlow Electronics Inc ....E 585 325-5323
Rochester (G-13462)

Hoff Associates Mfg Reps Inc ....E 585 398-2000
Farmington (G-4773)

Lyntronics Inc ....E 631 205-1061
Yaphank (G-16265)

North Hills Signal Proc Corp ....E 631 244-7393
Bohemia (G-1054)

Paal Technologies Inc ....G 631 319-6262
Ronkonkoma (G-13990)

Sturges Elec Pdts Co Inc ....E 607 844-8604
  Dryden (G-4041)
Sturges Electronics LLC ....F 607 844-8604
  Dryden (G-4042)
TCS Electronics Inc ....E 585 337-4301
  Farmington (G-4779)
Tony Baird Electronics Inc ....G 315 422-4430
  Syracuse (G-15014)

HARNESSES, HALTERS, SADDLERY & STRAPS

Equicenter Inc ....E 585 742-2522
  Honeoye Falls (G-6071)
Import-Export Corporation ....F 718 707-0880
  Long Island City (G-7246)
Jaclyn LLC ....D 201 909-6000
  New York (G-9963)
Unique Overseas Inc ....G 516 466-9792
  Great Neck (G-5429)

HEADPHONES: Radio

Gotenna Inc ....F 718 360-4988
  Brooklyn (G-1901)

HEALTH AIDS: Exercise Eqpt

Gym Store Inc ....G 718 366-7804
  Maspeth (G-7621)
Hypoxico Inc ....G 212 972-1009
  New York (G-9844)
Physicalmind Institute ....F 212 343-2150
  New York (G-10832)
TDS Foundry Corporation ....G 607 733-6789
  Elmira (G-4371)

HEARING AIDS

Atlantic Er Inc ....E 516 294-3200
  New Hyde Park (G-8252)
Beltone Corporation ....G 716 565-1015
  Williamsville (G-16122)
Benway-Haworth-Lwlr-Iacosta He .....F 518 432-4070
  Albany (G-47)
Buffalo Hearg & Speech ....E 716 558-1105
  West Seneca (G-15845)
Family Hearing Center ....G 845 897-3059
  Fishkill (G-4800)
Roner Inc ....G 718 392-6020
  Long Island City (G-7346)
Roner Inc ....C 718 392-6020
  Long Island City (G-7347)
Todt Hill Audiological Svcs ....G 718 816-1952
  Staten Island (G-14722)
Widex Usa Inc ....D 718 360-1000
  Hauppauge (G-5800)
William H Shapiro ....G 212 263-7037
  New York (G-11758)

HEAT EXCHANGERS

Aerco International Inc ....C 845 580-8000
  Blauvelt (G-925)
Costanzos Welding Inc ....E 716 282-0845
  Niagara Falls (G-11917)
Fross Industries Inc ....E 716 297-0652
  Niagara Falls (G-11930)
Schwabel Fabricating Co Inc ....E 716 876-2086
  Tonawanda (G-15138)
Yula Corporation ....E 718 991-0900
  Bronx (G-1398)

HEAT EXCHANGERS: After Or Inter Coolers Or Condensers, Etc

American Precision Inds Inc ....C 716 691-9100
  Amherst (G-210)
API Heat Transf Thermasys Corp ....C 716 684-6700
  Buffalo (G-2638)
API Heat Transfer Company ....F 716 684-6700
  Buffalo (G-2639)
API Heat Transfer Inc ....C 585 496-5755
  Arcade (G-368)
Nitram Energy Inc ....E 716 662-6540
  Orchard Park (G-12368)
Slantco Manufacturing Inc ....G 516 484-2600
  Greenvale (G-5465)

HEAT TREATING: Metal

A1 International Heat Treating ....G 718 863-5552
  Bronx (G-1188)
B & W Heat Treating Company ....G 716 876-8184
  Tonawanda (G-15088)
Bodycote Thermal Proc Inc ....E 585 436-7876
  Rochester (G-13276)
BSV Metal Finishers Inc ....E 585 747-7070
  Rochester (G-13285)
Buffalo Armory LLC ....G 716 935-6346
  Buffalo (G-2670)
Burke Frging Heat Treating Inc ....E 585 235-6060
  Rochester (G-13287)
Burton Industries Inc ....E 631 643-6660
  West Babylon (G-15697)
Cpp - Steel Treaters ....E 315 736-3081
  Oriskany (G-12388)
Expedient Heat Treating Corp ....G 716 433-1177
  North Tonawanda (G-12066)
Gibraltar Industries Inc ....D 716 826-6500
  Buffalo (G-2775)
Graywood Companies Inc ....A 585 738-8889
  Rochester (G-13450)
Great Lakes Metal Treating ....F 716 694-1240
  Tonawanda (G-15107)
Hercules Heat Treating Corp ....E 718 625-1266
  Brooklyn (G-1932)
International Ord Tech Inc ....D 716 664-1100
  Jamestown (G-6518)
Jasco Heat Treating Inc ....E 585 388-0071
  Fairport (G-4501)
Parfuse Corp ....E 516 997-8888
  Westbury (G-15916)
Rochester Steel Treating Works ....F 585 546-3348
  Rochester (G-13699)
Rough Brothers Holding Co ....G 716 826-6500
  Buffalo (G-2965)

HEATERS: Space, Exc Electric

American Comfort Direct LLC ....E 201 364-8309
  New York (G-8548)

HEATERS: Unit, Domestic

Chicken Hawk Racing Inc ....G 845 758-0700
  Red Hook (G-13072)
Roberts-Gordon LLC ....D 716 852-4400
  Buffalo (G-2957)

HEATING & AIR CONDITIONING EQPT & SPLYS WHOLESALERS

North Pk Innovations Group Inc ....E 716 699-2031
  Ellicottville (G-4315)
Pronto Gas Heating Sups Inc ....G 718 292-0707
  Bronx (G-1345)
Siemens Industry Inc ....E 585 797-2300
  Rochester (G-13728)
Split Systems Corp ....E 516 223-5511
  North Baldwin (G-12008)

HEATING & AIR CONDITIONING UNITS, COMBINATION

Colburns AC Rfrgn ....F 716 569-3695
  Frewsburg (G-5050)
Daikin Applied Americas Inc ....D 315 253-2771
  Auburn (G-472)
Enviromaster International LLC ....D 315 336-3716
  Rome (G-13848)
John F Krell Jr ....G 315 492-3201
  Syracuse (G-14918)
Keeler Services ....G 607 776-5757
  Bath (G-636)
Northern Air Systems Inc ....E 585 594-5050
  Rochester (G-13584)
Pro Metal of NY Corp ....G 516 285-0440
  Valley Stream (G-15353)

HEATING EQPT & SPLYS

A Nuclimate Qulty Systems Inc ....F 315 431-0226
  East Syracuse (G-4192)
Carrier Corporation ....B 315 432-6000
  Syracuse (G-14844)
Chentronics LLC ....E 607 334-5531
  Norwich (G-12117)
CIDC Corp ....F 718 342-5820
  Glendale (G-5222)

Dandelion Energy Inc ....F 603 781-2663
  New York (G-9163)
Economy Pump & Motor Repr Inc ....G 718 433-2600
  Astoria (G-418)
Embassy Industries Inc ....C 631 435-0209
  Hauppauge (G-5647)
Fisonic Corp ....G 212 732-3777
  Long Island City (G-7225)
Fisonic Corp ....F 716 763-0295
  New York (G-9507)
Fulton Volcanic Inc ....D 315 298-5121
  Pulaski (G-12999)
Juniper Elbow Co Inc ....C 718 326-2546
  Middle Village (G-7881)
Omega Heater Company Inc ....D 631 588-8820
  Ronkonkoma (G-13986)
RE Hansen Industries Inc ....C 631 471-2900
  Saint James (G-14113)
Slant/Fin Corporation ....B 516 484-2600
  Greenvale (G-5464)
Vincent Genovese ....G 631 281-8170
  Mastic Beach (G-7675)

HEATING EQPT: Complete

A Nuclimate Qulty Systems Inc ....F 315 431-0226
  East Syracuse (G-4192)
Coil Craft Inc ....G 718 369-1210
  Ozone Park (G-12459)
Dundas-Jafine Inc ....E 716 681-9690
  Alden (G-168)
Siemens Industry Inc ....E 716 568-0983
  Buffalo (G-2982)
Specified Air Solutions LLC ....E 716 852-4400
  Buffalo (G-2991)
Thomson Industries Inc ....E 716 691-9100
  Amherst (G-248)

HEATING EQPT: Induction

Ambrell Corporation ....F 585 889-0236
  Rochester (G-13227)
Ultraflex Power Technologies ....G 631 467-6814
  Ronkonkoma (G-14021)

HEATING SYSTEMS: Radiant, Indl Process

Radiant Pro Ltd ....G 516 763-5678
  Oceanside (G-12186)

HEATING UNITS & DEVICES: Indl, Electric

Concealed Baseboard Htg Co LLC ....F 212 378-6710
  New York (G-9075)
Cvd Equipment Corporation ....F 631 582-4365
  Central Islip (G-3272)
Fulton Volcanic Inc ....D 315 298-5121
  Pulaski (G-12999)

HELICOPTERS

CIC International Ltd ....D 212 213-0089
  Brooklyn (G-1663)

HELMETS: Athletic

Cascade Helmets Holdings Inc ....G 315 453-3073
  Liverpool (G-7006)
Performance Lacrosse Group Inc ....G 315 453-3073
  Liverpool (G-7032)

HIGH ENERGY PARTICLE PHYSICS EQPT

Advance Energy Systems NY LLC ....G 315 735-5125
  Utica (G-15237)

HIGHWAY SIGNALS: Electric

BNo Intl Trdg Co Inc ....G 716 487-1900
  Jamestown (G-6499)
Traffic Lane Closures LLC ....F 845 228-6100
  Carmel (G-3192)

HOBBY & CRAFT SPLY STORES

Paper House Productions Inc ....E 845 246-7261
  Saugerties (G-14207)

HOBBY, TOY & GAME STORES: Ceramics Splys

Corning International Corp ....G 607 974-9000
  Corning (G-3711)

HOBBY, TOY & GAME STORES: Toys & Games

Minted Green Inc................................G...... 845 458-1845
Airmont (G-14)

HOISTS

Columbus McKinnon Corporation ....C...... 716 689-5400
Getzville (G-5174)

Columbus McKinnon Corporation ....C...... 716 689-5400
Getzville (G-5175)

Columbus McKinnon Corporation ....C...... 716 689-5400
Getzville (G-5176)

Mannesmann Corporation ....D...... 212 258-4000
New York (G-10348)

Marros Equipment & Trucks ....F...... 315 539-8702
Waterloo (G-15555)

Mohawk Resources Ltd ....D...... 518 842-1431
Amsterdam (G-339)

Reimann & Georger Corporation..........E...... 716 895-1156
Buffalo (G-2951)

Thego Corporation ....G...... 631 776-2472
Bellport (G-808)

HOLDING COMPANIES: Banks

Flavors Holdings Inc.............................F...... 212 572-8677
New York (G-9509)

HOLDING COMPANIES: Investment, Exc Banks

Ample Hills Holdings Inc......................G...... 347 725-4061
Brooklyn (G-1508)

Asp Blade Intrmdate Hldngs Inc...........A...... 212 476-8000
New York (G-8650)

Chemprene Inc ....C...... 845 831-2800
Beacon (G-749)

Geritrex Holdings Inc...........................G...... 914 668-4003
Mount Vernon (G-8142)

Global Video LLC.................................D...... 516 222-2600
Woodbury (G-16172)

Graphic Controls Holdings Inc.............F...... 716 853-7500
Buffalo (G-2781)

Hw Holdings Inc...................................G...... 212 399-1000
New York (G-9841)

Pii Holdings Inc....................................G...... 716 876-9951
Buffalo (G-2919)

Skip Hop Holdings Inc.........................G...... 212 868-9850
New York (G-11260)

HOLDING COMPANIES: Personal, Exc Banks

Spf Holdings II LLC..............................G...... 212 750-8300
New York (G-11320)

HOME DELIVERY NEWSPAPER ROUTES

Nyt Capital LLC....................................F...... 212 556-1234
New York (G-10669)

HOME ENTERTAINMENT EQPT: Electronic, NEC

Request Inc..E...... 518 899-1254
Halfmoon (G-5497)

Request Serious Play LLC....................G...... 518 899-1254
Halfmoon (G-5498)

Shyk International Corp ....G...... 212 663-3302
New York (G-11222)

Sing Trix ....F...... 212 352-1500
New York (G-11249)

HOME FURNISHINGS WHOLESALERS

Feldman Company Inc..........................F...... 212 966-1303
New York (G-9482)

Lifetime Brands Inc..............................B...... 516 683-6000
Garden City (G-5104)

HOME HEALTH CARE SVCS

Curemdcom Inc.....................................E...... 212 509-6200
New York (G-9134)

HOMEBUILDERS & OTHER OPERATIVE BUILDERS

Hope International Productions ....F...... 212 247-3188
New York (G-9811)

HOMEFURNISHING STORES: Beddings & Linens

Duxiana Dux Bed ....G...... 212 755-2600
New York (G-9282)

Metro Mattress Corp ....E...... 716 205-2300
Niagara Falls (G-11951)

HOMEFURNISHING STORES: Lighting Fixtures

David Weeks Studio..............................F...... 212 966-3433
New York (G-9184)

Edison Power & Light Co Inc................F...... 718 522-0002
Brooklyn (G-1783)

Maxsun Corporation ....F...... 718 418-6800
Maspeth (G-7628)

Rapid-Lite Fixture Corporation.............F...... 347 599-2600
Brooklyn (G-2327)

Serway Bros Inc ....G...... 315 337-0601
Rome (G-13872)

Sir Industries Inc ....G...... 631 234-2444
Hauppauge (G-5767)

HOMEFURNISHING STORES: Mirrors

Global Glass Corp.................................G...... 516 681-2309
Hicksville (G-5912)

HOMEFURNISHING STORES: Towels

Himatsingka America Inc ....E...... 212 824-2949
New York (G-9787)

HOMEFURNISHING STORES: Vertical Blinds

Pj Decorators Inc ....E...... 516 735-9693
East Meadow (G-4139)

HOMEFURNISHING STORES: Wicker, Rattan, Or Reed

House Ur Home Inc...............................G...... 347 585-3308
Monroe (G-8023)

HOMEFURNISHING STORES: Window Furnishings

Blinds To Go (us) Inc...........................E...... 718 477-9523
Staten Island (G-14627)

Wallace Home Design Ctr ....G...... 631 765-3890
Southold (G-14546)

HOMEFURNISHINGS & SPLYS, WHOLESALE: Decorative

House Ur Home Inc...............................G...... 347 585-3308
Monroe (G-8023)

Mistdoda Inc...E...... 919 735-7111
New York (G-10483)

Secret Celebrity Licensing LLC............G...... 212 812-9277
New York (G-11175)

HOMEFURNISHINGS, WHOLESALE: Bedspreads

Ess Bee Industries Inc ....E...... 718 894-5202
Brooklyn (G-1814)

HOMEFURNISHINGS, WHOLESALE: Blinds, Venetian

D & D Window Tech Inc ....G...... 212 308-2822
New York (G-9145)

HOMEFURNISHINGS, WHOLESALE: Blinds, Vertical

Pj Decorators Inc ....E...... 516 735-9693
East Meadow (G-4139)

HOMEFURNISHINGS, WHOLESALE: Carpets

Albert Menin Interiors Ltd ....F...... 212 876-3041
Bronx (G-1200)

HOMEFURNISHINGS, WHOLESALE: Curtains

Baby Signature Inc ....G...... 212 686-1700
New York (G-8710)

HOMEFURNISHINGS, WHOLESALE: Draperies

Reynolds Drapery Service Inc ....F...... 315 845-8632
Newport (G-11899)

HOMEFURNISHINGS, WHOLESALE: Fireplace Eqpt & Access

Blackstone International Inc ....G...... 631 289-5490
Holtsville (G-6045)

HOMEFURNISHINGS, WHOLESALE: Kitchenware

Lifetime Chimney Supply LLC...............G...... 516 576-8144
Plainview (G-12696)

Madison Lifestyle Ny LLC ....G...... 212 725-4002
New York (G-10315)

Vanity Fair Bathmart Inc ....F...... 718 584-6700
Bronx (G-1389)

HOMEFURNISHINGS, WHOLESALE: Linens, Table

Lintex Linens Inc..................................B...... 212 679-8046
New York (G-10222)

HOMEFURNISHINGS, WHOLESALE: Pillowcases

Anhui Skyworth LLC..............................D...... 917 940-6903
Hempstead (G-5831)

HOMEFURNISHINGS, WHOLESALE: Rugs

Lorena Canals USA Inc ....G...... 844 567-3622
Hastings On Hudson (G-5575)

HOMEFURNISHINGS, WHOLESALE: Stainless Steel Flatware

Utica Cutlery Company ....D...... 315 733-4663
Utica (G-15298)

HOMEFURNISHINGS, WHOLESALE: Window Covering Parts & Access

Chf Industries Inc................................E...... 212 951-7800
New York (G-8984)

P E Guerin..D...... 212 243-5270
New York (G-10733)

HOMEFURNISHINGS, WHOLESALE: Wood Flooring

Wego International Floors LLC..............F...... 516 487-3510
Great Neck (G-5431)

HOMES, MODULAR: Wooden

Best Mdlr HMS Afrbe P Q&S In ....F...... 631 204-0049
Southampton (G-14527)

Bill Lake Homes Construction...............D...... 518 673-2424
Sprakers (G-14564)

House Ur Home Inc...............................G...... 347 585-3308
Monroe (G-8023)

Westchester Modular Homes Inc ....C...... 845 832-9400
Wingdale (G-16160)

Whitley East LLC..................................D...... 718 403-0050
Brooklyn (G-2582)

HOMES: Log Cabins

Alta Industries Ltd ....F...... 845 586-3336
Halcottsville (G-5487)

Beaver Mountain Log Homes Inc ....G...... 607 467-2700
Hancock (G-5534)

Northern Design & Bldg Assoc ....E...... 518 747-2200
Queensbury (G-13050)

Timberbuilt Inc ....F...... 716 337-0012
North Collins (G-12029)

HONES

09 Flshy Bll/Dsert Sunrise LLC.............G...... 518 583-6638
Saratoga Springs (G-14161)

HORMONE PREPARATIONS

American Hormones Inc........................F...... 845 471-7272
Poughkeepsie (G-12943)

Erika T Schwartz MD PC....................G........ 212 873-3420
New York (G-9395)

HORSE & PET ACCESSORIES: Textile

Saratoga Horseworks Ltd ....E...... 518 843-6756
Amsterdam (G-347)

Triple E Manufacturing ....F....... 716 761-6996
Sherman (G-14401)

HORSE ACCESS: Harnesses & Riding Crops, Etc, Exc Leather

Hampton Transport Inc.....................F....... 631 716-4445
Coram (G-3693)

Stonegate Stabless ....G........ 518 746-7133
Fort Edward (G-4944)

HOSE: Automobile, Plastic

Deer Park Driveshaft & Hose ....G...... 631 667-4091
Deer Park (G-3860)

HOSE: Fire, Rubber

Cataract Hose Co............................E....... 914 941-9019
Ossining (G-12402)

HOSE: Flexible Metal

TI Group Auto Systems LLC ....G....... 315 568-7042
Seneca Falls (G-14373)

HOSE: Plastic

Jain Irrigation Inc..........................D...... 315 755-4400
Watertown (G-15573)

TI Group Auto Systems LLC ....G....... 315 568-7042
Seneca Falls (G-14373)

HOSE: Pneumatic, Rubber Or Rubberized Fabric, NEC

Moreland Hose & Belting Corp ....G........ 631 563-7071
Oakdale (G-12154)

HOSE: Rubber

Mason Industries Inc ....C...... 631 348-0282
Hauppauge (G-5708)

Mercer Rubber Co.............................C...... 631 348-0282
Hauppauge (G-5713)

HOSE: Vacuum Cleaner, Rubber

Anchor Tech Products Corp ....E....... 914 592-0240
Elmsford (G-4393)

HOSES & BELTING: Rubber & Plastic

Flex Enterprises Inc ....E....... 585 742-1000
Victor (G-15409)

Habasit America Inc ....D...... 716 824-8484
Buffalo (G-2787)

Hitachi Cable America Inc ....F...... 914 694-9200
Purchase (G-13004)

Index Incorporated..........................F...... 440 632-5400
Bronx (G-1280)

Jed Lights Inc...................................F...... 516 812-5001
Deer Park (G-3888)

Peraflex Hose Inc.............................F...... 716 876-8806
Buffalo (G-2913)

Standard Motor Products Inc ....B...... 718 392-0200
Long Island City (G-7364)

Troy Belting and Supply Co ....D...... 518 272-4920
Watervliet (G-15609)

WF Lake Corp..................................E....... 518 798-9934
Queensbury (G-13060)

HOSIERY KITS: Sewing & Mending

V Technical Textiles Inc ....G........ 315 597-1674
Palmyra (G-12494)

HOSPITALS: Cancer

Actinium Pharmaceuticals Inc.............E...... 646 677-3870
New York (G-8451)

HOSPITALS: Medical & Surgical

Norcorp Inc......................................E...... 914 666-1310
Mount Kisco (G-8100)

HOT TUBS

D & M Enterprises Incorporated............G........ 914 937-6430
Port Chester (G-12816)

HOT TUBS: Plastic & Fiberglass

D & M Enterprises Incorporated............G........ 914 937-6430
Port Chester (G-12816)

Independent Home Products LLC ....E........ 718 541-1256
West Hempstead (G-15770)

HOUSEHOLD APPLIANCE STORES: Air Cond Rm Units, Self-Contnd

RE Hansen Industries Inc....................C....... 631 471-2900
Saint James (G-14113)

HOUSEHOLD APPLIANCE STORES: Fans, Electric

A & C/Furia Electric Motors ....F...... 914 949-0585
White Plains (G-15968)

HOUSEHOLD ARTICLES: Metal

Di Highway Sign Structure Corp ....E....... 315 736-8312
New York Mills (G-11831)

Hatfield Metal Fab Inc ....E....... 845 454-9078
Poughkeepsie (G-12961)

L D Flecken Inc..................................F...... 631 777-4881
Yaphank (G-16264)

New York Manufactured Products........F...... 585 254-9353
Rochester (G-13570)

Ulster County Iron Works LLC.............G........ 845 255-0003
New Paltz (G-8312)

HOUSEHOLD FURNISHINGS, NEC

388 Associates Inc ....G........ 267 367-0990
Brooklyn (G-1414)

AEP Environmental LLC....................F....... 716 446-0739
Buffalo (G-2625)

Area Inc ....G........ 212 924-7084
New York (G-8620)

August Silk Inc ....E....... 212 643-2400
New York (G-8678)

August Silk Inc ....G........ 212 643-2400
New York (G-8679)

Caddy Concepts Inc ....F...... 516 570-6279
Great Neck (G-5372)

Creative Scents USA Inc ....G........ 718 522-5901
Brooklyn (G-1698)

Dico Products Corporation ....F...... 315 797-0470
Utica (G-15255)

Ess Bee Industries Inc.......................E....... 718 894-5202
Brooklyn (G-1814)

Kartell Us Inc ....G........ 212 966-6665
New York (G-10070)

Kim Seybert Inc ....F...... 212 564-7850
New York (G-10101)

Medline Industries Inc ....B...... 845 344-3301
Middletown (G-7919)

Mgk Group Inc ....E....... 212 989-2732
New York (G-10448)

Moga Trading Company Inc ....G........ 718 760-2966
Corona (G-3746)

Nationwide Tarps Incorporated ....D...... 518 843-1545
Amsterdam (G-341)

Nbets Corporation ....G........ 516 785-1259
Wantagh (G-15487)

Paramount Textiles Inc ....F...... 212 966-1040
New York (G-10756)

Performance Sourcing Group Inc ....E....... 914 636-2100
Scarsdale (G-14240)

Q Squared Design LLC......................G........ 212 686-8860
New York (G-10942)

Richloom Fabrics Corp ....G........ 212 685-5400
New York (G-11042)

Silly Phillie Creations Inc ....G........ 718 492-6300
Brooklyn (G-2413)

Skil-Care Corporation ....C...... 914 963-2040
Yonkers (G-16348)

Sleepable Sofas Ltd ....D...... 973 546-4502
New York (G-11267)

Sleeping Partners Intl Inc ....F...... 212 254-1515
Brooklyn (G-2426)

Sure Fit Inc ....E....... 212 395-9340
New York (G-11398)

Terbo Ltd ....G........ 718 847-2860
Richmond Hill (G-13127)

William Harvey Studio Inc ....G........ 718 599-4343
Brooklyn (G-2586)

HOUSEWARE STORES

Swissmar Inc....................................G........ 905 764-1121
Niagara Falls (G-11983)

HOUSEWARES, ELECTRIC, EXC COOKING APPLIANCES & UTENSILS

Bino Products LLC ....E....... 212 886-6899
New York (G-8795)

Brumis Imports Inc ....D...... 646 845-6000
New York (G-8864)

World Trading Center Inc ....G........ 631 273-3330
Hauppauge (G-5803)

HOUSEWARES, ELECTRIC: Cooking Appliances

Peek A Boo USA Inc...........................G........ 201 533-8700
New York (G-10784)

HOUSEWARES, ELECTRIC: Extractors, Juice

Goodnature Products Inc ....E....... 800 875-3381
Buffalo (G-2779)

Sundance Industries Inc ....G........ 845 795-5809
Milton (G-7953)

HOUSEWARES, ELECTRIC: Fryers

Abbott Industries Inc ....B...... 718 291-0800
Jamaica (G-6423)

HOUSEWARES, ELECTRIC: Heaters, Space

Valad Electric Heating Corp ....F...... 888 509-4927
Montgomery (G-8068)

HOUSEWARES, ELECTRIC: Heating, Bsbrd/Wall, Radiant Heat

Vincent Genovese...............................G........ 631 281-8170
Mastic Beach (G-7675)

HOUSEWARES, ELECTRIC: Humidifiers, Household

Dampits International Inc ....G........ 212 581-3047
New York (G-9160)

Remedies Surgical Supplies.................G........ 718 599-5301
Brooklyn (G-2339)

HOUSEWARES, ELECTRIC: Massage Machines, Exc Beauty/Barber

Advanced Response Corporation.........G........ 212 459-0887
New York (G-8482)

Quality Life Inc ....F...... 718 939-5787
College Point (G-3561)

HOUSEWARES: Dishes, China

Jill Fagin Enterprises Inc ....G........ 212 674-9383
New York (G-10003)

Korin Inc ....E....... 212 587-7021
New York (G-10128)

Oneida International Inc ....G........ 315 361-3000
Oneida (G-12249)

Oneida Silversmiths Inc ....G........ 315 361-3000
Oneida (G-12252)

HOUSEWARES: Dishes, Earthenware

Ceramica Varm ....G........ 914 381-6215
New Rochelle (G-8324)

HOUSEWARES: Dishes, Plastic

Digitac Inc...F...... 732 215-4020
Brooklyn (G-1744)

Etna Products Co Inc.........................F...... 212 989-7591
New York (G-9413)

Howard Charles Inc ....G........ 917 902-6934
Woodbury (G-16173)

J M R Plastics Corporation ....G........ 718 898-9825
Middle Village (G-7879)

Madison Lifestyle Ny LLC ....G........ 212 725-4002
New York (G-10315)

Novelty Crystal Corp ....D...... 718 458-6700
Long Island City (G-7310)

Ocala Group LLC ....F 516 233-2750
New Hyde Park (G-8286)
Peek A Boo USA Inc ....G 201 533-8700
New York (G-10784)
Robinson Knife ....F 716 685-6300
Buffalo (G-2958)
Senior Brands LLC ....G 212 213-5100
New York (G-11190)
Villeroy & Boch Usa Inc ....F 212 213-8149
New York (G-11684)

HOUSEWARES: Kettles & Skillets, Cast Iron

Field Wares LLC ....G 508 380-6545
Brooklyn (G-1841)
S M S C Inc ....G 315 942-4394
Boonville (G-1110)

HUMIDIFIERS & DEHUMIDIFIERS

Alfa Laval Kathabar Inc ....A 716 875-2000
Tonawanda (G-15083)
MSP Technologycom LLC ....G 631 424-7542
Centerport (G-3257)

HYDRAULIC EQPT REPAIR SVC

Mooradian Hydraulics & Eqp Co ....F 518 766-3866
Castleton On Hudson (G-3203)

Hard Rubber & Molded Rubber Prdts

Apple Rubber Products Inc ....C 716 684-7649
Lancaster (G-6796)
Mason Industries Inc ....C 631 348-0282
Hauppauge (G-5708)
Prince Rubber & Plas Co Inc ....E 225 272-1653
Buffalo (G-2931)

ICE

Adirondack Ice & Air Inc ....F 518 483-4340
Malone (G-7481)
Annies Ice ....G 585 593-5605
Wellsville (G-15666)
Arctic Glacier Newburgh Inc ....G 718 456-2013
Brooklyn (G-1525)
Arctic Glacier Newburgh Inc ....F 845 561-0549
Newburgh (G-11858)
Maplewood Ice Co Inc ....E 518 499-2345
Whitehall (G-16076)
South Shore Ice Co Inc ....F 516 379-2056
Roosevelt (G-14033)

ICE CREAM & ICES WHOLESALERS

Four Brothers Italian Bakery ....G 914 741-5434
Hawthorne (G-5812)
Fresh Ice Cream Company LLC ....F 347 603-6021
Brooklyn (G-1868)
Macedonia Ltd ....F 718 462-3596
Brooklyn (G-2100)
Purity Ice Cream Co Inc ....F 607 272-1545
Ithaca (G-6408)
Ralphs Famous Italian Ices ....G 718 605-5052
Staten Island (G-14698)
Washburns Dairy Inc ....E 518 725-0629
Gloversville (G-5299)

IDENTIFICATION TAGS, EXC PAPER

Ketchum Manufacturing Co Inc ....F 518 696-3331
Lake Luzerne (G-6765)

IGNEOUS ROCK: Crushed & Broken

Barrett Paving Materials Inc ....F 315 737-9471
Clayville (G-3454)
Peckham Materials Corp ....E 518 747-3353
Hudson Falls (G-6192)

IGNITION APPARATUS & DISTRIBUTORS

Magnum Shielding Corporation ....E 585 381-9957
Pittsford (G-12648)
Martinez Specialties Inc ....G 607 898-3053
Groton (G-5483)
Taro Manufacturing Company Inc ....F 315 252-9430
Auburn (G-498)

IGNITION SYSTEMS: High Frequency

Standard Motor Products Inc ....B 718 392-0200
Long Island City (G-7364)

Zenith Autoparts Corp ....E 845 344-1382
Middletown (G-7939)

IGNITION SYSTEMS: Internal Combustion Engine

Zierick Manufacturing Corp ....D 800 882-8020
Mount Kisco (G-8108)

INCINERATORS

Thermal Process Cnstr Co ....E 631 293-6400
Farmingdale (G-4754)

INDICATORS: Cabin Environment

Excelsior Mlt-Cltural Inst Inc ....F 706 627-4285
Flushing (G-4850)

INDL & PERSONAL SVC PAPER WHOLESALERS

Felix Schoeller North Amer Inc ....D 315 298-8425
Pulaski (G-12994)
Josh Packaging Inc ....E 631 822-1660
Hauppauge (G-5681)
Stanley Paper Co Inc ....F 518 489-1131
Albany (G-131)

INDL & PERSONAL SVC PAPER, WHOL: Bags, Paper/Disp Plastic

Dawn Paper Co Inc ....F 516 596-9110
East Rockaway (G-4172)
Dory Enterprises Inc ....F 607 565-7079
Waverly (G-15620)
Dynamic Packaging Inc ....F 718 388-0800
Brooklyn (G-1768)
Elara Fdsrvice Disposables LLC ....G 877 893-3244
Jericho (G-6577)
Garb-O-Liner Inc ....G 914 235-1585
New Rochelle (G-8334)
Golden Group International Ltd ....G 845 440-1025
Patterson (G-12517)
Jay Bags Inc ....G 845 459-6500
Spring Valley (G-14573)
M C Packaging Corporation ....E 631 643-3763
Babylon (G-522)
Paramount Equipment Inc ....E 631 981-4422
Ronkonkoma (G-13991)
Poly Craft Industries Corp ....E 631 630-6731
Hauppauge (G-5744)
Primo Plastics Inc ....F 718 349-1000
Brooklyn (G-2286)
Westrock Rkt LLC ....C 631 586-6000
Deer Park (G-3953)

INDL & PERSONAL SVC PAPER, WHOL: Boxes, Corrugtd/Solid Fiber

Cattaraugus Containers Inc ....E 716 676-2000
Franklinville (G-4966)
Technical Packaging Inc ....F 516 223-2300
Baldwin (G-537)

INDL & PERSONAL SVC PAPER, WHOL: Container, Paper/Plastic

Pactiv LLC ....C 585 394-5125
Canandaigua (G-3138)

INDL & PERSONAL SVC PAPER, WHOL: Cups, Disp, Plastic/Paper

S J McCullagh Inc ....E 716 856-3473
Buffalo (G-2970)

INDL & PERSONAL SVC PAPER, WHOLESALE: Paperboard & Prdts

G F Labels LLC ....F 518 798-6643
Queensbury (G-13039)

INDL & PERSONAL SVC PAPER, WHOLESALE: Press Sensitive Tape

Edco Supply Corporation ....D 718 788-8108
Brooklyn (G-1782)
Tape-It Inc ....E 631 243-4100
Bay Shore (G-721)

INDL & PERSONAL SVC PAPER, WHOLESALE: Sanitary Food

Carry Hot Inc ....E 212 279-7535
New York (G-8925)

INDL EQPT SVCS

Burnett Process Inc ....G 585 254-8080
Rochester (G-13288)
Eis Legacy LLC ....E 585 426-5330
Rochester (G-13380)
Keyes Machine Works Inc ....G 585 426-5059
Gates (G-5141)
Oliver Gear Inc ....E 716 885-1080
Buffalo (G-2896)
R & B Fabrication Inc ....F 315 640-9901
Cicero (G-3423)

INDL GASES WHOLESALERS

Haun Welding Supply Inc ....G 607 846-2289
Elmira (G-4356)

INDL MACHINERY & EQPT WHOLESALERS

Accurate Industrial Machining ....E 631 242-0566
Holbrook (G-5983)
Advanced Photonics Inc ....F 631 471-3693
Ronkonkoma (G-13891)
Analog Digital Technology LLC ....G 585 698-1845
Rochester (G-13235)
Anderson Instrument Co Inc ....D 518 922-5315
Fultonville (G-5077)
Anthony Manufacturing Inc ....G 631 957-9424
Lindenhurst (G-6940)
Arbe Machinery Inc ....F 631 756-2477
Farmingdale (G-4586)
Brinkman Products Inc ....B 585 235-4545
Rochester (G-13282)
Brooklyn Brew Shop LLC ....F 718 874-0119
Brooklyn (G-1612)
Buflovak LLC ....E 716 895-2100
Buffalo (G-2685)
Charles Ross & Son Company ....D 631 234-0500
Hauppauge (G-5614)
Conrad Blasius Equipment Co ....G 516 753-1200
Plainview (G-12672)
DI Manufacturing Inc ....E 315 432-8977
North Syracuse (G-12040)
Dorsey Metrology Intl Inc ....E 845 229-2929
Poughkeepsie (G-12951)
Filling Equipment Co Inc ....F 718 445-2111
College Point (G-3542)
Genesee Manufacturing Co Inc ....G 585 266-3201
Rochester (G-13435)
Goulds Pumps LLC ....A 315 568-2811
Seneca Falls (G-14362)
Halpern Tool Corp ....G 914 633-0038
New Rochelle (G-8338)
Hunter Douglas Inc ....D 845 664-7000
Pearl River (G-12533)
Innotech Graphic Eqp Corp ....G 845 268-6900
Valley Cottage (G-15316)
ITT Goulds Pumps Inc ....A 914 641-2129
Seneca Falls (G-14366)
John N Fehlinger Co Inc ....F 212 233-5656
New York (G-10018)
Khk Usa Inc ....G 516 248-3850
Mineola (G-7984)
Kps Capital Partners LP ....E 212 338-5100
New York (G-10133)
Makerbot Industries LLC ....C 347 334-6800
Brooklyn (G-2104)
Mark - 10 Corporation ....E 631 842-9200
Copiague (G-3664)
N E Controls LLC ....F 315 626-2480
Syracuse (G-14949)
Noresco Industrial Group Inc ....E 516 759-3355
Glen Cove (G-5197)
Rapid Fan & Blower Inc ....F 718 786-2060
Long Island City (G-7339)
Riverside Machinery Company ....E 718 492-7400
Brooklyn (G-2349)
Rs Automation ....F 585 589-0199
Albion (G-160)
Simmons Machine Tool Corp ....C 518 462-5431
Menands (G-7848)
Specialty Steel Fabg Corp ....F 718 893-6326
Bronx (G-1368)
Thread Check Inc ....D 631 231-1515
Hauppauge (G-5784)

Troy Belting and Supply Co ....D...... 518 272-4920
  Watervliet (G-15609)
Uneeda Enterprizes Inc ....C...... 800 431-2494
  Spring Valley (G-14585)
Unicell Body Company Inc ....F...... 716 853-8628
  Schenectady (G-14313)
Viatran Corporation ....E...... 716 564-7813
  Tonawanda (G-15152)
Vibration & Noise Engrg Corp ....G...... 716 827-4959
  Orchard Park (G-12382)
Ward Industrial Equipment Inc ....G...... 716 856-6966
  Buffalo (G-3041)

INDL MACHINERY REPAIR & MAINTENANCE

Alternative Service Inc ....F...... 631 345-9500
  Bellport (G-793)
Atlantic Industrial Tech Inc ....E...... 631 234-3131
  Shirley (G-14415)
Dairy Conveyor Corp ....D...... 845 278-7878
  Brewster (G-1146)
Demartini Oil Equipment Svc................G...... 518 463-5752
  Glenmont (G-5236)
Excel Conveyor LLC ....F...... 718 474-0001
  Rockaway Beach (G-13822)
General Oil Equipment Co Inc ....E...... 716 691-7012
  Amherst (G-225)
Konecranes Inc ....G...... 585 359-4450
  Henrietta (G-5857)
Locker Masters Inc ....F...... 518 288-3203
  Granville (G-5349)
Prim Hall Enterprises Inc ....F...... 518 561-7408
  Plattsburgh (G-12772)
Tchnologies N MRC Ameerica LLC ....G...... 716 822-4300
  Buffalo (G-3003)

INDL PATTERNS: Foundry Patternmaking

G Haynes Holdings Inc ....G...... 607 538-1160
  Bloomville (G-953)
Studio One Leather Design Inc.............F...... 212 760-1701
  New York (G-11379)

INDL PROCESS INSTRUMENT: Potentiomtrc Self-Bal, Exc XY Plot

Betapast Holdings LLC ....D...... 631 582-6740
  Hauppauge (G-5603)

INDL PROCESS INSTRUMENTS: Analyzers

Cosa Xentaur Corporation ....F...... 631 345-3434
  Yaphank (G-16258)
Vibro-Laser Instrs Corp LLC.................G...... 518 874-2700
  Glens Falls (G-5269)

INDL PROCESS INSTRUMENTS: Control

Automation Evolution LLC ....G...... 585 241-6010
  Webster (G-15631)
Conax Technologies LLC ....C...... 716 684-4500
  Buffalo (G-2708)
Electrcal Instrumentation Ctrl...............F...... 518 861-5789
  Delanson (G-3959)
Inficon Inc ....C...... 315 434-1100
  East Syracuse (G-4220)
Inficon Holding AG ....G...... 315 434-1100
  East Syracuse (G-4221)
Nidec Indus Automtn USA LLC ....E...... 716 774-1193
  Grand Island (G-5338)
Rwb Controls Inc ....G...... 716 897-4341
  Buffalo (G-2967)

INDL PROCESS INSTRUMENTS: Controllers, Process Variables

Anderson Instrument Co Inc.................D...... 518 922-5315
  Fultonville (G-5077)
Applied Power Systems Inc ....E...... 516 935-2230
  Hicksville (G-5883)
Classic Automation LLC ....E...... 585 241-6010
  Webster (G-15635)
Digitronik Labs Inc...............................F...... 585 360-0043
  Rochester (G-13346)
New Scale Technologies Inc ....E...... 585 924-4450
  Victor (G-15420)
Ormec Systems Corp ....E...... 585 385-3520
  Rochester (G-13592)
Schneider Electric Usa Inc ....G...... 631 567-5710
  Bohemia (G-1073)

INDL PROCESS INSTRUMENTS: Digital Display, Process Variables

Display Logic USA Inc ....G...... 631 406-1922
  Hauppauge (G-5639)
Webinfinity Americas Inc ....F...... 516 331-5180
  Huntington (G-6234)

INDL PROCESS INSTRUMENTS: Elements, Primary

Aalborg Instrs & Contrls Inc ....D...... 845 398-3160
  Orangeburg (G-12304)

INDL PROCESS INSTRUMENTS: Fluidic Devices, Circuit & Systems

ITT Corporation ....D...... 315 568-2811
  Seneca Falls (G-14364)
ITT Inc ....C...... 914 641-2000
  White Plains (G-16017)
ITT LLC ....D...... 914 641-2000
  Seneca Falls (G-14368)
ITT LLC ....B...... 914 641-2000
  White Plains (G-16020)
Swagelok Western NY ....G...... 585 359-8470
  West Henrietta (G-15805)

INDL PROCESS INSTRUMENTS: Indl Flow & Measuring

Computer Instruments Corp ....E...... 516 876-8400
  Westbury (G-15874)
Select Controls Inc ....E...... 631 567-9010
  Bohemia (G-1076)

INDL PROCESS INSTRUMENTS: Level & Bulk Measuring

Gizmo Products Inc ....G...... 585 301-0970
  Stanley (G-14611)

INDL PROCESS INSTRUMENTS: On-Stream Gas Or Liquid Analysis

Calibrated Instruments Inc....................F...... 914 741-5700
  Manhasset (G-7532)

INDL PROCESS INSTRUMENTS: Temperature

Weiss Instruments Inc ....D...... 631 207-1200
  Holtsville (G-6058)

INDL PROCESS INSTRUMENTS: Water Quality Monitoring/Cntrl Sys

Blue Tee Corp ....G...... 212 598-0880
  New York (G-8820)
Danaher Corporation ....C...... 516 443-9432
  New York (G-9162)
Roessel & Co Inc ....G...... 585 458-5560
  Rochester (G-13703)

INDL SALTS WHOLESALERS

American Rock Salt Company LLC ....E...... 585 991-6878
  Retsof (G-13094)

INDL SPLYS WHOLESALERS

Allstate Gasket & Packing Inc ....F...... 631 254-4050
  Deer Park (G-3835)
Applince Installation Svc Corp...............E...... 716 884-7425
  Buffalo (G-2642)
Bfg Marine Inc ....F...... 631 586-5500
  Bay Shore (G-656)
D K Machine Inc ....F...... 518 747-0626
  Fort Edward (G-4938)
Executive Mirror Doors Inc ....G...... 631 234-1090
  Ronkonkoma (G-13937)
Flex Enterprises Inc ....E...... 585 742-1000
  Victor (G-15409)
Ford Regulator Valve Corp ....G...... 718 497-3255
  Brooklyn (G-1858)
Jar Metals Inc ....F...... 845 425-8901
  Nanuet (G-8200)
Lee Spring Company LLC ....C...... 888 777-4647
  Brooklyn (G-2058)
Macinnes Tool Corporation ....E...... 585 467-1920
  Rochester (G-13527)

Peraflex Hose Inc ....F...... 716 876-8806
  Buffalo (G-2913)
Rollers Inc ....G...... 716 837-0700
  Buffalo (G-2961)
SAS Industries Inc ....F...... 631 727-1441
  Manorville (G-7553)
Troy Belting and Supply Co ....D...... 518 272-4920
  Watervliet (G-15609)

INDL SPLYS, WHOL: Fasteners, Incl Nuts, Bolts, Screws, Etc

Fastener Dimensions Inc ....E...... 718 847-6321
  Ozone Park (G-12461)
Reddi Car Corp ....G...... 631 589-3141
  Sayville (G-14231)
SD Christie Associates Inc ....G...... 914 734-1800
  Peekskill (G-12557)

INDL SPLYS, WHOLESALE: Abrasives

Barton Mines Company LLC ....C...... 518 798-5462
  Glens Falls (G-5242)
Sunbelt Industries Inc ....F...... 315 823-2947
  Little Falls (G-6993)
Uneeda Enterprizes Inc ....C...... 800 431-2494
  Spring Valley (G-14585)
Warren Cutlery Corp ....F...... 845 876-3444
  Rhinebeck (G-13103)

INDL SPLYS, WHOLESALE: Adhesives, Tape & Plasters

Xto Incorporated ....D...... 315 451-7807
  Liverpool (G-7050)

INDL SPLYS, WHOLESALE: Bearings

Raydon Precision Bearing Co ....G...... 516 887-2582
  Lynbrook (G-7436)

INDL SPLYS, WHOLESALE: Bins & Containers, Storage

McIntosh Box & Pallet Co Inc ....E...... 315 446-9350
  Rome (G-13855)

INDL SPLYS, WHOLESALE: Brushes, Indl

Braun Bros Brushes Inc........................G...... 631 667-2179
  Valley Stream (G-15336)

INDL SPLYS, WHOLESALE: Clean Room Splys

Air Crafters Inc ....C...... 631 471-7788
  Ronkonkoma (G-13893)
Knf Clean Room Products Corp ....E...... 631 588-7000
  Ronkonkoma (G-13958)

INDL SPLYS, WHOLESALE: Fasteners & Fastening Eqpt

American Pride Fasteners LLC...............E...... 631 940-8292
  Bay Shore (G-649)
General Galvanizing Sup Co Inc............D...... 718 589-4300
  Bronx (G-1266)

INDL SPLYS, WHOLESALE: Gears

Khk Usa Inc ....G...... 516 248-3850
  Mineola (G-7984)

INDL SPLYS, WHOLESALE: Knives, Indl

Save O Seal Corporation Inc.................G...... 914 592-3031
  Elmsford (G-4427)

INDL SPLYS, WHOLESALE: Mill Splys

Polymag Tek Inc ....F...... 585 235-8390
  Rochester (G-13628)

INDL SPLYS, WHOLESALE: Rubber Goods, Mechanical

Tattersall Industries LLC ....E...... 518 381-4270
  Schenectady (G-14311)
Triangle Rubber Co Inc ....E...... 631 589-9400
  Bohemia (G-1089)

PRODUCT

INDL SPLYS, WHOLESALE: Seals

American Casting and Mfg Corp ....D 800 342-0333
Plainview (G-12662)

Web Seal Inc ....E 585 546-1320
Rochester (G-13800)

INDL SPLYS, WHOLESALE: Sewing Thread

V Technical Textiles Inc ....G 315 597-1674
Palmyra (G-12494)

INDL SPLYS, WHOLESALE: Tools

Dinosaw Inc ....E 518 828-9942
Hudson (G-6154)

INDL SPLYS, WHOLESALE: Valves & Fittings

John N Fehlinger Co Inc ....F 212 233-5656
New York (G-10018)

McWane Inc ....B 607 734-2211
Elmira (G-4362)

Trident Valve Actuator Co ....F 914 698-2650
Mamaroneck (G-7526)

INDUCTORS

Island Audio Engineering ....G 631 543-2372
Commack (G-3593)

INFORMATION RETRIEVAL SERVICES

Alternative Technology Corp ....G 914 478-5900
Hastings On Hudson (G-5571)

Aquifer Drilling & Testing Inc ....D 516 616-6026
Mineola (G-7958)

Avalon Copy Centers Amer Inc ....D 315 471-3333
Syracuse (G-14823)

Avalon Copy Centers Amer Inc ....E 716 995-7777
Buffalo (G-2651)

Data Key Communication LLC ....F 315 445-2347
Fayetteville (G-4783)

IAC Search LLC ....E 212 314-7300
New York (G-9850)

Iac/Interactivecorp ....A 212 314-7300
New York (G-9851)

New York Times Company ....B 212 556-1234
New York (G-10604)

Realtimetraderscom ....E 716 632-6600
Buffalo (G-2950)

INFRARED OBJECT DETECTION EQPT

Infrared Components Corp ....E 315 732-1544
Utica (G-15277)

INGOT: Aluminum

Novelis Inc ....E 315 349-0121
Oswego (G-12418)

INK OR WRITING FLUIDS

American Electronic Products ....F 631 924-1299
Yaphank (G-16255)

F M Group Inc ....F 845 589-0102
Congers (G-3614)

Specialty Ink Co Inc ....F 631 586-3666
Blue Point (G-957)

INK: Letterpress Or Offset

Bishop Print Shop Inc ....G 607 965-8155
Edmeston (G-4294)

INK: Printing

Atlas Coatings Corp ....D 718 402-2000
Bronx (G-1207)

Calchem Corporation ....G 631 423-5696
Ronkonkoma (G-13920)

Flint Group US LLC ....E 585 458-1223
Rochester (G-13413)

Gotham Ink & Color Co Inc ....E 845 947-4000
Stony Point (G-14744)

Intrinsiq Materials Inc ....E 585 301-4432
Rochester (G-13483)

INX International Ink Co ....E 716 366-6010
Dunkirk (G-4059)

Micro Powders Inc ....E 914 332-6400
Tarrytown (G-15048)

Millennium Rmnfctred Toner Inc ....F 718 585-9887
Bronx (G-1314)

Mitsubishi Chemical Amer Inc ....E 212 223-3043
New York (G-10484)

Specialty Ink Co Inc ....F 631 586-3666
Blue Point (G-957)

Superior Printing Ink Co Inc ....G 716 877-0250
Tonawanda (G-15142)

Wikoff Color Corporation ....F 585 458-0653
Rochester (G-13805)

INK: Screen process

Standard Screen Supply Corp ....E 212 627-2727
New York (G-11346)

INSECTICIDES

Island Marketing Corp ....G 516 739-0500
Mineola (G-7981)

Noble Pine Products Co Inc ....F 914 664-5877
Mount Vernon (G-8165)

INSECTICIDES & PESTICIDES

Green Amazon LLC ....G 585 300-1319
Rochester (G-13451)

INSPECTION & TESTING SVCS

Cs Automation Inc ....F 315 524-5123
Ontario (G-12286)

INSTR, MEASURE & CONTROL: Gauge, Oil Pressure & Water Temp

Make-Waves Instrument Corp ....E 716 681-7524
Buffalo (G-2860)

INSTRUMENTS & METERS: Measuring, Electric

Pulsafeeder Inc ....C 585 292-8000
Rochester (G-13653)

S R Instruments Inc ....E 716 693-5977
Tonawanda (G-15136)

Schlumberger Technology Corp ....C 607 378-0105
Horseheads (G-6136)

INSTRUMENTS, LABORATORY: Differential Thermal Analysis

East Cast Envmtl Rstration Inc ....G 631 600-2000
Farmingdale (G-4622)

Timtronics LLC ....G 631 345-6509
Yaphank (G-16274)

INSTRUMENTS, LABORATORY: Magnetic/Elec Properties Measuring

CTB Enterprise LLC ....F 631 563-0088
Holbrook (G-5994)

MMC Enterprises Corp ....G 800 435-1088
Hauppauge (G-5721)

INSTRUMENTS, LABORATORY: Mass Spectrometers

Advion Inc ....E 607 266-9162
Ithaca (G-6361)

INSTRUMENTS, LABORATORY: Protein Analyzers

Elementar Americas Inc ....G 856 787-0022
Ronkonkoma (G-13934)

INSTRUMENTS, LABORATORY: Spectrometers

Spectra Vista Corporation ....G 845 471-7007
Poughkeepsie (G-12983)

INSTRUMENTS, MEASURING & CNTRL: Radiation & Testing, Nuclear

L N D Incorporated ....E 516 678-6141
Oceanside (G-12179)

Mirion Tech Conax Nuclear Inc ....E 716 681-1973
Buffalo (G-2867)

Mirion Technologies Ist Corp ....D 607 562-4300
Horseheads (G-6128)

VJ Technologies Inc ....E 631 589-8800
Bohemia (G-1096)

INSTRUMENTS, MEASURING & CNTRL: Testing, Abrasion, Etc

Magnetic Analysis Corporation ....D 914 530-2000
Elmsford (G-4415)

INSTRUMENTS, MEASURING & CNTRLG: Aircraft & Motor Vehicle

James A Staley Co Inc ....F 845 878-3344
Carmel (G-3187)

Magtrol Inc ....E 716 668-5555
Buffalo (G-2859)

INSTRUMENTS, MEASURING & CNTRLG: Stress, Strain & Measure

Mechanical Technology Inc ....E 518 218-2550
Albany (G-99)

MTI Instruments Inc ....F 518 218-2550
Albany (G-103)

INSTRUMENTS, MEASURING & CNTRLG: Tensile Strength Testing

Andor Design Corp ....G 516 364-1619
Syosset (G-14777)

INSTRUMENTS, MEASURING & CNTRLG: Thermometers/Temp Sensors

Darkpulse Inc ....G 800 436-1436
New York (G-9170)

Qhi Group Incorporated ....G 646 512-5727
New York (G-10943)

INSTRUMENTS, MEASURING & CONTROLLING: Gas Detectors

Industrial Test Eqp Co Inc ....E 516 883-6423
Port Washington (G-12888)

INSTRUMENTS, MEASURING & CONTROLLING: Magnetometers

Vector Magnetics LLC ....E 607 273-8351
Ithaca (G-6417)

INSTRUMENTS, MEASURING & CONTROLLING: Photogrammetrical

Elsag North America LLC ....G 877 773-5724
Brewster (G-1148)

INSTRUMENTS, MEASURING & CONTROLLING: Toll Booths, Automatic

Highway Toll ADM LLC ....F 516 684-9584
Roslyn Heights (G-14051)

INSTRUMENTS, MEASURING & CONTROLLING: Ultrasonic Testing

Aurora Technical Services Ltd ....G 716 652-1463
East Aurora (G-4083)

U E Systems Incorporated ....E 914 592-1220
Elmsford (G-4438)

INSTRUMENTS, MEASURING/CNTRL: Hydrometers, Exc Indl Process

Mobius Labs Inc ....G 518 961-2600
Rexford (G-13095)

Peyser Instrument Corporation ....E 631 841-3600
West Babylon (G-15736)

INSTRUMENTS, MEASURING/CNTRLG: Fare Registers, St Cars/Buses

Cubic Trnsp Systems Inc ....F 212 255-1810
New York (G-9129)

INSTRUMENTS, MEASURING/CNTRLNG: Med Diagnostic Sys, Nuclear

Amarantus Bscence Holdings Inc ....F 917 686-5317
New York (G-8536)

Eastern Niagra Radiology ....E 716 882-6544
Buffalo (G-2737)

H D M Labs Inc ....G...... 516 431-8357
Island Park *(G-6318)*

Nuclear Diagnostic Pdts NY Inc ......G...... 516 575-4201
Plainview *(G-12705)*

Oyster Bay Pump Works Inc ....F...... 516 933-4500
Hicksville *(G-5937)*

INSTRUMENTS, OPTICAL: *Borescopes*

Machida Incorporated......................G...... 845 365-0600
Orangeburg *(G-12323)*

INSTRUMENTS, OPTICAL: *Elements & Assemblies, Exc Ophthalmic*

Applied Coatings Holding Corp............G...... 585 482-0300
Rochester *(G-13240)*

Lightforce Technology Inc ....G...... 585 292-5610
Rochester *(G-13518)*

Photon Gear Inc ....F...... 585 265-3360
Ontario *(G-12297)*

INSTRUMENTS, OPTICAL: *Gratings, Diffraction*

Newport Rochester Inc ....D...... 585 262-1325
Rochester *(G-13575)*

INSTRUMENTS, OPTICAL: *Grinding, Lens Exc Ophthalmic*

Apti Pro Systems 2000 Inc ....D...... 585 265-0160
Ontario *(G-12283)*

INSTRUMENTS, OPTICAL: *Lenses, All Types Exc Ophthalmic*

21st Century Optics Inc......................E...... 347 527-1079
Long Island City *(G-7140)*

Advanced Glass Industries Inc............D...... 585 458-8040
Rochester *(G-13210)*

Double Helix Optics Inc ....G...... 917 689-6490
Rochester *(G-13355)*

Enplas America Inc ....G...... 646 892-7811
New York *(G-9381)*

Jml Optical Industries LLC.................D...... 585 248-8900
Rochester *(G-13492)*

Lens Triptar Co Inc ....G...... 585 473-4470
Rochester *(G-13515)*

Optics Technology Inc ....G...... 585 586-0950
Pittsford *(G-12653)*

Optimax Systems Inc ....C...... 585 265-1020
Ontario *(G-12295)*

Rochester Precision Optics LLC ....B...... 585 292-5450
West Henrietta *(G-15802)*

Spectrum Thin Films Inc ....E...... 631 901-1010
Hauppauge *(G-5772)*

INSTRUMENTS, OPTICAL: *Mirrors*

Hudson Mirror LLC ....E...... 914 930-8906
Peekskill *(G-12553)*

INSTRUMENTS, OPTICAL: *Prisms*

Ariel Optics Inc ....G...... 585 265-4820
Ontario *(G-12284)*

INSTRUMENTS, OPTICAL: *Spyglasses*

Digitac Inc......................................F...... 732 215-4020
Brooklyn *(G-1744)*

INSTRUMENTS, OPTICAL: *Test & Inspection*

Quality Vision Intl Inc ....B...... 585 544-0450
Rochester *(G-13660)*

Videk Inc ....E...... 585 377-0377
Fairport *(G-4528)*

INSTRUMENTS, SURGICAL & MEDICAL: *Blood & Bone Work*

Drive Medical Spv LLC ....G...... 516 998-4600
Port Washington *(G-12875)*

Future Diagnostics LLC ....E...... 347 434-6700
Brooklyn *(G-1871)*

Manhattan Eastside Dev Corp ....F...... 212 305-3275
New York *(G-10343)*

INSTRUMENTS, SURGICAL & MEDICAL: *Blood Pressure*

American Diagnostic Corp ....D...... 631 273-6155
Hauppauge *(G-5589)*

N Y B P Inc ....G...... 585 624-2541
Mendon *(G-7851)*

W A Baum Co Inc ....D...... 631 226-3940
Copiague *(G-3689)*

INSTRUMENTS, SURGICAL & MEDICAL: *Catheters*

Nasco Enterprises Inc ....G...... 516 921-9696
Syosset *(G-14795)*

Novamed-Usa Inc ....E...... 914 789-2100
Elmsford *(G-4420)*

Vante Inc ....F...... 716 778-7691
Newfane *(G-11896)*

INSTRUMENTS, SURGICAL & MEDICAL: *IV Transfusion*

Sigma Intl Gen Med Apprtus LLC ....B...... 585 798-3901
Medina *(G-7747)*

INSTRUMENTS, SURGICAL & MEDICAL: *Inhalation Therapy*

Beacon Spch Lnge Pthlgy Phys............F...... 516 626-1635
Roslyn *(G-14039)*

Moogs Medical Devices Group............G...... 716 652-2000
Buffalo *(G-2872)*

INSTRUMENTS, SURGICAL & MEDICAL: *Inhalators*

Ip Med Inc ....G...... 516 766-3800
Oceanside *(G-12176)*

INSTRUMENTS, SURGICAL & MEDICAL: *Knives*

Huron TI Cutter Grinding Inc ....E...... 631 420-7000
Farmingdale *(G-4646)*

INSTRUMENTS, SURGICAL & MEDICAL: *Lasers, Surgical*

Aerolase Corporation ....D...... 914 345-8300
Tarrytown *(G-15039)*

Clerio Vision Inc ....F...... 617 216-7881
Rochester *(G-13318)*

INSTRUMENTS, SURGICAL & MEDICAL: *Muscle Exercise, Ophthalmic*

Biodex Medical Systems Inc...............C...... 631 924-9000
Shirley *(G-14417)*

Biodex Medical Systems Inc...............E...... 631 924-3146
Shirley *(G-14418)*

INSTRUMENTS, SURGICAL & MEDICAL: *Ophthalmic*

Corning Tropel Corporation ....C...... 585 377-3200
Fairport *(G-4494)*

Sonomed Inc ....E...... 516 354-0900
New Hyde Park *(G-8294)*

INSTRUMENTS, SURGICAL & MEDICAL: *Physiotherapy, Electrical*

Fabrication Enterprises Inc................E...... 914 591-9300
Elmsford *(G-4409)*

INSTRUMENTS, SURGICAL & MEDICAL: *Skin Grafting*

Skyler Brand Ventures LLC.................G...... 646 979-5904
New York *(G-11265)*

INSTRUMENTS, SURGICAL & MEDICAL: *Suction Therapy*

Njr Medical Devices ....E...... 440 258-8204
Cedarhurst *(G-3243)*

Repro Med Systems Inc ....D...... 845 469-2042
Chester *(G-3383)*

INSTRUMENTS: *Analytical*

A S A Precision Co Inc.......................G...... 845 482-4870
Jeffersonville *(G-6569)*

Advanced Mtl Analytics LLC................G...... 321 684-0528
Vestal *(G-15369)*

Awe Technologies LLC.......................G...... 631 747-8448
Bay Shore *(G-654)*

Bristol Instruments Inc ....G...... 585 924-2620
Victor *(G-15395)*

Brookhaven Instruments Corp ....E...... 631 758-3200
Holtsville *(G-6046)*

Carl Zeiss Inc..................................C...... 914 747-1800
White Plains *(G-15990)*

Ceres Technologies Inc......................D...... 845 247-4701
Saugerties *(G-14198)*

Chromosense LLC ....G...... 646 541-2302
Rye Brook *(G-14087)*

Corning Incorporated ....A...... 607 974-9000
Painted Post *(G-12473)*

Dantec Dynamics Inc ....G...... 631 654-1290
Holtsville *(G-6049)*

East Hills Instrument Inc ....F...... 516 621-8686
Westbury *(G-15879)*

Equine Imaging LLC ....F...... 414 326-0665
Port Washington *(G-12878)*

General Microwave Corporation...........F...... 516 802-0900
Syosset *(G-14789)*

High Voltage Inc ....E...... 518 329-3275
Copake *(G-3642)*

Ion-Tof Usa Inc ....G...... 845 352-8082
Spring Valley *(G-14572)*

Life Technologies Corporation ....D...... 716 774-6700
Grand Island *(G-5336)*

Multiwire Laboratories Ltd ....G...... 607 257-3378
Ithaca *(G-6399)*

Nanotronics Imaging Inc ....E...... 212 401-6209
Brooklyn *(G-2186)*

Nikon Instruments Inc ....D...... 631 547-4200
Melville *(G-7810)*

Nikon Instruments Inc ....G...... 631 845-7620
Edgewood *(G-4276)*

Photonics Industries Intl Inc ....D...... 631 218-2240
Ronkonkoma *(G-13994)*

Quality Vision Intl Inc ....E...... 585 544-0400
Rochester *(G-13661)*

Rheonix Inc.....................................D...... 607 257-1242
Ithaca *(G-6409)*

Smartpill Corporation ....E...... 716 882-0701
Buffalo *(G-2984)*

Thermo Fisher Scientific Inc...............E...... 585 899-7780
Penfield *(G-12575)*

Thermo Fisher Scientific Inc...............G...... 716 774-6700
Grand Island *(G-5345)*

Thermo Fisher Scientific Inc...............B...... 585 458-8008
Rochester *(G-13765)*

Thermo Fisher Scientific Inc...............A...... 585 899-7610
Rochester *(G-13766)*

Veeco Instruments Inc.......................C...... 516 677-0200
Woodbury *(G-16184)*

Velp Scientific Inc ....G...... 631 573-6002
Bohemia *(G-1095)*

INSTRUMENTS: *Colonoscopes, Electromedical*

Gravity East Village Inc ....G...... 212 388-9788
New York *(G-9667)*

INSTRUMENTS: *Combustion Control, Indl*

Aureonic ....G...... 518 791-9331
Gansevoort *(G-5083)*

INSTRUMENTS: *Electrocardiographs*

Integrated Medical Devices.................G...... 315 457-4200
Liverpool *(G-7016)*

INSTRUMENTS: *Electrolytic Conductivity, Indl*

Mark - 10 Corporation ....E...... 631 842-9200
Copiague *(G-3664)*

INSTRUMENTS: *Endoscopic Eqpt, Electromedical*

Elizabeth Wood ....G...... 315 492-5470
Syracuse *(G-14885)*

P
R
O
D
U
C
T

INSTRUMENTS: Flow, Indl Process

Schneider Elc Systems USA Inc ....F 214 527-3099
New York (G-11155)

INSTRUMENTS: Function Generators

Allied Motion Technologies Inc ....C 716 242-8634
Amherst (G-207)

INSTRUMENTS: Generators Tachometer

Make-Waves Instrument Corp ....E 716 681-7524
Buffalo (G-2860)

INSTRUMENTS: Indl Process Control

Ametek Inc ....D 585 263-7700
Rochester (G-13234)

Betatronix Inc ....E 631 582-6740
Ronkonkoma (G-13916)

Ceres Technologies Inc ....D 845 247-4701
Saugerties (G-14198)

Defelsko Corporation ....D 315 393-4450
Ogdensburg (G-12204)

Digital Analysis Corporation ....F 315 685-0760
Skaneateles (G-14449)

Dyna-Empire Inc ....C 516 222-2700
Garden City (G-5096)

East Hills Instrument Inc ....F 516 621-8686
Westbury (G-15879)

Electronic Machine Parts LLC ....F 631 434-3700
Hauppauge (G-5645)

Emerson Electric Co ....E 212 244-2490
New York (G-9361)

Emerson Process MGT Lllp ....F 585 214-8340
Rochester (G-13386)

Eni Mks Products Group ....F 585 427-8300
Rochester (G-13394)

Esensors Inc ....F 716 837-8719
Buffalo (G-2748)

Flexim Americas Corporation ....F 631 492-2300
Edgewood (G-4267)

Fts Systems Inc ....D 845 687-5300
Stone Ridge (G-14735)

Gurley Precision Instrs Inc ....C 518 272-6300
Troy (G-15170)

Hilliard Corporation ....B 607 733-7121
Elmira (G-4357)

Hilliard Corporation ....G 607 733-7121
Elmira (G-4358)

Integrated Control Corp ....E 631 673-5100
Huntington (G-6207)

Koehler Instrument Company Inc ....D 631 589-3800
Holtsville (G-6050)

Magtrol Inc ....E 716 668-5555
Buffalo (G-2859)

Mausner Equipment Co Inc ....C 631 689-7358
Setauket (G-14380)

Mks Instruments Inc ....E 585 292-7472
Rochester (G-13554)

Nautilus Controls Corp ....G 917 676-7005
New York (G-10554)

Nutec Components Inc ....F 631 242-1224
Deer Park (G-3913)

Orthstar Enterprises Inc ....D 607 562-2100
Horseheads (G-6130)

Parrington Instruments ....G 518 373-8420
Rexford (G-13096)

Pcb Group Inc ....E 716 684-0001
Depew (G-3992)

Poseidon Systems LLC ....F 585 239-6025
Rochester (G-13630)

Pulsafeeder Inc ....C 585 292-8000
Rochester (G-13653)

R K B Opto-Electronics Inc ....F 315 455-6636
Syracuse (G-14970)

Rosemount Inc ....G 585 424-2460
Rochester (G-13706)

Rotronic Instrument Corp ....G 631 427-3898
Huntington (G-6222)

Sixnet Holdings LLC ....G 518 877-5173
Ballston Lake (G-564)

Solar Metrology LLC ....G 845 247-4701
Holbrook (G-6021)

Telog Instruments Inc ....E 585 742-3000
Victor (G-15437)

Thread Check Inc ....D 631 231-1515
Hauppauge (G-5784)

Transtech Systems Inc ....E 518 370-5558
Latham (G-6878)

Vacuum Instrument Corporation ....D 631 737-0900
Ronkonkoma (G-14023)

Veeco Instruments Inc ....C 516 677-0200
Woodbury (G-16184)

Vertiv Corporation ....G 516 349-8500
Plainview (G-12727)

Winters Instruments Inc ....E 281 880-8607
Buffalo (G-3050)

Xentaur Corporation ....E 631 345-3434
Yaphank (G-16279)

INSTRUMENTS: Laser, Scientific & Engineering

Cambridge Manufacturing LLC ....G 516 326-1350
New Hyde Park (G-8255)

Gemprint Corporation ....E 212 997-0007
New York (G-9586)

Medpod Inc ....G 631 863-8090
Melville (G-7802)

Micro Photo Acoustics Inc ....G 631 750-6035
Ronkonkoma (G-13973)

Porous Materials Inc ....F 607 257-5544
Ithaca (G-6406)

Uptek Solutions Corp ....F 631 256-5565
Bohemia (G-1094)

INSTRUMENTS: Measurement, Indl Process

Riverhawk Company LP ....E 315 624-7171
New Hartford (G-8244)

INSTRUMENTS: Measuring & Controlling

Aspex Incorporated ....E 212 966-0410
New York (G-8652)

Awe Technologies LLC ....E 631 747-8448
Bay Shore (G-654)

Biodesign Inc of New York ....F 845 454-6610
Carmel (G-3184)

Carl Zeiss Inc ....C 914 747-1800
White Plains (G-15990)

Circor Aerospace Inc ....D 631 737-1900
Hauppauge (G-5615)

Computer Instruments Corp ....E 516 876-8400
Westbury (G-15874)

Cosense Inc ....G 516 364-9161
Syosset (G-14782)

Dayton T Brown Inc ....B 631 589-6300
Bohemia (G-1001)

Defelsko Corporation ....D 315 393-4450
Ogdensburg (G-12204)

Dispersion Technology Inc ....G 914 241-4777
Bedford Hills (G-768)

Dyna-Empire Inc ....C 516 222-2700
Garden City (G-5096)

Dynamic Systems Inc ....E 518 283-5350
Poestenkill (G-12802)

East Hills Instrument Inc ....F 516 621-8686
Westbury (G-15879)

Electrical Controls Link ....E 585 924-7010
Victor (G-15406)

Electro-Optical Products Corp ....G 718 456-6000
Ridgewood (G-13145)

Erbessd Reliability LLC ....E 518 874-2700
Glens Falls (G-5248)

Fougera Pharmaceuticals Inc ....C 631 454-7677
Melville (G-7785)

Freeman Technology Inc ....E 732 829-8345
Bayside (G-737)

Gei International Inc ....E 315 463-9261
East Syracuse (G-4212)

Hci Engineering ....G 315 336-3450
Rome (G-13850)

Helmel Engineering Pdts Inc ....F 716 297-8644
Niagara Falls (G-11935)

Hipotronics Inc ....C 845 279-8091
Brewster (G-1151)

Images Si Inc ....F 718 966-3694
Staten Island (G-14664)

Imaginant Inc ....E 585 264-0480
Pittsford (G-12643)

Itin Scale Co Inc ....E 718 336-5900
Brooklyn (G-1974)

Kem Medical Products Corp ....G 631 454-6565
Farmingdale (G-4665)

Kistler Instrument Corporation ....D 716 691-5100
Amherst (G-228)

Kld Labs Inc ....E 631 549-4222
Hauppauge (G-5685)

Liberty Controls Inc ....G 718 461-0600
College Point (G-3551)

Machine Technology Inc ....G 845 454-4030
Poughkeepsie (G-12968)

Mason Industries Inc ....C 631 348-0282
Hauppauge (G-5708)

North Pk Innovations Group Inc ....E 716 699-2031
Ellicottville (G-4315)

Orolia Usa Inc ....D 585 321-5800
Rochester (G-13593)

Pcb Piezotronics Inc ....F 716 684-0001
Depew (G-3993)

Peerless Instrument Co Inc ....E 631 396-6500
Farmingdale (G-4704)

Poseidon Systems LLC ....F 585 239-6025
Rochester (G-13630)

Precision Design Systems Inc ....E 585 426-4500
Rochester (G-13635)

Pronto Gas Heating Sups Inc ....G 718 292-0707
Bronx (G-1345)

Qualitrol Company LLC ....C 586 643-3717
Fairport (G-4516)

Quality Vision Intl Inc ....E 585 544-0400
Rochester (G-13661)

Research Frontiers Inc ....G 516 364-1902
Woodbury (G-16181)

Riverhawk Company LP ....E 315 624-7171
New Hartford (G-8244)

RJ Harvey Instrument Corp ....F 845 359-3943
Tappan (G-15038)

Schenck Corporation ....D 631 242-4010
Deer Park (G-3932)

Schenck USA Corp ....D 631 242-4010
Deer Park (G-3933)

Schott Corporation ....D 914 831-2200
Elmsford (G-4428)

Teledyne Lecroy Inc ....C 845 425-2000
Chestnut Ridge (G-3399)

Telog Instruments Inc ....E 585 742-3000
Victor (G-15437)

Vacuum Instrument Corporation ....D 631 737-0900
Ronkonkoma (G-14023)

Videk Inc ....E 585 377-0377
Fairport (G-4528)

Weiss Instruments Inc ....D 631 207-1200
Holtsville (G-6058)

Xeku Corporation ....F 607 761-1447
Vestal (G-15388)

York Industries Inc ....E 516 746-3736
Garden City Park (G-5126)

Zomega Terahertz Corporation ....F 585 347-4337
Webster (G-15664)

INSTRUMENTS: Measuring Electricity

Agilent Technologies Inc ....A 877 424-4536
New York (G-8494)

American Quality Technology ....F 607 777-9488
Binghamton (G-853)

Ametek Inc ....D 585 263-7700
Rochester (G-13234)

C Speed LLC ....E 315 453-1043
Liverpool (G-7004)

C-Flex Bearing Co Inc ....F 315 895-7454
Frankfort (G-4948)

Cetek Inc ....E 845 452-3510
Poughkeepsie (G-12948)

East Hills Instrument Inc ....F 516 621-8686
Westbury (G-15879)

Ems Development Corporation ....D 631 924-4736
Yaphank (G-16259)

Enertiv Inc ....G 646 350-3525
New York (G-9376)

Interntnal Elctronic Mchs Corp ....E 518 268-1636
Troy (G-15173)

L3harris Technologies Inc ....A 631 630-4200
Amityville (G-288)

Larry Kings Corporation ....G 718 481-8741
Rosedale (G-14036)

Lecroy Corporation ....E 845 425-2000
Spring Valley (G-14575)

Logitek Inc ....D 631 567-1100
Bohemia (G-1035)

Ludl Electronic Products Ltd ....E 914 769-6111
Hawthorne (G-5818)

Magnetic Analysis Corporation ....D 914 530-2000
Elmsford (G-4415)

Magtrol Inc ....E 716 668-5555
Buffalo (G-2859)

Messer LLC ....D 716 773-7552
Grand Island (G-5337)

North Atlantic Industries Inc ....E 631 567-1100
Bohemia (G-1052)

Peerless Instrument Co Inc ....C 631 396-6500
Farmingdale (G-4704)

R K B Opto-Electronics Inc ....F 315 455-6636
Syracuse (G-14970)

Scientific Components Corp ....E 631 243-4901
Deer Park (G-3934)

Transcat Inc ....B 585 352-7777
Rochester (G-13772)

Trek Inc ....F 716 438-7555
Lockport (G-7114)

Viatran Corporation ....E 716 564-7813
Tonawanda (G-15152)

Zumbach Electronics Corp ....D 914 241-7080
Mount Kisco (G-8109)

INSTRUMENTS: Measuring, Electrical Energy

Apogee Power Usa Inc ....F 202 746-2890
Hartsdale (G-5567)

Quadlogic Controls Corporation ....D 212 930-9300
Long Island City (G-7334)

INSTRUMENTS: Measuring, Electrical Power

Allied Motion Systems Corp ....F 716 691-5868
Amherst (G-206)

Primesouth Inc ....F 585 567-4191
Fillmore (G-4794)

INSTRUMENTS: Medical & Surgical

A Titan Instruments Inc ....F 716 667-9211
Orchard Park (G-12335)

Advanced Back Technologies ....G 631 231-0076
Hauppauge (G-5579)

Aktina Corp ....E 845 268-0101
Congers (G-3606)

Ala Scientific Instruments Inc ....F 631 393-6401
Farmingdale (G-4577)

Alconox Inc ....G 914 948-4040
White Plains (G-15970)

AM Bickford Inc ....F 716 652-1590
Wales Center (G-15465)

Ambulatory Monitoring Inc ....G 914 693-9240
Ardsley (G-385)

Angiodynamics Inc ....E 518 798-1215
Queensbury (G-13031)

Angiodynamics Inc ....B 518 975-1400
Queensbury (G-13032)

Angiodynamics Inc ....B 518 792-4112
Glens Falls (G-5241)

Angiodynamics Inc ....B 518 742-4430
Queensbury (G-13033)

Angiodynamics Inc ....B 518 795-1400
Latham (G-6848)

Argon Medical Devices Inc ....G 585 321-1130
Henrietta (G-5855)

Astra Tool & Instrument Mfg ....E 914 747-3863
Hawthorne (G-5809)

Beyond Air Inc ....F 516 665-8200
Garden City (G-5091)

Bioresearch Inc ....G 212 734-5315
Pound Ridge (G-12991)

Boehm Surgical Instrument Corp ....F 585 436-6584
Rochester (G-13277)

Buffalo Filter LLC ....D 716 835-7000
Lancaster (G-6799)

Buxton Medical Equipment Corp ....E 631 957-4500
Lindenhurst (G-6943)

C R Bard Inc ....B 518 793-2531
Queensbury (G-13035)

C R Bard Inc ....A 518 793-2531
Glens Falls (G-5244)

C R Bard Inc ....D 518 793-2531
Queensbury (G-13036)

Caire Inc ....E 716 691-0202
Amherst (G-215)

Caliber Imging Diagnostics Inc ....E 585 239-9800
Rochester (G-13292)

CN Group Incorporated ....A 914 358-5690
White Plains (G-15994)

Cognitiveflow Sensor Tech ....G 631 513-9369
Stony Brook (G-14737)

Conmed Corporation ....D 315 797-8375
Utica (G-15247)

Daxor Corporation ....F 212 330-8500
New York (G-9190)

Delcath Systems Inc ....E 212 489-2100
New York (G-9197)

Derm-Buro Inc ....E 516 694-8300
Plainview (G-12678)

Designs For Vision Inc ....C 631 585-3300
Bohemia (G-1006)

Elliquence LLC ....F 516 277-9000
Baldwin (G-530)

Endovor Inc ....G 214 679-7385
New York (G-9370)

Endovor LLC ....G 214 679-7385
New York (G-9371)

Esc Control Electronics LLC ....E 631 467-5328
Sayville (G-14225)

Extek Inc ....E 585 533-1672
Rush (G-14070)

Eyeglass Service Industries ....G 914 666-3150
Bedford Hills (G-769)

Flexbar Machine Corporation ....E 631 582-8440
Islandia (G-6332)

Flowmedica Inc ....F 800 772-6446
Queensbury (G-13038)

Fluorologic Inc ....G 585 248-2796
Pittsford (G-12640)

Ftt Medical Inc ....G 585 444-0980
Rochester (G-13425)

Gaymar Industries Inc ....B 800 828-7341
Orchard Park (G-12353)

Harmac Medical Products Inc ....B 716 897-4500
Buffalo (G-2793)

Hogil Pharmaceutical Corp ....F 914 681-1800
White Plains (G-16014)

Hurryworks LLC ....D 516 998-4600
Port Washington (G-12885)

Incredible Scents Inc ....G 516 656-3300
Greenvale (G-5462)

Integer Holdings Corporation ....E 716 937-5100
Alden (G-171)

J H M Engineering ....E 718 871-1810
Brooklyn (G-1978)

J Jamner Surgical Instrs Inc ....E 914 592-9051
Hawthorne (G-5814)

Jaracz Jr Joseph Paul ....G 716 533-1377
Orchard Park (G-12358)

Liberty Install Inc ....F 631 651-5655
Huntington (G-6211)

Medical Depot Inc ....C 516 998-4600
Port Washington (G-12905)

Medical Technology Products ....G 631 285-6640
Greenlawn (G-5455)

Medline Industries Inc ....B 845 344-3301
Middletown (G-7919)

Medsource Technologies LLC ....D 716 662-5025
Orchard Park (G-12365)

Misonix Opco Inc ....D 631 694-9555
Farmingdale (G-4687)

Modular Medical Corp ....E 718 829-2626
Bronx (G-1317)

Moog Inc ....A 716 805-2604
Elma (G-4321)

Nano Vibronix Inc ....G 516 374-8330
Cedarhurst (G-3242)

Navilyst Medical Inc ....A 800 833-9973
Glens Falls (G-5261)

Ocala Group LLC ....F 516 233-2750
New Hyde Park (G-8286)

Orics Industries Inc ....E 718 461-8613
Farmingdale (G-4697)

Ortho Medical Products ....E 212 879-3700
New York (G-10712)

Orthocon Inc ....G 914 357-2600
Irvington (G-6312)

P-Ryton Corp ....F 718 937-7052
Long Island City (G-7316)

Pall Corporation ....A 607 753-6041
Cortland (G-3779)

Pall Corporation ....A 516 484-5400
Port Washington (G-12913)

Parace Bionics LLC ....G 877 727-2231
New York (G-10752)

Parkchester Dps LLC ....C 718 823-4411
Bronx (G-1332)

Pavmed Inc ....G 212 949-4319
New York (G-10775)

Peter Digioia ....G 516 644-5517
Plainview (G-12707)

Precimed Inc ....E 716 759-5600
Clarence (G-3440)

Professional Medical Devices ....F 914 835-0614
Harrison (G-5558)

Progressive Orthotics Ltd ....G 631 732-5556
Selden (G-14355)

Rdd Pharma Inc ....G 302 319-9970
New York (G-10991)

Reichert Inc ....C 716 686-4500
Depew (G-3996)

Responselink Inc ....G 518 424-7776
Latham (G-6875)

Retia Medical LLC ....G 914 594-1986
Valhalla (G-15308)

Robert Bosch LLC ....E 315 733-3312
Utica (G-15292)

SeedIngs Lf Scnce Ventures LLC ....G 917 913-8511
New York (G-11178)

Seneca TEC Inc ....G 585 381-2645
Fairport (G-4521)

Sensodx II LLC ....G 585 202-4552
Victor (G-15429)

Simulaids Inc ....D 845 679-2475
Saugerties (G-14212)

Soniquence LLC ....F 516 267-6400
Baldwin (G-535)

St Silicones Corporation ....E 518 406-3208
Clifton Park (G-3475)

Striker Orthopedics ....E 585 381-1773
Rochester (G-13749)

Symmetry Medical Inc ....G 845 368-4573
Hillburn (G-5971)

Tril Inc ....G 631 645-7989
Copiague (G-3685)

Vaso Corporation ....F 516 997-4600
Plainview (G-12722)

Viterion Corporation ....F 914 333-6033
Elmsford (G-4439)

Vizio Medical Devices LLC ....F 646 845-7382
New York (G-11700)

Welch Allyn Inc ....G 503 530-7500
Skaneateles Falls (G-14462)

Wyeth Holdings LLC ....D 845 602-5000
Pearl River (G-12543)

INSTRUMENTS: Meteorological

Climatronics Corp ....F 541 471-7111
Bohemia (G-987)

INSTRUMENTS: Microwave Test

Hamilton Marketing Corporation ....G 585 395-0678
Brockport (G-1176)

INSTRUMENTS: Optical, Analytical

Applied Image Inc ....E 585 482-0300
Rochester (G-13241)

INSTRUMENTS: Oscillographs & Oscilloscopes

Teledyne Lecroy Inc ....C 845 425-2000
Chestnut Ridge (G-3399)

INSTRUMENTS: Pressure Measurement, Indl

Taber Acquisition Corp ....D 716 694-4000
North Tonawanda (G-12094)

Viatran Corporation ....E 716 564-7813
Tonawanda (G-15152)

INSTRUMENTS: Radar Testing, Electric

Anmar Acquisition LLC ....G 585 352-7777
Rochester (G-13238)

INSTRUMENTS: Radio Frequency Measuring

Omni-ID Usa Inc ....E 585 299-5990
East Rochester (G-4168)

T & C Power Conversion Inc ....F 585 482-5551
Rochester (G-13755)

W D Technology Inc ....G 914 779-8738
Eastchester (G-4250)

INSTRUMENTS: Standards & Calibration, Electrical Measuring

Ah Elctronic Test Eqp Repr Ctr ....F 631 234-8979
Central Islip (G-3260)

INSTRUMENTS: Telemetering, Indl Process

Medsafe Systems Inc ....G 516 883-8222
Port Washington (G-12906)

INSTRUMENTS: Temperature Measurement, Indl

Rotronic Instrument Corp ....F 631 348-6844
Hauppauge (G-5755)
Springfield Control Systems.................G 718 631-0870
Douglaston (G-4029)
Tel-Tru Inc ....E 585 295-0225
Rochester (G-13763)

INSTRUMENTS: Test, Electronic & Electric Measurement

Advanced Testing Tech Inc ....C 631 231-8777
Hauppauge (G-5580)
Avanel Industries Inc ....F 516 333-0990
Westbury (G-15871)
Clayton Dubilier & Rice Fun ....E 212 407-5200
New York (G-9029)
Comtech PST Corp ....C 631 777-8900
Melville (G-7770)
John Ramsey Elec Svcs LLC ....G 585 298-9596
Victor (G-15414)
Millivac Instruments Inc ....G 518 355-8300
Schenectady (G-14289)
Nas CP Corp ....E 718 961-6757
College Point (G-3556)
Northeast Metrology Corp ....F 716 827-3770
Depew (G-3990)
Optimized Devices Inc ....F 914 769-6100
Pleasantville (G-12797)
Photonix Technologies Inc ....F 607 786-4600
Endicott (G-4471)
Precision Filters Inc.......................E 607 277-3550
Ithaca (G-6407)
Ramsey Electronics LLC ....E 585 924-4560
Victor (G-15426)
Scj Associates Inc ....E 585 359-0600
Rochester (G-13719)

INSTRUMENTS: Test, Electronic & Electrical Circuits

Automated Control Logic Inc...............F 914 769-8880
Thornwood (G-15067)
Automation Correct LLC ....G 315 299-3589
Syracuse (G-14821)
Avcom of Virginia Inc ....D 585 924-4560
Victor (G-15392)
Clarke Hess Communication RES........G 631 698-3350
Medford (G-7704)
General Microwave Corporation...........F 516 802-0900
Syosset (G-14789)
Hipotronics Inc ....C 845 279-8091
Brewster (G-1151)
Iet Labs Inc ....F 516 334-5959
Roslyn Heights (G-14052)
Lexan Industries Inc ....F 631 434-7586
Bay Shore (G-690)
Pulsar Technology Systems Inc ....G 718 361-9292
Long Island City (G-7331)

INSTRUMENTS: Testing, Semiconductor

Pragmatics Technology Inc ....G 845 795-5071
Milton (G-7951)

INSTRUMENTS: Thermal Conductive, Indl

Ktk Thermal Technologies Inc.............E 585 678-9025
Macedon (G-7466)

INSTRUMENTS: Vibration

SKF USA Inc ....D 716 661-2600
Falconer (G-4556)

INSTRUMENTS: Viscometer, Indl Process

Beauty America LLC.......................E 917 744-1430
Great Neck (G-5370)

INSULATION & CUSHIONING FOAM: Polystyrene

C P Chemical Co Inc ....G 914 428-2517
White Plains (G-15987)
Carlisle Construction Mtls LLC ....D 386 753-0786
Montgomery (G-8059)
Foam Products Inc.......................E 718 292-4830
Bronx (G-1260)

New York State Foam Enrgy LLC ....G 845 534-4656
Cornwall (G-3730)
Shelter Enterprises Inc ....D 518 237-4100
Cohoes (G-3516)
Soundcoat Company Inc ....D 631 242-2200
Deer Park (G-3938)
Thermal Foams/Syracuse Inc ....G 716 874-6474
Buffalo (G-3009)

INSULATION MATERIALS WHOLESALERS

Regional MGT & Consulting Inc ....F 718 599-3718
Brooklyn (G-2336)

INSULATION: Felt

Shannon Global Enrgy Solutions.........D 716 693-7954
North Tonawanda (G-12090)

INSULATION: Fiberglass

Burnett Process Inc ....G 585 254-8080
Rochester (G-13288)
Elliot Industries Inc ....G 716 287-3100
Ellington (G-4316)
Fbm Galaxy Inc ....G 315 463-5144
East Syracuse (G-4210)
Richlar Industries Inc ....F 315 463-5144
East Syracuse (G-4234)

INSULATORS & INSULATION MATERIALS: Electrical

Gerome Technologies Inc ....D 518 463-1324
Menands (G-7843)
J H C Fabrications Inc ....E 718 649-0065
Brooklyn (G-1977)
Varflex Corporation ....C 315 336-4400
Rome (G-13876)
Volt Tek Inc ....F 585 377-2050
Fairport (G-4529)
Von Roll Usa Inc ....C 518 344-7100
Schenectady (G-14316)
Von Roll USA Holding Inc ....C 518 344-7200
Schenectady (G-14317)

INSULATORS, PORCELAIN: Electrical

Lapp Insulator Company LLC ....G 585 768-6221
Le Roy (G-6902)
Pfisterer Lapp LLC ....C 585 768-6221
Le Roy (G-6906)
Victor Insulators Inc ....C 585 924-2127
Victor (G-15440)

INTEGRATED CIRCUITS, SEMICONDUCTOR NETWORKS, ETC

Akoustis Inc ....E 585 919-3073
Canandaigua (G-3124)
Artemis Inc ....G 631 232-2424
Hauppauge (G-5594)
Central Semiconductor Corp ....D 631 435-1110
Hauppauge (G-5612)
Dionics-Usa Inc ....G 516 997-7474
Westbury (G-15876)
Elite Semi Conductor Products ....G 631 884-8400
Lindenhurst (G-6952)
Globalfoundries US Inc ....F 408 462-3900
Ballston Spa (G-574)
LSI Computer Systems ....E 631 271-0400
Melville (G-7801)
Philips Medical Systems Mr ....B 518 782-1122
Latham (G-6872)
Plures Technologies Inc ....G 585 905-0554
Canandaigua (G-3140)
Pvi Solar Inc ....G 212 280-2100
New York (G-10938)
RSM Electron Power Inc ....C 631 586-7600
Deer Park (G-3931)

INTERCOMMUNICATIONS SYSTEMS: Electric

Andrea Systems LLC......................E 631 390-3140
Farmingdale (G-4585)
Apple Core Electronics Inc ....F 718 628-4068
Brooklyn (G-1519)
AVI-Spl Employee ....B 212 840-4801
New York (G-8691)
Capstream Technologies LLC ....G 716 945-7100
Olean (G-12227)

Curbell Medical Products Inc ....F 716 667-2520
Orchard Park (G-12349)
Curbell Medical Products Inc ....C 716 667-2520
Orchard Park (G-12350)
Frequency Electronics Inc ....C 516 794-4500
Uniondale (G-15229)
Goddard Design Co ....G 718 599-0170
Brooklyn (G-1895)
McDowell Research Co Inc ....D 315 332-7100
Newark (G-11845)
Mkj Communications Inc ....E 212 206-0072
Brooklyn (G-2164)
Nu2 Systems LLC ....F 914 719-7272
White Plains (G-16035)
Response Care Inc ....G 585 671-4144
Webster (G-15651)
Roanwell Corporation ....E 718 401-0288
Bronx (G-1352)
Simrex Corporation ....G 716 206-0174
Buffalo (G-2983)
Telebyte Inc ....E 631 423-3232
Hauppauge (G-5783)
Telephonics Corporation ....A 631 755-7000
Farmingdale (G-4752)
Tokenize Inc ....F 585 981-9919
Rochester (G-13769)
TX Rx Systems Inc ....C 716 549-4700
Angola (G-361)
Visiontron Corp ....E 631 582-8600
Hauppauge (G-5797)

INTERIOR DECORATING SVCS

Furniture Doctor Inc ....G 585 657-6941
Bloomfield (G-947)

INTERIOR DESIGNING SVCS

Exhibit Corporation America ....E 718 937-2600
Long Island City (G-7217)

INTERIOR REPAIR SVCS

Auto-Mat Company Inc....................E 516 938-7373
Hicksville (G-5886)

INTRAVENOUS SOLUTIONS

Mercer Milling Co ....E 315 701-1334
Liverpool (G-7025)
Zenith Solutions ....G 718 575-8570
Saugerties (G-14217)

INVERTERS: Nonrotating Electrical

Applied Power Systems Inc ....E 516 935-2230
Hicksville (G-5883)

INVERTERS: Rotating Electrical

IEC Holden Corporation ....F 518 213-3991
Plattsburgh (G-12752)

INVESTMENT ADVISORY SVCS

Value Line Inc ....D 212 907-1500
New York (G-11637)

INVESTMENT FUNDS: Open-Ended

Altius Aviation LLC ....G 315 455-7555
Syracuse (G-14813)
Kps Capital Partners LP ....E 212 338-5100
New York (G-10133)

INVESTORS: Security Speculators For Own Account

Acf Industries Holding LLC.................G 212 702-4363
New York (G-8447)

IRON & STEEL PRDTS: Hot-Rolled

A-1 Iron Works Inc ....G 718 927-4766
Brooklyn (G-1439)
Bebitz USA Inc ....G 516 280-8378
Hicksville (G-5889)
Hudson Valley Steel Products ....G 845 565-2270
Newburgh (G-11871)
Image Iron Works Inc ....G 718 592-8276
Corona (G-3740)
N C Iron Works Inc ....G 718 633-4660
Brooklyn (G-2184)

IRON & STEEL: Corrugating, Cold-Rolled

Renco Group Inc ....G...... 212 541-6000
New York (G-11012)

IRON ORE MINING

Essar Steel Minnesota LLC ....F 212 292-2600
New York (G-9399)

IRON OXIDES

Applied Minerals Inc ....F 212 226-4265
Brooklyn (G-1520)

IRONING BOARDS

Garment Care Systems LLC ....G...... 518 674-1826
Averill Park (G-507)

IRRADIATION EQPT: Nuclear

R M F Health Management L L C ......E....... 718 854-5400
Wantagh (G-15488)

IRRIGATION SYSTEMS, NEC Water Distribution Or Sply Systems

Sigelock Systems LLC ....G...... 888 744-3562
Oceanside (G-12190)

JANITORIAL & CUSTODIAL SVCS

New Dynamics Corporation ....E 845 692-0022
Middletown (G-7923)
R H Crown Co Inc ....E 518 762-4589
Johnstown (G-6626)

JANITORIAL EQPT & SPLYS WHOLESALERS

Emulso Corp ....G...... 716 854-2889
Tonawanda (G-15102)
Nationwide Sales and Service ....F 631 491-6625
Farmingdale (G-4691)

JEWELERS' FINDINGS & MATERIALS

Boucheron Joaillerie USA Inc ....G...... 212 715-7330
New York (G-8839)
Goldmark Inc ....E 718 438-0295
Brooklyn (G-1899)
Nathan Berrie & Sons Inc ....G...... 516 432-8500
Island Park (G-6320)
New York Findings Corp ....F 212 925-5745
New York (G-10597)
Renco Manufacturing Inc ....E 718 392-8877
Long Island City (G-7342)

JEWELERS' FINDINGS & MATERIALS: Castings

A J M Enterprises ....F 716 626-7294
Buffalo (G-2615)
Allstar Casting Corporation ....E 212 563-0909
New York (G-8520)
Ampex Casting Corporation ....F 212 719-1318
New York (G-8566)
Asco Castings Inc ....G...... 212 719-9800
Long Island City (G-7167)
Asur Jewelry Inc ....G...... 718 472-1687
Long Island City (G-7170)
Carrera Casting Corp ....C 212 382-3296
New York (G-8924)
Frank Billanti Casting Co Inc ....F 212 221-0440
New York (G-9531)
Jaguar Casting Co Inc ....E 212 869-0197
New York (G-9968)
Karbra Company ....C 212 736-9300
New York (G-10069)
Satco Castings Service Inc ....E 516 354-1500
New Hyde Park (G-8291)

JEWELERS' FINDINGS & MATERIALS: Parts, Unassembled

Asa Manufacturing Inc ....E 718 853-3033
Brooklyn (G-1538)
Kemp Metal Products Inc ....E 516 997-8860
Westbury (G-15902)

JEWELERS' FINDINGS & MTLS: Jewel Prep, Instr, Tools, Watches

D R S Watch Materials ....E 212 819-0470
New York (G-9148)
Times One Inc ....G...... 718 686-8988
Brooklyn (G-2505)
Zak Jewelry Tools Inc ....F 212 768-8122
New York (G-11815)

JEWELERS' FINDINGS/MTRLS: Gem Prep, Settings, Real/Imitation

Jim Wachtler Inc ....G...... 212 755-4367
New York (G-10004)
Nyman Jewelry Inc ....G...... 212 944-1976
New York (G-10665)

JEWELRY & PRECIOUS STONES WHOLESALERS

Ace Diamond Corp ....G...... 212 730-8231
New York (G-8446)
Adg Jewels LLC ....F 212 888-1890
New York (G-8458)
Clyde Duneier Inc ....D 212 398-1122
New York (G-9040)
Dabby-Reid Ltd ....F 212 356-0040
New York (G-9150)
Gemoro Inc ....G...... 212 768-8844
Great Neck (G-5392)
Jayden Star LLC ....E 212 686-0400
New York (G-9982)
Justperfectmsp Ltd ....E 877 201-0005
New York (G-10047)
Lali Jewelry Inc ....G...... 212 944-2277
New York (G-10166)
Leo Schachter Diamonds LLC ....D 212 688-2000
New York (G-10202)
Mark King Jewelry Inc ....G...... 212 921-0746
New York (G-10363)
Mer Gems Corp ....G...... 212 714-9129
New York (G-10432)
Midura Jewels Inc ....G...... 213 265-8090
New York (G-10462)
Neil Savalia Inc ....F 212 869-0123
New York (G-10561)
Precision International Co Inc ....G...... 212 268-9090
New York (G-10875)
William Goldberg Diamond Corp ....E 212 980-4343
New York (G-11756)

JEWELRY APPAREL

Ale Viola LLC ....D 212 868-3808
New York (G-8510)
All The Rage Inc ....G...... 516 605-2001
Hicksville (G-5881)
Ateliers Tamalet Corp ....E 929 325-7976
New York (G-8661)
CJ Jewelry Inc ....F 212 719-2464
New York (G-9022)
Eastern Jewelry Mfg Co Inc ....E 212 840-0001
New York (G-9304)
Efron Designs Ltd ....G...... 718 482-8440
Long Island City (G-7212)
Fam Creations ....E 212 869-4833
New York (G-9466)
Fuzion Creations Intl LLC ....E 718 369-8800
Brooklyn (G-1873)
Gramercy Jewelry Mfg Corp ....E 212 268-0461
New York (G-9657)
H C Kionka & Co Inc ....F 212 227-3155
New York (G-9702)
Jaguar Jewelry Casting NY Inc ....G...... 212 768-4848
New York (G-9969)
Jayden Star LLC ....E 212 686-0400
New York (G-9982)
JC Crystal Inc ....E 212 594-0858
New York (G-9987)
Jewelry By Sarah Belle ....G...... 518 793-1626
Fort Ann (G-4933)
Jr Licensing LLC ....G...... 212 244-1230
New York (G-10033)
Le Hook Rouge LLC ....E 212 947-6272
Brooklyn (G-2052)
Leo Schachter & Co Inc ....D 212 688-2000
New York (G-10201)
Love Bright Jewelry Inc ....E 516 620-2509
Oceanside (G-12180)

MB Plastics Inc ....E 718 523-1180
Greenlawn (G-5454)
Park West Jewelery Inc ....G...... 646 329-6145
New York (G-10763)
R & R Grosbard Inc ....E 212 575-0077
New York (G-10966)
Riva Jewelry Manufacturing Inc ....C 718 361-3100
Brooklyn (G-2347)
Thomas Sasson Co Inc ....G...... 212 697-4998
New York (G-11472)
Watertown 1785 LLC ....G...... 315 785-0062
Watertown (G-15591)

JEWELRY FINDINGS & LAPIDARY WORK

Christopher Designs Inc ....E 212 382-1013
New York (G-9002)
Creative Tools & Supply Inc ....G...... 212 279-7077
New York (G-9121)
Danhier Co LLC ....F 212 563-7683
New York (G-9164)
Gemini Manufactures ....F 716 633-0306
Cheektowaga (G-3350)
Kaprielian Enterprises Inc ....D 212 645-6623
New York (G-10068)
Leo Schachter Diamonds LLC ....D 212 688-2000
New York (G-10202)
Magic Novelty Co Inc ....E 212 304-2777
New York (G-10325)
Max Kahan Inc ....F 212 575-4646
New York (G-10391)
ME & Ro Inc ....G...... 212 431-8744
New York (G-10405)
R G Flair Co Inc ....E 631 586-7311
Bay Shore (G-703)
Townley Inc ....G...... 212 779-0544
New York (G-11524)
Via America Fine Jewelry Inc ....G...... 212 302-1218
New York (G-11674)
Zirconia Creations Intl ....G...... 212 239-3730
New York (G-11826)

JEWELRY FINDINGS WHOLESALERS

Cardona Industries USA Ltd ....G...... 516 466-5200
Great Neck (G-5373)
D R S Inc ....E 212 819-0237
New York (G-9147)
New York Findings Corp ....F 212 925-5745
New York (G-10597)

JEWELRY REPAIR SVCS

Burke & Bannayan ....G...... 585 723-1010
Rochester (G-13286)
Carr Manufacturing Jewelers ....G...... 518 783-6093
Latham (G-6852)
Richards & West Inc ....D 585 461-4088
East Rochester (G-4169)

JEWELRY STORES

Burke & Bannayan ....G...... 585 723-1010
Rochester (G-13286)
Carr Manufacturing Jewelers ....G...... 518 783-6093
Latham (G-6852)
Charles Perrella Inc ....E 845 348-4777
Nyack (G-12138)
Diamond Boutique ....G...... 516 444-3373
Port Washington (G-12872)
Golden Integrity Inc ....E 212 764-6753
New York (G-9642)
Henry Dunay Designs Inc ....E 212 768-9700
New York (G-9765)
Iriniri Designs Ltd ....F 845 469-7934
Sugar Loaf (G-14769)
Joan Boyce Ltd ....G...... 212 867-7474
New York (G-10012)
Jr Licensing LLC ....G...... 212 244-1230
New York (G-10033)
Julius Cohen Jewelers Inc ....G...... 212 371-3050
Brooklyn (G-2012)
Love Bright Jewelry Inc ....E 516 620-2509
Oceanside (G-12180)
Mimi So International LLC ....E 212 300-8600
New York (G-10473)
Neil Savalia Inc ....F 212 869-0123
New York (G-10561)
Nyman Jewelry Inc ....G...... 212 944-1976
New York (G-10665)
Royal Jewelry Mfg Inc ....E 212 302-2500
Great Neck (G-5419)

PRODUCT

Stanmark Jewelry Inc ....G....... 212 730-2557
  New York (G-11347)
Suna Bros Inc ....E....... 212 869-5670
  New York (G-11392)

JEWELRY STORES: Precious Stones & Precious Metals

Aaron Group LLC ....D....... 718 392-5454
  Mount Vernon (G-8119)
Atr Jewelry Inc ....F....... 212 819-0075
  New York (G-8673)
Bourghol Brothers Inc ....G....... 845 268-9752
  Congers (G-3610)
David S Diamonds Inc ....F....... 212 921-8029
  New York (G-9182)
Harry Winston Inc ....C....... 212 399-1000
  New York (G-9732)
Hw Holdings Inc ....G....... 212 399-1000
  New York (G-9841)
Jim Wachtler Inc ....G....... 212 755-4367
  New York (G-10004)
Mellem Corporation ....F....... 607 723-0001
  Binghamton (G-897)
Midura Jewels Inc ....G....... 213 265-8090
  New York (G-10462)
Nicolo Raineri ....G....... 212 925-6128
  New York (G-10625)
Peter Atman Inc ....F....... 212 644-8882
  New York (G-10813)
Reinhold Brothers Inc ....E....... 212 867-8310
  New York (G-11002)
Richards & West Inc ....D....... 585 461-4088
  East Rochester (G-4169)
Shining Creations Inc ....G....... 845 358-4911
  New City (G-8230)

JEWELRY STORES: Silverware

Kingold Jewelry Inc ....F....... 212 509-1700
  New York (G-10109)

JEWELRY STORES: Watches

I-Tem Brand LLC ....F....... 718 790-6927
  Bronx (G-1277)

JEWELRY, PREC METAL: Mountings, Pens, Lthr, Etc, Gold/Silver

Leo Ingwer Inc ....E....... 212 719-1342
  New York (G-10199)

JEWELRY, PRECIOUS METAL: Bracelets

Alex Sepkus Inc ....E....... 212 391-8466
  New York (G-8512)
Hammerman Bros Inc ....G....... 212 956-2800
  New York (G-9715)
Jacoby Enterprises LLC ....G....... 718 435-0289
  Brooklyn (G-1987)
Julius Cohen Jewelers Inc ....G....... 212 371-3050
  Brooklyn (G-2012)
Lokai Holdings LLC ....F....... 646 979-3474
  New York (G-10245)

JEWELRY, PRECIOUS METAL: Cases

Albea Cosmetics America Inc ....E....... 212 371-5100
  New York (G-8507)

JEWELRY, PRECIOUS METAL: Cigar & Cigarette Access

Cigar Oasis LLC ....G....... 516 520-5258
  Farmingdale (G-4599)

JEWELRY, PRECIOUS METAL: Earrings

Indonesian Imports Inc ....D....... 855 725-5656
  New York (G-9882)
Jay-Aimee Designs Inc ....C....... 718 609-0333
  Great Neck (G-5396)
Richline Group Inc ....E....... 212 643-2908
  New York (G-11039)

JEWELRY, PRECIOUS METAL: Medals, Precious Or Semiprecious

Eagle Regalia Co Inc ....F....... 845 425-2245
  Spring Valley (G-14567)

Jacmel Jewelry Inc ....C....... 718 349-4300
  New York (G-9964)

JEWELRY, PRECIOUS METAL: Mountings & Trimmings

Shining Creations Inc ....G....... 845 358-4911
  New City (G-8230)

JEWELRY, PRECIOUS METAL: Necklaces

Feldman Jewelry Creations Inc ....G....... 718 438-8895
  Brooklyn (G-1837)
Iridesse Inc ....F....... 212 230-6000
  New York (G-9940)

JEWELRY, PRECIOUS METAL: Pearl, Natural Or Cultured

Clyde Duneier Inc ....D....... 212 398-1122
  New York (G-9040)
Dweck Industries Inc ....G....... 718 615-1695
  Brooklyn (G-1765)
Lali Jewelry Inc ....G....... 212 944-2277
  New York (G-10166)
Robin Stanley Inc ....G....... 212 871-0007
  New York (G-11064)

JEWELRY, PRECIOUS METAL: Pins

M H Manufacturing Incorporated 212 461-6900
  New York (G-10294)

JEWELRY, PRECIOUS METAL: Rings, Finger

Alfred Butler Inc ....F....... 516 829-7460
  Great Neck (G-5361)
Carbon6 LLC ....G....... 607 229-3611
  Brooklyn (G-1646)
D R S Inc ....E....... 212 819-0237
  New York (G-9147)
Grandeur Creations Inc ....G....... 212 643-1277
  New York (G-9661)
Hjn Inc ....F....... 212 398-9564
  New York (G-9795)
Jeff Cooper Inc ....F....... 516 333-8200
  New York (G-9992)
Standard Wedding Band Co ....G....... 516 294-0954
  Garden City (G-5117)
W & B Mazza & Sons Inc ....E....... 516 379-4130
  North Baldwin (G-12012)

JEWELRY, PRECIOUS METAL: Rosaries/Other Sm Religious Article

Rand & Paseka Mfg Co Inc ....E....... 516 867-1500
  Freeport (G-5019)
Yofah Religious Articles Inc ....F....... 718 435-3288
  Brooklyn (G-2601)

JEWELRY, PRECIOUS METAL: Settings & Mountings

Gold & Diamonds Wholesale Outl ....G....... 718 438-7888
  Brooklyn (G-1896)
Golden Integrity Inc ....E....... 212 764-6753
  New York (G-9642)
Kaprielian Enterprises Inc ....D....... 212 645-6623
  New York (G-10068)
Reinhold Brothers Inc ....E....... 212 867-8310
  New York (G-11002)

JEWELRY, PRECIOUS METAL: Trimmings, Canes, Umbrellas, Etc

Houles USA Inc ....G....... 212 935-3900
  New York (G-9821)

JEWELRY, WHOLESALE

Aaron Group LLC ....D....... 718 392-5454
  Mount Vernon (G-8119)
American Originals Corporation ....G....... 212 836-4155
  New York (G-8557)
Anatoli Inc ....F....... 845 334-9000
  West Hurley (G-15808)
Classic Medallics Inc ....E....... 718 392-5410
  Mount Vernon (G-8131)
Crown Jewelers Intl Inc ....G....... 212 420-7800
  New York (G-9124)
Diana Kane Incorporated ....G....... 718 638-6520
  Brooklyn (G-1739)

Formart Corp ....F....... 212 819-1819
  New York (G-9516)
Fuzion Creations Intl LLC ....E....... 718 369-8800
  Brooklyn (G-1873)
J & H Creations Inc ....E....... 212 465-0962
  New York (G-9952)
J R Gold Designs Ltd ....F....... 212 922-9292
  New York (G-9957)
Jr Licensing LLC ....G....... 212 244-1230
  New York (G-10033)
Keith Lewis Studio Inc ....G....... 845 339-5629
  New Paltz (G-8307)
Love Bright Jewelry Inc ....E....... 516 620-2509
  Oceanside (G-12180)
Magic Novelty Co Inc ....E....... 212 304-2777
  New York (G-10325)
Marlborough Jewels Inc ....G....... 718 768-2000
  Brooklyn (G-2116)
Mgd Brands Inc ....E....... 516 545-0150
  Plainview (G-12702)
Michael Bondanza Inc ....E....... 212 869-0043
  New York (G-10452)
Mimi So International LLC ....E....... 212 300-8600
  New York (G-10473)
Mwsi Inc ....D....... 914 347-4200
  Hawthorne (G-5819)
Pesselnik & Cohen Inc ....G....... 212 925-0287
  New York (G-10811)
Q Ed Creations ....G....... 212 391-1155
  New York (G-10941)
R M Reynolds ....G....... 315 789-7365
  Geneva (G-5161)
Richline Group Inc ....E....... 212 764-8454
  New York (G-11040)
Royal Jewelry Mfg Inc ....E....... 212 302-2500
  Great Neck (G-5419)
Samuel B Collection Inc ....F....... 516 466-1826
  Great Neck (G-5421)
Select Jewelry Inc ....D....... 718 784-3626
  Long Island City (G-7354)
Shah Diamonds Inc ....F....... 212 888-9393
  New York (G-11202)
Shanu Gems Inc ....F....... 212 921-4470
  New York (G-11205)
Sol Savransky Diamonds Inc ....F....... 212 730-4700
  New York (G-11287)
UNI Jewelry Inc ....G....... 212 398-1818
  New York (G-11582)

JEWELRY: Decorative, Fashion & Costume

Allure Jewelry and ACC LLC ....F....... 646 226-8057
  New York (G-8521)
Anatoli Inc ....F....... 845 334-9000
  West Hurley (G-15808)
Beth Ward Studios LLC ....F....... 646 922-7575
  New York (G-8769)
Bnns Co Inc ....G....... 212 302-1844
  New York (G-8825)
Carvin French Jewelers Inc ....F....... 212 755-6474
  New York (G-8927)
Columbus Trading Corp ....F....... 212 564-1780
  New York (G-9063)
Ema Jewelry Inc ....G....... 212 575-8989
  New York (G-9355)
Eu Design LLC ....G....... 212 420-7788
  New York (G-9416)
Five Star Creations Inc ....E....... 845 783-1187
  Monroe (G-8020)
Formart Corp ....F....... 212 819-1819
  New York (G-9516)
Greenbeads Llc ....G....... 212 327-2765
  New York (G-9673)
Holbrooke Inc ....F....... 646 397-4674
  New York (G-9801)
I Love Accessories Inc ....G....... 212 239-1875
  New York (G-9845)
International Inspirations LLC ....E....... 212 465-8500
  New York (G-9920)
J J Creations Inc ....E....... 718 392-2828
  Long Island City (G-7251)
Jill Fagin Enterprises Inc ....G....... 212 674-9383
  New York (G-10003)
K2 International Corp ....G....... 212 947-1734
  New York (G-10053)
Mataci Inc ....D....... 212 502-1899
  New York (G-10381)
Maurice Max Inc ....E....... 212 334-6573
  New York (G-10386)
Mel Bernie and Company Inc ....E....... 212 889-8570
  New York (G-10427)

Nes Jewelry Inc .... D 212 502-0025
New York (G-10565)

Noir Jewelry LLC .... G 212 465-8500
New York (G-10637)

Pearl Erwin Inc .... E 212 889-7410
New York (G-10777)

Pepe Creations Inc .... F 212 391-1514
New York (G-10797)

Reino Manufacturing Co Inc .... F 914 636-8990
New Rochelle (G-8352)

Rush Gold Manufacturing Ltd ..... D 516 781-3155
Bellmore (G-788)

Sanoy Inc .... E 212 695-6384
New York (G-11133)

Sarina Accessories LLC .... F 212 239-8106
New York (G-11139)

Shira Accessories Ltd .... F 212 594-4455
New York (G-11216)

Swarovski North America Ltd ...... G 212 695-1502
New York (G-11405)

Toho Shoji (new York) Inc .... F 212 868-7466
New York (G-11505)

Vetta Jewelry Inc .... E 212 564-8250
New York (G-11669)

Yacoubian Jewelers Inc .... E 212 302-6729
New York (G-11804)

JEWELRY: Precious Metal

1ktgold Inc .... F 212 302-8200
White Plains (G-15967)

A & V Castings Inc .... G 212 997-0042
New York (G-8412)

A Jaffe Inc .... C 212 843-7464
New York (G-8418)

Aaron Group LLC .... D 718 392-5454
Mount Vernon (G-8119)

Abraham Jwly Designers & Mfrs ... F 212 944-1149
New York (G-8434)

Abrimian Bros Corp .... F 212 382-1106
New York (G-8435)

Adamor Inc .... G 212 688-8885
New York (G-8454)

Adg Jewels LLC .... F 212 888-1890
New York (G-8458)

Alart Inc .... G 212 840-1508
New York (G-8505)

Alchemy Simya Inc .... E 646 230-1122
New York (G-8508)

Alexander Primak Jewelry Inc ...... D 212 398-0287
New York (G-8513)

Almond Jewelers Inc .... F 516 933-6000
Port Washington (G-12862)

Alpine Creations Ltd .... G 212 308-9353
New York (G-8531)

Altr Inc .... E 212 575-0077
New York (G-8532)

Ambras Fine Jewelry Inc .... E 718 784-5252
Long Island City (G-7154)

American Craft Jewelers Inc .... G 718 972-0945
Brooklyn (G-1498)

American Originals Corporation ... G 212 836-4155
New York (G-8557)

Anatoli Inc .... F 845 334-9000
West Hurley (G-15808)

Anima Group LLC .... G 917 913-2053
New York (G-8589)

Apicella Jewelers Inc .... E 212 840-2024
New York (G-8603)

AR & AR Jewelry Inc .... E 212 764-7916
New York (G-8614)

Arrangement International Inc ...... G 347 323-7974
Flushing (G-4840)

Art-TEC Jewelry Designs Ltd .... E 212 719-2941
New York (G-8632)

Ateret LLC .... G 212 819-0777
New York (G-8662)

Atlantic Precious Metal Cast .... G 718 937-7100
Long Island City (G-7171)

Atr Jewelry Inc .... F 212 819-0075
New York (G-8673)

B K Jewelry Contractor Inc .... E 212 398-9093
New York (G-8704)

Barber Brothers Jewelry Mfg .... F 212 819-0666
New York (G-8726)

Baroka Creations Inc .... G 212 768-0527
New York (G-8731)

Bartholomew Mazza Ltd Inc .... E 212 935-4530
New York (G-8735)

Bellataire Diamonds Inc .... F 212 687-8881
New York (G-8751)

Benlee Enterprises LLC .... F 212 730-7330
Long Island City (G-7176)

BH Multi Com Corp .... E 212 944-0020
New York (G-8778)

Bielka Inc .... G 212 980-6841
New York (G-8783)

Billanti Casting Co Inc .... E 516 775-4800
New Hyde Park (G-8254)

Bourghol Brothers Inc .... G 845 268-9752
Congers (G-3610)

Bral Nader Fine Jewelry Inc .... G 800 493-1222
New York (G-8846)

Brannkey Inc .... D 212 371-1515
New York (G-8847)

Brilliant Jewelers/Mjj Inc .... C 212 353-2326
New York (G-8854)

Brilliant Stars Collection Inc .... G 516 365-9000
Great Neck (G-5371)

Bristol Seamless Ring Corp .... F 212 874-2645
New York (G-8855)

Burke & Bannayan .... G 585 723-1010
Rochester (G-13286)

Carlo Monte Designs Inc .... G 212 935-5611
New York (G-8918)

Carr Manufacturing Jewelers .... G 518 783-6093
Latham (G-6852)

Carvin French Jewelers Inc .... E 212 755-6474
New York (G-8927)

Chaindom Enterprises Inc .... G 212 719-4778
New York (G-8967)

Chameleon Gems Inc .... F 516 829-3333
Great Neck (G-5375)

Charis & Mae Inc .... G 212 641-0816
New York (G-8972)

Charles Krypell Inc .... E 212 752-3313
New York (G-8974)

Charles Perrella Inc .... E 845 348-4777
Nyack (G-12138)

Christopher Designs Inc .... E 212 382-1013
New York (G-9002)

Concord Jewelry Mfg Co LLC .... E 212 719-4030
New York (G-9077)

Creative Gold LLC .... E 718 686-2225
Brooklyn (G-1697)

Crown Jewelers Intl Inc .... G 212 420-7800
New York (G-9124)

Csi International Inc .... E 800 441-2895
Niagara Falls (G-11919)

D M J Casting Inc .... G 212 719-1951
New York (G-9146)

David Friedman Chain Co Inc .... F 212 684-1760
New York (G-9178)

David Howell Product Design .... E 914 666-4080
Bedford Hills (G-767)

David S Diamonds Inc .... F 212 921-8029
New York (G-9182)

David Weisz & Sons USA LLC .... G 212 840-4747
New York (G-9185)

David Yurman Enterprises LLC ..... G 914 539-4444
White Plains (G-15999)

David Yurman Enterprises LLC ..... B 212 896-1550
New York (G-9186)

David Yurman Enterprises LLC ..... G 845 928-8660
Central Valley (G-3298)

David Yurman Retail LLC .... G 877 226-1400
New York (G-9187)

Diamond Distributors Inc .... G 212 921-9188
New York (G-9220)

Diana Kane Incorporated .... G 718 638-6520
Brooklyn (G-1739)

Dimoda Designs Inc .... E 212 355-8166
New York (G-9230)

Discover Casting Inc .... G 212 398-5050
New York (G-9234)

Donna Distefano Ltd .... G 212 594-3757
New York (G-9248)

Doris Panos Designs Ltd .... G 631 245-0580
Melville (G-7776)

Duran Jewelry Inc .... G 212 431-1959
New York (G-9280)

Earring King Jewelry Mfg Inc .... G 718 544-7947
New York (G-9300)

Echo Group Inc .... F 917 608-7440
New York (G-9315)

Eclipse Collection Jewelers .... G 212 764-6883
New York (G-9317)

Ed Levin Inc .... E 518 677-8595
Cambridge (G-3095)

Elegant Jewelers Mfg Co Inc .... F 212 869-4951
New York (G-9337)

Ema Jewelry Inc .... D 212 575-8989
New York (G-9355)

Emsaru USA Corp .... G 212 459-9355
New York (G-9363)

Eternal Line .... G 845 856-1999
Sparrow Bush (G-14547)

Euro Bands Inc .... F 212 719-9777
New York (G-9419)

F M Abdulky Inc .... F 607 272-7373
Ithaca (G-6380)

F M Abdulky Inc .... G 607 272-7373
Ithaca (G-6381)

Fantasia Jewelry Inc .... E 212 921-9590
New York (G-9471)

Fiesta Jewelry Corporation .... G 212 564-6847
New York (G-9492)

First Image Design Corp .... E 212 221-8282
New York (G-9500)

Five Star Creations Inc .... E 845 783-1187
Monroe (G-8020)

Frank Blancato Inc .... F 212 768-1495
New York (G-9532)

Gemoro Inc .... G 212 768-8844
Great Neck (G-5392)

Gemveto Jewelry Company Inc ..... E 212 755-2522
New York (G-9587)

George Lederman Inc .... G 212 753-4556
New York (G-9601)

Giovane Ltd .... E 212 332-7373
New York (G-9613)

Global Gem Corporation .... G 212 350-9936
New York (G-9628)

Goldarama Company Inc .... G 212 730-7299
New York (G-9638)

Goldmark Products Inc .... E 631 777-3343
Farmingdale (G-4639)

Gorga Fehren Fine Jewelry LLC .... G 646 861-3595
New York (G-9646)

Gottlieb & Sons Inc .... E 212 575-1907
New York (G-9649)

Grinnell Designs Ltd .... E 212 391-5277
New York (G-9679)

Guild Diamond Products Inc .... F 212 871-0007
New York (G-9695)

Gumuchian Fils Ltd .... F 212 588-7084
New York (G-9698)

Hanna Altinis Co Inc .... E 718 706-1134
Long Island City (G-7238)

Hansa Usa LLC .... G 646 412-6407
New York (G-9723)

Harry Winston Inc .... C 212 399-1000
New York (G-9732)

Haskell Jewels Ltd .... E 212 764-3332
New York (G-9735)

Henry Design Studios Inc .... G 516 801-2760
Locust Valley (G-7126)

Henry Dunay Designs Inc .... E 212 768-9700
New York (G-9765)

Horo Creations LLC .... G 212 719-4818
New York (G-9813)

Hw Holdings Inc .... G 212 399-1000
New York (G-9841)

Ilico Jewelry Inc .... G 516 482-0201
Great Neck (G-5393)

Imena Jewelry Manufacturer Inc ... F 212 827-0073
New York (G-9867)

Incon Gems Inc .... F 212 221-8560
New York (G-9875)

Inori Jewels .... F 347 703-5078
New York (G-9900)

Intentions Jewelry LLC .... G 845 226-4650
Lagrangeville (G-6749)

Iriniri Designs Ltd .... F 845 469-7934
Sugar Loaf (G-14769)

J C Continental Inc .... G 212 643-2051
Long Island City (G-7250)

J J Creations Inc .... E 718 392-2828
Long Island City (G-7251)

J R Gold Designs Ltd .... F 212 922-9292
New York (G-9957)

Jacobs & Cohen Inc .... E 212 714-2702
New York (G-9966)

Jaguar Casting Co Inc .... E 212 869-0197
New York (G-9968)

Jane Bohan Inc .... G 212 529-6090
New York (G-9973)

Jasani Designs Usa Inc .... G 212 257-6465
New York (G-9978)

Jay Strongwater Holdings LLC ...... A 646 657-0558
New York (G-9980)

P
R
O
D
U
C
T

Jcco Enterprises	F	716 626-0892	
Buffalo (G-2818)			
Jewels By Star Ltd	E	212 308-3490	
New York (G-9996)			
Jeweltex Mfg Corp	F	212 921-8188	
New York (G-9997)			
Jimmy Crystal New York Co Ltd	E	212 594-0858	
New York (G-10006)			
JK Manufacturing Inc	G	212 683-3535	
Locust Valley (G-7127)			
Joan Boyce Ltd	G	212 867-7474	
New York (G-10012)			
Jotaly Inc	A	212 886-6000	
New York (G-10030)			
JSA Jewelry Inc	F	212 764-4504	
New York (G-10036)			
Justin Ashley Designs Inc	G	718 707-0200	
Long Island City (G-7259)			
Justperfectmsp Ltd	E	877 201-0005	
New York (G-10047)			
Justyna Kaminska NY Inc	G	917 423-5527	
New York (G-10048)			
Karbra Company	C	212 736-9300	
New York (G-10069)			
Keith Lewis Studio Inc	G	845 339-5629	
New Paltz (G-8307)			
Kingold Jewelry Inc	F	212 509-1700	
New York (G-10109)			
Krainz Creations Inc	E	212 583-1555	
New York (G-10134)			
Krasner Group Inc	G	212 268-4100	
New York (G-10136)			
Kurt Gaum Inc	F	212 719-2836	
New York (G-10145)			
La Fina Design Inc	G	212 689-6725	
New York (G-10157)			
Le Vian Corp	C	516 466-7200	
Great Neck (G-5400)			
Leon Mege Inc	F	212 768-3868	
New York (G-10203)			
Leser Enterprises Ltd	G	212 832-8013	
Yonkers (G-16327)			
M & S Quality Co Ltd	F	212 302-8757	
New York (G-10291)			
M A R A Metals Ltd	G	718 786-7868	
Long Island City (G-7283)			
M Heskia Company Inc	G	212 768-1845	
New York (G-10295)			
M S Riviera Inc	E	212 391-0206	
New York (G-10300)			
Magnum Creation Inc	F	212 869-2600	
New York (G-10330)			
Manny Grunberg Inc	E	212 302-6173	
New York (G-10349)			
Marina Jewelry Co Inc	G	212 354-5027	
New York (G-10361)			
Mark King Jewelry Inc	G	212 921-0746	
New York (G-10363)			
Mark Robinson Inc	G	212 223-3515	
New York (G-10366)			
Markowitz Jewelry Co Inc	E	845 774-1175	
Monroe (G-8026)			
Marlborough Jewels Inc	G	718 768-2000	
Brooklyn (G-2116)			
Martin Flyer Incorporated	E	212 840-8899	
Manhasset (G-7537)			
Max Header	E	680 888-9786	
New York (G-10389)			
Maxine Denker Inc	G	212 689-1440	
Staten Island (G-14679)			
ME & Ro Inc	G	212 431-8744	
New York (G-10405)			
Mellem Corporation	F	607 723-0001	
Binghamton (G-897)			
Mer Gems Corp	G	212 714-9129	
New York (G-10432)			
Mgd Brands Inc	E	516 545-0150	
Plainview (G-12702)			
Michael Bondanza Inc	E	212 869-0043	
New York (G-10452)			
Midura Jewels Inc	G	213 265-8090	
New York (G-10462)			
Mimi So International LLC	E	212 300-8600	
New York (G-10473)			
Min Ho Designs Inc	G	212 838-3667	
New York (G-10474)			
Monelle Jewelry	G	212 977-9535	
New York (G-10499)			
Mwsi Inc	D	914 347-4200	
Hawthorne (G-5819)			

N Y Bijoux Corp	G	212 244-9585	
Port Washington (G-12909)			
Neil Savalia Inc	F	212 869-0123	
New York (G-10561)			
Nicolo Raineri	G	212 925-6128	
New York (G-10625)			
Oscar Heyman & Bros Inc	E	212 593-0400	
New York (G-10714)			
Overnight Mountings Inc	D	516 865-3000	
New Hyde Park (G-8287)			
Parijat Jewels Inc	G	212 302-2549	
New York (G-10759)			
Patuga LLC	G	716 204-7220	
Williamsville (G-16136)			
Pearl Erwin Inc	E	212 889-7410	
New York (G-10777)			
Pesselnik & Cohen Inc	G	212 925-0287	
New York (G-10811)			
Peter Atman Inc	F	212 644-8882	
New York (G-10813)			
Photograve Corporation	E	718 667-4825	
Staten Island (G-14688)			
Pink Box Accessories LLC	G	718 435-2821	
Brooklyn (G-2260)			
Pronto Jewelry Inc	E	212 719-9455	
New York (G-10912)			
Q Ed Creations	G	212 391-1155	
New York (G-10941)			
R Klein Jewelry Co Inc	D	516 482-3260	
Massapequa (G-7649)			
R M Reynolds	G	315 789-7365	
Geneva (G-5161)			
Renaissance Bijou Ltd	E	212 869-1969	
New York (G-11010)			
Richards & West Inc	D	585 461-4088	
East Rochester (G-4169)			
Richline Group Inc	C	212 764-8454	
New York (G-11040)			
Richline Group Inc	C	914 699-0000	
New York (G-11041)			
Ritani LLC	E	888 974-8264	
White Plains (G-16056)			
Robert Bartholomew Ltd	E	516 767-2970	
Port Washington (G-12919)			
Roberto Coin Inc	E	212 486-4545	
New York (G-11062)			
Rosy Blue Inc	E	212 687-8838	
New York (G-11086)			
Royal Jewelry Mfg Inc	E	212 302-2500	
Great Neck (G-5419)			
Royal Miracle Corp	E	212 921-5797	
New York (G-11089)			
Rubinstein Jewelry Mfg Co	F	718 784-8650	
Long Island City (G-7348)			
Rudolf Friedman Inc	F	212 869-5070	
New York (G-11097)			
Rumson Acquisition LLC	F	718 349-4300	
New York (G-11098)			
Ryan Gems Inc	E	212 697-0149	
New York (G-11102)			
S Kashi & Sons Inc	F	212 869-9393	
Great Neck (G-5420)			
S Scharf Inc	F	516 541-9552	
Massapequa (G-7650)			
Samuel B Collection Inc	E	516 466-1826	
Great Neck (G-5421)			
Sanoy Inc	E	212 695-6384	
New York (G-11133)			
Satco Castings Service Inc	E	516 354-1500	
New Hyde Park (G-8291)			
Satellite Incorporated	G	212 221-6687	
New York (G-11140)			
Select Jewelry Inc	D	718 784-3626	
Long Island City (G-7354)			
Shah Diamonds Inc	F	212 888-9393	
New York (G-11202)			
Shanu Gems Inc	F	212 921-4470	
New York (G-11205)			
Sharodine Inc	E	516 767-3548	
Port Washington (G-12926)			
Shiro Limited	E	212 780-0007	
New York (G-11217)			
Simka Diamond Corp	E	212 921-4420	
New York (G-11242)			
Sol Savransky Diamonds Inc	F	212 730-4700	
New York (G-11287)			
Somerset Manufacturers Inc	E	516 626-3832	
Roslyn Heights (G-14057)			
Spark Creations Inc	F	212 575-8385	
New York (G-11308)			

Stanley Creations Inc	C	718 361-6100	
Long Island City (G-7365)			
Stanmark Jewelry Inc	G	212 730-2557	
New York (G-11347)			
Stone House Associates Inc	G	212 221-7447	
New York (G-11365)			
Sube Inc	E	212 243-6930	
New York (G-11383)			
Sumer Gold Ltd	G	212 354-8677	
New York (G-11388)			
Suna Bros Inc	E	212 869-5670	
New York (G-11392)			
Sunrise Jewelers of NY Inc	G	516 541-1302	
Massapequa (G-7651)			
Tambetti Inc	G	212 751-9584	
New York (G-11427)			
Tamsen Z LLC	E	212 292-6412	
New York (G-11428)			
Tanagro Jewelry Corp	E	212 753-2817	
New York (G-11429)			
Technical Service Industries	E	212 719-9800	
Jamaica (G-6478)			
Teena Creations Inc	G	516 867-1500	
Freeport (G-5027)			
Temple St Clair LLC	E	212 219-8664	
New York (G-11452)			
Tiga Holdings Inc	E	845 838-3000	
Beacon (G-757)			
Trianon Collection Inc	E	212 921-9450	
New York (G-11542)			
Ultra Fine Jewelry Mfg	E	516 349-2848	
Plainview (G-12721)			
UNI Jewelry Inc	G	212 398-1818	
New York (G-11582)			
Unique Designs Inc	F	212 575-7701	
New York (G-11594)			
United Brothers Jewelry Inc	E	212 921-2558	
New York (G-11597)			
Valentin & Kalich Jwly Mfg Ltd	E	212 575-9044	
New York (G-11633)			
Valentine Jewelry Mfg Co Inc	E	212 382-0606	
New York (G-11634)			
Verragio Ltd	E	212 868-8181	
New York (G-11662)			
Viktor Gold Enterprise Corp	G	212 768-8885	
New York (G-11683)			
Von Musulin Patricia	G	212 206-8345	
New York (G-11704)			
Weisco Inc	F	212 575-8989	
New York (G-11737)			
William Goldberg Diamond Corp	E	212 980-4343	
New York (G-11756)			
Xomox Jewelry Inc	E	212 944-8428	
New York (G-11801)			
Zeeba Jewelry Mfg Inc	G	212 997-1009	
New York (G-11819)			
Zelman & Friedman Jwly Mfg Co	E	718 349-3400	
Long Island City (G-7412)			

JIGS & FIXTURES

Knise & Krick Inc	E	315 422-3516	
Syracuse (G-14927)			
Manhasset Tool & Die Co Inc	F	716 684-6066	
Lancaster (G-6816)			
Prime Tool & Die LLC	G	607 334-5435	
Norwich (G-12127)			

JOB PRINTING & NEWSPAPER PUBLISHING COMBINED

Adirondack Publishing Co Inc	E	518 891-2600	
Saranac Lake (G-14156)			
Albion-Holley Pennysaver Inc	E	585 589-5641	
Albion (G-153)			
Empire State Weeklies Inc	E	585 671-1533	
Webster (G-15640)			
Thousand Islands Printing Co	G	315 482-2581	
Alexandria Bay (G-180)			

JOB TRAINING & VOCATIONAL REHABILITATION SVCS

Avcom of Virginia Inc	D	585 924-4560	
Victor (G-15392)			

JOINTS: Ball Except aircraft & Auto

Advanced Thermal Systems Inc	E	716 681-1800	
Lancaster (G-6790)			

York Industries Inc ....E 516 746-3736
Garden City Park *(G-5126)*

JOINTS: Expansion

Adsco Manufacturing Corp ....D 716 827-5450
Buffalo *(G-2623)*

Mageba USA LLC ....E 212 317-1991
New York *(G-10321)*

Mount Vernon Iron Works Inc ....G 914 668-7064
Mount Vernon *(G-8163)*

Vulcraft of New York Inc ....C 607 529-9000
Chemung *(G-3366)*

Watson Bowman Acme Corp ....C 716 691-8162
Amherst *(G-253)*

JOINTS: Expansion, Pipe

Advanced Thermal Systems Inc ....E 716 681-1800
Lancaster *(G-6790)*

KEYS, KEY BLANKS

International Key Supply LLC ....F 631 983-6096
Farmingdale *(G-4652)*

KITCHEN CABINET STORES, EXC CUSTOM

Carefree Kitchens Inc ....G 631 567-2120
Holbrook *(G-5988)*

Custom Design Kitchens Inc ....F 518 355-4446
Duanesburg *(G-4044)*

Joseph Fedele ....G 718 448-3658
Staten Island *(G-14672)*

Michael P Mmarr ....G 315 623-9380
Constantia *(G-3636)*

Mind Designs Inc ....G 631 563-3644
Farmingville *(G-4782)*

Serway Bros Inc ....G 315 337-0601
Rome *(G-13872)*

KITCHEN CABINETS WHOLESALERS

Capital Kit Cab & Door Mfrs ....G 718 886-0303
College Point *(G-3539)*

Carefree Kitchens Inc ....G 631 567-2120
Holbrook *(G-5988)*

Central Kitchen Corp ....F 631 283-1029
Southampton *(G-14528)*

Custom Design Kitchens Inc ....F 518 355-4446
Duanesburg *(G-4044)*

Dak Mica and Wood Products ....G 631 467-0749
Ronkonkoma *(G-13929)*

Deer Pk Stair Bldg Mllwk Inc ....E 631 363-5000
Blue Point *(G-956)*

Di Fiore and Sons Custom Wdwkg ....G 718 278-1663
Long Island City *(G-7201)*

Hennig Custom Woodwork Corp ....G 516 536-3460
Oceanside *(G-12174)*

Johnny Mica Inc ....G 631 225-5213
Lindenhurst *(G-6953)*

Joseph Fedele ....G 718 448-3658
Staten Island *(G-14672)*

M & C Furniture ....G 718 422-2136
Brooklyn *(G-2091)*

Metro Kitchens Corp ....F 718 434-1166
Brooklyn *(G-2147)*

Rochester Countertop Inc ....G 585 338-2260
Rochester *(G-13687)*

Triad Counter Corp ....E 631 750-0615
Bohemia *(G-1088)*

KITCHEN TOOLS & UTENSILS WHOLESALERS

Ashco Management Inc ....F 212 960-8428
Brooklyn *(G-1540)*

KITCHEN UTENSILS: Bakers' Eqpt, Wood

Charles Freihofer Baking Co ....G 518 463-2221
Albany *(G-60)*

KITCHEN UTENSILS: Food Handling & Processing Prdts, Wood

Channel Manufacturing Inc ....E 516 944-6271
Port Washington *(G-12866)*

KITCHEN UTENSILS: Wooden

Abbott Industries Inc ....B 718 291-0800
Jamaica *(G-6423)*

Catskill Craftsmen Inc ....D 607 652-7321
Stamford *(G-14607)*

Imperial Frames & Albums LLC ....G 718 832-9793
Brooklyn *(G-1953)*

Thomas Matthews Wdwkg Ltd ....F 631 287-3657
Southampton *(G-14539)*

Thomas Matthews Wdwkg Ltd ....G 631 287-2023
Southampton *(G-14540)*

KITCHENWARE STORES

Lalique North America Inc ....E 212 355-6550
New York *(G-10167)*

Lifetime Brands Inc ....B 516 683-6000
Garden City *(G-5104)*

Nash Metalware Co Inc ....F 315 339-5794
Rome *(G-13858)*

Roger & Sons Inc ....G 212 226-4734
New York *(G-11074)*

KITCHENWARE: Plastic

L K Manufacturing Corp ....E 631 243-6910
West Babylon *(G-15724)*

KNIT GOODS, WHOLESALE

A & B Finishing Inc ....E 718 522-4702
Brooklyn *(G-1427)*

North Star Knitting Mills Inc ....G 718 894-4848
Glendale *(G-5230)*

Premier Knits Ltd ....F 718 323-8264
Ozone Park *(G-12466)*

KNIVES: Agricultural Or indl

Lancaster Knives Inc ....E 716 683-5050
Lancaster *(G-6814)*

Woods Knife Corporation ....E 516 798-4972
Massapequa *(G-7653)*

LABELS: Paper, Made From Purchased Materials

Accent Label & Tag Co Inc ....G 631 244-7066
Ronkonkoma *(G-13885)*

Apexx Omni-Graphics Inc ....D 718 326-3330
Maspeth *(G-7591)*

Master Image Printing Inc ....G 914 347-4400
Elmsford *(G-4416)*

Precision Label Corporation ....F 631 270-4490
Hauppauge *(G-5747)*

Quadra Flex Corp ....G 607 758-7066
Cortland *(G-3785)*

Quality Circle Products Inc ....D 914 736-6600
Montrose *(G-8078)*

Stoney Croft Converters Inc ....F 718 608-9800
Staten Island *(G-14715)*

Tri-Flex Label Corp ....E 631 293-0411
Farmingdale *(G-4758)*

Web-Tech Packaging Inc ....F 716 684-4520
Lancaster *(G-6839)*

LABELS: Woven

Colonial Tag & Label Co Inc ....F 516 482-0508
Great Neck *(G-5377)*

Imperial-Harvard Label Co ....F 212 736-8420
New York *(G-9869)*

Itc Mfg Group Inc ....F 212 684-3696
New York *(G-9947)*

Label Source Inc ....F 212 244-1403
New York *(G-10159)*

Labels Inter-Global Inc ....F 212 398-0006
New York *(G-10160)*

R-Pac International Corp ....E 212 465-1818
New York *(G-10968)*

LABORATORIES, TESTING: Forensic

Siemens Hlthcare Dgnostics Inc ....E 914 631-0475
Tarrytown *(G-15059)*

LABORATORIES, TESTING: Product Testing, Safety/Performance

Custom Sports Lab Inc ....G 212 832-1648
New York *(G-9135)*

LABORATORIES: Biological Research

Advance Biofactures Corp ....E 516 593-7000
Lynbrook *(G-7423)*

Cleveland Biolabs Inc ....F 716 849-6810
Buffalo *(G-2699)*

Eyenovia Inc ....E 917 289-1117
New York *(G-9453)*

Folia Water Inc ....G 412 802-5083
New York *(G-9514)*

Neurotrope Inc ....G 973 242-0005
New York *(G-10574)*

Synergy Pharmaceuticals Inc ....G 212 227-8611
New York *(G-11413)*

LABORATORIES: Biotechnology

Acorda Therapeutics Inc ....C 914 347-4300
Ardsley *(G-383)*

Albany Molecular Research Inc ....B 518 512-2000
Albany *(G-34)*

Anavex Life Sciences Corp ....F 844 689-3939
New York *(G-8575)*

Checkpoint Therapeutics Inc ....G 781 652-4500
New York *(G-8979)*

LABORATORIES: Commercial Nonphysical Research

Ubm Inc ....A 212 600-3000
New York *(G-11574)*

LABORATORIES: Dental

Marotta Dental Studio Inc ....E 631 249-7520
Farmingdale *(G-4677)*

Martins Dental Studio ....G 315 788-0800
Watertown *(G-15582)*

LABORATORIES: Dental Orthodontic Appliance Production

Vincent Martino Dental Lab ....F 716 674-7800
Buffalo *(G-3037)*

LABORATORIES: Electronic Research

C & D Assembly Inc ....E 607 898-4275
Groton *(G-5481)*

GE Aviation Systems LLC ....D 513 243-9104
Bohemia *(G-1016)*

Intrinsiq Materials Inc ....G 585 301-4432
Rochester *(G-13483)*

Mark - 10 Corporation ....E 631 842-9200
Copiague *(G-3664)*

Millennium Antenna Corp ....F 315 798-9374
Utica *(G-15284)*

Terahertz Technologies Inc ....G 315 736-3642
Oriskany *(G-12398)*

LABORATORIES: Medical

Immco Diagnostics Inc ....G 716 691-0091
Buffalo *(G-2807)*

LABORATORIES: Noncommercial Research

American Institute Physics Inc ....C 516 576-2410
Melville *(G-7760)*

Human Life Foundation Inc ....G 212 685-5210
New York *(G-9837)*

LABORATORIES: Physical Research, Commercial

Advanced Biomedical Tech Inc ....G 718 766-7898
New York *(G-8476)*

Albany Molecular Research Inc ....G 518 512-2234
Albany *(G-33)*

Conmed Corporation ....D 315 797-8375
Utica *(G-15247)*

Danisco US Inc ....D 585 256-5200
Rochester *(G-13337)*

Delphi Powertrain Systems LLC ....B 585 359-6000
West Henrietta *(G-15792)*

Durata Therapeutics Inc ....G 646 871-6400
New York *(G-9281)*

Easton Pharmaceuticals Inc ....G 347 284-0192
Lewiston *(G-6920)*

Fujitsu Ntwrk Cmmnications Inc ....F 845 731-2000
Pearl River *(G-12531)*

Grumman Field Support Services ....D 516 575-0574
Bethpage *(G-835)*

Interdgital Communications LLC ....C 631 622-4000
Melville *(G-7795)*

PRODUCT

International Aids Vaccine Ini ....D...... 646 381-8066
Brooklyn *(G-1964)*
International Aids Vccne Inttv ....D...... 212 847-1111
New York *(G-9917)*
International Paper Company ....C...... 845 986-6409
Tuxedo Park *(G-15217)*
Islechem LLC ....E...... 716 773-8401
Grand Island *(G-5334)*
Momentive Performance Mtls Inc ....D...... 914 784-4807
Tarrytown *(G-15049)*
Northrop Grumman Systems Corp ....A...... 516 575-0574
Bethpage *(G-842)*
Nouryon Surface Chemistry ....C...... 914 674-5008
Dobbs Ferry *(G-4018)*
OSI Pharmaceuticals LLC ....G...... 631 962-2000
Farmingdale *(G-4701)*
Starfire Systems Inc ....F...... 518 899-9336
Glenville *(G-5273)*
Transtech Systems Inc ....E...... 518 370-5558
Latham *(G-6878)*
Xactiv Inc ....F...... 585 288-7220
Fairport *(G-4531)*

LABORATORIES: Testing

Ken-Ton Open Mri PC ....G...... 716 876-7000
Kenmore *(G-6654)*

LABORATORIES: Testing

A & Z Pharmaceutical Inc ....D...... 631 952-3802
Hauppauge *(G-5576)*
B & H Electronics Corp ....E...... 845 782-5000
Monroe *(G-8015)*
Bga Technology LLC ....E...... 631 750-4600
Bohemia *(G-981)*
Dayton T Brown Inc ....B...... 631 589-6300
Bohemia *(G-1001)*
G E Inspection Technologies LP ....C...... 315 554-2000
Skaneateles *(G-14451)*
Kyra Communications Corp ....F...... 516 783-6244
Seaford *(G-14349)*
Laser & Electron Beam Inc ....G...... 603 626-6080
New York *(G-10175)*
Northeast Metrology Corp ....F...... 716 827-3770
Depew *(G-3990)*
Stetron International Inc ....F...... 716 854-3443
Buffalo *(G-2993)*

LABORATORY APPARATUS & FURNITURE

Biodesign Inc of New York ....F...... 845 454-6610
Carmel *(G-3184)*
Dynamica Inc ....F...... 212 818-1900
New York *(G-9288)*
Fungilab Inc ....G...... 631 750-6361
Hauppauge *(G-5655)*
Healthalliance Hospital ....G...... 845 338-2500
Kingston *(G-6693)*
Hyman Podrusnick Co Inc ....G...... 718 853-4502
Brooklyn *(G-1949)*
Instrumentation Laboratory Co ....C...... 845 680-0028
Orangeburg *(G-12321)*
Integrted Work Envronments LLC ....G...... 716 725-5088
East Amherst *(G-4078)*
Itin Scale Co Inc ....E...... 718 336-5900
Brooklyn *(G-1974)*
Maripharm Laboratories ....F...... 716 984-6520
Niagara Falls *(G-11949)*
Nalge Nunc International Corp ....A...... 585 498-2661
Rochester *(G-13565)*
Newport Corporation ....E...... 585 248-4246
Rochester *(G-13574)*
Radon Testing Corp of America ....F...... 914 345-3380
Elmsford *(G-4423)*
S P Industries Inc ....D...... 845 255-5000
Gardiner *(G-5130)*
Staplex Company Inc ....E...... 718 768-3333
Brooklyn *(G-2451)*

LABORATORY APPARATUS: Furnaces

Crystal Linton Technologies ....F...... 585 444-8784
Rochester *(G-13330)*

LABORATORY APPARATUS: Pipettes, Hemocytometer

Vistalab Technologies Inc ....E...... 914 244-6226
Brewster *(G-1160)*

LABORATORY APPARATUS: Shakers & Stirrers

Scientific Industries Inc ....E...... 631 567-4700
Bohemia *(G-1074)*

LABORATORY EQPT, EXC MEDICAL: Wholesalers

Ankom Technology Corp ....E...... 315 986-8090
Macedon *(G-7459)*
Enzo Life Sciences Inc ....E...... 631 694-7070
Farmingdale *(G-4625)*
Eugenia Selective Living Inc ....F...... 631 277-1461
Islip *(G-6352)*
Integrted Work Envronments LLC ....G...... 716 725-5088
East Amherst *(G-4078)*
Lab Crafters Inc ....E...... 631 471-7755
Ronkonkoma *(G-13961)*
Magic Touch Icewares Intl ....G...... 212 794-2852
New York *(G-10329)*
TEC Glass & Inst LLC ....G...... 315 926-7639
Marion *(G-7576)*

LABORATORY EQPT: Chemical

Integrated Liner Tech Inc ....E...... 518 621-7422
Rensselaer *(G-13089)*

LABORATORY EQPT: Clinical Instruments Exc Medical

Next Advance Inc ....F...... 518 674-3510
Troy *(G-15174)*

LABORATORY EQPT: Measuring

East Hills Instrument Inc ....F...... 516 621-8686
Westbury *(G-15879)*

LABORATORY EQPT: Sterilizers

Steriliz LLC ....G...... 585 415-5411
Rochester *(G-13746)*

LACE GOODS & WARP KNIT FABRIC DYEING & FINISHING

Eagle Lace Dyeing Corp ....F...... 212 947-2712
New York *(G-9297)*
Gehring Tricot Corporation ....D...... 315 429-8551
Dolgeville *(G-4022)*
Somerset Dyeing & Finishing ....E...... 518 773-7383
Gloversville *(G-5291)*

LADDERS: Metal

Brakewell Stl Fabricators Inc ....E...... 845 469-9131
Chester *(G-3371)*

LADDERS: Portable, Metal

Metallic Ladder Mfg Corp ....F...... 716 358-6201
Randolph *(G-13063)*

LADDERS: Wood

Babcock Co Inc ....E...... 607 776-3341
Bath *(G-630)*
Putnam Rolling Ladder Co Inc ....F...... 212 226-5147
New York *(G-10932)*
Putnam Rolling Ladder Co Inc ....F...... 718 381-8219
Brooklyn *(G-2308)*

LAMINATED PLASTICS: Plate, Sheet, Rod & Tubes

American Acrylic Corporation ....E...... 631 422-2200
West Babylon *(G-15687)*
Architctral Dsign Elements LLC ....G...... 718 218-7800
Brooklyn *(G-1523)*
Displays By Rioux Inc ....G...... 315 458-3639
North Syracuse *(G-12039)*
Favorite Plastic Corp ....C...... 718 253-7000
Brooklyn *(G-1834)*
Griffon Corporation ....E...... 212 957-5000
New York *(G-9676)*
Inland Paper Products Corp ....E...... 718 827-8150
Brooklyn *(G-1960)*
Iridium Industries Inc ....E...... 516 504-9700
Great Neck *(G-5395)*

Jaguar Industries Inc ....F...... 845 947-1800
Haverstraw *(G-5805)*
Nalge Nunc International Corp ....A...... 585 498-2661
Rochester *(G-13565)*
Strux Corp ....E...... 516 768-3969
Lindenhurst *(G-6976)*

LAMINATING SVCS

Copy Room Inc ....F...... 212 371-8600
New York *(G-9099)*
Hennig Custom Woodwork Corp ....G...... 516 536-3460
Oceanside *(G-12174)*

LAMP & LIGHT BULBS & TUBES

Kreon Inc ....G...... 516 470-9522
Bethpage *(G-837)*
La Mar Lighting Co Inc ....E...... 631 777-7700
Farmingdale *(G-4668)*
Led Waves Inc ....F...... 347 416-6182
Brooklyn *(G-2056)*
Lowel-Light Manufacturing Inc ....E...... 718 921-0600
Brooklyn *(G-2087)*
Make-Waves Instrument Corp ....E...... 716 681-7524
Buffalo *(G-2860)*
Oledworks LLC ....E...... 585 287-6802
Rochester *(G-13589)*
Philips Elec N Amer Corp ....C...... 607 776-3692
Bath *(G-639)*
Ric-Lo Productions Ltd ....E...... 845 469-2285
Chester *(G-3384)*
Satco Products Inc ....D...... 631 243-2022
Edgewood *(G-4282)*
Siemens Corporation ....F...... 202 434-7800
New York *(G-11226)*
Siemens USA Holdings Inc ....B...... 212 258-4000
New York *(G-11228)*
Welch Allyn Inc ....A...... 315 685-4347
Skaneateles Falls *(G-14461)*

LAMP BULBS & TUBES, ELECTRIC: For Specialized Applications

Boehm Surgical Instrument Corp ....F...... 585 436-6584
Rochester *(G-13277)*

LAMP BULBS & TUBES, ELECTRIC: Light, Complete

Emitled Inc ....G...... 516 531-3533
Westbury *(G-15882)*
Goldstar Lighting LLC ....F...... 646 543-6811
New York *(G-9643)*

LAMP BULBS & TUBES/PARTS, ELECTRIC: Generalized Applications

General Electric Company ....A...... 518 385-4022
Schenectady *(G-14266)*
Lighting Holdings Intl LLC ....A...... 845 306-1850
Purchase *(G-13006)*
Saratoga Lighting Holdings LLC ....G...... 212 906-7800
New York *(G-11136)*

LAMP FRAMES: Wire

Lyn Jo Enterprises Ltd ....G...... 716 753-2776
Jamestown *(G-6530)*

LAMP SHADES: Glass

Depp Glass Inc ....F...... 718 784-8500
Long Island City *(G-7200)*
Somers Stain Glass Inc ....F...... 631 586-7772
Deer Park *(G-3937)*

LAMP SHADES: Metal

Judis Lampshades Inc ....G...... 917 561-3921
Brooklyn *(G-2009)*

LAMP STORES

Custom Lampshades Inc ....F...... 718 254-0500
Brooklyn *(G-1711)*
Lighting Holdings Intl LLC ....A...... 845 306-1850
Purchase *(G-13006)*

LAMPS: Arc Units, Electrotherapeutic

Isimulate LLC ....G...... 877 947-2831
Albany *(G-90)*

LAMPS: Floor, Residential

Adesso Inc ....E 212 736-4440
New York *(G-8456)*

LAMPS: Fluorescent

K & H Industries Inc ....E 716 312-0088
Hamburg *(G-5511)*

LAMPS: Table, Residential

Jimco Lamp & Manufacturing Co ....G 631 218-2152
Islip *(G-6353)*
Two Worlds Arts Ltd ....G 212 929-2210
New York *(G-11566)*

LAMPS: Ultraviolet

Atlantic Ultraviolet Corp ....E 631 234-3275
Hauppauge *(G-5597)*

LAND SUBDIVIDERS & DEVELOPERS: Commercial

Micro Instrument Corp ....D 585 458-3150
Rochester *(G-13545)*

LANGUAGE SCHOOLS

Japan America Learning Ctr Inc ....F 914 723-7600
Scarsdale *(G-14237)*

LANTERNS

Mjk Enterprises LLC ....G 917 653-9042
Brooklyn *(G-2163)*

LAPIDARY WORK & DIAMOND CUTTING & POLISHING

Engelack Gem Corporation ....G 212 719-3094
New York *(G-9377)*
Fischer Diamonds Inc ....F 212 869-1990
New York *(G-9503)*
Sunshine Diamond Cutter Inc ....G 212 221-1028
New York *(G-11394)*

LAPIDARY WORK: Contract Or Other

Dweck Industries Inc ....E 718 615-1695
Brooklyn *(G-1766)*

LAPIDARY WORK: Jewel Cut, Drill, Polish, Recut/Setting

Classic Creations Inc ....G 516 498-1991
Great Neck *(G-5376)*
Diamond Boutique ....G 516 444-3373
Port Washington *(G-12872)*
Perma Glow Ltd Inc ....F 212 575-9677
New York *(G-10805)*
Stephen J Lipkins Inc ....G 631 249-8866
Farmingdale *(G-4741)*
Touch Adjust Clip Co Inc ....G 631 589-3077
Bohemia *(G-1086)*

LARD: From Slaughtering Plants

Bliss-Poston The Second Wind ....G 212 481-1055
New York *(G-8813)*

LASER SYSTEMS & EQPT

Advanced Photonics Inc ....F 631 471-3693
Ronkonkoma *(G-13891)*
Bare Beauty Laser Hair Removal ....G 718 278-2273
New York *(G-8728)*
Gb Group Inc ....G 212 594-3748
New York *(G-9576)*
LMD Power of Light Corp ....D 585 272-5420
Rochester *(G-13519)*
Navitar Inc ....D 585 359-4000
Rochester *(G-13568)*
Uptek Solutions Corp ....F 631 256-5565
Bohemia *(G-1094)*

LASERS: Welding, Drilling & Cutting Eqpt

Empire Plastics Inc ....E 607 754-9132
Endwell *(G-4479)*
Trident Precision Mfg Inc ....D 585 265-2010
Webster *(G-15658)*

LAUNDRY & GARMENT SVCS, NEC: Fur Cleaning, Repairing/Storage

Anastasia Furs International ....F 212 868-9241
New York *(G-8574)*

LAUNDRY & GARMENT SVCS, NEC: Garment Alteration & Repair

Connie French Cleaners Inc ....G 516 487-1343
Great Neck *(G-5379)*

LAUNDRY EQPT: Commercial

Autarkic Holdings Inc ....D 516 371-4400
Inwood *(G-6290)*
G A Braun Inc ....E 315 475-3123
Syracuse *(G-14897)*
Trio Clean LLC ....F 518 627-4055
Amsterdam *(G-350)*

LAUNDRY EQPT: Household

AES Electronics Inc ....G 212 371-8120
New York *(G-8488)*
Coinmach Service Corp ....A 516 349-8555
Plainview *(G-12670)*
CSC SW Holdco Inc ....D 516 349-8555
Plainview *(G-12677)*
Penn Enterprises Inc ....F 845 446-0765
West Point *(G-15834)*
Spin Holdco Inc ....G 516 349-8555
Plainview *(G-12715)*

LAUNDRY SVC: Wiping Towel Sply

Hygrade ....G 718 488-9000
Brooklyn *(G-1948)*
Yankee Corp ....F 718 589-1377
Bronx *(G-1397)*

LAWN & GARDEN EQPT

Chapin International Inc ....C 585 343-3140
Batavia *(G-608)*
Chapin Manufacturing Inc ....C 585 343-3140
Batavia *(G-609)*
Clopay Ames True Temper ....F 212 957-5096
New York *(G-9035)*
Fradan Manufacturing Corp ....F 914 632-3653
New Rochelle *(G-8332)*
Rhett M Clark Inc ....G 585 538-9570
Caledonia *(G-3072)*

LAWN & GARDEN EQPT STORES

Nelson Holdings Ltd ....G 607 772-1794
Binghamton *(G-901)*

LAWN & GARDEN EQPT: Tractors & Eqpt

Eaton Brothers Corp ....G 716 649-8250
Hamburg *(G-5505)*
Saxby Implement Corp ....F 585 624-2938
Mendon *(G-7852)*

LAWN & GARDEN EQPT: Trimmers

Capital E Financial Group ....F 212 319-6550
New York *(G-8911)*

LAWN MOWER REPAIR SHOP

Nelson Holdings Ltd ....G 607 772-1794
Binghamton *(G-901)*

LEAD & ZINC

Hh Liquidating Corp ....A 646 282-2500
New York *(G-9779)*
T L Diamond & Company Inc ....G 212 249-6660
New York *(G-11416)*

LEAD PENCILS & ART GOODS

Aakron Rule Corp ....C 716 542-5483
Akron *(G-15)*
R & F Handmade Paints Inc ....F 845 331-3112
Kingston *(G-6707)*

LEASING & RENTAL SVCS: Cranes & Aerial Lift Eqpt

R & B Fabrication Inc ....F 315 640-9901
Cicero *(G-3423)*

LEASING & RENTAL SVCS: Earth Moving Eqpt

Duke Company ....G 607 347-4455
Ithaca *(G-6379)*

LEASING & RENTAL: Computers & Eqpt

IBM World Trade Corporation ....G 914 765-1900
Armonk *(G-397)*
Systems Trading Inc ....G 718 261-8900
Melville *(G-7827)*

LEASING & RENTAL: Construction & Mining Eqpt

Christian Fabrication LLC ....G 315 822-0135
West Winfield *(G-15857)*

LEASING & RENTAL: Other Real Estate Property

Beardslee Realty ....G 516 747-5557
Mineola *(G-7960)*

LEASING: Laundry Eqpt

Thermopatch Corporation ....D 315 446-8110
Syracuse *(G-15012)*

LEASING: Shipping Container

A R Arena Products Inc ....E 585 277-1680
Rochester *(G-13195)*
Shiprite Services Inc ....F 315 427-2422
Utica *(G-15294)*

LEATHER GOODS, EXC FOOTWEAR, GLOVES, LUGGAGE/BELTING, WHOL

Pan American Leathers Inc ....G 978 741-4150
New York *(G-10744)*

LEATHER GOODS: Belt Laces

McM Products USA Inc ....E 646 756-4090
New York *(G-10401)*

LEATHER GOODS: Belting & Strapping

Fahrenheit NY Inc ....G 212 354-6554
New York *(G-9462)*

LEATHER GOODS: Boxes

Kamali Leather LLC ....G 518 762-2522
Johnstown *(G-6621)*

LEATHER GOODS: Cases

Slim Line Case Co Inc ....F 585 546-3639
Rochester *(G-13733)*

LEATHER GOODS: Corners, Luggage

Deluxe Travel Store Inc ....G 718 435-8111
Brooklyn *(G-1736)*

LEATHER GOODS: Cosmetic Bags

Baker Products Inc ....G 212 459-2323
White Plains *(G-15978)*
Jaclyn LLC ....D 201 909-6000
New York *(G-9963)*
M G New York Inc ....F 212 371-5566
New York *(G-10293)*
Penthouse Manufacturing Co Inc ....B 516 379-1300
Freeport *(G-5014)*

LEATHER GOODS: Desk Sets

Star Desk Pad Co Inc ....E 914 963-9400
Yonkers *(G-16350)*

LEATHER GOODS: Garments

Billykirk ....G 212 217-0679
New York *(G-8794)*

P
R
O
D
U
C
T

Dvf Studio LLC..................D...... 212 741-6607
New York *(G-9283)*

Dvf Studio LLC..................G...... 646 576-8009
New York *(G-9284)*

East West Global Sourcing Inc....G.... 917 887-2286
Brooklyn *(G-1775)*

First Manufacturing Co Inc.......E...... 516 763-0400
Oceanside *(G-12172)*

Tucano Usa Inc..................G...... 212 966-9211
New York *(G-11557)*

LEATHER GOODS: Holsters

Adirondack Leather Pdts Inc.....F...... 607 547-5798
Fly Creek *(G-4908)*

Courtlandt Boot Jack Co Inc.....E...... 718 445-6200
Flushing *(G-4846)*

Helgen Industries Inc...........C...... 631 841-6300
Amityville *(G-269)*

LEATHER GOODS: Key Cases

Atlantic Specialty Co Inc........E...... 845 356-2502
Monsey *(G-8036)*

Form A Rockland Plastics Inc....G.... 315 848-3300
Cranberry Lake *(G-3801)*

LEATHER GOODS: NEC

Leather Outlet.................G...... 518 668-0328
Lake George *(G-6757)*

LEATHER GOODS: Personal

Astucci US Ltd..................F...... 718 752-9700
Long Island City *(G-7169)*

Datamax International Inc.......E...... 212 693-0933
New York *(G-9175)*

Elco Manufacturing Co Inc.......F...... 516 767-3577
Port Washington *(G-12877)*

Excelled Sheepskin & Lea Coat...F...... 212 594-5843
New York *(G-9443)*

Fahrenheit NY Inc...............G...... 212 354-6554
New York *(G-9462)*

First Manufacturing Co Inc......E...... 516 763-0400
Oceanside *(G-12172)*

Grownbeans Inc.................G...... 212 989-3486
New York *(G-9686)*

Helgen Industries Inc...........C...... 631 841-6300
Amityville *(G-269)*

Hemisphere Novelties Inc........E...... 914 378-4100
Yonkers *(G-16318)*

House of Portfolios Co Inc......E...... 212 206-7323
New York *(G-9824)*

House of Portfolios Co Inc......F...... 212 206-7323
New York *(G-9825)*

Just Brass Inc..................G...... 212 724-5447
New York *(G-10045)*

Leather Artisan.................G...... 518 359-3102
Childwold *(G-3401)*

Merzon Leather Co Inc...........C...... 718 782-6260
Brooklyn *(G-2144)*

Mhg Studio Inc..................G...... 212 674-7610
New York *(G-10449)*

Neumann Jutta New York Inc.....F...... 212 982-7048
New York *(G-10572)*

Tapestry Inc....................B...... 212 594-1850
New York *(G-11434)*

LEATHER GOODS: Wallets

Randa Accessories Lea Gds LLC...D...... 212 354-5100
New York *(G-10979)*

Trafalgar Company LLC..........G...... 212 768-8800
New York *(G-11531)*

LEATHER TANNING & FINISHING

Aston Leather Inc...............G...... 212 481-2760
New York *(G-8656)*

Corium Corporation.............F...... 914 381-0100
Mamaroneck *(G-7505)*

Cromwell Leather Company Inc...F.... 914 381-0100
Mamaroneck *(G-7506)*

Edsim Leather Co Inc............E...... 212 695-8500
New York *(G-9323)*

Hastings Hide Inc...............G...... 516 295-2400
Inwood *(G-6295)*

Legendary Auto Interiors Ltd....E...... 315 331-1212
Newark *(G-11843)*

Pearl Leather Finishers Inc.....F...... 518 762-4543
Johnstown *(G-6624)*

Studio One Leather Design Inc...F...... 212 760-1701
New York *(G-11379)*

LEATHER, LEATHER GOODS & FURS, WHOLESALE

Carville National Leather Corp...F...... 518 762-1634
Johnstown *(G-6613)*

Leather Artisan.................G...... 518 359-3102
Childwold *(G-3401)*

Tandy Leather Factory Inc.......G...... 845 480-3588
Nyack *(G-12146)*

LEATHER: Accessory Prdts

Adam Scott Designs Inc.........E...... 212 420-8866
New York *(G-8453)*

Ariel Tian LLC..................G...... 212 457-1266
Forest Hills *(G-4917)*

Automotive Leather Group LLC....F...... 516 627-4000
Great Neck *(G-5368)*

Centric Brands Inc..............D...... 646 582-6000
New York *(G-8955)*

Justin Gregory Inc..............G...... 631 249-5187
Deer Park *(G-3890)*

Kamali Group Inc................G...... 516 627-4000
Great Neck *(G-5399)*

Tandy Leather Factory Inc.......G...... 845 480-3588
Nyack *(G-12146)*

Vic Demayos Inc.................G...... 845 626-4343
Accord *(G-1)*

LEATHER: Artificial

Beckmann Converting Inc........E...... 518 842-0073
Amsterdam *(G-318)*

LEATHER: Bag

Givi Inc........................E...... 212 586-5029
New York *(G-9616)*

Hat Attack Inc..................E...... 718 994-1000
Bronx *(G-1273)*

Jaclyn LLC......................D...... 201 909-6000
New York *(G-9963)*

LEATHER: Bookbinders'

Graphic Image Associates LLC....D...... 631 249-9600
Melville *(G-7787)*

System of AME Binding..........G...... 631 390-8560
Central Islip *(G-3290)*

LEATHER: Case

Baker Products Inc..............G...... 212 459-2323
White Plains *(G-15978)*

LEATHER: Colored

Mohawk River Leather Works......F...... 518 853-3900
Fultonville *(G-5080)*

LEATHER: Cut

A-1 Products Inc................G...... 718 789-1818
Brooklyn *(G-1440)*

Hohenforst Splitting Co Inc.....G...... 518 725-0012
Gloversville *(G-5285)*

LEATHER: Die-cut

John Gailer Inc.................E...... 212 243-5662
Long Island City *(G-7254)*

LEATHER: Embossed

Rainbow Leather Inc.............F...... 718 939-8762
College Point *(G-3562)*

LEATHER: Finished

Androme Leather Inc............F...... 518 773-7945
Gloversville *(G-5277)*

Arrow Leather Finishing Inc.....E...... 518 762-3121
Johnstown *(G-6610)*

Carville National Leather Corp...F...... 518 762-1634
Johnstown *(G-6613)*

Pan American Leathers Inc.......G...... 978 741-4150
New York *(G-10744)*

LEATHER: Glove

Shadal LLC......................G...... 212 319-5946
New York *(G-11200)*

LEATHER: Handbag

Street Smart Designs Inc........G...... 646 865-0056
New York *(G-11370)*

LEATHER: Indl Prdts

Leather Hub Worldwide LLC.......C...... 310 386-2247
New York *(G-10186)*

LEATHER: Processed

Pearl Leather Group LLC.........E...... 516 627-4047
Great Neck *(G-5412)*

LEATHER: Upholstery

Kamali Automotive Group Inc.....F...... 516 627-4000
Great Neck *(G-5398)*

LEGAL & TAX SVCS

Westchester Law Journal Inc.....G...... 914 948-0715
White Plains *(G-16072)*

LEGAL OFFICES & SVCS

Dick Bailey Service Inc..........F...... 718 522-4363
Brooklyn *(G-1742)*

Thomson Reuters Corporation.....A...... 646 223-4000
New York *(G-11475)*

Wave Publishing Co Inc..........F...... 718 634-4000
Rockaway Beach *(G-13823)*

LEGITIMATE LIVE THEATER PRODUCERS

Abkco Music & Records Inc.......E...... 212 399-0300
New York *(G-8430)*

LENS COATING: Ophthalmic

Equicheck LLC..................G...... 631 987-6356
Patchogue *(G-12500)*

Optisource International Inc.....E...... 631 924-8360
Bellport *(G-805)*

LENSES: Plastic, Exc Optical

Bin Optics......................G...... 604 257-3200
Ithaca *(G-6367)*

LESSORS: Landholding Office

Rock Mountain Farms Inc.........G...... 845 647-9084
Ellenville *(G-4311)*

LIFESAVING & SURVIVAL EQPT, EXC MEDICAL, WHOLESALE

Aero Healthcare (us) LLC........G...... 855 225-2376
Valley Cottage *(G-15312)*

LIGHT SENSITIVE DEVICES

Nsi Industries LLC..............C...... 800 841-2505
Mount Vernon *(G-8166)*

Tork Inc........................D...... 914 664-3542
Mount Vernon *(G-8183)*

LIGHTING EQPT: Flashlights

Psg Innovations Inc.............F...... 917 299-8986
Valley Stream *(G-15354)*

LIGHTING EQPT: Motor Vehicle, Headlights

Licenders......................G...... 212 759-5200
New York *(G-10210)*

LIGHTING EQPT: Motor Vehicle, NEC

Mobile Fleet Inc................E...... 631 206-2920
Hauppauge *(G-5722)*

LIGHTING EQPT: Outdoor

Exc Holdings I Corp.............A...... 212 644-5900
New York *(G-9438)*

Exc Holdings II Corp............A...... 212 644-5900
New York *(G-9439)*

Exc Holdings LP.................G...... 212 644-5900
New York *(G-9440)*

Northern Air Technology Inc.....G...... 585 594-5050
Rochester *(G-13585)*

LIGHTING EQPT: Reflectors, Metal, For Lighting Eqpt

Island Lite Louvers Inc ....E 631 608-4250
Amityville (G-278)

LIGHTING EQPT: Streetcar Fixtures

Power and Cnstr Group Inc ....E 585 889-6020
Scottsville (G-14342)

LIGHTING EQPT: Strobe Lighting Systems

Star Headlight Lantern Co Inc ....C 585 226-9500
Avon (G-516)

LIGHTING FIXTURES WHOLESALERS

Expo Furniture Designs Inc ....F 516 674-1420
Glen Cove (G-5192)
Global Lighting Inc ....G 914 591-4095
Yonkers (G-16313)
Lighting Holdings Intl LLC ....A 845 306-1850
Purchase (G-13006)
Matov Industries Inc ....E 718 392-5060
Long Island City (G-7291)
Quality HM Brands Holdings LLC ....G 718 292-2024
Bronx (G-1347)
Quoizel Inc ....E 631 436-4402
Hauppauge (G-5752)
Solarwaterway Inc ....E 888 998-5337
Brooklyn (G-2438)

LIGHTING FIXTURES, NEC

Cooper Industries LLC ....F 315 477-7000
Syracuse (G-14864)
Creative Stage Lighting Co Inc ....E 518 251-3302
North Creek (G-12031)
Edison Power & Light Co Inc ....F 718 522-0002
Brooklyn (G-1783)
Fabbian USA Corp ....G 973 882-3824
New York (G-9459)
General Led Corp ....G 516 280-2854
Mineola (G-7976)
Goddard Design Co ....G 718 599-0170
Brooklyn (G-1895)
Gordon S Anderson Mfg Co ....G 845 677-3304
Millbrook (G-7942)
Illumination Technologies Inc ....F 315 463-4673
Liverpool (G-7013)
J M Canty Inc ....E 716 625-4227
Lockport (G-7084)
Jag Lighting ....G 917 226-3575
Maspeth (G-7624)
Jaquith Industries Inc ....E 315 478-5700
Syracuse (G-14916)
Jed Lights Inc ....F 516 812-5001
Deer Park (G-3888)
Jt Roselle Lighting & Sup Inc ....F 914 666-3700
Mount Kisco (G-8095)
Julian A McDermott Corporation ....E 718 456-3606
Ridgewood (G-13148)
La Mar Lighting Co Inc ....E 631 777-7700
Farmingdale (G-4668)
Light Blue USA LLC ....G 718 475-2515
Brooklyn (G-2070)
Lighting N Beyond LLC ....G 718 669-9142
Blauvelt (G-930)
Lighting Sculptures Inc ....F 631 242-3387
Deer Park (G-3898)
Lilibrand LLC ....G 212 239-8230
Brooklyn (G-2073)
Luminescent Systems Inc ....B 716 655-0800
East Aurora (G-4091)
Olive Led Lighting Inc ....G 718 746-0830
College Point (G-3557)
Revolution Lighting LLC ....E 518 779-3655
Glens Falls (G-5266)
Rodac USA Corp ....E 716 741-3931
Clarence (G-3442)
Saratoga Lighting Holdings LLC ....G 212 906-7800
New York (G-11136)
Sensio America ....F 877 501-5337
Clifton Park (G-3472)
Sensio America LLC ....F 877 501-5337
Clifton Park (G-3473)
Shakuff LLC ....G 212 675-0383
Brooklyn (G-2401)
Strider Global LLC ....G 212 726-1302
New York (G-11374)

Tecnolux Incorporated ....G 718 369-3900
Brooklyn (G-2497)
Times Square Stage Ltg Co Inc ....E 845 947-3034
Stony Point (G-14749)
Truck-Lite Co LLC ....B 716 665-6214
Falconer (G-4560)
Vertex Innovative Solutions ....F 315 437-6711
Syracuse (G-15021)
Vincent Conigliaro ....F 845 340-0489
Kingston (G-6722)
Vivid Rgb Lighting LLC ....G 718 635-0817
Peekskill (G-12558)

LIGHTING FIXTURES: Airport

Cooper Crouse-Hinds Mtl Inc ....C 315 477-7000
Syracuse (G-14863)

LIGHTING FIXTURES: Decorative Area

Enchante Lites LLC ....G 212 602-1818
New York (G-9367)
Secret Celebrity Licensing LLC ....G 212 812-9277
New York (G-11175)

LIGHTING FIXTURES: Fluorescent, Commercial

La Mar Lighting Co Inc ....E 631 777-7700
Farmingdale (G-4668)
Legion Lighting Co Inc ....E 718 498-1770
Brooklyn (G-2059)
Lite Brite Manufacturing Inc ....F 718 855-9797
Brooklyn (G-2079)
Spectronics Corporation ....C 516 333-4840
Westbury (G-15926)
Vision Quest Lighting Inc ....E 631 737-4800
East Setauket (G-4190)

LIGHTING FIXTURES: Fluorescent, Residential

Eaton Corporation ....E 315 579-2872
Syracuse (G-14882)

LIGHTING FIXTURES: Indl & Commercial

AEP Environmental LLC ....F 716 446-0739
Buffalo (G-2625)
Aesthonics Inc ....D 646 723-2463
Brooklyn (G-1469)
Altman Stage Lighting Co Inc ....C 914 476-7987
Yonkers (G-16283)
Apparatus Studio ....E 646 527-9732
New York (G-8606)
Aquarii Inc ....G 315 672-8807
Camillus (G-3107)
Aristocrat Lighting Inc ....F 718 522-0003
Brooklyn (G-1530)
Arlee Lighting Corp ....G 516 595-8558
Inwood (G-6288)
Big Shine Worldwide Inc ....G 845 444-5255
Newburgh (G-11859)
Canarm Ltd ....G 800 267-4427
Ogdensburg (G-12203)
Coldstream Group Inc ....F 914 698-5959
Mamaroneck (G-7504)
Contemporary Visions LLC ....G 845 926-5469
Wappingers Falls (G-15490)
Cooper Industries LLC ....F 315 477-7000
Syracuse (G-14864)
Cooper Lighting LLC ....G 516 470-1000
Hicksville (G-5896)
Dreyfus Ashby Inc ....E 212 818-0770
New York (G-9271)
Edison Price Lighting Inc ....C 718 685-0700
Long Island City (G-7209)
Edison Price Lighting Inc ....D 718 685-0700
Long Island City (G-7210)
Electric Lighting Agencies ....E 212 645-4580
New York (G-9334)
Energy Conservation & Sup Inc ....E 718 855-5888
Brooklyn (G-1805)
G&G Led LLC ....E 800 285-6780
Clifton Park (G-3464)
Green Energy Concepts Inc ....G 845 238-2574
Chester (G-3379)
Hudson Valley Lighting Inc ....D 845 561-0300
Wappingers Falls (G-15497)
Ideoli Group Inc ....F 212 705-8769
Port Washington (G-12887)

Jesco Lighting Inc ....E 718 366-3211
Port Washington (G-12892)
Jesco Lighting Group LLC ....E 718 366-3211
Port Washington (G-12893)
LDI Lighting Inc ....G 718 384-4490
Brooklyn (G-2051)
Light Waves Concept Inc ....F 212 677-6400
Brooklyn (G-2072)
Lighting By Dom Yonkers Inc ....G 914 968-8700
Yonkers (G-16328)
Lighting Services Inc ....D 845 942-2800
Stony Point (G-14746)
Linear Lighting Corporation ....C 718 361-7552
Long Island City (G-7274)
Litelab Corp ....G 718 361-6829
Long Island City (G-7276)
Litelab Corp ....C 716 856-4300
Buffalo (G-2851)
Lukas Lighting Inc ....E 800 841-4011
Long Island City (G-7281)
Luminatta Inc ....G 914 664-3600
Mount Vernon (G-8159)
Luminescent Systems Inc ....B 716 655-0800
East Aurora (G-4091)
Lynne B Enterprises Inc ....E 631 254-6975
Deer Park (G-3901)
Magniflood Inc ....E 631 226-1000
Amityville (G-294)
Matov Industries Inc ....E 718 392-5060
Long Island City (G-7291)
Modulightor Inc ....F 212 371-0336
New York (G-10491)
Mtz Enterprises Inc ....F 347 834-2716
Brooklyn (G-2181)
North American Mfg Entps Inc ....E 718 524-4370
Staten Island (G-14684)
Nulux Inc ....E 718 383-1112
Ridgewood (G-13153)
Oledworks LLC ....E 585 287-6802
Rochester (G-13589)
Preciseled Inc ....F 516 418-5337
Valley Stream (G-15352)
Primelite Manufacturing Corp ....G 516 868-4411
Freeport (G-5017)
Rapid-Lite Fixture Corporation ....F 347 599-2600
Brooklyn (G-2327)
Remains Lighting ....E 212 675-8051
New York (G-11008)
S E A Supplies Ltd ....F 516 694-6677
Plainview (G-12712)
Saratoga Lighting Holdings LLC ....G 212 906-7800
New York (G-11136)
Savwatt Usa Inc ....G 646 478-2676
New York (G-11142)
Selux Corporation ....C 845 691-7723
Highland (G-5963)
Signify North America Corp ....C 646 265-7170
New York (G-11237)
Solarpath Inc ....G 201 490-4499
New York (G-11289)
Solarwaterway Inc ....E 888 998-5337
Brooklyn (G-2438)
Swivelier Company Inc ....D 845 353-1455
Blauvelt (G-934)
Twinkle Lighting Inc ....G 718 225-0939
Flushing (G-4902)
Versaponents Inc ....F 631 242-3387
Deer Park (G-3950)
Vital Vio Inc ....F 914 245-6048
Troy (G-15194)
Xeleum Lighting LLC ....F 954 617-8170
Mount Kisco (G-8107)
Zumtobel Lighting Inc ....C 845 691-6262
Highland (G-5965)

LIGHTING FIXTURES: Motor Vehicle

Copy Cat ....G 718 934-2192
Brooklyn (G-1686)
Wolo Mfg Corp ....E 631 242-0333
Deer Park (G-3955)

LIGHTING FIXTURES: Ornamental, Commercial

LDI Lighting Inc ....G 718 384-4490
Brooklyn (G-2050)
Rle Industries LLC ....E 973 276-1444
New York (G-11055)

PRODUCT

LIGHTING FIXTURES: Public

CEIT Corp ....F 518 825-0649
Plattsburgh *(G-12741)*

Tarsier Ltd ....C 646 880-8680
New York *(G-11436)*

USA Illumination Inc ....E 845 565-8500
New Windsor *(G-8385)*

LIGHTING FIXTURES: Residential

Aesthonics Inc ....D 646 723-2463
Brooklyn *(G-1469)*

Artemis Studios Inc ....D 718 788-6022
Brooklyn *(G-1536)*

Canarm Ltd ....G 800 267-4427
Ogdensburg *(G-12203)*

Cooper Lighting LLC ....C 516 470-1000
Hicksville *(G-5896)*

David Weeks Studio ....F 212 966-3433
New York *(G-9184)*

E-Finnergy Group LLC ....G 845 547-2424
Suffern *(G-14760)*

ER Butler & Co Inc ....E 212 925-3565
New York *(G-9392)*

Hudson Valley Lighting Inc ....D 845 561-0300
Wappingers Falls *(G-15497)*

Jamaica Lamp Corp ....E 718 776-5039
Queens Village *(G-13023)*

Litelab Corp ....C 716 856-4300
Buffalo *(G-2851)*

Matov Industries Inc ....E 718 392-5060
Long Island City *(G-7291)*

Modulightor Inc ....F 212 371-0336
New York *(G-10491)*

New Generation Lighting Inc ......F 212 966-0328
New York *(G-10582)*

Nulux Inc ....E 718 383-1112
Ridgewood *(G-13153)*

Philips Elec N Amer Corp ....C 607 776-3692
Bath *(G-639)*

Pompian Manufacturing Co Inc ...G 914 476-7076
Yonkers *(G-16343)*

Preciseled Inc ....F 516 418-5337
Valley Stream *(G-15352)*

Prestigeline Inc ....D 631 273-3636
Bay Shore *(G-701)*

Quality HM Brands Holdings LLC ...G 718 292-2024
Bronx *(G-1347)*

Quoizel Inc ....E 631 436-4402
Hauppauge *(G-5752)*

Rapid-Lite Fixture Corporation ...F 347 599-2600
Brooklyn *(G-2327)*

Remains Lighting ....E 212 675-8051
New York *(G-11008)*

Saratoga Lighting Holdings LLC ...G 212 906-7800
New York *(G-11136)*

Savwatt Usa Inc ....G 646 478-2676
New York *(G-11142)*

Solarwaterway Inc ....E 888 998-5337
Brooklyn *(G-2438)*

Swarovski Lighting Ltd ....C 518 563-7500
Plattsburgh *(G-12783)*

Swivelier Company Inc ....D 845 353-1455
Blauvelt *(G-934)*

Tarsier Ltd ....C 646 880-8680
New York *(G-11436)*

Tudor Electrical Supply Co Inc ....G 212 867-7550
New York *(G-11558)*

Ulster Precision Inc ....E 845 338-0995
Kingston *(G-6717)*

Vaughan Designs Inc ....F 212 319-7070
New York *(G-11649)*

Vision Quest Lighting Inc ....E 631 737-4800
East Setauket *(G-4190)*

Wainland Inc ....E 718 626-2233
Astoria *(G-444)*

LIGHTING FIXTURES: Residential, Electric

Expo Furniture Designs Inc ....F 516 674-1420
Glen Cove *(G-5192)*

Serway Bros Inc ....G 315 337-0601
Rome *(G-13872)*

LIGHTING FIXTURES: Street

Eluminocity US Inc ....G 651 528-1165
New York *(G-9353)*

Power and Cnstr Group Inc ....E 585 889-6020
Scottsville *(G-14342)*

LIGHTS: Trouble lights

Lyn Jo Enterprises Ltd ....G 716 753-2776
Jamestown *(G-6530)*

LIME

Lime Energy Co ....G 704 892-4442
Buffalo *(G-2849)*

LIME: Agricultural

Masick Soil Conservation Co ....F 518 827-5354
Schoharie *(G-14322)*

LIMESTONE & MARBLE: Dimension

Domoteck Interiors Inc ....G 718 433-4300
Woodside *(G-16204)*

Minerals Technologies Inc ....E 212 878-1800
New York *(G-10476)*

LIMESTONE: Crushed & Broken

Barrett Paving Materials Inc ....F 315 737-9471
Clayville *(G-3454)*

Buffalo Crushed Stone Inc ....E 716 826-7310
Buffalo *(G-2672)*

Buffalo Crushed Stone Inc ....E 716 632-6963
Clarence *(G-3427)*

Cayuga Crushed Stone Inc ....E 607 533-4273
Lansing *(G-6840)*

Cobleskill Stone Products Inc ......F 518 295-7121
Schoharie *(G-14321)*

Cobleskill Stone Products Inc ......F 518 234-0221
Cobleskill *(G-3498)*

Cobleskill Stone Products Inc ......F 607 637-4271
Hancock *(G-5535)*

Hanson Aggregates PA Inc ....E 315 858-1100
Jordanville *(G-6632)*

Hanson Aggregates PA LLC ....E 315 469-5501
Jamesville *(G-6560)*

Hanson Aggregates PA LLC ....E 315 685-3321
Skaneateles *(G-14455)*

Hanson Aggregates PA LLC ....E 585 624-1220
Honeoye Falls *(G-6074)*

Hanson Aggregates PA LLC ....E 315 821-7222
Oriskany Falls *(G-12400)*

Hanson Aggregates PA LLC ....E 315 789-6202
Oaks Corners *(G-12162)*

Jml Quarries Inc ....E 845 932-8206
Cochecton *(G-3502)*

John Vespa Inc ....F 315 788-6330
Watertown *(G-15575)*

Jointa Lime Company ....A 518 580-0300
Wilton *(G-16156)*

Lilac Quarries LLC ....G 607 867-4016
Mount Upton *(G-8118)*

Patterson Materials Corp ....E 845 832-6000
New Windsor *(G-8377)*

Shelby Crushed Stone Inc ....E 585 798-4501
Medina *(G-7746)*

Upstone Materials Inc ....E 518 891-0236
Saranac Lake *(G-14160)*

LIMESTONE: Cut & Shaped

Hanson Aggregates East LLC ......F 315 493-3721
Great Bend *(G-5358)*

Minerals Technologies Inc ....E 212 878-1800
New York *(G-10476)*

LIMESTONE: Dimension

New York Quarries Inc ....F 518 756-3138
Alcove *(G-163)*

LIMESTONE: Ground

Hanson Aggregates PA Inc ....F 518 568-2444
Saint Johnsville *(G-14117)*

Hanson Aggregates PA LLC ....F 315 393-3743
Ogdensburg *(G-12205)*

LINEN SPLY SVC: Apron

White Plains Coat Apron Co Inc ...G 914 736-2610
Peekskill *(G-12563)*

LINEN SPLY SVC: Coat

Maple Grove Corp ....E 585 492-5286
Arcade *(G-377)*

LINENS & TOWELS WHOLESALERS

American Country Quilts & Lin ......G 631 283-5466
Southampton *(G-14526)*

David King Linen Inc ....F 718 241-7298
New York *(G-9180)*

E & F Home Fashions Inc ....G 718 968-9719
Brooklyn *(G-1770)*

Paramount Textiles Inc ....F 212 966-1040
New York *(G-10756)*

LINENS: Napkins, Fabric & Nonwoven, From Purchased Materials

Bardwil Industries Inc ....C 212 944-1870
New York *(G-8727)*

LINENS: Tablecloths, From Purchased Materials

Josie Accessories Inc ....D 212 889-6376
New York *(G-10029)*

Michael Stuart Inc ....E 718 821-0704
Brooklyn *(G-2151)*

Premier Skirting Products Inc ......F 516 239-6581
Lawrence *(G-6890)*

Repellem Consumer Pdts Corp .....F 631 273-3992
Bohemia *(G-1070)*

Tablecloths For Granted Ltd ....F 518 370-5481
Schenectady *(G-14310)*

University Table Cloth Company ...F 845 371-3876
Spring Valley *(G-14586)*

LINERS & COVERS: Fabric

Kragel Co Inc ....G 716 648-1344
Hamburg *(G-5512)*

Meyco Products Inc ....E 631 421-9800
Melville *(G-7804)*

Vinyl Works Inc ....E 518 786-1200
Latham *(G-6880)*

LINERS & LINING

Themis Chimney Inc ....F 718 937-4716
Brooklyn *(G-2502)*

LINERS: Indl, Metal Plate

Lifetime Chimney Supply LLC ......G 516 576-8144
Plainview *(G-12696)*

LINGERIE WHOLESALERS

Naked Brand Group Inc ....G 212 851-8050
New York *(G-10531)*

LINIMENTS

Ges Ges ....G 631 291-9624
Hauppauge *(G-5660)*

LININGS: Apparel, Made From Purchased Materials

Bpe Studio Inc ....G 212 868-9896
New York *(G-8843)*

LININGS: Fabric, Apparel & Other, Exc Millinery

Amoseastern Apparel Inc ....F 212 730-6350
New York *(G-8565)*

Pangea Brands LLC ....G 617 638-0001
New York *(G-10746)*

Polkadot Usa Inc ....G 914 835-3697
Mamaroneck *(G-7520)*

LIP BALMS

Lotta Luv Beauty LLC ....F 646 786-2847
New York *(G-10268)*

LIPSTICK

Precision Cosmetics Mfg Co ....G 914 667-1200
Mount Vernon *(G-8171)*

LIQUEFIED PETROLEUM GAS DEALERS

Praxair Distribution Inc ....G 315 457-5821
Liverpool *(G-7034)*

LIQUID CRYSTAL DISPLAYS

Apollo Display Tech Corp ....E 631 580-4360
  Ronkonkoma *(G-13908)*

Dimension Technologies Inc ....G 585 436-3530
  Rochester *(G-13347)*

Orthogonal ....G 585 254-2775
  Rochester *(G-13598)*

Plura Broadcast Inc ....G 516 997-5675
  Massapequa *(G-7647)*

W D Technology Inc ....G 914 779-8738
  Eastchester *(G-4250)*

LOCK & KEY SVCS

Advanced Door Solutions Inc ....G 631 773-6100
  Holbrook *(G-5984)*

LOCKERS

Locker Masters Inc ....F 518 288-3203
  Granville *(G-5349)*

LOCKERS: Refrigerated

Carrier Corporation ....B 315 432-3844
  East Syracuse *(G-4203)*

LOCKS

A & L Doors & Hardware LLC ....F 718 585-8400
  Bronx *(G-1184)*

Delta Lock Company LLC ....F 631 238-7035
  Bohemia *(G-1002)*

Dortronics Systems Inc ....E 631 725-0505
  Sag Harbor *(G-14098)*

Eazy Locks LLC ....G 718 327-7770
  Far Rockaway *(G-4563)*

G Marks Hdwr Liquidating Corp ....D 631 225-5400
  Amityville *(G-263)*

Safe Skies LLC ....G 888 632-5027
  New York *(G-11114)*

LOCKS: Coin-Operated

American Lckr SEC Systems Inc ....E 716 699-2773
  Ellicottville *(G-4312)*

LOCKS: Safe & Vault, Metal

Secureit Tactical Inc ....F 800 651-8835
  Syracuse *(G-14991)*

LOCKSMITHS

A & L Doors & Hardware LLC ....F 718 585-8400
  Bronx *(G-1184)*

LOCOMOTIVES & PARTS

Higher Power Industries Inc ....G 914 709-9800
  Yonkers *(G-16319)*

LOG LOADING & UNLOADING SVCS

Bart Ostrander Trckg Log Corp ....G 518 661-6535
  Mayfield *(G-7681)*

Seaway Timber Harvesting Inc ....D 315 769-5970
  Massena *(G-7671)*

LOGGING

Attica Package Company Inc ....F 585 591-0510
  Attica *(G-456)*

B & B Forest Products Ltd ....F 518 622-0811
  Cairo *(G-3063)*

Bart Ostrander Trckg Log Corp ....G 518 661-6535
  Mayfield *(G-7681)*

C J Logging Equipment Inc ....E 315 942-5431
  Boonville *(G-1106)*

Central Timber Co Inc ....G 518 638-6338
  Granville *(G-5348)*

Chad Pierson ....G 518 251-0186
  Bakers Mills *(G-529)*

Daniel & Lois Lyndaker Logging ....G 315 346-6527
  Castorland *(G-3207)*

Davis Logging & Lumber ....G 315 245-1040
  Camden *(G-3100)*

Donald Snyder Jr ....F 315 265-4485
  Potsdam *(G-12936)*

Ed Beach Forest Management ....G 607 538-1745
  Bloomville *(G-952)*

Finger Lakes Timber Co Inc ....G 585 346-2990
  Livonia *(G-7054)*

Got Wood ....G 315 405-3384
  Constableville *(G-3634)*

Guldenschuh Logging & Lbr LLC ....G 585 538-4750
  Caledonia *(G-3070)*

Harris Logging Inc ....E 518 792-1083
  Queensbury *(G-13042)*

Kevin Regan Logging Ltd ....G 315 245-3890
  Camden *(G-3103)*

Mountain Forest Products Inc ....G 518 597-3674
  Crown Point *(G-3810)*

Peters LLC ....G 607 637-5470
  Hancock *(G-5538)*

Russell Bass ....F 607 637-5253
  Hancock *(G-5539)*

Schaefer Logging Inc ....F 607 467-4990
  Deposit *(G-4003)*

Seaway Timber Harvesting Inc ....D 315 769-5970
  Massena *(G-7671)*

Tim Cretin Logging & Sawmill ....F 315 946-4476
  Lyons *(G-7453)*

Timothy L Simpson ....G 518 234-1401
  Sharon Springs *(G-14384)*

Van Cpeters Logging Inc ....G 607 637-3574
  Hancock *(G-5540)*

LOGGING CAMPS & CONTRACTORS

Baker Logging & Firewood ....G 585 374-5733
  Naples *(G-8206)*

Couture Timber Harvesting ....G 607 836-4719
  Mc Graw *(G-7687)*

Decker Forest Products Inc ....G 607 563-2345
  Sidney *(G-14433)*

George Chilson Logging ....G 607 732-1558
  Elmira *(G-4353)*

Homer Logging Contractor ....G 607 753-8553
  Homer *(G-6065)*

J & S Logging Inc ....E 315 262-2112
  South Colton *(G-14503)*

Klein & Sons Logging Inc ....F 845 292-6682
  Wht Sphr Spgs *(G-16108)*

Lizotte Logging Inc ....F 518 359-2200
  Tupper Lake *(G-15210)*

Matteson Logging Inc ....G 585 593-3037
  Wellsville *(G-15672)*

Murray Logging LLC ....G 518 834-7372
  Keeseville *(G-6644)*

Northern Timber Harvesting LLC ....F 585 233-7330
  Alfred Station *(G-185)*

Oak Valley Logging Inc ....G 518 622-8249
  Cairo *(G-3067)*

Paul J Mitchell Logging Inc ....E 518 359-7029
  Tupper Lake *(G-15212)*

Richard Bauer Logging ....G 585 343-4149
  Alexander *(G-179)*

Richards Logging LLC ....F 518 359-2775
  Tupper Lake *(G-15213)*

Smoothbore International Inc ....G 315 754-8124
  Red Creek *(G-13070)*

Snyder Logging ....F 315 265-1462
  Potsdam *(G-12941)*

Wadsworth Logging Inc ....F 518 863-6870
  Gloversville *(G-5298)*

LOGGING: Timber, Cut At Logging Camp

GL & RL Logging Inc ....F 518 883-3936
  Broadalbin *(G-1174)*

Lyndaker Timber Harvesting LLC ....F 315 346-1328
  Castorland *(G-3208)*

Tonche Timber LLC ....G 845 389-3489
  Amsterdam *(G-348)*

LOGGING: Wood Chips, Produced In The Field

Chip It All Ltd ....G 631 473-2040
  Port Jefferson *(G-12840)*

LOGGING: Wooden Logs

Westrock Container LLC ....D 518 842-2450
  Amsterdam *(G-353)*

LOOSELEAF BINDERS

Consolidated Loose Leaf Inc ....E 212 924-5800
  New York *(G-9087)*

Sellco Industries Inc ....E 607 756-7594
  Cortland *(G-3788)*

LOTIONS OR CREAMS: Face

Abbe Laboratories Inc ....F 631 756-2223
  Farmingdale *(G-4571)*

Distribio USA LLC ....G 212 989-6077
  New York *(G-9240)*

EL Erman International Ltd ....G 212 444-9440
  Brooklyn *(G-1789)*

Fsr Beauty Ltd ....G 212 447-0036
  New York *(G-9546)*

Gassho Body & Mind Inc ....G 518 695-9991
  Schuylerville *(G-14324)*

Nea Naturals Inc ....G 845 522-8042
  New Windsor *(G-8373)*

Restorsea LLC ....G 212 828-8878
  New York *(G-11022)*

LOTIONS: SHAVING

Glacee Skincare LLC ....G 212 690-7632
  New York *(G-9617)*

LOUDSPEAKERS

Global Market Development Inc ....E 631 667-1000
  Edgewood *(G-4269)*

Speaqua Corp ....E 858 334-9042
  Deer Park *(G-3939)*

LOUVERS: Ventilating

Airflex Industrial Inc ....E 631 752-1234
  Farmingdale *(G-4575)*

Airflex Industrial Inc ....D 631 752-1234
  Farmingdale *(G-4576)*

Imperial Damper & Louver Co ....E 718 731-3800
  Bronx *(G-1279)*

LUBRICANTS: Corrosion Preventive

Engineering Maint Pdts Inc ....F 516 624-9774
  Oyster Bay *(G-12447)*

Reliance Fluid Tech LLC ....E 716 332-0988
  Niagara Falls *(G-11972)*

LUBRICATING EQPT: Indl

Advanced Tchncal Solutions Inc ....F 914 214-8230
  Mahopac *(G-7473)*

LUBRICATING OIL & GREASE WHOLESALERS

Chemlube International LLC ....F 914 381-5800
  Harrison *(G-5550)*

Chemlube Marketing Inc ....F 914 381-5800
  Harrison *(G-5551)*

LUBRICATION SYSTEMS & EQPT

Bowen Products Corporation ....G 315 498-4481
  Nedrow *(G-8214)*

LUGGAGE & BRIEFCASES

Adam Scott Designs Inc ....E 212 420-8866
  New York *(G-8453)*

Atlantic Specialty Co Inc ....E 845 356-2502
  Monsey *(G-8036)*

Bragley Mfg Co Inc ....E 718 622-7469
  Brooklyn *(G-1605)*

Deluxe Travel Store Inc ....G 718 435-8111
  Brooklyn *(G-1736)*

Fish & Crown Ltd ....D 212 707-9603
  New York *(G-9506)*

Goyard NM Beverly Hills LLC ....G 212 355-3872
  New York *(G-9652)*

Hornet Group Inc ....D 845 858-6400
  Port Jervis *(G-12850)*

Prepac Designs Inc ....G 914 524-7800
  Yonkers *(G-16344)*

Rhino Trunk & Case Inc ....F 585 244-4553
  Rochester *(G-13671)*

Trunk & Trolley LLC ....G 212 947-9001
  New York *(G-11551)*

LUGGAGE & LEATHER GOODS STORES: Leather, Exc Luggage & Shoes

House of Portfolios Co Inc ....E 212 206-7323
  New York *(G-9824)*

Tandy Leather Factory Inc ....G 845 480-3588
  Nyack *(G-12146)*

PRODUCT

LUGGAGE WHOLESALERS

Deluxe Travel Store Inc ....G 718 435-8111
Brooklyn *(G-1736)*

LUGGAGE: Traveling Bags

Carry-All Canvas Bag Co Inc ....G 718 375-4230
Brooklyn *(G-1649)*
Lo & Sons Inc ....F 917 775-4025
Brooklyn *(G-2082)*

LUGGAGE: Wardrobe Bags

Goyard Inc ....G 212 813-0005
New York *(G-9650)*
Goyard Miami LLC ....G 212 813-0005
New York *(G-9651)*

LUMBER & BLDG MATLS DEALER, RET: Garage Doors, Sell/Install

Amarr Company ....F 585 426-8290
Rochester *(G-13226)*
EZ Lift Operator Corp ....F 845 356-1676
Spring Valley *(G-14568)*
L & L Overhead Garage Doors ....G 718 721-2518
Long Island City *(G-7267)*

LUMBER & BLDG MATRLS DEALERS, RET: Bath Fixtures, Eqpt/Sply

Vaire LLC ....G 631 271-4933
Huntington Station *(G-6265)*

LUMBER & BLDG MTRLS DEALERS, RET: Windows, Storm, Wood/Metal

All United Window Corp ....E 718 624-0490
Brooklyn *(G-1487)*
Express Building Supply Inc ....E 516 608-0379
Oceanside *(G-12171)*

LUMBER & BUILDING MATERIAL DEALERS, RETAIL: Roofing Material

Hri Metals LLC ....G 518 822-1013
Hudson *(G-6161)*

LUMBER & BUILDING MATERIALS DEALER, RET: Door & Window Prdts

City Store Gates Mfg Corp ....E 718 939-9700
College Point *(G-3540)*
D D & L Inc ....F 607 729-9131
Binghamton *(G-870)*
Executive Mirror Doors Inc ....G 631 234-1090
Ronkonkoma *(G-13937)*
Lif Industries Inc ....E 718 767-8800
Whitestone *(G-16097)*
M & D Installers Inc ....D 718 782-6978
Brooklyn *(G-2092)*
Thompson Overhead Door Co Inc ....F 718 788-2470
Brooklyn *(G-2503)*

LUMBER & BUILDING MATERIALS DEALER, RET: Masonry Matls/Splys

Afco Precast Sales Corp ....D 631 924-7114
Middle Island *(G-7873)*
Cranesville Block Co Inc ....G 315 384-4000
Norfolk *(G-11998)*
Ferrara Bros LLC ....E 718 939-3030
Flushing *(G-4851)*
Guardian Concrete Products Inc ....F 518 372-0080
Schenectady *(G-14277)*
Nicolia Concrete Products Inc ....D 631 669-0700
Lindenhurst *(G-6965)*
Palumbo Block Co Inc ....E 845 832-6100
Dover Plains *(G-4033)*

LUMBER & BUILDING MATERIALS DEALERS, RETAIL: Brick

Barrasso & Sons Trucking Inc ....E 631 581-0360
Islip Terrace *(G-6358)*
Brick-It Inc ....G 631 244-3993
Hauppauge *(G-5607)*

LUMBER & BUILDING MATERIALS DEALERS, RETAIL: Countertops

Nlr Counter Tops LLC ....G 347 295-0410
New York *(G-10632)*
NY Cabinet Factory Inc ....F 718 256-6541
Brooklyn *(G-2224)*

LUMBER & BUILDING MATERIALS DEALERS, RETAIL: Paving Stones

Pallette Stone Corporation ....E 518 584-2421
Gansevoort *(G-5084)*
Unilock New York Inc ....G 845 278-6700
Brewster *(G-1159)*

LUMBER & BUILDING MATERIALS DEALERS, RETAIL: Sand & Gravel

Champion Materials Inc ....G 315 493-2654
Carthage *(G-3196)*

LUMBER & BUILDING MATERIALS DEALERS, RETAIL: Tile, Ceramic

Amendola MBL & Stone Ctr Inc ....D 914 997-7968
White Plains *(G-15972)*
Glen Plaza Marble & Gran Inc ....G 516 671-1100
Glen Cove *(G-5195)*

LUMBER & BUILDING MATERIALS RET DEALERS: Millwork & Lumber

Andike Millwork Inc ....G 718 894-1796
Maspeth *(G-7590)*
Attica Package Company Inc ....F 585 591-0510
Attica *(G-456)*
Island Street Lumber Co Inc ....G 716 692-4127
North Tonawanda *(G-12072)*
Meltz Lumber Co of Mellenville ....E 518 672-7021
Hudson *(G-6170)*
Metalocke Industries Inc ....G 718 267-9200
Woodside *(G-16213)*
Pella Corporation ....C 631 208-0710
Calverton *(G-3083)*
Pgs Millwork Inc ....D 518 828-2608
Hudson *(G-6175)*
Stephenson Lumber Company Inc ....G 518 548-7521
Speculator *(G-14548)*

LUMBER & BUILDING MATLS DEALERS, RET: Concrete/Cinder Block

Cranesville Block Co Inc ....E 518 684-6154
Amsterdam *(G-323)*
Duke Concrete Products Inc ....E 518 793-7743
Queensbury *(G-13037)*
Fort Miller Service Corp ....F 518 695-5000
Greenwich *(G-5472)*
Taylor Concrete Products Inc ....E 315 788-2191
Watertown *(G-15589)*

LUMBER: Dimension, Hardwood

Norton-Smith Hardwoods Inc ....G 716 945-0346
Salamanca *(G-14125)*

LUMBER: Fiberboard

Niagara Fiberboard Inc ....E 716 434-8881
Lockport *(G-7097)*

LUMBER: Fuelwood, From Mill Waste

GM Palmer Inc ....F 585 492-2990
Arcade *(G-374)*
PA Pellets LLC ....F 814 848-9970
Pittsford *(G-12654)*

LUMBER: Furniture Dimension Stock, Softwood

Hennig Custom Woodwork Corp ....G 516 536-3460
Oceanside *(G-12174)*

LUMBER: Hardwood Dimension

A D Bowman & Son Lumber Co ....E 607 692-2595
Castle Creek *(G-3199)*
Carlson Wood Products Inc ....F 716 287-2923
Sinclairville *(G-14444)*

LUMBER: Hardwood Dimension & Flooring Mills

B & B Lumber Company Inc ....C 866 282-0582
Jamesville *(G-6555)*
Clements Burrville Sawmill ....G 315 782-4549
Watertown *(G-15565)*
Donver Incorporated ....F 716 945-1910
Kill Buck *(G-6669)*
Fibron Products Inc ....E 716 886-2378
Buffalo *(G-2752)*
H B Millwork Inc ....E 631 289-8086
Medford *(G-7709)*
Horizon Floors I LLC ....G 212 509-9686
New York *(G-9812)*
J & J Log & Lumber Corp ....D 845 832-6535
Dover Plains *(G-4032)*
J A Yansick Lumber Co Inc ....E 585 492-4312
Arcade *(G-376)*
Petteys Lumber ....G 518 792-5943
Fort Ann *(G-4934)*
Potter Lumber Co Inc ....E 716 373-1260
Allegany *(G-190)*
Premier Hardwood Products Inc ....E 315 492-1786
Jamesville *(G-6561)*
S Donadic Inc ....D 718 361-9888
Sunnyside *(G-14774)*
Tupper Lake Hardwoods Inc ....E 518 359-8248
Tupper Lake *(G-15215)*
Wagner Millwork Inc ....D 607 687-5362
Owego *(G-12439)*

LUMBER: Kiln Dried

Carlson Wood Products Inc ....F 716 287-2923
Sinclairville *(G-14444)*
Mallery Lumber LLC ....G 607 637-2236
Hancock *(G-5537)*
Salamanca Lumber Company Inc ....E 716 945-4810
Salamanca *(G-14126)*

LUMBER: Plywood, Hardwood

Veneer One Inc ....E 516 536-6480
Oceanside *(G-12196)*

LUMBER: Plywood, Hardwood or Hardwood Faced

Kings Quartet Corp ....G 845 986-9090
Warwick *(G-15516)*

LUMBER: Plywood, Prefinished, Hardwood

Geonex International Corp ....G 212 473-4555
New York *(G-9599)*

LUMBER: Plywood, Softwood

H B Millwork Inc ....E 631 289-8086
Medford *(G-7709)*
Stone Boss Industries Inc ....F 718 278-2677
Woodside *(G-16229)*

LUMBER: Poles, Wood, Untreated

3b Timber Company Inc ....F 315 942-6580
Boonville *(G-1102)*

LUMBER: Siding, Dressed

Weather Tight Exteriors ....G 631 375-5108
Ridge *(G-13135)*

LUMBER: Silo Stock, Sawn

Machina Deus Lex Inc ....G 917 577-0972
Jamaica *(G-6455)*

LUMBER: Treated

Donver Incorporated ....F 716 945-1910
Kill Buck *(G-6669)*
Northeast Treaters Inc ....E 518 945-2660
Athens *(G-447)*

LUNCHROOMS & CAFETERIAS

Wired Coffee and Bagel Inc ....F 518 506-3194
Malta *(G-7498)*

MACHINE PARTS: Stamped Or Pressed Metal

Allen Machine Products Inc ....E 631 630-8800
  Hauppauge *(G-5584)*

Belrix Industries Inc..........................G 716 821-5964
  Buffalo *(G-2661)*

Cgs Fabrication LLC........................F 585 347-6127
  Webster *(G-15634)*

Colonial Precision Machinery ....G 631 249-0738
  Farmingdale *(G-4601)*

Creative Design and Mch Inc ....E 845 778-9001
  Rock Tavern *(G-13820)*

Custom Metal Incorporated ....F 631 643-4075
  Farmingdale *(G-4610)*

Electric Motors and Pumps Inc ....G 718 935-9118
  Brooklyn *(G-1790)*

Forkey Construction & Fabg Inc ....E 607 849-4879
  Cortland *(G-3766)*

G A Richards & Co Inc.....................F 516 334-5412
  Westbury *(G-15888)*

German Machine & Assembly Inc ....E 585 546-4200
  Rochester *(G-13437)*

Lancaster Knives Inc ....E 716 683-5050
  Lancaster *(G-6814)*

M F Manufacturing Enterprises ....G 516 822-5135
  Hicksville *(G-5924)*

Maehr Industries Inc 631 924-1661
  Bellport *(G-802)*

Mega Tool & Mfg Corp ....E 607 734-8398
  Elmira *(G-4363)*

Pervi Precision Company Inc ....G 631 589-5557
  Bohemia *(G-1061)*

Reynolds Manufacturing Inc ....F 607 562-8936
  Big Flats *(G-848)*

Sharon Manufacturing Co Inc ....G 631 242-8870
  Deer Park *(G-3936)*

Solidus Industries Inc......................D 607 749-4540
  Homer *(G-6067)*

Twinco Mfg Co Inc ....E 631 231-0022
  Hauppauge *(G-5789)*

Vosky Precision Machining Corp ....F 631 737-3200
  Ronkonkoma *(G-14025)*

Wessie Machine Inc ....G 315 926-4060
  Marion *(G-7578)*

Zeta Machine Corp ....G 631 471-8832
  Ronkonkoma *(G-14029)*

MACHINE SHOPS

Acad Design Corp...........................F 585 254-6960
  Rochester *(G-13198)*

Applied Technology Mfg Corp ....E 607 687-2200
  Owego *(G-12428)*

Architectural Coatings Inc ....F 718 418-9584
  Brooklyn *(G-1524)*

Bms Manufacturing Co Inc ....E 607 535-2426
  Watkins Glen *(G-15613)*

Centerless Technology Inc ....F 585 436-2240
  Rochester *(G-13305)*

Conesus Lake Association Inc ....E 585 346-6864
  Lakeville *(G-6774)*

David Fehlman ....G 315 455-8888
  Syracuse *(G-14875)*

Elite Precise Manufacturer LLC ....G 518 993-3040
  Fort Plain *(G-4946)*

Engineering Mfg Tech LLC ....D 607 754-7111
  Endicott *(G-4453)*

Euro Gear (usa) Inc ....G 518 578-1775
  Plattsburgh *(G-12746)*

Everfab Inc ....D 716 655-1550
  East Aurora *(G-4086)*

Fortech Inc 315 478-2048
  Syracuse *(G-14894)*

Globe Grinding Corp ....F 631 694-1970
  Copiague *(G-3655)*

Harwitt Industries Inc ....F 516 623-9787
  Freeport *(G-5002)*

Hohl Machine & Conveyor Co Inc ....E 716 882-7210
  Buffalo *(G-2799)*

Indian Springs Mfg Co Inc ....F 315 635-6101
  Baldwinsville *(G-549)*

Industrial Services of Wny ....G 716 799-7788
  Niagara Falls *(G-11941)*

ISO Plastics Corp...........................D 914 663-8300
  Mount Vernon *(G-8152)*

Kal Manufacturing Corporation ....E 585 265-4310
  Webster *(G-15644)*

Knise & Krick Inc ....E 315 422-3516
  Syracuse *(G-14927)*

M & S Precision Machine Co LLC..........F 518 747-1193
  Queensbury *(G-13048)*

Magellan Aerospace Bethel Inc ....C 203 798-9373
  Corona *(G-3743)*

Mar-A-Thon Filters Inc ....G 631 957-4774
  Lindenhurst *(G-6957)*

Ms Spares LLC ....G 607 223-3024
  Clay *(G-3451)*

Optics Technology Inc ....G 585 586-0950
  Pittsford *(G-12653)*

Precision Metals Corp ....E 631 586-5032
  Bay Shore *(G-700)*

Premier Prcision Machining LLC ....E 716 665-5217
  Falconer *(G-4551)*

Pronto Tool & Die Co Inc ....E 631 981-8920
  Ronkonkoma *(G-13997)*

Roccera LLC ....F 585 426-0887
  Rochester *(G-13678)*

Saturn Industries Inc ....E 518 828-9956
  Hudson *(G-6177)*

Sick Inc ....E 585 347-2000
  Webster *(G-15653)*

Source Technologies ....F 718 708-0305
  Brooklyn *(G-2443)*

Tobeyco Manufacturing Co Inc ....F 607 962-2446
  Corning *(G-3722)*

Triple Point Manufacturing ....G 631 218-4988
  Bohemia *(G-1091)*

Twinco Mfg Co Inc ....E 631 231-0022
  Hauppauge *(G-5789)*

Van Thomas Inc............................E 585 426-1414
  Rochester *(G-13795)*

Verns Machine Co Inc ....E 315 926-4223
  Marion *(G-7577)*

Village Decoration Ltd ....E 315 437-2522
  East Syracuse *(G-4248)*

MACHINE TOOL ACCESS: Balancing Machines

Schenck Corporation ....D 631 242-4010
  Deer Park *(G-3932)*

Schenck USA Corp ....D 631 242-4010
  Deer Park *(G-3933)*

MACHINE TOOL ACCESS: Cams

Designatronics Incorporated ....G 516 328-3300
  Hicksville *(G-5902)*

MACHINE TOOL ACCESS: Cutting

Ameri-Cut Tool Grinding Inc ....G 716 692-3900
  North Tonawanda *(G-12051)*

Boro Park Cutting Tool Corp ....E 718 720-0610
  Staten Island *(G-14629)*

Circo File Corp ....G 516 922-1848
  Oyster Bay *(G-12445)*

Dura-Mill Inc ....E 518 899-2255
  Ballston Spa *(G-573)*

Genesee Manufacturing Co Inc ....G 585 266-3201
  Rochester *(G-13435)*

Griffin Manufacturing Company ....E 585 265-1991
  Webster *(G-15641)*

Macinnes Tool Corporation ....E 585 467-1920
  Rochester *(G-13527)*

Morgood Tools Inc ....D 585 436-8828
  Rochester *(G-13560)*

Rota File Corporation ....E 516 496-7200
  Syosset *(G-14802)*

Steiner Technologies Inc ....F 585 425-5910
  Fairport *(G-4523)*

MACHINE TOOL ACCESS: Diamond Cutting, For Turning, Etc

Advance D Tech Inc ....F 845 534-8248
  Cornwall *(G-3724)*

MACHINE TOOL ACCESS: Dies, Thread Cutting

Brinkman Intl Group Inc ....G 585 429-5000
  Rochester *(G-13281)*

C J Winter Machine Tech ....E 585 429-5000
  Rochester *(G-13290)*

MACHINE TOOL ACCESS: Dressing/Wheel Crushing Attach, Diamond

Scomac Inc ....F 585 494-2200
  Bergen *(G-820)*

MACHINE TOOL ACCESS: Drills

Truebite Inc ....F 607 786-3184
  Endicott *(G-4476)*

MACHINE TOOL ACCESS: Knives, Shear

Lancaster Knives Inc ....E 716 683-5050
  Lancaster *(G-6814)*

MACHINE TOOL ACCESS: Sockets

Socket Products Mfg Corp ....G 631 232-9870
  Islandia *(G-6344)*

MACHINE TOOL ACCESS: Tool Holders

New Market Products LLC ....G 607 292-6226
  Wayne *(G-15628)*

Robert J Faraone ....E 585 232-7160
  Rochester *(G-13677)*

MACHINE TOOL ACCESS: Tools & Access

Advent Tool & Mold Inc ....C 585 254-2000
  Rochester *(G-13214)*

Fred M Velepec Co Inc ....E 718 821-6636
  Glendale *(G-5225)*

Huron Tl Cutter Grinding Inc ....E 631 420-7000
  Farmingdale *(G-4646)*

JD Tool Inc ....G 607 786-3129
  Endicott *(G-4462)*

Methods Tooling & Mfg Inc ....E 845 246-7100
  Mount Marion *(G-8111)*

Roechling Medical Rochester LP ....D 585 254-2000
  Rochester *(G-13702)*

MACHINE TOOL ATTACHMENTS & ACCESS

Curran Manufacturing Corp ....E 631 273-1010
  Hauppauge *(G-5633)*

Curran Manufacturing Corp ....E 631 273-1010
  Hauppauge *(G-5634)*

Flexbar Machine Corporation ....E 631 582-8440
  Islandia *(G-6332)*

Innovative Automation Inc ....F 631 439-3300
  Farmingdale *(G-4649)*

Jem Tool & Die Corp ....F 631 539-8734
  West Islip *(G-15811)*

Prz Technologies Inc ....F 716 683-1300
  Lancaster *(G-6827)*

Thuro Metal Products Inc ....E 631 435-0444
  Brentwood *(G-1128)*

Velmex Inc ....E 585 657-6151
  Bloomfield *(G-950)*

MACHINE TOOLS & ACCESS

Ale-Techniques Inc ....F 845 687-7200
  High Falls *(G-5954)*

American Linear Manufacturers ....F 516 333-1351
  Westbury *(G-15867)*

Baldwin Machine Works Inc ....G 631 842-9110
  Copiague *(G-3649)*

Bdp Industries Inc ....E 518 695-6851
  Greenwich *(G-5468)*

Bnm Product Service........................G 631 750-1586
  Holbrook *(G-5986)*

Custom Service Solutions Inc ....E 585 637-3760
  Brockport *(G-1175)*

Dinosaw Inc ....E 518 828-9942
  Hudson *(G-6154)*

Dock Hardware Incorporated ....F 585 266-7920
  Rochester *(G-13352)*

Everfab Inc ....D 716 655-1550
  East Aurora *(G-4086)*

Gardei Industries LLC ....F 716 693-7100
  North Tonawanda *(G-12069)*

Graywood Companies Inc ....A 585 738-8889
  Rochester *(G-13450)*

J H Robotics Inc ....E 607 729-3758
  Johnson City *(G-6603)*

Kps Capital Partners LP ....E 212 338-5100
  New York *(G-10133)*

M & S Precision Machine Co LLC..........F 518 747-1193
  Queensbury *(G-13048)*

Make-Waves Instrument Corp ....E 716 681-7524
  Buffalo *(G-2860)*

Messer LLC ....D 716 773-7552
  Grand Island *(G-5337)*

Michael Fiore Ltd ....G 516 561-8238
  Valley Stream *(G-15348)*

Myles Tool Company Inc ....E 716 731-1300
  Sanborn (G-14146)
Omega Tool Measuring Mchs Inc ....E 585 598-7800
  Fairport (G-4510)
Parlec LLC ....D 585 425-4400
  Fairport (G-4513)
Precision Mechanisms Corp ....E 516 333-5955
  Westbury (G-15919)
Production Metal Cutting Inc ....F 585 458-7136
  Rochester (G-13650)
Ross JC Inc ....G 716 439-1161
  Lockport (G-7103)
S & S Machinery Corp ....D 718 492-7400
  Brooklyn (G-2370)
S S Precision Gear & Instr ....G 718 457-7474
  Corona (G-3749)
Seneca Falls Machine Tool Co ....D 315 568-5804
  Seneca Falls (G-14371)
Sinn-Tech Industries Inc ....F 631 643-1171
  Bohemia (G-1079)
Strippit Inc ....C 716 542-4511
  Akron (G-22)
Transport National Dev Inc ....E 716 662-0270
  Orchard Park (G-12380)
Trident Precision Mfg Inc ....D 585 265-2010
  Webster (G-15658)
Universal Tooling Corporation ....F 716 985-4691
  Gerry (G-5172)
Vandilay Industries Inc ....E 631 226-3064
  West Babylon (G-15755)

MACHINE TOOLS, METAL CUTTING: Centering

Rush Machinery Inc ....G 585 554-3070
  Rushville (G-14075)

MACHINE TOOLS, METAL CUTTING: Exotic, Including Explosive

High Speed Hammer Company Inc ...F 585 266-4287
  Rochester (G-13468)

MACHINE TOOLS, METAL CUTTING: Grind, Polish, Buff, Lapp

Hartchrom Inc ....F 518 880-0411
  Watervliet (G-15603)
Mortech Industries Inc ....G 845 628-6138
  Mahopac (G-7475)

MACHINE TOOLS, METAL CUTTING: Lathes

Zyp Precision LLC ....G 315 539-3667
  Waterloo (G-15557)

MACHINE TOOLS, METAL CUTTING: Numerically Controlled

Omega Tool Measuring Mchs Inc ......E 585 598-7800
  Fairport (G-4510)
Ppi Corp ....E 585 880-7277
  Rochester (G-13632)
Ppi Corp ....D 585 243-0300
  Rochester (G-13633)
Precise Tool & Mfg Inc ....D 585 247-0700
  Rochester (G-13634)
Wazer Inc ....E 201 580-6486
  Brooklyn (G-2577)

MACHINE TOOLS, METAL CUTTING: Tool Replacement & Rpr Parts

Advanced Machine Design Co Inc ...E 716 826-2000
  Buffalo (G-2624)
Welch Machine Inc ....G 585 647-3578
  Rochester (G-13801)

MACHINE TOOLS, METAL FORMING: Die Casting & Extruding

Raloid Tool Co Inc ....F 518 664-4261
  Mechanicville (G-7694)

MACHINE TOOLS, METAL FORMING: Electroforming

Precision Eforming LLC ....F 607 753-7730
  Cortland (G-3783)

MACHINE TOOLS, METAL FORMING: Forging Machinery & Hammers

Special Metals Corporation ....D 716 366-5663
  Dunkirk (G-4067)
Trueforge Global McHy Corp ....G 516 825-7040
  Rockville Centre (G-13839)

MACHINE TOOLS, METAL FORMING: Headers

American Racing Headers Inc ....E 631 608-1427
  Deer Park (G-3837)

MACHINE TOOLS, METAL FORMING: High Energy Rate

Arconic Inc ....G 716 358-6451
  Falconer (G-4534)
Smart High Voltage Solutions ....F 631 563-6724
  Bohemia (G-1080)

MACHINE TOOLS, METAL FORMING: Presses, Hyd & Pneumatic

Servotec Usa LLC ....G 518 671-6120
  Hudson (G-6179)

MACHINE TOOLS, METAL FORMING: Pressing

Mpi Incorporated ....C 845 471-7630
  Poughkeepsie (G-12972)

MACHINE TOOLS, METAL FORMING: Punching & Shearing

Manhasset Tool & Die Co Inc ....F 716 684-6066
  Lancaster (G-6816)

MACHINE TOOLS, METAL FORMING: Rebuilt

Uhmac Inc ....F 716 537-2343
  Holland (G-6032)

MACHINE TOOLS, METAL FORMING: Spinning, Spline Rollg/Windg

Gemcor Automation LLC ....D 716 674-9300
  West Seneca (G-15848)

MACHINE TOOLS: Metal Cutting

Abtex Corporation ....E 315 536-7403
  Dresden (G-4034)
Alpine Machine Inc ....F 607 272-1344
  Ithaca (G-6362)
Alternative Service Inc ....F 631 345-9500
  Bellport (G-793)
Alton Manufacturing Inc ....D 585 458-2600
  Rochester (G-13225)
Ascension Industries Inc ....C 716 693-9381
  North Tonawanda (G-12054)
Aztec Mfg of Rochester ....G 585 352-8152
  Spencerport (G-14552)
Brinkman Products Inc ....B 585 235-4545
  Rochester (G-13282)
Bystronic Inc ....G 631 231-1212
  Hauppauge (G-5609)
Coastel Cable Tools Inc ....E 315 471-5361
  Syracuse (G-14855)
Dinosaw Inc ....E 518 828-9942
  Hudson (G-6154)
Dunlap Machine LLC ....F 315 926-1013
  Marion (G-7568)
Folam Tool Co Inc ....G 716 688-1347
  Buffalo (G-2756)
Gallery of Machines LLC ....G 607 849-6028
  Marathon (G-7557)
Gb Aero Engine LLC ....B 914 925-9600
  Rye (G-14078)
Genco John ....G 716 483-5446
  Jamestown (G-6512)
Gleason Corporation ....A 585 473-1000
  Rochester (G-13444)
H S Assembly Inc ....G 585 266-4287
  Rochester (G-13455)
Halpern Tool Corp ....E 914 633-0038
  New Rochelle (G-8338)
Hardinge Inc ....B 607 734-2281
  Elmira (G-4355)

IPC/Razor LLC ....D 212 551-4500
  New York (G-9938)
J Vogler Enterprise LLC ....F 585 247-1625
  Rochester (G-13486)
Jalex Industries Ltd ....F 631 491-5072
  West Babylon (G-15718)
Kodiak Cutting Tools LLC ....G 800 892-1006
  Syracuse (G-14928)
Kps Capital Partners LP ....E 212 338-5100
  New York (G-10133)
Kyocera Precision Tools Inc ....E 607 687-0012
  Owego (G-12431)
Lancaster Knives Inc ....E 716 683-5050
  Lancaster (G-6814)
Lk Industries Inc ....G 716 941-9202
  Glenwood (G-5274)
Montrose Equipment Sales Inc ....F 718 388-7446
  Brooklyn (G-2170)
Multimatic Products Inc ....D 800 767-7633
  Ronkonkoma (G-13977)
Munson Machinery Company Inc ....E 315 797-0090
  Utica (G-15286)
Myles Tool Company Inc ....E 716 731-1300
  Sanborn (G-14146)
Nifty Bar Grinding & Cutting ....E 585 381-0450
  Penfield (G-12571)
Omega Consolidated Corporation ......E 585 392-9262
  Hilton (G-5974)
P & R Industries Inc ....E 585 266-6725
  Rochester (G-13604)
Producto Corporation ....C 716 484-7131
  Jamestown (G-6538)
R Steiner Technologies Inc ....E 585 425-5912
  Fairport (G-4518)
Rapid Precision Machining Inc ....D 585 467-0780
  Rochester (G-13669)
S & S Machinery Corp ....D 718 492-7400
  Brooklyn (G-2370)
S & S Machinery Corp ....E 718 492-7400
  Brooklyn (G-2371)
Selflock Screw Products Co Inc ....E 315 541-4464
  Syracuse (G-14992)
Seneca Falls Capital Inc ....G 315 568-5804
  Seneca Falls (G-14370)
Seneca Falls Machine Tool Co ....D 315 568-5804
  Seneca Falls (G-14371)
Simmons Machine Tool Corp ....C 518 462-5431
  Menands (G-7848)
Teka Precision Inc ....G 845 753-1900
  Nyack (G-12147)
Transport National Dev Inc ....E 716 662-0270
  Orchard Park (G-12379)
Truemade Products Inc ....G 631 981-4755
  Ronkonkoma (G-14018)
Verns Machine Co Inc ....E 315 926-4223
  Marion (G-7577)
World LLC ....F 631 940-9121
  Deer Park (G-3956)
Zwack Incorporated ....E 518 733-5135
  Stephentown (G-14732)

MACHINE TOOLS: Metal Forming

Adaptive Mfg Tech Inc ....E 631 580-5400
  Ronkonkoma (G-13888)
Advanced Machine Design Co Inc ......E 716 826-2000
  Buffalo (G-2624)
Austin Industries Inc ....F 585 589-1353
  Albion (G-154)
Bdp Industries Inc ....E 518 695-6851
  Greenwich (G-5468)
Brinkman Intl Group Inc ....G 585 429-5000
  Rochester (G-13281)
Buffalo Machine Tls of Niagara ....F 716 201-1310
  Lockport (G-7062)
C & T Tool & Instrument Co ....E 718 429-1253
  Woodside (G-16199)
C J Winter Machine Tech ....E 585 429-5000
  Rochester (G-13290)
Commodore Manufacutring Corp ....E 718 788-2600
  Brooklyn (G-1678)
Dover Global Holdings Inc ....F 212 922-1640
  New York (G-9257)
Dunlap Machine LLC ....F 315 926-1013
  Marion (G-7568)
Ecko Fin & Tooling Inc ....F 716 487-0200
  Jamestown (G-6507)
Gh Induction Atmospheres LLC ....E 585 368-2120
  Rochester (G-13440)
Hawthorne Garden Company ....F 516 883-6550
  Port Washington (G-12882)

Hydramec Inc ....E 585 593-5190
Scio (G-14325)

Lourdes Systems Inc ....F 631 234-7077
Hauppauge (G-5701)

Miller Mechanical Services Inc ....E 518 792-0430
Glens Falls (G-5259)

Prim Hall Enterprises Inc ....F 518 561-7408
Plattsburgh (G-12772)

Producto Corporation ....C 716 484-7131
Jamestown (G-6538)

Schaefer Machine Co Inc ....E 516 248-6880
Mineola (G-8000)

Standard Paper Box Machine Co ....E 718 328-3300
Bronx (G-1370)

Strippit Inc ....C 716 542-4511
Akron (G-22)

Taumel Metalforming Corp ....G 845 878-3100
Patterson (G-12521)

MACHINERY & EQPT, AGRICULTURAL, WHOLESALE: Dairy

Brook North Farms Inc ....F 315 834-9390
Auburn (G-469)

MACHINERY & EQPT, AGRICULTURAL, WHOLESALE: Landscaping Eqpt

Scotts Company LLC ....E 631 816-2831
Yaphank (G-16269)

Upstone Materials Inc ....F 315 265-8036
Plattsburgh (G-12788)

MACHINERY & EQPT, AGRICULTURAL, WHOLESALE: Lawn & Garden

Rhett M Clark Inc ....G 585 538-9570
Caledonia (G-3072)

MACHINERY & EQPT, INDL, WHOL: Controlling Instruments/Access

Unimar Inc ....F 315 699-4400
Syracuse (G-15017)

MACHINERY & EQPT, INDL, WHOL: Recording Instruments/Access

His Productions USA Inc ....G 212 594-3737
New York (G-9793)

MACHINERY & EQPT, INDL, WHOLESALE: Conveyor Systems

Vetra Systems Corporation ....G 631 434-3185
Hauppauge (G-5796)

MACHINERY & EQPT, INDL, WHOLESALE: Countersinks

Empire Fabricators Inc ....G 585 235-3050
Rochester (G-13387)

Nlr Counter Tops LLC ....G 347 295-0410
New York (G-10632)

MACHINERY & EQPT, INDL, WHOLESALE: Fans

Canarm Ltd ....G 800 267-4427
Ogdensburg (G-12203)

MACHINERY & EQPT, INDL, WHOLESALE: Food Manufacturing

Vr Food Equipment Inc ....F 315 531-8133
Farmington (G-4780)

MACHINERY & EQPT, INDL, WHOLESALE: Food Product Manufacturng

ET Oakes Corporation ....E 631 232-0002
Hauppauge (G-5648)

Hobart Corporation ....E 631 864-3440
Commack (G-3592)

MACHINERY & EQPT, INDL, WHOLESALE: Heat Exchange

Aavid Niagara LLC ....E 716 297-0652
Niagara Falls (G-11900)

MACHINERY & EQPT, INDL, WHOLESALE: Hydraulic Systems

Ener-G-Rotors Inc ....G 518 372-2608
Schenectady (G-14262)

Triumph Actuation Systems LLC ....D 516 378-0162
Freeport (G-5030)

MACHINERY & EQPT, INDL, WHOLESALE: Indl Machine Parts

Alternative Service Inc ....F 631 345-9500
Bellport (G-793)

Rpb Distributors LLC ....G 914 244-3600
Mount Kisco (G-8105)

MACHINERY & EQPT, INDL, WHOLESALE: Instruments & Cntrl Eqpt

Carl Zeiss Inc ....C 914 747-1800
White Plains (G-15990)

Winters Instruments Inc ....E 281 880-8607
Buffalo (G-3050)

MACHINERY & EQPT, INDL, WHOLESALE: Machine Tools & Access

Cementex Latex Corp ....F 212 741-1770
New York (G-8944)

Curran Manufacturing Corp ....E 631 273-1010
Hauppauge (G-5633)

S & S Machinery Corp ....E 718 492-7400
Brooklyn (G-2371)

MACHINERY & EQPT, INDL, WHOLESALE: Measure/Test, Electric

Mausner Equipment Co Inc ....C 631 689-7358
Setauket (G-14380)

MACHINERY & EQPT, INDL, WHOLESALE: Packaging

Millwood Inc ....F 518 233-1475
Waterford (G-15539)

Modern Packaging Inc ....D 631 595-2437
Deer Park (G-3907)

MACHINERY & EQPT, INDL, WHOLESALE: Pneumatic Tools

U S Air Tool Co Inc ....E 631 471-3300
Ronkonkoma (G-14019)

MACHINERY & EQPT, INDL, WHOLESALE: Power Plant Machinery

Ultravolt Inc ....D 631 471-4444
Ronkonkoma (G-14022)

MACHINERY & EQPT, INDL, WHOLESALE: Processing & Packaging

National Equipment Corporation ....F 718 585-0200
Harrison (G-5556)

National Equipment Corporation ....E 718 585-0200
Bronx (G-1321)

MACHINERY & EQPT, INDL, WHOLESALE: Robots

Automated Cells & Eqp Inc ....E 607 936-1341
Painted Post (G-12471)

MACHINERY & EQPT, INDL, WHOLESALE: Safety Eqpt

Traffic Logix Corporation ....G 866 915-6449
Spring Valley (G-14583)

MACHINERY & EQPT, INDL, WHOLESALE: Textile

John A Eberly Inc ....G 315 449-3034
Syracuse (G-14917)

MACHINERY & EQPT, INDL, WHOLESALE: Tire Recapping Machinery

Loomis Root Inc ....F 716 564-7668
Amherst (G-230)

MACHINERY & EQPT, INDL, WHOLESALE: Water Pumps

Air Flow Pump Corp ....G 718 241-2800
Brooklyn (G-1472)

MACHINERY & EQPT, INDL, WHOLESALE: Woodworking

Putnam Rolling Ladder Co Inc ....F 212 226-5147
New York (G-10932)

MACHINERY & EQPT, WHOLESALE: Construction, General

Zwack Incorporated ....E 518 733-5135
Stephentown (G-14732)

MACHINERY & EQPT, WHOLESALE: Crushing, Pulverizng & Screeng

American Material Processing ....F 315 318-0017
Phoenix (G-12615)

MACHINERY & EQPT, WHOLESALE: Masonry

Arnan Development Corp ....D 607 432-8391
Oneonta (G-12257)

Duke Concrete Products Inc ....E 518 793-7743
Queensbury (G-13037)

Inwood Material ....F 516 371-1842
Inwood (G-6296)

Palumbo Block Co Inc ....E 845 832-6100
Dover Plains (G-4033)

MACHINERY & EQPT, WHOLESALE: Road Construction & Maintenance

Ducon Technologies Inc ....B 631 694-1700
New York (G-9278)

MACHINERY & EQPT: Electroplating

Caswell Inc ....F 315 946-1213
Lyons (G-7447)

Digital Matrix Corp ....E 516 481-7990
Farmingdale (G-4616)

Precision Process Inc ....D 716 731-1587
Niagara Falls (G-11969)

Sonicor Inc ....F 631 920-6555
West Babylon (G-15748)

Technic Inc ....F 516 349-0700
Plainview (G-12718)

MACHINERY & EQPT: Farm

Asp Blade Intrmdate Hldngs Inc ....A 212 476-8000
New York (G-8650)

Don Beck Inc ....G 585 493-3040
Castile (G-3198)

Eastern Welding Inc ....G 631 727-0306
Riverhead (G-13174)

Growtech Industries LLC ....G 315 335-9692
Buffalo (G-2786)

Haines Equipment Inc ....E 607 566-8531
Avoca (G-510)

House of The Foaming Case Inc ....G 718 454-0101
Saint Albans (G-14105)

Landpro Equipment LLC ....E 716 665-3110
Falconer (G-4549)

Oxbo International Corporation ....D 585 548-2665
Byron (G-3062)

Plant-Tech2o Inc ....G 516 483-7845
Hempstead (G-5847)

Road Cases USA Inc ....E 631 563-0633
Bohemia (G-1071)

Zappala Farms AG Systems Inc ....E 315 626-6293
Cato (G-3209)

MACHINERY & EQPT: Gas Producers, Generators/Other Rltd Eqpt

Audubon Machinery Corporation ....D 716 564-5165
North Tonawanda (G-12055)

P R O D U C T

MACHINERY & EQPT: Liquid Automation

Javlyn Process Systems LLC ....E 585 424-5580
Rochester *(G-13491)*

MACHINERY & EQPT: Metal Finishing, Plating Etc

Cameo Metal Products Inc ....E 718 788-1106
Brooklyn *(G-1641)*

P K G Equipment Incorporated ....E 585 436-4650
Rochester *(G-13605)*

Qes Solutions Inc ....D 585 783-1455
Rochester *(G-13656)*

R & B Machinery Corp ....G 716 894-3332
Buffalo *(G-2946)*

Witt Preparations LLC ....G 716 948-4002
Cheektowaga *(G-3365)*

MACHINERY BASES

American Standard Mfg Inc ....E 518 868-2512
Central Bridge *(G-3259)*

Kefa Industries Group Inc ....G 718 568-9297
Rego Park *(G-13079)*

Machinery Mountings Inc ....F 631 851-0480
Hauppauge *(G-5703)*

MACHINERY, COMMERCIAL LAUNDRY: Dryers, Incl Coin-Operated

Maxi Companies Inc ....G 315 446-1002
De Witt *(G-3824)*

MACHINERY, COMMERCIAL LAUNDRY: Washing, Incl Coin-Operated

G A Braun Inc ....C 315 475-3123
North Syracuse *(G-12041)*

Lynx Product Group LLC ....E 716 751-3100
Wilson *(G-16153)*

MACHINERY, EQPT & SUPPLIES: Parking Facility

Automotion Parking Systems LLC ....G 516 565-5600
West Hempstead *(G-15767)*

Park Assist LLC ....D 646 666-7525
New York *(G-10762)*

Parkmatic Car Prkg Systems LLC ....G 516 224-7700
Long Island City *(G-7319)*

Parkmatic Car Prkg Systems LLC ....G 800 422-5438
College Point *(G-3558)*

MACHINERY, FLOOR SANDING: Commercial

Hubco Inc ....G 716 683-5940
Alden *(G-170)*

MACHINERY, FOOD PRDTS: Beverage

Brooklyn Brew Shop LLC ....F 718 874-0119
Brooklyn *(G-1612)*

Kedco Inc ....F 516 454-7800
Farmingdale *(G-4663)*

US Beverage Net Inc ....F 315 579-2025
Syracuse *(G-15019)*

MACHINERY, FOOD PRDTS: Choppers, Commercial

Mary F Morse ....G 315 866-2741
Mohawk *(G-8006)*

MACHINERY, FOOD PRDTS: Confectionery

National Equipment Corporation ....F 718 585-0200
Harrison *(G-5556)*

National Equipment Corporation ....E 718 585-0200
Bronx *(G-1321)*

MACHINERY, FOOD PRDTS: Cutting, Chopping, Grinding, Mixing

ET Oakes Corporation ....E 631 232-0002
Hauppauge *(G-5648)*

Janel Corporation ....G 516 256-8143
Lynbrook *(G-7432)*

MACHINERY, FOOD PRDTS: Dairy & Milk

Chemicolloid Laboratories Inc ....F 516 747-2666
New Hyde Park *(G-8256)*

MACHINERY, FOOD PRDTS: Dairy, Pasteurizing

Goodnature Products Inc ....E 800 875-3381
Buffalo *(G-2779)*

MACHINERY, FOOD PRDTS: Food Processing, Smokers

Los Olivos Ltd ....C 631 773-6439
Farmingdale *(G-4673)*

MACHINERY, FOOD PRDTS: Juice Extractors, Fruit & Veg, Comm

Acai of America Inc ....G 862 205-9334
New York *(G-8438)*

MACHINERY, FOOD PRDTS: Milk Processing, NEC

Delaval Inc ....F 585 599-4696
Corfu *(G-3702)*

MACHINERY, FOOD PRDTS: Mixers, Commercial

Expert Industries Inc ....E 718 434-6060
Brooklyn *(G-1823)*

MACHINERY, FOOD PRDTS: Oilseed Crushing & Extracting

Caravella Food Corp ....F 646 552-0455
Whitestone *(G-16090)*

MACHINERY, FOOD PRDTS: Ovens, Bakery

Home Maide Incorporated ....F 845 837-1700
Harriman *(G-5544)*

Mohawk Valley Manufacturing ....G 315 797-0851
Frankfort *(G-4954)*

MACHINERY, FOOD PRDTS: Packing House

Desu Machinery Corporation ....D 716 681-5798
Depew *(G-3979)*

MACHINERY, FOOD PRDTS: Presses, Cheese, Beet, Cider & Sugar

Blue Toad Hard Cider ....E 585 424-5508
Rochester *(G-13274)*

MACHINERY, FOOD PRDTS: Roasting, Coffee, Peanut, Etc.

Wired Coffee and Bagel Inc ....F 518 506-3194
Malta *(G-7498)*

MACHINERY, MAILING: Canceling

Action Technologies Inc ....G 718 278-1000
Long Island City *(G-7145)*

MACHINERY, MAILING: Postage Meters

Neopost USA Inc ....E 631 435-9100
Hauppauge *(G-5726)*

Pitney Bowes Inc ....E 212 564-7548
New York *(G-10846)*

Pitney Bowes Inc ....E 203 356-5000
New York *(G-10847)*

Pitney Bowes Inc ....E 516 822-0900
Jericho *(G-6589)*

MACHINERY, METALWORKING: Assembly, Including Robotic

Alliance Automation Systems ....C 585 426-2700
Rochester *(G-13218)*

Hover-Davis Inc ....C 585 352-9590
Rochester *(G-13471)*

Manufacturing Resources Inc ....E 631 481-0041
Rochester *(G-13532)*

Mold-A-Matic Corporation ....E 607 433-2121
Oneonta *(G-12276)*

MACHINERY, METALWORKING: Cutting & Slitting

Expert Metal Slitters Corp ....G 718 361-2735
Long Island City *(G-7219)*

MACHINERY, OFFICE: Perforators

Cummins - Allison Corp ....D 718 263-2482
Kew Gardens *(G-6662)*

MACHINERY, OFFICE: Stapling, Hand Or Power

Staplex Company Inc ....E 718 768-3333
Brooklyn *(G-2451)*

MACHINERY, OFFICE: Time Clocks &Time Recording Devices

Gradual LLC ....F 347 293-0974
Long Island City *(G-7232)*

Widmer Time Recorder Company ....F 212 227-0405
New York *(G-11754)*

MACHINERY, PACKAGING: Canning, Food

Reynolds Packaging McHy Inc ....D 716 358-6451
Falconer *(G-4554)*

MACHINERY, PACKAGING: Carton Packing

Niagara Scientific Inc ....E 315 437-0821
East Syracuse *(G-4228)*

MACHINERY, PACKAGING: Packing & Wrapping

Fourteen Arnold Ave Corp ....F 315 272-1700
Utica *(G-15264)*

Turbofil Packaging Mchs LLC ....F 914 239-3878
Mount Vernon *(G-8189)*

Vetroelite Inc ....G 925 724-7900
New York *(G-11668)*

MACHINERY, PAPER INDUSTRY: Converting, Die Cutting & Stampng

Fbm Galaxy Inc ....F 315 463-5144
East Syracuse *(G-4210)*

Gailer Stamping Diecutting LLC ....F 212 243-5662
Long Island City *(G-7227)*

Richlar Industries Inc ....F 315 463-5144
East Syracuse *(G-4234)*

Rsb Associates Inc ....F 518 281-5067
Altamont *(G-199)*

MACHINERY, PAPER INDUSTRY: Paper Mill, Plating, Etc

Sonicor Inc ....F 631 920-6555
West Babylon *(G-15748)*

MACHINERY, PRINTING TRADES: Copy Holders

Copy4les Inc ....F 212 487-9778
New York *(G-9100)*

Exacta LLC ....G 716 406-2303
Clarence Center *(G-3445)*

MACHINERY, PRINTING TRADES: Plates

C M E Corp ....F 315 451-7101
Syracuse *(G-14839)*

Csw Inc ....F 585 247-4010
Rochester *(G-13331)*

Impressions International Inc ....G 585 442-5240
Rochester *(G-13477)*

Rubber Stamps Inc ....E 212 675-1180
Mineola *(G-7998)*

Standard Bots Company ....G 646 876-2687
Locust Valley *(G-7129)*

Tessy Plastics Corp ....B 315 689-3924
Skaneateles *(G-14457)*

Van Blarcom Closures Inc ....C 718 855-3810
Brooklyn *(G-2551)*

MACHINERY, PRINTING TRADES: Plates, Offset

Apexx Omni-Graphics Inc ....D.... 718 326-3330
Maspeth **(G-7591)**

MACHINERY, PRINTING TRADES: Presses, Envelope

AC Envelope Inc ....G...... 516 420-0646
Farmingdale **(G-4572)**

MACHINERY, PRINTING TRADES: Printing Trade Parts & Attchts

Lexar Global LLC ....G.... 845 352-9700
Valley Cottage **(G-15318)**
Rollers Inc ....G.... 716 837-0700
Buffalo **(G-2961)**

MACHINERY, PRINTING TRADES: Sticks

Bmp America Inc ....C.... 585 798-0950
Medina **(G-7730)**

MACHINERY, SEWING: Sewing & Hat & Zipper Making

Cvd Equipment Corporation ....E...... 845 246-3631
Saugerties **(G-14199)**

MACHINERY, TEXTILE: Card Cutting, Jacquard

Mjk Cutting Inc ....F.... 718 384-7613
Brooklyn **(G-2162)**

MACHINERY, TEXTILE: Embroidery

Herrmann Group LLC ....G...... 716 876-9798
Kenmore **(G-6651)**

MACHINERY, TEXTILE: Silk Screens

Angel Textiles Inc ....G.... 212 532-0900
New York **(G-8582)**
Big Apple Sign Corp ....E.... 631 342-0303
Islandia **(G-6326)**
Screen Team Inc ....F.... 718 786-2424
Long Island City **(G-7353)**

MACHINERY, TEXTILE: Thread Making Or Spinning

Thread Check Inc ....D.... 631 231-1515
Hauppauge **(G-5784)**

MACHINERY, WOODWORKING: Bandsaws

Phoenix Wood Wrights Ltd ....F.... 631 727-9691
Riverhead **(G-13184)**

MACHINERY, WOODWORKING: Cabinet Makers'

901 D LLC ....E.... 845 369-1111
Airmont **(G-9)**
Hat Factory Furniture Co ....G.... 914 788-6288
Peekskill **(G-12552)**

MACHINERY, WOODWORKING: Furniture Makers

Downtown Interiors Inc ....F.... 212 337-0230
New York **(G-9262)**

MACHINERY, WOODWORKING: Lathes, Wood Turning Includes Access

Hardinge Inc ....B.... 607 734-2281
Elmira **(G-4355)**

MACHINERY, WOODWORKING: Pattern Makers'

Corbett Stves Pttern Works Inc ....E.... 585 546-7109
Rochester **(G-13326)**

MACHINERY, WOODWORKING: Sanding, Exc Portable Floor Sanders

US Sander LLC ....G...... 518 875-9157
Esperance **(G-4485)**

MACHINERY: Ammunition & Explosives Loading

Eastend Enforcement Products ....G.... 631 878-8424
Smithtown **(G-14477)**

MACHINERY: Assembly, Exc Metalworking

Alliance Automation Systems ....C.... 585 426-2700
Rochester **(G-13218)**
Distech Systems Inc ....G.... 585 254-7020
Rochester **(G-13349)**
Dynamasters Inc ....G.... 585 458-9970
Rochester **(G-13359)**
Hubco Inc ....G.... 716 683-5940
Alden **(G-170)**
New Vision Industries Inc ....F.... 607 687-7700
Endicott **(G-4466)**
Quality Manufacturing Sys LLC ....G.... 716 763-0988
Lakewood **(G-6783)**
Rfb Associates Inc ....F.... 518 271-0551
Fort Edward **(G-4943)**
Trident Precision Mfg Inc ....D.... 585 265-2010
Webster **(G-15658)**
Veeco Process Equipment Inc ....C.... 516 677-0200
Plainview **(G-12726)**

MACHINERY: Automotive Maintenance

Blue Star Products Inc ....F.... 631 952-3204
Hauppauge **(G-5606)**
T-Rex Supply Corporation ....G.... 516 308-0505
Hempstead **(G-5850)**

MACHINERY: Automotive Related

B&K Precision Corporation ....G.... 631 369-2665
Manorville **(G-7551)**
Eltee Tool & Die Co ....F.... 607 748-4301
Endicott **(G-4449)**
Hitachi Metals America Ltd ....E.... 914 694-9200
Purchase **(G-13005)**
Reefer Tek Llc ....F.... 347 590-1067
Bronx **(G-1350)**
Rfb Associates Inc ....F.... 518 271-0551
Fort Edward **(G-4943)**
Riverview Associates Inc ....F.... 585 235-5980
Rochester **(G-13674)**

MACHINERY: Billing

Gary Roth & Associates Ltd ....E.... 516 333-1000
Westbury **(G-15889)**

MACHINERY: Brewery & Malting

Kings Cnty Brwers Cllctive LLC ....F.... 917 207-2739
Brooklyn **(G-2031)**
Singlecut Beersmiths LLC ....F.... 718 606-0788
Astoria **(G-440)**

MACHINERY: Bridge Or Gate, Hydraulic

Island Automated Gate Co LLC ....G.... 631 425-0196
Huntington Station **(G-6250)**

MACHINERY: Concrete Prdts

Nycon Diamond & Tools Corp ....G.... 855 937-6922
Bohemia **(G-1056)**

MACHINERY: Construction

AAAA York Inc ....F.... 718 784-6666
Long Island City **(G-7142)**
Air-Flo Mfg Co Inc ....D.... 607 733-8284
Elmira **(G-4340)**
Asp Blade Intrmdate Hldngs Inc ....A.... 212 476-8000
New York **(G-8650)**
BW Elliott Mfg Co LLC ....B.... 607 772-0404
Binghamton **(G-865)**
Ceno Technologies Inc ....G.... 716 885-5050
Buffalo **(G-2694)**
Construction Robotics LLC ....E.... 585 742-2004
Victor **(G-15400)**
Cooper Industries LLC ....F.... 315 477-7000
Syracuse **(G-14864)**

Diamond Coring & Cutting Inc ....G.... 718 381-4545
Maspeth **(G-7606)**
Dover Global Holdings Inc ....F.... 212 922-1640
New York **(G-9257)**
ET Oakes Corporation ....E.... 631 232-0002
Hauppauge **(G-5648)**
Line Ward Corporation ....G.... 716 675-7373
Buffalo **(G-2850)**
Northrock Industries Inc ....E.... 631 924-6130
Bohemia **(G-1055)**
Oswald Manufacturing Co Inc ....E.... 516 883-8850
Port Washington **(G-12910)**
Penn State Mtal Fbrctors No 2 ....E.... 718 786-8814
Brooklyn **(G-2253)**
Pier-Tech Inc ....E.... 516 442-5420
Oceanside **(G-12184)**
Precision Product Inc ....G.... 718 852-7127
Brooklyn **(G-2278)**
Rockland Manufacturing Co ....G.... 845 358-6000
West Nyack **(G-15832)**
Ziegler Truck & Diesl Repr Inc ....G.... 315 782-7278
Watertown **(G-15593)**

MACHINERY: Cryogenic, Industrial

Cryomech Inc ....D.... 315 455-2555
Syracuse **(G-14868)**
General Cryogenic Tech LLC ....F.... 516 334-8200
Westbury **(G-15890)**

MACHINERY: Custom

Accede Mold & Tool Co Inc ....D.... 585 254-6490
Rochester **(G-13199)**
Adaptive Mfg Tech Inc ....E.... 631 580-5400
Ronkonkoma **(G-13888)**
Aloi Solutions LLC ....E.... 585 292-0920
Rochester **(G-13223)**
American Linear Manufacturers ....F.... 516 333-1351
Westbury **(G-15867)**
Armstrong Mold Corporation ....D.... 315 437-1517
East Syracuse **(G-4197)**
Auburn Bearing & Mfg Inc ....D.... 315 986-7600
Macedon **(G-7460)**
Calvary Design Team Inc ....C.... 585 347-6127
Webster **(G-15632)**
Chocovision Corporation ....F.... 845 473-8003
Poughkeepsie **(G-12949)**
Converter Design Inc ....G.... 518 745-7138
Glens Falls **(G-5245)**
Danfoss Silicon Power LLC ....F.... 515 239-6376
Utica **(G-15252)**
Duetto Integrated Systems Inc ....F.... 631 851-0102
Islandia **(G-6331)**
Dynak Inc ....F.... 585 271-2255
Churchville **(G-3411)**
Endicott Precision Inc ....C.... 607 754-7076
Endicott **(G-4451)**
Finesse Creations Inc ....F.... 718 692-2100
Brooklyn **(G-1846)**
Hebeler Process Solutions LLC ....E.... 716 873-9300
Tonawanda **(G-15112)**
Interactive Instruments Inc ....G.... 518 347-0955
Scotia **(G-14332)**
International Climbing Mchs ....G.... 607 288-4001
Ithaca **(G-6388)**
Jet Sew Corporation ....F.... 315 896-2683
Barneveld **(G-592)**
Keller Technology Corporation ....C.... 716 693-3840
Tonawanda **(G-15117)**
Keyes Machine Works Inc ....G.... 585 426-5059
Gates **(G-5141)**
McGuigan Inc ....E.... 631 750-6222
Bohemia **(G-1045)**
Modern Packaging Inc ....D.... 631 595-2437
Deer Park **(G-3907)**
Ms Machining Inc ....G.... 607 723-1105
Binghamton **(G-900)**
Northern Tier Cnc Inc ....G.... 518 236-4702
Mooers Forks **(G-8080)**
R E F Precision Products ....F.... 631 242-4471
Deer Park **(G-3925)**
Rand Machine Products, Inc. ....C.... 716 665-5217
Falconer **(G-4552)**
Roboshop Inc ....G.... 315 437-6454
Syracuse **(G-14977)**
Tricon Machine LLC ....G.... 585 671-0679
Webster **(G-15657)**
Voss Manufacturing Inc ....D.... 716 731-5062
Sanborn **(G-14153)**
W H Jones & Son Inc ....F.... 716 875-8233
Kenmore **(G-6655)**

PRODUCT

W J Albro Machine Works Inc...............G... 631 345-0657
  Yaphank (G-16278)
Washburn Manufacturing Tech...........G... 607 387-3991
  Trumansburg (G-15202)
Wendt Corporation ....D... 716 391-1200
  Buffalo (G-3044)

MACHINERY: Drill Presses

Baldwin Machine Works Inc.............G... 631 842-9110
  Copiague (G-3649)

MACHINERY: Electronic Component Making

CBA Group LLC ....A... 607 779-7522
  Conklin (G-3622)
Designatronics Incorporated ....G... 516 328-3300
  Hicksville (G-5902)
James Morris ....E... 315 824-8519
  Hamilton (G-5527)
Sj Associates Inc ....E... 516 942-3232
  Jericho (G-6595)
Ui Acquisition Holding Co..............G... 607 779-7522
  Conklin (G-3631)
Ui Holding Company ....G... 607 779-7522
  Conklin (G-3632)
Universal Instruments Corp ....C... 800 842-9732
  Conklin (G-3633)

MACHINERY: Engraving

Bartizan Data Systems LLC ....E... 914 965-7977
  Yonkers (G-16290)

MACHINERY: Extruding

Kobe Steel USA Holdings Inc ....G... 212 751-9400
  New York (G-10120)

MACHINERY: Gear Cutting & Finishing

Gleason Works.........................A... 585 473-1000
  Rochester (G-13445)

MACHINERY: General, Industrial, NEC

Markpericom...........................G... 516 208-6824
  Oceanside (G-12182)

MACHINERY: Glassmaking

Emhart Glass Manufacturing Inc.......C... 607 734-3671
  Horseheads (G-6122)
Wilt Industries Inc ....G... 518 548-4961
  Lake Pleasant (G-6769)

MACHINERY: Grinding

Connex Grinding & Machining ....G... 315 946-4340
  Lyons (G-7448)
Stephen Bader Company Inc ....F... 518 753-4456
  Valley Falls (G-15331)

MACHINERY: Ice Cream

Pic Nic LLC ....G... 914 245-6500
  Amawalk (G-200)

MACHINERY: Ice Crushers

American Material Processing.........F... 315 318-0017
  Phoenix (G-12615)

MACHINERY: Ice Making

Hoshizaki Nrtheastern Dist Ctr ....G... 516 605-1411
  Plainview (G-12687)
Mgr Equipment Corp ....E... 516 239-3030
  Inwood (G-6298)

MACHINERY: Industrial, NEC

Exigo Precision Inc ....G... 585 254-5818
  Rochester (G-13406)
Fabtechny LLC ....F... 845 338-2000
  Kingston (G-6691)
Northeast Hardware Specialties ....F... 516 487-6868
  Mineola (G-7992)
Semi-Linear Inc ....G... 212 243-2108
  New York (G-11189)

MACHINERY: Jewelers

Arbe Machinery Inc...................F... 631 756-2477
  Farmingdale (G-4586)

MACHINERY: Marking, Metalworking

Autostat Corporation ....F... 516 379-9447
  Roosevelt (G-14030)

MACHINERY: Metalworking

Advanced Machine Design Co Inc ......E... 716 826-2000
  Buffalo (G-2624)
Bartell Machinery Systems LLC ....C... 315 336-7600
  Rome (G-13843)
Charles A Rogers Entps Inc ....E... 585 924-6400
  Victor (G-15397)
Duall Finishing Inc ....G... 716 827-1707
  Buffalo (G-2731)
Esm II Inc ....E... 716 446-8888
  Amherst (G-223)
Hardinge Inc ....B... 607 734-2281
  Elmira (G-4355)
Hje Company Inc ....G... 518 792-8733
  Queensbury (G-13043)
Mono-Systems Inc ....E... 716 821-1344
  Buffalo (G-2871)
Mtwli Precision Corp ....G... 631 244-3767
  Bohemia (G-1049)
Munson Machinery Company Inc........E... 315 797-0090
  Utica (G-15286)
Pems Tool & Machine Inc ....E... 315 823-3595
  Little Falls (G-6990)
Precision Systems Mfg Inc ....E... 315 451-3480
  Liverpool (G-7035)
Reelex Packaging Solutions Inc........E... 845 878-7878
  Patterson (G-12519)
Riverside Machinery Company ....E... 718 492-7400
  Brooklyn (G-2349)
S & S Machinery Corp ....D... 718 492-7400
  Brooklyn (G-2370)
S & S Machinery Corp ....E... 718 492-7400
  Brooklyn (G-2371)
Serge Duct Designs Inc ....E... 718 783-7799
  Brooklyn (G-2396)
Strippit Inc ....C... 716 542-4511
  Akron (G-22)
Voss Manufacturing Inc ....D... 716 731-5062
  Sanborn (G-14153)
Xto Incorporated ....D... 315 451-7807
  Liverpool (G-7050)

MACHINERY: Milling

Five Star Tool Co Inc ....E... 585 328-9580
  Rochester (G-13412)
Omc2 LLC ....G... 415 580-0262
  Peekskill (G-12554)

MACHINERY: Mining

Flatcut LLC ....G... 212 542-5732
  Brooklyn (G-1850)
Universal Metal Fabricators ....F... 845 331-8248
  Kingston (G-6719)

MACHINERY: Optical Lens

Optipro Systems LLC ....D... 585 265-0160
  Ontario (G-12296)
Universal Thin Film Lab Corp ....G... 845 562-0601
  Newburgh (G-11891)

MACHINERY: Ozone

Queenaire Technologies Inc ....G... 315 393-5454
  Ogdensburg (G-12210)

MACHINERY: Packaging

A & G Heat Sealing ....G... 631 724-7764
  Smithtown (G-14472)
All Packaging McHy & Sups Corp ....F... 631 588-7310
  Ronkonkoma (G-13897)
Automecha International Ltd ....E... 607 843-2235
  Oxford (G-12441)
Crandall Filling Machinery Inc..........G... 716 897-3486
  Buffalo (G-2712)
Dover Global Holdings Inc ....F... 212 922-1640
  New York (G-9257)
Elmar Industries Inc ....D... 716 681-5650
  Depew (G-3980)
Global Packaging Services LLC ....G... 646 648-0355
  Glen Head (G-5206)
Haines Equipment Inc ....E... 607 566-8531
  Avoca (G-510)

MACHINERY: Marking, Metalworking

Kabar Manufacturing Corp............E... 631 694-6857
  Farmingdale (G-4660)
Millwood Inc ....F... 518 233-1475
  Waterford (G-15539)
Modern Packaging Inc ....D... 631 595-2437
  Deer Park (G-3907)
National Equipment Corporation........E... 718 585-0200
  Bronx (G-1321)
Orics Industries Inc ....E... 718 461-8613
  Farmingdale (G-4697)
Overhead Door Corporation ....D... 518 828-7652
  Hudson (G-6173)
Pacemaker Packaging Corp...........E... 718 458-1188
  Woodside (G-16218)
Packaging Dynamics Ltd ....F... 631 563-4499
  Bohemia (G-1058)
Rfb Associates Inc ....F... 518 271-0551
  Fort Edward (G-4943)
Rota Pack Inc ....F... 631 274-1037
  Farmingdale (G-4727)
Save O Seal Corporation Inc...........G... 914 592-3031
  Elmsford (G-4427)
Utleys Incorporated ....E... 718 956-1661
  Woodside (G-16232)
Volckening Inc ....E... 718 748-0294
  Brooklyn (G-2568)

MACHINERY: Paper Industry Miscellaneous

Automecha International Ltd ....E... 607 843-2235
  Oxford (G-12441)
Cyclotherm of Watertown Inc ....E... 315 782-1100
  Watertown (G-15568)
GL&v USA Inc ....C... 518 747-2444
  Hudson Falls (G-6188)
Haanen Packard Machinery Inc ....G... 518 747-2330
  Hudson Falls (G-6190)
Jacob Inc ....E... 646 450-3067
  Brooklyn (G-1985)
Johnston Dandy Company ....G... 315 455-5773
  Syracuse (G-14919)
Kadant Inc ....F... 518 793-8801
  Glens Falls (G-5253)
Lake Image Systems Inc ....F... 585 321-3630
  Henrietta (G-5858)
Sinclair International Company ....D... 518 798-2361
  Queensbury (G-13057)
Verso Corporation....................B... 212 599-2700
  New York (G-11665)

MACHINERY: Pharmaciutical

George Ponte Inc ....G... 914 243-4202
  Jefferson Valley (G-6567)
Gordon S Anderson Mfg Co ....G... 845 677-3304
  Millbrook (G-7942)
Innovation Associates Inc.............C... 607 798-9376
  Johnson City (G-6602)
Michael Benalt Inc....................E... 845 628-1008
  Mahopac (G-7474)

MACHINERY: Photographic Reproduction

Qls Solutions Group Inc ....E... 716 852-2203
  Buffalo (G-2939)
Xerox Corporation....................A... 585 422-4564
  Webster (G-15663)

MACHINERY: Plastic Working

Addex Inc.............................G... 781 344-5800
  Newark (G-11837)
Haanen Packard Machinery Inc ....G... 518 747-2330
  Hudson Falls (G-6190)
Illinois Tool Works Inc ....C... 716 681-8222
  Lancaster (G-6811)
Kabar Manufacturing Corp.............E... 631 694-1036
  Farmingdale (G-4661)
Kabar Manufacturing Corp.............E... 631 694-6857
  Farmingdale (G-4660)
Pearl Technologies Inc.................E... 315 365-3742
  Savannah (G-14220)
Quality Strapping Inc ....D... 718 418-1111
  Brooklyn (G-2312)
Ultrepet LLC ....D... 781 275-6400
  Albany (G-140)
Valplast International Corp ....F... 516 442-3923
  Westbury (G-15937)

MACHINERY: Printing Presses

Advance Grafix Equipment Inc.........G... 917 202-4593
  Wyandanch (G-16242)

Halm Instrument Co Inc ....D 516 676-6700
  Glen Head (G-5207)

MACHINERY: Recycling

Adirondack Plas & Recycl Inc ....E 518 746-9212
  Argyle (G-391)
Andela Tool & Machine Inc ....G 315 858-0055
  Richfield Springs (G-13105)
Ben Weitsman of Albany LLC ....E 518 462-4444
  Albany (G-46)
Crumbrubber Technology Inc ....F 718 468-3988
  Hollis (G-6042)

MACHINERY: Riveting

High Speed Hammer Company Inc ......F 585 266-4287
  Rochester (G-13468)

MACHINERY: Road Construction & Maintenance

City of Jamestown ....D 716 483-7545
  Jamestown (G-6501)
Professional Pavers Corp ....E 718 784-7853
  Rego Park (G-13081)

MACHINERY: Rubber Working

Curtin-Hebert Co Inc ....F 518 725-7157
  Gloversville (G-5282)

MACHINERY: Screening Eqpt, Electric

Innovation In Motion Inc ....G 407 878-7561
  Long Beach (G-7137)

MACHINERY: Semiconductor Manufacturing

Cvd Equipment Corporation ....F 631 582-4365
  Central Islip (G-3272)
Globalfoundries US Inc ....E 512 457-3900
  Hopewell Junction (G-6095)
SPX Corporation ....E 585 436-5550
  Rochester (G-13740)
Veeco Instruments Inc ....B 516 677-0200
  Plainview (G-12725)

MACHINERY: Separation Eqpt, Magnetic

Innovative Cleaning Solutions ....G 716 731-4408
  Sanborn (G-14143)

MACHINERY: Sheet Metal Working

Factory East ....E 718 280-1558
  Brooklyn (G-1828)
U S Air Tool Co Inc ....E 631 471-3300
  Ronkonkoma (G-14019)

MACHINERY: Specialty

Force Dynamics Inc ....F 607 546-5023
  Trumansburg (G-15201)

MACHINERY: Textile

Aglika Trade LLC ....F 727 424-1944
  Middle Village (G-7877)
Corbertex LLC ....G 212 971-0008
  New York (G-9101)
Eastman Machine Company ....C 716 856-2200
  Buffalo (G-2738)
Herr Manufacturing Co Inc ....E 716 754-4341
  Tonawanda (G-15113)
Mohawk Valley Knt McHy Co Inc ....F 315 736-3038
  New York Mills (G-11835)
Rfb Associates Inc ....F 518 271-0551
  Fort Edward (G-4943)
Schwabel Fabricating Co Inc ....E 716 876-2086
  Tonawanda (G-15138)
Simtec Industries Corporation ....G 631 293-0080
  Farmingdale (G-4732)

MACHINERY: Tire Shredding

Northeast Data ....G 845 331-5554
  Kingston (G-6705)
Shred Center ....G 716 664-3052
  Jamestown (G-6540)

MACHINERY: Wire Drawing

Carpenter Manufacturing Co ....E 315 682-9176
  Manlius (G-7544)

MGS Manufacturing Inc ....E 315 337-3350
  Rome (G-13856)

MACHINERY: Woodworking

James L Taylor Mfg Co ....E 845 452-3780
  Poughkeepsie (G-12964)
James L Taylor Mfg Co ....E 845 452-3780
  Poughkeepsie (G-12965)
Merritt Machinery LLC ....E 716 434-5558
  Lockport (G-7090)
Oneida Air Systems Inc ....E 315 476-5151
  Syracuse (G-14956)
Wood-Mizer Holdings Inc ....G 315 564-5722
  Hannibal (G-5543)

MACHINES: Forming, Sheet Metal

Cetek Inc ....E 845 452-3510
  Poughkeepsie (G-12948)
Product Integration & Mfg Inc ....E 585 436-6260
  Rochester (G-13649)

MACHINISTS' TOOLS: Measuring, Precision

Mausner Equipment Co Inc ....C 631 689-7358
  Setauket (G-14380)

MACHINISTS' TOOLS: Precision

Drt Aerospace LLC ....G 585 247-5940
  Rochester (G-13357)
Egli Machine Company Inc ....E 607 563-3663
  Sidney (G-14434)
Hubbard Tool and Die Corp ....E 315 337-7840
  Rome (G-13851)
Jasco Tools LLC ....D 585 254-7000
  Rochester (G-13490)
Melland Gear Instr of Huppauge ....E 631 234-0100
  Hauppauge (G-5712)
Miller Metal Fabricating Inc ....E 585 359-3400
  Rochester (G-13549)
Novatech Inc ....E 716 892-6682
  Cheektowaga (G-3358)
Park Enterprises Rochester Inc ....C 585 546-4200
  Rochester (G-13611)
Ppi Corp ....D 585 243-0300
  Rochester (G-13633)
Precision Grinding & Mfg Corp ....C 585 458-4300
  Rochester (G-13636)
Ptc Precision LLC ....E 607 748-8294
  Endwell (G-4483)
Streamline Precision Inc ....G 585 421-9050
  Fairport (G-4524)
Streamline Precision Inc ....G 585 421-9050
  Fairport (G-4525)
Townline Machine Co Inc ....E 315 462-3413
  Clifton Springs (G-3481)
Trimaster/Htech Holding LLC ....G 212 257-6772
  New York (G-11545)
Xactra Technologies Inc ....D 585 426-2030
  Rochester (G-13810)

MAGAZINES, WHOLESALE

Economist Newspaper NA Inc ....E 212 554-0676
  New York (G-9319)
Global Finance Media Inc ....F 212 447-7900
  New York (G-9626)

MAGNETIC INK & OPTICAL SCANNING EQPT

Peoples Choice M R I ....F 716 681-7377
  Buffalo (G-2912)
Symbol Technologies LLC ....F 631 218-3907
  Holbrook (G-6025)

MAGNETIC RESONANCE IMAGING DEVICES: Nonmedical

Finger Lakes Radiology LLC ....G 315 787-5399
  Geneva (G-5154)
Islandia Mri Associates PC ....F 631 234-2828
  Central Islip (G-3280)

MAGNETIC TAPE, AUDIO: Prerecorded

Roadrunner Records Inc ....E 212 274-7500
  New York (G-11058)
Universal Mus Group Hldngs Inc ....E 212 333-8000
  New York (G-11608)

MAGNETOHYDRODYNAMIC DEVICES OR MHD

Passive-Plus Inc ....F 631 425-0938
  Huntington (G-6216)

MAGNETS: Ceramic

Arnold Magnetic Tech Corp ....C 585 385-9010
  Rochester (G-13246)
Eneflux Armtek Magnetics Inc ....G 516 576-3434
  Medford (G-7707)
Hitachi Metals America Ltd ....E 914 694-9200
  Purchase (G-13005)

MAGNETS: Permanent

Arnold Magnetic Tech Corp ....C 585 385-9010
  Rochester (G-13246)
Carpentier Industries LLC ....F 585 385-5550
  East Rochester (G-4160)
Magnaworks Technology Inc ....G 631 218-3431
  Bohemia (G-1042)
Magnetic Aids Inc ....G 845 863-1400
  Marlboro (G-7580)
Polymag Inc ....E 631 286-4111
  Bellport (G-807)
Precision Magnetics LLC ....E 585 385-9010
  Rochester (G-13639)
Truebite Inc ....E 607 785-7664
  Vestal (G-15386)

MAIL-ORDER BOOK CLUBS

Global Video LLC ....D 516 222-2600
  Woodbury (G-16172)
Station Hill of Barrytown 845 758-5293
  Barrytown (G-597)

MAIL-ORDER HOUSE, NEC

American Country Quilts & Lin ....G 631 283-5466
  Southampton (G-14526)
Chocolat Moderne LLC 212 229-4797
  New York (G-8996)
Collinite Corporation ....G 315 732-2282
  Utica (G-15245)
Hamtronics Inc ....G 585 392-9430
  Rochester (G-13457)
Hubray Inc ....F 800 645-2855
  North Baldwin (G-12006)
Quaker Boy Inc ....E 716 662-3979
  Springville (G-14596)
TRM Linen Inc ....G 718 686-6075
  Brooklyn (G-2524)

MAIL-ORDER HOUSES: Book & Record Clubs

Oxford University Press LLC ....B 212 726-6000
  New York (G-10727)
Oxford University Press LLC ....G 212 726-6000
  New York (G-10728)

MAIL-ORDER HOUSES: Books, Exc Book Clubs

Anthroposophic Press Inc ....G 518 851-2054
  Clifton Park (G-3461)
Looseleaf Law Publications Inc ....F 718 359-5559
  Flushing (G-4873)
Rizzoli Intl Publications Inc ....E 212 387-3400
  New York (G-11051)
Syracuse Cultural Workers Prj 315 474-1132
  Syracuse (G-15006)
Trusted Media Brands Inc ....A 914 238-1000
  New York (G-11553)
Trusted Media Brands Inc ....F 914 244-5244
  White Plains (G-16067)

MAIL-ORDER HOUSES: Cards

Color Card LLC ....F 631 232-1300
  Central Islip (G-3269)

MAIL-ORDER HOUSES: Clothing, Exc Women's

Cockpit Usa Inc ....F 212 575-1616
  New York (G-9046)

MAIL-ORDER HOUSES: Computer Eqpt & Electronics

Gim Electronics Corp ....F 516 942-3382
  Hicksville *(G-5911)*

MAIL-ORDER HOUSES: Cosmetics & Perfumes

Borghese Inc ....E 212 659-5318
  New York *(G-8837)*

MAIL-ORDER HOUSES: Fitness & Sporting Goods

KD Dids Inc ....E 718 402-2012
  Bronx *(G-1289)*

MAIL-ORDER HOUSES: Food

Sbk Preserves Inc ....E 800 773-7378
  Bronx *(G-1361)*

MAIL-ORDER HOUSES: Furniture & Furnishings

Charles P Rogers Brass Beds ....F 212 675-4400
  New York *(G-8975)*
Wink Inc ....E 212 389-1382
  New York *(G-11767)*

MAIL-ORDER HOUSES: Gift Items

Jomar Industries Inc ....E 845 357-5773
  Airmont *(G-13)*

MAIL-ORDER HOUSES: Jewelry

Indonesian Imports Inc ....D 855 725-5656
  New York *(G-9882)*

MAIL-ORDER HOUSES: Magazines

Dlc Comprehensive Medical PC ....F 718 857-1200
  Brooklyn *(G-1752)*

MAILING LIST: Brokers

Luria Communications Inc ....G 631 329-4922
  East Hampton *(G-4125)*

MAILING LIST: Compilers

Select Information Exchange ....F 212 496-6435
  New York *(G-11186)*

MAILING SVCS, NEC

Data Palette Info Svcs LLC ....D 718 433-1060
  Port Washington *(G-12871)*
Dispatch Graphics Inc ....F 212 307-5943
  New York *(G-9236)*
DP Murphy Co Inc ....D 631 673-9400
  Deer Park *(G-3865)*
Five Star Prtg & Mailing Svcs ....F 212 929-0300
  New York *(G-9508)*
Hugh F McPherson Inc ....G 716 668-6107
  Cheektowaga *(G-3354)*
PDQ Shipping Services ....G 845 255-5500
  New Paltz *(G-8310)*
Westchester Mailing Service ....E 914 948-1116
  White Plains *(G-16073)*

MANAGEMENT CONSULTING SVCS: Automation & Robotics

Cs Automation Inc ....F 315 524-5123
  Ontario *(G-12286)*
Javlyn Process Systems LLC ....E 585 424-5580
  Rochester *(G-13491)*

MANAGEMENT CONSULTING SVCS: Business

Hargrave Development ....F 716 877-7880
  Kenmore *(G-6650)*
Security Letter ....G 212 348-1553
  New York *(G-11177)*
Universal Mus Group Hldngs Inc ....E 212 333-8000
  New York *(G-11608)*
Yale Robbins Inc ....D 212 683-5700
  New York *(G-11805)*

MANAGEMENT CONSULTING SVCS: Construction Project

Darrell Mitchell ....G 646 659-7075
  Arverne *(G-407)*

MANAGEMENT CONSULTING SVCS: Distribution Channels

Standard Analytics Io Inc ....G 917 882-5422
  New York *(G-11344)*

MANAGEMENT CONSULTING SVCS: Food & Beverage

Marley Spoon Inc ....C 866 228-4513
  New York *(G-10372)*
SPX Flow Us LLC ....A 716 692-3000
  Getzville *(G-5182)*

MANAGEMENT CONSULTING SVCS: Industrial

GE Global Research ....A 518 387-5000
  Niskayuna *(G-11995)*

MANAGEMENT CONSULTING SVCS: Industrial & Labor

Terahertz Technologies Inc ....G 315 736-3642
  Oriskany *(G-12398)*

MANAGEMENT CONSULTING SVCS: Industry Specialist

ER Butler & Co Inc ....E 212 925-3565
  New York *(G-9392)*

MANAGEMENT CONSULTING SVCS: New Products & Svcs

L D Weiss Inc ....G 212 697-3023
  New York *(G-10150)*

MANAGEMENT CONSULTING SVCS: Real Estate

SC Building Solutions LLC ....D 800 564-1152
  New York *(G-11145)*

MANAGEMENT CONSULTING SVCS: Training & Development

Calia Technical Inc ....E 718 447-3928
  Staten Island *(G-14636)*

MANAGEMENT SERVICES

A & Mt Realty Group LLC ....F 718 974-5871
  Brooklyn *(G-1429)*
Arnan Development Corp ....D 607 432-8391
  Oneonta *(G-12257)*
Central Coca-Cola Btlg Co Inc ....B 914 789-1100
  Elmsford *(G-4399)*
Fonar Corporation ....C 631 694-2929
  Melville *(G-7784)*
International Center For Postg ....G 607 257-5860
  Ithaca *(G-6387)*
Quoizel Inc ....E 631 436-4402
  Hauppauge *(G-5752)*

MANAGEMENT SVCS: Administrative

Supermedia LLC ....D 212 513-9700
  New York *(G-11397)*
Tdk USA Corporation ....D 516 535-2600
  Uniondale *(G-15233)*

MANAGEMENT SVCS: Circuit, Motion Picture Theaters

Dolomite Products Company Inc ....E 315 524-1998
  Rochester *(G-13354)*

MANAGEMENT SVCS: Construction

Darrell Mitchell ....G 646 659-7075
  Arverne *(G-407)*
Sg Blocks Inc ....F 646 240-4235
  Brooklyn *(G-2399)*

MANAGEMENT SVCS: Restaurant

D R M Management Inc ....E 716 668-0333
  Depew *(G-3978)*

MANDRELS

Carl Safina Center Inc ....G 808 888-9440
  Setauket *(G-14378)*

MANHOLES COVERS: Concrete

Jefferson Concrete Corp ....D 315 788-4171
  Watertown *(G-15574)*

MANICURE PREPARATIONS

Angel Tips Nail Salon ....G 718 225-8300
  Little Neck *(G-6996)*
Essie Cosmetics Ltd ....D 212 818-1500
  New York *(G-9405)*

MANIFOLDS: Pipe, Fabricated From Purchased Pipe

M Manastrip-M Corporation ....G 518 664-2089
  Clifton Park *(G-3467)*

MANNEQUINS

Adel Rootstein (usa) Inc ....E 718 499-5650
  Brooklyn *(G-1460)*
Genesis Mannequins USA II Inc ....G 212 505-6600
  New York *(G-9592)*
Lifestyle-Trimco ....E 718 257-9101
  Brooklyn *(G-2069)*
Siegel & Stockman Inc ....G 212 633-1508
  New York *(G-11224)*

MANUFACTURING INDUSTRIES, NEC

A & W Metal Works Inc ....F 845 352-2346
  Garnerville *(G-5133)*
A Fire Inc ....G 631 897-9449
  Ronkonkoma *(G-13883)*
A&M Model Makers LLC ....G 626 813-9661
  Macedon *(G-7457)*
Accessible Bath Tech LLC ....F 518 937-1518
  Albany *(G-26)*
AFP Manufacturing Corp ....E 516 466-6464
  Great Neck *(G-5360)*
Anu Industries LLC ....G 201 735-7475
  Brooklyn *(G-1514)*
Avoomo Power LLC ....F 718 344-0404
  Brooklyn *(G-1553)*
B F G Elcpltg and Mfg Co ....E 716 362-0888
  Blasdell *(G-917)*
Bee Green Industries Inc ....G 516 334-3525
  Carle Place *(G-3171)*
Bushwick Bottling LLC ....F 929 666-3618
  Brooklyn *(G-1630)*
Cemecon Inc ....E 607 562-2363
  Horseheads *(G-6118)*
Ceylan & Co LLC ....G 646 858-3022
  New York *(G-8963)*
Consolidated Spring LLC ....F 845 391-8855
  Newburgh *(G-11862)*
Dolmen ....F 912 596-1537
  Conklin *(G-3623)*
Dyco Manufacturing LLC ....D 607 324-2030
  Hornell *(G-6105)*
E-Z Global Wholesale Inc ....G 888 769-7888
  Brooklyn *(G-1774)*
Energy Ahead Inc ....G 718 813-7338
  Brooklyn *(G-1804)*
Essex Industries ....G 518 942-6671
  Mineville *(G-8004)*
Everstone Industries LLC ....E 347 777-8150
  New York *(G-9429)*
Fun Industries of NY ....F 631 845-3805
  Farmingdale *(G-4634)*
Hudson Eastern Industries Inc ....G 917 295-5818
  Whitestone *(G-16094)*
Ilc Industries Inc ....E 631 567-5600
  Bohemia *(G-1022)*
Impressart ....F 631 940-9530
  Edgewood *(G-4271)*
John Prior ....G 516 520-9801
  East Meadow *(G-4138)*
Just Right Carbines LLC ....G 585 261-5331
  Canandaigua *(G-3135)*
K Dymond Industries Inc ....G 631 828-0826
  Medford *(G-7715)*

Kafko (us) Corp ....G...... 877 721-7665
  Latham (G-6861)
Kaylon Industries LLC ....G...... 315 303-2119
  Baldwinsville (G-550)
Lois Kitchen LLC ....G...... 216 308-9335
  New York (G-10244)
Madison Mfg & Mch Inc ....G...... 315 922-4476
  Erieville (G-4484)
Mitco Manufacturing ....G...... 516 745-9236
  Garden City (G-5110)
Ogd V-Hvac Inc ....E...... 315 858-1002
  Van Hornesville (G-15363)
Omicron Technologies Inc ....E...... 631 434-7697
  Holbrook (G-6015)
Oriskany Manufacturing LLC ....F...... 315 732-4962
  Yorkville (G-16377)
Oso Industries Inc ....G...... 917 709-2050
  Brooklyn (G-2237)
Performance Precision Mfg LLC ....G...... 518 993-3033
  Fort Plain (G-4947)
Quest Manufacturing Inc ....E...... 716 312-8000
  Hamburg (G-5519)
Rockwell Video Solutions LLC ....F...... 631 745-0582
  Southampton (G-14536)
Rutcarele Inc ....G...... 347 830-5353
  Corona (G-3748)
Select Industries New York Inc ....F...... 800 723-5333
  New York (G-11185)
Shenzhen Xnhdingsheng Tech Ltd ......E...... 510 506-5753
  Flushing (G-4892)
Sonaal Industries Inc ....G...... 718 383-3860
  Brooklyn (G-2441)
Specialists Ltd ....F...... 212 941-7696
  Ridgewood (G-13161)
Stasi Industries Inc ....G...... 516 334-2742
  Old Bethpage (G-12220)
Talisman Industries LLC ....G...... 908 433-7116
  New York (G-11426)
Tii Industries Inc ....F...... 631 789-5000
  Copiague (G-3683)
Tiki Industries Inc ....G...... 516 779-3629
  Riverhead (G-13190)
Topoo Industries Incorporated ....G...... 718 331-3755
  Brooklyn (G-2511)
Unistel LLC ....D...... 585 341-4600
  Webster (G-15660)
Unlimited Industries Inc ....G...... 631 665-5800
  Deer Park (G-3947)
Water Splash Inc ....G...... 800 936-3430
  Champlain (G-3321)
Woodfalls Industries ....F...... 518 236-7201
  Plattsburgh (G-12792)
Zmz Mfg Inc ....G...... 518 234-4336
  Warnerville (G-15502)

MAPS

Mapeasy Inc ....F...... 631 537-6213
  Wainscott (G-15455)

MARBLE BOARD

Amendola MBL & Stone Ctr Inc ....D...... 914 997-7968
  White Plains (G-15972)

MARBLE, BUILDING: Cut & Shaped

Dicamillo Marble and Granite ....E...... 845 878-0078
  Patterson (G-12515)
GDi Custom Marble & Gran Inc ....F...... 718 996-9100
  Brooklyn (G-1881)
International Stone Accessrs ....G...... 718 522-5399
  Brooklyn (G-1966)
Monroe Industries Inc ....G...... 585 226-8230
  Avon (G-514)
Unique MBL Gran Orgnztion Corp ....G...... 718 482-0440
  Long Island City (G-7387)
White Plains Marble Inc ....G...... 914 347-6000
  Elmsford (G-4441)

MARBLE: Crushed & Broken

Sparclean MBL Refinishing Inc ....G...... 718 445-2351
  Ridgewood (G-13160)

MARINAS

Meeco Sullivan LLC ....C...... 800 232-3625
  Warwick (G-15520)

MARINE HARDWARE

Bfg Marine Inc ....F...... 631 586-5500
  Bay Shore (G-656)
Dover Marine Mfg & Sup Co Inc ....G...... 631 667-4300
  Deer Park (G-3864)
Rollson Inc ....E...... 631 423-9578
  Huntington (G-6221)

MARINE RELATED EQPT

Kyntec Corporation ....G...... 716 810-6956
  Buffalo (G-2840)

MARINE SVC STATIONS

Accurate Marine Specialties ....G...... 631 589-5502
  Bohemia (G-963)

MARKERS

Mark Dri Products Inc ....C...... 516 484-6200
  Bethpage (G-838)

MARKETS: Meat & fish

Schaller Manufacturing Corp ....D...... 718 721-5480
  New York (G-11149)

MARKING DEVICES

Bianca Group Ltd ....G...... 212 768-3011
  New York (G-8779)
C M E Corp ....F...... 315 451-7101
  Syracuse (G-14839)
East Coast Thermographers Inc ....E...... 718 321-3211
  College Point (G-3541)
Hampton Art LLC ....E...... 631 924-1335
  Medford (G-7710)
Hodgins Engraving Co Inc ....D...... 585 343-4444
  Batavia (G-618)
Kelly Foundry & Machine Co ....E...... 315 732-8313
  Utica (G-15279)
Krengel Manufacturing Co Inc ....F...... 212 227-1901
  Fulton (G-5069)
Samoss Group Ltd ....E...... 212 239-6677
  New York (G-11125)
Tech Products Inc ....E...... 718 442-4900
  Staten Island (G-14721)
Ul Corp ....G...... 201 203-4453
  Bayside (G-743)
United Sttes Brnze Sign of Fla ....E...... 516 352-5155
  New Hyde Park (G-8300)

MARKING DEVICES: Date Stamps, Hand, Rubber Or Metal

Koehlr-Gibson Mkg Graphics Inc ....E...... 716 838-5960
  Buffalo (G-2838)
Long Island Stamp & Seal Co ....F...... 718 628-8550
  Ridgewood (G-13150)

MARKING DEVICES: Embossing Seals & Hand Stamps

A & M Steel Stamps Inc ....G...... 516 741-6223
  Mineola (G-7954)
Cannizzaro Seal & Engraving Co ....G...... 718 513-6125
  Brooklyn (G-1644)
Joseph Treu Successors Inc ....G...... 212 691-7026
  New York (G-10028)
New York Marking Devices Corp ....G...... 585 454-5188
  Rochester (G-13572)
New York Marking Devices Corp ....F...... 315 463-8641
  Syracuse (G-14951)
Rubber Stamp X Press ....G...... 631 423-1322
  Huntington Station (G-6258)

MARKING DEVICES: Embossing Seals, Corporate & Official

Sales Tax Asset Rceivable Corp ....G...... 212 788-5874
  New York (G-11119)

MARKING DEVICES: Figures, Metal

Thermopatch Corporation ....D...... 315 446-8110
  Syracuse (G-15012)

MARKING DEVICES: Letters, Metal

I & I Systems ....G...... 845 753-9126
  Tuxedo Park (G-15216)

MARKING DEVICES: Numbering Machines

National Time Recording Eqp Co ....F...... 212 227-3310
  New York (G-10547)

MARKING DEVICES: Pads, Inking & Stamping

Dab-O-Matic Corp ....D...... 914 699-7070
  Mount Vernon (G-8137)
Specialty Ink Co Inc ....F...... 631 586-3666
  Blue Point (G-957)
United Silicone Inc ....D...... 716 681-8222
  Lancaster (G-6837)

MARKING DEVICES: Postmark Stamps, Hand, Rubber Or Metal

Rubber Stamps Inc ....E...... 212 675-1180
  Mineola (G-7998)

MARKING DEVICES: Screens, Textile Printing

Michael Todd Stevens ....G...... 585 436-9957
  Rochester (G-13544)
Ward Sales Co Inc ....G...... 315 476-5276
  Syracuse (G-15023)

MASKS: Gas

Go Blue Technologies Ltd ....G...... 631 404-6285
  North Babylon (G-12001)

MASQUERADE OR THEATRICAL COSTUMES STORES

D-C Theatricks ....G...... 716 847-0180
  Buffalo (G-2719)
Moresca Clothing and Costume ....F...... 845 331-6012
  Ulster Park (G-15219)

MASTIC ROOFING COMPOSITION

Savage & Son Installations LLC ....E...... 585 342-7533
  Rochester (G-13716)

MATERIALS HANDLING EQPT WHOLESALERS

Four-Way Pallet Corp ....E...... 631 351-3401
  Huntington Station (G-6247)
George Ponte Inc ....G...... 914 243-4202
  Jefferson Valley (G-6567)
Koke Inc ....E...... 800 535-5303
  Queensbury (G-13047)
Nerak Systems Inc ....F...... 914 763-8259
  Fishkill (G-4803)
Overhead Door Corporation ....D...... 518 828-7652
  Hudson (G-6173)
Raymond Sales Corporation ....G...... 607 656-2311
  Greene (G-5449)
Tri-Boro Shelving Inc ....F...... 718 782-8527
  Ridgewood (G-13165)

MATS & MATTING, MADE FROM PURCHASED WIRE

Brook North Farms Inc ....F...... 315 834-9390
  Auburn (G-469)

MATS OR MATTING, NEC: Rubber

Seaway Mats Inc ....G...... 518 483-2560
  Malone (G-7490)

MATS, MATTING & PADS: Auto, Floor, Exc Rubber Or Plastic

Auto-Mat Company Inc ....E...... 516 938-7373
  Hicksville (G-5886)

MATS, MATTING & PADS: Nonwoven

Daniels Bath & Beyond ....G...... 718 765-1915
  Brooklyn (G-1724)
North Sunshine LLC ....F...... 307 027-1634
  Valley Cottage (G-15320)

MATS: Blasting, Rope

T M International LLC ....G....... 718 842-0949
Bronx **(G-1377)**

MATTRESS STORES

Otis Bedding Mfg Co Inc ....E....... 716 825-2599
Buffalo **(G-2900)**

MEAT & FISH MARKETS: Fish

Sea Breeze Fish & Seafood of S...........F....... 718 984-0447
Staten Island **(G-14707)**

MEAT & MEAT PRDTS WHOLESALERS

Brooklyn Bangers LLC ....F....... 718 875-3535
Brooklyn **(G-1611)**
Elmgang Enterprises I Inc ....F....... 212 868-4142
New York **(G-9350)**
Tri-Town Packing Corp ....F....... 315 389-5101
Brasher Falls **(G-1113)**

MEAT CUTTING & PACKING

A To Z Kosher Meat Products Co ....E....... 718 384-7400
Brooklyn **(G-1436)**
Caribbean Foods Delight Inc ....D....... 845 398-3000
Tappan **(G-15034)**
Chefs Delight Packing Co ....F....... 718 388-8581
Brooklyn **(G-1662)**
Crescent Duck Farm Inc ....E....... 631 722-8700
Aquebogue **(G-365)**
Domestic Casing Co ....G....... 718 522-1902
Brooklyn **(G-1756)**
DRG New York Holdings Corp ....D....... 914 668-9000
Mount Vernon **(G-8138)**
Frank Wardynski & Sons Inc ....E....... 716 854-6083
Buffalo **(G-2759)**
Gold Medal Packing Inc ....D....... 315 337-1911
Oriskany **(G-12391)**
Ives Farm Market ....G....... 315 592-4880
Fulton **(G-5065)**
Kamerys Wholesale Meats Inc ....G....... 716 372-6756
Olean **(G-12237)**
Orleans Custom Packing Inc ....G....... 585 314-8227
Holley **(G-6036)**
Side Hill Farmers Coop Inc ....G....... 315 697-9862
Canastota **(G-3157)**
The Smoke House of Catskills...............G....... 845 246-8767
Saugerties **(G-14215)**
Tri-Town Packing Corp ....F....... 315 389-5101
Brasher Falls **(G-1113)**
Tyson Deli Inc ....B....... 716 566-3189
Buffalo **(G-3024)**
We Work ....G....... 877 673-6628
New York **(G-11733)**

MEAT MARKETS

Ives Farm Market ....G....... 315 592-4880
Fulton **(G-5065)**
Lancaster Quality Pork Inc ....F....... 718 439-8822
Brooklyn **(G-2046)**
Mineo & Sapio Meats Inc ....G....... 716 884-2398
Buffalo **(G-2866)**
The Smoke House of Catskills...............G....... 845 246-8767
Saugerties **(G-14215)**
Wilson Beef Farms LLC...............F....... 607 545-8308
Canaseraga **(G-3148)**

MEAT PRDTS: Boneless Meat, From Purchased Meat

Tower Isles Frozen Foods Ltd ....D....... 718 495-2626
Brooklyn **(G-2515)**

MEAT PRDTS: Dried Beef, From Purchased Meat

Patla Enterprises Inc ....F....... 315 367-0237
Sherrill **(G-14405)**

MEAT PRDTS: Frankfurters, From Purchased Meat

Marathon Enterprises Inc ....D....... 718 665-2560
Bronx **(G-1306)**
White Eagle Packing Co Inc...............F....... 518 374-4366
Schenectady **(G-14318)**

MEAT PRDTS: Frozen

Caribbean Foods Delight Inc ....D....... 845 398-3000
Tappan **(G-15034)**
Life Earth Company ....G....... 310 751-0627
New York **(G-10211)**
Original Crunch Roll Fctry LLC ....G....... 716 402-5030
Amherst **(G-240)**
Prime Food Processing Corp ....D....... 718 963-2323
Brooklyn **(G-2284)**

MEAT PRDTS: Meat By-Prdts, From Slaughtered Meat

Cni Meat & Produce Inc ....G....... 516 599-5929
Valley Stream **(G-15338)**
Robert & William Inc ....G....... 631 727-5780
Riverhead **(G-13187)**
Sam A Lupo & Sons Inc ....G....... 800 388-5352
Endicott **(G-4472)**

MEAT PRDTS: Meat Extracts, From Purchased Meat

Reliable Brothers Inc ....E....... 518 273-6732
Green Island **(G-5441)**

MEAT PRDTS: Pork, From Slaughtered Meat

Hilltown Pork Inc ....F....... 518 781-4050
Canaan **(G-3119)**

MEAT PRDTS: Prepared Beef Prdts From Purchased Beef

Alle Processing Corp ....C....... 718 894-2000
Maspeth **(G-7587)**
Julian Freirich Company Inc ....E....... 718 361-9111
Long Island City **(G-7256)**

MEAT PRDTS: Prepared Pork Prdts, From Purchased Meat

Lancaster Quality Pork Inc ....F....... 718 439-8822
Brooklyn **(G-2046)**
Schaller Manufacturing Corp ....D....... 718 721-5480
New York **(G-11149)**
Syracuse Casing Co Inc ....F....... 315 475-0309
Syracuse **(G-15003)**

MEAT PRDTS: Sausage Casings, Natural

Brooklyn Casing Co Inc ....G....... 718 522-0866
Brooklyn **(G-1613)**
Camellia General Provision Co...............E....... 716 893-5352
Buffalo **(G-2691)**
Domestic Casing Co ....G....... 718 522-1902
Brooklyn **(G-1756)**
Frank Wardynski & Sons Inc ....E....... 716 854-6083
Buffalo **(G-2759)**
Niagara Tying Service Inc ....E....... 716 825-0066
Buffalo **(G-2888)**
Rapa Independent North America ....G....... 518 561-0513
Plattsburgh **(G-12774)**

MEAT PRDTS: Sausages & Related Prdts, From Purchased Meat

Dinos Sausage & Meat Co Inc ....F....... 315 732-2661
Utica **(G-15257)**
Elmgang Enterprises I Inc ....F....... 212 868-4142
New York **(G-9350)**

MEAT PRDTS: Sausages, From Purchased Meat

Arnolds Meat Food Products...............E....... 718 384-8071
Brooklyn **(G-1532)**
Buffalo Provisions Co Inc ....F....... 718 292-4300
Elmhurst **(G-4332)**
De Ans Pork Products Inc ....E....... 718 788-2464
Brooklyn **(G-1731)**
Grossglockner Inc ....G....... 585 266-4960
Canandaigua **(G-3134)**
Salarinos Italian Foods Inc ....F....... 315 697-9766
Canastota **(G-3156)**
Schonwetter Enterprises Inc ....E....... 518 237-0171
Cohoes **(G-3515)**
Zweigles Inc ....D....... 585 546-1740
Rochester **(G-13816)**

MEAT PRDTS: Sausages, From Slaughtered Meat

Sahlen Packing Company Inc...............D....... 716 852-8677
Buffalo **(G-2973)**

MEAT PRDTS: Snack Sticks, Incl Jerky, From Purchased Meat

Big Johns Adirondack Inc...............G....... 518 587-3680
Saratoga Springs **(G-14166)**
Provisionaire & Co LLC...............E....... 646 681-8600
Brooklyn **(G-2304)**

MEAT PROCESSED FROM PURCHASED CARCASSES

Alps Provision Co Inc ....E....... 718 721-4477
Astoria **(G-414)**
Bianca Burgers LLC ....F....... 516 764-9591
Rockville Centre **(G-13826)**
Brooklyn Bangers LLC ....F....... 718 875-3535
Brooklyn **(G-1611)**
Cni Meat & Produce Inc ....G....... 516 599-5929
Valley Stream **(G-15338)**
Hanzlian Sausage Incorporated ....G....... 716 891-5247
Cheektowaga **(G-3353)**
Hilltown Pork Inc...............F....... 518 781-4050
Canaan **(G-3119)**
Jacks Gourmet LLC ....F....... 718 954-4681
Brooklyn **(G-1983)**
Milan Provision Co Inc ....E....... 718 899-7678
Corona **(G-3745)**
Mineo & Sapio Meats Inc ....G....... 716 884-2398
Buffalo **(G-2866)**
Mr Pierogi LLC ....F....... 718 499-7821
Brooklyn **(G-2177)**
Muddy Trail Jerky Co ....G....... 518 642-2194
Granville **(G-5353)**
Orchard Sausages Inc ....F....... 718 381-9388
Brooklyn **(G-2233)**
Picone Meat Specialties Ltd...............G....... 914 381-3002
Mamaroneck **(G-7519)**
Pork King Sausage Inc ....E....... 718 542-2810
Bronx **(G-1341)**
Rosina Food Products Inc ....C....... 716 668-0123
Buffalo **(G-2962)**
Rosina Holding Inc ....G....... 716 668-0123
Buffalo **(G-2963)**
Schaller Manufacturing Corp...............F....... 212 879-3047
New York **(G-11150)**
Schrader Meat Market...............F....... 607 869-6328
Romulus **(G-13879)**
Sun Ming Jan Inc ....F....... 718 418-8221
Brooklyn **(G-2469)**
Wilson Beef Farms LLC...............F....... 607 545-8308
Canaseraga **(G-3148)**

MED, DENTAL & HOSPITAL EQPT, WHOL: Incontinent Prdts/Splys

Koregon Enterprises Inc ....G....... 450 218-6836
Champlain **(G-3314)**

MEDIA BUYING AGENCIES

Selby Marketing Associates Inc ....F....... 585 377-0750
Rochester **(G-13722)**
Silverlight Digital LLC...............G....... 646 650-5330
New York **(G-11240)**
Ubm LLC...............D....... 516 562-7800
New Hyde Park **(G-8298)**

MEDIA: Magnetic & Optical Recording

Aarfid LLC...............G....... 716 992-3999
Eden **(G-4253)**
BMA Media Services Inc...............E....... 585 385-2060
Rochester **(G-13275)**
Digiday Media LLC ....E....... 646 419-4357
New York **(G-9224)**
Ember Media Corporation ....F....... 212 695-1919
New York **(G-9357)**
Next Big Sound Inc ....G....... 646 657-9837
New York **(G-10618)**
Stamper Technology Inc ....G....... 585 247-8370
Rochester **(G-13743)**

MEDICAL & HOSPITAL EQPT WHOLESALERS

AEP Environmental LLC......................F 716 446-0739
Buffalo (G-2625)

Allied Pharmacy Products Inc ....G 516 374-8862
Hicksville (G-5882)

Awe Technologies LLC........................G 631 747-8448
Bay Shore (G-654)

Boehm Surgical Instrument Corp.........F 585 436-6584
Rochester (G-13277)

Hogil Pharmaceutical Corp ....F 914 681-1800
White Plains (G-16014)

Moogs Medical Devices Group.............G 716 652-2000
Buffalo (G-2872)

Occunomix International LLC ....E 631 741-1940
Port Jeff STA (G-12837)

Precimed Inc.......................................E 716 759-5600
Clarence (G-3440)

Progressive Orthotics Ltd ....G 631 732-5556
Selden (G-14355)

Roner Inc ....G 718 392-6020
Long Island City (G-7346)

TSS Foam Industries Corp ....F 585 538-2321
Caledonia (G-3074)

MEDICAL & HOSPITAL SPLYS: Radiation Shielding Garments

Biodex Medical Systems Inc................C 631 924-9000
Shirley (G-14417)

Biodex Medical Systems Inc................E 631 924-3146
Shirley (G-14418)

Xylon Industries Inc............................G 631 293-4717
Farmingdale (G-4766)

MEDICAL & SURGICAL SPLYS: Bandages & Dressings

Aero Healthcare (us) LLC....................G 855 225-2376
Valley Cottage (G-15312)

Euromed Inc ....D 845 359-4039
Orangeburg (G-12315)

MEDICAL & SURGICAL SPLYS: Braces, Orthopedic

Complete Orthopedic Svcs Inc.............E 516 357-9113
East Meadow (G-4133)

Eschen Prosthetic & Orthotic L.............E 212 606-1262
New York (G-9396)

Langer Biomechanics Inc ....D 800 645-5520
Ronkonkoma (G-13965)

Lorelei Orthotics Prosthetics................G 212 727-2011
New York (G-10263)

MEDICAL & SURGICAL SPLYS: Clothing, Fire Resistant & Protect

Crye Precision LLC.............................C 718 246-3838
Brooklyn (G-1705)

Elwood Specialty Products Inc.............F 716 877-6622
Buffalo (G-2741)

Hakson Safety Wears Inc ....F 613 667-3015
Buffalo (G-2790)

Salsa Professional Apparel LLC...........G 212 575-6565
New York (G-11122)

MEDICAL & SURGICAL SPLYS: Cotton & Cotton Applicators

Advanced Enterprises Inc....................F 845 342-1009
Middletown (G-7892)

MEDICAL & SURGICAL SPLYS: Ear Plugs

Cirrus Healthcare Products LLC ....E 631 692-7600
Cold Spring Harbor (G-3526)

Hearos LLC..G 844 432-7327
Latham (G-6858)

New Dynamics Corporation ....E 845 692-0022
Middletown (G-7923)

MEDICAL & SURGICAL SPLYS: Foot Appliances, Orthopedic

Brannock Device Co Inc.......................E 315 475-9862
Liverpool (G-7002)

Fiber Foot Appliances Inc ....F 631 465-9199
Farmingdale (G-4631)

Schuster & Richard Labortories............G 718 358-8607
College Point (G-3563)

MEDICAL & SURGICAL SPLYS: Gynecological Splys & Appliances

Cityscape Ob/Gyn PLLC......................F 212 683-3595
New York (G-9020)

Womens Health Care PC ....G 718 850-0009
Richmond Hill (G-13128)

MEDICAL & SURGICAL SPLYS: Limbs, Artificial

Center For Orthotic & Prosthet.............G 607 215-0847
Elmira (G-4343)

Creative Orthotics & Prosthet ....F 607 734-7215
Elmira (G-4347)

Creative Orthotics Prosthetics ....G 607 771-4672
Binghamton (G-868)

Gfh Orthotic & Prosthetic Labs.............G 631 467-3725
Bohemia (G-1017)

Great Lakes Orthpd Labs Inc ....G 716 893-4116
Buffalo (G-2782)

Green Prosthetics & Orthotics ....G 716 484-1088
Jamestown (G-6514)

Hanger Prsthetcs & Ortho Inc...............G 607 771-4672
Binghamton (G-881)

Hanger Prsthetcs & Ortho Inc...............G 315 472-5200
Syracuse (G-14908)

Hanger Prsthetcs & Ortho Inc...............D 607 795-1220
Elmira (G-4354)

Hanger Prsthetcs & Ortho Inc...............G 315 789-4810
Geneva (G-5158)

J-K Prosthetics & Orthotics ....E 914 699-2077
Mount Vernon (G-8153)

Lehneis Orthotics Prosthetic ....G 516 790-1897
Hauppauge (G-5691)

Lehneis Orthotics Prosthetic ....G 631 369-3115
Riverhead (G-13178)

Mark Goldberg Prosthetic ....F 631 689-6606
East Setauket (G-4180)

National Prosthetic Orthot ....G 718 767-8400
Bayside (G-740)

New England Orthotic & Prost...............G 212 682-9313
New York (G-10581)

North Shore Orthtics Prsthtics..............G 631 928-3040
Port Jeff STA (G-12836)

Orthocraft Inc ....G 718 951-1700
Brooklyn (G-2235)

Orthopedic Arts Laboratory Inc.............G 718 858-2400
Brooklyn (G-2236)

Orthopedic Treatment Facility ....G 718 898-7326
Woodside (G-16217)

Progressive Orthotics Ltd ....G 631 732-5556
Selden (G-14355)

Prosthetic Rehabilitation Ctr ....G 845 565-8255
Newburgh (G-11885)

Prosthetics By Nelson Inc....................F 716 894-6666
Cheektowaga (G-3359)

Robert Cohen ....G 718 789-0996
Ozone Park (G-12467)

Rochester Orthopedic Labs...................G 585 272-1060
Rochester (G-13691)

Sampsons Prsthtic Orthotic Lab............E 518 374-6011
Schenectady (G-14300)

Stafford Labs Orthotics/Prosth ....F 845 692-5227
Middletown (G-7932)

Tonawanda Limb & Brace Inc ....G 716 695-1131
Tonawanda (G-15146)

MEDICAL & SURGICAL SPLYS: Orthopedic Appliances

Advanced Orthotics & Prostheth ....F 518 472-1023
Albany (G-29)

Advantage Orthotics Inc ....G 631 368-1754
East Northport (G-4141)

Apollo Orthotics Corp ....G 516 333-3223
Carle Place (G-3170)

Arimed Orthotics Prosthetics ....F 718 875-8754
Brooklyn (G-1528)

Arimed Orthotics Prosthetics ....F 718 979-6155
Staten Island (G-14620)

Church Communities NY Inc ....E 518 589-5103
Elka Park (G-4302)

Church Communities NY Inc ....E 518 589-5103
Elka Park (G-4303)

Community Products LLC......................C 845 658-8799
Rifton (G-13167)

Community Products LLC......................F 845 572-3433
Chester (G-3374)

Cranial Technologies Inc ....G 914 472-0975
Scarsdale (G-14234)

Creative Orthotics & Prosthet................F 607 431-2526
Oneonta (G-12270)

Custom Sports Lab Inc ....G 212 832-1648
New York (G-9135)

East Cast Orthtics Prosthetics ....F 716 856-5192
Buffalo (G-2736)

East Coast Orthoic & Pros Cor..............D 516 248-5566
Deer Park (G-3867)

East Coast Orthoic & Pros Cor..............F 212 923-2161
New York (G-9302)

Hersco-Orthotic Labs Corp ....E 718 391-0416
Long Island City (G-7242)

Higgins Supply Company Inc ....D 607 836-6474
Mc Graw (G-7688)

Klemmt Orthotics & Prosthetics ....G 607 770-4400
Johnson City (G-6604)

La Torre Orthopedic Laboratory............F 518 786-8655
Latham (G-6864)

Latorre Orthopedic Laboratory..............F 518 786-8655
Latham (G-6869)

M H Mandelbaum Orthotic ....F 631 473-8668
Port Jefferson (G-12842)

Medi-Ray Inc.......................................D 877 898-3003
Tuckahoe (G-15205)

Ortho Medical Products ....E 212 879-3700
New York (G-10712)

Orthotics & Prosthetics Dept ....F 585 341-9299
Rochester (G-13599)

Premier Brands America Inc ....F 718 325-3000
Bronx (G-1343)

Profoot Inc..D 718 965-8600
Brooklyn (G-2298)

Progressive Orthotics Ltd ....F 631 447-3860
East Patchogue (G-4155)

Rehabilitation Tech of Syracuse............G 315 426-9920
Syracuse (G-14976)

Stj Orthotic Services Inc ....F 631 956-0181
Lindenhurst (G-6975)

MEDICAL & SURGICAL SPLYS: Personal Safety Eqpt

Bio-Chem Barrier Systems LLC ....G 631 261-2682
Northport (G-12099)

Fk Safety Gear Inc...............................G 516 233-9628
East Rockaway (G-4173)

Hygrade ....G 718 488-9000
Brooklyn (G-1948)

Kem Medical Products Corp ....G 631 454-6565
Farmingdale (G-4665)

Lakeland Industries Inc ....C 631 981-9700
Ronkonkoma (G-13963)

NY Orthopedic Usa Inc ....D 718 852-5330
Brooklyn (G-2225)

Occunomix International LLC ....E 631 741-1940
Port Jeff STA (G-12837)

Queue Solutions LLC ....F 631 750-6440
Bohemia (G-1069)

MEDICAL & SURGICAL SPLYS: Prosthetic Appliances

Advanced Prosthetics Orthotics ....F 516 365-7225
Manhasset (G-7530)

Center For Prosthetic ....G 845 336-7762
Kingston (G-6684)

Flo-Tech Orthotic & Prosthetic ....G 607 387-3070
Trumansburg (G-15200)

New York Rhbilitative Svcs LLC ....F 516 239-0990
Valley Stream (G-15349)

Peak Performance Design LLC.............G 518 302-9198
Cohoes (G-3512)

Syracuse Prosthetic Center Inc.............G 315 476-9697
Syracuse (G-15009)

Ultrapedics Ltd ....G 718 748-4806
Brooklyn (G-2534)

MEDICAL & SURGICAL SPLYS: Respiratory Protect Eqpt, Personal

Monaghan Medical Corporation ....G 315 472-2136
Syracuse (G-14946)

MEDICAL & SURGICAL SPLYS: Sponges

Medical Action Industries Inc................C 631 231-4600
Hauppauge (G-5711)

PRODUCT

MEDICAL & SURGICAL SPLYS: Suspensories

Ortho Rite Inc ....E 914 235-9100
Mamaroneck (G-7517)

MEDICAL & SURGICAL SPLYS: Technical Aids, Handicapped

Orcam Inc ....F 800 713-3741
New York (G-10704)

Thomas F Egan ....E 607 669-4822
Binghamton (G-913)

MEDICAL EQPT REPAIR SVCS, NON-ELECTRIC

Med Services Inc ....D 631 218-6450
Bohemia (G-1046)

MEDICAL EQPT: Diagnostic

Advantage Plus Diagnostics Inc ....G 631 393-5044
Melville (G-7755)

American Bio Medica Corp ....D 518 758-8158
Kinderhook (G-6670)

Becton Dickinson and Company ....B 845 353-3371
Nyack (G-12136)

Biochemical Diagnostics Inc ....E 631 595-9200
Edgewood (G-4263)

E-Z-Em Inc ....E 609 524-2864
Melville (G-7777)

Ken-Ton Open Mri PC ....G 716 876-7000
Kenmore (G-6654)

Memory Md Inc ....G 917 318-0215
New York (G-10430)

Nanobionovum LLC ....F 518 581-1171
Saratoga Springs (G-14186)

Nasiff Associates Inc ....G 315 676-2346
Central Square (G-3295)

Ortho-Clinical Diagnostics Inc ....B 585 453-4771
Rochester (G-13595)

Ortho-Clinical Diagnostics Inc ....F 585 453-5200
Rochester (G-13596)

Ovitz Corporation ....G 585 967-2114
Rochester (G-13601)

Praxis Powder Technology Inc ....E 518 812-0112
Queensbury (G-13052)

Proactive Medical Products LLC ....G 845 205-6004
Mount Vernon (G-8174)

RJ Harvey Instrument Corp ....F 845 359-3943
Tappan (G-15038)

Vasomedical Solutions Inc ....D 516 997-4600
Plainview (G-12723)

Welch Allyn Inc ....A 315 685-4100
Skaneateles Falls (G-14459)

Welch Allyn Inc ....A 315 685-4100
Skaneateles Falls (G-14460)

Welch Allyn Inc ....A 315 685-4347
Skaneateles Falls (G-14461)

MEDICAL EQPT: Electromedical Apparatus

Biofeedback Instrument Corp ....G 212 222-5665
New York (G-8797)

Conmed Andover Medical Inc ....F 315 797-8375
Utica (G-15246)

Conmed Corporation ....B 315 797-8375
Utica (G-15248)

Health Care Originals Inc ....G 585 471-8215
Rochester (G-13463)

Qrs Technologies Inc ....G 315 457-5300
Liverpool (G-7037)

MEDICAL EQPT: Electrotherapeutic Apparatus

Complex Biosystems Inc ....G 315 464-8007
Baldwinsville (G-545)

MEDICAL EQPT: Heart-Lung Machines, Exc Iron Lungs

Advd Heart Phys & Surgs ....F 212 434-3000
New York (G-8484)

Gary Gelbfish MD ....G 718 258-3004
Brooklyn (G-1878)

Jarvik Heart Inc ....E 212 397-3911
New York (G-9977)

MEDICAL EQPT: Laser Systems

Buffalo Filter LLC ....D 716 835-7000
Lancaster (G-6799)

Ddc Technologies Inc ....G 516 594-1533
Oceanside (G-12169)

Juvly Aesthetics Inc ....D 614 686-3627
New York (G-10049)

Laser and Varicose Vein Trtmnt ....G 718 667-1777
Staten Island (G-14676)

New Primecare ....G 516 822-4031
Hewlett (G-5872)

New York Laser & Aestheticks ....G 516 627-7777
Roslyn (G-14044)

University of Rochester ....B 585 275-3483
Rochester (G-13786)

MEDICAL EQPT: MRI/Magnetic Resonance Imaging Devs, Nuclear

City Sports Imaging Inc ....E 212 481-3600
New York (G-9019)

Philips Medical Systems Mr ....B 518 782-1122
Latham (G-6872)

MEDICAL EQPT: PET Or Position Emission Tomography Scanners

Nirx Medical Technologies LLC ....F 516 676-6479
Glen Head (G-5211)

MEDICAL EQPT: Patient Monitoring

Equivital Inc ....E 646 513-4169
New York (G-9391)

Novamed-Usa Inc ....E 914 789-2100
Elmsford (G-4420)

Ocean Cardiac Monitoring ....G 631 777-3700
Deer Park (G-3916)

Quadrant Biosciences Inc ....G 315 614-2325
Syracuse (G-14969)

MEDICAL EQPT: Sterilizers

Getinge Group Logistics Ameri ....C 585 475-1400
Rochester (G-13439)

SPS Medical Supply Corp ....F 585 968-2377
Cuba (G-3814)

Steriliz LLC ....G 585 415-5411
Rochester (G-13746)

MEDICAL EQPT: Ultrasonic Scanning Devices

Empire Open Mri ....G 914 961-1777
Yonkers (G-16307)

Global Instrumentation LLC ....F 315 682-0272
Manlius (G-7547)

Imacor Inc ....E 516 393-0970
Jericho (G-6583)

MEDICAL EQPT: Ultrasonic, Exc Cleaning

Nanovibronix Inc ....F 914 233-3004
Elmsford (G-4419)

MEDICAL EQPT: X-Ray Apparatus & Tubes, Radiographic

Genesis Digital Imaging Inc ....G 310 305-7358
Rochester (G-13436)

Quantum Medical Imaging LLC ....D 631 567-5800
Rochester (G-13663)

Siemens Corporation ....F 202 434-7800
New York (G-11226)

Siemens USA Holdings Inc ....B 212 258-4000
New York (G-11228)

MEDICAL EQPT: X-Ray Apparatus & Tubes, Therapeutic

Community Products LLC ....C 845 658-8799
Rifton (G-13167)

MEDICAL PHOTOGRAPHY & ART SVCS

Burns Archive Phtgraphic Distr ....G 212 889-1938
New York (G-8870)

MEDICAL, DENTAL & HOSPITAL EQPT, WHOL: Dentists' Prof Splys

Crosstex International Inc ....D 631 582-6777
Hauppauge (G-5631)

MEDICAL, DENTAL & HOSPITAL EQPT, WHOL: Hosptl Eqpt/Furniture

Creative Orthotics & Prosthet ....F 607 734-7215
Elmira (G-4347)

Medical Action Industries Inc ....C 631 231-4600
Hauppauge (G-5711)

MEDICAL, DENTAL & HOSPITAL EQPT, WHOL: Surgical Eqpt & Splys

Medline Industries Inc ....B 845 344-3301
Middletown (G-7919)

Paramount Textiles Inc ....F 212 966-1040
New York (G-10756)

MEDICAL, DENTAL & HOSPITAL EQPT, WHOLESALE: Diagnostic, Med

Memory Md Inc ....G 917 318-0215
New York (G-10430)

MEDICAL, DENTAL & HOSPITAL EQPT, WHOLESALE: Med Eqpt & Splys

Ala Scientific Instruments Inc ....F 631 393-6401
Farmingdale (G-4577)

Basil S Kadhim ....G 888 520-5192
New York (G-8736)

Brinkman Precision Inc ....D 585 429-5001
West Henrietta (G-15788)

Lehneis Orthotics Prosthetic ....G 516 790-1897
Hauppauge (G-5691)

Lehneis Orthotics Prosthetic ....G 631 369-3115
Riverhead (G-13178)

Peter Digioia ....G 516 644-5517
Plainview (G-12707)

Quantum Medical Imaging LLC ....D 631 567-5800
Rochester (G-13663)

MEDICAL, DENTAL & HOSPITAL EQPT, WHOLESALE: Medical Lab

Integrted Work Envronments LLC ....G 716 725-5088
East Amherst (G-4078)

MELAMINE RESINS: Melamine-Formaldehyde

Hexion Inc ....E 518 792-8040
South Glens Falls (G-14513)

Queen City Manufacturing Inc ....G 716 877-1102
Buffalo (G-2944)

MEMBERSHIP ORGANIZATIONS, PROFESSIONAL: Health Association

Curemdcom Inc ....E 212 509-6200
New York (G-9134)

MEMBERSHIP ORGS, BUSINESS: Growers' Marketing Advisory Svc

Atlantic Farm & Food Inc ....F 718 441-3152
Richmond Hill (G-13108)

MEMBERSHIP ORGS, CIVIC, SOCIAL/FRAT: Educator's Assoc

Modern Language Assn Amer Inc ....C 646 576-5000
New York (G-10488)

MEMORY DEVICES: Magnetic Bubble

Dynamic Photography Inc ....G 516 381-2951
Roslyn (G-14042)

MEN'S & BOYS' CLOTHING ACCESS STORES

A Bogen Enterprises Inc ....G 718 951-9533
Brooklyn (G-1432)

Broadway Knitting Mills Inc ....G 716 692-4421
North Tonawanda (G-12059)

Giliberto Designs Inc ....E 212 695-0216
New York (G-9610)

Swank Inc ....B 212 867-2600
New York (G-11403)

MEN'S & BOYS' CLOTHING STORES

By Robert James ....G 212 253-2121
New York (G-8876)

Elie Tahari Ltd ....G 212 763-2000
New York (G-9339)

Grunt Apparel Inc ....G 646 878-6171
New York (G-9689)

Hugo Boss Usa Inc ....D 212 940-0600
New York (G-9835)

Kcp Holdco Inc ....F 212 265-1500
New York (G-10086)

Kenneth Cole Productions Inc ......B 212 265-1500
New York (G-10089)

Mee Accessories LLC ....B 917 262-1000
New York (G-10421)

Mega Sourcing Inc ....G 646 682-0304
Merrick (G-7861)

Michael Andrews LLC ....F 212 677-1755
New York (G-10451)

Perry Ellis Menswear LLC ......C 212 221-7500
New York (G-10809)

Phillips-Van Heusen Europe ....F 212 381-3500
New York (G-10829)

Pvh Corp ....D 212 381-3500
New York (G-10933)

Pvh Corp ....G 212 549-6000
New York (G-10934)

Sanctuary Brands LLC ....F 212 704-4014
New York (G-11129)

MEN'S & BOYS' CLOTHING WHOLESALERS, NEC

A Bogen Enterprises Inc ....G 718 951-9533
Brooklyn (G-1432)

Billion Tower Intl LLC ....F 212 220-0608
New York (G-8791)

D-C Theatricks ....G 716 847-0180
Buffalo (G-2719)

Enzo Manzoni LLC ....G 212 464-7000
Brooklyn (G-1807)

G-III Apparel Group Ltd ....B 212 403-0500
New York (G-9560)

Halabieh Group Inc ....F 347 987-8263
New York (G-9710)

Herrmann Group LLC ....G 716 876-9798
Kenmore (G-6651)

Kate Spade Holdings LLC ......B 212 354-4900
New York (G-10076)

Kenmar Shirts Inc ....E 718 824-3880
Bronx (G-1291)

M Hidary & Co Inc ....D 212 736-6540
New York (G-10296)

Moresca Clothing and Costume ......F 845 331-6012
Ulster Park (G-15219)

Mountain T-Shirts Inc ....G 518 943-4533
Catskill (G-3215)

Onia LLC ....E 646 701-0008
New York (G-10693)

Penfli Industries Inc ....F 212 947-6080
Great Neck (G-5413)

Ryba General Merchandise Inc ....G 718 522-2028
Brooklyn (G-2368)

Sanctuary Brands LLC ....F 212 704-4014
New York (G-11129)

United Knitwear International ....G 212 354-2920
New York (G-11598)

Universal Mus Group Hldngs Inc ....E 212 333-8000
New York (G-11608)

Wp Lavori USA Inc ....G 212 244-6074
New York (G-11790)

MEN'S & BOYS' SPORTSWEAR CLOTHING STORES

Authentic Brands Group LLC ......C 212 760-2410
New York (G-8680)

Cockpit Usa Inc ....F 212 575-1616
New York (G-9046)

Foot Locker Retail Inc ....F 516 827-5306
Hicksville (G-5908)

Herrmann Group LLC ....G 716 876-9798
Kenmore (G-6651)

Mainly Monograms Inc ....E 845 624-4923
West Nyack (G-15827)

Royal Tees Inc ....G 845 357-9448
Suffern (G-14766)

MEN'S & BOYS' SPORTSWEAR WHOLESALERS

Bandit International Ltd ....F 718 402-2100
Bronx (G-1210)

Cockpit Usa Inc ....F 212 575-1616
New York (G-9046)

Mee Accessories LLC ....B 917 262-1000
New York (G-10421)

MEN'S SUITS STORES

Kozinn+sons Merchant Tailors ....E 212 643-1916
New York (G-10132)

Royal Clothing Corp ....G 718 436-5841
Brooklyn (G-2358)

MERCHANDISING MACHINE OPERATORS: Vending

Worksman Trading Corp ....G 718 322-2000
Ozone Park (G-12469)

MESSAGE CONCENTRATORS

Gac Express Inc ....G 718 438-2227
Brooklyn (G-1876)

METAL & STEEL PRDTS: Abrasive

Datum Alloys Inc ....G 607 239-6274
Endicott (G-4448)

Pellets LLC ....G 716 693-1750
North Tonawanda (G-12081)

Raulli and Sons Inc ....G 315 479-2515
Syracuse (G-14974)

METAL COMPONENTS: Prefabricated

Precision Fabrication LLC ....G 585 591-3449
Attica (G-458)

METAL CUTTING SVCS

Elmsford Sheet Metal Works Inc ....D 914 739-6300
Cortlandt Manor (G-3794)

Knise & Krick Inc ....E 315 422-3516
Syracuse (G-14927)

S & S Prtg Die-Cutting Co Inc ....F 718 388-8990
Brooklyn (G-2372)

METAL FABRICATORS: Architechtural

A & T Iron Works Inc ....E 914 632-8992
New Rochelle (G-8315)

A1 Ornamental Iron Works Inc ....G 718 265-3055
Brooklyn (G-1445)

Accurate Welding Service Inc ......G 516 333-1730
Westbury (G-1730)

Aero-Data Metal Crafters Inc ....C 631 471-7733
Ronkonkoma (G-13892)

Airflex Corp ....D 631 752-1219
Farmingdale (G-4574)

Aldos Iron Works Inc ....G 718 834-0408
Brooklyn (G-1481)

All American Metal Corporation ......G 516 623-0222
Freeport (G-4983)

Babylon Iron Works Inc ....F 631 643-3311
West Babylon (G-15692)

Bobrick Washroom Equipment Inc ....D 518 877-7444
Clifton Park (G-3463)

Cabezon Design Group Inc ....G 718 488-9868
Brooklyn (G-1638)

Caliper Studio Inc ....E 718 302-2427
Brooklyn (G-1640)

Cianfarani Armando ....G 518 393-7755
Schenectady (G-14256)

Creative Metal Fabricators ....G 631 567-2266
Bohemia (G-993)

E F Iron Works & Construction ....G 631 242-4766
Bay Shore (G-677)

Ej Group Inc ....G 315 699-2601
Cicero (G-3419)

Elevator Accessories Mfg ....F 914 739-7004
Peekskill (G-12550)

Flushing Iron Weld Inc ....E 718 359-2208
Flushing (G-4853)

Forest Iron Works Inc ....G 516 671-4229
Locust Valley (G-7125)

Giumenta Corp ....E 718 832-1200
Brooklyn (G-1889)

Global Steel Products Corp ....C 631 586-3455
Deer Park (G-3878)

Grillmaster Inc ....E 718 272-9191
Howard Beach (G-6140)

Hi-Tech Metals Inc ....E 718 894-1212
Maspeth (G-7622)

ITR Industries Inc ....E 914 964-7063
Yonkers (G-16321)

Jerry Cardullo Iron Works Inc ....F 631 242-8881
Bay Shore (G-685)

Kenal Services Corp ....G 315 788-9226
Watertown (G-15576)

Keuka Studios Inc ....G 585 624-5960
Rush (G-14073)

Kms Contracting Inc ....F 718 495-6500
Brooklyn (G-2033)

M B C Metal Inc ....F 718 384-6713
Brooklyn (G-2095)

Martin Orna Ir Works II Inc ....G 516 354-3923
Elmont (G-4386)

Material Process Systems Inc ....F 718 302-3081
Brooklyn (G-2124)

Mestel Brothers Stairs & Rails ....E 516 496-4127
Syosset (G-14794)

Metalworks Inc ....E 718 319-0011
Bronx (G-1312)

Milgo Industrial Inc ....D 718 388-6476
Brooklyn (G-2153)

Milgo Industrial Inc ....G 718 387-0406
Brooklyn (G-2154)

Mison Concepts Inc ....G 516 933-8000
Hicksville (G-5930)

Modern Art Foundry Inc ....E 718 728-2030
Astoria (G-430)

Morgik Metal Designs ....F 212 463-0304
New York (G-10503)

Moro Corporation ....E 607 724-4241
Binghamton (G-899)

New Dimensions Office Group ....D 718 387-0995
Brooklyn (G-2203)

Old Dutchmans Wrough Iron Inc ....G 716 688-2034
Getzville (G-5180)

Peconic Ironworks Ltd ....F 631 204-0323
Southampton (G-14535)

Phoenix Metal Designs Inc ......G 516 597-4100
Brooklyn (G-2256)

Pk30 System LLC ....F 212 473-8050
Stone Ridge (G-14736)

Railings By New Star Brass ....E 516 358-1153
Brooklyn (G-2324)

Raulli and Sons Inc ....D 315 479-6693
Syracuse (G-14972)

Riverside Iron LLC ....D 315 535-4864
Gouverneur (G-5322)

Rollson Inc ....E 631 423-9578
Huntington (G-6221)

Roman Iron Works Inc ....F 516 621-1103
Greenvale (G-5463)

Royal Metal Products Inc ....G 518 966-4442
Surprise (G-14776)

S A Baxter LLC ....G 845 469-7995
Chester (G-3385)

Steel Sales Inc ....E 607 674-6363
Sherburne (G-14395)

Steel Work Inc ....G 585 232-1555
Rochester (G-13744)

Steps Plus Inc ....D 315 432-0885
Syracuse (G-15000)

Studio 40 Inc ....G 212 420-8631
Brooklyn (G-2465)

Superior Metal & Woodwork Inc ....E 631 465-9004
Farmingdale (G-4744)

Tonys Ornamental Ir Works Inc ....E 315 337-3730
Rome (G-13874)

Tropical Driftwood Originals ....G 516 623-0980
Roosevelt (G-14034)

United Iron Inc ....E 914 667-5700
Mount Vernon (G-8191)

Universal Steel Fabricators ....F 718 342-0782
Brooklyn (G-2546)

Village Wrought Iron Inc ....F 315 683-5589
Fabius (G-4488)

Waverly Iron Corp ....G 631 732-2800
Medford (G-7726)

West End Iron Works Inc ....G 518 456-1105
Albany (G-141)

Z-Studios Dsign Fbrication LLC ....G 347 512-4210
Brooklyn (G-2604)

METAL FABRICATORS: *Plate*

Acro Industries Inc ....C 585 254-3661
Rochester *(G-13204)*

Aero-Data Metal Crafters Inc ....C 631 471-7733
Ronkonkoma *(G-13892)*

Allstate Gasket & Packing Inc ....F 631 254-4050
Deer Park *(G-3835)*

American Boiler Tank Wldg Inc ....E 518 463-5012
Albany *(G-39)*

API Heat Transfer Inc ....B 716 684-6700
Buffalo *(G-2640)*

Atlantic Industrial Tech Inc ....E 631 234-3131
Shirley *(G-14415)*

Blackstone Advanced Tech LLC........C 716 665-5410
Jamestown *(G-6498)*

Breton Industries Inc ....C 518 842-3030
Amsterdam *(G-320)*

Bridgehampton Steel & Wldg Inc ....F 631 537-2486
Bridgehampton *(G-1164)*

Bruce Pierce ....G 716 731-9310
Sanborn *(G-14138)*

Buflovak LLC ....E 716 895-2100
Buffalo *(G-2685)*

Charles Ross & Son Company ....D 631 234-0500
Hauppauge *(G-5614)*

Chart Industries Inc ....E 716 691-0202
Amherst *(G-218)*

Cigar Box Studios Inc ....F 845 236-9283
Marlboro *(G-7579)*

Contech Engnered Solutions LLC......F 716 870-9091
Orchard Park *(G-12348)*

Direkt Force LLC ....E 716 652-3022
East Aurora *(G-4085)*

Easco Boiler Corp ....E 718 378-3000
Bronx *(G-1249)*

ECR International Inc ....D 315 797-1310
Utica *(G-15260)*

ECR International Inc ....C 716 366-5500
Dunkirk *(G-4056)*

Endicott Precision Inc ....D 607 754-7076
Endicott *(G-4451)*

Fulton Boiler Works Inc ....C 315 298-5121
Pulaski *(G-12996)*

Fulton China LLC ....G 315 298-0112
Pulaski *(G-12997)*

Global Steel Products Corp ....C 631 586-3455
Deer Park *(G-3878)*

Inex Inc ....G 716 537-2270
Holland *(G-6029)*

J D Cousins Inc ....E 716 824-1098
Buffalo *(G-2815)*

Jaquith Industries Inc ....E 315 478-5700
Syracuse *(G-14916)*

Manning Lewis Div Rubicon Inds .....E 908 687-2400
Brooklyn *(G-2110)*

Marex Aquisition Corp ....C 585 458-3940
Rochester *(G-13536)*

Methods Tooling & Mfg Inc ....E 845 246-7100
Mount Marion *(G-8111)*

Mitsubishi Chemical Amer Inc ....E 212 223-3043
New York *(G-10484)*

Niagara Cooler Inc ....G 716 434-1235
Lockport *(G-7096)*

Pfaudler US Inc ....C 585 235-1000
Rochester *(G-13618)*

Roemac Industrial Sales Inc ....G 716 692-7332
North Tonawanda *(G-12088)*

Rosenwach Tank Co Inc ....E 212 972-4411
Astoria *(G-439)*

Seibel Modern Mfg & Wldg Corp ....D 716 683-1536
Lancaster *(G-6834)*

Slant/Fin Corporation ....B 516 484-2600
Greenvale *(G-5464)*

SPX Cooling Technologies Inc ....G 914 697-5030
Irvington *(G-6314)*

Weslor Industries Inc ....E 315 871-4405
Lyons *(G-7454)*

METAL FABRICATORS: *Sheet*

A & L Shtmtl Fabrications Corp ....E 718 842-1600
Bronx *(G-1185)*

Accra Sheetmetal LLC ....G 631 643-2100
Wyandanch *(G-16241)*

Acme Architectural Pdts Inc ....D 718 384-7800
Brooklyn *(G-1456)*

Acro-Fab Ltd ....E 315 564-6688
Hannibal *(G-5542)*

Advanced Precision Technology ....F 845 279-3540
Brewster *(G-1138)*

Advantage Metalwork Finshg LLC ......D 585 454-0160
Rochester *(G-13212)*

Advantech Industries Inc ....C 585 247-0701
Rochester *(G-13213)*

Aero Trades Mfg Corp ....E 516 746-3360
Mineola *(G-7955)*

Aeroduct Inc ....E 516 248-9550
Mineola *(G-7956)*

AFP Enterprises Inc ....C 585 254-1128
Rochester *(G-13215)*

Aj Genco Mch Sp McHy Rdout Svc .....F 716 664-4925
Falconer *(G-4532)*

Albany Mtal Fbrcation Holdings ....G 518 463-5161
Albany *(G-35)*

Aldo Frustacci Iron Works Inc ....F 718 768-0707
Brooklyn *(G-1480)*

Aleta Industries Inc ....F 718 349-0040
Brooklyn *(G-1482)*

All Metal Specialties Inc ....F 716 664-6009
Jamestown *(G-6492)*

All Star Carts & Vehicles Inc ....D 631 666-5581
Bay Shore *(G-646)*

All Star Sheet Metal Inc ....F 718 456-1567
Farmingdale *(G-4579)*

Allen Machine Products Inc ....E 631 630-8800
Hauppauge *(G-5584)*

Alliance Welding & Steel Fabg ....F 516 775-7600
Floral Park *(G-4806)*

Allure Metal Works Inc ....F 631 588-0220
Ronkonkoma *(G-13899)*

Alpine Machine Inc ....F 607 272-1344
Ithaca *(G-6362)*

Alternative Service Inc ....F 631 345-9500
Bellport *(G-793)*

American Std Shtmtl Sup Corp ....F 718 888-9350
Flushing *(G-4839)*

Arcadia Mfg Group Inc ....E 518 434-6213
Green Island *(G-5432)*

Arcadia Mfg Group Inc ....G 518 434-6213
Menands *(G-7840)*

Art Precision Metal Products ....F 631 842-8889
Copiague *(G-3647)*

Ascension Industries Inc ....C 716 693-9381
North Tonawanda *(G-12054)*

Atech-Seh Metal Fabricator ....E 716 895-8888
Buffalo *(G-2645)*

Atlantis Equipment Corporation ....F 518 733-5910
Stephentown *(G-14730)*

Auburn Tank & Manufacturing Co ......F 315 255-2788
Auburn *(G-463)*

B & R Sheet ....G 718 558-5544
Jamaica *(G-6428)*

Bargold Storage Systems LLC ....E 718 247-7000
Long Island City *(G-7175)*

Batavia Enclosures Inc ....G 585 344-1797
Arcade *(G-369)*

Berjen Metal Industries Ltd ....G 631 673-7979
Huntington *(G-6201)*

Best Tinsmith Supply Inc ....G 518 863-2541
Northville *(G-12113)*

Bhv Sheet Mtal Fabricators Inc ....E 607 797-1196
Vestal *(G-15371)*

Billings Sheet Metal Inc ....G 716 372-6165
Olean *(G-12224)*

Blackstone Advanced Tech LLC.........C 716 665-5410
Jamestown *(G-6498)*

Bmg Systems ....F 716 432-5160
Depew *(G-3972)*

Broadway Neon Sign Corp ....F 908 241-4177
Ronkonkoma *(G-13918)*

Brzozka Industries Inc ....F 631 588-8164
Holbrook *(G-5987)*

C & T Tool & Instrument Co ....E 718 429-1253
Woodside *(G-16199)*

C J & C Sheet Metal Corp ....F 631 376-9425
West Babylon *(G-15699)*

Cannon Industries Inc ....D 585 254-8080
Rochester *(G-13294)*

CBM Fabrications Inc ....E 518 399-8023
Ballston Lake *(G-559)*

Celtic Sheet Metal Inc ....E 845 267-3400
Congers *(G-3611)*

Center Sheet Metal Inc ....C 718 378-4476
Bronx *(G-1222)*

Chamtek Mfg Inc ....F 585 328-4900
Rochester *(G-13311)*

Chutes and Compactors of NY ....F 718 494-2247
Staten Island *(G-14638)*

City Cooling Enterprises Inc ....G 718 331-7400
Brooklyn *(G-1664)*

Clark Specialty Co Inc ....E 607 776-3193
Bath *(G-632)*

Contractors Sheet Metal LLC ....C 718 786-2505
Long Island City *(G-7191)*

Crown Die Casting Corp ....E 914 667-5400
Mount Vernon *(G-8135)*

Cutting Edge Metal Works ....E 631 981-8333
Holtsville *(G-6048)*

Cw Metals Inc ....E 917 416-7906
Long Island City *(G-7196)*

D & G Sheet Metal Co Inc ....F 718 326-9111
Maspeth *(G-7603)*

Dawson Metal Company Inc ....C 716 664-3811
Jamestown *(G-6506)*

Dimar Manufacturing Corp ....E 716 759-0351
Clarence *(G-3428)*

Dj Acquisition Management Corp ....D 585 265-3000
Ontario *(G-12288)*

Doortec Archtctural Met GL LLC ....E 718 567-2730
Brooklyn *(G-1758)*

Dundas-Jafine Inc ....E 716 681-9690
Alden *(G-168)*

Elevator Accessories Mfg ....F 914 739-7004
Peekskill *(G-12550)*

Empire Air Specialties Inc ....E 518 689-4440
Albany *(G-75)*

Endicott Precision Inc ....C 607 754-7076
Endicott *(G-4451)*

Engineering Mfg Tech LLC ....D 607 754-7111
Endicott *(G-4453)*

Expert Industries Inc ....E 718 434-6060
Brooklyn *(G-1823)*

F M L Industries Inc ....G 607 749-7273
Homer *(G-6062)*

Falso Industries Inc ....E 315 463-0266
Syracuse *(G-14892)*

Federal Sheet Metal Works Inc ....E 315 735-4730
Utica *(G-15263)*

Five Star Industries Inc ....E 716 674-2589
West Seneca *(G-15847)*

Fred A Nudd Corporation ....E 315 524-2531
Ontario *(G-12289)*

Goergen-Mackwirth Co Inc ....E 716 874-4800
Buffalo *(G-2778)*

Greene Technologies Inc ....D 607 656-4166
Greene *(G-5446)*

H Klein & Sons Inc ....E 516 746-0163
Mineola *(G-7978)*

Hana Sheet Metal Inc ....G 914 377-0773
Yonkers *(G-16317)*

Hansen Steel ....E 585 398-2020
Farmington *(G-4772)*

Hergo Ergonomic Support Syst ....E 888 222-7270
Oceanside *(G-12175)*

Hermann Gerdens Inc ....G 631 841-3132
Copiague *(G-3658)*

Hi-Tech Industries NY Inc ....E 607 217-7361
Johnson City *(G-6601)*

Hrd Metal Products Inc ....E 631 243-6700
Deer Park *(G-3881)*

Hunter Douglas Inc ....D 845 664-7000
Pearl River *(G-12533)*

I Rauchs Sons Inc ....E 718 507-8844
East Elmhurst *(G-4107)*

IEC Electronics Corp ....D 585 647-1760
Rochester *(G-13474)*

Industrial Fabricating Corp ....E 315 437-3353
East Syracuse *(G-4218)*

Intellimetal Inc ....D 585 424-3260
Rochester *(G-13481)*

J&T Metal Inc ....G 631 471-5335
Ronkonkoma *(G-13952)*

Jamestown Advanced Pdts Corp ....E 716 483-3406
Jamestown *(G-6519)*

Jaquith Industries Inc ....E 315 478-5700
Syracuse *(G-14916)*

Jar Metals Inc ....F 845 425-8901
Nanuet *(G-8200)*

Kal Manufacturing Corporation ....E 585 265-4310
Webster *(G-15644)*

Kassis Superior Sign Co Inc ....E 315 463-7446
Syracuse *(G-14924)*

Kellys Sheet Metal Inc ....F 718 774-4750
Brooklyn *(G-2023)*

Ksm Group Ltd ....G 716 751-6006
Newfane *(G-11894)*

L&B Fabricators LLC ....F 585 265-2731
Ontario *(G-12292)*

Leader Sheet Metal Inc ....F 347 271-4961
Bronx *(G-1298)*

(G-0000) Company's Geographic Section entry number

Manufacturing Resources Inc ....E 631 481-0041
Rochester *(G-13532)*

Marex Aquisition Corp ....C ... 585 458-3940
Rochester *(G-13536)*

Mariah Metal Products Inc ....G 516 938-9783
Hicksville *(G-5926)*

McHone Industries Inc ....D ... 716 945-3380
Salamanca *(G-14122)*

MD International Industries ....E 631 254-3100
Deer Park *(G-3906)*

Melto Metal Products Co Inc ....E 516 546-8866
Freeport *(G-5007)*

Met Weld International LLC ....D 518 765-2318
Altamont *(G-196)*

Metal Solutions Inc ....C 315 732-6271
Utica *(G-15281)*

Metallogix Design Fabrication ....E 315 738-4554
Utica *(G-15282)*

Metalsmith Inc ....G 631 467-1500
Holbrook *(G-6011)*

Methods Tooling & Mfg Inc ....E 845 246-7100
Mount Marion *(G-8111)*

Metro Duct Systems Inc ....F 718 278-4294
Long Island City *(G-7294)*

Mitsubishi Chemical Amer Inc ....E 212 223-3043
New York *(G-10484)*

Monarch Metal Fabrication Inc ....G 631 563-8967
Bohemia *(G-1047)*

Monroe Piping & Shtmtl LLC ....D 585 482-0200
Rochester *(G-13558)*

Ms Spares LLC ....G 607 223-3024
Clay *(G-3451)*

N & L Instruments Inc ....F 631 471-4000
Ronkonkoma *(G-13978)*

Nci Group Inc ....D ... 315 339-1245
Rome *(G-13859)*

North Coast Outfitters Ltd ....E 631 727-5580
Riverhead *(G-13183)*

Northeast Fabricators LLC ....D ... 607 865-4031
Walton *(G-15476)*

Northern Awning & Sign Company ....G 315 782-8515
Watertown *(G-15585)*

Olympic Manufacturing Inc ....E 631 231-8900
Hauppauge *(G-5733)*

Omc Inc ....C 718 731-5001
Bronx *(G-1328)*

Pathfinder Industries Inc ....E 315 593-2483
Fulton *(G-5075)*

Phoenix Envmtl Svcs Corp ....F 718 381-8100
Glendale *(G-5231)*

Pirnat Precise Metals Inc ....G 631 293-9169
Farmingdale *(G-4709)*

Plattsburgh Sheet Metal Inc ....E 518 561-4930
Plattsburgh *(G-12770)*

Precision Fabrication LLC ....G 585 591-3449
Attica *(G-458)*

Precision Metals Corp ....E 631 586-5032
Bay Shore *(G-700)*

Precision Mtal Fabricators Inc ....F 718 832-9805
Brooklyn *(G-2277)*

Precision Systems Mfg Inc ....E 315 451-3480
Liverpool *(G-7035)*

Protofast Holding Corp ....G 631 753-2549
Copiague *(G-3671)*

R & J Sheet Metal Distributors ....G 518 433-1525
Albany *(G-120)*

Reynolds Manufacturing Inc ....F 607 562-8936
Big Flats *(G-848)*

Rigidized Metals Corporation ....E 716 849-4703
Buffalo *(G-2955)*

Robert E Derecktor Inc ....D ... 914 698-0962
Mamaroneck *(G-7522)*

Rochester Colonial Mfg Corp ....D ... 585 254-8191
Rochester *(G-13686)*

Rollson Inc ....E 631 423-9578
Huntington *(G-6221)*

Royal Metal Products Inc ....E 518 966-4442
Surprise *(G-14776)*

S & J Sheet Metal Supply ....G 718 384-0800
Brooklyn *(G-2369)*

Savaco Inc ....G 716 751-9455
Newfane *(G-11895)*

Service Mfg Group Inc ....E 716 893-1482
Buffalo *(G-2981)*

Simmons Fabricating Svc Inc ....G 845 635-3755
Pleasant Valley *(G-12794)*

Smg Metal Products LLC ....G 716 633-6439
Cheektowaga *(G-3361)*

Solidus Industries Inc ....D ... 607 749-4540
Homer *(G-6067)*

Standard Industrial Works Inc ....F 631 888-0130
Bay Shore *(G-717)*

Steel Sales Inc ....E 607 674-6363
Sherburne *(G-14395)*

Steel Work Inc ....G 585 232-1555
Rochester *(G-13744)*

Sterling Industries Inc ....E 631 753-3070
Farmingdale *(G-4742)*

T Lemme Mechanical Inc ....E 518 436-4136
Menands *(G-7849)*

Tatra Mfg Corporation ....F 631 691-1184
Copiague *(G-3682)*

TCS Industries Inc ....D ... 585 426-1160
Rochester *(G-13759)*

Themis Chimney Inc ....F 718 937-4716
Brooklyn *(G-2502)*

Tri-Technologies Inc ....E 914 699-2001
Mount Vernon *(G-8187)*

Trident Precision Mfg Inc ....D ... 585 265-2010
Webster *(G-15658)*

Tripar Manufacturing Co Inc ....G 631 563-0855
Bohemia *(G-1090)*

Truform Manufacturing Corp ....D ... 585 458-1090
Rochester *(G-13776)*

Trylon Wire & Metal Works Inc ....E 718 542-4472
Bronx *(G-1384)*

Ucr Steel Group LLC ....F 718 764-3414
Ronkonkoma *(G-14020)*

Unadilla Silo Company Inc ....D ... 607 369-9341
Sidney *(G-14438)*

Universal Shielding Corp ....E 631 667-7900
Deer Park *(G-3945)*

Vance Metal Fabricators Inc ....D ... 315 789-5626
Geneva *(G-5165)*

Voss Manufacturing Inc ....D ... 716 731-5062
Sanborn *(G-14153)*

Wainland Inc ....E 718 626-2233
Astoria *(G-444)*

Wenig Corporation ....E 718 542-3600
Bronx *(G-1396)*

Weslor Industries Inc ....E 315 871-4405
Lyons *(G-7454)*

Wg Sheet Metal Corp ....F 718 235-3093
Brooklyn *(G-2581)*

William Kanes Mfg Corp ....G 718 346-1515
Brooklyn *(G-2587)*

Xli Manufacturing LLC ....E 585 436-2250
Rochester *(G-13812)*

Zahk Sales Inc ....G 631 851-0851
Islandia *(G-6347)*

METAL FABRICATORS: Structural, Ship

Cameron Bridge Works LLC ....E 607 734-9456
Horseheads *(G-6116)*

Miller Metal Fabricating Inc ....G 585 359-3400
Rochester *(G-13549)*

METAL FINISHING SVCS

ABS Metal Corp ....G 646 302-9018
Hewlett *(G-5868)*

Alta Metal Finishing Corp ....G 914 946-1916
White Plains *(G-15971)*

D & I Finishing Inc ....G 631 471-3034
Bohemia *(G-998)*

D & W Enterprises LLC ....F 585 590-6727
Medina *(G-7733)*

Eastside Oxide Co ....E 607 734-1253
Elmira *(G-4349)*

Ever-Nu-Metal Products Inc ....F 646 423-5833
Brooklyn *(G-1818)*

First Impressions Finishing ....G 631 467-2244
Ronkonkoma *(G-13938)*

Halmark Architectural Finshg ....E 718 272-1831
Brooklyn *(G-1919)*

L W S Inc ....F 631 580-0472
Ronkonkoma *(G-13960)*

Maracle Industrial Finshg Co ....E 585 387-9077
Rochester *(G-13534)*

Master Craft Finishers Inc ....E 631 586-0540
Deer Park *(G-3904)*

McAlpin Industries Inc ....E 585 544-5335
Rochester *(G-13539)*

Multitone Finishing Co Inc ....G 516 485-1043
West Hempstead *(G-15776)*

North East Finishing Co Inc ....F 631 789-8000
Copiague *(G-3666)*

Oerlikon Blzers Cating USA Inc ....E 716 564-8557
Buffalo *(G-2895)*

Rainbow Powder Coating Corp ....G 631 586-4019
Deer Park *(G-3926)*

Saccomize Inc ....G 818 287-3000
Bronx *(G-1358)*

Surface Finish Technology ....E 607 732-2909
Elmira *(G-4369)*

Vibra Tech Industries Inc ....F 914 946-1916
White Plains *(G-16069)*

METAL RESHAPING & REPLATING SVCS

Elmsford Sheet Metal Works Inc ....D ... 914 739-6300
Cortlandt Manor *(G-3794)*

Miscellnous Ir Fabricators Inc ....E 518 355-1822
Schenectady *(G-14290)*

METAL SERVICE CENTERS & OFFICES

Albea Cosmetics America Inc ....E 212 371-5100
New York *(G-8507)*

Aufhauser Corporation ....F 516 694-8696
Plainview *(G-12665)*

Cannon Industries Inc ....D ... 585 254-8080
Rochester *(G-13294)*

Specialty Steel Fabg Corp ....F 718 893-6326
Bronx *(G-1368)*

Steel Sales Inc ....E 607 674-6363
Sherburne *(G-14395)*

METAL SPINNING FOR THE TRADE

Acme Archictectural Products ....B 718 360-0700
Brooklyn *(G-1455)*

American Metal Spinning Pdts ....G 631 454-6276
West Babylon *(G-15688)*

Art Precision Metal Products ....F 631 842-8889
Copiague *(G-3647)*

Bridgeport Metalcraft Inc ....G 315 623-9597
Constantia *(G-3635)*

Gem Metal Spinning & Stamping ....G 718 729-7014
Long Island City *(G-7230)*

Hy-Grade Metal Products Corp ....G 315 475-4221
Syracuse *(G-14912)*

Koch Metal Spinning Co Inc ....D ... 716 835-3631
Buffalo *(G-2837)*

Long Island Metalform Inc ....F 631 242-9088
Deer Park *(G-3899)*

Russco Metal Spinning Co Inc ....F 516 872-6055
Baldwin *(G-534)*

S D Z Metal Spinning Stamping ....F 718 778-3600
Brooklyn *(G-2376)*

METAL STAMPING, FOR THE TRADE

4m Precision Industries Inc ....E 315 252-8415
Auburn *(G-459)*

Albest Metal Stamping Corp ....E 718 388-6000
Brooklyn *(G-1477)*

Alton Manufacturing Inc ....D ... 585 458-2600
Rochester *(G-13225)*

American Mtal Stmping Spinning ....F 718 384-1500
Brooklyn *(G-1499)*

Belmet Products Inc ....E 718 542-8220
Bronx *(G-1212)*

Cep Technologies Corporation ....E 914 968-4100
Yonkers *(G-16295)*

Charles A Rogers Entps Inc ....E 585 924-6400
Victor *(G-15397)*

Crosby Company ....E 716 852-3522
Buffalo *(G-2713)*

D-K Manufacturing Corp ....E 315 592-4327
Fulton *(G-5057)*

Dayton Industries Inc ....E 718 542-8144
Bronx *(G-1237)*

Dayton Rogers New York LLC ....D ... 585 349-4040
Rochester *(G-13339)*

Die-Matic Products LLC ....E 516 433-7900
Plainview *(G-12679)*

Gasser & Sons Inc ....C 631 543-6600
Commack *(G-3589)*

Gay Sheet Metal Dies Inc ....G 716 877-0208
Buffalo *(G-2768)*

Genesee Metal Stampings Inc ....G 585 475-0450
West Henrietta *(G-15795)*

Great Lakes Pressed Steel Corp ....E 716 885-4037
Buffalo *(G-2784)*

P & G Steel Products Co Inc ....D ... 716 896-7900
Buffalo *(G-2901)*

Quality Metal Stamping LLC ....G 516 255-9000
Rockville Centre *(G-13835)*

R G Flair Co Inc ....E 631 586-7311
Bay Shore *(G-703)*

Richter Metalcraft Corporation ....G 845 895-2025
Wallkill *(G-15472)*

PRODUCT

Rolite Mfg Inc ....E 716 683-0259
  Lancaster (G-6831)
S & S Prtg Die-Cutting Co Inc ....F 718 388-8990
  Brooklyn (G-2372)
Smithers Tools & Mch Pdts Inc ....D 845 876-3063
  Rhinebeck (G-13101)
Square Stamping Mfg Corp ....E 315 896-2641
  Barneveld (G-596)
Stamped Fittings Inc ....E 607 733-9988
  Elmira Heights (G-4380)
Tooling Enterprises Inc ....F 716 842-0445
  Buffalo (G-3014)
Tools & Stamping Corp ....G 718 392-4040
  Brooklyn (G-2510)
Trico Holding Corporation ....A 716 852-5700
  Buffalo (G-3019)
Trident Precision Mfg Inc ....D 585 265-2010
  Webster (G-15658)
Van Reenen Tool & Die Inc ....F 585 288-6000
  Rochester (G-13794)
Volkert Precision Tech Inc ....E 718 464-9500
  Queens Village (G-13027)
W & H Stampings Inc ....E 631 234-6161
  Hauppauge (G-5798)

METAL STAMPINGS: Patterned

Corbett Stves Pttern Works Inc ....E 585 546-7109
  Rochester (G-13326)

METAL STAMPINGS: Perforated

Erdle Perforating Holdings Inc ....D 585 247-4700
  Rochester (G-13397)
National Wire & Metal Tech Inc ....E 716 661-9180
  Jamestown (G-6534)
Pall Corporation ....A 607 753-6041
  Cortland (G-3779)

METAL STAMPINGS: Rigidized

Rigidized Metals Corporation ....E 716 849-4703
  Buffalo (G-2955)

METAL TREATING COMPOUNDS

Foseco Inc ....F 914 345-4760
  Tarrytown (G-15044)
Technic Inc ....F 516 349-0700
  Plainview (G-12718)

METAL, TITANIUM: Sponge & Granules

Saes Smart Materials Inc ....E 315 266-2026
  New Hartford (G-8245)

METAL: Heavy, Perforated

Perforated Screen Surfaces ....E 866 866-8690
  Conklin (G-3627)

METALLIC ORES WHOLESALERS

Umicore USA Inc ....E 919 874-7171
  Glens Falls (G-5268)

METALS SVC CENTERS & WHOL: Structural Shapes, Iron Or Steel

Blue Tee Corp ....G 212 598-0880
  New York (G-8820)
GCM Metal Industries Inc ....F 718 386-4059
  Brooklyn (G-1879)
Reliable Welding & Fabrication ....G 631 758-2637
  Patchogue (G-12511)
Universal Steel Fabricators ....F 718 342-0782
  Brooklyn (G-2546)

METALS SVC CENTERS & WHOLESALERS: Cable, Wire

Samzong Inc ....G 718 475-1843
  Monsey (G-8047)
Ultra Clarity Corp ....G 719 470-1010
  Spring Valley (G-14584)

METALS SVC CENTERS & WHOLESALERS: Iron & Steel Prdt, Ferrous

Apollo Management V LP ....E 914 467-6510
  Purchase (G-13001)

METALS SVC CENTERS & WHOLESALERS: Misc Nonferrous Prdts

Amt Incorporated ....E 518 284-2910
  Sharon Springs (G-14382)

METALS SVC CENTERS & WHOLESALERS: Nonferrous Sheets, Etc

Umicore USA Inc ....E 919 874-7171
  Glens Falls (G-5268)

METALS SVC CENTERS & WHOLESALERS: Pipe & Tubing, Steel

Accord Pipe Fabricators Inc ....E 718 657-3900
  Jamaica (G-6424)
ASAP Rack Rental Inc ....G 718 499-4495
  Brooklyn (G-1539)

METALS SVC CENTERS & WHOLESALERS: Sheets, Metal

Hatfield Metal Fab Inc ....E 845 454-9078
  Poughkeepsie (G-12961)

METALS SVC CENTERS & WHOLESALERS: Steel

Asm USA Inc ....F 212 925-2906
  New York (G-8649)
DAgostino Iron Works Inc ....G 585 235-8850
  Rochester (G-13335)
Hitachi Metals America Ltd ....G 914 694-9200
  Purchase (G-13005)
Nathan Steel Corp ....F 315 797-1335
  Utica (G-15287)
R & S Machine Center Inc ....E 518 563-4016
  Plattsburgh (G-12773)
Ta Chen International Inc ....F 845 352-5300
  Monsey (G-8051)

METALS SVC CENTERS & WHOLESALERS: Tin & Tin Base Metals

Tin Box Company of America Inc ....E 631 845-1600
  Farmingdale (G-4757)

METALS SVC CENTERS & WHOLESALERS: Tubing, Metal

Tube Fabrication Company Inc ....F 716 673-1871
  Fredonia (G-4971)

METALS: Honeycombed

Unicel Corporation ....E 760 741-3912
  Deer Park (G-3944)

METALS: Precious NEC

All American Funding & Ref LLC ....G 516 978-7531
  Farmingdale (G-4578)
Dennis Metals Inc ....G 516 487-5747
  Great Neck (G-5381)
Doral Refining Corp ....E 516 223-3684
  Freeport (G-4992)
Handy & Harman Ltd ....A 212 520-2300
  New York (G-9720)
Sph Group Holdings LLC ....F 212 520-2300
  New York (G-11321)
Starfuels Inc ....G 914 289-4800
  White Plains (G-16062)
Wallace Refiners Inc ....G 212 391-2649
  New York (G-11718)

METALS: Precious, Secondary

Encore Refining and Recycleing ....G 631 319-1910
  Holbrook (G-5999)
Sabin Metal Corporation ....F 631 329-1695
  East Hampton (G-4127)
Sabin Metal Corporation ....C 585 538-2194
  Scottsville (G-14343)

METALS: Primary Nonferrous, NEC

Ames Goldsmith Corp ....F 518 792-7435
  Glens Falls (G-5239)
Billanti Casting Co Inc ....E 516 775-4800
  New Hyde Park (G-8254)

Goldmark Products Inc ....E 631 777-3343
  Farmingdale (G-4639)
Marina Jewelry Co Inc ....G 212 354-5027
  New York (G-10361)
Materion Advanced Materials ....G 800 327-1355
  Brewster (G-1154)
S & W Metal Trading Corp ....G 212 719-5070
  Brooklyn (G-2375)
Sabin Metal Corporation ....C 585 538-2194
  Scottsville (G-14343)
Sigmund Cohn Corp ....D 914 664-5300
  Mount Vernon (G-8180)
Tdy Industries LLC ....E 716 433-4411
  Lockport (G-7110)

METALWORK: Miscellaneous

Abasco Inc ....E 716 649-4790
  Hamburg (G-5501)
Accurate Metal Weather Strip ....G 914 668-6042
  Mount Vernon (G-8121)
Coral Management Corp ....G 718 893-9286
  Bronx (G-1231)
Empire Metal Finishing Inc ....E 718 545-6700
  Astoria (G-421)
Halmark Architectural Finshg ....E 718 272-1831
  Brooklyn (G-1919)
Hornet Group Inc ....G 845 858-6400
  Port Jervis (G-12850)
Janed Enterprises ....F 631 694-4494
  Farmingdale (G-4657)
Jpl Designs Ltd ....G 212 689-7096
  New York (G-10032)
Kal Manufacturing Corporation ....E 585 265-4310
  Webster (G-15644)
Kraman Iron Works Inc ....F 212 460-8400
  New York (G-10135)
Lane Enterprises Inc ....E 518 885-4385
  Ballston Spa (G-579)
Longstem Organizers Inc ....G 914 777-2174
  Jefferson Valley (G-6568)
Metal Products Intl LLC ....E 716 215-1930
  Niagara Falls (G-11950)
Northern Metalworks Corp ....G 646 523-1689
  Selden (G-14354)
Orange County Ironworks LLC ....E 845 769-3000
  Montgomery (G-8064)
Orbital Holdings Inc ....G 951 360-7100
  Buffalo (G-2899)
Paragon Aquatics ....G 845 452-5500
  Lagrangeville (G-6752)
Ppi Corp ....E 585 880-7277
  Rochester (G-13632)
Risa Management Corp ....E 718 361-2606
  Maspeth (G-7637)
Riverside Iron LLC ....F 315 535-4864
  Gouverneur (G-5322)
Semans Enterprises Inc ....F 585 444-0097
  West Henrietta (G-15803)
Signature Metal MBL Maint LLC ....D 718 292-8280
  Bronx (G-1365)
Sims Steel Corporation ....E 631 587-8670
  Lindenhurst (G-6972)
Tebbens Steel LLC ....F 631 208-8330
  Calverton (G-3089)
Tonys Ornamental Ir Works Inc ....E 315 337-3730
  Rome (G-13874)
United Iron Inc ....E 914 667-5700
  Mount Vernon (G-8191)
Weslor Industries Inc ....E 315 871-4405
  Lyons (G-7454)
West Metal Works Inc ....E 716 895-4900
  Buffalo (G-3045)

METALWORK: Ornamental

Allied Bronze Corp (del Corp) ....E 646 421-6400
  New York (G-8517)
Arcadia Mfg Group Inc ....E 518 434-6213
  Green Island (G-5432)
Arcadia Mfg Group Inc ....E 518 434-6213
  Menands (G-7840)
Armento Incorporated ....G 716 875-2423
  Kenmore (G-6648)
Duke of Iron Inc ....G 631 543-3600
  Smithtown (G-14476)
Giumenta Corp ....E 718 832-1200
  Brooklyn (G-1888)
Iron Art Inc ....G 914 592-7977
  Elmsford (G-4412)
Kendi Iron Works Inc ....E 718 821-2722
  Brooklyn (G-2024)

Kleinfelder John ....G....... 716 753-3163
  Mayville (G-7683)
Koenig Iron Works Inc ....E....... 718 433-0900
  Long Island City (G-7263)
Kryten Iron Works Inc ....G....... 914 345-0990
  Hawthorne (G-5816)
Raulli Iron Works Inc ....F....... 315 337-8070
  Rome (G-13866)
Tensator Inc ....D....... 631 666-0300
  Bay Shore (G-722)

METALWORKING MACHINERY WHOLESALERS

S & S Machinery Corp ....D....... 718 492-7400
  Brooklyn (G-2370)

METER READERS: Remote

Quadlogic Controls Corporation ....D....... 212 930-9300
  Long Island City (G-7334)

METERING DEVICES: Flow Meters, Impeller & Counter Driven

SPX Flow Us LLC ....D....... 585 436-5550
  Rochester (G-13742)
Turbo Machined Products LLC ....E....... 315 895-3010
  Frankfort (G-4957)

METERING DEVICES: Water Quality Monitoring & Control Systems

Gurley Precision Instrs Inc ....C....... 518 272-6300
  Troy (G-15170)
Vepo Solutions LLC ....G....... 914 384-2121
  Cross River (G-3804)

METERS: Elasped Time

Curtis Instruments Inc ....C....... 914 666-2971
  Mount Kisco (G-8089)
Frequency Electronics Inc ....C....... 516 794-4500
  Uniondale (G-15229)

METERS: Liquid

Walter R Tucker Entps Ltd ....E....... 607 467-2866
  Deposit (G-4004)

METHANOL: Natural

Oci USA Inc ....G....... 646 589-6180
  New York (G-10677)
Ocip Holding LLC ....G....... 646 589-6180
  New York (G-10678)

MICA PRDTS

Fra-Rik Formica Fabg Co Inc ....G....... 718 597-3335
  Bronx (G-1262)
Reliance Mica Co Inc ....G....... 718 788-0282
  Rockaway Park (G-13825)
S & J Trading Inc ....G....... 718 347-1323
  Floral Park (G-4820)

MICROCIRCUITS, INTEGRATED: Semiconductor

Aeroflex Incorporated ....B....... 516 694-6700
  Plainview (G-12660)
Cobham Long Island Inc ....B....... 516 694-6700
  Plainview (G-12669)
Imperium Partners Group LLC ....C....... 212 433-1360
  New York (G-9870)
Microchip Technology Inc ....G....... 631 233-3280
  Hauppauge (G-5717)
Park Aerospace Corp ....D....... 631 465-3600
  Melville (G-7814)
Standard Microsystems Corp ....D....... 631 435-6000
  Hauppauge (G-5774)
Telephonics Tlsi Corp ....C....... 631 470-8854
  Huntington (G-6228)

MICROFILM EQPT

Mekatronics Incorporated ....E....... 516 883-6805
  Port Washington (G-12907)

MICROPHONES

Andrea Electronics Corporation ....G....... 631 719-1800
  Bohemia (G-973)

New Audio LLC ....E....... 212 213-6060
  New York (G-10576)
Theodore A Rapp Associates ....G....... 845 469-2100
  Chester (G-3391)

MICROPROCESSORS

Adco Circuits Inc ....G....... 716 668-6600
  Buffalo (G-2620)
Eversan Inc ....F....... 315 736-3967
  Whitesboro (G-16080)
Hippo International LLC ....G....... 617 230-0599
  New York (G-9791)
I E D Corp ....F....... 631 348-0424
  Islandia (G-6334)
INTEL Corporation ....D....... 408 765-8080
  Getzville (G-5177)

MICROWAVE COMPONENTS

Antenna & Radome Res Assoc ....E....... 631 231-8400
  Bay Shore (G-651)
Cobham Holdings Inc ....F....... 716 662-0006
  Orchard Park (G-12345)
Frequency Electronics Inc ....C....... 516 794-4500
  Uniondale (G-15229)
General Microwave Corporation ....F....... 516 802-0900
  Syosset (G-14789)
L3 Foreign Holdings Inc ....C....... 212 697-1111
  New York (G-10153)
L3 Technologies Inc ....G....... 631 289-0363
  Patchogue (G-12506)
L3 Technologies Inc ....B....... 212 697-1111
  New York (G-10154)
Lexan Industries Inc ....F....... 631 434-7586
  Bay Shore (G-690)
Microwave Filter Company Inc ....E....... 315 438-4700
  East Syracuse (G-4226)
Passive-Plus Inc ....F....... 631 425-0938
  Huntington (G-6216)
Sendec Corp ....E....... 585 425-5965
  Fairport (G-4520)
Transistor Power Tech Inc ....G....... 631 491-0265
  Stony Brook (G-14742)
Werlatone Inc ....G....... 845 278-2220
  Patterson (G-12522)

MICROWAVE OVENS: Household

Toshiba America Inc ....E....... 212 596-0600
  New York (G-11519)

MILITARY INSIGNIA

Baldwin Ribbon & Stamping Corp ....F....... 718 335-6700
  Woodside (G-16196)

MILITARY INSIGNIA, TEXTILE

Skd Tactical Inc ....E....... 845 897-2889
  Highland Falls (G-5966)
Tulmar Manufacturing Inc ....G....... 315 393-7191
  Ogdensburg (G-12212)

MILL PRDTS: Structural & Rail

Matrix Steel Company Inc ....G....... 718 381-6800
  Brooklyn (G-2125)

MILLINERY SUPPLIES: Veils & Veiling, Bridal, Funeral, Etc

Paula Varsalona Ltd ....E....... 212 570-9100
  New York (G-10772)

MILLING: Grains, Exc Rice

ADM Milling Co ....D....... 716 849-7333
  Buffalo (G-2621)

MILLWORK

Adams Interior Fabrications ....F....... 631 249-8282
  Massapequa (G-7644)
Amstutze Woodworking ....G....... 518 946-8206
  Upper Jay (G-15235)
Antique Lumber Modrn Mllwk LLC ....G....... 631 726-7026
  Wainscott (G-15454)
Architctral Mllwk Installation ....E....... 631 499-0755
  East Northport (G-4142)
Architectural Enhancements Inc ....F....... 845 343-9663
  Middletown (G-7893)
Armada New York LLC ....F....... 718 852-8105
  Brooklyn (G-1531)

Attica Millwork Inc ....F....... 585 591-2333
  Attica (G-455)
Auburn Custom Millwork Inc ....G....... 315 253-3843
  Auburn (G-460)
Bloch Industries LLC ....D....... 585 334-9600
  Rochester (G-13272)
BNC Innovative Woodworking ....F....... 718 277-2800
  Brooklyn (G-1598)
Braga Woodworks ....G....... 845 342-4636
  Middletown (G-7895)
Broadway Neon Sign Corp ....F....... 908 241-4177
  Ronkonkoma (G-13918)
Carob Industries Inc ....F....... 631 225-0900
  Lindenhurst (G-6945)
Champion Millwork Inc ....E....... 315 463-0711
  Syracuse (G-14847)
Christiana Millwork Inc ....E....... 315 492-9099
  Jamesville (G-6557)
City Store Gates Mfg Corp ....E....... 718 939-9700
  College Point (G-3540)
Clearwood Custom Carpentry and ....E....... 315 432-8422
  East Syracuse (G-4204)
Columbus Woodworking Inc ....G....... 607 674-4546
  Sherburne (G-14389)
Concepts In Wood of CNY ....E....... 315 463-8084
  Syracuse (G-14858)
Cousins Furniture & Hm Imprvs ....F....... 631 254-3752
  Deer Park (G-3854)
Craftsmen Woodworkers Ltd ....E....... 718 326-3350
  Maspeth (G-7601)
Crown Mill Work Corp ....G....... 845 371-2200
  Nanuet (G-8199)
Crown Woodworking Corp ....G....... 718 974-6415
  Brooklyn (G-1702)
Cuan Corp ....G....... 917 579-3774
  Roslyn Heights (G-14049)
Custom Door & Mirror Inc ....E....... 631 414-7725
  Farmingdale (G-4609)
Dbs Interiors Corp ....F....... 631 491-3013
  West Babylon (G-15706)
Dimaio Millwork Corporation ....E....... 914 476-1937
  Yonkers (G-16301)
Duncan & Son Carpentry Inc ....E....... 914 664-4311
  Mount Vernon (G-8139)
Ed Negron Fine Woodworking ....G....... 718 246-1016
  Brooklyn (G-1781)
Efj Inc ....D....... 518 234-4799
  Cobleskill (G-3499)
EM Pfaff & Son Inc ....F....... 607 739-3691
  Horseheads (G-6121)
Five Star Millwork LLC ....F....... 845 920-0247
  Pearl River (G-12530)
Grace Ryan & Magnus Mllwk LLC ....D....... 914 665-0902
  Mount Vernon (G-8144)
Gw Manufacturing ....E....... 718 386-8078
  Poughkeepsie (G-12960)
H Arnold Wood Turning Inc ....E....... 914 381-0801
  Tarrytown (G-15045)
H B Millwork Inc ....G....... 631 289-8086
  Medford (G-7709)
H B Millwork Inc ....G....... 631 924-4195
  Yaphank (G-16263)
Highland Organization Corp ....G....... 631 991-3240
  Deer Park (G-3880)
Hulley Holding Company Inc ....F....... 716 332-3982
  Kenmore (G-6653)
Humboldt Woodworking ....G....... 718 707-0022
  Long Island City (G-7244)
I Meglio Corp ....E....... 631 617-6900
  Hauppauge (G-5674)
Island Street Lumber Co Inc ....G....... 716 692-4127
  North Tonawanda (G-12072)
J Percoco Industries Inc ....G....... 631 312-4572
  Bohemia (G-1025)
Jacobs Woodworking LLC ....G....... 315 427-8999
  Syracuse (G-14915)
James King Woodworking Inc ....G....... 518 761-6091
  Queensbury (G-13044)
Jays Furniture Products Inc ....E....... 716 876-8854
  Buffalo (G-2816)
JEm Wdwkg & Cabinets Inc ....F....... 518 828-5361
  Hudson (G-6165)
John Langenbacher Co Inc ....G....... 718 328-0141
  Bronx (G-1288)
KB Millwork Inc ....G....... 516 280-2183
  Levittown (G-6916)
Living Doors Inc ....F....... 631 924-5393
  Medford (G-7717)
Mack Wood Working ....G....... 845 657-6625
  Shokan (G-14429)

PRODUCT

Mason Woodworks LLC .... G 917 363-7052
  Brooklyn (G-2121)
Masonite International Corp .... F 607 775-0615
  Binghamton (G-895)
Medina Millworks LLC .... G 585 798-2969
  Medina (G-7740)
Mensch Mill & Lumber Corp .... E 718 359-7500
  Bronx (G-1309)
Metalocke Industries Inc .... G 718 267-9200
  Woodside (G-16213)
Michbi Doors Inc .... D 631 231-9050
  Farmingdale (G-4683)
Millco Woodworking LLC .... F 585 526-6844
  Hall (G-5500)
Millwright Wdwrk Installetion .... E 631 587-2635
  West Babylon (G-15732)
Northern Forest Pdts Co Inc .... G 315 942-6955
  Boonville (G-1107)
Ohana Metal & Iron Works Inc ..... F 845 344-7520
  Montgomery (G-8063)
Old Souls Inc .... G 845 809-5886
  Cold Spring (G-3522)
P & B Woodworking Inc .... F 845 744-2508
  Pine Bush (G-12626)
Pella Corporation .... C 631 208-0710
  Calverton (G-3083)
Peter Productions Devivi Inc .... F 315 568-8484
  Waterloo (G-15556)
Piccini Industries Ltd .... E 845 365-0614
  Orangeburg (G-12325)
Professional Cab Detailing Co ...... F 845 436-7282
  Woodridge (G-16194)
Quality Woodworking Corp .... F 718 875-3437
  Brooklyn (G-2313)
Ragnatelli Inc .... E 718 765-4050
  Brooklyn (G-2321)
Randolph Dimension Corporation ... F 716 358-6901
  Randolph (G-13064)
Richard Anthony Corp .... E 914 922-7141
  Yorktown Heights (G-16371)
Roode Hoek & Co Inc .... F 718 522-5921
  Brooklyn (G-2354)
S Donadic Inc .... D 718 361-9888
  Sunnyside (G-14774)
Shawmut Woodworking & Sup Inc .. C 212 920-8900
  New York (G-11209)
Specialty Services .... G 585 728-5650
  Wayland (G-15627)
Syracuse Industrial Sls Co Ltd ..... F 315 478-5751
  Syracuse (G-15007)
TDS Woodworking Inc .... F 718 442-5298
  Staten Island (G-14719)
Tiedemann Waldemar Inc .... F 716 875-5665
  Buffalo (G-3010)
Unicenter Millwork Inc .... G 716 741-8201
  Clarence Center (G-3450)
Universal Custom Millwork Inc ...... D 518 330-6622
  Amsterdam (G-351)
Upbeat Upholstery & Design LLC ... G 347 480-3980
  Brooklyn (G-2547)
Wagner Millwork Inc .... D 607 687-5362
  Owego (G-12439)
Wolfe Lumber Mill Inc .... G 716 772-7750
  Gasport (G-5140)
Xylon Industries Inc .... G 631 293-4717
  Farmingdale (G-4766)
Zanzano Woodworking Inc .... F 914 725-6025
  Scarsdale (G-14243)

MINE DEVELOPMENT SVCS: Nonmetallic Minerals

Resource Capital Funds LP .... G 631 692-9111
  Jericho (G-6592)

MINERAL ABRASIVES MINING SVCS

Capital Gold Corporation .... G 212 668-0842
  New York (G-8912)

MINERAL MINING: Nonmetallic

Hargrave Development .... F 716 877-7880
  Kenmore (G-6650)

MINERAL PRODUCTS

American Crmic Process RES LLC ... G 315 828-6268
  Phelps (G-12601)

MINERAL WOOL

Owens Corning Sales LLC .... B 518 475-3600
  Feura Bush (G-4792)
Soundcoat Company Inc .... D 631 242-2200
  Deer Park (G-3938)
Unifrax I LLC .... C 716 696-3000
  Tonawanda (G-15149)

MINERAL WOOL INSULATION PRDTS

Unifrax Corporation .... E 716 278-3800
  Niagara Falls (G-11987)

MINERALS: Ground Or Otherwise Treated

Minerals Technologies Inc .... E 212 878-1800
  New York (G-10476)
Nutech Biosciences Inc .... F 315 505-6500
  Oneida (G-12248)

MINERALS: Ground or Treated

Allied Aero Services Inc .... G 631 277-9368
  Brentwood (G-1114)
DSM Nutritional Products LLC ...... C 518 372-5155
  Schenectady (G-14261)
DSM Nutritional Products LLC ...... E 518 372-5155
  Glenville (G-5271)
Northeastern Solite Corporation .... E 845 246-2646
  Saugerties (G-14205)
Northeast Solite Corporation .... E 845 246-2177
  Mount Marion (G-8112)
Oro Avanti Inc .... G 516 487-5185
  Great Neck (G-5409)

MINIATURES

Islip Miniture Golf .... G 631 940-8900
  Bay Shore (G-684)

MINING EXPLORATION & DEVELOPMENT SVCS

Advanced Biomedical Tech Inc ...... G 718 766-7898
  New York (G-8476)
Bedrock Industries .... G 202 400-0839
  New York (G-8749)
Coremet Trading Inc .... G 212 964-3600
  New York (G-9103)

MINING SVCS, NEC: Lignite

US Pump Corp .... G 516 303-7799
  West Hempstead (G-15781)

MIRROR REPAIR SHOP

D Best Service Co Inc .... G 718 972-6133
  Brooklyn (G-1715)

MIRRORS: Motor Vehicle

Rosco Inc .... C 718 526-2601
  Jamaica (G-6471)

MIXING EQPT

Munson Machinery Company Inc .... E 315 797-0090
  Utica (G-15286)

MIXTURES & BLOCKS: Asphalt Paving

Advanced Pavement Group Corp .... G 631 277-8400
  Islip (G-6349)
Barrett Paving Materials Inc .... E 315 652-4585
  Liverpool (G-7000)
Barrett Paving Materials Inc .... F 315 788-2037
  Watertown (G-15559)
Bross Quality Paving .... G 845 532-7116
  Ellenville (G-4305)
C & C Ready-Mix Corporation ...... F 607 687-1690
  Owego (G-12429)
Callanan Industries Inc .... C 518 374-2222
  Albany (G-55)
Callanan Industries Inc .... E 845 331-6868
  Kingston (G-6683)
Canal Asphalt Inc .... F 914 667-8500
  Mount Vernon (G-8127)
Cofire Paving Corporation .... E 718 463-1403
  Flushing (G-4845)
Cold Mix Manufacturing Corp .... F 718 463-1444
  Mount Vernon (G-8132)

Deans Paving Inc .... G 315 736-7601
  Marcy (G-7564)
Doctor Pavers .... G 516 342-6016
  Commack (G-3586)
Dolomite Products Company Inc .... F 585 352-0460
  Spencerport (G-14555)
Gernatt Asphalt Products Inc .... G 716 496-5111
  Springville (G-14591)
Grace Associates Inc .... G 718 767-9000
  Harrison (G-5554)
Graymont Materials Inc .... G 518 561-5200
  Plattsburgh (G-12749)
Hanson Aggregates East LLC .... E 585 343-1787
  Stafford (G-14604)
J Pahura Contractors .... G 585 589-5793
  Albion (G-156)
Jet-Black Sealers Inc .... G 716 891-4197
  Buffalo (G-2822)
John T Montecalvo Inc .... G 631 325-1492
  Speonk (G-14563)
Kal-Harbour Inc .... F 518 266-0690
  Albany (G-93)
Lafarge North America Inc .... E 518 756-5000
  Ravena (G-13069)
McConnaughay Technologies .... G 607 753-1100
  Cortland (G-3778)
Nicolia Concrete Products Inc .... D 631 669-0700
  Lindenhurst (G-6965)
Northeastern Sealcoat Inc .... F 585 544-4372
  Rochester (G-13583)
Patterson Blacktop Corp .... G 845 628-3425
  Carmel (G-3189)
Patterson Blacktop Corp .... G 914 949-2000
  White Plains (G-16040)
Patterson Materials Corp .... F 914 949-2000
  White Plains (G-16041)
Peckham Asphalt Resale Corp ...... F 914 949-2000
  White Plains (G-16043)
Peckham Asphalt Resale Corp ...... G 518 945-1120
  Athens (G-449)
Peckham Industries Inc .... E 518 945-1120
  Athens (G-450)
Peckham Materials Corp .... E 518 945-1120
  Athens (G-451)
Peckham Materials Corp .... F 518 494-2313
  Chestertown (G-3394)
Peckham Materials Corp .... E 518 747-3353
  Hudson Falls (G-6192)
Peckham Road Corp .... E 518 792-3157
  Queensbury (G-13051)
Rochester Seal Pro LLC .... E 585 594-3818
  Rochester (G-13695)
Sheldon Slate Products Co Inc ...... E 518 642-1280
  Middle Granville (G-7870)
Suit-Kote Corporation .... F 315 735-8501
  Oriskany (G-12396)
Suit-Kote Corporation .... E 607 535-2743
  Watkins Glen (G-15616)
Thalle Industries Inc .... E 914 762-3415
  Briarcliff Manor (G-1162)
Tilcon New York Inc .... D 845 638-3594
  Haverstraw (G-5808)
Tilcon New York Inc .... G 845 562-3240
  New Windsor (G-8384)
Tri City Highway Products Inc .... E 607 722-2967
  Binghamton (G-914)
Tri-City Highway Products Inc .... E 518 294-9964
  Richmondville (G-13130)
Twin County Recycling Corp .... F 516 827-6900
  Westbury (G-15935)
Unilock New York Inc .... G 845 278-6700
  Brewster (G-1159)
Universal Ready Mix Inc .... G 516 746-4535
  New Hyde Park (G-8301)
Upstone Materials Inc .... G 518 873-2275
  Lewis (G-6918)
Zielinskis Asphalt Inc .... F 315 306-4057
  Oriskany Falls (G-12401)

MOBILE COMMUNICATIONS EQPT

2p Agency Usa Inc .... G 212 203-5586
  Brooklyn (G-1413)
Andrea Electronics Corporation ..... G 631 719-1800
  Bohemia (G-973)
Cmb Wireless Group LLC .... B 631 750-4700
  Bohemia (G-989)
Elite Cellular Accessories Inc .... E 877 390-2502
  Deer Park (G-3869)
Flycell Inc .... D 212 400-1212
  New York (G-9511)

Icell Incorporated ....C....... 516 590-0007
Hempstead (G-5839)
Innovation In Motion Inc ....G....... 407 878-7561
Long Beach (G-7137)
Toura LLC ....F....... 646 652-8668
Brooklyn (G-2514)

MOBILE HOMES

All Star Carts & Vehicles Inc ....D....... 631 666-5581
Bay Shore (G-646)
Champion Home Builders Inc ....C....... 315 841-4122
Sangerfield (G-14155)
Leatherstocking Mobile Home PA ....G....... 315 839-5691
Sauquoit (G-14219)

MOBILE HOMES WHOLESALERS

Century Ready Mix Inc ....G....... 631 888-2200
West Babylon (G-15700)

MODELS

Copesetic Inc ....F....... 315 684-7780
Morrisville (G-8085)
Tri-Force Sales LLC ....E....... 732 261-5507
New York (G-11538)

MODELS: General, Exc Toy

Active Manufacturing Inc ....F....... 607 775-3162
Kirkwood (G-6728)
Creative Models & Prototypes ....G....... 516 433-6828
Hicksville (G-5899)
J T Systematic ....G....... 607 754-0929
Endwell (G-4480)

MODULES: Computer Logic

Intech 21 Inc ....F....... 516 626-7221
Port Washington (G-12889)

MODULES: Solid State

Data Device Corporation ....B....... 631 567-5600
Bohemia (G-999)

MOLDED RUBBER PRDTS

Apple Rubber Products Inc ....C....... 716 684-6560
Lancaster (G-6795)
Buffalo Lining & Fabricating ....G....... 716 883-6500
Buffalo (G-2676)
Enviroform Recycled Pdts Inc ....G....... 315 789-1810
Geneva (G-5152)
Moldtech Inc ....E....... 716 685-3344
Lancaster (G-6818)
SD Christie Associates Inc ....G....... 914 734-1800
Peekskill (G-12557)
Short Jj Associates Inc ....F....... 315 986-3511
Macedon (G-7470)
Traffic Logix Corporation ....G....... 866 915-6449
Spring Valley (G-14583)
Triangle Rubber Co Inc ....E....... 631 589-9400
Bohemia (G-1089)

MOLDING COMPOUNDS

Craftech ....D....... 518 828-5011
Chatham (G-3330)
Hanet Plastics Usa Inc ....G....... 518 324-5850
Plattsburgh (G-12750)
Jrlon Inc ....D....... 315 597-4067
Palmyra (G-12489)
Majestic Mold & Tool Inc ....F....... 315 695-2079
Phoenix (G-12617)
Plaslok Corp ....E....... 716 681-7755
Buffalo (G-2921)
Spectra Polymers & Color Spc ....F....... 631 694-6943
Farmingdale (G-4738)

MOLDINGS, ARCHITECTURAL: Plaster Of Paris

Foster Reeve & Associates Inc ....G....... 718 609-0090
Brooklyn (G-1861)

MOLDINGS: Picture Frame

AC Moore Incorporated ....G....... 516 796-5831
Bethpage (G-831)
Amci Ltd ....D....... 718 937-5858
Long Island City (G-7155)

Drummond Framing Inc ....F....... 212 647-1701
New York (G-9273)
Frame Shoppe & Art Gallery ....G....... 516 365-6014
Manhasset (G-7534)
General Art Company Inc ....F....... 212 255-1298
New York (G-9588)
Julius Lowy Frame Restoring Co ....E....... 212 861-8585
New York (G-10039)
Lco Destiny LLC ....B....... 315 782-3302
Watertown (G-15581)
P B & H Moulding Corporation ....E....... 315 455-1756
Fayetteville (G-4785)
Quattro Frameworks Inc ....F....... 718 361-2620
Astoria (G-435)
Sky Frame & Art Inc ....E....... 212 925-7856
New York (G-11263)
Structural Industries Inc ....C....... 631 471-5200
Bohemia (G-1082)

MOLDS: Indl

Advent Tool & Mold Inc ....C....... 585 254-2000
Rochester (G-13214)
Allmetal Chocolate Mold Co Inc ....F....... 631 752-2888
West Babylon (G-15685)
American Orthotic Lab Co Inc ....G....... 718 961-6487
College Point (G-3536)
Blue Chip Mold Inc ....F....... 585 647-1790
Rochester (G-13273)
Century Mold Company Inc ....D....... 585 352-8600
Rochester (G-13306)
Chenango Valley Tech Inc ....E....... 607 674-4115
Sherburne (G-14388)
East Pattern & Model Corp ....E....... 585 461-3240
Rochester (G-13362)
G N R Plastics Inc ....G....... 631 724-8758
Smithtown (G-14478)
Gatti Tool & Mold Inc ....F....... 585 328-1350
Rochester (G-13429)
Globmarble LLC ....G....... 347 717-4088
Brooklyn (G-1891)
HNST Mold Inspections LLC ....G....... 845 215-9258
Sloatsburg (G-14471)
Hy-Tech Mold Inc ....F....... 585 247-2450
Rochester (G-13472)
J T Systematic ....G....... 607 754-0929
Endwell (G-4480)
James B Crowell & Sons Inc ....G....... 845 895-3464
Wallkill (G-15470)
Nicoform Inc ....E....... 585 454-5530
Rochester (G-13577)
Nordon Inc ....D....... 585 546-6200
Rochester (G-13578)
Nordon Inc ....E....... 585 546-6200
Rochester (G-13579)
Nordon Inc ....E....... 585 546-6200
Rochester (G-13580)
PMI Industries LLC ....E....... 585 464-8050
Rochester (G-13627)
Polyshot Corporation ....E....... 585 292-5010
West Henrietta (G-15801)
Rochester Tool and Mold Inc ....F....... 585 464-9336
Rochester (G-13701)
Roechling Medical Rochester LP ....D....... 585 254-2000
Rochester (G-13702)
Royal Molds Inc ....F....... 718 382-7686
Brooklyn (G-2361)
Sb Molds LLC ....D....... 845 352-3700
Monsey (G-8048)
Specialty Model & Mold Inc ....G....... 631 475-0840
Ronkonkoma (G-14012)
Star Mold Co Inc ....G....... 631 694-2283
Farmingdale (G-4740)
Stuart Tool & Die Inc ....G....... 716 488-1975
Falconer (G-4559)
Sweet Tooth Enterprises LLC ....E....... 631 752-2888
West Babylon (G-15752)
T A Tool & Molding Inc ....G....... 631 293-0172
Farmingdale (G-4748)
W N R Pattern & Tool Inc ....G....... 716 681-9334
Lancaster (G-6838)

MOLDS: Plastic Working & Foundry

A & D Tool Inc ....G....... 631 243-4339
Dix Hills (G-4008)
Accede Mold & Tool Co Inc ....D....... 585 254-6490
Rochester (G-13199)
Clifford H Jones Inc ....F....... 716 693-2444
Tonawanda (G-15097)
Inter Molds Inc ....G....... 631 667-8580
Bay Shore (G-682)

Moldcraft Inc ....E....... 716 684-1126
Depew (G-3988)
Northern Design Inc ....G....... 716 652-7071
East Aurora (G-4095)
Universal Tooling Corporation ....F....... 716 985-4691
Gerry (G-5172)

MONUMENTS & GRAVE MARKERS, EXC TERRAZZO

Galle & Zinter Inc ....G....... 716 833-4212
Buffalo (G-2765)

MONUMENTS: Concrete

Presbrey-Leland Inc ....G....... 914 949-2264
Valhalla (G-15307)
St Raymond Monument Co ....G....... 718 824-3600
Bronx (G-1369)

MONUMENTS: Cut Stone, Exc Finishing Or Lettering Only

Dominic De Nigris Inc ....E....... 718 597-4460
Bronx (G-1241)
Suffolk Granite Manufacturing ....E....... 631 226-4774
Lindenhurst (G-6977)

MOPS: Floor & Dust

Cpac Inc ....E....... 585 382-3223
Leicester (G-6908)
Ingenious Designs LLC ....C....... 631 254-3376
Ronkonkoma (G-13948)
National Wire & Metal Tech Inc ....E....... 716 661-9180
Jamestown (G-6534)

MORTGAGE BANKERS

Caithness Equities Corporation ....E....... 212 599-2112
New York (G-8888)

MOTION PICTURE & VIDEO PRODUCTION SVCS

Crain Communications Inc ....C....... 212 210-0100
New York (G-9118)
Laird Telemedia ....C....... 845 339-9555
Mount Marion (G-8110)
North Six Inc ....F....... 212 463-7227
New York (G-10643)

MOTION PICTURE & VIDEO PRODUCTION SVCS: Non-Theatrical, TV

Scholastic Corporation ....G....... 212 343-6100
New York (G-11160)

MOTION PICTURE PRODUCTION & DISTRIBUTION

21st Century Fox America Inc ....D....... 212 852-7000
New York (G-8396)
Historic TW Inc ....E....... 212 484-8000
New York (G-9794)
Sony Broadband Entertainment ....F....... 212 833-6800
New York (G-11294)
Time Warner Companies Inc ....D....... 212 484-8000
New York (G-11494)

MOTION PICTURE PRODUCTION & DISTRIBUTION: Television

Martha Stewart Living ....C....... 212 827-8000
New York (G-10374)

MOTION PICTURE PRODUCTION ALLIED SVCS

Yam TV LLC ....G....... 917 932-5418
New York (G-11806)

MOTION PICTURE PRODUCTION SVCS

Abkco Music & Records Inc ....E....... 212 399-0300
New York (G-8430)

MOTOR & GENERATOR PARTS: Electric

Allied Motion Technologies Inc ....C....... 315 782-5910
Watertown (G-15558)

Employee Codes: A=Over 500 employees, B=251-500
C=101-250, D=51-100, E=20-50, F=10-19, G=5-9

2020 Harris
New York Manufacturers Directory

PRODUCT

1159

Ems Development Corporation ....D 631 924-4736
Yaphank (G-16259)
Hes Inc ....G 607 359-2974
Addison (G-5)
Moley Magnetics Inc ....F 716 434-4023
Lockport (G-7095)
Power and Composite Tech LLC ....D 518 843-6825
Amsterdam (G-345)
Stature Electric Inc ....F 716 242-7535
Amherst (G-244)

MOTOR HOMES

Authority Transportation Inc ....F 888 933-1268
Dix Hills (G-4010)

MOTOR REPAIR SVCS

Accurate Marine Specialties ....G 631 589-5502
Bohemia (G-963)
Premco Inc ....F 914 636-7095
New Rochelle (G-8350)
RC Entps Bus & Trck Inc ....G 518 568-5753
Saint Johnsville (G-14120)

MOTOR SCOOTERS & PARTS

Piaggio Group Americas Inc ....E 212 380-4400
New York (G-10833)
Ying Ke Youth Age Group Inc ....F 929 402-8458
Dix Hills (G-4017)

MOTOR VEHICLE ASSEMBLY, COMPLETE: Autos, Incl Specialty

Auto Sport Designs Inc ....F 631 425-1555
Huntington Station (G-6239)
Cabot Coach Builders Inc ....G 516 625-4000
Roslyn Heights (G-14048)
Marcovicci-Wenz Engineering ....G 631 467-9040
Ronkonkoma (G-13970)
Medical Coaches Incorporated ....E 607 432-1333
Oneonta (G-12275)
Troyer Inc ....F 585 352-5590
Rochester (G-13774)

MOTOR VEHICLE ASSEMBLY, COMPLETE: Buses, All Types

Leonard Bus Sales Inc ....G 607 467-3100
Rome (G-13854)
Prevost Car (us) Inc ....C 518 957-2052
Plattsburgh (G-12771)

MOTOR VEHICLE ASSEMBLY, COMPLETE: Cars, Armored

Armor Dynamics Inc ....F 845 658-9200
Kingston (G-6679)
Empire Emergency Apparatus Inc ....E 716 348-3473
Niagara Falls (G-11923)

MOTOR VEHICLE ASSEMBLY, COMPLETE: Fire Department Vehicles

AB Fire Inc ....G 917 416-6444
Brooklyn (G-1446)
Global Fire Corporation ....E 888 320-1799
New York (G-9627)
Kovatch Mobile Equipment Corp ....F 518 785-0900
Latham (G-6863)
Scehenvus Fire Dist ....D 607 638-9017
Schenevus (G-14320)

MOTOR VEHICLE ASSEMBLY, COMPLETE: Military Motor Vehicle

CIC International Ltd ....D 212 213-0089
Brooklyn (G-1663)

MOTOR VEHICLE ASSEMBLY, COMPLETE: Motor Buses

Daimler Buses North Amer Inc ....A 315 768-8101
Oriskany (G-12389)

MOTOR VEHICLE ASSEMBLY, COMPLETE: Snow Plows

Brothers-In-Lawn Property ....G 716 279-6191
Tonawanda (G-15094)

Sabre Enterprises Inc ....G 315 430-3127
Syracuse (G-14983)
Smart Systems Inc ....E 607 776-5380
Bath (G-640)

MOTOR VEHICLE ASSEMBLY, COMPLETE: Truck & Tractor Trucks

Dejana Trck Utility Eqp Co LLC ....C 631 544-9000
Kings Park (G-6672)
Tee Pee Auto Sales Corp ....F 516 338-9333
Westbury (G-15928)

MOTOR VEHICLE ASSEMBLY, COMPLETE: Trucks, Pickup

Dejana Trck Utility Eqp Co LLC ....E 631 549-0944
Huntington (G-6204)

MOTOR VEHICLE DEALERS: Automobiles, New & Used

Cabot Coach Builders Inc ....G 516 625-4000
Roslyn Heights (G-14048)
Split Rock Trading Co Inc ....G 631 929-3261
Wading River (G-15452)

MOTOR VEHICLE PARTS & ACCESS: Acceleration Eqpt

Lemans Corporation ....G 518 885-7500
Ballston Spa (G-580)

MOTOR VEHICLE PARTS & ACCESS: Air Conditioner Parts

GM Components Holdings LLC ....G 716 439-2237
Lockport (G-7078)
Titanx Engine Cooling Inc ....B 716 665-7129
Jamestown (G-6550)

MOTOR VEHICLE PARTS & ACCESS: Axel Housings & Shafts

Mohawk Innovative Tech Inc ....F 518 862-4290
Albany (G-100)

MOTOR VEHICLE PARTS & ACCESS: Bearings

Fcmp Inc ....F 716 692-4623
Tonawanda (G-15103)

MOTOR VEHICLE PARTS & ACCESS: Body Components & Frames

Johnson Controls Inc ....C 585 724-2232
Rochester (G-13495)

MOTOR VEHICLE PARTS & ACCESS: Cylinder Heads

M2 Race Systems Inc ....G 607 882-9078
Ithaca (G-6393)

MOTOR VEHICLE PARTS & ACCESS: Electrical Eqpt

Katikati Inc ....G 585 678-1764
West Henrietta (G-15798)

MOTOR VEHICLE PARTS & ACCESS: Engines & Parts

ARC Remanufacturing Inc ....D 718 728-0701
Long Island City (G-7162)
Curtis L Maclean L C ....B 716 898-7800
Buffalo (G-2715)
Marcovicci-Wenz Engineering ....G 631 467-9040
Ronkonkoma (G-13970)
Standard Motor Products Inc ....B 718 392-0200
Long Island City (G-7364)

MOTOR VEHICLE PARTS & ACCESS: Fuel Systems & Parts

Kearney-National Inc ....F 212 661-4600
New York (G-10087)
TI Group Auto Systems LLC ....G 315 568-7042
Seneca Falls (G-14373)

MOTOR VEHICLE PARTS & ACCESS: Gears

Enplas America Inc ....G 646 892-7811
New York (G-9381)
Gleason Works ....A 585 473-1000
Rochester (G-13445)

MOTOR VEHICLE PARTS & ACCESS: Power Steering Eqpt

CRS Remanufacturing Co Inc ....F 718 739-1720
Jamaica (G-6439)

MOTOR VEHICLE PARTS & ACCESS: Propane Conversion Eqpt

Kurtz Truck Equipment Inc ....F 607 849-3468
Marathon (G-7558)

MOTOR VEHICLE PARTS & ACCESS: Sanders, Safety

Smith Metal Works Newark Inc ....E 315 331-1651
Newark (G-11851)
Vehicle Safety Dept ....F 315 458-6683
Syracuse (G-15020)
Zwack Incorporated ....E 518 733-5135
Stephentown (G-14732)

MOTOR VEHICLE PARTS & ACCESS: Tops

Electron Top Mfg Co Inc ....E 718 846-7400
Richmond Hill (G-13112)

MOTOR VEHICLE PARTS & ACCESS: Transmissions

Banner Transmission & Eng Co ....F 516 221-9459
Melville (G-7762)

MOTOR VEHICLE PARTS & ACCESS: Wheel rims

Extreme Auto Accessories Corp ....F 718 978-6722
Mineola (G-7973)

MOTOR VEHICLE PARTS & ACCESS: Wiring Harness Sets

Agri Services Co ....G 716 937-6618
Alden (G-164)

MOTOR VEHICLE SPLYS & PARTS WHOLESALERS: New

American Auto ACC Incrporation ....E 718 886-6600
Flushing (G-4838)
K M Drive Line Inc ....G 718 599-0628
Brooklyn (G-2018)
Knorr Brake Holding Corp ....G 315 786-5356
Watertown (G-15578)
Trading Services International ....F 212 501-0142
New York (G-11530)
Walter R Tucker Entps Ltd ....E 607 467-2866
Deposit (G-4004)

MOTOR VEHICLE: Hardware

Wolo Mfg Corp ....E 631 242-0333
Deer Park (G-3955)
Zip Products Inc ....F 585 482-0044
Rochester (G-13815)

MOTOR VEHICLE: Radiators

API Heat Transf Thermasys Corp ....C 716 684-6700
Buffalo (G-2638)

MOTOR VEHICLE: Steering Mechanisms

Automotive Accessories Group ....B 212 736-8100
New York (G-8682)
Biltron Automotive Products ....E 631 928-8613
Port Jeff STA (G-12833)
Steering Columns Galore Inc ....G 845 278-5762
Mahopac (G-7479)

MOTOR VEHICLES & CAR BODIES

Antonicelli Vito Race Car ....G 716 684-2205
Buffalo (G-2637)

Jtekt Torsen North America ....F 585 464-5000
Rochester (G-13498)

Ranger Design Us Inc ....E 800 565-5321
Ontario (G-12299)

Siemens Mobility Inc ....F 212 672-4000
New York (G-11227)

Tesla Motors Inc ....A 212 206-1204
New York (G-11455)

Transprttion Collaborative Inc ....E 845 988-2333
Warwick (G-15522)

MOTOR VEHICLES, WHOLESALE: Recreational, All-Terrain

Adirondack Power Sports ....G 518 481-6269
Malone (G-7482)

MOTOR VEHICLES, WHOLESALE: Truck bodies

Smart Systems Inc ....E 607 776-5380
Bath (G-640)

MOTORCYCLE ACCESS

Chicken Hawk Racing Inc ....G 845 758-0700
Red Hook (G-13072)

MOTORCYCLE DEALERS

Se-Mar Electric Co Inc ....E 716 674-7404
West Seneca (G-15853)

Split Rock Trading Co Inc ....G 631 929-3261
Wading River (G-15452)

MOTORCYCLE DEALERS: Bicycles, Motorized

Bignay Inc ....G 786 346-1673
New York (G-8789)

MOTORCYCLE PARTS: Wholesalers

J & D Walter Distributors Inc ....F 518 449-1606
Glenmont (G-5238)

MOTORCYCLES & RELATED PARTS

Golub Corporation ....E 518 943-3903
Catskill (G-3211)

Golub Corporation ....E 518 899-6063
Malta (G-7496)

Golub Corporation ....E 315 363-0679
Oneida (G-12244)

Golub Corporation ....E 607 336-2588
Norwich (G-12122)

Golub Corporation ....E 518 583-3697
Saratoga Springs (G-14177)

Golub Corporation ....E 518 822-0076
Hudson (G-6158)

Golub Corporation ....E 845 344-0327
Middletown (G-7913)

Ihd Motorsports LLC ....F 979 690-1669
Binghamton (G-886)

Indian Larry Legacy ....G 718 609-9184
Brooklyn (G-1955)

Orange County Choppers Inc ....G 845 522-5200
Newburgh (G-11878)

Robs Cycle Supply ....G 315 292-6878
Syracuse (G-14978)

Sumax Cycle Products Inc ....F 315 768-1058
Oriskany (G-12397)

Super Price Chopper Inc ....F 716 893-3323
Buffalo (G-2996)

MOTORS: Electric

Allied Motion Technologies Inc ....C 716 242-8634
Amherst (G-207)

ARC Systems Inc ....E 631 582-8020
Hauppauge (G-5592)

Cobham Long Island Inc ....B 516 694-6700
Plainview (G-12669)

Current Applications Inc ....E 315 788-4689
Watertown (G-15567)

Elton El Mantle Inc ....G 315 432-9067
Syracuse (G-14886)

Empire Division Inc ....D 315 476-6273
Syracuse (G-14888)

Faradyne Motors LLC ....F 315 331-5985
Palmyra (G-12485)

Island Components Group Inc ....F 631 563-4224
Holbrook (G-6003)

John G Rubino Inc ....E 315 253-7396
Auburn (G-482)

Nidec Motor Corporation ....F 315 434-9303
East Syracuse (G-4229)

Sopark Corp ....D 716 822-0434
Buffalo (G-2987)

Worldwide Electric Corp LLC ....E 800 808-2131
Rochester (G-13809)

MOTORS: Generators

Allied Motion Control Corp ....G 716 242-7535
Amherst (G-205)

American Precision Inds Inc ....C 716 691-9100
Amherst (G-210)

Ametek Inc ....G 631 467-8400
Ronkonkoma (G-13904)

Ametek Inc ....D 607 763-4700
Binghamton (G-854)

Ametek Inc ....D 585 263-7700
Rochester (G-13234)

Cobham Long Island Inc ....C 631 231-9100
Hauppauge (G-5619)

D & D Motor Systems Inc ....E 315 701-0861
Syracuse (G-14871)

Designatronics Incorporated ....B 516 328-3300
New Hyde Park (G-8261)

Emes Motor Inc ....G 718 387-2445
Brooklyn (G-1799)

Ener-G-Rotors Inc ....G 518 372-2608
Schenectady (G-14262)

Eni Technology Inc ....B 585 427-8300
Rochester (G-13395)

Felchar Manufacturing Corp ....A 607 723-4076
Binghamton (G-877)

General Electric Company ....B 518 385-2211
Schenectady (G-14270)

General Electric Intl Inc ....G 518 385-2211
Schenectady (G-14273)

Generation Power LLC ....G 315 234-2451
Syracuse (G-14903)

Got Power Inc ....G 631 767-9493
Ronkonkoma (G-13944)

Kaddis Manufacturing Corp ....G 585 624-3070
Honeoye Falls (G-6077)

Lcdrives Corp ....E 860 712-8926
Potsdam (G-12937)

Makerbot Industries LLC ....C 347 334-6800
Brooklyn (G-2104)

Modular Devices Inc ....D 631 345-3100
Shirley (G-14425)

Premco Inc ....F 914 636-7095
New Rochelle (G-8350)

Protective Power Systms & Cntr ....F 845 721-1875
Staatsburg (G-14600)

Ruhle Companies Inc ....E 914 287-4000
Valhalla (G-15309)

Sima Technologies LLC ....G 412 828-9130
Hauppauge (G-5766)

Supergen Products LLC ....G 315 573-7887
Newark (G-11853)

Troy Belting and Supply Co ....D 518 272-4920
Watervliet (G-15609)

W J Albro Machine Works Inc ....G 631 345-0657
Yaphank (G-16278)

MOTORS: Torque

Aeroflex Incorporated ....B 516 694-6700
Plainview (G-12660)

MOVIE THEATERS, EXC DRIVE-IN

Sony Broadband Entertainment ....F 212 833-6800
New York (G-11294)

MOWERS & ACCESSORIES

Benishty Brothers Corp ....G 646 339-9991
Woodmere (G-16190)

MULTIPLEXERS: Telephone & Telegraph

Toshiba America Inc ....E 212 596-0600
New York (G-11519)

MUSEUMS

R H Guest Inc ....G 718 675-7600
Brooklyn (G-2319)

MUSEUMS & ART GALLERIES

Njf Publishing Corp ....G 631 345-5200
Shirley (G-14426)

MUSIC BROADCASTING SVCS

Michael Karp Music Inc ....G 212 840-3285
New York (G-10453)

MUSIC COPYING SVCS

Boosey and Hawkes Inc ....E 212 358-5300
New York (G-8836)

MUSIC DISTRIBUTION APPARATUS

Nykon Inc ....G 315 483-0504
Sodus (G-14492)

Tunecore Inc ....E 646 651-1060
Brooklyn (G-2527)

MUSIC LICENSING & ROYALTIES

Warner Music Group Corp ....C 212 275-2000
New York (G-11722)

MUSIC LICENSING TO RADIO STATIONS

Historic TW Inc ....E 212 484-8000
New York (G-9794)

Time Warner Companies Inc ....D 212 484-8000
New York (G-11494)

MUSIC RECORDING PRODUCER

Euphorbia Productions Ltd ....G 212 533-1700
New York (G-9418)

MUSICAL ENTERTAINERS

Wmg Acquisition Corp ....F 212 275-2000
New York (G-11771)

MUSICAL INSTRUMENT PARTS & ACCESS, WHOLESALE

Carl Fischer LLC ....E 212 777-0900
New York (G-8917)

MUSICAL INSTRUMENT REPAIR

Guitar Specialist Inc ....G 914 401-9052
Goldens Bridge (G-5303)

Sadowsky Guitars Ltd ....F 718 433-1990
Long Island City (G-7351)

MUSICAL INSTRUMENTS & ACCESS: Carrying Cases

Roadie Products Inc ....E 631 567-8588
Holbrook (G-6018)

MUSICAL INSTRUMENTS & ACCESS: NEC

DAddario & Company Inc ....E 718 599-6660
Brooklyn (G-1717)

DAndrea Inc ....E 516 496-2200
Syosset (G-14783)

Dimarzio Inc ....E 718 442-6655
Staten Island (G-14646)

Elsener Organ Works Inc ....G 631 254-2744
Deer Park (G-3870)

Magic Reed ....F 914 630-4006
Larchmont (G-6842)

Muzet Inc ....F 315 452-0050
Syracuse (G-14948)

Nathan Love LLC ....F 212 925-7111
New York (G-10537)

Paulson & Co Inc ....C 212 956-2221
New York (G-10773)

Roli USA Inc ....F 412 600-4840
New York (G-11076)

Samson Technologies Corp ....D 631 784-2200
Hicksville (G-5946)

Sound Source Inc ....G 585 271-5370
Rochester (G-13737)

Steinway Musical Instrs Inc ....E 781 894-9770
New York (G-11355)

MUSICAL INSTRUMENTS & ACCESS: Pianos

Steinway Inc ....A 718 721-2600
Long Island City (G-7367)

PRODUCT

Steinway and Sons ....C 718 721-2600
  Long Island City (G-7368)

MUSICAL INSTRUMENTS & ACCESS: Pipe Organs

Kerner and Merchant ....G 315 463-8023
  East Syracuse (G-4225)

MUSICAL INSTRUMENTS & PARTS: Brass

Siegfrieds Call Inc ....G 845 765-2275
  Beacon (G-756)

MUSICAL INSTRUMENTS & PARTS: String

DAddario & Company Inc ....D 631 439-3300
  Melville (G-7773)
Sadowsky Guitars Ltd ....F 718 433-1990
  Long Island City (G-7351)

MUSICAL INSTRUMENTS & SPLYS STORES

Albert Augustine Ltd ....D 718 913-9635
  Mount Vernon (G-8122)
Barbera Transduser Systems ....F 718 816-3025
  Staten Island (G-14624)
Carl Fischer LLC ....E 212 777-0900
  New York (G-8917)
DAndrea Inc ....E 516 496-2200
  Syosset (G-14783)
Hipshot Products Inc ....F 607 532-9404
  Interlaken (G-6284)

MUSICAL INSTRUMENTS & SPLYS STORES: Pianos

Steinway Inc ....A 718 721-2600
  Long Island City (G-7367)
Steinway and Sons ....C 718 721-2600
  Long Island City (G-7368)

MUSICAL INSTRUMENTS WHOLESALERS

Samson Technologies Corp ....D 631 784-2200
  Hicksville (G-5946)

MUSICAL INSTRUMENTS: Electric & Electronic

New Sensor Corporation ....D 718 937-8300
  Long Island City (G-7308)

MUSICAL INSTRUMENTS: Guitars & Parts, Electric & Acoustic

Barbera Transduser Systems ....F 718 816-3025
  Staten Island (G-14624)
DAddario & Company Inc ....A 631 439-3300
  Farmingdale (G-4612)
Guitar Specialist Inc ....G 914 401-9052
  Goldens Bridge (G-5303)
Hipshot Products Inc ....F 607 532-9404
  Interlaken (G-6284)
J D Calato Manufacturing Co ....E 716 285-3546
  Niagara Falls (G-11942)
Stuart Spector Designs Ltd ....G 845 246-6124
  Saugerties (G-14214)

MUSICAL INSTRUMENTS: Harmonicas

Jason Ladanye Guitar Piano & H ......E 518 527-3973
  Albany (G-91)

MUSICAL INSTRUMENTS: Heads, Drum

Evans Manufacturing LLC ....D 631 439-3300
  Farmingdale (G-4627)

MUSICAL INSTRUMENTS: Organs

Gluck Orgelbau Inc ....G 212 233-2684
  New York (G-9634)
Leonard Carlson ....G 518 477-4710
  East Greenbush (G-4115)

MUSICAL INSTRUMENTS: Strings, Instrument

Albert Augustine Ltd ....D 718 913-9635
  Mount Vernon (G-8122)
E & O Mari Inc ....D 845 562-4400
  Newburgh (G-11863)

Mari Strings Inc ....F 212 799-6781
  New York (G-10359)

NAIL SALONS

Angel Tips Nail Salon ....G 718 225-8300
  Little Neck (G-6996)

NAME PLATES: Engraved Or Etched

Advanced Graphics Company Inc ......F 607 692-7875
  Whitney Point (G-16105)
C & M Products Inc ....G 315 471-3303
  Syracuse (G-14838)
Harold Wood Co Inc ....G 716 873-1535
  Buffalo (G-2794)
Nameplate Mfrs of Amer ....E 631 752-0055
  Farmingdale (G-4690)
Precision Design Systems Inc ....E 585 426-4500
  Rochester (G-13635)
The Gramecy Group ....G 518 348-1325
  Clifton Park (G-3476)
Tricor Direct Inc ....E 716 626-1616
  Williamsville (G-16145)

NAMEPLATES

Decal Makers Inc ....E 516 221-7200
  Bellmore (G-781)
Island Nameplate Inc ....G 845 651-4005
  Florida (G-4825)
Modern Decal Co ....G 315 622-2778
  Liverpool (G-7027)
Signature Name Plate Co Inc ....G 585 321-9960
  Rochester (G-13730)

NATIONAL SECURITY FORCES

Universal Armor Systems Corp ....E 631 838-1836
  Levittown (G-6917)

NATURAL BUTANE PRODUCTION

Center State Propane LLC ....G 315 841-4044
  Waterville (G-15594)
Green Buffalo Fuel LLC ....F 716 768-0600
  Tonawanda (G-15108)

NATURAL GAS COMPRESSING SVC, On-Site

Archrock Inc ....F 716 763-1553
  Lakewood (G-6777)

NATURAL GAS LIQUIDS PRODUCTION

Nfe Management LLC ....F 212 798-6100
  New York (G-10620)
Okra Energy LLC ....G 206 495-7574
  New York (G-10683)
Western Oil and Gas JV Inc ....G 914 967-4758
  Rye (G-14086)

NATURAL GAS PRODUCTION

County Energy Corp ....G 718 626-7000
  Brooklyn (G-1692)
Flownet LLC ....G 716 685-4036
  Lancaster (G-6807)
Green Buffalo Fuel LLC ....F 716 768-0600
  Tonawanda (G-15108)
Repsol Oil & Gas Usa LLC ....G 607 562-4000
  Horseheads (G-6133)
Reserve Gas Company Inc ....G 716 937-9484
  Alden (G-173)

NATURAL GAS TRANSMISSION & DISTRIBUTION

Lenape Energy Inc ....G 585 344-1200
  Alexander (G-177)
Lenape Resources Inc ....F 585 344-1200
  Alexander (G-178)

NATURAL GASOLINE PRODUCTION

20 Bliss St Inc ....G 716 326-2790
  Westfield (G-15943)

NAVIGATIONAL SYSTEMS & INSTRUMENTS

Lockheed Martin Corporation ....A 315 456-0123
  Liverpool (G-7021)

NET & NETTING PRDTS

Apex Texicon Inc ....E 516 239-4400
  New York (G-8602)

NETS: Laundry

Sky Laundromat Inc ....E 718 639-7070
  Jamaica (G-6473)

NEW & USED CAR DEALERS

Auto Sport Designs Inc ....F 631 425-1555
  Huntington Station (G-6239)

NEWS DEALERS & NEWSSTANDS

Chronicle Express ....F 315 536-4422
  Penn Yan (G-12580)

NEWS FEATURE SYNDICATES

New York Times Company ....B 212 556-1234
  New York (G-10604)

NEWS PICTURES GATHERING & DISTRIBUTING SVCS

Kraus Organization Limited ....D 212 686-5411
  New York (G-10138)

NEWS SYNDICATES

Thomson Reuters Corporation ....A 646 223-4000
  New York (G-11475)

NEWSPAPERS & PERIODICALS NEWS REPORTING SVCS

Dow Jones & Company Inc ....E 212 597-5983
  New York (G-9259)

NEWSPAPERS, WHOLESALE

Nyt Capital LLC ....F 212 556-1234
  New York (G-10669)

NICKEL ALLOY

Nickel City Studios Photo Jour ....G 716 200-0956
  Buffalo (G-2889)

NONCURRENT CARRYING WIRING DEVICES

Chase Corporation ....F 631 827-0476
  Northport (G-12101)
Complete SEC & Contrls Inc ....F 631 421-7200
  Huntington Station (G-6243)
Lapp Insulator Company LLC ....G 585 768-6221
  Le Roy (G-6902)
Pfisterer Lapp LLC ....C 585 768-6221
  Le Roy (G-6906)
Von Roll Usa Inc ....E 203 562-2171
  Schenectady (G-14315)
Zierick Manufacturing Corp ....D 800 882-8020
  Mount Kisco (G-8108)

NONFERROUS: Rolling & Drawing, NEC

Arlon Viscor Ltd ....A 914 461-1300
  White Plains (G-15976)
Continental Cordage Corp ....D 315 655-9800
  Cazenovia (G-3225)
Cpp-Syracuse Inc ....E 315 687-0014
  Chittenango (G-3406)
Handy & Harman Holding Corp ....D 914 461-1300
  White Plains (G-16013)
Medi-Ray Inc ....D 877 898-3003
  Tuckahoe (G-15205)
Nationwide Precision Pdts Corp ....B 585 272-7100
  Rochester (G-13567)
Selectrode Industries Inc ....D 631 547-5470
  Huntington Station (G-6260)

NONMETALLIC MINERALS: Support Activities, Exc Fuels

CB Minerals LLC ....F 914 777-3330
  Mamaroneck (G-7502)
Crystal Ceres Industries Inc ....D 716 283-0445
  Niagara Falls (G-11918)

NOTARIES PUBLIC

Chesu Inc..............................F..... 239 564-2803
East Hampton *(G-4119)*

NOTEBOOKS, MADE FROM PURCHASED MATERIALS

Anne Taintor Inc......................G..... 718 483-9312
Brooklyn *(G-1512)*

NOTIONS: Button Blanks & Molds

Connection Mold Inc...................G..... 585 458-6463
Rochester *(G-13323)*

NOTIONS: Pins, Straight, Steel Or Brass

Karp Overseas Corporation.............E..... 718 784-2105
Maspeth *(G-7625)*

NOTIONS: Studs, Shirt, Exc Precious/Semi Metal/Stone

Columbia Button Nailhead Corp..........F..... 718 386-3414
Brooklyn *(G-1676)*

NOVELTIES

Best Priced Products Inc..............G..... 914 345-3800
Elmsford *(G-4395)*
Fish & Crown Ltd......................D..... 212 707-9603
New York *(G-9506)*
Jacobs Juice Corp.....................G..... 646 255-2860
Brooklyn *(G-1986)*
Orlandi Inc...........................D..... 631 756-0110
Farmingdale *(G-4698)*
Orlandi Inc...........................E..... 631 756-0110
Farmingdale *(G-4699)*

NOVELTIES & SPECIALTIES: Metal

Buttons & Trimcom Inc.................F..... 212 868-1971
New York *(G-8874)*
Criterion Bell & Specialty............E..... 718 788-2600
Brooklyn *(G-1701)*
Polich Tallix Inc.....................D..... 845 567-9464
Rock Tavern *(G-13821)*
Split Rock Trading Co Inc.............G..... 631 929-3261
Wading River *(G-15452)*
Stylebuilt Accessories Inc............F..... 917 439-0578
East Rockaway *(G-4175)*

NOVELTIES: Paper, Made From Purchased Materials

National Advertising & Prtg...........G..... 212 629-7650
New York *(G-10540)*
P C I Paper Conversions Inc...........F..... 315 437-1641
Syracuse *(G-14961)*

NOVELTIES: Plastic

Buttons & Trimcom Inc.................F..... 212 868-1971
New York *(G-8874)*
GPM Associates LLC....................E..... 585 335-3940
Dansville *(G-3819)*
Kling Magnetics Inc...................E..... 518 392-4000
Chatham *(G-3331)*
Pelican Products Co Inc...............E..... 718 860-3220
Bronx *(G-1334)*
Pleasure Chest Sales Ltd..............F..... 212 242-2158
New York *(G-10854)*
Skd Distribution Corp.................E..... 718 525-6000
Jericho *(G-6596)*

NOVELTY SHOPS

Mgd Brands Inc........................E..... 516 545-0150
Plainview *(G-12702)*

NOZZLES & SPRINKLERS Lawn Hose

Artys Sprnklr Svc Instllation.........F..... 516 538-4371
East Meadow *(G-4131)*

NOZZLES: Spray, Aerosol, Paint Or Insecticide

Sono-Tek Corporation..................D..... 845 795-2020
Milton *(G-7952)*

NUCLEAR REACTORS: Military Or Indl

Energy Nuclear Operations.............E..... 315 342-0055
Oswego *(G-12410)*

NURSERIES & LAWN & GARDEN SPLY STORES, RETAIL: Fertilizer

Scotts Company LLC....................E..... 631 816-2831
Yaphank *(G-16269)*

NURSERIES & LAWN & GARDEN SPLY STORES, RETAIL: Sod

E F Lippert Co Inc....................F..... 716 373-1100
Allegany *(G-187)*

NURSERIES & LAWN & GARDEN SPLY STORES, RETAIL: Top Soil

East Coast Mines Ltd..................E..... 631 653-5445
East Quogue *(G-4156)*
Grosso Materials Inc..................F..... 845 361-5211
Montgomery *(G-8061)*
Hampton Sand Corp.....................G..... 631 325-5533
Westhampton *(G-15955)*

NURSERY & GARDEN CENTERS

Birkett Mills.........................G..... 315 536-3311
Penn Yan *(G-12578)*

NUTS: Metal

Buckley Qc Fasteners Inc..............E..... 716 662-1490
Orchard Park *(G-12341)*
Dependable Acme Threaded Pdts.........G..... 516 338-4700
Westbury *(G-15875)*
Zierick Manufacturing Corp............D..... 800 882-8020
Mount Kisco *(G-8108)*

NYLON RESINS

Sk Capital Partners II LP.............F..... 212 826-2700
New York *(G-11254)*
Sk Titan Holdings LLC.................F..... 212 826-2700
New York *(G-11255)*

OFFICE EQPT WHOLESALERS

Automecha International Ltd...........E..... 607 843-2235
Oxford *(G-12441)*
DAF Office Networks Inc...............G..... 315 699-7070
Cicero *(G-3418)*
Finesse Creations Inc.................F..... 718 692-2100
Brooklyn *(G-1846)*

OFFICE EQPT, WHOLESALE: Duplicating Machines

Media Technologies Ltd................F..... 631 467-7900
Eastport *(G-4252)*

OFFICE FIXTURES: Exc Wood

Air Crafters Inc......................C..... 631 471-7788
Ronkonkoma *(G-13893)*
Evans & Paul LLC......................E..... 516 576-0800
Plainview *(G-12684)*

OFFICE FIXTURES: Wood

Bauerschmidt & Sons Inc...............D..... 718 528-3500
Jamaica *(G-6429)*

OFFICE FURNITURE REPAIR & MAINTENANCE SVCS

Davies Office Refurbishing Inc........C..... 518 449-2040
Albany *(G-69)*
Jim Quinn.............................F..... 518 356-0398
Schenectady *(G-14282)*
Roberts Office Furn Cncpts Inc........E..... 315 451-9185
Liverpool *(G-7038)*

OFFICE SPLY & STATIONERY STORES

American Office Supply Inc.............F..... 516 294-9444
Westbury *(G-15868)*
Flynns Inc............................E..... 212 339-8700
New York *(G-9512)*
Tripi Engraving Co Inc................E..... 718 383-6500
Brooklyn *(G-2522)*

OFFICE SPLY & STATIONERY STORES: Office Forms & Splys

Datagraphic Business Systems..........G..... 516 485-9069
Brentwood *(G-1118)*
Grant Hamilton........................F..... 716 652-0320
East Aurora *(G-4089)*
House Ur Home Inc.....................G..... 347 585-3308
Monroe *(G-8023)*
J P Printing Inc......................G..... 516 293-6110
Farmingdale *(G-4655)*
Kleer-Fax Inc.........................D..... 631 225-1100
Amityville *(G-286)*
Richard Ruffner......................F..... 631 234-4600
Central Islip *(G-3287)*
Rmd Holding Inc.......................G..... 845 628-0030
Mahopac *(G-7478)*
Short Run Forms Inc...................D..... 631 567-7171
Bohemia *(G-1078)*
Tannens...............................G..... 718 292-4646
Bronx *(G-1378)*

OFFICE SPLYS, NEC, WHOLESALE

DAF Office Networks Inc...............G..... 315 699-7070
Cicero *(G-3418)*
Rike Enterprises Inc..................F..... 631 277-8338
Islip *(G-6356)*
Robert Tabatznik Assoc Inc............F..... 845 336-4555
Kingston *(G-6708)*

OFFICES & CLINICS OF DENTISTS: Prosthodontist

Mark Goldberg Prosthetic..............F..... 631 689-6606
East Setauket *(G-4180)*

OFFICES & CLINICS OF DRS, MED: Specialized Practitioners

Erika T Schwartz MD PC................G..... 212 873-3420
New York *(G-9395)*

OFFICES & CLINICS OF HEALTH PRACTITIONERS: Nutrition

Nyb Distributors Inc..................G..... 516 937-0666
Jericho *(G-6587)*

OFFICES & CLINICS OF HEALTH PRACTITIONERS: Nutritionist

Everlast Worldwide Inc................E..... 212 239-0990
New York *(G-9428)*

OIL & GAS FIELD MACHINERY

Basin Holdings LLC....................E..... 212 695-7376
New York *(G-8738)*
Derrick Corporation...................C..... 716 683-9010
Buffalo *(G-2727)*
Schlumberger Technology Corp..........C..... 607 378-0105
Horseheads *(G-6136)*
Smith International Inc................F..... 585 265-2330
Ontario *(G-12303)*

OIL FIELD MACHINERY & EQPT

Anchor Commerce Trading Corp..........G..... 516 881-3485
Atlantic Beach *(G-452)*
Desmi-Afti Inc........................E..... 716 662-0632
Orchard Park *(G-12351)*

OIL FIELD SVCS, NEC

Alba Fuel Corp........................G..... 718 931-1700
Bronx *(G-1199)*
Bass Oil & Chemical Llc...............F..... 718 628-4444
Brooklyn *(G-1564)*
Bluebar Oil Co Inc....................F..... 315 245-4328
Blossvale *(G-955)*
Dlh Energy Service LLC................G..... 716 410-0028
Lakewood *(G-6782)*
Fuel Energy Services USA Ltd..........E..... 607 846-2650
Horseheads *(G-6124)*
Gas Field Specialists Inc.............D..... 716 378-6422
Horseheads *(G-6125)*
Grit Energy Services Inc..............G..... 212 701-4500
New York *(G-9680)*
Marcellus Energy Services LLC.........E..... 607 236-0038
Candor *(G-3162)*

P
R
O
D
U
C
T

Petro Inc .... G 516 686-1900
Hicksville **(G-5944)**

Schneider Amalco Inc .... F 917 470-9674
New York **(G-11154)**

U S Energy Development Corp .... D 716 636-0401
Getzville **(G-5183)**

OIL ROYALTY TRADERS

Schneider Amalco Inc .... F 917 470-9674
New York **(G-11154)**

OILS & GREASES: Blended & Compounded

Battenfeld Grease Oil Corp NY .... E 716 695-2100
North Tonawanda **(G-12058)**

Battenfeld-American Inc .... E 716 822-8410
Buffalo **(G-2658)**

Remcoda LLC .... G 212 354-1330
New York **(G-11009)**

Tribology Inc .... E 631 345-3000
Yaphank **(G-16275)**

OILS & GREASES: Lubricating

Baums Castorine Company Inc .... G 315 336-8154
Rome **(G-13844)**

Beka World LP .... G 716 685-3717
Buffalo **(G-2660)**

Castoleum Corporation .... F 914 664-5877
Mount Vernon **(G-8128)**

Chemlube International LLC .... F 914 381-5800
Harrison **(G-5550)**

Chemlube Marketing Inc .... F 914 381-5800
Harrison **(G-5551)**

Commercial Lubricants Moove .... E 718 720-3434
Staten Island **(G-14641)**

Finish Line Technologies Inc .... E 631 666-7300
Hauppauge **(G-5650)**

Inland Vacuum Industries Inc .... F 585 293-3330
Churchville **(G-3412)**

Loobrica International Corp .... G 347 997-0296
Staten Island **(G-14677)**

Oil and Lubricant Depot LLC .... F 631 841-5000
Wyandanch **(G-16246)**

Polycast Industries Inc .... G 631 595-2530
Bay Shore **(G-699)**

Specialty Silicone Pdts Inc .... D 518 885-8826
Ballston Spa **(G-587)**

Summit Lubricants Inc .... E 585 815-0798
Batavia **(G-626)**

US Global Lubricants Inc .... F 845 271-4277
Stony Point **(G-14750)**

OILS: Anise

Von Roll Usa Inc .... E 203 562-2171
Schenectady **(G-14315)**

OILS: Essential

Natures Warehouse .... F 800 215-4372
Philadelphia **(G-12612)**

Torre Products Co Inc .... G 212 925-8989
Mount Vernon **(G-8184)**

OILS: Lubricating

Oil Solutions Intl Inc .... G 631 608-8889
Amityville **(G-300)**

R H Crown Co Inc .... E 518 762-4589
Johnstown **(G-6626)**

OILS: Lubricating

Black Bear Company Inc .... E 718 784-7330
Valley Stream **(G-15335)**

Blaser Production Inc .... F 845 294-3200
Goshen **(G-5306)**

Blaser Swisslube Holding Corp .... F 845 294-3200
Goshen **(G-5307)**

Mdi Holdings LLC .... A 212 559-1127
New York **(G-10404)**

Monroe Fluid Technology Inc .... E 585 392-3434
Hilton **(G-5973)**

OILS: Orange

Solvents Company Inc .... F 631 595-9300
Kingston **(G-6709)**

OINTMENTS

Easton Pharmaceuticals Inc .... G 347 284-0192
Lewiston **(G-6920)**

Perrigo New York Inc .... F 718 901-2800
Bronx **(G-1337)**

Perrigo New York Inc .... B 718 960-9900
Bronx **(G-1338)**

ON-LINE DATABASE INFORMATION RETRIEVAL SVCS

Endava Inc .... F 212 920-7240
New York **(G-9369)**

Informa Media Inc .... B 212 204-4200
New York **(G-9889)**

News Corporation .... C 212 416-3400
New York **(G-10612)**

Optionline LLC .... E 516 218-3225
Garden City **(G-5111)**

Sparta Commercial Services Inc .... F 212 239-2666
New York **(G-11309)**

OPEN PIT GOLD MINING

Surtic Mining Company LLC .... F 718 434-0477
Brooklyn **(G-2481)**

OPERATOR: Apartment Buildings

Gallagher Printing Inc .... E 716 873-2434
Buffalo **(G-2764)**

Hospitality Inc .... E 212 268-1930
New York **(G-9817)**

OPHTHALMIC GOODS

21st Century Optics Inc .... E 347 527-1079
Long Island City **(G-7140)**

Alden Optical Laboratory Inc .... F 716 937-9181
Lancaster **(G-6794)**

Bausch & Lomb Holdings Inc .... G 585 338-6000
New York **(G-8741)**

Bausch & Lomb Incorporated .... D 585 338-6000
Rochester **(G-13262)**

Bausch & Lomb Incorporated .... B 585 338-6000
Rochester **(G-13263)**

Designs For Vision Inc .... C 631 585-3300
Bohemia **(G-1006)**

Doug Lambertson Od .... G 718 698-9300
Staten Island **(G-14647)**

Esc Control Electronics LLC .... E 631 467-5328
Sayville **(G-14225)**

Lens Lab .... G 718 379-2020
Bronx **(G-1302)**

Lens Lab Express .... G 718 921-5488
Brooklyn **(G-2062)**

Lens Lab Express Southern Blvd ...... G 718 626-5184
Astoria **(G-428)**

Luxottica of America Inc .... C 516 484-3800
Port Washington **(G-12902)**

North Bronx Retinal & Ophthlmi ...... G 347 535-4932
Bronx **(G-1326)**

Surgical Design Corp .... F 914 273-2445
Armonk **(G-403)**

Wyeth Holdings LLC .... D 845 602-5000
Pearl River **(G-12543)**

OPHTHALMIC GOODS WHOLESALERS

21st Century Optics Inc .... E 347 527-1079
Long Island City **(G-7140)**

Lens Lab Express Southern Blvd ...... B 718 626-5184
Astoria **(G-428)**

Winchester Optical Company .... E 607 734-4251
Elmira **(G-4372)**

OPHTHALMIC GOODS, NEC, WHOLESALE: Frames

Luxottica of America Inc .... C 516 484-3800
Port Washington **(G-12902)**

OPHTHALMIC GOODS: Eyewear, Protective

Provision Supply LLC .... F 347 623-0237
Brooklyn **(G-2303)**

OPHTHALMIC GOODS: Frames & Parts, Eyeglass & Spectacle

Art-Craft Optical Company Inc .... E 585 546-6640
Rochester **(G-13249)**

His Vision Inc .... E 585 254-0022
Rochester **(G-13469)**

Zyloware Corporation .... D 914 708-1200
Port Chester **(G-12831)**

OPHTHALMIC GOODS: Frames, Lenses & Parts, Eyeglasses

Moscot Wholesale Corp .... G 212 647-1550
New York **(G-10507)**

Optika Eyes Ltd .... G 631 567-8852
Sayville **(G-14230)**

Winchester Optical Company .... E 607 734-4251
Elmira **(G-4372)**

OPHTHALMIC GOODS: Lenses, Ophthalmic

Co-Optics America Lab Inc .... E 607 432-0557
Oneonta **(G-12264)**

Tri-Supreme Optical LLC .... D 631 249-2020
Farmingdale **(G-4759)**

OPHTHALMIC GOODS: Spectacles

Modo Retail LLC .... E 212 965-4900
New York **(G-10489)**

Spectacle Optical Inc .... G 646 706-1015
Rego Park **(G-13082)**

OPHTHALMIC GOODS: Temples & Fronts, Ophthalmic

Kathmando Valley Preservation .... F 212 727-0074
New York **(G-10078)**

OPTICAL GOODS STORES

Hart Specialties Inc .... D 631 226-5600
Amityville **(G-267)**

Match Eyewear LLC .... E 516 877-0170
Westbury **(G-15908)**

Optika Eyes Ltd .... G 631 567-8852
Sayville **(G-14230)**

Parker Warby Retail Inc .... D 646 517-5223
New York **(G-10764)**

OPTICAL GOODS STORES: Opticians

Eyeglass Service Industries .... G 914 666-3150
Bedford Hills **(G-769)**

Lens Lab Express .... G 718 921-5488
Brooklyn **(G-2062)**

OPTICAL INSTRUMENTS & APPARATUS

Aeroflex Incorporated .... B 516 694-6700
Plainview **(G-12660)**

Applied Image Inc .... E 585 482-0300
Rochester **(G-13241)**

Carl Zeiss Inc .... C 914 747-1800
White Plains **(G-15990)**

Exc Holdings I Corp .... A 212 644-5900
New York **(G-9438)**

Exc Holdings II Corp .... A 212 644-5900
New York **(G-9439)**

Exc Holdings LP .... A 212 644-5900
New York **(G-9440)**

Gradient Lens Corporation .... E 585 235-2620
Rochester **(G-13449)**

Halo Optical Products Inc .... D 518 773-4256
Gloversville **(G-5284)**

Hart Specialties Inc .... D 631 226-5600
Amityville **(G-267)**

Kevin Freeman .... G 631 447-5321
Patchogue **(G-12505)**

Leica Microsystems Inc .... G 716 686-3000
Depew **(G-3987)**

Lumetrics Inc .... F 585 214-2455
Rochester **(G-13524)**

Plx Inc .... E 631 586-4190
Deer Park **(G-3919)**

RPC Photonics Inc .... F 585 272-2840
Rochester **(G-13708)**

Spectral Systems LLC .... E 845 896-2200
Hopewell Junction **(G-6101)**

Stefan Sydor Optics Inc .... E 585 271-7300
Rochester **(G-13745)**

Tele-Vue Optics Inc .... E 845 469-4551
Chester **(G-3390)**

Westchester Technologies Inc .... E 914 736-1034
Peekskill **(G-12561)**

       (G-0000) Company's Geographic Section entry number

OPTICAL INSTRUMENTS & LENSES

Accu Coat Inc ....G...... 585 288-2330
Rochester **(G-13200)**
Anorad Corporation ....C...... 631 344-6600
Shirley **(G-14412)**
Apollo Optical Systems Inc ....E...... 585 272-6170
West Henrietta **(G-15784)**
Binoptics LLC ....E...... 607 257-3200
Ithaca **(G-6368)**
Caliber Imging Diagnostics Inc ....E...... 585 239-9800
Rochester **(G-13292)**
Carl Zeiss Microscopy LLC ....B...... 914 681-7840
White Plains **(G-15991)**
Carl Zeiss Sbe LLC ....E...... 914 747-1132
White Plains **(G-15992)**
CK Coatings ....G...... 585 502-0425
Le Roy **(G-6897)**
Cobham Long Island Inc ....B...... 516 694-6700
Plainview **(G-12669)**
Corning Tropel Corporation ....C...... 585 377-3200
Fairport **(G-4494)**
Cross Bronx Optical ....G...... 917 667-6611
Bronx **(G-1233)**
Dorsey Metrology Intl Inc 845 229-2929
Poughkeepsie **(G-12951)**
Dynamic Laboratories Inc ....E...... 631 231-7474
Ronkonkoma **(G-13931)**
Edroy Products Co Inc ....G...... 845 358-6600
Nyack **(G-12143)**
Germanow-Simon Corporation ......E...... 585 232-1440
Rochester **(G-13438)**
Gurley Precision Instrs Inc ....C...... 518 272-6300
Troy **(G-15170)**
Keon Optics Inc ....F...... 845 429-7103
Stony Point **(G-14745)**
Match Eyewear LLC ....E...... 516 877-0170
Westbury **(G-15908)**
Micatu Inc ....G...... 888 705-8836
Horseheads **(G-6126)**
Navitar Inc ....D...... 585 359-4000
Rochester **(G-13568)**
Optipro Systems LLC ....D...... 585 265-0160
Ontario **(G-12296)**
Planar Optics Inc ....G...... 585 671-0100
Webster **(G-15647)**
QED Technologies Intl Inc ....E...... 585 256-6540
Rochester **(G-13655)**
Rochester Photonics Corp ....D...... 585 387-0674
Rochester **(G-13694)**
Santa Fe Manufacturing Corp ....G...... 631 234-0100
Hauppauge **(G-5757)**
Schneider Optics Inc ....E...... 631 761-5000
Hauppauge **(G-5761)**
Schott Corporation ....D...... 315 255-2791
Auburn **(G-494)**
Steven John Opticians ....G...... 718 543-3336
Bronx **(G-1372)**
Surgical Design Corp ....F...... 914 273-2445
Armonk **(G-403)**
Va Inc ....E...... 585 385-5930
Rochester **(G-13791)**
Welch Allyn Inc ....A...... 315 685-4100
Skaneateles Falls **(G-14460)**

OPTICAL SCANNING SVCS

Kjckd Inc ....G...... 518 435-9696
Latham **(G-6862)**
Printech Business Systems Inc ......F...... 212 290-2542
New York **(G-10897)**

ORAL PREPARATIONS

Good Home Co Inc ....G...... 212 352-1509
New York **(G-9644)**
Robell Research Inc ....G...... 212 755-6577
New York **(G-11059)**
Vitiprints LLC ....G...... 646 591-4343
New York **(G-11697)**

ORDNANCE

Dyno Nobel Inc ....D...... 845 338-2144
Ulster Park **(G-15218)**
Island Ordnance Systems LLC ......F...... 516 746-2100
Mineola **(G-7982)**
Magellan Aerospace NY Inc ....C...... 718 699-4000
Corona **(G-3744)**

ORGAN TUNING & REPAIR SVCS

Kerner and Merchant ....G...... 315 463-8023
East Syracuse **(G-4225)**

ORGANIZATIONS, NEC

New York State Assoc ....F...... 518 434-2281
Albany **(G-104)**

ORGANIZATIONS: Medical Research

Encsyive Pharmaceuticals Inc ......E...... 212 733-2323
New York **(G-9368)**

ORGANIZATIONS: Professional

Physicalmind Institute ....F...... 212 343-2150
New York **(G-10832)**
Public Relations Soc Amer Inc ......E...... 212 460-1400
New York **(G-10922)**

ORGANIZATIONS: Religious

Albany Catholic Press Assoc ....G...... 518 453-6688
Albany **(G-31)**
American Jewish Congress Inc ....E...... 212 879-4500
New York **(G-8554)**
Nationwide Custom Services ....G...... 845 365-0414
Tappan **(G-15036)**
Seneca Media Inc ....D...... 607 324-1425
Hornell **(G-6110)**
United Synggue Cnsrvtive Jdism ....E...... 212 533-7800
New York **(G-11602)**

ORGANIZATIONS: Research Institute

Alo Acquisition LLC ....G...... 518 464-0279
Albany **(G-38)**
Katikati Inc ....G...... 585 678-1764
West Henrietta **(G-15798)**

ORGANIZATIONS: Scientific Research Agency

Loobrica International Corp ....G...... 347 997-0296
Staten Island **(G-14677)**

ORGANIZERS, CLOSET & DRAWER Plastic

Plascoline Inc ....F...... 917 410-5754
New York **(G-10852)**

ORNAMENTS: Christmas Tree, Exc Electrical & Glass

Criterion Bell & Specialty ....E...... 718 788-2600
Brooklyn **(G-1701)**

ORTHOPEDIC SUNDRIES: Molded Rubber

Certified Health Products Inc ....E...... 718 339-7498
Brooklyn **(G-1658)**
Newyork Pedorthic Associates ....G...... 718 236-7700
Brooklyn **(G-2214)**

OUTLETS: Electric, Convenience

99cent World and Variety Corp ......G...... 212 740-0010
New York **(G-8409)**
Another 99 Cent Paradise ....G...... 718 786-4578
Sunnyside **(G-14770)**
Bronx New Way Corp ....G...... 347 431-1385
Bronx **(G-1218)**
Dollar Popular Inc ....G...... 914 375-0361
Yonkers **(G-16302)**
RE 99 Cents Inc ....G...... 718 639-2325
Woodside **(G-16222)**

OVENS: Paint Baking & Drying

Specified Air Solutions LLC ....E...... 716 852-4400
Buffalo **(G-2991)**

PACKAGE DESIGN SVCS

Dolco LLC ....E...... 585 657-7777
Bloomfield **(G-946)**
Force Digital Media Inc ....G...... 631 243-0243
Deer Park **(G-3874)**
Hornet Group Inc ....D...... 845 858-6400
Port Jervis **(G-12850)**
Titherington Design & Mfg ....F...... 518 324-2205
Plattsburgh **(G-12785)**

PACKAGED FROZEN FOODS WHOLESALERS, NEC

Bagelovers Inc ....F...... 607 844-3683
Dryden **(G-4037)**
Rhosey LLC ....G...... 718 382-1226
Brooklyn **(G-2343)**

PACKAGING & LABELING SVCS

Atlantic Essential Pdts Inc ....D...... 631 434-8333
Hauppauge **(G-5596)**
Bfma Holding Corporation ....G...... 607 753-6746
Cortland **(G-3755)**
Ccmi Inc ....G...... 315 781-3270
Geneva **(G-5148)**
Elite Roasters Inc ....E...... 716 626-0307
East Amherst **(G-4077)**
F M Howell & Company ....D...... 607 734-6291
Elmira **(G-4351)**
Klg Usa LLC ....A...... 845 856-5311
Port Jervis **(G-12853)**
Marietta Corporation ....B...... 607 753-0982
Cortland **(G-3776)**
Marietta Corporation ....A...... 323 589-8181
Cortland **(G-3777)**
Nice-Pak Products Inc ....B...... 845 365-1700
Orangeburg **(G-12324)**
Nutra Solutions USA Inc ....E...... 631 392-1900
Deer Park **(G-3914)**
Orlandi Inc ....D...... 631 756-0110
Farmingdale **(G-4698)**
Orlandi Inc ....E...... 631 756-0110
Farmingdale **(G-4699)**
Paul Michael Group Inc ....G...... 631 585-5700
Ronkonkoma **(G-13993)**
Princeton Label & Packaging ....E...... 609 490-0800
Patchogue **(G-12510)**
Professnal Dsposables Intl Inc ......E...... 800 999-6423
Orangeburg **(G-12329)**
Sugar Foods Corporation ....E...... 212 753-6900
New York **(G-11385)**
Universal Packg Systems Inc ....A...... 631 543-2277
Hauppauge **(G-5792)**
Valentine Packaging Corp ....F...... 718 418-6000
Maspeth **(G-7641)**
Weather Products Corporation ....G...... 315 474-8593
Syracuse **(G-15024)**

PACKAGING MATERIALS, INDL: Wholesalers

Philpac Corporation ....E...... 716 875-8005
Buffalo **(G-2917)**

PACKAGING MATERIALS, WHOLESALE

Farm To Table Community Inc ....E...... 845 383-1761
Kingston **(G-6692)**
National Paper Converting Inc ....G...... 607 687-6049
Owego **(G-12434)**
Patco Tapes Inc ....G...... 718 497-1527
Maspeth **(G-7634)**
Technical Library Service Inc ....F...... 212 219-0770
Brooklyn **(G-2495)**
Technical Packaging Inc ....F...... 516 223-2300
Baldwin **(G-537)**
Terphane Holdings LLC ....G...... 585 657-5800
Bloomfield **(G-948)**
W N Vanalstine & Sons Inc ....D...... 518 237-1436
Cohoes **(G-3520)**

PACKAGING MATERIALS: Paper

Anasia Inc ....G...... 718 588-1407
Bronx **(G-1205)**
Apexx Omni-Graphics Inc ....D...... 718 326-3330
Maspeth **(G-7591)**
Ares Box LLC ....D...... 718 858-8760
Brooklyn **(G-1526)**
Berry Plastics Corporation ....B...... 315 986-6270
Macedon **(G-7463)**
CCL Label Inc ....C...... 716 852-2155
Buffalo **(G-2693)**
Classic Labels Inc ....E...... 631 467-2300
Patchogue **(G-12498)**
Colad Group LLC ....D...... 716 961-1776
Buffalo **(G-2703)**
Craft Packaging Inc ....G...... 718 633-4045
Brooklyn **(G-1694)**
Depot Label Company Inc ....G...... 631 467-2952
Patchogue **(G-12499)**

Dolco LLC ....E 585 657-7777
  Bloomfield (G-946)

General Fibre Products Corp ....D ... 516 358-7500
  New Hyde Park (G-8270)

General Trade Mark La ....E ... 718 979-7261
  Staten Island (G-14655)

International Paper Company ....C ... 585 663-1000
  Rochester (G-13482)

K Sidrane Inc ....E ... 631 393-6974
  Farmingdale (G-4659)

Multi Packaging Solutions Inc ....C ... 516 488-2000
  Hicksville (G-5932)

Multi Packaging Solutions Inc ....E ... 646 885-0005
  New York (G-10519)

Nameplate Mfrs of Amer ....E ... 631 752-0055
  Farmingdale (G-4690)

Nova Packaging Ltd Inc ....E ... 914 232-8406
  Katonah (G-6637)

Pactiv LLC ....C ... 518 562-6101
  Plattsburgh (G-12766)

Penta-Tech Coated Products LLC ....F ... 315 986-4098
  Macedon (G-7468)

Pliant LLC ....B ... 315 986-6286
  Macedon (G-7469)

Printex Packaging Corporation ....D ... 631 234-4300
  Islandia (G-6343)

Quality Circle Products Inc ....D ... 914 736-6600
  Montrose (G-8078)

Saint-Gobain Prfmce Plas Corp ....C ... 518 642-2200
  Granville (G-5355)

Shaant Industries Inc ....E ... 716 366-3654
  Dunkirk (G-4066)

Time Release Sciences Inc ....E ... 716 823-4580
  Buffalo (G-3011)

Transcntinental Ultra Flex Inc ....B ... 718 272-9100
  Brooklyn (G-2516)

Valley Industrial Products Inc ....E ... 631 385-9300
  Huntington (G-6231)

Westrock Mwv LLC ....C ... 212 688-5000
  New York (G-11748)

PACKAGING MATERIALS: Paper, Coated Or Laminated

American Packaging Corporation ....C ... 585 537-4650
  Churchville (G-3408)

American Packaging Corporation ....G ... 585 254-2002
  Rochester (G-13229)

American Packaging Corporation ....C ... 585 254-9500
  Rochester (G-13230)

Cove Point Holdings LLC ....E ... 212 599-3388
  New York (G-9113)

De Luxe Packaging Corp ....E ... 416 754-4633
  Saugerties (G-14200)

Patco Tapes Inc ....G ... 718 497-1527
  Maspeth (G-7634)

Tri-Plex Packaging Corporation ....E ... 212 481-6070
  New York (G-11539)

PACKAGING MATERIALS: Paper, Thermoplastic Coated

F M Howell & Company ....D ... 607 734-6291
  Elmira (G-4351)

Smart USA Inc ....F ... 631 969-1111
  Bay Shore (G-715)

PACKAGING MATERIALS: Plastic Film, Coated Or Laminated

Allied Converters Inc ....E ... 914 235-1585
  New Rochelle (G-8319)

Brook & Whittle Limited ....F ... 716 691-4348
  Amherst (G-214)

Brook & Whittle Limited ....C ... 716 853-1688
  Buffalo (G-2666)

Folene Packaging LLC ....G ... 917 626-6740
  Brooklyn (G-1857)

Mason Transparent Package Inc ....E ... 718 792-6000
  Bronx (G-1307)

RMS Packaging Inc ....F ... 914 205-2070
  Peekskill (G-12556)

Universal Packg Systems Inc ....A ... 631 543-2277
  Hauppauge (G-5792)

W E W Container Corporation ....E ... 718 827-8150
  Brooklyn (G-2572)

PACKAGING MATERIALS: Polystyrene Foam

ABI Packaging Inc ....E ... 716 677-2900
  West Seneca (G-15843)

Barclay Brown Corp ....F ... 718 376-7166
  Brooklyn (G-1563)

Chesu Inc ....F ... 239 564-2803
  East Hampton (G-4119)

Fedex Ground Package Sys Inc ....G ... 800 463-3339
  Plattsburgh (G-12747)

First Qlty Packg Solutions LLC ....F ... 516 829-3030
  Great Neck (G-5387)

Interntnal Bus Cmmncations Inc ......E ... 516 352-4505
  New Hyde Park (G-8275)

Jamestown Container Corp ....C ... 716 665-4623
  Falconer (G-4547)

Jem Container Corp ....F ... 800 521-0145
  Plainview (G-12692)

Knoll Printing & Packaging Inc ....E ... 516 621-0100
  Syosset (G-14791)

Lamar Plastics Packaging Ltd ....D ... 516 378-2500
  Freeport (G-5004)

Orcon Industries Corp ....D ... 585 768-7000
  Le Roy (G-6905)

Printex Packaging Corporation ....D ... 631 234-4300
  Islandia (G-6343)

R D A Container Corporation ....E ... 585 247-2323
  Gates (G-5142)

Shell Containers Inc ....E ... 516 352-4505
  New Hyde Park (G-8292)

Snow Craft Co Inc ....E ... 516 739-1399
  New Hyde Park (G-8293)

Technical Packaging Inc ....F ... 516 223-2300
  Baldwin (G-537)

TSS Foam Industries Corp ....F ... 585 538-2321
  Caledonia (G-3074)

W Stuart Smith Inc ....E ... 585 742-3310
  Victor (G-15441)

Walnut Packaging Inc ....E ... 631 293-3836
  Farmingdale (G-4764)

PACKAGING MATERIALS: Resinous Impregnated Paper

Cameo Process Corp ....G ... 914 948-0082
  White Plains (G-15988)

PACKAGING: Blister Or Bubble Formed, Plastic

Di Domenico Packaging Co Inc ....G ... 718 727-5454
  Staten Island (G-14645)

Formatix Corp ....E ... 631 467-3399
  Ronkonkoma (G-13939)

PACKING & CRATING SVC

Precision Techniques Inc ....D ... 718 991-1440
  Stony Point (G-14747)

PACKING & CRATING SVCS: Containerized Goods For Shipping

New York Air Brake LLC ....E ... 315 786-5576
  Watertown (G-15583)

PACKING MATERIALS: Mechanical

Bag Arts Ltd ....G ... 212 684-7020
  New York (G-8715)

Gaddis Industrial Equipment ....F ... 516 759-3100
  Glen Cove (G-5194)

Technical Packaging Inc ....F ... 516 223-2300
  Baldwin (G-537)

Unique Packaging Corporation ....G ... 514 341-5872
  Champlain (G-3319)

PACKING: Metallic

Commercial Gaskets New York ....F ... 212 244-8130
  New York (G-9067)

PADDING: Foamed Plastics

Arm Rochester Inc ....F ... 585 354-5077
  Rochester (G-13245)

Philpac Corporation ....E ... 716 875-8005
  Buffalo (G-2917)

PADS: Desk, Exc Paper

Star Desk Pad Co Inc ....E ... 914 963-9400
  Yonkers (G-16350)

PADS: Desk, Paper, Made From Purchased Materials

General Diaries Corporation ....F ... 516 371-2244
  Inwood (G-6294)

PADS: Mattress

Continental Quilting Co Inc ....E ... 718 499-9100
  New Hyde Park (G-8259)

Excellent Art Mfg Corp ....F ... 718 388-7075
  Inwood (G-6292)

PAGERS: One-way

Bayside Beepers & Cellular ....G ... 718 343-3888
  Glen Oaks (G-5214)

PAINT STORE

Atlas Coatings Group Corp ....D ... 718 469-8787
  Brooklyn (G-1549)

Mercury Paint Corporation ....D ... 718 469-8787
  Brooklyn (G-2141)

Nautical Marine Paint Corp ....E ... 718 462-7000
  Brooklyn (G-2193)

Starlite Pnt & Varnish Co Inc ....G ... 718 292-6420
  Bronx (G-1371)

PAINTING SVC: Metal Prdts

Aircraft Finishing Corp ....F ... 631 422-5000
  West Babylon (G-15684)

Buffalo Finishing Works Inc ....G ... 716 893-5266
  Buffalo (G-2673)

Buffalo Metal Finishing Co ....F ... 716 883-2751
  Buffalo (G-2679)

D & I Finishing Inc ....G ... 631 471-3034
  Bohemia (G-998)

Duzmor Painting Inc ....G ... 585 768-4760
  Le Roy (G-6900)

Industrial Paint Services Corp ....F ... 607 687-0107
  Owego (G-12430)

Js Coating Solutions Inc ....G ... 585 471-8354
  Rochester (G-13497)

Keymark Corporation ....A ... 518 853-3421
  Fonda (G-4911)

Mac Artspray Finishing Corp ....F ... 718 649-3800
  Brooklyn (G-2098)

Rims Like New Inc ....F ... 845 537-0396
  Middletown (G-7930)

Tailored Coatings Inc ....E ... 716 893-4869
  Buffalo (G-3002)

PAINTS & ADDITIVES

Atlas Coatings Group Corp ....D ... 718 469-8787
  Brooklyn (G-1549)

Fougera Pharmaceuticals Inc ....C ... 631 454-7677
  Melville (G-7785)

General Coatings Tech Inc ....E ... 718 821-1232
  Ridgewood (G-13146)

Liberty Panel Center Inc ....F ... 718 647-2763
  Brooklyn (G-2067)

Mercury Paint Corporation ....D ... 718 469-8787
  Brooklyn (G-2141)

Reddi Car Corp ....G ... 631 589-3141
  Sayville (G-14231)

Sml Brothers Holding Corp ....D ... 718 402-2000
  Bronx (G-1366)

Starlite Pnt & Varnish Co Inc ....G ... 718 292-6420
  Bronx (G-1371)

T C Dunham Paint Company Inc ....E ... 914 969-4202
  Yonkers (G-16351)

T J Ronan Paint Corp ....E ... 718 292-1100
  Bronx (G-1376)

PAINTS & ALLIED PRODUCTS

A & B Color Corp ....G ... 718 441-5482
  Kew Gardens (G-6660)

Akzo Nobel Coatings Inc ....G ... 631 242-6020
  Deer Park (G-3832)

Angiotech Biocoatings Corp ....E ... 585 321-1130
  Henrietta (G-5854)

Atc Plastics LLC ....E ... 212 375-2515
  New York (G-8660)

B & F Architectural Support Gr ....E ... 212 279-6488
  New York (G-8702)

Barson Composites Corporation ....E ... 516 752-7882
  Old Bethpage (G-12215)

Benjamin Moore & Co ....E ... 518 736-1723
  Johnstown (G-6611)

Cytec Industries Inc ....D 716 372-9650
  Olean (G-12231)
Eric S Turner & Company Inc ....F 914 235-7114
  New Rochelle (G-8329)
Fayette Street Coatings Inc ....F 315 488-5401
  Liverpool (G-7010)
Garco Manufacturing Corp Inc ....G 718 287-3330
  Brooklyn (G-1877)
Heany Industries Inc ....D 585 889-2700
  Scottsville (G-14340)
Jrlon Inc ....D 315 597-4067
  Palmyra (G-12489)
Nautical Marine Paint Corp ....E 718 462-7000
  Brooklyn (G-2193)
Nortek Powder Coating LLC ....F 315 337-2339
  Rome (G-13861)
Peter Kwasny Inc ....G 727 641-1462
  Hauppauge (G-5740)
Philadelphia Coatings LLC ....G 917 929-4738
  New York (G-10826)
Yewtree Millworks Corp ....G 914 320-5851
  Yonkers (G-16358)

PAINTS, VARNISHES & SPLYS, WHOLESALE: Paints

A & B Color Corp ....G 718 441-5482
  Kew Gardens (G-6660)
Benjamin Moore & Co ....E 518 736-1723
  Johnstown (G-6611)

PALLET REPAIR SVCS

Four-Way Pallet Corp ....E 631 351-3401
  Huntington Station (G-6247)

PALLETS

A D Bowman & Son Lumber Co ....E 607 692-2595
  Castle Creek (G-3199)
Best Pallet & Crate LLC ....G 518 438-2945
  Albany (G-49)
Four-Way Pallet Corp ....E 631 351-3401
  Huntington Station (G-6247)
Just Wood Pallets Inc ....G 718 644-7013
  New Windsor (G-8370)
North Shore Pallet Inc ....G 631 673-4700
  Huntington Station (G-6256)
Pooran Pallet Inc ....G 718 938-7970
  Bronx (G-1340)
Sanjay Pallets Inc. ....G 347 590-2485
  Bronx (G-1359)
Steven Coffey Pallet S Inc ....G 585 261-6783
  Rochester (G-13747)

PALLETS & SKIDS: Wood

Dimensional Mills Inc ....G 518 746-1047
  Hudson Falls (G-6185)
McIntosh Box & Pallet Co Inc ....F 315 789-8750
  Geneva (G-5159)
McIntosh Box & Pallet Co Inc ....E 315 446-9350
  Rome (G-13855)
Nefab Packaging North East LLC ....E 518 346-9105
  Scotia (G-14334)
Ongweoweh Corp ....D 607 266-7070
  Ithaca (G-6403)
Pallet Services Inc ....C 716 873-7700
  Clarence (G-3438)
Reuter Pallet Pkg Sys Inc ....E 845 457-9937
  Montgomery (G-8066)

PALLETS: Wood & Metal Combination

Pallet Division Inc ....G 585 328-3780
  Rochester (G-13606)

PALLETS: Wooden

Abbot & Abbot Box Corp ....F 888 930-5972
  Long Island City (G-7143)
B & B Lumber Company Inc ....C 866 282-0582
  Jamesville (G-6555)
B&B Albany Pallet Company LLC ....E 315 492-1786
  Jamesville (G-6556)
Berry Industrial Group Inc ....G 845 353-8338
  Nyack (G-12137)
CDF Indstrial Pckg Sltions Inc ....F 716 672-2984
  Fredonia (G-4968)
Clements Burrville Sawmill ....G 315 782-4549
  Watertown (G-15565)
Custom Shipping Products Inc ....F 716 355-4437
  Clymer (G-3496)

Dwa Pallet Inc ....G 518 746-1047
  Hudson Falls (G-6186)
Essex Box & Pallet Co Inc ....E 518 834-7279
  Keeseville (G-6641)
G & H Wood Products LLC ....F 716 372-0341
  Olean (G-12236)
Great Lakes Specialites ....E 716 672-4622
  Fredonia (G-4970)
Lindley Wood Works Inc ....E 607 523-7786
  Lindley (G-6986)
McIntosh Box & Pallet Co Inc ....D 315 675-8511
  Bernhards Bay (G-826)
McNeilly Wood Products Inc ....E 845 457-9651
  Campbell Hall (G-3118)
Neville Mfg Svc & Dist Inc ....E 716 834-3038
  Cheektowaga (G-3357)
Northeast Pallet & Cont Co Inc ....E 518 271-0535
  Troy (G-15176)
Orleans Pallet Company Inc ....F 585 589-0781
  Albion (G-158)
Pallet Services Inc ....E 585 647-4020
  Rochester (G-13607)
Pallets Inc ....E 518 747-4177
  Fort Edward (G-4941)
Pallets R US Inc ....E 631 758-2360
  Bellport (G-806)
Paul Bunyan Products Inc ....E 315 696-6164
  Cortland (G-3782)
Peco Pallet Inc. ....E 914 376-5444
  Irvington (G-6313)
Peter C Herman Inc ....E 315 926-4100
  Marion (G-7573)
Taylor Brothers Inc ....F 607 625-2828
  Apalachin (G-362)
Vansantis Development Inc ....G 315 461-0113
  Liverpool (G-7046)
Wolfe Lumber Mill Inc ....G 716 772-7750
  Gasport (G-5140)

PANEL & DISTRIBUTION BOARDS: Electric

Allied Circuits LLC ....E 716 551-0285
  Buffalo (G-2627)
Claddagh Electronics Ltd ....F 718 784-0571
  Long Island City (G-7186)

PANELS: Building, Wood

Bandec LLC ....G 516 627-1971
  Jericho (G-6572)
Harvest Homes Inc ....E 518 895-2341
  Delanson (G-3960)

PANELS: Cardboard, Die-Cut, Made From Purchased Materials

Hubray Inc ....F 800 645-2855
  North Baldwin (G-12006)

PAPER & BOARD: Die-cut

All Out Die Cutting Inc ....E 718 346-6666
  Brooklyn (G-1486)
American Dsplay Die Ctters Inc. ....E 212 645-1274
  New York (G-8549)
Art Industries of New York ....E 212 633-9200
  New York (G-8628)
Borden & Riley Paper Co Inc ....E 718 454-9494
  Hollis (G-6040)
Dia ....G 212 675-4097
  New York (G-9216)
General Die and Die Cutng Inc ....D 516 665-3584
  Massapequa Park (G-7655)
General Fibre Products Corp ....D 516 358-7500
  New Hyde Park (G-8270)
Kleer-Fax Inc ....D 631 225-1100
  Amityville (G-286)
Leather Indexes Corp ....D 516 827-1900
  Hicksville (G-5923)
Manufacturers Indexing Pdts ....G 631 271-0956
  Halesite (G-5488)
New York Cutting & Gumming Co ....E 212 563-4146
  Middletown (G-7924)
Norampac New York City Inc ....C 718 340-2100
  Maspeth (G-7630)
Paperworld Inc ....E 516 221-2702
  Bellmore (G-785)
Premier Packaging Corporation ....E 585 924-8460
  Victor (G-15424)
S & S Prtg Die-Cutting Co Inc ....F 718 388-8990
  Brooklyn (G-2372)

Spectrum Prtg Lithography Inc ....E 212 255-3131
  New York (G-11316)

PAPER CONVERTING

Aigner Label Holder Corp ....F 845 562-4510
  New Windsor (G-8358)
Beetins Wholesale Inc ....F 718 524-0899
  Staten Island (G-14625)
Eagles Nest Holdings LLC ....E 513 874-5270
  New York (G-9298)
Gardei Industries LLC ....F 716 693-7100
  North Tonawanda (G-12069)
Gavin Mfg Corp ....E 631 467-0040
  Farmingdale (G-4636)
Global Tissue Group Inc ....E 631 924-3019
  Medford (G-7708)
Graphic Cntrls Acqisition Corp ....B 716 853-7500
  Buffalo (G-2780)
Graphic Controls Holdings Inc ....F 716 853-7500
  Buffalo (G-2781)
Katz Group Americas Inc ....E 716 995-3059
  Sanborn (G-14144)
Lydall Performance Mtls US Inc ....F 315 346-3100
  Beaver Falls (G-760)
Marketing Group International ....G 631 754-8095
  Northport (G-12109)
Noteworthy Industries Inc ....E 518 842-2662
  Amsterdam (G-344)
P C I Paper Conversions Inc ....E 315 437-1641
  Syracuse (G-14958)
Pack America Corp ....E 212 508-6666
  New York (G-10740)
RB Converting Inc. ....G 607 777-1325
  Binghamton (G-905)
Sappi North America Inc ....D 914 696-5544
  White Plains (G-16060)
Trinity Packaging Corporation ....F 914 273-4111
  Armonk (G-404)
Waymor1 Inc ....E 518 677-8511
  Cambridge (G-3097)

PAPER MANUFACTURERS: Exc Newsprint

Albany International Corp ....E 518 445-2230
  Menands (G-7838)
Ampac Paper LLC ....G 845 713-6600
  Walden (G-15456)
Atlas Recycling LLC ....E 212 925-3280
  New York (G-8672)
Burrows Paper Corporation ....D 315 823-2300
  Little Falls (G-6987)
Carta Usa LLC ....E 585 436-3012
  Rochester (G-13297)
Cascades New York Inc ....C 716 285-3681
  Niagara Falls (G-11912)
Cascades New York Inc ....C 585 527-8110
  Rochester (G-13299)
Cascades New York Inc ....C 518 346-6151
  Schenectady (G-14254)
Cascades New York Inc ....E 716 681-1560
  Depew (G-3976)
Cascades New York Inc ....E 518 689-1020
  Albany (G-58)
Cascades Tssue Group-Sales Inc ....D 518 238-1900
  Waterford (G-15533)
Cascades USA Inc ....E 518 880-3600
  Waterford (G-15535)
Clearwater Paper Corporation ....D 315 287-1200
  Gouverneur (G-5319)
Daniel O Reich Incorporated ....F 718 748-6000
  Brooklyn (G-1723)
Dunmore Corporation ....D 845 279-5061
  Brewster (G-1147)
Easm Machine Works LLC ....E 518 747-5326
  Fort Edward (G-4939)
Essity Prof Hygiene N Amer LLC ....C 518 583-2785
  Saratoga Springs (G-14173)
Euro Fine Paper Inc ....E 516 238-5253
  Garden City (G-5098)
Fibercel Packaging LLC ....E 716 933-8703
  Portville (G-12934)
Freeport Paper Industries Inc ....D 631 851-1555
  Central Islip (G-3276)
Georgia-Pacific LLC ....A 518 561-3500
  Plattsburgh (G-12748)
International Paper Company ....A 518 585-6761
  Ticonderoga (G-15074)
International Paper Company ....C 845 986-6409
  Tuxedo Park (G-15217)
International Paper Company ....C 315 797-5120
  Utica (G-15278)

Employee Codes: A=Over 500 employees, B=251-500
C=101-250, D=51-100, E=20-50, F=10-19, G=5-9

2020 Harris
New York Manufacturers Directory

1167

P R O D U C T

Lenaro Paper Co Inc .... F 631 439-8800
  Central Islip (G-3282)
Minimill Technologies Inc .... F 315 692-4557
  Syracuse (G-14944)
Mohawk Fine Papers Inc .... B 518 237-1740
  Cohoes (G-3510)
Omniafiltra LLC .... E 315 346-7300
  Beaver Falls (G-761)
Paper Solutions Inc .... G 718 499-4666
  Brooklyn (G-2244)
Plastirun Corporation .... D 631 273-2626
  Brentwood (G-1126)
Potsdam Specialty Paper Inc .... D 315 265-4000
  Potsdam (G-12939)
Twin Rivers Paper Company LLC .... B 315 823-2300
  Little Falls (G-6994)
US Alliance Paper Inc .... C 631 254-3030
  Edgewood (G-4290)
Verso Corporation .... B 212 599-2700
  New York (G-11665)

PAPER PRDTS: Feminine Hygiene Prdts

Corman USA Inc .... G 718 727-7455
  Staten Island (G-14643)
Maxim Hygiene Products Inc .... F 516 621-3323
  Mineola (G-7988)
Rochester Midland Corporation ...... C 585 336-2200
  Rochester (G-13690)

PAPER PRDTS: Infant & Baby Prdts

Kas Direct LLC .... E 516 934-0541
  Westbury (G-15901)
Kimberly-Clark Corporation .... D 212 554-4252
  New York (G-10103)
Skip Hop Inc .... E 646 902-9874
  New York (G-11259)
Skip Hop Holdings Inc .... G 212 868-9850
  New York (G-11260)

PAPER PRDTS: Napkin Stock

Essity Prof Hygiene N Amer LLC ..... E 518 692-8434
  Greenwich (G-5470)

PAPER PRDTS: Napkins, Sanitary, Made From Purchased Material

Precare Corp .... G 631 667-1055
  Hauppauge (G-5746)

PAPER PRDTS: Pattern Tissue

Stephen Singer Pattern Co Inc ...... F 212 947-2902
  New York (G-11359)

PAPER PRDTS: Pressed Pulp Prdts

Huhtamaki Inc .... A 315 593-5311
  Fulton (G-5064)

PAPER PRDTS: Sanitary

Attends Healthcare Inc .... A 212 338-5100
  New York (G-8675)
Becks Classic Mfg Inc .... D 631 435-3800
  Brentwood (G-1116)
Cellu Tissue - Long Island LLC ..... C 631 232-2626
  Central Islip (G-3267)
Crosstex International Inc .... D 631 582-6777
  Hauppauge (G-5631)
First Quality Products Inc .... F 516 829-4949
  Great Neck (G-5388)
Georgia-Pacific LLC .... A 518 561-3500
  Plattsburgh (G-12748)
Monthly Gift Inc .... G 888 444-9661
  New York (G-10501)
Nice-Pak Products Inc .... B 845 365-1700
  Orangeburg (G-12324)
Nutek Disposables Inc .... G 516 829-3030
  Great Neck (G-5406)
Professnal Dsposables Intl Inc ..... E 800 999-6423
  Orangeburg (G-12329)
Sqp Inc .... C 518 831-6800
  Schenectady (G-14307)
US Nonwovens Corp .... D 631 952-0100
  Brentwood (G-1132)
Waymor1 Inc .... E 518 677-8511
  Cambridge (G-3097)

PAPER PRDTS: Sanitary Tissue Paper

Kimberly-Clark Corporation .... D 212 554-4252
  New York (G-10103)

PAPER PRDTS: Tampons, Sanitary, Made From Purchased Material

Alyk Inc .... E 866 232-0970
  New York (G-8535)
L VII Resilient LLC .... F 631 987-5819
  Medford (G-7716)

PAPER PRDTS: Toilet Paper, Made From Purchased Materials

Deluxe Packaging Corp .... F 845 246-6090
  Saugerties (G-14201)

PAPER PRDTS: Toweling Tissue

Crosstex International Inc .... D 631 582-6777
  Hauppauge (G-5631)

PAPER PRDTS: Towels, Napkins/Tissue Paper, From Purchd Mtrls

Florelle Tissue Corporation .... E 647 997-7405
  Brownville (G-2607)
HFC Prestige Intl US LLC .... A 212 389-7800
  New York (G-9778)
N3a Corporation .... D 516 284-6799
  Inwood (G-6299)
Select Products Holdings LLC .... E 631 421-6000
  Huntington (G-6224)

PAPER, WHOLESALE: Fine

Lenaro Paper Co Inc .... F 631 439-8800
  Central Islip (G-3282)

PAPER, WHOLESALE: Printing

Chesu Inc .... F 239 564-2803
  East Hampton (G-4119)
Malone Industrial Press Inc .... G 518 483-5880
  Malone (G-7488)

PAPER: Absorbent

Cascades Tssue Group-Sales Inc ..... E 819 363-5100
  Waterford (G-15534)
National Paper Converting Inc ...... G 607 687-6049
  Owego (G-12434)

PAPER: Adding Machine Rolls, Made From Purchased Materials

Gaylord Bros Inc .... D 315 457-5070
  North Syracuse (G-12042)
Paperworld Inc .... E 516 221-2702
  Bellmore (G-785)

PAPER: Adhesive

CCL Label Inc .... C 716 852-2155
  Buffalo (G-2693)
Cove Point Holdings LLC .... E 212 599-3388
  New York (G-9113)
Oaklee International Inc .... D 631 436-7900
  Ronkonkoma (G-13985)
Rochester 100 Inc .... C 585 475-0200
  Rochester (G-13679)

PAPER: Art

Donne Dieu Paper Mill Inc .... D 212 226-0573
  Brooklyn (G-1757)

PAPER: Bristols

Bristol Core Inc .... F 585 919-0302
  Canandaigua (G-3126)
Bristol/White Plains .... G 914 681-1800
  White Plains (G-15984)

PAPER: Building, Insulating & Packaging

CCT (us) Inc .... F 716 297-7509
  Niagara Falls (G-11913)
Howard J Moore Company Inc .... E 631 351-8467
  Plainview (G-12688)

PAPER: Business Form

Bigrow Paper Mfg Corp .... F 718 624-4439
  Brooklyn (G-1584)
Datagraphic Business Systems .... G 516 485-9069
  Brentwood (G-1118)

PAPER: Card

Lion Die-Cutting Co Inc .... E 718 383-8841
  Brooklyn (G-2077)

PAPER: Chemically Treated, Made From Purchased Materials

Micro Essential Laboratory .... E 718 338-3618
  Brooklyn (G-2152)

PAPER: Cigarette

Schweitzer-Mauduit Intl Inc .... C 518 329-4222
  Ancram (G-355)

PAPER: Cloth, Lined, Made From Purchased Materials

Albany International Corp .... D 518 447-6400
  Menands (G-7839)

PAPER: Coated & Laminated, NEC

A-One Laminating Corp .... G 718 266-6002
  Brooklyn (G-1442)
C & R De Santis Inc .... E 718 447-5076
  Staten Island (G-14633)
Classic Labels Inc .... E 631 467-2300
  Patchogue (G-12498)
Clp Holdings LLC .... G 917 846-5094
  New York (G-9038)
Dunmore Corporation .... D 845 279-5061
  Brewster (G-1147)
Felix Schoeller North Amer Inc ..... D 315 298-8425
  Pulaski (G-12994)
Greenbush Tape & Label Inc .... E 518 465-2389
  Albany (G-82)
K Sidrane Inc .... E 631 393-6974
  Farmingdale (G-4659)
Liberty Label Mfg Inc .... F 631 737-2365
  Holbrook (G-6006)
Mohawk Fine Papers Inc .... B 518 237-1740
  Cohoes (G-3510)
Neenah Northeast LLC .... E 315 376-3571
  Lowville (G-7419)
New York Cutting & Gumming Co ...... E 212 563-4146
  Middletown (G-7924)
P C I Paper Conversions Inc .... C 315 437-1641
  Syracuse (G-14958)
S & S Prtg Die-Cutting Co Inc ...... F 718 388-8990
  Brooklyn (G-2372)
Uniflex Holdings LLC .... F 516 932-2000
  Hauppauge (G-5790)

PAPER: Coated, Exc Photographic, Carbon Or Abrasive

Janice Moses Represents .... G 212 898-4898
  New York (G-9975)

PAPER: Corrugated

General Fibre Products Corp .... D 516 358-7500
  New Hyde Park (G-8270)

PAPER: Envelope

Tag Envelope Co Inc .... E 718 389-6844
  College Point (G-3567)

PAPER: Filter

Andex Corp .... E 585 328-3790
  Rochester (G-13236)
Hollingsworth & Vose Company .... C 518 695-8000
  Greenwich (G-5473)
Knowlton Technologies LLC .... C 315 782-0600
  Watertown (G-15580)

PAPER: Kraft

APC Paper Company Inc .... D 315 384-4225
  Norfolk (G-11997)
Scalamandre Wallpaper Inc .... B 631 467-8800
  Hauppauge (G-5760)

Westrock Container LLC ....D...... 518 842-2450
  Amsterdam *(G-353)*

PAPER: Packaging

Elgreco Gt Inc ....G....... 718 777-7922
  Astoria *(G-420)*

PAPER: Parchment

Palisades Paper Inc ....G...... 845 354-0333
  Spring Valley *(G-14580)*

PAPER: Printer

International Paper Company ....C...... 607 775-1550
  Conklin *(G-3625)*
Summit Fincl Disclosure LLC ....E...... 212 913-0510
  New York *(G-11390)*

PAPER: Specialty

Cottrell Paper Company Inc ....E...... 518 885-1702
  Rock City Falls *(G-13817)*
Dunn Paper - Natural Dam Inc ....D...... 315 287-1200
  Gouverneur *(G-5320)*
Gratitude & Company Inc ....G...... 607 277-3188
  Ithaca *(G-6383)*

PAPER: Tissue

Burrows Paper Corporation ....D...... 315 823-2300
  Little Falls *(G-6988)*
Morcon Inc ....D...... 518 677-8511
  Eagle Bridge *(G-4072)*
North End Paper Co Inc ....G...... 315 593-8100
  Fulton *(G-5073)*
Precare Corp ....G...... 631 667-1055
  Hauppauge *(G-5746)*
Twin Rivers Paper Company LLC ....E...... 315 348-8491
  Lyons Falls *(G-7456)*

PAPER: Wrapping

Flower Cy Tissue Mills Co Inc ....D...... 585 458-9200
  Rochester *(G-13417)*

PAPER: Wrapping & Packaging

Gooding Co Inc ....E...... 716 266-6252
  Lockport *(G-7082)*

PAPER: Writing

Automation Papers Inc ....G...... 315 432-0565
  Syracuse *(G-14822)*

PAPERBOARD

Alpine Paper Box Co Inc ....E...... 718 345-4040
  Brooklyn *(G-1492)*
American Wire Tie Inc ....E...... 716 337-2412
  North Collins *(G-12023)*
Lydall Performance Mtls US Inc ....D...... 518 686-3400
  Hoosick Falls *(G-6085)*
Ms Paper Products Co Inc ....G...... 718 624-0248
  Brooklyn *(G-2180)*
Niagara Fiberboard Inc ....E...... 716 434-8881
  Lockport *(G-7097)*
Professional Packg Svcs Inc ....E...... 518 677-5100
  Eagle Bridge *(G-4073)*
Westrock Rkt LLC ....F...... 315 487-6111
  Camillus *(G-3114)*

PAPERBOARD CONVERTING

Allied Converters Inc ....E...... 914 235-1585
  New Rochelle *(G-8319)*
Mid-York Press Inc ....D...... 607 674-4491
  Sherburne *(G-14392)*
Setterstix Inc ....E...... 716 257-3451
  Cattaraugus *(G-3222)*

PAPERBOARD PRDTS: Building Insulating & Packaging

Shell Containers Inc ....E...... 516 352-4505
  New Hyde Park *(G-8292)*

PAPERBOARD PRDTS: Container Board

Pactiv LLC ....E...... 585 248-1213
  Pittsford *(G-12655)*
Westrock - Solvay Llc ....C...... 315 484-9050
  Syracuse *(G-15025)*

Westrock Container LLC ....D...... 518 842-2450
  Amsterdam *(G-353)*
Westrock Cp LLC ....D...... 315 484-9050
  Syracuse *(G-15026)*

PAPERBOARD PRDTS: Folding Boxboard

Burt Rigid Box Inc ....F...... 607 433-2510
  Oneonta *(G-12262)*
Di Domenico Packaging Co Inc ....G...... 718 727-5454
  Staten Island *(G-14645)*
Enterprise Folding Box Co Inc ....E...... 716 876-6421
  Buffalo *(G-2747)*
Paper Box Corp ....D...... 212 226-7490
  New York *(G-10748)*
Westrock Rkt Company ....C...... 770 448-2193
  Syracuse *(G-15027)*

PAPERBOARD PRDTS: Kraft Linerboard

Continental Kraft Corp ....G...... 516 681-9090
  Jericho *(G-6575)*

PAPERBOARD PRDTS: Packaging Board

Farrington Packaging Corp ....E...... 315 733-4600
  Utica *(G-15262)*

PAPERBOARD: Boxboard

Prestige Box Corporation ....E...... 516 773-3115
  Great Neck *(G-5415)*

PAPERBOARD: Liner Board

Greenpac Mill LLC ....C...... 716 299-0560
  Niagara Falls *(G-11933)*
Westrock Mwv LLC ....C...... 212 688-5000
  New York *(G-11748)*

PAPIER-MACHE PRDTS, EXC STATUARY & ART GOODS

Specialty Quality Packg LLC ....D...... 914 580-3200
  Scotia *(G-14337)*

PARACHUTES

National Parachute Industries ....E...... 908 782-1646
  Palenville *(G-12479)*

PARKING LOTS

Deans Paving Inc ....G...... 315 736-7601
  Marcy *(G-7564)*

PARTITIONS & FIXTURES: Except Wood

All American Metal Corporation ....E...... 516 623-0222
  Freeport *(G-4983)*
American Standard Mfg Inc ....E...... 518 868-2512
  Central Bridge *(G-3259)*
Avf Group Inc ....F...... 951 360-7111
  Cheektowaga *(G-3339)*
Bobrick Washroom Equipment Inc ....D...... 518 877-7444
  Clifton Park *(G-3463)*
Bridge Metal Industries LLC ....C...... 914 663-9200
  Mount Vernon *(G-8125)*
Core Group Displays Inc ....E...... 845 876-5109
  Rhinebeck *(G-13098)*
Dakota Systems Mfg Corp ....G...... 631 249-5811
  Farmingdale *(G-4613)*
E-Systems Group LLC ....E...... 607 775-1100
  Conklin *(G-3624)*
Fifty Door Partners LLC ....E...... 845 562-3332
  New Windsor *(G-8367)*
Hergo Ergonomic Support Syst ....E...... 888 222-7270
  Oceanside *(G-12175)*
Inscape Inc ....E...... 716 665-6210
  Falconer *(G-4545)*
Joldeson One Aerospace Inds ....D...... 718 848-7396
  Ozone Park *(G-12463)*
Mass Mdsg Self Selection Eqp ....E...... 631 234-3300
  Bohemia *(G-1044)*
Maximum Security Products Corp ....E...... 518 233-1800
  Waterford *(G-15538)*
Milton Merl & Associates Inc ....G...... 212 634-9292
  New York *(G-10470)*
Mobile Media Inc ....E...... 845 744-8080
  Pine Bush *(G-12625)*
Modu-Craft Inc ....G...... 716 694-0709
  Tonawanda *(G-15123)*
Sturdy Store Displays Inc ....E...... 718 389-9919
  Brooklyn *(G-2467)*

Traco Manufacturing Inc ....G...... 585 343-2434
  Batavia *(G-628)*

PARTITIONS: Nonwood, Floor Attached

All American Metal Corporation ....G...... 516 223-1760
  Freeport *(G-4982)*
Global Steel Products Corp ....C...... 631 586-3455
  Deer Park *(G-3878)*
Inscape (new York) Inc ....D...... 716 665-6210
  Falconer *(G-4544)*
Knickerbocker Partition Corp ....E...... 516 546-0550
  Melville *(G-7799)*

PARTITIONS: Wood & Fixtures

Artone LLC ....D...... 716 664-2232
  Jamestown *(G-6495)*
Custom Countertops Inc ....G...... 716 685-2871
  Depew *(G-3977)*
Dbs Interiors Corp ....F...... 631 491-3013
  West Babylon *(G-15706)*
Deakon Homes and Interiors ....E...... 518 271-0342
  Troy *(G-15165)*
Encore Retail Systems Inc ....E...... 718 385-3443
  Mamaroneck *(G-7509)*
Farrington Packaging Corp ....E...... 315 733-4600
  Utica *(G-15262)*
Fina Cabinet Corp ....E...... 718 409-2900
  Mount Vernon *(G-8141)*
Gaughan Construction Corp ....G...... 718 850-9577
  Richmond Hill *(G-13114)*
Greenleaf Cabinet Makers LLC ....E...... 315 432-4600
  Syracuse *(G-14905)*
Hamlet Products Inc ....F...... 914 665-0307
  Mount Vernon *(G-8147)*
Heartwood Specialties Inc ....G...... 607 654-0102
  Hammondsport *(G-5529)*
Home Ideal Inc ....G...... 718 762-8998
  Flushing *(G-4860)*
Industrial Support Inc ....D...... 716 662-2954
  Buffalo *(G-2809)*
Integrated Wood Components Inc ....E...... 607 467-1739
  Deposit *(G-4000)*
Inter State Laminates Inc ....E...... 518 283-8355
  Poestenkill *(G-12803)*
Michael P Mmarr ....G...... 315 623-9380
  Constantia *(G-3636)*
New Dimensions Office Group ....D...... 718 387-0995
  Brooklyn *(G-2203)*
Old Souls Inc ....G...... 845 809-5886
  Cold Spring *(G-3522)*
Premier Woodworking Inc ....E...... 631 236-4100
  Hauppauge *(G-5749)*
Steelcraft Manufacturing Co ....F...... 718 277-2404
  Brooklyn *(G-2456)*
Stein Industries Inc ....E...... 631 789-2222
  Amityville *(G-307)*
Universal Designs Inc ....G...... 718 721-1111
  Long Island City *(G-7389)*
Winerackscom Inc ....E...... 845 658-7181
  Tillson *(G-15078)*

PARTITIONS: Wood, Floor Attached

Steeldeck Ny Inc ....F...... 718 599-3700
  Brooklyn *(G-2457)*

PARTS: Metal

All-State Diversified Pdts Inc ....E...... 315 472-4728
  Syracuse *(G-14810)*
Ross Metal Fabricators Inc ....E...... 631 586-7000
  Deer Park *(G-3930)*
Zone Fabricators Inc ....F...... 718 272-0200
  Ozone Park *(G-12470)*

PARTY & SPECIAL EVENT PLANNING SVCS

Proof 7 Ltd ....F...... 212 680-1843
  New York *(G-10913)*

PATENT OWNERS & LESSORS

Compositech Ltd ....C...... 516 835-1458
  Woodbury *(G-16168)*
Eagle Telephonics Inc ....F...... 631 471-3600
  Bohemia *(G-1007)*
General Microwave Corporation ....F...... 516 802-0900
  Syosset *(G-14789)*
Rainforest Inc ....F...... 212 575-7620
  New York *(G-10973)*

P R O D U C T

PATTERNS: Indl

A & T Tooling LLC ....G 716 601-7299
Lancaster *(G-6788)*

Armstrong Mold Corporation ....E 315 437-1517
East Syracuse *(G-4196)*

Armstrong Mold Corporation ....D 315 437-1517
East Syracuse *(G-4197)*

Bianca Group Ltd ....G 212 768-3011
New York *(G-8779)*

City Pattern Shop Inc ....F 315 463-5239
Syracuse *(G-14850)*

K & H Precision Products Inc ....E 585 624-4894
Honeoye Falls *(G-6076)*

Speyside Foundry Holdings LLC ....G 212 994-0308
New York *(G-11319)*

W N R Pattern & Tool Inc ....G 716 681-9334
Lancaster *(G-6838)*

Wolff & Dungey Inc ....E 315 475-2105
Syracuse *(G-15029)*

Woodward Industries Inc ....F 716 692-2242
Tonawanda *(G-15154)*

PAVERS

Lomin Construction Company ....G 516 759-5734
Glen Head *(G-5209)*

Technopaving New York Inc ....G 631 351-6472
Huntington Station *(G-6263)*

PAVING MATERIALS: Prefabricated, Concrete

Copeland Coating Company Inc ....F 518 766-2932
Nassau *(G-8213)*

PAVING MIXTURES

Dolomite Products Company Inc ....E 315 524-1998
Rochester *(G-13354)*

Dolomite Products Company Inc ....F 607 324-3636
Hornell *(G-6103)*

Dolomite Products Company Inc ....F 585 768-7295
Le Roy *(G-6898)*

Iroquois Rock Products Inc ....F 585 381-7010
Rochester *(G-13484)*

PENCILS & PENS WHOLESALERS

Mark Dri Products Inc ....C 516 484-6200
Bethpage *(G-838)*

Pda Panache Corp ....G 631 776-0523
Bohemia *(G-1060)*

PENS & PARTS: Ball Point

Mercury Pen Company Inc ....G 518 899-9653
Ballston Lake *(G-561)*

PENS & PARTS: Cartridges, Refill, Ball Point

STS Refill America LLC ....G 516 934-8008
Hicksville *(G-5949)*

PENS & PENCILS: Mechanical, NEC

Aakron Rule Corp ....C 716 542-5483
Akron *(G-15)*

Harper Products Ltd ....C 516 997-2330
Westbury *(G-15894)*

Pelican Products Co Inc ....E 718 860-3220
Bronx *(G-1334)*

Pintrill LLC ....F 718 782-1000
Brooklyn *(G-2261)*

PENS: Fountain, Including Desk Sets

Universal Luxury Brands Inc ....G 646 248-5700
New York *(G-11607)*

PERFUME: Concentrated

Inter Parfums Usa LLC ....G 212 983-2640
New York *(G-9912)*

Nr Fragrances & Cosmetics Inc ....G 212 686-4006
New York *(G-10651)*

Takasago Intl Corp USA ....D 845 751-0622
Harriman *(G-5547)*

Thompson Ferrier LLC ....G 212 244-2212
New York *(G-11473)*

PERFUME: Perfumes, Natural Or Synthetic

Christian Dior Perfumes LLC ....E 212 931-2200
New York *(G-8999)*

Delbia Do Company Inc ....G 718 585-2226
Bronx *(G-1238)*

Elias Fragrances Inc ....F 718 693-6400
Rye Brook *(G-14088)*

PERFUMES

Alan F Bourguet ....F 516 883-4315
Port Washington *(G-12861)*

Cassini Parfums Ltd ....G 212 753-7540
New York *(G-8929)*

Coty US LLC ....C 212 389-7000
New York *(G-9108)*

Coty US LLC ....B 212 389-7000
Uniondale *(G-15225)*

Delbia Do Company Inc ....F 718 585-2226
Bronx *(G-1239)*

Editions De Prfums Madison LLC ....G 646 666-0527
New York *(G-9321)*

Estee Lauder Inc ....D 631 531-1000
Melville *(G-7781)*

F L Demeter Inc ....E 516 487-5187
Great Neck *(G-5384)*

Fragrance Acquisitions LLC ....D 845 534-9172
Newburgh *(G-11865)*

Hogan Flavors & Fragrances ....E 212 598-4310
New York *(G-9800)*

Jean Philippe Fragrances LLC ....D 212 983-2640
New York *(G-9990)*

JP Filling Inc ....D 845 534-4793
Mountainville *(G-8194)*

Le Labo Holding LLC ....E 646 490-6200
Brooklyn *(G-2053)*

Le Labo Holding LLC ....E 646 719-1740
Brooklyn *(G-2054)*

Memo America Inc ....E 646 356-0460
New York *(G-10429)*

Perfumers Workshop Intl Ltd ....E 212 644-8950
New York *(G-10803)*

Selective Beauty Corporation ....F 585 336-7600
New York *(G-11187)*

Sixthscents Paper Products Ltd ....E 212 627-5066
Long Island City *(G-7358)*

PERLITE: Processed

Skyline LLC ....E 631 403-4131
East Setauket *(G-4187)*

PERSONAL APPEARANCE SVCS

Womens Health Care PC ....G 718 850-0009
Richmond Hill *(G-13128)*

PERSONAL CREDIT INSTITUTIONS: Consumer Finance Companies

Steel Partners Holdings LP ....D 212 520-2300
New York *(G-11352)*

PEST CONTROL SVCS

Hawthorne Garden Company ....F 516 883-6550
Port Washington *(G-12882)*

PET COLLARS, LEASHES, MUZZLES & HARNESSES: Leather

Finger Lakes Lea Crafters LLC ....F 315 252-4107
Auburn *(G-475)*

Max 200 Performance Dog Eqp ....E 315 776-9588
Port Byron *(G-12810)*

PET SPLYS

Animal Pantry ....G 631 673-3666
Huntington *(G-6199)*

Clara Papa ....G 315 733-2660
Utica *(G-15243)*

Four Paws Products Ltd ....D 631 436-7421
Ronkonkoma *(G-13940)*

Grand Island Animal Hospital ....E 716 773-7645
Grand Island *(G-5332)*

Image Tech ....F 716 635-0167
Buffalo *(G-2806)*

Kittywalk Systems Inc ....G 516 627-8418
Port Washington *(G-12895)*

Skaffles Group LLC ....F 212 944-9494
New York *(G-11256)*

PET SPLYS WHOLESALERS

Clara Papa ....G 315 733-2660
Utica *(G-15243)*

Soggy Doggy Productions LLC ....G 877 504-4811
Larchmont *(G-6843)*

Spectrum Brands Inc ....B 631 232-1200
Hauppauge *(G-5771)*

Unique Petz LLC ....E 212 714-1800
New York *(G-11595)*

PET SPLYS WHOLESALERS

Clara Papa ....G 315 733-2660
Utica *(G-15243)*

PETROLEUM & PETROLEUM PRDTS, WHOLESALE Engine Fuels & Oils

Bass Oil Company Inc ....E 718 628-4444
Brooklyn *(G-1565)*

PETROLEUM & PETROLEUM PRDTS, WHOLESALE Fuel Oil

Alba Fuel Corp ....G 718 931-1700
Bronx *(G-1199)*

PETROLEUM & PETROLEUM PRDTS, WHOLESALE: Bulk Stations

Hess Corporation ....B 212 997-8500
New York *(G-9771)*

PETROLEUM PRDTS WHOLESALERS

Industrial Raw Materials LLC ....F 212 688-8080
Plainview *(G-12689)*

PEWTER WARE

Quest Bead & Cast Inc ....G 212 354-1737
New York *(G-10955)*

Silver City Group Inc ....G 315 363-0344
Sherrill *(G-14407)*

PHARMACEUTICAL PREPARATIONS: Adrenal

Central Islip Pharmacy Inc ....G 631 234-6039
Central Islip *(G-3268)*

PHARMACEUTICAL PREPARATIONS: Barbituric Acid

872 Hunts Point Pharmacy Inc ....G 718 991-3519
Bronx *(G-1183)*

PHARMACEUTICAL PREPARATIONS: Digitalis

Intstrux LLC ....E 646 688-2782
New York *(G-9932)*

PHARMACEUTICAL PREPARATIONS: Druggists' Preparations

Advance Pharmaceutical Inc ....D 631 981-4600
Holtsville *(G-6044)*

American Regent Inc ....B 631 924-4000
Shirley *(G-14410)*

Asence Inc ....E 347 335-2606
New York *(G-8644)*

Biomed Pharmaceuticals Inc ....G 914 592-0525
Hawthorne *(G-5810)*

Biotie Therapies Inc ....F 650 244-4850
Ardsley *(G-386)*

Bristol-Myers Squibb Company ....E 315 432-2000
East Syracuse *(G-4201)*

Century Grand Inc ....F 212 925-3838
New York *(G-8960)*

Cognigen Corporation ....D 716 633-3463
Buffalo *(G-2701)*

Flushing Pharmacy Inc ....C 718 260-8999
Brooklyn *(G-1856)*

Fougera Pharmaceuticals Inc ....C 631 454-7677
Melville *(G-7785)*

Fougera Pharmaceuticals Inc ....C 631 454-7677
Hicksville *(G-5909)*

Global Alliance For Tb ....E 212 227-7540
New York *(G-9622)*

Hospira Inc ....C 716 684-9400
Buffalo *(G-2801)*

Ima Life North America Inc ....C 716 695-6354
Tonawanda *(G-15114)*

Jerome Stvens Phrmcuticals Inc...F... 631 567-1113
Bohemia *(G-1028)*
JRS Pharma LP...E... 845 878-8300
Patterson *(G-12518)*
Kingston Pharma LLC...D... 315 705-4019
Massena *(G-7668)*
Marietta Corporation...B... 607 753-6746
Cortland *(G-3775)*
Nutrascience Labs Inc...E... 631 247-0660
Farmingdale *(G-4696)*
Ony Inc Baird Researchpark...E... 716 636-9096
Buffalo *(G-2898)*
P & L Development LLC...D... 631 693-8000
Copiague *(G-3667)*
Pace Up Pharmaceuticals LLC...G... 631 450-4495
Lindenhurst *(G-6969)*
Par Pharmaceutical Inc...B... 845 573-5500
Chestnut Ridge *(G-3396)*
Pharbest Pharmaceuticals Inc...E... 631 249-5130
Farmingdale *(G-4705)*
Pharmavantage LLC...G... 631 321-8171
Babylon *(G-523)*
Puracap Laboratories LLC...G... 270 586-6386
Laurelton *(G-6885)*
Strativa Pharmaceuticals...F... 201 802-4000
Spring Valley *(G-14582)*
Wavodyne Therapeutics Inc...G... 954 632-6630
West Henrietta *(G-15807)*

PHARMACEUTICAL PREPARATIONS: Medicines, Capsule Or Ampule

AMP Nutraceuticals Inc...G... 631 676-5537
Ronkonkoma *(G-13906)*
Futurebiotics LLC...E... 631 273-6300
Hauppauge *(G-5656)*
Nanorx Inc...G... 914 671-0224
Chappaqua *(G-3326)*
Oova Inc...G... 215 880-3125
New York *(G-10696)*

PHARMACEUTICAL PREPARATIONS: Penicillin

G C Hanford Manufacturing Co...C... 315 476-7418
Syracuse *(G-14898)*

PHARMACEUTICAL PREPARATIONS: Pills

A & Z Pharmaceutical Inc...D... 631 952-3802
Hauppauge *(G-5576)*

PHARMACEUTICAL PREPARATIONS: Powders

Athenex Pharmaceutical Div LLC...F... 877 463-7823
Buffalo *(G-2647)*

PHARMACEUTICAL PREPARATIONS: Procaine

Glaxosmithkline LLC...D... 518 239-6901
East Durham *(G-4102)*

PHARMACEUTICAL PREPARATIONS: Proprietary Drug PRDTS

Ip Med Inc...G... 516 766-3800
Oceanside *(G-12176)*
Time-Cap Laboratories Inc...C... 631 753-9090
Farmingdale *(G-4756)*

PHARMACEUTICAL PREPARATIONS: Solutions

Container Tstg Solutions LLC...F... 716 487-3300
Jamestown *(G-6504)*
Container Tstg Solutions LLC...G... 716 487-3300
Sinclairville *(G-14445)*
Guosa Life Sciences Inc...F... 718 813-7806
New York *(G-9699)*
Kent Chemical Corporation...E... 212 521-1700
New York *(G-10094)*
Medek Laboratories Inc...E... 845 943-4988
Monroe *(G-8027)*
Pall Corporation...A... 516 484-5400
Port Washington *(G-12913)*
Sterrx LLC...E... 518 324-7879
Plattsburgh *(G-12781)*
Zitomer LLC...G... 212 737-5560
New York *(G-11827)*

PHARMACEUTICAL PREPARATIONS: Tablets

Aiping Pharmaceutical Inc...G... 631 952-3802
Hauppauge *(G-5581)*
Bli International Inc...C... 631 940-9000
Deer Park *(G-3847)*
Chartwell Pharma Nda B2 Holdin...G... 845 268-5000
Congers *(G-3612)*
Innovative Labs LLC...D... 631 231-5522
Hauppauge *(G-5676)*
Invagen Pharmaceuticals Inc...C... 631 949-6367
Central Islip *(G-3278)*

PHARMACEUTICALS

3v Company Inc...E... 718 858-7333
Brooklyn *(G-1417)*
5th Avenue Pharmacy Inc...G... 718 439-8585
Brooklyn *(G-1420)*
888 Pharmacy Inc...F... 718 871-8833
Brooklyn *(G-1425)*
Abbott Laboratories...F... 716 633-1904
Williamsville *(G-16117)*
Abeona Therapeutics Inc...E... 646 813-4712
New York *(G-8429)*
Abh Pharma Inc...D... 866 922-4669
Edgewood *(G-4259)*
Abraxis Bioscience LLC...G... 716 773-0800
Grand Island *(G-5324)*
Actinium Pharmaceuticals Inc...E... 646 677-3870
New York *(G-8451)*
Affymax Inc...G... 650 812-8700
New York *(G-8491)*
Alaska Spring Phrmcuticals Inc...E... 516 205-6020
Westbury *(G-15865)*
Alfred Khalily Inc...F... 516 504-0059
Great Neck *(G-5362)*
Allied Pharmacy Products Inc...G... 516 374-8862
Hicksville *(G-5882)*
Altaire Pharmaceuticals Inc...C... 631 722-5988
Aquebogue *(G-364)*
Amarantus Bscence Holdings Inc...F... 917 686-5317
New York *(G-8536)*
American Bio Medica Corp...D... 518 758-8158
Kinderhook *(G-6670)*
Amneal Pharmaceuticals LLC...E... 908 231-1911
Brookhaven *(G-1405)*
Amneal Pharmaceuticals LLC...E... 631 952-0214
Brookhaven *(G-1406)*
Amneal Pharmaceuticals NY LLC...G... 631 952-0214
Commack *(G-3576)*
Amneal Pharmaceuticals NY LLC...E... 908 947-3120
Brookhaven *(G-1407)*
Anacor Pharmaceuticals Inc...E... 212 733-2323
New York *(G-8570)*
Anavex Life Sciences Corp...F... 844 689-3939
New York *(G-8575)*
Angiogenex Inc...G... 347 468-6799
New York *(G-8584)*
Anterios Inc...G... 212 303-1683
New York *(G-8596)*
Apothecus Pharmaceutical Corp...F... 516 624-8200
Oyster Bay *(G-12444)*
Aratana Therapeutics Inc...G... 212 827-0020
New York *(G-8617)*
Ascent Pharmaceuticals Inc...D... 631 851-0550
Central Islip *(G-3262)*
Athenex Inc...D... 716 427-2950
Buffalo *(G-2646)*
Athenex Pharma Solutions LLC...G... 877 463-7823
Clarence *(G-3426)*
Auri Nutrascience Inc...G... 631 454-0020
Farmingdale *(G-4587)*
Auven Therapeutics MGT LP...F... 212 616-4000
New York *(G-8683)*
Avenue Therapeutics Inc...G... 781 652-4500
New York *(G-8689)*
Axim Biotechnologies Inc...F... 212 751-0001
New York *(G-8697)*
Azurrx Biopharma Inc...F... 646 699-7855
Brooklyn *(G-1554)*
Barc Usa Inc...E... 516 719-1052
New Hyde Park *(G-8253)*
Bausch & Lomb Holdings Inc...G... 585 338-6000
New York *(G-8741)*
Baxter Healthcare Corporation...B... 800 356-3454
Medina *(G-7729)*
Beyondspring Inc...D... 646 305-6387
New York *(G-8775)*
Beyondspring Phrmceuticals Inc...F... 646 305-6387
New York *(G-8776)*
Biospecifics Technologies Corp...G... 516 593-7000
Lynbrook *(G-7428)*
Bristol-Myers Squibb Company...A... 212 546-4000
New York *(G-8856)*
Bristol-Myers Squibb Company...C... 516 832-2191
Garden City *(G-5093)*
Bristol-Myers Squibb Intl Corp...E... 212 546-4000
New York *(G-8857)*
Caligor Rx Inc...E... 212 988-0590
New York *(G-8891)*
Campbell Alliance Group Inc...E... 212 377-2740
New York *(G-8899)*
Canbiola Inc...G... 954 253-4443
Hicksville *(G-5892)*
Cas Biosciences LLC...C... 844 227-2467
New York *(G-8928)*
Cellectis Inc...F... 347 809-5980
New York *(G-8942)*
Cerovene Inc...F... 845 359-1101
Orangeburg *(G-12308)*
Cerovene Inc...F... 845 267-2055
Valley Cottage *(G-15314)*
Chartwell Pharmaceuticals LLC...D... 845 268-5000
Congers *(G-3613)*
Checkpoint Therapeutics Inc...G... 781 652-4500
New York *(G-8979)*
Chembio Diagnostics Inc...D... 631 924-1135
Medford *(G-7702)*
Citypharma Inc...G... 917 832-6035
Jackson Heights *(G-6419)*
Cleveland Biolabs Inc...F... 716 849-6810
Buffalo *(G-2699)*
Combe Incorporated...C... 914 694-5454
White Plains *(G-15995)*
Contract Pharmacal Corp...E... 631 231-4610
Hauppauge *(G-5625)*
Contract Pharmacal Corp...C... 631 231-4610
Hauppauge *(G-5626)*
Contract Pharmacal Corp...E... 631 231-4610
Hauppauge *(G-5627)*
Contract Pharmacal Corp...D... 631 231-4610
Hauppauge *(G-5628)*
Contract Pharmacal Corp...F... 631 231-4610
Hauppauge *(G-5630)*
Coopersurgical Inc...F... 716 693-6230
North Tonawanda *(G-12064)*
CRS Nuclear Services LLC...F... 716 810-0688
Cheektowaga *(G-3342)*
Delcath Systems Inc...E... 212 489-2100
New York *(G-9197)*
Devos Ltd...C... 800 473-2138
Holbrook *(G-5996)*
Dr Reddys Laboratories NY Inc...E... 518 827-7702
Middleburgh *(G-7886)*
Edlaw Pharmaceuticals Inc...E... 631 454-6888
Farmingdale *(G-4623)*
Eli Lilly and Company...F... 516 622-2244
New Hyde Park *(G-8265)*
Emilior Phrm Compounding Inc...E... 646 350-0033
Bronx *(G-1254)*
Emphascience...G... 585 348-9415
Pittsford *(G-12639)*
Encysive Pharmaceuticals Inc...E... 212 733-2323
New York *(G-9368)*
Enumeral Biomedical Corp...G... 347 227-4787
New York *(G-9384)*
Enzo Life Sciences Inc...E... 631 694-7070
Farmingdale *(G-4625)*
Enzo Life Sciences Intl Inc...E... 610 941-0430
Farmingdale *(G-4626)*
Eon Labs Inc...F... 516 478-9700
New Hyde Park *(G-8267)*
Epic Pharma LLC...C... 718 276-8600
Laurelton *(G-6882)*
Eyenovia Inc...E... 917 289-1117
New York *(G-9453)*
Fera Pharmaceuticals LLC...F... 516 277-1449
Locust Valley *(G-7123)*
Forest Laboratories LLC...D... 212 421-7850
Hauppauge *(G-5654)*
Forest Labs...G... 631 755-1185
Farmingdale *(G-4632)*
Forest Research Institute Inc...F... 631 858-5200
Commack *(G-3588)*
Fortress Biotech Inc...E... 781 652-4500
New York *(G-9517)*
Fresenius Kabi Usa LLC...B... 716 773-0053
Grand Island *(G-5330)*
Fresenius Kabi USA LLC...E... 716 773-0800
Grand Island *(G-5331)*

PRODUCT

Company		Phone	Location
Gemini Pharmaceuticals Inc	B	631 543-3334	Commack (G-3590)
Generic Pharmaceutical Svcs	E	631 348-6900	Hauppauge (G-5658)
Genzyme Corporation	D	212 698-0300	New York (G-9596)
Geritrex LLC	E	914 668-4003	Middletown (G-7912)
Geritrex Holdings Inc	G	914 668-4003	Mount Vernon (G-8142)
Glaxosmithkline LLC	E	845 341-7590	Montgomery (G-8060)
Glaxosmithkline LLC	E	845 797-3259	Wappingers Falls (G-15495)
Glaxosmithkline LLC	E	585 738-9025	Rochester (G-13443)
Glaxosmithkline LLC	E	716 913-5679	Buffalo (G-2776)
Glaxosmithkline LLC	E	518 852-9637	Mechanicville (G-7692)
Glycobia Inc	G	607 339-0051	Ithaca (G-6382)
Greenkissny Inc	G	914 304-4323	White Plains (G-16011)
Greentree Pharmacy Inc	F	718 768-2700	Brooklyn (G-1911)
Health Care Products	G	631 789-8228	Amityville (G-268)
Healthone Pharmacy Inc	F	718 495-9015	Brooklyn (G-1928)
Hi-Tech Pharmacal Co Inc	C	631 789-8228	Amityville (G-270)
Hi-Tech Pharmacal Co Inc	E	631 789-8228	Amityville (G-271)
Hi-Tech Pharmacal Co Inc	F	631 789-8228	Amityville (G-272)
Hi-Tech Pharmacal Co Inc	C	631 789-8228	Amityville (G-273)
Hitech Pharm	G	631 789-8228	Amityville (G-274)
Hoffmann-La Roche Inc	G	973 890-2291	New York (G-9799)
Hogil Pharmaceutical Corp	F	914 681-1800	White Plains (G-16014)
Hookipa Pharma Inc	D	431 890-6360	New York (G-9810)
Ibio Inc	E	302 355-0650	New York (G-9852)
Ichor Therapeutics Inc	G	315 677-8400	La Fayette (G-6738)
Innogenix Inc	F	631 450-4704	Amityville (G-276)
Intercept Pharmaceuticals Inc	D	646 747-1000	New York (G-9914)
Intra-Cellular Therapies Inc	E	646 440-9333	New York (G-9929)
Invagen Pharmaceuticals Inc	B	631 231-3233	Hauppauge (G-5678)
Irx Therapuetics Inc	G	347 442-0640	Brooklyn (G-1970)
Iveric Bio Inc	E	212 845-8200	New York (G-9949)
Izun Pharmaceuticals Corp	F	212 618-6357	New York (G-9951)
Kadmon Corporation LLC	F	212 308-6000	New York (G-10055)
Kadmon Holdings Inc	D	212 308-6000	New York (G-10056)
Kaneka America LLC	D	212 705-4340	New York (G-10066)
Kannalife Sciences Inc	G	516 669-3219	Lloyd Harbor (G-7056)
Kbl Healthcare LP	G	212 319-5555	New York (G-10084)
Klg Usa LLC	A	845 856-5311	Port Jervis (G-12853)
Life Pill Laboratories LLC	G	914 682-2146	White Plains (G-16025)
Liptis Pharmaceuticals USA Inc	A	845 627-0260	Spring Valley (G-14576)
LNK International Inc	D	631 435-3500	Hauppauge (G-5694)
LNK International Inc	D	631 435-3500	Hauppauge (G-5695)
LNK International Inc	D	631 435-3500	Hauppauge (G-5696)
LNK International Inc	D	631 543-3787	Hauppauge (G-5697)
LNK International Inc	D	631 435-3500	Hauppauge (G-5698)
LNK International Inc	D	631 231-4020	Hauppauge (G-5699)
Maks Pharma & Diagnostics Inc	G	631 270-1528	Baldwin (G-532)
Medtech Products Inc	F	914 524-6810	Tarrytown (G-15047)
Mtc Industries Inc	F	631 274-4818	Hauppauge (G-5724)
Mustang Bio Inc	E	781 652-4500	New York (G-10522)
Mylan Health Management LLC	G	917 262-2950	New York (G-10526)
Neurotrope Inc	G	973 242-0005	New York (G-10574)
Norwich Pharmaceuticals Inc	B	607 335-3000	Norwich (G-12125)
Novartis Corporation	D	718 276-8600	Laurelton (G-6883)
Novartis Pharmaceuticals Corp	G	888 669-6682	New York (G-10649)
Novartis Pharmaceuticals Corp	G	718 276-8600	Laurelton (G-6884)
Noven Pharmaceuticals Inc	E	212 682-4420	New York (G-10650)
Nutratech Labs Inc	G	315 695-2256	Phoenix (G-12618)
NY Phrmacy Compounding Ctr Inc	G	201 403-5151	Astoria (G-432)
Ony Biotech Inc	E	716 636-9096	Amherst (G-239)
Orenova Group LLC	G	914 517-3000	White Plains (G-16036)
Ortho-Clinical Diagnostics Inc	F	585 453-3000	Rochester (G-13594)
Ovid Therapeutics Inc	E	646 661-7661	New York (G-10721)
P & L Development LLC	E	516 986-1700	Westbury (G-15913)
P & L Development LLC	D	516 986-1700	Westbury (G-15914)
P & L Development LLC	D	516 986-1700	Westbury (G-15915)
Par Phrmceutical Companies Inc	E	845 573-5500	Chestnut Ridge (G-3397)
Par Sterile Products LLC	E	845 573-5500	Chestnut Ridge (G-3398)
Parmed Pharmaceuticals LLC	D	716 773-1113	Niagara Falls (G-11963)
Pedinol Pharmacal Inc	G	800 733-4665	Farmingdale (G-4703)
Pfizer HCP Corporation	F	212 733-2323	New York (G-10820)
Pfizer Inc	B	518 297-6611	Rouses Point (G-14066)
Pfizer Inc	C	914 437-5868	White Plains (G-16052)
Pfizer Inc	C	937 746-3603	New York (G-10822)
Pfizer Inc	D	212 733-6276	New York (G-10823)
Pfizer Overseas LLC	G	212 733-2323	New York (G-10824)
PH David J Rossi	G	585 455-1160	Rochester (G-13619)
Polygen Pharmaceuticals Inc	E	631 392-4044	Edgewood (G-4278)
Precision Pharma Services Inc	C	631 752-7314	Melville (G-7817)
Prestige Brands Intl LLC	F	914 524-6800	Tarrytown (G-15053)
Prestige Consmr Healthcare Inc	D	914 524-6800	Tarrytown (G-15054)
Prime Pack LLC	F	732 253-7734	New York (G-10890)
Progenics Pharmaceuticals Inc	D	646 975-2500	New York (G-10905)
Protein Sciences Corporation	F	203 686-0800	Pearl River (G-12538)
Quogue Capital LLC	G	212 554-4475	New York (G-10959)
Rasna Therapeutics Inc	G	646 396-4087	New York (G-10982)
Regeneron Pharmaceuticals Inc	B	914 847-7000	Tarrytown (G-15056)
Regeneron Pharmaceuticals Inc	E	518 488-6000	Rensselaer (G-13091)
Regenron Hlthcare Slutions Inc	A	914 847-7000	Tarrytown (G-15057)
Relmada Therapeutics Inc	E	646 677-3853	New York (G-11004)
Retrophin LLC	G	646 564-3680	New York (G-11024)
Rij Pharmaceutical Corporation	E	845 692-5799	Middletown (G-7929)
Rk Pharma Inc	G	646 884-3765	Pearl River (G-12540)
Rls Holdings Inc	G	716 418-7274	Clarence (G-3441)
Roche Tcrc Inc	G	800 626-3553	New York (G-11067)
Rocket Pharmaceuticals Inc	E	646 440-9100	New York (G-11068)
Ropack USA Inc	F	631 482-7777	Commack (G-3596)
Salutem Group LLC	G	347 620-2640	New York (G-11123)
Saptalil Pharmacuetical Inc	G	631 231-2751	Hauppauge (G-5758)
Saptalis Pharmaceuticals LLC	E	631 231-2751	Hauppauge (G-5759)
Scarguard Labs LLC	F	516 482-8050	Great Neck (G-5422)
Sciarra Laboratories Inc	G	516 933-7853	Hicksville (G-5947)
Scienta Pharmaceuticals LLC	G	845 589-0774	Valley Cottage (G-15323)
Seelos Corporation	G	646 998-6475	New York (G-11179)
Seelos Therapeutics Inc	F	646 998-6475	New York (G-11180)
Seidlin Consulting	G	212 496-2043	New York (G-11183)
Sellas Life Sciences Group Inc	F	917 438-4353	New York (G-11188)
Shrineeta Pharmacy	G	212 234-7959	New York (G-11219)
Shrineeta Pharmacy Inc	G	212 234-7959	New York (G-11220)
Siga Technologies Inc	E	212 672-9100	New York (G-11230)
Silver Oak Pharmacy Inc	F	718 922-3400	Brooklyn (G-2414)
Sincerus LLC	G	800 419-2804	Brooklyn (G-2420)
Skills Alliance Inc	G	646 492-5300	New York (G-11258)
Specgx LLC	A	607 538-9124	Hobart (G-5979)
Stemline Therapeutics Inc	E	646 502-2311	New York (G-11356)
Steri-Pharma LLC	E	315 473-7180	Syracuse (G-15001)
Sunquest Pharmaceuticals Inc	F	855 478-6779	Hicksville (G-5950)
Syntho Pharmaceuticals Inc	G	631 755-9898	Farmingdale (G-4747)
Tg Therapeutics Inc	D	212 554-4484	New York (G-11457)
Tmp Technologies Inc	D	716 895-6100	Buffalo (G-3012)
Tocare LLC	F	718 767-0618	Whitestone (G-16101)
Tongli Pharmaceuticals USA Inc	F	212 842-8837	Flushing (G-4900)
Tonix Pharmaceuticals Inc	G	917 288-8908	New York (G-11513)
Tonix Phrmceuticals Holdg Corp	G	212 980-9155	New York (G-11514)
Topiderm Inc	C	631 226-7979	Amityville (G-312)
Topix Pharmaceuticals Inc	C	631 226-7979	Amityville (G-313)
Tyme Technologies Inc	F	212 461-2315	New York (G-11569)
Ultra-Tab Laboratories Inc	E	845 691-8361	Highland (G-5964)
United-Guardian Inc	E	631 273-0900	Hauppauge (G-5791)
Unither Manufacturing LLC	C	585 475-9000	Rochester (G-13783)
Unither Manufacturing LLC	F	585 274-5430	Rochester (G-13784)
Urogen Ltd	G	646 768-9780	New York (G-11619)
Urogen Pharma Inc	F	646 506-4663	New York (G-11620)
Vaccinex Inc	E	585 271-2700	Rochester (G-13792)
Ventrus Biosciences Inc	G	646 706-5208	New York (G-11655)

Verona Pharma Inc ....F 914 797-5007
White Plains (G-16068)
Viropro Inc ....E 650 300-5190
New York (G-11688)
Vitalis LLC ....G 646 831-7338
New York (G-11695)
Vitane Pharmaceuticals Inc ....E 845 267-6700
Congers (G-3620)
Viwit Pharmaceuticals Inc ....G 201 701-9787
Castleton On Hudson (G-3205)
Vvs International Inc ....G 212 302-5410
New York (G-11710)
Wyeth Holdings LLC ....D 845 602-5000
Pearl River (G-12543)
X-Gen Pharmaceuticals Inc ....G 607 562-2700
Big Flats (G-849)
X-Gen Pharmaceuticals Inc ....E 631 261-8188
Northport (G-12112)
Xstelos Holdings Inc ....G 212 729-4962
New York (G-11802)
Y-Mabs Therapeutics Inc ....F 917 817-2992
New York (G-11803)
Ys Marketing Inc ....E 718 778-6080
Brooklyn (G-2603)

PHARMACEUTICALS: Mail-Order Svc

Greentree Pharmacy Inc ....F 718 768-2700
Brooklyn (G-1911)
Natures Bounty Co ....D 631 244-2021
Ronkonkoma (G-13980)

PHARMACEUTICALS: Medicinal & Botanical Prdts

Accredo Health Incorporated ....G 718 353-3012
Flushing (G-4833)
Albany Molecular Research Inc ....F 518 433-7700
Rensselaer (G-13085)
Albany Molecular Research Inc ....F 518 512-2000
Rensselaer (G-13086)
Alo Acquisition LLC ....G 518 464-0279
Albany (G-38)
Bi Nutraceuticals Inc ....G 631 533-4934
Islandia (G-6325)
Conversion Labs Inc ....F 866 351-5907
New York (G-9094)
Great Life Elixirs LLC ....D 332 204-1953
New York (G-9669)
Kannalife Sciences Inc ....G 516 669-3219
Lloyd Harbor (G-7056)
Nbty Inc ....G 631 200-2062
Holbrook (G-6014)
Setauket Manufacturing Co ....G 631 231-7272
Ronkonkoma (G-14008)

PHARMACIES & DRUG STORES

Biomed Pharmaceuticals Inc ....G 914 592-0525
Hawthorne (G-5810)
Emilior Phrm Compounding Inc ....E 646 350-0033
Bronx (G-1254)
Far Rockaway Drugs Inc ....F 718 471-2500
Far Rockaway (G-4565)
J P R Pharmacy Inc ....F 718 327-0600
Far Rockaway (G-4566)
Nucare Pharmacy Inc ....F 212 426-9300
New York (G-10653)
Nucare Pharmacy West LLC ....F 212 462-2525
New York (G-10654)

PHONOGRAPH NEEDLES

Grado Laboratories Inc ....F 718 435-5340
Brooklyn (G-1905)

PHONOGRAPH RECORDS WHOLESALERS

Hope International Productions ....F 212 247-3188
New York (G-9811)
Sony Music Holdings Inc ....A 212 833-8000
New York (G-11299)

PHONOGRAPH RECORDS: Prerecorded

Abkco Music & Records Inc ....E 212 399-0300
New York (G-8430)
Eks Manufacturing Inc ....F 917 217-0784
Brooklyn (G-1787)
Hope International Productions ....F 212 247-3188
New York (G-9811)
Warner Music Inc ....D 212 275-2000
New York (G-11723)

PHOSPHATES

International Ord Tech Inc ....D 716 664-1100
Jamestown (G-6518)
Mdi Holdings LLC ....A 212 559-1127
New York (G-10404)

PHOTOCOPY MACHINES

Cannon Industries Inc ....D 585 254-8080
Rochester (G-13294)
Facsimile Cmmncations Inds Inc ....D 212 741-6400
New York (G-9460)

PHOTOCOPYING & DUPLICATING SVCS

A Q P Inc ....G 585 256-1690
Rochester (G-13194)
Apple Press ....G 914 723-6660
White Plains (G-15975)
Avalon Copy Centers Amer Inc ....D 315 471-3333
Syracuse (G-14823)
Avalon Copy Centers Amer Inc ....E 716 995-7777
Buffalo (G-2651)
Business Never Stops LLC ....G 888 479-3111
South Richmond Hill (G-14522)
Capital Dst Print & Imaging ....G 518 456-6773
Schenectady (G-14251)
Carges Entps of Canandaigua ....G 585 394-2600
Canandaigua (G-3128)
Chakra Communications Inc ....E 607 748-7491
Endicott (G-4446)
Clarsons Corp ....F 585 235-8775
Rochester (G-13317)
Constas Printing Corporation ....D 315 474-2176
Syracuse (G-14859)
Excellent Photo Copies ....G 718 384-7272
Brooklyn (G-1819)
Fairmount Press ....G 212 255-2300
New York (G-9465)
Fambus Inc ....G 607 785-3700
Endicott (G-4455)
Fedex Office & Print Svcs Inc ....G 718 982-5223
Staten Island (G-14653)
Graphic Fabrications Inc ....G 516 763-3222
Rockville Centre (G-13828)
Graphicomm Inc ....G 716 283-0830
Niagara Falls (G-11932)
Jon Lyn Ink Inc ....G 516 546-2312
Merrick (G-7857)
Kjckd Inc ....G 518 435-9696
Latham (G-6862)
Leader Printing Inc ....F 516 546-1544
Merrick (G-7859)
Mercury Print Productions Inc ....C 585 458-7900
Rochester (G-13542)
Multiple Imprssons of Rchester ....G 585 546-1160
Rochester (G-13563)
National Reproductions Inc ....E 212 619-3800
New York (G-10544)
North Delaware Printing Inc ....G 716 692-0576
Tonawanda (G-15128)
Persch Service Print Inc ....G 716 366-2677
Dunkirk (G-4063)
R & L Press of SI Inc ....G 718 667-3258
Staten Island (G-14697)
Rapid Print and Marketing Inc ....G 585 924-1520
Victor (G-15427)
Shipmtes/Printmates Holdg Corp ....D 518 370-1158
Scotia (G-14336)
Shiprite Services Inc ....G 315 427-2422
Utica (G-15294)
Silver Griffin Inc ....F 518 272-7771
Troy (G-15189)
Twin Counties Pro Printers Inc ....F 518 828-3278
Hudson (G-6181)
William J Ryan ....G 585 392-6200
Hilton (G-5975)
Woodbury Printing Plus + Inc ....G 845 928-6610
Central Valley (G-3302)

PHOTOELECTRIC DEVICES: Magnetic

Truebite Inc ....E 607 785-7664
Vestal (G-15386)

PHOTOENGRAVING SVC

Koehlr-Gibson Mkg Graphics Inc ....E 716 838-5960
Buffalo (G-2838)
Rapid Service Engraving Co ....G 716 896-4555
Buffalo (G-2948)

PHOTOFINISHING LABORATORIES

Digital Evolution Inc ....E 212 732-2722
New York (G-9227)
Eastman Kodak Company ....B 585 724-4000
Rochester (G-13367)

PHOTOGRAPHIC EQPT & CAMERAS, WHOLESALE

Ingenious Ingenuity Inc ....F 800 834-5279
Webster (G-15642)

PHOTOGRAPHIC EQPT & SPLY: Sound Recordg/Reprod Eqpt, Motion

Kelmar Systems Inc ....F 631 421-1230
Huntington Station (G-6252)

PHOTOGRAPHIC EQPT & SPLYS

Astrodyne Inc ....G 516 536-5755
Oceanside (G-12166)
AVI-Spl Employee ....B 212 840-4801
New York (G-8691)
Carestream Health Inc ....B 585 627-1800
Rochester (G-13296)
Cpac Inc ....E 585 382-3223
Leicester (G-6908)
Creatron Services Inc ....E 516 437-5119
Floral Park (G-4813)
Eastman Kodak Company ....E 585 724-4000
Rochester (G-13377)
Ebsco Industries Inc ....E 585 398-2000
Farmington (G-4770)
Emda Inc ....F 631 243-6363
Plainview (G-12683)
Garys Loft ....E 212 244-0970
New York (G-9575)
Henrys Deals Inc ....E 347 821-4685
Brooklyn (G-1931)
Kodak Alaris Inc ....B 888 242-2424
Rochester (G-13504)
Kodak Graphic Communications ....F 585 724-4000
Rochester (G-13505)
Labgrafix Printing Inc ....G 516 280-8300
Lynbrook (G-7433)
Lowel-Light Manufacturing Inc ....E 718 921-0600
Brooklyn (G-2087)
Mirion Technologies Ist Corp ....D 607 562-4300
Horseheads (G-6128)
Norazza Inc ....F 716 706-1160
Buffalo (G-2890)
Rockland Colloid Corp ....G 845 359-5559
Piermont (G-12622)
Stallion Technologies Inc ....G 315 622-1176
Liverpool (G-7041)
Thermo Cidtec Inc ....E 315 451-9410
Liverpool (G-7045)
Tiffen Company LLC ....G 631 273-2500
Hauppauge (G-5785)
Tiffen Company LLC ....C 631 273-2500
Hauppauge (G-5786)
Vishay Thin Film LLC ....C 716 283-4025
Niagara Falls (G-11990)
Xerox Corporation ....C 585 264-5584
Rochester (G-13811)

PHOTOGRAPHIC EQPT & SPLYS WHOLESALERS

AVI-Spl Employee ....B 212 840-4801
New York (G-8691)
Rockland Colloid Corp ....G 845 359-5559
Piermont (G-12622)

PHOTOGRAPHIC EQPT & SPLYS, WHOLESALE: Motion Picture

Doar Inc ....G 516 872-8140
Lynbrook (G-7430)

PHOTOGRAPHIC EQPT & SPLYS: Cameras, Aerial

Fluxdata Incorporated ....G 800 425-0176
Rochester (G-13418)
Geospatial Systems Inc ....F 585 427-8310
West Henrietta (G-15796)

P
R
O
D
U
C
T

PHOTOGRAPHIC EQPT & SPLYS: Editing Eqpt, Motion Picture

Avid Technology Inc ....E 212 983-2424
  New York (G-8692)
Kyle Editing LLC ....G 212 675-3464
  New York (G-10147)

PHOTOGRAPHIC EQPT & SPLYS: Film, Sensitized

Eastman Kodak Company ....D 585 722-2187
  Rochester (G-13366)
Eastman Kodak Company ....B 585 724-4000
  Rochester (G-13367)
Eastman Kodak Company ....D 585 724-5600
  Rochester (G-13368)
Eastman Kodak Company ....D 585 722-9695
  Pittsford (G-12638)
Eastman Kodak Company ....D 585 726-6261
  Rochester (G-13369)
Eastman Kodak Company ....D 585 724-4000
  Rochester (G-13370)
Eastman Kodak Company ....F 800 698-3324
  Rochester (G-13371)
Eastman Kodak Company ....D 585 722-4385
  Rochester (G-13372)
Eastman Kodak Company ....D 585 588-5598
  Rochester (G-13373)
Eastman Kodak Company ....C 585 726-7000
  Rochester (G-13374)
Eastman Kodak Company ....G 585 722-4007
  Rochester (G-13375)
Eastman Kodak Company ....D 585 588-3896
  Rochester (G-13376)
Eastman Park Micrographics Inc ....G 866 934-4376
  Rochester (G-13378)
Truesense Imaging Inc ....C 585 784-5500
  Rochester (G-13775)

PHOTOGRAPHIC EQPT & SPLYS: Graphic Arts Plates, Sensitized

Gpc International Inc ....C 631 752-9600
  Melville (G-7786)

PHOTOGRAPHIC EQPT & SPLYS: Plates, Sensitized

Apexx Omni-Graphics Inc ....D 718 326-3330
  Maspeth (G-7591)

PHOTOGRAPHIC EQPT & SPLYS: Printing Eqpt

Jack L Popkin & Co Inc ....G 718 361-6700
  Kew Gardens (G-6666)

PHOTOGRAPHIC EQPT & SPLYS: Shutters, Camera

Va Inc ....E 585 385-5930
  Rochester (G-13791)

PHOTOGRAPHIC EQPT & SPLYS: Toners, Prprd, Not Chem Plnts

Efam Enterprises LLC ....E 718 204-1760
  Long Island City (G-7211)
Hilord Chemical Corporation ....E 631 234-7373
  Hauppauge (G-5671)
Lasertech Crtridge RE-Builders ....G 518 373-1246
  Clifton Park (G-3466)
Toner-N-More Inc ....G 718 232-6200
  Brooklyn (G-2509)

PHOTOGRAPHIC EQPT/SPLYS, WHOL: Cameras/Projectors/Eqpt/Splys

Bescor Video Accessories Ltd ....F 631 420-1717
  Farmingdale (G-4592)

PHOTOGRAPHIC LIBRARY SVCS

Kraus Organization Limited ....D 212 686-5411
  New York (G-10138)

PHOTOGRAPHIC PEOCESSING CHEMICALS

Champion Photochemistry Inc ....D 585 760-6444
  Rochester (G-13310)

PHOTOGRAPHIC PROCESSING EQPT & CHEMICALS

Air Techniques Inc ....B 516 433-7676
  Melville (G-7758)
Cine Magnetics Inc ....E 914 667-6707
  Mount Vernon (G-8130)
Seneca TEC Inc ....G 585 381-2645
  Fairport (G-4521)
Sima Technologies LLC ....G 412 828-9130
  Hauppauge (G-5766)

PHOTOGRAPHIC SENSITIZED GOODS, NEC

Turner Bellows Inc ....E 585 235-4456
  Rochester (G-13778)

PHOTOGRAPHIC SVCS

Labgrafix Printing Inc ....G 516 280-8300
  Lynbrook (G-7433)

PHOTOGRAPHY SVCS: Commercial

Cobico Productions Inc ....G 347 417-5883
  New York (G-9045)
Untitled Media ....E 212 780-0960
  New York (G-11611)

PHOTOGRAPHY SVCS: Portrait Studios

Classic Album ....E 718 388-2818
  Brooklyn (G-1670)
Classic Album LLC ....D 718 388-2818
  Brooklyn (G-1671)

PHOTOGRAPHY SVCS: Still Or Video

Dynamic Photography Inc......................G 516 381-2951
  Roslyn (G-14042)

PHOTOTYPESETTING SVC

Digital Color Concepts Inc ....E 212 989-4888
  New York (G-9226)

PHOTOVOLTAIC Solid State

Besicorp Ltd ....F 845 336-7700
  Kingston (G-6680)
Onyx Solar Group LLC ....G 917 951-9732
  New York (G-10695)
Solar Thin Films Inc ....G 212 629-8260
  Cedarhurst (G-3244)

PHYSICAL FITNESS CENTERS

Womens Health Care PC ....G 718 850-0009
  Richmond Hill (G-13128)

PHYSICIANS' OFFICES & CLINICS: Medical doctors

M H Mandelbaum Orthotic ....F 631 473-8668
  Port Jefferson (G-12842)

PICTURE FRAMES: Metal

Access Display Group Inc......................F 516 678-7772
  Freeport (G-4979)
Bristol Gift Co Inc ....F 845 496-2821
  Washingtonville (G-15523)
Custom Frame & Molding Co ....F 631 491-9091
  West Babylon (G-15705)
Dobrin Industries Inc ....G 800 353-2229
  Lockport (G-7069)
Elias Artmetal Inc ....F 516 873-7501
  Mineola (G-7970)
Frame Shoppe & Art Gallery ....G 516 365-6014
  Manhasset (G-7534)
Inter Pacific Consulting Corp ....G 718 460-2787
  Flushing (G-4861)
Jay Strongwater Holdings LLC..............A 646 657-0558
  New York (G-9980)
Picture Perfect Framing ....G 718 851-1884
  Brooklyn (G-2257)
Structural Industries Inc.......................C 631 471-5200
  Bohemia (G-1082)

PICTURE FRAMES: Wood

Apf Manufacturing Company LLC............E 914 963-6300
  Yonkers (G-16287)

FG Galassi Moulding Co Inc ....G...... 845 258-2100
  Goshen (G-5308)
Fred M Lawrence Co Inc ....E 631 617-6853
  Bay Shore (G-681)
Fruit Fresh Up Inc ....E 716 683-3200
  Depew (G-3983)
Galas Framing Services ....F 718 706-0007
  Long Island City (G-7228)
Grant-Noren ....G 845 726-4281
  Westtown (G-15966)
Hubray Inc ....F 800 645-2855
  North Baldwin (G-12006)
Interntonal Consmr Connections ....F 516 481-3438
  West Hempstead (G-15771)
New Heydenryk LLC ....F 212 206-9611
  Long Island City (G-7307)
Picture Perfect Framing ....G 718 851-1884
  Brooklyn (G-2257)

PICTURE FRAMING SVCS, CUSTOM

Frame Shoppe & Art Gallery ....G 516 365-6014
  Manhasset (G-7534)
Galas Framing Services ....F 718 706-0007
  Long Island City (G-7228)
Interntonal Consmr Connections ....F 516 481-3438
  West Hempstead (G-15771)
Timeless Decor LLC ....C 315 782-5759
  Watertown (G-15590)

PICTURE PROJECTION EQPT

Just Lamps of New York Inc ....F 716 626-2240
  Buffalo (G-2826)

PIECE GOODS & NOTIONS WHOLESALERS

Hedaya Home Fashions Inc ....C 212 889-1111
  New York (G-9761)
Hpk Industries LLC ....F 315 724-0196
  Utica (G-15271)
J & M Textile Co Inc ....F 212 268-8000
  New York (G-9953)
Prym Fashion Americas LLC ....D 212 760-9660
  New York (G-10917)

PIECE GOODS, NOTIONS & DRY GOODS, WHOL: Textile Converters

Bank-Miller Co Inc................................E 914 227-9357
  Pelham (G-12565)
Klauber Brothers Inc ....E 212 686-2531
  New York (G-10114)
La Lame Inc ....G 212 921-9770
  New York (G-10158)

PIECE GOODS, NOTIONS & DRY GOODS, WHOL: Textiles, Woven

Kowa American Corporation ....E 212 303-7800
  New York (G-10131)
Mutual Sales Corp................................E 718 361-8373
  Long Island City (G-7300)
Shengkun North America Inc.................F 212 217-2460
  New York (G-11211)
Zorlu USA Inc ....D 212 689-4622
  New York (G-11830)

PIECE GOODS, NOTIONS & DRY GOODS, WHOL: Trimmings, Apparel

Rhino Sports & Leisure LLC ....E 844 877-4466
  Tarrytown (G-15058)

PIECE GOODS, NOTIONS & DRY GOODS, WHOLESALE: Fabrics, Knit

Continental Knitting Mills......................G 631 242-5330
  Deer Park (G-3853)

PIECE GOODS, NOTIONS & DRY GOODS, WHOLESALE: Fabrics, Lace

Penn & Fletcher Inc ....F 212 239-6868
  Long Island City (G-7324)
Super-Trim Inc ....E 212 255-2370
  New York (G-11396)

PIECE GOODS, NOTIONS & DRY GOODS, WHOLESALE: Sewing Access

Bfma Holding Corporation ....G....... 607 753-6746
Cortland **(G-3755)**

Marietta Corporation ....A 323 589-8181
Cortland **(G-3777)**

PIECE GOODS, NOTIONS & OTHER DRY GOODS, WHOLESALE: Bridal

Alvina Vlenta Couture Collectn ....F 212 921-7058
New York **(G-8534)**

PIECE GOODS, NOTIONS & OTHER DRY GOODS, WHOLESALE: Buttons

Emsig Manufacturing Corp ....F 518 828-7301
Hudson **(G-6155)**

Hemisphere Novelties Inc ....E 914 378-4100
Yonkers **(G-16318)**

PIECE GOODS, NOTIONS & OTHER DRY GOODS, WHOLESALE: Fabrics

Creation Baumann USA Inc ....E 516 764-7431
Rockville Centre **(G-13827)**

Eu Design LLC ....G 212 420-7788
New York **(G-9416)**

Pearl River Textiles Inc ....G 212 629-5490
New York **(G-10778)**

Sifonya Inc ....G 212 620-4512
New York **(G-11229)**

PIECE GOODS, NOTIONS & OTHER DRY GOODS, WHOLESALE: Woven

Citisource Industries Inc ....E 212 683-1033
New York **(G-9015)**

PIECE GOODS, NOTIONS/DRY GOODS, WHOL: Drapery Mtrl, Woven

Richloom Fabrics Corp ....F 212 685-5400
New York **(G-11042)**

Scalamandre Silks Inc ....D 212 980-3888
New York **(G-11147)**

PIECE GOODS, NOTIONS/DRY GOODS, WHOL: Linen Piece, Woven

Simple Elegance New York Inc ....F 718 360-1947
Brooklyn **(G-2419)**

PIECE GOODS, NOTIONS/DRY GOODS, WHOL: Sewing Splys/Notions

Artistic Ribbon Novelty Co Inc ....E 212 255-4224
New York **(G-8637)**

PILLOW FILLING MTRLS: Curled Hair, Cotton Waste, Moss

American Home Mfg LLC ....G....... 212 643-0680
New York **(G-8551)**

PILLOWS: Sponge Rubber

Schlegel Systems Inc ....C 585 427-7200
Rochester **(G-13718)**

PINS

Pin Pharma Inc ....G....... 212 543-2583
New York **(G-10841)**

Pins N Needles ....F 212 535-6222
New York **(G-10845)**

Pni Capital Partners ....G....... 516 466-7120
Westbury **(G-15917)**

PIPE & FITTING: Fabrication

Accord Pipe Fabricators Inc ....E 718 657-3900
Jamaica **(G-6424)**

Advanced Thermal Systems Inc ....E 716 681-1800
Lancaster **(G-6790)**

Arcadia Mfg Group Inc ....E 518 434-6213
Green Island **(G-5432)**

Arcadia Mfg Group Inc ....G....... 518 434-6213
Menands **(G-7840)**

Cobey Inc ....C 716 362-9550
Buffalo **(G-2700)**

Daikin Applied Americas Inc ....D 315 253-2771
Auburn **(G-472)**

Flatcut LLC ....G...... 212 542-5732
Brooklyn **(G-1850)**

J D Steward Inc ....G...... 718 358-0169
Flushing **(G-4864)**

James Woerner Inc ....G...... 631 454-9330
Farmingdale **(G-4656)**

Juniper Elbow Co Inc ....C 718 326-2546
Middle Village **(G-7881)**

Juniper Industries Florida Inc ....G...... 718 326-2546
Middle Village **(G-7882)**

Leo International Inc ....E 718 290-8005
Brooklyn **(G-2063)**

Leroy Plastics Inc ....D 585 768-8158
Le Roy **(G-6903)**

Long Island Pipe Supply Inc ....G...... 718 456-7877
Flushing **(G-4872)**

Long Island Pipe Supply Inc ....G...... 518 270-2159
Troy **(G-15160)**

Micromold Products Inc ....E 914 969-2850
Yonkers **(G-16333)**

Miles Moss of Albany Inc ....E 516 222-8008
Garden City **(G-5108)**

Miles Moss of New York Inc ....E 516 222-8008
Garden City **(G-5109)**

Tag Flange & Machining Inc ....G...... 516 536-1300
Oceanside **(G-12194)**

Total Piping Solutions Inc ....E 716 372-0160
Olean **(G-12243)**

Truly Tubular Fitting Corp ....F 914 664-8686
Mount Vernon **(G-8188)**

PIPE & FITTINGS: Cast Iron

Dragon Trading Inc ....G...... 212 717-1496
New York **(G-9265)**

PIPE & FITTINGS: Pressure, Cast Iron

Acme Nipple Mfg Co Inc ....G...... 716 873-7491
Buffalo **(G-2618)**

Penner Elbow Company Inc ....F 718 526-9000
Elmhurst **(G-4337)**

PIPE CLEANERS

R V Dow Enterprises Inc ....F 585 454-5862
Rochester **(G-13667)**

PIPE JOINT COMPOUNDS

Continental Buchanan LLC ....D 703 480-3800
Buchanan **(G-2608)**

PIPE: Concrete

Binghamton Precast & Sup Corp ....E 607 722-0334
Binghamton **(G-859)**

Roman Stone Construction Co ....E 631 667-0566
Bay Shore **(G-709)**

PIPE: Extruded, Aluminum

North American Pipe Corp ....F 516 338-2863
East Williston **(G-4249)**

PIPE: Plastic

BMC LLC ....G...... 716 681-7755
Buffalo **(G-2665)**

Hancor Inc ....D 607 565-3033
Waverly **(G-15622)**

Micromold Products Inc ....E 914 969-2850
Yonkers **(G-16333)**

National Pipe & Plastics Inc ....C 607 729-9381
Vestal **(G-15381)**

North American Pipe Corp ....F 516 338-2863
East Williston **(G-4249)**

Prince Rubber & Plas Co Inc ....E 225 272-1653
Buffalo **(G-2931)**

PIPE: Sheet Metal

Lane Enterprises Inc ....E 518 885-4385
Ballston Spa **(G-579)**

PIPES & TUBES: Steel

Coventry Manufacturing Co Inc ....E 914 668-2212
Mount Vernon **(G-8134)**

Liberty Pipe Incorporated ....G...... 516 747-2472
Mineola **(G-7986)**

Markin Tubing LP ....F 585 495-6211
Buffalo **(G-2861)**

McHone Industries Inc ....D 716 945-3380
Salamanca **(G-14122)**

Micromold Products Inc ....E 914 969-2850
Yonkers **(G-16333)**

Stony Brook Mfg Co Inc ....E 631 369-9530
Calverton **(G-3086)**

Tricon Piping Systems Inc ....F 315 697-8787
Canastota **(G-3159)**

Welded Tube Usa Inc ....D 716 828-1111
Lackawanna **(G-6746)**

PIPES & TUBES: Welded

Oriskany Mfg Tech LLC ....E 315 732-4962
Yorkville **(G-16378)**

PIPES: Steel & Iron

Lino International Inc ....G...... 516 482-7100
Great Neck **(G-5401)**

PIPES: Tobacco

Ryers Creek Corp ....E 607 523-6617
Corning **(G-3720)**

PISTONS & PISTON RINGS

Fcmp Inc ....F 716 692-4623
Tonawanda **(G-15103)**

PLACEMATS: Plastic Or Textile

Baby Signature Inc ....G...... 212 686-1700
New York **(G-8710)**

Hedaya Home Fashions Inc ....C 212 889-1111
New York **(G-9761)**

NY Cutting Inc ....G...... 646 434-1355
Suffern **(G-14763)**

Sterling Shelf Liners Inc ....G...... 631 676-5175
Holbrook **(G-6022)**

PLANING MILLS: Independent, Exc Millwork

Embassy Millwork Inc ....F 518 839-0965
Amsterdam **(G-326)**

PLANING MILLS: Millwork

Mind Designs Inc ....G...... 631 563-3644
Farmingville **(G-4782)**

PLANT CARE SVCS

Plant-Tech2o Inc ....G...... 516 483-7845
Hempstead **(G-5847)**

PLAQUES: Clay, Plaster/Papier-Mache, Factory Production

B & R Promotional Products ....G...... 212 563-0040
New York **(G-8703)**

PLAQUES: Picture, Laminated

B & R Promotional Products ....G...... 212 563-0040
New York **(G-8703)**

Donorwall Inc ....F 212 766-9670
New York **(G-9253)**

Kelly Foundry & Machine Co ....E 315 732-8313
Utica **(G-15279)**

PLASMAS

Coral Blood Service ....F 800 483-4888
Elmsford **(G-4403)**

D C I Plasma Center Inc ....G...... 914 241-1646
Mount Kisco **(G-8090)**

Lake Immunogenics Inc ....F 585 265-1973
Ontario **(G-12293)**

PLASTER WORK: Ornamental & Architectural

American Wood Column Corp ....G...... 718 782-3163
Brooklyn **(G-1503)**

B & F Architectural Support Gr ....E 212 279-6488
New York **(G-8702)**

P R O D U C T

PLASTIC PRDTS

Castino Corporation ....G 845 229-0341
Hyde Park *(G-6270)*

G and G Service ....G 518 785-9247
Latham *(G-6857)*

Global Hanger & Display Inc ....G 631 475-5900
East Patchogue *(G-4153)*

ITW Deltar ....G 860 435-2574
Millerton *(G-7949)*

Kc Tag Co ....G 518 842-6666
Amsterdam *(G-332)*

PLASTIC PRDTS REPAIR SVCS

All Spec Finishing Inc ....E 607 770-9174
Binghamton *(G-852)*

PLASTICIZERS, ORGANIC: Cyclic & Acyclic

Wecare Organics LLC ....E 315 689-1937
Jordan *(G-6631)*

PLASTICS FILM & SHEET

Albert F Stager Inc ....G 315 434-7240
East Syracuse *(G-4193)*

Astra Products Inc ....G 631 464-4747
Copiague *(G-3648)*

Dunmore Corporation ....D 845 279-5061
Brewster *(G-1147)*

Farber Trucking Corp ....E 516 378-4860
Freeport *(G-4995)*

Favorite Plastic Corp ....C 718 253-7000
Brooklyn *(G-1834)*

Integument Technologies Inc ....F 716 873-1199
Tonawanda *(G-15116)*

Kings Film & Sheet Inc ....E 718 624-7510
Brooklyn *(G-2032)*

Maco Bag Corporation ....C 315 226-1000
Newark *(G-11844)*

PLASTICS FILM & SHEET: Polyethylene

Clear View Bag Company Inc ....C 518 458-7153
Albany *(G-61)*

Nationwide Tarps Incorporated ....D 518 843-1545
Amsterdam *(G-341)*

Pace Polyethylene Mfg Co Inc ....E 914 381-3000
Harrison *(G-5557)*

Potential Poly Bag Inc ....G 718 258-0800
Brooklyn *(G-2272)*

PLASTICS FILM & SHEET: Polyvinyl

Shaant Industries Inc ....E 716 366-3654
Dunkirk *(G-4066)*

PLASTICS FILM & SHEET: Vinyl

Ace Canvas & Tent Corp ....F 631 981-9705
Ronkonkoma *(G-13886)*

Latham International Inc ....F 518 346-5292
Schenectady *(G-14286)*

Latham International Inc ....G 518 783-7776
Latham *(G-6865)*

Orafol Americas Inc ....E 585 272-0309
Henrietta *(G-5859)*

Plascal Corp ....G 516 249-2200
Farmingdale *(G-4710)*

Robeco/Ascot Products Inc ....E 516 248-1521
Garden City *(G-5114)*

Vinyl Materials Inc ....E 631 586-9444
Deer Park *(G-3951)*

PLASTICS FINISHED PRDTS: Laminated

Clear Cast Technologies Inc ....E 914 945-0848
Ossining *(G-12403)*

Inter State Laminates Inc ....E 518 283-8355
Poestenkill *(G-12803)*

Synthetic Textiles Inc ....F 716 842-2598
Buffalo *(G-2999)*

Unico Special Products Inc. ....E 845 562-9255
Newburgh *(G-11890)*

PLASTICS MATERIAL & RESINS

American Acrylic Corporation ....E 631 422-2200
West Babylon *(G-15687)*

Ampacet Corporation ....A 914 631-6600
Tarrytown *(G-15040)*

Ashley Resin Corp ....G 718 851-8111
Brooklyn *(G-1541)*

Atc Plastics LLC ....E 212 375-2515
New York *(G-8660)*

Bairnco Corporation ....E 914 461-1300
White Plains *(G-15977)*

Bamberger Polymers Inc ....E 516 622-3600
Jericho *(G-6571)*

Ccmi Inc ....G 315 781-3270
Geneva *(G-5148)*

Clarence Resins and Chemicals ....G 716 406-9804
Clarence Center *(G-3444)*

CN Group Incorporated ....A 914 358-5690
White Plains *(G-15994)*

Cytec Industries Inc ....D 716 372-9650
Olean *(G-12231)*

Dice America Inc ....E 585 869-6200
Victor *(G-15405)*

Durez Corporation ....F 716 286-0100
Niagara Falls *(G-11921)*

E I Du Pont De Nemours & Co ....E 716 876-4420
Buffalo *(G-2734)*

Eastman Chemical Company ....D 585 722-2905
Rochester *(G-13365)*

Endurart Inc ....E 212 473-7000
New York *(G-9373)*

GE Plastics ....G 518 475-5011
Selkirk *(G-14357)*

General Vy-Coat LLC ....E 718 266-6002
Brooklyn *(G-1882)*

Global Plastics LLC ....E 800 417-4605
New York *(G-9631)*

Hazen Holdings LLC ....G 607 542-9365
Jericho *(G-6581)*

Imbibitive Tech Amer Corp ....G 888 843-2323
Niagara Falls *(G-11936)*

Imbibitive Technologies Corp ....G 888 843-2323
Niagara Falls *(G-11937)*

International Casein Corp Cal ....G 516 466-4363
Great Neck *(G-5394)*

Macneil Polymers Inc ....F 716 681-7755
Buffalo *(G-2856)*

Maviano Corp ....G 845 494-2598
Monsey *(G-8040)*

MB Plastics Inc ....E 718 523-1180
Greenlawn *(G-5454)*

Mega Plastic Group Inc ....E 347 737-8444
Brooklyn *(G-2134)*

Mitsui Plastics Inc ....E 914 287-6800
White Plains *(G-16031)*

Momentive Performance Mtls Inc ....D 914 784-4807
Tarrytown *(G-15049)*

Nationwide Tarps Incorporated ....D 518 843-1545
Amsterdam *(G-341)*

Pac Plastics LLC ....G 631 545-0382
White Plains *(G-16038)*

Parker-Hannifin Corporation ....E 315 926-4211
Marion *(G-7572)*

Plasticycle Corporation ....E 914 997-6882
White Plains *(G-16053)*

Polycast Industries Inc ....G 631 595-2530
Bay Shore *(G-699)*

Polymers Merona Inc ....F 631 862-8010
Saint James *(G-14112)*

Sabic Innovative Plas US LLC ....B 518 475-5011
Selkirk *(G-14360)*

Sabic Innovative Plastics ....E 713 448-7474
East Greenbush *(G-4116)*

Saint-Gobain Prfmce Plas Corp ....C 518 686-7301
Hoosick Falls *(G-6088)*

Saint-Gobain Prfmce Plas Corp ....G 518 642-2200
Granville *(G-5355)*

Solepoxy Inc ....D 716 372-6300
Olean *(G-12241)*

Solid Surfaces Inc ....E 585 292-5340
Rochester *(G-13736)*

Telechemische Inc ....G 845 561-3237
Newburgh *(G-11889)*

Terphane Holdings LLC ....E 585 657-5800
Bloomfield *(G-948)*

Tmp Technologies Inc ....D 716 895-6100
Buffalo *(G-3012)*

Toray Holding (usa) Inc ....E 212 697-8150
New York *(G-11516)*

Toray Industries Inc ....E 212 697-8150
New York *(G-11517)*

Transpo Industries Inc ....E 914 636-1000
New Rochelle *(G-8356)*

Tri-Seal Holdings Inc ....D 845 353-3300
Blauvelt *(G-936)*

Urethane Technology Co Inc ....F 845 561-5500
Newburgh *(G-11892)*

Wilsonart Intl Holdings LLC ....E 516 935-6980
Bethpage *(G-846)*

WR Smith & Sons Inc ....G 845 620-9400
Nanuet *(G-8205)*

PLASTICS MATERIALS, BASIC FORMS & SHAPES WHOLESALERS

Fibre Materials Corp ....E 516 349-1660
Plainview *(G-12685)*

Imbibitive Tech Amer Corp ....G 888 843-2323
Niagara Falls *(G-11936)*

Imbibitive Technologies Corp ....G 888 843-2323
Niagara Falls *(G-11937)*

Plastic-Craft Products Corp ....E 845 358-3010
West Nyack *(G-15831)*

PLASTICS PROCESSING

A & G Heat Sealing ....G 631 724-7764
Smithtown *(G-14472)*

A-1 Products Inc ....G 718 789-1818
Brooklyn *(G-1440)*

Adirondack Plas & Recycl Inc ....E 518 746-9212
Argyle *(G-391)*

American Visuals Inc ....G 631 694-6104
Farmingdale *(G-4584)*

Billie-Ann Plastics Pkg Corp ....E 718 497-3409
Brooklyn *(G-1585)*

Centro Inc ....B 212 791-9450
New York *(G-8959)*

Continental Latex Corp ....F 718 783-7883
Brooklyn *(G-1683)*

CSP Technologies Inc ....E 518 627-0051
Amsterdam *(G-324)*

Dacobe Enterprises LLC ....F 315 368-0093
Utica *(G-15251)*

Dawnex Industries Inc ....F 718 384-0199
Brooklyn *(G-1729)*

Farber Plastics Inc ....E 516 378-4860
Freeport *(G-4994)*

Fbm Galaxy Inc ....F 315 463-5144
East Syracuse *(G-4210)*

Fei Products LLC ....E 716 693-6230
North Tonawanda *(G-12067)*

Formed Plastics Inc ....D 516 334-2300
Carle Place *(G-3173)*

Genpak LLC ....C 845 343-7971
Middletown *(G-7911)*

Germanow-Simon Corporation ....E 585 232-1440
Rochester *(G-13438)*

Jamestown Plastics Inc ....D 716 792-4144
Brocton *(G-1181)*

L I C Screen Printing Inc ....E 516 546-7289
Merrick *(G-7858)*

Major-IPC Inc ....G 845 292-2200
Liberty *(G-6925)*

Mettowee Lumber & Plastics Co ....C 518 642-1100
Granville *(G-5352)*

Mold-A-Matic Corporation ....E 607 433-2121
Oneonta *(G-12276)*

Nalge Nunc International Corp ....A 585 498-2661
Rochester *(G-13565)*

Patmian LLC ....B 212 758-0770
New York *(G-10769)*

Prince Rubber & Plas Co Inc ....E 225 272-1653
Buffalo *(G-2931)*

Richlar Industries Inc ....F 315 463-5144
East Syracuse *(G-4234)*

Rimco Plastics Corp ....E 607 739-3864
Horseheads *(G-6134)*

Royce Associates A Ltd Partnr ....G 516 367-6298
Jericho *(G-6593)*

Shamrock Plastic Corporation ....G 585 328-6040
Rochester *(G-13726)*

Silvatrim Corp ....C 212 675-0933
New York *(G-11239)*

Structural Industries Inc ....C 631 471-5200
Bohemia *(G-1082)*

Toray Industries Inc ....E 212 697-8150
New York *(G-11517)*

United Plastics Inc ....G 718 389-2255
Brooklyn *(G-2539)*

Vinyl Materials Inc ....E 631 586-9444
Deer Park *(G-3951)*

Zone Fabricators Inc. ....F 718 272-0200
Ozone Park *(G-12470)*

PLASTICS SHEET: Packing Materials

Edco Supply Corporation ....D 718 788-8108
Brooklyn *(G-1782)*

PLASTICS: Blow Molded

Bst United Corp ....F...... 631 777-2110
   Farmingdale *(G-4594)*
Confer Plastics Inc ....C...... 800 635-3213
   North Tonawanda *(G-12063)*

PLASTICS: Cast

Albest Metal Stamping Corp ....E...... 718 388-6000
   Brooklyn *(G-1477)*
Miller Technology Inc ....G...... 631 694-2224
   Farmingdale *(G-4684)*

PLASTICS: Extruded

Albany International Corp ....C...... 607 749-7226
   Homer *(G-6060)*
Burnham Polymeric Inc ....G...... 518 792-3040
   Fort Edward *(G-4937)*
Certainteed Corporation ....B...... 716 827-7560
   Buffalo *(G-2695)*
Christi Plastics Inc ....G...... 585 436-8510
   Rochester *(G-13314)*
E & T Plastic Mfg Co Inc ....E...... 718 729-6226
   Long Island City *(G-7208)*
East Cast Clor Compounding Inc ....G...... 631 491-9000
   West Babylon *(G-15708)*
Eastern Industrial Steel Corp ....F...... 845 639-9749
   New City *(G-8226)*
Finger Lakes Extrusion Corp ....E...... 585 905-0632
   Canandaigua *(G-3132)*
Kleer-Fax Inc ....D...... 631 225-1100
   Amityville *(G-286)*
Pawling Engineered Pdts Inc ....C...... 845 855-1000
   Pawling *(G-12527)*
Precision Extrusion Inc ....E...... 518 792-1199
   Glens Falls *(G-5265)*

PLASTICS: Finished Injection Molded

A R V Precision Mfg Inc ....G...... 631 293-9643
   Farmingdale *(G-4569)*
Alliance Precision Plas Corp ....C...... 585 426-5310
   Rochester *(G-13219)*
Alliance Precision Plas Corp ....D...... 585 426-5310
   Rochester *(G-13220)*
Alliance-Mcalpin Ny LLC ....F...... 585 426-5310
   Rochester *(G-13221)*
Aluminum Injection Mold Co LLC ....G...... 585 502-6087
   Le Roy *(G-6895)*
Anna Young Assoc Ltd ....C...... 516 546-4400
   Freeport *(G-4985)*
Colonie Plastics Corp ....C...... 631 434-6969
   Bay Shore *(G-665)*
Epp Team Inc ....D...... 585 454-4995
   Rochester *(G-13396)*
Everblock Systems LLC ....G...... 844 422-5625
   New York *(G-9424)*
H & H Hulls Inc ....G...... 518 828-1339
   Hudson *(G-6159)*
Harbec Inc ....D...... 585 265-0010
   Ontario *(G-12290)*
J T Systematic ....G...... 607 754-0929
   Endwell *(G-4480)*
Joe Pietryka Incorporated ....E...... 845 855-1201
   Pawling *(G-12526)*
K & H Precision Products Inc ....E...... 585 624-4894
   Honeoye Falls *(G-6076)*
Leidel Corporation ....E...... 631 244-0900
   Bohemia *(G-1034)*
M & M Molding Corp ....C...... 631 582-1900
   Central Islip *(G-3283)*
Pietryka Plastics LLC ....E...... 845 855-1201
   Pawling *(G-12528)*
PMI Industries LLC ....E...... 585 464-8050
   Rochester *(G-13627)*
Primoplast Inc ....F...... 631 750-0680
   Bohemia *(G-1066)*
Shamrock Plastics & Tool Inc ....G...... 585 328-6040
   Rochester *(G-13727)*
Specialty Products Inc ....E...... 866 869-4335
   Center Moriches *(G-3248)*
Sterling Molded Products Inc ....E...... 845 344-4546
   Middletown *(G-7933)*

PLASTICS: Injection Molded

Aaron Tool & Mold Inc ....G...... 585 426-5100
   Rochester *(G-13197)*
Advent Tool & Mold Inc ....C...... 585 254-2000
   Rochester *(G-13214)*
American Casting and Mfg Corp ....D...... 800 342-0333
   Plainview *(G-12662)*
American Casting and Mfg Corp ....E...... 516 349-7010
   Plainview *(G-12663)*
Anka Tool & Die Inc ....E...... 845 268-4116
   Congers *(G-3607)*
Armstrong Mold Corporation ....E...... 315 437-1517
   East Syracuse *(G-4196)*
Armstrong Mold Corporation ....D...... 315 437-1517
   East Syracuse *(G-4197)*
Auburn Vacuum Forming Co Inc ....F...... 315 253-2440
   Auburn *(G-464)*
Autronic Plastics Inc ....C...... 516 333-7577
   Central Islip *(G-3263)*
Avanti Advanced Mfg Corp ....F...... 716 791-9001
   Buffalo *(G-2652)*
Avanti U S A Ltd ....F...... 716 695-5800
   Tonawanda *(G-15087)*
Aztec Tool Co Inc ....E...... 631 243-1144
   Edgewood *(G-4262)*
Barton Tool Inc ....G...... 716 665-2801
   Falconer *(G-4535)*
Brandys Mold and Tool Ctr Ltd ....F...... 585 334-8333
   West Henrietta *(G-15787)*
Buffalo Polymer Processors Inc ....E...... 716 537-3153
   Holland *(G-6028)*
Cambridge Security Seals LLC ....E...... 845 520-4111
   Pomona *(G-12806)*
Carolina Precision Plas LLC ....D...... 631 981-0743
   Ronkonkoma *(G-13922)*
Cast-All Corporation ....E...... 516 741-4025
   Mineola *(G-7965)*
Cdj Stamping Inc ....G...... 585 224-8120
   Rochester *(G-13301)*
Century Mold Company Inc ....D...... 585 352-8600
   Rochester *(G-13306)*
Century Mold Mexico LLC ....G...... 585 352-8600
   Rochester *(G-13307)*
Champlain Plastics Inc ....D...... 518 297-3700
   Rouses Point *(G-14065)*
Chenango Valley Tech Inc ....E...... 607 674-4115
   Sherburne *(G-14388)*
Clifford H Jones Inc ....F...... 716 693-2444
   Tonawanda *(G-15097)*
CPI of Falconer Inc ....E...... 716 664-4444
   Falconer *(G-4537)*
Craftech Industries Inc ....E...... 518 828-5001
   Hudson *(G-6151)*
Currier Plastics Inc ....D...... 315 255-1779
   Auburn *(G-471)*
Custom Lucite Creations Inc ....F...... 718 871-2000
   Brooklyn *(G-1712)*
Custom Molding Solutions Inc ....E...... 585 293-1702
   Churchville *(G-3410)*
Cy Plastics Works Inc ....D...... 585 229-2555
   Honeoye *(G-6068)*
Dolco LLC ....E...... 585 657-7777
   Bloomfield *(G-946)*
Dutchland Plastics LLC ....C...... 315 280-0247
   Sherrill *(G-14404)*
East Pattern & Model Corp ....F...... 585 461-3240
   Rochester *(G-13363)*
East Pattern & Model Corp ....E...... 585 461-3240
   Rochester *(G-13362)*
Eck Plastic Arts Inc ....E...... 607 722-3227
   Binghamton *(G-873)*
Em-Kay Molds Inc ....G...... 716 895-6180
   Buffalo *(G-2742)*
Ernie Green Industries Inc ....D...... 585 295-8951
   Rochester *(G-13398)*
Ernie Green Industries Inc ....C...... 585 647-2300
   Rochester *(G-13399)*
Ernie Green Industries Inc ....D...... 585 647-2300
   Rochester *(G-13400)*
Extreme Molding LLC ....E...... 518 326-9319
   Watervliet *(G-15601)*
Faro Industries Inc ....F...... 585 647-6000
   Rochester *(G-13408)*
Felchar Manufacturing Corp ....A...... 607 723-4076
   Binghamton *(G-877)*
G N R Plastics Inc ....G...... 631 724-8758
   Smithtown *(G-14478)*
Galt Industries Inc ....G...... 212 758-0770
   New York *(G-9568)*

Gen-West Associates LLC ....G...... 315 255-1779
   Auburn *(G-477)*
Hansa Plastics Inc ....F...... 631 269-9050
   Kings Park *(G-6673)*
Ilion Plastics Inc ....F...... 315 894-4868
   Ilion *(G-6278)*
Illinois Tool Works Inc ....D...... 860 435-2574
   Millerton *(G-7948)*
Imco Inc ....E...... 585 352-7810
   Spencerport *(G-14556)*
Innovative Plastics Corp ....C...... 845 359-7500
   Orangeburg *(G-12320)*
Inteva Products LLC ....B...... 248 655-8886
   New York *(G-9927)*
K & H Industries Inc ....E...... 716 312-0088
   Hamburg *(G-5511)*
Kobe Steel USA Holdings Inc ....G...... 212 751-9400
   New York *(G-10120)*
Mam Molding Inc ....G...... 607 433-2121
   Oneonta *(G-12274)*
Mdi East Inc ....E...... 518 747-8730
   South Glens Falls *(G-14514)*
Midbury Industries Inc ....F...... 516 868-0600
   Freeport *(G-5009)*
Milne Mfg Inc ....F...... 716 772-2536
   Gasport *(G-5139)*
Minico Industries Inc ....G...... 631 595-1455
   Bay Shore *(G-693)*
Mold-Rite Plastics LLC ....G...... 518 561-1812
   Plattsburgh *(G-12759)*
Natech Plastics Inc ....E...... 631 580-3506
   Ronkonkoma *(G-13979)*
New York Manufactured Products ....F...... 585 254-9353
   Rochester *(G-13570)*
Nordon Inc ....D...... 585 546-6200
   Rochester *(G-13578)*
Nordon Inc ....E...... 585 546-6200
   Rochester *(G-13579)*
Nordon Inc ....E...... 585 546-6200
   Rochester *(G-13580)*
Oneida Molded Plastics LLC ....C...... 315 363-7980
   Oneida *(G-12250)*
P M Plastics Inc ....E...... 716 662-1255
   Orchard Park *(G-12369)*
Peninsula Plastics Ltd ....D...... 716 854-3050
   Buffalo *(G-2911)*
Plastic-Craft Products Corp ....E...... 845 358-3010
   West Nyack *(G-15831)*
Polymer Engineered Pdts Inc ....D...... 585 426-1811
   Rochester *(G-13629)*
Precision Techniques Inc ....D...... 718 991-1440
   Stony Point *(G-14747)*
Pylantis New York LLC ....G...... 310 429-5911
   Groton *(G-5484)*
Richardson Molding LLC ....D...... 716 282-1261
   Niagara Falls *(G-11973)*
Roechling Medical Rochester LP ....D...... 585 254-2000
   Rochester *(G-13702)*
Romold Inc ....F...... 585 529-4440
   Rochester *(G-13705)*
RSC Molding Inc ....E...... 516 351-9871
   Freeport *(G-5020)*
Russell Plastics Tech Co Inc ....E...... 631 963-8602
   Lindenhurst *(G-6971)*
Southern Tier Plastics Inc ....D...... 607 723-2601
   Binghamton *(G-909)*
Staroba Plastics Inc ....E...... 716 537-3153
   Holland *(G-6031)*
Stuart Mold & Manufacturing ....F...... 716 488-9765
   Falconer *(G-4558)*
Surprise Plastics Inc ....C...... 718 492-6355
   Brooklyn *(G-2480)*
Syntec Technologies Inc ....D...... 585 768-2513
   Rochester *(G-13754)*
Syracuse Plastics LLC ....C...... 315 637-9881
   Liverpool *(G-7043)*
T A Tool & Molding Inc ....F...... 631 293-0172
   Farmingdale *(G-4748)*
Termatec Molding Inc ....F...... 315 483-4150
   Sodus *(G-14493)*
Tessy Plastics Corp ....B...... 315 689-3924
   Skaneateles *(G-14457)*
Tessy Plastics Corp ....A...... 315 689-3924
   Elbridge *(G-4298)*
Titherington Design & Mfg ....F...... 518 324-2205
   Plattsburgh *(G-12785)*
Toolroom Express Inc ....D...... 607 723-5373
   Conklin *(G-3630)*
Trico Holding Corporation ....A...... 716 852-5700
   Buffalo *(G-3019)*

PLASTICS: Injection Molded (continued)

Trimac Molding Services ....G..... 607 967-2900
Bainbridge *(G-527)*
Unifab Inc ....G..... 585 235-1760
Rochester *(G-13782)*
Unifuse LLC ....F..... 845 889-4000
Staatsburg *(G-14601)*
Usheco Inc ....F..... 845 658-9200
Kingston *(G-6721)*
Viele Manufacturing Corp ....B..... 718 893-2200
Bronx *(G-1392)*
W Kintz Plastics Inc ....F..... 518 296-8513
Howes Cave *(G-6144)*

PLASTICS: Molded

Abr Molding Andy LLC ....F..... 212 576-1821
Ridgewood *(G-13138)*
Ace Molding & Tool Inc ....G..... 631 567-2355
Bohemia *(G-965)*
Baird Mold Making Inc ....G..... 631 667-0322
Bay Shore *(G-655)*
Craftech ....D..... 518 828-5011
Chatham *(G-3330)*
Egli Machine Company Inc ....E..... 607 563-3663
Sidney *(G-14434)*
Form-Tec Inc ....E..... 516 867-0200
Freeport *(G-4996)*
ISO Plastics Corp ....D..... 914 663-8300
Mount Vernon *(G-8152)*
K2 Plastics Inc ....G..... 585 494-2727
Bergen *(G-816)*
Mechanical Rubber Pdts Co Inc ....F..... 845 986-2271
Warwick *(G-15519)*
Mercury Plastics Corp ....E..... 718 498-5400
Brooklyn *(G-2142)*
Mirage Moulding Mfg Inc ....F..... 631 843-6168
Farmingdale *(G-4686)*
Monarch Plastics Inc ....E..... 716 569-2175
Frewsburg *(G-5051)*
Msi-Molding Solutions Inc ....E..... 315 736-2412
Rome *(G-13857)*
Niagara Fiberglass Inc ....E..... 716 822-3921
Buffalo *(G-2884)*
P V C Molding Technologies ....F..... 315 331-1212
Newark *(G-11849)*
Pawling Corporation ....C..... 845 373-9300
Wassaic *(G-15525)*
Peconic Plastics Inc ....F..... 631 653-3676
Quogue *(G-13061)*
Pii Holdings Inc ....G..... 716 876-9951
Buffalo *(G-2919)*
Piper Plastics Corp ....E..... 631 842-6889
Copiague *(G-3668)*
Piper Plastics Corp ....G..... 631 842-6889
Copiague *(G-3669)*
Plastic Works ....G..... 914 576-2050
New Rochelle *(G-8349)*
Polymer Conversions Inc ....D..... 716 662-8550
Orchard Park *(G-12372)*
Protective Industries Inc ....B..... 716 876-9951
Buffalo *(G-2936)*
Pulse Plastics Products Inc ....E..... 718 328-5224
Bronx *(G-1346)*
Pvc Container Corporation ....C..... 518 672-7721
Philmont *(G-12614)*
Seal Reinforced Fiberglass Inc ....E..... 631 842-2230
Copiague *(G-3676)*
Seal Reinforced Fiberglass Inc ....G..... 631 842-2230
Copiague *(G-3677)*
Sonoco-Crellin Intl Inc ....B..... 518 392-2000
Chatham *(G-3333)*
Thermold Corporation ....C..... 315 697-3924
Canastota *(G-3158)*

PLASTICS: Polystyrene Foam

Berry Plastics Corporation ....B..... 315 986-6270
Macedon *(G-7463)*
Burnett Process Inc ....G..... 585 254-8080
Rochester *(G-13288)*
Dura Foam Inc ....E..... 718 894-2488
Maspeth *(G-7608)*
General Vy-Coat LLC ....E..... 718 266-6002
Brooklyn *(G-1882)*
Great American Industries Inc ....G..... 607 729-9331
Vestal *(G-15379)*
J & M Packaging Inc ....F..... 631 608-3069
Hauppauge *(G-5679)*
Latham International Inc ....G..... 518 783-7776
Latham *(G-6865)*
Latham Pool Products Inc ....E..... 260 432-8731
Latham *(G-6868)*

Par-Foam Products Inc ....C..... 716 855-2066
Buffalo *(G-2905)*
Plastpac Inc ....E..... 908 272-7200
Brooklyn *(G-2265)*
Pliant LLC ....B..... 315 986-6286
Macedon *(G-7469)*
Professional Packg Svcs Inc ....E..... 518 677-5100
Eagle Bridge *(G-4073)*
Rimco Plastics Corp ....E..... 607 739-3864
Horseheads *(G-6134)*
Saint-Gobain Prfmce Plas Corp ....C..... 518 642-2200
Granville *(G-5355)*
Skd Distribution Corp ....E..... 718 525-6000
Jericho *(G-6596)*
Strux Corp ....E..... 516 768-3969
Lindenhurst *(G-6976)*
Thermal Foams/Syracuse Inc ....E..... 315 699-8734
Cicero *(G-3424)*
Tmp Technologies Inc ....D..... 716 895-6100
Buffalo *(G-3012)*

PLASTICS: Thermoformed

Bo-Mer Plastics LLC ....E..... 315 252-7216
Auburn *(G-468)*
Cjk Manufacturing LLC ....F..... 585 663-6370
Rochester *(G-13316)*
Marval Industries Inc ....D..... 914 381-2400
Mamaroneck *(G-7514)*
Pactiv Corporation ....C..... 518 743-3100
Glens Falls *(G-5263)*
Plastitel Usa Inc ....G..... 800 667-2313
Chazy *(G-3335)*
Specialty Model & Mold Inc ....G..... 631 475-0840
Ronkonkoma *(G-14012)*
Weather Products Corporation ....G..... 315 474-8593
Syracuse *(G-15024)*

PLATE WORK: Metalworking Trade

West Metal Works Inc ....E..... 716 895-4900
Buffalo *(G-3045)*

PLATEMAKING SVC: Color Separations, For The Printing Trade

Absolute Color Corporation ....G..... 212 868-0404
New York *(G-8436)*
Eastern Color Stripping Inc ....F..... 631 563-3700
Bohemia *(G-1008)*
Lazer Incorporated ....E..... 336 744-8047
Rochester *(G-13514)*
Leo P Callahan Inc ....F..... 607 797-7314
Binghamton *(G-894)*
Micro Publishing Inc ....G..... 212 533-9180
New York *(G-10456)*

PLATEMAKING SVC: Gravure, Plates Or Cylinders

Charles Henricks Inc ....F..... 212 243-5800
New York *(G-8973)*
Miroddi Imaging Inc ....G..... 516 624-6898
Oyster Bay *(G-12450)*

PLATES

Circle Press Inc ....D..... 212 924-4277
New York *(G-9011)*
Csw Inc ....F..... 585 247-4010
Rochester *(G-13331)*
David Fehlman ....G..... 315 455-8888
Syracuse *(G-14875)*
Dowd - Witbeck Printing Corp ....F..... 518 274-2421
Troy *(G-15166)*
Gallant Graphics Ltd ....E..... 845 868-1166
Stanfordville *(G-14610)*
Gazette Press Inc ....E..... 914 963-8300
Rye *(G-14077)*
Karr Graphics Corp ....E..... 212 645-6000
Long Island City *(G-7261)*
Mutual Engraving Company Inc ....D..... 516 489-0534
West Hempstead *(G-15777)*
P & H Thermotech Inc ....G..... 585 624-1310
Lima *(G-6934)*
Rigidized Metals Corporation ....E..... 716 849-4703
Buffalo *(G-2955)*
Rotation Dynamics Corporation ....E..... 585 352-9023
Spencerport *(G-14559)*
Syracuse Computer Forms Inc ....E..... 315 478-0108
Syracuse *(G-15005)*

Tobay Printing Co Inc ....E..... 631 842-3300
Copiague *(G-3684)*
Tripi Engraving Co Inc ....E..... 718 383-6500
Brooklyn *(G-2522)*

PLATES: Paper, Made From Purchased Materials

Amscan Inc ....F..... 845 469-9116
Chester *(G-3370)*
Apexx Omni-Graphics Inc ....D..... 718 326-3330
Maspeth *(G-7591)*
Hadp LLC ....F..... 518 831-6824
Scotia *(G-14331)*
Pactiv LLC ....C..... 518 562-6101
Plattsburgh *(G-12766)*

PLATES: Plastic Exc Polystyrene Foam

Apexx Omni-Graphics Inc ....D..... 718 326-3330
Maspeth *(G-7591)*

PLATES: Truss, Metal

Steele Truss and Panel LLC ....E..... 518 562-4663
Plattsburgh *(G-12779)*

PLATING & FINISHING SVC: Decorative, Formed Prdts

Jay Strongwater Holdings LLC ....A..... 646 657-0558
New York *(G-9980)*

PLATING & POLISHING SVC

Abetter Processing Corp ....F..... 718 252-2223
Brooklyn *(G-1448)*
Epner Technology Incorporated ....E..... 718 782-8722
Brooklyn *(G-1809)*
Praxair Surface Tech Inc ....C..... 845 398-8322
Orangeburg *(G-12327)*
Qos Enterprises LLC ....G..... 585 454-0550
Rochester *(G-13657)*
Square One Coating Systems LLC ..G..... 315 790-5921
Oriskany *(G-12395)*
Tcmf Inc ....D..... 607 724-1094
Binghamton *(G-912)*

PLATING COMPOUNDS

Coventya Inc ....F..... 315 768-6635
Oriskany *(G-12387)*
Mdi Holdings LLC ....A..... 212 559-1127
New York *(G-10404)*

PLATING SVC: Chromium, Metals Or Formed Prdts

West Falls Machine Co Inc ....F..... 716 655-0440
East Aurora *(G-4097)*

PLATING SVC: Electro

Airmarine Electroplating Corp ....G..... 516 623-4406
Freeport *(G-4980)*
Astro Electroplating Inc ....E..... 631 968-0656
Bay Shore *(G-653)*
Bfg Manufacturing Services Inc ....E..... 716 362-0888
Buffalo *(G-2663)*
Deming Electro-Plating Corp ....G..... 585 968-2355
Cuba *(G-3812)*
Dura Spec Inc ....F..... 718 526-3053
North Baldwin *(G-12004)*
Electro Plating Service Inc ....F..... 914 948-3777
White Plains *(G-16001)*
Epner Technology Incorporated ....E..... 718 782-5948
Brooklyn *(G-1808)*
Eric S Turner & Company Inc ....F..... 914 235-7114
New Rochelle *(G-8329)*
Finest Cc Corp ....G..... 917 574-4525
Bronx *(G-1257)*
General Plating LLC ....E..... 585 423-0830
Rochester *(G-13433)*
Greene Technologies Inc ....D..... 607 656-4166
Greene *(G-5446)*
Hamburg Finishing Works Inc ....G..... 716 362-0888
Buffalo *(G-2791)*
John Larocca & Son Inc ....G..... 631 423-5256
Huntington Station *(G-6251)*
Key Tech Finishing ....E..... 716 832-1232
Buffalo *(G-2832)*

PLATING SVC: NEC (continued)

Keystone Corporation ....E 800 880-9747
Buffalo (G-2834)

Precious Plate Inc ....D 716 283-0690
Niagara Falls (G-11967)

Rayco of Schenectady Inc ....F 518 212-5113
Amsterdam (G-346)

Sandys Bumper Mart Inc ....G 315 472-8149
Syracuse (G-14985)

T & M Plating Inc ....E 212 967-1110
New York (G-11414)

Tompkins Metal Finishing Inc ....D 585 344-2600
Batavia (G-627)

Tripp Plating Works Inc ....G 716 894-2424
Buffalo (G-3021)

Tronic Plating Co Inc ....F 516 293-7883
Farmingdale (G-4760)

Victoria Plating Co Inc ....D 718 589-1550
Bronx (G-1391)

PLATING SVC: Gold

Empire Metal Finishing Inc ....E 718 545-6700
Astoria (G-421)

Sherrill Manufacturing Inc ....C 315 280-0727
Sherrill (G-14406)

PLATING SVC: NEC

21st Century Finishes Inc ....F 516 221-7000
North Bellmore (G-12013)

Aircraft Finishing Corp ....F 631 422-5000
West Babylon (G-15684)

Buffalo Metal Finishing Co ....F 716 883-2751
Buffalo (G-2679)

Coating Technology Inc ....E 585 546-7170
Rochester (G-13320)

Galmer Ltd ....G 718 392-4609
Long Island City (G-7229)

Hartchrom Inc ....F 518 880-0411
Watervliet (G-15603)

Metal Man Restoration ....F 914 662-4218
Mount Vernon (G-8161)

Nas CP Ccrp ....E 718 961-6757
College Point (G-3556)

Nassau Chromium Plating Co Inc ....E 516 746-6666
Mineola (G-7990)

Premier Finishing Inc ....F 716 484-6271
Jamestown (G-6537)

Reynolds Tech Fabricators Inc ....E 315 437-0532
East Syracuse (G-4233)

Rochester Overnight Pltg LLC ....D 585 328-4590
Rochester (G-13692)

Silverman & Gorf Inc ....G 718 625-1309
Brooklyn (G-2415)

US Electroplating Corp ....G 631 293-1998
West Babylon (G-15754)

Vernon Plating Works Inc ....F 718 639-1124
Woodside (G-16233)

PLAYGROUND EQPT

Bears Management Group Inc ....F 585 624-5694
Lima (G-6929)

Billy Beez Usa LLC ....F 315 741-5099
Syracuse (G-14829)

Billy Beez Usa LLC ....F 646 606-2249
New York (G-8793)

Billy Beez Usa LLC ....E 845 915-4709
West Nyack (G-15818)

Billy Beez Usa LLC ....G 315 235-3121
New Hartford (G-8237)

Eastern Jungle Gym Inc ....E 845 878-9800
Carmel (G-3185)

PLEATING & STITCHING FOR THE TRADE: Decorative & Novelty

A Trusted Name Inc ....F 716 326-7400
Westfield (G-15944)

PLEATING & STITCHING FOR TRADE: Permanent Pleating/Pressing

Stylist Pleating Corp ....F 718 384-8181
Brooklyn (G-2468)

PLEATING & STITCHING SVC

Athletic Cap Co Inc ....E 718 398-1300
Staten Island (G-14621)

Pass Em-Entries Inc ....F 718 392-0100
Long Island City (G-7321)

Todd Walbridge ....G 585 254-3018
Rochester (G-13768)

PLEATING & TUCKING FOR THE TRADE

Vogue Too Plting Stitching EMB ....F 212 354-1022
New York (G-11703)

PLUGS: Electric

K & H Industries Inc ....E 716 312-0088
Hamburg (G-5511)

PLUMBING & HEATING EQPT & SPLY, WHOL: Htg Eqpt/Panels, Solar

Vincent Genovese ....G 631 281-8170
Mastic Beach (G-7675)

PLUMBING & HEATING EQPT & SPLY, WHOLESALE: Hydronic Htg Eqpt

Flushing Boiler & Welding Co ....F 718 463-1266
Brooklyn (G-1855)

PLUMBING & HEATING EQPT & SPLYS WHOLESALERS

Bobrick Washroom Equipment Inc ....D 518 877-7444
Clifton Park (G-3463)

Pronto Gas Heating Sups Inc ....G 718 292-0707
Bronx (G-1345)

Siemens Industry Inc ....E 585 797-2300
Rochester (G-13728)

PLUMBING & HEATING EQPT & SPLYS, WHOL: Fireplaces, Prefab

Blackstone International Inc ....G 631 289-5490
Holtsville (G-6045)

PLUMBING & HEATING EQPT & SPLYS, WHOL: Plumbing Fitting/Sply

Great American Industries Inc ....G 607 729-9331
Vestal (G-15379)

Miles Moss of Albany Inc ....E 516 222-8008
Garden City (G-5108)

P E Guerin ....D 212 243-5270
New York (G-10733)

PLUMBING & HEATING EQPT & SPLYS, WHOL: Plumbng/Heatng Valves

Flow-Safe Inc ....E 716 662-2585
Orchard Park (G-12352)

PLUMBING & HEATING EQPT & SPLYS, WHOL: Water Purif Eqpt

Empire Division Inc ....D 315 476-6273
Syracuse (G-14888)

Neptune Soft Water Inc ....F 315 446-5151
Syracuse (G-14950)

Pure Planet Waters LLC ....F 718 676-7900
Brooklyn (G-2306)

PLUMBING & HEATING EQPT & SPLYS, WHOLESALE: Boilers, Steam

Great Rock Automation Inc ....F 631 270-1508
Farmingdale (G-4640)

PLUMBING & HEATING EQPT & SPLYS, WHOLESALE: Brass/Fittings

Coronet Parts Mfg Co Inc ....E 718 649-1750
Brooklyn (G-1689)

PLUMBING FIXTURES

Corona Plumbing & Htg Sup Inc ....G 718 424-4133
Corona (G-3736)

ER Butler & Co Inc ....E 212 925-3565
New York (G-9392)

G Sicuranza Ltd ....G 516 759-0259
Glen Cove (G-5193)

L A S Replacement Parts Inc ....F 718 583-4700
Bronx (G-1296)

Liberty Brass Turning Co Inc ....E 718 784-2911
Westbury (G-15904)

Malyn Industrial Ceramics Inc ....G 716 741-1510
Clarence Center (G-3448)

P E Guerin ....D 212 243-5270
New York (G-10733)

Roccera LLC ....F 585 426-0887
Rochester (G-13678)

Toto USA Inc ....G 917 237-0665
New York (G-11521)

Watermark Designs Holdings Ltd ....D 718 257-2800
Brooklyn (G-2576)

PLUMBING FIXTURES: Brass, Incl Drain Cocks, Faucets/Spigots

A B S Brass Products Inc ....F 718 497-2115
Brooklyn (G-1431)

Acme Parts Inc ....E 718 649-1750
Brooklyn (G-1457)

Coronet Parts Mfg Co Inc ....E 718 649-1750
Brooklyn (G-1689)

Coronet Parts Mfg Co Inc ....E 718 649-1750
Brooklyn (G-1690)

PLUMBING FIXTURES: Plastic

An-Cor Industrial Plastics Inc ....D 716 695-3141
North Tonawanda (G-12052)

Bow Industrial Corporation ....D 518 561-0190
Champlain (G-3309)

Gms Hicks Street Corporation ....E 718 858-1010
Brooklyn (G-1894)

H Rindustries ....G 516 487-3825
Mineola (G-7979)

Quality Enclosures Inc ....E 631 234-0115
Central Islip (G-3286)

POINT OF SALE DEVICES

Kenney Manufacturing Displays ....F 631 231-5563
Bay Shore (G-686)

Powa Technologies Inc ....E 347 344-7848
New York (G-10872)

POLISHING SVC: Metals Or Formed Prdts

Apti Pro Systems 2000 Inc ....D 585 265-0160
Ontario (G-12283)

Barnes Metal Finishing Inc ....F 585 798-4817
Medina (G-7728)

Control Electropolishing Corp ....F 718 858-6634
Brooklyn (G-1684)

POLYESTERS

Perfect Poly Inc ....E 631 265-0539
Nesconset (G-8220)

Terphane LLC ....D 585 657-5800
Bloomfield (G-949)

POLYETHYLENE CHLOROSULFONATED RUBBER

Snow Craft 216 Inc ....F 718 757-6121
Freeport (G-5026)

POLYETHYLENE RESINS

APS American Polymers Svcs Inc ....G 212 362-7711
New York (G-8613)

POLYTETRAFLUOROETHYLENE RESINS

Saint-Gobain Prfmce Plas Corp ....C 518 686-7301
Hoosick Falls (G-6089)

POLYVINYL CHLORIDE RESINS

Adam Scott Designs Inc ....E 212 420-8866
New York (G-8453)

Kent Chemical Corporation ....E 212 521-1700
New York (G-10094)

Newmat Northeast Corp ....F 631 253-9277
West Babylon (G-15734)

POPCORN & SUPPLIES WHOLESALERS

Terrells Potato Chip Co Inc ....D 315 437-2786
Syracuse (G-15011)

PORCELAIN ENAMELED PRDTS & UTENSILS

Revol Usa LLC...........F 678 456-8671
New York (G-11029)

POSTERS

Candid Worldwide LLC............G 212 799-5300
Farmingdale (G-4597)

POTTERY: Laboratory & Indl

Saint Gobain Grains & Powders...........A 716 731-8200
Niagara Falls (G-11976)
Saint-Gbain Advnced Crmics LLC...........C 716 278-6066
Niagara Falls (G-11977)

POULTRY & POULTRY PRDTS WHOLESALERS

Vineland Kosher Poultry Inc...........F 718 921-1347
Brooklyn (G-2560)

POULTRY & SMALL GAME SLAUGHTERING & PROCESSING

Advanced Frozen Foods Inc...........E 516 333-6344
Westbury (G-15861)
Campanellis Poultry Farm Inc ....G 845 482-2222
Bethel (G-828)
Goya Foods Inc ....D...... 716 549-0076
Angola (G-359)
Hoskie Co Inc ....D...... 718 628-8672
Brooklyn (G-1944)
JW Consulting Inc ....G 845 325-7070
Monroe (G-8024)
MB Food Processing Inc ....B 845 436-5001
South Fallsburg (G-14509)
Murray Bresky Consultants Ltd ....B 845 436-5001
South Fallsburg (G-14510)
Vineland Kosher Poultry Inc ....F 718 921-1347
Brooklyn (G-2560)

POULTRY SLAUGHTERING & PROCESSING

Alle Processing Corp...........C 718 894-2000
Maspeth (G-7587)
Hlw Acres LLC...........G 585 591-0795
Attica (G-457)

POWDER PUFFS & MITTS

Penthouse Manufacturing Co Inc...........B 516 379-1300
Freeport (G-5014)

POWDER: Aluminum Atomized

Aip Mc Holdings LLC...........G 212 627-2360
New York (G-8502)

POWDER: Metal

Buffalo Tungsten Inc ....D...... 716 683-9170
Depew (G-3975)
Cws Powder Coatings Company LP ....G 845 398-2911
Blauvelt (G-927)
Hje Company Inc...........G 518 792-8733
Queensbury (G-13043)
Oerlikon Metco (us) Inc...........G 716 270-2228
Amherst (G-238)
Reed Systems Ltd...........F 845 647-3660
Ellenville (G-4310)
Tam Ceramics Group of Ny LLC...........D...... 716 278-9400
Niagara Falls (G-11984)
Trico Holding Corporation...........A 716 852-5700
Buffalo (G-3019)

POWDER: Silver

Ames Advanced Materials Corp...........D...... 518 792-5808
South Glens Falls (G-14511)
Ames Goldsmith Corp...........F 518 792-7435
Glens Falls (G-5239)

POWER GENERATORS

Independent Field Svc LLC ....G 315 559-9243
Syracuse (G-14913)
Intelligen Power Systems LLC...........G 212 750-0373
Old Bethpage (G-12218)
Power Gneration Indus Engs Inc...........E 315 633-9389
Bridgeport (G-1168)

POWER SPLY CONVERTERS: Static, Electronic Applications

Albatros North America Inc ....E 518 381-7100
Ballston Spa (G-567)
Orbit International Corp ....D...... 631 435-8300
Hauppauge (G-5735)

POWER SUPPLIES: All Types, Static

3835 Lebron Reqp & Sup Inc...........E 212 942-8258
New York (G-8402)
Applied Concepts Inc ....E 315 696-6676
Tully (G-15207)
Applied Power Systems Inc ....E 516 935-2230
Hicksville (G-5883)
Arstan Products International ....F 516 433-1313
Hicksville (G-5885)
BC Systems Inc ....E 631 751-9370
Setauket (G-14377)
Hipotronics Inc ....C 845 279-8091
Brewster (G-1151)
Orbit International Corp ....D...... 631 435-8300
Hauppauge (G-5734)
Ultravolt Inc ....D...... 631 471-4444
Ronkonkoma (G-14022)
Walter G Legge Company Inc ....G 914 737-5040
Peekskill (G-12560)

POWER SUPPLIES: Transformer, Electronic Type

Applied Power Systems Inc...........G 516 935-2230
Hicksville (G-5883)
Bright Way Supply Inc ....F 718 833-2882
Brooklyn (G-1609)
Fil-Coil International LLC ....F 631 467-5328
Sayville (G-14227)
Hammond Manufacturing Co Inc...........F 716 630-7030
Cheektowaga (G-3352)
National Energy Audits LLC ....G 631 883-3407
Holbrook (G-6013)

POWER SWITCHING EQPT

Switching Power Inc ....D...... 631 981-7231
Ronkonkoma (G-14016)

POWER TOOLS, HAND: Grinders, Portable, Electric Or Pneumatic

P & F Industries Inc ....E 631 694-9800
Melville (G-7813)

POWER TOOLS, HAND: Hammers, Portable, Elec/Pneumatic, Chip

Rbhammers Corp ....F 845 353-5042
Blauvelt (G-932)

POWER TRANSMISSION EQPT WHOLESALERS

Peerless-Winsmith Inc...........C 716 592-9311
Springville (G-14594)
United Richter Electrical Mtrs ....F 716 855-1945
Buffalo (G-3030)

POWER TRANSMISSION EQPT: Aircraft

Precision Gear Incorporated...........C 718 321-7200
College Point (G-3560)

POWER TRANSMISSION EQPT: Mechanical

Babbitt Bearings Incorporated ....D...... 315 479-6603
Syracuse (G-14825)
Champlain Hudson Power Ex Inc...........G 518 465-0710
Albany (G-59)
Designatronics Incorporated ....B 516 328-3300
New Hyde Park (G-8261)
Eaw Electronic Systems Inc ....G 845 471-5290
Poughkeepsie (G-12953)
Hudson Power Transmission Co...........G 718 622-3869
Brooklyn (G-1946)
Huron TI Cutter Grinding Inc ....E 631 420-7000
Farmingdale (G-4646)
Kaddis Manufacturing Corp ....G 585 624-3070
Honeoye Falls (G-6077)
Ls Power Equity Partners LP ....G 212 615-3456
New York (G-10276)

Metallized Carbon Corporation

Metallized Carbon Corporation...........C 914 941-3738
Ossining (G-12404)
On Line Power Technologies...........G 914 968-4440
Yonkers (G-16336)
Package One Inc ....D...... 518 344-5425
Schenectady (G-14294)
Sepac Inc ....E 607 732-2030
Elmira (G-4367)
Watson Bowman Acme Corp ....C 716 691-8162
Amherst (G-253)

PRECAST TERRAZZO OR CONCRETE PRDTS

Accurate Precast...........F 718 345-2910
Brooklyn (G-1452)
Coral Cast LLC ....E 516 349-1300
Plainview (G-12674)
Diamond Precast Products Inc...........F 631 874-3777
Center Moriches (G-3245)
Key Cast Stone Company Inc ....E 631 789-2145
Amityville (G-285)
Northeast Concrete Pdts Inc...........F 518 563-0700
Plattsburgh (G-12762)
Superior Aggregates Supply LLC ....E 516 333-2923
Lindenhurst (G-6979)
Superior Walls Upstate NY Inc...........E 585 624-9390
Lima (G-6936)
Superior Wlls of Hdson Vly Inc...........E 845 485-4033
Poughkeepsie (G-12986)

PRECIOUS METALS

Sigmund Cohn Corp ....D...... 914 664-5300
Mount Vernon (G-8180)

PRECIOUS METALS WHOLESALERS

Wallace Refiners Inc ....G 212 391-2649
New York (G-11718)

PRECIOUS STONES & METALS, WHOLESALE

Jacoby Enterprises LLC...........G 718 435-0289
Brooklyn (G-1987)
S Kashi & Sons Inc ....F 212 869-9393
Great Neck (G-5420)

PRECIOUS STONES WHOLESALERS

Gumuchian Fils Ltd ....F 212 588-7084
New York (G-9698)
Incon Gems Inc ....F 212 221-8560
New York (G-9875)
Jim Wachtler Inc ....G 212 755-4367
New York (G-10004)

PRECIPITATORS: Electrostatic

Beltran Technologies Inc ....E 718 338-3311
Brooklyn (G-1573)

PRERECORDED TAPE, CD & RECORD STORES: Video Discs/Tapes

Sony Broadband Entertainment...........F 212 833-6800
New York (G-11294)

PRERECORDED TAPE, CD/RECORD STORES: Video Tapes, Prerecorded

Society For The Study...........G 212 822-8806
New York (G-11283)

PRERECORDED TAPE, COMPACT DISC & RECORD STORES: Records

Motema Music LLC...........G 212 860-6969
New York (G-10508)

PRESSED FIBER & MOLDED PULP PRDTS, EXC FOOD PRDTS

Avco Industries Inc ....F 631 851-1555
Central Islip (G-3264)
Interntnal Bus Cmmncations Inc...........E 516 352-4505
New Hyde Park (G-8275)

PRESSES

Win Set Technologies LLC ....F 631 234-7077
   Centereach *(G-3253)*

PRIMARY METAL PRODUCTS

Bridge Components Inc ....G 716 731-1184
   Sanborn *(G-14136)*

Cintube Ltd ....F 518 324-3333
   Plattsburgh *(G-12742)*

Specialty Fabricators ....F 631 433-0258
   Oakdale *(G-12155)*

PRINT CARTRIDGES: Laser & Other Computer Printers

Cartridge Evolution Inc ....G 718 788-0678
   Brooklyn *(G-1651)*

Guttz Corporation of America ....F 914 591-9600
   Irvington *(G-6309)*

Northeast Toner Inc ....G 518 899-5545
   Ballston Lake *(G-562)*

Qls Solutions Group Inc ....E 716 852-2203
   Buffalo *(G-2939)*

Smartoners Inc ....G 718 975-0197
   Brooklyn *(G-2430)*

Summit Technologies LLC ....E 631 590-1040
   Holbrook *(G-6023)*

PRINTED CIRCUIT BOARDS

A A Technology Inc ....D 631 913-0400
   Ronkonkoma *(G-13882)*

Adco Circuits Inc ....G 716 668-6600
   Buffalo *(G-2620)*

Advance Circuit Technology Inc ....E 585 328 2000
   Rochester *(G-13208)*

Advance Micro Power Corp ....F 631 471-6157
   Ronkonkoma *(G-13889)*

Advanced Digital Info Corp ....E 607 266-4000
   Ithaca *(G-6360)*

Advanced Manufacturing Svc Inc ....E 631 676-5210
   Ronkonkoma *(G-13890)*

American Quality Technology ....F 607 777-9488
   Binghamton *(G-853)*

American Tchncal Ceramics Corp ....B 631 622-4700
   Huntington Station *(G-6237)*

Ansen Corporation ....G 315 393-3573
   Ogdensburg *(G-12202)*

Badger Technologies Inc ....D 585 869-7101
   Farmington *(G-4768)*

BCM Electronics Manuf Services ....G 631 580-9516
   Ronkonkoma *(G-13914)*

Bsu Inc ....E 607 272-8100
   Ithaca *(G-6373)*

C & D Assembly Inc ....E 607 898-4275
   Groton *(G-5481)*

Chautauqua Circuits Inc ..../.........G 716 366-5771
   Dunkirk *(G-4050)*

Cygnus Automation Inc ....E 631 981-0909
   Bohemia *(G-997)*

Della Systems Inc ....F 631 580-0010
   Ronkonkoma *(G-13930)*

Duro Business Solutions Inc ....G 646 577-9537
   Bronx *(G-1245)*

Electronic Coating Tech Inc ....F 518 688-2048
   Cohoes *(G-3506)*

Ems Technologies Inc ....E 607 723-3676
   Binghamton *(G-875)*

Ensil Technical Services Inc ....E 716 282-1020
   Niagara Falls *(G-11924)*

Entertron Industries Inc ....E 716 772-7216
   Lockport *(G-7074)*

Falconer Electronics Inc ....D 716 665-4176
   Falconer *(G-4541)*

Geometric Circuits Inc ....D 631 249-0230
   East Setauket *(G-4179)*

Hazlow Electronics Inc ....E 585 325-5323
   Rochester *(G-13462)*

I 3 Manufacturing Services Inc ....G 607 238-7077
   Binghamton *(G-883)*

I3 Assembly LLC ....C 607 238-7077
   Binghamton *(G-884)*

I3 Electronics Inc ....C 607 238-7077
   Binghamton *(G-885)*

I3 Electronics Inc ....D 607 238-7077
   Endicott *(G-4459)*

IEC Electronics Corp ....B 315 331-7742
   Newark *(G-11841)*

Irtronics Instruments Inc ....F 914 693-6291
   Ardsley *(G-389)*

Isine Inc ....E 631 913-4400
   Melville *(G-7797)*

Kingboard Holdings Limited ....A 705 844-1993
   New York *(G-10108)*

Marco Manufacturing Inc ....E 845 485-1571
   Poughkeepsie *(G-12969)*

Mpl Inc ....E 607 266-0480
   Ithaca *(G-6398)*

NEa Manufacturing Corp ....E 516 371-4200
   Inwood *(G-6300)*

Oakdale Industrial Elec Corp ....E 631 737-4092
   Ronkonkoma *(G-13984)*

Ormec Systems Corp ....E 585 385-3520
   Rochester *(G-13592)*

Park Aerospace Corp ....D 631 465-3600
   Melville *(G-7814)*

Performance Technologies Inc ....E 585 256-0200
   Rochester *(G-13615)*

Photonamics Inc ....F 585 247-8990
   Rochester *(G-13622)*

Procomponents Inc ....E 516 683-0909
   Westbury *(G-15921)*

Rce Manufacturing LLC ....E 631 856-9005
   Hauppauge *(G-5753)*

Rochester Industrial Ctrl Inc ....D 315 524-4555
   Ontario *(G-12300)*

Rumsey Corp ....G 914 751-3640
   Yonkers *(G-16347)*

S K Circuits Inc ....F 703 376-8718
   Canastota *(G-3155)*

Sag Harbor Industries Inc ....E 631 725-0440
   Sag Harbor *(G-14101)*

Sopark Corp ....D 716 822-0434
   Buffalo *(G-2987)*

Stetron International Inc ....F 716 854-3443
   Buffalo *(G-2993)*

Surf-Tech Manufacturing Corp ....F 631 589-1194
   Ronkonkoma *(G-14015)*

Transistor Devices Inc ....E 631 471-7492
   Ronkonkoma *(G-14017)*

Vexos Inc ....F 855 711-3227
   New York *(G-11670)*

Windsor Technology LLC ....F 585 461-2500
   Rochester *(G-13806)*

PRINTERS & PLOTTERS

Blue Skies ....G 631 392-1140
   Deer Park *(G-3848)*

CNy Business Solutions ....G 315 733-5031
   Utica *(G-15244)*

Mdi Holdings LLC ....A 212 559-1127
   New York *(G-10404)*

Mg Imaging ....G 212 704-4073
   New York *(G-10447)*

Peak Performance Design LLC ....G 518 302-9198
   Cohoes *(G-3512)*

X Brand Editions ....G 718 482-7646
   Long Island City *(G-7408)*

PRINTERS' SVCS: Folding, Collating, Etc

JP Signs ....G 518 569-3907
   Chazy *(G-3334)*

Shield Press Inc ....G 212 431-7489
   New York *(G-11213)*

PRINTERS: Computer

Control Logic Corporation ....G 607 965-6423
   West Burlington *(G-15758)*

Future Star Digatech ....F 718 666-0350
   Brooklyn *(G-1872)*

Lsc Peripherals Incorporated ....G 631 244-0707
   Bohemia *(G-1038)*

Transact Technologies Inc ....D 607 257-8901
   Ithaca *(G-6414)*

PRINTERS: Magnetic Ink, Bar Code

Advanced Barcode Tech Inc ....F 516 570-8100
   Great Neck *(G-5359)*

Jadak Technologies Inc ....C 315 701-0678
   North Syracuse *(G-12047)*

PRINTING & BINDING: Book Music

Bridge Enterprises Inc ....G 718 625-6622
   Brooklyn *(G-1607)*

PRINTING & BINDING: Books

Book1one LLC ....G 585 458-2101
   Rochester *(G-13278)*

Hamilton Printing Company Inc ....C 518 732-2161
   Troy *(G-15171)*

Logical Operations Inc ....C 585 350-7000
   Rochester *(G-13522)*

Syracuse Cultural Workers Prj ....F 315 474-1132
   Syracuse *(G-15006)*

PRINTING & BINDING: Pamphlets

Bmg Printing and Promotion LLC ....G 631 231-9200
   Bohemia *(G-982)*

PRINTING & EMBOSSING: Plastic Fabric Articles

Acorn Products Corp ....F 315 894-4868
   Ilion *(G-6276)*

Mountain T-Shirts Inc ....G 518 943-4533
   Catskill *(G-3215)*

Patrick Rohan ....G 718 781-2573
   Monticello *(G-8072)*

Starline Usa Inc ....C 716 773-0100
   Grand Island *(G-5344)*

PRINTING & ENGRAVING: Card, Exc Greeting

Abigal Press Inc ....D 718 641-5350
   Ozone Park *(G-12457)*

Printery ....G 516 922-3250
   Oyster Bay *(G-12454)*

Proof 7 Ltd ....F 212 680-1843
   New York *(G-10913)*

PRINTING & ENGRAVING: Financial Notes & Certificates

Doremus FP LLC ....E 212 366-3800
   New York *(G-9255)*

Merrill New York Company Inc ....C 212 229-6500
   New York *(G-10438)*

Superior Print On Demand ....G 607 240-5231
   Vestal *(G-15384)*

Table Tops Paper Corp ....G 718 831-6440
   Brooklyn *(G-2489)*

PRINTING & ENGRAVING: Invitation & Stationery

Batavia Press LLC ....E 585 343-4429
   Batavia *(G-603)*

Jon Lyn Ink Inc ....G 516 546-2312
   Merrick *(G-7857)*

Kurtskraft Inc ....G 516 944-4449
   Port Washington *(G-12898)*

Lion In The Sun Park Slope Ltd ....G 718 369-4006
   Brooklyn *(G-2078)*

Print Mall ....G 718 437-7700
   Brooklyn *(G-2289)*

Shade Tree Greetings Inc ....F 585 442-4580
   Rochester *(G-13725)*

PRINTING & ENGRAVING: Plateless

K & B Stamping Co Inc ....G 914 664-8555
   Mount Vernon *(G-8154)*

PRINTING & ENGRAVING: Poster & Decal

BDR Creative Concepts Inc ....F 516 942-7768
   Farmingdale *(G-4591)*

Stickershopcom Inc ....G 631 563-4323
   Bayport *(G-731)*

PRINTING & STAMPING: Fabric Articles

Casual Friday Inc ....F 585 544-9470
   Rochester *(G-13300)*

PRINTING & WRITING PAPER WHOLESALERS

Argo Lithographers Inc ....E 718 729-2700
   Long Island City *(G-7166)*

Shipmtes/Printmates Holdg Corp ....D 518 370-1158
   Scotia *(G-14336)*

Table Tops Paper Corp ....G 718 831-6440
   Brooklyn *(G-2489)*

P
R
O
D
U
C
T

PRINTING EQPT & SUPPLIES: Illustration & Poster Woodcuts

Patrick Rohan ....G 718 781-2573
Monticello *(G-8072)*

PRINTING INKS WHOLESALERS

I N K T Inc ....F 212 957-2700
New York *(G-9846)*

Won & Lee Inc ....E 516 222-0712
Garden City *(G-5119)*

PRINTING MACHINERY

A-Mark Machinery Corp ....F 631 643-6300
West Babylon *(G-15678)*

Anand Printing Machinery Inc ....G 631 667-3079
Deer Park *(G-3839)*

Awt Supply Corp ....G 516 437-9105
Elmont *(G-4383)*

Castlereagh Printcraft Inc ....D 516 623-1728
Freeport *(G-4989)*

Daige Products Inc ....F 516 621-2100
Albertson *(G-147)*

Davis International Inc ....F 585 421-8175
Fairport *(G-4496)*

Hodgins Engraving Co Inc ....D 585 343-4444
Batavia *(G-618)*

Innotech Graphic Eqp Corp ....G 845 268-6900
Valley Cottage *(G-15316)*

International Imaging Mtls Inc ....B 716 691-6333
Amherst *(G-227)*

Mekatronics Incorporated ....E 516 883-6805
Port Washington *(G-12907)*

Micro Powders Inc ....E 914 332-6400
Tarrytown *(G-15048)*

Package Print Technologies ....F 716 871-9905
Buffalo *(G-2904)*

Perretta Graphics Corp ....E 845 473-0550
Poughkeepsie *(G-12978)*

Prim Hall Enterprises Inc ....F 518 561-7408
Plattsburgh *(G-12772)*

Skandacor Direct Inc ....G 585 265-9020
Webster *(G-15654)*

Southern Graphic Systems LLC ....E 315 695-7079
Phoenix *(G-12621)*

Specilty Bus Mchs Holdings LLC ..E 212 587-9600
New York *(G-11314)*

Sterling Toggle Inc ....F 631 491-0500
West Babylon *(G-15749)*

Super Web Inc ....E 631 643-9100
West Babylon *(G-15751)*

Universal Metal Fabricators ....F 845 331-8248
Kingston *(G-6719)*

Vits International Inc ....E 845 353-5000
Blauvelt *(G-938)*

Voodoo Manufacturing Inc ....E 646 893-8366
Brooklyn *(G-2569)*

Woerner Industries Inc ....E 585 436-1934
Rochester *(G-13807)*

PRINTING MACHINERY, EQPT & SPLYS: Wholesalers

Boxcar Press Incorporated ....E 315 473-0930
Syracuse *(G-14833)*

Davis International Inc ....F 585 421-8175
Fairport *(G-4496)*

Info Label Inc ....F 518 664-0791
Halfmoon *(G-5493)*

Super Web Inc ....E 631 643-9100
West Babylon *(G-15751)*

PRINTING TRADES MACHINERY & EQPT REPAIR SVCS

Efam Enterprises LLC ....E 718 204-1760
Long Island City *(G-7211)*

Jack L Popkin & Co Inc ....G 718 361-6700
Kew Gardens *(G-6666)*

PRINTING, COMMERCIAL Newspapers, NEC

Buffalo Newspress Inc ....C 716 852-1600
Buffalo *(G-2681)*

Expedi-Printing Inc ....C 516 513-0919
Great Neck *(G-5383)*

Kim Jae Printing Co Inc ....G 212 691-6289
Roslyn Heights *(G-14053)*

Stellar Printing Inc ....D 718 361-1600
Long Island City *(G-7369)*

Webster Printing Corporation ....F 585 671-1533
Webster *(G-15662)*

PRINTING, COMMERCIAL: Announcements, NEC

Kates Paperie Ltd ....G 212 966-3904
New York *(G-10077)*

PRINTING, COMMERCIAL: Bags, Plastic, NEC

Bags Unlimited Inc ....E 585 436-6282
Rochester *(G-13258)*

Dynamic Packaging Inc ....F 718 388-0800
Brooklyn *(G-1768)*

PRINTING, COMMERCIAL: Business Forms, NEC

Data Flow Inc ....G 631 436-9200
Medford *(G-7705)*

Empire Business Forms Inc ....F 845 562-7780
Newburgh *(G-11864)*

General Business Supply Inc ....D 518 720-3939
Watervliet *(G-15602)*

Kinaneco Inc ....E 315 468-6201
Syracuse *(G-14926)*

McAuliffe Paper Inc ....E 315 453-2222
Liverpool *(G-7024)*

Select-A-Form Inc ....D 631 981-3076
Holbrook *(G-6020)*

Short Run Forms Inc ....D 631 567-7171
Bohemia *(G-1078)*

United Print Group Inc ....F 718 392-4242
Woodside *(G-16231)*

Vez Inc ....G 718 273-7002
Staten Island *(G-14726)*

Yoman Madeo Fano ....G 631 438-0246
Patchogue *(G-12514)*

PRINTING, COMMERCIAL: Calendars, NEC

Won & Lee Inc ....E 516 222-0712
Garden City *(G-5119)*

PRINTING, COMMERCIAL: Cards, Visiting, Incl Business, NEC

Create-A-Card Inc ....G 631 584-2273
Saint James *(G-14108)*

PRINTING, COMMERCIAL: Circulars, NEC

Linda Campbell ....G 718 994-4026
Bronx *(G-1303)*

PRINTING, COMMERCIAL: Coupons, NEC

Ad Publications Inc ....F 585 248-2888
Pittsford *(G-12635)*

PRINTING, COMMERCIAL: Decals, NEC

Love Unlimited NY Inc ....E 718 359-8500
Westbury *(G-15907)*

Modern Decal Co ....G 315 622-2778
Liverpool *(G-7027)*

Seri Systems Inc ....E 585 272-5515
Rochester *(G-13724)*

PRINTING, COMMERCIAL: Envelopes, NEC

Argo Envelope Corp ....D 718 729-2700
Long Island City *(G-7164)*

Design Distributors Inc ....D 631 242-2000
Deer Park *(G-3863)*

Diversified Envelope Ltd ....F 585 615-4697
Rochester *(G-13350)*

Dupli Graphics Corporation ....G 315 422-4732
Syracuse *(G-14878)*

Dupli Graphics Corporation ....C 315 234-7286
Syracuse *(G-14877)*

Eagle Envelope Company ....G 607 387-3195
Trumansburg *(G-15199)*

Ehs Group LLC ....G 914 937-6162
Port Chester *(G-12819)*

Federal Envelope Inc ....F 212 243-8380
New York *(G-9480)*

Hudson Envelope Corporation ....G 212 473-6666
New York *(G-9831)*

Matt Industries Inc ....C 315 472-1316
Syracuse *(G-14938)*

Poly-Flex Corp ....F 631 586-9500
Edgewood *(G-4277)*

Precision Envelope Co Inc ....G 631 694-3990
Farmingdale *(G-4715)*

Shipman Printing Inds Inc ....E 716 504-7700
Niagara Falls *(G-11980)*

PRINTING, COMMERCIAL: Imprinting

Burr & Son Inc ....G 315 446-1550
Syracuse *(G-14836)*

Imprint Branded Content LLC ....G 212 888-8073
New York *(G-9872)*

Issacs Yisroel ....G 718 851-7430
Brooklyn *(G-1971)*

Total Solution Graphics Inc ....G 718 706-1540
Long Island City *(G-7383)*

PRINTING, COMMERCIAL: Invitations, NEC

Alpine Business Group Inc ....F 212 989-4198
New York *(G-8530)*

Color Card LLC ....F 631 232-1300
Central Islip *(G-3269)*

PRINTING, COMMERCIAL: Labels & Seals, NEC

American Casting and Mfg Corp .....D 800 342-0333
Plainview *(G-12662)*

Citation Healthcare Labels LLC ......G 631 293-4646
Hauppauge *(G-5616)*

Classic Labels Inc ....E 631 467-2300
Patchogue *(G-12498)*

Crisray Printing Corp ....E 631 293-3770
Farmingdale *(G-4605)*

Franklin Packaging Inc ....G 631 582-8900
Northport *(G-12104)*

General Trade Mark La ....E 718 979-7261
Staten Island *(G-14655)*

Greenbush Tape & Label Inc ....E 518 465-2389
Albany *(G-82)*

Hammer Packaging Corp ....B 585 424-3880
West Henrietta *(G-15797)*

Info Label Inc ....F 518 664-0791
Halfmoon *(G-5493)*

Janco Press Inc ....F 631 563-3003
Bohemia *(G-1027)*

Labels Inter-Global Inc ....F 212 398-0006
New York *(G-10160)*

Magazines & Brochures Inc ....G 716 875-9699
Buffalo *(G-2857)*

Master Image Printing Inc ....G 914 347-4400
Elmsford *(G-4416)*

Niagara Label Company Inc ....G 716 542-3000
Akron *(G-18)*

Ontario Label Graphics Inc ....F 716 434-8505
Lockport *(G-7100)*

Precision Label Corporation ....F 631 270-4490
Hauppauge *(G-5747)*

Quadra Flex Corp ....G 607 758-7066
Cortland *(G-3785)*

Tri Star Label Inc ....G 914 237-4800
Mount Vernon *(G-8186)*

PRINTING, COMMERCIAL: Letterpress & Screen

Quist Industries Ltd ....F 718 243-2800
Brooklyn *(G-2316)*

PRINTING, COMMERCIAL: Literature, Advertising, NEC

Bizbash Media Inc ....D 646 638-3602
New York *(G-8804)*

Grado Group Inc ....G 718 556-4200
Staten Island *(G-14658)*

Landlord Guard Inc ....F 212 695-6505
New York *(G-10169)*

Nomad Editions LLC ....F 212 918-0992
Bronxville *(G-1402)*

North American DF Inc ....G 718 698-2500
Staten Island *(G-14683)*

PRINTING, COMMERCIAL: Magazines, NEC

Aspect Printing Inc ....E 347 789-4284
Brooklyn *(G-1542)*

L & M Uniserv Corp ....G...... 718 854-3700
Brooklyn *(G-2040)*

PRINTING, COMMERCIAL: Periodicals, NEC

Willis Mc Donald Co Inc ....F...... 212 366-1526
New York *(G-11761)*

PRINTING, COMMERCIAL: Post Cards, Picture, NEC

4 Over 4com Inc ....G...... 718 932-2700
Astoria *(G-412)*

PRINTING, COMMERCIAL: Promotional

Bobley-Harmann Corporation ....G...... 516 433-3800
Ronkonkoma *(G-13917)*

Cooper & Clement Inc ....E...... 315 454-8135
Syracuse *(G-14861)*

Excell Print & Promotions Inc ....G...... 914 437-8668
White Plains *(G-16004)*

Fulcrum Promotions & Prtg LLC ....G...... 203 909-6362
New York *(G-9550)*

Gary Stock Corporation ....G...... 914 276-2700
Croton Falls *(G-3805)*

Medallion Associates Inc ....E...... 212 929-9130
New York *(G-10408)*

PDQ Shipping Services ....G...... 845 255-5500
New Paltz *(G-8310)*

Printech Business Systems Inc ....F...... 212 290-2542
New York *(G-10897)*

Scancorp Inc ....G...... 315 454-5596
Syracuse *(G-14986)*

Sherwood Group Inc ....G...... 240 731-8573
New York *(G-11212)*

Swift Multigraphics LLC ....G...... 585 442-8000
Rochester *(G-13752)*

Syracuse Letter Company Inc ....F...... 315 476-8328
Bridgeport *(G-1169)*

Xpress Printing Inc ....G...... 516 605-1000
Plainview *(G-12729)*

PRINTING, COMMERCIAL: Publications

Advance Finance Group LLC ....D...... 212 630-5900
New York *(G-8468)*

Baffler Foundation Inc ....G...... 203 362-8147
New York *(G-8714)*

Beis Moshiach Inc ....E...... 718 778-8000
Brooklyn *(G-1571)*

Check-O-Matic Inc ....G...... 845 781-7675
Monroe *(G-8018)*

Dental Tribune America LLC ....F...... 212 244-7181
Forest Hills *(G-4919)*

Glenn Horowitz Bookseller Inc ....G...... 212 691-9100
New York *(G-9620)*

Graphic Printing ....G...... 718 701-4433
Bronx *(G-1269)*

Graphics 247 Corp ....G...... 718 729-2470
Long Island City *(G-7233)*

Merchandiser Inc ....G...... 315 462-6411
Clifton Springs *(G-3479)*

New York Christan Times Inc ....G...... 718 638-6397
Brooklyn *(G-2204)*

Nys Nyu-Cntr Intl Cooperation ....E...... 212 998-3680
New York *(G-10668)*

Sephardic Yellow Pages ....E...... 718 998-0299
Brooklyn *(G-2395)*

PRINTING, COMMERCIAL: Screen

A Promos USA Inc ....F...... 516 377-0186
Freeport *(G-4978)*

A Tradition of Excellence Inc ....G...... 845 638-4595
New City *(G-8223)*

Acme Screenprinting LLC ....G...... 716 565-1052
Buffalo *(G-2619)*

Active World Solutions Inc ....G...... 718 922-9404
Brooklyn *(G-1459)*

Ad Image Inc ....E...... 914 476-0000
Yonkers *(G-16280)*

Advanced Graphics Company Inc ....F...... 607 692-7875
Whitney Point *(G-16105)*

Albert Siy ....G...... 718 359-0389
Flushing *(G-4836)*

Alicia F Herdlein ....G...... 585 344-4411
Batavia *(G-599)*

AMA Precision Screening Inc ....F...... 585 293-0820
Churchville *(G-3407)*

Arca Ink LLC ....G...... 518 798-0100
South Glens Falls *(G-14512)*

Arena Graphics Inc ....G...... 516 767-5108
Port Washington *(G-12864)*

Artscroll Printing Corp ....E...... 212 929-2413
New York *(G-8640)*

Artwill Group LLC ....E...... 845 826-3692
Blauvelt *(G-926)*

Barnaby Prints Inc ....F...... 845 477-2501
Greenwood Lake *(G-5479)*

Bartolomeo Publishing Inc ....G...... 631 420-4949
West Babylon *(G-15693)*

Beebie Printing & Art Agcy Inc ....G...... 518 725-4528
Gloversville *(G-5279)*

Bidpress LLC ....G...... 267 973-8876
New York *(G-8782)*

Bkny Printing Corp ....E...... 718 875-4219
Brooklyn *(G-1591)*

C & C Athletic Inc ....G...... 845 713-4670
Walden *(G-15457)*

Cnyshirts ....G...... 315 432-1789
Syracuse *(G-14854)*

Con-Tees Custom Printing Ltd ....G...... 914 664-0251
Mount Vernon *(G-8133)*

Control Research Inc ....G...... 631 225-1111
Amityville *(G-259)*

Custom 101 Prints Inc ....F...... 718 708-4425
Bronx *(G-1234)*

Custom Sportswear Corp ....G...... 914 666-9200
Bedford Hills *(G-766)*

D B F Associates ....G...... 718 328-0005
Bronx *(G-1235)*

DEW Graphics Inc ....E...... 212 727-8820
New York *(G-9213)*

Dkm Sales LLC ....E...... 716 893-7777
Buffalo *(G-2730)*

Drns Corp ....E...... 718 369-4530
Brooklyn *(G-1763)*

Effective Sling Solutions LLC ....G...... 716 771-8503
Lake View *(G-6772)*

Efs Designs LLC ....G...... 718 852-9511
Brooklyn *(G-1785)*

First2print Inc ....G...... 212 868-6886
New York *(G-9502)*

Freeport Screen & Stamping ....E...... 516 379-0330
Freeport *(G-4998)*

Fresh Prints LLC ....F...... 917 826-2752
New York *(G-9539)*

Fulton Screen Printing ....G...... 315 593-2220
Fulton *(G-5060)*

Graph-Tex Inc ....F...... 607 756-7791
Cortland *(G-3767)*

Graph-Tex Inc ....G...... 607 756-1875
Cortland *(G-3768)*

Graphics For Industry Inc ....E...... 212 889-6202
New York *(G-9665)*

Graphics Plus Printing Inc ....E...... 607 299-0500
Cortland *(G-3769)*

Gruber Display Co Inc ....F...... 718 882-8220
Bronx *(G-1270)*

Handone Studios Inc ....G...... 585 421-8175
Fairport *(G-4498)*

Herrmann Group LLC ....G...... 716 876-9798
Kenmore *(G-6651)*

Human Technologies Corporation ....F...... 315 735-3532
Utica *(G-15273)*

Island Silkscreen Inc ....G...... 631 757-4567
East Northport *(G-4147)*

J Kendall LLC ....E...... 646 739-4956
Yonkers *(G-16322)*

J M L Productions Inc ....D...... 718 643-1674
Brooklyn *(G-1980)*

J N White Associates Inc ....D...... 585 237-5191
Perry *(G-12598)*

J T Printing 21 ....G...... 718 484-3939
Staten Island *(G-14668)*

Kenmar Shirts Inc ....E...... 718 824-3880
Bronx *(G-1291)*

Knucklehead Embroidery Inc ....G...... 607 797-2725
Johnson City *(G-6605)*

L I C Screen Printing Inc ....E...... 516 546-7289
Merrick *(G-7858)*

Logomax Inc ....G...... 631 420-0484
Farmingdale *(G-4671)*

Loremanss Embroidery Engrav ....F...... 518 834-9205
Keeseville *(G-6643)*

Mart-Tex Athletics Inc ....E...... 631 454-9583
Farmingdale *(G-4678)*

Mastercraft Decorators Inc ....E...... 585 223-5150
Fairport *(G-4506)*

Mastro Graphic Arts Inc ....E...... 585 436-7570
Rochester *(G-13537)*

Matthew-Lee Corporation ....F...... 631 226-0100
Lindenhurst *(G-6959)*

Metro Creative Graphics Inc ....E...... 212 947-5100
New York *(G-10444)*

Mixture Screen Printing ....G...... 845 561-2857
Newburgh *(G-11873)*

Multi Packaging Solutions Inc ....E...... 646 885-0005
New York *(G-10519)*

Mv Corp Inc ....C...... 631 273-8020
Bay Shore *(G-695)*

Nathan Printing Express Inc ....G...... 914 472-0914
Scarsdale *(G-14239)*

New Art Signs Co Inc ....G...... 718 443-0900
Glen Head *(G-5210)*

New Buffalo Shirt Factory Inc ....G...... 716 436-5839
Buffalo *(G-2881)*

Northwind Graphics ....G...... 518 899-9651
Ballston Spa *(G-584)*

Okey Enterprises Inc ....G...... 212 213-2640
New York *(G-10682)*

One In A Million Inc ....E...... 516 829-1111
Valley Stream *(G-15350)*

Paratore Signs Inc ....G...... 315 455-5551
Syracuse *(G-14962)*

Park Avenue Imprints LLC ....G...... 716 822-5737
Buffalo *(G-2906)*

Patrick Kraft ....G...... 315 343-9376
Oswego *(G-12419)*

PDM Studios Inc ....G...... 716 694-8337
Tonawanda *(G-15131)*

Penny Lane Printing Inc ....D...... 585 226-8111
Avon *(G-515)*

Personal Graphics Corporation ....G...... 315 853-3421
Westmoreland *(G-15961)*

Peter Papastrat ....G...... 607 723-8112
Binghamton *(G-904)*

Premier Ink Systems Inc ....E...... 845 782-5802
Harriman *(G-5546)*

Print Shoppe ....G...... 315 792-9585
Utica *(G-15291)*

Printing Max New York Inc ....G...... 718 692-1400
Brooklyn *(G-2292)*

R R Donnelley & Sons Company ....D...... 518 438-9722
Albany *(G-121)*

Rainbow Lettering ....G...... 607 732-5751
Elmira *(G-4366)*

Regal Screen Printing Intl ....G...... 845 356-8181
New City *(G-8229)*

Richs Sttches EMB Screenprint ....G...... 845 621-2175
Mahopac *(G-7477)*

Ross L Sports Screening Inc ....F...... 716 824-5350
Buffalo *(G-2964)*

Round Top Knit & Screening ....G...... 518 622-3600
Round Top *(G-14064)*

Royal Tees Inc ....G...... 845 357-9448
Suffern *(G-14766)*

S L C Industries Incorporated ....F...... 607 775-2299
Binghamton *(G-907)*

Sand Hill Industries Inc ....G...... 518 885-7991
Ballston Spa *(G-586)*

Screen The World Inc ....F...... 631 475-0023
Holtsville *(G-6052)*

Shore Line Monogramming Inc ....F...... 914 698-8000
Mamaroneck *(G-7523)*

Sign Shop Inc ....G...... 631 226-4145
Copiague *(G-3678)*

Silk Screen Art Inc ....G...... 518 762-8423
Johnstown *(G-6627)*

Sino Printing Inc ....F...... 212 334-6896
New York *(G-11250)*

Special Tees ....E...... 718 980-0987
Staten Island *(G-14711)*

Spst Inc ....G...... 607 798-6952
Vestal *(G-15383)*

Stromberg Brand Corporation ....F...... 914 739-7410
Valley Cottage *(G-15327)*

T L F Graphics Inc ....D...... 585 272-5500
Rochester *(G-13757)*

T-Shirt Factory Inc ....F...... 845 454-2255
Poughkeepsie *(G-12987)*

Tara Rific Screen Printing Inc ....G...... 718 583-6864
Bronx *(G-1379)*

Todd Walbridge ....G...... 585 254-3018
Rochester *(G-13768)*

U All Inc ....E...... 518 438-2558
Albany *(G-138)*

Universal Screening Associates ....F...... 718 232-2744
Brooklyn *(G-2545)*

Unlimited Ink Inc ....E...... 631 582-0696
Hauppauge *(G-5793)*

P
R
O
D
U
C
T

Viking Athletics Ltd............E....631 957-8000
Lindenhurst *(G-6982)*
Voss Signs LLC............E....315 682-6418
Manlius *(G-7550)*
Zacks Enterprises Inc............E....800 366-4924
Orangeburg *(G-12333)*

PRINTING, COMMERCIAL: Stamps, Trading, NEC

Ashton-Potter USA Ltd............C....716 633-2000
Williamsville *(G-16120)*

PRINTING, COMMERCIAL: Tags, NEC

Actioncraft Products Inc............G....516 883-6423
Port Washington *(G-12859)*
Colonial Tag & Label Co Inc............F....516 482-0508
Great Neck *(G-5377)*
Industrial Test Eqp Co Inc............E....516 883-6423
Port Washington *(G-12888)*
Itc Mfg Group Inc............F....212 684-3696
New York *(G-9947)*

PRINTING, LITHOGRAPHIC: Advertising Posters

V C N Group Ltd Inc............G....516 223-4812
North Baldwin *(G-12010)*

PRINTING, LITHOGRAPHIC: Calendars

Redi Records Payroll............F....718 854-6990
Brooklyn *(G-2335)*

PRINTING, LITHOGRAPHIC: Color

Crawford Print Shop Inc............G....607 359-4970
Addison *(G-4)*
Create-A-Card Inc............G....631 584-2273
Saint James *(G-14108)*
Raith America Inc............E....518 874-3000
Troy *(G-15182)*
Select-A-Form Inc............D....631 981-3076
Holbrook *(G-6020)*
Spectrum Prtg Lithography Inc............E....212 255-3131
New York *(G-11316)*

PRINTING, LITHOGRAPHIC: Decals

Aro-Graph Corporation............G....315 463-8693
Syracuse *(G-14817)*
Decal Makers Inc............E....516 221-7200
Bellmore *(G-781)*
Decal Techniques Inc............G....631 491-1800
Bay Shore *(G-671)*
Paper House Productions Inc............E....845 246-7261
Saugerties *(G-14207)*

PRINTING, LITHOGRAPHIC: Forms & Cards, Business

Batavia Press LLC............E....585 343-4429
Batavia *(G-603)*
Color Card LLC............F....631 232-1300
Central Islip *(G-3269)*
Miller Place Printing Inc............G....631 473-1158
Miller Place *(G-7945)*
Perfect Forms and Systems Inc............F....631 462-1100
Smithtown *(G-14484)*
U Invite Limited............G....212 739-0620
New York *(G-11570)*
Webb-Mason Inc............E....716 276-8792
Buffalo *(G-3043)*

PRINTING, LITHOGRAPHIC: Forms, Business

Artina Group Inc............E....914 592-1850
Elmsford *(G-4394)*
Precision Envelope Co Inc............G....631 694-3990
Farmingdale *(G-4715)*

PRINTING, LITHOGRAPHIC: Letters, Circular Or Form

Brooklyn Circus............F....718 858-0919
Brooklyn *(G-1614)*
F & D Services Inc............F....718 984-1635
Staten Island *(G-14652)*

PRINTING, LITHOGRAPHIC: Menus

Ready Check Glo Inc............G....516 547-1849
East Northport *(G-4151)*

PRINTING, LITHOGRAPHIC: Offset & photolithographic printing

Ace Printing & Publishing Inc............F....718 939-0040
Flushing *(G-4834)*
Iron Horse Graphics Ltd............G....631 537-3400
Bridgehampton *(G-1166)*
Kaymil Printing Company Inc............G....212 594-3718
New York *(G-10082)*
Mdi Holdings LLC............A....212 559-1127
New York *(G-10404)*
Nova Inc............G....212 967-1139
New York *(G-10648)*
Progressive Color Graphics............E....212 292-8787
Great Neck *(G-5416)*
Remsen Graphics Corp............G....718 643-7500
Brooklyn *(G-2340)*
Rgm Signs Inc............G....718 442-0598
Staten Island *(G-14703)*
Superior Print On Demand............G....607 240-5231
Vestal *(G-15384)*

PRINTING, LITHOGRAPHIC: On Metal

A I P Printing & Stationers............G....631 929-5529
Wading River *(G-15448)*
Challenge Graphics Svcs Inc............E....631 586-0171
Deer Park *(G-3851)*
David Helsing............G....607 796-2681
Horseheads *(G-6120)*
Denton Printing Corporation............F....631 586-4333
Bohemia *(G-1003)*
Hks Printing Company Inc............F....212 675-2529
New York *(G-9797)*
Mansfield Press Inc............F....212 265-5411
New York *(G-10352)*
Messenger Press............G....518 885-9231
Ballston Spa *(G-582)*
Seneca West Printing Inc............G....716 675-8010
West Seneca *(G-15854)*

PRINTING, LITHOGRAPHIC: Post Cards, Picture

Anne Taintor Inc............G....718 483-9312
Brooklyn *(G-1512)*

PRINTING, LITHOGRAPHIC: Promotional

21st Century Fox America Inc............D....212 852-7000
New York *(G-8396)*
China Imprint LLC............G....585 563-3391
Rochester *(G-13313)*
Gmp LLC............D....914 939-0571
Port Chester *(G-12821)*
In-Step Marketing Inc............F....212 797-3450
New York *(G-9874)*
R & L Press Inc............G....718 447-8557
Staten Island *(G-14696)*

PRINTING, LITHOGRAPHIC: Publications

Canyon Publishing Inc............F....212 334-0227
New York *(G-8908)*
Hudson Park Press Inc............G....212 929-8898
New York *(G-9833)*
Post Road............F....203 545-2122
New York *(G-10871)*

PRINTING, LITHOGRAPHIC: Tags

Kwik Ticket Inc............F....718 421-3800
Brooklyn *(G-2038)*

PRINTING, LITHOGRAPHIC: Tickets

Worldwide Ticket Craft............D....516 538-6200
Merrick *(G-7865)*

PRINTING, LITHOGRAPHIC: Transfers, Decalcomania Or Dry

Royal Tees Inc............G....845 357-9448
Suffern *(G-14766)*

PRINTING: Books

Cct Inc............G....212 532-3355
New York *(G-8940)*
Kravitz Design Inc............G....212 625-1644
New York *(G-10139)*
North Country Books Inc............G....315 735-4877
Utica *(G-15288)*
Twp America Inc............G....212 274-8090
New York *(G-11567)*
Vicks Lithograph & Prtg Corp............C....315 272-2401
Yorkville *(G-16380)*

PRINTING: Books

450 Ridge St Inc............G....716 754-2789
Lewiston *(G-6919)*
Bedford Freeman & Worth............C....212 576-9400
New York *(G-8745)*
Centrisource Inc............G....716 871-1105
Tonawanda *(G-15096)*
E Graphics Corporation............G....718 486-9767
Brooklyn *(G-1772)*
Experiment LLC............G....212 889-1659
New York *(G-9447)*
Flare Multicopy Corp............E....718 258-8860
Brooklyn *(G-1849)*
Hudson Valley Paper Works Inc............F....845 569-8883
Newburgh *(G-11870)*
In-House Inc............F....718 445-9007
College Point *(G-3544)*
Literary Classics of US............E....212 308-3360
New York *(G-10226)*
Panzarella Prtg & Packg Inc............G....716 853-4480
Amherst *(G-241)*
Printing Factory LLC............F....718 451-0500
Brooklyn *(G-2291)*
Promotional Sales Books LLC............G....212 675-0364
New York *(G-10909)*
Royal Fireworks Prtg Co Inc............F....845 726-3333
Unionville *(G-15234)*
Steffen Publishing Inc............D....315 865-4100
Holland Patent *(G-6034)*
Sterling Pierce Company Inc............E....516 593-1170
East Rockaway *(G-4174)*
Stop Entertainment Inc............F....212 242-7867
Monroe *(G-8031)*
Tobay Printing Co Inc............E....631 842-3300
Copiague *(G-3684)*
Vicks Lithograph & Prtg Corp............C....315 736-9344
Yorkville *(G-16381)*
Worzalla Publishing Company............C....212 967-7909
New York *(G-11788)*

PRINTING: Broadwoven Fabrics. Cotton

Mountain T-Shirts Inc............G....518 943-4533
Catskill *(G-3215)*

PRINTING: Checkbooks

Datamax International Inc............E....212 693-0933
New York *(G-9175)*
Deluxe Corporation............B....845 362-4054
Spring Valley *(G-14566)*

PRINTING: Commercial, NEC

2 1 2 Postcards Inc............E....212 767-8227
New York *(G-8391)*
461 New Lots Avenue LLC............G....347 303-9305
Brooklyn *(G-1419)*
5 Stars Printing Corp............F....718 461-4612
Flushing *(G-4831)*
A & A Graphics Inc II............G....516 735-0078
Seaford *(G-14348)*
A Graphic Printing Inc............G....212 233-9696
New York *(G-8416)*
AC Envelope Inc............G....516 420-0646
Farmingdale *(G-4572)*
Academy Printing Services Inc............G....631 765-3346
Southold *(G-14542)*
Accel Printing & Graphics............G....914 241-3369
Mount Kisco *(G-8086)*
Action Envelope & Prtg Co Inc............F....631 225-3900
Melville *(G-7754)*
Adirondack Pennysaver Inc............E....518 563-0100
Plattsburgh *(G-12731)*
Allsafe Technologies Inc............D....716 691-0400
Amherst *(G-208)*
Alpina Copyworld Inc............F....212 683-3511
New York *(G-8529)*

Company	Code	Phone
American Office Supply Inc	F	516 294-9444
Westbury (G-15868)		
Amerikom Group Inc	D	212 675-1329
New York (G-8562)		
Amstead Press Corp	G	347 416-2373
New York (G-8569)		
Apple Enterprises Inc	E	718 361-2200
Long Island City (G-7160)		
Argo Lithographers Inc	E	718 729-2700
Long Island City (G-7166)		
Arista Innovations Inc	E	516 746-2262
Mineola (G-7959)		
Artistic Typography Corp	F	212 463-8880
New York (G-8638)		
Asn Inc	E	718 894-0800
Maspeth (G-7593)		
Balajee Enterprises Inc	G	212 629-6150
New York (G-8721)		
Bedford Freeman & Worth	C	212 576-9400
New York (G-8745)		
Benchemark Printing Inc	D	518 393-1361
Schenectady (G-14249)		
Berkshire Business Forms Inc	F	518 828-2600
Hudson (G-6150)		
Bestmade Printing LLC	G	718 384-0719
Brooklyn (G-1580)		
Bestype Digital Imaging LLC	F	212 966-6886
New York (G-8767)		
Big Apple Sign Corp	D	212 629-3650
New York (G-8785)		
Body Builders Inc	G	718 492-7997
Brooklyn (G-1601)		
Bondy Printing Corp	G	631 242-1510
Bay Shore (G-659)		
BP Beyond Printing Inc	G	516 328-2700
Hempstead (G-5834)		
Bradley Marketing Group Inc	G	212 967-6100
New York (G-8844)		
Bridge Fulfillment Inc	G	718 625-6622
Brooklyn (G-1608)		
Brooks Litho Digital Group Inc	G	631 789-4500
Deer Park (G-3850)		
Cama Graphics Inc	F	718 707-9747
Long Island City (G-7183)		
Century Direct LLC	C	212 763-0600
Islandia (G-6328)		
Chakra Communications Inc	E	607 748-7491
Endicott (G-4446)		
Christian Bus Endeavors Inc	F	315 788-8560
Watertown (G-15564)		
Chroma Communications Inc	G	631 289-8871
Medford (G-7703)		
Classic Album	E	718 388-2818
Brooklyn (G-1670)		
Colad Group LLC	D	716 961-1776
Buffalo (G-2703)		
Colonial Label Systems Inc	E	631 254-0111
Bay Shore (G-664)		
Comgraph Sales Service	G	716 601-7243
Elma (G-4317)		
Commercial Press Inc	G	315 274-0028
Canton (G-3164)		
Copy Room Inc	F	212 371-8600
New York (G-9099)		
Copy X/Press Ltd	D	631 585-2200
Ronkonkoma (G-13925)		
D G M Graphics Inc	F	516 223-2220
Merrick (G-7854)		
D3 Repro Group Inc	G	347 507-1075
Long Island City (G-7197)		
Dash Printing Inc	G	212 643-8534
New York (G-9171)		
Delft Printing Inc	G	716 683-1100
Lancaster (G-6802)		
Digital Evolution Inc	E	212 732-2722
New York (G-9227)		
Dit Prints Incorporated	G	518 885-4400
Ballston Spa (G-572)		
Division Den-Bar Enterprises	G	914 381-2220
Mamaroneck (G-7508)		
Donald Bruhnke	F	212 600-1260
New York (G-9247)		
Dutchess Plumbing & Heating	G	845 889-8255
Staatsburg (G-14599)		
E&I Printing	F	212 206-0506
New York (G-9293)		
Elm Graphics Inc	G	315 737-5984
New Hartford (G-8239)		
Enterprise Press Inc	C	212 741-2111
New York (G-9382)		
Evergreen Corp Central NY	F	315 454-4175
Syracuse (G-14890)		
Exotic Print and Paper Inc	F	212 807-0465
New York (G-9446)		
Fedex Office & Print Svcs Inc	G	718 982-5223
Staten Island (G-14653)		
Fleaheart Inc	F	718 521-4958
Brooklyn (G-1852)		
Flp Group LLC	F	315 252-7583
Auburn (G-476)		
Folder Factory Inc	F	540 477-3852
Melville (G-7783)		
Force Digital Media Inc	G	631 243-0243
Deer Park (G-3874)		
Freeville Publishing Co Inc	F	607 844-9119
Freeville (G-5033)		
Gallant Graphics Ltd	E	845 868-1166
Stanfordville (G-14610)		
Garrett J Cronin	G	914 761-9299
White Plains (G-16008)		
Gatehouse Media LLC	B	585 598-0030
Pittsford (G-12641)		
GE Healthcare Fincl Svcs Inc	G	212 713-2000
New York (G-9584)		
Gem Reproduction Services Corp	G	845 298-0172
Wappingers Falls (G-15494)		
Genie Instant Printing Co Inc	F	212 575-8258
New York (G-9595)		
Grand Meridian Printing Inc	E	718 937-3888
Maspeth (G-7619)		
Graphics Service Bureau Inc	F	212 684-3600
Long Island City (G-7234)		
Haig Press Inc	E	631 582-5800
Hauppauge (G-5665)		
Hi-Tech Packg World-Wide LLC	G	845 947-1912
New Windsor (G-8369)		
Horace J Metz	G	716 873-9103
Kenmore (G-6652)		
Hospitality Inc	E	212 268-1930
New York (G-9817)		
I N K T Inc	F	212 957-2700
New York (G-9846)		
Image Typography Inc	G	631 218-6932
Holbrook (G-6000)		
Impress Graphic Technologies	F	516 781-0845
Westbury (G-15896)		
Incodema3d LLC	E	607 269-4390
Freeville (G-5035)		
Integrated Graphics Inc	G	212 592-5600
New York (G-9908)		
Iron Horse Graphics Ltd	G	631 537-3400
Bridgehampton (G-1166)		
Jack J Florio Jr	G	716 434-9123
Lockport (G-7085)		
Japan Printing & Graphics Inc	G	212 406-2905
New York (G-9976)		
Joed Press	G	212 243-3620
New York (G-10015)		
John Auguliaro Printing Co	G	718 382-5283
Brooklyn (G-1997)		
Jomar Industries Inc	E	845 357-5773
Airmont (G-13)		
Jomart Associates Inc	F	212 627-2153
Islandia (G-6339)		
Kallen Corp	G	212 242-1470
New York (G-10061)		
Kenan International Trading	G	718 672-4922
Corona (G-3742)		
Lake Placid Advertisers Wkshp	E	518 523-3359
Lake Placid (G-6767)		
Lennons Litho Inc	F	315 866-3156
Herkimer (G-5866)		
Leo Paper Inc	G	917 305-0708
New York (G-10200)		
Levon Graphics Corp	D	631 753-2022
Deer Park (G-3897)		
Linden Forms & Systems Inc	E	212 219-1100
Brooklyn (G-2076)		
Loy L Press Inc	G	716 634-5966
Buffalo (G-2853)		
M C Packaging Corporation	E	631 643-3763
Babylon (G-522)		
Mason Transparent Package Inc	E	718 792-6000
Bronx (G-1307)		
Measurement Incorporated	F	914 682-1969
White Plains (G-16028)		
Mega Graphics Inc	G	914 962-1402
Yorktown Heights (G-16368)		
Merrill Communications LLC	G	212 620-5600
New York (G-10435)		
Merrill Corporation	D	917 934-7300
New York (G-10436)		
Middletown Press	G	845 343-1895
Middletown (G-7920)		
Mimeocom Inc	B	212 847-3000
New York (G-10472)		
Mini Graphics Inc	D	516 223-6464
Hauppauge (G-5720)		
Mpe Graphics Inc	F	631 582-8900
Bohemia (G-1048)		
Msm Designz Inc	G	914 909-5900
Tarrytown (G-15050)		
New Deal Printing Corp	E	718 729-5800
New York (G-10578)		
New York Legal Publishing	G	518 459-1100
Menands (G-7847)		
Niagara Sample Book Co Inc	F	716 284-6151
Niagara Falls (G-11954)		
Noble Checks Inc	G	212 537-6241
Brooklyn (G-2218)		
North American Graphics Inc	F	212 725-2200
New York (G-10641)		
North Six Inc	F	212 463-7227
New York (G-10643)		
Nyc Vinyl Screen Printing Inc	G	718 784-1360
Cold Spring Harbor (G-3528)		
Nyc Vinyl Screen Printing Inc	G	718 784-1360
Long Island City (G-7312)		
Pace Editions Inc	G	212 643-6353
New York (G-10736)		
Paris Art Label Co Inc	D	631 467-2300
Patchogue (G-12508)		
Paulin Investment Company	E	631 957-8500
Amityville (G-302)		
Photo Agents Ltd	G	631 421-0258
Huntington (G-6217)		
Pony Farm Press & Graphics	G	607 432-9020
Oneonta (G-12280)		
Presstek Printing LLC	F	585 266-2770
Rochester (G-13643)		
Print City Corp	F	212 487-9778
New York (G-10894)		
Printfacility Inc	G	212 349-4009
New York (G-10898)		
Printing Resources Inc	E	518 482-2470
Albany (G-119)		
Printworks Printing & Design	G	315 433-8587
Syracuse (G-14968)		
Quality Impressions Inc	G	646 613-0002
Long Island City (G-7336)		
Quality Offset LLC	G	347 342-4660
Long Island City (G-7337)		
R & M Graphics of New York	F	212 929-0294
New York (G-10963)		
R R Donnelley & Sons Company	F	716 763-2613
Lakewood (G-6784)		
R R Donnelley & Sons Company	D	716 773-0647
Grand Island (G-5341)		
R R Donnelley & Sons Company	G	646 755-8125
New York (G-10967)		
Rfn Inc	F	516 764-5100
Bay Shore (G-705)		
Richard Ruffner	F	631 234-4600
Central Islip (G-3287)		
Rike Enterprises Inc	F	631 277-8338
Islip (G-6356)		
RIT Printing Corp	F	631 586-6220
Bay Shore (G-707)		
Rose Graphics LLC	F	516 547-6142
West Babylon (G-15743)		
Salamanca Press Penny Saver	E	716 945-1500
Salamanca (G-14127)		
Scan-A-Chrome Color Inc	G	631 532-6146
Copiague (G-3675)		
Shapeways Inc	C	914 356-5816
New York (G-11206)		
Shapeways Inc	G	646 470-3576
Long Island City (G-7356)		
Silver Griffin Inc	F	518 272-7771
Troy (G-15189)		
Spaulding Law Printing Inc	G	315 422-4805
Syracuse (G-14997)		
Spectrum Prtg Lithography Inc	E	212 255-3131
New York (G-11316)		
St James Printing Inc	G	631 981-2095
Ronkonkoma (G-14014)		
Standwill Packaging Inc	E	631 752-1236
Farmingdale (G-4739)		
Starfire Printing Inc	G	631 736-1495
Holtsville (G-6053)		

Structured 3d Inc ....G...... 346 704-2614
  Amityville (G-308)
Syracuse Label Co Inc ....D...... 315 422-1037
  Syracuse (G-15008)
T S O General Corp ....E...... 631 952-5320
  Brentwood (G-1127)
T&K Printing Inc ....F...... 718 439-9454
  Brooklyn (G-2487)
T-Base Communications USA Inc ....E...... 315 713-0013
  Ogdensburg (G-12211)
Takeout Printing LLC ....G...... 845 564-2609
  Newburgh (G-11888)
Tapemaker Supply Company LLC ....G...... 914 693-3407
  Hartsdale (G-5569)
Tc Transcontinental USA Inc ....G...... 818 993-4767
  New York (G-11439)
Tcmf Inc ....D...... 607 724-1094
  Binghamton (G-912)
Tele-Pak Inc ....E...... 845 426-2300
  Monsey (G-8053)
The Gramecy Group ....G...... 518 348-1325
  Clifton Park (G-3476)
Toppan Merrill USA Inc ....C...... 212 596-7747
  New York (G-11515)
Toprint Ltd ....G...... 718 439-0469
  Brooklyn (G-2512)
Tri-State Envelope Corporation ....F...... 212 736-3110
  New York (G-11541)
USA Custom Pad Corp ....E...... 607 563-9550
  Sidney (G-14439)
Varick Street Litho Inc ....G...... 646 843-0800
  New York (G-11644)
Venus Printing Company ....F...... 212 967-8900
  Hewlett (G-5875)
Veterans Offset Printing Inc ....G...... 585 288-2900
  Rochester (G-13796)
Waterhouse Publications Inc ....E...... 716 662-4200
  Orchard Park (G-12383)
Weicro Graphics Inc ....E...... 631 253-3360
  Brooklyn (G-2578)
Were Forms Inc ....G...... 585 482-4400
  Rochester (G-13802)
Westypo Printers Inc ....G...... 914 737-7394
  Peekskill (G-12562)
Willco Fine Art Ltd ....F...... 718 935-9567
  New York (G-11755)
William J Ryan ....G...... 585 392-6200
  Hilton (G-5975)
Wilson Press LLC ....E...... 315 568-9693
  Seneca Falls (G-14374)
Worldwide Ticket Craft ....D...... 516 538-6200
  Merrick (G-7865)
X Myles Mar Inc ....E...... 212 683-2015
  New York (G-11795)
X Press Screen Printing ....G...... 716 679-7788
  Dunkirk (G-4068)
XI Graphics Inc ....E...... 212 929-8700
  New York (G-11800)

PRINTING: Engraving & Plate

Allstate Sign & Plaque Corp ....F...... 631 242-2828
  Deer Park (G-3836)
Custom House Engravers Inc ....G...... 631 567-3004
  Bohemia (G-995)
D & A Offset Services Inc ....F...... 212 924-0612
  New York (G-9144)
New Dimension Awards Inc ....G...... 718 236-8200
  Brooklyn (G-2202)

PRINTING: Flexographic

Marlow Printing Co Inc ....E...... 718 625-4948
  Brooklyn (G-2117)
Transcntinental Ultra Flex Inc ....B...... 718 272-9100
  Brooklyn (G-2516)
W N Vanalstine & Sons Inc ....D...... 518 237-1436
  Cohoes (G-3520)

PRINTING: Gravure, Business Form & Card

Alamar Printing Inc ....F...... 914 993-9007
  White Plains (G-15969)
Alfa Card Inc ....G...... 718 326-7107
  Glendale (G-5217)

PRINTING: Gravure, Color

Kinaneco Inc ....E...... 315 468-6201
  Syracuse (G-14926)

PRINTING: Gravure, Forms, Business

American Print Solutions Inc ....G...... 718 208-2309
  Brooklyn (G-1502)
Macadame Inc ....G...... 212 477-1930
  Brooklyn (G-2099)

PRINTING: Gravure, Imprinting

C C Industries Inc ....F...... 518 581-7633
  Saratoga Springs (G-14167)

PRINTING: Gravure, Job

Sommer and Sons Printing Inc ....F...... 716 822-4311
  Buffalo (G-2986)

PRINTING: Gravure, Labels

Janco Press Inc ....F...... 631 563-3003
  Bohemia (G-1027)
Liberty Label Mfg Inc ....F...... 631 737-2365
  Holbrook (G-6006)
Niagara Label Company Inc ....F...... 716 542-3000
  Akron (G-18)
Trust of Colum Unive In The Ci ....F...... 212 854-2793
  New York (G-11552)

PRINTING: Gravure, Rotogravure

Color Industries LLC ....G...... 718 392-8301
  Long Island City (G-7190)
Copy Corner Inc ....G...... 718 388-4545
  Brooklyn (G-1687)
Foleys Graphic Center Inc ....F...... 914 245-3625
  Yorktown Heights (G-16364)
Gruner + Jahr USA Group Inc ....B...... 866 323-9336
  New York (G-9688)
Jack J Florio Jr ....F...... 716 434-9123
  Lockport (G-7085)
McG Graphics Inc ....G...... 631 499-0730
  Dix Hills (G-4012)
Mod-Pac Corp ....D...... 716 447-9013
  Buffalo (G-2870)
Paya Printing of NY Inc ....G...... 516 625-8346
  Albertson (G-149)
SRC Liquidation Company ....G...... 716 631-3900
  Williamsville (G-16141)
Tele-Pak Inc ....E...... 845 426-2300
  Monsey (G-8053)

PRINTING: Gravure, Stamps, Trading

Ashton-Potter USA Ltd ....C...... 716 633-2000
  Williamsville (G-16120)

PRINTING: Gravure, Stationery

Karr Graphics Corp ....E...... 212 645-6000
  Long Island City (G-7261)
Mrs John L Strong & Co LLC ....F...... 212 838-3775
  New York (G-10514)
Mutual Engraving Company Inc ....D...... 516 489-0534
  West Hempstead (G-15777)

PRINTING: Laser

Batavia Legal Printing Inc ....F...... 585 768-2100
  Le Roy (G-6896)
Data Palette Info Svcs LLC ....D...... 718 433-1060
  Port Washington (G-12871)
Diamond Inscription Tech ....F...... 646 366-7944
  New York (G-9221)
Doctor Print Inc ....E...... 631 873-4560
  Hauppauge (G-5640)
Miller Place Printing Inc ....G...... 631 473-1158
  Miller Place (G-7945)

PRINTING: Letterpress

6727 11th Ave Corp ....F...... 718 837-8787
  Brooklyn (G-1421)
Amax Printing Inc ....F...... 718 384-8600
  Maspeth (G-7588)
Bella Figura Letterpress ....G...... 866 699-6040
  Syracuse (G-14827)
Brodock Press Inc ....D...... 315 735-9577
  Utica (G-15242)
Chenango Union Printing Inc ....G...... 607 334-2112
  Norwich (G-12116)
Craig Envelope Corp ....G...... 718 786-4277
  Hicksville (G-5898)
Curtis Prtg Co The Del Press ....G...... 518 477-4820
  Castleton On Hudson (G-3201)

Eastwood Litho Impressions LLC ....F...... 315 437-2626
  Syracuse (G-14881)
Efficiency Printing Co Inc ....F...... 914 949-8611
  White Plains (G-16000)
F & B Photo Offset Co Inc ....G...... 516 431-5433
  Island Park (G-6317)
Fairmount Press ....G...... 212 255-2300
  New York (G-9465)
Forward Enterprises Inc ....F...... 585 235-7670
  Rochester (G-13421)
Frederick Coon Inc ....E...... 716 683-6812
  Elma (G-4318)
Gazette Press Inc ....E...... 914 963-8300
  Rye (G-14077)
Golos Printing Inc ....G...... 607 732-1896
  Elmira Heights (G-4377)
Grover Cleveland Press Inc ....F...... 716 564-2222
  Amherst (G-226)
H T L & S Ltd ....F...... 718 435-4474
  Brooklyn (G-1916)
Harmon and Castella Printing ....F...... 845 471-9163
  Hyde Park (G-6271)
HI Speed Envelope Co Inc ....F...... 718 617-1600
  Mount Vernon (G-8148)
Johnnys Ideal Printing Co ....G...... 518 828-6666
  Hudson (G-6166)
Judith Lewis Printer Inc ....F...... 516 997-7777
  Westbury (G-15900)
Kaufman Brothers Printing ....F...... 212 563-1854
  New York (G-10079)
Kaymil Printing Company Inc ....G...... 212 594-3718
  New York (G-10082)
Linco Printing Inc ....E...... 718 937-5141
  Long Island City (G-7273)
Louis Heindl & Son Inc ....G...... 585 454-5080
  Rochester (G-13523)
M T M Printing Co Inc ....F...... 718 353-3297
  College Point (G-3552)
Malone Industrial Press Inc ....G...... 518 483-5880
  Malone (G-7488)
Mark T Westinghouse ....G...... 518 678-3262
  Catskill (G-3214)
Maspeth Press Inc ....G...... 718 429-2363
  Maspeth (G-7626)
Midgley Printing Corp ....G...... 315 475-1864
  Syracuse (G-14942)
Mines Press Inc ....G...... 888 559-2634
  Cortlandt Manor (G-3797)
Moore Printing Company Inc ....G...... 585 394-1533
  Canandaigua (G-3136)
P & W Press Inc ....E...... 646 486-3417
  New York (G-10732)
Patrick Ryans Modern Press ....F...... 518 434-2921
  Albany (G-112)
S & S Prtg Die-Cutting Co Inc ....F...... 718 388-8990
  Brooklyn (G-2372)
Scotti Graphics Inc ....E...... 212 367-9602
  Long Island City (G-7352)
Seneca West Printing Inc ....G...... 716 675-8010
  West Seneca (G-15854)
Soho Letterpress Inc ....F...... 718 788-2518
  Brooklyn (G-2435)
Source Envelope Inc ....G...... 866 284-0707
  Farmingdale (G-4735)
Star Press Pearl River Inc ....G...... 845 268-2294
  Valley Cottage (G-15325)
Starcraft Press Inc ....G...... 718 383-6700
  Long Island City (G-7366)
Stony Point Graphics Ltd ....G...... 845 786-3322
  Stony Point (G-14748)
Tannens ....G...... 718 292-4646
  Bronx (G-1378)
Tovie Asarese Royal Prtg Co ....G...... 716 885-7692
  Buffalo (G-3016)
Tri Kolor Printing & Sty ....F...... 315 474-6753
  Syracuse (G-15015)
Weeks & Reichel Printing Inc ....G...... 631 589-1443
  Sayville (G-14232)
William Charles Prtg Co Inc ....E...... 516 349-0900
  Plainview (G-12728)

PRINTING: Lithographic

1 800 Postcards Inc ....D...... 212 741-1070
  New York (G-8387)
12pt Printing LLC ....G...... 718 376-2120
  Brooklyn (G-1410)
2 1 2 Postcards Inc ....E...... 212 767-8227
  New York (G-8391)
2 X 4 Inc ....E...... 212 647-1170
  New York (G-8392)

450 Ridge St Inc G 716 754-2789
Lewiston *(G-6919)*
518 Prints LLC G 518 674-5346
Averill Park *(G-505)*
A M & J Digital G 518 434-2579
Menands *(G-7836)*
A National Printing Co Inc G 631 243-3395
Bohemia *(G-958)*
AC Envelope Inc G 516 420-0646
Farmingdale *(G-4572)*
Add Associates Inc G 315 449-3474
Cicero *(G-3415)*
Adirondack Publishing Co Inc E 518 891-2600
Saranac Lake *(G-14156)*
Advance Publications Inc D 718 981-1234
New York *(G-8475)*
Advanced Business Group Inc F 212 398-1010
New York *(G-8477)*
Advanced Copy Center Inc G 212 388-1001
New York *(G-8478)*
Advanced Digital Printing LLC E 718 649-1500
New York *(G-8479)*
Albert Siy G 718 359-0389
Flushing *(G-4836)*
All Color Business Spc Ltd G 516 420-0649
Deer Park *(G-3833)*
Alpina Copyworld Inc F 212 683-3511
New York *(G-8529)*
Alpine Business Group Inc F 212 989-4198
New York *(G-8530)*
Amax Printing Inc F 718 384-8600
Maspeth *(G-7588)*
American Business Forms Inc E 716 836-5111
Amherst *(G-209)*
Amsterdam Printing & Litho Inc F 518 842-6000
Amsterdam *(G-316)*
Amsterdam Printing & Litho Inc E 518 842-6000
Amsterdam *(G-317)*
Andrew J George G 518 462-4662
Albany *(G-40)*
Ansun Graphics Inc F 315 437-6869
Syracuse *(G-14814)*
Answer Printing Inc F 212 922-2922
New York *(G-8595)*
April Printing Co Inc G 212 685-7455
New York *(G-8612)*
Argo Envelope Corp D 718 729-2700
Long Island City *(G-7164)*
Art Digital Technologies LLC F 646 649-4820
Brooklyn *(G-1535)*
Artscroll Printing Corp E 212 929-2413
New York *(G-8640)*
Asn Inc E 718 894-0800
Maspeth *(G-7593)*
Avm Printing Inc F 631 351-1331
Hauppauge *(G-5599)*
B D B Typewriter Supply Works E 718 232-4800
Brooklyn *(G-1557)*
Baum Christine and John Corp G 585 621-8910
Rochester *(G-13261)*
Beastons Budget Printing Inc G 585 244-2721
Rochester *(G-13264)*
Bennett Multimedia Inc F 718 629-1454
Brooklyn *(G-1575)*
Bernard Hall G 585 425-3340
Fairport *(G-4489)*
Billing Coding and Prtg Inc G 718 827-9409
Brooklyn *(G-1586)*
Bittner Company LLC F 585 214-1790
Rochester *(G-13270)*
Bk Printing Inc G 315 565-5396
East Syracuse *(G-4200)*
Bklynfavors Party Print G 718 277-0233
Brooklyn *(G-1590)*
Boka Printing Inc G 607 725-3235
Binghamton *(G-862)*
Bondy Printing Corp G 631 242-1510
Bay Shore *(G-659)*
Brodock Press Inc D 315 735-9577
Utica *(G-15242)*
Brooklyn Printers Inc G 718 511-7994
Brooklyn *(G-1619)*
Business Card Express Inc E 631 669-3400
West Babylon *(G-15698)*
C To C Design & Print Inc F 631 885-4020
Ronkonkoma *(G-13919)*
Canandaigua Msgnr Incorporated C 585 394-0770
Canandaigua *(G-3127)*
Carlara Group Ltd G 914 769-2020
Pleasantville *(G-12795)*
Castlereagh Printcraft Inc D 516 623-1728
Freeport *(G-4989)*
Catskill Delaware Publications F 845 887-5200
Callicoon *(G-3075)*
Cazar Printing & Advertising G 718 446-4606
Corona *(G-3735)*
Chromagraphics Press Inc G 631 367-6160
Melville *(G-7766)*
Circle Press Inc D 212 924-4277
New York *(G-9011)*
CK Printing Corp G 718 965-0388
Brooklyn *(G-1669)*
Classic Business Solutions G 212 563-9100
New York *(G-9023)*
Classic Color Graphics Inc G 516 822-9090
Hicksville *(G-5894)*
Cloud Printing G 212 775-0888
New York *(G-9036)*
Cobico Productions Inc G 347 417-5883
New York *(G-9045)*
Colad Group LLC D 716 961-1776
Buffalo *(G-2703)*
Color-Aid Corporation G 212 673-5500
Hudson Falls *(G-6184)*
Community Media LLC E 212 229-1890
New York *(G-9070)*
Community Newspaper Group LLC E 607 432-1000
Oneonta *(G-12267)*
Creative Juices Prtg Graphics F 631 249-2211
Deer Park *(G-3855)*
Cronin Enterprises Inc G 914 345-9600
Elmsford *(G-4405)*
Custom Prtrs Guilderland Inc F 518 456-2811
Guilderland *(G-5485)*
Daily Record F 585 232-2035
Rochester *(G-13336)*
Datorib Inc G 631 698-6222
Selden *(G-14352)*
Dawn Paper Co Inc F 516 596-9110
East Rockaway *(G-4172)*
Denton Publications Inc D 518 873-6368
Elizabethtown *(G-4299)*
Dependable Lithographers Inc F 718 472-4200
Long Island City *(G-7199)*
Design Distributors Inc D 631 242-2000
Deer Park *(G-3863)*
Designlogocom Inc G 212 564-0200
New York *(G-9208)*
Digital Color Concepts Inc E 212 989-4888
New York *(G-9226)*
Direct Print Inc G 212 987-6003
New York *(G-9232)*
Discover Casting Inc G 212 398-5050
New York *(G-9234)*
Diversified Envelope Ltd F 585 615-4697
Rochester *(G-13350)*
Donnelley Financial LLC D 212 351-9000
New York *(G-9252)*
Downright Printing Corp G 516 619-7200
Bellerose *(G-774)*
DPM of Western New York LLC D 716 775-8001
Grand Island *(G-5327)*
DPM of Western New York LLC D 716 684-3825
Cheektowaga *(G-3346)*
Dupli Graphics Corporation C 315 234-7286
Syracuse *(G-14877)*
Dyenamix Inc G 212 941-6642
New York *(G-9287)*
E B B Graphics Inc F 516 750-5510
Westbury *(G-15877)*
E W Smith Publishing Co Inc F 845 562-1218
New Windsor *(G-8366)*
East Coast Business Forms Inc G 631 231-9300
Saint James *(G-14110)*
East Coast Thermographers Inc E 718 321-3211
College Point *(G-3541)*
Eastwood Litho Impressions LLC F 315 437-2626
Syracuse *(G-14881)*
Efficiency Printing Co Inc F 914 949-8611
White Plains *(G-16000)*
Electronic Printing Inc G 631 218-2200
Hauppauge *(G-5646)*
Endeavor Printing LLC G 718 570-2720
Long Island City *(G-7214)*
Entermarket G 914 437-7268
Mount Kisco *(G-8092)*
Enterprise Press Inc C 212 741-2111
New York *(G-9382)*
Evenhouse Printing G 716 649-2666
Hamburg *(G-5508)*
Excellent Printing Inc G 718 384-7272
Brooklyn *(G-1821)*
Excelsus Solutions LLC E 585 533-0003
Rochester *(G-13405)*
F5 Networks Inc G 888 882-7535
New York *(G-9458)*
Figueroa Claribell G 718 772-8521
Bronx *(G-1256)*
Final Touch Printing Inc F 845 352-2677
Spring Valley *(G-14569)*
First Displays Inc F 347 642-5972
Long Island City *(G-7224)*
Flower City Printing Inc G 585 512-1235
Rochester *(G-13416)*
Flynns Inc E 212 339-8700
New York *(G-9512)*
Foleys Graphic Center Inc E 914 245-3625
Yorktown Heights *(G-16364)*
G F Labels LLC F 518 798-6643
Queensbury *(G-13039)*
Gannett Stllite Info Ntwrk LLC E 845 578-2300
West Nyack *(G-15821)*
Gatehouse Media LLC D 585 394-0770
Canandaigua *(G-3133)*
Gazette Press Inc E 914 963-8300
Rye *(G-14077)*
Global Graphics Inc F 718 939-4967
Flushing *(G-4854)*
Gotham T-Shirt Corp G 516 676-0900
Sea Cliff *(G-14345)*
Government Data Publication E 347 789-8719
Brooklyn *(G-1904)*
GPM Associates LLC E 585 335-3940
Dansville *(G-3819)*
Grafconect Corp G 212 714-1795
New York *(G-9655)*
Graphic Fabrications Inc G 516 763-3222
Rockville Centre *(G-13828)*
Graphic Lab Inc E 212 682-1815
New York *(G-9664)*
Graphicomm Inc G 716 283-0830
Niagara Falls *(G-11932)*
Green Girl Prtg & Msgnr Inc G 212 575-0357
New York *(G-9672)*
Hearst Corporation A 518 454-5694
Albany *(G-85)*
Holdens Screen Supply Corp G 212 627-2727
New York *(G-9802)*
Hooek Produktion Inc G 212 367-9111
New York *(G-9809)*
Horne Organization Inc F 914 572-1330
Yonkers *(G-16320)*
Huckleberry Inc G 631 630-5450
Hauppauge *(G-5673)*
Hugh F McPherson Inc G 716 668-6107
Cheektowaga *(G-3354)*
Image Sales & Marketing Inc G 516 238-7023
Massapequa Park *(G-7656)*
Ink Well G 718 253-9736
Brooklyn *(G-1959)*
Instant Again LLC E 585 436-8003
Rochester *(G-13479)*
Instant Stream Inc E 917 438-7182
New York *(G-9904)*
Insty-Prints of Buffalo Inc G 716 853-6483
Buffalo *(G-2812)*
J A T Printing Inc G 631 427-1155
Huntington *(G-6208)*
J F B & Sons Lithographers D 631 467-1444
Lake Ronkonkoma *(G-6771)*
J P Printing Inc G 516 293-6110
Farmingdale *(G-4655)*
J V Haring & Son F 718 720-1947
Staten Island *(G-14669)*
J3 Printing Inc G 516 304-6103
Queens Village *(G-13022)*
Jam Printing Publishing Inc G 914 345-8400
Elmsford *(G-4413)*
Japan Printing & Graphics Inc G 212 406-2905
New York *(G-9976)*
Jon Lyn Ink Inc G 516 546-2312
Merrick *(G-7857)*
Joseph Paul G 718 693-4269
Brooklyn *(G-2001)*
Kaleidoscope Imaging Inc E 212 631-9947
New York *(G-10058)*
Karr Graphics Corp E 212 645-6000
Long Island City *(G-7261)*
Key Brand Entertainment Inc C 212 966-5400
New York *(G-10095)*

Kim Jae Printing Co Inc ....G 212 691-6289
  Roslyn Heights *(G-14053)*

Kling Magnetics Inc ....E 518 392-4000
  Chatham *(G-3331)*

Kurtskraft Inc ....G 516 944-4449
  Port Washington *(G-12898)*

L & K Graphics Inc ....G 631 667-2269
  Deer Park *(G-3893)*

Label Gallery Inc ....E 607 334-3244
  Norwich *(G-12124)*

Lake Placid Advertisers Wkshp ....E 518 523-3359
  Lake Placid *(G-6767)*

Laser Printer Checks Corp ....G 845 782-5837
  Monroe *(G-8025)*

Lb Graph-X & Printing Inc ....G 212 246-2600
  Smithtown *(G-14482)*

Leigh Scott Enterprises Inc ....G 718 343-5440
  Bellerose *(G-775)*

LI Script LLC ....E 631 321-3850
  Woodbury *(G-16176)*

Liberty Label Mfg Inc ....F 631 737-2365
  Holbrook *(G-6006)*

Litmor Publishing Corp ....F 516 931-0012
  Garden City *(G-5105)*

Lmg National Publishing Inc ....E 585 598-6874
  Fairport *(G-4505)*

Logo Print Company ....G 607 324-5403
  Hornell *(G-6109)*

Loudon Ltd ....G 631 757-4447
  East Northport *(G-4149)*

Love Unlimited NY Inc ....E 718 359-8500
  Westbury *(G-15907)*

Magazines & Brochures Inc ....G 716 875-9699
  Buffalo *(G-2857)*

Marlow Printing Co Inc ....E 718 625-4948
  Brooklyn *(G-2117)*

Master Image Printing Inc ....G 914 347-4400
  Elmsford *(G-4416)*

McG Graphics Inc ....G 631 499-0730
  Dix Hills *(G-4012)*

Mdr Printing Corp ....G 516 627-3221
  Manhasset *(G-7538)*

Merrill New York Company Inc ....C 212 229-6500
  New York *(G-10438)*

Mickelberry Communications Inc ....G 212 832-0303
  New York *(G-10455)*

Minuteman Press Inc ....G 845 623-2277
  Nanuet *(G-8202)*

Minuteman Press Intl Inc ....E 631 249-1370
  Farmingdale *(G-4685)*

Minuteman Press Intl Inc ....G 718 343-5440
  Jamaica *(G-6461)*

Mod-Pac Corp ....D 716 447-9013
  Buffalo *(G-2870)*

Monarch Graphics Inc ....F 631 232-1300
  Central Islip *(G-3284)*

Moneast Inc ....G 845 298-8898
  Wappingers Falls *(G-15498)*

Multiple Imprssons of Rchester ....G 585 546-1160
  Rochester *(G-13563)*

Mutual Engraving Company Inc ....D 516 489-0534
  West Hempstead *(G-15777)*

Nameplate Mfrs of Amer ....E 631 752-0055
  Farmingdale *(G-4690)*

Nasco Printing Corporation ....G 212 229-2462
  New York *(G-10534)*

Nash Printing Inc ....F 516 935-4567
  Plainview *(G-12704)*

NCR Corporation ....C 607 273-5310
  Ithaca *(G-6400)*

New Goldstar 1 Printing Corp ....G 212 343-3909
  New York *(G-10583)*

Northern NY Newspapers Corp ....C 315 782-1000
  Watertown *(G-15586)*

Observer Daily Sunday Newsppr ....D 716 366-3000
  Dunkirk *(G-4062)*

Office Grabs NY Inc ....G 212 444-1331
  Brooklyn *(G-2229)*

Orlandi Inc ....D 631 756-0110
  Farmingdale *(G-4698)*

Orlandi Inc ....E 631 756-0110
  Farmingdale *(G-4699)*

P D R Inc ....G 516 829-5300
  Plainview *(G-12706)*

Pace Editions Inc ....G 212 643-6353
  New York *(G-10736)*

Paladino Prtg & Graphics Inc ....G 718 279-6000
  Flushing *(G-4883)*

Pama Enterprises Inc ....G 516 504-6300
  Great Neck *(G-5411)*

Parkside Printing Co Inc ....F 516 933-5423
  Jericho *(G-6588)*

Paya Printing of NY Inc ....G 516 625-8346
  Albertson *(G-149)*

Phillip Tissicher ....F 718 282-3310
  Brooklyn *(G-2255)*

Photo Agents Ltd ....G 631 421-0258
  Huntington *(G-6217)*

Positive Promotions Inc ....C 631 648-1200
  Hauppauge *(G-5745)*

Pre Cycled Inc ....G 845 278-7611
  Brewster *(G-1158)*

Presstek Printing LLC ....F 585 266-2770
  Rochester *(G-13643)*

Pricet Printing ....G 315 655-0369
  Cazenovia *(G-3234)*

Print Better Inc ....G 347 348-1841
  Ridgewood *(G-13156)*

Print Center Inc ....G 718 643-9559
  Cold Spring Harbor *(G-3529)*

Print Cottage LLC ....F 516 369-1749
  Massapequa Park *(G-7660)*

Print House Inc ....D 718 443-7500
  Brooklyn *(G-2288)*

Print It Here ....G 516 308-7785
  Massapequa *(G-7648)*

Print It Inc ....G 845 371-2227
  Monsey *(G-8044)*

Print Management Group Inc ....G 212 213-1555
  New York *(G-10895)*

Print Market Inc ....G 631 940-8181
  Deer Park *(G-3922)*

Print On Demand Initiative Inc ....F 585 239-6044
  Rochester *(G-13644)*

Print Seforim Bzul Inc ....G 718 679-1011
  Brooklyn *(G-2290)*

Print Tech Inc ....E 585 202-3888
  Webster *(G-15648)*

Printech Business Systems Inc ....F 212 290-2542
  New York *(G-10897)*

Printed Image ....G 716 821-1880
  Buffalo *(G-2932)*

Printing Prep Inc ....E 716 852-5011
  Buffalo *(G-2933)*

Printing Prmtnal Solutions LLC ....F 315 474-1110
  Syracuse *(G-14967)*

Printing Resources Inc ....E 518 482-2470
  Albany *(G-119)*

Printz and Patternz LLC ....E 518 944-6020
  Schenectady *(G-14296)*

Professional Solutions Print ....G 631 231-9300
  West Islip *(G-15812)*

Psychonomic Society Inc ....E 512 381-1494
  New York *(G-10919)*

Publimax Printing Corp ....G 718 366-7133
  Ridgewood *(G-13157)*

Rapid Service Engraving Co ....G 716 896-4555
  Buffalo *(G-2948)*

Richard Ruffner ....F 631 234-4600
  Central Islip *(G-3287)*

Richmar Printing Inc ....G 631 617-6915
  Bay Shore *(G-706)*

Rmf Printing Technologies Inc ....E 716 683-7500
  Lancaster *(G-6830)*

Rosen Mandell & Immerman Inc ....E 212 691-2277
  New York *(G-11083)*

Rv Printing ....G 631 567-8658
  Holbrook *(G-6019)*

Sample News Group LLC ....D 315 343-3800
  Oswego *(G-14420)*

Seaboard Graphic Services LLC ....E 315 652-4200
  East Syracuse *(G-4237)*

Sentine Printing Inc ....E 516 334-7400
  Westbury *(G-15925)*

Sign Shop Inc ....G 631 226-4145
  Copiague *(G-3678)*

Sign World Inc ....E 212 619-9000
  Brooklyn *(G-2410)*

Sloane Design Inc ....G 212 539-0184
  Brooklyn *(G-2429)*

Source Envelope Inc ....G 866 284-0707
  Farmingdale *(G-4735)*

Sputnick 84 LLC ....G 844 667-7468
  New York *(G-11340)*

St James Printing Inc ....G 631 981-2095
  Ronkonkoma *(G-14014)*

St Lawrence County Newspapers ....D 315 393-1003
  Canton *(G-3167)*

Steffen Publishing Inc ....D 315 865-4100
  Holland Patent *(G-6034)*

Sterling Pierce Company Inc ....E 516 593-1170
  East Rockaway *(G-4174)*

Stony Brook University ....E 631 632-6434
  Stony Brook *(G-14741)*

Studio 22 Print ....G 212 679-2656
  New York *(G-11377)*

Sun Printing Incorporated ....E 607 337-3034
  Norwich *(G-12128)*

Syracuse Computer Forms Inc ....E 315 478-0108
  Syracuse *(G-15005)*

Taylor Communications Inc ....G 718 361-1000
  Long Island City *(G-7378)*

Technipoly Manufacturing Inc ....E 718 383-0363
  Brooklyn *(G-2496)*

Teller Printing Corp ....G 718 486-3662
  Brooklyn *(G-2499)*

Thomson Press (india) Limited ....G 646 318-0369
  Long Island City *(G-7382)*

Tobay Printing Co Inc ....E 631 842-3300
  Copiague *(G-3684)*

Torsaf Printers Inc ....G 516 569-5577
  Hewlett *(G-5873)*

Transaction Printer Group ....G 607 274-2500
  Ithaca *(G-6415)*

Transcntinental Ultra Flex Inc ....B 718 272-9100
  Brooklyn *(G-2516)*

Transcontinental Printing GP ....G 716 626-3078
  Amherst *(G-249)*

Tripi Engraving Co Inc ....G 718 383-6500
  Brooklyn *(G-2522)*

Troy Sign & Printing ....G 718 994-4482
  Bronx *(G-1382)*

Vicks Lithograph & Prtg Corp ....G 315 736-9344
  Yorkville *(G-16381)*

Vicks Lithograph & Prtg Corp ....C 315 272-2401
  Yorkville *(G-16380)*

VIP Printing ....G 718 641-9361
  Howard Beach *(G-6142)*

Virgil Mountain Inc ....G 212 378-0007
  New York *(G-11686)*

Wallkill Valley Publications ....E 845 561-0170
  Newburgh *(G-11893)*

Wappingers Falls Shopper Inc ....E 845 297-3723
  Wappingers Falls *(G-15501)*

Waterhouse Publications Inc ....E 716 662-4200
  Orchard Park *(G-12383)*

Webster Printing Corporation ....F 585 671-1533
  Webster *(G-15662)*

Westmore Litho Corp ....G 718 361-9403
  Long Island City *(G-7400)*

Whitestone Dev Group LLC ....G 585 482-7770
  Rochester *(G-13804)*

William Boyd Printing Co Inc ....C 518 339-5832
  Latham *(G-6881)*

William J Kline & Son Inc ....D 518 843-1100
  Amsterdam *(G-354)*

Won & Lee Inc ....E 516 222-0712
  Garden City *(G-5119)*

Wynco Press One Inc ....G 516 354-6145
  Glen Oaks *(G-5215)*

X Myles Mar Inc ....E 212 683-2015
  New York *(G-11795)*

X-L Envelope and Printing Inc ....F 716 852-2135
  Buffalo *(G-3051)*

Zenger Group Inc ....E 716 871-1058
  Tonawanda *(G-15156)*

PRINTING: Offset

514 Adams Corporation ....G 516 352-6948
  Deer Park *(G-3825)*

6727 11th Ave Corp ....F 718 837-8787
  Brooklyn *(G-1421)*

A & M Litho Inc ....E 516 342-9727
  Bethpage *(G-829)*

A Esteban & Company Inc ....E 212 989-7000
  New York *(G-8414)*

A Q P Inc ....G 585 256-1690
  Rochester *(G-13194)*

Accuprint ....G 518 456-2431
  Albany *(G-27)*

Act Communications Group Inc ....F 631 669-2403
  West Islip *(G-15809)*

Ad-Vantage Printing Inc ....F 718 820-0688
  Kew Gardens *(G-6661)*

Ads-N-Color Inc ....E 718 797-0900
  Brooklyn *(G-1463)*

Advanced Printing New York Inc ....G 212 840-8108
  New York *(G-8481)*

Advantage Quick Print Inc ....G 212 989-5644
  New York *(G-8483)*

Advertising Lithographers	F	212 966-7771	
Long Island City *(G-7146)*			
Agrecolor Inc	F	516 741-8700	
Mineola *(G-7957)*			
Ahw Printing Corp	F	516 536-3600	
Oceanside *(G-12165)*			
Alamar Printing Inc	F	914 993-9007	
White Plains *(G-15969)*			
Albany Letter Shop Inc	G	518 434-1172	
Albany *(G-32)*			
All Time Products Inc	G	718 464-1400	
Queens Village *(G-13016)*			
All-Color Offset Printers Inc	G	516 420-0649	
Deer Park *(G-3834)*			
Allen William & Company Inc	C	212 675-6461	
Glendale *(G-5218)*			
Allied Reproductions Inc	E	212 255-2472	
New York *(G-8518)*			
Allstatebannerscom Corporation	G	718 300-1256	
Long Island City *(G-7150)*			
Alpha Printing Corp	F	315 454-5507	
Syracuse *(G-14812)*			
Alpina Color Graphics Inc	G	212 285-2700	
New York *(G-8528)*			
Always Printing	G	914 481-5209	
Port Chester *(G-12814)*			
American Print Solutions Inc	G	718 246-7800	
Brooklyn *(G-1501)*			
Amsterdam Printing & Litho Inc	F	518 792-6501	
Queensbury *(G-13030)*			
Apple Press	G	914 723-6660	
White Plains *(G-15975)*			
Ares Printing and Packg Corp	C	718 858-8760	
Brooklyn *(G-1527)*			
Argo Lithographers Inc	E	718 729-2700	
Long Island City *(G-7166)*			
Arista Innovations Inc	E	516 746-2262	
Mineola *(G-7959)*			
Arnold Printing Corp	F	607 272-7800	
Ithaca *(G-6363)*			
Arnold Taylor Printing Inc	G	516 781-0564	
Bellmore *(G-779)*			
Art Scroll Printing Corp	F	212 929-2413	
New York *(G-8631)*			
At Copy Inc	G	718 624-6136	
Brooklyn *(G-1543)*			
Atlantic Color Corp	E	631 345-3800	
Shirley *(G-14414)*			
Atlas Print Solutions Inc	E	212 949-8775	
New York *(G-8671)*			
B & P Jays Inc	G	716 668-8408	
Buffalo *(G-2654)*			
B Q P Inc	G	518 793-4999	
Queensbury *(G-13034)*			
Ballantrae Lithographers Inc	G	914 592-3275	
White Plains *(G-15979)*			
Barone Offset Printing Corp	G	212 989-5500	
Mohegan Lake *(G-8008)*			
Bartolomeo Publishing Inc	G	631 420-4949	
West Babylon *(G-15693)*			
Bates Jackson Engraving Co Inc	E	716 854-3000	
Buffalo *(G-2657)*			
Beacon Press Inc	G	212 691-5050	
White Plains *(G-15980)*			
Beehive Press Inc	G	718 654-1200	
Bronx *(G-1211)*			
Bel Aire Offset Corp	G	718 539-8333	
College Point *(G-3537)*			
Benchmark Printing Inc	D	518 393-1361	
Schenectady *(G-14249)*			
Benchmark Graphics Ltd	F	212 683-1711	
New York *(G-8756)*			
Beyer Graphics Inc	D	631 543-3900	
Commack *(G-3579)*			
Bishop Print Shop Inc	G	607 965-8155	
Edmeston *(G-4294)*			
Bluesoho	F	646 805-2583	
New York *(G-8822)*			
Bmg Printing and Promotion LLC	G	631 231-9200	
Bohemia *(G-982)*			
Boncraft Inc	D	716 662-9720	
Tonawanda *(G-15091)*			
Boulevard Printing	G	716 837-3800	
Tonawanda *(G-15092)*			
Boxcar Press Incorporated	E	315 473-0930	
Syracuse *(G-14833)*			
BP Beyond Printing Inc	G	516 328-2700	
Hempstead *(G-5834)*			
Brennans Quick Print Inc	G	518 793-4999	
Glens Falls *(G-5243)*			
Bridge Printing Inc	G	212 243-5390	
Long Island City *(G-7181)*			
Brigar X-Press Solutions Inc	D	518 438-7817	
Albany *(G-52)*			
Brooks Litho Digital Group Inc	G	631 789-4500	
Deer Park *(G-3850)*			
C & R De Santis Inc	E	718 447-5076	
Staten Island *(G-14633)*			
Cabba Printing Incorporated	E	212 319-4747	
New York *(G-8883)*			
Caboodle Printing Inc	G	716 693-6000	
Williamsville *(G-16125)*			
Canaan Printing Inc	E	718 729-3100	
Bayside *(G-736)*			
Canastota Publishing Co Inc	G	315 697-9010	
Canastota *(G-3151)*			
Candid Litho Printing Ltd	D	212 431-3800	
Farmingdale *(G-4596)*			
Canfield & Tack Inc	D	585 235-7710	
Rochester *(G-13293)*			
Capital Dst Print & Imaging	E	518 456-6773	
Schenectady *(G-14251)*			
Carges Entps of Canandaigua	G	585 394-2600	
Canandaigua *(G-3128)*			
Carnels Printing Inc	G	516 883-3355	
Great Neck *(G-5374)*			
Carr Communications Group LLC	F	607 748-0481	
Vestal *(G-15375)*			
Cathedral Corporation	C	315 338-0021	
Rome *(G-13846)*			
Cayuga Press Cortland Inc	G	888 229-8421	
Liverpool *(G-7007)*			
Cedar Graphics Inc	D	631 467-1444	
Ronkonkoma *(G-13923)*			
Cedar West Inc	D	631 467-1444	
Ronkonkoma *(G-13924)*			
Chakra Communications Inc	E	607 748-7491	
Endicott *(G-4446)*			
Chenango Union Printing Inc	G	607 334-2112	
Norwich *(G-12116)*			
Cherry Lane Lithographing Corp	E	516 293-9294	
Plainview *(G-12668)*			
CHv Printed Company	F	516 997-1101	
East Meadow *(G-4132)*			
Cilyox Inc	F	716 853-3809	
Buffalo *(G-2697)*			
Clarsons Corp	F	585 235-8775	
Rochester *(G-13317)*			
Classic Color Graphics Inc	G	516 822-9090	
Hicksville *(G-5893)*			
Cody Printing Corp	G	718 651-8854	
Woodside *(G-16202)*			
Coe Displays Inc	G	718 937-5658	
Long Island City *(G-7189)*			
Cohber Press Inc	D	585 475-9100	
West Henrietta *(G-15789)*			
Color Carton Corp	D	718 665-0840	
Bronx *(G-1228)*			
Colorfast	F	212 929-2440	
New York *(G-9056)*			
Colorfully Yours Inc	F	631 242-8600	
Bay Shore *(G-666)*			
Combine Graphics Corp	G	212 695-4044	
Forest Hills *(G-4918)*			
Commerce Offset Ltd	G	914 769-6671	
Thornwood *(G-15068)*			
Commercial Press Inc	G	315 274-0028	
Canton *(G-3164)*			
Commercial Print & Imaging	E	716 597-0100	
Buffalo *(G-2705)*			
Compass Printing Plus	G	518 523-3308	
Saranac Lake *(G-14157)*			
Complemar Print LLC	F	716 875-7238	
Buffalo *(G-2707)*			
Composite Forms Inc	G	914 937-1808	
Port Chester *(G-12815)*			
Compucolor Associates Inc	E	516 358-0000	
New Hyde Park *(G-8258)*			
Concept Printing Inc	G	845 353-4040	
Nyack *(G-12139)*			
Consolidated Color Press Inc	F	212 929-8197	
New York *(G-9086)*			
Constas Printing Corporation	G	315 474-2176	
Syracuse *(G-14859)*			
Copy Stop Inc	G	914 428-5188	
White Plains *(G-15996)*			
Coral Color Process Ltd	E	631 543-5200	
Commack *(G-3585)*			
Coral Graphic Services Inc	C	516 576-2100	
Hicksville *(G-5897)*			
Cosmos Communications Inc	C	718 482-1800	
Long Island City *(G-7193)*			
Courier Printing Corp	E	607 467-2191	
Deposit *(G-3999)*			
Craig Envelope Corp	E	718 786-4277	
Hicksville *(G-5898)*			
Crater Service Group Inc	G	585 482-7770	
Rochester *(G-13328)*			
Creative Forms Inc	G	212 431-7540	
New York *(G-9119)*			
Creative Printing Corp	G	212 226-3870	
New York *(G-9120)*			
D W S Associates Inc	E	631 667-6666	
Deer Park *(G-3858)*			
Dan Trent Company Inc	G	716 822-1422	
Buffalo *(G-2720)*			
Dark Star Lithograph Corp	G	845 634-3780	
New City *(G-8224)*			
Deanco Digital Printing LLC	E	212 371-2025	
Sunnyside *(G-14771)*			
Dell Communications Inc	G	212 989-3434	
New York *(G-9198)*			
Delta Press Inc	G	212 989-3445	
High Falls *(G-5955)*			
Design Lithographers Inc	F	212 645-8900	
New York *(G-9206)*			
Dick Bailey Service Inc	E	718 522-4363	
Brooklyn *(G-1742)*			
Digital United Color Prtg Inc	G	845 986-9846	
Warwick *(G-15512)*			
Dispatch Graphics Inc	E	212 307-5943	
New York *(G-9236)*			
Distinctive Printing Inc	G	212 727-3000	
New York *(G-9239)*			
Doco Quick Print Inc	G	315 782-6623	
Watertown *(G-15569)*			
Donmar Printing Co	F	516 280-2239	
Mineola *(G-7969)*			
Dowd - Witbeck Printing Corp	F	518 274-2421	
Troy *(G-15166)*			
DP Murphy Co Inc	D	631 673-9400	
Deer Park *(G-3865)*			
Dupli Graphics Corporation	G	315 422-4732	
Syracuse *(G-14878)*			
Eagle Graphics Inc	G	585 244-5006	
Rochester *(G-13361)*			
Earth Enterprises Inc	E	212 741-3999	
New York *(G-9301)*			
East Ridge Quick Print	F	585 266-4911	
Rochester *(G-13364)*			
Eastern Hills Printing	G	716 741-3300	
Clarence *(G-3431)*			
Echo Appellate Press Inc	G	516 432-3601	
Long Beach *(G-7136)*			
Edwards Graphic Co Inc	G	718 548-6858	
Bronx *(G-1252)*			
Empire Press Co	G	718 756-9500	
Brooklyn *(G-1801)*			
Engrav-O-Type Press Inc	F	585 262-7590	
Rochester *(G-13393)*			
Excel Graphics Services Inc	F	212 929-2183	
New York *(G-9441)*			
Excellent Photo Copies	G	718 384-7272	
Brooklyn *(G-1819)*			
Excelsior Graphics Inc	G	212 730-6200	
New York *(G-9444)*			
F & B Photo Offset Co Inc	G	516 431-5433	
Island Park *(G-6317)*			
F J Remey Co Inc	E	516 741-5112	
Mineola *(G-7974)*			
Fambus Inc	G	607 785-3700	
Endicott *(G-4455)*			
Fasprint	G	518 483-4631	
Malone *(G-7485)*			
Federal Envelope Inc	F	212 243-8380	
New York *(G-9480)*			
Finer Touch Printing Corp	F	516 944-8000	
Port Washington *(G-12879)*			
First Line Printing Inc	F	718 606-0860	
Woodside *(G-16207)*			
Five Star Prtg & Mailing Svcs	F	212 929-0300	
New York *(G-9508)*			
Flare Multicopy Corp	E	718 258-8860	
Brooklyn *(G-1849)*			
Flower City Printing Inc	C	585 663-9000	
Rochester *(G-13415)*			
Flp Group LLC	F	315 252-7583	
Auburn *(G-476)*			
Folder Factory Inc	F	540 477-3852	
Melville *(G-7783)*			

PRODUCT

Fort Orange Press Inc ......E 518 489-3233	Jacobs Press Inc ......F 315 252-4861	Mercury Print Productions Inc......C 585 458-7900
Albany **(G-78)**	Auburn **(G-481)**	Rochester **(G-13542)**
Forward Enterprises Inc ......F 585 235-7670	James Conolly Printing Co ......E 585 426-4150	Michael K Lennon Inc ......E 631 288-5200
Rochester **(G-13421)**	Rochester **(G-13488)**	Westhampton Beach **(G-15957)**
Francis Emory Fitch Inc ......E 212 619-3800	Jane Lewis ......G 607 722-0584	Microera Printers Inc......E 585 783-1300
New York **(G-9529)**	Binghamton **(G-890)**	Rochester **(G-13547)**
Frederick Coon Inc ......E 716 683-6812	JDS Graphics Inc ......F 973 330-3300	Mid Atlantic Graphics Corp ......E 631 345-3800
Elma **(G-4318)**	New York **(G-9989)**	Shirley **(G-14424)**
Freeville Publishing Co Inc ......F 607 844-9119	Johnnys Ideal Printing Co ......G 518 828-6666	Mid-York Press Inc ......D 607 674-4491
Freeville **(G-5033)**	Hudson **(G-6166)**	Sherburne **(G-14392)**
Fulton Newspapers Inc ......E 315 598-6397	Judith Lewis Printer Inc ......G 516 997-7777	Middletown Press ......G 845 343-1895
Fulton **(G-5059)**	Westbury **(G-15900)**	Middletown **(G-7920)**
G & P Printing Inc ......G 212 274-8092	Jurist Company Inc ......G 212 243-8008	Midgley Printing Corp ......G 315 475-1864
New York **(G-9557)**	Long Island City **(G-7257)**	Syracuse **(G-14942)**
G W Canfield & Son Inc ......G 315 735-5522	Just Press Print LLC ......G 585 783-1300	Midstate Printing Corp ......E 315 475-4101
Utica **(G-15265)**	Rochester **(G-13500)**	Liverpool **(G-7026)**
Gallagher Printing Inc ......E 716 873-2434	Kas-Ray Industries Inc ......F 212 620-3144	Mikam Graphics LLC ......D 212 684-9393
Buffalo **(G-2764)**	New York **(G-10071)**	New York **(G-10464)**
Gallant Graphics Ltd ......E 845 868-1166	Kaufman Brothers Printing ......G 212 563-1854	Miller Printing & Litho Inc ......G 518 842-0001
Stanfordville **(G-14610)**	New York **(G-10079)**	Amsterdam **(G-336)**
Gateway Prtg & Graphics Inc ......E 716 823-3873	Keeners East End Litho Inc ......G 631 324-8565	Mines Press Inc ......C 888 559-2634
Hamburg **(G-5509)**	East Hampton **(G-4124)**	Cortlandt Manor **(G-3797)**
Gem Reproduction Services Corp ......G 845 298-0172	Keller Bros & Miller Inc ......E 716 854-2374	Mitchell Prtg & Mailing Inc ......F 315 343-3531
Wappingers Falls **(G-15494)**	Buffalo **(G-2831)**	Oswego **(G-12414)**
General Business Supply Inc ......D 518 720-3939	Kent Associates Inc ......G., ... 212 675-0722	MJB Printing Corp ......G 631 581-0177
Watervliet **(G-15602)**	New York **(G-10093)**	Islip **(G-6355)**
Geneva Printing Company Inc ......G 315 789-8191	Kenyon Press Inc ......G 607 674-9066	Monte Press Inc ......G 718 325-4999
Geneva **(G-5156)**	Sherburne **(G-14391)**	Bronx **(G-1319)**
Glens Falls Printing LLC ......F 518 793-0555	Kinaneco Inc ......G 315 468-6201	Moore Printing Company Inc ......G 585 394-1533
Glens Falls **(G-5251)**	Syracuse **(G-14926)**	Canandaigua **(G-3136)**
Gn Printing ......E 718 784-1713	Kingsbury Printing Co Inc ......G 518 747-6606	Multimedia Services Inc ......E 607 936-3186
Long Island City **(G-7231)**	Queensbury **(G-13046)**	Corning **(G-3718)**
Golos Printing Inc ......G 607 732-1896	L I F Publishing Corp ......D 631 345-5200	Nesher Printing Inc ......G 212 760-2521
Elmira Heights **(G-4377)**	Shirley **(G-14423)**	New York **(G-10566)**
Gooding Co Inc ......E 716 266-6252	L K Printing Corp ......G 914 761-1944	New Horizon Graphics Inc ......E 631 231-8055
Lockport **(G-7082)**	White Plains **(G-16023)**	Hauppauge **(G-5727)**
Grand Meridian Printing Inc ......E 718 937-3888	L M N Printing Company Inc ......E 516 285-8526	New York Digital Print Ctr Inc ......E 718 767-1953
Maspeth **(G-7619)**	Valley Stream **(G-15345)**	Whitestone **(G-16098)**
Grand Prix Litho Inc ......E 631 242-4182	Lake View Graphics Inc ......G 607 687-7033	New York Typing & Printing Co ......G 718 268-7900
Hauppauge **(G-5663)**	Owego **(G-12432)**	Forest Hills **(G-4925)**
Graphics Plus Printing Inc ......E 607 299-0500	Lee Printing Inc ......G 718 237-1651	Newburgh Envelope Corp ......G 845 566-4211
Cortland **(G-3769)**	Brooklyn **(G-2057)**	Newburgh **(G-11877)**
Great Eastern Color Lith ......C 845 454-7420	Lehmann Printing Company Inc ......G 212 929-2395	Newport Graphics Inc ......E 212 924-2600
Poughkeepsie **(G-12959)**	New York **(G-10193)**	New York **(G-10610)**
Grover Cleveland Press Inc ......F 716 564-2222	Lennons Litho Inc ......F 315 866-3156	North Delaware Printing Inc ......G 716 692-0576
Amherst **(G-226)**	Herkimer **(G-5866)**	Tonawanda **(G-15128)**
Guaranteed Printing Svc Co Inc ......E 212 929-2410	Leonardo Printing Corp ......G 914 664-7890	Northeast Commercial Prtg Inc ......E 518 459-5047
Long Island City **(G-7236)**	Mount Vernon **(G-8157)**	Albany **(G-107)**
H T L & S Ltd ......F 718 435-4474	Levon Graphics Corp ......D 631 753-2022	Northeast Prtg & Dist Co Inc ......E 518 563-8214
Brooklyn **(G-1916)**	Deer Park **(G-3897)**	Plattsburgh **(G-12765)**
H&E Service Corp ......D 646 472-1936	Litho Dynamics Inc ......G 914 769-1759	Official Offset Corporation ......E 631 957-8500
Garden City **(G-5101)**	Hawthorne **(G-5817)**	Amityville **(G-299)**
Haig Press Inc ......E 631 582-5800	Lithomatic Business Forms Inc......G 212 255-6700	Orbis Brynmore Lithographics ......G 212 987-2100
Hauppauge **(G-5665)**	New York **(G-10227)**	New York **(G-10703)**
Harmon and Castella Printing ......F 845 471-9163	Louis Heindl & Son Inc ......G 585 454-5080	Orffeo Printing & Imaging Inc ......E 716 681-5757
Hyde Park **(G-6271)**	Rochester **(G-13523)**	Lancaster **(G-6819)**
Hempstead Sentinel Inc ......F 516 486-5000	Loy L Press Inc ......G 716 634-5966	Ozipko Enterprises Inc ......G 585 424-6740
Hempstead **(G-5838)**	Buffalo **(G-2853)**	Rochester **(G-13602)**
Heritage Printing Center ......E 518 563-8240	Lynmar Printing Corp ......G 631 957-8500	P & W Press Inc ......E 646 486-3417
Plattsburgh **(G-12751)**	Amityville **(G-292)**	New York **(G-10732)**
HI Speed Envelope Co Inc ......F 718 617-1600	M L Design Inc ......G 212 233-0213	Panther Graphics Inc ......E 585 546-7163
Mount Vernon **(G-8148)**	New York **(G-10298)**	Rochester **(G-13608)**
High End Print Solutions Inc ......F 585 325-5320	M T M Printing Co Inc ......F 718 353-3297	Park Slope Copy Center ......F 718 783-0268
Rochester **(G-13465)**	College Point **(G-3552)**	Brooklyn **(G-2249)**
Hillside Printing Inc ......F 718 658-6719	M&M Printing Inc ......F 516 796-3020	Parrinello Printing Inc ......F 716 633-7780
Jamaica **(G-6448)**	Carle Place **(G-3177)**	Buffalo **(G-2908)**
Hospitality Graphics Inc ......G 212 643-6700	Madison Printing Corp ......G 607 273-3535	Patrick Ryans Modern Press ......F 518 434-2921
New York **(G-9816)**	Ithaca **(G-6394)**	Albany **(G-112)**
Hudson Envelope Corporation ......E 212 473-6666	Mahin Impressions Inc ......G 212 871-9777	Paul Michael Group Inc ......G 631 585-5700
New York **(G-9831)**	Riverhead **(G-13182)**	Ronkonkoma **(G-13993)**
Hudson Printing Co Inc ......E 718 937-8600	Malone Industrial Press Inc ......G 518 483-5880	PBR Graphics Inc ......G 518 458-2909
New York **(G-9834)**	Malone **(G-7488)**	Albany **(G-113)**
I 2 Print Inc ......F 718 937-8800	Manifestation-Glow Press Inc ......G 718 380-5259	Peachtree Enterprises Inc ......E 212 989-3445
Long Island City **(G-7245)**	Jamaica **(G-6457)**	Long Island City **(G-7322)**
Impala Press Ltd ......G 631 588-4262	Marcal Printing Inc ......F 516 942-9500	Persch Service Print Inc ......G 716 366-2677
Ronkonkoma **(G-13947)**	Hicksville **(G-5925)**	Dunkirk **(G-4063)**
In-House Inc ......F 718 445-9007	Marcy Printing Inc ......F 718 935-9100	Petit Printing Corp ......G 716 871-9490
College Point **(G-3544)**	Brooklyn **(G-2114)**	Getzville **(G-5181)**
Ink-It Printing Inc ......G 718 229-5590	Mark T Westinghouse ......G 518 678-3262	Phoenix Graphics Inc ......E 585 232-4040
College Point **(G-3545)**	Catskill **(G-3214)**	Rochester **(G-13621)**
Inland Printing Company Inc ......E 516 367-4700	Marsid Group Ltd ......G 516 334-1603	Pic A Poc Enterprises Inc ......G 631 981-2094
Woodbury **(G-16174)**	Carle Place **(G-3179)**	Ronkonkoma **(G-13995)**
International Newsppr Prtg Co ......E 516 626-6095	Master Printing USA Inc ......F 718 456-0962	Pine Bush Printing Co Inc ......G 518 456-2431
Glen Head **(G-5208)**	Island Park **(G-6319)**	Albany **(G-116)**
Iver Printing Inc ......G 718 275-2070	Mc Squared Nyc Inc ......F 212 947-2260	Pioneer Printers Inc ......F 716 693-7100
New Hyde Park **(G-8276)**	New York **(G-10395)**	North Tonawanda **(G-12082)**
J & J Printing Inc ......F 315 458-7411	McPc Inc ......G 212 583-6000	PIP Inc ......G 518 861-0133
Syracuse **(G-14914)**	New York **(G-10403)**	Latham **(G-6873)**
Jack J Florio Jr ......G 716 434-9123	Medallion Associates Inc ......E 212 929-9130	Pixos Print ......G 585 500-4600
Lockport **(G-7085)**	New York **(G-10408)**	Rochester **(G-13625)**

Advertising Lithographers	F	212 966-7771	
Long Island City *(G-7146)*			
Agrecolor Inc	F	516 741-8700	
Mineola *(G-7957)*			
Ahw Printing Corp	F	516 536-3600	
Oceanside *(G-12165)*			
Alamar Printing Inc	F	914 993-9007	
White Plains *(G-15969)*			
Albany Letter Shop Inc	G	518 434-1172	
Albany *(G-32)*			
All Time Products Inc	G	718 464-1400	
Queens Village *(G-13016)*			
All-Color Offset Printers Inc	G	516 420-0649	
Deer Park *(G-3834)*			
Allen William & Company Inc	C	212 675-6461	
Glendale *(G-5218)*			
Allied Reproductions Inc	E	212 255-2472	
New York *(G-8518)*			
Allstatebannerscom Corporation	G	718 300-1256	
Long Island City *(G-7150)*			
Alpha Printing Corp	F	315 454-5507	
Syracuse *(G-14812)*			
Alpina Color Graphics Inc	G	212 285-2700	
New York *(G-8528)*			
Always Printing	G	914 481-5209	
Port Chester *(G-12814)*			
American Print Solutions Inc	G	718 246-7800	
Brooklyn *(G-1501)*			
Amsterdam Printing & Litho Inc	F	518 792-6501	
Queensbury *(G-13030)*			
Apple Press	G	914 723-6660	
White Plains *(G-15975)*			
Ares Printing and Packg Corp	C	718 858-8760	
Brooklyn *(G-1527)*			
Argo Lithographers Inc	E	718 729-2700	
Long Island City *(G-7166)*			
Arista Innovations Inc	E	516 746-2262	
Mineola *(G-7959)*			
Arnold Printing Corp	F	607 272-7800	
Ithaca *(G-6363)*			
Arnold Taylor Printing Inc	G	516 781-0564	
Bellmore *(G-779)*			
Art Scroll Printing Corp	F	212 929-2413	
New York *(G-8631)*			
At Copy Inc	G	718 624-6136	
Brooklyn *(G-1543)*			
Atlantic Color Corp	E	631 345-3800	
Shirley *(G-14414)*			
Atlas Print Solutions Inc	E	212 949-8775	
New York *(G-8671)*			
B & P Jays Inc	G	716 668-8408	
Buffalo *(G-2654)*			
B Q P Inc	G	518 793-4999	
Queensbury *(G-13034)*			
Ballantrae Lithographers Inc	G	914 592-3275	
White Plains *(G-15979)*			
Barone Offset Printing Corp	G	212 989-5500	
Mohegan Lake *(G-8008)*			
Bartolomeo Publishing Inc	G	631 420-4949	
West Babylon *(G-15693)*			
Bates Jackson Engraving Co Inc	E	716 854-3000	
Buffalo *(G-2657)*			
Beacon Press Inc	G	212 691-5050	
White Plains *(G-15980)*			
Beehive Press Inc	G	718 654-1200	
Bronx *(G-1211)*			
Bel Aire Offset Corp	G	718 539-8333	
College Point *(G-3537)*			
Benchemark Printing Inc	D	518 393-1361	
Schenectady *(G-14249)*			
Benchmark Graphics Ltd	F	212 683-1711	
New York *(G-8756)*			
Beyer Graphics Inc	D	631 543-3900	
Commack *(G-3579)*			
Bishop Print Shop Inc	G	607 965-8155	
Edmeston *(G-4294)*			
Bluesoho	F	646 805-2583	
New York *(G-8822)*			
Bmg Printing and Promotion LLC	G	631 231-9200	
Bohemia *(G-982)*			
Boncraft Inc	D	716 662-9720	
Tonawanda *(G-15091)*			
Boulevard Printing	G	716 837-3800	
Tonawanda *(G-15092)*			
Boxcar Press Incorporated	E	315 473-0930	
Syracuse *(G-14833)*			
BP Beyond Printing Inc	G	516 328-2700	
Hempstead *(G-5834)*			
Brennans Quick Print Inc	G	518 793-4999	
Glens Falls *(G-5243)*			
Bridge Printing Inc	G	212 243-5390	
Long Island City *(G-7181)*			
Brigar X-Press Solutions Inc	D	518 438-7817	
Albany *(G-52)*			
Brooks Litho Digital Group Inc	G	631 789-4500	
Deer Park *(G-3850)*			
C & R De Santis Inc	E	718 447-5076	
Staten Island *(G-14633)*			
Cabba Printing Incorporated	G	212 319-4747	
New York *(G-8883)*			
Caboodle Printing Inc	G	716 693-6000	
Williamsville *(G-16125)*			
Canaan Printing Inc	E	718 729-3100	
Bayside *(G-736)*			
Canastota Publishing Co Inc	G	315 697-9010	
Canastota *(G-3151)*			
Candid Litho Printing Ltd	D	212 431-3800	
Farmingdale *(G-4596)*			
Canfield & Tack Inc	D	585 235-7710	
Rochester *(G-13293)*			
Capital Dst Print & Imaging	G	518 456-6773	
Schenectady *(G-14251)*			
Carges Entps of Canandaigua	G	585 394-2600	
Canandaigua *(G-3128)*			
Carnels Printing Inc	G	516 883-3355	
Great Neck *(G-5374)*			
Carr Communications Group LLC	F	607 748-0481	
Vestal *(G-15375)*			
Cathedral Corporation	C	315 338-0021	
Rome *(G-13846)*			
Cayuga Press Cortland Inc	E	888 229-8421	
Liverpool *(G-7007)*			
Cedar Graphics Inc	D	631 467-1444	
Ronkonkoma *(G-13923)*			
Cedar West Inc	D	631 467-1444	
Ronkonkoma *(G-13924)*			
Chakra Communications Inc	E	607 748-7491	
Endicott *(G-4446)*			
Chenango Union Printing Inc	G	607 334-2112	
Norwich *(G-12116)*			
Cherry Lane Lithographing Corp	E	516 293-9294	
Plainview *(G-12668)*			
CHv Printed Company	F	516 997-1101	
East Meadow *(G-4132)*			
Cilyox Inc	F	716 853-3809	
Buffalo *(G-2697)*			
Clarsons Corp	F	585 235-8775	
Rochester *(G-13317)*			
Classic Color Graphics Inc	G	516 822-9090	
Hicksville *(G-5893)*			
Cody Printing Corp	G	718 651-8854	
Woodside *(G-16202)*			
Coe Displays Inc	G	718 937-5658	
Long Island City *(G-7189)*			
Cohber Press Inc	D	585 475-9100	
West Henrietta *(G-15789)*			
Color Carton Corp	D	718 665-0840	
Bronx *(G-1228)*			
Colorfast	F	212 929-2440	
New York *(G-9056)*			
Colorfully Yours Inc	F	631 242-8600	
Bay Shore *(G-666)*			
Combine Graphics Corp	G	212 695-4044	
Forest Hills *(G-4918)*			
Commerce Offset Ltd	G	914 769-6671	
Thornwood *(G-15068)*			
Commercial Press Inc	G	315 274-0028	
Canton *(G-3164)*			
Commercial Print & Imaging	E	716 597-0100	
Buffalo *(G-2705)*			
Compass Printing Plus	G	518 523-3308	
Saranac Lake *(G-14157)*			
Complemar Print LLC	F	716 875-7238	
Buffalo *(G-2707)*			
Composite Forms Inc	F	914 937-1808	
Port Chester *(G-12815)*			
Compucolor Associates Inc	E	516 358-0000	
New Hyde Park *(G-8258)*			
Concept Printing Inc	G	845 353-4040	
Nyack *(G-12139)*			
Consolidated Color Press Inc	F	212 929-8197	
New York *(G-9086)*			
Constas Printing Corporation	G	315 474-2176	
Syracuse *(G-14859)*			
Copy Stop Inc	G	914 428-5188	
White Plains *(G-15996)*			
Coral Color Process Ltd	E	631 543-5200	
Commack *(G-3585)*			
Coral Graphic Services Inc	C	516 576-2100	
Hicksville *(G-5897)*			
Cosmos Communications Inc	C	718 482-1800	
Long Island City *(G-7193)*			
Courier Printing Corp	E	607 467-2191	
Deposit *(G-3999)*			
Craig Envelope Corp	E	718 786-4277	
Hicksville *(G-5898)*			
Crater Service Group Inc	G	585 482-7770	
Rochester *(G-13328)*			
Creative Forms Inc	G	212 431-7540	
New York *(G-9119)*			
Creative Printing Corp	G	212 226-3870	
New York *(G-9120)*			
D W S Associates Inc	E	631 667-6666	
Deer Park *(G-3858)*			
Dan Trent Company Inc	G	716 822-1422	
Buffalo *(G-2720)*			
Dark Star Lithograph Corp	G	845 634-3780	
New City *(G-8224)*			
Deanco Digital Printing LLC	F	212 371-2025	
Sunnyside *(G-14771)*			
Dell Communications Inc	G	212 989-3434	
New York *(G-9198)*			
Delta Press Inc	E	212 989-3445	
High Falls *(G-5955)*			
Design Lithographers Inc	F	212 645-8900	
New York *(G-9206)*			
Dick Bailey Service Inc	F	718 522-4363	
Brooklyn *(G-1742)*			
Digital United Color Prtg Inc	G	845 986-9846	
Warwick *(G-15512)*			
Dispatch Graphics Inc	F	212 307-5943	
New York *(G-9236)*			
Distinctive Printing Inc	G	212 727-3000	
New York *(G-9239)*			
Doco Quick Print Inc	G	315 782-6623	
Watertown *(G-15569)*			
Donmar Printing Co	F	516 280-2239	
Mineola *(G-7969)*			
Dowd - Witbeck Printing Corp	F	518 274-2421	
Troy *(G-15166)*			
DP Murphy Co Inc	D	631 673-9400	
Deer Park *(G-3865)*			
Dupli Graphics Corporation	G	315 422-4732	
Syracuse *(G-14878)*			
Eagle Graphics Inc	G	585 244-5006	
Rochester *(G-13361)*			
Earth Enterprises Inc	E	212 741-3999	
New York *(G-9301)*			
East Ridge Quick Print	F	585 266-4911	
Rochester *(G-13364)*			
Eastern Hills Printing	G	716 741-3300	
Clarence *(G-3431)*			
Echo Appellate Press Inc	G	516 432-3601	
Long Beach *(G-7136)*			
Edwards Graphic Co Inc	G	718 548-6858	
Bronx *(G-1252)*			
Empire Press Co	G	718 756-9500	
Brooklyn *(G-1801)*			
Engrav-O-Type Press Inc	F	585 262-7590	
Rochester *(G-13393)*			
Excel Graphics Services Inc	F	212 929-2183	
New York *(G-9441)*			
Excellent Photo Copies	G	718 384-7272	
Brooklyn *(G-1819)*			
Excelsior Graphics Inc	G	212 730-6200	
New York *(G-9444)*			
F & B Photo Offset Co Inc	G	516 431-5433	
Island Park *(G-6317)*			
F J Remey Co Inc	E	516 741-5112	
Mineola *(G-7974)*			
Fambus Inc	G	607 785-3700	
Endicott *(G-4455)*			
Fasprint	G	518 483-4631	
Malone *(G-7485)*			
Federal Envelope Inc	F	212 243-8380	
New York *(G-9480)*			
Finer Touch Printing Corp	F	516 944-8000	
Port Washington *(G-12879)*			
First Line Printing Inc	F	718 606-0860	
Woodside *(G-16207)*			
Five Star Prtg & Mailing Svcs	F	212 929-0300	
New York *(G-9508)*			
Flare Multicopy Corp	E	718 258-8860	
Brooklyn *(G-1849)*			
Flower City Printing Inc	C	585 663-9000	
Rochester *(G-13415)*			
Flp Group LLC	F	315 252-7583	
Auburn *(G-476)*			
Folder Factory Inc	F	540 477-3852	
Melville *(G-7783)*			

P
R
O
D
U
C
T

Fort Orange Press Inc ....E .... 518 489-3233 Albany *(G-78)*	Jacobs Press Inc ....F .... 315 252-4861 Auburn *(G-481)*	Mercury Print Productions Inc ....C .... 585 458-7900 Rochester *(G-13542)*
Forward Enterprises Inc ....F .... 585 235-7670 Rochester *(G-13421)*	James Conolly Printing Co ....E .... 585 426-4150 Rochester *(G-13488)*	Michael K Lennon Inc ....E .... 631 288-5200 Westhampton Beach *(G-15957)*
Francis Emory Fitch Inc ....E .... 212 619-3800 New York *(G-9529)*	Jane Lewis ....G .... 607 722-0584 Binghamton *(G-890)*	Microera Printers Inc ....E .... 585 783-1300 Rochester *(G-13547)*
Frederick Coon Inc ....E .... 716 683-6812 Elma *(G-4318)*	JDS Graphics Inc ....F .... 973 330-3300 New York *(G-9989)*	Mid Atlantic Graphics Corp ....E .... 631 345-3800 Shirley *(G-14424)*
Freeville Publishing Co Inc ....F .... 607 844-9119 Freeville *(G-5033)*	Johnnys Ideal Printing Co ....E .... 518 828-6666 Hudson *(G-6166)*	Mid-York Press Inc ....D .... 607 674-4491 Sherburne *(G-14392)*
Fulton Newspapers Inc ....E .... 315 598-6397 Fulton *(G-5059)*	Judith Lewis Printer Inc ....G .... 516 997-7777 Westbury *(G-15900)*	Middletown Press ....G .... 845 343-1895 Middletown *(G-7920)*
G & P Printing Inc ....G .... 212 274-8092 New York *(G-9557)*	Jurist Company Inc ....E .... 212 243-8008 Long Island City *(G-7257)*	Midgley Printing Corp ....G .... 315 475-1864 Syracuse *(G-14942)*
G W Canfield & Son Inc ....G .... 315 735-5522 Utica *(G-15265)*	Just Press Print LLC ....G .... 585 783-1300 Rochester *(G-13500)*	Midstate Printing Corp ....G .... 315 475-4101 Liverpool *(G-7026)*
Gallagher Printing Inc ....E .... 716 873-2434 Buffalo *(G-2764)*	Kas-Ray Industries Inc ....G .... 212 620-3144 New York *(G-10071)*	Mikam Graphics LLC ....D .... 212 684-9393 New York *(G-10464)*
Gallant Graphics Ltd ....E .... 845 868-1166 Stanfordville *(G-14610)*	Kaufman Brothers Printing ....G .... 212 563-1854 New York *(G-10079)*	Miller Printing & Litho Inc ....G .... 518 842-0001 Amsterdam *(G-336)*
Gateway Prtg & Graphics Inc ....E .... 716 823-3873 Hamburg *(G-5509)*	Keeners East End Litho Inc ....G .... 631 324-8565 East Hampton *(G-4124)*	Mines Press Inc ....C .... 888 559-2634 Cortlandt Manor *(G-3797)*
Gem Reproduction Services Corp ....G .... 845 298-0172 Wappingers Falls *(G-15494)*	Keller Bros & Miller Inc ....G .... 716 854-2374 Buffalo *(G-2831)*	Mitchell Prtg & Mailing Inc ....F .... 315 343-3531 Oswego *(G-12414)*
General Business Supply Inc ....D .... 518 720-3939 Watervliet *(G-15602)*	Kent Associates Inc ....G .... 212 675-0722 New York *(G-10093)*	MJB Printing Corp ....G .... 631 581-0177 Islip *(G-6355)*
Geneva Printing Company Inc ....G .... 315 789-8191 Geneva *(G-5156)*	Kenyon Press Inc ....G .... 607 674-9066 Sherburne *(G-14391)*	Monte Press Inc ....G .... 718 325-4999 Bronx *(G-1319)*
Glens Falls Printing LLC ....F .... 518 793-0555 Glens Falls *(G-5251)*	Kinaneco Inc ....G .... 315 468-6201 Syracuse *(G-14926)*	Moore Printing Company Inc ....G .... 585 394-1533 Canandaigua *(G-3136)*
Gn Printing ....E .... 718 784-1713 Long Island City *(G-7231)*	Kingsbury Printing Co Inc ....G .... 518 747-6606 Queensbury *(G-13046)*	Multimedia Services Inc ....E .... 607 936-3186 Corning *(G-3718)*
Golos Printing Inc ....G .... 607 732-1896 Elmira Heights *(G-4377)*	L I F Publishing Corp ....D .... 631 345-5200 Shirley *(G-14423)*	Nesher Printing Inc ....G .... 212 760-2521 New York *(G-10566)*
Gooding Co Inc ....E .... 716 266-6252 Lockport *(G-7082)*	L K Printing Corp ....G .... 914 761-1944 White Plains *(G-16023)*	New Horizon Graphics Inc ....E .... 631 231-8055 Hauppauge *(G-5727)*
Grand Meridian Printing Inc ....E .... 718 937-3888 Maspeth *(G-7619)*	L M N Printing Company Inc ....E .... 516 285-8526 Valley Stream *(G-15345)*	New York Digital Print Ctr Inc ....G .... 718 767-1953 Whitestone *(G-16098)*
Grand Prix Litho Inc ....E .... 631 242-4182 Hauppauge *(G-5663)*	Lake View Graphics Inc ....G .... 607 687-7033 Owego *(G-12432)*	New York Typing & Printing Co ....G .... 718 268-7900 Forest Hills *(G-4925)*
Graphics Plus Printing Inc ....E .... 607 299-0500 Cortland *(G-3769)*	Lee Printing Inc ....G .... 718 237-1651 Brooklyn *(G-2057)*	Newburgh Envelope Corp ....G .... 845 566-4211 Newburgh *(G-11877)*
Great Eastern Color Lith ....C .... 845 454-7420 Poughkeepsie *(G-12959)*	Lehmann Printing Company Inc ....G .... 212 929-2395 New York *(G-10193)*	Newport Graphics Inc ....E .... 212 924-2600 New York *(G-10610)*
Grover Cleveland Press Inc ....F .... 716 564-2222 Amherst *(G-226)*	Lennons Litho Inc ....F .... 315 866-3156 Herkimer *(G-5866)*	North Delaware Printing Inc ....G .... 716 692-0576 Tonawanda *(G-15128)*
Guaranteed Printing Svc Co Inc ....E .... 212 929-2410 Long Island City *(G-7236)*	Leonardo Printing Corp ....G .... 914 664-7890 Mount Vernon *(G-8157)*	Northeast Commercial Prtg Inc ....G .... 518 459-5047 Albany *(G-107)*
H T L & S Ltd ....F .... 718 435-4474 Brooklyn *(G-1916)*	Levon Graphics Corp ....D .... 631 753-2022 Deer Park *(G-3897)*	Northeast Prtg & Dist Co Inc ....E .... 518 563-8214 Plattsburgh *(G-12765)*
H&E Service Corp ....D .... 646 472-1936 Garden City *(G-5101)*	Litho Dynamics Inc ....G .... 914 769-1759 Hawthorne *(G-5817)*	Official Offset Corporation ....G .... 631 957-8500 Amityville *(G-299)*
Haig Press Inc ....E .... 631 582-5800 Hauppauge *(G-5665)*	Lithomatic Business Forms Inc ....G .... 212 255-6700 New York *(G-10227)*	Orbis Brynmore Lithographics ....G .... 212 987-2100 New York *(G-10703)*
Harmon and Castella Printing ....F .... 845 471-9163 Hyde Park *(G-6271)*	Louis Heindl & Son Inc ....G .... 585 454-5080 Rochester *(G-13523)*	Orffeo Printing & Imaging Inc ....G .... 716 681-5757 Lancaster *(G-6819)*
Hempstead Sentinel Inc ....F .... 516 486-5000 Hempstead *(G-5838)*	Loy L Press Inc ....G .... 716 634-5966 Buffalo *(G-2853)*	Ozipko Enterprises Inc ....G .... 585 424-6740 Rochester *(G-13602)*
Heritage Printing Center ....G .... 518 563-8240 Plattsburgh *(G-12751)*	Lynmar Printing Corp ....G .... 631 957-8500 Amityville *(G-292)*	P & W Press Inc ....E .... 646 486-3417 New York *(G-10732)*
HI Speed Envelope Co Inc ....F .... 718 617-1600 Mount Vernon *(G-8148)*	M L Design Inc ....G .... 212 233-0213 New York *(G-10298)*	Panther Graphics Inc ....E .... 585 546-7163 Rochester *(G-13608)*
High End Print Solutions Inc ....F .... 585 325-5520 Rochester *(G-13465)*	M T M Printing Co Inc ....F .... 718 353-3297 College Point *(G-3552)*	Park Slope Copy Center ....F .... 718 783-0268 Brooklyn *(G-2249)*
Hillside Printing Inc ....F .... 718 658-6719 Jamaica *(G-6448)*	M&M Printing Inc ....F .... 516 796-3020 Carle Place *(G-3177)*	Parrinello Printing Inc ....F .... 716 633-7780 Buffalo *(G-2908)*
Hospitality Graphics Inc ....G .... 212 643-6700 New York *(G-9816)*	Madison Printing Corp ....G .... 607 273-3535 Ithaca *(G-6394)*	Patrick Ryans Modern Press ....F .... 518 434-2921 Albany *(G-112)*
Hudson Envelope Corporation ....E .... 212 473-6666 New York *(G-9831)*	Mahin Impressions Inc ....G .... 212 871-9777 Riverhead *(G-13182)*	Paul Michael Group Inc ....G .... 631 585-5700 Ronkonkoma *(G-13993)*
Hudson Printing Co Inc ....E .... 718 937-8600 New York *(G-9834)*	Malone Industrial Press Inc ....G .... 518 483-5880 Malone *(G-7488)*	PBR Graphics Inc ....G .... 518 458-2909 Albany *(G-113)*
I 2 Print Inc ....F .... 718 937-8800 Long Island City *(G-7245)*	Manifestation-Glow Press Inc ....F .... 718 380-5259 Jamaica *(G-6457)*	Peachtree Enterprises Inc ....E .... 212 989-3445 Long Island City *(G-7322)*
Impala Press Ltd ....G .... 631 588-4262 Ronkonkoma *(G-13947)*	Marcal Printing Inc ....G .... 516 942-9500 Hicksville *(G-5925)*	Persch Service Print Inc ....G .... 716 366-2677 Dunkirk *(G-4063)*
In-House Inc ....F .... 718 445-9007 College Point *(G-3544)*	Marcy Printing Inc ....G .... 718 935-9100 Brooklyn *(G-2114)*	Petit Printing Corp ....G .... 716 871-9490 Getzville *(G-5181)*
Ink-It Printing Inc ....G .... 718 229-5590 College Point *(G-3545)*	Mark T Westinghouse ....G .... 518 678-3262 Catskill *(G-3214)*	Phoenix Graphics Inc ....E .... 585 232-4040 Rochester *(G-13621)*
Inland Printing Company Inc ....G .... 516 367-4700 Woodbury *(G-16174)*	Marsid Group Ltd ....G .... 516 334-1603 Carle Place *(G-3179)*	Pic A Poc Enterprises Inc ....G .... 631 981-2094 Ronkonkoma *(G-13995)*
International Newsppr Prtg Co ....E .... 516 626-6095 Glen Head *(G-5208)*	Master Printing USA Inc ....F .... 718 456-0962 Island Park *(G-6319)*	Pine Bush Printing Co Inc ....G .... 518 456-2431 Albany *(G-116)*
Iver Printing Inc ....G .... 718 275-2070 New Hyde Park *(G-8276)*	Mc Squared Nyc Inc ....F .... 212 947-2260 New York *(G-10395)*	Pioneer Printers Inc ....G .... 716 693-7100 North Tonawanda *(G-12082)*
J & J Printing Inc ....F .... 315 458-7411 Syracuse *(G-14914)*	McPc Inc ....D .... 212 583-6000 New York *(G-10403)*	PIP Inc ....G .... 518 861-0133 Latham *(G-6873)*
Jack J Florio Jr ....G .... 716 434-9123 Lockport *(G-7085)*	Medallion Associates Inc ....E .... 212 929-9130 New York *(G-10408)*	Pixos Print ....G .... 585 500-4600 Rochester *(G-13625)*

2020 Harris
New York Manufacturers Directory

(G-0000) Company's Geographic Section entry number

Platinum Printing & Graphics ....G.... 631 249-3325
  Farmingdale (G-4711)
Pollack Graphics Inc ....G.... 212 727-8400
  New York (G-10861)
Pop Printing Incorporated ....F.... 212 808-7800
  Brooklyn (G-2270)
Positive Print Litho Offset ....G.... 212 431-4850
  New York (G-10870)
Preebro Printing ....G.... 718 633-7300
  Brooklyn (G-2279)
Presstek Printing ....G.... 585 266-2770
  Rochester (G-13641)
Presstek Printing LLC ....F.... 585 467-8140
  Rochester (G-13642)
Prestige Envelope & Lithograph ....F.... 631 521-7043
  Merrick (G-7863)
Print & Graphics Group ....G.... 518 371-4649
  Clifton Park (G-3470)
Print Early LLC ....E.... 718 915-7368
  Westbury (G-15920)
Print Media Inc ....D.... 212 563-4040
  New York (G-10896)
Print Solutions Plus Inc ....G.... 315 234-3801
  Liverpool (G-7036)
Printcorp Inc ....E.... 631 696-0641
  Ronkonkoma (G-13996)
Printers 3 Inc ....F.... 631 351-1331
  Hauppauge (G-5750)
Printing Sales Group Limited ....E.... 718 258-8860
  Brooklyn (G-2293)
Printing Spectrum Inc ....F.... 631 689-1010
  East Setauket (G-4185)
Printing X Press Ions.........................G.... 631 242-1992
  Dix Hills (G-4014)
Printinghouse Press Ltd ....G.... 212 719-0990
  New York (G-10899)
Printout Copy Corp ....E.... 718 855-4040
  Brooklyn (G-2294)
Printroc Inc ....F.... 585 461-2556
  Rochester (G-13645)
Printutopia ....F.... 718 788-1545
  Brooklyn (G-2295)
Pro Printing ....G.... 516 561-9700
  Lynbrook (G-7435)
Profile Printing & Graphics ....F.... 631 273-2727
  Hauppauge (G-5751)
Progressive Graphics & Prtg ....G.... 315 331-3635
  Newark (G-11850)
Prompt Printing Inc ....G.... 631 454-6524
  Farmingdale (G-4716)
Quad/Graphics Inc ....A.... 518 581-4000
  Saratoga Springs (G-14189)
Quad/Graphics Inc ....C.... 212 672-1300
  New York (G-10947)
Quad/Graphics Inc ....A.... 212 206-5535
  New York (G-10948)
Quad/Graphics Inc ....A.... 212 741-1001
  New York (G-10949)
Quality Graphics Tri State ....G.... 845 735-2523
  Pearl River (G-12539)
Quicker Printer Inc ....G.... 607 734-8622
  Elmira (G-4365)
Quickprint ....G.... 585 394-2600
  Canandaigua (G-3141)
R & J Graphics Inc ....F.... 631 293-6611
  Farmingdale (G-4721)
R & L Press of SI Inc ....G.... 718 667-3258
  Staten Island (G-14697)
R D Printing Associates Inc ....F.... 631 390-5964
  Farmingdale (G-4722)
R Hochman Papers Incorporated ....F.... 516 466-6414
  Brooklyn (G-2320)
Rapid Print and Marketing Inc ....G.... 585 924-1520
  Victor (G-15427)
Rapid Rays Printing & Copying ....G.... 716 852-0550
  Buffalo (G-2947)
Rapid Reproductions LLC ....G.... 607 843-2221
  Oxford (G-12442)
Rasco Graphics Inc ....G.... 212 206-0447
  New York (G-10981)
Reflex Offset Inc ....G.... 516 746-4142
  Deer Park (G-3927)
Register Graphics Inc ....E.... 716 358-2921
  Randolph (G-13065)
REM Printing Inc ....G.... 518 438-7338
  Albany (G-126)
Resonant Legal Media LLC ....D.... 800 781-3591
  New York (G-11019)
RIT Printing Corp ....F.... 631 586-6220
  Bay Shore (G-707)

Rmd Holding Inc ....G.... 845 628-0030
  Mahopac (G-7478)
Rmf Print Management Group ....F.... 716 683-4351
  Depew (G-3997)
Robert Tabatznik Assoc Inc ....F.... 845 336-4555
  Kingston (G-6708)
Rosemont Press Incorporated ....E.... 212 239-4770
  New York (G-11082)
Ryan Printing Inc ....E.... 845 535-3235
  Blauvelt (G-933)
Sand Hill Industries Inc ....G.... 518 885-7991
  Ballston Spa (G-586)
Sanford Printing Inc ....G.... 718 461-1202
  Flushing (G-4891)
Scotti Graphics Inc ....E.... 212 367-9602
  Long Island City (G-7352)
Searles Graphics Inc ....E.... 631 345-2202
  Yaphank (G-16270)
Sharp Printing Inc ....G.... 716 731-3994
  Sanborn (G-14149)
Shield Press Inc ....G.... 212 431-7489
  New York (G-11213)
Shipman Printing Inds Inc ....E.... 716 504-7700
  Niagara Falls (G-11980)
Shipman Printing Inds Inc ....F.... 716 504-7700
  Sanborn (G-14150)
Shipmtes/Printmates Holdg Corp ......D.... 518 370-1158
  Scotia (G-14336)
Shoreline Publishing Inc ....G.... 914 738-7869
  Pelham (G-12568)
Sizzal LLC ....E.... 212 354-6123
  Long Island City (G-7359)
Solarz Bros Printing Corp ....G.... 718 383-1330
  Brooklyn (G-2439)
South Bridge Press Inc ....G.... 212 233-4047
  New York (G-11305)
Speedway Press Inc ....G.... 315 343-3531
  Oswego (G-12421)
Speedy Enterprise USA Corp ....G.... 718 463-3000
  Flushing (G-4894)
Standwill Packaging Inc ....E.... 631 752-1236
  Farmingdale (G-4739)
Star Press Pearl River Inc ....G.... 845 268-2294
  Valley Cottage (G-15325)
Star Quality Printing Inc ....F.... 631 273-1900
  Hauppauge (G-5775)
Sterling North America Inc ....E.... 631 243-6933
  Hauppauge (G-5776)
Steval Graphics Concepts Inc ....F.... 516 576-0220
  Plainview (G-12716)
Stevens Bandes Graphics Corp ....F.... 212 675-1128
  New York (G-11361)
Stevenson Printing Co Inc ....G.... 516 676-1233
  Glen Cove (G-5202)
Stony Point Graphics Ltd ....G.... 845 786-3322
  Stony Point (G-14748)
Stubbs Printing Inc ....G.... 315 769-8641
  Massena (G-7672)
Studley Prtg Publications Inc ....F.... 518 563-1414
  Plattsburgh (G-12782)
Stylistic Press Inc ....F.... 212 675-0797
  New York (G-11382)
Suffolk Copy Center Inc ....G.... 631 665-0570
  Bay Shore (G-718)
Summit MSP LLC ....G.... 716 433-1014
  Lockport (G-7108)
Summit MSP LLC ....G.... 716 433-1014
  Lockport (G-7109)
T C Peters Printing Co Inc ....G.... 315 724-4149
  Utica (G-15296)
The Kingsbury Printing Co Inc ....G.... 518 747-6606
  Queensbury (G-13058)
Thomas Group Inc ....F.... 212 947-6400
  New York (G-11467)
Tom & Jerry Printcraft Forms ....G.... 914 777-7468
  Mamaroneck (G-7525)
Total Concept Graphic Inc ....G.... 212 229-2626
  New York (G-11520)
Tovie Asarese Royal Prtg Co ....G.... 716 885-7692
  Buffalo (G-3016)
Trade Mark Graphics Inc ....G.... 718 306-0001
  Staten Island (G-14724)
Tremont Offset Inc ....G.... 718 892-7313
  Bronx (G-1380)
Tri Kolor Printing & Sty ....F.... 315 474-6753
  Syracuse (G-15015)
Tri-Star Offset Corp ....E.... 718 894-5555
  Maspeth (G-7639)
Tri-Town News Inc ....E.... 607 561-3515
  Sidney (G-14436)

Triad Printing Inc ....G.... 845 343-2722
  Middletown (G-7936)
True Type Printing Co Inc ....G.... 718 706-6900
  Amityville (G-315)
Tucker Printers Inc ....D.... 585 359-3030
  Henrietta (G-5861)
Twenty-First Century Press Inc ....F.... 716 837-0800
  Buffalo (G-3023)
Twin Counties Pro Printers Inc ....F.... 518 828-3278
  Hudson (G-6181)
Upstate Printing Inc ....F.... 315 475-6140
  Syracuse (G-15018)
V & J Graphics Inc ....G.... 315 363-1933
  Oneida (G-12255)
Vanguard Graphics LLC ....C.... 607 272-1212
  Ithaca (G-6416)
Variable Graphics LLC ....G.... 212 691-2323
  New York (G-11643)
Veterans Offset Printing Inc ....G.... 585 288-2900
  Rochester (G-13796)
Vincys Printing Ltd ....F.... 518 355-4363
  Schenectady (G-14314)
Vivona Business Printers Inc ....G.... 516 496-3453
  Syosset (G-14805)
Walnut Printing Inc ....G.... 718 707-0100
  Long Island City (G-7397)
Warren Printing Inc ....F.... 212 627-5000
  Long Island City (G-7398)
Wayne Printing Inc ....F.... 914 761-2400
  White Plains (G-16071)
Weeks & Reichel Printing Inc ....G.... 631 589-1443
  Sayville (G-14232)
Weicro Graphics Inc ....E.... 631 253-3360
  Brooklyn (G-2578)
Westchester Mailing Service ....E.... 914 948-1116
  White Plains (G-16073)
Westypo Printers Inc ....G.... 914 737-7394
  Peekskill (G-12562)
William Charles Prtg Co Inc ....E.... 516 349-0900
  Plainview (G-12728)
William J Ryan ....G.... 585 392-6200
  Hilton (G-5975)
Wilson Press LLC ....E.... 315 568-9693
  Seneca Falls (G-14374)
Winner Press Inc ....G.... 718 937-7715
  Long Island City (G-7404)
Winson Surnamer Inc ....G.... 718 729-8787
  Long Island City (G-7405)
Woodbury Printing Plus + Inc ....G.... 845 928-6610
  Central Valley (G-3302)
Zacmel Graphics LLC ....G.... 631 944-6031
  Deer Park (G-3957)
Zenger Partners LLC ....E.... 716 876-2284
  Kenmore (G-6656)

PRINTING: Pamphlets

Willis Mc Donald Co Inc ....F.... 212 366-1526
  New York (G-11761)

PRINTING: Photo-Offset

Academy Printing Services Inc ....G.... 631 765-3346
  Southold (G-14542)
D G M Graphics Inc ....F.... 516 223-2220
  Merrick (G-7854)
Genie Instant Printing Co Inc ....F.... 212 575-8258
  New York (G-9595)
Kjckd Inc ....G.... 518 435-9696
  Latham (G-6862)
Leader Printing Inc ....F.... 516 546-1544
  Merrick (G-7859)
National Reproductions Inc ....E.... 212 619-3800
  New York (G-10544)
Pronto Printer ....G.... 914 737-0800
  Cortlandt Manor (G-3798)
Scriven Duplicating Service ....E.... 518 233-8180
  Troy (G-15187)
Three Star Offset Printing ....F.... 516 867-8223
  Freeport (G-5029)

PRINTING: Photogravure

Dijifi LLC ....F.... 646 519-2447
  Brooklyn (G-1746)

PRINTING: Photolithographic

BP Digital Imaging LLC ....G.... 607 753-0022
  Cortland (G-3757)

PRODUCT

PRINTING: Rotary Photogravure

Mastro Graphic Arts Inc ....E 585 436-7570
Rochester *(G-13537)*

PRINTING: Rotogravure

American Packaging Corporation ....C 585 254-9500
Rochester *(G-13230)*

PRINTING: Screen, Broadwoven Fabrics, Cotton

Dynamic Screenprinting ....G 518 487-4256
Albany *(G-72)*
Loremanss Embroidery Engrav ....F 518 834-9205
Keeseville *(G-6643)*
Mezzoprint LLC ....G 347 480-9199
Valley Stream *(G-15347)*
Printery ....G 315 253-7403
Auburn *(G-491)*
Santee Print Works ....B 212 997-1570
New York *(G-11134)*
Sciane Enterprises Inc ....G 845 452-2400
Poughkeepsie *(G-12982)*
Steve Poli Sales ....G 315 487-0394
Camillus *(G-3110)*
Tramwell Inc ....G 315 789-2762
Geneva *(G-5164)*
Ward Sales Co Inc ....G 315 476-5276
Syracuse *(G-15023)*

PRINTING: Screen, Fabric

Apple Imprints Apparel Inc ....E 716 893-1130
Buffalo *(G-2641)*
Apsco Sports Enterprises Inc ....D 718 965-9500
Brooklyn *(G-1522)*
Aro-Graph Corporation ....G 315 463-8693
Syracuse *(G-14817)*
Creative Images & Applique ....D 718 821-8700
Maspeth *(G-7602)*
Dirt T Shirts Inc ....E 845 336-4230
Kingston *(G-6689)*
Galli Shirts and Sports AP ....G 845 226-7305
Stormville *(G-14751)*
Human Technologies Corporation ....F 315 735-3532
Utica *(G-15273)*
Irene Cerone ....G 315 668-2899
Brewerton *(G-1136)*
J M L Productions Inc ....D 718 643-1674
Brooklyn *(G-1980)*
Kevin J Kassman ....G 585 529-4245
Rochester *(G-13502)*
Mezzoprint LLC ....G 347 480-9199
Valley Stream *(G-15347)*
Original Tube Tshirt ....G 845 291-7031
Goshen *(G-5312)*
Printz and Patternz LLC ....G 518 944-6020
Schenectady *(G-14296)*
Rainbow Lettering ....G 607 732-5751
Elmira *(G-4366)*
Randy Sixberry ....G 315 265-6211
Potsdam *(G-12940)*
Viewsport International Inc ....G 585 259-1562
Penfield *(G-12576)*
Wicked Smart LLC ....F 518 459-2855
Watervliet *(G-15612)*

PRINTING: Screen, Manmade Fiber & Silk, Broadwoven Fabric

Dyenamix Inc ....G 212 941-6642
New York *(G-9287)*
Efs Designs LLC ....G 718 852-9511
Brooklyn *(G-1785)*
Intertex USA Inc ....F 212 279-3601
New York *(G-9925)*
Mv Corp Inc ....C 631 273-8020
Bay Shore *(G-695)*
Rescuestuff Inc ....G 718 318-7570
Peekskill *(G-12555)*
Screen Gems Inc ....G 845 561-0036
New Windsor *(G-8382)*
Valley Stream Sporting Gds Inc ....E 516 593-7800
Lynbrook *(G-7442)*

PRINTING: Thermography

Bco Industries Western NY Inc ....E 716 877-2800
Tonawanda *(G-15089)*

Business Card Express Inc ....E 631 669-3400
West Babylon *(G-15698)*
East Coast Thermographers Inc ....E 718 321-3211
College Point *(G-3541)*
Fineline Thermographers Inc ....G 718 643-1100
Brooklyn *(G-1845)*
Karr Graphics Corp ....E 212 645-6000
Long Island City *(G-7261)*

PROFESSIONAL EQPT & SPLYS, WHOLESALE: Analytical Instruments

Peyser Instrument Corporation ....E 631 841-3600
West Babylon *(G-15736)*

PROFESSIONAL EQPT & SPLYS, WHOLESALE: Engineers', NEC

Advanced Tchncal Solutions Inc ....F 914 214-8230
Mahopac *(G-7473)*

PROFESSIONAL EQPT & SPLYS, WHOLESALE: Optical Goods

Carl Zeiss Inc ....C 914 747-1800
White Plains *(G-15990)*
Dynamic Laboratories Inc ....E 631 231-7474
Ronkonkoma *(G-13931)*
Lens Lab Express ....G 718 921-5488
Brooklyn *(G-2062)*
Moscot Wholesale Corp ....G 212 647-1550
New York *(G-10507)*
Spectrum Thin Films Inc ....E 631 901-1010
Hauppauge *(G-5772)*
Tri-Supreme Optical LLC ....D 631 249-2020
Farmingdale *(G-4759)*

PROFESSIONAL EQPT & SPLYS, WHOLESALE: Scientific & Engineerg

Avanel Industries Inc ....F 516 333-0990
Westbury *(G-15871)*
Scientifics Direct Inc ....F 716 773-7500
Tonawanda *(G-15139)*

PROFESSIONAL EQPT & SPLYS, WHOLESALE: Theatrical

Steeldeck Ny Inc ....F 718 599-3700
Brooklyn *(G-2457)*

PROFILE SHAPES: Unsupported Plastics

Chelsea Plastics Inc ....F 212 924-4530
New York *(G-8980)*
Franklin Poly Film Inc ....E 718 492-3523
Brooklyn *(G-1865)*
Howard J Moore Company Inc ....E 631 351-8467
Plainview *(G-12688)*
Mitsui Chemicals America Inc ....E 914 253-0777
Rye Brook *(G-14092)*
Ontario Plastics Inc ....E 585 663-2644
Rochester *(G-13591)*

PROGRAM ADMIN, GOVT: Air, Water & Solid Waste Mgmt, Local

City of Kingston ....F 845 331-2490
Kingston *(G-6686)*

PROTECTION EQPT: Lightning

Heary Bros Lghtning Protection ....E 716 941-6141
Springville *(G-14593)*
Tii Technologies Inc ....E 516 364-9300
Edgewood *(G-4287)*

PUBLIC RELATIONS & PUBLICITY SVCS

Studley Prtg Publications Inc ....F 518 563-1414
Plattsburgh *(G-12782)*

PUBLISHERS: Art Copy

Classic Collections Fine Art ....G 914 591-4500
White Plains *(G-15993)*

PUBLISHERS: Art Copy & Poster

Luminary Publishing Inc ....F 845 334-8600
Kingston *(G-6701)*

Pace Editions Inc ....E 212 421-3237
New York *(G-10735)*
Space 150 ....C 612 332-6458
Brooklyn *(G-2445)*

PUBLISHERS: Atlases

Directory Major Malls Inc ....G 845 348-7000
Nyack *(G-12141)*

PUBLISHERS: Book

A Lesley Dummett ....G 646 541-1168
Saint Albans *(G-14104)*
Abbeville Press Inc ....E 212 366-5585
New York *(G-8426)*
Advance Publications Inc ....D 718 981-1234
New York *(G-8475)*
Alm Media LLC ....B 212 457-9400
New York *(G-8524)*
Alm Media Holdings Inc ....B 212 457-9400
New York *(G-8525)*
American Inst Chem Engners Inc ....D 646 495-1355
New York *(G-8552)*
Amplify Education Inc ....B 212 213-8177
Brooklyn *(G-1509)*
Assouline Publishing Inc ....F 212 989-6769
New York *(G-8655)*
Ateres Publishing & Bk Bindery ....F 718 935-9355
Brooklyn *(G-1546)*
Atlas & Company LLC ....G 212 234-3100
New York *(G-8669)*
Bedrock Communications ....G 212 532-4150
New York *(G-8748)*
Benchmark Education Co LLC ....D 914 637-7200
New Rochelle *(G-8320)*
Bloomsbury Publishing Inc ....D 212 419-5300
New York *(G-8815)*
Bobley-Harmann Corporation ....G 516 433-3800
Ronkonkoma *(G-13917)*
Burns Archive Phtgraphic Distr ....G 212 889-1938
New York *(G-8870)*
Byliner Inc ....E 415 680-3608
New York *(G-8879)*
Canopy Books LLC ....G 516 354-4888
Massapequa *(G-7645)*
CCC Publications Inc ....F 718 306-1008
Brooklyn *(G-1656)*
Changdu Technology (usa) Co ....F 917 340-1976
North Bellmore *(G-12015)*
Curriculum Associates LLC ....F 978 313-1355
Brooklyn *(G-1709)*
Der Yid Inc ....E 718 797-3900
Brooklyn *(G-1737)*
Divine Phoenix LLC ....A 585 737-1482
Skaneateles *(G-14450)*
Eagle Art Publishing Inc ....G 212 685-7411
New York *(G-9296)*
F P H Communications ....G 212 528-1728
New York *(G-9455)*
Fairchild Publications Inc ....A 212 630-4000
New York *(G-9463)*
Family Publishing Group Inc ....E 914 381-7474
Mamaroneck *(G-7510)*
Feminist Press Inc ....E 212 817-7915
New York *(G-9483)*
Franklin Report LLC ....G 212 639-9100
New York *(G-9533)*
Gq Magazine ....G 212 286-2860
New York *(G-9653)*
Grey House Publishing Inc ....E 518 789-8700
Amenia *(G-202)*
Grolier International Inc ....G 212 343-6100
New York *(G-9682)*
Guilford Publications Inc ....G 800 365-7006
New York *(G-9697)*
Harpercollins Publishers LLC ....E 212 553-4200
New York *(G-9728)*
Houghton Mifflin Harcourt Co ....G 212 420-5800
New York *(G-9819)*
Informa Business Media Inc ....F 914 949-8500
White Plains *(G-16015)*
Kwesi Legesse LLC ....G 347 581-9872
Brooklyn *(G-2037)*
Learningexpress LLC ....E 646 274-6454
New York *(G-10185)*
Legal Strategies Inc ....G 516 377-3940
Merrick *(G-7860)*
Living Well Innovations Inc ....G 646 517-3200
Hauppauge *(G-5693)*
Macmillan College Pubg Co Inc ....F 212 702-2000
New York *(G-10307)*

Martha Stewart Living ....C 212 827-8000
New York *(G-10374)*
Mathisen Ventures Inc ....G 212 986-1025
New York *(G-10384)*
McGraw-Hill Globl Edcatn Hldng.....D 800 338-3987
New York *(G-10398)*
Mediaplanet Publishing Hse Inc......E 646 922-1400
New York *(G-10414)*
Meegenius Inc ....G 212 283-7285
New York *(G-10422)*
Micro Publishing Inc ....G 212 533-9180
New York *(G-10456)*
N A R Associates Inc ....G 845 557-8713
Barryville *(G-598)*
NC Audience Exchange LLC.........F 212 416-3400
New York *(G-10559)*
New Press ....E 212 629-8802
New York *(G-10588)*
New York Legal Publishing ....G 518 459-1100
Menands *(G-7847)*
New York Qrtrly Foundation Inc.....F 917 843-8825
Brooklyn *(G-2211)*
News Corporation ....C 212 416-3400
New York *(G-10612)*
Nova Science Publishers Inc.........F 631 231-7269
Hauppauge *(G-5728)*
Osprey Publishing Inc ....G 212 419-5300
New York *(G-10715)*
Oxford University Press LLC ....G 212 726-6000
New York *(G-10728)*
Ozmodyl Ltd ....G 212 226-0622
New York *(G-10730)*
Pace Walkers of America Inc ....F 631 444-2147
Port Jefferson *(G-12843)*
Pearson Education Inc ....G 845 340-8700
Kingston *(G-6706)*
Pearson Education Inc ....F 212 782-3337
New York *(G-10779)*
Pearson Education Inc ....E 212 366-2000
New York *(G-10780)*
Pearson Education Inc ....F 201 236-7000
West Nyack *(G-15829)*
Pegasus Books NY Ltd ....G 646 343-9502
New York *(G-10789)*
Poetry Mailing List Marsh Hawk....G 516 766-1891
Oceanside *(G-12185)*
Poets House Inc ....F 212 431-7920
New York *(G-10860)*
Powerhouse Cultural Entrmt Inc.....F 212 604-9074
Brooklyn *(G-2273)*
Preserving Chrstn Publications ......G 315 942-6617
Boonville *(G-1108)*
Rda Holding Co ....E 914 238-1000
New York *(G-10990)*
Readers Dgest Yung Fmilies Inc....E 914 238-1000
Pleasantville *(G-12798)*
Repertoire International De Ll........E 212 817-1990
New York *(G-11015)*
Rizzoli Intl Publications Inc...........F 212 387-3572
New York *(G-11052)*
S P Books Inc ....G 212 431-5011
New York *(G-11109)*
Scholastic Inc ....E 212 343-6100
New York *(G-11162)*
Scholium International Inc ....G 516 883-8032
Port Washington *(G-12923)*
Sheridan House Inc ....G 914 725-5431
Scarsdale *(G-14242)*
Simon Schuster Digital Sls Inc.....D 212 698-4391
New York *(G-11246)*
Springer Nature ....D 212 460-1500
New York *(G-11335)*
Springer Nature Cust Serv Cent....B 212 460-1500
New York *(G-11337)*
Station Hill of Barrytown ....G 845 758-5293
Barrytown *(G-597)*
Steffen Publishing Inc ....D 315 865-4100
Holland Patent *(G-6034)*
Stonesong Press LLC ....G 212 929-4600
New York *(G-11366)*
Storybooks Forever ....F 716 822-7845
Buffalo *(G-2994)*
Studio Fun International Inc ....E 914 238-1000
White Plains *(G-16064)*
Sweet Mouth Inc ....E 800 433-7758
New York *(G-11407)*
Targum Press USA Inc ....G 248 355-2266
Brooklyn *(G-2493)*
Thornwillow Press Ltd ....G 212 980-0738
New York *(G-11476)*

TI Gotham Inc ....E 212 522-1212
New York *(G-11479)*
Time Home Entertainment Inc ....E 212 522-1212
New York *(G-11489)*
Verso Inc ....G 718 246-8160
Brooklyn *(G-2554)*
W W Norton & Company Inc ....G 212 354-5500
New York *(G-11714)*
Woodward/White Inc ....F 718 509-6082
Brooklyn *(G-2594)*
Ziff Davis Publishing LLC.............D 212 503-3500
New York *(G-11824)*
Zinepak LLC ....F 212 706-8621
New York *(G-11825)*

PUBLISHERS: *Book Clubs, No Printing*

Humana Press Inc ....E 212 460-1500
New York *(G-9838)*

PUBLISHERS: *Books, No Printing*

Aip Publishing LLC ....C 516 576-2200
Melville *(G-7757)*
Alba House Publishers ....E 718 698-2759
Staten Island *(G-14616)*
Amereon Ltd ....G 631 298-5100
Mattituck *(G-7676)*
American Institute Physics Inc.......C 516 576-2410
Melville *(G-7760)*
Amherst Media Inc ....G 716 874-4450
Buffalo *(G-2633)*
Annuals Publishing Co Inc ....G 212 505-0950
New York *(G-8594)*
Anthroposophic Press Inc ....E 518 851-2054
Clifton Park *(G-3461)*
Barrons Educational Series Inc......C 631 434-3311
Hauppauge *(G-5602)*
Bertelsmann Pubg Group Inc ....A 212 782-1000
New York *(G-8765)*
Bicker Inc ....F 212 688-0085
New York *(G-8781)*
Bmg Rights Management (us) LLC..E 212 561-3000
New York *(G-8824)*
Boardman Simons Publishing ....E 212 620-7200
New York *(G-8827)*
British American Publishing ....D 518 786-6000
Latham *(G-6849)*
Cambridge University Press ....G 212 337-5000
New York *(G-8897)*
Campus Course Paks Inc ....G 516 877-3967
Garden City *(G-5094)*
Castle Connolly Medical Ltd ....E 212 367-8400
New York *(G-8931)*
CB Publishing LLC ....G 516 354-4888
Floral Park *(G-4811)*
Central Cnfrnce of Amrcn Rbbis.....F 212 972-3636
New York *(G-8951)*
Chain Store Age Magazine ....G 212 756-5000
New York *(G-8966)*
Church Publishing Incorporated .....G 212 592-1800
New York *(G-9004)*
Cinderella Press Ltd ....G 212 431-3130
New York *(G-9006)*
Columbia University Press ....E 212 459-0600
New York *(G-9060)*
Columbia University Press ....E 212 459-0600
New York *(G-9061)*
Columbia University Press ....E 212 459-0600
New York *(G-9062)*
Confrtrnity of Precious Blood ....G 718 436-1120
Brooklyn *(G-1681)*
Continuum Intl Pubg Group Inc......F 646 649-4215
New York *(G-9092)*
Daheshist Publishing Co Ltd ....F 212 581-8360
New York *(G-9151)*
Definition Press Inc ....F 212 777-4490
New York *(G-9195)*
Delaney Books Inc ....F 516 921-8888
Syosset *(G-14785)*
Demos Medical Publishing LLC......F 516 889-1791
New York *(G-9200)*
Edwin Mellen Press Inc ....E 716 754-2796
Lewiston *(G-6921)*
Egmont US Inc ....G 212 685-0102
New York *(G-9328)*
Four M Studios ....D 515 284-2157
New York *(G-9523)*
Foxhill Press Inc ....E 212 995-9620
New York *(G-9527)*
Frank Merriwell Inc ....F 516 921-8888
Syosset *(G-14788)*

French Publishers Agency Inc ....G 212 254-4540
New York *(G-9538)*
Ggp Publishing Inc ....F 914 834-8896
Harrison *(G-5553)*
Government Data Publication ....E 347 789-8719
Brooklyn *(G-1904)*
Grand Central Publishing ....C 212 364-1200
New York *(G-9658)*
Graphis Inc ....F 212 532-9387
New York *(G-9666)*
Guilford Publications Inc ....D 212 431-9800
New York *(G-9696)*
Hachette Book Group Inc ....B 800 759-0190
New York *(G-9704)*
Hachette Book Group USA ....E 212 364-1200
New York *(G-9705)*
Harpercollins ....F 212 207-7000
New York *(G-9726)*
Harpercollins Publishers LLC ....A 212 207-7000
New York *(G-9727)*
Harry N Abrams Incorporated ....D 212 206-7715
New York *(G-9731)*
Hearst Corporation ....E 212 649-2275
New York *(G-9754)*
Henry Holt and Company LLC ....D 646 307-5095
New York *(G-9766)*
Highline Media LLC......................C 859 692-2100
New York *(G-9784)*
Hudson Park Press Inc ....G 212 929-8898
New York *(G-9833)*
Infobase Holdings Inc ....D 212 967-8800
New York *(G-9886)*
Infobase Publishing Company ....G 212 967-8800
New York *(G-9887)*
Ir Media Group (usa) Inc ....E 212 425-9649
New York *(G-9939)*
Jonathan David Publishers Inc.......F 718 456-8611
Middle Village *(G-7880)*
Judaica Press Inc ....G 718 972-6202
Brooklyn *(G-2008)*
Juris Publishing Inc ....F 631 351-5430
Huntington *(G-6209)*
K T A V Publishing House Inc ....E 201 963-9524
Brooklyn *(G-2019)*
Kaplan Inc ....E 212 752-1840
New York *(G-10067)*
Kensington Publishing Corp ....D 212 407-1500
New York *(G-10092)*
Kodansha USA Inc ....G 917 322-6200
New York *(G-10122)*
Le Book Publishing Inc ....G 212 334-5252
New York *(G-10180)*
Lee & Low Books Incorporated......F 212 779-4400
New York *(G-10189)*
Lippincott Massie McQuilkin L........F 212 352-2055
New York *(G-10224)*
Literary Classics of US ....E 212 308-3360
New York *(G-10226)*
Little Bee Books Inc ....E 212 321-0237
New York *(G-10228)*
Liveright Publishing Corp ....G 212 354-5500
New York *(G-10234)*
Looseleaf Law Publications Inc......F 718 359-5559
Flushing *(G-4873)*
Macmillan Publishers Inc ....A 646 307-5151
New York *(G-10309)*
Macmillan Publishing Group LLC....G 212 674-5145
New York *(G-10310)*
Malhame Publs & Importers Inc .....E 631 694-8600
Bohemia *(G-1043)*
Marshall Cavendish Corp ....E 914 332-8888
Rye Brook *(G-14091)*
Mary Ann Liebert Inc ....D 914 740-2100
New Rochelle *(G-8347)*
McGraw-Hill Education Inc ....D 646 766-2000
New York *(G-10397)*
McGraw-Hill School Education H ....B 646 766-2000
New York *(G-10399)*
Medikidz Usa Inc ....G 646 895-9319
New York *(G-10418)*
Melcher Media Inc ....E 212 727-2322
New York *(G-10428)*
Merkos Llnyonei Chinuch Inc ....E 718 778-0226
Brooklyn *(G-2143)*
Mesorah Publications Ltd ....G 718 921-9000
Brooklyn *(G-2145)*
Michel Design Works Ltd ....F 914 763-2244
Katonah *(G-6635)*
Modern Language Assn Amer Inc....E 646 576-5000
New York *(G-10488)*

Monacelli Press LLC...........................G.....212 229-9925
New York (G-10497)
Mondo Publishing Inc..........................F.....212 268-3560
New York (G-10498)
Moznaim Publishing Co Inc..................G.....718 853-0525
Brooklyn (G-2173)
Mud Puddle Books Inc.........................G.....212 647-9168
New York (G-10517)
NBM Publishing Inc.............................G.....646 559-4681
New York (G-10558)
New City Press Inc..............................G.....845 229-0335
Hyde Park (G-6273)
New Directions Publishing....................F.....212 255-0230
New York (G-10579)
North Shore Home Improver..................F.....631 474-2824
Port Jeff STA (G-12835)
Other Press LLC..................................G.....212 414-0054
New York (G-10716)
Oxford University Press LLC................B.....212 726-6000
New York (G-10727)
P J D Publications Ltd...........................G.....516 626-0650
New Hyde Park (G-8288)
Palgrave Macmillan Ltd........................G.....646 307-5028
New York (G-10742)
Papercutz Inc......................................G.....646 559-4681
New York (G-10751)
Parachute Publishing LLC.....................E.....212 337-6743
New York (G-10753)
Penguin Putnam Inc.............................G.....212 366-2000
New York (G-10791)
Penguin Random House LLC..................E.....212 782-1000
New York (G-10792)
Penguin Random House LLC..................B.....212 782-9000
New York (G-10793)
Penguin Random House LLC..................A.....212 572-6162
New York (G-10794)
Penguin Random House LLC..................C.....212 366-2377
Albany (G-114)
Peter Mayer Publishers Inc..................F.....212 673-2210
New York (G-10815)
Peter Pauper Press Inc.........................E.....914 681-0144
White Plains (G-16051)
Phaidon Press Inc................................E.....212 652-5400
New York (G-10825)
Philipp Feldheim Inc.............................G.....845 356-2282
Nanuet (G-8203)
Picador USA...F.....646 307-5629
New York (G-10835)
Prestel Publishing LLC.........................G.....212 995-2720
New York (G-10884)
Princton Archtctural Press LLC.............F.....518 671-6100
Hudson (G-6176)
Prometheus Books Inc.........................E.....716 691-0133
Buffalo (G-2935)
PSR Press Ltd......................................F.....716 754-2266
Lewiston (G-6923)
Quarto Group Inc.................................E.....212 779-0700
New York (G-10953)
Rapid Intellect Group Inc......................F.....518 929-3210
Chatham (G-3332)
Relx Inc...E.....212 309-8100
New York (G-11005)
Research Centre of Kabbalah................G.....718 805-0380
Richmond Hill (G-13121)
Richard C Owen Publishers Inc.............F.....914 232-3903
Somers (G-14500)
Rizzoli Intl Publications Inc...................E.....212 387-3400
New York (G-11051)
Rosen Publishing Group Inc..................C.....212 777-3017
New York (G-11084)
Ryland Peters & Small Inc.....................G.....646 791-5410
New York (G-11103)
Scholastic Corporation.........................G.....212 343-6100
New York (G-11160)
Scholastic Inc......................................A.....212 343-6100
New York (G-11161)
Second Chance Press Inc......................G.....631 725-1101
Sag Harbor (G-14102)
Seven Stories Press Inc........................G.....212 226-8760
New York (G-11196)
Simon & Schuster Inc..........................D.....212 698-7000
New York (G-11244)
Skyhorse Publishing Inc.......................E.....212 643-6816
New York (G-11264)
Social Register Association....................F.....646 612-7314
New York (G-11281)
Soho Press Inc.....................................G.....212 260-1900
New York (G-11286)
Springer Adis Us LLC...........................F.....212 460-1500
New York (G-11333)

Springer Publishing Co LLC..................E.....212 431-4370
New York (G-11338)
Springer Scnce + Bus Media LLC..........D.....212 460-1500
New York (G-11339)
Square One Publishers Inc...................F.....516 535-2010
Garden City Park (G-5124)
STf Services Inc..................................E.....315 463-8506
East Syracuse (G-4239)
Suny At Binghamton.............................D.....607 777-2316
Binghamton (G-910)
Syracuse University Press Inc...............E.....315 443-5534
Syracuse (G-15010)
Tom Doherty Associates Inc................E.....212 388-0100
New York (G-11508)
Trusted Media Brands Inc....................A.....914 238-1000
New York (G-11553)
Trusted Media Brands Inc....................F.....914 244-5244
White Plains (G-16067)
Unisystems Inc....................................E.....212 826-0850
New York (G-11596)
United Synggue Cnsrvtive Jdism...........E.....212 533-7800
New York (G-11602)
Vaad LHafotzas Sichoes.......................F.....718 778-5436
Brooklyn (G-2550)
Vandam Inc..F.....212 929-0416
Long Island City (G-7391)
Vaultcom Inc..E.....212 366-4212
New York (G-11650)
William H Sadlier Inc.............................C.....212 233-3646
New York (G-11757)
William S Hein & Co Inc........................C.....716 882-2600
Getzville (G-5184)
William S Hein & Co Inc........................D.....716 882-2600
Buffalo (G-3049)
Wolters Kluwer US Inc..........................F.....212 894-8920
New York (G-11774)
Workman Publishing Co Inc...................C.....212 254-5900
New York (G-11779)
Workman Publishing Co Inc...................C.....212 254-5900
New York (G-11780)
YS Publishing Co Inc...........................G.....212 682-9360
New York (G-11813)

PUBLISHERS: Catalogs

Christopher Anthony Pubg Co................F.....516 826-9205
Wantagh (G-15483)
Select Information Exchange...................F.....212 496-6435
New York (G-11186)

PUBLISHERS: Comic Books, No Printing

Archie Comic Publications Inc...............D.....914 381-5155
Pelham (G-12564)
Clp Pb LLC..E.....212 340-8100
New York (G-9039)
Continuity Publishing Inc.......................F.....212 869-4170
New York (G-9090)
Valiant Entertainment LLC.....................E.....212 972-0361
New York (G-11635)

PUBLISHERS: Directories, NEC

Black Book Photography Inc.................F.....212 979-6700
New York (G-8806)
Catholic News Publishing Co.................F.....914 632-7771
Mamaroneck (G-7501)
Easy Book Publishing Inc......................G.....518 459-6281
Albany (G-73)
Foundation Center Inc...........................C.....212 620-4230
New York (G-9519)
Hearst Business Media..........................D.....516 227-1300
Uniondale (G-15230)
Highline Media LLC...............................C.....859 692-2100
New York (G-9784)
Leadership Connect Inc........................D.....212 627-4140
New York (G-10182)
Supermedia LLC...................................D.....212 513-9700
New York (G-11397)
Thomas Publishing Company LLC.........B.....212 695-0500
New York (G-11468)

PUBLISHERS: Directories, Telephone

Associated Publishing Company............E.....325 676-4032
Buffalo (G-2644)
Hola Publishing Co................................G.....718 424-3129
Long Island City (G-7243)

PUBLISHERS: Guides

Family Publications Ltd.........................F.....212 947-2177
New York (G-9467)

Fredonia Pennysaver Inc.......................G.....716 679-1509
Fredonia (G-4969)
Metro Group Inc...................................G.....716 434-4055
Lockport (G-7092)
Mt Morris Shopper Inc..........................G.....585 658-3520
Mount Morris (G-8114)

PUBLISHERS: Magazines, No Printing

21st Century Fox America Inc..............D.....212 852-7000
New York (G-8396)
2600 Enterprises Inc.............................F.....631 474-2677
Saint James (G-14107)
A Guideposts Church Corp....................C.....212 251-8100
New York (G-8417)
Abp International Inc.............................E.....212 490-3999
New York (G-8433)
Adirondack Life Inc..............................F.....518 946-2191
Jay (G-6565)
Adirondack Life Inc..............................G.....518 946-2191
Jay (G-6566)
Advance Magazine Publs Inc.................C.....212 450-7000
New York (G-8473)
Advanced Research Media Inc...............F.....631 751-9696
Setauket (G-14376)
Adventure Publishing Group..................E.....212 575-4510
New York (G-8485)
Aeon America Inc.................................G.....914 584-0275
Brooklyn (G-1468)
Alm Media LLC....................................B.....212 457-9400
New York (G-8524)
Alm Media Holdings Inc........................B.....212 457-9400
New York (G-8525)
American Inst Chem Engnrs Inc.............D.....646 495-1355
New York (G-8552)
American Jewish Committee...................G.....212 891-1400
New York (G-8553)
American Towman Network Inc..............F.....845 986-4546
Warwick (G-15510)
Analysts In Media (aim) Inc..................E.....212 488-1777
New York (G-8572)
Animal Fair Media Inc...........................F.....212 629-0392
New York (G-8590)
Athlon Spt Communications Inc.............F.....212 478-1910
New York (G-8665)
Atlantic Monthly Group Inc...................E.....202 266-7000
New York (G-8666)
Backstage LLC....................................E.....212 493-4243
Brooklyn (G-1559)
Bedford Communications Inc.................E.....212 807-8220
New York (G-8747)
Bellerophon Publications Inc................E.....212 627-9977
New York (G-8752)
Bertelsmann Pubg Group Inc................A.....212 782-1000
New York (G-8765)
Beverage Media Group Inc...................F.....212 571-3232
New York (G-8772)
Blue Horizon Media Inc........................F.....212 661-7878
New York (G-8819)
Bnei Aram Soba Inc..............................F.....718 645-4460
Brooklyn (G-1599)
Buffalo Spree Publishing Inc................E.....716 783-9119
Buffalo (G-2683)
C Q Communications Inc.......................E.....516 681-2922
Hicksville (G-5890)
Capital Partners LLC.............................D.....212 935-4990
New York (G-8913)
Carol Group Ltd....................................G.....212 505-2030
New York (G-8921)
Centennial Media LLC...........................F.....646 527-7320
New York (G-8948)
Center For Inquiry Inc..........................F.....716 636-4869
Amherst (G-217)
Cfo Publishing LLC...............................E.....212 459-3004
New York (G-8964)
Coda Media Inc....................................G.....917 478-2565
New York (G-9047)
College Calendar Company.....................F.....315 768-8242
Whitesboro (G-16079)
Commonweal Foundation Inc.................F.....212 662-4200
New York (G-9068)
Consumer Reports Inc ....B.....914 378-2000
Yonkers (G-16297)
Cosmopolitan Magazine.........................G.....212 649-2000
New York (G-9106)
Crain Communications Inc.....................C.....212 210-0100
New York (G-9118)
Daily Beast Company LLC......................E.....212 445-4600
New York (G-9152)
Data Key Communication LLC................F.....315 445-2347
Fayetteville (G-4783)

Dennis Publishing Inc ....D 646 717-9500
New York *(G-9204)*

Discover Media LLC ....E 212 624-4800
New York *(G-9235)*

Dissent Magazine ....F 212 316-3120
New York *(G-9238)*

Dj Publishing Inc ....E 516 767-2500
Port Washington *(G-12873)*

Doctorow Communications Inc ....F 845 708-5166
New City *(G-8225)*

Dotto Wagner ....G 315 342-8020
Oswego *(G-12409)*

Dow Jones & Company Inc ....E 212 597-5983
New York *(G-9259)*

E C Publications Inc ....F 212 728-1844
New York *(G-9289)*

E W Williams Publications ....G 212 661-1516
New York *(G-9292)*

Earl G Graves Pubg Co Inc ....D 212 242-8000
New York *(G-9299)*

Essence Communications Inc ....C 212 522-1212
Brooklyn *(G-1815)*

Essence Ventures LLC ....C 212 522-1212
New York *(G-9400)*

Executive Business Media Inc ....E 516 334-3030
Westbury *(G-15883)*

Faces Magazine Inc ....F 201 843-4004
Poughkeepsie *(G-12954)*

Fader Inc ....F 212 741-7100
New York *(G-9461)*

Fahy-Williams Publishing Inc ....F 315 781-6820
Geneva *(G-5153)*

Family Publishing Group Inc ....E 914 381-7474
Mamaroneck *(G-7510)*

Formula 4 Media LLC ....F 516 305-4709
Great Neck *(G-5390)*

Four M Studios ....F 212 499-2000
New York *(G-9522)*

Fridge Magazine Inc ....G 212 997-7673
New York *(G-9541)*

Frozen Food Digest Inc ....G 212 557-8600
New York *(G-9543)*

Fun Media Inc ....E 646 472-0135
New York *(G-9552)*

Future Media Group Inc ....D 646 854-1375
New York *(G-9555)*

Getting The Word Out Inc ....G 518 891-9352
Saranac Lake *(G-14158)*

Golfing Magazine ....G 516 822-5446
Hicksville *(G-5914)*

Graphis Inc ....F 212 532-9387
New York *(G-9666)*

Gruner + Jahr Prtg & Pubg Co ....C 212 463-1000
New York *(G-9687)*

Guernica Inc ....F 646 327-7138
New York *(G-9692)*

Halcyon Business Publications ....F 800 735-2732
Westbury *(G-15892)*

Hamptons Media LLC ....G 631 283-6900
Southampton *(G-14532)*

Harpers Magazine Foundation ....E 212 420-5720
New York *(G-9729)*

Hart Energy Publishing Lllp ....G 212 621-4621
New York *(G-9734)*

Haymarket Group Ltd ....F 212 239-0855
New York *(G-9737)*

Haymarket Media Inc ....C 646 638-6000
New York *(G-9738)*

Hearst Business Media ....D 516 227-1300
Uniondale *(G-15230)*

Hearst Business Publishing Inc ....F 212 969-7500
New York *(G-9742)*

Hearst Communications Inc ....C 212 649-2000
New York *(G-9745)*

Hearst Corporation ....E 212 649-3100
New York *(G-9746)*

Hearst Corporation ....B 212 767-5800
New York *(G-9748)*

Hearst Corporation ....D 516 382-4580
New York *(G-9749)*

Hearst Corporation ....D 212 649-4271
New York *(G-9750)*

Hearst Corporation ....D 212 649-3204
New York *(G-9753)*

Hearst Corporation ....E 212 649-2275
New York *(G-9754)*

Hearst Holdings Inc ....F 212 649-2000
New York *(G-9756)*

Herman Hall Communications ....F 718 941-1879
Brooklyn *(G-1933)*

Historic TW Inc ....E 212 484-8000
New York *(G-9794)*

Icd Publications Inc ....E 631 246-9300
Islandia *(G-6335)*

Imek Media LLC ....E 212 422-9000
New York *(G-9866)*

Impressions Inc ....G 212 594-5954
New York *(G-9871)*

Informa Business Media Inc ....C 212 204-4200
New York *(G-9888)*

Informa Media Inc ....B 212 204-4200
New York *(G-9889)*

Ink Publishing Corporation ....G 347 294-1220
Brooklyn *(G-1958)*

Intellignc The Ftr Cmptng Nwsl ....F 212 222-1123
New York *(G-9909)*

Intellitravel Media Inc ....E 646 695-6700
New York *(G-9910)*

Interhellenic Publishing Inc ....G 212 967-5016
New York *(G-9916)*

Interview New York ....E 857 928-4120
New York *(G-9926)*

Irish America Inc ....E 212 725-2993
New York *(G-9941)*

JSD Communications Inc ....E 914 588-1841
Bedford *(G-763)*

Kids Discover LLC ....G 212 677-4457
New York *(G-10096)*

L I F Publishing Corp ....D 631 345-5200
Shirley *(G-14423)*

Lagardere North America Inc ....E 212 477-7373
New York *(G-10164)*

Locations Magazine ....G 212 288-4745
New York *(G-10240)*

Mac Fadden Holdings Inc ....E 212 979-4805
New York *(G-10303)*

Macfadden Cmmnctions Group LLC ....C 212 979-4800
New York *(G-10306)*

Macmillan Holdings LLC ....E 212 576-9428
New York *(G-10308)*

Mag Inc ....E 607 257-6970
Ithaca *(G-6395)*

Manhattan Media LLC ....F 212 268-8600
New York *(G-10344)*

Mann Publications Inc ....E 212 840-6266
New York *(G-10347)*

Mansueto Ventures LLC ....C 212 389-5300
New York *(G-10353)*

Maritime Activity Reports ....E 212 477-6700
New York *(G-10362)*

Mark Levine ....F 212 677-4457
New York *(G-10364)*

Martha Stewart Living ....C 212 827-8000
New York *(G-10374)*

Martha Stewart Living Omni LLC ....B 212 827-8000
New York *(G-10375)*

Martinelli Holdings LLC ....E 302 504-1361
Harrison *(G-5555)*

Mass Appeal Magazine ....G 718 858-0979
Brooklyn *(G-2122)*

Mergent Inc ....B 212 413-7700
New York *(G-10433)*

Miami Media LLC ....F 212 268-8600
New York *(G-10450)*

Modern Farmer Media Inc ....F 518 828-7447
Hudson *(G-6172)*

Music & Sound Retailer Inc ....E 516 767-2500
Port Washington *(G-12908)*

Nation Company LLC ....E 212 209-5400
New York *(G-10538)*

Nation Magazine ....E 212 209-5400
New York *(G-10539)*

National Review Inc ....E 212 679-7330
New York *(G-10545)*

New Art Publications Inc ....F 718 636-9100
Brooklyn *(G-2200)*

New York Media LLC ....C 212 508-0700
New York *(G-10599)*

New York Moves Magazine LLC ....F 212 396-2394
New York *(G-10600)*

Next Step Publishing Inc ....F 585 742-1260
Victor *(G-15422)*

Nickelodeon Magazines Inc ....G 212 541-1949
New York *(G-10624)*

Nova Science Publishers Inc ....F 631 231-7269
Hauppauge *(G-5728)*

Nsgv Inc ....E 212 367-3100
New York *(G-10652)*

Nyemac Inc ....G 631 668-1303
Montauk *(G-8057)*

Nylon LLc ....E 212 226-6454
New York *(G-10663)*

Nyrev Inc ....E 212 757-8070
New York *(G-10667)*

Outdoor Sportsman Group ....G 323 791-7190
New York *(G-10718)*

Paper Publishing Company Inc ....E 212 226-4405
New York *(G-10750)*

Parade Publications Inc ....E 212 450-7000
New York *(G-10754)*

Parents Guide Network Corp ....E 212 213-8840
New York *(G-10757)*

Penhouse Media Group Inc ....C 212 702-6000
New York *(G-10795)*

Periodical Services Co Inc ....F 518 822-9300
Hudson *(G-6174)*

Photo Industry Inc ....F 516 364-0016
Woodbury *(G-16179)*

Preparatory Magazine Group ....D 718 761-4800
Staten Island *(G-14694)*

Prescribing Reference Inc ....D 646 638-6000
New York *(G-10881)*

Professnal Spt Pblications Inc ....D 212 697-1460
New York *(G-10904)*

Promenade Magazines Inc ....F 212 888-3500
New York *(G-10908)*

Q Communications Inc ....E 212 594-6520
New York *(G-10940)*

Quartz Media LLC ....E 646 539-6604
New York *(G-10954)*

Quest Media Llc ....F 646 840-3404
New York *(G-10956)*

Raharney Capital LLC ....G 212 220-9084
Brooklyn *(G-2323)*

Ralph Martinelli ....E 914 345-3055
Elmsford *(G-4424)*

Ramholtz Publishing Inc ....D 718 761-4800
Staten Island *(G-14699)*

Readers Digest Assn Incthe ....F 414 423-0100
New York *(G-10993)*

Real Estate Media Inc ....E 212 929-6976
New York *(G-10994)*

Relx Inc ....E 212 463-6644
New York *(G-11006)*

Rfp LLC ....E 212 838-7733
New York *(G-11032)*

Risk Society Management Pubg ....E 212 286-9364
New York *(G-11048)*

Rough Draft Publishing LLC ....F 212 741-4773
New York *(G-11087)*

Rsl Media LLC ....G 212 307-6760
New York *(G-11094)*

Ruby Newco LLC ....G 212 852-7000
New York *(G-11096)*

S C Magazine ....G 646 638-6018
New York *(G-11107)*

Sandow Media LLC ....F 646 805-0200
New York *(G-11131)*

Scholastic Corporation ....G 212 343-6100
New York *(G-11160)*

Scholastic Inc ....A 212 343-6100
New York *(G-11161)*

Shoreline Publishing Inc ....G 914 738-7869
Pelham *(G-12568)*

Simmons-Boardman Pubg Corp ....G 212 620-7200
New York *(G-11243)*

Smart & Strong LLC ....E 212 938-2051
New York *(G-11271)*

Smooth Magazine ....F 212 925-1150
New York *(G-11277)*

Society For The Study ....G 212 822-8806
New York *(G-11283)*

Sound Communications Inc ....E 516 767-2500
Port Washington *(G-12927)*

Spin Magazine Media ....E 212 231-7400
New York *(G-11323)*

Sports Illustrated For Kids ....E 212 522-1212
New York *(G-11326)*

Spotlight Publications LLC ....G 914 345-9473
Elmsford *(G-4435)*

Staten Island Parent Magazine ....G 718 761-4800
Staten Island *(G-14713)*

Suburban Publishing Inc ....F 845 463-0542
Fishkill *(G-4804)*

Testa Communications Inc ....E 516 767-2500
Port Washington *(G-12929)*

Thomas Publishing Company LLC ....G 212 695-0500
New York *(G-11470)*

TI Gotham Inc ....E 212 522-1633
New York *(G-11480)*

P
R
O
D
U
C
T

TI Gotham Inc	A	212 522-1212
New York (G-11481)		
TI Gotham Inc	E	212 522-0361
New York (G-11482)		
Time Inc Affluent Media Group	G	212 382-5600
New York (G-11490)		
Time Warner Companies Inc	D	212 484-8000
New York (G-11494)		
Trusted Media Brands Inc	A	914 238-1000
New York (G-11553)		
Trusted Media Brands Inc	F	914 244-5244
White Plains (G-16067)		
TV Guide Magazine Group Inc	D	212 852-7500
New York (G-11562)		
U S Japan Publication NY Inc	G	212 252-8833
New York (G-11571)		
Ulster Publishing Co Inc	E	845 334-8205
Kingston (G-6718)		
Untitled Media	E	212 780-0960
New York (G-11611)		
US Weekly LLC	D	212 484-1616
New York (G-11628)		
Value Line Inc	D	212 907-1500
New York (G-11637)		
Vending Times Inc	F	516 442-1850
Rockville Centre (G-13840)		
Veranda Publications Inc	G	212 903-5206
New York (G-11658)		
Visionaire Publishing LLC	E	646 434-6091
New York (G-11693)		
Weider Publications LLC	C	212 545-4800
New York (G-11736)		
Welcome Magazine Inc	F	716 839-3121
Amherst (G-254)		
Wenner Media LLC	C	212 484-1616
New York (G-11743)		
Western New York Family Mag	G	716 836-3486
Buffalo (G-3046)		
Wine & Spirits Magazine Inc	G	212 695-4660
New York (G-11764)		
Womens E News Inc	G	212 244-1720
New York (G-11775)		
Working Mother Media Inc	D	212 351-6400
New York (G-11778)		
World Guide Publishing	E	800 331-7840
New York (G-11781)		
Wsn Inc	G	212 924-7620
New York (G-11792)		

PUBLISHERS: Maps

Vandam Inc	F	212 929-0416
Long Island City (G-7391)		

PUBLISHERS: Miscellaneous

212 Media LLC	E	212 710-3092
New York (G-8394)		
Abkco Music Inc	F	212 399-0300
New York (G-8431)		
ABRA Media Inc	G	518 398-1010
Pine Plains (G-12632)		
Absolute Color Corporation	G	212 868-0404
New York (G-8436)		
Adcomm Graphics Inc	E	212 645-1298
West Babylon (G-15681)		
Ahae Press Inc	G	914 471-8671
Mount Kisco (G-8087)		
Albany Student Press Inc	E	518 442-5665
Albany (G-36)		
Albion-Holley Pennysaver Inc	E	585 589-5641
Albion (G-153)		
Alfred Mainzer Inc	E	718 392-4200
Long Island City (G-7148)		
America Press Inc	E	212 581-4640
New York (G-8542)		
American Hsptals Patient Guide	F	518 346-1099
Schenectady (G-14245)		
American Society of Composers	B	212 621-6000
New York (G-8558)		
Amy Pak Publishing Inc	G	585 964-8188
Holley (G-6035)		
Art Asiapacific Publishing LLC	G	212 255-6003
New York (G-8627)		
Award Publishing Limited	G	212 246-0405
New York (G-8696)		
Blood Moon Productions Ltd	G	718 556-9410
Staten Island (G-14628)		
Brownstone Publishers Inc	E	212 473-8200
New York (G-8863)		
Bulkley Dunton	E	212 863-1800
New York (G-8866)		

Burdick Publications Inc	G	315 685-9500
Skaneateles (G-14447)		
Business Expert Press LLC	F	212 661-8810
New York (G-8871)		
Bys Publishing LLC	G	315 655-9431
Cazenovia (G-3224)		
Cambridge Whos Who Pubg Inc	E	516 833-8440
Uniondale (G-15224)		
Catapult LLC	G	303 717-0334
New York (G-8935)		
Cayuga Press Cortland Inc	E	888 229-8421
Liverpool (G-7007)		
Cherry Lane Magazine LLC	D	212 561-3000
New York (G-8982)		
City Post Express Inc	G	718 995-8690
Jamaica (G-6435)		
Cnhi LLC	D	716 282-2311
Niagara Falls (G-11916)		
Coastal Publications Inc	F	631 725-1700
Sag Harbor (G-14097)		
Community Cpons Frnchising Inc	E	516 277-1968
Glen Cove (G-5190)		
Complete Publishing Solutions	G	212 242-7321
New York (G-9073)		
Comps Inc	F	516 676-0400
Glen Cove (G-5191)		
Consumer Reports Inc	B	914 378-2000
Yonkers (G-16297)		
CT Publications Co	G	718 592-2196
Whitestone (G-16092)		
D C I Technical Inc	F	516 355-0464
Franklin Square (G-4960)		
Dailycandy Inc	E	646 230-8719
New York (G-9158)		
Dapper Dads Inc	G	917 903-8045
Brooklyn (G-1725)		
Dezawy LLC	G	917 436-8820
New York (G-9214)		
DK Publishing	F	212 366-2000
New York (G-9241)		
Dlc Comprehensive Medical PC	F	718 857-1200
Brooklyn (G-1752)		
Draper Associates Incorporated	F	212 255-2727
New York (G-9266)		
Dryve LLC	G	646 279-3648
Bronx (G-1242)		
Dwell Life Inc	E	212 382-2010
New York (G-9285)		
Enjoy City North Inc	D	607 584-5061
Binghamton (G-876)		
Ethis Communications Inc	G	212 791-1440
White Plains (G-16003)		
Experiment Publishing LLC	G	212 889-1273
New York (G-9448)		
Fantasy Sports Media Group Inc	E	416 917-6002
New York (G-9472)		
First Games Publr Netwrk Inc	D	212 983-0501
New York (G-9499)		
Fitzgerald Publishing Co Inc	G	914 793-5016
Yonkers (G-16309)		
Galison Publishing LLC	E	212 354-8840
New York (G-9566)		
Gannett Co Inc	D	607 352-2702
Johnson City (G-6600)		
Gen Publishing Inc	G	914 834-3880
New Rochelle (G-8335)		
Genius Media Group Inc	F	509 670-7502
Brooklyn (G-1883)		
Glassview LLC	E	646 844-4922
New York (G-9619)		
Global Grind Digital	E	212 840-9399
New York (G-9630)		
Government Data Publication	G	347 789-8719
Brooklyn (G-1904)		
Grants Financial Publishing	F	212 809-7994
New York (G-9663)		
Grey House Publishing Inc	E	518 789-8700
Amenia (G-202)		
Guest Informat LLC	F	212 557-3010
New York (G-9693)		
Guilford Publications Inc	D	212 431-9800
New York (G-9696)		
Guilford Publications Inc	G	800 365-7006
New York (G-9697)		
Hagedorn Communications Inc	G	914 636-7400
New York (G-9708)		
Hampton Press Incorporated	G	646 638-3800
New York (G-9717)		
Harborside Press	G	631 470-4967
Huntington (G-6206)		

Helium Media Inc	G	917 596-4081
New York (G-9763)		
Helvetica Press Incorporated	G	212 737-1857
New York (G-9764)		
Hibert Publishing LLC	G	914 381-7474
Rye (G-14080)		
Holmes Group The Inc	G	212 333-2300
New York (G-9806)		
Humor Rainbow Inc	E	646 402-9113
New York (G-9840)		
International Society For Medl	G	520 820-8594
Tarrytown (G-15046)		
Intuition Publishing Limited	G	212 838-7115
New York (G-9933)		
Jewish Heritage For Blind	G	718 338-4999
Brooklyn (G-1993)		
Jobson Medical Information LLC	C	212 274-7000
New York (G-10013)		
John Szoke Graphics Inc	G	212 219-8300
New York (G-10019)		
Kalel Partners LLC	F	347 561-7804
Flushing (G-4866)		
Korangy Publishing Inc	C	212 260-1332
New York (G-10127)		
Kraus Organization Limited	D	212 686-5411
New York (G-10138)		
Kyra Communications Corp	G	516 783-6244
Seaford (G-14349)		
Language and Graphics Inc	G	212 315-5266
New York (G-10172)		
Lightbulb Press Inc	E	212 485-8800
New York (G-10218)		
Lino Press Inc	E	718 665-2625
Bronx (G-1304)		
Llcs Publishing Corp	F	718 569-2703
Brooklyn (G-2081)		
Lucky Peach LLC	G	212 228-0031
New York (G-10280)		
Mailers-Pblsher Wlfare Tr Fund	G	212 869-5986
New York (G-10332)		
Market Partners International	G	212 447-0855
New York (G-10369)		
Marketresearchcom Inc	F	212 807-2600
New York (G-10371)		
Mary Ann Liebert Inc	D	914 740-2100
New Rochelle (G-8347)		
Media Transcripts Inc	E	212 362-1481
New York (G-10411)		
Medical Information Systems	G	516 621-7200
Syosset (G-14793)		
Mens Journal LLC	A	212 484-1616
New York (G-10431)		
Menucha Publishers Inc	F	718 232-0856
Brooklyn (G-2138)		
Merrill Corporation	D	212 620-5600
New York (G-10437)		
Millennium Medical Publishing	F	212 995-2211
New York (G-10466)		
Minyanville Media Inc	E	212 991-6200
New York (G-10480)		
Morey Publishing	E	516 284-3300
Farmingdale (G-4689)		
Mortgage Press Ltd	E	516 409-1400
Wantagh (G-15486)		
Mtm Publishing Inc	G	212 242-6930
New York (G-10516)		
Multi-Health Systems Inc	D	800 456-3003
Cheektowaga (G-3356)		
National Health Prom Assoc	E	914 421-2525
White Plains (G-16032)		
National Rding Styles Inst Inc	F	516 921-5500
Syosset (G-14797)		
National RES Mktg Council Inc	G	914 591-4297
Irvington (G-6311)		
Nature Publishing Co	G	212 726-9200
New York (G-10553)		
New York Legal Publishing	G	518 459-1100
Menands (G-7847)		
New York Times Company	G	212 556-1200
New York (G-10605)		
Newbay Media LLC	D	212 378-0400
New York (G-10609)		
Nigun Music	F	718 977-5700
Brooklyn (G-2216)		
O Val Nick Music Co Inc	G	212 873-2179
New York (G-10671)		
Oakwood Publishing Co	G	516 482-7720
Great Neck (G-5407)		
One Story Inc	G	917 816-3659
Brooklyn (G-2232)		

Openroad Integrated Media Inc	E	212 691-0900	
New York *(G-10698)*			
Outreach Publishing Corp	G	718 773-0525	
Brooklyn *(G-2239)*			
Oyster Bay Publications LLC	G	516 922-1300	
Oyster Bay *(G-12453)*			
Pace Editions Inc	G	212 643-6353	
New York *(G-10736)*			
Per Annum Inc	E	212 647-8700	
New York *(G-10800)*			
Press Express	G	914 592-3790	
Elmsford *(G-4422)*			
Primary Wave Publishing LLC	E	212 661-6990	
New York *(G-10889)*			
Professnal Spt Pblications Inc	E	516 327-9500	
Elmont *(G-4387)*			
Publicis Health LLC	E	212 771-5500	
Long Island City *(G-7330)*			
Publishers Clearing House LLC	E	516 249-4063	
Melville *(G-7818)*			
Pwxyz LLC	E	212 377-5500	
New York *(G-10939)*			
Qtalk Publishing LLC	G	877 549-1841	
New York *(G-10946)*			
Quality Patterns Inc	D	212 704-0355	
New York *(G-10950)*			
R W Publications Div of Wtrhs	E	716 714-5620	
Elma *(G-4325)*			
Rda Holding Co	E	914 238-1000	
New York *(G-10990)*			
Refinery 29 Inc	D	212 966-3112	
New York *(G-11000)*			
Reliable Press II Inc	F	718 840-5812	
Hempstead *(G-5849)*			
Repertoire International De LI	E	212 817-1990	
New York *(G-11015)*			
Rizzoli Intl Publications Inc	F	212 308-2000	
New York *(G-11053)*			
Rolling Stone Magazine	G	212 484-1616	
New York *(G-11077)*			
Rosemont Press Incorporated	G	212 239-4770	
Deer Park *(G-3929)*			
Rough Guides US Ltd	D	212 414-3635	
New York *(G-11088)*			
Rsl Media LLC	G	212 307-6760	
New York *(G-11094)*			
Sacks and Company New York	E	212 741-1000	
New York *(G-11113)*			
Sag Harbor Express	G	631 725-1700	
Sag Harbor *(G-14100)*			
Seabay Media Holdings LLC	G	212 457-7790	
New York *(G-11172)*			
Selby Marketing Associates Inc	F	585 377-0750	
Rochester *(G-13722)*			
Sephardic Yellow Pages	E	718 998-0299	
Brooklyn *(G-2395)*			
Sharedbook Inc	E	646 442-8840	
New York *(G-11208)*			
Sing Tao Newspapers NY Ltd	E	212 699-3800	
New York *(G-11248)*			
Slosson Eductl Publications	F	716 652-0930	
East Aurora *(G-4096)*			
Social Science Electronic Pubg	F	585 442-8170	
Rochester *(G-13734)*			
Sony Music Holdings Inc	A	212 833-8000	
New York *(G-11299)*			
Southampton Town Newspapers	E	631 283-4100	
Southampton *(G-14538)*			
Springer Nature America Inc	B	212 726-9200	
New York *(G-11336)*			
Stephen Singer Pattern Co Inc	F	212 947-2902	
New York *(G-11359)*			
STf Services Inc	E	315 463-8506	
East Syracuse *(G-4239)*			
Straight Arrow Publishing Co	C	212 484-1616	
New York *(G-11368)*			
Student Lifeline Inc	E	516 327-0800	
Franklin Square *(G-4964)*			
Summit Communications	G	914 273-5504	
Armonk *(G-402)*			
Super Express USA Pubg Corp	F	212 227-5800	
Richmond Hill *(G-13126)*			
Tablet Publishing Company Inc	E	718 965-7333	
Brooklyn *(G-2490)*			
Tango Publishing Corporation	E	646 773-3060	
New York *(G-11430)*			
Taylor & Francis Group LLC	C	212 216-7800	
New York *(G-11437)*			
Te Neues Publishing Co LP	F	212 627-9090	
New York *(G-11441)*			

Thomson Reuters Corporation	F	212 393-9461	
New York *(G-11474)*			
Thomson Reuters Corporation	A	646 223-4000	
New York *(G-11475)*			
Trader Interntnal Publications	G	914 631-6856	
Sleepy Hollow *(G-14464)*			
Tradewins Publishing Corp	G	631 361-6916	
Saint James *(G-14115)*			
Treiman Publications Corp	G	607 657-8473	
Berkshire *(G-822)*			
Tribune Entertainment Co Del	E	203 866-2204	
New York *(G-11543)*			
Tribune Media Services Inc	B	518 792-9914	
Queensbury *(G-13059)*			
Triumph Learning LLC	E	212 652-0200	
New York *(G-11549)*			
Trusted Media Brands Inc	A	914 238-1000	
New York *(G-11553)*			
Trusted Media Brands Inc	F	914 244-5244	
White Plains *(G-16067)*			
Tunecore Inc	E	646 651-1060	
Brooklyn *(G-2528)*			
Turbo Express Inc	G	718 723-3686	
Jamaica *(G-6483)*			
Two Palms Press Inc	F	212 965-8598	
New York *(G-11565)*			
Ucc Guide Inc	F	518 434-0909	
Albany *(G-139)*			
Underline Communications LLC	F	212 994-4340	
New York *(G-11581)*			
USA Custom Pad Corp	F	607 563-9550	
Sidney *(G-14439)*			
Value Line Inc	D	212 907-1500	
New York *(G-11637)*			
Vending Times Inc	F	516 442-1850	
Rockville Centre *(G-13840)*			
Vendome Group LLC	D	646 795-3899	
New York *(G-11654)*			
Viamedia Corporation	F	718 485-7792	
Brooklyn *(G-2555)*			
Viewfinder Inc	G	212 831-0939	
New York *(G-11681)*			
Vincys Printing Ltd	F	518 355-4363	
Schenectady *(G-14314)*			
Watchanish LLC	F	917 558-0404	
New York *(G-11728)*			
Wayuga Community Newspapers	E	315 754-6229	
Red Creek *(G-13071)*			
Welcome Rain Publishers LLC	E	212 686-1909	
New York *(G-11738)*			
Won & Lee Inc	E	516 222-0712	
Garden City *(G-5119)*			
Worldwide Media Svcs Group Inc	B	212 545-4800	
New York *(G-11784)*			
Yam TV LLC	G	917 932-5418	
New York *(G-11806)*			

PUBLISHERS: Music Book

Boydell & Brewer Inc	F	585 275-0419	
Rochester *(G-13279)*			
Congress For Jewish Culture	G	212 505-8040	
New York *(G-9083)*			
Simmons-Boardman Pubg Corp	G	212 620-7200	
New York *(G-11243)*			

PUBLISHERS: Music Book & Sheet Music

Alphonse Lduc - Rbert King Inc	G	508 238-8118	
New York *(G-8527)*			
Boosey and Hawkes Inc	E	212 358-5300	
New York *(G-8836)*			
C F Peters Corp	E	718 416-7800	
Glendale *(G-5221)*			
Franklin-Douglas Inc	F	516 883-0121	
Port Washington *(G-12880)*			
Lagunatic Music & Filmworks	F	212 353-9600	
Brooklyn *(G-2044)*			
Lefrak Entertainment Co Ltd	G	212 586-3600	
New York *(G-10192)*			
Reservoir Media Management Inc	F	212 675-0541	
New York *(G-11018)*			
Sony/Atv Music Publishing LLC	E	212 833-7730	
New York *(G-11300)*			

PUBLISHERS: Music, Book

Euphorbia Productions Ltd	G	212 533-1700	
New York *(G-9418)*			
G Schirmer Inc	G	212 254-2100	
New York *(G-9559)*			

G Schirmer Inc	E	845 469-4699	
Chester *(G-3378)*			
Music Sales Corporation	G	212 254-2100	
New York *(G-10521)*			
Peer International Corp	E	212 265-3910	
New York *(G-10785)*			
Peermusic III Ltd	F	212 265-3910	
New York *(G-10787)*			
Peermusic Ltd	F	212 265-3910	
New York *(G-10788)*			

PUBLISHERS: Music, Sheet

Abkco Music & Records Inc	E	212 399-0300	
New York *(G-8430)*			
Bourne Music Publishers	F	212 391-4300	
New York *(G-8841)*			
Charing Cross Music Inc	G	212 541-7571	
New York *(G-8971)*			
Historic TW Inc	E	212 484-8000	
New York *(G-9794)*			
Integrated Copyright Group	E	615 329-3999	
New York *(G-9907)*			
Ludlow Music Inc	F	212 594-9795	
New York *(G-10281)*			
Michael Karp Music Inc	G	212 840-3285	
New York *(G-10453)*			
Mom Dad Publishing Inc	E	646 476-9170	
New York *(G-10495)*			
Screen Gems-EMI Music Inc	D	212 786-8000	
New York *(G-11170)*			
Shapiro Bernstein & Co Inc	F	212 588-0878	
New York *(G-11207)*			
Time Warner Companies Inc	D	212 484-8000	
New York *(G-11494)*			

PUBLISHERS: Newsletter

Alm Media LLC	B	212 457-9400	
New York *(G-8524)*			
Alm Media Holdings Inc	B	212 457-9400	
New York *(G-8525)*			
Energy Intelligence Group Inc	E	212 532-1112	
New York *(G-9375)*			
Fischler Hockey Service	F	212 749-4152	
New York *(G-9505)*			
Grant Hamilton	F	716 652-0320	
East Aurora *(G-4089)*			
Hart Energy Publishing LIlp	G	212 621-4621	
New York *(G-9734)*			
London Theater News Ltd	F	212 517-8608	
New York *(G-10247)*			
Mathisen Ventures Inc	G	212 986-1025	
New York *(G-10384)*			
Neu Group Inc	F	914 232-4068	
Katonah *(G-6636)*			
Redspring Communications Inc	E	518 587-0547	
Saratoga Springs *(G-14191)*			

PUBLISHERS: Newspaper

Advance Magazine Publs Inc	C	212 450-7000	
New York *(G-8473)*			
Advertiser Perceptions Inc	E	212 626-6683	
New York *(G-8486)*			
Albany Student Press Inc	E	518 442-5665	
Albany *(G-36)*			
All Times Publishing LLC	E	315 422-7011	
Syracuse *(G-14809)*			
Bangla Patrika Inc	G	718 482-9923	
Long Island City *(G-7174)*			
Brooklyn Rail Inc	F	718 349-8427	
Brooklyn *(G-1620)*			
Bureau of National Affairs Inc	E	212 687-4530	
New York *(G-8868)*			
Business Journals	F	212 790-5100	
New York *(G-8873)*			
China Daily Distribution Corp	E	212 537-8888	
New York *(G-8987)*			
China Newsweek Corporation	F	212 481-2510	
New York *(G-8992)*			
Chinese Medical Report Inc	G	718 359-5676	
Flushing *(G-4842)*			
Citywire LLC	F	646 503-2216	
New York *(G-9021)*			
Country Folks	G	585 343-9721	
Batavia *(G-612)*			
Digital One USA Inc	F	718 396-4890	
Flushing *(G-4848)*			
Economist Newspaper NA Inc	E	212 554-0676	
New York *(G-9319)*			

PRODUCT

Fairchild Publications Inc ....A 212 630-4000
New York *(G-9463)*

Gallagher Printing Inc ....E 716 873-2434
Buffalo *(G-2764)*

Gannett Co Inc ....D 607 798-1234
Vestal *(G-15377)*

General Media Strategies Inc ....G 212 586-4141
New York *(G-9590)*

Hagedorn Communications Inc..........G 914 636-7400
New York *(G-9708)*

Haitian Times Inc ....G 718 230-8700
New Rochelle *(G-8337)*

Hearst Corporation ....A 518 454-5694
Albany *(G-85)*

Informa Uk Ltd..............................G 646 957-8966
New York *(G-9892)*

Jewish Journal ....G 718 630-9350
Brooklyn *(G-1994)*

Long Islander Newspapers LLC ....G 631 427-7000
Huntington *(G-6213)*

Los Angles Tmes Cmmnctions LLC ...F 212 692-7170
New York *(G-10265)*

Market Place Publications................E 516 997-7909
Carle Place *(G-3178)*

Merchandiser Inc ....G 315 462-6411
Clifton Springs *(G-3479)*

Mortgage Press Ltd ....E 516 409-1400
Wantagh *(G-15486)*

Newspaper Delivery Solutions ....G 718 370-1111
Staten Island *(G-14682)*

Noticia Hispanoamericana Inc...........E 516 223-5678
Bayside *(G-741)*

Observer Daily Sunday Newsppr ....D 716 366-3000
Dunkirk *(G-4062)*

Panagraphics Inc ....G 716 312-8088
Orchard Park *(G-12370)*

Pearson Inc ....D 212 641-2400
New York *(G-10782)*

Realtimetraderscom ....E 716 632-6600
Buffalo *(G-2950)*

Record Advertiser ....E 716 693-1000
North Tonawanda *(G-12085)*

Republican Registrar Inc ....G 315 497-1551
Moravia *(G-8083)*

Rochester Democrat & Chronicle........E 585 232-7100
Rochester *(G-13688)*

Rvc Inc ....G 330 631-8320
Syracuse *(G-14981)*

Sag Harbor Express.........................G 631 725-1700
Sag Harbor *(G-14100)*

Salamanca Press Penny Saver............E 716 945-1500
Salamanca *(G-14127)*

Saugerties Delicioso Inc ....G 845 217-5072
Saugerties *(G-14211)*

Schneps Media LLC ....G 718 224-5863
Brooklyn *(G-2387)*

Sing Tao Newspapers NY Ltd ....F 212 431-9030
Brooklyn *(G-2422)*

SM News Plus Incorporated ....G 212 888-0153
New York *(G-11270)*

Star Sports Corp ....E 516 773-4075
Great Neck *(G-5426)*

Stratconglobal Inc...........................G 212 989-2355
New York *(G-11369)*

Straus Newspapers Inc ....E 845 782-4000
Chester *(G-3389)*

Syracuse Catholic Press Assn ....G 315 422-8153
Syracuse *(G-15004)*

Tegna Inc ....C 716 849-2222
Buffalo *(G-3005)*

Tenney Media Group.........................D 315 853-5569
Clinton *(G-3486)*

The Sandhar Corp............................G 718 523-0819
Jamaica *(G-6480)*

Tompkins Weekly Inc ....G 607 539-7100
Ithaca *(G-6413)*

Tryp Times Square ....G 212 246-8800
New York *(G-11554)*

Ubm Inc ....A 212 600-3000
New York *(G-11574)*

Ubm LLC ....G 516 562-7800
New Hyde Park *(G-8298)*

Urdu Times ....G 718 297-8700
Jamaica *(G-6485)*

Wallkill Lodge No 627 F&Am ....F 845 778-7148
Walden *(G-15464)*

Webster Ontrio Wlwrth Pnnysver.........F 585 265-3620
Webster *(G-15661)*

Weekly Ajkal ....F 718 565-2100
Jackson Heights *(G-6422)*

West Seneca Bee Inc ....D 716 632-4700
Williamsville *(G-16146)*

PUBLISHERS: Newspapers, No Printing

A C J Communications Inc ....F 631 587-5612
Babylon *(G-517)*

Advertiser Publications Inc.................F 845 783-1111
Chester *(G-3369)*

Afro Times Newspaper ....F 718 636-9500
Brooklyn *(G-1470)*

Albany Catholic Press Assoc ....G 518 453-6688
Albany *(G-31)*

Algemeiner Journal Inc ....G 718 771-0400
Brooklyn *(G-1483)*

Alm Media LLC ....B 212 457-9400
New York *(G-8524)*

Alm Media Holdings Inc ....B 212 457-9400
New York *(G-8525)*

American City Bus Journals Inc ....E 716 541-1654
Buffalo *(G-2629)*

American Sports Media LLC ....G 585 377-9636
Rochester *(G-13232)*

Angel Media and Publishing ....G 845 727-4949
West Nyack *(G-15816)*

Architects Newspaper LLC ....F 212 966-0630
New York *(G-8618)*

Auburn Publishing Co ....D 315 253-5311
Auburn *(G-462)*

Bee Publications Inc..........................D 716 632-4700
Williamsville *(G-16121)*

Belsito Communications Inc...............F 845 534-9700
New Windsor *(G-8360)*

Blue and White Publishing Inc ....F 215 431-3339
New York *(G-8817)*

Boonville Herald Inc ....G 315 942-4449
Boonville *(G-1104)*

Brown Publishing LLC ....G 585 484-0432
Rochester *(G-13284)*

Buffalo Law Journal ....G 716 541-1600
Buffalo *(G-2675)*

Business First of New York ....E 716 854-5822
Buffalo *(G-2686)*

Business First of New York ....E 518 640-6800
Albany *(G-54)*

Camden News Inc ....G 315 245-1849
Camden *(G-3098)*

Canandaigua Msgnr Incorporated........C 585 394-0770
Canandaigua *(G-3127)*

Catskill Mountain Publishing...............F 845 586-2601
Arkville *(G-394)*

Cnhi LLC..D 716 693-1000
Niagara Falls *(G-11915)*

Cnhi LLC..D 716 282-2311
Niagara Falls *(G-11916)*

Cnhi LLC..E 716 439-9222
Lockport *(G-7065)*

CNY Business Review Inc ....F 315 472-3104
Syracuse *(G-14853)*

Community Newspaper Group LLC .....E 607 432-1000
Oneonta *(G-12267)*

Cortland Standard Printing Co ....D 607 756-5665
Cortland *(G-3764)*

Courier-Life Inc ....C 718 260-2500
Brooklyn *(G-1693)*

Daily Cornell Sun ....E 607 273-0746
Ithaca *(G-6378)*

Daily Orange Corporation ....E 315 443-2314
Syracuse *(G-14873)*

Dale Press Inc ....E 718 543-6200
Bronx *(G-1236)*

Danet Inc ....F 718 266-4444
Brooklyn *(G-1722)*

Dans Paper Inc ....D 631 537-0500
Southampton *(G-14529)*

Das Yidishe Licht Inc ....G 718 387-3166
Brooklyn *(G-1726)*

Dbg Media ....G 718 599-6828
Brooklyn *(G-1730)*

Delaware County Times Inc ....G 607 746-2176
Delhi *(G-3963)*

Dray Enterprises Inc ....F 585 768-2201
Le Roy *(G-6899)*

Ecclesiastical Communications ....F 212 688-2399
New York *(G-9314)*

Ecuador News Inc ....F 718 205-7014
Woodside *(G-16205)*

Empire Publishing Inc ....F 516 829-4000
Far Rockaway *(G-4564)*

Expositor Newspapers Inc ....G 585 427-2468
Rochester *(G-13407)*

Five Islands Publishing Inc ....F 631 583-5345
Bronx *(G-1258)*

Four Directions Inc ....E 315 829-8388
Vernon *(G-15365)*

French Morning LLC ....G 646 290-7463
New York *(G-9537)*

FT Publications Inc ....E 212 641-2420
New York *(G-9548)*

Fulton Newspapers Inc ....E 315 598-6397
Fulton *(G-5059)*

Gannett Stllite Info Ntwrk Inc ....E 914 965-5000
Yonkers *(G-16312)*

Gannett Stllite Info Ntwrk LLC ....E 845 578-2300
West Nyack *(G-15821)*

Good Health Healthcare Newsppr ....F 585 421-8109
Victor *(G-15411)*

Guest of A Guest Inc ....G 212 206-0397
New York *(G-9694)*

Hagedorn Communications Inc...........D 914 636-7400
New Rochelle *(G-8336)*

Highline Media LLC............................C 859 692-2100
New York *(G-9784)*

Hudson Valley Black Press ....F 845 562-1313
Newburgh *(G-11868)*

Impremedia LLC................................D 212 807-4600
Brooklyn *(G-1954)*

India Abroad Publications Inc ....E 212 929-1727
New York *(G-9880)*

Irish Echo Newspaper Corp ....F 212 482-4818
New York *(G-9942)*

Jewish Press Inc ....C 718 330-1100
Brooklyn *(G-1995)*

Jewish Week Inc ....E 212 921-7822
New York *(G-9998)*

John Lor Publishing Ltd......................E 631 475-1000
Patchogue *(G-12504)*

Johnson Newspaper Corporation ....E 518 483-4700
Malone *(G-7486)*

Journal Register Company ....D 518 584-4242
Saratoga Springs *(G-14184)*

Korea Times New York Inc ....D 718 784-4526
Long Island City *(G-7266)*

Korea Times New York Inc ....G 718 961-7979
Flushing *(G-4868)*

L & M Publications Inc........................E 516 378-3133
Garden City *(G-5103)*

Lee Enterprises Incorporated ....C 518 792-3131
Glens Falls *(G-5255)*

Local Media Group Inc ....B 845 341-1100
Middletown *(G-7915)*

Local Media Group Inc ....E 845 341-1100
Middletown *(G-7916)*

Local Media Group Inc ....F 845 340-4910
Kingston *(G-6700)*

Manchester Newspaper Inc.................E 518 642-1234
Granville *(G-5350)*

Manhattan Media LLC ....F 212 268-8600
New York *(G-10344)*

Manhattan Times Inc ....F 212 569-5800
New York *(G-10346)*

Massapequa Post..............................E 516 798-5100
Massapequa Park *(G-7659)*

McClary Media Inc.............................G 800 453-6397
Amsterdam *(G-334)*

Miami Media LLC..............................F 212 268-8600
New York *(G-10450)*

Nassau County Publications ....G 516 481-5400
Hempstead *(G-5846)*

National Herald Inc ....E 718 784-5255
Long Island City *(G-7303)*

Neighbor To Neighbor News Inc...........G 585 492-2525
Arcade *(G-378)*

New Ski Inc.......................................E 607 277-7000
Ithaca *(G-6401)*

New York Cvl Srvc Emplys Pblsh ....F 212 962-2690
New York *(G-10593)*

New York Daily Challenge Inc ....E 718 636-9500
Brooklyn *(G-2205)*

New York IL Bo Inc ....E 718 961-1538
Flushing *(G-4878)*

News Communications Inc ....F 212 689-2500
New York *(G-10611)*

News Report Inc ....E 718 851-6607
Brooklyn *(G-2213)*

Newspaper Publisher LLC ....F 607 775-0472
Conklin *(G-3626)*

Nordic Press Inc...............................G 212 686-3356
New York *(G-10639)*

North Country This Week Inc ....E 315 265-1000
Potsdam *(G-12938)*

Northern NY Newspapers Corp ....C 315 782-1000
Watertown (G-15586)
Northern Tier Publishing Corp ....F 914 962-4748
Yorktown Heights (G-16369)
Novoye Rsskoye Slovo Pubg Corp ....D 646 460-4566
Brooklyn (G-2222)
Nyc Community Media LLC ....F 212 229-1890
Brooklyn (G-2226)
Page Front Group Inc ....G 716 823-8222
Lackawanna (G-6742)
Patchogue Advance Inc ....E 631 475-1000
Patchogue (G-12509)
Peace Times Weekly Inc ....G 718 762-6500
Flushing (G-4886)
Publishing Group America Inc ....F 646 658-0550
New York (G-10923)
Putnam Cnty News Recorder LLC ....F 845 265-2468
Cold Spring (G-3523)
Quality Guides ....G 716 326-3163
Westfield (G-15948)
Rochester Area Mdia Prtners LL ....F 585 244-3329
Rochester (G-13680)
Rochester Business Journal ....E 585 546-8303
Rochester (G-13683)
Rochester Catholic Press ....F 585 529-9530
Rochester (G-13684)
S I Communications Inc ....F 914 725-2500
Scarsdale (G-14241)
School News Nationwide Inc ....G 718 753-9920
Brooklyn (G-2388)
Sing Tao Newspapers NY Ltd 212 699-3800
New York (G-11248)
Southampton Town Newspapers ....E 631 283-4100
Southampton (G-14538)
Southampton Town Newspapers ....F 631 288-1100
Westhampton Beach (G-15959)
Spartacist Publishing Co ....E 212 732-7860
New York (G-11310)
Steffen Publishing Inc ....D 315 865-4100
Holland Patent (G-6034)
Tablet Publishing Company Inc ....E 718 965-7333
Brooklyn (G-2490)
Thestreet Inc ....D 212 321-5000
New York (G-11465)
Times Beacon Record Newspapers .....F 631 331-1154
East Setauket (G-4188)
Times Review Newspaper Corp ....E 631 354-8031
Mattituck (G-7680)
Tioga County Courier ....G 607 687-0108
Owego (G-12438)
Tri-Village Publishers Inc ....D 518 843-1100
Amsterdam (G-349)
Tribco LLC ....E 718 357-7400
Whitestone (G-16102)
Tricycle Foundation Inc ....G 800 873-9871
New York (G-11544)
Ulster Publishing Co Inc ....E 845 334-8205
Kingston (G-6718)
Ulster Publishing Co Inc ....F 845 255-7005
New Paltz (G-8313)
Wallkill Valley Publications ....E 845 561-0170
Newburgh (G-11893)
Wappingers Falls Shopper Inc ....E 845 297-3723
Wappingers Falls (G-15501)
Wave Publishing Co Inc ....F 718 634-4000
Rockaway Beach (G-13823)
Westfair Communications Inc ....E 914 694-3600
West Harrison (G-15763)
Westside News Inc ....F 585 352-3411
Spencerport (G-14560)
William J Kline & Son Inc ....D 518 843-1100
Amsterdam (G-354)
Worldwide Media Svcs Group Inc ....B 212 545-4800
New York (G-11784)
Yonkers Time Publishing Co ....F 914 965-4000
Yonkers (G-16360)

PUBLISHERS: Pamphlets, No Printing

Spartacist Publishing Co ....E 212 732-7860
New York (G-11310)

PUBLISHERS: Periodical, With Printing

Artifex Press LLC ....F 212 414-1482
New York (G-8635)
Bizbash Media Inc ....D 646 638-3602
New York (G-8804)
Canopy Canopy Canopy Inc ....F 347 529-5182
New York (G-8905)
Eidosmedia Inc ....E 646 795-2100
New York (G-9329)

Frost Publications Inc ....G 845 726-3232
Westtown (G-15965)
Gruner + Jahr USA Group Inc ....B 866 323-9336
New York (G-9688)
H W Wilson Company Inc ....B 718 588-8635
Bronx (G-1271)
Impact Journals LLC ....G 800 922-0957
Orchard Park (G-12354)
The PRS Group Inc ....F 315 431-0511
East Syracuse (G-4242)
Yale Robbins Inc ....D 212 683-5700
New York (G-11805)

PUBLISHERS: Periodicals, Magazines

21st Century Fox America Inc ....D 212 447-4600
New York (G-8397)
American Agora Foundation Inc ....E 212 590-6870
New York (G-8543)
Annointed Buty Ministries LLC ....G 646 867-3796
Brooklyn (G-1513)
Bedford Freeman & Worth ....C 212 576-9400
New York (G-8745)
Binah Magazines Corp ....E 718 305-5200
Brooklyn (G-1587)
BJ Magazines Inc ....G 212 367-9705
New York (G-8805)
Cambridge University Press ....D 212 337-5000
New York (G-8897)
Choice Magazine Listening Inc ....G 516 883-8280
Port Washington (G-12868)
CNY Business Review Inc ....F 315 472-3104
Syracuse (G-14853)
Cornell University ....E 607 254-2473
Ithaca (G-6377)
Delaware County Times Inc ....G 607 746-2176
Delhi (G-3963)
Denton Publications Inc ....E 518 561-9680
Plattsburgh (G-12744)
Dow Jones Aer Company Inc ....A 212 416-2000
New York (G-9260)
Downtown Media Group LLC ....F 646 723-4510
New York (G-9263)
Envy Publishing Group Inc ....G 212 253-9874
New York (G-9385)
Fairchild Publications Inc ....A 212 630-4000
New York (G-9463)
Fairchild Publishing LLC ....G 212 286-3897
New York (G-9464)
Fashion Calendar International ....G 212 289-0420
New York (G-9477)
Frontiers Unlimited Inc ....G 631 283-4663
Southampton (G-14530)
Global Finance Magazine ....G 212 524-3223
New York (G-9625)
Global Finance Media Inc ....F 212 447-7900
New York (G-9626)
Healthy Way of Life Magazine ....G 718 616-1681
Brooklyn (G-1929)
Her Money Media Inc ....G 917 882-3284
Briarcliff Manor (G-1161)
I On Youth ....G 716 832-6509
Buffalo (G-2804)
Jerome Levy Forecasting Center ....G 914 244-8617
Mount Kisco (G-8094)
Laurtom Inc ....E 914 273-2233
Mount Kisco (G-8098)
Lucky Magazine ....F 212 286-6220
New York (G-10279)
Magazine I Spectrum E ....E 212 419-7555
New York (G-10320)
Magnificat Inc ....F 914 502-1820
Yonkers (G-16330)
Media Press Corp ....E 212 791-6347
New York (G-10410)
Njf Publishing Corp ....G 631 345-5200
Shirley (G-14426)
Northeast Group ....D 518 563-8214
Plattsburgh (G-12763)
Northeast Prtg & Dist Co Inc ....G 514 577-3545
Plattsburgh (G-12764)
Paris Review Foundation Inc ....G 212 343-1333
New York (G-10760)
Pearson Education Inc ....F 201 236-7000
West Nyack (G-15829)
Professnal Spt Pblications Inc ....D 516 327-9500
Elmont (G-4388)
Rda Holding Co ....E 914 238-1000
New York (G-10990)
Readers Digest Sls & Svcs Inc ....C 914 238-1000
Pleasantville (G-12799)

Relx Inc ....B 212 633-3900
New York (G-11007)
Rolling Stone Magazine ....G 212 484-1616
New York (G-11077)
Rye Record ....G 914 713-3213
Rye (G-14085)
Small Business Advisors Inc ....F 516 374-1387
Atlantic Beach (G-454)
Standard Analytics Io Inc ....G 917 882-5422
New York (G-11344)
Steffen Publishing Inc ....D 315 865-4100
Holland Patent (G-6034)
Surface Magazine ....E 646 805-0200
New York (G-11400)
Swaps Monitor Publications Inc ....F 212 742-8550
New York (G-11404)
Time Out New York Partners LP ....D 646 432-3000
New York (G-11492)
Trend Pot Inc ....E 212 431-9970
New York (G-11536)
Ubm Inc ....A 212 600-3000
New York (G-11574)
US China Magazine ....E 212 663-4333
New York (G-11622)
Vickers Stock Research Corp ....E 212 425-7500
New York (G-11676)
Wallkill Valley Publications ....E 845 561-0170
Newburgh (G-11893)
Westfair Communications Inc ....E 914 694-3600
West Harrison (G-15763)
Winsight LLC ....G 646 708-7309
New York (G-11769)
Ziff Davis Publishing LLC ....D 212 503-3500
New York (G-11824)

PUBLISHERS: Periodicals, No Printing

Academy of Political Science ....G 212 870-2500
New York (G-8437)
Alcoholics Anonymous Grapevine ....F 212 870-3400
New York (G-8509)
Association For Cmpt McHy Inc ....D 212 869-7440
New York (G-8654)
Bernhard Arnold & Company Inc ....G 212 907-1500
New York (G-8763)
Boardman Simons Publishing ....E 212 620-7200
New York (G-8827)
Brownstone Publishers Inc ....E 212 473-8200
New York (G-8863)
Capital Reg Wkly Newsppr Group ....F 518 674-2841
Averill Park (G-506)
Conference Board Inc ....C 212 759-0900
New York (G-9081)
Congress For Jewish Culture ....G 212 505-8040
New York (G-9083)
Creative Magazine Inc ....G 516 378-0800
Merrick (G-7853)
Economist Intelligence Unit NA ....D 212 554-0600
New York (G-9318)
Francis Emory Fitch Inc ....E 212 619-3800
New York (G-9529)
Global Entity Media Inc ....G 631 580-7772
Ronkonkoma (G-13943)
Government Data Publication ....E 347 789-8719
Brooklyn (G-1904)
Hearst Corporation ....A 518 454-5694
Albany (G-85)
Highline Media LLC ....G 859 692-2100
New York (G-9784)
Human Life Foundation Inc ....G 212 685-5210
New York (G-9837)
International Center For Postg ....G 607 257-5860
Ithaca (G-6387)
Leadership Connect Inc ....D 212 627-4140
New York (G-10182)
Mathisen Ventures Inc ....G 212 986-1025
New York (G-10384)
Optionline LLC ....E 516 218-3225
Garden City (G-5111)
Pati Inc ....F 718 244-6788
Jamaica (G-6464)
Pointwise Information Service ....F 315 457-4111
Liverpool (G-7033)
Psychonomic Society Inc ....E 512 381-1494
New York (G-10919)
Real Est Book of Long Island ....F 516 364-5000
Syosset (G-14801)
Shugar Publishing ....G 631 288-4404
Westhampton Beach (G-15958)
Suffolk Community Council Inc ....G 631 434-9277
Deer Park (G-3940)

PRODUCT

Swift Fulfillment Services .... G 516 593-1198
Lynbrook (G-7440)
Thestreet Inc .... D 212 321-5000
New York (G-11465)
Trader Interntnal Publications .... G 914 631-6856
Sleepy Hollow (G-14464)
Ubm LLC .... D 516 562-7800
New Hyde Park (G-8298)
Value Line Publishing LLC .... C 201 842-8054
New York (G-11638)

PUBLISHERS: Posters

History Publishing Company LLC .... G 845 398-8161
Palisades (G-12481)

PUBLISHERS: Sheet Music

Carl Fischer LLC .... E 212 777-0900
New York (G-8917)
Kendor Music Inc .... F 716 492-1254
Delevan (G-3962)
Warner Music Inc .... D 212 275-2000
New York (G-11723)

PUBLISHERS: Shopping News

Freeville Publishing Co Inc .... F 607 844-9119
Freeville (G-5033)
Service Advertising Group Inc .... F 718 361-6161
Long Island City (G-7355)
Skylark Publications Ltd .... G 607 535-9866
Watkins Glen (G-15615)
Sneaker News Inc .... G 347 687-1588
New York (G-11278)

PUBLISHERS: Technical Manuals

Dayton T Brown Inc .... B 631 589-6300
Bohemia (G-1001)
Elsevier Inc .... B 212 989-5800
New York (G-9352)
Mosby Holdings Corp .... G 212 309-8100
New York (G-10505)

PUBLISHERS: Technical Manuals & Papers

Cambridge Info Group Inc .... F 301 961-6700
New York (G-8896)
Clearstep Technologies LLC .... G 315 952-3628
Camillus (G-3108)

PUBLISHERS: Technical Papers

Humana Press Inc .... E 212 460-1500
New York (G-9838)

PUBLISHERS: Telephone & Other Directory

Auto Market Publications Inc .... G 631 667-0500
Deer Park (G-3844)
Business Directory Inc .... F 718 486-8099
Brooklyn (G-1632)
Fashiondex Inc .... G 914 271-6121
New York (G-9478)
Golf Directories USA Inc .... G 516 365-5351
Manhasset (G-7535)
Israeli Yellow Pages .... E 718 520-1000
Kew Gardens (G-6665)
Korean Yellow Pages .... F 718 461-0073
Flushing (G-4869)
Long Islands Best Inc .... G 855 542-3785
Bohemia (G-1036)
Yellow Pages Inc .... G 845 639-6060
New City (G-8231)

PUBLISHERS: Textbooks, No Printing

Allworth Communications Inc .... F 212 777-8395
New York (G-8522)
Amsco School Publications Inc .... D 212 886-6500
New York (G-8568)
Bedford Freeman & Worth .... D 212 375-7000
New York (G-8746)
Bedford Freeman & Worth .... C 212 576-9400
New York (G-8745)
Booklinks Publishing Svcs LLC .... G 718 852-2116
Brooklyn (G-1602)
Brown Publishing Network Inc .... G 212 682-3330
New York (G-8862)
Cornell University .... D 607 277-2338
Ithaca (G-6376)
E W Williams Publications .... G 212 661-1516
New York (G-9292)

Hippocrene Books Inc .... G 212 685-4371
New York (G-9792)
Houghton Mifflin Harcourt Pubg .... E 212 420-5800
New York (G-9820)
Houghton Mifflin Harcourt Pubg .... C 914 747-2709
Thornwood (G-15070)
Oxford Book Company Inc .... C 212 227-2120
New York (G-10723)
Peter Lang Publishing Inc .... F 212 647-7700
New York (G-10814)
Project Energy Savers LLC .... F 718 596-6448
Brooklyn (G-2300)
W W Norton & Company Inc .... C 212 354-5500
New York (G-11713)
Waldman Publishing Corporation .... F 212 730-9590
New York (G-11716)
Worth Publishers Inc .... C 212 475-6000
New York (G-11787)

PUBLISHERS: Trade journals, No Printing

Access Intelligence LLC .... A 212 204-4269
New York (G-8440)
American Institute Physics Inc .... C 516 576-2410
Melville (G-7760)
American Physical Society .... D 631 591-4025
Ridge (G-13132)
BNP Media Inc .... D 646 849-7100
New York (G-8826)
Demos Medical Publishing LLC .... F 516 889-1791
New York (G-9200)
Direct Mktg Edctl Fndation Inc .... G 212 790-1512
New York (G-9231)
Elmont North Little League .... G 516 775-8210
Elmont (G-4384)
Hatherleigh Company Ltd .... G 607 538-1092
Hobart (G-5978)
Humana Press Inc .... E 212 460-1500
New York (G-9838)
International Data Group Inc .... E 212 331-7883
New York (G-9918)
Japan America Learning Ctr Inc .... F 914 723-7600
Scarsdale (G-14237)
Luria Communications Inc .... G 631 329-4922
East Hampton (G-4125)
Mary Ann Liebert Inc .... D 914 740-2100
New Rochelle (G-8347)
McMahon Group LLC .... D 212 957-5300
New York (G-10402)
NCM Publishers Inc .... G 212 691-9100
New York (G-10560)
Public Relations Soc Amer Inc .... E 212 460-1400
New York (G-10922)
Relx Inc .... E 212 309-8100
New York (G-11005)
Security Letter .... G 212 348-1553
New York (G-11177)
Springer Adis Us LLC .... F 212 460-1500
New York (G-11333)
Springer Healthcare LLC .... E 212 460-1500
New York (G-11334)
Springer Publishing Co LLC .... E 212 431-4370
New York (G-11338)
Springer Scnce + Bus Media LLC ...... D 212 460-1500
New York (G-11339)
Thomas Publishing Company LLC .... B 212 695-0500
New York (G-11468)
Westchester Law Journal Inc .... G 914 948-0715
White Plains (G-16072)

PUBLISHING & BROADCASTING: Internet Only

Ai Media Group Inc .... F 212 660-2400
New York (G-8500)
Aleteia Usa Inc .... G 914 502-1855
Yonkers (G-16281)
Bdg Media Inc .... E 917 551-6510
New York (G-8743)
Bright Line Eting Slutions LLC .... E 585 245-2956
Pittsford (G-12637)
Business Never Stops LLC .... G 888 479-3111
South Richmond Hill (G-14522)
Buzzoole Inc .... G 347 964-0120
New York (G-8875)
Byliner Inc .... E 415 680-3608
New York (G-8879)
Classpass Inc .... E 888 493-5953
New York (G-9027)
East Meet East Inc .... G 646 481-0033
New York (G-9303)

Elite Daily Inc .... F 212 402-9097
New York (G-9343)
Epost International Inc .... G 212 352-9390
New York (G-9388)
Gds Publishing Inc .... F 212 796-2000
New York (G-9583)
Golden Eagle Marketing LLC .... G 212 726-1242
New York (G-9641)
Hearst Digital Studios Inc .... E 212 969-7552
New York (G-9755)
Heed LLC .... E 646 708-7111
New York (G-9762)
Her Money Media Inc .... G 917 882-3284
Briarcliff Manor (G-1161)
Kitcheco Inc .... G 917 388-7479
New York (G-10110)
Media Trust LLC .... G 212 802-1162
New York (G-10412)
Medical Daily Inc .... E 646 867-7100
New York (G-10416)
Mindbodygreen LLC .... E 347 529-6952
Brooklyn (G-2156)
Napean LLC .... G 917 968-6757
New York (G-10533)
Narratively Inc .... E 203 536-0332
Brooklyn (G-2188)
News Now Waverly .... G 607 296-6769
Waverly (G-15624)
Nimbletv Inc .... F 646 502-7010
New York (G-10629)
Pictoure Inc .... G 212 641-0098
New York (G-10836)
Pro Publica Inc .... D 212 514-5250
New York (G-10901)
Qworldstar Inc .... G 212 768-4500
New York (G-10962)
Renegade Nation Online LLC .... G 212 868-9000
New York (G-11014)
Riot New Media Group Inc .... G 604 700-4896
Brooklyn (G-2346)
Sagelife Parenting LLC .... G 315 299-5713
Syracuse (G-14984)
Shepherds PI LLC .... G 516 647-8151
Valley Stream (G-15359)
Sportsgrid Inc .... F 646 849-4085
New York (G-11330)
Standard Analytics Io Inc .... G 917 882-5422
New York (G-11344)
Statebook LLC .... G 845 383-1991
Kingston (G-6711)
Thehuffingtonpostcom Inc .... E 212 245-7844
New York (G-11460)
Theskimm Inc .... F 646 213-4754
New York (G-11464)
Total Webcasting Inc .... G 845 883-0909
New Paltz (G-8311)
Trading Edge Ltd .... G 347 699-7079
Ridgewood (G-13164)
Vinous Group LLC .... G 917 275-5184
New York (G-11685)
Zazoom LLC .... F 212 321-2100
New York (G-11817)

PUBLISHING & PRINTING: Art Copy

Avalon Copy Centers Amer Inc .... D 315 471-3333
Syracuse (G-14823)
Avalon Copy Centers Amer Inc .... E 716 995-7777
Buffalo (G-2651)
Color Unlimited Inc .... G 212 802-7547
New York (G-9055)

PUBLISHING & PRINTING: Book Clubs

Dreams To Print .... G 718 483-8020
Brooklyn (G-1761)
National Learning Corp .... F 516 921-8888
Syosset (G-14796)

PUBLISHING & PRINTING: Book Music

Ai Entertainment Holdings LLC .... F 212 247-6400
New York (G-8499)
Faces Magazine Inc .... D 845 454-7420
Poughkeepsie (G-12955)
Kobalt Music Pubg Amer Inc .... D 212 247-6204
New York (G-10119)

PUBLISHING & PRINTING: Books

450 Ridge St Inc .... G 716 754-2789
Lewiston (G-6919)

Adir Publishing Co	F	718 633-9437	
Brooklyn (G-1461)			
Apollo Investment Fund VII LP	G	212 515-3200	
New York (G-8605)			
Bertelsmann Inc	E	212 782-1000	
New York (G-8764)			
Booklyn Artists Alliance Inc	G	718 383-9621	
Brooklyn (G-1603)			
Callaway Arts & Entrmt Inc	F	646 465-4667	
New York (G-8892)			
Crabtree Publishing Inc	E	212 496-5040	
New York (G-9115)			
D C I Technical Inc	F	516 355-0464	
Franklin Square (G-4960)			
H W Wilson Company Inc	B	718 588-8635	
Bronx (G-1271)			
James Morgan Publishing	G	212 655-5470	
New York (G-9971)			
Klutz	E	650 687-2600	
(G-10115)			
McGraw-Hill School Educatn LLC	A	646 766-2060	
New York (G-10400)			
Metro Creative Graphics Inc	E	212 947-5100	
New York (G-10444)			
Multi Packaging Solutions Inc	G	646 885-0005	
New York (G-10519)			
Nationwide Custom Services	G	845 365-0414	
Tappan (G-15036)			
Natural E Creative LLC	F	516 488-1143	
New Hyde Park (G-8283)			
News India USA Inc	F	212 675-7515	
New York (G-10614)			
Pearson Inc	D	212 641-2400	
New York (G-10782)			
Pearson Longman LLC	C	917 981-2200	
New York (G-10783)			
Pearson Longman LLC	E	212 641-2400	
White Plains (G-16042)			
Samuel French Inc	E	212 206-8990	
New York (G-11126)			
T G S Inc	G	516 629-6905	
Locust Valley (G-7130)			
Windows Media Publishing LLC	E	917 732-7892	
Brooklyn (G-2591)			

PUBLISHING & PRINTING: Catalogs

Global Video LLC	D	516 222-2600	
Woodbury (G-16172)			
Gooding & Associates Inc	F	631 749-3313	
Shelter Island (G-14386)			
Thomas Publishing Company LLC	D	212 695-0500	
New York (G-11469)			

PUBLISHING & PRINTING: Comic Books

Medikidz Usa Inc	G	646 895-9319	
New York (G-10418)			

PUBLISHING & PRINTING: Directories, NEC

Hibu Inc	C	516 730-1900	
East Meadow (G-4137)			
Want-Ad Digest Inc	F	518 279-1181	
Troy (G-15196)			

PUBLISHING & PRINTING: Magazines: publishing & printing

Advance Magazine Publs Inc	G	212 286-8582	
New York (G-8469)			
Advance Magazine Publs Inc	A	212 286-2860	
New York (G-8470)			
Advance Magazine Publs Inc	D	212 790-4422	
New York (G-8471)			
Advance Magazine Publs Inc	D	212 286-2860	
New York (G-8472)			
Advance Magazine Publs Inc	D	212 697-0126	
New York (G-8474)			
Advance Publications Inc	D	718 981-1234	
New York (G-8475)			
Alpha Media Group Inc	B	212 302-2626	
New York (G-8526)			
American Graphic Design Awards	G	212 696-4380	
New York (G-8550)			
American Intl Media LLC	F	845 359-4225	
White Plains (G-15973)			
American Jewish Congress Inc	E	212 879-4500	
New York (G-8554)			
Archaelogy Magazine	E	718 472-3050	
Long Island City (G-7163)			

Artnews Ltd	F	212 398-1690	
New York (G-8639)			
Aspire One Communications LLC	F	201 281-2998	
Cornwall (G-3725)			
Aspire One Communications Inc	G	845 534-6110	
Cornwall (G-3726)			
Bazaar	G	212 903-5497	
New York (G-8742)			
Bertelsmann Inc	E	212 782-1000	
New York (G-8764)			
Blackbook Media Corp	E	212 334-1800	
New York (G-8807)			
Bust Inc	G	212 675-1707	
Brooklyn (G-1634)			
Bz Media LLC	F	631 421-4158	
Melville (G-7763)			
Capco Marketing	F	315 699-1687	
Baldwinsville (G-544)			
City and State Ny LLC	E	212 268-0442	
New York (G-9016)			
City Real Estate Book Inc	G	516 593-2949	
Valley Stream (G-15337)			
Civil Svc Rtred Employees Assn	F	718 937-0290	
Long Island City (G-7185)			
CMX Media LLC	G	917 793-5831	
New York (G-9042)			
Commentary Inc	F	212 891-1400	
New York (G-9066)			
Complex Media Inc	E	917 793-5831	
New York (G-9074)			
Conde Nast Entertainment LLC	A	212 286-2860	
New York (G-9079)			
Convenience Store News	G	214 217-7800	
New York (G-9093)			
Credit Union Journal Inc	G	212 803-8200	
New York (G-9122)			
Davler Media Group LLC	E	212 315-0800	
New York (G-9188)			
Distinction Magazine Inc	E	631 843-3522	
Melville (G-7775)			
Dow Jones & Company Inc	B	609 627-2999	
New York (G-9258)			
Ebner Publishing International	G	646 742-0740	
New York (G-9311)			
Elite Traveler LLC	F	646 430-7900	
New York (G-9346)			
Entrepreneur Media Inc	F	646 502-5463	
New York (G-9383)			
Equal Opprtnity Pblcations Inc	F	631 421-9421	
Melville (G-7778)			
Essential Publications US LLC	G	646 707-0898	
New York (G-9401)			
Excelsior Publications	G	607 746-7600	
Delhi (G-3964)			
Foleon Inc	F	347 727-6809	
New York (G-9513)			
Fortune Media USA Corporation	C	212 522-1212	
New York (G-9518)			
Foundtion For A Mndful Soc Inc	G	902 431-8062	
New York (G-9520)			
Four M Studios	F	212 557-6600	
New York (G-9521)			
Four M Studios	D	515 284-2157	
New York (G-9523)			
Glamour Magazine	G	212 286-2860	
New York (G-9618)			
Green Apple Courage Inc	G	716 614-4673	
Buffalo (G-2785)			
Hearst Corporation	E	212 903-5366	
New York (G-9747)			
Hearst Corporation	D	212 204-4300	
New York (G-9751)			
Hearst Corporation	D	212 903-5000	
New York (G-9752)			
Homesell Inc	F	718 514-0346	
Staten Island (G-14661)			
Icarus Enterprises Inc	G	917 969-4461	
New York (G-9854)			
Index Magazine	G	212 243-1428	
New York (G-9879)			
Informa Media Inc	G	212 204-4200	
New York (G-9890)			
Intercultural Alliance Artists	G	917 406-1202	
Flushing (G-4862)			
Jobson Medical Information LLC	C	212 274-7000	
New York (G-10013)			
Kbs Communications LLC	F	212 765-7124	
New York (G-10085)			
Latina Media Ventures LLC	E	212 642-0200	
New York (G-10177)			

Livid Magazine	F	929 340-7123	
Brooklyn (G-2080)			
Ltb Media (usa) Inc	D	212 447-9555	
New York (G-10278)			
Luminary Publishing Inc	F	845 334-8600	
Kingston (G-6701)			
M Shanken Communications Inc	C	212 684-4224	
New York (G-10301)			
Marie Claire USA	D	212 841-8493	
New York (G-10360)			
Metrosource Publishing Inc	F	212 691-5127	
New York (G-10446)			
Mishpacha Magazine Inc	G	718 686-9339	
Brooklyn (G-2158)			
National Ggraphic Partners LLC	G	212 656-0726	
New York (G-10543)			
Nautilusthink Inc	G	646 239-6858	
New York (G-10555)			
New Hope Media LLC	G	646 366-0830	
New York (G-10585)			
New York Fshion Week Guide LLC	F	646 757-9119	
New York (G-10598)			
Niche Media Holdings LLC	E	702 990-2500	
New York (G-10621)			
Northside Media Group LLC	F	917 318-6513	
Brooklyn (G-2220)			
Nylon Media Inc	E	212 226-6454	
New York (G-10664)			
Odyssey Mag Pubg Group Inc	C	212 545-4800	
New York (G-10681)			
Pensions & Investments	E	212 210-0763	
New York (G-10796)			
Playbill Incorporated	E	212 557-5757	
New York (G-10853)			
Ragozin Data	E	212 674-3123	
Long Island City (G-7338)			
Redbook Magazine	F	212 649-3331	
New York (G-10997)			
Rnd Enterprises Inc	G	212 627-0165	
New York (G-11056)			
Romantic Times Inc	F	718 237-1097	
Brooklyn (G-2353)			
Ross Communications Associates	F	631 393-5089	
Melville (G-7820)			
Saveur Magazine	E	212 219-7400	
New York (G-11141)			
Scoutnews LLC	F	203 855-1400	
Melville (G-7821)			
Sky Art Media Inc	G	917 355-9022	
New York (G-11262)			
Source Media LLC	C	212 803-8200	
New York (G-11304)			
Stuff Magazine	G	212 302-2626	
New York (G-11380)			
Summit Professional Networks	D	212 557-7480	
New York (G-11391)			
Surface Media LLC	G	212 229-1500	
New York (G-11401)			
Sussex Publishers LLC	E	212 260-7210	
New York (G-11402)			
T V Trade Media Inc	F	212 288-3933	
New York (G-11420)			
Thomas Publishing Company LLC	G	212 695-0500	
New York (G-11471)			
TI Gotham Inc	E	212 522-1212	
New York (G-11479)			
Time Out America LLC	C	646 432-3000	
New York (G-11491)			
Towse Publishing Co	F	914 235-3095	
New Rochelle (G-8355)			
Trans-High Corporation	E	212 387-0500	
New York (G-11532)			
TV Guide Magazine LLC	G	800 866-1400	
New York (G-11561)			
Ubm LLC	F	516 562-5000	
New York (G-11575)			
Universal Cmmncations of Miami	C	212 986-5100	
New York (G-11604)			
Uptown Media Group LLC	E	212 360-5073	
New York (G-11614)			
Urbandaddy Inc	F	212 929-7905	
New York (G-11618)			
US News & World Report Inc	C	212 716-6800	
New York (G-11626)			
Valassis Communications Inc	G	585 627-4138	
Rochester (G-13793)			
Vanity Fair	F	212 286-7919	
New York (G-11640)			
Vibe Media Group LLC	D	212 448-7300	
New York (G-11675)			

PRODUCT

Wall Street Reporter Magazine ....D 212 363-2600
  New York (G-11717)
Watch Journal LLC ....G 212 229-1500
  New York (G-11727)
World Business Media LLC.................F 212 344-0759
  Massapequa Park (G-7662)

PUBLISHING & PRINTING: Music, Book

Atlas Music Publishing LLC ....G 646 502-5170
  New York (G-8670)
Princess Music Publishing Co...........E 212 586-0240
  New York (G-10892)
Spirit Music Group Inc ....E 212 533-7672
  New York (G-11324)
Universal Edition Inc ....D 917 213-2177
  New York (G-11605)
Wmg Acquisition Corp ....F 212 275-2000
  New York (G-11771)

PUBLISHING & PRINTING: Newsletters, Business Svc

An Group Inc ....G 631 549-4090
  Melville (G-7761)
Answer Printing Inc ....F 212 922-2922
  New York (G-8595)
Ceo Cast Inc ....F 212 732-4300
  New York (G-8961)
Church Bulletin Inc ....F 631 249-4994
  West Babylon (G-15703)
Froebe Group LLC ....G 646 649-2150
  New York (G-9542)
Portfolio Media Inc ....C 646 783-7100
  New York (G-10868)
Scholastic Inc ....D 212 343-7100
  New York (G-11163)
Ubm Inc ....A 212 600-3000
  New York (G-11574)

PUBLISHING & PRINTING: Newspapers

21st Century Fox America Inc ....G 212 782-8000
  New York (G-8395)
50+ Lifestyle ....G 631 286-0058
  Bellport (G-791)
A Zimmer Ltd ....D 315 422-7011
  Syracuse (G-14808)
Advance Publications Inc ....D 718 981-1234
  New York (G-8475)
After 50 Inc ....G 716 832-9300
  Lancaster (G-6791)
All Island Media Inc.......................C 631 698-8400
  Edgewood (G-4261)
All Island Media Inc.......................E 516 942-8400
  Hicksville (G-5880)
American Sports Media ....G 585 924-4250
  Victor (G-15391)
Amnews Corporation ....E 212 932-7400
  New York (G-8564)
Angola Penny Saver Inc ....F 716 549-1164
  Angola (G-358)
AR Publishing Company Inc.............F 212 482-0303
  New York (G-8615)
Asahi Shimbun America Inc ....F 212 398-0257
  New York (G-8643)
Beth Kobliner Company LLC ....G 212 501-8407
  New York (G-8768)
BNH Lead Examiner Corp ....G 718 807-1365
  Brooklyn (G-1600)
Bradford Publications Inc ....C 716 373-2500
  Olean (G-12226)
Brasilans Press Pblcations Inc...........E 212 764-6161
  New York (G-8848)
Brooklyn Journal Publications ....E 718 422-7400
  Brooklyn (G-1618)
Buffalo News Inc ....A 716 849-4401
  Buffalo (G-2680)
Canarsie Courier Inc ....F 718 257-0600
  Brooklyn (G-1642)
Capital Region Wkly Newspapers ......E 518 877-7160
  Albany (G-56)
Chester West County Press ....G 914 684-0006
  Mount Vernon (G-8129)
Christian Press Inc ....G 718 886-4400
  Flushing (G-4843)
Chronicle Express ....F 315 536-4422
  Penn Yan (G-12580)
Citizen Publishing Corp ....F 845 627-1414
  Nanuet (G-8198)
Cnhi LLC ....E 585 798-1400
  Medina (G-7732)

Columbia Daily Spectator ....E 212 854-9550
  New York (G-9058)
Community Media Group Inc ....D 315 789-3333
  Geneva (G-5151)
Community Media Group LLC ....G 518 439-4949
  Delmar (G-3968)
Community Media LLC ....E 212 229-1890
  New York (G-9070)
Community Newspaper Group LLC ....E 518 565-4114
  Plattsburgh (G-12743)
Copia Interactive LLC ....F 212 481-0520
  New York (G-9098)
Daily Freeman ....F 845 331-5000
  Kingston (G-6688)
Daily Mail & Greene Cnty News ....F 518 943-2100
  Hudson (G-6152)
Daily Muse Inc ....E 646 357-3201
  New York (G-9153)
Daily Racing Form Inc ....C 212 366-7600
  New York (G-9155)
Daily Racing Form LLC ....F 212 514-2180
  New York (G-9156)
Daily Record ....F 585 232-2035
  Rochester (G-13336)
Der Blatt Inc ....F 845 783-1148
  Monroe (G-8019)
Document Journal Inc ....G 646 586-3099
  New York (G-9244)
DOT Publishing ....F 315 593-2510
  Fulton (G-5058)
Dow Jones & Company Inc ....B 609 627-2999
  New York (G-9258)
Dow Jones & Company Inc ....E 212 597-5983
  New York (G-9259)
East Hampton Ind News Inc ....E 631 324-2500
  East Hampton (G-4120)
El Diario LLC ....C 212 807-4600
  Brooklyn (G-1788)
Event Journal Inc ....F 516 470-1811
  Jericho (G-6578)
Evercore Partners Svcs E LLC ....A 212 857-3100
  New York (G-9425)
Exhibits & More ....E 585 924-4040
  Victor (G-15408)
Finger Lakes Media Inc ....F 607 243-7600
  Dundee (G-4046)
Firefighters Journal ....E 718 391-0283
  Long Island City (G-7223)
First Choice News Inc......................G 212 477-2044
  New York (G-9498)
Francepress LLC ....F 646 202-9828
  New York (G-9528)
Fredonia Pennysaver Inc ....G 716 679-1509
  Fredonia (G-4969)
FT Publications Inc ....D 212 641-6500
  New York (G-9547)
Gannett Co Inc ....D 585 232-7100
  Rochester (G-13428)
Gannett Co Inc ....E 914 278-9315
  New Rochelle (G-8333)
Gannett Stllite Info Ntwrk Inc ....D 585 798-1400
  Medina (G-7735)
Gannett Stllite Info Ntwrk LLC ....C 845 454-2000
  Poughkeepsie (G-12956)
Gannett Stllite Info Ntwrk LLC ....F 914 381-3400
  Mamaroneck (G-7511)
Gatehouse Media LLC ....B 585 598-0030
  Pittsford (G-12641)
Gatehouse Media LLC ....E 315 792-5000
  Utica (G-15267)
Gatehouse Media LLC ....G 607 776-2121
  Bath (G-633)
Gatehouse Media LLC ....F 315 866-2220
  Utica (G-15268)
Gatehouse Media LLC ....D 607 936-4651
  Corning (G-3715)
Gatehouse Media LLC ....D 585 394-0770
  Canandaigua (G-3133)
Gatehouse Media LLC ....F 607 324-1425
  Hornell (G-6107)
Gleaner Company Ltd......................G 718 657-0788
  Jamaica (G-6444)
Glens Falls Newspapers Inc ....E 518 792-3131
  Glens Falls (G-5250)
Guardian News & Media LLC ....E 917 900-4663
  New York (G-9691)
Guidance Group Inc ....F 631 756-4618
  Melville (G-7788)
Hamodia Corp ....G 718 338-5637
  Brooklyn (G-1921)

Hamodia Corp ....F 718 853-9094
  Brooklyn (G-1922)
Hearst Communications Inc ....A 212 649-2000
  New York (G-9743)
Hearst Communications Inc ....G 212 247-1014
  New York (G-9744)
Hearst Corporation ....E 212 649-2275
  New York (G-9754)
Herald Publishing Company LLC ....G 315 470-2022
  New York (G-9767)
High Ridge News LLC ....G 718 548-7412
  Bronx (G-1276)
Hudson Group (hg) Inc ....G 212 971-6800
  New York (G-9832)
IMG The Daily ....G 212 541-5640
  New York (G-9868)
Investmentnews LLC ....E 212 210-0100
  New York (G-9935)
Investors Business Daily Inc ....F 212 626-7676
  New York (G-9936)
Irish Tribune Inc ....F 212 684-3366
  New York (G-9943)
Irwin Futures LLC ....G 518 884-9008
  Ballston Spa (G-577)
Jobs Weekly Inc ....F 716 648-5627
  Hamburg (G-5510)
Journal News ....G 914 694-5000
  White Plains (G-16021)
Journal News ....G 845 578-2324
  West Nyack (G-15825)
Korea Central Daily News Inc ....D 718 361-7700
  Long Island City (G-7265)
Lee Newspapers Inc ....F 518 673-3237
  Palatine Bridge (G-12477)
Lee Publications Inc ....D 518 673-3237
  Palatine Bridge (G-12478)
Litmor Publishing Corp ....F 516 931-0012
  Garden City (G-5105)
Livingston County News ....G 585 243-1234
  Geneseo (G-5144)
Lmg National Publishing Inc ....E 585 598-6874
  Fairport (G-4505)
Local Media Group Inc ....F 845 794-3712
  Monticello (G-8070)
Long Island Business News ....E 631 737-1700
  Ronkonkoma (G-13967)
Long Island Cmnty Nwsppers Inc ......F 631 427-7000
  Huntington (G-6212)
Los Angles Tmes Cmmnctions LLC ....E 212 418-9600
  New York (G-10266)
Louis Vuitton North Amer Inc ....G 212 644-2574
  New York (G-10271)
Macandrews & Forbes Inc................C 212 572-8600
  New York (G-10305)
Made Fresh Daily ....G 212 285-2253
  New York (G-10313)
Main Street Connect LLC ....F 203 803-4110
  Armonk (G-400)
Mark I Publications Inc ....E 718 205-8000
  Glendale (G-5228)
Melmont Fine Pringng/Graphics..........G 516 939-2253
  Bethpage (G-839)
Mid-York Press Inc ....D 607 674-4491
  Sherburne (G-14392)
Ming Pao (new York) Inc ....F 212 334-2220
  New York (G-10477)
Minority Reporter Inc ....E 585 225-3628
  Rochester (G-13550)
Minority Reporter Inc ....F 585 301-4199
  Rochester (G-13551)
Moneypaper Inc ....F 914 925-0022
  Rye (G-14083)
NC Audience Exchange LLC.............F 212 416-3400
  New York (G-10559)
New Living Inc ....G 631 751-8819
  Patchogue (G-12507)
New Media Investment Group Inc ......B 212 479-3160
  New York (G-10586)
New Republic ....G 212 989-8200
  New York (G-10589)
New York Daily News ....G 212 248-2100
  New York (G-10594)
New York Press Inc ....E 212 268-8600
  New York (G-10601)
New York Times Company ....B 212 556-1234
  New York (G-10604)
New York Times Company ....F 212 556-4300
  New York (G-10606)
New York University ....E 212 998-4300
  New York (G-10607)

2020 Harris
New York Manufacturers Directory

(G-0000) Company's Geographic Section entry number

New York1 News Operations ....F 212 379-3311
New York (G-10608)

News Corporation ....C 212 416-3400
New York (G-10612)

News India USA Inc ....F 212 675-7515
New York (G-10614)

News Now Waverly ....F 607 296-6769
Waverly (G-15624)

Newsday LLC ....C 631 843-3135
Melville (G-7809)

Newspaper Times Union ....F 518 454-5676
Albany (G-105)

Newsweek LLC ....G 646 867-7100
New York (G-10616)

Newsweek Media Group Inc ....D 646 867-7100
New York (G-10617)

Nick Lugo Inc ....F 212 348-2100
New York (G-10623)

Nikkei America Inc ....E 212 261-6200
New York (G-10627)

Nikkei America Holdings Inc ....D 212 261-6200
New York (G-10628)

Nyp Holdings Inc ....D 718 260-2500
Brooklyn (G-2227)

Nyt Capital LLC ....F 212 556-1234
New York (G-10669)

Nytimes Corporate ....G 212 556-1234
New York (G-10670)

Oak Lone Publishing Co Inc ....E 518 792-1126
Glens Falls (G-5262)

Observer Media LLC ....E 212 755-2400
New York (G-10674)

Oneida Publications Inc ....E 315 363-5100
Oneida (G-12251)

Ottaway Newspapers Inc ....G 845 343-2181
Middletown (G-7925)

Owego Pennysaver Press Inc ....F 607 687-2434
Owego (G-12436)

Pearson Longman LLC ....E 212 641-2400
White Plains (G-16042)

Pennysaver Group Inc ....F 914 966-1400
Yonkers (G-16340)

Pennysaver Group Inc ....F 845 627-3600
New City (G-8228)

Permanent Observer Mission ....G 212 883-0140
New York (G-10806)

Post-Standard CNY Department ....G 315 470-2188
Syracuse (G-14966)

Prospect News Inc ....F 212 374-2800
New York (G-10916)

Queens Ldgr/Grenpoint Star Inc ....F 718 639-7000
Maspeth (G-7636)

R W Publications Div of Wtrhs ....E 716 714-5620
Elma (G-4325)

R W Publications Div of Wtrhs ....E 716 714-5620
Elma (G-4326)

Record Review LLC ....F 914 244-0533
Katonah (G-6638)

Richner Communications Inc ....G 516 569-4000
Lawrence (G-6891)

Rocket Communications Inc.................F 716 873-2594
Buffalo (G-2959)

Rome Main Street Alliance Inc.............G 315 271-8356
Rome (G-13868)

Royal News Corp ....F 212 564-8972
New York (G-11090)

Ruby Newco LLC ....G 212 852-7000
New York (G-11096)

Russkaya Reklama Inc ....G 718 769-3000
Brooklyn (G-2367)

S G New York LLC ....F 631 698-8400
Edgewood (G-4281)

S G New York LLC ....E 631 665-4000
Bohemia (G-1072)

Sample News Group LLC ....D 315 343-3800
Oswego (G-12420)

Sb New York Inc ....D 212 457-7790
New York (G-11144)

Schneps Publications Inc ....G 718 260-2500
Bayside (G-742)

Seabay Media Holdings LLC.................G 212 457-7790
New York (G-11172)

Second Amendment Foundation ....G 716 885-6408
Buffalo (G-2978)

Seneca Media Inc ....D 607 324-1425
Hornell (G-6110)

Service Advertising Group Inc ....F 718 361-6161
Long Island City (G-7355)

Shelter Island Reporter Inc ....G 631 749-1000
Shelter Island (G-14387)

Sing Tao Newspapers NY Ltd ....E 718 821-0123
Brooklyn (G-2423)

Spartan Publishing Inc ....F 716 664-7373
Jamestown (G-6541)

Sports Pblications Prod NY LLC ....D 212 366-7700
New York (G-11327)

Sports Reporter Inc ....G 212 737-2750
New York (G-11329)

Ssrja LLC ....F 718 725-7020
Jamaica (G-6474)

Star Community Publishing...................C 631 843-4050
Melville (G-7824)

Star-Gazette Fund Inc ....C 607 734-5151
Elmira (G-4368)

Straus Communications........................F 845 782-4000
Chester (G-3388)

Stuart Communications Inc ....F 845 252-7414
Narrowsburg (G-8211)

Sun-Times Media Group Inc ....E 716 945-1644
Salamanca (G-14131)

Tech Times LLC ....G 646 599-7201
New York (G-11444)

Terrance Brown ....G 716 648-6171
Hamburg (G-5523)

The Earth Times Foundation ....G 718 297-0488
Brooklyn (G-2501)

Tri-Town News Inc ....E 607 561-3515
Sidney (G-14436)

Tribune Entertainment Co Del ....E 203 866-2204
New York (G-11543)

Trilake Three Press Corp......................E 518 359-2462
Tupper Lake (G-15214)

Unified Media Inc ....F 917 595-2710
New York (G-11584)

USA Today International Corp ....G 703 854-3400
New York (G-11630)

Village Herald ....G 516 569-4403
Lawrence (G-6894)

Vpj Publication Inc ....E 718 845-3221
Howard Beach (G-6143)

W H White Publications Inc..................G 914 725-2500
Dobbs Ferry (G-4021)

W M T Publications Inc ....F 585 244-3329
Rochester (G-13798)

Wayuga Community Newspapers ....E 315 754-6229
Red Creek (G-13071)

Wayuga Community Newspapers ....G 315 594-2506
Wolcott (G-16165)

Weekly Business News Corp ....G 212 689-5888
New York (G-11735)

Westbury Times ....D 516 747-8282
Mineola (G-8003)

World Journal LLC ....C 718 746-8889
Whitestone (G-16104)

World Journal LLC ....F 718 871-5000
Brooklyn (G-2596)

Wp Company LLC ....G 212 445-5050
New York (G-11789)

PUBLISHING & PRINTING: Patterns, Paper

Royalty Network Inc ....G 212 967-4300
New York (G-11092)

PUBLISHING & PRINTING: Posters

Enhance A Colour Corp ....E 212 490-3620
New York (G-9379)

Kjckd Inc ....G 518 435-9696
Latham (G-6862)

Panzarella Prtg & Packg Inc ....G 716 853-4480
Amherst (G-241)

PUBLISHING & PRINTING: Shopping News

Adirondack Pennysaver Inc ....E 518 563-0100
Plattsburgh (G-12731)

City of New York ....E 718 965-8787
Brooklyn (G-1665)

S G New York LLC ....E 631 665-4000
Bohemia (G-1072)

Salamanca Press Penny Saver ....E 716 945-1500
Salamanca (G-14127)

PUBLISHING & PRINTING: Technical Manuals

Dohnsco Inc ....G 516 773-4800
Manhasset (G-7533)

Service Education Incorporated............G 585 264-9240
Victor (G-15431)

PUBLISHING & PRINTING: Textbooks

Bright Kids Nyc Inc...............................E 917 539-4575
New York (G-8852)

Codesters Inc ....G 646 232-1025
New York (G-9048)

Iat Interactive LLC ....E 914 273-2233
Mount Kisco (G-8093)

Pearson Education Holdings Inc ....A 201 236-6716
New York (G-10781)

Peri-Facts Academy..............................G 585 275-6037
Rochester (G-13616)

Warodean Corporation ....G 718 359-5559
Flushing (G-4905)

PUBLISHING & PRINTING: Trade Journals

Beer Marketers Insights Inc ....G 845 507-0040
Suffern (G-14758)

Forum Publishing Co ....G 631 754-5000
Centerport (G-3255)

Guilford Publications Inc ....D 212 431-9800
New York (G-9696)

H F W Communications Inc ....F 315 703-7979
East Syracuse (G-4214)

Institute of Electrical and El.................E 212 705-8900
New York (G-9905)

Lockwood Trade Journal Co Inc............E 212 391-2060
Long Island City (G-7278)

Med Reviews LLC ....E 212 239-5860
New York (G-10407)

PUBLISHING & PRINTING: Yearbooks

Herff Jones LLC ....E 607 936-2366
Corning (G-3716)

Visant Secondary Holdings Corp ....E 914 595-8200
Armonk (G-405)

PULP MILLS

APC Paper Company Inc ....D 315 384-4225
Norfolk (G-11997)

Cenibra Inc ....G 212 818-8242
New York (G-8947)

Easm Machine Works LLC ....E 518 747-5326
Fort Edward (G-4939)

Georgia-Pacific LLC..............................E 631 924-7401
Yaphank (G-16262)

International Paper Company ....C 607 775-1550
Conklin (G-3625)

ITT Industries Holdings Inc ....G 914 641-2000
White Plains (G-16018)

Parsons & Whittemore Inc ....B 914 937-9009
Port Chester (G-12827)

Parsons Whittemore Entps Corp............E 914 937-9009
Port Chester (G-12828)

PULP MILLS: Mech Pulp, Incl Groundwood & Thermomechanical

Norton Pulpstones Incorporated...........G 716 433-9400
Lockport (G-7099)

PULP MILLS: Mechanical & Recycling Processing

Central Nat Pulp & Ppr Sls Inc ....A 914 696-9000
Purchase (G-13003)

Hamlin Bottle & Can Return Inc.............G 585 259-1301
Brockport (G-1177)

Suffolk Indus Recovery Corp.................D 631 732-6403
Coram (G-3700)

PULP MILLS: Soda Pulp

R D S Mountain View Trucking ....G 315 823-4265
Little Falls (G-6992)

PUMICE

A&B Conservation LLC ....G 845 282-7272
Monsey (G-8033)

PUMP GOVERNORS: Gas Machines

Dormitory Authority - State NY ....G 631 434-1487
Brentwood (G-1120)

PUMPS

Air Flow Pump Corp ....G 718 241-2800
Brooklyn (G-1472)

PRODUCT

Air Techniques Inc ....B 516 433-7676
  Melville *(G-7758)*
API International Group LLC ....G 877 215-0017
  Yonkers *(G-16288)*
Curaegis Technologies Inc ....E 585 254-1100
  Rochester *(G-13333)*
Daikin Applied Americas Inc ....D 315 253-2771
  Auburn *(G-472)*
Fisonic Corp ....F 716 763-0295
  New York *(G-9507)*
Fluid Handling LLC ....G 716 897-2800
  Cheektowaga *(G-3349)*
Fluid Metering Inc ....E 516 922-6050
  Syosset *(G-14787)*
Goulds Pumps LLC ....A 315 568-2811
  Seneca Falls *(G-14362)*
Goulds Pumps LLC ....E 315 568-2811
  Seneca Falls *(G-14363)*
ITT Corporation ....D 315 568-2811
  Seneca Falls *(G-14364)*
ITT Goulds Pumps Inc ....A 914 641-2129
  Seneca Falls *(G-14366)*
John N Fehlinger Co Inc ....F 212 233-5656
  New York *(G-10018)*
Ketcham Pump Co Inc ....F 718 457-0800
  Woodside *(G-16210)*
Lanco Manufacturing Co ....G 516 292-8953
  West Hempstead *(G-15774)*
Mannesmann Corporation ....D 212 258-4000
  New York *(G-10348)*
McWane Inc ....B 607 734-2211
  Elmira *(G-4362)*
Messer LLC ....D 716 773-7552
  Grand Island *(G-5337)*
Oyster Bay Pump Works Inc ....F 516 933-4500
  Hicksville *(G-5937)*
Pumpcrete Corporation ....G 716 667-7867
  Orchard Park *(G-12374)*
Voss Usa Inc ....C 212 995-2255
  New York *(G-11707)*
Wastecorp Pumps LLC ....F 888 829-2783
  New York *(G-11726)*
Xylem Inc ....D 315 239-2499
  Seneca Falls *(G-14375)*
Xylem Inc ....B 914 323-5700
  Rye Brook *(G-14095)*

PUMPS & PARTS: Indl

Armstrong Pumps Inc ....D 716 693-8813
  North Tonawanda *(G-12053)*
Century-Tech Inc ....F 718 326-9400
  Hempstead *(G-5835)*
Federal Pump Corporation ....E 718 451-2000
  New York *(G-9481)*
Fisonic Corp ....G 212 732-3777
  Long Island City *(G-7225)*
Gardner Dnver Oberdorfer Pumps ...E 315 437-0361
  Syracuse *(G-14900)*
Oberdorfer Pumps Inc ....E 315 437-0361
  Syracuse *(G-14952)*
Pulsafeeder Inc ....C 585 292-8000
  Rochester *(G-13653)*
Stavo Industries Inc ....F 845 331-4552
  Kingston *(G-6712)*
Westmoor Ltd ....F 315 363-1500
  Sherrill *(G-14409)*

PUMPS & PUMPING EQPT REPAIR SVCS

A & C/Furia Electric Motors ....F 914 949-0585
  White Plains *(G-15968)*
Daves Electric Motors & Pumps .....G 212 982-2930
  New York *(G-9176)*
Fuel Energy Services USA Ltd ....E 607 846-2650
  Horseheads *(G-6124)*
Sunset Ridge Holdings Inc ....G 716 487-1458
  Jamestown *(G-6546)*

PUMPS & PUMPING EQPT WHOLESALERS

Cummins-Wagner-Siewert LLC .....E 585 482-9640
  Rochester *(G-13332)*
Electric Motors and Pumps Inc .....G 718 935-9118
  Brooklyn *(G-1790)*

PUMPS, HEAT: Electric

Economy Pump & Motor Repr Inc ...G 718 433-2600
  Astoria *(G-418)*

PUMPS: Domestic, Water Or Sump

Flow Control LLC ....C 914 323-5700
  Rye Brook *(G-14089)*
Geopump Inc ....G 585 798-6666
  Medina *(G-7736)*
Liberty Pumps Inc ....C 800 543-2550
  Bergen *(G-817)*
Pentair Water Pool and Spa Inc ....E 845 452-5500
  Lagrangeville *(G-6753)*
Trench & Marine Pump Co Inc ....E 212 423-9098
  Bronx *(G-1381)*
Water Cooling Corp ....G 718 723-6500
  Rosedale *(G-14038)*

PUMPS: Fluid Power

Parker-Hannifin Corporation ....C 716 686-6400
  Lancaster *(G-6821)*

PUMPS: Measuring & Dispensing

Aptargroup Inc ....C 845 639-3700
  Congers *(G-3608)*
Charles Ross & Son Company ....D 631 234-0500
  Hauppauge *(G-5614)*
Economy Pump & Motor Repr Inc ...G 718 433-2600
  Astoria *(G-418)*
Pulsafeeder Inc ....C 585 292-8000
  Rochester *(G-13653)*
Schlumberger Technology Corp .....C 607 378-0105
  Horseheads *(G-6136)*
Valois of America Inc ....C 845 639-3700
  Congers *(G-3619)*

PUMPS: Vacuum, Exc Laboratory

Graham Corporation ....B 585 343-2216
  Batavia *(G-616)*
Precision Plus Vacuum Parts ....D 716 297-2039
  Sanborn *(G-14147)*

PUNCHES: Forming & Stamping

Arro Manufacturing LLC ....F 716 763-6203
  Lakewood *(G-6778)*
Pivot Punch Corporation ....D 716 625-8000
  Lockport *(G-7101)*
Precise Punch Corporation ....F 716 625-8000
  Lockport *(G-7102)*

PURIFICATION & DUST COLLECTION EQPT

Hilliard Corporation ....B 607 733-7121
  Elmira *(G-4357)*
Hilliard Corporation ....B 607 733-7121
  Elmira *(G-4358)*
Low-Cost Mfg Co Inc ....G 516 627-3282
  Carle Place *(G-3176)*
Oneida Air Systems Inc ....E 315 476-5151
  Syracuse *(G-14956)*

PURSES: Women's

Formart Corp ....F 212 819-1819
  New York *(G-9516)*

PUSHCARTS & WHEELBARROWS

Truxton Corp ....G 718 842-6000
  Bronx *(G-1383)*

QUICKLIME

Minerals Technologies Inc ....E 212 878-1800
  New York *(G-10476)*

RACE TRACK OPERATION

P S M Group Inc ....E 716 532-6686
  Forestville *(G-4932)*

RACKS & SHELVING: Household, Wood

American Epoxy and Metal Inc ......G 718 828-7828
  Scarsdale *(G-14233)*

RACKS: Garment, Exc Wood

ASAP Rack Rental Inc ....G 718 499-4495
  Brooklyn *(G-1539)*
Lifestyle-Trimco ....E 718 257-9101
  Brooklyn *(G-2069)*
Millennium Stl Rack Rntals Inc ......G 718 965-4736
  Brooklyn *(G-2155)*

RACKS: Garment, Wood

Lifestyle-Trimco ....E 718 257-9101
  Brooklyn *(G-2069)*

RACKS: Pallet, Exc Wood

Frazier Industrial Company ....D 315 539-9256
  Waterloo *(G-15552)*

RADAR SYSTEMS & EQPT

Artemis Inc ....G 631 232-2424
  Hauppauge *(G-5594)*
ITT Corporation ....D 315 568-2811
  Seneca Falls *(G-14364)*
ITT Inc ....C 914 641-2000
  White Plains *(G-16017)*
ITT LLC ....B 914 641-2000
  White Plains *(G-16020)*
ITT LLC ....D 914 641-2000
  Seneca Falls *(G-14368)*
Laufer Wind Group LLC ....F 212 792-3912
  New York *(G-10178)*
Penetradar Corporation ....F 716 731-2629
  Niagara Falls *(G-11964)*
Systems Drs C3 Inc ....B 716 631-6200
  Buffalo *(G-3000)*
Telephonics Corporation ....A 631 755-7000
  Farmingdale *(G-4752)*
Traffic Logix Corporation ....G 866 915-6449
  Spring Valley *(G-14583)*

RADIO & TELEVISION COMMUNICATIONS EQUIPMENT

Airnet Communications Corp ....F 516 338-0008
  Westbury *(G-15864)*
Ashly Audio Inc ....E 585 872-0010
  Webster *(G-15630)*
AVI-Spl Employee ....B 212 840-4801
  New York *(G-8691)*
Benchmark Media Systems Inc .....F 315 437-6300
  Syracuse *(G-14828)*
Chyronhego Corporation ....D 631 845-2000
  Melville *(G-7767)*
CJ Component Products LLC ....G 631 567-3733
  Oakdale *(G-12149)*
Clever Devices Ltd ....E 516 433-6100
  Woodbury *(G-16167)*
Electro-Metrics Corporation ....E 518 762-2600
  Johnstown *(G-6614)*
Eni Technology Inc ....B 585 427-8300
  Rochester *(G-13395)*
Fujitsu Ntwrk Cmmnications Inc ....F 845 731-2000
  Pearl River *(G-12531)*
GE Mds LLC ....C 585 242-9600
  Rochester *(G-13430)*
Griffon Corporation ....E 212 957-5000
  New York *(G-9676)*
Gurley Precision Instrs Inc ....C 518 272-6300
  Troy *(G-15170)*
It Commodity Sourcing Inc ....G 718 677-1577
  Brooklyn *(G-1972)*
L3 Technologies Inc ....A 631 436-7400
  Hauppauge *(G-5687)*
L3harris Technologies Inc ....A 585 244-5830
  Rochester *(G-13507)*
L3harris Technologies Inc ....B 585 244-5830
  Rochester *(G-13512)*
L3harris Technologies Inc ....F 718 767-1100
  Whitestone *(G-16096)*
L3harris Technologies Inc ....B 585 244-5830
  Rochester *(G-13513)*
L3harris Technologies Inc ....A 631 630-4200
  Amityville *(G-288)*
Listec Video Corp ....G 631 273-3029
  Hauppauge *(G-5692)*
Mark Peri International ....F 516 208-6824
  Oceanside *(G-12181)*
Mini-Circuits Fort Wayne LLC ....B 718 934-4500
  Brooklyn *(G-2157)*
Mirion Tech Imaging LLC ....C 607 562-4300
  Horseheads *(G-6127)*
Mitel Networks Inc ....G 877 654-3573
  Rochester *(G-13553)*
Motorola Solutions Inc ....C 518 869-9517
  Albany *(G-101)*
Motorola Solutions Sls & Svcs ......E 716 633-5022
  Williamsville *(G-16134)*
Movin On Sounds and SEC Inc .....E 516 489-2350
  Franklin Square *(G-4962)*

Navitar Inc ....D...... 585 359-4000
  Rochester *(G-13568)*

Quanta Electronics Inc ....F...... 631 961-9953
  Centereach *(G-3252)*

Quintel Usa Inc ....E...... 585 420-8364
  Rochester *(G-13665)*

Ruhle Companies Inc ....E...... 914 287-4000
  Valhalla *(G-15309)*

Sdr Technology Inc ....G...... 716 583-1249
  Alden *(G-174)*

Telephonics Corporation ....A...... 631 755-7000
  Farmingdale *(G-4752)*

Telxon Corporation ....E...... 631 738-2400
  Holtsville *(G-6056)*

US Space LLC ....G...... 646 278-0371
  New York *(G-11627)*

Whirlwind Music Distrs Inc ....D...... 800 733-9473
  Rochester *(G-13803)*

Zetek Corporation ....F...... 212 668-1485
  New York *(G-11821)*

RADIO & TELEVISION REPAIR

NCR Corporation ....C...... 516 876-7200
  Jericho *(G-6586)*

RADIO BROADCASTING & COMMUNICATIONS EQPT

Apex Airtronics Inc ....E...... 718 485-8560
  Brooklyn *(G-1516)*

Appairent Technologies Inc ....G...... 585 214-2460
  West Henrietta *(G-15785)*

Fleetcom Inc ....F...... 914 776-5582
  Yonkers *(G-16310)*

Hamtronics Inc ....G...... 585 392-9430
  Rochester *(G-13457)*

L3 Technologies Inc ....D...... 631 436-7400
  Hauppauge *(G-5689)*

Motorola Solutions Inc ....C...... 518 348-0833
  Halfmoon *(G-5495)*

North American MBL Systems Inc .....E...... 718 898-8700
  Sea Cliff *(G-14346)*

Wireless Communications Inc ....G...... 845 353-5921
  Nyack *(G-12148)*

RADIO BROADCASTING STATIONS

Iheartcommunications Inc ....C...... 585 454-4884
  Rochester *(G-13475)*

New York Times Company ....B...... 212 556-1234
  New York *(G-10604)*

RADIO RECEIVER NETWORKS

Cntry Cross Communications LLC .....F...... 386 758-9696
  Jamestown *(G-6503)*

Iheartcommunications Inc ....C...... 585 454-4884
  Rochester *(G-13475)*

RADIO, TELEVISION & CONSUMER ELECTRONICS STORES: Eqpt, NEC

Electrotech Service Eqp Corp ....E...... 718 626-7700
  Astoria *(G-419)*

Pass & Seymour Inc ....B...... 315 468-6211
  Syracuse *(G-14963)*

Sound Source Inc ....G...... 585 271-5370
  Rochester *(G-13737)*

RADIO, TV & CONSUMER ELEC STORES: Automotive Sound Eqpt

Ghostek LLC ....F...... 855 310-3439
  Brooklyn *(G-1885)*

RADIO, TV & CONSUMER ELECTRONICS: VCR & Access

Elite Cellular Accessories Inc ....E...... 877 390-2502
  Deer Park *(G-3869)*

RADIO, TV/CONSUMER ELEC STORES: Antennas, Satellite Dish

L3 Technologies Inc ....D...... 631 231-1700
  Hauppauge *(G-5688)*

RAILINGS: Prefabricated, Metal

D V S Iron & Aluminum Works ....G...... 718 768-7961
  Brooklyn *(G-1716)*

Paragon Aquatics ....E...... 845 452-5500
  Lagrangeville *(G-6752)*

RAILINGS: Wood

Blooming Grove Stair Co ....G...... 845 783-4245
  Monroe *(G-8016)*

Blooming Grove Stair Co ....G...... 845 791-4016
  Monticello *(G-8069)*

D K P Wood Railings & Stairs ....F...... 631 665-8656
  Bay Shore *(G-669)*

Deer Pk Stair Bldg Mllwk Inc ....E...... 631 363-5000
  Blue Point *(G-956)*

Rockaway Stairs Ltd ....G...... 718 945-0047
  Far Rockaway *(G-4567)*

Stairworld Inc ....G...... 718 441-9722
  Fresh Meadows *(G-5046)*

RAILROAD CAR RENTING & LEASING SVCS

Acf Industries Holding LLC ....G...... 212 702-4363
  New York *(G-8447)*

Highcrest Investors LLC ....D...... 212 702-4323
  New York *(G-9783)*

Starfire Holding Corporation ....E...... 914 614-7000
  New York *(G-11350)*

RAILROAD CAR REPAIR SVCS

Acf Industries Holding LLC ....G...... 212 702-4363
  New York *(G-8447)*

Ebenezer Railcar Services Inc ....D...... 716 674-5650
  West Seneca *(G-15846)*

Highcrest Investors LLC ....D...... 212 702-4323
  New York *(G-9783)*

Starfire Holding Corporation ....E...... 914 614-7000
  New York *(G-11350)*

RAILROAD CARGO LOADING & UNLOADING SVCS

Brook & Whittle Limited ....C...... 716 853-1688
  Buffalo *(G-2666)*

RAILROAD EQPT

Bombardier Mass Transit Corp ....B...... 518 566-0150
  Plattsburgh *(G-12737)*

CAF Usa Inc ....D...... 607 737-3004
  Elmira Heights *(G-4375)*

Cox & Company Inc ....C...... 212 366-0200
  Plainview *(G-12676)*

Eagle Bridge Machine & TI Inc ....E...... 518 686-4541
  Eagle Bridge *(G-4071)*

Ebenezer Railcar Services Inc ....D...... 716 674-5650
  West Seneca *(G-15846)*

Gray Manufacturing Inds LLC ....F...... 607 281-1325
  Hornell *(G-6108)*

Horne Products Inc ....G...... 631 293-0773
  Farmingdale *(G-4645)*

Hudson Machine Works Inc ....C...... 845 279-1413
  Brewster *(G-1152)*

Knorr Brake Holding Corp ....G...... 315 786-5356
  Watertown *(G-15578)*

Matrix Railway Corp ....G...... 631 643-1483
  West Babylon *(G-15730)*

Peck & Hale LLC ....E...... 631 589-2510
  West Sayville *(G-15842)*

Semec Corp ....F...... 518 825-0160
  Plattsburgh *(G-12776)*

Strato Transit Components LLC ....C...... 518 686-4541
  Eagle Bridge *(G-4075)*

Transco Railway Products Inc ....E...... 716 825-1663
  Buffalo *(G-3018)*

Twinco Mfg Co Inc ....E...... 631 231-0022
  Hauppauge *(G-5789)*

Westcode Incorporated ....E...... 607 766-9881
  Binghamton *(G-916)*

RAILROAD EQPT & SPLYS WHOLESALERS

Horne Products Inc ....G...... 631 293-0773
  Farmingdale *(G-4645)*

RAILROAD EQPT, EXC LOCOMOTIVES

Bombardier Transportation ....D...... 607 324-0216
  Hornell *(G-6102)*

Kawasaki Rail Car Inc ....C...... 914 376-4700
  Yonkers *(G-16323)*

Transco Railway Products Inc ....F...... 716 824-1219
  Blasdell *(G-923)*

RAILROAD EQPT: Brakes, Air & Vacuum

Knorr Brake Company LLC ....G...... 518 561-1387
  Plattsburgh *(G-12756)*

Knorr Brake Truck Systems Co ....B...... 315 786-5200
  Watertown *(G-15579)*

New York Air Brake LLC ....E...... 315 786-5576
  Watertown *(G-15583)*

New York Air Brake LLC ....C...... 315 786-5219
  Watertown *(G-15584)*

Westinghouse A Brake Tech Corp ......D...... 518 561-0044
  Plattsburgh *(G-12791)*

RAILROAD EQPT: Cars & Eqpt, Dining

Acf Industries Holding LLC ....G...... 212 702-4363
  New York *(G-8447)*

Highcrest Investors LLC ....D...... 212 702-4323
  New York *(G-9783)*

Starfire Holding Corporation ....E...... 914 614-7000
  New York *(G-11350)*

RAILROAD EQPT: Cars & Eqpt, Rapid Transit

Seisenbacher Inc ....F...... 585 730-4960
  Rochester *(G-13721)*

Westinghouse A Brake Tech Corp ......F...... 914 347-8650
  Elmsford *(G-4440)*

RAILROAD EQPT: Cars, Maintenance

Koshii Maxelum America Inc ....E...... 845 471-0500
  Poughkeepsie *(G-12966)*

RAILROAD EQPT: Cars, Motor

Siemens Mobility Inc ....F...... 212 672-4000
  New York *(G-11227)*

RAILROAD EQPT: Locomotives & Parts, Indl

Rand Machine Products, Inc. ....C...... 716 665-5217
  Falconer *(G-4552)*

RAILROAD RELATED EQPT: Railway Track

Applied Technology Mfg Corp ....E...... 607 687-2200
  Owego *(G-12428)*

Railworks Transit Systems Inc ....F...... 212 502-7900
  New York *(G-10972)*

RAILS: Steel Or Iron

Artistic Iron Works Inc ....G...... 631 665-4285
  Bay Shore *(G-652)*

RAMPS: Prefabricated Metal

Landmark Group Inc ....E...... 845 358-0350
  Valley Cottage *(G-15317)*

RAZORS, RAZOR BLADES

HFC Prestige Intl US LLC ....A...... 212 389-7800
  New York *(G-9778)*

RAZORS: Electric

Harrys Inc ....D...... 888 212-6855
  New York *(G-9733)*

REAL ESTATE AGENCIES & BROKERS

Yale Robbins Inc ....D...... 212 683-5700
  New York *(G-11805)*

REAL ESTATE AGENTS & MANAGERS

Directory Major Malls Inc ....G...... 845 348-7000
  Nyack *(G-12141)*

REAL ESTATE OPERATORS, EXC DEVELOPERS: Apartment Hotel

Atlas Bituminous Co Inc ....F...... 315 457-2394
  Syracuse *(G-14820)*

REAL ESTATE OPERATORS, EXC DEVELOPERS: Commercial/Indl Bldg

Bertelsmann Inc ....E...... 212 782-1000
  New York *(G-8764)*

E F Thresh Inc ....G...... 315 437-7301
  East Syracuse *(G-4208)*

PRODUCT

Penhouse Media Group Inc..............C...... 212 702-6000
New York (G-10795)

RECEIVERS: Radio Communications

Harris Globl Cmmunications Inc ....A...... 585 244-5830
Rochester (G-13460)

RECLAIMED RUBBER: Reworked By Manufacturing Process

Hti Recycling LLC ....E...... 716 433-9294
Lockport (G-7083)
Rubberform Recycled Pdts LLC...........F...... 716 478-0404
Lockport (G-7105)

RECORD BLANKS: Phonographic

Chesky Records Inc ....F...... 212 586-7799
New York (G-8983)
Europadisk LLC ....E...... 718 407-7300
Long Island City (G-7216)

RECORDING HEADS: Speech & Musical Eqpt

Fine Sounds Group Inc ....F...... 212 364-0219
New York (G-9496)

RECORDS & TAPES: Prerecorded

Columbia Records Inc ....F...... 212 833-8000
New York (G-9059)
Cult Records LLC ....G...... 718 395-2077
New York (G-9131)
Emusiccom Inc..............................D...... 212 201-9240
New York (G-9365)
Extreme Group Holdings LLC...........F...... 212 833-8000
New York (G-9450)
High Quality Video Inc ....F...... 212 686-9534
New York (G-9782)
His Productions USA Inc...................G...... 212 594-3737
New York (G-9793)
Lefrak Entertainment Co Ltd ....G...... 212 586-3600
New York (G-10192)
Pete Levin Music Inc........................G...... 845 247-9211
Saugerties (G-14209)
Pivot Records LLC ....F...... 718 417-1213
Brooklyn (G-2264)
Recorded Anthology of Amrcn Mus ....F...... 212 290-1695
Brooklyn (G-2333)
Side Hustle Music Group LLC ....F...... 800 219-4003
New York (G-11223)
Sony Broadband Entertainment...........F...... 212 833-6800
New York (G-11294)
Sony Music Entertainment ....A...... 212 833-8000
New York (G-11297)
Sony Music Entertainment Inc...........A...... 212 833-8000
New York (G-11298)
Sony Music Holdings Inc ....A...... 212 833-8000
New York (G-11299)
Universal Music Group Inc ....F...... 212 333-8237
New York (G-11609)
Warner Music Group Corp ....C...... 212 275-2000
New York (G-11722)

RECORDS OR TAPES: Masters

Bridge Records Inc ....G...... 914 654-9270
New Rochelle (G-8322)
Masterdisk Corporation.....................F...... 212 541-5022
Elmsford (G-4417)
Peer-Southern Productions Inc ....E...... 212 265-3910
New York (G-10786)
Sterling Sound Inc ....E...... 212 604-9433
New York (G-11360)
Wea International Inc ....D...... 212 275-1300
New York (G-11734)

RECOVERY SVC: Iron Ore, From Open Hearth Slag

Robert J Deluca Associates...............G...... 845 357-3212
New York (G-11061)

RECOVERY SVCS: Metal

Island Recycling Corp ....G...... 631 234-6688
Central Islip (G-3279)

RECREATIONAL & SPORTING CAMPS

Steel Excel Inc................................G...... 914 461-1300
White Plains (G-16063)

RECTIFIERS: Electrical Apparatus

Ems Development Corporation ....D...... 631 924-4736
Yaphank (G-16259)
Solid Sealing Technology Inc ....E...... 518 874-3600
Watervliet (G-15606)

RECTIFIERS: Solid State

Electronic Devices Inc ....E...... 914 965-4400
Yonkers (G-16306)

RECYCLABLE SCRAP & WASTE MATERIALS WHOLESALERS

Metalico Aluminum Recovery Inc...........E...... 315 463-9500
Syracuse (G-14940)

RECYCLING: Paper

Advanced Recovery & Recycl LLC ....F...... 315 450-3301
Baldwinsville (G-540)
Andritz Inc ....E...... 518 745-2988
Glens Falls (G-5240)
Fcr LLC ....G...... 845 926-1071
Beacon (G-752)
Georgia-Pacific Corrugared LLC ....D...... 585 343-3800
Batavia (G-615)
Harvest Technologies Inc...................G...... 518 899-7124
Ballston Spa (G-576)
Repapers Corporation ....G...... 305 691-1635
Hicksville (G-5945)
Sierra Processing LLC ....F...... 518 433-0020
Schenectady (G-14305)

REELS: Cable, Metal

Hannay Reels Inc ....C...... 518 797-3791
Westerlo (G-15941)
Reelcology Inc.................................F...... 845 258-1880
Pine Island (G-12630)

REFINERS & SMELTERS: Aluminum

Metalico Aluminum Recovery Inc..........E...... 315 463-9500
Syracuse (G-14940)

REFINERS & SMELTERS: Antimony, Primary

Zerovalent Nanometals Inc ....G...... 585 298-8592
Rochester (G-13814)

REFINERS & SMELTERS: Cobalt, Primary

Umicore USA Inc.............................E...... 919 874-7171
Glens Falls (G-5268)

REFINERS & SMELTERS: Copper

Sherburne Metal Sales Inc ....F...... 607 674-4441
Sherburne (G-14393)
Tecnofil Chenango SAC ....E...... 607 674-4441
Sherburne (G-14396)

REFINERS & SMELTERS: Copper, Secondary

Ben Weitsman of Albany LLC ....E...... 518 462-4444
Albany (G-46)

REFINERS & SMELTERS: Gold

Electro Alloy Recovery Inc.................G...... 631 879-7530
Bohemia (G-1012)
General Refining & Semlt Corp ....G...... 516 538-4747
Hempstead (G-5836)
General Refining Corporation..............G...... 516 538-4747
Hempstead (G-5837)

REFINERS & SMELTERS: Nonferrous Metal

Advanced Precision Technology...........F...... 845 279-3540
Brewster (G-1138)
Amt Incorporated.............................E...... 518 284-2910
Sharon Springs (G-14382)
Cora Materials Corp ....F...... 516 488-6300
New Hyde Park (G-8260)
General Refining & Semlt Corp ....G...... 516 538-4747
Hempstead (G-5836)
Germanium Corp America Inc ....F...... 315 853-4900
Clinton (G-3482)
Karbra Company ....C...... 212 736-9300
New York (G-10069)
Parfuse Corp ....E...... 516 997-8888
Westbury (G-15916)

Pluribus Products Inc.......................E...... 718 852-1614
Bayville (G-747)
S & W Metal Trading Corp ....G...... 212 719-5070
Brooklyn (G-2375)
Sims Group USA Holdings Corp ....D...... 718 786-6031
Long Island City (G-7357)
Special Metals Corporation.................D...... 716 366-5663
Dunkirk (G-4067)

REFINERS & SMELTERS: Platinum Group Metal Refining, Primary

AAA Catalytic Recycling Inc ....F...... 631 920-7944
Farmingdale (G-4570)
Marco Industries Ltd.........................G...... 212 798-8100
New York (G-10356)

REFINERS & SMELTERS: Silicon, Primary, Over 99% Pure

Globe Metallurgical Inc.....................D...... 716 804-0862
Niagara Falls (G-11931)

REFINERS & SMELTERS: Silver

Rochester Silver Works LLC...............G...... 585 743-1610
Rochester (G-13697)
Umicore Elec Mtls USA Inc ....C...... 518 792-7700
Glens Falls (G-5267)

REFINERS & SMELTERS: Zinc, Primary, Including Slabs & Dust

Hh Liquidating Corp ....A...... 646 282-2500
New York (G-9779)

REFINING LUBRICATING OILS & GREASES, NEC

Industrial Oil Tank Service ....F...... 315 736-6080
Oriskany (G-12392)
Safety-Kleen Systems Inc ....F...... 716 855-2212
Buffalo (G-2972)

REFINING: Petroleum

California Petro Trnspt Corp................G...... 212 302-5151
New York (G-8889)
Hess Corporation.............................B...... 212 997-8500
New York (G-9771)
Hess Oil Virgin Island Corp................A...... 212 997-8500
New York (G-9774)
Hess Pipeline Corporation..................C...... 212 997-8500
New York (G-9775)
Iep Energy Holding LLC ....A...... 212 702-4300
New York (G-9859)
Koch Supply & Trading LP ....G...... 212 319-4895
New York (G-10121)
Motiva Enterprises LLC.....................G...... 516 371-4780
Lawrence (G-6889)
Petre Alii Petroleum ....G...... 315 785-1037
Watertown (G-15587)

REFRACTORIES: Alumina Fused

Global Alumina Services Co ....B...... 212 309-8060
New York (G-9623)

REFRACTORIES: Brick

Capitol Restoration Corp ....G...... 516 783-1425
North Bellmore (G-12014)

REFRACTORIES: Brick

Saint-Gobain Strl Ceramics ....A...... 716 278-6233
Niagara Falls (G-11979)

REFRACTORIES: Clay

Filtros Ltd ....E...... 585 586-8770
East Rochester (G-4163)
Upstate Refractory Svcs Inc ....E...... 315 331-2955
Newark (G-11855)

REFRACTORIES: Graphite, Carbon Or Ceramic Bond

Blasch Precision Ceramics Inc............D...... 518 436-1263
Menands (G-7841)
Surmet Ceramics Corporation.............F...... 716 875-4091
Buffalo (G-2997)

REFRACTORIES: Nonclay

Filtros Ltd ....E 585 586-8770
East Rochester *(G-4163)*

Lucideon ....F 518 382-0082
Schenectady *(G-14287)*

Monofrax LLC ....C 716 483-7200
Falconer *(G-4550)*

Rembar Company LLC ....E 914 693-2620
Dobbs Ferry *(G-4019)*

Saint-Gobain Dynamics Inc ....F 716 278-6007
Niagara Falls *(G-11978)*

Unifrax I LLC ....C 716 696-3000
Tonawanda *(G-15149)*

Zircar Ceramics Inc ....E 845 651-6600
Florida *(G-4827)*

Zircar Refr Composites Inc ....G 845 651-4481
Florida *(G-4829)*

Zircar Zirconia Inc ....E 845 651-3040
Florida *(G-4830)*

REFRACTORY MATERIALS WHOLESALERS

Upstate Refractory Svcs Inc ....E 315 331-2955
Newark *(G-11855)*

REFRIGERATION & HEATING EQUIPMENT

A&S Refrigeration Equipment ....G 718 993-6030
Bronx *(G-1187)*

Besicorp Ltd ....F 845 336-7700
Kingston *(G-6680)*

Bombardier Trnsp Holdings USA ....D 607 776-4791
Bath *(G-631)*

Carrier Corporation ....A 315 432-6000
Syracuse *(G-14845)*

Carrier Corporation ....B 315 432-6000
Syracuse *(G-14844)*

Cold Point Corporation ....E 315 339-2331
Rome *(G-13847)*

Columbia Pool Accessories Inc ....G 718 993-0389
Bronx *(G-1229)*

Environmental Temp Systems LLC .....G 516 640-5818
Mineola *(G-7971)*

Fts Systems Inc ....D 845 687-5300
Stone Ridge *(G-14735)*

GM Components Holdings LLC ....B 716 439-2463
Lockport *(G-7079)*

GM Components Holdings LLC ....B 716 439-2011
Lockport *(G-7080)*

Healthway Products Company ....E 315 207-1410
Oswego *(G-12411)*

Hydro-Air Components Inc ....C 716 827-6510
Buffalo *(G-2803)*

Kedco Inc ....F 516 454-7800
Farmingdale *(G-4663)*

Nationwide Coils Inc ....G 914 277-7396
Mount Kisco *(G-8099)*

Northwell Health Inc ....A 646 665-6000
New York *(G-10646)*

Parker-Hannifin Corporation ....D 716 685-4040
Lancaster *(G-6823)*

Pfannenberg Manufacturing LLC ....D 716 685-6866
Lancaster *(G-6826)*

Storflex Holdings Inc ....C 607 962-2137
Corning *(G-3721)*

Supermarket Equipment Depo Inc ......G 718 665-6200
Bronx *(G-1373)*

Trane US Inc ....D 718 721-8844
Long Island City *(G-7386)*

Trane US Inc ....G 914 593-0303
Elmsford *(G-4436)*

Trane US Inc ....E 315 234-1500
East Syracuse *(G-4244)*

Trane US Inc ....E 518 785-1315
Latham *(G-6877)*

Trane US Inc ....E 585 256-2500
Rochester *(G-13771)*

Trane US Inc ....E 716 626-1260
Buffalo *(G-3017)*

Trane US Inc ....E 631 952-9477
Plainview *(G-12719)*

Universal Parent and Youth ....F 917 754-2426
Brooklyn *(G-2544)*

York International Corporation ....D 718 389-4152
Long Island City *(G-7410)*

REFRIGERATION EQPT & SPLYS WHOLESALERS

Maplewood Ice Co Inc ....E 518 499-2345
Whitehall *(G-16076)*

REFRIGERATION EQPT: Complete

Atmost Refrigeration Co Inc ....G 518 828-2180
Hudson *(G-6149)*

Cleanroom Systems Inc ....E 315 452-7400
North Syracuse *(G-12038)*

Foster Refrigerators Entp ....F 518 671-6036
Hudson *(G-6703)*

Millrock Technology Inc ....E 845 339-5700
Kingston *(G-6703)*

S & V Restaurant Eqp Mfrs Inc ....E 718 220-1140
Bronx *(G-1356)*

REFRIGERATION REPAIR SVCS

Colburns AC Rfrgn ....F 716 569-3695
Frewsburg *(G-5050)*

REFRIGERATION SVC & REPAIR

Foster Refrigerators Entp ....F 518 671-6036
Hudson *(G-6157)*

Medi-Ray Inc ....D 877 898-3003
Tuckahoe *(G-15205)*

REFUSE SYSTEMS

APC Paper Company Inc ....D 315 384-4225
Norfolk *(G-11997)*

Fabco Industries Inc ....G 631 393-6024
Farmingdale *(G-4628)*

REGULATORS: Power

Trac Regulators Inc ....E 914 699-9352
Mount Vernon *(G-8185)*

REGULATORS: Transmission & Distribution Voltage

Telephone Sales & Service Co ....E 212 233-8505
New York *(G-11449)*

REGULATORS: Transmission & Distribution Voltage

Precision Electronics Inc ....F 631 842-4900
Copiague *(G-3670)*

RELAYS & SWITCHES: Indl, Electric

Jit International Inc ....G 631 761-5551
Islandia *(G-6338)*

Select Controls Inc ....E 631 567-9010
Bohemia *(G-1076)*

RELAYS: Electronic Usage

Dri Relays Inc ....D 631 342-1700
Hauppauge *(G-5641)*

Hasco Componets ....E 516 328-9292
New Hyde Park *(G-8273)*

Precision Electronics Inc ....F 631 842-4900
Copiague *(G-3670)*

RELIGIOUS SPLYS WHOLESALERS

Cathedral Candle Co ....D 315 422-9119
Syracuse *(G-14846)*

Leiter Sukkahs Inc ....G 718 436-0303
Brooklyn *(G-2061)*

Malhame Publs & Importers Inc ....E 631 694-8600
Bohemia *(G-1043)*

Rose Solomon Co ....E 718 855-1788
Brooklyn *(G-2355)*

REMOVERS & CLEANERS

G & M Dege Inc ....F 631 475-1450
Patchogue *(G-12501)*

Rapid Removal LLC ....F 716 665-4663
Falconer *(G-4553)*

RENTAL CENTERS: General

Grayhawk Leasing LLC ....G 914 767-6000
Somers *(G-14498)*

RENTAL SVCS: Business Machine & Electronic Eqpt

Neopost USA Inc ....E 631 435-9100
Hauppauge *(G-5726)*

Pitney Bowes Inc ....E 212 564-7548
New York *(G-10846)*

Pitney Bowes Inc ....E 203 356-5000
New York *(G-10847)*

Pitney Bowes Inc ....E 516 822-0900
Jericho *(G-6589)*

RENTAL SVCS: Costume

Rubies Costume Company Inc ....B 718 846-1008
Richmond Hill *(G-13122)*

Rubies Costume Company Inc ....D 631 777-3300
Bay Shore *(G-711)*

Rubies Costume Company Inc ....C 631 951-3688
Bay Shore *(G-712)*

Rubies Costume Company Inc ....C 718 846-1008
Richmond Hill *(G-13124)*

RENTAL SVCS: Electronic Eqpt, Exc Computers

Sentry Technology Corporation ....E 631 739-2000
Ronkonkoma *(G-14006)*

RENTAL SVCS: Eqpt, Theatrical

Mutual Sales Corp ....E 718 361-8373
Long Island City *(G-7300)*

Production Resource Group LLC ....D 877 774-7088
Armonk *(G-401)*

Production Resource Group LLC ....E 845 567-5700
New Windsor *(G-8378)*

RENTAL SVCS: Invalid Splys

Konrad Prosthetics & Orthotics ....F 516 485-9164
West Hempstead *(G-15773)*

RENTAL SVCS: Live Plant

Plant-Tech2o Inc ....G 516 483-7845
Hempstead *(G-5847)*

RENTAL SVCS: Pallet

Peco Pallet Inc ....E 914 376-5444
Irvington *(G-6313)*

RENTAL SVCS: Tent & Tarpaulin

Ace Canvas & Tent Corp ....F 631 981-9705
Ronkonkoma *(G-13886)*

Classic Awnings Inc ....F 716 649-0390
Hamburg *(G-5503)*

RENTAL SVCS: Work Zone Traffic Eqpt, Flags, Cones, Etc

Traffic Lane Closures LLC ....F 845 228-6100
Carmel *(G-3192)*

RENTAL: Video Tape & Disc

Simulaids Inc ....D 845 679-2475
Saugerties *(G-14212)*

REPEATERS: Passive

Innovative Power Products Inc ....E 631 563-0088
Holbrook *(G-6002)*

REPRODUCTION SVCS: Video Tape Or Disk

Bertelsmann Inc ....E 212 782-1000
New York *(G-8764)*

Professional Tape Corporation ....G 516 656-5519
Glen Cove *(G-5199)*

RESEARCH, DEV & TESTING SVCS, COMM: Chem Lab, Exc Testing

Advanced Polymer Solutions LLC ......G 516 621-5800
Port Washington *(G-12860)*

RESEARCH, DEVELOPMENT & TEST SVCS, COMM: Business Analysis

Economist Intelligence Unit NA ....D 212 554-0600
New York *(G-9318)*

PRODUCT

RESEARCH, DEVELOPMENT & TEST SVCS, COMM: Cmptr Hardware Dev

Argon Corp .... F 516 487-5314
Great Neck *(G-5367)*

Digitronik Labs Inc .... F 585 360-0043
Rochester *(G-13346)*

Mitsui Chemicals America Inc .... E 914 253-0777
Rye Brook *(G-14092)*

Tokenize Inc .... F 585 981-9919
Rochester *(G-13769)*

RESEARCH, DEVELOPMENT & TEST SVCS, COMM: Research, Exc Lab

Dowa International Corp .... F 212 697-3217
New York *(G-9261)*

Intra-Cellular Therapies Inc .... E 646 440-9333
New York *(G-9929)*

RESEARCH, DEVELOPMENT & TESTING SVCS, COMM: Research Lab

MTI Instruments Inc .... F 518 218-2550
Albany *(G-103)*

RESEARCH, DEVELOPMENT & TESTING SVCS, COMMERCIAL: Medical

Athenex Inc .... D 716 427-2950
Buffalo *(G-2646)*

Health Care Originals Inc .... G 585 471-8215
Rochester *(G-13463)*

RESEARCH, DVLPMT & TESTING SVCS, COMM: Merger, Acq & Reorg

Toppan Merrill USA Inc .... C 212 596-7747
New York *(G-11515)*

RESEARCH, DVLPT & TEST SVCS, COMM: Mkt Analysis or Research

International Data Group Inc .... E 212 331-7883
New York *(G-9918)*

RESIDENTIAL REMODELERS

Andike Millwork Inc .... G 718 894-1796
Maspeth *(G-7590)*

Di Fiore and Sons Custom Wdwkg ...... G 718 278-1663
Long Island City *(G-7201)*

Majestic Home Imprvs Distr .... G 718 853-5079
Brooklyn *(G-2103)*

RESINS: Custom Compound Purchased

Advance Chemicals Usa Inc .... G 718 633-1030
Brooklyn *(G-1464)*

Atc Plastics LLC .... E 212 375-2515
New York *(G-8660)*

Cryovac LLC .... C 585 436-3211
Rochester *(G-13329)*

Lahr Recycling & Resins Inc .... F 585 425-8608
Fairport *(G-4502)*

Marval Industries Inc .... D 914 381-2400
Mamaroneck *(G-7514)*

Polyset Company Inc .... E 518 664-6000
Mechanicville *(G-7693)*

Si Group Inc .... C 518 347-4200
Schenectady *(G-14304)*

RESISTORS

Betapast Holdings LLC .... D 631 582-6740
Hauppauge *(G-5603)*

Microgen Systems Inc .... G 585 214-2426
Fairport *(G-4507)*

Micropen Technologies Corp .... D 585 624-2610
Honeoye Falls *(G-6078)*

Passive-Plus Inc .... F 631 425-0938
Huntington *(G-6216)*

Stetron International Inc .... F 716 854-3443
Buffalo *(G-2993)*

Vishay Thin Film LLC .... C 716 283-4025
Niagara Falls *(G-11990)*

RESISTORS & RESISTOR UNITS

Micropen Technologies Corp .... D 585 624-2610
Honeoye Falls *(G-6078)*

RESORT HOTELS

Quinn and Co of NY Ltd .... D 212 868-1900
New York *(G-10958)*

RESPIRATORS

Caire Inc .... E 716 691-0202
Amherst *(G-215)*

RESTAURANT EQPT REPAIR SVCS

Applince Installation Svc Corp .... E 716 884-7425
Buffalo *(G-2642)*

Hobart Corporation .... E 631 864-3440
Commack *(G-3592)*

Ronbar Laboratories Inc .... F 718 937-6755
Long Island City *(G-7345)*

RESTAURANT EQPT: Carts

A-Plus Restaurant Equipment .... E 718 522-2656
Brooklyn *(G-1444)*

All Star Carts & Vehicles Inc .... D 631 666-5581
Bay Shore *(G-646)*

S & V Restaurants Corp .... E 718 220-1140
Bronx *(G-1357)*

RESTAURANT EQPT: Food Wagons

Carts Mobile Food Eqp Corp .... E 718 788-5540
Brooklyn *(G-1652)*

Kinplex Corp .... G 631 242-4800
Edgewood *(G-4274)*

Restaurant 570 8th Avenue LLC .... F 646 722-8191
New York *(G-11021)*

Tao Group LLC .... G 646 625-4818
New York *(G-11431)*

RESTAURANT EQPT: Sheet Metal

Building New Bridges LLC .... F 315 960-1242
Remsen *(G-13083)*

E G M Restaurant Equipment Mfg .... G 718 782-9800
Brooklyn *(G-1771)*

Middleby Corporation .... E 631 226-6688
Lindenhurst *(G-6960)*

Shanghai Stove Inc .... F 718 599-4583
Brooklyn *(G-2403)*

RESTAURANTS:Full Svc, American

Empire Brewing Company Inc .... D 315 925-8308
Syracuse *(G-14887)*

RESTAURANTS:Full Svc, Mexican

Tortilla Heaven Inc .... E 845 339-1550
Kingston *(G-6715)*

RESTAURANTS:Full Svc, Seafood

Fire Island Sea Clam Co Inc .... G 631 589-2199
West Sayville *(G-15840)*

RESTAURANTS:Limited Svc, Coffee Shop

Aphrodities .... G 718 224-1774
Whitestone *(G-16087)*

Jonathan Brose .... G 716 417-8978
Lockport *(G-7086)*

RESTAURANTS:Limited Svc, Ice Cream Stands Or Dairy Bars

Blue Pig Ice Cream Factory .... G 914 271-3850
Croton On Hudson *(G-3806)*

Purity Ice Cream Co Inc .... F 607 272-1545
Ithaca *(G-6408)*

RESTAURANTS:Limited Svc, Lunch Counter

Roslyn Bread Company Inc .... E 516 625-1470
Roslyn Heights *(G-14056)*

RETAIL BAKERY: Bagels

999 Bagels Inc .... G 718 915-0742
Brooklyn *(G-1426)*

A T A Bagel Shoppe Inc .... G 718 352-4948
Bayside *(G-733)*

Bagel Grove Inc .... E 315 724-8015
Utica *(G-15240)*

M & M Bagel Corp .... F 516 295-1222
Cedarhurst *(G-3240)*

Mds Hot Bagels Deli Inc .... G 718 438-5650
Brooklyn *(G-2129)*

RETAIL BAKERY: Bread

Addeo Bakers Inc .... F 718 367-8316
Bronx *(G-1197)*

Giovanni Bakery Corp .... F 212 695-4296
New York *(G-9614)*

Harrison Bakery West .... E 315 422-1468
Syracuse *(G-14909)*

Rock Hill Bakehouse Ltd .... E 518 743-1627
Gansevoort *(G-5086)*

Roslyn Bread Company Inc .... E 516 625-1470
Roslyn Heights *(G-14056)*

RETAIL BAKERY: Cookies

Mannys Cheesecake Inc .... G 315 732-0639
Utica *(G-15280)*

RETAIL FIREPLACE STORES

Blackstone International Inc .... G 631 289-5490
Holtsville *(G-6045)*

RETAIL LUMBER YARDS

Axtell Bradtke Lumber Co .... G 607 265-3850
Masonville *(G-7583)*

Deer Pk Stair Bldg Mllwk Inc .... E 631 363-5000
Blue Point *(G-956)*

Georgia-Pacific LLC .... E 631 924-7401
Yaphank *(G-16262)*

Guldenschuh Logging & Lbr LLC .... G 585 538-4750
Caledonia *(G-3070)*

Lowville Farmers Coop Inc .... E 315 376-6587
Lowville *(G-7417)*

Mensch Mill & Lumber Corp .... E 718 359-7500
Bronx *(G-1309)*

RETAIL STORES, NEC

Exhibits & More .... G 585 924-4040
Victor *(G-15408)*

Mark F Rosenhaft N A O .... G 516 374-1010
Cedarhurst *(G-3241)*

RETAIL STORES: Alarm Signal Systems

Lifewatch Inc .... F 800 716-1433
Hewlett *(G-5871)*

Table Tops Paper Corp .... G 718 831-6440
Brooklyn *(G-2489)*

RETAIL STORES: Alcoholic Beverage Making Eqpt & Splys

DAgostino Iron Works Inc .... G 585 235-8850
Rochester *(G-13335)*

Dutch Spirits LLC .... F 518 398-1022
Pine Plains *(G-12633)*

Foster - Gordon Manufacturing .... G 631 589-6776
Bohemia *(G-1013)*

RETAIL STORES: Aquarium Splys

C B Management Services Inc .... F 845 735-2300
Pearl River *(G-12529)*

RETAIL STORES: Art & Architectural Splys

Patrick Mackin Custom Furn .... G 718 237-2592
Brooklyn *(G-2250)*

RETAIL STORES: Artificial Limbs

Creative Orthotics & Prosthet .... F 607 734-7215
Elmira *(G-4347)*

Green Prosthetics & Orthotics .... G 716 484-1088
Jamestown *(G-6514)*

Hanger Inc .... G 718 575-5504
Forest Hills *(G-4920)*

Konrad Prosthetics & Orthotics .... F 516 485-9164
West Hempstead *(G-15773)*

Lehneis Orthotics Prosthetic .... G 516 790-1897
Hauppauge *(G-5691)*

Lehneis Orthotics Prosthetic .... G 631 369-3115
Riverhead *(G-13178)*

M H Mandelbaum Orthotic .... F 631 473-8668
Port Jefferson *(G-12842)*

Mark Goldberg Prosthetic .... F 631 689-6606
East Setauket *(G-4180)*

North Shore Orthtics Prsthtics ....G...... 631 928-3040
  Port Jeff STA *(G-12836)*
Prosthetic Rehabilitation Ctr ....G...... 845 565-8255
  Newburgh *(G-11885)*
Ultrapedics Ltd ....G...... 718 748-4806
  Brooklyn *(G-2534)*

RETAIL STORES: Audio-Visual Eqpt & Splys

Audio Video Invasion Inc ....F 516 345-2636
  Plainview *(G-12664)*
Tony Baird Electronics Inc ....G...... 315 422-4430
  Syracuse *(G-15014)*

RETAIL STORES: Awnings

Acme Awning Co Inc ....F 718 409-1881
  Bronx *(G-1195)*
Alley Cat Signs Inc........................F 631 924-7446
  Middle Island *(G-7874)*
Awning Mart Inc ....G...... 315 699-5928
  Cicero *(G-3416)*
City Signs Inc ....G...... 718 375-5933
  Brooklyn *(G-1667)*
Dart Awning Inc............................G...... 516 544-2082
  Freeport *(G-4991)*
Di Sanos Creative Canvas Inc ....G...... 315 894-3137
  Frankfort *(G-4949)*
Graphic Signs & Awnings Ltd..........G...... 718 227-6000
  Staten Island *(G-14659)*
Kenan International Trading ....G...... 718 672-4922
  Corona *(G-3742)*
Lanza Corp ....G...... 914 937-6360
  Port Chester *(G-12824)*
Lotus Awnings Enterprises Inc ....G...... 718 965-4824
  Brooklyn *(G-2086)*
Mauceri Sign Inc...........................F 718 656-7700
  Jamaica *(G-6458)*
Proof Industries Inc ....G...... 631 694-7663
  Farmingdale *(G-4717)*
Rainbow Awning Co Inc ....G...... 716 297-3939
  Niagara Falls *(G-11970)*
Rgm Signs Inc ....G...... 718 442-0598
  Staten Island *(G-14703)*
Space Sign..................................F 718 961-1112
  College Point *(G-3565)*
Steinway Awning II LLC..................G...... 718 729-2965
  Astoria *(G-442)*

RETAIL STORES: Cake Decorating Splys

Pfeil & Holing Inc ....D...... 718 545-4600
  Woodside *(G-16219)*

RETAIL STORES: Canvas Prdts

Brock Awnings Ltd ....F 631 765-5200
  Hampton Bays *(G-5533)*
Geordie Magee Uphl & Canvas.............G...... 315 676-7679
  Brewerton *(G-1135)*

RETAIL STORES: Cleaning Eqpt & Splys

Collinite Corporation ....G...... 315 732-2282
  Utica *(G-15245)*
Empire Division Inc ....D...... 315 476-6273
  Syracuse *(G-14888)*
Mortech Industries Inc....................G...... 845 628-6138
  Mahopac *(G-7475)*

RETAIL STORES: Cosmetics

Malin + Goetz Inc ....F 212 244-7771
  New York *(G-10336)*
New Avon LLC ....B...... 212 282-6000
  New York *(G-10577)*

RETAIL STORES: Educational Aids & Electronic Training Mat

Logical Operations Inc ....C...... 585 350-7000
  Rochester *(G-13522)*

RETAIL STORES: Electronic Parts & Eqpt

G B International Trdg Co Ltd............C...... 607 785-0938
  Endicott *(G-4457)*
I Trade Technology Ltd ....E...... 615 348-7233
  Airmont *(G-12)*
Industrial Support Inc ....D...... 716 662-2954
  Buffalo *(G-2809)*
Ross Electronics Ltd ....E...... 718 569-6643
  Haverstraw *(G-5807)*

RETAIL STORES: Engine & Motor Eqpt & Splys

Electric Motors and Pumps Inc ....G...... 718 935-9118
  Brooklyn *(G-1790)*

RETAIL STORES: Farm Eqpt & Splys

Birkett Mills....................................G...... 315 536-3311
  Penn Yan *(G-12578)*

RETAIL STORES: Fiberglass Materials, Exc Insulation

Architectural Fiberglass Corp ....E...... 631 842-4772
  Copiague *(G-3645)*

RETAIL STORES: Fire Extinguishers

C E King & Sons Inc ....G...... 631 324-4944
  East Hampton *(G-4118)*
Sausbiers Awning Shop Inc..................G...... 518 828-3748
  Hudson *(G-6178)*

RETAIL STORES: Gravestones, Finished

Woodside Granite Industries ....G...... 585 589-6500
  Albion *(G-162)*

RETAIL STORES: Hearing Aids

Benway-Haworth-Lwlr-Iacosta He........F 518 432-4070
  Albany *(G-47)*

RETAIL STORES: Ice

Henry Newman LLC ....F 607 273-8512
  Dryden *(G-4038)*
South Shore Ice Co Inc.....................F 516 379-2056
  Roosevelt *(G-14033)*

RETAIL STORES: Infant Furnishings & Eqpt

Mam USA Corporation......................F 914 269-2500
  Purchase *(G-13007)*

RETAIL STORES: Medical Apparatus & Splys

Goodman Main Stopper Mfg Co ....F 718 875-5140
  Brooklyn *(G-1900)*
Medical Action Industries Inc ....C...... 631 231-4600
  Hauppauge *(G-5711)*
NY Orthopedic Usa Inc ....D...... 718 852-5330
  Brooklyn *(G-2225)*

RETAIL STORES: Mobile Telephones & Eqpt

2p Agency Usa Inc ....G...... 212 203-5586
  Brooklyn *(G-1413)*
Sima Technologies LLC ....G...... 412 828-9130
  Hauppauge *(G-5766)*

RETAIL STORES: Monuments, Finished To Custom Order

Presbrey-Leland Inc.......................G...... 914 949-2264
  Valhalla *(G-15307)*
St Raymond Monument Co ....G...... 718 824-3600
  Bronx *(G-1369)*

RETAIL STORES: Motors, Electric

A & C/Furia Electric Motors ....F 914 949-0585
  White Plains *(G-15968)*
Economy Pump & Motor Repr Inc........G...... 718 433-2600
  Astoria *(G-418)*
Emes Motor Inc ....G...... 718 387-2445
  Brooklyn *(G-1799)*

RETAIL STORES: Orthopedic & Prosthesis Applications

Arimed Orthotics Prosthetics ....F 718 875-8754
  Brooklyn *(G-1528)*
Creative Orthotics Prosthetics ....G...... 607 771-4672
  Binghamton *(G-868)*
Klemmt Orthotics & Prosthetics..........G...... 607 770-4400
  Johnson City *(G-6604)*
Ortho Medical Products ....E...... 212 879-3700
  New York *(G-10712)*
Orthocraft Inc ....G...... 718 951-1700
  Brooklyn *(G-2235)*
Progressive Orthotics Ltd ....F 631 447-3860
  East Patchogue *(G-4155)*

Progressive Orthotics Ltd....................G...... 631 732-5556
  Selden *(G-14355)*
Prosthetics By Nelson Inc ....F 716 894-6666
  Cheektowaga *(G-3359)*
Sampsons Prsthtic Orthotic Lab ....E 518 374-6011
  Schenectady *(G-14300)*

RETAIL STORES: Religious Goods

A-1 Skull Cap Corp ....E 718 633-9333
  Brooklyn *(G-1441)*
J Lowy Co ....G...... 718 338-7324
  Brooklyn *(G-1979)*
Moznaim Publishing Co Inc ....G...... 718 853-0525
  Brooklyn *(G-2173)*
Y & A Trading Inc ....F 718 436-6333
  Brooklyn *(G-2598)*

RETAIL STORES: Stones, Crystalline, Rough

Amendola MBL & Stone Ctr Inc............D...... 914 997-7968
  White Plains *(G-15972)*
Hanson Aggregates PA LLC ....E 585 624-1220
  Honeoye Falls *(G-6074)*

RETAIL STORES: Telephone Eqpt & Systems

ABS Talkx Inc ....G...... 631 254-9100
  Bay Shore *(G-642)*

RETAIL STORES: Tents

Leiter Sukkahs Inc ....G...... 718 436-0303
  Brooklyn *(G-2061)*

RETAIL STORES: Water Purification Eqpt

Neptune Soft Water Inc ....F 315 446-5151
  Syracuse *(G-14950)*
Pure Planet Waters LLC ....F 718 676-7900
  Brooklyn *(G-2306)*

RETAIL STORES: Welding Splys

Haun Welding Supply Inc..................G...... 607 846-2289
  Elmira *(G-4356)*

REUPHOLSTERY & FURNITURE REPAIR

Furniture Doctor Inc ....G...... 585 657-6941
  Bloomfield *(G-947)*
KPP Ltd ....G...... 516 338-5201
  Jericho *(G-6585)*

REUPHOLSTERY SVCS

Anthony Lawrence of New York ....E 212 206-8820
  Long Island City *(G-7159)*
Upbeat Upholstery & Design LLC ....G...... 347 480-3980
  Brooklyn *(G-2547)*

RIBBONS & BOWS

Artistic Ribbon Novelty Co Inc ....E 212 255-4224
  New York *(G-8637)*

RIBBONS, NEC

Essential Ribbons Inc......................G...... 212 967-4173
  New York *(G-9402)*
Fashion Ribbon Co Inc.....................E 718 482-0100
  Long Island City *(G-7221)*

RIBBONS: Machine, Inked Or Carbon

International Imaging Mtls Inc ....B...... 716 691-6333
  Amherst *(G-227)*

RIDING APPAREL STORES

Robert Viggiani ....G...... 914 423-4046
  Yonkers *(G-16346)*

RIVETS: Metal

John Hassall LLC...........................D...... 516 334-6200
  Westbury *(G-15898)*

ROAD MATERIALS: Bituminous, Not From Refineries

Alliance Paving Materials Inc................G...... 315 337-0795
  Rome *(G-13841)*
R Schleider Contracting Corp................G...... 631 269-4249
  Kings Park *(G-6676)*

PRODUCT

Rochester Asphalt Materials..................G......585 381-7010
Rochester (G-13681)

ROBOTS: Assembly Line

Automated Cells & Eqp Inc ....E......607 936-1341
Painted Post (G-12471)

Honeybee Robotics Ltd ....E......212 966-0661
Brooklyn (G-1942)

J H Robotics Inc ....E......607 729-3758
Johnson City (G-6603)

McHone Industries Inc.................D......716 945-3380
Salamanca (G-14122)

ROCK SALT MINING

American Rock Salt Company LLC....E......585 991-6878
Retsof (G-13094)

Steel City Salt LLC ....G......716 532-0000
Collins (G-3572)

ROCKET LAUNCHERS

CIC International Ltd.................D......212 213-0089
Brooklyn (G-1663)

ROCKETS: Space & Military

Lockheed Martin Corporation..............A......315 456-0123
Liverpool (G-7021)

RODS: Extruded, Aluminum

Jem Threading Specialties Inc ....G......718 665-3341
Bronx (G-1285)

RODS: Plastic

Comco Plastics Inc ....E......718 849-9000
Huntington Station (G-6242)

Great Lakes Plastics Co Inc.................E......716 896-3100
Buffalo (G-2783)

RODS: Steel & Iron, Made In Steel Mills

Mardek LLC ....G......585 735-9333
Pittsford (G-12649)

RODS: Welding

Aufhauser Corporation..................F......516 694-8696
Plainview (G-12665)

Aufhauser Manufacturing Corp............E......516 694-8696
Plainview (G-12666)

ROLL COVERINGS: Rubber

Finzer Holding LLC ....E......315 597-1147
Palmyra (G-12486)

ROLL FORMED SHAPES: Custom

Inscape (new York) Inc ....D......716 665-6210
Falconer (G-4544)

Lakeside Capital Corporation..............E......716 664-2555
Jamestown (G-6528)

Rolite Mfg Inc ....E......716 683-0259
Lancaster (G-6831)

Rollform of Jamestown Inc.................F......716 665-5310
Jamestown (G-6539)

ROLLED OR DRAWN SHAPES, NEC: Copper & Copper Alloy

Sherburne Metal Sales Inc ....F......607 674-4441
Sherburne (G-14393)

ROLLERS & FITTINGS: Window Shade

Windowtex Inc ....F......877 294-3580
New Hyde Park (G-8303)

ROLLING MILL MACHINERY

Anthony Manufacturing Inc ....G......631 957-9424
Lindenhurst (G-6940)

Ivy Classic Industries Inc ....E......914 632-8200
New Rochelle (G-8343)

Johnston Dandy Company ....G......315 455-5773
Syracuse (G-14919)

Mannesmann Corporation ....D......212 258-4000
New York (G-10348)

Polymag Tek Inc.................F......585 235-8390
Rochester (G-13628)

ROLLS & BLANKETS, PRINTERS': Rubber Or Rubberized Fabric

Enbi Indiana Inc ....E......585 647-1627
Rochester (G-13389)

Package Print Technologies ....F......716 871-9905
Buffalo (G-2904)

Rli Schlgel Specialty Pdts LLC.............G......585 627-5919
Rochester (G-13675)

ROLLS: Rubber, Solid Or Covered

Idg LLC ....E......315 797-1000
Utica (G-15274)

Rotation Dynamics Corporation.......E......585 352-9023
Spencerport (G-14559)

ROOFING MATERIALS: Asphalt

Countryside Truss LLC ....G......315 985-0643
Saint Johnsville (G-14116)

Johns Manville Corporation ....E......518 565-3000
Plattsburgh (G-12755)

Marathon Roofing Products Inc ....F......716 685-3340
Orchard Park (G-12364)

ROOFING MATERIALS: Sheet Metal

Brothers Roofing Supplies Co.................E......718 779-0280
East Elmhurst (G-4104)

Hri Metals LLC ....G......518 822-1013
Hudson (G-6161)

Pal Aluminum Inc ....G......516 937-1990
Hicksville (G-5939)

ROPE

Gladding Braided Products LLC ....E......315 653-7211
South Otselic (G-14520)

ROTORS: Motor

Taro Manufacturing Company Inc ....F......315 252-9430
Auburn (G-498)

RUBBER

API International Group LLC................G......877 215-0017
Yonkers (G-16288)

David Fehlman ....G......315 455-8888
Syracuse (G-14875)

Integrated Liner Tech Inc ....E......518 621-7422
Rensselaer (G-13089)

Release Coatings New York Inc.............G......585 593-2335
Wellsville (G-15674)

RUBBER PRDTS: Automotive, Mechanical

Bridgestone APM Company.................D......419 423-9552
Sanborn (G-14137)

RUBBER PRDTS: Mechanical

Apple Rubber Products Inc.................C......716 684-7649
Lancaster (G-6796)

Delford Industries Inc ....D......845 342-3901
Middletown (G-7904)

Finzer Holding LLC ....E......315 597-1147
Palmyra (G-12486)

Mechanical Rubber Pdts Co Inc ....F......845 986-2271
Warwick (G-15519)

Moldtech Inc ....E......716 685-3344
Lancaster (G-6818)

Ms Spares LLC ....G......607 223-3024
Clay (G-3451)

Pawling Corporation.................G......845 373-9300
Wassaic (G-15525)

Pawling Engineered Pdts Inc.................C......845 855-1000
Pawling (G-12527)

Pilot Products Inc ....F......718 728-2141
Long Island City (G-7326)

R & A Industrial Products.................G......716 823-4300
Buffalo (G-2945)

The Centro Company Inc ....G......914 533-2200
South Salem (G-14525)

Triangle Rubber Co Inc ....E......631 589-9400
Bohemia (G-1089)

RUBBER PRDTS: Oil & Gas Field Machinery, Mechanical

Camso Manufacturing Usa Ltd ....D......518 561-7528
Plattsburgh (G-12740)

RUBBER PRDTS: Reclaimed

Cementex Latex Corp ....F......212 741-1770
New York (G-8944)

RUBBER PRDTS: Silicone

Canton Bio-Medical Inc ....E......518 283-5963
Poestenkill (G-12801)

Depco Inc.................F......631 582-1995
Hauppauge (G-5635)

Silicone Products & Technology ....C......716 684-1155
Lancaster (G-6835)

Specialty Silicone Pdts Inc ....D......518 885-8826
Ballston Spa (G-587)

Vasquez Tito ....F......212 944-0441
New York (G-11648)

RUBBER PRDTS: Sponge

Tmp Technologies Inc ....D......716 895-6100
Buffalo (G-3012)

RUBBER PRDTS: Wet Suits

Great American Industries Inc.................G......607 729-9331
Vestal (G-15379)

RUBBER STRUCTURES: Air-Supported

Continental Latex Corp ....F......718 783-7883
Brooklyn (G-1683)

RUGS : Hand & Machine Made

Mark Nelson Designs LLC.................F......646 422-7020
New York (G-10365)

Mgk Group Inc.................E......212 989-2732
New York (G-10448)

Renaissnce Crpt Tapestries Inc............F......212 696-0080
New York (G-11011)

Safavieh Inc.................A......516 945-1900
Port Washington (G-12920)

RULERS: Metal

Gei International Inc ....E......315 463-9261
East Syracuse (G-4212)

SAFES & VAULTS: Metal

Gardall Safe Corporation ....E......315 432-9115
Syracuse (G-14899)

SAFETY EQPT & SPLYS WHOLESALERS

Human Condition Safety Inc.................F......646 867-0644
New York (G-9836)

SAILBOAT BUILDING & REPAIR

Allen Boat Co Inc ....G......716 842-0800
Buffalo (G-2626)

SAILS

Allen Boat Co Inc ....G......716 842-0800
Buffalo (G-2626)

Melbourne C Fisher Yacht Sails ....G......631 673-5055
Huntington Station (G-6253)

Ulmer Sales LLC ....F......718 885-1700
Port Chester (G-12830)

SALES PROMOTION SVCS

Platinum Sales Promotion Inc ....G......718 361-0200
Long Island City (G-7327)

SALT

Morton Salt Inc.................F......585 493-2511
Silver Springs (G-14443)

Real Co Inc ....G......347 433-8549
Valley Cottage (G-15321)

Roto Salt Company Inc.................E......315 536-3742
Penn Yan (G-12593)

Topaz Industries Inc ....F......631 207-0700
Holtsville (G-6057)

US Salt LLC ....D......607 535-2721
Watkins Glen (G-15617)

US Salt LLC ....F......888 872-7258
Watkins Glen (G-15618)

SAMPLE BOOKS

Federal Sample Card Corp ....D 718 458-1344
   Elmhurst (G-4334)
Niagara Sample Book Co Inc ....F 716 284-6151
   Niagara Falls (G-11954)

SAND & GRAVEL

110 Sand Company ....E 631 694-2822
   Melville (G-7751)
110 Sand Company ....F 631 694-2822
   West Babylon (G-15677)
A Colarusso and Son Inc ....E 518 828-3218
   Hudson (G-6146)
Barrett Paving Materials Inc ....E 607 723-5367
   Binghamton (G-856)
Belangers Gravel & Stone Inc ....G 585 728-3906
   Wayland (G-15625)
Callanan Industries Inc ....E 845 331-6868
   Kingston (G-6683)
Carver Sand & Gravel LLC ....E 518 355-6034
   Altamont (G-193)
D & A Sand & Gravel Inc ....E 516 248-9444
   Mineola (G-7967)
Dalrymple Grav & Contg Co Inc ....F 607 739-0391
   Pine City (G-12627)
Dalrymple Holding Corp ....E 607 737-6200
   Pine City (G-12628)
E Tetz & Sons Inc ....D 845 692-4486
   Middletown (G-7905)
East Coast Mines Ltd...................E 631 653-5445
   East Quogue (G-4156)
Genoa Sand & Gravel Lnsg............G 607 533-4551
   Freeville (G-5034)
Gernatt Asphalt Products Inc ....E 716 532-3371
   Collins (G-3571)
Greenebuild LLC ....F 917 562-0556
   Brooklyn (G-1910)
Hanson Aggregates East LLC ....E 315 548-4913
   Phelps (G-12604)
Johnson S Sand & Gravel Inc ....G 315 771-1450
   La Fargeville (G-6734)
Lafarge North America Inc ....E 716 651-9235
   Lancaster (G-6813)
Lafarge North America Inc ....E 518 756-5000
   Ravena (G-13069)
McEwan Trucking & Grav Produc ......G 716 609-1828
   East Concord (G-4100)
Milestone Construction Corp...........G 718 459-8500
   Flushing (G-4875)
Mitchell Stone Products LLC..........G 518 359-7029
   Tupper Lake (G-15211)
Northeast Solite Corporation..........E 845 246-2177
   Mount Marion (G-8112)
Northern Crushing LLC.................G 518 365-8452
   Averill Park (G-509)
R G King General Construction.........G 315 583-3560
   Adams Center (G-3)
R J Valente Gravel Inc ....D 518 432-4470
   Troy (G-15181)
R J Valente Gravel Inc ....E 518 279-1001
   Cropseyville (G-3803)
R J Valente Gravel Inc ....F 518 432-4470
   Rensselaer (G-13090)
Rd2 Construction & Dem LLC ....G 718 980-1650
   Staten Island (G-14700)
Republic Construction Co Inc ....G 914 235-3654
   New Rochelle (G-8353)
Robinson Concrete Inc.................E 315 253-6666
   Auburn (G-493)
Seneca Stone Corporation.............G 607 737-6200
   Pine City (G-12629)
Speyside Holdings LLC.................E 845 928-2221
   Highland Mills (G-5969)
Tilcon New York Inc ....D 845 358-3100
   West Nyack (G-15833)
Titus Mountain Sand & Grav LLC ......G 518 483-3740
   Malone (G-7492)
Tri City Highway Products Inc ....E 607 722-2967
   Binghamton (G-914)
Tri-City Highway Products Inc ....E 518 294-9964
   Richmondville (G-13130)
Troy Sand & Gravel Co Inc ....F 518 674-2854
   West Sand Lake (G-15837)
United Materials LLC...................G 716 662-0564
   Orchard Park (G-12381)
US Allegro Inc ....E 347 408-6601
   Maspeth (G-7640)

SAND MINING

Country Side Sand & Gravel ....G 716 988-3271
   Collins (G-3569)
Dicks Concrete Co Inc ....E 845 374-5966
   New Hampton (G-8234)
H L Robinson Sand & Gravel ....F 607 659-5153
   Candor (G-3161)
Hampton Sand Corp ....G 631 325-5533
   Westhampton (G-15955)
Rush Gravel Corp ....G 585 533-1740
   Honeoye Falls (G-6079)
Sparrow Mining Co 718 519-6600
   Bronx (G-1367)
Tilcon New York Inc ....E 845 942-0602
   Tomkins Cove (G-15079)
Troy Sand & Gravel Co Inc ....G 518 203-5115
   West Sand Lake (G-15836)

SAND: Hygrade

New Jersey Pulverizing Co Inc ....G 516 921-9595
   Syosset (G-14798)
Precision Elctro Mnrl Pmco Inc ....E 716 284-2484
   Niagara Falls (G-11968)

SANDSTONE: Crushed & Broken

County Line Stone Co Inc ....E 716 542-5435
   Akron (G-16)
Shelby Crushed Stone Inc ....E 585 798-4501
   Medina (G-7746)

SANITARY SVCS: Environmental Cleanup

Hygrade...................................G 718 488-9000
   Brooklyn (G-1948)

SANITARY SVCS: Waste Materials, Recycling

Crumbrubber Technology Inc ....F 718 468-3988
   Hollis (G-6042)
Hampton Sand Corp ....G 631 325-5533
   Westhampton (G-15955)
Ivi Services Inc ....D 607 729-5111
   Binghamton (G-889)
Kore Infrastructure LLC ....G 646 532-9060
   Glen Cove (G-5196)
Twin County Recycling Corp ....F 516 827-6900
   Westbury (G-15935)

SANITARY WARE: Metal

Advance Tabco Inc ....D 631 242-8270
   Hauppauge (G-5578)
Kenbenco Inc ....F 845 246-3066
   Saugerties (G-14203)
Metpar Corp ....D 516 333-2600
   Westbury (G-15910)

SANITATION CHEMICALS & CLEANING AGENTS

Bennett Manufacturing Co Inc ....C 716 937-9161
   Alden (G-166)
Cleanse TEC ....E 718 346-9111
   Hauppauge (G-5617)
Colgate-Palmolive Company ....A 212 310-2000
   New York (G-9051)
Crosstex International Inc ....D 631 582-6777
   Hauppauge (G-5631)
James Richard Specialty Chem.........G 914 478-7500
   Hastings On Hudson (G-5574)
Micro Powders Inc ....E 914 332-6400
   Tarrytown (G-15048)
Olin Chlor Alkali Logistics ....C 716 278-6411
   Niagara Falls (G-11961)
P S M Group Inc ....E 716 532-6686
   Forestville (G-4932)
Pure Green LLC ....G 800 306-9122
   Oyster Bay (G-12455)
Rochester Midland Corporation.........C 585 336-2200
   Rochester (G-13690)
Safetec of America Inc ....D 716 895-1822
   Buffalo (G-2971)
Tribology Inc ....E 631 345-3000
   Yaphank (G-16275)
US Nonwovens Corp ....C 631 236-4491
   Brentwood (G-1130)
US Nonwovens Corp ....C 631 232-0001
   Hauppauge (G-5794)
US Nonwovens Corp ....B 631 952-0100
   Commack (G-3600)

US Nonwovens Corp ....C 631 952-0100
   Brentwood (G-1131)
US Nonwovens Corp ....D 631 952-0100
   Brentwood (G-1132)

SASHES: Door Or Window, Metal

A G M Deco Inc ....F 718 624-6200
   Brooklyn (G-1433)
A G M Deco Inc ....D 718 624-6200
   Brooklyn (G-1434)
Hopes Windows Inc ....C 716 665-5124
   Jamestown (G-6516)
Revival Sash & Door LLC ....G 973 500-4242
   New York (G-11025)
Thermal Tech Doors Inc ....E 516 745-0100
   Garden City (G-5118)

SATCHELS

Barclay Brown Corp ....F 718 376-7166
   Brooklyn (G-1563)

SATELLITES: Communications

Geosync Microwave Inc ....G 631 760-5567
   Hauppauge (G-5659)
Icon Enterprises Intl Inc ....E 718 752-9764
   Mohegan Lake (G-8010)
Loral Space & Commnctns Holdng ....E 212 697-1105
   New York (G-10255)
Loral Space Communications Inc ......E 212 697-1105
   New York (G-10256)
Loral Spacecom Corporation...........E 212 697-1105
   New York (G-10257)
Orbcomm Inc ....F 703 433-6396
   Utica (G-15290)
Village Video Productions Inc ....G 631 752-9311
   West Babylon (G-15756)

SAW BLADES

Allway Tools Inc ....D 718 792-3636
   Bronx (G-1202)
Amana Tool Corp ....D 631 752-1300
   Farmingdale (G-4582)
Diamond Saw Works Inc ....E 716 496-7417
   Chaffee (G-3305)
Dinosaw Inc ....E 518 828-9942
   Hudson (G-6154)
Suffolk McHy & Pwr Tl Corp ....G 631 289-7153
   Patchogue (G-12512)

SAWDUST & SHAVINGS

Bono Sawdust Supply Co Inc ....G 718 446-1374
   Corona (G-3734)

SAWDUST, WHOLESALE

Attica Package Company Inc ....F 585 591-0510
   Attica (G-456)

SAWING & PLANING MILLS

A D Bowman & Son Lumber Co ....E 607 692-2595
   Castle Creek (G-3199)
Angelica Forest Products Inc ....G 585 466-3205
   Angelica (G-356)
Axtell Bradtke Lumber Co................G 607 265-3850
   Masonville (G-7583)
B & J Lumber Co Inc ....G 518 677-3845
   Cambridge (G-3091)
Bissel-Babcock Millwork Inc............F 716 761-6976
   Sherman (G-14399)
Cannonsville Lumber Inc ....G 607 467-3380
   Deposit (G-3998)
Capital Sawmill Service ....E 518 479-0729
   Nassau (G-8212)
Clements Burrville Sawmill ....G 315 782-4549
   Watertown (G-15565)
Curran Renewable Energy LLC ....E 315 769-2000
   Massena (G-7667)
Dlr Enterprises LLC ....G 315 813-2911
   Sherrill (G-14403)
Donver Incorporated ....F 716 945-1910
   Kill Buck (G-6669)
Farney Lumber Corporation ....F 315 346-6013
   Lowville (G-7415)
Gutchess Hardwoods Inc ....G 607 753-3393
   Cortland (G-3770)
Gutchess Lumber Co Inc ....E 716 492-2824
   Freedom (G-4975)

PRODUCT

J & J Log & Lumber Corp...................D...... 845 832-6535
  Dover Plains *(G-4032)*
McDonough Hardwoods Ltd ....E...... 315 829-3449
  Vernon Center *(G-15368)*
Meltz Lumber Co of Mellenville ....E...... 518 672-7021
  Hudson *(G-6170)*
Mettowee Lumber & Plastics Co ....C...... 518 642-1100
  Granville *(G-5352)*
Owletts Saw Mills...............................G...... 607 525-6340
  Woodhull *(G-16189)*
Pallets Inc ....E...... 518 747-4177
  Fort Edward *(G-4941)*
Piccini Industries Ltd ....E...... 845 365-0614
  Orangeburg *(G-12325)*
Rudy Stempel & Family Sawmill ....G...... 518 872-0431
  East Berne *(G-4098)*
Russell Bass ....F...... 607 637-5253
  Hancock *(G-5539)*
S Donadic Inc ....D...... 718 361-9888
  Sunnyside *(G-14774)*
Scotts Company LLC ....E...... 631 816-2831
  Yaphank *(G-16269)*
Sirianni Hardwoods Inc ....E...... 607 962-4688
  Painted Post *(G-12476)*
Spiegel Woodworks Inc ....F...... 845 336-8090
  Kingston *(G-6710)*
St Lawrence Lumber Inc ....G...... 315 649-2990
  Three Mile Bay *(G-15072)*
Swanson Lumber ....G...... 716 499-1726
  Gerry *(G-5171)*
Tri State Hardwoods Ltd ....G...... 845 687-7814
  Kingston *(G-6716)*
Tupper Lake Hardwoods Inc ....E...... 518 359-8248
  Tupper Lake *(G-15215)*
Wagner Hardwoods LLC ....G...... 607 594-3321
  Cayuta *(G-3223)*
Wagner Hardwoods LLC ....G...... 607 229-8198
  Friendship *(G-5053)*
Wagner Millwork Inc ....D...... 607 687-5362
  Owego *(G-12439)*
Wagner Nineveh Inc ....F...... 607 693-2689
  Afton *(G-8)*

SAWING & PLANING MILLS: Custom

Gutchess Freedom Inc ....D...... 716 492-2824
  Freedom *(G-4974)*

SCALES & BALANCES, EXC LABORATORY

Buffalo Scale and Sup Co Inc.............G...... 716 847-2880
  Buffalo *(G-2682)*
Circuits & Systems Inc ....E...... 516 593-4301
  East Rockaway *(G-4171)*
Itin Scale Co Inc ....E...... 718 336-5900
  Brooklyn *(G-1974)*

SCALES: Baby

Scale-Tronix Inc ....E...... 914 948-8117
  Skaneateles *(G-14456)*

SCALP TREATMENT SVCS

British Science Corporation ....G...... 212 980-8700
  Staten Island *(G-14631)*

SCANNING DEVICES: Optical

Broadnet Technologies Inc ....F...... 315 443-3694
  Syracuse *(G-14834)*
Symbol Technologies LLC ....A...... 631 737-6851
  Holtsville *(G-6054)*
T&K Printing Inc................................F...... 718 439-9454
  Brooklyn *(G-2487)*

SCHOOLS & EDUCATIONAL SVCS, NEC

Codesters Inc ....G...... 646 232-1025
  New York *(G-9048)*

SCIENTIFIC EQPT REPAIR SVCS

Transcat Inc ....B...... 585 352-7777
  Rochester *(G-13772)*

SCISSORS: Hand

Klein Cutlery LLC ....D...... 585 928-2500
  Bolivar *(G-1101)*

SCRAP & WASTE MATERIALS, WHOLESALE: Ferrous Metal

Blue Tee Corp....................................G...... 212 598-0880
  New York *(G-8820)*

SCRAP & WASTE MATERIALS, WHOLESALE: Metal

All American Funding & Ref LLC ....G...... 516 978-7531
  Farmingdale *(G-4578)*
Umicore USA Inc ....E...... 919 874-7171
  Glens Falls *(G-5268)*

SCRAP & WASTE MATERIALS, WHOLESALE: Plastics Scrap

Fiber USA Corp ....G...... 718 888-1512
  Flushing *(G-4852)*

SCRAP & WASTE MATERIALS, WHOLESALE: Rags

Yankee Corp ....F...... 718 589-1377
  Bronx *(G-1397)*

SCREENS: Projection

Dnp Electronics America LLC ....D...... 212 503-1060
  New York *(G-9242)*

SCREENS: Window, Metal

Alumil Fabrication Inc ....F...... 845 469-2874
  Long Island City *(G-7153)*
It Windows & Doors Inc ....G...... 646 220-8398
  Rye Brook *(G-14090)*
Window Tech Systems Inc ....E...... 518 899-9000
  Ballston Spa *(G-589)*

SCREENS: Woven Wire

Star Wire Mesh Fabricators ....G...... 212 831-4133
  New York *(G-11349)*

SCREW MACHINE PRDTS

Acme Precision Screw Pdts Inc ....F...... 585 328-2028
  Rochester *(G-13203)*
Action Machined Products Inc ....F...... 631 842-2333
  Copiague *(G-3643)*
Albert Gates Inc ....D...... 585 594-9401
  North Chili *(G-12021)*
All Type Screw Machine Pdts ....G...... 516 334-5100
  Westbury *(G-15866)*
Alpha Fasteners Corp ....G...... 516 867-6188
  Freeport *(G-4984)*
American-Swiss Products Co Inc.........G...... 585 292-1720
  Pittsford *(G-12636)*
Anderson Precision Inc ....D...... 716 484-1148
  Jamestown *(G-6494)*
Andros Manufacturing Corp ....G...... 585 663-5700
  Rochester *(G-13237)*
Brinkman Intl Group Inc ....G...... 585 429-5000
  Rochester *(G-13281)*
C R C Manufacturing Inc ....F...... 585 254-8820
  Rochester *(G-13291)*
C&C Automatics Inc ....E...... 315 331-1436
  Newark *(G-11838)*
CAM-Tech Industries Inc ....E...... 585 425-2090
  Fairport *(G-4491)*
Century Metal Parts Corp ....E...... 631 667-0800
  Bay Shore *(G-661)*
Craftech Industries Inc ....D...... 518 828-5001
  Hudson *(G-6151)*
Curtis Screw Co Inc ....E...... 716 898-7800
  Buffalo *(G-2716)*
Emory Machine & Tool Co Inc ....E...... 585 436-9610
  Farmington *(G-4771)*
Five Star Tool Co Inc ....E...... 585 328-9580
  Rochester *(G-13412)*
Gem Manufacturing Inc ....G...... 585 235-1670
  Rochester *(G-13431)*
Globe Electronic Hardware Inc............F...... 718 457-0303
  Woodside *(G-16209)*
Gsp Components Inc ....D...... 585 436-3377
  Rochester *(G-13452)*
Hanco Metal Products Inc ....F...... 212 787-5992
  Brooklyn *(G-1924)*
J & J Swiss Precision Inc ....E...... 631 243-5584
  Deer Park *(G-3884)*

Kaddis Manufacturing Corp ....G...... 585 624-3070
  Honeoye Falls *(G-6077)*
Lexington Machining LLC ....D...... 585 235-0880
  Rochester *(G-13516)*
Lexington Machining LLC ....C...... 585 235-0880
  Rochester *(G-13517)*
Liberty Brass Turning Co Inc ....E...... 718 784-2911
  Westbury *(G-15904)*
M Manastrip-M Corporation ....G...... 518 664-2089
  Clifton Park *(G-3467)*
Manacraft Precision Inc ....F...... 914 654-0967
  Pelham *(G-12567)*
Manth-Brownell Inc ....E...... 315 687-7263
  Kirkville *(G-6724)*
Marmach Machine Inc ....G...... 585 768-8800
  Le Roy *(G-6904)*
Micro Threaded Products Inc ....G...... 585 288-0080
  Rochester *(G-13546)*
Muller Tool Inc ....E...... 716 895-3658
  Buffalo *(G-2874)*
Multimatic Products Inc ....D...... 800 767-7633
  Ronkonkoma *(G-13977)*
Murphy Manufacturing Co Inc ....G...... 585 223-0100
  Fairport *(G-4509)*
Norwood Screw Machine Parts ....F...... 516 481-6644
  Mineola *(G-7993)*
Park-Ohio Inds Trsry Co Inc ....E...... 212 966-3310
  Albany *(G-111)*
Ppi Corp ....D...... 585 243-0300
  Rochester *(G-13633)*
Ranney Precision ....F...... 716 731-6418
  Niagara Falls *(G-11971)*
Selflock Screw Products Co Inc ....E...... 315 541-4464
  Syracuse *(G-14992)*
Supreme Screw Products Inc ....D...... 718 293-6600
  Plainview *(G-12717)*
T & L Automatics Inc ....C...... 585 647-3717
  Rochester *(G-13756)*
TAC Screw Products Inc ....F...... 585 663-5840
  Rochester *(G-13758)*
Taylor Metalworks Inc ....C...... 716 662-3113
  Orchard Park *(G-12378)*
Teale Machine Company Inc ....D...... 585 244-6700
  Rochester *(G-13761)*
Thuro Metal Products Inc ....E...... 631 435-0444
  Brentwood *(G-1128)*
Tri-Technologies Inc ....E...... 914 699-2001
  Mount Vernon *(G-8187)*
Trihex Manufacturing Inc ....G...... 315 589-9331
  Williamson *(G-16114)*
Triple Point Manufacturing..................G...... 631 218-4988
  Bohemia *(G-1091)*
Umbro Machine & Tool Co Inc ....E...... 845 876-4669
  Rhinebeck *(G-13102)*
Vanguard Metals Inc ....F...... 631 234-6500
  Central Islip *(G-3292)*
Verns Machine Co Inc ....E...... 315 926-4223
  Marion *(G-7577)*
Xli Manufacturing LLC ....E...... 585 436-2250
  Rochester *(G-13812)*

SCREW MACHINES

Johnson Mch & Fibr Pdts Co Inc.........F...... 716 665-2003
  Jamestown *(G-6527)*
Swiss Specialties Inc ....F...... 631 567-8800
  Wading River *(G-15453)*

SCREWS: Metal

Anthony Manno & Co Inc ....G...... 631 445-1834
  Deer Park *(G-3840)*
John F Rafter Inc ....E...... 716 992-3425
  Eden *(G-4256)*
Kinemotive Corporation ....E...... 631 249-6440
  Farmingdale *(G-4666)*
Radax Industries Inc ....E...... 585 265-2055
  Webster *(G-15650)*
Socket Products Mfg Corp ....G...... 631 232-9870
  Islandia *(G-6344)*
Tamperproof Screw Company Inc ....F...... 516 931-1616
  Hicksville *(G-5951)*

SEALANTS

Deal International Inc ....E...... 585 288-4444
  Rochester *(G-13341)*
J M Canty Inc ....E...... 716 625-4227
  Lockport *(G-7084)*
R-Co Products Corporation ....F...... 800 854-7657
  Lakewood *(G-6785)*

Saint-Gobain Prfmce Plas Corp.............C...... 518 642-2200
Granville **(G-5355)**
Walsh & Hughes Inc ....G...... 631 427-5904
Huntington Station **(G-6266)**

SEARCH & DETECTION SYSTEMS, EXC RADAR

Frequency Electronics Inc ....C...... 516 794-4500
Uniondale **(G-15229)**
Saab Defense and SEC USA LLC ....F...... 315 445-5009
East Syracuse **(G-4235)**
U S Tech Corporation ....F...... 315 437-7207
Skaneateles **(G-14458)**
Virtualapt Corp ....F...... 917 293-3173
Brooklyn **(G-2562)**
VJ Technologies Inc ....F...... 631 589-8800
Bohemia **(G-1096)**

SEARCH & NAVIGATION SYSTEMS

Accipiter Radar Corporation ....G...... 716 508-4432
Orchard Park **(G-12336)**
American Aerospace Contrls Inc ....E...... 631 694-5100
Farmingdale **(G-4583)**
Ametek Inc ....D...... 585 263-7700
Rochester **(G-13234)**
Aventura Technologies Inc ....E...... 631 300-4000
Commack **(G-3577)**
Bae Systems Info & Elec Sys ....E...... 603 885-4321
Rome **(G-13842)**
Bae Systems Info & Elec Sys ....F...... 631 912-1525
Greenlawn **(G-5452)**
Bae Systems PLC ....E...... 631 261-7000
Greenlawn **(G-5453)**
Boeing Distribution Svcs Inc ....F...... 845 534-0401
Cornwall **(G-3727)**
C Speed LLC ....E...... 315 453-1043
Liverpool **(G-7004)**
C-Flex Bearing Co Inc ....F...... 315 895-7454
Frankfort **(G-4948)**
CIT Aerospace LLC ....G...... 212 461-5200
New York **(G-9013)**
Clayton Dubilier & Rice Fun ....E...... 212 407-5200
New York **(G-9029)**
Cobham Management Services Inc ....A...... 716 662-0006
Orchard Park **(G-12346)**
Cobham Mission Systems ....B...... 716 662-0006
Orchard Park **(G-12347)**
Computer Instruments Corp ....E...... 516 876-8400
Westbury **(G-15874)**
Cox & Company Inc ....C...... 212 366-0200
Plainview **(G-12676)**
Dyna-Empire Inc ....C...... 516 222-2700
Garden City **(G-5096)**
Flightline Electronics Inc ....D...... 585 924-4000
Victor **(G-15410)**
GE Aviation Systems LLC ....D...... 513 243-9104
Bohemia **(G-1016)**
Inficon Inc ....C...... 315 434-1100
East Syracuse **(G-4220)**
Joldeson One Aerospace Inds ....D...... 718 848-7396
Ozone Park **(G-12463)**
Kerns Manufacturing Corp ....C...... 718 784-4044
Long Island City **(G-7262)**
L3 Foreign Holdings Inc ....C...... 212 697-1111
New York **(G-10153)**
L3 Technologies Inc ....B...... 212 697-1111
New York **(G-10154)**
L3harris Technologies Inc ....A...... 631 630-4200
Amityville **(G-288)**
Lockheed Martin Corporation ....G...... 212 953-1510
New York **(G-10241)**
Lockheed Martin Corporation ....E...... 315 456-3386
Liverpool **(G-7020)**
Lockheed Martin Corporation ....C...... 516 228-2000
Uniondale **(G-15231)**
Lockheed Martin Corporation ....A...... 607 751-2000
Owego **(G-12433)**
Lockheed Martin Corporation ....D...... 212 697-1105
New York **(G-10242)**
Lockheed Martin Corporation ....E...... 716 297-1000
Niagara Falls **(G-11948)**
Lockheed Martin Global Inc ....E...... 315 456-2982
Liverpool **(G-7022)**
Lockheed Martin Integrtd Systm ....E...... 315 456-3333
Syracuse **(G-14935)**
Logitek Inc ....D...... 631 567-1100
Bohemia **(G-1035)**
Magellan Aerospace NY Inc ....C...... 718 699-4000
Corona **(G-3744)**

Metro Dynamics Scie ....F...... 631 842-4300
West Babylon **(G-15731)**
Mirion Technologies Ist Corp ....D...... 607 562-4300
Horseheads **(G-6128)**
Moog Inc ....C...... 716 805-8100
East Aurora **(G-4094)**
Moog Inc ....F...... 716 687-7825
Elma **(G-4323)**
Northrop Grumman Corporation ....A...... 703 280-2900
Bethpage **(G-841)**
Northrop Grumman Systems Corp ....D...... 716 626-4600
Buffalo **(G-2893)**
Northrop Grumman Systems Corp ....G...... 631 423-1014
Huntington **(G-6215)**
Northrop Grumman Systems Corp ....C...... 516 346-7100
Bethpage **(G-843)**
Orthstar Enterprises Inc ....E...... 607 562-2100
Horseheads **(G-6130)**
Transistor Devices Inc ....E...... 631 471-7492
Ronkonkoma **(G-14017)**
Tusk Manufacturing Inc ....F...... 631 567-3349
Bohemia **(G-1092)**
U E Systems Incorporated ....E...... 914 592-1220
Elmsford **(G-4438)**
Vacuum Instrument Corporation ....D...... 631 737-0900
Ronkonkoma **(G-14023)**
Worldwide Arntcal Cmpnents Inc ....E...... 631 842-3780
Copiague **(G-3690)**
Worldwide Arntcal Cmpnents Inc ....G...... 631 842-3780
Copiague **(G-3691)**

SEATING: Bleacher, Portable

E & D Specialty Stands Inc ....E...... 716 337-0161
North Collins **(G-12025)**

SECRETARIAL SVCS

New York Typing & Printing Co ....G...... 718 268-7900
Forest Hills **(G-4925)**

SECURITY CONTROL EQPT & SYSTEMS

Aabacs Group Inc ....F...... 718 961-3577
College Point **(G-3532)**
Albatros North America Inc ....E...... 518 381-7100
Ballston Spa **(G-567)**
Altronix Corp ....D...... 718 567-8181
Brooklyn **(G-1494)**
Ameta International Co Ltd ....G...... 416 992-8036
Buffalo **(G-2632)**
Atlantic Electronic Tech LLC ....G...... 800 296-2177
Brooklyn **(G-1547)**
C & G Video Systems Inc ....G...... 315 452-1490
Liverpool **(G-7003)**
Comsec Ventures International ....G...... 518 523-1600
Lake Placid **(G-6766)**
Detekion Security Systems Inc ....F...... 607 729-7179
Vestal **(G-15376)**
Eyelock Corporation ....F...... 855 393-5625
New York **(G-9451)**
Eyelock LLC ....F...... 855 393-5625
New York **(G-9452)**
Fire Fox Security Corp ....G...... 917 981-9280
Brooklyn **(G-1847)**
Forte Network ....E...... 631 390-9050
East Northport **(G-4146)**
Innovative Video Tech Inc ....F...... 631 388-5700
Hauppauge **(G-5677)**
Issco Corporation ....F...... 212 732-8748
Garden City **(G-5102)**
Napco Security Tech Inc ....C...... 631 842-9400
Amityville **(G-297)**
National Security Systems Inc ....E...... 516 627-2222
Manhasset **(G-7539)**
Protex International Corp ....D...... 631 563-4250
Bohemia **(G-1068)**
Red Hawk Fire & Security LLC ....G...... 518 877-7616
Albany **(G-125)**
Roo Inc ....F...... 212 905-6100
New York **(G-11081)**
Security Dynamics Inc ....F...... 631 392-1701
Bohemia **(G-1075)**
Shield Security Doors Ltd ....G...... 202 468-3308
Brooklyn **(G-2405)**

SECURITY DEVICES

Custom Sound and Video ....E...... 585 424-5000
Rochester **(G-13334)**
Dyson-Kissner-Moran Corp ....E...... 212 661-4600
Poughkeepsie **(G-12952)**

Fairview Bell and Intercom ....G...... 718 627-8621
Brooklyn **(G-1829)**
Fiber Instrument Sales Inc ....C...... 315 736-2206
Oriskany **(G-12390)**
Hampton Technologies LLC ....E...... 631 924-1335
Medford **(G-7711)**
Highlander Realty Inc ....E...... 914 235-8073
New Rochelle **(G-8341)**
Home Tech LLC ....G...... 914 301-5408
Katonah **(G-6633)**
Intellicheck Inc ....E...... 516 992-1900
Melville **(G-7794)**
LTS Ny Inc ....G...... 646 558-3888
Port Washington **(G-12901)**
Manhole Brrier SEC Systems Inc ....E...... 516 741-1032
Kew Gardens **(G-6668)**
News/Sprts Microwave Rentl Inc ....E...... 619 670-0572
New York **(G-10615)**
Parabit Systems Inc ....E...... 516 378-4800
Bellmore **(G-786)**
Scorpion Security Products Inc ....F...... 607 724-9999
Vestal **(G-15382)**
Security Defense System ....G...... 718 769-7900
Whitestone **(G-16100)**

SECURITY EQPT STORES

Mod-Pac Corp ....C...... 716 898-8480
Buffalo **(G-2869)**

SECURITY PROTECTIVE DEVICES MAINTENANCE & MONITORING SVCS

Basil S Kadhim ....G...... 888 520-5192
New York **(G-8736)**
Security Defense System ....G...... 718 769-7900
Whitestone **(G-16100)**

SECURITY SYSTEMS SERVICES

Indegy Inc ....E...... 866 801-5394
New York **(G-9878)**
Intralinks Holdings Inc ....G...... 212 543-7700
New York **(G-9930)**
Synergx Systems Inc ....D...... 516 433-4700
Woodside **(G-16230)**
Verint Systems Inc ....C...... 631 962-9600
Melville **(G-7834)**
World Business Media LLC ....F...... 212 344-0759
Massapequa Park **(G-7662)**

SEMICONDUCTOR & RELATED DEVICES: Read-Only Memory Or ROM

Monolithic Coatings Inc ....G...... 914 621-2765
Sharon Springs **(G-14383)**

SEMICONDUCTOR DEVICES: Wafers

Thermoaura Inc ....F...... 518 813-4997
Albany **(G-136)**

SEMICONDUCTORS & RELATED DEVICES

Able Electronics Inc ....F...... 631 924-5386
Bellport **(G-792)**
Accumetrics Associates Inc ....F...... 518 393-2200
Latham **(G-6847)**
Advis Inc ....G...... 585 568-0100
Caledonia **(G-3068)**
Aeroflex Holding Corp ....A...... 516 694-6700
Plainview **(G-12659)**
Air Liquide Electronics ....G...... 518 605-4936
Malta **(G-7494)**
Applied Materials Inc ....G...... 518 245-1400
Ballston Spa **(G-569)**
Applied Materials Inc ....E...... 845 227-5000
Hopewell Junction **(G-6090)**
Atlantis Energy Systems Inc ....G...... 916 438-2930
Poughkeepsie **(G-12946)**
Beech Grove Technology Inc ....G...... 845 223-6844
Hopewell Junction **(G-6091)**
Bga Technology LLC ....E...... 631 750-4600
Bohemia **(G-981)**
Ceres Technologies Inc ....D...... 845 247-4701
Saugerties **(G-14198)**
Cobham Long Island Inc ....C...... 631 231-9100
Hauppauge **(G-5619)**
Cold Springs R & D Inc ....F...... 315 413-1237
Syracuse **(G-14857)**
Compositech Ltd ....C...... 516 835-1458
Woodbury **(G-16168)**

PRODUCT

Convergent Med MGT Svcs LLC ....G...... 718 921-6159
　Brooklyn *(G-1685)*
Cooper Power Systems LLC..............B...... 716 375-7100
　Olean *(G-12230)*
Corning Incorporated ....E...... 607 248-1200
　Corning *(G-3708)*
Corning Incorporated ....A...... 607 974-9000
　Corning *(G-3705)*
Corning Incorporated ....A...... 607 974-9000
　Painted Post *(G-12473)*
Corning Specialty Mtls Inc ....G...... 607 974-9000
　Corning *(G-3713)*
Crystalonics of New York Inc ....F...... 631 981-6140
　Ronkonkoma *(G-13928)*
Curtiss-Wright Controls ....F...... 631 756-4740
　Farmingdale *(G-4606)*
Cvd Equipment Corporation ....C...... 631 981-7081
　Central Islip *(G-3271)*
Cypress Semiconductor Corp ....F...... 631 261-1358
　Northport *(G-12102)*
Endicott Interconnect Tech Inc.........A...... 866 820-4820
　Endicott *(G-4450)*
Energy Materials Corporation..........G...... 315 247-0880
　Rochester *(G-13392)*
Excel Technology Inc ....G...... 718 423-7262
　Fresh Meadows *(G-5040)*
General Semiconductor Inc ....G...... 631 300-3818
　Hauppauge *(G-5657)*
Globalfoundries US 2 LLC ....C...... 512 457-3900
　Hopewell Junction *(G-6094)*
Globalfoundries US Inc ....E...... 512 457-3900
　Hopewell Junction *(G-6095)*
Gurley Precision Instrs Inc ....C...... 518 272-6300
　Troy *(G-15170)*
H K Technologies Inc. ....G...... 718 255-1898
　Long Island City *(G-7237)*
Hi-Tron Semiconductor Corp ....E...... 631 231-1500
　Hauppauge *(G-5670)*
Hipotronics Inc ....C...... 845 279-8091
　Brewster *(G-1151)*
Ilc Holdings Inc ....G...... 631 567-5600
　Bohemia *(G-1021)*
Ilc Industries LLC ....F...... 631 567-5600
　Bohemia *(G-1023)*
International Bus Mchs Corp ....C...... 800 426-4968
　Hopewell Junction *(G-6097)*
Intex Company Inc ....D...... 516 223-0200
　Freeport *(G-5003)*
Isine Inc ....E...... 631 913-4400
　Melville *(G-7797)*
J H Rhodes Company Inc.................F...... 315 829-3600
　Vernon *(G-15367)*
Kionix Inc ....C...... 607 257-1080
　Ithaca *(G-6391)*
KLA Corporation ....F...... 845 897-1723
　Hopewell Junction *(G-6098)*
Lightspin Technologies Inc..............G...... 301 656-7600
　Endwell *(G-4481)*
LMD Power of Light Corp.................D...... 585 272-5420
　Rochester *(G-13519)*
Logitek Inc ....D...... 631 567-1100
　Bohemia *(G-1035)*
M C Products ....E...... 631 471-4070
　Holbrook *(G-6008)*
Marcon Services ....G...... 516 223-8019
　Freeport *(G-5006)*
Marktech International Corp ....E...... 518 956-2980
　Latham *(G-6870)*
Materion Brewster LLC....................D...... 845 279-0900
　Brewster *(G-1155)*
McG Electronics Inc ....E...... 631 586-5125
　Deer Park *(G-3905)*
Micro Contract Manufacturing..........D...... 631 738-7874
　Medford *(G-7719)*
Micro Semicdtr Researches LLC ......G...... 646 863-6070
　New York *(G-10457)*
Microchip Technology Inc ....C...... 607 785-5992
　Endicott *(G-4465)*
Micromem Technologies ....F...... 212 672-1806
　New York *(G-10458)*
Mini-Circuits Fort Wayne LLC...........B...... 718 934-4500
　Brooklyn *(G-2157)*
Mosaic Microsystems LLC ....G...... 585 314-7441
　Rochester *(G-13561)*
Moser Baer Technologies Inc ....F...... 585 749-0480
　Fairport *(G-4508)*
Navitar Inc....................................D...... 585 359-4000
　Rochester *(G-13568)*
Optimum Semiconductor Tech ....G...... 914 287-8500
　Tarrytown *(G-15051)*

Procomponents Inc ....E...... 516 683-0909
　Westbury *(G-15921)*
Riverhawk Company LP ....E...... 315 624-7171
　New Hartford *(G-8244)*
RSM Electron Power Inc ....C...... 631 586-7600
　Hauppauge *(G-5756)*
Ruhle Companies Inc ....E...... 914 287-4000
　Valhalla *(G-15309)*
Sanrex Corporation ....F...... 516 625-1313
　Port Washington *(G-12922)*
Schott Corporation ....D...... 315 255-2791
　Auburn *(G-494)*
Schott Lithotec USA Corp ....G...... 845 463-5300
　Elmsford *(G-4430)*
Semitronics Corp ....E...... 516 223-0200
　Freeport *(G-5023)*
Sinclair Technologies Inc ....E...... 716 874-3682
　Hamburg *(G-5521)*
Solid Cell Inc ....F...... 585 426-5000
　Rochester *(G-13735)*
Spectron Glass & Electronics ....F...... 631 582-5600
　Hauppauge *(G-5769)*
Spectron Systems Technology ....F...... 631 582-5600
　Hauppauge *(G-5770)*
Spellman High Vltage Elec Corp ....D...... 914 686-3600
　Valhalla *(G-15310)*
Stetron International Inc ....F...... 716 854-3443
　Buffalo *(G-2993)*
Sumitomo Elc USA Holdings Inc.......G...... 212 490-6610
　New York *(G-11389)*
Super Conductor Materials Inc..........F...... 845 368-0240
　Suffern *(G-14767)*
Swissbit Na Inc ....G...... 914 935-1400
　Port Chester *(G-12829)*
Symwave Inc ....G...... 949 542-4400
　Hauppauge *(G-5780)*
Tel Technology Center Amer LLC ......E...... 512 424-4200
　Albany *(G-135)*
Telephonics Corporation ....E...... 631 549-6000
　Huntington *(G-6226)*
Thales Laser SA ....D...... 585 223-2370
　Fairport *(G-4527)*
Tlsi Incorporated ....D...... 631 470-8880
　Huntington *(G-6229)*
Tokyo Electron America Inc ....E...... 518 289-3100
　Malta *(G-7497)*
Tokyo Electron America Inc ....G...... 518 292-4200
　Albany *(G-137)*
Vgg Holding LLC ....E...... 212 415-6700
　New York *(G-11672)*
Viking Technologies Ltd ....E...... 631 957-8000
　Lindenhurst *(G-6983)*
Washington Foundries Inc ....G...... 516 374-8447
　Hewlett *(G-5876)*
Zastech Inc ....E...... 516 496-4777
　Syosset *(G-14806)*

SENSORS: Temperature For Motor Windings

Irtronics Instruments Inc ....F...... 914 693-6291
　Ardsley *(G-389)*

SENSORS: Temperature, Exc Indl Process

Titan Controls Inc ....F...... 516 358-2407
　New York *(G-11499)*

SEPARATORS: Metal Plate

Motivair Corporation.......................E...... 716 691-9222
　Amherst *(G-233)*

SEPTIC TANKS: Concrete

Bistrian Cement Corporation............F...... 631 324-1123
　East Hampton *(G-4117)*
H F Cary & Sons ....G...... 607 598-2563
　Lockwood *(G-7120)*

SEPTIC TANKS: Plastic

Roth Global Plastics Inc ....E...... 315 475-0100
　Syracuse *(G-14979)*

SERVOMOTORS: Electric

Magna Products Corp......................E...... 585 647-2280
　Rochester *(G-13529)*

SEWAGE & WATER TREATMENT EQPT

City of Kingston ....F...... 845 331-2490
　Kingston *(G-6686)*

Ferguson Enterprises Inc.................E...... 800 437-1146
　New Hyde Park *(G-8269)*
Yr Blanc & Co LLC ....G...... 716 800-3999
　Buffalo *(G-3053)*

SEWAGE TREATMENT SYSTEMS & EQPT

Environment-One Corporation...........C...... 518 346-6161
　Schenectady *(G-14264)*

SEWER CLEANING EQPT: Power

Dyna-Vac Equipment Inc ....F...... 315 865-8084
　Stittville *(G-14734)*
Pathfinder 103 Inc..........................G...... 315 363-4260
　Oneida *(G-12253)*

SEWING CONTRACTORS

TSS Foam Industries Corp ....F...... 585 538-2321
　Caledonia *(G-3074)*

SEWING MACHINES & PARTS: Indl

Herbert Jaffe Inc ....G...... 718 392-1956
　Long Island City *(G-7240)*
Tompkins Srm LLC ....G...... 315 422-8763
　Syracuse *(G-15013)*

SEWING, NEEDLEWORK & PIECE GOODS STORE: Needlework Gds/Sply

Viking Athletics Ltd ....E...... 631 957-8000
　Lindenhurst *(G-6982)*

SEWING, NEEDLEWORK & PIECE GOODS STORES: Sewing & Needlework

Great Adirondack Yarn Company........F...... 518 843-3381
　Amsterdam *(G-329)*

SHADES: Lamp & Light, Residential

Custom Lampshades Inc ....F...... 718 254-0500
　Brooklyn *(G-1711)*
Dreyfus Ashby Inc ....E...... 212 818-0770
　New York *(G-9271)*

SHADES: Lamp Or Candle

Artemis Studios Inc ....D...... 718 788-6022
　Brooklyn *(G-1536)*
Blanche P Field LLC ....E...... 212 355-6616
　New York *(G-8809)*
Diane Studios Inc ....D...... 718 788-6007
　Brooklyn *(G-1740)*
Jamaica Lamp Corp ....E...... 718 776-5039
　Queens Village *(G-13023)*
Jimco Lamp & Manufacturing Co ....G...... 631 218-2152
　Islip *(G-6353)*
Our Own Candle Company Inc ....F...... 716 769-5000
　Findley Lake *(G-4795)*
Ray Gold Shade Inc ....F...... 718 377-8892
　Brooklyn *(G-2329)*

SHADES: Window

Mechoshade Systems Inc ....C...... 718 729-2020
　Long Island City *(G-7292)*
Solar Screen Co Inc ....G...... 718 592-8222
　Corona *(G-3750)*
Windowcraft Inc ....F...... 516 294-3580
　Garden City Park *(G-5125)*

SHAFTS: Flexible

BW Elliott Mfg Co LLC ....B...... 607 772-0404
　Binghamton *(G-865)*

SHALE MINING, COMMON

Callahan & Nannini Quarry Inc ....G...... 845 496-4323
　Salisbury Mills *(G-14134)*
Grosso Materials Inc.......................F...... 845 361-5211
　Montgomery *(G-8061)*

SHALE: Expanded

Norlite LLC....................................B...... 518 235-0030
　Cohoes *(G-3511)*

SHAPES & PILINGS, STRUCTURAL: Steel

Empire Steel Works Inc ....F...... 516 561-3500
　Hicksville *(G-5905)*

Markin Tubing Inc ....C 585 495-6211
  Wyoming (G-16251)
Rochester Structural LLC ....E 585 436-1250
  Rochester (G-13700)

SHEATHING: Paper

Sabin Robbins Paper Company ....E 513 874-5270
  New York (G-11112)

SHEET METAL SPECIALTIES, EXC STAMPED

Aberdeen Blower & Shtmtl Works........G 631 661-6100
  West Babylon (G-15680)
Aero-Data Metal Crafters Inc.................C 631 471-7733
  Ronkonkoma (G-13892)
All Island Blower & Shtmtl ....F 631 567-7070
  Bohemia (G-969)
Apparatus Mfg Inc ....G 845 471-5116
  Poughkeepsie (G-12944)
Architctral Shetmetal Pdts Inc.............G 518 381-6144
  Scotia (G-14328)
Arlan Damper Corporation ....E 631 589-7431
  Bohemia (G-976)
Asm USA Inc ....F 212 925-2906
  New York (G-8649)
Asp Industries Inc ....E 585 254-9130
  Rochester (G-13253)
Avalanche Fabrication Inc ....F 585 545-4000
  Ontario (G-12285)
B & B Sheet Metal Inc ....E 718 433-2501
  Long Island City (G-7173)
B & H Precision Fabricators ....F 631 563-9620
  Bohemia (G-977)
Banner Metalcraft Inc ....D 631 563-7303
  Ronkonkoma (G-13913)
Boss Precision Ltd ....D 585 352-7070
  Spencerport (G-14553)
Custom Sheet Metal Corp ....G 315 463-9105
  Syracuse (G-14870)
Dayton T Brown Inc ....B 631 589-6300
  Bohemia (G-1001)
Elmsford Sheet Metal Works Inc ....D 914 739-6300
  Cortlandt Manor (G-3794)
Franchet Metal Craft Inc......................G 718 658-6400
  Jamaica (G-6443)
Hatfield Metal Fab Inc ....E 845 454-9078
  Poughkeepsie (G-12961)
Incodema Inc ....E 607 277-7070
  Ithaca (G-6385)
K Barthelmes Mfg Co Inc ....E 585 328-8140
  Rochester (G-13501)
McAlpin Industries Inc.........................E 585 266-3060
  Rochester (G-13538)
Metal Tek Products ....G 516 586-4514
  Plainview (G-12700)
P R B Metal Products Inc ....F 631 467-1800
  Ronkonkoma (G-13989)
PDQ Manufacturing Co Inc ....E 845 889-3123
  Rhinebeck (G-13100)
Prokosch and Sonn Sheet Metal ....E 845 562-4211
  Newburgh (G-11884)
Read Manufacturing Company Inc........E 631 567-4487
  Holbrook (G-6016)
S & B Machine Works Inc ....E 516 997-2666
  Westbury (G-15924)
S & T Machine Inc ....F 718 272-2484
  Brooklyn (G-2373)
Service Mfg Group Inc ....F 716 893-1482
  Buffalo (G-2980)
Technimetal Precision Inds...................E 631 231-8900
  Hauppauge (G-5782)
Tri-Metal Industries Inc ....E 716 691-3323
  Amherst (G-250)
Ulster Precision Inc ....E 845 338-0995
  Kingston (G-6717)
Universal Precision Corp ....E 585 321-9760
  Rochester (G-13785)
Vin Mar Precision Metals Inc ....F 631 563-6608
  Copiague (G-3688)
VM Choppy & Sons LLC......................E 518 266-1444
  Troy (G-15195)

SHEET MUSIC STORES

Golfing Magazine ....G 516 822-5446
  Hicksville (G-5914)

SHEET MUSIC, WHOLESALE

Carl Fischer LLC ....E 212 777-0900
  New York (G-8917)

SHEETING: Laminated Plastic

Advanced Structures Corp ....F 631 667-5000
  Deer Park (G-3830)
Allred & Associates Inc ....E 315 252-2559
  Elbridge (G-4296)

SHEETS & STRIPS: Aluminum

Alcoa Fastening Systems ....G........ 585 368-5049
  Rochester (G-13216)
Arconic Inc ....G........ 315 764-4011
  Massena (G-7666)

SHEETS: Fabric, From Purchased Materials

Elegant Linen Inc ....E 718 492-0297
  Brooklyn (G-1793)

SHELVES & SHELVING: Wood

Forecast Consoles Inc.........................E 631 253-9000
  Hauppauge (G-5653)
Karp Associates Inc............................D 631 768-8300
  Melville (G-7798)

SHELVING: Office & Store, Exc Wood

Abaco Steel Products Inc ....G 631 589-1800
  Bohemia (G-960)
Amscor Inc ....F 800 825-9800
  West Babylon (G-15689)
Jack Luckner Steel Shelving Co............D 718 363-0500
  Maspeth (G-7623)
Lucia Group Inc ....G 631 392-4900
  Deer Park (G-3900)
Sterling Shelf Liners Inc ....D 631 676-5175
  Holbrook (G-6022)
Tri-Boro Shelving Inc ....F 718 782-8527
  Ridgewood (G-13165)
Your Furniture Designers Inc................G 845 947-3046
  West Haverstraw (G-15765)

SHERARDIZING SVC: Metals Or Metal Prdts

Superior Metals & Processing..............G 718 545-7500
  Long Island City (G-7375)

SHIELDS OR ENCLOSURES: Radiator, Sheet Metal

Interior Metals ....E 718 439-7324
  Brooklyn (G-1963)
Radiation Shielding Systems.................F 888 631-2278
  Suffern (G-14765)
Rand Products Manufacturing Co..........G 518 374-9871
  Schenectady (G-14297)
Steelcraft Manufacturing Co ....F 718 277-2404
  Brooklyn (G-2456)

SHIMS: Metal

McD Metals LLC ....F 518 456-9694
  Albany (G-98)
Romac Electronics Inc ....E 516 349-7900
  Plainview (G-12711)

SHIP BUILDING & REPAIRING: Cargo Vessels

Reynolds Shipyard Corporation............F 718 981-2800
  Staten Island (G-14702)

SHIP BUILDING & REPAIRING: Cargo, Commercial

Steelways Inc ....E 845 562-0860
  Newburgh (G-11887)

SHIP BUILDING & REPAIRING: Ferryboats

Robert E Derecktor Inc ....D 914 698-0962
  Mamaroneck (G-7522)

SHIP BUILDING & REPAIRING: Rigging, Marine

Dragon Trading Inc ....G........ 212 717-1496
  New York (G-9265)

SHIP BUILDING & REPAIRING: Tankers

McQuilling Partners Inc ....E 516 227-5718
  Garden City (G-5107)

SHIPBUILDING & REPAIR

Caddell Dry Dock & Repr Co Inc ....C 718 442-2112
  Staten Island (G-14635)
Excelco Developments Inc ....E 716 934-2651
  Silver Creek (G-14441)
Excelco/Newbrook Inc..........................D 716 934-2644
  Silver Creek (G-14442)
Gmd Shipyard Corp ....E 718 260-9202
  Brooklyn (G-1893)
Huntington Ingalls Inc ....E 518 884-3834
  Saratoga Springs (G-14182)
May Ship Repair Contg Corp ....E 718 442-9700
  Staten Island (G-14680)
Metalcraft Marine Us Inc ....F 315 501-4015
  Cape Vincent (G-3168)
Moran Shipyard Corporation ....C 718 981-5600
  Staten Island (G-14681)
Port Everglades Machine Works ....F 516 367-2280
  Plainview (G-12708)
Viking Mar Wldg Ship Repr LLC ....E 718 758-4116
  Brooklyn (G-2558)
World Maritime News ....G 212 477-6700
  New York (G-11782)

SHIPPING AGENTS

Hastings Hide Inc...............................G 516 295-2400
  Inwood (G-6295)

SHOCK ABSORBERS: Indl

Kyntec Corporation ....E 716 810-6956
  Buffalo (G-2840)
Taylor Devices Inc..............................C 716 694-0800
  North Tonawanda (G-12095)

SHOE & BOOT ACCESS

Randall Loeffler Inc............................E 212 226-8787
  New York (G-10980)

SHOE MATERIALS: Counters

Counter Evolution ....G 212 647-7505
  New York (G-9109)
Custom Countertops Inc ....G 716 685-2871
  Depew (G-3977)
Custom Design Kitchens Inc ....F 518 355-4446
  Duanesburg (G-4044)

SHOE MATERIALS: Plastic

311 Industries Corp............................G 607 846-4520
  Endicott (G-4442)

SHOE MATERIALS: Quarters

Priscilla Quart Co Firts........................G 516 365-2755
  Manhasset (G-7540)

SHOE MATERIALS: Sole Parts

MBA Orthotics Inc...............................G 631 392-4755
  Bay Shore (G-691)

SHOE REPAIR SHOP

Arimed Orthotics Prosthetics...............F 718 875-8754
  Brooklyn (G-1528)

SHOE STORES

GH Bass & Co.....................................E 646 768-4600
  New York (G-9607)
Givi Inc ....F 212 586-5029
  New York (G-9616)
Jag Footwear ACC & Ret Corp ....A 800 999-1877
  New York (G-9967)
Kcp Holdco Inc....................................F 212 265-1500
  New York (G-10086)
Kenneth Cole Productions Inc.............B 212 265-1500
  New York (G-10089)

SHOE STORES: Children's

Jakes Sneakers Inc.............................G 718 233-1132
  Brooklyn (G-1988)

SHOE STORES: Orthopedic

Arimed Orthotics Prosthetics..............F 718 875-8754
  Brooklyn (G-1528)

PRODUCT

SHOE STORES: Women's

Lsil & Co Inc ....G...... 914 761-0998
   White Plains (G-16026)

SHOES & BOOTS WHOLESALERS

Ashko Group LLC ....F...... 212 594-6050
   New York (G-8645)
Bh Brand Inc ....E...... 212 239-1635
   New York (G-8777)
Jag Footwear ACC & Ret Corp ....A...... 800 999-1877
   New York (G-9967)

SHOES: Athletic, Exc Rubber Or Plastic

Custom Sports Lab Inc ....G...... 212 832-1648
   New York (G-9135)
Kicks Closet Sportswear Inc ....G...... 347 577-0857
   Bronx (G-1292)
Mango Usa Inc ....E...... 718 998-6050
   Brooklyn (G-2106)
Mayberry Shoe Company Inc ....G...... 315 692-4086
   Manlius (G-7549)
McM Products USA Inc ....E...... 646 756-4090
   New York (G-10401)
Vsg International LLC ....G...... 718 300-8171
   Brooklyn (G-2571)

SHOES: Ballet Slippers

La Strada Dance Footwear Inc ....G...... 631 242-1401
   Deer Park (G-3895)

SHOES: Canvas, Rubber Soled

Inkkas LLC ....G...... 646 845-9803
   New York (G-9895)
Little Eric Shoes On Madison ....G...... 212 717-1513
   New York (G-10229)
Mango Usa Inc ....E...... 718 998-6050
   Brooklyn (G-2106)
Vans Inc ....F...... 631 724-1011
   Lake Grove (G-6762)

SHOES: Infants' & Children's

Everlast Worldwide Inc ....E...... 212 239-0990
   New York (G-9428)
GH Bass & Co ....E...... 646 768-4600
   New York (G-9607)
Steven Madden Ltd ....B...... 718 446-1800
   Long Island City (G-7370)

SHOES: Men's

Air Skate & Air Jump Corp ....G...... 212 967-1201
   New York (G-8503)
Air Skate & Air Jump Corp ....F...... 212 967-1201
   Brooklyn (G-1473)
Bh Brand Inc ....E...... 212 239-1635
   New York (G-8777)
Detny Footwear Inc ....G...... 212 423-1040
   New York (G-9210)
GH Bass & Co ....E...... 646 768-4600
   New York (G-9607)
Kcp Holdco Inc ....F...... 212 265-1500
   New York (G-10086)
Kenneth Cole Productions Inc ....B...... 212 265-1500
   New York (G-10089)
Lake View Manufacturing LLC ....F...... 315 364-7892
   King Ferry (G-6671)
Nicholas Kirkwood LLC ....F...... 646 559-5239
   New York (G-10622)
Phillips-Van Heusen Europe ....F...... 212 381-3500
   New York (G-10829)
Pvh Corp ....D...... 212 381-3500
   New York (G-10933)
Pvh Corp ....G...... 212 549-6000
   New York (G-10934)
Steven Madden Ltd ....B...... 718 446-1800
   Long Island City (G-7370)
T O Dey Service Corp ....F...... 212 683-6300
   New York (G-11418)
Tapestry Inc ....B...... 212 594-1850
   New York (G-11434)
Tic TAC Toes Mfg Corp ....D...... 518 773-8187
   Gloversville (G-5296)

SHOES: Men's, Sandals

Neumann Jutta New York Inc ....F...... 212 982-7048
   New York (G-10572)

SHOES: Men's, Work

Artisan Boot & Shoe Co LLC ....F...... 585 813-2825
   Batavia (G-602)

SHOES: Orthopedic, Men's

Jerry Miller Molded Shoes Inc ....F...... 716 881-3920
   Buffalo (G-2820)
Pedifix Inc ....E...... 845 277-2850
   Brewster (G-1157)
Tru Mold Shoes Inc ....F...... 716 881-4484
   Buffalo (G-3022)

SHOES: Orthopedic, Women's

Jerry Miller Molded Shoes Inc ....F...... 716 881-3920
   Buffalo (G-2820)
Pedifix Inc ....E...... 845 277-2850
   Brewster (G-1157)
T O Dey Service Corp ....F...... 212 683-6300
   New York (G-11418)
Tru Mold Shoes Inc ....F...... 716 881-4484
   Buffalo (G-3022)

SHOES: Plastic Or Rubber

Anthony L & S LLC ....E...... 212 386-7245
   New York (G-8597)
Detny Footwear Inc ....G...... 212 423-1040
   New York (G-9210)
Great Shoes Inc ....F...... 718 813-1945
   Islandia (G-6333)
Homegrown For Good LLC ....F...... 857 540-6361
   New Rochelle (G-8342)
Nike Inc ....E...... 631 960-0184
   Islip Terrace (G-6359)
Nike Inc ....G...... 716 298-5615
   Niagara Falls (G-11955)
Timing Group LLC ....F...... 646 878-2600
   New York (G-11497)

SHOES: Plastic Or Rubber Soles With Fabric Uppers

Soludos LLC ....F...... 212 219-1101
   New York (G-11292)

SHOES: Women's

Bh Brand Inc ....E...... 212 239-1635
   New York (G-8777)
Detny Footwear Inc ....G...... 212 423-1040
   New York (G-9210)
Everlast Worldwide Inc ....E...... 212 239-0990
   New York (G-9428)
GH Bass & Co ....E...... 646 768-4600
   New York (G-9607)
Kenneth Cole Productions Inc ....B...... 212 265-1500
   New York (G-10089)
Lake View Manufacturing LLC ....F...... 315 364-7892
   King Ferry (G-6671)
Nicholas Kirkwood LLC ....F...... 646 559-5239
   New York (G-10622)
Steven Madden Ltd ....B...... 718 446-1800
   Long Island City (G-7370)
Tapestry Inc ....B...... 212 594-1850
   New York (G-11434)
Tic TAC Toes Mfg Corp ....D...... 518 773-8187
   Gloversville (G-5296)

SHOES: Women's, Dress

Adl Design Inc ....G...... 516 949-6658
   Huntington (G-6198)
Attitudes Footwear Inc ....G...... 212 754-9113
   New York (G-8676)
Mango Usa Inc ....E...... 718 998-6050
   Brooklyn (G-2106)
Scott Silverstein Llc ....G...... 212 781-1818
   New York (G-11169)

SHOES: Women's, Sandals

Neumann Jutta New York Inc ....F...... 212 982-7048
   New York (G-10572)

SHOPPING CENTERS & MALLS

Northpoint Trading Inc ....F...... 212 481-8001
   New York (G-10645)

SHOT PEENING SVC

Metal Improvement Company LLC ....D...... 607 533-7000
   Lansing (G-6841)

SHOWCASES & DISPLAY FIXTURES: Office & Store

Aarco Products Inc ....F...... 631 924-5461
   Yaphank (G-16254)
Abbott Industries Inc ....B...... 718 291-0800
   Jamaica (G-6423)
Four S Showcase Manufacturing ....G...... 718 649-4900
   Brooklyn (G-1863)
Glaro Inc ....D...... 631 234-1717
   Hauppauge (G-5661)
Ledan Inc ....E...... 631 239-1226
   Northport (G-12107)
Ludwig and Larsen ....G...... 718 369-0999
   Ridgewood (G-13151)
Manhattan Display Inc ....G...... 718 392-1365
   Long Island City (G-7289)
Steven Kraus Associates Inc ....G...... 631 923-2033
   Huntington (G-6225)
Visual Millwork & Fix Mfg Inc ....D...... 718 267-7800
   Deer Park (G-3952)

SHOWER STALLS: Metal

ITR Industries Inc ....E...... 914 964-7063
   Yonkers (G-16321)

SHOWER STALLS: Plastic & Fiberglass

ITR Industries Inc ....E...... 914 964-7063
   Yonkers (G-16321)

SIDING & STRUCTURAL MATERIALS: Wood

Builders Firstsource Inc ....E...... 860 528-2293
   Middletown (G-7897)
Gutchess Lumber Co Inc ....C...... 607 753-3393
   Cortland (G-3771)
L J Valente Inc ....G...... 518 674-3750
   Averill Park (G-508)
Mohawk Metal Mfg & Sls ....G...... 315 853-7663
   Westmoreland (G-15960)
One Tree Dist ....G...... 315 701-2924
   Syracuse (G-14955)
Tri-State Brick & Stone NY Inc ....D...... 212 366-0300
   New York (G-11540)
Upstate Increte Incorporated ....G...... 585 254-2010
   Rochester (G-13788)

SIDING: Precast Stone

Creative Stone Mfg Inc ....G...... 718 386-7425
   Brooklyn (G-1699)

SIGN LETTERING & PAINTING SVCS

Sign Shop Inc ....G...... 631 226-4145
   Copiague (G-3678)

SIGN PAINTING & LETTERING SHOP

Clinton Signs Inc ....G...... 585 482-1620
   Webster (G-15636)
Lanza Corp ....G...... 914 937-6360
   Port Chester (G-12824)
Paratore Signs Inc ....G...... 315 455-5551
   Syracuse (G-14962)
Ray Sign Inc ....F...... 518 377-1371
   Schenectady (G-14298)

SIGNALING APPARATUS: Electric

Intelligent Traffic Systems ....G...... 631 567-5994
   Bohemia (G-1024)
L3 Foreign Holdings Inc ....C...... 212 697-1111
   New York (G-10153)
L3 Technologies Inc ....B...... 212 697-1111
   New York (G-10154)

SIGNALING DEVICES: Sound, Electrical

Sensor Films Incorporated ....E...... 585 738-3500
   Victor (G-15430)

SIGNALS: Railroad, Electric

Alstom Signaling Inc ....B...... 585 783-2000
   West Henrietta (G-15782)

Star Headlight Lantern Co Inc ....C 585 226-9500
Avon *(G-516)*
Twinco Mfg Co Inc ....E 631 231-0022
Hauppauge *(G-5789)*

SIGNALS: Traffic Control, Electric

Apex Signal Corporation ....D 631 567-1100
Bohemia *(G-974)*
Comet Flasher Inc ....G 716 821-9595
Buffalo *(G-2704)*
Power Line Constructors Inc ....E 315 853-6183
Clinton *(G-3484)*

SIGNS & ADVERTISING SPECIALTIES

A M S Sign Designs ....G 631 467-7722
Centereach *(G-3249)*
Aakron Rule Corp ....C 716 542-5483
Akron *(G-15)*
Accurate Signs & Awnings Inc ....F 718 788-0302
Brooklyn *(G-1453)*
Acme Signs of Baldwinsville ....G 315 638-4865
Baldwinsville *(G-539)*
Ad Makers Long Island Inc ....F 631 595-9100
Deer Park *(G-3829)*
Allied Maker ....F 516 200-9145
Glen Cove *(G-5188)*
Allstar Graphics Ltd ....E 718 740-2240
Queens Village *(G-13017)*
Aric Signs & Awnings Inc ....G 516 350-0409
Hempstead *(G-5832)*
Artscroll Printing Corp ....E 212 929-2413
New York *(G-8640)*
Asi Sign Systems Inc ....G 646 742-1320
New York *(G-8646)*
Asi Sign Systems Inc ....G 716 775-0104
Grand Island *(G-5325)*
BC Communications Inc ....G 631 549-8833
Huntington Station *(G-6240)*
Bedford Precision Parts Corp ....E 914 241-2211
Bedford Hills *(G-765)*
Bmg Printing and Promotion LLC ....G 631 231-9200
Bohemia *(G-982)*
Buckeye Corrugated Inc ....D 585 924-1600
Victor *(G-15396)*
Central Rede Sign Co Inc ....G 716 213-0797
Tonawanda *(G-15095)*
Chautauqua Sign Co Inc ....G 716 665-2222
Falconer *(G-4536)*
Climax Packaging Inc ....C 315 376-8000
Lowville *(G-7414)*
Coe Displays Inc ....G 718 937-5658
Long Island City *(G-7189)*
Colad Group LLC ....D 716 961-1776
Buffalo *(G-2703)*
Colonial Redi Record Corp ....E 718 972-7433
Brooklyn *(G-1675)*
Community Products LLC ....E 845 658-8351
Rifton *(G-13168)*
Custom Display Manufacture ....G 516 783-6491
North Bellmore *(G-12018)*
Data Display USA Inc ....C 631 218-2130
Holbrook *(G-5995)*
Designplex LLC ....G 845 358-6647
Nyack *(G-12140)*
Eastern Metal of Elmira Inc ....D 607 734-2295
Elmira *(G-4348)*
Elderlee Incorporated ....C 315 789-6670
Oaks Corners *(G-12161)*
Exhibit Corporation America ....E 718 937-2600
Long Island City *(G-7217)*
Fastsigns ....F 518 456-7446
Albany *(G-76)*
First Signs Saratoga Springs ....G 518 306-4449
Saratoga Springs *(G-14174)*
Five Star Prtg & Mailing Svcs ....F 212 929-0300
New York *(G-9508)*
Forrest Engraving Co Inc ....F 845 228-0200
New Rochelle *(G-8331)*
Fortuna Visual Group Inc ....G 646 383-8682
Brooklyn *(G-1860)*
G I Certified Inc ....G 212 397-1945
New York *(G-9558)*
Grant Graphics LLC ....G 518 583-2818
Saratoga Springs *(G-14178)*
Graphitek Inc ....F 518 686-5966
Hoosick Falls *(G-6083)*
Greyline Signs Inc ....G 716 947-4526
Derby *(G-4005)*
Gupp Signs Inc ....G 585 244-5070
Rochester *(G-13453)*
Hollywood Advg Banners Inc ....E 631 842-3000
Copiague *(G-3659)*
Hollywood Banners Inc ....E 631 842-3000
Copiague *(G-3660)*
Hollywood Signs Inc ....G 917 577-7333
Brooklyn *(G-1938)*
Hospitality Graphic Systems ....F 212 563-9334
New York *(G-9815)*
Ideal Signs Inc ....G 718 292-9196
Bronx *(G-1278)*
Image360 ....G 585 272-1234
Rochester *(G-13476)*
Impressive Imprints Inc ....G 631 293-6161
Farmingdale *(G-4648)*
Innovative Signage Systems Inc ....F 315 469-7783
Nedrow *(G-8215)*
Jaf Converters Inc ....E 631 842-3131
Copiague *(G-3661)*
Jal Signs Inc ....F 516 536-7280
Baldwin *(G-531)*
Jay Turoff ....F 718 856-7300
Brooklyn *(G-1990)*
JP Signs ....G 518 569-3907
Chazy *(G-3334)*
Kenan International Trading ....G 718 672-4922
Corona *(G-3742)*
Kennyetto Graphics Inc ....E 518 883-6360
Gloversville *(G-5287)*
KP Industries Inc ....F 516 679-3161
North Bellmore *(G-12020)*
Kraus & Sons Inc ....F 212 620-0408
New York *(G-10137)*
L I C Screen Printing Inc ....E 516 546-7289
Merrick *(G-7858)*
L Miller Design Inc ....G 631 242-1163
Deer Park *(G-3894)*
Lanco Corporation ....C 631 231-2300
Ronkonkoma *(G-13964)*
Landmark Signs Elec Maint Corp ....F 212 262-3699
New York *(G-10170)*
Landmark Signs Elec Maint Corp ....F 212 354-7551
New York *(G-10171)*
Letterama Inc ....G 516 349-0800
West Babylon *(G-15725)*
Lifestyle-Trimco ....E 718 257-9101
Brooklyn *(G-2069)*
Marigold Signs Inc ....F 516 433-7446
Hicksville *(G-5927)*
Mekanism Inc ....E 212 226-2772
New York *(G-10426)*
Millennium Signs & Display Inc ....E 516 292-8000
Hempstead *(G-5845)*
Mixture Screen Printing ....G 845 561-2857
Newburgh *(G-11873)*
Monasani Signs Inc ....G 631 266-2635
East Northport *(G-4150)*
Morris Brothers Sign Svc Inc ....G 212 675-9130
New York *(G-10504)*
Movinads & Signs LLC ....G 518 378-3000
Halfmoon *(G-5496)*
Mr Sign Usa Inc ....F 718 218-3321
Brooklyn *(G-2178)*
Nameplate Mfrs of Amer ....E 631 752-0055
Farmingdale *(G-4690)*
New Art Signs Co Inc ....G 718 443-0900
Glen Head *(G-5210)*
New Kit On The Block ....G 631 757-5655
Bohemia *(G-1051)*
Noel Assoc ....G 516 371-5420
Inwood *(G-6301)*
Norampac New York City Inc ....C 718 340-2100
Maspeth *(G-7630)*
Northeastern Sign Corp ....G 315 265-6657
South Colton *(G-14504)*
Northern Awning & Sign Company ....G 315 782-8515
Watertown *(G-15585)*
Nysco Products LLC ....D 718 792-9000
Hawthorne *(G-5820)*
On The Mark Digital Printing & ....G 716 823-3373
Hamburg *(G-5515)*
Orlandi Inc ....D 631 756-0110
Farmingdale *(G-4698)*
Orlandi Inc ....E 631 756-0110
Farmingdale *(G-4699)*
Outer Image LLC ....G 914 420-3097
Brooklyn *(G-2238)*
Pierrepont Visual Graphics ....G 585 305-9672
Rochester *(G-13624)*
Promotional Development Inc ....D 718 485-8550
Brooklyn *(G-2301)*
Quick Sign F X ....F 516 249-6531
Farmingdale *(G-4720)*
Reflective Image ....G 631 477-3368
Greenport *(G-5457)*
Resonant Legal Media LLC ....D 800 781-3591
New York *(G-11019)*
Riverwood Signs By Dandev Desi ....G 845 229-0282
Hyde Park *(G-6274)*
Rpf Associates Inc ....G 631 462-7446
Commack *(G-3597)*
Saxton Corporation ....E 518 732-7705
Castleton On Hudson *(G-3204)*
Seifert Graphics Inc ....F 315 736-2744
Oriskany *(G-12394)*
Sellco Industries Inc ....E 607 756-7594
Cortland *(G-3788)*
Seneca Signs LLC ....G 315 446-9420
Syracuse *(G-14993)*
Sign A Rama Inc ....G 631 952-3324
Hauppauge *(G-5764)*
Sign City of New York Inc ....G 718 661-1118
College Point *(G-3564)*
Sign Company ....G 212 967-2113
New York *(G-11233)*
Sign Guys New York City Inc ....G 718 414-2310
West Hempstead *(G-15779)*
Sign Heaven Corp ....G 718 499-4423
Brooklyn *(G-2409)*
Sign Here Enterprises LLC ....G 914 328-3111
Hartsdale *(G-5568)*
Sign World Inc ....E 212 619-9000
Brooklyn *(G-2410)*
Signexpo Enterprises Inc ....F 212 925-8585
New York *(G-11236)*
Signs Inc ....G 518 483-4759
Malone *(G-7491)*
Signworks ....F 518 745-0700
South Glens Falls *(G-14518)*
Smith Graphics Inc ....G 631 420-4180
Farmingdale *(G-4734)*
Specialty Signs Co Inc ....F 212 243-8521
New York *(G-11313)*
Speedy Sign A Rama USA Inc ....G 516 783-1075
Bellmore *(G-790)*
Stamps & Signs Online Corp ....G 718 218-0050
Brooklyn *(G-2450)*
Starlite Media LLC ....E 212 909-7700
New York *(G-11351)*
Stepping Stones One Day Signs ....G 518 237-5774
Waterford *(G-15547)*
Swell LLC ....F 646 738-8981
New York *(G-11408)*
Tech Products Inc ....E 718 442-4900
Staten Island *(G-14721)*
Three Gems Inc ....G 516 248-0388
New Hyde Park *(G-8297)*
Tj Signs Unlimited LLC ....C 631 273-4800
Hicksville *(G-5952)*
Todd Walbridge ....G 585 254-3018
Rochester *(G-13768)*
Tru-Art Sign Co Inc ....F 718 658-5068
Jamaica *(G-6482)*
United Sttes Brnze Sign of Fla ....E 516 352-5155
New Hyde Park *(G-8300)*
USA Signs of America Inc ....D 631 254-6900
Deer Park *(G-3948)*
Vez Inc ....G 718 273-7002
Staten Island *(G-14726)*
Viana Signs Corp ....F 516 887-2000
Oceanside *(G-12197)*
Visual ID Source Inc ....F 516 307-9759
Mineola *(G-8002)*
Visual Impact Graphics Inc ....G 585 548-7118
Batavia *(G-629)*
Voss Signs LLC ....E 315 682-6418
Manlius *(G-7550)*
Westchester Signs Inc ....G 914 666-7446
Mount Kisco *(G-8106)*
Wings For Wheels Inc ....G 914 961-0276
Yonkers *(G-16357)*
Wl Concepts & Production Inc ....E 516 565-5151
Freeport *(G-5032)*
Woodbury Printing Plus + Inc ....G 845 928-6610
Central Valley *(G-3302)*
Yellowpagecitycom ....F 585 410-6688
Rochester *(G-13813)*
Z-Car-D Corp ....E 631 424-2077
Huntington Station *(G-6267)*

SIGNS & ADVERTISING SPECIALTIES:
Artwork, Advertising

Adstream America LLC ....E 212 804-8498
  New York (G-8465)
Liberty Awnings & Signs Inc ....G 347 203-1470
  East Elmhurst (G-4109)
National Prfmce Solutions Inc ....D 718 833-4767
  Brooklyn (G-2190)
Pereira & ODell LLC ....G 212 897-1000
  New York (G-10802)
Rsquared Ny Inc ....D 631 521-8700
  Edgewood (G-4280)
Sizmek Dsp Inc ....F 212 594-8888
  New York (G-11253)
United Print Group Inc ....F 718 392-4242
  Woodside (G-16231)
Whispr Group Inc ....F 212 924-3979
  New York (G-11750)

SIGNS & ADVERTISING SPECIALTIES:
Displays, Paint Process

Chameleon Color Cards Ltd ....D 716 625-9452
  Lockport (G-7064)
Faster-Form Corp ....D 800 327-3676
  New Hartford (G-8240)
Props Displays & Interiors ....F 212 620-3840
  New York (G-10915)

SIGNS & ADVERTISING SPECIALTIES:
Letters For Signs, Metal

Stickershopcom Inc ....G 631 563-4323
  Bayport (G-731)

SIGNS & ADVERTISING SPECIALTIES:
Novelties

Amsterdam Printing & Litho Inc ....F 518 842-6000
  Amsterdam (G-316)
Amsterdam Printing & Litho Inc ....E 518 842-6000
  Amsterdam (G-317)
Dkm Sales LLC ....E 716 893-7777
  Buffalo (G-2730)
Jomar Industries Inc ....E 845 357-5773
  Airmont (G-13)
Kling Magnetics Inc ....E 518 392-4000
  Chatham (G-3331)
Mastercraft Manufacturing Co ....G 718 729-5620
  Long Island City (G-7290)
National Advertising & Prtg ....G 212 629-7650
  New York (G-10540)
Northeast Promotional Group In ....G 518 793-1024
  South Glens Falls (G-14515)
Pama Enterprises Inc ....G 516 504-6300
  Great Neck (G-5411)
Sign Men ....G 718 227-7446
  Staten Island (G-14710)
Tempo Industries Inc ....G 516 334-6900
  Westbury (G-15929)
Von Pok & Chang New York Inc ....G 212 599-0556
  New York (G-11705)

SIGNS & ADVERTISING SPECIALTIES:
Scoreboards, Electric

Eversan Inc ....F 315 736-3967
  Whitesboro (G-16080)

SIGNS & ADVERTISING SPECIALTIES: Signs

ABC Windows and Signs Corp ....F 718 353-6210
  College Point (G-3533)
Adirondack Sign Company LLC ....F 518 409-7446
  Saratoga Springs (G-14162)
Allstate Sign & Plaque Corp ....F 631 242-2828
  Deer Park (G-3836)
Art Parts Signs Inc ....G 585 381-2134
  East Rochester (G-4159)
Big Apple Sign Corp ....E 631 342-0303
  Islandia (G-6326)
Big Apple Sign Corp ....D 212 629-3650
  New York (G-8785)
Cab Signs Inc ....E 718 479-2424
  Brooklyn (G-1637)
Checklist Boards Corporation ....G 585 586-0152
  Rochester (G-13312)
City Signs Inc ....G 718 375-5933
  Brooklyn (G-1667)

Crown Sign Systems Inc ....F 914 375-2118
  Mount Vernon (G-8136)
Decree Signs & Graphics Inc ....F 973 278-3603
  Floral Park (G-4814)
Dura Engraving Corporation ....E 718 706-6400
  Long Island City (G-7205)
East End Sign Design Inc ....G 631 399-2574
  Mastic (G-7674)
Eastern Concepts Ltd ....F 718 472-3377
  Sunnyside (G-14772)
Executive Sign Corp ....G 212 397-4050
  Cornwall On Hudson (G-3733)
Executive Sign Corporation ....G 212 397-4050
  New York (G-9445)
Flado Enterprises Inc ....G 716 668-6400
  Depew (G-3982)
Fossil Industries Inc ....G 631 254-9200
  Deer Park (G-3876)
Graphic Signs & Awnings Ltd ....G 718 227-6000
  Staten Island (G-14659)
Hanson Sign Screen Prcess Corp ....E 716 661-3900
  Falconer (G-4543)
Hermosa Corp ....E 315 768-4320
  New York Mills (G-11834)
HI Tech Signs of NY Inc ....G 516 794-7880
  East Meadow (G-4136)
L S Sign Co Inc ....G 718 469-8600
  Ridgewood (G-13149)
Linear Signs Inc ....F 631 532-5330
  Lindenhurst (G-6955)
Mauceri Sign Inc ....G 718 656-7700
  Jamaica (G-6458)
Modulex New York Inc ....G 646 742-1320
  New York (G-10490)
Mohawk Sign Systems Inc ....E 518 842-5303
  Amsterdam (G-340)
Nas Quick Sign Inc ....G 716 876-7599
  Buffalo (G-2879)
Poncio Signs ....G 718 543-4851
  Bronx (G-1339)
Precision Signscom Inc ....D 631 841-7500
  Amityville (G-304)
Quorum Group LLC ....G 585 798-8888
  Medina (G-7744)
Rapp Signs Inc ....F 607 656-8167
  Greene (G-5447)
Rgm Signs Inc ....G 718 442-0598
  Staten Island (G-14703)
Rome Sign & Display Co ....G 315 336-0550
  Rome (G-13869)
Sign Center Inc ....F 212 967-2113
  New York (G-11232)
Sign Impressions Inc ....G 585 723-0420
  Rochester (G-13729)
Sign Language Inc ....G 585 237-2620
  Perry (G-12599)
Sign Studio Inc ....F 518 266-0877
  Cohoes (G-3517)
Sign Works Incorporated ....E 914 592-0700
  Elmsford (G-4433)
Signature Industries Inc ....F 516 771-8182
  Freeport (G-5025)
Signs of Success Ltd ....F 516 295-6000
  Lynbrook (G-7438)
Snyders Neon Displays Inc ....G 518 857-4100
  Colonie (G-3575)
Spanjer Corp ....G 347 448-8033
  Long Island City (G-7361)
Suma Industries Inc ....G 646 436-5202
  New York (G-11387)
Terrabilt Inc ....G 914 341-1500
  Mamaroneck (G-7524)
Timely Signs of Kingston Inc ....F 845 331-8710
  Kingston (G-6714)
Universal 3d Innovation Inc ....F 516 837-9423
  Valley Stream (G-15362)
Universal Signs and Svc Inc ....E 631 446-1121
  Deer Park (G-3946)
Valley Creek Side Inc ....G 315 839-5526
  Clayville (G-3458)
Victory Signs Inc ....G 315 762-0220
  Canastota (G-3160)
Vital Signs & Graphics Co Inc ....G 518 237-8372
  Cohoes (G-3519)
Wizard Equipment Inc ....G 315 414-9999
  Syracuse (G-15028)

SIGNS & ADVERTSG SPECIALTIES:
Displays/Cutouts Window/Lobby

American Visuals Inc ....G 631 694-6104
  Farmingdale (G-4584)
Creative Solutions Group Inc ....B 914 771-4200
  Yonkers (G-16299)
Display Marketing Group Inc ....E 631 348-4450
  Islandia (G-6330)
Display Presentations Ltd ....D 631 951-4050
  Brooklyn (G-1749)
Display Producers Inc ....C 718 904-1200
  New Rochelle (G-8327)
DSI Group Inc ....C 800 553-2202
  Maspeth (G-7607)
Edge Display Group Entp Inc ....F 631 498-1373
  Bellport (G-798)
Flair Display Inc ....D 718 324-9330
  Bronx (G-1259)
Hadley Exhibits Inc ....D 716 874-3666
  Buffalo (G-2788)
Joseph Struhl Co Inc ....F 516 741-3660
  New Hyde Park (G-8277)
King Displays Inc ....F 212 629-8455
  New York (G-10107)
Lamar Plastics Packaging Ltd ....D 516 378-2500
  Freeport (G-5004)
Miller Mohr Display Inc ....G 631 941-2769
  East Setauket (G-4181)
Mystic Display Co Inc ....G 718 485-2651
  Brooklyn (G-2183)
Nationwide Exhibitor Svcs Inc ....F 631 467-2034
  Central Islip (G-3285)
New Style Signs Limited Inc ....F 212 242-7848
  New York (G-10590)
Newline Products Inc ....C 972 881-3318
  New Windsor (G-8376)
Platinum Sales Promotion Inc ....G 718 361-0200
  Long Island City (G-7327)
Polyplastic Forms Inc ....E 631 249-5011
  Farmingdale (G-4712)
R & J Displays Inc ....E 631 491-3500
  West Babylon (G-15740)
Royal Promotion Group Inc ....D 212 246-3780
  New York (G-11091)
Signs & Decal Corp ....E 718 486-6400
  Brooklyn (G-2411)
Steel-Brite Ltd ....F 631 589-4044
  Oakdale (G-12156)
Substrate LLC ....E 212 913-9600
  Long Island City (G-7373)
Timely Signs Inc ....G 516 285-5339
  Elmont (G-4390)
Unique Display Mfg Corp ....G 516 546-3800
  Freeport (G-5031)
Visual Citi Inc ....C 631 482-3030
  Lindenhurst (G-6985)

SIGNS, EXC ELECTRIC, WHOLESALE

Fedex Office & Print Svcs Inc ....G 718 982-5223
  Staten Island (G-14653)
Mixture Screen Printing ....G 845 561-2857
  Newburgh (G-11873)
New Kit On The Block ....G 631 757-5655
  Bohemia (G-1051)

SIGNS: Electrical

A B C Mc Cleary Sign Co Inc ....F 315 493-3550
  Carthage (G-3193)
Adirondack Sign Perfect Inc ....G 518 409-7446
  Saratoga Springs (G-14163)
All Signs ....G 973 736-2113
  Staten Island (G-14618)
Alley Cat Signs Inc ....F 631 924-7446
  Middle Island (G-7874)
Allied Decorations Co Inc ....G 315 637-0273
  Syracuse (G-14811)
American Car Signs Inc ....G 518 227-1173
  Duanesburg (G-4043)
Architectural Sign Group Inc ....G 516 326-1800
  Elmont (G-4382)
Clinton Signs Inc ....G 585 482-1620
  Webster (G-15636)
Flexlume Sign Corporation ....G 716 884-2020
  Buffalo (G-2755)
Gloede Neon Signs Ltd Inc ....F 845 471-4366
  Poughkeepsie (G-12958)
ID Signsystems Inc ....E 585 266-5750
  Rochester (G-13473)

Jax Signs and Neon Inc ....G...... 607 727-3420
Endicott (G-4461)
Jem Sign Corp ....G... 516 867-4466
Hempstead (G-5840)
Lanza Corp ....G...... 914 937-6360
Port Chester (G-12824)
M Santoliquido Corp ....F...... 914 375-6674
Yonkers (G-16329)
Metropolitan Signs Inc ....F...... 315 638-1448
Baldwinsville (G-551)
Motion Message Inc ....F...... 631 924-9500
Bellport (G-804)
North Shore Neon Sign Co Inc ....E...... 718 937-4848
Flushing (G-4881)
Olson Sign Company Inc ....G...... 518 370-2118
Schenectady (G-14292)
Premier Sign Systems LLC ....E...... 585 235-0390
Rochester (G-13640)
Ray Sign Inc ....F...... 518 377-1371
Schenectady (G-14298)
Sign & Signs ....G...... 718 941-6200
Brooklyn (G-2407)
Sign Design Group New York Inc ....F... 718 392-0779
Hauppauge (G-5765)
Sign Group Inc ....E...... 718 438-7103
Brooklyn (G-2408)
Signs Ink Ltd ....F...... 914 739-9059
Yorktown Heights (G-16372)
Space Sign ....F...... 718 961-1112
College Point (G-3565)
Spectrum On Broadway ....F...... 718 932-5388
Woodside (G-16226)
Spectrum Signs Inc ....E...... 631 756-1010
Woodside (G-16227)
Strategic Signage Sourcing LLC ....F... 518 450-1093
Saratoga Springs (G-14194)
T J Signs Unlimited LLC ....E...... 631 273-4800
Islip (G-6357)
Trans-Lux Corporation ....D...... 800 243-5544
New York (G-11533)
Ultimate Signs & Designs Inc ....E...... 516 481-0800
Hempstead (G-5851)
Unilumin North America Inc ....G...... 732 904-2037
New York (G-11590)
Valle Signs and Awnings ....G...... 516 408-3440
Copiague (G-3686)
Wedel Sign Company Inc ....G...... 631 727-4577
Riverhead (G-13192)

SIGNS: Neon

Bannerboy Corporation ....G...... 646 691-6524
Brooklyn (G-1562)
Broadway Neon Sign Corp ....F...... 908 241-4177
Ronkonkoma (G-13918)
K & B Stamping Co Inc ....G...... 914 664-8555
Mount Vernon (G-8154)
Super Neon Light Co Inc ....G...... 718 236-5667
Brooklyn (G-2471)
Turoff Tower Graphics Inc ....F...... 718 856-7300
Brooklyn (G-2529)
Ulrich Sign Co Inc ....E...... 716 434-0167
Lockport (G-7116)
Yost Neon Displays Inc ....G...... 716 674-6780
West Seneca (G-15856)

SILICA MINING

American Minerals Inc ....F...... 646 747-4222
New York (G-8556)
St Silicones Inc ....G...... 518 664-0745
Mechanicville (G-7695)

SILICON & CHROMIUM

Medima LLC ....C...... 716 741-0400
Clarence (G-3436)

SILICON WAFERS: Chemically Doped

Isonics Corporation ....G...... 212 356-7400
New York (G-9946)

SILICONE RESINS

George M Dujack ....G...... 518 279-1303
Troy (G-15169)
Meliorum Technologies Inc ....G...... 585 313-0616
Rochester (G-13541)
Mom Holding Company ....G...... 518 233-3330
Waterford (G-15540)
Momentive Performance Mtls Inc ......E... 518 233-3330
Waterford (G-15542)

Mpm Holdings Inc ....G...... 518 233-3330
Waterford (G-15543)
Pawling Corporation ....C...... 845 373-9300
Wassaic (G-15525)

SILICONES

Crown Delta Corporation ....E...... 914 245-8910
Yorktown Heights (G-16363)
Mom Holding Company ....G...... 518 233-3330
Waterford (G-15540)
Momentive Performance Mtls Inc ......E... 518 233-3330
Waterford (G-15542)
Mpm AR LLC ....G...... 518 233-3397
Albany (G-102)
Mpm Holdings Inc ....G...... 518 233-3330
Waterford (G-15543)
Mpm Intermediate Holdings Inc ....G... 518 237-3330
Waterford (G-15544)
Mpm Silicones LLC ....A...... 518 233-3330
Waterford (G-15545)
Specialty Silicone Pdts Inc ....D...... 518 885-8826
Ballston Spa (G-587)

SILK SCREEN DESIGN SVCS

Buffalo Circuits Inc ....G...... 716 662-2113
Orchard Park (G-12342)
Mainly Monograms Inc ....E...... 845 624-4923
West Nyack (G-15827)

SILVER ORES

Global Gold Corporation ....F...... 914 925-0020
Rye (G-14079)

SILVER ORES PROCESSING

Rochester Silver Works LLC ....E...... 585 477-9501
Rochester (G-13696)

SILVERSMITHS

DWH&s Inc ....E...... 718 993-6405
Bronx (G-1246)
R Goldsmith ....F...... 718 239-1396
Bronx (G-1349)

SILVERWARE

Studio Silversmiths Inc ....E...... 718 418-6785
Ridgewood (G-13162)

SILVERWARE & PLATED WARE

Oneida International Inc ....G...... 315 361-3000
Oneida (G-12249)
Oneida Silversmiths Inc ....G...... 315 361-3000
Oneida (G-12252)

SILVERWARE, SILVER PLATED

Sherrill Manufacturing Inc ....C...... 315 280-0727
Sherrill (G-14406)

SIMULATORS: Flight

BSC Associates LLC ....F...... 607 321-2980
Binghamton (G-864)
Northrop Grumman Intl Trdg Inc ......G... 716 626-7233
Buffalo (G-2892)

SINKS: Vitreous China

Kraus USA Inc ....F...... 800 775-0703
Port Washington (G-12897)

SKYLIGHTS

Citros Building Materials Co ....E...... 718 779-0727
East Elmhurst (G-4105)
Gottlieb Schwartz Family ....E...... 718 761-2010
Staten Island (G-14657)

SLAB & TILE: Precast Concrete, Floor

Duranm Inc ....G...... 914 774-3367
Cortlandt Manor (G-3793)
Rain Catchers Seamless Gutters ....G... 516 520-1956
Bethpage (G-844)

SLABS: Steel

Safespan Platform Systems Inc ....E... 716 694-1100
Tonawanda (G-15137)

SLATE PRDTS

Evergreen Slate Company Inc ....D...... 518 642-2530
Middle Granville (G-7867)
North American Slate Inc ....G...... 518 642-1702
Granville (G-5354)
Northeast Solite Corporation ....E...... 845 246-2177
Mount Marion (G-8112)
Sheldon Slate Products Co Inc ....E...... 518 642-1280
Middle Granville (G-7870)

SLATE: Crushed & Broken

Western Slate Inc ....E...... 802 287-2210
Granville (G-5356)

SLATE: Dimension

Vermont Multicolor Slate ....G...... 518 642-2400
Middle Granville (G-7871)

SLAUGHTERING & MEAT PACKING

Dinewise Inc ....G...... 631 694-1111
Farmingdale (G-4617)

SLINGS: Rope

All-Lifts Incorporated ....E...... 518 465-3461
Albany (G-37)

SLIP RINGS

Princetel Inc ....F...... 914 579-2410
Hawthorne (G-5822)

SLIPPERS: House

RG Barry Corporation ....E...... 212 244-3145
New York (G-11033)

SMOKE DETECTORS

Fuel Watchman Sales & Service ....F... 718 665-6100
Bronx (G-1263)
Nrd LLC ....E...... 716 773-7634
Grand Island (G-5339)

SNOW PLOWING SVCS

Northeastern Sealcoat Inc ....F...... 585 544-4372
Rochester (G-13583)

SOAPS & DETERGENTS

Aura Detergent LLC ....G...... 718 824-2162
Bronx (G-1208)
Baums Castorine Company Inc ....G...... 315 336-8154
Rome (G-13844)
Bocks Inc ....F...... 833 437-3363
New York (G-8828)
Colgate-Palmolive Company ....A...... 212 310-2000
New York (G-9051)
Colgate-Palmolive Nj Inc ....E...... 212 310-2000
New York (G-9052)
Cosco Enterprises Inc ....E...... 718 383-4488
Ridgewood (G-13143)
Cosco Interprises Inc ....E...... 718 417-8995
Ridgewood (G-13144)
Cpac Inc ....E...... 585 382-3223
Leicester (G-6908)
Crosstex International Inc ....D...... 631 582-6777
Hauppauge (G-5631)
Dr Jacobs Naturals LLC ....E...... 718 265-1522
Brooklyn (G-1759)
Ecolab Inc ....F...... 716 683-6298
Cheektowaga (G-3347)
Enviro Service & Supply Corp ....F... 347 838-6500
Staten Island (G-14651)
H & H Laboratories Inc ....F...... 718 624-8041
Brooklyn (G-1914)
H & H Laboratories Inc ....G...... 718 624-8041
Brooklyn (G-1915)
Medtech Products Inc ....F...... 914 524-6810
Tarrytown (G-15047)
Monroe Fluid Technology Inc ....E...... 585 392-3434
Hilton (G-5973)
Natures Warehouse ....F...... 800 215-4372
Philadelphia (G-12612)
Pro-Line Solutions Inc ....G...... 914 664-0002
Mount Vernon (G-8173)
RAD Soap Co LLC ....F...... 518 461-9667
Albany (G-122)

PRODUCT

Robert Racine..................E......518 677-0224
  Cambridge (G-3096)
Sunfeather Natural Soap Co Inc..........G......315 265-1776
  Potsdam (G-12942)

SOAPS & DETERGENTS: Textile

T S Pink Corp..................F......607 432-1100
  Oneonta (G-12282)

SOCIAL SERVICES INFORMATION EXCHANGE

Human Life Foundation Inc..................G......212 685-5210
  New York (G-9837)

SOCIAL SVCS, HANDICAPPED

Choice Magazine Listening Inc..........G......516 883-8280
  Port Washington (G-12868)

SOCIAL SVCS: Individual & Family

Maramont Corporation..................B......718 439-8900
  Brooklyn (G-2112)
Suffolk Community Council Inc..........G......631 434-9277
  Deer Park (G-3940)

SOFT DRINKS WHOLESALERS

Load/N/Go Beverage Corp..................F......585 218-4019
  Rochester (G-13521)
Pepsi-Cola Metro Btlg Co Inc..........C......585 454-5220
  Rochester (G-13614)
Save More Beverage Corp..................G......518 371-2520
  Halfmoon (G-5499)

SOFTWARE PUBLISHERS: Application

30dc Inc..................F......212 962-4400
  New York (G-8400)
Advanced Comfort Systems Inc..........F......518 884-8444
  Ballston Spa (G-566)
Aimsun Inc..................G......917 267-8534
  New York (G-8501)
Amcom Software Inc..................G......212 951-7600
  New York (G-8537)
Ansa Systems of USA Inc..................G......718 835-3743
  Valley Stream (G-15333)
Automated & MGT Solutions LLC..........G......518 833-0315
  East Greenbush (G-4113)
Big White Wall Holding Inc..................F......917 281-2649
  New York (G-8788)
Bigwood Systems Inc..................G......607 257-0915
  Ithaca (G-6366)
Birdsigns Inc..................G......201 388-7613
  New York (G-8800)
Braze Inc..................D......504 327-7269
  New York (G-8849)
Bull Street LLC..................G......212 495-9855
  New York (G-8867)
C S I G Inc..................G......845 383-3800
  Kingston (G-6682)
Callaway Digital Arts Inc..................E......212 675-3050
  New York (G-8893)
Capital Programs Inc..................G......212 842-4640
  New York (G-8914)
Catalyst Group Inc..................G......212 243-7777
  New York (G-8933)
Catch Ventures Inc..................F......347 620-4351
  New York (G-8936)
Cbord Group Inc..................C......607 257-2410
  Ithaca (G-6375)
Ceipal LLC..................G......585 584-1316
  Rochester (G-13303)
Citic Intl (usa) Travel Inc..................G......718 888-9577
  Flushing (G-4844)
Cloud Rock Group LLC..................G......516 967-6023
  Roslyn (G-14040)
Compelld Inc..................G......917 494-4462
  New York (G-9072)
Contactive Inc..................E......646 476-9059
  New York (G-9089)
Cordis Solutions Inc..................F......917 909-2002
  New York (G-9102)
Customshow Inc..................G......800 255-5303
  New York (G-9137)
Dbase LLC..................G......607 729-0234
  Binghamton (G-871)
Deephaven Data Labs LLC..................G......855 828-8445
  New York (G-9194)
Document Strategies LLC..................F......585 506-9000
  Rochester (G-13353)

Dwnld Inc..................E......484 483-6572
  New York (G-9286)
Eft Analytics Inc..................G......212 290-2300
  New York (G-9327)
Elepath Inc..................G......347 417-4975
  Brooklyn (G-1795)
Empire Innovation Group LLC..................F......716 852-5000
  Buffalo (G-2744)
Evocate Media LLC..................G......646 361-3014
  New York (G-9430)
Exchange My Mail Inc..................F......516 605-1835
  Jericho (G-6579)
Express Checkout LLC..................G......646 512-2068
  New York (G-9449)
Filestream Inc..................F......516 759-4100
  Locust Valley (G-7124)
Financial Technologies 360 Inc..................G......646 588-8853
  Whitestone (G-16093)
Freshop Inc..................E......585 738-6035
  Rochester (G-13424)
Galaxy Software LLC..................G......631 244-8405
  Oakdale (G-12151)
Geoweb3d Inc..................F......607 323-1114
  Vestal (G-15378)
Grantoo LLC..................G......646 356-0460
  New York (G-9662)
Gresham Technologies (us) Inc..................F......646 943-5955
  New York (G-9674)
High Performance Sftwr USA Inc..................E......866 616-4958
  Valley Stream (G-15343)
Hinge Inc..................F......214 576-9352
  New York (G-9790)
Hvr Mso LLC..................G......833 345-6974
  Poughkeepsie (G-12962)
Hydrogen Technology Corp..................E......800 315-9554
  New York (G-9842)
Incentivise Health LLC..................G......518 469-8491
  Saratoga Springs (G-14183)
Incycle Software Corp..................F......212 626-2608
  New York (G-9877)
Innofun Digital Entrmt LLC..................F......347 708-0078
  New York (G-9896)
INTEL Corporation..................D......408 765-8080
  Getzville (G-5177)
Intraworlds Inc..................G......631 602-5333
  New York (G-9931)
Jvl Ventures LLC..................D......212 365-7555
  New York (G-10050)
Kik Us Inc..................F......519 505-7616
  New York (G-10099)
Kitcheco Inc..................G......917 388-7479
  New York (G-10110)
Lighf Inc..................G......917 803-3323
  Katonah (G-6634)
Live Vote II Inc..................G......646 343-9053
  New York (G-10233)
Lookbooks Media Inc..................F......646 737-3360
  New York (G-10252)
Lubbu Inc..................G......917 693-9600
  Sag Harbor (G-14099)
Luluvise Inc..................E......914 309-7812
  New York (G-10283)
Madhat Inc..................G......518 947-0732
  New York (G-10314)
Mall Inc..................G......315 751-9490
  Cazenovia (G-3230)
Marcus Goldman Inc..................F......212 431-0707
  New York (G-10358)
Masterlibrarycom LLC..................F......585 270-6676
  Pittsford (G-12650)
Medaptive Health Inc..................G......646 541-7389
  New York (G-10409)
Medidata Solutions Inc..................B......212 918-1800
  New York (G-10417)
Medscale Plus LLC..................G......212 218-4070
  New York (G-10420)
Microsoft Corporation..................A......914 323-2150
  White Plains (G-16030)
Microsoft Corporation..................F......212 245-2100
  New York (G-10459)
Microsoft Corporation..................D......516 380-1531
  Hauppauge (G-5718)
Microstrategy Incorporated..................F......888 537-8135
  New York (G-10460)
Mml Software Ltd..................E......631 941-1313
  East Setauket (G-4182)
Molabs Inc..................G......310 721-6828
  New York (G-10494)
Nervve Technologies Inc..................E......716 800-2250
  New York (G-10564)

New York State Assoc..................F......518 434-2281
  Albany (G-104)
Nook Media LLC..................G......212 633-3300
  New York (G-10638)
Omx (us) Inc..................A......646 428-2800
  New York (G-10688)
One-Blue LLC..................G......212 223-4380
  New York (G-10692)
Oova Inc..................G......215 880-3125
  New York (G-10696)
P&C Group Inc..................G......212 425-9200
  New York (G-10734)
P8h Inc..................E......212 343-1142
  Brooklyn (G-2241)
Paperstreet Technology Inc..................G......704 773-5689
  Brooklyn (G-2245)
Pexip Inc..................F......703 338-3544
  New York (G-10819)
Piano Software Inc..................E......646 350-1999
  New York (G-10834)
Pingmd Inc..................G......212 632-2665
  New York (G-10842)
Piwik Pro LLC..................E......888 444-0049
  New York (G-10848)
Plectica LLC..................F......646 941-8822
  New York (G-10855)
Pts Financial Technology LLC..................E......844 825-7634
  New York (G-10921)
Quovo Inc..................E......212 643-0695
  New York (G-10961)
Raleigh & Drake Pbc..................G......212 625-8212
  New York (G-10974)
Revivn Public Benefit Corp..................F......347 762-8193
  Brooklyn (G-2342)
Robot Fruit Inc..................F......631 423-7250
  Huntington (G-6220)
Runs Inc..................E......212 618-1201
  New York (G-11099)
SC Building Solutions LLC..................D......800 564-1152
  New York (G-11145)
Signpost Inc..................C......877 334-2837
  New York (G-11238)
Splacer Inc..................G......646 853-9789
  New York (G-11325)
Spring Inc..................G......646 732-0323
  New York (G-11332)
Streetcred Nyc LLC..................G......646 675-0073
  New York (G-11372)
Striata Inc..................D......212 918-4677
  New York (G-11373)
Synced Inc..................G......917 565-5591
  New York (G-11411)
Taazu Inc..................E......212 618-1201
  New York (G-11421)
Tabi Inc..................G......347 701-1051
  Flushing (G-4897)
Theirapp LLC..................E......212 896-1255
  New York (G-11461)
Thing Daemon Inc..................G......917 746-9895
  New York (G-11466)
Tpa Computer Corp..................F......877 866-6044
  Carmel (G-3191)
Trac Medical Solutions Inc..................G......518 346-7799
  Schenectady (G-14312)
Tradeblock Inc..................A......212 231-8353
  New York (G-11529)
Treauu Inc..................G......703 731-0196
  New York (G-11535)
Unacast Inc..................G......917 670-7852
  New York (G-11580)
Usq Group LLC..................G......212 777-7751
  New York (G-11632)
Vhx Corporation..................F......347 689-1446
  New York (G-11673)
Virtual Frameworks Inc..................G......646 690-8207
  New York (G-11690)
Vision Logic Inc..................G......212 724-4606
  New York (G-11692)
Vuniverse Inc..................G......212 206-1041
  New York (G-11709)
West Internet Trading Company..................G......415 484-5848
  New York (G-11744)
Whiteboard Ventures Inc..................F......855 972-6346
  New York (G-11751)
Winesoft International Corp..................G......914 400-6247
  Yonkers (G-16356)
Wink Inc..................E......212 389-1382
  New York (G-11767)
Wink Labs Inc..................E......844 946-5277
  New York (G-11768)

Xborder Entertainment LLC ....G...... 518 726-7036
Plattsburgh **(G-12793)**

Zipari Inc ....E...... 855 558-7884
Brooklyn **(G-2605)**

SOFTWARE PUBLISHERS: Business & Professional

Aarfid LLC ....G...... 716 992-3999
Eden **(G-4253)**

Abacus Labs Inc ....E...... 917 426-6642
New York **(G-8424)**

Abel Noser Solutions LLC ....E...... 646 432-4000
New York **(G-8428)**

Adfin Solutions Inc ....F...... 650 464-0742
New York **(G-8457)**

Adgorithmics Inc ....G...... 646 277-8728
New York **(G-8459)**

Adl Data Systems Inc ....E...... 914 591-1800
Elmsford **(G-4392)**

Agrinetix Cmpt Systems LLC ......F...... 877 978-5477
Henrietta **(G-5853)**

Amplience Inc ....G...... 917 410-7189
New York **(G-8567)**

Andigo New Media Inc ....G...... 212 727-8445
New York **(G-8577)**

Appfigures Inc ....F...... 212 343-7900
New York **(G-8609)**

Application Security Inc ....D...... 212 912-4100
New York **(G-8611)**

Apprenda Inc ....D...... 518 383-2130
Troy **(G-15163)**

Articulate Global Inc ....C...... 800 861-4880
New York **(G-8634)**

Aspen Research Group Ltd ....G...... 212 425-9588
New York **(G-8651)**

Augury Inc ....E...... 866 432-0976
New York **(G-8677)**

Automated Office Systems Inc ....F...... 516 396-5555
Valley Stream **(G-15334)**

Aycan Medical Systems LLC ......F...... 585 271-3078
Rochester **(G-13255)**

Ayehu Inc ....G...... 408 930-5823
New York **(G-8699)**

B601 V2 Inc ....G...... 646 391-6431
New York **(G-8709)**

Beyondly Inc ....E...... 646 658-3665
New York **(G-8774)**

Big Data Bizviz LLC ....G...... 716 803-2367
West Seneca **(G-15844)**

Blue Wolf Group LLC ....D...... 866 455-9653
New York **(G-8821)**

Broadway Technology LLC ....E...... 646 912-6450
New York **(G-8859)**

Business Integrity Inc ....G...... 718 238-2008
New York **(G-8872)**

Business Management Systems ....F...... 914 245-8558
Brooklyn **(G-1633)**

Ca Inc ....A...... 800 225-5224
New York **(G-8882)**

Ca Inc ....G...... 800 225-5224
Islandia **(G-6327)**

Caminus Corporation ....D...... 212 515-3600
New York **(G-8898)**

Candex Solutions Inc ....G...... 215 650-3214
New York **(G-8902)**

Careconnector ....G...... 919 360-2987
Brooklyn **(G-1648)**

Chequedcom Inc ....E...... 888 412-0699
Saratoga Springs **(G-14169)**

Clearview Social Inc ....G...... 801 414-7675
Buffalo **(G-2698)**

Cloudscale365 Inc ....G...... 888 608-6245
Jericho **(G-6574)**

Condeco Software Inc ....E...... 408 508-7330
New York **(G-9080)**

Confiant Inc ....F...... 646 397-4198
New York **(G-9082)**

Continuity Software Inc ....E...... 646 216-8628
New York **(G-9091)**

Cross Border Transactions LLC ....F...... 646 767-7342
Tarrytown **(G-15042)**

Crunched Inc ....G...... 415 484-9909
New York **(G-9125)**

Cuffs Planning & Models Ltd ......G...... 914 632-1883
New Rochelle **(G-8325)**

Curaegis Technologies Inc ....E...... 585 254-1100
Rochester **(G-13333)**

Cureatr Inc ....E...... 212 203-3927
New York **(G-9133)**

Dartcom Incorporated ....G...... 315 790-5456
New Hartford **(G-8238)**

Diligent Corporation ....C...... 212 741-8181
New York **(G-9229)**

Dow Jones & Company Inc ....E...... 212 597-5983
New York **(G-9259)**

Dropcar Operating Company Inc ....G...... 646 342-1595
New York **(G-9272)**

Eastnets Americas Corp ....F...... 212 631-0666
New York **(G-9307)**

Ebrevia Inc ....E...... 203 870-3000
New York **(G-9312)**

Eccella Corporation ....E...... 718 612-0451
New York **(G-9313)**

Efront Financial Solutions Inc ....E...... 212 220-0660
New York **(G-9326)**

Elodina Inc ....G...... 646 402-5202
New York **(G-9351)**

Emx Digital LLC ....G...... 212 792-6810
New York **(G-9366)**

Endava Inc ....F...... 212 920-7240
New York **(G-9369)**

Equilend Holdings LLC ....E...... 212 901-2200
New York **(G-9389)**

Exact Solutions Inc ....F...... 212 707-8627
New York **(G-9437)**

EZ Systems US Inc ....C...... 929 295-0699
Brooklyn **(G-1826)**

F-O-R Software LLC ....E...... 914 220-8800
White Plains **(G-16005)**

Fastnet Software Intl Inc ....F...... 888 740-7790
East Northport **(G-4145)**

Findmine Inc ....F...... 925 787-6181
New York **(G-9493)**

Flextrade Systems Inc ....C...... 516 627-8993
Great Neck **(G-5389)**

Frazer Computing Inc ....E...... 315 379-3500
Canton **(G-3166)**

Gifts Software Inc ....F...... 904 438-6000
New York **(G-9608)**

Globalquest Solutions Inc ....F...... 716 601-3524
Buffalo **(G-2777)**

Happy Software LLC ....G...... 518 584-4668
Saratoga Springs **(G-14181)**

Hovee Inc ....F...... 646 249-6200
New York **(G-9827)**

Igambit Inc ....G...... 631 670-6777
Smithtown **(G-14479)**

Innroad Inc ....E...... 631 458-1437
New York **(G-9898)**

Inprotopia Corporation ....F...... 917 338-7501
New York **(G-9901)**

Inturn ....G...... 212 639-9675
New York **(G-9934)**

Ivalua Inc ....F...... 650 930-9710
Brooklyn **(G-1975)**

Kaazing Corporation ....E...... 212 572-4859
New York **(G-10054)**

Kasisto Inc ....E...... 917 734-4750
New York **(G-10073)**

Kindling Inc ....F...... 212 400-6296
New York **(G-10105)**

Krux Digital Inc ....F...... 646 476-6261
New York **(G-10140)**

Kryon Systems Inc ....C...... 800 618-4318
New York **(G-10141)**

Latchable Inc ....C...... 917 338-3915
New York **(G-10176)**

Liftforward Inc ....E...... 917 693-4993
New York **(G-10215)**

Live Up Top Inc ....F...... 866 333-1332
New York **(G-10232)**

Livetiles Corp ....F...... 917 472-7887
New York **(G-10235)**

Loyaltyplant Inc ....F...... 551 221-2701
Forest Hills **(G-4922)**

Market Factory Inc ....F...... 212 625-9988
New York **(G-10367)**

Medius Software Inc ....F...... 877 295-0058
New York **(G-10419)**

Micro Systems Specialists Inc ....G...... 845 677-6150
Millbrook **(G-7943)**

Mobo Systems Inc ....D...... 212 260-0895
New York **(G-10487)**

Navatar Group Inc ....E...... 212 863-9655
New York **(G-10557)**

Network Infrstructure Tech Inc ....G...... 212 404-7340
New York **(G-10571)**

Neverware Inc ....F...... 516 302-3223
New York **(G-10575)**

Nift Group Inc ....G...... 504 505-1144
Brooklyn **(G-2215)**

Nikish Software Corp ....G...... 631 754-1618
Northport **(G-12110)**

Ninth Wave Inc ....E...... 212 401-6381
New York **(G-10631)**

Noetic Partners Inc ....F...... 212 836-4351
New York **(G-10636)**

Numerix LLC ....D...... 212 302-2220
New York **(G-10655)**

Olb Group Inc ....G...... 212 278-0900
New York **(G-10684)**

Operative Media Inc ....D...... 212 994-8930
New York **(G-10699)**

Oracle Corporation ....C...... 212 508-7700
New York **(G-10701)**

Orangenius Inc ....F...... 631 742-0648
New York **(G-10702)**

Ordergroove Inc ....E...... 866 253-1261
New York **(G-10709)**

Orthstar Enterprises Inc ....D...... 607 562-2100
Horseheads **(G-6130)**

Os33 Inc ....G...... 708 336-3466
Brooklyn **(G-10713)**

Ougra Inc ....G...... 646 342-4575
Long Island City **(G-7314)**

Pb Mapinfo Corporation ....A...... 518 285-6000
Troy **(G-15177)**

Pegasystems Inc ....E...... 212 626-6550
New York **(G-10790)**

Pilot Inc ....F...... 212 951-1133
New York **(G-10839)**

Pilot Inc ....G...... 212 951-1133
New York **(G-10840)**

Pitney Bowes Software Inc ....F...... 518 285-6000
Troy **(G-15179)**

Pointman LLC ....G...... 716 842-1439
Buffalo **(G-2923)**

Powa Technologies Inc ....E...... 347 344-7848
New York **(G-10872)**

Premier Heart LLC ....G...... 516 883-3383
Port Washington **(G-12915)**

Pricing Engine Inc ....F...... 917 549-3289
New York **(G-10887)**

Principia Partners LLC ....D...... 212 480-2270
New York **(G-10893)**

Purebase Networks Inc ....G...... 646 670-8964
New York **(G-10929)**

Qmetis Inc ....G...... 212 500-5000
New York **(G-10945)**

Quality and Asrn Tech Corp ......G...... 646 450-6762
Ridge **(G-13133)**

Rational Retention LLC ....E...... 518 489-3000
Albany **(G-124)**

Ray Theta Inc ....G...... 646 757-4956
New York **(G-10987)**

Reactivecore LLC ....G...... 631 944-1618
New York **(G-10992)**

Reality Analytics Inc ....G...... 347 363-2200
New York **(G-10995)**

Retina Labs (usa) Inc ....F...... 866 344-2692
New York **(G-11023)**

Ringlead Inc ....F...... 310 906-0545
Melville **(G-7819)**

Rision Inc ....G...... 212 987-2628
New York **(G-11047)**

Ritnoa Inc ....G...... 212 660-2148
Bellerose **(G-776)**

RPS Holdings Inc ....E...... 607 257-7778
Ithaca **(G-6410)**

Sakonnet Technology LLC ....E...... 212 849-9267
New York **(G-11116)**

Sales Hacker Inc ....G...... 516 660-2836
New York **(G-11118)**

Sapphire Systems Inc ....F...... 212 905-0100
New York **(G-11135)**

Sefaira Inc ....E...... 855 733-2472
New York **(G-11181)**

Serraview America Inc ....D...... 800 903-3716
New York **(G-11194)**

Servicenow Inc ....G...... 914 318-1168
New York **(G-11195)**

Shake Inc ....F...... 650 544-5479
New York **(G-11204)**

Siemens Product Life Mgmt Sftw ....E...... 585 389-8699
Fairport **(G-4522)**

Skystem LLC ....G...... 877 778-3320
New York **(G-11266)**

Solve Advisors Inc ....G...... 646 699-5041
Rockville Centre **(G-13837)**

PRODUCT

Stop N Shop LLC ....G..... 518 512-9657
Albany (G-133)

Structured Retail Products ....G..... 212 224-3692
New York (G-11375)

Structuredweb Inc ....E..... 201 325-3110
New York (G-11376)

Styleclick Inc ....D..... 212 329-0300
New York (G-11381)

Symphony Talent LLC ....D..... 212 999-9000
New York (G-11409)

Synergy Resources Inc ....D..... 631 665-2050
Central Islip (G-3289)

Team Builders Inc ....F..... 718 979-1005
Staten Island (G-14720)

Tech Software LLC ....G..... 516 986-3050
Melville (G-7829)

Technology Partners Inc ....E..... 518 621-2993
Slingerlands (G-14468)

Telmar Information Services ....E..... 212 725-3000
New York (G-11451)

Tika Mobile Inc ....G..... 646 650-5545
New York (G-11487)

Touchcare P LLC ....F..... 646 824-5373
New York (G-11522)

Traddle LLC ....G..... 646 330-0436
New York (G-11528)

Transportgistics Inc ....F..... 631 567-4100
Mount Sinai (G-8117)

Trueex LLC ....E..... 646 786-8526
New York (G-11550)

Trustfort LLC ....G..... 781 787-0906
Holbrook (G-6027)

Tyme Global Technologies LLC ....E..... 212 796-1950
New York (G-11568)

UI Information & Insights Inc ....E..... 518 640-9200
Latham (G-6879)

Ullink Inc ....F..... 646 565-6675
New York (G-11579)

Unqork Inc ....E..... 844 486-7675
New York (G-11610)

Varnish Software Inc ....G..... 201 857-2832
New York (G-11645)

Varsity Monitor LLC ....G..... 212 691-6292
New York (G-11647)

Virtual Facility Inc ....F..... 646 891-4861
New York (G-11689)

Virtuvent Inc ....G..... 855 672-8677
Brooklyn (G-2563)

Whentech LLC ....F..... 212 571-0042
New York (G-11749)

Wochit Inc ....G..... 212 979-8343
New York (G-11773)

Xenial Inc ....E..... 845 920-0800
Pearl River (G-12544)

Ypis of Staten Island Inc ....G..... 718 815-4557
Staten Island (G-14729)

Zoomifier Corporation ....D..... 800 255-5303
New York (G-11829)

SOFTWARE PUBLISHERS: Computer Utilities

Vline Inc ....G..... 512 222-5464
Brooklyn (G-2567)

SOFTWARE PUBLISHERS: Education

Accelify Solutions LLC ....E..... 888 922-2354
New York (G-8439)

Amplify Education Inc ....B..... 212 213-8177
Brooklyn (G-1509)

Assessment Technologies Inc ....G..... 646 530-8666
New York (G-8653)

Brainpop LLC ....E..... 212 574-6017
New York (G-8845)

Classroom Inc ....E..... 212 545-8400
New York (G-9028)

Coalition On Positive Health ....F..... 212 633-2500
New York (G-9044)

Cognotion Inc ....G..... 347 692-0640
New York (G-9049)

Educational Networks Inc ....G..... 866 526-0200
New York (G-9324)

Empirical Resolution Inc ....F..... 510 671-0222
New York (G-9362)

Health Care Compliance ....F..... 516 478-4100
Jericho (G-6582)

Hopscotch Technologies Inc ....G..... 313 408-4285
Brooklyn (G-1943)

Jumprope Inc ....G..... 347 927-5867
New York (G-10041)

Learningateway LLC ....G..... 212 920-7969
Brooklyn (G-2055)

Maven Marketing LLC ....G..... 615 510-3248
New York (G-10387)

Nemaris Inc ....E..... 646 794-8648
New York (G-10562)

Parlor Labs Inc ....G..... 866 801-7323
New York (G-10765)

Playfitness Corp ....G..... 917 497-5443
Staten Island (G-14690)

Prime Research Solutions LLC ....F..... 917 836-7941
Flushing (G-4889)

Processing Foundation Inc ....G..... 415 748-2679
Brooklyn (G-2296)

Qlogix Entertainment LLC ....G..... 215 459-6315
New York (G-10944)

San Jae Educational Resou ....G..... 845 364-5458
Pomona (G-12808)

Scholastic Corporation ....G..... 212 343-6100
New York (G-11160)

Scholastic Inc ....A..... 212 343-6100
New York (G-11161)

Schoolnet Inc ....C..... 646 496-9000
New York (G-11164)

Sciterra LLC ....G..... 646 883-3724
New York (G-11167)

Skillsoft Corporation ....F..... 585 240-7500
Rochester (G-13732)

Skyop LLC ....G..... 585 598-4737
Canandaigua (G-3143)

Socialed Inc ....F..... 516 297-2172
New York (G-11282)

Special Circle Inc ....G..... 516 595-9988
New Hyde Park (G-8295)

Specialneedsware Inc ....F..... 646 278-9959
New York (G-11312)

Teachergaming LLC ....F..... 866 644-9323
New York (G-11442)

Teachley LLC ....G..... 347 552-1272
New York (G-11443)

Tequipment Inc ....D..... 516 922-3508
Huntington Station (G-6264)

Time To Know Inc ....G..... 212 230-1210
New York (G-11493)

Virtusphere Inc ....F..... 607 760-2207
Binghamton (G-915)

SOFTWARE PUBLISHERS: Home Entertainment

Avalanche Studios New York Inc ....D..... 212 993-6447
New York (G-8685)

Boulevard Arts Inc ....G..... 917 968-8693
New York (G-8840)

Clever Goats Media LLC ....G..... 917 512-0340
New York (G-9031)

E H Hurwitz & Associates ....G..... 718 884-3766
Bronx (G-1248)

Magic Numbers Inc ....G..... 646 839-8578
New York (G-10326)

Mdcare911 LLC ....G..... 917 640-4869
Brooklyn (G-2128)

Reentry Games Inc ....G..... 646 421-0080
New York (G-10999)

Remarkety Inc ....G..... 800 570-7564
Brooklyn (G-2338)

Urthworx Inc ....G..... 646 373-7535
New York (G-11621)

Vizbee Inc ....G..... 650 787-1424
New York (G-11699)

SOFTWARE PUBLISHERS: NEC

2k Inc ....G..... 646 536-3007
New York (G-8398)

30dc Inc ....F..... 212 962-4400
New York (G-8399)

A K A Computer Consulting Inc ....G..... 718 351-5200
Staten Island (G-14613)

A2ia Corp ....G..... 917 237-0390
New York (G-8421)

Ableton Inc ....G..... 646 723-4586
New York (G-8432)

Accela Inc ....F..... 631 563-5005
Ronkonkoma (G-13884)

Adobe Inc ....E..... 212 471-0904
New York (G-8461)

Adobe Systems Inc ....E..... 212 471-0904
New York (G-8462)

Adobe Systems Incorporated ....C..... 212 592-1400
New York (G-8463)

Adtech Us Inc ....C..... 212 402-4840
New York (G-8466)

Advanced Cmpt Sftwr Consulting ....G..... 718 300-3577
Bronx (G-1198)

Ahmazing Boutique Inc ....G..... 631 828-1474
Port Jeff STA (G-12832)

Altana Technologies Inc ....G..... 516 263-0633
Brooklyn (G-1493)

Amenity Analytics Inc ....E..... 646 786-8316
New York (G-8538)

American Ctr For Edmocracy LLC ....G..... 716 803-1118
Cheektowaga (G-3338)

Anju Sylogent LLC ....F..... 480 326-2358
New York (G-8591)

Answermgmt LLC ....G..... 914 318-1301
Albany (G-41)

Appguard Inc ....F..... 703 786-8884
New York (G-8610)

Application Resources Inc ....G..... 516 636-6200
Great Neck (G-5365)

Appsbidder Inc ....G..... 917 880-4269
Brooklyn (G-1521)

APS Enterprise Software Inc ....E..... 631 784-7720
Huntington (G-6200)

Arumai Technologies Inc ....F..... 914 217-0038
Armonk (G-395)

Asite LLC ....D..... 203 545-3089
New York (G-8648)

AT&T Corp ....F..... 212 317-7048
New York (G-8659)

Atomic Information Systems ....E..... 716 713-5402
Unadilla (G-15221)

Attachmate Corporation ....G..... 646 704-0042
New York (G-8674)

AVM Software Inc ....F..... 646 381-2468
New York (G-8694)

Axiom Software Ltd ....F..... 914 769-8800
Valhalla (G-15302)

Aydata Management LLC ....G..... 585 271-6133
Rochester (G-13256)

Base Systems Inc ....G..... 845 278-1991
Brewster (G-1142)

Bespoke Software Inc ....F..... 518 618-0746
Albany (G-48)

Billing Blocks Inc ....F..... 718 442-5006
Staten Island (G-14626)

Bluebird Transportation LLC ....F..... 716 395-0000
Williamsville (G-16123)

Brainworks Software Dev Corp ....E..... 631 563-5000
Sayville (G-14223)

Brigadoon Software Inc ....G..... 845 624-0909
Nanuet (G-8196)

Brightidea Incorporated ....D..... 212 594-4500
New York (G-8853)

Buncee LLC ....F..... 631 591-1390
Speonk (G-14561)

Byte Consulting Inc ....G..... 646 500-8606
New York (G-8880)

California US Holdings Inc ....A..... 212 726-6500
New York (G-8890)

Calypso Technology Inc ....E..... 212 905-0735
New York (G-8895)

Cdml Computer Services Ltd ....G..... 718 428-9063
Fresh Meadows (G-5038)

Ceipal LLC ....G..... 585 351-2934
Rochester (G-13302)

Celonis Inc ....G..... 941 615-9670
Brooklyn (G-1657)

Celonis Inc ....G..... 973 652-8821
New York (G-8943)

Cgi Technologies Solutions Inc ....F..... 212 682-7411
New York (G-8965)

Chronicles Systems Inc ....G..... 516 992-2553
North Baldwin (G-12003)

Cinch Technologies Inc ....G..... 212 266-0022
New York (G-9005)

Cinedigm Software ....G..... 212 206-9001
New York (G-9008)

Clayton Dubilier & Rice Fun ....E..... 212 407-5200
New York (G-9029)

Cloudsense Inc ....G..... 917 880-6195
New York (G-9037)

Cmnty Corporation ....G..... 646 712-9949
New York (G-9041)

Commercehub Inc ....F..... 518 810-0700
Albany (G-68)

Comprehensive Dental Tech ....G..... 607 467-4456
Hancock (G-5536)

Construction Technology Inc ....E..... 914 747-8900
Chappaqua (G-3323)

Coocoo SMS Inc ....F 646 459-4260
  Huntington (G-6203)
CTI Software Inc ....F 631 253-3550
  Deer Park (G-3856)
Cultureiq Inc ....E 212 755-8633
  New York (G-9132)
Curemdcom Inc ....E 212 509-6200
  New York (G-9134)
Cybersports Inc ....G 315 737-7150
  Utica (G-15250)
Dakota Software Corporation ....G 216 765-7100
  Victor (G-15403)
Dashlane Inc ....E 212 596-7510
  New York (G-9172)
Data Implementation Inc ....G 212 979-2015
  New York (G-9173)
Datadog Inc ....C 866 329-4466
  New York (G-9174)
Davel Systems Inc ....G 718 382-6024
  Brooklyn (G-1727)
Defran Systems Inc ....G 212 727-8342
  New York (G-9196)
Deniz Information Systems ....G 212 750-5199
  New York (G-9202)
Diligent Board Member Svcs LLC .....E 212 741-8181
  New York (G-9228)
Docuware Corporation ....D 845 563-9045
  New Windsor (G-8365)
Dynamic Applications Inc ....G 518 283-4654
  Troy (G-15167)
Easy Analytic Software Inc ....G 718 740-7930
  Flushing (G-4849)
Ebeling Associates Inc ....F 518 688-8700
  Halfmoon (G-5492)
Econometric Software Inc ....G 516 938-5254
  Plainview (G-12682)
Electronic Arts Inc ....G 212 672-0722
  New York (G-9335)
Elevondata Labs Inc ....E 470 222-5438
  New York (G-9338)
Emblaze Systems Inc ....C 212 371-1100
  New York (G-9358)
English Computer Consulting ....G 212 764-1717
  New York (G-9378)
Enterprise Tech Group Inc ....F 914 588-0327
  New Rochelle (G-8328)
Ert Software Inc ....G 845 358-5721
  Blauvelt (G-928)
Ex El Enterprises Ltd ....F 212 489-4500
  New York (G-9434)
EZ Newsletter LLC ....F 412 943-7777
  Brooklyn (G-1825)
F R A M Technologies Inc ....G 718 338-6230
  Brooklyn (G-1827)
F-O-R Software LLC ....F 212 231-9506
  New York (G-9457)
Fatwire Corporation ....E 516 247-4500
  Mineola (G-7975)
Fidelus Technologies LLC ....D 212 616-7800
  New York (G-9489)
Fidesa US Corporation ....B 212 269-9000
  New York (G-9490)
Flogic Inc ....F 914 478-1352
  Hastings On Hudson (G-5572)
Formats Unlimited Inc ....F 631 249-9200
  Deer Park (G-3875)
Fruit St Hlth Pub Benefit Corp ....G 347 960-6400
  New York (G-9545)
Fuel Data Systems Inc ....G 800 447-7870
  Middletown (G-7909)
Gameclub Inc ....G 415 359-5742
  New York (G-9570)
Games For Change Inc ....G 212 242-4922
  New York (G-9571)
Glitch Inc ....G 866 364-2733
  New York (G-9621)
Glitnir Ticketing Inc ....G 516 390-5168
  Levittown (G-6915)
Global Applctions Solution LLC ....G 212 741-9595
  New York (G-9624)
Great Dane Parent LLC ....G 518 810-0700
  Albany (G-81)
Group Commerce Inc ....F 646 346-0598
  New York (G-9684)
Hailo Network Usa Inc ....G 646 561-8552
  New York (G-9709)
Hallmark Hlth Care Sltions LLC ....F 516 513-0959
  Hauppauge (G-5666)
Healthix Inc ....F 877 695-4749
  New York (G-9741)

Heineck Associates Inc ....G 631 207-2347
  Bellport (G-800)
Hourglass Interactive LLC ....F 954 254-2853
  New York (G-9823)
Hudson Software Corporation ....E 914 773-0400
  Elmsford (G-4410)
Human Condition Safety Inc ....F 646 867-0644
  New York (G-9836)
IAC Search LLC ....E 212 314-7300
  New York (G-9850)
Iac/Interactivecorp ....A 212 314-7300
  New York (G-9851)
Indegy Inc ....E 866 801-5394
  New York (G-9878)
Infinity Augmented Reality Inc ....G 917 677-2084
  New York (G-9884)
Info Quick Solutions ....E 315 463-1400
  Liverpool (G-7015)
Infobase Holdings Inc ....D 212 967-8800
  New York (G-9886)
Infobase Publishing Company ....G 212 967-8800
  New York (G-9887)
Informa Solutions Inc ....E 516 543-3733
  New York (G-9891)
Informatica LLC ....F 212 845-7650
  New York (G-9893)
Informerly Inc ....G 646 238-7137
  New York (G-9894)
Innovation MGT Group Inc ....F 800 889-0987
  Shirley (G-14422)
Insight Unlimited Inc ....G 914 861-2090
  Chappaqua (G-3325)
Insight Venture Partners IV ....C 212 230-9200
  New York (G-9902)
Inspired Entertainment Inc ....F 646 565-3861
  New York (G-9903)
International Bus Mchs Corp ....E 914 499-2000
  Armonk (G-398)
International Identity LLC ....G 787 864-0379
  Brooklyn (G-1965)
International MGT Netwrk ....F 646 401-0032
  New York (G-9921)
Internodal International Inc ....E 631 765-0037
  Southold (G-14544)
Intralinks Holdings Inc ....E 212 543-7700
  New York (G-9930)
Invision Inc ....G 212 557-5554
  New York (G-9937)
Ipsidy Inc ....F 516 274-8700
  Long Beach (G-7138)
Irv Inc ....E 212 334-4507
  New York (G-9944)
Joseph A Filippazzo Software ....G 718 987-1626
  Staten Island (G-14671)
Kaseya US LLC ....F 415 694-5700
  New York (G-10072)
Kastor Consulting Inc ....G 718 224-9109
  Bayside (G-739)
Keynote Systems Corporation ....G 716 564-1332
  Buffalo (G-2833)
Knoa Software Inc ....E 212 807-9608
  New York (G-10117)
Kronos Incorporated ....E 518 459-5545
  Albany (G-96)
Lincdoc LLC ....G 585 563-1669
  East Rochester (G-4167)
Lmt Technology Solutions ....F 585 784-7470
  Rochester (G-13520)
Magic Software Inc ....F 646 827-9788
  New York (G-10327)
Market Logic Software Inc ....F 646 405-1041
  New York (G-10368)
Matrixcare Inc ....G 518 583-6400
  New York (G-10385)
Mealplan Corp ....G 909 706-8398
  New York (G-10406)
Mediamorph Inc ....G 212 643-0762
  New York (G-10413)
Microcad Trning Consulting Inc ....G 617 923-0500
  Lagrangeville (G-6751)
Microcad Trning Consulting Inc ....G 631 291-9484
  Hauppauge (G-5716)
Microsoft Corporation ....G 631 760-2340
  Huntington Station (G-6254)
Midas Mdici Group Holdings Inc ....G 212 792-0920
  New York (G-10461)
Mitel Networks Inc ....G 877 654-3573
  Rochester (G-13553)
Mobileapp Systems LLC ....G 716 667-2780
  Buffalo (G-2868)

Mongodb Inc ....C 646 727-4092
  New York (G-10500)
Mymee Inc ....F 917 476-4122
  New York (G-10527)
Netologic Inc ....E 212 269-3796
  New York (G-10569)
Netsuite Inc ....G 646 652-5700
  New York (G-10570)
New Triad For Collaborative ....E 212 873-9610
  New York (G-10591)
New York Computer Consulting ....G 516 921-1932
  Woodbury (G-16178)
Nortonlifelock Inc ....D 646 487-6000
  New York (G-10647)
Olympic Software & Consulting ....G 631 351-0655
  Melville (G-7811)
Openfin Inc ....G 917 450-8822
  New York (G-10697)
Operateit Inc ....G 631 259-4777
  Ronkonkoma (G-13988)
Oracle America Inc ....D 518 427-9353
  Albany (G-109)
Oracle America Inc ....D 585 317-4648
  Fairport (G-4511)
Orchard App Inc ....E 888 217-2718
  New York (G-10705)
Orchard Platform Advisors LLC ....G 888 217-2718
  New York (G-10707)
Overture Media Inc ....G 917 446-7455
  New York (G-10720)
Pap Chat Inc ....G 516 350-1888
  Brooklyn (G-2243)
Par Technology Corporation ....D 315 738-0600
  New Hartford (G-8242)
Pareteum Corporation ....E 212 984-1096
  New York (G-10758)
Peer Software Incorporated ....G 631 979-1770
  Hauppauge (G-5739)
Perry Street Software Inc ....G 415 935-1429
  New York (G-10810)
Platform Experts Inc ....G 646 843-7100
  Brooklyn (G-2266)
Portfolio Decisionware Inc ....E 212 947-1326
  New York (G-10867)
Portware LLC ....D 212 425-5233
  New York (G-10869)
Quartet Financial Systems Inc ....F 845 358-6071
  New York (G-10952)
Radnor-Wallace ....G 516 767-2131
  Port Washington (G-12917)
Ramsey Solutions LLC ....F 888 329-1055
  New York (G-10977)
Real Factors Inc ....G 206 963-6661
  Astoria (G-438)
Red Oak Software Inc ....G 585 454-3170
  Rochester (G-13670)
Reliant Security ....E 917 338-2200
  New York (G-11003)
Robly Digital Marketing LLC ....G 917 238-0730
  New York (G-11065)
Robocom Us LLC ....F 631 861-2045
  Farmingdale (G-4725)
Rockport Pa LLC ....G 212 482-8580
  New York (G-11069)
Ryba Software Inc ....G 718 264-9352
  Fresh Meadows (G-5045)
Safe Passage International Inc ....F 585 292-4910
  Rochester (G-13711)
Secured Services Inc ....G 866 419-3900
  New York (G-11176)
Segovia Technology Co ....F 212 868-4412
  New York (G-11182)
Seriesone Inc ....G 212 385-1552
  New York (G-11193)
Sharemethods LLC ....F 877 742-7366
  Brooklyn (G-2404)
Shiprite Services Inc ....F 315 427-2422
  Utica (G-15294)
Siemens Product Life Mgmt Sftw ......B 631 549-2300
  Melville (G-7822)
Similarweb Inc ....F 347 685-5422
  New York (G-11241)
Slidebean Incorporated ....F 866 365-0588
  New York (G-11269)
Slyde Inc ....F 917 331-2114
  Long Island City (G-7360)
Sneakers Software Inc ....F 800 877-9221
  New York (G-11279)
Social Bicycles LLC ....E 917 746-7624
  Brooklyn (G-2432)

SOFTWARE PUBLISHERS: NEC (continued)

Softlink International ....E 914 574-8197
  White Plains (G-16061)
Software & General Services Co ....G 315 986-4184
  Walworth (G-15479)
Software Engineering Amer Inc ....D 516 328-7000
  Garden City (G-5116)
Somml Health Inc ....G 518 880-2170
  Albany (G-130)
Soroc Technology Corp ....G 716 849-5913
  Buffalo (G-2988)
Sparta Commercial Services Inc ....F 212 239-2666
  New York (G-11309)
SS&c Financial Services LLC ....C 914 670-3600
  Harrison (G-5560)
Stensul Inc ....G 212 380-8620
  New York (G-11357)
Strada Soft Inc ....G 718 556-6940
  Staten Island (G-14716)
Street Smarts Vr Inc ....G 413 438-7787
  New York (G-11371)
Successware Inc ....F 716 565-2338
  Williamsville (G-16142)
Suite Solutions Inc ....E 716 929-3050
  Amherst (G-245)
Sutton Place Software Inc ....G 631 421-1737
  Melville (G-7826)
Synco Technologies Inc ....G 212 255-2031
  New York (G-11412)
Syrasoft LLC ....F 315 708-0341
  Baldwinsville (G-556)
Systems Trading Inc ....G 718 261-8900
  Melville (G-7827)
Tap2play LLC ....G 914 960-6232
  New York (G-11432)
Tapinator Inc ....G 914 930-6232
  New York (G-11435)
Targetprocess Inc ....F 877 718-2617
  Amherst (G-247)
Tecsys US Inc ....G 800 922-8649
  New York (G-11447)
Tel Tech International ....E 516 393-5174
  Melville (G-7830)
Terranua US Corp ....F 212 852-9028
  New York (G-11454)
Thomson Reuters Corporation ....A 646 223-4000
  New York (G-11475)
Tibco Software Inc ....G 646 495-2600
  New York (G-11483)
Total Defense Inc ....D 631 257-3258
  Hauppauge (G-5787)
Ttg LLC ....G 917 777-0959
  New York (G-11556)
Tunaverse Media Inc ....G 631 778-8350
  Hauppauge (G-5788)
U X World Inc ....G 914 375-6167
  Hawthorne (G-5824)
United Data Systems Inc ....G 631 549-6900
  Huntington (G-6230)
Upstate Records Management LLC ....G 518 834-1144
  Keeseville (G-6646)
Value Spring Technology Inc ....F 917 705-4658
  Harrison (G-5564)
Varonis Systems Inc ....C 877 292-8787
  New York (G-11646)
Vehicle Tracking Solutions LLC ....E 631 586-7400
  Commack (G-3601)
Verint Americas Inc ....F 631 962-9334
  Melville (G-7832)
Verint SEC Intelligence Inc ....D 631 962-9300
  Melville (G-7833)
Verint Systems Inc ....C 631 962-9600
  Melville (G-7834)
Verris Inc ....G 201 565-1648
  New York (G-11663)
Vertana Group LLC ....G 646 430-8226
  New York (G-11666)
Viridis Learning Inc ....G 347 420-9181
  New York (G-11687)
Vormittag Associates Inc ....G 800 824-7776
  Ronkonkoma (G-14024)
Water Oracle ....G 845 876-8327
  Rhinebeck (G-13104)
Wetpaintcom Inc ....E 206 859-6300
  Floral Park (G-4818)
Wizq Inc ....F 586 381-9048
  New York (G-11770)
Woodbury Systems Group Inc ....G 516 364-2653
  Woodbury (G-16186)
Wrkbook LLC ....F 914 355-1293
  White Plains (G-16075)

X Function Inc ....E 212 231-0092
  New York (G-11794)
Zedge Inc ....D 330 577-3424
  New York (G-11818)
Zydoc Med Transcription LLC ....F 631 273-1963
  Islandia (G-6348)

SOFTWARE PUBLISHERS: Operating Systems

Advanced Cyber Security Corp ....E 866 417-9155
  Bohemia (G-966)
J9 Technologies Inc ....E 412 586-5038
  New York (G-9959)
Reason Software Company Inc ....F 646 664-1038
  New York (G-10996)

SOFTWARE PUBLISHERS: Publisher's

Boeing Digital Solutions Inc ....G 212 478-1200
  New York (G-8830)
Catholic News Publishing Co ....F 914 632-7771
  Mamaroneck (G-7501)
Ceros Inc ....E 347 744-9250
  New York (G-8962)
Digital Associates LLC ....G 631 983-6075
  Smithtown (G-14475)
Hyperlaw Inc ....F 212 873-6982
  New York (G-9843)
Maz Systems Inc ....F 855 629-3444
  New York (G-10393)
Mediapost Communications LLC ....E 212 204-2000
  New York (G-10415)
Mnn Holding Company LLC ....F 404 558-5251
  Brooklyn (G-2165)
On Demand Books LLC ....G 212 966-2222
  New York (G-10689)
Spektrix Inc ....G 646 741-5110
  New York (G-11317)
Vortex Ventures Inc ....F 516 946-8345
  North Baldwin (G-12011)

SOFTWARE PUBLISHERS: Word Processing

Cegid Corporation ....F 212 757-9038
  New York (G-8941)

SOFTWARE TRAINING, COMPUTER

Logical Operations Inc ....C 585 350-7000
  Rochester (G-13522)
Microcad Trning Consulting Inc ....G 617 923-0500
  Lagrangeville (G-6751)

SOLAR CELLS

Atlantis Energy Systems Inc ....F 845 486-4052
  Poughkeepsie (G-12945)
Ely Beach Solar LLC ....G 718 796-9400
  New York (G-9354)
Idalia Solar Technologies LLC ....G 212 792-3913
  New York (G-9856)
Nationwide Tarps Incorporated ....D 518 843-1545
  Amsterdam (G-341)
Renewable Energy Inc ....G 718 690-2691
  Little Neck (G-6998)
Schott Solar Pv LLC ....G 888 457-6527
  Elmsford (G-4432)
Warner Energy LLC ....G 315 457-3828
  Liverpool (G-7048)

SOLAR HEATING EQPT

Atlantis Energy Systems Inc ....G 916 438-2930
  Poughkeepsie (G-12946)
General Electric Intl Inc ....G 518 385-2211
  Schenectady (G-14273)
Integrated Solar Tech LLC ....G 914 249-9364
  Binghamton (G-888)
Mx Solar USA LLC ....C 732 356-7300
  New York (G-10523)
Nanopv Corporation ....G 609 851-3666
  Liverpool (G-7028)
New Energy Systems Group ....C 917 573-0302
  New York (G-10580)
Prism Solar Technologies Inc ....E 845 883-4200
  Highland (G-5962)
Solar Energy Systems LLC ....F 718 389-1545
  Brooklyn (G-2437)

SOLDERS

Braze Alloy Inc ....G 718 815-5757
  Staten Island (G-14630)
Indium Corporation of America ....E 800 446-3486
  Clinton (G-3483)
Indium Corporation of America ....G 315 793-8200
  Utica (G-15275)
Indium Corporation of America ....G 315 381-2330
  Utica (G-15276)
Jewelers Solder Supply Inc ....F 718 637-1256
  Brooklyn (G-1992)

SOLVENTS

Solvents Company Inc ....F 631 595-9300
  Kingston (G-6709)

SONAR SYSTEMS & EQPT

Lockheed Martin Corporation ....E 315 456-6604
  Syracuse (G-14934)
Lockheed Martin Overseas ....F 315 456-0123
  Liverpool (G-7023)

SOUND EQPT: Electric

Audible Difference Inc ....E 212 662-4848
  Brooklyn (G-1551)
Isolation Technology Inc ....G 631 253-3314
  West Babylon (G-15714)
Magic Tech Co Ltd ....G 516 539-7944
  West Hempstead (G-15775)

SOUND EQPT: Underwater

L-3 Cmmnctons Ntronix Holdings ....D 212 697-1111
  New York (G-10152)

SOUND REPRODUCING EQPT

Samson Technologies Corp ....D 631 784-2200
  Hicksville (G-5946)
Vtb Holdings Inc ....G 914 345-2255
  Valhalla (G-15311)

SPACE VEHICLE EQPT

Gb Aero Engine LLC ....B 914 925-9600
  Rye (G-14078)
GKN Aerospace Monitor Inc ....B 562 619-8558
  Amityville (G-264)
L3 Foreign Holdings Inc ....C 212 697-1111
  New York (G-10153)
L3 Technologies Inc ....A 631 436-7400
  Hauppauge (G-5687)
L3 Technologies Inc ....B 212 697-1111
  New York (G-10154)
Lockheed Martin Corporation ....E 716 297-1000
  Niagara Falls (G-11948)
Magellan Aerospace NY Inc ....C 718 699-4000
  Corona (G-3744)
Moog Inc ....A 716 805-2604
  Elma (G-4321)
Saturn Industries Inc ....E 518 828-9956
  Hudson (G-6177)
Servotronics Inc ....C 716 655-5990
  Elma (G-4327)
SKF USA Inc ....D 716 661-2869
  Falconer (G-4555)
SKF USA Inc ....D 716 661-2600
  Falconer (G-4557)
Turbine Engine Comp Utica ....A 315 768-8070
  Whitesboro (G-16084)
Unison Industries LLC ....B 607 335-5000
  Norwich (G-12130)

SPARK PLUGS: Internal Combustion Engines

Karlyn Industries Inc ....F 845 351-2249
  Southfields (G-14541)

SPAS

461 New Lots Avenue LLC ....G 347 303-9305
  Brooklyn (G-1419)
Epic Beauty Co LLC ....G 212 327-3059
  New York (G-9387)
Skincare Products Inc ....G 917 837-5255
  Williamsville (G-16139)

SPEAKER SYSTEMS

Accent Speaker Technology Ltd ....G...... 631 738-2540
Holbrook (G-5982)

Covington Sound....................................G...... 646 256-7486
Bronx (G-1232)

L A R Electronics Corp ....G...... 716 285-0555
Niagara Falls (G-11945)

Professional Technology Inc ....G...... 315 337-4156
Rome (G-13864)

Pure Acoustics Inc ....G...... 718 788-4411
Brooklyn (G-2305)

Widgetworks Unlimited LLC ....G...... 914 666-6395
Chappaqua (G-3327)

SPECIAL EVENTS DECORATION SVCS

Allied Decorations Co Inc ....F...... 315 637-0273
Syracuse (G-14811)

Ubm LLC ....D...... 516 562-7800
New Hyde Park (G-8298)

SPECIALTY FOOD STORES: Coffee

Anandsar Inc ....E...... 551 556-5555
Oakland Gardens (G-12159)

Death Wish Coffee Company LLC........E...... 518 400-1050
Ballston Spa (G-571)

Orens Daily Roast Inc ....G...... 212 348-5400
New York (G-10710)

Pintail Coffee Inc..................................G...... 631 396-0808
Farmingdale (G-4708)

SPECIALTY FOOD STORES: Health & Dietetic Food

Ajes Pharmaceuticals LLC....................E...... 631 608-1728
Copiague (G-3644)

Cosmic Enterprise ....G...... 718 342-6257
Brooklyn (G-1691)

Matys Healthy Products LLC ....G...... 585 218-0507
Pittsford (G-12651)

Natures Bounty Co ....D...... 631 244-2021
Ronkonkoma (G-13980)

Only Natural Inc ....F...... 516 897-7001
Oceanside (G-12183)

Setauket Manufacturing Co ....G...... 631 231-7272
Ronkonkoma (G-14008)

SPECIALTY FOOD STORES: Juices, Fruit Or Vegetable

Mayer Bros Apple Products Inc............D...... 716 668-1787
West Seneca (G-15852)

Schutt Cider Mill..................................F...... 585 872-2924
Webster (G-15652)

SPECIALTY FOOD STORES: Tea

Harney & Sons Tea Corp ....C...... 518 789-2100
Millerton (G-7947)

SPECIALTY FOOD STORES: Vitamin

Natures Warehouse ....F...... 800 215-4372
Philadelphia (G-12612)

SPERM BANK

Daxor Corporation ....F...... 212 330-8500
New York (G-9190)

SPONGES, ANIMAL, WHOLESALE

Finger Lakes Lea Crafters LLC..............F...... 315 252-4107
Auburn (G-475)

SPONGES: Plastic

3M Company ....B...... 716 876-1596
Tonawanda (G-15080)

SPOOLS: Fiber, Made From Purchased Materials

Syraco Products Inc ....F...... 315 476-5306
Syracuse (G-15002)

SPOOLS: Indl

McIntosh Box & Pallet Co Inc ....E...... 315 446-9350
Rome (G-13855)

SPORTING & ATHLETIC GOODS: Bags, Golf

Athalon Sportgear Inc ....G...... 212 268-8070
New York (G-8664)

SPORTING & ATHLETIC GOODS: Bowling Pins

Qubicaamf Worldwide LLC ....C...... 315 376-6541
Lowville (G-7420)

SPORTING & ATHLETIC GOODS: Bows, Archery

Perfect Form Manufacturing LLC ....G...... 585 500-5923
West.Henrietta (G-15800)

SPORTING & ATHLETIC GOODS: Boxing Eqpt & Splys, NEC

Everlast Worldwide Inc ....E...... 212 239-0990
New York (G-9428)

SPORTING & ATHLETIC GOODS: Camping Eqpt & Splys

Adirondack Outdoor Center LLC..........G...... 315 369-2300
Old Forge (G-12221)

J R Products Inc....................................G...... 716 633-7565
Clarence Center (G-3446)

SPORTING & ATHLETIC GOODS: Cartridge Belts

Car Doctor Motor Sports LLC ....G...... 631 537-1548
Water Mill (G-15528)

SPORTING & ATHLETIC GOODS: Driving Ranges, Golf, Electronic

Paddock Chevrolet Golf Dome ....E...... 716 504-4059
Tonawanda (G-15130)

SPORTING & ATHLETIC GOODS: Dumbbells & Other Weight Eqpt

TDS Fitness Equipment Corp ....F...... 607 733-6789
Elmira (G-4370)

SPORTING & ATHLETIC GOODS: Fishing Bait, Artificial

Fishing Valley LLC ....G...... 716 523-6158
Lockport (G-7075)

Makiplastic..G...... 716 772-2222
Gasport (G-5138)

SPORTING & ATHLETIC GOODS: Fishing Eqpt

Fly-Tyers Carry-All LLC ....G...... 607 821-1460
Charlotteville (G-3328)

Rome Specialty Company Inc..............E...... 315 337-8200
Rome (G-13870)

SPORTING & ATHLETIC GOODS: Fishing Tackle, General

Sea Isle Custom Rod Builders..............G...... 516 868-8855
Freeport (G-5022)

SPORTING & ATHLETIC GOODS: Game Calls

Quaker Boy Inc......................................E...... 716 662-3979
Springville (G-14596)

SPORTING & ATHLETIC GOODS: Hockey Eqpt & Splys, NEC

Hart Sports Inc ....G...... 631 385-1805
Huntington Station (G-6248)

Kohlberg Sports Group Inc..................G...... 914 241-7430
Mount Kisco (G-8097)

SPORTING & ATHLETIC GOODS: Lacrosse Eqpt & Splys, NEC

Maverik Lacrosse LLC..........................A...... 516 213-3050
New York (G-10388)

SPORTING & ATHLETIC GOODS: Bags, Golf

Tosch Products Ltd ....G...... 315 672-3040
Camillus (G-3111)

SPORTING & ATHLETIC GOODS: Pools, Swimming, Exc Plastic

Charm Mfg Co Inc ....E...... 607 565-8161
Waverly (G-15619)

Imperial Pools Inc ....C...... 518 786-1200
Latham (G-6860)

Latham International Mfg Corp..............B...... 800 833-3800
Latham (G-6866)

Latham Pool Products Inc ....B...... 518 951-1000
Latham (G-6867)

Polytech Pool Mfg Inc ....F...... 718 492-8991
Brooklyn (G-2268)

SPORTING & ATHLETIC GOODS: Pools, Swimming, Plastic

Florida North Inc ....F...... 518 868-2888
Sloansville (G-14469)

Hinspergers Poly Industries ....E...... 585 798-6625
Medina (G-7738)

Swimline Corp ....C...... 631 254-2155
Edgewood (G-4284)

Wilbar International Inc ....D...... 631 951-9800
Hauppauge (G-5801)

SPORTING & ATHLETIC GOODS: Shooting Eqpt & Splys, General

Otis Products Inc ....C...... 315 348-4300
Lyons Falls (G-7455)

SPORTING & ATHLETIC GOODS: Skateboards

Blades ....F...... 212 477-1059
New York (G-8808)

SPORTING & ATHLETIC GOODS: Skates & Parts, Roller

Chapman Skateboard Co Inc ....G...... 631 321-4773
Deer Park (G-3852)

SPORTING & ATHLETIC GOODS: Snow Skis

Bomber LLC ....G...... 212 980-2442
New York (G-8833)

SPORTING & ATHLETIC GOODS: Target Shooting Eqpt

Devin Mfg Inc..F...... 585 496-5770
Arcade (G-372)

SPORTING & ATHLETIC GOODS: Team Sports Eqpt

Adpro Sports LLC ....D...... 716 854-5116
Buffalo (G-2622)

SPORTING & ATHLETIC GOODS: Tennis Eqpt & Splys

Rottkamp Tennis Inc............................E...... 631 421-0040
Huntington Station (G-6257)

SPORTING & REC GOODS, WHOLESALE: Camping Eqpt & Splys

Adirondack Outdoor Center LLC..........G...... 315 369-2300
Old Forge (G-12221)

Johnson Outdoors Inc..........................C...... 607 779-2200
Binghamton (G-891)

SPORTING & RECREATIONAL GOODS & SPLYS WHOLESALERS

Everlast Sports Mfg Corp......................E...... 212 239-0990
New York (G-9427)

Graph-Tex Inc ....G...... 607 756-1875
Cortland (G-3768)

Walsh & Hughes Inc ....G...... 631 427-5904
Huntington Station (G-6266)

SPORTING & RECREATIONAL GOODS, WHOL: Sharpeners, Sporting

Dead Ringer LLC ....G...... 585 355-4685
Rochester **(G-13340)**

SPORTING & RECREATIONAL GOODS, WHOLESALE: Bicycle

Worksman Trading Corp ....G...... 718 322-2000
Ozone Park **(G-12469)**

SPORTING & RECREATIONAL GOODS, WHOLESALE: Boat Access & Part

Brock Awnings Ltd ....F...... 631 765-5200
Hampton Bays **(G-5533)**
Di Sanos Creative Canvas Inc ....G...... 315 894-3137
Frankfort **(G-4949)**
Katherine Blizniak ....G...... 716 674-8545
West Seneca **(G-15850)**

SPORTING & RECREATIONAL GOODS, WHOLESALE: Exercise

TDS Fitness Equipment Corp ....F...... 607 733-6789
Elmira **(G-4370)**

SPORTING & RECREATIONAL GOODS, WHOLESALE: Fishing

Cortland Line Mfg LLC ....E...... 607 756-2851
Cortland **(G-3760)**
Fly-Tyers Carry-All LLC ....G...... 607 821-1460
Charlotteville **(G-3328)**

SPORTING & RECREATIONAL GOODS, WHOLESALE: Fishing Tackle

Hemisphere Novelties Inc ....E...... 914 378-4100
Yonkers **(G-16318)**

SPORTING & RECREATIONAL GOODS, WHOLESALE: Hot Tubs

Charm Mfg Co Inc ....E...... 607 565-8161
Waverly **(G-15619)**

SPORTING & RECREATIONAL GOODS, WHOLESALE: Skiing

Sundown Ski & Sport Shop Inc ....D...... 631 737-8600
Lake Grove **(G-6761)**

SPORTING & RECREATIONAL GOODS, WHOLESALE: Watersports

Great American Industries Inc ....G...... 607 729-9331
Vestal **(G-15379)**

SPORTING GOODS

Absolute Fitness US Corp ....D...... 732 979-8582
Bayside **(G-734)**
Apparel Production Inc ....E...... 212 278-8362
New York **(G-8608)**
Azibi Ltd ....F...... 212 869-6550
New York **(G-8701)**
Burnt Mill Smithing ....G...... 585 293-2380
Churchville **(G-3409)**
Burton Corporation ....D...... 802 862-4500
Champlain **(G-3310)**
City Sports Inc ....G...... 212 730-2009
New York **(G-9018)**
Cy Plastics Works Inc ....D...... 585 229-2555
Honeoye **(G-6068)**
Everlast Sports Mfg Corp ....E...... 212 239-0990
New York **(G-9427)**
Excellent Art Mfg Corp ....F...... 718 388-7075
Inwood **(G-6292)**
Fitsmo LLC ....G...... 585 519-1956
Fairport **(G-4497)**
Good Show Sportwear Inc ....F...... 212 334-8751
New York **(G-9645)**
Grand Slam Safety LLC ....F...... 315 301-4039
Croghan **(G-3802)**
Hermann Group LLC ....G...... 716 876-9798
Kenmore **(G-6651)**
Johnson Outdoors Inc ....C...... 607 779-2200
Binghamton **(G-891)**

Nalge Nunc International Corp ....A...... 585 498-2661
Rochester **(G-13565)**
North Coast Outfitters Ltd ....E...... 631 727-5580
Riverhead **(G-13183)**
Pilates Designs LLC ....G...... 718 721-5929
Astoria **(G-434)**
PNC Sports ....G...... 516 665-2244
Deer Park **(G-3920)**
PRC Liquidating Company ....E...... 212 823-9626
New York **(G-10873)**
Rawlings Sporting Goods Co Inc ....D...... 315 429-8511
Dolgeville **(G-4025)**
Rising Stars Soccer Club CNY ....F...... 315 381-3096
Westmoreland **(G-15962)**
Sportsfield Specialties Inc ....E...... 607 746-8911
Delhi **(G-3967)**
Stephenson Custom Case Company ....E...... 905 542-8762
Niagara Falls **(G-11982)**
Swimways Corp ....C...... 757 460-1156
Long Island City **(G-7377)**
Viking Athletics Ltd. ....E...... 631 957-8000
Lindenhurst **(G-6982)**
Watson Adventures LLC ....E...... 212 564-8293
New York **(G-11731)**
World Best Sporting Goods Inc ....F...... 800 489-0908
Westbury **(G-15940)**

SPORTING GOODS STORES, NEC

A Trusted Name Inc ....F...... 716 326-7400
Westfield **(G-15944)**
Arena Graphics Inc ....E...... 516 767-5108
Port Washington **(G-12864)**
Burnt Mill Smithing ....G...... 585 293-2380
Churchville **(G-3409)**
Glenda Inc ....G...... 718 442-8981
Staten Island **(G-14656)**
Graph-Tex Inc ....F...... 607 756-1875
Cortland **(G-3768)**
Great American Bicycle LLC ....E...... 518 584-8100
Saratoga Springs **(G-14179)**
Pda Panache Corp ....G...... 631 776-0523
Bohemia **(G-1060)**
Shore Line Monogramming Inc ....F...... 914 698-8000
Mamaroneck **(G-7523)**
Vic Demayos Inc ....G...... 845 626-4343
Accord **(G-1)**

SPORTING GOODS STORES: Camping Eqpt

Johnson Outdoors Inc ....C...... 607 779-2200
Binghamton **(G-891)**

SPORTING GOODS STORES: Fishing Eqpt

Cortland Line Mfg LLC ....E...... 607 756-2851
Cortland **(G-3760)**
Sea Isle Custom Rod Builders ....G...... 516 868-8855
Freeport **(G-5022)**

SPORTING GOODS STORES: Playground Eqpt

Eastern Jungle Gym Inc ....E...... 845 878-9800
Carmel **(G-3185)**

SPORTING GOODS STORES: Skateboarding Eqpt

Chapman Skateboard Co Inc ....G...... 631 321-4773
Deer Park **(G-3852)**

SPORTING GOODS STORES: Tennis Goods & Eqpt

Walsh & Hughes Inc ....G...... 631 427-5904
Huntington Station **(G-6266)**

SPORTING GOODS: Archery

Copper John Corporation ....F...... 315 258-9269
Auburn **(G-470)**
Outdoor Group LLC ....C...... 877 503-5483
West Henrietta **(G-15799)**
Shehawken Archery Co Inc ....F...... 607 967-8333
Bainbridge **(G-526)**

SPORTING GOODS: Fishing Nets

Koring Bros Inc ....G...... 888 233-1292
New Rochelle **(G-8346)**

Osprey Boat ....G...... 631 331-4153
Mount Sinai **(G-8116)**

SPORTING GOODS: Sailboards

Alternatives For Children ....E...... 631 271-0777
Dix Hills **(G-4009)**

SPORTING GOODS: Surfboards

Bungers Surf Shop ....G...... 631 244-3646
Sayville **(G-14224)**
Pilgrim Surf & Supply ....G...... 718 218-7456
Brooklyn **(G-2258)**

SPORTING/ATHLETIC GOODS: Gloves, Boxing, Handball, Etc

Fownes Brothers & Co Inc ....E...... 800 345-6837
New York **(G-9525)**
Fownes Brothers & Co Inc ....E...... 518 752-4411
Gloversville **(G-5283)**
Olympia Sports Company Inc ....F...... 914 347-4737
Elmsford **(G-4421)**

SPORTS APPAREL STORES

Gametime Sportswear Plus LLC ....G...... 315 724-5893
Utica **(G-15266)**
Hanesbrands Inc ....G...... 212 576-9300
New York **(G-9721)**
JM Studio Inc ....F...... 646 546-5514
New York **(G-10011)**
Unlimited Ink Inc ....E...... 631 582-0696
Hauppauge **(G-5793)**

SPORTS PROMOTION SVCS

Professnal Spt Pblications Inc ....D...... 212 697-1460
New York **(G-10904)**

SPOUTING: Plastic & Fiberglass Reinforced

Saint-Gobain Prfmce Plas Corp ....E...... 518 283-5963
Poestenkill **(G-12804)**

SPRAYING & DUSTING EQPT

Spfm Corp ....G...... 718 788-6800
Brooklyn **(G-2446)**

SPRAYING EQPT: Agricultural

Fountainhead Group Inc ....C...... 315 736-0037
New York Mills **(G-11832)**

SPRAYS: Self-Defense

Pom Industries LLC ....G...... 800 695-4791
New York **(G-10864)**

SPRINGS: Coiled Flat

Angelica Spring Company Inc ....F...... 585 466-7892
Angelica **(G-357)**
Whiting Door Mfg Corp ....D...... 716 542-3070
Akron **(G-24)**

SPRINGS: Leaf, Automobile, Locomotive, Etc

Red Onyx Industrial Pdts LLC ....G...... 516 459-6035
Huntington **(G-6219)**
Whitesboro Spring & Alignment ....F...... 315 736-4441
Whitesboro **(G-16085)**

SPRINGS: Mechanical, Precision

Lee Spring Company LLC ....C...... 888 777-4647
Brooklyn **(G-2058)**
Unimex Corporation ....C...... 718 236-2222
Brooklyn **(G-2537)**

SPRINGS: Precision

Fennell Spring Company LLC ....D...... 607 739-3541
Horseheads **(G-6123)**
Kinemotive Corporation ....E...... 631 249-6440
Farmingdale **(G-4666)**

SPRINGS: Sash Balances

Pullman Mfg Corporation ....G...... 585 334-1350
Rochester **(G-13652)**

SPRINGS: Steel

Isolation Dynamics Corp ....E 631 491-5670
Farmingdale (G-4653)
Lee Spring Company LLC ....C 888 777-4647
Brooklyn (G-2058)
Midstate Spring Inc ....E 315 437-2623
Syracuse (G-14943)
Temper Corporation ....E 518 853-3467
Fonda (G-4912)

SPRINGS: Wire

Ajax Wire Specialty Co Inc ....F 516 935-2333
Hicksville (G-5879)
Barnes Group Inc ....G 315 457-9200
Syracuse (G-14826)
Commerce Spring Corp ....F 631 293-4844
Farmingdale (G-4602)
Commercial Communications LLC ....G 845 343-9078
Middletown (G-7900)
Midstate Spring Inc ....E 315 437-2623
Syracuse (G-14943)
Teka Precision Inc ....G 845 753-1900
Nyack (G-12147)
The Caldwell Manufacturing Co ....D 585 352-3790
Rochester (G-13764)
The Caldwell Manufacturing Co ....E 585 352-2803
Victor (G-15438)
Unimex Corporation ....D 800 886-0390
New York (G-11591)

SPRINKLING SYSTEMS: Fire Control

Allied Inspection Services LLC ....F 716 489-3199
Falconer (G-4533)
Reliable Autmtc Sprnklr Co Inc ....B 800 431-1588
Elmsford (G-4426)
Sentry Automatic Sprinkler ....F 631 723-3095
Riverhead (G-13189)
Tyco Simplexgrinnell ....E 315 437-9664
East Syracuse (G-4245)

STAGE LIGHTING SYSTEMS

Altman Stage Lighting Co Inc ....C 914 476-7987
Yonkers (G-16283)
Methods Tooling & Mfg Inc ....E 845 246-7100
Mount Marion (G-8111)
Ric-Lo Productions Ltd ....E 845 469-2285
Chester (G-3384)
Sir Industries Inc ....G 631 234-2444
Hauppauge (G-5767)

STAINLESS STEEL

Allvac ....F 716 433-4411
Lockport (G-7059)
American Chimney Supplies Inc ....G 631 434-2020
Hauppauge (G-5588)
Dakota Systems Mfg Corp ....G 631 249-5811
Farmingdale (G-4613)
Dunkirk Specialty Steel LLC ....C 716 366-1000
Dunkirk (G-4055)
Nucor Steel Auburn Inc ....B 315 253-4561
Auburn (G-488)
Quality Stainless Steel NY Inc ....F 718 748-1785
Brooklyn (G-2311)
Quest Manufacturing Inc ....E 716 312-8000
Hamburg (G-5518)
Sims Group USA Holdings Corp ....D 718 786-6031
Long Island City (G-7357)
Tdy Industries LLC ....E 716 433-4411
Lockport (G-7110)
Viraj - USA Inc ....G 516 280-8380
Hicksville (G-5953)

STAIRCASES & STAIRS, WOOD

A W Hamel Stair Mfg Inc ....F 518 346-3031
Schenectady (G-14244)
Adirondack Stairs Inc ....F 845 246-2525
Saugerties (G-14196)
Bennett Stair Company Inc ....G 518 384-1554
Ballston Lake (G-558)
Capital District Stairs Inc ....G 518 383-2449
Halfmoon (G-5491)
Custom Stair & Millwork Co ....G 315 839-5793
Sauquoit (G-14218)
Ideal Wood Products Inc ....E 315 823-1124
Little Falls (G-6989)
Island Stairs Corp ....G 347 645-0560
Staten Island (G-14666)

Mestel Brothers Stairs & Rails ....C 516 496-4127
Syosset (G-14794)
Monroe Stair Products Inc ....E 845 783-4245
Monroe (G-8028)
Monroe Stair Products Inc ....G 845 791-4016
Monticello (G-8071)
Quality Stair Builders Inc ....F 631 694-0711
Farmingdale (G-4719)
R C Henderson Stair Builders ....F 516 876-9898
Westbury (G-15922)
S R Sloan Inc ....D 315 736-7730
Whitesboro (G-16082)
Staten Island Stair Inc ....G 718 317-9276
Staten Island (G-14714)
United Rockland Holding Co Inc ....E 845 357-1900
Suffern (G-14768)

STAMPED ART GOODS FOR EMBROIDERING

Dirt T Shirts Inc ....E 845 336-4230
Kingston (G-6689)

STAMPING SVC: Book, Gold

Mines Press Inc ....C 888 559-2634
Cortlandt Manor (G-3797)

STAMPINGS: Automotive

P R B Metal Products Inc ....F 631 467-1800
Ronkonkoma (G-13989)
Thyssenkrupp Materials NA Inc ....D 585 279-0000
West Seneca (G-15855)

STAMPINGS: Metal

Able National Corp ....E 718 386-8801
Brooklyn (G-1450)
Acro Industries Inc ....C 585 254-3661
Rochester (G-13204)
Advanced Structures Corp ....F 631 667-5000
Deer Park (G-3830)
Albest Metal Stamping Corp ....E 718 388-6000
Brooklyn (G-1478)
All Out Die Cutting Inc ....E 718 346-6666
Brooklyn (G-1486)
Arnell Inc ....G 516 486-7098
Hempstead (G-5833)
Arro Manufacturing LLC ....F 716 763-6203
Lakewood (G-6778)
Arro Tool & Die Inc ....F 716 763-6203
Lakewood (G-6779)
B & R Tool Inc ....G 718 948-2729
Staten Island (G-14622)
B H M Metal Products Co ....G 845 292-5297
Kauneonga Lake (G-6640)
Bailey Manufacturing Co LLC ....E 716 965-2731
Forestville (G-4930)
Barnes Group Inc ....G 315 457-9200
Syracuse (G-14826)
Barron Metal Products Inc ....E 914 965-1232
Yonkers (G-16289)
Bcs Access Systems Us LLC ....B 315 258-3469
Auburn (G-466)
Bowen Products Corporation ....G 315 498-4481
Nedrow (G-2757)
C & H Precision Tools Inc ....E 631 758-3806
Holtsville (G-6047)
Cameo Metal Products Inc ....E 718 788-1106
Brooklyn (G-1641)
Cannon Industries Inc ....D 585 254-8080
Rochester (G-13294)
Check-Mate Industries Inc ....E 631 491-1777
West Babylon (G-15701)
Cobbe Industries Inc ....E 716 287-2661
Gerry (G-5170)
Coil Stamping Inc ....F 631 588-3040
Holbrook (G-5991)
Compar Manufacturing Corp ....E 212 304-2777
New York (G-9071)
Dunkirk Metal Products Wny LLC ....E 716 366-2555
Dunkirk (G-4054)
Endicott Precision Inc ....C 607 754-7076
Endicott (G-4451)
Engineering Mfg Tech LLC ....D 607 754-7111
Endicott (G-4453)
Forsyth Industries Inc ....E 716 652-1070
Buffalo (G-257)
Freeport Screen & Stamping ....E 516 379-0330
Freeport (G-4998)

Gleason Works ....A 585 473-1000
Rochester (G-13445)
Greene Technologies Inc ....D 607 656-4166
Greene (G-5446)
International Ord Tech Inc ....D 716 664-1100
Jamestown (G-6518)
Johnson & Hoffman LLC ....D 516 742-3333
Carle Place (G-3175)
Magic Novelty Co Inc ....E 212 304-2777
New York (G-10325)
Mantel & Mantel Stamping Corp ....G 631 467-1916
Ronkonkoma (G-13969)
Marex Aquisition Corp ....G 585 458-3940
Rochester (G-13536)
Matov Industries Inc ....E 718 392-5060
Long Island City (G-7291)
McHone Industries Inc ....D 716 945-3380
Salamanca (G-14122)
National Die & Button Mould Co ....E 201 939-7800
Brooklyn (G-2189)
OEM Solutions Inc ....G 716 864-9324
Clarence (G-3437)
P R B Metal Products Inc ....F 631 467-1800
Ronkonkoma (G-13989)
Phoenix Metal Products Inc ....F 516 546-4200
Freeport (G-5015)
Precision Photo-Fab Inc ....D 716 821-9393
Buffalo (G-2928)
Pronto Tool & Die Co Inc ....E 631 981-8920
Ronkonkoma (G-13997)
Richter Charles Metal STMp&sp ....E 845 895-2025
Wallkill (G-15471)
Rochester Stampings Inc ....F 585 467-5241
Rochester (G-13698)
Simplex Manufacturing Co Inc ....F 315 252-7524
Auburn (G-495)
Stampcrete International Ltd ....E 315 451-2837
Liverpool (G-7042)
Stever-Locke Industries Inc ....G 585 624-3450
Honeoye Falls (G-6081)
Tri-Technologies Inc ....E 914 699-2001
Mount Vernon (G-8187)
Universal Shielding Corp ....E 631 667-7900
Deer Park (G-3945)
Web Associates Inc ....G 716 883-3377
Buffalo (G-3042)
WR Smith & Sons Inc ....G 845 620-9400
Nanuet (G-8205)

STANDS & RACKS: Engine, Metal

Devin Mfg Inc ....F 585 496-5770
Arcade (G-372)

STARTERS: Motor

Con Rel Auto Electric Inc ....E 518 356-1646
Schenectady (G-14259)

STATIC ELIMINATORS: Ind

Nrd LLC ....E 716 773-7634
Grand Island (G-5339)

STATIONARY & OFFICE SPLYS, WHOLESALE: Blank Books

Foster - Gordon Manufacturing ....G 631 589-6776
Bohemia (G-1013)

STATIONARY & OFFICE SPLYS, WHOLESALE: Stationery

F J Remey Co Inc ....E 516 741-5112
Mineola (G-7974)
One In A Million Inc ....G 516 829-1111
Valley Stream (G-15350)
Tripi Engraving Co Inc ....E 718 383-6500
Brooklyn (G-2522)

STATIONER'S SUNDRIES: Rubber

Hampton Art LLC ....E 631 924-1335
Medford (G-7710)
Rubber Stamps Inc ....E 212 675-1180
Mineola (G-7998)

STATIONERY & OFFICE SPLYS WHOLESALERS

Argo Lithographers Inc ....E 718 729-2700
Long Island City (G-7166)

PRODUCT

Atlaz International Ltd ....F...... 516 239-1854
  Freeport *(G-4986)*
Kas-Ray Industries Inc ....F...... 212 620-3144
  New York *(G-10071)*
Labels Inter-Global Inc ....F...... 212 398-0006
  New York *(G-10160)*

STATIONERY PRDTS

Drimark ....F...... 516 484-6200
  Bethpage *(G-834)*
Innovative Designs LLC ....E...... 212 695-0892
  New York *(G-9897)*
Kleer-Fax Inc ....D...... 631 225-1100
  Amityville *(G-286)*
Leather Indexes Corp ....D...... 516 827-1900
  Hicksville *(G-5923)*
P C I Paper Conversions Inc ....C...... 315 437-1641
  Syracuse *(G-14958)*
Paper Magic Group Inc ....B...... 631 521-3682
  New York *(G-10749)*
Princton Archtctural Press LLC ....F...... 518 671-6100
  Hudson *(G-6176)*
Westrock Mwv LLC ....C...... 212 688-5000
  New York *(G-11748)*

STATIONERY: Made From Purchased Materials

Allen William & Company Inc ....C...... 212 675-6461
  Glendale *(G-5218)*

STATUES: Nonmetal

Dream Statuary Inc ....G...... 718 647-2024
  Brooklyn *(G-1760)*
Jonas Louis Paul Studios Inc ....G...... 518 851-2211
  Hudson *(G-6168)*

STEAM SPLY SYSTEMS SVCS INCLUDING GEOTHERMAL

Caithness Equities Corporation .....E...... 212 599-2112
  New York *(G-8888)*

STEAM, HEAT & AIR CONDITIONING DISTRIBUTION SVC

P & G Steel Products Co Inc ....D...... 716 896-7900
  Buffalo *(G-2901)*

STEEL & ALLOYS: Tool & Die

B H M Metal Products Co ....G...... 845 292-5297
  Kauneonga Lake *(G-6640)*
Fuller Tool Incorporated ....F...... 315 891-3183
  Newport *(G-11898)*
Spin-Rite Corporation ....F...... 585 266-5200
  Rochester *(G-13739)*

STEEL FABRICATORS

760 NI Holdings ....E...... 716 821-1391
  Buffalo *(G-2614)*
A & T Iron Works Inc ....E...... 914 632-8992
  New Rochelle *(G-8315)*
A-Fab Initiatives Inc ....F...... 716 877-5257
  Buffalo *(G-2616)*
A/C Design & Fabrication Corp ......G...... 718 227-8100
  Staten Island *(G-14615)*
AAA Welding and Fabrication of ....G...... 585 254-2830
  Rochester *(G-13196)*
Abalon Precision Mfg Corp ....E...... 914 665-7700
  Mount Vernon *(G-8120)*
Acadia Stairs ....G...... 845 765-8600
  Fishkill *(G-4797)*
Accucut Inc ....G...... 631 567-2868
  West Sayville *(G-15838)*
Ackroyd Metal Fabricators Inc ......F...... 518 434-1281
  Menands *(G-7837)*
Advanced Thermal Systems Inc .....E...... 716 681-1800
  Lancaster *(G-6790)*
Aero-Data Metal Crafters Inc ....C...... 631 471-7733
  Ronkonkoma *(G-13892)*
Aldo Frustacci Iron Works Inc ....F...... 718 768-0707
  Brooklyn *(G-1480)*
Alken Industries Inc ....E...... 631 467-2000
  Ronkonkoma *(G-13896)*
All-City Metal Inc ....E...... 718 937-3975
  Maspeth *(G-7586)*
Alloy Metal Works Inc ....G...... 631 694-8163
  Farmingdale *(G-4580)*

Alpha Iron Works LLC ....F...... 585 424-7260
  Rochester *(G-13224)*
American Aerogel Corporation ......E...... 585 328-2140
  Rochester *(G-13228)*
Asp Industries ....E...... 585 254-9130
  Rochester *(G-13253)*
Atlantis Equipment Corporation ....F...... 518 733-5910
  Stephentown *(G-14730)*
B H M Metal Products Co ....G...... 845 292-5297
  Kauneonga Lake *(G-6640)*
Barber Welding Inc ....E...... 315 834-6645
  Weedsport *(G-15665)*
Barker Steel LLC ....E...... 518 465-6221
  Albany *(G-44)*
Barry Steel Fabrication Inc ....E...... 716 433-2144
  Lockport *(G-7061)*
Bear Metal Works Inc ....F...... 716 824-4350
  Buffalo *(G-2659)*
Bellmore Steel Products Corp ....F...... 516 785-9667
  Bellmore *(G-780)*
Bennett Manufacturing Co Inc ....C...... 716 937-9161
  Alden *(G-166)*
Bereza Iron Works Inc ....F...... 585 254-6311
  Rochester *(G-13266)*
Blackstone Advanced Tech LLC .....C...... 716 665-5410
  Jamestown *(G-6498)*
Bms Manufacturing Co Inc ....E...... 607 535-2426
  Watkins Glen *(G-15613)*
Bob Murphy Inc ....F...... 607 729-3553
  Vestal *(G-15373)*
Bombardier Transportation ....D...... 607 324-0216
  Hornell *(G-6102)*
Bombardier Trnsp Holdings USA .....D...... 607 776-4791
  Bath *(G-631)*
Bristol Metals Inc ....F...... 585 657-7665
  Bloomfield *(G-941)*
Buffalo Metal Fabricating Corp ......F...... 716 892-7800
  Buffalo *(G-2678)*
Buffalo Structural Steel Inc ....E...... 814 827-1350
  Syracuse *(G-14835)*
Burnt Hills Fabricators Inc ....F...... 518 885-1115
  Ballston Spa *(G-570)*
C & C Custom Metal Fabricators .....G...... 631 235-9646
  Hauppauge *(G-5610)*
C & C Metal Fabrications Inc ....E...... 315 598-7607
  Fulton *(G-5055)*
C & T Tool & Instrument Co ....E...... 718 429-1253
  Woodside *(G-16199)*
Cameron Mfg & Design Inc ....C...... 607 739-3606
  Horseheads *(G-6117)*
Carpenter Industries Inc ....F...... 315 463-4284
  Syracuse *(G-14843)*
CBM Fabrications Inc ....E...... 518 399-8023
  Ballston Lake *(G-559)*
Chautauqua Machine Spc LLC ....F...... 716 782-3276
  Ashville *(G-409)*
Christian Fabrication LLC ....G...... 315 822-0135
  West Winfield *(G-15857)*
Cives Corporation ....C...... 315 287-2200
  Gouverneur *(G-5318)*
Cobbe Industries Inc ....E...... 716 287-2661
  Gerry *(G-5170)*
Cobra Operating Industries LLC .....F...... 607 639-1700
  Afton *(G-7)*
Coco Architectureal Grilles ....G...... 631 482-9449
  Farmingdale *(G-4600)*
Computerized Metal Bending Ser ...F...... 631 249-1177
  West Babylon *(G-15704)*
Cottonwood Metals Inc ....E...... 646 807-8674
  Bohemia *(G-991)*
County Fabricators ....F...... 914 741-0219
  Pleasantville *(G-12796)*
Cyncal Steel Fabricators Inc ....F...... 631 254-5600
  Bay Shore *(G-668)*
Dennies Manufacturing Inc ....E...... 585 393-4646
  Canandaigua *(G-3130)*
Diversified Manufacturing Inc ....F...... 716 681-7670
  Lancaster *(G-6803)*
Donald Stefan ....G...... 716 492-1110
  Chaffee *(G-3306)*
Duquettes Steel & Structural F .....F...... 518 563-3161
  Plattsburgh *(G-12745)*
E B Atlas Steel Corp ....F...... 716 876-0900
  Buffalo *(G-2733)*
Eastern Manufacturing Inc ....E...... 716 741-4572
  Clarence *(G-3432)*
Eastern Welding Inc ....E...... 631 727-0306
  Riverhead *(G-13174)*
Elevator Accessories Mfg ....F...... 914 739-7004
  Peekskill *(G-12550)*

Elite Steel Fabricators Inc ....G...... 631 285-1008
  Ronkonkoma *(G-13935)*
Empire Industrial Systems Corp .....F...... 631 242-4619
  Bay Shore *(G-678)*
Empire Metal Fabricators Inc ....E...... 585 288-2140
  Rochester *(G-13388)*
Empro Niagara Inc ....G...... 716 433-2769
  Lockport *(G-7073)*
Eps Iron Works Inc ....E...... 516 294-5840
  Mineola *(G-7972)*
Erie Engineered Products Inc ....E...... 716 206-0204
  Lancaster *(G-6805)*
Everfab Inc ....D...... 716 655-1550
  East Aurora *(G-4086)*
Excel Industries Inc ....E...... 716 542-5468
  Clarence *(G-3434)*
Farmingdale Iron Works Inc ....G...... 631 249-5995
  Farmingdale *(G-4629)*
Feinstein Iron Works Inc ....E...... 516 997-8300
  Westbury *(G-15885)*
Fence Plaza Corp ....G...... 718 469-2200
  Brooklyn *(G-1838)*
Five Corners Repair Inc ....F...... 585 322-7369
  Bliss *(G-939)*
Flagpoles Incorporated ....D...... 631 751-5500
  East Setauket *(G-4178)*
Fort Miller Group Inc ....B...... 518 695-5000
  Greenwich *(G-5471)*
FPL Fbrctors Erctors Group LLC .....G...... 917 334-6968
  Howard Beach *(G-6139)*
Framing Technology Inc ....E...... 585 464-8470
  Rochester *(G-13422)*
Frazier Industrial Company ....D...... 315 539-9256
  Waterloo *(G-15552)*
Fred Santucci Inc ....F...... 716 483-1411
  Jamestown *(G-6511)*
Gasport Welding & Fabg Inc ....F...... 716 772-7205
  Gasport *(G-5137)*
Genesee Metal Products Inc ....E...... 585 968-6000
  Wellsville *(G-15671)*
George Industries LLC ....G...... 607 748-3371
  Endicott *(G-4458)*
Gibraltar Industries Inc ....D...... 716 826-6500
  Buffalo *(G-2775)*
Glenridge Fabricators Inc ....F...... 718 456-2297
  Glendale *(G-5227)*
Hansen Steel ....E...... 585 398-2020
  Farmington *(G-4772)*
Hebeler LLC ....C...... 716 873-9300
  Tonawanda *(G-15111)*
Homer Iron Works LLC ....G...... 607 749-3963
  Homer *(G-6064)*
Industrial Fabricating Corp ....E...... 315 437-3353
  East Syracuse *(G-4218)*
Industrial Support Inc ....D...... 716 662-2954
  Buffalo *(G-2809)*
Inscape (new York) Inc ....D...... 716 665-6210
  Falconer *(G-4544)*
Inter Metal Fabricators Inc ....F...... 718 852-4000
  Brooklyn *(G-1962)*
Irony Limited Inc ....G...... 631 329-4065
  East Hampton *(G-4123)*
Irv Schroder & Sons Inc ....E...... 518 828-0194
  Stottville *(G-14753)*
J F M Sheet Metal Inc ....E...... 631 737-8494
  Ronkonkoma *(G-13950)*
J M Haley Corp ....C...... 631 845-5200
  Farmingdale *(G-4654)*
Jaab Precision Inc ....C...... 631 218-3725
  Ronkonkoma *(G-13953)*
James Woerner Inc ....G...... 631 454-9330
  Farmingdale *(G-4656)*
Jaxson LLC ....E...... 631 842-7775
  Amityville *(G-279)*
Jbs LLC ....E...... 518 346-0001
  Scotia *(G-14333)*
Jentsch & Co Inc ....G...... 716 852-4111
  Buffalo *(G-2819)*
Joy Edward Company ....E...... 315 474-3360
  Syracuse *(G-14921)*
Jpw Structural Contracting Inc ....E...... 315 432-1111
  Syracuse *(G-14922)*
K & E Fabricating Company Inc ....F...... 716 829-1829
  Buffalo *(G-2827)*
Kal Manufacturing Corporation ......E...... 585 265-4310
  Webster *(G-15644)*
KDO Industries Inc ....G...... 631 608-4612
  Amityville *(G-284)*
King Steel Iron Work Corp ....F...... 718 384-7500
  Brooklyn *(G-2030)*

Kleinfelder John	G	716 753-3163
Mayville (G-7683)		
Knj Fabricators LLC	F	347 234-6985
Bronx (G-1294)		
Koenig Iron Works Inc	E	718 433-0900
Long Island City (G-7263)		
Kryten Iron Works Inc	G	914 345-0990
Hawthorne (G-5816)		
L&B Fabricators LLC	F	585 265-2731
Ontario (G-12292)		
Lindenhurst Fabricators Inc	G	631 226-3737
Lindenhurst (G-6954)		
M & E Mfg Co Inc	D	845 331-7890
Kingston (G-6702)		
M & L Steel & Ornamental Iron	F	718 816-8660
Staten Island (G-14678)		
Major-IPC Inc	G	845 292-2200
Liberty (G-6925)		
Marex Aquisition Corp	C	585 458-3940
Rochester (G-13536)		
Mason Industries Inc	C	631 348-0282
Hauppauge (G-5708)		
Maspeth Welding Inc	E	718 497-5430
Maspeth (G-7627)		
Metal Crafts Inc	G	718 443-3333
Brooklyn (G-2146)		
Metal Fab LLC	G	607 775-3200
Binghamton (G-898)		
Metal Works of NY Inc	G	718 525-9440
Jamaica (G-6459)		
Metro Iron Corp	G	631 842-5929
Amityville (G-296)		
Miscellnous Ir Fabricators Inc	E	518 355-1822
Schenectady (G-14290)		
Mobile Mini Inc	F	315 732-4555
Utica (G-15285)		
Modern Mechanical Fab Inc	G	518 298-5177
Champlain (G-3315)		
Nathan Steel Corp	F	315 797-1335
Utica (G-15287)		
Nb Elctrcal Enclsures Mfrs Inc	G	718 272-8792
Brooklyn (G-2194)		
Nci Group Inc	D	315 339-1245
Rome (G-13859)		
Neversink Steel Corp	E	845 292-4611
Liberty (G-6926)		
New Age Ironworks Inc	F	718 277-1895
Brooklyn (G-2199)		
New Vision Industries Inc	F	607 687-7700
Endicott (G-4466)		
New York Manufactured Products	F	585 254-9353
Rochester (G-13570)		
North E Rggers Erectors NY Inc	E	518 842-6377
Amsterdam (G-342)		
Northeast Fabricators LLC	D	607 865-4031
Walton (G-15476)		
Oehlers Wldg & Fabrication Inc	F	716 821-1800
Buffalo (G-2894)		
Orange County Ironworks LLC	E	845 769-3000
Montgomery (G-8064)		
Oriskany Mfg Tech LLC	E	315 732-4962
Yorkville (G-16378)		
P K G Equipment Incorporated	E	585 436-4650
Rochester (G-13605)		
Patsy Strocchia & Sons Iron Wo	F	516 625-8800
Albertson (G-148)		
Pcx Aerostructures LLC	E	631 467-2632
Farmingdale (G-4702)		
Penasack Machine Company Inc	E	585 589-7044
Albion (G-159)		
Peralta Metal Works Inc	G	718 649-8661
Brooklyn (G-2254)		
Perma Tech Inc	E	716 854-0707
Buffalo (G-2915)		
Pierce Industries LLC	E	585 458-0888
Rochester (G-13623)		
Pierce Steel Fabricators	F	716 372-7652
Olean (G-12240)		
Pirod Inc	E	631 231-7660
Hauppauge (G-5742)		
Precision Metals Corp	E	631 586-5032
Bay Shore (G-700)		
Precision Polish LLC	E	315 894-3792
Frankfort (G-4955)		
Precision Spclty Fbrctions LLC	E	716 824-2108
Buffalo (G-2929)		
Prime Materials Recovery Inc	G	315 697-5251
Canastota (G-3154)		
Productand Design Inc	F	718 858-2440
Brooklyn (G-2297)		

Pwf Enterprise LLC	F	315 695-2223
Phoenix (G-12620)		
Raulli and Sons Inc	D	315 479-6693
Syracuse (G-14972)		
REO Welding Inc	F	518 238-1022
Cohoes (G-3514)		
Risa Management Corp	E	718 361-2606
Maspeth (G-7637)		
RJ Precision LLC	G	585 768-8030
Stafford (G-14605)		
Robert E Derecktor Inc	D	914 698-0962
Mamaroneck (G-7522)		
Roman Iron Works Inc	F	516 621-1103
Greenvale (G-5463)		
Romar Contracting Inc	G	845 778-2737
Walden (G-15461)		
Roth Design & Consulting Inc	E	718 209-0193
Brooklyn (G-2357)		
Rothe Welding Inc	E	845 246-3051
Saugerties (G-14210)		
Rough Brothers Holding Co	G	716 826-6500
Buffalo (G-2965)		
Rs Automation	F	585 589-0199
Albion (G-160)		
Rus Industries Inc	E	716 284-7828
Niagara Falls (G-11975)		
Salit Specialty Rebar Inc	E	716 299-1990
Buffalo (G-2974)		
Schneider Brothers Corporation	E	315 458-8369
Syracuse (G-14988)		
Schuler-Subra Inc	E	716 893-3100
Buffalo (G-2975)		
Seibel Modern Mfg & Wldg Corp	D	716 683-1536
Lancaster (G-6834)		
Sentry Metal Blast Inc	E	716 285-5241
Lockport (G-7106)		
Silverstone Shtmtl Fbrications	G	718 422-0380
Brooklyn (G-2416)		
Specialty Steel Fabg Corp	F	718 893-6326
Bronx (G-1368)		
Specialty Wldg & Fabg NY Inc	D	315 426-1807
Syracuse (G-14998)		
Steel Tech SA LLC	G	845 786-3691
Thiells (G-15065)		
Stone Well Bodies & Mch Inc	E	315 497-3512
Genoa (G-5168)		
Team Fabrication Inc	G	716 655-4038
West Falls (G-15762)		
Tms Structures Inc	C	646 740-7646
New York (G-11503)		
Triton Builders Inc	E	631 841-2534
Amityville (G-314)		
Tropical Driftwood Originals	G	516 623-0980
Roosevelt (G-14034)		
Tymetal Corp	E	518 692-9930
Fort Edward (G-4945)		
Tymetal Corp	E	518 692-9930
Greenwich (G-5477)		
Ulster Precision Inc	E	845 338-0995
Kingston (G-6717)		
United Iron Inc	E	914 667-5700
Mount Vernon (G-8191)		
United Structure Solution Inc	F	347 227-7526
New York (G-11601)		
Universal Metal Works LLC	F	315 598-7607
Fulton (G-5076)		
Vance Metal Fabricators Inc	D	315 789-5626
Geneva (G-5165)		
Vulcan Iron Works Inc	G	631 395-6846
Manorville (G-7555)		
Welding Metallurgy Inc	D	631 586-5200
Edgewood (G-4293)		
Werok LLC	F	845 675-7710
Valley Cottage (G-15329)		
Whitacre Engineering Company	G	315 622-1075
Liverpool (G-7049)		
Winters Railroad Service Inc	G	716 337-2668
North Collins (G-12030)		
Xli Manufacturing LLC	E	585 436-2250
Rochester (G-13812)		

STEEL MILLS

Albaluz Films LLC	G	347 613-2321
New York (G-8506)		
Baker Tool & Die	G	716 694-2025
North Tonawanda (G-12056)		
Belmet Products Inc	E	718 542-8220
Bronx (G-1212)		
CFS Enterprises Inc	E	718 585-0500
Bronx (G-1223)		

China Industrial Steel Inc	G	646 328-1502
New York (G-8989)		
Coventry Manufacturing Co Inc	E	914 668-2212
Mount Vernon (G-8134)		
David Fehlman	G	315 455-8888
Syracuse (G-14875)		
Hmi Metal Powders	C	315 839-5421
Clayville (G-3456)		
Jaquith Industries Inc	E	315 478-5700
Syracuse (G-14916)		
Juniper Elbow Co Inc	C	718 326-2546
Middle Village (G-7881)		
Kenbenco Inc	F	845 246-3066
Saugerties (G-14203)		
L&B Fabricators LLC	F	585 265-2731
Ontario (G-12292)		
Niagara Specialty Metals Inc	E	716 542-5552
Akron (G-19)		
Republic Steel Inc	B	716 827-2800
Blasdell (G-920)		
Samuel Son & Co (usa) Inc	G	716 856-6500
Blasdell (G-921)		
Tms International LLC	G	315 253-8925
Auburn (G-499)		

STEEL, COLD-ROLLED: Sheet Or Strip, From Own Hot-Rolled

Renco Group Inc	G	212 541-6000
New York (G-11012)		

STEEL, COLD-ROLLED: Strip NEC, From Purchased Hot-Rolled

Worthington Industries Inc	D	315 336-5500
Rome (G-13877)		

STEEL, HOT-ROLLED: Sheet Or Strip

Jfe Engineering Corporation	F	212 310-9320
New York (G-9999)		
Jfe Steel America Inc	G	212 310-9320
New York (G-10000)		

STEEL: Cold-Rolled

Aero-Data Metal Crafters Inc	C	631 471-7733
Ronkonkoma (G-13892)		
Clover Wire Forming Co Inc	E	914 375-0400
Yonkers (G-16296)		
Gibraltar Industries Inc	D	716 826-6500
Buffalo (G-2775)		
Northeast Cnstr Inds Inc	F	845 565-1000
Montgomery (G-8062)		
Rough Brothers Holding Co	G	716 826-6500
Buffalo (G-2965)		

STEEL: Galvanized

Elderlee Incorporated	C	315 789-6670
Oaks Corners (G-12161)		

STEEL: Laminated

Advantech Industries Inc	C	585 247-0701
Rochester (G-13213)		

STENCIL BOARD: Die-Cut, Made From Purchased Materials

Precision Diecutting Inc	G	315 776-8465
Port Byron (G-12811)		

STENCILS

Crafters Workshop Inc	G	914 345-2838
Elmsford (G-4404)		

STONE: Cast Concrete

Alp Stone Inc	F	718 706-6166
Long Island City (G-7151)		
Corinthian Cast Stone Inc	E	631 920-2340
Wyandanch (G-16244)		

STONE: Crushed & Broken, NEC

Labrador Stone Inc	G	570 465-2120
Binghamton (G-893)		

Employee Codes: A=Over 500 employees, B=251-500
C=101-250, D=51-100, E=20-50, F=10-19, G=5-9

2020 Harris
New York Manufacturers Directory

1229

PRODUCT

STONE: Dimension, NEC

Dominic De Nigris Inc ....E 718 597-4460
Bronx (G-1241)

Suffolk Granite Manufacturing ....E 631 226-4774
Lindenhurst (G-6977)

STONE: Quarrying & Processing, Own Stone Prdts

Callanan Industries Inc ....E 845 331-6868
Kingston (G-6683)

Dalrymple Holding Corp ....E 607 737-6200
Pine City (G-12628)

Graymont Materials Inc ....E 518 561-5200
Plattsburgh (G-12749)

Hanson Aggregates PA LLC ....E 315 789-6202
Oaks Corners (G-12162)

Iroquois Rock Products Inc ....F 585 381-7010
Rochester (G-13484)

Thalle Industries Inc ....E 914 762-3415
Briarcliff Manor (G-1162)

STONEWARE CLAY MINING

Devonian Stone New York Inc ....E 607 655-2600
Windsor (G-16157)

STORE FIXTURES, EXC REFRIGERATED: Wholesalers

Alrod Associates Inc ....F 631 981-2193
Ronkonkoma (G-13900)

Artistry In Wood of Syracuse.........E 315 431-4022
Syracuse (G-14819)

Leo D Bernstein & Sons Inc ....E 212 337-9578
New York (G-10198)

STORE FIXTURES: Exc Wood

Alrod Associates Inc ....F 631 981-2193
Ronkonkoma (G-13900)

Fixtures 2000 Inc ....B 631 236-4100
Hauppauge (G-5651)

Hamlet Products Inc ....F 914 665-0307
Mount Vernon (G-8147)

Yaloz Mould & Die Co Inc ....E 718 389-1131
Brooklyn (G-2599)

STORE FIXTURES: Wood

Abbott Industries Inc ....B 718 291-0800
Jamaica (G-6423)

Alrod Associates Inc ....F 631 981-2193
Ronkonkoma (G-13900)

Custom Wood Inc ....G 718 927-4700
Brooklyn (G-1713)

Falvo Manufacturing Co Inc ....F 315 724-7925
Utica (G-15261)

L & J Interiors Inc ....G 631 218-0838
Bohemia (G-1031)

Longo Commercial Cabinets Inc ....E 631 225-4290
Lindenhurst (G-6956)

Madjek Inc ....D 631 842-4475
Amityville (G-293)

STORE FRONTS: Prefabricated, Metal

Eastern Storefronts & Mtls Inc ....F 631 471-7065
Ronkonkoma (G-13933)

Empire Archtctural Systems Inc........E 518 773-5109
Johnstown (G-6615)

Gamma North Corporation.............E 716 902-5100
Alden (G-169)

Pk30 System LLC ....F 212 473-8050
Stone Ridge (G-14736)

STORE FRONTS: Prefabricated, Wood

Empire Archtctural Systems Inc........E 518 773-5109
Johnstown (G-6615)

STORES: Auto & Home Supply

Bartell Machinery Systems LLC ....C 315 336-7600
Rome (G-13843)

STRAPPING

Gibraltar Industries Inc ....D 716 826-6500
Buffalo (G-2775)

Rough Brothers Holding Co ....G 716 826-6500
Buffalo (G-2965)

STRAPS: Bindings, Textile

Ambind Corp ....G 716 836-4365
Buffalo (G-2628)

New York Binding Co Inc ....E 718 729-2454
Long Island City (G-7309)

STRAPS: Braids, Textile

La Lame Inc ....G 212 921-9770
New York (G-10158)

STRAPS: Cotton Webbing

Sturges Manufacturing Co Inc ....D 315 732-6159
Utica (G-15295)

STRAWS: Drinking, Made From Purchased Materials

Plastirun Corporation ....D 631 273-2626
Brentwood (G-1126)

Sqp Inc ....C 518 831-6800
Schenectady (G-14307)

STRINGING BEADS

Toho Company Limited ....G 212 391-9058
New York (G-11504)

STRUCTURAL SUPPORT & BUILDING MATERIAL: Concrete

Cossitt Concrete Products Inc ....F 315 824-2700
Hamilton (G-5526)

Geotech Associates Ltd ....G 631 286-0251
Brookhaven (G-1408)

STUDIOS: Artist's

Donne Dieu Paper Mill Inc ....G 212 226-0573
Brooklyn (G-1757)

Eskayel Inc ....G 347 703-8084
Brooklyn (G-1812)

STUDIOS: Sculptor's

Surving Studios ....F 845 355-1430
Middletown (G-7934)

STUDS & JOISTS: Sheet Metal

Studco Building Systems US LLC.........D 585 545-3000
Webster (G-15655)

SUBSCRIPTION FULFILLMENT SVCS: Magazine, Newspaper, Etc

Time Inc Affluent Media Group............G 212 382-5600
New York (G-11490)

SUGAR SUBSTITUTES: Organic

American Hlth Formulations Inc...........G 631 392-1756
Hauppauge (G-5590)

Cumberland Packing Corp ....B 718 858-4200
Brooklyn (G-1708)

Dulcette Technologies LLC ....G 631 752-8700
Lindenhurst (G-6951)

Flavors Holdings Inc ....F 212 572-8677
New York (G-9509)

Sugar Foods Corporation ....E 212 753-6900
New York (G-11385)

SUNDRIES & RELATED PRDTS: Medical & Laboratory, Rubber

Hutchinson Industries Inc ....E 716 852-1435
Buffalo (G-2802)

Impladent Ltd ....G 718 465-1810
Jamaica (G-6449)

Jamestown Scientific Inds LLC ....F 716 665-3224
Jamestown (G-6525)

Life Medical Technologies LLC ....F 845 894-2121
Hopewell Junction (G-6099)

Remedies Surgical Supplies ....G 718 599-5301
Brooklyn (G-2339)

Tmp Technologies Inc ....D 585 495-6231
Wyoming (G-16253)

United Rubber Supply Co Inc ....G 212 233-6650
New York (G-11600)

SUNGLASSES, WHOLESALE

Luxottica of America Inc ....C 516 484-3800
Port Washington (G-12902)

SUNROOMS: Prefabricated Metal

Latium USA Trading LLC................D 631 563-4000
Holbrook (G-6004)

Sunbilt Solar Pdts By Sussman ....D 718 297-0228
Jamaica (G-6477)

SUPERMARKETS & OTHER GROCERY STORES

Ives Farm Market......................G 315 592-4880
Fulton (G-5065)

Melita Corp ....C 718 392-7280
Astoria (G-429)

Ravioli Store Inc ....G 718 729-9300
Long Island City (G-7340)

TLC-Lc Inc ....E 212 756-8900
New York (G-11501)

SURFACE ACTIVE AGENTS

Bigsky Technologies LLC ....G 585 270-5282
Rochester (G-13269)

Halmark Architectural Finshg ....E 718 272-1831
Brooklyn (G-1919)

Momentive Performance Mtls Inc ......D 914 784-4807
Tarrytown (G-15049)

Suit-Kote Corporation ....F 716 683-8850
Buffalo (G-2995)

SURFACE ACTIVE AGENTS: Oils & Greases

Comander Terminals LLC ....F 516 922-7600
Oyster Bay (G-12446)

SURGICAL & MEDICAL INSTRUMENTS WHOLESALERS

Derm-Buro Inc ....E 516 694-8300
Plainview (G-12678)

Ppi Corp ....D 585 243-0300
Rochester (G-13633)

SURGICAL APPLIANCES & SPLYS

Proficient Surgical Eqp Inc ....G 516 487-1175
Port Washington (G-12916)

SURGICAL APPLIANCES & SPLYS

ACS Custom USA LLC ....G 646 559-5642
New York (G-8450)

Argon Medical Devices Inc ....G 585 321-1130
Henrietta (G-5855)

Avanti U S A Ltd ....F 716 695-5800
Tonawanda (G-15087)

Backtech Inc ....G 973 279-0838
New York (G-8712)

Byer California ....G 212 944-8989
New York (G-8878)

Centinel Spine LLC ....G 212 583-9700
New York (G-8949)

Community Products LLC..............E 845 658-7720
Chester (G-3373)

Community Products LLC..............G 518 589-5103
Elka Park (G-4304)

Cy Plastics Works Inc ....D 585 229-2555
Honeoye (G-6068)

Derm-Buro Inc ....E 516 694-8300
Plainview (G-12678)

Eschen Prsthetic Orthotic Labs ....F 516 871-0029
Hicksville (G-5906)

Far Rockaway Drugs Inc ....F 718 471-2500
Far Rockaway (G-4565)

Flexible Lifeline Systems Inc ....E 716 896-4949
Buffalo (G-2754)

Grand Slam Holdings LLC ....E 212 583-5000
New York (G-9660)

Hanger Inc ....E 518 435-0840
Albany (G-84)

Hanger Inc ....F 607 431-2526
Oneonta (G-12272)

Hanger Inc ....E 518 438-4546
East Syracuse (G-4215)

Hanger Inc ....G 718 575-5504
Forest Hills (G-4920)

Hanger Prosthetics & ....G 315 492-6608
Syracuse (G-14907)

Hanger Prsthetcs & Ortho Inc...............G..... 516 338-4466
Westbury (G-15893)
Hanger Prsthetcs & Ortho Inc...............G..... 718 892-1103
Bronx (G-1272)
Hanger Prsthetcs & Ortho Inc...............F..... 607 277-6620
Ithaca (G-6384)
Hanger Prsthetcs & Ortho Inc...............G..... 607 776-8013
Bath (G-634)
Howmedica Osteonics Corp...................G..... 518 783-1880
Latham (G-6859)
Howmedica Osteonics Corp...................G..... 516 484-0897
Port Washington (G-12884)
Instrumentation Laboratory Co...............C..... 845 680-0028
Orangeburg (G-12321)
Integer Holdings Corporation.................D..... 716 759-5200
Clarence (G-3435)
J P R Pharmacy Inc.............................F..... 718 327-0600
Far Rockaway (G-4566)
Konrad Prosthetics & Orthotics..............F..... 516 485-9164
West Hempstead (G-15773)
Mayflower Splint Co............................E..... 631 549-5131
Dix Hills (G-4011)
Medline Industries Inc........................B..... 845 344-3301
Middletown (G-7919)
Monaghan Medical Corporation..............D..... 518 561-7330
Plattsburgh (G-12760)
Nucare Pharmacy Inc..........................F..... 212 426-9300
New York (G-10653)
Nucare Pharmacy West LLC...................F..... 212 462-2525
New York (G-10654)
Overhead Door Corporation...................D..... 518 828-7652
Hudson (G-6173)
Pall Biomedical Inc.............................C..... 516 484-3600
Port Washington (G-12912)
Pall Corporation................................A..... 607 753-6041
Cortland (G-3779)
Pall Corporation................................A..... 607 753-6041
Cortland (G-3780)
Pall Corporation................................A..... 516 484-2818
Port Washington (G-12914)
Pall Corporation................................A..... 607 753-6041
Cortland (G-3781)
Premier Brands America Inc...................C..... 914 667-6200
White Plains (G-16054)
Scientific Plastics Inc.........................F..... 212 967-1199
New York (G-11166)
Silipos Holding LLC............................G..... 716 283-0700
Niagara Falls (G-11981)
SPS Medical Supply Corp......................D..... 585 359-0130
Rush (G-14074)
Steris Corporation.............................G..... 845 469-4087
Chester (G-3387)
Synthes Usa LLC...............................C..... 607 271-2500
Horseheads (G-6138)
Tumble Forms Inc..............................C..... 315 429-3101
Dolgeville (G-4027)
Turbine Engine Comp Utica...................A..... 315 768-8070
Whitesboro (G-16084)
Wyeth Holdings LLC............................D..... 845 602-5000
Pearl River (G-12543)

SURGICAL EQPT: See Also Instruments

Abyrx Inc..F..... 914 357-2600
Irvington (G-6305)
Avery Biomedical Devices Inc................F..... 631 864-1600
Commack (G-3578)
Conmed Corporation...........................B..... 315 797-8375
Utica (G-15248)
Integer Holdings Corporation.................D..... 716 759-5200
Clarence (G-3435)
Lake Region Medical Inc.......................C..... 716 662-5025
Orchard Park (G-12361)
Medipoint Inc....................................F..... 516 294-8822
Mineola (G-7989)
Schilling Forge Inc.............................E..... 315 454-4421
Syracuse (G-14987)
Surgical Design Corp..........................F..... 914 273-2445
Armonk (G-403)
T G M Products Inc.............................G..... 631 491-0515
Wyandanch (G-16247)

SURGICAL IMPLANTS

Agnovos Healthcare LLC......................F..... 646 502-5860
New York (G-8495)
Bionic Eye Technologies Inc..................G..... 845 505-5254
Ithaca (G-6369)
Paradigm Spine LLC............................E..... 888 273-9897
New York (G-10755)
Rigicon Inc......................................G..... 631 676-3376
Ronkonkoma (G-14003)

SURVEYING SVCS: Aerial Digital Imaging

Systems Drs C3 Inc............................B..... 716 631-6200
Buffalo (G-3000)

SVC ESTABLISHMENT EQPT & SPLYS WHOLESALERS

Architectural Textiles USA Inc................E..... 212 213-6972
New York (G-8619)
Licenders.......................................G..... 212 759-5200
New York (G-10210)

SVC ESTABLISHMENT EQPT, WHOL: Cleaning & Maint Eqpt & Splys

Jad Corp of America...........................E..... 718 762-8900
College Point (G-3548)

SVC ESTABLISHMENT EQPT, WHOLESALE: Beauty Parlor Eqpt & Sply

Ivy Enterprises Inc............................B..... 516 621-9779
Port Washington (G-12890)

SVC ESTABLISHMENT EQPT, WHOLESALE: Firefighting Eqpt

Johnson Controls...............................G..... 845 774-4120
Harriman (G-5545)

SVC ESTABLISHMENT EQPT, WHOLESALE: Laundry Eqpt & Splys

Coinmach Service Corp.........................A..... 516 349-8555
Plainview (G-12670)
CSC SW Holdco Inc.............................D..... 516 349-8555
Plainview (G-12677)
G A Braun Inc...................................C..... 315 475-3123
North Syracuse (G-12041)
Low-Cost Mfg Co Inc...........................G..... 516 627-3282
Carle Place (G-3176)
Spin Holdco Inc.................................G..... 516 349-8555
Plainview (G-12715)

SWEEPING COMPOUNDS

Bono Sawdust Supply Co Inc..................G..... 718 446-1374
Corona (G-3734)

SWIMMING POOL ACCESS: Leaf Skimmers Or Pool Rakes

Swimline International Corp...................C..... 631 254-2155
Edgewood (G-4285)

SWIMMING POOL EQPT: Filters & Water Conditioning Systems

Pentair Water Pool and Spa Inc..............E..... 845 452-5500
Lagrangeville (G-6753)
Pleatco LLC.....................................D..... 516 609-0200
Glen Cove (G-5198)

SWIMMING POOL SPLY STORES

Clean All of Syracuse LLC.....................G..... 315 472-9189
Syracuse (G-14852)

SWIMMING POOLS, EQPT & SPLYS: Wholesalers

Imperial Pools Inc.............................C..... 518 786-1200
Latham (G-6860)

SWITCHBOARDS & PARTS: Power

Electric Swtchbard Sltions LLC..............G..... 718 643-1105
New Hyde Park (G-8264)

SWITCHES

Sector Microwave Inds Inc....................D..... 631 242-2245
Deer Park (G-3935)

SWITCHES: Electric Power

Adeptronics Incorporated.....................G..... 631 667-0659
Bay Shore (G-643)
Marquardt Switches Inc........................C..... 315 655-8050
Cazenovia (G-3231)

Nsi Industries LLC.............................C..... 800 841-2505
Mount Vernon (G-8166)
Tork Inc...D..... 914 664-3542
Mount Vernon (G-8183)
Transistor Devices Inc.........................E..... 631 471-7492
Ronkonkoma (G-14017)

SWITCHES: Electric Power, Exc Snap, Push Button, Etc

Atlas Switch Co Inc............................E..... 516 222-6280
Garden City (G-5090)

SWITCHES: Electronic

Dortronics Systems Inc........................E..... 631 725-0505
Sag Harbor (G-14098)
Kearney-National Inc..........................F..... 212 661-4600
New York (G-10087)
NEa Manufacturing Corp.......................E..... 516 371-4200
Inwood (G-6300)
Scientific Components Corp....................E..... 718 934-4500
Brooklyn (G-2390)
Spectron Glass & Electronics.................F..... 631 582-5600
Hauppauge (G-5769)

SWITCHES: Electronic Applications

Dortronics Systems Inc........................E..... 631 725-0505
Sag Harbor (G-14098)
Machine Components Corp.....................E..... 516 694-7222
Plainview (G-12698)
Switches and Sensors Inc......................F..... 631 924-2167
Yaphank (G-16273)

SWITCHES: Silicon Control

Senera Co Inc...................................F..... 516 639-3774
Valley Stream (G-15358)

SWITCHES: Starting, Fluorescent

Monarch Electric Products Inc................G..... 718 583-7996
Bronx (G-1318)

SWITCHES: Time, Electrical Switchgear Apparatus

Ems Development Corporation...............D..... 631 924-4736
Yaphank (G-16259)

SWITCHGEAR & SWITCHBOARD APPARATUS

All City Switchboard Corp.....................E..... 718 956-7244
Long Island City (G-7149)
Cooper Power Systems LLC....................B..... 716 375-7100
Olean (G-12230)
Inertia Switch Inc..............................E..... 845 359-8300
Orangeburg (G-12319)
Marquardt Switches Inc........................C..... 315 655-8050
Cazenovia (G-3231)
Schneider Electric Usa Inc....................C..... 646 335-0220
New York (G-11157)
Select Controls Inc............................E..... 631 567-9010
Bohemia (G-1076)
Sinclair Technologies Inc......................E..... 716 874-3682
Hamburg (G-5521)

SWITCHGEAR & SWITCHGEAR ACCESS, NEC

Cooper Industries LLC.........................F..... 315 477-7000
Syracuse (G-14864)
Electrotech Service Eqp Corp.................E..... 718 626-7700
Astoria (G-419)

SWORDS

Starfire Swords Ltd Inc........................E..... 607 589-7244
Spencer (G-14550)

SYNTHETIC RESIN FINISHED PRDTS, NEC

General Composites Inc........................E..... 518 963-7333
Willsboro (G-16151)
Kaneka America LLC...........................D..... 212 705-4340
New York (G-10066)

SYRUPS, DRINK

Pepsi-Cola Metro Btlg Co Inc.................G..... 914 767-6000
White Plains (G-16047)

P
R
O
D
U
C
T

SYRUPS, FLAVORING, EXC DRINK

3v Company Inc ....E 718 858-7333
  Brooklyn (G-1417)
Fox 416 Corp ....E 718 385-4600
  Brooklyn (G-1864)
Mapleland Farms LLC ....G 518 854-7669
  Salem (G-14133)

SYSTEMS INTEGRATION SVCS

Binghamton Simulator Co Inc ....E 607 321-2980
  Binghamton (G-860)
Medsim-Eagle Simulation Inc ....F 607 658-9354
  Endicott (G-4464)
New Media Investment Group Inc ...B 212 479-3160
  New York (G-10586)
Telxon Corporation ....E 631 738-2400
  Holtsville (G-6056)

SYSTEMS INTEGRATION SVCS: Local Area Network

Sphere Cables & Chips Inc ....E 212 619-3132
  New York (G-11322)

SYSTEMS SOFTWARE DEVELOPMENT SVCS

Ex El Enterprises Ltd ....F 212 489-4500
  New York (G-9434)
Inprotopia Corporation ....F 917 338-7501
  New York (G-9901)
Napco Security Tech Inc ....C 631 842-9400
  Amityville (G-297)
Sale 121 Corp ....D 240 855-8988
  New York (G-11117)
Schoolnet Inc ....C 646 496-9000
  New York (G-11164)
Verint Systems Inc ....C 631 962-9600
  Melville (G-7834)

TABLE OR COUNTERTOPS, PLASTIC LAMINATED

Allegany Laminating and Supply ....G 716 372-2424
  Allegany (G-186)
Contempra Design Inc ....G 718 984-8586
  Staten Island (G-14642)
Kitchen Specialty Craftsmen ....G 607 739-0833
  Elmira (G-4361)
Red White & Blue Entps Corp ....G 718 565-8080
  Woodside (G-16223)
Wilsonart Intl Holdings LLC ....E 516 935-6980
  Bethpage (G-846)

TABLECLOTHS & SETTINGS

Broder Mfg Inc ....G 718 366-1667
  Brooklyn (G-1610)
E & F Home Fashions Inc ....G 718 968-9719
  Brooklyn (G-1770)
Royal Copenhagen Inc ....F 845 454-4442
  Poughkeepsie (G-12980)

TABLES: Lift, Hydraulic

Columbus McKinnon Corporation ....C 716 689-5400
  Getzville (G-5174)
Columbus McKinnon Corporation ....C 716 689-5400
  Getzville (G-5175)
Columbus McKinnon Corporation ....C 716 689-5400
  Getzville (G-5176)

TABLETS & PADS: Book & Writing, Made From Purchased Material

Duck Flats Pharma ....G 315 689-3407
  Elbridge (G-4297)
USA Custom Pad Corp ....E 607 563-9550
  Sidney (G-14439)

TABLEWARE OR KITCHEN ARTICLES: Commercial, Fine Earthenware

Green Wave International Inc ....G 718 499-3371
  Brooklyn (G-1909)
Korin Inc ....E 212 587-7021
  New York (G-10128)

TABLEWARE: Plastic

Pactiv LLC ....A 585 393-3149
  Canandaigua (G-3139)
Q Squared Design LLC ....E 212 686-8860
  New York (G-10942)

TAGS & LABELS: Paper

Auto Data Systems Inc ....E 631 667-2382
  Deer Park (G-3843)
Depot Label Company Inc ....G 631 467-2952
  Patchogue (G-12499)
Gooding Co Inc ....G 716 266-6252
  Lockport (G-7082)
K Sidrane Inc ....E 631 393-6974
  Farmingdale (G-4659)
Stickershopcom Inc ....G 631 563-4323
  Bayport (G-731)

TAGS: Paper, Blank, Made From Purchased Paper

Jerry Tomaselli ....F 718 965-1400
  Brooklyn (G-1991)
Tag Envelope Co Inc ....E 718 389-6844
  College Point (G-3567)

TAILORS: Custom

Adrian Jules Ltd ....D 585 342-5886
  Rochester (G-13207)

TALLOW: Animal

Baker Commodities Inc ....E 585 482-1880
  Rochester (G-13259)

TANK COMPONENTS: Military, Specialized

Tecmotiv (usa) Inc ....E 716 282-1211
  Niagara Falls (G-11986)

TANK REPAIR SVCS

David Isseks & Sons Inc ....E 212 966-8694
  New York (G-9179)
Tecmotiv (usa) Inc ....E 716 282-1211
  Niagara Falls (G-11986)

TANK TOWERS: Metal Plate

Vertarib Inc ....G 561 683-0888
  Jericho (G-6597)

TANKS & OTHER TRACKED VEHICLE CMPNTS

Lourdes Industries Inc ....D 631 234-6600
  Hauppauge (G-5700)

TANKS: Concrete

Preload Concrete Structures ....E 631 231-8100
  Hauppauge (G-5748)

TANKS: Cryogenic, Metal

North American Svcs Group LLC ....F 518 885-1820
  Ballston Spa (G-583)

TANKS: Fuel, Including Oil & Gas, Metal Plate

Cardinal Tank Corp ....E 718 625-4350
  Brooklyn (G-1647)
Crown Tank Company LLC ....F 855 276-9682
  Horseheads (G-6119)
Stutzman Management Corp ....F 800 735-2013
  Lancaster (G-6836)

TANKS: Lined, Metal

Amherst Stnless Fbrication LLC ....E 716 691-7012
  Amherst (G-211)
General Oil Equipment Co Inc ....E 716 691-7012
  Amherst (G-225)
Modutank Inc ....F 718 392-1112
  Long Island City (G-7298)

TANKS: Plastic & Fiberglass

An-Cor Industrial Plastics Inc ....D 716 695-3141
  North Tonawanda (G-12052)

Chem-Tek Systems Inc

Chem-Tek Systems Inc ....F 631 253-3010
  Bay Shore (G-662)
Norwesco Inc ....F 607 687-8081
  Owego (G-12435)

TANKS: Standard Or Custom Fabricated, Metal Plate

Expert Industries Inc ....E 718 434-6060
  Brooklyn (G-1823)
Feldmeier Equipment Inc ....D 315 823-2000
  Syracuse (G-14893)
Gasport Welding & Fabg Inc ....F 716 772-7205
  Gasport (G-5137)
K Industries Inc ....G 631 897-2125
  Bellport (G-801)
Stainless Metals Inc ....F 718 784-1454
  Woodside (G-16228)
Stavo Industries Inc ....F 845 331-4552
  Kingston (G-6712)
Steelways Inc ....E 845 562-0860
  Newburgh (G-11887)
Taylor Tank Company Inc ....E 718 434-1300
  Brooklyn (G-2494)

TANKS: Storage, Farm, Metal Plate

Bigbee Steel and Tank Company ....E 518 273-0801
  Watervliet (G-15597)

TANKS: Water, Metal Plate

David Isseks & Sons Inc ....E 212 966-8694
  New York (G-9179)
Jbren Corp ....F 716 332-5928
  Buffalo (G-2817)
Water Cooling Corp ....G 718 723-6500
  Rosedale (G-14038)

TANKS: Wood

Rosenwach Tank Co Inc ....E 212 972-4411
  Astoria (G-439)

TANNERIES: Leather

Colonial Tanning Corporation ....F 518 725-7171
  Gloversville (G-5281)
Myers Group LLC ....G 973 761-6414
  New York (G-10525)
Simco Leather Corporation ....E 518 762-7100
  Johnstown (G-6628)
Tradition Leather Inc ....E 518 725-2555
  Gloversville (G-5297)
Wood & Hyde Leather Co Inc ....E 518 725-7105
  Gloversville (G-5301)

TAPES, ADHESIVE: MedicaL

Eis Legacy LLC ....E 585 426-5330
  Rochester (G-13380)
Tape Systems Inc ....F 914 668-3700
  Mount Vernon (G-8181)

TAPES: Audio Range, Blank

Orpheo USA Corp ....G 212 464-8255
  New York (G-10711)

TAPES: Coated Fiberglass, Pipe Sealing Or Insulating

GM Insulation Corp ....F 516 354-6000
  Elmont (G-4385)

TAPES: Gummed, Cloth Or Paper Based, From Purchased Matls

Patco Tapes Inc ....G 718 497-1527
  Maspeth (G-7634)

TAPES: Magnetic

Professional Tape Corporation ....G 516 656-5519
  Glen Cove (G-5199)

TAPES: Pressure Sensitive

Berry Specialty Tapes LLC ....C 631 727-6000
  Riverhead (G-13172)
Kleen Stik Industries Inc ....F 718 984-5031
  Staten Island (G-14674)

2020 Harris
New York Manufacturers Directory
(G-0000) Company's Geographic Section entry number

Merco Hackensack Inc ....G...... 845 357-3699
  Hillburn (G-5970)
T L F Graphics Inc ....D...... 585 272-5500
  Rochester (G-13757)
Tape-It Inc ....E...... 631 243-4100
  Bay Shore (G-721)
Valley Industrial Products Inc ....E...... 631 385-9300
  Huntington (G-6231)

TARGET DRONES

Enlighten Air Inc ....G...... 917 656-1248
  New York (G-9380)

TARPAULINS

Breton Industries Inc ....C...... 518 842-3030
  Amsterdam (G-320)

TELECOMMUNICATION SYSTEMS & EQPT

Aines Manufacturing Corp ....E...... 631 471-3900
  Islip (G-6350)
Alcatel-Lucent USA Inc ....D...... 516 349-4900
  Plainview (G-12661)
Clayton Dubilier & Rice Fun ....E...... 212 407-5200
  New York (G-9029)
Corning Incorporated ....E...... 607 248-1200
  Corning (G-3708)
Corning Incorporated ....A...... 607 974-9000
  Painted Post (G-12473)
Corning Incorporated ....A...... 607 974-9000
  Corning (G-3705)
ESi Cases & Accessories Inc ....E...... 212 883-8838
  New York (G-9397)
Forerunner Technologies Inc ....E...... 631 337-2100
  Edgewood (G-4268)
Interdgital Communications LLC ....C...... 631 622-4000
  Melville (G-7795)
Kelta Inc ....E...... 631 789-5000
  Edgewood (G-4273)
L3 Technologies Inc ....A...... 631 436-7400
  Hauppauge (G-5687)
L3harris Technologies Inc ....E...... 585 244-5830
  Rochester (G-13511)
Mitel Networks Inc ....G...... 877 654-3573
  Rochester (G-13553)
Parabit Systems Inc ....E...... 516 378-4800
  Bellmore (G-786)
Performance Technologies Inc ....E...... 585 256-0200
  Rochester (G-13615)
Snake Tray International LLC ....E...... 631 674-0004
  Bay Shore (G-716)
Telephonics Corporation ....D...... 631 755-7659
  Farmingdale (G-4751)
Telephonics Corporation ....A...... 631 755-7000
  Farmingdale (G-4752)
Tii Technologies Inc ....E...... 516 364-9300
  Edgewood (G-4287)

TELECOMMUNICATIONS CARRIERS & SVCS: Wired

Forerunner Technologies Inc ....E...... 631 337-2100
  Edgewood (G-4268)
Human Electronics Inc ....G...... 315 724-9850
  Utica (G-15272)

TELEMARKETING BUREAUS

S & H Uniform Corp ....D...... 914 937-6800
  White Plains (G-16057)

TELEMETERING EQPT

L3 Foreign Holdings Inc ....C...... 212 697-1111
  New York (G-10153)
L3 Technologies Inc ....B...... 631 231-1700
  Hauppauge (G-5686)
L3 Technologies Inc ....D...... 631 231-1700
  Hauppauge (G-5688)
L3 Technologies Inc ....B...... 212 697-1111
  New York (G-10154)

TELEPHONE ANSWERING SVCS

Milne Mfg Inc ....F...... 716 772-2536
  Gasport (G-5139)

TELEPHONE BOOTHS, EXC WOOD

Clark Specialty Co Inc ....E...... 607 776-3193
  Bath (G-632)

Parabit Systems Inc ....E...... 516 378-4800
  Bellmore (G-786)

TELEPHONE EQPT INSTALLATION

Telecommunication Concepts ....G...... 315 736-8523
  Whitesboro (G-16083)

TELEPHONE EQPT: Modems

Simrex Corporation ....G...... 716 206-0174
  Buffalo (G-2983)

TELEPHONE EQPT: NEC

ABS Talkx Inc ....G...... 631 254-9100
  Bay Shore (G-642)
Audio-Sears Corp ....D...... 607 652-7305
  Stamford (G-14606)
Avaya Services Inc ....G...... 866 462-8292
  New York (G-8688)
Call Forwarding Technologies ....G...... 516 621-3600
  Greenvale (G-5460)
Eagle Telephonics Inc ....F...... 631 471-3600
  Bohemia (G-1007)
I D Tel Corp ....F...... 718 876-6000
  Staten Island (G-14662)
Luxcore Networks Inc ....F...... 212 618-1724
  New York (G-10285)
Polycom Inc ....E...... 212 372-6960
  New York (G-10862)
R I R Communications Systems ....E...... 718 706-9957
  Mount Vernon (G-8175)
Siemens AG ....G...... 212 946-2440
  New York (G-11225)
Siemens Corporation ....F...... 202 434-7800
  New York (G-11226)
Siemens USA Holdings Inc ....B...... 212 258-4000
  New York (G-11228)
Telecommunication Concepts ....G...... 315 736-8523
  Whitesboro (G-16083)
Toshiba Amer Info Systems Inc ....B...... 949 583-3000
  New York (G-11518)

TELEPHONE SVCS

Tempo Industries Inc ....G...... 516 334-6900
  Westbury (G-15929)

TELEPHONE SWITCHING EQPT

Redcom Laboratories Inc ....C...... 585 924-6567
  Victor (G-15428)

TELEPHONE: Autotransformers For Switchboards

Astrocom Electronics Inc ....D...... 607 432-1930
  Oneonta (G-12258)

TELEPHONE: Fiber Optic Systems

Fiber Instrument Sales Inc ....C...... 315 736-2206
  Oriskany (G-12390)
Fiberwave Corporation ....C...... 718 802-9011
  Brooklyn (G-1840)
Fujitsu Ntwrk Cmmnications Inc ....F...... 845 731-2000
  Pearl River (G-12531)
Photonstring Inc ....G...... 917 966-5717
  Godeffroy (G-5302)
Sandstone Technologies Corp ....G...... 585 785-5537
  Rochester (G-13713)
Sandstone Technologies Corp ....G...... 585 785-5537
  Rochester (G-13714)
Splice Technologies Inc ....G...... 631 924-8108
  Manorville (G-7554)
Terahertz Technologies Inc ....G...... 315 736-3642
  Oriskany (G-12398)

TELEPHONE: Headsets

Quality One Wireless LLC ....C...... 631 233-3337
  Ronkonkoma (G-13999)
U2o Usa LLC ....G...... 516 813-9500
  Plainview (G-12720)

TELEPHONE: Sets, Exc Cellular Radio

Maia Systems LLC ....G...... 718 206-0100
  Jamaica (G-6456)
Powermate Cellular ....G...... 718 833-9400
  Brooklyn (G-2274)

TELEVISION BROADCASTING & COMMUNICATIONS EQPT

Basil S Kadhim ....G...... 888 520-5192
  New York (G-8736)
Prime View USA Inc ....G...... 212 730-4905
  New York (G-10891)

TELEVISION BROADCASTING STATIONS

21st Century Fox America Inc ....D...... 212 852-7000
  New York (G-8396)
General Electric Company ....A...... 518 385-4022
  Schenectady (G-14266)
New York Times Company ....B...... 212 556-1234
  New York (G-10604)
Tegna Inc ....C...... 716 849-2222
  Buffalo (G-3005)
Tribune Entertainment Co Del ....E...... 203 866-2204
  New York (G-11543)

TELEVISION SETS

Jwin Electronics Corp ....C...... 516 626-7188
  Port Washington (G-12894)
Toshiba America Inc ....E...... 212 596-0600
  New York (G-11519)

TELEVISION: Closed Circuit Eqpt

Click It Inc ....D...... 631 686-2900
  Hauppauge (G-5618)
Sartek Industries Inc ....G...... 631 473-3555
  East Setauket (G-4186)
Sentry Technology Corporation ....F...... 800 645-4224
  Ronkonkoma (G-14007)

TELEVISION: Monitors

Home Tech LLC ....G...... 914 301-5408
  Katonah (G-6633)

TEMPERING: Metal

Elmira Heat Treating Inc ....E...... 607 734-1577
  Elmira (G-4350)

TENT REPAIR SHOP

Custom Canvas Manufacturing Co ....E...... 716 852-6372
  Buffalo (G-2717)

TENTS: All Materials

Air Structures Amercn Tech Inc ....E...... 914 937-4500
  Port Chester (G-12812)
AMS Star Structures Inc ....G...... 914 584-0898
  Nyack (G-12135)
Dhs Systems LLC ....F...... 845 359-6066
  Orangeburg (G-12312)
Johnson Outdoors Inc ....C...... 607 779-2200
  Binghamton (G-891)
Kraus & Sons Inc ....F...... 212 620-0408
  New York (G-10137)
Leiter Sukkahs Inc ....E...... 718 436-0303
  Brooklyn (G-2061)
Select Fabricators Inc ....F...... 585 393-0650
  Canandaigua (G-3142)
Toptec Products LLC ....F...... 631 421-9800
  Melville (G-7831)

TERMINAL BOARDS

Veja Electronics Inc ....D...... 631 321-6086
  Deer Park (G-3949)

TERRA COTTA: Architectural

Boston Valley Pottery Inc ....C...... 716 649-7490
  Orchard Park (G-12340)

TEST KITS: Pregnancy

Ithaca Pregancy Center ....G...... 607 753-3909
  Cortland (G-3772)
Northeast Doulas ....G...... 845 621-0654
  Mahopac (G-7476)
Working Family Solutions Inc ....G...... 845 802-6182
  Saugerties (G-14216)

TESTERS: Battery

Sorfin Yoshimura Ltd ....G...... 516 802-4600
  Woodbury (G-16183)

Walter R Tucker Entps Ltd ....E 607 467-2866
Deposit (G-4004)

TESTERS: Environmental

Caltex International Ltd ....E 315 425-1040
Syracuse (G-14840)
Nexgen Enviro Systems Inc..................G 631 226-2930
Lindenhurst (G-6964)
Niagara Scientific Inc..........................E 315 437-0821
East Syracuse (G-4228)

TESTERS: Integrated Circuit

Epoch Microelectronics Inc ....G 914 332-8570
Valhalla (G-15303)
Xelic Incorporated.................................F 585 415-2764
Pittsford (G-12658)

TESTERS: Physical Property

G E Inspection Technologies LP ....C 315 554-2000
Skaneateles (G-14451)
Gleason Corporation ....A 585 473-1000
Rochester (G-13444)
Gleason Works ....A 585 473-1000
Rochester (G-13445)
Gurley Precision Instrs Inc ....C 518 272-6300
Troy (G-15170)

TESTERS: Water, Exc Indl Process

Industrial Municipal Equipment............F 631 665-6712
Brightwaters (G-1171)

TEXTILE & APPAREL SVCS

Crye Precision LLC ....C 718 246-3838
Brooklyn (G-1705)
Newcastle Fabrics Corp ....G 718 388-6600
Brooklyn (G-2212)
RAK Finishing Corp................................E 718 416-4242
Howard Beach (G-6141)

TEXTILE BAGS WHOLESALERS

Adam Scott Designs Inc.........................E 212 420-8866
New York (G-8453)
Nochairs Inc...G 917 748-8731
New York (G-10635)

TEXTILE CONVERTERS: Knit Goods

Bank-Miller Co Inc.................................E 914 227-9357
Pelham (G-12565)
Sextet Fabrics Inc ....F 516 593-0608
Roosevelt (G-14032)

TEXTILE FABRICATORS

Dream Green Productions ....G 917 267-8920
Warwick (G-15513)

TEXTILE FINISH: Chem Coat/Treat, Fire Resist, Manmade

American Spray-On Corp.......................E 212 929-2100
New York (G-8559)
Beckmann Converting Inc.....................E 518 842-0073
Amsterdam (G-318)

TEXTILE FINISHING: Chemical Coating Or Treating

Reynolds Drapery Service Inc...............F 315 845-8632
Newport (G-11899)

TEXTILE FINISHING: Decorative, Man Fiber & Silk, Broadwoven

Toltec Fabrics Inc..................................C 212 706-9310
New York (G-11506)

TEXTILE FINISHING: Dyeing, Broadwoven, Cotton

B & K Dye Cutting Inc............................G 718 497-5216
Brooklyn (G-1556)
Dyenamix Inc..G 212 941-6642
New York (G-9287)

TEXTILE FINISHING: Dyeing, Finishing & Printng, Linen Fabric

American Country Quilts & Lin.............G 631 283-5466
Southampton (G-14526)
China Ting Fshion Group USA LL........G 212 716-1600
New York (G-8993)
Duck River Textiles Inc.........................F 212 679-2980
New York (G-9277)

TEXTILE FINISHING: Dyeing, Manmade Fiber & Silk, Broadwoven

Eastern Silk Mills Inc ....G 212 730-1300
New York (G-9305)

TEXTILE FINISHING: Embossing, Cotton, Broadwoven

Lee Dyeing Company NC Inc ....F 518 736-5232
Johnstown (G-6622)

TEXTILE FINISHING: Embossing, Man Fiber & Silk, Broadwoven

Knucklehead Embroidery Inc ....G 607 797-2725
Johnson City (G-6605)

TEXTILE FINISHING: Silk, Broadwoven

Raxon Fabrics Corp...............................F 212 532-6816
New York (G-10984)

TEXTILE FINISHING: Sponging, Cotton, Broadwoven, Trade

Basiloff LLC...G 646 671-0353
New York (G-8737)

TEXTILE: Finishing, Cotton Broadwoven

All About Art Inc ....F 718 321-0755
Flushing (G-4837)
Carolyn Ray Inc ....G 914 476-0619
Yonkers (G-16294)
Central Textiles Inc ....F 212 213-8740
New York (G-8953)
Marcel Finishing Corp ....E 718 381-2889
Plainview (G-12699)
Prismatic Dyeing & Finshg Inc ....D 845 561-1800
Newburgh (G-11883)

TEXTILE: Finishing, Raw Stock NEC

Hosel & Ackerson Inc ....G 212 575-1490
New York (G-9814)
Majestic Rayon Corporation ....E 212 929-6443
New York (G-10334)
Marcel Finishing Corp ....E 718 381-2889
Plainview (G-12699)
National Spinning Co Inc ....E 212 382-6400
New York (G-10546)
Newcastle Fabrics Corp ....G 718 388-6600
Brooklyn (G-2212)
Prismatic Dyeing & Finshg Inc ....D 845 561-1800
Newburgh (G-11883)
Skin Prints Inc ....G 845 920-8756
Pearl River (G-12541)

TEXTILE: Goods, NEC

Southern Adrndck Fbr Prdcrs CP ....G 518 692-2700
Greenwich (G-5476)

TEXTILES

Stern & Stern Industries Inc..................D 607 324-4485
Hornell (G-6111)

TEXTILES: Bagging, Jute

Ivi Services Inc ....D 607 729-5111
Binghamton (G-889)

TEXTILES: Fibers, Textile, Rcvrd From Mill Waste/Rags

Ace Drop Cloth Canvas Pdts Inc..........E 718 731-1550
Bronx (G-1193)

TEXTILES: Flock

J Rettenmaier USA LP ....D 716 693-4040
North Tonawanda (G-12074)
J Rettenmaier USA LP ....D 716 693-4009
North Tonawanda (G-12075)

TEXTILES: Linen Fabrics

David King Linen Inc ....F 718 241-7298
New York (G-9180)
Novita Fabrics Furnishing Corp ....F 516 299-4500
Mineola (G-7994)
Sabbsons International Inc ....F 718 360-1947
Brooklyn (G-2379)
Sam Salem & Son LLC ....F 212 695-6020
New York (G-11124)
Simple Elegance New York Inc ....F 718 360-1947
Brooklyn (G-2419)
TRM Linen Inc..G 718 686-6075
Brooklyn (G-2524)

TEXTILES: Mill Waste & Remnant

Dean Trading Corp.................................F 718 485-0600
Brooklyn (G-1732)
S Hellerman Inc......................................F 718 622-2995
Brooklyn (G-2377)

TEXTILES: Tops & Top Processing, Manmade Or Other Fiber

Jo-Vin Decorators Inc...........................E 718 441-9350
Woodhaven (G-16187)

THEATRICAL LIGHTING SVCS

Creative Stage Lighting Co Inc.............E 518 251-3302
North Creek (G-12031)

THEATRICAL PRODUCERS & SVCS

Congress For Jewish Culture ....G 212 505-8040
New York (G-9083)
Peermusic Ltd ....F 212 265-3910
New York (G-10788)

THEATRICAL SCENERY

Costume Armour Inc ....F 845 534-9120
Cornwall (G-3728)
King Displays Inc ....F 212 629-8455
New York (G-10107)
Production Resource Group LLC...........D 877 774-7088
Armonk (G-401)
Production Resource Group LLC...........E 845 567-5700
New Windsor (G-8378)
Stiegelbauer Associates Inc ....E 718 624-0835
Brooklyn (G-2461)

THERMOMETERS: Indl

Kessler Thermometer Corp....................G 631 841-5500
West Babylon (G-15722)
Oden Machinery Inc...............................E 716 874-3000
Tonawanda (G-15129)

THERMOMETERS: Medical, Digital

Accuvein Inc...D 816 997-9400
Medford (G-7697)

THERMOPLASTIC MATERIALS

Bso Energy Corp....................................F 212 520-1827
New York (G-8865)

THERMOPLASTICS

ADC Acquisition Company ....E 518 377-6471
Niskayuna (G-11994)
On Time Plastics Inc ....G 516 442-4280
Freeport (G-5011)

THERMOSETTING MATERIALS

Empire Plastics Inc ....E 607 754-9132
Endwell (G-4479)

THIN FILM CIRCUITS

CAM Touchview Products Inc................F 631 842-3400
Sag Harbor (G-14096)

THREAD: All Fibers

Albany International Corp ....C...... 607 749-7226
  Homer (G-6060)
United Thread Mills Corp ....G...... 516 536-3900
  Oceanside (G-12195)
V Technical Textiles Inc ....G...... 315 597-1674
  Palmyra (G-12494)

THREAD: Embroidery

American Quality Embroidery ....G...... 631 467-3200
  Ronkonkoma (G-13903)
One In A Million Inc ....G....... 516 829-1111
  Valley Stream (G-15350)

TICKET OFFICES & AGENCIES: Theatrical

London Theater News Ltd ....F...... 212 517-8608
  New York (G-10247)

TIES, FORM: Metal

American Wire Tie Inc ....E...... 716 337-2412
  North Collins (G-12023)

TILE: Asphalt, Floor

Shenfield Studio LLC.....................F...... 315 436-8869
  Syracuse (G-14994)

TILE: Brick & Structural, Clay

Stone and Bath Gallery ....G...... 718 438-4500
  Brooklyn (G-2462)

TILE: Drain, Clay

Bistrian Cement Corporation ....F...... 631 324-1123
  East Hampton (G-4117)

TILE: Fireproofing, Clay

Certified Flameproofing Corp............G...... 631 265-4824
  Smithtown (G-14474)
Noroc Enterprises Inc....................C...... 718 585-3230
  Bronx (G-1325)

TILE: Stamped Metal, Floor Or Wall

Surving Studios ....F...... 845 355-1430
  Middletown (G-7934)

TILE: Terrazzo Or Concrete, Precast

Foro Marble Co Inc ....E...... 718 852-2322
  Brooklyn (G-1859)
Walter G Legge Company Inc ....G...... 914 737-5040
  Peekskill (G-12560)

TILE: Vinyl, Asbestos

Adore Floors Inc ....G...... 631 843-0900
  Farmingdale (G-4573)

TILE: Wall & Floor, Ceramic

Aremco Products Inc ....F...... 845 268-0039
  Valley Cottage (G-15313)
Dal-Tile Corporation ....G...... 914 835-1801
  Harrison (G-5552)
Lazer Marble & Granite Corp ....G...... 718 859-9644
  Brooklyn (G-2049)

TILE: Wall & Floor, clay

Quality Components Framing Sys ....F...... 315 768-1167
  Whitesboro (G-16081)

TIMBER PRDTS WHOLESALERS

Guldenschuh Logging & Lbr LLC ....G...... 585 538-4750
  Caledonia (G-3070)

TIMING DEVICES: Electronic

Eversan Inc ....F...... 315 736-3967
  Whitesboro (G-16080)
Infitec Inc ....D...... 315 433-1150
  East Syracuse (G-4222)

TIN

Mustard Tin ....G...... 315 769-8409
  Massena (G-7669)

Tin Rage Productions Inc.................G...... 718 398-0787
  Brooklyn (G-2506)

TIRE & INNER TUBE MATERIALS & RELATED PRDTS

Handy & Harman Ltd ....A...... 212 520-2300
  New York (G-9720)
Roli Retreads Inc..........................E...... 631 694-7670
  Farmingdale (G-4726)
Sph Group Holdings LLC ....F...... 212 520-2300
  New York (G-11321)

TIRE & TUBE REPAIR MATERIALS, WHOLESALE

Loomis Root Inc............................F...... 716 564-7668
  Amherst (G-230)

TIRE CORD & FABRIC

Albany International Corp ....C...... 518 445-2230
  Menands (G-7838)
Designatronics Incorporated ....B...... 516 328-3300
  New Hyde Park (G-8261)
Haines Equipment Inc ....E...... 607 566-8531
  Avoca (G-510)
York Industries Inc ....E...... 516 746-3736
  Garden City Park (G-5126)

TIRE INFLATORS: Hand Or Compressor Operated

Vac Air Service Inc ....F...... 716 665-2206
  Jamestown (G-6552)

TIRES & INNER TUBES

East Coast Intl Tire Group Inc ....G...... 718 386-9088
  Maspeth (G-7610)
East Coast Intl Tire Inc ....F...... 718 386-9088
  Maspeth (G-7611)

TIRES: Auto

McCarthy Tire Svc Co NY Inc.............F...... 518 449-5185
  Menands (G-7845)

TITANIUM MILL PRDTS

Titanium Dem Remediation Group........F...... 716 433-4100
  Lockport (G-7112)

TOBACCO & TOBACCO PRDTS WHOLESALERS

Kk International Trading Corp ....E...... 516 801-4741
  Syosset (G-14790)

TOBACCO LEAF PROCESSING

Schweitzer-Mauduit Intl Inc.................C...... 518 329-4222
  Ancram (G-355)

TOBACCO: Chewing

National Tobacco Company LP ....F...... 212 253-8185
  New York (G-10548)
Standard Diversified Inc.................E...... 302 248-1100
  Mineola (G-8001)

TOBACCO: Chewing & Snuff

Elab Smokers Boutique...................G...... 585 865-4513
  Rochester (G-13381)

TOBACCO: Cigarettes

East End.....................................F...... 716 532-2622
  Collins (G-3570)
Jacobs Tobacco Company ....E...... 518 358-4948
  Hogansburg (G-5980)
Kk International Trading Corp ....E...... 516 801-4741
  Syosset (G-14790)
Onondaga Nation ....G...... 315 469-3230
  Nedrow (G-8216)
Philip Morris Globl Brands Inc ....G...... 917 663-2000
  New York (G-10827)
Philip Morris Intl Inc......................D...... 917 663-2000
  New York (G-10828)
PMI Global Services Inc ....E...... 917 663-2000
  New York (G-10858)

R J Reynolds Tobacco Company ....C...... 716 871-1553
  Tonawanda (G-15135)
Schweitzer-Mauduit Intl Inc................C...... 518 329-4222
  Ancram (G-355)
Seneca Manufacturing Company ....G...... 716 945-4400
  Salamanca (G-14128)
Seneca Nation Enterprise ....F...... 716 934-7430
  Irving (G-6304)
Vector Group Ltd ....C...... 212 409-2800
  New York (G-11651)

TOBACCO: Cigars

American Cigar ....G...... 718 969-0008
  Fresh Meadows (G-5037)
Mafco Consolidated Group Inc ....F...... 212 572-8600
  New York (G-10318)

TOBACCO: Smoking

Mafco Consolidated Group Inc.............F...... 212 572-8600
  New York (G-10318)

TOILET FIXTURES: Plastic

Metpar Corp................................D...... 516 333-2600
  Westbury (G-15910)

TOILET PREPARATIONS

H & H Laboratories Inc ....F...... 718 624-8041
  Brooklyn (G-1914)
H & H Laboratories Inc ....G...... 718 624-8041
  Brooklyn (G-1915)
King Research Inc ....E...... 718 788-0122
  Brooklyn (G-2028)
MZB Accessories LLC....................D...... 718 472-7500
  Long Island City (G-7301)

TOILETRIES, COSMETICS & PERFUME STORES

Bastide Inc.................................D...... 646 356-0460
  New York (G-8739)
Estee Lauder Inc ....D...... 631 531-1000
  Melville (G-7781)
US Nonwovens Corp ....D...... 631 952-0100
  Brentwood (G-1132)

TOILETRIES, WHOLESALE: Hair Preparations

EL Erman International Ltd ....G...... 212 444-9440
  Brooklyn (G-1789)

TOILETRIES, WHOLESALE: Perfumes

Elias Fragrances Inc......................F...... 718 693-6400
  Rye Brook (G-14088)
Elite Parfums Ltd ....D...... 212 983-2640
  New York (G-9345)
Eternal Love Parfums Corp................F...... 516 921-6100
  Syosset (G-14786)
Scent-A-Vision Inc ....E...... 631 424-4905
  Huntington Station (G-6259)
Sundial Fragrances & Flavors ....E...... 631 842-8800
  Amityville (G-310)

TOILETRIES, WHOLESALE: Toilet Preparations

Quality King Distributors Inc ....C...... 631 439-2027
  Ronkonkoma (G-13998)

TOILETRIES, WHOLESALE: Toiletries

Bfma Holding Corporation ....G...... 607 753-6746
  Cortland (G-3755)
Gassho Body & Mind Inc.................G...... 518 695-9991
  Schuylerville (G-14324)
Marietta Corporation ....A...... 323 589-8181
  Cortland (G-3777)
Nea Naturals Inc ....G...... 845 522-8042
  New Windsor (G-8373)
Robell Research Inc......................G...... 212 755-6577
  New York (G-11059)

TOMBSTONES: Terrazzo Or Concrete, Precast

Eaton Brothers Corp......................G...... 716 649-8250
  Hamburg (G-5505)

TOOL & DIE STEEL

Baker Tool & Die & Die ....G 716 694-2025
North Tonawanda (G-12057)

TOOLS: Carpenters', Including Levels & Chisels, Exc Saws

Nyc District Council Ubcja ....G 212 366-7500
New York (G-10660)

TOOLS: Hand

Allway Tools Inc ....D 718 792-3636
Bronx (G-1202)
Ames Companies Inc ....E 607 739-4544
Pine Valley (G-12634)
Best Way Tools By Anderson Inc ....G 631 586-4702
Deer Park (G-3845)
Coastel Cable Tools Inc ....E 315 471-5361
Syracuse (G-14855)
Dead Ringer LLC ....G 585 355-4685
Rochester (G-13340)
Dresser-Argus Inc ....G 718 643-1540
Brooklyn (G-1762)
Huron TI Cutter Grinding Inc ....E 631 420-7000
Farmingdale (G-4646)
Hydramec Inc ....E 585 593-5190
Scio (G-14325)
Ivy Classic Industries Inc ....E 914 632-8200
New Rochelle (G-8343)
Robinson Tools LLC ....G 585 586-5432
Penfield (G-12573)
Schilling Forge Inc ....E 315 454-4421
Syracuse (G-14987)
Snyder Manufacturing Inc ....E 716 945-0354
Salamanca (G-14129)
U S Air Tool Co Inc ....E 631 471-3300
Ronkonkoma (G-14019)
Winters Railroad Service Inc ....G 716 337-2668
North Collins (G-12030)
York Industries Inc ....E 516 746-3736
Garden City Park (G-5126)

TOOLS: Hand, Engravers'

Edward C Lyons Company Inc ....G 718 515-5361
Bronx (G-1250)
Edward C Muller Corp ....F 718 881-7270
Bronx (G-1251)

TOOLS: Hand, Jewelers'

Boucheron Joaillerie USA Inc ....G 212 715-7330
New York (G-8839)
Empire Devleopment ....G 716 789-2097
Mayville (G-7682)

TOOLS: Hand, Mechanics

Classic Tool Design Inc ....E 845 562-8700
New Windsor (G-8363)

TOOLS: Hand, Plumbers'

Design Source By Lg Inc ....E 212 274-0022
New York (G-9207)
Metro City Group Inc ....G 516 781-2500
Bellmore (G-784)

TOOLS: Hand, Power

Allied Motion Technologies Inc ....C 315 782-5910
Watertown (G-15558)
Awt Supply Corp ....G 516 437-9105
Elmont (G-4383)
Black & Decker (us) Inc ....B 914 235-6300
Brewster (G-1143)
Black & Decker (us) Inc ....G 631 952-2008
Hauppauge (G-5605)
Black & Decker Corporation ....G 718 335-1042
Woodside (G-16198)
Dynabrade Inc ....C 716 631-0100
Clarence (G-3430)
Huck International Inc ....C 845 331-7300
Kingston (G-6694)
Ivy Classic Industries Inc ....E 914 632-8200
New Rochelle (G-8343)
Meritool LLC ....E 716 699-6005
Salamanca (G-14123)
Reimann & Georger Corporation ....E 716 895-1156
Buffalo (G-2951)

Stature Electric Inc ....F 716 242-7535
Amherst (G-244)
Thomas C Wilson LLC ....E 718 729-3360
Long Island City (G-7381)

TOOTHBRUSHES: Electric

Quip Nyc Inc ....G 917 331-3993
Brooklyn (G-2315)

TOOTHBRUSHES: Exc Electric

Colgate-Palmolive Company ....A 212 310-2000
New York (G-9051)

TOOTHPASTES, GELS & TOOTHPOWDERS

Colgat-Plmolive Centl Amer Inc ....F 212 310-2000
New York (G-9050)
Colgate-Palmolive Company ....A 212 310-2000
New York (G-9051)
Colgate-Palmolive Company ....B 718 506-3961
Queens Village (G-13018)
Quip Nyc Inc ....G 917 331-3993
Brooklyn (G-2315)

TOWELS: Indl

Blu Sand LLC ....G 212 564-1147
New York (G-8816)

TOWELS: Linen & Linen & Cotton Mixtures

Blc Textiles Inc ....E 844 500-7900
Mineola (G-7962)

TOWERS, SECTIONS: Transmission, Radio & Television

Fred A Nudd Corporation ....E 315 524-2531
Ontario (G-12289)

TOYS

Buffalo Games LLC ....D 716 827-8393
Buffalo (G-2674)
Church Communities NY Inc ....E 518 589-5103
Elka Park (G-4302)
Church Communities NY Inc ....E 518 589-5103
Elka Park (G-4303)
Creative Kids Far East Inc ....C 844 252-7263
Spring Valley (G-14565)
Dana Michele LLC ....G 917 757-7777
New York (G-9161)
Drescher Paper Box Inc ....F 716 854-0288
Clarence (G-3429)
First Brands LLC ....E 646 432-4366
Merrick (G-7855)
Glitter Slimes LLC ....G 845 772-1113
Goshen (G-5309)
Haba USA ....G 800 468-6873
Skaneateles (G-14453)
Habermaass Corporation ....F 315 729-0070
Skaneateles (G-14454)
Kling Magnetics Inc ....E 518 392-4000
Chatham (G-3331)
Master Juvenile Products Inc ....F 845 647-8400
Ellenville (G-4308)
Matel LLC ....G 646 825-6760
New York (G-10382)
Mattel Inc ....E 310 252-2000
East Aurora (G-4092)
Sandbox Brands Inc ....G 212 647-8877
New York (G-11130)
Swimways Corp ....C 757 460-1156
Long Island City (G-7377)
Toymax Inc ....G 212 633-6611
New York (G-11525)
Vogel Applied Technologies ....G 212 677-3136
New York (G-11702)
Way Out Toys Inc ....G 212 689-9094
New York (G-11732)

TOYS & HOBBY GOODS & SPLYS, WHOLESALE: Arts/Crafts Eqpt/Sply

Multi Packaging Solutions Inc ....E 646 885-0005
New York (G-10519)

TOYS & HOBBY GOODS & SPLYS, WHOLESALE: Balloons, Novelty

OH How Cute Inc ....G 347 838-6031
Staten Island (G-14687)

TOYS & HOBBY GOODS & SPLYS, WHOLESALE: Educational Toys

Global Video LLC ....D 516 222-2600
Woodbury (G-16172)
Ingenious Ingenuity Inc ....F 800 834-5279
Webster (G-15642)

TOYS & HOBBY GOODS & SPLYS, WHOLESALE: Toys & Games

Minted Green Inc ....G 845 458-1845
Airmont (G-14)
Way Out Toys Inc ....G 212 689-9094
New York (G-11732)

TOYS & HOBBY GOODS & SPLYS, WHOLESALE: Toys, NEC

Toymax Inc ....G 212 633-6611
New York (G-11525)

TOYS & HOBBY GOODS & SPLYS, WHOLESALE: Video Games

Barron Games Intl Co LLC ....F 716 630-0054
Buffalo (G-2655)

TOYS, HOBBY GOODS & SPLYS WHOLESALERS

Creative Kids Far East Inc ....C 844 252-7263
Spring Valley (G-14565)
Fierce Fun Toys LLC ....G 646 322-7172
New York (G-9491)
Habermaass Corporation ....F 315 729-0070
Skaneateles (G-14454)

TOYS: Dolls, Stuffed Animals & Parts

Community Products LLC ....E 518 589-5103
Elka Park (G-4304)
Dana Michele LLC ....G 917 757-7777
New York (G-9161)
First Brands LLC ....E 646 432-4366
Merrick (G-7855)
Jupiter Creations Inc ....G 917 493-9393
New York (G-10043)
Minted Green Inc ....G 845 458-1845
Airmont (G-14)
Naito International Corp ....F 718 309-2425
Rockville Centre (G-13832)

TOYS: Electronic

Littlebits Electronics Inc ....D 917 464-4577
New York (G-10231)
Wobbleworks Inc ....E 718 618-9904
New York (G-11772)

TOYS: Video Game Machines

C T A Digital Inc ....F 718 963-9845
Brooklyn (G-1636)
C T A Digital Inc ....E 845 513-0433
Monroe (G-8017)

TRADE SHOW ARRANGEMENT SVCS

212kiddish Inc ....G 718 705-7227
Brooklyn (G-1411)
Alm Media LLC ....B 212 457-9400
New York (G-8524)
Alm Media Holdings Inc ....B 212 457-9400
New York (G-8525)
International Data Group Inc ....E 212 331-7883
New York (G-9918)
Relx Inc ....E 212 309-8100
New York (G-11005)

TRADERS: Commodity, Contracts

De Meo Brothers Inc ....G 212 268-1400
New York (G-9192)

TRAILERS & PARTS: Boat

Performance Custom Trailer ....G...... 518 504-4021
  Lake George *(G-6758)*

TRAILERS & PARTS: Truck & Semi's

Cross Country Mfg Inc ....F 607 656-4103
  Greene *(G-5444)*
Davis Trailer World LLC ....F 585 538-6640
  York *(G-16362)*
General Welding & Fabg Inc ....G...... 716 652-0033
  Elma *(G-4319)*
Rolling Star Manufacturing Inc.............E 315 896-4767
  Barneveld *(G-595)*
Seneca Truck & Trailer Inc ....G...... 315 781-1100
  Geneva *(G-5163)*
Stone Well Bodies & Mch Inc...............E 315 497-3512
  Genoa *(G-5168)*

TRAILERS: Semitrailers, Truck Tractors

Blue Tee Corp ....G...... 212 598-0880
  New York *(G-8820)*

TRANSDUCERS: Electrical Properties

Pcb Group Inc ....E 716 684-0001
  Depew *(G-3992)*
Ruhle Companies Inc ....E 914 287-4000
  Valhalla *(G-15309)*

TRANSDUCERS: Pressure

Dylix Corporation ....E 716 773-2985
  Grand Island *(G-5328)*
Kinemotive Corporation ....E 631 249-6440
  Farmingdale *(G-4666)*

TRANSFORMERS: Control

Current Controls Inc ....C...... 585 593-1544
  Wellsville *(G-15668)*

TRANSFORMERS: Distribution

Electron Coil Inc...............................D...... 607 336-7414
  Norwich *(G-12121)*
Ems Development Corporation ....D...... 631 345-6200
  Yaphank *(G-16260)*
Kepco Inc.......................................D...... 718 461-7000
  Flushing *(G-4867)*
Schneider Electric It Corp ....F 646 335-0216
  New York *(G-11156)*

TRANSFORMERS: Distribution, Electric

Hale Electrical Dist Svcs Inc ....G...... 716 818-7595
  Wales Center *(G-15466)*
Siemens Corporation.........................F 202 434-7800
  New York *(G-11226)*
Siemens USA Holdings Inc ....B 212 258-4000
  New York *(G-11228)*
Supreme Lighting Design LLC ....F 718 812-3347
  Brooklyn *(G-2477)*

TRANSFORMERS: Electric

Niagara Transformer Corp ....D....... 716 896-6500
  Buffalo *(G-2887)*
Schneider Electric Usa Inc ....G...... 631 567-5710
  Bohemia *(G-1073)*
Transistor Devices Inc ....E 631 471-7492
  Ronkonkoma *(G-14017)*

TRANSFORMERS: Electronic

Atlantic Transformer Inc......................F 716 795-3258
  Barker *(G-590)*
Data Device Corporation ....B 631 567-5600
  Bohemia *(G-999)*
Esc Control Electronics LLC ....E 631 467-5328
  Sayville *(G-14225)*
Exxelia-Raf Tabtronics LLC ....E 585 243-4331
  Piffard *(G-12624)*
NEa Manufacturing Corp ....E 516 371-4200
  Inwood *(G-6300)*
Todd Systems Inc ....D....... 914 963-3400
  Yonkers *(G-16352)*
Urban Technologies Inc ....G...... 716 672-2709
  Fredonia *(G-4972)*

TRANSFORMERS: Ignition, Domestic Fuel Burners

Frederick Cowan & Company Inc..........F 631 369-0360
  Wading River *(G-15449)*

TRANSFORMERS: Power Related

Arstan Products International ....F 516 433-1313
  Hicksville *(G-5885)*
Berkshire Transformer ....G....... 631 467-5328
  Central Islip *(G-3265)*
Beta Transformer Tech Corp ....E 631 244-7393
  Bohemia *(G-980)*
Buffalo Power Electronics Ctr ....F 716 651-1600
  Depew *(G-3974)*
Caddell Burns Manufacturing Co ....E 631 757-1772
  Northport *(G-12100)*
Cooper Power Systems LLC.................B 716 375-7100
  Olean *(G-12230)*
Equus Power I LP ....G...... 847 908-2878
  West Babylon *(G-15710)*
Exxelia-Raf Tabtronics LLC ....E 585 243-4331
  Piffard *(G-12624)*
K Road Power Management LLC............G...... 212 351-0535
  New York *(G-10051)*
Piller Power Systems Inc ....F 845 695-6658
  Middletown *(G-7926)*
Ram Transformer Technologies ....F 914 632-3988
  New Rochelle *(G-8351)*
Sag Harbor Industries Inc ....E 631 725-0440
  Sag Harbor *(G-14101)*
Schneider Electric Usa Inc ....F 585 377-1313
  Penfield *(G-12574)*
Spence Engineering Company Inc.........C...... 845 778-5566
  Walden *(G-15462)*
Sunward Electronics Inc ....F 518 687-0030
  Troy *(G-15191)*
Switching Power Inc ....D...... 631 981-7231
  Ronkonkoma *(G-14016)*
Veeco Instruments Inc ....C...... 516 349-8300
  Plainview *(G-12724)*

TRANSFORMERS: Signaling Transformers, Electric

Railworks Corporation ....G...... 904 296-5055
  Farmingdale *(G-4723)*

TRANSFORMERS: Specialty

Dyco Electronics Inc.........................D...... 607 324-2030
  Hornell *(G-6104)*
Mitchell Electronics Corp....................E 914 699-3800
  Mount Vernon *(G-8162)*

TRANSLATION & INTERPRETATION SVCS

Language and Graphics Inc.................G...... 212 315-5266
  New York *(G-10172)*

TRANSMISSIONS: Motor Vehicle

A-Line Technologies Inc......................F 607 772-2439
  Binghamton *(G-850)*
Pro Torque ....E 631 218-8700
  Bohemia *(G-1067)*

TRANSPORTATION EPQT & SPLYS, WHOLESALE: Acft/Space Vehicle

Nell-Joy Industries Inc.......................E 631 842-8989
  Copiague *(G-3665)*

TRANSPORTATION EQPT & SPLYS WHOLESALERS, NEC

Worldwide Arntcal Cmpnents Inc..........G...... 631 842-3780
  Copiague *(G-3691)*
Zebra Technologies Entp Corp.............E 800 722-6234
  Holtsville *(G-6059)*

TRANSPORTATION EQUIPMENT, NEC

Truck-Lite Sub Inc ....G...... 800 888-7095
  Falconer *(G-4561)*

TRANSPORTATION: Local Passenger, NEC

Hampton Transport Inc ....F 631 716-4445
  Coram *(G-3693)*

TRAP ROCK: Crushed & Broken

Dolomite Products Company Inc ....E 585 586-2568
  Penfield *(G-12570)*
Tilcon New York Inc ....E 845 778-5591
  Walden *(G-15463)*
Tilcon New York Inc ....D...... 845 358-3100
  West Nyack *(G-15833)*

TRAPS: Animal & Fish, Wire

Cuba Specialty Mfg Co Inc...................E 585 567-4176
  Fillmore *(G-4793)*

TRAPS: Stem

John N Fehlinger Co Inc.....................F 212 233-5656
  New York *(G-10018)*

TRAVEL AGENCIES

Citic Intl (usa) Travel Inc.....................G...... 718 888-9577
  Flushing *(G-4844)*
Mapeasy Inc....................................F 631 537-6213
  Wainscott *(G-15455)*
Quinn and Co of NY Ltd ....D...... 212 868-1900
  New York *(G-10958)*
Rfp LLC ....E 212 838-7733
  New York *(G-11032)*

TRAVEL TRAILERS & CAMPERS

All Star Carts & Vehicles Inc ....D...... 631 666-5581
  Bay Shore *(G-646)*

TRAYS: Cable, Metal Plate

Mono-Systems Inc ....E 716 821-1344
  Buffalo *(G-2871)*

TRAYS: Plastic

Commodore Machine Co Inc ....E 585 657-6916
  Bloomfield *(G-943)*
SAV Thermo Inc ....F 631 249-9444
  West Babylon *(G-15746)*
Tully Products Inc ....G...... 716 773-3166
  Grand Island *(G-5346)*

TROPHIES, NEC

All American Awards Inc ....F 631 567-2025
  Bohemia *(G-968)*
Dwm International Inc........................F 646 290-7448
  Long Island City *(G-7207)*
Endurart Inc....................................E 212 473-7000
  New York *(G-9373)*

TROPHIES, PEWTER

Valerie Bohigian................................G...... 914 631-8866
  Sleepy Hollow *(G-14465)*

TROPHIES, PLATED, ALL METALS

Csi International Inc...........................E 800 441-2895
  Niagara Falls *(G-11919)*

TROPHIES, SILVER

Atlantic Trophy Co Inc.......................E 212 684-6020
  New York *(G-8668)*

TROPHIES: Metal, Exc Silver

C & M Products Inc ....G...... 315 471-3303
  Syracuse *(G-14838)*
Classic Medallics Inc........................E 718 392-5410
  Mount Vernon *(G-8131)*
New Dimension Awards Inc ....G...... 718 236-8200
  Brooklyn *(G-2202)*

TROPHY & PLAQUE STORES

Jem Sign Corp..................................G...... 516 867-4466
  Hempstead *(G-5840)*
Stamps & Signs Online Corp................G...... 718 218-0050
  Brooklyn *(G-2450)*

TRUCK & BUS BODIES: Ambulance

Jeffersonville Volunteer ....E 845 482-3110
  Jeffersonville *(G-6570)*

P
R
O
D
U
C
T

TRUCK & BUS BODIES: Motor Vehicle, Specialty

Kurtz Truck Equipment Inc ....F 607 849-3468
Marathon (G-7558)
Rexford Services Inc ....G...... 716 366-6671
Dunkirk (G-4065)

TRUCK & BUS BODIES: Truck, Motor Vehicle

Demartini Oil Equipment Svc.............G 518 463-5752
Glenmont (G-5236)
Eastern Welding Inc ....G 631 727-0306
Riverhead (G-13174)
Marros Equipment & Trucks ....F 315 539-8702
Waterloo (G-15555)
Renaldos Sales & Service Ctr ....G 716 337-3760
North Collins (G-12028)
Unicell Body Company Inc ....E 716 853-8628
Buffalo (G-3027)
Unicell Body Company Inc ....F 716 853-8628
Schenectady (G-14313)
Unicell Body Company Inc ....F 585 424-2660
Rochester (G-13781)
USA Body Inc ....G 315 852-6123
De Ruyter (G-3823)
Weld-Built Body Co Inc ....E 631 643-9700
Wyandanch (G-16248)

TRUCK BODIES: Body Parts

Brunner International Inc ....C 585 798-6000
Medina (G-7731)
Concrete Mixer Supplycom Inc ....G 716 375-5565
Olean (G-12229)
Ekostinger Inc ....F 585 739-0450
East Rochester (G-4161)
General Welding & Fabg Inc ....F 585 697-7660
Rochester (G-13434)
Tectran Mfg Inc.................................D 800 776-5549
Buffalo (G-3004)

TRUCK GENERAL REPAIR SVC

Bick & Heintz Inc..............................F 315 733-7577
Utica (G-15241)
Riverview Industries Inc.....................G 845 265-5284
Cold Spring (G-3524)

TRUCK PAINTING & LETTERING SVCS

Jem Sign Corp...................................G 516 867-4466
Hempstead (G-5840)
Monasani Signs Inc ....G 631 266-2635
East Northport (G-4150)

TRUCK PARTS & ACCESSORIES: Wholesalers

Unicell Body Company Inc...................E 716 853-8628
Buffalo (G-3027)

TRUCKING & HAULING SVCS: Garbage, Collect/Transport Only

Suffolk Indus Recovery Corp...............D 631 732-6403
Coram (G-3700)

TRUCKING, DUMP

Alice Perkins ....G 716 378-5100
Salamanca (G-14121)
Ribble Lumber Inc.............................G 315 536-6221
Penn Yan (G-12592)

TRUCKING: Except Local

Platinum Sales Promotion Inc ....G 718 361-0200
Long Island City (G-7327)

TRUCKING: Local, Without Storage

Clark Concrete Co Inc ....G 315 478-4101
Syracuse (G-14851)
Haley Concrete Inc............................F 716 492-0849
Delevan (G-3961)
J & S Logging Inc ....E 315 262-2112
South Colton (G-14503)
Little Valley Sand & Gravel..................G 716 938-6676
Little Valley (G-6999)

TRUCKS & TRACTORS: Industrial

ASAP Rack Rental Inc ....G...... 718 499-4495
Brooklyn (G-1539)
Channel Manufacturing Inc..................E 516 944-6271
Port Washington (G-12866)
Ducon Technologies Inc......................B 631 694-1700
New York (G-9278)
Ducon Technologies Inc......................E 631 420-4900
Farmingdale (G-4618)
E-One Inc ....D 716 646-6790
Hamburg (G-5504)
Raymond Corporation ....E 315 643-5000
East Syracuse (G-4232)

TRUCKS: Forklift

Continental Lift Truck Inc ....F 718 738-4738
South Ozone Park (G-14521)
Raymond Sales Corporation ....G 607 656-2311
Greene (G-5449)
Stanley Industrial Eqp LLC ....G 315 656-8733
Kirkville (G-6726)

TRUCKS: Indl

Meteor Express Inc ....F 718 551-9177
Jamaica (G-6460)
Pb08 Inc ....G 347 866-7353
Hicksville (G-5941)
W W Trading Co Inc ....E 718 935-1085
Brooklyn (G-2573)
Ward Lafrance Truck Corp ....F 518 893-1865
Saratoga Springs (G-14195)

TRUNKS

Junk In My Trunk Inc ....G 631 420-5865
Farmingdale (G-4658)
Rose Trunk Mfg Co Inc ....F 516 766-6686
Oceanside (G-12187)

TRUSSES & FRAMING: Prefabricated Metal

Countryside Truss LLC ....G 315 985-0643
Saint Johnsville (G-14116)

TRUSSES: Wood, Roof

Faulkner Truss Company Inc................G 315 536-8894
Dresden (G-4035)
Pdj Components Inc ....E 845 469-9191
Chester (G-3382)
Proof Industries Inc ....G 631 694-7663
Farmingdale (G-4717)
Rochester Lumber Company ....E 585 924-7171
Farmington (G-4778)
S R Sloan Inc ....D 315 736-7730
Whitesboro (G-16082)
Steele Truss Company Inc ....E 518 562-4663
Plattsburgh (G-12780)
Structural Wood Corporation ....E 315 388-4442
Waddington (G-15447)
Ufp New York LLC ....E 716 496-5484
Chaffee (G-3308)
Ufp New York LLC ....E 518 828-2888
Hudson (G-6182)
Ufp New York LLC ....E 315 253-2758
Auburn (G-501)

TUBE & TUBING FABRICATORS

Albany Nipple and Pipe Mfg.................E 518 270-2162
Troy (G-15157)
Coventry Manufacturing Co Inc............E 914 668-2212
Mount Vernon (G-8134)
Ram Fabricating LLC ....E 315 437-6654
Syracuse (G-14971)
Spinco Metal Products Inc ....D 315 331-6285
Newark (G-11852)
Star Tubing Corp ....G 716 483-1703
Jamestown (G-6543)
Tube Fabrication Company Inc.............F 716 673-1871
Fredonia (G-4971)

TUBES: Finned, For Heat Transfer

CMS Heat Transfer Division Inc............E 631 968-0084
Bohemia (G-990)

TUBES: Generator, Electron Beam, Beta Ray

E-Beam Services Inc..........................G 516 622-1422
Hicksville (G-5903)

TUBES: Paper

Caraustar Industries Inc ....G 716 874-0393
Buffalo (G-2692)

TUBES: Paper Or Fiber, Chemical Or Electrical Uses

Industrial Paper Tube Inc ....F 718 893-5000
Bronx (G-1281)

TUBES: Steel & Iron

Markin Tubing LP ....F 585 495-6211
Buffalo (G-2861)
TI Group Auto Systems LLC ....G 315 568-7042
Seneca Falls (G-14373)

TUBES: Vacuum

New Sensor Corporation ....D 718 937-8300
Long Island City (G-7308)

TUBES: Wrought, Welded Or Lock Joint

Markin Tubing LP ....C 585 495-6211
Wyoming (G-16250)
Markin Tubing Inc ....C 585 495-6211
Wyoming (G-16251)
Thyssenkrupp Materials NA Inc ....G 585 279-0000
West Seneca (G-15855)

TUBING: Flexible, Metallic

Conrad Blasius Equipment Co ....G 516 753-1200
Plainview (G-12672)

TUBING: Glass

Gray Glass Inc...................................E 718 217-2943
Queens Village (G-13020)

TUBING: Plastic

Finger Lakes Extrusion Corp................E 585 905-0632
Canandaigua (G-3132)
Hancor Inc ....D 607 565-3033
Waverly (G-15622)

TUBING: Seamless

TI Group Auto Systems LLC ....G 315 568-7042
Seneca Falls (G-14373)

TUNGSTEN CARBIDE

Buffalo Tungsten Inc ....D 716 683-9170
Depew (G-3975)
Niagara Refining LLC ....E 716 706-1400
Depew (G-3989)

TUNGSTEN CARBIDE POWDER

Golden Egret LLC ....G 516 922-2839
East Norwich (G-4152)

TURBINE GENERATOR SET UNITS: Hydraulic, Complete

Hdm Hydraulics LLC...........................D 716 694-8004
Tonawanda (G-15110)
Signa Chemistry Inc ....F 212 933-4101
New York (G-11234)

TURBINES & TURBINE GENERATOR SET UNITS: Gas, Complete

General Electric Company ....B 518 385-3716
Schenectady (G-14269)
General Electric Company ....B 518 385-2211
Schenectady (G-14270)
General Electric Intl Inc ....B 518 385-2211
Schenectady (G-14273)

TURBINES & TURBINE GENERATOR SETS

Awr Energy Inc..................................F 585 469-7750
Plattsburgh (G-12733)
Cooper Turbocompressor Inc...............B 716 896-6600
Buffalo (G-2711)
Dresser-Rand Company ....A 585 596-3100
Wellsville (G-15670)
Dresser-Rand Group Inc ....D 716 375-3000
Olean (G-12232)

GE Global Research ....A 518 387-5000
Niskayuna *(G-11995)*

General Electric Company ....B 518 385-2211
Schenectady *(G-14267)*

General Electric Company ....B 203 373-2756
Schenectady *(G-14268)*

General Electric Company ....B 518 387-5000
Schenectady *(G-14271)*

General Electric Company ....G 518 385-3439
Schenectady *(G-14272)*

Mission Critical Energy Inc ....G 716 276-8465
Getzville *(G-5178)*

Prime Turbine Parts LLC ....G 518 306-7306
Saratoga Springs *(G-14188)*

Stork H & E Turbo Blading Inc ....C 607 277-4968
Ithaca *(G-6411)*

Tgp Flying Cloud Holdings LLC ....E 646 829-3900
New York *(G-11458)*

Tuthill Corporation ....B 631 727-1097
Riverhead *(G-13191)*

Weaver Wind Energy LLC ....G 607 379-9463
Freeville *(G-5036)*

Worldwide Gas Turbine Pdts Inc ....G 518 877-7200
Clifton Park *(G-3478)*

TURBINES & TURBINE GENERATOR SETS & PARTS

Intersource Management Group..........G 518 372-6798
Halfmoon *(G-5494)*

Intersource Management Group..........E 518 372-6798
Schenectady *(G-14281)*

Siemens Government Tech Inc............B 585 593-1234
Wellsville *(G-15676)*

Turbine Engine Comp Utica ....A 315 768-8070
Whitesboro *(G-16084)*

Turbo Machined Products LLC ....E 315 895-3010
Frankfort *(G-4957)*

TURBINES: Hydraulic, Complete

Atlantic Projects Company Inc ....F 518 878-2065
Clifton Park *(G-3462)*

Frontier Hydraulics Corp...................F 716 694-2070
Buffalo *(G-2762)*

TURBINES: Steam

General Electric Company ....A 518 385-4022
Schenectady *(G-14266)*

General Electric Company ....E 518 385-7620
Niskayuna *(G-11996)*

TURBO-GENERATORS

Mannesmann Corporation ....D 212 258-4000
New York *(G-10348)*

TYPESETTING SVC

514 Adams Corporation ....G 516 352-6948
Deer Park *(G-3825)*

Act Communications Group Inc ....F 631 669-2403
West Islip *(G-15809)*

Advance Publications Inc ....D 718 981-1234
New York *(G-8475)*

Agrecolor Inc................................F 516 741-8700
Mineola *(G-7957)*

Alabaster Group Inc........................G 516 867-8223
Freeport *(G-4981)*

Albion-Holley Pennysaver Inc ....E 585 589-5641
Albion *(G-153)*

Arista Innovations Inc ....E 516 746-2262
Mineola *(G-7959)*

Art Resources Transfer Inc ....G 212 255-2919
New York *(G-8630)*

Artscroll Printing Corp ....E 212 929-2413
New York *(G-8640)*

Bates Jackson Engraving Co Inc ....E 716 854-3000
Buffalo *(G-2657)*

Baum Christine and John Corp ....G 585 621-8910
Rochester *(G-13261)*

Bco Industries Western NY Inc...........E 716 877-2800
Tonawanda *(G-15089)*

Beastons Budget Printing Inc............G 585 244-2721
Rochester *(G-13264)*

Beehive Press Inc ....G 718 654-1200
Bronx *(G-1211)*

Benchemark Printing Inc...................D 518 393-1361
Schenectady *(G-14249)*

Bernard Hall ....G 585 425-3340
Fairport *(G-4489)*

Beyer Graphics Inc ....D 631 543-3900
Commack *(G-3579)*

Boncraft Inc ....D 716 662-9720
Tonawanda *(G-15091)*

Bondy Printing Corp ....G 631 242-1510
Bay Shore *(G-659)*

Brodock Press Inc ....D 315 735-9577
Utica *(G-15242)*

Brooks Litho Digital Group Inc ....G 631 789-4500
Deer Park *(G-3850)*

Bytheway Publishing Services ....F 607 334-8365
Norwich *(G-12114)*

Carlara Group Ltd ....G 914 769-2020
Pleasantville *(G-12795)*

Carnels Printing Inc ....G 516 883-3355
Great Neck *(G-5374)*

Castlereagh Printcraft Inc ....G 516 623-1728
Freeport *(G-4989)*

Chakra Communications Inc ....E 607 748-7491
Endicott *(G-4446)*

Challenge Graphics Svcs Inc.............G 631 586-0171
Deer Park *(G-3851)*

Clarsons Corp ....F 585 235-8775
Rochester *(G-13317)*

Cohber Press Inc ....D 585 475-9100
West Henrietta *(G-15789)*

Consolidated Color Press Inc ....F 212 929-8197
New York *(G-9086)*

Cortland Standard Printing Co ....D 607 756-5665
Cortland *(G-3764)*

Cosmos Communications Inc ....C 718 482-1800
Long Island City *(G-7193)*

Csw Inc ....F 585 247-4010
Rochester *(G-13331)*

D G M Graphics Inc ....F 516 223-2220
Merrick *(G-7854)*

Desktop Publishing Concepts ....F 631 752-1934
Farmingdale *(G-4614)*

Digital Page LLC ....F 518 446-9129
Albany *(G-70)*

Dispatch Graphics Inc ....F 212 307-5943
New York *(G-9236)*

Dowd - Witbeck Printing Corp ....F 518 274-2421
Troy *(G-15166)*

DP Murphy Co Inc ....D 631 673-9400
Deer Park *(G-3865)*

Draper Associates Incorporated ....F 212 255-2727
New York *(G-9266)*

E B B Graphics Inc ....F 516 750-5510
Westbury *(G-15877)*

Eastwood Litho Impressions LLC ....F 315 437-2626
Syracuse *(G-14881)*

Empire Press Co ....G 718 756-9500
Brooklyn *(G-1801)*

Flare Multicopy Corp ....E 718 258-8860
Brooklyn *(G-1849)*

Flp Group LLC ....F 315 252-7583
Auburn *(G-476)*

Foleys Graphic Center Inc ....E 914 245-3625
Yorktown Heights *(G-16364)*

Fort Orange Press Inc ....E 518 489-3233
Albany *(G-78)*

Fulton Newspapers Inc ....G 315 598-6397
Fulton *(G-5059)*

Gallant Graphics Ltd ....E 845 868-1166
Stanfordville *(G-14610)*

Gateway Prtg & Graphics Inc ....E 716 823-3873
Hamburg *(G-5509)*

Gazette Press Inc ....E 914 963-8300
Rye *(G-14077)*

Gg Design and Printing ....G 718 321-3220
New York *(G-9606)*

Graphic Fabrications Inc ....G 516 763-3222
Rockville Centre *(G-13828)*

Graphicomm Inc ....G 716 283-0830
Niagara Falls *(G-11932)*

Hks Printing Company Inc ....F 212 675-2529
New York *(G-9797)*

Hugh F McPherson Inc ....G 716 668-6107
Cheektowaga *(G-3354)*

In-House Inc ....F 718 445-9007
College Point *(G-3544)*

Jack J Florio Jr ....G 716 434-9123
Lockport *(G-7085)*

James Conolly Printing Co ....G 585 426-4150
Rochester *(G-13488)*

Jane Lewis ....G 607 722-0584
Binghamton *(G-890)*

Johnnys Ideal Printing Co ....G 518 828-6666
Hudson *(G-6166)*

Jon Lyn Ink Inc ....G 516 546-2312
Merrick *(G-7857)*

L M N Printing Company Inc ....E 516 285-8526
Valley Stream *(G-15345)*

Lake Placid Advertisers Wkshp..........E 518 523-3359
Lake Placid *(G-6767)*

Leigh Scott Enterprises Inc ....E 718 343-5440
Bellerose *(G-775)*

Litmor Publishing Corp ....F 516 931-0012
Garden City *(G-5105)*

Loudon Ltd ....G 631 757-4447
East Northport *(G-4149)*

Louis Heindl & Son Inc ....E 585 454-5080
Rochester *(G-13523)*

Loy L Press Inc ....G 716 634-5966
Buffalo *(G-2853)*

Mechon Beiss Uvas ....G 718 436-1489
Brooklyn *(G-2131)*

Medallion Associates Inc ....E 212 929-9130
New York *(G-10408)*

Mercury Print Productions Inc............C 585 458-7900
Rochester *(G-13542)*

Midgley Printing Corp ....G 315 475-1864
Syracuse *(G-14942)*

Mines Press Inc ....C 888 559-2634
Cortlandt Manor *(G-3797)*

Moneast ....G 845 298-8898
Wappingers Falls *(G-15498)*

Multiple Imprssons of Rchester ....G 585 546-1160
Rochester *(G-13563)*

Mutual Engraving Company Inc ....D 516 489-0534
West Hempstead *(G-15777)*

News India USA Inc ....F 212 675-7515
New York *(G-10614)*

Newspaper Publisher LLC ....F 607 775-0472
Conklin *(G-3626)*

Official Offset Corporation ....E 631 957-8500
Amityville *(G-299)*

P D R Inc ....G 516 829-5300
Plainview *(G-12706)*

Panagraphics Inc ....G 716 312-8088
Orchard Park *(G-12370)*

Patrick Ryans Modern Press ....E 518 434-2921
Albany *(G-112)*

Presstek Printing LLC ....F 585 467-8140
Rochester *(G-13642)*

Prestige Envelope & Lithograph ....F 631 521-7043
Merrick *(G-7863)*

Printery ....G 516 922-3250
Oyster Bay *(G-12454)*

Printing Resources Inc ....E 518 482-2470
Albany *(G-119)*

Pro Printing ....G 516 561-9700
Lynbrook *(G-7435)*

Progressive Graphics & Prtg ....G 315 331-3635
Newark *(G-11850)*

Publishing Synthesis Ltd ....G 212 219-0135
New York *(G-10924)*

Quad/Graphics Inc ....A 518 581-4000
Saratoga Springs *(G-14189)*

Quicker Printer Inc ....G 607 734-8622
Elmira *(G-4365)*

Rmd Holding Inc ....G 845 628-0030
Mahopac *(G-7478)*

Scotti Graphics Inc ....E 212 367-9602
Long Island City *(G-7352)*

Sentine Printing Inc ....E 516 334-7400
Westbury *(G-15925)*

Stone Crest Industries Inc ....G 607 652-2665
Stamford *(G-14609)*

Syracuse Computer Forms Inc ....E 315 478-0108
Syracuse *(G-15005)*

Thomas Group Inc ....F 212 947-6400
New York *(G-11467)*

Times Review Newspaper Corp..........E 631 354-8031
Mattituck *(G-7680)*

Tobay Printing Co Inc ....E 631 842-3300
Copiague *(G-3684)*

Tom & Jerry Printcraft Forms ....E 914 777-7468
Mamaroneck *(G-7525)*

Torsaf Printers Inc ....E 516 569-5577
Hewlett *(G-5873)*

Tri Kolor Printing & Sty ....F 315 474-6753
Syracuse *(G-15015)*

Tripi Engraving Co Inc ....G 718 383-6500
Brooklyn *(G-2522)*

Voss Signs LLC ....E 315 682-6418
Manlius *(G-7550)*

Wallkill Valley Publications ....E 845 561-0170
Newburgh *(G-11893)*

PRODUCT

TYPESETTING SVC (continued)

Waterhouse Publications Inc ....E 716 662-4200
  Orchard Park **(G-12383)**
Webster Printing Corporation ....F 585 671-1533
  Webster **(G-15662)**
Westchester Mailing Service ....E 914 948-1116
  White Plains **(G-16073)**
Wilson Press LLC ....E 315 568-9693
  Seneca Falls **(G-14374)**
Woodbury Printing Plus + Inc ....G 845 928-6610
  Central Valley **(G-3302)**
Worldwide Ticket Craft ....D 516 538-6200
  Merrick **(G-7865)**
Wynco Press One Inc ....G 516 354-6145
  Glen Oaks **(G-5215)**
X Myles Mar Inc ....E 212 683-2015
  New York **(G-11795)**
Zenger Partners LLC ....E 716 876-2284
  Kenmore **(G-6656)**

TYPESETTING SVC: Computer

Star Composition Services Inc ....G 212 684-4001
  Brooklyn **(G-2452)**

TYPOGRAPHY

Artistic Typography Corp ....F 212 463-8880
  New York **(G-8638)**
Rubber Stamps Inc ....E 212 675-1180
  Mineola **(G-7998)**

ULTRASONIC EQPT: Cleaning, Exc Med & Dental

Alexy Associates Inc ....E 845 482-3000
  Bethel **(G-827)**
Branson Ultrasonics Corp ....E 585 624-8000
  Honeoye Falls **(G-6070)**
Tectran Inc ....G 800 776-5549
  Cheektowaga **(G-3364)**

UMBRELLAS & CANES

Essex Manufacturing Inc ....D 212 239-0080
  New York **(G-9404)**
Gustbuster Ltd ....G 631 391-9000
  Farmingdale **(G-4642)**

UMBRELLAS: Garden Or Wagon

Zip-Jack Industries Ltd ....E 914 592-2000
  Tarrytown **(G-15064)**

UNIFORM STORES

Craft Clerical Clothes Inc ....G 212 764-6122
  New York **(G-9116)**

UNIVERSITY

Cornell University ....D 607 277-2338
  Ithaca **(G-6376)**
Cornell University ....E 607 254-2473
  Ithaca **(G-6377)**
New York University ....E 212 998-4300
  New York **(G-10607)**
Suny At Binghamton ....D 607 777-2316
  Binghamton **(G-910)**
Trust of Colum Unive In The Ci ....F 212 854-2793
  New York **(G-11552)**
University of Rochester ....B 585 275-3483
  Rochester **(G-13786)**

UNSUPPORTED PLASTICS: Floor Or Wall Covering

Pacific Designs Intl Inc ....G 718 364-2867
  Bronx **(G-1331)**

UPHOLSTERY FILLING MATERIALS

Global Resources Sg Inc ....F 212 686-1411
  New York **(G-9632)**
Manrico Usa Inc ....G 212 794-4200
  New York **(G-10351)**

UPHOLSTERY MATERIALS, BROADWOVEN

Scalamandre Silks Inc ....D 212 980-3888
  New York **(G-11147)**

UPHOLSTERY WORK SVCS

August Studios ....G 718 706-6487
  Long Island City **(G-7172)**
Bettertex Inc ....F 212 431-3373
  New York **(G-8771)**
Dine Rite Seating Products Inc ....E 631 226-8899
  Lindenhurst **(G-6950)**
Elan Upholstery Inc ....F 631 563-0650
  Bohemia **(G-1011)**
Terbo Ltd ....G 718 847-2860
  Richmond Hill **(G-13127)**

URANIUM ORE MINING, NEC

Global Gold Corporation ....F 914 925-0020
  Rye **(G-14079)**

USED CAR DEALERS

A Zimmer Ltd ....D 315 422-7011
  Syracuse **(G-14808)**
Want-Ad Digest Inc ....F 518 279-1181
  Troy **(G-15196)**

USED MERCHANDISE STORES: Building Materials

Veeco Instruments Inc ....C 516 349-8300
  Plainview **(G-12724)**

USED MERCHANDISE STORES: Rare Books

Glenn Horowitz Bookseller Inc ....G 212 691-9100
  New York **(G-9620)**

UTENSILS: Cast Aluminum, Cooking Or Kitchen

August Thomsen Corp ....E 516 676-7100
  Glen Cove **(G-5189)**
Mehr Foil Corp ....G 631 648-9742
  Ronkonkoma **(G-13972)**
Smart USA Inc ....F 631 969-1111
  Bay Shore **(G-715)**

UTENSILS: Household, Cooking & Kitchen, Metal

Corning Vitro Corporation ....A 607 974-8605
  Corning **(G-3714)**
Lb Furniture Industries LLC ....C 518 828-1501
  Hudson **(G-6169)**
Nash Metalware Co Inc ....F 315 339-5794
  Rome **(G-13858)**
Oxo International Inc ....C 212 242-3333
  New York **(G-10729)**
Progressus Company Inc ....F 516 255-0245
  Rockville Centre **(G-13834)**

UTENSILS: Household, Cooking & Kitchen, Porcelain Enameled

Hyman Podrusnick Co Inc ....G 718 853-4502
  Brooklyn **(G-1949)**

UTENSILS: Household, Porcelain Enameled

Seneca Ceramics Corp ....G 315 781-0100
  Phelps **(G-12607)**

UTILITY TRAILER DEALERS

J D Handling Systems Inc ....F 518 828-9676
  Ghent **(G-5185)**

VACUUM CLEANER STORES

Nationwide Sales and Service ....F 631 491-6625
  Farmingdale **(G-4691)**

VACUUM CLEANERS: Household

American Comfort Direct LLC ....E 201 364-8309
  New York **(G-8548)**
D & C Cleaning Inc ....F 631 789-5659
  Copiague **(G-3650)**
Global Resources Sg Inc ....F 212 686-1411
  New York **(G-9632)**
Nationwide Sales and Service ....F 631 491-6625
  Farmingdale **(G-4691)**
Tri County Custom Vacuum ....G 845 774-7595
  Monroe **(G-8032)**

VACUUM CLEANERS: Indl Type

Empire Division Inc ....D 315 476-6273
  Syracuse **(G-14888)**
Key High Vacuum Products Inc ....E 631 584-5959
  Nesconset **(G-8219)**
National Vac Envmtl Svcs Corp ....E 518 743-0563
  Glens Falls **(G-5260)**

VACUUM SYSTEMS: Air Extraction, Indl

Adams Sfc Inc ....E 716 877-2608
  Tonawanda **(G-15082)**
Edwards Vacuum LLC ....D 800 848-9800
  Sanborn **(G-14140)**

VALUE-ADDED RESELLERS: Computer Systems

Graphics Slution Providers Inc ....F 845 677-5088
  Lagrangeville **(G-6748)**
Vision Logic Inc ....G 212 729-4606
  New York **(G-11692)**

VALVES

ITT Engineered Valves LLC ....D 662 257-6982
  Seneca Falls **(G-14365)**

VALVES & PIPE FITTINGS

A K Allen Co Inc ....C 516 747-5450
  Melville **(G-7753)**
Aalborg Instrs & Contrls Inc ....D 845 398-3160
  Orangeburg **(G-12304)**
Anderson Precision Inc ....D 716 484-1148
  Jamestown **(G-6494)**
Curtiss-Wright Flow Control ....C 631 293-3800
  Farmingdale **(G-4607)**
Devin Mfg Inc ....F 585 496-5770
  Arcade **(G-372)**
Dynamic Products Inc ....G 631 270-4833
  Farmingdale **(G-4619)**
Flomatic Corporation ....E 518 761-9797
  Glens Falls **(G-5249)**
Ford Regulator Valve Corp ....G 718 497-3255
  Brooklyn **(G-1858)**
Goodman Main Stopper Mfg Co ....F 718 875-5140
  Brooklyn **(G-1900)**
Holyoke Fittings Inc ....F 718 649-0710
  Brooklyn **(G-1939)**
J H Robotics Inc ....E 607 729-3758
  Johnson City **(G-6603)**
Key High Vacuum Products Inc ....E 631 584-5959
  Nesconset **(G-8219)**
Kingston Hoops Summer ....G 845 401-6830
  Kingston **(G-6696)**
Lance Valves ....G 716 681-5825
  Lancaster **(G-6815)**
M Manastrip-M Corporation ....G 518 664-2089
  Clifton Park **(G-3467)**
Make-Waves Instrument Corp ....E 716 681-7524
  Buffalo **(G-2860)**
Micromold Products Inc ....E 914 969-2850
  Yonkers **(G-16333)**
Rand Machine Products, Inc. ....C 716 665-5217
  Falconer **(G-4552)**
Ross Valve Mfg ....G 518 274-0961
  Troy **(G-15184)**
Sigmamotor Inc ....E 716 735-3115
  Middleport **(G-7890)**
Spence Engineering Company Inc .....C 845 778-5566
  Walden **(G-15462)**
Steel & Obrien Mfg Inc ....D 585 492-5800
  Arcade **(G-381)**
Sure Flow Equipment Inc ....E 800 263-8251
  Tonawanda **(G-15143)**
Westchester Valve & Fitting Co ....G 914 762-6600
  Clifton Park **(G-3477)**
William E Williams Valve Corp ....E 718 392-1660
  Long Island City **(G-7401)**
William E Williams Valve Corp ....E 718 392-1660
  Long Island City **(G-7402)**

VALVES & REGULATORS: Pressure, Indl

Spence Engineering Company Inc .....C 845 778-5566
  Walden **(G-15462)**
Total Energy Fabrication Corp ....G 580 363-1500
  North Salem **(G-12037)**

VALVES Solenoid

Jeg Online Ventures LLC ....F 800 983-8230
   Islandia (G-6337)

VALVES: Aerosol, Metal

Chapin International Inc ....C .. 585 343-3140
   Batavia (G-608)
Chapin Manufacturing Inc ....C .. 585 343-3140
   Batavia (G-609)
Jordan Panel Systems Corp ....E .. 631 754-4900
   East Northport (G-4148)
Mpl Metal Inc ....G .. 718 338-4952
   Brooklyn (G-2174)
Peak Motion Inc ....G .. 716 534-4925
   Clarence (G-3439)
Peelle Company ....G .. 631 231-6000
   Hauppauge (G-5738)

VALVES: Aircraft

Valvetech Inc ....E .. 315 548-4551
   Phelps (G-12610)

VALVES: Aircraft, Control, Hydraulic & Pneumatic

Young & Franklin Inc ....D .. 315 457-3110
   Liverpool (G-7051)

VALVES: Aircraft, Fluid Power

Dmic Inc ....G .. 716 743-4360
   North Tonawanda (G-12065)
Moog Inc ....A .. 716 805-2604
   Elma (G-4321)
Tactair Fluid Controls Inc ....C .. 315 451-3928
   Liverpool (G-7044)

VALVES: Control, Automatic

ADC Industries Inc ....E .. 516 596-1304
   Valley Stream (G-15332)

VALVES: Electrohydraulic Servo, Metal

Servotronics Inc ....C .. 716 655-5990
   Elma (G-4327)

VALVES: Engine

Helio Precision Products Inc ....E .. 585 697-5434
   Rochester (G-13464)

VALVES: Fluid Power, Control, Hydraulic & pneumatic

Aerco International Inc ....C .. 845 580-8000
   Blauvelt (G-925)
BW Elliott Mfg Co LLC ....B .. 607 772-0404
   Binghamton (G-865)
Direkt Force LLC ....E .. 716 652-3022
   East Aurora (G-4085)
Dynamic Sealing Tech Inc ....G .. 716 376-0708
   Olean (G-12233)

VALVES: Gas Cylinder, Compressed

Caithness Equities Corporation ....E .. 212 599-2112
   New York (G-8888)

VALVES: Hard Rubber

Inflation Systems Inc ....E .. 914 381-8070
   Mamaroneck (G-7512)

VALVES: Indl

Air System Products Inc ....F .. 716 683-0435
   Lancaster (G-6792)
Byelocorp Scientific Inc ....E .. 212 785-2580
   New York (G-8877)
Curtiss-Wright Flow Control ....C ., 631 293-3800
   Farmingdale (G-4607)
Curtiss-Wright Flow Ctrl Corp ....C .. 631 293-3800
   Farmingdale (G-4608)
Dresser-Rand Company ....A .. 585 596-3100
   Wellsville (G-15670)
Flow-Safe Inc ....E .. 716 662-2585
   Orchard Park (G-12352)
Hy Cert Services Inc ....G .. 631 231-7005
   Brentwood (G-1122)

J H Buscher Inc ....G 716 667-2003
   Orchard Park (G-12357)
McWane Inc ....B .. 607 734-2211
   Elmira (G-4362)
Murphy Manufacturing Co Inc ....G .. 585 223-0100
   Fairport (G-4509)
Plattco Corporation ....E .. 518 563-4640
   Plattsburgh (G-12768)
Precision Valve & Automtn Inc ....C .. 518 371-2684
   Cohoes (G-3513)
Syraco Products Inc ....E .. 315 476-5306
   Syracuse (G-15002)
Trac Regulators Inc ....G .. 914 699-9352
   Mount Vernon (G-8185)
William E Williams Valve Corp ....E .. 718 392-1660
   Long Island City (G-7402)

VALVES: Plumbing & Heating

Lemode Plumbing & Heating ....E .. 718 545-3336
   Astoria (G-427)
Venco Sales Inc ....E .. 631 754-0782
   Huntington (G-6233)

VALVES: Regulating & Control, Automatic

Curtiss-Wright Electro- ....E .. 585 596-3482
   Wellsville (G-15669)
Digital Home Creations Inc ....G .. 585 576-7070
   Webster (G-15638)
Tyco Simplexgrinnell ....E .. 315 437-9664
   East Syracuse (G-4245)

VALVES: Water Works

Flomatic Corporation ....E .. 518 761-9797
   Glens Falls (G-5249)

VARNISHES, NEC

John C Dolph Company ....E .. 732 329-2333
   Schenectady (G-14283)
Royce Associates A Ltd Partnr ....G .. 516 367-6298
   Jericho (G-6593)
Si Group Inc ....C .. 518 347-4200
   Rotterdam Junction (G-14061)

VEGETABLE STANDS OR MARKETS

Lakeside Cider Mill Farm Inc ....G .. 518 399-8359
   Ballston Lake (G-560)

VEHICLES: All Terrain

Kens Service & Sales Inc ....F .. 716 683-1155
   Elma (G-4320)

VEHICLES: Recreational

Adirondack Power Sports ....G .. 518 481-6269
   Malone (G-7482)
Bullet Industries Inc ....G .. 585 352-0836
   Spencerport (G-14554)

VENDING MACHINES & PARTS

Cubic Trnsp Systems Inc ....F .. 212 255-1810
   New York (G-9129)
Distributors Vending Corp ....F .. 914 472-8981
   Ardsley (G-388)
Green Enviro Machine LLC ....G .. 407 461-6412
   Schenectady (G-14276)
Vengo Inc ....G .. 866 526-7054
   Bethpage (G-845)

VENTILATING EQPT: Metal

Air Louver & Damper Inc ....F .. 718 392-3232
   Long Island City (G-7147)
Duravent Inc ....E .. 518 463-7284
   Albany (G-71)
Imperial Damper & Louver Co ....E .. 718 731-3800
   Bronx (G-1279)
Spence Engineering Company Inc ....C .. 845 778-5566
   Walden (G-15462)

VENTILATING EQPT: Sheet Metal

Empire Ventilation Eqp Co Inc ....F .. 718 728-2143
   Florida (G-4823)
Lambro Industries Inc ....D .. 631 842-8088
   Amityville (G-290)

VENTURE CAPITAL COMPANIES

Capital E Financial Group ....F .. 212 319-6550
   New York (G-8911)
Circle Peak Capital MGT LLC ....E .. 646 230-8812
   New York (G-9010)

VETERINARY PHARMACEUTICAL PREPARATIONS

Ark Sciences Inc ....G .. 646 943-1520
   Islandia (G-6324)
H W Naylor Co Inc ....F .. 607 263-5145
   Morris (G-8084)

VIBRATORS: Concrete Construction

Ozteck Industries Inc ....E .. 516 883-8857
   Port Washington (G-12911)

VIDEO & AUDIO EQPT, WHOLESALE

Listec Video Corp ....G .. 631 273-3029
   Hauppauge (G-5692)
Professional Tape Corporation ....G .. 516 656-5519
   Glen Cove (G-5199)
Video Technology Services Inc ....F .. 516 937-9700
   Syosset (G-14804)

VIDEO CAMERA-AUDIO RECORDERS: Household Use

Bayit Home Automation Corp ....E .. 973 988-2638
   Brooklyn (G-1568)
Digitac Inc ....F .. 732 215-4020
   Brooklyn (G-1744)
Digitac LLC ....G .. 732 669-7637
   Brooklyn (G-1745)
Keemotion LLC ....G .. 914 458-3900
   Brooklyn (G-2022)

VIDEO EQPT

Video Technology Services Inc ....F .. 516 937-9700
   Syosset (G-14804)

VIDEO PRODUCTION SVCS

Amherst Media Inc ....G .. 716 874-4450
   Buffalo (G-2633)
Scholastic Inc ....A .. 212 343-6100
   New York (G-11161)
Wochit Inc ....G .. 212 979-8343
   New York (G-11773)

VIDEO REPAIR SVCS

Video Technology Services Inc ....F .. 516 937-9700
   Syosset (G-14804)

VIDEO TAPE PRODUCTION SVCS

NCM Publishers Inc ....G .. 212 691-9100
   New York (G-10560)
Physicalmind Institute ....F .. 212 343-2150
   New York (G-10832)

VINYL RESINS, NEC

Manufacturers Indexing Pdts ....G .. 631 271-0956
   Halesite (G-5488)

VITAMINS: Natural Or Synthetic, Uncompounded, Bulk

Abh Natures Products Inc ....E .. 631 249-5783
   Edgewood (G-4258)
Ajes Pharmaceuticals LLC ....E .. 631 608-1728
   Copiague (G-3644)
Gemini Pharmaceuticals Inc ....B .. 631 543-3334
   Commack (G-3590)
Healthee Endeavors Inc ....G .. 718 653-5499
   Bronx (G-1274)
Healthy N Fit Intl Inc ....F .. 800 338-5200
   Brewster (G-1150)
Lyteline LLC ....G .. 657 333-5983
   New York (G-10290)
Natures Bounty Co ....F .. 631 472-2817
   Bayport (G-729)
Natures Bounty Co ....D .. 631 244-2021
   Ronkonkoma (G-13980)
Nbty Manufacturing LLC ....E .. 631 567-9500
   Ronkonkoma (G-13982)

PRODUCT

Nutra Solutions USA Inc ....E 631 392-1900
Deer Park (G-3914)
Nutraqueen LLC ....F 347 368-6568
New York (G-10657)
Only Natural Inc ....F 516 897-7001
Oceanside (G-12183)
Plant Science Laboratories LLC ....G 716 228-4553
Buffalo (G-2920)
Supplement Mfg Partner Inc ....F 516 368-2656
Edgewood (G-4283)
Vitalize Labs LLC ....G 212 966-6130
New York (G-11696)
Wellquest International Inc ....G 212 689-9094
New York (G-11740)

VITAMINS: Pharmaceutical Preparations

American Hlth Formulations Inc ....G 631 392-1756
Hauppauge (G-5590)
Atlantic Essential Pdts Inc ....D 631 434-8333
Hauppauge (G-5596)
Bactolac Pharmaceutical Inc ....C 631 951-4908
Hauppauge (G-5600)
Bactolac Pharmaceutical Inc ....E 631 951-4908
Hauppauge (G-5601)
Bi Nutraceuticals Inc ....D 631 232-1105
Central Islip (G-3266)
Contract Pharmacal Corp ....C 631 231-4610
Hauppauge (G-5629)
FB Laboratories Inc ....E 631 963-6450
Hauppauge (G-5649)
Kabco Pharmaceuticals Inc ....G 631 842-3600
Amityville (G-283)
Natural Organics Labs Inc ....B 631 957-5600
Melville (G-7807)
Natures Bounty Inc ....G 631 567-9500
Bohemia (G-1050)
Natures Bounty Inc ....A 631 200-2000
Ronkonkoma (G-13981)
Natures Value Inc ....B 631 846-2500
Coram (G-3695)
Nutraceutical Wellness Inc ....G 888 454-3320
New York (G-10656)
Premium Processing Corp ....D 631 232-1105
Babylon (G-525)
Sciegen Pharmaceuticals Inc ....D 631 951-4908
Hauppauge (G-5762)
Tishcon Corp ....C 516 333-3056
Westbury (G-15930)
Tishcon Corp ....C 516 333-3056
Westbury (G-15931)
Tishcon Corp ....C 516 333-3050
Westbury (G-15932)
Tishcon Corp ....C 516 333-3050
Westbury (G-15933)
Unipharm Inc ....D 212 594-3260
New York (G-11592)
Wellmill LLC ....E 631 465-9245
Commack (G-3603)

WALL COVERINGS WHOLESALERS

Scalamandre Wallpaper Inc ....B 631 467-8800
Hauppauge (G-5760)

WALLBOARD: Decorated, Made From Purchased Materials

Aniiwe Inc ....G 347 683-1891
Brooklyn (G-1511)

WALLPAPER & WALL COVERINGS

Adelphi Paper Hangings ....G 518 284-9066
Sharon Springs (G-14381)
Eskayel Inc ....G 347 703-8084
Brooklyn (G-1812)
Flavor Paper Ltd ....F 718 422-0230
Brooklyn (G-1851)
Gerald McGlone ....G 518 482-2613
Colonie (G-3574)
Larkin Anya Ltd ....G 718 361-1827
Long Island City (G-7268)
Sunnyside Decorative Prints Co ....G 516 671-1935
Glen Cove (G-5203)

WALLS: Curtain, Metal

A&B McKeon Glass Inc ....G 718 525-2152
Staten Island (G-14614)
Metalsigma Usa Inc ....G 212 731-4346
New York (G-10443)

WAREHOUSE CLUBS STORES

Brucci Ltd ....E 914 965-0707
Yonkers (G-16292)

WAREHOUSING & STORAGE FACILITIES, NEC

Acme Signs of Baldwinsville ....G 315 638-4865
Baldwinsville (G-539)
Cambridge University Press ....D 212 337-5000
New York (G-8897)
Eastern Welding Inc ....G 631 727-0306
Riverhead (G-13174)
Medical Action Industries Inc ....C 631 231-4600
Hauppauge (G-5711)

WAREHOUSING & STORAGE, REFRIGERATED: Frozen Or Refrig Goods

Adirondack Ice & Air Inc ....F 518 483-4340
Malone (G-7481)

WAREHOUSING & STORAGE: General

Avanti U S A Ltd ....F 716 695-5800
Tonawanda (G-15087)
Ivi Services Inc ....D 607 729-5111
Binghamton (G-889)
Lighting Holdings Intl LLC ....A 845 306-1850
Purchase (G-13006)
Platinum Sales Promotion Inc ....G 718 361-0200
Long Island City (G-7327)
Wayuga Community Newspapers ....G 315 594-2506
Wolcott (G-16165)

WAREHOUSING & STORAGE: General

Canfield & Tack Inc ....D 585 235-7710
Rochester (G-13293)
Dayleen Intimates Inc ....E 914 969-5900
Yonkers (G-16300)

WAREHOUSING & STORAGE: Refrigerated

Crescent Duck Farm Inc ....E 631 722-8700
Aquebogue (G-365)

WARM AIR HEATING & AC EQPT & SPLYS, WHOLESALE Air Filters

R P Fedder Corp ....E 585 288-1600
Rochester (G-13666)

WARM AIR HEATING/AC EQPT/SPLYS, WHOL Dehumidifiers, Exc Port

MSP Technologycom LLC ....G 631 424-7542
Centerport (G-3257)

WARM AIR HEATING/AC EQPT/SPLYS, WHOL: Ventilating Eqpt/Sply

DI Manufacturing Inc ....E 315 432-8977
North Syracuse (G-12040)

WASHCLOTHS

1510 Associates LLC ....G 212 828-8720
New York (G-8389)

WASHERS: Metal

Superior Washer & Gasket Corp ....D 631 273-8282
Hauppauge (G-5778)

WASHERS: Plastic

Fibre Materials Corp ....E 516 349-1660
Plainview (G-12685)

WATCH STRAPS, EXC METAL

International Time Products ....G 516 931-0005
Jericho (G-6584)
Roma Industries LLC ....E 212 268-0723
New York (G-11078)

WATCHCASES

American Time Mfg Ltd ....F 585 266-5120
Rochester (G-13233)

WATCHES

Croton Watch Co Inc ....E 800 443-7639
West Nyack (G-15820)
E Gluck Corporation ....C 718 784-0700
Little Neck (G-6997)
First Sbf Holding Inc ....E 845 425-9882
Valley Cottage (G-15315)
Geneva Watch Company Inc ....E 212 221-1177
New York (G-9594)
Life Watch Technology Inc ....E 917 669-2428
Flushing (G-4871)

WATCHES & PARTS, WHOLESALE

E Gluck Corporation ....C 718 784-0700
Little Neck (G-6997)
I-Tem Brand LLC ....F 718 790-6927
Bronx (G-1277)

WATER PURIFICATION EQPT: Household

Airgle Corporation ....E 866 501-7750
Ronkonkoma (G-13894)
Atlantic Ultraviolet Corp ....E 631 234-3275
Hauppauge (G-5597)
Water Energy Systems LLC ....G 844 822-7665
New York (G-11729)

WATER TREATMENT EQPT: Indl

Bolton Point Wtr Trtmnt Plant ....G 607 277-0660
Ithaca (G-6370)
Business Advisory Services ....G 718 337-3740
Far Rockaway (G-4562)
City of Olean ....G 716 376-5694
Olean (G-12228)
City of Oneonta ....G 607 433-3470
Oneonta (G-12263)
Clearcove Systems Inc ....F 585 734-3012
Victor (G-15398)
Fabco Industries Inc ....G 631 393-6024
Farmingdale (G-4628)
Integrated Water Management ....G 607 844-4276
Dryden (G-4039)
Metro Group Inc ....D 718 729-7200
Long Island City (G-7295)
Neptune Soft Water Inc ....F 315 446-5151
Syracuse (G-14950)
New Windsor Waste Water Plant ....F 845 561-2550
New Windsor (G-8374)
Ossining Village of Inc ....G 914 202-9668
Ossining (G-12406)
R C Kolstad Water Corp ....G 585 216-2230
Ontario (G-12298)

WATER: Mineral, Carbonated, Canned & Bottled, Etc

Alpha Wolf LLC ....G 516 778-5812
Carle Place (G-3169)
Global Brands Inc ....G 845 358-1212
Nyack (G-12144)
Just Beverages LLC ....F 480 388-1133
Glens Falls (G-5252)
New York Spring Water Inc ....E 212 777-4649
New York (G-10602)
Nirvana Inc ....C 315 942-4900
Forestport (G-4928)
Saratoga Spring Water Company ....E 518 584-6363
Saratoga Springs (G-14193)

WATER: Pasteurized & Mineral, Bottled & Canned

Mayer Bros Apple Products Inc ....D 716 668-1787
West Seneca (G-15852)

WATER: Pasteurized, Canned & Bottled, Etc

Alpine Water USA LLC ....G 203 912-9723
Dayton (G-3822)
Crystal Rock LLC ....E 716 626-7460
Buffalo (G-2714)
Just Goods Inc ....F 855 282-5878
New York (G-10046)
Soto Sake Corporation ....G 305 781-3906
Brooklyn (G-2442)

WATERPROOFING COMPOUNDS

Penetron International Ltd ....F 631 941-9700
East Setauket (G-4183)

WAVEGUIDES & FITTINGS

M W Microwave Corp ....F 516 295-1814
Lawrence (G-6887)

WAXES: Mineral, Natural

Koster Keunen Waxes Ltd ....F 631 589-0400
Sayville (G-14229)

WAXES: Paraffin

Industrial Raw Materials LLC ....F 212 688-8080
Plainview (G-12689)
Kent Chemical Corporation ....E 212 521-1700
New York (G-10094)

WAXES: Petroleum, Not Produced In Petroleum Refineries

Premier Ingridients Inc ....G 516 641-6763
Great Neck (G-5414)

WEATHER STRIPS: Metal

Accurate Metal Weather Strip ....G 914 668-6042
Mount Vernon (G-8121)

WEAVING MILL, BROADWOVEN FABRICS: Wool Or Similar Fabric

Loomstate LLC ....E 212 219-2300
New York (G-10254)

WEDDING CHAPEL: Privately Operated

Silver Griffin Inc ....F 518 272-7771
Troy (G-15189)

WEIGHING MACHINERY & APPARATUS

Measupro Inc ....F 845 425-8777
Spring Valley (G-14579)
S R Instruments Inc ....E 716 693-5977
Tonawanda (G-15136)
Weighing & Systems Tech Inc ....G 518 274-2797
Troy (G-15197)

WELDING & CUTTING APPARATUS & ACCESS, NEC

McAllisters Precision Wldg Inc ....F 518 221-3455
Menands (G-7844)

WELDING EQPT

Lynne B Enterprises Inc ....E 631 254-6975
Deer Park (G-3901)
Riverview Industries Inc ....G 845 265-5284
Cold Spring (G-3524)
Vante Inc ....F 716 778-7691
Newfane (G-11896)

WELDING EQPT & SPLYS WHOLESALERS

Haun Welding Supply Inc ....G 315 592-5012
Fulton (G-5063)
Jacksons Welding LLC ....G 607 756-2725
Cortland (G-3773)

WELDING EQPT: Electrical

3krf LLC ....G 516 208-6824
Oceanside (G-12163)

WELDING MACHINES & EQPT: Ultrasonic

Sonicor Inc ....F 631 920-6555
West Babylon (G-15748)

WELDING REPAIR SVC

A & J Machine & Welding Inc ....F 631 845-7586
Farmingdale (G-4568)
AAA Welding and Fabrication of ....G 585 254-2830
Rochester (G-13196)
Accurate Welding Service Inc ....G 516 333-1730
Westbury (G-15860)
Acro-Fab Ltd ....E 315 564-6688
Hannibal (G-5542)
Airweld Inc ....G 631 924-6366
Ridge (G-13131)
Aj Genco Sp McHy Rdout Svc ....F 716 664-4925
Falconer (G-4532)

Allen Tool Phoenix Inc ....E 315 463-7533
East Syracuse (G-4194)
Alliance Services Corp ....F 516 775-7600
Floral Park (G-4805)
Alliance Welding & Steel Fabg ....F 516 775-7600
Floral Park (G-4806)
Alpine Machine Inc ....F 607 272-1344
Ithaca (G-6362)
Alumi-Tech LLC ....G 585 663-7010
Penfield (G-12569)
American Metal Works Inc ....G 914 682-2979
White Plains (G-15974)
Andersens Spring & Wldg Corp ....G 516 785-7337
Bellmore (G-778)
ARC TEC Wldg & Fabrication Inc .....G 718 982-9274
Staten Island (G-14619)
Atlantis Equipment Corporation ....F 518 733-5910
Stephentown (G-14730)
Barber Welding Inc ....E 315 834-6645
Weedsport (G-15665)
Benemy Welding & Fabrication ....G 315 548-8500
Phelps (G-12602)
Bms Manufacturing Co Inc ....E 607 535-2426
Watkins Glen (G-15613)
Boilermatic Welding Inds Inc ....E 631 654-1341
Medford (G-7700)
Bracci Ironworks Inc ....F 718 629-2374
Brooklyn (G-1604)
Brenseke George Wldg Ir Works ......G 631 271-4870
Deer Park (G-3849)
Broadalbin Manufacturing Corp ....G 518 883-5313
Broadalbin (G-1172)
Bruce Pierce ....G 716 731-9310
Sanborn (G-14138)
C G & Son Machining Inc ....G 315 964-2430
Williamstown (G-16115)
CBM Fabrications Inc ....E 518 399-8023
Ballston Lake (G-559)
Competicion Mower Repair ....G 516 280-6584
Mineola (G-7966)
Cs Automation Inc ....F 315 524-5123
Ontario (G-12286)
Custom Laser Inc ....E 716 434-8600
Lockport (G-7066)
D & G Welding Inc ....G 716 873-3088
Buffalo (G-2718)
DC Fabrication & Welding Inc ....G 845 295-0215
Ferndale (G-4788)
Deck Bros Inc ....E 716 852-0262
Buffalo (G-2723)
Dennies Manufacturing Inc ....E 585 393-4646
Canandaigua (G-3130)
Donald Stefan ....G 716 492-1110
Chaffee (G-3306)
Dorgan Welding Service ....G 315 462-9030
Phelps (G-12603)
E B Industries LLC ....E 631 293-8565
Farmingdale (G-4620)
E B Industries LLC ....E 631 293-8565
Farmingdale (G-4621)
Eagle Welding Machine ....G 315 594-1845
Wolcott (G-16163)
Etna Tool & Die Corporation ....F 212 475-4350
New York (G-9414)
Excelco/Newbrook Inc ....D 716 934-2644
Silver Creek (G-14442)
F M L Industries Inc ....G 607 749-7273
Homer (G-6062)
Flushing Boiler & Welding Co ....G 718 463-1266
Brooklyn (G-1855)
Formac Welding Inc ....G 631 421-5525
Huntington Station (G-6246)
Fred Santucci Inc ....F 716 483-1411
Jamestown (G-6511)
G & C Welding Co Inc ....G 516 883-3228
Port Washington (G-12881)
Gasport Welding & Fabg Inc ....F 716 772-7205
Gasport (G-5137)
Gc Mobile Services Inc ....G 914 736-9730
Cortlandt Manor (G-3795)
Genco John ....G 716 483-5446
Jamestown (G-6512)
General Welding & Fabg Inc ....G 716 652-0033
Elma (G-4319)
Guthrie Heli-Arc Inc ....G 585 548-5053
Bergen (G-815)
Hadfield Inc ....F 631 981-4314
Saint James (G-14111)
Hadleys Fab-Weld Inc ....G 315 926-5101
Marion (G-7570)

Hansen Steel ....E 585 398-2020
Farmington (G-4772)
Hartman Enterprises Inc ....D 315 363-7300
Oneida (G-12245)
Haskell Machine & Tool Inc ....F 607 749-2421
Homer (G-6063)
Haun Welding Supply Inc ....G 607 846-2289
Elmira (G-4356)
Haun Welding Supply Inc ....G 315 592-5012
Fulton (G-5063)
Homer Iron Works LLC ....G 607 749-3963
Homer (G-6064)
Ingleside Machine Co Inc ....D 585 924-3046
Farmington (G-4774)
Jacksons Welding LLC ....G 607 756-2725
Cortland (G-3773)
Kon Tat Group Corporation ....G 718 207-5022
Brooklyn (G-2035)
L & S Metals Inc ....E 716 692-6865
North Tonawanda (G-12076)
Lagasse Works Inc ....G 315 946-9202
Lyons (G-7450)
Linita Design & Mfg Corp ....E 716 566-7753
Lackawanna (G-6741)
M M Welding ....E 315 363-3980
Oneida (G-12247)
Maple Grove Corp ....E 585 492-5286
Arcade (G-377)
Maria Dionisio Welding Inc ....G 631 956-0815
Lindenhurst (G-6958)
Maspeth Welding Inc ....F 718 497-5430
Maspeth (G-7627)
Meades Welding and Fabricating ......G 631 581-1555
Islip (G-6354)
Mega Tool & Mfg Corp ....E 607 734-8398
Elmira (G-4363)
Miller Metal Fabricating Inc ....G 585 359-3400
Rochester (G-13549)
Mooradian Hydraulics & Eqp Co ......F 518 766-3866
Castleton On Hudson (G-3203)
Ms Spares LLC ....G 607 223-3024
Clay (G-3451)
NY Iron Inc ....F 718 302-9000
Long Island City (G-7311)
Phillip J Ortiz Manufacturing ....G 845 226-7030
Hopewell Junction (G-6100)
Phoenix Welding & Fabg Inc ....G 315 695-2223
Phoenix (G-12619)
Precision Laser Technology LLC ....F 585 458-6208
Rochester (G-13637)
Pro-Tech Wldg Fabrication Inc ....E 585 436-9855
Rochester (G-13647)
Quality Industrial Services ....F 716 667-7703
Orchard Park (G-12376)
R & B Fabrication Inc ....F 315 640-9901
Cicero (G-3423)
Reliable Welding & Fabrication ....G 631 758-2637
Patchogue (G-12511)
REO Welding Inc ....F 518 238-1022
Cohoes (G-3514)
Rini Tank & Truck Service ....F 718 384-6606
Brooklyn (G-2345)
Rj Welding & Fabricating Inc ....G 315 523-1288
Clifton Springs (G-3480)
Robert M Brown ....F 607 426-6250
Montour Falls (G-8076)
Rothe Welding Inc ....G 845 246-3051
Saugerties (G-14210)
Ryans Mobile Welding Svc LLC ....G 315 769-5699
Massena (G-7670)
S & D Welding Corp ....G 631 454-0383
West Babylon (G-15744)
S J B Fabrication ....F 716 895-0281
Buffalo (G-2969)
Sierson Crane Inc ....F 315 723-6914
Westmoreland (G-15964)
Smithers Tools & Mch Pdts Inc ....D 845 876-3063
Rhinebeck (G-13101)
Strecks Inc ....E 518 273-4410
Watervliet (G-15607)
Tomahawk Welding Svcs & Insptn ....G 903 249-4451
Norwich (G-12129)
Tracey Welding Co Inc ....G 518 756-6309
Coeymans (G-3505)
Ub Welding Corp ....G 347 688-5196
Bronx (G-1386)
Walters & Walters Inc ....G 347 202-8535
Bronx (G-1395)
Watkins Welding and Mch Sp Inc ......G 914 949-6168
White Plains (G-16070)

PRODUCT

WELDING REPAIR SVC

Welding Chapter of New York ....G .. 212 481-1496
New York *(G-11739)*

Welding Guys LLC ....G .. 518 898-8323
Menands *(G-7850)*

West Metal Works Inc ....E .. 716 895-4900
Buffalo *(G-3045)*

WELDING SPLYS, EXC GASES: *Wholesalers*

Austin Industries Inc ....F 585 589-1353
Albion *(G-154)*

WELDING TIPS: *Heat Resistant, Metal*

JE Monahan Fabrications LLC ....F .. 518 761-0414
Queensbury *(G-13045)*

National Maint Contg Corp ....D .. 716 285-1583
Niagara Falls *(G-11953)*

WELDMENTS

Glenridge Fabricators Inc ....F .. 718 456-2297
Glendale *(G-5227)*

Industrial Fabricating Corp ....E .. 315 437-8234
East Syracuse *(G-4219)*

Miller Metal Fabricating Inc ....G .. 585 359-3400
Rochester *(G-13549)*

WHEELBARROWS

Clopay Ames True Temper ....F .. 212 957-5096
New York *(G-9035)*

WHEELCHAIR LIFTS

S & H Enterprises Inc ....G .. 888 323-8755
Queensbury *(G-13055)*

Thomas F Egan ....E .. 607 669-4822
Binghamton *(G-913)*

WHEELCHAIRS

Gadabout USA Wheelchairs Inc ....F .. 585 338-2110
Rochester *(G-13427)*

Palmer Industries Inc ....G .. 607 754-8741
Endicott *(G-4468)*

Palmer Industries Inc ....E .. 607 754-2957
Endicott *(G-4469)*

Palmer Industries Inc ....G .. 607 754-8741
Endicott *(G-4470)*

Skil-Care Corporation ....C .. 914 963-2040
Yonkers *(G-16348)*

Vcp Mobility Inc ....B .. 718 356-7827
Staten Island *(G-14725)*

VSM Investors LLC ....G .. 212 351-1600
New York *(G-11708)*

WHEELS & PARTS

Bam Enterprises Inc ....G .. 716 773-7634
Grand Island *(G-5326)*

Factory Wheel Warehouse Inc ....G .. 516 605-2131
Commack *(G-3587)*

Motor Components LLC ....D .. 607 737-8011
Elmira Heights *(G-4378)*

WHEELS: *Abrasive*

Jta USA Inc ....G .. 718 722-0902
Brooklyn *(G-2007)*

WHEELS: *Buffing & Polishing*

Barker Brothers Incorporated ....D .. 718 456-6400
Ridgewood *(G-13140)*

Dimanco Inc ....G .. 315 797-0470
Utica *(G-15256)*

Divine Brothers Company ....C .. 315 797-0470
Utica *(G-15259)*

WHEELS: *Iron & Steel, Locomotive & Car*

Nitro Wheels Inc ....F .. 716 337-0709
North Collins *(G-12027)*

WIGS & HAIRPIECES

M and J Hair Center Inc ....F .. 516 872-1010
Garden City *(G-5106)*

Moti Inc ....F .. 718 436-4280
Brooklyn *(G-2172)*

WIND TUNNELS

United Wind Inc ....E .. 888 313-3353
Brooklyn *(G-2541)*

WINDINGS: *Coil, Electronic*

American Precision Inds Inc ....C .. 716 691-9100
Amherst *(G-210)*

American Precision Inds Inc ....D .. 716 652-3600
East Aurora *(G-4081)*

American Precision Inds Inc ....D .. 585 496-5755
Arcade *(G-367)*

Caddell Burns Manufacturing Co ......E .. 631 757-1772
Northport *(G-12100)*

Mohawk Electro Techniques Inc ....D .. 315 896-2661
Barneveld *(G-594)*

Precision Electronics Inc ....F .. 631 842-4900
Copiague *(G-3670)*

WINDMILLS: *Electric Power Generation*

EDP Renewables North Amer LLC ....G .. 518 426-1650
Albany *(G-74)*

WINDOW & DOOR FRAMES

Action Bullet Resistant ....F .. 631 422-0888
West Islip *(G-15810)*

D D & L Inc ....F .. 607 729-9131
Binghamton *(G-870)*

Interstate Window Corporation ....D .. 631 231-0800
Brentwood *(G-1123)*

J Sussman Inc ....E .. 718 297-0228
Jamaica *(G-6450)*

Jaidan Industries Inc ....F .. 516 944-3650
Port Washington *(G-12891)*

Kasson & Keller Inc ....A .. 518 853-3421
Fonda *(G-4910)*

Munschauer Inc ....F .. 716 895-8888
Buffalo *(G-2877)*

New Bgnnngs Win Door Dstrs LLC ....F .. 845 214-0698
Poughkeepsie *(G-12974)*

Sunrise Door Solutions ....G .. 631 464-4139
Copiague *(G-3680)*

WINDOW BLIND REPAIR SVCS

Window-Fix Inc ....E .. 718 854-3475
Brooklyn *(G-2589)*

WINDOW FRAMES & SASHES: *Plastic*

Hart To Hart Industries Inc ....G .. 716 492-2709
Chaffee *(G-3307)*

JSM Vinyl Products Inc ....F .. 516 775-4520
New Hyde Park *(G-8278)*

WINDOW FRAMES, MOLDING & TRIM: *Vinyl*

Eastern Enterprise Corp ....F .. 718 727-8600
Staten Island *(G-14650)*

Kasson & Keller Inc ....A .. 518 853-3421
Fonda *(G-4910)*

Northeast Windows Usa Inc ....E .. 516 378-6577
Merrick *(G-7862)*

Pvc Industries Inc ....E .. 518 877-8670
Clifton Park *(G-3471)*

Tri-State Window Factory Corp ....D .. 631 667-8600
Deer Park *(G-3942)*

Vinyline Window and Door Inc ....F .. 914 476-3500
Yonkers *(G-16355)*

Window Tech Systems Inc ....E .. 518 899-9000
Ballston Spa *(G-589)*

WINDOW TRIMMING SVCS

New Business Solutions Inc ....E .. 631 789-1500
Amityville *(G-298)*

WINDOWS: *Wood*

Kelly Window Systems Inc ....E .. 631 420-8500
Farmingdale *(G-4664)*

Pella Corporation ....B .. 607 223-2023
Johnson City *(G-6607)*

Pella Corporation ....B .. 516 385-3622
Albertson *(G-150)*

Pella Corporation ....B .. 516 385-3622
Albertson *(G-151)*

Royal Windows Mfg Corp ....E .. 631 435-8888
Bay Shore *(G-710)*

Stealth Archtctral Windows Inc ....F .. 718 821-6666
Brooklyn *(G-2454)*

WINE & DISTILLED ALCOHOLIC BEVERAGES WHOLESALERS

Constellation Brands Inc ....D .. 585 678-7100
Victor *(G-15399)*

Liquid Management Partners LLC ......F .. 516 775-5050
New Hyde Park *(G-8280)*

Murphs Famous Inc ....G .. 516 398-0417
Rockville Centre *(G-13831)*

WINE CELLARS, BONDED: *Wine, Blended*

Solstars Inc ....G .. 212 605-0430
New York *(G-11290)*

Wine Services Inc ....G .. 631 722-3800
Riverhead *(G-13193)*

WIRE

Bekaert Corporation ....E .. 716 830-1321
Amherst *(G-212)*

EB Acquisitions LLC ....D .. 212 355-3310
New York *(G-9309)*

Island Industries Corp ....G .. 631 451-8825
Coram *(G-3694)*

Liberty Fabrication Inc ....G .. 718 495-5735
Brooklyn *(G-2066)*

Spectrum Cable Corporation ....E .. 585 235-7714
Rochester *(G-13738)*

Tappan Wire & Cable Inc ....C .. 845 353-9000
Blauvelt *(G-935)*

Web Associates Inc ....G .. 716 883-3377
Buffalo *(G-3042)*

WIRE & CABLE: *Aluminum*

Irtronics Instruments Inc ....F .. 914 693-6291
Ardsley *(G-389)*

SI Partners Inc ....G .. 516 433-1415
Hicksville *(G-5948)*

WIRE & CABLE: *Nonferrous, Aircraft*

Tdg Acquistion Co LLC ....E .. 585 500-4625
Henrietta *(G-5860)*

WIRE & WIRE PRDTS

369 River Road Inc ....E .. 716 694-5001
North Tonawanda *(G-12050)*

Abbott Industries Inc ....B .. 718 291-0800
Jamaica *(G-6423)*

Albest Metal Stamping Corp ....E .. 718 388-6000
Brooklyn *(G-1477)*

American Wire Tie Inc ....E .. 716 337-2412
North Collins *(G-12023)*

Angelica Spring Company Inc ....F .. 585 466-7892
Angelica *(G-357)*

Bayshore Wire Products Corp ....F .. 631 451-8825
Coram *(G-3692)*

Better Wire Products Inc ....E .. 716 883-3377
Buffalo *(G-2662)*

Bison Steel Incorporated ....G .. 716 683-0900
Depew *(G-3971)*

Cable Management Solutions Inc ....E .. 631 674-0004
Bay Shore *(G-660)*

Clover Wire Forming Co Inc ....E .. 914 375-0400
Yonkers *(G-16296)*

Compar Manufacturing Corp ....E .. 212 304-2777
New York *(G-9071)*

Continental Cordage Corp ....D .. 315 655-9800
Cazenovia *(G-3225)*

Cuddeback Machining Inc ....G .. 585 392-5889
Hilton *(G-5972)*

Engineering Mfg Tech LLC ....D .. 607 754-7111
Endicott *(G-4453)*

Flanagans Creative Disp Inc ....E .. 845 858-2542
Port Jervis *(G-12848)*

Flatcut LLC ....G .. 212 542-5732
Brooklyn *(G-1850)*

Hanes Supply Inc ....F .. 518 438-0139
Albany *(G-83)*

Interstate Wood Products Inc ....E .. 631 842-4488
Amityville *(G-277)*

Kehr-Buffalo Wire Frame Co Inc ....E .. 716 897-2288
Buffalo *(G-2830)*

Magic Novelty Co Inc ....E .. 212 304-2777
New York *(G-10325)*

Oneida Sales & Service Inc ....E .. 716 822-8205
Buffalo *(G-2897)*

Owl Wire & Cable LLC ....C .. 315 697-2011
Canastota *(G-3153)*

Peck & Hale LLC ....E 631 589-2510
West Sayville (G-15842)

Quality Industrial Services ....F 716 667-7703
Orchard Park (G-12376)

Rose Fence Inc ....F 516 223-0777
Baldwin (G-533)

SCI Bore Inc ....G 212 674-7128
New York (G-11165)

Selectrode Industries Inc ....D 631 547-5470
Huntington Station (G-6260)

Sigmund Cohn Corp ....D 914 664-5300
Mount Vernon (G-8180)

Teka Precision Inc ....G 845 753-1900
Nyack (G-12147)

Trylon Wire & Metal Works Inc ....E 718 542-4472
Bronx (G-1384)

Utility Engineering Co ....F 845 735-8900
Pearl River (G-12542)

WIRE CLOTH & WOVEN WIRE PRDTS, MADE FROM PURCHASED WIRE

G Bopp USA Inc ....G 845 296-1065
Wappingers Falls (G-15493)

Sinclair International Company ....D 518 798-2361
Queensbury (G-13057)

WIRE FABRIC: Welded Steel

Technical Wldg Fabricators LLC ....F 518 463-2229
Albany (G-134)

WIRE FENCING & ACCESS WHOLESALERS

Master-Halco Inc ....F 631 585-8150
Yaphank (G-16266)

WIRE MATERIALS: Copper

Camden Wire Co Inc ....A 315 245-3800
Camden (G-3099)

International Wire Group ....F 315 245-3800
Camden (G-3101)

Jaguar Industries Inc ....F 845 947-1800
Haverstraw (G-5805)

Omega Wire Inc ....D 315 689-7115
Jordan (G-6630)

Omega Wire Inc ....B 315 245-3800
Camden (G-3104)

Owi Corporation ....G 315 245-4305
Camden (G-3105)

WIRE MATERIALS: Steel

American Wire Tie Inc ....E 716 337-2412
North Collins (G-12023)

Continental Cordage Corp ....D 315 655-9800
Cazenovia (G-3225)

Hohmann & Barnard Inc ....E 631 234-0600
Hauppauge (G-5672)

Lee Spring Company LLC ....C 888 777-4647
Brooklyn (G-2058)

Omega Wire Inc ....D 315 689-7115
Jordan (G-6630)

Rolling Gate Supply Corp ....G 718 366-5258
Glendale (G-5232)

Rose Fence Inc ....F 516 223-0777
Baldwin (G-533)

Sigmund Cohn Corp ....D 914 664-5300
Mount Vernon (G-8180)

WIRE PRDTS: Ferrous Or Iron, Made In Wiredrawing Plants

Forsyth Industries Inc ....E 716 652-1070
Buffalo (G-2757)

WIRE PRDTS: Steel & Iron

Handy & Harman Ltd ....A 212 520-2300
New York (G-9720)

Sph Group Holdings LLC ....F 212 520-2300
New York (G-11321)

WIRE WHOLESALERS

Awt Supply Corp ....G 516 437-9105
Elmont (G-4383)

WIRE: Barbed

Cobra Systems Inc ....F 845 338-6675
Bloomington (G-951)

WIRE: Barbed & Twisted

Cobra Manufacturing Corp ....G 845 514-2505
Lake Katrine (G-6763)

WIRE: Communication

Caldwell Bennett Inc ....E 315 337-8540
Oriskany (G-12385)

Corning Optcal Cmmncations LLC ......F 607 974-7543
Corning (G-3712)

WIRE: Mesh

Aeroflex Incorporated ....B 516 694-6700
Plainview (G-12660)

WIRE: Nonferrous

C S Business Systems Inc ....E 716 886-6521
Buffalo (G-2688)

Camden Wire Co Inc ....A 315 245-3800
Camden (G-3099)

Colonial Wire & Cable Co Inc ....D 631 234-8500
Hauppauge (G-5621)

Colonial Wire Cable Co NJ ....G 631 234-8500
Hauppauge (G-5622)

Continental Cordage Corp ....D 315 655-9800
Cazenovia (G-3225)

Convergent Cnnctivity Tech Inc ....G 845 651-5250
Florida (G-4822)

Cortland Cable Company Inc ....E 607 753-8276
Cortland (G-3758)

Fiberall Corp ....F 516 371-5200
Inwood (G-6293)

International Wire Group Inc ....B 315 245-2000
Camden (G-3102)

Jaguar Industries Inc ....F 845 947-1800
Haverstraw (G-5805)

Leviton Manufacturing Co Inc ....B 631 812-6000
Melville (G-7800)

Performance Wire & Cable Inc ....F 315 245-2594
Camden (G-3106)

Rdi Inc ....F 914 773-1000
Mount Kisco (G-8104)

Remee Products Corp ....D 845 651-4431
Florida (G-4826)

Rockland Insulated Wire Cable ....G 845 429-3103
Haverstraw (G-5806)

Siemens Corporation ....F 202 434-7800
New York (G-11226)

Siemens USA Holdings Inc ....B 212 258-4000
New York (G-11228)

Sinclair Technologies Inc ....E 716 874-3682
Hamburg (G-5521)

Steelflex Electro Corp ....D 516 226-4466
Lindenhurst (G-6973)

Tappan Wire & Cable Inc ....C 845 353-9000
Blauvelt (G-935)

United Wire Technologies Inc ....F 315 623-7203
Constantia (G-3637)

Universal Builders Supply Inc ....F 845 758-8801
Red Hook (G-13074)

Whirlwind Music Distrs Inc ....D 800 733-9473
Rochester (G-13803)

WIRE: Nonferrous, Appliance Fixture

Kris-Tech Wire Company Inc ....E 315 339-5268
Rome (G-13853)

WIRE: Steel, Insulated Or Armored

Able Industries Inc ....F 914 739-5685
Cortlandt Manor (G-3792)

Aerospace Wire & Cable Inc ....E 718 358-2345
College Point (G-3534)

WOMEN'S & CHILDREN'S CLOTHING WHOLESALERS, NEC

Alpha 6 Distributions LLC ....F 516 801-8290
Locust Valley (G-7121)

Arteast LLC ....E 646 859-6020
New York (G-8633)

Bilco Industries Inc ....F 917 783-5008
New York (G-8790)

D-C Theatricks ....G 716 847-0180
Buffalo (G-2719)

Design Archives Inc ....G 212 768-0617
New York (G-9205)

Eb Couture Ltd ....E 212 912-0190
New York (G-9310)

Grand Knitting Mills Inc ....E 631 226-5000
Amityville (G-265)

Halmode Apparel Inc ....A 212 819-9114
New York (G-9712)

Hampshire Sub II Inc ....D 631 321-0923
New York (G-9716)

JM Originals Inc ....C 845 647-3003
Ellenville (G-4307)

Kate Spade Holdings LLC ....B 212 354-4900
New York (G-10076)

Kenmar Shirts Inc ....E 718 824-3880
Bronx (G-1291)

Lloyds Fashions Inc ....D 631 435-3353
Brentwood (G-1125)

M Hidary & Co Inc ....C 212 736-6540
New York (G-10296)

Mango Usa Inc ....F 718 998-6050
Brooklyn (G-2106)

Moresca Clothing and Costume ....F 845 331-6012
Ulster Park (G-15219)

Nlhe LLC ....E 212 594-0012
Brooklyn (G-2217)

Onia LLC ....E 646 701-0008
New York (G-10693)

Only Hearts Ltd ....E 212 268-0886
New York (G-10694)

Penfli Industries Inc ....F 212 947-6080
Great Neck (G-5413)

Soho Apparel Ltd ....G 212 840-1109
New York (G-11285)

United Knitwear International ....G 212 354-2920
New York (G-11598)

Universal Mus Group Hldngs Inc ....E 212 333-8000
New York (G-11608)

Ying Ke Youth Age Group Inc ....F 929 402-8458
Dix Hills (G-4017)

WOMEN'S & GIRLS' SPORTSWEAR WHOLESALERS

Argee America Inc ....G 212 768-9840
New York (G-8621)

Casuals Etc Inc ....D 212 838-1319
New York (G-8932)

Danice Stores Inc ....F 212 665-0389
New York (G-9166)

F & J Designs Inc ....G 212 302-8755
New York (G-9454)

Jaxis Inc ....G 212 302-7611
Brooklyn (G-1989)

Lollytogs Ltd ....D 212 502-6000
New York (G-10246)

Morelle Products Ltd ....F 212 391-8070
New York (G-10502)

Noah Enterprises Ltd ....E 212 736-2888
New York (G-10634)

Planet Gold Clothing Co Inc ....C 646 432-5100
New York (G-10851)

S2 Sportswear Inc ....F 347 335-0713
Brooklyn (G-2378)

WOMEN'S CLOTHING STORES

6 Shore Road LLC ....G 212 274-9666
New York (G-8406)

Amj DOT LLC ....G 718 775-3288
Brooklyn (G-1505)

Caribbean Fashion Group Inc ....G 212 706-8851
New York (G-8916)

Elie Tahari Ltd ....G 212 763-2000
New York (G-9339)

Joseph (uk) Inc ....G 212 570-0077
New York (G-10026)

Kozinn+sons Merchant Tailors ....E 212 643-1916
New York (G-10132)

Mee Accessories LLC ....B 917 262-1000
New York (G-10421)

Mega Sourcing Inc ....G 646 682-0304
Merrick (G-7861)

Uniqlo USA LLC ....F 877 486-4756
New York (G-11593)

WOMEN'S CLOTHING STORES: Ready-To-Wear

Ferris USA LLC ....G 617 895-8100
New York (G-9485)

Hillary Merchant Inc ....G 646 575-9242
New York (G-9785)

Phillips-Van Heusen Europe ....F 212 381-3500
New York (G-10829)

PRODUCT

WOMEN'S CLOTHING STORES: Ready-To-Wear (continued)

Pvh Corp ....D 212 381-3500
New York *(G-10933)*

Pvh Corp ....G 212 549-6000
New York *(G-10934)*

Stallion Inc ....E 718 706-0111
Long Island City *(G-7362)*

WOMEN'S SPECIALTY CLOTHING STORES

Dvf Studio LLC ....D 212 741-6607
New York *(G-9283)*

Dvf Studio LLC ....G 646 576-8009
New York *(G-9284)*

JBS Limited ....E 212 764-4600
New York *(G-9984)*

WOMEN'S SPORTSWEAR STORES

Central Apparel Group Ltd ....F 212 868-6505
New York *(G-8950)*

Mainly Monograms Inc ....E 845 624-4923
West Nyack *(G-15827)*

Royal Tees Inc ....G 845 357-9448
Suffern *(G-14766)*

WOOD FENCING WHOLESALERS

Interstate Wood Products Inc ....E 631 842-4488
Amityville *(G-277)*

Master-Halco Inc ....F 631 585-8150
Yaphank *(G-16266)*

WOOD PRDTS: Beekeeping Splys

Betterbee Inc ....F 518 314-0575
Greenwich *(G-5469)*

Northast Ctr For Bekeeping LLC ....F 800 632-3379
Greenwich *(G-5474)*

WOOD PRDTS: Clothespins

Green Renewable Inc ....E 518 658-2233
Berlin *(G-824)*

WOOD PRDTS: Display Forms, Boot & Shoe

Encore Retail Systems Inc ....F 718 385-3443
Mamaroneck *(G-7509)*

WOOD PRDTS: Engraved

Lanwood Industries Inc ....E 718 786-3000
Bay Shore *(G-688)*

WOOD PRDTS: Furniture Inlays, Veneers

American Woods & Veneers Works ....E 718 937-2195
Long Island City *(G-7157)*

WOOD PRDTS: Jalousies, Glass, Wood Framed

Paul David Enterprises Inc ....G 646 667-5530
New York *(G-10770)*

WOOD PRDTS: Ladders & Stepladders

York Ladder Inc ....F 718 784-6666
Long Island City *(G-7411)*

WOOD PRDTS: Laundry

Grohe America Inc ....G 212 206-8820
New York *(G-9681)*

WOOD PRDTS: Moldings, Unfinished & Prefinished

Adriatic Wood Products Inc ....E 718 922-4621
Brooklyn *(G-1462)*

Deerfield Millwork Inc ....F 631 726-9663
Water Mill *(G-15529)*

Fire Island Sea Clam Co Inc ....G 631 589-2199
West Sayville *(G-15840)*

Old World Mouldings Inc ....G 631 563-8660
Bohemia *(G-1057)*

Scanga Woodworking Corp ....E 845 265-9115
Cold Spring *(G-3525)*

Spiegel Woodworks Inc ....F 845 336-8090
Kingston *(G-6710)*

WOOD PRDTS: Mulch Or Sawdust

Premium Mulch & Materials Inc ....F 631 320-3666
Coram *(G-3698)*

Wholesale Mulch & Sawdust Inc ....G 607 687-2637
Owego *(G-12440)*

WOOD PRDTS: Novelties, Fiber

Cowee Forest Products Inc ....E 518 658-2233
Berlin *(G-823)*

Graphics Slution Providers Inc ....F 845 677-5088
Lagrangeville *(G-6748)*

Ryers Creek Corp ....E 607 523-6617
Corning *(G-3720)*

WOOD PRDTS: Outdoor, Structural

Amish Structure ....F 607 257-1070
Dryden *(G-4036)*

Wolski Wood Works Inc ....G 718 577-9816
Flushing *(G-4906)*

WOOD PRDTS: Panel Work

Empire Building Products Inc ....G 518 695-6094
Schuylerville *(G-14323)*

WOOD PRDTS: Pedestals & Statuary

Mrp Supports LLC ....F 716 332-7673
Orchard Park *(G-12367)*

WOOD PRDTS: Rulers & Rules

Aakron Rule Corp ....C 716 542-5483
Akron *(G-15)*

WOOD PRDTS: Shavings & Packaging, Excelsior

RWS Manufacturing Inc ....G 518 361-1657
Queensbury *(G-13054)*

WOOD PRDTS: Shoe Trees

R P M Industries Inc ....E 315 255-1105
Auburn *(G-492)*

WOOD PRDTS: Signboards

Paramount Graphix ....G 845 367-5003
Port Jervis *(G-12854)*

Sentine Printing Inc ....E 516 334-7400
Westbury *(G-15925)*

WOOD PRDTS: Silo Staves

Unadilla Silo Company Inc ....D 607 369-9341
Sidney *(G-14438)*

WOOD PRDTS: Trophy Bases

Cherry Creek Woodcraft Inc ....E 716 988-3211
South Dayton *(G-14506)*

M A Moslow & Bros Inc ....E 716 896-2950
Buffalo *(G-2854)*

WOOD PRDTS: Window Backs, Store Or Lunchroom, Prefabricated

Vitarose Corp of America ....G 718 951-9700
Brooklyn *(G-2565)*

WOOD PRODUCTS: Reconstituted

Bedford Wdwrk Instllations Inc ....G 914 764-9434
Bedford *(G-762)*

Northeastern Products Corp ....E 518 623-3161
Warrensburg *(G-15505)*

Zircar Refr Composites Inc ....F 845 651-2200
Florida *(G-4828)*

WOOD TREATING: Creosoting

Colorspec Coatings Intl Inc ....F 631 472-8251
Holbrook *(G-5992)*

Osmose Holdings Inc ....A 716 882-5905
Depew *(G-3991)*

WOOD TREATING: Flooring, Block

Wego International Floors LLC ....F 516 487-3510
Great Neck *(G-5431)*

WOOD TREATING: Structural Lumber & Timber

Genesee Reserve Buffalo LLC ....E 716 824-3116
Buffalo *(G-2774)*

Northeast Treaters NY LLC ....E 518 945-2660
Athens *(G-448)*

WOODWORK & TRIM: Interior & Ornamental

Beaver Creek Industries Inc ....G 607 545-6382
Canaseraga *(G-3147)*

Inform Studio Inc ....F 718 401-6149
Bronx *(G-1282)*

Miller Blaker Inc ....D 718 665-0500
Bronx *(G-1315)*

P H Custom Woodworking Corp ....E 917 801-1444
Bronx *(G-1330)*

Props Displays & Interiors ....F 212 620-3840
New York *(G-10915)*

RB Woodcraft Inc ....E 315 474-2429
Syracuse *(G-14975)*

Vander Heyden Woodworking ....G 212 242-0525
New York *(G-11639)*

Wood Innovations of Suffolk ....G 631 698-2345
Oceanside *(G-12198)*

WOODWORK: Carved & Turned

Lanza Corp ....G 914 937-6360
Port Chester *(G-12824)*

Superior Wood Turnings ....F 716 483-1254
Jamestown *(G-6549)*

WOODWORK: Interior & Ornamental, NEC

A Losee & Sons ....E 516 676-3060
Glen Cove *(G-5186)*

American Wood Column Corp ....G 718 782-3163
Brooklyn *(G-1503)*

Arbr Studios LLC ....F 585 254-7607
Rochester *(G-13242)*

Bauerschmidt & Sons Inc ....D 718 528-3500
Jamaica *(G-6429)*

Brauen Constrution ....G 585 492-0042
Arcade *(G-371)*

Custom Wood Inc ....G 718 927-4700
Brooklyn *(G-1713)*

DAngelo Home Collections Inc ....G 917 267-8920
Warwick *(G-15511)*

DC Contracting & Building Corp ....F 631 385-1117
Huntington Station *(G-6244)*

Ignelzi Interiors Inc ....E 718 464-0279
Queens Village *(G-13021)*

Kng Construction Co Inc ....F 212 595-1451
Warwick *(G-15517)*

Michael Bernstein Design Assoc ....E 718 456-9277
Brooklyn *(G-2150)*

Nordic Interior Inc ....C 718 456-7000
Brooklyn *(G-2219)*

Pgs Millwork Inc ....D 518 828-2608
Hudson *(G-6175)*

WOVEN WIRE PRDTS, NEC

Joldeson One Aerospace Inds ....D 718 848-7396
Ozone Park *(G-12463)*

WRITING FOR PUBLICATION SVCS

Mosby Holdings Corp ....G 212 309-8100
New York *(G-10505)*

X-RAY EQPT & TUBES

Air Techniques Inc ....B 516 433-7676
Melville *(G-7758)*

American Access Care LLC ....F 631 582-9729
Hauppauge *(G-5587)*

Biodex Medical Systems Inc ....C 631 924-9000
Shirley *(G-14417)*

Dra Imaging PC ....E 845 296-1057
Wappingers Falls *(G-15491)*

Flow X Ray Corporation ....D 631 242-9729
Deer Park *(G-3873)*

Mitegen LLC ....G 607 266-8877
Ithaca *(G-6397)*

Multiwire Laboratories Ltd ....G 607 257-3378
Ithaca *(G-6399)*

New York Imaging Service Inc ....F 716 834-8022
Tonawanda *(G-15125)*

Phantom Laboratory Inc ....F 518 692-1190
Greenwich *(G-5475)*

Photo Medic Equipment Inc ....D 631 242-6600
Deer Park *(G-3918)*

Surescan Corporation ....E 607 321-0042
Binghamton *(G-911)*

VJ Technologies Inc ....E 631 589-8800
Bohemia *(G-1096)*

Wolf X-Ray Corporation ....D 631 242-9729
Deer Park *(G-3954)*

YARN & YARN SPINNING

Advanced Yarn Technologies Inc ....E 518 239-6600
Durham *(G-4069)*

Colortex Inc ....G 212 564-2000
New York *(G-9057)*

Missiontex Inc ....G 718 532-9053
Brooklyn *(G-2161)*

National Spinning Co Inc ....E 212 382-6400
New York *(G-10546)*

United Thread Mills Corp ....G 516 536-3900
Oceanside *(G-12195)*

YARN MILLS: Twisting

Majestic Rayon Corporation ....E 212 929-6443
New York *(G-10334)*

YARN WHOLESALERS

Colortex Inc ....G 212 564-2000
New York *(G-9057)*

Great Adirondack Yarn Company ....F 518 843-3381
Amsterdam *(G-329)*

National Spinning Co Inc ....E 212 382-6400
New York *(G-10546)*

YARN: Embroidery, Spun

Printz and Patternz LLC ....G 518 944-6020
Schenectady *(G-14296)*

YARN: Natural & Animal Fiber, Spun

Great Adirondack Yarn Company ....F 518 843-3381
Amsterdam *(G-329)*

YARN: Specialty & Novelty

A Thousand Cranes Inc ....F 212 724-9596
New York *(G-8419)*

K F I Inc ....G 516 546-2904
Roosevelt *(G-14031)*

La Lame Inc ....G 212 921-9770
New York *(G-10158)*

YARN: Weaving, Twisting, Winding Or Spooling

Marsha Fleisher ....F 845 679-6500
Woodstock *(G-16236)*

YOGURT WHOLESALERS

Fage USA Holdings ....G 518 762-5912
Johnstown *(G-6617)*

Kesso Foods Inc ....G 718 777-5303
East Elmhurst *(G-4108)*

PRODUCT